P RAMANATHA AIYAR

CONCISE LAW DICTIONARY

First Edition	1940
With Supplement	1947
Reprint	1987
Reprint	1988
Reprint	1990
Reprint	1992
Reprint	1993
Reprint	1994
Reprint	1995
Reprint	1996
Second Edition	1997
Reprint	2002
Reprint	2003
Reprint	2004
Third Edition	2005
Reprint	2006
Reprint	2007
Reprint	2008
Reprint	2009
Fourth Edition	2012
Fifth Edition	2014
Reprint	2015
Reprint	2016
Reprint	2017
Sixth Edition	2018
Reprint	2019
Seventh Edition	2020
Reprint	2021
Reprint	2022
Reprint	2023
Eighth Edition	2024
Reprint	**2025**

P RAMANATHA AIYAR

CONCISE LAW DICTIONARY

With Legal Maxims, Latin Terms and Words & Phrases

Eighth Edition

LexisNexis

LexisNexis®

This book is a publication of LexisNexis
(A Division of RELX India Pvt Ltd)
14th floor, Building No 10, Tower–B, DLF Cyber City, Phase-II,
Gurgaon–122002, Haryana, India.
Tel : + 91 124 4774444 Fax: + 91 124 4774100
Website : www.lexisnexis.co.in / E-mail : help.in@lexisnexis.com

---

P Ramanatha Aiyar: *Concise Law Dictionary*, Eighth Edition, 2024

ISBN: 978-81-19403-68-4

Printed by: Saurabh Printers Pvt. Ltd.

THE AUTHOR

— An Immortal Soul —

The late Shri P Ramanatha Aiyar

A very simple, religious and pious man popularly called Vakil Baba.

He was born in 1873 at Pinayur in Chingleput district of Tamil Nadu. After studying law, he started writing and editing encyclopaedic works and voluminous series of law books at the Madras Law Journal Office. With his flawless brilliance, all his writings proved ultimate in power and perfection, he spent most part of his life in Mylapore, Madras, editing and writing law books.

He took *sanyasam* in 1954 with the blessings from Paramacharya of Kanchi Mutt at Kashi (Varanasi). After sanyasam, he was renamed Shree Ramabrahmendra Swamigal Saraswati but was affectionately called Vakil Baba and lived upto the last day of his life as a sanyasi.

He passed away at the age of 87 years on Chitrapurnima day in April 1960 at Varanasi.

His grandchildren built-up "Dhyana Mandapam" (Meditation Hall) in his memory at his birthplace where even today people perform "Aradhana" in his fond memory on every Chitrapurnima day.

He authored several well known titles including *Principles and Precedents on the Art of Cross Examination, The Law of Benami Transactions, Law of Costs, Law of Receivers, Law of Interest in British India, Statute Law relating to Marriage and Divorce in British India, Commentaries on the Codes of Civil and Criminal Procedure, The Indian Limitation Act, The Easement Act, The Provincial Small Cause Courts Act, The Court-Fees and Suits Valuation Act, The Law of Minors and Guardianship, The Contract Act, The Current Index of Indian Cases, The Civil Court Manual, The Criminal Court Manual, The All-India Digest, Civil and Criminal,* etc.

Publisher's Note

P Ramanatha Aiyar *Concise Law Dictionary* has withstood the test of time, since its first publication in 1940, and continues to ably serve the legal profession and everyone associated with it. This legal dictionary provides the precise meaning of legal words, Latin terms, and phrases in common usage under varied areas of law. It defines terms applicable to general and personal laws, as well as terms from specialized fields such as information technology, intellectual property, insolvency and bankruptcy, forensic medicine, mercantile, maritime, military et al. Words, phrases, and expressions commonly found in English Statutes, decisions and treatises have been succinctly explained. In addition, references to relevant statutes and judgments have also been provided to illustrate the usage of words and phrases.

This new edition is up to date and exhaustive in its coverage and scope; comprising important judicial pronouncements, so far as words and phrases defined by the Courts, the Latin Maxims occurring its judgments, the words defined by the legal authorities along with the Regional Legal Terms cited in its judgments, are concerned. Statutory definitions from Central Acts, Ordinances and Codes as well as words defined in Rules and Regulations have been appropriately incorporated. Important terms from latest statutes viz., The Bhartiya Nyaya Sanhita, 2023, The Bharatiya Sakshya Adhiniyam, 2023, The Bhartiya Nagarik Suraksha Sanhita, 2023, Digital Personal Data Protection Act, 2023, and Mediation Act, 2023 have also been included in this edition.

As hard as it is, a sincere effort has been made to ensure that this work continues to be dependable and all-encompassing, upholding its glory of being one of the oldest and most trusted law dictionaries in India. We are confident this new edition will be an indispensable reference for legal professionals, jurists, academicians, researchers, as well as civil and judicial services aspirants.

Editorial Board

Abbreviations

A

A.	Arabic
A. & E.	Adolphus and Ellis (1834-1841)
A.2d.	Atlantic Reporter, 2nd Series
A.C. (preceded by date)	Law Reports, Appeal Cases
A.D.	Anno Domini in the year of the Lord
A.D. (Delhi)	Apex Decisions (Delhi)
A.D.	Apex Decisions
A.I.R. (N.O.C)	All India Reporter (Notes of Cases) (All. Andh Pra. etc.)
A.I.R. (n.U.C.) (All) (Andh)	All India Reporter (Notes of Unreported Cases) (Allahabad, Andh. Pra. etc.)
AIR	All India Reporter, Allahabad (All), Bombay (Bom) etc., sections
A.L.J.R.	Allahabad Law Journal Reports
A.L.J.R.	Australian Law Journal Reports
A.L.R.	Argus Law Reports (1895-1981)
	Australian Law Reports
	Amity Law Review
A.L.T.	Andhra Law Times
A.LJ./Austr. L.J.	Australian Law Journal
A.M.L.J.	Ajmer Merwara Law Journal
A.W.N.	Allahabad Weekly Notes (1881-1908)
A.W.R.	Andhra Weekly Reporter
Abbot L. Dict.	Abbot Law Dictionary
Abbott	Abbott on Merchant Ships and Seamen.
Abbr.	Abbreviation
Adam's Gloss/Adams	Adam's Glossary
Adject.	Adjective
Affd.	affirmed
AIHCC	All India High Court Cases
Ala.	Alabama Reports
All E.R. (preceded by date)	All England Law Reports
All ER	All England Reports
All L.W.	Allahabad Law Weekly
All or ILR. All	Indian Law Reports, Allahabad Series
All. Cr.R.	Allahabad Criminal Reports
All. Cri. Rul.	Allahabad Criminal Rulings
All. L.J.	Allahabad Law Journal. (Published by AIR)
All. L.T./ ALT	Allahabad Law Times
All. W.R.	Allahabad Weekly Reporter

All.	...	Indian Law Reports Allahabad Series (1876)
Am. Dec.	...	American Decisions
Am. Rep.	...	American Reports
Am. St. Rep.	...	American State Papers
Ame. Rul. Case Law	...	American Ruling Case Law
Amer. Cyc.	...	American Heritage Dictionary
And.	...	Anderson (1558-1603)
Anderson L. Dict.	...	Anderson Law Dictionary
Andh. W.R.	...	Andhra Weekly Reporter
Andhra/ AP	...	Indian Law Reports, Andhra Series (1955)
Ann. Pr.	...	Annual Practice
AP	...	Andhra Pradesh
App. Cas.	...	Law Reports, Appeal Cases (Note. In and since 1891 these reports are cited
App. D.C.	...	Appeal Cases, District of Columbia
App.	...	appendix
Arn./Arnold, Mar. Ins.	...	Arnould on Marine Insurance
Art.	...	Article
AS	...	Accounting Standard
Assam / Ass.	...	Indian Law Reports, Assam Series (1949)
Atk.	...	Atkyns (1736-1755)
Att. Gen./ AG	...	Attorney-General
AWN / All. W.N.	...	Allahabad Weekly Notes

B

B. & C. / Barn. & Cress.	...	Barnewall and Cresswell (1822-1830)
Bacon Abr.	...	Bacon's Abridgement of the Law. A new Abridgment of the Law by Matthew Bacon With considerable additions by Henry Gwillim and with the additions of later English and American decisions. This book is generally cited by the page and sometimes by the title
Bell.	...	Bell's Dictionary and Digest of the Law of Scotland
Ben.	...	Bengali
Beng	...	Bengal
Bishop Cr. Proc.	...	Bishops Criminal Procedure
Bl. H.	...	Blackstone, Henry (1788-1796)
Black. Rep.	...	Blackford's Reports
Black/ Black's Law Dictionary	...	Black's Law Dictionary
Blackf	...	Blackford's Reports (1871-1898) Indiana.
Blackstone	...	Blackstone's Legal Dictionary
Bouv. Law Dict./ Bouvier	...	Bouvier Law Dictionary
Brac/Bract/Bracton	...	Bracton de Legibus et Consuetudinibus
Bract.	...	Bracton's Treatise on the Laws and Customs of England
Brewst.	...	Brewster's Pennsylvania Reports

		Geo. III. 1794, by William Brown in 4 Volumes
Broom/Broom. Max.	...	Brooms Legal Maxims
Brown L. Dict.	...	Brown Law Dictionary
Brown P.C.	...	Brown's Parliamentary Cases (1702-1800)
Bulls	...	Bullstrode's Reports, 1609-1639. K.B.
Bulst.	...	Bulstrode (1603-1649)
Bur.	...	Burma
Burr.	...	Burrow (1756-1772)
Burrill, L. Dict./ Burrill	...	Burrill Law Dictionary
Bushnell, Nat. and the Supernat	...	Nature and the Supernatural by Horace Bushnell
Byrne	...	A Dictionary of the English Law by W.J. Byrne

C

C.	...	Column (of Digest)
C.A.	...	Court of Appeal
C.C.A.	...	Court of Criminal Appeal
C.C.R.	...	County Court Rules
C.J.	...	Chief Justice
C.L.C.	...	Corporate Law Cases (Published by AIR)
C.L.J.	...	Calcutta Law Journal Reports (1905)
	...	Cambridge Law Journal
	...	Consumer Law Journal
C.L.R.	...	Commonwealth Law Reports
C.P.	...	Central Provinces
CPC	...	Code of Civil Procedure (1908)
Cal.	...	Calcutta
Cal. App.	...	California Appellate Reports
Cal. L.J. / CLJ	...	Calcutta Law Journal
Cal. or I.L.R. Cal.	...	Indian Law Reports Calcutta Series
Cali.	...	California Reports
Callis	...	The Reading of Robert Callis on the Statute of Sewers, 23 Hen. 8, c. 5, delivered by him at Gray's Inn, August, 1622
Car.	...	Carolus
Cent. Dict.	...	Century Dictionary
Cf.	...	confer; compare
Challis	...	Challis on Real Property
Chalmers	...	Chalmers on Bills of Exchange
Chap./Ch.	...	Chapter (of Act of Parliament)
Chit.	...	Chitty's Reports
Chitty	...	Chitty (Vol. 1, 1819, Vol. II, 1770-1822)
Chitty. Cri. Law	...	Chitty's Criminal Law
Chron.	...	The Chronological Study Bible
CJEC	...	Court of Justice of the European Communities
Cl. & F.	...	Clark and Finelly's Reports

Cl. & F.	...	Clarke and Finelly (1831-1846)
Cl.	...	clause
Co. Litt./ Coke Litt.	...	Coke upon Littleton, the edition here used being the 18th by Hargrave & Butler
Coke	...	Coke's Reports, (1752-1816)
Colloq.	...	colloquial
Colo.	...	Colorado Reports
Com Cases	...	Company Cases
Com. Cas.	...	Commercial Cases
Comp. L.J./C.L.J.	...	Company Law Journal
Comyn. Contr.	...	Comyn on Contracts
Conn.	...	Connecticut Reports
Const.	...	Constitution of India
Contr.	...	Contract
Cowel	...	Cowel's Interpreter by Tho. Tanley, 1672
Cowell	...	Cowell's Law Dictionary Cowell's Interpreter
Cp. Rep.	...	Common Pleas Reporter
Cp.	...	Compare.Cr. or Cri L.J.
	...	Criminal Law Journal (Published by AIR)
Cr PC	...	Criminal Procedure Code, Act V of 1898
CrPC	...	Code of Criminal Procedure (1973)
Crim. L.R.	...	Criminal Law Review
Cro.	...	Croke's Reports
Cro. Car.	...	Croke, reports during the reign of Charles I (1581-1641)
Cyc. Dic./ Cyc. Law Dict.	...	Cyclopedia Law Dictionary
Cyc./ Cyclop. L.D.	...	Cyclopaedia of Law and Procedure

D

D.	...	Dictum
D.	...	Digest of Justinian
D.	...	Dialogue
D.C.	...	District Court
D.C.	...	District of Columbia Reports
D.C.	...	Divisional Court
DB	...	Division Bench
Dict.	...	Dictionary
Dig.	...	Digest; Digest of Justinian; Digest of Writs
Dillon	...	Dillon's United States Circuit Court Reports
Dis.	...	Discussed
DOC	...	Digest of Cases
Dyer	...	Dyer's Reports, 1513-1538. Q.B.
Dyer. or Dy.	...	Dyer (1513-1582)

E

E.C.R.	...	Excise and Customs Reporters
E.G.	...	Estate Gazette
e.g.	...	for example
E.P. or East Punj	...	East Punjab
Eccl.	...	Ecclesiastical
Ency. Brit./ Encyc.	...	Encyclopaedia Britannica
Ency of the Laws of England	...	Encyclopedia of the Laws of England
excep.	...	exception
Expln.	...	explanation
Ed.	...	Edition
Ed. note	...	Editors' Note
El. & Bl.	...	Ellis and Blackburn's English Queen's Bench Reports
Eliz.	...	Elizabeth
Ex. Rep./Exch./E.	...	Exchequer Reports (1847-1856)
E.& B./ El. & Bl.	...	Ellis and Blackburn (1852-1858)
Ex. D	...	Law Reports, Exchequer Division (1875-1880)

F

F. Supp.	...	Federal Supplement, US-Alaska
F. Supp. 2d	...	Federal Supplement, 2nd, US-Alaska
F.	...	Federal Reporter
F.2d	...	Federal Reporter, 2nd Series, US-Alaska
FB	...	Full Bench
Fed. Cas.	...	Federal Cases
Fed. Rep.	...	Federal Reporter
Fifth Report	...	Fifth Report from the Select Committee of the House of Commons on "The Affairs of the East India Company," 28th July 1812
Foll.	...	Followed
Foster	...	Foster's Crown Law Cases (1708-1760)
Fr.	...	French

G

G. & D.	...	Gale & Davison (1841-1843)
G. / Geo.	...	George
Guj. L.R./G.L.R.	...	Gujarat Law Reporter

H

H.	...	Hindustani
H.	...	Hebrew
H.L.	...	House of Lords
H.P. or I.L.R. Him. Pra.	...	India Law Reports., Himachal Pradesh Series
Hale P.C.	...	Hale's Please of the Crown

Halk. Max./Halkerston Max. No.3.	...	Halkerton's Latin Maxims
Halsbury	...	Halsbury's Laws of England
HCR	...	High Court Reports
Hed.	...	Hedges's Reports, vols. 2-6 Montana
Hen.	...	Henry
Hob.	...	Hobart's Reports
Houst.	...	Houston's Delaware Reports
HTML	...	Hyper Text Markup Language
HTTP	...	Hyper Text Transfer Protocol

I

I.	...	The Institute of Justinian
I.A./ Ind. App.	...	Law Reports Indian Appeals (P.C.)
	...	Indian Appeals
I.C./ Ind. Cas.	...	Indian Cases
i.e.	...	that is
ILR Assam.	...	India Law Reports, Assam Series
ILR Cut.	...	Indian Law Reports, Cuttack Series
ILR E.P. or East Punj.	...	Indian Law Reports. East Punjab Series
ILR Guj.	...	Indian Law Reports, Gujarat Series
ILR M.P.	...	Indian Law Reports. Madhya Pradesh
ILR Madh. B.	...	Indian Law Reports. Madhya Bharat Series
ILR Patiala.	...	Indian Law Reports, Patiala Series
ILR Punj.	...	Indian Law Reports, Punjab Series
ILR Raj.	...	Indian Law Reports, Rajasthan Series
ILR Trav.-Co. or T.C.	...	Indian Law Reports. Travancore-Cochin Series
ILR	...	Indian Law report
I.L.R.	...	Insurance Law Reporter
I.L.T.R.	...	Irish Law Times Reports
IPC	...	Indian Penal Code
I.T.R.	...	Income-tax Reports
I.T.R.	...	Industrial Tribunal Reports
Ibid., ib.	...	Same as above
ill.	...	illustration
Imp. Dict.	...	Imperial Dictionary
Inst.	...	Coke's Institutes

J

Jac.	...	Jacob (1821-1822)
Jacob L. Dict.	...	Jacob Law Dictionary
Jacob	...	Jacob's Law Dictionary "enlarged and improved" by Tomlins and brought by him "to the end of the reign of our late venerated Sovereign George the Third", 3rd. quartoed Sometimes this book is cited as Tomlins, or Tomlins Law Dictionary

Jur. N.S.	...	Jurist, New Series (1854-1866)
Jur.	...	Jurist (1837-1854)

K

K.B. (preceded by date)	...	Law Reports, King's Bench, see now Q.B. (1901-1952)
K.B.D.	...	King's Bench Division
KLT	...	Kerala Law Times
Kan.	...	Kannad
Kan.	...	Kansas
Kan./Kansas. App.	...	Kansas Appeal Reports
Kant or ILR Kant	...	Indian Law Reports, Karnataka Series
Kant. L.J./K.L.J.	...	Karnataka Law Journal
Kant. Serve. L.J.	...	Karnataka Service Law Journal
Karachi or I.L.R. Karachi	...	Indian Law Reports, Karachi Series
Karn.		Karnataka
Kent/Kent Comm.	...	Kent's Commentaries on American Law

L

L.C.J. or C.J.	...	Lord Chief Justice
L.L.J.	...	Labour Law Journal
L.Q.R.	...	Law Quarterly Review
L.R. Eq.	...	Law Reports, Equity (1865-1875)
L.R. Ex.	...	Law Reports, Exchequer (1865-1875)
L.R. Ind. App.	...	Law Reports, Indian Appeals
La. Ann.	...	Louisiana Annual Reports
Lab. I.C.	...	Labour and Industrial Cases (Published by A.I.R.)
Lat.	...	Latin
Lewin	...	Lewin on Trusts
Litt. Rep.	...	Littleton (1626-1632)
Litt.	...	Littleton's Tenures, the version used being that in the edition of Co. Litt. here used
LJQB	...	Law Journal Reports, New Series, Queen's Bench - 1831-1946
LLJ	...	Labour Law Journal
Lloyd's Rep (preceded by date)	...	Lloyd's List Reports
Lofft	...	Lofft (1772-1774)
Lofft. Append.	...	Lofft's Maxims, appended to Lofft's Reports

M

M. & W.	...	Meeson & Welsby (1836-1847)
M.	...	Morison Dictionary of Decisions
M.B.	...	Indian Law Reports, Madhya Bharat Series (1952-56)
M.P.	...	Indian Law Reports, Madhya Pradesh Series (1956)
Macaulay	...	Thomas Babington Macaulay, Lord Macaulay (1800-1859)

Macaulay, Hist. Eng.	...	History of England by Lord Thomas Babington Macaulay
Macn. Mah. Law	...	Mac Naughten's Mohammadan Law
Mad. L.J./M.L.J.	...	Madras Law Journal
Maine's Anc. Law	...	Ancient law by Henry James Sumner Maine
Mal.	...	Malyne's Lex Mercatoria
Mal.	...	Malayalam
Man. & G.	...	Manning and Granger's Reports
Mani.	...	Manipur cases in All India Reports and Indian Law Reports
Mar.	...	Marathi
Mass.	...	Massachusetts Reports
Med. Jur.	...	Medical Jurisprudence
Mit.	...	Mitakshara on the Yajnavalkya Smriti
Mo. App.	...	Missouri Appeal Reports - Kansas City
Mo.	...	Missouri Reports
Moore Mal. Law	...	Moore's Malabar Law
Morgn. Leg Max.	...	Morgan Legal Maxims
Mys. H.C.R.	...	Mysore High Court Reports
Mys. L.J.	...	Mysore Law Journal
Mys.	...	Indian Law Reports, Mysore Series (1951)

N

N. D.	...	North Dakota
N. H.	...	New Hampshire Reports
N. Y.	...	New York Court of Appeals
N. Y. Suppl.	...	New York Supplement
n.	...	Note
N.E.2d	...	Indiana Cases (West)
N.Y.R.	...	New York Reports
Nag. L.J.	...	Nagpur Law Journal
Nag./ Nag. ILR	...	Indian Law Reports, Nagpur Series
NDPS	...	Narcotic Drugs and Psychotropic Substances
NE 2d	...	North Eastern Reporter, Second Series - West
Neb.	...	Nebraska Reports
Nev.	...	Nevada
NJL	...	New Jersey Law Reports
No.	...	Number
Noy	...	Noy (1559-1649)
Noy Max	...	Noy's maxims
NS	...	New Series
NW 2d	...	North Western Reporter, Second Series

O

O.	...	Order
O.C.	...	Oudh Cases (1898-1926)
O.E.D.	...	Oxford English Dictionary
O.W.N.	...	Oudh Weekly Notes (1924-1947)
Ohio St.	...	Ohio State Reports
Ohio	...	Ohio Reports
Ohio. App.	...	Ohio Appellate Reports
Old Eng.	...	Old English Law
Ori.	...	Orissa cases in All India Reports and Indian Law Reports
Orissa J.D./O.J.D.	...	Orissa Judicial Decisions
Oudh. Cas	...	Oudh. Cases
Oudh. L.J. / OLJ	...	Oudh. Law Journal
Oxf. Dict.	...	Oxford Dictionary

P

P& H	...	Punjab and Haryana cases
P.	...	Pacific Reporter
P.	...	Punjabi
P. & M./ Poll. & Maitl. Hist.	...	Pollock and Maitland's History of English Law
P. H.C.C.	...	Patna High Court Cases
P. W.N.	...	Patna Weekly Notes
P.	...	Law Reports, Probate Division (1891)
P.2d	...	Pacific Reporter, 2nd Series, US-Alaska
P.C.	...	Privy Council
P.J./ Pj.	...	Punjab
P.R.	...	Punjab Record (1866-1919)
P.W.N.	...	Patna Weekly Notes (1936)
Pac. Rep.	...	Pacific Reporter
Pak.	...	Pakistan
Para.	...	Paragraph
Park	...	Park on Marine Insurance
Park. Ins.	...	Parkers Insurance
Pat. L. Tim./Pat.L.T.	...	Patna Law Times
Pat. L.W./P.L.W.	...	Patna Law Weekly
Pat.	...	Indian Law Reports, Patna Series (1922)
Per.	...	Persian
PLD	...	Pakistan Legal Decisions
Plowd. Rep.	...	Plowden Report
Plowd.	...	Plowden (1550-1580)
Pom. Eq. Jur.	...	Pomeroy's Equity Jurisprudence
Prov.	...	proviso
pt.	...	part
Pun. L.R./P.L.R.	...	Punjab Law Reporter

Pun. W.R./ PWR	...	Punjab Weekly Reporter
Punj. L.J.	...	Punjab Law Journal

Q

Q.B. (preceded by date)	...	Law Reports, Queen's Bench (1891-1901, 1952)
Q.B.	...	Queen's Bench Reports (1841-1852)
Q.B.D.	...	Law Reports, Queen's Bench Division (1875-1890)
QD	...	Quinquennial Digest

R

R., r.	...	Rule.
R.D.	...	Revenue Decisions
R.P.C.	...	Reports of Patent, Design, and Trade Mark Cases
R.R.	...	Revised Reports by Sir Fredrick Pollock
R.S.C.	...	Revised Statutes of Canada
R.S.C.	...	Rules of the Supreme Court
R.T.R.	...	Road Traffic Reports
Rae, Contem. Socialism	...	Contemporary Socialism by John Rae
Raj. Cri. C.	...	Rajasthan Criminal Cases
Raj. L.W./R.L.W.	...	Rajasthan Law Weekly
Raj.	...	Indian Law Reports, Rajasthan Series (1951)
Rang. L.R.	...	Rangoon Law Reports
Rang. or I.L.R. Rang.	...	Indian Law Reports, Rangoon Series
Rapalje & L.L. Dict.	...	Rapalje & Law Latin Dictionary
RCL	...	Ruling case law
Re. C.R./R.C.R	...	Rent Control Reports
Ref.	...	referred
Reg.	...	Regulation
Rel. on	...	Relied on
Rep.	...	Coke's Reports (1572-1617)
Rettie	...	The same as Session Cases, Scottish, 4th series (1873-1898)
Rev. L.R.	...	Revenue Law Reporter
Rev. Rul.	...	Revenue Rulings
Ry. & Can. Traffic Cases	...	Railway and Canal Traffic Cases: cp. B. & Macn. (see Traffic Cas.) (1855-1950)

S

S. Ct	...	Supreme Court Reporter
S. E.	...	South Eastern Reporter
S.	...	Sanskrit
S.	...	Section (of Act of Parliament)
SCC	...	Supreme Court Cases
S.C.J.	...	Supreme Court Journal
S.C.R.	...	Canada Law Reports (Supreme Court)

S.C.R.	...	Supreme Court Reports
S.C.T.	...	Service Cases Today
SCW	...	Supreme Court Weekly
S.J.	...	Solicitor's Journal
S.L.R.	...	Services Law Reporter
S.R.A.	...	Specific Relief Act (1 of 1877)
STC	...	Sales Tax Cases
S.T.C.	...	Simon's Tax Cases
Salk.	...	Salkeld (1689-1712)
SC	...	Supreme Court
Sch., Sched.	...	Schedule
Shumaker	...	The Cyclopedic Law Dictionary
ss.	...	sections
Stat.	...	Statutes
Steele, Tattler	...	Sir Richard Steel's journal, "The Tatler"
Steph. Com./Steph. Comm.	...	Stephen's Commentaries on English Law
Steph. Cr. Law	...	Stephen's Digest of the Criminal Law
Steph. Pl.	...	Stephen on Pleading
Stimson L. Gloss.	...	Stimson Law Glossary
Str.	...	Stranger's Reports (1795) K.B.
Stroud	...	Stroud's Dictionary of Words and Phrases
Stubbs, Const. Hist.	...	The Constitutional History of England by William Stubbs
Sug. Pow.	...	Sugden on Powers
Sug. V. & P.	...	Sugden on Vendors and Purchasers
Sund./Sundaram Iyer Mal. Law	...	Sundaram Iyer's Malabar Law
Sup. Ct. R.	...	Supreme Court Rules
Supp	...	Supplementary
Supreme	...	Supreme Today
Sweet Dict.	...	Sweet Dictionary
Syn.	...	Synonyms

T

T.C.	...	Tax Cases
T.C.	...	Travancore-Cochin
T.C.L.R. or Trav.-Co. L.R.	...	Travancore Cochin Law Reports
T.L.R. (preceded by date)	...	Times Law Reports
T.P. Act	...	Transfer of Property Act, 1882
T.R.	...	Taxation Reports
T.R.	...	Term Reports, same as Durnford and East (1785-1800)
Tam.	...	Tamil
Tam	...	Tamlyn's English Rolls Court Reports
Tax. L.R. (NOC) (All) (Bom)	...	Taxation Law Reports (Notes of Cases) Allahabad, Bombay (Published by A.I.R.)

Tax. L.R.	...	Taxation Law Reports
Tel.	...	Telugu
Tel	...	The Telegram, London
Termes de la Ley	...	Terms de la Ley—The edition being used was published in London and printed by Jo. Beale & Ric. Hearne for the benefit of all that are studious in the Common Laws of this Realme, 1641; "a book of great antiquity and accuracy" (per Bayley J., 5 B. & C. 229). If any word is not found in the edition mentioned, then refer to that of 1721
Tidd's Prac.	...	Tidd's Practice
Tit.	...	Title
TLR	...	Texas Law Review
Tomlin	...	Tomlin Law Dictionary
Touch	...	The Touch-Stone, commonly cited as Shep Touch

U

U.P.	...	Uttar Pradesh
U.S.	...	United States Supreme Court Reports
Uttar.	...	Uttaranchal Cases

V

v.	...	Versus
V.C.	...	Vice-Chancellor
V.R.	...	Victorian Reports
Vin. Abr	...	Viner's Abridgment
Vol.	...	Volume

W

W. Va.	...	West Virginia Reports
W.L.N. (U.C.)	...	Weekly Law Notes (Unreported Cases)
W.L.N.	...	Weekly Law Notes
W.L.R. (preceded by date)	...	Weekly Law Reports
Wallace, or Wall.	...	Wallace's United States Supreme Court Reports
Washb. R.P.	...	Washburn on Real Property
Webs. Dict.	...	Websters Dictionary
Webs. Imp. Dictionary	...	Websters Imperial Dictionary
Webs.	...	Webesters
Weir. / Weir Cr. Rul.	...	Weir's Criminal Rulings
Wend./ Wend N.Y.	...	Wendell's New York Reports
Wharton	...	Wharton Law Lexicon
Wharton. Cr. L.	...	Wharton's Criminal Law
WTO	...	World Trade Organisation
www.	...	World Wide Web

Contents

The Author: An Immortal Soul v
Publisher's Note vii
Abbreviations ix

A 1
B 127
C 179
D 349
E 447
F 529
G 595
H 625
I 655
J 757
K 781
L 791
M 843
N 915
O 953
P 997
Q 1139
R 1149
S 1227
T 1333
U 1389
V 1413
W 1435
X 1465
Y 1467
Z 1469

CONCISE LAW DICTIONARY

A

A aver et tener. (*Fr. Law*) To have and to hold.

A capite ad calcem. From top to bottom; from head to heel.

A case open to appeal. Means not only a case in which an appeal is always provided, but also a case where appeal is provided on certain grounds. [CPC (5 of 1908), O. XLIII, R. 1(*d*)]

A coelo usque ad centrum. (*Lat.*) From the heavens to the centre of the earth.

A communi observantia non est recedendum. From common observance there should be no departure. (*Burrill, L. Dict*, 2 Coke, 74)

A contrario sensu. (*Lat.*) Literally, in the opposite sense or view; equivalent to the common expression, on the other hand.

A Corporation established by or under a Central, Provincial or State Act. The phrase 'a Corporation established by or under a Central, Provincial or State Act' is a standard phrase used in several enactments to denote a statutory corporation established or brought into existence by or under statute. For example, it is used in section 21(12)(b) of the Indian Penal Code, 1860 and section 2(c)(iii) of the Prevention of Corruption Act, 1988 and both these statutes provide that a person in the service of a 'Corporation established by or under a Central, Provincial or State Act' is a public servant.

In short the term refers to a statutory corporation as contrasted from a non-statutory corporation incorporated or registered under the Companies Act. *Dalco Engineering Private Ltd.* v. *Shree Satish Prabhakar Padhye*, AIR 2010 SC 1576.

A facto ad jus non datur consequentia. The inference from the fact to the law is not allowed. (*Halkerston Max. No.* 3; *Adam's Gloss.*)

A fortiori. An argument which concludes that something does take place, because causes much weaker than those which operate to bring it about are effective in another case.

By a stronger reason; much more; used to denote an argument to the effect that because one ascertained fact exists, therefore another, which is included in it, or analogous to it, and which is less improbable, must also necessarily exist. All the more; from a stronger reason.

A judgment in *personam* and a judgment in *rem*. The difference between "a judgment in *personam*" and "a judgment in *rem*" was pointed out by Chief Justice Holmes in *Tyler* v. *Judges of the Court of Registration,* (1990) 175 Mass 71 : 179 US 405, where he said : If the technical object of the suit is to establish a claim against some particular person, with a judgment which generally, in theory at least, binds his body, or to bar some individual claim or objection, so that only certain persons are entitled to be heard in defence, the action is in *personam*, although it may concern the right to, or possession of, a tangible thing. If, on the other hand, the object is to bar indifferently all who might be minded to make an object of any sort against the right sought to be established, and if any one in the world has a right to be heard on the strength of alleging facts which, if true, show an inconsistent interest, the proceeding is in *rem*. *Sankaran Govindan* v. *Lakshmi Bharathi,* AIR 1974 SC 1764, 1778 : (1975) 3 SCC 351.

A-la-carte. With reference to offering of a TV channel means offering the channel individually on a standalone basis. [Standards of Quality of Service (Digital Addressable Cable TV Systems) Regulations (12 of 2012), Regn. 2(c); Telecommunication (Broadcasting and Cable Services) Interconnection (Digital Addressable Cable Television Systems) Regulations, 2012, Regn. 2(d)].

A latere. Collateral. Used in this sense in speaking of the succession to property from, on, or at the side collaterally.

A mensa et thoro. From table and bed; from bed and board. A kind of divorce, which is rather a separation of the parties by law, than a dissolution of the marriage, and what is called judicial separation in Indian Law. (*Bouvier*)

Judicial separation; descriptive of a limited form of divorce.

'A mensa at thoro' (from table to bed) describes a partial divorce in a case in which the marriage was just and lawful; but, for some supervening cause, such as the commission of adultery or cruelty by the husband or wife, it becomes improper or impossible for them to live together. It only caused the separation of husband and wife; but did not dissolve the marriage. *R.S. Manual Raju* v. *Mary Sava,* AIR 1982 Kant 235, 236. [Indian Divorce Act (4 of 1869), S. 22]

A morte testatoris. (*Lat.*) From the death of the testator. A legacy or bequest does not vest in the legatee or beneficiary until this event takes place; and therefore, where the legatee predeceases the testator, the legacy lapses, and the legatee's successor takes no benefit under the bequest, unless there be a conditional institution of the legatee's heirs. (*Trayner*)

A multo fortiori. By far the stronger reason, right or equity.

A non posse ad non esse sequitur argumentum necessarie negative, licet non affirmative. A maxim meaning, from the impossibility of a thing you may infer its nonexistence, but not from the possibility of a thing, its existence.

A pari. (*Lat.*) Equally; In like manner.

A person. In view of S. 13, General Clauses Act (10 of 1897), the presence of the words, 'a person' in singular does not exclude the possibility of a joint information by two or more persons. *Nathu* v. *State,* AIR 1958 All 467, 471.

A person who has been a judge. The phrase 'a person who has been a Judge' means a person who has, at some time, held office as a judge, but that it does not necessarily mean that the person must be holding office as a judge at the time of his appointment as a member of the tribunal. *Mubarak Mazdoor* v. *K.K. Banerji,* AIR 1958 All 323, 324. [Representation of the People Act (43 of 1951), S. 86(3)]

A piratis et latronibus capta dominium non mutant. (*Maxim*) Things taken or captured by pirates and robbers do not change their ownership. (*Adam*)

A posteriori. (*Lat.*) Argument from the consequence to the antecedent.

A prendre. A right to take something out of the soil of another is a profit *a prendre*.

Rightfully taken from the soil; used in the phrase *profit a prendre* which differs from easement which confers no interest in the land itself.

A priori. An argument founded on analogy, or abstract considerations.

Deductive; from earlier *i.e.* original or antecedent; argument from antecedent to the consequent; not empirical.

From the cause to the effect; from what goes before— deductive reasoning— "an argument derived from considerations of an abstract character or which has but a remote and possibly indirect (though none the less real) bearing upon the point under discussion, is called an argument a *priori*, whereas an argument derived from actual observation, or other direct consideration is called an argument a *posteriori*. (*Mozley and Whiteley*)

A-shares. Shares with rights different from those legally attached to *ordinary shares*. There are also B-shares, C-shares, *etc.* The term is frequently used to describe *nonvoting shares*. (*Banking*)

A spoliatus debet ante omnia restitui. (*Broom*). A maxim meaning "a person who is wrongfully deprived of his property is entitled to the restitution of his property before all others."

A tempore cujus contrarii memoria non existet. From time of which memory to the contrary does not exist.

A verbis legis non est recedendum. (*Maxim*) You must not vary the words of a statute. (*Byrne*)

From the words of the law there is not any departure. A Court of law will not make any interpretation contrary to the express letter of a statute. "Nothing is more unfortunate than a disturbance of the plain language of the Legislature by the attempt to use equivalent words".

A vinculo matrimonii. Divorce which effects a complete dissolution of the marriage contract.

Aadhaar ecosystem. "Aadhaar ecosystem" includes enrolling agencies, Registrars, requesting entities, offline verification-seeking entities and any other entity or group of entities as may be specified by regulations. [Aadhaar (Targeted Delivery of Financial and other Subsidies and Services) Act (18 of 2016), section 2(*aa*)].

Aadhaar number means a 12 digit unique identification number generated and issued to an individual by the Unique Identification Authority of India (UIDAI) after deduplication of demographic and biometric information pertaining to that individual. [Right to Fair Compensation and Transparency in Land Acquisition, Rehabilitation and Resettlement (Compensation, Rehabilitation and Resettlement and Development Plan) Rules, 2015, R. 2(a)].

Aadhaar number holder. Means an individual who has been issued an Aadhaar number under this Act. [Aadhaar (Targeted Delivery of Financial and other Subsidies, Benefits and Services) Act (18 of 2016), S. 2(b)].

"Aadhar". Means, in english, "foundation" or "base". [*K.S. Puttaswamy* v. *Union of India,* (2019) 1 SCC 1, para 1].

"Aadhaar Letter". Means a document for conveying the Aadhaar number to a resident. [Aadhaar (Sharing of Information) Regulations, 2016, Regn. 2(1)(b)].

Ab abusu ad usum non valet consequentia. From the abuse of a thing you can draw no conclusion as to its legitimate use. (*Byrne; Broom*)

Ab antiquo. Of old; of an ancient date.

Ab assuetis. If a person neglects to insist on his right, he is deemed to have abandoned it.

Ab assuetis non fit injuria. (*Maxim*) From things to which we are accustomed, no legal wrong results. (*Wharton; Ame. Cyc.; Broom*)

Ab initio. From the beginning; from the first act; from the inception. An agreement is said to be "void *ab initio*" if it has at no time had any legal validity. (*Black*)

Ab intestato. From an intestate, in case of intestacy; used as the opposite of *ex testamento* (from, by, or under a will).

'Succession *ab intestato*' means succession to the property of a person who has not made his will.

ABA transit number. The code number assigned to a bank pursuant to the numerical transit system devised by the American Bankers Association to facilitate collection of transit items (cheques and other items on out-of-town banks). (*Banking*)

Abadi deh. It refers to cultivable lands which are inhabited by the villagers. These areas are also called *phirni*. They are usually demarcated on the revenue maps/*shajra* in red ink or lal dora, within which a departure from the prescription of strictly agricultural user is permitted. *Sarjeet Singh* v. *Hari Singh*, (2015) 1 SCC 760, para 5.

Abandon. To withdraw ourselves from an object totally; to lay aside all care for it; to forsake, to renounce.

To give up; to leave without help; to surrender control or possession, frequently with the knowledge that the thing abandoned is left for the mercy of someone or something else. [T. P. Act (4 of 1882), S. 68 (2)].

Abandon (a child). "Abandon or expose" as child "includes a wilful omission to take charge of the child on the part of a person legally bound to do so, and any mode of dealing with it calculated to leave it exposed to risk without protection."

Abandoned. In the context in which it occurs in S. 418(1), the meaning which can reasonably be attached to the word "abandoned" is "let loose" in the sense of being 'left unattended' and certainly not 'ownerless'. *Kanwar Singh* v. *Delhi Administration*, AIR 1965 SC 871, 874. [Delhi Municipal Corporation Act (66 of 1957), S. 418(1)]

Abandoned animal. An animal was "abandoned" within the meaning of section 1(1) of the Protection of Animals Act, 1911 (c. 27), as applied by the Abandonment of Animals Act, 1960, if the owner, at the time of leaving the animal, had totally disregarded his duty to make arrangements for the welfare of the animal. (*Hunt v Duckering, The Times,* March 23, 1993)

Abandoned child. It means a child deserted by his biological or adoptive parents or guardians, who has been declared as abandoned by the Committee after due inquiry. [Juvenile Justice (Care and Protection of Children) Act, 2015 (2 of 2016), S. 2(1)].

Abandoned property. The expression 'abandoned property' or to use the more familiar term '*bona vacantia*' comprises properties of two different kinds, those which come in by escheat and those over which no one has a claim. *Bombay Dyeing* v. *State of Bombay*, AIR 1958 SC 328, 339.

Abandonment. Abandonment means the giving up of a thing; the external act by which the intention is carried into effect. Abandonment is the relinquishment of a right, the giving up of something to which one is entitled.

'Abandonment' means the act of intentionally relinquishing a known right absolutely and unconditionally and without reference to any particular person or persons. When the expression 'abandonment' is used in relation to property, it signifies the complete relinquishment of title, possession or claim, virtually indicating that the property is being thrown away. Abandonment is not equivalent to inaction. *Kanhiya Shanker* v. *Mohabata Sedhu,* AIR 1960 Pun 494.

The action of abandoning. [Gift-tax Act (18 of 1958), S. 4(c) and Constitution of India, Art. 39(*f*)].

HINDU LAW—The inactivity or the passive attitude of a person has never in law been interpreted as an act of abandonment. Abandonment is a positive act. A man must expressly say that he gives up his right. If he remains quiet it cannot be said that he is forsaking his title to property or his interest in any other manner.

INTENTION IN ABANDONMENT. In determining whether one has abandoned his property the intention is the first and paramount object of inquiry. There can be no abandonment without the intention to abandon. Thus, property sunk in a steamboat and unclaimed for twenty-three years is derelict.

AS APPLIED TO A HOLDING—Among tenants mere long absence and settling abroad does not amount to "Abandonment."

AS APPLIED TO EASEMENTS—it is the voluntary and permanent relinquishment by the dominant owner of a right of easement.

IN PATENT LAW—As applied to inventions abandonment is the giving up of his rights by the inventor.

OF A TRADE-MARK—It can be inferred only from intention; intention to abandon must be shown : mere evidence of non-user is insufficient.

IN THE CUSTOMS LAW—Abandonment is the giving up of an article by the importer to avoid payment of the duty.

Abandonment and non-user. The abandonment of an easement necessarily implies non-user. But non-user by itself does not create abandonment how long it continues.

Abandonment of copyright. A copyright holder like an author can surrender his rights in his work and allow the public to enjoy it.

Abandonment of invention. An inventor's abandonment of his right to a patent may be evidenced by the express and voluntary declaration of the inventor. It may be inferred from negligence or unexplained delay in making application for patent, or it may be declared as a consequence of the inventor's concealing his invention and delaying application for patent in an endeavor to extend the term of the patent protection beyond the period fixed by statute. *Electric Storage Battery Co.* v. *Shimadzu,* 307 US 5 : 83 LED 1071 : 59 SCT 675.

Abandonment of plea. CPC (5 of 1908), S. 115, O. XLI, R. 1. It is not enough for a party to raise objections in the memorandum of appeal or revision. The objections should also be pressed at the time of hearing arguments and if they are not pressed, the presumption is that they were abandoned by the party. *Rodu* v. *Board of Revenue*, AIR 1953 Raj 155, 157.

Abatable nuisance. A nuisance, practically susceptible of being suppressed, or extinguished, or rendered harmless, and whose continued existence is unauthorized.

Abate. To diminish or take away.

To put an end to; to curtail [CPC (5 of 1908), O. XXII, R. 1] to come to naught. [Sick Textile Undertakings (Taking Over of Management) Act (72 of 1972), S. 14].

Abatement. Removal or destruction, (as) of a nuisance; failure; premature end, suspension or diminution, (as) of an action or of a legacy.

"ABATEMENT" means, in respect of any chargeable accounting period, ending on or before the 31st day of March, 1947 a sum which bears to a sum equal to—

(a) in the case of a company, not being a company deemed for the purposes of Section 9 to be a firm, six per cent of the capital of the company on the first day of the said period computed in accordance with Schedule II, or one lakh of rupees, whichever is greater, or

(b) in the case of a firm having—

(i) not more than two working partners, one lakh of rupees, or

(ii) three working partners, one and a half of rupees, or

(iii) four or more working partners, two lakh of rupees, or

(c) in the case of a Hindu undivided family, two lakhs of rupees, or

(d) in any other case, one lakh of rupees,— The same proportion as the said period bears to the period of one year and, in respect of any chargeable accounting period beginning after the 31st day of March, 1947, such sum as may be fixed by the annual Finance Act. [Business Profits Tax Act (21 of 1947), S. 2(1)]

The action of abating; being abated. [CPC (5 of 1908), O. XXII, R. 1]; decrease [Specific Relief Act (47 of 1963), S. 12(3)(b)(i)].

OF AN ACTION OR SUIT : In civil law an abatement of a suit is a complete termination of it. Abatement of a matter or cause is caused by the same becoming defective on account of the death of the parties materially interested. (*Ency. of the Laws of England*)

A suspension or termination of proceedings for want of proper parties or due to some technical defect.

The abatement of the main action abates proceedings ancillary or collateral to it.

IN CRIMINAL LAW : Abatement of proceedings connotes their termination without any decision on merits and without the assent of the prosecutor. (*Ency. of the Laws of England*)

IN REVENUE LAW : Abatement is a deduction from or refunding of duties on goods damaged during importation or in store.

Abatement of action/suit. A suspension or termination of proceedings in an action for want of proper parties or owing to a technical defect.

Abatement of freehold. The entry of a stranger upon land after the owner's death, prior to the entry of the heir.

Abatement of legacies. The proportional diminution or reduction of the pecuniary legacies when the funds or assets out of which such legacies are payable are not sufficient to pay them in full.

Abatement of nuisance. Removal or destruction of a nuisance and not its mere prevention.

Abatement, Plea in. A plea taken with reference to actions at law to the effect that the action is utterly dead and cannot be revived except by commencing a new action.

Abator. An occupier without legal title.

Abbreviation. The act of abbreviating, shortening, reducing or contracting; the means used to abbreviate.

A shortened form of a written word or phrase used for brevity in place of the whole. [Indian Evidence Act (1 of 1872), S. 98].

ABC agreement. In a US brokerage company, an agreement with an employee detailing the rights of the company if it buys a membership of the New York Stock Exchange on his or her behalf. (*Investment*)

Abdicate. To renounce; discard; disclaim; refuse anything.

"The word 'abdicate' doth naturally and properly signify entirely to renounce, throw off, disown, relinquish anything, so as to have nothing further to do with it; and that whether it be done by express words, or in writing, or by doing such acts as are inconsistent with the holding and retaining of the thing." (Speech of Lord SOMERS delivered in 1688 with reference to the abdication or vacating the throne by James II of England.)

Abdication. Abdicate is to renounce, discard, disclaim, or refuse anything. Abdication is the renunciation or giving up of an office by a magistrate or person in office before the term of service has expired. (*Jacob; Tomlin*)

Abduct. To take away (especially a person) by fraud or force; to induce a person to go from any place, by force or deceitful means. [IPC (45 of 1860), S. 362]

Abduction. Abduction in general signifies the act of illegally taking or leading away, carrying off by force a child, ward, voter or wife. This may be by fraud, persuasion, or open violence. (*Blackstone cited in Webster*)

In a more restricted sense it is confined to the taking of females for the purpose of marriage, concubinage, or prostitution. (*Bouvier*)

Whoever by force compels or by any deceitful means induces, any person to go from any place, is said to abduct that person. [IPC (45 of 1860), S. 362] [(w.e.f. 1-7-2024) repealed and replaced by Bharatiya Nyaya Sanhita, 2023 (45 of 2023), section 138]

The action of abducting. [IPC (45 of 1860), S. 362].

Abductor. One who abducts.

Abearance. Conduct; behaviour; demenour.

Aberration, Mental. Unsoundness of the mind, especially unsoundness insufficient to constitute insanity.

Abet. To aid, to encourage, countenance,—formerly used in a good, but now chiefly in a bad sense (*Webs*).—The word "abet" is generally used with the word "aid," as in the phrase "to aid and to abet." (*Burrill L. Dict.*). (See Indian Penal Code (45 of 1860), Ss. 107 to 114; General Clauses Act (10 of 1897), S. 3).

"ABET," with its grammatical variations and cognate expressions, includes,—

(i) the communication or association with any person or class of persons who is engaged in assisting in any manner terrorists or disruptionists;

(ii) the passing on, or publication of, without any lawful authority, any information likely to assist the terrorists or disruptinists, and the passing on, or publication of, or distribution of, any document or matter obtained from terrorists or disruptionists;

(iii) the rendering of any assistance, whether financial or otherwise, the terrorists or disruptionists. [TADA Act (28 of 1987) (*repealed*), S. 2(1)(a)].

SYNONYMOUS WITH "AID"—The words "aid" and "abet", in legal phrase, are pretty nearly synonyms of each other. They comprehend all assistance rendered by acts, words of encouragement or support, or by presence, actual or constructive, to render assistance, should it become necessary. "Aid" does not imply guilty knowledge. "Abet" includes knowledge of wrongful purpose.

To instigate or encourage the commission of a crime. [IPC (45 of 1860), S. 107;General Clauses Act (10 of 1897), S. 3(1) and Income-tax Act (43 of 1961), S. 278].

Abetment. The action or fact of abetting. [*Expln.*, Indian Evidence Act (1 of 1872), S. 30; Income-tax Act (43 of 1961), S. 278 and IPC (45 of 1860), Ss. 89, fourthly, 107, 132, 135 and 138].

"Abetment" means certain amount of active suggestion or support to do the act. [*Pavan Kumar* v. *State of H.P.*, (2017) 7 SCC 780, para 34].

A mere reprimand or a word in a fit of anger will not earn the status of abetment. There be positive action that creates a situation for the victim to put an end to life. [*Pawan Kumar* v. *State of H.P.*, (2017) 7 SCC 780, para 43].

Abetment of an offence. A person abets an offence, who—

First.—Instigates any person to that offence; or

Secondly.—Engages with one or more other person or persons in any conspiracy for the doing of that offence, if an act or illegal omission takes place in pursuance of that conspiracy, and in order to the doing of that offence; or

Thirdly.—Intentionally aids, by any act or illegal omission, the doing of that offence.

Explanation I.—A person who, by wilful misrepresentation, or by wilful concealment of a material fact, which he is bound to disclose, voluntarily causes or procures, or attempts to cause or procure a thing to be done, is said to instigate the doing of that offence.

Explanation II.—Whoever, either prior to or at the time of commission of an act, does anything in order to facilitate the commission of that act, and thereby facilitates the commission thereof, is said to aid the doing of that act.

Explanation III.—Whoever employs, harbours, receives or transports a child, by means of threat or use of force or other forms of coercion, abduction, fraud, deception, abuse of power or of a position, vulnerability or giving or receiving of payments or benefits to achieve the consent of a person having control over another person, for the purpose of any offence under this Act, is said to aid the doing of that act. [Protection of Children from Sexual Offences Act (32 of 2012), S. 16].

Abettor. One who abets the commission of a crime. [IPC (45 of 1860), Ss. 108 and 445, firstly]

One who promotes or procures the commission of a crime. (*Bouvier*)

The words "ABETTOR", "ACCOMPLICE", "ACCESSORY" and "AIDER" are often used indiscriminately and interchangeably by Courts and text-book writers on criminal law. But an "ACCOMPLICE" may be one of the principal actors, or an aider and abettor, or an accessory before the fact. The word includes in its meaning all persons who participate in the commission of a crime, whether they so participate as principals, aiders and abettors, or accessories before the fact. It is commonly applied to a witness, and is not so often used in describing a person accused of crime. Usually when persons are spoken of by Courts in connection with the commission of an offence, they are mentioned as principals, accessories, or aiders or abettors, but if in the course of the trial, either of these persons is put upon the witness-stand, and a question comes up as to the necessity of corroborating his testimony, he will be spoken of as an accomplice, although he may in fact be a joint principal, or an accessory or an aider and abettor. (*Ame. Rul. Case Law*)

Abeyance, or abbayance is what is in expectation, suspense, remembrance, and intendment of law. By a principle of law, in every land there is a fee-simple in somebody, or it is in abeyance; that is, though for the present it be in no man, yet it is in expectancy, belonging to him that is next to enjoy the land (1 Inst. 342) (See *Plowd Rep.* 547; *Tomlin* See also 1 Ency. 27.)

Abeyance of seisin. An interruption in the tenancy of a freehold.

Abeyance or **abbayance** is what is in expectation, suspense, remembrance, and intendment of law. (*Tomlin*)

"Abeyance" means "in expectation", to "expect" for when a person dieth, we say that the freehold is in abeyance, because a successor is in expectation to take it. So it is a maxim, in law, that "of every land there is Fee Simple in some man, or else it lies in abeyance." (*Cowell; Termes de la Ley*)

Abide. To await; to acquiesce in; to conform to; to accept as valid; to take the consequences of.

Abide by. To adhere; to obey; to accept the consequences of; to stand to; acquiesce in; conform to.

Abide by decision. The words 'abide by decision' without more, were to imply an abandonment or giving up of the right of appeal. *Edapalli Kotamma* v. *Nallapaneni Mangamma,* AIR 1957 AP 700, 704. [CPC (5 of 1908), S. 96]

Ability. In a broad sense "ability" means the state or condition of being able; power or capacity to do an act or competence in any occupation; capacity, skill, means, or other qualifycation for doing an act (*Cent. Dict.*) but sometimes used in statutes to mean rather "pecuniary ability".

Abjuration. A forswearing or renouncing by oath.

Abjure. To retract, to renounce or abnegate a position upon oath. (*Wharton*)

Able-bodied seaman. In maritime law, a merchant seaman who is qualified for all seaman's duties.

Abnegation. Self denial; adjuration; renunciation.

Abnormal. Not conforming to rule; contrary to any law or system.

Abnormality of mind. Means a state of mind so different from that of ordinary human beings that the reasonable man would term it abnormal. Abnormality substantially impairs the mental responsibility.

"Abnormality of mind" has to be contrasted with "defect of reason" in the "McNaughten rules". (*R.* v. *McNaughten*, 10 Cl. & F. 200).

Abnormally dangerous activity. An undertaking that cannot be performed safely even if reasonable care is used while performing it, and for which the actor may face strict liability for any harm caused.

Abode. Place where a person dwells.

One's place of residence or habitation for the time being; a place of stay, or dwelling, a habitation.

Abolish. To annul or destroy; to make void; to terminate, or put an end to (as) to abolish laws; to abolish slavery. *Abolish, Repeal, Abrogate, Revoke, Nullify, Annul.* As to distinguishing these words, see *Webs. Dict.*

To demolish or destroy (mainly of institutions, customs and practices).

Abolition. Act of abolishing; an annulling; abrogation (as) the abolition of laws or ordinances. (*Bouvier*)

To destroy, extinguish, abrogate or annihilate.

Abominable crime. Crime of sodomy or bestiality.

Abortion. The delivery or expulsion of the human foetus prematurely, (*i.e.,*) before it is yet capable of sustaining life (*Abbot L. Dict.*) *i.e.*, at any period of gestation short of the full term. [*See* IPC (45 of 1860), S. 312]

To cause an abortion is unlawful, unless it is done in good faith for the purpose of saving the life of the mother. (As to the medical aspects of abortion. [*see* Luff. Forensic Medicine, (1895), Vol. II, pp. 173-187; Taylor, Medical Jurisp., 5th Ed. (1905)]

DISTINGUISHED FROM MISCARRIAGE. The word "miscarriage" is often used as synonymous with and equivalent to "abortion." (*Abbott*)

It has been applied to the expulsion of the foetus at any time during the period of gestation. "Miscarriage," signifies, in the strict medical sense, an expulsion of the foetus from the womb within the first six weeks after conception. (*Abbott*)

Criminal abortion is premeditated or intentional abortion procured, at any period of pregnancy, by artificial means, and solely for the purpose of preventing the birth of a living child, the same not being necessary to save the mother's life.

Abortive. Fruitless; unsuccessful; miscarrying; failing in its effect (as) abortive attempt.

Fruitless. [Indian Telegraph Act (13 of 1885), S. 7(2)(i)(b)]

Abortive trial. The term is used to denote a trial where the case has gone off and no verdict has been pronounced without the fault, contrivance, or management of the parties.

Above-the-line expenditure. Alternative name for *current expenditure*, so called because these items are recorded before the total in a statement of account. (*Banking*)

Abrasion. (*Med. Jur.*) The breaking of the skin.

Superficial injury to skin or mucous membrane from scrapping or rubbing.

Abridge. To abridge is to curtail; to shorten; to make shorter in words, so as to retain the sense and substance. (*Tomlin*)

To make shorter; to curtail; to diminish. [Constitution of India, Art. 13(2) and Art. 31(B)].

Abridged prospectus. Means a memorandum containing such salient features of a prospectus as may be specified by the Securities and Exchange Board by making regulations in this behalf. [S. 2(1) of the Companies Act, 2013 (18 of 2013)]

Abridgment. A large work contracted into a narrow compass.

Abrogate. To put an end to; to set aside; revoke.

To abolish by official, authoritative or formal action; to annul a formal law by an act of the legislative power. [Navy Act (62 of 1957), S. 4].

Abrogation. Means the act of abrogating; the annulment or repeal of a law by authority of the legislative power. (*Burril*) To abrogate is to annul or take away anything. To abrogate a law is to lay aside or repeal it. (*Tomlin*)

A law is *abrogated* when it is totally annulled; it is *derogated* from when only a part is abrogated. (*Bouvier*)

Abscond. To hide; to depart clandestinely.

It is an act of insolvency if done with intent to defeat or delay creditors.

To hide away, especially to escape arrest; to go out of the jurisdiction of the Court; to conceal oneself in order to avoid legal process or to escape arrest. [Indian Evidence Act (1 of 1872), S. 8 ill. (h)].

If a person before the legal process could be issued somehow or other comes to know of the issue of such a process or anticipates the issue of the process and quits the country he can be said to have absconded. *K.T.M.S. Abdul Cader* v. *Union of India,* AIR 1977 Mad 386, 399 (FB). [CrPC 1973, (2 of 1974), S. 82(1)]

The term "abscond" has been considered as equivalent to the term "conceal". It is not synonymous with absent.

Absconder. One who absconds; one who hides to escape a legal process.

Absconding. "Absconding" does not necessarily mean absconding from one's residence although usually when a person is hiding from his place of residence he is said to abscond. The primary meaning of the word is "to hide". A person may hide even in his place of residence or away from it and in either case he will be absconding when he does so.

Absconding by person released on bail. Failure, without reasonable cause, by one who has been released on bail in criminal proceedings, to surrender to custody.

Absconding person. A person against whom a warrant has been issued and who has absconded so that such warrant cannot be executed. [CrPC, 1973 (2 of 1974), Ss. 82 and 83]

Absence. Means non-appearance; opposed to presence.

(1) The state of being away from one's usual place of residence.

(2) A failure to appear, or to be available and reachable, when expected.

(3) Louisiana law. The state of being on absent person.—Also termed (in sense 3) absentia." [Black's Law Dictionary as cited in *Abuzar Hossain* v. *State of West Bengal*, (2012) 10 SCC 489, para 45].

Being away from a place or person; time of being away; nonexistence or lack of; inattention due to thought of other things. [Concise Oxford Dictionary as cited in *Abuzar Hossain* v. *State of W.B.*, (2012) 10 SCC 489, para 45].

With regard to a lawsuit, it means non-appearance in the suit, and not absence without knowledge or notice of the suit.

The word "absence" under Section 498, IPC (45 of 1860), means absence from the place and cannot be extended to include a case where the husband is present but is unable, owing to illness, to institute the prosecution himself. 'Absence' is opposed to 'appearance at a specified time'.

Being wanting or non-existing [T.P. Act (4 of 1882), S. 109]; the state of being absent or away. [IPC (45 of 1860), S. 108, *Expln*. 3, ill. (b) and S. 109, ill. (c)].

Absent. "Absent" does not connote that the person referred to was ever previously present. It denotes the act of not being in a particular place at the time referred to.

Not present; being away in another place [Representation of the People Act (43 of 1951), S. 26(1), *Prov.*]; a subordinate or a minor occupation [Industrial Disputes Act (14 of 1947), S. 2(j)]; being elsewhere [Navy Act (62 of 1957), S. 93(3)(a)].

Absent-mindedness. Preoccupied; Inattentive.

Absente reo. (*Lat.*) The defendant being absent.

Absentee landlord. A landlord who does not live on the leased premises and usually who lives far away.

Absentee voting. Practice of allowing a qualified voter who was unable to appear at the polls on election day, to vote.

Absentia ejus qui reipublicae causa abest neque ei neque alii damnosa esse debet. (*Lat.*) His absence, who is absent on account of the State, ought not to be injurious to him, or to another; or (less literally) no one should take injury or disadvantage from an absence occasioned by the service of the State.

Absoluta sententia expositore non indiget. (*Maxim*) Plain words require no explanation". "A Court may construe an Act of

Parliament but it may not distort it to make it accord with what the Court thinks to be reasonable. (*Altrincham Electric Supply Co. Ltd.* v. *Sale U.D.C.*, (1936), 154 LTR 379, p. 388, *per* Lord MACMILLAN.) (*Latin for Lawyers*)

Absolute. Complete, perfect, final, without any condition or limitation.

Unqualified; free from external restraint or limitation [T.P. Act (4 of 1882), S. 58 (c)]; free from doubt [Army Act (46 of 1950), S. 132(1)]; complete and outright [Indian Easements Act (5 of 1882), S. 15, para 4]; final and not liable to modification or termination. [Income-tax Act (43 of 1961), Second Sch., Item 6(2)].

Absolute assignment. The assignment that transfers the entire interest of assignor.

Absolute contraband. Munitions and other primary materials of war as distinguished from conditional contraband and free goods.

Absolute delivery. A delivery which is complete upon the actual transfer of the instrument from the grantor's possession. Usually it does not depend on recordation.

Absolute discharge. A mode of dealing with a person convicted of an offence where the Court, having regard to the circumstances, the nature of the offence, and the character of the offender, regards punishment as inexpedient and discharges him unconditionally. (*Britain*)

Absolute discretion. It was suggested that an absolute discretion was the equivalent of a right to make a purely arbitrary demand. It is not so. A discretion, although absolute, is nonetheless a discretion to be exercised with reference to the true position and with perhaps even a greater sense of responsibility in that it is within final limits. [*Diwan Chand Kirpa Ram & Co.* v. *Weld & Co.*, 88 IC 54 : 1925 PC 150 (154) : 1925 MWN 459; *State of Gujarat* v. *Krishna Cinema,* AIR 1971 SC 1650, 1653 : (1970) 2 SCC 744. [Bombay Cinemas (Regulation) Act, 1953, S. 5(2)].

A discretion, although absolute, is none the less a discretion to be exercised with reference to the true position and with perhaps even a greater sense of responsibility in that it is within limits final.

Absolute duties. Duties to which there are no corresponding rights.

Absolute estate. Means a full and complete estate.

Absolute law. Supposed law of nature which though thought to be unchanging in principle, may vary in its application circumstantially.

Absolute liability. Liability irrespective of intention or negligence such as liability for the escape of dangerous things. Strict liability.

Absolute majority. A majority comprising more than half of the total number of votes. [Army Act (46 of 1950), S. 132(1)].

Absolute novelty. An invention which has not been published anywhere; prior publication destroys the novelty of a patent. (Patents)

Absolute owner. Person capable of disposing the whole interest in immoveable property although it is charged or encumbered. [First Sch., App. A, No. 13(2) and No. 35, CPC (5 of 1908)]

Absolute power. Unrestricted power.

Absolute privilege. A statement is said to be absolutely privileged when it is of such a nature that no action will lie for it, however false and defamatory it may be, and even though it is made maliciously, that is to say, from some improper motive.

Absolute privilege renders defendant absolutely immune from civil liability for his defamatory statements.

Absolute property. Means property uncontrolled by any conditions, complete in all its parts, free from any limitations.

Absolute right. A right set out in the European Convention on Human Rights that cannot be interfered with lawfully, no matter how important the public interest in doing so might be. Absolute rights include freedom of thought, conscience, and religion and the prohibitions on torture, inhuman treatment or punishment, and degrading treatment or punishment. (*Oxford Law Dictionary, 5th Edn., 2003*)

Absolute sententia expositore not indiget. Plain language does not need an interpreter.

Absolute title. Means complete title; a title which excludes all others not compatible with it.

Absolutely. In an absolute manner or degree; without condition or limitation. [T.P. Act (4 of 1882), Ss. 7, 67 and 135]; [Army Act (46 of 1950), S. 8(2)].

Absolution. Setting free from guilt or "release from a penalty. Absolution is, at any rate, a theological concept which implies an act of forgiving the sinner of his sins upon confession. [*MSR Leathers* v. *S. Palaniappan,* (2013) 1 SCC 177, para 26].

Absolutism. State or quality of being absolute.

Absolve. To release; to set free from some debt, obligation or responsibility. To absolve an offender means a remission of his punishment.

Absorb. To take in; to assimilate.

"**Absorbent cotton**" means cotton which is used for cleaning the skin or bathing wounds. [Oxford Dictionary of English as cited in *Mamta Surgical Cotton Industries, Rajasthan* v. *Assistant Commissioner (Anti-Evasion), Bhilwara, Rajasthan,* (2014) 4 SCC 87, para 46].

"Absorbent cotton" means "Cotton that has had the natural wax removed, making it absorbent and suitable for medical and cosmetic use as dressings or swabs". [Enearta Dictionary as cited in *Mamta Surgical Cotton Industries, Rajasthan* v. *Assistant Commissioner (Anti-Evasion) Bhilwara, Rajasthan,* (2014) 4 SCC 87, para 46].

Absorption. Absorption means to take in. On absorption an employee becomes part and parcel of the department absorbing him and partakes the same colour and character of the existing employees of the department.

Absque hoc. (*Lat.*) Without this.

Absque impetitione vasti. (*Lat.*) Without liability for waste.

Abstain. To keep oneself away (from); to with-old oneself from (participation or action). [Indian Contract Act (9 of 1872), S. 2(a)]

Abstention. The action of abstaining. [Employees State Insurance Act (34 of 1946), S. 2(20)].

Abstinence. The action or practice of abstaining. [Indian Contract Act (9 of 1872), S. 2(a)].

Abstract. A summary or an epitome. [Mines Act (35 of 1952), S. 62 and Companies Act (1 of 1956) replaced with Companies Act, 2013, S. 165(3)(c)].

Abstract of title. Means a memorandum a memorandum or concise statement of the conveyances and encumbrances which appear on the public records affecting the title to real property. The object of an abstract of title is to enable the purchaser, or his counsel, to pass readily upon the validity of the title in question.

Abstraction. 'Abstraction' means taking or appropriating. Energy may be dishonestly abstracted by artificial means or unauthorised devices. *Jaganath Singh* v. *Ramaswamy*, AIR 1966 SC 849, 851. [Indian Electricity Act (9 of 1910), S. 39] Act 9 of 1910 repealed and replaced by Act 36 of 2003.

Taking from with intent to injure or defraud. "Wrongful abstraction" is unauthorised and illegal taking or withdrawing of funds, *etc.*, and appropriation thereof to taker's benefit. (*Black*)

Absurd. Anything which is irrational, unnatural, or inconvenient obviously and flatly opposed to the manifest truth; inconsistent with the plain dictates of common sense.

Abundans cautela non nocet. (*Maxim*) Extreme caution does no harm. (*Abbott*), *Heydon's Case* 11 Co. Rep. 5a at 6b.

Abuse. That which is contrary to good order or established usage.

The word 'abuse' has a very wide meaning. Everything which is contrary to good order established by usage amount to 'abuse'. Physical or mental maltreatment also is an abuse. *Gaurav Jain* v. *Union of India,* (1997) 8 SCC 114, 127 : AIR 1997 SC 3021.

The word "abuse" means, misuse i.e. using his (public servant) position for something for which it is not intended. [*Edmund S. Lyngdoh* v. *State of Meghalaya,* (2016) 15 SCC 572, para 31].

As a noun "abuse" in its largest sense signifies ill use or improper treatment of another; application to wrong purpose (as) abuse of civil rights; abuse of power or of liberty; a corrupt practice (as) abuses of Government; abuse of the law; *as a verb* it signifies to injure, diminish in value, or wear away, by using improperly; to violate, ravish (as, abuse of woman—(*Webs.*)

The verb "abuse" is sometimes used as synonymous with "ravish", and as a noun "abuse" is defined as "violation", "rape." (*Webs.*)

The word "abuse" includes "misuse."

Abuse means misuse, *i.e.,* using his position for something for which it is not intended. *M. Narayan* v. *State of Kerala*, AIR 1963 SC 1116, 1118.

Misuse; improper use; perversion [CrPC 1973 (2 of 1974), S. 482]; to misuse; to take bad advantage of [Constitution of India, Art. 39(e)].

Abuse of discretion. An abuse of discretion is merely a discretion exercised to an end or purpose not justified by and clearly against reason and evidence.

It implies that the reasons given by the Court for its action are clearly untenable and unreasonable, that its action clearly amounts to denial of justice or is against conscience, reason and evidence. Discretion is abused when the judicial action is arbitrary, fanciful or unreasonable.

Abuse of female child. Is synonymous with rape or ravish.

Abuse of position. Abuse of position must necessarily be dishonest, so that it may be proved that the accused caused deliberate loss to the Department.

Abuse of process. Means the frivolous and vexatious use of legal proceedings.

Abuse of process of Court. Is the malicious and improper use of some regular legal proceedings to obtain an unfair advantage over an opponent.

The term is generally used in connection with action for using some process of the Court maliciously to the injury of another person.

Abuse of process of Court generally applies to proceeding wanting in bonafide and which is frivolous, vexatious or oppressive. Making use of the process of Court as a devise to help the jurisdiction of a civil Court is an abuse of the process of the Court.

Improper use of a regular legal process by which an unfair advantage is obtained by a party to the proceeding over an opponent. [CrPC 1973 (2 of 1974), S. 482]

Abusive. Tending to deceive; practicing abuse; prone to ill-treat by coarse, insulting words or harmful acts using ill treatment; injurious; improper; hurtful; offensive; reproachful.

Abusive tax shelter. Type of limited partnership in the USA that, according to the Internal Revenue Service, claims illegal deductions of tax, usually by inflating the real value of property that has been purchased. (*Business Term*)

Abut. To reach; to touch (*Abbot*); to touch at the end; be contiguous; join at a boundary. (*Webs.*)

Abuttals. The buttings and boundings of lands, east, west, north or south, with respect to the places by which they are limited and bounded. (*Jacob; Tomlin*)

Academic. Pertaining to college, university, or preparatory school. A question or issue which is not relevant to case or is premature or hypothetical. (*Black*)

Academic Council. Means the Academic Council of the University. [S. 2(a) of the Rajiv Gandhi National Aviation University Act, 2013 (26 of 2013); S. 3(a) of the Rani Lakshmi Bai Central Agricultural University Act, 2014 (10 of 2014); S. 3(a) of University of Allahabad Act, 2005 (26 of 2005)]

Academic freedom. Right to teach as one sees fit, but not necessarily the right to teach evil. The term encompasses much more than teaching-related speech rights of teachers.

Academic question. An issue which does not require answer or adjudication by Court. A hypothetical or moot question.

Academic staff. Means such categories of staff as are designated as academic staff by the Ordinances.

[S. 2(b) of the Rajiv Gandhi National Aviation University Act, 2013 (26 of 2013); S. 3(b) of the Rani Lakshmi Bai Central Agricultural University Act, 2014 (10 of 2014)]

Academy. Institution for learning. An association of experts in some particular branch of art, literature or science. (*Bouvier*)

Accedas ad curiam. (*Law Lat.*) You are to go to the Court.

Accede. To agree; ascent; consent, to a proposition on terms proposed by another.

Accelerated Cost Recovery System (ACRS). In the USA, an Internal Revenue Service system that permits an arbitrary recovery period to be employed in calculating deductions for depreciation, rather than an item's useful life. By allowing quicker recovery of the cost of an asset it encourages capital investment. (*International Accounting*)

Accelerated succession. Succession accelerated by surrender or extinction of any prior interests.

Acceleration. The shortening of the time for the vesting in possession of an expectant interest. (*Wharton; Bouvier 95*)

Acceleration clause. A provision or clause in a mortgage, note, bond, deed of trust, or other credit agreement, that required the maker, drawer or other obligor to pay part or all of the balance sooner than the date or dates specified for payment upon the occurrence of some event or circumstances described in the contract. Such clause operates when there has been a default such as non-payment of principal, interest, or failure to pay insurance premiums.

Acceleration of an estate. Is the shortening of the time for the vesting in possession of an expectant interest in an estate. (*Wharton*)

Accept. To take or receive with consenting mind. [Indian Contract Act (9 of 1872), S. 2(b)]

Acceptance. "Acceptance" is the receipt of a thing offered by another with an intention to retain it, as acceptance of a gift.

The action or fact of accepting; in its widest sense it is the act of assenting to an offer. [T.P. Act (4 of 1882), Ss. 35 and 112].

Acceptance of bill. The signification by the drawee of his assent to the order of a drawer.

Acceptance of bills of exchange. Implies a promise to pay the bill in money when due.

When a person on whom a bill is drawn puts his signature across the bill, with or without the word "accepted", he thereby engages to pay the bill when due.

Acceptance supra protest. Acceptance for honour. Situation that occurs when a bill of exchange is turned down (or protested) and is then accepted by another party, thereby saving honour of the drawer.

Acceptare. To accept; to assent; to assent to a promise made by another. (*Black*)

Acceptor. One who accepts a bill of exchange.

Acceptor for honour. When a bill of exchange has been noted or protested for nonacceptance or for better security and any person accepts it *supra protest* for honour of the drawer or of any one of the endorsers, such person is called an "acceptor for honour". [Negotiable Instruments Act (26 of 1881), S. 7].

Acceptor of bill of exchange. After the drawee of a bill has signed his assent upon the bill, or, if there are more parts thereof than one, upon one of such parts, and delivered the same or given notice of such signing to the holder or to some person on his behalf he is called the "acceptor". [Negotiable Instruments Act (26 of 1881), S. 7].

The person who accepts a bill of exchange (generally the drawee) or who engages to be primarily responsible for its payment. [Negotiable Instruments Act (26 of 1881), Ss. 41 and 42 and Indian Evidence Act (1 of 1872), S. 14].

Acceptor supra protest. One who accepts a protested bill of exchange on which he is not already liable for the honour of some party to the bill, the acceptor, being liable to the holder and all parties subsequent to the one for whose honour he accepts. [Negotiable Instruments Act (26 of 1881), S. 7].

Access. Access literally means approach or the means or power of approaching.

ACCESS with its grammatical variations and cognate expressions means gaining entry into, instructing or communicating with the logical, arithmetical, or memory function resources of a computer, computer system, computer network. [Information Technology Act (21 of 2000), S. 2(1)(a)]

"Access" means collecting, procuring or possessing any biological resource occurring in or obtained from India or traditional knowledge associated thereto, for the purposes of research or bio-survey or commercial utilization. [Biological Diversity Act, 2002 (18 of 2002), section 2(a)]

Approach, or the means, power, or opportunity of approaching; an opportunity for sexual intercourse [Indian Evidence Act (1 of 1872), S. 112 and CPC (5 of 1908), S. 55(1)]

In Matrimonial law, access is understood in the sense of sexual intercourse; or the opportunity of communicating together so that sexual intercourse may have taken place. A man who can readily be in company with his wife is said to have access to her; and in that case her issue is presumed to be his issue. But this presumption may be rebutted by positive evidence that no sexual intercourse took place.

Access and non access. 'Access' and 'non access' means the existence or non-existence of opportunities for sexual intercourse; it does not mean actual 'cohabitation' *Gautam Kundu* v. *State of W.B.*, AIR 1993 SC 2295. [Indian Evidence Act (1 of 1872), S. 112]

Access easement. Right to use another's land to get to a nearby road.

Access control. The method of restricting access to various resources of a computer system, programs or computer networks only to the legitimate users. (*Information Technology*)

Access Control List (ACL). Access Control List means by which access to a computer network security system is controlled. It lists the services available and the hosts allowed to use them. (*Information Technology*)

"Access Facilitation". Means access or interconnection, as the case may be, to the essential facilities (including landing facilities for submarine cable) at cable landing station. [International Telecommunication Cable Landing Stations Access Facilitation Charges and Co–location Charges Regulations, 2012, Regn. 2(a)].

Access provider. A company that sells Internet connection. Known variously as Internet access or service providers (IAPs or ISPs), *e.g.* Demon, CompuServe or America Online. (*Information Technology*)

Accessary or Accessory. One guilty of an offence, not principally but by participation; as by command, advice, or concealment *etc.* (*Tomlin*)

BEFORE THE FACT. One who is absent at the time of the commission of a criminal offence yet procures or counsels another to it.

AFTER THE FACT. One who knowing a fellow has committed a criminal offence receives, or assist the felon.

DURING THE FACT. One who stands by without interfering or giving such help as may be in his power to prevent the commission of a criminal offence.

Accessible. Means capable of access without any reasonable let or hindrance.

Capable of being reached [Beedi and Cigar Workers (Conditions of Employment) Act (32 of 1966), S. 12]; easy to approach.

Accessio. (*Lat.*) An increase or addition to a thing; that which arises or is produced from the principal thing.

Accessio cedit principali. An accessory thing when annexed to a principal thing becomes part of the principal thing.

Accession. Accession is a mode of acquiring property as an addition to existing property by natural growth or by application of human labour.

In Oxford Dictionary "accession" has been defined and relevant portion is extracted thus:

> A new item added to an existing collection of books, paintings, or artefacts. An amount added to an existing quantity of something; substantial accessions of gold. Verb [with obj.] (usu. Be accessioned) record the addition of (a new item) to a library, museum, or other collection. ORIGIN late 16th cent. (in the general sense 'something added'): from Latin accession(n-), from the verb accedere 'approach, come to ' (see ACCEDE) Emphasis is on addition to the existing property, quality or title. [Oxford Dictionary as cited in *Maharaji Educational Trust* v. *Housing and Urban Development Corporation Ltd.,* 2017 (6) SCALE 4, para 34.]

Black's Law Dictionary defines the expression "accession" with respect to property thus: The acquisition of title to personal property by bestowing labor on a raw material to convert it to another thing. Also termed in Roman law '*accessio*'. See Adjunction (2). Accessio is the combination of two chattels belonging to different persons into a single article: as when A's cloth is used to patch B's coat, or a vehicle let on hire-purchase has new accessories fitted to it." R.F.V. Heuston, Salmond on the Law of Torts 113 (17th ed. 1977). *Maharaji Educational Trust* v. *Housing and Urban Development Corporation Ltd.*, 2017 (6) SCALE 4, para 30.

Coming to as an addition; the mode of acquiring property by which the owner of a corporeal substance (as land or cattle) becomes the owner of addition by growth, increase or labour; any property so acquired. [T.P. Act (4 of 1882), S. 63]; coming to the throne [Indian Evidence Act (1 of 1872), S. 57(5)]; coming to an office [Indian Evidence Act (1 of 1872), S. 57(7)]; increase by something added; assent [Geneva Conventions Act (6 of 1960), Art. 57].

In International Law, 'accession' is occasionally used as a technical expression denoting the absolute or conditional acceptance by one or several states, of a treaty already concluded between other sovereigns.

Accessories. The term 'accessories' is used to describe goods which may have been manufactured for use and an aid or addition.

'Accessories' are not necessarily confined to particular machineries for which they may serve as aids. The same item may be an accessory of more than one kind of instrument. *Annapurna Carbon Industries* v. *State of A.P.*, AIR 1976 SC 1418, 1421.

Accessorium non ducit sed sequitur suum principale. (*Maxim*) That which is the accessory or incident does not lead, but follows its principal. The incident does not draw, but follows, its principal. (*Broom*; *Coke Litt. 125-a*)

Accessorium non trahit principale. "The accessory does not draw the principal." (*Adam*) *e.g.*, The release of a surety is not the release of his principal, although the release of the principal is a release of the surety also. (*Byrne*)

Accessorium principale sequitur. (*Lat.*) An accessory follows the principal to which it is an accessory. Where two things stand in such intimate connection, that the one depends upon, or is derived from the other, the accessory belongs to him who has right to the principal subject. (*Trayner*)

Accessorium sequitur naturam rei cui accedit. The accessory follows the nature of the thing to which it relates. (*Stimson*)

Accessorium sequitur suum principale. That which is the accessory or incident follows *i.e.* goes with, its principal.

Accessorium sequiture principale. The accessory follows its principal. (*Adam*)

Where there is no principal there can be no accessory.

The accessory does not carry the principal. (*Latin for Lawyers*)

The accessory right does not lead, but follows its principal.

Accessorius sequitur naturam sui principalis. "An accessory follows the nature of his principal." An application of the maxim results in the proposition that an accessary cannot be guilty of a higher crime than his principal. (*Broom 497*)

Accessory. (*as a noun*) is one who is guilty of a crime, not by committing the offence in person as a principal, but by having in some way concerned therein (as) by advising. "An accessory is one who participates in an offence too remotely to be deemed a principal." (*Bishop Cr. Proc.*)

An object or device not essential in itself but that adds to the convenience or effectiveness of something else; an adjunct or accompaniment [Essential Commodities Act (10 of 1955), S. 2(a)(iii) and Income-tax Act (43 of 1961), fifth Sch., item 8]; subsidiary; present along with something more important [Indian Easements Act (5 of 1882), S. 33]; one who aids or gives countenance to a crime [Explosive Substances Act (6 of 1908), S. 6].

Anything which is joined to another thing as an ornament, or to render it more perfect, or which accompanies it, or is connected with it as an incident, or as subordinate to it, or which belongs to or with it. Adjunct or accompaniment…A thing of subordinate importance, aiding or contributing in secondary way or assisting in or contributing to as a subordinate." [Black's Law Dictionary as cited in *Commissioner of Sales Tax, U.P., Lucknow* v. *Akzo Nobel India Limited*, (2014) 16 SCC 242, para 12.3].

An object or device that is not essential in itself but that adds to the beauty, convenience, or effectiveness of something else. [Webster's Third New International Dictionary as cited in *Commissioner of Sales Tax, U.P., Lucknow* v. *Akzo Nobel India Limited*, (2014) 16 SCC 242, para 13].

"Accessory" means "a person or thing that aids subordinately; an adjunct; appurtenance; accompaniment (2) such items of apparel as complete an outfits, as gloves, a scarf, hat or handbag. (3) A person who, even if not present, is concerned, either before or after, in the perpetration of a felony below the crime of treason. Adj. (1) Aiding the principal design, or assisting subordinately the chief agent, as in the commission of crime. (2) contributory; supplemental; additional; accessory nerves." [Webster's Comprehensive Dictionary (International), Vol. I as cited in *State of Punjab* v. *Nokia India Private Limited*, (2014) 16 SCC 410, para 17].

"Accessory" means "a thing which can be added to something else in order to make it more useful, versatile, or attractive".[Oxford Advanced Learner's Dictionary as cited in *Commissioner of Sales Tax, U.P. Lucknow* v. *Akzo Nobel India Limited*, (2014) 16 SCC 242, para 12.1].

"Accessory" means "something added to something else to make it more useful, attractive, or effective". [Merriam–Webster Dictionary as cited in *Commissioner of Sales Tax, U.P., Lucknow* v. *Akzo Nobel India Limited*, (2014) 16 SCC 242, para 12.2]

ACCOMPLICES AND ABETTORS also come in some measure under the name of accessories. An abettor is one who stirs up, incites, instigates, or encourages or who, commands counsels or procures another to commit a crime. An accomplice is one of many equally concerned in a felony and is generally applied to those who are admitted to give evidence against their fellow criminals, for the furtherance of justice, which might otherwise be eluded.

Accessory after the fact. An accessory who knows that a crime has been committed and who helps the principal to escape arrest or punishment

Accessory at the fact. One who is principal in the second degree under the principal.

Accessory before the fact. One who helps or encourages another to commit a crime but is not present at the time of the commission of the offence.

Accessory licence. A licence necessary for the enjoyment of any interest or the exercise of any right. [Indian Easements Act (5 of 1882), S. 55].

Accessory obligation. An obligation subordinate to the main or principal one.

Accessory right. A right supplementary or secondary to a right of greater or primary importance. [Indian Easements Act (5 of 1882), S. 24]

Accident. An undersigned, sudden or unexpected event; mishap; misfortune; disaster. (*See* Workmen's Compensation Act (8 of 1923), Ss. 2 and 3)

An unintended and unforeseen injurious occurrence; something that does not occur in the usual course of events or that could not be reasonably anticipated. [Black's Law Dictionary as cited in *State* v. *Sanjeev Nanda*, (2012) 8 SCC 450, para 32].

The word "accident" generally denotes an event that takes place without one's foresight or expectation; an event which proceeds from an unknown cause, or is an unusual effect of a known cause, and therefore not expected; chance, casualty, contingency. (*Webster's Dict.*)

An event happening without the concurrence of the will of the person by whose agency it was caused.

The word "accident" is derived from the Latin verb "accidere" signifying "fall upon, befall, happen, chance." In an etymological sense anything that happens may be said to be an accident and in this sense, the word has been defined as befalling a chance; a happening; an incident; an occurrence or event. In its most commonly accepted meaning, or in its ordinary or popular sense, the word may be defined as meaning : a fortuitous circumstance, event, or happening; an event happening without any human agency, or if happening wholly or partly through human agency, an event which under the circumstances is unusual and unexpected by the person to whom it happens; an unusual, fortuitous, unexpected, unforeseen or unlooked for event, happening or occurrence; an unusual or unexpected result attending the operation or performance of a usual or necessary act or event; chance or contingency; fortune, mishap : some sudden and unexpected event taking place without expectation, upon the instant, rather than something which continues, progresses or develops; something happening by chance; something unforeseen unexpected, unusual, extraordinary or phenomenal, taking place not according to the usual course of things or events, out of the range of ordinary calculations; that which exists or occurs abnormally, or an uncommon occurrence.

A sudden event occurring without intent or volition whether through negligence, carelessness, unawareness, ignorance or a combination of causes and producing an unfortunate result; an unexpected happening causing loss or injury which is not due to the fault of the person [IPC (45 of 1860), S. 80]; anything that happens.

The ordinary meaning of the word 'accident' is an unintended occurrence which had an adverse physical result.

Death by drowning, though in shallow water whilst in a state of insensibility, is an "accident" within a life insurance policy.

Sun-stroke is not an accident within a policy. Misfortunes in business are not accidents.

"ACCIDENT" means an occurrence associated with the operation of an aircraft which,—

(*i*) in the case of a manned aircraft, takes place between the time any person boards the aircraft with the intention of flight until such time as all such persons have disembarked; or

(*ii*) in the case of an unmanned aircraft, takes place between the time the aircraft is ready to move with the purpose of flight until such time as it comes to rest at the end of the flight and the primary propulsion system in shut down, in which—

(*a*) a person is fatally or seriously injured as a result of—

(*i*) being in the aircraft; or

(*ii*) direct contact with any part of the aircraft, including parts which have become detached from the aircraft; or

(*iii*) direct exposure to jet blast,

Except when the injuries are from natural causes, self-inflicted or inflicted by other persons, or when the injuries are to stowaways hiding outside the areas normally available to the passengers and crew; or

(*b*) the aircraft sustains damage or structural failure which—

(*i*) adversely affects the structural strength, performance or flight characteristics of the aircraft; and

(*ii*) would normally require major repair or replacement of the affected component,

Except for engine failure or damage, when the damage is limited to a single engine, (including its cowlings or accessories), to propellers, wingtips, antennas, probes, vanes, tires, brakes, wheels, fairings, panels, landing gear doors, wind screens, the aircraft skin (such as small dents or puncture holes), or for minor damages to main rotor blades, tail rotor blades, landing gear, and those resulting from hail or bird strike (including holes in the radome); or

(*c*) the aircraft is missing or is completely inaccessible.

Note 1.—For the purpose of this clause, the guidance for the determination of aircraft damage is at Schedule B.

Note 2.—For the purposes of this clause, only unmanned aircraft which have design or operational approval given by a State to be considered. [Aircraft (Investigation of Accidents and Incidents) Rules, 2017, R. 2(1)].

Accident arising out of or in the course of employment. There should be a direct, intimate and causal connection between the accident and the employment so as to eliminate any possible conclusion that the accident was something which had no relation whatsoever to the sphere of the duties of the deceased. *Jayathilal Dhanji & Co.* v. *Employees State Insurance Corporation,* AIR 1963 AP 210, 212. [Employees' State Insurance Act (34 of 1948), S. 2(8) & 6]

Accident in course of employment. An accident cannot be said to arise out of and in the course of employment if it takes place on a public road in the absence of any circumstance showing that the nature of the employment of the workmen required him to be there. *Commissioner Port of Calcutta* v. *Kanez Fatema,* AIR 1961 Cal 310, 313. [Workmen's Compensation Act (8 of 1923), S. 3(1)]

Accident insurance. It is a contract to pay a fixed sum in case of death resulting from accident, either generally, or limited to accidents of a particular kind. (*Rapalje; Bouvier; Brown*)

Though accidents to property may be made the subject of insurance, the term has been more often applied to insurance against accidents resulting in bodily harm.

Accidental. Happening by chance or unexpectedly taking place, not according to the usual course of things; Unintentional, something unforeseen and unexpected and casual.

Accidental death benefit. The provision in the insurance policy allowing for a payment (often double the face value of the policy) if the insured dies an accidental death.

Accidental falling of a passenger from a train carrying passengers. It is possible that two interpretations can be given to the expression 'accidental falling of a passenger from a train carrying passengers', *the first* being that it only applies when a person has actually got inside the train and thereafter falls down from the train, while *the second* being that it includes a situation where a person is trying to board the train and falls down while trying to do so. *UOI* v. *Prabhakaran Vijaya Kumar,* AIR 2009 SC (Supp) 383.

Accidental killing. Death caused by misadventure.

Accidental slip (or omission). An error due to careless mistake or omission unintentionally made. [*Master Construction Co. (P) Ltd.* v. *State of Orissa*, AIR 1966 SC 1047 as cited in *Srihari* v. *Syed Maqdoom*, (2015) 1 SCC 607, para 14].

Accidentally. In an accidental manner; without intention or design. [Representation of the People Act (43 of 1951), S. 58(i)(a)]

Accipere quid ut justitiam facias, not est tam accipere quam extorquere. (*Maxim*) To accept anything as a reward for doing justice is extortion and not acceptance.

Accommodated party. A person who signs a negotiable instrument for the purpose of being a surety for another party.

Accommodation. The act of accommodating; in mercantile language is used for a loan of money; pecuniary aid in an emergency; money loan either directly or by standing surety for the repayment of sums advanced by another. It also signifies a friendly agreement or composition of differences. (*Abbott*)

Anything which serves the need of residence [CPC (5 of 1908), S. 55(1)]; room space [Plantations Labour Act (69 of 1951), S. 11(2)(b)]; provision of what is needful or desirable for convenience, such as, accommodation by way of loan or other pecuniary assistance in emergency [Negotiable Instruments Act (26 of 1881), S. 44, ill.]; lodging [Companies Act (1 of 1956) replaced with Companies Act, 2013, S. 198(4), *Expln.* (a)]; quarters [Companies Act (1 of 1956) replaced with Companies Act, 2013, Sch. 1, table D, 3rd item]; convenience [Indian Railways Act (9 of 1890), S. 7(1)]; supplying of wants especially, housing [Indian Railways Act (9 of 1890), S. 50(d)].

The word "accommodation" cannot simply mean premises in which a person and his family are personally lodging. The accommodation must be such that it is reasonable for the applicant and his family to continue to occupy it, having regard to the general circumstances prevailing in relation to housing in the area of the housing authority to whom he has applied.

Accommodation means a building or part of a building which is used for residential or nonresidential purposes, but not as a factory or for an industrial purpose. *Sitaram Shasan* v. *Johrimal*, AIR 1972 All 317, 319.

A garage which is a permanent roofed structure and which is part of a building would come within the purview of 'accommodation'. *R.N. Gupta* v. *Sarla Khandelwal*, AIR 1974 All 376, 377.

The construction of a 'chhapper' and a latrine on a vacant plot will not convert the land into accommodation. *Abdul Sami* v. *Mohd. Noor*, AIR 1966 All 39, 41.

A land surrounded on three sides by boundary walls cannot be said to be an accommodation within the meaning of the Act. *Mewa Lal* v. *Tara Mani*, AIR 1973 All 165, 168. [U.P. (Temporary) Control of Rent and Eviction Act (3 of 1947), S. 2]

Accommodation bill. A bill of exchange or note, *etc.*, drawn, accepted or indorsed by one or more parties to enable another or others to obtain credit by or raise money on it, and not given like business paper in payment of a debt, but merely intended to accommodate the drawer.

Accommodation credit. A credit with recourse finance facility used by large-scale exporters and importers. They can draw a bill of exchange on their own or another bank discounted 'at a fine rate' (*i.e.* cheaper). (*Trade Finance*)

Accommodation note or bill. A note or bill made, drawn, accepted or endorsed by one person for another without consideration to enable that other to raise money or obtain credit thereby. [Negotiable Instruments Act (26 of 1881), S. 59, *Prov.*]

Accommodation paper. Promissory notes or bills of exchange made, accepted, or endorsed without any consideration therefor.

Accommodation party. The person signing a negotiable instrument to become a surety for another party.

Accommodation works. Works which a railway company is required to make and maintain for the accommodation of the owners or occupiers of land adjoining the railway, such as gates, culverts *etc.*

Accomplice. A person who commits a crime, either as a perpetrator or accessory along with one or more other persons.

"One who is in some way concerned in the commission of a crime, though not as principal."

One concerned with another or others in the commission of offence; an associate in crime or guilt. [Indian Evidence Act (1 of 1872), Ss. 114, ill. (b), 133 and IPC (45 of 1860), S. 192, ill. (c)]

An accomplice shall be a competent witness against an accused person; and a conviction is not illegal if it proceeds upon the corroborated testimony of an accomplice. [(w.e.f. 1-7-2024) Bharatiya Sakshya Adhiniyam, 2023 (47 of 2023), section 138]

Accord. It is an agreement between two or more persons, where any one is injured by a trespass, or offence done, or on a contract, to satisfy him with some recompense, which accord, if executed and performed, shall be a good bar in law, if the other party after the accord performed brings an action for the same trespass etc. (*Termes de la ley*; *Tomlin*)

An agreement between two or more persons. To furnish or grant; to agree.

Accord and satisfaction. Is an agreement between two at the least to satisfy an offence that the one hath made to the other, when a man hath done a trespass, or such like, unto another for which he hath agreed with him to satisfy and content him with some recompense, which, if it be executed and performed, then, because that this recompense is a full satisfaction for the offence, it shall be a good bar in law, if the other, after the accord performed, should sue again any action for the same trespass. (*Termes de la ley*) is an agreement to give and accept something in satisfaction of a right which one has against the other, which when performed is a bar to all actions upon this account.

Mutual agreement and fulfilment of obligation.

Accordance. Agreement; harmony; concord; conformity.

According to law. To act according to law is to act in conformity with legal formalities.

According to the form. The expression 'according to the form' does mean 'in the form' that is, a verbal and literal following of the form set out in the Third Schedule. It means the substantial following of the form. In other words, the Article means that the form set out in the Third Schedule or any form as near thereto as circumstances admit, shall be used in taking an oath or affirmation under the Article. *Anand Bihari Mishra* v. *Ram Sahay,* AIR 1952 MB 31. [Constitution of India, Art. 188]

Accordingly. The word "accordingly" means in a similar manner. *National Insurance Co.* v. *LIC of India,* AIR 1963 SC 1911, 1913. [Life Insurance Corporation Act (31 of 1956), S. 2(3)(*i*)]

Account. A detailed statement of the mutual demands in the nature of debit and credit between parties.

A statement of moneys received and paid with calculation of balance; a formal record of debits and credits relating to the person named or caption placed at the head of the ledger account; computation; reckoning; a statement of facts or occurrences.

Account assigned. A pledge of an account receivable to a bank or factor as a security for a loan.

Account book. Is a book kept by a merchant, trader, mechanic, or other person, in which are entered from time to time the transactions of his trade or business.

Account current. The amount of money a person has deposited at a bank or which he can draw from or add to as may be desired, generally no interest being chargeable on either side.

Account for. In respect of moneys means "to render an account of" and "to be responsible for."

To furnish substantial reasons or convincing explanation, make clear or reveal basic causes.

To give an account of; to answer for [Indian Contract Act (9 of 1872), S. 195, ill. (b) and Emigration Act (7 of 1922), S. 27C(2)]; to give a reason for; to tell the cause of [Indian Evidence Act (1 of 1872), S. 114, ill. (a)]; to render accounts [CPC (5 of 1908), Sch. I, App. F, Form No. 10 and Indian Contract Act (9 of 1872), S. 143, ill. (a)].

Account of profits. A remedy that a claimant can claim as an alternative to damages in certain circumstances, *e.g.,* in an action for breach of copyright.

Account payable. An account showing a balance to a creditor.

Account receivable. A debt owed to an enterprise arising out of the normal course of business dealings.

Account rendered. is one which is drawn up in form and delivered by the creditor to the debtor as an exhibition of the former's demand. (*Abbott L. Dict.*)

Account settled. A settled account is a statement of the accounts between two parties, which is agreed to and accepted by both as correct. It must be in writing; and it must be final, that is, it must show clearly what balance is due, or that no balance is due. An informal release of all demands may be settled account. The fact that it is stated with the qualification "errors excepted" will not prevent its being a good settled account. It is not enough for the accounting party merely to deliver his account; there must be some evidence, that the other party accepted it as correct. But such acceptance need not be express.

Account stated. Account stated is an agreement by both parties that all the items are true.

Account stated is an agreed balance of account (*i.e.*) an account which has been examined and accepted by the parties.

The expression 'accounts stated' means (1) a claim to payment made by one party and admitted by the other to be correct and (2) striking of a balance after adjusting items of credit and debit making the account.

Accounts rendered which by implied or express acceptance have been agreed upon by both the parties as correct. [Limitation Act (36 of 1963), Sch, Art. 26].

Account, Take into. To notice; to calculate.

Accountability. 'Accountability' refers to the formal or legal locus of 'responsibility'. Accountability, which concerns the formal relationship between administration and the legislative and judicial branches, can never be shared. In general, the bureaucracy is regarded as accountable to elected representatives and to the Courts who give meaning to the rule of law doctrine. Within the executive branch, accountability is sought through a hierarchy of offices and duties and makes possible a 'line of command' from top to bottom. The Council of Ministers is accountable for the entire administrative branch. [*Scheduled Castes and Scheduled Tribes Officers' Welfare Council* v. *State of U.P.*, (1996) 8 SCALE 22]

Accountable. Being liable to account.

Accountable person. "PERSON ACCOUNTABLE" or "ACCOUNTABLE PERSON" means the person accountable for estate duty within the meaning of this Act, and, includes every person in respect of whom any proceeding under this Act has been taken for the assessment of the principal value of the estate of the deceased. [Estate duty Act (34 of 1953), S. 2(12A)]

Accountable receipt. Receipt for money or goods in respect of which the giver of the receipt is subsequently accountable.

Accountant. One whose vocation or function it is to keep or adjust accounts; also a person who renders an account in a particular case. (*Abbott*)

An officer in charge of the accounts; one who professionally makes up accounts. [Public Accountants' Default Act (12 of 1850), S. 2]

"ACCOUNTANT" in this section, "accountant" means a chartered accountant within the meaning of the Chartered Accountants Act, 1949 (38 of 1949), and includes, in relation to any State, any person who by virtue of the provisions of sub-section (2) of section 226 of the Companies Act, 1956 (1 of 1956) replaced with Companies Act, 2013, is entitled to be appointed to act as an auditor of companies registered in that State. [*Explanation* below S. 288(2) of Income Tax Act, 1961 (43 of 1961)]

"ACCOUNTANT" means—

(*i*) a chartered accountant within the meaning of clause (*b*) of sub-section (1) of Section 2 of the Chartered Accountant's Act, 1949 (38 of 1949); or

(*ii*) a person who by virtue of the provisions of Section 141 of the Companies Act, 2013 (18 of 2013), is entitled to be appointed to act as an auditor of companies registered; or

(*iii*) a cost accountant within the meaning of the Cost and works Accountants Act, 1959 (23 of 1959); or

(*iv*) a person referred to in Section 139 and Section 143 of the Companies Act, 2013 (18 of 2013). [Andaman and Nicobar Islands Value Added Tax Regulations (6 of 2017), S. 2(1)(a)].

Accountant-client privilege. Protection which is afforded to the client from unauthorized disclosure by his or her accountant of materials submitted to or prepared by the accountant.

Accountant-General. A superior officer who has charge of the finances of the Government. (*Tomlin*)

Accountants chartered. Persons skilled in the keeping and examination of accounts, who are employed for the purpose of examining and certifying to the correctness of accounts of corporations and others.

Accounting. Accounting is the rendering or delivering a statement of one's dealings. Giving an account of receipts and expenses.

Accounting cushion. The US practice of making a larger provision for expenses in a particular year, so that they can be minimized in future years. In other words, earnings are initially understated, and then overstated later. (*International Accounting*)

Accounting for profits. A restitutionary remedy based upon avoiding unjust enrichment.

Accounting method. System for determining income and expenses for tax purposes.

Accounting period. Period for which accounts are prepared.

Accounting period. For the purposes of this clause, it is hereby declared that "accounting period" means each period of twelve months ending with the 31st day of March:

Provided that where a company or an entity, referred to in *Explanation 5*, regularly adopts a period of twelve months ending on a day other than the 31st day of March for the purpose of—

(i) complying with the provisions of the tax laws of the territory, of which it is a resident, for tax purposes; or

(ii) reporting to persons holding the share or interest,

then, the period of twelve months ending with the other day shall be the accounting period of the company or, as the case may be, the entity:

Provided further that the first accounting period of the company or, as the case may be, the entity shall begin from the date of its registration or incorporation and end with the 31st day of March or such other day, as the case may be, following the date of such registration or incorporation, and the later accounting period shall be the successive periods of twelve months:

Provided also that if the company or the entity ceases to exist before the end of accounting period, as aforesaid, then, the accounting period shall end immediately before the company or, as the case may be, the entity, ceases to exist. [Income-tax Act (43 of 1961), section 9(1)(i), *Explanation 6(c)*]

Accounting records. Records that disclose and explain a company's financial position at any time and enable its directors to prepare its accounts.

Accounting standards. Means the standards of accounting or any addendum thereto for companies or class of companies referred to in section 133 of the Companies Act, 2013 (18 of 2013). [S. 2(2) of the Companies Act, 2013 (18 of 2013)]

"Accounting Standards" means the standards of accounting, or any addendum thereto for companies or class of companies as specified in rule 3. [Companies (Indian Accounting Standards) Rules, 2015, rule 2(1)(a)]

"Accounting Standards" means the standards of accounting or any addendum thereto as specified in rule 3. [Companies (Accounting Standards) Rules, 2021, rule 2(1)(a)]

Accounting value. For the purposes of rule 8 of the Companies (Share Capital & Debentures) Rules, 2014, it is hereby clarified that the 'accounting value' shall be the fair value of the sweat equity shares as determined by a registered value under rule 8(6) of the Companies (Share Capital & Debentures) Rules, 2014. [*Explanation* to rule 8(12) of the Companies (Share Capital & Debentures) Rules, 2014]

Accounting year. For the purposes of this section "ACCOUNTING YEAR" means,—

(*i*) a previous year, in a case where the parent entity or alternate reporting entity is resident in India; or

(*ii*) an annual accounting period, with respect to which the parent entity of the international group prepares its financial statements under any law for the time being in force or the applicable accounting standards of the country or territory of which such entity is resident, in any other case. [Income-tax Act (43 of 1961), S. 286, *Explanation* (*a*)].

"ACCOUNTING YEAR" means,—

(i) in relation to a corporation, the year ending on the day on which the books and accounts of the corporation are to be closed and balanced

(ii) in relation to a company, the period in respect of which any profit and loss account of the company laid before it in annual general meeting is made up, whether that period is a year or not;

(iii) in any other case—

(a) the year commencing on the 1st day of April; or

(b) if the accounts of an establishment maintained by the employer thereof are closed and balanced on any day other than 31st day of March, then, at the option of the employer, the year ending on the day on which its accounts are so closed and balanced.

Provided that an option once exercised by the employer under paragraph (b) of this sub clause shall not again be exercised except with the previous permission in writing of the prescribed authority and upon such conditions as that authority may think fit. [Payment of Bonus Act (21 of 1965), S. 2(a)]

A period of one year for which accounts are separately closed and balanced. [Payment of Bonus Act (21 of 1965), S. 2(1) and Agricultural Refinance and Development Corporation Act (10 of 1963), S. 29(1)].

Accredit. (*In international Law*) To acknowledge; send "an envoy" with credentials.

Accreditation. A formal declaration by the Controller that a particular information system, professional or other employee or contractor, or organization is approved to perform certain duties and to operate in a specific security mode, using a prescribed set of safeguards. (*Information Technology*)

Accredited. Furnished with credentials; officially vouched for. [Citizenship Act (57 of 1955), S. 3(2)(a)]

Accredited representative. In relation to service of process, a person with general authority to act.

Accretion, is the increase of land or estate by the addition of portions of soil through the operation of natural causes, to that already in possession of the owner. *(Washburn Real Property, 5th Ed., p. 50)*

The principle of accretion is, that land formed gradually and imperceptibly by the action of water goes to the owner of the adjacent soil, such newly formed land being said to become his property.

The word 'Accretion' is also applied to the state of circumstances which arises when a person having no right, or only an imperfect right to property, makes a grant, and subsequently has his right perfected.

To fall (to any one) as a natural growth or increment; to come as an accession or advantage; to come into existence as an enforceable claim. [T.P Act (4 of 1882), Ss. 24, 55(1)(g) and Indian Trusts Act (2 of 1882), S. 24]

Accroach. To usurp power; to exercise power without authority.

Accrocher un proces. (*Fr.*) To stay the proceedings in a suit.

Accrual. Recognition of revenues and costs as they are earned or incurred.

Accrual accounting. Method of accounting in which revenue is entered when it is earned (but not yet necessarily received) and expenses are recognized when they are incurred (but not necessarily paid for). It thus differs fundamentally from *cash-flow accounting*. (*International Accounting*)

Accrual basis. A method of accounting that reflects expenses incurred and income earned for anyone tax year. (*Black*)

Accrual, clause of. A clause in a deed of gift or will, providing that in the event of death of one, his share shall vest in the survivors.

Accrual of income. Income may accrue to an assesse without the actual receipt of the same. If the assesse acquires a right to receive the income, the income can be said to have accrued to him though it may be received later, on its being ascertained. The basic conception is that he must have acquired a right to receive the income.

Accrue. Accrue means to arise (as) cause of action accruing; to grow; or to be added to (as) accruing rent, accruing debt, accruing dividend.

In the past tense the word "accrued" is used in the sense of due and payable; vested; and existed (as, rights accrued).

Accrue means to arise, to happen, to come into force or existence, to vest.

A title "accrues" when the instrument creating it, or the fact constituting it, first becomes operative.

Accrue and arise. The two words — 'accrue' and 'arise' — are used to contra-distinguish the word 'receive'. Income is said to be received when it reaches the assessee; when the right to receive the income becomes vested in the assessee, it is said to accrue or arise. *C.I.T.* v. *Ashokbai Chimanbai*, (1965) 56 ITR 42, 45 (SC). [Income-tax Act (43 of 1961), S. 5]

Accrued compensation. Remuneration, earned but not paid yet.

Accrued expense. Expenses actually been incurred but not yet paid.

Accrued holiday remuneration. For the purposes of this section, the expression "accrued holiday remuneration" includes, in relation to any person, all sums which, by virtue either of his contract of employment or of any enactment including any order made or direction given thereunder, are payable on account of the remuneration which would, in the ordinary course, have become payable to him in respect of a period of holiday, had his employment with the company continued until he became entitled to be allowed the holiday. [Companies Act (18 of 2013), section 327, *Expln. (a)*]

Accrued income. Though a person has got only a right to receive commission during a year and it is actually computed only in the next year, it is said to have accrued in the first year itself. The computation of the profits whenever it may take place cannot be allowed to suspend their accrual.

Accrued interest. An interest payment that is due, but not yet received.

Accrued right. A matured right; a right that is ripe for enforcement (as through).

A right which has finally vested in a person.

"ACCRUED RIGHT" liberty to apply for a right is not in itself an 'accrued right' or privilege. *Vinod Gurudas Raikar* v. *National Insurance Co. Ltd.*, AIR 1991 SC 2156 : 1991 AIR SCW 2503.

Accruing dividend. In a Public Co., is dividend in process of being earned, but not yet declared.

Accruing interest. Means running or accumulating interest as distinguished from accrued or matured interest.

Accumulate. To collect or bring together [Indian Trusts Act (2 of 1882), S. 23, ill, (f)]; to grow or increase; to go on increasing.

Accumulated. The expression "accumulated" means that the income is set apart during the year for future spending on the specified purposes. *H.E.H. Nizam's Religious Endorsement Trust* v. *Commissioner of Income Tax*, (1966) 59 ITR 582, 588 (SC). [Income-tax Act (43 of 1961), S. 1]

Accumulated-earning tax. A tax imposed as a penalty on a corporation which retains its earnings, instead of distributing them to shareholders as dividends, so as to avoid income taxes paid by the shareholders on those dividends.

Accumulated loss. For the purposes of this section,—

"ACCUMULATED LOSS" means so much of the loss of the amalgamating banking company under the head "Profits and gains of business or profession" (not being a loss sustained in a speculation business) which such amalgamating banking company, would have been entitled to carry forward and set-off under the provisions of section 72 if the amalgamation had not taken place. [Income-tax Act (43 of 1961), S. 72AA, *Expln.* (i) as inserted by Finance Act (18 of 2005), S. 19]

Accumulated profits. Profit that has accrued but not yet been distributed; earned surplus. Also called as *undivided profit*.

The words 'accumulated profits' cannot be construed to include current profits. *I.T. Commissioner* v. *Damodaran*, AIR 1980 SC 478, 481.

"ACCUMULATED PROFITS" signifies, firstly that there must have been profits in earlier years and secondly, that amount out of such profits have been accumulated from time to time, with the result that there is some amount of accumulated profits in the possession of the company just before the commencement of the accounting year. *Navnitlal C. Jhaveri* v. *CIT,* (1931) 80 ITR 582, 586 (Bom). [Income-tax Act (43 of 1961), S. 2 (22)]

Earned surplus or undivided profits. (*Black*)

Accumulated surplus. The fund which a corporation has in excess of its capital stock after payment of its debts.

Accumulating shares. Additional ordinary shares issued to equity holders *in lieu* of a dividend. They are consequently attractive for capital growth, rather than for regular income. Tax is normally deducted from the declared dividend as usual and then the net dividend is used to purchase additional ordinary shares. (*Trade Finance*)

Accumulation, (of income). The putting by of dividends, rents, profits or other income and converting it into principal by investing it and again capitalizing the income arising from the new principal, and so on. The capital and accrued interest is called the accumulations.

The action of accumulating [T.P. Act (4 of 1882), S. 17(2)]; growing of increasing in quantity or number; heaping up; a heap or mass. [Factories Act (63 of 1948), S. 11(1)(a)].

Accumulation clause. The clause which provides for a slight increase in policy benefits when policy premiums have been paid. It rewards persistency. (*Insurance*)

Accumulative judgment. A second or additional judgment or sentence given against one who has already been convicted, to take effect after the expiration of the first. (*Wharton*)

Accumulative legacy. Additional legacy; a legacy given in addition to another given by the same instrument or by another instrument.

A legacy which is given in addition to previously made bequest.

Accumulative sentence. A sentence of imprisonment which commences at the end of another sentence already imposed.

Accuracy. Precision. [Air Force Act (45 of 1950), S. 63(a)]; correctness [Trade and Merchandise Marks Act (43 of 1958), S. 2(1)(c)]; [Chartered Accountants Act (38 of 1949), S. 33] (Repealed *by the Repealing and Amending Act, 1952 (48 of 1952), sec. 2 and Sch. I (w.e.f. 2-8-1952);* [Indian Fisheries Act (4 of 1897), S. 7(1)(b)].

Accusare nemo debet se nisi coram deo. No one is obliged to accuse himself, except before God.

Accusare nemo se debet. No one is bound to accuse himself.

Accusation. The charging of a person with a crime. (*Jacob*)

An allegation against a person that he has committed an offence. [IPC (45 of 1860), Ss. 389 and 499, *Except*. 8]

Accusator post rationabile tempus non est audiendus, nisi se bene de omissione excusaverit. (*Maxim*) An accuser ought not to be heard after the expiration of a reasonable time, unless he can account satisfactorily for his delay. (*Abbott*)

Accusatorial procedure. A system of criminal justice in which conclusions as to liability are reached by the process of prosecution and defence.

Accuse. To charge or impute to a person the commission of crime. To "accuse", "or threaten to accuse" of a crime is not restricted to the narrow meaning of accuse by course of law, but means, to allege, or threaten to charge, before any third person (*Per* PATTESON, J. *R.* v. *Robinson*, 2 M. & Rob. 14 at p. 16)

Accused. A person against whom an allegation has been made that he has committed an offence, or who is charged with an offence [IPC (45 of 1860), Ss. 212 and 216 and Indian Evidence Act (1 of 1872), S. 3, ill. to *Expln.*].

In this section, "accused" includes a person in relation to whom any proceeding under Chapter IX has been commenced under this Sanhita. [(w.e.f. 1-7-2024) Bharatiya Nagarik Suraksha Sanhita, 2023 (46 of 2023), section 308, *Explanation*]

One who is charged with a crime.

The term "accused," in Criminal Procedure Code means a 'person over whom a Magistrate or other "Criminal" Court is exercising jurisdiction'.

The protection of Article 20(3) becomes available to a person as soon as he is named as an accused either in a First Information Report made under section 154, CrPC 1973 (2 of 1974) or in a complaint instituted against him in Court. *Subedar* v. *State*, AIR 1957 All 396, 398. [Constitution of India, Art. 20(3)]

Until a complaint is filed under S. 137 with the sanction of the Collector of Customs, the person against whom an enquiry is commenced under the Customs Act does not stand in the character of a person accused of an offence. *Ramesh Chandra* v. *State of West Bengal*, AIR 1970 SC 940, 951. [Customs Act (52 of 1962), S. 135]

The word 'accused' or 'accused person' is used only in a generic sense in Sec. 167(1) & (2) denoting the 'person' whose liberty is actually restrained on his arrest by a competent authority on well-founded information or formal accusation or indictment. *Directorate of enforcement* v. *Deepak Mahajan*, AIR 1994 SC 1775, 1796. [CrPC 1973 (2 of 1974), S. 167 (1) & (2)]

Accused of an offence. Where evidence oral or circumstantial points to the guilt of a person and he is taken in custody and interrogated on that basis, he becomes a person accused of an offence. The mere fact that his name was not mentioned as an accused in the first information report will not take him out of the category of persons accused of an offence. *Amin* v. *State,* AIR 1958 All 293, 302. [Constitution of India, Art. 20(3)]

Accused of any offence. "Only a person against whom a formal accusation relating to the commission of an offence has been levelled, which in the normal course may result in his prosecution, would fall within the ambit of the term "accused of any offence." *Veera Ibrahim* v. *State of Maharashtra*, AIR 1976 SC 1167 at p. 1169.

The expression 'accused of any offence' is description of the person against whom evidence relating to information alleged to be given by him is made probable under S. 27. It does not predicate a formal accusation against him at the time of making the statement sought to be proved as a condition of its applicability. *State of U.P.* v. *Deoman*, AIR 1960 SC 1125, 1132. [Indian Evidence Act (1 of 1872), S. 87]

Accused person. The expression 'accused person' connotes a person against whom evidence is sought to be led in a criminal proceeding and it does not predicate a condition of that person at the time of making the statement. *Abraham Verghese* v. *State of Kerala,* AIR 1965 Ker 175, 176. [Indian Evidence Act (1 of 1872), S. 24]

Acid. For the purposes of section 326A and section 326B of Act 45 of 1860, 'acid' includes any substance which has acidic or corrosive character or burning nature, that is capable of causing bodily injury leading to scars or disfigurement or temporary or permanent disability. [*Explanation* 1 to S. 326B of IPC, 1860 (45 of 1860), as inserted by the Criminal Laws (Amendment) Act, 2013 (13 of 2013)]

For the purposes of this section, "acid" includes any substance which has acidic or corrosive character or burning nature, that is capable of causing bodily injury leading to scars or disfigurement or temporary or permanent disability. [(w.e.f. 1-7-2024) Bharatiya Nyaya Sanhita, 2023 (45 of 2023), section 124, *Explanation 1*]

Acid rain. The expression "acid rain" means acidification of the ecosystem by natural boiler which evaporates water from the sea, lakes and rivers and sends it down in the form of rain. Once the pure vapour enters the atmosphere, it condenses on solid particles and reaches equilibrium with atmospheric gases. In the main, carbon dioxide, sulphur oxides, nitrogen oxides, and chlorine from stationery and mobile sources (industries, power plants, and automobiles) are emitted into the atmosphere which combine with water vapour (in the presence of sunlight which acts as catalyst) and get transformed into carbonic acid, sulphuric acid, nitric acid, and hyrochloric acid respectively. Acid rain is a transboundary problem. Each country gets part of its acid fallout from its own pollutants but receives the rest on the winds from the neighboring countries. (*Environment*)

Acknowledge. To admit as true; to admit a claim or liability; to avow or assent to in legal form; to own as genuine or valid in law. [Registration Act (16 of 1908), S. 17(1)(c); IPC (45 of 1860), Ss. 30 and 467].

Acknowledgment. Means a proceeding whereby a person who has executed an instrument may, by declaring it to be his act and deed, entitle it to be received in evidence without further proof of execution, or oath. (*Cent. Dict.*)

The action of acknowledging; a thing done or given in recognition of something received. [T.P. Act (4 of 1882), Ss. 3 and 60 and Indian Evidence Act (1 of 1872), S. 32(2)].

Acknowledgement of debt. An admission in writing that a debt is due or that some claim or liability is sill in existence. [Indian Stamp Act (2 of 1899), Sch. 1, item 1]

Acknowledgment of service. A response by a defendant to a claim.

Acknowledgment of signature. Acknowledgment by a testator of the signature to his will:—

(a) "the signature" to be acknowledged may be made by the testator, or by another for him.

(b) "A testator" whether speechless or not, may acknowledge his signature by gestures.

(c) "There is no sufficient acknowledgement" unless the witness either saw, or might have seen, the signature.

(d) "When the witness" either saw, or might have seen the signature, an express acknowledgment of the signature itself is not necessary, a mere statement that the paper is his Will, or direction to them to put their names under his, or even the request by the testator, or by some person in his presence, to sign the paper is sufficient." Jarman on Wills. Jarman on Wills. See Indian Succession Act (39 of 1925), S. 63, Cl (c).

Acquaint. To inform; to make aware. [Indian Contract Act (9 of 1872), S. 143, ill. (a)].

Acquainted. Having personal knowledge of.

Having personal, familiar, knowledge of a person, event, or thing.

"Acquaintance" expresses less than familiarity; familiarity less than intimacy. Acquaintance springs from occasional intercourse, familiarity from daily intercourse, intimacy from unreserved intercourse. To be "personally acquainted with," and to "know personally" are equivalent terms.

Being aware of; having personal knowledge. [Registration Act (16 of 1908), S. 63(2)].

Acquiesce. To give silent or passive assent to; to tacitly agree to; resting satisfied with any state of things. [Indian Trusts Act (2 of 1882), S. 23 and CPC (5 of 1908), S. 20(b)].

Acquiescence. A resting satisfied with or submission to an existing state of things. The term implies both knowledge and power to contract on the part of the person acquiescing.

The action or condition of acquiescing; the assent to an infringement of rights, either express or implied from conduct, by which the rights to equitable or discretionary relief may be lost [Indian Contract Act (9 of 1872), S. 39]; a consent inferred from silence; a tacit encouragement.

Acquiescence imports full knowledge.

Acquiescence is the common element in a somewhat indefinite group of equitable estoppels, constituted by the fact that the person entitled has, as it is said, "slept upon his rights," and by his conduct at the time of a breach of them, or subsequently thereto, has, with full knowledge, both of his own rights and of the acts which infringe them, led that person responsible for the infringement to believe that he has waived or abandoned his rights. (*Ency. of the Laws of England*)

Acquire (*in the law of Contracts and Descents*), is to become the owner of property; to make property one's own.

The word 'acquire' must and can only mean acquisition for the first time under any of the instruments there mentioned or under a decree. When the female has already by reason of law or otherwise an interest in the property then she does not "acquire" any interest in it by reason of the instrument or the decree. [Hindu Succession Act (30 of 1956), S. 14(2)]

The word 'acquire' may include the power to purchase by agreement but is wide enough to enable the corporation to request the State Government to acquire property under the Land Acquisition Act 1 of 1894 in order to provide living accommodation for its employees. *State of Bombay* v. *R.S. Nanji*, AIR 1956 SC 294, 298. [Road Transport Corporation Act (64 of 1950), S. 19]

To gain as one's own; to receive; to come into possession of. [T.P. Act (4 of 1882)]; [S. 23, IPC (45 of 1860), S. 3(c), *Expln.* 1 and S. 44].

Acquired. The word 'acquired' signifies the obtaining of title as a result of a positive act done by the acquirer and will not apply to a case, where, on account of death, the right devolves upon the heirs of the deceased lessee.

The imposition, of a compulsory Governmental agency for the purpose of managing the forest with liability imposed to account for the income as laid down by the statute (Bihar Private Forests Act, 9 of 1928) is not an acquisition of the property itself within Section 299(2) of the Government of India Act, 1935. *Guru Datta Sharma* v. *State of Bihar*, AIR 1961 SC 1684, 1697.

The word 'acquired' means "come into possession; or gain by oneself." *Kamuri Sri Sankara Rao* v. *Kanuri Rajka Lakshmma,* AIR 1961 AP 241, 244. [Hindu Succession Act (30 of 1956), S. 14(1)]

"Acquired territory" means so much of the territories comprised in the India-Bangladesh agreement and its protocol and referred to the First Schedule as are demarcated for the purpose of being acquired by India from Bangladesh in pursuance of the agreement and its protocol referred to in clause (c). [Constitution (One Hundredth Amendment) Act, 2015, S. 2(a)].

See also Appointed Day.

Acquirer. Means any person who, directly or indirectly, acquires or agrees to acquire shares or voting rights in the target company, or acquires or agrees to acquire control over the target company, either by himself or with any person acting in concert with the acquirer [S. 2(1)(b) of the Securities and Exchange Board of India (Substantial Acquisition of Shares and Takeovers) Regulations, 1997; Also see *Explanation* to section 236(8) of the Companies Act, 2013 (18 of 2013)]

"ACQUIRER" means any person who, directly or indirectly, acquires or agrees to acquire whether by himself, or through, or with persons acting in connect with him, shares or voting rights in, or control over a target company [S. 2(1)(a) of the Securities and Exchange Board of India (Substantial Acquisition of Shares and Takeovers) Regulation, 2011]

Acquis communautaire. The body of law which is represented by the legislation adopted by the European community.

Acquisition. Gaining of possession or control. In India, if the State acquires property for a public purpose under statutory powers, this is described as the acquisition of land.

"ACQUISITION", with its grammatical variations and cognate expressions, includes hiring, borrowing, or accepting as a gift. [Arms Act (54 of 1959), S. 2(1)(a)].

"ACQUISITION" means, directly or indirectly, acquiring or agreeing to acquire—

(i) shares, voting rights or assets of any enterprise; or

(ii) control over management or control over assets of any enterprise. [Competition Act, 2003 (12 of 2003), S. 2(a)].

The act by which a person acquires the property in a thing. The word "acquisition" as used in S. 23, Land Acquisition Act (1 of 1894) (repealed), includes the purpose for which the land is taken as well as the actual taking.

'Acquisition' in every case must mean transfer of ownership. *Dwarkadas* v. *Sholapur S & W Co.*, AIR 1951 Bom 86, 91. [Constitution of India, Art. 31(2)]

The act by which a person acquires the property in a thing. The word "acquisition" as used in Land Acquisition Act (1 of 1894)(repealed), S. 23, includes the purpose for which the land is taken as well as the actual taking. (*Collector of Dinajpore* v. *Girja Nath Roy*, 25 Cal 346)

The word 'acquisition' in Art 31, Constitution of India has quite a wide concept meaning the procuring of property or the taking of it permanently or temporarily. It does not necessarily imply the acquisition of legal title by the State in the property taken in possession. *Dwarkadar Shrinivas* v. *Sholapur Spinning & Weaving Co. Ltd.*, AIR 1954 SC 119.

Acquisition and **deprivation.** By 'deprivation' it is meant to take away or seize the rights of another person whereas by 'acquisition' it is meant to acquire something from another person and to have it vested in another whether it is the ownership of the proprietory rights or other rights. *Joshi Jayantilal* v. *Gujarat State,* AIR 1962 Guj 297, 303. [Constitution of India, Art. 31]

Acquisition and **possession**—Distinction. Acquisition means and implies the acquiring of the entire title of the expropriated owner, whatever the nature and extent of that title might be. In taking possession, the title to the property admittedly remains in the original holder, though he is excluded from possession or enjoyment of the property. *Chiranjit Lal* v. *Union of India*, AIR 1951 SC 41, 54. [Constitution of India, Art. 31(2)]

Acquisition and requisition. Acquisition means acquiring of entire title of expropriated owner.

Requisition involves merely taking of domain or control over property without acquiring rights of ownership for temporary duration. It cannot be continued indefinitely. *H.D. Vora* v. *State of Maharashtra,* AIR 1984 SC 866, 869; *Grahak Sanstha Manch* v. *State of Maharashtra,* AIR 1994 SC 2319, 2327 : (1994) 4 SCC 192.

The concept of acquisition has an air of permanence and finally in that there is transference of the title of the original holder to the acquiring authority or the Government. The concept of requisition merely involves taking of domain or control over property without acquiring rights of ownership. From the very nature of things, it is only of a temporary duration. *Brij Narian* v. *UOI,* AIR 1998 Del 116, 119. [Income-tax Act (43 of 1961), S. 4]

Acquisition and taking possession. The expression "taking possession of" or "acquisition" convey the same meaning as conveyed by the word 'deprivation'. *Nand Ram* v. *Kishori Raman Singh,* AIR 1962 All 521, 530. [Constitution of India, Art 31]

Acquisition by the State. If the State has in substance acquired all the rights in the land for its own purposes, even if the title remains with the owner, it cannot be said that it is not an acquisition within the second proviso to Article 31-A. *Ajit Singh* v. *State of Punjab*, AIR 1967 SC 856, 861. [Constitution of India, Art. 31A]

Acquisition of gain. Both the expressions 'business' and 'acquisition of gain' are to be given the widest possible meaning : charitable, religious, scientific and other associations not having for their object the acquisition of gain being alone excluded. *I.R.C.* v. *Horean Syndicate Ltd.,* (1921) 3 KB 258. [Companies Act (1 of 1956) replaced with Companies Act, 2013, S. 11]

Acquisition of property. The mere enhancement of land revenue does not amount to acquisition of property. *Raghavaraju* v. *Revenue Inspector*, AIR 1962 AP 415, 416. [Constitution of India, Art. 31]

Acquisitive prescription. Prescription whereby a right is acquired.

Acquit. To set free or deliver from the charge of an offence after trial [CrPC 1973 (2 of 1974), S. 237(3) and Emigration Act (7 of 1922), S. 27C(1)].

Acquittal. The word 'acquittal' is *verbum equivocum*, and may in ordinary language be used to express the formal judgment of the Court, that the prisoner is not guilty.

The word "acquittal" does not mean that the trial must have ended in a complete acquittal but would also include the case where an accused has been acquitted of the charge of murder and has been convicted of a lesser offence. *Tarachand Dansu Sutar* v. *State of Maharashtra*, AIR 1962 SC 130, 132. [Constitution of India, Art. 134(1)(*a*)]

Acquittance. A discharge in writing of a sum of money or duty which ought to be paid or done. [IPC (45 of 1860), S. 467]; a release or discharge in respect of any debt or obligation.

Acre. A piece of land containing 4,840 square yards or 43,560 square feet.

Acretion. Acreited land is the ground which is added to the estate so gradually and imperceptibly that none could judge as to how much is added in each moment of time. [*Justiman Institute Let II Tite 1020*].

Act. The word "ACT" denotes as well a series of acts as a single act. [IPC (45 of 1860), S. 33] now (w.e.f. 1-7-2024) repealed & replaced by Bharatiya Nyaya Sanhita, 2023 (45 of 2023), section 2(1)]

"ACT" used with reference to an offence or a civil wrong shall include a series of acts, and words which refer to acts done extend also to illegal omissions. [General Clauses Act (10 of 1897), S. 3(2)].

In a general sense, something done; the exercise of power, or an effect produced thereby. (*Abbott, L. Dict.*) It also means an instrument in writing to verify facts. (*Webster*). In a more special sense the word is used to denote the result of a public deliberation, the decision of the Sovereign, of a legislative body, of a council, court of justice, or magistrate. Also a decree, edict, law, judgment, resolve, award, determination. (*Bouvier*; *Burrill*)

ACT IN LEGISLATION is a statute, or law made by a legislative body.

"ACT" when used in a statute is wide enough to cover a judicial or *quasi*-judicial act.

ACT OR OMISSION, "The word 'ACT' denotes as well a series of acts as a single act; the word "omission" denotes as well a series of omissions as a single omission." [IPC (45 of 1860), S. 33]

ACT, in CPC (5 of 1908), S. 80 includes tortious Acts. *Cecil Gray* v. *Cantonment Committee of Poona,* 12 Bom LR 615.

"Act includes illegal omission." *Amalgamated Electricity Co. (Belgaum) Ltd.* v. *Municipal Committee, Ajmer*, AIR 1969 SC 227 at 231. [CPC (5 of 1908), S. 80]

The word "act" appearing in the order was not such as would include the act of pleading, and was intended to cover only such acts as are capable of being done in the act of acting for a litigant. The word 'act' in O. III, R. 1 is preceded by the words "appearance and application". The term 'act' there appears to have been used in the technical sense and not in the ordinary sense as being referable to any action by any party. *Anglo French Drug Co.* v. *R.D. Tinaikar*, AIR 1959 Bom 21, 24. [CPC (5 of 1908), O. III, R.1]

A law made by a competent legislature [IPC (45 of 1860), Ss. 1 and 5]; a thing done; the process of doing; action [IPC (45 of 1860), S. 33 and General Clauses Act (10 of 1897), S. 3(2)]; to perform [Army Act (46 of 1950), S. 3(x) and Constitution of India, Art. 124(7)]; to perform as on the stage.

ACT, BILL, LAW. "A bill is a draft or form of an act presented to the legislature, but not enacted." The word 'law' is peculiarly inappropriate, for a portion of any Act may be law as well as the whole of the Act.

Act done under colour of office. To be able to say that an act was done under the colour of an office one must discover a reasonable connection between the act alleged and the duty or authority imposed by the statutory enactment. *State of Maharashtra* v. *Narhar Rao*, AIR 1966 SC 1783, 1785.

Act in law. "Act in law" or, as it is sometimes expressed "act of law" is something done by law, or by force of law, whether, if by force of law, the hand that does it is willing or not : e.g. a sale of land by the owner to a body which has statutory compulsory powers to acquire it (Co. Litt. 215 a : *Winter's Case* 3 Dyer 308 b).

An act which one is compelled to do, or does under statutory compulsion, is an "act of law" and it cannot properly be limited to such matters and things as were probably the only acts in law at the time when Lord COKE was writing (*Per* EVE J., *Piggott* v. *Middlesex County Council,* [1909] 1 Ch. 134, at p. 142; cp. By LAW).

Act in pais, means literally an act in the country, *i.e.*, an ordinary conveyance as distinguished from an act done in Court which is a matter of record.

A judicial or other act performed out of Court and not a matter of record.

Act judicially. To exercise the functions of a judicial or quasi-judicial character; to do judicial work. [IPC (45 of 1860), S. 20].

Act of God. (*Vis Major*). An event which happens independently of human action and which no human foresight or skill could reasonably be expected to anticipate [Motor Transport Workers Act (27 of 1961), S. 13 (2nd prov.) and Railways Act (24 of 1989), S. 93(a)].

(*Vis Major*) It may be defined to be any accident, due directly and exclusively to natural causes without human intervention, which by no amount of foresight, pains or care, reasonably to have been expected, could have been prevented.

The storms, lightning, and tempests, are Acts of God as they could not happen by the intervention of man.

Permanent illness is an "Act of God."

Act of Law. The operation of legal rules upon given facts.

Act of Parliament. A written law formally enacted by the legislature into a law, as distinguished from a bill which is in the form of draft of a law or legislative proposal presented to the legislature for enactment, in India, a bill passed by the two Houses of Parliament and assented to by the President and in the absence of an express provision to the contrary, operative from the date of notification in the Gazette.

Act of State. Where a territory is acquired by a sovereign state for the first time that is an Act of State. It matters not how the acquisition has been brought about. It may be by conquest; it may be by cession following on treaty; it may be by occupation of territory hitherto unoccupied by a recognized ruler.

'Act of State' is the taking over of sovereign powers by a State in respect of territory which was not till then a part of its territory either by conquest, treaty or cession or otherwise, and may be said to have taken place on a particular date, if there is proclamation or other public declaration of such taking over. *Promod Chandra Deb* v. *State of Orissa*, AIR 1962 SC 1288, 1289.

Acts of Courts and acts of judicial officers come within the purview of the expression 'Act of state'. [Constitution of India, Art. 19(1)(*g*)]

The term 'act of state' also means an act in respect of which there is an official declaration. *Roman Catholic Mission* v. *State of Madras*, AIR 1966 SC 1457, 1464.

Act of State Doctrine. Doctrine that one government will not judge the legality of acts of another government committed within the latter's territory.

Act of terrorism. See "Acts of terrorism".

Act of violence. Includes any of the following acts committed by any person against a healthcare service personnel serving during an epidemic, which causes or may cause—

(i) harassment impacting the living or working conditions of such healthcare service personnel and preventing him from discharging his duties;

(ii) harm, injury, hurt, intimidation or danger to the life of such healthcare service personnel, either within the premises of a clinical establishment or otherwise;

(iii) obstruction or hindrance to such healthcare service personnel in the discharge of his duties, either within the premises of a clinical establishment or otherwise; or

(iv) loss or damage to any property or documents in the custody of, or in relation to, such healthcare service personnel. [Epidemic Diseases Act, 1897 (3 of 1897), section 1A(a)]

Act purporting to be done. The expression 'act purporting to be done' according to one interpretation which is strictly grammatical, takes in part acts as well as future acts. The other interpretation based upon an idiomatic interpretation of the language is that it would be restricted to part acts. *State of Madras* v. *Chitturi Venkata Durga Prasadrao*, AIR 1957 AP 675, 677. [CPC (5 of 1908), S. 80]

Acta exteriora indicant interiora secreta. External acts indicate undisclosed thoughts. External actions show internal secrets. Intention may be inferred from external actions.

Acta in uno judicio non probant in alio nisi inter easiem personas. (*Maxim*) Things done in one action cannot be taken as evidence in another unless it be between the same parties.

Acta publica. (*Lat.*) Things of general knowledge and concern; matters transacted before certain public officers.

Acted illegally or with material irregularity. This phrase occurring in CPC (5 of 1908), S. 115, is not limited to cases of procedure only, but includes cases of decisions vitiated by an error so gross and palpable as to lead to grave and manifest injustice.

Acting. A term employed to designate one performing the duties of an office to which he does not himself claim title; (as) acting appointment. The word is also sometimes used in the sense of "operating" (as) in a provision that one of two companies should be the "acting and controlling" company.

The mechanical act of handing over an appeal to the clerk of Court or another officer appointed for receiving appeals does not amount to "acting" as contemplated by O. III, R. 4, CPC (5 of 1908), it is only a ministerial work and similar in nature to the payment of process fee, *etc.*, which the clerks of counsel usually do.

Performing [IPC (45 of 1860), S. 20]; holding a temporary position; performing services temporarily; an assumed or a dramatic part.

Acting and **applying.** "Applying" is included in the meaning of the word 'acting' and a pleader who files an application on behalf of a party 'acts' for him. *Nadella Satyanarayana* v. *Yamanoori Venkata Subbiah,* AIR 1957 AP 172, 179 (FB). [CPC (5 of 1908), O. III, R. 1, 4]

Acting in any manner prejudicial to the security of state or maintenance of public order. The expression 'Acting in any manner prejudicial to the security of State or maintenance of public order' includes the commission of the offence of mischief by fire on any property of the Govt. or educational institution where the commission of such mischief disturbs or is likely to disturb public order. *Keshab Roy* v. *State of West Bengal*, AIR 1972 SC 926, 927.

Causing insult to the Indian National Flag or to any other object of public generation is such a situation as reasonably exposes the act, causing such insult, to the view of those, who hold these objects in veneration or to the public view. *State of W.B.* v. *Ashok Dey etc.*, AIR 1972 SC 1660, 1667.

If a threat to kill is administered to a person on account of refusal to rub out the anti-naxalite slogans written on the wall of his house 'terrorised the common public and as such they could not pursue the normal avocations of life and further more, disturbed public order, this offence of threatening would come within the expression "acting in any manner prejudicial to the maintenance of public order." *Joydeb Gorai* v. *State of W.B.*, AIR 1972 SC 2173, 2174.

Defiling an object of public veneration like the statute of Rabindra Nath Tagore, in public view amounts to disturbance of 'public order'. *Deb Sadhan Roy* v. *The State of West Bengal*, AIR 1972 SC 1924, 1932.

Acting partner. A partner who habitually acts in the business of the firm. [Indian Partnership Act (9 of 1932), S. 24].

Acting upon the licence. A person would be 'acting upon the licence, within S. 60(*b*) only when he executes a work of a permanent character upon the land of a licensor. *Deep Chand Sao* v. *Kasturi Devi,* AIR 1975 Pat 17, 20. [Indian Easement Act (5 of 1882), S. 60(*b*)]

Actio. An action.

Actio contrario. A counter or cross action.

Actio damni injuria. An action for damages.

Actio in personam. A personal action seeking redress against a particular individual.

Actio in rem. An action for the recovery of the very thing; an action for the enforcement of a right against all the world.

Actio nihil aluid est quam jus prosequendi in judicio quod alicui debetur. An action is nothing else than the right of pursuing in a Court of justice, that which is due to one.

Actio non datur non damnificato. (*Maxim*) An action is not given to one who is not injured. (*Burrill*)

Actio personalis moritur cum persona. (*Maxim*) A personal action dies with the person. This maxim expresses the law in regard to the surviving of personal actions. The maxim does not apply in the case of civil death.

A personal right of action dies with the person. In other words, the personal action dies with a man. [*I. Pedasubhayya* v. *Akkamma*, AIR 1958 SC 1043; *B. Gajapathi Rao* v. *State of Andhra Pradesh*, AIR 1964 SC 1645].

Arbitration Act (10 of 1940), Sec. 6(3) is founded on this maxim.

The maxim has application only when the action is one for damages for a personal wrong, and as a suit for partition is a suit for property, the rule in question has no application to it. *Kakumanu Pedasubhayya* v. *Kakumanu Akkamma*, AIR 1958 SC 1042, 1050.

The maxim does not apply to the death of a person liable to render an account for the property received by him, not affecting the liability of his estate. *Girijanandhini* v. *Bijendra Narain*, AIR 1967 SC 1124, 1131. [CPC (5 of 1908), O. XXII, R. 1]

Actio poenalis in haeredem non datur nisi forte ex domno locupletior haeres factussit. (*Maxim*) A penal action is not given against an heir, unless, indeed, such heir is benefitted by the wrong. (*Wharton*)

Actio quaelibet it sua via. Every action follows its prescribed course.

Every action is to follow its prescribed course in law. [*Ramlila Maidan Incident, In Re,* (2012) 5 SCC 1, para 270].

Action. The form of a suit given by law for recovery of that which is one's due; or it is a legal demand of a man's right. (*Co. Lit.* 285. *Tomlin.* See to the same effect *Justinian Inst.* 4, 6).

ACTION, generally means a litigation in a civil Court for the recovery of individual right or redress of individual wrong.

A proceeding. [CrPC 1973 (2 of 1974), S. 2(d)]; A judicial proceeding for the enforcement or protection of a right, the redress or prevention of a wrong or the punishment of an offence [Negotiable Instruments Act (26 of 1881), S. 134, ill]; [Indian Contract Act (9 of 1872), S. 145, ill. (b) and Arbitration Act (10 of 1940), S. 36]; doing; operating; a thing done [Dakshina Bharat Hindi Prachar Sabha Act(14 of 1964), S. 6]; something done or doing [Arms Act (54 of 1959), S. 2(1)(e)]; active operation against enemy [Army Act (46 of 1950), S. 34(g)]; a deliberative or authoritative proceeding [Representation of the People Act (43 of 1951), S. 146C].

Action by husband for loss of society of his wife. A husband has an action for loss of society or consortium of his wife caused by enticement, harbouring, inducing her to live away from him.

Action, cause of. The term "cause of action" in law, is generally understood as meaning the whole cause of action; that is, every fact which it is necessary to establish in order to support the right to judicial relief. As otherwise defined, it consists of a right in the plaintiff, a correlative duty or obligation resting on the defendant, and some act or omission done by the latter in violation of the right.

"SUBJECT OF ACTION" is a code term used in the stead of what was formerly known as "subject-matter of the action" and describes the physical facts, the things, real or personal, the money, land, chattel, and the like, in relation to which the suit is prosecuted.

"CIVIL ACTION", is one which has for its object the recovery of private or civil rights, or of compensation for their infraction.

"CRIMINAL ACTION", is one instituted by, or in the name of, the Sovereign power of the State against one or more individuals for the purpose of punishing or preventing a criminal offence. (*Black; Bouvier*)

TO TAKE ACTION is to take steps in regard to anything; to institute legal proceedings.

Actionable. Subject to, or affording ground for, an action or suit at law; as, slander is actionable.

Affording ground for an action at law. [T.P. Act (4 of 1882), Ss. 8 and 130].

Actionable claim. "ACTIONABLE CLAIM" means a claim to any debt, other than a debt secured by mortgage of immovable property of by hypothecation or pledge of movable property or to any beneficial interest in movable property not in the possession, either actual or constructive, of the claimant, which the Civil Courts recognize as affording grounds for relief, whether such debt or beneficial interest be existent, accruing. conditional or contingent. [T.P. Act (4 of 1882), S. 3].

"Actionable claim" in S. 130 of the Transfer of Property Act (4 of 1882) refers only to claims capable of enforcement, at the time of assignment, by suit in the Civil Court. It does not include a claim in respect of which the cause of action had not arisen at the time of the transfer, but which, in future, will mature into a claim so as to be enforceable at once; in other words, a claim could not be treated as an actionable one unless, at the date of the transfer, an action could have been brought therein.

A decretal debt is an actionable claim. The words 'right to sue' do not connote the same meaning as the words 'actionable claim'. *Ambica Prasad Singh* v. *Ram Charitar Singh,* AIR 1951 Pat 415. [T.P. Act (4 of 1882), Ss. 3 & 130]

A debt secured by a charge on immovable property, is an actionable claim.

Actionable wrong. The term "actionable wrong" is an illegal or unauthorised act infringing a legal right of another affording him a ground for action in law.

A wrong in respect of which an action lies in law. [Indian Evidence Act (1 of 1872), S. 10].

Actionare. (From actio an action) To bring an action; to prosecute; or sue. (*Black*)

Actiones nominatae. (*Lat.*) Common law writs having their origin before 1285; writs specifically named as distinguished from writs on the case.

Active concealment. An act of concealing what ought to be revealed, requiring or implying action or execution. [Indian Contract Act (9 of 1872), S. 17(2)].

Active duty. Means the duty to restore and preserve order in any local area in the event of any disturbance therein. [Central Reserve Police Force Act (66 of 1949), S. 2(a)]

"ACTIVE DUTY" in relation to a person subject to this Act, means any duty as a member of the Security Guard during the period in which such person is attached to or forms part of a unit of the Security Guard. (i) which is engaged in operations against terrorists or any person in arms against the Union; or (ii) which is operating at a picket or engage on patrol or any other duty in relation to combating terrorist activity. [National Security Guard Act (47 of 1986), S. 2(a)]

"ACTIVE DUTY" in relation to a person subject to this act, means any duty as a member of the Force during the period in which such person is attached to, or forms part of, a unit of the Force. (i) which is engaged in operations against an enemy, or (ii) which is operating at a picket or engaged on patrol or other guard duty along the borders of India, and includes duty by such person during any period declared by the Central Government by order as a period of active duty with reference to any area in which any person or class of persons subject to this Act may be serving. [Indo Tibetan Border Police Act (35 of 1992), S. 2(a)]

"ACTIVE DUTY" in relation to a member of the Group means any duty as such member during the period when he is posted to physically protect the Prime Minister of India and the members of his immediate family or former Prime Minister and the member of his immediate family, wherever he or they may be. [Special Protection Group Act, (34 of 1988), S. 2(a)]

Active euthanasia. Euthanasia provided by a physician who not only provides the means of death but also carries out the final act of causing death.

Active member. Means a member who fulfils the quantum and period of patronage of the Producer Company as may be required by the articles. [(Repealed and replaced) Companies Act (1 of 1956), section 581A(a); Companies Act (18 of 2013), section 378A(a)]

Active partner. A member of a partnership, actively and openly taking part in the management of the business of the firm; as distinguished from a dormant or silent partner.

Active politics. 'Active politics' means almost whole time in politics. Company job and active politics cannot go together. *Pyare Lal Sharma* v. *Managing Director, J & K Industries*, AIR 1989 SC 1854, 1859.

Active service. ACTIVE SERVICE means service or duty—

(a) during the period of operation of a Proclamation of Emergency issued under clause (1) of Article 352 of the Constitution; or

(b) during any period declared by the Central Government........as a period of active service with reference to any area in which any person or class of persons subject to naval law may be serving. [Navy Act (62 of 1957), S. 3(1)(a), (b)]

"ACTIVE SERVICE", as applied to a person subject to the Air Force Act, 1950, or the Army Act, 1950, means The time during which such person—

(a) is attached to, or forms part of, a force which is engaged in operations against an enemy, or

(b) is engaged in air force operations or is on the line of march to, a country or place wholly or partly occupied by an enemy, or

(c) is attached to, or forms part of a force which is in military occupation of any foreign country. [Air Force Act (45 of 1950), S. 4(i)(a), (b) and (c) and Army Act (46 of 1950), S. 3(i), (a), (b) and (c)]

Active trust. Trust in which the trustee is not a mere passive depository of the estate, but is required to exert himself actively in the execution of the settlor's intention.

Activities. Instances of being active as in an occupation, recreation *etc.* [Agricultural Refinance Corporation Act (10 of 1963), S. 2(a), *Expln.*].

Activity. An occupation or pursuit in which person is active.

Activity-Based Budgeting (ABB). Assigning resource to activities within a budget by identifying those activities and how they interact and incur cost. (*International Accounting*)

Activity-Based Costing (ABC). Alternative to *absorption costing* which acknowledges that every *activity* within an organization incurs cost and therefore the products or users of that activity should bear its cost. (*International Accounting*)

Actore incumbit onus probandi. (*Maxim*) The burden of proof lies on the plaintiff or the complainant. (*Morgan; Broom*)

Actore non probante reus absolvitur. (*Maxim*) The plaintiff not proving (his demand) the defendant is discharged or acquitted.

Actori incumbit onus probandi. The burden of proof lies on the plaintiff or the prosecution. [*Dahyabhai Chhaganbhai Thakkar* v. *State of Gujarat*, AIR 1964 SC 1563 (1566)].

Acts endangering sovereignty, unity and integrity of India. Whoever, purposely or knowingly, by words, either spoken or written, or by signs, or by visible representation, or by electronic communication or by use of financial mean, or otherwise, excites or attempts to excite, secession or armed rebellion or subversive activities, or encourages feelings of separatist activities or endangers sovereignty or unity and integrity of India; or indulges in or commits any such act shall be punished with imprisonment for life or with imprisonment which may extend to seven years, and shall also be liable to fine.

Explanation.—Comments expressing disapprobation of the measures, or administrative or other action of the Government with a view to obtain their alteration by lawful means without exciting or attempting to excite the activities referred to in this section do not constitute an offence under this section. [(w.e.f. 1-7-2024) Bharatiya Nyaya Sanhita, 2023 (45 of 2023), section 152]

Acts in *pari materia*. Acts are regarded to be in *pari materia* when they deal with the same person or thing or class; it is not enough that they deal with a similar subject-matter. [MAXWELL on *Interpretation of Statutes*, 12th Edn., p. 66]

"**Acts of terrorism**" means "criminal acts directed against a State and intended or calculated to create a state of terror in the minds of particular persons, a group of persons or the general public." [The League of Nations took the initiative to formulate the first Global Convention on Preventing Terrorism and, accordingly, adopted the 1937 Convention for the Prevention and Punishment of Terrorism as cited in *Yakub Abdul Razak Memon* v. *State of Maharashtra*, (2013) 13 SCC 1, para 814]. "Acts of unlawful interference"

"**Acts of unlawful interference**" means acts or attempted acts to jeopardise the safety of civil aviation and air transport, including—

(i) unlawful seizure of aircraft in flight;

(ii) unlawful seizure of aircraft on the ground;

(iii) hostage-taking on board aircraft or on aerodromes;

(iv) forcible intrusion on board an aircraft at an aerodrome or on the premises of an aeronautical facility;

(v) introduction on board an aircraft or at an aerodrome of a weapon or hazardous device or material intended for criminal purposes;

(vi) communication of false information with a view to jeopardise the safety of an aircraft in flight or on the ground, of passengers, crew, ground personnel or the general public, at an aerodrome on the premises of a civil aviation facility. [Aircraft (Security) Rules, 2011, R. 2(e)].

Actual. Real; existing in act as opposed to constructive or theoretical, or speculative.

Real, existing in act or fact. [T.P. Act (4 of 1882), S. 3(c)].

Actual authority. The authority, the prince-pal intentionally confers upon the agent, or intentionally, or by want of ordinary care, allows the agent to believe himself to possess.

Actual bailment. Bailment, arising from an actual or constructive delivery of property.

Actual bodily harm. Any hurt or injury calculated to interfere with the health or comfort of the victim.

Actual capital sum assured. For the purposes of section 80C(3A) of Act 43 of 1961, 'actual capital sum assured' in relation to a life insurance policy shall mean the minimum amount assured under the policy on happening of the insured event at any time during the term of the policy, not taking into account—(i) the value of any premium agreed to be returned; or (ii) any benefit by way of bonus or otherwise over and above the sum actually assured, which is to be or may be received under the policy by any person. [*Explanation* to section 80C(3A) of the Income-tax Act, 1961 (43 of 1961) as inserted (w.e.f. 1-4-2013) by the Finance Act, 2012]

Actual cash value. "Contemplates the value, represented by the price obtainable in a sale by a willing vendor to a willing purchaser both alive to commercial realities, for cash and not upon extended or unsecured terms"

Price at which a seller is ready and willing to sell and buyer is ready and willing to buy on the open market and in an arm's length transaction.

Actual cause. Cause without which an event could not occur.

Actual cost. Real price paid upon a genuine *bona fide* purchase. It is said not to include interest, commission paid, incidental expenses or wasted expenditure. In the expression "actual costs and expenses" or "disbursements", profit or trade allowances will not be included.

Government subsidy is an incentive not for the specific purpose of meeting a portion of the costs of the assets, though quantifies as or geared to a percentage of such cost. So it does not partake of the character of a payment intended either directly or indirectly to meet the actual cost. *Commissioner of Income Tax Hyderabad* v. *P.J. Chemicals Ltd.*, AIR 1994 SC 2727, 2733. [Income-tax Act (43 of 1961), S. 43(1)]

Actual damages. Damages awarded for a loss or injury actually sustained as distinguished from damages implied by law or those awarded by way of penalty.

Actual delivery. Delivery in which real and immediate possession is given to the buyer or buyer's agent.

Actual delivery of goods. The expression 'actual delivery of goods' means physical delivery of the goods at the place of destination and not any constructive delivery to the common carrier.

Actual entry. An actual entry upon land is made as soon as the person desiring to make an entry has any part of his body upon the land, and such entry is complete and effectual even though he should immediately afterwards be dragged off by force.

Actual eviction. Expelling a person physically from land or rental property.

Actual fraud. A concealment or misrepresentation of truth through a statement or conduct which causes injury to another.

Actual income must mean income-tax income.

Actual knowledge. Direct and clear knowledge.

Actual loss. As capture of a ship followed by condemnation by the sentence of a Prize Court of competent jurisdiction extinguishing the title of the owner will be actual loss of the owner. *A. Akooji Jadwat Ltd.* v. *Oriental Fire and General Insurance Co. Ltd.*, AIR 1972 Cal 228, 240. [Marine Insurance Act (11 of 1963), S. 60]

Actual malice. Deliberate intent of committing an injury, as evidenced by external circumstances.

Actual market value. In custom laws, the price at which merchandise is freely offered for sale to all purchasers; the price which the manufacturer or owner would have received for merchandise, sold in the ordinary course of trade in the usual wholesale quantities. (*Black*)

Actual notice. Notice which is given to a party directly or presumed to be received personally because the evidence within the knowledge of the party is sufficient to put him or her on inquiry.

Actual occupation. 'Actual occupation' *prima facie* means physical presence on land, no doubt mere temporary presence is not enough, there must be some degree of permanence; secondly, a person may be in occupation through another, thirdly, that occupation may be shared and fourthly, that the actual occupier is not required to do anything to protect his rights.

Actual possession. Occupation or having control over property.

Actual residence. "Actual residence" means that the person should be residing at the place in fact and in reality at the commencement of the suit and not constructively. *Jaichand Lal* v. *Firm Keshri Chand Bhanwarlal,* AIR 1962 Raj 88, 89. [CPC (5 of 1908), S. 20]

Actual seisin. Actual possession of a freehold estate in land.

Actual service. Actual delivery of legal notice to the person to whom it is directed.

Actual total loss. A term, used in marine insurance to describe the situation "where the subject-matter is destroyed or so damaged as to cease to be a thing of the kind insured or where the assured is irretrievably deprived thereof."

Actual value. Emergency Risks (Factories) Insurance Scheme, Para 7, Cl (*a*). The actual value which was the insurable value could only be the market value and not the actual cost to the owner. *Aluminum Corporation of India Ltd.* v. *Union of India*, AIR 1988 SC 751, 752.

Actually. In fact; really; indeed. [T.P. Act (4 of 1882), S. 3(c)].

Actually and **voluntarily resides.** In interpreting the phrase "actually and voluntarily resides", the words "actually" and "voluntarily" must be taken together; the word "actually" means "in fact." A person cannot be said to be "voluntarily residing" in a place where he is confined in a jail.

The adverb 'actually' before the word 'resides' has been used to exclude an idea of domicile or constructive residence. The place of a person's abode where he ordinarily lives, is to be taken as the place of his residence and his short visits to other places will not make him a resident of those places. *Mulk Baj* v. *Thakat Mal,* AIR 1965 All 72, 75, 76. [Displaced persons (Debts Adjustments) Act (70 of 1951), S. 5]

Actually delivered. The expression 'actually delivered' can only mean physical delivery of the goods or such action as puts the goods in the possession of the purchaser, it does not contemplate mere symbolical or notional delivery *e.g.* by entrusting the goods to a common carrier, or even delivery of documents of title like railway receipts. *Bajarang Jute Mills Ltd.* v. *State of Andhra Pradesh*, AIR 1966 S.C. 376, 379. [Constitution of India, Art. 286(1)]

Actuarial calculation. Calculation determined by actuaries; calculation relating to statistics especially of life expectancy.

Actuarial table. Organised statistical data which indicates life expectancies.

Actuary. A person skilled in calculating the value of life interests, annuities and insurances, or an officer appointed to keep savings bank accounts, or the manager of an insurance company. (*Ency. of the Laws of England*)

One whose profession is to solve monetary problems depending on interest and probability in connection with life, fire or other accidents *etc.* [Insurance Act (4 of 1938), S. 2(1)].

Actus curiae neminem gravabit. (*Maxim*) An act of the Court shall prejudice no man.

A maxim meaning "an act of the court shall prejudice no man." **Applied** in *Srihari* v. *Syed Maqdoom Shah*, (2015) 1 SCC 607, para 23.

This maxim "is founded upon justice and good sense, and affords a safe and certain guide for the administration of the law".

Maxim applied in *In Re Biyamma*, AIR 1963 Mys 326, 328; *Union of India* v. *Kamal Kumar Goswami,* AIR 1974 Cal 231, 238; *Oil and Natural Gas Corporation Limited* v. *Modern Construction and Company*, (2014) 1 SCC 648, para 19].

An act of the Court (judge) shall prejudice no one. *State of Gujarat* v. *Jagan Bhai*, AIR 1966 SC 1631. [IPC (45 of 1860), S. 77].

Actus dei nemini est damnosus. (*Maxim*) The act of God is hurtful to no one, (*i.e.*, a person cannot be held responsible for an accident occurring without his fault and attributable to *vis major* or act of God. (*Black; Burrill*)

Actus dei nemini facit injuriam. (*Maxim*) The act of God does injury to no one.

Actus incaeptus cujus perfectio pendet ex voluntate partium revocari potest, si autem pendet ex voluntate tertie persanoe vel ex contingenti revocari non potest. (*Bacon*) (*Maxim*) An act already begun, the completion of which depends upon the will of the parties, may be revoked; but if it depends on the will of a third person, or on a contingency, it cannot be revoked. (*Burrill; Bacon*)

Actus judiciarius coram non judice irritus habetur de ministeriali autem a quocunque provenit ratum esto. (*Maxim*) A judicial act done without authority is void; not so a ministerial act." (*Morgan*) "When an act is done without or in excess of jurisdiction, the act will be invalid if it is a judicial act, but if it is a ministerial act, the question as to whether it is valid or invalid depends on circumstances. (*Byrne*)

Actus legis nemini est damnosus. (*Maxim*) The act of the law is hurtful to no one; it shall prejudice no body.

Actus legis nemini facit injuriam. (*Maxim*) The act of the law injures no one.

Actus legitimi non recipiunt modum. (*Maxim*) Legal actions do not admit a limitation (*Morgan*) *i.e.*, acts required to be done by law do not admit of qualification or limitation.

Actus me invito factus non est meus actus. (*Maxim*) An act done by me against my will is not my act.

Actus non facit reum, nisi mens sit rea. (*Maxim*) The act itself does not make a man guilty unless his intention were so.

An act does not make one guilty unless the mind is also guilty.

The act itself does not constitute guilt unless done with a guilty intent. An act is not a crime unless it is committed with a particular criminal intention (*mens rea*). What constitutes the *mens rea* is laid down in the case of offences defined in the Indian Penal Code (45 of 1860) [*State of Maharashtra* v. *Mayer Hans George*, AIR 1965 SC 722 (731)].

Actus novus interveniens. A new act which intervenes to break the chain of causation.

Actus repugnum non potest in esse produce. (*Maxim*) A repugnant act cannot be brought into being *i.e.* it cannot be made effectual. (*Plowden*)

Actus reus. Wrongful Act; guilty act.

Actus reus non facit reum nisi mens sit rea. (*Lat.*) An act does not make a person guilty of his crime unless his mind also be guilty.

Actus servi in lis quibus opera ejus communitur adhihita actus domini habetur. (*Maxim*) The act of a servant in those things in which he is usually employed is considered the acts of his master.

Ad colligenda bona. (*Lat.*) To collect the goods.

Ad colligendum bona defuncti. To collect the goods of the deceased.

Ad damnum clause. A clause in a prayer for relief mentioning the amount of damages claimed.

Ad diem. At the day or at a day.

Ad ea quae frequentius accidunt jura adaptantur. The laws are adapted to those cases which more frequently occur.

Ad filum aquae. To the thread or middle of a stream.

Ad filum viae. (Lat.) To the middle of the way.

Ad hoc. For particular purpose.

Made, established, acting or concerned with a particular end or purpose.

Ad hoc. The expression "ad hoc" means "something which is formed for a particular purpose". [Black's Law Dictionary as cited in *Rita Wahal and Ors.* v. *Chancellor, King George's Medical University and Ors.*, 2017 (6) ADJ 652, para 52]

Ad hoc employee. The term 'ad hoc employee' is conveniently used for a wholly temporary employee engaged either for a particular period or for a particular purpose and one whose services can be terminated with the maximum of ease. *S.K. Varma* v. *State of Punjab,* AIR 1979 P&H 149, 151 (FB). [Constitution of India, Art. 311]

Ad hominem. Appeal to personal perjuries rather than to reason.

Ad idem. With a common understanding.

Ad infinitum. To infinity; endlessly; on and on without end; through an infinite series. Without limit; forever.

Ad interim. In the interval (as) *ad interim* injunction. In the meantime.

Ad litem. (*Lat.*) For the suit.

Ad litum, ad litem. For the suit. Every Court has the power to appoint a guardian *ad litum.* For the suit *e.g.* guardian *ad litem.* [CPC (5 of 1908), O. XXXI, R. 3].

Ad medium filum acquae. To the middle thread of the stream.

Ad medium filum viae. To the middle thread of the way.

Where the boundary between two properties is a non-navigable river, a road or a ditch, the respective proprietors are presumed to have control up to an imaginary line or thread (*filum*), drawn through the center of such river, road, or ditch. The same rule applied whether the properties on both the sides be private property of individuals or corporations or villages, or municipalities.

Ad officium justiciariorum spectat, unicuique coram eis placitanti justitiam exhibere. It is the duty of justices to administer justice to everyone seeking it from them. (*Latin for Lawyers*)

Ad proximum antecedents fiat relatio nisi impediatur sententia. (*Maxim*) Relative words refer to the next antecedent unless by such a construction the meaning of the sentence would be impaired. (*Broom*)

The antecedent has relation to that which next follows unless thereby the meaning of the sentence would be impaired. But although this general proposition is true in strict grammatical construction, yet there are numerous examples in the best writers to show that the context often requires a deviation from the rule, and that the relative may refer to nouns which go before the last antecedent, and either take from it or give to it some qualification. (*Latin for Lawyers*)

Ad questionem facti non respondent judices; ad questionem juris non respondent juratores. To questions of fact judges do not answer; to questions of law the jury do not answer.

Ad questionem legis respondent judices. To questions of law the judges answer.

Ad quaestiones facti non respondent judices; ad quaestiones legis non respondent juratores. (*Maxim*) As regards cases tried by a judge and jury, the Judge does not decide questions of fact and the jury do not decide questions of law. (*Byrne*)

In other words : "it is the office of the judge to instruct the jury in points of law—of the jury to decide on matters of fact." (*Broom*)

Ad referendum. (*Lat.*) For further consideration.

Ad sectam. At the suit of.

Ad valorem. According to the valuation. *Ad valorem* duties are always estimated at a certain per cent on the valuation of the property, as opposed to fixed or specific duties.

In proportion to the value. [Indian Forest Act (16 of 1927), S. 39(2)].

Ad vim majorem vel ad casus fortuitos non tenetur quis, nisi sua culpa intervenerit. (*Maxim*) No one is held to answer for the effects of a superior force, or of accidents unless his own fault has contributed to it.

Adalat. (Udalut, corruptly, Adawlut) : Court of justice; justice; equity. Under the Mohammadan Government, the Adalats, or Courts of Justice, were four : (1) *Nizamat Adalat.*—The Supreme Court of Criminal Justice, nominally presided over by the Nazim or Viceroy of the province. This was subdivided into the *Roz-a-adalat* or Court held on a Sunday by the Nazim for the trial of capital offenders, and the *Adalat ul Aaliyat* the High Court in which affrays, quarrels, and cases regarding personal property were tried : this was usually presided over by the Nizam's Deputy, or Darogha. (2) *Diwani Adalat.*—The Civil Court of the Diwan, the chief officer in charge of the revenue of the principality. (3) *Faujdari Adalat.*—The Court of the Faujdar, or chief of the magistracy and police of a district; the Subordinate, or District Criminal Court. (4) *Adalatul Kazi.* The Court of the Kazi, the Chief Judge of a town or district in civil causes and questions regarding the Mohammadan religion. Under him the *Muhtasib* held a Court for the adjudication of offences against morals—as drunkenness, gambling, *etc.* Under the British Government these Courts were continued, with some modifications, until 1793, when the judicial and revenue departments were separated, and Zila and Provincial Courts were established, subordinate to one Supreme Adalat at the Presidency, distinguished as the Sadar or Sudder Adalat, High Court of Justice, or Court of Final Decision, subdivided into *Sadar-diwani Adalat*, High Court of Civil Jurisdiction and *Sadar Nizamat or Faujdari Adalat*, High Court of Criminal Justice. (*Bengal Reg.* iii, ix, xii, xiii, 1793; ii, 1795, ii, 1801; viii, 1803)

Adapt. To make suitable; to fit or suit; to adjust; to alter so as to fit for a new use; to change by adaptation—often followed by to, or for.

Adaptable. Capable of being adapted.

Adaptation. Act or process of adapting, or state of being adapted.

The word adaptation carries with it the idea of modification for new uses or a change in form or structure.

Process of modifying a thing so as to suit new condition. The expression must mean alterations of the phraseology of an enactment in order to bring the enactment into accord with the changed constitutional position. *Gulab Singh* v. *District Magistrate, Dehradun,* AIR 1950 All 11, 17 (FB). [Independence Act, 1947, S. 18(3)]

The action or process of adapting. [Copyright Act (14 of 1957), S. 2(a); Constitution of India, Art. 35(b) and Art. 118(2)].

Adaptation means—

(i) in relation to a dramatic work, the conversion of the work into a non-dramatic work;

(ii) in relation to a literary work or an artistic work, the conversion of the work into a dramatic work by way of performance in public or otherwise;

(iii) in relation to a literary or dramatic work, any abridgement of the work or any version of the work in which the story or action is conveyed wholly or mainly by means of pictures in a form suitable for reproduction in a book, or in a newspaper, magazine or similar periodical; (iv) in relation to a musical work, any arrangement or transcription of the work; and (v) in relation to any work, any use of such work involving its re-arrangement or alteration; [The Copyright Act, 1957, S. 2(a)].

Adaptation right. The exclusive right of the copyright holder to prepare derivative works on the basis of the protected work.

Adapted. Means "fit and apt for the purposes." "Adapted" also means "suitable."

Adapted, Best. Best suited. [Mines Act (35 of 1952), S. 61(4)(c)].

Adapted for sale. Adapting for sale points clearly to something being done to the article in question which, in some way, makes it in itself a little different from what it was before. Conversion of sea water into salt amounts to adapting it for sale. *Ardeshir* v. *Bombay State*, AIR 1962 SC 29, 34. [Factories Act (63 of 1948), S. 2(*h*)]

Adapted for use. The words 'adapted for use' must be construed as 'suitable for use'. *Bolani Ores* v. *State of Orissa*, AIR 1975 SC 17, 26.

"Adapted vehicle". Means a motor vehicle either specially designed and constructed, or to which alterations have been made under sub-section (2) of section 52, for the use of a person suffering from any physical defect or disability, and used solely by or for such person. [Motor Vehicles Act, 1988 (59 of 1988), section 2(1)]

Add. To attach, annex or subjoin as an augmentation or accretion.

Add, Attach, Affix, Annex. These words agree in denoting the increasing of a thing by something additional. *Add* is the most general term, but it may denote an intimate union of the things combined, the formation of a whole in which the parts lose their individuality : as, to add water to a decoction; to add one sum to another. This idea is not expressed by any of the others. *Attach* (as also *annex* and *affix*) denotes a more external combination. It implies the possibility of detaching that which is attached, as to attach a locomotive to a train. Hence we do not attach, but add, one fluid to another. It generally retains its original notion of a strong connection physical, moral or other; as, to attach a condition to a gift. *Affix* may be used either of that which is essential to the value or completeness of the whole, or of something that is wholly extrinsic or unrelated : as, to affix a signature or seal to an instrument; to *affix* a notice to a post. To *annex* sometimes brings the parts into vital relation : as, to *annex* territory, a codicil to a will, or a penalty to a prohibition. (*Cent. Dict.*)

Addendum. A thing that is added or is to be added. [Companies Act (1 of 1956), S. 217(3) replaced by Companies Act, 2013].

Addicere. In the civil law, to adjudge or condemn; to assign, allot, or deliver; to sell. (*Black*)

Addict. "ADDICT" means a person who has dependence on any narcotic drug or psychotropic substance. [Narcotic Drugs and Psychotropic Substance Act (61 of 1985), S. 2(i)]

To be an addict, means something more than being merely accustomed to drink. It is certainly not a term of art, and giving to it its plain natural meaning the expression 'addict' does carry with it a sense of moral obloquy. *State of Bombay* v. *P.V. Balsara*, AIR 1951 SC 319, 331.

The expression 'addict' is applicable to a person who habitually is given to a practice. *Sunder Dumanna Shetty* v. *K.D. Billimoria*, AIR 1959 Bom 346, 355.

Addictive drug. Any natural or synthetic drug which causes periodic or chronic intoxication when consumed repeatedly.

Addition. In this Act, unless there is anything repugnant in the subject or context,— "ADDITION" means the place of residence, and the profession, trade, rank and title (if any) of a person described as the son of his mother, then his mother's name. [Registration Act (16 of 1908), S. 2(1)].

Title; designation [Registration Act (16 of 1908), S. 2(1)]; [Negotiable Instruments Act (26 of 1881), S. 124]; the act or process of adding [CPC (5 of 1908), Or. XXVII, A, R. 3].

Existing in addition; added. [Constitution of India, Art. 115, margin]; existing in addition (when used with reference to designations).

Additional Commissioner. A person appointed to be an Additional Commissioner of Income-tax under sub-section (1) of section 117. [Income-tax Act (43 of 1961), section 2(1C)]

Additional Director. A person appointed to be an Additional Director of Income-tax under sub-section (1) of section 117. [Income-tax Act (43 of 1961), section 2(1D)]

Additional evidence. Evidence let in appeal after the trial has closed in the lower Court,—a privilege allowed only under special circumstances. The legitimate occasion for the admission of additional evidence in appeal is where, on looking into the evidence as it stands, some inherent lacuna or defect becomes evident.

Additional insured. Specially named assured party under an insurance policy.

Additional trading floor. Means a trading ring or trading facility offered by a recognized stock exchange outside its area of operation to enable the investors to buy and sell securities through such trading floor under the regulatory framework of that stock exchange. [Securities Contracts (Regulations) Act (42 of 1956), S. 13-A, *Expln*]

Additional voluntary contribution. Extra sum paid into an occupational pension scheme by an employee, to increase the size of the pension.

Address. Direction or superscription of a letter [Inland Vessels Act (1 of 1917), S. 19L(1)]; to direct a written message or spoken words to [Jawaharlal Nehru University Act (53 of 1966), S. 8(5)]; a formal speech or written statement directed to a person or group of persons [Copyright Act (14 of 1957), S. 2(n) and Constitution of India, art. 86(1)]; [Army Act (46 of 1950), S. 143(1)].

Address for service. "ADDRESS FOR SERVICE" shall mean the address furnished by a party or his authorised agent, or his legal practitioner at which service of summons, notices or other processes may be effected. [Debts Recovery Tribunal Regulations of Practices Act, 1997, S. 3(i)]

"Address for service" shall mean the address furnished by a party or his authorised representative at which service of summons, notices or other processes may be effected under these rules. [National Company Law Tribunal Rules, 2016, R. 2(2)].

The address, which a party to Court proceedings gives to the Court and/or the other party, to which all the formal documents relating to the proceedings should be delivered. Notices delivered at that address (which may be, for example, the address of his solicitors) are binding on the party concerned.

For the purposes of this section, "Addressable system" means an electronic device (which includes hardware and its associated software) or more than one electronic devices put in an integrated system through which signals of television network can be sent in encrypted form, which can be decoded by the device or devices, having an activated Conditional Access System at the premises of the subscriber within the limits of authorization made, through the Conditional Access System and the Subscriber Management System, on explicit choice and request of such subscriber, by the cable operator to the subscriber. [Cable Television Networks (Regulation) Act (7 of 1995), S 4-A, Explanation (a) as substituted by Amending Act (21 of 2011), S. 5; Telecommunication (Broadcasting and Cable Services) Interconnection (Digital Addressable Cable Television Systems) Regulations, 2012, Regn. 2(b)].

Address of delivery. "Address of delivery" means the address of the recipient of goods or services or both indicated on the tax invoice issued by a registered person for delivery of such goods or services or both [The Central Goods and Services Tax Act, 2017 (12 of 2017), S. 2(2)]

Address on record. "Address on record" means the address of the recipient as available in the records of the supplier [The Central Goods and Services Tax Act, 2017 (12 of 2017), S. 2(3)]

Address, President's/Presidential. In India, prepared speech delivered by the President of India to both Houses of Parliament assembled together at the commencement of the first session after each general election to Lok Sabha and the commencement of the first session of each year informing Parliament of the causes of its summons which is later laid before and discussed on a formal Motion of Thanks in each House of Parliament or an address by the President of India to either House of Parliament or both Houses assembled together on any other occasion.

Address to. At the address of [CrPC 1973 (2 of 1974), S. 63]; directed to [Indian Evidence Act (1 of 1872), S. 47, *Expln*.].

Addressable system.

Means an electronic device (which includes hardware and its associated software) or more than one electronic device put in an integrated system through which signals of cable television network can be sent in encrypted form, which can be decoded by the device or devices, having an activated Conditional Access System at the premises of the subscriber within the limit of authorisation made, through the Conditional Access System and the subscriber management system, on the explicit choice and request of such subscriber, by the cable operator to the subscriber. [Cable Television Networks (Regulation) Act (7 of 1995), S. 4A, Explanation (a)].

Addressee. "ADDRESSEE" means a person who is intended by the originator to receive the electronic record but does not include any intermediary. [Information Technology Act (21 of 2000), S. 2(1)(b)]

One who is addressed; specifically one to whom anything is addressed.

"The postmaster shall also, at the time of its arrival, notify the addressee thereof that such a letter or package has been received." (*Postal Rules*.)

A person to whom a document, *etc.*, is addressed. [Indian Post Office Act (6 of 1898), S. 3(a)].

Adduce. To bring forward; advance; cite; name or cite as authority or evidence for what one advances.

Adduce evidence. The right to adduce evidence would take in a right to cross-examine the witnesses, adopting all legal means to get at all possible and relevant evidentiary materials and putting forward arguments analysing the entire evidence on record so as to produce the required conviction in the mind of the Court. *Victoria Zavier* v. *Greater Cochin Development Authority,* AIR 1993 Ker 95, 103. [CPC (5 of 1908), O. I, R. 9]

Adeem. To revoke, as a legacy, grant *etc.*, or to satisfy by some other gift.

Ademption. To take away.

Ademption of legacy. If anything which has been specifically questioned does not belong to the testator at the time of his death, or has been converted into property of a different kind, the legacy is adeemed; that is, it cannot take effect, by reason of the subject matter having been withdrawn from the operation of the will; division of legacy. [margin, Indian Succession Act (39 of 1925), S. 152].

Adequate. "Adequate" means commensurate in fitness, sufficient, suitable "sufficient" means—Sufficiency, adequate, especially in amount or number to the need, enough, adequate quantity. The expression "adequately represented in the service" means that reservations may be made in order to make the number of any backward class sufficient in the services under the State. *General Manager Southern Railway* v. *Rangachari*, AIR 1962 SC 36, 46. [Constitution of India, Art. 16(4)]

The word "adequate" is commensurate in fitness, sufficient, suitable, equal in magnitude and extent, and fully. [*State of Rajasthan* v. *Vinod Kumar,* (2012) 6 SCC 770, para 9].

Commensurate in fitness; fully sufficient; legally sufficient; lawfully and reasonably sufficient. [Minimum Wages Act (11 of 1948), S. 32(2)(e)].

The dictionary meanings of the word "adequate" are commensurate to fitness, sufficient, suitable, equal in magnitude and extent, and fully. [*State of Rajasthan* v. *Vinod Kumar*, (2012) 6 SCC 770, para 9].

The word means 'equal to'; 'sufficient'.

If the appeal filed is defective, it need not be turned in toto. A memo for rectifying the defects is 'adequate'. [VXL Ltd (OCM Woollen Mills) v CC (1991) 52 ELT 545, 39 ECR 299]

Adequate Consideration. The word 'adequate consideration' denote consideration other than mere love and affection, which, in the case of a wife may be presumed. [Tulsidas Kalichand v CIT AIR 1961 SC 1023, (1962) 2 SCJ 500 pp 503–504, (1962) 2 SCA 1, (1962) 1 Ker LR 242, (1962) 2 Mad LJ 123, (1961) 42 ITR 1, (1961) CrLJ 7, (1961) 2 Guj LR (SC) 1, (1962) 2 Andh WR (SC) 123].

Notice must be given to enable the directors to participate in the meeting in whatever way it is going to be held.

Notice sent by facsimile is an 'adequate notice'. [*Ferrucio Sias v Jai Manga Ram Mukhi* (1994) 1 Comp LJ 345 (Del)]

Reason for condoning the delay. Bona fide pursuit of writ petition was held 'adequate reason for condoning the delay' in filing of appeal. [*Bremels Rubber Industries v CCE* (1991) 56 ELT 604, 38 ECR 141]

Reason for reducing the sentence of imprisonment. Delay in trial amounting to 6 and ½ years is not 'adequate reason for reducing the sentence of imprisonment'. [*Balkrishna Chhaganlal Soni v State of W B* (1974) Cr LJ 280 : (1974) 3 SCC 567 : AIR 1974 SC 120 : (1983) 13 ELT 1527 (SC)]

Reasons for taking a lenient view. Poor health of the accused, lapses of over 12 years were not 'adequate reasons for taking a lenient view. [*Udai Kant Jha v UOI,* (2000) 121 ELT 6 (SC)]

Adequate compensation. Just value of property taken under power of eminent domain, payable in money. Market value of property when taken. It may include interest and may include the cost or value of the property to the owner for the purposes for which he designed it.

Adequate consideration. The words 'adequate consideration' denote consideration other than mere love and affection which in the case of wife may be presumed. They may be good consideration to support a contract but adequate consideration to avoid tax is quite a different thing. *Provat Kumar Mitter* v. *Commissioner of Income Tax,* AIR 1961 SC 1019, 1026.

The words 'adequate consideration' clearly postulate that consideration must be capable of being measured in terms of money value and it excludes a gift. *Sonia Bhatia* v. *State of U.P.*, AIR 1981 SC 1274, 1281. [U.P. Imposition of Ceiling on Land Holdings Act (1 of 1961), S. 5(6); Indian Contract Act (9 of 1872), S. 2(*d*)]

Adequate notice. Notice reasonably calculated to apprise a person of an action, proceeding, or motion. Notice sufficient to permit an objection or defense. *U.S.* v. *San Juan Lumber Co.*, D.C. Colo., 313 F. Supp. 703, 709.

Notice reasonably calculated, in all circumstances of given proceeding, to apprise all interested parties of action and opportunity to present their objections. *U.S.* v. *San Juan Lumber Co.*, D.C. Colo., 313 F. Supp. 703, 709.

"Adheenadha". Means control, domination, command, manage, etc. [*Mathai Samuel* v. *Eapen Eapen*, (2012) 13 SCC 80, para 26].

Adherence. The character of being fixed in attachment, fidelity; steady attachment : as, an adherence to a party or opinions : as, a rigid adherence to rules.

Continued observance. [Assam Reorganisation (Meghalaya) Act (55 of 1969), S. 29(d) and Constitution of India, Art. 102(1)(d)].

Adherent. One who adheres; clinging; attached.

Adhesion contract. A standard-form printed contract prepared by the more powerful party and submitted the weaker on a take it or leave it basis.

Adhesive. Sticky; tenacious, as glutinous substances : of the nature of adhesion as, adhesive stamps. (*See* Indian Stamp Act (2 of 1899), S. 11)

Having a gummed back. [Court-fees Act (7 of 1870), S. 26].

Adhesive stamp. A stamp having a gummed back. [Employees' State Insurance Act (34 of 1948), S. 43(b)].

Adhyahara. In Mimansa, *casus omissus* is known as adhyahara. The adhyahara principle permits us to add words to a legal text. However, the superiority of the Mimansa Principles over Maxwell's Principles in this respect is shown by the fact that Maxwell does not go into further detail and does not mention the sub-categories coming under the general category of *casus omissus*. In the Mimansa system, on the other hand, the general category of adhyahara has under it several sub-categories, *e.g.*, anusanga, anukarsha, vakyashesha, etc. *Dr. Rajbir Singh Dalal* v. *Chaudhari Devi Lal University*, AIR 2009 SC (Supp) 768.

Adhyapak. Includes a Professor, Reader, Lecturer, and any other person engaged in imparting instruction in relation to any learning process and designated as an adyapak by the ordinances. [Visva-Bharati Act (29 of 1951), S. 3(c)]

Adjacent. Close; contiguous but not necessarily touching.

Adjacent means close to or nearby or lying by. Lying near to; adjoining. [CrPC 1973 (2 of 1974), S. 133(1)(e)]. 2 All ER 239, 243 (CA).

Adjective Law. Law regulating Procedure (as) the law as to pleading, practice, evidence *etc.*

Adjoining. The word in its etymological sense means touching or contiguous, as distinguished from lying near to or adjacent. To be in contact with; to abut upon.

Adjacent; contiguous; in the closest relative position to.

One meaning of the word is "neighboring" and all that the context seems to require is that the premises of the adjoining occupiers should be near enough to be affected by the tenant's conduct on the demised premises.

Adjourn. To put off or defer; a formal intermission of business; to suspend a sitting meeting, or transaction till another day, or transfer it to another place, usually said to Courts, legislatures, or other formally organised bodies : as, the legislature adjourned at four o'clock, the meeting adjourned to another place. Adjourn, is also used in its popular sense, *i.e.*, "deferring or postponing as inquiry to a future day."

To put off or defer proceedings to another day; to defer or put off [CrPC 1973 (2 of 1974), S. 309(2) and Constitution of India, Art. 101(4), P*rov*.].

Adjourn sine die. To adjourn without setting a time to reconvene or recommence business or sit again; specifically to adjourn without intending or expecting to sit again.

The act of postponing a meeting of any private or public body or any business until another time or indefinitely.

Adjournamentum est ad diem dicere seu diem dare. An adjournment is to appoint a day or to give a day. This refers to Parliament, and distinguishes adjournment from prorogation. (*Latin for Lawyers*)

Adjourned for hearing. When the entirety of "hearing" of the suit was completed and the Court being competent to pronounce the judgment then and there, adjourns the suit merely for the purpose of pronouncing judgment. *Arjun Singh* v. *Mohinder Kumar*, AIR 1964 SC 993. [CPC (5 of 1908), O. IX, R. 7].

Adjourned for the day. It means hearing is postponed for the day. *Chandrakant Khaire* v. *Shantaram Kale*, AIR 1988 SC 1665.

Adjournment. A putting off until another time or transferring to a different place (*Tomlin*). Act of adjourning or state of being adjourned; also, the time or interval for which a body adjourns.

ADJOURNMENT, RECESS, PROROGATION, DISSOLUTION, "*Adjournment* is the act by which an assembly suspends its session in virtue of authority inherent in itself; it may be also the time or interval of such suspension. A *recess* is a customary suspension of business, as during the period of certain recognised or legal holidays. Recess is also popularly used for a brief suspension of business for any reason : as, it was agreed that there be a recess of ten minutes. This may be a short interval for the purpose of repose or refreshment. A *prorogation* is the adjournment of the sittings of a legislative body at the instance of the authority which called it together; during a prorogation it can hold no sittings, but in order to resume business it must be again summoned : the close of a session of the Parliament is called a prorogation. *Dissolution* is the Act by which the body, as such, is broken up, and its members are finally discharged from their duties. The dissolution of the Parliament necessitates a new election."

"An adjournment is the act of postponement."

Unless the object of the context or inquiry otherwise warrants the term 'adjournment' refers only to a meeting which has already convened and which is thereafter postponed and not to a case where a notice concerning a meeting is cancelled and subsequently a notice for holding the same meeting on a later date is issued. *J.M. Patel* v. *A.S. Mehta*, AIR 1989 SC 1289, 1294.

An action of adjourning. [CPC (5 of 1908), O. XLV, R. 7, 2nd prov.].

Adjournment motion. A motion for discussing "a specific and important matter that should have urgent consideration". It can be moved by any member of the House legislature and is in the nature of emergency motion of censure upon the Government.

Adjournment of the House. Suspend (proceedings) for the day; to put off until a future day. In Lok Sabha, the Speaker determines when sitting of House is to adjourn *sine die* or to a particular day or to an hour or part of same day. Sitting of Lok Sabha is normally adjourned at 6.00 P.M. Sitting does not conclude automatically but only when Speaker makes announcement to that effect. Change in time of adjournment beyond the normal hour is made by Speaker after taking sense of House. House may be adjourned before normal time if business or agenda is exhausted; if there is lack of quorum or uncontrollable disorder; due to death of a sitting member or of a distinguished national or world leader or to express sorrow or sympathy at the death of common people in a tragedy, *etc*.

During session, House is adjourned at close of sitting to meet again at 11.00 A.M. on next working day as per calender of sittings. On last day of session, Speaker adjourns the House *sine die.*

Adjudge. To decide or pass upon or determine judicially; to settle; decree; to determine in the exercise of judicial power; to decide or determine judicially, to adjudicate; as, the case was adjudged. Adjudge does not necessarily imply a final judgment, but is used as well of awards or decisions of arbitrators or other judicial officers, interlocutory orders or decrees of a Court.

To decide judicially. [CPC (5 of 1908), S. 34(1)].

Adjudicate. To hear or try and determine, as a Court; to settle by judicial decree; to adjudge (as) the Court "*adjudicated*" upon the case.

To award judicially; to try and determine judicially. [CPC (5 of 1908), O. I, R. 10(2)].

Adjudication. The act of adjudicating; the process of trying and determining a case judicially. The application of the law to the facts and an authoritative declaration of the result.

ADJUDICATION, ARBITRATION. Adjudication is used of the determination of matters in dispute by the decision of a competent Court; arbitration of the determination of such matters by the decision of arbitrators, whose decision may not be binding until confirmed by a higher Court or assented to by the parties.

FORMER ADJUDICATION, is previous judicial decision between the same parties or those whom they succeed, available or sought to be made available, as a bar to subsequent litigation involving the same point.

"Adjudicatory Board". Means the Board constituted by the Central Government under sub-section (1) of section 54. [Major Port Authorities Act, 2021 (1 of 2021), section 2(1)(a)]

Adjunct. Added or attached as an accompanying object or circumstance.

Adjunctio. The act by which the owner of one thing attatches to or includes in his own property a thing belonging to another.

Adjuration. A swearing or binding upon oath.

Adjure. To charge or entreat solemnly.

Adjust. To put in order; to fit; to make exact; to regulate or reduce to a system; to bring to a proper state or position; to *adjust* accounts.

To arrange, compose, harmonise; to arrange suitably in relation to something.

Adjustable rate mortgage. A mortgage whose rate of interest rises and falls along with interest rates in general.

Adjusted basis. Basis which is increased by capital improvements and decreased by depreciation deductions.

Adjusters. Persons who investigate and settle losses for an insurance carrier.

Adjusting entry. Accounting entry, made at the end of an accounting period, to record previously unrecognized revenue and expenses, as well as changes in assets and liabilities.

Adjustment. That which serves to adjust or adapt one thing to another or to a particular service.

Where matters in dispute are referred by the parties to arbitration without the intervention of the Court and subsequently the award is accepted by them, such acceptance is an "adjustment" within the meaning of R. 3, O. XXIII of the CPC (5 of 1908).

An arrangement whereby things are adjusted; the process of adjusting. [CPC (5 of 1908), S. 44A(2)].

Adjustment of suits. The settlement of the claims in suits by a lawful agreement or compromise. [CPC (5 of 1908), O. XXIII].

Admeasurement. The process of measuring.

Administer. To direct or manage; to furnish; to give; to dispense; to tender (as) persons having authority to *administer* an oath; to fulfil the functions of or perform the duties of an administrator.

The term is also applied to the management of public affairs (as) to administer the government.

In *criminal law*, 'to administer' means to cause or procure a person to take some drug or other substance into his or her system; to direct and cause a medicine, poison, or drug to be taken into the system.

To manage the affairs of [General Clauses Act(10 of 1897), S. 3(47)]; [IPC (45 of 1860), S. 263A(4)]; to manage the property of a person who dies intestate *i.e.* without a will or whose will incompletely dispose of his property or whose will lacks a competent executor; to give as a remedial measure, as medicine *etc.* [IPC (45 of 1860), S. 37, ill. (a)].

Administer poison. To give poison. [IPC (45 of 1860), S. 37, ill. (a)]

Administratio aedificare in tuo proprio solo non licet quod alteri noceat. It is not permitted to build upon one's own land what may be injurious to another.

Administratio durante absentia. That which subsists during the absence of the executor, and until he has proved the will.

Administratio durante minori aetate. That which is granted when the executor is a minor. It continues until the minor attains his lawful age to act.

Administratio pendente lite. That which is granted pending the controversy respecting an alleged will or the right of appointment. An officer of the Court is appointed to take care of the estate only till the suit terminates.

Administration. Dispensation (as) Administration of Justice.

'Administration' means management of the affairs of the institution. *State of Kerala* v. *Mother Provincial*, AIR 1970 SC 2079, 2082. [Constitution of India, Art. 30(1)]

Management; the managing or conduct of an office, employment or institution; the management of public affairs; the executive part of the government; the management and disposal of the estate of a deceased person by an executor or administrator. [T.P. Act (4 of 1882), S. 69A(10)]

"Administration" means proceedings of the nature of placing under administration and includes imposition of moratorium, reorganisation, winding up, liquidation (including any compulsory winding up procedure or proceeding), insolvency, bankruptcy, composition with creditors, receivership, conservatorship or any proceedings of nature similar to or resulting in any of the foregoing, initiated or commenced under any law for the time being in force, against a qualified financial market participant. [Bilateral Netting of Qualified Financial Contracts Act, 2020 (30 of 2020), section 2(1)(a)]

Administration bond. The bond which must be given (with or without) sureties by any person to whom the letters of administration are granted.

A bond (for due performance of duties) given by a person to whom the administration of another's property is entrusted. [Guardians and Wards Act (8 of 1890), S. 35]

Administration, letters of. The instrument or authority by which an administrator is authorised by Court, to have the charge and administration of the goods of an intestate.

Administration of justice. The expression "administration of justice" must necessarily include the power to try suits and proceedings of civil as well as criminal nature, irrespective of who the parties to the suit or proceedings or what its subject-matter may be. This power must necessarily include the power of defining, enlarging, altering, amending and diminishing the jurisdiction of the Courts and defining their jurisdiction territorially and pecuniary. *State of Bombay* v. *Narotamdas*

Jethabai, AIR 1951 SC 69, 70. [Constitution of India, Sch. VII, List II, Entry 3]

"Administration practitioner". Means the liquidator, receiver, trustee, conservator, resolution professional or any other person or entity, by whatever name called, which administers the affairs of a party subject to administration under any law for the time being in force. [Bilateral Netting of Qualified Financial Contracts Act, 2020 (30 of 2020), section 2(1)(b)]

Administration suit. A suit brought by anyone interested, for administration of a decedent's estate when there is doubt as to its solvency.

A suit to secure due administration of any property, particularly that of a deceased person. [CPC (5 of 1908), O. XX, R. 13(2)]

Administrative. Of, or pertaining to administration; administering; executive; as, administrative law; an administrative body.

Pertaining to administration; executive as distinguished from judicial. [IPC (45 of 1860), S. 124, *Expln.* 3]

Administrative adjudication, is the process which an administrative agency uses to issue regulations through an adversary proceeding.

Administrative authority. The power of an agency or its head to carry out the terms of the law creating the agency as well as to make regulations for the conduct of business before the agency; distinguishable from legislative authority to make laws.

Administrative body. An administrative body is not always a judicial body though it might act, on various occasions or always, in accordance with strict judicial principles. In the case of an administrative tribunal, however, the emphasis is on policy, expediency and discretion to enable it to achieve the object for which it was set up. If, on the other hand, an administrative body, in arriving at its decision, had before it at no stage any form of *lis* and throughout has to consider the question from the point of view of policy and expediency, it cannot be said that it is under a duty at any time to act judicially.

Administrative decision. "In the case of administrative decision, there is no legal obligation upon the person charged with duty of making the decision to consider and weigh submissions and arguments, or to collect any evidence or solve any issue. The grounds upon which he acts, and the means which he takes to inform himself before acting, are left entirely to his discretion."

Administrative discretion. This term refers to the latitude that governments, governmental agencies, and public administrators possess in the interpretation and implementation of public laws and programmes.

Administrative hearing. A proceeding of an administrative agency in which evidence is offered for argument or trial.

Administrative law. That branch of public law which deals with the various organs of the Sovereign power considered as in motion, and "prescribes in detail the manner of their activity, being concerned with such topics as the collection of the revenue, the regulation of the military and naval forces, citizenship and naturalization, sanitary measures, public safety and morals". See *Holland Jurisprudence* 305-307.

That branch of public law which deals with the various organs of the Sovereign power. It relates to the organisation, powers and duties of administrative authorities and consists of body of rules governing the detailed exercise of executive functions by the officers or the public authorities. It is judge made law.

"ADMINISTRATIVE LAW" is a growing branch of Indian jurisprudence with a mission. Where the trellis work of technical procedures and rules of evidence usually applicable to ordinary courts under the Code contains too many taboos regarding pleadings and too many prescriptions regarding trials, administrative bodies, manned by lay and legal men, charged with duties which are wider than decision of individual disputes between specific parties and operating quasi-judicially at the public-interest level, have to enjoy more liberal powers and less formal and more flexible processes if they are to fulfill the statutory behest efficaciously. To overjudicialize is to undermine. *B. Prabhakara Rao* v. *Desari Panakala Rao*, AIR 1976 SC 1803.

Administrative or executive. The term 'Administrative' or 'executive' refers to broad areas of government activities in which the repositories of power exercise every class of statutory functions.

Administrative order. An administrative order would be one which is directed to the regulation or supervision of matters as distinguished from an order which decides the rights of parties or confers or refuses to confer rights to property which are the subject of adjudication before the Court. *Shankharlal Aggarwal* v. *Shankharlal Poddar*, AIR 1965 SC 507, 511. [Companies Act (7 of 1913), Ss. 183(3) & 184]

Administrative overheads. "Administrative overheads" means the expenses incurred by the company for 'general management and administration' of Corporate Social Responsibility functions in the company but shall not include the expenses directly incurred for the esigning, implementation, monitoring, and evaluation of a particular Corporate Social Responsibility project or programme. [Companies (Corporate Social Responsibility Policy) Rules, 2014, rule 2(1)(b)]

Administrative power. The powers upon which principles of fairness and natural justice are not applicable.

Discretionary powers of an executive nature that are conferred by legislation on government ministers, public and local authorities, and other bodies and persons for the purpose of giving detailed effect to broadly defined policy.

Administrative procedure. The course of procedure followed by administrative departments and authorities in the exercise of quasi-judicial functions, in deciding claims or controversies brought before them, or the appropriate tribunal or person, for adjudication. Administrative procedure lacks the formality, and carefully formulated course of happenings, laid own for civil and criminal Courts. The only requisites appear to be that any rules of procedure laid down for the particular tribunal or process or adjudication should be observed, and that the rules of natural justice be observed. But to a large extent controversies have been entrusted to administrative tribunals to avoid the formalism of Court procedure and the development of formalism is contrary to the spirit of the legislation. Appeal is frequently limited, and frequently lies to a special appellate tribunal, or to a Minister, rather than to ordinary Court. (*Walker*)

Administrative proceeding. A proceeding in or before an administrative body, as distinguished from a proceeding in a court. [1 Am J2d Adm L 158]. Any proceeding before an administrative agency which is not of such specific nature as to give it a more particular designation. (*Ballentine's Law Dictionary, 3rd Edn.*)

Administrative tribunal. The tribunals which are concerned with administrative law. They have quasi-judicial powers.

"Administrative Tribunal", in relation to a State, means the Administrative Tribunal for the State or, as the case may be, the Joint Administrative Tribunal for that State and any other State or States [Administrative Tribunals Act, 1985 (13 of 1985), section 3(aa)]

Administrator. "ADMINISTRATOR" means a person appointed by competent authority to administer the estate of a deceased person when there is no executor. [Indian Succession Act (39 of 1925), S. 2]

One who administers; a manager or conductor of affairs, especially of another. (*Kendrick*)

The person to whom Letters of Administration are granted. (*Tomlin*)

A person appointed by Court to administer the estate when there is no executor; one who administers; one who has the faculty of organising. [Wealth-tax Act (27 of 1957), S. 2(i)]

"ADMINISTRATOR" means a person or a body of persons appointed as Administrator under section 7 [S. 2(a) of the Unit Trust of India (Transfer of Undertaking and Repeal) Act, 2002 (58 of 2002); Also see Income Tax Act 1961 (43 of 1961), S. 10(35) and Income-tax Act 1961 (43 of 1961), *Explanation* (*i*) to section 115R(2)]

"ADMINISTRATOR" means an officer appointed for the purpose of rehabilitation and resettlement of affected families under section 43(1) of Act 30 of 2013. [S. 3(a) of the Right to Fair Compensation & Transparency in Land Acquisition, Rehabilitation & Resettlement Act, 2013 (30 of 2013)]

Administratrix. A woman who administers the estate of an intestate.

Admiralty. Is that branch or department of law which relates to maritime property, affairs, and transactions, whether civil or criminal. In a more limited sense it is the tribunal exercising jurisdiction over maritime causes and administering the maritime law by a procedure peculiar to itself and to some extent, and in respects, distinct from that followed by other Courts.

The maritime branch of the administration of justice. [Indian Evidence Act (1 of 1872), S. 41]; pertaining to navy. [CPC (5 of 1908), S. 140(1)]

Admiralty Court. Court having jurisdiction on civil actions related to ships and sea.

Admiralty Proceeding. "admiralty proceeding" means any proceeding before a High Court, exercising admiralty jurisdiction. [The Admiralty (Jurisdiction and Settlement of Maritime Claims) Act, 2017 (22 of 2017), S. 2(1)(b)]

Admissibility. Allowability as judicial proof; the quality of being admissible. [App. C, form No. 10, CPC (5 of 1908)]

Admissibility of evidence. The principles determining whether or not particular items of evidence may be received by the Court.

Admissible. Allowable as judicial proof; worthy of being admitted or received. [IPC (45 of 1860), S. 197]; capable of being allowed or conceded. [Employees' State Insurance Act (34 of 1948), S. 62]

Admissible evidence. As applied in evidence, the term means that the evidence introduced is of such a character that the Court or judge is bound to receive it; that is, allow it to be introduced at trial. To be "admissible" the evidence must be relevant, and, *inter alia*, to be "relevant" it must tend to establish material proposition.

Admission. An ADMISSION is a statement, oral or documentary or contained in electronic form, which suggests any inference as to any fact in issue or relevant fact, and which is made by any of the persons, and under the circumstances, herein after mentioned. [Indian Evidence Act (1 of 1872), section 17] [(w.e.f. 1-7-2024) repealed and replaced by Bharatiya Sakshya Adhiniyam, 2023 (47 of 2023), section 15]

Statements made by a party to the proceeding, or by an agent to any such party, whom the Court regards, under the circumstances of the case, as expressly or impliedly authorised by him to make them, are admissions. Statements made by—(i) parties to suits suing or sued in a representative character, are not admissions, unless they were made while the party making them held that character are admissions, if they are made during the continuance of the interest of the persons making the statements; or (ii)(a) persons who have any proprietary or pecuniary interest in the subject matter of the proceeding, and who make the statement in their character of persons so interested are admissions, if they are made during the continuance of the interest of the persons making the statements; or (ii)(b) persons from whom the parties to the suit have derived their interest in the subject matter of the suit are admissions, if they are made during the continuance of the interest of the persons making the statements [(w.e.f. 1-7-2024) Bharatiya Sakshya Adhiniyam, 2023 (47 of 2023), section 16]

Statements made by persons whose position or liability, it is necessary to prove as against any party to the suit, are admissions, if such statements would be relevant as against such persons in relation to such position or liability in a suit brought by or against them, and if they are made whilst the person making them occupies such position or is subject to such liability. [(w.e.f. 1-7-2024) Bharatiya Sakshya Adhiniyam, 2023 (47 of 2023), section 17]

Statements made by persons to whom a party to the suit has expressly referred for information in reference to a matter in dispute are admissions. [(w.e.f. 1-7-2024) Bharatiya Sakshya Adhiniyam, 2023 (47 of 2023), section 18]

'ADMISSION' includes admission as a spectator or as one of an audience and admission for the purpose of amusement by taking part in an entertainment. [Kerala (Local Authorities) Entertainment Tax Act (20 of 1961), S. 2(1)]

"ADMISSION" means formal permission given by the pre-school authority to a child to attend the pre-school center on the working days during the academic year. [1998 (1) Mah LJ]

The term "admission" in S. 70, Indian Evidence Act, relates only to the admission of a party in the course of the trial of a suit, and not to the attestation of a document by the admission of the party executing it.

Admission must be 'conscious and deliberate act' and not something which was not intended.

The admitting of anything as true [Indian Evidence Act (1 of 1872), S. 17]; the act of accepting or the fact of being accepted for the purpose of consideration; the fact of being admitted to a place, society, body or institution.

Admission capacity. For the purpose of this section, "ADMISSION CAPACITY", in relation to any course of study or training (including a post-graduate course of study or training) in an authority or institution granting recognised dental qualification, means the maximum number of students that may be fixed by the Council from time to time for being admitted to such course or training. [Dentists Act (16 of 1948), S. 10A, *Expl.* 2; Indian Medical Council Act (102 of 1956), S. 10A *Expl.* 2]

For the purposes of this section, "ADMISSION CAPACITY", in relation to any course of study or training (including post-graduate course of study or training) in a medical institution, means the maximum number of students as may be decided by the Central Council from time to time for being admitted to such course or training. [Homoeopathy Central Council Act (59 of 1973), S. 12A(1) *Expl.* 2]

Admission in criminal cases. An admission in a criminal case, commonly called a confession, is any statement made by an accused person of his guilt, or of any fact or circumstance tending to prove it.

Admission of appeal. The acceptance by Court of an appeal for the purpose of consideration. [CPC (5 of 1908), O. XLI, R. 9]

Admission of claim. The claim or part thereof which a defendant may admit, under O. IX, R. 8, CPC (5 of 1908), must be the claim as laid down in the plaint and for the amount stated therein and not simply of the cause of action. The words "*admits the claim or part thereof*" in the said rule apply to a case where, on examining the plaint and the defendant's admission in the written statement, it can be considered that he, there and then, agreed to pay the money or to submit to the relief claimed in the plaint.

Admit. To accept for the purpose of consideration; to admit anything as true; to let in.

Admit as a minor. Allow to join (a firm) as a minor. [Indian Partnership Act (9 of 1932), S. 30(6)]

Admittance. Entrance. [CrPC 1973 (2 of 1974), S. 47(2)]

Admitted. "Admitted" as a member of a company is equivalent to being "elected" as such (when election is the mode prescribed for admission of a new member). All allegations in the pleadings which are not specifically denied are taken to have been "admitted" [CPC (5 of 1908), O. VIII, R. 5] but the terms debts "*admitted*" or "*established*," in S. 26 of the Indian Insolvency Act, mean admitted in the Schedule or established on proof, and not that it has been alleged and not denied.

The expression 'appeal admitted before the commencement of S. 38 of CPC (5 of 1908) Amendment Act means appeals already accepted by the High Court to be heard. [CPC Amendment Act (104 of 1976), Ss. 38 and 97(2)(*m*)]

Admitted against the plaintiffs. An endorsement that a document is "admitted against the plaintiff" or "admitted against the defendants" means that the document is admitted in evidence as proved.

Admitted in evidence. The expression "admitted in evidence" in S. 36 of the Indian Stamp Act (2 of 1899) means the act of letting the document in as part of the evidence, as a result of the judicial determination of the question whether the document is admissible or not for want of stamp. In other words, the Court admitting it must have applied its mind consciously to the question whether the document is admissible or not. Where a document which is not admissible for want of stamp is allowed by the Court to go in, the question of stamp escaping its notice as well as the attention of the parties, the admission is a judicial determination of the question, because the Court let in the document on its view that there was nothing against its admission.

Admixture. The act of mixing; the compound formed by the mixture of different substances. Improper admixture of foodstuffs would be an offence against laws relating to prevention of adulteration of food and drink.

Admonish. To counsel against wrong practice; to warn mildly; to give a gentle caution or advice.

Admonition. Gentle or friendly reproof or warning; counselling against a fault or error; expression of authoritative advice or warning.

A censure; which if not obeyed, may be followed by punishment.

An expression of authoritative warning; a gentle reproof to a convict *in lieu* of punishment. [Children Act (60 of 1960), S. 21(1)(a) (*repealed*)]

A punishment administered by the Presiding Officer of a legislature to an offender for breach of privilege or contempt of the House in case of an offence which is not so grave as to warrant his committal; it is the mildest form of punishment.

Adolescence. That age which follows puberty & precedes the age of majority. (*Wharton; Bouvier*)

State or process of growing up from childhood to manhood or womanhood; youth, generally considered to be in the male sex from fourteen to twenty-five years of age, and in the female sex from twelve to twenty-one.

Adolescence is the penumbral period (presently between 18 years and 23 years) when, for good reason, a person is not perceived and treated as an adult for the purposes of incarceration. [*Nagoor Pichai* v. *State,* (2013) 10 SCC 668, para 4].

Adolescent. "ADOLESCENT" means a person who has completed his fifteenth year of age but has not completed his eighteenth year. [Plantations Labour Act (69 of 1951), S. 2(a); Motor Transport Workers Act (27 of 1961), S. 2(a); Factories Act (63 of 1948), S. 2(b)]

"**Adolescent**" means a person who has completed his fourteenth year of age but has not completed his eighteenth year. [Child Labour (Prohibition and Regulation) Act (61 of 1986), S. 2(i) as inserted by Amending Act (35 of 2016].

A person in an age of adolescence *i.e.* grown from childhood to maturity. [Mines Act (35 of 1952), S. 2(1)(a) and Minimum Wages Act (11 of 1948), S. 2(a)]

"Adolescent" shall have the same meaning as assigned to it in clause (*i*) of section 2 of the Child and Adolescent Labour (Prohibition and Regulation) Act, 1986 (61 of 1986). [Occupational Safety, Healthy & Working Conditions Code, 2020 (37 of 2020), section 2(1)(a)]

'**Adolescent offender**' means any person who has been convicted of any offence punishable with imprisonment or who having been ordered to give security under section 118 of the Code of Criminal Procedure has failed to do so and who at the time of such conviction or failure to give security is not less than 16 in the case of a boy and not less than 18 in the case of a girl, but not more than 21 years of the age in either case. [T.N. Borstal Schools Act, 1925 (5 of 1926), S. 2(1) as cited in *Nagoor Pichai* v. *State*, (2013) 10 SCC 668, para]

Adopt. To take and receive as one's own that which is not naturally so; to take into one's family as son and heir to the adopting person.

To take as one's son or daughter [Registration Act (16 of 1908), S. 40]; to endorse and assume responsibility for [Indian Contract Act (9 of 1872), S. 215, ill. (b)]; [Constitution of India, Preamble]

Adopted child. A child in respect of which an adoption order has been made.

Adoption. "Adoption" shall have the same meaning as assigned to it in clause (2) of section 2 of the Juvenile Justice (Care and Protection of Children) Act, 2015 (2 of 2016) [Registration of Births & Deaths Act, 1969 (18 of 1969), section 2(1)(aa)]

Act by which relations of paternity and affiliation are recognized, as legally existing between persons not so related by nature; the act of adopting. "The legal act whereby an adult person takes a minor into the relation of child, and thereby acquires the rights and incurs the responsibilities of a parent in respect to such minor." (*Abbott*)

The action of adopting a child. [Indian Majority Act (9 of 1875), S. 2(a) and General Clauses Act (10 of 1897), S. 3(20)]; taking as one's own [Companies Act (1 of 1956) replaced with Companies Act, 2013, S. 303(1), *Expln.* 3(i)]; endorsing and assuming responsibility for [Income-tax Act (43 of 1961), S. 80C(2)(b), *Expln.* (ii)]

Adoption agency. A licensed agency where a biological parent can voluntarily surrender a child for adoption.

Adoption of contract. A contract whose acceptance is binding, notwithstanding some defect which entitles the party to repudiate it.

Adoption of Hindu Law. "Adoption has been spoken of as "new birth" in many cases, a term sanctioned by the theory of Hindu Law. Nor is the expression a mere figure of speech. The theory itself involves the principle of a complete severance of the child adopted from the family in which he is born and complete substitution into the adoptive family, as if he were born in it." "The fundamental idea is that the boy given in adoption gives up the natural family and everything connected with that family."

The adopted son has in his new family precisely the same rights as a natural born son, save only when the question is one that raises a competition between the natural and the adopted son.

ADOPTION—REVOCATION OF. Once a person makes an adoption, he has no power subsequently to revoke the adoption.

ADOPTION OF GIRLS. Adoption of girls is not known to the general law of Hindus. A local, tribal or family custom of adoption of girls must be proved by those who allege it.

ADOPTION—MAHANT AND CHELA. *Adoption* in Cl. 5 of S. 32 of the Indian Evidence Act (1 of 1872) is not to be interpreted in a restricted sense. The *relationship between a 'mohunt' and his 'chela'* is a relationship by "adoption" within the meaning of that clause.

Adoptive father. The father who has taken a child in adoption. [General Clauses Act (10 of 1897), S. 3(20)]

Adoptive mother. The mother who has taken a child in adoption. [Hindu Minority and Guardianship Act (32 of 1956), S. 7]

ADR map. A chart portraying the various alternative dispute resolution mechanisms/ processes in the order of (i) *consensual processes* such as negotiation and mediation, (ii) *advisory processes* such as expert appraisal and early neutral evaluation, (iii) *determinative processes* such as arbitration and rent-a-judge, and (iv) *hybrid processes* such as med-arb and mini-trial. Prudent disputants would use the ADR processes in the order given in the ADR map unless the nature of the dispute warrants a departure from the order. (*Arbitration*)

ADR net. It is a network of ADR practitioners, comprising of solicitors and counsel, organized under the patronage of IDR Europe Limited. (Alternative Dispute Resolution)

ADRCI. ADR Chambers International ('ADRCI') is the leading Canadian organisation that specializes in International Arbitration and Mediation. Through the use of the UNCITRAL Arbitration Rules as supplemented by its own state of the art rules, ADRCI provides practitioners and their clients uniformity and credibility in the field of the international arbitration and mediation. (*Arbitration*)

Adult. Means a person who has completed his eighteen years. [Cinematograph Act (37 of 1952), S. 2(a) and Factories Act (63 of 1948), S. 2(a)]

One who has attained the full age of majority. "The expression 'ADULT', means a person who, in the opinion of the Court before whom he is brought, is of the age of majority." See also Act (8 of 1923), S. 2, Act (25 of 1934), S. 2.

Adult consumption unit. Means the consumption unit of male above the age of fourteen years; and the consumption unit of a female above the age of fourteen years; and that of a child below the age of fourteen years shall be calculated at the rates of 8 and 6 respectively of one adult consumption unit. [Factories Act (63 of 1948), S. 80(2), *Expln.* (2)]

Adulterant. A person or thing that adulterates.

"ADULTERANT" means any material which is or could be employed for making the food unsafe or sub-standard or misbranded or containing extraneous matter. [S. 3(1)(a) of the Food Safety & Standards Act, 2006 (34 of 2006)]

Adulterate. Articles are adulterated to increase their weight or bulk or to improve or change their appearance or flavour in imitation of an article of higher grade or different kind. (*Cent. Dict.*)

To corrupt, debase or make impure by the addition of a foreign substance. [IPC (45 of 1860), S. 272]

Adulterated. An article of food shall be deemed to be adulterated—

(a) if the article sold by a vendor is not of the nature, substance or quality demanded by the purchaser and is to his prejudice, or is not of the nature, substance or quality which it purports or is represented to be;

(b) if the article contains any other substance which affects, or if the article is so processed as to affect, injuriously the nature, substance or quality thereof;

(c) if any inferior or cheaper substance has been substituted wholly or in part for the article so as to affect injuriously the nature, substance or quality thereof;

(d) if any constituent of the article has been wholly or in part abstracted so as to affect injuriously the nature, substance or quality thereof;

(e) if the article had been prepared, packed or kept under insanitary conditions whereby it has become contaminated or injurious to health;

(f) if the article consists wholly or in part of any filthy putrid, rotten, decomposed or diseased animal or vegetable substance or is insect-infested or is otherwise unfit for human consumption;

(g) if the article is obtained from a diseased animal;

(h) if the article contains any poisonous or other ingredient which renders it injurious to health;

(i) if the container of the article is composed, whether wholly or in part, of any poisonous or deleterious substance which renders its contents injurious to health;

(j) if any colouring matter other than that prescribed in respect thereof is present in the article, or if the amounts of the prescribed colouring matter which is present in the article are not within the prescribed limits of variability;

(k) if the article contains any prohibited preservative or permitted preservative in excess of the prescribed limits;

(l) if the quality or purity of the article falls below the prescribed standard or its constituents are present in quantities not within the prescribed limits of variability, which renders it injurious to health;

(m) if the quality or purity of the article falls below the prescribed standard or its constituents are present in quantities not within the prescribed limits of variability but which does not render it injurious to health;

Provided that, where the quality or purity of the article, being primary food, has fallen below the prescribed standards or its constituents are present in quantities not within the prescribed limits of variability, in either case, solely due to natural causes and beyond the control of human agency, then, such article shall not be deemed to be adulterated within the meaning of this sub-clause.

Explanation.—Where two or more articles of primary food are mixed together and the resultant article of food—

(a) is stored, sold or distributed under a name which denotes the ingredients thereof; and

(b) is not injurious to health, then, such resultant article shall not be deemed to be adulterated within the meaning of this clause. [Prevention of Food Adulteration (37 of 1954), S. 2(ia)].

Adulterated food. Various categories of 'adulterated food' mentioned in section 2(1)(f) of the Prevention of Food Adulteration Act, 1954 (37 of 1954), broadly fall into two kinds of adulteration : *firstly*, where the constituent elements make the food obnoxious to human health or the existence of the particular composition of it, itself makes the food adulterated, and *secondly*, where the adulteration is constituted by the fact that the prescribed standard has not been observed in selling what purports to be a food of that standard or quality. *Municipal Corporation of Delhi* v. *Tek Chand Bhatia*, AIR 1980 SC 360.

Adulteration. Means the infusion of some foreign substance." The term is generally applied to the act of mixing up with food or drink, intended to be sold, other matters of an inferior quality and usually of a more or less deleterious character.

Adulteration is the mixing with any substance intended for sale any ingredient which is injurious to health, or which makes the nature or quality of such substance other than that for which it is to be sold or passed. An article of food is "adulterated" when any substance, other than which the article purports to be, is mixed with, or added to, or placed upon it, either to increase the bulk or weight or apparent size of the article, or to give it a deceptive appearance.

The action of adulterating, the condition of being so adulterated; an adulterated substance. [IPC (45 of 1860), S. 272]

Adulterer. One, specially a man who commits adultery.

One who has sexual intercourse with a person who is and whom he knows or has reason to believe to be the wife of another man without the consent or connivance of that man. [Special Marriage Act (43 of 1954), S. 41(2)(a)]

Adulteress. A woman who commits adultery.

Adulterine. Proceeding from adulterous intercourse. Hence : spurious; without the support of law; illegal; a child issuing from an adulterous connection. (*Bouvier*)

Adultery. "Whoever has sexual intercourse with a person who is and whom he knows or has reason to believe to be the wife of another man, without the consent or connivance of that man; such sexual intercourse not amounting to the offence of rape, is the offence of adultery." [Indian Penal Code (45 of 1860), S. 497]

Adultery is the wilful violation of the marriage bed. Adultery is the offence of incontinence by married persons.

Advance. Means an advance, whether in cash or in kind, or partly in cash or partly in kind, made by one person (hereinafter referred to as the creditor) to another person (hereinafter referred to as the debtor). [Bonded Labour System (19 of 1976), S. 2(a)]

Advance (*as a noun*) means something that precedes; something paid in advance; such as a payment of money made before it is due.

"ADVANCE" does not mean an advance in money only; an advance may be in money or goods.

An act of approach. The word 'advance' conveys the idea of furnishing, tendering or offering something which may be returned in the same form.

Money in whole or in part, forming the consideration of an agreement paid before the same is completely payable [Indian Partnership Act (9 of 1932), S. 13(d)]; a loan [Indian Contract Act (9 of 1872), S. 141, ill (b)]; to lend; to make payment in anticipation [Industrial Finance Corporation Act (15 of 1948), S. 23(1)(e), (*Repealed by Act 23, 1993*)]; to improve [North-Eastern Hill University Act (24 of 1973), S. 4].

Advance freight. Freight payable at a time before the goods are delivered at the place of destination in the contract of carriage.

Advance money. To make payment of money in advance. [IPC (45 of 1860), S. 415, *Expln*, ill. (g)].

Advance note. When a seaman signs his articles of agreement, he may receive an ADVANCE NOTE for a month's wages. The note is drawn upon the owner of the vessel and is payable three days after the ship has sailed, to the person named in the note. If the seaman fails to join the ship, the advance note will not, of course, be paid. They were made legal, for sums not exceeding one month's wages. [Merchant Shipping Act, 1958, S. 135]

Advance pricing agreement (APA). Under the APA Scheme, taxpayers can enter into an agreement with the tax administration in respect of the arm's length price to be used in a proposed transaction. [Parthasarthi Shome, *Taxation Principles and Applications A compendium*, 2014, LexisNexis, at p. 541].

Advance ruling. Means the determination, by the authority of a question of law or fact specified in the application regarding the liability to pay duty in relation to an activity proposed to be undertaken, by the applicant. [Central Excise Act (1 of 1944), S. 23A(b)]

"ADVANCE RULING" means—

(i) a determination by the Authority in relation to a transaction which has been undertaken or is proposed to be undertaken by a non-resident applicant; or

(ii) a determination by the Authority in relation to a transaction which has been undertaken or is proposed to be undertaken by a resident applicant with a non-resident, and such determination shall include the determination of any question of law or of fact specified in the application;

(iii) a determination or decision by the Authority in respect of an issue relating to computation of total income which is pending before any income-tax authority or the Appellate Tribunal and such determination or decision shall include the determination or decision of any question of law or of fact relating to such computation of total income specified in the application.

Provided that where an advance ruling has been pronounced before the date on which the Finance Bill, 2003 receives the assent of the President, by the Authority in respect of an application by a resident applicant referred to in sub-clause (ii) of the clause as it stood immediately before such date, such ruling shall be binding on the person specified in Section 245S. [Income-tax Act (43 of 1961), S. 245N(a)]

Advance sheets. Sheets of a book unbound and furnished before publication, as for review or reproduction.

Advance tax. Means the tax paid in advance during the previous year when the income is in the process of being earned.

Advancement. Means a gift establishing a young person in life, or in the case of an older person, as meeting some particular need, expansion of business *etc.*

The promotion in life [Indian Trusts Act (2 of 1882), S. 41]; improvement [Guardians and Wards Act (8 of 1890), S. 34(e)]; [Aligarh Muslim University Act (40 of 1920), S. 5(1)]; furtherance [Income-tax Act (43 of 1961), S. 2(15)]; going forward. [Salarjung Museum Act (26 of 1961), S. 15(2)(a)].

Advancement in life. Promotion in life. [Indian Trusts Act (2 of 1882), S. 41].

Advances. The expression means something due to a person but which is paid to him ahead of the time when it is due to be paid. *C.I.T.* v. *E. Srinivasan,* (1963) 50 ITR 788, 797. [Income-tax Act (43 of 1961), S. 2(22)]

Moneys paid before or in advance of the proper time of payment; money or commodities furnished on credit; money advanced to be repaid conditionally.

Advantage. Benefit, profit or gain of any kind. [IPC (45 of 1860), S. 268].

Adventure. A mercantile or speculative enterprise of hazard; a venture; a shipment of goods by a merchant on his own account; sending goods abroad under charge of a supercargo or other agent, which are to be disposed of to the best advantage for the benefit of the owners; the goods themselves so sent.

A pecuniary venture. [Income-tax Act (43 of 1961), S. 2(13)].

Adventure in the nature of trade. In considering whether a transaction is or is not an adventure in the nature of trade, the problem must be approached in the light of the intention of the assesse having regard to the "legal requirements which are associated with the concept of trade or business." *Ramnarian Sons (P) Ltd.* v. *I.T. Commissioner*, AIR 1961 SC 1141, 1143. [Income-tax Act (43 of 1961), S. 2(13).

The expressions "adventure in the nature of trade" clearly suggests that the transaction cannot properly be regarded as trade or business. It is allied to transactions that constitute trade or business itself. It is characterised by some of the essential features that make up trade or business but not by all of them and so even an isolated transaction can satisfy the description of an "adventure in the nature of trade". *Estate Investment Co. Ltd.* v. *Commissioner of Income Tax*, (1980) 121 ITR 580, 591 (Bom). [Income-tax Act (43 of 1961), S. 28]

Adversary. One turned against another or others with a design to oppose or resist them; a member of an opposing or hostile party; an opponent; an antagonist; an enemy; foe.

Adversary proceeding. A proceeding involving a dispute between opposing parties.

Adverse. Having opposing interests; having interests for the preservation for which opposition is essential. The words "adverse party" (as to competency of witnesses) are not limited to adversary positions of plaintiff and defendant, but affect any party, whether plaintiff or defendant, whose interests are actually adverse to those of another party to the action. (*Kansas. App. 841*)

Acting in a contrary direction; opposing. [CPC (5 of 1908), O. XXXII, R. 4(1)].

Adverse claim. A claim put forward against the interest of another person.

Adverse easement. Creation of an easement from an open, adverse and continuous use over a statutory period.

Adverse enjoyment. The possession or exercise of an easement or right or privilege under a claim of right against the owner.

Adverse event. Means any untoward medical occurrence (including a symptom or disease or an abnormal laboratory finding) during treatment with an investigational drug or a pharmaceutical product in a patient or a trial subject that does not necessarily have a relationship with the treatment being given. [New Drugs and Clinical Trials Rules, 2019, R. 2(1)(d)].

Adverse interest. This is an interest claimed or asserted by one against the interest of other the party.

Adverse occupation. Occupation of premises by a trespasser to the exclusion of the owner or lawful occupier.

Adverse possession. May be defined as "holding possession under a claim of title inconsistent with that of the true owner". (*Ency. of the Laws of England*)

Possession may be adverse *ab initio* or may become adverse subsequently. (24 CWN 659 : 68 IC 745)

Other definitions. "Adverse Possession" designates a possession in opposition to the true title and real owner; and implies that it commenced in wrong and is maintained against right. (*Alexander* v. *Polk*, 39 Miss. 755).

Adverse possession, generally speaking, is a possession of another's land which, when accompanied by certain facts and circumstances, will vest title in the possessor. (*Black; Bouvier L Dict.*)

Decisions and text-books are unanimous in declaring that the possession must be actual, visible, exclusive, hostile, and continued, during the time necessary to create a bar under a statute of limitations.

For the purpose of acquiring title by adverse possession, the nature of the *animus possidendi* is material, whether the *animus* is based on real, false or pretended title. The title acquired cannot be higher than what it would be if the pretence or falsehood were true. (*Mithale Veetil Raman* v. *Puthulal Ambu* 24 IC 95). Possession in order to be adverse must be adequate in continuity, in publicity and extent (12 years under the Limitations Act (36 of 1963), Art. 65.

The mere act of tethering cattle and throwing cow dung on the land of another without the assertion of any adverse right does not by itself constitute adverse possession. (*Mahabir Misser* v. *Nanda Kishore Misser*, 27 IC 640).

A person cannot acquire a title by prescription to a land which remains covered with the flood-water of a river for a few months every year, as he must be deemed to have been dispossessed by *vis major* during the time of the flood and possession, during such period remains in the person who has the title to the land. *Baldeo Thakurain* v. *Ugra Nath Misra*, 29 IC 278.

Storing straw ricks upon a land, a part of the Gramanatham which is the property of Government will not by itself give a person any title as against Government by adverse possession.

By "adverse possession" is meant possession which is hostile, under a claim or colour of title, actual, open, uninterrupted, notorious, exclusive and continuous. Adverse possession is made out by the co-existence of two distinct ingredients:

first, such as little as will afford colour, and second, such possession under it as will be adverse to the right of the true owner and title by adverse possession becomes complete only when the possession of the trespasser continues uninterruptedly for the full statutory period. [*Tapasi Rani Das* v. *Sajal Das*, AIR 2013 Gau 100, para 13].

When a person in bringing an action relied on the existence of a contract for sale to support his continued occupation of the property and since he could have set up the contract as a valid defence to any proceedings brought against him for possession, he could not thereafter assert that he had obtained a title by adverse possession, that he had been squatting, unlawfully on the property or that he had a right to remain on the property other than by virtue of the contract to purchase. *Hyde* v. *Pearce*, (1982) 1 All ER 1029. [Limitation Act, 1939, Ss. 4(3), 10] Adverse witness

Adverse witness. Is a witness whose mind discloses a bias hostile to the party examining him. (*Brown L. Dict.*)

A witness hostile to the party calling him.

Adversely. Being in a contrary direction. [CPC (5 of 1908), S. 88].

Adversus extraneous vitiosa possessio prodesse soiet. Prior possession is a good title of ownership against all who cannot show a better.

An imperfect possession is accustomed to prevail as against outsiders claiming adversely.

Advertise. To give public notice of; to announce publicly; especially by a printed notice; as, to advertise goods for sale, for a lost article. The sailing day of a vessel, a public meeting.

To make publicly known by announcement in a journal, paper *etc.* [Indian Partnership Act (9 of 1932), S. 55(2)].

Advertisement. Notice given in a manner designed to attract public attention; information communicated to the public, or to an individual concerned, by means of hand bills or the newspaper. The meaning of the word is not however confined to notices printed in newspapers. (*Com.* v. *Hooper*, 5 Pick. Mass. 42)

An advertisement is a form of speech but its true character is reflected by the object for the promotion of which it is employed. It assumes the attributes and elements of the activity under Art 19(1) which it seeks to aid by bringing it to the notice of the public. When it takes the form of a commercial advertisement it no longer falls within the concept of freedom of speech. *Hamdard Dawakhana* v. *Union of India*, AIR 1950 SC 554, 563. [Constitution of India, Art. 19(1)]

The action of advertising; a public notice or announcement of a thing [S. 171-H of IPC (45 of 1860), and S. 76(1)(e) of Trade and Merchandise Marks Act (43 of 1958),].

"Advertisement" means any audio or visual publicity, representation, endorsement or pronouncement made by means of light, sound, smoke, gas, print, electronic media, internet or website and includes any notice, circular, label, wrapper, invoice or such other documents. [Consumer Protection Act, 2019 (35 of 2019), section 2(1)]

"Advertisement" means any audio or visual publicity, representation or pronouncement made by means of any light, sound, smoke, gas, print, electronic media, internet or website or social media and includes through any notice, circular, label, wrapper, invoice or other document or device. [Prohibition of Electronic Cigarettes (Production, Manufacture, Import, Export, Transport, Sale, Distribution, Storage & Advertisement) Act, 2019 (42 of 2019), section 3(a)]

"Advertisements, (Indecent)" Includes any picture or printed or written matter of an obscene nature, or indecent advertisement, exhibited to public view or placed so as to be visible to persons passing along a public highway or using an urinal, or is given away or offered to such persons, or is delivered to any one for the purpose of being so exhibited. Indecent Advertisement Act, 1889, 52 & 53, Vict. c. 18 S. 3.

"ADVERTISEMENT" means any audio or visual publicity, representation or pronouncement made by means of any light, sound, smoke, gas, print, electronic media, internet or website and includes through any notice, circular, label, wrapper, invoice or other documents. [S. 3(1)(b) of the Food Safety & Standards Act, 2006 (34 of 2006)]

Advice. Counsel given or an opinion expressed as to the wisdom of future conduct; (*Abbott*). *Inmercantile usage*, direction given by a correspondent (*Burrill*); information given by letter by one merchant or banker to another in regard to some business transaction which concerns him. (*Cyc. Law Dict.*)

It is also known as Letter of Advice.

"Advice" means "the way in which a matter is looked at; opinion; judgement". [New Shorter Oxford English Dictionary as cited in *Manoj Narula* v. *Union of India*, (2014) 9 SCC 1, para 95].

"Advice" means encouragement or dissuation; counsel; suggestion". [Webster Comprehensive Dictionary International Edn., as cited in *Manoj Narula* v. *Union of India*, (2014) 9 SCC 1, para 95].

An opinion given or offered as to action [T.P. Act (4 of 1882), S. 69A(10)]; [Children Act (60 of 1960), S. 21(1)(a)]; information.

Advice and counsel. Advice implies real or pretended knowledge, often professional or technical on the part of the one who gives it, and may apply to any of the affairs of life; as, advice, regarding the choice of books, the conduct of a business, legal or medical advice. Counsel is rather the fruit of wisdom or deliberation, and usually presupposes weightier occasions than advice, as, to seek counsel in an emergency, in affairs of state; in matters of litigation. "Counsel of perfection". (*Cent. Dict.*)

TO TAKE ADVICE : To consult with others; specifically to consult one who has a special knowledge of a subject; take the opinion of a professional or skilled person, as a physician, lawyer or the like.

Advice, letter of. A letter by one merchant or banker to another concerning a business transaction in which both are engaged.

Advice note. A document accompanying a delivery of goods which advises as to the kind, quality and quantity of goods delivered.

Advice of counsel. A lawyer's guidance to his client.

Advise. To give advice; to inform.

Advisement. Careful consideration.

Adviser. One who gives advice or counsel; one who advises; one designated to give advice. [Indian Evidence Act (1 of 1872), S. 129 and Oil Industry (Development) Act (47 of 1974), S. 18(2)(a)].

"ADVISER" MEANS a person appointed by a State, on the basis of his or her qualifications, for the purpose of assisting its accredited representative in an investigation. [Aircraft (Investigation of Accidents and Incidents) Rules, 2012, R. 2(d); Aircraft (Investigation of Accident and Incidents) Rules, 2017, R. 2(5)].

Advisory arbitration. An effort to resolve specific issues in a dispute by an arbitrator who renders an award which merely recommends possible solutions and is therefore not binding on the parties.

Advocacy. The act of pleading for, supporting or recommending; acting espousal.

Advocare. To defend; to call to one's aid; to vouch; to warrant.

Advocate. "ADVOCATE" in the Bar Council's Act means an advocate entered in the roll of advocates of a High Court under the provisions of that Act. [Bar Councils Act (38 of 1926), S. 2(*a*).

(From *advocare*), to summon to one's assistance; one who pleads the cause of another in a Court of law, or other judicial tribunal. His duty is two-fold—to advise his client before going into Court, and to act for him when in Court. He is a person learned in the law and duly admitted to practice, who assists his client with advice and pleads for him in open Court.

An advocate entered in the roll of advocates can mean only one whose name continues to be entered in that roll. *Jethanand Betab* v. *Judges of the Punjab High Court*, AIR 1962 SC 742, 744. [Indian Bar Councils Act (38 of 1926), S. 2]

One who is qualified to plead before the higher Courts of law [Advocates Act (25 of 1961), S. 2(a)]; to support or recommend publicly [Unlawful Activities (Prevention) Act (37 of 1967),

S. 13(1)(b)]; [Indian Evidence Act (1 of 1872), S. 10, ill].

'Advocate' means a person whose name has been entered in the roll of advocates prepared and maintained by the Bar Council under section 17 of the Advocates Act, 1961 (Central Act 25 of 1961) and who is a member of a Bar Association or an Advocates Association. [Tamil Nadu Advocates' Welfare Fund Act (49 of 1987), S. 2(a) as cited in *S. Seshachalam* v. *Bar Council of T.N.*, (2014) 16 SCC 72, para 12].

Advocate-General. "ADVOCATE-GENERAL" includes, where there is no Advocate-General, the Government Advocate and, such officer as the Local Government may declare to be the Advocate-General for the purposes of this Act. Act XXXVIII of 1926 (Indian Bar Councils Act) S. 2, cl. (*b*); Act II of 1911, S. 2(1); Criminal Procedure Code; 1898, S. 4.

The adviser of the government. He is the principal law officer of the government.

See, Art. 165, The Constitution of India

Advocate-on-record. Means an advocate who is entitled under these rules to act as well as to plead for a party in the Court. [Supreme Court Rules, 1966, R. 2(1)(b)]

Advocate, senior. A 'Senior Advocate' means an Advocate so designated under sub-section (2) of Section 16 of the Advocates Act, 1961 (25 of 1961) and all such Advocates whose names were borne on the role of Senior Advocates of the Court immediately before the commencement of Chapter III of the Advocates Act 1961. [Supreme Court Rules, 1966, Order 1, R. 2(q)]

Aedificare in tuo proprio solo non licet quod alteri noceat. (*Maxim*) It is not lawful to build on one's own land what may injure another. (*Burrill; Broom; Coke 3rd inst.*)

Aedificatum solo, solo cedit. (*Maxim*) What is built upon the land goes with the land. (*Abbott; Coke Litt. 4-a; Broom stln. 2, 1, 29*)

Aedificia solo cedunt. (*Maxim*) Buildings go with the land. (*Black; Ency. Law Dict.; Fleta. Lib. 3, Ch. 2, S. 12*)

Aequior est dispositio legis quam hominis. (*Maxim*) The disposition of the law is more equitable or impartial than that of man. (*Black; 8 Coke 152; Bracton, fol. 3-a*)

Aequitas agit in personam. (*Maxim*) Equity acts in person. (*4 Bouvier Inst. Note 3733; Cyc. Law Dict.*)

Aequitas curiae cancellarie, quasi filia conscientiae, obtemperat secundum regulas curaie. (*Maxim*) The equity of the Court of chancery, as if it were the daughter of conscience, conforms to the rules of Court. (*Adam*)

Aequitas defectus supplet. (*Maxim*) Equity supplies defects. (*Morgan*)

Aequitas erroribus medatur. (*Maxim*) Equity rectifies errors. (*Adam*)

Aequitas est aequalitas. (*Maxim*) Equity is equality. (*Morgan*)

Aequitas est correctio legis generaliter latae qua parte deficit. Equity is the correction of that wherein the law by reason of its generality, is deficient. (*Plowd. 375; Black*)

Aequitas est correctio quaedam legi adhibita, quia ab ea abest aliquid propter generalem sine exceptione comprehensionem. (*Maxim*) Equity is a certain correction applied to law, because on account of its general comprehensiveness, without an exception, something is absent from it. (*Plowd. 467*)

Aequitas est perfecta quaedam ratio quae jus scriptum interpretatur et emendat; nulla scriptura comprehensa sed sola ratione consistens. (*Maxim*) Equity is a certain perfect reason, which interprets and amends the written law, comprehended in no writing, but consisting in right reason alone.

Aequitas est quasi aequalitas. Equity is as it were equality; equity is a species of equality or equalization.

Aequitas est virtus voluntatis, correctrix ejus in quo lex propter universa litatem deficit. (*Maxim*) Equity is a virtue of the will, the corrector of that wherein the law, by reason of its universality, is deficient. (*Adam*)

Aequitas ex lege generliter lata aliquid excipit. (*Maxim*) Equity generally excepts something from a widespread or diffuse law. (*Lofft Max. 362*)

Aequitas factum habet quod fieri oportuit. Equity regards as done that which ought to have been done. Equity treats a contract to do a thing as producing the state of affairs which the parties intended should exist when the contract had been duly performed.

Aequitas ignorantiae opitulatur, oscitantiae non item. (*Maxim*) Equity assists ignorance, but not carelessness. (*Ame. Cyc.*)

Aequitas in paribus causis paria jure desiderat. (*Maxim*) Equity in like cases requires like laws. (*Morgan; Plowden 385*)

Aequitas naturam rei non mutat. (*Maxim*) Equity does not change the nature of a thing." (*Adam*)

Aequitas neminem juvat cum injuria alterius. (*Maxim*) Equity aids no man to the injury of another. (*Adam*)

Aequitas non facit jus sed juri auxilatur. (*Maxim*) Equity does not make law, but assists law.

Aequitas non medetur defectu eorum quae jure positivo requisita allium. Equity does not supply the deficiency of those things which are required by positive law.

Aequitas non supplet ea quae in manu orantis esse possunt. "Equity does not supply those things which may be in the hand of an applicant." (*Lofft. Max.* 391)

Aequitas non vaga atque incert est sed terminos habet atque limites praefinites. (*Maxim*) Equity is not vague and uncertain, but has certain determined boundaries and definite limits. (*Adam*)

Aequitas nunquam contravenit legis. (*Maxim*) Equity never counteracts the law. (*Rapalje*)

Aequitas sequitur legem. (*Maxim*) Equity follows the law. (*Burrill*)

Equity does not claim to over-ride the law. Equity generally operates by recognising the legal rule and adding some further rule, remedy or other machinery of its own.

Aequitas supervacua odit. Equity abhors superfluous things.

Aequitas uxoribus, liberis, creditoribus maxime favet. Equity favours wives and children, creditors most of all.

Aequitas vult omnibus modis, ad veritatem parvenire. (*Maxim*) Equity wishes by every possible means to arrive at the truth. (*Adam*)

Aequitas vult spoliatos, vel deceptos, vel lapsos ante omnia restitui. (*Maxim*) Equity desires the plundered, the deceived, and the ruined, above all things, to have restitution. (*Lofft. Max. 374*)

Aequum et bonum. In equity and good conscience.

Aequum et bonum est lex legum. (*Maxim*) What is equitable and good is the law of laws. (*Burrill*; 1 *Ame. Cyc.* 1157-1158)

Aerial. "Belonging or pertaining to the air or atmosphere inhabiting or frequenting the air; existing or happening in the air." (as, *Aerial Railway*)

Aerodrome. 'AERODROME' means any definite or limited ground or water area intended to be used, either wholly or in part, for the landing or departure of aircraft, and includes all buildings, sheds, vessels, piers and other structures thereon or appertaining thereto. [Aircraft Act (22 of 1934), S. 2(2)]

"AERODROME" means aerodrome as defined for the purposes of the enactments relating to airways, aircraft and air navigation. [Constitution of India, Art. 364(2)(b)].

Aerodrome reference point. in relation to any aerodrome, means a designated point established in the horizontal plane at or near the geometric center of that part of the aerodrome reserved for the departure or landing of aircraft. [Aircraft Act (22 of 1934), S. 2(2A)].

Aeronautical communication station. Means a station in the aeronautical communication service which includes aeronautical practicing service, aeronautical fixed service, aeronautical mobile service ánd aeronautical radio communication service. [Airports Authority of India Act (55 of 1994), S. 2(a)]

Aestimatio praeteriti delicti ex postremo facto nunquam crescit. (*Maxim*) The weight of a past offence is never increased by a subsequent fact. (*Wharton; Bacon*)

Affair. Business of any kind, commercial, professional or public; something to be transacted, matter, concern.

Affairs. Used to mean public affairs or the administration of the State (as) "At the head of affairs". Matters of interest or concern; particular doings or interests; specifically pecuniary interests or relations : as, to meddle with a neighbour's affairs; his affairs are in an embarrassed state.

Business of any kind, commercial, professional or public. [Indian Partnership Act (9 of 1932), S. 44(d)]; [Jayanti Shipping Company (Taking Over of Management) Act (63 of 1971), S. 12(1)(d)]; matters; concern [Indian Evidence Act (1 of 1872), S. 32(6)]; [Prevention of Corruption Act (2 of 1947), S. 6(1)(a)].

Affairs of family. Matters of interest or concern to the family. [Indian Evidence Act (1 of 1872), S. 32(6)].

Affairs of State. The words "affairs of State" have acquired a secondary meaning, namely, those matters of State whose disclosure would cause injury to the public interest. *State of Punjab* v. *Sodhi Sukhdev Singh*, AIR 1961 SC 493, 502, 527. [Indian Evidence Act(1 of 1872), S. 123]

The words 'affairs of State' are not confined only to matters which will be prejudicial to the public interest or injurious to national defence or detrimental to good diplomatic relations. It may cover the case of documents in respect of which the practice of keeping them secret is necessary for the proper functioning of the public service. *S.B. Chowdhary* v. *I.P. Changakati*, AIR 1960 Ass 210, 216.

The term 'affairs of the State' is of very wide amplitude and it will cover every business activity of the State in every day to day routine administration as also highly confidential matters, pertaining to defence, foreign affairs, Cabinet minutes and advice or notes exchanged between Ministers and other Heads of Departments of the Government. *Raj Narain* v. *Indira Nehru Gandhi*, AIR 1974 All 324, 335.

Matters of public nature with which the State is concerned. [Indian Evidence Act (1 of 1872), S. 123].

Affect. To have an effect upon; to influence.

The word 'affect' is a word of wide import and it must be construed to mean 'touch' or relate to or 'concern'. *Daniraiji Urajlaji* v. *Chandra Prabha*, AIR 1975 SC 784, 788. [Hindu Adoption and Maintenance Act (78 of 1956), S. 30]

To act or produce an effect upon. [T.P. Act (4 of 1882), Ss. 2 and 5].

Affect and effect are sometimes confused. To affect is to influence, concern; to effect is to accomplish or bring about. (*Cent. Dict.*)

Affected area. Means such area as may be notified by the appropriate Government for the purposes of land acquisition. [S. 3(b) of the Right to Fair Compensation & Transparency in Land Acquisition, Rehabilitation & Resettlement Act, 2013 (30 of 2013)]

Affected family. Includes—(i) a family whose land or other immovable property has been acquired; (ii) a family which does not own any land but a member or members of such family may be agricultural labourers, tenants including any form of tenancy or holding of usufruct right, share-croppers or artisans or who may be working in the affected area for three years prior to the acquisition of the land, whose primary source of livelihood stand affected by the acquisition of land; (iii) the Scheduled Tribes and other traditional forest dwellers who have lost any of their forest rights recognised under the Scheduled Tribes and Other Traditional Forest Dwellers (Recognition of Forest Rights) Act, 2006 (2 of 2007) due to acquisition of land; (iv) family whose primary source of livelihood for three years prior to the acquisition of the land is dependent on forests or water bodies and includes gatherers of forest produce, hunters, fisher folk and boatmen and such livelihood is affected due to acquisition of land; (v) a member of the family who has been assigned land by the State Government or the Central Government under any of its schemes and such land is under acquisition; (vi) a family residing on any land in the urban areas for preceding three years or more prior to the acquisition of the land or whose primary source of livelihood for three years prior to the acquisition of the land is affected by the acquisition of such land. [S. 3(c) of the Right to Fair Compensation & Transparency in Land Acquisition, Rehabilitation & Resettlement Act, 2013 (30 of 2013)]

"Affected person". Means a user of the inter-State transmission system who is affected due to non–adherence to the Standards of Performance specified in these regulations by the inter–State transmission licensee. [Central Electricity Regulatory Commission (Standards of Performance of Inter-State Transmission Licensees) Regulations, 2012, Regn. 3(1)(b)].

Affectio tua nomen imponit operi tuo. (*Maxim*) The affection of a person gives a name to his work. (*Wharton L. Lex.*)

One's intention gives character to one's act". (*Burrill*)

Affectus punitur licet non sequatur effectus. The intention is punished even if the object is not achieved.

Affiant. One who makes an affidavit.

Affidavit. "AFFIDAVIT" shall include affirmation and declaration in the case of persons by law allowed to affirm or declare instead of swearing. [General Clauses Act (10 of 1897), S. 3(3)].

A declaration on oath, reduced to writing, affirmed or sworn to by an affiant before some person who has authority to administer oaths. (*Bouvier; Wharton; Burrill*)

"An affidavit is an oath in writing signed by the party deposing, sworn before and attested by him who hath authority to administer the same". A written declaration under oath, made without notice to the adverse party."

A written statement in the name of a person, called the deponent by whom it is voluntarily signed and sworn to or affirmed. [General Clauses Act (10 of 1897), S. 3(3) and Oaths Act (44 of 1969), S. 3(3)].

Affidavit by several. Several persons may swear to and sign the same statement of facts in a single affidavit.

Affidavit by insane persons—Before the affidavit of an insane person can be received there must first be an inquiry into his mental capacity to make such affidavit.

Affidavit, Deposition, Complaint. Affidavit is always made *ex parte* and without cross-examination and in this it differs from a *deposition* which is evidence given by a witness under interrogatories, oral or written and usually written down by an official person; while an affidavit is the mere voluntary act of the party making the oath, and may be, and generally is taken without the cognizance of the one against whom it is to be used." A *complaint* in a criminal prosecution is not necessarily equivalent to an affidavit, although, on oath since it need not necessarily be certified by the magistrate and may be merely formal and made by one having little, if any, knowledge of the facts, while an affidavit is understood to be a sworn statement of facts or a deposition in writing, including a jurat or certificate of the magistrate showing that it was sworn to before him.

Affiliate. To connect or associate oneself.

Affiliated College. The term "affiliated college" means an institution affiliated to the University. "Institution" does not mean classes.

Persons who only prepare students for a diploma which was not recognised by the University could not be considered as teachers of an affiliated college.

Affiliation. "AFFILIATION" together with its grammatical variations, includes in relation to a college, recognition of such college by, association of such college with, and admission of such college to the privileges of, a University. [University Grants Commission Act (3 of 1956), S. 12A(a)]

The act of affiliating (*Wharton*); adoption; association in the same family or society. (*Cent. Dict.*)

"Affiliation" is meant to prepare and present the students for public examination.

Affiliation of college. To university means such a connection between an existing university and a college as shall be entered into by their mutual consent, under the conditions approved by the University Commissioners or other proper authorities.

Affinis dictur, cum due cognationes, inter se divise, per nuptias copulantur, et altera ad alterius fines

accidit. Persons are said to be bound by affinity when two families, divided from one another, are united by marriage, and each approaches the confines of the other. (*Latin for Lawyers*)

Affinity. The tie which arises from the marriage between the husband and the blood relations of the wife, and between the wife and the blood relations of the husband.

Affirm. To make firm, confirm, establish, ratify (as) a higher Court affirming the judgment of the lower Court. (*Burrill; Abbott*)

To make a solemn affirmation [Indian Evidence Act (1 of 1872), S. 9, ill. (b)]; [CPC (5 of 1908), O. XIV, R. 1(1)]; to confirm or ratify.

Affirmance. Confirmation; ratification.

Affirmanti non neganti incumbit probatio. (*Maxim*) The burden of proof rests upon him who affirms, not upon him who denies. (*Abott; Wharton; Broom*)

The reason for this rule is not that it is impossible to prove a negative, but that a negative does not admit of the simple and direct proof of which an affirmative is capable. See, Taylor on Evidence, 12th Edn., Vol. I, p. 525. (*Latin for Lawyers*)

Affirmantis est probare. He who affirms must prove.

Affirmation. Confirmation; ratification; establishment of something of prior origin. (*Hooker*)

A solemn declaration without oath. [General Clauses Act (10 of 1897), S. 3(3)].

Affirmative action. The positive steps designed for the elimination of existing and continuing discrimination.

Affirmative pregnant. A positive statement that ambiguously implies a negative.

Affirmative warranty. A warranty in which facts are stated at the beginning of policy period.

Affix. To fix, fasten, join or attach; conjoin, add.

Affixing digital signature. Affixing digital signature with its grammatical variations and cognate expressions means adoption of any methodology or procedure by a person for the purpose of authenticating an electronic record by means of digital signature. [Information Technology Act (21 of 2000) (as stood before the IT Amendment Act of 2008), S. 2 (1)(d)]

Affixing electronic signature. With its grammatical variations and cognate expressions means adoption of any methodology or procedure by a person for the purpose of authenticating an electronic record by means of electronic signature. [Information Technology Act, 2000, S. 2 (1)(d)].

Affluent. The raw sewage entering a disposal plant; flowing in abundance.

Afford him earliest opportunity of making representation. These words imply that as and when representation is made it should be dealt with properly. *Bimal Chandra Dutta* v. *State of West Bengal*, AIR 1972 SC 2605, 2606. Constitution of India, Article 22(5).

Afford him the earliest opportunity. The words 'afford him the earliest opportunity' in article 22(5) have been interpreted by the apex court in *Abdul Karim* v. *State of West Bengal*, [1969] 3 SCR 479 : AIR 1969 SC 1028 to imply that the State Government to whom the representation is made should properly consider it as expeditiously as possible. *Niranjan Singh* v. *State of M. P.*, AIR 1972 SC 2215.

Afforest. To turn a ground into a forest. When forest ground is turned from forest to other uses, it is called *disafforested.* (*Tomlin; Termes de la ley*)

Affray. When two or more persons, by fighting in a public place disturb the public peace, they are said to commit an affray. [IPC (45 of 1860), S. 159]. [(w.e.f. 1-7-2024) repealed and replaced by Bharatiya Nyaya Sanhita, 2023 (45 of 2023), section 194(1)]

AFFRAY signifies a skirmish or fighting in a public place between two or more, and there must be a stroke given or offered, or a weapon drawn, otherwise it is not an affray. "If the fighting be in private, it is not an affray, but an assault". (*Rose Cr. 241; Termes de la Ley; Jacob*)

Distinguished from riot. Affray is distinguished from riot or rioting in that the latter offence must be committed by a number of persons and is of a somewhat more public nature.

Affreight. To hire or charter a ship for transportation of goods.

Affreightment. Is the freight or lading of a ship (*Cowell*); the contract by which a vessel, or the use of it, is let out to hire. (*Bouvier; Tomlin*); The contract may be made by a charter party or by a bill of Lading.

The hiring of a ship to carry cargo.

Afloat. Borne on the water. [Navy Act (62 of 1957), S. 98].

Aforesaid. Before mentioned, already said; before indicated; previously mentioned (*Plowden 67*); recited, or said (*Burrill*); mentioned in a previous part of the same writing, document or discourse. (*Imp. Dict.; Webs.; Cent Dict.*)

Said or mentioned before. [T.P. Act (4 of 1882), Ss. 51, 59 and 126].

Afforestation. The act of turning ground into a forest or woodland or subjecting it to forest law; the territory afforested.

Aforethought. (In criminal law) Deliberate; planned; premeditated; (as, malice aforethought).

After-born children. A bequest to "after-born children" would generally mean a bequest to those born after the date of the will and before the death of the testator.

"Aftercare". Means making provision of support, financial or otherwise, to persons, who have completed the age of eighteen years but have not completed the age of twenty-one years, and have left any institutional care to join the mainstream of the society. [Juvenile Justice (Care and Protection of Children) Act, 2015 (2 of 2016), S. 2(5)].

After date. Written on a *bill of exchange,* after date indicates that the bill will become due a certain (specified) period after the date on the bill. Hence, the bill might read, "60 days after date, we promise to pay . . ."

After her life time. (*Will-construction*) The words 'after the lifetime' indicate that the interest referred to was a terminable one — a life interest. These words indicate that the persons designated by the words that followed were to take an interest after her, *i.e.* in succession and not jointly with the first interest. *Ramachandra* v. *Hilda Brite*, AIR 1954 SC 1323, 1328, 1329.

After presentment for sight. After being presented for being seen (by the maker of a promissory note). [Negotiable Instruments Act (26 of 1881), S. 21].

After the execution of the warrant. The expression 'execution of warrant' includes unsuccessful execution of warrant yielding no fruits and the Magistrate can award the sentence even after the unsuccessful execution of warrant. *Moddari Bin* v. *Sukded Bin,* AIR 1967 Cal 136, 140.

Afternoon. This word has two senses. It may mean the whole time from noon to midnight; or it may mean the earlier part of that time, as distinguished from the evening. When used in a statute its meaning must be determined by the context and the circumstances of the subject matter.

Afterthought. A later or second thought. Reflection after an act; some consideration that occurs to one's mind too late, or after the performance of the act to which it refers.

Afterthought is the opposite of forethought.

'Against her will' mean that the act must have been done inspite of the opposition of the woman. [*Kaini Rajan* v. *State of Kerala*, (2013) 9 SCC 113, para 12]. [Indian Penal Code (45 of 1860), S. 375].

Age. The time that anything or person has existed or lived. [IPC (45 of 1860), S. 6, ill. (a) and Constitution of India, Art. 124 (2A)]; the time of life at which one becomes naturally or conventionally qualified for something. [T.P. Act (4 of 1882), S. 14].

Age of capacity. The age at which a person becomes legally capable of entering into a contract, executing a will, maintaining a law suit *etc.*

Age of consent. The age of at which a person becomes legally capable of agreeing to marriage or to sexual intercourse.

Age of majority. The age at which a person attains full legal rights.

Age of reason. The age at which a person becomes able to distinguish between right and wrong.

Agency. The relation which exists between one person called 'the principal' and another person called 'the agent' who, by his authority, express or implied, acts on his behalf. (*Wharton's Law Lexicon, 15th Edn.*)

An agent acts on behalf of his principal and often uses his name and his acts in that capacity are attributable to the principal.

The area comprising the jurisdiction of (political) agent [CPC (5 of 1908), S. 1(3), prov.]; the office or function of an agent. [Indian Contract Act (9 of 1872), S. 185].

"AGENCY" means any agency, other than a local authority, which may undertake sanitation facilities in an area and includes a contractor or a firm or a company which engages in development and maintenance of real estate. [S. 2(1)(a) of the Prohibition of Employment as Manual Scavengers & Their Rehabilitation Act, 2013 (25 of 2013)]

Agency of a State. Would ordinarily mean an instrumentality of a State. It must be a separate legal entity. A statutory authority does not answer the description of an agency under the control of the State. 'Agency of a State' would mean a body which exercises public functions. It would itself be a 'State' within the meaning of Article 12 of the Constitution of India. *Deewan Singh* v. *Rajendra Pd. Ardevi*, AIR 2007 SC 767 : 2007 AIR SCW 461.

Agency of necessity. Agency of necessity arises where the persons authorised to act as an agent for another without any regard to the consent of the principal act in certain circumstances and the law creates an agency of necessity. A wife becomes an agent of necessity. Where after the parties have created a constructed relationship the law, in view of some emergency, confers upon one party, authority to act for another, or allows an agent to exceed the authority which has been conferred upon him. *Mohd. Serajuddin* v. *State of Orissa*, AIR 1975 SC 1564, 1574.

Agenda. A list of business to be transacted.

Agent."AGENT" means a person, including a factor, broker, commission agent, arhatia, del credere agent, an auctioneer or any other mercantile agent, by whatever name called, who carried on the business of supply or receipt of goods or services or both on behalf of another. [Central Goods and Services Tax Act (12 of 2017), S. 2(5)].

An "AGENT" is a person employed to do any act for another or to represent another in dealings with third persons. The person for whom such act is done, or who is so represented, is called the "principal." [Indian Contract Act (9 of 1872), S. 182].

The expression "AGENT" includes an election agent, a polling agent and any person, who is held to have acted as an agent in connection with the election with the consent of the candidate. [Representation of the People Act (43 of 1951), S. 123(1)]

"agent" means a person, including a factor, broker, commission agent, arhatia, del credere agent, an auctioneer or any other mercantile agent, by whatever name called, who carries on the business of supply or receipt of goods or services or both on behalf of another [The Central Goods and Services Tax Act, 2017 (12 of 2017), S. 2(5)]

"Agent" when used in relation to an establishment, means every person, whether appointed as such or not, who acting or purporting to act on behalf of the owner, takes part in the management, control, supervision or direction of such establishment or part thereof. [Code on Social Security, 2020 (36 of 2020), section 2(1)]

"Agent" when used in relation to a mine, means every person, whether appointed as such or not, who, acting or purporting to act on behalf of the owner, takes part in the management, control, supervision or direction of such mine or of any part thereof. [Occupational Safety, Healthy & Working Conditions Code, 2020 (37 of 2020), section 2(1)(c)]

A person employed to do any act for another or to represent another in dealings with third persons. [Mines Act (35 of 1952), S. 2(1)(c)].

"AGENT". For the purposes of section 342(5) of Act 18 of 2013, the expression 'agent', in relation to a company, shall include any banker or legal adviser of the company and any person employed by the company as auditor. [*Explanation* to section 342(5) of the Companies Act, 2013 (18 of 2013)]

Agent provocateur. Person who entraps or entices another to break the law and then inform against the other as a law breaker.

Agent : Servant. An agent is not under direct control or supervision of the principal whereas the servant is under direct control or supervision of the Principal. *Qamar Shaffi Tyaliys* v. *Commr. of Excess Profit Tax*, AIR 1960 SC 1269.

Agentes et consentientes pari poena plectentur. (*Maxim*) Acting and consenting parties are liable to the same punishment. (*Morgan*)

Agent's lien on goods. It arises when the agent pays for such goods on behalf of the principal. *Ramprasad* v. *State of M.P.*, AIR 1970 SC 1818.

Aggravate. To make more grave or heavy; increase the weight or pressure of; intensify, as anything evil.

To make worse, more severe or more serious. [Army Act (46 of 1950), S. 46(b)]; [Navy Act (62 of 1957), S. 61].

Aggravated assault. A criminal assault which is accompanied by circumstances making it more severe, *e.g.* use of a deadly weapon, intent to cause serious bodily harm.

Aggravated battery. A criminal battery which is accompanied by circumstances making it more severe, such as the use of deadly weapon.

Aggravated burglary. Burglary committed by a person who had deadly weapons with him.

Aggravated damages. Damages that are awarded when the defendant's conduct or surrounding circumstances increase the injury to the claimant by subjecting him to humiliation, distress, embarrassment, false imprisonment and defamation.

Aggravated penetrative sexual assault. :

(a) Whoever, being a police officer commits penetrative sexual assault on a child—
   (i) within the limits of the police station or premises at which is appointed; or
   (ii) in the premises of any station house, whether or not situated in the police station to which he is appointed; or
   (iii) in the course of his duties or otherwise; or
   (iv) where he is known as, or identified as, a police officer; or

(b) Whoever being a member of the armed forces or security forces commits penetrative sexual assault on a child–
   (i) within the limits of the area to which the person is deployed; or
   (ii) in any areas under the command of the forces or armed forces; or
   (ii) in the course of his duties or otherwise; or
   (iv) where the said person is known or identified as a member of the security or armed forces; or

(c) Whoever being a public servant commits penetrative sexual assault on a child; or

(d) Whoever being on the management or on the staff of a jail, remand home, protection home, observation home, or other place of custody or care and protection established by or under any law for the time being in force, commits penetrative sexual assault on a child, being inmate of such jail, remand home, protection home, observation home, or other place of custody or care and protection; or

(e) Whoever being on the management or staff of a hospital, whether Government or private, commits penetrative sexual assault on a child in that hospital;

(f) Whoever being on the management or staff of an educational institution or religious institution commits penetrative sexual assault on a child in that institution; or

(g) Whoever commits gang penetrative sexual assault on a child.

   Explanation.—When a child is subjected to sexual assault by one or more persons of a group in furtherance of common intention, each of such persons shall be deemed to have committed gang penetrative sexual assault within the meaning of this clause and each of such person shall be liable for that act in the same manner as if it were done by him alone; or

(h) Whoever commits penetrative sexual assault on a child using deadly weapons, fire, heated substance or corrosive substance; or

(i) Whoever commits penetrative sexual assault causing grievous hurt or causing bodily harm or injury or injury to the sexual organ of the child; or

(j) Whoever commits penetrative sexual assault on a child, which—

(i) physically incapacitates the child or causes the child to become mentally as defined under clause (b) of section 2 of the Mental Health Act, 1987 (14 of 1987) or causes impairment of any kind so as to render the child unable to perform regular tasks, temporarily or permanently; or

(ii) in the case of female child, makes the child pregnant as a consequence of sexual assault; or

(iii) inflicts the child with Human Immunodeficiency Virus or any other life threatening disease or infection which may either temporarily or permanently impair the child by rendering him physically incapacitated, or mentally ill to perform regular tasks; or

(k) Whoever, taking advantage of a child's mental or physical disability, commits penetrative sexual assault on the child; or

(l) Whoever commits penetrative sexual assault on the child more than once or repeatedly; or

(m) Whoever commits penetrative sexual assault on a child below twelve years; or

(n) Whoever being the relative of the child through blood or adoption or marriage or guardianship or in foster care or having a domestic relationship with a parent of the child or who is living in the same or shared household with the child, commits penetrative sexual assault or such child; or

(o) Whoever being, in the ownership or management, or staff, of any institution providing services to the child, commits penetrative sexual assault on the child; or

(p) Whoever being in a position of trust or authority of a child commits penetrative sexual assault on the child in an institution or home of the child or anywhere else; or

(q) Whoever commits penetrative sexual assault on a child knowing the child is pregnant; or

(r) Whoever commits penetrative sexual assault on a child and attempts to murder the child; or

(s) Whoever commits penetrative sexual assault in the course of communal or sectarian violence; or

(t) Whoever commits penetrative sexual assault on a child and who has been previously convicted of having committed any offence under this Act or any sexual offence punishable under any other law for the time being in force; or

(u) Whoever commits penetrative sexual assault on a child and makes the child to strip or parade naked in public, is said to commit aggravated penetrative sexual assault.

[Protection of Children from Sexual Offences Act (32 of 2012), S. 5].

Aggravated robbery. Robbery accompanied by inflicting of bodily injury on someone.

Aggravating circumstances. Circumstances attending the commission of a crime or tort which increase its guilt or enormity or add to its injurious consequences. Instances of these are : malice, gross recklessness, violence of language or wantonly harmful kind of imputation calculated to outrage feelings and cause mental pain to the plaintiff excessive publicity, repetition of the libel, publishing fresh libels before or after suit; refusal or neglect to retract or apologies, conduct of the defendant during the trial of the action, an unsuccessful plea of justification, persisting in that plea with knowledge that it cannot be proved.

Aggravation. Any circumstance attending the commission of a crime or tort, which increases its guilt or enormity or adds to its injurious consequences.

Aggregate. Entire number, sum, mass, or quantity of something; total amount; complete whole. (*Black*)

Aggregate concept. In taxing business organisations, an approach, where the organisation is viewed as a collection of its individual owners rather than a separate taxable entity.

Aggregate income. The total income of husband and wife given in their joint income tax return.

Aggregate Turnover. "aggregate turnover" means the aggregate value of all taxable supplies (excluding the value of inward supplies on which tax is payable by a person on reverse charge basis), exempt supplies, exports of goods or services or both and inter-State supplies of persons having the same Permanent Account Number, to be computed on all India basis but excludes central tax, State tax, Union territory tax, integrated tax and cess [The Central Goods and Services Tax Act, 2017 (12 of 2017), S. 2(6)]

"Aggregate turnover". Means the aggregate value of all taxable supplies (excluding the value of inward supplies on which tax is payable by a person on reverse charge basis), exempt supplies, exports of goods or services or both and inter-State supplies of persons having the same Permanent Account Number, to be computed on all India basis but excludes Central tax, State tax, Union Territory tax, integrated tax and cess. [Central Goods and Services Tax Act (12 of 2017), S. 2(6)].

For the purposes of this section, the expression "AGGREGATE TURNOVER" shall include all supplies made by the taxable person, whether on his own account or made on behalf of all his principals. [Central Goods and Services Tax Act (12 of 2017), S. 22, *Explanation* (*i*)].

Aggregatio mentium. Literally "the meeting of the minds". The moment when a contract is complete.

Aggregator. Means a digital intermediary or market place for a passenger to connect with a driver for the purpose of transportation. [Motor Vehicles Act, 1988 (59 of 1988), section 2(1A)]

Means a digital intermediary or a market place for a buyer or user of a service to connect with the seller or the service provider. [Code on Social Security, 2020 (36 of 2020), section 2(2)]

Aggression. The act of proceeding to hostilities or invasion; a breach of the peace or right of another or others; an assault, inroad, or encroachment; hence, any offensive action or procedure; as, an aggression upon a country, or upon vested rights or liberties.

Aggrieved. A person who has suffered a legal grievance—a man against whom a decision has been pronounced which has wrongfully deprived him of something or wrongfully refused him something or wrongfully affected his title to something.

Injuriously affected; having a grievance. [CPC (5 of 1908), Ss. 97 and 114].

"AGGRIEVED" means a stakeholder who has filed a grievance with the Board on failing to get his grievance redressed from the concerned service provider. [Insolvency and Bankruptcy Board of India (Grievance and Complaint Handling Procedure) Regulations, 2017, Regn. 2(1)(d)].

Aggrieved parties. The persons whose right are adversely affected by a judgment, decree or order.

Aggrieved person. It means affected person. *P. Lal* v. *Union of India*, (2003) 3 SCC 393.

"AGGRIEVED PERSON" means any woman who is, or has been, in a domestic relationship with the respondent and who alleges to have been subjected to any act of domestic violence by the respondent. [S. 2(a) of the Protection of Women from Domestic Violence Act, 2005 (43 of 2005)]

Aggrieved person (in criminal law). Where a libelious statement in a newspaper is true as regards the complainant though untrue as regards others, the complainant is not an "aggrieved person" within the meaning of Section 198 of the CrPC 1973 (2 of 1974).

In the offence of Bigamy committed by the husband, the wife is the "aggrieved party', and not relatives, however closely related to the wife. *State of Mysore* v. *Gangamma*, AIR 1965 Mysore 235, 236. [CrPC 1973 (2 of 1974), S. 198]

Aggrieved woman. Means—(i) in relation to a workplace, a woman, of any age, whether employed or not, who alleges to have been subjected to any act of sexual harassment by the respondent; (ii) in relation to a dwelling place or house, a woman of any age who is employed in such a dwelling place or house. [S. 2(a) of the Sexual Harassment of Women at Workplace (Prevention, Prohibition & Redressal) Act, 2013 (14 of 2013)]

"AGGRIEVED WOMAN" means, in relation to the Supreme Court, any female, of any age, whether employed or not, who claims to have been subjected to any act of sexual harassment by any person in the Supreme Court of India precincts, but does not include any female who is already governed by the Supreme Court service regulations [Gender Sensitisation and Sexual Harassment of Women at the Supreme Court of India (Prevention, Prohibition and Redressal) Regulation, 2013, Regn. 2(a)].

"AGGRIEVED WOMAN" means in relation to work place, a woman of any age whether reemployed or not, who alleges to have been subjected to any act of sexual harassment by the respondent. [All India Council for Technical Education (Gender Sensitization, Prevention and Prohibition of Sexual Harassment of Women Employees and Students and Redressal of Grievances in Technical Educational Institutions) Regulations, 2016, Regn. 2(a)].

"'Aghadi' or 'front'. means a group of persons who have formed themselves into a party for the purpose of setting up candidates for election to a local authority." [*Jeevan Chandrabhan Idani* v. *Divisional Commissioner, Konkan Bhavan*, (2012) 2 SCC 794, para 15] [Maharashtra Local Authority Members' Disqualification Act, 1968, s. 2(a)].

Agistment. A contract of bail man for the benefit of both bailor and bailee.

Agitate. To engage in agitation; arouse or attempt to arouse public interest as in some political or social question.

Agnate. A descendant by male links from a common male ancestor. [Hindu Succession Act (30 of 1956), S. 3(1)(a)].

Agnates or agnati. Relatives whose relationship can be traced exclusively through males, (*Abbott*). Relations on the father's side as distinguished from cognates, (*i.e.*,) relations on the mother's side. (*Smith Dict. of Antiq- Tit Cognates, see also Maine's Anc. Law 142; Tomlin*)

Agnatus. n. (*Lat.*) A person related through the male line.

Agrarian. Relating to land or to a distribution or division of land (*Burrill; Black*) or agrarian laws; agrarian outrage *i.e.*, outrage resulting from some dispute relating to land or occupancy of land. (*Imp. Dict.*)

Agrarian reform. A legislation to improve the standard of living and working in villages in the context in which the general good of the village agricultural community will be covered, is agrarian reform.

Agree. To concur; to come to a mutual assent; to come into harmony; to promise; to contract; to assent; to unite in mental action; to acquiesce in. (*Ame. Cyc.*)

To enter into an agreement [T.P. Act (4 of 1882), S. 58(b)]; to concur. [Indian Evidence Act (1 of 1872), S. 23].

Agreed rent. Means the rent agreed between the parties and not any unilateral demand to which the tenant has not consented. *S. Venkataramanaswamy Ayyer* v. *S. Abdul Wahab*, AIR 1969 Mad 473, 476.

Agreement.

"AGREEMENT" means a combination of all of the following agreements, namely—

(*i*) an agreement entered into under sub-section (1) of Section 90 or sub-section (1) of Section 90-A; and

(*ii*) an agreement for exchange of the report referred to in sub-section (2) and notified by the Central Government. [Income-tax Act (43 of 1961), S. 286(9)(b) as substituted by Finance Act (13 of 2018)].

"AGREEMENT" for the purpose of these regulations means an agreement entered into between an Insurance Web Aggregator and an Insurer. [Insurance Regulatory and Development Authority of India (Insurance Web Aggregators) Regulations, 2017, Regn. 2(b)].

'AGREEMENT' means the agreement for the establishment and operation of the international body known as the Asian Development Bank. [Asian Development Bank Act (18 of 1966), S. 2(a)]

Every promise and every set of promises, forming the consideration for each other, is an AGREEMENT. [Indian Contract Act (9 of 1872), S. 2(e)]

"AGREEMENT" includes any arrangement or understanding whether or not it is intended that such agreement shall be enforceable (apart from any provision of this Act) by legal proceedings. [Monopolies and Restrictive Trade Practices Act (54 of 1969), S. 2(a)(Repealed)]

"AGREEMENT" means the Air Services Agreements or Air Transport Agreements entered into by India with parties to the convention. [Foreign Aircraft Exemption from Taxes and Duties on Fuel and Lubricants Act (36 of 2002), S. 2(a)]

"AGREEMENT" includes any arrangement or understanding or action in concert,—

(i) whether or not, such arrangement, understanding or action is formal or in writing; or

(ii) whether or not such arrangement, understanding or action is intended to be enforceable by legal proceedings. [Competition Act, 2002 (12 of 2003), S. 2(b)]

"AGREEMENT" means an agreement (whether written or oral, or partly written and partly oral) between a debtor and creditor, and includes an agreement providing for forced labour, the existence of which is presumed under any social custom prevailing in the concerned locality. [Bonded Labour System (Abolition) Act (19 of 1976), S. 2(b)]

A coming together of parties in opinion or final determination; the union of two or more minds in a thing done or to be done; a mutual assent to do a thing. The joining together of two or more minds in respect of the same matter.

AGREEMENT : CONTRACT : PROMISE. The term "Agreement" is often used as synonymous with "contract". Properly speaking, however it is a wider term than "contract". An agreement might not be a contract, because of not fulfilling some requirement of the law of the place in which it is made. The distinction between agreements and contracts is apparent from S. 2 of the Indian Contract Act (9 of 1872); by its cl. (*e*) every promise and every set of promises forming the consideration for each other is an agreement, and by its cl. (*h*) an agreement enforceable by law is a contract. "Agreement" is seldom applied to specialties; "contract" is generally confined to simple contracts; and "promise" refers to the engagement of a party without reference to the reasons or considerations for it, or the duties of other parties. "Agreement" is not synonymous with "promise" or "undertaking" but, in its more proper and correct sense, signifies a mutual contract between two or more parties, and implies a consideration. (*Black*)

The word "agreement" as used in Sec. 2, Indian Contract Act (9 of 1872) refers both to a promise and a set of promises forming the consideration for each other.

"Agreement" or "concerted practice". The "agreement" or "concerted practice" is the means through which enterprise or association of enterprises or person or association of persons restrict competition. [*Competition Commission of India* v. *Coordination Committee of Artists and Technicians of West Bengal Film and Television*, (2017) 5 SCC 17, para 45].

Agreement of indemnity. An agreement by which one party agrees to save the other from loss caused to him by the conduct of the promisor himself or by the conduct of any other person. [CPC (5 of 1908), Sch., App. A, form No. 20].

Agreement of rescission. An agreement by contracting parties so as to discharge all remaining duties of performance and terminate the contract.

Agreement on Trade-Related Aspects of Intellectual Property Rights (TRIPS). International agreement (one of the World Trade Organization's multilateral agreements) that establishes a comprehensive set of rights and obligations governing international trade in intellectual property. (*Cyber Law*)

Agreement to sell. A contract of sale in which the transfer of the property in the goods is to take place at a future time.

Agricultural drought is usually triggered by meteorological and hydrological droughts and occurs when soil moisture and rainfall are inadequate during the crop growing season causing extreme crop stress and wilting. Plant water demand depends on prevailing weather conditions, biological characteristics of the specific plant, its stage of growth and the physical and biological properties of the soil.

Agricultural drought arises from variable susceptibility of crops during different stages of crops development, from emergence to maturity. In India, it is defined as a period of four consecutive weeks (of severe meteorological drought) with a rainfall deficiency of more than 50% of the long-term average or with a weekly rainfall of 5 cm or less from mid-May to mid-October (the Kharif season) when 80% of India's total crop is planted or six such consecutive weeks during the rest of the year. [*Swaraj Abhiyan* v. *Union of India*, (2016) 7 SCC 498, para 36].

"Agricultural or horticultural produce" shall not include such produce as has been subjected to any physical, chemical or other process for being made fit for consumption, save mere cleaning, grading, sorting or dying. [T.N. Value Added Tax, 2006, S. 41, *Explanation I* as cited in *Jayam and Company* v. *Assistant Commissioners,* (2016) 15 SCC 125, para 8].

Agricultural holding. Land cultivated for profit in some way and not to natural grass land.

Agricultural income. Is the revenue received by direct association with the land which is used for agricultural purposes and not by indirectly extending it to cases where that revenue or part thereby changes hands either by way of distribution of dividends or otherwise.

"AGRICULTURAL INCOME" means—

(a) any rent or revenue derived from land which is situated in India and is used for agricultural purposes;

(b) any income derived from such land by—

(i) agriculture; or

(ii) the performance by a cultivator or receiver of rent-in-kind of any process ordinarily employed by a cultivator or receiver of rent-in-kind to render the produce raised or received by him fit to be taken to market; or

(iii) the sale by a cultivator or receiver of rent-in-kind of the produce raised or received by him, in respect of which no process has been performed other than a process of the nature described in paragraph (*ii*) of this sub-clause;

(c) any income derived from any building owned and occupied by the receiver of the rent or revenue of any such land, or occupied by the cultivator or the receiver of rent-in-kind, of any land with respect to which, or the produce of which, any process mentioned in paragraphs (ii) and (iii) of sub-clause (b) is carried on :

Provided that—

(i) the building is on or in the immediate vicinity of the land, and is a building which the receiver of the rent or revenue or the cultivator, or the receiver of rent-in-kind, by reason of his connection with the land, requires as a dwelling house, or as a store-house, or other outbuilding, and

(ii) the land is either assessed to land revenue in India or is subject to a local rate assessed and collected by officers of the Government as such or where the land is not so assessed to land revenue or subject to a local rate, it is not situated—

(*A*) in any area which is comprised within the jurisdiction of a municipality (whether known as a municipality, municipal corporation, notified area committee, town area committee, town committee or by any other name) or a cantonment board and which has a population of not less than ten thousand; or

(*B*) in any area within the distance, measured aerially,—

(I) not being more than two kilometres, from the local limits of any municipality or cantonment board referred to in item (*A*) and which has a population of more than ten thousand but not exceeding one lakh; or

(II) not being more than six kilometres, from the local limits of any municipality or cantonment board referred to in item (*A*) and which has a population of more than one lakh but not exceeding ten lakh; or

(III) not being more than eight kilometres, from the local limits of any municipality or cantonment board referred to in item (*A*) and which has a population of more than ten lakh.

Explanation 1.—For the removal of doubts, it is hereby declared that revenue derived from land shall not include and shall be deemed never to have included any income arising from the transfer of any land referred to in item (*a*) or item (*b*) of sub-clause (*iii*) of clause (*14*) of this section.

Explanation 2.—For the removal of doubts, it is hereby declared that income derived from any building or land referred to in sub-clause (*c*) arising from the use of such building or land for any purpose (including letting for residential purpose or for the purpose of any business or profession) other than agriculture falling under sub-clause (*a*) or sub-clause (*b*) shall not be agricultural income.

Explanation 3.—For the purposes of this clause, any income derived from saplings or seedlings grown in a nursery shall be deemed to be agricultural income.

Explanation 4.—For the purposes of clause (*ii*) of the proviso to sub-clause (*c*), "population" means the population according to the last preceding census of which the relevant figures have been published before the first day of the previous year. [Income-tax Act (43 of 1961), section 2(1-A)]

"Agricultural income-tax law". Means any law for the time being in force relating to the levy of tax on agricultural income. [Payment of Bonus Act (21 of 1965), section 2(3)]

"Agricultural income tax law" means any law for the time being in force relating to the levy of tax on agricultural income. [Code on Wages, 2019 (29 of 2019), section 2(c)]

Agricultural land. The term 'agriculture' cannot be defined by the nature of products cultivated, but should be defined rather by the circumstances in which the cultivation is carried on. The mere fact that an industry has some connection with or is in some way dependent on land is not sufficient to bring it within the scope of the term. The term 'agricultural' should be construed in its primary sense as meaning the art or science of cultivating the ground. The expression "land used for agricultural purposes" cannot extend to forests of spontaneous growth, where nothing is done to prepare the soil for trees to be planted therein, and where the growth of the trees is not fostered by tillage.

All forest lands are not agricultural lands in the sense that they can be prudently and profitably exploited for agricultural purposes. *Controller Estate Duty Kerala* v. *V. Venugopala Varama Rajah*, AIR 1977 SC 121, 126. [Estate Duty Act (34 of 1953), S. 5, 34]

It is an open land which is either cultivated or which is fit for cultivation. "A land left barren but capable of being cultivated is also agricultural land unless the said land is actually put to some other non-agricultural purpose, like construction of building or an aerodrome, runway etc. thereon, which alters the physical character of the land rendering it unfit for immediate cultivation." *Sir Vicar-ul-umra Hyderabad* v. *The Commissioner of Wealth Tax*, AIR 1969 AP 345, 349, 355 (FB).

A land which is used as an air-strip and which has been used for non-agricultural purpose for over 15 years cannot be an agricultural land. *Krishna Rao L. Balekai* v. *Third Wealth Tax Officer*, AIR 1963 Mys 111, 112. [Wealth Tax Act (27 of 1957), S. 2]

Agricultural land connotes land pertaining to or connected with agriculture and the agricultural land includes water tank and roads in tea garden. *Tea Estates India Ltd.* v. *Wealth-tax Commr.*, AIR 1966 Cal 9, 11, 13. [Wealth-tax Act (27 of 1957), S. 2(*e*), (i)]

Field or soil pertaining to farming or capable for the purpose of agriculture or tilling [Wealth-tax Act (27 of 1957), S. 2(e)(1)(i), and CPC (5 of 1908), S. 4(2)].

"AGRICULTURAL LAND" for the purposes of section 194-IA of Act 43 of 1961, 'agricultural land' means agricultural land in India, not being a land situate in any area referred to in sections 2(14)(iii)(a) and 2(14)(iii)(b). [(w.e.f. 1-6-2013) *Explanation* (*a*) to section 194-IA of the Income-tax Act, 1961 (43 of 1961)]

"AGRICULTURAL LAND" means land used for the purpose of—(i) agriculture or horticulture; (ii) dairy farming, poultry farming, pisciculture, sericulture, seed farming, breeding of livestock or nursery growing medicinal herbs; (iii) raising of crops, trees, grass or garden produce; and (iv) land used for the grazing of cattle. [S. 3(d) of the Right to Fair Compensation & Transparency in Land Acquisition, Rehabilitation & Resettlement Act, 2013 (30 of 2013)]

The expression 'agricultural lands' must be taken to include lands which are used or are capable of being used for raising any valuable plants or trees or for any other purpose of husbandry. *Paramananda Das* v. *Shankar Rath*, AIR 1951 Ori 11.

Agricultural land, in the Agricultural Rates Act, 1896 (59 & 60 Vict, c. 16), does not include glass-houses, in or on a market-garden if they are buildings. *Smith* v. *Richmond*, (1898), App. Cas. 448.

Agricultural marketing society. Means a cooperative society the objects of which include the marketing of agricultural produce. [State Agricultural Credit Corporation Act (60 of 1968), S. 2(a)]

Agricultural operations. "AGRICULTURAL OPERATION" includes animal husbandry, dairy farming, pisciculture and poultry-farming. [State Agricultural Credit Corporation Act (60 of 1968), S. 2(b)]

Agricultural produce. "AGRICULTURAL PRODUCE" includes all produce of agriculture or horticulture and all articles of food or drink wholly or partly manufactured from any such produce, and fleeces and the skins of animals. [Agricultural Produce (Grading & Marking) Act (1 of 1937), S. 2(a)]

"AGRICULTURAL PRODUCE" means any of the following classes of commodities, namely,—

(i) foodstuffs, including edible oil-seeds;
(ii) cattle fodder, including oil-cakes and other concentrates;
(iii) raw cotton, whether ginned or unginned, and cotton seed;
(iv) raw jute; and
(v) vegetable oils. [Warehousing Corporations Act (58 of 1962), S. 2(a)]

"AGRICULTURAL PRODUCE" includes the following:—

(i) edible and non-edible oil seeds;
(ii) cattle feed, including oilcakes and other ingredients;
(iii) produce of horticulture and animal husbandry;
(iv) produce of forestry;

(v) produce of poultry farming;

(vi) produce of pisciculture; and

(vii) produce of other allied activities, whether or not undertaken jointly with agriculture. [National Co-operative Development Corporation Act (26 of 1962), S. 2(a)]

"AGRICULTURAL PRODUCE" means any produce resulting from cultivation or plantation, on which either no further processing is done or such processing is done by the cultivator like tending, pruning, cutting, harvesting, drying which does not alter its essential characteristics but makes it only marketable and includes all cereals, pulses, fruits, nuts and vegetables, spices, copra, sugar cane, jaggery, raw vegetable fibers such as cotton, flax, jute, indigo, unmanufactured tobacco, betel leaves, tendu leaves, rice, coffee and tea but does not include manufactured products such as sugar, edible oils, processed food and processed tobacco. [Central Excise Tariff Act, 1985 (5 of 1986), Appendix IX, Service Tax (c), *Expln.* 2(ii)]

"Agricultural produce" means all produce whether processed or non-processed, manufactured or not, of agriculture, horticulture, plantation, animal husbandry, forest, sericulture, pisciculture and includes livestock or poultry as specified in the schedule." [Bihar Agricultural Produce Market Act 1960, Section 2(1)(a)] as cited in *Lipton India Ltd., Calcutta* v. *Bihar State Agrl. Marketing Board*, AIR 1998 Pat 58, para 5.]

'AGRICULTURAL PRODUCE' means all produce of agriculture, horticulture, animal husbandry, apiculture, pisciculture, or forest as specified in this Schedule [M.P. Krishi Upaj Mandi Adhiniyam, 1972, S. 2(1)(a)] as cited in *Krishi Upaj Mandi Samiti, Narsinghpur* v. *Shiv Shakti Khansari Udyog*, (2012) 9 SCC 368, Para 20].

The term 'agricultural produce' as used in the CPC is confined to growing crop standing on the land on which it has grown and cut crop lying on the threshing floor or fodder stock. *Bhaboot Singh* v. *Ghanshyam Durga Prasad,* AIR 1962 Raj 82, 83. [CPC (5 of 1908), O. XXI, R. 44]

Agricultural produce is agricultural Produce, whether it is stocked on the thrashing floor or stored in a house, or godown. *UOI* v. *D. Venkataramaiah,* AIR 1985 AP 375, 376. [CPC (5 of 1908), O. XXXVIII, R. 12]

The term 'agricultural produce' is not only confined to agricultural produce alone but also an industrial product by processing of agricultural produce. *Swagat Stores* v. *State*, AIR 1993 Pat 82, 86.

Anything produced by agriculture [State Agricultural Credit Corporations Act (60 of 1968), S. 2(a) and Income-tax Act (43 of 1961), Sch. II, pt. 2, item 24].

Agricultural product or product of agriculture. The term 'AGRICULTURAL PRODUCT' OR 'PRODUCT OF AGRICULTURE' is required to be construed liberally so as to include not merely the primary product as it actually grows but also a product which undergoes a simple operation so as to make it more saleable or more usable. The rice and the husk though separated remain as they were produced and hence continue to be 'agricultural product' or 'product of agriculture'. *CIT* v. *Cynamid India Ltd.,* (1999) 3 SCC 727, para 6 : AIR 1999 SC 1346. [Income-tax Act (43 of 1961), S. 35-C]

Agricultural property. Means, agricultural land, pasture, and woodland; and also includes such cottages, farm buildings, farm houses and mansion-houses, (together with the lands occupied therewith) as are of a character appropriate to the property.

Agricultural purpose. The purpose pertaining to agriculture [IPC (45 of 1860), S. 430]; [Income-tax Act (43 of 1961), S. 2(1)(a); CPC (5 of 1908), S. 5(2) and T.P. Act (4 of 1882), S. 37, para 3].

The words "agricultural purposes" refer to tilling and cultivation for purposes of raising crops.

Agricultural year. "Agricultural year" means the year commencing on the sixteenth day of June, or on such other date as the State Government may by notification appoint for any local area. Punjab Act XVII of 1887 (Land Revenue) S. 3, cl. 14. In the definition given in S. 3 of U.P. Act XIX 1873, cl. 8 the term "agricultural year" means a year commencing on the Ist day of July and ending on the 30th day of June.

Agriculture. "AGRICULTURE" includes horticulture, but does not include—

(i) raising of grass

(ii) dairy farming

(iii) poultry farming

(iv) breeding of live-stock and

(v) such cultivation, or the growing of such plant, as may be prescribed. [Urban Land (Celling and Regulation) Act (33 of 1976), S. 2(o)(ii), *Expln* (A)]

"AGRICULTURE" includes horticulture, animal husbandry, forestry, dairy and poultry farming, pisciculture, and other allied activities, whether or not undertaken jointly with agriculture and the expression "agricultural operation" shall be construed accordingly. [National Bank for Agriculture and Rural Development Act (61 of 1981), S. 2(a)].

"AGRICULTURE" means the basic and applied sciences of the soil and water management, crop production including production of all garden crops, control of plants, pests and diseases, horticulture including floriculture, animal husbandry including veterinary and dairy science, fisheries, forestry including farm forestry, home-science, agricultural engineering and technology, marketing and processing of agricultural and animal husbandry products, land use and management. [Central Agricultural University Act, 1992 (40 of 1992), S. 2(c)]; [Rani Lakshmi Bai Central Agricultural University Act (10 of 2014), s. 3(c)].

The ordinary meaning of "agriculture" is the raising of annual or periodical grain crops through the operation of ploughing, sowing *etc.*

The science or art of cultivating soil, harvesting crops, and raising livestock.

'Agriculture' includes horticulture, the raising of crops, grass or garden produce, the use by an agriculturist of the land held by him or part thereof for grazing but does not include—

(i) the use of any land, whether or not an appendage to rice or paddy land, for the purpose of rab manure;

(ii) the cutting of wood, only;

(iii) dairy farming;

(iv) poultry farming;

(v) breeding of livestock; and

(vi) such other pursuits as may be prescribed.

Explanation—If any question arises as to whether any land or part thereof is used for any of the pursuits specified in any of the sub-clauses (i) to (vi), such question shall be decided by the tribunal. [Gujarat Agricultural Lands Ceiling Act, 1960 (27 of 1961), s. 2(1) as cited in *State of Gujrat* v. *Manoharsinhji Pradyumansinhji Jadeja*, (2013) 2 SCC 300, para 33].

'Agriculture' includes—

(a) horticulture;

(b) the raising of crops, grass or garden produce;

(c) the use by an agriculturist of the land held by him or part thereof for grazing. [Gujrat Agricultural Lands Ceiling Act, 1960 (After the Amendment), s. 2(1) as cited in *State of Gujrat* v. *Manoharsinhji Pradyumansinhji Jadeja*, (2013) 2 SCC 300, para 34].

Agriculturist. A student of the science of agriculture, or one who engages himself in the occupation of agriculture. See 11 B. 469 : 4 B. 624 : 11 CPLR 30.

The proper test to be applied in deciding whether a particular person is an *'Agriculturist'* is to see whether his main source of income is derived from cultivation or not. The term 'agriculturist' is used with reference to one who is so by profession. 1944 R.D. 226 : 1944 AWR (Rev.) 119.

Even if it is not necessary that a person must till the land with his own hands to come within the meaning of the word 'agriculturist' he must at least show that he was really dependent for his living on tilling the said land, was unable to maintain himself otherwise. *Appasaheb* v. *Bhalchandra*, AIR 1961 SC 589, 595. [CPC (5 of 1908), S. 60(1), *Proviso*].

"AGRICULTURIST" means an individual or a Hindu Undivided Family who undertakes cultivation of land—

(*a*) by own labour, or

(*b*) by the labour of family, or

(*c*) by servants on wages payable in cash or kind or by hired labour under personal supervision or the personal supervision of any member of the family. Central Goods and Services Tax Act (12 of 2017), S. 2(7)].

A person making his living by agriculture. [CPC (5 of 1908), S. 60(1)(b)].

'Agriculturist' means a person who cultivates lands personally. [Gujrat Agricultural Lands Ceiling Act, 1960 (27 of 1961), s. 2(3) as cited in *State of Gujrat* v. *Manoharsinhji Pradyumansinhji Jadeja*, (2013) 2 SCC 300, para 33].

A person who has a saleable interest in any agricultural or horticultural land or one who holds interest in such land under a landholder as tenant, ryot or under tenure holder. *Sri Ranga Nilayam Rama Krishna Rao* v. *Kandokori Chellayamma*, AIR 1953 SC 425, 429]

A member of a joint Hindu family can rank as an 'agriculturist' though the land of the family is recorded in the revenue papers only in the name or names of other member or members of the family. AIR 1942 All 19 (FB).

Residence in the village plus cultivation is strong proof that a person has not abandoned his calling of agriculturist, whatever his other sources of income. *Shiamlal* v. *Sahodra Devi*, AIR 1960 All 429, 430.

If he engages personally in agriculture in order to earn his livelihood, i.e., not as a hobby and devotes most of his time, energy and skill to agriculture then he would normally be entitled to be classed as an agriculturist. *Chandrawati Tewari* v. *U.P. Government*, AIR 1961 All 183, 198 (FB); *Keshav Wandan* v. *Bank of Behar*, AIR 1977 Pat 185, 187; Prabu Dayal v. Ram Nik Lal, AIR 1979 All 193, 196; *Maheshkumar v Addl. Collector Hoshangabad*, AIR 1988 MP 210, 212.

Agriculturist in 'Dekkhan Agriculturists' Act (XVII of 1879), S. 2 means a person who by himself or by his servants or by his tenants earns his livelihood wholly or principally by agriculture; or who ordinarily engages personally in agricultural labour within those limits. *Sawantarawa* v. *Giriappa*, 21 IC 4 at p.5 (per SCOTT, C.J.); Purshotam v. Bhavanji, 4 Bom 360; *Dwarkojiray* v. *Balachandra*, 19 Bom 255; *Damodar* v. *Manubai*, 34 Bom 65; *Chunilal* v. *Vinayak*, 33 Bom 376; *Bijhumal* v. *Khiomal,* 6 IC 855.

If a person who was having agricultural lands was attending to agricultural operations he is an agriculturist. *State Bank of Travancore* v. *C.T. George*, AIR 1975 Ker 169, 171. [Usurious Loans Act (10 of 1918), S. 3]

A firm of money lenders cannot be an agriculturist. AIR 1941 Mad 537.

Where a person owning extensive lands grows plantains and coffee on the lands personally supervising the cultivation of his lands, he is a person following the calling of an agriculturist. The fact that the produce on the lands is grown for the purpose of sale in his own shops and thus carrying on of business, does not make him a person other than an agriculturist. He is still an 'agriculturist' for the purposes of the Act. 56. LW 718 : 1943 MWN 695 : (1943) 2 MLJ 504.

'Agriculturist' or **'producer'** means a person, who, by his own labour or by the labour of any member of his family or by the labour of hired labour or otherwise, is engaged in the production and growth of agricultural produce, but it does not include any market functionary like a trader, broker (dalal), Commission agent (*arhatiya*) or who is otherwise ordinarily engaged in the business of storage of agricultural produce. [Uttarakhand Agricultural Produce Marketing (Development and Regulation) Act (9 of 2011), sections 2(ii) **as cited in** *Gujarat Ambuja Exports Ltd v State of Uttarakhand*, (2016) 3 SCC 601, para 30.2].

Aid. To support, help or assist.

The word 'aid' used is Art. 29(2) and Art. 30(2) will cover the "grant" under Art. 337. The amount received by the Anglo-Indian institutions as grant under Art. 337 must be construed as "aid". *In re the Kerala Education Bill*, 1957, AIR 1958 SC 956, 980. [Constitution of India, Art. 29(2)].

Succour; anything helpful [Iron Ore Mines Labour Welfare Cess Act (55 of 1976), S. 3(c)]; to give support to; [IPC (45 of 1860), S. 130].

Aid and abet. To assist or facilitate the commission of an offence, or to promote its accomplishment.

Aid and advise. See, Constitution of India, Art. 74.

The expression "aid and advise" in Art. 74 may apparently suggest that it is left to the President to accept the advice or ignore the same and thus the decision on all matters will be of the President himself. In re *K. Jayarama Iyer*, AIR 1958 AP 643, 644. [Constitution of India, Art. 74]

It would be difficult to conclude that "AID AND ADVICE" can be treated synonymous with a binding "direction", an irrevocable "command" or a conclusive "mandate." Surely, the term "aid and advice" cannot individually be construed as an imperative dictate which had to be obeyed under all circumstances. In common parlance, a process of consultation is realty the process of "aid and advice". [*Supreme Court Advocates-on-Record Association* v. *Union of India*, (2016) 5 SCC 1, para 130] [Constitution of India, Art. 74].

Aid the doing of acts. The IPC defines the expression as "whoever, either prior to or at the time of the commission of an act, does anything in order to facilitate the commission of that act, and thereby facilitates the commission thereof, is said to aid the doing of that act." [IPC (45 of 1860), S.107, *Expln.* 2].

AIDS. (*abbr.*), Acquired Immuno Deficiency Syndrome. A group of symptoms and signs caused by the Human Immune Deficiency Virus (HIV).

Aiel. A grandfather.

Air force. That branch of a country's defence force, consisting of aeroplanes and personnel to fight in the air either in the offensive or in defence. [Air Force Act (45 of 1950), S. 4(iv)].

Air pollution. "AIR POLLUTION" means the presence in the atmosphere of any air pollutant. [Air (Prevention and Control of Pollution) Act (14 of 1981), S. 2(h)]

Any harmful substance or energy emitted directly or indirectly into the air, especially if the harm is to the environment or to the public health or welfare.

Air service. Service of a State analogous to or a part of the military and naval services charged with the operation of aircraft [IPC (45 of 1860), S. 140]; mail, passenger and freight service provided by the operation of aircraft.

Air traffic service. Includes flight information service, alerting service, air traffic advisory service, air traffic control service, area control service, approach control service and airport control service. [Airports Authority of India Act (55 of 1994), S. 2(d)]

"**Air traffic service**" means the flight information service, altering service and air traffic advisory service and air traffic control service (area control service, approach control service or aerodrome control service). [Aircraft Rules, 1937, R. 3(1-F)].

Air transport service. Means any service for any kind of remuneration, whatsoever, for the transport by air of persons, mails or any other thing, animate or inanimate whether such service relates to a single flight or series of flights. [Airports Authority of India Act (55 of 1994), S. 2(e)]

"AIR TRANSPORT SERVICE" means a service for the transport by air of persons, mails or any other thing, animate or inanimate, for any kind of remuneration whatsoever, whether such service consists of a signals of a single flight or a series of flights. [Air Corporations Act (27 of 1953), S. 2(ii)]

Air travel agent. Means any person engaged in providing any service connected with the booking of passage for travel by air. [Finance Act (32 of 1994), S. 65(4) as amended by Act (32 of 2003), S. 159 (now repealed by Central Goods and Services Tax, 2017)]

Aircraft. "AIRCRAFT" means any machine which can derive support in the atmosphere from reaction of the air other than reactions of the air against the earth surface and includes balloons, whether fixed or free, airships, kites, gliders and flying machines. [Aircraft Act (22 of 1934), section 2(1); Air Corporation Act (27 of 1953), section 2(i)].

"AIRCRAFT" includes aeroplanes, kites, balloons, airships, gliders or other machines for flying. [Air Force Act (45 of 1950), section 4(ii)]

"AIRCRAFT" means any craft, whether or not registered in India, other than a military aircraft or an aircraft used in customs or police service. [Suppression of Unlawful Acts Against Safety of

Civil Aviation Act (66 of 1982), S. 2(a); Anti-Hijacking Act (65 of 1982), S. 2(a)]

Aircraft material. Includes any engines, fittings, guns, gear, instruments or apparatus for use in connection with aircraft and any of its components and accessories and petrol, oil and any other substance used for providing motive power for planes. [Air Force Act (45 of 1950), S. 4(iii)]

Aircraft operator. Means any commercial concern which provides the service of transport of goods by aircraft. [Finance Act (32 of 1994), S. 65(3b) (Inserted by Finance (No. 2) Act (23 of 2004), S. 90 (now repealed by Central Goods and Services Tax Act, 2017)]

Aircraft papers. Includes all books, passes, charter parties, bills of lading, customs receipts, manifests, certificates, licences lists, tickets, notes, letters and other documents and writings delivered up or found on board a captured aircraft. [Naval And Aircraft Prize Act (59 of 1971), S. 2(b)]

Airport. Means a landing and taking off area for aircrafts, usually with runways and aircraft maintenance and passenger facilities and includes aerodrome as defined in clause (2) of Section 2 of the Aircraft Act 1934. [Airports Authority of India Act (55 of 1994), S. 2(b)]

Airport premises. "AIRPORT PREMISES" means any premises—

(i) belonging to airport;

(ii) taken on lease for the purposes of airport;

(iii) acquired for the Authority under the provisions of the Land Acquisition Act (1 of 1894) (repealed) or any other corresponding law for the time being in force.

Explanation.—For the removal of doubts, it is hereby declared that for the purposes of this clause, "airport" includes private airport. [Airport Authority of India (Amendment) Act (43 of 2003), S. 8(a)]

Airports authority. Means the Airports Authority of India constituted under Section 3 of the Airports Authority of India Act, 1994 and also includes any person having the charge of management of an airport or a civil enclave. [Finance Act (32 of 1994), S. 65(3d) (Inserted by Finance (No. 2) Act (23 of 2004), S. 90 (now repealed by Central Goods and Services Tax Act, 2017)]

"Airside" means the movement area of an aerodrome, adjacent terrain and buildings or portions thereof access to which is controlled. [Aircraft (Security) Rules, 2011, R. 2(f)].

Airstrip. Means an area used for intended to be used for the landing and take-off the aircrafts with short take-off and landing characteristics and includes all buildings and structures thereon or appertaining thereto. [Airports Authority of India Act (55 of 1994), S. 2(c)]

Alarm. Fear or terror arising from a sudden sense of danger [Defence and Internal Security of India Act (42 of 1971), S. 3(2)(5)]; a sound or signal giving notice of danger or calling attention to some event or condition. [IPC (45 of 1860), Ss. 503 and 505(b)].

Alcohol. A liquid formed by the fermentation of aqueous sugar-solutions or by the destructive distillation of organic bodies, as wood.

Alcoholism. (*Medical jurisprudence*) The pathological effect (as distinguished from physiological effect) of excessive indulgence in intoxicating liquors. Delirium tremens and alcoholic homicidal maniac are examples of this form.

Alcoholometer. A device used to measure the blood-alcohol content of a person's breath sample.

Alderman. A member of the corporation or common council of a city or corporate town, elected by and representing the inhabitants of a ward. (*Burrill*)

Aleatory contract. A wagering contract.

Aliaenormia. Other wrongs.

Alias. Literally, "otherwise called" or "otherwise". A term used to denote a second or further description of a person who has gone by two or more names. (*Burrill*).

An assumed or additional name by which a person is known.

Alias subpoena. Issue of subpoena after the failure of initial subpoena.

Alias writ. A second writ.

Alibi. Elsewhere.

The plea of *alibi* postulates the physical impossibility of the presence of the accused at the scene of offence by reason of his presence at another place. It should be shown that the accused was so far away at the relevant time that he could not be present at the place where the crime was committed. *Dudh Nath Pandey* v. *State of U.P.*, AIR 1981 SC 911, 916. [Indian Evidence Act (1 of 1872), Ss. 11 & 3]

Alibi, plea of. A plea by a person accused of an offence that he was elsewhere—that having regard to the time and place when and where he is alleged to have committed the offence, he could not have been present.

Alien. Generally speaking, one born in a foreign country.

The word 'alien' which is synonymous with 'foreigner' is said to be : "a person belonging to a foreign country, or without the country or jurisdiction under consideration."

(*Verb*). To transfer or make over to another; to covey or transfer the property or a thing from one person to another; to alienate; usually applied to the transfer of lands and tenements.

Alien (ami) amy. An alien who is a citizen or subject of a friendly power.

Alien enemy. A person owing allegiance to an adverse belligerent State; a person owing allegiance to a country which is at war with India. [CPC (5 of 1908), S. 83].

Alien friend. A person owing allegiance to a country which is in alliance; a person owing allegiance to a country which is at peace with India. [CPC (5 of 1908), S. 83].

Alienable. Capable of being transferred.

Alienate. Is to transfer property from one person to another. The word "alienate" in CPC (5 of 1908), Sch. III, para II is used *ejusdem generis* with the words preceding it, namely, mortgage, charge and lease, and manifestly contemplates a transfer which would have a present effect and not a devise which can only have operation after the death of the testator.

To transfer one's interest to another.

Alienatio rei praefertur juri accrescendi. (*Maxim*) Alienation is favoured by the law rather than accumulation. (*Broom*)

Alienation. The action of transferring property or any interest therein to another. [CPC (5 of 1908), S. 64].

Alienee. One to whom an alienation, conveyance, or transfer of property is made. (*Anderson*)

Alieni juris. Under the mastership of another.

Alignment. (in Mit. law) the line on which troops are formed in battle order.

The act of aligning or the state of being aligned. [Indian Electricity Act (9 of 1910), Sch., item (xvi)]; a line of things arranged.

Alii per allium non acquiritur obligatio. One man cannot incur a liability through another, unless the other is his duly authorised agent.

Alike. In the same manner; equally.

Alimony. The allowance made to the wife out of her husband's estate for her support, either during a matrimonial suit, or at its termination, when she proves herself entitled to a separate maintenance.

Maintenance allowance payable by the husband or wife, as the case may be, for other's support on separation. [Hindu Marriage Act (25 of 1955), S. 25].

Alimony pendente lite. Alimony granted temporarily by the Court during the pendency of proceeding for divorce or separation.

Alio intuitu. (*Lat.*) Under a different aspect; in a different view, with respect to another case or condition.

Aliquis non debet esse judex in propria causa, quia non potest esse judex et pars. (*Maxim*) A person ought not to be a judge in his own cause, because he cannot act as judge and party both. (*Broom*)

Aliquot. Of, relating to; or being a fraction or percentage of a whole.

Aliter. (*Lat.*) Otherwise; it would be otherwise.

Aliud est celare, aliud tacere. (*Maxim*) Silence is not equivalent to concealment. The maxim applies to the sale of goods, with regard to which there is no warranty either express or implied. The seller in such cases, is entitled to be silent as to the defects, but not to conceal the defects for the purposes of the sale.

To conceal is one thing, to be silent another.

Aliud est distinctio, aliud separatio. (*Maxim*) Distinction is one thing; separation is another.

Aliud est possidere, aliud esse in possessione. (*Maxim*) It is one thing to possess; it is another to be in possession. (*Wharton; Broom*)

Aliud est vendere, aliud vendenti consentire. To sell is one thing; to consent to sell is another. (*Burrill; Black*)

Aliunde. From elsewhere, from another source or quarter (*Burrill*); from outside : (as) evidence *aliunde* (*i.e.* from without or outside of the will or other document) may be admitted to explain ambiguity in a will.

From another place; independent of.

Alive. Living. [IPC (45 of 1860), S. 315].

All and singular. Collectively and individually.

All cases. All cases, does not mean the goods of specified description to mean goods identified by destination of the goods. *Hoare Millers & Co. Ltd.* v. *Asst. Collector of Customs,* AIR 1975 Cal 440 444. [Imports and Exports (Control) Act (18 of 1947), S. 3(1)]

All-current rate method. A foreign currency translation method. All items denominated in foreign currency are translated at current exchange rates. Sometimes called the closing rate method or current rate method but not to be confused with the current non-current rate method.

All disciplinary matters affecting a person. The phrase 'all disciplinary matters affecting a person' is sufficiently comprehensive to include any kind of disciplinary action proposed to be taken in respect of a particular person. *Pradyat Kumar* v. *Chief Justice of Calcutta High Court*, AIR 1956 SC 285, 292. [Constitution of India, Art. 320(3)(c)]

All fours. To be in substantial agreement with each other.

A metaphorical expression used to describe cases which are alike in all the circumstances which affect their determination, and which are said to be, or run, upon all-fours. (*Abbott*)

All offences under any other law. The words "all offences under any other law" in S. 5 of the CrPC 1973 (2 of 1974) cannot be intended to include a contempt of the High Court by a libel published out of Court when the Court is not sitting for which offence no provision is made by the Code.

All other leases. A lease not from year to year nor for a term exceeding one year nor a contract of lease reserving yearly rent falls under the expression 'all other leases' and it could be entered into by oral agreement accompanied by delivery of possession. A lease under which rent was payable on the expiry of the three months comes within this expression. *Gordhan* v. *Ali Bux,* AIR 1981 Raj 206, 209. [T.P. Act (4 of 1882), S. 107]

All previous parties. The words "all previous parties" appearing in S. 83 of the Negotiable Instruments Act, (26 of 1881), should be construed as including the drawer.

All proceedings. The words 'all proceedings' are significant, and mean "each and every" proceeding in respect of the debt of the displaced debtor. *Shyamlal Ramkrishna Agarwal* v. *Thakhatmal Bodhraj*, AIR 1957 MP 98, 101. [Displaced Persons (Debts Adjustment) Act (70 of 1951), S. 15]

All proceedings in respect of the said notice. For the purposes of Section 73 and this section, (*i*) the expression "ALL PROCEEDINGS IN RESPECT OF THE SAID NOTICE" shall not include proceedings under Section 132';

(*ii*) where the notice under the same proceedings is issued to the main person liable to pay tax and some other persons, and such proceedings against the main person have been concluded under Section 73 or Section 74, the proceedings against all the persons liable to pay penalty under Sections 122, 125, 129 and 130 are deemed to be concluded. [Central Goods and Service Tax Act (12 of 2017), S. 74, *Explanation 1*].

All rights reserved. A printed intimation in a literary work, notifying that the owner of the copy right has legal protection of his rights against infringement.

All risk insurance. Insurance designed to protect the insured against loss or damage however caused.

All sorts. The words "all sorts" mean that the "vegetable non-essential oils" whether raw or refined and from whatever raw material produced will be liable to excise duty. Refined oil is one sort; raw oil is another sort. *Union of India* v. *Delhi Cloth and General Mills*, AIR 1963 SC 781, 795. [Central Excises and Salt Act (1 of 1944), Scheduled I, Item 12]

All the component units thereof. Where two or more political parties have federated into a new political party while retaining their separate identity instead of merging themselves with the new political party, in such a case, they retain their separate identity, and will be deemed to be component units of the new-party. *Rameshankar Kaushik* v. *Election Commission of India*, AIR 1974 SC 445, 452. [Election Symbols (Reservation and Allotment) Order (168), Paras 16(1)(2)]

All the contesting candidates. The expression "all the contesting candidates" means all those who took part in the contest at the poll and all those who may have under S. 55-A retired from the contest. [Representation of the People Act (43 of 1951), Ss. 82(a), 55-A]

All the law in force. The expression 'all the law in force' extends even to customary law, personal law like the Hindu and Mohammeddan Law. *Naresh Chandra Bose* v. *Sachindra Nath Deb,* AIR 1956 Cal 222, 224. [Constitution of India, Art. 372(1)]

All the parties interested. In S. 21 of the Act the words 'all the parties interested' mean parties interested in the specific dispute referred to arbitration and not in the subjectmatter of the whole suit and where the two are not identical. *Laxmi Narain* v. *Raghbir Singh,* AIR 1956 Punj 249, 250. [Arbitration Act (10 of 1940) (*repealed*), S. 21]

All the property. The word 'all the property' in S. 211(1) shall have to be restricted only to the property covered by the will. [Indian Succession Act (39 of 1925), S. 211(1)]

All the questions. Referred to in O. I, R. 10(2), CPC (5 of 1908), must be questions between the plaintiff and the defendant, and not questions which may arise between co-defendants or between co-plaintiffs *inter se.* Questions having to be decided incidentally during an appeal, such as who the legal representative of a deceased party, was, are not among those contemplated by the section.

All the questions involved in the suit. All the questions involved in the suit, cannot be read as questions involved between the parties to the suit. *Bindeshwari Chaudhary* v. *Sheo Nandan Upedhya,* AIR 1973 Pat 347, 351. [CPC (5 of 1908), O. I, R. 10(2)]

All waste lands and all uncultivated lands. A waste land is uncultivable or unfit for cultivation. Uncultivated means cultivable but not cultivated. *State of Gujarat* v. *Gujarat Revenue Tribunal,* AIR 1980 SC 91. [Registration Act (16 of 1908), S. 2(6) and (9) and 17, CPC (5 of 1908), O. XLI, R. 2]

Allegans contraria non est audiendus. (*Maxim*) He is not to be heard who alleges things contrary to each other. (*Broom*).

The doctrine of estoppel is mainly based on this maxim.

He who alleges contradictory things is not to be heard. A man shall not be permitted to "blow hot and cold" with reference to the same transaction or insist, at different times, on the truth of each of two conflicting allegations, to suit his private interests. [*Nagubai Ammal* v. *B. Sharma Rao*, AIR 1956 SC 593 (601)].

Maxim considered in Indian Evidence Act (1 of 1872), S. 115.

Allegans suam turpitudinem non est audiendus. (*Maxim*) He is not to be heard who alleges his own infamy. (*Black*; 4 Inst. 279; *Broom; Wharton*)

A maxim meaning "He is not to be heard who alleges his own infamy." 4 Inst. 279; *Broom; Wharton*). "A person boasting of his own wrong is not to be heard." (*Max.*)

A person alleging his own infamy is not to be heard. The meaning is that no one shall be heard in a Court of justice to allege his own turpitude as a foundation of a right or claim; not that a man shall not be heard who testifies to his own turpitude, however much of his testimony may be discredited by his character. (Latin for Lawyers)

If a party has committed a wrong, he cannot be permitted to take the benefit of his own wrong.

[*Bhartiya Seva Samaj Trust* v. *Yogeshbhai Ambalal Patel*, (2012) 9 SCC 310, para 28].

One of the exceptions to this maxim is where the fraudulent transaction still remains executory and the purpose of the fraud has not been effected. *Narayanan* v. *Sankaran,* AIR 1963 Ker 79, 80. [T.P. Act (4 of 1882), S. 53]

Allegari non debuit quod probatum non relevat. (*Maxim*) That ought not to be alleged which, if proved, is not relevant. (*Burrill;* 1 Ch. Cas. 45; *Broom*)

Allegatio contra factum non est admittenda. (*Maxim*) Where a man has entered into a solemn engagement under his hand and seal as to certain facts he shall not be permitted to deny any matter which he has so asserted. This is the basis of the doctrine of estoppel by deed.

An allgation contrary to a deed is not admissible. The rule of evidence contained in this maxim is that of estoppel by deed. Parties and privies to a deed are estopped from denying statements in the deed which, on its true construction, are intended to be statements by them. (*Latin for Lawyers*)

Allegation. Assertion, declaration, an asserted fact or statement of a party to an action, made in a pleading, setting out what he expects or undertakes to prove. (*Black*)

An action of alleging; that which is alleged.

'Allegation' in relation to a public servant means any affirmation that such public servant—

(i) has abused his position as such to obtain any gain or favour to himself or to any other person or to cause undue harm to any person;

(ii) was actuated in the discharge of his functions as such public servant by improper or corrupt motives;

(iii) is guilty of corruption; or

(iv) is in possession of pecuniary resources or property disproportionate to his known source of income and such pecuniary resources or property is held by the public servant personally or by any member of his family or by some other person on his behalf. [Madhya Pradesh Lokayukta Evam Uplokayukta Act, 1981 (37 of 1981), s. 2(b) as cited in *Lokayukta, Justice Ripusudan Dayal* v. *State of Madhya Pradesh*, (2014) 4 SCC 473, para 17].

'ALLEGATION' in relation to a public servant means any affirmation that such public servant—

(i) has abused his position as such public servant to obtain any gain or favour to himself or to any other person or to cause undue harm or hardship to any other person.

(ii) was actuated in the discharge of his functions as such public servant by personal interest or improper or corrupt motives; or

(iii) is guilty of corruption, favourtism, nepotism or lack of integrity in his capacity as such public servant. [Kerala Lok Ayukta Act (8 of 1999), S. 2(b) as cited in *Nitin Norbert* v. *University of Kerala*, AIR 2009 Ker 60, 63, para 8]

Allege. To pronounce with positiveness; declare, affirm; assert; as, to allege a fact.

To state positively. [Indian Evidence Act (1 of 1872), S. 8, *Expln.*, 2, ill. (b)].

Allegiance. The obligation of fidelity which the individual owes to the government or to the sovereign under which he lives in return for the protection he receives.

The natural, lawful and faithful obedience that every subject owes to the sovereign or a citizen owes to the State and its Constitution; loyalty to a person or cause. [Constitution of India, Art. 69].

Allegiance, Loyalty, Fealty.—Terms distinguished. Allegiance is the most formal and official of these words, it is a matter of principle and applies especially to conduct, the oath of allegiance covers conduct only. Loyalty is a matter of both principle and sentiment, conduct and feeling. It implies enthusiasm and devotion, and hence is most frequently chosen for figurative uses, as, a loyalty to a lover, husband, family, clan, friends, old traditions, religion. Fealty has escaped less completely from this earliest sense, but has permissible use in the sense of fidelity under obligation of various kinds. (*Cent. Dict.*)

Alliance. (*From Lat, alligo*) To tie or unite together; the state of connection or union with another; the union or connection of two persons or families by marriage. (as) alliance by marriage. (*Bouvier*)

In INTERNATIONAL LAW, a union between two or more nations, contracted by compact, treaty, or league. (*Burrill*)

Allocable area. In this scheme, unless the context otherwise requires,—

"ALLOCABLE AREA" means,—

(i) in the case of an industrial park referred to in sub-paragraph (*b*) of paragraph 4, the net floor area available for allocation but excluding the built-up space used for providing common facilities;

(ii) in any other case, the net area available for allocation for industrial, commercial or residential purpose but excluding the areas used for providing common facilities.

Allocable surplus. "ALLOCABLE SURPLUS" means—

(a) in relation to an employer, being a company (other than a banking company) which has not made the arrangements prescribed under the Income-tax Act for the declaration and payment within India of the dividends payable out of its profits in accordance with the provision of Section 194 of that Act, sixty-seven per cent of the available surplus in an accounting year;

(b) in any other case, sixty per cent of such available surplus. [Payment of Bonus Act (21 of 1965), S. 2(4)]

A surplus which is available for distribution. [Payment of Bonus Act (21 of 1965), S. 2(4)].

Allocation. The act of allocating, allotting or assigning. Allotment, assignment, apportionment (as) the allocation of shares in a public company.

An allowance made upon accounts in the English exchequer (Wharton); or placing or adding to a thing (Ency. Lond.; Cowell.). The act of allocating, allotting or assigning; allotment, assignment, apportionment (as) the allocation of shares in a public company

Allotment. [State Financial Corporation Act (63 of 1951), S. 4(4) and Constitution of India, Art. 77(3)].

Allocatur. (*Law Lat.*) "It is allowed".

Allocutus : Allocution. The formal address of the judge to a prisoner asking him why the Court should not proceed to judgment against him, or why sentence should not be pronounced.

Allodium. Land which is the absolute property of the owner.

Allograph. A document not written by any of the parties thereto.

Allonge. A piece of paper which is attached to a note or other negotiable instrument to make room for further indorsements.

Allot. To divide or distribute, as by lot; to apportion or distribute or parcel out; (as) to allot shares in a public company; to grant; assign; set apart; appropriate; (as) to allot a sum of money for some specific purpose.

To appropriate to a special purpose or person; to assign shares authoritatively. [CPC (5 of 1908), O. XXVI, R. 14(1)].

Allotment. The act of allotting or distribution by lot. That which is allotted; a share, or portion granted or distributed; the thing or portion which is assigned by lot.

IN COMPANY LAW 'allotment' means the appropriation out of the previously unappropriated capital of a company, of a certain number of shares to a person. *Sri Gopal Jalan & Co.* v. *Calcutta Stock Exchange Association Ltd.*, AIR 1964 SC 250, 252. [Companies Act (1 of 1956) replaced with Companies Act, 2013, S. 75(1)].

'Allotment' means the grant in writing by or on behalf of the State Government of a right of use and occupation of any Government premises to any person but does not include a grant by way of lease. [Bihar Govt. Premises (Rent Recovery and Eviction) Act (20 of 1956), S. 2(a) as cited in *Amrit Varsha Hindi Dainik* v. *Bihar State Agricultural Marketing Board*, AIR 2000 Pat 192, 194, para 10

The expression "allotment" means a formal administrative decision of the Authority to lease a particular piece of land in favour of an appellant who is decisions of establishing industry thereon. [*Tata Steel Limited* v. *State of Jharkhand*, (2015) 15 SCC 55, para 33].

The action of allotting. [State Financial Corporations Act (63 of 1951), S. 4(4)].

Allotment letter. A letter denoting allotment of a land, plot or premises on rent or hire purchase.

"Allotment list". Means a list containing details of allotment of the securities intimated by the issuer to the depository under sub-section (2) of section 8 of the Depositories Act, 1996 (22 of 1996). [Indian Stamp Act, 1899 (2 of 1899), section 2(1)]

Allottee. A person to whom land under an enclosure act or shares in a public undertaking are allotted. (*Wharton*)

A person to whom allotment has been made.

"ALLOTTEE," in relation to an apartment, means the person to whom such apartment has been allotted, sold or otherwise transferred by the promoter. [Delhi Apartment Ownership Act, (58 of 1986), section 2(b)]

"ALLOTTEE" in relation to a real estate project, means the person to whom a plot, apartment or building, as the case may be, has been allotted, sold (whether as freehold or leasehold) or otherwise transferred by the promoter, and includes the person who subsequently acquires the said allotment through sale, transfer or otherwise but does not include a person to whom such plot, apartment or building, as the case may be, is given on rent. [Real Estate (Regulation and Development) Act (16 of 2016), section 2(d)].

'Allottee' means a person in whose favour an order under section 8 of the Act has been made for purpose of purchase of molasses from the occupier of a sugar factory. [U.P. Sheera Niyantran Niyamawali, 1974, rule 2(b) **as cited in** *Commr., Central Excise, Lucknow v Chhota Sugar Co Ltd,* AIR 2004 SC 3005, 3015, para 35]

'ALLOTTEE' means a person to whom a property has been allotted by way of sale or hire-purchase or lease or in such manner as prescribed by the Board. [Chandigarh Housing Board (Allotment, Management, and Sale of Tenements) Regulations, 1979, Regn. 2(3) **as cited in** *Ajay Kashyap v Mohini Nijhawan,* AIR 2004 P&H 193, 197, para 17]

Allow. To grant, permit or approve (as) to allow an account; to allow an appeal.

To permit [T.P. Act (4 of 1882), Ss. 2(b), 6(g) and 34]; to accept as true of correct [CrPC 1973 (2 of 1974), S. 84(1)].

Allow for. To take into account; to admit of.

Allowance. Something given as a compensation, abatement, or deduction; a portion or a gift or gratuity to a child or other dependent; "allowance." as "a payment beyond the agreed salary of the officer, for additional services rendered by him."

A sum granted as a reimbursement or a bounty or as appropriate for any purpose. [CPC (5 of 1908),

Const., S. 57 and Art. 59(3)]; a reduction from the stated price, a concession; rebate.

Allowance pendente lite. Alimony temporarily ordered by the Court pending an action for divorce or separation.

Allowed. The word means "fixed, taken into account, set apart, granted." It takes in perquisites given in cash or in kind or in money or money's worth and also amenities which are not convertible into money. It implies that a right is conferred on the employee in respect of those perquisites. *Commissioner of Income Tax* v. *L.W. Russel*, (1964) 53 ITR 91, 97 (SC). [Income Tax Act (43 of 1961), S. 15(b), 17(1)(iv)].

Allowing and wilfully suffering (a person to do thing). It means allowing by negligence or without any volition on the part of the offender. *Om Prakash Gupta* v. *State of U.P.*, AIR 1957 SC 458.

Alloy. A substance composed of two or more metals ultimately mixed and united, usually by being fused together and dissolving in each other when molten. [Gold (Control) Act (45 of 1968), S. 2(e) (*repealed*)].

Allure. Seduce; attract; coax.

Alluvial land. In the sense of land gradually gained from the river, which has no other owner, and which belongs by way of accretion to the lands of the adjoining proprietor.

Alluvial soils. Soils having good water holding capacity, fertile, more suitable for irrigation and easy for tillage.

Alluvion. An imperceptibly gradual deposit of soil from a river or sea forming new land. [T.P. Act (4 of 1882), Ss. 70, ill. (a) and 108(d)].

Alluvium. Accumulation of land by natural action such as alluvium added to land by the action of a river or sea. Land added by accretion usually belongs to the owner of the land to which accretion takes place.

Ally. A person associated with another by kinship, treaty or league; a confederate; more particularly, a sovereign or state connected with another by treaty, offensive and defensive, or a subject or citizen of such sovereign or state.

Alma mater. A fond mother. An epithet bestowed by students on the university in which they received their education.

Almshouse. A house appropriated for poor.

Alter. (*verb.*) To make a change in; to modify; to vary in some degree.

"ALTER" shall include the making of additions. [Companies Act (1 of 1956) replaced with Companies Act, 2013, S. 2(1)]

To make otherwise or different in some respect without changing the thing itself; to modify. [Companies Act (1 of 1956) replaced with Companies Act, 2013, S. 2(1) and Constitution of India, Art. 114(2)]

"ALTER" includes the making of additions, omissions and substitutions. [S. 2(3) of the Companies Act, 2013 (18 of 2013)]

Alter : Change : Amend. "This term (alter) is to be distinguished from its synonyms "change" and "amend". To change may import the substitution of an entirely different thing, while to alter is to operate upon a subject matter which continues objectively the same while modified in some particular. To "amend" implies that the modification made in the subject improves it, which is not necessarily the case with an alteration. An amendment always involves an alteration, but an alteration does not always amend." (*Black*)

Alter ego. (*Lat.*) Second self; a person or entity vicariously liable for another (as an agent).

Alteration. For the purpose of this section, "ALTERATION" means a change in the structure of a vehicle which results in change in its basic feature. [Motor Vehicles Act (59 of 1988), S. 52, *Expln*].

"ALTERATION" shall include omissions. [Companies Act (1 of 1956), S. 2(1)]

(*Changing*) A change or substitution of one thing for another.

The action of altering; a modification or change made in altering anything. [Companies Act (1 of 1956), S. 2(1) and Constitution of India, Art. 110(1)(a)].

"ALTERATION" includes the making of additions, omissions and substitutions. [S. 2(3) of the Companies Act, 2013 (18 of 2013)]

Alteration of building. The term "alteration" includes changes and additions as well.

Alteration of instruments. An alteration of an instrument is something by which its meaning or language is changed, either in a material or an immaterial particular.

Alternate. One that takes the place of another who is unable to perform his duty; a person that takes his turn often at regular intervals with another or equal rank in an occupation or in performing a duty.

Alternate legacy. Giving of two or more items by the testator to the legatee without designating which one to be taken.

Alternative. The one or the other of two things; of two things such that one or the other may be chosen, the choice of either involving the rejection of another; that which is in the alternative; either of two courses open to choose between; offering a choice of two or more things; expressing a choice or choices.

Alternative and cumulative remedy. Where a new remedy is created in addition to an existing one, it is called alternative if only one can be enforced; if both can be enforced it is called cumulative. (*Wharton*)

Alternative dispute resolution. (ADR). It is a procedure for settling a dispute by means other than litigation, such as arbitration, mediation.

This term covers an agglomeration of dispute resolution procedures which are alternatives to litigation. They usually entail helping the parties to arrive at a negotiated agreement, often but not necessarily using a third party neutral. Arbitration is sometimes included in the term ADR : but as it is now in the mainstream of adjudicatory processes and as it is adversarial rather than consensual, the term ADR often excludes arbitration, sometimes but not invariably being used to refer only to consensual processes. (*Arbitration*)

Alternative remedy. It means other remedies. *Ram Shyam & Co.* v. *State of Haryana*, AIR 1985 SC 1147.

Alternative verdict. A verdict not guilty of the offence actually charged.

Altruistic surrogacy. Means the surrogacy in which no charges, expenses, fees, remuneration or monetary incentive of whatever nature, except the medical expenses and such other prescribed expenses incurred on surrogate mother and the insurance coverage for the surrogate mother, are given to the surrogate mother or her dependents or her representative. [Surrogacy (Regulation) Act, 2021 (47 of 2021), section 2(1)(b)]

Aluminum undertaking, in relation to the company, means the undertaking of the company located at Jay-Kay Nagar, near Asansol (West Bengal), being the industrial undertaking referred to in the order of the Government of India in the Ministry of Industry (Department of Industrial Development) NO. S.O. 293 (E)/18AA/IDRA/ 78, dated the 1st day of May, 1978. [Aluminum Corporation of India Ltd. (Acquisition and Transfer of Undertaking) Act (43 of 1984), S. 2(a)]

Alumnus. A person educated at a school or college.

Amalgamate. To merge into a single body; to mix; to unite. [Companies Act (1 of 1956) replaced with Companies Act, 2013, S. 17(1)(g)].

A power to a company to "amalgamate" with any other company does not enable the directors to compel a share-holder to become a member of any such other company.

Amalgamation. "AMALGAMATION", in relation to companies, means the merger of one or more companies with another company or the merger of two or more companies to form one company (the company or companies which so merge being referred to as the amalgamating company or companies and the company with which they merge or which is formed as a result of the merger, as the amalgamated company) in such a manner that—

(i) all the property of the amalgamating company or companies immediately before the amalgamation becomes the property of the amalgamated company by virtue of the amalgamation;

(ii) all the liabilities of the amalgamating company or companies immediately before the amalgamation become the liabilities of the amalgamated company by virtue of the amalgamation;

(iii) shareholders holding not less than [three-fourths] in value of the shares in the amalgamating company or companies (other than shares already held therein immediately before the amalgamation by, or by a nominee for, the amalgamated company or its subsidiary) become share-holders of the amalgamated company by virtue of the amalgamation, otherwise than as a result of the acquisition of the property of one company by another company pursuant to the purchase of such property by the other company or as a result of the distribution of such property to the other company after the winding up of the first-mentioned company. [Income-tax Act (43 of 1961), S. 2(1B)]

The act or process of amalgamating or the state of being amalgamated. [Specific Relief Act (47 of 1963), S. 15(g)]; [Constitution of India, Art 31A(1)(c)].

Amalgamation of companies. The term "amalgamation" means a state of things under which either two companies are so joined as to form a third entity or one is absorbed into or blended with another.

Amalphitan Code. A collection of sea laws, compiled about the end of the 11th century by the people of Amalphi, consisting of the laws on maritime subjects which were or had been in force in countries bordering on the Mediterranean and which for a long time was received as authority in those countries. (*Wharton*)

Ambassador. A public minister or officer of the highest rank clothed with high diplomatic powers, sent abroad by a sovereign State or prince with a legal commission and authority to transact business on behalf of his country with the government or Court of the country to which he is sent. [Diplomatic and Consular Officers (Oaths and Fees) Act (41 of 1948), S. 2(6) as before it was amended by (Act 2 of 1973)].

Ambassador, Agent, Consul. An agent represents the affairs only of his master; but an ambassador ought to represent the greatness of his master, and his affair. It is said there can be no ambassador without letters of credence from his Sovereign, to another that hath Sovereign authority : and if a person be sent from a King or absolute potentate, though in his letters of credence he is termed an agent, yet he is an ambassador, he being for the Public. (*Tomlin*)

A consul is a commercial agent appointed by a government to reside in a foreign country, and permitted by the government of the latter country so to do, to watch over the commercial rights and privileges of the nation, deputing him, and to protect the interests of its subjects. (*Abbott; Bouvier*)

Ambigua responsio contra proferentem est accipienda. (*Maxim*) An ambiguous answer is to be interpreted against the party who delivers it. (*Burrill; 10 Coke 59; Broom*)

Ambiguitas. From *ambiguas*, doubtful, uncertain, obscure. Ambiguity; uncertainty of meaning.

Ambiguitas contra stipulatorem est. Doubtful words will be construed most strongly against the party using them. (*Black*)

Ambiguitas latens. A latent ambiguity. Not apparent on the face of the deed.

Ambiguitas patens. A patent ambiguity, apparent on the face of the deed.

Ambiguitas verborum latens verificatione suppletur nam quod ex facto oritur ambiguum verificatione facti tollitur. Latent ambiguity of words may be removed by parole evidence, for an ambiguity arising upon proof of extraneous fact may be removed in like manner. [Indian Evidence Act (1 of 1872), S. 96].

Ambiguitas verborum patens nulla verificatione excluditur. (*Maxim*) A patent ambiguity cannot be cleared up by extrinsic evidence. [Indian Evidence Act. (1 of 1872), S. 93].

Ambiguity. Doubtfulness; double meaning; the quality or state of being ambiguous; uncertainty, particularly of signification.

Ambiguities are of two kinds, patent and latent. A patent ambiguity, —*ambiguitas patens* — is one which appears on the face of the instrument. A *latent ambiguity* is one which arises from some collateral circumstance, or extrinsic matter, in cases where the instrument is itself sufficiently certain and intelligible.

Ambiguous. Doubtful or uncertain, particularly in respect of signification; equivocal; indeterminate; indefinite; unsettled; indistinct.

Open to more than one interpretation. [Indian Evidence Act (1 of 1872), S. 93].

Ambiguum pactum contra venditorem interpretandum est. An ambiguous contract is to be interpreted against the seller.

Ambiguum placitum interpretari debet contra proferentem. (*Maxim*) An ambiguous pleading ought to be construed against the party offering or delivering it. (*Broom; Wharton; Co. Litt. 303 b*)

Ambit. A circuit; compass or circumference.

Ambulatoria est voluntas defuncti usque ad vitae supremum exitum. (*Maxim*) The will of a deceased person is ambulatory (changeable) until the last moment of life. (*Burrill; Broom*)

Ambulatory. Revocable, subject to change. (*Abbott*)

Ambulatory automatism. Describes the pathological impulse to purposeless and irresponsible wanderings from place to place often characteristic of patients suffering from loss of memory with dissociation of personality.

Ameliorate. To make better.

Ameliorating waste. Alteration made by tenant to improve the land he leases.

Amelioration. Improvement; the action of making better; being made better.

Amenable. Answerable under law; liable to be brought to judgment.

Amend. A word derived from the French word signifying 'to make better'; 'to change for the better.'

To alter formally by some addition, omission or substitution. [Preamble, T. P. Act (4 of 1882)].

Amend : Emend : Correct : Rectify : Reform. All these words convey the idea of making a thing better or bringing things into a more perfect state. We *correct* when we conform things to some standard or rule; as to *correct* proof sheets. We amend by removing faults or errors as to amend a decree or a law. Emend is another form of *amend* and is mostly applied to editions of books. To *reform* is to put into a new and better form, as, to reform one's life. *Rectify* is to make right, as, to rectify a mistake, to rectify an abuse.

The amendment of a law may in a proper case include the deletion of any one or more of the provisions of the law and substitution in their place of new provisions. An amendment of the Constitution which is the subject-matter of the power conferred by Art. 368, may include modifications or change of the provisions or even an amendment which makes the said provisions inapplicable in certain cases. *Sajjan Singh* v. *State of Rajasthan*, AIR 1965 SC 845, 854. [Constitution of India, Art. 368]

Amendment. The correction of an error : *In practice* the correction of any error in any process, pleading, or proceeding at law, either by consent of the parties, or upon motion to the Court in which the proceeding is pending. (*Burrill; 3 Bl. Camm. 407, 448; 1Tidd. Pr. 696*)

In legislation : A modification or alteration to be made in a bill on its passage or in an enacted law; modification or change in an existing act or statute.

Amendment means any addition or change in any of the provisions of the Constitution within the broad contours of the Preamble and the Constitution to carry out the objective in the Preamble and Directive principles. *His Holiness Kesavananda Bharati Sripandagalvam* v. *State of Kerala*, AIR 1973 SC 1461, 1535. [Constitution of India, Article 368]

The action or result of amending; any alteration made or proposed by adding, deleting or substituting something. [CPC (5 of 1908), O. I, R. 4].

Amendment of plaint. A cause of action which did not accrue at the date of the institution of the suit, and which related to a property which was not originally the subject-matter of the suit, could be brought in by way of amendment of the plaint.

Amended return. A return which is filed after the original return so as to correct error in the original.

Amends. Compensation for a loss or injury; recompense; satisfaction; equivalent.

Amenities. Things that conduce to physical or material comfort or convenience or to a pleasant and agreeable life. [Industrial Disputes Act (14 of 1947), S. 2(rr)(ii)].

Amenity. ''Amenity' means roads, streets, open spaces, parks, recreational grounds, playgrounds, gardens, water supply, electric supply, street lighting, sewerage, drainage, public works and other utilities, services and conveniences.

[Development Control Regulations for Greater Bombay, Regn. 3(7) as cited in *Godrej & Boyce Mfg. Co. Ltd.* v. *State of Maharashtra*, (2009) 5 SCC 24, 34, para 27]

'AMENITY' includes road, street, lighting, drainage, public works and such other conveniences as the Government may, by notification, specify to be an amenity for the purposes of this Act. [Bangalore Development Authority Act, 12 of 1976, s. 2(b) as cited in *Bangalore Development Authority* v. *Aircraft Employees' Cooperative Society Limited*, (2012) 3 SCC 442, para 9].

In real property law, such circumstances, in regard to situation, view, location, access to a water course, or the like, as enhance the pleasantness or desirability of the property for purposes of residence, or contribute to the pleasure and enjoyment of the occupants, rather than to their indispensable needs. Extras or intangible items often associated with property. They may be tangible. Often amenities in a condominium include swimming pools, landscaping, and tennis Court.

In the law of *easements,* an "amenity" consists in restraining the owner from doing that on his property which, but for the grant or covenant, he might otherwise lawfully have done. Sometimes called a "negative easement" as distinguished from that class of easements which compel the owner to suffer something to be done on his property by another.

Amentia. Imbecility, idiocy or insanity; absence of mind.

Amercement. A fine or damages imposed at the discretion of the Court.

Amerciament. (*amerciamentum*) Signifies the pecuniary punishment of an offender.

Amicable. Friendly; mutually forbearing; agreed or assented to by parties having conflicting interests (opposed to, hostile or adversary).

Friendly; done with mutual goodwill. [Industrial Disputes Act (14 of 1947), S. 12(2)].

Amicus curiae. Friend of the Court; one who voluntarily or on invitation of the Court, and not on the instructions of any party helps the Court in any judicial proceedings.

Amidships. The middle of the length of the load water-line, as measured from the fore side of the stem to the aft side of the stern post.

Amity. Friendship, harmony; good understanding, especially between nations; political friendship; as, a treaty of amity and commerce.

Ammunition. "AMMUNITION" means ammunition for any firearm, and includes—

(i) rockets, bombs, grenades, shells and other missiles,

(ii) articles designed for torpedo service and submarine mining,

(iii) other articles containing, or designed or adapted to contain, explosive, fulminating or fissionable material or noxious liquid, gas or other such thing, whether capable of use with firearms or not,

(iv) charges for firearms and accessories for such charges,

(v) fuses and friction tubes,

(vi) parts of, and machinery for manufacturing, ammunition, and

(vii) such ingredients or ammunition as the Central Government may, by notification in the Official Gazette, specify in this behalf. [Arms Act (54 of 1959), S. 2(1)(b)]

Military stores; provision for attack or defence. Includes also all articles specially designed for torpedo service and submarine mining, rockets, gun-cotton, dynamite, lithofracteur and other explosive or fulminating material, gun-flints, gun-wads, percussion caps, fuses and friction-tubes, all parts of ammunition and all machinery for manufacturing ammunition, but does not include lead, sulphur or saltpeter.

Amnesia. Loss of memory as a result of organic trauma, delirium lesions of the diencephalon area of the brain, hysteria or epilepsy.

Amnesty. The word 'amnesty' properly belongs to international law, and is applied to treaties of peace following a state of war, and signifies there the burial in oblivion of the particular cause of the strife, so that shall not be again a cause for war between the parties. And so amnesty is applied to rebellions which by their magnitude are brought within the rules of international law, and in which multitudes of men are the subjects of the clemency of the Government.

The meaning of the word "amnesty" is a general pardon.

Amortisation. Redemption of stock by a sinking fund.

Amortisation of loan. The 'amortisation of loan' is the rate at which the principal balance will be paid down over a period of time. It is a process of decreasing or accounting for an amount over a period of time. Shorter periods will have higher amounts amortised. It is allocation of a lump sum amount to different time periods, particularly for loans and other forms of finances. [*Morirku Ut India (P) Ltd.* v. *State of U.P.,* (2008) 4 SCC 548, 553, para 11]

Amortised loan. A loan which calls for periodic payments that are applied first to interest and then to principal as provided by the terms of the note.

Amortised mortgage. Payment of interest as well as the portion of the principal in the periodic payment by the mortgagor.

Amortizing loan. Loan for which the repayments are made as a series of instalments. (*International Accounting*)

Amotion. A moving or carrying away; removal from office.

Amount. The substance, or result of a thing; the total or aggregate sum.

Aggregate sum; quantity; to come upto; resulting; equaling in effect.

Amount claimed. The expression "amount claimed", in a decree which states that "the amount claimed with costs be decreed" should be construed applying to the principal and interest claimed in the plaint and is not applicable to a general and unascertained sum of future interest.

Amount covered. (*In insurance*). The amount that is insured and for which underwriters are liable for loss under the policy of insurance.

Amount in controversy. Extent of damages which are claimed or demanded for relief.

Amount standing. For the purposes of this sub-section "amount standing" shall include principal, interest and any others dues payable by the borrower to the secured creditor in respect of secured asset as per the books of account of the secured creditor. [Securitisation and Reconstruction of Assets and Enforcement of Security Interest Act (54 of 2002), S. 13(9), *Explanation* (b)].

Amount of consideration. The words "the amount of the consideration" contemplates the consideration of the property which is subject-matter of sale under the agreement. *Saroj Gupta* v. *IV Addl. Dist. Judge, Etah*, AIR 1994 All 22, 24. [Court Fees Act (7 of 1870), S. 7(x)(a)]

Amount of loss incurred by the assesse in the activity of owning and maintaining race horses. Means—

(i) in a case where the assesse has no income by way of stake money, the amount of expenditure (not being in the nature of capital expenditure) laid out or expended by him wholly and exclusively for the purposes of maintaining race horses;

(ii) in a case where the assesse has income by way of stake money, the amount by which such income falls short of the amount of expenditure (not being in the nature of capital expenditure) laid out or expended by the assesse wholly and exclusively for the purposes of maintaining race horses. [Income-tax Act (43 of 1961), S. 74A(3) *Expln.* (a)]

Amounting to murder. Being equivalent to murder in the eyes of law. [IPC (45 of 1860), S. 300, excep., thirdly, *Expln.*].

Amplification. The word "amplification" means increase or enlarge. If by the word 'particulars' is meant details of facts already stated, then 'amplification' would mean giving more details of those facts. But if by the word 'particulars' is meant 'instances', then 'amplification of instances' can only mean "giving more instances". *Sangappa* v. *Shivamurthy Swami,* AIR 1950 Mys 320, 324. [Representation of the People Act (43 of 1951), S. 90(5)]

Amputation. Cutting off a limb.

Amusement. Entertainment; diversion; pastime; sport.

The words "entertainments" and "amusements" are wide enough to include theatres, dramatic performances, cinemas, sports and the like. *Y.V. Srinivasamurthy* v. *State of Mysore*, AIR 1959 SC 894, 896. [Constitution of India, Sch. VII, List II, Entries 33, 62; List I, Entry 60]

"**Amusement facility**" means a facility where fun or recreation is provided by means of rides, gaming devices or bowling alleys in amusement parks, amusement arcades, water parks, theme parks or such other places but does not include a place within such facility where other services are provided [Finance Act (32 of 1994), s. 65-B(9) (now repealed by Central Goods and Services Tax Act, 2017)].

Amy. (amicus) In law *prochein amy* is the next friend to be trusted for an infant. Infants are to sue by *prochein amy* (*i.e.*) next friend and defended by guardian.

Anaerobic digestion. Means a controlled process involving microbial decomposition of organic matter in the absence of oxygen. [Rule 2(1), Municipal Solid Wastes (Management and Handling) Rules, 2000]

Analogous. Having analogy; bearing some resemblance or proportion to something else.

Analogous to trade or business. The expression "analogous to trade or business" could reasonably mean only activity which results in goods made or manufactured or services rendered which are capable of being converted into saleable ones. *Bangalore Water Supply and Sewerage Board* v. *A. Rajappa*, AIR 1978 SC 548, 555.

Analogy. A term in logic meaning identity or similarity of proportion. (*Wharton* cited in 2 Cys. 285) Where there is no judicial precedent in point on the same subject, lawyers have recourse to cases on a different subject-matter, but governed by the same general principles. This is called reasoning by analogy or analogical extension of the principle of a decision.

Analysis. A detailed exmaination of anything complex made in order to understand its nature or to determine its essential features. [Drugs and Cosmetics Act (23 of 1940), S. 6(2)(d)].

Analytical jurisprudence. A method of legal study which examines law purely in its existing structure.

Anarchy. Lawlessness.

Anatomical examination. The examination by dissection of a body for purposes of teaching or studying, or researching into.

Anatomical gift. Testamentary donation of bodily organs for medical transplant.

Ancestor. One who has gone before in a family. One who has preceded another in a direct line of descent; a lineal ascendant.

In Hindu Law, it is used only as signifying a direct ascendant in the paternal or maternal line, and more technically as signifying the paternal grandfather and his ascendants in the male line.

One from whom a person is descended. [Hindu Marriage Act (25 of 1955), S. 3(c)].

Ancestral. What relates to or has been done by one's ancestors : as homage ancestral, *etc.* (*Tomlin*)

Belonging to or inherited from an ancestor. [CPC (5 of 1908), S. 53].

Ancestral estate. An estate which is acquired by descent or by operation of law with no other consideration than that of blood.

Ancestral property. Any property inherited upto four generations of male lineage from the father, father's father or father's father's father i.e. father, grandfather etc., is termed as ancestral property. In other words, property inherited from mother, grandmother, male and even brother is not ancestral property. In ancestral property, the right of property accrues to the coparcener or on birth. [*Management* v. *T.B. Raju,* (2018) 15 SCC 662, para 11].

If property came to a son as gift from his father, it cannot be regarded as his ancestral property. Ancestral property in the ordinary sense must mean property of the father which is inherited.

IN HINDU LAW. "Ancestral property" in Hindu law is to be limited to property which has come from certain male lineal ancestor.

The word "ancestral" is here employed in the sense of "paternal", that is, as meaning property of the father, in whatsoever manner, or by whatsoever title, the father had acquired it. Therefore "ancestral" property here means property derived from the father, at least immovable property.

Anchorage. Anchoring ground; place where ships anchor, customary place for anchoring; a duty imposed on ships for anchoring in a harbour; anchorage dues.

Ancient. Old. Belonging to times long past. Ancient is a correlative term, and has for its correlative, as standing in the opposition, the term, 'modern'.

Ancient document. It is probably, impossible to define what an "Ancient document" is. It should be, at least, "one or two centuries" old. [See also Evidence Act (1 of 1872), S. 90].

Ancient light. An ancient light is a defined aperture in a building, through which there has been actually enjoyed, peaceably and as of right, an access and use of light "for the full statutory prescriptive period without interruption." *Gale,* Part 3, Ch. 2; *Goddard on Easements,* 5th Ed., 49—57. [Indian Easements Act (5 of 1882), S. 15].

Ancient monument. "ANCIENT MONUMENT" means any structure, erection or monuments, or any tumulus or place of interment, or any cave, rock-sculpture, inscription or monolith, which is of historical, archaeological or artistic interest, or any remains thereof, and includes—

(a) the site of an ancient monument;

(b) such portion of land adjoining the site of an ancient monument as may be required for fencing or covering in or otherwise preserving such monument; and

(c) the means of access to and convenient inspection of an ancient monument. [Ancient Monuments Preservation Act (7 of 1904), S. 2(1)]

"ANCIENT MONUMENTS" means any structure, erection or monument, or any tumulus or place of interment, or any cave, rock sculpture, inscription or monolith, which is of historical, archaeological or artistic interest and which has been in existence for not less than one hundred years, and includes (i) the remains of an ancient monument, (ii) such portion of land adjoining the site of an ancient monument, (iii) such portion of land adjoining the site of an ancient monument as may be required for fencing or covering in or otherwise preserving such monument, and (iv) the means of access to, and convenient inspection of an ancient monument. [Karnataka Ancient and Historical Monuments and Archaeological Sites and Remains Act, 1961 (7 of 1962), S. 2 (1) as cited in *K. Guruprasad Rao* v. *State of Karnataka*, (2013) 8 SCC 418, para 20].

The words 'ancient monument' mean any monument which is very old having historic past or record. It can also be a stone, a post, a river, *etc.* The 'Brahm Sarover' would come within the expression. *Ram Sarup* v. *State of Haryana*, AIR 1993 SC 201, 206.

Ancient writings. Documents upward of thirty years old. [Indian Evidence Act (1 of 1872), S. 90]

Ancillary. Aiding, auxiliary; subordinate; attendant upon; that which aids or promotes a proceeding regarded as the principal (*Abbott*) as ancillary administration; ancillary attachment; ancillary action. (*Ency. Lond.*)

Subservient, related and supplementary. [Coal mines Provident Funds and Miscellaneous Provisions Act (46 of 1948), S. 2(b)(xiii)].

Ancillary jurisdiction. Jurisdiction which is incident to the main cause pending before the Court.

Ancillary service. Means any subsidiary service which provides amenities or facilities to persons making use of any road transport service of a Corporation. [Road Transport Corporation Act (64 of 1950), S. 2(a)]

Ancipitis usus. (*Lat.*) Of doubtful use.

And. (*Abbr.* *&*). "The word "and" is normally conjunctive but sometimes it is read as disjunctive to give effect to the manifest intention of the legislature as disclosed from the context". "And" may legitimately be construed as 'or' when the intention of the legislature is clear and when any other construction would tend to defeat such intention. [CPC (5 of 1908), Preamble]

The word 'And' should be understood in a disjunctive sense. *S. Krishnan* v. *State of Madras*, AIR 1951 SC 301, 304. [Constitution of India, Art. 22(7)]

The word 'and' has not been used in cumulative sense rather it has been used in a disjunctive sense. The word 'and' occurring in Art. 236(b) should be read as 'or'. [Constitution of India, Art. 236(b)].

The use of the word 'and' in the expression "goods and passengers", does not mean that the tax cannot be levied on one to the exclusion of the other.

And for any other purpose. The expression cannot be interpreted to mean a purpose other than protection of the legal rights of a person. It is not the Courts province to decide questions of academic importance. *In re Chakkarai Chettiar,* AIR 1953 Mad 96, 97. [Constitution of India, Art. 226]

And in any case. Held to mean "in every case".

And other documents. In a charge of an offence under S. 471, IPC (45 of 1860), the use of the expression "*and other documents*" without specifying them is improper because, the accused can have no idea of the case he has to meet and to which particular documents the reference is made.

Anesthesia. *In medical jurisprudence.* (1) Loss of sensation, or insensibility to pain, caused by the administration of certain drugs, such as either nitrous oxide gas, or cocaine. (2) More or less complete insensibility to pain, existing in various parts of the body as a result of certain diseases of the nervous system. (*Black*)

Anew. A fresh; as a new action. [Inland Vessels Act (1 of 1917), S. 19J(3)].

Anganwadi. Means a child care and development center set up under the Integrated Child Development Services Scheme of the Central Government to render services covered under section 4, section 5(1)(a) and section 6. [S. 2(1) of the National Food Security Act, 2013 (20 of 2013)]

"Angel fund" means a sub-category of Venture Capital Fund under Category I Alternative Investment Fund that raises funds from angel investors and invests in accordance with the provisions of this chapter. [Securities and Exchange Board of India (Alternative Investment Funds) Regulations, 2012, Chap. III-A, Regn. 19-A(1) as inserted by Amending Regulations, 2013].

"**Angel investor**" means any person who proposes to invest in any angel fund and satisfies one of the following conditions, namely,—

(a) an individual investor who has net tangible assets of at least two crore rupees excluding value of his principal residence, and who:

(i) has early stage investment experience; or

(ii) has experience as serial entrepreneur; or

(iii) is a senior management professional with at least ten years of experience;

Explanation.—For the purposes of this clause, 'early-stage investment experience' shall mean prior experience in investing in start-up or emerging or early-state ventures and 'serial entrepreneur' shall mean a person who has promoted or co-promoted more than one start-up venture.

(b) a body corporate with a net worth of a least ten crore rupees; or

(c) an Alternative Investment Fund registered under these regulations or a Venture Capital Fund registered under the SEBI (Venture Capital Funds) Regulations, 1996. [Securities and Exchange Board of India (Alternative Investment Funds) Regulation, 2012, Chap. III-A, Regn. 19-A(2) as inserted by Amending Regulations, 2013].

Angling. Fishing.

Anglo-Indian. "ANGLO-INDIAN" means a person whose father or any of whose other male progenitors in the male line is or was of European descent but who is domiciled within the territory of India and is or was born within such territory of parents habitually resident therein and not established there for temporary purposes only. [Constitution of India, Art. 366(2)]

Animal. The word ANIMAL denotes any living creature, other than a human being. [IPC (45 of 1860), S. 47] now (w.e.f. 1-7-2024) repealed & replaced by Bharatiya Nyaya Sanhita, 2023 (45 of 2023), section 2(2), same definition in new Sanhita]

"ANIMAL" means animal useful to human beings and includes fish and fowl, and such kind of wildlife as the Central Government may, by notification in the Official Gazette, specify, being king which in its opinion it is desirable to protect or preserve. [Insecticides Act (46 of 1968), S. 3(a)]

"ANIMAL" includes Amphibians, birds, mammals and reptiles and their young, and also includes, in the case of birds and reptiles, their eggs. [Wild Life (Protection) Act (53 of 1972), S. 2(1)]

The word 'animals' in law includes any animate being, which is not human, endowed with the power of voluntary motion. (*Bouvier*)

It includes all living creatures not human.

ANIMALS, PREVENTION OF CRUELTY TO. So long as an animal is *ferae naturae* and it is not brought under subjugation and control of man it stands upon a wholly different ground, but when it is captured or domesticated the law protects it from cruelty if such cruelty is practiced at a place or in the manner laid down in the Act.

Animal : Fish. Fish is also an animal but of different kind. *ITC Ltd.* v. *Person-in charge Agricultural Marketing Committee, Kavinander*, (2004) 2 SCC 794.

Animalia fera, si facta sint mansueta et ex consuetudine cunt et redeunt, volant et revolant, utcervi, cygni, etc, eo usque notsra sunt, et ita intelliguntur quamdiu habuerunt animum revertendi. (*Maxim*) Wild animals, if they be made tame, and are accustomed to go out and return, fly away and fly back, as stags, swans, *etc.*, are considered to belong to us so long as they have the intention of returning to us.

Animalia ferae naturae. Animals of a wild and untamable disposition.

Liability of Animals. The owner's liability for damages caused by his animals.

Animo. With the intention.

Animo defamandi. (*Lat.*) With the intention of defaming.

Animo furandi. (Co. 3rd inst. 107) With an intention of stealing.

Animo or animus furandi. With an intention of stealing. In order to constitute larceny, the thief must take the property *Animo furandi*; for when the taking of property is lawful, although it may afterwards be converted *animo furandi* to the taker's use, it is not larceny. (*Latin for Lawyers*)

Animo or animus testandi. With the intention of making a will. *Animus testandi* is required to make a valid will. An idiot can make no will, for he can have no intention. (*Latin for Lawyers*)

Animo testandi. With the intention of making a will.

Animus. Mind; design; will; intention; disposition (*Burrill*); hostility; ill will; hatred.

This word "animus" is used in various combinations.

Animus ad se omne jus ducit. It is to the intention that all law applies.

Animus belligerandi. The intention to wage war.

Animus cancellandi. Intention to destroy or cancel.

Animus dedicandi. Intention of dedicating.

Animus defamandi. The intention to defame.

Animus deserendi. Intention to desert.

Animus donandi. Intention of giving.

Animus et factum. Combination of intention with the act.

Animus felonico. Intention of committing a felony.

Animus furandi. Intention of stealing.

Animus hominis est anima scripti. (*Maxim*) The intent of a man is the soul of his writing. (*Morgan's Leg. Max.; Black;* 3 *Bulstr.* 67) In order to give life or effect to an instrument, it is necessary to look to the intention of the individual who executed the same.

Animus injurandi. Intention of injuring.

Animus manendi. Intention of remaining.

Animus possidendi. The intention of possessing.

Animus quo. The intention with which.

Animus revertendi. The intention of returning.

Animus revocandi. The intention of revoking.

Animus testandi. (*Lat.*) Testamentary intention.

Annex. Is to attach at the end; sub-join; affix; as to annex a codicil to a will. In law it implies physical connection which, however, is often dispensed with when not reasonably practicable. To unite, as a smaller thing to a greater; join; make an integral part of : as, to annex a conquered province to a kingdom.

To unite materially as an accessary.

Annexation. Is the act of annexing or uniting one thing with another; the act of adding as a smaller thing to a greater; the act of connecting; conjunction, addition. (*Tomlin*)

It occurs when the occupying power acquires and makes the occupied territory as its own. Annexation gives a *de jure* right to administer the territory. It means not only possession but also uncontested sovereignty over the territory. *R. Monteiro* v. *State of Goa*, AIR 1970 SC 329 at 336. [Geneva Conventions Act (6 of 1960), Sch. IV, Art. 6]

Annexed to the land. Connotes fastened to the land. Mere juxtaposition to, or the lying of a thing on the land, does not amount to annexation.

See T.P. Act (4 of 1882), S. 40 "annexed to the ownership of property."

Annexure. Annexure is something which is added, joined, or attached, affixed, or appended. [Representation of the People Act (43 of 1951), S. 81(3)]

Anni nubiles. The marriageable age of woman.

Annihilate. To destroy the form or peculiar distinctive properties of, so that the specific thing no longer exists; as, to annihilate a forest by cutting and carrying away the trees; to annihilate an army; to annihilate a house by demolishing the structure.

Anniversary. The yearly return of any remarkable date; the day on which some event is annually celebrated. [Indian Majority Act (9 of 1875), S. 4].

Anno Domini. The year of Lord.

Annotation. The act of annoting or marking notes.

Announce. To make public or give official intimation of. [Sale of Goods Act (3 of 1930), S. 64(2)].

Announcement. The action of announcing; public or official notification. [Sale of Goods Act (3 of 1930), S. 64(2)].

Annoy. To affect so as to ruffle, trouble, vex. [Indian Evidence Act (1 of 1872), S. 152].

(1) to irritate or displease, (2) to harass with repeated attacks. [Collin's Dictionary as cited in *Shreya Singhal* v. *Union of India*, (2015) 5 SCC 1, para 54].

Annoyance. In law it includes any hurt done to a place, public or private, by placing anything thereon that may breed infection, or by encroachment or such like means.

The state of feeling caused by that which annoys; the state of being annoyed. [Air Force Act (45 of 1950), S. 63(c)].

(1) the feeling of being annoyed, (2) the act of annoying. [Collin's Dictionary as cited in *Shreya*

Singhal v. *Union of India*, (2015) 5 SCC 1, para 54].

Annual. Pertaining or relating to a year, yearly; as the annual growth of a tree; annual profits; annual rent; relating to the events or transactions of a year; as, an annual report.

The word 'annual' means something which is reckoned by the year. *National Insurance* v. *Life Insurance Corporation of India*, AIR 1963 SC 1171, 1778. [Life Insurance Corporation Act (31 of 1956), Sch. I, Part A, Para I]

Annual accretion. In relation to the balance to the credit of an employee, means the increase to such balance in any year, arising from contributions and interest. [Income-tax Rules (1962), Sch. IV, Part A, R. 2(e)]

Annual charge. The words "annual charge" mean a charge to secure an annual liability.

The word 'annual', as used in taxing statutes, must be taken to mean payments, in whatever kind of instalments paid, made every year in discharge of a liability incident to that year, if it has to be made during more than one year, whether consecutively or otherwise.

Annual depreciation. The annual loss, not restored by current maintenance.

Annual financial statement. A statement of the estimated receipts and expenditure of the Government of India or that of a State Government in respect of any financial year which the President causes to be laid before both the Houses of Parliament and the Governor before the State Legislature respectively. [Constitution of India, Arts. 112(1) and 202(1)]

Annual general meeting. (***AGM***) Every company shall in each year hold, in addition to any other meetings a general meeting as is annual general meeting and shall specify the meeting as such in the notices calling it and not more than fifteen months shall elapse between the date of one annual general meeting of a company and that of the next. [Companies Act (1 of 1956) replaced with Companies Act, 2013, S. 166]

Share holders meeting, required by law to be held yearly by every public company.

Annual letting value. Means the annual rent for which any building or land, exclusive of furniture or machinery contained or situated therein or thereon, might reasonably be expected to let from year to year. [Bom. Act (3 of 1901) (Dist. Muni.), S. 3(11)]

Annual loading. Means the provision made for future expenses and profits [Insurance Act (4 of 1938), Fifth Sch, Part I(5)(a) now omitted].

Annual payments. The annual payments which are to be treated as an element to be taken into account in computing the profits of the recipient, are not to be regarded as annual payments.

Annual percentage rate. Actual cost of borrowing money.

Annual report. A document required by law to be released by public companies, describing the company's activities during the previous year.

Annual return. A document, accompanied by a copy of the auditor's report and balance sheet which a limited company must file annually with the Registrar of the Companies.

Annual value. The phrase 'annual value' whether in income-tax acts, or wherever else it appears in connection with rating or taxation means the same thing, *i.e.,* the sum at which the property may reasonably be expected to let from year to year.

"ANNUAL VALUE" means—

(a) in the case of railway stations, hotels, colleges, schools, hospitals, factories and any other building which a Board decides to assess under this clause, one-twentieth of the sum obtained by adding the estimated present cost of erecting the building to the estimated value of the land appertaining thereto, and

(b) in the case of a building or land not assessed under clause (a), the gross annual rent for which such building (exclusive of furniture or machinery therein) or such land is actually let or, where the building or land is not let or in the opinion of the Board is let for a sum less than its fair letting value, might reasonably be expected to let from year to year :

Provided that, where the annual value of any building is by reason of exceptional circumstances in the opinion of the Board may fix the annual value at any less amount which appears to it to be just. [Cantonments Act (2 of 1924), S. 64]

"Annual value", in relation to any property, means its annual value as determined under S. 23. [Income-tax Act (43 of 1961), S. 2(2)]

'Annual value' notwithstanding anything contained in any other law for the time being in force, means—

(a) in the case of land, the gross annual rent

(i) to be calculated on the basis of fair rent fired under the law relating to rent restriction for the time being in force; or

(ii) where no fair rent referred to in item (i) is fixed, at which it is expected to be let or it is actually let, whichever is greater. [Haryana Municipal Act (24 of 1973), S. 2(1)]

'Annual value' means—

(a) in the case of land or building which is in the occupation of a tenant, the gross annual rent at which the land or building has actually been let.

(b) in the case of land or building which is occupied by the owner, the annual value shall be five per cent on the sum obtained by adding the present market value of the land and estimated cost of erecting the building less ten per cent depreciation. [Punjab Municipal Act (3 of 1911), S. 3(1)]

'Annual value' means—

(a) in the case of railway stations, hotels, colleges, schools, hospitals, factories and other such buildings, a proportion not exceeding five per centum to be fixed by rule made in this behalf of the sum obtained by adding the estimated present cost of erecting the building to the estimated value of the land appurtenant thereto; and

(b) in the case of a building or land not falling within the provisions of clause (a) the gross annual rent for which such building, exclusive of furniture or machinery therein, or such land is actually let or where the building or land is not let or in the opinion of the Board is let for a sum less than its fair letting value might reasonably be expected to let from year to year" [U.P. Municipality Act 1940, S. 140(f)]

Annualized percentage rate (APR). Also known as annual percentage rate, the rate of interest charged on a monthly basis (*e.g.* on a *hire purchase* transaction) shown as a yearly *compound interest* rate. (*Investment; International Accounting*)

Annuitant. One who holds or receives an annuity.

Annuity, in its strict sense, is a yearly payment of a certain sum of money, granted to another for life or for years, and chargeable only on the person of the grantor. (*Black*)

ANNUITY includes any series of payments, whether interconnected or not, whether of the same or of varying amounts, and whether payable at regular intervals or otherwise, and payments of dividends or interest on shares in or debentures of a company shall be treated for the purposes of this section as a series of payments constituting an annuity limited to cease on the death if the payments are liable to cease on the death or the amounts thereof are liable to be reduced on the death, by reason directly or indirectly of the extinguishment of any alteration of rights attaching to, or of the issue of any shares in or debentures of a company. [Estate Duty Act (34 of 1953), S. 27(7)(iii)]

It is a periodical payment of money bequeathed as a gift or secured by the personal covenant or bond of the payer. (*Termes de la Ley* 44 *Reg. Orig.* 158 : *Co. Litt.* 144b : *Tomlin*)

In order to constitute an annuity, the payment to be made periodically should be a fixed or pre-determined one, and it should not be liable to any variation depending upon or on any ground relating to the general income of the fund or estate which is charged for such payment. *Commissioner of Wealth Tax* v. *P.K. Banerjee*, AIR 1981 SC 401, 409.

An amount specially of money payable yearly (or by extention at other regular intervals, as quarterly) for a certain or uncertain period. [T.P. Act (4 of 1882), S. 36].

Annuity Deposit Certificate. In this scheme, unless the context otherwise requires,—

"ANNUITY DEPOSIT CERTIFICATE" means a Ten Year Annuity Deposit Certificate the form of which has been prescribed by the Central Government in the Government of India, Ministry of Finance (Department of Economic Affairs) Notification No. G.S.R. 1313, dated the 10th September, 1964, and which is issued as evidence of annuity deposit. [Annuity Deposit Scheme, 1964, S. 2(1)(b)].

Annul. To make void; to destroy; to cancel (as to annul a judgment; nullify; abrogate; abolish; do away with; used especially of laws, decrees, edicts, decisions of Courts, or other established rules, usages and the like.

To make void or of no effect; to nullify. [T.P. Act (4 of 1882), S. 115]; [North-Eastern Hill University Act (24 of 1973), S. 8(10)].

Annulment. The act of annulling; the act of making void retrospectively as well as prospectively : (as) annulment of adjudication order in insolvency.

The act of annulling; being annulled. [Wealth-tax Act (27 of 1957), S. 46(4)].

Annus et dies. (*Lat.*) A year and a day.

Anomalous mortgage. A mortgage, neither purely simple nor exclusively usufructuary but a mixture of two. *Munni Lal* v. *Phuddi Singh*, AIR 1987 All 155, 158. [T.P.A. (4 of 1882), S. 58(g)]

Anomaly. Irregularity; deviation from the common or natural order. [Companies (Profits) Surtax Act (7 of 1964), S. 24].

Anomaly detection. A label for the class of intrusion-detection tactics that seek to identify potential intrusion attempts by virtue of their being (presumably) sufficiently deviant (anomalous) in comparison with expected or authorized activities. Phrased another way, anomaly detection begins with a positive model of expected system operations and flags potential intrusions on the basis of their deviation (as particular events or actions) from this presumed norm. (*Cyber law*)

Anonymous. Nameless; without name; a term applied to the reported cases in which the names of the parties are not given, or which are without the usual title. (*Burrill*)

Often abbreviated as "anon." "An," or "A". (*Wharton*)

An anonymous publication is a publication withholding the name of the author.

Of unknown name; of unknown authorship. [IPC (45 of 1860), S. 507].

Anonymous and **pseudonymous works.** Article 7(3)(5) of Berne Convention contains special provisions as to anonymous and pseudonymous works concerning term and identity of the author. (*Copyright*)

Anonymous FTP. Allows visitors to upload and/or download predetermined files from designated directories without usernames or passwords. For example, distribute your latest software package by allowing visitors to download it through anonymous

FTP (File Transfer Protocol). This is different than a regular FTP account. (*Cyber Law*)

Anonymous FTP server. A remote computer, with publicly accessible file archives, that accepts 'anonymous' as the log-in name and an e-mail address as the password. (*Information Technology*)

Another civil proceeding. The words "another civil proceeding" occurring in Sec. 14 of the Limitation Act (36 of 1963), will include execution proceedings in another suit. The expression "civil proceeding" is of wide import, and again, no distinction can properly be made as to the applicability of the principle underlying S. 14 between the steps which a litigant has to take after he has obtained a decree and those which he takes prior to it. *Shyam Sunder* v. *Chand Bai,* AIR 1962 Raj 968. [Limitation Act (36 of 1963), S. 14]

Another Court. The expression 'another Court' in Section 39(1), does not connote another Court of equal jurisdiction as the Court which passed the decree. *Chandravathi* v. *Payapathiliath,* AIR 1966 Ker 318. [CPC (5 of 1908), S. 39(1)]

Another person. The expression 'another person' in S. 11(4) (i) should not be read with the remaining words of the clause as to render the meaning that the Chief Justice must nominate a person other than himself, who is or had been a Judge. *Shabbir Fatima* v. *Allahabad University,* AIR 1966 All 45, 50. [Allahabad University Act (3 of 1921), S. 11(4)(i)(b)]

Answer. Something said or written in reply; to give reply; to be in conformity.

Answerable. Capable of being answered; admitting of a satisfactory reply; liable. "Unanswerable is a boastful word. His best reasons are answerable; his worst are not worthy of being answered." (*Jeremy Collier,* Moral Subjects). Liable to give an account or to be called to account; responsible; amenable; as, an agent is answerable to his principal. "Answerable" is merely an equivalent for liable' *River Wear Commissioners* v. *Wear Adamson*, 2 App. Cas. 743 at 775) Liable to be called to account. [T.P. Act (4 of 1882), S. 37, *Prov.*].

Answering statement. A reply in writing by the party who has not initiated the arbitration. (*Arbitration*)

Ante. Before; when used in a report or legal text book it refers the reader to a previous part of the book.

Ante-date. To date a document before the day of its signature or execution.

To date before the true time; to give an earlier date than the real one; thus, to antedate a deed or bond is to give to it a date anterior to the true time of its execution.

Ante litem motam. (*Lat.*) Before litigation was in contemplation.

Ante mortem. (*Lat.*) Before death.

Ante-natal. Happening before birth; pertaining or relating to terms, occurrence or conditions previous to birth.

Ante-natus. A child born before the marriage of its parents.

Ante-nuptial. Occurring before marriage; existing, or done before marriage; preceding marriage; as, an ante-nuptial agreement; ante-nuptial children. (*Wharton*)

Ante-nuptial settlements. Settlements of property on the wife or upon the wife and children made before or in contemplation of marriage.

Antecedent. Pre-existing; previous; earlier.

Antecedent claim. A pre-existing claim. In law of negotiable instruments, a holder takes for value if he takes the instrument for an antecedent claim against any person whether or not the claim is due. (*Black*)

Antecedent debt. (*In Hindu Law*) The expression "antecedent debt" means with regard to a mortgage, debt "antecedent to the transaction," and, in the case of a proceeding by suit, "debt antecedent to the institution of the suit." An "antecedent debt," to support a sale or mortgage for such debt, is a debt which is not for the first time incurred at the time of a sale or mortgage, that is, presently incurred, but a debt which existed prior to, and independently of such sale or mortgage. See *Mayne's Hindu Law.*

Antecedent debt means a debt antecedent in fact as well as in time, *i.e.* the debt must be truly independent of the subsequent mortgage debt which is impeached. *Virdhachalam Pillai* v. *Chaldean Bank*, AIR 1964 SC 1425, 1430; *Prasad* v. *Govindasami Mudaliar*, AIR 1982 SC 84, 96.

"Anthropocentrism". Consider humans to be the most important factor and value in the universe and states that humans have greater intrinsic value than other species. Resultantly, any species that are of potential use to humans can be a reserve to be exploited which leads to the point of extinction of biological reserves. Further that principle highlights human obligations towards environment arising out of instrumental, educational, scientific, cultural recreational and asthetic values that forests have to offer to humans. Under this approach, environment is only protected as a consequence of and to extent needed to protect human well-being. [*T.N. Godavarman Thirumulpad* v. *Union of India*, (2012) 4 SCC 362, para 31].

Anthropometry. (*In criminal law and medical jurisprudence*). The measurement of the human body; a system of measuring the dimensions of the human body both absolutely and in their proportion to each other, the facial, cranial, and other angles, the shape and size of the skull, *etc.*, for purposes of comparison with corresponding measurements of other individuals, and serving for the identification of the subject in cases of doubtful or disputed identity.

Anti-Doping Rule Violation. Means the circumstance, act or conduct specified in section 4. [National Anti-Doping Act, 2022 (15 of 2022), section 2(b)]

"Anti-fouling system". Means a coating, point, surface treatment, surface or device that is used on a ship to control or prevent attachment of unwanted organism. [Merchant Shipping Act (44 of 1958), Part XI-B, S. 356-Q(a) as inserted by Amending Act (31 of 2014)].

Anti-national. The word 'anti-national' covers acts prejudicial to the defence of India and efficient conduct of military operations. *Subba Rao* v. *State of A.P.*, AIR 1967 AP 202, 207. [Defence of India Rules (1962), R. 7]

Anti-social element. The persons who take law in their own hands and the persons who are acting against the will of the society. *Vijay Narain Singh* v. *State of Bihar*, AIR 1984 SC 1334.

Anti-suit injunction. The expression 'anti-suit injunction' means an injunction granted by a Court restraining a party to a suit, from instituting or prosecuting a case in another Court, including a foreign Court. *Modi Entertainment Network* v. *W.S.G. Cricket PTE Ltd.*, (2003) 4 SCC 341, para 10 : AIR 2003 SC 1177. [CPC (5 of 1908), O. XXXIX, R. 1; Specific Relief Act (47 of 1963), S. 38]

When a court restrains a party to a suit/proceeding before it from instituting or prosecuting a case in another court including a foreign court, it is called anti-suit injunction. The courts in India like the courts in England are courts of both law and equity. The principles governing grant of injunction: an equitable relief: by a court will also govern grant of anti-suit injunction which is but a species of injunction. V K Ahuja, *Intellectual Property Rights in India*, 2015, LexisNexis Butterworths at p. 720.

The courts in India have power to issue anti-suit injunction to a party over whom it has personal jurisdiction. This is because courts of equity exercise jurisdiction in personam. However, having regard to the rule of comity, this power will be exercised sparingly because such an injunction though directed against a person, in effect causes interference in the exercise of jurisdiction by another court. *Modi Entertainment Network* v. *WSG Cricket Pvt Ltd,* (2003) 4 SCC 341.

Antiseptic. (*Med. Jur.*) Anything which destroys the micro-organism of disease, putrefaction, or fermentation, or which restricts their growth and multiplication.

Anticipated. The word "anticipated" should be construed as including "likely." It may, however, mean "anticipated by the person making the statement". "Proceedings were anticipated" means "proceedings were regarded as likely" or as "reasonably probable".

Anticipation, (*in conveyancing*) means the act of assigning, charging or otherwise dealing with income before it becomes due.

A prior knowledge [IPC (45 of 1860), S. 464, *Expln.* 1, ill. (e)]; expectation. [T.P. Act (4 of 1882), S. 55(6)(b)]

Anticipatory bail. Bail taken in apprehension of arrest. *Samunder Singh* v. *State of Rajasthan*, (1987) 1 SCR 979.

Anticipatory breach. Breach of contract which is caused by a party's anticipatory repudiation.

If a party to a contract, before the time for performance of a contract has either refused or made it impossible for him to perform the contract, the other party may treat the act as a case of anticipatory breach, and act as if the breach has taken place.

Anticipatory nuisance. An activity, which, although not yet at the level of nuisance, is very likely to become one, so that the party obtains an injunction prohibiting the activity.

Anticipatory offence. It is a step towards the commission of another crime.

Anticipatory repudiation. Repudiation of contractual duty before the time for performance, giving an immediate right to damages for total breach to the injured party, as well as discharging the remaining duties of performance of the injured party.

Anticipatory search warrant. A warrant which is based on an affidavit showing probable cause that evidence of a certain crime (such as the delivery of illegal drugs) will be located at the specific place in the future.

Anticybersquatting Consumer Protection Act (ACPA). US legislation which protects registered trademark holders from online cyber-piracy (registering as domain names another person or company's trademark). (*Cyber Law*)

Antidumping law. Statute designed for protection of domestic companies by preventing the sale of foreign goods at less than fair value.

Antidumping tarrif. A tarrif which equals the difference between the price at which the product is sold in the exporting country and the price at which the importer will sell the product in the importing country.

Antigen. Any substance that the body regards as foreign and against which it produces an antibody. Viruses, bacteria and fungi are regarded by the body as antigens. The HIV contains a number of different antigens.

Antinomy. A contradiction in law or logic.

Antiquarian. Of or belonging to old times. [Arms Act (54 of 1959), S. 45(c)].

Antique (or vetera) statuta. Antique statutes.

Antiquities. A relic or monument of ancient times; a thing of antiquity.

Antiquity. Includes :

(i) any coin, sculpture, epigraph or other work of art or craftsmanship;

(ii) any article, object or thing detached from a building or cave.;

(iii) any article, object or thing illustrative of science, arts, crafts, literature, religion, customs, morals or politics in bygone ages.

(iv) any article, object or thing of historical interest, and

(v) any article, object or thing declared by the Central Government, by notification in the official Gazette, to be an antiquity for the purposes of this Act which has been in existence for not less than one hundred years. [Ancient Monuments and Archaeological Sites and Remains Act (24 of 1958), S. 2(b)]

Antitrust law. Those laws which are designed to prevent abuse of monopoly rights. (*Patents*)

Antivirus. Software that detects, repairs, cleans, or removes virus-infected files from a computer. (*Cyber Law*)

Anton pillar order. Generally an *ex-parte* Court order allowing the premises of an alleged infringer to be searched for evidence of infringement. (*Patents*)

Court injunction that permits a person to enter named premises to copy certain specified documents. It is generally used to prevent someone from destroying documentary evidence. (*International Accounting*)

A court order that provides the right to search and seize evidence without prior warning. This prevents destruction of incriminating evidence, particularly in cases of alleged trademark, copyright or patent infringement.

An *Anton Piller* order is *ex parte,* interlocutory mandatory injunction which usually basically orders the defendant to allow the plaintiff to enter his premises for the purposes of searching for, inspecting, and seizing property infringing the plaintiffs rights or documents relevant to the plaintiff's claim against the defendant. It is given where speed and secrecy are vital to prevent the defendant destroying or disposing of such property or documents. [Clerk & Lindsell on Torts, 17th Edn., 1995, C. 28, para 28-22, p. 1522]

An order restraining a person from handing over the property in his possession along with the documents to the judgment debtor and keeping the documents in safe custody of the Court would amount to 'anton pillar order'. [*Mohit Bhargava* v. *Bharat Bhushan Bhargava,* (2007) 4 SCC 795, 801, para 10]

Antyodaya Anna Yojana. For the purpose of section 3 of Act 20 of 2013, the 'Antyodaya Anna Yojana' means, the scheme by the said name launched by the Central Government on the 25th day of December, 2000; and as modified from time to time. [*Explanation* to section 3(1) of the National Food Security Act, 2013 (20 of 2013)]

Any. The word "any" may have one of several meanings, according to the circumstances, it may mean "all"; "each"; "every"; "some"; "or one or more out of several." (*Ame Cyc.*)

ANY is used in the sense of any body, any person.

The word 'any' means 'one or same or all'. The use of the word 'any' in the context it has been used in clause (o) indicates that it has been used in wider sense extending from one to all. *Lucknow Development Authority* v. *M.K. Gupta*, AIR 1994 SC 787, 793. [Consumer Protection Act (68 of 1986), S. 2(10)]

The word 'any' has the following meaning—some, one out of many; an infinite number, one indiscriminately of whatever kind or quantity; or may be employed to indicate 'all' or 'every' as well as 'some' or 'one'. It is often synonymous with 'either' 'every' or 'all'—Extracted from Black's Dictionary Fifth Edition. *Shri Balaganesan Metals* v. *M.N. Shanmugam Chetty*, AIR 1987 SC 1668, 1674. [Tamil Nadu Buildings (Lease and Rent Control) Act, 1960, S. 10(3)(c)]

'Word "any" has a diversity of meaning and may be employed to indicate "all" or "every" as well as "some" or "one" and its meaning in a given statute depends upon the context and the subject-matter of the statute.' [*LDA* v. *M.K. Gupta*, (1994) 1 SCC 243, para 4 as cited in *Narne Construction Private Limited* v. *Union of India*, (2012) 5 SCC 359, para 4].

Any act. Term 'any Act' under Sec. 511 excludes the notion that the final act short of actual commission is alone punishable. *Sudhir Kumar Mukherjee and Sham Lal Shad* v. *State of W.B.*, AIR 1973 SC 2655, 2657. [IPC (45 of 1850), S. 511]

Any amount that the buyer is liable to pay to. The expression "any amount that the buyer is liable to pay to" is of significance. This expression shows that, apart from price of goods, the buyer should also be liable to pay an additional amount to the manufacturer/seller. In other words, the sale of the goods would not be made unless the buyer is also to pay an additional amount to the manufacturer, apart from the price of the goods. [*Commissioner of Central Excise, Mysore* v. *TVS Motors Company Limited,* (2015) 16 SCC 319, para 14] [(Repealed and replaced) Central Excise Act (1 of 1944), S. 4(3)(d)].

Any authority or other body of the university. The expression 'any authority or other body of the university' does not comprehend the Selection Committee. *Kashi Nath Misra* v. *Chancellor, University of Allahabad,* AIR 1967 All 101, 110. [Allahabad University Act (3 of 1921), S. 45]

Any candidate. The words 'any candidate' are qualified by 'at such election'. They cannot obviously include a person who withdrew himself from the contest before the election was over. *Sheo Kumar* v. *V.J. Oak,* AIR 1953 All 633, 636. [Representation of the People Act (43 of 1951), S. 81]

Any candidate essentially means a candidate in the constituency and not a candidate in the entire process of election to Parliament or Assembly. *Yeshwant Sitaram Desai* v. *Jaising Rao A. Rane,*

AIR 1974 Goa 4, 8. [Representation of the People Act (43 of 1951), S. 81]

Any candidate against whom allegations of any corrupt practice is made. The expression "any candidate against whom allegations of any corrupt practice are made" is to be construed as "any candidate who is alleged to have committed corrupt practices." *S.B. Adityan* v. *S. Kandaswamy,* AIR 1958 Mad 171, 173. [Representation of the People Act (43 of 1951), S. 82(b)]

Any child. The words 'ANY CHILD' include plural also and it means 'children'. *Shanti* v. *Bhagwani,* AIR 1984 P&H 313, 315. [Indian Succession Act (39 of 1925), S. 109]

Any claim. The expression 'any claim' in S. 446(2)(b) means any claim enforceable at law. *Faridabad Cold Storage* v. *Ammonia Supplies,* AIR 1978 Del 158, 161 (FB). [Companies Act (1 of 1956) replaced with Companies Act, 2013, S. 446(2)(b)]

Any Court. In O. XXI, R. 2, C.P. Code (5 of 1908), the words "any Court" have been construed to mean only "any Civil Court."

Any director. Any director in R. 3 need not be the same director who has signed and verified a pleading or on whom summons has been served. He can be any one of the directors who will be in a position to answer material questions relating to the suit. *Ramchand and Sons Sugar Mills* v. *Kanhayalal*, AIR 1966 SC 1899, 1902. [CPC (5 of 1908), O. XXIX, R.3]

Any election. While ascertaining the meaning of the words, 'any election' it is only the constituency from which the election is to be held is to be taken into consideration and not the entire body to which the elections are to be held.

Any interest. The words 'Any interest' in O. XXII, R. 10, CPC (5 of 1908), include any transferable 'right to sue' spoken of in the earlier rule of the order which provide for its devolution in case of death. *Pritimby Sen Gupta* v. *Giribala Devi,* AIR 1957 Tri 10.

Any interest in the estate of the deceased. Means any interest in the estate in respect of which the deceased is alleged to have executed a testament. *G. Jayakumar* v. *R. Ramaratnam,* AIR 1972 Mad 212, 214. [Indian Succession Act (39 of 1925), S. 283(1)(c)]

Any law. The words "any law" as mentioned in S. 23 of the Indian Contract Act (9 of 1872) refer to some substantive law and not an adjective law such as the CPC (5 of 1908), O. VI, R. 15(1), is. The term 'any law' includes the Special Law or procedure prescribed in O. XXXVII, R. 1, CPC (5 of 1908). *State of Bihar* v. *Gopal Saran,* AIR 1967 Pat 295, 296.

Any money due. Before an order for payment can be made under S. 469, the applicant must show that the amount is due, and if under the law of limitation governing actions for recovery of money, the claim would be barred, it cannot be said that the amount is a sum due within the meaning of Sec. 469. *Malabar Petroleum Co.* v. *Continental Oil Co. Ltd.,* AIR 1963 Mad 307, 308. [Companies Act (1 of 1956) replaced with Companies Act, 2013, S. 469(1)]

Any object held sacred by any class of persons. Any object however trivial or destitute or real value in itself, if regarded as sacred by any class of persons would come within the meaning of penal section. The object need not have been actually worshipped. An object may be held sacred by a class of persons without being worshipped by them. *Veerabhadran Chettiar* v. *Ramaswami Naicker*, AIR 1958 SC 1032, 1035. [IPC (45 of 1860), S. 295]

Any one. The word "any one" means everyone. *Chief Inspector of Mines* v. *Karam Chand Thapar*, AIR 1961 SC 838.

Any order. The term 'any order' comprehends appealable as well as non-appealable orders. *Sankara Menon* v. *Gowri Kutty Amma,* AIR 1978 Ker 211, 214. [CPC (5 of 1908), S. 105]

Any organization. For the purposes of section 52(1)(zb) of Act 14 of 1957, 'any organisation' includes an organization registered under section 12A of the Income-tax Act, 1961 (43 of 1961), and working for the benefit of persons with disability or recognized under Chapter X of the Persons with Disabilities (Equal Opportunities, Protection or Rights and full Participation) Act, 1995 (1 of 1996) or receiving grants from the Government for facilitating access to persons with disabilities or an educational institution or library or archives recognized by the Government. [*Explanation* to S. 52(1)(zb) of the Copyright Act, 1957 (14 of 1957) as inserted (w.e.f. 21-6-2012) by the Copyright (Amendment) Act, 2012 (27 of 2012)]

Any other candidate. If there are allegations of corrupt practice against any candidate other than, the returned candidate, he would have to be made a party as 'any other candidate'. *Harswarup* v. *Brij Bhushan*, AIR 1967 SC 836, 838. [Representation of the People Act (43 of 1951), Ss. 79(b), 82 (b), 82(a), 87, 123, 80]

Any other charges. The expression 'any other charges' includes a charge for carriage of any commodity between places other than two stations. *Union of India* v. *Indian Sugar Mills Association*, AIR 1968 SC 22, 26. [(Repealed and replaced) Indian Railways Act (9 of 1890), Ss. 41(2) and 29]

Any other establishment. The expression 'any other establishment' means an establishment which is a non-factory establishment. *Radhakrishnan* v. *R.P.P. Commissioner,* AIR 1967 MP 157, 160. [Employees Provident Funds Act (19 of 1952), Ss. (1)(3)(a) and (b), 4 and Sch. 1]

Any other matter. These words refer to the matters contained in each of the Entries 1 to 96. It cannot be interpreted to mean a topic mentioned by way of exclusion. *Union of India* v. *Harbhajan Singh*

Dhillon, AIR 1972 SC 1061, 1069. [Constitution of India, Art. 246(1), 248 and Sch. 7, List 1, Entry 97]

Any other person. The words "any other person" would not include creditors who might be injuriously affected by a transfer of property. Guardians and Wards Act (8 of 1890), S. 30.

When a section of an Act of Parliament after enumerating several office-holders proceeds to add the words 'any other person or persons whatever,' the doctrine of '*ejusdem generis*' applies. Any 'other person' means any one who holds an office in the Government of a similar kind to those enumerated.

Administration of Evacuee Property Act (31 of 1950), S. 10(1), (2)(m). The expression 'any other person' is not restricted to persons who are members of the family of the evacuee; they include other persons as well who are entitled to receive money from the evacuee. *Bhanu Pratap* v. *Asst. Custodian, E.P.*, AIR 1966 SC 245, 247.

The expression "any other person" has reference to those other persons, who have been mentioned in the preceding rules of Order V, who according to those rules, are entitled, to receive service on behalf of the parties to a litigation. *Sundrabai Dalichand* v. *Moneshwar Mahadeo Gokhale,* AIR 1959 Bom 178, 179. [CPC (5 of 1908), O. V, R. 16]

Any other public purpose. Though every State purpose or Union purpose must be a public purpose, it is easy to think of cases where the purpose of the acquisition or requisition is neither the one nor the other but a public purpose. Acquisition of sites for the building of hospitals or educational institutions by private benefactors will be a public purpose, though it will not strictly be a State or Union purpose. *State of Bombay* v. *Ali Gulshan*, AIR 1955 SC 810.

Any other purpose. The words 'any other purpose' in Art. 226 of the Constitution of India must be construed to refer to all purposes for which at English Common law the high prerogative writs are issued for the protection of the rights of the individuals, to check excess or abuse of powers. *Harendranath* v. *State of M.B.,* AIR 1950 MB 46, 51.

The words 'any other purpose' mean nothing more than any other purpose ancillary to the enforcement of any of the rights conferred by Part III of the Constitution. They cannot mean 'for the enforcement of any legal right and the performance of any legal duty'. *Prasad Srivastava* v. *State of Bhopal,* AIR 1952 Bhopal 52.

The expression "for any other purpose" would suggest that the aid of the Court may also be invoked by a person for the protection of his or her ordinary legal rights, interests and privileges or for the prevention of legal wrongs or injuries to him or her. *Parkasho* v. *State of U.P.*, AIR 1962 All 151.

The words must be read in context of what precedes the same so that the breach of the legal right or of a provision of law or of the Constitution as alleged and proved will come under 'any other purpose'.

Where the tenancy is for 'residential and manufacturing purposes' as distinguished from 'manufacturing purposes'. these 'mixed and multiple purposes' would take it outside the earlier clause and bring it within the later residuary clause 'for any other purpose'. *L.A. Saunders* v. *Land Corporation of Bengal Ltd.,* AIR 1955 Cal 169. [Transfer of Property Act (4 of 1882), S. 106]

Any other reasonable cause. The words "any other reasonable cause", in Section 13 Clause (*f*) of the Legal Practitioners Act (18 of 1879), are not confined to misconduct of which a practitioner is guilty in his professional capacity, but embrace all causes which in the opinion of the Court, may afford reasonable ground for his suspension or dismissal.

Any other relevant factor. Would mean a circumstance which is relevant and affords justification for refusal of a telephone connection. *Ginni Vitreous* v. *UOI,* AIR 1994 Ori 151, 155. [Telegraph Rules, 1951, Rule 416(2)(b)]

Any other shareholder applies for leave to buy at a valuation. The words employed, therein simply mean that the other shareholder has to inform the Court or to notify to it that he is prepared to buy at a valuation the share of the party asking for sale. *R. Ramamurthi Iyer* v. *Raja V. Rajeswara Rao*, AIR 1977 SC 643, 650. [Petition Act (4 of 1893), S. 3(1)]

Any other steps. A request for adjournment, before the filing of written statement, for the purpose of effecting a compromise cannot be held to be a step in the progress of the suit. *Daman Anand* v. *Hiralal,* AIR 1974 Punj 232, 234. [Arbitration Act (10 of 1940) (*repealed*), S. 34]

Any other substantial cause. The words "any other substantial cause" in O. XLVII, R. 27, CPC (5 of 1908), are not to be understood in a wide and unrestricted sense, but as referring to the same class of cases as the one specifically named.

Any other sufficient reason. The words "*any other sufficient reason,*" in CPC (5 of 1908), O. XLVII, R. 1 mean a reason sufficient on the grounds at least analogous to those specified immediately previously. *Ajit Kumar Rath* v. *State of Orissa,* AIR 2000 SC 85.

Any other undertaking. In the Phrase 'any other undertaking' occurring in S. 23(1) the word 'undertaking' is used in the meaning given to it in S. 2(v)—an undertaking which is engaged in production, supply, distribution or control of goods of any description or the provision of service of any kind. *Union of India* v. *Tata Engineering and Locomotive Co. Ltd.,* AIR 1972 Bom 301, 305. [(Repealed and replaced) Monopolies and Restrictive Trade Practices Act (54 of 1969), S. 2(v) and 23(1)(a)]

Any other wife living. The words "any other wife living" in clause (d) of S. 18 must be given their ordinary meaning. They are words of wide connotation and include wives except the one claiming relief and cannot be limited to any particular wife. *Mutyala Jaggamuna* v. *Mutyala Satyanarayanamurthy,* AIR 1958 AP 582, 585. [Hindu Adoptions and Maintenance Act (78 of 1956), S. 18(2)(d)]

Any party bound by the award. The expression 'any party bound by the award' refers to all workmen bound by the award, notice to terminate the said award can be given not by an individual workman but by a group of workmen acting collectively either through their union or otherwise and it is not necessary that such a group or the union through which it acts should represent the majority of workmen bound by the award. *Associated Cement Companies* v. *Their Workmen*, AIR 1960 SC 777, 781. [Industrial Disputes Act (14 of 1947), S. 19(6)]

Any person. The words "any person" would not include an absolute stranger who had no connection in the remotest degree with the prosecution and whose desire to help the prosecution was based on a personal grudge only.

The expression "any person", looking at the context in which Section 195 has been placed, would mean any person who is a resident in India. [*Vodafone International Holdings BV* v. *Union of India*, (2012) 6 SCC 613, para 419] [Income–tax Act (43 of 1961), S. 195].

The expression "any person" would mean any person who is a resident in India. [*Vodafone International Holdings BV* v. *Union of India*, (2012) 6 SCC 613, para 419] [Income-tax Act (43 of 1961), S. 195].

The expression "any person" occurring in Art. 14 may not include Government only in respect of those functions which are incidental to the ordinary functions of the Government. *Nabin Chandra Gantayet* v. *State of Orissa*, AIR 1957 Ori 56, 60. [Constitution of India, Art. 14]

The words 'any person' includes a person accused of an offence. There are no words limiting the section to persons other than a person accused of an offence and in the absence of any such limiting words it is not open to the court to read them into the section. *Sailendra Nath Sinha* v. *The State*, AIR 1955 Cal 247. [Indian Evidence Act (1 of 1872), S. 73]

The words 'any person' could only mean those persons in whom the workmen themselves were directly and substantially interested. *E. Sefton & Co.* v. *Textile Mill Mazdoor Union*, AIR 1958 All 80, 89. [Industrial Disputes Act (14 of 1947) 1947, S. 2(k)]

The expression "any person" means a person in whose employment or non-employment, or terms of employment, or conditions of labour, the workmen as a class have a direct or substantial interest—with whom they have a community of interest. *Michael Villavarayar* v. *Boatmen's Union*, AIR 1962 Mad 205, 209. [Industrial Disputes Act (14 of 1947), S. 2(k)]

"Any person" in the last part of the sub-section of Section 31 of Guardians and Wards Act (8 of 1890), does not mean a friend or relative only, but is wide enough to cover an application by persons other than relatives or friends of the minor the words 'any person' in S. 24 can only mean a person whose properties have been declared to be evacuee properties by the custodian or a person who moved the custodian to get the properties so declared or any other such aggrieved person. The words 'any person aggrieved' in the context of the Act cannot include any custodian as defined in the Act. *Md Sharfuddin* v. *RP Singh*, AIR 1961 SC 1312, 1314. [Administration of Evacuee Property Act (31 of 1950), S. 24]

The expression "any person" cannot be restricted to those on the managerial or administrative staff only. *Central Bank of India* v. *Their Workmen*, AIR 1960, SC 12, 23. [Banking Companies Act (10 of 1949), S. 10]

The expression "any persons" or "class of persons" are very general and are applicable not only to the creditors or debenture holders of a company but also to every person whose interests may be affected. *Orient Paper Mills Ltd.* v. *State,* AIR 1957 Ori 232, 234.

The expression "any person" occurring in Art. 14 may not include Government only in respect of those functions which are incidental to the ordinary functions of the Government. *Nabin Chandra Gentajit* v. *State of Orissa,* AIR 1957 Ori 56, 60. [Constitution of India, Art. 14]

'Any person' refers only to a person who is guilty of misappropriation or wilful waste of the funds of the institution etc.

It obviously refers to a trustee or some other person in management of the institution who is guilty of misappropriation. *Sri Vedagiri Lakshmi Narasimha Swami Temple* v. *Induru Pattabhirami Reddi*, AIR 1967 SC 781, 788. [Madras Hindu Religious and Charitable Endowments Act (19 of 1951), S. 74(5)]

Prima facie, such a person (any person) mentioned in S. 41(a) is expected to have a present and subsisting interest in the property. *Thayammal* v. *Adhimoolam Servai*, AIR 1956 Mad 304, 305. [Transfer of Property Act (4 of 1882), S. 91(a)]

The expression "any person" must be confined to a person intimately connected with the assessment of the year under appeal or revision. *I.T.O., A. Ward, Sitapur* v. *Murlidhar Bhagwan Das*, AIR 1965 SC 342, 349; *IT Commissioner* v. *Joharmal Parsuram*, AIR 1967 Pat 49, 53; *Daffadar Bhagar Singh and Sons* v. *Income Tax Officer, A Ward Ferozepure*, AIR 1969 SC 340, 342; *Ramkrishna Ramnath* v. *G. Lakshmi Narsimhan*, AIR 1970 Bom 30, 40; *Commissioner of Income Tax* v. *Ambala Flour Mills*, AIR 1972 SC 83, 87.

The words 'any person' will not include the liquidator himself. *Sailendra Nath Sinha (Dr.)* v. *State*, AIR 1955 Cal 29, 38.

The expression "any persons" or "class of persons" are very general and are applicable not only to the creditors or debenture holders of a company but also to every person whose interests may be affected. *Orient Paper Mills Ltd.* v. *The State*, AIR 1957 Ori 232, 234.

The words 'any person' are wide enough to include landlords, tenants, agents or middlemen. These words cover all who may be concerned with grant, renewal or continuance of protected tenancies; prohibiting the requiring of a sum as a condition, assignment of protected tenancies etc. *Farrell* v. *Alexander*, (1976) 2 All ER 721, 724, 726 (HL) [Rent Act, 1968, S. 85(1)(2)]

The expression includes a person who is subsequently arrayed as an accused in the trial in respect of smuggled gold. *Balakrishna Chhaganlal Soni* v. *State of West Bengal*, AIR 1974 SC 120, 124. [Customs Act (52 of 1962), S. 107-135(b)]

The words 'any person' includes a person accused of an offence. There are no words limiting the section to persons other than a person accused of an offence and in the absence of any such limiting words it is not open to the Court to read them into the section. *Shailendra Nath Sinha* v. *State,* AIR 1955 Cal 247. [Indian Evidence Act (1 of 1872), S. 73]

The words 'any person' could only mean those persons in whom the workmen themselves were directly and substantially interested. *E. Sefton & Co.* v. *Textile Mill Mazdoor Union,* AIR 1958 All 80, 89. [Industrial Disputes Act (14 of 1947), S. 2(k)]

The expression "any person" means a person in whose employment or non-employment, or terms of employment, or conditions of labour, the workmen as a class have a direct or substantial interest—with whom they have a community of interest. *Michael Villavarayar* v. *Boatmen's Union,* AIR 1962 Mad 205, 209. [Industrial Disputes Act (14 of 1947), S. 2(k)]

Prima facie, such a person (any person) mentioned in S. 41(a) is expected to have a present and subsisting interest in the property. A contingent interest not being a vested interest is not present or a subsisting interest in the property. *Thayammal* v. *Adhimoolam Servai,* AIR 1956 Mad 304, 305. [T.P. Act (4 of 1882), S. 91(a)]

Any person claiming under him. The expression 'any person claiming under him' means only the person who has derived any interest from or through the transfer, namely, assignee or legal representative of the transferor. *Raju Roy* v. *Kasinath Roy,* AIR 1956 Pat 308, 311. [T.P. Act (4 of 1882), S. 53-A]

Any person in whom any of the director of the company is interested. For the purposes of this sub-section, the expression "any person in whom any of the director of the company is interested" means—

(a) any private company of which any such director is a director or member;

(b) any body corporate at a general meeting of which not less than twenty-five per cent of the total voting power may be exercised or controlled by any such director, or by two or more such directors, together; or

(c) any body corporate, the Board of directors, managing director or manager, whereof is accustomed to act in accordance with the directions or instructions of the Board, or of any director or directors, of the lending company. [Companies Act (18 of 2013), section 185(2), *Expln.*]

Any person interested. The 'person interested in the objection' would seem to cover primarily persons who are likely to be adversely affected by the success of the objection. *Mohd. Ibrahim Sahib* v. *Land Acquisition Officer,* AIR 1958 AP 226, 229. [Land Acquisition Act (1 of 1894), S. 18(repealed)]

Any person who is not duly licensed. The expression 'any person who is not duly licensed' means a person who does not hold permit or authority, by whatever name called, granted in accordance with law by licensing authority, (and as such a person who holds a driving licence or a learner's driving licence does not come under the expression).

Any person whose interests are affected by sale. The expression does not include any creditor of the judgment-debtor who has even obtained a decree against the judgment-debtor. *S.K. Sundaram* v. *M. Joshi Rajamannar Chettiar,* AIR 1973 Mad 166, 167. [CPC (5 of 1908), O. XXI, R. 90]

Any proceeding. The expression 'any proceeding' occurring under section 633 of the Companies Act, 1956 (1 of 1956) replaced with Companies Act, 2013, cannot be read out of context and treated in isolation. It must be construed in the light of the penal provisions. Otherwise what will happen is the penal clauses under the various other Acts would be rendered ineffective by application of said section 633. Again, if Parliament intended section 633 to have a coverage wider than the Act, it would have specifically provided for it as, otherwise, it is a sound rule of construction to confine the provisions of a statute to itself. *Rabindra Chamria* v. *Registrar of Companies*, AIR 1992 SC 398.

Any proceeding under the Act. The right of appeal is one conferred under the Act and therefore it is a proceeding under the Act. Any proceeding under the Act is a proceeding in respect of a right conferred under the Act. *Jalasutram Annapurnamma* v. *Jalasutram Ramakrishnan Sastry,* AIR 1959 AP 49. [Hindu Marriage Act (25 of 1955), Ss. 24 and 28]

Any property. The words 'any property' are wide enough to include paddy lands. *Upendra Das* v. *Krishna Sahu,* AIR 1972 Ori 12, 13. [CPC (5 of 1908), O. XXXIX, R. (1)]

Any property possessed by a female Hindu. If a contingent interest created by a Hindu dying prior to Hindu Succession Act fails and the property reverts to his estate, it may very well develop as a limited estate on a female heir by virtue of the provisions of the Hindu Law in force prior into the coming to force of the Hindu Succession Act. *Jegannathan Pillai* v. *Kunjithapatham Pillai,* AIR 1972 Mad 390, 398. [Hindu Succession Act (30 of 1956), S. 14(1)]

Word 'possessed' means lawfully possessed and does not refer to a case where the person in possession is a trespasser.

Any structure. The word "any structure" relates to structure erected or acquired by purchase or gift on such land for a residential, manufacturing or business purpose. [*Nemai Chandra Kumar* v. *Mani Square Limited*, (2015) 14 SCC 203, para 36].

Any structure. The words 'any structure' occurring in Section 2(5) of the Calcutta Thika Act would ordinarily include a pucca structure. But the Calcutta Thika is a special Act and the general law regulating relationship of landlord and tenant, including the tenant, is contained in Chapter V of the Transfer Property Act, in Section 108(p) of which there is a prohibition against the lessee raising pucca or permanent structures on the land of the tenancy, without lessor's consent. The Calcutta Thika Tenancy Act is not a complete Code. It deals only with some aspects or incidents of thika tenancy. In respect of matters which are not governed by the Thika Tenancy Act, Transfer of Property Act applies. For the rights and liabilities of the tenants, therefore, one has to look into the provisions of Section 108, T.P. Act. The provisions contained in Section 2(5) of the Calcutta Thika Tenancy Act and those in Section 108(p) of the Transfer of Property Act, 1882 are not necessarily repugnant. It is possible to harmonise the provisions contained in the two sections if it be held that the expression 'any structure' in Section 2(5) of the Calcutta Tenancy Act means any structure other than the type of structure referred to in Section 108 of the Transfer of Property Act, the construction whereof is prohibited under the latter section. The expression 'any structure' in Section 2(5) must therefore be held not to include a permanent structure. *Manmatho Nath Mukherjee* v. *Banarsi*, MLJ : QD (1956-1960) Vol. IV C2201 : 63 Cal WN 824.

Any surety. The term "any surety" will include not only a surety who has given some security but also one who has given only a personal guarantee. *Maharashtra State Financial Corpn.* v. *Jaycee Drugs and Pharmaceuticals Pvt. Ltd.*, (1991) 1 SCC 637, 653.

Anyone. The word 'anyone' should be interpreted as 'everyone', (*Chief Inspector of Mines* v. *Karam Chand Thaper*, AIR 1961 SC 838 Followed). *Banwarilal Agarwalla* v. *State of Bihar*, AIR 1961 SC 849, 850. [Mines Act (35 of 1952), S. 76]

Anyone accident. A person looking at the occurrence subjectively, like the one who is injured in the collision, will say that he met with an accident, 'Anyone accident' means 'accident to anyone'. *Motor Owners Insurance Co. Ltd.* v. *J.K. Modi*, AIR 1981 SC 2059, 2064.

Anyone of the directors. The expression "anyone of the directors" means "everyone of the directors". *Chief Inspector of Mines* v. *Karam Chand Thapar*, AIR 1961 SC 838, 849. [Mines Act (35 of 1952), S. 76]

Anything. The word 'anything' is of the widest import and is equivalent to 'everything'. *Tej Kiran Jain* v. *Sanjiva Reddy*, AIR 1970 SC 1573, 1574. [Constitution of India, Art. 105(2)]

Anything said in Parliament. It means during the sitting of Parliament. *Tej Kiran Jain* v. *Sanjeeva Reddy*, AIR 1970 SC 1573.

Apartheid. Policy by discrimination and segregation; racial segregation.

"Apartment". Means a part of the property intended for any type of independent use, including one or more rooms or enclosed spaces located on one or more floors or part or parts thereof, in a building, intended to be used for residential purposes and with a direct exit to a public street, road or highway or to a common area leading to such street, road or highway. [Haryana Apartment Ownership Act (10 of 1983), S. 3(a) as cited in DLF Limited v. Manmohan Lowe, (2014) 12 SCC 231, para 41].

"Apartment owner". "Apartment owner" means the person or persons owning an apartment and undivided interest in the common area and facilities in the percentage specified and established in the declaration. [Haryana Apartment Ownership Act (10 of 1983), S. 3(b) as cited in *DLF Limited* v. *Manmohan Lowe*, (2014) 12 SCC 231, para 42].

Apex. The summit or highest point of anything; the top.

Apex Court. The highest Court.

Apices juris non sunt jura. (*Maxim*) Extreme points of law are not laws.

Apologize. To excuse oneself; to make an apology or excuse; acknowledge or express regret for a fault.

Apology. There cannot be both justification and an apology. The two things are incompatible. An apology is not a weapon of defence to purge the guilty of their offence; nor is it intended to operate as a universal panacea, but it is intended to be evidence of real contriteness. *M.Y. Shareef* v. *Judges of Nagpur High Court*, AIR 1955 SC 19, 23. [Contempt of Courts Act, 1952, S. 4]

The apology means a regretful acknowledgement or an excuse for failure. An explanation offered to a person affected by one's action that no offence was intended, coupled with the expression of regret for any that may have been given. Apology should be unquestionable in sincerity. It should be tampered with a sense of genuine remorse and repentance, and not a calculated strategy to avoid punishment. [*Bal Kishan Giri* v. *State of U.P.*, (2014) 7 SCC 280, para 15].

Apothecary. A person who professes to be judge of internal disease by its symptoms, and applies himself to cure that disease by medicines.

Apparel of the ship. The equipment of a ship (such as masts, sails, rigging and anchors). [Naval and Aircraft Prize Act (59 of 1971), S. 2(1)].

Apparent. Evident; clear; obvious to eye or mind [Indian Easements Act (5 of 1882), S. 5]; seeming, as distinct from (though not necessarily opposed to) what really is. [Indian Contract Act (9 of 1872), S. 16(2)(a)].

Apparent agent. Reasonable appearance of a person, having authority to act for another, regardless of whether actual authority has been conferred.

Apparent authority. In the law of agency, such authority as the principal knowingly or negligently permits the agent to assume, or which he holds the agent out as possessing. Such authority as a reasonably prudent man, using diligence and discretion in view of the principal's conduct, would naturally suppose the agent to possess. (*Black*) JOHN ALAN APPLEMAN & JEAN APPLEMAN, *Insurance Law and Practice,* S. 8674 (1981).

Apparent consideration. In this Chapter, unless the context otherwise requires "APPARENT CONSIDERATION",—

(1) in relation to any immovable property transferred, being immovable property of the nature referred to in sub-clause (i) of clause (e), means,—

(i) if the transfer is by way of sale, the consideration for such transfer as specified in the instrument of transfer;

(ii) if the transfer is by way of exchange,—

(A) in a case where the consideration for the transfer consists of a thing or things only the price that such thing or things would ordinarily fetch on sale in the open market on the date of execution of the instrument of transfer;

(B) in a case where the consideration for the transfer consists of a thing or things and a sum of money, the aggregate of the price that such thing or things would ordinarily fetch on sale in the open market on the date of execution of the instrument of transfer and such sum;

(iii) if the transfer is by way of lease,—

(A) in a case where the consideration for the transfer consists of premium only, the amount of premium as specified in the instrument of transfer;

(B) in a case where the consideration for the transfer consists of rent only, the aggregate of the moneys (if any) payable by way of rent and the amounts for the service or things forming part of or constituting the rent, as specified in the instrument of transfer;

(C) in a case where the consideration for the transfer consists of premium and rent, the aggregate of the amount of the premium, the moneys (if any) payable by way of rent and the amounts for the service or things forming part of or constituting the rent, as specified in the instrument of transfer, and where the whole or any part of the consideration for such transfer is payable on any date or dates falling after the date of such transfer, the value of the consideration payable after such date shall be deemed to be the discounted value of such consideration, as on the date of such transfer, determined by adopting the rate of interest at eight per cent. per annum.

(2) in relation to any immovable property transferred, being immovable property of the nature referred to in sub-clause (ii) of clause (e), means,—

(i) in a case where the consideration for the transfer consists of a sum of money only, such sum;

(ii) in a case where the consideration for the transfer consists of a thing or things only, the price that such thing or things would ordinarily fetch on sale in the open market on the date of the transfer;

(iii) in a case where the consideration for the transfer consists of a thing or things and a sum of money, the aggregate of the price that such things or things would ordinarily fetch on sale in the open market on the date of the transfer and such sum, and where the whole or any part of the consideration for such transfer is payable on any date or dates falling after the date of such transfer, the value of the consideration payable after such date shall be deemed to be the discounted value of such consideration, as on the date of such transfer, determined by adopting the rate of interest at eight per cent. per annum. [Income-tax Act (43 of 1961), S. 269A(a)]

Apparent easement. "An apparent easement is one the existence of which is shown by some permanent sign which, upon careful inspection by a competent person, would be visible to him." [Indian Easements Act (5 of 1882), S. 5]

Apparent easements are "not only those which must necessarily be seen, but those which may be seen and known on a careful inspection by a person ordinarily conversant with the subject." (GALE on *Easements, 2nd Fd. 100*)

Apparent error. An apparent error means a patent 'mistake', an error which one could point put without any elaborate argument. *K.C. Thapar Bros* v. *State of U.P.*, AIR 1976 SC 2101, 2107. [U.P. Sales Tax Act (15 of 1948), S. 22]

Appeal. Is the right of entering a superior Court and invoking its aid and interposition to redress the error of the Court below. (*per* WESTBURY. C., *AG* v. *Sillem*, 10 HLC 704 : 33 LJ Ex. 209.)

Appeal. quoted in Dayawalti v. Inderjit AIR 1966 SC 1423.

An 'appeal' is an application by a party to an appellate Court asking it to set aside or revise a decision of a subordinate Court. *Nagendra Nath Dey* v. *Suresh Chandra Dey,* AIR 1932 PC 165 : 59 (IA) 283 **as referred in** *Tirupati Balaji Developers (P.) Ltd.* v. *State of Bihar,* (2004) 5 SCC 1, 15 para 11.

A proceeding taken before a superior Court or authority for reversing or modifying decision of an inferior Court or authority on ground of error; a case so appealed. [CPC (5 of 1908), O. XLI, R. 1(1)]; a call for help; a language addressed to or likely to influence some particular principle, faculty *etc.*; to make an appeal; appeal from (a Court); appeal from (a decree); appeal to (a person); appeal to (a Court or tribunal); accusation.

An appeal must be against a decree as pronounced and though it may be rested on an argument directed to special items, it must be against the decree and the decree alone. [Constitution of India, Art. 133(1)]

Appeal and memorandum of appeal. The appeal is the judicial examination; the memorandum of appeal contains the grounds on which the judicial examination is invited. *Lakshmiratan Engineering Works Ltd.* v. *Assistant Commissioner* (*Judicial*) *I, Sales Tax*, AIR 1968 SC 488, 492.

Appeal in forma pauperis. An appeal by an indigent party for whom costs of the Court are waived.

Appealable. Liable to be appealed against; capable of being appealed; admitting of appeal; removable to a higher tribunal for decision.

Appealable decision. Decree or order which is sufficiently final to receive appellate review.

Appealed from. No decree can be treated as a decree "appealed from" so long as there is before the Court nothing more than an application by a party to be declared entitled to appeal. [CPC (5 of 1908), O. XLV, R. 13(2)(*c*)]

Appeals Court. Court created to review appeals from inferior Courts or administrative agencies. It is also called as Appellate Court.

See also Appellate Court.

Appear. To enter or make appearance; to stand in presence, as parties or advocates before a Court.

A party cannot be held to have appeared under CPC (5 of 1908), O. IX, R. 13 merely because he is alleged to have been seen within the premises of the Court on the day of the trial.

Where counsel has done some act amounting to participation at the hearing, so that the same constitutes appearance of the party through counsel, the withdrawal of the counsel after refusal of an adjournment sought, does not amount to non-appearance of the party. *Rama Rao* v. *Shabtibai,* AIR 1977 MP 222, 235. [CPC (5 of 1908), O. XVII, Rr. 2 and 3]

The word 'appear' includes voluntary appearance of the accused, even in the absence of any summons or warrant. *State of Karnataka* v. *Baswanth Rao,* 1966 Mys 71, 72.

To present oneself formally before a tribunal, hence also to act as a counsel; to seem [IPC (45 of 1860), S. 161, ill. (b)]; to come forth into view; to be present.

Appearance. The coming into a Court as a party in a suit or other proceeding, whether as plaintiff or defendant; ordinarily, the word is used particularly to signify the act by which a person against whom a suit has been commenced submits himself to the jurisdiction of the Court.

Appearance, in CPC (5 of 1908), O. XLI, Rr. 17, 19, means effective appearance.

Appearance in a proceeding may be either in person or by pleader, attorney or recognized agent; or by next friend or by guardian *ad litem* or committee in lunacy.

The action of appearing formally [CrPC 1973 (2 of 1974), S. 88]; [Registration Act (16 of 1908), S. 34(2)]; looks [IPC (45 of 1860), S. 248].

Appearance docket. List of the participating lawyers and parties, in an action, together with a brief abstract of the successive steps in the action.

Appearing. Plainly set forth in a document; seeming; coming in view; being manifest.

Appears. The appropriate meaning of the word 'appears' is 'seems'. *Pyarelal* v. *State of Rajasthan*, AIR 1963 SC 1094, 1095. [Indian Evidence Act (1 of 1872), S. 24]

Appears to have been committed. The expression 'appears to have been committed' means that at the present stage there should be *prima facie* material before the Court to indicate that the offences complained of are likely to have-been committed. *Kapoor* v. *Pratap Singh Kaison,* AIR 1966 All 66, 68.

Appellant. Is one who appeals against a decision, or removes a cause from a lower to a higher tribunal.

One who makes an appeal. [CPC (5 of 1908), O. XLI, R. 10(1)].

"Appellant". Means—

(i) a person in whose case an appeal or a writ petition or special leave petition has been filed either by him or by the income-tax authority or by both, before an appellate forum and such appeal or petition is pending as on the specified date;

(ii) a person in whose case an order has been passed by the Assessing Officer, or an order has been passed by the Commissioner (Appeals) or the Income Tax Appellate Tribunal in an appeal, or by the High Court in a writ petition, on or before the specified date, and the time for filing any appeal or special leave petition against such order by that person has not expired as on that date;

(iii) a person who has filed his objections before the Dispute Resolution Panel under section 144C of the Income-tax Act, 1961 (43 of 1961) and the Dispute Resolution Panel has not issued any direction on or before the specified date;

(iv) a person in whose case the Dispute Resolution Panel has issued direction under sub-section (5) of section 144C of the Income-tax Act and the Assessing Officer has not passed any order under sub-section (13) of that section on or before the specified date;

(v) a person who has filed an application for revision under section 264 of the Income-tax Act and such application is pending as on the specified date.

Explanation.—For the removal of doubts, it is hereby clarified that the expression "appellant" shall not include and shall be deemed never to have been included a person in whose case a writ petition or special leave petition or any other proceeding has been filed either by him or by the income-tax authority or by both before an appellate forum, arising out of an order of the Settlement Commission under Chapter XIX-A of the Income-tax Act, and such petition or appeal is either pending or is disposed of. [Direct Tax Vivad se Vishwas Act, 2020 (3 of 2020), section 2(1)(a)]

Appellate. Pertaining to appeals; having cognizance of appeals; as an appellate Court; appellate jurisdiction.

Appellate stands in contradistinction to original jurisdiction; and as the former implies that the appeal must be to a superior Court, so the latter implies that the case must commence in an inferior Court, not having final jurisdiction; and, therefore, liable to be carried up to a higher Court, for final decision.

Pertaining to appeal; taking cognizance of appeals. [CPC (5 of 1908), S. 108].

"Appellate Authority" means the authority specified in, or under, sub-section (1) of section 15. [Foreign Trade (Development and Regulation) Act (22 of 1992), section 2(b)]

'Appellate authority' means the Deputy Commissioner (Appeals), the Commissioner (Appeals) or the Appellate Tribunal. [Income-tax Act (43 of 1961), section 158A, *Expln.* (a)] [Wealth-tax Act, 1957, section 18C, *Expln.* (a)]

"Appellate authority" means an authority appointed by the appropriate Government to exercise such functions in such area as may be specified by that Government by notification in the Official Gazette. [Industrial Relations Code, 2020 (35 of 2020), section 2(a)]

"Appellate court". Would not only include the first appellate court, but also include the second appellate court and the Supreme Court, once the Supreme Court has granted leave to file appeal to the appellant. [*Karedla Parthasaradhi* v. *Gangula Ramanamma*, (2014) 15 SCC 789, para 32].

Appellate court-house. A place, hall or chamber where an appellate Court functions. [CPC (5 of 1908), O. XLI, R. 14(1)].

Appellate decree. A decree passed on an appeal. [CPC (5 of 1908, S. 108(a)].

Appellate jurisdiction is the cognisance which a superior Court takes of a case removed to it, by appeal or otherwise from the decision of an inferior Court.

Jurisdiction to hear and dispose of appeals [CPC (5 of 1908), Ss. 105(1), 106 and Constitution of India, Art. 132, margin].

Appellate Tribunal. Means the National Company Law Appellate Tribunal constituted under section 410 of the Companies Act, 2013 (18 of 2013). [S. 2(4) of the Companies Act, 2013 (18 of 2013)]

"Appellate Tribunal" means the Appellate Tribunal constituted under section 347A of the Delhi Municipal Corporation Act, 1957. [Delhi Fire Prevention and Fire Safety Act (56 of 1986), section 2(b)]

Appellate Tribunal" means the Appellate Tribunal established under section 30 [Prohibition of Benami Property Transactions Act (45 of 1988), section 2(3)]

"Appellate Tribunal" means the Appellate Tribunal referred to in sub-section (1) of section 33C [Aadhaar (Targeted Delivery of Financial & Other Subsidies, Benefits & Services) Act (18 of 2016), section 2(bb)]

"Appellate Tribunal" means the Telecom Disputes Settlement and Appellate Tribunal established under section 14 of the Telecom Regulatory Authority of India Act, 1997 (24 of 1997). [Digital Personal Data Protection Act, 2023 (22 of 2023), section 2(a)]

"Appellate Tribunal" means the Competition Appellate Tribunal established under sub-section (1) of section 53-A of the Act. [Competition Commission of India (Form and Time of Preparation of Annual Report) Rules, 2008 rule 2(c);

Competition Appellate Tribunal (Form and Fee for filing an appeal and Fee for filing compensation Applications Rules, 2009, rule 2(1)(c); Competition Act, 2002 (12 of 2003), section 53-A(1)]

Appendant. Attached or belonging to property as an additional but subsidiary right.

Appendant easement. Easement created for the benefit of another tract of land, the use of which is incident to the ownership of the land. Also called as Appurtenant easement.

Appendix. Something added; an adjunct, concomitant, appendage, or accessory.

An addition subjoined to a document or book having some contributory value but not essential to completeness. [CPC (5 of 1908), O. XLVIII, R. 3].

Appertaining. Belonging to; to have relation to; usually occupied with, or lying to; peculiar to. (*Burrill*)

Belonging as part to the whole; relating.

Appliance. A household or office apparatus.

Applicable. Capable of being applied; fit; suitable or right to be applied. [T.P. Act (4 of 1882), S. 55 and IPC (45 of 1860), S. 41].

Applicable tax. For the purposes of the rules under the provisions of this Chapter, the "APPLICABLE TAX" shall include central tax and State tax or central tax and the Union territory tax, as the case may be and the cess, if any, payable under the Goods and Services Tax (Compensation to States) Act, 2017 (15 of 2017). [Central Goods and Services Tax Rules, 2017, R. 140, *Explanation*].

Applicant. "APPLICANT" includes—

(i) a petitioner;

(ii) any person from or through whom an applicant derives his right to apply;

(iii) any person whose estate is represented by the applicant as executor, administrator or other representative. [Limitation Act (36 of 1963), S. 2(a)]

"APPLICANT" means—

(i) (a) a non-resident setting up a joint venture in India in collaboration with a non-resident or a resident; or

(b) a resident setting up a joint venture in India in collaboration with a non-resident; or

(c) a wholly owned subsidiary Indian company, of which the holding company is a foreign company, who or which, as the case may be, proposes to undertake any business activity in India;

(ii) a joint venture in India; or

(iii) a resident falling within any such class or category of persons, as the Central Government may, by notification in the Official Gazette, specify in this behalf, and which or who, as the case may be, makes application for advance ruling under sub-section (*l*) of Section 28H. [Customs Act (52 of 1962, S. 28E(c) *as substituted by Finance Act (18 of 2005), S. 65(a)]*

"APPLICANT" means a non-resident setting up a joint venture in India in collaboration with a non-resident or resident, or a resident setting up a joint venture in India in collaboration with a non-resident, making application. [Central Excise Act (1 of 1944), S. 23A(c)]

"APPLICANT" means a person or an organization that applies, in Form 1, for granting of authorization to perform specific activities connected with handling of hazardous waste. [Air (Prevention and Control of Pollution) Act (14 of 1981), S. 2(c)]

One who makes an application to Court.

Applicatio est vita regulae. (*Maxim*) Application is the life of a rule. (*Burrill*)

Application. "APPLICATION" includes a petition. [Limitation Act (36 of 1963), S. 2(b)]

"APPLICATION" means and includes original application (O.A.), instituted under Section 19 of the Act, Review Application (R.A.), Transferred Application (T.A.), Miscellaneous Application (M.A.) and Petition for Transfer (P.T.) but not any interlocutory application instituted in the case already instituted before the Tribunal. [Debts Recovery Tribunal Regulations of Practice, 1997, S. 3(ii)]

A petition to Court; a request to a judicial officer; the act of making or preferring a request. (*Burrill*)

If an application could be understood in a generic sense as a prayer made to an authority for some relief to set aside an order of another authority and such an application is under the Statute, it would amount to an Appeal. [Companies Act (1 of 1956) replaced with Companies Act, 2013, S. 111].

"Application" means the practical use or relevance (of something to something); the application of a statutory provision, therefore, is by definition case related and as opposed to interpretation, the application or non-application of a statutory provision would always depend on the exact facts of a given case. Anyone associated with the process of adjudication fully knows that even the slightest difference in the facts of two cases can make a world of difference on the question whether or not a statutory provision can be fairly and reasonably applied to it. [*Sudevanand* v. *State through CBI*, (2012) 3 SCC 387, para 28.2].

The action of applying; a petition or request; the putting of anything to use; practical operation.

"APPLICANT" means—

(A) any person who—

(I) is a non-resident referred to in sub-clause (*i*) of clause (*a*); or

(II) is a resident referred to in sub-clause (*ii*) of clause (*a*); or

(III) is a resident referred to in sub-clause (*ii-a*) of clause (*a*) falling within any such class or category of persons as the

Central Government may, by notification in the Official Gazette, specify; or

(IV) is a resident falling within any such class or category of persons as the Central Government may, by notification in the Official Gazette, specify in this behalf; or

(V) is referred to in sub-clause (*iv*) of clause (*a*)

and makes an application under sub-section (1) of Section 245-Q;

(B) an application as defined in clause (*c*) of Section 28-E of the Customs Act, 1962 (52 of 1962);

(C) an application as defined in clause (*c*) of Section 23-A of the Central Excise Act, 1944 (1 of 1944);

(D) an applicant as defined in clause (*b*) of Section 96-A of the Finance Act, 1994 (32 of 1994). [Income-tax Act (43 of 1961), S. 245-N as substituted by Finance Act (7 of 2017)].

"APPLICANT" means any person,—

(*i*) holding a valid Importer-exporter Code Number granted under Section 7 of the Foreign Trade (Development and Regulation) Act, 1992 (22 of 1992); or

(*ii*) exporting any goods to India; or

(*iii*) with a justifiable cause to the satisfaction of the Authority, who makes an application for advance ruling under Section 28-H. [Customs Act (52 of 1962), S. 28-E(c) as substituted by Finance Act (13 of 2018)].

"APPLICANT" means a petitioner or an appellant or any other person or entity capable of making an application including an interlocutory application or a petition or an appeal under the Act. [National Company Law Tribunal Rules, 2016, R. 2(4)].

Application for execution of a decree. Application for execution of a decree includes application by an auction-purchaser for delivery of possession. [Limitation Act (36 of 1963), S. 15(1) & Article 134]

Application gateway. If a person other than one entitled applies for execution, or if the person entitled applies for execution in a mode and for a relief outside the decree, the application is "not in accordance with law". [*Bando Krishna Kunbargi* v. *Narasimha Konher Deshpande*, 14 Bom LR 861 : (1913) ILR 37 Bom 42 : 17 Ind. Cas. 210 (212). *Per* CHANDAUARKAR, J].

One form of a firewall in which valid application-level data must be checked or confirmed before allowing a connection. In the case of an FTP connection, the application gateway appears as a FTP server to the client and a FTP client to the server. (*Cyber Law*)

If a person other than one entitled applies for execution, or if the person entitled applies for execution in a mode and for a relief outside the decree, the application is 'not in accordance with law'. [*Bando Krishna* v. *Narasinha*, 14 Bom LR 861 : 37 Bom 42 : 17 Ind Cas 210 (212). *Per* Chandauarkar, J]

Application is entertained. Merely because an application made by an employed person is taken on file or numbered, it cannot be said that it has been legally entertained. If the application is dismissed on the ground that the subject-matter of the claim would not fall within the Act, it cannot be said that the application is entertained. *Madras Provincial Type Foundary Worker's Union* v. *Ramalinga Mudaliar,* AIR 1957 Mad 68, 69. [Payment of Wages Act (4 of 1936), S. 15(3)]

Application for registration of a trade mark. Includes the trade mark for goods or services contained in it. [Trade Marks Rules, 2017, R. 2(1)(c)].

Application of mind. Consideration implies 'application of mind' in respect of granting sanction for prosecution under Section 19 of the Act. The order of sanction must *ex facie* disclose that the sanctioning authority had considered the evidence and other material placed before it. *State (Anti-Corruption Branch), Govt. of N.C.T. of Delhi* v. *R.C. Anand (Dr.)*, AIR 2004 SC 3693 : (2004) 4 SCC 615, 621, para 13. [Prevention of Corruption Act (49 of 1988), S. 19]

"**Application program interface (API)**" means a set of routines, protocols, and tools for building software applications. [Information Technology (Preservation and Retention of Information by Intermediaries Providing Digital Locker Facilities) Rules, 2016, R. 2(1)(c)].

Application server. *Server* software that manages one or more other pieces of software in a way that makes the managed software available over a network, usually to a *Web* server. By having a piece of software manage other software packages it is possible to use resources like memory and database access more efficiently than if each of the managed packages responded directly to requests. *(Matisse Enzer-Glossary of Internet Terms)*

Application software. It is a software written for or by an end user that performs a service or relates to the user's work. (*Information Technology*)

'Application software' such as word processing programs, databases, *etc*., which perform the tasks for which we use computers. [*Commr. of Customs* v. *Hewlett Packard India Sales (P). Ltd.,* (2007) 8 SCC 404, 410, para 17]

Application system. A group of wares designed to offer solutions for commercial data processing, office and communications environments, as well as to provide simple, consistent programmer and end user interfaces for businesses of all sizes. (*Information Technology*)

Applied. The word "applied" need not necessarily imply "spent". Even if an amount is irretrievably ear-marked and allocated for the charitable or religious purpose or purposes, it may be said to have been "applied" to the purpose(s). *CIT* v. *Radhaswami Sabha,* (1964) 25 ITR 472, 522 (All). [Income Tax Act (43 of 1961), S. 11]

Applied art. Works of art used for industrial or commercial purposes. Article 2(1) of Berne Convention allows its Member States to determine the extent of the application of their laws as well as the conditions under which works of applied art, industrial designs and models shall be protected. (*Copyright*)

Apply. To have practical operation; to have a valid reference to [IPC (45 of 1860), S. 4]; to use or employ for a particular purpose; to appropriate and devote to a particular use, object, demand, or subject-matter [T.P. Act (4 of 1882), S. 11]; to make request or application [IPC (45 of 1860), S. 92, ill. (c)]; to lay or put in contract; to lay on as applique [Trade and Merchandise Marks Act (43of 1958), S. 76(1) (repealed)].

Applying in accordance with law. The expression "Applying in accordance with law" means "applying to the Court to do something which, by law, the Court is competent to do." It does not mean applying to the Court to do something which either to the decree-holder's direct knowledge of facts, or his presumed knowledge of law, it is incompetent to do.

Appoint. To designate a person to discharge the duties of an office or trust to nominate; to fix by a decree, order, command, resolve, decision or mutual agreement; to settle.

Appoint means to ordain or nominate to an office", (and even if the arbitrator or the umpire as such does not accept then also the fact of appointment has happened and is independent of the subsequent acceptance or refusal of the arbitrator or the umpire as such). *Keshav Singh Dwarka Das* v. *Indian Engineering Co.,* AIR 1969 Bom 227, 229. [Arbitration Act, (10 of 1940) (*repealed*), S. 8(1)(b)]

Appointed. The regular employment of a person in a particular function, is equivalent to his being "appointed" to it, unless some special mode of appointment is prescribed. (*Frost* v. *Bolland*, 5 B & C 611)

Appointed date. For the purposes of this section, "APPOINTED DATE" means the date which the Securities and Exchange Board of India may, by notification in the Official Gazette, appoint and different appointed dates may be appointed for different recognised stock exchanges. [Securities Contracts (Regulation) Act (42 of 1956), S. 4A, *Expln. as inserted by Securities Contracts (Regulation) Act (42 of 1956), S. 3]*

Appointed day. Means such date as the Central Government may, by notification in Official Gazette, appoint for the merger of the acquired territories under Section 3, after causing the territories to be acquired demarcated for the purpose, and different dates may be appointed for the merger of such territories into different states. [Acquired Territories (Merger) Act (64 of 1960), S. 2(b)]

Appointee. One who is appointed.

Appointing authority. It must be understood as authority who appointed the person concerned. *Omprakash* v. *Union of India*, AIR 1975 SC 1265. [Appointing Authority Central Civil Services (Temporary Service) Rules, 1965, S. 2(a)].

Appointment. For the purposes of this Chapter, "appointment" includes re-appointment. [Companies Act (18 of 2013), Chapter X, section 139(1), *Expln.*]

For the purposes of this Sanhita, "appointment" does not include the first appointment, posting or promotion of a person by the Government to any Service, or post in connection with the affairs of the Union or of a State, where under any law, such appointment, posting or promotion is required to be made by the Government. **[Bharatiya Nagarik Suraksha Sanhita, 2023 (46 of 2023), section 8, *Explanation*]**

In international trade, the action of designating an agent to act on someone's behalf. The appointment can either be formally by deed, in writing, or even verbal

The designation of a person to discharge the duties of an office or trust by the person or persons having authority therefor.

The word 'appointment' in Art. 229(1) is to be construed according to the *axiom* that the greater includes the less. The power of appointment conferred by Art. 229(1) includes the power to suspend, dismiss, remove or compulsorily retire from service. *Chief Justice, A.P.* v. *L.V.A. Dikshitulu*, AIR 1979 SC 193, 199. [Constitution of India, Art. 229(1)]

Appointment just like the word 'Manager' is not a term of art. and therefore has to receive its ordinary actual and normal meaning. *State Wakf Board, Madras* v. *Subramanyam,* AIR 1977 Mad 79, 82. [Limitation Act (36 of 1963), Art. 96; Wakfs Act (29 of 1954), S. 15]

The action of nominating to or placing in an office; the office itself. [Constitution of India, Art. 16(4)]; fixing.

"APPOINTMENT" for the purposes of Chapter X of Act 18 of 2013, 'appointment' includes reappointment. [*Explanation* to section 139(1) of the Companies Act, 2013 (18 of 2013)]

Apportion. To divide or partition or assign in just proportion; to distribute; to allot.

To divide and distribute proportionately [Industrial Finance Corporation Act (15 of 1948), S. 30(a), prove. (*Repealed by Act 23, 1993*)].

Apportionable. Capable of being apportioned; liable to be apportioned. [T.P. Act (4 of 1882), S. 36].

Apportionment. The act of apportioning; dividing or making into parts (*Burrill*); the dividing into just proportions or shares.

The action of apportioning; the division of rights or liabilities among several persons entitled or liable to them in accordance with their respective interests. [State Financial Corporations Act (63 of 1951), S. 3A(2)(d)].

Appraisal. An act of estimating or evaluating especially by one fitted to judge.

Appraisal clause. Provision of an insurance policy which allows either the insurer or the insured to demand an independant estimation of a claimed loss.

Appraise. To estimate; to value in current money; to set a price upon; used especially of the action of a person or persons appointed for the purpose under direction of law or by agreement of parties interested : as to appraise the goods and estate of a deceased person; or to appraise the value of a jewel offered as pledge.

Appraisement. Valuation of goods or property, particularly of goods seized in execution, or by distraint, or under the order of a Court.

Appraiser. To appraise is to set a price or fix a value upon a thing, and an appraiser is one, who appraises. A person appointed by competent authority to ascertain and state the true value of property submitted to his inspection, and who is usually sworn to perform such duty conscientiously and to the best of his ability. (*Burrill*)

Appreciate. To rise in value; to understand; to recognize the value in a person or a thing. (*Ballentine's Law Dictionary, 3rd Edn.*)

To estimate justly; to set a price or value on when used with reference to the nature and effect of an act, "appreciate" may be synonymous with "know" or "understand" or "realize". (*Black*)

Appreciation. The act of valuing or estimating.

Apprehend. To seize under process of law; to take into custody; make prisoner; arrest by legal warrant or authority. "The robber was apprehended selling his plunder".

To seize in the name of law; to arrest; to lay hold upon; [Companies Act (1 of 1956) replaced with Companies Act, 2013, S. 477(4)]; to anticipate (especially with anxiety, dread or fear).

Apprehension (of a person)**.** The seizing or taking hold of a man; the act of arresting or seizing under process of law; arrest; (as) the apprehension of criminals. "Apprehension", may include detention.

Being apprehended or seized in the name of justice or authority. [IPC (45 of 1860), S. 52A]; anticipation, chiefly of a thing adverse. [Oil Industry (Development) Act (47 of 1974), S. 9(1)(b)].

Apprehension and arrest. The term "apprehension" seems to be more peculiarly appropriate to seizure on criminal process; while "arrest" may apply to either a civil or criminal action, but is perhaps better confined to the former.

Apprentice. "APPRENTICE" means a person who is undergoing apprenticeship training in pursuance of a contract of apprenticeship. [Apprentices Act (52 of 1961), S. 2(a)]

A learner; one who is taken to learn a trade; a person, usually a minor, bound, in form of law, under a contract of apprenticeship, to a master to learn from him his art, trade, or business, and to serve him during his time of the apprenticeship. (*Tomlin*)

Apprentice at law. A student at law learning practice under a qualified legal practitioner.

Apprenticeship. The service or legal condition of an apprentice, the method or process of gaining knowledge of some trade, art, or profession from the instruction of a master; the term during which one is an apprentice.

Status as an apprentice; the time during which an apprentice serves [Workmen's Compensation Act (8 of 1923), S. 2(1)(e) and Copyright Act (14 of 1957), S. 17, prov. (a)].

Apprenticeship training. Means a course of training in any industry or establishment undergone in pursuance of a contract of apprenticeship and under prescribed terms and conditions which may be different for different categories of apprentices. [Apprentices Act (52 of 1961), S. 2(aaa)]

Apprenticii ad legem. Apprentices to the law.

Approach. To come near; to go near; to advance nearer; to make advance.

(As a noun) passage or avenue by which buildings are approached.

(*In international law*) The right of a ship of war, upon the high sea, to visit another vessel for the purpose of ascertaining the nationality of the latter.

Approbans non reprobat. (*Lat.*) One approbating cannot reprobate.

Approbate and Reprobate. To *approve* and reject; to take advantage of one part, and reject the rest.

A man cannot both affirm and disaffirm the same transaction, show its true nature for his own relief, and insist on its apparent character to prejudice his adversary.

The maxim that a person cannot 'approbate and reprobate' is only one application of the doctrine of election, and its operation must be confined to reliefs claimed in respect of the same transaction and to the persons who are parties thereto. *Nagerbai* v. *B. Sharma Rao*, AIR 1956 SC 593, 602. [Indian Evidence Act (1 of 1872), S. 115]

The doctrine of 'approbate and reprobate' is only a species of estoppel; it applies only to the conduct of parties. As in the case of estoppel it cannot operate against the provisions of a statute.

There is no rule that a "judgment is indivisible" so that a party cannot accept a part and appeal against the rest. The doctrine of "approbate and reprobate" rests on the same basis as the equitable doctrine of election and applies only when an interest is conferred as an act of bounty by some instrument.

Approbation. The act of approving; the assenting to the propriety of a thing.

Approving; formal or authoritative approval. [App. D, Form No. 17, para 11, CPC (5 of 1908)].

Appropriate. To make a thing one's own; to set apart for, or assign for a particular use to the exclusion of all other uses; to claim or use as by an exclusive right; to make peculiar, as to appropriate words to ideas; to take from another to one's self, with or without violence; necessary and proper (as) "appropriate words and expressions". "Appropriate" is said to be "to allot", assign, set apart, or apply anything to the use of a particular person or thing, or for a particular purpose".

To assign for a special purpose; to prescribe a particular use for particular moneys, or for the payment of a particular demand. [T.P. Act (4 of 1882), S. 58(d)]; specially suitable [IPC (45 of 1860), Ss. 54 and 55].

Appropriate authority. A public authority on whose behalf the land is designed for a public purpose in any plan or scheme and which it is authorised to acquire. [*Manohar Joshi* v. *State of Maharashtra*, (2012) 3 SCC 619, para 106] [Maharashtra Regional and Town Planning Act (37 of 1966), S. 2(3)].

"Appropriate authority" means the Appropriate Authority appointed under Section 13. [Transplantation of Human Organs Act (42 of 1994), S. 2(b)]

Appropriate fraction. Means the fraction which represents the extent to which the income derived from the capital asset transferred was immediately before such transfer applicable to charitable or religious purposes. [Income-tax Act (43 of 1961), S. 11(1A) *Expln.* (i)]

"APPROPRIATE FRACTION" means the fraction the numerator of which is one and the denominator of which is the number of the relevant previous years. [Income-tax Act (43 of 1961), S. 35A(1) *Expln.* (ii)]

Appropriate Government. The proper government as indicated in a statute or rule [Indian Electricity Act (9 of 1910), S. 2(a); Collection of Statistics Act (32 of 1953), S. 2(a); Apprentices Act (52 of 1961), S. 2(d) and State Agricultural Credit Corporations Act (60 of 1968), S. 2(e)].

"APPROPRIATE GOVERNMENT" in relation to Cantonment Boards, railway lands, and lands and buildings owned by the Central Government, a Central Public Sector Undertaking or an autonomous body wholly or substantially funded by the Central Government, means the Central Government and in all other cases, the State Government. [S. 2(1)(b) of the Prohibition of Employment as Manual Scavengers & Their Rehabilitation Act, 2013 (25 of 2013)]

"APPROPRIATE GOVERNMENT" means in respect of matters relating to,—(i) a Union territory without Legislature, the Central Government; (ii) the Union territories with Legislature, the Government of the National Capital Territory of Delhi or, as the case may be, the Government of Union territory of Puducherry; (iii) a State, the State Government. [S. 2(1)(a) of the Street Vendors (Protection of Livelihood and Regulation of Street Vending) Act, 2014 (7 of 2014)]

"APPROPRIATE GOVERNMENT" means—(i) in relation to a workplace which is established, owned, controlled or wholly or substantially financed by funds provided directly or indirectly—(A) by the Central Government or the Union Territory administration, the Central Government; (B) by the State Government, the State Government; (ii) in relation to any workplace not covered under sub-clause (i) and falling within its territory, the State Government. [S. 2(b) of the Sexual Harassment of Women at Workplace (Prevention, Prohibition & Redressal) Act, 2013 (14 of 2013)]

"APPROPRIATE GOVERNMENT" means,—(i) in relation to acquisition of land situated within the territory of, a State, the State Government; (ii) in relation to acquisition of land situated within a Union Territory (except Puducherry), the Central Government; (iii) in relation to acquisition of land situated within the Union Territory of Puducherry, the Government of Union Territory of Puducherry; (iv) in relation to acquisition of land for public purpose in more than one State, the Central Government, in consultation with the concerned State Governments or Union Territories; and (v) in relation to acquisition of land for the purpose of the Union as may be specified by notification, the Central Government: Provided that in respect of a public purpose in a district for an area not exceeding such as may be notified by the appropriate Government, the Collector of such district shall be deemed to be the appropriate Government. [S. 3(e) of the Right to Fair Compensation & Transparency in Land Acquisition, Rehabilitation & Resettlement Act, 2013 (30 of 2013)]

For the purposes of this section the expression "appropriate Government" means,—

(a) in cases where the sentence is a sentence of death or is for an offence against any law relating to a matter to which the executive power of the Union extends, the Central Government; and

(b) in cases where the sentence (whether of death or not) is for an offence against any law relating to a matter to which the executive power of the State extends, the Government of the State within which the offender is sentenced. [(w.e.f. 1-7-2024) Bharatiya Nayaya Sanhita, 2023 (45 of 2023), section 5, *Explanation*]

Appropriate laboratory. Means a laboratory or organisation—

(i) recognised by the Central Government;

(ii) recognised by a State Government, subject to such guidelines as may be issued by the Central Government in this behalf; or

(iii) established by or under any law for the time being in force, which is maintained, financed or aided by the Central Government or a State Government for carrying out analysis or test of any goods with a view to determining whether such goods suffer from any defect. [Consumer Protection Act (35 of 2019), section 2(2)]

Appropriate proceedings. The expression 'appropriate proceedings' has reference to proceedings which may be appropriate having regard to the nature of the order, direction, or writ. The appropriateness of the proceedings would depend upon the particular writ or order which a person claims. *Daryao* v. *State of U.P.*, AIR 1961 SC 1457, 1461. [Constitution of India, Art. 32]

Appropriate State. Means—

(i) in relation to a dealer who has one or more places of business situate in the same State, that State;

(ii) in relation to a dealer who has places of business situate in different States, every such State with respect to the place or places of business situate within its territory. [Central Sales Tax Act (74 of 1956), S. 2(a)]

Appropriation. The act of setting apart, or assigning a thing or substance to a particular use or person to the exclusion of others; application to a special use or purpose; an authority from the legislature, given at the proper time and in legal form, to the proper officers, to apply sums of money in the public treasury, in a given year, to specified objects or demands against the state.

The action of appropriating; the thing or amount appropriated. [Indian Contract Act (9 of 1872), S. 61 and Constitution of India, Art. 110(1)(d)]; [Indian Easements Act (5 of 1882), S. 4, *Expln.*].

Appropriation account. Means accounts which relate the expenditure brought to account during a financial year, to the several items specified in the law made in accordance with the provisions of the Constitution or of the Government of Union Territories Act, 1963, for the appropriation of moneys out of the Consolidated Fund of India or of a State, or of a Union Territory having a Legislative, as the case may be. [Comptroller and Auditor General's (Duties, Powers and Conditions of Service) Act (56 of 1971), S. 2(b)]

An account which shows how net profits are appropriated. On the one side appears the total sum available for division, and on the other side the manner in which that sum is appropriated, for payment of dividend, transfers to reserve fund, *etc.*

Appropriation bill. A bill authorizing governmental expenditures.

Appropriation of payments. "Where the purchaser owes more than one debt to the vendor, and makes a payment, it is his right to apply (or in technical language 'appropriate') the payment to whichever debt he pleases'.

Approval. The action of approving. [CPC (5 of 1908), S. 126, prov. 1].

'Approval' and **'permission'.** Ordinarily the difference between approval and permission is, that in the first the act holds goods until disapproved, while in the other case it does not become effective until permission is obtained. But permission subsequently obtained may all the same validate the previous Act. *Shakir Hussain* v. *Chandoo Lal*, AIR 1931 All 567 (FB).

Approve. To accept as good or sufficient for the purpose intended. (*Black; Burrill; Anderson*)

To pronounce good; admit the propriety or excellence of; be pleased with; commend; as on trial the goods were approved; to approve the policy of administration; to turn to one's own profit; augment the value of profits of, as of waste land, by inclosing and cultivating; improve.

"Approved". Means approved or accepted by the directorate. [Merchant Shipping (Seafarer Accommodation) Rules, 2016, R. 2(1)(b)].

Approved appliances. Means any equipment or gadget used for the bringing of any combustible material or for generating or consuming any fume, gas of particulate matter and approved by the State Board for the purpose of this Act. [Air (Prevention and Control of Pollution) Act (14 of 1981), S. 2(c)]

Approved bill. A bill to which no reasonable objection could be made, and which ought to be approved.

Approved deferred share trust (ADST). A trust fund in which a company buys shares in itself for the benefit of its employees. A reduced rate of tax is paid on the shares, and then only after they are sold. (*Investment*)

Approved equipment. Means the devices and instruments necessary for the performance of the inspection team's duties that have been certified by the Technical Secretariat in accordance with regulations prepared by the Technical Secretariat pursuant to Part II, paragraph 27 of this Annex. Such equipment may also refer to the administrative supplies or recording materials that would be used by the inspection team. [Chemical Weapons Convention Act (34 of 2000), (Verification Annex) 1]

Approved gratuity fund. Means a gratuity fund which has been and continues to be approved by the Principal Chief Commissioner or Chief Commissioner or Principal Commissioner in accordance with the rules contained in Part C of the Fourth Schedule. [Income-tax Act (43 of 1961), S. 2(5)]

Approved institution. "APPROVED INSTITUTION" means a hospital, health centre or other such institution recognised by a University as an institution in which a person may undergo the training, if any, required by his course of study before the award of any medical qualification to him. [Indian Medical Council Act (102 of 1956), S. 2(a)]

"APPROVED INSTITUTION" means—

(i) a housing finance institution which has been granted a certificate of registration under sub-section (5) of Section 29A;

(ii) a scheduled bank;

(iii) National Housing Bank acting as trustee or otherwise in a transaction of securitisation of housing mortgages undertaken by the National Housing Bank;

(iv) such other institutions as the Central Government may, on the recommendation of the National Housing Bank, by notification, specify. [National Housing Bank Act (53 of 1987), S. 36C(b)]

"APPROVED INSTITUTION" means a teaching institution, health centre or hospital recognised by a University or Board as an institution in which a person may undergo the training, if any, required by his course of study before the award of any medical qualification to him. [Indian Medicine Central Council Act (48 of 1970), S. 2(a)]

Approved intermediary. "APPROVED INTERMEDIARY" means a person duly registered by the Board under the guidelines/ scheme through whom the lender will deposit the securities for lending and the borrower will borrow the securities. [Securities Lending Scheme, 1997, S. 3(a)]

Approved launching device. Means a device approved by the Administration, capable of launching from the embarkation position a life raft fully loaded with the number of persons it is permitted to carry and with its equipment. [International Conference on safety of life at sea, 1974, Part A, Reg. 2(c)]

Approved securities. "APPROVED SECURITIES" means—

(i) Government securities and other securities charged on the revenues of the Central Government or of the Government of a [* * *] State of guaranteed fully as regards principal and interest by the Central Government, or the Government of any [* * *] State;

(ii) Debentures or other securities for money issued under the authority of any Central Act or Act of a State Legislature by or on behalf of a port trust or municipal corporation or city improvement trust in any presidency town;

(iii) Shares of a corporation established by law and guaranteed fully by the Central Government or the Government of a [* * *] State as to the repayment of the principal and the payment of dividends;

(iv) Securities issued or guaranteed fully as regards principal and interest by the Government of any Part B State and specified as approved securities for the purposes of this Act by the Central Government by notification in the official Gazette; and

(v) Subject to the limitations contained in the proviso hereto, securities guaranteed fully as regards principal and interest by a provincial Government in Pakistan or charged on the revenues of any part of that Dominion; and debentures or other securities for money issued by or on behalf of the trustees of the port of Karachi.

Provided that securities or debentures specified in item (v) shall be recognised as approved securities only for such purposes and for such period and such conditions as may be prescribed;

Explanation.—In sub-clauses (i) and (ii) "Government of a State" in relation to any period before the 1st November, 1956, means the Government of a part A state. [Insurance Act (4 of 1938), S. 2(3)]

"APPROVED SECURITIES" means securities of any State Government or of the Central Government and such bonds, both the principal whereof and the interest whereon shall have been fully and unconditionally guaranteed by any such Government. [National Housing Bank Act (53 of 1987), S. 29B *Expln.* (1); R.B.I. Act (2 of 1934), S. 45-IB, *Expln.* 1]

"APPROVED SECURITIES" means—

(i) securities in which a trustee may invest money under clause (a), clause (b), clause (bb), clause (c) or clause (d) of section 20 of the Indian Trusts Act, 1882 (2 of 1882);

(ii) such of the securities authorised by the Central Government under clause (f) of section 20 of the Indian Trusts Act, 1882 (2 of 1882), as may be prescribed; [S. 5(a) of the Banking Regulation Act, 1949 (10 of 1949]

"APPROVED SECURITIES" means the securities issued by the Central Government or any State Government or such other securities as may be specified by the Reserve Bank from time to time [S. 5(a) of the Banking Regulation Act, 1949 (10 of 1949) as substituted by the Banking Laws (Amendment) Act, 2012 (4 of 2013)]

Approved superannuation fund. Means a superannuation fund or any part of a superannuation fund which has been and continues to be approved by the Principal Chief Commissioner or Chief Commissioner or Principal Commissioner in accordance with the rules contained in Part B of the Fourth Schedule. [Income tax Act (43 of 1961), S. 2(6)]

Approver. One that, confessing felony committed by himself accuses others to be guilty of the same crime. (*Tomlin*)

'Approver' is he who hath committed some felony which he confessed, and now approved; that is to say, accused others who were helpers with him in doing the same or other felonies, which thing he will approve. (*Termes de La Ley; Cowell; Jacob*)

A person who confesses offence and who turns State's evidence.

Approving authority. "Approving Authority" means an Additional Commissioner or a Joint Commissioner as defined in clauses (1C) and (28C) respectively of section 2 of the Income-tax Act, 1961 (43 of 1961). [Prohibition of Benami Property Transactions Act (45 of 1988), section 2(4)]

For the purpose of this regulation 'APPROVING AUTHORITY' means EXIM bank of India or the authorised dealer. [Foreign Exchange Management (Export of Goods and Services) Regulations, 2000, Regn. 18, *Explanation* as substituted by Second Amending Regulations, 2014].

Approximate. The word approximate means very near, closely resembling or fairly correct. *Om Prakash* v. *Mayaram*, AIR 1964 All 430, 431.

Nearest; approaching correctness, very nearly exact. [Cotton Ginning and Pressing Factories Act (12 of 1925), S. 5(1)].

Approximately. Nearly. [CPC (5 of 1908), O. VII, R. 2].

Appurtenance. A thing that belong to another.

Appurtenant. Literally the word 'Appurtenant' means pertaining to or belonging to. It does not mean adjacent to. *Harnam Singh* v. *Bibi Kimbar Singh,* AIR 1980 All 50, 52. [Indian Easement Act (5 of 1882), S. 4]

Annexed or belonging legally to some more important thing. [Salaries and Allowances of Ministers Act (58 of 1952), S. 4, *Expln.*].

Aqua cedit solo. The water goes with the ground.

Aquae et ignis interdicto. (*Roman law*) Forbidding the use of air and water.

Arable. There is no definition of the word 'arable' in the original Land Acquisition Act. A local amendment includes garden lands in the expansion. Now lands are of different kinds: there is waste-land, desert-land, pasture-land, meadow-land, grass-land, woodland, marshy-land, hilly-land, etc., and arable land. The *Oxford Dictionary* gives the meaning of the term 'arable' as capable of being ploughed, fit for tillage, opposed to pastureland or wood-land and gives the root as *arablis* in Latin. Arable is *arvum* as Cicero spoke of *prata et arva* (meadows and arable lands). *Ishwarlal Girdharlal Joshi* v. *State of Gujarat*, AIR 1968 SC 870.

Arable and wasteland. The expression "arable land" must be construed to mean "lands" which are mainly used for ploughing and for raising crops and the expression "waste land" would mean "land which is unfit for cultivation or habitation"; desolate and barren land with little or no vegetation thereon. *Raja Anand Brahma Shah* v. *State of U.P.*, AIR 1967 SC 1081. [Land Acquisition Act (1 of 1894), S. 17(1)(repealed)].

Arable land. Land fit for tillage [Land Acquisition Act (1 of 1894), S. 35 and

Agriculturists' Loans Act (12 of 1884), S. 4].

Arbiter. An arbitrator; a private extra judicial Judge; a referee. (*Wharton; 3 Cys. 567*)

Arbitrage. The principle of profiting from the difference in price which the same thing may have at different places at the same time. [Income-tax Act (43 of 1961), S. 43(5)(c)].

Arbitral immunity. Arbitrators are protected from suits arising out of their *quasi* judicial conduct in arbitration proceedings. This privilege of the arbitrator is known as arbitral immunity.

Arbitral institution. Means an arbitral institution designated by the Supreme Court or a High Court under this Act. [Arbitration & Conciliation Act (26 of 1996), section 2(1)(ca)]

Arbitral procedure. The procedure, which is required to be followed by the arbitrators, should also be in accordance with the agreement of the parties. If there is no such agreement then it should be in accordance with the procedure prescribed in Part I of the Arbitration and Conciliation Act (26 of 1996) *i.e.,* Sections 2 to 43.

Arbitral situs. Place of arbitration.

Arbitral tribunal. Arbitral tribunal means a sole arbitrator or a panel of arbitrators. [Arbitration and Conciliation Act (26 of 1996), S. 2(d)]

An 'Arbitral Tribunal' is not a 'Court' within the meaning of Section 2(e) of the Act. *Ranjul Baruah* v. *Numaligarh Refinery Ltd.,* AIR 2002 Gau 85, 88, para 14. [Arbitration and Conciliation Act (26 of 1996), S. 2(e)]

Arbitrament. Determination or decision of arbitrators upon a claim or matter of dispute which has been submitted to them.

Arbitramentum acquum tribuit cuique suum. (*Maxim*) A fair judgment gives to each his due. (*Latin for Lawyers*)

Arbitrarily. In an arbitrary manner; according to one's pleasure or caprice; capriciously; without fair, solid, and substantial cause and without reason given. Judicial discretion ought not to be used arbitrarily.

Arbitrariness. Adjudging or doing according to one's or discretion; Despotic; Capricious; Uncontrolled.

Arbitrary. Depending on will or pleasure; based on mere opinion or preference, hence capricious. [Specific Relief Act (47 of 1963), S. 20].

Arbitrary and capricious. Characterization of a decision or action taken by an administrative agency or inferior court meaning wilful and unreasonable action without consideration or in disregard of facts of law or without determining principle.

An action is said to be arbitrary and capricious, where a person, in particular, a person in authority does any action based on individual discretion by ignoring prescribed rules, procedure as law and the action or decision is founded on prejudice or preference rather than reason or fact. To be termed as arbitrary and capricious, the action must be illogical and whimsical, something without any reasonable explanation. When an action or procedure seeks to achieve a specific objective in furtherance of education in a bona fide manner, by adopting a process which is uniform and nondiscriminatory, it cannot be described as arbitrary or capricious or mala fide. [*Sanchit Bansal* v. *Joint Admission Board*, (2012) 1 SCC 157, para 28].

Arbitration. Means any arbitration whether or not administered by permanent arbitral institution. [Arbitration and Conciliation Act (26 of 1996), S. 2(a)]

An arbitration is a reference to the decision of one or more persons, either with or without an umpire, of a particular matter in difference between the parties. (*Termes de la Ley*)

The submitting of a disputed matter to the judgment of one or more persons called arbitrators. (*Wharton*)

Arbitration agreement. A written agreement to submit present or future differences to arbitration, whether an arbitrator is name therein or not.

Arbitration Agreement/Clause. An agreement between parties agreeing to refer disputes which have already arisen, or which may arise in future, to arbitration.

Arbitration award. An 'arbitration award' can not be treated a 'decree' of Civil Court during pendency of application under Section 34 of the Act, for the purpose of execution. [*Gurbax Singh* v. *Punjab State Civil Supply Corporation Ltd.*, AIR 2007 (NOC) 1024 (P & H)] [Arbitration and Conciliation Act (26 of 1996), S. 34]

Arbitration clause. A clause inserted in a contract providing for compulsory arbitration in case of dispute as to the rights or liabilities arising under it.

Arbitration proceedings. Arbitration proceedings do not commence from the time an arbitration agreement is made, but they commence only on the arbitrator getting authority to arbitrate in that behalf. *Baby Paul* v. *Hindustan Paper Corporation,* AIR 1978 Ker 223, 227. [Arbitration Act (10 of 1940) (*repealed*), S. 41(b)]

Arbitrator. The arbitrator is the person to whose attention the matters in dispute are submitted—a judge of the parties' own choosing, whose functions are judicial and whose duties are not those of a mere partisan agent, but of an impartial judge, to dispense equal justice to all the parties, and to decide the law and facts involved in the matters submitted, with a view to determining and finally ending the controversy.

A person or one of two or more persons chosen by parties or according to their agreement to decide the dispute between them. [S. 2(aa), Industrial Disputes Act (14 of 1947) and S. 1, Indian Evidence Act (1 of 1872)].

"Arbitrator" includes an umpire. [Industrial Relations Code, 2020 (35 of 2020), section 2(c)]

Arbitrator and umpire. *An umpire*, in the common signification of the word, denotes one who is to decide the controversy in case the original arbitrators cannot agree.

SPECIAL ARBITRATOR AND UMPIRE. A special arbitrator is one who is called in to act only after a disagreement between other arbitrators, not alone, however, but only in conjunction with the others so as to enable a majority of them to render an award. Likewise, an umpire is one who is called in to act only after a disagreement; but the nature of his authority differs from that of a special arbitrator in the fact that he acts not with the other arbitrators, for the making of a majority award, but alone, and that his sole award determines the matters submitted to him. (3 *Ame. Cyc.* 655)

Arbitrium est judicium. The award of an arbitrator has the same force and effect as a judgment.

Arbitrium est judicium boni viri, secundum aequum et bonum. (*Maxim*) An award is the judgment of a good man, according to justice.

Arbor consanguinitatis. A geneological table in the shape of a tree.

Archaeological officer. Means an officer of the Department of Archaeology of the Government of India not lower in rank than Assistant Superintendent of Archaeology. [Ancient Monuments and Archaeological Sites and Remains Act (24 of 1958), S. 2(c)]

Archaeological site and remains. Means any area which contains or is reasonably believed to contain ruins or relics of historical or archaeological importance which have been in existence for not less than one hundred years, and include—

(i) such portion of land adjoining the area as may be required for fencing or covering in or otherwise preserving it, and

(ii) the means of access to, and convenient inspection of, the area. [Ancient Monuments & Archaeological Sites, and Remains Act (24 of 1958), S. 2(d)]

Archipelago. A collection of islands (including parts of islands, interconnecting waters, and other natural features) so closely interrelated that they form an intrinsic geographical, economic and political entity, or which historically have been regarded as such.

Architect's certificate. A certificate from an architect certifying that a structure has been built in accordance with the specifications and plans of the contract.

Archives. A place in which public or institutional records are systematically preserved.

Arduous. Hard to accomplish or achieve. [Maternity Benefit Act (53 of 1961), S. 4(3)]. A particular extent of surface range; scope. [CPC (5 of 1908), S. 1(3)(a)].

Area. A particular extent of surface range; scope. [CPC (5 of 1908), S. 4(3)(a)].

Arguable issue. A point raises 'arguable issues' if the Court has some doubt upon the question raised or there are obscure points which require elucidation and upon which two views may reasonably be held. *Jatin Chakraborty* v. *Mr. Justice Himansu Kumar Bose*, AIR 1964 Cal 500, 503.

Argue. To offer an argument.

Arguendo. In arguing; in the course of the argument. A statement or observation made by a judge as a matter of argument or illustration, but not directly bearing upon the case at the bar, or only incidentally involved in it, is said (in the reports) to be made arguendo. (*Black*)

Argument. An inference drawn from premises, the truth of which is indisputable, or at least highly probable; a statement of fact tending to produce belief concerning a matter in doubt; a premise or premises set forth in order to prove an assumption or conclusion.

A connected series of statements intended to establish or subvert a proposition or any specific statement therein; the discussion by a counsel of the evidence in a suit and placing of various authorities for legal positions before a judge arrives at a decision. [CPC (5 of 1908), O. XV, R. 3(1)].

Argument and Argumentation. Argument is the bare proof advanced by a person to prove the truth of his assertion; "argumentation is the whole reasoning itself, or what form so ever it be, comprehending both the question and also the proof thereof." (*Blundeville,* 1619)

Argumenta ignota et obscura ad lucem rationis proferunt et reddunt splendida. (*Maxim*) Arguments bring things hidden and obscure to the light of reason and render them clear. (*Adam*)

Argumentation. The setting forth of reasons together with the conclusion drawn from them; also the premises and conclusion so set forth.

Argumentative affidavit. An affidavit which contains not only allegations of facts but also arguments as to the bearing of those facts on the matter in dispute.

Argumentative matter. Matter containing arguments (rather than facts). [CPC (5 of 1908), O. XIX, R. 3(2)].

Argumentative plea. A plea, not concise, direct and positive.

Argumentum a communiter accidentibus in jure frequens est. (*Maxim*) An argument drawn from common understanding of a thing is common in law. (*Morgan*)

An agreement from things commonly happening is frequent in law. (*Latin for Lawyers*)

Argumentum a divisione est fortissimum in jure. (*Maxim*) An argument from division is of the greatest force in law.

Argumentum a majori ad minus negative non valet, valet e converso. (*Maxim*) An argument from the greater to the less is of no force negatively; affirmatively it is. (*Morgan; Latin for Lawyers*))

"You cannot argue in the negative from the greater to the less, but you can argue in the negative from the less to the greater". (*Byrne*)

Argumentum a simili valet in lege. (*Maxim*) An argument from analogy is good in law. (*Burrill*)

An argument from a like case avails in law. (*Latin for Lawyers*)

An argument from a like or analogous case is good in law. The binding effect or decision does not depend upon whether a particular argument was considered therein or not, provided that the point with reference to which an argument was subsequently advanced was actually decided. [*Somawanti* v. *State of Punjab*, AIR 1963 SC 151 (160)].

Argumentum ab auctoritate est fortissimum in lege. (*Maxim*) An argument from authority is the strongest in law. (*Burrill*)

Argumentum ab impossibili plurimum valet in lege. (*Maxim*) An argument from an impossibility is of weight in law. (*Abbott; Coke Litt. 92a; Broom*)

Argumentum ab inconvenient. Argument from being caught in inconvenience is no answer.

Argumentum ab inconvenienti est validum in lege; quia lex non permittit aliquod inconveniens. An argument drawn from what is inconvenient is good in law, because the law will not permit any inconvenience. (*Co. Litt.* 66a. 258)

Argumentum ab inconvenienti plurimum valet in lege. An argument from inconvenience avails much in law. Arguments of inconvenience are sometimes of great value upon the question of intention. If there be in any instrument, equivocal expressions, and great inconvenience must necessarily follow from one construction, it is strong to show that such construction is not according to the true intention of the grantor; but where there is no equivocal expression in the instrument, and the words used admit only of one meaning, arguments of inconvenience prove only want of foresight in the parties. (*Latin for Lawyers*)

Arise. To spring forth from its source; to come into existence [Employment of Children Act (26 of 1938), S. 3C]; [T.P. Act (4 of 1882), Ss. 6(dd) and 21, *Excep.*].

Arising out of. If the parties to a contract make provision in it as to their rights should certain events occur in the course of the contract and a dispute arises between them as to their rights following the occurrence of those events then that dispute as to their rights arises out of the contract. *Union of India* v. *Aabuy's Redere,* (1974) 2 All ER 874, 884 (HL), Supreme Court Act, 1981, S. 20(2)(h). The words 'arising out of' are to be given a wider meaning 'connected with' than a narrow meaning 'arising under'. *The Antonis P. Lemos*, (1985) 1 All ER 695, 703 (HL)

The words 'arising out of' have been used in the sense that they comprise purchase of shares and lands from income arising out of the Kanpur Undertaking. *Doypack Systems Pvt. Ltd.* v. *Union of India*, AIR 1988 SC 782, 799. [Swadeshi Cotton Mills Co. Ltd. (Acquisition and Transfer Undertakings) Act (30 of 1986), S. 3]

Arising out of and in the course of his employment. The words indicate that any accident which occurred while going to the place of employment or for the purpose of employment, cannot be said to have arisen out of his employment, there being no casual connection between the accident and the employment. *Regional Director E.S.I. Corpn.* v. *Francis De Costa*, (1996) 6 SCC 1, 6.

Arising out of employment. The words 'arising out of employment' are vide enough so as to cover a case where there may not necessarily be a direct connection between the injury caused as a result of an accident and the employment of the workman. *PWD Bhopal* v. *Kausa,* AIR 1961 MP 297, 298. [Workmen's Compensation Act (8 of 1923), S. 3]

Arising out of employment. The words "arising out of employment" are understood to mean that during the course of employment, the injury has resulted from some risk incidental to duties. [*Daya Kishan Joshi* v. *Dynemech Systems Private Limited,* (2018) 11 SCC 642, para 9].

The accident must be connected with the employment and must arise out of it. There must be a causal connection or association between the employment and the accidental injury.

Where a driver of a bus service when going home from the depot or coming to the depot uses a bus belonging to the same bus service and an accident occurs to him, it is an accident in the course of employment. *B.E.S.T. Undertaking* v. *Agnes*, AIR 1964 SC 193, 201.

Aristocracy. Government by the best men in the state; a governing body composed of the best men in the state. (*Macaulay*)

Aristocracy and Oligarchy. Aristocracy is a form of Government in which the supreme power is exercised by those members of the state who are distinguished by their rank, wealth and opulence. When the ruling power is exercised by a very few of this class to the exclusion of all others, the Government becoming an oligarchy.

Aristocrat. A member of the aristocracy or a man of rank in a community; hence a person having the traits supposed to be characteristic of an aristocracy. One who favours an aristocracy; one who is an advocate of an aristocratic form of Government.

Arithmetic mean. Average; the total of a series of values divided by the number of values.

Arm. Any thing which a man takes in his hand in anger to strike or assault another, or to do physical harm to another.

A weapon primarily intended for domestic and agricultural purposes, even if it can be used for purposes of offence and defence, is not 'arm' within the meaning of the Arms Act. It is the intention of the manufacturer, and not of the possessor of a weapon as to the use to which it is to be put, which determines whether a weapon is an arm or not.

A means of offence or defence. [Arms Act (45 of 1959), S. 2(1)(c)]; a combat branch. [Army Act (46 of 1950), S. 142(2)].

ARM; ARMS. A weapon, in this sense most commonly used in the plural and when used in the singular for the most part referring rather to a particular kind of weapon than to an individual piece.

Arm, Weapon. Arm is especially applied to those things which are designed for fighting and recognised as such; it includes means of defence as well as of offence. Weapon applies to any means of offence made for the purpose or (as a scythe, chisel, or hammer) used for the nonce.

Arma in armatos sumere jura sinunt. (*Maxim*) The laws permit us to take up arms against the armed. (*Adam*)

Armament. Munitions of war; arms and accessory equipment of a combat or defence unit. [Arms Act (54 of 1959), S. 45(a)].

Armed. Supported by arms, carried on or maintained by force or readiness for military action : as, an armed force; an armed inroad; armed peace; or neutrality.

Armed forces. "ARMED FORCES" means the military forces and the air forces operating as land forces, and includes any other armed forces of the Union so operating. [Armed Forces (Assam & Manipur) Special Powers Act (28 of 1958), S. 2(a)]

The expression "ARMED FORCES" means the military, naval and air forces, operating as land forces and includes any other armed forces of the Union so operating. [Cr PC, 1973 (2 of 1974), section 132(3)(a)] [Now (w.e.f. 1-7-2024) repealed & replaced by Bharatiya Nagarik Suraksha Sanhita, 2023 (46 of 2023)]

In this section and in the preceding sections of this Chapter, the expression "armed forces" means the army, naval and air forces, operating as land forces and includes any other armed forces of the Union so operating. [(w.e.f. 1-7-2024) Bharatiya Nagarik Suraksha Sanhita, 2023 (46 of 2023), section 151(3)(a)]

"ARMED FORCES" means the naval, military and air forces and includes any other armed forces of the Union. [Protection of Human Rights Act, 1993 (10 of 1994), S. 2(1)(a)]

For the purposes of this section, "ARMED FORCES" means an armed force of the Union constituted under an Act of Parliament and includes a member of the police force constituted under Section 3 of the Delhi Police Act, 1978. [Delhi Rent Act (33 of 1995), S. 24 *Expln.*]

Military force of a country. [Constitution of India, Art. 136(2)].

"ARMED FORCES" means the naval, military and air forces and includes any member of the Armed Forces constituted under any law for the time being in force, including the paramilitary forces and any auxiliary forces that are under the control of the Central Government, or the State Government. [*Explanation* (a) to S. 376(2) of IPC, 1860 (45 of 1860), as substituted by the Criminal Laws (Amendment) Act, 2013 (13 of 2013)] Now (w.e.f. 1-7-2024) repealed & replaced by Bharatiya Nayaya Sanhita, 2023 (45 of 2023), section 64(2), Explanation (a), same definition in new Sanhita]

Armed forces or security forces. Means armed forces of the Union or security forces or police forces, as specified in the Schedule. [(w.e.f. 14-11-2012) S. 2(1)(c) of the Protection of Children from Sexual Offences Act, 2012 (32 of 2012)].

Armed insurrection. The action of rising in arms or open resistance (with arms) against established authority or governmental restraint; an incipient or limited rebellion. [Indian Evidence Act (1 of 1872), S. 6, ill. (b)].

Armed robbery. Robbery which is committed by carrying a dangerous weapon, regardless of whether the weapon is revealed or not.

Armistice. Truce; a suspending or cessation of hostilities between belligerent nations or forces for a considerable time; a temporary suspension of hostilities by convention or agreement of opposing forces.

A short truce; a suspension of hostilities, truce. [Ist Sch., Art. 15, Geneva Conventions Act (6 of 1960)].

Armistice and peace. While an armistice is an interval in war and supposes a return to it, a peace is a return to a state of amity and intercourse, implying no intention to recommence hostilities. An armistice again leaves the questions of the war unsettled, but a peace implies in its terms that redress of wrongs has been obtained, or that the intention is renounced of seeking to obtain it.

Armless. Without arms; destitute of weapons; defenceless.

Armour. A defensive arm; covering worn to protect the person against offensive weapons.

Armoury. A place where arms are kept. [Navy Act (62 of 1957), S. 2(1)(b)(ii) and Arms Act (54 of 1959), S. 21, *Expln.*].

Arm's length transaction. In section 188(1) of Act 18 of 2013, the expression 'arm's length transaction' means a transaction between two related parties that is conducted as if they were unrelated, so that there is no conflict of interest. [*Explanation* (*b*) to Section 188(1) of the Companies Act, 2013 (18 of 2013)]

Arms. "ARMS" means articles of any description designed or adapted as weapons for offence or defence, and includes firearms, sharp-edged and other deadly weapons and parts of, and machinery for manufacturing arms, but does not include articles designed solely for domestic or agricultural uses such as a *lathi* or an ordinary walking stick and weapons incapable of being used otherwise than as toys or of being converted into serviceable weapons. [Arms Act (54 of 1959), S. 2 (1)(c)]

Weapons of offence or defence [IPC (45 of 1860), S. 52-A and Arms Act (54 of 1959), S. 2(1)(c)].

Anything that a man wears for his defence, or takes in his hands or uses for attack to cast at or strike at another.

"ARMS" includes fire-arms, bayonets, swords, daggers, spears, spear-heads and bows and arrows, also cannon and parts of arms, and machinery for manufacturing arms.

Arms, in. Armed; ready to fight.

Army. The national armed forces intended for military service on land. "The term 'army' or 'armies' has never been used so as to include the navy or marines."

The national armed forces intended for military service on land. [Army Act (46 of 1950), S. 142(2)].

Arrack. A fermented liquor made from the juice of the palm, or from rice, an excisable article.

Arraign. To put upon trial; to accuse publicly. To call a prisoner by name and to read to him the substance of the indictment in the Court, and ask him whether he pleads guilty or not guilty.

Arraignment. The act of arraigning; the act of calling and setting a prisoner before a Court to answer to an accusation.

Accusation; indictment. [Navy Act (62 of 1957), S. 105].

Arrange. To make preparation; [Presidency-Towns Insolvency Act (3 of 1909), S. 44(2)]; [Now repealed by Act 31 of 2016] to place in a desired order.

A settlement of mutual relations, claims or matters in dispute [Workmen's Compensation Act (8 of 1923), S. 35]; the disposition of measures for a particular purpose. [CPC (5 of 1908), O. XXI, R. 45(1)].

Arrangement. The disposition of measures for a particular purpose.

A settlement of mutual relations, claims or matters in dispute [S. 35, Workmen's Compensation Act (8 of 1923)]; the disposition of measures for a particular purpose. [O. XXI, R. 45(1), CPC (5 of 1908)].

In this chapter, unless the context otherwise requires, "ARRANGEMENT" means any step in, or a part or whole of, any transaction, operation, scheme, agreement or understanding, whether enforceable or not, and includes the alienation of any property in such transaction, operation, scheme, agreement or understanding. [Income-tax Act (43 of 1961), Chap. XA, S. 102(1)].

"ARRANGEMENT" for the purposes of section 230(1) of Act 18 of 2013, 'arrangement' includes a reorganisation of the company's share capital by the consolidation of shares of different classes or by the division of shares into shares of different classes, or by both of those methods. [*Explanation* to Section 230(1) of the Companies Act, 2013 (18 of 2013)]

"ARRANGEMENT" means any step in, or a part or whole of, any transaction, operation, scheme, agreement or understanding, whether enforceable or not, and includes the alienation of any property in such transaction, operation, scheme, agreement or understanding. [(w.e.f. 1-4-2016) S. 102(1) of the Income-tax Act, 1961 (43 of 1961); (still-born) Section 102(1) of the Income-tax Act, 1961 (43 of 1961) as inserted (w.e.f. 1-4-2014) by the Finance Act, 2012 (23 of 2012) and omitted (w.e.f. 1-4-2014) by the Finance Act, 2013 (17 of 2013)]

Arrangement to lack commercial substance. An 'arrangement shall be deemed to lack commercial substance', if—(a) the substance or effect of the arrangement as a whole, is inconsistent with, or differs significantly from, the form of its individual steps or a part; or (b) it involves or includes—(i) round trip financing; (ii) an accommodating party; (iii) elements that have effect of offsetting or cancelling each other; or (iv) a transaction which is conducted through one or more persons and disguises the value, location, source, ownership or control of funds which is the subject matter of such transaction; or (c) it involves the location of an asset or of a transaction or of the place of residence of any party which is without any substantial commercial purpose other than obtaining a tax benefit (but for the provisions of Chapter X-A of Act 43 of 1961) for a party; or (d) it does not have a significant effect upon the business risks or net cash flows of any party to the arrangement apart from any effect attributable to the tax benefit that would be obtained (but for the provisions of Chapter X-A of Act 43 of 1961). [(w.e.f. 1-4-2016) S. 97(1) of the Income-tax Act, 1961 (43 of 1961)]

Arrangement with creditors. Agreement between a debtor and creditors for settlement of claims. [Indian Contract Act (9 of 1872), S. 63, ill. (e)].

Array. To place or dispose in order, as troops for battle; marshal; draw up in hostile order; often used figuratively. An orderly collection or assemblage; especially a body of men in order of battle or prepared for battle; hence, military force; soldiery troops.

Arrear. That which remains unpaid though due. [T.P. Act (4 of 1882), S. 8].

Arrear of rent. The expression 'ARREARS OF RENT' means arrears of rent legally recoverable which are to be paid or tendered by the tenant within two months of the service of a notice of demand. [Delhi Rent Control Act (59 of 1958), S. 14(1)(a)]

'Arrears of rent' means arrears of rent lawfully payable.

Arrears. The definition of "arrears" involves the idea not merely of money unpaid, but of money unpaid at the due time. The term "arrears" involves the existence of some default on the part of the debtor.

Arrears of any kind. Arrears of any kind means arrears of every kind. Amount which a person is liable to pay or under a duty to pay, but has defaulted in payment thereof even after the expiry.

Arrears of interest. It means arrears of interest up to the date of the decree. *K. Manikchand* v. *Elias Saleh Mohd. Sait*, AIR 1969 SC 671. [Mysore Money-Lenders Act, 1939, S. 17]

Arrest. A restraint of a man's person, obliging him to be obedient to the law; and it is defined to be the execution of the command of some Court of record or officer of justice. An arrest is the beginning of imprisonment, where a man is first taken and restrained of his liberty by power or colour of lawful warrant. (*Tomlin*)

"ARREST" means detention or restriction for removal of a vessel by order of a High Court to secure a maritime claim including seizure of a vessel in execution or satisfaction of a judgment or order. [Admiralty (Jurisdiction and Settlement of Maritime Claims) Act (22 of 2017), S. 2(c)].

An arrest of a person, by a duly authorised officer, is accomplished if the officer lawfully touches him; the power of affecting actual capture is not essential.

An arrest *in a civil cause* is defined to be the apprehending or restraining one's person by process in execution of the command of some Court, or officers of justice. (*Tomlin*) [CPC (5 of 1908), S. 55 and Order XXI, Rr. 37-40].

When a person was summoned to answer a charge of a complaint under S. 474, IPC (45 of 1860), in the summons he was only required to appear in person before the Magistrate. When he did appear before the Magistrate, and was released on bail, this was not tantamount to arrest. *Dhanji Ram Sharma* v. *Union of India,* AIR 1960 Punj 605, 606.

The expression 'arrest' appearing in Art. 22, Constitution of India, is a comprehensive term which is designed to cover all cases in which a person is apprehended by legal authority and is not confined to cases in which a person is apprehended by or under the orders of a civil or criminal Court. It covers not only cases of punitive and preventive detention but also cases of what may, for convenience, be called protective detention. *Ajaib Singh* v. *State of Punjab,* AIR 1952 Punj 309, 320 (FB).

"Arrest consists of the actual seizure or touching of a person's body with a view to his detention. The mere pronouncing of words of arrest is not an arrest, unless the person sought to be arrested submits to the process and goes with the arresting officer." [Halsbury's Laws of England, 4th Edn., Vol. 2, para 99 as cited in *Sundeep Kumar Bafna* v. *State of Maharashtra*, (2014) 16 SCC 623, para 11].

The restraining of the liberty of man's person in order to compel obedience to the order of a Court of justice, or to prevent the commission of a crime, or to ensure that a person charged or suspected of a crime may be forthcoming to answer it. [Indian Evidence Act (1 of 1872), S. 132].

AS APPLIED TO CRIMINAL PROCEEDINGS. The word 'arrest' signifies the apprehension or detention of the person or stopping, seizing or apprehending him and restraining his liberty in order to bring him to answer for an alleged or suspected crime, or to prevent the commission of criminal offence. (*Black*)

NECESSITY OF ASSUMING CONTROL OF PERSON. To constitute an arrest it is necessary that the officers should assume custody and control over the party, either by force or with his consent, and it has been held that neither the utterance of words indicating an intention to arrest on the part of the person uttering them, nor the reading of the warrant is of itself sufficient.

Arrest and apprehension. "*Apprehension*" is more properly used in criminal cases, "*arrest*" in civil cases. (*3 Ame. Cyc. 873*)

Arrest and commit. By arrest is to be understood to take the party into custody. *To commit* is the separate and distinct act of carrying the party to prison, after having taken him into custody by force of the execution.

Arrest and custody. The word 'arrest' is derived from the French word 'Arreter' meaning "to stop or stay" and signifies a restraint of the person. Lexicologically, the meaning of the word 'arrest' is given in various dictionaries depending upon the circumstances in which the said expression is used. In every arrest, there is custody but not *vice versa* and that both the words 'custody' and 'arrest' are not synonymous terms. Though 'custody' may amount to an arrest in certain circumstances but not under all circumstances. If these two terms are interpreted as synonymous, it is nothing but an *ultra* legalist interpretation which if under all circumstances accepted and adopted, would lead to a startling anomaly resulting in serious consequences. *Directorate of Enforcement* v. *Deepak Mahajan,* AIR 1994 SC 1775, 1788.

Arrest and detention. The physical restraint put upon an abducted person in the process of recovery and taking the person into custody without any allegation is not arrest but detention. *State of Punjab* v. *Ajaib Singh,* AIR 1953 SC 10. [Constitution of India, Art. 22]

Arrest of judgment. Stay of judgment after its entry.

Arrest warrant. Warrant, issued on a probable cause, directing a law enforcer to arrest a person and bring him to Court.

Arret. Judgment, sentence or decree of a competent Court.

Arretted. Accused imputed.

Arrive. To reach or come to a particular place of destination by travelling towards it.

Arrogation. Claiming or taking something unrightfully.

Arsenal. A repository of magazine of arms and military stores of all kinds, whether for land or naval service.

A storehouse or source of supply of arms, ammunition and other military equipment; an establishment often maintained by the government, for the manufacture, repair, storage or issue of arms and other military equipment.

Arson. "The wilful and malicious, burning of the house or the outhouse of another". House burning; the wilful setting fire to anything maliciously. (3 *Just* 66)

Arson clause. An insurance-policy provision which excludes coverage of a loss because of fire if the insured intentionally started the fire.

Art. Human skill; application of skill to subjects of taste, as poetry, music *etc.*; skill as the result of knowledge and practice; certain branches of learning, which are of the nature of instruments for more advanced studies or for the work of life. [Indian Evidence Act (1 of 1872), S. 45 and Constitution of India, Art. 80(3)].

Art : Science. The essential difference between an art and a science is in aim. "Science and Art may be said to be investigations of truth, but science inquires for the sake of knowledge, art for the sake of production." (*Karslake*). Hence, they differ somewhat in that with which they are concerned. "An art directly and immediately concerns itself with a faculty. It fastens upon that, and keeps it ever in its view as it teaches how that may be developed, trained and gained. A science, on the other hand, regards rather the product of faculty, and, keeping its view directly upon that, proceeds to unfold its nature and proper characteristics." (*H.N. Day, Art of Discourse,* 1)

Article.

"Article" means in the Patents and Designs Act (as respects designs) any article of manufacture and any substance, artificial or natural, or partly artificial and partly natural. [Patents and Designs (2 of 1911), S. 2(2)] [Now repealed by Act 39 of 1970]

"ARTICLE" means any substance, artificial or natural, or partly artificial or partly natural, whether raw or partly or wholly processed or manufactured or handmade within India or imported into India. [Bureau of Indian Standards Act (11 of 2016), S. 2(1)].

(from articulas, a joint or division) One thing of many; divisions or paragraphs of a document or agreement; one item of several; distinct portion or part. The word is also sometimes construed as meaning 'a joint or part or member' or clause or item (as) articles of an agreement or articles of association of a company; a point of faith, doctrine, or duty (as) 'articles of faith'; "each article of human duty" (Parley); a complete, independent or partly independent portion of a literary publication especially in a periodical, magazine, review, or magazine (as) contributing articles to the London Times a particular substance or commodity (as) articles of merchandise.

"It is a word of separation to individualize and distinguish some particular thing from the general thing or whole of which it forms a part, as an article in an agreement, an article of faith, an article of a newspaper, or an article of merchandise." (3 Cyc 1012)

One thing of many; divisions or paragraphs of a document or agreement; one item of several; distinct portion or part. The word is also sometimes construed as meaning 'a joint or part or member" or clause or item (as) articles of an agreement or articles of association of a company; a point of faith, doctrine, or duty (as) 'articles of faith"; "each article of human duty"; a complete, independent or partly independent portion of a literary publication especially in a periodical, review, or magazine, a particular substance or commodity (as) articles of merchandise.

A division of a document or statute (designated as such) [S. 26(1), Specific Relief Act (47 of 1963)]; (in plural) a formal agreement; a thing [S. 51, Cr PC 1973 (2 of 1974)]; [App. A, form No. 4, CPC (5 of 1908)]; a generally short non-fictional prose composition usually forming an independent protion of a publication (as a newspaper or magazine).

In the Companies Act, unless there is anything repugnant in the subject or context "ARTICLES" means the article of association of a company as originally framed or as altered by special resolution, including, so far as they apply to the company, the prescribed regulations.

Articles. A particular item of business. [Shorter Oxford English Dictionary as cited in *Escorts Limited* v. *Commissioner of Central Excise, Faridabad*, (2015) 9 SCC 109, para 89].

A machine is a tangible thing which can be both seen and felt and so it is an article". *Zaffar Md.* v. *State of W.B.*, AIR 1976 SC 171 at 172. [Drugs and Magic Remedies (Objectionable Advertisements) Act (21 of 1954), S. 2(b)(iii)]

A division of a document or statute (designated as such) [Specific Relief Act (47 of 1963), S. 26(1)]; (in plural) a formal agreement; a thing [CrPC 1973 (2 of 1974), S. 51]; [CPC (5 of 1908), App. A, form No. 4]; a generally short non-fictional prose composition usually forming an independent protion of a publication (as a newspaper or magazine).

Articles. Means the articles of association of a company as originally framed or as altered from time to time or applied in pursuance of any previous company law or of the Companies Act, 2013 (18 of 2013). [S. 2(5) of the Companies Act, 2013 (18 of 2013)]

Articles of Association. (or Articles of Incorporation) The certificate filed, in conformity with law by persons who desire to become a corporation and setting forth the rules and conditions upon which the association or corporation is founded.

A written agreement prescribing regulations for the governance of a company. [Companies Act (1 of 1956) replaced with Companies Act, 2013, S. 2(2) and Specific Relief Act (47 of 1963), S. 26(1)].

Articles of partnership. A written agreement by which the parties enter into a partnership upon the conditions therein mentioned. (*Bouvier*)

Rules and regulations drawn up for the conduct of partnership. [CPC (5 of 1908), Sch. I, App. A, form No. 49].

Articles of the peace. An obligation to keep the peace for a certain time, under a penalty, and with or without sureties, imposed upon an individual against whom someone has preferred a complaint that there is just cause to fear that the party complained of will commit some crime or do him some bodily harm, or procure a third person to do it.

Articles of war. A code of regulation or rules for the Government and discipline of the army and navy.

The rules for the government of troops on active service (issued under the prerogative of the Crown, prior to the Mutiny Act, 1803). [Indian Evidence Act (1 of 1872), S. 57(3)].

Articulated pleading. Pleading which states each allegation in a separate paragraph.

Articuli magnae chartae. The preliminary articles upon which the Magna Carta was founded.

Artificer. "An 'artificer' is a skilled workman". One who is a master in his art and whose employment consists chiefly in manual labour. (*Cunningham*)

Artificial. (*Opposed to natural*) Created by art, or by law; existing only by force of or in contemplation of law.

Opposite to natural; made by or resulting from art or artifice; made by art in imitation or as a substitute for, what is natural or real. [IPC (45 of 1860), S. 431].

Artificial insemination. A method by which a female is made pregnant by injecting semen from a donor other than her husband; and other than through sexual intercourse.

Artificial insemination by donor. Introduction of semen into the uterus by other than natural means.

Artificial persons. Such as are created and devised by human laws, for the purposes of society and government, which are called corporations or bodies politic. Corporations, companies, or other bodies of men. (*Wharton*)

"The plain and broad distinction between a *natural and an artificial person* is, that whilst the former may do any act which is not prohibited by law from doing, the later can do none which the charter giving its existence does not expressly, or by fair inference, to enable it to perform its functions, authorize it to do".

Artificial presumptions (Or "legal presumptions"). Those which derive their force and effect from the law, rather than their natural tendency to produce belief.

Artillery. (*Milit. Law*) Implements of war. The particular troups employed in the service of fire arms.

Mounted projectile; firing guns [Arms Act (54 of 1959), S. 2(1)(e)(i)]; that branch of an army which manages the cannons in war.

Artisan. Artificer; one skilled in some kind of mechanical craft or art. A skilled mechanic. (*Black*; *Stroud*)

The expression 'artisan' must be restricted to handicraftsman or artificer who is employed in any of the industrial arts. *T.R. Pannavanam* v. *U. Muthuswami,* AIR 1962 Mad 444, 447. [CPC (5 of 1908), S. 60(1) Proviso., Cl (b)]

The word 'artisan' is used often a synonymous with a mechanic, who is a person who has such special knowledge of some mechanism as to enable him to operate it and to set it right when it goes wrong. A motor driver is not necessarily a mechanic and is not an artisan.

A carpenter who might have been utilised only for the purposes of making tea chests will come under the definition of 'artisan'. *Cachar Cha Sramik Union* v. *Manager Manjhegram Tea Estate,* AIR 1960 Ass 123, 126. [Minimum Wages Act (11 of 1948), S. 3]

One skilled in some kind of mechanical art or craft. [Emigration Act (7 of 1972), S. 2(1)(o)(iv)].

Artist. One who professes or practices an art in which conception and execution are governed by imagination and taste; one whose vocation involves drawing, painting, designing or layout work.

Artistic work. Means,—(i) a painting, a sculpture, a drawing (including diagram, map, chart or plan), an engraving or a photograph, whether or not any such work possesses artistic quality; (ii) an architectural work of art; and (iii) any other work of artistic craftsmanship. [Copyright Act (14 of 1957), S. 2(c)]

As. In that way; after the manner of; in the character or capacity of.

As a whole. The expression 'as a whole' in "net value of the assets of the business as a whole", means to ascertain the value of the assets of the business as a whole, after taking into account the liabilities of the business. *Commissioner of Wealth Tax* v. *Raipur Mfg. Co.,* AIR 1964 Guj 154, 171. [Wealth Tax Act (27 of 1957), S. 2(n)]

As far as it can be made applicable. The words "as far as it can be made applicable" make it clear that, in applying the various provisions of the code to proceedings other than those of a suit, the Court must take into account the nature of those proceedings and the relief sought. *Babubhai Mujibai Patel* v. *Nandalal Khodidas Barob,* AIR 1974 SC 2105, 2110. [CPC (5 of 1908), S. 141]

As far as possible. This phrase really means that the principles are to be observed unless it is not possible to follow them in the particular circumstances of a case.

Calling not less than two persons enjoined in the sub-section is only 'as far as possible' and no more. If it is not possible then it cannot vitiate the search or the seizure. *Gopalpur Tea Co.* v. *Calcutta Corporation,* AIR 1966 Cal 51, 53. [Prevention of Food Adulteration Act (37 of 1954), S. 10(7)]

The expression "as far as may be", occurring in Section 343(1), does not foreclose wholly, the discretion of the Magistrate, if he genuinely feels necessary, to get additional material on record for his necessary satisfaction to proceed thereafter as required in the law. [*State of Goa* v. *Jose Maria Albert Vales,* (2018) 11 SCC 659, para 54] [Code of Criminal Procedure, 1973 (1 of 1974), S. 343(1)].

As if. The words "as if" are used in sub-section (1) to make the whole scheme of O. XXI applicable in respect of execution of decrees of foreign Courts mentioned in sub-sec. (1) — The words 'as if' have no wider meaning. *Morlays (B'Ham) Ltd.* v. *Roshanlal Ramsahai,* AIR 1961 Bom 156. [CPC (5 of 1908), S. 44-A]

As if he were. The legal effect of the words 'as if he were' in the definition of owner is that, although the petitioners were not the owners they bring the contractors for the working of the mine in question, they were to be treated as such though in fact, they were not so. *Industrial Supplies (P) Ltd.* v. *Union of India,* AIR 1980 SC 1858, 1864. [Coking Coal Mines (Nationalisation) Act (36 of 1972), S. 3(ii)]

As if he were a civil Court. The words 'as if he were a civil Court' occurring in S. 75(4) of the Registration Act attracts all the provisions of the civil procedure code in respect of summoning and enforcing attendance of witnesses and the provisions of O. XVI, R. 14 CPC (5 of 1908) apply with full force to any enquiry before the Sub-registrar for compulsory registration of documents presented before him. *Kuppa Gaunder* v. *Joint Sub-Registrar,* AIR 1960 Mad 401, 403. [Registration Act (16 of 1908), S. 75(4)]

As it deems fit. The expression confers a jurisdiction of widest amplitude on the *quasi*-judicial tribunal. But that does not mean that such tribunal can pass any order in total disregard of the statutory provisions under which the *quasi*-judicial tribunal is created and is conferred jurisdiction to resolve disputes arising in the implementation of the statute. *Narendra Singh* v. *Chhotey Singh,* AIR 1983 SC 990, 994.

As it thinks fit. The expression "pass such orders thereon as it thinks fit" does not give any arbitrary power. The expression is intended to define the jurisdiction of the tribunal to deal with and determine questions which arise out of the subject matter of the appeal in the light of evidence and consistent with the justice of the case. *Commissioner of Income Tax* v. *Walchand & Co.*, AIR 1967 SC 1435, 1437. [Income Tax Act (11 of 1922) S. 33(4)]

The expression "as it thinks fit" confers a very wide jurisdiction enabling it to take an entirely different view on the same set of facts and has the same connotation, unless context otherwise indicates, 'as he deems fit' which means to make an order in terms of the statute, which would give effect to a right which the Act has elsewhere conferred. *Babulal Nagar* v. *Shree Synthetics Ltd.,* AIR 1984 SC 1164. [M.P. Industrial Relations Act, 1960, S. 66]

As may seem necessary to satisfy the decree. The words clearly indicate that no sale can be allowed beyond the decretal amount mentioned in the sale proclamation. *Takkaseela Pedda Subba Reddi* v. *Pujari Palmavathamma*, AIR 1977 SC 1789, 1791. [CPC (5 of 1908), O. XXI, R. 64].

As nearly as may be. The expression suggests that direction is meant not to be mandatory but directory. The expression as used in the proviso to clause (1) of Art. 316 of the Constitution suggests that the proportion of 50% of the service members in not to be mandatory but directory. The proviso does not, in terms, say that in no case and no point of time, the said proportion should either go above or fall below 50%. *Jai Shankar Prasad* v. *State of Bihar*, AIR 1993 SC 1906, 1912.

As of. On; at.

As of right. The expression 'as of right' means that the enjoyment of the right should not be secret or by stealth or by sufferance or the leave and licence of another person. By virtue of a legal entitlement. [Indian Easements Act (5 of 1882), S. 15]

The Indian expression 'as of right' means that the enjoyment of the light should not be secret or by stealth or by sufferance or the leave and licence of another person. *Suresh Chand* v. *Hindu Mal*, AIR 1994 HP 56, 58. [Indian Easements Act (5 of 1882), S. 15]

The expression "as of right" in S. 26, Limitation Act XV of 1877 does not and cannot mean a user enjoyed from time to time at the will and pleasure of the owner of the property over which the user is sought. *Kyinan* v. *Set Lan*, 8 Ind Cas 1196 : 3 Bur LT 100 (*per* JUSTICE TWOMEY). [See also Indian Easements Act (5 of 1882), S. 15]

As per. In accordance with.

As soon as. This term has a relative meaning according to the thing which is to be done. It may denote merely a reasonable time; or may be equivalent to "whenever", or may mean "immediately."

As soon as may be. The phrase "as sŏon as may be" does not exclude reasonable time for formulating the grounds on the material in the possession of the authority. *B. Santhamma* v. *State of Hyderabad,* AIR 1951 Hyd 128. [Constitution of India, Art. 22(5)]

"As soon as may be" means "as soon as practicable". *Ashok Kumar* v. *Delhi Administration*, AIR 1982 SC 1143, 1146. [National Security Act (65 of 1980), S. 3(2) and 8]

The period of 5 days provided in Sec. 7 is an absolute one and is independent of the period which is permissible under the expression 'as soon as may be', which must, by its very nature, be indefinite depending on the facts and circumstances of the case. *Keshav Nilkanth Joglekar* v. *Commissioner of Police*, AIR 1957 SC 28, 33.

"Where the State Government took only less than a week to send the report to Central Government it may be regarded as soon as may be". *Bidya Deb Barma* v. *District Magistrate*, *Tripura Agartala*, AIR 1969 SC 323 at 326.

Quite clearly the period of time predicted by the phrase 'as soon as may be' begins to run from the time the detention in pursuance of the detention order begins. It may not be possible in many cases to affirmatively say or to precisely quantify the period of time by reference to hours, days or months : nevertheless it is possible having regard to the circumstances of the cases, to say whether the thing done was or was not done 'as soon as may be', *i.e.*, within the time which was reasonably convenient or requisite. *Abdul Jabar Butt* v. *Sate of Jammu & Kashmir*, AIR 1957 SC 281, 283.

Promptly and with due diligence; as soon as was reasonably possible; within a reasonable time; as soon as possible; forthwith; as soon as they conveniently can.

As soon as possible. "To do a thing "as soon as possible" means to do it within a reasonable time, with an understanding to do it within the shortest possible time".

As soon as practicable means reasonable time. These words are not synonymous with "as soon as possible", they mean ordinarily as soon as reasonably can be expected in the particular circumstances; or "in due time". But the words have also been construed as practically synonymous with speedily.

As the case may be. The phrase 'as the case may be' means that one out of the various alternatives would apply to one out of the various situations and not otherwise.

Ascend. To go up; to pass up or upwards; to go or pass in the ascending line.

Ascendant. A relation in the ascending line; one who precedes in geneological order. [Hindu Marriage Act (25 of 1955), S. 3(f)(ii)].

Ascendant, Lineal. An ascendant in direct line of ascent [Hindu Marriage Act (25 of 1955), S. 3(f)(ii)].

Ascending degree. A degree counted in the order of ascent. [Hindu Succession Act (30 of 1956), S. 13(1)].

Ascent. Line of ascent, in genealogy, ancestry. The transmission of an estate from the ancestor to the heir in the ascending line. (*Burrill*)

Ascertain : Ascertained.—These words have two meanings, (1) 'known', (2) "made certain"; to free from obscurity, doubt or chance; to fix; to settle or determine. (*Cent. Dict.*)

To render certain or definite, to estimate and determine; to clear of doubt or obscurity. To insure as a certainty. To find out by investigations.

To find out or learn for a certainty; to make sure of; get to know. [Indian Evidence Act (1 of 1872), S. 73].

Ascertained by taxation. Made sure by assessment. [CPC (5 of 1908), S. 118].

Ascertained money. The expression "ascertained money" as used in section 2(1)(d) of the 1983 Act will include not only the amount already ascertained but also the amount which may be ascertained during the proceedings on the basis of claims/counterclaims of the parties. [*Gangotri Enterprises Limited* v. *M.P. Road Development Corporation,* (2018) 16 SCC 296, para 3] [M.P. Madhyasthan Adhikaran Adhiniyam, 1963, Section 2(1)(d)].

Ascertained goods. Goods the identity of which has by some means or other been determined. [Sale of Goods Act (3 of 1930), S. 58].

Ask price. The price at which one can buy an asset.

Asking price. Value at which a seller lists property for sale, often suggesting a willingness to sell for less.

Aspect. View; object; implies the existence of alternative. (As) a "contingency with a double aspect".

A way in which a thing may be viewed or regarded.

Asphyxia. (*In medical jurisprudence*) A morbid condition of swooning, suffocation, or suspended animation, resulting in death if not relieved, produced by any serious interference with normal respiration, (as) the obstruction of the air passages by inhalation of poisonous gases or too rarified air, choking or drowning, with a consequent deficiency of oxygen in the blood.

Asportation. An asportation is a carrying away : and is, generally, spoken of the carrying away of goods; feloniously taken.

Taking the thing away from the plaintiff's possession.

Assailant. One who assaults. [IPC (45 of 1860), Ss. 100 and 101].

Assassin. A murderer.

Assassination is the murdering of a person without provocation or cause of resentment given to the murderer. (*Scotch Dict.; Tomlin*)

Assault. "Whoever makes any gesture, or any preparation, intending or knowing it to be likely that such gesture or preparation will cause any person present to apprehend that he who makes that gesture or preparation is about to use criminal force, to that person, is said to commit an assault.

Explanation.—Mere words do not amount to an assault. But the words which a person uses may give to his gestures or preparation such a meaning as may make those gestures or preparations amount to an assault". [IPC (45 of 1860), S. 351][(w.e.f. 1-7-2024) repealed and replaced by Bharatiya Nyaya Sanhita, 2023 (45 of 2023), section 130] An onset with hostile intent [IPC (45 of 1860), S. 351]; to make an assault [Children Act (60 of 1960), S. 41(1) (*repealed*)].

An attempt with force and violence, to do corporal hurt to another as by striking at him, with or without a weapon. (*Tomlin*)

Assault and Battery. "A *battery* is an assault whereby any physical force of adverse nature is actually applied to the person of another, or to the dress worn by him, directly or indirectly". "Battery is the unlawful beating of another". "Every battery includes an assault". (*Ame. Cyc.*) But not *vice versa.*

Assay. The proof or trial, by chemical experiments, of the purity or fineness of metals— especially of the precious metals, as gold or silver.

To make a trial of metals by touch, fire *etc.* [Gold (Control) Act (45 of 1968), S. 2(s) (*Repealed*)].

Assayer. One whose business it is to make assays of the precious metals.

"Assaying and hallmarking centre" means a testing and marking centre recognised by the Bureau to determine the purity of precious metal articles and to apply hallmark on the precious metal articles in a manner as may be determined by regulations. [Bureau of Indian Standard Act (11 of 2016), S. 2(2)]

Assemble. To bring together; to collect in one place or as one body; to convene; to congregate.

Assembling. Fitting together various parts so as to make into an operative whole [Collection of Statistics Act (32 of 1953), S. 2(d)]; meeting; bringing or summoning together into an assembly. [Navy Act (62 of 1957), S. 101(3)].

Assembly. A company of persons assembled together in one place usually for a common purpose— generally, for deliberation, legislation, worship or social entertainment.

An "Assembly" of persons would seem to mean three or more (*Stroud*); the concourse or meeting together of a considerable number of persons at the same place; also the persons so gathered. (*Black*)

The concourse or meeting together of a considerable number of persons at the same place. Also the persons so gathered. [Black's Law Dictionary, 6th Edn. as cited in *State of Haryana* v. *Shakuntala*, (2012) 5 SCC 171, para 31].

For the purpose of S. 296, IPC (45 of 1860), three persons gathered together for purpose of worship in a temple would be sufficient to constitute an "assembly."

'Assembly, unlawful'. The congregating of people which results in antisocial behavior of the group i.e. blocking a sidewalk, obstructing traffic, littering streets; but, a law which makes such congregating a crime because people may be annoyed is violative of the right of free assembly. [Black's Law Dictionary, 6th Edn. as cited in *State of Haryana* v. *Shakuntala*, (2012) 5 SCC 171, para 31].

Assembly of persons. A company of persons collected together in one place usually for some common purpose. [IPC (45 of 1860), S. 141].

Assent. The act of the mind in admitting or agreeing to the truth of a proposition proposed for acceptance; consent, agreeing to; to admit, yield, or concede; to express an agreement of the mind to what is alleged or proposed, (as) President's or Governor's assent to an enactment passed in the Parliament or the Legislature

MUTUAL ASSENT is the meeting of the minds of both or all the parties to a contract.

Agreement, approval, or permission.

Assent, consent, concurrence, acquiescence, acceptance, adherence. "*Assent* is primarily an act of the understanding; *consent* is distinctly the act of the will; Assent is not yet altogether excluded from the field of the will, but tends to express a feebler action of the will than consent does. *Concurrence* is a running of minds in the same channel, an agreement in opinion or decision. *Acquiescence* is a state or act of quiet submission to a decision; an act, or the prevalence of an opinion, because it is near enough to one's wishes, or not worth resisting, or impossible to resist, but not because it is entirely acceptable". (*Cent. Dict.*)

An official, judicial or formal sanction; the concurrence of one's will. [Constitution of India, Art. 31 A, *prov.*]; to give assent; to express one's agreement.

Assent to bill. Assent of the head of the executive to the bill passed by legislature.

Assert : To vindicate, maintain or defend with words (as) to assert our rights and liberties.

To aver; to affirm [Indian Evidence Act (1 of 1872), S. 3, *Expln.*].

Assertion. The action of asserting; the thing asserted. [Indian Trusts Act (2 of 1882), S. 13].

Assess. To rate or ascertain, to apportion or fix the amount of a tax to be paid or contributed; to make a valuation or official estimate of property for the purpose of taxation; to adjust or apportion; to fix or settle a sum to be levied or paid (as) assessed taxes; or revenue assessed on land.

Assess is a comprehensive word, in a taxing statute. It often means the computation of the income of the assesse, the determination of the tax payable by him, and the procedure for collecting or recovering the tax. *Bhopal Sugar Industries Ltd.* v. *State of M.P.*, AIR 1979 SC 537, 540.

To fix or settle a sum to be levied or paid; to make a valuation or official estimate (of property or income) for the purpose of taxation; to fix or determine the rate or amount of [Wealth-tax Act (27 of 1957), S. 17(b)].

Assessed tax. Tax, the amount or rate of which is assessed or fixed in each case, *e.g.*, Income tax.

Assessee. (*in Income-tax Act*) means a person by whom income-tax is payable.

"ASSESSEE" means a person by whom any tax or any other sum of money is payable under this Act, and includes—

(a) every person in respect of whom any proceeding under this Act has been taken for the assessment of his income or assessment of fringe benefits or of the income of any other person in respect of which he is assessable, or of the loss sustained by him or by such other person, or of the amount of refund due to him or to such other person;

(b) every person who is deemed to be an assessed under any provision of this Act;

(c) every person who is deemed to be an assessed in default under any provision of this Act. [Income-tax Act (43 of 1961), S. 2(7)]

"Assessee" means a person,—

(a) being a resident in India within the meaning of section 6 of the Income-tax Act, 1961 (43 of 1961) in the previous year; or

(b) being a non-resident or not ordinarily resident in India within the meaning of clause (6) of section 6 of the Income-tax Act, 1961 (43 of 1961) in the previous year, who was resident in India either in the previous year to which the income referred to in section 4 relates; or in the previous year in which the undisclosed asset located outside India was acquired:

Provided that the previous year, in case of acquisition of undisclosed asset outside India, shall be determined without giving effect to the provisions of clause (c) of section 72. [Black Money (Undisclosed Foreign Income and Assets) and Imposition of Tax Act (22 of 2015), section 2(2)]

"ASSESSEE" means the person who is liable to pay the duty of excise under this Act and includes his agent. [Central Excise Act (1 of 1944), S. 4(3)(a) S. 2(5)]

"ASSESSEE" means a person by whom surtax or any other sum of money is payable under this Act and includes every person in respect of whom any proceeding under this Act has been taken for the assessment of his chargeable profits or of the amount of refund due to him or of the chargeable profits of any other person in respect of which he is assessable or of the amount of refund due to such other person. [Companies (Profits) Surtax Act (7 of 1964), S. 2(1-A)]

"ASSESSEE" means a person liable to pay the service tax and incudes his agent. [Finance Act (32 of

1994), S. 65(7), as amended by Act (32 of 2003), S. 159 (now repealed by Central Goods and Services Tax, 2017)]

One upon whom a payment is assessed. [Income-tax Act (43 of 1961), S. 2(7), Companies (Profits) Surttax Act (7 of 1964), S. 2(1) and Gift-tax Act (18 of 1958), S. 2(iii)].

The word "assesse" refers to the person whose income, profits or gains in respect of a particular source had been once assessed to tax. *Commissioner of Income Tax* v. *Kanchanbai*, AIR 1970 SC 691, 693.

The word 'assesse' will not include the legal representative of the assesse.

"**Assessing authority**" means, any person appointed by the State Government or the Commissioner to perform all or any of the functions of the assessing authority under this Act. [Uttar Pradesh Trade Tax Act, 1948 (15 of 1948), S. 2(a) as cited in *State of U.P.* v. *Systematic Conscom Limited*, (2014) 13 SCC 627, para 10].

Assessing Officer. Means the Assistant Commissioner or Deputy Commissioner or Assistant Director or Deputy Director or the Income-tax Officer who is vested with the relevant jurisdiction by virtue of directions or orders issued under sub-section (1) or sub-section (2) of S. 120 or any other provision of this Act, and the Joint Commissioner or Joint Director who is directed under clause (b) of sub-section (4) of that section to exercise or perform all or any of the powers and functions conferred on, or assigned to, an Assessing Officer under this Act. [Income-tax Act (43 of 1961), S. 2(7A)]

"ASSESSING OFFICER" includes an income-tax authority who is assigned the duty of allotting permanent account numbers. [Income-tax Act (43 of 1961), S. 139A(8) Expl. (a)]

"ASSESSING OFFICER" means the Income-tax Officer or Assistant Commissioner of Income-tax or Deputy Commissioner of Income-tax or Joint Commissioner of Income-tax or Additional Commissioner of Income-tax who is authorised by the Board to exercise or perform all or any of the powers and functions conferred on, or assigned to, an Assessing Officer under this Chapter. [Finance Act (18 of 2005), Ch. VII, S. 94(2)].

Assessment. Determining the value of man's property or occupation for the purpose of levying a tax; determining share of a tax to be paid by each individual (*Bouvier*); levying a tax (as) land revenue assessment.

"Assessment" includes reassessment. [Income-tax Act (43 of 1961), S. 2(8)]

"Assessment" means determination of tax liability under this Act and includes self-assessment, re-assessment, provisional assessment, summary assessment and best judgment assessment [The Central Goods and Services Tax Act, 2017 (12 of 2017), S. 2(11)]

Assessment is popularly used as a synonym for taxation in the general, — the authoritative imposition of a rate or duty to be paid.

The word assessment has been used in the sense of 'computation of income'. At best the word is used in the sense of 'the determination of the amount of tax payable'.

Assessment is the official determination of liability of a person to pay a particular tax.

The word assessment is used in a comprehensive sense and includes all proceedings, starting with the filing of the return or issue of notice and ending with the determination of the tax payable by assesse. *S. Sankarappa* v. *Income Tax Officer*, AIR 1968 SC 816, 818.

The word 'assessment' can comprehend the whole procedure for ascertaining and imposing liability upon the tax-payer. *Kalamati Devi* v. *Commissioner of Income Tax*, AIR 1968 SC 162, 167. [Income-tax Act (43 of 1961), S. 297(2)(a)]

The action of assessing; official valuation of property or income for the purposes of taxation; the amount assessed. [Customs Act (52 of 1962), S. 2(2); Wealth-tax Act (27 of 1957), S. 2(ca); Gift-tax Act (18 of 1958), S. 2(iv) and Income-tax Act (43 of 1961), S. 2(8)].

"ASSESSMENT" means determination of the dutiability of any goods and the amount of the duty, tax, cess or any other sum so payable, if any, under this Act or under the Customs Tariff Act, 1975 (51 of 1975) (hereinafter referred to as the Customs Tariff Act) or under any other law for the time being in force, with reference to—

(*a*) the tariff classification of such goods as determined in accordance with the provisions of the Customs Tariff Act;

(*b*) the value of such goods as determined in accordance with the provisions of this Act and the Customs Tariff Act;

(*c*) exemption of concession of duty, tax, cess or any other sum, consequent upon any notification issued therefor under this Act or under the Customs Tariff Act or under any other law for the time being in force;

(*d*) the quantity, weight, volume, measurement or other specifies is here such duty, tax, cess or any other sum is leviable on the basis of the quantity, weight, volume, measurement or other specifies of such goods;

(*e*) the origin of such goods, determined in accordance with the provisions of the Customs Tariff Act or the rules made thereunder, if the amount of duty, tax, cess or any other sum is affected by the origin of such goods;

(*f*) any other specific factor which affects the duty, tax, cess or any other sum payable on such goods,

and includes provisional assessment, self-assessment, re-assessment and any assessment in which the duty assessed in nil. [Customs Act (52 of 1962), S. 2 as substituted by Finance Act (13 of 2018)].

"ASSESSMENT" means determination of tax liability under this Act and includes self-assessment, reassessment, provisional assessment, summary assessment and best judgment assessment. [Central Goods and Services Tax Act (12 of 2017), S. 2(11)].

"ASSESSMENT" includes self-assessment of duty made by the assese under Rule 6 and provisional assessment under Rule 7. [Central Excise Rules, 2017, R. 2(1)(b)].

Assessment year. Means the period of twelve months commencing on the 1st day on April every year. [Income-tax Act (43 of 1961), section 2(9); Wealth-tax Act (27 of 1957), section 2(d); Black Money (Undisclosed Foreign Income and Assets) and Imposition of Tax Act (22 of 2015), section 2(4)]

Assessor. A person associated with the judge of a Court to advise and direct the decision of such judge; a person appointed to ascertain or fix the value of taxes, rates *etc.* [CPC (5 of 1908), S. 140; Indian Evidence Act (1 of 1872), S. 166 and Cinematograph Act (37 of 1952), S. 3A].

Asset. An asset must be one for which a market value can be ascertained. A right to personal services under a contract of service is unassignable, it cannot be bought or sold. It cannot survive the demise of either of the parties. It can have no actual marketable value and so it cannot be an asset. *O' Brien (Inspector of Taxes)* v. *Bensons Hosiery (Holdings) Ltd.*, (1978) 3 All ER, 1057, 1063. [Financial Act, 1965, S. 22 (1)(3)(c)]

If the employer is able to exact from the employee a substantial sum as a term of releasing him from his obligations to serve, the rights of the employer appear to bear quite sufficiently the mark of an asset of the employer, something which he can turn to account, notwithstanding that his ability to turn it to account is by a type of disposal limited by the nature of the asset. *O'Brieu* v. *Benson's Hosiery Ltd.*, (1979 3 All ER 652, 656 (HL).

The right to trade freely and to compete in the market place is not an asset. *Kirby* v. *Thorn Emi Plc.*, (1988) 2 All ER 947, 959 (CA).

"ASSET" includes property, or right, of any kind. [(w.e.f. 1-4-2016) S. 102(2) of the Income-tax Act, 1961 (43 of 1961) (still-born) Section 102(2) of the Income-tax Act, 1961 (43 of 1961) as inserted (w.e.f. 1-4-2014) by the Finance Act, 2012 and omitted (w.e.f. 1-4-2014) by the Finance Act, 2013]

Asset allocation. The allocation of investments, such as stocks and shares, to make up an investment portfolio.

Asset allocation mutual fund. A mutual fund (such as a unit trust) in which the fund manager moves investments among various securities to achieve the best return at the least risk. (*Investment*)

Asset acquisition. Acquisition of a corporation by purchasing all its assets directly from the corporation itself, instead of purchasing shares from its shareholders.

Asset-backed fund. A fund consisting of investments that are related to *tangible assets* (such as property or shares), so that the investment participates in growth and can be regarded as a hedge against inflation. (*Investment; International Accounts*)

Asset-based financing. Loans secured on a company's assets, especially its accounts receivable or stock. (*Investment*)

Asset-based swap. An interest rate or cross-currency interest rate swap entered into by a party to convert the coupon on an asset to another rate or another currency rate basis. (*Finance*)

Asset construction. 'Asset reconstruction' means acquisition by any securitisation company or reconstruction company of any right or interest of any bank or financial institution in any financial assistance for the purpose of realisation of such financial assistance. [Securitisation and Reconstruction of Financial Assets and Enforcement of Security Interest Act (54 of 2002), S. 2(b)]

Asset dividend. Payment of a dividend in the form of property, usually the company's product, rather than in cash or stock.

Asset Liability Management. Denotes a scientific way of measuring, monitoring and managing the various risks banks or financial institutions are exposed during the course of their operations. Risk management involves continuous process of planning, organizing and controlling the volumes, maturities, rates and yields of assets and liabilities. [*M L Tannan Banking Law & Practice in India*, 2021, LexisNexis, Dictionary of Banking Terminology].

Asset reconstruction. Asset reconstruction means acquisition by any securitisation company or reconstruction company of any right or interest of any bank or financial institution in any financial assistance for the purpose of realisation of such financial assistance. [Securitisation and Reconstruction of Financial Assets and Enforcement of Security Interest Act (54 of 2002), S. 2(1)(b)]

The expression 'asset reconstruction' means acquisition by asset reconstruction company or asset management company of any right or interest created in favour of any bank or financial institution in any loan or advance granted or created in any debentures or bonds subscribed or guarantee given to the bank or financial institution or rights created in favour of the bank or financial institution under letters of credit. [*Transcore* v. *Union of India,* (2008), 1 SCC 125, 141, para 20]

Asset securitization. It is a process by which non-tradable assets are converted into tradable securities. [*M L Tannan Banking Law & Practice in India*, 2021, LexisNexis, Dictionary of Banking Terminology].

Asset stripping. A process whereby a company acquires a controlling interest in another company for the purpose of disposing of its assets. The opportunity arises where the management of the company taken over has underutilised the assets so that the share price is below the market value of the underlying assets. Asset stripping makes a quick profit for the company engaging in it but brings to an end the business of the company taken over. (*Stock Market*)

Selling off the assets of a company for quick profit, rather than running the company for steady gain. The asset stripper is usually left with a shell company which he keeps alive, not for regular business, but for other, usually dishonest purposes, such as tax evasion. (*Stock Market*)

Practice (which is normally frowned upon) whereby a company is bought merely so that the buyer may sell off its assets for immediate gain. It is also known colloquially as unbundling. (*Business Term*)

Asset value. The value of the assets of a company less its liability.

Assets. "ASSETS" means all the property, movable and immovable, of a deceased person, which is chargeable with and applicable to the payment of his debts and legacies, or available for distribution among his heirs and next-of-kin. [Administrators-General Act (45 of 1963), S. 2(a)]

"ASSET" means a resource controlled by the company and from which future economic benefits are expected to flow to the company. [Unlisted Companies (Issue of Sweat Equity Shares) Rules, 2003, S. 2(i)]

Any item of use or value.

The word "assets" means, a man's property, of whatever kind, which may be used to satisfy debts or demands existing against him.

The expression 'assets' in S. 73, CPC (5 of 1908), must be understood as referring only to money. *Maddu Venkata Subbaiah* v. *Alane Adinarayana,* AIR 1954 Andh 44.

The word 'assets' is 'property in general; all that one owns, considered as applicable to the payment of his debts'.

As a singular, any portion of one's property or effects so considered. *D.G. Gouse* & Co. v. *State of Kerala*, AIR 1980 SC 271, 275. [Constitution of India, Sch. 7, List 1, Entry 86]

The propety of a person available for the inheritance of an heir or for the payment of his debts or legacies; property in general; all that one owns [Wealth-tax Act (52 of 1962), S. 2(e); CPC (5 of 1908), S. 64, *Expln.* and Income-tax Act (43 of 1961), S. 93(4)(a)].

The word "assets" in S. 73, CPC (5 of 1908), means the proceeds of the sale of the property which is sold in execution of a decree. The "assets" referred to in S. 73, CPC (5 of 1908), should be assets held in process of execution, and do not include money paid into Court under O. XXI, R. 55. *Sorabji* v. *Kala Raghunath,* 13 Bom LR 1193.

Assets are real, or personal. Where a man hath lands and dies seized thereof, the lands which come to his heir are assets real; and where he dies possessed of any personal estate, the goods which come to the executors are assets personal. (*Tomlin*)

Assets held by a Court. Assets held by a Court mean any fund in possession of a Court or at its disposal which may be applied by it for the payment of Judgment-debtor's debt. *Vijay Raj* v. *Lalchand,* AIR 1966 Raj 194, 197. [CPC (5 of 1908), S. 73]

Assets (in insolvency law). Realisable property possessed by insolvent at the material moment is 'assets' which however does not include future earnings as they cannot be sold.

Assets in India. Shall be deemed to include export bills drawn in, and import bills drawn on and payable in India and expressed in such currencies as the Reserve Bank may approve in this behalf and also such securities as the Reserve Bank may approve in this behalf, notwithstanding that all or any of the said bills or securities are held outside India. [Banking Regulation Act (10 of 1949), S. 25(3)]

Assets of partnership. Is an expression to denote the aggregate of the several items of property belonging to the partnership".

Assets of the firm. The phrase 'assets of the firm' in S. 29(2), Indian Partnership Act (9 of 1932), means nothing else but the amount that remains after meeting the debts and liabilities of the partnership out of the sale proceeds of the property belonging to the partnership and other amounts in the hands of the partnership. *Bhola Naith* v. *Mt. Kaso Deve,* AIR 1951 All 601.

Assets of the company. If a floating charge has been crystalised at the making of a winding order, the proceeds of realisation of the assets of the company comprised in it, to the extent that those proceeds are required to meet preferential debts and the claims of the debenture holders, are no longer assets of the company in a subsequent winding up any more than if they had initially been subject to a fixed charge. *Re Christorette International Ltd.* (1982) 3 All ER 225, 230. [Companies Act, 1948, Ss. 94(1), 319]

Assets of the Interim Pension Fund Regulatory and Development Authority. The 'assets of the Interim Pension Fund Regulatory and Development Authority' shall be deemed to include all rights and powers, all properties, whether movable or immovable, including, in particular, cash balances, deposits and all other interests and rights in, or arising out of, such properties as may be in the possession of the Interim Pension Fund Regulatory and Development Authority and all books of account and other documents relating to the same; and liabilities shall be deemed to include all debts, liabilities and obligations of whatever kind. [*Explanation* to section 13(a) of the Pension Fund

Regulatory & Development Authority Act, 2013 (23 of 2013)]

Asseverate. To affirm, or declare solemnly.

Assign (*Verb*)**.** To grant; to convey; to make an assignment; to point out (*Bouvier*); to transfer or make over to another the right one has in any object, as in an estate, chose in action, or reversion especially in trust for the security of creditors; rarely applied to testamentary transfers. To show or set forth with particularity; as, to assign error in a writ; to point out or substantiate as a charge; as, perjury cannot be assigned on an oath taken without the jurisdiction of the officer administering it.

To make over or set over to another. [Constitution of India, Art. 76(2)]; to transfer, as to assign property or some interest therein. [Presidency-towns Insolvency Act (3 of 1909), Ss. 4 and 8(2)(a)].

Assignable. That may be assigned or transferred; transferable; negotiable, as a bill of exchange.

Assigned account. Pledge of an account receivable to a bank a security for loan.

Assigned counsel. Appointment of an attorney by the Court to represent an indigent person.

Assigned risk. One who is a poor risk for insurance but whom an insurance company is forced to insure because of state law *e.g.* an accident prone driver.

Assignee. "ASSIGNEE" includes an assignee of the assignee and the legal representative of a deceased assignee and references to the assignee of any person include references to the assignee of the legal representative or assignee of that person. [Patents Act (39 of 1970), S. 2(ab)]

One to whom rights have been transmitted, by particular title, such as conveyance, gift, legacy or other transfer.

Those who are assigned, deputed or appointed by the act of the party, or the operation of law, to do any act, or enjoy any benefit on their own account and risk—an *assignee* not being one that possesses a thing in his own right; but a *deputy*, he that acts in right of another.

A person to whom an assignment is made [T.P Act (4 of 1882), S. 135, and Copyright Act (14 of 1957), S. 18(3)].

"ASSIGNEE" for the purposes of section 339 of Act 18 of 2013, the expression 'assignee' includes any person to whom or in whose favour, by the directions of the person liable, the debt, obligation, mortgage or charge was created, issued or transferred or the interest was created, but does not include an assignee for valuable consideration, not including consideration by way of marriage, given in good faith and without notice of any of the matters on the ground of which the declaration is made. [*Explanation* (*a*) to section 339 of the Companies Act, 2013 (18 of 2013)]

For the purposes of this section, "assignee" includes a person to whom or in whose favour, by the directions of the person held liable under clause (*a*) the debt, obligation, mortgage or charge was created, issued or transferred or the interest created, but does not include an assignee for valuable consideration given in good faith and without notice of any of the grounds on which the directions have been made. [Insolvency and Bankruptcy Code (31 of 2016), section 67(1), *Explanation*]

"ASSIGNEE" means a factor in whose favour the receivable is transferred. [S. 2(b) of the Factoring Regulation Act, 2011 (12 of 2012)]

Assignment. Transferring the interest a man hath in any thing to another. (*Tomlin*)

The term assignment, as ordinarily used, signifies the transfer, between living parties, of all kinds of property, real, personal and mixed, whether in possession or action, and whether made by delivery, indorsement, transfer in writing, or by parole, and includes as well the instruments by which the transfer is made as the transfer itself.

The action of assigning; the document effecting an assignment [Gift-tax Act (18 of 1958), S. 2(xxiv); Indian Forest Act (16 of 1927), S. 28(1), and T.P. Act (4 of 1882), S. 135]; [Esso (Acquisition of Undertakings in India) Act (4 of 1974), S. 9(1)].

The word "assignment" cannot mean "appointment". *Oriental Metal Pressing Works (P) Ltd.* v. *Bhaskar Kashivath Thakoor*, AIR 1961 SC 573, 575. [Companies Act (1 of 1956) replaced with Companies Act, 2013, S. 312]

Assignment means the transfer of the claim, right or property to another. *Commissioner Gift Tax* v. *Getty Chattiar*, AIR 1971 SC 2410, 2413. [Gift Tax Act (18 of 1958), S. 2(xxiv)].

Assignment means an assignment in writing by act of the parties concerned. [Trade Mark Act, 1999, S. 2(1)(b)].

"ASSIGNMENT" means transfer by agreement, of undivided interest of any assignor in any receivable due from any debtor in favour of a factor and includes an assignment where either the assignor or the debtor, are situated or established outside India. *Explanation.*—For the purposes of this clause, undivided interest of any assignor in any receivable shall not include creation of rights in receivables as security for loans and advances or other obligations by a bank or a financial institution. [S. 2(a) of the Factoring Regulation Act, 2011 (12 of 2012)]

"Assignment" means any assignment of an insolvency professional as interim resolution professional, resolution professional, liquidator, bankruptcy trustee, authorised representative or in any other role under the Code. [Insolvency and Bankruptcy Board of India (Insolvency Professionals) Regulations, 2016, Regn. 2(1)(a)]

Assignment, creation or devolution of any interest. During the pendency of the suit, if the mortgagee or the mortgagor becomes insolvent the receiver has a right to be substituted under the order. *Dharam Chand* v. *Ramchand,* AIR 1972 P&H 203, 204. [CPC (5 of 1908), O. XXII, R. 10]

Assignment of contract. Liabilities under a contract can be assigned with the consent of other party to the contract and the parties may make them assignable, expressly or impliedly and the right and benefits under it may be assigned by legal assignment, equitable assignment, or by operation of law.

Assignment of rents clause. A separate agreement or mortgage provision which entitles the mortgagee to collect rents from the mortgaged premises if the mortgagor defaults.

Assignatus utitur jure auctoris. (*Maxim*) An assignee is clothed with the rights of his principal. (*Broom*)

Assignor. One who assigns or transfers property to another. (*Perkins; Tomlin*)

One who makes an assignment. [CPC (5 of 1908), O. XXI, R. 18(2)].

"ASSIGNOR" means any person who is the owner of any receivable. [S. 2(c) of the Factoring Regulation Act, 2011 (12 of 2012)]

Assigns of copyright. 'Assigns' shall be construed to mean and include every person in whom the interest of an author in copyright shall be vested—whether derived from such author before or after the publication of any book, and whether acquired by sale, gift, bequest, or by operation of law, or otherwise.

Assisa cadere. To be non-suited.

Assisa continuanda. An ancient writ addressed to the justices of assize for the continuation of a cause, when certain facts put in issue could not have been proved in time by the party alleging them. (*Black*)

Assise (See, *Assize*). Anciently signified a Legislative Enactment *e.g.* The Assise of Clarendon, The Assise of the Forest, The Assise of Arms. An assise passed in the reign of Henry II provided for the trial of questions of seizing and title to land by an enquiry of the men sworn to speak the truth; hence the proceedings and the jurors themselves became known as the assises.

Assist. To aid; succour; help; lend encouragement to.

Merely using stolen goods in the possession of another could not constitute the offence of assisting in their retention. Mere verbal representations dishonestly made for the benefit of another to conceal that goods were stolen, even if unsuccessful, could constitute 'assisting' in the retention of the stolen goods.

To give support to in some undertaking or effort.

Assistance. The act of assisting; help; aid; succour; support.

The action of assisting; the help afforded; aid; relief [IPC (45 of 1860), Ss. 105 and 187].

Assistant. Acting as an officer or official subordinate to another whom he assists; officer of a grade below the highest.

Helper; an employee whose duty is to help his superiors, to whom he must look for authority to act. [Indian Evidence Act (1 of 1872), S. 57(12)].

Assistant Commander. Means a person appointed or in pay as an Assistant Commander Grade I, Assistant Commander Grade II or Assistant Commander Grade III. [National Security Guard Act (47 of 1986), S. 2(b)]

Assisted areas. Parts of the UK in which companies receive government grants as an incentive to locate there.

"Assisted reproductive technology". With its grammatical variations and cognate expressions, means all techniques that attempt to obtain a pregnancy by handling the sperm or the oocyte outside the human body and transferring the gamete or the embryo into the reproductive system of a woman. [Assisted Reproductive Technology (Regulation) Act, 2021 (42 of 2021), section 2(1)(a)]

"Assisted reproductive technology bank". Means an organisation which shall be responsible for collection of gametes, storage of gametes and embryos and supply of gametes to the assisted reproductive technology clinics or their patients [Assisted Reproductive Technology (Regulation) Act, 2021 (42 of 2021), section 2(1)(b)]

"Assisted reproductive technology clinic". Means any premises equipped with requisite facilities and medical practitioners registered with the National Medical Commission for carrying out the procedures related to the assisted reproductive technology. [Assisted Reproductive Technology (Regulation) Act, 2021 (42 of 2021), section 2(1)(c)]

Assisted self determination. Intentional act to provide a person with the medical means or the medical knowledge to commit suicide. Also called as *Assisted suicide*.

Assize (See, *Assise*). Assembly of judges; a legislative assembly; decree, edict, ordinance (as) assize of arms, a jury trial; also the jury.

Assize of Clarendon (1166). It provided that 12 legal men of every 104 legal men from every township must present to the judges the crimes which were in their knowledge. Accused were punished if they failed to clear by ordeal. Virtually, this was the origin of the Grand Jury.

Associate. A forfeiture of a wife's annuity, if she shall "associate, continue to keep company with, or cohabit, or criminally correspond with, may result", if F (named person) calls at her house and leaves his card like any other visitor, and still more if he is sometimes admitted; the meaning of such a condition is "that there should be no communication whatever between the parties" (*per* MANSFIELD C.J.), "the receiving a man's visits, whenever he chooses to call, is 'associating with' him." (*per* CURIAM, *Dormer* v. *Knight*, (1809) 1 Taunt. 417, 418).

"ASSOCIATE" in relation to either of the corporations means any subsidiary of the corporation or any person with whom the corporation has made an agreement in accordance with clause (h) of sub-section (2) of S. 7. [Air Corporation Act (27 of 1953), S. 2(iii)]

"ASSOCIATE" in relation to a person whose property is liable to be forfeited under this Chapter, includes—

(i) any individual who had been or is managing the affairs or keeping the accounts of such person;

(ii) any association of persons, body of individuals, partnership firm or private company within the meaning of the Companies Act, 1956 of which such person had been or is a member, partner or director;

(iii) any individual who had been or is a member, partner or director of an association of persons, body of individuals, partnership firm or private company referred to in sub-clause (ii) at any time when such person had been or is a member, partner or director of such association, body, partnership firm or private company;

(iv) any person, who had been or is managing the affairs, or keeping the accounts of any association of persons, body of individuals, partnership firm or private company referred to in sub-clause (iii);

(v) the trustee of any trust, where,—

(1) the trust has been created by such person; or

(2) the value of the assets contributed by such person (including the value of the assets, if any, contributed by him earlier) to the trust amounts on the date on which contribution is made, to not less than twenty per cent. of the value of the assets of the trust on that date;

(vi) where the competent authority, for reasons to be recorded in writing, considers that any properties of such person are held on his behalf by any other person, such other person. [Wild Life Protection Act (53 of 1972), S. 58B(b)]

One who is united to another by community of interest; a partner, comrade, companion or colleague [IPC (45 of 1860), S. 94, expln. 1]; joined in companionship, function or dignity [Companies Act (1 of 1956) replaced with Companies Act, 2013, S. 2(3)]; to join in any action or in companionship for a common purpose.; to accompany; to be with.

"Associate" in relation to a creditor, a resolution professional or professionals engaged by resolution professional, as the case may be, shall have the same meaning as assigned to it in relation to a debtor in sub-section (2) of section 79. [Insolvency and Bankruptcy Board of India (Insolvency Resolution Process for Personal Guarantors to Corporate Debtors) Regulations, 2019, Regn. 3(a)]

"Associate" in relation to a creditor, a bankruptcy trustee or professionals appointed by the bankruptcy trustee shall have the same meaning as assigned to it in relation to a debtor in sub-section (2) of section 79, as may be applicable. [Insolvency and Bankruptcy Board of India (Bankruptcy Process for Personal Guarantors to Corporate Debtors) Regulations, 2019, Regn. 2(a)]

Associate company. In relation to another company, means a company in which that other company has a significant influence, but which is not a subsidiary company of the company having such influence and includes a joint venture company. *Explanation.*—For the purposes of this clause, "significant influence" means control of at least twenty per cent of total share capital, or of business decisions under an agreement. [S. 2(6) of the Companies Act, 2013 (18 of 2013)]

Associate enterprise. Means a company, whether incorporated or not, which,—(i) is a holding company or a subsidiary company of the applicant; or (ii) is a joint venture of the applicant; or (iii) controls the composition of the board of directors or other body governing the applicant; or (iv) exercises, in the opinion of the Reserve Bank, significant influence on the applicant in taking financial or policy decisions; or (v) is able to obtain economic benefits from the activities of the applicant. [S. 12B(1), *Explanation* 1(a) of the Banking Regulation Act, 1949 (10 of 1949) as inserted by the Banking Laws (Amendment) Act, 2012 (4 of 2013)]

Associated. Joined in companionship [IPC (45 of 1860), S. 310]; joined in loose combination; [Haryana and Punjab Agricultural University Act (16 of 1970), S. 13(2) (d) (iii)].

Associated operation. In relation to any transfer, means an operation of any kind effected by any person in relation to—

(i) any of the assets transferred, or

(ii) any assets representing, whether directly or indirectly, any of the assets transferred, or

(iii) the income arising from any such assets, or

(iv) any assets representing, whether directly or indirectly, the accumulations of income arising from any such assets. [Income-tax Act (43 of 1961), S. 93(4)(b)]

"ASSOCIATED OPERATIONS" means any two or more operations of any kind being—

(a) operations which affect the same property, or one of which affects some property and the other or others of which affects property which represents, whether directly or indirectly, the property, or income arising from that property, or any property representing accumulations of any such income; or

(b) any two operations of which one is effected with reference to the other, or with a view to enabling it to be effected or to facilitating its being effected, and any third operation having a like relation to either of those two, and any fourth operation having a life relation to any of those three, and so on; whether those operations are effected by the same person or by different persons, whether they are connected otherwise than as aforesaid or not, and whether they are contemporaneous or any of them precedes or follows any other. [Estate Duty Act (34 of 1953), S. 27(7)(iv)]

Associated person. In relation to a person, means—(a) any relative of the person, if the person is an individual; (b) any director of the company or any relative of such director, if the person is a company; (c) any partner or member of a firm or association of persons or body of individuals or any relative of such partner or member if the person is a firm or association of persons or body of individuals; (d) any member of the Hindu undivided family or any relative of such member, if the person is a Hindu undivided family; (e) any individual who has a substantial interest in the business of the person or any relative of such individual; (f) a company, firm or an association of persons or a body of individuals, whether incorporated or not, or a Hindu undivided family having a substantial interest in the business of the person or any director, partner, or member of the company, firm or association of persons or body of individuals or family, or any relative of such director, partner or member; (g) a company, firm or association of persons or body of individuals, whether incorporated or not, or a Hindu undivided family, whose director, partner, or member have a substantial interest in the business of the person, or family or any relative of such director, partner or member; (h) any other person who carries on a business, if—(i) the person being an individual, or any relative of such person, has a substantial interest in the business of that other person; or (ii) the person being a company, firm, association of persons, body of individuals, whether incorporated or not, or a Hindu undivided family, or any director, partner or member of such company, firm or association of persons or body of individuals or family, or any relative of such director, partner or member, has a substantial interest in the business of that other person. [(still-born) Section 102(3) of the Income-tax Act, 1961 (43 of 1961) as inserted (w.e.f. 1-4-2014) by the Finance Act, 2012 and omitted (w.e.f. 1-4-2014) by the Finance Act, 2013]

"Associated person", in relation to a person, means—

(a) any relative of the person, if the person is an individual;

(b) any director of the company or any relative of such director, if the person is a company;

(c) any partner or member of a firm or association of persons or body of individuals or any relative of such partner or member if the person is a firm or association of persons or body of individuals;

(d) any member of the Hindu Undivided Family or any relative of such member, if the person is a Hindu Undivided Family;

(e) any individual who has substantial interest in the business of the person or any relative of such individual;

(f) a company, firm or an association of persons or a body of individuals, whether incorporated or not, or a Hindu Undivided Family having a substantial interest in the business of the person or any director, partner or member of the company, firm or association of persons or body of individuals or family, or any relative of such director, partners or member;

(g) a company, firm or association of persons or body of individuals, whether incorporated or not or a Hindu Undivided Family, whose director, partner or member have a substantial interest in the business of the person or family or any relative of such director, partner or member;

(h) any other person who carries on a business, if—

(i) the person being an individual, or any relative of such person, has a substantial interest in the business of that other person; or

(ii) the person being a company, firm, association of persons, body of individuals, whether incorporated or not, or a Hindu Undivided Family, or any director, partner or member of such, firm or association of persons or body of individuals or family, or any relative of such director, partner or member has a substantial interest in the business of that other person. [Income-tax Act (43 of 1961), Chap. XA, S. 102(3)].

Associated personnel. Means the employees of each of the three companies associated with its power transmission system. [NTPC Act (24 of 1993), S. 2(b)]

"ASSOCIATED PERSONNEL" means the employees of each of the three companies associated with its power transmission system. [National Thermal Power Corporation Limited, National Hydroelectric Power Corporation Limited and the North Eastern Electric Power Corporation Limited (acquisition and Transfer of Power Transmission System) Act (24 of 1993), S. 2(b)]

"ASSOCIATED PERSONNEL" means the employees of the company associated with its power transmission system. [Neyveli Lignite Corporation Limited (Acquisition and Transfer of Power Transmission System) Act (56 of 1994), S. 2(b)]

Associated trade mark. Means a trademark deemed to be, or required to be registered as associated trade mark under this Act. [Trade & Merchandise Marks

Act (43 of 1958), S. 2(1)(b) and Trade Marks Act (47 of 1999), S. 2(1)(c)]

Associated with. The expression "Associated with" means being connected with or in relation to.

Association. "ASSOCIATION" means anybody of individuals whether incorporated or not, constituted for the purpose of regulating and controlling the business of the sale or purchase of any goods. [Forward Contract (Regulation) Act (74 of 1952), S. 2(a)] [Now repealed by s. 132 of the Finance Act, 2015]

"ASSOCIATION" means the National Association for Supplying Medical Aid by Women to the Women of India, being a society registered under the Societies Registration Act, 1860. [Countess of Dufferin's Fund Act (63 of 1957), S. 2(a)]

"ASSOCIATION" means any association, exchange, organization or body of individuals, whether incorporated or not, established for the purpose of regulating and controlling business of the sale or purchase of, or other transactions relating to, any goods or marketable securities. [Bombay Stamp Act (60 of 1958), S. 2(a)]

"ASSOCIATION" means any combination or body of individuals. [Unlawful Activities (Prevention) Act (37 of 1967), S. 2(1)(a) as amended by Unlawful Activities (Prevention) Amendment Act (29 of 2004), S. 4]

An association may be defined to be a body of persons acting together, upon the methods and forms used by incorporated bodies, for the prosecution of some common enterprise.

Body of persons associated for a common purpose [Gift-tax Act (18 of 1958), S. 2(xxi)(a), Income-tax Act (43 of 1961), S. 2(17)(iii), and T.P. Act (4 of 1882), S. 5]; joining in any action or in companionship for a common purpose.

Association of persons. Association of persons can be formed only when two or more individuals voluntarily combine together for a certain purpose. *G. Murugesan & Brothers* v. *Commissioner of Income Tax, Madras*, AIR 1973 SC 2369, 2372.

The term 'association of persons' means an association in which two or more persons join in a common purpose or common action, and as the words occur in a section which imposes a tax on income, the association must be one, the object of which is to produce income, profits or gains. *M.V. Shanmugam* v. *I.T. Commissioner*, AIR 1970 SC 1707, 1710.

An association of persons must be one in which two or more persons join in a common purpose or common action, and as the words occur in a section which imposes a tax on income, the association must be one the object of which is to produce income, profits or gains. *Commissioner of Income Tax* v. *Indira Balakrishnan*, AIR 1960 SC 1172, 1174. [Income Tax Act (11 of 1922), S. 3]

When the business of the import and distribution of cloth was done by a group on a joint basis, when the sales and the profits were ascertained on a joint basis and then distributed according to the capital contributed by each member of the group, the fact that the Deputy Commissioner of the district had appointed the members constituting of the group to import and distribute the cloth in the district does not make any difference in finding this group as the "association of persons." *Commissioner of Income Tax* v. *Buldana District Main Cloth Importers Group*, AIR 1961 SC 1261, 1263.

Assume. To take upon one's self; to undertake; (as to assume responsibility) to engage; to promise; to pretend to possess; to take in appearance; to arrogate; to usurp; to affect; to presume.

Assumed character. A pretended simulated appearance. [IPC (45 of 1860), S. 170].

Asumed name. The name under which a business is operated; alias.

Assumpsit. Is taken for a voluntary promise, by which a man assumes or takes upon him to perform or pay anything to another; it comprehends any verbal promise, made upon consideration. (*Termes de la Ley*)

Assumpsit is an undertaking, either express or implied to perform an oral or written agreement.

Assumpsit in the law of contracts, is a promise or undertaking, either express or implied, made either orally or in writing, not under seal. (*Rapalje*)

Assumption. The act of assuming or taking upon one's self; the undertaking or adopting of a debt or obligation resting upon another. (*Black*)

The action of assuming, taking or seizing [Railway (Employment of Members of the Armed Forces) Act (40 of 1965), S. 4]; [Estate Duty Act (34 of 1953), S. 17(4)(ii)(c)].

Assumption of the risk. The principle that one who has taken on oneself the risk of loss, injury or damage consequently cannot maintain an action against the party having caused the loss.

Assurance. A deed or instrument of conveyance, the legal evidences of transfer of property.

Insurance, the action of insuring or securing the value of property in the event of it being lost or of securing the payment of a specified sum in the event of a person's death [Indian Evidence Act (1 of 1872), S. 14, ill. (m)]; the deed of conveyance of property [T.P. Act (4 of 1882), S. 59]; a positive declaration intended to give confidence.

Assurance and Insurance. There is a tendency to use "Assurance" for contracts of life insurance companies and "Insurance" for risks upon property.

"Recent writers have sought to establish distinctions of a novel character between them (assurance and insurance). One of these is that a person insures his life, his house or his ships and the office assures to him in each of these cases a sum of money payable in certain contingencies. Another is that assurance represents the principle and insurance the practice". (*Ency. Brit.* XIII 169)

Assured. A person who has been insured by some insurance company, or underwriter, against losses or perils mentioned in the policy of insurance; a person in whose favour an insurance policy stands.

Assurer. An insurer against certain perils and dangers; an underwriter, an indemnifier.

Asterisk. The figure of a (*), used in printing and writing (*a*) as a reference to a passage or note in the margin; (*b*) to distinguish words or phrases as conjectural, theoretical, unverified, obscure, or as having some other specified character; (*c*) to mark the omission of words or letters; and (*d*) arbitrarily, as a mark of classification. Something in the shape of or resembling an asterisk.

Asura form of marriage. (*Hindu Law*) *Asura* Marriage is a marriage where the bride's father or any other person entitled to give away the bride takes '*Sulka*' or price for giving the bride in marriage. *Veerappa* v. *Michael*, AIR 1963 SC 933, 943.

Asylee. An asylum seeker.

Asylum. Means primarily a place in which there is safety from pursuit and is defined as "a sanctuary or place of refuge and protection where criminals and debtors found shelter, and from which they could not be taken without sacrilege"; an institution for the protection and relief of unfortunates. (*Ame. Cyc.*)

'Asylum' according to its original derivation and in its widest meaning, simply signifies a refuge, — a place of retreat and security.

"Asylum" means an asylum or mental hospital for lunatics established or licensed by Government.

A Criminal seeking an "asylum", means going to a place where the matter may not be tried.

In extradition treaties, "asylum" means a place where the matter may not be tried.

Asymmetric cryptography. An encryption/decryption system in which it is impossible to derive the decryption key from the encryption key or the other way around. (*Information Technology*)

Asymmetric crypto system. Asymmetric crypto system means a system of a secure key pair consisting of a private key for creating a digital signature and a public key to verify the digital signature'. [Information Technology Act, 2000, S. 2(1)(d)].

Asynchronous attacks. Attacks that take advantage of dynamic system actions—especially by exploiting an ability to manipulate the timing of those actions. (*Cyber Law*)

At a time. The words 'at a time' do not mean that the controller can artificially break and issue successive orders imposing restrictions on the manufacture of the milk product and thus convert temporary restrictions into almost restriction. *Daily Foods* v. *Union of India,* AIR 1993 Del 278, 285. [Essential Commodities Act (10 of 1955), S. 3]

At all times hereafter. The words 'at all times hereafter' in the agreement are capable of meaning 'at all times hereafter during the subsistence of the agreement'.

At any stage. The word "at any stage" of the case presupposes that proceedings are actually pending.

The expression 'at any stage' means any stage previous to the delivery of the judgment in the case. *Alekh Pradesh* v. *Bhavamar Pal,* AIR 1978 Ori 58, 59. [CPC (5 of 1908), O.XCVIII, R. 2(4)]

The expression 'at any stage' means that once a document has been admitted in evidence, it is not open to the trial Court or to a Court of appeal or revision to go behind that order. *Rajendra Prasad* v. *Siba Devi,* AIR 1982 Pat 65, 66. [Indian Stamp Act (2 of 1899), S. 36]

At any time. Though it is open to a Court, under S. 153 of the CPC (5 of 1908), to amend a judgment, decree or order at any time, it is manifest that the judgment, decree or order when it is amended must be in full operation, and must not have become merged in or cancelled by the decree of a superior Court of Appeal.

The expression 'at any time' must be given its full force and effect which requires the recognition of the committee's power to amend an assessment list even after the expiry of the year following the one in which the list was finalised by due authentication. *New Delhi Municipality* v. *L.I.C. of India*, AIR 1977 SC 2134, 2139. [Punjab Municipal Act (3 of 1911), S. 67]

The word "at any time" must be understood as within a reasonable time depending on the facts and circumstances of each case in the absence of prescribed period of limitation. [*ACC Limited* v. *Global Cements Limited*, (2012) 7 SCC 71, para 24].

DEED CONSTRUCTION. The words "at any time" can only mean at any time the party concerned likes. *Central Bank of India* v. *H.F. Insurance Co.*, AIR 1965 SC 1288, 1290.

The words 'at any time' have not to be limited to the year of assessment. *The State of Assam* v. *Deva Prasad Banua*, AIR 1969 SC 831, 834. [Assam Agricultural Income Tax Act (1939), S. 19]

The expression 'at any time' in S. 10(2) could only mean "at any time" when the pawn brokers' premises are normally kept open for business." *M. Kevalchand Sowcar* v. *State of Madras*, AIR 1957 Mad 514, 520. [Madras Pawn Brokers Act (23 of 1943), S. 10]

The use of the words 'at any time' in Section 42 does not place limitation on the exercise of the power of revision. *Haqiqat Singh* v. *Additional Director, Consolidation of Holdings*, AIR 1981 P & H 204, 210. [East Punjab Holdings (Consolidation and Prevention of Fragmentation) Act (50 of 1948), S. 42]

The words 'at any time' are of wide amplitude and read without reference to the context, admit of no limitation. The phrase has sometime been construed "within reasonable time", "after a certain time", "after the fulfilment of a certain condition or" subject to the restrictions in the Act", "at all times", "at any one time" or "from time to time." *National Industrial Corporation Ltd.* v. *Registrar of Companies*, AIR 1963 Punj 239, 241. [Companies Act (1 of 1956) replaced with Companies Act, 2013, S. 18(4)]

The words 'at any time' in S. 10(1) refer to a period which commences with the issue of demand notice or with any other legal steps by which the proceedings are initiated for making a reference to a labour court or tribunal and which period terminates with an order either making a reference or declining to make it for any reason. *Gowdhara Transport Co.* v. *State of Punjab*, AIR 1966 Pun 354, 360. [Industrial Disputes Act (14 of 1947), S. 10(1)]

The expression 'at any time' is intended to have some effective and practical limitation in point of duration. The reasonable time limit for the exercise of power under S. 42, according to the statutory scheme, purpose and object, would be up to the time when the consolidation is completed and when it becomes immune from challenge under the Act. *Nar Singh* v. *State of Punjab*, AIR 1967 Pun 111, 124 (FB). [East Punjab Holdings (Consolidation and Prevention of Fragmentation) Act, Ss. 36, 42]

Though it is open to a Court, under S. 153 of the CPC (5 of 1908), to amend a judgment, decree or order at any time, it is manifest that the judgment, decree or order when it is amended must be in full operation, and must not have become merged in or cancelled by the decree of a superior Court of Appeal. (11 All 267 (FB); 24 Cal 759; 22 Mad 293 and 30 All 290. foll) *Abhas Khan* v. *Niharani Dassi*, 11 CLJ 159 : 5 IC 261.The expression 'at any time' occurring in Section 34(1)(a) of the Act would mean that the action may be taken without any time limit. [*S.C. Prashar* v. *Vasantsen Dwarkadas*, (1963) 49 ITR (SC)] [Indian Income-tax Act (11 of 1922), S. 34(1)(a) (as amended in 1959)]

The words 'at any time' have not to be limited to the year of assessment'. *State of Assam* v. *Deva Prasad Bania*, AIR 1969 SC 831 at 834.

The words 'at any time' are of wide amplitude and read without reference to the context, admit of no limitation. The phrase has sometime been construed as "within reasonable time", "after a certain time", "after the fulfilment of a certain condition" or subject to the restrictions in the Act", "at all times", "at any one time" or "from time to time". *National Industrial Corporation Ltd.* v. *Registrar of Companies,* AIR 1963 Raj 239, 241. [Companies Act (1 of 1956) replaced with Companies Act, 2013, S. 18(4)]

The words 'at any time' in S. 10(1) refer to a period which commences with the issue of demand notice or with any other legal steps by which the proceedings are initiated for making a reference to a labour Court or Tribunal and which period terminates with an order either making a reference or declining to make it for any reason. *Godhara Transport Co.* v. *State of Punjab,* AIR 1966 Punj 354, 360. [Industrial Disputes Act (14 of 1947), S. 10(1)]

DEED CONSTRUCTION. The words "at any time" can only mean at any time the party concerned likes. *Central Bank of India* v. *H.F. Ince Co.*, AIR 1965 SC 1288, 1290.

At any time before the filing of a written statement. The expression "at any time before the filing of a written statement" must mean "before actually filing the same" and not "before the expiry of the time to file the same". *Pragati Engineering (P.) Ltd.* v. *T.N. Water Supply and Drainage Board,* AIR 1992 Cal 139, 145. [Arbitration Act (10 of 1940), S. 34]

At arm's length. When a person is not under the influence or control of another.

At Bar. Before the Court; before the bar.

At equity. According to equity.

At his discretion. According to his discretion. [Indian Contract Act (9 of 1872), S. 60].

At large. Free; unrestrained.

At law. According to law; by law; in law. (*Burrill*)

At least. Where time is to be computed as so many days, "at least" means so many clear days.

At least seven days before the election. The use of the words 'at least seven days before the election' clearly indicates that the law contemplates exclusion of the interval of 7 days for the purpose. Seven 'clear days' interval is required between the date of announcement of the notice and the date of election.

At liberty. Free to act, think, move *etc.*

At once. Means as soon as is reasonably practicable.

At or about the time. The main test is whether the statement was made as early as can reasonably be expected in the circumstances of the case and before there was opportunity for tutoring or concoction. *Rameshwar* v. *State of Rajasthan*, AIR 1952 SC 54, 58. [Indian Evidence Act (1 of 1872), S. 157]

At or about the time of marriage. "At" means the actual time of marriage. 'About the time of marriage" means 'near or round about the time of marriage and not subsequently'. *M.D. Krishnan* v. *M.C. Padma,* AIR 1988 Mys 226 at 228, 229. [Hindu Marriage Act (25 of 1955), S. 27]

At or before such settlement. Means that the application shall be filed either before the settlement of issues or simultaneously with the settlement of issues.

At par. At the face value. [Indian Trusts Act (2 of 1882), S. 20A(1), *Prov.*].

At-risk rules. Statutory limitations of a taxpayers deductible losses to the amount the taxpayer could actually lose, so as to prevent them from sheltering income.

At sea. Out of the limits of any port or harbour; on the sea coast; on the open sea.

At sight. A term applies to bills or notes that are payable on demand without allowing days of grace.

At sight—"After sight". In a promissory note or bill of exchange the expressions "at sight" and "on presentment" mean on demand. The expression "after sight" means, in a promissory note, after presentment for sight and in a bill of exchange, after acceptance, or noting for non-acceptance or protest for non-acceptance. [Negotiable Instruments Act (26 of 1881), S. 21].

At the commencement of the constitution. It means only the 26th January, 1950. [Constitution of India, Art. 5, 394]

At the commencement of the proceeding. The words "at the commencement of the proceeding" mean the commencement of proceeding in which question, as to conclusive character of the registration as laid down in Sec. 32 arises. *Mohd. Rafiq* v. *Modi Sugar Mills Ltd.,* AIR 1972 Del 46, 48. [Trade and Merchandise Marks Act (43 of 1958), S. 32(c)]

At the cost of. The expense to be met by. [T.P. Act (4 of 1882), S. 60].

At the election. The words 'at the election' have reference to the actual time when the voting takes place. Assuming election to be a continuous process with nomination as a preliminary requisite for standing as a candidate, the words 'at the election' would seem 'in the context in which they are used' in Section 82, to refer to the period when the actual polling takes place. *Sheo Kumar* v. *V.G. Oak,* AIR 1953 All 633, 635. [Representation of the People Act (43 of 1951), S. 82]

At the expense of. By putting (someone) to loss [Indian Trusts Act (2 of 1882), S. 17]; [Companies Act (1 of 1956) replaced with Companies Act, 2013, S. 188(1)].

At the instance of. On being urged by.

At the instance of either party. Examining the scheme of the statute and the purpose for which such a provision has been made it is held that the words 'either party' would also cover the legal heirs who have stepped into the shoes of the spouses under the law and such persons would also be competent to ask for variation, modification or rescission of the order for maintenance. That term would also include the holders of the estate with lawful title for the time being. *Aruna Basu* v. *Dorothea Mitra*, AIR 1983 SC 916, 920. [Special Marriage Act (43 of 1954), S. 37(2)]

At the pleasure of. As or when one pleases.

At the time of execution. The expression 'at the time of execution' is to be construed as required affixing of the stamp in close proximity in point of time to the affixing of the signature. If immediately after the signature is affixed, the requisite stamp is affixed, such act do constitute affixing of the stamp at the time of execution of the document. *Devendrappa* v. *Kallaya,* AIR 1979 Kant 21, 23. [Indian Stamp Act (2 of 1899), S. 17]

At the time of partition. It means that at the time when parties effect a severance in status. *Jalaja Sheothi and Others* v. *Lakshmi Shedthi*, AIR 1973, SC 2658, 2665.

At the trial. Means during or immediately at the end of the trial, and not after a lapse of an hour and a half after the judgment given.

At will. Subject to one's discretion; as one wishes or chooses.

"Athlete". Means any person who competes in any sport at the national level or international level or participates in any competition or event to which this Act applies. [National Anti-Doping Act, 2022 (15 of 2022), section 2(d)]

"Athlete support personnel". Means any coach, trainer, manager, agent, team staff, official, medical or paramedical personnel or such other person working with or treating or assisting an athlete who is participating in, or preparing for, a competition or event at the national level or international level or to which this Act applies. [National Anti-Doping Act, 2022 (15 of 2022), section 2(e)]

Atmosphere. The air in any particular place, especially as affected by heat, cold, purifying influences *etc.* [IPC (45 of 1860), S. 278]; a conditioning surrounding influence, mental or moral environment.

Atomic energy. The energy released from atomic nuclei as a result of any process, including the fission process. The term does not include energy released in any process of natural transmutation or radio-active decay which is not accelerated or influenced by external means. [Atomic Energy Act (29 of 1948), S. 3(a), 2(a) now repealed by Atomic Energy Act, 1962].

"ATOMIC ENERGY" means energy released from atomic nuclei as a result of any process, including the fission and fusion process. [Atomic Energy Act (33 of 1962), S. 2(d)]

Atomic minerals. Means the minerals included in atomic minerals specified in Part B of the First Schedule to the Mines and Minerals (Development and Regulation) Act, 1957. [Offshore Areas Minerals (Development and Regulation) Act, 2002 (17 of 2003), S. 4(b)]

Ats. At the time of.

Attach. "Attach", is a taking, seizing or apprehending property by order of Court". (*Termes de la Ley*)

To seize (property) by authority of a writ of attachment; to take property into the custody of law.

Attache. A person attached to a foreign legation.

Attached. (*Attached to premises*). In referring to the statement that whatever is 'attached' to premises has to be estimated for the purpose of ascertaining its rating value. The word 'attached' there, means attached by some physical fastening such as screws or bolts, a thing weighing tons, which cannot be and never was intended to be lifted, would not be taken into account, if not fastened to some part of the building; whereas if it were fastened it would. That would be a monstrous consequence so the word 'attached' does there mean 'physically fastened', so as to determine whether the thing is to be taken into account or not". Hence heavy machinery kept in a fixed position by its own weight has to be taken into account in assessing the ratable value of the premises.

Shop or outhouse or warehouse "*attached*" *to a dwelling-house,* does not mean, mere contact of some part of the two structures, but means attached for use with the dwelling-house.

Fastened to another; subjected to attachment.

Attached decree. A decree subjected to attachment. [CPC (5 of 1908), O. XXI, R. 53(6)].

Attached in execution of a decree. CPC (5 of 1908), O. XXI, R. 57. The expression 'attached in execution of a decree' does not cover attachments effected before judgement. *State of Haryana* v. *Bharat Trimmee Store,* AIR 1977 P&H 312, 314.

Attached to earth. The definition of the word 'attached to earth' has meaning 'embedded in the earth'. It clearly indicates that the attachment must be for the permanent beneficial enjoyment of that to which it is attached. The machinery which is embedded in the earth for its own enjoyment, the attachment is for the beneficial use of the machinery. [*Industrial Weaver's Co-operative Society Ltd.* v. *The Collector, Hardoi,* MLJ : YD (1983), p. 385 : 1982 AWC 347]. [Transfer of Property Act (4 of 1882), S. 3]

"ATTACHED TO THE EARTH" means—

(a) rooted in the earth, as in the case of trees and shrubs;

(b) imbedded in the earth, as in the case of walls or buildings; or

(c) attached to what is so imbedded for the permanent beneficial enjoyment of that to which it is attached. [T.P. Act (4 of 1882), S. 3].

Attachiamenta bonorum. A distress formerly taken upon goods and chattels, by the attchiators or bailiffs, as security to an answer an action.

Attaching creditor. A creditor at whose instance an attachment is made. [App. E, form No. 36. CPC (5 of 1908)].

Attaching officer. An officer, who effects an attachment. [CPC (5 of 1908), O. XXI, R. 43].

Attachment. The word *attachment* has been defined as "taking into the custody of the law the person or property of one already before the Court, or of one whom it is sought to bring before it; a writ issued at the institution or during the progress of an action, commanding the sheriff or other proper officer to attach the property, rights, credits, or effects of the defendant to satisfy the demands of the plaintiff".

Attachment. According to dictionary meaning, "attachment" means "act of attaching", "state of being attached". In law, it is seizure of property or person by legal authority, especially seizure of defendant's property to prevent its dissipation before trial. [Oxford Webster's Encyclopedic Unabridged Dictionary, (1994), p. 95; Justice C.K. Thakker: Encyclopedic Law Lexicon, (2009) as cited in *SESA International Limited* v. *Avani Projects and Infrastructure Limited and Ors.* GA No. 1919, 1705, 2282 and 113 of 2017, decided on 5-9-2017 (Cal HC), para 80]

In general attachments may be used for two purposes : (1) To compel the appearance of a defendant; (2) to seize and hold his property for the payment of the debt.

"Attachment" means the prohibition of transfer, conversion, disposition or movement of property, by an order issued under this Act [Prohibition of Benami Property Transactions Act (45 of 1988), section 2(5)]

The word 'attachment' in S. 51 *Proviso* (*b*) *Explanation*—CPC (5 of 1908), contemplates both attachment simpliciter and attachment as a preliminary step to a sale in execution of the decree. *Amalya Chandra Roy* v. *Pashupathi Nath,* AIR 1951 Cal 48 (FB).

The action of attaching or the fact of being attached. [CPC (5 of 1908), O. XXI, R. 30]; [Factories Act (63 of 1948), S. 28(2)(a)].

Attachment bond. Bond which a defendant gives to recover attached property.

Attachment lien. Lien on property seized by prejudgment attachment.

Attachment of debts does not constitute a "wrongful seizure of movable property under legal process" within the meaning of the Article 29, Sch. 1 of Indian Limitation Act (9 of 1908). *Yellammal* v. *Ayyappa Naick*, 22 IC 870 (872).

Attachment of earnings. A Court may make an attachment of earnings order to secure payment of an order of the Court.

Attack. To assault; fall upon with force or violence; assail; to begin hostilities against.

The falling upon with force of arms; to make an attack.

Attain majority. Arrive at an age at which one becomes legally capable of conducting his own affairs. [CPC (5 of 1908), O. XXXII, R. 4(1)].

Attainable. Capable of being attained or obtained. [Navy Act (62 of 1957), S. 97(19)].

Attainder. The act in which a person's civil rights are extinguished when he is sentenced to death or declared an outlaw for committing a felony or treason.

Attempt. "Attempt"—defined. S. 511, IPC (45 of 1860).

"An attempt to commit a crime is an act done with intent to commit that crime, and forming part of a series of acts which would constitute its actual commission if it were not interrupted".

Attempt. To make an effort or try to do something specially something difficult; to endeavor; an effort or endeavor to effect the accomplishment of an act..." [Oxford Advanced Learner's Dictionary as cited in *Abhinav Pandey* v. *Guru Gobind Singh Indraprastha University and Ors.* W.P.(C) 2028/2016 and C.M. No. 8746/2016, decided on 23-1-2018 (Del HC), para 15]

There may be an attempt at theft by trying to pick an empty pocket.

An intentional act which a person does towards the commission of an offence but which fails in its object through circumstances independent of the volition of that person is "attempt". [IPC (45 of 1860), S. 511]

Preparation to commit an offence is not attempt. Covert or overt acts preceding to committing an offence with an intention to commit the offence amount to attempt. Intention to commit a particular offence, some act necessarily done towards the commission of the offence and proximity of such act to the intended result constitute 'attempt'. *State of Maharasthra* v. *Mohd. Yakub*, AIR 1980 SC 1111, 1115, 1117.

An effort or endeavor to do something; to try to accomplish or attain any action or object.

Attempt to commit culpable homicide. Whoever does any act with such intention or knowledge and under such circumstances that, if he by that act caused death, he would be guilty of culpable homicide not amounting to murder. [(w.e.f. 1-7-2024) Bharatiya Nyaya Sanhita, 2023 (45 of 2023), section 110]

Attempt to murder. Whoever does any act with such intention or knowledge, and under such circumstances that, if he by that act caused death, he would be guilty of murder. [(w.e.f. 1-7-2024) Bharatiya Nyaya Sanhita, 2023 (45 of 2023), section 109(1)]

Attend. To present oneself at a meeting *etc.* in order to take part in the proceedings; to perform; to look after; to take care.

Attend diligently to duties. To apply steadily to one's duties. [Indian Partnership Act (9 of 1932), S. 12(b)].

Attend on. To look after; to take care of [Mines Act (35 of 1952), S. 25(2)].

Attendance. The action or state of attending.

Attendant. One who attends or accompanies as a servant or keeper.

Attention. Earnest direction of the mind. [Indian Evidence Act (1 of 1872), S. 145]; [Indian Succession Act (39 of 1925), S. 61, ill. (viii)].

Attest. To bear witness to; to certify; to affirm to be true or genuine; to make a solemn declaration in words or writing to support a fact; to certify to the verity of a copy of a public document. (*Abbott*)

Where an instrument is required to be "attested", the meaning is, that a witness shall be present at its execution and shall testify on it that it has been executed by the proper person.

"To attest" is to bear witness to a fact, and it is not necessary that the witness attesting a document should sign his name personally.

"To attest is to bear witness to a fact, the witnesses must have seen the executant sign or receive personal acknowledgement of his signature and they should sign with *animo attestandi* in the presence of the executant. *M.L. Abdul Jabbar Sahib* v. *H. Venkata Sastri*, AIR 1969 SC 1147 at 1151.

A deed required by law to be attested is properly executed when the signatures of the witnesses are affixed for them to the deed by another person, with their consent, they being illiterate and not able to write. It is not necessary that the witnesses should put their mark on the deed themselves, any such mark on the deed not being implied in the word 'attest'.

To affirm to be true or genuine; to witness and authenticate by signing as a witness. [T.P. Act (4 of 1882), S. 3, and Indian Evidence Act (1 of 1872), Ss. 70 and 72].

Attestation. See T.P. Act (4 of 1882), S. 3.

The act of witnessing the signature of an instrument and subscribing the name of the witness in testimony of such fact; the certification by the keeper of a record of the verity of a copy. (*Ame. Cyc.*)

Attestation means that what is said to be attested happened in the presence of the attesting witness.

The action of attesting [T.P. Act (4 of 1882), S. 3]; the proof or evidence by which something is attested. [Indian Evidence Act (1 of 1872), S.69].

Attestation and **Acknowledgment** are different acts. 'Attestation' is the act of witnessing the actual execution of a paper and subscribing one's name as a witness to that fact. 'Acknowledgment' is the act of a grantor in going before some competent officer and declaring the paper to be his deed." (4 *Cyc.* 888).

Attestation and attesting witness. By attestation is meant the signing of a document to signify that the attestor is a witness to the execution of the document. An attesting witness is one who signs the document in the presence of the executant after seeing the execution of the document or after receiving a personal acknowledgement from the executant as regards the execution of the document. *Beni Chand* v. *Kamala Kunwar*, AIR 1977 SC 63, 67. [Indian Evidence Act (1 of 1872), S. 68]

Attestation clause. That clause in which the witnesses certify that the instrument has been executed before them, and the manner of its execution. (*4 Cyc.* 888)

Attestation of a deed. Does not by itself estop the person attesting from denying that he knew of its contents or that he consented to the transaction which it effects.

Attested. "The word 'attested' when used with reference to judicial writings, or copies thereof, as copies of records or judicial process, means an authentication by the clerk of the Court so as to make them receivable in evidence".

"ATTESTED", in relation to an instrument, means and shall be deemed always to have meant attested by two or more witnesses each of whom has seen the executant sign or affix his mark to the instrument, or has seen some other person sign the instrument in the presence, and by the direction of the executant, or has received from the executant a personal acknowledgment of his signature or mark, or of the signature of such other person, and each of whom has signed the instrument in the presence of the executant; but it shall not be necessary that more than one of such witnesses shall have been present at the same time, and no particular form of attestation shall be necessary". [T.P. Act (4 of 1882), S. 3]

Attested copy. A copy of a document verified as correct.

Attesting witness. One who signs his name to an instrument, at the request of the party or parties, for the purposes of proving or identifying it.

A witness who has attested the document. [Indian Evidence Act (1 of 1872), Ss. 69 and 71].

Attorn. To transfer of turn over to another; to consent to a transfer; to make attornment. (*Burrill*)

To agree to become tenant to one as owner or landlord of an estate previously held of another; (in case of a bailee) to acknowledge that he holds a property on behalf of a new party.

Attorney. In its broadest sense, an attorney is one put in place of another; one acting for another; an agent; but, when not coupled with any qualifying expression, the word is usually construed as meaning attorney at law. "Attorney, is one that is appointed by another man to do anything in his absence.

One duly appointed or constituted to act for another in business or legal matters; a properly qualified legal agent who conducts litigation, preparing the case for barristers. [Indian Evidence Act (1 of 1872), Ss. 126, 127, 128; CPC (5 of 1908), S. 119 and Companies Act (1 of 1956) replaced with Companies Act, 2013, S. 60(3)].

Attorney-client privilege. A client's privilege against disclosure of his confidential communication between him and his attorney.

Attorney General. The first ministerial Law Officer of the state.

Attorney General for India. A legal counsel to the government of India. [Constitution of India, Art 76]

Attorney of record. Appearance of lawyer for a party in a law suit and his entitlement to receive, on the party's behalf, all pleadings and other formal documents from the Court and from other parties.

Attorney's fees. Charge made to a client for the services performed for him.

Attorney's lien. Right of an attorney to retain money or property of a client or to encumber money payable to the client in the Court's possession until his (attorney's) fees has been properly determined and paid.

Attornment. Attornment means an agreement or acknowledgement by a tenant that he holds the tenement of a new person as a landlord. *Madanlal* v. *Manackchand,* AIR 1971 Raj 55, 59. [Indian Evidence Act (1 of 1872), S. 116]

Where a person in whose favour the attornment has been made has no title, a mere paper attornment would not be enough to establish, as against third parties, the possession of the person attorned. The possession should be effective in the sense that the person who attorned has paid the rent voluntarily or under a decree to the person attorned. *V. Satyanarayanaraju* v. *Hanumayamma*, AIR 1967 SC 174, 177. [Transfer of Property Act (4 of 1882), Ss. 105, 108]

Acknowledgement by a tenant or bailee to attorney for a new owner or party.

"Attornment" by the tenant would mean acceptance of the new owner as the landlord. "Attornment" also implies continuity of tenancy, though landlord might change when title of the property passes by sale or otherwise. *Mohd. Ilyas* v. *Mohd. Adil,* AIR 1994 Del 212, 218. [Transfer of Property Act (4 of 1882), S. 109]

Attributable to. The expression 'attributable to' is wider in import than the expression 'derived from' and so it follows that the legislature intended to cover receipts from sources other than the actual conduct of the business of generation and distribution of electricity. *Cambay Electric Supply Industrial Co. Ltd.* v. *Commissioner of Income Tax*, AIR 1978 SC 1099, 1105. [Income Tax Act (43 of 961), S. 80-E]

Attribute. Any property, quality, or characteristic that can be ascribed to a person or thing.

Auction. A public sale of land, or goods by public outcry to the higher bidder. Auction is very generally defined as a sale to the highest bidder, and this is the usual meaning. There may, however be a sale to the lowest bidder, as where land is sold for non-payment of taxes to whomsoever will take it for the shortest term; or where a contract is offered to the one who will perform it at the lowest price. And these appear fairly included in the term "auction" (*Abbott*; 5 MIA 109).

Auction ring. A group of buyers who agree not to compete against each other at an auction with a view to purchasing articles for less than the open market value.

Auction sale. A sale by auction. [Sale of Goods Act (3 of 1930), S. 64].

Auctioneer. A person authorized by law or engaged to sell lands or goods of other persons at public auction; one who sells at auction.

One who conducts sale by auction. [Indian Contract Act (9 of 1872), S. 194, ill. (a)].

Auctoritates Philosophorum? Medicoam et poetarum, Sunt in causis Alleganoae et tenendae. The opinions of philosophers, physicians, and poets are to be alleged and received in causes. (*Ballentine's Law Dictionary, 3rd Edn.*)

Aucupia verborum sunt Judice indigna. (*Maxim*) Quibbles are beneath the dignity of a Judge. (*Latin for Lawyers*)

Audi alteram partem. "Hear the other side; "Hear both sides "an injunction which means that no man should be condemned unheard" (*Byrne*).

'Audi alteram partem' is as much a principle of African, as it is of English legal procedure" a popular Yoruba saying is : 'wicked and iniquitous is he who decides a case upon the testimony of only one party to it.' [T.O. Elias, The Nature of African Customary Law as cited in *National Textile Workers Union* v. *P.R. Ramakrishnan*, (1983) 1 SCC 228, para 16 : 1983 SCC (L&S) 72 : 1983 SCC (Tax) 2]. See also *Manohar Lal Sharma* v. *Principal Secretary*, (2014) 9 SCC 614, para 16].

Both sides should be heard before a decision is arrived at.

It is obligatory on the part of the Tribunal to hear, expressly or by implication by giving an opportunity to be heard as a natural justice otherwise, the impugned act or order was never valid. *Nawabkhan Abbaskhan* v. *State of Gujarat*, AIR 1974 SC 1471, 1480.

No decision shall be given against a party without affording him a reasonable hearing. [*Manohar* v. *State of Maharashtra,* (2012) 13 SCC 14, para 18]. [*Rajendra Shankar Shukla* v. *State of Chhattisgarh*, (2015) 10 SCC 400, para 39] [See also A.*K. Kraipak* v. *Union of India*, (1969) 2 SCC 262, para 20].

If any reliance is placed on evidence or record against a person then that evidence or record must be placed before him for his information, comment and criticism. That is all that is meant by the doctrine of audi alteram partem, that no party should be condemned unheard. *Kishanlal Agarwalla* v. *Collector of Land Customs*, AIR 1967 Cal 80.

The maxim 'audi alteram partem' means—no one shall be condemned, punished or deprived of his property in any judicial proceeding unless he has had an opportunity of being heard. *Ramjibhai Ukabhai Parmar* v. *Manilal Purushottam Solanki*, AIR 1960 Guj 19, 21

The maxim means that a person should not be condemned on ex parte statements. No order of removal or discharge should be passed against a government servant unless he has been given a real and effective opportunity of refuting the statements upon which his notice of discharge is based. *Gopi Kishore Prasad* v. *State of Bihar*, AIR 1955 Pat 372. Audi alteram partem

A communication of the information or substance of the anticorruption reports, which were hostile or contained severe criticism of the petitioner, is a sufficient compliance with the principle embodied in the maxim 'audi alteram partem'. *Punit Lall Saha* v. *State of Bihar,* AIR 1957 Pat 357, 360. [Constitution of India, Art. 311]

The principle of audi alteram partem meaning also hear the other party, has been treated as of fundamental nature laying down the norm which is to be implemented even by the international tribunals in their proceedings. *Bhikhan Bobla* v. *Punjab State*, AIR 1963 P&H 255, 268.

Ganapathi Muthiriyar v. *Narayanaswami Vaithiar*, AIR 1957 Mad 405, 408; Rajah Yenumula Suryanarayana *Murthy Dora* v. *State of Madras*, AIR 1959 AP 487, 491. [Pensions Act (23 of 1871), S. 7]

It has long been a received rule that no one is to be condemned, punished, or deprived of property in any judicial or quasi-judicial proceeding, unless he has had an opportunity of being heard. *Cooper* v. *Wands worth Board of Works* (1863), 14 CB (NS) 180; *Errington* v. *Minister of Health*, [1935] 1 KB 249. But this only applies where there is a duty to act judicially (*Franklin* v. *Minister of Town and Country Planning*, [1948] AC 87). (Latin for Lawyers)

"Audio-video electronic". Means shall include use of any communication device for the purposes of video conferencing, recording of processes of identification, search and seizure or evidence, transmission of electronic communication and for such other purposes and by such other means as the State Government may, by rules provide. [Bharatiya Nagarik Suraksha Sanhita, 2023 (46 of 2023), section 2(1)(a)]

Audio-visual. Production with both sound and images which may or may not be moving.

"audio-visual production" means audio-visual produced wholly or partly in India and includes—

(i) animation, cartoon depiction, audio-visual advertisement;

(ii) digital production or any of the activities in respect of making thereof; and

(iii) features films, non-feature films, television, web-based serials, talk shows, reality shows and sport shows. [Code on Social Security, 2020 (36 of 2020), section 2(4)]

"Audio-visual production". Means audio-visual produced wholly or partly in India and includes—

(i) animation, cartoon depiction, audio-visual advertisement;

(ii) digital production or any of the activities in respect of making thereof; and

(iii) features films, non-feature films, television, web-based serials, talk shows, reality shows and sport shows. [Occupational Safety, Healthy & Working Conditions Code, 2020 (37 of 2020), section 2(1)(e)]

"Audio-visual worker". Means a person, who is employed, directly or through any contractor, in or in connection with the audio-visual production to work as an artist including actor, musician, singer, anchor, news reader, dancer, dubbing artist or stunt person or to do any work, skilled, unskilled, manual, supervisory, technical, artistic or otherwise, and his remuneration with respect to such employment in or in connection with the production of audio-visual does not exceed, where remuneration is by way of monthly wages or where such remuneration is by way of lump sum, in each case, such amount as may be notified by the Central Government. [Occupational Safety, Healthy & Working Conditions Code, 2020 (37 of 2020), section 2(1)(f)]

Audit. An official examination of accounts with verification by reference to witness and vouchers [Dakshina Bharat Hindi Prachar Sabha Act (14 of 1964), S. 5, and Constitution of India, art. 110(1)(of)]; to examine (accounts) officially; a calling to account generally.

As a verb; to draw up or present an account; to make an official investigation and examination of accounts and vouchers.

'AUDIT' means examination of bills of entry, shipping bills, invoices, packing lists, import licences, books of account, and other records of transaction relating to imported and export goods, and may include inspection of goods at the premises, if available and where necessary, drawl of samples. [On-site Post Clearance Audit at the Premises of Importers and Exporters Regulations, 2011, Regn. 2(a)].

"Audit" means the examination of records, returns and other documents maintained or furnished by the registered person under this Act or the rules made thereunder or under any other law for the time being in force to verify the correctness of turnover declared, taxes paid, refund claimed and input tax credit availed, and to assess his compliance with the provisions of this Act or the rules made thereunder [The Central Goods and Services Tax Act, 2017 (12 of 2017), S. 2(13)]

Audit, in the Public Health Act, 1875 (38 & 39 Vict. c. 55, S. 246). See *Thomas* v. *Devonport Corporation*, (1900) 1 QB 16.

Audit trail. A system by which each stage of a transaction is formally documented and recorded, so that they can be examined during an audit.

In computer security systems, a chronological record of when users log-in, how long they are engaged in various activities, what they were doing, and whether any actual or attempted security violations occurred. An automated or manual set of chronological records of system activities that may enable the reconstruction and examination of a sequence of events and/or changes in an event. (*Cyber Law*)

A system by means of which each stage of a transaction is formally documented and recorded, so that they can be examined during an audit. (*Investment*)

Audita querela. (*Law Latin*). The complaint having been heard.

Audietur et altera pars. Hear the other side.

Auditing standards. Means the standards of auditing or any addendum thereto for companies or class of companies referred to in section 143(10) of the Companies Act, 2013 (18 of 2013). [S. 2(7) of the Companies Act, 2013 (18 of 2013)]

Auditor. A person appointed and authorized to audit accounts—usually employed for the official examination of public accounts as well as those of large corporations, banks, societies, *etc.*

One who audits or whose business it is to audit.

For the purposes of this Chapter, the word "auditor" includes a firm of auditors. [Companies Act (18 of 2013), Chapter X, section 140, *Expln. II*]

Augusta legibus soluta non est. "The wife of the Emperor is subject to the laws."

Aula regis. The King's Court or Curia Regis.

Auter droit. Another (in another's) right : thus, one who acts not on his own behalf, but as trustee or representative or another, is said to act in *auter droit.*

Authentic. Real; of genuine origin; being what it purports to be; opposed to pretended or imaginary fictitious, counterfeit, apocryphal, or unauthorised : as, authentic documents. Executed with all due formalities; executed by the proper person and legally attested before the proper authorities; as, authentic deed.

Authentic act. Act which has been executed before a notary or public officer, duly authorised, or which is testified by a public seal, or has been rendered public by the authority of a competent magistrate, or which is certified at being a copy of a public register.

Authenticate. To give legal validity to; to establish the genuineness of; to make an authentication *i.e.* an attestation made by a proper officer by which he certifies that the record is in due form of law, and that the person who certifies it, is the officer appointed to do so. [IPC (45 of 1860), Ss. 21(4) and 21(10)]; [Constitution of India, Art. 77(2)].

Authenticity. The quality of being authentic, or entitled to acceptance as authoritative, genuine, true or correct : as, the authenticity of scriptures or of a document; the authenticity of a portrait : the authenticity of a statement.

Author. "AUTHOR" means,—

(i) in relation to a literary or dramatic work, the author of the work;

(ii) in relation to musical work, the composer;

(iii) in relation to an artistic work other than a photograph, the artist;

(iv) in relation to a photograph, the person taking the photograph;

(v) in relation to a cinematograph film, the owner of the film at the time of its completion;

(vi) and in relation to a record, the owner of the original plate from which the record is made, at the time of making of the plate. [Copyright Act (14 of 1957), S. 2(d)]

AUTHOR includes a joint author. [Income-tax Act (43 of 1961), S. 80QQB, *Expln.* (a)].

One who composes or writes a book, as distinguished from an editor, translator or compiler; one who produces, by his own intellectual labour applied to the materials of his composition, an arrangement or compilation new in itself. The original composer of a book or writing of any kind, as distinguished from a compiler, translator, editor, or copyist.

Creator; originator; maker; he who gives rise to an action, event, circumstance or state of things; the writer or composer of treatise or book.

Author of the trust. The person who reposes or declares the confidence of trust is called the author of the trust. (See Trusts Act, 2 of 1882, S. 3).

Authorization. 'AUTHORIZATION' means permission for collection, reception, treatment, transport, storage and disposal of hazardous wastes granted by the competent authority on Form 2. [Rule 2(c) of the Hazardous Waste (Management and Handling) Rules, 1989]

"AUTHORIZATION" means the consent given by the Board or Committee to the "operator of a facility". [Rule 2(11) the Municipal Solid Wastes (Management and Handling) Rules, 2000]

'AUTHORISATION' means permission granted by the prescribed authority for the generation, collection, reception, storage, transportation, treatment, disposal and/or any other form of handling of bio-medical waste in accordance with these rules and any guidelines issued by the Central Government. [Rule 3(3), Batteries (Management and Handling) Rules, 2001]

'Authorisation', refers to the permission of the licensee to use of electricity, subject to the terms and conditions for such use and the law governing the subject. [*Execution Engineer Southern Electricity Supply Company of Orissa Limited (SOUTHCO)* v. *Sri Seetaram Rice Mill,* (2012) 2 SCC 108, para 27].

The action of authorising [Working Journalists (Fixation of Rates of Wages) Act (29 of 1958), S. 10]; sanction; warrant [State Financial Corporations Act (63 of 1951), S. 19(5)(a)]; to authorise [Copyright Act (14 of 1957), S. 32(4)(b)].

Authorisation for assignment. "Authorisation for assignment" means an authorisation to undertake an assignment, issued by an insolvency professional agency to an insolvency professional, who is its professional member, in accordance with its bye-laws. [Insolvency and Bankruptcy Board of India (Insolvency Professionals) Regulations, 2016, Regn. 2(1)(aa)]

Authorise. To empower; to give right or authority to act; to clothe with authority, warrant or legal power. [T.P. Act (4 of 1882), S. 67(d)].

To empower; to give a right or authority to act. To endow with authority or effective legal power, warrant, or right. To permit a thing to be done in the future. It has a mandatory effect or meaning, implying a direction to act.

Authorised absence. The absence of a worker who is on legal strike, would amount to an 'authourised absence' and he would be deemed to continue in service. U.P. State Bridge Corpn. Ltd. v. U.P. Rajya Setu Nigam S. Karmchari Sangh, (2004) 4 SCC 268, 279, para 21.

Authorised Bank. Means a bank including co-operative bank (other than an authorised dealer) authorised by the Reserve Bank to maintain an account of a person resident outside India. [Foreign Exchange Management (Deposit) Regulations, 2000, Reg. 2(ii); Foreign Exchange Management (Borrowing and Lending in Rupees) Regulations, 2000, Reg. 2(b) and Foreign Exchange Management (Investment in Firm or Proprietary Concern in India) Regulations, 2000, Reg. 2(ii)]

"AUTHORISED BANK" means a bank, other than an authorised dealer, authorised by the Reserve Bank to accept deposits from persons resident outside India. [Foreign Exchange Management (Manner of Receipt and Payment) Regulations, 2000, Reg. 2(iii)]

Authorised by law. The expression 'authorised by law' means sanctioned by law while 'according to law' means in conformity with law. *S.K. Jadhav* v. *State of Maharastra*, AIR 1971 SC 840, 844.

Authorised capital. Means such capital as is authorised by the memorandum of a company to be the maximum amount of share capital of the company. [S. 2(8) of the Companies Act, 2013 (18 of 2013)]

"Authorised insurer". Means any insurance company carrying on any class of marine insurance business, which is registered or recognised by the Central Government under any law for the time being in force in India. [Inland Vessels Act, 2021 (24 of 2021), section 3(a)]

Authorised officer. Means, within his local limits of jurisdiction—

(i) a District Magistrate, or

(ii) a Sub-divisional Magistrate, or

(iii) a Commissioner of Police, and includes any other officer notified in the Official Gazette, by the Central Government or the State Government, to be an authorised officer for such local limits of jurisdiction as may be determined by that Government. [Cable

Television Networks (Regulation) Act (7 of 1995), S. 2(a)]

"AUTHORISED OFFICER" means an officer not less than a chief manager of a public sector bank or equivalent, as specified by the Board of Directors or Board of Trustees of the secured creditor or any other person or authority exercising powers of superintendence, direction and control of the business or affairs of the secured creditor, as the case may be, to exercise the rights of a secured creditor under the Ordinance. [Security Interest (Enforcement) Rules (3 of 2002), R. 2(a)]

"Authorised Officer" means such officer of the Central Board, or as the case may be, of the Corporation notified by the Central Government. [Code on Social Security, 2020 (36 of 2020), section 2(5)]

Authorised person. Means a person or body of persons or trustees of any trust authorised by the Central Government under Section 7. [Acquisition of certain Area at Ayodhya (33 of 1993), S. 2(b)]

"AUTHORISED PERSON" means an authorised dealer, money changer, off-shore banking unit or any other person for the time being authorised under sub-section (1) of Section 10 to deal in foreign exchange or foreign securities. [Foreign Exchange Management Act (42 of 1999), S. 2(c)]

"AUTHORIZED PERSON" means a person or an organization authorized by the competent authority to collect, treat, transport, store or dispose of hazardous waste in accordance with the guidelines to be issued by the competent authority from time to time. [Rule 2(d) the Hazardous Wastes (Management and Handling) Rules, 1989]

In these regulations, unless the context otherwise requires,—

"AUTHORISED PERSON" means,—

(i) a Custom House Agent who holds a permanent licence under the Custom House Agents Licensing Regulations, 1984 and is authorised by the Commissioner of Customs with a user identification; or

(ii) an importer who holds a valid Import Export Code Number and is specially authorised by the Commissioner of Customs with a user identification for the purpose of obtaining clearance of goods imported by him. [Bill of Entry (Electronic Declaration) Regulation, 1995, Reg. 2(a)]

"AUTHORIZED PERSON" means an occupier or operator authorized by the prescribed authority to generate, collect, receive, store, transport, treat, dispose or handle biomedical waste in accordance with these rules and any guidelines issued by the Central Government. [Rule 3(4) of the Batteries (Management and Handling) Rules, 2001]

Authorised physician. Means any person registered under any Central Act or State Act providing for the maintenance of a register of medical practitioners or in any area where no such last mentioned Act is in force, any person declared by State Government by notification in the Official Gazette to be a qualified medical practitioner. [Rule (c) of the, 1991]

Authorised representative. For the purposes of this section, "AUTHORISED REPRESENTATIVE" means a person authorised by the assesse in writing to appear on his behalf, being—

(i) a person related to the assesse in any manner, or a person regularly employed by the assesse; or

(ii) any officer of a Scheduled Bank with which the assesse maintains a current account or has other regular dealings; or

(iii) any legal practitioner who is entitled to practise in any civil Court in India; or

(iv) an accountant; or

(v) any person who has passed any accountancy examination recognised in this behalf by the Board; or

(vi) any person who has acquired such educational qualifications as the Board may prescribe for this purpose; or

(*via*) any person who, before the coming into force of this Act in the Union Territory of Dadra and Nagar Haveli, Goa, Daman and Diu, or Pondicherry, attended before an Income-tax authority in the said territory on behalf of any assesse otherwise than in the capacity of an employee or relative of that assesse; or

(vii) any other person who, immediately before the commencement of this Act, was an Income-tax practitioner within the meaning of clause (*iv*) of sub-section (2) of Section 61 of the Indian Income-tax Act, 1922 (XI of 1922), and was actually practicing as such. [Income-tax Act (43 of 1961), S. 288(2)]

For the purposes of this section, "authorised representative" in relation to—

(i) the Initiating Officer, means a person authorised by the Central Government;

(ii) any other party to the proceedings, means a person authorised by the party

in writing to appear on his behalf, being—

(i) a person related to the party in any manner, or a person regularly employed by the party; or

(ii) any officer of a scheduled bank with which the party maintains an account or has other regular dealings; or

(iii) any legal practitioner who is entitled to practice in any civil court in India; or

(iv) any person who has passed any accountancy examination recognised in this behalf by the Board; or

(v) any person who has acquired such educational qualifications as the Board may prescribe for this purpose. [Prohibition of Benami Property Transactions Act (45 of 1988), section 48, *Expln.*]

In this section, "authorised representative" means a person authorised by the assessee in writing to appear on his behalf, being—

(a) a person related to the assessee in any manner, or a person regularly employed by the assessee;

(b) any officer of a scheduled bank with which the assessee maintains a current account or has other regular dealings;

(c) any legal practitioner who is entitled to practice in any civil court in India;

(d) an accountant;

(e) any person who has passed any accountancy examination recognised in this behalf by the Board; or

(f) any person who has acquired such educational qualifications as may be prescribed. [Black Money (Undisclosed Foreign Income and Assets) and Imposition of Tax Act (22 of 2015), section 78(3)]

"AUTHORISED REPRESENTATIVE" means,—

(a) in relation to an applicant, except where such applicant is required under any of the provisions of Chapter XIX-A of the Act to attend in person, a person who would be entitled to represent him before any income-tax authority or the Appellate Tribunal under Section 288.

(b) in relation to a Commissioner, a person—

(i) authorised in writing by the Commissioner or the Chief Commissioner, or

(ii) duly appointed by the Central Government as authorised representative or duly authorised by the Central Board of Direct Taxes.

To appear, plead and act for the Commissioner in any proceeding before the Commission. [Income-tax Settlement Commission (Procedure) Rules, 1997, S. 2(iv)]

In this rule—

"AUTHORISED REPRESENTATIVE" means a person who represents any other person, on payment of any fee or remuneration, before any tribunal or authority constituted or appointed by or under any law for the time being in force, but does not include an employee of the person so represented or a person carrying on legal profession or a person carrying on the profession of accountancy. [Income-tax Rules, 1962, R. 6F(2) *Expln.* (a)]

"AUTHORISED REPRESENTATIVE" in relation to any proceedings before the Tribunal means,—

(i) a person authorised by the person referred to in sub-section (1) of Section 146A of the Customs Act, or, as the case may be, sub-section (1) of Section 35Q of the Central Excises Act or sub-section (1) of Section 101A of the Gold (Control) Act, to appear on his behalf in such proceedings; or

(ii) a person duly appointed by the Central Government or by an officer duly authorised in this behalf as authorised representative to appear, plead and act for the Commissioner or Administrator, in such proceedings. [, R. 2(c)]

'AUTHORISED REPRESENTATIVE' means a person duly appointed and authorised by, a complainant or a party to an arbitration proceeding, as the case may be, to act on his behalf and represent him, in the proceedings under the Scheme before a Banking Ombudsman for consideration of his complaint, claim or counter claim. [Banking Ombudsman Scheme, 2002, S. 3(2)]

Authorised service station. Means any service station, or centre, authorised by any motor vehicle manufacturer, to carry out any service or repair of any motor car, light motor vehicle or two wheeled motor vehicle manufactured by such manufacturer. [Finance Act (32 of 1994), S. 65(9) *as substituted by Act (32 of 2003), S. 159* (now repealed by Central Goods and Sevice Tax, 2017)]

Authorities. Statutes, rules, precedents. judicial decisions, official declarations or opinions, and recognized text-books cited in arguments on questions of law or in the trial of causes before a Court, in support of the legal positions contended for.

Authority. A person or persons, or a body, exercising power of command; generally in the plural : as, the civil and military authorities. Power or admitted right to command or to act, whether original or delegated : as, the authority of parents over children; the authority of an agent to act for his principal. An authority is *general* when it extends to all acts, or all connected with a particular employment, and *special* when confined to a single act.

"AUTHORITY, is nothing but a power to do something; it is sometimes given by word, and sometimes by writing : also it is by writ, warrant, commission, letter of attorney, &c. and sometimes by law. The authority that is given must be to do a thing lawful; for if it be for the doing anything against law, as to beat a man, take away his goods, or disseize him of his lands this will not be a good authority to justify him that doth it." (*Dyer* 102; *Tomlin*)

'AUTHORITY' means and includes any authority or officer authorized by the Central Government, or as the case may be, the State Government, in accordance with the laws in force and includes a District Magistrate, Police Commissioner, or any other officer not below the rank of the Deputy Superintendent of Police designated for the maintenance of the ambient air quality standards in respect of noise under any law for the time being in force. [Rule 2(c) of the Noise Pollution (Regulation and Control) Rules, 2000]

(*In contracts*) The lawful delegation of power by one person to another.

(*In administrative law*) a body having jurisdiction in certain matters of a public nature.

Person or officer having authority as Cantonment-authority; Chief controlling revenue authority; Local Authority; Municipal authority; Police authority; Road authority; Telegraph authority, Express authority, Implied authority.

If a statutory corporate body or other authority is an instrumentality or agency of the Government, it would be an 'Authority' and therefore "State" within the meaning of the expression in Art. 12 of the Constitution. *Som Prakash Rekhi* v. *Union of India*, (1981) 51 Com. Cases 71 : AIR 1981 SC 212. [Companies Act (1 of 1956) replaced with Companies Act, 2013, S. 617]

The U.P. Warehousing Corporation is a statutory body wholly controlled and managed by the government and it is therefore 'authority', within the meaning of Art. 12. *U.P. Warehousing Corporation* v. *Vijay Narain*, AIR 1980 SC 840, 843. [Constitution of India, Art. 12]

In India, a corporation deemed to be authority, would not be subject to the constitutional limitation of fundamental rights in the performance of all its functions, and the application of 'authority' would stick to such Corporation, irrespective of the functional context. *M.C. Mehta* v. *Union of India*, AIR 1987 SC 1086, 1097.

As the Army Welfare Housing Organisation is not an instrumentality or agency of the Government as is clear from the State Government not finding the source of the organisation, the State not exercising plenary control over the organisation and also from the organisation out-discharging public function, the organisation is not authority within the meaning of Art. 226 of the Constitution. *N.C. Rastogi* v. *UOI*, AIR 1986 Del 128, 136. [Constitution of India, Art. 226]

The word 'authority' in S. 3(3) includes Central and State Governments. *Harkishan Singh* v. *State of Punjab*, AIR 1966 P&H 248, 254. *Mohd. Anwar Allai* v. *State of J&K*, AIR 1967 J&K 32, 35. [Defence of India Act (1962), S. 443(3)]

A right; an official or judicial command; also a legal power to do an act given by one man to another; the person or body having the authority; weight of testimony [Companies Act (1 of 1956) replaced with Companies Act, 2013, S. 59(2)]; body having authority.

Authority concerned. The expression 'authority concerned', means the authority before which the application for approval was made, *viz.*, authority before which the proceeding is pending. *A and C Corporation of India* v. *VII Industrial Tribunal*, AIR 1967 Cal 114, 117. [Industrial Disputes Act (14 of 1947), S. 33(2)(*b*), proviso]

Authority controlled By State Government. A Co-operative Society has its own independent existence and the management of the Society vests in a body and not in the State, though in the said body the State might have its own nominated members. Therefore, the State Government has no deep and pervasive control over the Co-operative Society. *Managing Director* v. *Natabar Mohanty*, AIR 1989 Ori 189. [Arbitration Act (10 of 1940) (*repealed*), S. 41A, as inserted by Orrisa Act 3 of 1982]

Authority in writing. A legal power in writing to do an act given by one man to another. [IPC (45 of 1860), S. 99, *Expln.* 2].

Authority making the order. The words 'authority making the order' do not mean the individual who made it. What is meant is, if the order is made by the Dist. Magistrate, the Dist. Magistrates; if it is by State, the State and so on. *In re. Maganlal Jirabhai Patel*, AIR 1951 Bom 33. [Preventive Detention Act 1950, S. 7]

Authority of law. 'Authority of law' means the permission under the law (say, statute law) to do a thing. When Art. 300-A says 'authority of law' all that the statute should prescribe is an enabling power leaving it open to the parties concerned neither of which may necessarily be the state, to make their own arrangement by way of contract, or a set of rules or conditions by one, which are accepted by the other party. *Ahmedali* v. *State of Madhya Pradesh*, AIR 1960 MP 282, 286. [Constitution of India, Art. 300-A]

Authority Revocation List. A list of revoked Certifying Authority Certificates. An ARL is a CRL for Certifying Authority Cross Certificates. (*Information Technology*)

Authority to contract and Capacity to contract. "Capacity to contract" means power to bind oneself by the contract and "authority to contract" means the authority to bind another by the contract. While capacity is part of the law of status, authority is part of the law of principal and agent. While capacity is usually a question of law, authority is usually a question of fact.

Authorize. To empower; to give right or authority to act; to clothe with authority; warrant or legal power.

Authorize. The word 'Authorize' as defined in Oxford Concise English Dictionary means to give an authority to a person or a body or to sanction or commission a person to do some act.' The Black's Law Dictionary defines the word 'Authorize' to mean to give legal authority or to empower the authorized person to act for the person giving such an authority. ' [As cited in *Ranvir Singh* v. *State of U.P.*, 2017 (6) AWC 6271 (All), para 10]

Authorized. Means "permitted" or "directed".

Authorized capital. The amount of capital that a company has been authorised to raise by way of equity and preference shares.

Authorized shares. The total number of shares of stock which the charter or articles of incorporation permit or corporation to sell. It is also called as *Authorized stock*.

Authorship. The state of being an author; the occupation of writing books or contributing articles to newspapers or journals.

Autism. Means a condition of uneven skill development primarily affecting the communication and social abilities of a person, marked by repetitive and ritualistic behaviour. [National Trust for Welfare of Persons with Autism, Cerebral Palsy,

Mental Retardation and Multiple Disabilities Act (44 of 1999), S. 2(a)]

Autocracy. Absolute supremacy; the name of an unlimited monarchical Government. A Government at the will of one man, (called an "autocrat,") unchecked by constitutional restrictions, conventions or limitations.

Autocratic. Pertaining to or of the nature of autocracy; absolute; uncontrolled; holding independent and unlimited powers of Government.

Automatic suspension. In bankruptcy, a bar against the debtor or debtor's property to all his judicial and extrajudicial collection efforts.

"Automated". Means any digital process capable of operating automatically in response to instructions given or otherwise for the purpose of processing data. [Digital Personal Data Protection Act, 2023 (22 of 2023), section 2(b)]

Automatism. State or quality of being automatic; an automatic habit of acting. *In medical jurisprudence*, this term is applied to actions or conduct of an individual apparently occurring without will, purpose, or reasoned intention on his part; a condition in which one who is not actually insane, suffers from an obscuration of the mental faculties, loss of volition or of memory, of kindred affections.

Automobile. Means any vehicle powered either by internal combustion engine or by any method of generating power to drive such vehicle by burning fuel. [Air (Prevention and Control of Pollution) Act (14 of 1981), S. 2(e)]

Autonomous. Possessing self-government. [Representation of the People Act (43 of 1951), S. 4(b)].

Autonomous Board. Means any of the Autonomous Boards constituted under section 16. [National Dental Commission Act, 2023 (21 of 2023), section 2(a)]

"Autonomous Board" means any of the Autonomous Boards constituted under section 16. [National Medical Commission Act, 2019 (30 of 2019), section 2(a)]

Autonomy. The quality or state of being autonomous, the power or right of self-government; the political independence of a nation.

Autonomous power—having definite powers, which cannot be encroached upon by the centre.

Autopsy. (*in Med. Jur.*) The dissection of a dead body for the purpose of inquiring into or ascertaining the cause of death; a postmortem examination.

Autre droit. An expression used where persons sue or are sued in another's right; as executors, administrators, *etc.*

Autre Droit, In. In right of another.

Autrefois acquit; Autre fois attaint; Autre fois convict.

AUTRE FOIS ACQUIT. "Formerly acquitted".

The principle underlying the plea of *autre fois acquit* is not fully stated merely by saying that an accused person should not be vexed twice by prosecution on the same set of facts.

AUTRE FOIS ATTAINT. "Formerly attainted". AUTRE FOIS CONVICT. "Formerly convicted" are all pleas in bar to a prosecution.

Formerly convicted. By this plea, a person charged with an offence pleads that he had been tried before and convicted of the same offence by a competent Court.

AUTRE FOIS ACQUIT "is a plea by a criminal, that he was heretofore acquitted of the same offence; for one shall not be brought in to danger of his life or liberty for the same offence more than once. (*Tomlin*)

Autre vie. (*Fr.*) Other law.

Auxiliary. One that aids or helps; an assistant; a confederate.

Assisting or supporting. [Army Act (46 of 1950), S. 12, prov.].

Auxilium. (*Lat.*) A form of compulsory aid or tribute, paid by the vassal to his lord, as an incident of the tenure.

Avail. A person can be stated to have availed himself of something, only if he has taken advantage or profited by that thing or utilized it to his benefit. *R.S. Mani* v. *A. Planimuthu,* AIR 1967 Mad 16, 19 [Indian Partnership Act (9 of 1932), S. 4]

Available. Capable of being turned to account; to one's disposal; within one's reach.

Availment. The act of taking advantage or making use of something for one's own benefit.

Avalanche. A hustling mass of snow, with ice and rock, descending a mountain side. [Indian Forest Act (16 of 1927), S. 35(1)(c)(i)].

Aver. To declare or assert; to avouch or verify; to offer to verify; to set out distinctly and formally; to allege as a fact. To assert or prove the truth of; to confirm, verify; to assert; to affirm with confidence; declare in a positive or peremptory manner.

To declare in a positive manner as in confidence of asserting the truth; to set out distinctly and formally. [Specific Relief Act (47 of 1963), S. 16(c)].

Average. In *Marine Insurance*. Loss or damage accidentally happening to a vessel or its cargo during a voyage.

An arithmetical mean.

"Average adjusted total income" means,—

(a) in a case where the total income of the assesse is assessable for each of the three assessment years immediately preceding the relevant assessment year, one-third of the aggregate amount of the adjusted total income in respect of the previous year's relevant to the aforesaid three assessment years;

(b) in a case where the total income of the assesse is assessable only for two of the aforesaid three assessment years, one-half of the aggregate amount of the adjusted total income in respect of the previous year's relevant to the aforesaid two assessment years;

(c) in a case where the total income of the assesse is assessable only for one of the aforesaid three assessment years, the amount of the adjusted total income in respect of the previous year relevant to that assessment year. [Income-tax Act (43 of 1961), S. 44C, *Expln.* (ii)]

Average basic wage. The expression 'average basic wage' can only mean the wage earned by a workman during a month divided by the number of days for which he has worked and multiplied by 26 in order to arrive at the monthly wage for the computation of gratuity payable. *DCM Ltd.* v. *Their Workmen*, AIR 1970 SC 919, 938. [Industrial Disputes Act (14 of 1947), Third Schedule, item 5]

Average clause. In marine and commercial insurance and some fire insurance policies, a clause in the policy that stipulates that certain items shall be subject to average if there is under insurance.

Average daily balance. Average amount of money in an account during a given period.

Average pay. Means the average of the wages payable to a workman—

(i) in the case of monthly paid workman, in the three complete calendar months,

(ii) in the case of weekly paid workmen, in the four complete weeks,

(iii) in the case of daily paid workman, in the twelve full working days, preceding the date on which the average pay becomes payable if the workman had worked for three complete calendar months or four complete weeks or twelve full working days, as the case may be, and where such calculation cannot be made, the average pay shall be calculated as the average of the wages payable to a workman during the period he actually worked. [Industrial Disputes Act (14 of 1947), S. 2(aaa)]

"Average pay" means the average of the wages payable to a worker,—

(i) in the case of monthly paid worker, in three complete calendar months;

(ii) in the case of weekly paid worker, in four complete weeks;

(iii) in the case of daily paid worker, in twelve full working days,

preceding the date on which the average pay becomes payable, if the worker had worked for three complete calendar months or four complete weeks or twelve full working days, as the case may be, and where such calculation cannot be made, the average pay shall be calculated as the average of the wages payable to a worker during the period he actually worked. [Industrial Relations Code, 2020 (35 of 2020), section 2(d)]

Average weekly earnings. Mentioned in the Workmen's Compensation Act (8 of 1923) have to be calculated on the basis of the weekly earnings during the one period of continuous employment immediately preceding the injury. *Jones* v. *Ocean Coal Company,* 1899 2 QB 124.

Averia. Beast of burden, such as oxen, horses *etc.* (*Latin for Lawyers*)

Averium. (*Lat.*) Goods; property. A beast of burden.

Averment. Act of averring; that which is averred; affirmation; positive assertion; a positive statement of facts, in opposition to argument or inference.

The action of averring; that which is averred. [CPC (5 of 1908), O. VI, R. 6].

Aviation Turbine Fuel (ATF). 'Aviation Turbine Fuel (ATF)' means any hydrocarbon oil conforming to the Indian Standards Specification of Bureau of Indian Standards IS : 1571 : 1992 : 2000; [Customs Tariff Act (51 of 1975), Sch, S. V, Chap. 27, Note 3, Supplementary Note (d); Central Excise Tariff Act, 1985 (5 of 1986), Sch. I, S.V, Ch. 27, Suppl. N. (d) as substituted by S. 3, Central Excise Tariff (Amendment) Act 2004, (5 of 2005)]

Avigational easement. An easement which permits free aircraft flights over the land in question.

Avocation. The Word 'avocation' means the principal occupation as well as the subsidiary pursuits of life of an individual. *M.A. Khan* v. *State of Maharashtra*, AIR 1967 Bom 254, 259. [Bombay Conditions of Detention Order, 1951, Cl. 16]

'Avocation' is defined in the Oxford Dictionary as that which has the effect of taking away or withdrawing one from his occupation. 'Avocation' is a word of wide signification meaning that to which a man passes his life or spends his time. 'Avocation' cannot be equated to profession or calling. *Workman, B. Somayajulu* v. *State of A.P.*, AIR 1961 AP 528, 532. [Working Journalists and other Newspaper Employees (Conditions of Service) Miscellaneous Provisions Act (45 of 1955), S. 2(f)]

Avoid. To escape; to evade; to keep out of the way; to make void; to annul; to expel (doubt).

Avoidable cause. A cause that can be obviated or get rid of. [Indian Contract Act (9 of 1872), S. 73, ill. (e)].

Avoidance. Avoidance. Setting aside or avoiding or vacating *e.g.*, avoidance of a fraudulent conveyance.

Avoided. "Avoided means escapement and not evasion". *Mansumkhilal* v. *C.I.T., Bombay City II, Bombay.* AIR 1969 SC 835 at p. 839.

Avoiding service, for the purpose of. For evading service of any process. [CPC (5 of 1908), O. V, R. 20(1)].

Avow. To declare openly; to own; to acknowledge and justify an act done (as) a man avows his principles or his crimes. Avow is to justify or maintain an act done, specifically a distress for rent taken in one's own right.

Avowal. An open declaration; offer of proof.

Avowry. In common law pleading, it is an acknowledgment in an answer to replevin action.

Avowtry. Adultery.

Avulsion. Avulsion is where lands are by an inundation or current torn off from the property to which they originally belonged, and gained to the estate of another person; or wherever a river changes its course, and in place of continuing to run betwixt two properties, cuts off part of one and joints it to the other property. The property of the part thus separated continues in the original proprietor, in which respect the term *avulsio* stands in contradistinction to the term *alluvio*, by which an addition is insensibly made to a property by the gradual washing down of river, and which addition becomes the property of the owner of the lands to which the addition is made (*Tomlin*). Avulsion is the removal of soil from the land of one man and its deposit on the land of another.

Avyavaharika. The term "Avyavaharika" has been variously translated as being that which is not lawful or what is not just or what is not admissible under the law or normal conditions. *S.M. Jakati* v. *S.M. Borkar*, AIR 1959 SC 282, 286.

Awaiting. "Awaiting his Trial," means, Committed for Trial. (*Stroud*)

Award. AWARD means an arbitration award. [Arbitration Act (10 of 1940), S. 2(b)].

"Award" means an interim or a final determination of any industrial dispute or of any question relating thereto by any Industrial Tribunal referred to in section 44 or National Industrial Tribunal referred to in section 46 and includes an arbitration award made under section 42. [Industrial Relations Code, 2020 (35 of 2020), section 2(e)]

The expression "award" means the amount of money that a court decides should be given to someone who has won a case; the decision to give money; to make an official decision to give something to someone as a payment, prize, etc. (See Oxford Advanced Learner's Dictionary, A.S. Hornby, 7th Edition.) The expression "award", n. is defined as a final judgment or decision, especially, one by an arbitrator or by a jury assessing damages. (See Black's Law Dictionary, Eighth Edition.) [As cited in *Shriram Transport Finance Co. Ltd.* v. *Naduvacheri Balakrishnan and Ors.* AIR 2017 Ker 252, para 16]

To adjudge to be due; assign, or bestow as of right, or give by judicial determination or deliberate judgment, especially upon arbitration or umpirage as, to award the prizes at a school examination; the arbitrators awarded him heavy damages.

The act by which parties refer any matter between them to the private decision of another party, (whether one person or more,) is called a *Submission*; the party to whom the reference is made, an *Arbitrator* or *Arbitrators*; when the reference is made to more than one, provision made, that in case they shall disagree, another shall decide, that other is called an *Umpire*. The judgment given or determination made by an arbitrator or arbitrators, is termed an *Award;* that by an umpire an *Umpirage,* or less correctly an award. (*Tomlin*)

An award is not a mere agreement but is equivalent to a judgment.

An *award* must be read in the light of the proceedings before the arbitrators.

The order discussing an application to get substituted or added as a party in the land acquisition proceeding is not an award. *Sundarlal* v. *Paramsukhadas*, AIR 1968 SC 366, 371.

Award means determination, final or interim of any question relating to an industrial dispute. *Cox and Kings (Agents) Ltd.* v. *Their Workmen and Others*, AIR 1977 SC 1666, 1670. [Industrial Disputes Act (14 of 1947), S. 19(3)(b)].

A decision given by an arbitrator or umpire; the document embodying it [Arbitration Act (10 of 1940), S. 2(b) (*repealed*)]; a sentence or decision after examination; the document embodying it [Requisitioning and Acquisition of Immovable Property Act (30 of 1952), S. 2(a)]; to adjudge; 'something that is conferred or bestowed upon a person [Jawaharlal Nehru University Act (53 of 1966), S. 17(1)(a)]; to give out (a degree *etc.* [Banaras Hindu University Act (16 of 1915), S. 18(1)(c)].

Award, error on the face of. An *error in law on the face of the award* means that one can find in the award or a document actually incorporated thereto, as for instance a note appended by the arbitrator stating the reason for his judgment some legal proposition which is the basis of the award and which one can then say is erroneous.

Award, making of. An a award is the judgment pronounced by the arbitrators, and *to make an award* is to announce and publish the judgment. It is a judicial act, and while sometime said to partake of the attributes of a contract, it is more nearly akin to a judgment of a regular tribunal, and is no more a contract than such judgment, being at the same time of a higher nature than a mere specialty. (*Ame. Cyc.*)

Award upon settlement. An award which the arbitrator makes at the request of the parties on the terms of the settlement which the parties have arrived at themselves during the course of the arbitration. (*Arbitration*)

Awardable. Fit to be awarded; rightly or law fully to be awarded. [Army Act (46 of 1950) Ss. 71 and 72].

Aware of, Be. To be cognizant or informed of [Arms Act (54 of 1959), S. 30(1)]

Away-going crop. A crop which has been sown or planted during a tenancy, but is no ready for gathering until after its expiration.

Axiom. A self-evident or apparent truth.

Ayurvedic, Siddha or Unani drug. Includes all medicine intended for internal or external use for or in the diagnosis, treatment, migration or prevention of disease or disorder human beings or animals, and manufactured exclusively in accordance with the formulae described in, the authoritative books Ayurvedic, Siddha and Unani (Tibb) system of medicine specified in the First Schedule [Drug and Cosmetics Act (23 of 1940) S. 3(a)]

B

Baby Doe. A generic pseudonym for a very young child involved in litigation, specially in the context of medical care.

Baby-snatching. Kidnapping of a baby or child, often without the element of force or fraud.

Baby walker. An article, given to babies to assist them in learning walking and encourage them to acquire manual and muscular dexterity and is to be taxed as a toy.

Bachelor. In the universities, there are bachelors of arts, of law, in divinity, in medicine & c. which is the first degree taken by students, before they come to greater dignity. (*Tomlin*)

A man (also a woman), who has never been married. [Hindu Adoptions and Maintenance Act (78 of 1956)].

Bachelor of Teaching. The B.T. course of studies is open only to graduates and in a dictionary manner of speaking, the degree of 'Bachelor of Teaching' may be said to be a post-graduate degree in the sense that the degree is obtainable only after graduation. *Smt. Juthika Bhattacharya* v. *State of M.P.*, AIR 1976 SC 2534.

Back. To indorse; to sign on the back; to sing generally by way of acceptance or approval.

Back-bencher. Private member who does not hold any ministerial office. In the Indian Parliament it is a more journalistic term than a procedural one.

Back bond. The bond of indemnity given to a surety.

Back carry. The crime of carrying on one's back, unlawfully killed game.

Back date. To put the date earlier than the actual date.

Back door. A hole in the security of a computer system deliberately left in place by designers or maintainers. Synonymous with trap door. A hidden software or hardware mechanism used to circumvent security controls. A breach created intentionally for the purpose of collecting, altering, or destroying data.

Back duty. Tax relating to a period in the past which was unpaid then because fraudulent or erroneous returns were made.

Back freight. Freight which consists of expenses claimed by the shipowner from the cargo owner where the master of the ship is not able to deliver goods to the consignee.

Backflush accounting. Way of avoiding the complications of *absorption costing* by keeping minimum levels of stock, so that stock valuation is less important. Profitability is established by apportioning actual costs between cost of sales and stocks held. *Work in progress* is not accounted for. (*International Accounting*)

Backhander. Informal term for a bribe or unofficial payment in cash for work done.

Backing a warrant. Where a warrant issued in one country is presented to a Magistrate of another country and he signs it for the purpose of making it executory in his country he is said to "back" it. (4 *Bl. Comm.* 291)

Backlog. Accumulation of unfilled orders.

Backward classes. "BACKWARD CLASSES" means such classes of citizens, other than the Scheduled Castes and the Scheduled Tribes, as may be notified—

(i) by the Central Government; or

(ii) by any State Government,

as the case may be, from time to time. [Income-tax Act (43 of 1961), S. 10(26B), *Expln.* (b)].

"BACKWARD CLASSES" means such backward classes of citizens other than the Scheduled Castes and the Scheduled Tribes as may be specified by the Central Government in the lists. [National Commission for Backward Classes Act (27 of 1993), S. 2(a)].

"BACKWARD CLASSES" means any of the backward classes specified from time to time by the Administrator and whose names are published in the Official Gazette. [Punjab Municipal Corporation Law (Extention to Chandigarh) Act (45 of 1994), S. 2(1A) Schedule, Part II].

The expression 'backward classes' means that the classes are socially and educationally backward and they are not adequately represented in the services under the state. *Trilokinath* v. *State of J & K*, AIR 1967 SC 1283, 1286. [Constitution of India, Art. 16(4) and 15(4)].

Backwardation or backadation (*in stock exchange*) is the condition existing when stock can be bought cheaper as a matter of account.

In securities transaction, payment of a fee by the seller so that the buyer will allow delayed delivery of the securities beyond their original date of delivery.

Bad character. A person whose general conduct and behaviour is bad or is not free from blemish. [Indian Evidence Act (1 of 1872), S. 54].

Bad cheque. A cheque which is dishonoured due to insufficient amount in the account, also when the account is not in existence.

Bad debt. Debt which cannot reasonably be collected.

A debt about which there is no reasonable expectation of recovery; debt believed to be unrecoverable. [Interest-tax Act (45 of 1974), S. 6(1)]; [Income-tax Act (43 of 1961), S. 36(1)(vii)].

Bad-debt reserve. Reserve used to cover losses on uncollectible accounts receivable.

Bad faith. The opposite of "good faith". Generally implying or involving actual or constructive fraud, or design to mislead or deceive another, or a neglect or refusal to fulfil some duty or some contractual obligation, not prompted by an honest mistake as to one's rights or duties, but some interested or sinister motive. [CPC (5 of 1908), S. 55(3)].

Bad in law. Not valid

Bad security. A security which is substantially defective. [Indian Contract Act (9 of 1872), S. 220, ill. (a)].

Bad title. One which conveys no property to the purchaser of the estate; one which is so radically defective that it is not marketable.

Badge. A distinctive or distinguishing mark, token, device or sign (of membership *etc.*) usually worn on the person. [Air Force Act (45 of 1950), S. 4(vii)].

Badger. A person who buys corn or victuals from one place and carries them to another place so as to sell and make profit by them.

Badli. A '*badli*' is one who is employed on the post of a permanent operative or probationer who is temporarily absent. [*Lalappa* v. *Laxmi Vishnu Textile Mills,* (1981) 2 SCC 238, 245, para 17].

Badli workman. A '*Badli* workman' only means a person who is employed as a casual workman in place of another. He is nothing but a substitute. *Radha Raman Samanta* v. *Bank of India*, (2004) 1 SCC 605, 611, para 17.

Badly drafted. The phrase 'badly drafted' was used to mean that the language of the entry was ambiguous. *ITC Ltd.* v. *CCE*, AIR 2005 SC 1370 : 2004 AIR SCW 7208.

Baffle. Something for deflecting, checking or otherwise regulating the flow. [Factories Act (63 of 1948), S. 37(2)].

Baggage. Such articles of necessity, or personal convenience, as are usually carried by passengers for their personal use.

Bail. To set at liberty a person arrested or imprisoned, on security being taken for his appearance on a day and a place certain, which security is called "bail". "Bail" means release of a person accused of or suspected of commission of an offence from the custody of law upon certain conditions imposed by an officer or Court on execution by such person of a bond or a bail bond. [Bharatiya Nagarik Suraksha Sanhita, 2023 (46 of 2023), section 2(1)(b)]

A delivery or bailment, of a person to his sureties, upon their giving (together with himself) sufficient security for his appearance.

Temporary release from imprisonment on furnishing surety or security to appear for trial; the security so given. [IPC (45 of 1860), S. 205]; to deliver (goods) in trust upon a contract.

Bail-bond. The bond or obligation entered into by the surety or sureties. (*Anderson; Rapalje & L.L.*

A bond given by a prisoner and his surety to ensure the appearance of the former in Court on a fixed day or when called upon [Indian Contract Act (9 of 1872), S. 74, excep.]; [CrPC 1973 (2 of 1974), S. 436(2)].

Bail bondsman. One who provides bail as a surety for the release of criminal defendant.

Bail-jumper. Accused who fails to appear in Court at the appointed time, even after posting a bail bond and promising to appear.

Bail jumping. Defaulting one's bail.

Bailable. Capable of being bailed; capable of being set free on giving a proper bail bond; admitting of bail; authorizing or requiring bail.

In which bail is to be granted as a matter of right. [Children Act (60 of 1960) (*repealed*), S. 18(1)].

Bailable action. Is one in which the defendant cannot be released from arrest except on furnishing bail.

Bailable offence. Is one for which the prisoner may be admitted to bail.

"BAILABLE OFFENCE" means an offence which is shown as bailable in the First Schedule, or which is made bailable by any other law for the time being in force. [CrPC, 1973 (2 of 1974), S. 2(a)]. [Now (w.e.f. 1-7-2024) repealed & replaced by Bharatiya Nagarik Suraksha Sanhita, 2023 (46 of 2023)]

"Bailable offence" means an offence which is shown as bailable in the First Schedule, or which is made bailable by any other law for the time being in force. [(w.e.f. 1-7-2024) Bharatiya Nagarik Suraksha Sanhita, 2023 (46 of 2023), section 2(1)(c)]

Bailee. The party of whom personal property is delivered under a contract of bailment. He has a temporary possession of them and a qualified property in them for such purpose only. (*Blackstone*)

The person to whom the goods are delivered is called the bailee. [Indian Contract Act (9 of 1872), S. 148].

When after a motor accident, the insurance company takes possession of the car and takes it to the nearest repairer, the Insurance Company would be the bailee and the repairer would be the sub-bailee. *N.R. Srinivasa Iyer* v. *New India Assurance Co. Ltd.*, AIR 1983 SC 899, 905.

One to whom goods are bailed. [Indian Contract Act (9 of 1872), S. 148].

Bailer or Bailor. One who delivers goods to another on bailment.

Bailiff. In a general sense, a person to whom some authority, care guardianship, or jurisdiction is delivered, committed, or intrusted: one who is deputed or appointed to take charge of another's affairs.

An officer entrusted with the duty of executing warrants *etc.* or making arrests under orders of Court. [IPC (45 of 1860), S. 300, *Excep.* I, ill. (e),].

Bailiwick. The area within which a bailiff exercises jurisdiction.

Bailment. A "bailment" is the delivery of goods by one person to another for some purpose, upon a contract that they shall, when the purpose is accomplished, be returned or otherwise disposed of according to the directions of the person delivering them. The person delivering the goods is called the "bailor". The person to whom they are delivered is called the "bailee". [Indian Contract Act (9 of 1872), S. 148].

Bailment of pledge. The bailment of goods as security for payment of a debt or performance of a promise. [Indian Contract Act (9 of 1872), S. 172].

Bailor. The party who bails or delivers goods to another under a contract of bailment. [Indian Contract Act (9 of 1872), S. 4].

Bailout. Rescuing an entity from financial trouble.

Bait and Switch. A deceptive sales practice. Such tactic usually involves advertising a low-priced product to lure customers to a store, then inducing them to buy higher-priced models by failing to stock sufficient quantities of the lower priced item to satisfy demand, or by disparaging the less expensive product. Such practices are prohibited by statue in most States.

Baiting. To harass by setting on dogs *etc.*, to worry and bite. [Prevention of Cruelty to Animals Act (11 of 1890), S. 6C].

Baiting animals. To provoke or harass animals; procuring them to be worried by dogs; as, to *bait* a bear with dogs.

Coursing rabbits with dogs in an inclosure from which they cannot escape, is not "baiting".

Balance. The conclusion or result of the debit and credit sides of an account; the amount remaining due from one person to another on a settlement of the accounts involving mutual dealings.

The difference between the debit and credit side of an account; the remainder. [TP Act (4 of 1882), S. 79] and Indian Contract Act (9 of 1872), S. 171; [Trade Unions Act (16 of 1926), S. 15(f)].

Balance confirmation. A statement issued periodically by a business organisation, and sent to all its customers an association, showing the balance of amount due from or payable to them. This exercise ensures accuracy in accounts and helps remove discrepancies if any. (*Banking*)

Balance due. The words "balance due" written by the debtor in the creditor's account do not form a promise required by S. 25, Cl 3, Indian Contract Act (9 of 1872), which is a promise to pay despite the consciousness that the debt is barred. *Ramaswami Pillai* v. *Kuppuswami Pillai*. 7 IC 901a : 20 MLJ 656.

Balance of payment. An account of all recorded financial exchanges made between the residents of a country and those of other countries. The balance of payments is divided into current and capital accounts. [*P. Ramanatha Aiyar's, The Major Law Lexicon*, 2010, LexisNexis].

Balance of probabilities. A concept in the law of evidence which relates to the standard of proof whereby the party upon whom the legal burden of proof rests is entitled to a verdict in his favour if he has established some preponderance of probability in his favour.

Balance of trade. Also known as visible balance, the difference in value between a country's visible imports and visible exports. When the total value of visible imports is more than the total value of visible exports, it is an adverse balance of trade. [*P. Ramanatha Aiyar's, The Major Law Lexicon*, 2010, LexisNexis].

Balance order. The order made by the Court for enforcing payment of calls in the winding up, whether voluntary, or compulsory of a company.

Balance-sheet. A statement which should exhibit all the balances of debits and credits, the value of merchandise, and the result of the whole made of merchants and others to show the true state of a particular business. Credit and debit entries of mercantile dealings exhibited together on a single page, and so grouped and arranged as to close into each other and be summed up in one general result, constitute the "balance-sheet." It is a statement designed to show the assets and liabilities and the profits and losses of a company. (*Marsh, Bank.*)

A statement in a summarized form of the balance of the ledger accounts remaining, after all revenue and expense accounts have been closed by transfer of revenue or profit and loss account. [Income-tax Act (43 of 1961), S. 5(2)(b), *Expln.* I and Food Corporations Act (37 of 1964), S. 34(1)].

Balance sheet and Profit and Loss Account. Means the consolidated balance sheet of the company as a whole and not of its departments, undertakings and branches separately. [Payment of Bonus Act (21 of 1965), S. 3].

Balance shelf-life. means the period between the date of import (Import General Manifest) and "Best Before" or "Date of expiry" as the case may be. [Food Safety and Standards (Import) Regulations, 2017, Regn. 2(1)(c)].

Balanced accounts. Accounts of which the balance had been struck. [Payment of Bonus Act (21 of 1965), S. 2(1)(iii)(b)].

Bale. Means any pressed package of cotton of whatever size or density. [Cotton Ginning & Pressing Factories Act (12 of 1925), S. 2(a)].

A pack or certain quantity of goods or merchandise wrapped or packed up in cloth and corded round very tightly for carriage or transportation.

Ballast. Means any solid or liquid placed in a ship to increase the draft to change the trim, to regulate the stability, or to maintain stress load within such limits as may be prescribed. [Merchant Shipping Act (44 of 1958), S. 356B(a) (*Substituted by Act (59 of 2003)*)].

Weight carried by a ship or boat for the purpose of insuring the proper stability, both to avoid risk of capsizing and to secure the greatest effectiveness of the propelling power.

Ballastage. Is a toll paid for the privilege of taking up ballast from the bottom of harbour or port.

Ballistic expert. Where the direct evidence is not satisfactory or disinterested or where the injuries are alleged to have been caused with a gun and they *prima facie* appear to have been inflicted by a rifle, undoubtedly the apparent inconsistency can be cured or the oral evidence can be carroborated by loading the evidence of a ballistic expert. *Gurcharan Singh* v. *State of Punjab*, AIR 1963 SC 340, 346. [Indian Evidence Act (1 of 1872), S. 45].

Ballistics. The science of the motion of projectiles, such as bullets; the study of a weapon's firing characteristics, especially to determine a gun's firing capacity and whether a particular gun fired a given bullet.

Balloon-payment mortgage. A mortgage which requires periodic payments for a specified time and lumpsum payment of the outstanding balance at maturity.

Ballot. (*In the law of elections*) A slip of paper bearing the names of the offices to be filled at the particular election and the names of the candidates for whom the elector desired to vote. A ballot ticket is folded in such a manner that nothing written or printed thereon can be seen. A casting of ballots; a vote by ballot; also, the whole number of votes cast or recorded.

The word "ballot" in its strict sense would not include voting by the use of voting machines. *A.C. Jose* v. *Sivan Pillai*, AIR 1984 SC 921, 928.

Ballot-box. A case or box for receiving ballots.

Ban. Legal prohibition. [Gold (Control) Act (45 of 1968), S. 12 (*Repealed*) by Act (18 of 1990)].

Band. A company of persons united in a common design—especially a body of armed men.

BAND, COMPANY, CREW, GANG. All these terms denote a small association for a particular object: a *band* is an association where men are bound together by some strong obligation, whether taken in a good or bad sense, as a *band* of soldiers, a *band* of robbers. A *company* marks an association for convenience without any particular obligation as a *company* of travellers, a *company* of strolling players. *Crew* marks an association collected together by some external power, or by coincidence of plan and motive: in the former case it is used for a ship's *crew*; in the latter and bad sense of the word it is employed for any number of evil-minded persons met together from different quarters, and co-operating for some bad purpose. *Gang* is used in a bad sense for an association of thieves, murderers, and depredators in general; or in a technical sense for those who work together.

Bandhu. A relation, a kinsman in general. In law, a cognate kinsman in a remote degree.

The term "*bandhu*" is defined in the Mitakshara (Ch. II, S. 5, Verse 3) as a "*binna gotra sapinda*", *i.e.* one sprung from a different family and connected by common corporeal particles, or by consanguinity.

Bandit. An outlaw; a man banned, or put under a ban; a lawless or desperate fellow; a brigand; a robber; especially, one of an organised band or lawless marauders.

Bangkok Agreement. "BANGKOK AGREEMENT" means the First Agreement on Trade Negotiations among Developing Member Countries of the Economic and Social Commission for Asia and the Pacific. [Customs Tariff (Determination of Origin of Goods Under The Bangkok Agreement) Rules, 1976].

Banishment. A punishment inflicted upon criminals, by compelling them to quit the country for a specified period of time, or for life; transportation or exile by way of punishment for crime: expulsion or deportation by the political authority on the ground of expediency. The act of banishing or compelling a citizen to leave his country or place of residence by political or judicial authority.

Banishment and **Exilement.** Are synonyms, and import a compulsory loss of one's country.

TO BANISH, EXILE. The idea of exclusion, or of a coercive removal from a place, is common to these terms: *banishment* includes the removal from any place, or the prohibition of access to any place, where one has been or where one is in the habit of going; *exile* signifies the removal from one's home: to *exile,* therefore, is to *banish*, but to *banish* is not always to *exile*.

Banjar or **Bunjar.** Waste or fallow land.

"Banjar" in common parlance mean fallow or barren or unproductive. *Sarjeet Singh* v. *Hari Singh*, (2015) 1 SCC 760, para 5.

Bank. An elevation or mound of earth; usually applied in this sense to the raised earth bordering the sides of a water-course (as) the bank of a river or stream.

"BANK" means—

(i) the State Bank of India constituted under the State Bank of India Act, 1955;

(ii) a subsidiary Bank as defined in the State Bank of India (Subsidiary Banks) Act, 1959;

(iii) a corresponding new bank constituted under Section 3 of the Banking Companies (Acquisition and Transfer of Undertakings) Act, 1970;

(iv) a corresponding new bank constituted under Section 3 of the Banking Companies (Acquisition and Transfer of Undertakings) Act, 1980;

(v) any other bank, being a scheduled bank as defined in clause (e) of Section 2 of the Reserve Bank of India Act, 1934. [Textile

Undertakings (Nationalisation) Act (39 of 1995), S. 2(b)].

"BANK" means—

(i) a banking company;

(ii) a corresponding new bank;

(iii) State Bank of India;

(iv) a subsidiary bank; or

(v) a Regional Rural Bank.

(vi) a multi-state co-operative bank. [Recovery of Debts Due to Banks and Financial Institutions Act, 1993 (51 of 1993), S. 2(d) (*Inserted by Act 1 of 2013 (w.e.f 15-1-2013)*].

"BANK" means—

(i) a banking company; or

(ii) a corresponding new bank; or

(iii) the State Bank of India; or

(iv) a subsidiary bank; or

(v) such other bank which the Central Government may, by notification, specify for the purposes of this Act. [Securitization and Reconstruction of Financial Assets and Enforcement of Security Interest Act (54 of 2002), S. 2 (1)(c)].

'BANK' means a banking company and includes a 'corresponding new bank', a 'Regional Rural Bank', 'State Bank of India', a 'Subsidiary Bank' as defined in Section 5 of the Banking Regulation Act, 1949 (Act 10 of 1949) or a 'Primary Co-operative Bank' as defined in clause (c) of Section 56 of that Act and included in the Second Schedule of the Reserve Bank of India Act, 1934 (Act 2 of 1934), having a place of business in India, whether such bank is incorporated in India or outside India. [Banking Ombudsman Scheme, 2006, S. 3(4) (*updated as on 14 July 2017)*].

'BANK' means a commercial bank, Regional Rural Bank, State Co-operative Bank, Central Co-operative Bank, Primary Co-operative Society, State Land Development Bank or Urban Co-operative Bank, or a financial institution, Khadi & Village Industries Board (KVIB). [Debt Relief Scheme for Borrowers in State of J&K, para 2(b) issued under J&K Debtors Relief Act (15 of 1976), S. 4].

Bank (*in commercial law*) signifies a place where a great sum of money is deposited, returned by exchange, or otherwise disposed of to profit. (*Tomlin*)

(*verb.*) To have an account with a banker; deposit money in a bank; transact business with a bank or as a bank; exercise of the trade or profession of a banker.

Any establishment which carries on the business of banking [Banker's Books Evidence Act (18 of 1891), S. 2(2)]; to keep an account with a banker] [Indian Contract Act (9 of 1872), S. 50, ill. (a)].

"BANK" means,—(*i*) a banking company; (*ii*) a corresponding new bank; (*iii*) the State Bank of India; (*iv*) a subsidiary bank; (*v*) such other bank which the Central Government may by notification specify for the purposes of this Act on the recommendations of the Reserve Bank; or (*vi*) a Multi-State Co-operative Society registered under the Multi-State Co-operative Societies Act, 2002 (39 of 2002) and licensed to undertake business of banking by the Reserve Bank under the provisions of the Banking Regulation Act, 1949 (10 of 1949). [S. 2(d) of the Factoring Regulation Act, 2011 (12 of 2012)]

Bank acceptance. Bill of exchange which is drawn on and accepted by a commercial bank.

Bank-account trust. A revocable trust which is created by one's deposit of money in one's own name as a trustee for another.

Bank Award Commission. Means the person appointed by the Resolution of the Government of India in the Ministry of Labour, No. L.R. 100(9)/55, dated the 25th day of February, 1955, to enquire into and report upon the term of reference specified in the Resolution of the Government of India in the Ministry of Labour No. 100(56)/54, dated the 17th day of September, 1954. [Industrial Disputes (Banking Companies) Decision Act (41 of 1955), S. 2(c)].

Bank charges. Means charges made by a bank in respect of bills and notes presented to it. This phrase, in an action on a Bill of Exchange would include "Expenses of Noting."

Bank-credit. A credit by which a person is allowed to draw amount from the bank to a certain extent, by giving proper security to the bank.

Bank deposit rate. Means the highest of the maximum rates at which interest may be paid on different classes of deposits (other than those maintained in saving account or those maintained by charitable or religious institutions) by different classes of scheduled banks in accordance with the directions given or issued to banking companies generally by the Reserve Bank of India under the Banking Regulation Act, 1949. [Compulsory Deposit Scheme (Income-tax Payers) Act (38 of 1974), S. 7(1) *Expln.*] [Now repealed by the Finance Act, 1995 (22 of 1995)]

Bank draft. A cheque, draft or other order for payment of money, drawn by an authorised officer of a bank upon either his own bank or some other bank in which funds of his bank are deposited. (*Black*)

Bank for International Settlements (BIS). means the body corporate established with the said name under the law of Switzerland in pursuance of an agreement dated the 20th January, 1930, signed at the Hague. [Reserve Bank of India Act (2 of 1934), S. 2(aiii)].

International bank that acts as agent and trustee for various international organizations. It is also a clearing house for interbank transactions using European currency. The Bank of England is the agent of BIS in London. BIS was originally established in Basle, Switzerland, for dealing with German war reparations after World War I.

Bank holiday. A secular day on which the law exempts the parties to negotiable paper from the obligation of presentment, payment *etc.*, and consequently allows bank to be closed. *See* Negotiable Instruments Act (26 of 1881), S. 25. Its effect on such paper differs from that of Sunday in the fact that the laws establishing such holidays usually, if not always, provide that paper falling due on such day is payable on the next following secular day while paper entitled by commercial usage to days of grace, and falling due on Sunday, is often made payable on Saturday.

Bank-note. A promissory note issued by a bank or authorised banker, payable to bearer on demand, and intended to circulate as money.

"Bank note" means a bank note issued by the bank, whether in physical or digital form, under section 22. [Reserve Bank of India Act, 1934 (2 of 1934), section 2(aiv)]

A promissory note or engagement for the payment of money to bearer on demand, issued by any person carrying on the business of banking in any part of the world, or issued by or under the authority of any State or Sovereign Power, and intended to be used as equivalent to, or as a substitute for money. [IPC (45 of 1860), S. 489A, *Expln.*]. [Now (w.e.f. 1-7-2024) repealed & replaced by Bharatiya Nyaya Sanhita, 2023 (45 of 2023)]

The expression "bank-note" means a promissory note or engagement for the payment of money to bearer on demand issued by any person carrying on the business of banking in any part of the world, or issued by or under the authority of any State or Sovereign Power, and intended to be used as equivalent to, or as a substitute for money. [(w.e.f. 1-7-2024) Bharatiya Nyaya Sanhita, 2023 (45 of 2023), section 178, *Explanation* (1)]

Bank of issue. A bank authorised to issue its own notes payable to bearer on demand.

Bank rate. The rate at which the bank grants loans or discount bills.

Bank sweep arrangement. Standing instruction to a bank to move funds between accounts (such as from a *deposit account* to a *current account*) as necessary without the need for specific instructions from the customer. (*Banking*)

Bankable. Receivable at a bank; receivable as the equivalent of cash at the bank; receivable for discount by a bank.

Bankbook. A book of depositor in which a bank records all the transactions an account.

Banker : Bank. "BANK" and "BANKER" means—

(a) any company carrying on the business of banking,

(b) any partnership of individual to whose books the provisions of this Act shall have been extended as hereinafter provided,

(c) any post office savings bank or money order office. [Bankers' Book Evidence Act (18 of 1891), S. 2(2)].

"BANKER" includes any person acting as a banker and any post office savings bank. [Negotiable Instruments Act (26 of 1881), S. 3].

"BANKER" means an association, a company or a person who accepts, for the purpose of lending or investment, deposit of money from the public, repayable on demand or otherwise and with drawable by cheque, draft, order or otherwise. [Bombay Stamp Act (60 of 1958), S. 2(b)].

BANKERS now are those private persons in whose hands money is deposited and lodged for safety, to be drawn out again as the owners have occasion for it. (*Tomlin*)

"Banker" means any person carrying on a banking undertaking as may be declared by order of the Treasury to be a banker. HALSBURY, 4th Edn., Vol. 3, para 2, p. 3.

By keeping funds of the society with him, the secretary of the society could not constitute himself a banker of the society. *State* v. *Raman Kalidas Panda*, AIR 1956 Bom 524, 526. [IPC (45 of 1860), Ss. 405 and 408].

A person, corporation or a company, who carries on the business of banking. [Bankers' Books Evidence Act (18 of 1891), S. 2(2)]; [T.P. Act (4 of 1882), S. 79, ill.].

Banker's acceptance. A bill of exchange drawn on and accepted by a bank.

Banker's books. Include ledgers, day-books, cash-books, account-books and all other records used in the ordinary business of the bank, whether these records are kept in written form or stored in a micro film, magnetic tape or in any other form of mechanical or electronic data retrieval mechanism, either onsite or at any offsite location including a back-up or disaster recovery site of both. [Banker's Books Evidence Act (18 of 1891), S. 2(3), *vide* Negotiable Instruments (Amendment and Miscellaneous Provisions) Act (55 of 2002), Chapter III].

Bankers' cheques. A cheque drawn by one bank on another.

Banker's clearing house. An organisation through which member banks exchange and settle cheques drawn on each other. In India, such organisations are working under the control of the Reserve Bank of India or its representative, the State Bank of India.

Banker's drafts. A draft which is payable on demand drawn by a banker on himself whether payable at the office or some other office of his bank.

Banker's lien. The right of a bank to satisfy a customer's matured debt by seizing the customer's money or property in the bank's possession.

Proceeds of fixed deposits of plaintiffs credited in cash credit account-balance can be adjustted by appropriating amount lying in separate account in exercised of lien. [See Indian Contract Act (9 of 1872), S. 171, *Krishna Kishore Kar* v. *United Commercial Bank Anr.*, AIR 1982 Cal 62]; Banker's lien— Cannot be exercise where there is express contract to the contrary.

Banker's note. A promissory note given by a private banker or banking institution, not incorporated, but in all other respects resembling a Bank Note.

Banking. In this Act, unless the context otherwise requires,—

"BANKING" means the accepting, for the purpose of lending or investment, of deposits of money from the public, repayable on demand or otherwise, and withdrawable by cheque, draft, order or otherwise. [Deposit Insurance and Credit Guarantee Corporation Act (47 of 1961), S. 2(a)].

Banking is defined as "the business or employment of a banker, the business of establishing a common fund for lending money, discounting notes, issuing bills, receiving deposits, collecting the money or notes deposited, negotiating bills of exchange." Pertaining to or conducted by a bank; as banking operations.

Accepting (for the purpose of lending or investment) deposits of money from the public repayable on demand or otherwise [Banking Companies Act (1949), S. 5(b)].

Banking and other financial services. Means—

(a) the following services provided by a banking company or a financial institution including a non-banking financial company or any other body corporate or commercial concern, namely:—

(i) financial leasing services including equipment leasing and hire-purchase;

Explanation:—For the purposes of this item, "financial leasing" means a lease transaction where—

(i) contract for lease is entered into between two parties for leasing of a specific asset;

(ii) such contract is for use and occupation of the asset by the lessee;

(iii) the lease payment is calculated so as to cover the full cost of the asset together with the interest charges; and

(iv) the lessee is entitled to own, or has the option to own, the asset at the end of the lease period after making the lease payment;]

(ii) Omitted

(iii) merchant banking services;

(iv) securities and foreign exchange (forex) broking;

(v) asset management including portfolio management, all forms of fund management, pension fund management, custodial, depository and trust services;

(iv) securities and foreign exchange (forex) broking, and purchase or sale of foreign currency, including money changing;

(vii) provision and transfer of information and data processing; and

(viii) banker to an issue services; and

(ix) other financial services, namely, lending, issue of pay order, demand draft, cheque, letter of credit and bill of exchange, transfer of money including telegraphic transfer, mail transfer and electronic transfer, providing bank guarantee, overdraft facility, bill discounting facility, safe deposit locker, safe vaults, operation of bank accounts;]

(b) foreign exchange broking and purchase or sale of foreign currency, including money changing provided by a foreign exchange broker or an authorised dealer in foreign exchange or an authorised money changer, other than those covered under sub-clause (a). [Finance Act (32 of 1994), S. 65(12) *as substituted by Finance Act, 2008* (now repealed by Central Goods and Services Tax Act, 2017)].

Banking cash transaction tax. 'Banking cash transaction tax' means tax leviable on the taxable banking transactions under the provisions of this Chapter. [Finance Act (18 of 2005), S. 94(3), Ch. VII].

Banking Company. "BANKING COMPANY" means any company which transacts business of banking in India.

Explanation.—Any company which is engaged in the manufacture of goods or carries on any trade and which accepts deposits of money from the public merely for the purpose of financing its business as such manufacturer or trader, shall not be deemed to transact the business of banking within the meaning of this clause. [Banking Regulation Act (10 of 1949), S. 5(c)].

For the purposes of this section "banking company" includes the Reserve Bank, the Exim Bank, the Reconstruction Bank, the National Housing Bank, the National Bank, the Small Industries Bank, the National Bank for Financing Infrastructure and Development or the other development financial institution, the State Bank of India, a corresponding new bank, a regional rural bank and a subsidiary bank. [Banking Regulation Act (10 of 1949), sections 34A(3) and 36AD(3)].

For the purposes of this section, the expression "banking company" shall include—

(i) in the case of a banking company incorporated outside India, all its branches in India; and

(ii) in the case of a banking company incorporated in India—

(a) all its subsidiaries formed for the purpose of carrying on the business of banking exclusively outside India; and

(b) all its branches whether situated in India or outside India. [Banking Regulation Act (10 of 1949), section 35, *Explanation*].

"BANKING COMPANY" [Also see S. 2(9) of the Companies Act, 2013 (18 of 2013); S. 2(e) of the Factoring Regulation Act, 2011 (12 of 2012)]

"BANKING COMPANY" means any company which transacts the business of banking in India and includes the State Bank and a subsidiary bank but does not include the Tamil Nadu Industrial Investment Corporation Limited;

Explanation.—Any company which is engaged in the manufacture of goods or carries on any trade and which accepts deposits of money from the public merely for the purpose of financing its business as such manufacturer or trader shall not be deemed to transact the business of banking within the meaning of the clause. [Deposit Insurance and Credit Guarantee Corporation Act (47 of 1961), S. 2(b)].

"BANKING COMPANY" means a banking company as defined in Section 5 of the Banking Companies Act, 1949, and includes the State Bank of India, any subsidiary bank as defined in the State Bank of India (Subsidiary Banks) Act, 1959, any corresponding new bank specified in the First Schedule to the Banking Companies (Acquisition and Transfer of Undertakings) Act, 1970 any corresponding new bank constituted under Section 3 of the Banking Companies (Acquisition and Transfer of Undertakings) Act, 1980, any co-operative bank as defined in clause (bii) of Section 2 of the Reserve Bank of India, Act, 1934 and any other banking institution which may be notified in this behalf by the Central Government. [Payment of Bonus Act (21 of 1965), S. 2(8)].

"BANKING COMPANY" means a banking company or a co-operative bank to which the Banking Regulation Act, 1949 applies and includes any bank or banking institution referred to in Section 51 of that Act. [Prevention of Money Laundering Act (15 of 2003), S. 2(1)(e)]. [Income-tax Act (43 of 1961), section 269SS, *Expln (i)*; Prohibition of Benami Property Transactions Act (45 of 1988), section 2(7)]

Governed by the Baking Regulation Act, a banking company's main business includes accepting deposits from general public under various schemes and investing such deposits in lending. (*Banking*)

The definition of Banking Company in the banking Companies Act does not mean that the Company must, at the time in question, be able to accept deposits of money from the public, It must mean that banking should be the primary business of the company even if, by reason of certain supervening causes, it is not able for the time being to carry on the work of receiving deposits and of making payments. *Jwala Bank Ltd.* v. *Shitla Prasad Singh,* AIR 1950 All 309.

The definition of banking in S. 5(1)(b) makes it clear that acceptance of deposits is '*sine qua non*' to constitute banking business. *Samyuktha Samajam* v. *Doly Kalyani*, AIR 1954 TC 50. [Banking Companies Act, 1949, S. 5(1)(b)].

A company which carries on the business of banking. [Deposit Insurance and Credit Guarantee Corporation Act (47 of 1961), S. 2(b) and Industrial Disputes Act (14 of 1947), S. 2(bb)].

"BANKING COMPANY". Co-operative banks established under the Maharashtra Co-operative Societies Act, 1960, the Andhra Pradesh Co-operative Societies Act, 1964, and the Multi-State Co-operative Societies Act, 2002, transacting the business of banking, do not fall within the meaning of the expression 'banking company' as defined in section 5(c) of the Banking Regulation Act, 1949. *Greater Bombay Co-operative Bank Ltd.* v. *United Yarn Tex. Pvt. Ltd.*, AIR 2007 SC 1584 : 2007 AIR SCW 2325.

Banking hours. Banking hours are those hours in the day when the bank is open to do its ordinary business over the counter. It does not include the time after the bank closes to public custom or business, but which is devoted by the employees or officials to setting up the affairs of the day, *etc.*

Banking Ombudsman. A person charged with investigating complaints against any of the member banks of the scheme made by individuals, group depositors or small businesses.

"Banking operations" would, *inter alia*, include accepting of loans and deposits, granting of loans and recovery of the debts due to the bank. [*Union of India* v. *Delhi High Court Bar Assn.,* (2002) 4 SCC 275, para 14 **as cited in** *State Bank of India* v. *Santosh Gupta,* (2017) 2 SCC 538, para 29].

Bankrupt. Means—

(*a*) a debtor who has been adjudged as bankrupt by a bankruptcy order under Section 126;

(*b*) each of the partners of a firm, where a bankruptcy order under Section 126 has been made against a firm; or

(*c*) any person adjudged as an undischarged insolvent. [Insolvency and Bankruptcy Code (31 of 2016), S. 79(3)].

A person who is unable to meet his financial obligations. A person who has committed an act of bankruptcy. A trader, who secretes himself, or does certain other acts, tending to defraud his creditors. (*Cowel; Tomlin*)

An insolvent person whose property is administered for, and distributed among his creditors in accordance with the provisions of a system of laws called bankrupt, bankruptcy or insolvent laws.

Bankrupt and Insolvent. The leading distinction between a bankrupt law and an insolvent law, in the proper technical sense of the words, consists in the character of the persons upon whom it is designed to operate, the former contemplating as its objects, traders of a certain description; the latter insolvents in general, or persons unable to pay their debts.

Bankrupt : Debtor, distinguished. A "bankrupt" is a debtor and something more. He is a debtor who has committed an act of bankruptcy declared to be such by the bankruptcy law. A debtor may or may not be a bankrupt. (*United States* v. *Pusy* (U.S.), 27 Feb. Cas 631, 632.)

Bankrupt's estate. It comprises of all property which belonged to or vested in the bankrupt at the commencement of the bankruptcy.

Bankruptcy. The state or condition of one who is a bankrupt; amenability to the bankrupt laws.

Bankruptcy debt. "BANKRUPTCY DEBT", in relation to a bankrupt, means—

(*a*) any debt owed by him as on the bankruptcy commencement date;

(*b*) any debt for which he may become liable after bankruptcy commencement date but before his discharge by reason of any transaction entered into before the bankruptcy commencement date; and

(*c*) any interest which is a part of the debt under Section 171. [Insolvency and Bankruptcy Code (31 of 2016), S. 79(5)].

Any debt or liability to which the bankrupt is subject at the commencement of the bankruptcy.

"Bankruptcy debt" in relation to a bankrupt, means—

(a) any debt owed by him as on the bankruptcy commencement date;

(b) any debt for which he may become liable after bankruptcy commencement date but before his discharge by reason of any transaction entered into before the bankruptcy commencement date; and

(c) any interest which is a part of the debt under section 171. [Insolvency and Bankruptcy Code, 2016, s. 79(5) *(Dictionary of International Insurance and Finance by John O E Clark, published by Routledge)*].

Bankruptcy estate. Legal and equitable interests of debtor.

Bankruptcy notice. A notice which is served by a creditor on a debtor requiring the debtor within a limited time to pay the debt or secure or compound for the same, non-compliance of which constitutes on act of bankruptcy.

Bannitus or Banniatus. A banished man; an outlaw.

Bar. A partition or railing running across a court-room intended to separate the general public from the space occupied by the judges, counsel, jury, and others concerned in the trial of a cause. The term also designates a particular part of the court-room; for example, the place where prisoners stand at their trial, whence the expression "prisoner at the bar." It further denotes the presence actual or constructive of the Court; the "case at bar" is the case now before the Court and under its consideration, the case being tried or argued. "At the bar of the Court" means "in open Court". The practising members of the legal profession in a given community, all those who have the right to plead in a Court are called the bar. The whole body of attorneys and counsellors or the members of the legal profession collectively, are figuratively called the "bar" from the place which they usually occupy in Court. They are thus distinguished from the "bench," which term denotes the whole body of judges.

Advocates, as representing the suitor or criminal whose case the Court is trying, used always to stand at the bar, by the client's side, and there plead his cause. From this last fact the phrase " the bar" has obtained secondary signification, and is used to describe those who practise the profession of advocacy. From the same fact, too, we get the word "barrister". (*Ency. of the Laws of England*)

That which obstructs entry or egress; excluding from consideration; a piece of wood, metal or other rigid material, long in proportion to its thickness and frequently used as a barrier fastening or obstruction; barristers and advocates collectively; an addition to a medal, a strip of metal below the clasp; to obstruct; to exclude from consideration.

Bar Associations. Associations of lawyers united for the purpose of furthering the interests of their profession.

Bar Council. 'BAR COUNCIL' means a Bar Council constituted under the Advocates Act. Act (25 of 1961), S. 2(d).

In India there are two Bar Councils—one for each State and the other for India.

Bar Council of India. 'BAR COUNCIL OF INDIA' means the Bar Council constituted under Section 4 of the Advocates Act for the territories to which the Advocates Act extends. [Advocates Act (25 of 1961), S. 2(e)].

Bar of the House. The place inside the House of a Legislature where the persons who commit a breach of privilege or contempt of the House are summoned for administering admonition or reprimand. In the House of Commons, the Bar consists of two rods which can be drawn across the end of the benches to form the boundary of the House opposite the Speaker's Chair, the offender is brought here by the Serjeant-at-Arms and is reprimanded or admonished by the Speaker in the name and by the authority of the House.

In Lok Sabha, the bar consists of a wooden bar placed between two pillars near the door which opens into the central aisle facing the speaker and which connects the benches on either side of the aisle. Before an offender is brought to the Bar of the House, the Speaker makes an announcement about it in the House and emphasizes the solemnity of the occasion and asks the members to keep total silence in order to maintain the dignity and authority of Parliament and to emphasise the significance of the reprimand. Thereafter he orders the Watch and Ward Officer (now Director, Security) to bring the offender in. He is brought in and he stands at the Bar. The Speaker then reads out the reprimand after which he asks the offender to withdraw.

Baratriam committit qui propter pecuniam justitiam baractat. (*Lat.*) He is guilty of barratry who for money sells justice. (*Bell.*)

Barbarian. A man in his rude or savage state; an uncivilized person (figuratively) a cruel or brutal person devoid of pity; a savage.

Barbarous. "Cruel and barbarous treatment, and indignities to the person endangering life or health" within the meaning of the divorce law, must consist of wilful and malicious acts or they would not come within the description of the terms. "Cruel" and "barbarous" are the words employing a merciless and savage disposition, taking pleasure in suffering, and without pity; while "indignities" involves an insulting and contemptuous purpose. The evil and malicious will must be present to constitute an act, cruel or barbarous, and an insulting intent to make it an indignity.

Barbell portfolio. A US term that describes an investment portfolio consisting mainly of short-term bonds and long-term bonds, with few of intermediate date. (*Investment*)

Bare licensee. A licensee whose presence on the premises is tolerated by the occupier, but is not approved by the occupier.

Bare trust (naked trust, simple trust). A trust in which the trustee has no obligation except to handover the trust property to a person entitled to it, at the latter's request.

Bare trustee. A trustee without any beneficial interest.

Bareboat charter. In this chapter unless the context otherwise requires,—

"BAREBOAT CHARTER" means hiring of a ship for a stipulated period on terms which give the charterer possession and control of the ship, including the right to appoint the master and crew. [Income-tax Act (43 of 1961), Chapter XIIG, S. 115V(a) (*Inserted by Finance (No. 2) Act (23 of 2004)*, S. 30)].

"Bareboat charter" means an arrangement for the hiring of a vessel without crew, where the charterer is responsible for appointing the crew and making other arrangements. [Inland Vessels Act, 2021 (24 of 2021), section 3(b)]

Bareboat charter cum demise. In this chapter unless the context otherwise requires,—

"BAREBOAT CHARTER-CUM-DEMISE" means a bareboat charter where the ownership of the ship is intended to be transferred after a specified period to the company to whom it has been chartered. [Income-tax Act (43 of 1961), Chapter XII G, S. 115V(b) (*Inserted by Finance Act (No.2) (23 of 2004)*, S. 30)].

"Bareboat charter-*cum*-demise" is a bareboat charter where the ownership of the vessel is intended to be transferred after a specified period to the company to which it has been chartered. [Inland Vessels Act, 2021 (24 of 2021), section 3(c)]

Bargadar. BARGADAR means any person who under the system generally known as *adhi, barga* or *bhag,* cultivates the land of another person on condition of delivering a share of the produce of such land to that person and includes a person who under the system generally known as *kisani or by any other description* cultivates the land of another person on condition of receiving a share of the produce of such land from that person but does not include a person who is related to the owner of the land as (a) wife, or; (b) husband, or (c) child, or (d) grandchild, or (e) parent, or (f) grandparent, or (g) brother, or (h) sister, or (i) brother's son or brother's daughter, or (j) sister's son or sister's daughter, or (k) daughter's husband, or (l) son's wife, or (m) wife's brother or wife's sister, or (ma) husband's brother, or (n) brother's wife, and

Explanation.—A bargadar shall continue to be a bargadar until cultivation by him is lawfully terminated under this Act;] [West Bengal Land Reforms Act, 1956, S. 2(2)].

Bargain. Mutual agreement; an agreement between persons concerning the loan, exchange or sale of property; a contract or agreement between two parties, the one to sell goods or lands, and the other to buy them. "A 'Bargain' is only another name for a 'Contract' ". The term is also used to denote the act of discussing the terms of a proposed agreement.

An agreement between two parties settling the part of each in a transaction between them; that which is acquired by bargain.

Bargain for vote. A bargain does not mean that the candidate or his agent makes an offer and the voter accepts it in the sense that he promises to vote. If a candidate or his agent pays money to a voter saying that he wants him to vote for him, it is a bargain. It is not necessary that the voter should say that he would vote and thereafter the candidate or his agent should pay the money. *Iqbal Singh* v. *Gurdas Singh*, AIR 1976 SC 27, 35. [Representation of the People Act (43 of 1951), S. 123(1)].

Bargaining unit. The group of employees for whom a labour union negotiates a collective bargaining agreement—called also *collective bargaining unit.*

Barge. A 'barge' is a large flat-bottomed boat used for transporting heavy burdens on canals and rivers but is not generally a ocean-going vessel. It may or may not be fitted with an engine depending on its calibration. *Pandurang Timblo Industries* v. *Union of India*, AIR 1992 SC 1194, 1198. Constitution of India, Sch. VII, List II, Entry 58.

Baron. A Lord or nobleman; the most general title of nobility in England. In ancient records, the word baron includes all the nobility of England, because regularly, all noblemen were barons, though they had a higher dignity. (*Tomlin*)

Baron et feme. Man and woman; husband and wife.

Baronet. An English name or title of dignity.

Barony. The rank or dignity of a baron.

Barrage. An artificial bar across a river. [Damodar Valley Corporation Act (14 of 1948), S. 22(2)(ii)].

Barratrous. Fraudulent.

Barratry or Barretry. The fraud or offence committed by a barrator. A vexatious and persistent inciting of others to law suits and litigation; a stirring up and maintaining of controversies and litigation.

(*In maritime law*) An act committed by the master or mariners of a vessel, for some unlawful or fraudulent purpose, contrary to their duty to the owners, whereby the latter sustain injury.

A fraudulent breach of duty or wilful act of known illegality on the part of the master of a ship or of the mariners to the injury of the owner of the ship or cargo and without his consent (as running away with the ship, sinking or deserting her or embezzling the cargo). [Marine Insurance Act (11 of 1963), S. 2(e)].

Barred. Subject to hindrance or obstruction by a bar or barrier which if interposed, will prevent legal redress or recovery.

Barred by law. Excluded from consideration or prohibited by any law.

Barred by limitation. "Barred" is the word in general use to characterize the effect of the statute of limitations. An action or a cause of action is commonly said to be "barred" by a statute.

Barrel. A measure of capacity equal to 35 imperial or 42 US gallons (about 159 litres.

Metal tube of a gun, through which the shot is discharged.

A cylindrical container ordinarily bulging out in the middle, conventionally made of wood with metal hoops around them, but which can be made of many other materials includeing metal and plastic.

Barrier. (*in mining law*) Is a wall of coal left between two mines.

A material obstruction which bars advance or prevents access. [Mines Act (35 of 1952), S. 57(m)].

"Barrier" means any factor including communicational, cultural, economic, environmental, institutional, political, social, attitudinal or structural factors which hampers the full and effective participation of persons with disabilities in society. [Rights of Persons with Disabilities Act (49 of 2016), section 2(c)].

Barrister. A person entitled to practise as an advocate or counsel in the Law Courts. (*Sweet*)

An advocate; one who has been called to the bar. A counsellor learned in the law who pleads at the bar of the Courts, and who is engaged in conducting the trial or argument of causes. A counsellor or an advocate learned in the law, admitted to plead at the bar in protection and defence of clients, called in full a barrister-at-law.

Barter. To exchange one commodity for another, (*Tomlin*).

Barter is exchange of wares for wares, (*Termes de la Ley; Cowell*). Also the thing given in exchange.

An exchange of goods for goods; to trade by exchanging one commodity for another, to exchange by bartering.

BARTER DIFFERS FROM SALE, in this—that in the latter transaction goods or property are always exchanged for money.

Base. Fraudulently debased in value; spurious; false as base coin.

(*In Military law.*) A track of country protected by fortification, strong by natural advantages, or for any other reason comparatively secure, from which, the operations of an army proceed, or from which supplies are obtained, called distinctively the *base of operations or the base of supply.* Base, in military operations, is simply a secure starting point, or rather tract of country behind which an army is in comparative safety, and in which the stores and reserves of men for the force is situated.

That on which something rests or stands [Payment of Bonus Act (21 of 1965), S. 34, *Expln.* II(a)]; debased; place from which operations are conducted. [Geneva Conventions Act (6 of 1960), Second Sch., Art. 43].

Base-born. Of base or low birth; born out of wedlock; of low or mean parentage or origin; spurious.

Base level. Means the quantity of ozone depleting substance produced or consumed, as the case may be, in the year or average of the years listed in column (3) of Schedule II and Schedule III. [Ozone Depleting Substance (Regulation) Rules, 2000, R. 2(c)].

Base metals. On commodity markets, copper, lead, tin and zinc (*i.e.* not *precious metals*). (*Investment*)

Baseball arbitration. Used in relation to the resolution of disagreements concerning the salaries of baseball players in the United States. (*Alternative Dispute Resolution*)

Based on. Derived from.

Based on religion. The expression means that the only or principal basis of a minority must be their adherence to one of the many religions and not a sect or a part of the religion. [Constitution of India, Article 30(1)].

Basel convention. 'Basel Convention' is the United Nations Environment Programme Convention on the Control of Transboundary Movement of Hazardous Wastes and their Disposal. [Hazardous Waste (Management, Handling and Transboundary Movement) Rules, 2008, R. 3(c)].

Baseline. In International law, the lines on the map of the coastline of a maritime state from which its territorial waters are measured and which limit its internal or national waters.

Basic. Forming a base.

Basic education. It means education up to the eighth class imparted in school other than high schools or intermediate colleges, and expression 'basic schools' shall be construed accordingly. Uttar Pradesh Basic Education Act, 1972, S. 2(b) as cited in *State of U.P.* v. *Pawan Kumar Divedi,* (2014) 9 SCC 692, para 24.

Basic service tier. Means a package of free-to-air channels to be offered by a cable operator to a subscriber with an option to subscribe, for a single price to subscribers of the area in which his cable television network is providing service; [Cable Television Networks (Regulation) Act (7 of 1995), S. 4A, Expl. (b) Substituted by Act 21 of 2011 (w.r.e.f. 25-10-2011)].

Basic wages. Means all emoluments which are earned by an employee while on duty or on leave or on holidays with wages in either case in accordance with the terms of the contract of employment and which are paid or payable in cash to him but does not include:

(i) the cash value of any food concessions;

(ii) any dearness allowance (that is to say, all cash payments by whatever name called paid to an employee on account of a rise in the cost of living), house rent allowance, overtime allowance, bonus, commission or any other similar allowance payable to the employee in respect of his employment or of work done in such employment;

(iii) any presents made by the employer. [Employees' Provident Funds and Miscellaneous Provisions Act (19 of 1952), S. 2(b)].

"Basic wages" means (1) a wage or salary based on the cost of living and used as a standard for calculating rates of pay; (2) a rate of pay for a standard work period exclusive of such additional payments as bonuses and overtime. Merriam-Webster Dictionary, as cited in *Kichha Sugar Company Limited* v. *Tarai Chini Mill Majdoor Union, Uttarakhand,* (2014) 4 SCC 37, para 9.

"Basic wage" means, those wages, which are universally, necessarily and ordinarily paid to all the employees across the board, are basic wage. Where the payment is available to those who avail the opportunity more than others, the amount paid for that cannot be included in the basic wage. *Kichha Sugar Company Limited* v. *Tarai Chini Mill Majdoor Union, Uttarakhand,* (2014) 4 SCC 37, para 10.

The expression "basic wages" does not include leave encashment. *Manipal Academy of Higher Education* v. *Provident fund Commissioner*, AIR 2008 SC 1951, 1954, para 12. Employees' Provident Funds and Miscellaneous Provisions Act (19 of 1952), S. 2(b)

The phrase 'basic wages' is ordinarily understood to mean that part of the price of labour, which the employer must pay to all workmen belonging to all categories, 'Basic Wage' never includes the additional emoluments which some workman may earn, on the basis of a system of bonuses related to the production. *Munir Mills Co. Ltd.* v. *Workmen*, AIR 1960 SC 985, 988.

Basin. A tract of country drained by rivers and its tributaries. [Damodar Valley Corporation Act (14 of 1948), S. 2(2)].

Basis. The basis of a thing is that on which it stands, and on the failure of which it falls: and when a document consisting partly of statements of fact and partly of undertakings for the future is made the basis of a contract of insurance, this must mean that the document is to be the very foundation of the contract, so that if the statements of fact are untrue, or the promissory statements are not carried out, the risk does not attach. (*Stroud*)

Basis point. One hundredth of one percent. These points are used in computing investment yields, and in apportioning costs and figuring interest rates in real-estate transaction.

Basic split-dollar plan. A plan to purchase life insurance that enables a more financially able relative, employer or associate to pay a substantial portion of another individual's insurance premiums. Under the basic plan, the insured pays the excess, if any, of the premium due over the annual increase in the cash value of the policy. (*Insurance*)

Basket purchase. Purchase of several assets for an all-in price, which then has to be split into several costs (one for each asset) for the purposes of accounting. (*International Accounting*)

Bastard. One whose father and mother were not lawfully married to each other, previous to his birth; or "one born out of lawful wedlock." (*Tomlin*)

Bastard eigne. An illegitimate son.

Bastardize. To declare, to prove to be a bastard; stigmatize as a bastard.

Bastardus non potest habere haeredem nisi de corpore suo legitime procreatum. (*Lat.*) A bastard can have no heir except one lawfully begotten of his own body. A bastard is regarded by the law as *filius nullius*.

Bastardus nullius est filius aut filius populi. (*Maxim*) A bastard is nobody's son, or the son of the people.

Batai. (From Sanskrit *Vut,* to divide). A share.

Division of the crop between the cultivator and the landlord or the Government in that capacity. Rent taken by division of produce.

Batch. Means—

(i) in the case of packages which have been stored, where the total number of such packages does not exceed 100, all such packages, and where the total number exceeds 100 but does not exceed 10,000 all the packages of the same production run;

(ii) in the case of packages which are on or at the end of the packing line, the maximum hourly output of packages. [Standards of Weights and Measures (Packaged Commodities) Rules, 1977, R. 2(b) now Clause (b) omitted by G.S.R. 425(E), dated 17th July,2006 (w.e.f. 13-1-2007)].

Battalion. "BATTALION" means a unit of the Force constituted as a battalion by the Central Government. [Indo Tibetan Border Police Force Act (35 of 1992), S. 2(1)(b)].

A considerable body of troops organized to act together; a tactical military unit composed basically of a headquarters and two or more companies, batteries, or similar units.

Battered child. A child who is suffering serious physical or emotional injury resulting from abuse inflicted upon him including sexual abuse, or from neglect, including malnutrition, or who is determined to be physically dependent upon an addictive drug at birth.

Battered-woman syndrome. Means the psychological symptoms exhibited by a woman repeatedly abused by a mate (as a husband). Battered Woman's syndrome is used as defense to violent criminal charges (as homicide). Evidence of repeated abuse is used to show that the defendant acted in self-defence even though the threat or danger was not imminent; Battered Woman's syndrome is also used as a mitigating factor in sentencing. (*Webster's Dictionary of Law, Indian Edn.* (*2005*))

Battery. Means lead acid battery which is a source of electrical energy and contains lead metal. [Batteries (Management and Handling) Rules, 2001, R. 3(e)].

If force is actually applied, directly or indirectly, unlawfully or without the consent of the person assaulted, the assault becomes a battery, however slight the force. A battery may or may not include an assault. HALSBURY, 4th Edn., Vol. 11, para 1210, p. 643.

Battery is the actual and intentional application of any physical force of an adverse nature to the person of another without his consent, or even with his consent, if it is obtained by fraud, or the consent is unlawful, as in the case of a prize-fighting.

A small division of artillery for tactical purposes [Army Act (46 of 1950), S. 89(1)]; this is the name given to the intentional application of force to a person without lawful justification, and corresponds to the offence known as the use of criminal force in the IPC. [(45 of 1860), S. 350].

Battle. A fight, hostile encounter, or engagement between opposing forces. This may occur on sea, land or air.

Battle, trial by. A method of trying guilt of an accused person or a dispute, by setting the two opposite parties to fight each other, the loser was punished or he lost his claim.

Battlefield visualization. The process whereby the commander develops a clear understanding of the current state with relation to the enemy and environment, envisions a desired end-state that represents mission accomplishment, and then subsequently visualizes the sequence of activity that moves the commander's force from its current state to the end-state. (*Cyber Law*)

Bawd. One who procures opportunities for persons of opposite sexes to cohabit in an illicit manner. (*Ame. Cye.*)

Bawdy-house. A house of ill fame, kept for the resort and commerce of lewd people of both sexes; a brothel. (*Tomlin*)

Bay. A well marked roughly semicircular indentation on a coast line.

BBS. Bulletin Board System. A computer system accessible by modem. Members can dial in and leave messages, send e-mail, play games, and trade files with other users. (*Information Technology*)

A little like an electronic notice board. You "post" messages to the board and everyone who subscribes to the board can view them.

(*abbr.*) A computerized meeting and announcement system that allows people to carry on discussions, upload and download files, and make announcements without the people being connected to the computer at the same time. In the early 1990's there were many thousands (millions?) of BBS's around the world, most are very small, running on a single IBM clone PC with 1 or 2 phone lines. Some are very large and the line between a BBS and a system like AOL gets crossed at some point, but it is not clearly drawn. (*Matisse Enzer-Glossary of Internet Terms*)

Be permitted to enter. The words "be permitted to enter" do not cast an absolute duty on the employer to prevent the entry and the mere fact that a person has entered a pit in which dangerous fumes are likely to be present, would not by itself prove that he had been permitted to enter the pit. *Chunubhai Haridas* v. *State*, AIR 1960 SC 37, 40. [Factories Act (63 of 1948), S. 36(3)].

Beach. The word "beach" must be deemed to designate land washed by the sea and its waves, and to be synonymous with "shore".

Beacon. A light-house, or sea-mark, formerly used to alarm the country in case of the approach of an enemy, but now used for the guidance of ships at sea.

Bear. One who intrigues for a fall in a market.

Bear market. A securities market which is characterized by falling prices over a prolonged period.

A weak or falling market characterized by the dominance of sellers. (*Capital Market*)

A situation in which share prices are falling (bears are speculators who sell shares in anticipation of falling prices). (*Investment*)

Prolonged period of falling share prices, dominated by selling pressure in the market place, brought about by bears, or adverse economic or political factors, *e.g.*, a change in the Industrial policy of the government, imposition of price control, drought or flood, free imports, *etc.*, or a change in the Government, Income Tax raids *etc.* (*Stock Market*)

Bearer. The "Bearer," of Bill or Note, "means the person in possession of a Bill or Note which is payable to Bearer."

"PAYABLE TO BEARER" "The use of the words payable 'to Bearer' has the effect of making the note pass from hand to hand free form any equities which might have attached to it as between the original parties thereto."

He who bears or carries. [Companies Act (1 of 1956), S. 219(1) replaced by Companies Act, 2013].

Bearer bond. Bond payable to a person holding it.

Bearer certificate. Means a certificate of title to securities by the delivery of which (with or without endorsement) the title to the securities is transferable. [Foreign Exchange Regulation Act (46 of 1973), S. 2(c)].

Bearer document. An instrument which is payable to the person who holds it instead of the order of a specific person.

Bearing on, Having. Having relation with.

Beast. An animal; a quadruped, such as may be used for food or in labour or for sport. Any four footed animal, as distinguished from fowls, insects, fishes, and man; as, beasts of burden; beasts of the chase; beasts of the forest. It is applied chiefly to large animals.

Beauty parlour. Means any establishment providing beauty treatment services. [Finance Act (32 of 1994), S. 65 (17), *as* substituted by Act 32 of 2003, S. 159 (now repealed by Central Goods and Services Tax Act, 2017)]

Beauty treatment. Means face and beauty treatment, cosmetic treatment, manicure, pedicure or counselling services on beauty, face care or make-up. [Finance Act (32 of 1994), S. 65(16), *as substituted by Act 32 of* 2003, S. 159 (now repealed by Central Goods and Services Tax Act, 2017)].

"BEAUTY TREATMENT" includes hair cutting, hair dyeing, hair dressing, face and beauty treatment, cosmetic treatment, manicure, pedicure or counselling services on beauty, face care or make-up or such other similar services. [Finance Act (32 of 1994), S. 65(17), as substituted by Finance Act (18 of 2005), S. 88(a)(iv) (now repealed by Central Goods and Services Tax Act, 2017)].

Become. The word "become" means change of conditions—that is the entering into a new state or condition by a change from some former state or condition.

Become vested. The expression "become vested" covers every possible manner in which the vesting can take place.

Becomes impossible. In commercial contracts, where the contract becomes impossible of performance by reason of a state of war or by an act of the executive government or the contract which would otherwise be expected to be ordinarily performed, is delayed by reason of certain regulations imposed by the Government making the performance of such contract dependent upon the grant of licence or permit, the parties need not wait for an indefinite period in the hope of the relaxing of the control orders or the granting of licence and permit. [Indian Contract Act (9 of 1872), S. 56].

Becomes void. Section 65 of Indian Contract Act (9 of 1872) has no application to the case where one of the parties was incompetent to contract by reason of his minority. Section 65 applies only to a contract between competent parties. *Shah Jethalal Lalchand* v. *Darbar Shri Amarwala Laxmanwala,* AIR 1953 Sau 177, 179.

Bed. (*In matrimonial law.*) The right of cohabitation or marital intercourse (*Ame. Cye.*) as in the phrase, "divorce from bed and board" a *mensa et thoro*.

Bedlam. A scene of wild uproar and confusion.

Beer. (In Excise law) A malt liquor; a fermented liquor made from any malted grain, a fermented liqour made from the malt of barley, and favoured with hops. (*Ame. Cye.*)

Before. In front of; in the presence of; under the jurisdiction or consideration of; in advance; ahead; earlier than.

Beg. To "beg" does not necessarily import spoken words. One who, to obtain alms, exhibits his need or infirmities, or attracts attention by signs or conduct to his desire to receive charity, is chargeable with a violation of a statute against begging, as fully, as if he had spoken.

Begar. The word may be loosely described as labour or service which a person is forced to give without receiving any remuneration for it. *People's Union for Democratic Rights* v. *Union of India*, AIR 1982 SC 1473, 1487. [Constitution of India, Art. 23].

Beget. To procreate; chiefly used of the father alone, but sometimes of both parents.

Beggary. The act of begging, especially as a livelihood.

Begging. Means—

(i) soliciting or receiving alms in a public place or entering into any private premises for the purpose of soliciting or receiving alms, whether under the pretence of singing, dancing, fortune-telling, performing tricks or selling articles or otherwise;

(ii) exposing or exhibiting, with the object of obtaining or extorting alms, any sore, wound, injury, deformity or disease, whether of himself or of any other person or of an animal;

(iii) allowing oneself to be used as an exhibit for the purpose of soliciting or receiving alms. [Juvenile Justice Act (53 of 1986), S. 2(a); See also Children's Act (60 of 1960].

In this section "begging" means—

(i) soliciting or receiving alms in a public place, whether under the pretence of singing, dancing, fortune telling, performing tricks or selling articles or otherwise;

(ii) entering on any private premises for the purpose of soliciting or receiving alms;

(iii) exposing or exhibiting, with the object of obtaining or extorting alms, any sore, wound, injury, deformity or disease, whether of himself or of any other person or of an animal;

(iv) using such child as an exhibit for the purpose of soliciting or receiving alms. [(w.e.f. 1-7-2024) Bharatiya Nyaya Sanhita, 2023 (45 of 2023), section 139(4)]

"Begging" means—

(i) soliciting or receiving alms in a public place or entering into any private premises for the purpose of soliciting or receiving alms, under any pretence;

(ii) exposing or exhibiting with the object of obtaining or extorting alms, any sore, wound injury, deformity or disease, whether of himself or of any other person or of an animal. [Juvenile Justice (Care and Protection of Children) Act, 2015 (2 of 2016), s. 2(8)].

Behalf. A witness testifies on "behalf" of the party who calls him, notwithstanding his evidence proves to be adverse to that party's case.

Behaviour. Manner of behaving whether good or bad; conduct; manners; mode of acting; deportment, as good behaviour; security for good behaviour.

The manner of conducting oneself [Children Act (60 of 1960), S. 22(1), prov.]; [Defence and Internal Security of India Act (42 of 1971), S. 9(5)]; the peculiar reaction of a thing (under given circumstances) [Trade and Merchandise Marks Act (43 of 1958), S. 2(1)(u)(iii)].

CARRIAGE, BEHAVIOUR, CONDUCT, DEPORT MENT, DEMEANOR, MANNERS all denote primarily outward manner of conduct. *Carriage,* the way of carrying one's self may be mere physical attitude or it may be personal manners, as expressing states of mind; we speak of a haughty or noble carriage, but not ordinarily of an ignoble, cringing or base carriage. *Behaviour* is the most general expression of one's mode of acting; it also refers particularly to comparatively conspicuous actions and conduct. *Conduct* is more applicable to actions viewed as connected into a course of life, especially to actions considered with reference to morality. *Deportment* is especially behaviour in the line of the proprieties or duties of life. *Demeanor* is most used for manners as expressing character; (as) judge's remarks on the demeanor of the witness. It is a more delicate word than the others and is generally used in a good sense. We may speak of lofty or gracious carriage; good, bad, wise, foolish, modest, conceited behaviour; exemplary conduct; grand, modest, correct deportment; quiet demeanor.

'Negative' as well as 'Positive' behaviour is capable of forming the basis of a decree of divorce and may include cases where the behaviour is caused by mental or physical injury or illness, and may be involuntary.

Behind. Surviving; as in the phrase 'leaving no issue behind him'.

Behindhand. Late; in arrear; in a state where expenditure exceeds the receipt of funds (*Webs.*); delayed beyond the proper time; behind the time set or expected.

Being a trader. The phrase, "being a trader," in the Bankruptcy Act, means "carrying on trade at the time when the act of insolvency in question is committed".

Being in charge of. To be in charge of the vehicle means something different (than driving) *viz.*, the vehicle being in the custody of the person who is said to be in charge of that vehicle and that person may be or may not be performing the function of driving.

Being partners. "Any two or more persons being partners" (who may proceed, or be proceeded against in the partnership name) does not connote that they must be partners at the time of the proceedings, but rather means, persons "who have had the relation-ship of partners for the purpose of the liability which is sought to be enforced'.' [*See* CPC (5 of 1908), O. XXX, R. 1 & 2].

Being the property of the assessee. The expression 'being the property of the assessee' means that the assessee owns the property and not the assessee has only acquired equitable interest in the property.

Belief. Confidence reposed in any person or thing; faith; trust: (as, a child's belief in his parents).

A persuasion of the truth, or an assent of the mind to the truth of a declaration, proposition, or alleged fact; a persuasion of the truth of a fact, formed in the way of inference from some other fact; an actual conclusion drawn from information; partial assurance without positive knowledge.

A conviction of the truth of a proposition, existing subjectively in mind; the mental action, condition, or habit of trusting to or confiding in a person or thing or statement. [Constitution of India, Preamble].

"BEST OF HIS BELIEF" means "In the full belief."

Belief and **Knowledge.** A belief will be inculcated in the mind of a person by various factors, by evidence of witnesses or by inferences from given premises. But not so with knowledge. Knowledge is gained by a person by making use of his perceptional faculties and is clearly distinguishable from belief.

Between "belief" and "knowledge", the difference is, after all nothing more than in the degree of certainty. With regard to the things which make not a very deep impression on the memory, it may be called "belief." "knowledge" is nothing more than a man's firm belief.

Knowledge and belief may differ not only in degree but in kind. Knowledge is a certainty founded upon insight; belief is certainly founded upon feeling.

Belief in good faith. "Belief in good faith" in S. 51 of the Transfer of Property Act (4 of 1882) means believing honestly and fairly after due inquiry. Where a man has consciously avoided making an inquiry on any matter he may, nevertheless, be said to have a belief on that matter, but such belief would in such a case not be a belief in good faith.

Believe. To put credit or confidence in the veracity of testimony; to apprehend; to have belief; to satisfy; to suppose; to think.

The word 'believe' occurring in S. 411, IPC (45 of 1860) is much stronger than 'suspect'.

To give credence to; to have confidence or faith in.

Believe and **hope.** 'To hope' means 'to want and expect', 'to look forward with expectation and desire'. The term 'believe' has 'logical confidence' or 'rational conviction' as its essential element. It imports a very high degree of expectation wrought by reason, a satisfaction fast-rooted in *terra firma*, free from doubt as to the truth of the fact perceived and believed. *Chandran* v. *State of Madras*, AIR 1978 SC 1574, 1581. [CrPC, 1973 (2 of 1974), S. 164].

Believe to be stolen. The word 'believe' is a very much stronger word than 'suspect' and it involves the necessity of showing that the circumstances were such that a reasonable man must have felt convinced in his mind that the property with which he was dealing must be stolen property. *State* v. *Jaigovind,* AIR 1951 Raj 89, 92. [IPC (45 of 1860), S. 411].

Belligerency. Position or status of a belligerent; the state of being actually engaged in war; waging war; as, "Belligerent powers", "Belligerent rights".

Belligerent. Warlike; waging war; characterized by a tendency to wage war.

BELLIGERENT literally means one waging war, in distinction to a neutral or one not taking part in a war. The term is also used to distinguish the regular forces in warfare from irregular combatants.

(*In International law.*) The term is used to designate either of two nations which are actually in a state of war with each other, as well as their allies actively co-operating; as distinguished from a nation which takes no part in the war and maintains a strict indifference as between the contending parties, called a 'neutral'.

Bello pacta cedunt reipublicae. Contracts of the State give way to war.

Bello parta cedunt republicae. (*Maxim*) "Things acquired in war belong to the state." (*Burrill; Broom; Kent. Com. 101*)

Bellum omnium contra omne. It means if we were all to have our way each person would be allowed to wage a war against every other person. *State of Gujarat* v. *Justice R.A. Mehta*, (2013) 3 SCC 1, para 56.

Belong. The word 'belong' denotes ownership. AIR 1942 Bom 183. [Merchant Shipping Act 1894, S. 686(1)].

Belonging. The word "belonging" may and very often does mean "ownership," but it may also mean that which is connected with a principal or greater thing; an appendage; an appurtenance.

Belonging to. The words 'belonging to' refers to owner. *Pheku Chamar* v. *Harish Chandra,* AIR 1953 All 406, 407. [U.P. Zamindari Abolition and Land Reforms Act, 1950 (1 of 1951), S. 9]

The word 'belonging to', though capable of denoting an absolute title, can also signify of even possession of an interest less than that of full ownership. The words 'belonging to me' do not amount to a disclaimer of the tenancy and a repudiation of the landlord's title. *Mohd. Amir* v. *Municipal Board. Sitapur*, AIR 1965 SC 1923, 1929.

Belonging to and occupied by. The term "belong" in S. 400, IPC (45 of 1860) implied something more than the idea of casual association; it involves the notion of continuity and indicates a more or less intimate connection with a body of persons extending over a period of time sufficiently long to warrant the inference that the person affected was identified with a band, the common purpose of which is the habitual commission of dacoity. *Sharaf Shah Khan* v. *State of A.P.*, AIR 1963 AP 314, 322.

Belongings. Personal effects. [Metal Cor-poration of India (Acquisition of Undertaking) Act (100 of 1976), S. 8].

Belongs to the Government. The use of the verb "belong" in the present tense indicates that the Government must be the owner of the servient tenement at the time when the right is claimed in the suit. The words "belong to the Government" cannot refer to the time during which the easement is enjoyed if plain meaning is given to them. *Kesarichand* v. *Chananmal,* AIR 1959 Raj 58, 59. [Indian Easements Act (5 of 1882), S. 15].

Below-the-line expenditure. Alternative term for *capital expenditure,* because such expenditure is listed below the line recording the total in a statement of account and is regarded as an additional cost. *See also above-the-line expenditure.* (*Banking*)

Benami. Nameless, fictitious, fraudulent; as a purchase under a false name, or land held in another name than that of the real proprietor. (*Wil Gloss. 70*)

A sale or purchase made in the name of some one other than the actual vendor or purchaser. (*Mac Naughten*)

The word '*benami*' is used to denote two classes of transactions which differ from each other in their legal character and incidents. In one sense, it signifies a transaction which is real, as for example, the *benami* purchase, *i.e.*, a real purchase by one in the name of another. Occasionally the word '*benami*' is used to refer to a sham transaction for example when 'A' purports to sell property to 'B' without intending that the title should pass to 'B'. *Sree Meenakshi Mills Ltd.* v. *Commissioner of Income Tax,* AIR 1957 SC 49, 66.

"Benami Transaction" means,—

(A) a transaction or an arrangement—

(a) where a property is transferred to, or is held by, a person, and the consideration for such property has been provided, or paid by, another person; and

(b) the property is held for the immediate or future benefit, direct or indirect, of the person who has provided the consideration, except when the property is held by—

(i) a Karta, or member of a Hindu Undivided Family, as the case may be, and the property is held for his benefit or the benefit of other members in the family and the consideration for such property has been provided or paid out of the known sources of the Hindu Undivided Family;

(ii) a person standing in a fiduciary capacity for the benefit of another person towards whom he stands in such capacity and includes a trustee, executor, partner, director of a company, a depository or a participant as an agent of a depository under the Depositories Act, 1996 (22 of 1996) and any other person as may be notified by the Central Government for this purpose;

(iii) any person being an individual in the name of his spouse or in the name of any child of such individual and the consideration for such property has been provided or paid out of the known sources of the individual;

(iv) any person in the name of his brother or sister or lineal ascendant or descendant, where the names of brother or sister or lineal ascendant or descendant and the individual appear as joint-owners in any document, and the consideration for such property has been provided or paid out of the known sources of the individual; or

(B) a transaction or an arrangement in respect of a property carried out or made in a fictitious name; or

(C) a transaction or an arrangement in respect of a property where the owner of the property is not aware of, or, denies knowledge of, such ownership;

(D) a transaction or an arrangement in respect of a property where the person providing the consideration is not traceable or is fictitious;

Explanation.—For the removal of doubts, it is hereby declared that benami transaction shall not include any transaction involving the allowing of possession of any property to be taken or retained in part performance of a contract referred to in Section 53A of the Transfer of Property Act, 1882 (4 of 1882), if, under any law for the time being in force,—

(i) consideration for such property has been provided by the person to whom possession of property has been allowed but the person who has granted possession thereof continues to hold ownership of such property;

(ii) stamp duty on such transaction or arrangement has been paid; and

(iii) the contract has been registered. [), Prohibition of Benami Property Transactions Act (45 of 1988), section 2(9)].

Transfer of property is *sine qua non* for attracting the definition of 'Benami transaction' under section 2(a) of the Act. *Canbank Financial Services Ltd v Custodian,* AIR 2004 SC 5123 : 5135, para 62 [Benami Transaction (Prohibition) Act (45 of 1988), section 2(a)]

"A benami transaction is one where one buys property in the name of another or gratuitously transfers his property to another, without indicating an intention to benefit the other. The benamidar, therefore, has no beneficial interest in the property or business that stands in his name; he represents in fact the real owner and so far as their relative legal position is concerned, he is a mere trustee for him. In other words, a benami purchase or conveyance leads to a resulting trust in India, just as a purchase or transfer under similar circumstances leads to a resulting trust in England. The general rule and principle of the Indian law as to resulting trusts differs but little if at all, from the general rule of English law upon the same subject." [*Treatise on Hindu Law* by MAYNE, 11th Edn., p. 953 as cited in *Controller of Estate Duty, Lucknow* v. *Aloke Mitra,* AIR 1981 SC 102].

Benamidar. One whose name appears in a *benami* transaction but who is not the real proprietor of the right indicated. A *benamidar* may be either a stranger whose name is used in order to conceal the real owner, or he may be a relative for the sake of whose reputation a nominal assignment of property is made.

A *benamidar* is an ostensible owner and if a person purchases from a benamidar, the real owner cannot recover unless he shows that the purchaser had actual or constructed notice of the real title. But from this it does not follow that the *benamidar* has real title to the property, he is merely an ostensible owner thereof. *Controller of Estate Duty* v. *Aloke Mitra,* AIR 1981 SC 102, 111.

One whose name appears in *benami* transaction but who is not the real proprietor of the right indicated. [Limitation Act (36 of 1963), S. 2(n)].

Bench. The seat where Judges sit in Court; the seat of justice.

The word 'Bench' includes a single Judge, and it does not necessarily mean two or more Judges. *Rajendra Prasad* v. *Sheel Bhadra,* AIR 1967 SC 1445, 1447.

"BENCH" means a bench of the Lokpal. [S. 2(1)(a) of the Lokpal & Lokayuktas Act, 2013 (1 of 2014)]

Bench warrant. An order issued by or from a bench for the attachment of property or arrest of a person; it may issue either in a case of a contempt, or where an indictment has been found.

Benedicta est expositio quando res redimitur a destructione. (*Maxim*) That is a blessed interpretation when a thing is saved from destruction. (*Burrill; Broom*)

Benefaction. The act of benefiting; a benefit conferred; the bestowal of money for a charitable purpose. [Aligarh Muslim University Act (40 of 1920), S. 8].

Benefice. An ecclesiastical living and promotion.

Beneficial. Conferring benefit; advantageous.

Beneficial enjoyment. The enjoyment which a man has in his own right and for his own benefit, and not as trustee for another. [Indian Easement Act (5 of 1882), S. 4].

Enjoyment in one's own right and for one's own benefit and not as a trustee of another. [Requisitioning and Acquisition of Immovable Property Act (30 of 1952), S. 2(e)(ii)].

Beneficial interest. The "beneficial interest" of the beneficiary is his right against the trustee as owner of the trust property. [Indian Trust Act (2 of 1882), S. 3].

The interest of a beneficial owner or beneficiary.

Beneficial interest in a share. For the purposes of this section and section 90, beneficial interest in a share includes, directly or indirectly, through any contract, arrangement or otherwise, the right or entitlement of a person alone or together with any other person to—

(i) exercise or cause to be exercised any or all of the rights attached to such share; or

(ii) receive or participate in any dividend or other distribution in respect of such share. [Companies Act (18 of 2013), section 89(10)]

Beneficial occupation. Occupation of land which is to the benefit of the occupier.

Beneficial owner. "BENEFICIAL OWNER" means a person whose name is recorded as such with a depository. [Depositories Act (22 of 1996), S. 2(a)].

One who, enjoys or is entitled to the benefit of the property

One who, though not having apparent legal title, is in equity entitled to enjoy the advantage of ownership.

"BENEFICIAL OWNER" means an individual who ultimately owns or controls a client of a reporting entity or the person on whose behalf a transaction is being conducted and includes a person who exercises ultimate effective control over a juridical person. [S. 2(1)(fa) of the Prevention of Money-Laundering Act, 2002 (15 of 2003) as inserted by the Prevention of Money-Laundering (Amendment) Act, 2012 (2 of 2013)]

"BENEFICIAL OWNERS" means a person, whether his identity is known or not, for whose benefit the benami property is held by a benamidar. Prohibition of Benami Property Transactions Act (45 of 1988), section 2(12)

Beneficial ownership. It means such a right to enjoyment of property as exists where the legal title is in one person and the right to such beneficial use or interest is in another and where such right is recognised by law and can be enforced by the Courts at the suit of such owner or of someone on his behalf. (*Associated Clothiers Ltd.* v. *Union of India,* AIR 1957 Pun 261, 264)

Beneficial use. The right of using property and all that makes that property desirable or habitable.

Beneficialis. Beneficial.

Beneficially entitled. Entitled to receive and appropriate. [Specific Relief Act (47 of 1963), S. 15(c)].

Beneficiary. "BENEFICIARY" means a person or object for whose benefit a *waqf* is created and includes religious, pious and charitable objects and any other objects of public utility sanctioned by the Muslim law. [Waqf Act (43 of 1995), S. 3(a) as substituted by Act 27 of 2013 (w.e.f. 1-11-2013)].

Beneficiaries are persons for whose benefit property is held by trustees, executors, *etc.*; persons named in insurance policies to whom the insurance is payable upon the happening of the event insured against. (*Bouvier*)

Where property is dedicated to an idol, it would be a "beneficiary".

"Beneficiary" is the person for whose benefit the confidence of the author of the trust is accepted by the trustee.[Indian Trusts Act (2 of 1882), S. 3]

"BENEFICIARY" means any person who enters into a contract with an energy service company empanelled with the Bureau for execution of an energy efficiency project in the premises in its possession, based on energy savings performance contract. [Energy Conservation (Partial Risk Guarantee Fund for Energy Efficiency) Rules, 2016, R. 2(1)(b)].

Beneficium invito non datur. A privilege or benefit is not granted against one's will.

Beneficium non datum nisi propter officium. A remuneration is not given, unless on account of a duty performed.

Beneficium non datur nisi officii causa. A benefice is not granted except on account or in consideration of duty.

Benefit. Advantage; profit; gain; interest; use; whatever contributes to promote prosperity or add value to property.

The word 'benefit' connotes benefits, express or otherwise, in terms of money but requiring computation. [*Kaliammal* v. *Andiammal*, AIR 1965 Mad 450, 451] [Industrial Disputes Act (14 of 1947), S. 33C(2)].

The word "benefit" denotes any form of advantage. Restatement of the Law of Restitution by American Law Institute, p. 12 as cited in *State of Gujarat* v. *Essar Oil Limited*, (2012) 3 SCC 522, para 63.

The word 'benefit' is not restricted to material benefit, but that is of wide significance comprehending whatever would be beneficial in any respect, material or otherwise.

Profit; good [IPC (45 of 1860), S. 88, ill.]; anything that is for the good of a person or thing.

"BENEFIT" includes a payment of any kind whether in tangible or intangible form. [(w.e.f. 1-4-2016) S. 102(3) of the Income-tax Act, 1961 (43 of 1961); (still-born) Section 102(4) of the Income-tax Act, 1961 (43 of 1961) as inserted (w.e.f. 1-4-2014) by the Finance Act, 2012 (23 of 2012) and omitted (w.e.f. 1-4-2014) by the Finance Act, 2013 (17 of 2013)]

"BENEFIT" means any advantage, gift, reward, relief, or payment, in cash or kind, provided to an individual or a group of individuals and includes such other benefits as may be notified by the Central Government. [Aadhaar (Targeted Delivery of Financial and Other Subsidies, Benefits and Services) Act (18 of 2016), section 2(f)].

Mere pecuniary benefit is not "BENEFIT" within the meaning of sections 26, 27 and 30 [(w.e.f. 1-7-2024) Bharatiya Nyaya Sanhita, 2023 (45 of 2023), section 30, *Expln.*]

Benefit claimers. Means the conservers of biological resources, their by-products, creators and holders of traditional knowledge associated thereto (excluding codified traditional knowledge only for Indians) and information relating to the use of such biological resources, innovations and practices associated with such use and application. [Biological Diversity Act, 2002 (18 of 2003), S. 2(a)].

Benefit of doubt. The advantage derived from doubt about guilt, a possible error or the weight of the evidence.

Benefit-of-the-bargain-rule. The principle that a defrauded buyer may recover from the seller as damages the difference between the misrepresented value of the property and the actual value received.

Benefit sharing. In relation to a variety, means such proportion of the benefit accruing to a breeder of such variety or such proportion of the benefit accruing to the breeder from an agent or a licensee of such variety, as the case may be, for which a claimant shall be entitled as determined by the Authority under S. 26. [Protection of Plant Varieties and Farmers' Right Act (53 of 2001), S. 2(b)].

Benefit to arise out of land. Future rents payable in respect of lands are "benefits to arise out of land" within the meaning of S. 2(6) of Registration Act (16 of 1908).

Benefit to estate. Under Hindu Law when from out sale proceeds of family properties the manager of the joint family purchased properties in a place to which the family migrated, it is a benefit to the estate.

Benevolences. An extraordinary aid.

Benevolent purposes. Purposes which are for the public good but not necessarily charitable.

Benige faciendae sunt interpretatione chartarum, ut res magls valeat quam pereat: et quae libet concesio fortissime contra donatorem interpretanda est. Deeds are to be liberally interpreted so that their purpose may stand rather than fall; and every grant is to be construed strictly against the grantor.

Benignae. Beneficially.

Benignae faciendae sunt interpretationes chartarum, ut res magis valet quam pereat. *(Maxim)* Benign (liberal) construction of documents is to be made, so that the instrument may avail rather than perish. (*Broom*)

Benignae faciendae sunt interpretationes, et verba intentioni debent inservire. Liberal interpretation should be the rule, and the words should be made to carry out the intention.

Benignae faciendae sunt interpretationes, propter, simplicitatem laicorum, ut res matgi valeaquam pereat; et verba intentioni, non e contra, debent inservire. (*Maxim*) A liberal construction should be put upon written instruments, so as to uphold them, if possible, and carry into the effect the intention of the parties.

Benigne sunt faciende imterpretationes cartarum, propter simplicitatem lalcorum, ut res magis valeat quam pereat; et verba intentioni, non e contra, debvent inservire. Liberal construction of written documents are to be made, because of the simplicity of the laity, and with a view to carry out the intention of the parties and uphold the document; and words ought to be made subservient, not contrary, to the intention.

Benignior sententia, in verbis generalibus seu dubiis, est proeferenda. (*Maxim*) Of general or doubtful words, the more liberal interpretation is preferred. (*Broom*)

This maxim proceeds upon the principle of carrying into effect, as far and as nearly as possible, the intention of the testator, and if there be a general and also a particular intention apparent on the will, and the particular intention cannot take effect, the words shall be so construed as to give effect to the general intention.

Benignius leges interpretandae sunt quo voluntas earum conservatur. (*Maxim*) Laws are to be more liberally interpreted, in order that their intent may be preserved. (*Burrill*)

Bequeath. To give by will; assign as a legacy. This word is properly applied only to personality, but in a will it avails to transmit real property also; "devise," however is the proper word.

To leave property by will to a person.

"SPECIFICALLY BEQUEATHED." means "bequeathed expressly and not by reference."

Bequest. A gift of personal property by will; a legacy; but it generally means "any gift by will whether it consists of personal or real property."

Bequest to class. Where there is a bequest to a class the essential thing to be determined first is the point of time, when the class has to be ascertained. The normal rule is that the date of death of the testator crystalises the class of legatees and those, who come within the class and are capable of taking on that date, obtain the benefit; the subsequent expansion of the class cannot diminish that benefit. *Narayanan* v. *ITC,* AIR 1963 Mad 172, 180. [Indian Succession Act (39 of 1925), S. 111].

Berne Convention Country. 'Berne Convention Country' means a country which is a member of the Berne Copyright Union, and includes a country mentioned either in Part I or in Part II of the Schedule of the International Copyright Order 1999. [International Copyright Order, 1999, S. 2(a)].

Berne Union. The union constituted by the member states of the Berne Convention. [Article 1, Berne Convention] (*Copyright*) Short form of *International Union of Credit and Investment Insurers* (because it is domiciled in Berne under the Swiss Civil Code). It is an international forum for discipline and consultation in export credit and investment insurance. (*Trade Finance*)

Berth. A post or an appointment; situation; employment; as, he has got a good berth at last.

Best efforts. Diligent efforts to carry out one's obligation.

Best-efforts underwriting. Underwriting in which an investment banker agrees to direct, but does not guarantee, the public sale of the issuer's securities.

Best evidence. Primary evidence, as distinguished from secondary; the best and highest evidence of which the nature of the case is susceptible.

Best evidence rule. A rule requiring that a party must call the best evidence that the nature of the case will allow.

There seems to be no reason for assuming that a rule requiring the best evidence producible to be produced has no application to Courts of which the Judges may be presumed to be, for want of professional training, less, capable than they are elsewhere of weighing the effect of evidence. [(1872) Sup. IA 10 : 12 BLR 120 : 18 WR 349 : 3 Sar 1 : 1 PR 1872 : 2 Suth 628].

Best interest of child. The basis for any decision taken regarding the child, to ensure fulfilment of his basic rights and needs, identity, social well-being and physical, emotional and intellectual development. [Juvenile Justice (Care and Protection of Children) Act, 2015 (2 of 2016), S. 2(9)].

Best judgment assessment. The assessing authority while making the "best judgment assessment" should arrive at its conclusion without any bias and on rational basis. That authority should not be vindictive or Capricious. If the estimate made by the assessing authority is a *bona fide* estimate and is based on a rational basis, the fact that there is no good proof in support of that estimate is immaterial. *Commissioner of Sales Tax, M.P.* v. *H.M. Esufali*, AIR 1973 SC 2266, 2269. [M.P. General Sales Tax Act (2 of 1958), S. 19(1)].

Best mode requirement. Best mode requirement of patent laws places an obligation on the applicant to describe the best way of carrying out the invention. (*Patents*)

Best of his knowledge and belief. The phrase 'to the best of deponent's knowledge and belief' imports the same as the phrase "so far as the deponent knows, and as he verily believes." Both imply that the deponent has information or evidence of the facts asserted, which, though it may not amount to certain knowledge, is, in his judgment, sufficient to justify a conclusion of the facts to which he swears.

Best rent. Rent which is the best *i.e.* most advantageous. [T.P. Act (4 of 1882), S. 65A(2)(b)].

Bestial. Belonging to a beast or to the class of beasts; animal; brutish.

Bestiality. The qualities or nature of a beast; conduct or mental condition unworthy of human nature; beastliness.

BESTIALITY is the carnal knowledge and connection against the order of nature by man or woman in any manner with a beast.

Carnal knowledge and connection by a man or woman with a beast. [Special Marriage Act (43 of 1954), S. 27(1A)(i)].

Bestiality : Sodomy : Buggery. We take it that there is a difference, in signification between the terms "bestiality, " and the "crime against nature". Bestiality is a connection between a human being and a brute of the opposite sex. Sodomy is a connection between two human beings of the same sex. Both may be embraced by the term "crime against nature." Buggery seems to include both sodomy and bestiality.

Bestow. To convey as a gift.

Bet. A wager, under which money or money's worth is made payable on the result of some future uncertain event.

Bet; Betting. To pledge as a forfeit to another who makes a similar pledge in return, on a future contingency, in support of an affirmation or opinion.

Beta shares (US beta stocks). Second-line shares, as opposed to the less numerous highly-capitalized alpha (first-line) or more numerous gamma (third-line) shares. (*Investment*)

Shares of companies having generally low capital; not frequently traded but listed shares. (*Depositories*).

Listed, but infrequently traded, shares of companies with a generally low equity capital. (*Stock Market*)

Beta stock. The designation used for the second rank of shares traded in on the stock market. They are less actively traded than those designated alpha stocks. (*Stock Market*)

Betray. To reveal or disclose in violation of confidence as, to betray a person's secrets or designs.

Betrayal. The act of betraying.

Betroth. To contract for a marriage; to give in marriage to another; promise or pledge one's troth for marriage.

Betrothal. The act of betrothing; betrothment; engagement for a marriage. A mutual promise or compact between two parties by which they bind themselves to marry. (*Burrill*)

Betterment. Making better; improvement. An improvement of real property which adds to its value.

Betting. Betting is a form of wagering contract in which money or money's worth is made payable by the parties on the result of an uncertain event, usually a game or sport. (*Ency.*)

"Betting or Gambling" means putting on stake something of value, particularly money, with consciousness of risk and hope of gain outcome of a game or a contest, whose result may be determined by chance or accident, or on the likelihood of anything occurring or not occurring. [Finance Act (32 of 1994), S. 65B(15) (now repealed by the Central Goods and Services Tax Act, 2017)].

Making of bets. [Income-tax Act (43 of 1961), S. 2(24)(ix)].

Between. In the intermediate space, without regard to distance; extending or passing from one place to another; belonging to two as a mutual relation. (*Bouvier*)

Between the parties to the suit. The expression "between the parties to the suit" in S. 47, CPC (5 of 1908), means parties opposed to one another and not necessarily those who are plaintiff and defendant in a suit respectively.

Beverage. A liquid for drinking, especially such liquid other than water. [Employees' Provident Funds and Miscellaneous Provisions Act (19 of 1952), Sch. I, item 13].

Beyond. Farther away; in addition to; past; later than.

Beyond a reasonable doubt. The phrase "proof beyond a reasonable doubt" is synonymous with the term "moral certainty."

Bharatia. Means any person by whom, or on whose account, rent is payable for any structure or part thereof, owned by a thika tenant or tenant of other lands in his holding or by a landlord in a bustee or his khas land. Calcutta Thika Other Tenancies and Lands (Acquisition and Regulation) Act, 1981 (37 of 1981), S. 3(1) as cited in *Ram Das Bansal* v. *Kharag Singh Baid*, (2012) 2 SCC 548, para 15.

Bhoomihin Kissan. The Bhoodan Yagna movement used generally an expression 'Bhoomihin Kissan' and it is this expression which gained momentum and virtually was understood to mean those agricultural labourers whose main source of livelihood is agriculture but who have no lands of their own or who have no lands (agricultural) recorded in their names in the revenue record. *U. P. Bhoodan Yagna Samiti* v. *Braj Kishore*, AIR 1988 SC 2239.

"Bhopal gas leak disaster" or **"disaster".** Means the occurrence on the 2nd and 3rd days of December, 1984, which involved the release of highly noxious and abnormally dangerous gas from a plant in Bhopal (being a plant of the Union Carbide India Limited, a subsidiary of the Union Carbide Corporation, U.S.A.) and which resulted in loss of life and damage to property on an extensive scale. [Bhopal Gas Leak Disaster (Processing of Claims) Act (21 of 1985), S. 2(a)].

Bhugut bandha mortgage. Means a transfer of the interest of a tenant in his tenancy, for the purpose of securing the payment of money advanced or to be advanced by way of loan, upon the condition that the loan, with all interest thereon, shall be deemed to be extinguished by the profits arising from the tenancy during the period of the mortgage. [Ben. Act VI of 1908 (Chota Nagpur Tenancy), S, 3 (2)]

Bi-cameral. By the provisions of the Government of India Act, 1935, it has been indicated that the Legislature at the Centre was 'bi-cameral'. The Lower Chamber was called 'House of Assembly'. The Upper Chamber was called 'Council of States'. *Kuldip Nayar* v. *UOI*, AIR 2006 SC 3127 : 2006 AIR SCW 4394.

Bi-cameral legislature. A legislature having two chambers. [CPC (5 of 1908), S. 135A(1)(a)].

Bi-cameral system. A term applied by Jeremy Bentham to the division of a legislative body into two chambers, as in the United States Congress (Senate and House of Representatives) and in Indian Parliament, Council of States (Rajya Sabha) and House of People (Lok Sabha).

Bi-partite. Of two parts.

Bias. A leaning of the mind; prepossession; inclination; propensity toward an object; bent of mind, a mental power, which sways the judgment; that which sways the mind toward one opinion rather than another; as, bias of arbitrator, of judge, or jury or witness.

A one-sided inclination of mind; any special influence that sways the mind.

The term "bias" is used to denote a departure from the standing of even-ended justice. *N.K. Bajpai* v. *Union of India*, (2012) 4 SCC 653, para 56.

"Bias" means general statements will not be sufficient for the purposes of indication of ill-will. There must be cogent evidence available on record to come to the conclusion as to whether in fact there was existing a bias which resulted in the miscarriage of justice. Stroud's Judicial Dictionary, 5th Edn., Vol. 3 as cited in *ABP Private Limited* v. *Union of India*, (2014) 3 SCC 327, para 37.

'Bias' may be of three kinds; pecuniary, personal and official. Pecuniary—A member of the Tribunal having a pecuniary interest in the subject-matter of the decision. Personal—The existence of close relationship between a member of the Tribunal and one of the parties. Official—an abnormal desire to uphold a particular departmental policy, which would prevent an impartial adjudication of the dispute.

"Bias" stands included within the attributes and broader purview of the word "malice", which in general connotation means and implies "spite" or "ill will". It is also a well-settled proposition that existence of the element of "bias" is to be inferred as per the standard and comprehension of a reasonable man. The bias may also be malicious act having some element of intention without just cause or excuse. In case of malice or ill-will, it may be an actual act conveying negatively but the element of bias could be apparent or reasonably seen without any negative result and could form part of a general public perception. *N.K. Bajpai* v. *Union of India*, (2012) 4 SCC 653, para 57.

A predisposition to decide for or against one party without proper regard to the true merits of the dispute is bias. Personal bias is one of the three major limbs of bias, namely, pecuniary bias, personal bias and official bias. *State of U.P.* v. *Mohd. Nooh,* AIR 1958 SC 86.

To incline to one side; condition of mind, which sways judgment and renders judge unable to exercise his functions impartially in particular case. *Secretary to Government Transport Department* v. *Munuswamy,* AIR 1988 SC 2232.

The words "bias" in popular English parlance stands included within the attributes and broader purview of the word "malice", which in common acceptation means and implies "spite" or "ill-will". (*Stroud*, 5th Edn., Vol. 3) and it is now well settled that mere general statements will not be sufficient for the purposes of indication of ill-will. There must be cogent evidence available on record to come to the conclusion as to whether in fact there was existing a bias which resulted in miscarriage of justice. *Kumaon Mandal Vikas Nigam Ltd.* v. *Girja Shankar Pant,* AIR 2001 SC 24 (28).

Bias and **prejudice.** Distinguished. "Bias" is not synonymous with 'prejudice'; . . . A man cannot be prejudiced against another, without being biased against him, but he may be biased without being prejudiced." (5 *Cyc.* 685)

Bias, judicial. No man can lawfully be a judge in his own cause. This is a clear rule of law as well as of natural equity and it is rigorously enforced. Hence, if a judge has any interest in the subject-matter of the litigation before him all proceedings will be stayed or set aside unless the parties, with full knowledge of the facts, have waived the objection.

Bid. An offer to give a price for an article about to be sold in auction.

An offer by an intending purchaser to pay a designated price for property which is about to be sold at auction; to make a bid.

A BID AT AN AUCTION is nothing more than an offer and can be withdrawn like all other offers before it is accepted by the other party which, in the case of an auction, is signified by the fall of the hammer.

Bid and asked. In securities transactions, it is a notation which describes the range of prices quoted in an over the counter stock exchange.

Bid document. The bid document is not a statutory instrument. Therefore, the rules of interpretation, which are applicable to the interpretation of statutes and statutory instruments are not applicable to the bid document. *Patel Engineering Limited* v. *Union of India*, (2012) 11 SCC 257, para 25.

Bid land. Such land as has been used by Barkhalidar for grazing his cattle or for cutting grass for the use of his cattle. Sourashtra Act (26 of 1951), S. 2(ii) as cited in *State of Gujarat* v. *Manoharsinhji Pradyumansinhji Jadeja*, (2013) 2 SCC 300, para 37.

"Bid land" means such land as has been used by the Girasdar for grazing his cattle or for cutting grass for the use of his cattle. Sourashtra Act (25 of 1951), S. 2(6) as cited in *State of Gujarat* v. *Manoharsinhji Pradyumansinhji Jadeja*, (2013) 2 SCC 300, para 36.

"Bid land" means such land as on 17-4-1951 was specifically reserved and was being used by a Girasdar or Barkhalidar for grazing cattle or for cutting grass. Sourashtra Act (3 of 1952), S. 2(a) as cited in *State of Gujarat* v. *Manoharsinhji Pradyumansinhji Jadeja*, (2013) 2 SCC 300, para 35.

Bid price. The highest price which a prospective buyer willing to pay for a security at a given time.

Bid rigging. For the purposes of this sub-section "bid rigging" means any agreement, between enterprises or persons referred to in sub-section (3) engaged in identical or similar production or trading of goods or provision of services, which has the effect of eliminating or reducing competition for bids or adversely affecting or manipulating the process for bidding. [Competition Act, 2002 (12 of 2003), S. 3(3) *Expl.*].

Bidder. A person who makes an offer at an auction.

One who makes a bid [Sale of Goods Act (3 of 1930), S. 64(2)].

Bidding ring. A group of dealers acting in concert in order to drive prices up or down. The practice is illegal. (*Investment*)

Biennial. Happening or appearing once in two years.

Bifurcated divorce. A divorce by which the marriage itself is dissolved but the issues incident to the divorce such as alimony, child custody, and visitation are reserved until a later proceeding.

Bigamus. A person who is married twice; one who has two wives. (*Latin for Lawyers*)

Bigamy. A double marriage; this word properly signifies the being twice married; but is now used by an almost universal corruption, to signify the offence of polygamy, or the having a plurality of wives or husbands at once. (*Tomlin.*)

It is the wilfully and knowingly contracting a second marriage when the contracting party knows that the first is still subsisting; the state of a man who has two wives, or of a woman who has two husbands, living at the same time. (*See also* IPC (45 of 1860), Ss. 494 and 495)

Entering into a marriage with one person while still legally married to another. [Indian Evidence Act (1 of 1872), S. 43, ill. (b)].

To constitute 'bigamy' under section 494 of IPC, 1860, the second marriage had to be a valid marriage duly solemnized and as it was not so solemnized it was not a marriage at all in the eye of law and, was, therefore, invalid. The essential ingredient constituting the offence of 'bigamy' is the marrying again during the lifetime of husband or wife in contrast to the ingredients of section 498A which, among other things, envisage subjecting the woman concerned to cruelty. The thrust is mainly marrying in section 494 of IPC, 1860 as against subjecting of the woman to cruelty in section 498A of that Act. *Koppisetti Subbharao alias Subramaniam* v. *State of A. P.*, AIR 2009 SC 2684.

Bigamy with adultery. Means adultery with the same woman with whom the bigamy was committed. [Indian Divorce Act (4 of 1869), S. 3(7) omitted by Act 51 of 2001, sec. 3(b) (w.e.f. 3-10-2001)].

Bigha. (*H.*) A measure of land, varying in extent in different parts of India. A standard area measure (of the Mughal Empire). In Upper India it is usually 3025 sq. yds., in Bengal=1600 sq. yds.

Bila lagan. Connotes either rent-free grant or one where the rent has not been fixed. *Sarjeet Singh* v. *Hari Singh*, (2015) 1 SCC 760, para 9.

Bilateral. Affecting or obligating both parties (a bilateral contract).

Bilateral contract. A contract in which both the parties are bound to fulfil obligations reciprocally towards each other

Bilateral discharge. The ending of contract by agreement, when neither party has yet performed his obligations under it.

Bilateral intervention. A concept used in the arena of dispute resolution of resolving the dispute by the disputants themselves without involving a third party's interventions *e.g.,* negotiation is based on the technique of bilateral intervention. (*Arbitration*)

Bilateral mistake. A mistake made by both the parties during the contract.

Bilateral monopoly. A hypothetical market condition in which there is only one buyer and one seller, which results in the delay of transaction because either party can hold out for better deal without fearing that other party will turn to a third party.

Bilinguis. Denotes properly one who has the command of two languages.

Bill. A formal statement or declaration of a thing in writing; an order drawn by one person on another to pay a third a certain sum of money, absolutely and at all events; a form or draft of a law, presented to a legislature, but not yet enacted, or before it is enacted; a proposed law. (*Ame. Cye.*)

The word "bill" in the proviso will not include an amendment of any of the clauses of the bill or any substantial amendment thereof. *Babulal Parate* v. *State of Bombay*, AIR 1960 SC 51, 55. [Constitution of India, Art. 3, proviso].

A bill of exchange; the draft submitted to the legislature for discussion and adoption as an Act; a written document; a note of charges for goods delivered or services rendered.

Bill of attainder. A legislative act, which indicted punishment without trial. "Acts of the supreme power, pronouncing sentences, where the legislature assumes judicial magistracy." "Bills of attainder" are such special acts of the Legislature as inflict capital punishment on all persons supposed to be guilty of high offences, such as treason and felony, without any conviction in the ordinary course of judicial proceedings." (*Ex parte Law* 15 *Feb. Cas.* 3)

An Act of Parliament whereby sentence of death was pronounced against the accused; bills of pains and penalties were acts denouncing milder punishments within the meaning of the U.S. Constitution, bill of attainder includes bills of pains and penalties.

Bill of entry. Means the electronic declaration accepted and assigned with a number by the Customs Computer System for further processing. [Bill of Entry (Electronic Declaration) Regulation, 1995, Reg. 2(b)].

Bill of entry is a certificate delivered to the Customs authorities by importers of goods, giving particulars of such goods, and the port or place from which they have been imported. The term is likewise applied to a somewhat similar certificate given on the exportation of goods.

Bill of exchange. A "BILL OF EXCHANGE" is an instrument in writing containing an unconditional order, signed by the maker, directing a certain person to pay a certain sum of money only to, or to the order of, a certain person or to the bearer of the instrument. [Negotiable Instruments (26 of 1881), S. 5].

"BILL OF EXCHANGE" means a bill of exchange as defined by the Negotiable Instruments Act, 1881, and includes also a *hundi,* and any other document entitling or purporting to entitle any person, whether named therein or not, to payment by any other person of, or to draw upon any other person for, any sum of money. [Indian Stamp Act (2 of 1899), S. 2(2)].

"BILL OF EXCHANGE" includes a *hundi* and a cheque. [Limitation Act (36 of 1963), S. 2(c)].

"A BILL OF EXCHANGE is an unconditional order in writing, addressed by one person to another, signed by the person giving it, requiring the person to whom it is addressed to pay, on demand, or at a fixed or determinable future time, a sum certain in money to, or to the order of, a specified person, or to bearer." [(English) Bills of Exchange Act, 1882, S. 3].

A form of negotiable instrument.

'Bill of exchange' and 'cheque'. A 'post-dated cheque' is not payable till the date which shown thereon arrives and will become 'cheque' on the said date and prior to that date it remains a bill of exchange. *Ashok Yashwant Badave* v. *Surendra Madhav Rao Nighojakar,* (2001) 2 SCC 726, para 19. [Negotiable Instruments Act (26 of 1881), Ss. 5 & 6].

Bill of exchange payable on demand. Includes—

(a) an order for the payment of any sum of money by a bill of exchange or promissory note, or for the delivery of any bill of exchange or promissory note in satisfaction of any sum of money, or for the payment of any sum of money out of any particular fund which may or may not be available, or upon any condition or contingency which may or may not be performed or happen;

(b) an order for the payment of any sum of money weekly, monthly, or at any other stated period; and

(c) a letter of credit, that is to say, any instrument by which one person authorizes another to give credit to the person in whose favour it is drawn. [Indian Stamp Act (2 of 1899), S. 2(3)]

The person who makes the bill is called the *drawer*; he to whom it is addressed, the *drawee*; and when he undertakes to pay the amount, he is then called the *acceptor*. The person to whom it is ordered to be paid is called the *payee*; and if he appoints another to receive the money, that other is called the *indorsee,* as the payee is with respect to him, the *indorser*; any one who happens, for the time, to be in possession of the bill, is called the *holder* of it." (*Tomlin*)

Bill of lading. "BILL OF LADING" includes a "through bill lading", but does not include a mate's receipt. [Indian Stamp Act (2 of 1899), S. 2(4)]

"BILL OF LADING" means a document which evidences a contract of carriage by sea and the taking over or loading of the goods by the carrier, and by which the carrier undertakes to deliver the goods against surrender of the document. A provision in the document that the goods are to be delivered to the order of a named person, or to order, or to bearer, constitutes such an undertaking. [United Nations Conference on the Carriage of goods by Sea, Part 1, Art. 1(7)].

Receipt for goods delivered to a carrier for transportation. A memorandum signed by masters of ships acknowledging the receipt of the merchant's goods, of which there usually are three parts, one kept by the consignor, one sent to the consignee, and one kept by the captain. (*Tomlin*)

An official detailed receipt given by the master of a vessel to the person consigning goods by which he makes himself responsible for the safe delivery to the consignee [Indian Stamp Act (2 of 1899), S. 2(4) and T.P. Act (4 of 1882), S. 137, *Expln.*].

Bill of rights. The title of "An Act of Parliament of 1689 declaring the rights and liberties of the subject, and settling the succession to the Crown of England."

Bill of sale. A written instrument effecting a transfer of moveable property, especially a document given as security for money borrowed authorising seizure of the property on default. [Indian Contract Act (9 of 1872), S. 139, ill. (b)].

Bill Payable; Bill receivable. A bill of exchange, promissory note, or other commercial paper. it is called a *bill payable* by the person who is to pay it, and a *bill receivable* by the person who holds it.

Separate accounts under these names are usually kept in mercantile books.

Billa vera. (*Lat.*) A true bill.

Billet. A small bar of metal. [Central Sales Tax Act (74 of 1956), S. 14(iv)(ii) repealed by Act No. 18 of 2017 (w.e.f 1-7-2017)].

Bilti. "*Bilti*" is the Hindi word for railway receipt. A *Bilticut* rate includes the cost of bagging, weighing, transport to the railway station, loading in wagons, and other station charges till the *Bilti* is issued. *Firm Shah Chandanmal Fatehraj* v. *Hazarilal*, AIR 1962 Raj 122. [Sale of Goods Act (3 of 1930), S. 25(1)].

Bind. To constrain, especially by legal authority. To impose legal duties.

Bind over. To bind by a bond or under legal obligation.

Binding. Obligatory; restrictive coercive. [Damodar Valley Corporation Act (14 of 1948), S. 49(2) and Constitution of India, Art. 141].

Binding agreement. An enforceable contract.

Binding contract. The words "binding contract" mean a contract which can be enforced by the vendor against the purchaser. *Peter Long & Partners* v. *Burns*, (1956) 3 All ER 207, 211.

Bioavailability. A property which enables a substance such as an insoluble or low-solubility substance to pass through the stomach into the blood stream and reach the target site, namely, receptors at which binding of the drug results in a chain of reactions which prevent proliferation of cells leading to cessation of cancer. *Novartis AG* v. *Union of India*, (2013) 6 SCC 1, para 4.2.9.

Bio-medical waste. Means any waste, which is generated during the diagnosis, treatment or immunisation of human beings or animals or research activities pertaining thereto or in the production or testing of biological or in health camps, including the categories mentioned in Schedule I appended to these rules. [Bio-Medical Waste (Management and Handling) Rules, 2016, R. 3(f)].

Bio-medical waste treatment and disposal facility. Means any facility wherein treatment, disposal of bio-medical waste or processes incidental to such treatment and disposal is carried out, and includes common bio-medical waste treatment facilities; [Bio-Medical Waste Management Rules, 2016, R. 3(g)].

Bio-survey and bio-utilisation. Means survey or collection of species, sub-species, genes, components and extracts of biological resource for any purpose and includes characterisation, inventorisation and bioassay. [Biological Diversity Act, 2002 (18 of 2003), S. 2(d)].

Biodegradable substance. Means a substance that can be degraded by microorganisms. [Municipal Solid Wastes (Management and Handling) Rules, 2000, R. 3(iii)].

Biodiversity. The variety of world's organisms, including their genetic make up and their communities and inter-relationships. Biodiversity can be considered at three levels; the genetic, species and ecosystem levels of biological diversity. Biodiversity is a valuable resource and its importance to mankind is traceable to Darwin theory for the survival of species. CHARLES DARWIN first identified the full significance of man's relationship to other species. The threats to biodiversity are such that the genetic variety within species, including many species with potential value to mankind, is being eroded; species, most of which have never been classified, are becoming extinct; and species rich ecosystems are being destroyed or degraded worldwide.

Biogeochemical cycles. The movement of massive amounts of carbon, nitrogen, oxygen, hydrogen, calcium, sodium, sulphur, phosphorus, and other elements among various living and non-living components of the environment—including the atmosphere, soils, aquatic systems, and biotic systems— through the processes of production and decomposition.

Biogeography. The scientific study of the geographic distribution of organisms.

Biologicals. Means any preparation made from organism or micro-organism or product of metabolism and biochemical reactions intended for use in the diagnosis, immunization or the treatment of human beings or animals or in research activities pertaining thereto. [Bio-Medical Waste (Management and Handling) Rules, 1998, R. 3(6)].

Biological diversity. Means the variability among living organisms from all sources and the ecological complexes of which they are part and includes diversity within species or between species and of eco-systems. [Biological Diversity Act, 2002 (18 of 2003), S. 2(b)].

Biological resources. Include genetic resources, organisms or parts thereof, populations, or any other biotic component of ecosystems with actual or potential use or value for humanity.

"BIOLOGICAL RESOURCES" means plants, animals and micro-organisms or parts thereof, their genetic material and by-products (excluding value added products) with actual or potential use or value, but does not include human genetic material. [Biological Diversity Act, 2002 (18 of 2003), S. 2(c)].

Biological weapons. "BIOLOGICAL WEAPONS" are—

(i) microbial or other biological agents, or toxins whatever their origin or method of production, of types and in quantities that have no justification for prophylactic, protective or other peaceful purposes; and

(ii) weapons, equipment or delivery systems specially designed to use such agents or toxins for hostile purposes or in armed conflict.

[Weapons of Mass Destruction and their Delivery Systems (Prohibition of Unlawful Activities) Act (21 of 2005), S. 4(a)].

Biomethanation. Means a process which entails enzymatic decomposition of the organic matter by microbial action to produce methane rich biogas. [Municipal Solid Wastes (Management and Handling) Rules, 2000, R. 3(iv)].

Biometrics. Identification technology such as finger-printing, retinal scanning, and DNA analysis.

Security technology designed to authentic-cate users by capturing human characteristics. (*Cyber Law*)

The technologies that measure and analyze human body characteristics, such as 'fingerprints,' 'eye retinas and irises,' 'voice patterns,' 'facial patterns,' 'hand measurements' and 'D.N.A. for authentication purposes.' [Guide to Enactment of the UNCITRAL Model Law on Electronic Signatures, 2001, R. 2(b)].

Biopsy. The removal and examination, usually microscopic, of tissue or other material from the human body, for purposes of diagnosis.

BIOS (Basic Input/Output System). Software that controls a computer's peripherals. The BIOS is usually held in one or more ROM chips and can be used by both the operating system and applications programs. (*Computer*)

Biotechnology. Means any technological application that uses biological systems, living organisms, or derivatives thereof to make or modify products or processes for specific use.

"BIOTECHNOLOGY" means the application of scientific and engineering principle to the processing materials by biological agents to produce goods and services. [Rules for the Manufacture, Use, Import, Export and Storage of Hazardous Micro Organisms, Genetically Engineered Organisms or Cells, 1989, R. 3(i)].

Birretum. The cap or coif of a judge.

Birth-mark. Some congenital mark or blemish on a person's body (as) a mole.

Bis idem exigi bona fides non patitur; et in satisfactionibus non permittitur amplius fieri quam semel factum est. Good faith does not allow the same thing to be exacted twice; and in satisfying claims, it is not permitted that more should be done after satisfaction has once been rendered.

Bissextile. Leap year.

Bisexual. Women who are attracted to both sexes, men who are attracted to both sexes. [Michael Kirby, former Judge of High Court of Australia **as cited in** *Navtej Singh Johar* v. *Union of India,* (2018) 10 SCC 1, para 151].

Biswa. (*H.*) A twentieth, but applied especially to the twentieth part of a *bigha*. The *biswa* is divided into twenty *biswansis*.

Black list. Is a list of persons or firms against whom its compiler would warn the public, or some section of the public; a list of persons unworthy of credit, or with whom it is not advisable to make contracts. A list of persons firms, companies *etc.* boycotted or punished.

"Blacklisting". Blacklisting has the effect of preventing a person from the privilege and advantage of entering into lawful relationship with the Government for purposes of gains. *Erusian Equipment & Chemicals Ltd.* v. *State of W.B.* (1975) 1 SCC 70, para 20 as cited in *Patel Engineering Limited* v. *Union of India*, (2012) 11 SCC 257, para 13].

Black market. Buying and selling goods which are subject to government rationing or control.

Illegal market that usually deals in scarce or stolen goods.

Black money. Money usually obtained illegally.

Blackleg. One who wins money at cards or betting by dishonest practices; one who continues to work during a strike.

Blackmail. Extortion of money, *etc.*, by threats of libel, prosecution, exposure or bodily harm. (*Ency. of the Laws of England*)

It usually implies that the payment is involuntary and the ground for demanding it unlawful or pretended and fraudulent.

Blank acceptance. An acceptance which is written on blank stamped paper, and which acts as a *prima facie* authority by the acceptor to complete a bill of exchange for any amount the stamp will cover.

Blank cheque. An inchoate instrument. This cheque need not have any details other than the signature of the drawer.

Blank indorsement. The signature of a payee without further restriction, converting the instrument to *bearer paper*.

Blank transfer. In the case of a "blank transfer" the name of the transferor is entered in the transfer form, and the transferor, signs the transfer with the share scrip annexed, and hands it over to the transferee who, if he chooses, may complete the transfer by entering his name and then apply to the company to register his name in the place of that of the transferor. *Howrah Trading Co. Ltd.* v. *C.I.T.*, AIR 1959 SC 775. [Companies Act (1 of 1956), S. 108 replaced by Companies Act, 2013].

Blanket insurance. A group health insurance policy covering a number of individuals who are not individually named but are exposed to the same hazards, such as members of an athletic team, company officials who are passengers in the same company plane, *etc.* (*Insurance*)

Blanket mortgage. A mortgage which covers two or more properties that are pledged to support a debt.

Blanket policy. An agreement to indemnify all property, regardless of location.

Blanket search warrant. A single search warrant which authorizes the search of more than one area.

Blanks. Vacant spaces. [Registration Act (16 of 1908), S. 20(1)].

Blasphemy. The offence of speaking against God.

Blended fund. Is the aggregate proceeds of the sale of real and personal estate.

Blind trust. A trust in which the investments are placed by the settlor under the control of an independant trustee usually to avoid a conflict of interest.

Blindness. Refers to a condition where a person suffers from any of the following conditions, namely:—

(i) total absence of sight; or

(ii) visual acuity not exceeding 6/60 or 20/200 (snellen) in the better eye with correcting lenses; or

(iii) limitation of the field of vision subtending an angle of 20 degree or worse; [Persons with Disabilities (Equal Opportunities, Protection of Rights and Full Participation) Act, 1995 (1 of 1996), S. 2(b)] [Now repealed & replaced by Act 49 of 2016]

'Blindness' contemplates total disability. *Lal Chand* v. *State of Haryana,* (1999) 6 SCC 760, para 5.

BLOB. Binary Large Object, used to describe any random large block of bits, usually a picture or sound file; can be stored in a database but normally not interpretable by a database program. Can be used as a mild hacker threat (mailbomb) when mailed. Can also be used to hide malicious logic code. (*Cyber Law*)

Bloc. Alignment of a group of persons or natons having common interest or purpose.

Block. A mass of stone, metal *etc.*; a connective group. [Trade and Merchandise Marks Act (43 of 1958), S. 78(c) Repealed by Act 47 of 1999] .

Block of assets. Means a group of assets falling within a class of assets comprising—

(a) tangible assets, being buildings, machinery, plant or furniture;

(b) intangible assets, being know-how, patents, copyrights, trade-marks, licences, franchises or any other business or commercial rights of similar nature, not being goodwill of a business or profession,

A single asset can form a block of assets under section 2(11) of the Act. User of asset for business is not important for the determination of the question whether the asset falls within the 'block of assets' or not. *Chhabria Trust v Asst. CIT*, (2003) 264 IRT (A.T.) 12 (Bom). [Income-tax Act (43 of 1961), section 2(11)]

Block period. Means the period comprising of ten previous years preceding the previous year in which the search was conducted under section 132 or any requisition was made under section 132A, and also includes the previous year in which such search was conducted or requisition made:

Provided that where the search is initiated or the requisition is made before the 1st day of June, 2001, the provisions of this clause shall have effect as if for the words "six assessment years", the words "ten assessment years" had been substituted; [Income-tax Act (43 of 1961), S. 158B(a)].

Blockade. The blocking of a harbour, port, or sea board by hostile ships, in order to prevent ingress or egress, and by stopping the supply of provisions or ammunition compel surrender without bombardment or siege.

Blockade, by international law, in order to be binding on any must be effective as to all. It must be maintained by a force sufficient really to prevent access to the coast of the enemy.

Blood. In law means (1) The relationship which enables a person to take by descent; (2) a number of persons connected by blood relationship, that is, by being descended for one or more common ancestors.

HALF-BLOOD, relationship through one parent only, as that of half-brothers, or sisters.

WHOLE BLOOD, relationship through both father and mother.

Blood fued. A fued between the members of different class or families arising out of a crime or violence (as a killing) committed by a member of one upon a member of the other and requiring a continuing series of alternative retaliation in kind. [Indian Evidence Act (1 of 1872), S. 153, ill. (d)].

Blood, Full. Two persons are said to be related to each other by full blood when they are descended from a common ancestor by the same wife.

Blood-money. Money paid as the price of blood. Compensation or reward for bringing about the death of another, either by bringing a capital charge against him or by giving such testimony as will lead to conviction.

Blood poisoning/septicemia. Introduction of virulent bacteria into the bloodstream, usually from a local infection such as a boil or wound and marked by chills, fever, and fatigue.

Blood relation. Persons descended from the same stock or ancestor are said to be blood relations.

Blood test. Test to determine the paternity of the child.

Blood, Uterine. Being descended from a common female; two persons are said to be related to each other by uterine blood when they are descended from a common ancestress but different husbands. [Hindu Succession Act (30 of 1956), S. 3(1)(e)].

Bloodwyte. A fine for shedding of blood, payable to the lord, or a part there of to the injured or, in case of death to, to his relatives.

Blot on title. A defect in title.

BlowFish. The 64-bit BlowFish block cipher developed by Bruce Schneier which uses a simplification of the principles used in DES to provide the same security with greater speed and efficiency than DES in software. BlowFish is the precursor to TwoFish.

Blue-book. A name applied to the reports and other papers printed by order of the British Parliament or issued by the Privy Council or other departments of Government because their covers are blue.

Blue chips. A corporate stock which is considered a safe investment because the corporation has a history of stability, consistent growth and reliable earnings.

Blue sky laws. A popular name for statutes providing for the regulation and super-vision of investment companies and securities. *(The Law Dictionary)*

Any state laws relating to the regulation of securities. (*Cyber Laws*)

The laws in some US states that are intended to protect investors, including broker licensing and the supervision of the issue of securities. (*Investment*)

Laws passed by the states in US to protect investors. The term traces its origin to a remark made by a Kansas legislator that unless a state passed effective legislation, promoters would try to sell shares in the blue sky to unsuspecting investors. (*Capital Market*)

Blunder. A mistake made through mental confusion; a gross or stupid mistake.

BLUNDER, ERROR, MISTAKE. An *error* is a wandering from truth primarily in impression, judgment, or calculation, and by the extension of the idea, in conduct. *A mistake* is a false judgment or erroneous choice; it does not, as error sometimes does, imply moral obliquity, the defect being placed wholly in the wisdom of the actor. *Blunder* is a stronger word, a gross error in action or speech.

BMC4I. Battle(-space) Management Command, Control, Communications, and Intelligence. Briefly stated, the overall label for those components and processes comprising the 'nervous system' of a modern military force in a theater of operations. The planing, tasking, and control of the execution of missions through an architecture of sensors, communications, automation, and intelligence support. (*Cyber Law*)

Board. "BOARD" means the board of directors or the governing body of a multi-state cooperative society by whatever name called, to which the direction and control of the management of the affairs of the society is entrusted. [Multi-State Co-operative Societies Act (39 of 2002), S. 3(b)].

A number of persons appointed or elected to sit in council for the management or investigation of a public or private business, trust or other organisation or institution. [Companies, (Profits) Surtax Act, S. 2(4) and Income-tax Act (43 of 1961), S. 2(12)].

"BOARD" in relation to a company, means the collective body of the directors of the company. [S. 2(10) of the Companies Act, 2013 (18 of 2013)]

Board, Free. The distance measured vertically downwards amid ships from the upper edge of the deck line to the upper edge of the related load line. [Merchant Shipping Act (44 of 1958), S. 3(14)].

Board of Approvals. Means the combined Board of Approvals for export oriented unit and Special Economic Zone units, as notified in the Official Gazette, from time to time by the Government of India in the Ministry of Commerce and Industry. [Central Excise Tariff Act, 1985 (5 of 1986), Appendix IX, Service Tax (D) *Expln.* (1)].

Board of Direct Taxes. "Board of Direct Taxes" means the Central Board of Direct Taxes constituted under the Central Boards of Revenue Act, 1963. [National Tax Tribunal Act (49 of 2005), section 2(b)] [Now held unconstitutional by the Supreme Court]

Board of directors. The governing body of a corporation elected by its shareholders.

"BOARD OF DIRECTORS". In relation to a company, means the collective body of the directors of the company. [S. 2(10) of the Companies Act, 2013 (18 of 2013)] "Board of Directors" or "Board" means the collective body of the directors appointed or nominated or deemed as such under section 4. [Life Insurance Corporation Act, 1956 (31 of 1956), section 2(1b)]

"Board of Discipline". Means the Board of Discipline constituted under sub-section (1) of section 21A. [Chartered Accountants Act, 1949 (38 of 1949), section 2(1)(ab)]

"Board of Discipline" means the Board of Discipline constituted under sub-section (1) of section 21A. [Company Secretaries Act, 1980 (56 of 1980), section 2(1)(ab)]

"Board of Discipline" means the Board of Discipline constituted under sub-section (1) of section 21A. [Cost Accountants Act, 1959 (23 of 1959), section 2(1)(ab)]

Board of Excise and Customs. "Board of Excise and Customs" means the Central Board of Excise and Customs constituted under the Central Boards of Revenue Act, 1963. [National Tax Tribunal Act (49 of 2005), section 2(b)] [Now held unconstitutional by the Supreme Court]

Board of trustees. The 'Board of Trustees' is a broad based body representing a cross-section of a variety of interests. It is the Board constituted that frames the Scale of Rates and Statement of Conditions under which the services shall or may be performed by it. Every scale and every statement of conditions framed by the Board has to be submitted to the Central Government for sanction under section 44 of the T. N. Port Trust Act 2 of 1905, and it is only when it is so sanctioned that it has the force of law. *Trustees of the Port of Madras* v. *Aminchand Pyarelal*, AIR 1975 SC 1935.

Board's report. The "board's report" shall include a statement showing the name of every employee of the company, who—(i) if employed throughout the financial year, was in receipt of remuneration for that year which, in the aggregate, was not less than sixty lakh rupees; (ii) if employed for a part of the financial year, was in receipt of remuneration for any part of that year, at a rate which, in the aggregate, was not less than five lakh rupees per month; (iii) if employed throughout the financial year or part thereof, was in receipt of remuneration in that year which, in the aggregate, or as the case may be, at a rate which, in the aggregate, is in excess of that drawn by the managing director or whole-time director or manager and holds by himself or along with his spouse and dependent children, not less than two per cent of the equity shares of the company. [R. 5(2) of the Companies (Appointment & Remuneration of Managerial Personnel) Rules, 2014]

Boarder. One who boards. One who gets his meals, or both meals and lodging, in the house of another for a price agreed upon.

Bodily. Pertaining to or concerning or belonging to the body or physical constitution as opposed to the mental (as) bodily harm or bodily injury.

Of or relating to the body.

Bodily harm. Physical injury, bodily harm is used in the sense in which hurt is defined in the IPC (45 of 1860), S. 319 and means bodily pain, disease or infirmity.

Bodily infirmity. An infirmity *i.e.* physical weakness especially from old age, some permanent disease, accident or something of that kind pertaining to the body.

Bodily injury. Injury to the body. [IPC (45 of 1860), S. 299]. The expression "bodily injury" in clause thirdly includes also its plural, so that the clause would cover a case where all the injuries intentionally caused by the accused are *cumulatively* sufficient to cause the death in the ordinary course of nature, even if none of those injuries *individually* measures-up to such sufficiency. [*State of A.P.* v. *Rayavarapu Punnayya,* (1976) 4 SCC 382, para 39 **as cited in** *State of M.P.* v. *Galoo Raikwar,* (2016) 12 SCC 139, para 4].

Bodily weakness. Weakness of the body.

Body. The main portion; the bulk of anything; the larger part; the majority: as, the body of the people are opposed to the measure. A number of things or particulars taken together, a general collection, a code; a system: as, a body of laws.

A number of individuals spoken of collectively, usually associated for a common purpose, joined in a certain cause or united by some common tie or occupation; the main-central or principal part [Constitution of India, Art. 110 (2)]; physical or material frame of a man or animal; gang of thieves *etc.*

Body corporate. A corporation.

"Body Corporate" or "Corporation" includes a company incorporated outside India, but does not include—

(i) a co-operative society registered under any law relating to co-operative societies; and

(ii) any other body corporate (not being a company as defined in this Act), which the Central Government may, by notification, specify in this behalf.

[Companies Act (18 of 2013), S. 2(11)].

"BODY CORPORATE" or "Corporation" includes a company incorporated outside India but does not include—

(a) a corporation sole;

(b) a co-operative society registered under any law relating to co-operative societies; and

(c) any other body corporate (not being a company as defined in this Act), which the Central Government may, by notification in the Official Gazette, specify in this behalf. [Companies Act (1 of 1956), S. 2(7) replaced by Companies Act, 2013].

"It is called a body corporate, because the persons are made into a body politic and are of capacity to take, grant, *etc.,* by a particular name."

The words "body corporate" are not equivalent to the words "incorporated company.' An incorporated company is a body corporate but many bodies corporate are not incorporated companies. *Madras Central Urban Bank* v. *Corporation of Madras*, (1932) 2 Com Cases 328, 332 (Mad) [Companies Act (1 of 1956), S. 2(7)].

A corporation aggregate; an incorporated body. [Ss. 2(17) and 10(23BBA), Income-tax Act (43 of 1961)].

"BODY CORPORATE" includes a company incorporated outside India, but does not include— (*i*) a co-operative society registered under any law relating to co-operative societies; and (*ii*) any other body corporate (not being a company as defined in this Act), which the Central Government may, by notification, specify in this behalf. [S. 2(11) of the Companies Act, 2013 (18 of 2013)]

Body of an instrument. The main and operative part consisting of the substantive provisions, as distinguished from the recitals, title, *etc.*

Body of deed. Operative part of a deed as distinguished from the recitals.

Bogus. Spurious; not genuine; sham; as, a bogus claim; a bogus government; bogus cheque.

Boiler. "BOILER" means any closed vessel exceeding 22.75 litres in capacity which is used expressly for generating steam under pressure and includes any mounting or other fitting attached to such vessel, which is wholly or partly under pressure when steam is shut off. [Boilers Act (5 of 1923), S. 2(b)].

A part of a steam generator in which water is converted into steam.

Boisterous. Turbulent; rough and noisy; clamorous: applied to persons or their actions: as, a boisterous man; a boisterous game.

Bomb. To attack with bombs.

An explosive projectile, consisting of a hollow ball, or spherical shell, generally of cast-iron, filled with a bursting charge, fired from a mortar, and usually exploded by means of a fuse or tube filled with a slow-burning compound, which is ignited by the exploding powder when the mortar is discharged. Bombs are now commonly termed shells, though shell in the sense of a projectile has a wider meaning. Also called bomb-shell.

Bombast. High-sounding words; extravagant language; speech too big and high-sounding for the occasion.

Bomb hoax. A deception, leading one or more people to believe that an explosion is likely to occur that will cause physical injury or damage to property.

Bon ami. (*Fr.*) A good friend.

Bona. (*Lat.*) Goods; property; possessions. In the Roman law, this term was used to designate all species of property, real, personal, and mixed, but was more strictly applied to real estate.

Bona confiscata. Goods confiscated or forfeited.

Bona et catalla. Goods and chattles; moveable property. This expression includes all personal things that belong to a man.

Bona fide. In good faith; without fraud or deception; honestly, as distinguished from bad faith; openly; sincerely.

Acting or done in good faith.

Bona fide holder. For value of a Bill or Note is "Holder in due course". [See Negotiable Instruments Act (26 of 1881), S. 9].

A holder in good faith. [T.P. Act (4 of 1882), S. 51].

Bona fide interest. Real and genuine interest, not fraudulent or colourable. [CPC (5 of 1908), O. XXXVI, R. 5(2)(b)].

Bona fide livelihood needs. Means fulfilment of livelihood needs of self and family through exercise of any of the rights specified in sub-section (1) of Section 3 of the Act and includes sale of surplus produce arising out of such rights. [Schedule Tribes and Other Traditional Forest Dwellers (Recognition of Forest Rights) Rules, 2008, R. 2(1)(b) as substituted by 2012 Amendment] [Schedule Tribes and Other Traditional Forest Dwellers (Recognition of Forest Rights) Act, 2006

Bona fide mistake. Means that the mistake is not made deliberately. Where a mistake is honestly made, it is a *bona fide* mistake."

A mistake committed in spite of good faith. [CPC (5 of 1908), O. I, R. 10(1)].

Bona fide need. Means the landlord has a genuine need to occupy the accommodation, that is, he must have necessity to occupy it and the necessity must be *bona fide* or genuine one. *Girija Debi* v. *R.C. & E. Officer*, AIR 1965 All 366, 367. [U.P. (Temporary) Control & Rent and Eviction Rules (1947), R. 6].

Bona fide occupational qualification. A characteristic required of employees as a matter of business necessity; it may justify an exemption from laws prohibiting discrimination based on religion, national origin or sex.

Bona fide purchaser. One who at the time of the purchase advances a new consideration, surrenders some security, or does some other act which leaves him in a worse position if his purchase should be set aside, and purchases in the honest belief that his vendor had a right to sell, without notice, actual or constructive of any adverse rights, claims, interest or equities of other in and to the property sold.

Bona fide requirement. There must be a sort of "must have" element in the need of the landlord and also that his want or need of the house must be honestly felt by him. *Naresh* v. *Kanai Lal*, AIR 1952 Cal 852, 853. [W.B. Premises Rent Control (Temporary Provisions) Act (38 of 1948), S. 11(1)(f)].

Bona fides. Good faith.

Bona fides exigit ut quod convenit fiat. Good faith demands that what is agreed upon shall be done.

Bona fides non patitur ut bis idem exigatur. (*Lat.*) Good faith does not allow us to demand twice the payment of the same thing.

Bona gestura. Good behaviour.

Bona mobilia. Moveables; those things which move themselves or can be transported from one place to another, and not permanently attached to a farm, heritage, or building.

Bona notabilia. (*Lat.*) Goods situated in another diocese to that in which a deceased had died.

Bona vacantia. (*Lat.*) Goods in which no one claims a property such as royal fish, ship-wrecks treasure trove, waifs, strays, *etc.*

The term "*bona vacantia*" comprises properties of two different kinds, those which come in by escheat and those over which no one has a claim. *Bombay Dying and Manufacturing Co.* v. *State of Bombay*, AIR 1958 SC 328, 339.

Bona waviata. (*Lat.*) Goods that are thrown away by a thief in his flight for fear of being apprehended.

Bonae fide possessor in id tantum quod ad se pervenerit, tenetur. A possessor in good faith is only liable for that which he himself has obtained.

Bonae fidei possessor in id tantum quod ad se pervenerit, tenetur. A possessor in good faith is only liable for that which he himself has obtained.

Bonae fidei emptor. A purchaser in good faith.

Bonae fidei non congruit de apicibus juris disputare. It is incompatible with good faith to insist on the extreme subtleties of the law.

Bonae fidei possessor in id tantum quod ad se pervenerit tenetur. A possessor in good faith is liable only for that which he himself has obtained (literally, what has come to him). 2 Co. Inst. 285.

Bonae fidei possessor in id tantum quod sese pervenerit tenetur. A person in possession in good faith is answerable only for that which he himself has obtained.

Bond. An agreement of engagement; a covenant between two or more persons. Technically a bond is a deed or obligatory instrument, in writing, whereby one doth bind himself to another, to pay a sum of money, or to do some other act; but in popular language any instrument in writing that legally binds a party to do a certain thing may be called a bond. (*Burrill*)

"BOND" as defined in the Indian Stamp Act includes—

(a) any instrument whereby a person obliges himself to pay money to another, on condition that the obligation shall be void if a specified act is performed, or is not performed, as the case may be;

(b) any instrument attested by a witness and not payable to order or bearer, whereby a person obliges himself to pay money to another; and

(c) any instrument so attested, whereby a person obliges himself to deliver grain or other agricultural produce to another but does not include a debenture [Indian Stamp Act (2 of 1899), S. 2(5)].

"BOND" includes—

(i) any instrument whereby a person obliges himself to pay money to another on condition that the obligation shall be void if a specified act is performed, or is not performed, as the case may be;

(ii) any instrument attested by a witness and not payable to order or bearer, whereby a person obliges himself to pay money to another; and

(iii) any instrument so attested whereby a person obliges himself to deliver grain or other agricultural produce to another;

Explanation.—Notwithstanding anything contained in any law for the time being in force, for the purposes of this clause, "attested", in relation to an instrument means attested by one or more witnesses each of whom has seen the executant sign or affix his mark to the instrument, or has some other person sign the instrument in the presence and by the direction of the executant, or has received from the executant a personal acknowledgement of his signature or mark or of the signature of such other person, and each of whom has signed the instrument in the presence of the executant; but it shall not be necessary that more than one of such witnesses shall have been present at the same time, and no particular form of attestation shall be necessary. [Maharashtra Stamp Act (60 of 1958), S. 2(c)].

"Bond" means a personal bond or an undertaking for release without surety. [(w.e.f. 1-7-2024) Bharatiya Nagarik Suraksha Sanhita, 2023 (46 of 2023), section 2(1)(e).

Bondage. In Chambers 20th Century Dictionary, (New Edition), "bondage" means "captivity" or "slavery" (the state of being a slave), in Merriam - Webster's Advanced Learner's English Dictionary, "bondage" means "Slavery". In Oxford Advanced Learner's Dictionary - 95th Edition, the meaning of the word "bondage", is the state of being a slave or prisoner and the synonym of the word "bondage" is "Slavery". Cited in *Nizamudhin vs. Station House Officer*, 2017 (3) KLT 244, para 7]

Bonded. Put or placed in bond; as, *bonded goods*. Encumbered, mortgaged: as, heavily *bonded property*. Secured by or consisting of bonds: as *bonded debt*.

Bonded debt. Means an advance obtained, or presumed to have been obtained, by a bonded labourer under, or in pursuance of the bonded labour system. [Bonded Labour System (Abolition) Act, 1976, S. 2(d)].

Bonded debt is that part of the entire indebtedness of a corporation, state, *etc.* which is represented by the bonds, it has issued, as distinguished from floating debt.

Bonded goods. Goods in a bonded warehouse, and not chargeable with duty until required for consumption.

Bonded indebtedness. Indebtedness lawfully contracted for governmental purposes by issuing bonds repayable after a specified term.

Bonded labour. Means any labour or service rendered under the bonded labour system. [Bonded Labour System (Abolition) Act (19 of 1976), S. 2(e)].

Bonded labour system. Means the system of forced labour under which a debtor enters, or has, or is presumed to have, entered into an agreement with the creditor to the effect that—

(i) in consideration of an advance obtained by him or by any of his lineal ascendants or descendants (whether or not such advance is evidenced by any document) and in consideration of the interest, if any, due on such advance, or

(ii) in pursuance of any customary or social obligation, or

(iii) in pursuance of an obligation developing on him by succession, or

(iv) for any economic consideration received by him or by any of his lineal ascendants or descendants, or

(v) by reason of his birth in any particular caste or community.

he would—

(1) render, by himself or through any member of his family, or any person dependant on him, labour or service to the creditor, or for the benefit of the creditor, for a specified period or for an unspecified period, either without wages or for nominal wages, or

(2) forfeit the freedom of employment or other means of livehood for specified period or for an unspecified period, or

(3) forfeit the right to move freely throughout the territory or India, or

(4) forfeit the right to appropriate or sell at market value any of his property or product of his labour or the labour of a member of his family or any person dependent on him, and includes the system of forced, or partly forced, labour under which surety for a debtor enter, or has, or is presumed to have, entered, into an agreement with the creditor to the effect that in the event of the failure of the debtor to repay the debt, he would render the bonded labour on behalf of the debtor;

Explanation—For the removal of doubts, it is hereby declared that any system of forced or partly forced labour under which any workman being contract labourer as defined in clause (b) of sub-section (1) of Section 2 of the Contract Labour (Regulation and Abolition) Act, 1970, or an inter-State migrant workman as defined in clause (e) of sub-section (1) of Section 2 of the Inter-State Migrant Workmen (Regulation of Employment and Conditions of Service) Act, 1979 is required to render labour or service in circumstances of the nature mentioned in sub-clause (1) of this clause or is subjected to all or any disabilities referred to in sub-clauses (2) to (4) is "bonded labour system" within the meaning of this clause. [Bonded Labour System (Abolition) Act (19 of 1976), S. 2(g)].

Bonded labourer. Means a labourer who incurs, or has, or is presumed to have, incurred a bonded debt. [Bonded Labour System (Abolition) Act (19 of 1976), S. 2(f)].

Bonded sugarcane. Notification issued under Supply of "bonded sugarcane" would mean supply of sugarcane which has been secured by a bond or an agreement. *Janki Sugar Mills & Co.* v. *Commissioner of Meerut Division*, AIR 1979 SC 616, 619 [U.P. Sugarcane (Regulation of Supply and Purchase) Act (24 of 1953)].

Bonded ware-house. A warehouse under bond to the government for payment of duties and taxes on goods stored or processed. [Medicinal and Toilet Preparations (Excise Duties) Act (16 of 1955), S. 3(2)(a)].

Bondsman. One who guarantees a bond; a surety.

Bone products. The expression 'bone products' merely means anything produced or obtained from bones. Whether such derivation is by a simple physical process or by a chemical reaction would seem to make no difference to the end product. The ossein and gelatine manufactured by the respondent can, without straining the expression used in the notification, be described as 'bone products'. *Collector of Central Excise* v. *Protein Products of India Ltd.*, AIR 1989 SC 627.

Bonfire. A fire kindled, usually in some high, open, and conspicuous place; such as a hilltop as an expression of public joy or exultation, or as a beacon.

Boni judicis est ampliare jurisdictionem. A good judge will extend the limits of his jurisdiction (not to be taken too literally).

Boni judicis est causas litium dirimere. (*Maxim*) It is the duty of a good Judge to remove the causes of litigation.

Boni judicis est judicium sine dilatione mandare executioni. (*Maxim*) It is the duty of a good Judge to cause judgment to be executed without delay.

Boni judicis est lites dirimere ne lis ex lite oritur. (4 Rep. 15). It is the duty of a good judge to prevent litigation lest suit arise from suit.

Boni judicis est lites dirimere, ne lis ex lite oritur, et interest reipublicae ut sint fines litium. (*Maxim*) It is the duty of a good judge to put an end to litigation, that suit may not grow out of suit; and it concerns the welfare of the state that an end be put to litigation.

Bonitas tota aestimabitur cum pars evincitur. (*Maxim*) The value of the whole may be estimated when a part is proved.

Bonorum emptio or venditio. The purchase or sale of an insolvent estate, by or to one that offers to satisfy the largest proportion of the claims of the creditors.

Bonorum possessio. Possession of goods.

Bonorum possessio contra tabulas. [*Latin* "possession of goods against the testament"] An order authorizing the applicant to take possession of an estate contrary to testator's will.

Bonum defendentis ex integra causa; malum ex quolibet defectu. The success of a defendant depends on a perfect case; his loss arises from some defect. (II. Coke 68a)

Bonum factum. (*Latin*) A good or proper act or deed.

Bonus. A gratuity; a premium or advantage; a sum paid for services or upon a consideration in addition to or in excess of that which would ordinarily be given. (*Ame. Cye.*)

Bonus in the industrial sense as understood in our country does come out of the available surplus of profit, and when paid, it fills the gap, wholly or in part, between the living wage and actual wage. It is labour's share in the profits and as it is a remuneration which takes the form of a share in profits. *Central Bank of India* v. *Workmen*, AIR 1960 SC 12, 25.

The claim for bonus cannot be effectively made unless two conditions are satisfied; the wages paid to workman fall short of what can be properly described as living wages; and the industry must be shown to have made profits which are partly the result of the contribution made by the workmen in increasing production. *Meenakshi Mills Ltd.* v. *Workmen*, AIR 1958 SC 153, 156. [Industrial Disputes Act (14 of 1947), Ss. 10 & 11].

A sum paid for services or upon some other consideration but in addition to or in excess of that which would ordinarily be given; an extra dividend paid out of surplus profits; a portion of the profits of an insurance company distributed *pro rata* to the policyholders. [Payment of Bonus Act (21 of 1965), S. 2(21)(iv)].

Bonus judex secundum aequum et bonum judicat, et aequitatem stricto juri praefert. (*Maxim*) A good judge decides according to justice and right, and prefers equity to strict law. (*Coke Litt. 34; Broom*)

Bonus-penalty contract. A type of contract under which the contractor is guaranteed a bonus, usually a fixed sum of money, for each day the project he has undertaken to construct is completed ahead of a specified date, while he agrees to pay a penalty for each day of delay in completing the works after the specified date.

Bonus share. A share which is given by a company free to a share holder, usually in proportion to his present shareholding.

Bonus stock. A stock share which is issued without any consideration, as an enticement to buy some other type or class of security.

Book. "BOOK" includes a portion of a book and also any number of sheets connected together with a view of forming a book or portion of a book. [Registration Act (16 of 1908), S. 2(2)].

"BOOK" includes every volume, part or division of a volume and pamphlet in any language, and every sheet of music, map, chart or plan separately printed or lithographed but does not include a newspaper in conformity with the provisions of Section 5 of the Press and Registration of Books Act, 1867. [Delivery of Books and Newspapers (Public Libraries) Act (27 of 1954), S. 2(a)].

"BOOKS" shall not include brochures, commentaries, diaries, guides, journals, magazines, newspapers, pamphlets, text books for schools, tracts and other publications of similar nature, by whatever name called. [Income-tax Act (43 of 1961), S. 80QQB, *Expln.* (b)].

"Book" has the same meaning as in the Press and Registration of Books Act, 1867 (25 of 1867). [(w.e.f. 1-7-2024) Bharatiya Nagarik Suraksha Sanhita, 2023 (46 of 2023), section 98(2)(a)]

The word book as defined in the Printing Presses and Books Act (25 of 1867) includes part of a volume or pamphlet. *Emperor* v. *Hari Govind Limay*, 13 IC 827 : 14 Bom LR 40.

The term "book" in S. 34 of Indian Evidence Act (1 of 1872) means a collection of sheets of paper bound together with the intention that such binding shall be permanent, and the papers used collectively in one volume, but unbound paper, in whatever quantity, though filled up with one continuous account, are not a book of account within the purview of S. 34. [*Mukandram* v. *Dayaram*, 23 Ind Cas 893 (894)].

A collection of sheets of paper or other substance, blank, written or printed, fastened together so as to form a material whole, especially that fastened together at the back and having a cover [Registration Act (16 of 1908), S. 2(2)]; a bound volume consisting of sheets of paper not printed, containing manuscript entries; a book of account; to write or enter in a book; to engage in advance; to make a reservation in advance.

Book account. A detailed statement of debits and credits which give a history of the business transactions of an enterprise.

Book and paper and Book or Paper. Include books of account, deeds, vouchers, writings, documents, minutes and registers maintained on paper or in electronic form. [S. 2(12) of the Companies Act, 2013 (18 of 2013)]

"Book and paper" and "book or paper". Includes accounts, deeds, vouchers, writing and documents. [Companies Act (1 of 1956), S. 2(8) replaced by Companies Act, 2013].

Book-debt. A debt standing against a person in an account book.

By a "book-debt" is meant a debt which is in some way connected with the trade of the person concerned. It should be one arising out of a transaction in the ordinary course of business and usually finds its way as an entry in his books of account. Ramaiya's Companies Act, 12th Edition, P. 653) [Companies Act (1 of 1956), S. 125(4)(d)].

Book-keeper. One who keeps accounts; one whose occupation is to make a formal balanced record of pecuniary transactions in account books.

One who keeps the accounts of a business or public office. [Indian Evidence Act (1 of 1872), S. 160, ill.].

Book-keeping. The art of recording pecuniary transactions in a regular and systematical manner.

Book, Memorandum. A book containing an informal record of something that one wishes to remember or preserve for future use; a book containing a brief or informal note in writing of some transaction or an outline of an intended instrument.

Book of account regularly kept in the course of business. It is only such books as are entered up from day to day or (as in banks) from hour to hour as transactions take place, that can be considered as "books regularly kept in the course of business" within the meaning of S. 34, Indian Evidence Act (1 of 1872).

Book of accounts. Books in which merchants, businessmen, and traders generally keep their accounts.

Unbound sheets of papers in whatever quantity, though filled up with one continuous account are not a "book of account".

(See also Books of accounts.)

Book-post. Postal arrangement by which books and printed matter are conveyed at certain reduced rates; the wrappers must be left open at the ends.

Book value. The value of an asset or liability as recorded in the books of a business [Air Corporations Act (27 of 1953), S. 24(1)(f)].

Bookmark or favourites. A way for storing one's favourite Internet sites on the computer under the "Favourites" directory on Internet Explorer, the application used to browse the internet. (*Internet*)

A Web browser's file used to store URLs. (*Information Technology*)

Books of account. Unbound sheets of papers in whatever quantity, though filled up with one continuous account are not a "book of account." A book which merely contains entries of items of which no account is made, is not a book of account. The term "book of account" signifies a collection of sheets of paper bound together with the intention that such binding shall be permanent and the papers used collectively in one volume. (*Makumd Ram* v. *Durga Ram*, 23 IC 839 : 10 NLR 44)

'BOOKS OF ACCOUNT' includes ledgers, day-books, cash-books, account-books and other accounts whether kept in the written or printed form and data stored on a floppy, disc, tape or any other form in electro-magnetic data storage device. [On-site Post Clearance Audit at the Premises of Importers and Exporters Regulations, 2011, Regn. 2(b)]

"BOOKS OF ACCOUNT" includes records maintained in respect of—(*i*) all sums of money received and expended by a company and matters in relation to which the receipts and expenditure take place; (*ii*) all sales and purchases of goods and services by the company; (*iii*) the assets and liabilities of the company; and (*iv*) the items of cost as may be prescribed under section 148 in the case of a company which belongs to any class of companies specified under that section. [S. 2(13) of the Companies Act, 2013 (18 of 2013)]

Books or books of account. Includes ledgers, day-books, cash books, account books and other books, whether kept in the written form or as print-outs of data stored in a floppy, disc, tape or any other form of electromagnetic data storage device. [Income-tax Act (43 of 1961), S. 2(12A)].

"Books of the corporate debtor" means—

(*i*) the books of account and the financial statements as defined in Sections 2(13) and 2(40) of the Companies Act, 2013,

(*ii*) the books of account as referred to in Section 34 of the Limited Liability Partnership Act, 2008, or

(*iii*) the books of accounts as specified under the applicable law, as the case may be. [Insolvency and Bankruptcy Board of India (Liquidation Process) Regulations, 2016, Regn 2(1)(a)].

Books or documents of reference. Encyclopaedia, dictionaries and other authoritative treatises on different subjects and important and authentic documents of which the Court may take judicial notice and to which it may refer without the same being formally proved. [Indian Evidence Act (1 of 1872), S. 57(13)].

Bookwright. Writer of books; an author.

Boom. To bring into prominence or public notice; push with vigour or spirit; a sudden increase of business; a rapid advance of prices.

Boot. To start up your computer. Because the computer gets itself up and going from an inert state, it could be said to lift itself up "by its own bootstraps"—this is where the term 'boot' originates.

Derived from the saying "to pull himself up by his boot-straps." In computers this refers to the process of starting up a computer, either by turning it on (a "cold boot") or by using a reset key or combination of keys (a "warm boot"). When a computer is turned on, a short program loads into memory the much larger programs that are required to operate it. (*Computer*)

Boot disk. The magnetic disk (usually a hard disk) from which an operating system kernel is loaded (or "bootstrapped"). MS-DOS and Microsoft® Windows® can be configured (in the BIOS) to try to boot off either floppy disk or hard disk, in either order (and on some modern systems even from CD or other removable media). A special floppy boot disk (often called a "System Rescue Disk") can be created, which will allow your computer to boot even if it cannot boot from the hard disk.

Boot record. Once the BIOS determines which disk to boot from, it loads the first sector of that disk into memory and executes it. Besides this loader program, the Boot Record contains the partition table for that disk. If the Boot Record is damaged, it can be a very serious situation!

Booth. A stall for the sale of goods or refreshments at a fair or market.

Bootleg. Unauthorized manufacture, reproduction or distribution of something.

Bootlegger. Bootlegger means a person who distils, manufactures, stores, transports, imports, exports, sells or distributes any liquor or a person knowingly expends any money or supplies animal or any other conveyance or material in support of doing any of the above things or a person who abets the doing of any such thing. *Ayub* v. *S.N. Sinha*, AIR 1960 SC

2069, 2071. [Gujarat Prevention of Anti Social Activities Act (16 of 1985), S. 2(b)].

Bootlegging. Illegal manufacture or sale of liquor, cigarettes, records, and the like to evade taming, licensing, copyright, etc, laws. (*Black*)

Bootstrap. To load and initialize the operating system on a computer. Often abbreviated to boot. (*Cyber Law*)

To make a success despite sparse resources; to reach an unsupported conclusion. Mostly used in the USA where *take-over* activity is most prevalent, to describe a cash offer for a controlling interest in a company which, if accepted, is followed by another offer (usually at a lower price) for the remainder of the shares. (*Banking*)

Bootstrap acquisition. Term used in connection with a friendly takeover. Threatened with a hostile takeover the target company exchanges some of its assets for shares held by dissident shareholders. Then the target company sells the rest of the company to a friendly acquirer. The friendly acquirer thus gets 100% of the target company for less than it would have paid otherwise. The target company has virtually helped finance part of the takeover. (*Stock Market*)

Booty. Property captured from the enemy in war on land as distinguished from "prize" which denotes property captured at sea.

Border. The line which separates one country, state, province or district from another; a frontier line.

Border search. A search which is conducted by immigration or customs officials at the border of the country to prevent and detect illegal entry of people or things.

Bore. The interior tube of a gun; to make a hole by boring.

Born alive. In an indictment for child murder, "born alive" means that the whole body must be brought into the world alive, and it is not sufficient that the child respires in the progress of the birth.

Born out of wedlock. A child born to a married woman, but begotten during the continuance of the marriage status by one other than her husband, is a child "born out of wedlock" within the purview of a statute making the father of a child so born liable for its maintenance, education, and support. *State* v. *Coliton,* 73 ND 582 : 17 NW2d 546 : 156 ALR 1403.

Borough. A town or city which was granted a charter of incorporation, became known as a borough, the corporation consisting of a mayor, alderman, and councillors. (*England*)

Borough Council. A Borough Council in England consists of the mayor, aldermen and councillors.

Borough Court. The Court of record. for an English borough, generally presided over by the recorder.

Borrow. "BORROW" includes the raising of money by the grant of annuities, and "loan" shall be construed accordingly. [Constitution of India, Art. 366(4)].

To take something on credit on the under-standing of returning it or an equivalent.

Borrowed capital. Term denoting various transaction between corporation and stockholders, but commonly referring to cash dividends declared by corporation and retained by it pursuant to agreement with stockholders for operating business successfully. Moneys due by corporation to another corporation used as its capital.

Borrowed money. The words "borrowed money" are used to indicate and denote money actually borrowed as a loan in the ordinary sense and not also to indicate and denote money which, though obtained on some other basis and in some other kind of transaction, could be, on the failure of such basis and such transaction, made out to be "borrowed money" in essence and in law.

The term "borrowed money" must be construed in its natural and ordinary meaning and implies a real borrowing and a real lending. *Lakshmanier & Sons* v. *Income Tax and Express Profits Tax Commissioner*, AIR 1953 SC 145, 147. [Excess Profits Tax Act (1940), Sch. II, R. 2-A].

Borrower. "BORROWER" means any person to whom any assistance has been given by an approved institution for the purposes of purchase, construction, repairs, extension or renovation of a residential house. (National Housing Bank Act (53 of 1987), S. 36C(d)].

"Borrower" means any person who, or a pooled investment vehicle as defined in clause (da) of section 2 of the Securities Contracts (Regulation) Act, 1956 (42 of 1956) which, has been granted financial assistance by any bank or financial institution or who has given any guarantee or created any mortgage or pledge as security for the financial assistance granted by any bank or financial institution and includes a person who, or a pooled investment vehicle which,] becomes borrower of an asset reconstruction company] consequent upon acquisition by it of any rights or interest of any bank or financial institution in relation to such financial assistance or who has raised funds through issue of debt securities.

"BORROWER" means a person who borrows the securities under the scheme through an approved intermediary. [Securities Lending Scheme, 1997, S. 3(1)(c)].

"BORROWER" means and individual, company, association or body of individuals, whether incorporated or not, to whom a loan has been advanced under this Act. [Rehabilitation Finance Administration Act (12 of 1948), S. 2(c)].

'BORROWER' means an individual, proprietary concern, partnership firm, Hindu undivided family or any other legal entity identified by the State Government of

Jammu and Kashmir for providing relief/rehabilitation assistance from a bank/financial institution and/or such borrowers of the banks/ financial institutions. [J&K Debtor's Relief Act (15 of 1976), S. 4. Debt Relief Scheme para 2(a)].

One who borrows; opposed to lender.

A Karta of a joint Hindu family can be a borrower in his representative capacity. *V.D. Deshpande* v. *Kusum Kulkarni*, AIR 1978 SC 1791, 1801. [Land Improvement Loans Act (19 of 1883), S. 7].

Borstal school. A school established by the State Government to detain adolescent offenders and give them such industrial training and other instruction and subject to such disciplinary measures and moral influences as will conduce to their reformation and the prevention of crime. [Bengal Borstal Schools Act (1 of 1928), S. 3(1)].

Bottling. Bottling means transferring liquor, from a cask or other vessel to a bottle, jar, flask or pot or similar receptacle of the purpose of sale whether any process of manufacture be employed or not and includes rebottling. *In Re Dr. A.L. Meganathan*, AIR 1951 Mad 996. [Madras Prohibition Act (10 of 1937), S. 4(2)(h)].

Bottomry. In marine law, the act of borrowing money and pledging the bottom of a ship, that is, the ship itself, as security for its payment.

Bottomry on the ship. A species of mortgage or hypothecation of a ship by which her keel or bottom is pledged, as security for the repayment of a sum of money. [IPC (45 of 1860), S. 425, ill. (f)].

BOTS. Programs that are installed covertly on a user's system which allows the attacker to remotely control the targeted computer through a communication channel such as Internet relay chat (IRC), peer-to-peer (P2P), or HTTP. [Symantec Global Internet Security Threat Report: Trends for 2009 (Vol. XV), April 2010 at p. 30].

Bought and sold. Bought and sold is one transaction resulting in buying on the one hand and selling on the other. *Krishna Coconut Co.* v. *E.G.C. & T.M. Committee*, AIR 1967 SC 973, 977.

Bought and sold notes. Documents which are usually delivered by brokers to their principals on the conclusion of a contract of sale and purchase, the bought note being delivered to the buyer, and the sold note to the seller.

Bought as seen. Means the purchaser has bought what he had seen.

Bound. Denotes the condition of being constrained by the obligations of a bond or a covenant.

"Bound by law", "Bound by law to pay". The words "bound by law" in Section 69, Indian Contract Act (9 of 1872) cannot restrict the section to statutory liabilities and exclude those arising out of contracts by parties.

The phrase "bound by law to pay" in S. 69 of the Indian Contract Act not only includes personal liability of the "other" but also liability on his property even when he was under no personal liability to pay.

The words 'bound by law to pay' in S. 69 of the Indian Contract Act do not exclude those obligations of law which arise inter parties whether by contract or tort and are not confined only to those public duties which are imposed by statute or general law. They extend to any obligations which is an effective bond in law.

"Bound to", "Bound for". In the law of shiping, these words denote that the vessel spoken of is designed to make a voyage to the place named.

Boundary. A visible mark indicating a dividing line or that line itself; it marks off a given thing from other things alike in kind, as one field or country from another.

Bounds. Boundaries.

Bounty. Gratuity, or an unusual or additional benefit conferred upon, or compensation paid to, a class of persons.

Bounty : Bounties. A sum of money or other things given, generally by the government, to certain persons for some service they have done or are about to do to the public.

An extra allowance to induce entry into the armed services. [Navy Act (62 of 1957), S. 49(2)(b)].

Boutique. A small specialty business; especially, a small law firm specializing in one particular aspect of law practice (a tax boutique).

Bovine. Of the oxlike; oxkind.

Bovine cattle. The expression 'species of bovine cattle' is wide enough to include and does in ordinary parlance include buffaloes (male or female, adults or calves). *M.H. Quareshi* v. *State of Bihar*, AIR 1958 SC 731, 737. [Bihar Preservation and Improvement of Animals Act (2 of 1956), S. 2].

Boycott. To combine in refusing to work for, buy from, sell to, give assistance to, or have any kind of dealings with.

Bracton. The common title of one of the earliest books of English law, *De Legibus et Consuetudinibus Angliae* (ca. 1250).

Brain death. The final stopping of activity in the central nervous system especially as indicated by a flat electro-encephalogram for a usually statutorily predetermined period of time.

Brainwash. To manipulate various psychological and morale factors so as to induce a person to reveal confidential information or to subscribe to false statements.

Branch. A division; a sub-division; a department; a component portion of an organisation or system.

BRANCH shall have the meaning assigned to it in sub-section (9) of Section 2 of the Companies Act, 1956. [Said sub-section (9) reads as follows:

"Branch of study". Means a branch of study leading to three principal levels of qualifications at bachelors (under graduate), masters (post graduate) and doctoral levels. [Central Educational Institutions (Reservation in Teachers' Cadre) Act, 2019 (10 of 2019), section 2(b)]

"Branch office". "BRANCH OFFICE", in relation to a banking company, means any branch or branch office, whether called a pay office or sub-pay office or by any other name, at which deposits are received, cheques cashed or moneys lent, and for the purposes of section 35 includes any place of business where any other form of business referred to in sub-section (1) of section 6 is transacted. [Banking Regulation Act (10 of 1949), section 5(cc)]

"BRANCH OFFICE

In relation to a company means—

(a) any establishment described as a branch by the company; or

(b) any establishment carrying on either the same or substantially the same activity as that carried on by the Head Office of the company; or

(c) any establishment engaged in any production, processing or manufacture,

but does not include any establishment specified in any order made by the Central Government under Section 8. [Foreign Exchange Management (Establishment in India of Branch or Office or Other Place of Business) Regulations, 2000, Reg. 2(c); Companies Act (1 of 1956), S. 2(9) replaced by Companies Act, 2013].

"BRANCH OFFICE" means—

(i) any establishment described as a branch by the opposite party; or

(ii) any establishment carrying on either the same or substantially the same activity as that carried on by the head office of the establishment. [Consumer Protection Act (68 of 1986), S. 2(1)(aa)] [Now repealed & replaced by Act 35 of 2019]

"Branch office" means—

(i) any office or place of work described as a branch by the establishment; or

(ii) any establishment carrying on either the same or substantially the same activity carried on by the head office of the establishment. [Consumer Protection Act, 2019 (35 of 2019), section 2(3)]

"BRANCH OFFICE" in relation to a company, means any establishment described as such by the company. [S. 2(14) of the Companies Act, 2013 (18 of 2013)]

Brand. To burn or impress or make a mark upon with a hot iron. A distinguishing name, design, or trade mark used for putting on goods or packages. It generally defines ownership, class, or quality of the goods.

Brand name. Name used to distinguish one product from its competitors. It can apply to a single, product, an entire product line, or even a company.

"Brand name" or "trade name" is defined to mean a brand name or trade name whether registered or not, that is to say a name or a mark, such as a symbol, monogram, label, signature or invented word or writing which is used in relation to such specified goods for the purpose of indicating or so as to indicate a connection in the course of trade between such specified goods and some person using such name or mark with or without any indication of the identity of that person. *Vir Rubber Products Private Limited* v. *Commissioner of Central Excise, Mumbai III,* (2015) 13 SCC 466, para 4.

Brawl : Brawling. In its original sense as a legal term, brawling meant creating a disturbance in a consecrated building or consecrated ground. In modern usage it means a clamorous or tumultuous quarrel in a public place.

Breach. The act of breaking: violation; infringement; now used only figuratively of the violation or neglect of a law, contract, or any other obligation, or of a custom.

Violation of a duty, or invasion of a right.

"BREACH". The term 'breach' is of great significance. The dictionary meaning of the term 'breach' is infringement or violation of a promise or obligation [*Collins English Dictionary*]. Also see, *Skandia Insurance Co. Ltd.* v. *Kokilaben Chandravadan*, AIR 1987 SC 1184.

Breach of confidence. Disclosure of confi-dential information without permission.

The disclosure by a person such as an employee who is in possession of confidential information to a person not authorised to receive such information. The employer can obtain Court orders restraining an employee from doing so if he can establish that the information was really confidential.

Breach of contract. The expression "BREACH OF CONTRACT" means breach of contract of service or employment and not a special contract not to go on strike. [Industrial Disputes Act (14 of 1947), S. 23].

Violation of contractual obligation.

Breach of duty. Violation of legal obligation. Failure to do one's duty.

Breach of law. The breaking or violating of a law, right, or duty, either by commission or omission. (*Burrill*)

Breach of privilege. Disregard of any of the privileges, rights and immunities either of the Members of Parliament individually or of either House of Parliament in its collective capacity or of its committees. It also includes action which obstruct the House in the performance of its functions and thereby lower its dignity and authority such as disobedience of its legitimate orders or libel upon itself, or its member or officers which are called contempt of the House. (*Constitutional and Parliamentary Term*)

Breach of promise. Not performing what one is bound to do under a contract; violation of one's word or undertaking; non-fulfilment of one's engagement: often used for breach of promise of marriage.

Breach of trust. A breach of any duty imposed on a trustee, as such, by any law for the time being in force, is called a "BREACH OF TRUST". [Indian Trusts Act (2 of 1882), S. 3].

It is violation or non-performance of the duty by a trustee, executor, administrator or any other person standing in a fiduciary position.

Any act done by a trustee contrary to the terms of his trust, or in excess of his authority and to the detriment of the trust; or the wrongful omission by a trustee of any act required of him by the terms of the trust.

Breach of the peace. Violation of the public peace, by riot, affray or any tumult contrary to law. *Breach of the peace* is an offence against the public peace.

"Peace", in this connection, means the tranquillity enjoyed by the citizens of a community.

Break. (*This word is used in many senses.*) To destroy the continuity of in any way; destroy the order or formation of. To open or force one's way into a house or a dwelling, store, *etc.*, burglariously. A house is *broken* by a burglar when any part or fastening of it is removed with intent to enter. To violate, as a contract or law, either by a positive act, neglect or non-fulfilment.

Break clause. A clause giving a party the right to terminate the contract at a particular point.

Break down. Collapse; failure.

Break-up value of shares. Net assets as shown in the company balance sheet divided by the number of shares.

The equity capital and reserves as reduced by intangible assets and revaluation reserves, divided by the number of equity shares of the investee company. [Non-Banking Financial Companies Prudential Norms (Reserve Bank) Direction, 1998, para 2(1)(i)].

Breakage. An allowance given by a manufacturer to a buyer for goods damaged during transit or storage.

Breakdown of marriage. Breakdown of marriage can be inferred, when an intolerable situation has been reached and partners are living with hostility for a considerable number of years. *Mohamed Usman* v. *Sainaba Umma,* AIR 1988 Ker 138, 139. [Dissolution of Muslim Marriage Act (8 of 1939), S. 2(*ix*)].

Breaking bulk. To remove, transfer or displace part of a load or cargo.

Breaking up or clearing for cultivation. The expression "breaking up or cleaning for cultivation" can only mean that what has been prohibited is reclaiming any portion of a protected forest for the purpose of cultivation, by breaking up the soils for the first time and it does not extend to the prohibition of cultivation of such land which has already been broken up or cleared and brought into cultivation. *State of Bihar* v. *Munshi Kahar,* AIR 1963 Pat 195, 196. [Forest Act (16 of 1927), S. 33(1)(c)].

Breath specimen. A specimen of breath for analysis taken from a person suspected of being drunk.

Breath test. In England a constable in uniform may require any person driving or attempting to drive a motor vehicle on a road or public place to provide a specimen of breath for a breath test if the constable has a reasonable cause to suspect him of having alcohol in his body or to suspect him of having committed a traffic offence while the vehicle was in motion. [Road Traffic Act, 1972, S. 8(1) and (2)].

Breeder. Means a person or group of persons or a farmer or a group of farmers or any institution which has bred, evolved or developed any variety. [Protection of Plant Varieties and Farmers' Right Act (53 of 2001), S. 2(c)].

Brethren. Brothers, specially those considered spiritual kins.

Breve de recto. A writ of right available to one who is dispossessed of an estate to recover the possession thereof.

Brew. The mixture formed by brewing; that which is brewed; a fermented liquor.

Brewery. A brew-house; an establishment in which the process of brewing is carried on. Brewers collectively; also applied to beer-trade.

Bribe. A reward or gift bestowed or promised with a view to perverting the judgment or corrupting the conduct of a judge or other officer, witness or other person. [IPC (45 of 1860), S. 171-B].

To give bribe to a person.

Bribee. One who receives a bribe.

Briber. One who offers a bribe.

Bribery. Whoever—

(i) gives a gratification to any person with the object of inducing him or any other person to exercise any electoral right or, of rewarding any person for having exercised any such right; or

(ii) accepts either for himself or for any other person any gratification as a reward for exercising any such right or for inducing or attempting to induce any other person to exercise any such right,

Commits the offence of bribery:

Provided that a declaration of public policy or a promise of public action shall not be an offence under this section. [IPC (45 of 1860), S. 171-B(1)] [(w.e.f. 1-7-2024) repealed and replaced by Bharatiya Nyaya Sanhita, 2023 (45 of 2023), section 170(1)]

"Bribery", that is to say,—

(A) any gift, offer or promise by a candidate or his agent or by any other person with the consent of a candidate or his agent of any gratification, to any person whatsoever, with the object, directly or indirectly of inducing,—

(a) a person to stand or not to stand as, or to withdraw or not to withdraw from being a candidate at an election, or

(b) an elector to vote or refrain from voting at an, or as a reward to

(i) a person for having so stood or not stood, or for having withdrawn or not having withdrawn his candidature; or

(ii) an elector for having voted or refrained from voting;

(B) The receipt of, or agreement to receive, and gratification, whether as a motive or reward—

(a) by a person for standing or not standing as, or for withdrawing or not withdrawing, from being, a candidate, or

(b) by any person whomsoever for himself or any other person for voting or refraining from voting, or inducing or attempting to induce any elector to vote or refrain from voting, or any candidate to withdraw or not to withdraw his candidature.

Explanation.—For the purpose of this clause, the term "gratification" is not restricted to pecuniary gratifications or gratifications estimable in money and it includes all forms of entertainment and all forms of employment for reward but it does not include the payment of any expenses *bona fide* incurred at or for the purpose of, any election and duly entered in the account of election expenses referred to in section 78.. [The Representation of the People Act, 1951, S. 123(1)]

BRIBERY, is a high offence, where a person, in a judicial place, or holding a public office takes any fee, gift, reward, or brokerage, for doing his office, or by colour of his office. (*Tomlin*)

Brick earth. 'Brick earth' is minor mineral within S. 3(*e*). *Sharma & Co.,* v. *State of U.P.,* AIR 1975 All 386, 389. [Mines and Minerals (Regulation and Development) Act (67 of 1957), S. 3(*e*)].

Bridge financing. Interim financing, before a long-term financing is put in place.

Bridging loan. It is a short term advance made by a bank to a customer pending the receipt by the customer of funds from some other source.

Brief. A summary of acts and points of law drawn up for counsel in charge of a case; concise; succinct.

To abridge; shorten; make a brief of: as, to brief pleadings.

Brigade. Division of troops or soldiers, whether cavalry or infantry, regulars or militia, consisting of several regiments, squadrons or battalions under the command of a brigadier, or brigadier-general.

A sub-division of army. [Army Act (46 of 1950), S. 8].

Brigade area. Means one of the Brigade areas, whether occupied by a brigade or not, into which India is for military purposes for the time being divided, and includes any area which the Central Government may, by notification in the Official Gazette, declare to be a Brigade area for all or any of the purposes of this Act. [Cantonments (House-Accommodation Act (6 of 1923), S. 2(a)].

Bring. To fetch or put forward before a tribunal; institute; as, to bring an action or a charge against one; the jury brought the prisoner in guilty. *See* 1936 ALJ 962 : 1936 All 743.

Bring into action. To bring into the battle. [Navy Act (62 of 1957), S. 34(a)].

Bring suit or action. To "bring" a suit is to initiate legal proceedings in a suit.

Bring to book. To arrest and to put to trial an offender.

British Officer. Means a person of non-Indian domicile holding a commission in His Majesty's Land forces or in the Royal Marines or in the Territorial Army and serving in the regular army. [Army Act (46 of 1950), S. 195(1) repealed by 37 of 1992 (w.e.f. 6-9-1992)].

"BRITISH OFFICER" means (1) a person of non-Indian domicile holding a commission in His Majesty's Air Force and serving in the Air Force; (2) The expression "superior officer" in this Act shall be deemed to include a British officer. [Air Force Act (45 of 1950), S. 193(1)].

British possession. "BRITISH POSSESSION" means any Part of His Majesty's Dominions other than British India, the United Kingdom and Ireland, and includes Protectorates and territories which are or may be administered by Dominion as a mandatory on behalf of the League of Nations. [Act III of 1924 (Immigration into India), S. 2, Cl. (*a*)].

"BRITISH POSSESSION" means any part of His Majesty's dominions and includes protectorate or other territory administered by a British possession a mandatory on behalf of the League of Nations, and where parts of those dominions are under both a central and a local Legislature, the expression shall mean either each part under a local Legislature or all parts under central legislature. [Reciprocity Act (9 of 1943), S. 2(a)].

British protected person. "BRITISH PROTECTED PERSON" means a person who is a member of a class of persons declared by Order in Council made in relation to any protectorate, protected state, mandated territory or trust territory to be for the purposes of this Act British protected persons by virtue of their connection with that protectorate, State or territory. [British Nationality Act, 1948 (11 and 12 Geo. VL.C. 56), Part II, (32)(1)].

One of a class of people defined as such by an order under the British Nationality Act 1981 or the Solomon Islands Act 1978 because of their connection with former protectorates, protected states, and trust territories.

Broad construction. In construing either the Constitution or a statute, that interpretation which, brushing aside minor objections and trivial technicalities, effectuates the intent of the act, is a broad construction.

Broadcast. Means communication to the public—

(i) by means of wireless diffusion, whether in any one or more of the forms of signs, sounds or visual images;

(ii) by wire,

and includes a re-broadcast. [Copyright Act (14 of 1957), S. 2(dd)].

Broadband. Broadband is a descriptive term for evolving digital technologies that provide consumers a signal switched facility offering integrated access to voice, high speed data service, video demand services, and interactive delivery services. (*Telecommunications*)

Broadcast. Means communication to the public—(*i*) by means of wireless diffusion, whether in any one or more of the forms of signs, sounds or visual images; (*ii*) by wire, and includes a re-broadcast. [Copyright Act (14 of 1957), S. 2(dd)].

Broadcaster. 'Broadcaster' means any person who provides a content broadcasting service and includes a broadcasting network service provider when he manages and operates his own television or radio channel service. [Sports Broadcasting Signals (Mandatory Sharing with Prasar Bharti) Act (11 of 2007), S. 2(1)(a)]

'Broadcaster' means any person including an individual, group of persons, body corporate, firm or any organisation or body, who, or which, is providing programming services and includes his authorised distribution agencies. [Standards of Quality of Service (Broadcasting and Cable Services) (Cable Television Non-CAS Areas) Regulations 2009, Regn. 2(e)].

Broadcasting. "BROADCASTING" means the dissemination of any form of communication like signs, signals, writing, pictures, images sounds of all kinds by transmission of electromagnetic waves through space or through cables intended to be received by the general public either directly or indirectly through the medium of relay stations and all its grammatical variations and cognate expressions shall be construed accordingly. [Prasar Bharati (Broadcasting Corpn. of India) Act (25 of 1990), S. 2(c)].

"BROADCASTING" has the meaning assigned to it in clause (c) of Section 2 of the Prasar Bharati (Broadcasting Corporation of India) Act, 1990 and also includes programme selection, scheduling or presentation of sound or visual matter on a radio or a television channel that is intended for public listening or viewing, as the case may be; and in the case of a broadcasting agency or organisation, having its head office situated in any place outside India, includes the activity of selling of time slots or obtaining sponsorships for broadcasting of any programme or collecting the broadcasting charges on behalf of the said agency or organisation, by its branch office or subsidiary or representative in India or any agent appointed in India or by any person who acts on its behalf in any manner. [Finance Act (32 of 1994), S. 65 (15) *as substituted by Finance Act (32 of 2003), S. 159* (now repealed by Central Goods and Services Tax Act, 2017)].

The act of transmitting speech and visual images *etc.* by radio or television.

Broadcasting agency or organization. Means any agency or organisation engaged in providing service in relation to broadcasting in any manner and, in the case of a broadcasting agency or organisation, having its head office situated in any place outside India, includes its branch office or subsidiary or representative in India or any agent appointed in India or any person who acts on its behalf in any manner, engaged in the activity of selling of time slots for broadcasting of any programme or obtaining sponsorships for programme or collecting broadcasting charges on behalf of the said agency or organisation. [Finance Act (32 of 2003), S. 159 substituted S. 65(16) of Finance Act (32 of 1994) (now repealed by Central Goods and Services Tax Act, 2017)].

Broadcasting networks service. 'Broadcasting networks service' means a service, which provides a network of infrastructure of cables or transmitting devices for carrying broadcasting content in electronic form on specified frequencies by means of guided or unguided electro-magnetic waves to multiple users, and includes the management and operation of any of the following: (*i*) Teleport/ Hub/Earth Station, (*ii*) Direct-to-Home (DTH) Broadcasting Network, (*iii*) Multi-system Cable Television Network, (*iv*) Local Cable Television Network, (*v*) Satellite Radio Broadcasting Network, (*vi*) any other network service as may be prescribed by the Central Government. [Sports Broadcasting Signals (Mandatory Sharing with Prasar Bharti) Act (11 of 2007), S. 2(1)(d)].

Broader than the invention. (Of a patent claim) having a scope that exceeds the limits of the invention disclosed in the application or patent.

Brocage. The wages or hire of a broker.

Brochures. A pamphlet; a booklet of salient facts on a subject.

Broker. "BROKER" means a broker of tea. [Tea Act (29 of 1953), S. 2(a)].

A middleman or agent who, for a commission on the value of the transaction, negotiates for others the purchase or sale of stocks, bonds, commodities, or property of any kind, or who attends to the doing of something for another.

Broker and **Factor.** A broker is an agent employed to negotiate and make contracts on behalf of his principal, and, in general, contracts of sale or purchase. He is not put into possession of the property to be sold as a factor.

Brokerage. The business of a broker; commission paid to a broker. [Companies Act (1 of 1956), S. 165(3)(h) replaced by Companies Act, 2013].

The wages or hire of a broker.

If the company employs a broker to act as a broker in the issue of the capital, the payment by the company to such broker of a proper commission or brokerage for placing shares is legitimate, and it is not necessary to look into the memorandum for authority to pay it. [Companies Act (1 of 1956), S. 77 replaced by Companies Act, 2013].

Broker's cover note. A note which is issued by a broker pending the preparation of the policy certifying that the insurance has been effected and setting out its terms.

Brothel. House of lewdness; a house appropriated to the purpose of prostitution. "Place, where people of opposite sexes are allowed to resort for prostitution."

The definition of 'Brothel' implies that the premises must have been used for the purpose of prostitution for the gain of another person or for the mutual gain of two or more persons. [Suppression of Immoral Traffic in Women and Girls Act (104 of 1956), S. 3(1)].

A house appropriated to the purpose of prostitution. [Children Act (60 of 1960), S. 2(d)].

Brother-german. A full brother; brother on both the father's and the mother's side.

Brought in transit. Means to bring goods from any country into India by land, air, or amphibious means of transportation, where the goods are to be taken out from India on the same conveyance on which they are brought into India without any landing in India, but does not include a conveyance in innocent passage through Indian territory, Indian territorial waters or Indian airspace of a foreign conveyance carrying goods.

Explanation I.—A conveyance is a foreign conveyance if it is not registered in India.

Explanation II.—A conveyance is in "innocent passage" if it is not engaged in relevant activity and passes through or above Indian territorial waters or airspace without stopping or anchoring in India. [Weapons of Mass Destruction and their Delivery Systems (Prohibition of Unlawful Activities) Act (21 of 2005), S. 4(6)].

Browser. A software program, such as Netscape Communicator or Microsoft's Internet Explorer, that allows you to read and download web documents. (*Information Technology*)

A *Client* program (software) that is used to look at various kinds of Internet resources. (*Matisse Enzer-Glossary of Internet Terms*)

Browsewrap agreement. Browsewrap terms do not require an express consent of the user and its terms are generally accessible through a hyperlink on the website. Merely by browsing a website if a user's consent is deemed, it forms a broswewrap agreement. [Karnika Seth, *Computers Internet and New Technology Laws*, 2021, LexisNexis, Glossary of Legal Terms]

Bruise. (*Medical jurisprudence.*) Contusion; superficial injury upon the flesh of a person with a blunt or heavy instrument without breaking the skin.

Brutal. Inhuman. Stupidly cruel. [Geneva Conventions Act (6 of 1960), III Sch., Art. 89].

Pertaining to, or resembling a brute; brutish; savage.

Bubo. (*in Med. Jur.*) An inflammatory swelling of a lymphatic gland, especially such as arises in the groin from otaliza infection.

Bucket-shop. A dishonest brokerage house.

Budapest Treaty. "BUDAPEST TREATY" means the Budapest Treaty on the International Recognition of the Deposit of Micro-organisms for the purposes of Patent Procedure done at Budapest on 28th day of April, 1977, as amended and modified from time to time. [Patents Act (39 of 1970), S. 2(1) (aba) *as inserted as by the Patents (Amendment) Act (15 of 2005), S. 2(a)*].

Budget. The annual financial statement of the Government presented to the Legislature. In making this statement the minister in charge gives a view of the general financial policy of the Government, and at the same time presents an estimate of the probable income and expenditure for the following 12 months, and a statement of what taxes it is intended to reduce or abolish, or what new ones it may be necessary to impose.

Budget deficit. When the estimated income falls short as against the budgeted expenditure.

Buffer. A person who takes pay to swear falsely; a hired perjurer.

(*In Railroad law*) An apparatus attached to railroad-cars to prevent injury from violent contact or collision.

Buffer state. One situated between more powerful neighbours which relies for its security largely on the fact that no one neighbouring state is prepared to let it be occupied by a third state.

Buffer stocks. Stocks of raw materials and commodities held for the purpose of reducing fluctuations in the prices of primary products. Buffer stocks may be used to match the supplies coming on to a market with the current demand in order to narrow the movement of prices. Usually a "ceiling" and a "floor" price is fixed for a commodity; when the ceiling price is reached, stocks are released on to the market and, conversely, when the floor price is reached stocks are increased.

Buffet. An error, such as a design flaw, in software or hardware. (*Computer*)

Bugger. One guilty of the unnautral crime of buggery; a sodomite.

Buggery or sodomy. A carnel intercourse against nature, and this is either by the confusion of species; that is to say, a man or a woman with a brute beast; a man with a man, or a man otalizator with a woman. (*Tomlin*)

"Buggery" is said to be synonymous with sodomy. [Stroud's Judicial Dictionary as cited in *Suresh Kumar Koushal* v. *Naz Foundation*, (2014) 1 SCC 1, para 59.9.

A carnal copulation against nature : a man or a woman with a brute beast, a man with a man, or man unnaturally with a woman. *Suresh Kumar Koushal* v. *Naz Foundation*, (2014) 1 SCC 1, para 48.

Bugging. An electronic device to intercept, overhear or record conversations.

Build. To construct. [Indian Contract Act (9 of 1872), S. 73, ill.(I)].

Building. "BUILDING" means a house, outhouse, stable latrine, urinal, sheet house, hut, wall (other than a boundary wall) or any other structure whether made of masonry, bricks, wood, mud, metal or other material. [Employment of Manual Scavengers and Construction of Dry Latrines Act (46 of 1993), S. 2(b); Delhi Fire Prevention and Fire Safety Act (56 of 1986), S. 2(c) and Manipur Municipalities Act (43 of 1994), S. 2(2)].

"Building" means 'a structure of edifice inclosing a space within its walls, and usually, but not necessarily, covered with a roof'. Black's Law Dictionary (5th Edn.) as cited in *Shaha Ratansi Khimji and Sons* v. *Kumbhar Sons Hotel Private Limited*, (2014) 14 SCC 1, para 18.

'Building' means 'an edifice, erected by art, and fixed upon or over the soil, composed of brick, marble, wood, or other proper substance, connected together, and designed for use in the position in which it is so fixed.' Bourvier's Law Dictionary (A Concise Encyclopaedia of the Law, Vol. 1, 3rd revision) as cited in *Shaha Ratansi Khimji and Sons* v. *Kumbhar Sons Hotel Private Limited*, (2014) 14 SCC 1, para 18.

'Building' means which is built; a structure, edifice : now a structure of the nature of a house built where it is to stand. Oxford Dictionary as cited in *Shaha Ratansi Khimji and Sons* v. *Kumbhar Sons Hotel Private Limited*, (2014) 14 SCC 1, para 18.

"BUILDING" means a house, out-house, stable, latrine, urinal, shed, hut, wall (other than a boundary wall) or any other structure, whether of masonry, bricks, wood, mud, metal or other material but does not include any portable shelter. [New Delhi Municipal Council Act (44 of 1994), S. 2(4)].

"BUILDING" as referred to in the definition of chemical weapons production facility in Article II comprises specialized buildings and standard buildings:

(a) "Specialized Building" means:

(i) Any building, including underground structures, containing specialized equipment in a production or filling configuration;

(ii) Any building, including underground structures, which has distinctive features which distinguish it from buildings normally used for chemical production or filling activities not prohibited under this Convention.

(b) "Standard Building" means any building, including underground structures, constructed to prevailing industry standards for facilities not producing any chemical specified in Article II, paragraph 8(a)(i), or corrosive chemicals. [Chemical Weapons Convention Act (34 of 2000), (Verification Annex) 2].

"BUILDING" means any structure or erection or part of structure or erection after the rules relating to energy conservation building codes have been notified under clause (p) of section 14 and clause (a) of section 15 and includes any existing structure or erection or part of structure or erection, which is having a connected load of 100 Kilowatt (kW) or contract demand of 120 Kilovolt Ampere (kVA) and above and is used or intended to be used for commercial purposes. [Energy Conversation Act (52 of 2001), S. 2(c) *Substituted by Act 28 of 2010*].

"BUILDING" means any work of construction done in any manner by use of any material and includes a farm building for agricultural purposes, plinth, doorstep, wall, drain, advertisement board and other things fixed with such building. [Control of National Highways (Land and Traffic) Act, 2002 (13 of 2003), S. 2(b)].

"BUILDING" means a house, outhouse, stable, latrine, shed, hut or other roofed structure, whether of masonry, brick, wood, mud, metal or other material, and any part thereof, and includes a well and a wall other than a boundary wall but does not include a tent or other portable and temporary shelter. [Cantonments Act (2 of 1924), S. 2(iv)].

"'Building' means any structure for whatsoever purpose and of whatsoever materials constructed and every part thereof whether used as human habitation or not and includes foundation, plinth, walls, floors, roofs, chimneys, plumbing and building services, fixed platforms, otaliza, balcony, cornice or projection, part of a building or anything affixed thereto or any wall enclosing or intended to enclose any land or space and signs and outdoor display structures;

Explanation—Tents, shamianas, tarpauline shelters, *etc.*, shall not be considered as building". [Regulation 2(12), Bhubaneshwar Development

Authority (Planning and Building Standards) Regulations 1993].

"BUILDING" means and includes any building, or part of a building, which is, or is intended to be, let separately for use as a residence or for commercial use or for any other purpose, and includes the garden, grounds and outhouses, if any, appertaining to such building or part of the building; any furniture supplied by the landlord for use in such building or part of the building, but doe not include a room in a hotel or lodging house. [Goa, Daman and Diu Buildings (Lease, Rent and Eviction) Control Act (2 of 1969), S. 2I].

'BUILDING' means any building or hut or part of a building or hut, let or to be let separately for residential or non-residential purposes and includes—

(a) the garden, grounds and outhouses, if any, appurtenant to such building, hut or part of such building or hut and let or to be let along with such building or hut,

(b) any furniture supplied by the landlord for use in such but does not include a room in a hotel or boarding house. [T.N. Building (Lease and Rent Control) Act (18 of 1960), S. 2(2)].

As a house, out house, garage or any other structure cannot be erected without the ground on which it is to stand, the expression "building" includes, the fabric of which it is composed, the ground upon which its walls stand and the ground within those walls. *D.G. Gouse & Co.* v. *State of Kerala*, AIR 1980 SC 271, 278.

The existence of a roof is not always necessary for a structure to be regarded as a building. Residential buildings ordinarily have roofs but there can be a non-residential building for which a roof is not necessary. *Ghanshiam Das* v. *Devi Prasad*, AIR 1966 SC 1998, 1999. [Income Tax Act (43 of 1961), S. 32].

The roads laid within the factory premises as links or providing approach to the buildings are necessary adjuncts to the factory buildings to carry on the business activity and they would be 'building' within the meaning of S. 32. *I.T. Commissioner, Bombay* v. *Gwalior Rayon Silk Manufacturing Co. Ltd.*, AIR 1992 SC 1782, 1788. [Income Tax Act (43 of 1961), S. 32].

'BUILDING' means a house, out-house, stable, latrine, urinal, shed, hut, wall (other than a boundary wall) or any other structure, whether masonry, bricks, wood, mud, metal or other material but does not include any portable shelter. *Gas Authority of India Ltd.* v. *Municipal Corporation of Delhi*, AIR 1999 Del 210, 215, para 18. [Delhi Municipal Corporation Act (66 of 1957), S. 2(3)].

A caravan kiosk used as a booth for selling goods to which electric light and power were supplied is a 'building'.

That which is built. [Constitution of India, Art. 31 A, Second prov.].

"BUILDING" is broadly defined as meaning any house or hut or a part of a house or a hut, let or to be let separately for residential or non-residential purposes. *S. Mohan Lal* v. *R. Kondiah*, AIR 1979 SC 1132.

'BUILDING' means any house or hut or a part of a house or hut, let or to be let separately for residential or non-residential purposes and includes:

(*a*) the gardens, grounds, garages and outhouses if any appurtenant to such house, but or part of such house or hut and let or to be let alongwith such house or hut or part of such house or hut,

(*b*) any furniture supplied or any fittings affixed by the landlord for use in such house or hut or part of a house or hut, but does not include a room in a hotel or boarding house. [*A.P. Buildings (Lease, Rent and Eviction) Control Act (15 of 1960), S. 2(iii)* **as cited in** *Noorunnissa Begum* v. *Brij Kishore Sanghi,* (2015) 17 SCC 128, para 12].

"Building" means any structure or erection or part of structure or erection–

(i) constructed after the rules relating to energy conservation and sustainable building codes have been notified by the Central Government under clause (p) of section 14 and by the State Government under clause (a) of section 15;

(ii) which has a minimum connected load of 100 Kilowatt (kW) or contract demand of 120 Kilovolt Ampere (kVA); and

(iii) which is used or intended to be used for commercial purpose or as an office building or for residential purpose:

Provided that the State Government may specify a lower connected load or contract demand than the load or demand specified above. [Energy Conservation Act, 2001 (52 of 2001), section 2(c)]

'BUILDING' includes a house, outhouse, shop, stable, latrine, shed (other than a cattle shed in an agricultural land), hut, wall and any other such structure whether of masonry, bricks, wood, mud, metal or other material whatsoever. [A.P. Panchayat Raj Act (13 of 1994), S. 2(3) **as cited in** *Indian Oil Corporation Limited* v. *A.P. Industrial Infrastructure Corporation Limited,* (2016) 14 SCC 655, para 10].

"BUILDING" includes a house, out house, stable, shed, but and other enclosure or structure whether of masonry, bricks, wood, mud, metal or any other material whatever whether used as a human dwelling or otherwise, and also includes verandahs, fixed platforms, plinth, doorsteps, walls including compound walls and fencing and the like. [Gujarat Provincial Municipal Corporation Act (59 of 1949), S. 2(5) **as cited in** *Ahmedabad Municipal Corpo-*

ration v. *GTL Infrastructure Limited,* (2017) 3 SCC 545, para 6].

Building bye-laws. Means bye-laws made under section 481 of the Delhi Municipal Corporation Act, 1957 (66 of 1957) or the bye-laws made under section 188, section 189(3) and section 190(1) of the Punjab Municipal Act, 1911 (Punjab Act 3 of 1911), as in force in New Delhi or the regulations made under section 57(1) of the Delhi Development Act, 1957 (61 of 1957), relating to buildings. [S. 2(1)(a) of the National Capital Territory of Delhi Laws (Special Provisions) Act, 2011 (5 of 2011)]

Building lease. A lease which is generally for a term of 99 years, at a rent known as a ground rent, under which the lessee convenants to erect certain specified buildings on the land demised by the lease and to insure and keep in repair such buildings during the term.

Building-line. Means a line (in rear of the street alignment) up to which the main wall of a building abutting on a street may lawfully extend. [Ben. Act III of 1899 (Municipal), S. 3, Cl. 3].

Building or other construction work. Means the construction, alteration, repairs, maintenance or demolition, of or, in relation to, buildings, streets, roads, railways, tramways, airfields, irrigation, drainage, embankment and navigation works, flood control works (including storm water drainage works), generation, transmission and distribution of power, water works (including channels for distribution of water), oil and gas installations, electric lines, wireless, radio, television, telephone, telegraph and overseas communications, dams, canals, reservoirs, watercourses, tunnels, bridges, viaducts, aqueducts, pipelines, towers, cooling towers, transmission towers and such other work as may be specified in this behalf by the appropriate Government, by notification but does not include any building or other construction work to which the provisions of the Factories Act, 1948, or the Mines Act, 1952 apply. [Building and Other Construction Workers (Regulation of Employment and Conditions of Service) Act (27 of 1996), S. 21(d)].

"Building or other construction work" means the construction, alteration, repairs, maintenance or demolition in relation to buildings, streets, roads, railways, tramways, airfields, irrigation, drainage, embankment and navigation works, flood control works (including storm water drainage works), generation, transmission and distribution of power, water works (including channels for distribution of water), oil and gas installations, electric lines, internet towers, wireless, radio, television, telephone, telegraph and overseas communications, dams, canals, reservoirs, watercourses, tunnels, bridges, viaducts, aqua-ducts, pipelines, towers, cooling towers, transmission towers and such other work as may be specified in this behalf by the Central Government, by notification, but does not include any building or other construction work which is related to any factory or mine or any building or other construction work employing less than ten workers in the preceding twelve months or where such work is related to own residential purposes of an individual or group of individuals for their own residence and the total cost of such work does not exceed fifty lakhs rupees or such higher amount and employing more than such number of workers as may be notified by the appropriate Government. [Code on Social Security, 2020 (36 of 2020), section 2(6)]

"Building or other construction work" means the construction, alteration, repairs, maintenance or demolition in relation to buildings, streets, roads, railways, tramways, airfields, irrigation, drainage, embankment and navigation works, flood control works (including storm water drainage works), generation, transmission and distribution of power, water works (including channels for distribution of water), oil and gas installations, electric lines, internet towers, wireless, radio, television, telephone, telegraph and overseas communications, dams, canals, reservoirs, watercourses, tunnels, bridges, viaducts, aqua-ducts, pipelines, towers, cooling towers, transmission towers and such other work as may be specified in this behalf by the Central Government, by notification, but does not include building or other construction work which is related to any factory or mine and the building or other construction work where such work is for own residential purposes of an individual or group of individuals for their own residence and the total cost of such work does not exceed rupees fifty lakhs or such higher amount and employing more than such number of workers as may be notified by the appropriate Government. [Occupational Safety, Healthy & Working Conditions Code, 2020 (37 of 2020), section 2(1)(h)]

Building regulations. Means the rules or regulations or bye-laws made under any law for the time being in force for the erection or re-erection of buildings or parts thereof and for the purpose of this Act includes Zoning Regulations framed under any law for the time being in force. [Punjab Apartment and Property Regulation Act (14 of 1995), S. 2(h)].

Building worker. Means a person who is employed to do any skilled, semi-skilled or unskilled, manual, supervisory, technical or clerical work for hire or reward, whether the terms of employment be expressed or implied, in connection with any building or other construction work but does not include any such person

(i) who is employed mainly in a managerial or administrative capacity; or

(ii) who, being employed in a supervisory capacity, draws wages exceeding one thousand six hundred rupees *per mensem* or exercises, either by the nature of the duties attached to the office or by reason of the powers vested in him, functions mainly of a managerial nature. [Building and Other Construction Workers (Regulation of Employment and Conditions of Service) Act (27 of 1996), S. 21(e)].

"Building worker" means a person who is employed to do any skilled, semi-skilled or unskilled, manual, technical or clerical work for hire or reward, whether the terms of such employment are express or implied, in connection with any building or other construction work, but does not include any such person who is employed mainly in a managerial or supervisory or administrative capacity. [Code on Social Security, 2020 (36 of 2020), section 2(7)]

"Building worker" means a person who is employed to do any highly skilled, skilled, semi-skilled or unskilled, manual, technical or clerical work for hire or reward, whether the terms of such employment are express or implied, in connection with any building or other construction work, but does not include any such person who is employed mainly in a managerial or supervisory or administrative capacity. [Occupational Safety, Healthy & Working Conditions Code, 2020 (37 of 2020), section 2(1)(i)]

"Building Workers' Welfare Board". Means the State Building and other Construction Workers' Welfare Board constituted under sub-section (*1*) of section 7. [Code on Social Security, 2020 (36 of 2020), section 2(8)]

Built-up area. means the inner measurements of the residential unit at the floor level, including projections and balconies, as increased by the thickness of the walls, but does not include the common areas shared with other residential units, including any open terrace so shared. [Income-tax Act (43 of 1961), S. 80-IBA(6)(a) as inserted by Finance Act (28 of 2016), s. 44 replaced by definition of "carpet area" by Finance Act, 2017 (w.e.f. 1-4-2018)].

Means the inner measurements of the residential unit at the floor level, including the projections and balconies, as increased by the thickness of the walls but does not include the common areas shared with other residential units. [Income-tax Act (43 of 1961), S. 80IB (14)(a) *substituted by Finance (No. 2) Act (23 of 2004), S. 18(g)(A)*].

For the purposes of this section, "BUILT-UP AREA" means the inner measurements of the residential unit at the floor level, including projections and balconies, as increased by the thickness of the walls, but does not include the common areas shared with other residential units, including any open terrace so shared. [Income-tax Act (43 of 1961), S. 80-IBA (6), *Explanation (a)*].

"BUILT-UP AREA" means the total covered areas on all floors of a building from the basement to all storeys covered by walls and parapet measured at the floor levels excluding parking. [Energy Conservation Building Code Rules, 2018, R. 291)(d)].

Bulk. The gross; the greater part; the main portion as, the bulk of a debt; the bulk of a nation; the bulk of one's fortune.

Volume [Coffee Act (7 of 1942), S. 3(h)]; the mass. [Naval and Aircraft Prize Act (59 of 1971), S. 8(1)].

Bulk buying. Purchasing in sufficient quantities to obtain a discount on the normal retail price.

Bulk cargo. Cargo or goods not in packages, boxes, *etc.* [Indian Dock Labourers Act (19 of 1934), S. 5(1)(a) repealed by Act 54 of 1986 (w.e.f 7-12-1986)].

Bulk consumer. Means a consumer such as the Departments of Central Government like Railways, Defence, Telecom, Posts and Telegraph, the Departments of State Government, the Undertakings, Boards and other agencies or companies who purchase hundred or more than hundred batteries per annum. [Batteries (Management and Handling) Rules, 2001, R. 3(f) substituted by the Batteries (Management and Handling) Amendment Rules, 2010].

Bulk drug. The drug capable of use by itself or as an ingredient in any formulation. *Balakrishna Pillai* v. *Matha Medicals,* (1991) 2 SCC 203, 207 : 1991 Cr LJ 691 (SC).

Bulk licensee. Means a licensee who otalizatosed by his licence to supply electricity to other licensees for distribution by them. [Electricity (Supply) Act (54 of 1948), S. 2(3) repealed by Act 36 of 2003 (w.e.f. 10-6-2003).] [Now repealed by Act 36 of 2003]

Bull. (*Stock Exchange term*) One who intrigues for a rise in the market; one who buys, or contracts, to buy shares in the expectation of rise in price and to sell at a higher price.

Bull-baiting. The practice of baiting or attacking bulls with dogs; a sport formerly very popular in England, but made illegal in 1835.

Bull-doze. To bully; to punish summarily with a bull-whip; especially in politics to coerce, to intimidate by violence or threats.

Bull market. Prolonged rise in the price of shares, sustained by buying pressure of actual investors. (*Depositories*)

A rising market with abundance of buyers and relatively few sellers. (*Capital Market*)

Condition in which share prices are rising. *Bulls* are speculators who buy shares in anticipation of rising prices. (*Banking*)

A market in which rises in commodity prices over several months or more have been accompanied by high levels of business. (*Trade Finance*)

A securities market which is characterized by falling prices over prolonged period.

Bulletin. An official report concerning some public event.

Bulletin-board. A board put up in a public place on which to placard important announcements, recent news, notices, *etc.*

One computer running software allowing multiple people to access the same information and to post information. Virtually all bulletin boards are text and graphics only, although they could become capable of displaying audio visual works. (*Information Technology*)

Web-based message forum where visitors can read, post, and reply to messages or questions left by other visitors.

Bullion. Uncoined gold or silver.

"BULLION", according to its plain ordinary meaning means gold or silver in the mass. It connotes gold or silver regarded as raw material and it may be either in the form of raw gold or silver or ingots or bars of gold or silver. *Deputy CST* v. *G. S. Pai & Co.*, AIR 1980 SC 611.

Bullion and specie. Bullion means gold or silver in the mass. Ornaments and other articles of gold cannot be regarded as 'bullion', because even if old and antiquated, they are not raw or unwrought gold or gold in the mass. The word 'specie' means any metallic coin which is used as currency. *Deputy Commissioner of Sales Tax* v. *Advani Coorlikon (P) Ltd.*, AIR 1980 SC 609, 612, 613; *Department Commissioner of Sales Tax (Law) Board of Revenue (Taxes Ernakulam)* v. *G.S. Pai & Co.*, AIR 1980 SC 611, 612.

Bullion market. A market at which precious metals and gold and silver coins are traded.

Bumper draw of a lottery. Means a special draw of lottery conducted on or during any festival or other special occasion wherein the prize money offered is greater than the prize money offered in the case of other ordinary draw of lotteries. [Lotteries (Regulation) Act (17 of 1998), S. 2(a)].

Bundoobust. A settlement of the amount of revenue to be paid or collected.

Buoy. To support; to sustain; keep afloat in a fluid; bear up or keep from sinking, as, in water or air. (*In Maritime Law*)

Buoyant apparatus. Means flotation equipment (other than lifeboats, liferafts, lifebuoys and life-jackets) designed to support a specified number of persons who are in the water and of such construction that it retains its shapes and properties. [International Conference on Safety of Life at Sea, 1974, Part A, Reg. 2(e)].

Burden. Duty; responsibility.

Burden of a contract. The liability to perform a contract or discharge the obligations of a contract for the benefit of the other party to the contract.

Burden of allegation. Duty of a party to plead a matter in order for that matter to be heard in the lawsuit.

Burden of production. Duty of a party to introduce enough evidence to have a given issue considered by the fact-finder in the case, instead of deciding it against him in a peremptory ruling such as summary judgment or a directed verdict or a non suit.

Burden of proof. The duty of a party to prove a disputed assertion or charge. The necessity which lies, now, on one party, now on the other, of calling evidence, to prevent judgment going against him. The onus frequently shifts as the case proceeds from the person on whom it rested at first to his opponent. This occurs whenever a *prima facie* case has been established on any issue of fact or whenever a rebuttable presumption of law has arisen. (*Ency. of the Laws of England*).

Whoever desires any Court to give judgment as to any legal right or liability dependent on the existence of facts which he asserts, must prove that those facts exist. [Indian Evidence Act (1 of 1872), S. 101] [(w.e.f. 1-7-2024) repealed and replaced by Bharatiya Sakshya Adhiniyam, 2023 (47 of 2023), section 104]

Burdensome buy-out clause. Where the *escalation clause* or an *indemnity clause* in a lease agreement becomes enforceable, the lessee may be provided with an alternative to avoid such clauses and purchase the asset at a price sufficiently higher than the *termination value.* Such clause is called *burdensome buy-out clause,* and such buy-out is called *burdensome buy-out.* (*Leasing*)

Bureau. An office for the transaction of business. A department of Government for the transaction of public business; generally confined to subordinate and inferior executive departments.

Bureaucracy. A system in which Government is carried on in departments, each under the control of a chief officer; Government by bureaus; specifically excessive multiplication of, and concentration of power in, administrative officers of departments.

Bureaucrat. An advocate of bureaucracy; a member of a bureaucracy.

Burglar. A house-breaker; thief; especially one who commits robbery by breaking into a house in the night.

Burglary. House-breaking by night, with an intent to commit a felony therein, whether such felony be actually committed or not. (*Chitty. Crim. Law*).

Burial. The act of depositing a dead body.

Burial-ground. A grave-yard or cemetery.

Burial place. Same as burial-ground.

Burial right. The residents of a village cannot in law acquire the right of burial either as easement by prescription or otherwise, or on a fiction of a lost grant.

Burkism. Murder committed with the object of selling the dead body for purposes of dissection, generally, by suffocating or strangling the victim.

Bury. To cover out of sight; to hide in oblivion; to cover out of sight the body of a deceased person, as in a grave.

Bush doctrine. The policy announced by President George W. Bush after the September 11, 2001 attacks on the World Trade Center and the Pentagon, to the effect that nations harbouring terrorists will be treated as terrorists themselves and may be subject to a first-strike strategy.

Business. "BUSINESS" includes any trade, commerce or manufacture or any adventure or concern in the nature of trade, commerce or manufacture. [Income-tax Act (43 of 1961), S. 2(13)].

"Business" means any activity that is continuous and systemic perceptions about what would constitute business may vary from public to private sector or from industrial financing to commercial banking sectors. What is certain is that any activity in order to constitute business must be systematic and continuous. A single transaction in circumstances like the one in the case at hand would not constitute business of both the parties to the transaction. *Bhanushali Housing Cooperative Society Limited* v. *Mangilal*, (2015) 10 SCC 277, para 24.

"Business" includes— (a) any trade, commerce, manufacture, profession, vocation, adventure, wager or any other similar activity, whether or not it is for a pecuniary benefit; (b) any activity or transaction in connection with or incidental or ancillary to sub-clause (a); (c) any activity or transaction in the nature of sub-clause (a), whether or not there is volume, frequency, continuity or regularity of such transaction; (d) supply or acquisition of goods including capital goods and services in connection with commencement or closure of business; (e) provision by a club, association, society, or any such body (for a subscription or any other consideration) of the facilities or benefits to its members; (f) admission, for a consideration, of persons to any premises; (g) services supplied by a person as the holder of an office which has been accepted by him in the course or furtherance of his trade, profession or vocation; (h) services provided by a race club by wotalizatorisator or a licence to book maker in such club ; and (i) any activity or transaction undertaken by the Central Government, a State Government or any local authority in which they are engaged as public authorities [The Central Goods and Services Tax Act, 2017 (12 of 2017), S. 2(17)]

"Business" includes—

(a) any trade, commerce or manufacture or any adventure or concern in the nature of trade, commerce, or manufacture, whether or not such trade, commerce, manufacture, adventure or concern is carried on with a motive to make gain or profit and whether or not any profit accrues from such trade, commerce, manufacture, adventure or concern; and

(b) any transaction in connection with, or incidental or ancillary to such trade, commerce, manufacture, adventure or concern." Kerala General Sales Tax Act (15 of 1963), S. 2(vi) as cited in *Assistant Commissioner, Ernakulam* v. *Hindustan Urban Infrastructure Limited*, (2015) 3 SCC 745, para 24.

"BUSINESS" includes every trade, occupation and profession. [Indian Partnership Act (9 of 1932), S. 2(b)].

The word "business" extends the covenant to all cases where work, involving the recourse of numerous persons to the premises, is done for payment, or even without payment where the result is in effect the same as if a charge were made. The making of profit is not essential to constitute a business; nor, on the other hand, does payment necessarily constitute one. HALSBURY, 4th Edn., Vol. 27, para 325, p. 273.

The word "business" is one of wide import and it means an activity carried on continuously and systematically by a person by the application of his labour or skill with a view to earning an income. *Barendera Prasad* v. *I.T. Officer*, AIR 1981 SC 1047, 1953. [Income-tax Act (43 of 1961), S. 9(1)(i)(a)].

Business has a very wide import. In its generic sense, it is any purposeful activity, any activity directed towards some end, an activity engaged in as normal, logical, or inevitable and usually extending over a period of time. In its narrow sense it is confined to activity of a commercial nature with a profit motivation.

The expression 'Business' means commercial business and not duties or functions of a sovereign character.

Plying of Motor Vehicles for hire on public roads is a business. [Constitution of India, Art. 19(1)(*g*)].

As the consideration of profit motive cannot be regarded as an essential constituent of the term 'business' we have to consider whether the other ingredients of the term 'business' *viz.* volume, frequency, continuity and regularity of transactions of sale and purchase are satisfied. *Revenue Board* v. *A.M. Awari*, AIR 1976 SC 1813, 1819.

The expression "business" though extensively used is a word of indefinite import, in taxing statutes it is used in the sense of an occupation, or profession which occupies the time, attention and labour of a person, normally with the object of making profit. *State of Andhra Pradesh* v. *H. Abdul Bakhi*, AIR 1965 SC 531, 532.

"Business" is a word of wide import. It has no definite meaning. Its perceptions differ form private to public sector or from industrial financing to commercial banking. *Mahesh Chandra* v. *Regional Manager U.P. Financial Corporation*, AIR 1993 SC 935, 939. [State Financial Corporation Act (63 of 1951), S. 24].

In general sense 'business' means practically anything which is an occupation distinguished from some pleasure. Agriculture will amount to a profession of cultivation which would fall within the meaning of 'business'.

Trade; commercial transaction or engagements; commercial enterprise as a going concern [Constitution of India, Art. 19(1)(g)]; that about which one is busy.

BUSINESS, TRADE, PROFESSION. These words are synonymous in the sense of a calling for the purpose of a livelihood; *business* is general, *trade* and *profession* are particular; all *trade* is *business*, but all *business* is not *trade*. Buying and selling of merchandise is inseparable from *trade*; but the exercise of one's knowledge and experience, for purpose of gain, constitutes a *business*; when learning or particular skill is required, it is a *profession*.

"BUSINESS" includes—

(*a*) any trade, commerce, manufacture, profession, vocation, adventure, wager or any other similar activity, whether or not it is for a pecuniary benefit;

(*b*) any activity or transaction in connection with or incidental or ancillary to sub-clause (*a*);

(*c*) any activity or transaction in the nature of sub-clause (*a*), whether or not there is volume, frequency, continuity or regularity of such transaction;

(*d*) supply or acquisition of goods including capital goods and services in connection with commencement or closure of business;

(*e*) provision by a club, association, society, or any such body (for a subscription or any other consideration) of the facilities or benefits to its members;

(*f*) admission, for a consideration, of persons to any premises;

(*g*) services supplied by a person as the holder of an office which has been accepted by him in the course or furtherance of his trade, profession or vocation;

(*h*) services provided by a race club by way of totalisator or a licence to book maker in such club; and

(*i*) any activity or transaction undertaken by the Central Government, a State Government or any local authority in which they are engaged as public authorities. [Central Goods and Services Tax Act (12 of 2017), S. 2(17)].

"BUSINESS" includes—

(*i*) the provision of any services, but excluding the services provided by an employee;

(*ii*) any trade, commerce or manufacture;

(*iii*) any adventure or concern in the nature of trade, commerce or manufacture;

(*iv*) any transaction in connection with, or incidental or ancillary to, such trade, commerce, manufacture, adventure or concern; and

(*v*) any occasional transaction in the nature of such service, trade, commerce, manufacture, adventure or concern whether or not there is a volume, frequency, continuity or regularity of such transaction,

whether or not such service, trade, commerce, manufacture, adventure or concern is carried on with a motive to make gain or profit and whether or not any gain or profit accrues from such service, trade, commerce, manufacture, adventure or concern. [Andaman and Nicobar Islands Value Added Tax Regulation (6 of 2017), S. 2(1)(e)].

"Business" and "goodwill". "The goodwill of a business is not the business but is one result springing out of it" (*6 Ame. Cye.* 259)

Business auxiliary service. Means any service in relation

(vii)(i) promotion or marketing or sale of goods produced or provided by or belonging to the client; or

(ii) promotion or marketing of service provided by the client; or

(iii) any customer care service provided on behalf of the client; or

(iv) procurement of goods or services, which are inputs for the client; or

(v) production of goods on behalf of the client; or

(vi) provision of service on behalf of the client; or

(vii) a service incidental or auxiliary to any activity specified in sub-clauses (*i*) to (*vi*), such as billing, issue or collection or recovery of cheques, payments, maintenance of accounts and remittance, inventory management, evaluation or development of prospective customer or vendor, public relation services, management or supervision, and includes services as a commission agent, but does not include any information technology service and any activity that amounts to "manufacture" within the meaning of clause (*f*) of Section 2 of the Central Excise Act, 1944.

Explanation.—For the removal of doubts, it is hereby declared that for the purposes of this clause "information technology service" means any service in relation to designing, developing or maintaining of computer software, or computerized data processing or system networking, or any other service primarily in relation to operation of computer systems. [Finance Act (32 of 1994), S. 65(19) *as substituted by Act (23 of 2004),S. 90* (now repealed by Central Goods and Services Tax Act, 2017)]

Business connection. For the removal of doubts, it is hereby declared that "business connection" shall include any business activity carried out through a person who, acting on behalf of the non-resident,–

(a) has and habitually exercises in India, an authority to conclude contracts on behalf of the non-resident or habitually concludes contracts or habitually plays the principal role leading to conclusion of contracts by that non-resident and the contracts are—

(i) in the name of the non-resident; or

(ii) for the transfer of the ownership of, or for the granting of the right to use, property owned by that non-resident or that non-resident has the right to use; or

(iii) for the provision of services by the non-resident; or

(b) has no such authority, but habitually maintains in India a stock of goods or merchandise from which he regularly delivers goods or merchandise on behalf of the non-resident; or

(c) habitually secures orders in India, mainly or wholly for the nonresident or for that non-resident and other non-residents controlling, controlled by, or subject to the same common control, as that non-resident :

Provided that such business connection shall not include any business activity carried out through a broker, general commission agent or any other agent having an independent status, if such broker, general commission agent or any other agent having an independent status is acting in the ordinary course of his business :

Provided further that where such broker, general commission agent or any other agent works mainly or wholly on behalf of a non-resident (hereafter in this proviso referred to as the principal non-resident) or on behalf of such non-resident and other non-residents which are controlled by the principal non-resident or have a controlling interest in the principal non-resident or are subject to the same common control as the principal non-resident, he shall not be deemed to be a broker, general commission agent or an agent of an independent status. [Income Tax Act 1961, *Explanation* 2 to S. 9(1)(i)]

For the removal of doubts, it is hereby declared that the significant economic presence of a non-resident in India shall constitute "business connection" in India. [Income-tax Act (43 of 1961), section 9(1)(i), *Explanation* 2A]

Business cycle. The recurrent expansion and contraction of economic activity.

Business enterprise. Means any enterprise or medium enterprise, micro enterprise or small enterprise as defined in clauses (*e*), (*g*), (*h*) and (*m*) of section 2 of the Micro, Small and Medium Enterprises Development Act, 2006 (27 of 2006), respectively engaged in any business activity. [S. 2(f) of the Factoring Regulation Act, 2011 (12 of 2012)]

Business exhibition. Means an exhibition,—

(a) to market; or

(b) to promote; or

(c) to advertise; or

(d) to showcase,

any product or service, intended for the growth in business of the producer or provider of such product or service, as the case may be. [Finance Act (32 of 1994), S. 65 (19a) (*Introduced by Finance (No. 2) Act (23 of 2004), S. 90*) (now repealed by Central Goods and Services Tax Act, 2017)].

Business in force. Means the total sum assured with bonuses, without taking into account reinsurances, ceded or accepted, by an insurer in respect of the whole of the life insurance business on the last working day of the calendar year or the period covered by the revenue account furnished by such insurer under clause (b) of sub-section (2) of Section 16, as the case may be, preceding the calendar year in question. [Insurance Act (4 of 1938), Sixth Sch., Part C(6) *Expln*].

Business-interruption insurance. An agreement which is done to protect against one or more kinds of loss from interruption of an ongoing business.

Business liability. Liability for a breach of obligations or duties arising in the course of business.

Business, manufacture and calling. Business means an enterprise which is an occupation as distinguished from pleasure. Manufacture is a kind of production in which the making of articles or material (often on a large scale) is by physical labour or mechanical power. Calling denotes the following of a profession or trade. *Madras Gymkhana Club Employee's Union* v. *Management of the Gymkhana Club*, AIR 1968 SC 554, 563. [Industrial Disputes Act (14 of 1947), S. 2(*j*)].

Business method patents. Patents covering systems and methods used in business, such as financial recordkeeping software. Considered to include any process involving data processing, calculations, conversions, and so on, used for business operations and management. (*Cyber Law*)

Business name. A name used by a person in the course of his business.

Business of a co-operative society. The expression "the business of a co-operative society" occurring in R. 26, Co-operative Societies Act, is not restricted to the dealings with the members of the society only but it includes business which the co-operative society is under the law empowered to transact. ILR (1945) Nag 677.

Business of a non-banking financial institution. Means carrying on of the business of a financial institution referred to in clause (c) and includes business of a non-banking financial company referred to in clause (f). [Reserve Bank of India Act (2 of 1934), S. 45-I(a)].

Business of financing of companies. For the purposes of section 186(11)(a) of the Companies Act, 2013 (18 of 2013), the expression 'business of financing of companies' shall include, with regard to a Non-Banking Financial Company registered with Reserve Bank of India, "business of giving of any loan to a person or providing any guaranty or security for due repayment of any loan availed by any person in the ordinary course of its business. [R. 11(2) of the Companies (Meetings of Board and its Powers) Rules, 2014]

Business of the House. The relative order of all the items of business in the House of a Legislature to be taken up on a particular day.

In the Indian Parliament, the business of the House is divided into (1) Government Business; and (2) Private Members' Business.

'Business' : 'profession'. The maintenance management and running in faces of race horses by an assessee, and his betting, do not in law constitute the 'business', 'profession', 'vocation', or 'occupation' of the assessee, nor any part of such 'business', 'profession', 'vocation', or 'occupation' and the receipts by the assessee from the said sources or any of them would not, if a profit had been derived therefrom have in law, constituted income, profits or gains of the assessee from 'other sources' within the meaning of S. 6(*vi*) of the Income-tax Act, 1922. ILR (1940) All 274 : 1940 ITR 187 : 1940 ALJ 129 : AIR 1940 All 154 (FB).

Business relationship. For the purpose of clause (e) of sub-section (3) of section 141, the term "business relationship" shall be construed as any transaction entered into for a commercial purpose, except—

(i) commercial transactions which are in the nature of professional services permitted to be rendered by an auditor or audit firm under the Act and the Chartered Accountants Act, 1949 and the rules or the regulations made under those Acts;

(ii) commercial transactions which are in the ordinary course of business of the company at arm's length price-like sale of products or services to the auditor, as customer, in the ordinary course of business, by companies engaged in the business of telecommunications, airlines, hospitals, hotels and such other similar businesses. [Companies (Audit and Auditors) Rules, 2014, rule 10(4)]

Business transaction. "Business transaction" is a generic expression used in the sense that it is a transaction which a businessman, in a commercial business, would enter into. Distribution of assets at the time of dissolution of partnership is a business transaction.

Business trust. A business organisation which is similar to a corporation, in which investors receive transferable certificate of beneficial interest.

Business Vertical. means a distinguishable component of an enterprise that is engaged in the supply of individual goods or services or a group of related goods or services which is subject to risks and returns that are different from those of the other business verticals

Explanation.—For the purposes of this clause, factors that should be considered in determining whether goods or services are related include—

(a) the nature of the goods or services;

(b) the nature of the production processes;

(c) the type or class of customers for the goods or services;

(d) the methods used to distribute the goods or supply of services; and

(e) the nature of regulatory environment (wherever applicable), including banking, insurance, or public utilities; [The Central Goods and Services Tax Act, 2017 (12 of 2017), S. 2(18)]

But-for cause. Cause without which the event could not have occurred.

Butter. Butter is a product prepared by a process out of milk whether the process involved is a simple or a complicated one and butter drawn form curd is a product prepared from milk. *M.V. Joshi* v. *M.V. Shimpi*, AIR 1961 SC 1494, 1497. Prevention of Food Adulteration Rules (1955), Appendix B, Rule A. 11.05.

Buy-back. For the purposes of section 115QA of Income-tax Act, 1961 (43 of 1961), 'buy-back' means purchase by a company of its own shares in accordance with the provisions of any law for the time being in force relating to companies [*Explanation* (*i*) to section 115QA(1) of the Income-tax Act, 1961 (43 of 1961) *Substituted vide Act No. 28 of 2016* (w.e.f 1-6-2016)]

Buyer. Means a person who buys, or agrees to buy goods. [Sale of Goods Act (3 of 1930), S. 2(1)].

"BUYER" means whoever buys any goods or receives any services from a supplier for consideration. [Interest on Delayed Payments to Small Scale and Ancillary Industrial Undertakings Act (32 of 1993), S. 2(c) repealed by Act 27 of 2006 (w.e.f. 2-10-2006)].

For the purposes of this section,—

"BUYER" means (i) a person who obtains in any sale, by way of auction, tender or any other mode, goods of the nature specified in the Table in sub-section (1) or the right to receive any such goods but does not include,—

(A) a public sector company, the Central Government, a State Government, and an embassy, a High Commission, legation, commission, consulate and the trade representation, of a foreign State and a club; or,

(B) a buyer in the further sale of such goods obtained in pursuance of such sale, or

(ii) Omitted

(iii) sub-section (1F) means a person who obtains in any sale, goods of the nature specified in the said sub-section, but does not include,—

(A) the Central Government, a State Government and an embassy, a High Commission, legation, commission, consulate and the trade representation of a foreign State; or

(B) a local authority as defined in *Explanation* to clause (20) of section 10; or

(C) a public sector company which is engaged in the business of carrying passengers.] [Income-tax Act (43 of 1961), S. 206 C (ii) *Expln.* (a), (iii) omitted by Finance Act, 2003].

A purchaser; one who buys.

A 'License' does not fall within the expression 'buyer' under Section 206-C of the Act. *Union of India* v. *Om Prakash S.S. & Co.*, (2001) 3 SCC 593, para 2 : AIR 2001 SC 1202. [Income-tax Act (43 of 1961), S. 206C].

The word 'buyer' occurring in Section 206-C would mean where a person by virtue of the payment gets a right to receive specific goods and not where he is merely permitted to carry on business in that trade. *Union of India* v. *Om Prakash SS & Co.* (2001) 3 SCC 593, para 2 : AIR 2001 SC 1202. [Income-tax Act (43 of 1961), Section 206C (1) and (II) & *Expln.* (a)].

Buyer's market. A market in which supply exceeds demand resulting in lowered prices.

Buying in. The buying of property at an auction or mortgage foreclosure sale by the original owner or an interested party.

Buyout. The purchase of controlling percentage of company's shares.

By. The expression "by" clearly indicates the utmost limit of time being the end or the expiry of the date or period indicated.

The word 'By' does not mean presentation by the candidate or the elector in person only, and it means also either on behalf of or instrumentality. *Bhanwar Singh* v. *Navrang Singh,* AIR 1987 Raj 63, 66. [Representation of the People Act (43 of 1951) S. 81(1)].

By any proprietor thereof. The expression "by any proprietor thereof" in S. 46 should not be restricted to the user by the proprietor himself or any registered user, but it should also be taken into account if it is used by *bona fide* authorised user. *Cycle Corporation of India Ltd.* v. *T.I. Baleigh Industries Pvt. Ltd.,* AIR 1995 Cal 73, 77. [Trade and Merchandise Marks Act (43 of 1958), S. 46] [Now repealed & replaced by Act 47 of 1999]

"By" and Act. Would mean by a provision directly enacted in the statute in question and which is gatherable from its express language or by necessary implication therefrom. [*Indramani Pyarelal Gupta* v. *W.R. Natu,* AIR 1963 SC 274, para 15]. See also *BSNL* v. *TRAI,* (2014) 3 SCC 222, para 90; *Lok Prahari* v. *Union of India,* (2018) 4 SCC 699, para 47.

By law or **Bye law.** "BYE-LAWS" means the registered bye-laws for the time being in force, and includes a registered amendment of the bye-laws. [Co-operative Societies Act (2 of 1912), S. 2(a)].

"BYE-LAWS" means the bye-laws for the time being in force which have been duly registered or deemed to have been registered under this Act and includes amendments thereto which have been duly registered or deemed to have been registered under this Act. [Multi-State Co-operative Societies Act (39 of 2002), S. 3(c)].

A rule of administrative provision which is adopted by an association or corporation for its internal governance.

"BYE-LAW" includes all orders, ordinances, regulations, rules, and statutes made by any authority subordinate to the Legislature. The subordinate authority must, of course, have power expressly or impliedly conferred on it to legislate on the matters to which the by-law relates.

"Bye-laws". Means regulatory framework notified by local body, census town and notified area townships for facilitating the implementation of these rules effectively in their jurisdiction. [Solid Waste Management Rules, 2016, R. 3(1)(9)].

"Bye-laws". Means the building bye-laws framed by a State Government or any authority under its control to regulate the building activities in its areas falling in the jurisdiction of—

(*i*) all Municipal authorities or Committees or Councils;

(*ii*) all Metropolitan areas or Nagar Panchayats;

(*iii*) all areas covered under the Development or Planning authorities;

under various development plans notified by a State Government and enforced by such authority in its jurisdiction in which the Energy Conservation Building Code complaint building shall be located and includes any regulation or rule framed by the State Government or any other authority having jurisdiction established by the State Government. [Energy Conservation Building Code Rules, 2018, R. 2(1)(e)].

By-legislation. Legislation by the executive department on subordinate or secondary matters; by-laws; or the making of by-laws.

By or under this Act or as may be prescribed. Though normally and in their signification the words 'under the Act' would include both rules framed under S. 28 as well as bye-laws under sections 11 or 12, the reference to rules might be eliminated as tautologous since they have been specifically provided by the words that follow, 'By an Act' would mean by a provision directly enacted in the statute in question. *Indiramani Pyarelal Gupta* v. *W.R. Natu*, AIR 1963 SC 274, 281, 282.

[Forward Contracts (Regulation) Act (47 of 1952), S. 4].

By parol. Given by word of mouth. [Companies Act (1 of 1956), S. 46(b) replaced by Companies Act, 2013].

By-product. Secondary product from a process which, although not the main purpose of the operation, is capable of yielding revenue.

By virtue of. By force of; by authority of; by reason of; because of. [Constitution of India, Art. 88].

Bypass. Means a road provided as a permanent diversion to a scheduled road, whether such diversion is situated within or without the limits of a local authority and whether it is çonstructed before or after the commencement of this Act. Punjab Scheduled Roads and Controlled Areas Restriction of Unregulated Development Act (41 of 1963), S. 2(3) as cited in *Women's Education Trust* v. *State of Haryana*, (2013) 8 SCC 99, para 16.

"Bypass" means a section of the national highway bypassing a town or city. [National Highways Fee (Determination of Rates and Collection) Rules, 2008, R. 2(c)]

Bystander. One who is present at the place of occurrence, but does not participate in it.

Byway. A secluded private or obscure way; an out-the-way path or course.

C

Cab. Means a motor cab or maxi cab. [Finance Act (32 of 1994), S. 65(20) (now repealed by Central Goods and Services Tax Act, 2017)]

Carriage for the conveyance of passengers which plies for hire and is not a stage carriage (or what is commonly known as an omnibus) that is, a carriage in which the passengers are charged separate fares for their seats.

"Cabin baggage" means a baggage intended for carriage in the cabin of an aircraft. [Aircraft (Security) Rules, 2011, R. 2(i)].

Cabinet. An advisory council to the head of the executive. The collective body of ministers who direct the Government of a country.

A council advising a sovereign or head of a State. [Salarjung Museum Act (26 of 1961), Sch. pt. 1].

In India Cabinet is an inner body within the Council of Ministers which is responsible for formulating the policy of the Government. The Council of Ministers is collectively responsible to Lok Sabha; it is headed by the Prime Minister who determines which of the Ministers should be members of the Cabinet.

Cable. A large strong rope or chain, such as is used to hold a vessel at anchor; submarine or electric or telegraph cable.

A heavy strong rope; a wire rope or metal chain of great strength. [Workmen's Compensation Act (8 of 1923), Sch. II(ix)]; [Income-tax Act (43 of 1961), Fifth Sch., Item 7].

Cable operator. Means any person who provides cable service through a cable television network or otherwise controls or is responsible for the management and operation of a cable television network. [Cable Television Network (Regulation) Act (7 of 1995), S. 2(a)]

Cable service. Means the transmission by cables of programmes including re-transmission by cables of any broadcast television signals. [Cable Television Networks (Regulation) Act (7 of 1995), S. 2(b)]

Cable service means the transmission by cables of programmes including re-transmission by cables of any broadcast television signals. [Cable Television Networks (Regulation) Act (7 of 1995), S. 2(b) and Telecommunication (Broadcasting and Cable Services) Interconnection Regulations (2004), Regn. 2(h); Standards of Quality of Service (Broadcasting and Cable Services) (Cable Television—Non—CAS Areas) Regulations, 2009, Regn. 2(g)]

'Cable service' means transmission or retransmission of programmes including broadcast television channel signals or satellite television channel signals or both through cables or by any other means. [W.B. Entertainment-Cum-Amusement Tax Act (6 of 1982), S. 4-A *Expln.* (4-c) **as referred in** *State of W.B.* v. *Purvi Communication (P.) Ltd.*, (2005) 3 SCC 711, 718, para 8]

Cable subscriber. 'Cable subscriber' means a subscriber who receives the signals of a cable service. [Standards of Quality of Service (Broadcasting and Cable Services) (Cable Television—Non-CAS Areas) Regulations, 2009, Regn. 2(h)]

Cable television network. Means any system consisting of a set of closed transmission paths and associated signal generation, control and distribution equipment, designed to provide cable service for reception by multiple subscribers. [Cable Television Network (Regulation) Act (7 of 1995), S. 2(c)]

Cache. (Internet Browser) The files and graphics saved locally from Web sites you have previously visited.

A section of RAM used to reduce the time the computer needs to perform certain operations. A *disk cache* stores information read from a disk so that less time will be required for the central processings unit (CPU) to obtain the information when it is needed. (*Computer*)

Cadit quaestio. (*Lat.*) The question is at the end.

Cadre. Means the strength of an establishment or service sanctioned as a separate unit and it does not mean "post" as defined by Rules 9 and 4 of the Fundamental Rules. [Constitution of India, Art. 311]

Cadre cannot be confined to permanent posts. It will also include a temporary post. *G.R. Luthora, Additional District Judge* v. *Lt. Governor, Delhi*, AIR 1974 SC 1908, 1919. [Delhi Higher Judicial Services Rules (1970), R. 6(3)]

In service jurisprudence, the term 'cadre' has a definite legal connotation. In the legal sense, the word 'cadre' is not synonymous with 'service'. Fundamental Rule 9(4) defines the word 'cadre' to mean the strength of a service or part of a service sanctioned as a separate unit. *Chakradhar* v. *State of Bihar*, AIR 1988 SC 959, 963.

Cadre post. "Cadre post" in the Fundamental Rules means a post as specified in the Schedule and includes a temporary post. *G.R. Luthra, Additional District Judge, Delhi* v. *Ltd. Governor, Delhi,* AIR 1974 SC 1908.

Caesarian operation. A surgical operation whereby the foetus, which can neither make its way into the world by the ordinary and natural passage, nor be extracted by the attempts of art, whether the mother and foetus be yet alive, or whether either of them be dead, is by a cautious and well timed operation taken from the mother with a view to save the lives of both, or either of them.

Cafeteria plan. Employee benefit plan allowing employees to select among various groups of life, disability, dental, medical expense and some other plans which best meet their particular needs. (*Insurance*)

US term for an arrangement whereby a company employee may chose from among several fringe benefits; that benefit is then not taxable. (*International Accounting*)

Calculate. To reckon; [Income-tax Act (43 of 1961), S. 2(10)]; plan or contrive to achieve a purpose.

Calculated. The word 'calculated' suggests design, forethought, or intention to accomplish a purpose; "calculated" primarily means to compute mathematically, but when applied to a human action, it is used in the sense of, to intend, to design, to plan, or to adopt to achieve a purpose. *Rattam Singh* v. *Moga Transport Company*, AIR 1959 Pun 196, 198. [Companies Act (1 of 1956), S. 67(3)(*a*)]

Calculated level of consumption. Shall be determined by adding together calculated levels of production and imports and subtractting calculated level of exports. [Ozone Depleting Substances (Regulation and Control) Rules, 2000, R. 2(h)]

Calculated level of production, sale, import or export. As the case may be, means level determined by multiplying quantity of the ozone depleting substance by its ozone depleting potential specified in column (5) of Schedule I [Ozone Depleting Substances (Regulation and Control) Rules, 2000, R. 2(e)].

Calculation. The action of reckoning. [CPC (5 of 1908), S. 51, *Expln.*].

Calendar. An orderly arrangement of the divisions of time into years, months, weeks and days, or a register of them.

Calendar year. "CALENDAR YEAR" means by the year commencing on the 1st day of January. [Copyright Act (14 of 1957), S. 2(e)]

"CALENDAR YEAR" means the period of twelve months beginning with the first day of January in any year. [Factories Act (43 of 1968), S. 2(bb)].

"CALENDAR YEAR" means the period starting from the 1st day of January and ending on the 31st day of December of the same year. [Customs Tariff Act (51 of 1975), Gen Exemption No. 28, *Expln.* (B)]

There are two principal modes of computing the calendar years. One is by the annual course of the Sun (solar year). The other is by the periodical revolutions of the Moon (lunar year). The solar year consists of 365 days 5 hours 48 minutes and 45 seconds. The lunar year consists of 354 days, 3 hours, 48 minutes and 39 seconds.

Calendering. Calendering involves assortment and variety of processes, representing a member of sub-species of operations which may or may not alter the nature of the 'grey' fabric. *Maftlal Firm Spinning of Manufacturing Co. Ltd.* v. *Collector, C.E., Bombay,* AIR 1989 SC 784, 787. [Central Excise Rules (1944), Rules 49A(1)(*b*) and (2)]

Calibration. Means all the operations which are necessary for the purpose of determining the values of the errors of a weight or measure and, if necessary, to determine the other metrological properties of such weight or measure, and includes the actual fixing of the positions of the gauge-marks or scale-marks of a weight or measure, or in some cases, of certain principal marks only, in relation to the corresponding values of the quantity to be measured.

Explanation.—Calibration may also be carried out with a view to permitting the use of a weight or measure as a standard. [Standards of Weights and Measures Act (60 of 1976), S. 2(a)]

Call. An official declaration that sums subscribed are required to be paid; a public claim or demand.

Demand; a demand upon the holder of partly paid up shares in a company for payment of the balance, or an instalment of it [T.P. Act (4 of 1882), S. 127, ill. (a)]; to demand; to summon by a call; to name, to address; an option to buy a certain amount of stock at a fixed price at or within a certain time. [Forward Contracts (Regulation) Act (74 of 1952), S. 2(g)] Now repealed by the Finance Act, 2015]

(*In company law*) An assessment on the stockholders of a corporation or a joint-stock company, or members of a mutual insurance company, usually for payment of instalments of their unpaid subscriptions, or for their promised contributions to pay losses. Instalment due on shares not fully paid, payable according to the terms of the prospectus or Articles of Association of a company.

Call centre. Means a commercial concern which provides assistance, help or information, through telephone, on behalf of another person. [Central Excise Tariff Act, 1985 (5 of 1986), Appendix IX, Service Tax (c)(xi), *Expln* (i)]

Call for. To demand. [CrPC 1973 (2 of 1974), S. 325(3); Art. 78(b) and Constitution of India, Art. 167(b)].

Call in. To collect or withdraw. [Indian Trusts Act (2 of 1882), S. 40].

Call price. Price at which a bond may be retired before its maturity date.

Call up. To summon for action or service. [Companies Act (1 of 1956), S. 99 (replaced by Companies Act 2013]; [Indian Reserve Forces Act (4 of 1888), S. 7(1)].

Call upon. To make a demand upon. [Requisitioning and Acquisition of Immovable Property Act (30 of 1952), S. 3(1)(a)].

Callable bond. A bond that may be called for payment before its maturity.

Callable security. A security which when presented to the issuer, entitles the holder to receive a share of the assets of issuer or the cash equivalent.

Called-up capital. Means such part of the capital, which has been called for payment. [S. 2(15) of the Companies Act, 2013 (18 of 2013)]

Called-up share capital. That part of the *subscribed share capital* which shareholders have been required to pay. (*Finance*)

Face value of a company's shares that the shareholders have actually paid for (*Business Term*)

Calligraphists. In order to come within the definition of 'calligraphists' three conditions have to be satisfied by an employee namely: (a) he must be an artist, (b) he should perform journalistic work and (c) he should also calligraph matters. From the discussion (contained in the judgment) it follows that the Katibs are artists who perform journalistic work and who also calligraph matters. Accordingly they satisfy the definition of 'Calligraphists' as per the Wage Board Recommendations and they are working journalists. *The Management of Daily Pratap* v. *Katibs,* AIR 1972 SC 1872.

Calling. Profession, trade or occupation; employment. The business of investment for interest resulting in gain is calling.

However extended the meaning be given to the expression 'undertaking' or 'calling', we cannot include within their concept the case of an individual who carries on a profession, dependent on his own intellectual skill. For example a doctor or a lawyer. *Brij Mohan Bagaria* v. *N.C. Chaterjee,* AIR 1958 Cal 460, 464. [Industrial Disputes Act (14 of 1947), S. 2(*j*) & (*k*)]

The word 'calling' is very wide and it means one's usual occupation, vocation, business or trade. *National Union of Commercial Employees* v. *M.R. Meher,* AIR 1960 Bom 22, 24.

Profession, trade or occupation. [Industrial Disputes Act (14 of 1947), S. 2(j)].

Calling attention. A parliamentary procedure to call the attention of the Government to a matter of urgent public importance. (*Constitutional and Parliamentary Term*)

Calling attention notice. A device to bring urgent matters to the attention of the government. A member of the Parliament, with previous permission of the Speaker/ Chairman, may call the attention of a minister to a matter of urgent public importance and request him to make a statement on the subject who may make a brief statement or ask for time to make the statement at a later date. (*Rules of Procedure of the Parliament*)

Calling upon a prisoner. The demand made upon a prisoner, after verdict of guilty found against him, whether he has any reason to give why sentence should not be passed.

Camera. A chamber; room or apartment; Judges chamber.

Camera proceedings. "The word 'proceeding' means the course of procedure in an action at law. Thus 'camera proceedings' would mean Chamber proceedings or in other words 'secret proceedings' wherefrom public is excluded."

Camouflage. The disguising or concealment of guns, ships, aircrafts, *etc.*, by obscuring with splashes of various colours, foliage, netting, smokescreens; any means of disguise or evasion. [*New Shorter Oxford English Dictionary, Thumb Index Edition, Vol. 1*]

Camp. Any place established under Section 4 as a camp where any body of volunteers is for the time being undergoing training. [Lok Sahayak Sena Act (53 of 1956), S. 2(a)].

Camphor. Camphor must be given its ordinary meaning and it includes drug camphor as much as non-drug camphor, natural or synthetic. [Import and Exports (Control) Act (18 of 1947). Import (Control) Order, 1955-Import Trade Control Schedule, Part IV, No. 131]

Campus. Means the unit established or constituted by the University for making arrangements for instruction, research, education and training. [S. 2(d) of the Rajiv Gandhi National Aviation University Act, 2013 (26 of 2013)]

Can. To have power, either physical or moral; to be able; having the necessary capacity (as, a witness *can* only speak of things which he had heard and seen).

Can, May. *Can* denotes possibility. *May* liberty and probability.

Canal. "CANAL" includes—

(a) all canals, channels and reservoirs constructed, maintained or controlled by the State Government for the supply or storage of water;

(b) all words, embankments, structures, supply and escape channels connected with such canals, channels or reservoirs;

(c) all water-courses as defined in the second clause of this section;

(d) any part of a river, stream, lake or natural collection of water or natural drainage-channel, to which the State Government has applied the provisions of Part II of this Act. [Northern India Canal and Drainage Act (8 of 1973), S. 3(1)]

'CANAL' includes any river, inland navigation or lake, and any other waters situated wholly or partly within a county, whether those waters are or are not within the ebb and flow of the tide. [(English) Public Health (Control of Disease) Act, 1984, S. 53]

An artificial water-course. [T.P. Act (4 of 1882)].

Canal boat. Means any vessel, however propelled, which is used for the conveyance of goods along a canal, not being—

(a) a sailing barge which belongs to the class generally known as 'Thames sailing barge' and is registered under the Merchant Shipping Acts, 1894 to 1983, either in the Port of London or elsewhere, or

(b) a sea-going ship so registered, or

(c) a vessel used for pleasure purposes only.

[(English) Public Health (Control of Disease) Act, 1984, S. 53]

A boat used in canals.

Cancellation. To destroy the force, effectiveness, or validity of. To annul, abrogate, or terminate. Defacement or mutilation of instrument. Words of revocation written across instrument.

The action or process of cancelling. [IPC (45 of 1860), S. 477 and Constitution of India, Art. 31A(e)].

Cancellation and non-renewal. Refusal to renew will not amount to cancellation. There is no justification for stretching the word 'cancellation' to cover the case of 'non-renewal'. Renewal means fresh grant. In the case of refusal to grant a licence, no reasons need be stated. For refusal to renew also no reasons need be recorded.

Cancellation of adhesive stamp. The true test for determining whether an adhesive stamp has been effectually cancelled is whether an ordinary man would, on seeing the stamp, believe that it had already been used so as to preclude him from using it again. *Narayana* v. *Sarojini Devi,* AIR 1963 AP 378. [Indian Stamp Act (2 of 1899), S. 12(3)]

Candidate. Means a person who has been nominated as a candidate at any election. [IPC (45 of 1860), S. 171-A] [Now (w.e.f. 1-7-2024) repealed & replaced by Bharatiya Nyaya Sanhita, 2023 (45 of 2023), section 169(a), same definition in new Sanhita]

One who seeks or aspires to some office or previlege, or who offers, himself for the same; a person offering himself to the suffrage of the electors; one put forward for election, whether with or against his own will.

Candidate means only a person who has either been duly nominated as a candidate at Vice-Presidential election; or a person who claims to have been duly nominated. *Charan Lal Sahu* v. *Giani Zail Singh*, AIR 1984 SC 309, 312. [Presidential and Vice-Presidential Election Act (31 of 1952), Ss. 13(*a*), 144, 14, 5(*b*)(1)(*a*)]

A person becomes a 'candidate' only when he has been duly nominated as a 'candidate'. *Raj Krushna* v. *Binod*, AIR 1954 SC 202, 204. [Representation of the People Act (43 of 1951), S. 79(*b*)]

The person referred to as a candidate in the clause should be a person who has been or claims to have been duly nominated as a candidate at an election and not one who is yet to be nominated. *Indira Nehru Gandhi* v. *Raj Narain*, AIR 1975 SC 2299, 2357. [Representation of the People Act (43 of 1951), S. 123(7)]

The word 'candidate' occurring in Section 82(b) of the Act includes a nominated candidate at the election who has withdrawn from the contest. *Gadnis Bhawani Shanker* v. *Falero Eduardo Martinho*, (2000) 7 SCC 472 para 8 : AIR 2000 SC 2502. [Representation of the People Act (43 of 1951), S. 82(b)]

One who seeks or offers himself, or is put forward by others for an office, privilege or honour. [IPC (45 of 1860), S. 171A].

Candidate against whom allegations of any corrupt practice are made. The expression "candidate against whom allegations of any corrupt practice are made" is to be construed as "any candidate who is alleged to have committed corrupt practices". *Aditya* v. *Kandaswami,* AIR 1958 Mad 171, 173. [Representation of the People Act (43 of 1951), S. 82(*b*)]

Candidate, Rejected. As opposed to a selected candidate.

Candidature. The term 'candidate' cannot be equated to the term 'candidature'. It has been used in conjunction with the words 'candidature of a candidate'. The word 'candidature' can only mean "the state of his being a candidate" or "the fact of his being a candidate". *Salara Devi* v. *Shriprat Amrit Dange,* AIR 1961 MP 127, 138. [Representa tion of the People Act (43 of 1951), S. 123(4)]

The act or fact of being a candidate. [Representation of the People Act (43 of 1951), S. 30(c)].

Cane. Means sugarcane. [Sugar Undertakings (Taking over of Management), (49 of 1978), S. 2]

Cannabis. "CANNABIS" (hemp) means—

(a) *charas,* that is the separated resin, in whatsoever form whether crude or purified, obtained from the cannabis plant and also includes concentrated preparation and resin known as *hashish* oil or liquid *hashish;*

(b) *ganja,* that is, the flowering or fruiting tops of the cannabis plant (excluding the seeds and leaves when not accompanied by the tops), by whatever name they may be known or designated; and

(c) any mixture, with or without any neutral material of any of the above forms of cannabis or any drink prepared therefrom. [N.D. & P.S. Act (61 of 1985), S. 2(iii)]

Cannabis plant. Means any plant of the Genus cannabis. [N.D. P.S. Act (61 of 1985), S. 2 (iv)].

Canned software. 'Canned software' means that it is not specifically created for a particular consumer. The sale or lease of, or granting a licence to use, canned software is not automatic data processing and computer services, but is the sale of tangible personal property. When a vendor, in a single transaction, sells canned software that has been modified or customized for that particular consumer, the transaction will be considered the sale of tangible personal property if the charge for the modification constitutes no more than half of the price of the sale.' [State-Case App-CT, OHTAXRPTR 402-978, Ohio Board of Tax Appeals, Aeroquip Cop. p. 9 of 12 **as referred in** *Tata Consultancy Services* v. *State of A.P.*, (2005) 1 SCC 308, 341, para 79]

Cannon. "CANNON" includes also all how-itzers, mortars, wall-pieces, mitrailleuses and other ordnance and machine-guns, all parts of the same, and all carriages, platforms and appliances for mounting, transporting and serving the same. [Arms Act (11 of 1878), S. 4].

(*Milit-Law*) Mounted gun for throwing project-tiles larger than bullets.

Canon. A law, rule or ordinance in general, and of the church in particular. (*Burrill*)

Rule of law or decree of the church, specially one laid down by an ecclesiastical council; general rule or principle.

Canon Law. A collection of ecclesiastical constitutions for the discipline of the church of Rome. (*Burrill L. Dict*)

THE CANON LAW consists partly of certain rules taken out of scripture: partly of the writings of the ancient fathers of the church; partly of the ordinance of the general and provincial councils; and partly of the decrees of the Popes in former ages. (*Tomlin*)

Canonicalisation. In relation to a xml digital signatures, means the process of converting electronic record that has more than one possible representation into a 'standard', 'normal', or 'canonical form' in which the variation in representation of electronic record shall be standardised by applying consistent rules, primarily as part of the xml digital signature creation and verification processes. [Digital Signature (End Entity) Rules, 2015, R. 2(1) (b)].

Cantonment. Place assigned to a body of troops for quarters; a more or less permanent shelter or place of rest for an army.

A permanent military station or military town often connected with a town or city. [Indian Electricity Act (9 of 1910), S. 3(2)(ii)] [Now repealed & replaced by Act 36 of 2003]

Cantonment authority. A local authority entrusted with the administration of a cantonment. [CPC (5 of 1908), S. 60, *Expln.* 3 (i)].

Canvass. In common parlance the term 'canvass' is used in the sense of soliciting support by interviewing each elector.

The employment of a municipal servant for painting posters and leading processions, though highly improper, does not amount to canvassing in the proper sense of the term, even though such acts may indirectly influence the votes of electors. *Kishanchand Sharma* v. *Bishabh Kumar*, AIR 1950 Nag 208.

Soliciting support or votes. [Representation of the People Act (43 of 1951), S. 130(1)(a)].

Capable. Susceptible; competent; qualified; fitting; possessing legal power or capacity. Able, fit or adapted for. (*Black*)

Possessing capacity. [T.P. Act (4 of 1882), S. 122].

Capable of being computed in terms of money. The word 'capable' means susceptible. By the word 'compute' it is meant to estimate or determine by arithmetical or mathematical reckoning. *Bombay Gas Company* v. *R.N. Kulkarni,* AIR 1965 Bom 172, 175. [Industrial Disputes Act (14 of 1947), S. 37-C(2)]

Capable of giving discharge. Though a suit filed by one of the presumptive reversioners is a representative suit and binds the entire body of reversioners and as such it can be held that the presumptive reversioner is capable of giving a discharge without the concurrence of others, yet the mere non-filing of a suit by the presumptive reversioner cannot bar the suit filed by the other reversioner before three years after attaining majority. *Netramani Debi* v. *Laxminarayan Kar,* AIR 1959 Ori 179, 185. [Limitation Act (36 of 1963), S. 7]

Capable of industrial application. In relation to an invention, means that the invention is capable of being made or used in an industry. [Patents Act (39 of 1970), S. 2(ac)]

Capacity. Legal qualification (*i.e.* legal age), competency, power of fitness. Mental ability to understand the nature and effects of one's acts. (*Black*)

Legal qualification, capability [Indian Evidence Act (1 of 1872), S. 92, prov. (1)]; a position enabling one to do something [IPC (45 of 1860), S. 466]; a container containing space, area or volume. [IPC (45 of 1860), S. 265].

Capacity of state to sue and be sued. The state is capable of suing and being sued but that is so not because the State is a person, but because Art. 300 has made an express provision in that behalf. It has prescribed the method by which proceedings can be instituted for the purpose of determining the rights between the State and the people of the State. *Shiv Prashad* v. *State of Punjab,* AIR 1957 Punj 150, 151. [Constitution of India, Art. 300]

Capacity to act. The words "capacity to act" in S. 2 are wide enough to include in it the institution of a suit by a minor who under her personal law may have attained majority, in matters of marriage, dower and divorce. *Sun Achia Khatoon* v. *Abdul Hai,* AIR 1952 Cal 381. [Majority Act (9 of 1875), S. 2]

Capacity to contract. Competence to enter into a legally binding agreement.

"Capacity to consent". Means ability of an individual, determined on an objective basis, to understand and appreciate the nature and consequences of a proposed action and to make an informed decision concerning such action. [Human Immunodeficiency Virus and Acquired Immune Deficiency Syndrome (Prevention and Control) Act (16 of 2017), S. 2(b)].

Capacity to manage himself and his affairs. The expression means the inadequate ability of a person to look after himself and his affairs according to accepted norms and standards and its meaning should not be equated with incapacity flowing from unsoundedness of mind. R. *Lingaraj* v. *Parvathi,* AIR 1975 Mad 285, 291. [Lunancy Act (4 of 1912) (*repealed*), S. 62]

Capax doli. The condition of one who has sufficient mind and understanding to be made responsible for his actions.

Capable of wrong-doing; able to commit fraud.

Capital. CAPITAL means equity shares, preference shares, convertible preference shares, and convertible debentures. [Foreign Exchange Management (Transfer or Issue of Security by a Person Resident Outside India) Regulations, 2000, Reg. 2(ii)].

Money actually contributed for employment in business [CPC (5 of 1908), O. XXI, R. 46(1)(b)]; principal [T.P. Act (4 of 1882), S. 57(2)(c)]; punishable with death.

"CAPITAL" for the purposes of section 43 of Act 18 of 2013, the term 'capital' shall be deemed to be preference capital, notwithstanding that it is entitled to either or both of the following rights, namely:—(*a*) that in respect of dividends, in addition to the preferential rights to the amounts specified in sub-clause (*a*) of clause (*ii*), it has a right to participate, whether fully or to a limited extent, with capital not entitled to the preferential right aforesaid; (*b*) that in respect of capital, in addition to the preferential right to the repayment, on a winding up, of the amounts specified in sub-clause (*b*) of clause (*ii*), it has a right to participate, whether fully or to a limited extent, with capital not entitled to that preferential right in any surplus which may remain after the entire capital has been repaid. [*Explanation (iii)* to section 43 of the Companies Act, 2013 (18 of 2013)]

Capital account. An account on the balancesheet of the partnership representing a partner's share of the partnership capital.

Capital account convertibility. Freedom to convert local financial assets into foreign financial assests and vice versa at market determined rates of exchange. [Tarapore Committee, RBI, 1997 quoted in *M L Tannan, Banking Law & Practice in India*, 2021, LexisNexis, Dictionary of Banking Terminology].

Capital account transaction. Means a transaction which alters the assets or liabilities, including contingent liabilities, outside India of persons resident in India or assets or liabilities in India of persons resident outside India, and includes transactions referred to in sub-section (3) of Section 6. [Foreign Exchange Management Act (42 of 1999), S. 2(e)]

Capital asset. Means property of any kind held by an assessee, whether or not connected with his business or profession, but does not include—

(a) any stock-in-trade, consumable stores or raw materials held for the purposes of his business or profession,

(b) any securities held by a Foreign Institutional Investor which has invested in such securities in accordance with the regulations made under the Securities and Exchange Board of India Act, 1992 (15 of 1992);

(c) any unit linked insurance policy to which exemption under clause (*10D*) of section 10 does not apply on account of the applicability of the fourth and fifth provisos thereof,

but does not include—

(i) any stock-in-trade other than the securities referred to in sub-clause (*b*), consumable stores or raw materials held for the purposes of his business or profession;

(ii) personal effects, that is to say, movable property (including wearing apparel and furniture) held for personal use by the assessee or any member of his family dependent on him, but excludes—

(a) jewellery;

(b) archaeological collections;

(c) drawings;

(d) paintings;

(e) sculptures; or

(f) any work of art.

Explanation.—For the purposes of this sub-clause, "jewellery" includes—

(a) ornaments made of gold, silver, platinum or any other precious metal or any alloy containing one or more of such precious metals, whether or not containing any precious or semi-precious stone, and whether or not worked or sewn into any wearing apparel;

(b) precious or semi-precious stones, whether or not set in any furniture, utensil or other article or worked or sewn into any wearing apparel;

(iii) agricultural land in India, not being land situate—

(a) in any area which is comprised within the jurisdiction of a municipality (whether known as a municipality, municipal corporation, notified area committee, town area committee, town committee, or by any other name) or a cantonment board and which has a population of not less than ten thousand; or

(b) in any area within the distance, measured aerially,—

(I) not being more than two kilometres, from the local

limits of any municipality or cantonment board referred to in item (*a*) and which has a population of more than ten thousand but not exceeding one lakh; or

(II) not being more than six kilometres, from the local limits of any municipality or cantonment board referred to in item (*a*) and which has a population of more than one lakh but not exceeding ten lakh; or

(III) not being more than eight kilometres, from the local limits of any municipality or cantonment board referred to in item (*a*) and which has a population of more than ten lakh.

Explanation.—For the purposes of this sub-clause, "population" means the population according to the last preceding census of which the relevant figures have been published before the first day of the previous year;

(iv) 6½ per cent Gold Bonds, 1977, [or 7 per cent Gold Bonds, 1980,] [or National Defence Gold Bonds, 1980,] issued by the Central Government;

(v) Special Bearer Bonds, 1991, issued by the Central Government;

(vi) Gold Deposit Bonds issued under the Gold Deposit Scheme, 1999 [or deposit certificates issued under the Gold Monetisation Scheme, 2015] notified by the Central Government.

Explanation 1.—For the removal of doubts, it is hereby clarified that "property" includes and shall be deemed to have always included any rights in or in relation to an Indian company, including rights of management or control or any other rights whatsoever.

Explanation 2.—For the purposes of this clause—

(a) the expression "Foreign Institutional Investor" shall have the meaning assigned to it in clause (a) of the *Explanation* to section 115AD;

(b) the expression "securities" shall have the meaning assigned to it in clause (h) of section 2 of the Securities Contracts (Regulation) Act, 1956 (42 of 1956). [Income-tax Act (43 of 1961), section 2(14)]

Capital charge. The expression "capital charge" in the clause in S. 9(1)(*iv*) Income-tax Act (11 of 1922) cannot connote a charge on the capital, that is, the property assessed. It means a charge credit for a capital sum, *i.e.* a charge to secure the discharge of a liability of a capital nature. *New Piece Goods Bazzar Co. Ltd.* v. *Commissioner of Income Tax*, AIR 1950 SC 165.

Capital contribution. Funds which are made available by a shareholder without increasing his or her stockholding.

Capital crime. An offence for which the punishment of death may be inflicted.

Capital employed. There can be no doubt that the expression 'capital employed' is susceptible of more than one interpretation and it may include long term borrowings, or it may not, depending on the context and the circumstances in which it may be used. *Lohia Machines Ltd.* v. *Union of India*, AIR 1985 SC 421, 438. [Income-tax Rules (1962), Rule 19-A]

If the funds of the assessee have been used to acquire assets for being used in the business of the assessee, that would be capital employed in the business within the meaning of the rule. *Jayaram Mills Ltd.* v. *Commr. of Excise Profits Tax,* AIR 1959 Mad 376, 377. [Excess Profits Tax Act (15 of 1940), Sch. II, R. 1(*i*)]

Capital employed in the business of the company. Means—

(i) in a case referred to in clause (*i*) of sub-section (1), the aggregate of the issued share capital, debentures and long-term borrowings as on the last day of the previous year in which the business of the company commences;

(ii) in a case referred to in clause (*ii*) of sub-section (1), the aggregate of the issued share capital, debentures and long-term borrowings as on the last day of the previous year in which the extension of the industrial undertaking is completed or, as the case may be, the new industrial unit commences production or operation, in so far as such capital, debentures and long-term borrowings have been issued or obtained in connection with the extension of the industrial undertaking or the setting up of the new industrial unit of the company. [Income-tax Act (43 of 1961), S. 35D *Expln.* (b)]

Capital expenditure and **revenue expenditure.** Where the expenditure is made for the initial outlay or for extension of a business or a substantial replacement of the equipment, it is a capital expenditure. If the expenditure is for running the business or working it with a view to produce the profits it is a revenue expenditure. *Assam Bengal Cement Co. Ltd.* v. *Commisisoner of Income Tax*, AIR 1955 SC 89. [Income-tax Act (11 of 1922), S. 10(2)(*v*)]

Capital gains. Gains accruing from the sale or exchange of capital assets. [Wealth-tax Act (27 of 1957), Sch. II(ii)].

Capital gains tax. Chargeable gains accruing to a person on the disposal of assets.

Capital gearing. Also called leverage, especially in the USA, the relationship between a company's funds derived from ordinary shares and long-term, fixed-interest rate funds such as preference shares and debentures. It is the ratio of the company's debts to total capital or shareholders' funds. High gearing, *i.e.* a high proportion of debt, generally represents a speculative investment. (*Business Term & International Accounting*)

Capital goods. means:

(a) machines, machinery, plant, equipment, apparatus, tools or appliances used for producing or processing of any goods or for bringing about any change in any substance for the manufacture of final products;

(b) components, spare parts and accessories of the aforesaid machines, machinery, plant, equipment, apparatus, tools or appliances used for aforesaid purpose; and

(c) moulds and dies, generating sets and weigh bridges used in the factory of the manufacturer. [Central Excise Rules, 1944, Rule 57-Q, *Expl.* (1)(a) now repealed by Central Goods and Services Tax Act, 2017].

"Capital goods" means goods, the value of which is capitalised in the books of account of the person claiming the input tax credit and which are used or intended to be used in the course or furtherance of business [The Central Goods and Services Tax Act, 2017 (12 of 2017), S. 2(19)]

"CAPITAL GOODS" means,—

(i) all goods falling under Chapter 82, Chapter 84, Chapter 85, Chapter 90, Heading No. 68.02 and sub-heading No. 6801.10 of the First Schedule to the Tariff Act;

(ii) pollution control equipment;

(iii) components, spares and accessories of the goods specified at (i) and (ii) above;

(iv) moulds and dies;

(v) refractories and refractory materials;

(vi) tubes and pipes and fittings thereof; and

(vii) storage tank,

used in the factory of the manufacturer of the final products, but does not include any equipment or appliance used in an office. [CENVAT Credit Rules, 2002, R. 2(b)]

Power cables and capacitors, control panels, cable distribution boards, switches, starters and air compressors and electric wires & cables in manufacturing companies, are 'capital goods' within the meaning of Rule 57 Q. *CCE* v. *Jawahar Mills Ltd*, (2001) 6 SCC 274, para 6 : AIR 2001 SC 2500. [Central Excise Rules, 1944, R. 57-Q]

Capital improvement. An outlay of funds so as to acquire or improve a fixed asset.

Capital loss. The loss which is realized on the sale or exchange of capital asset.

Capital market. The market which exclusively involves sale and purchase of shares, securities, debentures *etc.*

Capital offence. A crime punishable with death. [IPC (45 of 1860), S. 214].

Capital paid in surplus. A no par value stock on the books, a portion of the consideration received therefor may be charged to 'Stated capital' and a portion to 'paid-in surplus". The item 'Paid-in surplus' must be carried in the balance-sheet as a separate item from "Earned Surplus" or "undivided profits". *I.T. Commissioner (Central) Calcutta* v. *Standard Vacuum Oil Co.*, AIR 1966 SC 1393, 1397.

Capital punishment. Punishment of death.

Capital stock. The common stock or fund of a company; the sum raised by subscription of stock-holders divided into shares.

Capital structure. The composition of the capital (of a company) [Payment of Bonus Act (21 of 1965), S. 32(ix)(g)(i)].

Capital sum. "CAPITAL SUM" means—

(i) any sum paid or payable by way of a loan or repayment of a loan; and

(ii) any other sum paid or payable otherwise than as income, being a sum which is not paid or payable for full consideration in money or money's worth. [Income-tax Act (43 of 1961), S. 93(4)(d)]

Capitalisation. Act of providing money to be used as capital in a commercial or other business undertaking; the conversion of profit or income into capital.

The profits of a company can be capitalised in accordance with the Articles of Association and the law. The most common example of capitalisation of profits is by issuance of bonus shares to the share-holders. Mere transferring a sum of money by debiting it to the profit and loss account did not amount to capitalisation of profits. *P.K. Badiani* v. *I.T. Commissioner*, *Bombay*, AIR 1977 SC 560, 565, 566.

Capitalisation shares. Bonus shares go by the modern name of 'capitalisation shares'. It would mean that the undistributed profits have been ploughed back into the business and converted into share capital. [*Khoday Distilleries Ltd.* v. *CIT*, (2008) 1 SCC 256, 263, para 19]

Capitation fee. 'Capitation fee' means any kind of donation or contribution or payment other than the fee notified by the School. S. 2(b), [Right of Children to Free and Compulsory Education Act (35 of 2009)]

'Capitation fee' means any amount, by whatever name called, whether in cash or kind, in excess of the prescribed or, as the case may be, approved, rates of fees. *Forum for Fairness in Education Western Suburbs* v. *State of Maharashtra*, AIR 1999 Bom 310, p. 312.

Capitation or **capitation tax.** A poll tax upon the person simply, without any reference to his property or to any business in which he may be engaged, or to any employment which he may follow.

A capitation tax is a tax on the poll, without regard to property, business, or other circumstances.

Caprice. A turn of mind without substantial cause, implying wilfulness or wantonness in some degree, *Waller* v. *Skelton*, 186 Tenn. 433, 211 SW2d 445. *(Ballentine's Law Dictionary, 3rd Edn.)*

Arbitrary or unfounded motivation.

Capricious. Not guided by steady judgment, intent or purpose. [Indian Succession Act (39 of 1925), S. 61, ill. (viii)].

Captain. A Chief head, the master or commander of a vessel of any kind. [Navy Act (62 of 1957), S. 62].

Caption. The act of taking or arresting a person by judicial process; the title of heading of a legal document.

Captive. One taken prisoner in war; one made prisoner by force or stratagem in war by an enemy. (*Ency. of the Laws of England*)

Captive animal. Means any animal (not being a domestic animal) which is in captivity or confinement, whether permanent or temporary, or which is subjected to any appliance or contrivance for the purpose of hindering or preventing its escape from captivity or confinement or which pinioned or which is or appears to be maimed. [Prevention of Cruelty to Animals Act (59 of 1960), S. 2(c)]

The expression 'CAPTIVE ANIMAL' means any animal (not being a domestic animal) of whatsoever kind or species, and whether a quadruped or not, including any bird, fish, or reptile, which is in captivity, or confinement, or which is maimed, pinioned, or subjected to any appliance or contrivance for the purpose of hindering or preventing its escape from captivity or confinement. [Protection of Animals Act, 1911, S. 15]

"CAPTIVE ANIMAL" means any animal, specified in Schedule I, Schedule II, Schedule III or Schedule IV, which is captured or kept or bred in captivity. [Wild Life (Protection) Act (53 of 1972), S. 2(5)]

Captive consumption. The expression 'captive consumption' would mean the generation of electricity for the use of the holder of the plant, may be one single person or a joint venture collectively by many as one unit. [*A.P. Gas Power Corpn. Ltd.* v. *A.P. State Regulatory Commission*, (2004) 10, SCC 511, 527, para 33]

The phrase 'captive consumption' would mean the consumption of anything which is manufactured or produced, by the manufacturer for the purpose of his own use or consumption. It would not go out of the hands of manufacturer. *A.P. Gas Power Corpn. Ltd.* v. *A.P. State Regulatory Commission*, AIR 2004 SC 3090. [Electricity Act (36 of 2003), S. 2(8)]

Captivity. State of being kept in confinement [Geneva Conventions Act (6 of 1960), 3rd Sch., Art. 14].

Captivity is neither a punishment inflicted on prisoners of war, nor an act of vengeance; it is merely a temporary detention which is devoid of all penal character.

Captor. One who takes or seizes property in times of war; one who takes the property of an enemy. In a stricter sense, one who takes a prize at sea. (*International Law*) (*Burrill*).

The term also designates a belligerent who has captured the person of an enemy.

One who takes by force a prisoner or a prize at sea. [Indian Trust Act (2 of 1882), S. 1]; [Naval and Aircraft Prize Act (59 of 1971), S. 9(1)].

Capture. The act of taking by force; arrest (as) the capture of an enemy; seizure as prize.

A taking or seizure of the goods of an enemy; a taking of prizes in times of war, particularly at sea. "Capture", is a hostile seizure by one country of the ships or goods of the subjects of another country with which it is in a state of war, with intent to keep or to deprive the owner of the thing seized. (*International Law*)

Capture is a taking by an enemy as prize in time of war with intent to deprive the owner of all property in the thing taken. (25 HALSBURY'S Laws (4th edn) para 157).

The fact of taking forcibly or by stratagem. [Indian Evidence Act (1 of 1872), S. 114, ill, (b)].

Carat. A measure of weight for diamonds and such other precious stones; a term also used in assessing the value of gold and precious stones.

A twenty-fourth part used in expressing the proportionate fineness of a gold alloy. [Gold (Control) Act (45 of 1968) (*repealed*), S. 2(e)].

Caravan. Any structure adapted for human habitation and capable of being moved from one place to another, either by being towed or being transported on a motor vehicle or trailer.

Carbon credit. For the purpose of this section, "CARBON CREDIT" in respect of one unit shall mean reduction of one tonne of carbon dioxide emissions or emissions of its equivalent gases which is validated by the United Nations Framework of Climate Change and which can be traded in market at its prevailing market price. [Income-tax Act (43 of 1961), section 115BBG, *Explanation*]

Carbon paper. As defined in "pulp and paper manufacture" 2nd Edn., Vol. II—Carbon paper is made by coating paper with a mixture consisting principally of a wax and a pigment. The colour is obtained from the pigment, usually a carbon black of low oil absorption, plus toners, usually like pigments, or oil soluble dyes which are added to increase the blackness. *Collector of Central Excise, Kanpur* v. *Krishna Carbon Paper Co.*, AIR 1988 SC 2223.

"CARBON PAPER" it is made by coating paper with a mixture consisting principally of a wax and a pigment. The color is obtained from the pigment, usually a carbon black of low oil absorption, plus toners, usually lake pigments or oil-soluble dyes, which are added to increase the blackness. The wax, which acts as a binder for the pigment, must have a viscosity low enough to permit slight penetration into the paper, but not so low that the wax strikes through or sweats oil. The principal wax used is carnauba, although some, ceresin, beeswax, candelilla, ozokerite, ouricury, and synthetic waxes are also used. Special grades of microcrystalline waxes may be added to soften the coating and improve the printing qualities. Oleic acid is sometimes used as a solvent for oil-soluble dyes. *Collector of Central Excise* v. *Krishna Carbon Paper Co.*, AIR 1988 SC 2223.

Carcase/Carcass. 'CARCASE' means whole carcases of livestock, and sides, quarters and other wholesale cuts of carcases. [Agriculture Act, 1967, S. 25].

Carcass is the body of an animal when dead.

Carcer ad homines custodiendos, non ad puniendos, dari debet. A prison should be used for keeping or detaining persons, not for punishing.

Carcer non supplicii causa sed custodiae constitutus. A prison is established not for the sake of punishment, but for detention under guard.

Card game and other game of any sort. Includes any game show, an entertainment programme on television or electronic mode, in which people compete to win prizes or any other similar game. [Income-tax Act (43 of 1961), S. 2(24)(ix), *Expl* (ii)]

Cardamom. Means the fruit of cardamom plant and includes green cardamom, bleached cardamom, bleachable white cardamom, sundried cardamom, cardamom seeds, powdered cardamom and oil extracted from cardamom. [Spices Boards Act (10 of 1986), S. 2(b)]

Cardamom plant. Means Elettaria Cardomomum Maton, Ammomum Subulatum Roxband any other plant which the Board may, by notification in the official Gazette, declare to be a cardamom for the purposes of this Act. [Spices Board Act (10 of 1986), S. 2(c)].

Carding. The process in which fibres (as cotton *etc.*) are manipulated into silver form prior to spinning. [Employees Provident Funds and Miscellaneous Provisions Act (19 of 1952), Sch. I, item 25(d)].

Care. Charge; responsibility for well-being; serious attention, especially attention accompanied by caution, wariness *etc.* [IPC (45 of 1860), S. 52].

Care and control. In divorce or matrimonial proceedings, the power and responsibility of parents or other person with whom a child lives; custody.

Care to be taken by bailee. In Mulla's Commentary to Section 151, Indian Contract Act (9 of 1872), it is mentioned that under the English law a gratuitous bailee is bound to take the same care of the property entrusted to him as a reasonable prudent and careful man may fairly be expected to take of his property of the like description. *Munnalal* v. *Ganga Prasad,* AIR 1955 VP 30, 31. [Indian Contract Act (9 of 1872), S. 151]

"Career centre". Means any office (including employment exchange, place or portal) established and maintained in the manner prescribed by the Central Government for providing such career services (including registration, collection and furnishing of information, either by the keeping of registers or otherwise, manually, digitally, virtually or through any other mode) as may be prescribed by the Central Government, which may, *inter alia*, relate generally or specifically to—

(i) persons who seek to employ employees;

(ii) persons who seek employment;

(iii) occurrence of vacancies; and

(iv) persons who seek vocational guidance and career counselling or guidance to start self-employment. [Code on Social Security, 2020 (36 of 2020), section 2(9)]

Care-giver. "Care-giver" means a person who resides with a person with mental illness and is responsible for providing care to that person and includes a relative or any other person who performs this function, either free or with remuneration [The Mental Healthcare Act, 2017 (10 of 2017), S. 2(1)(e)]

Careless driving. An offence of driving a motor vehicle on a road without due care in disregard of the safety of other persons using the road.

Carelessness. Negligence; heedlessness, inattention; the state or quality of being careless; lack of ordinary care.

Cargo. "Cargo" includes anything carried or to be carried in a ship or other vessel. [Dock Workers (Safety, Health and Welfare Act (54 of 1986), S. 2(b)]

"Cargo" includes anything carried or to be carried in a ship or other vessel, or vehicle. [Occupational Safety, Healthy & Working Conditions Code, 2020 (37 of 2020), section 2(1)(j)]

"CARGO" includes ballast and ship's stores and fuel. [Merchant Shipping Act (44 of 1958), S. 356B(a)]

The lading of a ship or vessel, of whatever it consists; the lading or freight of a ship; the goods merchandise, or whatever is conveyed in a ship or other merchant vessel.

Goods shipped for carriage. [Dock Workers (Regulation of Employment) Act (9 of 1948), S. 2(aa)]

Cargo and **personal luggage.** The term "cargo" is used in contradistinction to personal luggage in the law relating to the carriage of goods. The latter has been defined as whatever a passenger takes with him for his personal use or convenience either with reference to his immediate necessities or for his personal needs at the end of the journey. *State of Maharashtra* v. *Mayer Hans George,* AIR 1965 SC 722.

Cargo handling service. Means loading, unloading, packing or unpacking of cargo and includes cargo handling services provided for freight in special containers or for non-containerised freight, services provided by a container freight terminal or any other freight terminal, for all modes of transport and cargo handling services incidental to freight, but does not include handling of export cargo or passenger baggage or mere transportation of goods. [Finance Act (32 of 1994), S. 65(23) (now repealed by Central Goods and Services Tax Act, 2017)]

Caricature. Gross representation of a person or thing by over-emphasis of certain characteristics.

Grotesque or lidicrous representation by exaggeration of parts, as in a portrait [Indian Evidence Act (1 of 1872), S. 3, ill. 3 and S. 32, ill. (n)].

Carnal. Pertaining to flesh; sensual.

Carnal intercourse Pertaining to the body, its passions and its appetites, animal; fleshy; sensual; impure; sexual. Black's Law Dictionary, 6th Edn., 1990 as cited in *Suresh Kumar Koushal* v. *Naz Foundation*, (2014) 1 SCC 1, para 48.

Carnal intercourse. Sexual intercourse. [IPC (45 of 1860), S. 377].

Carnal knowledge. Sexual intercourse; bodily connection by a man with a woman. In the definition of rape, "'Carnal knowledge,' means the penetration even to the slightest degree of the organ known as the male organ of generation." *Bhupinder Sharma* v. *State of H.P.*, AIR 2003 SC 4684. [IPC (45 of 1860), Ss. 375 and 376].

Coitus; copulation, the act of a man having sexual bodily connections with a woman; sexual intercourse. Carnal knowledge of a child is unlawful sexual intercourse with a female child under the age of consent. It is a statutory crime, usually a felony. Such offense is popularly known as 'statutory rape'. [Black's Law Dictionary, 6th Edn, 1990 as cited in Suresh Kumar Koushal v. Naz Foundation, (2014) 1 SCC 1, para 48].

It is not necessary that the vagina be entered or that the hymen be ruptured; the entering of the vulva or labia is sufficient. Black's Law Dictionary (6th Edn., 1990) as cited in *De Armond* v. *State*, 285 P2d 236 (Okl Cr 1955)] . See also *Suresh Kumar Koushal* v. *Naz Foundation,* (2014) 1 SCC 1, para 48].

While penetration is an essential element, there is 'carnal knowledge' if there is the slightest penetration of the sexual organ of the female by the sexual organ of the male. State v. Cross, 2000 SE2d 27, p. 29 : 284 NC 174 (1973) as cited in *Suresh Kumar Koushal* v. *Naz Foundation*, (2014) 1 SCC 1, para 48.

Carnally knew. A technical phrase to charge a person with the crime of rape.

Carnivore/DCS-1000. Computer system that the FBI has installed onto ISPs' servers, in order to read and analyze packets of data sent to or received by suspects in criminal investigations.

Carnivore Software. A software that uses packet sniffing at the Internet Service Provider (ISP) level to monitor data flow through ISPs. Carnivore is designed to monitor email and electronic communications. It is known as a customized packet sniffer which can be used to monitor all of the internet traffic of a particular user. Aparna Viswanathan, *Cyber Law: Indian & International Perspectives,* 2012, LexisNexis Butterworths at p. 151

Carpet area. Means the net usable floor area of an apartment, excluding the area covered by external walls, areas under services shafts, exclusive balcony or verandah area and exclusive open terrace area, but includes the area covered by the internal partition walls of the apartment.

Explanation.—For the purpose of this clause, the expression "exclusive balcony or verandah area" means the area of the balcony or verandah, as the case may be, which is appurtenant to the net usable floor area of an apartment, meant for the exclusive use of the allottee; and "exclusive open terrace area" means the area of open terrace which is appurtenant to the net usable floor area of an apartment, meant for the exclusive use of the allottee. [Real Estate (Regulation and Development) Act (16 of 2016), s. 2(k)].

Carriage. "CARRIAGE" means the carriage of passengers or goods by a railway administration. [Railways Act (24 of 1989), S. 2(2)]

"CARRIAGE" includes any carriage, wagon, cart, truck, vehicle or other means of conveying goods, or passengers by land. In whatever manner the same may be propelled. [Explosives Act (4 of 1884), S. 4].

"CARRIAGE" in the case of a tramway on which steam-power or any other mechanical power or electrical power is used, includes an engine worked on the tramway for the purpose of producing or utilizing that power. [Indian Tramways Act (11 of 1886), S. 3(9)]

Means of conveyance especially a wheeled vehicle. [Explosives Act (4 of 1884), S. 4], [Indian Railways Act (9 of 1890), S. 3(10)]; the act of carrying.

Carriage fee. 'Carriage fee' means any fee paid by a broadcaster to a distributor of TV channels, for carriage of the channels or bouquets of channels of that broadcaster on the distribution platform owned or operated by such distributor of TV channels, without specifying the placement of various channels of the broadcaster *vis-à-vis* channels of other broadcasters. [Telecommunication (Broadcasting and Cable Services) Interconnection Regulations (13 of 2004), Regn. 2(ia) (inserted by Fifth Amendment, Regulations, 2009)]

Carriage of goods. (by sea) covers the period from the time when the goods are loaded on to the time when they are discharged from the ship. [Indian Carriage of Goods by Sea Act (26 of 1925), Schedule, Art. 1, Cl. (e)]

"Carriage of goods" includes haulage of goods. HALSBURY, 4th Edn., Vol. 40, para 730, p. 554.

Carried. The entry makes no mention of the agency through which goods are carried. Goods may be carried by a vehicle belonging to the producer or by a hired vehicle. They would be carried even if the vehicle is not hired. Therefore goods even when carried without the employment of common or public carriers, would fall within the ambit of the entry. *H.P. Barua* v. *State of Assam,* AIR 1955 Ass 249, 260. [Constitution of India, Sch. VII, List II, Entry 56]

Carrier. One who carries; one employed or engaged in the business of carrying goods for hire by land water or air. [Indian Carriage of Goods by Sea Act (26 of 1925), Preamble].

"CARRIER" means a person who is engaged in the business of transporting for hire goods by road, rail, inland waterways or sea. [Multimodal Transportation of Goods Act (28 of 1993), S. 2(a)]

"CARRIER" means a person who performs or undertakes to perform for hire, the carriage or part thereof, of goods by road, rail, inland waterways sea or air. [Multimodal Transportation of Goods Act (28 of 1993), S. 2(a)]

"CARRier" means a person who is engaged in the business of transporting passengers by water or air and includes any association of persons, whether incorporated or not, by whom the aircraft or the ship is owned or chartered. [Immigration (Carriers Liability) Act (52 of 2000), S. 2(1)(a)]

"CARRIER" includes the owner or the charterer who enters into a contract of carriage with a shipper. [Indian Carriage of Goods by Sea Act (26 of 1925), Sch. Art. 1(a)]

Carrier of articles of special value. The expression "carrier of articles of special value" in the marginal note has reference to the totality of the articles in the parcel and not to the special value of each. *Bhukandas* v. *UOI,* AIR 1963 Guj 150. [Indian Railways Act (9 of 1890), S. 75]

Carry. "To carry" a person includes putting him in a position to be carried.

To convey. [Army Act (46 of 1950), S. 4].

A ship will be considered to "carry" goods from the moment when they were loaded on board.

Carry forward. To transfer to the succeeding column, page or book or to the next account. [Mines Act (35 of 1952), S. 52(4), prov. II].

Carry on business. A person carries on a trade or business when he "habitually does and contracts to do a thing capable of producing profit", but it has been said that it is not necessary in order to constitute the carrying on of a trade that the persons engaged in it should make or desire to make a profit by it. HALSBURY, 4th Edn., Vol. 27, para 540, p. 437.

In getting their ships repaired by the appellant the non-resident companies cannot be said to carry on business with them in the real sense of that word. *Mazagaon Dock Ltd.* v. *Commissioner of Income Tax and Excess Profits Tax*, AIR 1958 SC 861, 866.

Carry on personal cultivation. "A person is said to carry on personal cultivation on a land when he contributes his own physical labour or that of the members of his family in the cultivation of that land". *S.N. Sudalaimuthu Chettiar* v. *Palaniandavan,* AIR 1966 SC 469.

Carry on profession. Even an assistant to a professional man like a surgeon or an architect will be considered as carrying on that profession.

Carry on trade or business. To conduct, prosecute or continue a particular avocation or business as a continuous operation or permanent occupation. The repetition of acts may be sufficient. To hold one's self out to others as engaged in the selling of goods or services.

Carry out. To carry into practice. [Plantations Labour Act (69 of 1951), S. 5(b)]; to execute. [Coal Mines Labour Welfare Fund Act (32 of 1947), S. 6(1)(b)]; to accomplish; to put into operation.

Carry over. Postponement of the completion of a contract to buy or sell shares.

Carrying. Taking back rice from mill amounts to 'carrying'. *Har Murat* v. *State,* AIR 1953 All 545. [U.P. Foodgrains Movement Control Order, 1949, Cl. 3(vii)]

Carrying arms or weapons. To constitute the offence of carrying arms, the weapons must be carried as arms. The intent with which the weapon is carried must be that of going armed or being armed.

Carrying on business. When a company is incorporated it may not necessarily come into existence for the purpose of carrying on a business. *Lakshminarayan Ram Gopal and Son Ltd.* v. *Government of Hyderabad,* AIR 1954 SC 364. [Income-tax Act (11 of 1922), S. 10]

The phrase 'carrying on' business implies a repetition or series of acts.

To keep up business [Companies Act (1 of 1956), S. 17(1)(a) (Replaced by Companies Act 2013) and Constitution of India, Art. 19(6)]; [Indian Partnership Act (9 of 1932), S. 6, *Expln.* 2].

A firm cannot be said to carry on business where it has only canvassers or agents for the purpose of obtaining offers of business and attending to matters ancillary to its business and that the business of the firm will be taken to be as being carried on where the contract relating to the business are entered into or wherefrom effective control is exercised. *Mohd. Kasim Haji Ahamed Kunju* v. *Shree Hanuman Industries,* AIR 1956 TC 200, 201. [CPC (5 of 1908), S. 20(a)]

The expression "carrying on business" implies that there must be some real and systematic or organized course of activity or conduct with a set purpose of making profit; there must exist the characteristics of volume, frequency, continuity and system indicating an intention to make profit. But no single test or group of tests is decisive of the intention to carry on a business. It must be decided in the circumstances of each particular case whether an inference could be raised that the assessee is carrying on the business of purchasing or selling goods within the meaning of the statute. *Director of Supplies & Disposals* v. *Member, Board of Revenue*, AIR 1967 SC 1826.

The government is carrying on business within the meaning of S. 20, CPC (5 of 1908), when it is providing transport of all descriptions in a country so vast as India. *Pratap Chandra Biswar* v. *Union of India,* AIR 1956 Ass 85, 94.

In getting their ships repaired by the appellant the non-resident companies cannot be said to carry on business with them in the real sense of that word. *Mazagaon Dock Ltd.* v. *Commissioner of Income Tax and Excess Profits Tax*, AIR 1958 SC 861, 866.

A "carrying on business" need not be personal carrying one.

A "carrying on of business" through an agent would be business carried on by the principal.

Carrying out the purposes of the act. (*Interpretation of Statutes*) In some statutes power is given to frame rules and when so framed they are made part of the Statute. In such a case, it might be permissible to supplement the provision of the Statute itself within limits. But where rules are to be framed for "carrying out the purpose of the Act", such rules cannot travel beyond the four corners of the Act itself.

Carrying over. A term, in stock exchange, used to signify the postponement of the settlement of an account over the proper settling day to the next. For such accommodation the speculator would have to pay backwardation and other charges.

Carryover basis. The basis of property which is transferred by gift or in trust.

Cart. "CART" in the Bengal Mun. Act means any cart, hackery or wheeled vehicle with or without springs ordinarily drawn by animals, and not included in the definition of "carriage." [Bengal Act III of 1884 (Municipal), S. 6, Cl. 2].

It does not include "gigs, dog carts, or gentlemen's carriages." *Per* LUSH, J., *Danby* v. *Hunter*, 49 LJMC 16.

Carte blanche. The signature of one or more individuals on a white paper, with a sufficient space left above it to write a note or other writing; blanksheet; authorization to do what one wills.

Cartel. "CARTEL" includes an association of producers, sellers, distributors, traders or service providers who, by agreement amongst themselves, limit, control or attempt to control the production, distribution, sale or price of, or, trade in goods or provision of services. [Competition Act, 2002 (12 of 2003), S. 2(c)]

(*Milit.*) A writing or agreement between states at war for exchange of prisoners.

The 'cartel' is an association of producers who by agreement among themselves attempt to control production, sale and prices of the product to obtain a monopoly in any particular industry or commodity. It amounts to an unfair trade practice which is not in the public interest. *Union of India* v. *Hindustan Development Corporation*, AIR 1994 SC 988, 1008.

Cartel ship. A ship used between belligerents under a cartel. A cartel ship sails under a safe conduct given by an officer called a commissary of prisoners, who resides in the country of the enemy. "She is protected from capture or molestation both when she has prisoners on board, and when she is upon a voyage to fetch prisoners of her own country, or is returning from handing over those belonging to the enemy". (*Hall International Law, 5th. Ed.*, p. 551).

Cartoon. Large illustrations, especially on politics and political events in comic papers.

Cartoonist. One who draws cartoons. [Working Journalists and Other Newspaper Employees (Conditions of Service) and Miscellaneous Provisions Act (45 of 1955), S. 2(f)].

Carving. Decorative sculpture. [Ancient Monuments and Archaeological Sites and Remains Act (24 of 1958), Preamble].

CAS Area. 'CAS Area' means the States, cities, towns or areas, where, in terms of a notification issued under sub-section (1) of Section 4-A of the Cable Television Networks (Regulation) Act, 1995 (7 of 1995), it is obligatory for every multi system operator or cable operator to transmit or retransmit programmes of any pay channel through an addressable system and the expression 'Non-CAS Area' shall be constructed accordingly. [Standards of Quality Service (Broadcasting and Cable Services) Cable Television-Non-CAS Areas) Regulations, 2009, Regn. 2(j)]

Case. "CASE" includes a suit or any proceeding before a Court. [Legal Services Authorities Act (39 of 1987), S. 2(1)(a)]

In this Chapter, unless the context otherwise requires,—

"CASE" means any proceeding under this Act for the assessment or reassessment of any person in respect of any year or years, or by way of appeal or revision in connection with such assessment or reassessment, which may be pending before an income-tax authority on the date on which an application under sub-section (1) of Section 245C is made:

Provided that where any appeal or application for revision has been preferred after the expiry of the period specified for the filing of such appeal or application for revision under this Act and which has not been admitted, such appeal or revision shall not be deemed to be a proceeding pending within the meaning of this clause. [Income-tax Act (43 of 1961), S. 245A(b)]

In a legal sense a state of facts which furnishes occasion for the exercise of the jurisdiction of a Court of Justice; a subject on which the judicial power is capable of acting and which has been submitted to it by a party in the forms required by law; a state of fact involving a question for discussion, especially a cause or suit in Court; a question contested before a Court of justice in an action or suit brought before it.

Condition; state of being; situation [Indian Partnership Act (9 of 1932), S. 44(a)]; a cause or suit; a state of things requiring discussion, decision or investigation [Income-tax Act (43 of 1961), S. 127(2), *Expln.*]; a decided case; covering; box [Trade and Merchandise Marks Act (43 of 1958), S. 2(1)(b)].

In common parlance it has a more extended meaning than the word 'suit,' or 'action', and may include application for divorce, applications for the establishment of high ways, applications for orders of support of relatives, and other special proceedings unknown to the common law.

The word "case" in S. 115 of CPC (5 of 1908) is not confined to a litigation in which there is a plaintiff who seeks to obtain particular relief in damages or otherwise against a defendant who is before the Court. It includes an *ex parte* application praying that persons in the position of trustees or officials should perform their trust or discharge their official duties. *Comunidade of Velguem of Bichoim* v. *Vassant Vithal Govekar*, AIR 1969 Goa 37 at p. 38.

The word 'case' in S. 115, CPC (5 of 1908), covers a finding on an issue. *Srinivasa Raw* v. *Kaliaperumal*, AIR 1966 Mad 321, 322.

It includes a proceeding in a civil Court in which the jurisdiction of the Court is invoked for the determination of some claim or right legally enforceable. *Jitnath Singh* v. *State of Bihar*, AIR 1974 Pat 28, 35.

It is a word of comprehensive import. It includes an entire proceeding and a part of it, a case is said to be decided if the Court adjudicates it for the purpose of suit, some right or obligation of the parties in controversy, every order of the Court cannot be regarded as case decided within the meaning of S. 115 of the CPC (5 of 1908) *I. T. Commissioner* v. *India Discourt Co.*, AIR 1970 SC 406 at p. 410.

Since the case before the Division bench was about the condonation of the delay in filing of the Memorandum of Appeal, it could not be said that the entire case was involved before the said bench. *State of Bihar* v. *Birla Gwalior P. Ltd.*, AIR 1974 Cal 202, 203. [Constitution of India, Art. 132(1), 133(1)]

'Case' means the case of each individual person. Though several persons may join in presenting a common Memorandum of Appeal, the appeal of each forms a separate 'case'. *Nar Singh* v. *State of Uttar Pradesh*, AIR 1954 SC 457, 458. [Constitution of India, Art. 134(1)(c)]

The word "case" is used in a more comprehensive sense of including (i) pending proceeding as well as, (ii) proceedings to be initiated in future, (iii) as also pretransfer completed proceedings. *C.I.T.* v. *Bidhu Bhusan Sarkar*, (1967) 63 ITR 278, 287 (SC). [Income-tax Act (43 of 1961), S. 127(i) *Expln.*]

'Case' means facts or events which furnish cause of action to party. *Kanti Prasad Garj* v. *Vice Chancellor, Jawaharlal Nehru Krishi Vishwa Vidyalaya, Jabalpur*, AIR 1971 MP 15. [States Reorganisation Act (37 of 1956), Section 51 (2)]

In criminal jurisdiction means ordinarily a proceeding for the prosecution of a person alleged to have committed an offence. In other contexts the word may represent other kinds of proceedings. *Bhimappa Bassappa Bhu Sannavar* v. *Laxman Shivarayappa Samagouda,* AIR 1970 SC 1153.

The word "case" is not limited in its import to the entirety of the matter in dispute in an action. To interpret the word "case" as an entire proceeding only and not a part of the proceeding imposes an unwarranted restriction on the exercise of powers of superintendence and may result in certain cases in denying relief to the aggrieved litigant where it is most needed and may result in the perpetration of gross injustice. *Baldevdas Shivlal* v. *Filmistan Distributors (India) (P.) Ltd.,* AIR 1970 SC 406.

The word 'case' in ordinary usage means "event", happening, situation, circumstances. The term "case" in legal sense means "a case" suit or proceeding in Court or Tribunal. *J.C. Yadav* v. *State of Haryana,* (1990) 2 SCC 189.

The term "case" is a word of comprehensive import; it includes civil proceedings other than suits, and is not restricted by anything contained in the section to the entirety of the proceeding in a civil Court. To interpret the term 'case' as an entire proceeding only and not a part of a proceeding would be to impose a restriction upon the exercise of powers of superintendence to which the jurisdiction to issue writs, and the supervisory jurisdiction are not, subject and may result in certain cases in denying relief to an aggrieved litigant where it is most needed, and may result in the perpetration of gross injustice. The term 'case' includes a suit, but in ascertaining the limits of the jurisdiction of the High Court, there would be no warrant for equating it with a suit alone. *R.S. Khanna* v. *F.I. Dillon*, AIR 1964 SC 497, paras 11 and 12; *Michael Mascarenhas* v. *John Mascarenhas*, AIR 1996 Kant 348, 352.

The word 'case' in S. 115, CPC should be construed to include the decision on any substantial question in controversy between the parties affecting their rights even though such order is passed in the course of the trial of the suit. *Niranjan Nath* v.

Sardar Mul, AIR 1950 Raj 31; *Nandkishore* v. *Mangilal*, AIR 1951 Raj 59.

The expression 'case' includes an interlocutory proceeding relating to the rights and obligation of the parties. *S.S. Khanna* v. *F.J. Dillon*, AIR 1964 SC 497, 500.

'Case' and 'Counter case'. When two criminal cases resulting from two different versions of the same incident are tried and disposed of by the same Court by pronouncing judgments on the same day, they are called 'Case' and 'Counter case'. *Sudhir* v. *State of MP*, (2001) 2 SCC 688, para 8 : AIR 2001 SC 826.

Case certified : Case referred. Where there is a difference of opinion between judges of a Division Bench they may certify or refer the question to the Full Bench; but it must be a distinct point or proposition of law so clearly stated that it can be answered without regard to the other issues of law or fact in the case.

Case decided. [See CPC (5 of 1908), S. 115]

The term 'case' which has been decided includes an interlocutory order of Court directing payment of additional Court fee on plaint. *Krishna Kumar* v. *Parmeshridevi*, AIR 1967 Punj 389, 391 (FB).

Where the Court exercises its judicial discretion in granting or refusing the leave to the defendant to serve interrogatories, it cannot be stated to be an adjudication of some right or obligation of the parties in controversy and so it is not a 'case decided'. *Y. Venkateswara Rao* v. *K. Nagamma*, AIR 1972 Mys 254, 255; *Maheswari Oil Mill* v. *Girjanath, Durga Saran*, AIR 1980 All 265, 266.

If some illegality or irregularity is committed by the trial Court in the matter of taking evidence before the plaintiffs have closed their case such an order will not come under one expression 'case decided'. *Ramgulam Chowdhry* v. *Nausir Choudhary*, AIR 1972 Pat 499, 502.

Passing of an *ex parte* interim order does not amount to case decided. It is only when a final order is passed deciding the application it can be said that a case has been decided. *Mahendra Pratap Kapur* v. *Burmah Shell Oil Storage & Distributing Co. Ltd.*, AIR 1973 All 109, 110.

Where the Court decides, that the suit is maintainable that the plaintiff has *locus standi* and that the Court has jurisdiction to try the suit, the decision is a 'case decided' for the purpose of revision. *Sohan Singh & Co.* v. *Mohammad Ashok Tyagi*, AIR 1973 HP 39, 41.

Proceeding to set aside an *ex parte* decree under O. IX, Rule 13 [CPC (5 of 1908)] amounts to 'case decided'. *Dhoba Naik* v. *Sabi Ders*, AIR 1973 Ori 182, 183.

The admission of a document is not a 'case decided'. *Parsuram Dubey* v. *Mahanth Laxman Das*, AIR 1974 Pat 278, 280; *Jai Singh* v. *Lala Ganesh*, AIR 1977 HP 68; *Sagarmal* v. *Gulab Chand*, AIR 1978 P&H 251, 252.

An order rejecting an application for the appointment of a commissioner is not a 'case decided'. *Harrinder Kaur* v. *Godharam*, AIR 1979 P&H 76, 79.

It is not always necessary that rights or obligations must be expressly decided. It is sufficient if an adjudication that has been made would have the "necessary effect of deciding the rights of obligations". *Media Nasuyamuna* v. *Choppela Lakshmanamma*, AIR 1992 AP 183, 188.

An interlocutory order not affecting any of the rights of the party, the subject-matter of decision in the suit, does not amount to 'case decided'. *Srisugli* v. *Collector/Dist. Magistrate*, AIR 1988 All 246, 247.

Rejection of an application for summoning of certain document does not amount to 'case decided' under Section 115 of CPC *I.I. of Science Employees Association* v. *Indian Institute of Science*, AIR 1999 Kant 307, 308, para 3. [CPC (5 of 1908), S. 115]

Orders/directions of taking cognizance, initiating inquisition proceedings, requiring production of lunatic before the Court and asking the Bank not to allow anyone to operate alleged lunatic's locker till further orders cannot be said to be 'Case (s) decided' under Section 115 of the Code. *Bashir Ahmad Mir* v. *Gh. Husain Wani*, AIR 1999 J & K 34, 36, para 10. [J. & K. CPC (10 of 1977 Smvt.), S. 115]

Case, Cause. The *case* is matter of fact; the *cause* is matter of question; a *cause* involves circumstances and consequences; a *cause* involves reasons and arguments: a *case* is something to be learned; *a cause* is something to be decided. A *case* needs only to be stated; a *cause* must be defended: a *cause* may include *cases*, but not *vice versa*: in all *causes* that are to be tried, there are many legal *causes* that must be cited.

Case instituted upon complaint. The words "in any case instituted upon complaint" appearing in the section mean "in any case of which the Court has taken cognizance upon complaint" and "complaint" does not include a police report. *K. Damodharan* v. *V.K. Sippi*, AIR 1960 Ker 389. [CrPC, (5 of 1898), S. 417(3) (now S. 378 (4) of 1974 Code)]

Case-law. The body of law created by judicial decisions, as distinguished from law derived from statutes and other sources. Law established by judicial decisions.

Case management. Case management means the proceedings of a case are managed effecttively by the Judge presiding over the Court and not controlled by the lawyers. (*Arbitration*)

Cases arising of original suits. A revision challenging an order passed during the hearing of the original suit, an application for restitution, review, execution or restitution of an appeal are all cases arising out of the original suit. *Phulwati* v.

Gursahai, AIR 1975 All 262, 265. [CPC (5 of 1908), S. 115]

Cash. For the purposes of this sub-section, "CASH" means—

(a) coins or notes in any currency;

(b) postal orders;

(c) traveller's cheques;

(d) banker's drafts; and

(e) such other monetary instruments as the Central Government or, as the case may be, the State Government may specify by an order made in writing.

[Unlawful Activities (Prevention) Act (37 of 1967), S. 25(5) Expln. as substituted by Unlawful Activities (Prevention) Amendment Act (29 of 2004), S. 7]

Cash means the actual coin of the country, or bank-notes, which are part of the currency, and are treated a equivalent to coin.

Ordinarily '*cash*' has a narrower meaning than money.

The expression "cash balance" has to be construed as the excess of credits over debits. *Custodian, Evacuee Property* v. *Rabia Bai*, AIR 1976 SC 2557, 2565. [Displaced Persons Compensation and Rehabilitation Act (44 of 1954), S. 14(1)(b)]

Cash accounting. Also called cash-flow accounting (CFA), an accounting system that keeps records only of a business's cash transactions (receipts and payments), as opposed to *accrual accounting* which records when expenses are incurred or money is earned. (*International Accounting*)

Cash-basis accounting method. A system which considers only cash actually received as income and only cash actually paid out as an expense.

Cash-book. In this rule—

"CASH BOOK" means a record of all cash receipts and payments, kept and maintained from day to day and giving the cash balance in hand at the end of each day or at the end of a specified period not exceeding a month. [Income-tax Rules, 1962, R. 6F(2), *Expln.* (b)]

Account-book in which is kept a record of all cash transactions.

Cash credit account. 'Cash credit account' is an account against credit granted by a bank and is operated like a current account on which an overdraft has been sanctioned. [*Raneeganj Coal Assn. Ltd.* v. *Union of India*, AIR 1990 SC 1879]

Cash delivery. Delivery of foreign exchange on the day of transaction. [Foreign Exchange Management (Foreign Exchange Derivative Contracts) Regulations, 2000, Reg. 2(iii)]

Cash discount. Cash discount is allowed when the purchaser makes payment promptly or within a period of credit allowed. It is a discount granted in consideration of expeditious payment. *Dy. Sales Tax Commissioner* v. *Advani Coorlikon*, AIR 1980 SC 609, 610. [Central Sales Tax Act (74 of 1956), S. 2(h)].

Cash equivalent. A short-term security which is liquid enough to be considered equivalent to cash.

Cash flow. Cash which is generated from a business or transaction.

Cash flow reporting. There are two methods of 'cash flow reporting' *i.e* direct and indirect. Both give identical results in the matter of the final total. They differ only in presentation of the data contained in the cash flows from operational activities. Indirect method is known as reconciliation method. [*Reliance Energy Ltd.* v. *Maharashtra State Road Development Corpn., Ltd.*, (2007) 8 SCC 1, 32, para 50]

Cash Reserve Ratio. Called in short CRR. Suppose a bank has total deposits of Rs. 100 Bn and is required to maintain a CRR of say 5%. This means that the bank should maintain in current accounts with the central bank or any other approved bank balances, not less than Rs. 5 Bn. This much amount is impounded and kept in the free form. And the bank cannot lend this money. This acts as a buffer to the bank. In India, the Reserve Bank of India decides the CRR from time to time.

Cash value. Of an article is measured by the amount of cash into which it can be converted.

Cashewnut. Is an edible seed or nut belonging to the family of anacardiaceae and grows mostly in tropical and sub-tropical regions where humidity is great. It is generally grown in the States of Kerala, Karnataka and Tamil Nadu, in India, in East Africa and in the tropics of Central and South America. *K. Janardhan Pillai* v. *UOI,* AIR 1981 SC 1485.

Cashier. An officer or agent whose business is mainly to take care of the money of an institution or a private person, or of a firm or public company. [IPC (45 of 1860), S. 499, 7th *Excep., Illustration*]; to dismiss with disgrace. [Army Act (46 of 1950), S. 2(2)].

To force a military personnel to leave or to dismiss him for he having done something seriously wrong.

Cast. Imposition upon a party litigant of costs in the suit.

To throw down; to drop; something that is formed by casting in mould or form [Copyright Act (14 of 1957), S. 2(za)]; the assignment of various parts of a play to several actors.

Cast iron. A commercial alloy of iron, carbon, and silicon cast in a mold, being hard, brittle, non-malleable, and incable of hammerwelded but more easily fusible than steel, contains usually 2.0 to 4.5 percent carbon and 1 to 4 percent silicon oand having a melting point of 1200 to 1500 C and weight per cubic foot of 425 to 475 pounds. Also see *Bengal Iron Corpn.* v. *CTO,* AIR 1993 SC 2414.

For the purpose of interpreting the provision of Section 14 of Central Sales Tax Act, the definition of cast iron must be considered in the manner in which it is understood by the trade and commerce. Molten metal which cannot be bought or sold in trade or commerce cannot be regarded as cast iron. *Vasantham Foundry* v. *Union of India,* AIR 1995 SC 2400.

Castaway. To throw away. One who is cast away; that which is cast away. A vessel "castaway" is one lost and irrecoverable by ordinary means.

Caste. A word applied to the distinctions of birth, tribe, and occupation. "A caste may be taken to be a combination of a number of persons governed by a body of usages which differentiate them from the others. The usage may refer to social or religious observances, to drink, food, ceremonials, pollution, occupation or marriage. Some of these usages may be common to others also. The caste is invariably known by a distinctive name or identification. It has its own rules for internal management, and has also got power of exclusion."

A caste is a horizontal segmental division of society spread over a district or a region or the whole state and also sometimes outside it. *K.C. Vasanth Kumar* v. *State of Karnataka*, AIR 1985 SC 1495, 1503.

Castigatory. Corrective; punitive.

An instrument or device of chastisement formerly used to punish women by repeatedly plunging them underwater.

Casting vote is the term used to denote the final and decisive vote which the law, in some cases, allows the chairman or the president of a meeting to give in case of an equality of votes; vote given by the chairman of a deliberative assembly.

The vote given by the Chairman or President of a deliberative assembly in case of equality of votes. [Army Act (46 of 1950), S. 132(4) and Constitution of India, Art. 100(1)].

Castration. The act of gelding; the act of depriving of the testicles. The consequences of castration, when complete, are impotence and sterility.

Casual. Occasional; incidental; accidental (as) casual expenses.

Subject to or produced as a result of chance; occasional.

Casual employment. Employment which is not regular or continuous. It is employment for short periods or for a limited or temporary purpose.

Casual pauper. A destitute wayfarer or wanderer who applied for relief.

Casual taxable person. "Casual taxable person" means a person who occasionally undertakes transactions involving supply of goods or services or both in the course or furtherance of business, whether as principal, agent or in any other capacity, in a State or a Union territory where he has no fixed place of business [The Central Goods and Services Tax Act, 2017 (12 of 2017), S. 2(20)]

Casual trader. 'CASUAL TRADER' means a person, other than a registered dealer, who has no fixed place of business in West Bengal and who,—

(a) as a consignor or consignee, brings into West Bengal any goods, other than those specified in Schedule I or Schedule IV or those notified under sub-section (2) of Section 10, from any place outside West Bengal for sale in West Bengal, or

(b) procures goods, other than those specified in Schedule I or Schedule IV, otherwise than by way of purchase from a person other than a registered dealer, for sale in West Bengal, or

(c) purchases any goods, other than those specified in Schedule I or Schedule IV, in West Bengal from any person, other than a registered dealer, for purposes other than his personal use or consumption of such goods in West Bengal, and includes whether he has a fixed place of business in West Bengal or not,—

(i) a transporter as defined in clause (a) of the *Explanation* of Section 72 and who while carrying such goods in his good vehicle fails to disclose the name and address of the consignor or consignee in West Bengal or fails to furnish any copy of invoice, challan, transport receipt or consignment note or document of like nature in respect of such goods, or

(ii) an owner or lessee of a warehouse where such goods are stored and who fails to disclose the name and address of the owner of such goods or fails to satisfy the Commissioner that such goods are for his personal use or consumption, and who for such failure shall be deemed to have brought such goods as specified in sub-clause (a) or procured such goods as specified in sub-clause (c) as the case may be, on his own account. [West Bengal Sales Tax Act (49 of 1994), S. 2(6)]

Casual vacancy. Means a vacancy occurring otherwise than by efflux of time.

Casualty. Inevitable accident; event not to be foreseen or provided against. (*Standard Dict.*).

What happens by chance or accident.

An unfortunate occurrence. [Inland Vessels Act (1 of 1917), S. 32(b)]; serious accident.

"Casualty" includes any vessel which—

(i) is lost, abandoned, materially damaged;

(ii) causes loss of material or damage to any other vessel;

(iii) causes any loss of life or personal injury;

(iv) causes pollution as a result of or in connection with its operation. [Inland Vessels Act, 2021 (24 of 2021), section 3(e)]

An "accident" or "casuality", according to the common understanding, proceeds from an unknown cause, or is the unusual effect of a known cause. Either may be said to occur by chance or unexpectedly.

Casualty insurance. An agreement made to indemnify against losses which result due to theft, accident, property damages and worker's compensation.

Casus fortuitus non est sperandus, et nemo tenetur divinare. (*Lat.*) A fortuitous event is not to be expected, and no man is bound to divine or foresee it.

This is another way of saying *nemo tenure ad impossibile*, for to foresee a fortuitous or unlooked for event is impossible, and this the law requires of no one. This maxim, however, would not excuse anyone from liability resulting reasonably from his act, although such liability was not foreseen by the party himself.

Casus major. (*Lat.*) An unusual accident.

Casus omissus. A point unprovided for by a statute. (*Wharton*)

Catalogue. A list of books *etc.* [Trade and Merchandise Marks Act (43 of 1958), S. 76(1)(c)]; a complete enumeration of items arranged systematically in a pamphlet. [Weekly Holidays Act (18 of 1942), S. 2(d)].

Catchment area. The entire area from which drainage is received by a body of water (as a reservoir, lake or river). [Punjab Reorganisation Act (31 of 1966), S. 48(5)(ii)]

Catchpole. A bailiff.

Category. A class, group or classification of any kind. [Industrial Disputes Act (14 of 1947), S. 25G].

Cater. It means 'to act as caterer, or purveyor of provisions; to provide a supply of food'. It also means "To occupy oneself in procuring or providing (requisites, things desired, etc.) and 'cater' is understood to mean 'Purvey food and other requisites'. Oxford Dictionary as cited in *Brihanmumbai Mahanagarpalika* v. *Willingdon Sports Club*, (2013) 16 SCC 260, para 26.

Caterer. Means any person who supplies, either directly or indirectly, any food, edible preparations, alcoholic or non-alcoholic beverages or crockery and similar articles or accoutrements for any purpose or occasion. [Finance Act (32 of 1994), S. 65(24) (now repealed by Central Goods and Services Tax Act, 2017)]

Catch-up rule. This judicially evolved rule enables a general category employee to regain his seniority over a reserved category employee promoted earlier. See also *M. Naraj* v. *U.O.I.*, (2006) 8 SCC 212, *Union of India* v. *Virpal Singh,* (1995) 6 SCC 684; *Ajit Singh (ii)* v. *State of Punjab,* (1999) 7 SCC 209; *Kamlesh Jaiswal* v. *The General Manager, Centaaur Hotel,* 91 (2001) DLT 161.

Cattle. The word "CATTLE" shall, besides horned cattle, include elephants, camels, horses, asses, mules, sheep, goats and swine. [Police Act (5 of 1861), S. 1)

"CATTLE" includes elephants, camels, buffaloes, horses, mares, geldings, ponies, colts, fillies, mules, asses, pigs, rams, ewes, sheep, lambs, goats and kids. [Forest Act (16 of 1972), S. 2 and Cattle-trespass Act (1 of 1871), S. 3]

Beasts subject to ownership; domestic animals useful for labour; live-stock; domestic quadrupeds which serve for tillage or other labour, or as food for man.

Cattle-fair. Means a periodical concourse of buyers and sellers in a place generally for sale and purchase of cattle at times or on occasions ordained by custom." *Municipal Committee, Amritsar* v. *State of Punjab*, AIR 1969 SC 1100 at p. 1104.

Cattle market. Means a place where the business of sale or purchase of cattle is regularly conducted. [Punjab Cattle Fairs (Regulation) Act, 1967, S. 2(bbb)]

Caucus. A meeting of the legal voters of any political party assembled for the purpose of choosing delegates, or for the nomination of candidates for office.

Caught. To say that a person was "caught" with his house girl, would import that he was discovered in such a position that adultery would be inferred.

Causa causans. The immediate cause as opposed to a remote cause; the "last link in the chain of causation."

Causa causans, or remota. The original or remote cause.

The immediate cause; the proximate or efficient cause, opposed to some remote cause.

Causa causataor proxima. The immediate or next cause.

Causa ecclesie publicis causis equiparatur; et summa est ratio que pro religione facit. The cause of the Church is equal to public causes; and for the best of reasons, it is the cause of religion. (*Latin for Lawyers*)

Causa et origio est materia negotii. (*Maxim*) The cause and origin is the substance of the thing.

Causa mortis. With reference to or in contemplation of death.

Causa proxima. The immediate cause.

Causa proxima et non remota spectatur. (*Maxim*) The immediate and not the remote cause is to be considered.

Causa proxima non remota spectatur. The immediate, not the memote cause, is to be considered.

Causa rei. Things accessory or appurtenant. (*Civil Law*)

Causa remota. Remote cause. A cause operating indirectly by the intervention of other causes.

Causa sine qua non. A cause without which a thing cannot exist.

A cause without which the effect would not have been caused.

Causa vaga et incerta non est causa rationabilis. (*Maxim*) "A vague and uncertain cause is not a reasonable cause."

Causae colesiac publicis aequiparatur : et summa est ratio quae pro religione facit. The cause of the church is equal to public cause; and paramount is the reason which makes for religion.

Causae dotis, vitae, libertatis, fasci, sunt inter favorabilia in lege. Causes of dower, liberty of life, revenue, are among the favourable things in law.

Causal relation. Causal relation means that the plaintiff should prove that the breach of duty by the defendant was the legal cause of the damage complained of by him.

Causality. The relation between cause and effect.

Cause. In a legal sense "a suit" or litigation; an action at law; case; prosecution; a judicial proceeding; any question, civil or criminal, contested before a Court of justice; the origin or foundation of a thing as of a suit or action; a ground of action; the subject of difference between the parties, as settled by the pleadings, whether oral or written.

A suit or litigation; an action of law; that which produces an effect or result [T.P. Act (4 of 1882), S. 69A(2)]; reason [Aligarh Muslim University Act (40 of 1920), Sch. item 40(3)]; to bring about an effect; to be the cause of [IPC (45 of 1860), S. 301]; to induce (to do).

CAUSE, REASON, MOTIVE. *Cause* respects the order and connection of things; *reason* the movements and operations of the mind and body. *Cause* is said of all inanimate objects: *reason* and *motive* of rational agents. Whatever happens in the world happens from some *cause* mediate or immediate; the primary or *first cause* of all is God: For whatever opinion a judge delivers he ought to be able to assign a substantial *reason;* and for all actions that men do, they generally have a sufficient *motive*. As the *cause* gives birth to the effect, so does the *reason* give birth to the conclusion, and the *motive* gives birth to the action.

TO CAUSE, OCCASION, CREATE. What is *caused* seems to follow naturally; what is *occasioned* follows incidentally, what is *created* receives its existence arbitrarily. Hurt *causes* pain; accidents *occasion* delay; Offences are *created* by statute.

CAUSE FOR REMOVAL FROM OFFICE. A cause which is sufficient to authorise a removal from office of an officer means legal cause, and not any cause which the council may think sufficient.

CAUSE OF ACCIDENT OR INJURY. "Ordinarily that condition is usually termed the cause of accident whose share in the matter is most conspicuous and is the most immediately preceding and proximate in the event." Everything which induces or influences an accident does not necessarily and legally cause it. It might be the agency, or medium or opportunity, or occasion or situation, or condition, as it is variously styled, through or by which the accident happened, but no part of it is real and controlling cause. Much must depend upon the circumstances of each particular case and upon the common sense of the thing.

Cause death. To effect or bring about death. [IPC (46 of 1860), S. 304].

Cause injury or loss to the plaintiff. The expression "cause injury or loss to the plaintiff" can only mean to do something wrongful which will result in loss or damage to the plaintiff. It can have no reference to any loss caused by a person pursuing his legitimate remedies. *A. Venkanna* v. *R. Venkata Rao,* AIR 1957 AP 453, 454. [CPC (5 of 1908), O. XXXIX, R. 1(c), Andhra Amendment]

Cause list. An official list of actions, petitions, appeals *etc.*, set down for trial or argument in open Court. Courts have their respective cause lists, in which are entered in succession, the various actions or matters set down for trial or hearing in open Court. The books which are kept for this purpose are extremely numerous and somewhat complicated, and the nature and extent of their contents are regulated by the rules prescribed for the Courts or groups of Courts for which such lists are kept.

Cause of action. The fact or combination of facts which gives rise to a right to sue. [CPC (5 of 1908), S. 20 and O. VII, R. 1(e)].

"CAUSE OF ACTION" for a suit is the sum total of the facts and circumstances which the plaintiff has to prove in order to entitle him to the relief claimed.

A 'cause of action' means every fact which if traversed, it would be necessary for the plaintiff to prove in order to support his right to a judgment of the Court. In other words it is a bundle of facts which taken with law applicable to them gives the plaintiff a right to relief against the defendant. It must include some act done by the defendant since in absence of such an act no cause of action can possibly accrue. It is not limited to the actual infringement of the right sued on but includes all the material facts on which it is founded. *Swamy Atmananda* v. *Ramkrishna Tapovanam*, AIR 2005 SC 2392 : (2005) 10 SCC 51.

A cause of action must include some act done by the defendant since in the absence of such an act no cause of action can possibly accrue. *Church of Christ Charitable Trust and Educational Charitable Society* v. *Ponniamman Educational Trust*, (2012) 8 SCC 706, para 13.

The expression 'cause of action' in S. 20, CPC (5 of 1908) may be defined as being the fact or facts which establish or give rise to a right of action or the existence of which entitles a party to seek redress in a Court of law. *Subhash Chandra* v. *Vidyat,* AIR 1978 All 234, 237.

Cause of action means an action for which the defendant is answerable to Court.

The performance of a contract is part of cause of action and a suit in respect of the breach can always be filed at the place where the contract should have been performed or its performance completed. *S.B.C. Laminant Pvt. Ltd.* v. *A.P. Agencies*, AIR 1989 SC 1239, 1243.

The expression "cause of action" does not mean "every fact which it is material to be proved to entitle the plaintiff to succeed. It only means a new claim made on a new basis constituted by new facts. *A.K. Gupta & Sons.* v. *Damodar Valley Corporation*, AIR 1967 SC 96, 98.

Cause of action includes the right which the plaintiff asserts and the infringement of that right by the defendant. Where the plaintiff's right is infringed by more persons than one and by different acts done separately by each of them, the plaintiff has a separate cause of action against each of these persons. *Ram Chandra* v. *Teia Bai,* AIR 1966 All 522, 523. [Court fees Act (7 of 1870), S. 17]

Any proceeding in a Court of Justice to enforce a demand, is a suit; the person, who applies to the Court, is a *suitor for relief* or *plaintiff*: the person who defends himself against the enforcement of the relief is a *defendant*: the claim, if recoverable, is a *cause of action*.

DISTINGUISHED FROM "REMEDY" AND "RELIEF"—"Cause of action" is to be distinguished from the "remedy", which is simply the means by which the obligation or the corresponding action is effectuated, and also from the "relief" sought. "A cause of action may be defined in general term to be a legal right, invaded without justification or sufficient excuse. Upon such invasion a *cause of action* arises, which entitles the party injured to some relief by the application of such remedies as the laws may afford. But the cause of action, and the *remedy*, sought, are entirely different matters. The one precedes and, it is true, gives rise to the other, but they are separate and distinct from each other, and are governed by different rules and principles.

Cause of salvage. A legal proceeding involving claim to a reward payable to those by whose exertions, ships or goods were saved from the danger of the sea, fire *etc.* [CPC (5 of 1908), S. 140].

Causing death. The accused sent some sweetmeats containing poison to one person. The sweetmeat was shared by some others but none of them died. The accused was guilty of attempting to cause death as his intention was to cause death although the quantity of arsenic was insufficient to cause death.

Causing the loss. That which causes loss. [Limitation Act (36 of 1963), Art. 44(b)].

Causus omissus. Even when there is *Causus omissus*—defect in phraseology used by the legislature— it is for others than the Courts to remedy the defect. *Nalinakha Bysak* v. *Shyam Sunder*, AIR 1953 SC 148, 152.

Caution. Avoidance of rashness; taking care. "The caution which the law requires a man to exercise in order to excuse homicide by misadventure is not the utmost caution that can be used. The law is not so extravagant as to require that a man should always do what is right to the very letter. It is sufficient that a reasonable precaution be taken, such as is usual and ordinary in similar cases, such as has been found by long experience, in the ordinary course of things to answer the end of safety of life and property.

The taking of heed. [IPC (45 of 1860), S. 80]; a precept or warning against evil of any kind.

Caveat. Literally, "Let him beware". A formal notice, or caution given by a party interested, to a Court, judge, or public officer, against the performance of certain judicial or ministerial acts; (*Burrill*); a caution entered in a competent Court, to stop probates, administrations, and such like, from being granted without the knowledge of the party that enters.

It is a caution registered in a public Court or office to indicate to the officials that they are not to act in the matter mentioned in the caveat without first giving notice to the caveator.

A legal notice given by an interested party to some officers not to do a certain act until the party is heard in opposition.

Caveat actor. (*Lat.*) Let the doer be on his guard.

Caveat emptor. It means "Let the purchaser beware". Disclaimer of responsibility for buyer's disappointment. It is one of the settled maxims, applying to a purchaser who is bound by actual as well as constructive knowledge of any defect in the thing purchased, which is obvious, or which might have been known by proper diligence.

Caveat emptor; qui ignorare non debuit quod jus alienum emit. (*Maxim*) Let a purchaser beware; who ought not to be ignorant that he is purchasing the rights of another.

The buyer according to the maxim has to be cautious, as the risk is his and not that of the seller.

Caveat venditor. (*Maxim*) Let the seller beware.

"If the seller wishes to secure himself from future responsibility in case the article sold should afterwards be found to be different in kind or quality from what the party supposed it to be, he must take care or provide against such responsibility by a particular agreement with the purchaser."

It applies to executory sales, to contracts for goods to be manufactured or produced or to sales where the buyer has no opportunity to inspect the article purchaised.

Caveat viator. The duty of a traveller on a highway to use due care to detect and avoid defects in the way.

Caveatee. One whose interest is challenged by a caveat.

Caveator. One who files a caveat.

CDMA. (*abbr.*) (Code Division Multiple access). A *protocol* for wireless data and voice communication, CMDA is widely used in cell phone networks, but also in many other data communications systems. CDMA uses a technique called 'Spread Spectrum' whereby the data being transmitted is spread across multiple radio frequencies, making more efficient use of available radio spectrum. There are a number of additional protocols built on top of CDMA, such as *1xRTT* (also called CMDA 2000). (*Matisse Enzer-Glossary of Internet Terms*).

CD-ROM drive. A peripheral that uses a CD-ROM (Compact disc-read only memory) for data storage. A type of optical disc, it is read by a mechanism designed to detect light from a laser reflected from the surface of the disc. (*Computer*)

Cease. To put an end to; to put a stop to; to come to an end; to stop doing.

Cease-and-desist notice. 'Cease-and-desist' notice means that the recipient is alleged to have infringed the rights of the sender of the notice to the copyright and as a result of such alleged infringement, the recipient is liable to institution of civil and/or criminal proceedings. *Exphar Sa* v. *Eupharma Laboratories Ltd.*, (2004) 3 SCC 688, 694, para 15.

Cease and desist orders. Court orders that a party must stop an activity such as unfair trade practices. (*Cyber Law*)

Cease fire. (*Milit.*) Order to troops to stop firing.

A suspension of active hostilities.

Cease to be. To discontinue; to become extinct. [Indian Partnership Act (9 of 1932), S. 36(1)(c)].

Cease to operate. A statute ceases to operate when it has passed out of existence, as if repealed by a valid Act of the legislature *(i.e)* when it ceases to have existence.

Cedant arma togae. (*Lat.*) Let military power be subject to military power.

Cede. To assign or transfer; to transfer territory. "Where one nation cedes territory to another, it hands over the title and sovereignty to goods against all the world, but this does not necessarily determine in what way it shall he held by the new sovereign."

Ceiling. The uppermost limit (of prices, wages, possession *etc.*) [Hindu Succession Act (30 of 1956), S. 4(2) and Constitution of India, Art. 31A, *Second Prov.*].

Ceiling price. The highest price at which the buyer is willing to buy.

Celebrate. Duly perform: "Celebrate" is equivalent to "solemnise."

TO CELEBRATE, COMMEMORATE. *Commemorate* is a species of *celebrating;* we always *commemorate* when we *celebrate,* but not *vice versa.* Every thing is *celebrated* which is distinguished by any marks of attention, without regard to the time of the event, whether present or past; but nothing is *commemorated* but what has been past. A marriage or a birthday is *celebrated;* the anniversary of any national event is *commemorated. Celebrating* is not limited to any species of events of circumstances; whatever interests any number of persons is *celebrated : commemorating* is confined to whatever is thought of sufficient importance to be borne in mind; whether of a public or private nature. The election of a favourite member is *celebrated* by those who have contributed to his success: a remarkable preservation whether national or individual, sometimes demands some signal act of *commemoration.*

Celibacy. The condition of a person not married.

Cell Bouncing Busy Hour. 'Cell Bouncing Busy Hour' means the one hour period in a day during which a cell in a cellular mobile telephone network experiences the maximum traffic. [Standards of Quality of Basic Telephone Service (Wire line) and Cellular Mobile Telephone Service Regulations, 2009, Regn. 2(1)(e)]

Cell hybridization. Means the formation of live cells with new combination of genetic material through the fusion of two or more cells by means of methods which do not occur naturally. [Rules for the Manufacture, Use, Import, Export and Storage of Hazardous Micro Organisms Genetically Engineered Organisms or Cells Rules, 1989, R. 3(11)]

Cellular confinement. CELLULAR CONFINEMENT means such confinement with or without labour as entirely excludes a prisoner from communication with, but not from right of, other prisoners. [Prisons Act (9 of 1894), S. 46(10), *Expln.*]

Cellular telephony. Cellular telephone is a type of short wave analogue or digital transmission in which a subscriber has a wireless connection from a mobile (terminal) to a nearby transmitter. The transmitter's area of coverage is called as *a cell.* In wireless telephony, a cell is the geographical area covered by a cellular telephone transmitter. The transmitter facility is called the *cell site.* When a subscriber enters into an agreement with a cellular telephone service provider, he is given access to the cell system of that provider, which is local. When travelling out of the range of the said cell system, the cell system can enable him to be transferred to a neighbouring company's cell system without the subscriber being aware of it. This is called *roaming service.* A cellular telephone is not to be confused with a cordless telephone, which is simply a phone with a very short wireless connection to a local phone outlet. [*Tata Teleservices Ltd.* v. *Bharat Sanchar Nigam Ltd.*, (2008) 10 SCC 556, 564(i)]

Cemetery. A cemetery is an area or place where the dead bodies of human beings are buried. Burial ground.

The words *"cemetery" and "burial place"* are synonymous in common parlance.

Censure. Expression of disapproval; the word "censure" is synonymous with the words "reproach" and "obloquy."

An unfavourable criticism [Navy Act (62 of 1957), S. 119(ii)]; to blame or condemn; to criticise unfavourably [Aligarh Muslim University Act (40 of 1920), Sch. 5(4)].

Censure motion. It can be moved by a member of Parliament against the Council of Ministers or an individual minister or a group of ministers for the failure to act or not to act or for their policy, and may express regret, indignation or surprise of the House at the such failure. The motion should be specific and self-explanatory with reasons for the censure. No leave of the House is required to move this motion. The government has the discretion to find time and to fix a date for its discussion. (*Rules of Procedure of the Parliament*).

Census. A census is an official enumeration of the inhabitants of a state or country, with details of sex, age, family, occupation, possessions, *etc.* (*Cent. Dict.*)

"An official numbering of the people of a country or district."

Central Act. 'CENTRAL ACT' shall mean an Act of Parliament, and shall include—

(a) an Act of the Dominion Legislature or of the Indian Legislature passed before the commencement of the Constitution, and

(b) an Act made before such commencement by the Governor-General in Council or the Governor-General acting in a legislative capacity. [General Clauses Act (10 of 1897), S. 3(7)]

An order of the President under Article 373 of the Constitution, for the purpose of construction with reference to the General Clauses Act is a Central Act. *Prahlad Jena* v. *State,* AIR 1950 Ori 157.

Rules 10 or Rule 10-A of Central Excise Rules, is not a 'Central Act' within the meaning of Section 3(7) of General Clauses Act (10 of 1897). *Kolhapur Canesugar Works Ltd.* v. *Union of India*, (2000) 2 SCC 536, para 36 : AIR 2000 SC 811.

Central bank. The official government-owned bank of a given country.

'CENTRAL BANK' means a cooperative Bank, the objects of which include the creation of funds to be loaned to other societies, but does not include the primary urban co-operative bank. [Maharashtra Co-operative Societies Act (1 of 1960), S. 2(6)]

Central Co-operative bank. Means the principal co-operative society in a district in a State, the primary object of which is the financing of other co-operative societies in that district:

Provided that in addition to such principal society in a district, or where there is no such principal society in a district, the State Government may declare any one or more co-operative societies caring on the business of financing other co-operative societies in that district to be also or to be a central co-operative bank or central co-operative banks within the meaning of this definition. [National Bank for A & R. Development (61 of 1991), S. 2(d)]

"Central Government debt". At any date means—

(*i*) the total outstanding liabilities of the Central Government on the security of the Consolidated Fund of India, including external debt valued at current exchange rates;

(*ii*) the total outstanding liabilities in the public account of India; and

(*iii*) such financial liabilities of any body corporate or other entity owned or controlled by the Central Government, which the Government is to repay or service from the annual financial statement, reduced by the cash balance available at the end of that date. [Fiscal Responsibility and Budget Management Act (39 of 2003), S. 2(aa) as substituted by Finance Act (13 of 2018)].

"Central Licensing Authority". Means the Drugs Controller General of India appointed by the Central Government. [Medical Devices Rules, 2017, R. 3(h)].

Central List. For the purposes of clauses (1) and (2), the expression "Central List" means the list of socially and educationally backward classes prepared and maintained by and for the Central Government. [Constitution of India, Article 342A(2), *Explanation*]

Central pool. Means the stock of foodgrains which is,—(*i*) procured by the Central Government and the State Governments through minimum support price operations; (*ii*) maintained for allocations under the Targeted Public Distribution System, other welfare schemes, including calamity relief and such other schemes; (*iii*) kept as reserves for schemes referred to in sub-clause (*ii*). [S. 2(2) of the National Food Security Act, 2013 (20 of 2013)]

"Central Provident Fund Commissioner". Means the Central Provident Fund Commissioner of the Central Board appointed under sub-section (*1*) of section 14. [Code on Social Security, 2020 (36 of 2020), section 2(11)]

Central recordkeeping agency. Means an agency registered under section 27 of Act 23 of 2013 to perform the functions of recordkeeping, accounting, administration and customer service for subscribers to schemes. [S. 2(1)(b) of the Pension Fund Regulatory & Development Authority Act, 2013 (23 of 2013)]

Central Vigilance Commission. Means the Central Vigilance Commission constituted under section 3(1) of the Central Vigilance Commission Act, 2003 (45 of 2003). [S. 2(1)(d) of the Lokpal & Lokayuktas Act, 2013 (1 of 2014)]

Centralisation. To draw to or concentrate at the centre.

"Centralised counseling". Means a common counselling and allotment of seats in colleges through a single window procedure by the Government or by any agency authorised by it for persons who have qualified in the common entrance test for the purpose of merit-based admission to medical colleges or institutions. [Kerala Medical Education (Regulation and Control of Admission to Private Medical Educational Institutions) Ordinance, 2017, S. 2(c) **as cited in** *Amina Marwa Salreen* v. *State of Kerala,* (2018) 14 SCC 193, para 3].

Cereal. 'CEREALS' are grains that are edible and fit for human consumption. [Karnataka Sales Tax Act (25 of 1957), S. 5(1), 1984 Tax LR (Noc) 151 (Kant)]

Cerebral palsy. Means a group of non-progressive conditions of a person characterised by abnormal motor control posture resulting from brain insult or injuries occurring in the pre-natal, peri-natal or infant period of development. [Persons with Disabilities (Equal Opportunities, Protection of Rights and Full Participation) Act, 1995 (1 of 1996), S. 2(e) and National Trust for Welfare of Persons with Autism, Cerebral Palsy, Mental Retardation and Multiple Disabilities Act (44 of 1999), S. 2(c)]

Ceremonials. Formal rites and ceremonies enjoined by law, protocol or customs for observance in religious worships, social affairs or Court procedure. [Navy Act (62 of 1957), S. 184(2)(k)].

Ceremonies. Outward rites or observances held sacred (used with reference to religion). [Guardians and Wards Act (8 of 1890), S. 34(e)].

Certain. Defined; Negotiable Instruments Act (26 of 1881), S. 5.

Reliable; sure to happen. In matters of obligetions, a thing is certain when its essence, quality and quantity are sufficiently described, such as one hundred rupees, such as a house, or such as a horse.

Fixed; exact; sure, inevitable; particular [Sale of Goods Act (3 of 1930), S. 25(1)]; some [CrPC 1973 (2 of 1974), S. 380]; [T.P. Act (4 of 1882), S. 70 ill. (a) and (b)].

Certain person. The words "a certain person", in Sections 4 and 5 of the Negotiable Instruments Act (26 of 1881) mean a person who is capable of being ascertained at the time when the promissory note is made.

Certainty. Distinctness; accuracy of statement; the fact of being certain; exemption from doubt.

CERTAINTY is a plain, clear, and distinct setting down of things so that they may be understood.

IN PLEADINGS. Certainty in pleadings includes both precision and particularity, but these words are used in a sense opposed to ambiguity and generality.

IN PROOF. It has been held that by the term "certainty" as applied to the degree of proof required, is meant generally that there must be sufficient positive facts proved to take the matter out of the realm of conjecture and presumption.

Certificate. "CERTIFICATE" means—

(i) a certificate of competency referred to in Section 78; or

(ii) a certificate of competency referred to in Section 86, which has been obtained by any person by availing of training facilities in any of the merchant navy training establishments in India or experience of sea service on board any Indian ship [Merchant Shipping Act (44 of 1958), S. 87A(b)].

"CERTIFICATE" means a certificate of registration granted or renewed by the Authority under these regulations. [Insurance Regulatory and Development Authority (Registration of Indian Insurance Companies) Regulations, 2000, R. 2(c)]

A Digital Signature Certificate issued by the relevant Certifying Authority. [*Information Technology*]

A writing so signed and authenticated as to be legal evidence. (*Standard Dict.*)

A writing by which an officer or other person bears testimony that a fact has or has not taken place, *etc.*; a written testimony to the truth of any fact [University of Hyderabad Act (39 of 1974), S. 5(2)].

The expression 'certificate' is used in relation to verification of the exactness of certain facts, and it does not involve the expression of any opinion. On the other hand, a report is a formal statement made after an enquiry and examination of specified matters and includes auditor's opinion thereon (See Guidance Note on Audit Reports and Certificates for Special Purposes, Research Committee, ICAI, New Delhi, 1984, para 2.2).

Certificate authorities (CAs). They issue and manage digital certificates and are centralized by industry with a wide range of applications, such as e-mail, browsers, and VPNs. (*Cyber Law*)

An issuer of *Security Certificates* used in *SSL* connections. (*Matisse Enzer-Glossary of Internet Terms*).

Certificate chain. A list of certificates comprising Certifying Authority Certificates and user subscriber certificate. (*Information Technology*)

Certificate class. A Digital Signature Certificate of a specified level of trust. (*Information Technology*)

Certificate expiration. The validity period comprising of time and date specified in the Digital Signature Certificate when the operational period ends. (*Information Technology*)

Certificate extension. An extension field to a Digital Signature Certificate which may convey additional information about the public key being certified, the certified Subscriber, the Digital Signature Certificate issued and/or the certification process. (*Information Technology*)

Certificate issuance. The actions performed by a Certifying Authority in creating a Digital Signature

Certificate and notifying the Digital Signature applicant (anticipated to become a subscriber) listing the Digital Signature Certificate of its contents. (*Information Technology*)

Certificate management. (*Management of Digital Signature Certificate*). Certificate management includes, but is not limited to, storage, distribution, dissemination, accounttng, publication, compromise, recovery, revocation, suspension and administration of Digital Signature Certificate. A Certifying Authority undertakes Digital Signature Certificate management functions by serving as a registration authority subscriber Digital Signature Certificates. A Certifying Authority designates issued and accepted Digital Signature Certificates as valid by publication. (*Information Technology*)

Certificate of administration. A document certifying that a person has been granted authority to administer a particular property or estate of a particular person. [Guardians and Wards Act (8 of 1890), S. 51].

Certificate of character. The expression "certificate of character" in S. 7, Legal Practitioners' Act (18 of 1879) means nothing more than a certificate that the presiding officer of the Court is not aware of any misconduct of the pleader justifying action under Ss. 12 to 14 of the Act.

Certificate of deposit. (*in banking*) A writing acknowledging that the person named has deposited in the bank a specified sum of money.

Certificate of discharge. A written statement of satisfaction made between two parties, which states that one party is satisfied and the other has discharged its obligation.

Certificate of incorporation. The instrument by which a private corporation is formed is called "articles of incorporation" or "certificate of incorporation".

It is a certificate issued by the Registrar of Joint-Stock Companies, after the registration of a company. The instrument by which a corporation or company is formed under the law of the land, setting forth the name, objects and other particulars of the company, and filed in some designated public office as evidence of its corporate existence.

Certificate of registration. Means the certificate issued by a competent authority to the effect that a motor vehicle has been duly registered in accordance with the provisions of Chapter IV. [Motor Vehicles Act (59 of 1988), S. 2(4)]

"Certificate of recognition". Means the certificate of recognition granted to a registered valuers organisation under sub-rule (5) of Rule 13 and the term "recognition" shall be construed accordingly. [Companies (Registered Valuers and Valuation) Rules, 2017, R. 2(1)(d)].

Certificate of sale. A certificate granted by the Court to a purchaser at a Court sale certifying the fact of purchase by him [CPC (5 of 1908), O. XXI, R. 96].

"Certified by Tribunal". Means in relation to a copy of a document, certified to be a true copy issued by the Registry or of a Bench of the Tribunal under its hand and seal and as provided in section 76 of the Indian Evidence Act, 1872 (1 of 1872). [National Company Law Tribunal Rules, 2016, R. 2(10)].

Certificate of title to a security. Means any document used in the ordinary course of business as proof of the possession or control of the security, or authorising or purporting to authorise, either by endorsement or by delivery, the possessor of the document to transfer or receive the security thereby represented. [FERA (46 of 1973), S. 2(d)]

Certification. The action of certifying. [Indian Evidence Act (1 of 1872), S. 86].

Certification authority. A trusted third party which binds the identity of a particular party to a particular public key and, by implication, a particular private key. (*Internet and E-commerce*)

Certification practice statement. Means a statement issued by a Certifying Authority to specify the practices that the Certifying Authority employs in issuing Digital Signature Certificates. [Information Technology Act (21 of 2000), S. 2(1)(h)]

'Certification practice statement means a statement issued by a Certifying Authority to specify the practices that the Certifying Authority employs in issuing Electronic Signature Certificates'. [Information Technology Act (21 of 2000), S. 2(1)(h)].

Certification trade mark. Means a mark adapted in relation to any goods to distinguish, in the course of trade, goods certified by any person in respect of origin, material, mode of manufacture, quality, accuracy or other characteristic, from goods not so certified and registrable as such under provisions of chapter VIII in respect of those goods in the name as proprietor of the certification trade mark of that person. [Trade and Merchandise Marks Act (43 of 1958), S. 2(1)(c)] [Now repealed & replaced by Act 47 of 1999]

"CERTIFICATION TRADE MARK" means a mark capable of distinguishing the goods or services in connection with which it is used in the course of trade which are certified by the proprietor of the mark in respect of origin, material, mode of manufacture of goods or performance of services, quality, accuracy or other characteristics from goods or services not so certified and registrable as such under Chapter IX in respect of those goods or services in the name, as proprietor of the certification trade mark, of that person. [Trade marks Act (47 of 1999), S. 2(1)(c)]

Certification trade mark means a mark capable of distinguishing the goods or services in connection with which it is used in the course of trade which are certified by the proprietor of the mark in respect of origin, material, mode of manufacture of goods or performance of services, quality, accuracy or other characteristics from goods or services not so certified and registrable as such under Chapter IX in respect of those goods or services in the name, as proprietor of the certification trade mark, of that person. [Trade Marks Act, 1999, S. 2(e)].

Certified. In the Insurance Company Act, unless there is anything repugnant in the subject or context,—

"CERTIFIED" in relation to any copy or translation of a document required to be furnished by or on behalf of an insurer or a provident society as defined in Part III means certified by a principal officer or such insurer or provident society to be a true copy or a correct translation, as the case may be. [Insurance Act (4 of 1938), S. 2(5)]

"CERTIFIED" in relation to any copy or translation of a document required to be furnished by or on behalf of an insurance company, means certified by a responsible officer of the company to be a true copy or a correct translation, as the case may be. Act XX of 1928, S. 6; *see also* Com. Act VII of 1913, S. 277, cl. (6).

Officially declared or informed.

Certified cheque. The cheque of a depositor drawn on a bank which guarantees the available funds for the cheque.

Certified copy. Every public officer having the custody of a public document, which any person has a right to inspect, shall give that person on demand a copy of it on payment of the legal fees therefor, together with a certificate written at the foot of such copy that it is a true copy of such document or part thereof, as the case may be, and such certificate shall be dated and subscribed by such officer with his name and his official title, and shall be sealed, whenever such officer is authorised by law to make use of a seal; and such copies so certified shall be called "certified copies". [(w.e.f. 1-7-2024) Bharatiya Sakshya Adhiniyam, 2023 (47 of 2023), section 75]

"CERTIFIED COPY" means when the books of a bank,—

(a) are maintained in written form, a copy of any entry in such books together with a certificate written at the foot of such copy that it is a true copy of such entry, that such entry is contained in one of the ordinary books of the bank and was made in the usual and ordinary course of business and that such book is still in the custody of the bank, and where the copy was obtained by a mechanical or other process which in itself ensured the accuracy of the copy, a further certificate to that effect, but where the book from which such copy was prepared has been destroyed in the usual course of the bank's business after the date on which the copy had been so prepared, a further certificate to that effect, each such certificate being dated and subscribed by the principal accountant or manager of the bank with his name and official title; and

(b) consist of printouts of data stored in a floppy, disc, tape or any other electro-magnetic data storage device, a printout of such entry or a copy of such printout together with such statements certified in accordance with the provisions of Section 2A.

(c) a printout of any entry in the books of a bank stored in a micro film, magnetic tape or in any other form of mechanical or electronic data retrieval mechanism obtained by a mechanical or other process which in itself ensures the accuracy of such printout as a copy of such entry and such printout contains the certificate in accordance with the provisions of section 2A. [Bankers' Books Evidence Act (18 of 1891), section 2(8).

In these rules, unless the context otherwise requires—

"CERTIFIED COPY" means the original copy of the order received by the party or a copy (including a photostat copy) thereof duly authenticated by the concerned department. [Customs, Excise and Gold (Control) Appellate Tribunal (Procedure) Rules, 1982, R. 2(f)]

A copy which is certified to be true. [Indian Evidence Act (1 of 1872), S. 76].

A copy of a document signed and certified as a true copy by the officer to whose custody the original is entrusted.

By long usage, the term, 'certified copy' has obtained a special meaning in view of the provision in S. 76 of the Indian Evidence Act (1 of 1872); and that term when used in connection with an appeal and with reference to the orders against which the appeal is filed, has always been understood as the copy which the party preferring the appeal obtains under S. 76 of the Indian Evidence Act on payment of the necessary fee. *Malayalam Plantations Ltd.* v. *Commissioner of Income Tax*, AIR 1959 Ker 34, 35. [Indian Evidence Act (1 of 1872), S. 76]

A certified copy is an authenticated copy and a certificate issued by an officer is only a written declaration of the fact that the copy is a true copy of the original. *Mohan Reddy* v. *Neelagiri Muralidhara Rao*, AIR 1958 AP 485, 488.

Certified copy and duplicate. The term "certified copy" is not synonymous with "duplicate." A duplicate must be executed by the same parties with the same formalities as the original.

A copy of a document is a certified copy when there is in it a certificate of a public officer that it is a true copy of a document contained in the office.

Certified purchaser. A purchaser to whom a certificate of sale has been granted. [CPC (5 of 1908), S. 66(2)].

Certifies. Ordinarily in a case which does not involve a substantial question of law or principle in an affirming judgment, the High Court would not be justified in granting a certificate under Art. 134(1) of Constitution. *Sundar Singh* v. *State of Uttar*

Pradesh, AIR 1956 SC 411, 412. [Constitution of India, Art. 134(1)(c)].

The word 'certifies' is a strong word. It indicated that the High Court must bring its mind to bear on the question and as in all cases of judicial orders and certificates, the reasons for the order must be apparent on the face of the record itself. The Supreme Court must be in a position to know first that the High Court has applied its mind to the matter and not acted mechanically, and secondly, exactly what question of outstanding difficulty or importance the High Court feels, this Court ought to settle. *Baladin* v. *State of Uttar Pradesh*, AIR 1956 SC 181, 188. [Constitution of India, Art. 134(1)(c)].

Certify. To give certain knowledge or information of; make evident; vouch for the truth of; attest; to make statement as to matter of fact; to testify in writing; give a certificate of; make a declaration about in writing under hand, or hand and seal; to make attestation either in writing or orally as to the truth or excellence of something.

To make a declaration in writing under hand or hand and seal, to make attestation in writing as to the truth of the facts or the result of the execution proceedings in the transferee Court and the circumstances thereof. *Shimoga Oil Mills by its Proprietor* v. *Radhakrishna Oil Mills,* AIR 1969 AP 263. [CPC (5 of 1908), S. 41].

The word "certify" is a strong word postulating, the exercise of judicial discretion in determining if the question requiring decision by the Supreme Court involves a matter of principle or a substantial question of law of great general importance. *State of Bihar* v. *Bhagirath*, AIR 1973 SC 2198, 2199.

To vouch for the truth; to attest; to testify in writing; to give a certificate of. [IPC (45 of 1860), S. 191, ill. (e)].

Certifying authority. Means a person who has been granted a licence to issue a Electronic Signature Certificate under section 24. [Information Technology Act (21 of 2000), S. 2(1)(g)].

"CERTIFYING AUTHORITY" for the purpose of 'Digital Signature Certificate' means a person who has been granted a licence to issue it under section 24 of the Information Technology Act, 2000 (21 of 2000). [R. 2(1)(c) of the Companies (Registration Offices and Fees) Rules, 2014; R. 2(1)(b) of the Companies (Specification of Definitions Details) Rules, 2014]

Certifying Authority Software. The cryptographic Software required to manage the keys of end entities. (*Information Technology*)

"**Certifying Officer**" means any officer appointed by the appropriate Government, by notification, to perform the functions of a certifying officer under the provisions of Chapter IV. [Industrial Relations Code, 2020 (35 of 2020), section 2(g)]

Certiorari. A writ issuing from a superior Court calling up the record of a proceeding in an inferior Court for review. [Constitution of India, Art. 32(2) and Art. 139].

CERTIORARI is a writ, issued from a superior Court directed to one of inferior jurisdiction, commanding the latter to certify and return to the former the record in the particular case. It differs from appeal in that it brings up the case on the record, while on appeal the case is brought up on the merits; and from *mandamus*, for by that writ the case is proceeded within the inferior Court, in accordance with the order of the Court granting it. In most cases and in modern practice a review is a substitute for and serves the purpose of *certiorari*. (*Ame. Cyc*)

Certiorarified mandamus. (Distinction). A writ of *certiorari* is available for the removal of any judicial or *quasi*-judicial act of an inferior tribunal, whereas a writ of *mandamus* is issued to compel the performance of duties of a public nature. The condition that the act complained of should be a judicial act applies to the former relief and not to the latter. The division of the *panchayat* into wards and the conduct of elections are administrative acts of the Government but that itself is not a ground for rejecting a writ petition against Government. *Lachhaiah* v. *District Panchayat Officer, Guntur*, MLJ : QD (1956-1960) Vol. II C114-115 : AIR 1960 AP 493. [Constitution of India, Art. 226]

A merger of two writs, *viz certiorari* and *mandamus* where *mandamus* comes to help *certiorari* [*Madhya Pradesh* v *Bhailal Bhai*, AIR 1964 SC 1006].

Certiorari and prohibition. A writ of '*certiorari*' is issued when the case is disposed of and there is apparent error while writ of 'prohibition' is issued in pending cases to stop exercise of jurisdiction. [*Hari Vishnu Kamath* v. *Syed Ahmad Ishaque*, AIR 1955 SC 233]

Certiorari, a writ of. A certiorari is an original writ issuing out of chancery, or the King's Bench, directed in the King's name, to the judges or officers of the inferior courts, commanding them to return the records of a cause pending before them, to the end the party may have more sure and speedy justice before him, or such other justices as he shall assign to determine the cause. [A New Abridgement of the Law, Seventh Edn. Vol. II, pp. 9 & 10 **as referred in** *Prabodh Verma* v. *State of U.P.*, (1984) 4 SCC 251, 275, para 32]

Certum est quod certum reddi potest. (*Lat.*) That is sufficiently certain which can be made certain.

Cess. "CESS" means a duty in the nature of duty of excise and customs, imposed and collected on motor spirit commonly known as petrol and high speed diesel oil for the purposes of this Act. [Central Road Fund Act (54 of 2000), S. 2(b)]

An assessment or tax.

The word '*Cess*' has a definite legal connotation, indicating tax allocated to a particular thing, not forming part of the general fund. The word '*cess*' is only tax and not a mere fee.

A cess may either be a tax or a fee. In Entry 49, List 2 of the Government of India Act the expression 'cesses' is used in the sense of 'taxes'. *Kunwar Ram Nath* v. *Municipal Board, Pilibhit*, AIR 1983 SC 930, 934. [Constitution of India, List 2, Entry 53; Government of India Act, List 2, Entry 49].

The word 'cess' means a tax and is generally used when the levy is for some special administrative expense which the name (health cess, education cess, road cess, *etc.*) indicates. *Shinde Brothers* v. *Hy. Commissioner, Raichur*, AIR 1967 SC 1512, 1525.

An assessment, tax or levy. [Cardamom Act (42 of 1965), S. 14(1)].

Cess and **Licence Fee.** A 'cess' is a tax levied for a specific purpose often with a prefixed word defining the object. A 'licence' on the other hand involves a permission to trade subject, to compliance with certain conditions.

Cessante causa, cessat effectus (*Lat.*) The cause ceasing the effect ceases also.

Cessante ratione legis cessat leg ipsa. (*Lat.*) When the very basis of a rule does not exist the rule itself ceases to exist.

Cessante ratione legis cessat ipsa lex. (*Lat. Maxim*) Reason is the soul of the law and when the reason of any particular law ceases so does the law itself.

Cessat ratio cessat lex. (*Lat.*) A rule becomes obsolete when the reason of the rule disappears through change of circumstances and environments in the society which was governed by that rule.

Cessation. Ceasing; discontinuance; stoppage. [Limitation Act (36 of 1963), S. 17(2)].

Cessation of motion. Stoppage of the process of moving. [IPC (45 of 1860), S. 349].

Cessation of practice. In relation to an advocate means discontinuance of practice by the Advocate by taking up any employment, trade calling or other similar engagement or discontinuance of practice on account of death or disability. [Goa Advocate Welfare Fund Act (2 of 1997), S. 2(g)]

"CESSATION OF PRACTICE" means removal of the name of an advocate from the State roll under Section 26A of the Advocates Act, 1961(Central Act 25 of 1961). Advocates' Welfare Fund Act (45 of 2001), S. 2 (c). Tamil Nadu Advocate, Welfare Act, 1987 (49 of 1987), S. 2(e) as cited in *S. Seshachalam* v. *Bar Council of T.N.*, (2014) 16 SCC 72, para 12].

Cesses. The expression 'cesses' in Entry 49 of List II of the Government of India Act was used in the sense of 'taxes' as used in Entry 52 of List II, the nature and content of the legislative power under both being the same. A cess may either be a tax or a fee. Whether a cess in a given context is a tax or a fee depends upon the purpose for which it is levied. *Kunwar Ram Nath* v. *Municipal Board Pilibhit,* (1983) 3 SCC 357.

Cession. A giving up; an assignment; transfer; relinquishment or abandonment of a right, or property.

Cession of a part of the territory of India. Includes admission of the claim of any foreign country to any such part. [Unlawful Activities (Prevention) Act (37 of 1967), S. 2(b)]

Cession of a part of the territory of India from the Union. Includes the assertion of any claim to determine whether such part will remain a part of the territory of India. [Unlawful Activities (Prevention) Act (37 of 1967), S. 2(d)]

Cession of territory. Where there is a dispute as to what in fact the territory of India is and that dispute is settled on the basis that certain territory never belonged to India, it does not entail any cessation of territory requiring a constitutional amendment.

Cestui que trust. A beneficiary under a trust, the person for whose benefit a trust is created.

"CESTUI QUE TRUST". A person in whose favour a trust operates, namely, the beneficially interested person is called cestui que trust and the person who holds the property is called trustee. [*M L Tannan, Banking Law & Practice in India*, 2021, LexisNexis, Dictionary of Banking Terminology].

Cestui que use. A person to whose use lands or other hereditaments were held by another person.

Cestui que vie. He for whose life any lands or tenements are granted.

Ceteris paribus. (*Lat.*) Other things remaining equal.

C.F.I. Contract or **"C.I.F." Contract.** Under a C.F.I. contract there is an absolute duty on the Vendor to procure the shipment of the goods under such a Bill of Lading as will, subject to its exceptions, ensure their delivery at the Port of Destination. (*Lecky* v. *Ogilvy*, 3 Com. Ca. 29.) *See also* C.I.F. Contract and also 5 LBR 144 : 4 IC 1037 : 40 Bom 11 : 17 Bom LR 249 : 28 IC 433.

CGI. (*abbr.*) Computer Graphical Interface. (Common Gateway Interface). A set of rules that describe how a *Web Server* communicates with another piece of software on the same machine, and how the other piece of software (the "CGI program") talks to the web server. Any piece of software can be a CGI program if it handles input and output according to the CGI standard.

Usually a CGI program is a small program that takes data from a web server and does something with it, like putting the content of a form into an e-mail message, or turning the data into a database query.

You can often see that a CGI program is being used by seeing "cgi-bin" in a URL, but not always. (*Matisse Enzer-Glossary of Internet Terms; Internet and E-commerce*).

CGI-BIN. CGI stands for "common gateway interface." It's simply a way for your visitor's computer to communicate with programs, such as shopping-cart scripts, on your server. The CGI-BIN is a special directory where you store executable programs, such as shopping-cart scripts and counters, on the server. If you don't have access to a CGIBIN directory, you can't run programs (scripts) on your website.

The most common name of a directory on a web server in which CGI programs are stored.

The "BIN" part of "CGI-BIN" is a shorthand version of "binary", because once upon a time, most programs were referred to as "binaries". In real life, most programs found in CGI-BIN directories are text files—scripts that are executed by binaries located elsewhere on the same machine. *(Internet and E-commerce).*

Chain, Fetter, Band, Shackle. All these terms designate the instrument by which animals or men are confined. *Chain* is general and indefinite; all the rest are species of *chains*; but there are many *chains* which do not come under the other names; a *chain* is indefinite as to its make; *fetters* are large, they consist of many stout *chains*. *Bands* are in general any thing which confines the body or the limbs; they may either be *chains* or even cords; *shackle* is that species of *chain* which goes on the legs to confine them; malefactors of the worst order have *fetters* on different part of their bodies, and *shackles* on their legs.

Chain of circumstances. The expression "chain of circumstances" in a criminal case, conveys substantially the same idea as that of "inculpatory facts". Where a chain of circumstances is the means by which the guilt of a defendant is to be established each necessary link in that chain must be established beyond a reasonable doubt, for the reason that the chain without the necessary links would be incomplete and ineffectual. To constitute a chain of circumstances sufficient to establish guilt, each independent fact in the chain relied on must be established to a moral certainty or beyond a reasonable doubt.

Chairman. The person who presides over a committee, convention, assembly, or other deliberative body.

Chairperson. In Chapter XXVII of Act 18 of 2013, unless the context otherwise requires, 'Chairperson' means the Chairperson of the Appellate Tribunal. [S. 407(a) of the Companies Act, 2013 (18 of 2013)]

"CHAIRPERSON" means the Chairperson of the Authority. [S. 2(1)(c) of the Pension Fund Regulatory & Development Authority Act, 2013 (23 of 2013)]

"CHAIRPERSON" means the Chairperson of the Lokpal. [S. 2(1)(b) of the Lokpal & Lokayuktas Act, 2013 (1 of 2014)]

"Chairperson" means the Chairperson of the National Dental Commission appointed under section 4. [National Dental Commission Act, 2023 (21 of 2023), section 2(b)]

"Chairperson" means the Chairperson referred to in clause (a) of sub-section (2) of section 4. [Life Insurance Corporation Act, 1956 (31 of 1956), section 2(1c)]

Chairperson of the Approving Panel. The 'Chairperson of the Approving Panel' shall be a person who is or has been a judge of a High Court, and—(i) one member shall be a member of Indian Revenue Service not below the rank of Chief Commissioner of Income-tax; and (ii) one member shall be an academic or scholar having special knowledge of matters, such as direct taxes, business accounts and international trade practices. [(w.e.f. 1-4-2016) S. 144BA(16) of the Income-tax Act, 1961 (43 of 1961)]

Challan. *Challan* is the traditional way of indicating initiation of prosecution *i.e.* a police charge sheet. It can only be the result of examination of records and enquiry into the facts and arriving at a satisfaction about the conduct of the person sought to be prosecuted.

Challenge. An objection to the right or capacity of a person.

A formal objection [Air Force Act (45 of 1950), S. 129(4)]; to call into question; to dispute especially as being unjust, invalid or outmoded. [Army Act (46 of 1050), S. 130(4)].

Chamber business. All business done out of Court by the judge. It is not necessary that chamber business should invariably be done in what is usually called "chambers". It may be done, and often is done, on the street, in the judge's own house, at the hotel where he stops, when absent from home, or it may be done in transit, on the cars, in going from one place to another within his territorial jurisdiction. For the purposes of jurisdiction, the chambers of the judge are wherever he happens to be in his circuit or district, when the exigencies of the case call for the transaction of chamber business, and a Judge is as clearly engaged in the discharge of the duties of his office, when going from one place of holding Court to another, for the purpose of holding Court. (*Black*)

Chamber, Chambers. Room or apartment; a private repository; the private room or office of a judge, where, for the convenience of parties, he hears such matters and transacts such business as a judge in vacation is authorized to hear, and which do not require a hearing by the judge sitting as a Court; the office or private rooms of a judge, where parties are heard and orders made, in matters not requiring to be brought before the full Court, and where costs are taxed, judgments signed, and similar business transacted. (*Burrill*)

Chamber of commerce. An association of the principal merchants, traders, and others, organised, for promoting the interests of trade. It is useful in obtaining and spreading statistical information, aiding commercial legislation, and otherwise. It is designed for convenience in buying, selling and exchanging goods and to foster the commercial and industrial interests of the people.

Champerty. Assistance to any person in action or suit upon condition to have paid of the things (be it lands or goods) when recovered. It is an unlawful act. It is that form of maintenance in which the intermeddler renders assistance by bargaining for a share of the profits of litigation.

Champion. One who fights for another or takes his place in a quarrel. (*Bracton*)

Chance. A possibility or probability as distinct from a certainty.

Chance : Accident. There is a wide difference between 'chance' and 'accident'. The one is the intervention of some unlooked for circumstances to prevent an expected result, the other is the uncalculated effect of mere luck. A shot discharged at random strikes its object by chance; that which is turned from its well directed aim by some unforeseen circumstance misses its mark by accident.

Chance : Hazard. Both these terms are employed to mark the course of future events, which is not discernible by the human eye. With the Deity there is neither *chance* nor *hazard*; His plans are the result of omniscience: but the designs and actions of men are all dependent on *chance* or *hazard*.

Chance may be favourable or unfavourable, more commonly the former: *hazard* is always unfavourable; it is properly a species of *chance*. In business transactions, there is always a *chance* either of gaining or losing. In speculation there is a *hazard* of losing. In most speculations the *chance* of succeeding scarcely outweighs the *hazard* of losing.

Chance witness. A person who witnesses a crime by sheer chance.

Chancellor. Judge or presiding judge of the Court of chancery. (*England*)

Chancellor of the Exchequer. The officer who formerly presided in the Exchequer. (*England*)

THE LORD HIGH CHANCELLOR is the highest judicial officer of the realm, supreme judge of the Court of Chancery, Keeper of the Great Seal and Privy Councillor. (*England*)

Chancery. "*Chancery jurisdiction*" is a judicial power to hear and determine all cases wherein the law, on account of its universality, could not afford adequate relief. (*England*)

Chancery Division. The division of the High Court of Justice created by the Judicature Acts 1873-75 to replace the Court of Chancery. The work of the Division is principally concerned with matters relating to real property, trusts, and the administration of estates but also includes cases concerned with company law, patents and other intellectual property, and confidentiality cases. The effective head of the Division is the Vice Chancellor, although the Lord Chancellor is nominally its president. It may hear some appeals. (*Oxford Law Dictionary, 5th Edn., 2003*)

Change. Exchange of money against money of a different denomination.

To become different, to transform or convert. *State of U.P.* v. *Systemetic Consom Limited,* (2014) 13 SCC 627, para 20.

(*Verb*). To exchange; to alter or make different; to cause to pass from one place to another.

A mere application for job, by a person who was alleged to have been wrongly declared as passed in the examination, cannot be said to have changed his position.

TO CHANGE, ALTER, VARY. We *change* a thing by putting another in its place; we *alter* a thing by making it different from what it was before; we *vary* it by *altering* it in different manners and at different times. We *change* our clothes whenever we put on others: the tailor *alters* clothes which are found not to fit; and he *varies* the fashion of making them to suit social conditions. A man *changes* his habits, *alters* his conduct and *varies* his manner of speaking and thinking, according to circumstances.

"CHANGE" for the purpose of Rule 13 of the Companies (Management & Administration) Rules, 2014, the 'change' means increase or decrease by two percent or more in the shareholding of each of the promoters and each of the top ten shareholders of the company. [*Explanation* to Rule 13 of the Companies (Management & Administration) Rules, 2014].

Change and rate. The ordinary meaning of change is to become different, to transform or convert and rate is the standard or measure. *State of Uttar Pradesh* v. *Systemetic Conscom Limited,* (2014) 13 SCC 627, para 20.

Change in the constitution of a licencee. In relation to,—

(*i*) a firm means change from proprietorship to partnership including Limited Liability Partnership or vice versa;

(*ii*) a company means—

(A) its conversion from a private to a public company, or from a public to a private company; or

(B) any change in the ownership of shares of more than fifty per cent. of the voting capital in the body corporate or in case of a body corporate not having a share capital, any change in its membership; and where the managing agent, being a body corporate is a subsidiary of another body corporate, includes a change in the constitution of that other body corporate within the meaning of this clause. [Medical Devices Rules, 2017, R. 3(j)].

Change in law of procedure. No person has a vested right in any course of procedure. He has only the right of prosecution or defence in the manner prescribed for the time being by or for the Court in which the case is pending and if by an Act of

Parliament the mode of procedure is altered he has no other right than to proceed according to the altered mode. *Anant Gopal Sheorey* v. *State of Bombay*, AIR 1958 SC 915, 917.

'Change in the rate of tax' would mean any such change in the already existing standard or measure of computing the tax payable but not the introduction of a yet another kind of tax for levy and collection of the tax from the dealers. *State of U.P.* v. *Systemetic Consom Limited*, (2014) 13 SCC 627, para 20

Change of venue. Change of the place of trial to another Court or country; transfer of the cause to another Court or Judge.

Channel. "CHANNEL" means a set of frequencies used for transmission of a programme. [Cable Television Networks (Regulation) Act (7 of 1995), S. 4A, *Expl.* (c) as it stood prior to substitution by Act 21 of 2011 (w.e.f. 25.10.2011)]

The word "CHANNEL" in the Canal's Act includes any river, canal, *khal, nala* or waterway, whether natural or artificial. [Ben. Act. V of 1964, S. 1]

A passage way between banks through which flow the waters of the stream; the bed of the stream over which its waters run.

The bed of a stream of water; the hollow course in which stream flows; the hollow bed of running water; a route through which anything passes or progresses.

Chapter. Shall mean a Chapter of the Act or Regulation in which the word occurs. [General Clauses Act (10 of 1897), S. 3(9)].

Main division of a book. [General Clauses Act (10 of 1897), S. 3(9)].

Character. In Sections 52, 53, 54 and 55, the word "CHARACTER" includes both reputetion and disposition; but except as provided in Section 54, evidence may be given only of general reputation, and not of particular acts by which reputation or disposition were shown. [Indian Evidence Act (1 of 1872), S. 55 *Expln.*]

In this section and sections 46, 47 and 49, the word "character" includes both reputation and disposition; but, except as provided in section 49, evidence may be given only of general reputation and general disposition, and not of particular acts by which reputation or disposition has been shown. [(w.e.f. 1-7-2024) Bharatiya Sakshya Adhiniyam, 2023 (47 of 2023), section 50, *Explanation*]

Estimation of a person by his community. Particular qualities impressed by nature or habit of a person which distinguish him from others.

Recognised official rank; position [Indian Evidence Act (1 of 1872), S. 18]; quality or capacity [IPC (45 of 1860), S. 205]; graphic symbol standing for sounds, syllables, notations, used in writing or printing; writing; printing [CPC (5 of 1908), S. 137(2)]; particular qualities impressed by nature or habit of a person which distinguish him from others.

A character is one of the set of symbols handled by the computer. Each letter of the alphabet may be included in the character set, as are numerals, punctuation, and special symbols. There are also control characters included in many character sets: these cause actions and are not shown on display screens and printers. Each character in the character set is represented by a unique binary code. (*Computer*)

Character certificate. In the means that the person certifying as to character is not aware of any misconduct.

Character evidence. Evidence regarding someone's personality traits.

Character : Reputation. *Character* lies in the man; it is the mark of what he is; it shows itself on all occasions; *reputation* depends upon others; it is what they think of him. A *character* is given particularly: a *reputation* is formed generally. Individuals give a *character* of another from personal knowledge: public opinion constitutes the *reputation. Character* has always some foundation; it is a positive description of something; *reputation* has more of conjecture in it; its source is hearsay. It is possible for a man to have a fair *reputation* who was not in reality a good *character;* although men of really good *character* are not likely to have a bad *reputation.*

Charas. CHARAS is the separated resin, in whatever form whether crude or purified, obtained from the cannabis plant and also includes concentrated preparation and resin known as hashish oil or liquid hashish. [Narcotic Drugs and Psychotropic Substances Act (61 of 1985), S. 2(iii)(a)]

Charge. "CHARGE" includes any head of charge when the charge contains more heads than one. [CrPC 1973 (2 of 1974), S. 2(b)] [Now (w.e.f. 1-7-2024) repealed & replaced by Bharatiya Nagarik Suraksha Sanhita, 2023 (46 of 2023), section 2(1)(f), same definition in new Sanhita]

Charge is the price required or demanded for services rendered, or less frequently for goods supplied. It is a word of very general and varied use. It also signifies a debt or liability. The word "charge" as a technical word of legal use, conveys the idea of obligation. It is also used in the sense of a lien, encumbrance or claim on property.

(IN CRIMINAL LAW) The expression "charged with" as applied to a crime, is sometimes used in a limited sense, intending the accusation of a crime which preceded a formal trial. In a fuller and more accurate sense the expression includes the responsibility for the crime.

An obligation, lien, encumbrance or claim on property; accusation of a crime which precedes a formal trial; and accusation, made in a legal manner of illegal conduct, either of omission or commission by the person charged. [CrPC 1973 (2 of 1974), Second Sch., form 32]; price required or demanded for services rendered, or less frequently for goods supplied. [T.P. Act (4 of 1882), S. 69A(6)]; control, custody or superintendence. [IPC (45 of 1860), S. 157]; the address of judge to jury instructing them upon the law relating to the matters before them in the case; the quantity of explosive used in single discharge; the load powder, fuel *etc.* for a gun [Arms Act (54 of 1959), S. 2(b)(iv)]; to subject a property to an encumbrance or pecuniary liability [Guardians and Wards Act (8 of 1890), S. 28]; to accuse formally; to frame a charge; to charge a sum or price. [CPC (5 of 1908), O. XXXIX, R. 9]; to address a charge to the jury; to restore the active materials in a storage battery by the passage of a direct current.

A charge is not an accusation made or information given in abstract but an accusation made against a person in respect of an act committed or omitted in violation of a penal law forbidding or commanding it. In other words it is an accusation made against a person in respect of an offence alleged to have been committed by him. *Birich Bhivan* v. *State of Bihar*, AIR 1963 SC 1120, 1123.

In S. 211, IPC (45 of 1860) the 'charge' must be one against any person with having committed an offence.

(AS FORMAL COMPLAINT). Charge signifies an accusation, made in a legal manner of legal conduct, either of omission or commission by the person charged.

"Charge" means expenditure. *H.H. Maharajadhiraja Madhav Rao Jivaji Rao Scindia Bahadur of Gwalior* v. *Union of India,* AIR 1971 SC 530.

The term "charge" is a broad one. As used here, it is not a technical term and has not been defined by the Act. It has, therefore, its ordinary dictionary meaning. It means any amount which may be demanded as a price for the rendering of some service or as price of some goods. *Gajanana Motor Transport Co. Ltd.* v. *The State of Karnataka,* AIR 1977 SC 418.

The term 'charges' in relation of fixation of price must be read *ejusdem generis* taking colour from the succeeding terms—rates, duties and taxes, under Cl. 2(d). *Nagrik Upbhokta M. Manch* v. *Union of India*, (2002) 5 SCC 466, para 12 : AIR 2002 SC 2405. [Kerosene (Restriction on Use and Fixation of Ceiling Price) Order, 1993, cl. 2(d)]

"CHARGE" means an interest or lien created on the property or assets of a company or any of its undertakings or both as security and includes a mortgage. [S. 2(16) of the Companies Act, 2013 (18 of 2013)]

Charge and discharge. A *charge* is said to be a thing done that bindeth him that doth it, or that which is his to the performance thereof; and *discharge* is the removal, or taking away of that charge. (*Termes de La Ley.; Tomlin*)

Charge d' Affaires. Persons invested with the affairs of their Government at the seat of a foreign Government; diplomatic agents, envoys, *etc.*

A diplomatic representative lower in rank to an ambassador or minister; an envoy to a State to which a diplomat of higher grade is not sent.

Charge holder. A person who holds a charge of another's property. [T.P. Act (4 of 1882), S. 101].

Charge-sheet. Charge-sheet is the form of sheet on which the officer in-charge of a police station or lock-up enters the accusations or charges against persons brought there in custody, whether arrested with or without warrant.

Chargeable. Means, as applied to an instrument executed or first executed after the commencement of this Act, chargeable under this Act, and, as applied to any other instrument, chargeable under the law in force in India when such instrument was executed or, where several persons executed the instrument at different times, first executed. [Indian Stamp Act (2 of 1899), S. 2(6)]

Liable to be charged with expenses. [Indian Stamp Act (2 of 1899), S. 2(6)].

Chargeable accounting period. Means—

(a) any accounting period falling wholly within the terms beginning on the first April 1946, and ending on the 31st day of March, 1949;

(b) where any accounting period falls partly within and partly without the said part of that accounting period as falls within the said term:

Provided that where an accounting period falls partly before, and partly after, the end of March, 1947, so much of that accounting period as falls before and so much of that accounting period as falls after, the end of March, 1947, shall be deemed each to be a separate chargeable accounting period. [Business Profits Tax Act (21 of 1947), S. 2(4)]

Charged. The word "charged" in S. 218, IPC (45 of 1860), is not restricted to the narrow meaning of "enjoined by a special provision of law."

Charged with. Having the charge of; having a charge against oneself. [IPC (45 of 1860),S . 216].

Charges. The word 'charges' denotes the accusations or imputations against member of the service. *Govinda Menon* v. *Union of India*, AIR 1967 SC 1274, 1283. [All India Services (Discipline and Appeal) Rules (1955), Rules 5, 2 and 7]

Charging and Levying. The words 'charging' in Cl. (b) and 'levying' in Cl. (c) are used in one and the same sense. They were not used to include 'collecting'. *Upper Doab Sugar Mills Ltd.* v. *Shabdara Saharanjan Light Railway Co. Ltd.*, AIR 1963 SC 217, 220. [Indian Railways Act (9 of 1890), S. 41(1)(b)(c)]

Charging order. An order obtained from a Court or judge by a decree-holder binding the stocks or funds of judgment debtor with decree debts. [CPC (5 of 1908), S. 128(2)(d)].

Charging section. A section of an Act by which a tax is charged.

Charitable. Having the character or purpose of a charity. The word "charitable", in a legal sense includes every gift for a general public use, to be applied consistent with existing laws, for benefit of an indefinite number of persons, and designed to benefit them from an educational, religious, moral, physical or social standpoint. This term is synonymous with "beneficent", "benevolent", and "eleemosnary". (*Black*)

"Charitable" means "of or relating to the assistance of those in need." Oxford English Dictionary as cited in *S.H. Medical Centre Hospital* v. *State of Kerala*, (2014) 11 SCC 381, para 17.

Connected with an object of charity; of the nature of charity. [, Indian Evidence Act (1 of 1872), S. 49 and CPC (5 of 1908), S. 92(1)].

Charitable institution. Under Hindu Law, a tank can be an object of charity and when a dedication is made in favour of a tank, the same is considered as a charitable institution. *Kamaraju Venkata Krishna Rao*. v. *Sub Collector Ongole*, AIR 1969 SC 563, at 566.

One which dispenses charity to all who need and apply for it, does not provide gain or profit in private sense to any person connected with it, and does not appear to place obstacles of any character in the way of those who need and would avail themselves of charitable benefits it dispenses. Distinctive features are that it has no capital stock or shareholders and earns no profits or dividends; but rather derives its funds mainly from public and private charity and holds them in trust for objects and purposes expressed in its charter. (*Black*)

Charitable object. Merely because education is imparted in the school, that by itself, cannot be regarded as charitable object. *Municipal Corporation of Delhi* v. *Children Book Trust*, AIR 1922 SC 1456, 1471. [Delhi Municipal Corporation Act (66 of 1957), S. 115(4)(a)]

Charitable purpose. In this Act "CHARITABLE PURPOSE" includes relief of the poor, education, medical relief and the advancement of any other object of general public utility, but does not include a purpose which related exclusively to religious teaching or worship. [Charitable Endowments Act (6 of 1890), S. 2].

'Charitable purpose' includes relief of the poor, education, yoga, medical relief, preservation of environment (including watersheds, forests and wildlife) and preservation of monuments or places or objects of artistic or historic interest, and the advancement of any other object of general public utility.

Provided that the advancement of any other object of general public utility shall not be a charitable purpose, if it involves the carrying on of any activity in the nature of trade, commerce or business, or any activity of rendering any service in relation to any trade, commerce or business, for a cess or fee or any other consi-deration, irrespective of the nature of use or application, or retention, of the income from such activity, unless—

(i) such activity is undertaken in the course of actual carrying out of such advancement of any other object of general public utility; and

(ii) the aggregate receipts from such activity or activities during the previous year, do not exceed twenty per cent of the total receipts, of the trust or institution undertaking such activity or activities, of that previous year. [Income-tax Act (43 of 1961), section 2(15)

"CHARITABLE PURPOSE" includes relief of the poor, education, medical relief, and the advancement of any other object of general public utility. [Income-tax Act (43 of 1961), S. 2(15); Foreign Trade (Regulation) Rules, 1993, R. 2(b)]

A charitable purpose which is not of a religious character must contain the element of benefiting the public. A trust, the object and scope of which is limited to the education of the members of a family would not come within the definition of a charitable purpose. Public utility must always be a matter of degree, so that circumstances must be examined to ascertain whether the section or class of the community to be benefitted can be said to be public as opposed to being private. A trust for the benefit of the members of a family or for the descendants of a named individual imports a conception or notion of something which is private and not something which is public.

"Charitable purposes" in S. 2(15) of the Income-tax Act (43 of 1961)) would include relief of the poor, education, medical relief and the advancement of any other object of general public utility. Trusts for the benefit of the inhabitants of a particular locality are regarded as charitable, but trusts for the benefit of a particular political party or for the advancement of particular political purposes or opinions are not regarded as charitable.

'Charitable purpose'—the dominant purpose of a State Bar Council is to ensure quality service of competent lawyers to the litigating public, to spread legal literacy, promote law reforms and provide legal assistance to the poor, such purpose is the advancement of the object of general public utility and it will be a charitable purpose. *C.I.T. Bombay* v. *Bar Council of Maharashtra*, AIR 1981 SC 1462, 1467. [Income-tax Act (43 of 1961), Ss. 2(15) and 11].

The test of 'charitable purpose' is satisfied by the proof of any of three conditions, namely, relief of the poor, education, or medical relief. *P.C. Rajaratnam Institution* v. *Municipal Corporation of Delhi*, AIR 1990 SC 816, 817. [Delhi Municipal Corporation Act (66 of 1957), S. 115(4)(a)].

A gift is for charitable purposes if it is for religious, scientific, charitable, literary, or educational purposes under tax law. (*Black*)

Charitable trust. Trust for charitable purpose; charitable trusts are public trusts.

Charitable trusts are those created for the benefit of an unascertained, uncertain and sometimes fluctuating body of individuals.

Charitable trust of public nature. Charitable trust of public nature means both charitable and public. In the Trust of public nature, the beneficiaries must be public, which though may not constitute the public at large, yet must be a classified section of it; no specified individuals, but must be unascertained persons.

Charity. In the broadest sense charity includes whatever proceeds from a sense of moral duty or from humane feelings towards others, uninfluenced by one's own advantage or pleasure. A charity is "a gift to a general public use, which may extend to the poor as well as to the rich." It embraces all that is usually understood by the words "benevolence," philanthropy" and "good will."

A trust created for a purpose such as the advancement of education, health, religion, or other purposes beneficial to the community. Such trusts are regulated by public officers.

"Charity" connotes altruism in thought and action involves an idea of benefiting others rather than oneself. *CIT* v. *Andhra Chambers of Commerce*, 1981 Supp SCC 81 : 1982 SCC (Tax) 103, (1965) 55 ITR 722 (SC) as cited in *Commissioner of Income Tax, Ujjain* v. *Dawoodi Bohra Jamat*, (2014) 16 SCC 222, para 32.

A benevolence, specially to the poor. [IPC (45 of 1860), S. 378, ill. (n)].

The word 'charity' in a legal sense includes every gift for educational, a general public use, to be applied consistent with existing laws for the benefit of an indefinite number of persons and signed to benefit them from a religious, moral, physical or social standpoint. *Pannalal Bansilal Pitti* v. *State of Andhra Pradesh,* AIR 1996 SC 1023.

CHARITY AND BENEVOLENCE. "Charity" is not synonymous with "benevolence." There can be no charitable purpose which is not also a benevolent purpose. But there may be a benevolent purpose which is not charitable in the strictly legal sense of the term.

Charity property. The purpose to which the property is dedicated, and not the source from which it is derived will determine whether or not any property is "charity property,"

Chart. A map, a draft or projection on paper of some part of the earth's surface; a sheet on which information is exhibited in a methodical or tabulated form (as) a historical chart.

A sheet bearing information of any kind arranged in a graphical or tabular form. [Delivery of Books and Newspapers (Public Libraries) Act (27 of 1954), S. 2(a)].

Charter. A written grant of rights by a sovereign or state, of certain privileges or rights, which, in case of doubt, is to be construed strongly against the grantee, but not against the state. *In Mercantile Law*, to hire a vessel for a voyage.

To hire. [Indian Evidence Act (1 of 1872), S. 32(8), ill. (d)]; to hire a ship under an agreement of charter party.

Charter of the United Nations. The constitution of the United Nations Organization, drafted at the U.N. Conference on International Organization, held at San Francisco in 1945. It comprises a preamble and 70 articles in 19 chapters, dealing respectively with (1) purposes and principles, (2) membership, (3) organs, (4) The General Assembly, (5) The Security Council, (6) pacific settlement of disputes, (7) action with respect to threats to the peace, breaches of the peace, and acts of aggression, (8) regional arrangements, (9) international economic and social co-operation, (10) the Economic and Social Council, (11) declaration regarding non-selfgoverning territories, (12) international trusteeship system, (13) the trusteeship council, (14) the International Court of Justice, (15) the Secretariat, (16) miscellaneous provisions, (17) transitional security arrangements, (18) amendments, and (19) ratification and signature.

Charter party. The common written form in which the contract of affreightment is expressed. [Naval and Aircraft Prize Act (59 of 1871), S. 2(k)].

It is a contract by which a ship, or some principal part thereof, is let to a merchant, for the conveyance of goods on a determined voyage to one or more places.

Chartered accountant. "CHARTERED ACCOUNTANT" means a person who is a member of the Institute (Institute of Chartered Accountants of India). [Chartered Accountants Act (38 of 1949), S. 2(b)]

Member of chartered institute of documents.

"CHARTERED ACCOUNTANT" for the purposes of rule 13 of the Companies (Accounts) Rules, 2014, the term 'Chartered Accountant' shall mean a Chartered Accountant whether engaged in practice or not. [*Explanation* (*ii*) to Rule 13(1) of the Companies (Accounts) Rules, 2014]

"CHARTERED ACCOUNTANT" means a chartered accountant as defined in section 2(1)(*b*) of the Chartered Accountants Act, 1949 (38 of 1949), who holds a valid certificate of practice under section 6(1) of that Act. [S. 2(17) of the Companies Act, 2013 (18 of 2013)]

Chartered company. A company created by the grant of a charter from Government and regulated by the terms of the charter.

Chartered in. For the purposes of this section, the term "CHARTERED IN" shall exclude a ship chartered in by the company on bareboat charter-cum-demise terms. [Income-tax Act (43 of 1961),

Chap. XII G, S. 115VV, *Expln.* (*Inserted by Finance (No 2) Act (23 of 2004), S. 30*)].

Chartered ship. A ship hired for freight; a ship which is the subject-matter of a charter-party.

Charterer. One who by contract acquires the right to use a vessel belonging to another. One who charters or hires or engages the whole or part of a ship under an agreement of charter-party for a voyage.

A person who charters or hires a ship under an agreement of charter party. [CPC (5 of 1908), O. V, R. 13(2)].

Chaste. Pure from all unlawful commerce of sexes. Applied to persons before marriage, it signifies pure from all sexual commerce; undefiled; applied to married persons true to the marriage bed.

Chaste with respect to a wife means (according to Hindu Smritis) one "who is well restrained and who by reason of her continence is competent to perform *vedic* and *smirta* ceremonies living with her husband."

Pure from unlawful sexual intercourse; virtuous. [Hindu Marriage Act (25 of 1955), S. 25(3)].

Chaste wife. The expression "chaste wife" in Hindu Law means *Sadhvi, i.e.,* "she who slights not her lord, but keeps her mind, speech and body to him."

Chastisement. Correction; punishment. No chastisement is legal unless it is given under authority of a competent Court or by a person having some recognised punitive authority over the person chastised.

Chastity. Chasteness; virtuous conduct; that virtue which prevents the unlawful commerce of the sexes, it relates to the question whether a woman has improper sexual relations with a man or not.

Chat room. A section of an on-line service where interactive textual communication occurs amongst a collection of people. (*Information Technology*)

Chattel : Chattels. Chattel is any article of personal property. It consists of movable property such as furniture and household goods generally, as distinct from fixture or land.

Personal property comprising goods. [Indian Contract Act (9 of 1872), S. 200, ill. (a)].

Chattel mortgage. A mortgage which covers the installment purchase of goods, where the seller transfers title to the buyer but retains a lien securing the unpaid balance.

Chattels. Moveable property or things.

Chattels and goods. "Chattels" is more comprehensive than "goods" and includes animate as well as inanimate property. "Every movable thing which can be weighed, measured or counted is included under the general term 'chattels.'

Cheat. A person who defrauds, deceives or tricks; to fool, to beguile; to practise fraud or deception. [IPC (45 of 1860), S. 415].

TO CHEAT, DEFRAUD, TRICK. These terms convey the idea of practising deception, but in different ways. One *cheats* by direct and gross falsehood or artifice; one *defrauds* by a settled plan or contrivance; one tricks by a sudden invention. *Cheating* and *tricking* are resorted to in the common dealing of men; both may be equally low in their ends, but may be equally base in their means. Tricking requires ingenuity, which is not wanted in the practice of cheating. *Defrauding* applies to the more serious concerns of life, and for the most part involves a breach of confidence, as to *defraud* one's creditors.

"CHEAT AND DEFRAUD", mean "every kind of trick and deception, from false representation and intimidation to suppression and concealment of any fact or information by which a party may be induced to part with his property for less than its value or to give more than its worth for the property of another."

Cheating. "Whoever, by deceiving any person, fraudulently or dishonestly induces the person so deceived to deliver any property to any person or to consent that any person shall retain any property, or intentionally induces the person so deceived to do or omit to do anything which he would not do or omit if he were not so deceived, and which act or omission causes or is likely to cause damage or harm to that person in body, mind, reputation, or property, is said to "cheat".

Explanation.—A dishonest concealment of facts is a deception within the meaning of this section." [IPC (45 of 1860), S. 415] [(w.e.f. 1-7-2024) repealed and replaced by Bharatiya Nyaya Sanhita, 2023 (45 of 2023), section 318(1)]

The main ingredients of the offence of cheating are:

(i) there should be fraudulent or dishonest inducement of a person by deceiving him;

(ii) (*a*) the person so induced should be intentionally induced to deliver any property to any person or to consent that any person shall retain any property, or

(*b*) the person so induced should be intentionally induced to do or to omit to do anything which he would not do or omit if he were not so deceived; and

(iii) in cases covered by the second part of (*ii*), the act or omission should be one which caused or is likely to cause damage or harm to the person induced in body, mind, reputation or property. *R.S. Nayak* v. *A.R. Antulay*, AIR 1986 SC 2045; *Ram Jas* v. *State of U.P.*, (1970) 2 SCC 740; *Kanumukkala Krishnamurthy* v. *State of A.P.*, AIR 1965 SC 333. [IPC (45 of 1860), Ss. 415 and 420]

Cheating by personation. A person is said to "cheat by personation" if he cheats by pretending to be some other person, or by knowingly substituting one person for another, or representing that he or any other person is a person other than he or such other person really is.

Explanation.—The offence is committed whether the individual personated is a real or imaginary person. [IPC (45 of 1860), S. 416] [(w.e.f. 1-7-2024) repealed and replaced by Bharatiya Nyaya Sanhita, 2023 (45 of 2023), section 319(1)]

Checks and balances. The theory of governmental power and functions whereby the three organs of the government check and control one another so that no single organ can control the entire government and the balance is maintained.

Chemical. Any substance used for producing a chemical effect, or one produced by a chemical process. It also denotes a chemical agent prepared for scientific or economic purposes. Drinks like soda or lemonade are not "chemicals."

Broadly and literally, it can be said that the rayon grade pulp is neither chemical industry nor textile industry nor paper industry. *(Member Secretary) A.P. Board for Water Pollution Control* v. *Andhra Pradesh Rayons Ltd.,* AIR 1989 SC 611.

Chemicals accident. Means an accident involving a fortuitous, or sudden or unintended occurrence while handling any hazardous chemicals resulting in continuous, intermittent or repeated exposure to death, or injury to, any person or damage to any property but does not include an accident by reason only of war or radio-activity. [Chemical Accidents (Emergency Planning, Preparedness, and Response) Rule, 1986, R. 2(a)]

Chemical Weapons. Means the following, together or separately:

(a) Toxic Chemicals and their precursors, except where intended for purposes not prohibited under this Convention, as long as the types and quantities are consistent with such purposes;

(b) Munitions and devices, specifically designed to cause death or other harm through the toxic properties of those toxic chemicals specified in sub-paragraph (a), which would be released as a result of the employment of such munitions and devices;

(c) Any equipment specifically designed for use directly in connection with the employment of munitions and devices specified in sub-paragraph (b). [Chemical Weapons Convention Act (34 of 2000), Art. II (1)]

"CHEMICAL WEAPONS" means—

(i) the toxic chemicals and their precursors, except where intended for purposes not prohibited under the Convention, as long as the types and quantities are consistent with such purposes;

(ii) the munitions and devices, specifically designed to cause death or other harm through the toxic properties of those Toxic Chemicals specified in sub-clause (i), which would be released as a result of the employment of such munitions and devices;

(iii) any equipment specifically designed for use directly in connection with the employment of munitions and devices specified in sub-clause (ii), together or separately. [Chemical Weapons Convention Act (34 of 2000), S. 2(b)]

"CHEMICAL WEAPONS" means,—

(i) the toxic chemicals and their precursors, except where intended for—

  (a) industrial, agricultural, research, medical, pharmaceutical or other peaceful purposes;

  (b) protective purposes, namely those purposes directly related to protection against toxic chemicals and to protection against chemical weapons;

  (c) military purposes not connected with the use of chemical weapons and not dependent on the use of the toxic properties of chemicals as a method of warfare; or

  (d) law enforcement including domestic riot control purposes;

as long as the types and quantities are consistent with such purposes;

(ii) the munitions and devices, specifically designed to cause death or other harm through the toxic properties of those toxic chemicals specified in sub-clause (*i*), which would be released as a result of the employment of such munitions and devices; and

(iii) any equipment specifically designed for use directly in connection with the employment of munitions and devices specified in sub-clause (*ii*), together or separately.

[Weapons of Mass Destruction and their Delivery System (Prohibition) of Unlawful Activities) Act (21 of 2005), S. 4(c)]

Chemical Weapons Production Facility.—

(a) Means any equipment, as well as any building housing such equipment, that was designed, constructed or used at any time since 1 January 1946:

  (i) As part of the stage in the production of chemicals (final technological stage) where the material flows would contain, when the equipment is in operation:

    (1) Any chemical listed in Schedule I in the Annex on Chemicals; or

    (2) Any other chemical that has no use, above 1 tonne per year on the territory of a State Party or in any other place under the jurisdiction or control of a State Party, for purposes not prohibited under this Convention, but can be used for Chemical Weapons purposes; or

  (ii) For filling Chemical Weapons, including, *inter alia,* the filling of chemicals listed in Schedule I into munitions, devices or bulk storage containers; the filling of chemicals into containers that form part of assembled binary munitions and devices or into chemical submunitions that form part of assembled unitary munitions and devices, and the loading of the containers and chemical submunitions into the respective munitions and devices;

(b) Does not mean:

(i) Any facility having a production capacity for synthesis of chemicals specified in sub-paragraph (a) (i) that is less than 1 tonne;

(ii) Any facility in which a chemical specified in sub-paragraph (a) (i) is or was produced as an un-avoidable by-product of activities for purposes not prohibited under this Convention, provided that the chemical does not exceed 3 per cent. of the total product and that the facility is subject to declaration and inspection under the Annex on Implementation and Verification (hereinafter referred to as "Verification Annex"); or

(iii) The single small-scale facility for production of chemicals listed in Schedule I for purposes not prohibited under this Convention as referred to in Part VI of the Verification Annex. [Chemical Weapons Convention Act (34 of 2000), Art. II 8].

Chemically pure. "Chemically pure" means absolutely pure. (69 *Fed.* 597. 608). It means a much greater degree of purity than that required for trade and commercial purposes.

Cheque. A "CHEQUE" is a bill of exchange drawn on a specified banker and not expressed to be payable otherwise than on demand and it includes the electronic image of a truncated cheque in the electronic form. [Negotiable Instruments Act (26 of 1881), S. 6A]

"CHEQUE" means a bill of exchange drawn on a specified banker and not expressed to be payable otherwise than on demand. [Indian Stamp Act (2 of 1899), S. 2(7)]

CHEQUE includes a travellers cheque. [Foreign Exchange Management (Encashment of Draft, Cheque, Instrument and Payment of Interest) Rules, 2000, Rule 2(d)].

A cheque is defined by the Bills of Exchange Act 1882, Section 73, as a bill of exchange drawn on a banker, payable on demand, and generally the provisions of that Act applicable to bills apply to cheques. HALSBURY, 4th Edn., Vol. 3, para 38, p. 32.

It is an order on a bank purporting to be drawn upon a deposit of funds for the payment of a specified sum of money, on presentation, to the person named in the document, or to him on his order or to the bearer. It is made payable instantly on demand.

Cheque book. A book containing blank cheques on a particular bank or banker with an inner margin, called a "stub" on which to note the number of each cheque its amounts and date and the payee's name and the memorandum of the balance in bank.

Cheque crossed. A cheque is crossed for protection. The crossing is usually done by the drawer, who writes, "& Co.," between two parallel transverse lines across the face of the cheque after which the cheque can only be realised by being passed through a bank. The simple "& Co.," crossing is called "general"; when the name of a particular bank is added it is called "special."

Cheque crossed generally. 'Where a cheque bears across its face an addition of the words "and company" or any abbreviation thereof, between two parallel transverse lines, the cheque shall be deemed to be crossed generally.' [Negotiable Instruments Act (26 of 1881), S. 123]

Cheque crossed specially. 'Where a cheque bears across its face an addition of the name of the banker, the cheque shall be deemed to be crossed specially and to be crossed to that banker.' [Negotiable Instruments Act (26 of 1881), S. 124]

Cheque dishonoured. When the amount specified on the cheque is not paid or clearance is not given, it is said that the cheque has been dishonoured.

Cheque in the electronic form. "A CHEQUE IN THE ELECTRONIC FROM" means a cheque which contains the exact mirror image of a paper cheque, and is generated, written and signed in a secure system ensuring the minimum safety standards with the use of digital signature (with or without biometrics signature) and asymmetric crypto system. [Negotiable Instruments Act (26 of 1881), S. 6A *Expl.* (1)(a)]

Cheque to bearer. A cheque payable to the person holding it without requiring endorsement.

Chief. A principal thing, as distinguished from that which is incidental or subordinate. (*Burrill*)

Chief agent. Means a person who, not being a salaried employee of an insurer in consideration of any commission—

(i) performs any administrative or organising functions for the insurer, and

(ii) procures life insurance business for the insurer by employing or causing to be employed insurance agents on behalf of the insurer. [Insurance Act (4 of 1938), S. 2(5A)]

Chief Controlling Revenue Authority. CHIEF CONTROLLING REVENUE AUTHORITY OR CHIEF REVENUE AUTHORITY shall mean—

(a) in a State where there is a Board of Revenue, that Board;

(b) in a State where there is a Revenue Commissioner, that Commissioner;

(c) in Punjab, the Financial Commissioner; and

(d) elsewhere, such authority as, in relation to matters enumerated in List I in the Seventh Schedule to the constitution, the Central Government, and in relation to other matters, the State Government, may, by notification in the Official Gazette appoint. [General Clauses Act (10 of 1897), S. 3 (10)].

Chief Election Commissioner. The Chairman of the Election Commission; appointed by the President of India. Under his supervision, the Election Commission superintends, directs and controls the preparation of the electoral rolls and conducts all elections to Parliament and to the legislature of every State and to the offices of President and Vice-President of India.

Chief executive. The highest executive responsible for directing, co-ordinating and controlling activities in a business enterprise so as to carry out effectively the general policy laid down by the Board, *e.g.,* Managing Director, General Manager.

Chief Executive Officer. In relation to a Municipality or Panchayat, means, its senior-most executive officer, by whatever name called. [S. 2(1)(c) of the Prohibition of Employment as Manual Scavengers & Their Rehabilitation Act, 2013 (25 of 2013)]

"CHIEF EXECUTIVE OFFICER" means an officer of a company, who has been designated as such by it. [S. 2(18) of the Companies Act, 2013 (18 of 2013)]

"CHIEF EXECUTIVE OFFICER" means a person appointed as the Chief Financial Officer of a company. [S. 2(19) of the Companies Act, 2013 (18 of 2013)]

Chief Justice. 'CHIEF JUSTICE' means the Chief Justice of India, and includes a Judge appointed under Article 126 of the Constitution to perform the duties of the Chief Justice. [Supreme Court Rules, 1966 Order 1, Rule 2(d)]

"CHIEF JUSTICE" includes senior Judge. [Parsi Marriage and Divorce Act (3 of 1936), S. 2]

The principal judge of a High Court or Supreme Court.

CHIEF JUSTICE includes Acting Chief Justice also. *Ram Rakh Vyas* v. *Union of India*, AIR 1977 Raj 243, 250. [States Reorganisation Act (1956), S. 51(2)]

CHIEF JUSTICE is the presiding or principal judge of a High Court.

Chief of the Air Staff. Means the officer commanding the Air Force [Air Force Act, 1950 (45 of 1950), section 4(xiv)]

Chief of the Naval Staff. Means the flag officer appointed by the President as Chief of the Naval Staff or, in his absence on leave or otherwise, an officer appointed by the Central Government to officiate as such, or, in the absence of such officiating appointment, the officer on whom the command devolves in accordance with the Regulations made under this Act. [Navy Act (62 of 1957), S. 3 (2)]

Chief Officer Incharge. Incharge of revenue administration of a division. [General Clauses Act (10 of 1897), S. 3(14)].

Chief whip. Chief of the persons appointed by a party in a legislature to enforce discipline among and ensure attendance of members at voting *etc.* [Parliament (Prevention of Disqualification) Act (10 of 1959), S. 3(b)].

"Child", "Children". A person who is under twelve years of age. [IPC (45 of 1860), Ss. 83, 89]. [Now (w.e.f. 1-7-2024) repealed & replaced by Bharatiya Nyaya Sanhita, 2023 (45 of 2023)]

"Child" means any person below the age of eighteen years. [(w.e.f. 1-7-2024) Bharatiya Nyaya Sanhita, 2023 (45 of 2023), section 2(3)]

"CHILD" means person who, if a male, has not completed twenty-one years of age, and if a female, has not completed eighteen years of age. [Child Marriage Restraint Act (19 of 1929), S. 2(a)]

"CHILD", in relation to an individual, includes a step-child and an adopted child of that individual. [Income-tax Act (43 of 1961), S. 2(15B)].

A person of tender years [IPC (45 of 1860), S. 82]; male or female descendant of the first degree. [T.P. Act (4 of 1882), S. 17(2)(ii)]; issue [Hindu Minority and Guardianship Act (32 of 1956), S. 3(1), *Expln.* (i)]; descendant [CrPC 1973 (2 of 1974), S. 127(1)].

The term 'child' includes an illegitimate child also. *Gurmit Singh* v. *Ajit Singh*, AIR 1977 P&H 381, 382. [Fatal Accidents Act (13 of 1855), S. 1-A]

"CHILD" means any person below the age of eighteen years and includes any adopted, step or foster child. [S. 2(b) of the Protection of Women from Domestic Violence Act, 2005 (43 of 2005)]

"CHILD" means any person below the age of eighteen years. [(w.e.f. 14-11-2012) S. 2(1)(d) of the Protection of Children from Sexual Offences Act, 2012 (32 of 2012)].

"Child" means a person who has not completed 18 years of age. [Aadhaar (Targeted Delivery of Financial & Other Subsidies, Benefits & Services) Act (18 of 2016), section 2(ia)]

"Child", for the purposes of Chapter VI, includes a stillborn child. [Code on Social Security, 2020 (36 of 2020), section 2(12)]

"CHILD" means a male or female child of the age of six to fourteen years. [Right of Children to Free and Compulsory Education Act 2009 (35 of 2009), S. 2(c)].

CHILDREN BY ADOPTION may be included in the term "children". They are the legal children of their adoptive parents.

A son adopted after the death of the deceased is not a "child" within the meaning of the term "child" in the Fatal Accidents Act (13 of 1855).

CHILDREN MADE LEGITIMATE BY MARRIAGE of their parents may be included in the term "children". [Indian Evidence Act (1 of 1872), S. 112]

BEQUEST TO "CHILDREN" *prima facie* means, if no intervening interest be given, a bequest to those who may be living at the date of the testator's death.

A bequest to "children" should not be construed as bequest to "sons" only.

In the law of negligence, and *in laws for the protection of children, etc.*, "child" is used as the opposite of "adult". (*Black*)

The word 'child' means a minor, whether under the Indian Majority Act (9 of 1875) or the Guardians and Wards Act (8 of 1890).

It is not concerned with age. The only quailfication is that the child should be unable to maintain itself, hence a child though not a minor is still a child as long as it is unable to maintain itself. *Nanak Chand* v. *Chandra Kishore*, AIR 1970 SC 446, at 449, 450.

"Child Adoption Resource Information and Guidance System". Means on online information system for facilitating, guiding and monitoring the adoption programme. [Adoption Regulations, 2017, Regn. 2(4)].

"Child affected by HIV". Means a person below the age of eighteen years, who is HIV-positive or whose parent or guardian (with whom such child normally resides) is HIV-positive or has lost a parent or guardian (with whom such child resided) due to AIDS or lives in a household fostering children orphaned by AIDS. [Human Immunodeficiency Virus and Acquired Immune Deficiency Syndrome (Prevention and Control) Act (16 of 2017), S. 2(c)].

Child abuse. Deprivation of the right to innocence, child prostitution, child pornography, torture, violence, economic exploitation including child labour, drug abuse, sexual exploitation and sexual abuse, sale, trafficking, abduction, discrimination, juvenile injustice, deprivation of liberty including any form of detention, imprisonment or placement in custodial settings, disrespect to their views, non-preservation of their identity, non-protection of their privacy, inhuman or degrading treatment or punishment.

Child en ventre sa mere. A child while yet unborn; child in the womb of the mother. From the time of conception the infant is *in esse* for the purpose of taking any estate which is for his interest, whether by descent or devise. *Children en ventre sa mere* are included within the meaning of the word "children".

An infant unborn, but *in esse* is deemed a person capable of taking by deed or other writing any estate whatever in the same manner as if he were born.

Child in need of care and protection. Means a child—

(i) who is found without any home or settled place or abode and without any ostensible means of subsistence,

(ii) who resides with a person (whether a guardian of the child or not) and such person—

(a) has threatened to kill or injure the child and there is a reasonable likelihood of the threat being carried out, or

(b) has killed, abused or neglected some other child or children and there is a reasonable likelihood of the child in question being killed, abused or neglected by that person,

(iii) who is mentally or physically challenged or ill children or children suffering from terminal diseases or incurable diseases having no one to support or look after.

(iv) who has a parent or guardian and such parent or guardian is unfit or incapacitated to exercise control over the child,

(v) who does not have parent and no one is willing to take care of or whose parents have abandoned him or who is missing and run away child and whose parents cannot be found after reasonable inquiry,

(vi) who is being or is likely to be grossly abused, tortured or exploited for the purpose of sexual abuse or illegal acts,

(vii) who is found vulnerable and is likely to be inducted into drug abuse or trafficking,

(viii) who is being or is likely to be abused for unconscionable gains,

(ix) who is victim of any armed conflict, civil commotion or natural calamity. [Juvenile Justice (Care and Protection of Children) Act (56 of 2000), S. 2(d)]

Child friendly. Means any behaviour, conduct practice, process, attitude, environment or treatment that is humane, considerate and in the best interest of the child. [Justice (Care and Protection of Children) Act, 2015 (2 of 2016), S. 2 (15)].

Child in need of care and protection. Means a child—

(i) who is found without any home or settled place of abode and without any ostensible means of subsistence, or

(ii) who is found working in contravention of the provisions of this Act or labour laws for the time being in force or is found begging, or living on the street; or

(iii) who resides with a person (whether a guardian of the child or not) and such person—(a) has injured, exploited, abused or neglected the child or have violated any other law for the time being in force meant for protection of child; or (b) has threatened to kill, injure or abuse the child and there is a reasonable likelihood of the threat being carried out; or

(c) has killed, abused, neglected or exploited some other child or children and there is a reasonable likelihood of the child in question being killed, abused, exploited or neglected by that person; or

(iv) who is mentally ill or mentally or physically challenged or suffering from terminal or insurable disease, having no one to support or look after or having parents and guardians unfit to take care, if found so by the Board or the Committee; or

(v) who has a parent or guardian and such parent or guardian is found to be unfit or incapacitated, by the Committee or the Board, to take care for and protect the safety and well-being of the child; or

(vi) who does not have parents and no one is willing to take care of, and protect or who is abandoned or surrendered; or

(vii) who is missing or run away child, or whose parents cannot be found after making reasonable inquiry in such manner as may be prescribed; or

(viii) who has been or is being or is likely to be abused, tortured or exploited for the purpose of sexual abuse or illegal acts; or

(ix) who is found vulnerable and has been or is being or is likely to be inducted into drug abuse or trafficking; or

(x) who is being or is likely to be abused for unconscionable gains; or

(xi) who is victim of or affected by any armed conflict, civil unrest or natural calamity; or

(xii) who is in imminent risk of marriage before attaining the age of marriage and whose parents, family members, guardian and any other persons are likely to be responsible for solemnisation of such marriage. Juvenile Justice (Care and Protection of Children) Act, 2015 (2 of 2016), S. 2 (14).

No one can deny that a child victim of sexual abuse or sexual assault or sexual harassment is a child in need of care and protection. Similarly in a given case, a child accused of an offence and brought before the Juvenile Justice Board or any other authority might also be a child in need of case and protection. [*Exploitation of Children in Orphanages in State of Tamil Nadu* v. *Union of India,* (2017) 7 SCC 578, para 63].

Child marriage. Means a marriage to which either of the contracting parties is a child. [Child Marriage Restraint Act (19 of 1929), S. 2(b)]

"Child pornography" means any visual depiction of sexually explicit conduct involving a child which include photograph, video, digital or computer generated image indistinguishable from an actual child and image created, adapted, or modified, but appear to depict a child. [Protection of Children from Sexual Offences Act, 2012 (32 of 2012), section 2(1)(da)]

Child support. A legal obligation of parent to contribute to the economic maintenance and education of a child.

Child Welfare Officer. Means an officer attached to a child care institution for carrying out the directions given by the Committee or, as the case may be, the Board with such responsibility as may be prescribed. [Juvenile Justice (Care and Protection of Children) Act, 2015 (2 of 2016), section 2(17)]

Child witness. It is imperative that the Court should test the competency of a child witness before examining him. It should test his intellectual capacity by putting a few simple and ordinary questions and also judge the competency of the witness during the course of his examination and say something to that effect after the statement is over. *Dhanna* v. *State*, AIR 1951 Raj 37, 42. [Indian Evidence Act (1 of 1872), S. 118]

Childish. "Childish" refers to mere simplicity or weakness of mind. A childish person is not *non compos mentis*; or an idiot.

Childless. Without a child. [Hindu Adoptions and Maintenance Act (78 of 1956), S. 20, *Expln*.].

Childline services. Means a twenty-four hours emergency outreach service for children in crisis which links them to emergency or long-term care and rehabilitation service [Juvenile Justice (Care and Protection of Children) Act, 2015 (2 of 2016), S. 2 (25)].

Children's home. A home which provides care and accommodation to children.

Chimney. "CHIMNEY" includes any structure with an opening or outlet from or through which any air pollutant may be emitted. [Air (Prevention and Control of Pollution) Act (14 of 1981), S. 2(h)]

In this Part of this Act the expression 'CHIMNEY' includes structures and openings of any kind from or through which smoke may be emitted. [(English) Public Health Act, 1936, S. 110]

'CHIMNEY' includes structures and openings of any kind from or through which smoke or (where the reference is to the chimney serving an oven) grit or dust may be emitted, and references to a chimney of a building include references to a chimney which serves the whole or a part of a building but is structurally separate therefrom. [(English) Clean Air Act, 1956, S. 34(1)]

Chirograph. A written deed, subscribed and witnessed.

Chirographum apud debitorem repertum praesumitur solutum. (*Maxim*) An evidence of debt found in the possession of the debtor is presumed to be paid. [*See* Indian Evidence Act (1 of 1872), S. 114]

A deed or bond found with the debtor is presumed to be paid. (*Latin for Lawyers*)

Chirographum non extans praesumitur solutum. An evidence of debt not existing is presumed to have been discharged. (*Black*)

Chit. 'CHIT' means a transaction whether called chit, chit fund, *chitty, kuri, fraternity fund, Rotating Savings & Credit Institution* or by any other name by or under which a person enters into an agreement with a specified number of persons that everyone of them shall subscribe a certain sum of money (or a certain quantity of grain instead) by way of periodical instalments over a definite period and that each such subscriber shall, in his turn, as determined by lot or by auction or by tender or in such other manner as may be specified in the chit agreement, be entitled to the net chit amount.

Explanation. A transaction is not a chit within the meaning of this clause, if in such transaction—

(i) some alone, but not all, of the subscribers get the prize amount without any liability to pay future subscriptions; or

(ii) all the subscribers get the chit amount by turns with a liability to pay future subscriptions. [R.B.I. Act (2 of 1934), S. 45-I(bb), *Expln.* and Chit Funds Act (40 of 1982), S. 2(b)]

Chit agreement. Means the document containing the articles of agreement between the foreman and the subscribers relating to the chit. [Chit Funds Act (40 of 1982), S. 2(c)]

Chit amount. Means the sum total of the subscriptions payable by all the subscribers for any instalment of a chit without any deduction of discount or otherwise. [Chit Funds Act (40 of 1982), S. 2(d)]

Chit business. Means the business of conducting of chit. [Chit Funds Act (40 of 1982), S. 2(a)]

Chit fund. A chit fund organisation is an organisation of a number of people who join together and subscribe amounts monthly so that that person or the subscriber who is in need of funds may draw the amount less discount. It is an organisation run on a co-operative basis for the benefit of the subscribers, the funds to be utilised by them as and when a particular subscriber needs it. It helps thrifty persons to invest their savings with good chances of profit. *Narasimleo* v. *Rajana,* ILR 1958 AP 409.

Chit fund company. Means a company managing, conducting or supervising, as foreman, agent or in any other capacity, chits as defined in Section 2 of the Chit Funds Act, 1982. [Prevention of Money Laundering Act (15 of 2003), S. 2(1)(h)]

Choate. Complete in and of itself; become perfected.

Choate lien. A lien where the holder of the lien, the property, and the monetary amount are established, so that the lien is perfected and nothing else is needed to make it enforceable.

Choose. Select out of a greater number; make choice; decide as between several alternatives. The word "*choose*" when used of a superior Government officer with power of appointing a person to office, is equivalent to the word "appoint".

To select; to make choice. [Indian Contract Act (9 of 1872), S. 195].

Chose. Means personal property; things in general.

Chose in action. The expression "chose in action" is now used to cover a miscellaneous assortment of rights and properties. Originally the phrase had a clear and definite meaning *viz.*, a present right to take proceedings in a Court of Law to recover a debt or damages. The term now includes all debts, and all claims for damages, for breach of contract, or for torts connected with contract, which cannot be enforced without action. "A chose or thing in action" is an expression in contradistinction to a chose or thing in possession and is applicable to cases where the title to the money or property is in one person and the possession is in another, which by contract he is bound to deliver to the owner."

Chronic. Pesistent. "In order to distinguish a disease as "chronic" it is necessary that it should have been of long standing. "Chronic" and "acute" are the antithesis of each other. An acute disease is one usually attended with violent symptoms, while a chronic disease is deep-seated and obstinate, threatening a long continuance."

Church. "CHURCH" includes any chapel or other building generally used for public Christian worship (Indian Christian Marriage Act (15 of 1872), S. 3).

A house set apart for public worship especially that of a parish [Gift-tax Act (18 of 1858), S. 5(va)(i)]; a body of Christian believers holding the same creed, observing the same rites, and acknowledging the same ecclesiastical authority regarded either as the only true representative of or as a separate branch of the church universal and often confined to territorial or historical limits.

Churning. A stock-broker's excessive trading of an account of a customer so as to earn more commission instead of furthering the interests of customer.

C.I.F. Contract. On a sale C.I.F. the seller undertakes to ship the goods sold on a vessel bound to the port mentioned and to deliver the goods on board such vessel by tendering to the buyer a bill of lading for them together with a policy of insurance covering their insurance to the port to which the goods are to go, and the seller must be ready and able to endorse the bill of lading and to transfer the policy to the buyer on receiving payment of the price. 4 IC 1037 : 5 LBR 144.

A C.I.F. contract is one under which the purchaser is bound to pay the stated price for the goods on tender of the documents showing that the goods have been shipped for transit to the port of destination, duly insured according to the terms of the contract and that freight has been paid. A C.I.F. purchaser is entitled to ask for a bill of lading for he is not bound to pay upon proof merely that the goods have arrived at the port of destination. *Nassim Isaal Bekhur* v. *Sultan Ali Shurtary,* 40 Bom 11 : 17 Bom LR 249 : 28 IC 433; *Messrs India Coffee and Tea Distributing Co.* v. *State of Madras*, AIR 1954 Mad 1030.

Cigarette. "CIGARETTE" includes,—

(i) any roll of tobacco wrapped in paper or in any other substance not containing tobacco,

(ii) any roll of tobacco wrapped in any substance containing tobacco, which, by reason of its appearance, the type of tobacco used in the filter, or its packaging and labelling is likely to be offered to or purchased by, consumers as cigarette, but does not include *beedi,* cheroot and cigar. [Cigarettes and Other Tobacco Products (Prohibitions of Advertisement and Regulation of Trade and Commerce, Production, Supply and Distribution) Act (34 of 2003), S. 3(b)]

Cylinder of cut tobacco rolled in paper for smoking.

Cine-worker. Means an individual—

(i) who has been employed, directly or through any contractor or in any other manner, in or in connection with the production of not less than five feature films to work as an artiste (including actor, musician or dancer) or to do any work, skilled, unskilled, manual, supervisory, technical, artistic or otherwise; and

(ii) whose remuneration with respect to such employment in or in connection with the production of each of any five feature films, has not exceeded, where such remuneration has been by way of monthly wages, a sum of one thousand and six hundred rupees per month, and where such remuneration has been by way of a lump sum, a sum, of eight thousand rupees. [Cine-Workers Welfare Fund Act (33 of 1981), S. 2(b)]

"CINE-WORKER" means an individual—

(i) who is employed, directly or through any contractor or other person, in or in connection with the production of a feature film to work as an artiste (including actor, musician or dancer) or to do any work, skilled, unskilled, manual, supervisory, technical, artistic or otherwise; and

(ii) whose remuneration with respect to such employment in or in connection with the production of such feature film does not exceed, where such remuneration is by way of monthly wages, a sum of one thousand six hundred rupees per month, and where such remuneration is by way of a lump sum, a sum of fifteen thousand rupees. [Cine-Workers & Cinema Theatre Workers (Regulation of Employment) Act (50 of 1981), S. 2(c)]

Cinema. The word 'cinema' is an abbreviated form of cinematograph and it includes a film exhibition theatre. *Nageena Traders Ltd.* v. *Regional Provident Fund Commr.,* AIR 1965 AP 200, 213.

Cinema house is not a public place. A privately owned cinema house is not a public place since no member of the public has a legal right of access. It is no more a public place than the inside of a grocer's shop or the consulting room of a dentist. *Calcutta Corporation* v. *Sarat Chandra,* AIR 1959 Cal 704, 711.

Cinema theatre. Means a place which is licensed under Part III of the Cinematograph Act, 1952, or under any other law for the time being in force in a state for exhibition of a cinematograph film. [Cine-Workers & Cinema Theatre Workers (Regulation of Employment) Act (50 of 1981), S. 2(a)]

Cinematograph. Includes any apparatus for the representation of moving pictures or series of pictures; [Cinematograph Act (37 of 1952), S. 2(*c*)]

The term 'cinematograph' includes any apparatus for representation of moving pictures or series of pictures. The VCR/VCP are within the ambit of the definition. *Laxmi Video Theatres* v. *State of Haryana,* AIR 1993 SC 2328, 2330. [Cinematograph Act (37 of 1952), S. 2(*c*)]

It is an apparatus producing pictures of motion by the rapid projection on a screen of a great number of photographs taken successively on a long film.

The expression 'cinematograph' includes any apparatus for representation of moving pictures or series of pictures. The VCR/VCP are within the ambit of the definition. *Laxmi Video Theatres* v. *State of Haryana,* AIR 1993 SC 2328, 2330. [Cinematograph Act (37 of 1952), S. 2(*c*)]

Cinematograph film. Means any work of visual recording on any medium produced through a process from which a moving image may be produced by any means and includes a sound recording accompanying such visual recording and "cinematograph" shall be construed as including any work produced by any process analogous to cinematography including video films. [Copyright Act (14 of 1957), S. 2(f)]

'Cinematograph film' means any work of visual recording on any medium produced through a process from which a moving image may be produced by any means and includes a sound recording accompanying such visual recording and 'cinematograph' shall be construed as including any work produced by any process analogous to cinematography including video films. [Copyright Act (14 of 1957), S. 2(f)]

A "cinematograph film" is to be taken to include the sounds embodied in a sound track which is associated with the film. Section 13 recognizes 'cinematograph film' as a distinct and separate class of 'work' and declares that copyright shall subsist therein throughout India. *Indian Performing Right Society Ltd.* v. *Eastern India Motion Picture*

Association, AIR 1977 SC 1443. [Copyright Act (14 of 1957), S. 13]

Circuit. A civil division of a country, state or kingdom. for the more convenient administration of justice (*Burill*). Circuits are certain divisions of the kingdom appointed for the judges to go at stated times every year, for administering of justice, in the several counties. (*Tomlin*)

Circuitus est evitandus, et boni judicis est lites dirimere, ne lis ex lite oriatur. Circuity is to be avoided and it is the duty of a good judge to determine litigation lest one lawsuit arises out of another.

Circular. An announcement or directive typically in the form of a printed leaflet intended to be sent to many persons, or otherwise distributed. [Trade and Merchandise Marks Act (43 of 1958), S. 120(1)] [Now repealed & replaced by Act 47 of 1999].

Circulate. The word "circulate" as per Oxford Concise Dictionary means, " to go round from one place or person, etc. to the next and so on or cause to go around and put into circulation". "Circulation" means a movement to and fro from and back to a starting point. Webster Dictionary defines "circulation" as under:- "cause to pass from place to place or from person to person; to spread"

It can, thus, be seen that "circulation" involves an act by a person, which facilitates or triggers the matter to go from one person to another and so on. [As cited in *Marconi Estevan Rodrigues* v. *The State of Goa*, Criminal Appeal No. 32 of 2013, decided on 3 April 2017.]

Circulation. A Bank-note is said to be "In Circulation," when it is passing from hand to hand as a Negotiable Instrument; and when returned to the Bank (or any of its branches), it ceases to be "In Circulation" or "Outstanding".

Passing from hand to hand. [IPC (45 of 1860), S. 292(a)].

Circumstance. Particulars which accompany an act; the surroundings of an act; the state of affairs surrounding and affecting an agent. [IPC (45 of 1860), S. 307].

A situation as regards wealth, property or assured income. [Professions Tax Limitation (Amendment and Validation) Act (61 of 1949), Preamble].

The "circumstances" include financial circumstances and in that view, the inquiry as to the change in the circumstances must extend to a change in the financial circumstances of the wife. *Shri Bhagwan Dutt* v. *Kamla Devi,* AIR 1975 SC 83. [Cr PC, 1973 (2 of 1974)]

"Circumstances" would ordinarily mean situations or events extraneous to the activities of a concerned person or a group of persons, such as riots, disorders, tension, religious, racial, regional or linguistic or other such commotions, which might by their pre-existence accentuate the impact of such activities effecting the security of the country or a part of it or the public order. *Sambhu Nath Sarkar* v. *State of West Bengal,* AIR 1973 SC 1425.

Circumstances of the transaction. The Indian Evidence Act is confined to only such statements as relate to matters so closely connected with the events which resulted in the death of the person that they may be said to relate to circumstances of the transaction which resulted in his death. *Ghazi* v. *State of U.P.,* AIR 1966 All 142, 145. [Indian Evidence Act (1 of 1872), S. 32(1)].

Circumstantial evidence. Evidence which tends to prove the ultimate fact in issue; presumptive evidence. Evidence derived from circumstances, as distinguished from direct and positive proof. It is the inference of a fact from other facts proved, and the fact thus inferred and assented to by the mind is said to be "presumed"; that is to say, it is taken for granted until the contrary is proved.

All evidence of indirect nature.

Circus. "CIRCUS" means an establishment, whether stationary or mobile, where animals are kept or used wholly or mainly for the purpose of performing tricks or manoeuvres [Wild Life (Protection) Act (53 of 1972), S. 2(7A)]

Anciently it was an edifice or inclosure used for the exhibition of games and shows to the people. It now means a circular inclosure for the exhibition of feats, horsemanship *etc.* Every building, space, tent or area where feats of horsemanship or acrobatic sports or theatrical performances are exhibited are regarded as a circus.

Citation. A reference to a legal precedent or authority such as a case, treatise or a statute.

A passage cited; quotation [General Clauses Act (10 of 1897), S. 28]; an official summons giving notice to a person to appear (as before a tribunal of justice) [Administrators General Act (43 of 1965), S. 14].

Citator. Volume or section of a volume containing table of cases or legislation that have been judicially noticed in subsequent cases.

Cite. To quote or refer to authorities in support of a proposition as, citing authorities in support of an argument in a case.

TO CITE, QUOTE. To *cite* is employed for persons or things; to *quote* for things only: authors are *cited,* passages from their works are *quoted*: we cite only by authority; we quote for general purposes of convenience. Historians ought to *cite* their authority in order to strengthen their evidence and inspire confidence; controversialists must *quote* the objectionable passages in those works which they wish to confute.

Citizen. Member or inhabitant of a state; one who, as a member of a nation or state, owes alliegance to and may claim reciprocal protection from its government. (*Abbot*)

A person who is either born within the State or born of parents who are citizens or one who has acquired the status of citizen by application of the laws of the

State providing for the naturalisation of persons born in another State.

"Citizen" can only be a natural person. The fact that corporations may be nationals of the country for purposes of international law will not make them citizens of this country for the purposes of municipal law or the constitution. *State Trading Corporation of India* v. *Commercial Tax Officer*, AIR 1963 SC 1811, 1821. [Citizenship Act (57 of 1955); Constitution of India, Art. 19]

The definition of 'citizen' is comprehensive and fundamental rights guaranteed by the constitution to citizens are available to corporations as well except where the language of the provision and the nature of the right compels an inference to the contrary. *Maharaja Kishangarh Mills Ltd.* v. *State of Rajasthan*, AIR 1953 Raj 188. [Constitution of India, Art. 19(1)]

"Citizen" can only be a natural person. The fact that corporations may be nationals of the country for purposes of international law will not make them citizens of this country for the purposes of municipal law or the constitution. *State Trading Corporation of India* v. *Commercial Tax Officer*, AIR 1963 SC 1811, 1821. [Citizenship Act (57 of 1955); Constitution of India, Art. 19]

Company is not a citizen and has no fundamental right under Art. 19 of the Constitution. *Barium Chemicals Ltd.* v. *Company Law Board,* AIR 1967 SC 295, 313 : (1966) 36 Com Cas 639.

A municipal committee not being a "Citizen" within the meaning of Art. 19 of the Constitution is not entitled to claim protection of any of the fundamental rights under Art. 19. *Municipal Committee, Amritsar* v. *State of Punjab,* AIR 1969 SC 1100.

'T.N. Outdoor Advertising Association' does not come within the ambit of the expression 'citizen' under Art. 19 of the Constitution. *T.N. Outdoor Advertising Association* v. *Union of India*, AIR 2003 Mad 340, 343, para 10. [Constitution of India, Art. 19]

Citizen and Subject. *Citizen* is a term usually employed under the republican form of government as the equivalent of subject in monarchies of feudal origin. (*Ency. of the Laws of England*)

Citizen of India. When once a person is admitted or held to be a "citizen of India", unless there is a decision of the Central Government under Section 9(2) of the Citizenship Act, 1955 that he has acquired the citizenship of a foreign country, he should be presumed to be an Indian citizen. Section 9 of the Citizenship Act, 1955 is a complete Code as regards the termination of Indian citizenship on the acquisition of the citizenship of a foreign country. *Bhagwati Prasad Dixit 'Ghorlwala'* v. *Rajeev Gandhi,* AIR 1986 SC 1534. [Citizenship Act (57 of 1955), S. 9(2)]

Citizenship. Status of being a citizen. Sex is not involved in citizenship. A woman is a citizen. Age or majority is not involved. A minor is a citizen.

The position or status of a citizen [Wealth-tax Act (27 of 1957), S. 19A(3) and main heading of Part II, Constitution of India].

Civic. Pertaining to a citizen, citizenship or city (as) civic rights or duties; civic institution; civil activity.

Civic amenity. 'Civic amenity' means—

(i) a market, a post office, a telephone exchange, a bank, a fair price shop, a milk booth, a school, a dispensary, a hospital, a pathological laboratory, a maternity home, a child care centre, a library, a gymnasium, a bus-stand or a bus depot;

(ii) a recreation centre run by the Government or the Corporation,

(iii) a centre for educational, social or cultural activities established by the Central Government or the State Government or by a body established by the Central Government or the State Government;

(iv) a centre for educational, religious, social or cultural activities or for philanthropic service run by a cooperative society registered under the Karnataka Cooperative Societies Act, 1959 (Karnataka Act 11 of 1959) or a society registered under the Karnataka Societies Registration Act, 1960 (Karnataka Act 17 of 1960) or by a trust created wholly for charitable, educational or religious purposes;

(v) a police station, an area office or a service station of the Corporation of the Bangalore Water Supply and Sewerage Board or the Karnataka Electricity Board; and

(vi) Such other amenity as the Government may, by notification, specify.

[Bangalore Development Authority Act, 1976 (12 of 1976) S. 2(bb) as cited in *Bangalore Development Authority* v. *Aircraft Employees' Cooperative Society Limited*, 2012 (1) SCALE 646, para 5].

Civic interest. Interest of the citizens. [Trade Unions Act (16 of 1926), S. 16(1)].

Civil. Pertaining to the private rights and remedies of a citizen, as distinguished from criminal, political *etc.*; legal, as distinguished from natural; pertaining to the ordinary life and affairs as a citizen, as distinguisned from ecclesiastical *etc.* [IPC (45 of 1860), S. 19 and Constitution of India, Art. 132(1), Art. 144 and Art. 320(3)(c)]; as distinguished from military; pertaining to citizens.

Civil action. A personal action which is instituted to compel payment, or the doing of some other thing which is purely civil. It is an action which deals with acts which constitute an infringement or privation of the private or civil rights belonging to individuals.

The words *"civil action"* or *"civil suit"* or a *"civil case"* mean more or less the samething, and is a proceeding in a Court of Justice by one party against another for the enforcement or protection of a private right, or for the redress or protection of a private wrong.

"Civil suit". Refers to a civil action instituted before a court of law for realisation of a right vested in a party by law. *General Officer Commanding, Rashtriya Rifles* v. *Central Bureau of Investigation*, (2012) 6 SCC 228, para 28.

A proceeding in a Court of justice by one party against another for the enforcement or protection of a private right, or for the redress or prevention of a private wrong. [IPC (45 of 1860), S. 43].

Civil and **civil nature.** The word "civil" according to dictionary means "relating to the citizen as an individual". The word 'nature' has been defined as "the fundamental qualities of a person or thing, identity or essential character, sort, kind, character". The word 'civil nature' is wider than the word 'civil proceeding,' *P.M.A. Metropolitan* v. *Moran Mar Marthoma*, AIR 1995 SC 2001, 2023. [CPC (5 of 1908), S. 9]

Civil and criminal procedure. That part of the law of the State as relates to the procedure in civil and criminal Courts [Indian Evidence Act (1 of 1872), S. 135].

Civil commotion. An insurrection of the people for general purposes, though it does not amount to rebellion.

Civil consequences. In its comprehensive connotation every thing that affects a citizen in his civil life inflicts a civil consequence. "Civil consequence" covers infraction of not merely property or personal right but of civil liberties, material deprivations and non-pecuniary damages. In *State of Orissa* v. *(Miss) Binapani Dei*, (1967) 2 SCR 625: AIR 1967 SC 1269: (1967) 2 LLJ 266 the Supreme Court of India held that even an administrative order which involves civil consequence must be made consistent with the rules of natural justice. [See also *D.K. Yadav* v. *J.M.A. Industries Limited*, (1993) 3 SCC 259].

Civil contempt. Means wilful disobedience to any judgment, decree, direction, order, writ or other process of a Court or wilful breach of an undertaking given to a Court. [Contempt of Courts Act (70 of 1971), S. 2(b)]

Contempts of Court which consist in failing to do something which the contemnor is ordered by the Court to do for the benefit or advantage of another party to the proceedings.

Civil contempt. Includes willful breach of an undertaking given to a court. *Board of Trustees of the Port of Mumbai* v. *Nikhil N. Gupta*, (2015) 10 SCC 139, para 8.

Civil contempt and criminal contempt distinguished. "There is a well defined distinction between "contempts" which are merely criminal or punitive, and those which are termed "civil contempts", the latter applying to such as are remedial in character. The two classes of contempts are often distinguished as "direct" and "constructive" or "consequential". Civil contempts are those quasi-contempts which consist in failing to do something which the contemnor is ordered by the Court to do for the benefit or advantage of another party to the prosecution before the Court, while criminal contempts are those acts in disrespect of the Court or its processes, or which obstruct the administration of justice or tend to bring the Court, into disrespect. Criminal contempts are those committed in the immediate view and presence of the Court, such as insulting language or acts of violence which interrupt the regular proceedings of the Court."

Civil Court. The Courts consolidated for deciding purely civil question between persons seeking their civil rights must be considered to be civil Courts, notwithstanding that they are created by special statute and are mentioned in that statute as distinct from civil Court. A Deputy Commissioner exercising highest revenue jurisdiction is a civil Court. *Arakhita Das* v. *Hari Mahapatra,* AIR 1963 Ori 162, 163. [Hindu Succession Act (30 of 1956), S. 14(2)]

The expression 'civil Courts' includes all Courts of civil judicature whose procedure is in essence governed by the Code of Civil Procedure and therefore includes also Revenue Courts in this State.

Civil death. Deprivation of all rights whose exercise or enjoyment depends upon some provision of positive law; the state of a person who, possessing natural life, has lost all his civil rights and as to them is considered as dead.

A person who was not heard for more than seven years was treated as having died a civil death. *Sheo Nand* v. *Deputy Director of Consolidation*, (2000) 3 SCC 103, para 6 : AIR 2000 SC 1141.

Civil defence. This term includes any measure not amounting to actual combat, for affording defence against any form of hostile attack by a foreign power or for depriving any form of hostile attack by a foreign power of its effect either wholly or in part, whether such measures are taken before, during or after the time of the attack. [Defence of India Act (51 of 1962), S. 2(a), Civil Defence Act, 1968, S. 2(a) and Defence of India Act, 1971, S. 2(a)]

Civil defence corps. Means the corps formed wholly or mainly to meet the needs of civil defence and includes an organisation deemed to be a Corps under the proviso to sub-section (1) of Section 4. [Civil Defence Act (27 of 1968), S. 2(b)]

Civil defence organization. Means any organisation established for civil defence purpose which is declared by a scheme to be a civil defence organisation for the purposes of this Act, and the scheme. [Personal Injuries (Emergency Provisions) Act (59 of 1962), S. 2(1)]

Civil defence services. The services formed wholly or mainly to meet the needs of civil defence. [Defence of India Act (51 of 1962), S. 2(b)]

Civil defence volunteer. In relation to an injury, means a person certified by an officer of a civil defence organisation authorised by the Central Government to grant such certificates, to have been a member of that organisation at the time when the injury was sustained. [Personal Injuries (Emergency Provisions) Act (59 of 1962), S. 2(2)]

Civil disabilities. Disqualification created by law. Minors, lunatics, proprietors of Zamindari estates under Court of Wards and other disqualified proprietors are persons under civil disabilities.

Civil disobedience. A non-violent but deliberate violation of law to call attention to a particular law or set of laws of questionable legitimacy or morality.

Civil disorder. A public disturbance involving three or more people who commit violent acts that cause immediate danger or injury to people or property.

Civil enclave. Means the area, if any allotted at an airport belonging to any armed force of the Union, for use by persons availing of any air transport services from such airport or for the handling of baggage or cargo by such service, and includes land comprising of any building and structure on such area. [Airports Authority of India Act (55 of 1994), S. 2(i) and National Airports Authority Act (64 of 1985), S. 2(i)]

'Civil enclave' means the area, if any allotted at an airport belonging to any armed force of the Union, for use by persons availing of any air transport services from such airport or for the handling of baggage or cargo by such service, and includes land comprising of any building and structure on such area. [Airports Authority of India Act (55 of 1994), S. 2(i) and National Airports Authority Act (64 of 1985), S. 2(i); Airports Economic Regulatory Authority of India Act (27 of 2008), S. 2(f)]

Civil injuries. Infringement or privation of the private or civil rights belonging to the individuals, considered as individuals. It is to be distinguished from a breach and violation of a public right or duty which affects the whole community, considered as a community, which is termed "crime or misdemeanor."

Civil Judicature, Court of. A Court of justice of a civil nature. [CPC (5 of 1908), Preamble].

Civil jurisdiction. Jurisdiction of Court which exists when the subject-matter is not of a criminal nature. It means jurisdiction to hear and determine civil actions.

The terms *"Civil" and "criminal"* when used, whether in reference to jurisdiction, or judicial proceedings generally, have respect to the nature and form of the remedy and the cause of action or occasion for instituting legal proceedings. Civil stands for the opposite of criminal, and hence, we have Courts known as Courts of civil jurisdiction and that of criminal jurisdiction, distinguished by the character of the prosecutions in each. (*Bacon Abr. Actions*)

Civil law. Private rights of action for redress, contrasted with criminal law; the family of legal systems where the influence of Roman law has been strong.

Civil liberty. Civil liberty consists in protecting the rights of individuals by the united force of society. It is natural liberty so far restrained by human laws as is necessary and expedient for the general advantage of the public; the power of doing whatever the laws permit.

Civil marriage. A wedding ceremony which is conducted by a governmental official, such as a judge or by some other authorized person.

Civil matters. Include all matters other than criminal.

Civil obligation. A legal obligation enforceable by a judicial tribunal.

CIVIL OBLIGATION AND NATURAL OBLIGATION. A civil obligation which gives the person in whose favour it is contracted a right of judicially enforcing it. A natural obligation is that which obliges the person in honour and conscience. Obligations are commonly both natural and civil. There are some, however, which are merely civil, and which the debtor may be judicially compelled to perform without being under any obligation to do so in point of conscience.

Civil offence. "CIVIL OFFENCE" means an offence which is triable by a Criminal Court or by a Special Judge appointed under the Criminal Law Amendment Act, 1952. [National Security Guard Act (47 of 1986), S. 2(c)]

"CIVIL OFFENCE" means an offence which is triable by a criminal Court. [Indo-Tibetan Border Police Force Act (35 of 1992), S. 2(1)(e)]

Every offence of which magistrates can take cognizance as a trial Court, or while holding inquiry before commitment to the Court of Session or to the High Court is a civil offence. *S.R. Tripathi* v. *State*, AIR 1964 All 371, 372. [Air Force Act (45 of 1950), Ss. 71 & 72]

Civil officer. Any officer holding appointment under the government, except in the military or naval service, whether the duties are executive or judicial, or in the highest or the lowest departments.

Civil post. A civil post means a post not connected with defence outside the regular civil services. *State of Assam* v. *Kanak Chandra*, AIR 1967 SC 884, 886; S. *Mohan Singh* v. *Patiala & East Punjab States Union*, AIR 1954 Pepsu 136; *Brojo Gopal Sarkar* v. *Commissioner of Police*, AIR 1955 Cal 556.

The word 'civil' used before the word 'post' in S. 240(1) is clearly meant to distinguish posts in the Defence Forces. All posts held by a public servant, if the posts did not belong to the Military Department or the Defence Forces, must be deemed to be civil posts under the crown. *Mohammed Matteen Qidwai* v. *G.G. in Council*, AIR 1953 All 17, 21. [Govt. of India Act (1935), S. 240(1)]

Civil post under a State. Civil post under a State means employment under the State Govt. A notary, not being paid salary or fee by the Government does not hold a civil post under a State. *Kashi Prasad* v. *State of U.P.*, AIR 1967 All 173, 177. [Constitution of India, Art. 311(1)]

The expression 'civil post' under a State means that the post is under the control of the State: that is the State can abolish the post if it so desires, or the State can regulate the conditions subject to which the post is or will be held. The real test is the immediate or ultimate control which is exercised by the State with regard to the post in question. *Chaturbhuj Sahai* v. *Bihar State Co-op. Bank Ltd.*, AIR 1955 Pat 223.

A person giving up Government service and joining his post under the State Co-operative Bank, Patna, cannot be said to hold a civil post under the State of Bihar within the meaning of Art. 311 of the Constitution of India. *Kumaran* v. *State*, AIR 1952 TC 264.

Civil prison. "CIVIL PRISON" means any jail or place used for the detention of any criminal prisoner under the Prisons Act, 1894, or under any other law for the time being in force. [Indo-Tibetan Border Police Force Act (35 of 1992), S. 2(1)(d); Air Force Act (45 of 1950), (2 xii), S. 4(xiii); Army Act (46 of 1950), S. 3(iii); Navy Act (62 of 1957), S. 3(4); National Security Guard Act (47 of 1986), S. 2(d)]

Detention in the Court-house cannot be said to be detention in a civil prison. (AIR 1937 Lah 253).

Civil prisoner. "CIVIL PRISONER" means any prisoner who is not a criminal prisoner. [Prison Act (9 of 1894), S. 3(4)]

Civil procedure. A particular method or practice which is used in carrying on a civi litigation.

Civil proceeding. A process for the recovery of individual right or redress of individual wrong. It is opposed to a criminal proceeding.

Any proceeding brought to establish and vindicate one's right to an office must be considered to be a civil proceeding. Merely because an act is purely ministerial does not take it out of the definition of the words "civil proceeding'. *Sardar Kapur Singh* v. *UOI*, AIR 1957 Pun 173, 182 (FB).

The words "a civil proceeding" are wide enough to cover any proceeding of a civil nature, whether it is being held by the High Court in its original jurisdiction or in its appellate jurisdiction or in its revisional jurisdiction. *Thakur Rudra Pratap Singh* v. *Thakur Mrityunjay Pratap Singh*, AIR 1957 All 28, 33; *Union of India* v. *R.D. Gupta*, AIR 1970 Tri 86 at 89. [Constitution of India, Arts. 132 & 133]

On its general acceptation, the term "proceeding" means the form in which the action is brought or defended, the manner of intervention by parties, the mode of deciding issues, or opposing judgment and of executing (*Bouvier's Law Dictionary*).

It follows that the expression "civil proceeding" of a High Court must be interpreted to mean the form of proceeding of the High Court in the exercise of its civil jurisdiction. *Collector of Monghyr* v. *Maharaja Pratap Singh Bahadur*, AIR 1957 Pat 102, 105 (FB).

Ordinarily 'civil proceedings' are proceedings relating to right to property, status of a person or right to an office.

The word 'civil' when prefixed before 'proceeding', 'action', 'suit', remedy', or other cognate expression relates to private rights and remedies given to individuals or corporations as members of the community in contradistinction to those which are public and relate to Government. *Kehar Singh Nihar Singh* v. *Custodian General Evacuee Property*, AIR 1959 Punj 58, 60. [Constitution of India, Arts. 133(1) and 226]

If the proceeding is in aid of establishing a civil right or for disputing one it would be a civil proceeding. If the proceedings taken establish or negative a man's office or status or would affect his right to property of any kind, it will be a civil proceeding. *Guru Gobinda Basu* v. *Sankari Prasad Ghosal*, AIR 1963 Cal 364, 366.

The proceedings for recovery of tax are civil proceedings. *Sheo Prasad* v. *State of U.P.*, AIR 1965 All 106, 114.

Civil proceeding may be defined as a judicial process to enforce a civil right and includes any remedy employed to vidicate that right. *Brij Lal Suri* v. *State of U.P.*, AIR 1958 All 621, 627.

Proceedings in revenue Court are proceedings of civil nature within the meaning of S. 14, Limitation Act (36 of 1963). *Yasin Mohammad* v. *Mirza Ashan Beg*, AIR 1954 Bho 21.

Income-tax Cases and Sales Tax Cases are not civil proceedings. *Allen Berry & Co. Ltd.* v. *ITO*, AIR 1956 Pat 175, 177.

Proceedings for assessment of income-tax are not proceedings relating to a civil right. The liability to income-tax is not a civil right enforceable as such in Courts of law. Such a proceeding is a revenue proceeding and not a civil proceeding. *ITO* v. *Jyoti Prasad Agarwal*, AIR 1960 All 84, 85.

Proceedings in a Court of justice by one party against another for the enforcement or protection of a private right or for the redress or prevention of a private wrong. [General Clauses Act (10 of 1897), S. 3(2)].

Civil proceeding in a Court of Appeal. A revision proceeding in the High Court under S. 115, CPC (5 of 1908), is a "civil proceeding in a Court of

Appeal" within the meaning of S. 14, Limitation Act (36 of 1963).

Civil process. Process issued by a Civil Court. We have civil process and criminal process just as we have civil jurisdiction and criminal jurisdiction.

An order of Court in a civil action [CPC (5 of 1908), S. 135(1)]; civil procedure.

Civil remedy. The remedy afforded by law, to a private person in the Civil Courts in so far as his private and individual rights have been injured by a tort or crime as distinguished from the remedy by criminal prosecution for the injury to the rights of the public. (*Black*; *Ame. Cyc.*)

Civil responsibility. The liability to be called upon to respond to an action at law for an injury caused by a civil wrong.

Civil rights are those which appertain to citizenship, and which may be enforced or redressed by a civil action. (*Burrill; Rapalje & L.L. Dict.*)

DISTINGUISHED FROM NATURAL RIGHTS. "By civil rights, are understood those rights which the municipal law will enforce, at the instance of private individuals, for the purpose of securing to them the enjoyment of their means of happiness. They are distinguishable from natural rights, which would exist even if there were no municipal law.

DISTINGUISHED FROM POLITICAL RIGHTS. 'A civil right, is, 'a right accorded to every member of a distinct community or nation,' while a political right is a 'right exercisable in the administration of government.' 'Political rights consist in the power to participate, directly or indirectly, in the establishment or management of the government. Every citizen has the right of voting for public officers, and of being elected; these are the political rights which the humblest citizen possesses. Civil rights are those which have no relation to the establishment, support or management of the government.

Civil service. The body of persons employed by the administrative branches of a government; the administrative branches of a government.

Service rendered to and paid for by the State, other than pertaining to armed forces. [IPC (45 of 1860), S. 415, ill. (a)].

Civil service of the State. The expression 'civil service of the State' remains more or less an amorphous expression as it has not been defined anywhere in the Constitution. Contrasted with it, the expressions 'judicial service of the State' and 'District Judge' have been specifically defined in article 236, and thus given a distinctive, definite meaning by the Constitution makers. *Chief Justice of A. P.* v. *L. V. A. Dikshitulu*, AIR 1979 SC 193 : 1978 LAB. I. C. 1672.

Civil side. Side of a Court which is devoted to the civil cases.

Civil war. An internecine war; war carried on between opposing masses of citizens of the same country, or nation.

Civil wrong. An infringement of a person's rights, for which the person wronged may sue for damages or some other remedy.

Civilian. A person who is not serving on the army or navy or air force.

Civilization. An advanced stage of social development; opposed to barbarism.

Civis. (*Lat.*) One entitled to the privileges of a city of which he is a member. There is a distinction between a citizen and an inhabitant in the same city, for "every inhabitant there, is not a citizen."

Civitas. (*Lat.*) A State having power to make and enforce laws for the governance of its subjects.

Claim. Is a word of very extensive signification, embracing every species of legal demand. It is one of the largest words of law and includes "demand" and "debt."

The term also signifies a 'demand made of a right or supposed right; a calling of another to pay something due or supposed to be due, as a "claim for wages or services." "Claim" is sufficiently comprehensive to embrace actions founded on tort as well as actions founded on contract.

The word 'claim' includes relief and also any grounds of obtaining the relief. [CPC (5 of 1908), O. XXIII, R. 1]

A demand for something as due; an assertion of a right to something [IPC (45 of 1860), S. 155]; to seek or ask for on the ground of right. [Indian Evidence Act (1 of 1872), S. 12].

The word 'claim' means something on which right is sought to be enforced for which there is a denial. *Probodh Chandra Ghosh* v. *Urmila Dassi*, (2000) 6 SCC, page 526, paras 10, 11 : AIR 2000 SC 2534. [Benami Transaction (Prohibition) Act (45 of 1988), S. 4(1)]

CLAIM AND CAUSE OF ACTION. In practice, the word 'claim', and the phrase 'cause of action' relate to the same thing and have one meaning. The plaintiff before suit may have 'a claim' for damages; and this, when stated in a complaint, is technically, a 'cause of action'.

"CLAIM" means any representation which states, suggests, or implies that a food has particular qualities relating to its origin, nutritional properties, nature, processing, composition or otherwise. [S. 3(1)(d) of the Food Safety & Standards Act, 2006 (34 of 2006)]

"CLAIM" means—

(*a*) a right to payment, whether or not such right is reduced to judgment, fixed, disputed, undisputed, legal, equitable, secured or unsecured;

(*b*) right to remedy for breach of contract under any law for the time being in force, if such breach gives rise to a right to payment, whether or not such right is reduced to judgment, fixed, matured, unmatured, disputed, undisputed, secured or unsecured; [Insolvency and Bankruptcy Code (31 of 2016), S. 3(6)].

Claim adversely. Asserting or demanding on the ground of right in opposition to the interest of some one. [CPC (5 of 1908), S. 88].

Claim against Government. The words "claim against Government relating to property or lands" may fairly be said to imply that relief of some kind is sought against Government.

Claim dilution. In bankruptcy law, the reducetion in the likelihood that a debtor's claimants will be fully repaid, including considerations of the time value of money.

Claim of right. The expression "claim of right" (used in respect of a person holding adversely) means nothing more than that the person holding intends to hold and use the land as his own to the *exclusion* of all others. It is not necessary that such person should enter under colour of title, or should either believe or assert that he had right to enter.

Claim of the privilege. Asking for a right, advantage or immunity granted to or enjoyed by a person or a class of persons beyond the common advantages of others. [CPC (5 of 1908), S. 133(3)].

Claim of title. Possession commenced under "claim of title," does not require that the possessor should think that the land belonged to him before entry, "but it is sufficient if the entry be hostile to all the world and he intends to hold the land as his own."

Claimable. The word "claimable," in S. 26, Indian Stamp Act (2 of 1899), means "claimable in a Court of Justice."

Claimant. A party making a claim in a law suit.

One who makes or enters a claim. [T.P. Act (4 of 1882), S. 3(c)].

"CLAIMANT" means a person who has acted in good faith and has suffered a quantifiable loss as a result of the offence of Money-laundering despite having taken all reasonable precautions, and is not involved in the offence of money-laundering. [Prevention of Money-laundering (Restoration of Confiscated Property) Rules, 2016, R.2(b)].

Claimed. The claim need not necessarily be made in the presence and to the knowledge of the person to be affected thereby. A claim can very well be made in the absence and without the knowledge of the person to be affected. [Indian Evidence Act (1 of 1872), S. 13(a)]

Claimed in common. The expression "claimed in common" occurring in S. 11, *Expln.* VI, CPC (5 of 1908), refers to persons who would be benefited by the granting of the relief claimed and have such an interest in the relief that they could be joined as coplaintiffs.

To claim for oneself alongwith others. [CPC (5 of 1908), S. 11, *Expln.* VI].

Claiming under. The words 'claiming under' in their ordinary meaning direct attention to the source of the rights.

The expression 'claiming under' includes cases of devolution and assignment of interest. *Brahm Dutt* v. *Life Insurance Corporation,* AIR 1966 All 474, 476. [CPC (5 of 1908), S. 146]

Claiming under him, Person. A person, putting forward a claim under the right derived from him. [T.P. Act (4 of 1882), S. 53A].

Claims tribunal. The 'Claims Tribunal' constituted under S. 110 of the Act (1929) is a mere Tribunal and not a Court. *Laxminarain Misra* v. *Kailash Narain Gupta*, AIR 1974 Raj 55, 60.

Clam delinquens, magis punitur quam palam. (*8 Rep. 127*): Secret offenders are more severely punished than open ones.

Clandestine. Secret, hidden; concealed.

CLANDESTINE, SECRET. *Clandestine* expresses more than *secret.* To do a thing *clandestinely* is to elude observation; to do a thing *secretly* is to do it without the knowledge of any one.

Clandestinely. Secretly. [Indian Trusts Act (2 of 1882), S. 88, ill. (e)].

Clarification. For the purposes of this sub-rule, the expression "clarification" includes modification or correction of particulars declared in the application for registration, other than Permanent Account Number and e-mail address declared in Part A of the GSR REG-01. [Central Goods and Services Tax Rules, 2017, R. 9(2) *Explanation*].

Class. A "class" as used in the law of wills is where several persons answering the said description sustain the same relation to the legacy so that one word describes them all.

The expression 'class' means a homogenous section of the people grouped together because of certain likenesses or common traits and who are identifiable by some common attributes such as status, rank, occupation, residence in a locality, race, religion and the like. *State of A.P.* v. *P. Sagar*, AIR 1968 SC 1379, 1382. [Constitution of India, Art. 15(4)]

The word 'class' is used in the sense of social class and not in the sense it is understood in marxist jargon. *Indra Sawhney* v. *Union of India,* AIR 1993 SC 477, 552. [Constitution of India, Art. 16(4)]

Order or rank according to which persons or things are arranged or assorted; a number of persons or things possessing common attributes and grouped together under a general or class name. [T.P. Act (4 of 1882), S. 69(1)(a); Constitution of India, Art. 16(3) and Art. 23(2)].

CLASS, ORDER, RANK, DEGREE. *Class* is more general than order; degree is more specific than *rank. Class* and *order* are said of the persons who are distinguished; *rank* and *degree* of the distinction itself; men belong to a certain *class* or *order*; they hold a certain *rank*; they are of a certain *degree*; there are the labouring class, the class of merchants, mechanics, *etc.* the general *orders* are divided into higher, lower, or middle, arising from the unequal distribution of wealth and power; the particular *orders* are those of the nobility, or the clergy.

Class action. A lawsuit by a single person or a small group of persons representing a class or a larger group by their litigation.

Class and **grade.** 'Class" is a group in which posts of a particular description are included by the order of Government and the grade has reference exclusively to scales of pay.

Class legislation. "Class legislation" is legislation which selects particular individuals from a class and imposes upon them special burdens from which others of the same class are exempt, and thus denies them the equal protection of the laws. "Class legislation is of two kinds, namely, that in which the classification is natural and reasonable, and that in which the classification is arbitrary, and capricious.

Class, or Section. The words "class or section" mean a definitely ascertainable body of individuals, not an indeterminate body or group having no clearly defined and nonvariable characteristics or criteria by which they may be distinguished from any other body or group.

Classes of income. The expression 'classes of income' means a category of income and is a much wider expression than 'heads of income".

Classification. The action or system of arranging into classes. [Industrial Finance Corporation Act (15 of 1948), (*Repealed by Act (23 of 1993*), S. 35(2)].

Classification means segregation of classes which have a systematic relation, usually found in common properties and characteristics. *Suraj Mall Mohta & Co.* v. *A.V. Viswanatha Sastri,* (1954) 26 ITR 1 (SC). [Constitution of India, Art. 14].

Classification of goods. Classification of goods in accordance with the rates of custom or excise duty applicable to them.

Classification—reasonableness. A classification must have reasonable relation to the object sought to be achieved. The standard of reasonableness is inextricably conditioned by the extent and nature of the evil and the urgency for eradicating the same. *Madhubai Amathalal Gandhi* v. *Union of India*, AIR 1961 SC 21, 28. [Constitution of India, Art. 14]

Clause. A single paragraph or sub-division of a legal document, such as contract, deed, will, constitution, or statute. Sometimes a sentence or part of a sentence.

A group of words containing a subject and a verb usually forming part of a compound or complex sentence; one of the sub-divisions of an instrument. [T.P. Act (4 of 1882), S. 55(6)(b)].

Clauses. A series of numbered parts into which a Bill is divided; a descriptive title printed in the margin of each clause. (*Constitutional and Parliamentary Term*)

Clausula generalis non refertur ad expressa. A general clause does not refer to things expressed/mentioned. (*Burrill 8 Coke*. 154)

Clausula quae abrogationem excludit ab initio non valet. (*Maxim*) A clause (in an Act) which precludes its abrogation, is void from the beginning. (*Burrill*; *Bacon's Max Reg.* 19, p. 89; 2 *Dwar St.* 673; *Broom*)

Clausulae inconsuetae semper indunt suspicionem. (*Maxim*) Unusual clauses (in an instrument) always excite suspicion. (*Wharton*)

Clean bill of lading. If, in a Bill of Lading, words are inserted in the Margin to the effect that the Weight, or Quality, or Quantity, unknown, that is not a Clean Bill of Lading, because that contains a qualification. Where, on the other hand, there is no such qualifycation inserted in the Margin, there the Bill of Lading is a clean one.

Broadly defined, a clean bill of lading is one which contains nothing, in addition to its usual clauses, indicating any qualification or the condition of the goods, their packing or the liability of the ship-owner. A clean bill of lading is which does not contain any reservation as to the apparent good order or condition of either the goods themselves, or their packing.

Clean break. The principle according to which, upon divorce, spouses should try to settle their financial affairs in a final manner, by a lumpsum order, rather than a continuous periodical payments order.

Clean hands. The maxim that one who comes into equity must come with "clean hands" is based on conscience and good faith. The maxim is confined to misconduct in regard to, or at all events connected with, the matter in litigation. "Clean hands" means a clean record with respect to the transaction with the defendant, and not with respect to any third person.

Cleaner. One employed to do cleaning, especially the interior of transportation vehicle. [Motor Transport Workers Act (27 of 1961), S. 2(h)].

Cleaning activity. "CLEANING ACTIVITY" means cleaning, including specialised cleaning services such as disinfecting, exterminating or sterilising of objects or premises, of—

(i) commercial or industrial buildings and premises thereof; or

(ii) factory, plant or machinery, tank or reservoir of such commercial or industrial buildings and premises thereof.

but does not include such services in relation to agriculture, horticulture, animal husbandry or dairying.

[Finance Act (32 of 1994), S. 65(24b) *as inserted by Finance Act (18 of 2005), S. 88(a)(vi)* (now repealed by Central Goods and Services Tax Act, 2017)]

Cleansing. Making clean. [Ancient Monuments and Archaeological Sites and Remains Act (24 of 1958), S. 2(f)].

Clear and convincing evidence. It has been described as evidence that produces in the mind of a trier of the fact an abiding conviction that the truth of the factual contentions is highly probable. [Corpus Juris Secundum, Evidence Section 1624 as cited in *Heinz India Private Limited* v. *State of U.P.*, (2012) 5 SCC 443, para 47].

Clear and positive proof. "Clear and positive proof" is such as, upon the case made, leaves no reasonable doubt as to the matter required to be proved, the truth of which it establishes to a moral certainty; and it is by the combined effect of the whole evidence that the Court has to judge, whether the proof is "clear and positive".

Clear and unambiguous. (*Interpretation*) If the language of the statute is clear and unambiguous and if two interpretations are not reasonably possible, it would be wrong to discard the plain meaning of the words used in order to meet a possible injustice. *C.I.T. Madras* v. *T.V. Sundram Iyengar (P) Ltd.*, AIR 1976 SC 255.

Clear days. Complete days (reckoned excluding the first and also the last days). [Arbitration Act (10 of 1940) (*repealed*), S. 9(b)].

Clear evidence of proof. These words and the words "clear and decisive proof", "clear and satisfactory evidence", "clear and convincing evidence", "clear and conclusive proof" and "conclusive proof" substantially convey the same idea, and require the same degree of proof, that is, facts must be established "by a fair preponderance of the proof". Proof must be clear of all reasonable doubt.

Clear profit. Means—the difference between the amount of income and the sum of expenditure plus specific appropriations, made up in each case as follows:—

(a) income derived from—

(i) gross receipts from sale of energy, less discounts applicable thereby;

(ii) rental of meters and other apparatus hired to consumers;

(iii) sale and repair of lamps and apparatus;

(iv) rents, less outgoings not otherwise provided for;

(v) transfer fees;

(vi) investments, fixed and call deposits, and bank balances;

(vii) other general receipts accountable in the assessment of Indian Income-tax and arising from and ancillary or incidental to the business of electricity supply.

(b) expenditure properly incurred of—

(i) generation and purchase of energy;

(ii) distribution and sale of energy;

(iii) rents, rates and taxes, other than all taxes on income and profits;

(iv) interest on loans advanced by the Board [***];

(iv-a) interest on loans borrowed from organisations or institutions approved by the State Government;

(iv-b) interest on debentures issued by the licensees;

(v) interest on security deposits;

(vi) legal charges;

(vii) bad debts;

(viii) auditors' fees;

(ix) management including managing agents remuneration as provided for in paragraph XIII;

(x) depreciation, computed as therein-before set out;

(xi) other expenses (excluding interest on debentures and loans) admissible under the law for the time being in force in the assessment of Indian Income-tax and arising from and ancillary or incidental to the business of electricity supply;

(xii) contributions to the provident fund, staff pension and gratuity computed under any law for the time being in force or any such scheme as is approved by the State Government;

(xii-a) expenses on apprentice and other training schemes;

(xiii) bonus paid to the employees of the undertaking—

(a) where, any dispute regarding such bonus has been referred to any Tribunal or other authority under any law for the time being in force relating to industrial or labour disputes, in accordance with the decision of such Tribunal or authority;

(b) in any other case, with the approval of the State Government;

(c) special appropriations sufficient to cover—

(i) previous losses (that is to say excess of expenditure over income) which have arisen from the business of electricity supply to the extent in any year permitted by the State Government;

(ii) all taxes on income and profits;

(iii) instalments of written down amounts in respect of

intangible assets and new capital issue expenses to the extent in any year actually appropriated for the purpose in the books of the undertaking:

Provided that the amounts so appropriated shall not exceed the amount found by dividing the written down cost of such assets by the number of complete years remaining before the next option of purchase under the license arises;

(iv) contributions to the Contingency Reserve, computed as hereinbefore set out;

(v) contributions towards arrears of depreciation;

(va) contributions to the Development Reserve referred to in paragraph V-A;

(vb) debt redemption obligation of the private licensees which may be done on a year to year basis, taking into account the requirements of debt redemption and resource generation through depreciation, retained surplus;

(vi) other special appropriations permitted by the State Government.

[Electricity (Supply) Act (54 of 1948), Sixth Sch., Para XVII, (2)]

Clear specification of the relief. Mentioning or specifying the relief in a clear manner. [CPC (5 of 1908), O. XLI, R. 35(2)].

Clearance. Certificate that ship has been cleared at the custom house; the action of clearing or making clear [Customs Act (52 of 1962), S. 47]; the off setting of cheques and other claims among banks through a clearing house. [Reserve Bank of India Act (2 of 1934), S. 58(2)]; the act of making clear of whatever may obstruct, occupy, encumber or hinder.

Clearances for home consumption. Wherever referred to in this notification, shall include clearances for export to Bhutan and Nepal. [Central Excise Tariff Act, 1985 (5 of 1986), Gen. Exemption No. 1(5) *Expln.* (G)]

Clearing a bill. To provide cash to satisfy a bill of exchange.

Clearing and forwarding agent. Means any person who is engaged in providing any service, either directly or indirectly, connected with the clearing and forwarding operations in any manner to any other person and includes a consignment agent. [Finance Act (32 of 1994), S. 65(25) (now repealed by Central Goods and Services Tax Act, 2017)]

Clearing house. An institution organised by the Banks of a city—the house through which bankers pass the bills and cheques they hold on other banks by a mutual arrangement. This is a place where bankers meet daily adjust balances of accounts and receive and pay differences. [Reserve Bank of India Act (2 of 1934), S. 58(2)(p)]

Clearing house stock exchange. deals with bonds and shares on much the same principle as that of the Banker's Clearing House in respect of cheques and bills.

Clearly. Decidely in a clear manner. [Beedi and Cigar Workers (Conditions of Employment) Act (32 of 1966), S. 22(1)].

Clemency. Disposition to treat with favour and kindness; to forgive and spare offenders; tenderness. The power of the President or a Governor to pardon or commute a sentence.

Clemency, Lenity, Mercy. All these terms agree in denoting the disposition or act of forbearing to inflict pain by the exercise of power. *Clemency* and *lenity* are employed only towards offenders; *mercy* towards all who are in trouble, whether from their own fault, or any other cause.

Clerical. Relating to clergy or a clerk or clerks involving copying out.

Clerical error. A mistake of a copyist in copying; a mistake in transcribing a written instrument; the mistake of a clerk in writing; error made by a clerk or by a transcriber. [Imperial Dict.; *See* CPC (5 of 1908), S. 152]

'CLERICAL ERROR' is one which is committed in the course of what may be called clerical duties.

Clerical errors are to be distinguished from errors of substance, of judgment, or of law.

By Rules of Court, the Court of a judge may at any stage of the proceedings allow the pleadings to be amended, and, clerical mistakes in judgments or orders, or other accidental slips or omissions therein, may at any time be corrected by the Court or a judge on its own motion or on petition. [*See* CPC (5 of 1908), S. 152].

An error made in copying or writing. [Trade and Merchandise Marks Act (43 of 1958), S. 23(4)].

Clerical mistake. An ordinary mistake made by a clerk in copying a legal document. The Court may correct it without the motion by the parties; an inadvertent omission or mistake made in transcribing or otherwise but capable of being corrected. [CPC (5 of 1908), S. 152].

Clerk. The term '*clerk*' as used, in its popular sense, denotes as one whose duties are clerical, and they may be of various kinds. (*In ecclesiastical law*), clerk is a person in holy orders; a clergyman. (*In*

Court practice), clerk is an officer of a Court who keeps its minutes, or records its proceedings, and has the custody of its records and seal *i.e.* the clerk of the Court. (*In commercial law*), one employed to keep records and accounts; a scribe, penman or accountant; (*Webster's Dict.*) one employed to write orders, letters, despatches, public or private papers, records, and the like.

One employed to keep records and accounts; a scribe. [IPC (45 of 1860), S. 27].

A person employed temporarily or on a particular occasion in the capacity of a clerk or servant, is a clerk or servant within the meaning of this sub-section. [(w.e.f. 1-7-2024) Bharatiya Nyaya Sanhita, 2023 (45 of 2023), section 3(3), *Expln.*]

Clerk of Court or **Court Clerk.** A clerk of the Court is included in the term "officer of the law". The clerk is not the Court. He is simply the scribe and custodian of its records. He is not an agent of the Court, nor has he any authority to act for or represent the Court in its absence.

Clerk or **Servant.** A person employed temporarily or on a particular occasion in the capacity of a clerk or servant, is a clerk or servant within the meaning of S. 27. [IPC (45 of 1860), S. 27, *Expln.*]

Click-wrap agreement. An agreement under which access to a website or installation of software is prevented unless the user clicks to accept the terms of the agreement; analogous to a *shrink-wrap agreement.* (*Cyber Law*)

An agreement in which the agreement is displayed in a separate window from which it cannot be downloaded or printed. (*Internet and E-commerce*).

Click-wrap license. A license that appears on a computer screen when software is first being installed; and which the purchaser must accept before the installation will proceed. (*Cyber Law*)

Client. One who applies to a lawyer or counsellor for advice and direction on a question of law, or commits his cause to his management in prosecuting a claim or defending a suit, in a Court of Justice.

A person who seeks advice of a lawyer or commits his cause to the management of one, in prosecuting or defending an action in a Court of justice. [Indian Evidence Act (1 of 1872), S. 111, ill. (a)].

"CLIENT" means a person who is engaged in a financial transaction or activity with a reporting entity and includes a person on whose behalf the person who engaged in the transaction or activity, is acting. [S. 2(1)(ha) of the Prevention of Money-Laundering Act, 2002 (15 of 2003) as inserted by the Prevention of Money-Laundering (Amendment) Act, 2012 (2 of 2013)]

Client's privilege. The right of client to refuse to disclose and to prevent any other person from disclosing confidential communications between the client and his or her attorney.

Clinic. A clinic is stated to be a premises with facilities for treatment of outdoor patients by a doctor. *Chairman and Chief Executive Officer, Noida Authority* v. *Mange Ram Sharma*, (2012) 7 SCC 65, para 6.

Clinical Psychologist. "Clinical psychologist" means a person—

(i) having a recognised qualification in Clinical Psychology from an institution approved and recognised, by the Rehabilitation Council of India, constituted under S. 3 of the Rehabilitation Council of India Act, 1992; or

(ii) having a Post-Graduate degree in Psychology or Clinical Psychology or Applied Psychology and a Master of Philosophy in Clinical Psychology or Medical and Social Psychology obtained after completion of a full time course of two years which includes supervised clinical training from any University recognised by the University Grants Commission established under the University Grants Commission Act, 1956 and approved and recognised by the Rehabilitation Council of India Act, 1992 or such recognised qualifications as may be prescribed [The Mental Healthcare Act, 2017 (10 of 2017), S. 2(1)(g)]

Clock. An electronic circuit that serves as a source of very accurately timed electrical pulses; the speed of a computer depends on the speed of the clock used with its central processing unit (CPU). Many computers contain one or more additional clocks for such purposes as keeping track of the date and time of day. (*Computer*)

Close. Bring to an end; finish; complete.

Close arrest. Means confinement within the force or a detachment of the force or a post quarter guard building or tent under the charge of a guard. [Central Reserve Police Force Act (66 of 1949), S. 2(b)]

Close season. A season in which hunting and fishing is prohibited.

Closed. The dictionary meaning of the word 'closed' is 'shut up, not open'. 'Open' means ready to receive or transact business with members of the public. When neither the presiding officer of the Court nor any officer authorised to receive any plaint is present in the Court on any day due to circumstances over which the person concerned has no control, it must be held that the Court is closed for the purpose of Limitation Act. *Basantha Kumar Nath* v. *Lakshma Maninath,* AIR 1968 Ass & Nag 57, 59. [Indian Limitation Act (36 of 1963), S. 4].

Closed : Dismissed. The distinction between 'closed' and 'dismissed' is well known and it cannot be argued that a petition which is closed has been dismissed so as to attract the mischief of O. XXI, R. 57, CPC (5 of 1908). *A.V. Sreenivasalu Naidu* v. *V.K. Nataraja Goundan*, AIR 1955 Mad 461, 465.

Closed holiday. A holiday on which shops and establishments are to be closed. *Basantha Kumar Nath* v. *Lakshma Maninath*, AIR 1968 Assam & Nagaland 57, 59. [Plantations Labour Act (69 of 1951), S. 20(2)].

Closing time. The time or hour at which public house or office has to be closed and business should be stopped.

Closure. 'Closure' means the permanent closing down of a place of employment or part thereof. [Industrial Disputes Act (14 of 1947), section 2(cc)]

"Closure" means the permanent closing down of a place of employment or part thereof. [Industrial Relations Code, 2020 (35 of 2020), section 2(h)]

Cloud Bursting. A process where a service provided by a private cloud can automatically access and use resources from a public cloud when it needs to ramp up and handle peak demand. [Saurabh Srivastava, *'Cloud Computing is a game changer for Indian Businesses'*, Financial Express, September 20, 2010]

Cloud on title. A cloud upon one's title is something which shows *prima facie* some right of a third person to it.

Club. A club is a definite association for social and other purposes.

Club or association. "CLUB OR ASSOCIATION" means any person or body of persons providing services, facilities or advantages, for a subscription or any other amount, to its members, but does not include—

(i) any body established or constituted by or under any law for the time being in force; or

(ii) any person or body of persons engaged in the activities of trade unions, promotion of agriculture, horticulture or animal husbandry; or

(iii) any person or body of persons engaged in any activity having objectives which are in the nature of public service and are of a charitable, religious or political nature; or

(iv) any person or body of persons associated with press or media.

[Finance Act (32 of 1994), S. 65(25a) *as insert ed by Finance Act (18 of 2005), S. 88(a)(vii)* (now repealed by Central Goods and Services Tax Act, 2017)]

Co-extensive. The word 'co-extensive' is an objective for the word 'extent' and it can relate only to the quantum of the principal debt. [Indian Contract Act (9 of 1872), S. 128]

Co-operative farming society. Means a co-operative society the objects of which include the cultivation of land on a cooperative basis. [State Agricultural Credit Corporation Act (60 of 1968), S. 2(h)]

Co-operative Life Insurance Society. Means an insurer being a society registered under the Co-operative Societies Act, 1912, or under an Act of a State Legislature governing the registration of Co-operative Societies which carries on the business of life insurance and which has no share capital on which dividend or bonus is payable and of which by its constitution only original members on whose application the society is registered and all policy-holders are members. [Insurance Act (4 of 1938), S. 95(1)(b)]

Co-operative principles. Means the co-operative principles specified in the First Schedule. [Multi-State Co-operative Societies Act (39 of 2002), S. 2(g)]

Co-operative society. A union of individuals, commonly labourers, farmers, businessmen, or small capitalists, formed for the prosecution in common of productive enterprise, the profits being shared in accordance with the amount of capital or labour contributed by each member. (*Century Dict.*)

"CO-OPERATIVE SOCIETY" means a co-operative society registered under the Co-operative Societies Act, 1912 (2 of 1912), or under any other law for the time being in force in any State for the registration of co-operative societies. [Income-tax Act (43 of 1961), S. 2(19) and Displaced Persons (Debt Adjustment) Act (70 of 1951), S. 2(4)]

"CO-OPERATIVE SOCIETY" means a society registered or deemed to be registered under the Co-operative Societies Act, 1912 or under the Multi-State Co-operative Societies Act, 1984 or under any other law with respect to co-operative societies for the time being in force in any State, which is engaged in any of the activities specified in sub-section (1) of Section 9 and includes a Co-operative Land Development Bank, by whatever name called. [National Co-operative Development Corporation Act (26 of 1962), S. 2(c)]

"CO-OPERATIVE SOCIETY" means a society registered or deemed to be registered under any law relating to co-operative societies for the time being in force in any State. [MultiState Co-operative Societies Act (39 of 2002), S. 2(h) and Payment of Bonus Act (21 of 1965), S. 2]

A society registered or deemed to be registered, under the Co-operative Societies Act, 1912, or under any other law for the time being in force in any State relating to co-operative societies which is engaged in any of the activities specified in Section 9(1) of the Agricultural Produce (Development and Warehousing) Corporations Act, 1956, and includes a Co-operative Land Mortgage Bank. [Agricultural Produce (Development and Warehousing) Corporation Act (28 of 1956), S. 2(e)]

A society registered or deemed to be registered under the Co-operative Societies Act, 1912, or under any other law with respect to co-operative societies which is engaged in any of the activities specified in Section 9(1) of the National Co-operative Development Corporation Act, 1962, and includes a Co-operative Land Mortgage Bank. [National Co-operative Development Corporation Act (26 of 1962), S. 2(c).

"CO-OPERATIVE SOCIETY" means a society registered, or deemed to be registered, under the Co-operative Societies Act, 1912 or any other law relating to co-operative societies for the time being in force in any State. [National Bank for Agricultural and Rural Development Act (61 of 1981), S. 2(f)]

"CO-OPERATIVE SOCIETY" means a society registered or deemed to be registered under the Co-operative Societies Act, 1912, or under any other law with respect to co-operative societies for the time being in force in any state, which is engaged in the processing, marketing, storage, export or import of agricultural produce or any notified commodity or in insurance business and includes a co-operative land mortgage bank. [Warehousing Corporations Act (58 of 1962), S. 2(d)]

"CO-OPERATIVE SOCIETY" means a society registered or deemed to have been registered under any Central Act for the time being in force relating to the multi-State co-operative societies, or any other Central or State law relating to co-operative societies for the time being in force;'; [Banking Regulation Act (10 of 1949), S. 56(*cciia*) (as amended by Banking Regulation (Amendment) and Miscellaneous Provisions Act (24 of 2004), S. 2(A))]

Co-operative year. In relation to any multiState co-operative society or class of such societies, means the year ending on the 30th day of June and where the accounts of such society or class of such societies are, with the previous sanction of the Central Registrar, balanced on any other day, the year ending on such day. [Multi-State Co-operative Societies Act (51 of 1984), S. 2(h)]

"CO-OPERATIVE YEAR", in relation to any multi-State co-operative society or class of such societies, means the year ending on the 31st day of March of the year and where the accounts of such society or class of such societies are, with the previous sanction of the Central Registrar, balanced on any other day, the year ending on such day. [Multi-State Co-operative Societies Act (39 of 2002), S. 2(i)]

A "co-operative year" means the year commencing on the first day of July and ending on the 30th June of next following. *Ziley Singh* v. *Registrar, Cane Co-operative Societies,* AIR 1972 SC 758.

Co-option. "CO-OPTION" involves consensus of the members in entirety or of the majority to be ascertained by a process of vote taking. [Tamil Nadu Panchayats Act (1958), S. 147]

Co-ordinate. To combine or integrate harmoniously. [North-Eastern Hill University Act (24 of 1973), S. 21(1)].

Co-ordination. According to the Dictionary meaning, the expression 'co-ordination' means 'to place in the same order, rank or division; to place in proper position relatively to each other and to the system of which they form parts; to act in combined order for the production of a particular result.' *Gujarat University* v. *Krishna*, AIR 1963 SC 703, 722. [Constitution of India, Schedule 7, List I, Entry 66].

Co-respondent. A joint defendant; specially in a suit for divorce, one charged with having committed adultery with the husband or from whom divorce is being sought.

Co-owner. A co-owner is as much an owner of the entire property as any sole owner of a property is. Now jurisprudentially it is not correct to say that a co-owner of property is not its owner. He owns every part of the composite property along with others and it cannot be said that he is only a part owner or a fractional owner of the property. The position will change only when partition takes place. *Ram Pasricha* v. *Jagannath,* AIR 1976 SC 2335; also see *Kanta Goel* v. *B.P. Pathak,* AIR 1977 SC 1599.

Co-trustee. A joint trustee. [Indian Trusts Act (2 of 1882), S. 10].

Coal. In an order to a miner for coal, the word is to be construed to mean coal of a merchantable character.

"COAL" includes anthracite, bituminous, lignite, peat and any other form of carbonaceous matter sold or marketed as coal and also coke. Auction by Competitive Bidding of Coal Mines Rules, 2012, R. 2(b).

"COAL" includes coke in all its forms but does not include lignite. [Coal Mines (Conservation and Safety) Act (28 of 1974), S. 3(c)]

"COAL" includes lignite. [Coal Mines Provident Fund & Miscellaneous Provisions Act (46 of 1948), S. 2(aa)]

When the language employed is so wide *viz.* 'coke in all its forms' petroleum coke which is a form of coke cannot possibly be excluded merely by reference to the word 'coal'. *India Carbon Ltd.* v. *Superintendent of Taxes, Gauhati,* AIR 1972 SC 154, 156. [Central Sales Tax Act (74 of 1956), S. 14(*ia*)]

"COAL" includes anthracite, bituminous coal, lignite, peat and any other form of carbonaceous matter sold or marketed as coal. [Clause 2(5) of the Coal Mines Regulations, 1957].

"COAL" the word 'coal' includes charcoal. *CST* v. *Jaswant Singh Charan Sing*, 19 STC 469 : AIR 1967 SC 1454. Also see, *Ganesh Trading Co.* v. *State of Haryana*, AIR 1974 SC 1362.

Coal mine. Consists of shafts, drifts, slopes, engines, machinery, platforms, cars, tracks, scales. *etc.*, as well as the hole in the ground.

"COAL MINE" means any excavation where any operation for the purpose of searching for or obtaining coal has been or is being carried on, and includes—

(i) all borings and bore holes;

(ii) all shafts, in or adjacent to and belonging to a coal mine, whether in the course of being sunk or not;

(iii) all levels and inclined planes in the course of being driven;

(iv) any open cast working or quarry, that is to say, an excavation where any operation, for the purpose of searching for or obtaining coal has been or is being carried on not being a shaft or an excavation which extends below superjacent ground;

(v) all conveyors or aerial rope-ways provided for the bringing into or removal from a coal mine of coal or other articles or for the removal of refuse therefrom;

(vi) all adits, levels, planes, machinery works, railways, tramways, and sidings, in or adjacent to and belonging to a coal mine;

(vii) all workshops situated within the precincts of a coal mine and under the same management and used for purposes connected with that coal mine or a number of coal mines under the same management;

(viii) any office of a coal mine;

(ix) all power stations for supplying electricity for the purpose of working the coal mine or a number of coal mines under the same management;

(x) any premises for the time being used for depositing refuse from a coal mine, or in which any operation in connection with such refuse is being carried on, being premises exclusively occupied by the employer of the coal mine;

(xi) all hospitals and canteens maintained for the benefit of the employees of a coal mine or a number of coal mines under the same management;

(xii) any coke oven or plant;

(xiii) any premises in or adjacent to and belonging to a coal mine, on which any plant or other machinery connected with a coal mine is situated or on which any process ancillary to the work of a coal mine is being carried on. [Coal Mines Provident Fund and Miscellaneous Provisions Act (46 of 1948), S. 2(b)]

"COAL MINE" means a mine in which there exists one or more seams of coal. [Coal Mines (Nationalisation) Act (26 of 1973), S. 2(b)]

The expression 'coal mine' includes a coking coal mine. *Mahindra Nath* v. *State of Bihar*, AIR 1980 SC 1308, 1311. [Coal Mines (Nationalisation) Act (26 of 1973), S. 2(*b*)]

Coalition. Fusion into one whole; temporary combination between parties retaining distinctive principles. (*In Diplomacy*), an alliance between States for combined action.

Union of political parties to secure a majority in Parliament over other groups; usually takes, place in multi-party system in which no single party is able to command support of a working majority. (*Constitutional and Parliamentary Term*)

Coalition Government. Government by a coalition of parties is formed when political parties unite to secure majority in Parliament over other groups or in times of war or other great national emergency when a majority party invites minority parties to form government in the interest of national unity; it tends to be unstable and weak as it lacks clear electoral mandate because it reflects diverse and partisan viewpoints; lacks cohesion of its membership; it has to necessarily accommodate minority view point for getting its Parliamentary support.

Coast. The land which bounds the sea.

Coast guard. A body of officers and men raised and equipped to defend the coast of the realm.

There shall be an armed force of the Union called the Coast Guard for ensurng the security of the maritime zones of India with a view to the protection of maritime and other national interests in such zones. [Coast Guard Act (30 of 1978), Ss. 2(d) and 4)(1)]

Coast Guard Court. A Coast Guard Court may be convened by the Central Government or the Director-General or by any officer empowered in this behalf by warrant of the Director-General (hereafter in this Act referred to as the convening authority). A Coast Guard Court consists of not less than live officers, each of whom has held the post of Assistant Commandant for not less than three years. [Coast Guard Act (30 of 1978), Ss. 2(e), 64 and 65].

Coast guard custody. Means the arrest or confinement of a member of the Coast guard according to rules. [Coast Guard Act (30 of 1978), S. 2(f).]

Coast protection work. Means any work of construction, alteration, improvement, repair, maintenance, demolition or removal for the purpose or the protection of any land, and includes the sowing or planting of vegetation for the said purpose. [(English) Coast Protection Act, 1949, S. 49)]

Coastal aquaculture. "COASTAL AQUACULTURE" means culturing, under controlled conditions in ponds, pens, enclosures or otherwise, in coastal areas, of shrimp, prawn, fish or any other aquatic life in saline or brackish water; but does not include fresh water aquaculture. [Coastal Aquaculture Authority Act (24 of 2005), S. 2(e)]

Coastal area. "COASTAL AREA" means the area declared as the Coastal Regulation Zone, for the time being, in the notification of the Government of India in the Ministry of Environment and Forests (Department of Environment, Forests and Wildlife) No. S.O. 114(E), dated the 19th February, 1991 and includes such other area as the Central Government may, by notification in the Official Gazette, specify. [Coastal Aquaculture Authority Act (24 of 2005), S. 2(d)]

Coastal goods. Means goods, other than imported goods, transported in a vessel from one part of India to another. [Customs Act (52 of 1962), S. 2(7)].

Coastal shipping. 'Coastal shipping' means the carrying of goods or passengers in ships by sea to or from any point in Great Britain from or to any point in the United Kingdom, the Isle of Man, the Channel Islands or the Republic of Ireland, but does not include the carrying of goods or passengers in the exercise of a right of ferry legally established whether by Act of Parliament or otherwise. [(English) Transport Act, 1962, S. 92)].

Coastal waters. "COASTAL WATERS" means any part of the territorial water of India, or any marine areas adjacent thereto over which India has, or, may hereafter have exclusive jurisdiction in regard to control of marine pollution under the Territorial Waters, Continental Shelf, Exclusive Economic Zone and other Maritime Zones Act, 1976, or any other law for the time being in force. [Merchant Shipping Act (44 of 1958), S. 356 B(c)]

'COASTAL WATERS' means waters within a distance of three nautical miles from any point on the coast measured from low water mark of ordinary spring tides. [(English) Public Health (Control of Disease) Act, 1984, S. 74)].

'COASTAL WATERS' means—

(a) in relation to the United Kingdom, the Channel Islands and the Isle of Man, so much of the waters adjoining those countries respectively as is within British fishery limits; and

(b) in relation to any other country, so much of the waters adjoining that country as is within the distance to which provisions of the law of that country corresponding to the provisions of this Act extend. [(English) Whaling Industry (Regulation) Act, 1934, S. 17, substituted by Fishery Limits Act, 1964, S. 3(3), Sch 1 and amended by the Fishery Limits Act, 1976, S. 9(1), Sch 2)]

Coasting ship. "COASTING SHIP" means a ship exclusively employed in trading between any port or place in India and any other port or place on the continent of India or between ports and places in India and ports and places in Ceylon or Burma. [Merchant Shipping Act (44 of 1958), S. 3(1A)]

Coasting trade of India. Means the carriage by sea of passengers or goods from any port or place in India to any other port or place on the sub-continent of India. [Merchant Shipping Act (44 of 1958), S. 3(2)]

Coated paper. The term 'coated paper' refers only to coated paper used for industrial purposes and not to coated varieties of printing and writing paper; waxed paper obviously means coated paper. *Rohit Pulp and Paper Mills Ltd.* v. *Collector of Central Excise, Baroda*, AIR 1991 SC 754, 759. [Central Excises and Salt Act (1 of 1944), First Sch, Item 17(1), Notification (24 of 1984), (25 of 1984) and (45 of 1985)]

Coca derivative. Means—

(a) crude cocaine, that is, any extract of coca leaf which can be used, directly or indirectly, for the manufacture of cocaine;

(b) ecgonine and all the derivatives of ecgonine from which it can be recovered;

(c) cocaine, that is, methyl ester of benzoyl ecgonine and its salts; and

(d) all preparation containing more than 0.1 per cent of cocaine. [Narcotic Drugs and Psychotropic Substances Act (61 of 1985), S. 2(v)]

Coca leaf. It means:

(i) the leaf and young twigs of any coca plant, that is, of the *Erythroxylon Coca* (*Lamak*) and the *Erythroxylon non-granatense* (*Hierrn*) and their varities, and of any other species of this genus which the Central Government may, by notification in the Official Gazette, declare to be coca plants for the purposes of the Dangerous Drugs Act, 1930; and

(ii) any mixture thereof, with or without neutral materials.

It does not include any preparations containing not more than O.1 of cocaine. [Dangerous Drugs Act (2 of 1930), S. 2(a)]

"COCA LEAF" means—

(a) the leaf of Coca plant except a leaf from which ecgonine, Cacaine and any other ecgonine alkaloid have been removed;

(b) any mixture thereof with or without any neutral material, but does not include any preparation containing not more that 0.1 percent of cocaine. [Narcotic Drugs and Psychotropic Substances Act (61 of 1985), S. 2(vi)]

COCA LEAF means the leaf of any plant of the genus *Erythroxylon* from whose leaves cocaine can be extracted either directly or by chemical transformation. [(English) Misuse of Drugs Act, 1971, Sch 2. Part IV)].

Coca plant. Means the plant of any species of the genus *Erythroxylon*. [Narcotic Drugs and Psychotropic Substances Act (61 of 1985), S. 2(vii)]

Cock-pit. A name which is used to be given to the Judicial Committee of the Privy Council, the council room being built on the old cockpit of Whitehall Place. (*Black, 7; Cyc.* 268)

Cocoa manufactured. (*in the Tariff Act*) Is not a commercial term, and is broad enough to include the preparations of chocolate.

Coconut. "COCONUT" means the fruit of coconut palm and includes green coconut, ripe coconut and copra. [Coconut Development Board Act (5 of 1979), S. 2(c)]

The word is understood in several forms, viz., tender coconut, watery coconut, dried coconut and copra, and all these come under the expression 'coconut'. Except in the case of tender coconut from which oil cannot be extracted, in all other cases, oil can be extracted and all of them are regarded in common parlance as 'oil seeds'. The argument that as copra cannot be sown and it does not germinate, it is not a seed within the strict dictionary meaning of the expression and as such copra is not an oil seed is not impressive. If such a strict construction is to be given, it would follow that the entire coconut with the outer shell which ripens and falls off from the tree can alone be considered to be a seed. *K.R. Sastry & Sons* v. *A.C.C.T.,* (1976) 37 STC 399 (AP).

Coconut industry. Does not include—

(i) Coir industry; or

(ii) an industry from which products (including by-products), out of coconut oil are manufactured. [Coconut Development Board Act (5 of 1979), S. 2(d)]

Code. A general collection or compilation of laws by public authority; a system of law; a systematic and complete body of law, on any subject such as Civil Procedure Code, Code of Criminal Procedure, Indian Penal Code, *etc.*

"Code" includes rules made under the Code. [CPC (5 of 1908), S. 2(1)]

A digest of the laws of a country, or of those relating to any subject. [Title, IPC (45 of 1860)]; any system of symbols for meaningful communication. [Official Secrets Act (19 of 1923), S. 3(1)(c)].

Code Napoleon. Was the name of the Code Civil under the empire. Codified Law of France. Under this name are often understood the five codes, the Civil Code (1804), Code of Civil Procedure (1806), Code of Commerce (1807), adopted in France during the first Napoleanic regime. In 1807 the Emperor altered the title of the first of these from Code of Civil *des francais* to Code Napoleon, but at the restoration of the legitimate dynasty the title became Code Civil simply and thereafter the practice grew up of using the term Code Napoleon as a short description of the whole of French codified law.

Code of Civil Procedure. That part of the laws of the state relating to procedure in Civil Courts.

Code of conduct. A written set of rules governing the behaviour of specified groups, such as lawyers, government employees, or corporate employees.

Code of Justinian. (*Roman law*) is a collection of imperial constitutions in Rome, compiled, under the order of that Emperor by a commission of ten eminent jurists, and promulgated in A.D. 529.

Co-defendant. One of several defendants impleaded in a suit.

Codex Gregorianus. (*Lat.*) The collection of laws made by the Roman jurist Gregorius in the fifth century.

Codicil. Means an instrument made in relation to a will, and explaining, altering or adding to its dispositions, and shall be deemed to form part of the will. [Indian Succession Act (39 of 1925), S. 2(b)]

A codicil is a part of the will. It is executed with the same formalities as any other testamentary disposition, and is to be carried out by the executors named in the will, and therefore, the same rules apply as would apply to the rights of the parties acquired under a will.

Codification. The process of consolidating the law of a country on any particular subject, or any portion of it, into a Code, whether that law consists of statutes, or case-laws, or customs, or all the three. (*Sweet*)

The Act of putting a body of laws so related to each other as to avoid inconsistency and overlapping.

Codify. To consolidate into a code. [Hindu Marriage Act (25 of 1955), Preamble].

Coercion. "Coercion" is the committing, or threatening to commit, any act forbidden by the Indian Penal Code (45 of 1860), or the unlawful detaining, or threatening to detain, any property to the prejudice of any person whatever, with the intention of causing any person to enter into an agreement. [Indian Contract Act (9 of 1872), S. 15]

To constitute coercion or duress, there must be some actual or threatened exercise of power, possessed or believed to be possessed, by the party coercing over the person and property of another. Actual violence is not necessary to constitute coercion; imaginary terrors may be sufficient for that purpose.

The word 'coercion" in S. 72, Indian Contract Act (9 of 1872), is used in its general and ordinary sense as an English word and its meaning is not controlled by the definition in S. 15 which is expressly inserted with the special object of applying to S. 14 of that Act where "free consent," such as is required to render an agreement a contract under S. 10 of the Act, is defined.

The application to another of such force either physical or moral as to constrain him to do against his will something he would not otherwise have done. [Indian Contract Act (9 of 1872), S. 15].

Coercion : coerce. Coerce is to restrain by force, especially by law or authority; to repress, to curb: to compel or constrain to any action. (*Standard Dict.*) "Coerce had at first only the negative sense of checking or restraining by force; as, to coerce a bad man by punishments, or a prisoner with fetters. It has now gained a positive sense, *viz.*, that of driving a person into the performance of some act which is required of him by another; as to coerce a man to sign a contract; to coerce obedience. In this sense (which is now the prevailing one), 'coerce' differs but little from 'compel', and yet there is a distinction between them". (*Webster*)

Coffee. "COFFEE" means the commodity derived from the fruit of *rubiaceous* plant known by that name and includes raw coffee, cured coffee, uncured coffee, roasted coffee and prepared coffee. [Coffee Act (7 of 1942), S. 3(b)]

In heading No. 09.01, 'COFFEE' means the seed of the coffee tree (coffea), but does not include the seed while still attached to the tree. This heading includes coffee in powder form. [Central Excise Tariff Act, 1985 (5 of 1986), I Sch., S. II, Chap. 9, Note 1]

The expression 'coffee' in S. 5(y) of the Madras General Sales Tax Act, 1939, would not include coffee blended with chicory, which is commonly known as French coffee. *Dy. C.C.T.* v. *Iyanar Coffee & Tea Co.,* (1962) 13 STC 457 (Mad).

Cogent. Compelling or convincing.

Cogitationis poenam nemo meretur. (*Maxim*) No man deserves punishment for a thought.

So long as an act rests in bare intention it is not punishable, yet when an act is done the law judges not only of the act itself but of the intent with which it was done.

Cogitationis poenam nemo patitur. The thoughts and intents of men are not punishable.

Cognate. The term 'cognate' is used in customary law in a very wide sense and it means blood relation other than an agnate and includes a female relation.

A class of heirs according to Hindu Law [Hindu Succession Act (30 of 1956), S. 3(1)(c)]; descended or borrowed from the same earlier form.

Cognates. Persons descended from a common ancestor.

Cognates or **cognati.** Relations by the mother's side (2 Bl. Comm. 235); relations by or through females. (Same as *Bhandus* in Hindu Law)

Cognati. Relations by the mother's side. Cognate. (*Latin for Lawyers*)

Cognatio. In the civil law, cognation; relationship or kindred generally. Relationship through females, as distinguished from *agnatio* or relationship through males.

Cognation. Relationship by blood rather than by marriage.

Cognition. Faculty of knowing.

Cognizable. Capable of being taken cognizance of. [CrPC 1973 (2 of 1974), S. 2(c)].

"Cognizable offence", "Cognizable case". "COGNIZABLE OFFENCE" means an offence for, and "*cognizable case*" means a case in which a police officer, within or without the presidency-towns may, in accordance with the First Schedule of the Code of Criminal Procedure or under any law for the time being in force, arrest without warrant. [CrPC 1973 (2 of 1974), S. 2(c)] Now (w.e.f. 1-7-2024) repealed & replaced by Bharatiya Nagarik Suraksha Sanhita, 2023 (46 of 2023), section 2(1)(g), same definition in new Sanhita]

Cognizance. Judicial notice or knowledge; the judicial recognition or hearing of a cause; jurisdiction, or right to try and determine causes. It is a word of the largest import: embracing all power, authority and jurisdiction. The word "cognizance" is used in the sense of "the right to take notice of and determine a cause." Taking cognizance does not involve any formal action, or indeed action of any kind, but occurs as soon as a Magistrate, as such, applies his mind to the suspected commission of an offence.

"Cognizance" means 'jurisdiction' or 'the exercise of jurisdiction' or 'power to try and determine causes'. Black's Law Dictionary as cited in *Subramanian Swamy* v. *Manmohan Singh*, (2012) 3 SCC 64, para 64.1.

The expression 'cognizance' has not been defined in the Code. But the word (cognizance) is of indefinite import. It has no esoteric or mystic significance in criminal law. It merely means 'become aware of' and when used with reference to a court or a Judge, it connotes 'to take notice of judicially'. It indicates the point when a court or Magistrate takes judicial notice of an offence with a view to initiating proceedings in respect of such offence said to have been committed by someone. *Chief Enforcement Officer* v. *Videocon International Limited*, (2008) 2 SCC 492, para 19 as cited in *Sarah Mathew* v. *Institute of Cardio Vascular Diseases*, (2014) 2 SCC 62, para 33.

Cognizance takes place at a point when a magistrate first takes judicial notice of an offence. This is the position whether the magistrate takes cognizance of an offence on a complaint, or on a police report, or upon information of a person other than a police officer. *Darshan Singh* v. *State of Maharashtra*, AIR 1971 SC 2372, 2374. [CrPC, 1973 (2 of 1974), S. 190(1)]

The word "cognizance" has no esoteric or mystic significance in criminal law or procedure. It merely means—become aware of and when used with reference to a Court or Judge to take notice of judicially. *Ajit Kumar* v. *State of W.B.*, AIR 1963 SC 765, 770. [CrPC, 1973 (2 of 1974), S. 190(1)]

The word 'cognizance' indicates the point when a Magistrate or a Judge first takes judicial notice of an offence. *State of W.B.* v. *Mohd. Khalid,* AIR 1995 SC 785.

The word 'cognizance' means jurisdiction or the 'exercise of jurisdiction' or 'power to try and determine causes'. In common parlance, it means taking notice of. *State of H.P.* v. *M.P. Gupta*, (2004) 2 SCC 349, 358, para 10.

Legal right to deal with a matter; jurisdiction; the hearing and trying of a cause. [Indian Evidence Act (1 of 1872), S. 40].

Cognizance judicial. Matters of which the Courts take *judicial cognizance* require no proof, although they are not formally admitted. They include matters of law and of fact.

Cognizance of an offence. In S. 190(*c*), CPC 1973 (2 of 1974), is not equivalent to cognizance of any offender, for the definition of complaint includes a complaint that some person unknown has committed an offence.

Cohabit. To dwell or live together; to inhabit the same place; to dwell or live together as husband and wife (usually of unmarried pair). If they live together in the same house, in like manner as respects bed and board, as marks the intercourse between husband and wife, they may be said to cohabit as husband and wife.

Cohabitation. Cohabitation does not mean merely living together, but is used in the law as relating to the living together of a man and woman, as husband and wife. Cohabitation implies sexual intercourse, which will be inferred from the fact of the living together of husband and wife.

Cohabitation means being together as husband and wife. Cohabitation does not necessarily depend upon whether there is sexual intercourse between the husband and wife. *Harvinder Kaur* v. *Harmander Singh Choudhry,* AIR 1984 Del 66, 78. [Hindu Marriage Act (25 of 1955), Ss. 9, 13(2)(iii)]

Living together as husband and wife, or as if husband and wife; coitus. [IPC (45 of 1860), S. 493].

Cohabiting together as husband and wife. Means living together publicly in the face of society as if the conjugal relation existed; living in the same house in like manner as marks the intercourse between husband and wife.

Cohaeredes una persona censentur, propter unitatem juris quod habent. Co-heirs are deemed as one body, *or* one person, on account of the unity of right which they possess.

Coils. Spirals. [Income-tax Act (43 of 1961), Sch. V, Item 17].

Coin. Coin is metal used for the time being as money, and stamped and issued by the authority of some State or Sovereign power in order to be so used. [IPC (45 of 1860), S. 230]. [Now (w.e.f. 1-7-2024) repealed & replaced by Bharatiya Nyaya Sanhita, 2023 (45 of 2023)]

"Coin" shall have the same meaning as assigned to it in section 2 of the Coinage Act, 2011 (11 of 2011) and includes metal used for the time being as money and is stamped and issued by or under the authority of any State or Sovereign Power intended to be so used. [(w.e.f. 1-7-2024) Bharatiya Nyaya Sanhita, 2023 (45 of 2023), section 178, *Explanation* (2)]

The coining and legitimation of money is an exclusive prerogative of the sovereign, but this prerogative has from the earliest times been both asserted and regulated by Acts of the Legislature.

As a verb 'coin' means 'to stamp metal and convert it into coin'. To emit stamped paper is not to "coin" money.

"COIN" means any coin which is made of any metal or any other material stamped by the Government or any other authority empowered by the Government in this behalf and which is a legal tender including commemorative coin and Government of India one rupee note. *Explanation.*—For the removal of doubts, it is hereby clarified that a 'coin' does not include the credit card, debit card, postal order and e-money issued by any bank, post office or financial institution. [S. 2(a) of the Coinage Act, 2011 (11 of 2011)]

COIN : MONEY. "Coin" differs from "money" as the species differs from the genus. "Money" is any matter, whether metal on paper, which has currency as a medium in commerce. "Coin" is a particular specie, always made of metal, and struck according to a certain process, called "coining."

COUNTERFEIT COIN. One in imitation of the genuine; not genuine.

FALSE COIN. Imitation of coin in base metal; spurious coin.

Coinage. The process or the function of coining metallic money; also used to denote the great mass of metallic money of the country in circulation at any particular period. The phrase "coining" cannot without violence, be applied to the issue of paper money.

The action of making coins.

Coincide. 'Coincide' means 'simultaneous.'

Coiner. Maker of counterfeit coins.

One who makes or mints a coin. [IPC (45 of 1860), S. 241, ill.].

"Coir" or "coir fibre". Means the fibre extracted from the husk of the cocoanut. [Coir Industry Act (45 of 1953), S. 3(c)].

Coir products. Means mats and mattings, rugs and carpets, ropes and other articles manufactured, wholly or partly from coir or coir yarn. [Coir Industry Act (45 of 1953), S. 3(d)].

Coir yarn. Means yarn obtained by the spinning of coir. [Coir Industry Act (45 of 1953), S. 3(e)].

Coition. Sexual copulation.

Coke. Solid residue of coal after distillation of volatile parts; it consists of coal, with some gases expelled.

Whereas coal is a stone-like product excavated from the earth, coke is the processed product of coal obtained by indirect heating in beehive ovens and by-product ovens which are commonly known as "coke oven plants". *Bharat Cooking Coal Ltd.* v. *Steel Abrasers & Allied Products Ltd.,* 1994 Supp (3) SCC 361, 363. [Colliery Control Order, 1945, Cl. 2(1), (2)]

The expression "Coke in all its forms" is so wide that petroleum coke which is a form of coke cannot possibly be excluded merely by reference to the word "Coal". *India Carbon Limited* v. *Superintendent of Taxes, Gauhati,* AIR 1972 SC 154. [Central Sales Tax Act (74 of 1956), S. 14(i)]

Coke oven plant. Means the plant and equipment with which the manufacture of hard coke has been, or is being, carried on and includes—

(i) all lands, buildings, works, machinery and equipment, vehicles, railways, tramways and sidings, adjacent to, and belonging to, or in the coke oven plant,

(ii) all workshops belonging to the coke oven plant including buildings, machinery, instruments, stores, equipment of such workshops and the lands on which such workshops stand,

(iii) all hard coke in stock or in transit or under production and other stores, stocks and instruments, belonging to the coke oven plant,

(iv) all power stations belonging to the coke oven plant or operated for supplying electricity for the purpose of working the coke oven plant,

(v) all lands, buildings and equipment adjacent to or belonging to, the coke oven plant where the washing of coal is carried on,

(vi) all other assets, movable or immovable, belonging to a coke oven plant, whether within its premises or outside including cash balances, reserve funds and investments in so far as they may relate to the coke oven plant and also any money lawfully due to the coke oven plant in relation to any period prior to the specified date. [Coking Coal Mines (Emergency Provisions) Act (64 of 1971), S. 3(b)].

"COKE OVEN PLANT" means the plant and equipment with which the manufacture of hard coke has been, or is being, carried on, and includes—

(i) all lands, buildings, works, machinery and equipment, vehicles, railway, tramways and sidings, belonging to, or in, the coke oven plant,

(ii) all workshops belonging to the coke oven plant, including buildings, machinery, instrument, stores, equipment of such workshops and the lands on which such workshops stand,

(iii) all coke in stock or under production, and other stores, stocks and instruments, belonging to the coke oven plant,

(iv) all power station belonging to the coke oven plant or operated for supplying electricity for the purpose of working of coke oven plant or a number of coke oven plants,

(v) all lands, buildings and equipment belonging to the coke oven plant where the washing of coal is carried on,

(vi) all other fixed assets movable or immovable, and current assets belonging to a coke oven plant, whether within its premises or outside.

Explanation.—The expression "current assets" does not include,—

(a) dues representing the sale of coal and coal products effected at any time before the appointed day and outstanding immediately before the said day;

(b) dues from the Coal Board, established under Section 4 of the Coal Mines (Conservation, Safety and Development) Act, 1952, prior to the repeal of the said Act, with respect to any period before the appointed day;

(c) dues from sundry debtors, loans and advances to other parties and investments, not being investments in the coke oven plant;

(d) security deposits made by the owners with the Coal Controller appointed by the Central Government or with the Railways for the fulfilment of contracts or with a State Electricity Board for the payment of bills;

(e) earnest money deposited by the owners with the Railways for obtaining contracts.] [Coking Coal Mines (Nationalisation) Act (36 of 1972), S. 3(b)]

Coking coal mine. Means a coal mine in which there exists one or more seams of coking coal, whether exclusively or in addition to any seam of other coal. [Coking Coal Mines (Emergency Provisions) Act (64 of 1971), S. 2(c) and Coking Coal Mines (Nationalisation) Act (36 of 1972), S. 3(c)]

In the Act of 1972, a "coking coal mine" included a "coke oven plant" in or about such coking coal mine. The separate provisions in Section 5 and Schedule II for the nationalisation of coke oven plants was necessary to cover those coke oven plants which were situated in or about the nationalised mines but which did not belong to the owners of those mines. *Sanjeev Coke Manufacturing Company* v. *Bharat Coking Coal Limited,* (1983) 1 SCC 147. [Coking Coal Mines (Nationalisation) Act (36 of 1972), S. 3(c)]

Cold-blood. A state of mind marked by premeditation and deliberateness.

Cold-blooded murder. Wilful, deliberate and premeditated homicide.

Cold chain facility. Means a chain of facilities for storage or transportation of agricultural produce under scientifically controlled conditions including refrigeration and other facilities necessary for the preservation of such produce. [Income-tax Act (43 of 1961), S. 80-IB(14) (aa)]

Cold-water-ordeal. The trial which was ordinarily used for the common sort of people, who, having a cord tied about them under their arms, were cast into a river; if they sank to the bottom until they were drawn up, which was in a very short time, then they were held guiltless; but such as did remain upon the water, were held culpable, being, as they said, of the water rejected and kept up. (*Wharton*)

Collaboration. The action or process of collaborating or working in combination. [Aligarh Muslim University Act (40 of 1920), S. 12(2)].

"COLLABORATION" for the purposes of these regulations, means an arrangement between an Indian Educational Institution and a Foreign Educational Institution, put into place through an instrument of written Agreement for the purposes of twinning leading to the award of degree(s). [University Grants Commission (Promotion and Maintenance of Standards of Academic Collaboration between Indian and Foreign Educational Institutions) Regulations, 2016, Regn. 2(d)]

Collapse. Collapse means falling; shrinking together; breaking down or giving way through external pressure or loss of support. It will not include demolition.

Collateral. By the side; at the side; attached upon the side.

The word "collateral" is of frequent use in law, where it bears its ordinary signification of "parallel" or "additional." It is used in a variety of connections, *e.g.,* we speak of a collateral agreement, collateral security, collateral relations, and collateral facts.

Descended from the same stock, but in a different line; lying aside from the main subject, action, issue *etc.*; situated or running side by side. [T.P. Act (4 of 1882), S. 38, ill.].

Collateral agreement. Is one related, but ancillary to the main contract come to between parties. "Collateral" means in effect not inconsistent with the terms of the agreement in question.

Collateral ancestors. Uncles, aunts, and others who are not "ancestors" in the sense of progenitors.

Collateral benefits. Benefits which are received from a third party by the victim of a tortious injury in consequence of injury such as social security benefits, loans, insurance money *etc.*.

Collateral consanguinity. Collateral consanguinity is that which subsists between two persons, who are descended from the same stock or ancestor, but neither of whom is descended in a direct line from the other. [Indian Succession Act (39 of 1925), S. 26].

Collateral contract. A contract prior to, or contemporaneous with, a deed, which, if not incorporated in the deed, is not effective to limit the estate conveyed or bind directly the use of the property included in the grant, but may be given effect as a personal covenant binding upon the parties and persons in privity of estate and having notice. (*Ballentine's Law Dictionary 3rd Edn.)*

Collateral estoppel. A doctrine which prevents litigating facts or issues which were previously resolved in another suit.

Collateral facts. In the law of evidence are those not bearing directly on the issue before the Court; facts which are not directly involved or connected with the principal issue or matter in dispute.

Collateral guaranty; collateral surety. In a "collateral guaranty" a guarantor undertakes, in the event the principal fails to do what he has promised, to pay damages incurred on such failure. A guarantor undertakes to pay such damages as a result of the principal's default. A surety undertaken to do the particular thing if the principal fails.

Collateral heirs. Heirs who are collaterals, as distinguished from those in the direct line. [T.P. Act (4 of 1882), S. 38, ill.].

Collateral obligation. A separate obligation attached to any other contract to guarantee its performance.

Collateral proceeding. Another proceeding, not for the direct purpose of impeaching the proceeding to which it is said to be collateral.

Collateral relations. Is used in opposition to "lineal relations". Collateral relations are those who are descended from the same stock or ancestor, but not, like lineal relations, descended the one from the other.

Collateral relationship. Words expressive of collateral relationship apply alike to relatives of full and of half blood. [Indian Succession Act (39 of 1925), S. 99(*h*)]

Collateral security. A security given in addition to the dircet security; an additional security given by the debtor to further safeguard the interests of the creditor [Registration Act (16 of 1908), S. 17(2)(ix)].

Collateral transaction. A "*collateral transaction*" within the meaning of the proviso to S. 49 of the Registration Act (16 of 1908) is a transaction other than the transaction affecting the immovable property but which is in some way connected with it.

Collateral transaction means a transaction which does not create rights in immovable property. *Kanbi Karshan Jaram* v. *Kanbi Harkha Hari,* AIR 1953 San 56. [Registration Act (16 of 1908), S. 49, Proviso]

A transaction which is collateral to the main transaction. [Registration Act (16 of 1908), S. 49(c)].

Collation. The action of collating or comparing in order to note points of agreement or disagreement.

Colleague. Member in a joint office (as) colleagues on the Bench or the Bar.

COLLEAGUE, PARTNER. Colleague is more noble than partner: men in the highest offices are *colleagues*; tradesmen, mechanics, and subordinate persons, are *partners*.

Collect—Collection. Assemble; accumulate; bring together.

To gather in [IPC (45 of 1860), S. 122]; to realize; to gather together.

Collection. "COLLECTION" means lifting and removal of solid wastes from collection points or any other location. [Municipal Solid Wastes (Management and Handling) Rules, 2000, R. 2(v)]

A group of things collected. [Gold (Control) Act (45 of 1968) (*Repealed*), S. 2(a)(iii)]; the action of collecting. [Collection of Statistics Act (32 of 1953), Preamble].

The term 'collection' means only recovery of tax already assessed and levied and in respect of which liability to pay has arisen.

Collective agreement. An agreement which is made by or on behalf of one or more trade unions and one or more employers or employers' association in relation to terms and conditions of employment, matters of discipline, membership or non-membership of trade union.

Collective bargaining. It means the negotiations taking place between the employer and the representatives of organized employees for the purpose of determining the conditions of the employment; *e.g,* wages, hours and fringe benefits.

As contemplated by National Labor Relations Act, is a procedure looking toward making of collective agreements between employer and accredited representative of union employees concerning wages, hours, and other conditions of employment, and requires that parties deal with each other with open and fair minds and sincerely endeavor to overcome obstacles existing between them to the end that employment relations may be stabilized and obstruction to free flow of commerce prevented. National Labor Relations Act $ 8(5), 29 USCA $ 158(5). *Rapid Roller Co.* v. *National Labor Relations Board*, CCA 7, 126 F. 2d 452, 460.

Collective mark. Means a trade mark distinguishing the goods or services of members of an association of persons (not being a partnership within the meaning of the Indian Partnership Act, 1932) which is the proprietor of the mark from those of others. [Trade Marks Act (47 of 1999), S. 2(1)(g)]

Collective mark means a trade mark distinguishing the goods or services of members of an association of persons (not being a partnership within the meaning of the Indian Partnership Act, 1932) which is the proprietor of the mark from those of others. [Trade Marks Act, 1999, S. 2(g)].

Collective naturalization. Is where the Government by treaty or cession, acquires the whole or a part of the territory of another nation, and takes to itself the inhabitants thereof.

Collective responsibility. The concept of 'collective responsibility' is essentially a political concept. It has two meanings: firstly it is that all members of a Government are unanimous in support of its policies and world exhibit that unanimity on public occasions although while formulating the policies, they might have different view in the meeting of cabinet, and secondly it is that the Ministers, who had an opportunity to speak for or against the policies in the Cabinet are thereby personally and morally responsible for its success and failure. *Common cause, a Registered Society* v. *Union of India*, AIR 1999 SC 2979.

The Council of Ministers is collectively responsible to the House of the People. [Constitution of India, Article 75]

Collectively. In a collective manner or capacity [Indian Partnership Act (9 of 1932), S. 4].

Collector. "COLLECTOR" means (1) any Revenue-officer in independent charge of a district, and (2) any officer appointed by the State Government to perform the functions of a Collector under this Act. [Indian Treasure Trove (6 of 1878), S. 3]

The expressions "COLLECTOR" means the Collector of a District and includes a Deputy Commissioner and any officer appointed by the appropriate Government to perform the function of a Collector under the Act. [Land Acquisition Act (1 of 1894), S. 3(c)] [Now repealed & replaced by Act 30 of 2013]

"COLLECTOR" shall mean, in a presidencytown, the collector of Calcutta, Madras or Bombay as the case may be, and elsewhere the chief officer-in-charge of the revenue administration of a district. [General Clauses Act (10 of 1897), S. 3(11)]

"COLLECTOR"—(*a*) means, within the limits of the towns of Calcutta, Madras and Bombay, the Collector of Calcutta, Madras and Bombay, respectively and, without those limits the Collector of a district; and (*b*) includes a Deputy Commissioner and any officer whom the Government may, by notification in the Official Gazette, appoint in this behalf. [Indian Stamp Act (2 of 1899), S. 2(9)].

"COLLECTOR" means the chief officer-incharge of the revenue administration of a district or any other officer not below the rank of a Deputy Collector as may be appointed by the State Government under Section 18B in this behalf. [Wild Life (Protection) Act (53 of 1972), S. 2(9)]

"COLLECTOR" means the Collector having jurisdiction over the area in which the accident occurs. [Public Liability Insurance Act (6 of 1991), S. 2(b)]

The collector is not the same as 'the Government'. *Bombay State* v. *Mulji Jeltha*, AIR 1955 SC 325, 328. [Bombay Land Revenue Code (5 of 1879), S. 67]

The word 'collector' should be interpreted to mean and include all Assistant Collectors, who have been invested with the powers of a collector for the purpose of entry 11, list II of Sch. 2. *Ramlal* v. *Ram Narain*, AIR 1953 All 467 (FB). [U.P. Tenancy Act (17 of 1939) Entry II, List II, Sch. 2]

Collector [In S. 80, CPC (5 of 1908)], means the Collector of the District in which the suit is instituted.

(*In the Land Acquisition Act*) it means the Collector of a District and includes a Deputy Commissioner and any officer empowered by the appropriate Government to perform the function of a Collector under the Act.

The term "Collector" in S. 93, CPC (5 of 1908), does not include "Assistant Collector" in-charge during the Collector's illness.

An officer who receives money due as taxes, customs *etc.* [General Clauses Act (10 of 1897), S. 3(11)].

MYSORE LAND REVENUE CODE. The Deputy Commissioner who is entrusted with the revenue administration of a District under the Mysore Land Revenue Code is a Collector within the meaning of the. [General Clauses Act (10 of 1897), S. 3(11)]. *D.C. Mills* v. *Dy. Commissioner Chitradurga*, AIR 1961 SC 1441, 1442.

"COLLECTOR" means the Collector of a Revenue District, and includes a Deputy Commissioner and any officer specially designated by the appropriate Government to perform the functions of a Collector under Act 30 of 2013. [S. 3(g) of the Right to Fair Compensation & Transparency in Land Acquisition, Rehabilitation & Resettlement Act, 2013 (30 of 2013)]

Collectorate. The word "Collectorate" in this Act means the *zila* or other district to which a Collector is appointed, and no lands situate beyond the limits of such *zila* or district shall be deemed to be situate within the collectorate by reason of their forming part of an estate paying revenue to the Collector thereof. [Ben. Act VI of 1853 (Rent Recovery), S. 3]

Collector's Office. The expression "COLLECTOR'S OFFICE" also includes the office of the Land Acquisition Officer. [Land Acquisition Act (1 of 1894), S. 12]

College. The term "COLLEGE" or "AFFILIATED COLLEGE" includes any collegiate institution affiliated to or maintained by the University. [Indian University Act (8 of 1904), S. 2, cl. (2)(*a*)]

"COLLEGE" means a college or teaching institution (other than a secondary, primary or infant school or pathasala) maintained by, or admitted to the privileges of, the University. [Banaras Hindu University Act (16 of 1915), S. 2(b)]

"COLLEGE" means a college or teaching institution (other than a University) established or maintained by a person or group of persons from amongst a minority community. [National Commission for Minority Educational Institution Act, 2004 (2 of 2005), S. 2(b)]

The term "*college*" is used in various senses, as a college of electors, a college of surgeons, or a college of cardinals.

In ordinary usage, a college is an institution of learning, which offers instruction in the liberal arts and in scientific branches. The word is applied to institutions which are confined to some special grades of instruction.

"COLLEGE" means a college maintained by or admitted to the privileges of the University for imparting education and training in aviation studies or in its associated disciplines. [S. 2(f) of the Rajiv Gandhi National Aviation University Act, 2013 (26 of 2013)]

"COLLEGE" means a constituent college of the University whether located at the headquarters, campus or elsewhere. [S. 3(h) of the Rani Lakshmi Bai Central Agricultural University Act, 2014 (10 of 2014)]

Colliery. A place where coals are dug. A mine, pit or place where coals are dug, together with machinery used in digging and raising of coal.

The word 'colliery' includes or may include all contiguous and connected veins and seams of coal which are worked as one concern, together with the workings and machinery necessary for working the minerals, and the business of selling the coal worked. HALSBURY, 4th Edn., Vol. 31, para 13, p. 16.

A coal mine and the building connected with it. [Coal Mines Labour Welfare Fund Act (32 of 947), S. 3(1)].

Collision. Violent encounter of moving bodies; a dashing or violently running together. In maritime law, "collision" is the act of ships or vessels striking or colliding together. In its strict sense collision means the impact of two vessels, both moving. (*Abbott; Burrill*)

By common usage the term "collision" is applied to cases where one vessel quite stationary is run into by another.

The action of colliding; violent encounter of a moving body with another. [Indian Railways Act (9 of 1890), S. 82A(1)].

Collusion. A secret agreement for a fraudulent purpose; a secret or dishonest arrangement in fraud of the rights of another; a secret agreement by two or more persons to obtain an unlawful object. An agreement between persons to obtain an object forbidden by law, or to obtain a lawful object by illegal means. The word 'collusion' when used in connection with judicial proceedings means a secret agreement between two persons that the one should institute a suit against the other in order to obtain the decision of a judicial tribunal for some sinister purpose or even in the wider sense of a deceitful agreement or compact between two or more persons to do some act in order to prejudice a third person or for some improper purpose.

More than one mind must be involved to constitute a collusion.

There are two kinds of collusion, positive and negative. The positive collusion is one where true facts are put forward in support of a false case or false facts in support of a true case. Negative collusion is an agreement between the parties to withhold relevant facts from the Court. *Clarance* v. *Racheel,* AIR 1964 Mys 67, 74. [Indian Divorce Act (4 of 1869), S. 12]

Collusion implies the existence of two or more parties who can deal with each other independently with the object or entering into an arrangement which may serve as a cloak to cover up the real state of affairs. When one party can dominate over the will of the other, it would not be a case of collusion but one of compulsion. *V.S. Rahi* v. *Ram Chambali*, AIR 1984 SC 595, 599. [Delhi Rent Control Act (59 of 1958), S. 21]

Collusion means agreement or understanding between the parties to make the Court believe in the existence or truth of the circumstances which the parties know to be non-existent or false and the existence or truth of which is necessary for the grant of relief claimed in the petition. *Tirukappa* v. *Kamalamma,* AIR 1966 Mys 1, 4. [Hindu Marriage Act (25 of 1955), S. 23(1)(c)]

The word 'collusion' means a secret agreement for illegal purposes or a conspiracy, implying that a person does something evil designedly. *Subhas Chandra* v. *Ganga Prasad*, AIR 1967 SC 878, 881, 882.

A secret agreement or understanding for a fraudulent or deceitful purpose. [Indian Evidence Act (1 of 1872), S. 44 and IPC (45 of 1860), S. 37, ill. (c)].

"Collusion" is synonymous with "conspiracy". Both are agreements for a wrongful purpose. Both are secret agreements by two or more persons to obtain an unlawful object.

Collusive. Fraudulent, concerted or devised, characterrised by collusion. [T.P. Act (4 of 1882), S. 52].

Collusive action. Fraudulently concerted or devised action.

Collusive and fraudulent. Collusion in judicial proceeding is a secret arrangement between two persons that the one should institute a suit against the other in order to obtain the decision of a judicial tribunal for some sinister purpose. (Wharton's Law Lexicon). *Nager Bai* v. *B. Shama Rao*, AIR 1956 SC 593, 599. [Transfer of Property Act (4 of 1882), S. 52]

There was a fundamental distinction between a collusive and a fraudulent proceeding in that while the former was the result of an understanding between the parties, both the claim and the contest being fictitious and the purpose to confound third parties, in the latter the contest was real, though the claim was untrue, and the purpose to injure the defendant by a verdict of the Court obtained by practising fraud in it. *Nagubai Ammal* v. *B. Shama Rao,* AIR 1956 SC 593.

'Coloniser' means an individual, company or association or body of individuals, whether incorporated or not, owning land for converting it into a colony and to whom a licence has been granted under this Act. Haryana Development and Regulation of Urban Areas Act (8 of 1975), S. 2(d) as cited in *DLF Limited* v. *Manmohan Lowe*, (2014) 12 SCC 231, para 23.

Colony. An overseas dependency of a State. [General Clauses Act (10 of 1897), S. 3(12)]; a settlement; a part of a town.

'Colony' means an area of land divided or proposed to be divided into plots or flats for residential, commercial, industrial, cyber city or cyber park purposes or for the construction of flats in the form of group housing or for the construction of integrated commercial complexes, but an area of land divided or proposed to be divided—

(i) for the purpose of agriculture; or

(ii) as a result of family partition, inheritance, succession or partition of joint holding not with the motive or earning profit; or

(iii) in furtherance of any scheme sanctioned under any other law; or

(iv) by the owner of a factory for setting up a housing colony for the labour or the employees working in the factory; provided there is no profit motive; or

(v) when it does not exceed one thousand square metres or such less area as may be decided from time to time in an urban area by Government for the purposes of this sub-clause, shall not be a colony. Haryana Development and Regulation of Urban Areas Act (8 of 1975), S. 2(c) as cited in *DLF Limited* v. *Manmohan Lowe,* (2014) 12 SCC 231, para 22.

"COLONY" means an area of land not less than one thousand square meters divided or proposed to be divided into plots for residential, commercial or industrial purpose, but does not include any area of *abadi deh* of a village falling inside its *Lal Lakir* or *phirny* or any area of land divided or proposed to be divided—

(i) for the purpose of agriculture; or

(ii) as a result of family partition, inheritance succession or partition of joint holdings not with the motive of earning profit; or

(iii) by the owner of a factory for setting up a housing colony for the labourers or the employees working in the factory:

Provided that there is no profit motive:

Explanation.—The term "agriculture" used in clause (i) shall include horticulture, dairy farming and poultry farming. [Punjab Apartment and Property Regulation Act (14 of 1995), S. 2(i)]

Colour. Any of the manifold phenomenon of light as green, red *etc.*; a hue or tinge noticeable. [Central Excises and Salt Act (1 of 1944), Sch. I, Item 14].

Colour of office is the right or authority by which an officer exercises the duties of his office, which might have been invalid for some reason. In general, it is a pretence of official right to do an act made by one who has no such right; an act wrongfully done by an officer under the pretended authority of his office. (*Bouvier*)

The words 'colour of office' should be carefully construed. They refer to irregular as distinguished from illegal acts. They show that the act was within the jurisdiction but that jurisdiction had been exercised irregularly or on insufficient grounds. *In re Ganapathia Pillai,* AIR 1953 Mad 936, 938. [IPC (45 of 1860), S. 99]

Semblance or appearance of official authority. [IPC (45 of 1860), S. 170].

Colourable. Designed to give colour or conceal; that which has or gives colour; that which is in appearance only, and not in reality, what it purports to be. (*Black*)

Colourable deviation. A certain device, which was a plain equivalent, performing the same function in a combination as that covered by the patent, is a mere colourable deviation. It is however, a smaller and more restricted term than 'equivalent' as used in its technical patent law sense. (*Patent Law*)

Colourable imitation. A mark can be said to be colourable imitation of another mark, when it is not really an imitation of any other mark but just appears to be so and can pass off as such. *Kundal Lal Agarwal* v. *State,* AIR 1958 All 643, 645. [IPC (45 of 1860), S. 486]

Alikeness which has the appearance of original. [CPC (5 of 1908), App., F. No. 8].

Colourable legislation. The idea conveyed by the expression "colourable legislation" is that although apparently the legislature in passing the statute purported to act within the limits of its powers, yet in substance and in reality transgressed these powers, the transgression being veiled by what appears on proper examination, to be a mere pretence or disguise.

A legislation which is in appearance only and not in reality, what it purports to be.

When the legislature is incompetent to enact a particular law although the label of competency is stuck on it, it is colourable legislation. *R.S. Joshi* v. *Ajit Mices*, AIR 1977 SC 2279, 2286. [Constitution of India, Art. 246]

Colourable transaction. Ordinarily, a transaction may be described as colourable when it is not what it purports to be, but when, as a matter of fact, a substantial part of the consideration appears to have been paid, the transaction cannot be described as colourable within the meaning of S. 53, T.P. Act (4 of 1882).

Colours, National. National flag, ensign or standard. [Geneva Conventions Act (6 of 1960), 2nd Sch., Art. 35].

Column. One of two or more upright sections, as of a page or table, separated by a line or a blank space. [Companies (Profits) Surtax Act (6 of 1964), 2nd Sch., Item I(v), *Expln.*].

Combat. An engagement; battle, forcible encounter between two or more individuals or bodies of men.

A fight encounter between individuals or groups. [Civil Defence Act (27 of 1968), S. 2(a)].

Combatant. One that engages in combat. [Army Act (46 of 1950), S. 16(a)].

Combatants. (*In Milit. Law*) It is usual to distinguish the men composing a regular belligerent army into combatants and non-combatants. On capture by the enemy both are entitled to the rights of prisoners of war.

COMBATANT, CHAMPION. A combatant fights for himself and for victory; a champion fights either for another, or in another's cause.

Combatised tradesman. Means a person appointed or in pay as a combatised tradesman. [National Security Guard Act (47 of 1986), S. 2(e)]

Combatting desertification. Includes activities which are part of the integrated development of land in arid, semi-arid and dry sub-humid areas for sustainable development which are aimed at:

(i) prevention and/or reduction of land degradation;

(ii) rehabilitation of partly degraded land; and

(iii) reclamation of desertified land. [Art. 1(b), United Nations: Convention to combat desertification in those countries experiencing serious drought and/or desertification, particularly in Africa (June 17, 1994)].

Combination. The result or product of combining. [Workmen's Compensation Act (8 of 1923), S. 2(1)(1), *Prov.*]; the quality or state of being combined. [Trade and Merchandise Marks Act (43 of 1958), S. 2(f)(iv)] [Now repealed & replaced by Act 47 of 1999]

Combination package. Means a package intended for retail sale, containing two or more individual packages, or individual pieces, of dissimilar commodities;

Illustration. A package containing dissimilar commodities such as, spoons, knives, forks, cups, napkins, or the like, is a combination package. [Standards of Weights and Measures (Comm Pack) Act, 1977, S. 2(c)]

Come : Comes. The word "comes" in S. 33(1), Indian Stamp Act (2 of 1899), is wide enough to include the production of documents under a search warrant.

Come of. To issue or proceed from as a descendant, (as) to *come of* a noble family.

Comfort. Support; solace; consolation; assistance; encouragement. The words "*support and comfort*" in a will giving property to a wife for life, for her "support and comfort" merely express the purpose and motive of the gift and do not make the gift conditional. The use of these words do not cut down the clearly expressed absolute gift to a qualified or conditional one. A provision in a will requiring the testator's executors to set aside so much of the income of his estate as is necessary for the *comfort* of testator's wife, is not satisfied by setting aside a sufficient sum to provide her with sufficient food and wearing apparel. The word embraces whatever is required for mental and spiritual enjoyment also; happy and agreeable prospects.

Comity of nations. It is the recognition which one state or nation allows within its territory to the legislative, executive, or judicial acts of another nation, having due regard both to international duty and covenence and to the rights of its own citizens, who are under the protection of its laws. It is a matter of political necessity under modern conditions. As the law of a State cannot be enforced beyond its territorial limits except by a favour of the State which, by its Courts of law, is asked to respect it, a voluntary recognition of foreign law is involved, and has been ascribed to a supposed "comity" or courtesy of nations towards each other.

Command. "COMMAND" means one of the Commands into which India is for military purposes for the time being divided, and includes any area which the Central Government may, by notification in the Official Gazette, declare to be a command for all or any of the purposes of this Act. [Cantonments Act (2 of 1924), S. 2(viii) and Cantonments (House Accommodation) Act (2 of 1923), S. 2(c)]

The word 'command' is used where a person having control over another, as a master over his servant, orders a thing to be done.

An authoritative order; mandate; injunction [IPC (45 of 1860), S. 151]; a body of troops or district under a commander; influence.

IN MILITARY LAW. A body of troops or any naval or military force under the command of a particular officer. (*Webster*)

In TESTAMENTARY LAW. The words "*wish*", "*desire*", "*command*" or "*direct*" are all apt words to be used in a will to show testator's intent to make a will or dispose of his property.

COMMAND, ORDER, INJUNCTION, PRECEPT. A *command* is an exercise of power or authority; it is imperative and must be obeyed: an order that serves to direct; it is instructive and must be executed. *Command* is properly the act of a superior or of one possessing power: *order* has more respect to the office than to the person.

Commandant. "COMMANDANT" means a person appointed by the Local Government to be a Commandant of Military Police, and includes a District Superintendent of Police, and an Assistant District Superintendent of Police in charge of the police of a district or of a sub-division [Bur. Act XV of 1887 (Military Police), S. 3, cl.(4)]

"COMMANDANT", when used in any provision of this Act with reference to any unit of the force, means the officer whose duty it is under the rules to discharge with respect to that unit, the functions of a commandant in regard to matter of the description referred to in the provision. [Border Security Force Act (47 of 1968), S. 2(f)]

A commander; a commanding officer of a place or of a body of forces.

Commander. The chief officer of an army or a division of it.

"COMMANDER", when used in any provision of this Act with reference to any unit of the Security Guard, means the officer whose duty it is to discharge with respect to that unit, the functions of a Commander in regard to matters of the description referred to in that provision. [National Security Guard Act (47 of 1986), S. 2(f)]

'COMMANDER', in relation to an aircraft, means the member of the flight crew designated as commander of that aircraft by the operator thereof, or, failing such a person, the person who is for the time being the pilot in command of the aircraft. [(English) Dumping at Sea Act, 1974, S. 12(1)]

'COMMANDER' in relation to an aircraft means the member of the crew designated as commander of that aircraft by the operator thereof, or, failing such a person, the person who is for the time being the pilot in command of the aircraft. [(English) Civil Aviation Act, 1982, S. 94(7)]

Commanding Officer. "COMMANDING OFFICER", when used in any relation of this Act, with reference to any separate portion of the regular army or to any department thereof, means the officer whose duty it is under the regulation of the regular army, or in the absence of any such regulations, by the customs of the service, to discharge with respect to that portion of the regular army or that department, as the case may be, the functions of a commanding officer in regard to matters of the description referred to in that provision. [Army Act (46 of 1950), S. 3(v)]

"COMMANDING OFFICER" used in relation to a person subject to this Act, means the officer for the time being in command of the unit or detachment to which such person belongs or is attached. [Air Force Act (45 of 1950), S. 4(xv)]

"COMMANDING OFFICER", used in relation to a person subject to this Act, means an officer for the time being in command of the unit or any separate portion of the Force to which such person belongs or is attached. [Indo- Tibetan Border Police Force Act (35 of 1992), S. 2(1)(e)]

In its military usage, the expression commanding officer includes an office in command of every species of military unit—a corps, a regiment, a battalion, a troop, and so on.

Commemorative coin. Means any coin stamped by the Government or any other authority empowered by the Government in this behalf to commemorate any specific occasion or event and expressed in Indian currency. [S. 2(b) of the Coinage Act, 2011 (11 of 2011)]

Commence. To originate; to cause to begin; perform the first act of; inter upon; to do the first act in anything; to take the first step.

To begin. [T.P. Act (4 of 1882), S. 52, *Expln.*].

Commence any business. "Commence any business" does not mean merely the business for which the company was started, but any transaction including, sale, purchase, *etc. Kishan Garh Electric Supply Co. Ltd.* v. *State of Rajasthan,* AIR 1960 Raj 49. [Companies Act (1 of 1956), S. 149].

Commencement. Beginning [General Clauses Act (10 of 1897), S. 3(13) and Constitution of India, Art. 394, margin].

Commencement of Act or Regulation. "Commencement", used with reference to an Act or Regulation shall mean the day on which the Act or Regulation comes into force. [General Clauses Act (10 of 1897), S. 3(13)]

Commencement of action or suit. Institution of process in a Court of Justice.

"Commencement of an Act" and "coming into operation of an Act in a particular area". Distinction. The date of coming into operation is not necessarily the date of commencement. An Act can only "commence" in a particular area on the date on which that Act is brought into force in that area. The mere fact that it was already in operation in other areas previously will not result in the Act having commenced in the Area where it had not yet been applied. *K. Manickchand* v. *Elias Saleh Mohamed Sait*, AIR 1969 SC 751, 761.

Commencement of criminal proceedings. A complaint or preliminary oath before a Magistrate on which a warrant is issued. (*Wharton*)

Commencement of tenancy. The words 'commencement of tenancy' must therefore be held to refer to the original or the first tenancy, under which the tenant or his predecessor-in-title entered into possession of the land as a tenant and since the time of which tenancy he and his predecessors-in-title have been in continuous and uninterrupted possession of the land.

Commencement of this Act. The words "commencement of this Act" used in a particular enactment mean commencement of that Act and not of an amending Act.

Commencement of trial. The trial commences with the performance of the first act or steps necessary or essential to proceed with the trial. *Union of India* v. *Madan Lal Yadav, (Maj. Gen.*), (1996) 4 SCC 127 para 19.

Initiation of a preliminary enquiry which is only to find out the existence of a case against the accused to initiate a trial would not amount to 'commencement of trial' under the B.S.F. Act. *Shiv Prasad Pandey* v. *C.B.I.*, (2003) 11 SCC 508, 517, para 23. [B.S.F. Act (47 of 1968), S. 77]

Commencing with immediate effect. The words 'commencing with immediate effect' in the notice mean commencing from the date on which the notice was served on the concerned person. *Harbhajan Singh* v. *Himachal Pradesh Government*, AIR 1965 Him Prad 55, 58. [Constitution of India, Art. 311]

Comment. Observations or remarks expressing an opinion or attitude concerning the subject at hand. [IPC (45 of 1860), S. 124A, *Explns*. 2 and 3]; [Aligarh Muslim University Act (40 of 1920), S. 28(6)].

Comments on public news. 'Comments on public news' means 'comments on some of the recent decisions'. *All India Reporter Karmachari Sangh* v. *AIR Ltd.*, AIR 1988 SC 1325, 1331. [Working Journalists and other Newspapers Employees (Conditions of Service) and Miscellaneous Act (45 of 1955), S. 2(b)].

Commerce. "Commerce" means 'financial transactions especially buying and selling of merchandise, on a large scale'. Concise Oxford Dictionary as cited in *National Seeds Corporation Limited* v. *M. Madhusudhan Reddy*, (2012) 2 SCC 506, para 72.

Commerce" is a term of the largest import. It comprehends intercourse for the purposes of trade in any and all its forms, including transportation, purchase, sale, and exchange of commodities between the citizens of one country and the citizens or subjects of other countries, and between the citizens of different provinces in the same state or country.

"COMMERCE" means the carrying of any trade, business or profession, sale or exchange of goods of any type whatsoever and includes the running of with a view to make profits, hospitals or nursing homes, infirmaries, educational institutions, and also includes hotels restaurants and boarding houses not attached to educational institutions and the expression 'commercial' shall be construed accordingly. [Punjab Regional and Town Planning and Development Act (11 of 1995), S. 2(k)]

Buying and selling together; exchange of merchandise especially on a large scale between different countries or districts; intercourse for the purpose of trade in any and all its forms [Income-tax Act (43 of 1961), S. 2(13)].

Commerce and **trade.** The Court does not feel at all embarrassed by the use of the words 'trade or commerce'. The word 'commerce' is undoubtedly, in its usual sense, a larger word than 'trade' in its usual sense. Sometimes 'commerce' is used to embrace less than 'trade', and sometimes 'trade' is used to embrace as much as 'commerce'.

Commercial. The agreement to render consultancy services is commercial in nature. *R.M. Investment and Trading Co. Pvt. Ltd.* v. *Boeing Co.*, AIR 1994 SC 1136, 1139. [Foreign Awards (Recognition and Enforcement) Act (45 of 1961), Section 2]

'Commercial' means 'connected with, or engaged in commerce; mercantile; having profit as the main aim'. Collins English Dictionary as cited in *National Seeds Corporation Limited* v. *M. Madhusudhan Reddy*, (2012) 2 SCC 506, para 72.

'Commercial' denotes 'pertaining to commerce'. Chambers Twentieth Century Dictionary as cited in *National Seeds Corporation Limited* v. *M. Madhusudhan Reddy*, (2012) 2 SCC 506, para 72.

Commercial action.

(1) 'Commercial action' includes any cause arising out of the ordinary transactions of merchants and traders and, without prejudice to the generality of the foregoing words any cause relating to the construction of a mercantile document, the export or import of merchandise, affreightment, insurance, banking, mercantile agency and mercantile usage. (2) An incorporated canal company whose profits arose from tolls, was held a 'commercial company' or a company associated for 'commercial purposes', and, as such, liable to become bankrupt under the Joint Stock Companies Act, 1844." Stroud's Judicial Dictionary as cited in *Punjab University* v. *Unit Trust of India*, (2015) 2 SCC, 669, para 22.

Commercial activity. The very concept of any activity which can justly be called a commercial activity must imply some investment of capital and the activity must run the risk of profit or loss.

Term includes any type of business or activity which is carried on for a profit. Activity relating to or connected with trade and traffic or commerce in general.

Commercial agent or broker. One who negotiates the sale of merchandise without possession or control of it; commission agent.

Commercial and Industrial monopolies. Constitution of India, List III, Entry 21.

The expression "commercial and Industrial monopolies" is wide enough to include grant or creation of commercial or industrial monopolies to the State and citizens as well as control of monopolies. *Khazan Singh* v. *State of U.P.*, AIR 1974 SC 669, 674.

Commercial Appellate Division. It means the commercial Appellate Division in a High Court Constituted under subsection (1) of Section 5 [Commercial Courts Act, 2015 (4 of 2016) (w.r.e.f. 3-5-2018, S. 2 (1)(a)].

Commercial concern. Means a public limited company or a co-operative society or a firm or any other person or body of persons engaged in trade or commerce, and includes—

(i) a concern engaged in banking or insurance;
(ii) a financial corporation;
(iii) a concern engaged in shipping and navigation;
(iv) a concern engaged in the business of brokers dealing in shares; stocks and securities and commodities;
(v) a concern engaged in the business advertising consultants;
(vi) a light railway;
(vii) a concern engaged in road transport service;
(viii) a concern engaged in air transport service;
(ix) a rubber, tea, coffee or chincona plantation;
(x) a concern engaged in the business of forwarding and clearing agents;
(xi) any other concern which, in the opinion of the Central Government, is a commercial concern and is declared to be such by that Government by notification in the Official Gazette, but does not include an industrial concern. [Collector of Statistics Act (32 of 1953), S. 2(b)]

"COMMERCIAL COURT" means the Commercial Court constituted under sub-section (1) of Section 3 [Commercial Courts, Commercial Division and Commercial Appellate Division of High Courts Act, 2015 (4 of 2016), S. 2(1)(b)].

"Commercial Court", for the purposes of any State, means a Commercial Court constituted under section 3, or the Commercial Division of a High Court constituted under section 4, of the Commercial Courts Act, 2015 (4 of 2016). [Copyright Act, 1957 (14 of 1957), section 2(fa)]

"Commercial dispute" means a dispute arising out of—

(i) ordinary transactions of merchants, bankers, financiers and traders such as those relating to mercantile documents, including enforcement and interpretation of such documents;
(ii) export or import of merchandise or services;
(iii) issues relating to admiralty and maritime law;
(iv) transactions relating to aircraft, aircraft engines, aircraft equipment and helicopters, including sales, leasing and financing of the same;
(v) carriage of goods;
(vi) construction and infrastructure contracts, including tenders;
(vii) agreements relating to immovable property used exclusively in trade or commerce;
(viii) franchising agreements;
(ix) distribution and licensing agreements;
(x) management and consultancy agreements;
(xi) joint venture agreements;
(xii) shareholders agreements;
(xiii) subscription and investment agreements pertaining to the services industry including outsourcing services and financial services;
(xiv) mercantile agency and mercantile usage;
(xv) partnership agreements;
(xvi) technology development agreements;
(xvii) intellectual property rights relating to registered and unregistered trademarks,

copyright, patent, design, domain names, geographical indications and semiconductor integrated circuits;

(xviii) agreements for sale of goods or provision of services;

(xix) exploitation of oil and gas reserves or other natural resources including electromagnetic spectrum;

(xx) insurance and re-insurance;

(xxi) contracts of agency relating to any of the above; and

(xxii) such other commercial disputes as may be notified by the Central Government.

Explanation.—A commercial dispute shall not cease to be a commercial dispute merely because—

(a) it also involves action for recovery of immovable property or for realization of monies out of immovable property given as security or involves any other relief pertaining to immovable property;

(b) one of the contracting parties is the State or any of its agencies or instrumentalities, or a private body carrying out public functions. [Commercial Courts, Commercial Division and Commercial Appellate Division of High Courts Act, 2015 (4 of 2016), S. 2(1)(c)].

Commercial Division. It means the Commercial Division in a High Court constituted under sub-section (1) of Section 4 [Commercial Courts, Commercial Division and Commercial Appellate Division of High Courts Act, 2015 (2 of 2016), S. 2(1)(d)].

Commercial employment. "COMMERCIAL EMPLOYMENT" means employment in any capacity under, or agency of, a person engaged in trading, commercial, industrial or financial business in any field and includes also a director of a company or partner of a firm and it also includes setting up practice either independently or as partner of a firm or as an adviser or a consultant. [Telecom Regulatory Authority of India Act (24 of 1997), S. 5, *Expl.*]

Commercial establishment. A place where commodities are exchanged, bought or sold. The term contemplates a profit-making establishment. (*Black*)

The office of a Chartered Accountant is not a commercial establishment.

The premises of the Federation of Indian Chambers of Commerce and Industry are a commercial establishment since the activity carried on by it is in the nature of trade or business. *Chief Commissioner, Delhi* v. *Federation of Indian Chambers of Commerce and Industries*, AIR 1974 SC 1527, 1533.

Commercial insurance. Has reference to "indemnity agreements, issued in the form of insurance bonds or policies, whereby parties to commercial contracts are protected against loss by reason of a breach of contractual obligations on the part of the other contracting party." The term would include "title insurance."

Commercial law. That branch of the law which comprises and includes rules established for the Governance of commercial transactions. A law not peculiar to one state or dependent upon local authority, but one arising out of the usages of the commercial world.

COMMERCIAL LAW AND LAW-MERCHANT. No municipal laws can be sufficient to order and determine the very extensive and complicated affairs of traffic and merchandise: neither can they have a proper authority for this purpose: for as these are transactions carried on between subjects of independent states, the municipal laws of one will not be regarded as binding by the other. For this reason the affairs of commerce are regulated by a law of their own, called the Lawmerchant or *Lex mercantoria,* which all nations agree in and take notice of. And in particular it is held to be part of the law of the land, which decides the causes of merchants by the general rules. (*Tomlin*)

Commercial letter of credit. 'A letter of credit' is termed 'commercial' when the underlying transaction involves the sale of goods and the credit becomes payable upon the presentation of documents showing that the seller has complied with the sales agreement. [*New Braunfels National Bank, Et Al. v James T Odiorne, Receiver of Southern International Insurance Co Ltd,* 780 SW 2d 313. See also *Fargo Freight Ltd v Commodities Exchange Corpn,* (2004) 7 SCC 203, 211, para 17].

Commercial loan. A loan which a financial institution gives to a business.

Commercial mark : trade mark : commercial name. A trade mark is not a commercial mark. The trade mark is specially or purely the mark of the manufacturer, or his, who creates the product or manufactures it; the commercial mark is that of the dealer, who receiving the product of the manufacturer, sells it in turn to the consumer. The commercial name is the name of an individual, or any name which is the property of the merchant, without reference to its use as a mark or trade mark in any distinctive form.

Commercial or industrial construction service. "COMMERCIAL OR INDUSTRIAL CONSTRUCTION SERVICE" means—

(a) construction of a new building or a civil structure or a part thereof; or

(b) construction of pipeline or conduit; or

(c) completion and finishing services such as glazing, plastering painting, floor and wall tiling, wall covering and wall papering, wood and metal joinery and carpentry, fencing and railing, construction of swimming pools, acoustic applications or fittings and other similar services, in relation to building or civil structure; or

(d) repair, alteration, renovation or restoration of, or similar services in relation to, building or civil structure, pipeline or conduit,

which it—

(i) used, or to be used, primarily for; or

(ii) occupied, or to be occupied, primarily with; or

(iii) engaged, or to be engaged, primarily in, commence or industry, or work intended for commerce or industry, but does not include such services provided in respect of roads, airports, railways, transport terminals, bridges, tunnels and dams. [Finance Act (32 of 1994), S. 65(25b) *as inserted of Finance Act (18 of 2005), S. 88(a)(vii)* (now repealed by Central Goods and Services Tax Act, 2017)]

"Commercial organisation". Means—

(*i*) a body which is incorporated in India and which carries on a business, whether in India or outside India;

(*ii*) any other body which is incorporated outside India and which carries on a business, or part of a business, in any part of India;

(*iii*) a partnership firm or any association of persons formed in India and which carries on a business whether in India or outside India; or

(*iv*) any other partnership or association of persons which is formed outside India and which carries on a business, or part of a business, in any part of India. [Prevention of Corruption Act (49 of 1988), Ss. 8 and 9 as substituted by Amending Act (16 of 2018)].

Commercial premises. "Commercial premises" in the context of the classification rules for electric supply by an electric licensee means nothing more than "premises used for purposes of business." The words cannot be read as being in contradiction to trade premises. Premises used for running a coffee-hotel must be regarded as "commercial premises" for the purpose of fixing rates for the supply of electric energy.

Commercial purpose. For the purposes of this clause, "commercial purpose" does not include use by a person of goods bought and used by him and services availed by him exclusively for the purposes of earning his livelihood by means of self-employment. [Consumer Protection Act (68 of 1986), S. 2(1)(d), *Expl.*] [Now repealed & replaced by Act 35 of 2019]

The words "Commercial purpose" would cover an undertaking the object of which is to make a profit out of the undertaking. *Punjab University* v. *Unit Trust of India*, (2015) 2 SCC 669, para 23.

Word has a wide connotation, in determining commercial purpose, scale of business, the investment involved, motive and intention behind the business, whether in the nature of earning a livelihood or earning substantial profits, currently as well as in future should be taken into consideration.

Commercial quantity. In relation to narcotic drugs and psychotropic substances, means any quantity greater than the quantity specified by the Central Government by notification in the Official Gazette. [Narcotic Drugs and Psychotropic Substance Act (61 of 1985), S. 2(viia)]

Commercial rental. Does not include the rental, lease or lending of a lawfully acquired copy of a computer programme, sound recording, visual recording or cinematography film for non-profit purposes by a non-profit library or non-profit educational institution.

Explanation.—For the purposes of this clause, a non-profit library or non-profit educational institution means a library or educational institution which receives grants from the Government or exempted from payment of tax under the Income-tax Act, 1961 (43 of 1961). [S. 2(fa) of the Copyright Act, 1957 (14 of 1957) as inserted (w.e.f. 21-6-2012) by the Copyright (Amendment) Act, 2012 (27 of 2012)] [Now s. 2(faa) by Act 33 of 2021]

Commercial subscriber. 'Commercial subscriber' means any subscriber who receives a programming service at place indicated by him to a service provider and uses signals of such service for the benefit of his clients, customers, members or any other class or group of persons having access to such place. [Standards of Quality Service (Broadcasting and Cable Services) Cable Television—Non-CAS Areas) Regulations, 2009, Regn. 2(k)]

Commercial transaction. Construction of Highways, bridges, *etc.* by Government cannot be treated as commercial transaction. *State of Maharashtra* v. *Saifuddin Mujaffarali Saifi,* AIR 1994 Bom 48. [CPC (5 of 1908), S. 34, *Proviso*]

Though the expression 'commercial transaction' is inclusive of 'industry trade and business' it is exclusive of "profession."

Commercial use. Includes the use of any land or part thereof for purposes of Commerce or for storage of goods as an office, whether attached to any industry or otherwise. [Punjab Regional and Town Planning and Development Act (11 of 1995), S. 2(l)]

Commercial utilization. Means end uses of biological resources for commercial utilization such as drugs, industrial enzymes, food flavours, fragrance, cosmetics, emulsifiers, oleoresins, colours, extracts and genes use for improving crops and livestock through genetic intervention, but does not include conventional breeding or traditional practices in use in any agriculture, horticulture, poultry, dairy farming, animal husbandry or bee keeping. [Biological Diversity Act, 2002 (18 of 2003), S. 2(f)]

Commercial vehicle. "Commercial vehicle" means "heavy goods vehicle", "heavy passenger motor vehicle" "light motor vehicle," "medium goods vehicle" and "medium passenger motor vehicle" but does not include "maxi-cab", "motor-cab", "tractor" and "road-roller". The expressions "heavy goods vehicle", "heavy passenger motor vehicle", "light motor vehicle", "medium goods vehicle," "medium passenger motor vehicle", "maxi-cab", "motor-cab", "tractor" and "road-roller" shall have the meanings respectively as assigned to them in Section 2 of the Motor Vehicles Act, 1988 (59 of 1988). [Income-tax Rules, 1962, App. I, Note (3A)]

For the purposes of this proviso,—

The expression "commercial vehicle" means "heavy goods vehicle", "heavy passenger motor vehicle", "light motor vehicle", "medium goods vehicle" and "medium passenger motor vehicle" but does not include "maxi-cab", "motor-cab", "tractor" and "road-roller"; [Income-tax Act (43 of 1961), S. 32(1) *Expln.* (a)]

Commission. The warrant which all persons exercising jurisdiction, either ordinary or extraordinary, have to authorize them to do certain acts of ministerial nature as to make enquiry or to hear or determine any cause or action. (*Tomlin*) (*See* CPC (5 of 1908), O. XXVI, Rr. 1-22). Any written appointment of a person to an office; written authority issued or granted by the government to a person appointed to an office, or conferring public authority or jurisdiction upon him; also in private affairs, the authority or instructions under which one person transacts business or negotiates for another.

"Commission" means the National Dental Commission constituted under section 3. [National Dental Commission Act, 2023 (21 of 2023), section 2(c)] Commission in common parlance has duly been understood to mean a fixed charge payable to an agent or a broker for providing services for facilitating a transaction. *Bangalore Turf Club Limited* v. *Regional Director, Employees' State Insurance Corporation*, (2014) 9 SCC 657, para 45.

In Commercial law, commission is a compensation to a factor or other agent for services to be rendered in making a sale or otherwise; a sum allowed as compensation to a servant, factor or agent who manages the affairs of others, in recompense for his services. It is generally calculated at a certain percentage on the amount of the transactions or on the profit to the principal.

In Criminal law, doing or perpetration; the performance of an act.

In army and other forces, the commission issued by the government to a person to serve as an officer in any of the land, sea or air forces of the state.

The word 'commission' as used in the Act, refers to payment of money, not only out of the capital of a company, but from its profit as well. *Madanlal Fakirchand Oudhedhiyas* v. *Changdeo Sugar Mills Ltd.,* AIR 1958 Bom 491, 497. [Companies Act (1 of 1956), S. 76(1)]

An employee may also be entitled to receive, as part of his remuneration, a commission to be calculated on the basis of a fixed percentage of the profits of the employer or to be calculated on any other basis. [Income-tax Act(43 of 1961), S. 17(1)(iv)]

An agent's remuneration [Companies Act (1 of 1956), S. 204(5)(Repealed by Companies Act 2015)]; an order or authority to do an act or exercise powers. [CrPC 1973 (2 of 1974), S. 285(1)]; a body of persons charged with some specific functions [University Grants Commission Act (3 of 1956), S. 2(a)]; the committing (of a crime *etc.*) [CrPC 1973 (2 of 1974), S. 220(2)].

Commission agent. "COMMISSION AGENT" means a person who causes sale or purchase of goods, on behalf of another person for a consideration which is based on the quantum of such sale or purchase. [Central Excise Tariff Act, 1985 (5 of 1986), Appendix IX, Service Tax (c)(xi), *Expln* 2(i)]

"COMMISSION AGENT" means any person who acts on behalf of another person and causes sale or purchase of goods, or provision of receipt of services, for a consideration, and includes any person who, while acting on behalf of another person—

(i) deals with goods or services or documents of title to such goods or services; or

(ii) collects payment of sale price of such goods or services; or

(iii) guarantees for collection or payment for such goods or services; or

(iv) undertakes any activities relating to such sale or purchase of such goods or services. [Finance Act (32 of 1994), S. 15(19) *Expln.* (a) *as substituted by Finance Act (18 of 2005), S. 88(a)(v)* (now repealed by Central Goods and Services Tax Act, 2017)]

One who sells or buys goods for another and receives by way of remuneration or commission a percentage upon the amount involved in each transaction. [Gold (Control) Act (45 of 1968) (*Repealed by Act 18 of 1990*), S. 2(d)(3)(c)].

Commission del credere. An absolute engagement to the principal from an insurance broker in effecting an insurance, and making him liable in the first instance, and at all events though the principal may resort to the underwriter as a collateral security.

Commission merchant. A term which is synonymous with factor.

It means one who receives goods, chattels, or merchandise for sale, exchange, or other disposition, and who is to receive a compensation for his services, to be paid by the owner, or derived from the sale, *etc.*, of the goods; one whose business is to receive and sell goods for a commission, being intrusted with the possession of the goods to be sold, and usually selling in his own name. (*Black*)

Commission of Oyer and Terminer. A commission especially granted to some eminent persons of the hearing and determining one or more causes; and it was the first and largest of the five commissions, by which the English Judges of Assize sat in their several circuits. (*Scotch; Tomlin*)

Commission or brokerage. For the purposes of this section,—

"Commission or brokerage" includes any payment received or receivable, directly or indirectly, by a person acting on behalf of another person for services rendered (not being professional services) or for any services in the course of buying or selling of goods or in relation to any transaction relating to any asset, valuable article or thing. [Income-tax Act (43 of 1961), S. 194 H *Expln.* (i)]

Commissioned. Furnished with a commission or legal warrant; empowered or entrusted with an office or duty. [CrPC (2 of 1974), S. 132(3)(b)].

Commissioned officer. "COMMISSIONED OFFICER" means a person holding a commission from the President in the Indian Navy or in the Indian Naval Reserve Forces. [Navy Act (62 of 1957), S. 3(5)]

An officer of the armed forces holding commission. [IPC 1973 (45 of 1860), S. 21 (second)].

A person in military service of a superior rank.

Commissioned work. Any work which is produced in response to a request and usually in consideration of payment of money for the making of the work; the initial owner of the copyright may or may not be a commissioner in a commissioned work. (*Copyright*)

Commissioner. A member of a commission. An administrative head.

"Commissioner" means, the Chief Officer in charge of the revenue administration of a division. *Archaeological Survey of India* v. *State of M.P.*, (2014) 12 SCC 34, para 42 [General Clauses Act, 1897, S. 3(14)].

"Commissioner" means, the Commissioner of Trade Tax appointed by the State Government. *State of U.P.* v. *Systematic Conscom Limited*, (2014) 13 SCC 627, para 10] [U.P. Trade Tax Act, 1948 (15 of 1948).

One appointed by commission to carry out some specified work; [General Clauses Act (10 of 1897), S. 3(14); Wealth-tax Act (27 of 1957), S. 2(g); Income-tax Act (43 of 1961), S. 2(16) and Gift-tax Act (18 of 1958), S. 2(vi)].

Commissioner of Food Safety. Means the Commissioner of Food Safety appointed under section 30 of Act 34 of 2006. [S. 3(1)(e) of the Food Safety & Standards Act, 2006 (34 of 2006)]

Commissioner of Police. "COMMISSIONER OF POLICE" includes a Deputy Commissioner of Police. [CrPC (5 of 1898), S. 4(g)].

The term "Commissioner of Police" in the Bombay Police Act, 1951, would include all officers who are executing or performing the functions of the Commissioner as defined or authorised under the Police Act. Section 6(2) of Police Act clearly mentions that the term "Commissioner of Police" would include an Assistant Commissioner. *Janardhan* v. *State of Maharashtra,* AIR 1978 SC 1234. [Bombay Police Act, 1951, S. 6(2)]

"Commissioning couple". Means an infertile married couple who approach an assisted reproductive technology clinic or assisted reproductive technology bank for obtaining the services authorised of the said clinic or bank. [Assisted Reproductive Technology (Regulation) Act, 2021 (42 of 2021), section 2(1)(e)]

Commissioning mother. "Commissioning mother" means a biological mother who uses her egg to create an embryo implanted in any other woman [The Maternity Benefit (Amendment) Act, 2017 (6 of 2017), S. 3(ba)]"Commissioning mother" means a biological mother who uses her egg to create an embryo implanted in any other woman. [Code on Social Security, 2020 (36 of 2020), section 2(13)]

Commit. To perpetrate; to do a fault; to be guilty of a crime (*Johnson Dict.*); to consign to custody by official warrant (*Century Dict.*); to send to prison; to imprison; to be put in any place to be kept safe.

Do; perform [Indian Trusts Act (2 of 1882), S. 18]; to give in charge or trust [IPC (45 of 1860), S. 19(d)].

Commit/Committal for trial. To entrust for trial. [CrPC 1973 (2 of 1974), S. 170(1)].

Commitment. The action of entrusting; giving in charge; being committed (especially for trial) [IPC (45 of 1860), S. 220]; an engagement by contract or purchase order to assume a financial obligation [Companies Act (1 of 1956), S. 217(1)(d) now replaced by the Companies Act, 2013]; the state of being obligated or bound. [Interest-tax Act (45 of 1974), S. 2(7)(a)].

"Commitment" means the commitment referred to in section 48B. [Competition Act, 2002 (12 of 2003), section 2(ea)]

Committed. Sent to jail or other proper prison, to be there detained and held to answer for a criminal offence preferred, against a person.

COMMITTED, SENTENCED, PUNISHED. "A person is '*committed*' to jail by a proper tribunal to answer for a criminal offence; upon conviction he is *sentenced* by the judgment of the Court to be imprisoned in jail as a *punishment*; and when put in jail, it is done in *execution of the judgment*."

Committee. "COMMITTEE" of co-operative society means the governing body of a registered society to whom the management of its affairs is entrusted. [Co-operative Societies Act (2 of 1912), S. 2(b)].

An assembly or board of persons to whom the consideration or management of any matter is committed.

"Committee" means the Managing Committee or other governing body of a society to which the direction and control of the management of the affairs of a society is entrusted to. Gujarat Cooperative Societies Act, 1961 (10 of 1962),

s. 2(5) as cited in *Vipulbhai M. Chaudhary* v. *Gujarat Cooperative Milk Marketing Federation Limited*, (2015) 8 SCC 1, para 33.

In parliamentary law, portion of a legislative body, comprising one or more members, who are charged with the duty of examining some matter specially referred to them by the house, or of deliberating upon it, and reporting to the house the result of their investtigations or recommending a course of action. (*Black*)

The expression 'Committee' takes in 'elected committee' and also a, 'nominated committee'. There is no difference between a nominated committee and appointed committee.

A body of persons appointed or elected for some specified business or function [CPC (5 of 1908), S. 135A(1)(b) and Army and Air Force (Disposal of Private Property) Act (40 of 1950), S. 2(1)]; a person to whom the charge of lunatic or an idiot is committed. [Registration Act (16 of 1908), S. 2(10)].

Committee on Private Members' Bills and Resolutions. A Parliamentary Committee to examine and classify all private members' Bills and to allot time for discussion of private members' Bills and resolutions (*Constitutional and Parliamentary Term*)

Committee on Subordinate Legislation. A Parliamentary Committee to scrutinize whether powers to make regulations, rules, sub-rules, bye-laws are being properly exercised within the sphere of delegation. (*Constitutional and Parliamentary Term*)

Committees, Parliamentary. *Committee on Absence of Members from Sittings of the House*—A Parliamentary Committee for considering applications from Members for leave of absence from sittings of the House. (*Constitutional and Parliamentary Term*)

Committing Magistrate. The Magistrate who commits an accused to trial under S. 322 or S. 323 is a committing Magistrate. *Banwari Lal* v. *State*, AIR 1956 All 385, 392. [CrPC, (5 of 1898), Ss. 213, 287, 346, 347]

Commodities transaction tax. Means tax leviable on the taxable commodities transaction under the provisions of this chapter. [S. 116(4) Chapter VII of the Finance Act, 2013 (17 of 2013). Also see (w.e.f. 1-4-2014) *Explanation* to section 36(1)(xvi) of the Income-tax Act, 1961 (43 of 1961)]

Commodity. (*In commerce*). Goods of any kind.

"COMMODITY" means —

(i) any essential commodity

(ii) any article manufactured or produced by any scheduled industry. [Jute Packaging Material (Compulsory use in Packing Commodities) Act (10 of 1987), S. 2(a)]

A thing of use or value; a thing that is an object of trade; a thing one deals in or makes use of [Shorter Oxford English Dictionary as cited in *Escorts Limited* v. *Commissioner of Central Excise, Faridabad*, (2015) 9 SCC 109, para 9].

"COMMODITY" means a specific item of goods. [Railway Act (24 of 1989), S. 2(7)]

Something of use. [Collection of Statistics Act (32 of 1953), S. 3(c)(i)]; an article of commerce.

COMMODITY, GOODS, MERCHANDIZE, WARE. Commodity is employed only for articles of the first necessity: it is the source of comfort and object of industry; goods is applied to everything belonging to tradesmen, for which there is a stipulated value; they are sold in retail, and are the proper objects of trade, merchandize applied to what belongs to merchants; it is the object of commerce; wares are manufactured, and may be either goods or merchandize; a country has its commodities; a shopkeeper his goods; a merchant his merchandise; a manufacturer his wares.

Commodity derivative. Means (i) a contract for delivery of goods which is not a ready delivery contract; or (ii) a contract for differences which derives its value from prices or indices of prices – (A) of such underlying goods or; (B) of related services and rights, such as warehousing and freight; or (C) with reference to weather and similar events and activities, having a bearing on the commodity sector. [S. 116(5) Chapter VII of the Finance Act, 2013; (w.e.f. 1-4-2014) *Explanation 2(i)* to section 43(5) of the Income-tax Act, 1961 (43 of 1961)]

"Commodity derivative" means a contract—

(i) for the delivery of such goods, as may be notified by the Central Government in the Official Gazette, and which is not a ready delivery contract, or

(ii) for differences, which derives its value from prices or indices of prices or such underlying goods or activities, services, rights, interests and events, as may be notified by the Central Government, in consultation with the Board, but does not include securities as referred to in sub-clauses (A) and (B) of clause (ac). [Securities Contracts (Regulation) Act (42 of 1956), S. 2 (bc) as inserted by Finance Act (20 of 2015), S. 133].

Commodum ex injuria sua nemo habere debet. No person ought to have advantage of his own wrong.

In other words no one can be allowed to benefit from his own wrongful act. *Mrutunjay Pan* v. *Narmada Bala Sasmal*, AIR 1961 SC 1353.

Common. Owned by several jointly; belonging to the public; general; universal. (*Worcester*)

Belonging to more than one; belonging to the community; marked by the same relationship to a number of persons or things; [Indian Railways Act (9 of 1890), S. 48]; held, enjoyed, experienced or participated in by a number of individuals.

Common areas and facilities. In relation to a multi-storeyed building, means—

(i) the land on which such building is located and all easements, rights and appurtenances belonging to the land and the building;

(ii) the foundations, columns, girders, beams, supports, main walls, roofs, halls, corridors, lobbies, stairs, stairways, fire-escapes and entrances and exits of the building;

(iii) the basements, cellars, yards, gardens, parking areas, shopping centres, schools and storage spaces;

(iv) the premises for the lodging of janitors or persons employed for the management of the property. [Delhi Apartment Ownership Act (58 of 1986), S. 2(j)]

"COMMON AREAS AND FACILITIES", in relation to a building, means all parts of the building or the land on which it is located and all easements, rights and appurtenances belonging to the land or the building, which are neither in the exclusive possession of an apartment owner in terms of his conveyance deed of apartment, nor are handed over or intended to be handed over to the local authority or other public service agency and shall include the limited common areas and facilities. [Punjab Apartment and Property Regulation Act (14 of 1995), S. 2(j)]

"Common areas" mean—

(i) the entire land for the real estate project or where the project is developed in phases and registration area under this Act is sought for a phase, the entire land for that phase;

(ii) the stair cases, lifts, staircase and lift lobbies, fire escapes and common entrances and exits of buildings;

(iii) the common basement, terraces, parks, play areas, open parking areas and common storage spaces;

(iv) the premises for the lodging of persons employed for the management of the property including accommodation for watch and ward staffs or for the lodging of the community service personnel;

(v) installations of central services such as electricity, gas, water and sanitation, air-conditioning and incinerating system for water conservation and renewable energy;

(vi) the water tanks, sumps, motors, fans, compressors, ducts and all apparatus connected with installation for common use;

(vii) all community and commercial facilities as provided in the real estate project;

(viii) all other portions of the project necessary or convenient for its maintenance, safety, etc., and in common use. [Real Estate Regulation and Development) Act (16 of 2016), S. 2(n)].

'Common areas and facilities' unless otherwise provided in the declaration or lawful amendments thereto means—

(1) the land on which the building is located;

(2) the foundation, columns, girders, beams, supports, main walls, roofs, halls, corridors, lobbies, stairs, stair ways, fire escapes and entrances and exits of the building;

(3) the basements, cellars, yards, gardens, parking area and storage spaces;

(4) the premises for the lodging of janitors or persons employed for management of the property;

(5) installation of central services such as power, light, gas, hot and cold water, heating refrigeration, air conditioning and incinerating;

(6) the elevators, tanks, pumps, motors, fans compressors, ducts and in general all apparatus and installations existing for common use;

(7) such community and commercial facilities as may be provided for in the declaration; and

(8) all other parts of the property necessary or convenient to its existing maintenance and safety or normally in common use. [Haryana Apartment Ownership Act, 1983 (10 of 1983), S. 3(f) as cited in *DLF Limited* v. *Manmohan Lowe*, (2014) 12 SCC 231, para 43].

'Common areas and facilities' as defined in Section 3(j) of the Act includes roof also. *Virmani, Roy & Kutty* v. *Ansal Properties and Industries Ltd.*, AIR 2003 Del 158, 160, para 9. [Delhi Apartment ownership Act (58 of 1986), S. 3(j)]

Common carelessness. Such want of care as is shared by several persons or by both the parties. [Indian Evidence Act (1 of 1872), S. 114, ill. (b)].

Common carrier. "COMMON CARRIER" denotes a person, other than the Government, engaged in the business of transporting for hire property from place to place, by land or inland navigation, for all persons indiscriminately. [Carriers Act (3 of 1865), S. 2].

Those who undertake the office of carrying goods or persons for hire and for all persons indifferently. [CPC (5 of 1908), Ist Sch., App. A, form 29 and long title, Carriers Act (3 of 1865), S. 2].

Common course, usual course. The usual succession of events. [Indian Evidence Act (1 of 1872), S. 114, ill. (f)].

Common entrance test. It means an entrance test, conducted for determination of merit of the candidates followed by centralized counselling for the purpose of merit-based admission to professional colleges or institutions through a single-window procedure by the State Government or by any agency authorized by it. [M.P. Niji Vyavsayik Shikshan Sanstha (Pravesh Ka

Viniyaman Evam Shulk ka Nirdharan) Adhiniyam, 2007, s. 3 (d) as cited in *Modern Dental College and Research Centre* v. *State of M.P.*, (2016) 7 SCC 353, para 9].

Common expenses. Means—

(i) all sums lawfully assessed against the apartment owners by the association for meeting the expenses of administration, maintenance, repair or replacement of the common areas and facilities;

(ii) expenses, declared by the provisions of this Act or by the bye-laws made by the association under the Punjab Apartment Ownership Act, 1995, or agreed upon by the association, as common expenses;

(iii) the Government and municipal taxes, including ground rent and property tax, which is not assessed separately for each apartment. [Punjab Apartment and Property Regulation Act (14 of 1995), S. 2(k)]

Common facilities. In this Scheme, unless the context otherwise requires,—

"COMMON FACILITIES" includes the facilities of air-conditioning, roads (including approach roads), water supply and sewerage, common effluent treatment facility, telecom network, generation and distribution of power used by two or more industrial units in an industrial park. [Industrial Park Scheme, 1999, S. 2(c)]

Common form. One of the two methods of obtaining probate.

Common gaming-house. Means any house, walled enclosure, room or place in which cards, dice, tables or other instruments of gaming are kept or used for the profit or gain of the person owning, occupying, using or keeping such house; enclosure, room or place, whether byway of charge for the use of the instruments of gaming, or of the house, enclosure, room or place, or otherwise howsoever, [Public Gambling Act (3 of 1867), S. 1].

"COMMON GAMING HOUSE" means—(i) in the case of gaming—(a) on the market price of cotton, opium or other commodity or on the digits of the number used is stating such price, or (b) on the amount of variation in the market price of any such commodity or on the digits of the number used in stating the amount of such variation, or (c) on the market price of any stock or share or on the digits of the number used in stating such price, or (d) on the occurrence or nonoccurrence of rain or other natural event, or (e) on the quantity of rainfall or on the digits of the number used in stating such quantity, or (f) on the pictures, digits or figures of one or more playing cards or other documents or objects bearing numbers, or on the total of such digits or figures, or on the basis of the occurrence or non-occurrence of any uncertain future event, or on the result of any draw, or on the basis of the sequence or any permutation or combination of such pictures, digits, figures, numbers, events or draws, any house, room or place whatsoever in which such gaming takes place or in which instruments of gaming are kept or used for such gaming: (ii) in the case of any other form of gaming, any house, room or place whatsoever in which any instruments of gaming are kept or used for the profit or gain of the person owning, occupying, using or keeping such house, room or place by way of charge for the use of such house, room or place or instrument or otherwise howsoever. [Bombay Prevention of Gambling Act (4 of 1887), S. 3(7)]

Common intention. The essence of liability under S. 34, IPC (45 of 1860), is to be found in the existence of a common intention animating the accused leading to the doing of a criminal act in furtherance of such intention. In order to invoke the section, it must be shown that the criminal act complained against was done by the accused persons in the furtherance of the common intention of all.

"*Common intention*" within the meaning of the section implies a pre-arranged plan and it should be proved that the criminal act was done in concert, pursuant to the pre-arranged plan. Care must be taken not to confuse same or similar intention with common intention. The distinction, though very thin is a real and substantial one.

The expression 'common intention' under Section 34 of the Code implies pre-arranged plan and acting in concert pursuant to the pre-arranged plan. It may develop on the spot as between the number of persons, but it must, be anterior in point of time to the commission of offence showing a prearranged plan and prior concert. *Parasa Raja Manikyala Rao* v. *State of A.P.*, AIR 2004 SC 132, 136, para 12. Also see *Krishna Govind Patil* v. *State of Maharashtra*, AIR 2004 SC 1413. [IPC (45 of 1860), S. 34]

An intention shared by all concerned. [IPC (45 of 1860), S. 34 and Indian Evidence Act (1 of 1872), S. 10].

Common interest. Where several persons claim an interest in the subject-matter of controversy, as members of a class or community or residents of a locality, they can be said to have common interest in respect of such subject-matter.

Common Key. Some systems of cryptographic hardware require arming through a secretsharing process and require that the last of these shares remain physically attached to the hardware in order for it to stay armed. In this case 'Common Key' refers to this last share. It is not assumed to be secret as it is not continually in an individual's possession. (*Information Technology*)

Common knowledge. A fact that is so generally known that a Court may accept it as true without proof.

"COMMON KNOWLEDGE" means a well known fact, quote, figure or information that is known to most of the people. [University Grants Commission (Promotion of Academic Integrity and Prevention of Plagiarism in Higher Educational Institutions) Regulations, 2018, Regn. 2(d)].

Common Law. "Common Law is taken in three manner of ways: First, it is taken as the law of the realm of England, dissevered from all other laws. And, under this manner taken, it is often times argued in the laws of England, what matters ought of right to be determined by the Common Law, and what by the Admiral's Court or by the spiritual Court, *etc.* Secondly, the Common Law is taken as the King's Courts, or the Common Law Courts (as distinguished from the Chancery Courts). Thirdly, by the Common Law is understood such things as were law before any statute made in that point that is in question."

The term, in its largest sense, now means the whole body of legal principles and usages which is common to all parts of England.

Judge-made law as distinct from legislation and the rules of equity; family of legal systems deriving from the law of England.

Common nuisance. A common nuisance is an act not warranted by law, or an omission to discharge a legal duty, which act or omission obstructs or causes inconvenience or damage to the public in the exercise of rights common to all. (*Stroud*)

Public nuisance. [IPC (45 of 1860), S. 268].

Common object. The phrase "common object" is the central fact on which the liability of persons other than the actual doer of the act depends. The word "object" means the purpose, intention or design, and in order to make it "common", it must be possessed by all. There must be a community of an object which may, however, exist up to a certain point only beyond which they may differ in their objects and the knowledge possessed by each member of what is likely to be committed in prosecution of the common object will vary not only according to the information at their command but also according to the extent to which he shares the community of objects. The common object has to be determined with reference to the facts and circumstances of each case.

The expression 'common object' occurring in Section 149 of the Code means the purpose or design which should be shared by all the persons who compose the assembly and they should all be aware of it. *State of Maharashtra* v. *Kashirao*, (2003) 10 SCC 434, 441, para 12. [IPC (45 of 1860), S. 149]

The word 'object' means the purpose or design and, in order to make it 'common', it must be shared by all. In other words, the object should be common to the persons, who compose the assembly, that is to say, they should all be aware of it and concur in it. [*Dani Singh* v. *State of Bihar*, (2004) 13 SCC 203, para 11 : 2005 SCC (Cri) 127 as cited in *Bharat Soni* v. *State of Chhattisgarh*, (2012) 12 SCC 657, para 17] [IPC (45 of 1860), S. 149].

The expression 'common object' under Section 149 of the Code would mean that the object should be common to the persons who compose the assembly. They should all be aware of it and concur in it. It may be formed by express agreement after mutual consultation at any stage by all or a few members of the assembly and other members just may join and adopt it. Once formed it need not continue to be the same. *Chander* v. *State of U.P.*, (2004) 5 SCC 141, 147, para 8. [IPC (45 of 1860), S. 149]

'Common object' is different from 'common intention' as it does not require a prior concert and a common meeting of minds before the attack. The 'common object' of an assembly is to be ascertained from the acts and the language and utterances of the members composing it, the nature of arms carried, and from a consideration of all surrounding circumstances. It may be gathered also from the course of conduct adopted by and behaviour of the members of the assembly at or before the actual conflict. *Madan Singh* v. *State of Bihar*, (2004) 4 SCC 622, 631, para 11.

An object shared by all concerned. [IPC (45 of 1860), S. 149].

"COMMON OBJECT VIS-À-VIS COMMON INTENTION." 'Common object' is different from a 'common intention' as it does not require a prior concert and a common meeting of minds before the attack. It is enough if each has the same object in view and their number is five or more and that they act as an assembly to achieve that object. *Shiyjee Singh* v. *State of Bihar*, AIR 2009 SC 417.

Common object of unwalful assembly. For determination of the 'common object of the unlawful assembly', the conduct of each of the members of the unlawful assembly, before and at the time of attck and thereafter, the motive for the crime, are some of the relevant considerations. What the common object of the unlawful assembly is at a particular stage of the incident is essentially a question of fact to be determined, keeping in view the nature of the assembly, the arms carried by the members, and the behaviours of the members at or near the scene of the incident. It is not necessary under law that in all cases of unlawful assembly, with an unlawful common object, the same must be translated into action or be successful. *Shivjee singh* v. *State of Bihar*, AIR 2009 SC 417.

Common original. An original in relation to several copies prepared therefrom. [Indian Evidence Act (1 of 1872), S. 62, *Expln.* 2].

Common parlance test. It is settled position in law that while interpreting the entry for the purpose of taxation recourse should not be made to scientific meaning of the terms or expressions used but to their popular meaning, that is to say, the meaning attached to them, by those dealing in them. It is known as 'common parlance test'. [*Trustful Safety Glass Industries* v. *CST,* (2007) 7 SCC (242, 246), para 13]

"Common portal". Means the Common Customs Electronic Portal referred to in section 154C. [Customs Act, 1962 (52 of 1962), section 2(7B)]

Common profits. This means the balance of all income, rents, profits and revenues from the common areas and facilities remaining after the deduction of the common expenses. [Haryana Apartment Ownership Act (10 of 1983), S. 3(h) as cited in *DLF Limited* v. *Manmohan Lowe*, (2014) 12 SCC 231, para 44].

Common property. Property held in common ownership without demarcation of shares characterised by the existence of a right in any common owner to compel a division of the common property. [T.P. Act (4 of 1882), S. 47].

Common question of law or fact. A question of law or fact which arises at more than one place *e.g.* in two different suits. [CPC (5 of 1908), O. I, R. l].

Common scold. A quarrelsome woman, whose conduct is a public nuisance to her neighbourhood.

Common working days. "Common working days" in respect of a State or Union territory shall mean such days in succession which are not declared as gazetted holidays by the Central Government or the concerned State or Union territory Government [The Central Goods and Services Tax Act, 2017 (12 of 2017), S. 2(27)]

Commoner. Person below the rank of a peer, member of the House of Commons (The lower house of the British Parliament).

Commonly intelligible characters. Writing or alphabets which are not ordinarily or generally capable of being read or understood. [Indian Evidence Act (1 of 1872), S. 98].

Commons. The common people; the lower house of Parliament, the House of Commons (*England*).

Commonwealth. The association of the United Kingdom and the self-governing nations whose territory originally formed the part of the British Empire.

Commonwealth country. A country which is member of the commonwealth. [Extradition Act (34 of 1962), S. 2(a)].

Commorientes. Persons dying together or simultaneously. (*Sweet*)

Persons dying together in the same place, or from the same cause. (*Adam; Webs.*)

Commorientes are persons who perish at the same time in consequence of the same calamity like shipwrecks, collisions, bomb explosions, conflagrations, earthquakes, fatalities during the war. *In the matter of Mahabir Singh* v. *Pirthi Singh Dhillon,* AIR 1963 Punj 66, 72. [Hindu Succession Act (30 of 1956), S. 21]

'Communal land'. Means—

(i) in relation to estates governed by the Madras Estates Land Act, 1908 (Madras Act 1 of 1908) land of the description mentioned in sub-clause (a) or sub-clause (b) of clause (16) of Section 3 of that Act; and

(ii) in relation to cases governed by the Orissa Tenancy Act, 1913 (B&O Act 2 of 1913) lands recorded as gochar, rakshit or sarbasadharan in the record of rights or wastelands which are either expressly or impliedly set apart for the common use of the villagers whether recorded as such in the record-of rights. [Orissa Communal, Forest and Private Lands (Prohibition of Alienation) Act, (1 of 1948), S. 2(a) as cited in *Chandradhoja Sahoo* v. *State of Orissa*, (2012) 13 SCC 419, para 14].

Communicable form. Of such form or nature as is communicated from one to another. [Hindu Marriage Act (25 of 1955), S. 13(1)(iv)].

Communicate. The expression 'communicate' is not synonymous with the expression 'publish' which means to make public; it means "to bestow, convey, make known, recount, to import as to communicate information to anyone".

It means to impart, confer or transmit information. Where a communication is sent by the authority and goes out of its control it must be held as having been communicated no matter whether the intended person actually received it or not. *State of Punjab* v. *Khemiram*, AIR 1970 SC 214 at p. 219.

To give by way of information; to make known. [Indian Contract Act (9 of 1872), S. 3 and Constitution of India, Art. 22(5)]; to speak; to convey information [Army Act (46 of 1950), S. 177(f)].

Communicate and Communications, in Official Secrets Act (19 of 1923) "include any communication, whether in whole or in part, and whether the document, sketch, plan, model, or information itself, or the substance or effect thereof only be communicated."

Communication. Common door or passage, or road or rail or telegraph or other connection between two or more places (as) road communication; telegraph communication, *etc.*

Communication must mean imparting to the detenue sufficient knowledge of all the grounds on which the order of detention is based. *Harikisan* v. *State of Maharashtra*, AIR 1962 SC 911, 913. [Constitution of India, Art. 22(5)]

Communication means imparting to the detenu sufficient and effective knowledge of the facts and circumstances in the language known to the detenu on which the detention order is based. [Constitution of India, Article 22(5)]

The action of communicating, imparting or exchange of information; sharing of knowledge by one with another; the thing communicated. [Indian Evidence Act (1 of 1872), S. 122]; access or means of access between two or more persons or places [Indian Contract Act (9 of 1872), S. 3 and 4 and Constitution of India, Art. 118(3)]; correspondence.

Communication device. 'Communication device' means cell phones, personal digital assistance or combination of both or any other device used to communicate, send or transmit any text, video or image. [Information Technology Act (21 of 2000), S. 2(ha) as inserted by amending Act No. 10 of 2000), S. 4A,]

Communication in official confidence. The words "communication in official confidence" used in S. 124, Indian Evidence Act (1 of 1872), import no special degree of secrecy and no pledge or direction for its maintenance, but include generally all matters communicated by one officer to another in the performance of their duties. The expression has the same meaning as "professional confidence" used in S. 126 of the Act.

Communication right. Generally limited to the cases of perception of the communicate material by 'the public', is a right to communicate the sound or images or other representation of a work, sound recording, film or broadcast or performance or cable transmission or retransmission. (*Copyright*)

Communication to the public. Means making any work or performance available for being seen or heard or otherwise enjoyed by the public directly or by means of display or diffusion other than by issuing physical copies of it, whether simultaneously or at places and times chosen individually, regardless of whether any member of the public actually sees, hears or otherwise enjoys the work or performance so made available.

Explanation.—For the purpose of this clause, communication through satellite or cable or any other means of simultaneous communication to more than one household or place of residence including residential rooms of any hotel or hostel shall be deemed to be communication to the public. [Copyright Act (14 of 1957), S. 2(ff)].

"COMMUNICATION TO THE PUBLIC" means making any work or performance available for being seen or heard or otherwise enjoyed by the public directly or by any means of display or diffusion other than by issuing physical copies of it, whether simultaneously or at places and times chosen individually, regardless of whether any member of the public actually sees, hears or otherwise enjoys the work or performance so made available. *Explanation.*—For the purposes of this clause, communication through satellite or cable or any other means of simultaneous communication to more than one household or place of residence including residential rooms of any hotel or hostel shall be deemed to be communication to the public. [S. 2(ff) of the Copyright Act, 1957 (14 of 1957) as substituted (w.e.f. 21-6-2012) by the Copyright (Amendment) Act, 2012 (27 of 2012)]

Communications. (*In Military law*) Connection between base and front.

Communications made to counsel. The immunity from disclosure which can be claimed by a client in respect of a communication made to his lawyer is not absolute but limited as prescribed by Section 126. Such a privilege can be claimed only by those clients who after committing a crime approach a lawyer for legal advice for defence. [Indian Evidence Act (1 of 1872), S. 126]

Communis error facit jus. (*Maxim*) Common error sometimes makes law. (*Black*)

The principle underlying the maxim 'communis error facit jus' is that 'the law so favours the public good, that it will in some cases permit a common error to pass for right.

Communis error non facit jus. A common error does not make law.

Communism. Communism of goods; a social system which makes the necessary provision for employment of capital, labour and distribution of profits.

Community. A society or body of people living in the same place, under the same law and regulations, and who have common rights and privileges; a corporation or body politic. *"The community"* means the public generally.

A body of people organised into a political, municipal or social unity. [IPC (45 of 1860), S. 12].

The word 'community' is wider than 'caste'— and 'backward communities' meant not only the castes—wherever they may be found but also other groups, classes and sections among the populace. *Indra Sawhney* v. *Union of India*, AIR 1993 SC 477, 552. [Constitution of India, Art. 16(4)]

In India a community is often organised on the basis of caste or religion. The word 'community' used in S. 123(3) has only to be confined to such an organisation which in effect divides the citizens of the country into groups sometimes opposed to one another. The word 'community' must be construed by reference to the words 'caste, race, and religion'. *Khilumal Topandas* v. *Arjundas Tulsidas,* AIR 1959 Raj 280, 283. [Representation of the People Act (43 of 1951), S. 123(3)]

The term 'community' cannot be confined to a religious community only.

"COMMUNITY" for the purposes of section 4 of Act 25 of 2013, 'community' in relation to railway authorities means passengers, staff and other authorised users of railways. [*Explanation* to section 4 of the Prohibition of Employment as Manual Scavengers & Their Rehabilitation Act, 2013 (25 of 2013)]

"Community mediator". Means a mediator for the purposes of conduct of community mediation under Chapter X. [Mediation Act, 2023 (32 of 2023), section 3(b)]

Community of assets. The sharing of ownership of matrimonial property, *e.g.;* the home and furniture, as an automatic consequence of marriage.

Community of interest. Term as applied to relation of joint adventure means interest common to both or all parties, that is, mixture or identity of interest in venture wherein each and all are reciprocally concerned and from which each and all derive material benefit and sustain a mutual responsibility. *Carboneau* v. *Peterson,* 1 Wash. 2d 347, 95 P. 23 1043, 1055.

Community : Society. Community in anything constitutes a *community*; a common interest, a common language, a common government, is the basis of that *community* which is formed by any number of individuals; the coming together of many and keeping together under given law and for given purposes constitutes a *society*; *societies* are either public or private according to the purpose: friends form *societies* for pleasure, persons form *societies* for business. The term *community* is appropriately applied to indefinite numbers, and *society* in cases where the number is restricted by the nature of the union.

Commutation. Alteration; change; exchange; substitution. (*Burrill*)

A substitution of a less thing for a greater, especially a substitution of one form of payment for another, or one payment for many, or a specific sum of money for conditional payments or allowances, *etc.*

The substitution of a lesser punishment for a greater one. [IPC (45 of 1860), S. 222]; substitution of a consolidated payment in place of payment in installments [Income-tax Act (43 of 1961), S. 10(10A)(i) and Workmen's Compensation Act (8 of 1923), S. 7]; change of one thing for another.

Commute. To substitute one punishment for another.

"Companies Act". Means the Companies Act, 2013 (18 of 2013) or any other previous company law as defined in clause (67) of section 2 of the said Act. [Company Secretaries Act, 1980 (56 of 1980), section 2(1)(b)]

Company. A company is a separate legal persona, and the fact that all the shares are owned by one person or a company has nothing to do with the existence of a separate company. *Vodafone International Holdings BV* v. *Union of India*, (2012) 6 SCC 613, para 105.

"COMPANY" means—

(i) any Indian company, or

(ii) any body corporate incorporated by or under the laws of a country outside India, or

(iii) any institution, association or body which is or was assessable or was assessed as a company for any assessment year under the Indian Income-tax Act, 1922 (11 of 1922), or which is or was assessable or was assessed under this Act as a company for any assessment year commencing on or before the 1st day of April, 1970, or

(iv) any institution, association or body, whether incorporated or not and whether Indian or non-Indian, which is declared by general or special order of the Board to be a company:

Provided that such institution, association or body shall be deemed to be a company only for such assessment year or assessment years (whether commencing before the 1st day of April, 1971, or on or after that date) as may be specified in the declaration. [Income-tax Act (43 of 1961), S. 2(17)]

"COMPANY" means any body corporate and includes a firm or other association of individuals. [Transplantation of Human Organs Act (42 of 1994), S. 21(a); Cable Television Networks (Regulation) Act (7 of 1995), S. 17 *Expl.* (a); National Environment Appellate Authority Act (22 of 1997), S. 20 *Expl.* (a); Foreign Exchange Management Act (42 of 1999), S. 42 *Expl.* and Semi-Conductor Integrated Circuit Layout-Design Act (37 of 2000), S. 63, *Expl.* (a)]

"COMPANY" means any body corporate, and includes—

(i) a firm; and

(ii) an association of persons or a body of individuals whether incorporated or not. [Insurance Act (41 of 1999), S. 105A, *Expl.* (9)]

"COMPANY means the Industrial Investment Bank of India Limited to be formed and registered under the Companies Act, 1956. [Industrial Reconstruction Bank Act, 1997 (7 of 1997), S. 2(b)]

"COMPANY" means the Neyveli Lignite Corporation Limited, a company incorporated and registered under the Companies Act, 1956 having its registered office at Neyveli-607801, South Arcot District, Tamil Nadu. [Neyveli Lignite Corporation Limited (Acquisition and Transfer of Power Transmission System) Act (56 of 1994), S. 2(e)]

"COMPANY" means "Indian Airlines Limited" or "Air India Limited" formed and registered under the Companies Act, 1956. [Air Corporations (Transfer of Undertakings and Repeal) Act (13 of 1994), S. 2(b)]

"COMPANY" means a company as defined in Section 3 of the Companies Act, 1956, and includes a foreign company within the meaning of Section 591 of that Act. [Coking Coal Mines (Nationalisation) Act (36 of 1972), S. 3(d) and Bankers' Books Evidence Act (18 of 1891), S. 2(1)]

"COMPANY" means—

(i) a company as defined in Section 3 of the Companies Act, 1956, other than a Government company referred to in clause (cc);

(ii) a society registered under the Societies Registration Act, 1860, or under any corresponding law for the time being in force in a state, other than a society referred to in clause (cc);

(iii) a co-operative society within the meaning of any law relating to a co-operative societies for the time being in force in any State, other than a co-operative society referred to in clause (cc). [Land Acquisition Act (1 of 1894), S. 3(e)]

A company as defined in Section 3 of the Companies Act (1 of 1956), including a foreign company within the meaning of Section 591 of that Act. Section 3(1)(*i*) of the Companies Act defines a 'company' as a company formed and registered under that Act, or a company formed and registered under any of the previous companies laws specified in Section 3(1)(ii) of that Act. [RBI Act (2 of 1934), S. 45-I(aa)]

The word 'company' imports an association of a number of individuals formed for some common purpose. Such an association may be incorporated (that is, a body corporate with perpetual succession and a common seal) or it may be unincorporated. An incorporated company is a legal person separate and distinct from the individual members of the company, whereas an unincorporated company has no such separate existence and is not in law distinguishable from its members. (HALSBURY, 4th Edn., Vol. 7, para 1, p. 11)

This word, apart from special definition in a particular statute, has no strictly technical meaning. It involves the ideas: (1) an association of persons too numerous to be described as a firm; (2) power of a member to transfer his interest without the consent of the other members.

A company according to the new socioeconomic thinking, is a social institution having duties and responsibilities towards the community in which it functions. *National Textile Workers' Union* v. *P.R. Ramakrishnan*, AIR 1983 SC 75, 82. [Companies Act (1 of 1956), S. 3]

A company incorporated by an Indian Law would be 'company'. Food Corporation of India created under S. 3(2) of the Food Corporation Act, 1964, is a 'company'. *State of Punjab* v. *Raja Ram*, AIR 1981 SC 1694, 1696. [Land Acquisition Act (1 of 1894), S. 3(e)]

Registered Co-operative Society comes within the meaning of 'Company'. *Principal Secretary to Govt. HMA & UD Department* v. *G. Adilakshmamma,* AIR 1989 AP 342, 346.

"COMPANY" a 'company' is not established under the Companies Act. A 'company' is incorporated and registered under the Companies Act. *Dalco Engineering Private Ltd.* v. *Shree Satish Prabhakar Padhye* : *Fancy Rehabilitation Trust* v. *UOI*, AIR 2010 SC 1576.

"COMPANY" means a company incorporated under this Act or under any previous company law. [S. 2(20) of the Companies Act, 2013 (18 of 2013)]

"COMPANY" for the removal of doubts, it is hereby declared that the 'company' shall include any limited liability partnership which has company as its partner for the purposes of section 25 of Act 38 of 1949. [*Explanation* to S. 25(1) of the Chartered Accountants Act, 1949 (38 of 1949) as inserted (w.e.f. 1-2-2012) by the Chartered Accountants (Amendment) Act, 2011 (3 of 2012)].

For purpose of this section "A COMPANY" means any body corporate and includes a firm, a trust, a cooperative society and other association of individuals. [Specified Bank Notes (Cessation of Liability) Act (2 of 2017), S. 8 *Explanation (a)*].

"COMPANY" means a company defined in sub-section (20) of Section 2 of the Act and includes 'corresponding new bank' as defined in sub-section (d) of Section 2 of the Banking Companies (Acquisition and Transfer of Undertaking) Act, 1970 (5 of 1970) and clause (b) of Section 2 of the Banking Companies (Acquisition and Transfer of Undertakings) Act, 1980 (40 of 1980) and 'subsidiary bank' as defined in clause (k) of Section 2 of State Bank of India (Subsidiary Bank) Act, 1959 (38 of 1959. [Investor Education and Protection Fund Authority (Accounting, Audit, Transfer and Refund) Rules, 2016, R. 2(1)(d) as substituted by Amending Rules, 2017]..

Company in which the public are substantially interested. A company is said to be a company in which the public are substantially interested—

(a) if it is a company owned by the Government or the Reserve Bank of India or in which not less than forty per cent of the shares are held (whether singly or taken together) by the Government or the Reserve Bank of India or a corporation owned by that bank; or

(aa) if it is a company which is registered under Section 25 of the Companies Act, 1956 (1 of 1956); or

(ab) if it is a company having no share capital and if, having regard to its objects, the nature and composition of its membership and other relevant considerations, it is declared by order of the Board to be a company in which the public are substantially interested:

Provided that such company shall be deemed to be a company in which the public are substantially interested only for such assessment year or assessment years (whether commencing before the 1st day of April, 1971, or on or after that date) as may be specified in the declaration; or

(ac) if it is a mutual benefit finance company, that is to say, a company which carries on, as its principal business, the business of acceptance of deposits from its members and which is declared by the Central Government under Section 620A of the Companies Act, 1956 (1 of 1956), to be a *Nidhi* or Mutual Benefit Society; or

(ad) if it is a company, wherein shares (not being shares entitled to a fixed rate of dividend whether with or without a further right to participate in profits) carrying not less than fifty per cent of the voting power have been allotted unconditionally to, or acquired unconditionally by, and were throughout the relevant previous year beneficially held by, one or more co-operative societies;

(b) if it is a company which is not a private company as defined in the Companies Act, 1956 (1 of 1956), and the conditions specified either in item (*A*) or in item (*B*) are fulfilled, namely:—

(A) shares in the company (not being shares entitled to a fixed rate of dividend whether with or without a further right to participate in profits) were, as on the last day of the relevant previous year, listed in a recognised stock exchange in India in accordance with the Securities Contracts (Regulation) Act, 1956 (42 of 1956), and any rules made thereunder;

(B) shares in the company (not being shares entitled to a fixed rate of dividend whether with or without a further right to participate in profits) carrying not less than fifty per cent of the voting power have been allotted unconditionally to, or acquired unconditionally by, and were throughout the relevant previous year beneficially held by—

(a) the Government, or

(b) a corporation established by a Central, State or Provincial Act, or

(c) any company to which this clause applies or any subsidiary company of such company if the whole of the share capital of such subsidiary company has been held by the parent company or by its nominees throughout the previous year.

Explanation.—In its application to an Indian company whose business consists mainly in the construction of ships or in the manufacture or processing of goods or in mining or in the generation or distribution of electricity or any other form of power, item (*B*) shall have effect as if for the words "not less than fifty per cent," the words "not less than forty per cent" had been substituted. [Income-tax Act (43 of 1961), S. 2(18)]

Company limited by guarantee. Means a company having the liability of its members limited by the memorandum to such amount as the members may respectively undertake to contribute to the assets of the company in the event of its being wound up. [S. 2(21) of the Companies Act, 2013 (18 of 2013); S.12(2)(b) of the Companies Act, 1956 (1 of 1956)]

Company limited by shares. Means a company having the liability of its members limited by the memorandum to the amount, if any, unpaid on the shares respectively held by them. [S. 2(22) of the Companies Act, 2013 (18 of 2013); S.12(2)(b) of the Companies Act, 1956 (1 of 1956)]

Company Liquidator. Means a person appointed by the Tribunal as the Company Liquidator in accordance with the provisions of section 275 for the winding up of a company under this Act

Company secretary. An officer of a company who deals with the running of its day to day and general administration.

"COMPANY SECRETARY" means a person who is a member of the Institute. [Company Secretaries Act 1980, S. 2(1)(c)]

"COMPANY SECRETARY" means a company secretary as defined in section 2(1)(c) of the Company Secretaries Act, 1980 (56 of 1980), who is appointed by a company to perform the functions of a company secretary under the Companies Act, 2013 (18 of 2013). [S. 2(24) of the Companies Act, 2013 (18 of 2013)]

Company secretary in practice. Save as otherwise provided in this Act, a member of the Institute shall be deemed "to be in practice" when, individually or in partnership with one or more members of the Institute in practice or in partnership with members of such other recognised professions as may be prescribed, he, in consideration of remuneration received or to be received,—

(a) engages himself in the practice of the profession of Company Secretaries to, or in relation to, any company; or

(b) offers to perform or performs services in relation to the promotion, forming incorporation, amalgamation, reconstruction, reorganiaation or winding up of companies; or

(c) offers to perform or performs such services as may be performed by—

(i) An authorized representative of a company with respect to filing, registering, presenting, attesting or verifying any documents (including forms, applications and returns) by or on behalf of the company,

(ii) A share transfer agent,

(iii) An issue house,

(iv) A share and stockbroker,

(v) A secretarial auditor or consultant,

(vi) An adviser to a company on management, including any legal or procedural matter falling under the Capital Issues (Control) Act, 1947 (29 of 1947), the Industries (Development and Regulation) Act, 1951 (65 of 1951), the Companies Act, Companies Act, 1956 (1 of 1956), the Securities Contracts (Regulation) Act, 1956 (42 of 1956), any of the rules or bye-laws made by a recognised stock exchange, the Monopolies and Restrictive Trade Practices Act, 1969 (54 of 1969), the Foreign Exchange Regulation Act, 1973

(46 of 1973), or under any other law for the time being in force,

(vii) issuing certificates on behalf of, or for the purposes of, a company; or

(d) holds himself out to the public as a Company Secretary in practice; or

(e) renders professional services or assistance with respect to matters of principle or detail relating to the practice of the profession of Company Secretaries; or

(f) renders such other services as, in the opinion of the Council, are or may be rendered by a Company Secretary in practice;

and the words "to be in practice" with their grammatical variations and cognate expressions, shall be construed accordingly. [Company Secretaries Act 1980, S. 2(2)]

"COMPANY SECRETARY IN PRACTICE" means a company secretary who is deemed to be in practice under section 2(2) of the Company Secretaries Act, 1980 (56 of 1980). [S. 2(25) of the Companies Act, 2013 (18 of 2013)]

Comparatives. "Comparatives" shall mean comparative figures for the preceding accounting period. [Companies (Indian Accounting Standards) Rules, 2015, rule 4(1), *Explanation 2*]

Compare. To mark the similarities and difference of. [CPC (5 of 1908), O. VII, R. 17(2)].

Compass. An instrument used in navigation, by the direction and assistance whereof vessels are steered to the most distant parts of the world.

Compassionate allowance. A "Compassionate allowance" is a voluntary bounty, and not income. (*Stroud*)

Compatriot. A fellow countryman. [Geneva Conventions Act (6 of 1960), 3rd. Sch., Art. 126].

Compel. To oblige; to force; to constrain. [IPC (45 of 1860), S. 94].

Compellable. One liable to be compelled. [Indian Contract Act (9 of 1872), S. 25(2)].

Compelled testimony. The expression "compelled testimony" means evidence procured not merely by physical threats or violence but by psychic torture, atmospheric pressure, environmental coercion, tiring interrogative prolixity, overbearing and intimidatory methods and the like. *Nandini Satpathy* v. *P. L. Dani*, AIR 1978 SC 1025, 1046. [Constitution of India, Art. 20(3)]

Compelled to give makes a distinction between those cases in which a witness voluntarily answers a question and those in which he is compelled to answer, and gives him a protection in the latter cases only. The insertion of those words shows that protection is afforded only to answers which a witness has objected to give or which he has asked to be excused from giving, and which is given when he has been so compelled by the Court to give. [Indian Evidence Act (1 of 1872), S. 132, *Proviso*]

Unless a person objects to any question the answer, to which is likely to criminate him, he cannot be said to have been compelled to give such answer within S. 132, proviso of the Indian Evidence Act (1 of 1872).

Giving evidence is a matter of duty and not of compulsion and the duty cannot be treated as compulsion within the meaning of the proviso. The main provisions lays down that if a witness begs to be excused from answering a question on the particular ground, his prayer shall be rejected. The proviso comes into operation after the prayer of the witness to be excused is rejected and he is made to answer the question; that is the occasion when he can be said to be compelled to answer it. The compulsion emanates from the presiding officer and not by operation of any law.

Compensation. "COMPENSATION" means any compensation paid, whether in cash or in kind, in respect of any immovable property in West Pakistan belonging to a displaced person under any general scheme arrived at in this behalf between the Government of India and the Government of Pakistan or framed by the Government of India. [Displaced Persons (Debt Adjustment) Act (70 of 1951), S. 2(3)]

"Compensation" means compensation as provided under Chapter VII. [Code on Social Security, 2020 (36 of 2020), section 2(15)]

An act which a Court orders to be done, or money which a Court orders to be paid, by a person whose acts or omissions have caused loss or injury to another in order that thereby the person damnified may receive equal value for his loss, or be made whole in respect of his injury; remuneration or satisfaction for injury or damage of every description; remuneration for loss of time, necessary expenditures, and for permanent disability if such be the result; remuneration for the injury directly and proximately caused by a breach of contract or duty; remuneration or wages given to an employee or officer. (*Black; Cyc. Law. Dict. Ame. Cyc.*)

The word "compensation" is the general term used also in the Indian Contract Act (9 of 1872), S. 73 to denote the payment which a party is entitled to claim on account of loss or damage arising from the breach of contract. It is used in the same sense in Art. 54, 55 of the Limitation Act (36 of 1963).

The word 'compensation' means anything given to make things equivalent, a thing given or to make amends for loss, recompense, remuneration or pay; it need not necessarily be in terms of money. *Divisional controller KSRTC* v. *Mahadeva Shetty,* (2003) 7 SCC 197, para 11.

Normally, compensation means the full market value of the property as existing on the relevant date exclusive of future potentiality. *Mohd. Amir* v. *Nagar Mahapalika Lucknow,* AIR 1965 All 599, 603. [Constitution of India, Art. 31-A].

The word 'compensation' cannot include the amount of interest which a person may be otherwise entitled to as of right on the amount of compensation.

The word 'compensation' includes money which has become due to a party after the contract has been breached.

A return for a loss or damage sustained; money payable for the loss sustained. [Workmen's Compensation Act (8 of 1923), S. 2(1)(c) and T.P. Act (4 of 1882), S. 73(2)].

COMPENSATION, DAMAGES—DISTINCTION. The expression compensation is not ordinarily used as an equivalent to damages, although compensation may often have to be measured by the same rule as damages in an action for a breach. The term compensation signifies that which is given in recompense, an equivalent rendered; damages, on the other hand, constitute the sum of money claimed or adjudged to be paid in compensation for loss or injury sustained.

COMPENSATION (*in respect of Land Acquisition*) is the word usually applied by lawyers to the satisfaction to be made to persons whose rights are interfered with or whose property is taken away in the exercise of statutory powers.

Compensation means any thing given to make things equivalent, a thing given to or to make amends for loss, recompense, remuneration or pay. It need not therefore necessarily be in terms of money. *State of Gujarat* v. *Shantilal Mangal Das*, AIR 1969 SC 634 at p. 644.

The expression 'compensation' means 'just equivalent of what the owner has been deprived of.' *Jeejeebhoy* v. *Asst. Collector, Thana*, AIR 1965 SC 1069, 1100. [Constitution of India, Art. 31(2) (*Omitted*)]

The word 'compensation' connotes equivalency, which adequately remunerates for a loss or deprivation, or for a service rendered, though under a statutory definition, it may indicate not what constitutes, but what by the Legislature is treated as equivalent. *CIT* v. *Sham Lal Narula,* AIR 1963 Punj 411, 414. [Land Acquisition Act (1 of 1894), S. 34]

The word 'compensation' under S. 8(1)(e) encompasses within its ambit the payment of solatium under the given facts and circumstances of the case. *Mancheddudin* v. *Collector, Hyderabad,* AIR 1984 AP 217, 225. [Requisitioning and Acquisition of Immovable Property Act (30 of 1952), S. 8(1)(e)]

Compensation as understood under the law of Eminent Domain, necessarily involves the idea of 'just compensation' carrying with it the following attributes: (1) market value payable on the footing of compulsory sale; (2) determination of compensation by a judicial tribunal, (3) payment of compensation (a) in cash and (b) on the date when possession is taken unless any other method and manner of payment is consented to by the dispossessed proprietor.

COMPENSATION PAYABLE FOR THE LAND. The words 'the compensation payable for the land' in S. 11 of the Land Acquisition Act (1 of 1894), cannot be paraphrased into 'compensation for those interests in the land which are not vested in the Government.'

Compensation : Damages. Compensation signifies that which is given in recompense, an equivalent rendered. Damages, on the other hand; constitute the sum of money claimed or adjudged to be paid in compensation for loss or injury sustained; the value estimated in money, of something lost or withheld. The term compensation etymologically suggest the image of balancing one thing against another; its primary signification is equivalence, and the secondary and more common meaning is something given or obtained as an equivalent…" *Jailabdeen* v. *Mohammed Basheer,* AIR 1992 Ker 31 (Page 35).

The expression compensation is not ordinarily used as an equivalent to damages, although compensation may often have to be measured by the same rule as damages in an action for a breach. The term compensation as pointed out in the Oxford Dictionary, signifies that which is given in recompense, an equivalent rendered; damages, on the other hand, constitute the sum of money claimed or adjudged to be paid in compensation for loss or injury sustained; The value estimated in money, of something lost or withheld. *Md. Mozaharal Ahmad* v. *Md Azimaddin,* AIR 1923 Cal 507; Y. *S Vivekananda Reddy* v. *Govt. of A.P.*, AIR 1996 AP 403, 412.

Compensation or **consideration.** For the purposes of this clause, the expression "COMPENSATION OR CONSIDERATION" includes the compensation or consideration enhanced or further enhanced by any Court, tribunal or other authority." [Income-tax Act (43 of 1961), S. 10(37) *Expln. (Inserted by Finance Act (23 of 2004), S. 5(h)*]

Compensation order. Means an order granted in terms of section 22 of Act 43 of 2005. [S. 2(c) of the Protection of Women from Domestic Violence Act, 2005 (43 of 2005)]

Compensatory. Compensating; giving compensation. [CPC (5 of 1908), S. 35A].

Compensatory afforestation. "Compensatory Afforestation" means afforestation done in lieu of the diversion of forest land for non-forestry use under the Forest (Conservation) Act, 1980 (69 of 1980). [Compensatory Afforestation Fund Act (38 of 2016), S. 2(d)].

Compensatory damages. Damages equivalent to the actual loss in respect to which they are allowed.

Compensatory tax. A working test for deciding whether a tax is compensatory or not is to enquire whether the trades people are having the use of certain facilities for the better conduct of their business and paying not patently much more than what is required for providing the facilities. It would be impossible to judge the compensatory nature of a tax by a meticulous test, and in the nature of things that cannot be done. *Automobile Transport* (*Rajasthan*) *Ltd* v. *State of Rajasthan*, AIR 1962 SC 1406, 1425. [Constitution of India, Arts. 301, 304(b)]

Competence. Sufficiency of qualification; legal capacity.

Competence of Court. Juridically speaking, the concept of jurisdiction of a Court comprehends (i) pecuniary jurisdiction. (ii) territorial jurisdiction, and (iii) jurisdiction of the subject-matter. *Church of South India Trust Association* v. *Telugu Church Council,* AIR 1996 SC 987.

Competence of Court means its jurisdiction.

Competency. Intelligence of one sufficient to understand the act one is performing.

Competency : Credibility—distinction. *Competency* differs from *credibility*. The *former* is a question which arises before considering the evidence given by the witness; the *latter* concerns the degree of credit to be given to his testimony. The *former* denotes the personal qualification of the witness; the *latter* his veracity. A witness may be competent, and yet give incredible testimony; he may be incompetent, and yet his evidence, if received, be perfectly credible. *Competency* is for the Court; *credibility* for the jury. Yet in some cases the term '*credible*' is used as an equivalent for '*competent*'. In law of contracts, of legal age without mental disability or incapacity.

Competency of witness. It means the evidence of the witness called for is receivable.

In the law of evidence, the presence of those characteristics, or the absence of those disabilities, which render a witness legally fit and qualified to give testimony in a Court of justice; applied, in the same sense, to documents or other written evidence. In law of contracts, the legal age without mental disability or incapacity.

Competent. Answering to all requirements; adequate; sufficient; suitable; capable; legally qualified as competent Court; competent judge; competent witness; fit; fitness or capability of performing the duties of the office.

The term 'competent' in Ss. 15, 24, CPC, (5 of 1908), means 'having jurisdiction, that is, with reference to the pecuniary value and nature of the suits which the Court has power to try.

Having competence, legally sufficient. [T.P. Act (4 of 1882), S. 7].

Competent authority. The expression "Competent authority" in R. 4(2), O. XXXII, CPC (5 of 1908), does not include a Hindu father appointing a person to act as a guardian to his son after his death.

"COMPETENT AUTHORITY" means any person or authority authorised by the Central Government, by notification in the Official Gazette, to perform the functions of the competent authority for such area as may be specified in the notification. [National Highways Act (48 of 1956), S. 3(a)]

"COMPETENT AUTHORITY" means the Reserve Bank of India or such other authority as is authorised under any law for the time being in force for regulating payments and dealings in foreign exchange. [Income-tax Act (43 of 1961), S. 80 QQB, *Expln.* (c)]

"COMPETENT AUTHORITY" means any authority authorised by the Central Government by notification in the Official Gazette to perform all or any of the functions of the competent authority under this Act. [Cine-Workers & Cinema Theatre Workers (Regulation of Employment) Act (50 of 1981), S. 2(d)]

For the purposes of this section, "COMPETENT AUTHORITY" means a Commissioner, a Director, a Principal Commissioner of Income-tax or a Principal Director of Income-tax as defined in clause (*16*), clause (*21*), clause (*34B*) and clause (*34C*), respectively, of section 2 of the Income-tax Act, 1961 (43 of 1961). [Prohibition of Benami Property Transactions Act (45 of 1988), section 55, *Expln.*]"COMPETENT AUTHORITY" means,—

(i) a Secretary in the Delhi Administration, or

(ii) the Vice-Chairman of the Delhi Development Authority, or

(iii) the Land and Development Officer of the Central Government.

who may be authorised by the Administrator, by notification in the Official Gazette, to perform the functions of the competent authority under this Act. [Delhi Apartment Ownership Act (58 of 1986), S. 2(m)]

"COMPETENT AUTHORITY" means any person or authority authorised by the Central Government, by notification in the Official Gazette, to perform the functions of the competent authority under this Act. [Multimodal Transportations of Goods Act (28 of 1993), S. 2(b)]

"COMPETENT AUTHORITY" means any person or authority appointed by the State Government, by notification in the Official Gazette, to exercise and perform all or any of the powers and functions of the competent authority under this Act and the rules made thereunder. [Punjab Apartment and Property Regulation Act (14 of 1995), S. 2(e)]

"COMPETENT AUTHORITY" means the civil authority appointed under sub-paragraph (2) of paragraph 2 of the Foreigners Order, 1948 made under the Foreigners Act, 1946 or any other officer notified by the Central Government in this behalf. [Immigration (Carriers Liability) Act (52 of 2000), S. 2(1)(b)]

"COMPETENT AUTHORITY" means in relation to children in need of care and protection a Committee and in relation to juveniles in conflict with law a

Board. [Juvenile Justice (Care and Protection of Children) Act (56 of 2000), S. 2(g)]

"COMPETENT AUTHORITY" in relation to—(i) the Prime Minister, means the House of the People; (ii) a member of the Council of Ministers, means the Prime Minister; (iii) a member of Parliament other than a Minister, means—(A) in the case of a member of the Council of States, the Chairman of the Council; and (B) in the case of a member of the House of the People, the Speaker of the House; (iv) an officer in the Ministry or Department of the Central Government, means the Minister in charge of the Ministry or Department under which the officer is serving; (v) a chairperson or members of any body or Board or corporation or authority or company or society or autonomous body (by whatever name called) established or constituted under any Act of Parliament or wholly or partly financed by the Central Government or controlled by it, means the Minister in charge of the administrative Ministry of such body or Board or corporation or authority or company or society or autonomous body; (vi) an officer of any body or Board or corporation or authority or company or society or autonomous body (by whatever name called) established or constituted under any Act of Parliament or wholly or partly financed by the Central Government or controlled by it, means the head of such body or Board or corporation or authority or company or society or autonomous body; (vii) in any other case not falling under sub-clauses (i) to (vi) above, means such Department or authority as the Central Government may, by notification, specify: *Provided* that if any person referred to in sub-clause (v) or sub-clause (vi) is also a member of Parliament, then, the competent authority shall be—(A) in case such member is a member of the Council of States, the Chairman of the Council; and (B) in case such member is a member of the House of the People, the Speaker of the House. [S. 2(1)(c) of the Lokpal & Lokayuktas Act, 2013 (1 of 2014)]

Competent Court. A civil or other Court having jurisdiction in the matter before it. In interpreting the meaning of "Competent Court" for the purposes of *res judicata*, it is essential to take notice of the pecuniary limit of jurisdiction.

The expression 'competent Court' in S. 24 must be taken as referring to pecuniary jurisdiction and not territorial jurisdiction. [CPC (5 of 1908), S. 24]

A Court having jurisdiction over the matter. [Indian Evidence Act (1 of 1872), S. 41].

Competent Government. Means the Central Government in respect of a Generating Company wholly or partly owned by it and in all other cases the Government of the State in which the generating station of a Generating Company is located or proposed to be located. [Electricity (Supply) Act (54 of 1948), S. 2(3A)])] [Now repealed & replaced by Act 36 of 2003]

Competent jurisdiction. The phrase 'competent jurisdiction' refers to pecuniary jurisdiction only and not jurisdiction over the subject-matter of the suit. [CPC (5 of 1908), 39(3) (as amended by U.P. Act 31 of 1978)]

Competent to contract. The use of the expression in S. 11 of the Indian Contract Act (9 of 1872), requiring that all contracting parties should be "competent to contract", has the effect of rendering the contracts entered into by incompetent person not voidable but void.

Every person is competent to contract who is of the age of majority according to the law to which he is subject, and who is of sound mind and is not disqualified from contracting by any law to which he is subject. [Indian Contract Act (9 of 1872), S. 11]

Competent to investigate. [in S. 157, Indian Evidence Act (1 of 1872)] Refers to the persons competent to hold the Police investigation into an alleged offence under Chapter XII of the Criminal Procedure Code 1973 (2 of 1974).

Competent to remove him from his office. When a person was appointed by the Chief Commissioner, the authority competent to remove him from his office would, by virtue of Art. 311 of the Constitution, be not one subordinate to the Chief Commissioner. *Brij Nath Prasad Tripathi* v. *State,* AIR 1956 Bho 36, 39. [Constitution of India, Art. 311]

Competent to try. The expression 'competent to try' refers to pecuniary jurisdiction and not territorial jurisdiction. *Mulraj Doshi* v. *Gangadhar Singhania,* AIR 1982 Ori 191, 194. [CPC (5 of 1908), S. 24(1)(a)]

Competent to try or dispose of the same. The expression 'competent to try or dispose of the same' means that the Court to which the suit, appeal or other proceeding could be transferred must be competent to try or dispose of the case in the sense that in addition to precuniary jurisdiction, it should have territorial jurisdiction. [CPC (5 of 1908), S. 24(1)(b)(ii)]

Competent witness. All persons shall be competent to testify unless the Court considers that they are prevented from understanding the questions put to them, or from giving rational answers to those questions, by tender years, extreme old age, disease, whether of body or mind, or any other cause of the same kind.

Explanation.—A lunatic is not incompetent to testify, unless he is prevented by his lunacy from understanding the questions put to him and giving rational answers to them. [Indian Evidence Act (1 of 1872), S. 118]

In all civil proceedings the parties to the suit, and the husband or wife of any party to the suit, shall be competent witnesses. In criminal proceedings against any person, the husband or wife of such person, respectively, shall be competent witness. [Indian Evidence Act (1 of 1872), S. 120]

Competing. Striving against each other. [Indian Partnership Act (9 of 1932), S. 16(b)].

Competition. Striving against each other for settling something desired or doing something desired or doing something in the best manner possible; a trial of ability. [Indian Trusts Act (2 of 1882), S. 15, ill. (d)].

Compilation. A bringing together of preexisting statues in the form in which they were enacted, with the removal of sections which have been repealed and the substitution of amendments in an arrangement designed to facilitate their use. A literary production composed of the works or selected extracts of others and arranged in methodical manner. (*Black*)

Complain. To express grief *etc.* [IPC (45 of 1860), S. 95]; to make a formal accusation in a Court of law.

Complainant. One who applies to the Courts for legal redress; one who files complaint; statement that one is aggrieved.

"Complainant". Means—

(i) a consumer; or

(ii) any voluntary consumer association registered under any law for the time being in force; or

(iii) the Central Government or any State Government; or

(iv) the Central Authority; or

(v) one or more consumers, where there are numerous consumers having the same interest; or

(vi) in case of death of a consumer, his legal heir or legal representative; or

(vii) in case of a consumer being a minor, his parent or legal guardian. [Consumer Protection Act, 2019 (35 of 2019), section 2(5)]

A person who makes a formal accusation in a Court of law. [CrPC 1973 (2 of 1974), S. 170(2)].

Complainant is one who makes an allegation or accusation or a charge in order to prosecute a person. A body corporate can be a complainant.

It can only mean person examined as complainant under S. 200, CrPC 1973 (2 of 1974). No other person can be deemed to be a complainant however much he may be interested in the prosecution. [CrPC 1973 (2 of 1974), S. 200]

Complaint. Means the allegation made orally or in writing to a Magistrate, with a view to his taking action under this Code, that some person, whether known or unknown, has committed an offence, but it does not include the report of a police-officer. [CrPC 1973 (2 of 1974), S. 4] [Now (w.e.f. 1-7-2024) repealed & replaced by Bharatiya Nagarik Suraksha Sanhita, 2023 (46 of 2023)]

"Complaint" means any allegation made orally or in writing to a Magistrate, with a view to his taking action under this Sanhita, that some person, whether known or unknown, has committed an offence, but does not include a police report.

Explanation.—A report made by a police officer in a case which discloses, after investigation, the commission of a non-cognizable offence shall be deemed to be a complaint; and the police officer by whom such report is made shall be deemed to be the complainant. [(w.e.f. 1-7-2024) Bharatiya Nagarik Suraksha Sanhita, 2023 (46 of 2023), section 2(1)(h)]

"COMPLAINT" means any allegation in writing made by a complainant that—

(i) as a result of any unfair trade practice adopted by any trader, the complainant has suffered loss or damage;

(ii) the goods mentioned in the complaint suffer from one or more defects;

(iii) the services mentioned in the complaint suffer from deficiency in any respect;

(iv) a trader has charged for the goods mentioned in the complaint a price in excess of the price fixed by or under any law for the time being in force or displayed on the goods or any package containing such goods, with a view to obtaining any relief provided by or under this Act. [Consumer Protection Act (68 of (1986), S. 2(1)(c)] [Now repealed & replaced by Act 35 of 2019]

"complaint" means any allegation in writing, made by a complainant for obtaining any relief provided by or under this Act, that—

(i) an unfair contract or unfair trade practice or a restrictive trade practice has been adopted by any trader or service provider;

(ii) the goods bought by him or agreed to be bought by him suffer from one or more defects;

(iii) the services hired or availed of or agreed to be hired or availed of by him suffer from any deficiency;

(iv) a trader or a service provider, as the case may be, has charged for the goods or for the services mentioned in the complaint, a price in excess of the price—

(a) fixed by or under any law for the time being in force; or

(b) displayed on the goods or any package containing such goods; or

(c) displayed on the price list exhibited by him by or under any law for the time being in force; or

(d) agreed between the parties;

(v) the goods, which are hazardous to life and safety when used, are being offered for sale to the public—

(a) in contravention of standards relating to safety of such goods as required to be complied with, by or under any law for the time being in force;

(b) where the trader knows that the goods so offered are unsafe to the public;

(vi) the services which are hazardous or likely to be hazardous to life and safety of the public when used, are being offered by a person who provides any service and who knows it to be injurious to life and safety;

(vii) a claim for product liability action lies against the product manufacturer, product seller or product service provider, as the case may be. [Consumer Protection Act, 2019 (35 of 2019), section 2(6)]

The word 'complaint' includes even an oral allegation. However, there must be an allegation which *prima facie* discloses the commission of an offence with the necessary facts for the Magistrate to take action. Section 190(1)(a) makes it necessary that the alleged facts must disclose the commission of an offence. *Bhimappa Bassappa Bhu Sannavar* v. *Laxman Shivarayappa Samagouda,* AIR 1970 SC 1153. [CrPC, 1973 (2 of 1974), S. 190]

The essence of the complaint is the statement of facts relied upon as constituting the offence. It is sufficient that the complainant shall state the true facts in his own language, and it is for the magistrate to apply the law to those facts.

It is a form of legal process which consists of a formal allegation or charge against a party, made or presented to the appropriate Court or officer, as for a wrong done or a crime committed; in the latter case generally under oath.

COMPLAINT is an allegation that a wrong has been done or a grievance suffered. This term is most generally used in law with reference to criminal Courts to describe the mode in which proceedings are to be instituted. The complaint need not be either in writing or on oath, unless required to be so by the particular enactment upon which it is framed.

A "*complaint*" is an allegation that some person has committed an offence and "an offence" is an act or omission made punishable by any law for the time being in force. An application under S. 107, CrPC (2 of 1974), is not a complaint where there is merely an allegation that a breach of the peace is likely.

The action of complaining; an utterance of grievance. [IPC (45 of 1860), Ss. 95 and 499, ill to 8th excep.]; a formal accusation in a Court of law. [CrPC 1973 (2 of 1974), S. 2(d)]; an ailment or disease of the body.

'COMPLAINT' DISTINGUISHED FROM 'INFORMATION'. A letter to a Magistrate informing him that a certain person used insulting language to the writer and asking the Magistrate to take action is a complaint.

Deposition made to a Magistrate in course of a trial is not a complaint.

A statement made by a person at a Police enquiry, which results in the institution of criminal proceedings against another, is not a 'complaint' made by him within the meaning of S. 250, CrPC 1973 (2 of 1974), when the case is not instituted either on his complaint or on information given by him as a result of enquiry by the Police.

"COMPLAINT" means a complaint, made in such form as may be prescribed, alleging that a public servant has committed an offence punishable under the Prevention of Corruption Act, 1988 (49 of 1988). [S. 2(1)(e) of the Lokpal & Lokayuktas Act, 2013 (1 of 2014)]

COMPLAINT, ACCUSATION. Both these terms are employed in regard to the conduct of others, but a *complaint* is mostly made in matters that personally affect the complainant; an *accusation* is made of matters in general but especially those of a moral nature. A *complaint* is made for the sake of obtaining redress; an *accusation* is made for the sake of ascertaining a fact or bringing to punishment. A *complaint* may be frivolous; an *accusation* false.

Complete. To finish; accomplish that which one starts out to do. Full; entire. (*Black*)

With no part, item or element lacking [Indian Contract Act (9 of 1872), S. 4]; [Sale of Goods Act (3 of 1930), S. 64(2)]; brought to an end; to accomplish.

Complete justice. Articles 32, 141 and 142 are couched in wide and elastic terms to enable the SC to declare law and to pass such orders or give such directions as are necessary for doing complete justice. [Constitution of India, Art. 142].

The phrase 'complete justice' engrafted in Article 142(1) of the constitution is the word of width couched with elasticity to meet myriad situations created by human ingenuity or cause or result of operation of statute law declared under Articles, 32, 136 and 141 of the constitution and cannot be cribbed or cabined within any limitations or phraseology. It is for the Apex Court to exercise its power to do complete justice or prevent injustice arising from the exigencies of the cause or matter before it. *Ashok Kumar Gupta* v. *State of U.P.,* (1997) 5 SCC 201, para 60. [Constitution of India, Art. 142(1)]

Complete specification. Complete specification is an elaborate description of the invention which completely describes the invention. (*Patents*)

Completion. The action of making complete. [T.P. Act (4 of 1882), S. 118]; becoming complete. [Sale of Goods Act (3 of 1930), S. 64(2)]; accomplishment. [CrPC 1973 (2 of 1974), S. 116(3)].

Complexity. Intricacy.

Compliance. Acting in accordance with a desire, condition *etc.* [T.P. Act (4 of 1882), S. 63A(2)]; be in agreement with.

"Compliance officer". Means a person of responsibility from the point of presence; designated as such and charged with the responsibility of monitoring compliance by the point of presence of the provisions of the Act or the rules or the regulations made or notifications, guidelines, circulars or instructions issued by the Authority thereunder. [Pension Fund Regulatory and Development Authority (Point of Presence) Regulations, 2018, Regn. 2(1)(e)].

Complicity. The state of being an accomplice in a crime. [Indian Evidence Act (1 of 1872), S. 10 ill.].

Comply with. To act in accordance with a request, demand, order, rule *etc.* [T.P. Act (4 of 1882), S. 26].

Component. "COMPONENTS" means lead bearing components of a lead acid battery. [Batteries (Management and Handling) Rules, 2001, R. 2(g)].

For an article to be called a component part, it is not necessary that even if it becomes part of another article, it should still retain its identity. All that is necessary to make an article a component part is that it goes into the composition of another article. If an article is an element in the composition of another article made out of it, such an article may well be described as a component part of another article. It may be that a final product made may be in the nature of a compound in which case, the elements forming component parts may not be capable of any more separate identification. Equally, it may be that when a machinery is assembled out of several parts forming that machinery, those machineries, those parts, even after their being filled may retain their individuality or identity. Encyclopedic Law Lexicon, Vol. 2008-09 Edn., by Justice C.K. Thakkar as cited in *Saraswati Sugar Mills* v. *Commissioner of Central Excise, Delhi-III*, (2014) 15 SCC 625, para 24.

"Component" means a "constituent part". Oxford Advanced Learner's Dictionary vol. 1 International Edn, as cited in *Saraswati Sugar Mills* v. *Commissioner of Central Excise, Delhi-III*, (2014) 15 SCC 625, para 23.

Component part of an article is an integral part necessary to the constitution of the whole article and without it, the article will not be complete. *Saraswati Sugar Mills* v. *Commissioner of Central Excise, Delhi-III*, (2014) 15 SCC 625, para 27.

Constituents. [Drugs and Cosmetics Act (23 of 1940), S. 3]; [Air Force Act (45 of 1950), S. 4(iii)].

Component parts. 'Component part' means a constituent part. Paper core is necessary for rewinding of paper and would come within the purview of the expression 'any process incidental or ancillary to the completion of a manufactured product' and for the same reason it is constituent part of paper and falls within the term 'component parts'. *Star Paper Mills Ltd.* v. *Collector, Central Excise, Meerut*, AIR 1988 SC 2066, 2071. [Central Excises and Salt Act (1 of 1944), S. 2(f), Sch. 1, item 68, Notification No. 201/79, dt. 4-6-79, as amended by Notification No.-105/82, dt. 28-2-1982]

Compos mentis. Of sound mind. "One qualified legally to execute a deed." (*Latin for Lawyer's*)

One who has use and control over one's own mental faculties.

Compose. To make up; construct of several elements.

Composer. 'Composer', in relation to a musical work, means the person who composes the music regardless of whether he records it in any form of graphical notation. [The Copyright Act, 1957, S. 2(ffa)].

Composing the Court, Judges. Judges, who at the time of hearing compose the Court. [CrPC 1973 (2 of 1974), S. 401(1)].

Composite insurer. Means an insurer carrying on in addition to controlled business any other kind of insurance business. [Life Insurance Corporation Act (31 of 1956), S. 2(2)]

Composite negligence. 'Composite negligence' refers to the negligence on the part of two or more persons. Where a person is injured as a result of negligence on the part of two or more wrongdoers, it is said that the person was injured on account of the 'composite negligence' of those wrongdoers. [*T.O. Anthony* v. *Karvaran,* (2008) 3 SCC 748, 750, para 6]

Composite offence. Means an act or conduct of a person occurred, wholly or in part, in a foreign State or in India but its effects or intended effects, taken as a whole, would constitute an extradition offence in India or in a foreign State, as the case may be. [Extradition Act (34 of 1962), S. 2(a)]

Composite property. Means any property which, or any property in which an interest, has been declared to be evacuee property, or has vested in the Custodian, under the Administration of Evacuee Property Act, 1950 and—

(i) in which the interest of the evacuee consists of an undivided share of the property held by him as a co-sharer or partner of any other person not being an evacuee; or

(ii) in which the interest of the evacuee is subject to mortgage in any form in favour of a person, not being an evacuee; or

(iii) in which the interest of a person, not being an evacuee, is subject to mortgage in any form in favour of an evacuee; or

(iv) in which an evacuee has such other interest jointly with any other person, not being an evacuee, as may be notified by the Central Government in the Official Gazette. [Evacuee Interest (Separation) Act (64 of 1951), S. 2(d)]

Composite Supply. "Composite supply" means a supply made by a taxable person to a recipient consisting of two or more taxable supplies of goods or services or both, or any combination thereof, which are naturally bundled and supplied in conjunction with each other in the ordinary course of business, one of which is a principal supply; Illustration.— Where goods are packed and transported with insurance, the supply of goods, packing materials, transport and insurance is a composite supply and supply of goods is a principal supply [The Central Goods and Services Tax Act, 2017 (12 of 2017), S. 2(30)]

Composite unit. A unit made of diverse elements. [Employees' Provident Funds and Miscellaneous Provisions Act (19 of 1952), Sch. I, item 4].

Composition. A written or literary work invented and set in order; a mixture or chemical combination of materials (*Black*); agreement or compromise between debtor and creditor.

A mixture or chemical combination of materials [IPC (45 of 1860), S. 244]; formation; construction [Aligarh Muslim University Act (40 of 1920), S. 24(1)]; a compounding of some claim or liability, especially an agreement by which a creditor accepts part of a debt in satisfaction from an insolvent debtor [Companies Act (1 of 1956), S. 267(b)]; compounding an offence; mutual settlement or agreement. [Presidency-towns Insolvency Act (3 of 1909), S. 28(1)].

Composition : Accord. "Composition" should be distinguished from "accord." The latter properly denotes an arrangement between a debtor and a single creditor for a discharge of the obligation by a part payment or on different terms. The former designates an arrangement between a debtor and the whole body of his creditors (or at least a considerable proportion of them) for the liquidation of their claims by the dividend offered.

Composition-deed. The expression "composition-deed" in S. 17(2)(*i*), Registration Act (16 of 1908), denotes a transaction entered into by a debtor, insolvent or in embarrassed circumstances, with his creditors with the object of paying the latter a composition upon their claims.

A composition deed does not mean any deed composing differences but means a deed by which a debtor compounds with his creditors.

A deed by which a debtor compounds with his creditor. [Indian Stamp Act (2 of 1899), Sch. I. item 12].

Composting. Means a controlled process involving microbial decomposition of organic matter. [Rule 2(vi) of the Municipal solid Wastes (Management and handling) Rules, 2000, R. 2(vi)]

Compound. Settle by mutual concession; to '*compound*' a *debt*, is to abate a part on receiving the residue.

To forbear from prosecution for consideration or any private motive. [CrPC 1973 (2 of 1974), S. 320]; to settle with a creditor [Income-tax Act (43 of 1961), S. 279(2)]; [Presidency-towns Insolvency Act (3 of 1909), S. 44(2)]; [Now repealed by Act 31 of 2016] with broken bone exposed; a mixture or chemical combination of materials [Factories Act (63 of 1948), Sch. I, Entry 1].

Compound interest. Interest computed in a manner that the unpaid interest is periodically added to the principal, besides the original capital and further interest is calculated on the total amount. [Indian Trusts Act (2 of 1882), S. 23(e)].

Compound offence. Offence committed, when more than one crime is committed in the same transaction.

Compoundable. Capable of being compounded.

Compoundable offence. An offence which is capable of being compounded. [CrPC 1973 (2 of 1974), S. 320(3)].

It is offence which the law allows to be compounded privately between the parties.

Compounding. Arranging; coming to terms; condone for money; arranging with his creditor to the satisfaction.

Compounding a crime. The making by one directly injured by the commission of a crime of an agreement not to inform against or prosecute the offender in return for a reward, bribe, or reparation for the injury. (*Ballentine's Law Dictionary, 3rd Edn.*)

Compounding authority. The persons authorised by the Central Government under sub-section (1) of Section 15 of the Act, namely:

(a) an officer of the Enforcement Directorate not below the rank of Deputy Director or Deputy Legal Advisor (DLA).

(b) an officer of the Reserve Bank of India not below the rank of Assistant General Manager. [Foreign Exchange (Compounding Proceedings) Rules, 2000, Rule 3].

Compounding of offences. Forbearing from prosecution of the offence for consideration or any private motive. Compounding of less serious offences can be permitted by Court. See CrPC 1973 (2 of 1974), S. 320.

Comprehensive policy. The expression 'comprehensive policy' means that apart from the loss or damage suffered to the vehicle, it also assumes responsibility for third party liability.

Comprise. To include; to contain. [Epidemic Diseases Act (3 of 1897), S. 1(2)].

Comprised in. Included in. [T.P. Act (4 of 1882), S. 1].

Compromise. To adjust by mutual concession; to settle without resort to the law; to compound. (*As noun*) An "adjustment of matters in dispute by mutual concessions." (*Abbott*)

The expression 'compromise' means settlement of differences by mutual concessions. It is an agreement reached by adjustment of conflicting or opposing claims by reciprocal modification of demands. [*State of Punjab* v. *Ganpat Raj*, (2006) 8 SCC 364 : AIR 2006 SC 3089 as cited in *Panna Lal Prasad* v. *Manoj Kumar Gupta*, AIR 2012 Pat 115, para 12].

"An agreement between two or more persons, who, to avoid a law suit, amicably settle their differences, on such terms as they can agree upon." (*Bouvier*)

The arrangement of a dispute by concessions on both sides; an adjustment between the parties to a dispute ending in a settlement; a joint promise or agreement made by contending parties to abide by the terms and conditions agreed. [Registration Act (16 of 1908), S. 17(2)(vi)].

A compromise is always bilateral and means a mutual adjustment. A compromise means agreement or adjustment for the settlement of a controversy by mutual concessions, often involving partial surrender. [CPC (5 of 1908), O. XXIII, R. 3]

Compromise : Arrangement. "Compromise" is an expression which implies the existence of a dispute such as relating to rights, which it seeks to settle, but the word "arrangement" is a term of very wide import, and its meaning is not to be limited to something analogous to a compromise. All modes of reorganizing the share capital, takeover of shares of one company by another including interference with preferential and other special rights attached to shares can properly form part of an arrangement with members. *Hindustan Commercial Bank Ltd.* v. *Hindustan General Electric Corporation*, AIR 1960 Cal 637.

Compromise and **Settlement.** A *compromise* is an agreement made between two or more parties as a *settlement* of matters in dispute.

The term 'compromise' means settlement of differences by mutual concessions. It is an agreement reached by adjustment of conflicting or opposing claims by reciprocal modification of demands. It is a mutual promise of two or more parties that are at controversy. *Union of India* v. *Ananto*, AIR 2007 SC 1561, 1562, para 7. Legal Services Authorities Act (39 of 1987), S. 20(3).

Comptroller (*Controller*). The term comptroller or controller signifies, in its widest and most general sense, one who examines and verifies the accounts of collectors of public money.

Comptroller and Auditor-general of India. An officer to look into the accounts of the Union and the States. (*See* Constitution of India, Articles 148-151).

Compulsion. Constraint; objective necessity; duress. Forcible inducement to the commission of an act. The act of compelling or the state of being compelled; the act of driving or urging by force or by physical or moral constraint; subjection to force.

Compulsory. Obligatory. [T.P. Act (4 of 1882), S. 73(2)]; [Registration Act (16 of 1908), S. 17].

"Compulsory" The word "compulsory" in the title of the Act stands for compulsion on the State and the parental duty to send children to school. *Society for Unaided Private Schools of Rajasthan* v. *Union of India*, (2012) 6 SCC 1, para 7. Rights of Children to Free and Compulsory Education Act (35 of 2009).

Compulsory acquisition. Where land or an interest in land is purchased or taken under statutory powers without the agreement of the owner it is said to have been compulsorily acquired, but where there is statutory power to take mere possession of the land without the acquisition of any estate or interest in it apart from the possession, it is said to have been requisitioned. [8 HALSBURY'S *Laws* (4th Edn.) para 1].

Compulsory arbitration. Arbitration required by law or forced by law on the parties.

Compulsory deposit. Means a subscription to, or deposit in, a Provident Fund which, under the rules of the Fund, is not, until the happening of some specified contingency, repayable on demand otherwise than for the purpose of the payment of premium in respect of a policy of life insurance or the payment of subscriptions or premia in respect of a family pension fund, and includes any contribution and any interest or increment which has accrued under the rules of the Fund on any such subscription, deposit or contribution, and also any such subscription, deposit, contribution, interest or increment remaining to the credit of the subscriber or depositor after the happening of any such contingency. [Provident Funds Act (19 of 1925), S. 2(a)]

Compulsory licence. A statutorily granted licence without previous authority of the right owner to do an act covered by an exclusive right. Berne Convention permits under certain conditions, States to introduce compulsory licences enabling sound recordings to be made of a musical work without the author's consent however, only where such recording has been duly authorised already. (*Copyright*)

An involuntary licence where the appropriate authority orders the patentee to grant the right to use the invention to another party. (*Patents*)

Compulsory retirement. A compulsory retirement does not amount to dismissal or removal and therefore does not attract Art. 311. *Shyamlal* v. *State of U.P.*, AIR 1954 SC 369, 375. [Constitution of India, Art. 311; Civil Services Regulations (1920); Art. 465-A. Note 1].

Compulsory retirement means retiring a person against his will. The Government has absolute right to retire any officer after he has completed 25 years of qualified service without giving any reasons and no claim to special compensation on this account is entertainable. This right is to be exercised only when it is in the public interest to dispense with the further service of a civil servant, as provided in Article 465 of Civil Service Regulations. *State of Bombay* v. *Doshi*, AIR 1957 SC 892.

"Compulsory retirement" does not involve civil consequence and Government servant has no right to be heard before such an Order is passed. *B. Venkateswararao Naidu* v. *Union of India,* AIR 1973 SC 698.

The heading of Rule 3.26 is "Compulsory retirement". Rule 3.26(a) has used the words "age of compulsory retirement" for the age of superannuation which is 58 years. But this does not indicate that Rule 3.26(c)(1) provides for reduction in the age of superannuation below 58 and above 50 years with regard to Class I Officers of PWD if they have not attained the rank of Superintending Engineer. The heading "compulsory retirement" is wide enough to include premature retirement within its fold. Compulsory retirement includes premature retirement. *S.C. Jain* v. *State of Haryana,* AIR 1986 SC 169. [Punjab Civil Services Rules, Part I, Rr. 3.26(a) and 3.26(c)(1)]

The expression 'compulsory retirement' has two meanings. Firstly, it is one of the penalties inflicted on a delinquent Government servant consequent upon a finding of guilt being recorded in disciplinary proceedings and secondly, under service rules one has to retire on attaining a particular age or on his having completed a certain number of years of service. *Bishwarnath Prasad Singh* v. *State of Bihar*, (2001) 2 SCC 305, para 12.

'Compulsory retirement' is a penalty that can be imposed on an employee under R. 9(v) of the Rules. *Board of Trustees of the Port of Calcutta* v. *Amal Kumar Ghosh*, (1998) 9 SCC 696, para 6. [Calcutta Port Commissioners Employees (Discipline & Appeal) Rules, R. 9(v)]

Compulsory winding-up. Winding-up of a company's affairs by the order and under the supervision of the Court.

Compurgation. (*Archaic*) A trial by which a defendant could have eleven witnesses (compurgators) to testify that they thought that he was telling the truth.

Computation. The act of computing, numbering, reckoning, or estimating.

Compute. To determine or ascertain by calculation with mathematical means [Unit Trust of India Act (52 of 1963), S. 32(1)(ba)].

Computer. "COMPUTER" means any electronic, magnetic, optical or other high-speed data processing device or system which performs logical, arithmetic, and memory functions by manipulations of electronic, magnetic or optical impulses, and includes all input, output, processing, storage, computer software, or communication facilities which are connected or related to the computer in a computer system or computer network. [Information Technology Act (21 of 2000), S. 2(1)(i)]

"COMPUTER" includes any electronic or similar device having information processing capabilities. [Copyright Act (14 of 1957), S. 2(ffb)]

An electronic contrivance which solves problems and does complicated calculations by processing data according to prescribed, programmed instructions and then produces and/or retains the outcome of these processes. (*Webster*)

Computer centre. An area covering the computer room, media library, network area, server area, programming and administration areas, other storage and support areas used to carry out the computer processing functions (*Information Technology*)

Computer contaminant. 'Computer contaminant means any set of computer instructions that are designed—(*a*) to modify, destroy, record, transmit data or programme residing within a computer, computer system or computer network; or (*b*) by any means to usurp the normal operation of the computer, computer system, or computer network.' [Information Technology Act (21 of 2000), S. 43].

Computer crime. Offences that at least partially involve computers. (*Cyber Law*)

Broadly defined as any illegal act that involves a computer, its systems, or its applications. (*Cyber Law*)

Computer database. Means a representation of information, knowledge, facts, concepts or instructions in text, image, audio, video that are being prepared or have been prepared in a formalised manner or have been produced by a computer, computer system or computer network and are intended for use in a computer, computer system or computer network.' [Information Technology Act (21 of 2000), S. 43].

Computer emergency response. This term means to coordinate action during cyber security emergencies, provide incident response services to users, publish alerts concerning vulnerabilities and threats, and offer information to help improve cyber security. [Information Technology (The Indian Computer Emergency Response Team and Manner of Performing Functions and Duties) Rules, 2013, R. 2(1)(c)].

Computer evidence. Is quite unique when compared to other forms of "documentary evidence." Unlike paper documentation, computer evidence is fragile and a copy of a document stored in a computer file is identical to the original. The legal 'best evidence' rules change when it comes to the processing of computer evidence. Another unique aspect of computer evidence is the potential for unauthorized copies to be made of important computer files without leaving behind a trace that the copy was made. This situation creates problems concerning the investigation of the theft of trade secrets (client lists, research materials, computer-aided design files, formulas, and proprietary software).

Computer forensics. Computer Forensics deals with the preservation, identification, extraction, and documentation of computer evidence. The field is relatively new to the private sector but it has been the mainstay of technology-related investigations and intelligence gathering in law enforcement and military agencies since the mid-1980s. Like any other forensic science, computer forensics involves the use of sophisticated technology tools and procedures, which must be followed to guarantee the accuracy of the presservation of evidence and the accuracy of results concerning computer-evidence processing. Typically, computer forensic tools exist in the form of computer software. Computer forensic specialists guarantee accuracy of evidence-processing results through the use of time-tested evidence-processing procedures and through the use of multiple software tools, developed by separate and independent developers. The use of different tools that have been developed independently to validate results is important to avoid inaccuracies introduced by potential software design flaws and software bugs. It is a serious mistake for a computer forensics specialist to put "all of their eggs in one basket" by using just one tool to preserve, identify, extract, and validate the computer evidence. Cross-validation through the use of multiple tools and techniques is standard in all forensic sciences. When this procedure is not used, it creates advantages for defense lawyers who may challenge the accuracy of the software tool used and thus the integrity of the results. Validation through the user of multiple software tools, computer specialists, and procedures eliminates the potential for errors and the destruction of evidence. (*Cyber Law*)

Computer Fraud and Abuse Act (CFAA of 1986). Federal law that provides civil and criminal penalties for unauthorized access or molestation of protected computer systems. (*Cyber Law*)

The pre-eminent stature used in prosecuting the range of computer crimes. (*Cyber Law*)

Computer Graphics. Illustrations created with the aid of a computer. (*Computer*)

Computer investigations. Computer investigations rely on evidence stored as data and the timeline of dates and times that files were created, modified, and/or last accessed by the computer user. Timelines of activity can be especially helpful when multiple computers and individuals are involved in the commission of a crime. The computer forensics investtigator should always consider timelines of computer usage in all computer-related investigations. The same is true in computer security reviews concerning potential access to sensitive and/or trade secret information stored in the form of computer files. (*Cyber Law*)

Computer network. Where there computers are connected with one another with the help of coxial cables, satellite, microwave, terrestrial lines or other communication media. (*Information Technology*)

"COMPUTER NETWORK" means the interconnection of one or more computers through—

(i) the use of satellite, microwave, terrestrial line or other communication media; and

(ii) terminals or a complex consisting of two or more interconnected computers whether or not the interconnection is continuously maintained. [Information Technology Act (21 of 2000), S. 2(1)(j)]

Computer peripheral. Various electronic devices which are connected with the computer, but do not form the part of computer, like scanner, mouse, printer. (*Information Technology*)

Computer programme (or computer program). Means a set of instructions expressed in words, codes, schemes or in any other form, including a machine readable medium, capable of causing a computer to perform a particular task or achieve a particular result. [Copyright Act (14 of 1957), S. 2(ffc)].

Computer-program. A 'computer program' is a set of statements or instructions to be used directly or indirectly in a computer in order to bring about a certain result. [U.S. Copyright Act, Section 101]

The term "Computer program" also includes preparatory design work leading to the development of a computer program, provided that the nature of the preparatory work is such that a computer program can result from it at a later stage. [*Svaz Softwarove Ochrange* v. *Ministerstvo Kultury*, Case No. C-393/09:2010 ECR I-0000, decided on 22-12-2010 (Czech Republic). European Council Directive 91/250, Preamble, recital 7th, phrase 2nd] see also *SAS Institute Inc.* v. *World Programming Limited*, (2012) 7 SCC (FJ) 1, para 35.

Computer-related forgery. Computer-related forgery involves the unauthorized creating or altering or manipulation of stored data so that they acquire a different evidentiary value in the course of legal transactions which relies on the authenticity of information contained in the data. Aparna Viswanathan, *Cyber Law: Indian & International Perspectives,* 2012, LexisNexis Butterworths at p. 106.

Computer-related fraud. The causing of loss of property to another person by manipulating or altering, deleting any computer data, with fraudulent or dishonest intention to gain an economic benefit without right, is considered as computer-related fraud. [The European Convention on Cyber Crime, Art. 7]

Computer resource. Means computer, computer system, computer network, data, computer data base or software. [Information Technology Act (21 of 2000), S. 2(1)(k)]

Computer software. "COMPUTER SOFTWARE" means—

(a) any computer programme recorded on any disc, tape, perforated media or other information storage device; or

(b) any customized electronic data or any product or service of similar nature, as may be notified by the Board, which is transmitted or exported from India to any place outside India by any means. [Income-tax Act (43 of 1961), S. 10A(9), *Expl.* 2]

For the purposes of this clause, "COMPUTER SOFTWARE" means any computer programme recorded on any disc, tape, perforated media or other information storage device and includes any such programme or any custommized electronic data. [Income-tax Act (43 of 1961), S. 9(1)(vi), *Expl.* 3]

According to WIPO Model Provisions, 'computer software' includes anyone or more of the following items:—

(i) computer program

(ii) program description

(iii) supporting material (*Copyright*)

Computer Software Copyright Act. Federal law protecting software, both source code and object code, as a literary work under copyright. (*Cyber Law*)

Computer source code. For the purposes of this section, "COMPUTER SOURCE CODE" means the listing of programmes, computer commands, design and layout and programme analysis of computer resource in any form. [Information Technology Act (21 of 2000), S. 65, *Expl.*]

Computer system. Means a device or collection of devices, including input and output support devices and excluding calculators which are not programmable and capable of being used in conjunction with external files, which contain computer programmes, electronic instructions, input data and output data, that performs logic, arithmetic, data storage and retrieval, communication control and other functions. [Information Technology Act (21 of 2000), S. 2(1)(l)]

For the purposes of this clause,—

"Computer system" means a device or collection of devices including input and output support devices and excluding calculators which are not programmmable and capable of being used in conjunction with external files, or more of which contain computer programmes, electronic instructtions, input data and output data, that performs functions including, but not limited to, logic, arithmetic, data storage and retrieval, communication and control. [Income-tax Act (43 of 1961), S. 36(1)(xi), *Expln. (a)*]

Computer virus. A specially written computer programme to destroy the data or adversely effect the performance of the computer. Certain virus are such which multiply if run on a computer network. (*Information Technology*)

Conceal. To hide or keep secret.

Conceal his presence. The words concealing his presence in S. 109(*a*), CrPC, 1973 (2 of 1974), are very wide. They are sufficient to cover the concealment of bodily presence in a house or grove or under a bridge, etc, but they are also sufficient to cover the case when a man conceals his appearance (*e.g.*) by wearing a mask or covering his face or disguising himself by a uniform or in some other manner.

TO CONCEAL, HIDE, SECRET. *Concealing* has simply the idea of not letting come to observation; *hiding* that of putting under cover; *secreting* that of setting at a distance or in unfrequented place; whatever is not seen is *concealed*, but whatever is *hidden* or *secreted* is intentionally put out of sight. A thief *conceals* himself behind a hedge; he *hides* his treasures in the earth; he secrets what he has stolen under his cloak.

Concealment. The suppression of, or neglect to communicate, a Material Fact within the knowledge of one of the parties which the other has not the means of knowing, or is not presumed to know. A 'Material Fact,' is one which is calculated, if communicated to the other of the parties, to induce him either to refrain altogether from the contract, or not to enter into it except on more favourable terms'. (*Insurance law*)

"CONCEALMENT" means the concealment or disguise of the nature, source, disposition, movement or ownership of property and includes the movement or conversion of such property by electronic transmission or by any other means. [Wild life (Protection) Act (53 of 1972), S. 58B(d) and Narcotic Drugs and Psychotropic Substances Act (61 of 1985), S. 68B(d)]

The meaning of the word "concealment" is "the intentional suppression of truth or fact known, to the injury or prejudice of another". *CIT* v. *J.K.A. Subravania Chettiar,* (1997) 110 ITR 602, 608 (Mad). [Income-tax Act (43 of 1961), S. 271(1)(c)].

The action of concealing [IPC (45 of 1860), S. 212, *Excep.*]; [Indian Contract Act (9 of 1872), S. 23, ill, (g)]; being concealed. [Indian Contract Act (9 of 1872), S. 17(2)].

Concealment of birth. If a person secretly buries or otherwise disposes of the dead body of a child, whether died during or after birth, intentionally conceals or endeavors to conceal birth of the child.

Concealment of evidence. If a person intentionally causes any evidence of the commission of an offence to disappear or with the intention of screening the offender from legal punishment and gives a false information respecting the offence, he is guilty of concealing evidence.

Concentrate. Concentrated substance. [Metal corporation of India (Acquisition of Undertaking) Act (36 of 1966), S. 4(1)]; to make denser [Two-Member Constituencies (Abolition) Act (1 of 1961), S. 63(c)].

Concept. A general notion, an idea of a class of objects; the product of the faculty of conception.

"Concept of restitution" The principle of 'doctrine of restitution' is that on the reversal of a decree, the law imposes an obligation on the party to the suit who received the benefit of the erroneous decree to make restitution to the other party for what he has lost. *Lal Bhagwant Singh* v. *Sri Kishen Das*, AIR 1953 SC 136 as cited in *Binayak Swain* v. *Ramesh Chandra Panigrahi*, AIR 1966 SC 948, para 4. See also *State of Gujrat* v. *Essar Oil Limited,* (2012) 3 SCC 522, para 60.

Concept of time-barred. 'Time-barred' means simply that a particular remedy, called suit, for the enforcement of a right is no longer available. The concept of 'time-barred' cannot be extended to proceedings outside the law Courts.

Conceptus. Means any product of conception at any stage of development from fertilisation until birth including extra embryonic membranes as well as the embryo or foetus. [Pre-Natal Diagnostic Techniques (Regulation and Prevention of Misuse) Act (57 of 1994), S. 2(ba)]

Concern. That which concerns one's affairs; that which relates or pertains to one; matter of concernment; business affair; firm or enterprise.

Something that relates or belongs to one. [Industrial Disputes Act (14 of 1947), S. 3(2)]; an organisation or establishment for business.

Concerned. That which relates to or pertains to one. [IPC (45 of 1860), S. 38; Indian Evidence Act (1 of 1872), S. 15 and T.P. Act (4 of 1882), S. 58(f)]; having or showing concern.

The words 'concerned in' mean interested in, involved in, and mixed up. The words 'deal with' mean to have something to do with, to concern one self, to make arrangement, and to negotiate with respect to something. *Asst. Collector of Customs, Calcutta* v. *Sitaram*, AIR 1966 SC 955, 963.

The word 'concern' is not a term of art, having a precise, fixed meaning, It has several names, and is used to convey diverse shades of meaning over a wide spectrum. It may mean 'to have a relation to or bearing on, be of interest or, importance,' or 'to have an anxiety, worry', 'concerned (as an adjective may mean 'interested', 'involved'. R. *Dalmia* v. *I.T. Commissioner, Delhi*, AIR 1977 SC 988, 992.

Concerned in such dispute. The expression 'concerned in such dispute' means really concerned or directly, personally or primarily concerned in such dispute and not merely interested in such dispute. The word 'concerned' connotes a kind of specific, direct interest, and in a given legal or quasi-legal proceedings, it implies a direct and personal interest which a party to the proceedings would have in the result of those proceedings, when the same are capable of directly affecting him in any adjudication beneficially or prejudicially, according to the result. *New Jehangir Vakil Mills Ltd.* v. *N.L. Vyas,* AIR 1959 Bom 248, 249. [Industrial Disputes Act (14 of 1947), S. 33(1)(a)].

Concerning. The word 'concerning' means 'about', 'regarding', 'pertaining to'. *Pradeep Kumar Tripathi* v. *Telecom District Manager,* AIR 1994 All 325, 328. [Indian Telegraph Act (13 of 1885), S. 7-B].

Concert. Combined state; to act in harmony; to plan together.

TO CONCERT, CONTRIVE, MANAGE. There is a secret understanding in concerting; invention in contriving; execution in managing. Measures are concerted, schemes are contrived, affairs are managed. Two parties at least are requisite in concerting, one is sufficient for contriving and managing. Concerting is always employed in all secret transaction; contrivance and management are used indifferently. Robbers who have determined on any scheme of plunder concert together the means of carrying their project into execution; they contrive various devices to elude the vigilance of the police; they manage everything in the dark.

Conciliation: Reconciliation: Mediation. The principal thrust of the law in family matters is to make an attempt for reconciliation before processing the dispute in the legal framework. Reconciliation is not mediation. Neither it is conciliation. No doubt, there is conciliation in reconciliation. But the concepts are totally different. Similarly, there is mediation in conciliation but there is no conciliation in mediation. In mediation, the role of mediator is only to evolve situations whereas in reconciliation, the duty-holders have to take a proactive role to assist the parties to reach an amicable solution. In conciliation, the conciliator persuades the parties to arrive at a solution as suggested by him in the course of discussion. In reconciliation, the duty holders remind the parties of the essential family values, the need to maintain a cordial relationship, both in the interest of the husband and the wife or the children, as the case may be, also to make a persuasive effort to make the parties reconcile to the reality and restore the relationship. Reconciliation is not always the restoration of *status quo ante,* it can as well be a solution acceptable to both parties. [*Santhini* v. *Vijaya Venkatesh,* (2018) 1 SCC 62, para 17].

Concert parties. Group of persons acting to acquire the shares of a company.

Concerted action. An action which has been planned, arranged and agreed on by parties acting together so as to further some scheme or cause, so that all involved are liable for the actions of one.

Concessio versus concedentem latam interpretationem habere debet. (*Maxim*) A grant ought to have a broad interpretation (to be liberally interpreted) against the grantor. (*Black*)

Concession. Concealing or thing conceded; a grant; ordinarily applied to a grant of specific privileges by government, a special privilege granted by a government, corporation or other authority.

Concession at the Bar. When counsells make a concession at the bar, it means that the point is so clear and unarguable that it must be taken as well settled and any decision based on a concession must be considered as a binding decision. [CPC (5 of 1908), O. III, R. 4].

Conciliation. Bringing of opposing parties or individuals into harmony to settle the dispute.

CONCILIATE, RECONCILE, *Conciliate and reconcile* are both employed in the sense of uniting men's affections, but under different circumstances. The conciliator gets the goodwill and affections for himself; the reconciler unites the affections of two persons to each other. Conciliate is mostly employed for men in public stations; reconcile is indifferently employed for those in public or private stations.

Concise. Brief.

Expressing much in brief form. Webster's Comprehensive Dictionary, International Edition, as cited in *Ashraf Kokkur* v. *K.V. Abdul Khader*, (2015) 1 SCC 129, para 12.

"Giving a lot of information clearly and in few words". Conscise Oxford Dictionary as cited in *Ashraf Kokkur* v. *K.V. Abdul Khader*, (2015) 1 SCC 129, para 12].

"Brief and Comprehensive". [Oxford Dictionary as cited in *Ashraf Kokkur* v. *K.V. Abdul Khader*, (2015) 1 SCC 129, para 12].

Conclude. Bring about; make (as) conclude treaty, peace or bargain.

Concluded. The word 'concluded' in S. 452(1) CrPC 1973 (2 of 1974) means, concluded after a full hearing with a final judgment or determination of the case against the accused.

Conclusion. The end; close; the act of concluding; judgment; arriving at judgment by reasoning.

The final part of a speech or writing (such as a jury argument or a pleading); A judgement arrived at by reasoning; an inferential statement; The closing, settling, or final arranging of a treaty, contract, deal, etc. Black's Law Dictionary as cited in *Anand Brothers Private Limited* v. *Union of India*, (2014) 9 SCC 212, para 13.

Conclusion of fact. An evidentiary inference.

Conclusive. Final, finishing, ending (as) conclusive argument; decisive; convencing; authoritative.

The term 'conclusive' is used in statutes with reference (1) To JUDGMENTS AND ORDERS or decisions of a Court or a public department or authority; (2) to evidence. Where a judgment or order of a Court is declared to be final or conclusive, it cannot be questioned by appeal or otherwise unless given with such disregard of the jurisdiction of the Court as not to be really a decision, in which case it may be treated as a nullity. (*Ency. of the Laws of England*.)

CONCLUSIVE, DECISIVE, CONVINCING. *Conclusive* applies either to practical or argumentative matters; *Decisive* to what is practical only; *Convincing* to what is argumentative only. It is necessary to be *conclusive* when we deliberate, and *decisive* when we command. What is *conclusive* puts an end to all discussion, and determines the judgment: what is *decisive* puts an end to all wavering, and determines the will.

Conclusive evidence. Absolute evidence of a fact for all purposes for which it is so made evidence.

When the law says that a particular kind of evidence would be conclusive as to the existence of a particular fact it implies that that fact can be proved either by that evidence or by some other evidence which the Court permits or requires to be advanced when evidence which is made conclusive is adduced, the Court has no option but to hold that the fact exists. *Somawanti* v. *State of Punjab*, AIR 1963 SC 151, 160. [Land Acquisition Act (1 of 1894), S. 6(3)].

Conclusive presumption. A presumption which cannot be overcome by any additional argument or evidence.

Conclusive proof. Is 'clear and positive proof.' When one fact is declared by this Act to be conclusive proof of another, the Court shall, on proof of the one fact, regard the other as proved, and shall not allow evidence to be given for the purpose of disproving it. [Indian Evidence Act (1 of 1872), S. 4].

"Conclusive proof" means when one fact is declared by this Adhiniyam to be conclusive proof of another, the Court shall, on proof of the one fact, regard the other as proved, and shall not allow evidence to be given for the purpose of disproving it. [(w.e.f. 1-7-2024) Bharatiya Sakshya Adhiniyam, 2023 (47 of 2023), section 2(1)(b)]

In several instances certificates or other such documents are by special Acts made conclusive evidence of the facts stated in them, for example, S. 381 of the Indian Succession Act (39 of 1925); S. 61 of the Indian Christian Marriage Act (15 of 1872) and S. 4, Indian Evidence Act (1 of 1872).

Conclusively determined. Determined in a conclusive manner.

Concoct. Fabricate; scheming in concert (as) *concocted* evidence.

Concomitant. Attendant; incidental; accompanying (as) concomitant circumstances.

Concord. An amicable arrangement which is made between parties, specially between peoples or nations.

Concubinage. The cohabiting of a man and a woman who are not legally married; the state of being a concubine; a comprehensive term covering any illicit intercourse. (*Wharton*)

The state of being kept as a concubine. [Indian Contract Act (9 of 1872), S. 23, ill. (k)]; the state of being a concubine.

Concubine. A woman who cohabits with a man without being his wife; a kept mistress; a sort of inferior wife. (*Black; Ame Cyc; Webs.*)

WHEN A WOMAN BECOMES A 'CONCUBINE.' When a single woman consents to unlawfully cohabit with a man generally, as though the marriage relation existed between them, without any limit as to the duration of such illicit intercourse, and actually commences cohabiting with him in pursuance of that understanding, she becomes his concubine, or, as it is usually expressed in modern times, 'his kept mistress' which amounts to the same thing.

Concur. Agree; coincide; express agreement in opinion (as) concurring judgment. Judicially, agreeing of one Court with the opinion of another Court.

Concurrence. The action of concurring. [Constitution of India, Art. 145(5)].

Concurrent. Having the same authority; existing together; agreeing in the same act; contributing to the same event; accompanying; conjoined; associate; concomitant.

Running together in time or space; covering the same ground.

Concurrent findings. Similar findings of two Courts on a question of fact.

It is general rule of practice on appeals in the Privy Council not to reverse the concurrent findings of two Courts on a question of fact. [*Hay* v. *Gordon*, (1872) LR 4 PC 337, 348]; and the question for the Privy Council is, not what conclusion their Lordships would have arrived at if the matter had for the first time come before them, but whether it has been established that the judgments of the Courts below were clearly wrong. *Allen* v. *Queen Warehouse Co*, (1886), 12 App Cas 101 : 56 LT 30 : 56 LJPC 6.

Concurrent interests. Interests in something held by two or more persons, at one and the same time.

Concurrent jurisdiction. The jurisdiction of several bodies, authorised to deal with the same subject matter.

Concurrent lease. Lease granted by a landlord to run at the same time as another lease of same premises.

Concurrent List. List III of the Seventh Schedule of the Constitution of India.

A list of subjects appended to a federal Constitution in respect of which the federal legislature and the state or regional legislatures have power to make laws, federal law prevailing in case of conflict. The object of a concurrent list of subjects over which the Centre and the units have concurrent powers is uniformity. Concurrent list in the Indian Constitution comprising 47 subjects over which both Union and States can legislate. Known also as List III. Union law prevails where state law is repugnant to it. The question of repugnancy arises in case of subjects enumerated in concurrent list.

Concurrent power. The power of the Parliament and the State Legislatures, each acting independently of the other, to make laws on the same subject-matter.

Concurrent sentences. Sentences are said to be concurrent when made to run from the same date in respect of convictions on several counts or indictments. The term is used in opposition to '*Consecutive or Cumulative Sentences*'.

Concussion. Violent shock.

Concussion of the brain is injury to the brain caused by a heavy blow.

Condemn. Censure; blame; doom to punishment; to give judgment against a prisoner.

Condemnation. Conviction; judically pronouncing someone guilty.

Condemned. Forfeited; pronounced unfit for use (as) condemned articles; doomed to punishment.

Condemned cell. Cell for the confinement of condemned men.

Condemned criminal. A culprit, who has been adjudged guilty.

Conditio beneficialis, quae statum construit, bonigne secundum verborum intentionem, est interpretandi odiosa autem quae statum destruit, stricte secundum verborum proprietatem accipienda. (*Maxim*) A beneficial condition which creates an estate, ought to be construed favourably, according to the intention of the words; but a condition which destroys an estate is odious and ought to be construed strictly according to the letter of the words.

Conditio ex parte extincta ex toto extinguitur. (*Maxim*) An agreement extinguished in part is wholly extinguished. (*Morgan*)

Conditio illicita hebetur pro non adjecta. (*Maxim*) An unlawful condition is deemed as not annexed. (*Black*)

Conditio liberum tenementum casans non per nuda verba sine charta valebit. (*Maxim*) A condition making void a free tenement will be of no value by bare words without writing.' (*Peloubet*)

Conditio neminem juvabit nisi qui pars fuerit aut privus. (*Maxim*) An agreement shall avail no one unless he shall have been a party or privy to it.' (*Morgan*)

Conditio Praecedens Adimpleri Debet Prius Quam Sequatur Effectus. (*Maxim*) A condition precedent must be fulfilled before the effect can follow.

Condition. Thing on whose fulfilment another thing or act is made to depend. "Condition" is a restraint or bridle annexed and joined to a thing, so that by the non-performance or not doing thereof the party to the condition shall receive prejudice and lose and; by the performance and doing of the same, profit and advantage.' (*Termes de la Ley*)

A provision or a stipulation as to leave and holidays would necessarily include a provision for the quantum of holidays and leave and this construction would be consistent with the meaning of the word 'condition' as employed in the preamble to the Act. *Bagalkot Cement Co. Ltd.* v. *R.K. Pathan*, AIR 1963 SC 439, 443. [Industrial Employment (Standing Orders) Act (20 of 1946), Sch. Cl. 5].

Something agreed upon as a requisite to the doing or taking effect of something else; a thing on whose fulfilment another thing or act is made to depend; a stipulation or provision [Constitution of India, Art. 15(2)]; mode or state of being; state in which a thing exists.

Condition and warranty. A stipulation in a contract of sale with reference to goods which are subject matter thereof may be a condition or a warranty. (2) A condition is a stipulation essential to the main purpose of the contract, the breach of which gives rise to treat the contract as repudiated. (3) A warranty is a stipulation collateral to the main purpose of the contract, the breach of which gives rise to a claim for damages but not to a right to reject the goods and treat the contract as repudiation. (4) Whether a stipulation in a contract of sale is a condition or a warranty depends in each case on the construction of the contract. A stipulation may be a condition, though called a warranty in the contract." [Sale of Goods Act (3 of 1930), S. 12].

Condition precedent. (*in a will*) Is a condition that must be fulfilled before a bequest becomes valid.

A condition whose fulfilment must precede the vesting of an estate, the taking effect of a contract or the accruing of a right. [T.P. Act (4 of 1882), S. 26].

In a conveyance or disposition of an estate, is a condition which must happen or be performed before the estate or interest can vest.

Condition subsequent. A condition which destroys or divests upon the happening of an event or not happening of an event. [T.P. Act (4 of 1882), S. 29].

Conditional. 'A promise or order to pay is not "conditional", within the meaning of this section.' [Negotiable Instruments Act (26 of 1881), S. 5].

Subject to or limited by one or more conditions.

Conditional attachment. The expression 'conditional attachment' might mean an attachment to be made conditionally on the security not being furnished nor cause shown by the prescribed day, or it might mean an immediate attachment of a provisional kind conditioned to become plenary if security should not be furnished, or cause shown according to the terms of the order.

Conditional bequest. A bequest whose continuation or effectiveness depends upon the occurrence or non-occurrence of a particular event.

Conditional discharge. An order which may be made by a criminal Court if it does not think that it is expedient to impose a punishment and a probation order is not appropriate. If the offender commits a further offence during the period fixed, he may be sentenced for the original offence. (*Walker*)

Conditional fee simple. A fee simple granted to a person with a condition that on the happening or non happening of the specified event, the grantor shall have the right to reenter the event.

Conditional interest. An interest which is liable to be forfeited, on the occurrence of a specified event, at the instance of a person who created it.

Conditional jump. An instruction in software that tests for the presence of a certain condition in the computer and, upon finding it, jumps to an instruction not in sequential order rather than performing the following instruction. (*Information Technology*)

Conditional legacy. A bequest whose existence depends upon the happening, or not happening, of some uncertain event, by which it is either to take place or be defeated.

Conditional legislation. A legislation to come into operation at all or in some particular area only upon an executive declaration or upon the happening of a particular event.

When operation of a legislation is made subject to fulfilment of certain conditions, it is conditional legislation. *Chandrakant Muljibhai Parekh* v. *State of Gujarat*, AIR 2001 Guj. 234, 242, para 10. Also see *Hamdard Dawakhana (Wakf) Lal Kuan, Delhi* v. *Union of India*, (1960) 2 SCR 671 : AIR 1960 SC 554. [Constitution of India, Art. 245]

Conditional Legislation and **Delegated Legislation**—distinction. The distinction between 'conditional legislation' and 'delegated legislation' is that in the former the delegate's power is that of determining when a Legislature declared rule of conduct shall become effective and the latter involves delegation of rules-making-power which constitutionally may be exercised by administrative agent. *Chandrakant Muljibhai Parikh* v. *State of Gujarat*, AIR 2001 Guj 234, 242, para 10. [Constitution of India, Art 245]

Conditional sale. A sale which is accompanied by an agreement to resell upon specified terms.

Conditions of sale. The regulations under which lands, houses, or goods are put up for sale by public auction, and by which purchasers are bound. It is usual for 'particulars and conditions of sale' to be printed and distributed prior to or at the sale in hand-bills or advertisements.

Conditions of service. Conditions of service, means all those conditions which regulate the holding of a post by a person, right from the time of his appointment till his retirement and even beyond retirement in matters like pension *etc. I.N. Subba Reddy* v. *Andhra University*, AIR 1976 SC 2049, 2053. [Andhra University Act (1926), S. 19(c)(iii)].

The expression 'conditions of service' includes everything from the stage of appointment to the stage of termination of service and even beyond and relates to matters pertaining to disciplinary action. *Lilliy Kurian* v. *Sr. Lewine*, AIR 1979 SC 52, 56. [Kerala University Act (14 of 1967), S. 19(i)].

The expression "conditions of service" would take in its fold, fixation of the age of superannuation. *State of A.P.* v. *S.K. Mohinuddin*, AIR 1994 SC 1474, 1477.

Conditions of service : Competent authority. The expression 'conditions of service' covers dismissal from service. The expression 'competent authority' in S. 116(2) means the appointing authority or an authority equivalent to or co-ordinate in rank with the appointing authority. *Mys. S.R.T. Corporation* v. *Mirja Khasim*, AIR 1977 SC 747, 752, 753. [States Reorganisation Act (37 of 1956), Ss. 115 (7) and 116(2)].

Conditions subsequent. A condition on the failure or non-performance of which an estate already vested may be defeated.

Condominium. A single real-estate unit in a multi-unit development in which a person has both a common interest and separate ownership of a unit.

Condonation. A pardon or forgiveness of a past wrong or fault; condonation means forgiveness of a conjugal offence with full knowledge of all the circumstances. The best evidence of condonation is the continuance or resumption of sexual intercourse by the husband after he has discovered the misconduct of his wife, a grave character such as adultery.

Condonation of delay. Overlooking by the Court of non-imitation of legal proceedings, appeal or revision within the prescribed time.

Condone. To forgive or overlook (an offence).

Conduce. Tend to produce effect. What has conduced an effect must in some sense have caused it, or contributed to it; and the conducing cause must be such as, if not directly at least indirectly might at the time be contemplated as likely somehow to contribute to that effect.

Conducive. Helpful, contributive.

Conduct. The word "CONDUCT" in this section does not include statements, unless those statements accompany and explain acts other than statements; but this explanation is to affect the relevancy of statements under any other section of this Act. [Indian Evidence Act (1 of 1872), S. 8, *Expln.* 1]

The word "conduct" in this section does not include statements, unless those statements accompany and explain acts other than statements; but this explanation is not to affect the relevancy of statements under any other section of this Adhiniyam. When the conduct of any person is relevant, any statement made to him or in his presence and hearing, which affects such conduct, is relevant. [(w.e.f. 1-7-2024) Bharatiya Sakshya Adhiniyam, 2023 (47 of 2023), section 6, *Explanations* 1 & 2]

Personal behaviour, whether by action or inaction; the manner in which a person behaves.

The standard of conduct the Members of Parliament are expected to observe in order to maintain the highest traditions in Parliamentary life.

The behaviour of the members of Parliament should be such as to enhance the dignity of Parliament and its Members in general. The extent and amplitude of the words "Conduct of a member" have not been defined exhaustively; it is within the powers of the House in each case to determine whether a member has acted in an unbecoming manner or has acted in a manner unworthy of a member of Parliament. A few illustrations bearing on the conduct of Members are given below:—

(i) a member should not try to secure business from government for a firm, company *etc.* with which he is directly or indirectly concerned;

(ii) a member should not unduly influence Government officials or Ministers in a case in which he is interested financially;

(iii) members should not receive hospitality of any kind for any work he does or proposes to do;

(iv) information given to members in confidence should not be divulged *etc.*

The expression 'conduct' is not used with reference to the character or reputation of the victim, but how the victim conducted in not telling any one about the crime committed on the victim for a certain period. *State of Haryana* v. *Prem Chand*, AIR 1990 SC 538, 540. [Indian Penal Code (45 of 1860), S. 376(2)].

Behaviour [CrPC 1973 (2 of 1974), S. 123(10) and IPC (45 of 1860), S. 499, second and third exceptions.]; to behave; direction or management; to manage; to direct; to carry on [Representation of the People Act (43 of 1951), S. 24]; [IPC (45 of 1860), S. 21 (11th)].

Management; conducting of an affair (as) conduct of business; conduct of a campaign; conduct of sale.

TO CONDUCT, MANAGE, DIRECT. *Conducting* requires most wisdom and knowledge; *managing* most action; *direction* most authority. A lawyer *conducts* the cause entrusted to him; a steward *manages* the mercantile concerns for his employer; a *superintendent* directs the movements of all the subordinate agents. A *conductor* conceives, plans, arranges and disposes; a *manager* acts or executes; a *director* commands. It is necessary to *conduct* with wisdom; to *manage* with diligence, attention, and skill; to *direct* with promptitude, precision, and clearness.

Conduct in the discharge of his public functions. If there is any defamatory statement concerning the behaviour of a public servant which can be reasonably associated with the discharge or non-discharge of his official duty even if not strictly necessary for that discharge, or relating to his conduct which bears such rational though not pretended or fanciful relation to the duty that it appears to have been displayed in the course of the performance or non-performance of the duty, the behaviour or conduct having reference *inter alia* to its moral quality, it would immediately attract the operation of S. 199(2). *Munneshwara Nand* v. *State,* AIR 1961 All 24, 36. [CrPC (2 of 1974), S. 199(2)].

Conduct the prosecution. Conducting the prosecution means taking charge of the entire proceedings free from guidance and control by anyone else. [CrPC 1973 (2 of 1974), S. 301(2)].

Conduct the search in person. S. 165(2), CrPC 1973 (2 of 1974), does not mean that an officer-in-charge of a Police Station (*i.e.*) investigating officer personally conducting a search must himself make the search, *e.g.,* ransack boxes, examine the roof, dig up the floor, or otherwise seek for the property. Nor is it necessary that all these processes must take place under his eye. The meaning of the section is that the officer should be present on the spot and exercise a general supervision over the search, in contradistinction to the cases where he is unable to go to the spot, and deputes a subordinate by a written order to conduct the search in his place.

Conductivity. The ratio of the current density in a conductor to the electric field causing the current to flow. It is the conductance between opposite faces of a cube of the material of one metre. edge. Reciprocal of resistivity.

Conductor. (*Lat.*) Lessee. In a contract of hiring, the conductor is he who pays the stipulated consideration for the subject let.

Official in charge of passengers or goods in a tramway or omnibus.

"CONDUCTOR", in relation to a stage carriage, means a person engaged in collecting fares from passengers, regulating their entrance into, or exit from, the stage carriage and performing such other functions as may be prescribed. [Motor Vehicles Act (59 of 1988), S. 2(5)]

Conductor's licence. Means the licence issued by a competent authority under Chapter III (of this Act) authorising the person specified therein to act as a conductor. [Motor Vehicles Act (59 of 1988), S. 2(6)]

Confectioner. As per dictionary meaning, 'confectioner' means dealer in sweets and pastries. *Pepsico India holding Pvt. Ltd.* v. *State of Punjab*, AIR 2012 P&H 163, para 13.

Confederacy. When two or more combine together to do any damages or injury to another, or to do any unlawful act.

Confederation. Permanent union of several independent states for common external action each retaining its sovereignty but delegating some powers to the confederation—the central authority.

Confer. To meet together; to take counsel; also to give (as) conferring titles.

TO CONFER, BESTOW. *Conferring* is an act of authority; *bestowing* that of charity or generosity. Princes and men in power *confer;* people in a private station *bestow.* Honours, dignities, privileges, and rank, are the things *conferred;* favours, kindness and pecuniary relief, are the things *bestowed.* Merit, favour, interest, caprice, or intrigue, gives rise to *conferring;* necessity, solicitation, and private affection, lead to *bestowing.*

Conference. A meeting of several persons for the interchange of opinions or for the removal of doubts or differences.

Confess. To own or admit as a fault. [IPC (45 of 1860), S. 205].

Confess judgment. To acknowledge that a claim is or is about to become due to another and consent that legal judgment may be entered for the amount when due and unpaid. [IPC (45 of 1860), S. 205].

Confessio, facta in judicio, omni probatione major est. (*Maxim*) A confession made in Court is of greater effect than any proof.

Confession. *Confession* is a direct admission or acknowledgment of his guilt by a person who has committed a crime. It may be judicial or extra-judicial.

CONFESSION in Section 25 of the Indian Evidence Act (1 of 1872); means, as in Section 24 of the same Act, a 'confession made by an accused person' which it is proposed to prove against him to establish an offence.

'Confession' in common acceptation means and implies acknowledgement of guilt. *State of Punjab* v. *Gurdeep Singh*, (1999) 7 SCC 714, para 3 : AIR 1999 SC 3724.

Confession and Admission. If a person admits all facts necessary to convict him, it is a confession. If such admission does not give all essential elements of the crime, it is only an admission and not confession.

Confessus in judicio pro judicato habetur, et quo dammodo sua sententia damnatur. (*Maxim*) A person confessing his guilt when arraigned is deemed to have been found guilty, and is, as it were condemned by his own sentence.

Confide. To have trust in.

TO CONFIDE, TRUST. *Confidence* is an extraordinary trust, but *trust* is always ordinary unless the term be otherwise qualified. *Confidence* involves communication of a man's mind to another, but *trust* is confined to matters of action. A *breach of trust* evinces a want of that common principle which keeps human society together; but a *breach of confidence* betrays a more than ordinary share of baseness and depravity.

Confidential. Imparted in confidence; confiding of secrets or in trust (as) confidential communications between husband and wife being privileged communications under the Indian Evidence Act (1 of 1872), S. 122.

Confidential communication. Privileged communications such as those between spouses, physician-patient, attorney-client, confessorpenitent, *etc.* Such are privileged at the option of the spouse-witness, client-witness and penitent-witness. Confidential communication is statement made under circumstances showing that speaker intended statement only for ears of person addressed; thus if communication is made in presence of third party whose presence in not reasonably necessary for the communication, it is not privileged. [*See*, Indian Evidence Act (1 of 1872), Ss. 122, 123, 124, 125, 126, 129].

Confidential report. A "confidential report" is intended to be a general assessment of work performed by a Government servant subordinate to the reporting authority, that such reports are maintained for the purpose of serving as data of comparative merit when questions of promotion, confirmation, etc. arise. They also show that such reports are not ordinarily to contain specific incidents upon which assessments are made except in cases where as a result of any specific incident a censure or a warning is issued and when such warning is by an order to be kept in the personal file of the Government servant. *R.L. Butail* v. *Union of India,* (1970) 2 SCC 876.

Confine. Imprison; hold in custody.

To keep within circumscribing limits. [CrPC 1973 (2 of 1974), S. 46(1)]; to restrict.

Confinement. Imprisonment, civil or criminal; also means child birth.

The action of confining; being confined. [IPC (45 of 1860), S. 6, ill. (b) and Army Act (46 of 1950), S. 80(c)]; being confined in child births [Employees' State Insurance Act (34 of 1948), S. 2(3)].

"Confinement" means labour resulting in the issue of a living child, or labour after twenty-six weeks of pregnancy resulting in the issue of a child whether alive or dead. [Code on Social Security, 2020 (36 of 2020), section 2(18)]

CONFINEMENT, IMPRISONMENT, CAPTIVITY. *Confinement* is the generic, the other two are specific terms. *Confinement and imprisonment* both imply the abridgement of one's personal freedom, but the former specifies no cause, which the latter does. We may be *confined* in a room by ill health, but we are never *imprisoned* but in some specific place appointed for the confinement of offenders, and always on some supposed offence. We are *captives* by the rights of war, when we fall into the hands of enemy.

Confinement in a prison. References to confinement in a prison, by whatever form of words include references to confinement or detention in a prison under any law providing for preventive detention. [Prisoners (Attendance in Courts) Act (32 of 1955), S. 2(a)]

Confirm. Make stronger; further establish; make secure; corroborate.

Sometimes, 'confirm' means merely 'verify' it is commonly used in that sense at the meetings of public bodies who 'confirm' the minutes of their last meeting, not meaning thereby that they give them force, but merely that they declare them accurate.

To make firm; to satisfy; to render valid by formal assent; to corroborate. [T.P. Act (4 of 1882), S. 35, ill.]; [Indian Evidence Act (1 of 1872), S. 158].

TO CONFIRM, TO CORROBORATE. The idea of strengthening is common to these terms, but under different circumstances; *confirm* is used generally, *corroborate* only in particular instances. What *confirms* serves to confirm the mind; what *corroborates* gives weight to the thing. An opinion is *confirmed;* an evidence is *corroborated.* What *confirms* removes all doubt; what *corroborates* only gives more strength than the thing had before. When the truth of a thing is confirmed, nothing more is necessary. The testimony of an accomplice may be so little credited that it wants frequent corroboration.

Confirmation est nulla ubi donum precedens est invadium. (*Maxim*) An illegal act cannot be rendered valid by a subsequent confirmation. (*Latin for Lawyers*)

Confirmatio omnes supplet defectus licet id quod actum est ab initio non valuit. (*Maxim*) Confirmation supplies all defects, though that which had been done was not valid at the beginning. (*Wharton*)

Confirmation. The word 'confirmed' etymologically comes from the old French and Latin 'conformere' meaning thereby to made firm or strengthen. Confirmation in such a case should include some element of application of mind and some consequential and necessary correction.

Confirmation, Court of. A Court which confirms a sentence or order passed by a lower Court, so as to give it full legal efficacy. [CrPC 1973 (2 of 1974), S. 454(3)].

Confiscate. To appropriate (private property) to the public treasury by way of penalty; to deprive of property as forfeited to the State.

Confiscation. The action of confiscating or the fact of being confiscated.

Conflict of interest. Term used in connection with public officials and fiduciaries and their relationship to matters of private interest or gain to them. Ethical problems connected therewith are covered by statutes in most jurisdictions and by federal statutes on the federal level. The Code of Professional Responsibility and Model Rules of Professional Conduct set forth standards for actual or potential conflicts of interest between attorney and client. Generally, when used to suggest disqualification of a public official from performing his sworn duty, term 'conflict of interest' refers to a clash between public interest and the private pecuniary interest of the individual concerned. *Gardner* v. *Nashville Housing Authority of Metropolitan Government of*

Nashville and Davison County, Tenn., CA Tenn., 514 F. 2d 38, 41. A situation in which regard for one duty tends to lead to disregard of another. *U.S.* v. *Miler, C.A. Mass.*, 463 F.2d 600, 602.

Conflict of laws. The discordance between the laws of one country and another, as applied to the same subject matter; *e.g.,* in the case of a contract made in one country and intended to be executed in another.

Conflict resolution. To truly resolve a conflict, the solution must go beyond just satisfying the parties' interests as in dispute settlement. To end or *resolve* a long-term conflict, a relatively stable solution that identifies and deals with the underlying sources of the conflict must be found. This is a more difficult task than simple dispute settlement, because resolution means going beyond negotiating interests to meet all sides' basic needs, while simultaneously finding a way to respect their underlying values and identities. (*Arbitration*)

Conflict transformation. The phrase 'conflict transformation', coined by *John Paul Lederach*, in *Preparing for Peace*: *Conflict Transformation Across Cultures*, means envisioning and responding to the ebb and flow of social conflict as life giving opportunities for creative constructive change processes that reduce violence, increase justice in direct interaction and social structures, and respond to real-life problems in human relationships. (*Arbitration*)

Conform. To make of the same form or character; to bring into harmony or correspondence; to adapt; to act in conformity or compliance.

Conformity. Correspondence in form or manner; agreement in character.

Congeable. Lawful; permissible; allowable.

Congenital. Born with the person; dating from birth.

Congregate. Collect or flock together; form into a crowd or mass.

Congregation. The act of congregating; the act of bringing together or assembling; aggregation. In ecclesiastical affairs, an assemblage or union of persons in society for some religious purpose, to unite in public worship; an assembly met or a body of persons who usually meet in some stated place for the worship of God and religious instruction and may or may not include a church or spiritual body. (*Cyc*)

Congress. A meeting of the representatives of the people to discuss and regulate common interests. The legislative body of the U.S.A.

Conjecture. Guess work; induction on scanty grounds; conjecture should not be the basis for the conviction of an accused charged with a grave criminal offence.

CONJECTURE, SUPPOSITION, SURMISE, All these terms convey an idea of something in the mind independent of the reality; but *conjecture* is founded less on rational inference than supposition; and *surmise* less than either: any circumstance, however trivial, may give rise to a *conjecture;* some reasons are requisite to produce a *supposition;* a particular state of feeling or train of thinking may of itself create a *surmise*. Although the same epithets are generally applicable to all these terms, yet we may with propriety say that a conjecture is idle: a supposition false; a surmise fanciful.

Conjointly. 'The word 'conjointly' used in a will is not inapplicable to a gift of property in equal shares so long as the property remains undivided. When applied in the phrase "conjointly and in the equal shares" the word cannot neutralize or control the plain meaning of the words 'in equal shares' by which it is immediately followed. '

Related to, made up of or carried on by two or more in combination. [Army Act (46 of 1950), S. 81(3)].

Conjugal. Between married people (as) conjugal society.

Conjugal rights. A suit for restitution of conjugal rights, is one of the species of matrimonial causes and is brought when either the husband or wife lives separate from the other without any sufficient reason; in which case the Court will compel them to come together again, if either party be weak enough to desire it, contrary to the inclination of the other. (*Tomlin;* Cooly on *Husband and Wife*)

Conjugal rights are not merely creature of statute. Such rights are inherent in the very institution of marriage itself. AIR 1984 SC 1562. [Hindu Marriage Act (25 of 1955), S. 9]

Conjunctio mariti et feminae est de jure naturae. (*Maxim*) The union of husband and wife is of the law of nature.

Conjuncture. Position of affairs at a particular moment.

Conjuration. Conferring with evil spirits; a plot or compact made by persons who swear to each other to do something that will result in public harm.

Connected. The word 'connected' means intimately connected or connected in a manner, so as to take pressure or be unable to act independently. [Allahabad University Act (3 of 1921),S. 11(4)(i)(a)].

Linked; related. [Indian Evidence Act (1 of 1872), Ss. 3 and 39].

Connected person. Means any person who is connected directly or indirectly to another person and includes,—(a) any relative of the person, if such person is an individual; (b) any director of the company or any relative of such director, if the person is a company; (c) any partner or member of a firm or association of persons or body of individuals or any relative of such partner or member, if the person is a firm or association of persons or body of individuals; (d) any member of the Hindu undivided family or any relative of such member, if the person is a Hindu undivided family; (e) any individual who has a substantial interest in the business of the person or any relative of such individual; (f) a company, firm or an association of persons or a body of individuals, whether incorporated or not, or a Hindu undivided family having a substantial interest in the business of the person or any director, partner, or member of the company, firm or association of persons or body of individuals or family, or any relative of such director, partner or member; (g) a company, firm or association of persons or body of individuals, whether incorporated or not, or a Hindu undivided family, whose director, partner, or member has a substantial interest in the business of the person, or family or any relative of such director, partner or member; (h) any other person who carries on a business, if—(i) the person being an individual, or any relative of such person, has a substantial interest in the business of that other person; or (ii) the person being a company, firm, association of persons, body of individuals, whether incorporated or not, or a Hindu undivided family, or any director, partner or member of such company, firm or association of persons or body of individuals or family, or any relative of such director, partner or member, has a substantial interest in the business of that other person. [(w.e.f. 1-4-2016) S. 102(4) of the Income-tax Act, 1961 (43 of 1961)]

"CONNECTED PERSON" means any person who is connected directly or indirectly to another person and includes associated person. [(still-born) Section 102(5) of the Income-tax Act, 1961 (43 of 1961) as inserted (w.e.f. 1-4-2014) by the Finance Act, 2012 (23 of 2013) and omitted (w.e.f. 1-4-2014) by the Finance Act, 2013 (17 of 2013)]

Connection. Act of uniting; state of being united.

Relationship; link; relation between things one of which is bound up with, or involved in, another; a relative.

"Connection" means a link or relationship between people or things or people with whom one has contact. Concise Oxford Dictionary (Indian Edition) as cited in *Chloro Controls India Private Limited* v. *Seven Trent Water Purification Inc.*, (2013) 1 SCC 641, para 145.

An act of reason coupled with deliberation. It denotes an active will in the mind of a person to permit the doing of an act complained of. *Kaini Rajan* v. *State of Kerala*, (2013) 9 SCC 113, para 12.

CONNECTION (CONNEXION), RELATION. These words are applied to two or more things to denote the manner in which they stand in regard to each other. A connexion denotes that which binds two objects, or the situation of being so bound by some tie; but relation denotes the situation of two or more objects in regard to each other, yet without defining what it is; a connexion is therefore a species of relation, but a relation may be something which does not amount to a connexion. Families are connected with each other by ties of blood or marriage; persons are connected with each other in the way of trade or business.

Connivance. A figurative expression, meaning voluntary blindness to some present act or conduct, to something going on before the eyes, and is inapplicable to anything past or future; an agreement or consent, directly or indirectly given that something unlawful shall be done by another; consent; passive consent; voluntary oversight. (*Ame. Cyc.*)

"Connivance," in *Matrimonial Law* is the willing consent to a conjugal offence or by way of acquiescence in a course of conduct reasonably likely to lead to the offence being committed.

To constitute 'connivance' something more than mere negligence is necessary. *Pothi Gollari* v. *Ghanni Mondal*, MLJ : QD (1961-1965) Vol IV C2282-2283 : 29 Cut LT 482 : 1963 Cri LJ 312 : (1962) 4 Orissa JD 359 : ILR (1962) Cut 941 : AIR 1963 Ori 60. [IPC (45 of 1860), S. 497].

Passive consent; a corrupt or guilty assent to wrong doing not involving actual participation in it, but implying knowledge of and failure to prevent or oppose it. [IPC (45 of 1860), Ss. 150 and 497].

Connivance and **Consent.** Connivance invariably and necessarily does not mean consent. It does not necessarily imply that parties are of one mind. Whereas consent implies that parties are *ad idem*. *Charan Lal Sahw* v. *Giani Zail Singh*, AIR 1984 SC 309, 316. [Presidential and Vice-Presidential Election Act (31 of 1952), Ss. 13(a), 14(A), 14, 5B(1)(a)].

"Connive" means to secretly allow a wrongdoing whereas "consent" is permission. Concise Oxford English Dictionary as cited in *Anvar P.V.* v. *P.K. Basheer*, (2014) 10 SCC 473, para 30.

Connotation. The word 'connotation' means the meaning of any word obtained by its association with other words. [*Heinz India Private Ltd.* v. *Glaxo SmithKline Consumer Healthcare,* AIR 2008 (NOC) 1228 (Cal)]

Conquer. To gain or acquire by force; to obtain success.

Conquest. Is the forcible appropriation by one power of territory belonging to another. The completion of the act of appropriation followed by a declaration of annexation, vesting the title of sovereignty in the conquering power. (*Ency. of the Laws of England.*)

Consanguine sister. A sister who has the same father, but a different mother.

Consanguineus. A blood relative; one descended from the same ancestor. (*Latin for Lawyers*)

Consanguineus est quasi eodem sanguine natus. (*Maxim*) A person related by consanguinity is, as it were, sprung from the same blood.

Consanguinity. "Kindred or consanguinity is the connection or relation of persons descended from the same stock or common ancestor. (S. 24)

"Lineal consanguinity is that which subsists between two persons, one of whom is descended in a direct line from the other, as between a man and his father, grandfather and great-grand father, and so upwards in the direct ascending line; or between a man and his son, grandson, great-grandson, and so downwards in the direct descending line. (S. 25)

"Collateral consanguinity is that which subsists between two persons, who are descended from the same stock or ancestor, but neither of whom is descended in a direct line from the other." [S. 26(1)].

CONSANGUINITY (*Consanguinitas*) is a kindred by blood or birth: as *affinity* is a kindred by marriage. (*Tomlin*)

Conscience. Moral sense of right or wrong as applied to one's own judgments and actions; the moral rule requiring justice and honest dealings between people.

'Conscience' is the moral sense of right and wrong of a person. Oxford English Dictionary as cited in *Manoj Narula* v. *Union of India*, (2014) 9 SCC 1, para 143.

Conscience of the Court. Equitable power of the Court to decide issues on the principles of fairness and equality.

Conscientia legalise lege fundatur. (*Maxim*) Legal conscience is founded upon the law. (*Morgan; Broom*)

Conscientia legi nunqum contravenit. (*Maxim*) Conscience never contravenes the law. (*Morgan*)

Conscientia legis ex lege pendet. (*Maxim*) The conscience of the law depends upon the law. (*Morgan*)

Conscientious. "Conscientious" means "wishing to do what is right, relating to a person's conscience". Concise Oxford English Dictionary as cited in *Manoj Narula* v. *Union of India*, (2014) 9 SCC 1, para 146.

Conscientiously. In a conscientious manner. [Delhi Administration Act (19 of 1966), Sch., form No. 3]; [Apprentices Act (52 of 1961), S. 12(a)].

As a matter of conscience; faithfully; accurately. (*Webster.*)

Conscionable. In accord with strict honesty, justice and good conscience.

Conscious. The word 'conscious' means awareness about a particular fact. It is a state of mind which is deliberate or intended. *Madanlal* v. *State of H.P.*, (2003) 7 SCC 465, para 23 : AIR 2003 SC 3642, 3646, para 24 and *Megh Singh* v. *State of Punjab*, (2003) 8 SCC 666, para 10 : AIR 2003 SC 3134. Also see 2003 SCC (Cri) 1664 : AIR 2003 SC 3642 as cited in *Gian Chand* v. *State of Haryana*, (2013) 14 SCC 420, para 17.

Conscious possession. Recovery of *charas* during the search of a car vehicle in which the accused persons were travelling would constitute that the *charas* was found within 'conscious possession' of the accused persons under Section 20 of the Act. *Madanlal* v. *State of H.P.*, (2003) 7 SCC 465, para 19. [N.D.P.S. Act (61 of 1985), S. 20]

Consecutive. Following in uninterrupted succession. [Constitution of India, Art. 164(4)].

The ordinary meaning of the word "consecutive" as given in the Oxford English Dictionary is "following continuously", "in sequence" "expressing consequence or result", "denoted intervals of same kind occurring in succession between two parts or voices". Oxford English Dictionary as cited in *Minati Chowdhury* v. *State of West Bengal and Ors.* AIR 2017 Cal 43, para 11.

Consecutive sentences. A sentence to be served at the time as one or more other sentences, when the accused has been convicted of more than one offence.

Consensus. Agreement of opinion on the part of all concerned.

Consensus ad idem. (*Maxim*) A meeting of minds; one of the essential requisites of the formation of a valid contract. (*Latin*)

Consensus facit jus. (*Lat.*) Consent makes law.

Consensus non concubitus, facit matrimonium. (*Maxim*) It is the consent of the parties, not their concubinage, which constitutes a valid marriage. (*Morgan; Broom*)

Consensus, non concubitus, facit nuptias vel matrimonium, et consentire non possunt ante annos nubiles. (*Maxim*) Consent, and not cohabitation (or coition), constitutes nuptials or marriage, and person cannot consent before marriageable years.

Consensus tollit errorem. (*Maxim*) Consent removes a mistake or the acquiescence of a party who might take advantage of an error obviates its effect. (*Broom; U.P. Mitra; Morgan*)

On this maxim depends the important doctrine of waiver—that is, the passing by of a thing—a doctrine which is of wide application both in the science of pleading and in those practical proceedings which are to be observed in the progress of a cause from the first issuing of a writ to the ultimate signing of judgment and execution. (*Latin for Lawyers*)

Consent. 'Consent' must imply a knowledge of the necessary facts and materials which leads to the consent, consent cannot be given in the abstract or *in vacuo*. *Walchandnagar Industries Ltd.* v. *Ratanchand Khimchand Motishaw*, AIR 1953 Bom 285, 286.

Consent supposes three things—a physical power, a mental power and a free and serious use of them. Hence it is that if consent be obtained by intimidation, force, meditated imposition, circumvention, surprise, or under influence, it is to be treated as a delusion, and not as a deliberate and free act of the mind. Jowitt's Dictionary of English Law as cited in *Dilip* v. *State of M.P.*, (2013) 14 SCC 331, para 19.

Defined, Indian Penal Code (45 of 1860), S. 90 and Indian Contract Act (9 of 1872), S. 13.

'Two or more persons are said to CONSENT when they agree upon the same thing in the same sense.' [Indian Contract Act (9 of 1872), S. 13]

A consent is not such a consent as is intended by any section of this Sanhita,—(a) if the consent is given by a person under fear of injury, or under a misconception of fact, and if the person doing the act knows, or has reason to believe, that the consent was given in consequence of such fear or misconception; or (b) if the consent is given by a person who, from unsoundness of mind, or intoxication, is unable to understand the nature and consequence of that to which he gives his consent; or (c) unless the contrary appears from the context, if the consent is given by a person who is under twelve years of age. [(w.e.f. 1-7-2024) Bharatiya Nyaya Sanhita, 2023 (45 of 2023), section 28]

"Consent" is an act of reason, accompanied with deliberation, the mind weighing, as in a balance, the good and evil on each side.

The 'consent' referred to in O. I, R. 10, CPC (5 of 1908), means an express consent.

If a client be present in Court, and stand by and see his solicitor enter into terms of an agreement, and makes no objection whatever to it, he is deemed to have consented to it and is not at liberty afterwards to repudiate it.

The word 'consent' referred to in the section need not necessarily be an express consent. An implied consent can be spelt out from the agreement itself. *Food Corporation of India* v. *S.K. Samanta,* AIR 1979 Cal 193, 194. [Arbitration Act (10 of 1940) (*repealed*), S. 8(1)(a)].

The word 'consent' as used in S. 30(2) Sale of Goods Act (3 of 1930) means 'agreeing on the same thing in the same sense' as defined in S. 13 of the Contract Act. *Central National Bank Ltd.* v. *United Industrial Bank Ltd.*, AIR 1954 SC 181, 184.

A concurrence of will. [Indian Contract Act (9 of 1872), S. 13].

"The consent (to a contract) is none the less 'genuine' and 'real', even though it be induced by fraud, mistake, or duress. Consent may be induced by a mistaken hope of gain or a mistaken estimate of value or by the lie of a third person, and yet there is a contract and we do not doubt the 'reality of the consent.' Fraud, mistake, and duress are merely collateral operative facts that co-exist with the expressions of consent and have a very important effect upon the resulting legal relations." WILLIAM R. ANSON. *Principles of the Law of Contract 199 n. 1* (Arthur 1. Cectic ed. 3d An ed. 1919."

For constituting 'consent', there must be exercise of intelligence based on the knowledge of the significance and moral effect of the act. A mentally deficient girl cannot be said in law to have suffered sexual intercourses with 'consent' under Section 376 of the Code. *Tulshidas Kanolkar* v. *State of Goa*, (2003) 8 SCC 590, para 6. [IPC (45 of 1860), S. 376]

Submission of her body by the prosecutrix for sexual act under the fear of terror does not amount to 'consent' under Sections 375 and 376 of the Code. *State of H.P.* v. *Mango Ram*, (2000) 7 SCC 224, para 13 : AIR 2000 SC 2798. [IPC (45 of 1860), Ss. 375 and 376]

"CONSENT" means an unequivocal voluntary agreement when the woman by words, gestures or any form of verbal or non-verbal communication, communicates willingness to participate in the specific sexual act: *Provided* that a woman who does not physically resist to the act of penetration shall not by the reason only of that fact, be regarded as consenting to the sexual activity. [*Explanation* 2 to S. 375 of IPC, 1860 (45 of 1860), as substituted by the Criminal Laws (Amendment) Act, 2013 (13 of 2013)]

Consent, Age of. The age at which one can enter into a contract of marriage without the consent of the parents or guardian.

Consent and approbation. Approbation in Matrimonial Law, subsequent to a marriage is not, in general, a sufficient compliance with a condition requiring 'consent'. (*Ld. Hardwicke* in *Burleton* v. *Humfrey*, Amb 256. See also *Clarke* v. *Parker*, 19 Ver. 21 : 2 Jarm. 55).

Consent and assent. 'Consent' in law means an affirmative, positive act and 'assent' means passivity or inaction.

Consent and Connive. Connivance is also consent in the legal sense. 'To consent' means according to the Concise Oxford Dictionary, 'to acquiesce' or 'to agree'. 'To connive' at a thing means, to wink at it. The word 'connive' is only used in connection with a thing which is unlawful or immoral which one ought to oppose. It implies knowledge and lack of opposition where there is a duty to oppose. *Sheopat Singh* v. *Narishchandra,* AIR 1958 Raj 324, 332. [Representation of the People Act (43 of 1951), S. 100].

Consent award. The award rendered as the result of a negotiated settlement between the parties at the interlocutory stage or during the hearing. The arbitrator will set out the terms of the settlement and incorporate them in his award. (*Arbitration*)

Consent based Aadhaar authentication service" means electronic authentication carried out by Unique Identification Authority of India (UIDAI), or agencies appointed by it, after matching the biometric information of an individual at his request or with his consent, with the information maintained by UIDAI in its own central servers, and includes a 'Yes/No' response, or a response containing the demographic information and photograph of that individual. Right to Fair Compensation and Transparency in Land Acquisition, Rehabilitation and Resettlement (Compensation, Rehabilitation and Resettlement and Development Plan) Rules, 2015, R. 2 (c).

Consent decree. An award decree need not be treated as consent decree. *Parkesh Chand Khurana Etc.* v. *Harnam Singh*, AIR 1973 SC 2065, 2070. [CPC (5 of 1908), O. XXIII, Rule 3].

Consent free and voluntary. 'Free and voluntary consent' is active consent, as distinguished from that consent which is said to be implied by silence.

"Consent Manager". Means a person registered with the Board, who acts as a single point of contact to enable a Data Principal to give, manage, review and withdraw her consent through an accessible, transparent and interoperable platform. [Digital Personal Data Protection Act, 2023 (22 of 2023), section 2(g)]

Consentientes et agentes pari poena plectentur. (*Maxim*) Those consenting and those perpetrating are embraced in the same punishment. (*Morgan*)

Consentire est facere. (*Maxim*) To consent to a thing is to do a thing. (*Morgan*)

Consentire matrimonio non possunt infra annos nubiles. (*Maxim*) Consent to a marriage is not possible in the parties before marriageable years. (*Morgan*)

Consequence. A thing or circumstance which follows as an effect or result from something preceding.

The word 'consequence' in CrPC 1973 (2 of 1974), S. 179, means a consequence which forms a part and parcel of the offence and does not mean a consequence which is not such a direct result of the act of the offender as to form no part of that offence.

Consequent failure of justice. Justice becoming unavailing, worthless or non-existent following or as a result of (something). [CPC (5 of 1908), S. 18(2)].

Consequentiae non est consequentia. (*Maxim*) The consequence of a consequence does not exist. (*Morgan; Broom*)

Consequential. Following as a consequence. [Constitution of India, Art. 4(1)].

Damages following an act, but not the direct and immediate result of it.

Consequential damage or injury. Is a damage or injury which arises by consequence to one person, from the culpable act or omission of another.

Consequential damages. Damages following an act, but not the direct and immediate result of it.

Consequential losses. It is a fundamental principle in law and reason, that he who does the first wrong shall answer for all conesquential damages. (*Tomlin*)

Consequential relief. Consequential relief means a substantial and immediate remedy in accordance with the title which the Court has been asked to declare. A futile and demurrable claim for injunction is excluded.

The expression 'consequential relief' means some relief, which would follow directly from the declaration given, the valuation of which is not capable of being definitely ascertained and which is not specifically provided for anywhere in the Act and cannot be claimed independently of the declaration as a substantial relief. *Purushotham Dass* v. *Har Narain,* AIR 1978 Del 114, 119 (FB). [Court Fees Act (7 of 1870), S. 7(iv)(*c*)].

Conservancy. Includes dredging, training, closure, diversion or abandoning channels; [Inland Waterways Authority of India Act (82 of 1985), S. 2(d)]

"CONSERVANCY" means the removal and disposal of sewage, offensive matter and rubbish. [Manipur Municipalities Act (43 of 1994), S. 2(6)]

Conservancy measures. Means measures for purposes of conservancy, but does not include measures for protection of banks against floods or for restricting banks which have become eroded mainly on account of reasons not connected with shipping and navigation. [Inland Waterways Authority of India Act (82 of 1985), S. 2(e)]

Conservation. Conservation means preservation and protection of existing forests and also re-afforestation. *Annapana Minerals* v. *UOI,* AIR 1986 AP 225, 237. [Forest (Conservation) Act (69 of 1980), S. 2].

Preservation from loss, injury, decay or waste. [Wealth-tax Act (27 of 1957), S. 5(1)(ix)].

Conservation and management measures. Means measures to conserve and manage one or more species of living marine resources that are adopted and applied consistent with the relevant rules of International Law as reflected in the Convention and the agreement. [UN Conference on Straddling Fish Stocks and Highly Migratory Fish Stocks, Art. (1)(b), 24 July 4 Aug., 1995]

Conservation area. An area which is designated as such by a local planning authority because it is of special architectural or historic interest the character of which ought to be preserved or enhanced.

Conservative. Of conserving tendency; opposed to change; moderate; member of the conservative party.

Consider. To think over; to regard as or deem to be.

The word "consider" merely connotes that there should be active application of the mind by the disciplinary authority after considering the entire circumstances of the case in order to decide the nature and extent of the penalty to be imposed on the delinquent employee on his conviction on a criminal charge. *Divisional Personal Officer Southern Railway* v. *T.R. Challpran*, AIR 1975 SC 2216, 2226.

"Consider" means "to think over", "to regard as", or "deem to be". *Chairman, Life Insurance Corporation of India* v. *A. Masilamani*, (2013) 6 SCC 530, para 19.

Considerable part. Pretty large part.

Consideration. "When, at the desire of the promisor, the promisee or any other person has done or abstained from doing, or does or abstains from doing, or promises to do or to abstain from doing, something, such act or abstinence or promise is called a CONSIDERATION for the promise." [Indian Contract Act (9 of 1872), S. 2(d)].

"Consideration" means 'a benefit to the party promising or a loss or detriment to the party to whom the promise is made ...' some benefit to the promisor, or some detriment to the promisee." Corpus Juris Secundum, (Vol. 17 pp. 420-21 and 425) as cited in *Commissioner of Central Excise, Mumbai* v. *Fiat India Private Limited*, (2012) 9 SCC 332, para 70].

"A consideration in its widest sense is the reason, motive or inducement, by which a man is moved to bind himself by an agreement. It is for nothing that he consents to impose an obligation upon himself, or to abandon or transfer a right. It is in consideration of such and such a fact that he agrees to bear new burdens or to forego the benefits which the law already allows him." [Salmond on Jurisprudence as cited in *Commissioner of Central Excise, Mumbai* v. *Fiat India Private Limited*, (2012) 9 SCC 332, para 71].

Currie v. *Misa*, (1875) LR 10 Ex. 162, defines valuable consideration as "A valuable consideration in the sense of the law may consist either in some right, interest, profit or benefit accruing to one party, or some forbearance, detriment loss, or responsibility, given, suffered or undertaken by the other." Also See *Chidambara Iyer* v. *P.S. Renga Iyer*, AIR 1966 SC 193; *Commissioner of Central Excise, Mumbai* v. *Fiat India Private Limited*, (2012) 9 SC 332, para 68.

"Consideration" in relation to the supply of goods or services or both includes—

(a) any payment made or to be made, whether in money or otherwise, in respect of, in response to, or for the inducement of, the supply of goods or services or both, whether by the recipient or by any other person but shall not include any subsidy given by the Central Government or a State Government;

(b) the monetary value of any act or forbearance, in respect of, in response to, or for the inducement of, the supply of goods or services or both, whether by the recipient or by any other person but shall not include any subsidy given by the Central Government or a State Government:

Provided that a deposit given in respect of the supply of goods or services or both shall not be considered as payment made for such supply unless the supplier applies such deposit as consideration for the said supply [The Central Goods and Services Tax Act, 2017 (12 of 2017), S. 2(31)]

'CONSIDERATION' in relation to a dwelling unit/flat or other built up property or any other property shall include the price fixed by the Board for allotment of such property by way of sale, hire-purchase or lease or in any other manner premium, hire purchase, lease money and ground rent. [Chandigarh Housing Board (Allotment, Management and Sale of Tenements) Regulations, 1979, Regn. 2(10)]

Anything regarded as compense or equivalent for what one does or undertakes for another's benefit [Indian Contract Act (9 of 1872), S. 2(d)]; careful thought.

CONSIDERATION, is the material cause of any contract, without which it will not generally be effectual or binding. (*Tomlin*)

It may take the form of a money payment, a delivery of goods or a promise of money payment. The definition of consideration in S. 2(*d*), Indian Contract Act (9 of 1872), shows that consideration means an act, abstinence or promise made by the promisee or some other person at the desire of the promisor. Surrender of a disputed title is a good consideration for a contract.

"Consideration" means a reasonable equivalent or other valuable benefit passed on by the promisor to the promise or by the transferor to the transferee. [*Commissioner of Central Excise, Mumbai* v. *Fiat India Private Limited*, (2012) 9 SCC 332, para 58].*Sonia Bhatia* v. *State of U.P.*, AIR 1981 SC 1274, 1280. [Indian Contract Act (9 of 1872), S. 2(*d*)].

"CONSIDERATION" in relation to the supply of goods or services or both includes—

(a) any payment made or to be made, whether in money or otherwise, in respect of, in response to, or for the inducement of, the supply of goods or services or both, whether by the recipient or by any other person but shall not include any subsidy given by the Central Government or a State Government;

(b) the monetary value of any act or forbearance, in respect of, in response to, or for the inducement of, the supply of goods or services or both, whether by the recipient or by any other person but shall not include any subsidy given by the Central Government or a State Government:

Provided that a deposit given in respect of the supply of goods or services or both shall not be considered as payment made for such supply unless the supplier applies such deposit as consideration for the said supply. [Central Goods and Services Tax Act (12 of 2017), S. 2(31)].

Consideration, For. In return of some consideration. [T.P. Act (4 of 1882), S. 45].

Consideration for promise. When, at the desire of the promisor, the promisee or any other person has done or abstained from doing, or does or abstains from doing, something, such act or abstinence or promise is called a consideration for the promise. [Indian Contract Act (9 of 1872), S. 2(d)]

Consideration or object. In a gift in favour of woman with whom the donor has adulterous cohabitation, the adulterous cohabitation is the motive and not the consideration or object of the gift. [Indian Contract Act (9 of 1872), S. 23].

Considerations. Something that is considered as ground of opinion or action. [Trade and Merchandise Marks Act (43 of 1958), S. 62(3)].

Considers it necessary. The words "considers it necessary" postulate that the authority concerned has thought over the matter deliberately and with care and it has been found necessary as a result of such thinking to pass the order. *Barium Chemicals* v. *A.J. Rana,* AIR 1972 SC 591, 595. [Foreign Exchange Regulation Act (7 of 1947), S. 19(2)] [Now repealed & replaced by Act 42 of 1999]

Consign. To transfer to another's charge or custody.

To deliver or to transmit (goods) for sale or custody, usually implying their transit by ship, railway *etc.*

Consigned to the record room. Where by an order execution proceedings are 'consigned to the record room', the order is tantamount to 'a dismissal' of the application concerned.

Consignee. A person to whom goods are consigned.

Consignment. "CONSIGNMENT" means the goods entrusted to a multimodal transport operator for multimodal transportation. [Multimodal Transportation of Goods Act (28 of 1993), S. 2(d)]

"CONSIGNMENT" means goods entrusted to a railway administration for carriage. [Railways Act (24 of 1989), S. 2(9)]

The act or process of consigning goods; the transportation of goods consigned.

Consignment note. A document to be filled up before despatching of goods by rail or through other common carrier.

Consignor. "CONSIGNOR" means the person named in a railway receipt as consignor, by whom or on whose behalf goods covered by the railway receipt are entrusted to a railway administration for carriage. [Railways Act (24 of 1989), S. 2(10)]

"CONSIGNOR" means the person, named in the multimodal transport contract as consignor, by whom or on whose behalf the goods covered by such contract are entrusted to a multimodal transport operator for multimodal transportation. [Multimodal Transportation of Goods Act (28 of 1993), S. 2(e)]

One who consigns goods to another.

Consistent. Compatable; not contradictory (as) Rules *consistent* with the provisions of a Code.

In harmony; in accord; compatible.

CONSISTENT WITH THE CODE.—The words "consistent with the Code" in S. 157 of the CPC (5 of 1908) mean only consistent with the sections of the Code and not with the rules in the first schedule which can be altered by the High Court.

Consolation. Comfort, contentment, ease, enjoyment, happiness, pleasure, satisfaction. (*Black*)

Consolidate. In a general sense, to unite or unify into one mass or body.

To combine compactly into one connected whole.

Consolidated plan. For the purposes of this clause, "CONSOLIDATED PLAN" means the plan with which the consolidating plan merges or which is formed as a result of such merger. [Income-tax Act (43 of 1961), S. 47(xix), *Explanation (b)*].

Consolidating plan. For the purposes of this clause, "CONSOLIDATING PLAN" means the plan within a scheme of a mutual fund which merges under the process of consolidation of the plans within a scheme of mutual fund in accordance with the Securities and Exchange Board of India (Mutual Funds) Regulations, 1996 made under the Securities and Exchange Board of India Act, 1992 (15 of 1992). [Income-tax Act (43 of 1961), S. 47(xix), *Explanation (a)*].

Consolidated Fund. The fund of money formed of all taxes and other government revenues.

Consolidated Fund of India. All revenues received by the Government of India, all loans raised by that Government by the issue of treasury bills, loans or ways and means advances and all moneys received by that Government in repayment of loans shall form one consolidated fund to be entitled "the Consolidated Fund of India." [Constitution of India, Art. 266].

Consolidated Fund of State. All revenues received by the Government of a State, all loans raised by that Government by the issue of treasury bills, loans or ways and means advances and all moneys received by that Government in repayment of loans shall form one consolidated fund to be entitled "the Consolidated Fund of the State." [Constitution of India, Art. 266].

Consolidation. Making strong by coherence of organization; combination (as) consolidation of companies; consolidation of statutes or of debts.

The state of being united; the act or process of uniting.

The word 'consolidation' means the consolidation of two pieces of land, which are contigeous to one another, which are owned by the same person and which can be cultivated as one piece of land.

Consolidation of Actions. Consolidation of actions may be defined generally as the union of two or more actions in one. (*Burrill*)

Consols. Government securities consolidated into a single stock.

Consort. Spouse.

"The idea implicit in 'consorting' suggests a more or less close personal relationship: at least some degree of familiarity or intimacy with persons, or attraction from or an enjoyment of some feature in common, that results in a tendency towards companionship".

Consortium. Consortium means companionship, love, affection, comfort, mutual services, sexual intercourse. All these things belongs to the married state. Taken together they make up consortium. *Hartinder Kaur* v. *Harmander Singh Choudhry*, AIR 1984 Del 66, 69. [Hindu Marriage Act (25 of 1955), Ss. 9, 13].

"Consortium" is the right of the spouse to the company, care, help, comfort, guidance, society, solace, affection and sexual relations with his or her mate. [*Rajesh* v. *Rajbir Singh*, (2013) 9 SCC 54, para 17].

'Consortium' connotes only the husband and the wife and the companionship, fellowship or togetherness of the husband and the wife. *Farooque* v. *Ahmedabad Municipality,* AIR 1985 Guj 114, 115. [Fatal Accidents Act (13 of 1855), S. 1-A].

Conjugal fellowship of husband and wife, and the right of each to the company, society, cooperation, affection, and aid of the other in every conjugal relation.

Loss of "consortium" consists of several elements, encompassing not only material services but such intangibles as society, guidance, companionship, and sexual relations.

Damages for loss of consortium are commonly sought in wrongful death actions, or when spouse has been seriously injured through the negligence of another, or by spouse against third person alleging that he or she has caused breaking-up of marriage. Cause of action for "consortium" occasioned by injury to marriage partner, is a separate cause of action belonging to the spouse of the injured married partner and though derivative in the sense of being occasioned by injury to spouse, is a direct injury to the spouse who has lost the consortium.

Conspicuous. Clearly visible, obvious or striking to the eye.

Conspicuous place. A "conspicuous place" means one which is reasonably calculated to impart the information in question. (*Black*)

Conspiracy. When two or more persons agree to commit any crime, they are guilty of conspiracy whether the crime is committed or not.

A planning and acting together secretly, especially for an unlawful or harmful purpose; the plan agreed on; plot.

It is a combination between two or more persons to do a criminal or an unlawful act or a lawful act by criminal or unlawful means.

In conspiracy the concert or agreement of the two minds is the offence, the overt act is but the outward and visible evidence of it.

A conspiracy means nothing more than a combination and agreement by persons to do some illegal act or acts.

Constable. An inferior officer to whom the service of maintaining the peace, and bringing to justice those by whom it is infringed, is more immediately committed.

Constabulary. The police force.

Constituency. A population-based geographical area for the election of a member of the parliament, state legislature or local bodies.

A geographical area for elections to Parliament and State Legislatures. Thus, an Assembly constituency is a constituency for elections to the Legislative Assembly of a State; Council Constituency is a constituency for electrons to the Legislative Council of a State and a Parliamentary constituency is a constituency for elections to the House of the People. [Representation of the People Act (43 of 1950), Ss. 2(b), (c) and (f)].

The Delimitation Commission is empowered to a stribute seats in the House of the People allocated to each State and the seats assigned to the Legislative Assembly of each State to single-member territorial constituencies and delimit them on the basis of the latest census figures. [Delimitation Act (76 of 1972), S. 9.]

Constituency, Territorial. Each state shall be divided into as many territorial constituencies as the members to be elected, in such a manner that the ratio between the population of each constituency and the number of seats allotted to it is, so far as practicable, the same throughout the state. [Constitution of India, Art. 81(2)(b) and 170(2)].

Constituent. Electing a representative (as constituent body); charged with making or changing a constitution (*as constituent assembly*). It is a word used as a correlative to "attorney", to denote one who constitutes another his agent or invests the other with authority to act for him. It is also used in the language of politics, as a correlative to "representative," the constitutes of a legislator being those whom he represents and whose interests he is to care for in public affairs; usually the electors of his district.

"Constituent" means "serving to form or compose as a necessary part". [*Saraswati Sugar Mills* v. *Commissioner of Central Excise, Delhi-III*, (2014) 15 SCC 625, para 23].

Constituting; empowered to appoint or elect a repesentative (as constituent body); charged with making or changing a constitution (*as constituent assembly*). Serving to make up a thing; component.

Constituent Assembly. A legislative body charged with the task of framing or revising a Constitution; set up for India after it became independent in 1947 for the purpose of framing its Constitution.

Constituent entity. For the purposes of this section, "CONSTITUENT ENTITY" means,

(i) any separate entity of an international group that is included in the consolidated financial statement of the said group for financial reporting purposes, or may be so included for the said purpose, if the equity share of any entity of the international group were to be listed on a stock exchange

(ii) any such entity that is excluded from the consolidated financial statement of the international group solely on the basis of size or materiality; or

(iii) any permanent establishment of any separate business entity of the international group included in clause (i) or clause (ii), if such business unit prepares a separate financial statement for such permanent establishment for financial reporting, regulatory, tax reporting or internal management control purposes;

"Constituent Institution". Means an institution operating under the administrative, academic and financial control of the sponsoring body and declared as such under the Notification. [UGC (Institutions Deemed to be Universities) Regulations, 2019, Regn. 2 (2.05)].

Constitute. To appoint, depute, elect; to establish.

To make (a thing) what it is; to frame; to compose; to appoint.

Constituted. The word "constituted" does not necessarily mean "created" or "set up" though it may mean that also. It also includes the idea of clothing the agreement in a legal form. The word in its wider significance, would include both the idea of creating or establishing, and the idea of giving a legal form to, a partnership. The words "constituted under an instrument of partnership "include not only firms which have been created by an instrument of partnership but also those which may have been created by word of (mouth) and have been subsequently clothed in legal form by reducing the terms and conditions of the partnership to writing. *R.C. Mitter and Sons* v. *Commissioner of Income Tax*, AIR 1959 SC 868, 873, 874.

Constitution. The system or body of fundamental principles according to which a nation, state or body politic is constituted and governed; the action of constituting; composition; to set up; to establish.

Constitution and **Statutes.** There is essential distinction between Constitution and statutes. Constitution is permanent and an organic statute and it grows by its own inherent force. *Golak Nath* v. *State of Punjab*, AIR 1967 SC 1643, 1666.

Constitutional Law. Constitutional Law is a branch of public law containing so much of the political constitution as is laid down in positive legal rules, and as including such subjects as the formation, powers, and privileges of the legislature, the executive functions and powers of the head of the executive, the existence and composition of the judicial establishment and the machinery of local government. (*Ency. of the Laws of England.*)

In the generally accepted use of the term it means the rules which regulate the structure of the principal organs of government and their relationship to each other, and determine their principal functions. In other words, it could be expected to contain only the basic framework. *State of Karnataka* v. *Union of India,* AIR 1978 SC 68.

"Constitutional culture", Is inherent in the concepts where words are transformed into concrete consequences. It is an interlocking system of practices, institutional arrangements, norms and habits of thought. It is the conceptual normative spirit that transforms the Constitution into a dynamic document. It is the constitutional culture that constantly enables the words to keep its stride with the rapid and swift changes occurring in the society. [*State (NCT of Delhi)* v. *Union of India,* (2018) 8 SCC 501, paras 161 and 162].

"Constitutional document". In relation to a corporate person, includes articles of association, memorandum of association of a company and incorporation document of a Limited Liability Partnership. [Insolvency and Bankruptcy Code (31 of 2016), S. 5(4)].

Constitutional safe-guards. Part III of Constitution sets out the safeguards for certain rights of the people and secures these rights from invasion by the State itself.

Constitutionality. The quality or state of being constitutional.

Constitutiones tempore posteriores potiores sunt his quae ipsas praecesserunt. (*Maxim*) Later laws prevail over those which preceded them. (*Black*)

Constitutions of Clarendon. Statutes enacted in 1164, during the reign of Henry II, by which the jurisdiction of the ecclesiastical Courts was limited and the clerics' exemptions from secular jurisdiction were greatly narrowed.

Constrain. To force; to compel.

Construct. With its grammatical variations, in relation to a building, means to construct, reconstruct, erect, re-erect, extend or alter structurally a building. [Control of National Highways (Land and Traffic) Act, 2002 (13 of 2003), S. 2(c)]

Construction. Thing constructed (as) construction of a building. Interpretation of or way of understanding particular words used in an Act or other document (as) construction of Acts, of deeds or of wills.

"Construction" of any structure includes additions to or alterations of an existing building. Karnataka Ancient and Historical Monuments and Archaeological Sites and Remains Rules, 1966, R. 2(b) as cited in *K. Guruprasad Rao* v. *State of Karnataka*, (2013) 8 SCC 418, para 21.

The construing, explaining or interpreting of a text, statement, action or words *etc.*; building.

Construction and Interpretation. "Interpretation" as applied to a written *constitution* means to determine the true sense of the words used in the text. In practice *construction includes interpretation*, and both terms are frequently used synonymously. (*Bouvier*)

"Construction documents". Means drawings or documents containing information pertaining to building construction processes and approvals, building materials and equipment specification, architectural details required by the authority having jurisdiction. [Energy Conservation Building Code Rules, 2018, R. 2(1)(j)].

Construction of complex. "CONSTRUCTION OF COMPLEX" means—

(a) construction of a new residential complex or a part thereof; or

(b) completion and finishing services in relation to residential complex such as glazing, plastering, painting, floor and wall tiling, wall covering and wall papering, wood and metal joinery and carpentry, fencing and railing, construction of swimming pools, acoustic applications or fittings and other similar services; or

(c) repair, alteration, renovation or restoration of, or similar services in relation to, residential complex.

[Finance Act (32 of 1994), S. 65(30a) *as substituted by Finance Act (18 of 2005), S. 88(a)(viii)* (now repealed by Central Goods and Services Tax Act, 2017)]

Construction service. Means,—

(a) construction of new building or civil structure or a part thereof; or

(b) repair, alteration or restoration of, or similar services in relation to, building or civil structure,

which is—

(i) used, or to be used, primarily for; or

(ii) occupied, or to be occupied, primarily with; or

(iii) engaged, or to be engaged, primarily in,

commerce or industry, or work intended for commerce or industry, but does not include road, airport, railway, transport terminal, bridge, tunnel, long distance pipeline and dam. [Finance Act (32 of 1994), S. 65(30), (30a) (*Inserted by Finance (No. 2) Act, 2004 (23 of 2004), S. 90*) (now repealed by Central Goods and Services Tax Act, 2017)]

Constructive. Derivative; inferential. That which has not the character assigned to it in its own nature, but acquires such character in consequence of the way in which it is regarded by a rule or policy of law; implied; by inference; made out by legal interpretation; "that which is established by the operation of the law in its act "construing facts, conduct, circumstances, or instruments". It also means, tending towards construction of a positive kind, as opposed to destructive or negative (as) constructive proposal; constructive criticism.

That which has not the character assigned to its own nature but acquires such character in consequence of the way in which it is regarded by a rule of or policy of law; inferential. [Agricultural Refinance and Development Corporation Act (10 of 1963), S. 8(2)].

Constructive assent. Implied assent; an assent or consent imputed to a party from a construction or interpretation of his conduct; as distinguished from one which he actually expresses.

Constructive contempt. A contempt which, without open insult or direct opposition, tends to induce a general disregard of the authority of a Court.

Constructive delivery. A delivery not actually made, but in the law regarded as made; symbolical delivery.

Constructive desertion. The test is not who left the matrimonial home first. If one spouse by his words and conduct compels the other spouse to leave the marital house, the former would be guilty of desertion, though it is the latter who has physically separated from the other and has been made to leave the marital home. In such a case, the husband is guilty of constructive desertion. *Bipindrandra Shah* v. *Prabhavati*, AIR 1957 SC 176, 188.

Constructive dismissal. A dismissal which is to be inferred from the fact that the employer's conduct is such that the employee has no choice but to resign.

Constructive fraud. Fraud inferred by law, fraud in law, as distinguished from fraud in fact.

S. 18, cl. (2) of the Indian Contract Act (9 of 1872) is probably intended to meet all those cases which are called cases of "constructive fraud." Where there is no intention to deceive, but the circumstances are such as to make the party, who derives a benefit from the transaction, equally answerable in effect, as if he had been actuated by motives of fraud and deceit, is a case of constructive fraud.

Constructive knowledge. If one by exercise of reasonable care would have known a fact, he is deemed to have had constructive knowledge of such fact; *e.g.* matters of public record. *Attoe* v. *State, Farm Mutual Auto, Ins. Co.*, 36 Wis. 2d 539, 153 NW 2d 575, 579.

Constructive malice. Malice inferred from the conduct of a person.

Constructive notice. Notice inferred by law, as distinguished from actual or formal notice; that which is held by law to amount to notice.

"Constructive notice" means that a man ought to have known a fact. A person to have notice of a fact when he actually knows a fact but for wilful abstention from inquiry or search which he ought to have made, or gross negligence he would have known it. Constructive notice is a notice inferred by law, as distinguished from actual or formal notice; that which is held by law to amount to notice. [*Rajasthan Housing Board* v. *New Pink City Nirman Sahkari Samiti Limited*, (2015) 7 SCC 601, para 16].

Constructive notice in legal fiction signifies that the individual person should know as a reasonable person would have. Even if they have no actual knowledge of it. Constructive notice means a man ought to have known a fact. A person is said to have notice of a fact when he actually knows a fact but for wilful abstention from inquiry or search which he ought to have made, or gross negligence he would have known it. Constructive notice is a notice inferred by law, as distinguished from actual or formal notice, that which is held by law amounts to notice. *Rajasthan Housing Board* v. *New Pinkcity Nirman Sahkari Samiti Limited* (2015) 7 SCC 601, para 16.

Constructive payment. Where the payee has made the payment but the payee has not credited it yet, it would be constructive payment, for example, the payment of rent made by cheque on the due date but not yet deposited by the landlord in his account.

Constructive possession. Possession in contemplation of law. By 'constructive possession' is generally meant possession, as distinguished from actual possession, through a tenant or agent. It has also been used in connection with property which is incapable of actual possession and is said to be in the constructive possession of the owner as waste lands or lands under water. If the person is the owner of a property but does not use it for some time, it cannot be said that he is in constructive possession of it. He is in actual possession so long as he has the power to bring it into use whenever he likes.

A person has constructive possession of property if he has power to control and intent to control such item exists where one does not have physical custody or possession, but is in a position to exercise dominion or control over a thing. (*Black*)

Constructive res judicata. In order to invoke in aid the doctrine of constructive *res judicata*, there must be a decision by the Court either in express terms or by necessary implication. *See also* CPC (5 of 1908), S. 11.

Constructive taking. The taking need not, unlike theft in the criminal law, be necessarily a physical moving or handling of the goods; it may be constructive as by a transfer in the books of a banker or warehouseman or endorsement of documents of title.

Constructive total loss. In marine insurance law, it is a law which entitles the insured to claim the whole amount of his insurance.

Constructive trust. A trust arising by operation of law apart from any intention to create a trust.

Constructive trustee. The person deemed to be a trustee in the case of a constructive trust.

Construe. To give the sense or meaning of; to interpret; to put a construction on.

Consuetudo debet esse certa; nam incerta pro nulla (nullius) habetur. (*Maxim*) A custom should be certain; for an uncertain custom is considered null. (*Broom*); [*Saraswathi Ammal* v. *Jagadambal*, AIR 1953, SC 201 (205)].

Consuetudo est altera lex. (*Maxim*) Custom is another law.

Consuetudo est optimus interpres legum. (*Maxim*) Custom is the best expounder (interpreter) of the laws. (*Black*)

Consuetudo loci est observanda. (*Maxim*) The custom of a place is to be observed.

A custom may be defined to be a usage which has obtained the force of law, and is, in truth, the binding law within a particular district or at a particular place, of the persons and things which it concerns. There are several requisites to the validity of a custom: it must be certain, reasonable in itself, have existed from times immemorial, have continued without any interruption, have been peaceably enjoyed and acquiesced in, be compulsory, be consistent with other local customs.

Consuetudo non trahitur in consequentiam. (*Maxim*) Custom is not drawn into consequence.

Consul. A consul is an official appointed by his Government to reside at a definite place abroad, and there fulfil certain duties in the interest of his country and fellow citizens.

An officer appointed by his government to reside at a definite place abroad and there fulfil certain duties in the interest of his country and fellow citizens. [General Clauses Act (10 of 1897), S. 3(16)].

Consular archives. Includes all the papers, documents, correspondence, book, films, tapes and registers of the Consular post, together with the ciphers and codes, the Card Indexes and any article of furniture intended for their protection or safe keeping. [Vienna Convention on Consular Relations, 1963, Art. 1(k)]

Consular district. Means the area assigned to consular post for the exercise of consular functions. [Vienna Convention on Consular Relations, 1963, Art. 1(b)]

Consular employee. Means any person employed in the administrative or technical service of a consular post. [Vienna Convention on Consular Relations, 1963, Art. 1(e)]

Consular officer. "CONSULAR OFFICER" shall include consul-general, consul, vice-consul, consular agent, pro-consul and any person for the time being authorised to perform the duties of consul-general, consul, vice-consul or consular agent. [General Clauses Act (10 of 1897), S. 3, Cl. 16].

"Consular Officer," when used in relation to a Foreign Country, means, the officer recognised by the government as a Consular Officer of that Foreign Country".

Consular premises. Means the buildings or parts of buildings and the land ancillary thereto, irrespective of ownership, used exclusively for the purposes of the consular post. [Vienna Convention on Consular Relations, 1963, Art. 1(j)]

Consulate. Consul's office or tenure of office; Consul's Official residence.

The office of consul. [S. 20(1), Registration of Births and Deaths Act (18 of 1969)].

Consult. Consult implies a conference of two or more persons or the impact of two or more minds brought about in respect of a topic with a view to evolve a correct or at least a satisfactory solution. It must be directed to the essential points of the subject under discussion and enable the consultor to consider the pros and cons before coming to a decision.

The word 'consult' is defined as under:-"consult - verb - seek information or advice from someone, especially an expert or professional" [Concise Oxford English Dictionary as cited in *M. Saraswathy vs. The District Collector, Vellore District and Ors.* 20172WritLR232, para 7]

Consultant. One who gives professional advice.

Consultation. Taking counsel.

The term "consultation" occurring in section 435(1) of the Code should be interpreted to mean "concurrence". *Union of India* v. *V. Sriharan*, (2014) 11 SCC 1, para 17 [Criminal Procedure Code, 1973 (2 of 1974), S. 435(1)].

An act of asking the advice or opinion of someone (such as a lawyer). It means a meeting in which a party consults or confers and eventually it results in human interaction that leads to rendering of advice. *GVK Industries Limited* v. *Income Tax Officer*, (2015) 11 SCC 734, para 39.

The scheme of 'consultation' under the Constitution varies. The word 'consult' as understood in ordinary parlance means to ask or seek advice or the views of a person on any given subject *i.e.* to take counsel from another but it does not convey that the consultant is bound by the advice. *S.C. Advocates-on Record Association* v. *Union of India*, AIR 1994 SC 268, 382. [Constitution of India, Arts. 124(2), 217(1)].

Consultation is a process which requires meeting of minds between the parties involved in the process of consultation on the material facts and points involved to evolve a correct or at least satisfactory solution. *Indian Administrative Service (S.C.S.) Assn.* v. *Union of India,* 1993 Supp (1) SCC 730, 752 to 754.

The word 'consultation' occurring in Arts. 233 and 234 means 'meaningful, effective and conscious consultation'. *Gauhati High Court* v. *Kuladhar Phukan*, (2002) 4 SCC 524, para 14 : AIR 2002 SC 1589. [Constitution of India, Arts. 233 & 234]

Consultation: Aid and advice—Distinction. The only distinction being that "consultation" is obtained whereas "aid and advice" may be tendered. [*Supreme Court Advocates-on-Record Association* v. *Union of India,* (2016) 5 SCC 1, para 130

Consultation committee. "CONSULTATION COMMITTEE" means the stakeholders' consultation committee constituted under sub-regulation (1) of regulation 31A. [Insolvency and Bankruptcy Board of India (Liquidation Process) Regulations, 2016, Regn. 2(1)(ba)]

Consulting engineer. Means any professionally qualified engineer or an engineering firm who, either directly or indirectly, renders any advice, consultancy or technical assistance in any manner to a client in one or more disciplines of engineering. [Finance Act (32 of 1994), S. 65(25) (now repealed by Central Goods and Services tax Act, 2017)]

Consumables. 'Consumables' means any item which participates in or is required for a manufacturing process, but does not form part of the end product, items which are substantially or totally consumed during a manufacturing process will be deemed to be consumables. The Export and Import Policy 1997-2002, 3.13 as cited in *Meridian Industries Limited* v. *Commissioner of Central, Excise*, (2015) SCC 469, para 15.

Consume. The word 'consume' means to drink or to otherwise use prohibited liquor.

Consumer. A purchaser of goods or services. [Oxford Dictionary as cited in *LDA* v. *M.K. Gupta*, (1994) 1 SCC 243, para 3] See also *Narne Construction Private Limited* v. *Union of India*, (2012) 5 SCC 359, para 3.

'Consumer' means 'one who consumes. Individuals who purchase, use, maintain, and dispose of products and services. A member of that broad class of people who are affected by pricing policies, financing practices, quality of goods and services, credit reporting, debt collection, and other trade practices for which State and federal consumer protection laws are enacted.' Black's Law Dictionary as cited in *LDA* v. *M.K. Gupta*, (1994) 1 SCC 243, para 3. See also *Narne Construction Private Limited* v. *Union of India*, (2012) 5 SCC 359, para 3.

"CONSUMER" means any person who,—

(i) buys any goods for a consideration which has been paid or promised or partly paid and partly promised, or under any system of the deferred payment and includes any user of such goods other than the person who buys such goods for consideration paid or promised or partly paid or partly promised, or under any system of deferred payment when such use is made with the approval of such person, but does not include a person who obtains such goods for resale or for any commercial purpose; or

(ii) hires any services for a consideration which has been paid or promised or partly paid and partly promised, or under any system of deferred payment and includes any beneficiary of such services other than the person who hires the services for consideration paid or promised, or partly paid and partly promised, or under any system of deferred payment, when such services are availed of with the approval of the first mentioned person.

Explanation.—For the purposes of subclause (i), "commercial purpose" does not include use by a consumer of goods bought and used by him exclusively for the purpose of earning his livelihood, by means of self-employment. [Consumer Protection Act (68 of 1986), S. 2(1)(d)]

"CONSUMER" means any person who—

(i) buys any goods for a consideration which has been paid or promised or partly paid and partly promised, or under any system of deferred payment and includes any user of such goods other than the person who buys such goods for consideration paid or promised or partly paid or partly promised, or under any system of deferred payment when such use is made with the approval of such person, whether such purchase of goods is for resale or for any commercial purpose or for personal use;

(ii) hires or avails of any services for a consideration which has been paid or promised or partly paid and partly promised, or under any system of deferred payment and includes any beneficiary of such services other than the person who hires or avails of the services for consideration paid or promised, or partly paid and partly promised, or under any system of deferred payment, when such services are availed of with the approval of the first-mentioned person whether such hiring or availing of services is for any commercial purpose or for personal use. [Competition Act 2002 (12 of 2003), S. 2(f)]

"Consumer" means any person who—

(i) buys any goods for a consideration which has been paid or promised or partly paid and partly promised, or under any system of deferred payment and includes any user of such goods other than the person who buys such goods for consideration paid or promised or partly paid or partly promised, or under any system of deferred payment, when such use is made with the approval of such person, but does not include a person who obtains such goods for resale or for any commercial purpose; or

(ii) hires or avails of any service for a consideration which has been paid or promised or partly paid and partly promised, or under any system of deferred payment and includes any beneficiary of such service other than the person who hires or avails of the services for consideration paid or promised, or partly paid and partly promised, or under any system of deferred payment, when such services are availed of with the approval of the first mentioned person, but does not include a person who avails of such service for any commercial purpose.

Explanation.—For the purposes of this clause,—

(a) the expression "commercial purpose" does not include use by a person of goods bought and used by him exclusively for the purpose of earning his livelihood, by means of self-employment;

(b) the expressions "buys any goods" and "hires or avails any services" includes offline or online transactions through electronic means or by teleshopping or direct selling or multi-level marketing. [Consumer Protection Act, 2019 (35 of 2019), section 2(7)]

"CONSUMER" means any person who is supplied with energy by a licensee or the Government or by any other person engaged in the business of supplying energy to the public under this Act or any other law for the time being in force and includes any person whose premises are for the time being connected for the purpose of receiving energy with the works of a licensee, the Government or such any person, as the case be. [Indian Electricity Act (9 of 1910), S. 2(c)] Act 9 of 1910 repealed and replaced by Act 36 of 2003.

It extends from a person who buys any commodity to consume either as eatable or otherwise from a shop, business house, corporation, store, fair price shop to use of private or public services. *LDA* v. *M.K. Gupta*, (1994) 1 SCC 243, p. 253, para 3 as cited in *Narne Construction Private Limited* v. *Union of India*, (2012) 5 SCC 359, para 3.

"CONSUMER" means a consumer of any article or process. [Bureau of Indian Standard Act (63 of 1986), S. 2(c)]

"CONSUMER" includes persons purchasing, consuming or using for the purpose or in course of trade or business or for public purposes; and references in this section to any one person include references to any two or more persons being inter-connected undertakings or individuals carrying on business in partnership with each other. [Monopolies and Restrictive Trade Practices Act (54 of 1969), S. 38(2)]

"CONSUMER" means a person or local authority by whom the cess under sub-section (1) Section 3 is payable under sub-section (2) of that section. [Water (Prevention and Control of Pollution) Cess Rules, 1978, R. 2(c)].

"CONSUMER" means a person using lead acid batteries excluding bulk consumers. [Batteries (Management and Handling) Rules, 2001, R. 2(h)]

In order to hold that a person is a "consumer" as defined by S. 2(*c*) of the Indian Electricity Act, it would *prima facie* be enough to prove either that energy was supplied for the use of that person, or that that person was the owner or occupier of premises connected up with the licensee's electric system. If either of these is proved that person is a consumer under R. 106 of the rules.

"CONSUMER" means persons and families purchasing and receiving food in order to meet their personal needs. [S. 3(1)(f) of the Food Safety & Standards Act, 2006 (34 of 2006)]

Owner of a building is not 'consumer', where the building is in the occupation of a tenant. *Fatechand Murlidhar* v. *M.E.S. Board, Nagpur,* AIR 1985 Bom 71, 74.

Co-owners, by reason of purchase of an undertaking, using electricity in the undertaking are consumers within the meaning of S. 2(*c*) of Indian Electricity Act (9 of 1910). *Ramchandra* v. *State of Bihar*, AIR 1967 SC 349, 353. [Now repealed & replaced by Act 36 of 2003]

Consumer dispute. Means a dispute where the person against whom a complaint has been made, denies or disputes the allegations contained in the complaint. [Consumer Protection Act (35 of 2019), section 2(8)]

Consumer Disputes Redressal Agencies. There shall be established for the purposes of this Act, the following agencies, namely:—

(a) a Consumer Disputes Redressal Forum to be known as the "District Forum" established by the State Government with the prior approval of the Central Government in each district of the State by notification;

(b) a Consumer Disputes Redressal Commission to be known as the "State Commission" established by the State Government with the prior approval of the Central Government in the State by notification; and

(c) a National Consumer Disputes Redressal Commission established by the Central Government by notification. [Consumer Protection Act (68 of 1986), S. 9]] [Now repealed & replaced by Act 35 of 2019

Consumer law. The law dealing with the rights of consumers, in particular their rights regarding commercial dealings with suppliers of goods and services, the obtaining of credit, and the liability of manufacturers and suppliers in respect of defective products.

"Consumer rights" includes,—

(i) the right to be protected against the marketing of goods, products or services which are hazardous to life and property;

(ii) the right to be informed about the quality, quantity, potency, purity, standard and price of goods, products or services, as the case may be, so as to protect the consumer against unfair trade practices;

(iii) the right to be assured, wherever possible, access to a variety of goods, products or services at competitive prices;

(iv) the right to be heard and to be assured that consumer's interests will receive due consideration at appropriate fora;

(v) the right to seek redressal against unfair trade practice or restrictive trade practices or unscrupulous exploitation of consumers; and

(vi) the right to consumer awareness. [Consumer Protection Act, 2019 (35 of 2019), section 2(9)]

Consumer sale. In this section 'consumer sale' means a sale of goods (other than a sale by auction or by competitive tender) by a seller in the course of a business where the goods (a) are of a type ordinarily bought for private use of consumption; and (b) are sold to a person who does not buy or hold himself out as buying them in the course of a business. [(English) Sale of Goods Act, 1979, Sch. 1, para 11]

Consummate. Of high perfection; complete (as) consummate skill in forgery.

Consummation. Putting finishing to a thing; perfection; completion.

CONSUMMATION OF MARRIAGE, is done by sexual union between husband and wife.

CONSUMMATION, COMPLETION. The arrival at a conclusion is comprehended in both these terms, but they differ principally in application; wishes are *consummated*; plans are *completed.*

Consummation of marriage. Cohabitation of the spouses. 4 Am J2d Annul § 1. The usual meaning of the term, in a common-law sense, is sexual intercourse between the parties after the marriage has been formally solemnized, or consent given, but statute has given the term a wider meaning in some jurisdictions. *Sharon* v. *Sharon*, 75 Cal 1, 16 P 345. (*Ballentine's Law Dictionary*, *3rd Edn.*)

Consumption. For the purposes of Article VI: 'CONSUMPTION' of a chemical means its conversion into another chemical via a chemical reaction. [Chemical Weapons Convention Act (34 of 2000), Art. II 12(c)]

"CONSUMPTION" with respect to any ozone depleting substance means the amount of that substance produced in India in addition to the amount imported, less the amount exported. [Ozone Depleting Substances (Regulation and Control) Rules, 2000, R. 2(d)]

The word 'consumption' in its primary sense means the act of consuming and in ordinary parlance means the use of an article in a way which destroys, wastes or uses up that article. But in some legal contexts, the word has a wider meaning. It is not necessary that the commodity must be destroyed or used up. Consumption consists in the act of taking such advantage of the commodities and services produced as constitutes the utilisation thereof. *Burmashell Co.* v. *Belgaum Municipality*, AIR 1963 SC 906, 911.

The word 'consumption' cannot be understood in the limited sense of eating but in the wider sense of using.

Conversion of a commodity by subjecting it to some processing, is consumption no less than the final act of user when no distinct commodity is being brought into existence but what was brought into existence is being used up. Whenever a commodity is so dealt with as to change it into another commercial commodity there is consumption of the first commodity. *Anwarkhan Mahbool Co.* v. *State of Bombay*, AIR 1961 SC 213, 217.

In a wider meaning 'consumption' means 'useup', 'spend'. *Jiyajeerao Cotton Mills* v. *State of Madhya Pradesh*, AIR 1963 SC 414, 416. [Constitution of India, Sch. VII, List II, Entry 53].

Consumption in the true economic sense does not mean only use of goods in the production of consumer's goods or final utilisation of consumers goods by consumers involving activities like eating of food, drinking of beverages, wearing of clothes or using of an automobile by its owner for domestic purposes. A manufacturer also consumes commodities which are ordinarily called raw materials when he produces semi-finished goods which have to undergo further processes of production before they can be transformed into consumers' goods. At every such intermediate stage of production, some utility or value is added to goods which are used as raw materials and at every such stage the raw materials are consumed. *State of Karnataka* v. *B. Raghurama Shetty*, AIR 1981 SC 1206, 1208. [Karnataka Sales Tax Act (25 of 1957), S. 6(*i*)]

The action or fact of consuming *i.e.* using up anything.

Contact. The state or condition of touching; the act of touching; the state of being in touch or association; association.

Contagious. Communicable by contact [Second Sch., item 79 (3), Income-tax Act (43 of 1961)]; carrying disease or other contagion.

Contagious disease. INFECTIOUS OR CONTAGIOUS disease means Cholera, leprosy, enteric fever, small-poxs tuberculosis, diphtheria, plague, influenza, venereal diseases, or any other epidemic, endemic or infectious disease which the Central Government may, by notification in the Official Gazette, declare to be an infectious or contagious disease for the purpose of this Act. [Cantonments Act (2 of 1924), S. 2(xvii)] Now repealed & replaced by Act 41 of 2006]

"CONTAGIOUS DISEASES" means a disease specified in the schedule to this Act and any other disease which the State Govt. may by notification in the Official Gazette, declare to be a contagious disease. [Assam Cattle Diseases Act (26 of 1948), S. 2(ii)]

A disease communicated by contact or touch. "CONTAGIOUS DISEASE," includes, venereal disease, including gonorrhoea."

Contain in. Comprise in.

Container. A vessel [Agricultural Produce (Grading and Marking) Act (1 of 1937), S. 2(c)]; anything that contains or can contain something.

'CONTAINER' means containers ordinarily intended for packaging of goods for sale, including collapsible tubes, casks, drums, cans, boxes, gas cylinders and pressure containers whether is assembled or unassembled condition and containers known commercially as flattened or folded containers. [Central Excises and Salt Act, 1944, *Explanation* I, Tariff Item 27(a)(i)] [Now repealed by Act 12 of 2017]

"CONTAINER" means a box, bottle, casket, tin barrel, case, receptacle, sack, bag, wrapper or other thing in which any article or thing is placed or packed. [Seeds Act (54 of 1966), S. 2(5)]

"CONTAINER" means a box, bottle, casket, tin, can, barrel, case, tube, receptacle, sack, wrapper or other thing in which any infant milk substitute, feeding bottle or infant food is placed or packed for sale or distribution. [Infant Milk Substitutes, Feeding Bottles and *etc.* Act (41 of 1992), S. 2(b)]

A large box for intermodal transport, containning many smaller boxes of different shapes and sizes as well as individual articles. [Glossary of Packaging Terms (Australia) as cited in *C.C.E. Madras* v. *I.T.C. Ltd., Bihar,* AIR 2003 SC 1484, 1487, para 6]

Any receptacle which holds, restrains or encloses any article or commodity or articles or commodities to be stored or transported. [Indian Standard Glossary of Terms: 1.5.4261-1967 as cited in *CCE Madras* v. *I.T.C. Ltd., Bihar,* AIR 2003 SC 1484, 1487, para 6]

Contaminant. Means any substance, whether or not added to food, but which is present in such food as a result of the production (including operations carried out in crop husbandry, animal husbandry or veterinary medicine), manufacture, processing, preparation, treatment, packing, packaging, transport or holding of such food or as a result of environmental contamination and does not include insect fragments, rodent hairs and other extraneous matter. [S. 3(1)(g) of the Food Safety & Standards Act, 2006 (34 of 2006)]

Contamination. The action of contaminating or condition of being contaminated; defilement; pollution; infection. [Insecticides Act (46 of 1968), S. 36(2)(q)].

Contemn. Feel contempt for; disregard with scorn.

To treat (as laws or Court orders) with contemptuous disregard.

Contemner. The person who commits contempt of Court.

Contemplation of death. The apprehension or expectation of approaching dissolution; not that general expectation which every mortal entertains, but the apprehension which arises from some presently existing sickness or physical condition or from some impending danger. As applied to transfers of property, the phrase "in contemplation of death" means that thought of death is the impelling cause of transfer and that motive which induces transfer is of sort which leads to testamentary disposition and is practically equivalent to "*causa mortis.*" *In re Cornell's Estate*, 66 AD 162, 73 NYS 32; *Nicholas* v. *Martin*, 128 NJ

Eq 344, 15 A. 2d 235, 243; *Pate* v. *C.I.R.* C.C.A 8, 149 F. 2d 669, 670. It has been further held however, that in determining whether transfer by decedent within three years prior to date of death was made in contemplation of death, phrase "contemplation of death" is not restricted in meaning to apprehension that death is imminent; inquiry is whether the "life" as opposed to "death" motives were the dominant controlling or impelling reasons for the transfer. *Bel* v. *U.S.*, D.C.La., 310 F .Supp. 1189, 1194.

Contemporanea consuetudo optimus interpres. (*Maxim*) Contemporary custom is the best interpretator. (*Broom*)

Contemporanea expositio. (*Maxim*) Contemporaneous exposition, or construction.

The maxim *contemporanea expositio* as laid down by Coke was applied to construing ancient statutes, but not to interpreting Acts which are comparatively modern. *Senior Electric Inspector* v. *Lakshminarayan Chopra*, AIR 1962 SC 159, 163.

The principle of *contemporanea exposito* means interpreting a statute or any other document by referring to the exposition it has received from contemporary authority. [*Desh Bandhu Gupta & Co.* v. *Delhi Stock Exchange Association Ltd.*, AIR 1979 SC 1049, 1054].

Contemporanea exposito est optima. (*Lat.*) The mere fact of the proceeds of any land being used for the support of an idol may not be proof that those lands formed an endowment for the purpose; but it is a fact that that may well be taken into consideration when, the intention of the founder has to be gathered from an ancient document expressed, to say the least, in ambiguous language.

Contemporanea expositio est optima et fortissima in lege. (*Lat.*) The best way to construe a document is to read it as it would have read when made.

Contemporaneous exposition. *Principles of Statutory Interpretation.* Contemporaneous Exposition applies only to the construction of ambiguous language in old statutes. *Doypack Systems (P) Ltd.* v. *Union of India*, AIR 1988 SC 782, 802.

Contempt. A wilful disregard or disobedience (of public authority); a mental attitude in which a thing is considered as vile and worthless. [Constitution of India, Art. 19(2)].

"Contempt" means "conduct that defies the authority or dignity of a court or legislature". Black's Law Dictionary (8th Edn., 1999) as cited in *Kalyaneshwari* v. *Union of India*, (2012) 12 SCC 599, para 11.

If an act or utterance or writing has the effect of scandalising the Court or the Judge, it would be within the mischief of the expression 'contempt'.

"Contempt" is disorderly conduct of a contemnor causing serious damage to the institution of justice administration. Such conduct, with reference to its adverse effects and consequences, can be discernibly classified into two categories: one which has a transient effect on the system and/or the person concerned and is likely to wither away by the passage of time while the other cause permanent damage to the institution and administration of justice. The latter conduct would normally be unforgivable. *Kalyaneshwari* v. *Union of India*, (2012) 12 SCC 599, para 5.

Contempt of court. "Contempt of courts" means civil contempt or criminal contempt. [Contempt of Courts, (70 of 1971), S. 2(a)].

Under the common law definition, "Contempt of Court" is defined as an act or omission calculated to interfere with the due administration of justice. This covers criminal contempt (that is, acts which so threaten the administration of justice that they require punishment) and civil contempt (disobedience of an order made in a civil cause). *Vinay Chandra Mishra,* in re*,* AIR 1995 SC 2348.

Scandalising Court or judge, undermining people's confidence in administration of justice and bringing or tending to bring the Court into disrepute or disrespect tantamount to criminal contempt. Scurrilous attack on a judge questioning his authority would amount to contempt. Dr. *D.C. Saxena* v. *Hon'ble The C.J.I., J.T.*, 1996 (6) SC 529.

Contempt, in the legal acceptation of the term, primarily signifies disrespect to that which is entitled to legal regard. In its origin all legal contempt will be found to consist of an offence more or less direct against the Sovereign himself as the fountain head of law and justice, or against the place where justice was administered. It is not, however, in its primary meaning of contempt of the sovereign, his person, government, or prerogative, but in its secondary or derivative meaning of an offence against Courts or persons to whom the judicial functions of the sovereign are delegated that the word contempt is understood when used in the technical or legal expression Contempt of Court. (*Ency. of the Laws of England.*)

CONTEMPT OF COURT is disobedience to the Court, by acting in opposition to the authority, justice and dignity thereof. It signifies a wilful disregard or disobedience of the Court's order; it also signifies such conduct as tends to bring the authority of the Court and the administration of the law into disrepute. *B. Mishra* v. *B. Dixit*, AIR 1972 SC 2466, 2468.

CONTEMPT OF COURT—CLASSIFICAITON OF. Contempts may be *direct* or *constructive*, *criminal* or *civil*.

A DIRECT CONTEMPT is an open insult in the presence of the Court to the person of the presiding Judge, or defiance in his presence to his powers or authority.

A CONSTRUCTIVE CONTEMPT is an act done not in the presence of the Court, but at a distance which tends to belittle, to degrade, or to obstruct, interrupt, prevent, or embarrass the administration of justice.

A CRIMINAL CONTEMPT is conduct that is directed against the dignity and authority of the Court. Acts punishable as criminal contempts are in the nature of crimes, in that they involve the idea of punishment as a penalty for the commission of unauthorised acts.

"Civil contempt" means wilful disobedience to any judgement, decree, direction, order, writ or other process of a Court or wilful breach of an undertaking given to a Court.

CIVIL CONTEMPT consists in failing to do something ordered to be done by a Court in a civil action for the benefit of the opposing party therein.

"Criminal contempt" means the publication (whether by words, spoken or written, or by signs, or by visible representations, or otherwise) of any matter or the doing of any other act, whatsoever which —

(i) scandilises or tends to scandalise, or lowers or tends to lower the authority of any Court; or

(ii) prejudices, or interfere with, the due course of any judicial proceeding; or

(iii) interferes or tends to interfere with, or obstruct, the administration of justice in any other manner. [Contempt of Courts Act (70 of 1971), S. 2]

EXAMPLES OF CONTEMPT. *Contempt may be shown either by language or manner.* Language not in itself contemptuous may become so if uttered in an insolent or defiant manner.

Abstracting papers and substituting others therefor or taking papers from Court files and refusing or neglecting to return them, is punishable as a contempt.

Wilful abuse of legal process, such as instituting, or procuring the institution of *unauthorised or fictitious proceedings or suits, obtaining Court orders by fraud or deceit*, or knowingly interposing false pleadings is contempt, where such acts obstruct or tend to impede the due administration of justice.

It is contempt to wilfully destroy, remove, conceal, or *dispose of, the subject-matter of the litigation* pending the proceedings.

Disobedience or resistance to, or an attempt to *prevent the execution of, a lawful order, judgment decree*, or mandate of a Court is an interference with, or an attempt to obstruct, the due administration of justice, and is therefore a contempt.

Contempt of the House. Wilful disregard of the authority of a Court or legislature.

In India, any misconduct in the presence of the House or any of its Committees by members of Parliament or by members of the Public admitted to the galleries of the House or to sittings of Committees as witnesses constitutes contempt of the House. Acts like interrupting the proceedings of the House, refusal by a witness to make as oath, giving false evidence, presenting false, forged or fabricated documents to either House or its Committee, constitute contempt of the House.

Contention. Dispute; controversy. [CPC (5 of 1908), O. XXXI, R. 1].

Contentious. Contested; adversary; involving a contention; litigated between adverse and contending parties; a judicial proceeding which is not *ex parte*.

Contents. That which is contained; the subject matter.

Contest. To assert a defence to an adverse claim in a Court proceeding. To oppose, resist, or dispute the case made by a plaintiff or prosecutor. To strive to win or hold. To controvert, litigate, call in question, challenge. To defend, as a suit or other proceeding.

The word 'contest' does not merely mean filing of written statement of defence, but means every stage of the proceedings till the culmination of the proceedings, that is, filing of written statement, cross-examination, leading defence evidence and arguments on merits before the final order is made.

Strife; conflict; to controvert; to defend as a suit; to oppose; to struggle for victory.

Contestatio litis eget terminos contradictorios. (*Maxim*) An issue requires terms of contradiction. To constitute an issue, there must be an affirmative on one side and a negative on the other.

Contesting candidate. A contesting candidate whose name was included in the list under S. 38, but who retires from the contest under S. 55-A(2) continues to be a contesting candidate for the purposes of the Act though by reason of such retirement it would be unnecessary for the constituency to cast its votes in his favour at the poll. *K. Kamaraj Nadar* v. *Kunju Thevan*, AIR 1958 SC 687, 695. [Representation of the People Act (43 of 1951), S. 38].

A contesting candidate is one who has not withdrawn his candidature under S. 37. *Har Swarup* v. *Brij Bhushan*, AIR 1967 SC 836, 838. [Representation of the People Act (43 of 1951), S. 37].

Context. What precedes and follows a word or passage as throwing light on its meaning.

Contiguous. Adjoining; adjacent. "What is contiguous must be fitted to touch entirely on one side: fields are adjoining to each other; houses contiguous to each other." (*Crabbe. Synonyms*)

Two houses opposite to one another and a street going between them would be strictly speaking "contiguous," because each would include the soil of the street *ad medium filum*.

Touching; adjoining.

Contiguous zone. "CONTIGUOUS ZONE" means the contiguous zone of India described, or notified as such for the time being under Section 5 of the Territorial Waters, Continental Shelf, Exclusive Economic Zone and other Maritime Zones Act, 1976 (80 of 1976). [Merchant Shipping Act (44 of 1958), S. 75A(a)]

Contiguous zone of India. The contiguous zone of India (hereinafter referred to as the contiguous zone) is an area beyond and adjacent to the territorial waters and the limit of the contiguous zone is the line every point of which is at a distance of twenty four nautical miles from the nearest point of the baseline referred to in sub-section (2) of S. 3. [The Territorial Waters, Continental Shelf, Exclusive Economic Zone and other Maritime Zones Act (80 of 1976), S. 5].

Continental Shelf of India. Shall have the meaning assigned to it in the Territorial Waters, Continental Shelf, Exclusive Economic Zone and other Maritime Zones Act, 1976. [Suppression of Unlawful Acts against Safety of Maritime Navigation And Fixed Plateform on Continental Shelf Act (69 of 2002), S. 2(b)]

Contingency. A situation in which an event may or may not happen.

An event conceived of possible occurrence in the future. [Constitution of India, Art. 70]; a chance event.

Contingency Fund of India. The fund at the disposal of the President to enable advances to be made by him out of such fund for the purposes of meeting unforeseen expenditure. [Constitution of India, Art. 267(1)].

Contingency Fund of State. The fund at the disposal of the Governor of a State to enable advances to be made by him out of such fund for the purposes of meeting unforeseen expenditure. [Constitution of India, Art. 267(2)].

Contingent. That which may happen or not; conditional; dependant on something else. Dependant on a probability; possible; unpredictable; uncertain; conditional.

Contingent contract. "CONTINGENT CONTRACT" is a contract to do or not to do something, if some event, collateral to such contract, does or does not happen. [Indian Contract Act (9 of 1872), S. 31]

Contingent debt. A debt which is not presently fixed but which may become fixed in the future with the occurrence of any event.

Contingent interest. Where, on a transfer of property, an interest therein is created in favour of a person to take effect only on the happening of a specified uncertain event, or if a specified uncertain event shall not happen, such person thereby acquires a contingent interest in the property. Such interest becomes a vested interest in the former case, on the happening of the event, in the latter, when the happening of the event becomes possible.

Exception.—Where under a transfer of property, a person becomes entitled to an interest therein upon attaining a particular age, and the transferor also gives to him absolutely the income to arise from such interest before he reaches that age, or directs the income or so much thereof as may be necessary to be applied for his benefit, such interest is not contingent. [T.P. Act (4 of 1882), S. 21].

CONTINGENT INTEREST is a future interest that is to depend upon an event that is uncertain, *e.g.*, a contingent remainder.

Contingent interest in personal property. A future interest not transmissible to the representatives of the party entitled thereto, in case he dies before it vests in possession. Thus, if a testator leaves the income of a fund to his wife for life, and the capital of the fund to be distributed among such of his children as shall be living at her death, the interest of each child during the widow's life-time is *contingent*, and in case of his death is not transmissible to his representative. (*Black*)

Contingent legacy. A legacy bequeathed on an expressed contingency.

Contingent liability. That which is not now fixed and absolute, but which may become so in case of the occurrence of some future event; a liability which may be discharged without any liability accruing.

An amount that may or may not be owed dependent on the outcome of a contingency. [Industrial Finance Corporations Act (15 of 1948) (*Repealed by Act 23 of 1993*), S. 21(1)].

Contingent remainder. An estate in remainder is limited to take effect, either to a dubious and uncertain person; or upon dubious and uncertain person; or upon dubious and uncertain event; so that the particular estate may chance to be determined, and the remainder never take effect. (*Tomlin*)

Contingent rights. Are rights which are only to come into existence on an event or condition which may not happen or be performed until some other event may prevent their vesting.

Continuance. The state of continuing.

Where the Court conceives it to be necessary for the more perfect attainment of justice it has the power, upon the application, of any party or on its own motion, to continue a case from one day to another.

Now the rule is well established that the trial Court acts within its own discretion in granting or refusing an application for a continuance in a criminal case, whether it be on behalf of the accused or of the state; which act will not be disturbed in the absence of a clear abuse of discretion.

Continue. To remain in existence or in the given place or condition; to persevere; to go on with.

Continue in force. [Arms Act (54 of 1959), S. 15(2)].

Continue in possession. To keep up possession.

Continued ill-health. "Continued ill-health" includes any physical defect or infirmity incapacitating a workman for future work for an indefinite period. *Burra Kur Coal Co. Ltd.* v. *Azimmuddin Ashraff,* AIR 1960 Pat 554, 556. [Industrial Disputes Act (14 of 1947), S. 2(oo)(*c*)].

Continuing. So far as 'breaches' and 'wrongs' are concerned, they give rise to a fresh cause of action *de die in diem* so long as the wrongful state of affairs subsists and so far as offences are concerned they give rise to a fresh offence *de die in diem* so long as the omission which has been made penal by the statute is not rectified. *State* v. *Umashankar Laxminarayan,* AIR 1962 MP 311, 314. [Limitation Act (36 of 1963), S. 22].

"Continuing" means 'enduring; not terminated by a single act or fact; subsisting for a definite period or intended to cover or apply to successive similar obligations or occurrences'. Black's Law Dictionary, (5th Edn., Special Deluxe) as cited in *Udai Shankar Awasthi* v. *State of U.P.*, (2013) 2 SCC 435, para 25.

Continuing Act. In those cases in which the law prescribes a period within which legal proceedings for an offence or an infraction of a civil right must be instituted, it is often necessary, for the purpose of ascertaining whether the remedy is statute-barred, to consider where the act or default in respect of which it is claimed was completed at a given date or is a continuing act or an act repeated from time to time, so that the time for pursuing the remedy can be computed from the last day on which the act or default took place, and not from the day on which a complete offence was committed or a right of action first accrued; that being the date from which a Statute of Limitation ordinarily runs. [Limitation Act (36 of 1963), S. 22; *Ency. of the Laws of England*].

Continuing breach. A breach of contract which endures for a considerable amount of time, or which is repeated at short intervals.

Continuing candidate. The definition of 'continuing candidate' in Rule 71(1) has two elements which must be satisfied before a candidate could be said to be such a continuing candidate. He should be a candidate not elected and further, he must not have been excluded from the poll at any given time. *Thiru John* v. *The Returning Officer,* AIR 1977 SC 1724. [Conduct of Election Rules, 1961, R. 71(1)]

Continuing guarantee. A guarantee which extends to a series of transactions is called a "continuing guarantee." [Indian Contract Act (9 of 1872), S. 129]

Continuing offence. The expression 'continuing offence' means that if an act or omission on the part of an accused constitutes an offence, and if that act or omission continues from day to day, then a fresh offence is committed on every day on which the act or omission continues.

"Continuing offence" means 'type of crime which is committed over a span of time'. As to period of statute of limitation in a continuing offence, the last act of the offence controls for commencement of the period. 'A continuing offence, such that only the last act thereof within the period of the statute of limitations need be alleged in the indictment or information, is one which may consist of separate acts or a course of conduct but which arises from that singleness of thought, purpose or action which may be deemed a single impulse'. [Black's Law Dictionary, (5th Edn., Special Deluxe) as cited in Udai Shankar Awasthi v. State of U.P., (2013) 2 SCC 435, para 25].

A continuing offence is one which is susceptible of continuance and is distinguishable from the one which is committed once and for all. It is one of those offences which arise out of a failure to obey or comply with a rule or its requirement and which involves a penalty, the liability for which continues until the rule or its requirement is obeyed or complied with. On every occasion that such disobedience or non-compliance occurs and reoccurs, there is the offence committed. The distinction between the two kinds of offences is between an act or omission which constitutes an offence once and for all and an act or omission which continues, and therefore, constitutes a fresh offence every time or occasion on which it continues. In the case of a continuing offence, there is thus the ingredient of continuance of the offence which is absent in the case of an offence which takes place when an act or omission is committed once and for all. [*State of Bihar* v. *Deokaran Nenshi*, (1972) 2 SCC 890, para 5 : 1973 SCC (Cri) 114 : AIR 1973 SC 908 as cited in *Gokak Patel Volkart Ltd.* v. *Dundayya Gurushiddaiah Hiremath*, (1991) 2 SCC 141 : 1991 SCC (Cri) 315]. See also *Udai Shankar Awasthi* v. *State of U.P.*, (2013) 2 SCC 435, para 26.

Using the premises as a factory without obtaining a licence constituted a continuing offence. *Public Prosecutor* v. *T.A. Rathanam Pillai,* AIR 1958 Mad 155, 157. [Factories Act (63 of 1948), S. 92].

Payment of tax deducted at source is an obligation and duty covered by statute and the default of such payment, which has been made an offence, continues from day to day till the payment is made. *V. Hallay Mathew* v. *State of Kerala,* (1971) 79 ITR 72, 79. [Income-tax Act (43 of 1961), S. 279].

Continuing offence is one which is susceptible of continuance and is distinguishable from the one which is committed once and for all. It is one of those offences which arises out of a failure to obey or comply with a rule or its requirement and which involves a penalty, the liability for which continues until the rule or its requirement is obeyed or complied with. On every occasion that such disobedience or non-compliance occurs and reoccurs, there is the offence committed. *State of Bihar* v. *Deokaran Nenshi*, AIR 1973 SC 908, 909. [Mines Act (35 of 1952), S. 66].

'Continuing offence' means an offence that continues from moment to moment without any interruption or break. The words "continuing offence" should be interpreted in the same manner as the words 'continuing breach of contract' and 'continuing the wrong independent of contract' occurring in S. 22 of the Limitation Act. *Trilok Chand* v. *C.N. Srivastava,* AIR 1961 All 88, 89.

Continuing partners. Partners remaining and carrying on a partnership after the retirement of one or more of their fellow partners.

"Continuing unlawful activity". Means an activity prohibited by law which is a cognizable offence punishable with imprisonment of three years or more, undertaken by any person, either singly or jointly, as a member of an organised crime syndicate or on behalf of such syndicate in respect of which more than one charge-sheets have been filed before a competent Court within the preceding period of ten years and that Court has taken cognizance of such offence, and includes economic offence. [(w.e.f. 1-7-2024) Bharatiya Nyaya Sanhita, 2023 (45 of 2023), section 111(1), *Explanation* (ii)]

Continuing wrong. It is the very essence of a continuing wrong that it is an act which escates a continuing source of injury and renders the doer of the act responsible and liable for the continuance of the said injury. If the wrongful act causes an injury, which is complete, there is no continuing wrong even though the damage resulting from the act may continue. If, however, a wrongful act is of such a character that the injury caused by it itself continues, then the act constitutes a continuing wrong. [Limitation Act (36 of 1963), S. 22].

Continuous. Going on without interruption; uninterrupted in time sequence or essence.

Continuous crime. "Continuous crime" means one consisting of a continuous series of act, which endures after the period of consummation, as, the offence of carrying concealed weapons. In the case of instantaneous crimes, the statute of limitation begins to run with the consummation, while in the case of continuous crimes it only begins with the cessation of the criminal conduct or act.' Black's Law Dictionary (5th Edn., Special Deluxe) as cited in *Udai Shankar Awasthi* v. *State of U.P.*, (2013) 2 SCC 435, para 25.

Continuous easement. "A continuous easement is one whose enjoyment is, or may be, continual without the act of man." [Indian Easements Act (5 of 1882), S. 5].

Continuous Journey. "Continuous journey" means a journey for which a single or more than one ticket or invoice is issued at the same time, either by a single supplier of service or through an agent acting on behalf of more than one supplier of service, and which involves no stopover between any of the legs of the journey for which one or more separate tickets or invoices are issued

Explanation.—For the purposes of this clause, the term "stopover" means a place where a passenger can disembark either to transfer to another conveyance or break his journey for a certain period in order to resume it at a later point of time [The Integrated Goods and Services Tax Act, 2017 (13 of 2017), S. 2(3)]

Continuous process plant. A plant which is required and designed to operate for twenty-four hours a day. [Companies Act (18 of 2013), Schedule II, Part C, Notes]

Continuous possession. (*In the Mad Pro. Est. Village Act*) The principle adopted appears to be that, in order that Government may have the right of resumption, the right to the land must either have, in the first instance, emanated from Government, or the continuance of the right must have been due to an act of Government. At any rate, there must have been recognition by Government of the right which could be set up by the holder in support of his possession. Mere sufferance by Government, or forbearance from taking steps which it might have been open to the Government to take, will not amount to a "continuance" by the Government of the land in respect of the office. Mere collateral expression of opinions which were not intended to be a recognition or confirmation of the right of the holder would equally be insufficient to amount to a continuance. (17 IC 373, 374)

Continuous residence. When a person is physically absent from his place of residence for time, if he has *animus revertendi,* his residence continues.

Continuous service. For the purposes of this Chapter,—

(1) a workman shall be said to be in continuous service for a period if he is, for that period, in uninterrupted service, including service which may be interrupted on account of sickness or authorised leave or an accident or a strike which is not illegal, or a lock-out or a cessation of work which is not due to any fault on the part of the workman;

(2) Where a workman is not in continuous service within the meaning of clause (1) for a period of one year or six months, he shall be deemed to be in continuous service under an employer—

 (a) for a period of one year, if the workman, during a period of twelve calendar months preceding the date with reference to which calculation is to be made, has actually worked under the employer for not less than—

  (i) one hundred and ninety days in the case of a workman employed below ground in a mine; and

  (ii) two hundred and forty days, in any other case;

 (b) for a period of six months, if the workman, during a period of six calendar months preceding the date with reference to which calculation is to be made, has actually worked under the employer for not less than—

  (i) ninety-five days, in the case of a workman employed below ground in a mine; and

  (ii) one hundred and twenty days, in any other case.

Explanation.—For the purposes of clause (2), the number of days on which the workman has actually worked under an employer shall include the days on which—

(i) he has been laid off under an agreement or as permitted by Standing Orders made under the Industrial Employment (Standing Orders) Act, 1946, or under this Act or under any other law applicable to the industrial establishment;

(ii) he has been on leave with full wages, earned in the previous years;

(iii) he has been absent due to temporary disablement caused by accident arising out of and in the course of his employment; and

(iv) in the case of a female, she has been on maternity leave; so, however, that the total period of such maternity leave does not exceed twelve weeks. [Industrial Disputes Act (14 of 1947), S. 25-B]

"CONTINUOUS SERVICE". For the purpose of this Act,—

(1) an employee shall be said to be in continuous service for a period if he has, for that period, be in uninterrupted service, including service which may be interrupted on account of sickness, accident, leave, absence from duty without leave (not being absence in respect of which an order treating the absence as break in service has been passed in accordance with the standing order, rules or regulations governing the employees of the establishment), lay off, strike or a lock-out or cessation of work not due to any fault of the employee, whether such interrupted service was rendered before or after commencement of this Act;

(2) Where an employee (not being an employee employed in a seasonal establishment) is not in continuous service within the meaning of clause (1), for any period of one year or six months, he shall be deemed to be in continuous service under the employer—

(a) for the said period of one year, if the employee during the period of twelve calender months preceding the date with reference to which calculation is to be made, has actually worked under the employer for not less than—

(i) one hundred and ninety days, in the case of an employee employed below the ground in a mine or in an establishment which works for less than six days in a week; and

(ii) two hundred and forty days, in any other case;

(b) for the said period of six months, if the employee during the period of six calendar months preceding the date with reference to which the calculation is to be made, has actually worked under the employer for not less than—

(i) ninety-five days, in the case of an employee employed below the ground in a mine or in an establishment which works for less than six days in a week; and

(ii) one hundred and twenty days, in any other case;

Explanations.—For the purposes of clause (2), the number of days on which an employee has actually worked under an employer shall include the days on which—

(i) he has been laid-off under an agreement or as permitted by standing orders made under the Industrial Employment (Standing Orders) Act, 1946, or under Industrial Disputes, 1947, or under any other law applicable to the establishment;

(ii) he has been on leave with full wages, earned in the previous year;

(iii) he has been absent due to temporary disablement caused by accident arising out of and in the course of his employment; and

(iv) in the case of a female, she has been on maternity leave; so, however, that the total period of such maternity leave does not exceed twelve weeks.

(c) Where an employee, employed in a seasonal establishment, is not in continuous service, within the meaning of clause (1), for any period of one year or six months, he shall be deemed to be in continuous service under the employer for such service if he has actually worked for not less than seventy-five percent of the number of days on which the establishment was in operation during such period. [Payment of Gratuity Act (39 of 1972), S. 2A]

"Continuous service" in the context of the scheme of gratuity framed by the Tribunal postulates the continuance of the relationship of master and servant between the employer and his employees. When a servant resigns or when the employer terminates the services of the employee or when the service of an employee is brought to an end by the operation of any law, the continuance of service is disrupted. *Jeewanlal (1929) Ltd.* v. *Workmen*, AIR 1961 SC 1567, 1569.

A workman shall be deemed to be in continuous service if he has "actually worked under the employer" for particular period. The expression "actually worked under the employer" cannot mean those days only when the workman worked with hammer, sickle or pen, but must necessarily comprehend all those days during which he was in the employment of the employer and for which he had been paid wages either under express or implied contract of service or by compulsion of statue, standing orders *etc.* Thus Sundays and other paid holidays should be taken into account for the purpose of reckoning the total number of days on which the workman could be said to have actually worked. *Workmen of American Express International Banking Corporation* v. *Management of American Express International Banking Corporation.* AIR 1986 SC 458. [Industrial Disputes Act (14 of 1947), S. 25-B(2)]

Counting back from the date of termination of the service, if a person had rendered service for a period of 240 days within a period of 12 months he will be deemed to be in continuous service for a period of one year. *Mohan Lal* v. *The Management of Bharat Electronics Ltd.*, AIR 1981 SC 1253, 1262. [Industrial Disputes Act (14 of 1947), S. 25-B(1) & (2)].

The *badli* employees who are nothing but substitutes due to their failure to report to duty are not covered by the substantive part of the definition of 'continuous service' in S. 2(*c*), and therefore they are not entitled to payment of gratuity for the *badli* period (*i.e.)* in respect of the years in which there was no work allotted to them. *Lalappa Lingappa* v. *Laxmi Vishnu Textile Mills*, AIR 1981 SC 852, 857. [Payment of Gratuity Act (39 of 1972), Ss. 2-A, 4(1)].

A person who served a university for a period of eight years and during that period he was without job for about 4 months and he worked in another university for 2 months and then he joined the first University on a permanent basis. This gap will not prevent the whole services from being considered as a continuous service. *Banaras Hindu University* v. *Indra Pratap Singh*, AIR 1992 SC 780, 784.

"Continuous service" is defined as "uninterrupted service", including service which may be interrupted on account of sickness or authorised leave or an accident or a strike which is not illegal, or a lockout or a cessation of work which is not due to any fault on the part of the workman. *U.P. State Bridge Corpn. Ltd.* v. *U.P.* Rajya *Setu Nigam,* (2004) 4 SCC 268, para 21. [Industrial Disputes Act (14 of 1947), S. 25-B(1)]

Continuous supply of goods. "continuous supply of goods" means a supply of goods which is provided, or agreed to be provided, continuously or on recurrent basis, under a contract, whether or not by means of a wire, cable, pipeline or other conduit, and for which the supplier invoices the recipient on a regular or periodic basis and includes supply of such goods as the Government may, subject to such conditions, as it may, by notification, specify [The Central Goods and Services Tax Act, 2017 (12 of 2017), S. 2(32)]

Continuous supply of services. "continuous supply of services" means a supply of services which is provided, or agreed to be provided, continuously or on recurrent basis, under a contract, for a period exceeding three months with periodic payment obligations and includes supply of such services as the Government may, subject to such conditions, as it may, by notification, specify [The Central Goods and Services Tax Act, 2017 (12 of 2017), S. 2(33)]

Continuous voyage. The doctrine that the voyage undertaken with contraband to the enemy port/country *via* a neutral port/country would be treated as a single continuous voyage.

Continuously. With continuity or continuation without interruption in space or time; unbrokenly; without break or interruption. It is almost, but not exactly, synonymous with "uninterruptedly".

"...It cannot legitimately be contended that the word 'continuously' has one definite meaning only to convey uninterruptedness in time sequences or essence and on the other hand the very word would also mean 'recurring at repeated intervals so as to be of repeated occurrence'. That apart, used as an adjective it draws colour from context too...." [*Raymond Ltd.* v. *M.P. Electricity Board*, (2001) 1 SCC 534, para 18 : AIR 2001 SC 238 as cited in *Udai Shankar Awasthi* v. *State of U.P.*, (2013) 2 SCC 435, para 27].

The word "continuously" is one definite means uninterruptedness in time sequence or essence and it would also mean "recurring at repeated intervals so as to be of repeated occurrence." *Raymond Ltd.* v. *M.P. Electricity Board,* AIR 2001 SC 238. [MP Electricity Board Agreement for High Tension Supply, cl. 23]

Contra. Thing that may be urged against a course; counter in operation; in opposition to; contrary to; on the opposite side; the contrary. It is a term constantly used in the reports, to denote the opposition of counsel in a cause; the disallowance by the Court of a point in argument; and the opposition of cases cited as establishing opposite doctrines. In some other older books, *contra* is used instead of *versus,* in the titles of causes. (*Burrill*)

Against; on the other hand.

Contra bonos mores. (*Lat.*) Against good morals; offensive to conscience and to a sense of justice.

Contra formam collationis. (*Lat.*) Against the form of the gift.

Contra formam statuti. (*Lat.*) Against the form of the statute.

Contra jus civilis regulas pacta conventa rata non habentur. (*Maxim*) Agreements made contrary to the civil law are not to be constrused as valid. (*Morgan*)

Contra legem facit, qui id facit, quod lex prohibit; in fraudem vero qui, salvis verbis legis, sententia eius circumvenit. (*Maxim*) He does contrary to the law who does what the law prohibits; he acts in fraud of the law who, the letter of the law being inviolate, uses the law contrary to its intention. (*Adams Gloss; Burrill*)

Contra spoliatorem omnia praesumuntur. (*Maxim*) All things are to be presumed in disfavour of the spoliator.

Contra veritatem lex nunquam aliquid permittit. (*Lat.*) (*2 Inst. 252*). The law never suffers/allows anything contrary to truth. (*Wharton; Morgan Leg. Max.*)

Contraband. Against law or treaty; prohibited, goods exported from or imported into a country against its laws; smuggling.

Contraband goods. Are those which are prohibited by law to be imported into, or exported out of, the realim to any other country. (*Tomlin*; *Cowell.*)

Contract. "An agreement enforceable by law is a CONTRACT." [Indian Contract Act (9 of 1872), S. 2(h)].

An enforceable covenant or agreement between two or more persons, with a lawful consideration or cause. (*Tomlin*)

Whilst it is probably impossible to give one absolute and universally correct definition of a contract, the most commonly accepted definition is "a promise or set of promises which the law will enforce". The expression "contract" may, however, be used to describe any or all of the following: (1) that series of promises or acts themselves constituting the contract; (2) the document or documents constituting or evidencing that series or promises or acts, or their performance; (3) the legal relations resulting from that series. HALSBURY, 4th Edn., Vol. 9, para 201, p. 80.

Contracts have been divided, according to the mode of their formation, into three classes: (1) contracts of record; (2) contracts under seal; and (3) simple contracts. Contracts of record, however, are not contracts in the sense in which that term is here employed but are judgments and recognisances which are enrolled in the record of the proceedings of a Court of record, and in law imply a debt though the obligation arises from the entry on the record and not from any agreement between the parties. Leaving aside contracts of record, all contracts may be divided into contracts under seal and simple contracts. HALSBURY, 4th Edn., Vol. 9, para 209, p. 86.

A licence granted to a company on certain conditions does not create contractual relationship.

The word 'contract' does not include a lease.

"A contract is a deliberate engagement between competent parties, upon a legal CONSIDERATION, to do or to abstain from doing some act".

BILATERAL AND UNILATERAL CONTRACTS. A bilateral contract is a contract in which there are reciprocal promises, so that there is something to be done or forborne on both sides, while a unilateral contract is one in which there is a promise on one side only, the consideration on the other side being executed.

COMMUTATIVE CONTRACTS. "Commutative contract" is a term used in the civil law to designate a contract in which each of the contracting parties gives and receives some equivalent.

EXPRESS CONTRACTS. An empress contract is one where the intention of the parties and terms of the agreement are declared or expressed by the parties, in writing or orally, at the time it is entered into. It is an express contract, although some of its terms are dependent upon the happening of a future event.

IMPLIED CONTRACTS. An implied contract, in the proper sense, is where the intention of the parties is not expressed, but an agreement in fact, creating an obligation, is implied or presumed from their acts, as, in the case where a person performs services for another, who accepts the same, the services not being performed under such circumstances as to show that they were intended to be gratuitous, or where a person performs services for another on request.

Contract carriage. A contract carriage is one engaged for the whole of the journey between two points for carriage of a person or persons hiring it; but it has not the right to pick up other passengers *en route*. *N. Krishnasami Chetty* v. *Licensing Officer, Dy. Transport Commissioner and Secy., RTA*, AIR 1988 Mad 274, 275. [Motor Vehicles Act (4 of 1939), S. 2(3)]

"CONTRACT CARRIAGE" means a motor vehicle which carries a passenger or passengers for hire or reward and is engaged under a contract, whether expressed or implied, for the use of such vehicle as a whole for the carriage of passengers mentioned therein and entered into by a person with a holder of a permit in relation to such vehicle or any person authorised by him in this behalf on a fixed or an agreed rate or sum—

(a) on a time basis, whether or not with reference to any route or distance; or

(b) from one point to another,

and in either case, without stopping to pick up or set down passengers not included in the contract anywhere during the journey, and includes—

(i) a maxicab; and

(ii) a motorcab notwithstanding that separate fares are charged for its passengers. [Motor Vehicles Act (59 of 1988), S. 2(7)]

Contract for hire. A contract for hire is one whereby "one person grants to another the enjoyment of a thing, or the use of the labour and industry, either himself or through servant, during a certain time for a stipulated compensation."

Contract for sale. An agreement to sell. [T.P. Act (4 of 1882), S. 54].

Contract in writing. The words "contract in writing" contemplate an agreement in writing signed by both the parties affected thereby. An agreement signed by only one of the parties to it does not satisfy the requirements of the law, unless the assent of the other party appears in any way from the agreement itself.

Contract labour. A workman shall be deemed to be employed as "CONTRACT LABOUR" in or in connection with the work of an establishment when he is hired in or in connection with such work by or through a contractor, with or without the knowledge of the principal employer. [Contract Labour (Regulation and Abolition) Act (37 of 1970), S. 2(b)]

"Contract labour" means a worker who shall be deemed to be employed in or in connection with the work of an establishment when he is hired in or in connection with such work by or through a contractor, with or without the knowledge of the principal employer and includes inter-State migrant worker but does not include a worker (other than part-time employee) who —

(i) is regularly employed by the contractor for any activity of his establishment and his employment is governed by mutually accepted standards of the conditions of employment (including engagement on permanent basis), and

(ii) gets periodical increment in the pay, social security coverage and other welfare benefits in accordance with the law for the time being in force in such employment. [Code on Wages, 2019 (29 of 2019), section 2(g)]

"Contract labour" means a worker who shall be deemed to be employed in or in connection with the work of an establishment when he is hired in or in connection with such work by or through a contractor, with or without the knowledge of the principal employer and includes inter-State migrant worker but does not include an employee (other than part time employee) who is regularly employed by the contractor for any activity of his establishment and his employment is governed by mutually accepted standards of the conditions of employment (including engagement on permanent basis), and gets periodical increment in the pay, social security coverage and other welfare benefits in accordance with the law for the time being in force in such employment. [Code on Social Security, 2020 (36 of 2020), section 2(19)]

"Contract labour" means a worker who shall be deemed to be employed in or in connection with the work of an establishment when he is hired in or in connection with such work by or through a contractor, with or without the knowledge of the principal employer and includes inter-State migrant worker but does not include a worker (other than part time employee) who is regularly employed by the contractor for any activity of his establishment and his employment is governed by mutually accepted standards of the conditions of employment (including engagement on permanent basis), and gets periodical increment in the pay, social security coverage and other welfare benefits in accordance with the law for the time being in force in such employment. [Occupational Safety, Healthy & Working Conditions Code, 2020 (37 of 2020), section 2(1)(m)]

"CONTRACT LABOUR" means a person engaged or employed in any premises by or through a contractor, with or without the knowledge of the employer, in any manufacturing process. [Beedi & Cigar workers (C.O.E) Act (32 of 1966), S. 2(e)]

Contract note. The note which is sent by a broker or agent to his principal advising him of the sale or purchase of any stock or marketable security.

Contract of affreightment. For the purposes of this sub-clause—

"CONTRACT OF AFFREIGHTMENT" means a service contract under which a tonnage tax company agrees to transport a specified quantity of specified products at a specified rate, between designated loading and discharging ports over a specified period. [Income-tax Act (43 of 1961), Chapter XII G., S. 115 V-I 2(A), *Expln.* (b) (*Inserted by Finance Act (23 of 2004), S. 30*)]

Contract of agency. The essence of agency to sell is the delivery of the goods to a person who is to sell them, not as his own property but as the property of the principal who continues to be the owner of the goods and will therefore be liable to account for the sale proceeds. *Sri T.V.T & Firm* v. *Commercial Tax Officer*, AIR 1968 SC 784, 787. [Sale of Goods Act (3 of 1930), S. 4].

Contract of carriage. (in the Carriage of Goods by Sea Act) Applies only to contracts of carriage covered by a bill of lading or any similar document of title, insofar as such document relates to the carriage of goods by sea, including any bill of lading or any similar document as aforesaid issued under or pursuant to a charterparty from the moment at which such bill of lading or similar document of title regulates the relations between carrier and a holder of the same. [Indian Carriage of Goods Act (26 of 1925), Art. 1(b); United States Carriage of Goods by Sea Act, 1936, S. 1(b)]

"CONTRACT OF CARRIAGE" applies only to contracts of carriage covered by a bill of lading or any similar document of title, in so far as such document relates to the carriage of goods by sea, including any bill of lading or any similar document as aforesaid issued under or pursuant to a charter party from the moment at which such bill of lading or similar document of title regulates the relations between a carrier and a holder of the same. [Hague-Visby Rules, Art. 1, R. (b)]

Contract of carriage by sea. Means any contract whereby the carrier undertakes against payment of freight to carry goods by sea from one port to another; however, a contract which involves carriage by sea and also carriage by some other means is deemed to be a contract of carriage by sea for the purposes of this Convention only in so far as it relates to the carriage by sea. [Hamburg Rules, Art. 1, R. (6)]

Contract of employment. The expression 'contract of employment' implies an employer, an employee and a contract therefor.

Contract of guarantee. A "CONTRACT OF GUARANTEE" is a contract to perform the promise, or discharge the liability, of a third person in case of his default. The person who gives the guarantee is called the "*surety*"; the person in respect of whose default the guarantee is given is called the "*principal debtor*", and the person to whom the guarantee is given is called the "*creditor*". A guarantee may be either oral or written. [Indian Contract Act (9 of 1872), S. 126].

"CONTRACT OF GUARANTEE", in relation to any hire-purchase agreement, means a contract whereby a person (in this Act referred to as the surety) guarantees the performance of all or any of the hirer's obligation under the hire-purchase guarantee. [Hire-Purchase Act (26 of 1972), S. 2(a)] [Now repealed by Act 31 of 2005]

Contract of indemnity. A contract by which one party promises to save the other from loss caused to him by the conduct of the promisor himself, or by the conduct of any other person, is called a "CONTRACT OF INDEMNITY". [Indian Contract Act (9 of 1872), S. 124].

Contract of sale. Includes an agreement to sell as well as a sale.

Contracted tenancy. A tenancy created under section 116, Transfer of Property Act itself is based on an offer and acceptance and thus it can be regarded as a contractual tenancy and if the terms of the old tenancy can be looked into as part of the terms of the new tenancy, there is no bar to the applicability of Section 5 to the tenancies created under section 116. [T.P. Act (4 of 1882), S. 116].

Contracting out. To remove oneself by contract from a right or obligation.

Contracting party. A party that enters or has entered into a contract.

Contracting party to a marriage. Means either of the parties whose marriage is or is about to be thereby solemnised. [Child Marriage Restraint Act (19 of 1929), S. 2(c)]

Contracting State. Means any country or place outside India in respect of which arrangements have been made by the Central Government with the Government of such country through a treaty or otherwise. [CrPC 1973 (2 of 1974), S. 105A(a)] [Now (w.e.f. 1-7-2024) repealed & replaced by Bharatiya Nagarik Suraksha Sanhita, 2023 (46 of 2023)]

In this Chapter, unless the context otherwise requires,--"contracting State" means any country or place outside India in respect of which arrangements have been made by the Central Government with the Government of such country through a treaty or otherwise. [(w.e.f. 1-7-2024) Bharatiya Nagarik Suraksha Sanhita, 2023 (46 of 2023), section 111(a)]

"CONTRACTING STATE" means a State which has consented to be bound by the treaty, whether or not the treaty has entered into force. [Vienna Convention on Succession of States in Respect of Treaties, 1978, Art. 2(k)]

"CONTRACTING STATE" means a Government of any country or place outside India in respect of which arrangement has been made by the Central Government with the Government of such country or place through a treaty or otherwise for transfer of prisoners from India to such country or place and *vice versa* and includes any other Government of such country or place specified by the Central Government, by notification in the Official Gazette, under sub-section (*l*) of Section 3. [Repatriation of Prisoners Act (49 of 2003), S. 2(a)]

Contractor. "CONTRACTOR" means a person who, in relation to manufacturing process, undertakes to produce a given result by executing the work through contract labour or who engages labour for any manufacturing process in a private dwelling house and includes a sub-contractor, agent, munshi, thekedar or sattedar. [Beedi and Cigar Workers Act (32 of 1966), S. 2(d)]

"CONTRACTOR", in relation to an establishment, means a person who undertakes (whether as an independent contractor, agents, employee or otherwise) to produce a given result for the establishment, other than a mere supply of goods or articles of manufacture to such establishment, by the employment of workmen or to supply workmen to the establishment, and includes a subcontractor, Khatadar, Sardar, agent or any other person, by whatever name called, who recruits or employs workmen. [Inter-state Migrant Workmen (Regulation of Employment and Conditions of Service) Act (30 of 1979), S. 2(b)]

"CONTRACTOR" means a person who furnishes or undertakes to furnish cine-workers for being employed in or in connection with the production of a feature film, and includes a sub-contractor or agent. [Cine-Workers & Cinema Theatre Workers (Regulation of Employment) Act (50 of 1981), S. 2(e)]

"CONTRACTOR" means a person who undertakes to produce a given result for any establishment, other than a mere supply of goods or articles of manufacture, by the employment of building workers or who supplies building workers for any work of the establishment; and includes a sub-contractor. [Building and other Construction Workers (Regulation of Employment and Conditions of Service) Act (27 of 1996), S. 2(1)(g)]

"Contractor", in relation to an establishment, means a person, who —

(i) undertakes to produce a given result for the establishment, other than a mere supply of goods or articles of manufacture to such establishment, through contract labour; or

(ii) supplies contract labour for any work of the establishment as mere human resource and includes a sub-contractor. [Code on Wages, 2019 (29 of 2019), section 2(f)]

"contractor", in relation to an establishment means a person, who—

(i) undertakes to produce a given result for the establishment, other than a mere supply of goods or articles of manufacture to such establishment through contract labour; or

(ii) supplies contract labour for any work of the establishment as mere human resource, and includes a sub-contractor. [Code on Social Security, 2020 (36 of 2020), section 2(20)]

"Contractor", in relation to an establishment, means a person, who—

(i) undertakes to produce a given result for the establishment, other than a mere supply of goods or articles of manufacture to such establishment, through contract labour; or

(ii) supplies contract labour for any work of the establishment as mere human resource, and includes a sub-contractor. [Occupational Safety, Healthy & Working Conditions Code, 2020 (37 of 2020), section 2(1)(n)]

A "contractor" is a person who, in the pursuit of an independent business, undertakes to do specific jobs or work for other persons, without submitting himself to their control in respect to the details of the work.

One who contracts to furnish supplies, or to perform any work or service at a certain price or rate; one who enters into a contract.

Contractual liability. Legal liability of another party that the business firm agrees to assume by a written or oral contract. (*Insurance*)

Contractual obligation. An obligation which arises from a contract.

Contractual voyage. The voyage from the port of loading to the port of discharge as declared in the charter-party or in the bill of lading.

Contractus ad mentem partium verbis notatum intelligences. (*Maxim*) A contract is to be understood according to the intention of the parties, expressed in words. (*Morgan*)

Contractus ex turpi causa vel contra bonos mores, est nullus. (*Maxim*) Contracts arising from a base consideration or against morality are void. (*Morgan; Broom*)

Contractus infantis invalidus, si in damnum sui spectet. (*Maxim*) The contract of a minor is invalid, if it tends to his loss.

Contractus legem ex contione accipient. (*Maxim*) Contracts take their law from the agreement of their parties.

Contradict. To affirm the contrary of; to declare untrue or erroneous.

An omission is not a contradiction unless what is actually said contradicts what is omitted to be said.

The meaning given to the word 'contradict' must include the case of an omission in a previous statement which by implication amounts to contradiction. *Tahshildar Singh* v. *State of U.P.*, AIR 1959 SC 1012, 1033. [Indian Evidence Act (1 of 1872), S. 145].

Contraria contrariis curantur. Opposites are cured by opposites.

Contrary. Opposite.

Contrary to law. Violating or not conforming to the provisions of law. The circumstances that a finding of a lower appellate Court is based mainly upon evidence which is explicitly referred to and avowedly reproduced in the judgment, but is not to be found anywhere in the record, vitiates the decision and renders it "contrary to law".

Violating or not confirming to the provisions of law.

Contrary to natural justice. A judgment will be contrary to natural justice if it is the result of bias or want of impartiality on the part of the judge. *Viswanathan* v. *Abdul Wajid*, AIR 1963 SC 1, 25.

Contravene. To go against; to violate: as, to contravene the constitution. (*Ballentine's Law Dictionary, 3rd Edn.*)

Contravention. 'In contravention of' sometimes means 'otherwise than in accordance with.'

The action of contravening; a transgression or violation.

Contrectatio rei alienae, animo furandi, est furtum. (*Maxim*) The touching another's property with intent to steal is theft. (*Stimson*)

Contribute. To give as contribution; to give or grant in common with others; give to a common stock or for a common purpose; furnish as a share or constituent part of anything, (as) contribute to a charitable fund; contribute articles to a newspaper.

Contributing institution. An institution that makes a contribution. [Unit Trust of India Act (52 of 1963), S. 2(b)].

Contributing oil. "CONTRIBUTING OIL" means crude oil and fuel oil.

Explanation. For the purposes of this clause,—

(i) "crude oil" means any liquid hydro carbon mixture occurring naturally in the earth whether or not treated to render it suitable for transportation and includes crude oils from which certain distillate fractions have been removed or to which certain distillate fractions have been added;

(ii) "fuel oil" means heavy distillates or residues from crude oil or blends of such materials intended for use as a fuel for the production of heat or power of a quality equivalent to the 'American Society for Testing and Materials'

Specification for Number Four Fuel Oil (Designation D 396-69)', or heavier. [Merchant Shipping Act (44 of 1958), S. 352S (Inserted by Merchant Shipping (Amendment) Act, 2002)]

Contribution. "CONTRIBUTION" means any amount credited in a Provident Fund, by [any authority administering the Fund], by way of addition to, (a subscription to, or deposit or balance at the credit of an individual account in), the Fund; and "Contributory Provident Fund" means a Provident Fund the rules of which provide for the crediting of contribution. [Provident Funds Act (19 of 1925), S. 2(b)]

"CONTRIBUTION" means the sum of money payable to the Corporation by the principal employer in respect of an employee and includes any amount payable by or on behalf of the employee in accordance with the provision of this Act. [Employer's State Insurance Act (34 of 1948), S. 2(4)]

"CONTRIBUTION" means the contribution payable in respect of a member under the Coal Mines Provident Fund Scheme framed under this Act of or the contribution payable in respect of an employee to whom the Insurance Scheme applies. [Coal Mines Provident Fund and Miscellaneous Provisions Act (46 of 1948), S. 2(c)]

The action of contributing; the payment by each of the parties interested in any common loss or liability; amount so payable; proportionate discharge of liability of properties jointly liable. [Income-tax Act (43 of 1961), S. 10(13)(iv)]

"CONTRIBUTION" has the meaning assigned to it under Section 293A, of the Companies Act, 1956 and includes any donation or subscription offered by any person to a political party. [Election and other Related Laws (Amendment Act (46 of 2003), S. 2 *Expln.*(c)]

"Contribution" means the sum of money payable by the employer, under this Code, to the Central Board and to the Corporation, as the case may be, and includes any amount payable by or on behalf of the employee in accordance with the provisions of this Code. [Code on Social Security, 2020 (36 of 2020), section 2(21)]

"CONTRIBUTION" means any sum credited by or on behalf of any employee out of his salary, or by an employer out of his own monies, to the individual account of an employee, but does not include any sum credited as interest. [Income-tax Act (43 of 1961), Sch. IV, Part A. R. 2(c)]

Contribution, General average. Where any loss or damage is voluntarily and properly incurred in repect of the goods or of the ship for the general safety of the ship and cargo, the loss is to be distributed between all the interested parties. [Marine Insurance Act (11 of 1963), S. 63(3)(ii)].

Contribution to the assets of society. This phrase refers to the liability of the members of the society to contribute to its assets in the event of the winding up of the society. [Co-operative Societies Act (2 of 1912), S. 42(4-A)].

Contributory. means a person liable to contribute towards the assets of the company in the event of its being wound up.

Explanation.—For the purposes of this clause, it is hereby clarified that a person holding fully paid-up shares in a company shall be considered as a contributory but shall have no liabilities of a contributory under the Act whilst retaining rights of such a contributory; [Companies Act, 2013, S. 2(26)]

The term "CONTRIBUTORY" means every person liable to contribute to the assets of a company in the event of its being wound up, and includes the holder of any shares which are fully paid up; and for the purposes of all proceedings for determining, and all proceedings prior to the final determination of, the persons who are to be deemed contributories, includes any person alleged to be a contributory. [Companies Act (1 of 1956), S. 428]

"CONTRIBUTORY" means a person liable to contribute towards the assets of the company in the event of its being wound up. *Explanation.*—For the purposes of this clause, it is hereby clarified that a person holding fully paid-up shares in a company shall be considered as a contributory but shall have no liabilities of a contributory under the Act whilst retaining rights of such a contributory. [S. 2(26) of the Companies Act, 2013 (18 of 2013)]

Contributory mortgage. A mortgage where the mortgage money is advanced by two or more persons separately.

Contributory negligence. The act or omission amounting to want of ordinary care on the part of the complaining party which concurring with defendant's negligence, is proximate cause of injury.

Contributory negligence: In case of contributory negligence, a person who has himself contributed to the accident cannot claim compensation for the injuries sustained by him in the accident to the extent of his own negligence, where as in the case of composite negligence, a person who has suffered has not contributed to the accident but due to the outcome of combination of negligence of two or more other persons. [*Khenyei* v. *New India Assurance Company Limited*, (2015) 9 SCC 273, para 15].

The contributory negligence of the plaintiff is no bar to his claim but will reduce the damages to which he is entitled. Where any person suffers damage as the result partly of his own fault and partly of the fault of any other person or persons, a claim in respect of the damage is not defeated by reason of the fault of the person suffering the damage, but the damages recoverable in respect of it will be reduced to such extent as the Court thinks just and equitable having regard to the claimant's in the responsibility for the damage. HALSBURY, 4th Edn., Vol. 12, para 1212, p. 499.

The act or omission amounting to want of ordinary care or in defiance of duty or obligation on the part of the complaining party which conjointly with the other party's negligence was the proximate cause of the accident, renders it one to be the result of contributory negligence. *Municipal Corpn of Greater Bombay* v. *Laxman Iyer,* (2003) 8 SCC 731, para 7.

The expression 'contributory negligence' does not mean breach of any duty. It only means the failure by a person to use reasonable care for the safety of either himself or his property, so that he becomes blameworthy in part as an 'author of his own wrong'. *Pramod Kumar Rasikbhai Jhavery* v. *Karmasey Kunvargi Tak,* (2002) 6 SCC 455, para 8 : AIR 2002 SC 2864.

Contributory provident fund. Means a Provident Fund the rules of which provide for the crediting of Contribution. [Provident Fund Act (19 of 1925), S. 2(b)]

Contrive. To make devices; to plan; to scheme; to invent.

Control. "CONTROL" shall include the right to appoint majority of the directors or to control the management or policy decisions exercisable by a person or persons acting individually or in concert, directly or indirectly, including by virtue of their shareholding or management rights or shareholders agreements or voting agreements or in any other manner. [Unlisted Public Companies (Preferential allotment) Rules, 2003, R. 3(3)]

"To exercise restraining or directing influence over; to regulate; restrain; dominate; curb; to hold from action; overpower; counteract; govern; power or authority to manage, direct superintend, restrict, regulate, govern. Administer or oversee. The ability to exercise a restraining or directing influence over something." [Black's Law Dictionary as cited in *The Thrissur District Co-Op. Bank* v. *The State Information Commission*, AIR 2017 Ker 120, para 45]

"The power to influence people's behaviour or the course of events; the restriction of an activity, tendency, or phenomenon. [Concise Oxford English Dictionary as cited in *The Thrissur District Co-Op. Bank* v. *The State Information Commission and Ors.*, AIR2017Ker120, para 45]

"Control" is a mixed question of law and fact. Ownership of shares has the character of a controlling interest in the management of the company. [*Vodafone International Holdings BV* v. *Union of India*, (2012) 6 SCC 613, para 159].

"Control" is an interest arising from holding a particular number of shares and the same cannot be separately acquired or transferred. Each share represents a vote in the management of the company and such a vole can be utilised to control the company. [*Vodafone International Holdings BV* v. *Union of India*, (2012) 6 SCC 613, para 276].

As a noun, power to check or restrain; superintendence; management. *As a verb,* to restrain; to check; to regulate; to govern; to keep under check; to hold in restraint; to dominate; to rule and direct; to counteract; to exercise a directing, restraining or governing influence over; to govern with reference thereto; to subject to authority; to have under command, and authority over; to have authority over the particular matter. (*Ame. Cyc.*)

Read with Articles 233 and 234, the word "control" used in Article 235 would indicate that although the Appointing Authority of the District Judge and officers other than District Judge is the Governor of the State, the words "control over district Courts and Courts subordinate thereto" which are words of wide connotation, vests in the High Court in other facets of service of those officers, namely, their confirmation on completion of probation period, their postings, transfers and disciplinary matters including power to recommend major punishments. Thus the "control" vested in High Court is complete control subject only to the powers of the Governor in the matter of appointment, initial posting and promotion to the post of District Judges. For imposing major punishment, including the punishment of dismissal, removal or reduction in rank, the High Court can, in exercise of its powers under Article 235 of the Constitution, hold disciplinary proceedings and recommend punishment to the Governor who alone is competent to impose such punishment having regard to the provisions of Articles 233 and 234. *Yoginath D. Bagde* v. *State of Maharashtra*, AIR 1999 SC 3734.

Control is not merely the power to arrange the day to day working of the Court but contemplates disciplinary jurisdiction over the presiding judge. . . . The word "control" in Art. 235 must have a different content. It includes something in addition to mere superintendence. It is control over the conduct and discipline of the judges . . . . *State of West Bengal* v. *Nripendranath Bagchi,* AIR 1966 SC 447. [Constitution of India, Art. 235]

The term 'control' includes the power to prohibit. *Kesho Ram* v. *State of Punjab,* AIR 1964 Punj 307, 311. [Defence of India Rules (1962), S. 125(2)].

The concept of control implies a dominant and a dominated undertaking. The controlling undertaking must be in a position to dominate the affairs of the controlled undertaking either in respect of the management of its affairs, or in respect of its finance or with regard to the capital structure. [Monopolies and Restrictive Trade Practices Act (54 of 1969), S. 2(*g*)(*iii*)].

The word 'control' is synonymous with superintendence, management or authority to direct, restrict or regulate. Control is exercised by a superior authority in exercise of its supervisory power. *S.V. Co-op. Bank* v. *K. Panduranga*, AIR 1972 SC 1248, 1250. [Multi-Unit Co-operative Societies Act (6 of 1942), S. 2(1)].

The word 'control' suggests check, restraint or influence. Control is intended to regulate and hold in check and restrain from action. *State of Mysore* v. *Karibasappa*, AIR 1974 SC 1863, 1866. [Mysore Co-operative Societies Act (11 of 1950), S. 54].

The word 'control' must include disciplinary jurisdiction. *State of W.B.* v. *Nripendra Nath Bagchi*, AIR 1966 SC 447, 453.

Control means something in addition to that mere superintendence of the Courts. The control is over the conduct and discipline of Judges. *Beradakanta Mishra* v. *The High Court of Orissa*, AIR 1976 SC 1899, 1902, 1903. [Constitution of India, Article 235]

The word 'control' occurring in Article 235 includes general superintendence of the working of the subordinate Courts. *Brij Mohan Lal* v. *Union of India,* (2002) 5 SCC 1, para 9 : AIR 2002 SC 2096. [Constitution of India, Art. 235]

The word 'control' occurring in Article 235 of the Constitution includes the control and superintendence of the High Court over the subordinate Courts. *Gauhati High Court* v. *Kuladhar Phukan,* (2002) 4 SCC 524 para 14 : AIR 2002 SC 1589. [Constitution of India, Art. 235]

The expression 'control' occurring in Article 235 of the Constitution would also include the administrative control of High Court. So also premature and compulsory retirement is also within the ambit of expression 'control' of High Court. *Madan Mohan Choudhary* v. *State of Bihar,* (1999) 3 SCC 396, para 25 : AIR 1999 SC 1018. [Constitution of India, Art. 235]

The word 'control' occurring in Article 235 of the Constitution includes general superintendence of the working of the subordinate Courts, disciplinary control over the presiding officers of the subordinate Courts and to recommend the imposition of punishment of dismissal, removal and reduction in rank or compulsory retirement and it would also include suspension of a member of judicial service for the purposes of holding a disciplinary inquiry, transfer, confirmation and promotion. *High Court of Judicature for Rajasthan* v. *Ramesh Chand Paliwal,* AIR 1998 SC 1079. [Constitution of India, Art. 235]

The word 'control' occurring in Section 264 of the Act includes the power of State Government to check the resolution of the municipality. *Girishbhai Maganlal Kotecha* v. *State of Gujarat,* AIR 2002 Guj 311, para 13. [Gujarat Municipalities Act (34 of 1964), S. 264]

"CONTROL" shall include the right to appoint majority of the directors or to control the management or policy decisions exercisable by a person or persons acting individually or in concert, directly or indirectly, including by virtue of their shareholding or management rights or shareholders agreements or voting agreements or in any other manner. [S. 2(27) of the Companies Act, 2013 (18 of 2013). Also see Nidhi Rules 2014, *Explanation* to rule 6(d).]

Control equipment. Means any apparatus, device, equipment or system to control the quality and the manner of emission of any air pollutant and includes any device used for securing the efficient operation of any industrial plant. [Air (Prevention and Control of Pollution) Act (14 of 1981), S. 2(i)]

Control of a company. Means control, direct or indirect, of more than one-half of the voting power attached to the total issued paid-up share capital of the company, or control vested by its Memorandum and Articles of Association otherwise than by reference to such voting power:

Provided that voting power attached to shares held by a nominee or trustee for any person shall be deemed for the purpose of this definition to be held by that person. [Business Profits Tax Act (21 of 1947), S. 2(6)]

Control over sub-ordinate Courts. Control means something in addition to that mere superintendence of the Courts. The control is over the conduct and discipline of Judges. *Beradakanta Mishra* v. *The High Court of Orissa*, AIR 1976 SC 1899, 1902, 1903. [Constitution of India, Art. 235].

A direction may mean an order issued to a particular individual or a precept which many may have to follow. *Kanhiya Lal Guar* v. *R.K. Trivedi*, AIR 1986 SC 111, 118. [Constitution of India, Art. 324].

Controlled business. The optical redemption business and the annuity of certain business must be included in the expresion "controlled business" even in the case of a composite insurer like the National Insurance Company. *National Insurance Co. Ltd.* v. *LIC of India*, AIR 1963 SC 1911, 1913. [Life Insurance Corporation Act (31 of 1956), S. 2(3)(*i*), *Expln.* 7(*i*)].

Controlled company. A company the majority of whose voting stock is held by an individual or corporation. For example, a subsidiary of a parent company. The level of control depends on the amount of stock owned. (*Black*)

Controlled delivery. Means the technique of allowing illicit or suspect consignments of narcotic drugs, psychotropic substances, controlled substances or substances substituted for them to pass out of, or through or into the territory of India with the knowledge and under the supervision of an officer empowered in this behalf or duly authorised under Section 50A with a view to identifying the persons involved in the commission of an offence under this Act. [Narcotic Drugs and Psychotropic Substances Act (61 of 1985), S. 2(viib)]

Controlled fund. Means—

(a) in the case of any insurer specified in sub-clause (a)(ii) or sub-clause (b) of clause (9) of

Section 2 and carrying on life insurance business—

(i) all his funds, if he carries on no other class of insurance business,

(ii) all the funds appertaining to his life insurance business if he carries on some other class of insurance business also; and

(b) in the case of any other insurer carrying on life insurance business,—

(i) all his funds in India, if he carries on no other class of insurance business;

(ii) all the fund in India appertaining to his life insurance business if he carries on some other class of insurance business also; but does not include any fund or portion thereof in respect of which the Controller is satisfied that such fund or portion thereof, as the case may be, is regulated by the law of any country outside India or in respect of which the Controller is satisfied that it would not be in the interest of the insurer to apply to provisions of this section. [Insurance Act (4 of 1938), S. 27A(14), *Expln.*]

Controlled industry. Means any industry the control of which by the Union has been declared by any Central Act to be expedient in the public interest. [Contract Labour (Regulation and Abolition) Act (37 of 1970), S. 2(d); Inter-State Migrant Workmen (Regulation of Employment and Conditions of Service) Act (30 of 1979), S. 2(c); Industries (Development and Regulation) Act (65 of 1951), S. 52]

"Controlled industry" means any industry the control of which by the Union has been declared by any Central Act to be expedient in the public interest. [Industrial Relations Code, 2020 (35 of 2020), section 2(k)]

Controlled price. Means the price of the relevant grade of levy sugar, determined from time to time under sub-section (3C) of Section 3 of the Essential Commodities Act, 1955, or under the Defence and Internal Security of India Rules, 1971, in relation to any year of production. [Levy Sugar Price Equalisation Fund Act (31 of 1976), S. 2(a)]

The mere fact that a commodity could be sold in the market below the price fixed by a notification fixing the maximum price by Government would not indicate that there was no control. Control of any of the article contemplated by the parties under the agreements was a control of the price of the articles. *Mohd. Rajab Gujari* v. *State of J&K.,* AIR 1974 SC 887.

Controlled substance. Means any substance which the central Government may, having regard to the available information as to its possible use in the production or manufacture of narcotic drugs or psychotropic substances or to the provisions of any International Convention, by notification in the official Gazette declare to be a controlled substance. [Narcotic Drugs and Psychotropic Substances Act (61 of 1985), S. 2(viia)]

Controller. "CONTROLLER" means the Controller General of Patents, Designs and Trade Marks appointed under sub-section (1) of Section 4 of the Trade and Merchandise Marks Act, 1958.] Now repealed & replaced by Act 37 of 1999]. [Designs Act (2 of 1911), section 2(3)] [Now repealed & replaced by Act 16 of 2000]

"CONTROLLER" means the Controller of Certifying Authorities appointed under sub-section (1) of Section 17. [Information Technology Act (21 of 2000), S. 2(1)(m)]

'CONTROLLER' means in respect of any local areas comprised within the limit of Sub-Division, the Sub-Divisional Officer Incharge of the Sub-Division, and includes any other Officer appointed in this behalf by the State Government to perform the functions of a Controller under this Act. [Bihar Buildings (Lease, Rent and Eviction) Control Act (4 of 1983), S. 2(c)]

Controller of Insurance. Means the officer appointed by the Central Government under Section 2B to exercise all the powers, discharge the functions and perform the duties of the Authority under this Act or the Life Insurance Corporation Act, 1956 or the General Insurance Business (Nationalisation) Act, 1972 or the Insurance Regulatory and Development Authority Act, 1999. [Insurance Act (4 of 1938), S. 2(5B)]

Controlling Interest. A controlling interest is an incident of ownership of shares in a company, something which flows out of the holding of shares. A controlling interest is, therefore, not an identifiable or distinct capital asset independent of the holding of shares. *Vodafone International Holdings BV* v. *Union of India*, (2012) 6 SCC 613, para 159.

Controversy. A dispute; a disputed question; a dispute arising between two or more persons; a lawsuit. (*Cent. Dict.; Webster; Burrill*)

Contention as to right, claims and the like, or on a matter of opinion; a disputed question.

Convene. Summon an assembly or meeting; convention.

"Convene" and **"Summon".** There is an obvious difference between 'convened' and 'summoned'. . . 'convened' is applied, properly, not to individuals but to aggregate bodies. A Board is 'convened'; an Assembly is 'convened'; a Senate is 'convened'; but a person is not 'convened', he is 'summoned, warned, or noticed.

Convenience. Personal comfort; material advantage.

Suited to one's personal ease or comfort or to one's easy performance of some act or function; affording convenience.

Conventio privatorum non potest publico juri derogare. (*Maxim*) A private agreement cannot derogate from public law. (*Trayner; Broom*)

Convention. "CONVENTION" means the International Convention on Standards of Training, Certification and Watchkeeping for Seafarers, 1978, signed at London on the 7th day of July, 1978, as amended from time to time. [Merchant Shipping Act (44 of 1958), S. 75A(b)]

"CONVENTION" means the Convention on Limitation of Liability for Maritime Claims, 1976 as amended from time to time. [Merchant Shipping Act (44 of 1958), S. 352(b)]

"CONVENTION" means a formal meeting or assembly which is not open to the general public, and does not include a meeting or assembly, the principal purpose of which is to provide any type of amusement, entertainment or recreation. [Finance Act (32 of 1994), S. 65(1)(26) (now repealed by Central Goods and Service Tax Act, 2017)]

"CONVENTION" means the Convention on the Prohibition of the Development, Production, Stockpiling and Use of Chemical Weapons and on their Destruction signed on behalf of the Government of India at Paris on the 14th day of January, 1993. [Chemical Weapons Convention Act (34 of 2000), S. 2(c)]

"CONVENTION" means the convention on International Civil Aviation opened for signatures at Chicago on the 7th December, 1944. [Foreign Aircraft Act (36 of 2002), S. 2(b)]

"CONVENTION" means the Convention for the Suppression of Unlawful Acts Against the Safety of Maritime Navigation, signed at Rome on the 10th day of March, 1988 as amended from time to time. [Suppression of Unlawful Acts Against Safety of Maritime Navigation and Fixed Platform on Continental Shelf Act (69 of 2002), S. 2(c)]

"CONVENTION" means the Vienna Convention for the Protection of the Ozone layer, adopted on 22 March 1985. [Montreal Protocol on Substances That Deplete the Ozone layer, 1987, Art. 1(1)]

Agreement; any temporary treaty; agreement between states of less formality or importance than a treaty; a generally accepted rule or practice; usage or custom.

Convention centre. Means a building of a prescribed area comprising of convention halls to be used for the purpose of holding conferences and seminars, being of such size and number and having such other facilities and amenities, as may be prescribed. [Income-tax Act (43 of 1961), S. 80IB(14)(aa)]

Convention country. "CONVENTION COUNTRY" means a Country in which the Hague Convention is for the time being in force. [Anti-Hijacking Act (65 of 1982), S. 2(c)]

"CONVENTION COUNTRY" means a country or a country which is member of a group of countries or a union of countries or an intergovernmental organisation notified as such under sub-section (1) of Section 133. [Patents Act (39 of 1970), S. 2(d)]

"CONVENTION COUNTRY" means a country which has acceded to an international convention for the protection of plant varieties to which India has also acceded, or a country which has a law on protection of plant varieties on the basis of which India has entered into an agreement for granting plant breeders' right to the citizens of both the countries. [Protection of Plant Varieties and Farmer's Right Act (53 of 2001), S. 2(f)]

Convention State. Means a State Party to the Convention. [Suppression of Unlawful Acts against Safety of Maritime Navigation and Fixed Plateform on Continental Shelf Act (69 of 2002), S. 2(c)]

Conventional. Depending on convention; not spontaneous; that which is produced by, or depends upon the agreement or mutual arrangement of parties. (*Burrill Law. Dict*)

Conventional chit. Means a transaction whether called chit, chit fund kuri or by any other name by or under which a person responsible for the conduct of the chit enters into an agreement with a specified number of persons that every one of them shall subscribe a certain sum of money (or certain quantity of grain instead) by way of periodical instalments for a definite period and that each such subscriber shall, in his turn, as determined by lot or by auction or by tender or in such other manner as may be provided for in the chit agreement, be entitled to a prize amount.

Explanation. In this clause the prize amount shall mean the amount, by whatever name called, arrived at by deducting from out of the total amount paid or payable at each instalment by all the subscribers, (i) the commission charged as service charges as a promoter or a foreman or an agent; and (ii) any sum which a subscriber agrees to forego, from out of the total subscriptions of each instalment, in consideration of the balance being paid to him. [Prize Chits and Money Circulation Schemes (Banning) Act (43 of 1978), S. 2(a)]

Conventional law. Law depending on, or arising from the mutual agreement of parties, as distinguished from legal, which means created by, or arising from the act of law; law based on established usage or custom.

Convergence. Different technologies available through a single source, like telephone, internet, television could be accessible through a single device.

CONVERGENCE has been recognised between broadcasting, information and communication sector which, until now, are separated. Regulation till date is seen as sector specific whereas Competition Law is more general. All over the world, the present approach is to stimulate a dynamic competition market for communication service, to consolidate the internal market in a converging environment, a restrict regulation to necessary minimum and to aim at technology neutrality and to accommodate converging market. (*Internet and E-commerce*).

Conversation. Communication of thoughts; familiar intercourse; an exchange of thoughts or sentiments. Oral exchange of ideas.

Conversational mode. A computer operating so as to accept English or "near English" statements directly from the user, normally from a keyboard/display unit, and to provide an immediate response that has meaning to the user without translation (*Computer*)

Conversion. "CONVERSION", with its grammatical variations, includes alteration or change of whatever nature. [Places of Worship (Special Provisions) Act (42 of 1991), S. 2(b)]

"CONVERSION" means "the change of an occupancy or change in building structure or part thereof, resulting into change of space or use requiring additional occupancy certificate". Noida Building Regulations and Directions, 2006, Regn. 3.22 as cited in *R. K. Mittal* v. *State of Uttar Pradesh*, para 25.

The transformation of one species of property into another, as money into land, or land into money.

The action of wrongfully converting something to one's own use; the action of converting or the fact of being converted.

Convert. To change one thing into another. Person converted from one religion to another.

To divert wrongfully; to appropriate and apply to one's use; to cause to turn to a religion or belief; one who is converted.

Convertible foreign exchange. Means foreign exchange which is for the time being treated by the Reserve Bank of India as convertible foreign exchange for the purposes of the Foreign Exchange Regulation Act, 1973 (46 of 1973), and any rules made thereunder or any other corresponding law for the time being in force. [Income-tax Act (43 of 1961), S. 10A(9), *Expln.* 2(ii)]

"Convertible note". Means an instrument issued by a startup company evidencing receipt of money initially as debt, which is repayable at the option of the holder, or which is convertible into such number of equity shares of such startup company, within a period not exceeding five years from the date of issue of the convertible note, upon occurrence of specified events as per the other terms and conditions agreed to and indicated in the instrument. [Foreign Exchange Management (Transfer of Issue or Security by a Person Resident Outside India) Regulations, 2000, Regn. 2(ii-A)].

For the purposes of this sub-clause, "CONVERTIBLE NOTE" means an instrument evidencing receipt of money initially as a debt, which is repayable at the option of the holder, or which is convertible into such number of equity shares of the start-up company upon occurrence of specified events and as per the other terms and conditions agreed to and indicated in the instrument. [Companies (Acceptance of Deposits) Rules, 2014, R. 2(1)(c), *Explanation II*].

'CONVERTIBLE NOTE' means an instrument issued by a startup company evidencing receipt of money initially as debt, which is repayable at the option of the holder, or which is convertible into such number of equity shares of such startup company, within a period not exceeding five years from the date of issue of the convertible note, upon occurrence of specified events as per the other terms and conditions agreed to and indicated in the instrument. [Foreign Exchange Management (Transfer or Issue of Security by a Person Resident outside India) Regulations, 2017, Regn. 2(vi)].

Convertible paper currency. One that can be converted into cash on demand, as a Bank of England note in England; Government Currency Notes in India.

Convertible securities. Securities that are marketable and convertible into money.

Converts to his own use. A sale of the property by the bailee, contrary to the terms of the bailment, and for his own benefit, is clearly a conversion.

Convey. To transport; to take from one place to another [IPC (45 of 1860), S. 282]; to transfer property by means of instrument and other formalities; to transport; to communicate.

Conveyance. "CONVEYANCE" includes a conveyance on sale and every instrument by which property, whether movable or immovable, is transferred *inter vivos* and which is not otherwise specifically provided for by Schedule I. [Indian Stamp Act (2 of 1899), S. 2(10)]

"Conveyance" includes a vessel, an aircraft and a vehicle [The Central Goods and Services Tax Act, 2017 (12 of 2017), S. 2(34)]

"CONVEYANCE" includes a vessel, vehicle, country-craft and an air-craft. [Emigration Act (31 of 1983), S. 2(b); Customs Act (52 of 1962), S. 2(9)]

"CONVEYANCE" includes a carrier vessel or a vehicle. [Marine Products Export Development Authority Act (13 of 1972), S. 3(c)]

"CONVEYANCE" means a conveyance of any description whatsoever and includes any aircraft, vehicle or vessel. [Narcotics Drugs and Psychotropic Substances Act (61 of 1985), S. 2(viii)]

"CONVEYANCE" means any vehicle, vessel, aircraft or any other means of transport including any animal. [Foreign Trade (Development & Regulation) Act (22 of 1992), S. 2(c)]

'CONVEYANCE' includes,—

(i) a conveyance on sale,

(ii) every instrument,

(iii) every decree or final order of any civil Court,

(iv) every order made by High Court under Section 394 of the Companies Act, 1956 in respect of amalgamation or reconstruction of companies; and every order made by the

Reserve Bank of India under Section 44A of the Banking Regulation Act, 1949 in respect of amalgamation or reconstruction of Banking companies by which property, whether movable or immovable, or any estate or interest in any property is transferred to, or vested in, other person, *inter vivos*, and which is not otherwise specifically provided for by Schedule I. [Bombay Stamp Act (60 of 1958), S. 2(g)]

'CONVEYANCE' includes,—

(i) a conveyance on sale,

(ii) every instrument,

(iii) every decree or final order of any civil Court,

(iv) every order made by the High Court under Section 394 of the Companies Act, 1956 in respect of amalgamation of companies,

by which property, whether movable or immovable, or any estate is transferred to, or vested in, any other person, and which not otherwise specifically provided for by schedule. [Karnataka Stamp Act (34 of 1957), S. 2(1)(d)]

An 'agreement to sell' an immovable property with transferring of possession without execution of any conveyance is deemed to be a 'conveyance' under Art. 25, *Expln.* I of the Act. *Veena Hasmukh Jain* v. *State of Maharashtra*, AIR 1999 SC 807. [Bombay Stamp Act (60 of 1958), Sch. I, Art. 25, *Expln.* 1]

A 'consent decree' comes within the ambit of 'conveyance' under Section 2(g) of the Act. *Hindustan Lever* v. *State of Maharashtra,* AIR 2004 SC 326, 330, para 6. Also see *Ruby Sale and Services (P.) Ltd.* v. *State of Maharashtra,* (1994) 1 SCC 531. [Bombay Stamp Act (60 of 1958), S. 2(g)]

An act by which property is conveyed or voluntarily transferred from one person to another by means of a written instrument and other formalities; the instrument itself; the writing that transfers property; the means of transportation.

Conveyance in Section 64 includes documents of sale, mortgage, charge, exchange and other transfer of property. *Jayanta Mohan Chatterjee* v. *Jagat Mohan Chatterjee,* AIR 1972 Cal 88, 94. [Indian Trusts Act (2 of 1882), S. 63, 64].

Conveyance means transfer of ownership. *Commissioner Gift Tax, Madras* v. *Getty Chettiar*, AIR 1971 SC 2410, 2413. [Gift Tax Act (18 of 1958), S. 2, cl. (*xxiv*)].

Conveyance includes a mortgage, charge, lease, assert, vesting declaration, vesting instrument, disclaimer, release and every other assurance of property or of any interest therein by any instrument except a will. *Official Assignee Madras* v. *Tehmina Dinshaw Tehrani,* AIR 1972 Mad 187, 188. [Transfer of Property Act (4 of 1882), S. 5].

Conveyance or assignment. In the Bankruptcy Act, 1883, (46 & 47 Vict., c. 52), S; 4, sub-s. 1(*a*) is limited to those particular modes of disposition of property, and means a formal conveyance or assignment properly so called of the whole, or substantially the whole, of the debtor's property, [Re *Spackman,* (1890) 24 QBD 741, FRY, LJ]. "Conveyance or assignment in an instrument under seal actually transferring the legal and equitable interest in the property, so as to take it out of the assignor and vest it in the assignees," LOPES, L.J.

Conveyance or sale. in the Stamp Act, 1891 (54 & 55 Vict., c. 39), Ss. 54, 57. See *Inland Revenue Commissioners* v. *Tod,* (1898) App. Cas 399; *Chesterfield Brewery Co.* v. *Inland Retenue Commissioners,* (1898) 2 QB 7; *Swayne* v. *Inland Revenue Commissioners,* (1898) 1 QB 335; (1900) 1 QB 172 (CA); *G.N.R* v. *Inland Revenue Commissioners*, (1901) 1 KB 416.

Conveyancer. One whose business is to draw deeds, *etc.*, or other legal papers.

Conveyancing. The science and art of transferring titles to real estate from one person to another; the framing of legal documents intended to create, define, transfer or extinguish rights. Drawing of deeds *etc.*

Convicia si irascaris tua divulgas; spreta exolescunt. (*Maxim*) If you be moved to anger by insults, you publish them, if despised, they are forgotten.

Convict. (As a verb) To condemn; to prove or find guilty of an offence or crime charged; to pronounce guilty as by legal decision.

CONVICT (as a noun) is one who has been condemned by a competent Court; one who has been convicted of a crime or misdemeanour.

A "convict" means declared to be guilty of criminal offence by the verdict of court of law. That declaration is made after the court finds him guilty of the charges which have been proved against him. *Shyam Narain Pandey* v. *State of U.P.*, (2014) 8 SCC 909, para 4.

Convict, Life. One who is convicted with a sentence of imprisonment for life. [IPC (45 of 1860), S. 307].

Convicted. Found guilty of the crime whereof one stands indicted.

The expression 'convicted' would mean by any Court, whether final or not. [Representation of the People Act (43 of 1951), S. 8(2)].

Convicted criminal prisoners. Means any criminal prisoner under sentence of a Court or Court-martial and includes a person detained under the provisions of Chapter VIII of the Code of Criminal Procedure, (2 of 1974) or under the Prisoners' Act, 1894. [Prisons Act (9 of 1894), S. 3(3)]

Conviction. The act of a legal tribunal adjudging a person guilty of an offence; finding of guilt; strong belief.

The word 'conviction' means that the person has been convicted finally. [Constitution of India, Art. 311(2), *Proviso* (*a*)].

Conviction and Convicted. Do not include or refer to a conviction which under foreign law is a conviction for contumacy, but the term "person accused" includes a person so convicted for contumacy. [Extradition Act (34 of 1962), S. 2(b)]

Convince. To satisfy the mind by proof; to bring to a belief; to produce conviction or belief.

Convocation. An assembly of people called together or summoned.

Convoy. A escort for courtesy's sake or for guidance or protection.

Cooked food. Biscuit is not a cooked food. *Annapurna Biscuit Manufacturing Co., Kanpur* v. *Commissioner of Sales Tax, U.P., Lucknow*, AIR 1981 SC 1656, 1657.

Cookie. A small file stored in the computer by an Internet Site visited by the user. Then when user again visits that site, the information related to that site is readily available. (*Internet*)

(Internet Browser)—Holds information on the times and dates you have visited Web sites. Other information can also be saved to your hard disk in these text files, including information about online purchases, validation information about you for members only Web sites, and more.

Small files placed on a Web user's hard drive when a website is visited; they may persist for years or disappear when the browser is closed.

The most common meaning of "Cookie" on the Internet refers to a piece of information sent by a Web *Server* to a Web *Browser* that the Browser software is expected to save and to send back to the Server whenever the browser makes additional requests from the Server.

Depending on the type of Cookie used, and the Browsers' settings, the Browser may accept or not accept the Cookie, and may save the Cookie for either a short time or long time.

Cookies might contain information such as login or Registration information, online "shopping cart" information, user preferences, *etc.*

When a Server receives a request from a Browser that includes a Cookie, the Server is able to use the information stored in the Cookie. For example, the server might customize what is sent back to the user, or keep a log of particular users' requests.

Cookies are usually set to expire after a predetermined amount of time and are usually saved in memory until the Browser software is closed down, at which time they may be saved to disk if their "expire time" has not been reached.

Cookies do not read your hard drive and send your life story to the CIA, but they can be used to gather more information about a user than would be possible without them. (*Matisse Enzer-Glossary of Internet Terms, Internet and E-commerce*)

A cookie is a text file which can be left, unseen, on the internet browser software of a visitor to a website. The cookie contains a unique identifier assigned by a website which enables it to recognize the repeat visitor and collect information regarding each of the user's visits. Aparna Viswanathan, *Cyber Law: Indian & International Perspectives*, 2012, LexisNexis Butterworths at p. 235.

Co-operate. To make joint effort; to act or operate jointly with another or others; to concur in action, effort or effect.

Co-operative. "A co-operative is autonomous association of persons united voluntarily to meet their common economic, social and cultural needs and aspirations through a jointly-owned and democratically-controlled enterprise". The International Cooperative Alliance Statement on the Co-operative Identity was adopted in Manchester, United Kingdom on 23-9-1995 as cited in *Vipulbhai M. Chaudhary* v. *Gujarat Cooperative Milk Marketing Federation Limited*, (2015) 8 SCC 1, para 4.

Co-operative credit society. "Co-operative credit society" means a co-operative society, the primary object of which is to provide financial accommodation to its members and includes a co-operative land mortgage bank. [Banking Regulation Act (10 of 1949), sections 5(ccii) and 56(c)(i)]

"Co-operative Ombudsman". Means the Ombudsman appointed by the Central Government under section 85A. [Multi-State Co-operative Societies Act, 2002 (39 of 2002), section 3(fa)]

Co-operative society. A union of individuals, commonly labourers, farmers, businessmen, or small capitalists, formed for the prosecution in common of productive enterprise, the profits being shared in accordance with the amount of capital or labour contributed by each member. (*Century Dict.*)

In this Part, unless the context otherwise requires, "COOPERATIVE SOCIETY" means a society registered or deemed to be registered under any law relating to co-operative societies for the time being in force in any state [Constitution of India, Part IX B, Article 243ZH(c)].

"Co-operative society" means a society registered or deemed to have been registered under any Central Act for the time being in force relating to the multi-State co-operative societies, or any other Central or State law relating to co-operative societies for the time being in force. [Banking Regulation Act (10 of 1949), sections 5(cciia) and 56(c)(i)]

"Co-operative society" means a society registered or deemed to be registered under the Co-operative Societies Act, 1912 (2 of 1912), or any other law for the time being in force relating to co-operative societies in any State. [Code on Wages, 2019 (29 of 2019), section 2(h)]

Coordinate. "Coordinate" means "make coordinate; bring (parts, movements, etc.) into proper relation, cause to function together or in proper order." [Oxford Concise Dictionary (7 Edn.) as cited in *Modern Dental Collage and Research Centre* v. *State of Madhya Pradesh*, (2016) 7 SCC 353, para 126].

Co-ordination. "Co-ordination" means harmonisation with a view to forge a uniform pattern for concerted action. [Entry 66 of the Union List as cited in *Modern Dental College and Research Centre* v. *Union of India*, (2016) 7 SCC 353, para 134]. "Co-ordination"

"Co-ordination" is the means through which determined norms or standards are kept in harmony with each other. [*Modern Dental College and Research Centre* v. *State of M.P.*, (2016) 7 SCC 353, para 126].

The expression "coordination" used in Entry 66 of the Union List of the Seventh Schedule to the Constitution does not merely mean evaluation. It means harmonisation with a view to forge a uniform pattern for a concerted action according to a certain design, scheme or plan of development. It, therefore, includes action not only for removal of disparities in standards but also for preventing the occurrence of such disparities. It would, therefore, also include power to do all things which are necessary to prevent what would make "coordination" either impossible or difficult. This power is absolute and unconditional and in the absence of any valid compelling reasons, it must be given it full effect according to its plain and express intention. *State of Tamil Nadu* v. *Adhiyaman Educational and Research Institute*, 1995 (4) SCC 104.

Coparcenary. Land is held in coparcenary when there is "unity of title, possession and interest".

Joint ownership; joint heirship; of or pertaining to coparceners. [Hindu Succession Act (32 of 1956), S. 6]

A Hindu coparcenary is, however, a narrower body than the joint family, only males who acquire by birth an interest in the joint or coparcenary property can be members of the coparcenary or coparceners. A male member of a joint family and his sons, grandsons and great grandsons constitute a coparcenary. *State of Maharashtra* v. *Narayan Rao Sham Rao Deshmukh,* AIR 1985 SC 716. [Hindu Succession Act (30 of 1956), S. 6)]

Coparcenary property. The expression 'coparcenary property' includes property in which the deceased husband had an interest as a joint owner during his life time and, therefore, ancestral property as the term is understood in the Punjab Customary law. *State of Maharashtra* v. *Narayan Rao Sham Rao Deshmukh,* AIR 1985 SC 716. [Hindu Adoption and Maintenance Act (78 of 1956), S. 19]

Coparcenary property means the property which consists of ancestral property, or of joint acquisitions, or of property thrown into the common stock, and accretions to such property.

Coparcener. One who shares (equally) with others in inheritance in the estate of a common ancestor. [Hindu Succession Act (32 of 1956), S. 6, *Expln.* 1]

Coparceners. Otherwise called Parceners, are such as have equal portion in the inheritance of an ancestor, or who come in equality to the lands of their ancestors.

Coparcenary property. "Coparcenary property" means the property which consists of ancestral property and a coparcener would mean a person who shares equally with others in inheritance in the estate of common ancestor. *Rohit Chauhan* v. *Surinder Singh,* (2013) 9 SCC 419, para 11.

Copartner. A member of a partnership.

Copulatio verborum indicat acceptationem in eodem sensu. (*Maxim*) The coupling of words together shows that they are to be understood in the same sense.

Copy. In a legal sense the transcript of an original writing.

An individual example of a manuscript or print; a transcript or reproduction of an original work; to make a copy or copies of; to write, print, engrave or paint after an original.

A copy is a full re-production of the original and it should be accurate or true. *Hindustan Construction Co.* v. *Union of India*, AIR 1967 SC 526, 527.

The word "copy" in sub-section (3) of S. 81 does not mean an absolutely exact copy, but means that the copy shall be so true that no body can by any possibility misunderstand it. *Murarka Radhey Shyam Ram Kumar* v. *Roop Singh*, AIR 1964 SC 1545, 1550. [Representation of the People Act (43 of 1951), S. 81(3)]

Copyright. The exclusive right given by law for a certain term of years to an author, composer *etc.* (Or his assignee or heirs) to print, publish and sell copies of his original work or translation thereof.

"COPYRIGHT" means the exclusive right to apply a design to any article in any class in which the design is registered. [Designs Act (2 of 1911), S. 2(4)]

"For the purpose of this Act "COPYRIGHT" means the exclusive right, by virtue of, and subject to the provisions of this Act,—

(a) in the case of a literary, dramatic or musical work, to do and authorise the doing of any of the following acts, namely:

(i) to reproduce the work in any material form;

(ii) to publish the work;

(iii) to perform the work in public;

(iv) to produce, reproduce, perform or publish any translation of the work;

(v) to make any cinematograph film or a record in respect of the work;

(vi) to communicate the work by broadcast or to communicate to the public by a loud-speaker or any other similar instrument the broadcast of the work;

(vii) to make any adaptation of the work;

(viii) to do in relation to a translation or adaptation of the work or any of the acts specified in relation to the work in clauses (i) to (vi);

(b) in the case of an artistic work, to do or authorise the doing of any of the following acts, namely:—

(i) to reproduce the work in any material form;

(ii) to publish the work;

(iii) to include the work in any cinematograph film;

(iv) to make any adaptation of the work;

(v) to do in relation to an adaptation of the work any of the acts specified in relation to work in clauses (i) to (iii);

(c) in the case of a cinematograph film, to do or authorise the doing of any of the following acts, namely:—

(i) to make the copy of the film;

(ii) to cause the film, in so far as it consists of visual images, to be seen in public and, in so far as it consists of sounds, to be heard in public;

(iii) to make any record embodying the recording in any part of the sound track associated with the film by utilising such sound track;

(iv) to communicate the film by broadcast;

(d) in case of a record, to do or authorise the doing of any of the following acts by utilising the record namely:—

(i) to make any record embodying the same recording;

(ii) to cause the recording embodied in the record to be heard in public;

(iii) to communicate the recording embodied in the record by broadcast." [Copyright Act (14 of 1957), S. 14]

Three meanings may be attributed to the term:—

(1) In its broadest sense, all that area of law or the right dealing with the protection of authors' works and of productions of modern technology incorporating such works, such as sound recordings, film recordings and broadcasts.

(2) In its narrower sense, meaning that branch of law or the right dealing with the authors' works in the traditional categories i.e., literary, dramatic, musical and artistic works, in contradistinction to the law dealing with rights of performers, producers, broadcasters etc.

(3) As descriptive of the system of law applying in the common law countries (United Kingdom, Commonwealth, United States *etc.*) for the protection of authors' works (and in some cases, other material), as distinct from the "authors right system" applied in countries of the civil law tradition (*e.g.* France, Germany). (by JAL STERLING, SWEET & MAXWELL (1998))

Copyright infringement. Unauthorized exercise of the rights which are reserved exclusively for the copyright owner.

Coram. (*Lat.*) Before; in the presence of.

Coram non judice. (*Lat.*) Not before a judge.

"Core services" means services rendered by an information utility for—

(a) accepting electronic submission of financial information in such form and manner as may be specified;

(b) safe and accurate recording or financial information;

(c) authenticating and verifying the financial information submitted by a person; and

(d) providing access to information stored with the information utility to persons as may be specified. [Insolvency and Bankruptcy Code, 2016, S. 3(9)].

Corollary. Consequence or result; easy inference.

Coroner. A judicial and ministerial officer of great importance in the middle ages and an office of great dignity under the earlier common law, but whose functions have gradually been diminished in importance by legislation, until today, where the office exists at all, the coroner has little, if anything to do except to serve some process in the absence of the sheriff and, in some jurisdictions, conduct an inquiry, sometimes with the aid of a jury, into the cause of death of persons who appear to have come to an end from other than natural causes formal words in the now obsolete replication. (*Ballentine's Law Dictionary, 3rd Edn.*)

"The office of coroner was established in September 1194, when the justices in eyre were required to see that three knights and one clerk were elected in every county as 'keepers of the pleas of the crown.' These were the first county coroners. . . . Throughout the Middle Ages the coroner could be ordered to perform almost any duty of an administrative or inquisitorial nature within his bailiwick, either alone or with the sheriff, but there were other duties which belonged more specifically to his office and which he performed without being ordered. These consisted of holding inquests upon dead bodies, receiving adjurations of the realm made by felons in sanctuary, hearing appeals, confessions of felons and appeals of approvers, and attending and sometimes organising exactions and outlawries promulgated in the county Court. These were the 'crown pleas' which the coroner had to 'keep' . . . ." R.F. HUNNISETT, *The Medieval Coroner* 1 (1961).

Corporal punishment. In its primary and restricted meaning, punishment upon the body, such as whipping, as distinguished from punishment of the body, such as imprisonment.

Corporate. Belonging to a corporation, as a corporate name; incorporated, as a corporate body.

Corporate authority. CORPORATE AUTHORITY means—

(i) any company or corporation referred to in sub-sec. (1); or

(ii) the corporation or any committee or the authority referred to in sub-sec (2), of cl. (*e*) of this section. [Public Premises (Eviction of Unauthorised Occupants) Act, 1971, S. 2(a). (*Omitted by Act 61 of 1980*)]

"Corporate applicant". Means—

(*a*) corporate debtor; or

(*b*) a member or partner of the corporate debtor who is authorised to make an application for the corporate insolvency resolution process under the constitutional document of the corporate debtor; or

(*c*) an individual who is in charge of managing the operations and resources of the corporate debtor; or

(*d*) a person who has the control and supervision over the financial affairs of the corporate debtor. [Insolvency and Bankruptcy Code (31 of 2016), S. 5(5)].

"Corporate debtor" means a corporate person who owes a debt to any person. [Insolvency and Bankruptcy Code (31 of 2016), S. 3(8)].

For the purposes of this section, a corporate debtor includes a corporate applicant in respect of such corporate debtor. [*Insolvency and Bankruptcy Code (31 of 2016), section 11, Explanation* I].

"Corporate debtor" means a corporate person for whom the guarantor has given a personal guarantee. [Insolvency and Bankruptcy Board of India (Insolvency Resolution Process for Personal Guarantors to Corporate Debtors) Regulations, 2019, Regn. 3(c); Insolvency and Bankruptcy Board of India (Bankruptcy Process for Personal Guarantors to Corporate Debtors) Regulations, 2019, Regn. 2(e)]

"Corporate person" means a company as defined in clause (20) of Section 2 of the Companies Act, 2013 (18 of 2013), a limited liability partnership, as defined in clause (*n*) of sub-section (1) of Section 2 of the Limited Liability Partnership Act, 2008 (6 of 2009), or any other person incorporated with limited liability under any law for the time being in force but shall not include any financial service provider. [Insolvency and Bankruptcy Code (31 of 2016), S. 3(7)].

Corporate benefit. In this scheme, unless the context otherwise requires,—

"CORPORATE BENEFITS" shall include dividends (gross), rights, bonus, redemption benefits, interest, or any other right or benefit accruing on the securities lent. [Securities Lending Scheme, 1997, S. 3(d)]

Corporate espionages. Also known as industrial espionages, it means spying activity for commercial reasons committed by companies or corporations including gathering trade secrets, acquiring intellectual property and proprietary information such as customer database, pricing and marketing strategies about competing entity. [Karnika Seth, *Computers Internet and New Technology Laws*, 2021, LexisNexis, Glossary of Legal Terms].

Corporate governance. "Corporate governance is a system by which business corporations are directed and controlled. The corporate governance structure specifies the distribution of rights and responsibilities among different participants in the corporation and other stockholders, and spells out the rules and procedures for making decisions or corporate affairs. By doing this, it also provides the structure through which the company objectives are set, and the means of attaining those objectives and monitoring performance." By the Organization for Economic Cooperation and Development (OECD) as cited in *Vodafone International Holdings BV* v. *Union of India*, (2012) 6 SCC 613, para 244.

Corporate Liquidation Account. Means the Corporate Liquidation Account operated and maintained by the Board under regulation 46. [Insolvency and Bankruptcy Board of India (Liquidation Process) Regulations, 2016, Regn. 2(1)(ca)]

Corporate personality. A personality distinct from those of its members.

Corporate structures. "Corporate structures" created for genuine business purposes are those which are generally created or acquired at the time when investment is being made; or further investments are being made; or the time when the group is undergoing financial or other overall restructuring; or when operations, such as consolidation, are carried out, to clean defused or over diversified. Sound commercial reasons like hedging business risk, hedging political risk, mobility of investment, ability to raise loans from diverse investments, often underlie creation of such structures. *Vodafone International Holdings BV* v. *Union of India*, (2012) 6 SCC 613, para 241.

Corporate veil. The assumption of law that the actions of the corporation are not the actions of the owners of the corporation, so that they are exempt from liability for the actions of the corporation.

Corporate Voluntary Liquidation Account. Means the Corporate Voluntary Liquidation Account operated and maintained by the Board under regulation 39. [*Insolvency and Bankruptcy Board of India (Voluntary Liquidation Process) Regulations, 2017, Regn. 2(1)(ba)]*

Corporation. "CORPORATION" means any body corporate established by or under Central, Provincial or State Act but does not include a company or a co-operative society. [Payment of Bonus Act (21 of 1965), S. 2(11)].

"CORPORATION" means a corporation incorporated by an Act of any legislature. [R.B.I. Act (2 of 1934), section 45-I (b)]

In this section, "corporation" means an incorporated company or other body corporate registered under the Companies Act, 2013 (18 of 2013) or a society registered under the Societies Registration Act, 1860 (21 of 1860). [(w.e.f. 1-7-2024) Bharatiya Nagarik Suraksha Sanhita, 2023 (46 of 2023), section 65(1), *Explanation*]

In this section, "corporation" means an incorporated company or other body corporate, and includes a society registered under the Societies Registration Act, 1860 (21 of 1860). [(w.e.f. 1-7-2024) Bharatiya Nagarik Suraksha Sanhita, 2023 (46 of 2023), section 342(1)]

"Corporation" means anybody corporate established by or under any Central Act, or State Act, but does not include a company or a co-operative society. [Code on Wages, 2019 (29 of 2019), section 2(i)]

"Corporation" means the Employees' State Insurance Corporation constituted under section 5. [Code on Social Security, 2020 (36 of 2020), section 2(22)]

Artificial persons established for prescribing in perpetual succession certain rights, which, if conferred on natural persons, would fail in process of time. A corporation is an artificial being, invisible, intangible and existing only in contemplation of law. Being, the mere creature of law it possesses only those properties which the charter of its creation confers upon it, either expressly or as incidental to its very existence. They enable a corporation to manage its own affairs, and to hold property without the perplexing intricacies, the hazardous and endless necessity, or perpetual conveyances for the purpose of transmitting it from hand to hand.

It is a body corporate legally authorised to act as a single person. [Constitution of India, Art. 19(6)(ii)].

The expression "corporation" must mean a corporation created by the legislature and not a body or society brought into existence by an act of a group of individuals. *S.S. Dhanos* v. *Delhi Municipality*, AIR 1981 SC 1395, 1398. [IPC (45 of 1860), S. 21, Twelfth (b)]

A co-operative society is a corporation. *Daman Singh* v. *State of Punjab*, AIR 1985 SC 973, 978. [Punjab Co-operative Societies Act (25 of 1961) S. 31-A(1)(*c*)]

"CORPORATION" includes a company incorporated outside India, but does not include—(*i*) a co-operative society registered under any law relating to co-operative societies; and (*ii*) any other body corporate (not being a company as defined in this Act), which the Central Government may, by notification, specify in this behalf. [S. 2(11) of the Companies Act, 2013 (18 of 2013)]

Corporation aggregate. A corporation consisting of several persons united into one body.

Corporation, If citizen. State Trading Corporation is not a citizen. The fact that corporations may be nationals of the country for purposes of international law will not make them citizens of this country for purposes of municipal law or the Constitution. *State Trading Corporation* v. *Commercial Tax Officer*, AIR 1963 SC 1811, 1821. [Constitution of India, Art. 19]

Corporation sole. A corporation consisting of a single person, who is made a body corporate and politic, in order to give him some legal capacities and advantages, and especially that of perpetuity which as an individual person he could not have.

Corporation tax (CT). "CORPORATION TAX" means any tax on income, so far as that tax is payable by companies and is a tax in the case of which the following conditions are fulfilled:—

(a) that it is not chargeable in respect of agricultural income;

(b) that no deduction in respect of the tax paid by companies is, by any enactments which may apply to the tax, authorised to be made from dividends payable by the companies to individuals;

(c) that no provision exists for taking the tax so paid into account in computing for the purposes of Indian Income-tax the total income of individuals receiving such dividends, or in computing the Indian Income-tax payable by, or refundable to, such individuals. [Constitution of India, Art. 366(6)]

Corporatisation. "CORPORATISATION" means the succession of a recognised stock exchange, being a body of individuals or a society registered under the Societies Registration Act, 1860, by another stock exchange, being a company incorporated for the purpose of assisting, regulating or controlling the business of buying, selling or dealing in securities carried on by such individuals or society. [Securities Contracts (Regulation) Act (42 of 1956), S. 2(aa) *as inserted by Securities Laws (Amendment) Act (1 of 2005), S. 5*]

Corporator. A member of a corporation.

Corporeal. Things which may be seen and touched.

Corporeal hereditaments. A material object in contrast to a right, *e.g.*; land, buildings, minerals, trees or fixtures.

Corporeal property. Such as affects the senses, and may be seen and handled, as opposed to incorporeal property, which cannot be seen or handled, and exists only in contemplation. Thus a house is corporeal, but the annual rent payable for its occupation is incorporeal. Corporeal property is, if movable, capable of manual transfer: if immovable, possession of it may be delivered up. But incorporeal property cannot be so transferred, but some other means must be adopted for its transfer, of which the most usual is an instrument in writing.

Corps. A body of persons organised under a common direction especially an organised sub-division of military establishment.

A battalion or a regiment is treated as a corps. *Prithi Lal Singh* v. *Union of India*, AIR 1982 SC 1413, 1428. [Army Rules (1954), R. 187]

Corpus. A body; human body.

Corpus corporatum ex uno potest consistere. (*Maxim*) One person may constitute a corporation.

Corpus delicti. The body of a crime; the body, substance or foundation of an offence.

The body of facts which constitue an offence; gist or substance of the offence.

Corpus juris. (*Lat.*) Body of law.

Corpus possessionis. (*Maxim*) The thing possessed.

Correct. "A meter shall be deemed to be "correct" if it registers the amount of energy supplied, or the electrical quantity contained in the supply, within the prescribed limits of error, and a maximum demand indicator or other apparatus referred to in sub-section (7) shall be deemed to be "correct" if it complies with such conditions as may be prescribed in the case of any such indicator or other apparatus." [Indian Electricity Act (9 of 1910), S. 26, *Expln.*] Act 9 of 1910 repealed and replaced by Act 36 of 2003.

(*As an adjective*), in accordance or agreement with a certain standard, model, or original; conformable to truth; rectitude or propriety; not faulty; free from error; accurate.

(*As a verb*), to make straight or right; remove error from; bring into accordance with a standared; point out errors in.

"Meter is correct" would mean that there is not fault or defect in the meter and the expression "meter is not correct" means meter is defective—there is fault in meter. *MP Electricity Board, Jabalpur* v. *Chhaganlal*, AIR 1981 MP 170, 173. [Indian Electricity Act (9 of 1910), S. 26(1) and (6)] Act 9 of 1910 repealed and replaced by Act 36 of 2003.

Correct income. Of a person, in relation to an assessment year, means—

(i) in a case where the person has furnished the return of income under Section 139 of the Income-tax Act, the total income exclusive of capital gains and income referred to in sub-section (ix) of clause (24) of Section 2 and in clause (c) of Section 115C of the Income-tax Act returned by him, as increased by the net agricultural income, if any, returned by him;

(ii) in a case where the person has failed to furnish the return of income under Section 139 of the Income-tax Act and assessment is made under Section 144 of that Act, the total income exclusive of capital gains and income referred to in sub-clause (ix) of clause (24) of Section 2 and in clause (c) of Section 115C of the Income-tax Act determined on assessments as increased by the net agricultural income, if any, determined on assessment.

Explanation—In this sub-section, "net agriculture income" has the meaning assigned to it in the *Explanation* to sub-section (3) of Section 4. [Compulsory Deposit Scheme (Income-tax Payers) Act (38 of 1974), S.6 (2)]

Correction. Making right what is wrong; punishment and treatment of an offender through a programme of imprisonment, parole and probation.

Correctional home. "Correctional home" means any place used permanently or temporarily under the orders of the State Government for detention of persons, whether under-trial or convicted, in accordance with any order for confinement under any law providing for preventive detention or any other law for the time being in force, but does not include a place for confinement of a person under the custody of the police.' [West Bengal Correctional Services Act, 1992 (32 of 1992), S. 2(c) as cited in *Life Convict Bangal* v. *B.K. Srivastava*, (2013) 3 SCC 425, para 6].

Correctional system. A network of governmental agencies that administer a jurisdiction's prisons and parole system.

Corrective institution. Means an institution, by whatever named called (being an institution established or licensed as such under Section 21), in which person, who are in need of correction, may be detained under this Act, and includes a shelter where undertrials may be kept in pursuance of this Act. [Immoral Traffic (Prevention) Act, 1956 (104 of 1956), S. 2(b)]

Correctness. The use of the word "correctness" in S. 105(2), CPC (5 of 1908), precludes the questioning of all material decisions in the judgment equally with the questioning of the decree itself.

"Correctness" and "propriety". The term "correctness" and "propriety" ordinarily convey the same meaning, that is, something which is legal and proper. In its ordinary meaning and substance, "correctness" is compounded of "legality" and "propriety" and that which is legal and proper is "correct". *Hindustan Petroleum Corporation Limited* v. *Dilbahar Singh*, (2014) 9 SCC 78, para 29.3.

Correctness of order. In substance, correctness is compounded of legality and propriety and that which is legal and proper is correct. *Moti Ram* v. *Union of India,* AIR 1965 Punj 318, 320. [Displaced Persons (Compensation and Rehabilitation) Act (14 of 1954), S. 26]

Correspond. To harmonize with; to be similar; to be equivalent; to hold correspondence; to have communication; to agree.

Correspondence. Identity; adaptation; making things agree; also means the interchange of written communications.

Correspondent. A person who has regular business relations with another; one employed to communicate news to a newspapaer or broadcasting company.

Corresponding. That which corresponds, *i.e.*, is similar to another in character or function.

Corresponding bank. Means,—

(i) in relation to the State Bank of Bikaner, the Bank of Bikaner, Limited;

(ii) in relation to the State Bank of Indore, the Bank of Indore, Limited;

(iii) ***

(iv) in relation to the State Bank of Mysore, the Bank of Mysore, Limited;

(v) in relation to the State Bank of Patiala, the Bank of Patiala;

(vi) in relation to the State Bank of Travancore, the Travancore Bank, Limited. [State Bank of India (Subsidiary) Act (38 of 1959), S. 2(b)]

Corresponding Institute. Means,—

(i) in relation to the society known as the Indian Institute of Technology, Bombay, the Indian Institute of Technology Bombay;

(a) in relation to the society known as the College of Engineering and Technology Delhi, the Indian Institute of Technology, Delhi;

(b) in relation to the society knows as the Indian Institute of Technology, Guwahati, Assam, the Indian Institute of Technology, Guwahati;

(ii) in relation to the society known as the Indian Institute of Technology (Kanpur) Society, the Indian Institute of Technology, Kanpur, and

(iii) in relation to the society known as the Indian Institute of Technology, Madras, the Indian Institute of Technology, Madras [Institutes of Technology Act (59 of 1961), S. 3(c)]

Corresponding jurisdiction. A jurisdiction comprising the same or similar powers.

Corresponding law. A law having the same purposes and objects.

The legislation made as part of the same social legislative canopy as that of an other legislation. *Krishan Prasad Gupta* v. *Controller, Printing & Stationery,* JT 1995 (7) SC 522 : 1995 (6) Scale 89.

"CORRESPONDING LAW" means any law of any foreign country corresponding to any of the provisions of Act 15 of 2003 or dealing with offences in that country corresponding to any of the scheduled offences. [S. 2(1)(ia) of the Prevention of Money-Laundering Act, 2002 (15 of 2003) as inserted by the Prevention of Money-Laundering (Amendment) Act, 2012 (2 of 2013)]

Corresponding new bank. "CORRESPONDING NEW BANK" means a corresponding new bank constituted under section 3 of the Banking Companies (Acquisition and Transfer of Undertakings) Act, 1970 (5 of 1970), or under section 3 of the Banking Companies (Acquisition and Transfer of Undertakings) Act, 1980 (40 of 1980). [Banking Regulation Act (10 of 1949), section 5(da)]

"CORRESPONDING NEW BANK" means,—

(i) in relation to the Bank of Bikaner, Limited, the State Bank of Bikaner;

(ii) in relation to the Bank of Indore, Limited, the State of Indore;

(iii) ***

(iv) in relation to the Bank of Mysore, Limited, the State Bank of Mysore;

(v) in relation to the Bank of Patiala, the State Bank of Patiala;

(vi) in relation to the Travacore Bank, Limited, the State Bank of Travancore. [State Bank of India (Subsidiary Banks) Act (38 of 1959), S. 2(c)]

"CORRESPONDING NEW BANK" means a corresponding new bank constituted under section 3 of the Banking Companies (Acquisition and Transfer of Undertakings) Act, 1970 (5 of 1970); or under section 3 of the Banking Companies (Acquisition and Transfer of Undertakings) Act, 1980 (40 of 1980). [Banking Regulation Act 1949, S. 5(da). Also See Factoring Regulation Act 2011 (12 of 2012), S. 2(g)]

Corresponding province. "CORRESPONDING PROVINCE", "corresponding Indian State" or 'corresponding State' means in cases of doubt such Province, Indian State or State as may be determined by the President to be the corresponding province, the corresponding Indian State or the corresponding State, as the case may be, for the particular purpose in question. [Constitution of India, Art. 366(7)]

Corresponding unit. In relation to—

(i) the integral Company, means that unit of the Integral Company which corresponds to the unit of the dissolved company or the transferred company in which the concerned officer or other employee was holding office before the transfer of the said unit;

(ii) a transferee company, means that unit of a transferee company which corresponds to the unit of the dissolved company in which the concerned officer or other employee was holding office before the transfer of the said unit. [Public Sector Iron & Steel Companies *etc*. Act (16 of 1978), S. 2(c)]

Corrigendum. A printing or typographic error detected after publication and corrected separately on an added page.

Corroborate. To support; To strengthen; to give support; to give additional strength; to make more certain; to add weight or credibility to a thing; to confirm; to concur in testimony.

Corroboration. The act of corroborating or strengthening or confirming; addition of strength; confirmation. As a general rule evidence of an accomplice is not acted upon by Courts without corroboration in material particulars.

'Corroboration' is nothing other than evidence which 'confirms' or 'supports' or 'strengthens' other evidence. It is, in short, evidence which renders other evidence more probable.

Corroborative evidence. Evidence which concurs with another evidence. [Indian Evidence Act (1 of 1872), S. 8, ill. (j)].

Corrupt. Unlawful; dishonest, without integrity; guilty of dishonesty, involving bribery.

Tainted with vice. [IPC (45 of 1860), S. 162]

The word "corrupt" does not necessarily include an element of bribe taking. It is used in a much larger sense as denoting conduct which is morally unsound or debased . . . The word corruptly was not synonymous with dishonestly or fraudulently but was much wider . . . it even included conduct which was neither fraudulent nor dishonest if it was otherwise blameworthy or improper. S. *Dutt* v. *State of U.P.,* AIR 1966 SC 523.

Corrupt and illegal practice. Rules under the words 'corrupt and illegal practices' have no standard meaning and it will be found that the expression has been defined variously in different Acts. The act in using loud-speakers and in conveying voters to the polling booths do not fall within the definition of corrupt and illegal practices. *Jaikumar Balasa Jain* v. *Survalal Chamilal*, AIR 1958 Bom 413, 414. [C.P. and Berar Local Government Act (38 of 1948)]

Corrupt, Corruptly. Tainted with vice; relating to bribery. "To corrupt" a voter means to do an act of bribery which was completed by acceptance of the bribe, whether subsequently the voter voted or not.

Corrupt practices. "The following shall be deemed to be corrupt practices for the purposes of this Act:—

(1) "Bribery", that is to say—

(A) any gift, offer or promise by a candidate or his agent or by any other person with the consent of a candidate or his election agent of any gratification, to any person whomsoever, with the object, directly or indirectly of inducing—

(a) a person to stand or not to stand or not to stand as, or to withdraw or not to withdraw from being a candidate of an election, or

(b) an elector to vote or refrain from voting at an election, or as a reward to—

(i) a person for having so stood or not stood, or for having withdrawn or not having withdrawn his candidature; or

(ii) an elector for having voted or refrained from voting.

(B) the receipt of, or agreement to receive, any gratification, whether as a motive or a reward—

(a) by a person for standing or not standing as, or for withdrawing or not withdrawing from being, a candidate; or

(b) by any person whomsoever for himself or any other person for voting, or refraining from voting, or inducing or attempting to induce any elector to vote or refrain from voting, or any candidate to withdraw or not to withdraw his candidature."

Explanation.—For the purposes of this clause the term "gratification" is not restricted to pecuniary gratifications or gratifications estimable in money and it includes all forms of entertainment and all forms of employment for reward but it does not include the payment of any expenses *bona fide* incurred at, or for the purpose of, any election and duly entered in the account of election expenses referred to in S. 78.

(2) Undue influence, that is to say, any direct or indirect interference or attempt to interfere on the part of the candidate or his agent, or of any other person with the consent of the candidate or his election agent, with the free exercise of any electoral right:

Provided that —

(a) without prejudice to the generality of the provisions of this clause any such person as is referred to there in who—

(i) threatens any candidate or any elector, or any person in whom a candidate or an elector is interested, with injury of any kind including social ostracism and excommunication or expulsion from any Caste or Community; or

(ii) induces or attempts to induce a candidate or elector to believe that he, or any person in whom he is interested, will become or will be rendered an object of divine displeasure or spiritual censure,

shall be deemed to interfere with the free exercise of electoral right of such candidate or elector within the meaning of this clause;

(b) a declaration of public policy, or a promise of public action, or the mere exercise of a legal right without intent to interfere with an electoral right, shall not be deemed to be interference within the meaning of this clause. [Representation of People Act (43 of 1951), S. 123]

If a candidate who has been elected is reported by an election Court personally guilty or guilty by his agents of any corrupt or illegal practice, his election is void. HALSBURY, 4th Edn., Vol. 15 para 808, p. 441,

The expression 'corrupt practice' occurring in Section 83(b) read with Section 123 of the Act would mean that there should be an independent appeal or canvassing for voters by the candidate or his agent or by any other person with the consent of the candidate or election agent for the furtherance of the prospects of the election of the candidate or prejudicially affecting the election of any candidate. The fact that a candidate obtains a certificate that he belonged to and is a member of the scheduled caste/Tribe to contest as one belonging to such Caste/Tribe, essential for contesting as a candidate in a reserved constituency, at any rate cannot amount to an appeal to vote and refrain from voting on ground of his Caste/tribe that, what was obligated by the statute upon anyone to be entitled to contest the election in such a reserved constituency, cannot be condemnable as corrupt practice. *Regu Mahesh* v. *Rajendra Pratap Bhanj Dev,* AIR 2004 SC 38, 42, para 8. [Representation of the People Act (43 of 1951), Ss. 83(b), 123]

Corrupt practices are defined in S. 123, Representation of People Act (43 of 1951). The expression "corrupt practice," means any one of the following offences:-(1) Bribery; (2) treating (3) undue influence; (4) personation and aiding, abetting, counselling, and procuring the commission of the offence of personation; and (5) knowingly making a false declaration as to election expenses.

The connivance at the employment of a servant of a municipal committee as an agent or for canvassing on behalf of the candidate concerned in a municipal election amounts to a 'corrupt practice'.

Corrupt practices are defined by the Elections Act as meaning bribery, treating and undue influence, or any such election offences, as defined by Act of Parliament or recognised by the law of the land. The Corrupt and illegal Practices Prevention Act, 1883, 46 & 47 Vict. c. 51, has effected considerable changes in the law relating to the prevention of corrupt and illegal practices at parliamentary elections.

The expression "corrupt practice," as used in that Act means (*see S.* 3) any one of the following offences:- (1) bribery; (2) treating (3) undue influence; (4) personation and aiding abetting, counselling, and procuring the commission of the offence of personation; and (5) knowingly making a false declaration as to election expenses, (*See* Rogers of Elections, O'Malley and Hardcastle's Reports of Election Petitions, Returns of Controverted Elections, printed by order of the House of Commons)

The charge of corrupt practices are *quasi*-criminal in character and allegations relating thereto must be sufficiently clear and precise to bring home the charges to the candidates.

Maganlal Radhakishan Bagdi v. *Hari Vishun Kamath*, AIR 1960 MP 362, 364. [Representation of the People Act (43 of 1951), S. 123]

Corruption. Something against law; something forbidden by law, as certain acts by arbitrators, election or other officers, trustees; an act done with intent to gain an advantage not consistent with official duty and the rights of others.

Corruption of public morals. Conduct which destructs the moral fabric of society.

Corruption of the blood. When any one is attained of felony or treason, then his blood is said to be corrupt.

Corum populo. (*Lat.*) Before the public.

Cosmetic. "COSMETIC" means any article intended to be rubbed, poured, sprinkled or sprayed on or introduced into, or otherwise applied to, the human body or any part thereof for cleansing, beautifying, promoting attractiveness, or altering the appearance, and includes any article intended for use as a component of cosmetic. [Drugs and Cosmetic Act (23 of 1940), S. 3(aaa)]

The term 'cosmetics' is a general term which would include all articles intended to beautify, adorn, protect or improve the skin, the human body or part thereof. It means a preparation designed to beautify hair, skin or complexion or to alter the appearance of the body or for cleansing, colouring, conditioning or protecting hair, skin, nails, eyes or teeth, "Dettol" antisepting cream, specifically formulated to "protect against germs in cuts, abrasions, minor burns and other infective skin conditions", could not be treated as a cosmetic covered by entry 70 of the list of taxable goods under the Orissa Sales Tax Act, 1947, but was taxable as a drug. *State of Orissa* v. *Reckitt and Colman of India Ltd.*, (1995) 97 STC 279 (Ori).

Cost. COST in relation to an election petition means all Costs, charges and expenses of, or incidental to the trail of, an election petition. [Kerala Panchayat Raj Act, Ker Act No. (13 of 1994), as amended by Act (7 of 1995)]

"COST" means the amount actually paid for acquiring specified securities and where no money has been paid, the cost shall be taken as *nil.* [Income-tax Act (43 of 1961), S. 17, *Expl.* (a)]

"COST", in relation to any long-term specified asset, means the amount invested in such specified asset out of capital gains received or accruing as a result of the transfer of the original asset. [Income-tax Act (43 of 1961), 54 EC, *Expl.* (a)]

The expenses; the price paid or payable for anything; outlay.

Cost accountant. Means a cost accountant as defined in clause (b) of sub-section (1) of section 2 of the Cost and Works Accountants Act, 1959 and who has obtained a certificate of practice under sub-section (1) of section 6 of that Act. [Companies Act (1 of 1956), section 10GD, *Expl.* (c); Airports Economic Regulatory Authority of India Act (27 of 2008), section 30(c); Limited Liability Partnership Act, 2008 (6 of 2009), section 2(h); Companies Act (18 of 2013), section 2(28)]

Cost and freight. A term used in a quoted sales price which indicates that the quoted price includes the cost of goods and freight charges, but not insurance or other special charges.

Cost auditing standards.

Cost auditing standards. For the purposes of this sub-section, the expression "cost auditing standards" mean such standards as are issued by the Institute of Cost Accountants of India, constituted under the Cost and Works Accountants Act, 1959 (23 of 1959), with the approval of the Central Government. [Companies Act (18 of 2013), section 148(3), *Expln.*]

Cost Inflation Index. For any year means such Index as the Central Government may, having regard to seventy-five per cent. of average rise in the Consumer Price Index for urban non-manual employees for that year, by notification in the Official Gazette, specify in this behalf. [Income-tax Act (43 of 1961), S. 48, *Expl.* (v)]

Cost of acquisition. Includes—(i) amount of compensation which includes solatium, any enhanced compensation ordered by the Land Acquisition and Rehabilitation and Resettlement Authority or the Court and interest payable thereon and any other amount determined as payable to the affected families by such authority or court; (ii) demurrage to be paid for damages caused to the land and standing crops in the process of acquisition; (iii) cost of acquisition of land and building for settlement of displaced or adversely affected families; (iv) cost of development of infrastructure and amenities at the resettlement areas; (v) cost of rehabilitation and resettlement as determined in accordance with the provisions of Act 30 of 2013; (vi) administrative cost,—(A) for acquisition of land, including both in the project site and out of project area lands, not exceeding such percentage of the cost of compensation as may be specified by the appropriate Government; (B) for rehabilitation and resettlement of the owners of the land and other affected families whose land has been acquired or proposed to be acquired or other families affected by such acquisition; (vii) cost of undertaking 'Social Impact Assessment study'. [S. 3(i) of the Right to Fair Compensation & Transparency in Land Acquisition, Rehabilitation & Resettlement Act, 2013 (30 of 2013)]

Cost of fuel. Means the sums expended for fuel consumed plus the cost of any transport, handling, preparation or treatment incurred in connection with the delivery of fuel to the boiler hoppers, furnaces or engines and in connection with the disposal of the products or residues of combustion, plus the proportion of salaries and wages and any contributions made by the owner of the station for pension, provident fund, superannuation and insurance of officers and servants properly attributable to such delivery or disposal less any sums received from the sale of any products or residues of combustion. [Electricity (Supply) Act (54 of 1948), Ninth Sch., Para I (d)]

Cost of land. Means the market value of the land as determined by the competent authority of the State Government or the Government of the Union territory appointed for such determination, as the case may be. [Control of National Highways (Land and Traffic) Act, 2002 (13 of 2003), S. 2(d)] [Now repealed by Act 36 of 2003]

Cost of living index number. In relation to employees in any scheduled employment in respect of which minimum rates of wages have been fixed, means the index number ascertained and declared by the competent authority by notification in the Official Gazette to be the cost of living index number applicable to employees in such employment. [Minimum Wages Act (11 of 1948), S. 2(d)]

Cost of maintenance. In an asylum includes the cost of lodging, maintenance, clothing, medicine and care of a lunatic and any expenditure incurred in removing such lunatic to and from an asylum. [Lunacy Act (4 of 1912) (*repealed*), S. 3].

"COST OF MAINTENANCE" in relation to a mentally ill person admitted in a psychiatric hospital or psychiatric nursing home, shall mean the cost of such items as the State Government may, by general or special order, specify in this behalf. [Mental Health Act (14 of 1987), S. 2(a)]

Cost of maintenance in an asylum. This term includes the cost of lodging, maintenance, clothing, medicine or care of a lunatic and any expenditure incurred in removing such lunatic to and from an asylum. [Indian Lunacy Act (4 of 1912), S. 2(2)]

Cost of oil, water and stores. Means the sums expended for oil, water and stores consumed. [Electricity (Supply) Act (54 of 1948), Ninth Sch., Para (I) (e)] [Now repealed by Act 36 of 2003]

Cost of production (COP). "COST OF PRODUCTION", in relation to a feature film, means the expenditure incurred on the production of the film, not being—

(a) the expenditure incurred for the preparation of the positive prints of the film; and

(b) the expenditure incurred in connection with the advertisement of the film after it is certified for release by the Board of Film Censors:

Provided that the cost of production of a feature film, shall be reduced by the subsidy received by the film producer under any scheme framed by the Government, where such amount of subsidy has not been included in computing the total income of the assessee for any assessment year. [Income-tax Rules, 1962, R. 9A, *Expln.* (ii)]

Cost of repairs, maintenance and renewals. Means the sum expended for repairs and maintenance and for renewals not chargeable to capital account, together with the proportion of salaries and wages and any contribution made by the owner of the station for pension, provident fund, superannuation and insurance of officers and other employees properly attributable to repairs, maintenance and renewals. [Electricity (Supply) Act (54 of 1948), Ninth Sch., Para I (e)] [Now repealed by Act 36 of 2003]

Cost of the transferred asset. Means the aggregate of the cost of acquisition (as ascertained for the purposes of Section 48 and 49) of the capital asset which is the subject of the transfer and the cost of any improvement thereto within the meaning assigned to that expression in sub-clause (*b*) of clause (1) of Section 55. [Income-tax Act (43 of 1961), S. 11 (IA) *Expln.* (ii)]

Costs. The expenses of litigation.

Costs of and incidental to any proceeding. The expression "costs of, and incidental to any proceeding" means costs of interlocutory applications *etc.* such costs as have been determined thereon, at the conclusion of the hearing. *Punjab National Bank Ltd.* v. *Ram Kunwar*, AIR 1957 SC 276, 278. [CPC (5 of 1908), S. 35]

Costs of any proceeding. The expression "costs of any proceeding" means cost of the entire proceeding as determined on its conclusion and not costs in a pending proceeding, nor costs to be incurred in future by a party. *Punjab National Bank* v. *Sriram Kunwar*, AIR 1957 SC 276, 278. [Industrial Disputes Act (14 of 1947), S. 11(7)]

Costs shall abide the event. The meaning of the expression 'costs shall abide the event' is quite clear and that is that the successful party must get the costs. [CPC (5 of 1908), S. 35]

Costs shall not follow the event. Costs not to be paid in accordance with the result of the suit. [CPC (5 of 1908), S. 35(2)]

Cottage industry. A cottage industry is one which is carried on by the artisan himself using his own equipment with the help of the members of his family. The idea of cottage industry is alien to the idea of industry where hired labour is engaged. *District Co-Operative Development Federation Ltd.* v. *C.I.T.*, (1973) 88 ITR 330 (All) [Income-tax Act (43 of 1961), S. 80(P)(2)(a)(ii)]

Cotton. COTTON means every kind of unmanufactured cotton, that is to say, ginned and unginned cotton, cotton waste and cottonseed. [Cotton Transport Act (3 of 1923), S. 2(c)].

COTTON means raw cotton, whether baled or loose, which has been ginned. [Indian Cotton Cess Act, 1923, S. 2(c)]

"Cotton wool/absorbent cotton/surgical cotton" means "absorbent cotton, purified cotton, bleached and sterilized cotton form". [Collins English Dictionary as cited in *Mamta Surgical Cotton Industries, Rajasthan* v. *Assistant Commissioner (Anti-Evasion), Bhilwara, Rajasthan*, (2014) 4 SCC 87, para 46].

Cotton fabrics. Means all varieties of fabrics manufactured either wholly or partly from cotton and includes, *dhoties, saries, chadars,* bed-sheets, bedspreads, counterpanes and table-cloths, but do not include any such fabric if it contains 60 per cent or more by weight of rayon or artificial silk. *Union of India* v. *Ahmedabad Manufacturing and Calico Printing Co. Ltd. (Calico Mills), Ahmedabad*, AIR 1986 SC 121.

Cotton ginning factory. Means any place where cotton is ginned or where cotton fibre is separated from cotton seed by any process whatever involving the use of steam, water or other mechanical power or of electrical power. [Cotton Ginning and Pressing Factories Act (12 of 1925), S. 2(c)]

Cotton textiles. Means yarn or fabrics made either wholly or partially of cotton. [Cotton Textile Companies (Management of Undertakings and Liquidation or Reconstruction) Act, 1967, S. 2(a)]

Cotton waste. Means droppings, strippings, fly or other waste products of a cotton mill or any cotton ginning factory or of a cotton pressing factory but does not include yarn waste. [Cotton Ginning and Pressing Factories Act (12 of 1925), S. 2(e) and Cotton Transport Act (3 of 1923), S. 2(c)]

Council. An assembly of persons for the purpose of concerting measures of State Policy.

"Council" means the Council of the Institute constituted under section 9. [Chartered Accountants Act, 1949 (38 of 1949), section 2(1)(c)]

"Council" means the Council of the Institute constituted under section 9. [Cost Accountants Act, 1959 (23 of 1959), section 2(1)(c)]

"Council" means the Dental Advisory Council constituted under section 11. [National Dental Commission Act, 2023 (21 of 2023), section 2(d)]

Council constituency. Means a constituency provided by law for the purpose of elections to the Legislative Council of a State. [Representation of the People Act (43 of 1950), S. 2(e)]

Council of Europe Convention on Cybercrime. International agreement that promotes cooperation and standardization among nations regarding crimes committed in cyberspace. (*Cyber Law*)

Council of Ministers. See Arts. 74 and 163. (*Constitution of India*)

A body of Ministers headed by the Prime Minister. It consists of Ministers belonging to categories of Cabinet Ministers, Ministers of State and Deputy Ministers and as per Constitution 91st Amendment, 2003, the total number of Ministers, including the P.M. must not exceed 15% of the total number of members of the House of People. The entire Council of Ministers rarely meets to transact any State business; Cabinet comprising selected Ministers from Council of Ministers appointed by Prime Minister acts and exercises all powers on behalf of Council of Ministers. (*Constitutional and Parliamentary Term*)

Council of Scientific and Industrial Research. Means a society registered by the name of the Council of Scientific and Industrial Research under the Societies Registration Act, 1860 (21 of 1860). [(w.e.f. 3-4-2012) S. 2(c) of the Academy of Scientific & Innovative Research Act, 2011 (13 of 2012)]

Counsel. A lawyer appointed or engaged to advise and represent in legal matters [Army Act (46 of 1950), S. 138(2)]; to advise. [Explosive Substances Act (6 of 1908), S. 6].

(*As a verb*) to give advice to; to admonish; to recommend.

A counsel's position is one of the utmost difficulty. He is not to speak of that which he knows; he is not called upon to consider whether the facts with which he is dealing are true or false. What he has to do, is to argue as best as he can, without degrading himself, in order to maintain the proposition which will carry with it either the protection or the remedy which he desires for his client.

Count. In this section, the expression 'COUNT' wherever it appears, means the size of grey yarn (excluding any sizing material) expressed in English count. For multiple fold yarn, 'count' means the count of the basic single yarn. Where the count is in fraction, then, if the fraction is one-half or more it shall be treated as one, and if such fraction is less than one-half, it shall be ignored. [Central Excise Tariff (5 of 1986), I Sch., S. XI, Note 11]

(*As a noun*) Reckoning; the act of numbering; also in pleading in an action; a declaration particularly in a real action; a statement of everything which is necessary to constitute a declaration; a part a section or division of a declaration embracing a distinct statement of a cause of action.

(*As a verb*). In pleading, to declare; to recite; to state a case; to narrate the facts constituting a plaintiff's cause of action; and in a special sense to set out the claim or count of the defendant in an action.

Counter. Contrary to; contrary way; opposetion to.

Counter-affidavit. An affidavit in opposition or contradiction to another affidavit.

Counter-claim. A claim set up against the plaintiff in the same suit, being based on a cause of action. [CPC (5 of 1908), S. 128(2)(c)]; [Limitation Act (36 of 1963), S. 3(2)(b)].

Counterdeed. A secret writing, either before a notary or under a private seal, which invalidates or alters another.

Counterfeit. "A person is said to "COUNTERFEIT" who causes one thing to resemble another thing, intending by means of that resemblance to practice deception, or knowing it to be likely that deception will thereby be practised.

Explanation 1.—It is not essential to counterfeiting that the imitation should be exact.

Explanation 2.—When a person causes one thing to resemble another thing, and the resemblance is such that a person might be deceived thereby, it shall be presumed, until the contrary is proved, that the person so causing the one thing to resemble the other thing intended by means of that resemblance to practice deception or knew it to be likely that deception would thereby be practised." [IPC (45 of 1860), S. (28)]

"COUNTERFEIT", in relation to a seal or stamp, means a seal or stamp which is so made as to resemble an authorised seal or stamp, as the case may be, intending by that resemblance to practise deception, or knowing it to be likely that deception will thereby be practised.

Explanation I.—It is not essential that the resemblance of the counterfeit seal or stamp to the authorised seal or stamp should be exact.

Explanation II.—When a person causes a counterfeit seal or stamp to resemble an authorised seal or stamp and the resemblance is such that if a person relies on such seal or stamp, he might be deceived thereby, it shall be presumed, until the contrary is proved, that the person so causing the seal or stamp to resemble the authorised seal or stamp intended by means of that resemblance to practice deception or knew it to be likely that deception would thereby be practised. [Standards of Weights and Measures (Enforcement) Act (54 of 1985), S. 3(d)]

Counterfeit coin. "Counterfeit coin" means coin not genuine, but resembling or apparently intended to resemble, or pass for genuine coin; and includes genuine coin prepared or altered so as to resemble or pass for a coin of a higher denomination. (Steph. Cr. (9th ed.), 416.

Counterfeit; Counterfeiting. (*As a noun*), A counterfeit is a likeness or resemblance, intended to deceive, and to be taken for that which is original and genuine. (*As a verb*) To counterfeit is to make something falsely and fraudulently in imitation or the semblance of that which is true.

Ordinarily counterfeiting implies the idea of an exact imitation; but for the purpose of the Indian Penal Code there can be counterfeiting even though the imitation is not exact and there are differences in detail between the original and the imitation so long as the resemblance is so close that deception may thereby be practised. *State of Uttar Pradesh* v. *Hafiz Mohd. Ismail*, AIR 1960 SC 669, 670. [IPC (45 of 1860), S. 28]

Imitated with intent to deceive. [IPC (45 of 1860), S. 28]; to make a fraudulent copy or replica of (something of value, such as a coin) [IPC (45 of 1860), S. 232]; something false or copied or that intends to be true or original.

Counterfeit Indian currency. Means the counterfeit currency as may be declared after examination by an authorized or notified forensic authority that such currency imitates or compromises with the key security features of Indian currency. [(w.e.f. 1-7-2024) Bharatiya Nyaya Sanhita, 2023 (45 of 2023), section 113(1), *Explanation* (b)]

Counterfeit trade mark. A counterfeit trade mark would be a trade mark which purports to be a genuine trade mark but is in reality not so and it would so purport only when it is a copy of the other though not an absolutely exact copy in every detail. [Indian Penal Code (45 of 1860), S. 486]

Counterfeiting A Government Stamp. "A person commits this offence who counterfeits by causing a genuine stamp of one denomination to appear like a genuine stamp of different denomination." [IPC (45 of 1860), S. 255, *Expln.*]

Counterfeiting coin. "A person commits this offence who intending to practise deception, or knowing to be likely that deception will thereby be practised, causes a genuine coin to appear like a different coin." [IPC (45 of 1860), S. 486, S. 231, *Expln.*] [Now (w.e.f. 1-7-2024) repealed & replaced by Bharatiya Nyaya Sanhita, 2023 (45 of 2023)]

The offence of "counterfeiting coin" includes diminishing the weight or alteration of the composition, or alteration of the appearance of the coin. [(w.e.f. 1-7-2024) Bharatiya Nyaya Sanhita, 2023 (45 of 2023), section 178, *Explanation* (5)]

Counterfeiting govt. stamp. A person commits this offence who counterfeits by causing a genuine stamp of one denomination to appear like a genuine stamp of a different denomination. [IPC (45 of 1860), S. 255, *Expln.*] [Now (w.e.f. 1-7-2024) repealed & replaced by Bharatiya Nyaya Sanhita, 2023 (45 of 2023), section 178, *Explanation* (3), same definition in new Sanhita]

Causing a genuine stamp of one denomination to appear like a genuine stamp of a different denomination. [IPC (45 of 1860), section 255, *Expln.*] [Now (w.e.f. 1-7-2024) repealed & replaced by Bharatiya Nyaya Sanhita, 2023 (45 of 2023)]

Counterfeiting Indian Coin. See IPC (45 of 1860), S. 232.

Counterfoil. A form giving main particulars of something treated in more detail on another and in detachable form.

Countermand. In practice, a new or opposite direction; an order made contrary to a former one, for the purpose of avoiding, or suspending it; the revocation of a thing done before, or directed to be done.

To command the opposite of; to revoke by a counter command.

Counterpart. Where an instrument of conveyance (as a lease) is executed in parts *i.e.* by having several copies or duplicates made and interchangeable, that which by the grantor is usually called the original and the rest are counterparts; the corresponding part of a duplicate. [Indian Evidence Act (1 of 1872), S. 62, *Expln.* I]; something or someone having the same use, role, office or characteristics, often in a different sphere or period.

In conveyancing, the corresponding part of an instrument; a duplicate or copy. Where an instrument of conveyance, as a lease, is executed in parts, that is by having several copies or duplicates made and interchangeable, that which is executed by the grantor is usually called the original and the rest are counterparts; although where all the parties execute every part this renders them all originals. (*Burrill*)

The meaning of "counter-part" is "duplicate"; when a deed is prepared in two or more identical forms, the part signed by the grantor is the original, the other parts are counterparts *Jayarama Iyer* v. *S. Ramanatha Iyer,* AIR 1976 Mad 147. See also *Shivkant Pandey* v. *Ishwari Singh,* AIR 1997 Raj 155, 157, para 14.

Countersecurity. A security given to one who has entered into a bond or become surety for another.

Countersign. Countersigning is an act of authentication of a previously signed document by an additional signature. The object is to authenticate the signature of another to the writing.

A sign in response to another sign; to add one's signature to a document already signed by another, for authentication or confirmation.

Countersignature. The signature put by way of countersigning.

"Counter signature" means a signature on a previous signature in a series of signatures, affixed after the verification signature on the electronic record and subsequent signatures on previous signatures serially. [Digital Signature (End Entity) Rules, 2015, R. 2(1)(c)].

Countertrade. A form of trading in which an exporter of goods or services undertakes to accept goods or services (rather than money) from the importer in exchange.

Countervailing. Action taken by the importing country, usually in the form of increased duties to offset subsidies given to producers or exporters in the exporting country. (*WTO*)

Countervailing duty. Under Section 2-A, any article which is imported into India shall be liable to customs duty equal to the excise duty for the time being leviable on a like article if produced or manufactured in India. Such customs duty in addition to the duty under the Tariff Act is known as countervailing duty. *Dunlop India Ltd.* v. *Union of India*, AIR 1977 SC 597, 599. [Indian Tariff Act 1934, S. 2-A]

Counties : County. Originally the term "county" designated the district or portion of a country under the immediate government of a count or earl. In modern use the word denotes a distinct portion of the country organised by itself for judicial and political purposes. "It may denote either the territory marked off to form a county or the citizens resident within such territory, taken collectively and considered as invested with political rights, or the county regarded as a municipal corporation possessing subordinate government powers or an organized rural society invested with specific rights and duties."

Counting agent. An agent appointed by a candidate to watch his interest and to represent him at the counting of votes.

Country. In its primary meaning, signifies place, and in a larger sense the territory or dominions occupied by a community or even waste and unpeopled sections or regions of the earth.

"COUNTRY" includes a group or union of countries or inter-governmental organisation. [Patents Act (39 of 1970), S. 133, *Expl.*]

"COUNTRY" means a country or territory declared to be other preferential area. [Customs Tariff (Determination of Origin of Other Preferential Areas) Rules, 1977 and Notification Issued Thereunder, R. 3(b)]

Country craft. An indigenous boat. [Seaward Artillery Practice Act (8 of 1949), S. 2(d)].

Country of origin. According to Article 5(4) of Berne Convention (1971), the Country of origin shall be considered to be:—

(1) in the case of works first published in a country of the Union, that country; in the case of works published simultaneously in several countries of the union which grant different terms of protection, the country whose legislation grants the shortest term of protection;

(2) in the case of works published simultaneously in a country outside the Union and in a country of the Union, the latter country;

(3) in the case of unpublished works or of works first published in a country outside the Union, without simultaneous publication in a country of the Union, the country of the Union of which the author is a national, provided that:

(a) when these are cinematographic works the maker of which has his head quarters or his habitual residence in a country of the Union, the country of origin shall be that country; and

(b) when these are works of architecture erected in a country of the Union or other artistic works incorporated in a building or other structure located in a country of the Union, the country of origin shall be that country. (*Jal Sterling 1998*) (*Copyright*)

Country of origin of genetic resources. Means the country which possesses these genetic resources in in-situ conditions. [Convention on Biological Diversity, 1992, Art. 2]

Country providing genetic resources. Means the country supplying genetic resources collected from in-situ sources, including populations of both wild and domesticated species, or taken from ex-situ resources, which may or may not have originated in that country. [Convention on Biological Diversity (1992), Art. (2)]

Country to which the safety convention applies. Means,—

(a) a country the Government of which has been declared under Section 283 to have accepted the Safety Convention and has not been declared to have denounced that convention;

(b) a territory to which it has been so declared that the Safety convention extends, not being a territory to which it has been so declared that that the convention has ceased to extend. [Merchant Shipping Act (44 of 1958), S. 3(6)]

Country to which the Load Line convention applies. Means,—

(a) a country the Government of which has been declared under Section 283 to have accepted the Load Line Convention and has not been so declared to have denounced the convention;

(b) a country to which it has been so declared that the Load Line Convention has been applied under the provisions of Article 32 thereof, not being a country to which it has been so declared that that the Convention has ceased to apply under the provisions of that article. [Merchant Shipping Act (44 of 1958), S. 3(5)]

County. [*see* Counties] Signifies the same with shire, the one coming from the French, the other from the Saxon. It contains a circuit or position of the realm, into which the whole land is divided for the better government of it, and the more easy administration of justice; so that there is no part of this kingdom that lies not within some county; and every county is governed by elected officers and the sheriff." (*Fortesque*, cap. 24; *Tomlin*)

County Council. Elected governing body of a council for administrative purposes.

County Court (*Curia Comitatus*). All administration of justice was at first in the King's hands but afterwards when by the increase of the people the burden grew too great for him, as the kingdom was divided into counties, hundreds, *etc.,* so the administration of justice was distributed amongst diverse Courts; of which the sheriff had the County-Court for government of the county, and lords of liberties had their Leets and Law-days, for the speedier and easier administering justice therein, *etc.* (*Tomlin*) At present it is a Court in England for civil actions, especially for recovery of small debts. (*See* Eng. Intr. Act of 1889, S. 63)

Coupon rate. Refers to the interest rate fixed to the bond/security. [*M L Tannan Banking Law & Practice in India*, 2021, LexisNexis, Dictionary of Banking Terminology]

Courier. A messenger, especially one who delivers parcels, packages, and the like.

"COURIER" for the purposes of section 20 of Act 18 of 2013, the term 'courier' means a person or agency which delivers the document and provides proof of its delivery. [*Explanation* to section 20 of the Companies Act, 2013 (18 of 2013)]

"COURIER" for the purposes of section 20(1) and 20(2) of Act 18 of 2013, 'courier' means a document sent through a courier which provides proof of delivery. [R. 35(5) of the Companies (Incorporation) Rules, 2014]

Courier agency. Means a commercial concern engaged in the door-to-door transporttation of time-sensitive documents, goods or articles utilising the services of a person, either directly or indirectly, to carry or accompany such documents, goods or articles. [Finance Act (32 of 1994), S. 65(27) (now repealed by Central Goods and Service Tax Act, 2017)]

"Courier agency" means any person engaged in the door-to door transportation of time sensitive documents, goods or articles utilising the services of a person, either directly or indirectly, to carry or accompany such documents, goods or articles. [Finance Act (32 of 1994), S. 65B(20) (now repealed by Central Goods and Services Tax Act, 2017)].

Course, Common. The usual succession of events. [Indian Evidence Act (1 of 1872), S. 114, ill. (f)].

Course of business. The usual custom in business or a particular line of business.

In worker's compensation acts, the usual course of business of the employer covers the normal operations which form part of the ordinary business carried on, and not including incidental and occasional operations having for their purpose the preservation of the premises or the appliances used in the business.

Course of business, ordinary. The usual course and routine of business.

Course of dealing. Usual custom or way or line of dealing.

An established pattern of conduct between the parties to a particular transaction.

Course of employment. Whatever may be incident to the employment.

These words as applied to compensation for injuries within the purview of workers' compensation acts, refer to the time, place, and circumstances under which the accident takes place. A worker is in course of employment when, within time covered by employment, he is doing something which he might reasonably do while so employed at proper place. Generally, in order that an injury may arise out of and in the course of employment, it must be received while the worker is doing the duty he is employed to perform and also as a natural incident of the work flowing therefrom as a natural consequence and directly connected therewith.

Course of natural events. The evidence about the conduct of an animal can be taken into account as being covered by the words— course of natural events. [Indian Evidence Act (1 of 1872), S. 114]

Course of nature. In natural course; in ordinary sequence or order.

Course of voyage. The path or route of journey by sea. [Marine Insurance Act (11 of 1963), S. 47(2)].

Court. "COURT" includes all Judges and Magistrates and all persons, except arbitrators, legally authorised to take evidence. [Indian Evidence Act (1 of 1872), S. 3] [Now (w.e.f. 1-7-2024) repealed & replaced by Bharatiya Sakshya Adhiniyam, 2023 (47 of 2023

"COURT" in Prisoners Act includes a *Coroner* and any officer lawfully exercising Civil, Criminal or Revenue jurisdiction. [Act 3 of 1900, S. 2].

'Courts' means courts of civil judicature and by 'tribunals', those bodies of men who are appointed to decide controversies arising under certain special laws. [*Harinagar Sugar Mills Limited* v. *Shyam Sundar Jhujhunwala*, AIR 1961 SC 1669, p. 1680, para 32 as cited in *Columbia Sportswear Company* v. *Director of Income Tax, Bangalore*, (2012) 11 SCC 224, para 9].

"COURT" means a Civil Court having jurisdiction to decide the questions forming the subject-matter of the references if the same had been the subject matter of a suit, but does not except for the purpose of arbitration proceedings under Section 21, include a small cause Court. [Arbitration Act (10 of 1940), S. 2(1)(c)] [Now repealed & replaced by the Arbitration & Conciliation Act, 1996 (26 of 1996)]

In this Chapter, unless the context otherwise requires:—

"Court" means a principal civil Court of original jurisdiction, unless the Central Government has appointed (as it is hereby authorised to do) any special judicial officer within any specified local limits to perform the functions of the Court under this Chapter. [Income–tax Act (43 of 1961), S. 269A(c)]

"COURT" means a civil, criminal or revenue Court and includes any tribunal or any other authority constituted under any law for the time being in force, to exercise judicial or *quasi*-judicial functions. [Legal Services Authorities Act (39 of 1987), S. 2(1)(aaa)]

"Court" means any civil court, revenue court or High Court having jurisdiction over the matters of liabilities and offences as provided in this Act including investigation and inquiry into claims arising out of causalities and accidents within its jurisdiction. [Inland Vessels Act, 2021 (24 of 2021), section 3(i)]

"Court" means a Judge who is empowered by law to act judicially alone, or a body of Judges which is empowered by law to act judicially as a body, when such Judge or body of Judges is acting judicially. [(w.e.f. 1-7-2024) Bharatiya Nyaya Sanhita, 2023 (45 of 2023), section 2(5)]

In clause (*b*) of sub-section (1), the term "Court" means a Civil, Revenue or Criminal Court, and includes a tribunal constituted by or under a Central or State Act if declared by that Act to be a Court for the purposes of this section. [(w.e.f. 1-7-2024) Bharatiya Nagarik Suraksha Sanhita, 2023 (46 of 2023), sections 215(3) and 379]

"COURT" means a principal Civil Court of original jurisdiction, and includes the Court of any Additional Judge, Subordinate Judge or Munsif whom the State Government may appoint, by name or by virtue of his office, to perform, concurrently with any such principal Civil Court, all or any of the functions of the Court under this Act within any specified local limits and, in the case of a Munsif, upto the limits of pecuniary jurisdiction with which he is vested under Section 19 of the Bengal, Agra and Assam Civil Courts. [Bengal Act (2 of 1934), S. 3]

'Court' means the Court having jurisdiction under CPC (5 of 1908), to entertain a suit by a landlord against a tenant for recovery of possession of building in respect of which a suit or application is filed under this Act. [Bihar Buildings (Lease, Rent and Eviction) Control Act (4 of 1983), S. 2(d)]

COURT means a criminal Court having jurisdiction, under the Code, to try offences under this Act. [Unlawful Activities (Prevention) Act (37 of 1967), S. 2(d)] *as substituted by Unlawful Activities (Prevention) Amendment Act (29 of 2004), S. 4*]

A Court is a body in the government to which the public administration of justice is delegated; an organized body, with defined powers, meeting at certain times, and places, for the hearing and decision of causes and other matters brought before it, and aided in this, its proper business, by its proper officers, *viz*., attorneys and counsel, to present and manage the business, clerks to record and attest its acts and decisions, and ministerial officers to execute its commands and secure order in its proceedings.

The word 'Court' has not been defined in any Act of the Legislature, but it may be presumed that an officer, to be a 'Court' must be competent to make a judicial decision.

COURT is "a tribunal empowered to hear and determine issues between parties upon pleadings either oral or written, and upon evidence to be adduced under well-defined and established rules, according to settled principles of law."

'COURT' is not confined to the Court room but is present at least when in session, in all parts of the place set apart for its own use or the use of its Judges and officers and of persons attending as witnesses, suitors or jurors.

The word 'Court' should include the appellate and revisional Court.

A place where justice is administered, the judge or judges who sit in a Court, an aggregate or separate Courts of judges.

"COURT" means the Court of the University. [S. 2(g) of the Rajiv Gandhi National Aviation University Act, 2013 (26 of 2013)]

"COURT" means—(*i*) the High Court having jurisdiction in relation to the place at which the registered office of the company concerned is situate, except to the extent to which jurisdiction has been conferred on any district court or district courts subordinate to that High Court under sub-clause (*ii*); (*ii*) the district court, in cases where the Central Government has, by notification, empowered any district court to exercise all or any of the jurisdictions conferred upon the High Court, within the scope of its jurisdiction in respect of a company whose registered office is situate in the district; (*iii*) the Court of Session having jurisdiction to try any offence under this Act or under any previous company law; (*iv*) the Special Court established under section 435; (*v*) any Metropolitan Magistrate or a Judicial Magistrate of the First Class having jurisdiction to try any offence under this Act or under any previous company law. [S. 2(29) of the Companies Act, 2013 (18 of 2013)]

Court-annexed arbitration. 'A form of Court annexed ADR in which an 'arbitrator' gives a preliminary decision which, in some circumstances, may thereafter become binding upon the parties (especially USA)'. This form of arbitration is approved by the Court. In various models of this form the neutral's finding is initially non-binding but it will become binding, if neither party seeks a rehearing by a Judge.

Court-annexed (or Court-ordered) mediation. Mediation ordered by or arranged through a Court, and undertaken by a judicial officer or a Court welfare officer, or by an outside third party approved by the Court. (*ADR : Brown & Marriat*)

Court-Baron. An ancient inferior Court of civil jurisdiction in England attached to a Manor, being an inseperable incident thereto, and holden by the Steward within the Manor.

Court before which such objection is raised. The expression "Court before which such objection is raised" in S. 167, Indian Evidence Act (1 of 1872), includes the reviewing on appellate Court.

Court Commissioners. A Court Commissioner is an officer possessing certain minor judicial or *quasi*-judicial powers. He is a sub-ordinate officer of the Court of which he is Commissioner.

Court-fee. A fee received under the Court-fees Act (7 of 1870) on plaints, petitions, *etc.*

Court having jurisdiction. Court within whose jurisdiction the defendant is residing will have jurisdiction. [Hindu Marriage Act (25 of 1955), S. 19 and 21]

Court house. A building in which Courts of law are held.

Court immediately below. The expression 'Court immediately below' must mean the Court from the decision of which an appeal has been filed to the High Court, whether such Court is a single Judge of the High Court or a Court subject to the superintendence of the High Court. *Ladli Parshad Jaiswal* v. *The Karual Distillary Co. Ltd.*, AIR 1963 SC 1279, 1286. [Constitution of India, Art. 133(1)]

Court martial. Courts-martial are Courts constituted under statutory authority with jurisdiction to try offences committed by persons subject to military law; and these offences may be either crimes under the ordinary law, or purely military offences against the law established for the governance and discipline of the army and navy.

A tribunal for the administration of military law. [Air Force Act (45 of 1950), S. 4(xvi) and Constitution of India, Art. 72(1)(a)].

It means a Court martial held under the Army Act, 1950 or the Navy Act, 1957 including the disciplinary Courts constituted under the Act or the Air Force Act, 1950. [Armed Forces Tribunal Act (55 of 2007), section 3(f)]

In this section—"Court-martial" includes any Tribunal with the powers similar to those of a Court-martial constituted under the relevant law applicable to the Armed Forces of the Union. [(w.e.f. 1-7-2024) Bharatiya Nagarik Suraksha Sanhita, 2023 (46 of 2023), section 521, *Explanation* (b)]

Court of Appeals. The phrase "COURT OF APPEAL, CONFIRMATION, REFERENCE OR REVISION" in S. 454(3), CrPC 1973 (2 of 1974), designates the Courts which can "modify, alter or annul" an order of a Subordinate Court, and does not specify the nature of the application which has to be made to them.

Court of civil judicature. A Court of justice of a civil nature. [CPC (5 of 1908), Preamble].

Court of Common Pleas. One of the three superior Courts of common law at Westminster.

Court of competent jurisdiction. It is the competency of the original Court which decided the former suit that must be looked to, and not that of the appellate Court in which the suit was ultimately decided on appeal for purposes of S. 11, CPC (5 of 1908).

The term "*Court of competent jurisdiction*" is wide enough to include a competent foreign Court. In adopting this form of expression, the Legislature did not intend to restrict the application of the section in any way.

Court of confirmation. A Court which confirms a sentence or order passed by a lower Court, so as to give it full legal efficacy. [CrPC 1973 (2 of 1974), S. 454(3)].

Court of Equity. A court having jurisdiction of suits in equity and in which equitable remedies are administered. (*Ballentine's Law Dictionary*, *3rd Edn.*)

Court of Exchequer. A superior Court of record in England administering justice on question of Law and Revenue.

Court of Exchequer Chamber. An English court of appeals for the correction of the errors of other jurisdictions. It also heard important matters of great difficulty which were suspended and submitted to it before any judgment was rendered in the court below. (*Ballentine's Law Dictionary*, *3rd Edn.*)

Court of final appellate jurisdiction. A Court which exercises final appellate jurisdiction.

Court of first instance. A Court of original jurisdiction in which legal proceedings may be instituted. [Suits Valuation Act (7 of 1887), S. 11(a)].

Court of inquiry. A Court to examine into the nature of any transaction of, or accusation or imputation against, any officer or soldier, which is provided for both in the army and navy.

Court of Justice. "The words "COURT OF JUSTICE" denote a Judge who is empowered by law to act judicially alone, or a body of Judges which is empowered by law to act, judicially as a body, when such Judge or body of Judges is acting judicially." [IPC (45 of 1860), S. 20].

Court of law. Court of law is a Tribunal dealing with and adjudicating upon civil disputes by the operation of law in a judicial manner untroubled by ulterior considerations or matters of executive policy and observing certain definite rules and procedure which are either defined by statute or recognised by practice. If any of these attributes is missing, the Tribunal falls short of a bearing on a Court of law. *Firm S. Mohd. Ali & Sons* v. *V.V. Madhavarao*, AIR 1964 AP 132, 136. [CPC (5 of 1908), S. 24; Andhra Pradesh (Lease Rent & Eviction) Control Rules (1961) Rr. 9, 12]

Court of limited jurisdiction. The expression 'Court of limited jurisdiction' means Courts other than the ordinary Courts. These Courts are Revenue Courts, Land Acquisition Courts, Administrative Courts, Insolvency Courts, Guardianship Courts, Probate

Courts *etc.* [CPC (5 of 1908), S. 11, *Expln.* VIII (introduced by Amendment Act (1976)]

Court of Original and Court of Appellate Jurisdiction. Courts of original jurisdiction are those in which an action has its first source or existence, and which do not take jurisdiction of it by appeal. Courts of appellate jurisdiction are those which review causes removed by appeal or error from another Court.

Court of original jurisdiction. A Court of first instance.

Court of Oyer and Terminer. A Court of criminal jurisdiction for the trial of cases of treason and felony. (*England*)

Court of Parliament. Is a Court, although many of its functions are not judicial. There are other Courts which are not Courts of Justice, but which are rather Courts of Investigation, *e.g.*, a Coroner's Court [*per* FRY, L.J., *Royal Aquarium* v. *Parkinson,* (1892), 1 QB 43]

Court of probate. A Court on which the testamentary jurisdiction is conferred.

Court of Queen's Bench. Until 1875, one of the three Courts of common law into which the *curia regis* was divided (the others being the Court of Common Pleas and the Court of Exchequer). Its principal functions were the trial of civil actions in contract and tort and the exercise of supervisory powers over inferior Courts. By the judicature Acts 1873-75 its jurisdiction was transferred to the Queen's Bench Division of the High Court. When the sovereign was a king, it was known as the *Court of King's Bench.* (*England*) (*Oxford Law Dictionary, 5th Edn., 2003*)

Court of record. A Court of record is "a Court where the acts and judicial proceedings are enrolled in parchment for a perpetual memorial and testimony, and which has power to fine and imprison for contempt of its authority."

Court of reference. *See* C.P. Code (5 of 1908), S. 113, O. XLVI.

A Court having jurisdiction to entertain and dispose of references from other Courts.

Court of review. A superior Court with jurisdiction to correct errors of trial Court; Court of appeal. *See* CPC (5 of 1908), S. 114, O. XLVII.

Court of revision. *See* C.P. Code (5 of 1908), S. 115.

A Court having jurisdiction to exercise the power of revision.

Court of session. The words "Court of session" occurring in S. 374(3) refers only to the Court of Session presided over by the Sessions Judge. *Kamleswar Singh* v. *Dharamdas Singh,* AIR 1957 Pat 375, 377. [CrPC 1973 (2 of 1974), S. 374(3)]

A Court established by a State Government for a sessions division. [Indian Evidence Act (1 of 1872), S. 121, ill. (b)].

Court of Small Causes. In this Act, unless there is something repugnant in the subject or context, "*Court of small Causes*" means a Court of Small Causes constituted under this Act, and includes any person exercising jurisdiction under this Act in any such Court. [Provincial Small Cause Courts Act (9 of 1887), S. 4].

A Court having jurisdiction over small cause suits. [Provincial Small Cause Courts Act (9 of 1887), S. 4 and Presidency Small Cause Courts Act (15 of 1882), S. 4].

Court of Star Chamber. A Court of very ancient origin, which once existed in England, consisting of diverse lords, spiritual and temporal, being privy councillors, together with two judges of the Courts of common law, without the intervention of the jury.

Court of summary jurisdiction. Means the Court of a Chief Presidency Magistrate or of a District Magistrate. [Maintenance Orders Enforcement Act (18 of 1921), S. 2]

Court of wards. A department for the superintendence of the persons and properties of disqualified proprietors [Indian Majority Act (9 of 1875), S. 3].

Court, Open. A sitting of Court at the transactions of which the public are free to be present [Indian Evidence Act (1 of 1872), S. 119].

Court or **tribunal.** By "Courts" is meant Courts of Civil Judicature and by 'Tribunals', those bodies of men who are appointed to decide controversies arising under certain special laws. *Harinagar Sugar Mills Ltd.* v. *Shyam Sunder Jhumphurwala*, AIR 1961 SC 1669, 1680.

The customs officer is not a Court or Tribunal though in adjudicating upon matters under S. 167 of the Sea Customs Act he has to act in a judicial manner. *Indo-China Steam Navigation Co. Ltd.* v. *Jasjit Singh*, AIR 1964 SC 1140, 1146.

Court subordinate to the High Court. A Judge of a High Court, sitting alone, is not a Court subordinate to the High Court within the meaning of S. 115, CPC (5 of 1908).

Agency Court constituted under the Scheduled District Act and the Andhra Pradesh Agency Rules framed thereunder is a Court subordinate to the High Court. [CPC (5 of 1908), S. 24]

Court, Superior. Higher Court; a Court having superior jurisdiction.

Court, Supreme. The highest Court of justice in India. [CrPC 1973 (2 of 1974), S. 2(e)(iii)].

Court which passed a decree. The expression "COURT WHICH PASSED A DECREE", or words to that effect, shall, in relation to the execution of decrees, unless there is anything repugnant in the subject or context, be deemed to include,—

(a) where the decree to be executed has been passed in the exercise of appellate jurisdiction, the Court of first instance, and

(b) where the Court of first instance has ceased to exist or to have jurisdiction to execute it, the Court which, if the suit wherein the decree was passed was instituted at the time of making the application for the execution of the decree, would have jurisdiction to try such suit.

Explanation.—The Court of first instance does not cease to have jurisdiction to execute a decree merely on the ground that after the institution of the suit wherein the decree was passed or after the passing of the decree, any area has been transferred from the jurisdiction of that Court to the jurisdiction of any other Court; but, in every such case, such other Court shall also have jurisdiction to execute the decree, if at the time of making the application for execution of the decree it would have jurisdiction to try the said suit. [CPC (5 of 1908), S. 37]

A Court did not cease to be "the Court which passed the decree," so as to be deprived of jurisdiction to entertain an application for execution, merely by reason of the headquarters having been moved to another place, or of the local limits of the jurisdiction of such Court having been altered.

Courts, jurisdiction of. The power conferred by law to determine causes concerning certain subjects, and between parties legally before the Court, by process and notice, actual or constructive; a power conferred by law upon a judge or magistrate to take cognizance of and determine causes according to law, and to carry his sentence into execution; the power and authority to expound and interpret the law; the right of administering justice through the laws; authority to judge or declare the law between parties brought into Court; the power to hear and determine the subject matter in controversy between parties to the suit; to adjudicate or exercise any judicial power over them.

LOCAL COURTS. Those which have jurisdiction of causes occurring in certain places only. SUPERIOR AND INFERIOR COURTS. A superior Court is a Court with controlling authority over some other Court or Courts, and with certain original jurisdiction of its own. An inferior Court is one which is subordinate to other Court or Courts or is one of a very limited jurisdiction.

ACT OF COURT. A Judge should always be vigilant not to allow the act of the Court itself to do wrong to the suitor.

The Court must at any rate not fall below the standard of honesty which it exacts form those on whom it has to pass judgment.

ARM OF COURT. The arm of the Court is long enough to reach the offender, whatever his position may be.

Courts of Assize and nisi prius. Courts in England, composed of two or more Commissioners, called Judges of Assize, who were sent by the Queen's special commission, on circuits all round the kingdom, to try by a jury, of the respective counties, the truth of such matters of fact as were then under dispute in the Courts of Westminster Hall. Eng. Int. Act (1889), S. 13(4).

Courts of common law jurisdiction or **"Common Law Courts".** Were such as exercised their powers according to the course of the common law. Courts which administer justice according to the principles and forms of the common law. (*Anderson)*

Courts of Magistrates. The expression 'Courts of Magistrates' refers only to Courts of Judicial Magistrates and does not include Executive Magistrates. [CrPC, 1973 (2 of 1974), S. 15].

'Courts of natural jurisdiction.' Where over one subject matter, more than one Courts have their jurisdiction, they are called 'Courts of natural jurisdiction' *Modi Entertainment Network v W.S.C. Cricket Pvt Ltd,* (2003) 4 SCC 341, para 11 : AIR 2003 SC 1177. [CPC (5 of 1908), section 16-20]

Courts of record. 'Courts of record' includes the Supreme Court and various inferior Courts. The essential feature of such Courts is that their proceedings can be proved only by their own official record, and that their judges possess the power to punish for contempt of Court. [CLERK & LINDSELL, 17th Edn., 1995, c. 16, para 16-03, p. 770]

Cousin. The word 'cousins' is sufficiently extensive to comprehend cousins of every description, whether they are first cousins of any degree, or second cousins, or third cousins. That is the general meaning of the word 'Cousin'.

According to the context, "cousins" may include those illegitimate as well as legitimate.

Any collateral relation except brothers and sisters and their descendants and the brothers and sisters of any ancestor [Indian Succession Act (39 of 1925), S. 99(e)].

Cousin german. This is synonym for the first cousin. [Indian Succession Act (39 of 1925), S. 28, ill. (i)].

Cousins. The words "cousins," or "first cousins" or "cousins-german," apply only to children of brothers or of sisters of the father or mother of the person whose "cousins," or "first cousins," or "cousins-german" are spoken of. [Indian Succession Act (39 of 1925), S. 99(*d*)].

Cousins, First. The words "first cousins once removed" apply only to children of cousinsgerman, or to cousins-german of a parent of the person whose "first cousins once removed" are spoken of. [Indian Succession Act (39 of 1925), S. 99(*e*)].

The child of one's uncle or aunt [Indian Succession Act (39 of 1925), S. 99(e)]

Cousins, Second. The words "second cousins" apply only to grandchildren of brothers or of sisters of the grandfather or grandmother of the person whose "second cousins" are spoken of. [Indian Succession Act (39 of 1925), S. 99(*f*)].

The grand child of one's great uncle. [Indian Succession Act (39 of 1925), S. 99(f)]

Covenant. A "Covenant" is an Agreement by Deed between two or more persons to do one or more thing or things, or to do, or give, or to prevent, or refrain from something; and it is either, (1) a Covenant in Law implied from the terms employed; or, (2) a Covenant in Fact, *i.e.*, that which is expressly agreed between the parties.

A covenant is an agreement under seal whereby the parties, or some or one of them, are or is bound to do or not to do a specified thing, as covenants in a lease under seal to pay rent or not to carry on certain trades; or whereby they undertake that a certain state of affairs exists, as a covenant in a conveyance that the grantor is entitled or that he has not incumbered. HALSBURY, 4th Edn., Vol. 12, para 1539, p. 661.

An agreement by deed between two or more persons to do one or more thing or things, to give, or to prevent, or to refrain from something; an agreement creating an obligation, contained in a deed, each of the terms of an agreement. [Constitution of India, Art. 131, *Prov.*]

Covenant running with land. A covenant which goes with the land, as being annexed to the estate, and which cannot be separated from the land, and transferred without it.

Covenants that touch and concern the land, as distinguished from collateral covenants, run with the land and bind the assignees. When there is no privity of contract and privity of estate between the original lessee and the sub-lessee, the sub-lessee will not be bound by the covenants of the principal lessee. *Jagdish Chandra* v. *Md. Bakhtiyan Shah,* AIR 1952 Pat 409, 415. [Transfer of Property Act (4 of 1882), Ss. 40, 108(j)]

Covenantee. The party to whom a covenant is made. The person to whom a promise in the form of a covenant is made.

Covenantor. The party who makes a covenant. One that makes a covenant.

Cover. "COVER" means an insurance contract whether in the form or a policy or a cover note or a Certificate of Insurance or any other form prevalent in the industry to evidence the existence of an insurance contract: [IRDA (Protection of Policyholders' Interest) Regulations, 2002, R. 2(1)(c)]

An envelope; a lid; anything which veils or conceals; a screen; disguise; cloak; that which is laid over something else; a covering.

That which covers or is intended to cover [Indian Standards Institution (Certification Marks) Act (36 of 1952), S. 2(b)]; to put or spread something on, over or about; to comprise.

"Cover" (in Stock Exchange dealings) "is a deposit made with a broker to secure him from being out of pocket in the event of the stocks falling against his client and the client not paying the difference."

Cover note. A note which is signed on the behalf of the insurers by the agent through whom proposal for insurance is submitted.

"Cover note" includes any note of undertaking issued by the insurer who promises to cover the liability and to indemnify the losses incurred by the insured as provided in the contract of insurance. [Inland Vessels Act, 2021 (24 of 2021), section 3(j)]

Cover version. For the purposes of section 31C of Act 14 of 1957, 'cover version' means a sound recording made in accordance with section 31C of Act 14 of 1957. [*Explanation* to S. 31C of the Copyright Act, 1957 (14 of 1957) as inserted (w.e.f. 21-6-2012) by the Copyright (Amendment) Act, 2012 (27 of 2012)]

Covering. "COVERING" includes any stopper, cask, bottle, vessel, box, crate, cover, capsule, case, frame, wrapper or other container. [Bureau of Indian Standards Act (63 of 1986), S. 2(d) and Indian Standard Institution (Certification Marks) (36 of 1952), S. 2(b)]

Something wrapped around a thing. [Agricultural Produce (Grading and Marking) Act (1 of 1937), S. 2(c)]; something laid over a thing.

Covering slip. A slip containing explanation, additional information, and often recommendation, accompanying a communication.

Covert. Not open; protected; sheltered; implied; inferred; under the disability of marriage; married.

Coverture. The legal status of a woman during marriage and under the cover, authority and protection of her husband. [Indian Divorce Act (4 of 1869), S. 39].

Covin. A secret conspiracy or agreement between two or more persons to injure or defraud another.

Cow. "COW" includes a heifer or a calf, whether male or female of a Cow. [Andhra Pradesh Prohibition of Cow Slaughter and Animal Preservation Act (11 of 1997), 3(iii)]

The female of the bovine genus of animals— female ox; chief source of milk.

Cowardice. Lack of courage to face danger, difficulty *etc.*

Cowl. Promise, agreement, contract, engagement. An engagement or lease of land.

Cowle. The word 'cowle' means a lease. *T.K. Lakshmana Iyer* v. *State of Madras*, AIR 1968 SC 1489, 1494.

"Cowle" ordinarily denoted a lease and not a mortgage.

Crackers. Paper containers with explosive that discharges when knocked down or caught with fire.

Craft. Some mechanical art in which the person practising may acquire and exhibit dexterity and skill; the occupation or employment itself; manual art; trade; a guild; also cunning art; skill or dexterity applied to bad purposes; subtlety; vessel of any kind for carriage by water or air (as) small crafts, air craft, coasting craft.

A ship or other vessel; an aircraft. [Antiquities and Art Treasures Act (52 of 1972), S. 2(1)(a)(1)(iii)].

Craftsman. One who practises a handicraft. [Apprentices Act (52 of 1961), S. 10(1)].

Craftmanship. Skill in any handicraft or art.

Crafty. Dexterous; skilful; cunning.

Cramp. A painful affection of the muscles, and frequently associated with an acute disease of the stomach or bowels; a sudden involuntary and highly painful contraction of a muscle or muscles.

Crane. A device for lifting and moving heavy weights.

Creamy layer. The 'creamy layer' in the backward class is to be treated on a par with the forward classes and is not entitled to benefit of reservation. This principle cannot be ignored even by making a law by the Legislature as it would be violative of the principle of separation of powers and of Articles 14, 16(1) and 16(4) of the Constitution of India. [*Indra Sawhney* v. *Union of India,* (2000) 1 SCC 168, 190-91, para 27 to 29]

Create. To bring into existence.

Creation. The action of creating; the fact of being created; thing created.

Creche. A nursery where children are cared for while their mothers work. [Plantations Labour Act (69 of 1951), S. 12].

Credibility. Worthiness of belief. The quality of being credible.

Credible. Worthy of credit.

Credible information. By credible information is not meant information which is in fact true. The words have the same meaning as is given to them in S. 41(1)(a) of the Criminal Procedure Code (2 of 1974) and include any information which in the judgment of the officer to whom it is given, appears entitled to credit in the particular instance. It has reference to the mental condition of the person receiving the information.

CREDIBLE INFORMATION need not be sworn information.

Credible witness. A witness whose testimony is believable.

Credit. (*In a commercial sense*) A good reputation and the confidence of the business community, in the borrower: confidence or trust reposed in one's ability to say what he may promise; the ability to borrow; the capacity of being trusted; the confidence reposed in the ability and intention of a purchaser or borrower to make payment at some future time. (*In Book Keeping*) The side of an account in which payments are entered is called the credit side as distinguished from the debit side. (*As a verb*) To enter upon the credit side of an account; give credit for.

Reputation of probity and solvency in business enabling person or body to be trusted; a sum placed in the credit side of an account; credit-side itself; a sum recoverable from another; (as used in 'on credit'); to place on the credit side; a deduction from an expense or asset account [Income-tax Act (43 of 1961), S. 219]; a debt legal or equitable owing or accruing [Indian Succession Act (39 of 1925), VIth and VIIth Sch.].

Credit broker. A person acting in the course of a business of credit-brokerage carried on by him.

Credit-brokerage. The business of putting person seeking loans of money or credit in touch with sources of finance.

Credit information company. 'Credit information company' means a company formed and registered under the Companies Act, 1956 and which has been granted a certificate of registration under subsection (*2*) of Section 5. [Credit Information Companies (Regulation) Act (30 of 2005), S. 2(e)]

Credit institution. Means—

(i) a banking company to which the Banking Regulation Act, 1949, applies (including any bank or banking institution referred to in Section 51 of that Act);

(ii) a public financial institution as defined in Section 4A of the Companies Act, 1956,

(iii) a State financial corporation established under Section 3 or Section 3A or an institution notified under Section 46 of the State Financial Corporations Act, 1951 and

(iv) any other financial company. [Interest Tax Act (45 of 1974), S. 25(a)].

"CREDIT INSTITUTION" means all or any of the following, namely:—

(i) a banking company;

(ii) a corresponding new bank;

(iii) a Regional Rural bank;

(iv) a co-operative bank;

(v) a financial institution. [Deposit Insurance and Credit Guarantee Corporation Act (47 of 1961), S. 2(cea)]

Credit insurance. Insurance done against risk of loss arising from the insolvency of debtors, or their failure to pay their debt when due.

Credit, letter of. An open or sealed letter from a bank, authorising payment to a person named of a specified sum, for which the sender assumes responsibility.

A letter written by one person to another requesting to advance money or entrust goods to a particular person for which the writer's credit is pledged. [Indian Stamp Act (2 of 1899), S. 2(3)(c)].

Credit rating agency. Means any commercial concern engaged in the business of credit rating of any debt obligation or of any project or programme requiring finance, whether in the form of debt or otherwise, and includes credit rating of any financial obligation, instrument or security, which has the purpose of providing a potential investor or any other person any information pertaining to the relative safety of timely payment of interest or principal. [Finance Act (32 of 1994), S. 65(28) (now repealed by Central Goods and Services Tax Act, 2017)]

Credit sale. A credit sale is made when the seller believes in the solvency and probity of the buyer and delivers his goods to him in confidence of it; or he delivers them on the reputation of his customer.

Credit-sale agreement. An agreement for the sale of goods, under which the purchase price or part of it is payable by installments, but which is not a conditional sale.

Credit swap. A swap whose value depends on underlying credit quality, preferably without bearing ordinary interest rate risk. [*M L Tannan Banking Law & Practice in India*, 2021, LexisNexis, Dictionary of Banking Terminology].

Creditable witnesses. Witnesses competent to testify and whose evidence is worthy of credit.

Creditor. The person to whom the guarantee is given is called the "CREDITOR". [Indian Contract Act (9 of 1872), S. 126]

"CREDITOR" includes a decree holder. [Presidency Towns Insolvency Act (3 of 1909), S. 2(a) and Provincial Insolvency Act (5 of 1920), S. 2(a)]

A person to whom a debt is owed by another person, is called the debtor. [Presidency-Towns Insolvency Act (5 of 1920), S. 2(a)]

Person or body to whom one owes money; one who has a right to require of another the fulfilment of a contract or obligation; one to whom another owes the performance of an obligation; one in whose favour an obligation exists, by reason of which he is or may become entitled to the payment of money. 'Creditor' signifies him that trusts another with any debt, be it money, wares or other things.

The term "creditors" in S. 53 of the T.P. Act (4 of 1882), includes not only the creditors of the transferor at the time or prior to the time of the assignment complained of, but also the subsequent creditors of the transferor.

The definition of 'creditor' in S. 2(*a*). Presidency Town Insolvency Act (3 of 1909) is an inclusive and not an exhaustive definition and it includes an assignee of a decree-holder.

"Creditor" includes decree holder. A person, though not a creditor on the date of the alleged act of insolvency but became a creditor before the filing of the application for adjudication, is also a creditor. *Ramu Chettiar* v. *B.R. Govindarajulu*, AIR 1987 Mad 3, 6. [Provincial Insolvency Act (5 of 1920), Ss. 2(*a*),16]

Credits, account of the. An account of credit side entries.

Creed. A system of religious belief; articles of faith; what a man believes; the common belief of a sect.

Creek. A narrow recess or inlet in the coast line of the sea.

Cremation. Burning as a method of disposing corpses.

The reduction of a corpse to ashes in lieu of interment.

Crew. Any body of men organised or associated for a purpose as a squad of workmen under a foreman; a gang of men under a petty officer or assigned for a particular duty.

Crew accommodation. It includes sleeping rooms, mess rooms, sanitary accommodation, store rooms and catering accommodation provided for the use of seamen.

Crew list. A list of the crew of a vessel; one of a ship's papers.

Crier. An officer of Court, whose duty is to make proclamation of opening and adjournment, to call parties, jurors and witnesses, to assist in the administration of oath, to impose silence, *etc.*

Crime. A crime is an act or omission which is prohibited by law as injurious to the public and punished by the state. An offence.

A crime is an act deemed by law to be harmful to society in general, even though its immediate victim is an individual. *P.S.R. Sadhanandham* v. *Arunachalam*, AIR 1980 SC 856, 862. [Constitution of India, Art 136, 21]

A crime is frequently a moral wrong in that it amounts to conduct which is inimical to the general moral sense of the community. It is, however, possible to instance many crimes which exhibit neither of the foregoing characteristics. An act may be made criminal by Parliament simply because it is criminal process, rather than civil, which offers the effective means of controlling the conduct in question." [Halsbury's Law of England, 4th Edn., Vol. 11, para 1, "Principles of Criminal Liability" as cited in *Subramanian Swamy* v. *Union of India*, (2016) 7 SCC 221, para 81]

"A crime is an unlawful act or default which is an offence against the public, rendering the guilty of such act or default liable to legal punishment. The process by which such person is punished for the unlawful act or default is carried on in the name of the Crown; although any private person, in the absence of statutory provision to the contrary, may commence a criminal prosecution. Criminal proceedings were formerly called pleas of the Crown, because the king, in whom centres the majesty of the whole community, is supposed by the law to be the person injured by every infraction of the public rights belonging to that community. Wherefore he is, in all cases, the proper prosecutor for every public offence." [Stephen, New Commentaries on the Laws of England (17th Edn., Vol. 4 Ch. I) 1-2 as cited in *Subramanian Swamy* v. *Union of India*, (2016) 7 SCC 221, para 83].

"A crime, or misdemeanour, is an act committed or omitted, in violation of a public law, either forbidding or commanding it. This general definition comprehends both crimes and misdemeanours; which, properly speaking, are mere synonym terms: though, in common usage, the word "crimes" is made to denote such offences as are of a deeper and more atrocious dye; while smaller faults, and omissions of less consequence, are comprised under the gentler name of "misdemeanours" only." [Blackstone, Commentaries on Laws of England, Edited by Wayne Morrison, Vol. 4, p. 5 as cited in *Subramanian Swamy* v. *Union of India*, (2016) 7 SCC 221, para 84.

CRIME, TORT. A tort or private wrong is "an infringement or privation of the civil rights which belong to individuals, considered merely as individuals" while crime or public wrong is a breach and violation of the public rights and duties due to the whole community, considered as a community, in its social aggregate capacity.

Crimen ex post facto non diluitur. Crime can not be expiated by after-acts.

Crimen falsi. (*Lat.*) Forgery, perjury or an offence of kindred character, the making of a false charter, false money.

Crimen laesae majestatis. (*Lat.*) The crime of injuring majesty; high treason.

Crimen omnia ex se nata vitiat. (*Maxim*) A crime vitiates all things proceeding from it.

Crimina morte extinguuntur. (*Maxim*) Crimes are extinguished by death.

Criminal. One who has committed a crime [Indian Evidence Act (1 of 1872), S. 114, ill. (b)]; relating to punishment of crime [Constitution of India, Art. 132(1)]; relating to or involving a crime.

Criminal act. An act which amounts to a crime. [IPC (45 of 1860), S. 34].

Criminal action. Opposed to civil action; action prosecuted by or in the name of the state against a person charged with a public offence for the punishment thereof.

Criminal appeal. Appeal from a judgment in a criminal case.

Criminal breach of contract. A breach of contract which amounts to an offence. [IPC (45 of 1860), Ch. 19].

Criminal breach of trust. "Whoever, being in any manner entrusted with property, or with any dominion over property, dishonestly uses or disposes of that property in violation of any direction of law prescribing the mode in which such trust is to be discharged, or of any legal contract, express or implied, which he has made touching the discharge of such trust, or wilfully suffers any person so to do, commits "CRIMINAL BREACH OF TRUST." [IPC (45 of 1860), S. 405] [(w.e.f. 1-7-2024) repealed and replaced by Bharatiya Nyaya Sanhita, 2023 (45 of 2023), section 316(1)]

Criminal case. The phrase in CrPC 1973 (2 of 1974), S. 407, does not mean only a "criminal case" arising out of an offence which has already been committed. It includes proceedings taken under S. 145 for the prevention of a crime.

A proceeding under S. 107 (relating to security proceedings) is "a criminal case".

A cause for the punishment or prevention of a crime. [CrPC 1973 (2 of 1974), S. 267].

Criminal charge. Charge of an offence [Prisoners (Attendance in Courts) Act (32 of 1955) and Art. 311(2), second prov., (a), Constitution of India].

Criminal code. A legislative code defining particular crimes and specific punishments.

Criminal, Condemned. A culprit who has been adjudged guilty.

Criminal conspiracy. "When two or more persons agree to do, or cause to be done,—(1) an illegal act, or (2) an act which is not illegal by illegal means, such an agreement is designated a criminal conspiracy."

Provided that no agreement except an agreement to commit an offence shall amount to a criminal conspiracy unless some act besides the agreement is done by one or more parties to such agreement in pursuance thereof." [IPC (45 of 1860), S. 120-A] [(w.e.f. 1-7-2024) repealed and replaced by Bharatiya Nyaya Sanhita, 2023 (45 of 2023), section 61(1)]

Criminal contempt. "CRIMINAL CONTEMPT" means the publication (whether by words, spoken or written, or by signs, or by visible representations, or otherwise) of any matter or the doing of any other act whatsoever which—

(i) scandalises or tends to scandalise, or lowers or tends to lower the authority of any Court; or

(ii) prejudices, or interferes or tends to interfere with, the due course of any judicial proceeding;

(iii) interferes or tends to interfere with, or obstructs or tends to obstruct, the administration of justice in any other manner. [Contempt of Courts Act (70 of 1971), S. 2(c)]

It is noteworthy, that in the categorisation of contempt in the three sub-clauses (i) to (iii), only category (ii) refers to "judicial proceeding". Sacandalising of Court in its administrative capacity will also be covered by sub-clauses (i) and (iii). The phrase "administration of justice" in sub-clause (iii) is far wider in scope than "course of any judicial proceeding". The last words "in any other manner" of sub-clause (iii) further extend its ambit and give it a residuary character. Although sub-clauses (i) to (iii) describe three distinct species of "criminal contempt", they are not always mutually exclusive. Interference or tendency to interfere with any judicial proceeding or administration of justice is a common element of sub-clauses (ii) and (iii). This element is not required to be established for a criminal tends to scandalise, or lowers or tends to lower the authority of any Court; or (ii) prejudices, or interferes or tends to interfere with, the due course of any judicial proceedings (iii) interferes or tends to interfere, or obstructs or tends to obstruct, the administration of justice in any other manner. *S. Abdul Karim* v. *M.K. Prakash,* AIR 1976 SC 859. [Contempt of Courts Act (70 of 1971), S. 2(c)]

Filing an application in Court calculated to obstruct the due course of a judicial proceeding and administration of justice is an abuse of the process of Court and a criminal contempt of Court. *Advocate General, Bihar* v. *M.P. Khair Industries*, AIR 1980 SC 946, 951. [Contempt of Courts Act (70 of 1971), S. 2(*c*)]

Criminal conversation. Illegal sexual-inter-course.

Criminal Court. "CRIMINAL COURT" means a Court having ordinary criminal jurisdiction.

"CRIMINAL COURT" means a Court having ordinary criminal jurisdiction in British India or such a Court established elsewhere by the authority of the Governor-General in Council. [Marine Act (14 of 1887), S. 2]

"CRIMINAL COURT" means a Court of ordinary criminal justice in any part of India. [Air Force Act (45 of 1950), S. 4(xvii) and Army Act (46 of 1950), S. 3(viii)]

"CRIMINAL COURT" means a Court of ordinary criminal justice in any part of India and includes a Court of a special Judge appointed under the Criminal Law Amendment Act, 1952. [Indo-Tibetan Border Police Force Act (35 of 1992), S. 2(f) and National Security Guard Act (47 of 1986), S. 2(g)]

Besides the High Court and the Courts constituted under any law, other than this Code, there shall be, in every State, the following classes of Criminal Courts, namely:—

(i) Courts of Session;

(ii) Judicial Magistrates of the first class and, in any metropolitan area, Metropolitan Magistrates;

(iii) Judicial Magistrates of the second class; and

(iv) Executive Magistrates. [CrPC 1973 (2 of 1974), S. 6]

Criminal damage. A person who without lawful excuse destroys or damages any property belonging to another.

Criminal force. "Whoever intentionally uses force to any person without that person's consent, in order to the committing of any offence, or intending by the use of such force to cause, or knowing it to be likely that by the use of such force he will cause injury, fear or annoyance to the person to whom the force is used, is said to "use criminal force to that other". [IPC (45 of 1860), S. 350] [(w.e.f. 1-7-2024) repealed and replaced by Bharatiya Nyaya Sanhita, 2023 (45 of 2023), section 129]

Criminal : Guilty. *Criminal* respects the character of the offence; *guilty* respects the fact of committing the offence. The *criminality* of a person is estimated by all the circumstances of his conduct which present themselves to observation; his *guilt* requires to be proved by evidence. The *criminality* is not a matter of inquiry, but of judgment; the *guilt* is often doubtful, if not positively concealed. The higher the rank of a person, the greater his *criminality* if he does not observe an upright and irreproachable conduct; where a number of individuals are concerned in any unlawful proceeding, the difficulty of attaching the *guilt* to the real offender is greatly increased. *Criminal* may be applied as an epithet either to the person or *his action; guilty* is properly applied to the person; a person, or his action, looks, thoughts, intentions, may be *criminal*; the person himself is *guilty* of whatever he actually commits.

Criminal intent. An intention to commit a crime. [IPC (45 of 1860), S. 81].

Criminal intimidation. "Whoever threatens another with any injury to his person, reputation or property or to the person or reputation of any one in whom that person is interested, with intent to cause alarm to that person, or to cause that person to do any act which he is not legally bound to do, or to omit to do any act which that person is legally entitled to do, as the means of avoiding the execution of such threats, commits criminal intimidation." [IPC (45 of 1860), S. 503] [(w.e.f. 1-7-2024) repealed and replaced by Bharatiya Nyaya Sanhita, 2023 (45 of 2023), section 351(1)]

Criminal investigation. Seeking all facts associated with a crime to determine the truth what happened and who is responsible. (*Criminal*)

Criminal jail. A prison house for keeping criminals.

Criminal jurisdiction. That which exists for the punishment of crimes. Jurisdiction of Court regarding cases of criminal nature.

Criminal Justice. "There is no difference between civil and criminal cases as to evidence; whatever is proper evidence in one case is in the other. With respect to criminal cases, if there is any doubt, one would lean in favour of a defendant, for the reason mentioned by my lord yesterday, because that is not to be set right afterwards." [*Laurence, J., Stone's Case* (1796), 25 How. St., Tr. 1314]

Criminal knowledge. A knowledge of facts which make the act an offence. [IPC (45 of 1860), S. 35].

Criminal law. Is that part of the law which deals with the definition, and punishment of crime and with the procedure for the trial of persons suspected or accused of crime; that branch or division of law which defines crimes, treats of their nature, and provides for their punishment. The term "criminal law" is sufficiently comprehensive to cover all of that branch of jurisprudence which deals in any way with crimes and punishments.

Criminal liability. A liability which is of a criminal nature. [CPC (5 of 1908), S. 35A(3)].

Criminal lunatic. "CRIMINAL LUNATIC" means any person for whose detention in, or removal to an asylum, jail or other place of safe custody an order has been made in accordance with the provisions of S. 466 or S. 471 of the CrPC (5 of 1898) (now Ss. 330, 335 and 336 of 1974 Code), or of S. 30 of the Prisoners Act (3 of 1900) or of S. 103-A of the Indian Army Act, 1911. (Lunacy Act 4 of 1912), S. 3).

Criminal misappropriation. A dishonest misappropriation of property which amounts to a crime. [IPC (45 of 1860), S. 403] [(w.e.f. 1-7-2024) repealed and replaced by Bharatiya Nyaya Sanhita, 2023 (45 of 2023), section 314]

Criminal misconduct. A public servant commits an offence of criminal misconduct in the discharge of his duty, if he, by corrupt or illegal means, or by otherwise abusing his position as a public servant, obtains for himself or for any other person, any valuable thing or pecunary advantage. *Bishanbhar Lal* v. *State of Punjab*, AIR 1966 Pun 175, 179. [Constitution of India, Art. 311]

Criminal negligence. Criminal negligence is gross and culpable neglect or failure to exercise that reasonable and proper care and to take precaution to guard against injury either to the public generally or to an individual in particular, which, having regard to all the circumstances attending the charge, it was the imperative duty of the accused person to have adopted. *A.W. Lazarus* v. *State,* AIR 1953 All 72, 74. [IPC (45 of 1860), S. 304-A]

'Criminal negligence' is the failure to exercise duty with reasonable and proper care and precaution guarding against injury to the public generally or to any individual in particular. It is imperative duty of the driver of a vehicle to adopt such reasonable and proper care and precaution. [*Mohammed Aynuddin* v. *State of Andhra Pradesh,* AIR 2000 SC 2511 : (2000) 7 SCC 72]

Criminal offence. Any act or omission made punishable by any law for the time being in force; includes any act in respect of which a complaint is made u/s. 20 of the Cattle Trespass Act (1 of 1871). [CrPC 1973 (2 of 1974), S. 2(n)]

Criminal prisoner. Means any prisoner duly committed to custody under the warrant or order of any Court or authority exercising criminal jurisdiction, or by order of a Courtmartial. [Prisons Act (9 of 1894), S. 3(2)].

Criminal procedure. The legal rules that govern the mechanism under which investigation, prosecution, adjudication and punishment of crime as well as protection of constitutional rights of the accused are effected.

Criminal proceeding. An action or proceeding instituted and prosecuted by the state in its own name against a person who is accused of a crime to punish him therefor. A proceeding instituted and conducted for the purpose either of preventing the commission of a crime or for fixing the guilt of a crime already committed and punishing the offender, as distinguished from a civil proceeding which is for the redress of a private injury.

The proceedings under Section 126 CrPC, 1973 (2 of 1974) falls within the contemplation of "Criminal proceedings" in the article 134 of the Constitution. *Harbajan Kaur* v. *Major Sant Singh,* AIR 1969 Del 298. [Constitution of India, Art. 134(1)]

Refusal of leave to appeal under S. 378(6), Cr.1P.C. 1973 (2 of 1974) is an order passed in criminal proceedings, as granting of special leave would expose the accused to jeopardy and would lead to proceedings in which, if the accused is found guilty, he would be convicted and sentenced. *Temption Jehangir* v. *Banchhoddas,* AIR 1966 Guj 166, 172. [Constitution of India, Art. 136]

When a man sets the criminal law in motion against a person by giving information to the Police that, that person has committed a cognizable offence, he institutes criminal proceeding against that person within the meaning of S. 211 of IPC [IPC (45 of 1860)] *Albert* v. *State of Kerala,* AIR 1966 Ker 11, 12 (FB).

The expression "criminal procedings" means a criminal inquiry or a trial before a Court. *L. Choraria* v. *State of Maharashtra*, AIR 1969 SC 938, 944. [Oaths Act (44 of 1969), S. 4(2)]

Criminal process. Process issued to compel a persons to answer for a crime, where punishment of some kind or other must be the consequence of conviction.

Criminal prosecution. A prosecution in a Court of justice against one accused of a crime. [Indian Evidence Act (1 of 1872), S. 32(3)].

Criminal purpose. The object involving a crime. [Indian Evidence Act (1 of 1872), S. 126, *Expln.*, ill. (a)].

Criminal rashness. In order to hold the existence of 'criminal rashness' or criminal negligence it shall have to be found out that the rashness was of such a degree as to amount to taking a hazard knowing that the hazard was of such a degree that the injury was most likely imminent. [*Jacob Mathew* v. *State of Punjab,* (2005) 6 SCC 1, para 14]

Criminal session. A session of a Court for the trail of criminal cases.

Criminal trespass. Whoever enters into or upon property in the possession of another with intent to commit an offence or to intimidate, insult or annoy any person in possession of such property, or having lawfully entered into or upon such property, unlawfully remains there with intent thereby to intimidate, insult, or annoy any such person, or with intent to commit an offence, is said to commit "criminal trespass." [IPC (45 of 1860), S. 441] [(w.e.f. 1-7-2024) repealed and replaced by Bharatiya Nyaya Sanhita, 2023 (45 of 2023), section 329(1)]

Criminal trial. A trail with the object of punishing the offender. [Indian Evidence Act (1 of 1872), S. 120].

Criminalis. Criminal.

Criminalization. The act of making a previously legal act criminal usually by passing a statute.

Criminate. Impute crime to; incriminate.

Criminology. Study of crimes, their nature, the causes, detection and prevention of crimes.

Criminosus. Blameworthy.

Criterion. Means of judging; standard of judgment.

Critical circumstances. Means circumstances in which there is clear evidence that imports have taken place in such increased quantities and under such circumstances as to cause or threaten to cause serious injury to the domestic industry and delay in imposition of provisional safeguard duty would cause irreparable damage to the domestic industry. [Customs Tariff (Identification And Assessment of Safeguard Duty) Rules, 1997, R. 2(b)]

Critical information. The data which is very important for the data owner. (*Information Technology*)

Critical Information Infrastructure. For the purposes of this section, 'Critical Information Infrastructure' means the computer resource, the incapacitation or destruction of which, shall have debilitating impact on national security, economy, public health or safety. [S. 35, Information Technology Act (21 of 2000), S. 70(1), *Expln.* as substituted by Amending Act (10 of 2009)].

Criticism. Judging on merit; fault finding; a discussion.

Crop; Crops. Yield of any cultivated plant. A crop is some product of the soil gathered during a single year.

"CROPS" includes all agricultural or horticultural crops (and all bushes, trees or plants). [Destructive Insects and Pests Act (2 of 1914), S. 2(a)]

"CROPS", includes products of agricultural operations. [National Bank for Agricultural and Rural Development Act (61 of 1981), S. 2(g)]

The word "crops" in S. 145(2), CrPC 1973 (2 of 1974), means not only standing crops but also includes cut and stored crops. AIR 1928 Sind 68.

The produce of the field either while growing or when gathered. [Destructive Insects and Pests Act (2 of 1914), S. 2(a)].

Crop or other product raised on land. The words 'crop or other product raised on land' means 'enablements'. 'Crop or enablements' means products of the soil annually planted, severed, and saved by manual labour as cereals, vegetables, grass, naturing for harvest or harvested *etc.* but not grass on land used for pasturage.

Trees which are cut and severed and lying on or near the land come within the expression 'crop or produce of land' in S. 145(2) CrPC 1973 (2 of 1974). *Rampur* v. *Subba Reddy,* AIR 1950 Mad 658.

Cross. In the inverse order; made by the opposite party.

To draw two parallel lines across the face of a cheque often with '& Co' written between them in order to indicate that payment is to be made only through a bank. [Negotiable Instruments Act (26 of 1881), S. 124].

Cross action. An action by a defendant in an action, against the plaintiff in the same action upon the same contract, or for the same tort.

Cross-appeal. An appeal against each other by both parties, not satisfied with the decree/ judgment.

Cross-border injunction. It is an injunction where an order of a Court in one country prohibits an infringement in another country. An exception as the operation of an order of a Court is outside its territorial jurisdiction. (*Patents*)

Cross-certificate. A certificate used to establish a mutual trust relationship between two Certifying Authorities. (*Information Technology*)

Cross-claim. A claim made by the defendant against the plaintiff and raised in the defendant's answer.

Cross complaint. One filed by the accused against the person starting the prosecution or co-accused in respect of same subject-matter.

Cross-decree. A decree against the holder of another decree and in favour of the judgment debtor in that other decree.

Cross examination. "The examination of a witness by the adverse party shall be called his cross-examination". [Indian Evidence Act (1 of 1872), S. 137] [(w.e.f. 1-7-2024) repealed and replaced by Bharatiya Sakshya Adhiniyam, 2023 (47 of 2023), section 142(2)]

The examination of a witness by the party opposed to the party who has first examined him, in order to test the truth of such first or direct examination, which is called examination-in-chief.

Cross-examine. To subject (A witness) to cross-examination. [Indian Evidence Act (1 of 1872), S. 33, prov.].

Cross-objection. An objection filed by the respondent in an appeal against the findings in the judgment appealed against.

Cross reference. Reference to another passage in or portion of the same book.

Cross-suit. A suit filed by the defendant against the plaintiff in regard to the same transaction [CPC (5 of 1908), O. VIII, R. 6(2)].

Cross voting. Voting by members of a party for the other side or against its own motion.

Crossed cheque. A cheque symbolically crossed so as to be payable to an account only.

A cheque crossed with two lines between which are written either the name of a bank or the words "and company" in full or abbreviated.

Crown. The British Sovereign.

Crude oil. Means any liquid hydro carbon mixture occurring naturally in the earth whether or not treated to render it suitable for transportation and includes crude oils from which certain distillate fractions have been removed or to which certain distillate fractions have been added. [Merchant Shipping Act (44 of 1958), S. 352 S(a), *Expln.* (i)]

Cruelty. For the purposes of this section, "CRUELTY" means—

(a) any wilful conduct which is of such a nature as is likely to drive the woman to commit suicide or to cause grave injury or danger to life, limb or health (whether mental or physical) of the woman; or

(b) harassment of the woman where such harassment is with a view to coercing her or any person related to her to meet any unlawful demand for any property or valuable security or is on account of failure by her or any person related to her to meet such demand. [IPC (45 of 1860), S. 498-A, *Expln.* (a)] [(w.e.f. 1-7-2024) repealed and replaced by Bharatiya Nyaya Sanhita, 2023 (45 of 2023), section 86]

For the purposes of this section, "cruelty" shall have the same meaning as in section 86 of the Bharatiya Nyaya Sanhita, 2023. [(w.e.f. 1-7-2024) Bharatiya Sakshya Adhiniyam, 2023 (47 of 2023), section 117, *Explanation*]

(*In Matrimonial law*) Mere austerity of temper, petulance of manners, rudeness of language, a want of civil attention and accommodation, even occasional sallies of passion, if they do not threaten bodily harm, do not amount to legal cruelty.

Cruelty which is a ground for dissolution of marriage may be defined as willful and unjustifiable conduct of such a character as to cause danger to life, limb or health, bodily or mental, or as to give rise to reasonable apprehension of such a danger. [The Law and Practice of Divorce and Matrimonial Causes, by D. Tolstoy, Sixth Edition, page 61 as cited in *Sangeeta* v. *Hitesh Kumar*, AIR 2013 Del 83, para 27]

Conduct of the husband during his insanity to strangulate wife's brothers and her young child amounts to cruelty, regardless of motive or intention to be cruel. *Bhagwat* v. *Bhagwat,* AIR 1967 Bom 80, 86. [Hindu Marriage Act (25 of 1955), S. 13(1)(*ia*)]

Cruelty is the very antithesis of love and affection and what may be cruelty in one case may not be treated as an act or cruelty in another case. Much depends on the social, economic and educational background of both the parties and also on the level of their tolerance. If observed, one would find ego based fights more amongst educated and urban families and less in poor and illiterate state of the society whereas in the latter category, economical factors may be mainly responsible to cause matrimonial discord. However, irrespective of the social, educational and economic background of the parties, none would tolerate an attack on their chastity or moral character. [*Memwanti Tripathi* v. *Harish Narain Tripathi*, AIR 2012 Del 1, para 13].

Harm or injury to health, reputation, the working career or the like would be an important consideration in determining whether there was cruelty. *Dastane* v. *Dastane*, AIR 1975 SC 1534, 1541.

Cruelty includes "every wilful act, omission or negligence whereby unjustifiable physical pain, suffering or death is caused or permitted. *Gopal Krishan* v. *Mithilesh Kumari,* AIR 1979 All 316, 323. [Hindu Marriage Act (25 of 1955), S. 13(1)(*ia*)]

The question whether a particular act or behaviour will amount to cruelty or not depends upon the character, way of the life of the parties, their social and economic conditions, their status, customs and traditions.

Harassment of a woman with a view to coerce her or any person related to her to meet any unlawful demand for any property or valuable security is cruelty. *Shobha Rani* v. *Madhukar Reddy*, AIR 1988 SC 121, 124, 125.

Physical violence is not absolutely essential to constitute cruelty. A consistent course of conduct inflicting immeasurable mental agoney and torture will constitute cruelty.

Conduct of such a character as to cause danger to life, limb or health (bodily or mental) or as to give rise to a reasonable apprehension of such danger; hard-heartedness.

"CRUELTY, ACT OF". Living with another woman may be an 'act of cruelty' on the part of the husband for the purpose of judicial separation or dissolution of marriage but the same would not attract the wrath of section 498A of the Indian Penal Code, 1860. U. Suvetha v. State, AIR 2009 SC (Supp) 1451.

Cruelty by conduct. Husband repeatedly accusing wife of a false charge of adultery in the presence of all and sundry is a clear case of cruelty by conduct, even if such conduct does not amount to physical ill-treatment.

Cryptographic algorithm. A cryptographic algorithm is a mathematical function that takes intelligible information (plain text) as input and changes it into unintelligible cipher text. (*Information Technology*)

An unambiguously specified mathematical process for computation, that produces a prescribed result. (*Information Technology*)

Cryptology. The scientific study of cryptography and cryptanalysis, crytography being the art or practice of preparing or reading massages in a form intended to prevent their being read by those not privy to secrets of the form.

The art of encoding and decoding secret papers; any system of codes or ciphers. Most ministries of foreign affairs have cryptograhic devices.

Cryptography is the science of keeping communications private. A central element of cryptography is encryption, which is the transformation of data into an unintelligible form. Encryption and decryption (the reverse of encryption) using computers requires the use of some information, usually called a key. Some encryption systems use the same key to encrypt and decrypt **(Symmetric cryptography)**, while others rely upon the two parties having different, but mathematically related keys **(Asymmetric cryptography).** (*Information Technology*)

The mathematical science used to secure the confidentiality and authentication of data by replacing it with a transferred version that can be reconverted to reveal the original data only by someone holding the proper crypto-graphic algorithm and key. (*Information Technology*).

Cryptography is a branch of applied mathematics enabling the transformation of messages by application of an algorithmic function into an unintelligible form (a string of alphanumeric characters) and then retransformation of the text back into the original form. Aparna Viswanathan, *Cyber Law: Indian & International Perspectives,* 2012, LexisNexis Butterworths at p. 53

Cui jurisdictio data est, ea quoque concessa ease videntur, sine quibus jurisdictio explicari non potest. (*Maxim*) To whomsoever a jurisdiction is given, those things are also supposed to be granted, without which the jurisdiction cannot be exercised.

Cui jus est donandi, eidem et vendendi et concedendi jus est. (*Maxim*) He who has a right to give has also a right to sell and to grant.

Cui licit quod majus non debet quod minus est non licere. (*Maxim*) He who has authority to do the more important act shall not be debarred from doing that of less importance.

Cuicunque aliquis quid concedit, concedere videtur et id, sine quo res ipsa esse non potuit. (*Maxim*) (The) Grantor of any thing to another grants that also without which the thing granted would be useless.

Cuilibet in sua arte perito est credendum. (*Maxim*) Credence should be given to one skilled in his peculiar profession.

Cuilibet licet juri pro se introducto renunciare. (*Maxim*) Any one may waive or renounce the benefit of a principle or rule of law that exists only for his protection.

Cuiques in sua arte perito credendum est. To each one skilled in his own art credence should be given. [Indian Evidence Act (1 of 1872), Ss. 45 and 56].

Cujus est commodum ejus debet esse incommodum. (*Maxim*) Whose is the advantage, his also should be the disadvantage.

Cujus est commodum ejus est onus. (*Maxim*) He who has the benefit has also the burden.

Cujus est dare ejus est disponere. (*Maxim*) The giver of a gift has the right to regulate its disposal.

Cujus est dominium ejus est pericu ulum. (*Maxim*) The risk lies upon the owner of the subject.

Cujus est instituere ejus est abrogare. (*Maxim*) Whose right is to institute, his right it is to abrogate.

Cujus est solum ejus est usque ad coelum. (*Maxim*) He who possesses land possesses also that which is above it.

Cujus est solum ejus est usque ad coelum et ad inferos. (*Maxim*) To whomsoever the soil belongs, he owns also to the sky and to the depths.

Cujus est solum ejus usque ad inferos. (*Lat.*) One who owns the soil, owns up to the water.

Cullibet in sua arte perito est credendum. (*Maxim*) Whosoever is skilled in his profession is to be believed.

Cullibet licet juri pro se introduce to renuntiare. (*Maxim*) One may waive a legal right existing in his favour.

Culibet/Cullibet licet renuntare juri pro se introducto. (*Lat.*) Anyone can waive the advantage of a law made solely for the protection and benefit of the individual in a private capacity as long as this does not infringe any public policy or right.

Culpa. An act of neglect causing damage, but not implying an intent to injure.

Culpa lata dolo aequiparatur. (*Maxim*) Gross neglect is equivalent to fraud.

Culpa levus. Slight negligence.

Culpa tenet suos auctores. (*Maxim*) A fault binds its own authors.

Culpability. Blameworthiness; possibility of being pronounced guilty of an offence.

Culpable. Criminal; censurable; blamable; blameworthy.

Culpable homicide. "Whoever causes death by doing an act with the intention of causing death, or with the intention of causing such bodily injury as is likely to cause death, or with the knowledge that he is likely by such act to cause death, commits the offence of culpable homicide." [IPC (45 of 1860), S. 299] [(w.e.f. 1-7-2024) repealed and replaced by Bharatiya Nyaya Sanhita, 2023 (45 of 2023), section 100]

Culpable homicide not amounting to murder. Defined, Act 45 of 1860 (Indian Penal Code), S. 300, Exceptions 1 to 5.

Culpable intoxication. A willing ingestion of alcohol or drugs to the point of impairment which is done with knowledge that physical and mental capability of a person would be impaired.

Culpable mental state. In this sub-section "culpable mental state" includes intention, motive or knowledge of a fact or belief in, or reason to believe, a fact. [Black Money (Undisclosed Foreign Income and Assets) and Imposition of Tax Act (22 of 2015), S. 54(1), *Explanation*].

Culpable negligence. Culpable negligence is failure to exercise that reasonable and proper care and to take precautions to guard against injury either to the public generally or to an individual in particular which, having regard to all the circumstances attending the charge, it was the imperative duty of the accused person to have adopted. *Chammanlal* v. *State*, AIR 1954 All 186, 187. [IPC (45 of 1860), S. 304-A]

"Culpable negligence" is acting without the consciousness that the illegal and mischievous effect will follow, but in circumstances which show that the actor has not exercised the caution incumbent upon him and if he had, he would have had the consciousness. The imputability arises from the neglect of civil duty of circumspection. In such a case the mere fact accident is prima facie evidence of such negligence. [Ref. Justice Rajesh Tandon's An Exhaustive Commentary on Motor Vehicles Act, 1988 (1st Edn., 2010) as cited in *Ravi Kapur* v. *State of Rajasthan*, (2012) 9 SCC 284, para 15].

Culpable rashness and negligence. (Distinction). Acting with the consciousness thatmischievous and illegal consequences may follows but with the hope that they will not follow is culpable rashness. Culpable negligence is acting without the consciousness that the illegal and mischievous effect will follow: 1953 NLJ 320, **Foll.** *Jumma* v. *State,* MLJ : QD (1956-1960) Vol. IV C905 : 1959 MPLJ (Notes) 138. [IPC (45 of 1860), S. 304-A]

"Culpable rashness" is acting with the consciousness that mischievous and illegal consequences may fallow but with the hope that they will not and after with the belief that the actor has taken sufficient precautions to prevent their happenings. The imputability arises acting despite consciousness (luxuries). [Ref. Justice Rajesh Tandon's An Exhaustive Commentary on Motor Vehicles Act, 1988 (1st Edn., 2010) as cited in *Ravi Kapur v.. State of Rajasthan*, (2012) 9 SCC 284, para 15].

Culpable tenet suos auctores. A fault binds its own authors.

Culpable vel poena ex equitate non intenditure. Blame or punishment does not proceed from equity.

Culpae poena par esto. (*Maxim*) Let the punishment be proportioned to the offence.

Culprit. A criminal; one in fault; a person accused but not yet tried.

Cultivable waste. "Cultivable waste" means cultivable land which has remained under uncultivated for a period of three years or more before 17-4-1951. [Saurashtra Act, (3 of 1952), S. 2(6) as cited in *State of Gujarat* v. *Monoharsinhji Pradyumansinhji Jadeja*, (2013) 2 SCC 300, para 35].

Cultivate. To improve the product of the earth by manual industry; to till or husband the ground to forward the product of the earth by general industry.

"To Cultivate" with its grammatical variations and cognate expressions means to till or husband the land for the purpose of raising or improving agricultural produce, whether by manual labour or by means of cattle or machinery, or to carry on any agricultural operation thereon; and the expression "uncultivate" shall be construed correspondingly.

Explanation: A person who takes up a contract to cut grass or together the fruits or other produce of trees on any land, shall not on that account only be deemed to cultivate such land. [Bombay Tenancy and Agricultural Lands Act, 1948, S. 2(5)]

Cultivate personally. "To Cultivate Personally" means to cultivate land on one's own account—

(i) by one's own labour, or

(ii) by the labour of any member of one's family, or

(iii) under the personal supervision of oneself or any member of one's family by hired labour or by servants on wages payable in cash or kind but not in crop share,

being land, the entire area of which—

(a) is situated within the limits of a single village, or

(b) is so situate that no piece of land is separated from another by distance of more than five miles, or

(c) forms one compact block." [Bombay Tenancy and Agricultural Lands Act, 1948, S. 2(6)].

"Cultivating personally" means to cultivate land on one's own account—

(i) by one's own labour or;

(ii) by the labour of any member of one's family; or

(iii) by hired labour or by servants on wages payable in cash or kind, but not in crop share, under the personal supervision of oneself or by member of one's family. [Karnataka Land Reforms Act, 1961 (10 of 1962), S. 2(A)(11) as cited in *Harsha V. Rai* v. *State of Karnataka*, (2013) 10 SCC 484, para 11].

Cultivable land. Means land permanently cultivable for all practical purposes and not land which might be occasionally cultivated.

Waste land covered with shrubs, jungle and the like cannot be held to be uncultivable merely on that account or on account of their being not cultivated for a long time. Land which can be brought under cultivation is cultivable land unless some provisions of law provide for holding it otherwise in certain circumstances. *Athmanathaswami Devasthanam* v. *K. Gopalaswami Ayyangar*, AIR 1965 SC 338, 340.

Cultivating tenant. In order to fall within the definition of cultivating tenant a person should carry on personal cultivation which again requires that he should contribute physical labour. The use of physical labour includes physical strain, the use of muscles and sinews. Mere supervision of work, or maintaining of accounts or distributing the wage will not be such contribution of physical labour. *Ganapathi Thevar* v. *S.W. Devasthanam*, AIR 1969 SC 764, 770.

Cultivating tenant is the person who cultivates a land belonging to another person under a tenancy agreement, express or implied. *Dondeti Gopi Reddy* v. *Shri Anjaneya Swamyvaru Agraharam,* AIR 1980 SC 105.

In order that a person should be 'a cultivating tenant' or a 'tenant', firstly he should not be the owner of land and secondly he should hold the land under a tenancy agreement express or implied.

Cultivation. Flowers and grass are as much the produce of the soil as rice, and the upkeep of a garden or a grass lawns is *cultivation*.

For the purpose of this sub-section, 'cultivation' includes cultivation of trees or plants of any species. [Kerala Private Forests (Vesting and Assignment) Act (26 of 1971), S. 3(2) *Explanation* as cited in *State of Kerala* v. *Abdul Ali*, (2013) 15 SCC 274, para 4].

Ploughing and preparing land for crops, or the raising of something that grows from the ground besides grass.

The tilling of land; husbandry. [CPC (5 of 1908), S. 61].

Cultivator. The "cultivator" connotes only those persons who actually cultivate the soil themselves, or who cultivate it by members of their household, or by their servants, or by hired labour, and with their own or hired stock, in other words the class of husbandmen or actual agriculturists; but not farmers, middlemen or lessees, even though cultivation may be carried on to some extent by such persons in an area covered by their lease.

A person who takes a lease of land for planting coconut trees is, in respect of that occupation, a "cultivator."

Cultivatory possession. A trespasser who has no right to be in possession by merely entering upon the land forcibly or surreptitiously cannot be said to be a person in 'cultivatory possession'. *Sonawati* v. *Sri Ram*, AIR 1969 SC 466, 469.

Cultured pearl. A natural pearl grown under controlled conditions.

Culvert. A water-way or water passage, whether of wood or stone, square or arched; a covered drain under a road, designated for the passage of water; and arched drain to carry water under a road from one side to the other; an arched drain for the passage of water under a road or canal; an arched passage or drain for water beneath a road, canal or railway.

Cum. (*As a preposition*) With. (*As an adverb*) When; whereas.

Cum adsunt testimonia rerum quid opus est verbis. (*Maxim*) When the proofs of facts are present, what need is there of words.

Cum aliquis renunciaverit societati solvitur societas. (*Maxim*) When any partner renounces the partnership, the partnership is dissolved.

Cum dividend. A transaction that carries with it the right of any profit to accrue from the ensuing drawing.

Cum duo inter se pugnantia reperiuntur in testamento ultimum ratum est. (*Maxim*) When two clauses are found in a will, contradictory of, or inconsistent with, each other, the last is confirmed.

Cum in testamento ambigue aut etiam perperam scriptum est, benigne interpretari debet et secundum id quod credible est cogitatum credendum est. Where an ambiguous, or even erroneous, expression occurs in a will, it should be construed liberally and in accordance with the testator's probable meaning. (*Latin for Lawyers*)

Cum legitimae nuptiae factae sunt patrem liberi sequuntur. (*Maxim*) Children born under the legitimate marriage follow the condition of the father.

Cum licet fugere ne quaere litem. (*Maxim*) Enter not into law if you can avoid it.

Cumulative. That arguments by addition, that is added to something else; in law, the arguments as evidence, facts or arguments of the same kind.

Cumulative evidence. Additional evidence of the same kind to the same point; additional evidence to support the same point, and which is of the same character with the evidence already given; additional evidence offered to establish a fact as which witnesses have already testified; additional evidence of the same general character to the same fact or point which was the subject of proof before; evidence which is additional to the other evidence already obtained.

Cumulative legacy. A legacy in addition to one already given.

Cumulative punishment. A punishment adjudged to be inflicted after the expiration of a prior punishment.

Cumulative sentence. A sentence passed on a person already under sentence for a crime.

An expression occasionally used as an equivalent for consecutive or successive sentences.

Curative statutes. Curative statutes are those which attempt to cure or correct errors and irregularities in judicial or administrative proceedings and when seek to give effect to contracts and other transactions between private persons which otherwise would fail to produce their intended consequences on account of some statutory disability or failure to comply with some technical requirement.

Curator. A keeper, a custodian.

Curator bonis. Trustees who are appointed to take care of the property and affairs of.

Cure. To restore to health; to subject to a preservative process.

Curfew. A regulation obliging persons to be indoors within certain hours.

Curia advisari vult. The Court wishes to be advised.

Curia regis. The king's Court. (*Latin for Lawyers*)

Curing. Means application to raw coffee of mechanical processes other than pulping for the purpose of preparing it for marketing. [Coffee Act (7 of 1942), S. 3(d)]

"CURING" includes wilting, drying, fermenting and any process for rendering an unmanufactured product fit for marketing or manufacture. [Central Excise & Salt Act (1 of 1944), S. 2(c)]

Curing establishment. Means any place to which raw coffee is sent by a registered owner for curing and includes any estate which the (Coffee) Board may declare to be a curing establishment, for the purposes of this Act. [Coffee Act (7 of 1942), S. 3(e)]

Currency. "CURRENCY" includes all coins, currency notes, bank notes, postal notes, postal orders, money orders, cheques, drafts, travellers's cheques, letters of credit, bills-of-exchange and promissory notes. [Foreign Exchange Regulation Act (46 of 1973), S. 2(f) repealed by Act 42 of 1999]

"CURRENCY" includes all currency notes, postal notes, postal orders, money orders, cheques, drafts, travellers cheques, letters of credit, bills of exchange and promissory notes, credit cards or such other similar instruments, as may be notified by the Reserve Bank. [Foreign Exchange Management Act (42 of 1999), S. 2(h)]

Anything which is used as a circulating medium and is generally accepted in trade as a representative of values of property. Whatever circulates conventionally on its own credit as a medium of exchange, whether it be bank notes, bills of exchange, or government securities; the circulating medium, the aggregate of coins, bills, notes *etc.*, in circulation; money current by law or paper equivalent in value circulating in the business community at par; money—coined money and paper money equally.

Currency account transaction. Means a transaction other than a capital account transaction and without prejudice to the generality of the foregoing such transaction includes,—

(i) payments due in connection with foreign trade, other current business, services, and short-term banking and credit facilities in the ordinary course of business,

(ii) payments due as interest on loans and as net income from investments,

(iii) remittances for living expenses of parents, spouse and children residing abroad, and

(iv) expenses in connection with foreign travel, education and medical care of parents, spouse and children. [Foreign Exchange Management Act (42 of 1999), S. 2(j)]

Currency note. "CURRENCY NOTES" means and includes cash in the form of coins and bank notes. [Foreign Exchange Management Act (42 of 1999), S. 2(i)]

Paper money in circulation.

Current. Running; now passing or present in its progress.

Current account. Account of money which a person has deposited at a bank, and on which he can draw from or add to as may be desired.

Current assets. "CURRENT ASSETS" means bank balances and cash, and includes such other assets or reserves as are expected to be realised in cash or sold or consumed within a period of not more than twelve months in the ordinary course of business, such as, stock-in-trade, amounts due from sundry debtors for sale of goods and for services rendered, advance tax payments and bills receivable, but does not include sums credited to a provident fund, a pension fund, a gratuity fund or any other fund for the welfare of the employees, maintained by a company owning an industrial undertaking. [Industries (Development and Regulation) Act (65 of 1951), S. 3(ab)]

An asset shall be classified as current when it satisfies any of the following criteria:—

(a) it is expected to be realised in, or is intended for sale or consumption in, the company's normal operating cycle;

(b) it is held primarily for the purpose of being traded;

(c) it is expected to be realised within twelve months after the reporting date; or

(d) it is cash or cash equivalent unless it is restricted from being exchanged or used to settle a liability for at least twelve months after the reporting date. [Companies Act (18 of 2013), Schedule III, Division I, Notes]

An entity shall classify an asset as current when—

(a) it expects to realise the asset, or intends to sell or consume it, in its normal operating cycle;

(b) it holds the asset primarily for the purpose of trading;

(c) it expects to realise the asset within twelve months after the reporting period; or

(d) the asset is cash or a cash equivalent unless the asset is restricted from being exchanged or used to settle a liability for at least twelve months after the reporting period. [Companies

Act (18 of 2013), Schedule III, Division II, Notes]

Current business. The business in progress.

Current coin. Coin lawfully current by virtue of any law, proclamation or otherwise.

Current expenses. Ordinary expenses; expenses incurred within a reasonable time.

Current income. For the purposes of this section, "CURRENT INCOME", in relation to an assessment year, means,—

(a) in a case where a statement is sent by the person under clause (a) of Section 209A of the Income-tax Act in the financial year immediately preceding that assessment year or where the Income-tax Officer has made an order under sub-section (1) or sub-section (3) of Section 210 of that Act requiring the person to pay advance tax during the financial year immediately preceding that assessment year and the person has not sent an estimate under Section 209A or, as the case may be, Section 212 of that Act;

(i) if the total income of the lastest previous year in respect of which the person has been assessed by way of regular assessment forms basis of computation of advance tax payable by him, such total income exclusive of capital gains and income referred to in sub-clause (ix) of clause (24) of Section 2 and in clause (c) of Section 115C of the Income-tax Act as increased by the net agricultural income, if any, which has been taken into account for the purposes of charging income-tax for the assessment year relevant to that previous year; or

(ii) if the total income of the previous year on the basis of which income-tax has been paid by the person under Section 140A of the Income-tax Act forms the basis of computation of advance tax, such total income exclusive of capital gains and income referred to in sub-clause (ix) of clause (24) of Section 2 and in clause (c) of Section 115C of the Income-tax Act as increased by the net agricultural income, if any, returned by the person in the return of income for the assessment year relevant to that previous year;

(b) in a case where an estimate in sent by the person under Section 209A or Section 212 of the Income-tax Act, the total income exclusive of capital gains and income referred to in sub-clause (ix) of clause (24) of Section 2 and in clause (c) of Section 115C of the Income-tax Act as estimated by him, of the period which would be the previous year for that assessment year, as increased by the net agricultural income, if any, of the period as estimated by him;

(c) in any other case, if the total income of the person, as estimated by him, of the period which would be the previous year for that assessment year exceeds the maximum amount not chargeable to Income-tax in his case, such total income exclusive of capital gains and income referred to in sub-clause (ix) of clause (24) of Section 2 and in clause (c) of Section 115C of the Income-tax Act as increased by the net agricultural income, if any, of that period as estimated by him.

Explanation.—In this sub-section, "net agricultural income" means the net agricultural income as defined in the Finance Act of the relevant year. [Compulsory Deposit Scheme (Income-tax Payers) Act (38 of 1974), S. 4(3) now repealed by the Finance Act, 1995 (22 of 1995).]

Current investment. An investment which is by its nature readily realisable and is intended to be held for not more than one year from the date on which such investment is made. [Non-Banking Financial Companies Prudential Norms (Reserve Bank) Directions, 1998, para 2(1)(iii)].

Current liabilities. Means liabilities which must be met on demand or within a period of twelve months from the date they are incurred, and includes any current liability which is suspended under Section 18FB. [Industries (Development and Regulation) Act (65 of 1951), S. 3(ac)]

"Current liabilities" means liabilities which must be met on demand or within a period of twelve months from the date they are incurred, and includes any current liability which is suspended under section 18FB. [Industries (Development and Regulation) Act, (65 of 1951), section 3(ac)]

A liability shall be classified as current when it satisfies any of the following criteria:—

(a) it is expected to be settled in the company's normal operating cycle;

(b) it is held primarily for the purpose of being traded;

(c) it is due to be settled within twelve months after the reporting date; or

(d) the company does not have an unconditional right to defer settlement of the liability for at least twelve months after the reporting date. Terms of a liability that could, at the option of the counterparty, result in its settlement by the issue of equity instruments do not affect its classification. [Companies Act (18 of 2013), Schedule III, Division I, Notes]

An entity shall classify a liability as current when—

(a) it expects to settle the liability in its normal operating cycle;

(b) it holds the liability primarily for the purpose of trading;

(c) the liability is due to be settled within twelve months after the reporting period; or

(d) it does not have an unconditional right to defer settlement of the liability for at least twelve months after the reporting period. Terms of a liability that could, at the option of the counterparty, result in its settlement by the issue of equity instruments do not affect its classification. [Companies Act (18 of 2013), Schedule III, Division II, Notes]

A liability that:

(*a*) is expected to be settled in the normal course of the enterprise's operating cycle; or

(*b*) is due to be settled within twelve months of the balance sheet date. (*IAS, Para 1.60*)

Liability including loans, deposits and bank overdraft which falls due for payment in a relatively short period, normally not more than twelve months.

An obligation of a corporation payable within one year or one operating cycle whichever is longer.

Money owed by a person or company that should be paid within a year of the date of the balance sheet (as opposed to a long-term liability).

An asset that is used by a company in its day-to-day operation, *e.g.* materials

Current month. The running month.

Current official scale of rates. The expression "current official scale of rates" means the official scale of rates current or prevalent from time to time during the currency of the agreement. *Gopisetti Venkataratnam* v. *Vijayawada Municipality,* AIR 1966 SC 353.

Current rate of exchange. The rate of exchange at which drafts are negotiated.

Current rate of interest. Means the highest of the maximum rates at which interest may be paid on different classes of deposits (other than those maintained in savings account or those maintained by charitable or religious institutions) by different classes of scheduled banks in accordance with the directions given or issued to banking companies generally by the Reserve Bank of India under the Banking Regulation Act, 1949.

Explanation.—In this clause "scheduled bank" means a bank, not being a co-operative bank, transacting any business authorised by the Banking Regulation Act, 1949. [Interest Act (14 of 1978), S. 2(b)]

Current relevant profit. For the purposes of Schedule V of Act 18 of 2013, 'current relevant profit' means the profit as calculated under section 198 of Act 18 of 2013 but without deducting the excess of expenditure over income referred to in section 4(1) of Act 18 of 2013 thereof in respect of those years during which the managerial person was not an employee, director or shareholder of the company or its holding or subsidiary companies. [*Explanation* VI(A) to section IV of Part II of Schedule V of the Companies Act, 2013 (18 of 2013)]

Current repairs. The expression 'current repairs' must be interpreted to mean 'repairs in the current accounting year'. In other words, 'current' is used in contradiction to past or arrear repairs.

Current topic. A current topic necessarily implies a topic relating to matters or events which are current. The words 'current topics' do not necessarily imply that it must relate to current events. Events, which have happened in the past, may have, due to certain circumstances, become of interest to the public. If the general public takes interest in any topic, such a topic can be regarded as a current topic, even though it may deal with events which happened in the past. *Kali Charan Garg* v. *Post Master General,* AIR 1956 All 87, 88. [Post Office Act (6 of 1898), S. 9(2)]

Current use. The use which is prevalent at the present time.

Curriculum. The set of studies for a particular period, appointed by a university.

Cursor. The indicator that shows where the next character to be entered will enter the system (sometimes a blinking underline or rectangle, sometimes a solid highlight). (*Computer*).

A movable marker—usually a flashing underline or rectangle, an arrow, or a vertical bar. A person uses a cursor on the screen to indicate to the computer where information is to be added or changed. (*Computer*)

Cursor keys. Some systems have keys with arrows that move the cursor up or down, right or left, depending on which key is pressed. If the key is held down, the cursor will continue to move in a given direction until the key is released. Other systems have keys with names that move the cursor forward or backward by character, by word, by sentence, by paragraph, or by page. Most systems have supershift combinations that enable you to move the cursor directly to a particular page in a long document, or to the start (top) or the end (bottom) of the document. By using "find" or "search" commands, you can move the cursor to particular words in your document. (*Computer*)

Cursus curiae est lex curiae. (*Maxim*) The Practice of the Court is the law of the Court.

Curtilage. The grounds immediately surrounding a dwelling.

Custodes pacis. Conservators or keepers of the peace.

Custodia Legis. Custody of the law.

Custodial torture –'Custodial torture' is a naked violation of human dignity and degradation which destroys, to a very large extent, the individual personality. It is a calculated assault on human dignity. [D.K. Basu v. State of W.B., (1997) 1 SCC 416: 1997 SCC (Cri) 92 : AIR 1997 SC 610, para 11 as cited in *Mehmood Nayyar Azam* v. *State of Chhattisgarh*, (2012) 8 SCC 1, para 18].

Custodian. One who has the care or custody of anything; a guardian; a caretaker.

Custody. Care keeping; charge (as parent or guardian having custody of children and minors); imprisonment; judicial or penal safe keeping (as custody of prisoner); defence from an enemy; preservation (as a fleet stationed for the *custody* of the narrow seas).

"Custody, within the meaning of statutes defining the crime, consists of the detention or restraint of a person against his or her will, or of the exercise of control over another to confine the other person within certain physical limits or a restriction of ability or freedom of movement." [Corpus Juris Secundum under to topic of Escape & Related Offences; Rescue" as cited in *Sundeep Kumar Bafna* v. *State of Maharashtra*, (2014) 16 SCC 623, para 9.8].

The care and control of a thing or a person. The keeping, guarding, care, watch, inspection, preservation or security of a thing, carrying with it the idea of the thing being within the immediate personal care and control of the person to whose custody it is subjected. Immediate charge and control, and not the final, absolute control of ownership, implying responsibility for the protection and preservation of the thing in custody. Also the detainer of a man's person by virtue of lawful process or authority. The term is very elastic and may mean actual imprisonment or physical detention or mere power, legal or physical, or imprisoning or of taking manual possession. Term 'custody' within statute requiring that petitioner be 'in custody' to be entitled to federal habeas corpus relief does not necessarily mean actual physical detention in jail or prison but rather is synonymous with restraint of liberty. *US ex rel Writz* v. *Sheeham*, 319 F Supp 146 at p. 147 (DC Wis 1970). Accordingly, persons on probation or released on own recognizance have held to be 'in custody' for purposes of habeas corpus proceedings." [Black's Law Dictionary, (5th Edn., 2009) as cited in *Sundeep Kumar Bafna* v. *State of Maharashtra*, (2014) 16 SCC 623, para 9.9].

"Custody" means imprisonment, detention, confinement, incarceration, internment, captivity; remand, duress, and durance. [Oxford Dictionary (online) as cited in *Sundeep Kumar Bafna* v. *State of Maharashtra*, (2014) 16 SCC 623, para 9.1].

"Custody" means "the condition of being held by the police; arrest or imprisonment; to take someone into custody to arrest them". [Chambers Dictionary (online) as cited in *Sundeep Kumar Bafna* v. *State of Maharashtra*, (2014) 16 SCC 623, para 9.4].

"Custody" means someone who is in custody or has been taken into custody or has been arrested and is being kept in prison until they get tried in a court or if someone is being held in a particular type of custody, they are being kept in a place that is similar to a prison. [Collins Cobuild English Dictionary for Advance Learners as cited in *Sundeep Kumar Bafna* v. *State of Maharashtra*, (2014) 16 SCC 6231, para 9.6].

"Custody" means "when someone is kept in prison until they go to court, because the police think they have committed a crime". [Longman Dictionary (online) as cited in *Sundeep Kumar Bafna* v. *State of Maharashtra*, (2014) 16 SCC 623, para 9.3].

When a person is in duress either because he is held by the investigating agency or other Police or allied authority or is under the control of the Court having been remanded by Judicial Orders, or having offered himself to the Courts jurisdiction and submitted to its orders by physical presence. This word is of elastic semantics, but its core meaning is that the law has taken control of the person. *Niranjan Singh* v. *Prabakar Rajaram Kharote*, AIR 1980 SC 785, 787. [CrPC (2 of 1974), S. 439(2)]

The word 'custody' in S. 27, Indian Evidence Act (1 of 1872) does not mean formal custody. An accused is in police custody when he is under surveillance of the police and cannot break away from the company of the police officer and get away.

The interpretation of the word 'custody' in various decisions has proceeded in so far as to suggest that police 'custody' in the terms of S. 27 might well include surveillance, interrogation before arrest *etc.* where a person submits himself to the custody of a police officer, with the consciousness that temporarily at least he is in such custody, or such control, whether formerly authorised in some manner or otherwise.

The word 'custody' as used in the section refers not only to actual but also to constructive or legal custody. [Guardians and Wards Act (8 of 1890), S. 25]

"Custody" merely denotes keeping at care. It cannot be denied that when the drivers are given the buses to be plied they are given to their care. During the time when the buses are being plied they are obviously in the care of the drivers. In this sense the buses are certainly in the custody of the drivers. [Payment of Wages Act (4 of 1936), S. 7(2)(*c*)]

The detaining of a man'a person by virtue of lawful process or authority; actual imprisonment; safe keeping; protection; charge; care, guardianship. [CrPC 1973 (2 of 1974), Ss. 167(2) and 51(a)].

Custody of child. Being in actual possession of the child's person, may be by one person or be shared by more other persons.

Custody of law. That custody which an officer has the right to assume over property by virtue of legal process.

Custody of parent. An infant is 'in the custody of a parent if he is, in point of fact, in the effective care and control of a parent.

Custody of property. The keeping of property by one who is charged with or assumes responsibility for its safety.

Custody order. Means an order granted in terms of section 21 of Act 43 of 2005. [S. 2(d) of the

Protection of Women from Domestic Violence Act, 2005 (43 of 2005)]

Custom. Is a law not written, established by long usage, and the consent of the ancestors. No law can oblige a free people without their consent: so wherever they consent and use a certain rule or method as a law, such rule *etc.*, gives it the power of a law.

A usage that has by long continuance acquired a legally binding force; usage [Constitution of India, Art. 13(3)(a)]; duties on exports and imports.

CUSTOM, USAGE, PRESCRIPTION. A usage in its most extensive meaning includes both custom and prescription; but in its narrower signification it refers to a general habit, mode or course of procedure. The words "custom" and "usage" are not synonymous. A usage need not possess the same degree of antiquity as a custom.

Custom frontiers. It cannot be construed to mean "Custom barriers". (Where sales were effected by transfer of document of title long after the goods had crossed the custom frontiers of India it is not a sale in the course of import). *State of Madras* v. *Davar and Co.*, AIR 1970 SC 165 at p. 167, 168. [Central Sales Tax Act (74 of 1956), S. 5(2)].

Customary easement. An easement may be acquired in virtue of a local custom. Such easements are called customary easements.

Customary law. A custom which by continuance has acquired the force of law.

Customary manner. A manner which has been followed as a matter of custom.

Customary rites and ceremonies. It means such '*sastric* ceremonies' which the caste or community to which the party belongs is customarily following, which must be definite and followed from ancient times. Where such rites include *saptapadi* the marriage becomes complete and binding when the seventh step is taken, if *Saptapadi Homam* is not a part of the customary rite, then it need not be performed. *Rabindra Nath Dutta* v. *State,* AIR 1969 Cal 55 at p. 58. [Hindu Marriage Act (25 of 1955), S. 7]

Custome serra prise stricte. (*Maxim*) Custom must be taken strictly.

Customer. A person with whom a business house or a business man, has regular or repeated dealings; a purchaser of goods; one who frequents any place of sale for the sake of purchasing or ordering goods.

Buyer; one who patronizes or uses the services; a person with whom a business-house or business-man has dealings.

In this section, "customer" includes a Government Department and a corporation incorporated by or under any law. [Banking Regulation Act (10 of 1949), section 45Z, *Explanation*]

Customer is a person who has the habit of resorting to the same place or person to do business. Customer of bank is a person, whose money has been accepted on the factory, that the banker will honour up to the amount standing to his credit irrespective of his connection being of short-standing or long standing. *Central Bank of India* v. *V. Gopinathan,* AIR 1970 Ker 74 at p. 80. [Negotiable Instrument Act (26 of 1881), S. 131]

Customer of a bank. A person who has habitual or consecutive business relation with a bank.

Customs and manners of the country. S. 132(1), CPC (5 of 1908). The customs and manners of the country mean the customs and manners of the different 'communities and classes and sections of the people in the country'. *Mohd. Ismail* v. *Wazir Bibi Saheba*, AIR 1951 Mad 311, 312.

Customs area. "CUSTOMS AREA" means the area of a customs station and includes any area in which imported goods or export goods are ordinarily kept before clearance by Customs Authorities. [Customs Act (52 of 1962), S. 2(11)]

Customs : Custom duties. Customs are duties charged upon commodities on their being imported into or exported from a country [*Union of India* v. *Nitdip Textile Processors Private Limited*, (2012) 1 SCC 226, para 44.

Customs declaration. A form to be filled up and signed by one who sends goods abroad, stating the nature, description, weight, and value of the goods.

Customs duty. A duty imposed on import of goods.

Customs station. Means any customs port, customs airport or land customs station [Customs Act (52 of 1962), S. 2(13)].

Custos statum haeredis in custodia existentis meliorem non deteriorem facere potest. (*Maxim*) A guardian can make the estate of an existing heir under his guardianship better, but not worse.

Cut motion. A motion or a proposal formally made in deliberative assembly for reduction of an expenditure. It may be moved in Parliament or State Legislature to reduce the amount of a demand. (*Constitutional and Parliamentary Term*)

In Indian Parliament, during the discussion on the demands for grants, motion can be moved to reduce the amount of a demand; such a motion is called cut motion.

Cut off. Cut off is a positive word, and applies where the withdrawal or deprivation of the essential supply of service is brought about by some direct and positive act or means on the part of landlord.

Cut-off date. A "cut-off-date" can be provided in terms of the provisions of the statute or executive order. If a "cut-off-date" can be fixed, indisputably those who fall within the purview thereof would form a separate class. Such a classification has a reasonable nexus with the object which the decision of the bank to promote its employee seeks to achieve. *Ramarao* v. *All Indian Backward Class Bank Employee Welfare Association,* JT (2004) 1 SC 331.

Cutcherry. Court of justice; also the public office where the rents are paid, and other business, respecting the revenue, transacted, (*Fifth Report*); a hall, office, or place where any public business is transacted.

Cutlery. Edged or cutting tools in general; all cutting tools made of steel, such as knives, forks, scissors, razors, shears, *etc.*

Cutting. The word 'cutting' in relation to land can only mean digging the land or making an incision into the land.

Cy pres. The practice of carrying out the wishes of a testator as closely as possible when these wishes are impossible, in practical, or illegal to administer exactly as directed.

(*Literally as near to*). A rule in equity which may be stated thus. when a definite function or duty is to be performed, and it cannot be done in exact conformity with the scheme of the person or persons who have provided for it, the duty may be performed with as close an approximation to that scheme as is reasonably practicable. "The Courts will not decree execution of a trust to a charity in a manner different from that intended by the author of the trust except so far as they see that the intention cannot be executed literally. In such a case another mode may be adopted, consistent with the general intention of the author. If the mode prescribed by the instrument of trust becomes, by subsequent circumstances, impossible, the general object is not to be defeated if it can be attained" by other means consistent with the intention for the author. [*per* ARDEN, M.R., *A.G.* v. *Boultbee*, 2 Ves. 387 : AIR 1937 PC 240 (PC)]

'*Cy pres*' means in some way as nearly as possible when the particular purpose for which a charitable trust is created fails, or it cannot be carried out in whole or in part, the Court would not allow the trust to fail but would execute it. '*Cy pres*' that is to say, in some way as nearly as possible to that which the author of the trust intended. *Ratilal Panachand Gandghi* v. *State of Bombay*, AIR 1954 SC 388, 394.

Cyber café. 'Cyber café' means any facility from where access to the internet is offered by any person in the ordinary course of business to the members of the public. [Information Technology Act (21 of 2000), S. 2(na) as inserted by Amending Act No (10 of 2009)]

Cyber incident. "Cyber incident" means any real or suspected adverse event that is likely to cause or causes an offence or contravention, harm to critical functions and services across the public and private sectors by impairing the confidentiality, integrity, or availability of electronic information, systems, services or networks resulting in unauthorised access, denial of service or disruption, unauthorised use of a computer resource, changes to data or information without authorisation; or threatens public safety, undermines public confidence, have a negative effect on the national economy, or diminishes the security posture of the nation. [Information Technology (The Indian Computer Emergency Response Team and Manner of Performing Functions and Duties) Rules, 2013, R. 2(1)(g)].

Cybercrime. Crime committed over the internet.

Computer crime committed over telecommunications networks. (*Cyber Law*)

Cyber notaries. Third-party certification authorities that attest to the identity of a signatory. (*Cyber Law*)

Cyber security. 'Cyber security' means protecting information, equipment, devices, computer, computer resource, communication device and information stored therein from unauthorised access, use, disclosure, disruption, modification or destruction. [Information Technology Act (21 of 2000), S. 4(D); S. 2 (nb) as inserted by Amending Act No (10 of 2009)]

"CYBER SECURITY" for the purposes of rule 20 of the Companies (Management & Administration) Rules, 2014, the expression 'cyber security' means protecting information, equipment, devices, computer, computer resource, communication device and information stored therein from unauthorised access, use, disclosures, disruption, modification or destruction. [*Explanation* (*iii*) to Rule 20(2) of the Companies (Management & Administration) Rules, 2014]

Cyber stalking. A form of *stalking* that involves telecommunications, such as intercepting the target's e-mail or interacting in chat rooms. (*Cyber Law*)

"CYBER STALKING" the use of internet and its services such as blog, e-mail, or chat services to harass, intimidate, defame, and stalk a person, threatening or causing mental agony or injury to a person. [Karnika Seth, *Computers Internet and New Technology Laws*, 2021, LexisNexis, Glossary of Legal Terms].

Cyber terrorism. Criminal activities committed against computer systems, such as theft of information, malicious destruction, spying, or fraud. (*Cyber Law*)

"CYBER TERRORISM" it means use of computers, computer networks, internet by criminals such as terrorists to spread terror and crime that threatens the integrity, sovereignty, defence systems and public safety of a nation. [Karnika Seth, *Computers Internet and New Technology Laws*, 2021, LexisNexis, Glossary of Legal Terms].

Cyber trespass. Invasion of another's property interest in an electronic database by physical acts on site or by remote access. (*Cyber Law*)

Cybercash. Used for secure processing of credit-card transactions. It actually takes the payment information and sends it via the banking gateways to obtain real-time approvals for credit cards and checks. (*Cyber Law*)

Cybernetics. The science of computers and computerized processes and study of their functioning and application. (*Copyright*)

Cyberporn. Obscene material transmitted over the Internet or through e-mail. (*Cyber Law*)

Cyberpunk. Cyberpunk was originally a cultural sub-genre of science fiction taking place in a not-so-distant, dystopian, over-industrialized society. The term grew out of the work of William Gibson and Bruce Sterling and has evolved into a cultural label encompassing many different kinds of human, machine, and punk attitudes. It includes clothing and lifestyle choices as well. (*Matisee Enzer-Glossary of Internet Terms*) (*Telecommunication*)

An antiestablishment rebel in the computer universe. Also refers to an entire counter-culture existing in cyberspace. (*Criminal*)

Cyber security breaches. "Cyber security breaches" means unauthorised acquisition or unauthorised use by a person as well as an entity of data or information that compromises the confidentiality, integrity or availability or information maintained in a computer resource. [Information Technology (The Indian Computer Emergency Response Team and Manner of Performing Functions and Duties) Rules, 2013, R. 2(1)(i)].

Cyber security incident. "Cyber security incident" means any real or suspected event in relation to cyber security that violates an explicitly or implicitly applicable security policy resulting in unauthorised access, denial of service or disruption, unauthorised use of a computer resource for processing or storage of information or changes to data, information without authorisation. [Information Technology (The Indian Computer Emergency Response Team and Manner of Performing Functions and Duties) Rules, 2013, R. 2(1)(h).

Cyberspace. A term coined by science fiction writer William Gibson, referring to the virtual world which exists within the marriage of computers, telecommunication networks, and digital media. (*Information Technology*)

Term originally used by William Gibson in his 1982 novel Neuromancer. The totality of all the world's computers, represented as a visual virtual three dimensional domain in which a user may move and act with the consequences in the real world. (*Cyber Law*)

Term originated by author William Gibson in his novel *Neuromancer* the word Cyberspace is currently used to describe the whole range of information resources available through computer networks. (*Matisse Enzer-Glossary of Internet Terms*) (*Telecommunication*)

Cybersquatting. Registering an Internet domain name for the purpose of reselling it for a profit. One of the more notable transactions was the domain name wallstreet.com, which was registered in 1994 for $70 and sold for one million in 1999. Some people have registered every common name and name combination they can think of with the hopes of making a profit. *(Computer desktop encyclopedia)*

The practice of acquiring domain names that suggest established firms and reselling them to those firms as a form of ransom. (*Cyber Law*)

Cycle. 'Cycle' means a bicycle, tricycle, or cycle having four or more wheels, not being in any case a motor vehicle. [(English) Road Traffic Act, 1972, S. 196(1)].

Cyclic redundancy check (CRC). A checking scheme in which all the data being considered as a block are processed by a complex mathematical equation and one or two check characters are formed as a result. The check characters are then attached to the data block when it is stored or transferred. The receiving unit or the unit retrieving the data block performs the same mathematical operation on the data block and compares its CRC characters with those received to check the accuracy of transmission or storage. (*Computer*)

D

Dacoit. One of any gang which commits dacoity.

Dacoity. When five or more persons conjointly commit or attempt to commit a robbery, or where the whole number of persons conjointly committing or attempting to commit a robbery, and persons present and aiding such commission or attempt amount to five or more, every person so committing, attempting or aiding is said to commit dacoity. [IPC (45 of 1860), S. 391] [(w.e.f. 1-7-2024) repealed and replaced by Bharatiya Nyaya Sanhita, 2023 (45 of 2023), section 310(1)]

Robbery committed by a gang of five or more persons. [IPC (45 of 1860), S. 391] [(w.e.f. 1-7-2024) repealed and replaced by Bharatiya Nyaya Sanhita, 2023 (45 of 2023), section 310(1)].

Dactylography. The scientific study of fingerprints as a method of identification.

Daily fine. Means a fine for each day on which an offence is continued after conviction therefor. [Indian Electricity Act (9 of 1910), S. 2(d)]

Daily newspaper. Means a newspaper which is published on not less than six days a week, and includes any supplement or special edition of such newspaper. [Newspaper (Price and Page) Act (45 of 1956), S. 2(a)]

Dairy. 'DAIRY' includes any farm, cattle-shed, milk-store, milk-shop or other place from which milk is supplied or in which milk is kept for purposes of sale or is manufactured for sale into butter, ghee, cheese or curd, and, in relation to a dairyman who does not occupy any premises for the sale of milk, includes any place in which he keeps the vessels used by him for the storage or sale of milk. [Cantonments Act (2 of 1924), S. 2(x)]

'DAIRY'—

(i) includes any farm, cowshed, milking house, milk store, milk shop or other premises from which milk is supplied on or for sale, or in which milk is kept or used for purposes of sale or for the purposes of manufacture into butter, cheese, dried milk or condensed milk for sale, or in which vessels used for the sale of milk are kept, but

(ii) does not include a shop from which milk is supplied only in the properly closed and unopened vessels in which it is delivered to the shop, or a shop or other place in which milk is sold for consumption on the premises only. [(English) Food Act, 1984, S. 32(1)(a)]

"DAIRY" includes any farm, farmhouse, cowshed, milk-store, milk-shop, or other place from which milk is kept, for purposes of sale." [(Eng.) Infec. Diseases Prevention Act, 1893, S. 2]

Dairy farm. 'DAIRY FARM'—

(i) means any premises (being a dairy) on which milk is produced from cows, but

(ii) does not include any part of any such premises on which milk is manufactured into other products unless the milk produced on the premises forms a substantial part of the milk so manufactured. [(English) Food Act, 1984, S. 32(1)(b)]

Dairyman. Includes the keeper of a cow, buffalo, goat, ass or other animal, the milk of which is offered or intended to be offered for sale for human consumption and any purveyor of milk and any occupier of a dairy. [Cantonments Act (2 of 1924), S. 2(xi)]

Dalal Street. Street on which the Bombay Stock Exchange is situated. Used synonymously for the Bombay Stock Exchange.

Dam. "A 'dam' is a structure composed of wood, earth or other material, erected in and usually extending across the entire channel at right angles to the thread of the stream, and intended to retard the flow of water by the barrier, or to retain it within the obstruction." [Words and Phrases, Permanent Edn. 11, as cited in *Morton* v. *Oregon Short Line Railway Co.*, (1906) 87P 151 : 40 or 444.] See also *State of A.P.* v. *State of Maharashtra*, (2013) 5 SCC 68, para 51.

"The word 'dam' is used in two different senses. It properly means a structure raised to obstruct the flow of water in a river, but by well-settled usage it is often applied to designate the pond of water created by its obstruction. The word is used in this conventional sense in some statutes, and it is evidently used in this sense in a statute giving power to raise the 'dam and water-works' to a height mentioned." [Words and Phrases, Permanent Edn. 11 as cited in *State of A.P.* v. *State of Maharashtra*, (2013) 5 SCC 68, para 51.1].

"A barrier constructed across a river or natural watercourse for the purpose of : (a) impounding water or creating reservoir; (b) diverting water there from into a conduct or channel for power generation and or irrigation purpose; (c) creating a head which can be used for generation of power; (d) improving river navigability; (e) retention of debris; (f) flood control; (g) domestic, municipal and induses; (h) preservation of wildlife and pisciculture, and (j) recreation, etc." [Indian Standard Glossary of Terms Relating to River Valley Projects, Part 8, Dams and Dam Sections (First Revision), Para 2.27 as cited in *State of A.P.* v. *State of Maharashtra*, (2013) 5 SCC 68, para 51.2].

The common meaning of the word 'dam' is the structure across the stream, including the abutment on the sides. The dam is an obstruction to the natural flow of the water of a river or a barrier to prevent the flowing water. A dam is built across a water course to confine and keep back flowing water. [State of *Andhra Pradesh* v. *State of Maharashtra*, (2013) 5 SCC 68, para 51].

Damage. Loss, or injury which results from an unlawful act; injury, or deterioration, caused by the negligence, design, or accident of one person to another; depreciation in value, whether such depreciation is caused by a wrongful or lawful act; "any hurt or hindrance a man receives in his person or property or estate." (*Tomlin*)

"DAMAGE" AND "DAMAGES". The word, "damage" is to be distinguished from its plural "damages," which means a compensation in money for a loss or damage caused by another's act.

Damage-feasant. Is when a stranger's beasts are found in another person's ground without his leave or licence, and without the fault of the possessor of the close (which may happen from his not repairing his fences) and there doing damage, by feeding, or otherwise on the grass, corn, woods, *etc.* In which case, the tenant whom they damage, may distrain and impound them, as well by night as in the day, lest the beasts escape before being taken. (*Tomlin: Termes de la Ley*)

Damaged. The word 'damaged' in the collection of the words 'lost or damaged' appearing both in sub-section (2) of Section 11 and in the proviso to sub-section (2-C) of Section 13, must take its colour from the context in which it appears and must be construed in furtherance of the purpose and object of inserting these provisions and in the light of the mischief sought to be avoided by the Legislature. *Charanji Lal* v. *State of Punjab*, AIR 1984 SC 80. [Prevention of Food Adulteration Act (37 of 1954), Ss. 11(2) and 13(2-C), Prov.]

Damages. Compensation for legal injury. "Damages" are the pecuniary recompense given by process of law to a person for the actionable wrong that another has done him. HALSBURY, 4th Edn., Vol. 12, para 1102, p. 412.

In current usage, "special damage" or "special damages" relate to past pecuniary loss calculable at the date of trial, whilst "general damage" or "general damages" relates to all other items of damage whether pecuniary or non-pecuniary. HALSBURY, 4th Edn., Vol,. 12, para 1113, p. 416.

The word 'damages' constitute the sum of money, claimed or adjudged to be paid in compensation for loss or injury sustained. *Divisional Controller, KSRTC* v. *Mahadeva Shetty,* (2003) 7 SCC 197, para 11.

The sum claimed or awarded in compensation for loss or injury sustained. [Indian Evidence Act (1 of 1872), S. 12].

Damages and injury. Distinguished. There is a material distinction between "damages" and "injury." Injury is the wrongful act or tort which causes loss or harm to another. Damages are allowed as an indemnity to the person who suffers loss or harm from the injury. The word "injury" denotes the illegal act. The term "damages" means the sum recoverable as amends for the wrong.

Damages & penalty. (Difference). The scope of the power under Section 14-B is to recover damages. Damages, it is well known, is totally different from penalty. Where a statute enjoins a person to do a particular thing and when he fails to do so he becomes liable to be penalised, in other words, the imposition of penalty arises in such cases. Parliament, under Section 14-B has clothed the authority to levy damages. Therefore, it would be incumbent upon the authority to find how the beneficiaries of the Provident Fund contribution had been damnified by the belated payment of the contributions. No doubt, the liability to contribute might be statutory, but nevertheless, merely because there was a delay or merely because there was a belated payment, it would not follow automatically that the liability for damages got attracted. It is not mere arithmetical computation or a rigid application of law by which damages could be recovered. There must be an exercise of mind and there must be an examination of merits of each case. Case-law discussed. [MOHAN, J] *The South Indian Flour Mills P. Ltd.* v. *The Regional Provident Fund Commissioner*, YD 1978 Suppl C 1006 : (1978) Lab IC 1187 : (1978) 1 Lab LJ 101 : 52 FJR 62 : (1978) 1 Lab LN 158 (Mad). [Employees' Provident Funds Act (1952), S 14-B]

Damages, exemplary. Awarded by the Court not only to compensate the plaintiff but also to punish defendant for the outrageous nature of his conduct.

Damages for loss of expectation of life. The Courts have now recognised loss of expectation of life as a distinct head of damages besides physical pain and suffering and pecuniary loss resulting from bodily harm. Where damages are awarded in respect of personal injuries or death, the damages may include a modest sum in respect of shortening of expectation of life.

Damnify. To cause hurt or injury; to cause loss.

Damnum absque injuria. (*Lat.*) A loss without a wrong; loss or hurt without injury in law (*i.e.*) without such injury as would give rise to an action for damages against the offending party. If one man keeps a school in such a place, another may do so likewise in the same place, though he draw away the scholars from the other school; and this is *damnum absque injuria*, a loss without an injury; but he must not do anything to disturb the other school. (3 Salk. 10; *Tomlin)*

Damnum absque injuria esse potest. (*Maxim*) There is such a thing as damage without injury. (*Morgan*)

Damnum fatale. (*Lat.*) Damage caused by an unavoidable circumstance.

Damnum sentit dominus. (*Lat.*) The owner suffers the damage.

Damnum sine injuria. The rule of law is that the exercise of an ordinary right is no wrong even if it causes damage. As a price of our free action, which the law permits, the other person must abide by some measure of inconvenience from equal freedom of one's neighbour.

Damage with injury, that is damage caused without legal wrong.

Damnum sine injuria esse potest. (*Maxim*) There may be damage or injury inflicted without any act of injustice. (*Cyclopaedic: Ame Cye.; Black; Morgan; Broom*)

Damodar valley. Includes the basin of the Damodar river and its tributaries. [Damodar Valley Corporation Act (14 of 1948) S. 2(2)]

Danger. Risk, hazard, peril or exposure to pain or injury. [CrPC 1973 (2 of 1974), S. 133(1)(e)].

"Danger" (1) the state of being vulnerable to injury, loss, or evil; risk; (2) a person or a thing that may cause injury, pain, etc. [Collins Dictionary as cited in *Shreya Singhal* v. *Union of India*, (2015) 5 SCC 1, para 51].

Dangerous. Fraught with danger or risk; perilous; hazardous; unsafe.

Dangerous animals. A person who keeps a dangerous animal does so at his peril.

Dangerous building. The words "*dangerous building*", apply to all structures which are in a dangerous state; the word is not confined to structures which are dangerous to passengers using a public way. *R* v. *Herring*, 63 LJMC 230.

Dangerous chattels. Things which are specially likely to cause injury to those persons into whose possession they may come.

Dangerous disease. "DANGEROUS DISEASE" means—

(a) cholera, plague, chicken-pox, small-pox, tuberculosis, leprosy, enteric fever, cerebrospinal meningitis and diptheria; and

(b) any other epidemic, endemic or infectious disease which the Chairperson may, by notification in the Official Gazette, declare to be a dangerous disease for the purposes of this Act. [New Delhi Municipal Council Act (44 of 1994), S. 2(10)]

"DANGEROUS DISEASE" includes cholera and endemic, epidemic or infectious disease by which the life of man is endangered. [Bom Act III of 1888 (City Bombay Municipal), S. 3, cl. (*aa*)]

"DANGEROUS DISEASE" means a disease specified in the Ninth schedule to the Kerala Municipalities Act, 20 of 1994 or any disease included in the said schedule by Government, from time to time, by notification in the Gazette. [Kerala Municipality Act (20 of 1994), S. 2(12)]

Dangerous driving. The offence in which one drives a motor vehicle in such a way as to fall far below the standard that would be expected of a competent and careful driver.

Dangerous drug. 'DANGEROUS DRUG' includes cocoa leaf, hemp and opium and all manufactured drugs. [Dangerous Drug Act, 1930 S. 2(h); Children's Act (60 of 1960), S. 2(i)]

Dangerous machine. Means a power thresher, and includes any machine intended to be used in the agricultural or rural sector as the Central Government, being of opinion that it is of such nature that any accident in the course of operation thereof is likely to cause to its operator death, dismemberment of any limb or other bodily injury, may by notification in the official Gazette, specify as dangerous machine. [Dangerous Machines (Regulation) Act (35 of 1983), S. 3(c)]

Dangerous parts of the machinery. The phrase 'All dangerous parts of the machinery,' is not confined to parts which are in themselves dangerous, but applies to all machinery from which, in the ordinary course of working it, danger may be reasonably anticipated, although such danger may arise only through careless working or external causes. (*Stroud*)

A machinery or part thereof is dangerous if in the ordinary course of its working danger may reasonably be anticipated from it when working, without protection, taking into account the various factors incidental to its working, including the carelessness of the workman. *J.B. Mangharam and Co.* v. *E.S.I. Corporation,* AIR 1969 MP 110 at p. 113. [Factories Act (63 of 1948), S. 21(1)(iv)(c)]

Dangerous person. 'Dangerous person' means a person who habitually commits or attempts to commit or abets commission of offences, either by himself or as a member of or leader of a gang. *Ayub* v. *S.N. Sinha*, AIR 1990 SC 2069, 2071.

Dangerous person means a person who either by himself or as a member of or leader of a gang, habitually commits or attempts to commit or abets the commission of offences, punishable under chapter XVI or chapter XVII or chapter XXII of the Indian Penal Code, 1860 or any of the offences punishable under chapter V of the Arms Act, 1959. *Rashidmiya Ahmedmiya* v. *Police Commissioner, Ahmedabad*, AIR 1989 SC 1703.

A person who is not alleged to have committed or abetted any of the offences punishable under Chapter-XVI or XVII of the Penal Code of under Chapter-V of Arms Act, cannot be called a dangerous person. *Musmkmiya Jabbarmiya Shaikh* v. *M.M. Mehta*, 1995 (3) SCC 237.

Dangerous weapon. A weapon likely to produce death or great bodily harm; a weapon capable of producing death or danger to life; one by which a fatal wound may be given.

Dangerously inflammable substance. Liquids or other substances, namely:—

(1) acetone, (2) calcium phosphide, (3) carbide of calcium, (4) cinematograph films having nitro cellulose base, (5) ethyl alcohol, (6) Methyl alcohol, (7) wood nephtha, are hereby declared to be dangerously inflammable. [Inflammable Substances Act (20 of 1952), S. 3]

Dastauvej. A voucher, a document, any legal paper, a note of hand, a bond, a title-deed, and the like.

Anything in writing producible in evidence, or by which a person may be bound in law. A certificate of any kind.

Data. "DATA" means a representation of information, knowledge, facts, concepts or instructions which are being prepared or have been prepared in a formalised manner, and is intended to be processed, is being processed or has been processed in a computer system or computer network, and may be in any form (including computer printouts magnetic or optical storage media, punched cards, punched tapes) or stored internally in the memory of the computer. [Information Technology Act (21 of 2000), S. 2(1)(o)]

"Data" means a representation of information, facts, concepts, opinions or instructions in a manner suitable for communication, interpretation or processing by human beings or by automated means. [Digital Personal Data Protection Act, 2023 (22 of 2023), section 2(h)]

Data centre. The facility covering the computer room, media library, network area, server area, programming and administration areas, other storage and support areas used to carry out the computer processing functions. Usually refers to the computer room and media centre. (*Information Technology*)

Data confidentiality. Where the secrecy of the data is maintained. (*Information Technology*)

Data Fiduciary. Means any person who alone or in conjunction with other persons determines the purpose and means of processing of personal data. [Digital Personal Data Protection Act, 2023 (22 of 2023), section 2(i)]

Data integrity. A condition in which data has not been altered or destroyed in an unauthorized manner. (*Information Technology*)

Data that has not been tampered with during a given period of time. (*Internet and E-commerce*).

Data interference. Means damaging, deletion, deterioration, alteration or suppression of computer data, intentionally and without a right to do so and input of malicious codes, such as viruses and Trojan horses. [Note 61, Explanatory Report on The European Convention on Cyber Crime]

Data preservation. Data preservation means keeping data, which already exists in a stored form, protected from anything that would cause its current quality or condition to change or deteriorate. Aparna Viswanathan, *Cyber Law: Indian & International Perspectives,* 2012, LexisNexis Butterworths at p. 109.

Data Principal. Means the individual to whom the personal data relates and where such individual is—

(i) a child, includes the parents or lawful guardian of such a child;

(ii) a person with disability, includes her lawful guardian, acting on her behalf. [Digital Personal Data Protection Act, 2023 (22 of 2023), section 2(j)]

Data privacy. Data in which a person or a legal entity has a continuing interest or right. (*Internet and E-commerce*).

Data processing. The sorting and organization of data in order to produce the desired information, generally according to standard procedures and generally using a computer. (*Trade Finance*)

Data Processor. Means any person who processes personal data on behalf of a Data Fiduciary. [Digital Personal Data Protection Act, 2023 (22 of 2023), section 2(k)]

Data protection measures. For the purpose of this section 'DATA PROTECTION MEASURES' shall include procedures for protecting information from disclosure, procedures for accessing information, provision for security systems to protect the information stored in any form and mechanisms to ensure accountability and liability of persons in the establishment. [Human Immunodeficiency Virus and Acquired Immune Deficiency Syndrome (Prevention and Control) Act (16 of 2017), S. 11, *Explanation*].

Data Protection Officer. Means an individual appointed by the Significant Data Fiduciary under clause (*a*) of sub-section (2) of section 10. [Digital Personal Data Protection Act, 2023 (22 of 2023), section 2(l)]

Data retention. Data retention means the accumulation of data in the present and the keeping or possession of it into a future time period. Aparna Viswanathan, *Cyber Law: Indian & International Perspectives,* 2012, LexisNexis Butterworths at p. 109.

Data security. The practice of protecting data from accidental or malicious modification, disclosure or destruction. (*Information Technology*)

Database. A large collection of organized, related data, as, for example, a telephone directory on a computer. A database is organized so that data can be rapidly retrieved from or added to it. A database program is a computer program designed for creating, maintaining, and using such a collection of data. (*Computer*)

A computerised filing system for storing, arranging and retrieving information.

Collections of works, data, or other materials arranged in a systematic or methodical way for retrieval or access by manual or electronic means.

The organized collection of data, generally stored and accessed in electronic form from a computer network. [Registration of Births & Deaths Act, 1969 (18 of 1969), section 2(1)(b)]

Date. The day or the precise time at which something takes place or is to take place [T.P. Act (4 of 1882), S. 14]; to put date.

Date fixed for the hearing. Means the day on which the hearing commences, and includes both that day and the day to which the hearing may be adjourned.

Date of acquisition. "DATE OF ACQUISITION" Means the date on which the ownership of financial assets is acquired by Securitisation Company or Reconstruction Company either on its own books or directly in the books of the trust. [Securitisation Companies and Reconstruction Companies (Reserve Bank) Guidelines and Directions, 2003, 3(1)(iii)]

Date of award. The date of the award referred to in proviso (b) of S. 18(2) is the date of its filing in the Collector's office and not the date on which the Collector has only written or signed it. *State of Travancore Cochin* v. *Narayani Amma Ponnamma,* AIR 1958 Ker 272, 278. [Land Acquisition Act (1 of 1894), S. 18(2), *Prov.* (b)] [Now repealed & replaced by Act 30 of 2013]

The expression 'date of the award' means either the date of the receipt of the notice of the award or the date of the knowledge of the award either actual or constructive. *Sukhdev* v. *State of U.P.,* AIR 1992 All 142, 144. [Land Acquisition Act (1 of 1894), S. 28A] [Now repealed & replaced by Act 30 of 2013]

Date of delivery. The natural meaning of the words 'from the date of delivery' can only be that the relevant date is the date on which goods are handed over to the railway for carriage.

Date of election. The date of election referred to in S. 81 is the date on which a candidate in an election is declared by the Returning Officer to be elected. *Bhaktibh Mondal* v. *Khagendra K. Bandopadya,* AIR 1968 Cal 69, 70. [Representation of the People Act (43 of 1951), S. 81]

Date of export. 'DATE OF EXPORT' in relation to the export of software in other than physical form, shall be deemed to be the date of invoice covering such export. [FEM (Export of Goods & Services) Regulations, 2000, Reg. 9 *Expln.*]

Date of finalisation of the duly audited accounts. Means the date on which the audited accounts of the company are adopted at the annual general meeting of the company. [Sick Industrial Companies (Special Provisions) Act 1985 (1 of 1986), S. 3(1)(da)]

Date of first hearing. The expression 'date of first hearing' is the date on which the Court proposed to apply its mind to determine the points in controversy between the parties to the suit and to frame issues, if necessary. *Suraj Ahmad Siddiqui* v. *Prem Nath Kapoor*, AIR 1993 SC 2525, 2528. [U.P. Urban Buildings (Regulation of Letting, Rent and Eviction) Act (13 of 1972), S. 20(4)]

Date of maturity. The date on which a pay ment becomes due.

Date of order. Where a Court passes an order in the absence of a party without having previously informed that party of the day on which it was going to pass the order, the date of passing the order cannot validly be made the starting point of limitation. *Saint Ram* v. *M.T. Mrawati,* AIR 1953 Bilaspur 9. [CPC (5 of 1908), S. 115]

The expression 'date of the order' must mean the date when the order was either actually communicated to the party or was known by it either actually or constructively.

Date of the succession of states. Means the date upon which the successor State replaced the predecessor State in respect of the res ponsibility for the International relations of the territory to which the succession of states relates. [Vienna Convention on Succession of States, 1978, Art. 2(e)]

Date of transfer. If the date of the execution of a document is different from the date on which it is registered, then the date on which it is registered shall constitute the starting point for the computation of time under section 54. *M. Narayanaswami* v. *A. Narayanaswami,* AIR 1953 Mad 682, 683. [Provincial Insolvency Act (5 of 1920), S. 54]

Date rape. A rape which is committed by someone known to the victim, specially by the social companion of the victim.

Date of receipt of payment. For the purposes of this section, "the date of receipt of payment" shall be the date on which the payment is entered in the books of account of the supplier or the date on which the payment is credited to his bank account, whichever is earlier. [Central Goods and Services Tax Act (12 of 2017), S. 14, *Explanation*].

Dated security. A security, such as a bill of exchange or a bond, that has a stated date for repayment (redemption date) of its nominal value. It may be described as short-dated or long-dated. (*Trade Finance*)

Daughter. "DAUGHTER" in the case of any one whose personal Law permits adoption, includes an adopted daughter. [Meghalaya Interpretation and General Clauses Act, 1972, S. 3(18)]

A female issue of a person. [T.P. Act (4 of 1882), S. 25 ill. (b)].

Day. "DAY" means a period of twenty-four hours beginning at midnight. [Dangerous Machines (Regulation) Act (35 of 1983), S. 3(d)]

"DAY" means a period of twenty-four hours beginning at midnight :

Provided that where a motor transport worker's duty commences before midnight but extends beyond midnight, the following day for him shall be deemed to be the period of twenty-four hours beginning when such duty ends, and the hours he has worked after midnight shall be counted in the previous day. [Motor Transport Workers Act (27 of 1961), S. 2(d)]

Daya Vibhaga. A digest on ancient Hindu Law written by Madhava.

Dayabhaga. A digest on ancient Hindu Law written by Jimutavahana; a work of para mount authority in Bengal.

Dayanandis. Dayanandis are Hindus forming a sect of the Arya Samajists. They believe in the supremacy of the Vedas.

Days of grace. "Every promissory note or bill of exchange which is not expressed to be payable on demand, at sight or on presentment, is at maturity on the third day after the day on which it is expressed, to be payable." [Negotiable Instruments Act (26 of 1881), S. 22]

The days of grace, strictly so called, are clearly the days before the expiry of which there is no right of action for the party, giving the days of grace.

In calculating the days of grace, the due date should be excluded.

Daysman. An arbiter.

De bonis non administratis. (*Lat.*) Of unadministered goods.

De die in diem. From day to day.

De facto. In fact, actually, frequently used in contradistinction to *de jure* meaning rightful, legitimate, lawful.

Of fact; founded in fact; in deed, in point of fact; actually, really. It is opposed to *de jure*. (*Tomlin*)

De facto government. A government *de facto*, in the proper legal sense, is the government that unlawfully gets the possession and con trol of the rightful legal government, and maintains itself there by force and arms against the will of the rightful legal government, and claims to exercise the powers thereof. (*Chisholm* v. *Coleman*, 94 Am. Dec. 677). *De facto* Governments are of two kinds. One of them is such as exists after it has expelled the regularly constituted authorities and established its own functionaries in their places, so as to represent in fact the sovereignty of the nation. Such was the government of England under the Commonwealth. As a rule, the rights acquired under such a government are respected after the restoration of the authorities which were expelled. The other kind of *de facto* government is such as exists where a portion of the inhabitants of a country have separated themselves from the parent state and established an independent government. If it succeeds, the validity of its acts from the commencement of its existence are upheld as those of an independent nation. If it fails, its acts are of no effect. (*Words and Phrases Jud. Dep.*)

De facto guardian. A guardian in point of fact. [Hindu Minority and Guardianship Act (32 of 1956), S. 11].

De facto possession. Legal possession is ordinarily associated with the '*de facto* possession', but legal possession may exist without *de facto* possession. '*De facto* possession' is not always regarded as possession in law. [*B. Gangadhar* v. *B.G. Rajalingam,* (1995) 5 SCC 238, 240-41, para 5]

De fide et officio judicis non recipitur quaestio; sed de scientia sive sit error juris sive facti. (*Maxim*) The *bona fides* and honesty of purpose of a judge cannot be questioned, but his decision may be impugned for error either of law or of fact.

De hors. Out of; without; beyond; foreign; unconnected with. Outside of; unrelated to.

De minimis non curat lex. (*Maxim*) The law does not concern itself with trifles.

De morte hominis nulla est cunctatio longa. (*Lat.*) (Co. Litt. 134) When the death of a human being is concerned, no delay is long.

De non apparentibus, et non existentibus eadem est ratio. (*Lat.*) (4 Rep. 47 a: 5 Id. 5b) As to things not apparent, and those not existing, the rule is the same".

De novo. Anew; afresh; a second time; again.

De novo trial. A *de novo* trial is not strictly speaking a new or fresh trial. All that it means is that the accused shall have the right to have all or any of the witnesses re-summoned and re-heard by the new Magistrate. [AIR 1937 Mad 448]

De proprio motu. Of one's own motion.

De similibus idem est judicium. (*Maxim*) In like cases or matters the judgment is to be the same. (*Ame. Cyc.*)

De son tort demesne. Of his own wrong.

De tempore cujus contrarium memoria hominum non existit. From time immemorial, from time whereof the memory of man does not exist to the contrary.

Dead body. A corpse; corpse has been defined to be the *dead body* of a human being. Although the dead body of a person is not property and therefore cannot be said to be owned by any one, yet in all ages and in all countries it has been deemed the right of certain near relatives of the dead to take possession of the corpse for the purpose of interring or making such other disposition of it as custom may prescribe. Though it has been said that there is a *quasi*-property in a dead body, and undoubtedly there are certain rights respecting it which the Courts recognize and protect, yet it is not property in any proper commercial sense. The custodian of it has a legal right to its possession for the purpose of preservation and burial, and any interference with that right by mutilating or otherwise disturbing the body is an actionable wrong. The person having charge of a body cannot be considered the owner of it; he holds it only as a trust for the benefit of those who may from family relationship or friendship have an interest in it.

Dead freight. Freight which is payable by a charterer in respect of cargo not shipped.

Dead letter. Law no longer observed; also letter not claimed and not deliverable by the Post Office.

Dead letter office. Office of the Postal Department where undeliverable letters are sent before the same are returned to the sender.

Dead lock. State of affairs in which it is impossible to advance or recede; a state of suspended animation in business affairs.

A state of inaction as a result of opposition or lack of compromise or agreement, as it so happens when the two Houses of the Parliament disagree in respect of an ordinary bill.

Dead rent. In order to ensure for the lessor a regular income, whether the mine is worked or not, a fixed amount is provided to be paid to him by the lessee. This is called "dead rent." *King Pal Singh* v. *State of Uttar Pradesh,* JT 1996 (10) SC 402 : 1996 (8) Scale 272.

Dead stock. "DEAD STOCK" means goods which have not been exported for two years after their manufacture in the hundred percent export oriented undertaking. [Central Excise Tariff Act (5 of 1986), Gen. Exemption No. 39, 1(ii)(i) *Expln.* (d)]

Deadly. Causing fatal injury.

Deadly weapon. A weapon causing or having the capacity to cause death. [IPC (45 of 1860), Ss. 144 and 158]. (*Black*)

Deadly weapon may include an axe, a club, a knife, a gun, sword, large knife, bar of iron, and any 'other heavy instrument' by a blow from which a grievous hurt would probably be inflicted, a pistol, and a sledge hammer, weapon with which a person may be wounded by cutting or stabbing.

There are some weapons which are not considered '*deadly'* as a pocket knife.

Deadly weapon per se. A weapon which of itself is deadly or one which would ordinarily result in death by its use; *e.g.* gun.

Deadly weapons distinguished **from dangerous weapon.** Deadly and dangerous are not equivalents. A dangerous weapon may possibly not be deadly, but a deadly weapon, one which is capable of causing death, must be dangerous. What is a dangerous and deadly weapon depends not so much on the article itself, as upon surrounding circumstances, the intent with which it is carried, and the manner in which it is used; it is necessarily, to some extent, a question of fact, not of law.

Deal in. To do business with a person in an article. [IPC (45 of 1860), S. 263A].

Deal with. The expression 'deal with' is all comprehensive and investigation, inquiry and trial are some aspects of 'dealing with' the offences. *Delhi Administration* v. *Ram Singh*, AIR 1962 SC 63, 67. [Suppression of Immoral Traffic in Women and Girls Act (104 of 1956), S. 13(3)]

To have dealing with; to do business with; to act in regard to; to discuss; to take action (as in regard to some object, problem or source of difficulty.

Deal with his security. The words 'deal with his security' in S. 17 Presidency Towns Insolvency Act (3 of 1909), refer to the rights which the mortgagees and pledgees may have of transferring or assigning the debt due to, and the security in the possession or at the disposal of, the said creditors.

Dealer. Seller of a specified articles (as, dealer in cotton). A person who buys to sell again and not one who buys to keep, one who trades, buys or sells; one whose business it is to buy and sell; one who buys to sell to others at a profit.

"DEALER" means any person who deals in rubber, whether wholesale or retail or holds stock stocks of rubber, and includes the representative or agent of a dealer. [Rubber (Production and Marketing) Act (24 of 1947), S. 3(b)]

"DEALER" means any person who carries on in Uttar Pradesh (whether regularly or otherwise) the business of buying, selling, supplying or distributing goods directly or indirectly, for cash or different payment or for commission, remuneration or other valuable consideration and includes—

(i) a local authority, body corporate, company, any cooperative society or other society, club, firm, Hindu Undivided Family or other association of persons which carries on such business;

(ii) a factor, broker, arhati, commission agent, del credere agent, or any other mercantile agent, by whatever name called and whether of the some description as herein before mentioned or not, who carries on the business of buying, selling, supplying or distributing goods belonging to any principal, whether disclosed or not;

(iii) an auctioneer who carries on the business of selling or auctioning goods belonging to any principal, whether disclosed or not, and whether the offer of the intending purchaser is accepted by him or by the principal or nominee of the principal;

(iv) a government which, whether in the course of business or otherwise buys, sells, supplies or distributes goods, directly or otherwise for cash or for deferred payment or for commission, remuneration or other valuable consideration;

(v) every person who acts within the State as an agent of a dealer residing outside the State, and buys, sells, supplies or distributes goods in the State or acts on behalf of such dealer as—

(A) a mercantile agent as defined in the Sale of Goods Act, 1930; or

(B) an agent for handling of goods or documents of title relating to goods; or

(C) an agent for the collection or the payment of the sale price of goods or as a guarantor for such collection or such payment;

(vi) a firm or a company or other body corporate, the principal office or headquarters whereof is outside the State having a branch or office in the State, in respect of purchases or sales, supplies or distribution of goods through such branch or office;

(vii) every person who carries on the business of transfer of property in goods (whether as goods or in some other farm) involved in the execution of a works contract;

(viii) every person who carries on the business of transfer of the right to use any goods for any purpose (whether or not for a specified period) for cash, deferred payment or other valuable consideration.

U.P. Trade Tax Act, 1948, S. 2(c) as cited in *State of U.P.* v. *Jaiprakash Associated Limited*, (2014) 4 SCC 720, para 22].

"DEALER" means a person carrying on, either personally or through any other person, the business of selling any drugs, whether wholesale or retail. [Drugs (Control) Act (26 of 1950), S. 2(a)]

"DEALER" means any person who carries on (whether regularly or otherwise) the business of buying, selling, supplying or distributing goods, directly or indirectly, for cash or for deferred payment, or for commission, remuneration or other valuable consideration, and includes—

(i) a local authority, a body corporate, a company, any co-operative society or other society, club, firm, Hindu undivided family or other association of persons which carries on such business;

(ii) a factor, broker, commission agent, del credere agent, or any other mercantile agent, by whatever name called, and whether of the same description as hereinbefore mentioned or not, who carries on the business of buying, selling, supplying or distributing, goods belonging to any principal whether disclosed or not; and

(iii) an auctioneer who carries on the business of selling or auctioning goods belonging to any principal, whether disclosed or not and whether the offer of the intending purchaser is accepted by him or by the principal or nominee of the principal.

Explanation 1.—Every person who acts as an agent, in any State, of a dealer residing outside that State and buys, sells, supplies, or distributes, goods in the State or acts on behalf of such dealer as—

(i) a mercantile agent as defined in the Sale of Goods Act, 1930, or

(ii) an agent for handling of goods or documents of title relating to goods, or

(iii) an agent for the collection or the payment of the sale price of goods or as a guarantor for such collection or payment,

and every local branch or office in a State of a firm registered outside that State or a company or other body corporate, the principal office or head-quarters whereof is outside that State, shall be deemed to be a dealer for the purposes of this Act.

Explanation 2.—A Government which, whether or not in the course of business, buys, sells, supplies or distributes, goods, directly or otherwise, for cash or for deferred payment or for commission, remuneration or other valuable consideration, shall, except in relation to any sale, supply or distribution of surplus, un-serviceable or old stores or materials or waste products or obsolete or discarded machinery or parts or accessories thereof, be deemed to be a dealer for the purposes of this Act. [Central Sales Tax (74 of 1956), S. 2(b), *Expln.* 1 and 2]

"DEALER" any person who carries on the business of buying and selling any captive animal, animal article, trophy, uncured trophy or meat or specified plant. [Wild Life Protection Act (53 of 1972), S. 2(11)]

"DEALER" in relation to any captive animal, animal article, trophy, uncured trophy, meat or specified plant, means a person, who carries on the business of buying or selling any such animal or article, and includes a person who undertakes business in any single transaction. [Wild Life (Protection) Act (53 of 1972), S. 2(11), (as amended)]

"DEALER", in relation to any weight or measure, means a person who, or a firm or a Hindu undivided family which, carries on, directly or otherwise, the business of buying, selling, supplying or distributing any weight or measure, whether for cash or for deferred payment or for commission, remuneration or other valuable consideration, and includes—

(i) a commission agent who carries on such business on behalf of any principal,

(ii) an importer who sells, supplies, distribute or otherwise delivers any weight or measure to any user, manufacturer, repairer, consumer or any other person,

but does not include a manufacturer who sells, supplied, distributes or otherwise delivers any weight or measure to any person or category of persons referred to in this clause.

Explanation.—For the removal of doubts, it is hereby declared that a manufacturer, who sells, supplies, distributes or otherwise delivers any weight or measure to any person other than a dealer, shall be deemed to be a dealer. [Standards of Weights and Measures Act (60 of 1976), S. 2(c)]

"DEALER", in relation to any dangerous machine or any part thereof, means a person who, or a firm or a Hindu undivided family which, carries on, directly or otherwise, the business of buying, selling, supplying or distributing any dangerous machine or any part thereof, whether for cash or for deferred payment or for commission, remuneration or other valuable consideration and includes—

(i) a commission agent who carries on such business on behalf of any principal;

(ii) an importer who sells, supplies, distributes or otherwise delivers any dangerous machine to any user, manufacturer, repairer, consumer or any other person, but does not include a manufacturer who sells, supplies, distributes or otherwise delivers any dangerous machine or any part thereof to any person or category of persons referred to in this clause. [Dangerous Machines (Regulation) Act (35 of 1983), S. 3(e)]

DEALER includes a person who is engaged—(a) in the manufacture of motor vehicles, [Sub-clause (a) omitted by Motor Vehicles Amendment Act, 1994] or (b) in building bodies for attachment to chassis; or (c) in the repair of motor vehicles; or (d) in the business of hypothecation, leasing or hire-purchase of motor vehicle. [Motor Vehicles Act (59 of 1988), S. 2(8)]

"DEALER" means a person who sells and receives lead acid batteries or components thereof to and from the consumers or other dealers or retailers on behalf of the manufacturers, importers, assemblers and re-conditioner or to otherwise. [Batteries (Management and Handling) Rules, 2001, R. 3(i)]

DEALER means any person who carries on the business of buying or selling or supplying goods in the state, whether on commission or for remuneration or otherwise, and includes the Central Government, a State Government or any of their departments in respect of any such business, a Hindu undivided family, and a society, club or any other association which buys goods from or sells or supplies goods, to its members;

Expln. Where a dealer who resides outside the State carries on the business of buying, selling, or supplying goods in the State through a manager or agent, the manager or agent shall, in respect of such business, be deemed to be a dealer for the purposes of this Act. [Rajasthan Sales Tax Act (24 of 1954), S. 2(f)]

'DEALER' means any person engaged in the business of purchase, movement, sale, supply, distribution or storage for sale of any scheduled article directly or otherwise including (i) casual traders (ii) commission agents (iii) brokers or auctioneers or any other mercantile agent engaged in such business and also persons engaged in house boiling to process paddy but does not include a person who stores for sale of paddy or rice or any other scheduled article in village or town as the case may be, produced by personal cultivation on land owned by him or held on lease. [Tamil Nadu Scheduled Article (Prescription of Standards) Order, 1977, S. 2(c) issued under S. 3 of E.C. Act (10 of 1955)]

'DEALER' means any person engaged in the business of purchase, movement, sale, supply, distribution or storage for sale of any essential trade article directly or otherwise including casual trader engaged in such business and also includes person engaged in house boiling to process paddy but does not include a bulk consumer or a person who stores for sale of essential trade articles in a village or town, as the case may be, produced by personal cultivation on land owned by him or held on lease. [T.N. Essential Trade Articles (Regulation of Trade) Order, 1984, cl. 2(i)]

One who deals in merchandise; a trader [Rubber Act (24 of 1947), S. 3(b)]; [Central Sales Tax Act (74 of 1956), S. 2(b)].

If a person carries on a business with a profit motive, whether profit is actually earned or not, he will be a dealer. *Govt. Medical Depot* v. *Supdt. of Taxes, Gauhati*, AIR 1985 SC 1748, 1751.

The sugar factories which bought sugarcane could be said to carry on the business of buying and selling sugarcane and the factories are dealers. *Salar Jung Sugar Mills Ltd.* v. *State of Mysore*, AIR 1972 SC 87, 101.

Disposal of the unclaimed goods by the railway can be regarded as necessarily incidential or ancillary to its business as carrier of the goods and so railway is a dealer. *Member, Board of Revenue, West Bengal.* v. *Controller of Stores, Eastern Railway*, AIR 1989 SC 1468, 1470. [Bengal Finance (Sales Tax) Act (6 of 1941), S. 2(c)]

The word 'dealer' under Section 2(c) of the Act includes all types of agents. *State of West Bengal* v. *O.P. Lodha,* (1997) 5 SCC 93, para 10 : AIR 1997 SC 2021. [Bengal Finance (Sales Tax) Act (6 of 1941), S. 2(c)]

The term 'dealer' under Section 2(c) of the Act includes the 'Collector of Customs' when he sold goods confiscated under the provisions of Customs Act, 1962 because of non-payment of customs duty thereon. *Collector of Customs* v. *State of West Bengal,* (1999) 1 SCC 192, para 1. [Bengal Finance (Sales Tax) Act (6 of 1941), S. 2(c)]

A co-operative Agriculture Service Society registered under Punjab Co-operative Societies Act, 1961, purchases fertiliser and supplies the same to its members on no-profit-no-loss basis under its bye-laws and is not involved in any business activity, hence it is not a dealer under cl. 2(f) of the Order. *State of Punjab* v. *Guno Majra Cooperative Agriculture Service Society Ltd.,* (2000) 9 SCC 210, para 3. [Fertiliser (Control) Order, 1985, cl. 2(f)]

"DEALER" A 'dealer' may be any person, whether he sells commodities to the general public or not. It is only the exception, which provides that an oil company storing its goods in its storage depot or installation wherefrom no sales are made to the general public shall not be a 'dealer'. The terms 'dealer' and 'distributor' can be used interchangeably. *Holani Auto Links Pvt. Ltd.* v. *State of M. P.*, AIR 2009 SC (Supp) 796.

"DISTRIBUTOR" The terms 'dealer' and 'distributor' can be used interchangeably. *Holani Auto Links Pvt. Ltd.* v. *State of M. P.*, AIR 2009 SC (Supp) 796.

'Dealer' and 'Merchant'. Distinguished. In *Kansas City* v. *Ferd Heim Brewing Co.*, 98 Mo. App. 590, 594 : 73 SW 302, the Court in construing the term 'merchant' as used in a city charter and in a statute said: 'It does not follow that because a merchant is a dealer, a dealer is also a merchant. A merchant must have a store, stand, or other place where he sells his goods. A dealer need not have such store, stand, or place to keep and sell his goods. He may buy and sell without such aids to his business. A merchant is not required to be a purchaser; but the dealer, at common law, is both a buyer and seller.'

'Dealer' and 'Trader'. In *State* v. *Barnes*, 126 NC 1063, 1064 : 35 SE 605, it is said:—'Our Revenue Acts appear to have used the words '*dealer*' and '*trader*' as synonymous.' *See also* 33 Am. Rep. 694.

Dealing with offences. The expression 'dealing with offences' is of wide import and will include any act which the police has to do in connection with the offences under the Act. *Delhi Administration* v. *Ram Singh*, AIR 1962 SC 63, 66. [Suppression of Immoral Traffic in Women and Girls Act (104 of 1956), S. 13]

Dean. A *Dean* is an ecclesiastical dignitary next in rank to the bishop.

The head of one of the divisions, faculties, colleges or schools of a university.

Dearness allowance. The whole purpose of dearness allowance being to neutralise a portion of the increase in the cost of living, it should ordinarily be on a sliding scale, and provide for an increase on a rise in the cost of living and a decrease on a fall in the cost of living. *Hindustan Times Ltd.* v. *Workmen*, AIR 1963 SC 1333, 1338.

Death. "The word 'DEATH' denotes the death of a human being, unless the contrary appears from the context". [Indian Penal Code (45 of 1860), S. 46] [Now (w.e.f. 1-7-2024) repealed & replaced by Bharatiya Nyaya Sanhita, 2023 (45 of 2023)]

Death means the death of a human being unless the contrary appears from the context. [(w.e.f. 1-7-2024) Bharatiya Nyaya Sanhita, 2023 (45 of 2023), section 2(6)]

"DEATH" means the permanent disappearance of all evidence of life at any time after live-birth has taken place. [Registration of Births and Deaths Act (18 of 1969), S. 2(b)]

The act or fact of dying; the final cessation of vital functions of an animal or plant.

'DEATH' has been defined as the end or termination of life.

Death-bed. A state of serious illness; sickness which ends in death.

Death-bed or **Dying Declarations** are constantly admitted in evidence. 'The principle of this exception to the general rule is founded partly on the awful situation of the dying person, which is considered to be as powerful over his conscience as the obligation of an oath, and partly on a supposed absence of interest in a person on the verge of the next world, which dispenses with the necessity of cross-examination. But before such declarations can be admitted in evidence against a prisoner, it must be satisfactorily proved that the deceased, at the time of making them, was conscious of his danger, and had given up all hope of recovery, and this may be collected from the nature and circumstances of the case, although the declarant did not express such an apprehension. It is not essential that the party should apprehend immediate dissolution; it is sufficient if he apprehends it to be impending. Much consideration should be given to the state of the mind of the person whose declarations are received. (*Phil. Evid.; Starkie's Evid.; Taylor on Evidence*).

Death by accident. Death from any unexpected event which happens, as by chance, or which does not take place according to the usual course of things.

Death by negligence—Liability of the Doctor. Where the doctor is a qualified person and administers a drug which after due research and experiment is expected on all hands as the appropriate remedy and the drug is also administered with due precautions indicated in the science, and the patient dies on account of a surprising and unexpected personal idiosyncrasy, the doctor would not be liable of any criminal offence. *Jugam Khan* v. *State,* AIR 1963 MP 102, 105. [IPC (45 of 1860), Ss. 302, 300]

Death certificate. A certificate issued by a public official to verify that a person has died, with such information as the time of death, the cause of death, and the signature of the attending physician or examining physician.

"Such certificate is issued by the Registrar of Births and Deaths under Section 23 of the [Births and Deaths & Marriages Registration Act (6 of 1886)]."

Death duties. The expression '*Death duties'* is used as the most compendious term for describing the taxation levied on the estates of deceased persons, or on persons to whom benefits accrue by the death of other persons.

Death penalty. Death as punishment for a crime—called also capital punishment.

Death-rate. Yearly number of deaths to 1000 of population.

Death, Unnatural. Death under circumstances not natural [Cr PC (2 of 1974), S. 40(1)(d)].

Death-warrant. Magistrate's warrant for the execution of a criminal sentenced to capital punishment.

Deathsman. The executioner; hangman; he that executes the extreme penalty of the law. (*Black*)

Debar. To exclude from admission or right; to preclude from doing certain acts.

Debate. Fight for; contend; discuss (as) parliamentary debates.

A discussion.

Debauch. To seduce, spoil and violate a woman; to ravish, deflower; to pervert from virtue.

Debenture. "DEBENTURE" includes debenture stock, bonds and any other securities of a company, whether constituting a charge on the assets of the company or not. [Company Act (1 of 1956), S. 2(12)].

"DEBENTURE" includes:

(i) debenture stock, bonds or any other instrument of a company evidencing a debt, whether constituting a charge on the assets of the company or not;

(ii) bonds in the nature of debenture issued by any incorporated company or body corporate;

(iii) certificate of deposit, commercial usance bill, commercial paper and such other debt instrument of original or initial maturity upto one year as the Reserve Bank of India may specify from time to time;

(iv) securitised debt instruments; and

(v) any other debt instruments specified by the Securities and Exchange Board of India from time to time. [Indian Stamp Act (2 of 1899), section 2(10A)]

"DEBENTURE" includes debenture stock, bonds or any other instrument of the company evidencing a debt, whether constituting a charge on the assets of the company or not.

Provided that—

(a) the instruments referred to in Chapter III-D of the Reserve Bank of India Act, 1934 (2 of 1934); and

(b) such other instrument, as may be prescribed by the Central Government in consultation with the Reserve Bank of India, issued by a company,

shall not be treated as debenture. [[Companies Act (18 of 2013), s. 2(30)].

A document or certificate signed by the officer of a corporation, or company acknowledging indebtedness for money lent and guaranteeing repayment with interest. [T.P. Act (4 of 1882), S. 137]

No precise definition of the word 'debenture' can be found, but various forms of instruments are called debentures. A debenture is a document which either creates or acknowledges a debt. A document may be a debenture although under its terms the debt is only to be repaid out of a part of the profits. The term 'debenture' is usually associated with a company of some kind, and most debentures are securities given by companies, but they are often granted by clubs and occasionally by individuals. HALSBURY, 4th Edn., Vol. 7, para 813, p. 482.

Debenture bonds. Bonds of a company engaging to repay a specified borrowed sum, with interest.

Debenture-holders' action. An action which is brought about by a debenture-holder on behalf of himself and all other debenture-holders of the same class to enforce their right under the debentures.

Debenture stock. A stock or fund representing money borrowed by a company or public body and charged on the whole of its property. It differs from debenture bonds in that it is usually irredeemable. The principal sum is registered in the owner's name, and the interest, which takes priority over dividends, is paid by warrant or coupons to the owner on owner's order.

Debenture stock is generally constituted and secured by a trust deed containing a charge upon the property of the company. A stock certificate is issued to each person, being an allottee or transferee to the stock, stating, *inter alia,* in the case of a registered stock, that the person named therein is the registered proprietor, or, in the case of bearer stock, that the bearer thereof is the proprietor of the amount of stock therein mentioned, and having printed therein the conditions on which the stock is issued and held. HALSBURY, 4th Edn., Vol. 7, para 823, p. 489.

Debenture is the form of a stock, the nominal capital of which represents a debt of which only the interest is secured by a perpetual annuity. [CPC (5 of 1908), S. 2(19)].

Debenture trust deed. A deed charging specific property of a company by a legal mortgage or legal charge in favour of trustees for the debenture-holders and charging the rest of the assets of the company by a floating charge.

Debet esse finis litium. (*Maxim*) There ought to be an end of law suits.

Debet quis juris subjacere ubi delinquit. (*Maxim*) Every one ought to be subjected to the law of the place where he offends.

Debet sua cuique domus esse perfugium tutissimum. (*Maxim*) Every man's house should be a perfectly safe refuge.

Debit. The left hand page of a ledger, to which all items are carried that are charged to an account; that which is charged as due or owing.

The amount debited against one; to charge as a debt against. [T.P. Act. (4 of 1882), S. 76(i)].

Debit against. To charge as a debt against. [T.P. Act (4 of 1882), S. 76(h)].

Debit card. A card used to pay for purchases by electronic transfer from the bank account of the purchaser.

Debitor non praesumitur donare. (*Lat.*) A debtor is not presumed to make gift..

Debitorum pactionibus creditorum petitio nec tolli nec minui potest. (*Maxim*) The rights of creditors can neither be taken away nor diminished by agreements among the debtors.

Debitum connexium. (*Lat.*) A debt which gives rise to a lien.

Debitum in praesenti, solvendum in futuro. (*Lat.*) A debt due at present to be paid in future.

Debt. "DEBT" includes any liability in respect of any obligation to repay capital sums by way of annuity and any liability under any guarantee, and "debt charges" shall be construed accordingly. [Constitution of India, Art. 266 (8)]

"DEBT" means any pecuniary, liability, whether payable presently or in future, or under a decree or order of a Civil or Revenue Court or otherwise, or whether ascertained or to be ascertained, which—

(a) in the case of displaced person who has left or been displaced from his place of residence in any area now forming part of West Pakistan, was incurred before he came to reside in any area now forming part of India;

(b) in the case of a displaced person who, before and after the 15th day of August, 1947, has been residing in any area now forming part of India, was incurred before the said date on the security of any immovable property situate in the territories now forming part of West Pakistan :

Provided that where any such liability was incurred on the security of immovable properties situate both in India and in West Pakistan, the liability shall be so apportioned between the said properties that the liability in relation to each of the said properties bears the same proportion to the total amount of the debts as the value of each of the properties as at the date of the transaction bears to the total value of the properties furnished as security, and the liability, for the purposes of this clause, shall be the liability which is relatable to the property in West Pakistan;

(c) is due to a displaced person from any other person (whether a displaced person or not) ordinarily residing in the territories to which this Act extends and includes;

any pecuniary liability incurred before the commencement of this Act by any such person as is referred to in this clause which is based on, and is solely by way of renewal of, any such liability as is referred to in sub-clause (a) or sub-clause (b) or sub-clause (c):

Provided that in the case of a loan, whether in cash or in kind, the amount originally advanced and not the amount for which the liability has been renewed shall be deemed to be the extent of the liability;

but does not include any pecuniary liability due under a decree passed after the 15th day of August, 1947 by any Court situate in West Pakistan or any pecuniary liability the proof of which depends merely on an oral agreement. [Displaced Persons (Debts Adjustment) Act (10 of 1951), S. 2(6)]

"DEBT" means any liability (inclusive of interest) which is claimed as due from any person or a pooled investment vehicle as defined in clause (da) of section 2 of the Securities Contracts (Regulation) Act, 1956 (42 of 1956) by a bank or a financial institution or by a consortium of banks or financial institutions during the course of any business activity undertaken by the bank of the financial institution or the consortium under any law for the time being in force, in cash or otherwise, whether secured or unsecured, or assigned, or whether payable under a decree or order of any civil Court or any arbitration award or otherwise or under a mortgage and subsisting on, and legally recoverable on, the date of the application and includes any liability towards debt securities which remains unpaid in full or part after notice of ninety days served upon the borrower by the debenture trustee or any other authority in whose favour security interest is created for the benefit of holders of debt securities. [Recovery of Debt Due to Banks and Financial Institution Act (51 of 1993), S. 2(g)]

A sum of money due under an express or implied agreement (as) a bond or bill or note; amount due or payable from one person to another in return for money, services, goods, or other obligation.

Debt comes into existence in the cases of accrued rent not paid to the landlord and pecuniary liability quantified or capable of quantification on the basis of admitted contract or principles embodied in law. *Dwarka Das Agarwal* v. *Dharam Chand Jain,* AIR 1954 Cal 583, 586. [Indian Contract Act (9 of 1872), S. 59]

Section 73 of the Indian Contract Act (9 of 1872) expressly provides that as soon as a breach of contract occurs, a liability to pay many compensation arises, and that the liability can only be described as pecuniary. It is therefore, a debt within the meaning of S. 2(6) of the Displaced Persons (Debts Adjustment) Act (70 of 1951). The case is exactly similar when the breach is not of a contract, strictly speaking, but of any obligation resembling a contract like a pledge. *Ram Lal Jain* v. *Central Bank of India,* AIR 1961 Punj 340, 352 (FB). [Indian Contract Act (9 of 1872), S. 73].

'Debt' could be defined as a liability to pay in present or in future unascertainable sum of money. On a deposit being made, the depositee, incurs a liability although the time for repayment would come only when a demand is made. *Ramanathan Chettiar* v. *Ramanathan Chettiar*, AIR 1968 SC 1047, 1049.

Claim against Insurance Company, the exact amount of which has yet to be ascertained, includes in the term 'debt'. *S.G. Insurance Co.* v. *Lala Bahali,* AIR 1966 All 385, 392. [Displaced Persons (Debts Adjustment) Act (10 of 1951), S. 2(6)]

'Debt' means a certain sum due from one person to another either by record under a speciality or deed or under simple contract by writing or oral. *Commissioner Wealth Tax* v. *Ahmad Tea Co.,* AIR 1967 Ass 63, 65. [Wealth Tax Act (27 of 1957), S. 2(m)]

Consideration which remains unpaid in respect of assets purchased by assessee from another company is a 'debt' due from assessee. *Commissioner of Wealth Tax, Madras*. v. *Spencer & Co. Ltd.*, AIR 1973 SC 2376, 2377.

Debt and Loan Distinguished**.** A *debt* is something quite different from a *loan.* A *loan* contracted creates a *debt,* but there may be a *debt* created without contracting a *loan*. A *debt* may be contracted without resorting to a *loan*.

Debt-equity ratio. The proportion of debt to equity, often expressed as a percentage. The higher this ratio, the greater the financial leverage of the firm. Also called as D:E ratio.

In its simplest terms, a company's total liabilities (long-term debt) divided by its total equities. It gives an indication of a company's *gearing*.

Debt-equity swap. A method by which a lender (such as a bank) disposes of a loan to a Third World country by converting it into a holding of equity in a company in that country. Venture capital may also be provided in exchange for equity in the company being financed. (*Investment*)

Debt instrument. A written promise to repay a debt, like promissory note, bill, bond and commercial paper.

Debt is property. That a debt is property is clear. It is a chose in action and is heritable and assignable and is treated as property under the Transfer of Property Act (4 of 1882) which calls it an actionable claim. *R.K. Dalmia* v. *Delhi Administration*, AIR 1962 SC 1821, 1834. [IPC (45 of 1860), Ss. 405, 409]

Debt owed. The words 'debts owed' mean ascertained or certain amount which is opposed to inchoate, contingent, future, unascertained, uncertain or imperfect obligetions.

Tax paid under S. 68 of the Finance Act should be treated as a 'debt owed' for purposes of determining net wealth as defined in Section 2 (m) of the Act. *Ahmed Ibrahim* v. *Wealth Tax Commissioner, Gujarat*, AIR 1981 SC 1562, 1570. [Wealth Tax Act (27 of 1957), S. 2(m)]

A certain sum set apart by the assessee for its tax liability less the amount of the last instalment of advance tax constitutes a debt owed by the assessee. *B. Sanjamma* v. *State of Andhra Pradesh*, AIR 1977 SC 784, 785.

Debt payable. The term 'payable' has two meanings (1) owing and (2) payable at a particular point of time, and when this expression is used without any qualification it generally means payable at once.

Debt pooling. An arrangement by which the debts of a person are consolidated and creditor's agree to accept lower monthly payments or to take less money.

Debt ratio. A total long-term and short-term liabilities of a corporation divided by the firm's total assets.

Debt securities. Means debt securities listed in accordance with regulations made by the Securities Exchange Board of India under the Securities and Exchange Board of India Act, 1992 (15 of 1992). [Recovery of Debts & Bankruptcy Act, 1993 (51 of 1993), section 2(ga)]

A security representing a loan by an investor to an issuer such as corporation, municipality, the federal government or a federal agency. In return for the loan, the issuer promises to repay the debt on a specified date and with interest. [*ML Tannan Banking Law & Practice in India*, 2021, LexisNexis, Dictionary of Banking Terminology].

Debt service. Payments of principal and interest on a loan. The amount of interest and principal payments due annually on long-term debt.

Debtor. One who owes a debt. The word debtor is used in a wide sense and would include a judgment-debtor.

'DEBTOR' means a person who is :

(i) a landless agricultural labourer; or

(ii) a person belonging to the weaker section of the people; or

(iii) a small farmer;

and from whom a debt is due. [Karnataka Debt Relief Act (29 of 1980), S. 2(6)()]

'DEBTOR' means any person from whom any debt is due. [Tamil Nadu Debt Relief Act (40 of 1979), S. 3(3)]

"DEBTOR" means any person liable to the assignor, whether under a contract or otherwise, to pay any receivable or discharge any obligation in respect of the receivable whether existing, accruing, future, conditional or contingent. [S. 2(h) of the Factoring Regulation Act, 2011 (12 of 2012)]

Debts provable. The expression 'debts provable' in the Act, means the debts whose proof are offered with a view to entitle the creditors to be included in the Schedule with a view of their participating in the assets of the insolvent and not the proof for any other purpose. *Yersamilli Radraraju* v. *Yavanamanda Suryanarayana Raju,* AIR 1960 AP 257, 258. [Provincial Insolvency Act (5 of 1920), Ss. 33, 34, 62(1)(a)] [Now repealed by Act 31 of 2016]

Decay, Subject to natural. Liable to deterioration which takes place in accordance with the ordinary course of nature. [CrPC 1973 (2 of 1974), S. 85(2)].

Deceased. Departed from life; dead.

A person who is dead [Estate Duty Act (34 of 1953), S. 2(6)]; dead [CPC (5 of 1908),S. 2(11)].

Deceased ancestor. An ancestor who is dead. [CPC (5 of 1908), S. 53].

Deceased partner. A partner who is dead. [Indian Partnership Act (9 of 1932), S. 28(2)].

Deceased person. "DECEASED PERSON" means a person in whom permanent disappearance of all evidence of life occurs, by reason of brain-stem death or in a cardio-pulmonary sense, at any time after live birth has taken place. [Transplantation of Human Organs Act (42 of 1994), S. 2(e)]

A person who is no more, who is dead and gone. [Estate Duty Act (34 of 1953), S. 2(6)].

Decedent. A deceased person. Decedent means a deceased person, that is, one dead; departed from this life, Hence one, though civilly dead, by reason of imprisonment for life, is not a decedent. The word 'decedent' means either a testator or a person dying intestate.

Deceit. Fraud; false representation made with intent to deceive.

'Deceit' is a false statement of a fact made by a person knowingly or recklessly with intent that it shall be acted upon by another who does act upon it and thereby suffers damage.

(1) The act of intentionally giving a false impression (the juror's deceit led the lawyer to believe that she was not biased). (2) A false statement of fact made by a person knowingly or recklessly (i.e. not caring whether it is true or false) with the intent that someone else will act upon it. Black's Law Dictionary (8th Edn.) as cited in *Ram Chandra Bhagat* v. *State of Jharkhand*, (2013) 1 SCC 562, para 4.

"Deceit", deceptio, fraus, dolus, is a subtle, wily shift or device, having no other name; hereto may be drawn all manner of craft, subtilly, guile, fraud, wilinesse, slight, cunning, covin, collusion, practice, and offence used to deceive another man by any means, which hath none other proper or particular name but offence'." Stroud's Judicial Dictionary (5th Edn.) as cited in *Ram Chandra Bhagat* v. *State of Jharkhand*, (2013) 1 SCC 562, para.

Any device or false representation by which one man misleads another to the injury of the latter. Deceit is a false statement of fact made by a person knowingly or recklessly with intent that it shall be acted upon by another who does act upon it and thereby suffers an injury. It is always a personal act and is intermediate when compared with fraud. Deceit is a sort of a trick or contrivance to defraud another. It is an attempt to deceive and includes any declaration that misleads another or causes him to believe what is false. [*Ram Chandra Bhagat* v. *State of Jharkhand*, (2013) 1 SCC 562, para 6].

Deceitful means. In Section 362 of the IPC (45 of 1860) is wide enough to include the inducing of a girl to leave her guardian's house by means of a representation that the person to whom, she went would either marry her himself or arrange for her marriage and that the accused was guilty of the offence of abduction. *Ramjilal* v. *State,* AIR 1951 Raj 33.

Deceive. To cause to believe what is false; to lead into error; to delude; to mislead; to defraud. [Indian Contract Act (9 of 1872), S. 17(1)]; [IPC (45 of 1860), S. 415].

Deceiver. One who deceives or practices deception upon another.

Decency. The recognized code of social propriety; opposite of indecency.

Propriety of demeanour; due regard to what is becoming. [Customs Act (52 of 1962), S. 11(2)(b)]; [Constitution of India, Art. 19(2)].

Decency and morality. The expressions "decency and morality" themselves are wide and variable contents. They are not static and are bound to change from place to place, from time to time, from people to people, and from age to age. The Courts concern and anxiety would be only to prevent the exhibition at public places of performances, which are immodest and indecent judged by the standards of our comity and of our time. [*K.P. Mohamed* v. *State of Kerala,* MLJ : Digest (1984), p. 491 : 1984 CrLJ 745]. [IPC (XLV of 1860), S. 294]

Deception. Act of deceiving or misleading.

The action of deceiving or cheating; that which deceives. [IPC (45 of 1860), S. 415, *Expln.*].

A dishonest concealment of facts is a DECEPTION within the meaning of this section. [(w.e.f. 1-7-2024) Bharatiya Nyaya Sanhita, 2023 (45 of 2023), section 318(1), *Explanation*]

Deceptis non decipientibus, jura subveniunt. (*Lat.*) The laws help persons who are deceived, not those deceiving.

Deceptive advertising. False and misleading advertising. Advertisement which contains any assertion, representation or statement of fact which is untrue or misleading. Where the public are not cautious or watchful in their buying habits and are likely to be misled, the legislature may require not only the absence of active deception in advertising, but also affirmative measures to prevent misunderstanding.

Deceptive marks. Marks that falsely connect a product with persons, institutions, or national symbols. (*Cyber Law*)

Deceptive resemblance. There will be deceptive resemblance of a trade mark if a trade mark is likely to deceive or cause confusion by its resemblance to another already on the Register of Trade Marks, if it is likely to do so in the course of its legitimate use in a market where the two marks are assumed to be in use by traders in that market. *Amritdhara Pharmacy* v. *Satya Deo*, AIR 1963 SC 449, 453.

Deceptive sales practices. The Federal Trade Commission and statutes in most states make deceptive sales practices unlawful. Historically, an act was deceptive if it had any tendency to deceive a non trival number of customers. A more recent reformulation of the test defines a deceptive act as one which is likely to deceive a consumer acting reasonable in the circumstances. See. *e.g.* Mass. G.L. C 93A, 21 (1) : 15 USCA 45 (a) (1).

Descriptive word. A term that portrays a general characteristic or function of a product or service. A descriptive word may not be registered as a trademark unless it has acquired secondary meaning in the minds of consumers so that it is directly associated with one brand.

Deceptively misdescriptive. A mark that makes a false inference about an important matter, such as the product's geographic origin.

Deceptively similar. A geographical indication shall be deemed to be "DECEPTIVELY SIMILAR" to another geographical indication if it so nearly resembles that other geographical indication as to be likely to deceive or cause confusion. [Geographical Indications of Goods (Registration and Protection) Act (48 of 1999), S. 2(1)(c)]

A mark shall be deemed to be DECEPTIVELY SIMILAR to another mark if it so nearly resembles that other mark as to be likely to deceive or cause confusion. [Trade and Merchandise Marks Act (43 of 1958), S. 2(d) and Trade Marks Act (47 of 1999), S. 2(1)(h)]

The expression 'deceptively similar', in S. 2(d) means that the similarity or resemblance must be such as it would be likely to deceive or cause confusion. *A.V. Rajadurai Nadar* v. *P. Ayya Nadar,* AIR 1977 Mad 237, 238. [Trade and Merchandise Marks Act (43 of 1958), S. 2(d)]

Decibel. A unit in which noise is measured. [Environment (Protection) Rules, 1986, Sch I, Sl. No. 111, Definitions (c)].

Decide. To determine (a question, controversy or cause); to form a definite opinion; to render judgment; to give judgment for or against a party to suit or other proceeding in Court.

Decide the suit forthwith. The words, '*decide the suit forthwith,*' in O. XVII, R. 3(a) of CPC (5 of 1908) pre-suppose and imply the presence before the Court of materials of some kind on which to base its decision. It is not the mere equivalent, in the case of a plaintiff who has adduced no evidence, of a *dismissal of the suit*.

Decided. Determined; ended; concluded; rendered judgment.

Decimal system. A system of calculation by tens, proceeding by tens. In Mathematics it is based on a unit of 10, and for purposes of calculation is much simpler than the English system. It is adopted in France and other European countries.

Decision. A word which has been used as signifying the judgment of the Court; a judgment given by a competent tribunal; the findings of fact; the finding by the Court upon which a decree or judgment may be entered; the result of the deliberations of a tribunal. The refusal of the judge to do a '*ministerial act*' can hardly, with propriety, be called a 'ruling' or 'decision.'

"Decision" means "a determination arrived at after consideration of facts, and, in legal context, law". [Black's Law Dictionary as cited in Natural Resources Allocation, In re, Special Reference No. 1 of 2012, (2012) 10 SCC 1, para 44].

"Decision : opinion". "Decision is not necessarily synonymous with 'opinion'. A decision of the court is its judgment; the opinion is the reasons given for that judgment, or the expression of the views of the Judge." [Black's Law Dictionary as cited in *Natural Resources Allocation, In Re, Special Reference No. 1 of 2012*, (2012) 10 SCC 1, para 44].

The decision under this rule means decision on merits.

The word 'decision' is equivalent to the word 'decree'. In other words, the word 'decision' embraces the final determination of the Court on all the claims put forward in controversy between the parties in a suit or a proceeding. *Kanhk Sunder Bibi* v. *Ram Lakhan Pandey,* AIR 1956 Pat 325, 328 (FB). [Constitution of India, Art. 133 (1)]

The word 'decision' should mean not a part of the decision or the grounds given for it but the decision of the suit as a whole. *T. Rajaram* v. *Radhakrishnayya*, AIR 1961 SC 1795, 1799. [Constitution of India, Art. 133(1)]

The term 'decision' implies the exercise of a judicial determination as the final and definite result of examining a question and as such an order granting extension of time is not a 'decision'. *Ratan & Co.* v. *P. Narayanan,* AIR 1977 Del 93, 96. [Trade and Merchandise Marks Act (43 of 1958), Ss. 91 and 97(c)]

The action of deciding a contest, question *etc.*; determination of a judgment. [IPC (45 of 1860), S. 21, sixthly].

A 'decision' does not merely mean the 'conclusion'. It embraces within it's fold the reasons which form the basis for arriving at the conclusions. *Mukhtiar Singh* v. *State of Punjab*, AIR 1995 SC 686, 690. [CrPC 1973 (2 of 1974), S. 354(1)(b)]

Decision being 'contrary to law'. Where the finding of a judge is based mainly upon evidence which is explicitly referred to and avowedly reproduced in the judgment but is not to be found anywhere in the record, this circumstance vitiates the decision and renders it 'contrary to law' within S. 100, CPC (5 of 1908).

Decision instruction. An instruction whose action depends upon the conditions it finds existing when it is executed. A "Branch on 0" instruction, for example, will branch if it finds that the accumulator contents are 0 but will not branch if they are not 0. (*Computer*)

Decision or order. The expression 'any decision or order' is of wide amplitude and would include all orders or decisions passed by the Company Law Board. The expression is wide enough to include Interlocutory orders passed by the Board. *M.S. Naina* v. *C.C.,* 1975 Tax LR 1351 (Cal). [Companies Act (1 of 1956), S. 10-F]

Decision upon the merits. Is a decision upon the justice of the cause as opposed to one upon technical grounds only.

Decisive oath. An oath upon which the cause rested where a party elected to leave the issue to the oath of his adversary.

Deck, Weather. A deck having no overhead protection from the weather. [Merchant Shipping Act (44 of 1958), S. 3(47B)].

Declarant. In these regulations, unless the context otherwise requires;—

"DECLARANT" means—

(i) the person in-charge of the conveyance in which the goods are imported, or his agent, or

(ii) the person authorised to tranship the goods by the exporter of the goods or by an agent acting on behalf of such exporter. [Goods Imported (Conditions of Transhipment) Regulations, 1995, R. 2(b)]

One who makes an evidentiary declaration. One who makes declaration.

A person who files declaration under section 4. [Direct Tax Vivad se Vishwas Act, 2020 (3 of 2020), section 2(1)(c)]

Declaration. "A declaration which is inadmissible merely upon the ground of some informality, is a declaration within the meaning of Sections 199 and 200." [IPC (45 of 1860), S. 200, *Expln.*]

"Declaration"' means the instrument to be executed and got registered in the prescribed form and includes the amended declaration [Haryana Apartment Ownership Act (10 of 1983), s. 3(j) as cited in *DLF Limited* v. *Manmohan Law*, (2014) 12 SCC 231, para 29,].

A formal announcement; a deliberate statement.

The order of the District Court acknowledging a person as the guardian of a minor is a declaration of such guardianship within the meaning of S. 7 of the Guardians and Wards Act (8 of 1890).

The act of declaring; something which is declared [Oaths Act (44 of 1969), S. 2]; a statement made.

Declaration. Means the declaration filed under section 4. [Direct Tax Vivad se Vishwas Act, 2020 (3 of 2020), section 2(1)(d)]

Declaration/Declaratory relief. An order of a Court merely declaring the rights of a party to a particular property or under a particular contract.

Declaration of Maritime Labour Compliance. "Declaration of Maritime Labour Compliance" means a declaration issued by the Director General of Shipping or by any officer, authority or organisation authorised by him in this behalf, in respect of a ship that it meets with the requirements and standards set out in the provisions of the Maritime Labour Convention. [Merchant Shipping Act (44 of 1958), s. 88-A(a) as inserted by Amendment Act (32 of 2014)].

Declaration of Paris. A state paper agreed upon at the conclusion of the Crimean War, by the representatives of Great Britain, France, Austria, Russia, Sardinia, and Turkey, (Feb. 26, 1856), in which the following agreements on maritime law were come to:— (1) Privateering is abolished. (2) The neutral flag covers enemy's goods save contraband of war. (3) Neutral goods save contraband of war are not liable to capture under enemy's flag. (4) Blockades to be binding must be real. *See also* Letters of Marque and Paper Blockades.

Declaration of rights. A clause in the constitution specifically reserving certain rights to the people. (Found in the American Constitution).

Declaration of solvency. The statutory decalration made by the Directors of a company, and delivered to the Registrar of the companies, that they are of opinion that the company will be able to pay its debts in full within the stipulated time from the commencement of winding up.

Declaration of status or right. Any person entitled to any legal character, or to any right as to any property, may institute a suit against any person denying, or interested to deny, his title to such character or right, and the Court may in its discretion make therein a declaration that he is so entitled, and the plaintiff need not in such suit ask for any further relief :

Provided that no Court shall make any such declaration where the plaintiff, being able to seek further relief than a mere declaration of title, omits to do so.

Explanation.—A trustee of property is a 'person interested to deny' a title adverse to the title of someone who is not in existence, and for whom, if in existence, he would be a trustee. [Specific Relief Act (47 of 1963), S. 34]

Declaration, Dying. A statement by a person as to the cause of his death or as to any of the circumstances of the transaction which resulted in his death; this is a statement that comes within the scope of Section 32(1) of the Indian Evidence Act (1 of 1872).

Declaration of unconstitutionality. Declaration of unconstitutionality represents an aspect of want of legislative power. A mere reference to the provisions of Article 13(2), and Articles 245 and 246 is sufficient to indicate that there is no competency in Parliament or a State legislature to make a law which comes into clash with Part III of the Constitution after the coming into force of the Constitution. *Behram Khurshid* v. *Bombay State*, AIR 1955 SC 123, 145. [Constitution of India, Arts. 13(1), 245 & 246]

Declaration of use or trust. A statement or admission that property is to be held to the use of or upon trust for a certain person.

Declaration shall be made. The act of 'making declaration' by the appropriate Government that any particular land is needed for any public purpose, includes the act of making it known to public, in official manner as prescribed under Section 6(2). *Jagrup Singh* v. *State,* AIR 1993 Raj 157, 176. [Land Acquisition Act (1 of 1894), S. 6(2)] [Now repealed & replaced by Act 30 of 2013]

Declaratory. Explanatory; clear; designed to fix or elucidate what before was uncertain or doubtful. (*Black*)

Having the nature or form of declaration. [Ch. VI, heading, Specific Relief Act (47 of 1963)].

Declaratory Act. Act which, by profession at least, declares no new law, but only the formerly existing law, removing certain doubts which have arisen on the subject. (*Ame. Cyc.*)

Declaratory and **Remedial Acts.** (*Interpretation of Statutes*) A declaratory Act is an Act to remove doubts existing as to the common law, or the meaning or effect of any statute. Such Acts are usually held to be retrospective. A remedial Act, on the contrary, is not necessarily retrospective; it may be either enlarging or restraining and it takes effect prospectively, unless it has retrospective effect by express terms or necessary intendment. *Central Bank of India* v. *Workmen*, AIR 1960 SC 12, 27.

Declaratory decree. A decree which simply declares the rights of the parties or expresses the opinion of the Court on any question without ordering to be done. [Court Fees Act (7 of 1870), S. 7(iv)(c)].

Declaratory judgment. A judgment which simply declares the rights of the parties, or expresses the opinion of the Court on a question of law (or also of fact) without ordering anything to be done.

Declaratory law. One whereby the rights to be observed and the wrongs to be eschewed are clearly defined and laid down.

Declaratory part of a decree. That part of a decree which declares the rights of the parties, as distinct from recitals, *etc.*

Declaratory statute. Statutes which only lay down the law as previously existing.

Declare. Announce formally; reveal one's intention or contemplated action. To state; to assert; to publish; to announce clearly some opinion or resolution; to make known, to assert to others. In pleading, to set forth in a formal writing, the cause of action and claim which plaintiff alleges against defendant.

To make known; to state publicly, formally or in explicit terms. [Constitution of India, Art. 101(4)].

An instrument does not fall within the meaning of the word declare in S. 17(1)(*b*) of the Registration Act (16 of 1908) unless it effects a definite change of legal relation to the property. Where a minor on attaining majority ratifies a registered sale-deed of his property executed by his guardian, the document of ratification effects no change in the legal rights to the property the title to which passed at the date of the sale. All it does is to make clear that he does not intend to exercise his privilege of setting aside the sale. Such a declaration does not require registration.

The expression 'declared' is wider than the words 'found or made'. To declare is to announce opinion. *Golak Nath* v. *State of Punjab*, AIR 1967 SC 1643, 1669. [Constitution of India, Art. 141]

Declared perimeter. Means the external boundary of the facility declared pursuant to Articles III, IV, V and VI. [Chemical Weapons Convention Act (34 of 2000), (Verifications Annex.), S. 21(d)]

Decline. To refuse.

Decompilation. Analysis of a computer program, particularly for determining its structure, for making other programs which will operate with the decompiled program or systems which are associated with this. (*Copyright*)

Decoration. A star cross, medal or other badge conferred and worn as a mark of honour. [Army Act (46 of 1950), S. 54(d)].

Decortication. The act of removal of cortex. [Employees' State Insurance Act (34 of 1948), S. 2()].

Decoy witness. The word 'decoy" means to allure into a net, ensnare, entice, entrap, to lead into danger by artifice. This term is used to denote a person employed by law enforcing agencies to obtain evidence upon which criminal prosecution is based. A decoy witness, therefore, means a witness who is set up by some agency to lure or entice another person to commit a crime with a view to involve him in that crime by participating in that unlawful transaction in such manner that they almost become partners therein and after the commission of the unlawful act he gets him caught up and then becomes a prosecution witness to secure his conviction."

Decrease. Diminution; to diminish.

Decree. 'DECREE,' means the formal expression of an adjudication which, so far as regards the Court expressing it, conclusively determines the rights of the parties with regard to all or any of the matters in controversy in the suit and may be either preliminary or final. It shall be deemed to include the rejection of a plaint and the determination of any question within S. 144, but shall not include—(*a*) any adjudication from which an appeal lies as an appeal from an order, or (*b*) any order of dismissal for default.

Explanation.—A decree is *preliminary* when further proceedings have to be taken before the suit can be completely disposed of. It is *final* when such adjudication completely disposes of the suit. It may be partly preliminary and partly final. [CPC (5 of 1908), S. 2(2)]

The word 'the decree' mean the whole decree made in the suit. The word 'decree' must be deemed to include the judgment on which the decree is based. Decrees, as a rule, should not be drawn up on the model of a steel frame and it is always desirable that the Court, under its inherent powers and in order to give full effect to its decision, should frame its decree in such an elastic form as would define the respective rights and liabilities of the several parties to the suit and thus to do substantial justice between all those who are concerned with the result of litigation.

DECREE, TEST OF. Order must conclusively determine rights of parties.

DECREE CONTAINING SEVERAL ADJUDICATION. Each adjudication is a decree.

DECREE, JUDGMENT. A Decree is the final order of a Court in a suit. It closely resembles, but is not identical with 'Judgment.' 'The final decision' in a proceeding is termed a 'Decree'; the proceeding itself is usually styled a 'Cause,' or 'Suit.' (*Stroud*)

The word decree would include both preliminary and final decrees. *State of Punjab* v. *A.K. Raha,* AIR 1968 Cal 152, 153. [Constitution of India, Art. 133(1)(a)]

A decree means expression of adjudication, dismissing or allowing of a suit or petition or giving or refusing a relief. *S. Jagannadha Prasad* v. *S. Lalithakumari,* AIR 1989 AP 8, 11. [Hindu Marriage Act (25 of 1955), Ss. 25, 23-A]

Order refusing to grant a request for set off consequential to the order for sale is not appealable decree within meaning of Section 8. *Alli Ammal* v. *Natraja Mudaliar,* AIR 1972 Mad 195, 196. [Partition Act (4 of 1893), S. 8]

An order for possession passed on an application made under Section 41 of the Act is not a decree. *Nalinakhya* v. *Shyam Sunder*, AIR 1953 SC 148, 151. [Presidency Small Causes Courts Act (15 of 1882), S. 43]

To pass a decree.

Decree absolute. A final and conclusive decree, which finally dissolves the marriage.

Decree appealed from. The words 'decree appealed from' included a decree against which a person seeks leave to appeal. *Baldeo Prashad* v. *Dwarika Pd.,* AIR 1957 All 334, 335. [Limitation Act (36 of 1963), S. 12(2)]

Decree, appellate. A decree passed on an appeal. [CPC (5 of 1908), S. 108(a)].

Decree-holder. Holder of decree; any person in whose favour a decree has been passed or order capable of execution has been made. [CPC (5 of 1908), S. 2(3)]; holder of a decree.

Decree nisi. A decree to be made final unless a contingency happens.

Decree of affirmance. Any variation in the trial Courts decree whether in favour of the intended appellant or otherwise would not be relevant in determining whether the appellate decree is one of affirmance or not. *Management Committee T.G. Ghosh's Academy* v. *T.C. Palit*, AIR 1984 SC 1495, 1499. [Constitution of India, Art. 133]

Decree of nullity. A decree declaring (a marriage) null and void. [Hindu Marriage Act (25 of 1955), S. 11].

Decree to possession of such property. It means a decree for the immoveable property from which any person other than the judgment-debtor is dispossessed. The expression does not refer to a decree for the possession of any immovable property. *R.L. Mitra* v. *Minti Mazumdar,* AIR 1975 All 424, 425. [CPC (5 of 1908), O. XXI, R. 100]

Decretal order. An order in the nature of a decree; such an order as finally determines some right between the parties.

Decretum est sententia lata super legem. A decree is a sentence made upon the law.

Decriminatization. Legislation to legalize an illegal act.

Dedicated. If a property is set apart for a definite purpose, such property would become "dedicated" for that purpose. *U.P. Sunni Central Board of Wakf* v. *Mazhar Hassan,* 2001 (6) SCC 289.

Deduct. To take away; withhold; not to be taken into account; not to reckon.

To take away or subtract from a sum. [T.P. Act (4 of 1882), S. 76(d)].

Deduct and **Deduction.** The word 'deduct' means the right to subtract and/or take off the duty in the process of calculation of and arriving at the contract price. Deduction means the amount as will be equivalent to the decrease of duty or remitted duty. *Central Hindustan Italian Trading Co. (P.) Ltd.* v. *Pity Bros. Pvt. Ltd.,* AIR 1962 Bom 222, 223. [Sale of Goods Act (3 of 1930), S. 64-A(b)]

Deduction. Act of deducting; amount deducted; deducing; inference from the general to the particular.

An amount pertaining to wages which ought to have been paid and which has not been paid, amounts to a deduction from wages. *B.C. Mills* v. *S.D. Magistrate,* AIR 1965 Raj 11, 14. [Payment of Wages Act (4 of 1936) *(as amended by Act (58 of 1957), S. 15(2)*]

Deduction of wages. The expression defined as deductions for absence from duty which indicated that such deduction can be total deduction. Deduction from wages may be the same thing as deduction of wages. *Dilbagh Rai Jerry* v. *Union of India*, AIR 1974 SC 130, 134. [Payment of Wages Act (4 of 1936), S. 15(2), *Proviso*]

Deed. A written or printed document between parties able to contract under the hand (and sometimes also seal) of the obliger.

An instrument in writing (or other legible representation of words on parchment or paper) purporting to effect some legal disposition. [Indian Evidence Act (1 of 1872), S. 21, ill. (a)].

A deed is nothing more than an instrument or agreement under seal. *Nathu Lal* v. *Mussamat Gunti Kuar,* LR 67 IA 318 (PC); *Kaliana Gounder* v. *Palani Gounder,* AIR 1970 SC 1942. See also *Janab M.H.M. Yakoob* v. *M. Krishnan,* AIR 1992 Mad 80, 88.

DEED DISTINGUISHED FROM WILL. If the instrument passes a present interest, although the right to its possession and enjoyment may not occur till some future time, it is a deed or contract; but if the instrument does not pass an interest or right till the death of the maker, it is a will or testamentary paper.

Deed, estoppel by. 'Estoppel by deed' is a bar which precludes one party to a deed and his privies from asserting as against the other party and his privies any right or title in derogation of the deed or from denying the truth of any material facts asserted in it. (*Black*)

Deed of arrangement. A deed of assignment or composition, whereby a debtor conveys his property, to a trustee for realisation and distribution among his creditors on terms specified.

Deed of covenant. A deed whereby one party covenants or contracts with another to do certain things.

Deed of defeasance. A collateral deed, which is made at the same time with a conveyance, containing certain conditions, on the performance of which the estate then created may be defeated or totally undone.

Deed poll. Deed of one part or executed by one party only, instead of between parties and in two or more parts.

Deemed. To treat a thing as being something which it is not, or having certain qualities which it does not have.

The word 'deemed' is used in various senses. Sometimes it means 'generally regarded', at other time it signifies "taken *prima facie* to be," while in other cases it means "taken conclusively to be.' Its various meanings are—To deem is to hold in belief, estimation, or opinion; to judge; adjudge; decide; consider to be; to have or to be of an opinion; to esteem; to suppose; to think, decide or believe on consideration; to account; to regard; to adjudge or decide; to conclude upon consideration. (*Worcester*)

The words 'deem' and 'deemed' when used in a statute state the meaning which some matter or thing has the way in which it is to be adjudged.

A deeming provision might be made to include what is obvious or what is uncertain or to impose for the purpose of a statute an artificial construction of a word or phrase that would not otherwise prevail. *Consolidated Coffee Ltd.* v. *Coffee Board*, AIR 1980 SC 1468, 1479. [Central Sales Tax Act (74 of 1956), S. 5(3)]

The word 'deemed' makes it clear that a thing is not what, in the eye of law, it is supposed to be. [CPC (5 of 1908), O. XXXIII, R. 8]

The word 'deemed' includes the obvious, the uncertain and the impossible. *Mahendra* v. *Controller of Estate Duty,* AIR 1965 Guj 9, 20. [Estate Duty Act (34 of 1953), Ss. 23, 6 to 16]

The use of the word 'deemed' in the rule indicates that the Government has the power to make a retrospective declaration because it is only after promotion that there is any occasion to consider whether the period of officiation prior to promotion will be counted for purposes of seniority. *Ramprakash* v. *S.A.F. Abbas*, AIR 1972 SC 2350, 2355. [Indian Administrative Service (Regulation of Seniority) Rules (1954), Rule 3(3)(b)]

Deemed dealer. An assessee of an Equitable Coal Company is a 'deemed dealer'. *State of Rajasthan* v. *Karamchand Thappar & Bros.*, AIR 1965 SC 913.

Deemed dividend. Where a loan is advanced by the company to a registered shareholder and the other conditions set out in Section 2(6-A)(e) are satisfied that the amount of the loan would be liable to be regarded as 'deemed dividend'. The amount of loan would not fall within the mischief of Section 2(6-A)(e) if it is granted to a beneficial owner of the shares who is not the registered shareholder. *Rameshwari Lal Sanwarmal* v. *Commissioner of Income Tax, Assam,* AIR 1980 SC 372. [Income-Tax Act (43 of 1961), S. 2(6-A)(e)].

Deemed tenancy. Payment of land revenue to the Government without any notice or acquiescence of landlord is of no consequence. *Hanmanta Daulappa Nimbal* v. *Babasaheb Dajisaheb Londhe,* AIR 1996 SC 223 : (1995) 6 SCC 58. [Bombay Tenancy and Agricultural Land Act, 1948 (67 of 1948), S. 4]

Deemed to accrue. The term 'deemed' brings within the net of chargeability income not actually accruing but which is supposed notionally to have accrued. By statutory fiction income which can in no sense be said to accrue at all may be considered as so accruing. Similarly, the fiction may relate to the place or the person or be in respect of the year of taxability. *I.T. Commissioner* v. *Bhogilal Laherchand*, AIR 1954 SC 155, 157.

Deemed to arise out of and in the course of employment. An accident happening while an insured person is, with the express or implied permission of his employer, travelling as a passenger by any vehicle to or from his place of work shall, not withstanding that he is under no obligation to his employer to travel by that vehicle, be deemed to arise out of and in the course of his employment, if (a) the accident would have been deemed so to have arisen had he been under such obligation; and (b) at the time of the accident, the vehicle

(i) is being operated by or on behalf of his employer or some other person by whom it is provided in persuance of arrangements made with his employer, and

(ii) is not being operated in the ordinary course of public transport service.

[Employees' State Insurance Act (34 of 1948) S. 51C(1)]

Deemed to be. When a person is 'deemed to be' something, the only meaning possible is that whereas he is not in reality that something, the Act requires him to be treated as if he were. *Malchand Agarwal* v. *Samtolal Agarwalla*, AIR 1954 Assam 177.

When a thing is 'deemed to be' something, the only meaning possible is that whereas it is not in reality that something, the Act directs that it should be treated as if it were that thing. *Darbari Lal* v. *Dharam Wati*, AIR 1957 All 541, 545 (FB).

The phrase 'deemed to be' means 'not in reality'. *State of Maharashtra* v. *Laljit Rajshi Shah*, (2000) 2 SCC 699, para 6 : AIR 2000 SC 937.

No doubt the phrase 'deemed to be' is commonly used in statutes to extend the application of a provision of law to a class not otherwise amenable to it.

Deemed to be a public servant. Every member of the Press Council and every officer or other employee appointed by the Council shall be deemed to be a public servant within the meaning of Section 21 of the Indian Penal Code (45 of 1960). [Press Council of India Act (37 of 1978), S. 24]

Deemed to commence. The word "deemed" means supposed, considered, construed, thought, taken to be, or presumed. The words "shall be deemed to commence" in Section 441 of the Companies Act (1 of 1956), show the intention of the legislature that although the winding up of a petition does not, in fact, commence at the time of presentation of the petition itself, but it shall be presumed to commence from that stage. *Rishab Agro Industries Ltd.* v. *PNB Capital Services Ltd.,* (2000) 3 Comp LJ 1 p.a. (SC). [Companies Act (1 of 1956), S. 441]

Deemed to have been surrendered by such person. It is clear from the words "deemed to have been surrendered by such person" that something more remains to be done. *Sreelatha Bhupal* v. *Govt. of A.P.,* AIR 1990 SC 294. [A.P. Ceiling on Agricultural Holdings Act, 1961]

Deemed vacancy. Where a landlord does not occupy a building or substantially removes his effects therefrom, or allows a person not being a member of his family to occupy the building the vacancy is a deemed vacancy. *Girja Shankar* v. *Hirdey Ranjan*, AIR 1989 SC 151, 154.

Deeming. In *Habib & Sons* v. *Commissioner of Income-Tax*, AIR 1947 Bom 380 STONE C.J. observed : 'deeming' a past event or thing to be something other than what it was or is, may be an interference with the course of nature, since it creates artificial date in the place of existing fact. But it is not in my opinion a retrospective changing of the statute law'. *Gulab Chand* v. *Kudi Lal*, AIR 1951 MB 1, 8 (FB). (*Interpretation of Statutes*)

Deeming fiction. A supposition of law that a thing is true without inquiring whether it be so or not, that it may have the effect of truth so far as it is consistent with justice.

Deeming provision. A provision of law which makes a supposition.

The deeming provision is intended to enlarge the meaning of a particular word or to include matters which otherwise may or may not fall within the main provisions. *Doy Pack System (Pvt.) Ltd.* v. *Union of India,* 1988 (36) ELT 201 (SC).

When a person is "deemed to be" something, the only meaning possible is that whereas he is not in reality that something, the Act of Parliament requires him to be treated as if he were. *CIT* v. *Bombay Trust Corporation,* AIR 1930 PC 54, 55.

Deems fit. The words 'as he deems fit' do not bestow a power to make any order on consideration *de hors* the statute which the authorities consider best according to their notions of justice. *R.M. Paranjpe* v. *A.M. Mali*, AIR 1962 SC 753, 758.

"Deems it necessary" obviously means that the proper officer must have good reason to subject imported goods to a chemical or other tests. [*Tata Chemicals Limited* v. *Commissioner of Customs (Preventive), Jamnagar*, (2015) 11 SCC 628, para 14]

Deep Packet Inspection. Interception of online data from emails, internet phone calls, as well as images and messages on social networking sites, such as Facebook and Twitter. Every digitized packet of online data is intercepted, de-constructed, examined for keywords and then reconstructed within a few milliseconds. [Christopher Rhoads and Loretta Chao, 'Iran's Web Spying Aided by Western Technology: European Gear used in Vast Effort to Monitor Communications,' Wall Street Journal, June 22, 2009]

Deep stream. In relation to the river Ganga or the river Ghaghra, means the deep stream there of as verified and agreed upon by the State Governments of Bihar and Uttar Pradesh after the 30th day of September of the year preceding the year in which the appointed day falls and before the 1st day of January of the year in which the appointed day falls and in default of agreement between the State Governments, as determined by such authority as may be specified by the Central Government. [Bihar & U.P. (Alteration of Boundaries) Act (24 of 1968), S. 2(c)]

Deface. "DEFACE", with its grammatical variations and cognate expressions, including clipping, filling, stamping, or such other alteration of the surface or shape of a coin as is readily distinguishable from the effects of reasonable wear. [Coinage Act (3 of 1906), S. 2(a)]

To mar the face or appearance of; to spoil the form or beauty of; to disfigure. [IPC (45 of 1860), Ss. 477].

"DEFACE" means any type of clipping, filing, stamping, or such other alteration of the surface or shape of a coin as is readily distinguishable from the effects of reasonable wear. [S. 2(c) of the Coinage Act, 2011 (11 of 2011)]

Defaced security. 'Defaced security' means a security which has become illegible or rendered undecipherable in material parts thereof; and the material parts of such security are those where—(*i*) the security, number, loan to which it belongs to and the face value of the security or payments of interest are recorded; or (*ii*) the endorsement or the name of the payee is written or the transfer is executed; or (*iii*) the renewal is recorded. [Government Securities Regulations, 2007, Regn. 2(b)]

Defacing. Impairing or effacing; blotting out; making illegible; erasing; obliterating; cancelling.

Defalcation. The act of a defaulter : embezzlement or misappropriation of public or trust funds; diminution, abatement, excision of any part of a customary allowance; a cutting off; a diminution by way of deficit.

Defamation. 'Whoever by words either spoken or intended to be read, or by signs or by visible representations, makes or publishes any imputation concerning any person intending to harm, or knowing or having reason to believe that such imputation will harm, the reputation of such person, is said, except in the cases excepted, to defame that person'. [IPC (45 of 1860), S. 499 and *Exceptions*]

Whoever, by words either spoken or intended to be read, or by signs or by visible representations, makes or publishes in any manner, any imputation concerning any person intending to harm, or knowing or having reason to believe that such imputation will harm, the reputation of such person, is said, except in the cases hereinafter excepted, to defame that person. [(w.e.f. 1-7-2024) Bharatiya Nyaya Sanhita, 2023 (45 of 2023), section 356(1) and *Exceptions*]

"Defamation" means to take away or destroy the good fame or reputation; to speak evil of; to charge falsely or to asperse. [Chambers Twentieth Century Dictionary as cited in *Subramanian Swamy* v. *Union of India*, (2016) 7 SCC 221, para 21.4].

"The wrong of defamation, consists in the publication of a false and defamatory statement concerning another person without lawful justification. The wrong has always been regarded as one in which the court should have the advantage of the personal presence of the parties if justice is to be done. Hence, not only does on action of defamation not survive for or against the estate of a deceased person, but a statement about a deceased person is not actionable at the suit of his relative." (Salmond). See also [Gatley's Libel and Slander (6th Edn., 1960) and Odger's Libel and Slander (6th Edn., 1929) as cited in *Subramanian Swamy* v. *Union of India*, (2016) 7 SCC 221, para 21.4].

"Defamation is the publication of a statement which tends to lower a person in the estimation of right thinking members of society generally; or which tends to make them shun or avoid that person." [Winfield & Jolowicz on Torts (Sweet and Maxwell, 17th Edn., 2006) as cited in *Subramanian Swamy* v. *Union of India*, (2016) 7 SCC 221, para 21.5].

"Defamation may be broadly defined as a false statement of which the tendency is to disparage the good name or reputation of another person." [The Law of Defamation, Richard O' Sullivan, QC and Ronald Brown as cited in *Subramanian Swamy* v. *Union of India*, (2016) 7 SCC 221, para 21.6].

"... A publication, without justification or lawful excuse, which is calculated to injure the reputation of another, by exposing him to hatred, contempt, or ridicule...." [*Parmiter* v. *Coupland*, (1840) 6 M&W 105 : 151 ER 340, p. 342 as cited in *Subramanian Swamy* v. *Union of India*, (2016) 7 SCC 221, para 21.7].

"A defamatory statement is a statement concerning any person which exposes him to hatred, ridicule or contempt or which causes him to be shunned or avoided or which has a tendency to injure him in his office, profession of trade." [by Fraser approved by Mc Cardie, J. in *Myroft* v. *Sleight*, (1921) 90 LJ KB 883 : 37 TLR 646 as cited in *Subramanian Swamy* v. *Union of India*, (2016) 7 SCC 227, para 21.8].

An intentional false communication, either published or publicly spoken, that injures another's reputation or good name, holding up of a person to ridicule, scorn or contempt in a respectable and considerable part of the community; may be criminal as well as civil. Includes both libel and slander.

"A defamatory statement is a statement which tends to lower a person in the estimation of right thinking members of society generally or to cause him to be shunned or avoided or to expose him to hatred, contempt or ridicule, or to convey an imputation on him disparaging or injurious to him in his office, profession, calling, trade or business." [Halsburys Laws of England, 4th Edn., Vol. 28, para 10 as cited in *Subramanian Swamy* v. *Union of India*, (2016) 7 SCC 221, para 21.2].

"A defamatory statement is one which has a tendency to injure the reputation of the person to whom it refers; which tends, that is to say, to lower him in the estimation of right thinking members of society generally and in particular to cause him to be regarded with feelings of hatred, contempt, ridicule, fear, dislike, or disesteem. The statement is judged by the standard of an ordinary, right thinking member of society. ..." [Salmond & Heuston on the Law of Torts, 20th Edn. As cited in *Bata India Limited* v. *A.M. Turaz*, (2013) 53 PTC 586 : 2012 SCC on Line Del 5387; *Pandey Surendra Nath Sinha* v. *Bageswari Pd.*, AIR 1961 Pat 164 : 1960 SCC on Line Pat 116] See also *Subramanian Swamy* v. *Union of India*, (2016) 7 SCC 221, para 21.1].

"Defamatory Statement" means "false statement about a man to his discredit". [by Cave, J. In *Scott* v. *Sampson*, (1882) LR 8 QBD 491 (DC) as cited in *Subramanian Swamy* v. *Union of India*, (2016) 7 SCC 221, 21.3].

The action of defaming; the fact of being defamed. [IPC (45 of 1860) and Art. 19(2), Constitution of India, S. 499].

Defamation in law. Defamation in law in Art. 19(2) means the entire law of defamation, Criminal and Civil. [Constitution of India, Art. 19(2)]

Defamatory. Containing defamation; tending to defame : calumnious; slanderous; libelous; injurious to reputation. The word '*defamatory*', does not, in its ordinary and proper signification, include, the element of malice.

"A statement is defamatory if it tends to harm the reputation of another so as to lower him or her in the estimation of the community or to deter third parties from associating or dealing with him or her." [American Law Institute in the Second Restatement of Torts, S. 559 as cited in *Gatley on Libel and Slander*, (9th Edn., 1998, para 2.1, p. 23]

Defamatory per se. Certain statements that are automatically considered defamatory without specific proof of damage to reputation.

Defame. To bring ill fame upon anyone. [Indian Evidence Act (1 of 1872), S. 14, *Expln.* 2 ill. (e)].

Default. Means non-payment of any principal debt or interest thereon or any other amount payable by a borrower to any secured creditor consequent upon which the account of such borrower is classified as non-performing asset in the books of account of the secured creditor in accordance with the directions or guidelines issued by the Reserve Bank. [Securitization and Reconstruction of Financial Assets and Enforcement of Security Interest Act (54 of 2002), S. 2(1)(j)]

"Default" means non-payment of debt when whole or any part or instalment of the amount of debt has become due and payable and is not paid by the debtor or the corporate debtor, as the case may be. *[Insolvency & Bankruptcy Code, 2016 (31 of 2016), section 3(12)]*

Default is commonly taken for non-appearance in Court, at a day assigned; though it extends to any omission of that which we ought to do. *Default* means omission, neglect or failure; a failure or omission to do something required; omission to do that which ought to have been done by one of the parties; non-performance of duty; a failure in the performance of an obligation; neglect or omission of a legal requirement; fault, transgression; not doing what is reasonable under the circumstances.

The word 'default' must mean 'failure in performance' or 'failure to act'. *Organo Chemical Industries* v. *Union of India,* AIR 1979 SC 1803.

Omission to issue or serve a notice under O. XXI, R. 66, CPC (5 of 1908), upon the judgment-debtor is a "*default*" within the meaning of O. XXI, R. 57. There is no reason for giving a restricted meaning to the word "default" in O XXI, R. 57, and confining it to default in appearance, in the payment of process fees or in the production of documents.

The word 'default' in O. XVII, R. (3) can be applied to every default referred to in the earlier part of the rule. *Budhulal* v. *Chotelal*, AIR 1977 MP 1, 7 (FB). [Civil Procedure Code (5 of 1908), S. 2(2) and O. XVII, R. 3]

Failure to perform some legal requirement or obligation; want; absence; to commit a default; defect.

Default in proceedings in Court. The word "default" in relation to proceedings in Court is generally used to signify the failure of one party or the other to take some step in the action on the proceeding at the proper time, whereby the party so failing becomes liable to certain consequences. Formerly the meaning of the word appears to have been restricted to non-appearance in Court but it has of late been used with a wider significance.

Defaulter. "DEFAULTER" means a person from whom an arrear of land-revenue or a sum recoverable, as an arrear of land-revenue is due, and includes a person who is responsible as surety for the payment of any such arrear or sum. [Revenue Recovery Act (1 of 1890), S. 2(3)]

One who commits default. [Inocme tax Act (43 of 1961), Sch. 2, item 1(b)]; [Estate Duty Act (34 of 1953), S. 18(2)].

Defaulting purchaser. A purchaser who fails to perform some legal requirement or obligation. [2nd Sch., item 14, Income-tax Act (43 of 1961)]; [first Sch., App. E, No. 29(8), CPC (5 of 1908)].

Defaulting subscriber. Means a subscriber who has defaulted in the payment of subscriptions due in accordance with the terms of the chit agreement. [Chit Funds Act (40 of 1982), S. 2(f)]

Defeasance. A 'defeasance' is an instrument which avoids or defeats the force and operation of some other deed. *Defeasance* is collateral deed, made at the same time with a conveyance, containing certain conditions, upon the performance of which the estate then created may be defeated or totally undone. (*Burrill; Ame Cyc.; Terms de la Ley*)

Defeasance : Condition. A *'Defeasance'* is something which defeats the operation of a deed or document. If it is contained in the same deed it is called a 'Condition". [TP Act (4 of 1882), S. 8]

Defeasible. That which may be annulled, abrogated, cancelled or made void; capable of defeating, destroying or impairing.

'Defeat the provisions of any law' must be taken as limited to defeating the intention which the legislature has expressed, or which is necessarily implied from the express terms of an Act. It is unlawful to contract to do that which it is unlawful to do; but an agreement will not be void, merely because it tends to defeat some purpose ascribed to the legislature by conjecture, or even appearing, as a matter of history, from extraneous evidence, such as legislative debates or preliminary memoranda, not forming part of the enactment. [Pollock & Mulla, Indian Contract and Specific Relief Acts, 13th Edn., Vol. 1, p. 668 as cited in *Union of India* v. *Colonel L.S.N. Murthy*, (2012) 1 SCC 718, para 9].

Defect. "DEFECT" means any fault, imperfection or shortcoming in the quality, quantity, potency, purity or standard which is required to be maintained by or under any law for the time being in force or under any contract express or implied, or as is claimed by the trader in any manner whatsoever in relation to any goods. [Consumer Protection Act (68 of 1986), S. 2(f)] [Now repealed & replaced by Act 35 of 2019]

"Defect" means any fault, imperfection or shortcoming in the quality, quantity, potency, purity or standard which is required to be maintained by or under any law for the time being in force or under any contract, express or implied or as is claimed by the trader in any manner whatsoever in relation to any goods or product and the expression "defective" shall be construed accordingly. [Consumer Protection Act, 2019 (35 of 2019), section 2(10)]

A want or absence of something necessary or essential for completeness or perfection; shortcoming; blemish.

'Defect' is a weak word and could according to its ordinary connotation, cover only omissions, irregularities or deficiencies but not also a fraudulent suppression of distinction of facts. *Manmatha Nath Chakravarthy* v. *Sachindra Kumar Chakravarthy,* AIR 1956 Cal 59, 61. [CPC (5 of 1908), O. XXI, R. 90, *Expln.*]

Defect, latent. A defect which is not apparently noticeable by ordinary examination [Indian Railways Act (9 of 1890), S. 73(h)] [Now repealed & replaced by Act 24 of 1989].

Defect in title. Where the vendor fails to convey through a defect of title the purchaser will not recover any damages for loss of bargain, for in this case, which is exceptional, he cannot recover by an action for breach of contract damages beyond the expenses he has actually incurred in investigating title. Such damages are commonly all that naturally and directly result from the breach, for a contract for the sale of land is made on the understanding that it may fail for defect of title. HALSBURY, 4th Edn., Vol. 12, para 1183, p. 468.

Defect of a substantial nature. The non-delivery of the nomination paper between the hours of eleven o'clock in the forenoon and the three o'clock in the afternoon is a defect of a substantial nature. *Harjit Singh* v. *S. Umrao Singh*, AIR 1980 SC 701, 704. [Representation of the people Act (43 of 1951), S. 36(4)]

DEFECTS—LATENT AND PATENT. *Patent,*—that is, such as may be discovered by ordinary vigilance. *Latent,*—that is, such as the greatest attention would not enable to discover. (*Stroud*)

Defect of character. Under S. 12 of the Legal Practitioners Act (18 of 1879), an advocate of the High Court, with his position as a member of a political organization which is out to break the law, cannot expect any privileges at the hands of the Court when he is out to break the law which the Court is to uphold. Though an advocate, like every one else, has a right to own political opinions, and to express those opinions in any peaceful and lawful way, he has no right to break the law or to disobey a lawful order merely because he does not happen to like it or thinks it unnecessary or even unwise. He is part of the machinery for upholding law and order. In that sense it is a much more serious thing for an advocate of the High Court or any legal practitioner deliberately to break a law or disobey a lawful order. An advocate who is convicted of an offence under the Police Act for deliberately disobeying an order issued by the District Magistrate comes within the provisions of the Legal Practitioners Act. Such deliberate commission of an offence shows a "defect of character" which makes him liable to punishment or to removal by the High Court.

The expression 'defect of character' as used in S. 12 of the Legal Practitioners Act (18 of 1879) includes not only moral turpitude, but also such defect in the character of a legal practitioner which renders him unfit to be a member of the honourable profession to which he belongs. *In the matter of Krishna Ojha Mukhtear,* AIR 1955 Pat 80.

Defect of form in the order by Government. Any defect of form in the order by Government would not necessarily make it illegal and the only consequence of the order not being in proper form is that the burden is thrown on the Government to show that the order was in fact passed by it. *State of Rajasthan* v. *Sripal Jain*, AIR 1963 SC 1323, 1326. [Constitution of India, Art. 166]

Defect of jurisdiction. The words "defect of jurisdiction" mean a defect of jurisdiction peculiar to the Court in which the proceedings were taken, and do not cover such mistakes as the presentation and prosecution of an appeal, which did not lie at all in any Court.

The 'defect of jurisdiction' goes to the root of the matter as the Court is incompetent to entertain the proceeding. There must be some preliminary objection which if it succeeds, the Court would be incompetent to entertain the proceeding on merits, such defect could be said to be 'of the like nature' as defect of jurisdiction. *Zafar Khan* v. *Board of Revenue*, AIR 1985 SC 39, 47. [Limitation Act (36 of 1963), S. 14]

Defect of parties. A defect of parties arises where from the statement of the cause of action, it appears that there are parties omitted who should have been made parties—plaintiff or defendant. "A defect of parties to an action" means the absence of one or more of the necessary parties and not merely the absence of proper parties.

A defect of parties is founded on the notion or fact that there are other persons interested in the controversy who should be brought before the Court, and whom the Court will order to be brought in where the objection is taken in time.

The phrase "defect of parties" does not include joinder of an improper party.

Defection. Crossing the Floor by a Member of a Legislature is called defection.

'Defection' is a malady defacing our democracy and if not checked would shake the very foundation of our democracy. [*Gyanendra Kumar Singh* v. *Bihar Legislative Assembly*, Patna, AIR 2015 Pat, para 41].

Defective. Incomplete; faulty; wanting in some essential particulars.

Having a defect or defects [Indian Evidence Act (1 of 1872), S. 93]; [Sale of Goods Act (3 of 1930), S. 38(2)].

Defective condition. An unreasonably dangerous condition which might well cause physical harm beyond that which would be contemplated by the ordinary user or consumer who purchases the product.

Defective in substance. 'Defective in substance' in cl. 9 of the Explanation to S. 263(a) Indian Succession Act (39 of 1925) must mean that the defect was of such a character as to substantially affect the regularity and correctness of the previous proceedings. *Anil Behari Ghosh* v. *Lalika Bala Dassi*, AIR 1955 SC 566, 572.

The expression means that the very foundation of the proceedings and the basis on which the proceedings started and proceeded were irregular and defective and such a defect goes to the root of the matter.

Defective pleading. A pleading that fails to meet the minimum standards of sufficiency or accuracy in form or substance.

Defective title. A title that cannot legally convey the property to which it applies.

Defence. Action against attack or challenge; the opposing or denial of the truth or validity of the prosecutor's complaint; the proceedings by a defendant or accused party (or his legal agents) for defending himself.

Defence of oneself or **self defence.** The defence of one's self, and the mutual and reciprocal defence of such as stand in the relations of husband and wife, parent and child, master and servant, is a right which belongs to every person. If a man, or one standing in any of these relations to him, be forcibly attacked in his person or property, it is lawful for him to repel force by force; and the breach of the peace which happens is chargeable upon him only who began the affray. *Self-defence*, therefore is justly called the primary law of nature, and it is not, neither can it be, in fact, taken away by the law of society.

Defence on the merits. The action of defending on the merits of (a case *etc.*) *i.e.* on intrinsic rights and wrongs of substance in distinction from matters of form.

Defence struck off. CPC (5 of 1908), O. XI, R. 21. Even when a defence is struck off the defendant is entitled to appear, cross-examine the plaintiff in witnesses and submit that even on the basis of the evidence on behalf of the plaintiff a decree cannot be passed against him. *Pardise Industrial Corporation* v. *K.P. Products*, AIR 1976 SC 309, 312.

Defence witness. Witness summoned on the request of the defending party.

Defend. To deny, repel, oppose (the plaintiff's plea) to appear, address the Court *etc.* in defence of; to take action against attack or challenge. [Constitution of India, Art. 60].

Defend : Protect. To *Defend* implies an active repelling of some adverse influence or power; *protect* a passive placing of something between the object and the power. A fortress is *defended* by its guns, and *protected* by its walls. A *defence* is successful or unsuccessful. A *protection* is adequate or inadequate.

Defendant. "DEFENDANT" includes—

(i) in any person from or through whom a defendant derives his liability to be sued;

(ii) any person whose estate is represented by the defendant as executor, administrator or other representative. [Limitation Act (36 of 1963), S. 2(e)]

A person sued in a Court of law. [Limitation Act (36 of 1963), S. 2(*e*)].

Defender. One who defends. [IPC. (45 of 1860), S. 106].

A lawyer who represents defendants.

Defer. To put off to some other time; to postpone.

"Deferment". The act of delaying; postponement (deferment of a indicial decision). [Black's Law Dictionary as cited in *State of Punjab* v. *Shreyans Industries Limited*, (2016) 4 SCC 769, para 11].

Deferred. Delayed; put off, postponed to a future time.

Deferred debt. A debt which has to be paid after the preferred debts and the ordinary debts have been paid in full.

Deferred income. Income received but not yet earned, *i.e.*, prepaid rent or insurance.

Deferred payment. Payment postponed, or not made when due. [State Financial Corporations Act (63 of 1951), S. 25(1)(*h*)].

Deferred sentence. A sentence that will not be carried out if the defendant meets certain requirements, such as complying with conditions of probation.

Deferred stock or shares. Stock as does not rank for dividend until after the ordinary, preference and guaranteed dividends have been paid off.

Defiance. The act of one who defies. Contempt. [Army Act (46 of 1950), S. 41(1)].

"Defibrillator". A defibrillator is a device that delivers electrical shock through paddles placed either directly across the heart or on the surface of the body during cardiac emergency resulting from ventricular fibrillation. [*B.P.L. Limited* v. *Commissioner of Central Excise, Cochin-II Commissionerate Calicut*, (2015) 13 SCC 220, para 3].

Deficiency. "DEFICIENCY" means any fault, imperfection, shortcoming or inadequacy in the quality, nature and manner of performance which is required to be maintained by or under any law for the time being in force or has been undertaken to be performed by a person in pursuance of a contract or otherwise in relation to any service. [Consumer Protection Act (68 of 1986), S. 2(g)] *Karnataka Power Transmission Corpn. Ltd.* v. *Ashok Iron Works Pvt. Ltd.* : *H. V. Balachandra Rao* v. *Karnataka Power Transmission Corpn.*, AIR 2009 SC 1905.

Shortage or insufficiency.

Want; lack. [Indian Succession Act (39 of 1925), S. 81].

"Deficiency" means any fault, imperfection, shortcoming or inadequacy in the quality, nature and manner of performance which is required to be maintained by or under any law for the time being in force or has been undertaken to be performed by a person in pursuance of a contract or otherwise in relation to any service and includes—

(i) any act of negligence or omission or commission by such person which causes loss or injury to the consumer; and

(ii) deliberate withholding of relevant information by such person to the consumer. [Consumer Protection Act, 2019 (35 of 2019), section 2(11)]

Deficiency in service. 'Deficiency' means any fault, imperfection, shortcoming or inadequacy in the quality, nature and manner of performance which is required to be maintained by or under any law for the time being in force or has been undertaken to be performed by a person in pursuance of a contract or otherwise in relation to any service. *Consumer Unity and Trust Society* v. *Bank of Baroda,* (1997) 2 Comp LJ 192, p. 194 (SC). [Consumer Protection Act (68 of 1986), S. 2(1)(g)] [Now repealed & replaced by Act 35 of 2019]

Supply of electricity by the Board or for that matter KPTC to a consumer would be covered under the provisions of section 2(1)(o) of the Consumer Protection Act, 1986, being 'service' and if the supply of electrical energy to a consumer is not provided in time as is agreed upon, then under the provisions of section (2)(1)(g) of the 1986 Act, there may be a case for 'deficiency in service'. *Karnataka Power Transmission Corpn. Ltd.* v. *Ashok Iron Works Pvt. Ltd.*, AIR 2009 SC 1905.

Deficiency of profits. Means—

(i) Where profits have been made in any chargeable accounting period, the amount by which such profits fall short of the abatement in respect of the period;

(ii) Where a loss has been made in any chargeable accounting period, the amount of the loss added to the abatement in respect of that period. [Business Profits Tax Act (21 of 1947), S. 2(7)]

Deficit. Want; deficiency in an account or a number. An excess of expenditures or liabilities over revenues or assets.

Defile. To pollute; to corrupt the chastity of; to debauch or to violate; also to make impure, foul or unclean.

To render ceremonially unclean. [IPC (45 of 1860), S. 295].

Define. To determine the end or limit; to mark out; to fix the boundary of a thing; to establish or prescribe authoritatively the limits of anything.

To determine the end or limit; to establish or prescribe authoritatively the limits of anything. [Coal Mines Provident Fund and Miscellaneous Provisions Act (46 of 1948)], S. 10(*i*); to give the definition of. [T.P. Act (4 of 1882), preamble].

Definite. Having fixed limits; bounded with precision; determinate. (*Cent. Dict.*)

'Definite' means something which is not vague. *State of J & K* v. *Bakshi Gulam Mohammed*, AIR 1967 SC 122, 128.

Definite conclusion. The words "definite conclusion" connote 'precise' or 'exact' conclusion and not a final conclusion. *Govind Shanker* v. *State of M.P.*, AIR 1963 MP 115, 119. [Constitution of India, Art. 311(2)]

Definite matter of public importance. Quite conceivably the conduct of an individual person or a company or a group of individual persons or companies may assume such a dangerous proportion and may so prejudicially affect or threaten to affect the public well-being so as to make such conduct a definite matter of public importance urgently calling for a full inquiry. *Ram Krishna Dalmia* v. *Justice S.R. Tendolkar*, AIR 1950 SC 538, 544. [Commissions of Inquiry Act (60 of 1952), S. 3(1)]

Definition. The act of defining; a declaration of the signification of a word or phrase; a precise statement of the essential nature of a thing [Constitution of India, Art. 12, margin, Art. 36, margin and Art. 152, margin]; the action of determining the limits.

Definitive judgment. A judgment that finally decides the controversy. [IPC (45 of 1860), S. 19].

Deflation. Decline in the price of goods and services.

Defloration. Seduction or debauching; the act by which a woman is deprived of her virginity.

Deflower. To deprive of virginity of a woman; to ravage.

Defraud. To deprive of some right, interest, or property by deceitful devices; to cheat; to overreach. "Defraud" always denotes some form of dishonesty. (*Standard Dict.*)

The word 'defraud' involves two elements, namely, deceit and injury to the person deceived. Injury is something other than economic loss and it will include any harm whatever caused to any person in body, mind, reputation or such others. Where a forged document is prepared with the intention to deceive and by means of deceit to obtain an advantage then there is a fraud. *State of U.P.* v. *Ranjit Singh,* (1999) 2 SCC 617, para 3 : AIR 1999 SC 1201.

To take or withhold from (a person) by fraud what is his by right [T.P. Act (4 of 1882), S. 53(2) and CPC (5 of 1908), O. XXXIX, R. 1(b)]; to cheat; to beguile.

Defraud, Intent to. The expression 'defraud' involves two elements, namely deceit and injury to the person deceived. Injury is something other than economic loss that is, deprivation of property, whether movable or immovable, or of money, and it will include any harm whatever caused to any person in body, mind, reputation or such others. *Vimla* v. *Delhi Administration*, AIR 1963 SC 1572, 1576.

Defray expenses. To meet the expenses; to pay out the expenses [Employees' State Insurance Act (34 of 1948), S. 2(22)(e) and CPC (5 of 1908), O. XVI, R. 2(1)].

Defunct. Dead; a decedent (as, a defunct company).

Defunct banking. "DEFUNCT BANKING" means a banking company—

(i) which has been prohibited from receiving fresh deposits; or

(ii) which has been ordered to be wound up; or

(iii) which has transferred all its deposit liabilities in India to any other institution; or

(iv) which has ceased to be a banking company within the meaning of sub-section (2) of Section 36A of [the Banking Regulation Act, 1949] (10 of 1949), or has converted itself into a non-banking company; or

(v) in respect of which a liquidator has been appointed in pursuance of resolution for the voluntary winding up of its affairs; or

(vi) in respect of which any scheme of compromise or arrangement or of reconstruction has been sanctioned by any competent authority and the said scheme does not permit the acceptance of fresh deposits; or

(vii) which has been granted a moratorium which is in operation; or

(viii) in respect of which an application for the winding up of its affairs is pending in a competent Court. [Deposit Insurance and Credit Guarantee Corporation Act (47 of 1961), S. 2(f)]

Defunct co-operative bank. "DEFUNCT CO-OPERATIVE BANK" means a co-operative bank—

(i) which has been prohibited from receiving fresh deposits; or

(ii) which has been ordered or directed to be wound up; or

(iii) which has transferred all its deposit liabilities in India to any other institution; or

(iv) which has ceased to be a co-operative bank within the meaning of sub-section (2) of Section 36A of the Banking Regulation Act 1949 (10 of 1949); or

(v) which has converted itself into a nonbanking co-operative society; or

(vi) in respect of which any scheme of compromise or arrangement or of reconstruction has been sanctioned under any law for the time being in force and such scheme does not permit the acceptance of fresh deposits; or

(vii) which has been granted a moratorium which is in operation; or

(viii) in respect of which an application for winding up is pending before the Registrar of Co-operative Societies or other competent authority under any law relating to co-operative societies for the time being in force in a State. [Deposit Insurance and Credit Guarantee Corporation Act (47 of 1967), S. 2(ff)]

Defunctus. Dead.

Degradation. A deprivation of dignity or dismissal from an office. An ecclesiastical censure, whereby a clergyman is divested of his holy orders. (*Seldon's Titles of Hon*. 787; *Tomlin*)

Degrading. Lowering a person in the estimation of the public, exposing to disgrace, dishonour, or contempt.

Degree. "DEGREE" means any such degree as may, with previous approval of the Central Government, be specified in this behalf by the University Grants Commission, by notification in the Official Gazette. [National Commission for Minority Educational Institutions Act, 2004 (2 of 2005), S. 2(d)]

A mark of distinction conferred upon a student for proficiency in some art or science; university diploma or specified proficiency. (*Rapalje & L.L. Dict.*)

The measure or amount of a quality, attribute or action; a step in direct line of ascent or descent; a title conferred, making a stage of proficiency in studies.

Degree of prohibited relationship. A man and any of the persons mentioned in Part I of the First Schedule and a woman and any of the persons mentioned in Part II of the said Schedule are within the degree of prohibited relationship;

Explanation I.—Relationship includes,—

(a) relationship by half or uterine blood as well as by full blood;

(b) illegitimate blood relationship as well as legitimate;

(c) relationship by adoption as well as by blood; new line and all terms of relationship in this Act shall be construed accordingly.

Explanation II.—"Full blood" and "half blood"—two persons are said to be related to each other by full blood when they are descended from a common ancestor by the same wife and by half blood when they are descended from a common ancestor but by different wives.

Explanation III.—"Uterine blood"— two persons are said to be related to each other by uterine blood when they are descended from a common ancestress but by different husbands.

Explanation IV.—In explanation II and III, "ancestor" includes the father and 'ancestress' the mother. [Special Marriage Act (43 of 1954), S. 2(b)]

"DEGREE OF PROHIBITED RELATIONSHIP". Two persons are said to be within the "degree of prohibited relationship"—

(i) If one is a lineal ascendant of the other; or

(ii) If one was the wife or husband of a lineal ascendant or descendant of the other; or

(iii) If one was the wife of the brother or of the father's or mother's brother or of the grandfather's or grandmother's brother of the other, or

(iv) If the two are brother and sister, uncle and niece, aunt and nephew, or children of brother and sister or of two brothers or of two sisters;

Explanation—For the purpose of clauses (f) and (g), relationship includes—

(i) relationship by half or uterine blood as well as by full blood;

(ii) illegitimate blood relationship as well as legitimate;

(iii) relationship by adoption as well as by blood; and all terms of relationship in those clauses shall be construed accordingly. [Hindu Marriage Act (25 of 1955), S. 3(g)]

Del credere. (*Lat.*) Of trust; credit.

In a confined sense, a commission *del credere* is an undertaking by an insurance broker, for an additional premium, to insure his principal against the contingency of the failure of the underwriter. See *Grove* v. *Dubois*, 1 Term Rep 112; *Begs* v. *Dickoson*, 1d. 285. (*Tomlin*)

Del credere agent. A mercantile agent who, in consideration of the payment of an extra remuneration, undertakes to be answerable to the principal for the due performance of the contracts made by him on his behalf. [Gold (Control) Act (45 of 1968), S. 2(h)(iii) (*repealed*)].

Del credere commission. An additional commission received by a factor in consideration of his engaging to insure to his principal not only the solvency of the debtor, but the punctual discharge of the debt.

Delay. To hinder; detain; keep back or retard; to arrest progress.

Procrastination; the time during which something is delayed; to cause delay; to prolong the time. [CPC (5 of 1908), O. XXXVIII, R. 1(a)].

Delay defeats equity. The maxim, that delay defeats equities should not be applied to a case where want of fair dealing and inequality have been proved to exist. [35 IC 243 (251)]

Delayed wages. The expression "delayed wages" can only mean wages which are admittedly due but the payment of which has been postponed on some excuse or the other. *Arumugham* v. *Jawahar Mills,* AIR 1956 Mad 79, 83. [Payment of Wages Act (4 of 1936), S. 1 5(3)]

Delectus personae. Every partnership is founded in a "delectus personae," which implies confidence and knowledge of the character, skill, and ability of the other associates, and their personal co-operation, advice, and aid in the management of the business.

Delegacy. A committee of a university entrusted with some branch of university business.

Delegata potestas non potest delegari. (*Maxim*) A delegated authority cannot be redelegated. (*Broom; Morgan.*)

Delegate. A person sent and empowered to act for another; one deputed to represent another.

Delegate. The ordinary dictionary meaning of the word 'Delegate' is to send or authorise a person as a representative or to depute (Oxford Concise English Dictionary). The word 'Delegate' in Black's Law Dictionary has been defined to mean to entrust another with the authority or empower another to act as an agent or a representative. [As cited in *Ranvir Singh* v. *State of U.P.,* 2017 6 AWC 6271 (All), para 10]

To assign or commit to another as an agent. [Companies Act (1 of 1956), S. 292(2)]; one who is delegated; a deputy or representative.

"*As a noun*, a person sent and empowered to act for another, one deputed to represent another in a more popular but less accurate sense, a regularly selected member of a regular party convention.

As a verb, in its general sense and as generally used, the term does not imply, or point to, a giving up of authority, but rather the conferring authority upon someone else.

At common law, it is transfer of authority by one person to another, the act of making or commissioning a delegate." *Corpus Juris Secundum*, Vol. 26, as cited in *Ishwar Singh* v. *State of Rajasthan*, (2005) 2 SCC 335 at 338.

"It is an accepted position in law that to "delegate" to another is not to denude yourself". *Ishwar Singh* v. *State of Rajasthan*, (2005) 2 SCC 335 at 338.

The word "delegate" means little more than an agent. An agent exercises no power of his own but only the powers of his principal. *Ishwar Singh* v. *State of Rajasthan*, (2005) 2 SCC 335, 338.

Delegated legislation. Legislation made by a person or body other than the Parliament, by virtue of powers conferred either by statute or by legislation which is itself made under statutory powers.

It is a fundamental principle of Constitutional Law that everything necessary to the exercise of a power is included in the grant of the power. A legislature can not strip itself of its essential functions and vest the same on an extraneous authority. The primary duty of law-making has to be discharged by the legislature itself but delegation may be resorted to as a subsidiary or an ancillary measure. *Edward Mill. Co.* v. *State of Ajmer*, AIR 1955 SC 25, 32. [Constitution of India, Art. 245]

Delegated legislation and **conditional legislation (Distinction).** The distinction between conditional legislation and delegated legislation is this, that in the former the delegate's power is that of determining when a legislative declared rule of conduct shall become effective, and the latter involves delegation of rule making power which constitutionally may be exercised by the administrative agent. By delegated legislation the delegate completes the legislation by supplying details within the limits prescribed by the statute and in the case of conditional legislation the power of legislation is exercised by the legislature conditionally leaving to the discretion of an external authority the time and manner of carrying its legislation into effect as also the determination of the area to which it is to extend. *Hamdard Dawakhan* v. *Union of India,* MLJ : QD (1956-1960) Vol. IV C2335 : 1960 MLJ (Cri) 358 : AIR 1960 SC 544. [Drugs and Magic Remedies (Objectionable Advertisements) Act (21 of 1954), S. 3(a)]

Delegatee. An agent or representative to whom a matter is delegated.

Delegation. The appointment of an attorney or proxy to do an act merely ministerial and involving no independent discretion is not a delegation within the meaning of this section. [Indian Trusts Act (2 of 1882), S. 47, *Expln.*]

'Delegation' is the act of making or commissioning a delegate. It generally means parting of powers by the person who grants the delegation and conferring of an authority to do thing which otherwise that person would have to do himself. *Sidhartha Sarawgi* v. *Board of Trustees for the Port of Kolkata*, (2014) 16 SCC 248, para 2.

"Delegation" means "The act of entrusting another with authority or empowering another to act as an agent or representative." [Black's Law Dictionary as cited in *Sidhartha Sarawgi* v. *Board of Trustees for the Port of Kolkata*, (2014) 16 SCC 248, para 2].

The word 'delegation' as generally used, does not imply a parting with powers by a person who grants the delegation, but points rather to the conferring of an authority to do things which otherwise that person would have to do himself. [Constitution of India, Art. 245]

The action of delegating or the fact of being delegated [CPC (5 of 1908), S. 128(2)(i)]; a body of delegates.

Delegation of power. The transfer of authority by one person to another.

Transfer of authority by one branch of government in which such authority is vested to some other branch or administrative agency. (*Black*)

Delegatus debitor est odiosus in lege. A delegate debtor is hateful in the law.

Delegatus non potest delegare. (*Maxim*) A delegate cannot delegate.

A delegated power cannot be further delegated. (*Latin for Lawyers*)

The delegatee can not delegate, (unless expressly authorised so to do).

The maxim means one who is himself a delegate cannot further delegate the task entrusted to him. S. 54 permits only one delegation *i.e.* delegation by the Deputy Commissioner to his Gazetted Assistant and hence there can be no further delegation by the Gazetted Assistant to any one else. *Puttakamaiah* v. *State of Karnataka,* AIR 1990 Kar 89, 90. [CPC (5 of 1908), S. 54]

Delete. To remove (erase) characters, words, pages, documents, or entire disks.

"Delete". Blot out, cancel, censor, cross off, cross out, cut, cut out, dele, discard, do away with, drop, edit out, efface, elide, eliminate, eradicate, erase, excise expunge, extirpate, get rid of, leave out, modify by excisions, obliterate, omit, remove, rub out, rule out, rule out, scratch out, strike off, take out, weed, wipe out. [William C Burton, 1979 Edition as cited in *Shree Bhagwati Steel Rolling Mills* v. *Commissioner of Central Excise*, (2016) 3 SCC 643, para 13].

Deleterious. Physically or morally harmful or injurious; noxious.

Deletion. Act of deleting. [Companies Act (1 of 1956), S. 21, prov.].

Delhi. Means the entire area of the National Capital Territory of Delhi except New Delhi and Delhi Cantonment as defined in clause (10) of Section 2 of the Delhi Municipal Corporation Act, 1957. [New Delhi Municipal Council Act (44 of 1994), S. 2(11)]

"DELHI" means the Union territory of Delhi. [Delhi Apartment Ownership Act (58 of 1986), S. 3(o)]

"DELHI" means the entire area of the National Capital Territory of Delhi except the Delhi Cantonment as defined in section 2(10) of the Delhi Municipal Corporation Act, 1957 (66 of 1957). [S. 2(1)(b) of the National Capital Territory of Delhi Laws (Special Provisions) Act, 2011 (5 of 2011)]

Delhi Special Police Establishment. Means the Delhi Special Police Establishment constituted under section 2(1) of the Delhi Special Police Establishment Act, 1946 (25 of 1946). [S. 2(1)(f) of the Lokpal & Lokayuktas Act, 2013 (1 of 2014)]

Deliberandum est diu quod statuendum est semel. (*Lat.*) (12 Rep. 74) That which is to be resolved once for all should long be deliberated upon. (*Morgan; Latin for Lawyers*)

Deliberate. (*As an Adjective*), Premeditated; formed with deliberation; not sudden or rash; carefully considering the probable consequences of a step; an act done after reflecting and weighing the matter well.

(*As a Verb*) To weigh in the mind; to consider and examine the reasons for and against; to consider maturely; to reflect upon; to reflect, with a view to make a choice.

Premeditated; done on set purpose. [IPC (45 of 1860), S. 298]; [Constitution of India, Art. 108(1)].

'Deliberate conduct of a person means that he knows what he is doing and intends to do the same. Therefore, there has to be a calculated action with evil motive on his part. *Ram Kishan* v. *Tarun Bajaj*, (2014) 16 SCC 204, para 10.

Deliberation. The action of deliberating; careful consideration with a view to decision.

Deliberative body. The term "deliberative body" as applied to a constituted body of individuals is properly applied to a meeting which "acts as such in determining all matters that may lawfully be determined by it.

Delimit. Assign boundaries; to mark or lay out the limits or boundary line of a territory or country.

Delimitation. The action of fixing boundaries. [Preamble, Representation of the People Act (43 of 1950)].

Delineate. Portray by drawing or description.

To draw a line; to represent with accuracy and minute attention to detail. [Trade and Merchandise Marks Act (43 of 1958), S. 81(3)(*a*)].

Delineation. The act of representing, portraying or depicting.

Delinquency. "Delinquency," when applied to a merchant, cannot mean anything less than that he has proved to be dishonest and attempted to evade the payment of his debts.

Delinquency, juvenile. A status in a juvenile characterised by anti-social behaviour, waywardness, incorrigibility; an offence committed by a person who is under 16 years of age.

Delinquens per iram provocatus, puniri debet nitius. A delinquent provoked by rage ought to be punished with less rigour.

Delinquent. A person who fails to do his duty or commits an offence.

Delinquent child. A legal infant who has either violated criminal laws or engaged in disobedient or indecent conduct, and is in need of treatment, rehabilitation, or supervision.

'Delinquent child' has been defined as meaning a child who has been found to have committed an offence. *Raghbir* v. *State of Haryana,* AIR 1981 SC 2037.

Delirious. Affected with delirium, especially as a result of symptom of disease; wandering in mind. [IPC (45 of 1860), S. 305]; [Indian Contract Act (9 of 1872), S. 12, ill. (b)].

Delirium. A condition in which the sufferer has confused ideas of the past and present circumstances.

A disordered state of the mental faculties resulting from disturbance of the functions of the brain and characterised by incoherent speech, hallucination, restlessness and frenzied excitement. [Indian Contract Act (9 of 1872), S. 12, ill. (b)].

Delirium tremens. Disorder with paroxysms of terror due to heavy drinking; a violent delirium induced by the excessive and prolonged use of intoxicating liquors; a disorder of the brain arising from inordinate and protracted use of ardent spirits, and therefore almost peculiar to drunkards; one of the forms of insanity consequent on excessive drinking.

Delisting. The suspension of the privileges of having a security listed on exchange for failure to meet the requirements of the listing.

Deliver. To give or transfer; to hand over possession of; to hand over to another; to give forth in action; to discharge.

The word "delivers" in S. 58(b), Transfer of Property Act (4 of 1882), does not necessarily mean "delivers immediately" and where the mortgagor is not in a position to give immediate delivery of possession, it is sufficient if he gives the right to possession though he cannot give delivery of possession.

Deliver possession. "It is a bilateral act and requires one side to give up possession and the other side to receive it or accept it." *The State* v. *Virchand Shah*, AIR 1969 Bom 348 at 350. [Bombay Rents. Hotel and Lodging House Rents Central Act (57 of 1947), S. 16]

Deliver up. To surrender. [IPC (45 of 1860), S. 390, ill. (c)].

Deliverable state. "Goods are said to be in a "DELIVERABLE STATE," when they are in such a state that the buyer would, under the contract, be bound to take delivery of them." [Sale of Goods Act (3 of 1930), S.(2)(3)]

Deliverance. The act of giving or transferring from one to another; setting free.

"Delivered" or **"delivery".** "Delivered" or "delivery" means physical delivery of cloth in bales or in pieces but not cloth which though paid for is still in the physical possession of the seller. *Seksaria Cotton Mills Ltd.* v. *State of Bombay,* AIR 1953 SC 278.

Delivers the judgment. The Judge who 'delivers' the judgement, or causes it to be delivered by a brother Judge, must be in existence as a member of the Court at the moment of delivery so that he can, if necessary, stop delivery and say that he has changed his mind. *Surendra Singh* v. *State of UP*., AIR 1954 SC 194, 196. [Criminal P.C. 1898, S. 369 (now S. 362 of 1974 code)]

Delivery. "DELIVERY" means voluntary transfer of possession from one person to another. [Sale of Goods Act (3 of 1930), S. 2(2)]

"DELIVERY," IN RELATION TO A LECTURE, includes delivery by means of any mechanical instrument or by broadcast. [Copyright Act (14 of 1957), S. 2(g)]

"DELIVERY" means,—

(i) in the case of a negotiable multimodal transport document, delivering of the consignment to, or placing the consignment at the disposal of, the consignee or any other person entitled to receive it;

(ii) in the case of a non-negotiable multimodal transport document, delivering of the consignment to, or placing the consignment at the disposal of, the consignee or any person authorised by the consignee to accept delivery of the consignment on his behalf. [Multimodal Transportation of Goods Act (28 of 1993), S. 2(f)]

The transfer of possession of a thing from one person to another; transmitting the possession of a thing from one person into the power or possession of another; the transferring of the thing sold into the power and possession of the buyer.

DELIVERY (IN RESPECT OF POSTAL LETTERS). Any of the periodical distributions of letters of goods by post office or firm.

'Delivery' contemplated therein is the delivery of one's property to another for no consideration. *Commissioner, Gift Tax* v. *Getty Chettiar*, AIR 1971 SC 2410, 2413. [Gift-tax Act (18 of 1958), S. 2, cl. (xxiv)]

The action of delivering up or over; giving birth to a child; a delivering specially of a speech; an act or instance of delivery.

Delivery bond. A bond that goods or their value will be delivered up to a certain time or upon certain conditions; an order drawn by the owner on the bailee of goods for their delivery to a third party.

Delivery of arms. Means such a delivery gives the person into whose possession the arm is delivered, control over the arm and the authority to use it as an arm.

Delivery of goods. Delivery means voluntary transfer of possession from one person to another. The term includes symbolical delivery and is not restricted to the physical transfer of the goods themselves, but covers also transfers of possession of documents of title to goods. Where the buyer takes possession pursuant to the leave of the seller, whether concurrent or antecedent, that is a voluntary transfer of possession. HALSBURY, 4th Edn., Vol. 41, para 757, p. 685.

Delivery (of goods sold). "Delivery of goods sold may be made by doing anything which the parties agree shall be treated as delivery or which has the effect of putting the goods in the possession of the buyer or of any person authorised to hold them on his behalf." [Sale of Goods Act (3 of 1930), S. 33]

Delivery of mail at the house or office of the addresee. The house should not be construed as the flat in a building but the house includes not only the building but the surrounding area of the building. A delivery of the mail in the mail box located on the ground floor of the building cannot by any stretch of imagination be considered as invalid delivery because mail is not delivered at the door of each flat holder. *Mahabir Prasad S. Deora* v. *Union of India*, AIR 1995 Bom 142, 145. [Indian Post Offices Act (6 of 1898), S. 3(c)]

Delivery of possession. The essence of delivery of possession is that the deliveree, by some apt and manifest act, puts the deliverer in the same possession of control over the thing, either directly through a custodian, which he held himself immediately before the act.

Delivery order. An order by the owner of goods to a person to hold them on his behalf, to deliver them to the person named in the order.

Delivery up order. It is an order of the Court to an infringer asking him to deliver infringing goods to the patentee for alteration or destruction. (*Patents*)

Delusion. A false belief; hallucination; a diseased state of the mind in which persons believe things to exist, which exist only in their own imagination, with the persuasion so fixed and firm, that neither evidence nor argument can convince them to the contrary.

The person believes delusions even after other people prove that the beliefs are not true or logical. They may also believe that people on television are directing special messages to them, or that radio stations are broadcasting their thoughts aloud to others. Sometimes they believe they are someone else, such as a famous historical figure. They may have paranoid delusions and believe that others are trying to harm them. [*Veer Pal Singh* v. *Secretary, Ministry of Defence*, (2013) 8 SCC 83, para 14.1].

Demand. The action of demanding; to ask for with legal right or authority; to ask for peremptorily, imperiously or urgently.

The word 'demand' ordinarily means something more than what is due; it means something which has been demanded, called for or asked for. *Mangoo Singh* v. *Election Tribunal*, AIR 1957 SC 871, 874.

Demand clause. A provision in a note which allows the holder to compel full payment if the maker fails to meet the installment.

Demand draft. Bill of exchange payable on demand. A draft payable on presentation.

Demand instrument. A negotiable instrument payable on demand (when presented).

Demand liabilities. Means liabilities which must be met on demand. [Banking Regulations Act (10 of 1949), S. 5(f)]

Demands (for grants). A requirement or claim, a strong or authoritative request; asking for what is due; request made as of right; any account upon which money or other thing is, or is claimed to be due; asking of anything with authority demands for grants refer to the anticipated financial requirements of the public service for the forthcoming financial year.

Demarcation. Division between adjacent areas. Determining and marking of boundaries.

Demat account. "Demat account" means an account opened with the depository participant in accordance with the guidelines laid down by the Securities and Exchange Board of India established under section 3 of the Securities and Exchange Board of India Act, 1992 (15 of 1992). [Rajiv Gandhi Equity Savings Scheme, 2012, Para 3(ii)].

Demeanour. Way of acting; conduct; behaviour.

Manner of comporting oneself towards others; bearing [CrPC 1973 (2 of 1974), S. 280; [CPC (5 of 1908), O. XVIII, R. 12].

THE DEMEANOUR OF AN ACCUSED person is entirely irrelevant for deciding the question of the guilt or innocence of the accused. It embraces such facts as the tone of voice in which a witness' statement is made, the hesitation or readiness with which his answers are given, the look of the witness, his carriage, his evidences of surprise, his gestures, his zeal, his bearing, his expression, his yawns, the use of his eyes, his furtive or meaning glances, or his shrugs, the pitch of his voice, his self-possession or embarrassment, his air of candor or seeming levity. (*Black*)

Dementia. In medical jurisprudence, that form of insanity which is characterized by mental weakness and decrepitude, and by total inability to reason, where the mental derangement is accompanied with a general derangement of the faculties; an extremely low condition of the mental function; profound general mental incapacity.

Demerged company. Means the company whose undertaking is transferred, pursuant to a demerger, to a resulting company. [Income tax Act (43 of 1961), S. 2(19AAA)]

Demesne. Possession of land with unrestricted right of use.

Demi. Half.

Demi-god. Half divine, half human; a worshipped person.

Demise. The conveyance of an estate [Companies Act (1 of 1956), S. 535(6), prov.]; death; end of existence or being.

Demised premises. The expression 'demised premises' means the premises transferred by way of lease or conveyance. *Delta International Ltd.* v. *Shyam Sunder Ganeriwala*, (1999) 4 SCC 545, para 23 : AIR 1999 SC 2607.

Democracy. One of the three forms of government; that in which the sovereign power is neither lodged in one man, as in a monarchy, nor in the nobles, as in an oligarchy, but in the collective body of the people; government by the people; state in which such a government prevails; the principle that all citizens have equal political rights.

Democrat. Advocate of democracy; member of a democratic state of party.

Democratic. Advocating or practising principles of democracy.

Demographic information. "Demographic information" Includes information relating to the name, date of birth, address and other relevant information of an individual, as may be specified by regulations for the purpose of issuing an Aadhaar number, but shall not include race, religion, caste, tribe, ethnicity, language, records of entitlement, income or medical history. [Aadhaar (Targated Delivery of Financial and Other Subsidies, Benefits and Services) Act (18 of 2016), S.2(k)].

Demolish. To throw or pull down; overthrow; crush to pieces; destroy the structural character of, as a building or wall; reduce to ruins.

Demolition and construction waste. Means wastes from building materials debris and rubble resulting from construction, re-modeling, repair and demolition operation. [Municipal Solid Wastes (Management and Handling) Rules, 2000, R. 3(VII)].

Demonetisation. The process of demonetizing or the state of being demonetized.

Demonstration. Demonstration always means expression of resentment by a number of persons grouped together.

A demonstration is a visible manifestation of the feelings or sentiments of an individual or a group. It is thus a communication of one's ideas to others to whom it is intended to be conveyed. It is in effect therefore a form of speech or of expression, because speech need not be vocal since signs made by a dumb person would also be a form of speech. *Kameshwar Prasad* v. *Union of India*, AIR 1962 SC 1166, 1170. [Constitution of India, Art. 19 (1) & (b)]

The act of making known or evident by visible or tangible means; an expression or display, show [Navy Act (62 of 1957), S. 19(2)]; a public display of group feeling especially towards a person, cause or action of public interest.

Demonstrative. Pointing out specifically; designating particularly. (*Anderson*)

Demonstrative evidence. That which established a fact beyond doubt; conclusive evidence.

Demonstrative legacy. "Where a testator bequeaths a certain sum of money, or a certain quantity of any other commodity, and refers to a particular fund or stock so as to constitute the same the primary fund or stock out of which payment is to be made, the legacy is said to be demonstrative." [Indian Succession Act (39 of 1925), S.150]

DEMONSTRATIVE LEGACY is general in its phrase but specific in its fund.

Demonstrative legacy is a gift by will of a certain sum directed to be paid out of a specific fund or asset. [Indian Succession Act (39 of 1925), S. 150, *Expln.*].

Demur. In pleading, to rest or pause; to interpose an objection which raises an issue of law.

Demurrage. DEMURRAGE" means the charge levied for the detention of any rolling stock after the expiry of free time, if any, allowed for such detention. [Railways Act (24 of 1989), S. 2(11)]

An extended freight, or reward to the vessel in compensation of the earnings she is caused to lose improperly; an allowance or compensation for the delay or detention of vessel; compensation for undue detention (*Ame. Cyc.*); also applied to payment made on account of delay in railroad equipment. (*Cyc. Law Dict.*) Charge for delay in clearing goods at place or destination. (*Spirit of Marine Laws; Tomlin*)

Rate of amount payable to ship-owner by charterer for failure to load or discharge ship within the time accorded; similar charge on railway. [Indian Railways Act (9 of 1890), S. 45(1)(b)] [Now repealed & replaced by Act 24 of 1989].

Demurrage is a charge and not a service., The Power of the Board is not limited to fixing rates of demurrage. Besides, it is plain that the Board has used expression 'demurrage' not in the strict mercantile sense but merely to signify a charge which may be levied on goods after the expiration of free days. *The Trustees of the Port of Madras*. v. *Aminchand Pyarelal*, AIR 1975 SC 1935, 1944. [Madras Port Trust Act (2 of 1905), S. 42, 43, 43A]

In the context of the goods remaining in the wharfage, 'demurrage' implies the charges which the port trust can levy at a particular rate if the goods remain on the docks beyond a specified time. *Sun Export Corporation* v. *Board of Trustees of the Port Bombay*, (1998) 1 SCC 142, para 14 : AIR 1998 SC 92.

Demurrage charges. "Demurrage charges" are levied in order to ensure quick clearance of the cargo from the harbour. and make it unprofitable for importers to use the port permises as a warehouse. *Board of Trustees of the Port of Bombay* v. *Jai Hind Oil Mills Co.,* AIR 1987 SC 622.

Demurrer. "A pleading stating that although the facts alleged in a complaint may be true, they are insufficient for the plaintiff to state a claim for relief and for the defendant to frame an answer..." [Black's Law Dictionary (Ninth Edition) as cited in *Angelo Brothers Ltd. vs. Bennett, Coleman and Co. Ltd. and Ors.* [2017] 203 CompCas180 (Cal), para 13]

"Demurrer means "an objection granting the factual basis of an opponent's point but dismissing it as irrelevant or invalid..." [Concise Oxford English Dictionary (Eleventh Edition) as cited in *Angelo Brothers Ltd. vs. Bennett, Coleman and Co. Ltd. and Ors.* [2017] 203 CompCas180 (Cal), para 13]

Demutualisation. "DEMUTUALISATION" means the segregation of ownership and management from the trading rights of the members of a recognised stock exchange in accordance with a scheme approved by the Securities and Exchange Board of India. [Securities Contracts (Regulation) Act (42 of 1956), S. 2(ab), as inserted by Securities Laws (Amendment) Act (1 of 2005), S. 2]

Denationalization. The act of returning government ownership and control of an industry or function to private ownership and control.

Ending of a Parliament with a view to have fresh election. In India, only the House of People, the lower house of Parliament, may be dissolved.

Denatured. To have the essential nature of a thing changed.

"DENATURED" is defined to mean "effectually and permanently rendered unfit for human consumption." [22 IC 425 (426), Bengal Excise Act, 1909, S. 2(6)]

Denial. Act of denying or refusing; a term which implies a contradiction of an assertion. Also a traverse in the pleading of one party of an allegation of fact set up by the other.

The act of denying; a disavowal [Indian Evidence Act (1 of 1872), S. 136, ill. (c)]

Denomination. "DENOMINATION", in relation to a variety or its propagating material or essentially derived variety or its propagating material, means the denomination of such variety or its propagating material or essentially derived variety or its propagating material, as the case may be, expressed by means of letters or a combination of letters and figures written in any language. [Protection of Plant Varieties and Farmers' Right Act (53 of 2001), S. 2(g)]

Denomination. The word 'denomination' has been defined to mean allocation of individuals classed together under the same name; a religious sect or body having a common faith and organization and designed by a distinctive name. As Art 26. Constitution of India contemplates not merely a religious denomination but also a section thereof, the math or the spiritual fraternity represented by it can legitimately come within the purview of this Article. [Oxford Dictionary as cited in *V.A. Kandasamy Mudaliar and Ors. vs. The Commissioner, Hindu Religious and Charitable Endowments, Madras* (2017) 5 MLJ 288, para 18(2)]

The Webster's Third New International Dictionary gives the meaning of "denomination" "a religious group of a community of believers called by the same name" [Webster's Third New International Dictionary as cited in *V.A. Kandasamy Mudaliar and Ors. vs. The Commissioner, Hindu Religious and Charitable Endowments, Madras* (2017) 5 MLJ 288, para 18(4)]

A class or collection of individuals called by the same name; a sect; a class of units in money (coins of small denomination); a distinctively named church or sect (as, elergy of all denominations).

The 'Hindus' do not come within the ambit of the expression 'denomination'. *Sri Adi Visheshwara of Kashi Vishwanath Temple* v. *State of U.P.*, (1997) 4 SCC 606, para 45.

As Art. 26, Constitution of India contemplates not merely a religious denomination but also a section thereof, the *math* or the spiritual fraternity represented by it can legitimately come within the purview of this Article. *Commissioner H.R.E.* v. *Lakshmindra Thirtha Swamiar of Shriruv Mutt*, AIR 1954 SC 282, 289.

A characteristic name given to a thing or class of things; that by which anything is called; [Reserve Bank of India (Amendment and Miscellaneous Provisions) Act (54 of 1953), S. 9]; a class or society of individuals called by the same name especially a religious group or a community of believers called by the same name.

Denomine proprio non est curandum cum in substantia non erretur quia nomina mutabilia sunt res autem immobiles. As to the proper name, it is not to be regarded where it errs not in substance; because names are changeable, but things are immutable.

Denote. To mean; to indicate; to stand for to signify.

Denotify. To withdraw a notification; to cancel a notification, to take out an entry out of a notification.

Denoting stamp. An embossed Revenue stamp on a document showing or "denoting" the amount of stamp duty paid and stamped on another document in respect of the same matter.

Denounce. To make formal or public accusation against; to condemn openly; to declare an act to be a crime and prescribe punishment for it; accuse; give notice of intention to withdraw from (as, treaty, *etc.*). An act or thing is "denounced" when the law declares it a crime and provides a punishment for it.

Dental Assessment and Rating Board. Means the Board constituted under section 16. [National Dental Commission Act, 2023 (21 of 2023), section 2(e)]

"Dental auxiliary" includes a dental hygienist or a dental mechanic or a dental operating room assistant or such other category as may be specified by the Commission. [National Dental Commission Act, 2023 (21 of 2023), section 2(f)]

Dental hygienist. Means a person, not being a dentist or a medical practitioner, who scales, cleans or polishes teeth and gives instructions in dental hygiene. [Dentists Act (16 of 1948), S. 2(b)]

"Dental hygienist" means a person not being a dentist or a medical practitioner who scales, cleans or polishes teeth, or gives instruction in dental hygiene. [National Dental Commission Act, 2023 (21 of 2023), section 2(g)]

Dental institution. Means any institution within or outside India which grants degrees, diplomas, certificates for certification courses or licences in dentistry and includes affiliated colleges, deemed to be Universities and institutions mentioned in the Schedule. [National Dental Commission Act, 2023 (21 of 2023), section 2(h)]

Dental mechanic. Means a person who makes or repairs denture and dental appliances. [Dentists Act (16 of 1948), S. 2(c)]"Dental mechanic" means a person qualified to perform laboratory work required for the prosthetic rehabilitation of dental and maxillofacial structures and orthodontic appliances. [National Dental Commission Act, 2023 (21 of 2023), section 2(i)]

"Dental operating room assistant". Means a person who assists the dentist in sterilising and handing over instruments as required by the dentist at the chair side. [National Dental Commission Act, 2023 (21 of 2023), section 2(j)]

Dentist. "DENTIST" means a person who practices dentistry. [Dentists Act (16 of 1948), S. 2(e)]

"Dentist" means a person who practices dentistry. [National Dental Commission Act, 2023 (21 of 2023), section 2(k)]

A dental surgeon; one who practices dentistry; one whose profession is to clean and extract teeth, repair them when diseased, and replace them when necessary, by artificial ones; one who performs manual or mechanical operations to preserve teeth, to cleanse, extract, insert or repair them, one who practices dental surgery and mechanical dentistry. A "dentist" is a dental surgeon. He performs surgical operations upon the teeth and jaw, and, as incidental thereto, upon the flesh connected therewith. His sphere of operations is included in the larger one of the physician and surgeon.

Dentistry. Includes—

(i) the performance of any operation on, and the treatment on any disease, deficiency or lesion of human teeth or jaws, and the performance of radio-graphic work in connection with human teeth or jaws or the oral cavity;

(ii) the giving of any anesthetic in connection with any such operation or treatment;

(iii) the mechanical construction or the renewal of artificial dentures or restorative dental appliances;

(iv) The performance of any operation on, or the giving of any treatment, advice or attendance to, any person preparatory to, or for the purpose of, or in connection with, the fitting, inserting, fixing, constructing, repairing or renewing of artificial dentures or restorative dental appliances, and the performance of any such operation and the giving of any such treatment, advice or attendance as is usually performed or given by dentists. [Dentists Act (16 of 1948), S. 2(d)]

"Dentistry" includes the science, practice and research in dental and oral health, directed towards—

(i) facilitating healthy development of dentition, jaws and dentofacial structures;

(ii) prevention of oral diseases and promotion of oral health;

(iii) diagnosis and use of diagnostic tests, investigations and procedure to decide the normal and abnormal state or diseases of teeth, gums, jaws and related tissues necessary for the functions of the oral cavity;

(iv) performing procedures for the optimisation of dental and oral health, which may include restoration, rehabilitation, surgery or a combination thereof, to restore the functions, structural anatomy and aesthetics of the stomatognathic system and the masticatory apparatus;

(v) creating awareness and working knowledge of the effects of systemic health on dentition and oral cavity and to perform the duties of an active member of the healthcare team, including basic life support;

(vi) promoting good systemic health through diagnosis and necessary interventions related to oral health conditions; and

(vii) bringing awareness of oral health related issues of the society and of nation and to facilitate implementation of the updated policies of the Government or Government bodies in this regard. [National Dental Commission Act, 2023 (21 of 2023), section 2(l)]

Deny. To contradict; to gainsay; disavow; repudiate.

To refuse to admit the truth of; to disown; to denounce; to withold the possession or an enjoyment of. [Constitution of India, Art. 14].

Deodand. An old English practice of forfeiting to the Crown the thing or the animal that had done a wrong.

A thing that by English law before 1846 was forfeited to the Crown and thence to pious uses because it had been the immediate cause of the death of a person. [Coroners Act (4 of 1871), S. 30].

Dolo malo pactum de non servaturum. A pact made with malicious intent will not be upheld.

Depart. To go away.

Departed from. Deviated from; from which one has diverged.

Department. A separate division of a complex whole; one of the separate divisions or branches of state or municipal administration. [Indian Evidence Act (1 of 1872), S. 123].

"DEPARTMENT" means a Department of Studies and includes a Centre of Studies. [S. 2(i) of the Rajiv Gandhi National Aviation University Act, 2013 (26 of 2013). Also see S. 3(i) of the Rani Lakshmi Bai Central Agricultural University Act, 2014 (10 of 2014)]

Department representative. In these Rules unless the context otherwise requires— "DEPARTMENT REPRESENTATIVE" in relation to the proceedings before the Tribunal means a person appointed by the Central Government or by an officer duly authorised in this behalf, as authorised representative to appear, plead and act for the designated authority in such proceedings. [Cegat (Countervaining Duty and Anti-Dumping Duty) Procedure Rules, 1996, R. 1(i)(g)]

Departmental inquiry. Means an inquiry held under and in accordance with—

(i) any law made by parliament or any rule made thereunder, or

(ii) any rule made under proviso to Article 309, or continued under Article 313 of the Constitution of India, into any allegation of lack of integrity against any person to whom this Act applies. [Departmental Inquiries (Enforcement of Attendance of Witnesses and Production of Documents) Act (18 of 1972), S. 3(a)]

"DEPARTMENTAL INQUIRY" is only an inter-regnum inquiry. *UOI* v. *Alok Kumar*, AIR 2010 SC 2735.

Departure. 'DEPARTURE', with its grammatical variations and cognate expressions, means departure from India by water, land or air. [Passports Act (15 of 1967), S. 2(a)]

Depend. To be contingent on, or conditioned by; to rest entirely on for support. [CPC (5 of 1908), S. 9].

Dependant/Dependent. "DEPENDENT" means any woman or child who is related to an emigrant and any aged or incapacitated relative of an emigrant. [Emigration Act (7 of 1922), S. 2(c)].

"DEPENDENT" means any of the following relatives of a deceased subscriber to, or a depositor in, a Provident Fund, namely, a wife, husband, parent, child, minor brother, unmarried sister and a deceased son's widow and child, and where no parent of the subscriber or depositor is alive, a paternal grandparent. [Provident Funds Act (19 of 1925), S. 2(c)]

"DEPENDENT" means any of the following relatives of a deceased insured person, namely:—

(i) a widow, minor legitimate or adopted son, an unmarried legitimate or adopted daughter;

(ia) a widowed mother.

(ii) if wholly dependant on the earnings of the insured person at the time of his death, a legitimate or adopted son or daughter who has attained the age of eighteen years and is infirm;

(iii) if wholly or in part dependent on the earnings of insured person at the time of his death,—

(a) a parent other than widowed mother,

(b) a minor illegitimate son, an unmarried illegitimate daughter or a daughter legitimate or adopted son or a daughter legitimate or adopted or illegitimate if married and a minor or if widowed and minor,

(c) a minor brother or an unmarried sister or a widowed sister if a minor,

(d) a widowed daughter-in-law,

(e) a minor child of a pre-deceased son.

(f) a minor child of a per-deceased daughter where no parent of the child is alive, or

(g) a parental grand-parent if no parent of the insured person in alive. [Employee's State Insurance Act (34 of 1948), S. 2(6A)]

"DEPENDENT" means—

(a) in the case of an individual, the spouse, children, parents, brothers and sisters of the individual or any of them,

(b) in the case of a Hindu undivided family, a member of the Hindu undivided family,

dependant wholly or mainly on such individual or Hindu undivided family for his support and maintenance. [Income-Tax Act (43 of 1961), S. 80DDB *Expln* (1)]

"DEPENDENT" means any person who is related to an emigrant and is dependent on that emigrant. [Emigration Act (31 of 1983), S. 2(c)]

"DEPENDENTS" means wife, husband, father, mother, unmarried daughter and minor child or such of them as exist. [Gujarat Advocates Welfare Fund Act (14 of 1991), S. 2(h)]

"DEPENDENTS" means the spouse, parents or minor children of a member of the Fund. [Advocates Welfare Fund Act (45 of 2001), 2(f)]

"DEPENDENT" means any of the following relatives of a deceased member, namely :—

(i) a minor legitimate son, and an unmarried legitimate daughter and a widowed mother; or

(ii) if wholly dependent on the earnings of the member at the time of his death, a son or a daughter who has attained the age of eighteen years and who is infirm; or

(iii) if wholly or in part dependent on the earnings of the member at the time of his death,—

(a) the parent; or

(b) a minor brother or an unmarried sister; or

(c) a widowed daughter-in-law; or

(d) a minor child of a pre-deceased son; or

(e) a minor child of a pre-deceased daughter where no parent of the child is alive; or

(f) the paternal grandparent if no parent of the member is alive; or

(g) such other person as may be specified by the rules made under Section 9 by the Joint Committee. [Salary, Allowances and Pension of Members of Parliament (Amendment) Act 2003 (9 of 2004), S. 2(aa)]

"DEPENDENTS" means such person as a person against whom a maintenance order is made is liable to maintain according to the law in force in the reciprocating territory in which the maintenance order is made. [Maintenance Order Enforcement Act (18 of 1921), S. 2].

A person who depends on another for support. [Employees' State Insurance Act (34 of 1948), S. 2(6A)].

Dependents mean such members of the workman's family, specified by S. 2(1)(d) of Workmen's Compensation Act (8 of 1923) as were wholly, or in part, dependent upon the earnings of the workman at the time of his death.

An illegitimate child though born of an adulterous intercourse is a "dependent" within the meaning of S. 2(1)(d) of the Workmen's Compensation Act when it appears that the child was supported by the putative father. A step-mother is not a dependent within the meaning of the Workmen's Compensation Act.

The Workmen's Compensation Act, includes in the term "dependent" without any further qualification, only the wife, minor, legitimate son, unmarried legitimate daughter of widowed mother. For a father of a deceased workman to be adjudged a dependent, he must show that he was wholly or in part dependent on the earnings of his son at the time of his death.

A married sister is not a 'dependent' within the meaning of S. 2(c) of the Provident Funds Act (19 of 1925); and having married, she cannot return to the status of an unmarried sister on widowhood so as to come within the meaning of the word "dependent".

Dependency. The state of being dependent for support.

A dependent or subordinate place or territory. [Extradition Act (34 of 1962), S. 2(a)].

Deplete. To reduce; to exhaust.

Depletion. An emptying, exhausting, or wasting of an asset, especially of a finite natural resource such as oil.

Deponent. One who bears witness or testimony; one who gives information on oath or affirmation respecting some fact known to him, before a Court or magistrate.

One who deposes or gives evidence; a witness. [CrPC 1973 (2 of 1974), S. 291(2) and CPC (5 of 1908), S. 139].

Deportation. The lawful expulsion of an undesired alien or other person from a state.

DEPORTATION, TRANSPORTATION, EXTRADITION. Strictly speaking, "transportation, extradition, and deportation," although each has the effect of removing a person from a country, are different things and for different purposes. *Transportation* is by way of punishment of one convicted of offence against the laws of the country: *extradition* is the surrender to another country of one accused of an offence against its laws, there to be tried, and, if found guilty, punished; *deportation* is the removing of an alien out of the country simply because his presence is deemed inconsistent with the public welfare, and without any punishment being imposed or contemplated, either under the laws of the country out of which he is sent, or under those of the country to which he is taken.

Depose. To give evidence; bear witness or testimony; to state or affirm some matter of fact in an affidavit or deposition; also to lay down; to lodge; to degrade from a throne or high station.

To state in evidence; to give evidence on oath in a Court of law. [Indian Evidence Act (1 of 1872), S. 27].

Deposit. Thing stored or entrusted for safe keeping.

"DEPOSIT" means a deposit of money. [Compulsory Deposit Scheme (21 of 1963), S. 3(b)]

"DEPOSIT" means a voluntary deposit made by any person with the National Housing Bank in accordance with the scheme on or after the commencement of this Act but before the specified date. [Voluntary Deposits (Immunities and Exemptions) Act (47 of 1991), S. 2(a)]

"DEPOSIT" includes and shall be deemed always to have included any receipt of money by way of deposit or loan or in any other form, but does not include,—

(i) amounts raised by way of share capital;

(ii) amounts contributed as capital by partners of a firm;

(iii) amounts received from a scheduled bank or a co-operative bank or any other banking company as defined in Section 5(*c*) of the Banking Regulation Act, 1949;

(iv) any amount received from, (*a*) the Industrial Development Bank of India or (*b*) a State Financial Corporation, or (*c*) any financial institution specified in or under Section 6A of the Industrial Development Bank of India Act, 1964, or (*d*) any other institution that may be specified by the Bank in this behalf;

(v) amounts received in the ordinary course of business, by way of (*a*) security deposit, or (*b*) dealership deposit, or (*c*) earnest money, or (*d*) advance against orders for goods, properties or services;

(vi) any amount received from an individual or a firm or an association of individuals not being a body corporate, registered under any enactment relating to money lending which is for the time being in force in any state; and

(vii) any amount received by way of subscription in respect of a chit.

Explanation I—"Chit" has the meaning assigned to it in clause (b) of Section 2 of the Chit Fund Act, 1982.

Explanation II—Any credit given by a seller to a buyer on the sale of any property (whether movable or immovable) shall not be deemed to be deposit for the purposes of this clause. [Reserve Bank of India (2 of 1934), S. 45-I (bb)]

"DEPOSIT" means—

(i) any moveable property in the custody or under the control of any Civil or Revenue Court in respect of any proceedings before it; or

(ii) any moveable property under the superintendence or in the custody of a Court of wards under any law for the time being in force whether such moveable property is in the actual custody of the Court of Wards, or in that of some other authority on its behalf; or

(iii) any moveable property in the custody or under the control of a manager;

and includes any securities, insurance policies and negotiable instruments in the custody or under the control of any such Civil or Revenue Court or under the Superintendence or in the custody of such Court of Wards or in the custody or under the control of such manager.

Explanation I—"Securities" include shares, scrips, stocks bonds, debentures, debenture stocks or other marketable securities of a like nature in or of any body corporates and also Government securities.

Explanation II—Where any deposit in the custody or under the control of any Civil or Revenue Court or under the superintendence or in the custody of a Court of Wards or in the custody or under the control of the manager has vested in the Custodian of Evacuee Property as evacuee property, such deposit shall, for the purpose of this Act, be deemed to be in the custody or under the control of such Civil or Revenue Court or under the superintendence or in the custody of the Court of Wards or in the custody or under the control of manager, as the case may be. [Transfer of Evacuee Deposit Act (15 of 1954), S. 2(b)]

"DEPOSIT" means the aggregate of the unpaid balances due to a depositor (other than a foreign Government, the Central Government, a State Government, corresponding new bank or a Regional Rural bank or a banking company or a co-operative bank in respect of all his accounts by whatever name called, with a corresponding new bank or with a Regional Rural Bank or with a banking company or a co-operative bank and includes credit balances in any cash credit account but does not include,—

(i) where a banking company or a Regional Rural Bank or a corresponding new bank at the commencement of this Act or where an eligible co-operative bank at the commencement of the Deposit Insurance Corporation (Amendment) Act, 1968 (56 of

1968) is working under a scheme of compromise or arrangement or of reconstruction sanctioned by any competent authority providing for the acceptance of fresh deposits any amount due to the depositor in respect of his deposit before the date of the coming into force of the scheme of the extent it is not credited after the said date under he provisions of that scheme; or

(ia) any amount due on account of any deposit with any insured bank which has been specially exempted in this behalf by the Corporation with the previous approval of the Reserve Bank; or

(ii) any amount due on account of any deposit received outside India. [Deposit Insurance and Credit Guarantee Corp-oration Act (47 of 1961), S. 2(g)]

"DEPOSIT" includes deposit of money with a bank, company, proprietary concern, partnership firm, corporate body, trust or any other person. [Foreign Exchange Management (Deposit) Regulations, 2000, Reg. 2(iv)]

The essence of a deposit is that there must be a liability to return it to the party by whom or on whose behalf it is made on the fulfilment of certain conditions. *C.I.T.* v. *Bazpur Co-Operative Sugar Factory Ltd.*, (1988) 172 ITR 321, 330 (SC).

Something deposited; sum deposited; the action of depositing; to commit to the charge of someone for safe keeping as pledge; natural accumulation.

"DEPOSIT" includes any receipt of money by way of deposit or loan or in any other form by a company, but does not include such categories of amount as may be prescribed in consultation with the Reserve Bank of India. [S. 2(31) of the Companies Act, 2013 (18 of 2013)]

"DEPOSIT" includes any receipt of money by way of deposit or loan or in any other form, by a company, but does not include—

(i) any amount received from the Central Government or a State Government, or any amount received from any other source whose repayment is guaranteed by the Central Government or a State Government, or any amount received from a local authority, or any amount received from a statutory authority constituted under an Act of Parliament or a State Legislature;

(ii) any amount received from foreign Governments, foreign or international banks, multilateral financial institutions (including, but not limited to, International Finance Corporation, Asian Development Bank, Commonwealth Development Corporation and International Bank for Industrial and Financial Reconstruction), foreign Governments owned development financial institutions, foreign export credit agencies, foreign collaborators, foreign bodies corporate and foreign citizens, foreign authorities or persons resident outside India subject to the provisions of Foreign Exchange Management Act, 1999 (42 of 1999) and rules and regulations made there under;

(iii) any amount received as a loan or facility from any banking company or from the State Bank of India or any of its subsidiary banks or from a banking institution notified by the Central Government under section 51 of the Banking Regulation Act, 1949 (10 of 1949), or a corresponding new bank as defined in section 2(d) of the Banking Companies (Acquisition and Transfer of Undertakings) Act, 1970 (5 of 1970) or in section 2(b) of the Banking Companies (Acquisition and Transfer of Undertakings) Act, 1980 (40 of 1980), or from a co-operative bank as defined in section 2(b-ii) of the Reserve Bank of India Act, 1934 (2 of 1934);

(iv) any amount received as a loan or financial assistance from Public Financial Institutions notified by the Central Government in this behalf in consultation with the Reserve Bank of India or any regional financial institutions or Insurance Companies or Scheduled Banks as defined in the Reserve Bank of India Act, 1934 (2 of 1934);

(v) any amount received against issue of commercial paper or any other instruments issued in accordance with the guidelines or notification issued by the Reserve Bank of India;

(vi) any amount received by a company from any other company;

(vii) any amount received and held pursuant to an offer made in accordance with the provisions of Act 18 of 2013 towards subscription to any securities, including share application money or advance towards allotment of securities pending allotment, so long as such amount is appropriated only against the amount due on allotment of the securities applied for.

Explanation.—For the purposes of this sub-clause, it is hereby clarified that—

(a) Without prejudice to any other liability or action, if the securities for which application money or advance for such securities was received cannot be allotted within sixty days from the date of receipt of the application money or advance for such securities and such application money or advance is not refunded to the subscribers within fifteen days from the date of completion of sixty days, such amount shall be treated as a deposit under these rules;

(b) any adjustment of the amount for any other purpose shall not be treated as refund;

(viii) any amount received from a person who, at the time of the receipt of the amount, was a director of the company:

Provided that the director from whom money is received, furnishes to the company at the time of giving the money, a declaration in writing to the effect that the amount is not being given out of funds acquired by him by borrowing or accepting loans or deposits from others;

(ix) any amount raised by the issue of bonds or debentures secured by a first charge or a charge ranking pari passu with the first charge on any assets referred to in Schedule III of Act 18 of 2013 excluding intangible assets of the company or bonds or debentures compulsorily convertible into shares of the company within five years:

Provided that if such bonds or debentures are secured by the charge of any assets referred to in Schedule III of the Act, excluding intangible assets, the amount of such bonds or debentures shall not exceed the market value of such assets as assessed by a registered valuer;

(x) any amount received from an employee of the company not exceeding his annual salary under a contract of employment with the company in the nature of non-interest bearing security deposit;

(xi) any non-interest bearing amount received or held in trust;

(xii) any amount received in the course of, or for the purposes of, the business of the company,—

(a) as an advance for the supply of goods or provision of services accounted for in any manner whatsoever provided that such advance is appropriated against supply of goods or provision of services within a period of three hundred and sixty five days from the date of acceptance of such advance:

Provided that in case of any advance which is subject matter of any legal proceedings before any court of law, the said time limit of three hundred and sixty five days shall not apply;

(b) as advance, accounted for in any manner whatsoever, received in connection with consideration for property under an agreement or arrangement, provided that such advance is adjusted against the property in accordance with the terms of agreement or arrangement;

(c) as security deposit for the performance of the contract for supply of goods or provision of services;

(d) as advance received under long term projects for supply of capital goods except those covered under item (b) above:

Provided that if the amount received under items (a), (b) and (d) above becomes refundable (with or without interest) due to the reasons that the company accepting the money does not have necessary permission or approval, wherever required, to deal in the goods or properties or services for which the money is taken, then the amount received shall be deemed to be a deposit under these rules.

Explanation.—For the purposes of this sub-clause, the amount referred to in the first proviso shall be deemed to be deposits on the expiry of fifteen days from the date they become due for refund;

(xiii) any amount brought in by the promoters of the company by way of unsecured loan in pursuance of the stipulation of any lending financial institution or a bank subject to fulfillment of the following conditions, namely:—

(a) the loan is brought in pursuance of the stipulation imposed by the lending institutions on the promoters to contribute such finance;

(b) the loan is provided by the promoters themselves or by their relatives or by both; and

(c) the exemption under this sub-clause shall be available only till the loans of financial institution or bank are repaid and not thereafter;

(xiv) any amount accepted by a Nidhi company in accordance with the rules made under section 406 of Act 18 of 2013. *Explanation.*—For the purposes of this clause, any amount,—

(a) received by the company, whether in the form of instalments or otherwise, from a person with promise or offer to give returns, in cash or in kind, on completion of the period specified in the promise or offer, or earlier, accounted for in any manner whatsoever, or

(b) any additional contributions, over and above the amount under item (a) above, made by the company as part of such promise or offer, shall be treated as a 'deposit'. [R. 2(1)(c) of the Companies (Acceptance of Deposits) Rules, 2014]

Deposit account. Accounts of deposits of money with bankers withdrawable only on giving a specified previous notice; an account of sums lodged with a bank not to be drawn upon by cheques, and usually not to be withdrawn except after a fixed notice.

The bank account of a depositor. [Additional Emoluments (Compulsory Deposit) Act (37 of 1974), S. 2(f)].

Deposit company. A company whose business is the safe keeping of securities or other valuables deposited in boxes or safes in its building.

Deposit in Bank. When moneys are deposited in a bank, the relationship that is constituted between the banker and the customer is one of debtor and creditor and not trustee and beneficiary. The banker is entitled to use the moneys without being called upon to account for such user, his only liability being to return the amount in accordance with the terms agreed between him and the customer. *Shanti Prasad* v. *Director of Enforcement*, AIR 1962 SC 1764, 1775.

Deposit in Court. If a specific fund in the possession of a party to a cause is the subject of conflicting claims, the Court may in certain cases either allow or compel him to pay it into Court subject to further orders of the Court in the cause. This is termed "Deposit in Court".

Deposit Office. Means any branch or branch office of the State Bank of India constituted under the State Bank of India Act, 1955 (23 of 1955), or of a subsidiary bank as defined in the State Bank of India (Subsidiary Banks) Act, 1959 (38 of 1959), or of a corresponding new bank constituted under Section 3 of the Banking Companies (Acquisition and Transfer of Undertakings) Act, 1970 (5 of 1970), or under Section 3 of the Banking Companies (Acquisition and Transfer of Undertakings) Act, 1980 (40 of 1980), authorised by the Central Government, by notification in the Official Gazette, to receive deposit and maintain account of the depositor, under this Scheme. [Capital Gains Accounts Scheme, 1988, S. 2(e)]

Deposit of title deeds. A method of pledging immoveable property as security for a loan by keeping the title deeds in the keeping of the lender as pledgee.

Deposition. The giving of testimony upon oath in a Court of law, or the testimony so given.

Deposition distinguished from affidavit. The distinction between an affidavit and a deposition is that the former is *ex parte* and voluntary, and the latter is made after notice and is compulsory. A deposition differs from an affidavit, in that the opposite party has an opportunity to cross-examine the witness who makes the former. "A *deposition* is evidence given by a witness under interrogatories, oral or written, and usually written down by an official person, while an affidavit is the mere voluntary act of the party making the oath, and may be, and generally is, taken without the cognizance of the one against whom it is to be used."

Deposition distinguished from an oath. "There is an obvious distinction between an *oath* and *deposition.* The ordinary and usual meaning of the word '*deposition*' is confined to written testimony, at least in legal proceedings." The *oath* is that which is administered to the witness before the deposition is taken. (*U.S.* v. *Clark*, 25, Fed. Cas. No. 14, 804)

Depositor. "DEPOSITOR" means a person by whom, or on whose behalf, money has been heretofore, or shall be hereafter, deposited in a Government Savings Bank and "deposit" means money so "deposited." [Government Savings Bank Act (5 of 1873), S. 3]

"Depositor" means any person who makes a deposit under this Act [Banning of Unregulated Deposit Schemes Act, 2019 (21 of 2019), section 2(5)]

"DEPOSITOR" means a retired employee of public sector company by whom or on whose behalf money is deposited in an account and deposit means money so deposited. [Deposit Scheme for Retiring Employees of Public Sector Companies, 1991, S. 3(c)]

"DEPOSITOR" means any person who has made a deposit with the housing finance company or a heir, legal representative, administrator or assignee of the depositor. [Housing Finance Companies (NHB) Directions, 2001, S. 2(g)]

In these rules, unless the context otherwise requires—
"DEPOSITOR" means :—

(i) an individual, or
(ii) a Hindu undivided family, or
(iii) an association of persons or a body of individuals consisting in either case, only of husband and wife governed by the system of community of property in force in the State of Goa and the Union Territories of Dadra and Nagar Haveli and Daman and Diu, by whom, or on whose behalf money, is deposited in an account and deposit means money so deposited. [National Saving Scheme Rules, 1992, R. 2(c)]

Any person who has made a deposit with a company; or a heir, legal representative, administrator or assignee of the depositor. [Non-Banking Financial Companies Acceptance of Public Deposit (Reserve Bank) Directions, 1998, Para 2(1)(i)]

"DEPOSITOR" means,—(i) any member of the company who has made a deposit with the company in accordance with the provisions of section 73(2) of the Companies Act, 2013 (18 of 2013), or (ii) any person who has made a deposit with a public company in accordance with the provisions of section 76 of Act 18 of 2013. [R. 2(1)(d) of the Companies (Acceptance of Deposits) Rules, 2014]

"DEPOSITOR" means an individual by whom, or on whose behalf moneys has been deposited in a Government Savings Bank and "deposit" means the money so deposited. [Government Savings Banks Act (5 of 1873), S. 3(e) as substituted by Finance Act (13 of 2018)].

Depository. "DEPOSITORY" means a company formed and registered under the Companies Act, 1956 and which has been granted a certificate of registration under sub-section (1A) of Section 12 of the Securities and Exchange Board of India Act, 1992. [Depositories Act (22 of 1996), S. 2(e)] Also see (w.e.f. 1-4-2014) *Explanation* (i) to section 10(23ED) of the Income-tax Act, 1961 (43 of 1961); S. 2(32) of the Companies Act, 2013 (18 of 2013)]

A place in which things are deposited for safe keeping.

Includes—

(a) a depository as defined in clause (e) of sub-section (1) of section 2 of the Depositories Act, 1996 (22 of 1996); and

(b) any other entity declared by the Central Government, by notification in the Official Gazette, to be a depository for the purposes of this Act. [Indian Stamp Act (2 of 1899), section 2(10B)]

Deprave. To defame; to corrupt morally; villify; exhibit contempt for. Corrupt, perverted or immoral state of mind. (*Black*)

Depraved. Marked by moral corruption or perversion as shown by a capacity for extreme and wanton physical cruelty.

Depravity. Corruption; wickedness.

The quality or state of being deprave or corrupt. [Special Marriage Act (43 of 1954), S. 29(1), *Prov.*].

Depreciable amount. The depreciable amount of an asset is the cost of an asset or other amount substituted for cost, less its residual value. [Companies Act (18 of 2013), Schedule II, Part A]

Depreciation. Depreciation is the systematic allocation of the depreciable amount of an asset over its useful life. For the purpose of this Schedule, the term depreciation includes amortisation. [Companies Act (18 of 2013), Schedule II, Part A]

Allowance made in valuation for wear and tear (as, allowance made for depreciation in the value of property for purposes of taxation).

A fall in value; reduction of worth. The deterioration, or the loss or lessening in value, arising from age, use, and improvements, due to better methods. A decline in value of property caused by wear or obsolescence and is usually measured by a set formula which reflects these elements over a given period of useful life of property….. Consistent gradual process of estimating and allocating cost of capital investments over estimated useful life of asset in order to match cost against earnings. [Black's Law Dictionary (5th Edn.) as cited in *Industrial Credit and Development Syndicate Limited* v. *Commissioner of Income Tax, Mysore*, (2013) 3 SCC 541, para 11].

As for building, depreciation is the measurement of wearing out through consumption, or use, or effluxion of time. [Principles and Practice of Valuation (5th Edn., p. 323 by Parks as cited in *Industrial Credit and Development Syndicate Limited* v. *Commissioner of Income Tax, Mysore*, (2013) 3 SCC 541, para 12].

Depreciation is an out-of-pocket cost as any other costs. He has further observed that the depreciation charge is merely the periodic operating aspect of fixed asset costs. [Accountants's Handbook (3rd Edn. by Paton as cited in *Industrial Credit and Development Syndicate Limited* v. *Commissioner of Income Tax, Mysore*, (2013) 3 SCC 541, para 12].

Depreciation is the monetary equivalent of the were and tear suffered by a capital asset that is set aside to facilitate its replacement when the asset becomes dysfunctional. *Industrial Credit and Development Syndicate Limited* v. *Commissioner of Income Tax, Mysore*, (2013) 3 SCC 541, para 10.

The expression 'depreciation' means a decrease in value of property through wear, deterioration or obsolescence. Depreciation is allowable as a deduction both according to accountancy principles and according to the Indian Income Tax Act. *I.T. Commissioner, Punjab* v. *Alps Theatre*, AIR 1967 SC 1437, 1439.

Depreciation represents the diminution in value, of a capital asset, when applied to the purpose of making profit or gain. *Workmen N.G. Bank* v. *N.G. Bank*, AIR 1976 SC 611, 616.

Generally speaking 'depreciation' is an allowance for the diminution in the value due to wear and tear of capital asset employed by an assessee in his business. *Union of India* v. *Savjiram*, (2004) 9 SCC 312, 317, para 10.

For building 'depreciation' is the measurement of wearing out through consumption, or use, or effluxion of time. [Parks in Principles and Practice of Valuation, 5th Edn., at p. 323, as cited in *Union of India* v. *Savjiram*, (2004) 9 SCC 312, 317, para 11]

Lowering of value; fall in the exchangeable value of money.

Depredation. Plundering; pillaging. [IPC (45 of 1860), S. 126].

Depression. A period of economic stress which persists over an extended period of time.

Deprivation. The action of being deprived.

Deprive. To take away; dispossess; strip one of office or dignity; injure or destroy; to take something from; to keep from acquiring, using or enjoying something.

"Deprive" conveys the idea of taking away that which one has or withholding that which one may have. To take something from; to keep from acquiring, using or enjoying something; to take away, end, injure, or destroy. *Mammath Nath Kayal* v. *District Manager, FCI*, AIR 1996 Cal 316, 322. [Constitution of India, Art. 300-A]

Deputation. The word 'deputation' means service outside the cadre or outside the parent department. *State of Punjab* v. *Inder Singh,* (1997) 8 SCC 372 (para 18) : AIR 1998 SC 7.

Depute. To appoint as a delegate or agent to ordain to act on another's behalf.

Deputy. The term "deputy" means "one who is appointed, designated, or deputed to act for another."

A second in command or assistant who usually takes charge when his superior is absent. [Army Act (46 of 1950), S. 3(xx)].

Deputy Speaker. The Officer of the House of a Legislature, who takes the Chair during the absence of the Speaker and performs his duties in relation to all proceedings in the House.

In Lok Sabha the Deputy Speaker is elected from amongst its members; he is not subordinate to the Speaker and holds and independent position; he is answerable to the House alone. In the absence of the Speaker, the Deputy Speaker is required to perform the duties of the Office of the Speaker and preside over the sitting of the House and the joint sitting of the Houses of Parliament and exercises the powers of the Speaker. (*Constitutional and Parliamentary Term*)

Derecognition. A process whereby notice is given to terminate union recognition in an establishment or company.

Derelict. Abandoned; deserted; cast away.

Dereliction. Abandonment; intentional or conscious neglect.

Derivatia protestas non potest esse major primitiva. (*Maxim*) Derived power cannot be greater than that from which it is derived. (*Broom*)

Derivative. Coming from another; taken from something preceding; secondary; source to which a thing's origin is traced.

"DERIVATIVE" includes—

(a) a security derived from a debt instrument, share, loan, whether secured or un-secured, risk instrument or contract for differences or any other form of security;

(b) a contact which derives its value from the prices, or index of prices, of underlying securities. [Securities Contracts (Regulation Act, 1956, S. 2(ac). Also see S. 2(33) of the Companies Act, 2013 (18 of 2013)]

"Derivative" means a naturally occurring biochemical compound or metabolism of biological resources, even if it does not contain functional units of heredity. [Biological Diversity Act, 2002 (18 of 2003)]

Derivative conveyance. A conveyance which presupposes some other conveyance precedent, and serves to enlarge, confirm, alter, restrain, restore or transfer the interest granted by such original conveyance.

Derivative deed. A deed which is supplemental to another, whose scope it alters, confirms, or extends.

Derivative of opium. Means—

(i) medicinal opium, that is, opium which has undergone the processes necessary to adapt it for medicinal use;

(ii) prepared opium, that is, any product of opium obtained by any series of operations designed to transform opium into an extract suitable for smoking, and the dross or other residue remaining after opium is smoked;

(iii) morphine, that is, the principal alkaloid of opium having the chemical formula $C_{17}H_{19}NO_3$, and its salts and its derivatives. [Medicinal & Toilet Preparations (Excise Duties) Act (16 of 1955), S. 2(bb)]

Derivative title. The principle, that a transferee of property acquires only the transferor's right therein.

Derivative work. A work based on a preexisting work, such as translation, musical arrangement, fictionalization, motion picture version, adbridgment or any other form in which a work may be recast, transformed or adapted.

Derive. To draw or receive, or obtain as from a source or origin, or by regular transmission.

Derogate. To lessen in estimation; to invalidate; degenerate; degrade.

Derogation. The action of derogating; detracttion. [CrPC 1973 (2 of 1974), S. 145(10)].

The act of annulling or breaking a law, or some part of it; impairment; partial surrender of a right.

The partial repeal or abrogation of a law by a later Act that limits its scope or impairs its utility and force. The Black's Law Dictionary as cited in *KSL and Industries Limited* v. *Arihant Threads Limited,* (2015) 1 SCC 166, para 37.

"Derogation" means, taking away, lessening or impairing the authority, position or dignity. *P.C. Joshi* v. *State of Uttar Pradesh*, AIR 1961 SC 387, 390.

Derogatory. Detracting; tending to lessen effect or estimation.

Descend. To go down; to pass down from the elder to be derived by the younger; to go over to; to pass; to pass or be transferred; to pass by descent or inheritance; or be inherited by; to pass from; to vest in; to be vested with. (*Ame. Cyc.*)

The word "descend" means ordinarily to go down, but in the law relating to the devolution of property rights "descend" may mean "ascend," as descending in the ascending line."

Descendant. Person descended from another; one who descends, as off-spring, however remotely; correlative to ancestor or an ascendant; one who has issued from an individual, including children, grandchildren and their children to the remotest degree; issue of the body of the person named of the very degree; issue of any degree; the issue of a deceased person; and person proceeding from an ancestor, in any degree.

One descended from an ancestor. [Income-tax Act (43 of 1961), S. 2(41)].

Descendant, lineal. A descendant in the direct line of descent [Hindu Marriage Act (25 of 1955), S. 3(g)(ii); Estate Duty Act (34 of 1953), S. 17(4)(ii)(c)(iii), *Expln.* (a)].

Descent. Derivation from an ancestor [Pensions Act (23 of 1871), S. 7(2)]; birth. [Constitution of India, Art. 16(2)].

DESCENTS, COLLATERAL AND LINEAL. Descents are of two sorts as from father or grandfather to son and grandson and collateral as from brother to brother, and cousin to cousin, *etc.*

Describe. To set forth in words by reference to characteristics; to give a detailed account.

Description. 'Description,' is a representation that gives to another a view of the thing intended to be represented. A description is a sketch or account of anything in words; a portraiture or representation in language. It is a representation by visible lines, marks, colours, *etc.*, the act of representing a thing by words or signs, or the account of writing containing such representation; and, as used in conveyances of real estate and in legal instruments in writing, it is the language which depicts the thing under consideration.

The year of the make and the particulars of the model of a motor vehicle are part of the description. *Subhash Chandra* v. *State of U.P.*, AIR 1980 SC 800, 801.

Description means the combination of qualities or features that marks out or describes a particular class, hence, a sort, kind or variety.

The combination of qualities or features that marks out or describes a particular class; hence a sort, species, kind or variety; the action of describing, verbal representation or portrait; a statement or passage that describes.

Description, sale by. Sale of goods by the description thereof under contract for sale of the goods with description implying that the goods shall correspond. [Sale of Goods Act (3 of 1930), S. 15].

Desecration. Taking away of sacred character.

Desegregation. The abrogation of policies which separates and place races into different institutions and facilities.

Desert. To abandon; cease to frequent; withdraw one's help or attendance.

To "DESERT", together with its grammatical variations and cognate expressions, means to desert the other party to a marriage without reasonable cause and without the consent, or against the will, of such party. [Parsi Marriage and Divorce Act (3 of 1936), S. 2(3)]

To forsake one's service, one's post or one's party. [T.P. Act (4 of 1882), S. 30, ill.]; [T.P. Act. (4 of 1882), S. 25, ill (d)].

Deserted woman. Merely because a decree for divorce was passed on the ground of desertion, the position of a deserted woman does not improve or the desertion disappears. So a deserted woman includes a woman against whom a decree for divorce on the ground of desertion was passed. *V. Shanthanalaxmi* v. *State of Tamil Nadu,* AIR 1995 Mad 219, 223. [Hindu Marriage Act (25 of 1955), Sec 13]

Deserter. One who deserts; one who quits a service without permission. [CrPC 1973 (2 of 1974), S. 41(1)(f)].

Desertification. "DESERTIFICATION" means land degradation in arid, semi-arid and dry sub-humid areas resulting from various factors, including climatic variations and human activities. [UN Convention to Combat desertification in those countries experiencing serious drought and/or desertification, particularly in Africa, (June 17, 1994), Art. 1(a)]

Desertion. The action of deserting [IPC (45 of 1860), S. 135].

Desertion. In general parlance, desertion means "The action of deserting, forsaking, or abandoning. Willful abandonment of one's duty or obligations, (b) to live with one's spouse. [Oxford English Dictionary Vol-1 as cited in *Rahul Verma vs. Kiran Verma and Ors.* 2017(7) ADJ 544, para 8]

In general, the act by which a person abandons and forsakes, without justification, a station or condition of public or social life, renouncing its responsibilities and evading its duties.

Desertion and absence without leave. Every absence without leave is not treated as desertion but absence without leave may be deemed to be desertion if the procedure prescribed by Section 106 is followed. Since every desertion necessarily implies absence without leave the distinction between desertion and absence without leave must necessarily depend on the animus. If there is *animus deserendi* the absence is straightway desertion. (*Virendra Kumar* v. *Chief of Army Staff, New Delhi,* AIR 1986 SC 1086). [Army Act (46 of 1950), S. 106]

Desertion in Maritime Law. Desertion is an unlawful and wilful abandonment of a vessel, during her voyage by her crew, without an intention of returning to their duty; a quitting of the ship and her service, not only without leave, and against the duty of the party, but with an intent not again to return to the ships duty.

The gist of desertion is the existence of an *animus* not to return to the ship or in other words, to go against the agreements under which the employment of seamen for sea voyages generally takes place.

Ibrahim v. *State of West Bengal*, AIR 1968 SC 731, 732. [Merchant Shipping Act (44 of 1958)]

Desertion in matrimonial law. In (*Matrimonial Law*) Desertion means continual absence from cohabitation contrary to the will, or without the consent, of the party charging it, and without reasonable cause.

"Desertion is not to be tested by merely ascertaining which party left the matrimonial home first. If one spouse is forced by the conduct of the other to leave home, it may be that the spouse responsible for the driving out is guilty of desertion. There is no substantial difference between the case of man who intends to cease cohabitation and leaves his wife, and the case of a man who compels his wife by his conduct, with the same intention, leave him. This is the doctrine by constructive desertion." [Rayden on Divorce, p. 155 as cited in *AS* v. *SNS*, AIR 2016 Del 43, para 18].

Desertion means abandonment, and implies an action of withdrawal from a cohabitation that exists. *Kako* v. *Ajit Singh*, AIR 1960 Punj 328, 330.

The expression "DESERTION" means the desertion of the petitioner by the other party to the marriage without reasonable cause and without the consent or against the wish of such party, and includes the wilful neglect of the petitioner by the other party to the marriage, and its grammatical variations and cognate expressions shall be construed accordingly. [Hindu Marriage Act (25 of 1955), S.13(1), *Explanation*]

"Desertion" has been defined in Section 2(b) of the Act in these terms:

Desertion means to desert without reasonable cause and without the consent or against the will of the spouse. [Bombay Hindu Divorce Act, 1947, S. 2(b)]

"Desertion" is the separation of one spouse from the other, with an intention on the part of the deserting spouse of bringing cohabitation permanently to an end without reasonable cause and with the consent of the other spouse, but the physical act of departure of one spouse does not necessarily make that spouse, the deserting party. (RAYDEN on *Divorce*, p. 128, 6th Edn.)

"Desertion" means the intentional permanent forsaking and abandonment of one spouse by the other without that other's consent, and without reasonable cause. It is a total repudiation of the obligations of marriage. (*Halsbury's Laws of England, 3rd Edn., Vol. 12, p. 241 to 243*)

It has two essential elements (i) Factum of separation (ii) Intention to bring marital life permanently to an end.

The offence of desertion commences when the fact of separation and the *animus deserendi* (the intention to bring cohabitation permanently to an end) co-exist. *Dhrubajyoti* v. *Dila,* AIR 1979 Ori 93, 94. [Special Marriage Act (43 of 1954), S. 27(1)(b)]

The word 'desertion' occurring in Section 13(1)(ib) of the Act, means the intentional permanent forsaking and abandonment of one spouse by the other without consent and reasonable cause. *Savitri Pandey* v. *Prem Chandra Pandey*, (2002) 2 SCC 73, para 8 : AIR 2002 SC 591. [Hindu Marriage Act (25 of 1955), S. 13(1)(ib)].

Desertion in Military Law. *See* Manual of Military Law (War Office), 1899; Manual of Naval Law by Stephens, Gifford and Smith 1901. A soldier is said to desert his post, a sailor his ship, an apprentice his master, when they depart from the service to which they are bound, without permission or contrary to orders.

A soldier is said to desert his post, a sailor his ship, an apprentice his master, when they depart from the service to which they are bound, without permission or contrary to orders.

Desertion of post. The word "desertion" does not simply mean leaving the post or mere departure from the post without permission. It means something more and that something more is the intention never to return to the post or to go away with the idea of avoiding hazardous duty, or shirking any important service. *State* v. *Rawat singh,* AIR 1957 Raj 26. [Rajasthan Armed Constabulary Act (12 of 1950), S. 6(e)]

Design. "DESIGN" means only the features of shape, configuration, pattern or ornament applied to any article by any industrial process or means, whether manual, mechanical or chemical, separate or combined, which in the financial article appeal to and are judged solely by the eye; but does not include any mode or principle of construction or anything which is in substance a mere mechanical, and does not include any trade mark as defined in clause (v) of sub-sec. (1) of S. 2 of the Trade and Merchandise Marks Act, 1958, or property mark as defined in Section 479 of the Indian Penal Code. [Designs Act (2 of 1911), S. 2(5)] or any artistic work as defined in cl. (c) of S. 2 of the Copyright Act, 1957. [Designs Act, 2000, S. 2(d)].

Design. "Design" means a rational, logical and sequential innovation process for the purposes of transferring culture to viable products and services in footwear and leather products, including fashion and retail thereof and for providing a competitive edge to products and services [The Footwear Design and Development Institute Act, 2017 (20 of 2017), S. 3(b)]

"Design", in relation to a product, means the intended or known physical and material characteristics of such product and includes any intended or known formulation or content of such product and the usual result of the intended manufacturing or other process used to produce such product. [Consumer Protection Act, 2019 (35 of 2019), section 2(12)]

Purpose or intention, combined with plan in the mind; aim; purpose; object; end in view; scheme; intention to be carried into effect.

A plan or scheme conceived in the mind of something to be done; a scheme formed to the detriment of another; a drawing or sketch.

The word 'design' in popular parlance is used as a synonym with 'plan' and includes 'a sketch'. It has within its ambit many facets including a criminal design which connotes an evil desire. *Commr. of Customs, New Delhi* v. *Parasram-puria Synthetics Ltd.*, (2001) 9 SCC 74, para 8.

Design marks. Trademarks that use non text elements such as borders, unique fonts, and geometric designs. (*Cyber Law*)

Design patent. A patent that protects the appearance of a product against infringement.

Designate. To call by a distinctive title; to point out a thing by distinguishing it from others; to express or declare; to indicate by description or by something known and determinate, to point out, or mark by some particular token; to specify. The word "designate", when used by the appointing power in making an appointment to office, is equivalent to the word "appointment".

To describe as; to call by the name of the office.

Designated authority. Shall mean such officer of the Central Government not below the rank of Joint Secretary to the Government, or such officer of the State Government not below the rank of Secretary to the Government, as the case may be, as may be specified by the Central Government or, as the case may be, the State Government, by a notification published in the Official Gazette. [Prevention of Terrorism Act (15 of 2002), S. 2(1)(b)]

"DESIGNATED AUTHORITY" means,—

(i) where the tax arrear is under any direct tax enactment, an officer not below the rank of Commissioner of Income-tax and notified by the Chief Commissioner for the purposes of this Scheme;

(ii) where the tax arrear payable is under any indirect tax enactment, an officer not below the rank of Commissioner of Customs or the Commissioner of Central Excise and notified by the Chief Commissioner for the purposes of this Scheme. [Finance Act (No. 2), (21 of 1998), S. 87(b)]

"DESIGNATED AUTHORITY" means such officer of the Central Government not below the rank of Joint Secretary to that Government, or such officer of the State Government not below the rank of Secretary to that Government, as the case may be, as may be specified by the Central Government or the State Government, by a notification published in the Official Gazette. [Unlawful Activities (Prevention) Act (37 of 1967), S. 2(1)(e) as amended by unlawful activities (Prevention) Amendment Act (29 of 2004), S. 4]

"Designated authority" means an officer not below the rank of a Commissioner of Income-tax notified by the Principal Chief Commissioner for the purposes of this Act. [Direct Tax Vivad se Vishwas Act, 2020 (3 of 2020), section 2(1)(e)]

"Designated authority" means the authorities appointed by State Government under sub-section (3) of section 5. [Inland Vessels Act, 2021 (24 of 2021), section 3(n)]

Designated Consumer. Means any consumer notified by the Central Government under clause (e) of Section 14 of the Energy Conservation Act, 2001 and for which a target is notified under the Statutory Orders issued by the Government of India from time to time. [Central Electricity Regulatory Commission (Terms and Conditions for Dealings in Energy Savings Certificates) Regulations, 2016, Regn. 2(1)(g)].

Designated collection centre. Means a collection centre established, individually or jointly by one or more manufacturers or importers, assemblers and reconditioners in pursuance of their responsibilities under Rule 4 of these rules, [Batteries (Management and Handling) Rules, 2001, R. 3(j)]

Designated partner. 'Designated partner' means any partner designated as such pursuant to Section 7. [Limited Liability Partnership Act, 2008 (6 of 2009), S. 2(j)]

Designated Partner Identification Number. 'Designated Partner Identification Number' (DPIN) means an identification number which the Central Government may allot to any individual or nominee of a body corporate, intending to be appointed as designated partner of a Limited Liability Partnership (LLP), for the purpose of his identification as such, and includes Directors Identification Number (DIN) issued under section 266A, 266B and 266E of the Companies Act, 1956 and rules made thereunder. [R. 2(iv), Limited Liability Partnership Rules, 2009]

Designated trade. 'DESIGNATED TRADE' means any trade or occupation or any subject field in engineering or technology or any vocational course which the Central Government after consultation with the Central Apprenticeship Council may, by notification in the Official Gazette, specify as a designated trade for the purposes of this Act. [Apprentices Act (52 of 1961), S. 2(e) as substituted by Amending Act (29 of 2014)]

Designation. That which designates; distinctive title; appellation; that which serves to distinguish; selection and appointment for a purpose; the act of designating or pointing out.

A descriptive name; appellation. [CrPC 1973 (2 of 1974), Sch. II, Form 2].

Designedly. With definite purpose. [Income Tax Act (43 of 1961), Sch. II, item 11(1), prov.].

Desirable. Worth seeking or doing as advantageous, beneficial or wise. [CrPC 1973 (2 of 1974), S. 91(1)].

Desire. To wish or long for; be solicitous for; have a wish for the possession, enjoyment, or being of; crave or covet.

A wish; craving; to wish.

Desist. To cease from; to stop; to leave off; to forbear; to discontinue. [CrPC 1973 (2 of 1974), S. 133(l)(f)(ii)].

Desktop Publishing (DTP). The creation of newsletters, books, promotional materials, annual reports, and other publications with a computer, typically with an applications program that gives the user direct control over the layout of text, illustrations, and other elements on the page, as well as the ability to select fonts, type sizes, and other typographic elements. (*Computer*)

Despatch. Haste; to send off.

Note sent by the Customs with dutiable goods and necessary to be produced at the place of destination.

Removal from the seam through the pit's mouth to the surface has to be considered as coming within the term 'despatch'. *N.C.D. Corporation* v. *State,* AIR 1976 Ori 159, 162. [Mines and Minerals (Regulation and Development) Act (67 of 1957), S. 9]

Desperate. Hopelessly bad, difficult, dangerous.

Driven to desperation; hence reckless, violent, ready to risk or do anything. [CrPC 1973 (2 of 1974), S. 110(g)].

Despoil. Plunder; strip; a word which involves in its signification, violence, or clandestine means, by which one is deprived of that which he possesses.

To strip; to rob. [Geneva Conventions Act (6 of 1960), Art. 15].

Despondency. Dejection. [Air Force Act (45 of 1950), S. 34(g)].

Despot. One who governs with unlimited authority.

Despotism. The rule of a despot; the exercise of absolute authority; tyranny; an absolute autocratic form of government.

Absolute power.

Destination. Place to which a person or thing is bound.

Destiny. The power that foreordains.

DESTINY, FATE, LOT, DOOM, *Destiny* is used in regard to one's station and walk in life; *fate* in regard to what one suffers; *lot* in regard to what one gets or possesses; and *doom* is the final destiny which terminates unhappily, and depends mostly upon the will of another.

Destitute. Bereft or divested [Children Act (60 of 1960) (*repealed*), S. 2(l)(ii)]; lacking possessions and resources of life especially the necessaries of life.

"Without resource, in want of necessaries". A person can be held destitute when no one is to support him and is found wandering without any settled place of abode and without visible means of subsistence. *Shivdev Kaur* v. *R.S. Grewal,* (2013) 4 SCC 636, para 14.

Destroy. To pull down; unbuild; demolish; to make away with; to reduce to nothing; to kill; slay.

Destruction. The fact or condition of being destroyed; the action of destroying. [Constitution of India, Art. 49].

DESTRUCTION, RUIN. *Destruction* is an act of immediate violence; *ruin* is a gradual process; a thing is *destroyed* by some external action upon it; a thing falls to *ruin* of itself.

Destructive. Having the quality of destroying; tending to destroy; deadly; annihilative. [T.P. Act (4 of 1882), S. 108(o)].

Desuetude. Discontinuance from use, practice, exercise or functioning.

Detach. To separate. [Navy Act (62 of 1957), S. 97(5)].

"Detached signature" means the signature that is stored independent of electronic record being signed. [Digital Signature (End Entity) Rules, 2015, R. 2(1)(d)].

Detain. To stop, to delay, to restrain from proceeding; keep in temporary custody.

To keep in confinement or custody. [Constitution of India, Art. 22(3)(b)].

The word "detains" in S. 498, IPC (45 of 1860) means "keeps back." There may be various ways of keeping back. It need not necessarily be by physical force; it may be by persuasion or by allurements and blandishments. But the use of the words does require that there should be something in the nature of control or influence which can properly be described as a keeping back of the woman. Therefore the mere fact that a man who picks a woman up in a brothel, takes her to his house to live with him is not by itself sufficient to establish detention within the meaning of the section.

The word "detains" may denote detention of a person against his or her will, but in the context of the section it is impossible to give this meaning to the said word. Detention in the context must mean keeping back a wife from her husband or any other person having the care of her on behalf of her husband with the requisite intention. Such keeping back may be by force, but it need not be by force. It can be the result of persuation, allurement or blandishment which may either have caused the willingness of the woman, or may have encouraged, or co-operated with her initial inclination, to leave her husband. *Alamgir* v. *State of Bihar*, AIR 1959 SC 436, 440. [IPC (45 of 1860), S. 498]

Detained. In this Order, "detained" includes detained under any law providing for preventive detention. [CPC (5 of 1908), O XXVI (A), rule 1]

In this Chapter,-- "detained" includes detained under any law providing for preventive detention. [(w.e.f. 1-7-2024) Bharatiya Nagarik Suraksha Sanhita, 2023 (46 of 2023), section 301(a)]

Detainee. A person who is detained; *especially* : a person held in custody prior to trial or hearing.

Detainer. The act of keeping something in one's possession.

Detect. To find out; to discover (a person) being or doing something; to discover the presence, existence or fact of something apt to elude notice.

Detection. The action of detecting. [IPC (45 of 1860), S. 330].

Detention. The action of detaining; the keeping in confinement or custody; a keeping from going on or proceeding.

The word 'detention' must mean keeping back a wife from her husband or any other person having the care of her on behalf of her husband with the requisite intention. *Alamgir* v. *State of Bihar*, AIR 1959 SC 436, 440. [IPC (45 of 1860), S. 498]

Detention, Preventive. Confinement or detention in a prison under the preventive law. [Prisoners (Attendance in Courts) Act (32 of 1955), S. 2(a)].

Detenu. The person detained under preventive measure.

Deter. Abstain from action.

To terrify; to keep (a person) from doing something through fear. [IPC (45 of 1860), S. 445, ill. (h)].

Detergent. A cleansing agent. [Factories Act (63 of 1948), S. 19(2)(c)].

Deterioration. (In *Railways Act*) The word "deterioration" does not cover the fall in the market value of the goods which is due to the delay in delivery.

The process of growing or making worse. [T.P. Act. (4 of 1882), S. 63A(2)].

The word 'deterioration' used in the above two sections is wide enough to include depreciation in value on account of a fall in the price of the goods. *Union of India* v. *Sheo Bux Satyanarayan,* AIR 1963 Ori 68, 70. [Indian Railways Act (9 of 1890), S. 72(1) and Contract Act (9 of 1872), S. 161]

The word deterioration used in the section refers to the physical and actual deterioration of goods. *Union of India* v. *S.S.H. Syndicate, Poona*, AIR 1976 SC 879, 886. [Indian Railways Act (9 of 1890), S. 76]

Determinable. The word "determinable" in S. 8 of the Suits Valuation Act (7 of 1887) applies as much to the final and exact and judicial determination made under S. 11 of the Court Fees Act (7 of 1870) as it does to the inexact and *ex parte* valuation in the plaint.

Capable of being determined *i.e.*, being put to an end to; capable of being decided.

Determinable interest. An estate or interest which may come to an end before its natural termination, or period limited, upon the happening of some contingency.

"Determinate" means "Having defined limits; fixed; definite". Black's Law Dictionary (10th Edn.) as cited in *Modern Dental College and Research Centre* v. *State of M.P.*, (2016) 7 SCC 353, para 115.

Determination. The expression, 'determination' signifies an effective expression of opinion which ends a controversy or a dispute by some authority to whom it is submitted under a valid law for disposal. *Jaswant Sugar Mills* v. *Lakshmi Chand*, AIR 1963 SC 677, 680. [Constitution of India, Art 136]

"Determination" means "the act of deciding something officially; especially, a final decision by a court or administrative agency." Black's Law Dictionary (10th Edn.) as cited in *Modern Dental College and Research Centre* v. *State of M.P.*, (2016) 7 SCC 353, para 115.

"Determination" means the official characterization of an expression. *Modern Dental College and Research Centre* v. *State of M.P.*, (2016) 7 SCC 353, para 115.

The expression 'determination' in the definition of award in the Act indicates only a coming to an end, may be in any way whatever, though it may require examination and choice. *Krishna Kutty Nair* v. *Industrial Tribunal,* AIR 1960 Ker 31, 34. [Industrial Disputes Act (14 of 1947), S. 2(b)]

The word 'determination' presupposes application of mind and expression of the conclusion. It connotes the official 'determination and not a mere opinion of finding. *Ashok Leyland* v. *State of T.N.*,(2004) 3 SCC 1, 38, para 94.

Determination of suit. Judicial or authoritative decision or settlement of suit. [Waste Lands (Claims) Act (23 of 1863), S. 18].

Determination or order. The expression "determination" signifies an effective expression of opinion which ends a controversy or a dispute by some authority to whom it is submitted under a valid law for disposal. The expression "order" must have also a similar meaning, except that it need not operate to end the dispute. Determination or order must be judicial or *quasi*-judicial. *Jaswant Sugar Mills* v. *Lakshmi Chand*, AIR 1963 SC 677, 680. [Constitution of India, Art. 136(1)]

The action of determining or deciding; a judicial or authoritative decision; ending; termination. [Constitution of India, Art 136(1)].

Determination, Points for. Points to be decided. [CPC (5 of 1908), O. XX, R. 4(1)].

Determine. To settle or decide; to come to a decision; to lay down decisively or authoritatively; to put an end to; to ascertain definitely.

The use of the words 'proceed to assess' and 'determine' would not lead to different consequences or result. *S.T. Officer* v. *Yengar and sons*, AIR 1970 SC 311 at 313, 314.

Deterrence. The act or process to discourage a certain behaviour, particularly by fear; in criminal law, prevention of criminal behaviour by fear of punishment.

Deterrent punishments/Sentence. Severe punishment, intended to prevent the offender from again committing the crime. The theory of deterrent punishments should be loosely put into force.

Deterrent theory. Awarding such punishment, to the offender so as to deter other persons from committing crimes.

Detriment. Harm done; loss or harm suffered in person or property.

The detriment suffered by a promisee in the case of promissory estoppel is not some prejudice suffered by the promisee by acting on the promise, but the prejudice which would be caused to the promisee, if the promisor were allowed to go back on the promise. *M.P. Sugar Mills* v. *State of U.P.*, AIR 1979 SC 621, 651. [Indian Evidence Act (1 of 1872), S. 115]

Loss or damage done to or sustained by any person or thing.

Detrimental. Harmful, undesirable.

Devaluation. Reduction in the value of one currency in relation to another.

Devasthan land. 'DEVASTHAN LAND' means a village portion of village, or land held under *Devasthan inam.* [Gujarat Devasthan Inams Abolition Act (16 of 1969), S. 2(7)]

Developed. For the purposes of this section, "DEVELOPED" means at least seventy-five per cent of the expenditure incurred in India by the eligible assesse for any invention in respect of which a patent is granted under the Patents Act, 1970 (39 of 1970) (herein referred to as the Patents Act). [Income-tax Act (43 of 1961), S. 115-BBF, *Explanation (d)*].

Developer. Means a person engaged in development or operation or maintenance of Special Economic Zone, and also includes any person authorised for such purpose by any such developer. [Central Excise Tariff Act, 1985 (5 of 1986), Appendix IX, Service Tax (D), *Expln.* (2)]

Development. "DEVELOPMENT" with its grammatical variations and cognate expressions means the carrying out of building, engineering, mining, quarring or other questions in, on, over or upper land, the cutting of a hill or any portion thereof or the making of any material change in any building or land or in the use of any building or land and includes re-development, a layout or subdivision of any land. [Punjab Regional and Town Planning and Development Act (Punjab Act No. 11 of 1995), S. 2(o)]

"Development" with its grammatical variations means the carrying out of building, engineering, or other operations in or over or under land or the making of any material change in any building or land and includes redevelopment. [Bangalore Development Authority Act, 1976 (12 of 1976), s. 2(j) as cited in Bangalore Development Authority v. Aircraft Employees' Cooperative Society Limited, (2012) 3 SCC 442, para 5].

"Development" means the systematic use of scientific and technical knowledge to meet specific objective or requirements and includes an extension of the theoretical or practical aspects of concepts, design, discovery and invention including business thereof [The Footwear Design and Development Institute Act, 2017 (20 of 2017), S. 3(c)]

"DEVELOPMENT" with its grammatical variations means the carrying out of building, engineering, mining or other operations in, on, over or under land or the making of any material change on any building, or land, or planting of any tree on land and includes redevelopment. [Delhi Metro Railway (Operation and Maintenance) Act (60 of 2002), S. 2(1)(c)]

The act, process or result of developing or growing or causing to grow; the state of being developed; happening.

The raising of further construction over the existing first floor of the hotel building comes within the expression of 'development' under Section 2(7) of the Act. *Hotel Sea Gull* v. *State of W.B.*, (2002) 4 SCC 1, para 20 : AIR 2002 SC 1506. [West Bengal Town and Country (Planning and Development) Act (13 of 1979), S. 2(7)]

Development charges. Means the cost of external development works and internal development works. [Punjab Apartment and Property Regulation Act (Punjab Act (14 of 1995), S. 2(m)]

Development plan. 'DEVELOPMENT PLAN' means a plan for the development or re-development or improvement of the entire area within the jurisdiction of a local authority prepared under Section 3. [Bombay Town Planning Act, 1954 (27 of 1955), S. 2(2)].

'Development plan' means a plan for the development or redevelopment of the area within the jurisdiction of a Planning Authority and includes revision of a development plan and proposal of a Special Planning Authority for development of land within its jurisdictions. [Maharashtra Regional and Town Planning Act (37 of 1966), S. 2(9) as cited in *Jayesh Dhanesh Goragandhi* v. *Municipal Corporation of Greater Mumbai*, (2012) 13 SCC 305, para 22].

Development work. "DEVELOPMENT WORKS" means internal development works and external development works. [Punjab Apartment and Property Regulation Act, (Punjab Act No. 14 of 1995), S. 2(n)]

The construction of underground market does not destroy the intrinsic character of the park as a public park but re-locate and re-develop the park as a place for public recreation and as such the construction of the underground market is a development work. *Calcutta Youth Front* v. *State of West Bengal*, AIR 1988 SC 436, 439. [Calcutta Municipal Corporation Act (59 of 1980), S. 353(2) *Expln*]

The construction of schools, hospitals and community centres and other community buildings do not come within the purview of the term 'development works' under Section 2(e) of

Haryana Development and Regulation of Urban Areas Act (8 of 1975). *DLF Qutub Enclave Complex Educational Charitable Trust* v. *State of Haryana*, (2003) 5 SCC 622, para 33.

Deviation. (*In Marine Insurance*) Alteration of course from that set down in marine policy, such a departure, unless it is made for avoiding sea perils, annuls the risk of the underwriters.

Deviation in the course of a ship under a contract of affreightment may be justified either by express permission in the contract or by necessity (as) to avoid danger as capture by hostile ships in time of war, to avoid other peculiar damages or risks to ship, cargo or persons, in order to save life in another ship in distress, *etc.*

Deflection; an act or instance of deviating [Indian Carriage of Goods by Sea Act (26 of 1925), Sch., Art IV(4)]; divergence.

Device. That which is devised or formed by design; a contrivance; an artificial contrivance. So also the term has been variously defined as meaning an invention; a stratagem; a project; a scheme, often a scheme to deceive; and artifice; also, used to denote hearing or emblematic representation or motto.

Something devised; an arrangement; plan; contrivance; often an underhand contrivance. [IPC (45 of 1860), S. 475]; [Workmen's Compensation Act (8 of 1923), S. 3(1), Prov. (b)(iii)]; [Trade and Merchandise Marks Act (43 of 1958), S. 2(j)].

Devise. (Primarily, a dividing or division.) In the law of wills *as a noun*, a gift of real property by will; a disposition by will; an instrument by which lands are conveyed by will; the direction of a testator of sound mind as to the disposition of his property after his death. *As a verb* to give or dispose of land or hereditaments by will; sometimes as a verb, to draw an instrument. (*Tomlin*)

To give by a will; a will or clause of a will disposing of property. [Companies Act (1 of 1956), S. 345(1) replaced by Companies Act, 2013].

Devisee. One to whom property is given by will.

The person to whom a devise is made. [Limitation Act (36 of 1963), Sch., Art 65, *Expln.* (a)].

Devisee and **legatee.** A devisee is one to whom immoveable property is given by will; and legatee is one whom moveable property is so given.

Devolution. The act of transferring or transmitting to another.

The passing of property to another on the death of a person. [Hindu Succession Act (30 of 1956), S. 4(2)].

The word 'devolution' connotes the accession of a right. *Mahimuddin* v. *Panu Sahani*, AIR 1952 Ori 64. [CPC (5 of 1908), O. XXII, R. 10]

Devolution of interest. The phrase "devolution of interest" in O. XXII, R. 10 of CPC (5 of 1908) is not confined in its meaning to devolutions by death. The Legislature intended by this section to provide for all cases not falling within the foregoing sections as to devolution by assignment, marriage or death.

Devolve. A term used where an estate devolves upon another by operation of law, and without any voluntary act of the previous owner, passes from one person to another. 'Devolve' means to pass from a person dying to a person living. *M.K. Balakrishna* v. *Asst. Commissioner Estate Duty*, AIR 1971 SC 2392, 2395. [Hindu Succession Act (30 of 1956), S. 7(3)]

Devotion to duty. The expression "devotion to duty" appears to have been used as something opposed to indifference to duty or easy-going or light-hearted approach to duty. *Union of India* v. *J. Ahmed*, AIR 1979, SC 1022, 1025. [All India Services (Death-cum-Retirement Benefits) Rules, (1958), R. 16(2)]

Dharmada. *Dharmada* means an endowment or gift for religious or charitable purpose. *I.T. Commissioner, New Delhi* v. *Bijli Cotton Mills*, AIR 1979 SC 346, 352. [Income-tax Act (11 of 1922), S. 4(3)(i)]

Dhoti. Any type of grey or bleached cloth of plain weave which—

(i) is manufactured by a mill either wholly from cotton or partly from cotton and partly from any other material;

(ii) contains coloured yarn on its borders;

(iii) has a width ranging between 28 inches and 54 inches; and

(iv) is commonly known by that name. [Dhoties (Additional Excise Duty) Act (39 of 1953) S. 2(a)]

Diagnosis. The art or act of identifying a disease from its signs and symptoms; also the decision reached. [Drugs and Cosmetics Act (23 of 1940), S. 3(b)(i)].

Diagnostic program. A program intended to test computer equipment and, through a logical process of testing and elimination, isolate failures to small sections of the machine. (*Computer*)

Diagram. A figure composed of lines, serving to illustrate a statement or to aid in a demonstration.

Dial around. Long distance services that require consumers to dial a long-distance provider's access code (or "10-10" number) before dialing a long-distance number to bypass or "dial around" the consumer's chosen long-distance carrier in order to get a better rate. (*Telecommunication*)

Dial-up. A term used to describe use of telephone lines or ISDN communication networks to connect a computer to the WWW.

Diarchy. Government by two independent authorities.

Diary. Daily record kept of events. Case diary is a book in which are entered the cases posted for a particular day, their disposal and other important matters connected therewith. "A man's diary is a record in youth of his sentiments; in middle age of his actions, in old age of his reflections." (*J.Q. Adams*)

Dictator. Person in the position of supreme irresponsible authority; statesman or soldier invested with absolute power to deal with a crisis.

Dictatorial. Despotic, absolute or free from all checks.

Dictatorship. The office or dignity of a dictator; a form of Government in which the supreme authority in the State is vested in one person, called the dictator.

Dictionary. A lexicon; a vocabulary; a word book with meanings and explanations.

Dictionary meaning, Value of. The dictionary meaning of a word cannot be looked at where that word has been statutorily defined or judicially interpreted but where there is no such definition or interpretation, the Court may take the aid of dictionaries to ascertain the meaning of a word in common parlance, bearing in mind that a word is used in different senses according to its context and a dictionary gives all the meanings of a word, and the Court has, therefore, to select the particular meaning which is relevant to the context in which it has to interpret that word. *State of Orissa* v. *Titaghur Paper Mills Co. Ltd.*, (1985) Tax LR 2948, 2984, 3006 (SC).

Dictionary meanings, however, helpful in understanding the general sense of the words, cannot control where the scheme of the statute considered as a whole clearly conveys a somewhat different shade of meaning. *Dy. Chief Controller* v. *K.T. Kosalram*, AIR 1971 SC 1283.

Dictum. An opinion expressed by a Court, but which not being necessarily involved in the case, lacks the force of an adjudication; an opinion of a judge which does not embody the determination of the Court, and made without argument, or full consideration of the point. The word is generally used as an abbreviated form of *obiter dictum*; a remark by the way.

Statements which are not necessary to the decision, which go beyond the occasion and lay down a rule that is unnecessary for the purpose in hand (usually termed dicta) have no binding authority on another Court, though they may have some merely persuasive efficacy. HALSBURY, 4th Edn., Vol. 26, para 574, p. 294.

Die intestate. "Dying intestate" means dying without making a valid will and operative disposition of one's property by will.

Differ. To be unlike; to be distinguishable; to have a different opinion.

Difference. The act of distinguishing; discrimination; distinction; disagreement; dispute. In an agreement for submission to arbitrating; "difference" means "disagreement" or "dispute".

Differences. Partly or totally unlike in nature, form or quality; various; several.

Different. Exhibiting differences; dissimilar.

Differential bonus. Bonus of a special nature. [Life Insurance Corporation of India Act (31 of 1956), S. 49(k)].

Differential pricing. The process of setting of the price of a product or service differently for different customers.

Differential scale. A scale showing the quantitative difference. [Coffee Act (7 of 1942), S. 25(4)].

Differential schedule. A schedule showing the difference. [Sugar Export Promotion Act (30 of 1958), S. 9(3)].

Differential voting rights. Include rights as to dividend or voting. [Companies (Issue of Share Capital with Differential Voting Rights) Rules, 2001, R. 2(b)]

Difficilem oportet aurum habere ad crimina. One should not lend an easy ear to criminal charges.

Difficult. Requiring effort or labour; hard; not easy. [Specific Relief Act (47 of 1963), S. 8(c)].

Difficulty. A difficult point or situation; embarrased state. A thing hard to do or over-come.

Diffusion. Spreading; dispersion. [Preamble, Societies Registration Act (21 of 1860)].

Digamy. A Second marriage entered into after the first marriage ends.

Digest. A compilation of the headnotes of decided cases, arranged alphabetically or systematically subject wise; collection of principles or rules of law, compiled privately.

Digital computer. A computer in which all quantities are represented by discrete numbers rather than variations in voltage or current level. A computer that uses voltage and current levels to represent quantities is an analog computer. (*Computer*)

Digital certificate. A digital certificate indicates the ownership of a public key by an individual or other entity. It allows verification of the claim that a given public key does in fact belong to a given individual. Certificates help prevent someone from using a phone key to impersonated someone else. In their simplest form digital certificates contain a public key and a name. More sophisticated versions also contain an expiration date, the name of the certifying authority that issues the certificate, a serial number, and the digital signature of the certificate issuer. The most widely accepted format for certificates is defined by the X. 509 international standard. Therefore certificates can be read or written by any application complying with X. 509. (*Cyber Law*)

Digital ID or passport, so that only those who can authenticate their identities may access the secure data. (*Cyber Law*)

Digital Certificate Applicant. An individual requesting the issuance of a public key Digital Signature Certificate by a Certifying Authority. (*Information Technology*)

Digital certificate application. An application from a Digital Signature Certificate applicant (or authorised agent) to a Certifying Authority for the issuance of a Digital Signature Certificate. (*Information Technology*)

Digital office. Means an office that adopts an online mechanism wherein the proceedings, from receipt of intimation or complaint or reference or directions or appeal, as the case may be, to the disposal thereof, are conducted in online or digital mode. [Digital Personal Data Protection Act, 2023 (22 of 2023), section 2(m)]

Digital personal data. Means personal data in digital form. [Digital Personal Data Protection Act, 2023 (22 of 2023), section 2(n)]

Digital signature. "DIGITAL SIGNATURE" means authentication of an electronic record by a subscriber by means of an electronic method or procedure in accordance with the provisions of Section 3. [Information Technology Act (21 of 2000), S. 2(1)(p)] [Also see R. 2(1)(d) of the Companies (Registration Offices and Fees) Rules, 2014; R. 2(1)(c) of the Companies (Specification of Definitions Details) Rules, 2014]

Digital Signature Certificate. Digital Signature Certificate means a Digital Signature Certificate issued under sub-sec. (*4*) of S. 35. [Information Technology Act (21 of 2000), S. 2(1)(q)]. [Also see R. 2(1)(e) of the Companies (Registration Offices and Fees) Rules, 2014; R. 2(1)(d) of the Companies (Specification of Definitions Details) Rules, 2014]

Digital Television (DTV). A new technology for transmitting and receiving broadcast television signals. DTV provides clearer resolution and improved sound quality. (*Telecommunication*)

Dilatory. Tending to cause delay.

Dilatory defence. A defence intended to defeat or delay a pending action without touching the merits of the case.

Dilatory motion. A motion which is intended to have a postponing or indefinitely delaying effect on debate; it seeks to put off further consideration of the business in hand for the time being. Motions for the adjournment of a debate, or of the House during any debate, or in Committee that the Chairman do report progress or do leave the Chair, are dilatory motions.

Dilatory plea. Dilatory pleas are distinguished from pleas to the action, and are defined to be such as tend merely to delay or put off the suit by questioning the propriety of the remedy, rather than by denying the injury; whereas pleas to the action are such as dispute the cause of action.

Diligently. With diligence. [Indian Partnership Act (9 of 1932), S. 12(b)].

Diluent. A diluting agent. [Prevention of Food Adulteration Act (37 of 1954), S. 23(m)(i)].

Dilution. Means in trademark law, where a business entity is using a deceptively similar or identical trademark as that of another entity in such a manner that it is likely to confuse general public as to an association between two entities and likely to derogate or cause injury to the reputation of the mark and genuine owner of the mark.

"DILUTION" use of an owner's mark by an outsider in such a way as to diminish the mark's value and diminish the owner's interest in maintaining brand image.

Diploma. Document conferring an honour or privilege.

Diplomacy. Management of international relations; skill in negotiation of affairs with a foreign state or country; tactful and adroit dealing, especially in international affairs; a knowledge of the interests of different states, and the policy of foreign Courts, &c. obtained by means of ambassadors, envoys, consuls &c.

Diplomatic agent. An agent employed by a State in its diplomatic service or in its intercourse or negotiations with other States. [Indian Evidence Act (1 of 1872), S. 78(6)].

Diplomatic asylum. Sanctuary given to persons seeking refuge from the State in which they are situated in cases of actual danger.

Diplomatic officer. "DIPLOMATIC OFFICER" means any ambassador, envoy, minister, charged' affairs or secretary of embassy or legation. [Diplomatic and Consuler Officers, (Oaths and Fees) Act (41 of 1948), S. 2(b)]

In this Section, "DIPLOMATIC OFFICER" means an ambassador, envoy, minister, high Commissioner, Commissioner, Charged' affairs or diplomatic representative or a Counsellor or secretary of an embassy, legation or high Commission. [Foreign Marriages Act (33 of 1969), S. 3, *Explanation*]

Diplomatic privileges. The exemption from ordinary law of an accredited representative of a foreign Sovereign.

Diplomatic protocol. Also called diplomatic ceremonial. A collection of norms concerning contacts of diplomats with state authorities or intergovernmental organizations to which they are accredited, codified by the Vienna Congress, 1815, the so-called Vienna Rules, modernized by the Vienna Convention on Diplomatic Relations, 1961.

Direct. Means "immediate; express; unambiguous; confessed; absolute"; immediate or proximate, as distinguished from remote; straightforward, not crooked, not winding, not circuitous, not sideways, also an epithet for the line of ascendants and descendants in genealogical succession, opposed to collateral.

It means command and in the section it refers to the order of the magistrate to the police to investigate when they are not engaged in investigation. [CrPC, 1973 (2 of 1974), S. 159]

DIRECT, CONDUCT, REGULATE. To *direct* as applied to the administration of affairs, is more authoritative than conduct, while *conduct* is more active or operative. We *direct* by ordering others in the way to a certain end, as to direct the movements of an army. We *conduct* by actually taking a practical part, as we speak of conducting an important or lucrative business. *Regulate* stands midway between, with less of the command of *direct*, and less of the activity of conduct; as, to regulate the proceedings of a public meeting. (*Smith. Syn. Des.*)

'Direct appointment' means an appointment made otherwise with by promotion within the service or by transfer of an official serving in another department of any State in India or the Government of India. [Punjab Educational Service Class III School Cadre Rules, 1955, R. 2(e) as cited in *State of Haryana* v. *Vijay Singh*, (2012) 8 SCC 633, para 10].

Direct and Proximate Cause. Means the cause which naturally leads to and might have been expected to be directly instrumental in producing the result complained of. The direct cause may not be the proximate cause, and the proximate cause may not be the direct cause.

Direct cause. That which sets in motion train of events which brings about result without intervention of any force operating or working actively from new and independent source; or, one without which the injury would not have happened.

Direct costs. Mean costs directly attributable to the trading goods exported out of India including the purchase price of such goods. [Income-tax Act (43 of 1961), S. 80HHC(3) *Expln.* (d)]

Direct evidence. Evidence given where witness testifies directly of his own knowledge as to the main fact or facts in dispute.

"Direct injury" and **"Consequential injury".** The phrases "direct injury" and "consequential injury" are not of the same meaning as "direct damages" and "consequential damages". The latter phrases are of the terminology of damages and measure of damages, while the former are not, but are of the terminology of injuries. To illustrate, a direct injury may, in addition to direct damages, give rise to consequential damages; and the latter are recoverable as well as the former, unless they be not "proximate" but "remote." In the case of a direct injury the measure of damages includes both direct and indirect or consequential damages, but in the case consequential injuries, there are not recoverable damages at all. Consequential damages can only result from a direct injury, while no actionable damages of any kind result from a consequential injury. (*Sadlier* v. *City of New York*, 40 Misc Rep 78)

Direct investment outside India. Means investment by way of contribution to the capital or subscription to the Memorandum of Association of a Foreign entity, but does not include portfolio investment or investment through stock exchange or by private placement in that entity. [Foreign Exchange Management (Transfer or Issue of any Foreign Security) Regulations, 2000, Reg. 2(e)]

Direct negotiation. Dispute resolution method with no neutral third party, disputants communicate and negotiate with each other directly. (*Arbitration*)

'Direct recruited fresh entrant' with reference to a post or a government servant means the post on which such government servant was recruited as a regular and direct recruitee in the Government service and is in continuous employment of Government since such recruitment. [Haryana Civil Services (Assured Career Progression) Rules, 1998, R. 3(6) as cited in *State of Haryana* v. *Sita Ram*, (2013) 16 SCC 677, para 3].

'Direct recruitment' means an appointment made otherwise than by promotion or by transfer of an official already in the service of the Government of India or any State Government. [Haryana State Prosecution Legal Service (Group C) Rules, 1979, R. 2(b) as cited in *Deepak Aggarwal* v. *Keshav Kaushik*, (2013) 5 SCC 277, para 75].

Direct recruitment. Means the process of appointing faculty by inviting applications against public advertisement from persons eligible to teach in a Central Educational Institution. [Central Educational Institutions (Reservation in Teachers' Cadre) Act, 2019 (10 of 2019), section 2(d)]

'Direct recruitment' means recruitment by open competition but does not include (a) appointment by promotion; or (b) appointment by transfer of an officer already in the service of any State Government of the Government of India. [Haryana Civil Service (Executive Branch) and Allied Services and other Services Common Combined Examination Act, 2002, S. 2(vii) as cited in *Jitendra Kumar* v. *State of Haryana*, (2008) 2 SCC 161, 172, para 17]

Direct selling. Means marketing, distribution and sale of goods or provision of services through a network of sellers, other than through a permanent retail location. [Consumer Protection Act, 2019 (35 of 2019), section 2(13)]

Direct tax. "DIRECT TAX" means—

(1) Any duty leviable or tax chargeable under—

(i) the Estate Duty Act, 1953;

(ii) the Wealth-tax Act, 1957;

(iii) the Expenditure-tax Act, 1957;

(iv) the Gift-tax Act, 1958;

(v) the Income-tax Act, 1961;

(vi) the Super Profits Tax Act, 1963;

(vii) The Interest tax Act, 1974; [and]

(viii) The Hotel-Receipts Tax Act, 1980;

(ix) The Expenditure Tax Act, 1987; and

(2) any other duty or tax which, having regard to its nature or incidence, may be declared by the Central Government, by notification in the

Official Gazette, to be a direct tax. [Central Boards of Revenue Act (54 of 1963), S. 2(c)]

'DIRECT TAX' means—

(a) any tax chargeable under—

(i) the Income-tax Act;

(ii) the Super Profits Tax Act, 1963;

(iii) the Companies (Profits) Surtax Act, 1964;

(iv) the agricultural income-tax law; and

(b) any other tax which, having regard to its nature or incidence, may be declared by the Central Government, by notification in the Official Gazette, to be a direct tax for the purposes of this Act. [Payment of Bonus Act (21 of 1965), S. 2(12)]

'DIRECT TAX' means—

(*i*) any tax chargeable under the—

(A) Income-tax Act, 1961 (43 of 1961);

(B) Companies (Profits) Surtax Act, 1964 (7 of 1964);

(C) Agricultural income-tax law; and

(ii) any other tax which, having regard to its nature or incidence, may be declared by the Central Government, by notification, to be a direct tax for the purposes of this Code. [Code on Wages, 2019 (29 of 2019), section 2(j)]

Direct tax: indirect tax. The expression "direct taxes" include those assessed upon the property, person, business, income, etc., of those who are to pay them, while indirect taxes are levied upon commodities before they reach the consumer, and are paid by those upon whom they ultimately fall, not as taxes, but as part of the market price of the commodity. [*Union of India* v. *Nitdip Textile Processors Private Limited*, (2012) 1 SCC 226, para 45].

Direct testimony. The term "direct testimony," or "positive testimony", is used to designate the testimony of those who speak of their own actual and personal knowledge of the fact in controversy.

Direct-to-Home (DTH) broadcasting service. 'Direct-to-Home (DTH) broadcasting service' means a service for multi-channel distribution of programmes direct to a subscriber's premises without passing through an intermediary such as a cable operator by uplinking to a satellite system. [Sports Broadcasting Signals Act (11 of 2007), S. 2(1)(j)]

Directed. Given directions; aimed fixedly at.

Direction. Instruction as to what one has to do.

In law 'direction' means guidance or command. [Air Corporation Act (27 of 1953), Ss. 34, 44, 45]

"Direction" means an order; an instruction on how to proceed. [Black's Law Dictionary (9th Edn., 2009) as cited in *Arun Kumar Aggarwal* v. *State of M.P.*, (2014) 13 SCC 707, para 19].

"The word 'direction' is of common usage, and is defined as meaning the act of governing, ordering, or ruling; the act of directing, authority to direct as circumstances may require; guidance; management; superintendence; 'prescription'; also a command, an instruction, an order, an order prescribed either verbally or written, or indicated by acts; that which is imposed by directing, a guiding or authoritative instruction; information as to method." [Corpus Juris Secundum, Vol. 26-A, pp. 955-56 as cited in *Arun Kumar Aggarwal* v. *State of M.P.*, (2014) 13 SCC 707, para 20].

"Direction" means a guiding or authoritative instruction, prescription, order, command. [Words and Phrases, Permanent Edn., Vol. 12-A as cited in *Arun Kumar Aggarwal* v. *State of M.P.*, (2014) 13 SCC 707, para 22].

"Direction" means a guiding authoritative instruction, prescription order, command. [Words and Phrases, Permanent Edn. Vol. 12-A as cited in *Arun Kumar Aggarwal* v. *State of M.P.*, (2014) 13 SCC 707, para 22].

The expression "direction" cannot be construed in vacuum. It could only refer to the directions which the Appellate Assistant Commissioner or other tribunals can issue under the powers conferred on him or them. *Daffdar Bhagat Singh and Sons*. v. *I.T.O., A Ward, Ferozepue*, AIR 1969 SC 340 at 342.; *Commissioner of Income Tax U.P.* v. *Mohd. Shakoor Mohd. Bashir*, AIR 1973 SC 2359, 2360. [Income-tax Act (43 of 1961), S. 153(3)(ii)]

The word 'direction' in S. 17(1) with reference to an appeal by an employed person must be construed as including a refusal to make a direction. *Ram Lubhaya Bhatia* v. *Divisional Superintendent Northern Railway,* AIR 1958 Punj 153, 154. [Payment of Wages Act (4 of 1936), Ss. 15(2), (3) and 17]

Direction; Sanction. For sanction to prosecute, all that is necessary for one to be satisfied about is the existence of a *prima facie* case; in the case of direction to prosecute a further element that the accused deserves to be prosecuted is involved. *Rameshwar Bhartia* v. *State of Assam*, AIR 1952 SC 405, 407.

An instruction how to proceed; an order; a precept. [Constitution of India, Art. 32(2) and Art. 39].

Directive principles of State Policy. See part IV of the Constitution of India.

Constitutional directions and principles fundamental in the governance of the country, broadly classified under three categories—(1) economic ideals which Sate should strive to attain, (ii) directions to the legislatures and executive regarding their exercise of powers, and (iii) certain rights of the citizens which the State has to secure by its legislative and administrative policy.

Directly and substantially in issue. *See* CPC (5 of 1908), S. 11.

Directly. In a direct manner.

The word 'directly' as applied to the time of doing an act, would mean IMMEDIATELY.

Directly attributable. Personal injury is directly attributable to any of the matters, if such matter is on the basis of all the relevant facts, a substantial cause of personal injury. It does not need to be the sole cause.

Directly or indirectly. The term 'directly or indirectly' shall include rendering of services by the auditor,—(*i*) in case of auditor being an individual, either himself or through his relative or any other person connected or associated with such individual or through any other entity, whatsoever, in which such individual has significant influence or control, or whose name or trade mark or brand is used by such individual; (*ii*) in case of auditor being a firm, either itself or through any of its partners or through its parent, subsidiary or associate entity or through any other entity, whatsoever, in which the firm or any partner of the firm has significant influence or control, or whose name or trade mark or brand is used by the firm or any of its partners. [*Explanation* to section 144 of the Companies Act, 2013 (18 of 2013)]

Director. "DIRECTOR", in relation to—

(i) a firm, means a partner in the firm;

(ii) an association of persons or a body of individuals, means any member controlling the affairs thereof. [Insurance Act (41 of 1999), S. 105A *Expln.* (a)]

One who directs; a superintendent; a member of the Board appointed to direct the affairs of an establishment. [Constitution of India, Art 31A(1)(d)].

'Director' means on officer appointed by the State Government as Director of Mandis and includes any other officer authorised by the Director to perform all or any of his functions under this Act. U.P. Krishi Utpadan Mandi Adhiniyam (25 of 1964), S. 2(h) as cited in *Heiny India Private Limited* v. *State of U.P.*, (2012) 5 SCC 443, para 33].

Reference to a Director is to an individual and not to a body corporate. *Sita Ram Singhania* v. *State of Orissa,* AIR 1972 Ori 217, 219. [State Finance Corporation Act (63 of 1951), S. 10(e)]

"DIRECTOR" for the purpose of section 25 of Act 12 of 2012, a 'director', in relation to a factor means any officer entrusted with the management of the whole or substantially the affairs of the factor. [*Explanation* to section 25 of the Factoring Regulation Act, 2011 (12 of 2012)]

"DIRECTOR" means a director appointed to the Board of a company. [S. 2(34) of the Companies Act, 2013 (18 of 2013)]

"Director", in relation to a co-operative society, includes a member of any committee or body for the time being vested with the management of the affairs of that society. [Banking Regulation Act (10 of 1949), sections 5(cciii) and 56(c)(i)]

Director-General. Unless there is anything repugnant in the subject or context, the expression "Director-General" means the Director General of Posts and Telegraphs. [Indian Post Office Act (6 of 1898), S. 2(a)].

"DIRECTOR-GENERAL" means the Director-General of Civil Aviation. [S. 2(j) of the Rajiv Gandhi National Aviation University Act, 2013 (26 of 2013)]

Director Identification Number (DIN). Means an identification number allotted by the Central Government to any individual, intending to be appointed as director or to any existing director of a company, for the purpose of his identification as a director of a company: *Provided* that the Director Identification Number (DIN) obtained by the individuals prior to the notification of these rules shall be the DIN for the purpose of the Companies Act, 2013: *Provided further* that Director Identification Number (DIN) includes the Designated Partnership Identification Number (DPIN) issued under section 7 of the Limited Liability Partnership Act, 2008 (6 of 2009) and the Rules made thereunder. [R. 2(1)(e) of the Companies (Specification of Definitions Details) Rules, 2014; Companies (Appointment and Qualification of Directors) Rules, 2014, rule 2(1)(d)]

Director of the Central Food Laboratory. Means the person appointed by the Central Government by notification in the official Gazette as the Director of the Central Food Laboratory and includes any person appointed by the Central Government in like manner to perform all or any of the functions of the Director under this Act. [Prevention of Food Adulteration Act (37 of 1954), S. 2(iv)]

Director's remuneration. 'DIRECTOR'S REMUNERATION' includes all remuneration payable by a company to a director thereof in respect of any services rendered to or employment with the company in any capacity whatsoever. [Business Profits Tax Act (2 of 1947) S. 2(8A)]

Directorate. The office of a director or of a body of directors.

Directorship. The office of a director [Industrial Finance Corporation Act (15 of 1948) (Repealed by Act 23 of 1993, S. 25(2)].

Directory. A statute or rule which is not mandatory or imperative, but specifies the way in which a thing should be done.

Directory or mandatory. If there is anything that makes it the duty of the person on whom the power is conferred to exercise that power, it is (directory) imperative, if not, the exercise is discretionary. *Maxwell on Interpretation of Statutes*, 9th (1946) edition, pages 249 and 250 as cited in *Balak Ram* v. *Sita Ram*, AIR 1954 HP 6, 10.

Directory statute. A statute or enactment which directs anything to be done or omitted, without invalidating acts or omissions in contravention of it.

Diriment impediments. Absolute bars to marriage which would make it null, *ab initio*.

Disability. For the purposes of this section,—"DISABILITY" shall have the meaning assignned to it in clause (*i*) of Section 2 of the Persons With Disabilities (Equal Opportunities, Protection of Rights and Full Participation) Act, 1995, and includes "autism", "cerebral palsy" and "multiple disabilities" referred to in clauses (*a*), (*c*) and (*h*) of Section 2 of the National Trust for Welfare of Persons with Autism, Cerebral Palsy, Mental Retardation and Multiple Disabilities Act, 1999. [Income-tax Act (43 of 1961), S. 80U, *Expln.* (a) (*Substituted by Finance (No. 2) Act (23 of 2004), S. 19 Expln. (a)*)]

"DISABILITY" means—

(i) blindness;

(ii) low vision;

(iii) leprosy-cured;

(iv) hearing impairment;

(v) locomotor disability;

(vi) mental retardation;

(vii) mental illness. [Person with Disabilities (Equal Opportunities *etc.*) Act, 1995 (1 of 1996), S. 2(i)]

The absence of legal capacity to do certain acts or enjoy certain legal rights [CPC (5 of 1908),S. 147 and Constitution of India, Art 15(2)]; incapacity [Personal Injuries (Compensation Insurance) Act (37 of 1963), S. 2(e), prov.]; inability to do something.

Disable. To incapacitate; make unable to act; to cause a disability; to do "something which creates a permanent disability and not merely a temporary injury".

Disablement. The state of being disabled. [Workmen's Compensation Act (8 of 1923), S. 2(1)(g) and Constitution of India, Art 41].

Disabling statute. A statute which restricts the right of a person.

Disadvantage. The fact of being without advantage [Trade Unions Act (16 of 1926), S. 16(3)]; injury to reputation, interest *etc.* [Arbitration Act (10 of 1940) (*repealed*), S. 43(2)]. Opposite of advantage.

Disaffection. "DISAFFECTION" includes disloyalty and all feelings of enmity. [IPC (45 of 1860), S. 124-A, *Expln.* 1 and Indian States (Protection against Disaffection) Act (1923), S. 2].

Absence or alienation of affection or goodwill especially towards the government. [IPC (45 of 1860), S. 124-A].

Disagree. To differ; to dissent. [Constitution of India, Art 108(1)(b)].

Disagreement. A want of agreement unanimity; unpleasantness; quarrel. The act or an instance of disagreeing; the state of being at variance with.

Disallow. To refuse to allow; to disapprove of.

Disappear. The mere removal of the dead body from the place of murder to another place and also hanging up the same on a tree do not amount to causing disappearance of the evidence of murder. [IPC (45 of 1860), S. 201]

Disappearance. Ceasing to be present or visible; passing away.

Disappointed. Having one's expectations frustrated, foiled or thwarted.

Disarm. Deprive of arms or weapons; abandon the maintenance of army or navy on a large scale.

Disarmament. Abandonment or reduction of warlike establishment.

Disaster management. 'Disaster management' means all aspects of planning, coordinating and implementing all measures which are necessary or desirable to prevent, minimize, overcome or to stop the spread of the disaster upon the people or, any property and includes all stages of rescue and immediate relief. *N.D. Jayal* v. *Union of India*, JT 2003 (Supp-2) SC 1 : 2003 (7) Scale 54 : 2003 (6) Supreme 572. [Constitution of India, Arts. 32 & 21; Environment Protection Act (29 of 1986), S. 3, and Environment Protection Rules, 1986, R. 5]

Disavow. To repudiate; to disclaim.

Disband. Same as dissolve.

To break up the organisation of; to dissolve. [National Cadet Corps Act (31 of 1948), S. 4]

Disbandment. The act of disbanding or the state of being disbanded. [National Cadet Corps Act (31 of 1948), S. 4].

Disbursement. DISBURSEMENT (BY EXECUTORS *etc.*). Money expended by an executor, guardian, trustee *etc.,* for the benefit of the estate in his hands or in connection with its administration.

Discard. To cast off as useless or as no longer of service; to put off; to dismiss from employment, confidence or favour; to reject.

To drop, dismiss, let go or get rid of as no longer useful, valuable or pleasurable.

Discharge. "DISCHARGE" shall include release. [Army Act (46 of 1950), S. 24(4) and Air Force Act (45 of 1950), S. 24(4)]

"DISCHARGE", in relation to oil or oily mixture, means any discharge or escape, however caused. [Merchant Shipping Act (44 of 1958), S. 356 B(m)]

Release, absolve, or acquit, as, of an obligation, claim, accusation, or service due; to exonerate; to relieve; to clear.

The word "discharge" connotes for any other reason *ejusdem generis* due to abolition of the post or course of study or such similar circumstances, except discharge due to misconduct. *State of Kerala*

v. *Mother Anesthasia Superior General,* AIR 1997 SC 1310. [Calicut University Act, 1975, S. 57(6)]

The word 'discharge' occurring in Section 138 would include cession of relationship of employer and employee, may be by retirement, resignation, dismissal or removal. *S.K. Sarma* v. *Mahesh Kumar Verma*, (2002) 7 SCC 505, para 11 : AIR 2002 SC 3294. [Indian Railways Act (9 of 1890), S. 138]

The act of freeing from obligation, liability or restraint; the act of clearing off a pecuniary liability; fulfilment; execution; to relieve of obligation; to exonerate; to cancel, annul (an order); to relieve from an appointment; to fire off; to shoot; the act of discharging; removal of a load; a flowing or issuing out.

Discharge from liability. The words "Discharged from liability", are apt to express an intention of total extinction of the liability, and should specially in view of the international character of the legislation, be construed in that sense. It is hereby necessary to add that once the liability is extinguished under this clause, there is no scope of any acknowledgment of liability thereafter. *East and West Steamship Co.* v. *S. K. Ramalingam Chettiar*, AIR 1960 SC 1058, 1065. [Carriage of Goods by Sea Act, 1925, Art. III, Paragraph 6, cl. 3].

DISCHARGE, ACQUITTAL. The discharge is a judgment upon an accused person, because the law has not exactly provided for the offence. The acquittal recognizes his innocence. In the former case the law is powerless to punish, in the latter powerful to absolve. (*Smith Syn. Dis.*)

Discharge of contract. End of contract.

Discharge of duty as public servant. The word 'discharge' has the same connotation as removal and should be construed so as to be included within the term 'dismissal'.

The use of the word 'discharged' is not conclusive. If in fact the petitioner had been removed by Government from its service as a punishment the use of the word 'discharge' would not absolve the Government from complying with the provisions of Art 311 (2). [Constitution of India, Art. 311]

The word "discharge" in S. 73(1) must in the context, be taken to be a discharge which is the result of a decision of the employer embodied in an order passed by him. It may conceivably also include the case of a discharge where discharge is provided for by a standing order. *Buckingham and Carnatic Co. Ltd.* v. *Venkatiah*, AIR 1964 SC 1272, 1278. [Employees State Insurance Act (34 of 1948), S. 73(1)]

'Discharge' means discharge of a person in a running or continuing business, not discharge of all workmen when the industry itself ceases to exist on a bonafide closure of business. *Banaras Ice Factory* v. *Its Workmen*, AIR 1957 SC 168, 172. [Industrial Disputes (Appellate Tribunal) Act, 1950, Ss. 22 and 23]

Discharge means to free from liability. The liability may be in respect of monetary claims, like debts; it may be in respect of possession of property; it may be in respect of taking some order as regards property; it may be in respect of many other matters. *Sarda Prasad* v. *Lala Jumna Prasad*, AIR 1961 SC 1074, 1076. [Limitation Act (36 of 1963), S. 7]

The word 'discharge' is ordinarily used only in the context of exonerating a person from liability or relieving him of his obligations and is not used in the sense of giving up rights.

The word 'discharge' means to relieve one of one's charge or office and one can be so relieved of charge or office either on retirement or on being dismissed by way of punishment on a charge being established against him. It embraces in its fold the fact of termination of contract of employment by some acts of parties or otherwise. [Indian Railways Act (9 of 1890), S. 138]

Discharge or escape. In relation to pollution damage, means the discharge or escape of oil carried by the ship. [Merchant Shipping Act (44 of 1958), S. 352S(b)]

Discharged employee. A temporary teacher in a leave vacancy can be considered as 'discharged employee' under Section 57(*b*) of the Act. 'Discharge' would connote for any other reason *ejusdem generis* due to abolition of the post or course of study or such similar circumstances except for discharge due to misconduct. [*State of Kerala* v. *Mother Anasthasia Superior General*, AIR 1997 SC 1310 : (1997) 10 SCC 79] [Calicut University Act, 1975, S. 57(b)]

Disciplinary authority. For the purposes of the Rules the 'disciplinary authority' is defined in Rule 2(c) of the Rules as the authority competent under the Rules to impose on a government servant any of the penalties under Rule 9 or Rule 10 of the Rules. [*Govt. of A.P.* v. *N. Ramanaiah*, (2009) 7 SCC 165, 171, para 18] [A.P. Civil Services (CCA) Rules, 1991, R. 2(c)]

Disciplinary proceeding. An action initiated to reprimand, suspend, or punish an official for his unethical or illegal conduct.

Discipline. Training, especially used of training which produces self-control, obedience, orderliness; maintenance of a proper subordination.

Discipline and misconduct. Breach of discipline or misconduct is as serious an offence as any other offence, and it may be punished with dismissal or suspension. Hunger strike, resorted to by a police office to redress any grievance, real or imaginary, is breach of discipline. *Hariprasad Raghuram* v. *State of Gujarat*, AIR 1965 Guj 283, 291, 192. [Bombay Police Act (22 of 1951), S. 25(1)]

Disciplinary Committee. Means the Disciplinary Committee constituted under sub-section (1) of section 21B. [Chartered Accountants Act, 1949 (38 of 1949), section 2(1)(cc)]

Means a committee of whole time member(s) constituted by the Board under sub-section (1) of Section 220 of the Code:

Provided that the whole time member(s) in the Disciplinary Committee shall not be associated with the investigation or inspection. [Insolvency and Bankruptcy Board of India (Inspection and Investigation) Regulations, 2017, Regn. 2(1)(c)].

Disciplinary Directorate. Means the Disciplinary Directorate established under sub-section (1) of section 21. [Chartered Accountants Act, 1949 (38 of 1949), section 2(1)(cd)]

Disclaim. To renounce a claim or title; disavow (intention, *etc.*).

To disavow all parts or shares; to renounce or repudiate a legal claim; to make a disclaim.

Disclaimer. Disclaimer is an express denial, or complete renouncing of one's legal right or claim. (*Tomlin*)

Disclose. Is to expose to view; to reveal.

(*In the Law of Contracts*) The word 'disclose' in S. 230 of the Indian Contract Act (9 of 1872) means to make known. But the essential point is knowledge, and, therefore, where there is actual knowledge, it is equivalent to disclosure.

Discloses himself. The words "discloses himself" in S. 231 of the Indian Contract Act (9 of 1872) must be construed strictly. They do not mean merely "is disclosed" or "appears upon the scene." The words really denote the fact of the principal disclosing himself, and not the fact of the existence of the principal becoming known by some source or other.

Disclosure. The act of uncovering, unwealing or discovering; revealing; opening; making known; telling that which has been kept concealed; on that which has not been apparent.

"Disclosure" means a complaint relating to—

(i) an attempt to commit or commission of an offence under the Prevention of Corruption Act, 1988 (49 of 1988);

(ii) wilful misuse of power or wilful misuse of discretion by virtue of which demonstrable loss is caused to the Government or demonstrable wrongful gain accrues to the public servant or to any third party;

(iii) attempt to commit or commission of a criminal offence by a public servant. [Whistle Blowers Protection Act, 2011 (17 of 2014), S. 3(d)].

Discontinue. To cause to cease; to put a stop to. [Indian Partnership Act (9 of 1932), S. 61].

Discontinuing operation. A component of an enterprise :

(a) that the enterprise, pursuant to a single plan, is :

(i) disposing of substantially in its entirety, such as by selling the component in a single transaction, by demerger or spin-off of ownership of the component to the enterprise's shareholders;

(ii) disposing of piecemeal, such as by selling off the component's assets and settling its liabilities individually, or

(iii) terminating through abandonment;

(b) that represents a separate major line of business or geographical area of operations; and

(c) that can be distinguished operationally and for financial reporting purposes. (*IAS, Para 35.2*)

Discontinuous easement. Is one that needs the act of man for its enjoyment. [Indian Easement Act (5 of 1882), S. 5]

Discount. "DISCOUNT" means the sum of money or the quantity of grain which a prized subscriber is, under the terms of a chit agreement, required to forego and which is set apart under the said agreement to meet the expenses of running the chit or for distribution among the subscribers or for both. [Chit Funds Act (40 of 1982), S. 2(g)]

'Discount' means the amount of money or quantity of grain or other commodity, which a prize winner has, under the terms of the variola, to forego for the payment of veethapalisa, foreman's commission or such other expenses as may be prescribed. [Kerala Chitties Act, 1975, s. 2(4) as cited in *State of Kerala* v. *Mar Appraem Kuri Company Limited*, (2012) 7 SCC 106, para 9].

"In a general sense, an allowance or deduction made from a gross sum on any account whatever. In a more limited and technical sense, the taking of interest in advance. A deduction from an original price or debt, allowed for paying promptly or in cash. Method of selling securities (e.g. treasury bills) which are issued below face value and redeemed at face value….. To purchase an instrument or other right to the payment of money usually for an amount less than the face amount or value of the right. [Black's Law Dictionary as cited in *Commissioner of Income Tax, Ahmedabad* v. *Ahmedabad Stamp Vendors Association*, (2014) 16 SCC 114, para 13: (2012) 254 CTR (SC) 111: [2012] 348 ITR 378 (SC)].

"DISCOUNT" means the difference between the amount received or receivable by the infrastructure capital company or infrastructure capital fund or public sector company issuing the bond and the amount payable by such company or fund or public sector company on maturity or redemption of such bond. [Income-tax Act (43 of 1961), S. 36(iiia) *Expln. (i) as inserted by Finance Act (18 of 2005), S. 12(a)*]

In a general sense (as a noun) A counting off, an allowance or deduction made from a gross sum on any account whatever; an allowance or deduction generally of so much per cent, made for prepayment or for prompt payment of a bill or account; a sum deducted in consideration of cash payment from the price of a thing usually sold on credit; any deduction from the customary price or from a sum due at a future time. *As a verb*, to abate in advance from the sum paid in a business transaction; to count back; to pay back.

Discover. To uncover that which was hidden, concealed, or unknown from every one.

To find out; to detect the presence of; to make known.

Discovered. A meaning can be given to the expression 'discovered' which does not necessarily confine it to the finding out of an already existing fact. One may also find out a fact which has come into existence for the first time. *Commissioner of Excess Profits Tax* v. *India United Mills Ltd.*, AIR 1953 Bom 88. [Excess Profits Tax Act (15 of 1940), S. 15]

Discovered to be void. The expression "discovered to be void" in S. 65 of the Indian Contract Act (9 of 1872) is appropriate only to cases where the agreement is void by reason of some fact not known to the parties at the time of making it.

An agreement discovered to be void *i.e.* not enforceable by law is one which is void from its very inception. *Sunderlal* v. *Laxman Prasad,* AIR 1949 Nag 292. [Indian Contract Act (9 of 1872), S. 65]

Discovers. The word 'discovers' in S. 15 of the Act is of sufficient amplitude to take in subsequent events which have a material bearing on the facts and circumstances on which assessment had been made or relief granted and is not limited to events which were in existence during the chargeable accounting period. *India United Mills Ltd.* v. *Commissioner of Excess Profits Tax*, AIR 1955 SC 79. [Excess Profits Tax Act (15 of 1940), S. 15] [Now repealed by Act 20 of 2000]

Discovert. Unmarried woman; widow; unprotected.

Discovery. Making known; disclosure by a party to an action at the instance of the other party, of facts or documents necessary to maintain his own title [Constitution of India, Art. 142(2)]; finding out; being found out.

The act of revealing or disclosing any matter by a defendant in his answer to a suit filed against him in a Court of law. To administer to the ends of justice, the Court, in many cases, compels a discovery. (*See* CPC (5 of 1908), O. XI); (*Tomlin*)

The expression 'discovery' implies recovery of an incriminating article in a real place of concealment and not in a place where the incrimating article could be recovered by most perfunctory search.

If the articles were not recovered from any hidden place and in the normal course of investigation, the investigating agency was bound to see them and take them in possession without the accused making any statement of pointing them out, it cannot be described as 'discovery'. *Amin* v. *State,* AIR 1958 All 293, 300. [Indian Evidence Act (1 of 1872), S. 27]

Discovery of fact. 'Discovery of a fact' cannot be equated with recovery of the object. On the statement of the accused that he had kept the fire arm concealed behind the old house in a heap of wood, the fact discovered by investigating officer was certainly not 'the gun'. The fact discovered is that 'accused had concealed the gun behind the old house under a heap of wood'. *Pandurang Kalu Patil* v. *State of Maharashtra*, AIR 2002 SC 733 : (2002) 2 SCC 490, 496, paras 14 & 15. [Indian Evidence Act (1 of 1872), S. 27]

'Discovery of fact' under Section 27 of the Act cannot be equated to the object produced or found. The 'discovery of fact' arises by reasons of the fact that the information given by the accused exhibited the knowledge or the mental consciousness of the informant accused in relation thereto. [*State (NCT of Delhi)* v. *Navjot Sandhu,* (2005) 11 SCC 600, 704, para 125] [Indian Evidence Act (1 of 1872), S. 27]

Discovery of new matter. Discovery of new matter is a good ground of review. [See CPC (5 of 1908), O. XLVII, R. 1]

Discovery rule. The statute of limitations for a cause of action does not begin to run until the time that the injured party discovers or reasonably should have discovered the injury.

Discrepancy. Difference.

'Discrepancy' and **'contradiction'.** Whereas the 'contradiction' in the statement of a witness is fatal for the case, but minor 'discrepancy' will not make the case doubtful. Contradictions mean material discrepancies. *State of H.P.* v. *Lekh Raj*, (2000) 1 SCC 247, para 7 : AIR 1999 SC 3916.

Discrete. Individual; separate; distinct.

Discrete organic chemical. Means any chemical belonging to the class of chemical compounds consisting of all compounds of carbon except for its oxides, sulfides and metal carbonates, identifiable by chemical name, by structural formula, if known, and by Chemical Abstracts Service registry number, if assigned. [Chemical Weapons Convention Act (34 of 2000), (Verification Annex) 4]

Discretio est discernere per legem quid sit justum. (*Maxim*) Discretion consists in knowing what is just in law. (*Broom*)

Discretion. When anything is left to any person, judge or magistrate to be done according to his discretion, the law intends it must be done with sound discretion, and in accordance with law. (*Tomlin*)

A "discretion", when applied to a court of justice means discretion guided by law. It must be governed by Rule, not by humor; it must not be arbitrary, vague and fanciful but legal and regular. [*R.* v. *Wilkes*, (1770) 4 Burr 2527 : (1558-1774) All ER Rep 570 (HL)].

Discretion is governed by rule and it must not be arbitrary, vague and fanciful. *Jaisinghani* v. *Union of India*, AIR 1967 SC 1427, 1434.

The word "discretion" standing single and unsupported by circumstances signifies exercise of judgment, skill or wisdom as distinguished from folly., unthinking or haste; evidently therefore a discretion cannot be arbitrary but must be a result of judicial thinking. The word in itself implies vigilant circumspection and care; therefore, where the Legislature concedes discretion it also imposes a heavy responsibility. *National Insurance Co. Ltd.* v. *Keshav Bahadur*, AIR 2004 SC 1581, 1584, para 10.

DISCRETION, undoubtedly, means judicial discretion and not whim, caprice or fancy of a Judge. Powers of review cannot be invoked unless it is shown that there is error apparent on the face of the record in the order sought to be reviewed. *Dhurandhar Prasad Singh* v. *Jai Prakash University,* AIR 2001 SC 2552. [CPC (5 of 1908) Ss. 96, 100, 115]

Discretion, abuse of. Numerous laws confer discretion on some executive agency. Granting of licences, for example, may involve some element of discretion even if the law lays down general rules to guide the authority. This is true of many exercises of statutory power, ranging from acquisition of land of the allotment of Government accommodation. Courts have evolved rules about how such discretionary power ought to be exercised. Broadly, the executive must act fairly and reasonably, and in conformity with the purpose of the law.

Discretion, judicial. Is a certain latitude or liberty accorded by statute or rules to a judge as distinguished from a ministerial or administrative official, in adjudicating on matters brought before him. The use of the word "judicial" limits and regulates the exercise of the discretion, and prevents it from being wholly absolute, capricious, or exempt from review. But the presence of the word "discretion" permits the judge to consider as a judge, what are vaguely termed, all the circumstances of the case and the purpose for which he is invested with the considerations of convenience or utility or saving of expense rather than on considerations of strict law or technicalities.

Discretion of Court. "Ability to discern by the right line of law, and not by the crooked cord of private opinion, which the vulgar call discretion"; freedom to act according to the judgment of the Court, or according to the rules of equity, and the nature of circumstances; judicial discretion regulated according to known rules of law; legal discretion, and not personal discretion sound discretion guided by fixed legal principles. Sound discretion guided by law; sound judgment to be exercised according to the rules of law.

Discretionary. Pertaining to or left to discretion.

Discretionary power. A term which involves an alternative power, *i.e.* a power to do or refrain from doing a certain thing.

Power of free decision or choice within certain legal bounds.

Discretionary trust. A discretionary trust is one which gives a beneficiary no right to any part of the income of the trust property, but vests in the trustees a discretionary power to pay him, or apply for his benefit, such part of the income as they think fit. The trustees must exercise their discretion as and when the income becomes available, but if they fail to distribute in due time, the power is not extinguished so that they can distribute later. They have no power to bind themselves for the future. The beneficiary thus has no more than a hope that the direction will be exercised in his favour. [Snell's Principles of Equity, 28th Edn., 138 as cited in *Commissioner of Wealth Tax, Rajkot* v. *Estate of Late HMM Vikramsinhji of Gondal*, (2015) 5 SCC 666, para 18].

Discriminate against. "Discriminate against" means "make an adverse distinction with regard to", 'distinguish unfavorable from others". *Dorairajan* v. *State of Madras,* AIR 1951 Mad 120, 125. [Constitution of India, Art. 15(1)]

Discrimination. The word 'discrimination' used in Art. 304(a), involves an element of intentional and purposeful differentiation thereby creating economic barrier and involves an element of an unfavourable bias. Discrimination implies an unfair classification. *Video Electronics Pvt. Ltd.* v. *State of Punjab*, AIR 1990 SC 820, 832. [Constitution of India, Art. 304(a)]

"Discrimination" means an unjust, an unfair action in favour of one and against another. It involves an element of intentional and purposeful differentiation and further an element of unfavourable bias; an unfair classification. [State of M.P. v. Narmada Bachao Andolan, (2011) 7 SCC 639, para 67 : (2011) 3 SCC (Civ) 875 : AIR 2011 SC 1989 as cited in *Rajasthan State Industrial Development and Investment Corporation* v. *Subhash Sindhi Cooperative Housing Society, Jaipur,* (2013) 5 SCC 427, para 67].

'Discrimination on the basis of disability' means any distinction, exclusion or restriction on the basis of disability which has the purpose or effect of impairing or nullifying the recognition, enjoyment or exercise, on an equal basis with others, of all human rights and fundamental freedoms in the political, economic, social, cultural, civil or any other field. It includes all forms of discrimination, including denial of reasonable accommodation. [U.N. Convention on Protection and Promotion of the Rights and Dignity of Persons with Disabilities, 2008, Article 2 as cited in Deaf Employees Welfare Association v. Union of India, (2014) 3 SCC 173, para 10].

Discrimination involves an element of unfavourable bias and it is in that sense the expression must be understood. If the statute indicates such bias, it will be violative of the Constitutional prohibition unless it is saved by one of the clauses to Article 15 and 16. *Kathi Raning Rawat* v. *State of Saurashtra*, AIR 1952 SC 123, 125 (Per Patanjali Sastri CJ).

"DISCRIMINATION" in relation to disability, means any distinction, exclusion, restriction on the basis of disability which is the purpose or effect of impairing or nullifying the recognition, enjoyment or exercise on an equal basis with others of all human rights and fundamental freedoms in the political, economic, social, cultural, civil or any other field and includes all forms of discrimination and denial of reasonable accommodation. [Rights of Persons with Disabilities Act (49 of 2016), S. 2(h)].

"DISCRIMINATION" means any act or omission which directly or indirectly, expressly or by effect, immediately or over a period of time,—

(i) imposes any burden, obligation, liability, disability or disadvantage on any person or category of persons, based on one or more HIV-related grounds; or

(ii) denies or withholds any benefit, opportunity or advantage from any person or category of persons, based on one or more HIV-related grounds, and the expression "discriminate" to be construed accordingly.

Explanation 1.—For the purposes of this clause, HIV-related grounds include—

(i) being an HIV-positive person;

(ii) ordinarily living, residing or cohabiting with a person who is HIV-positive person;

(iii) ordinarily lived, resided or cohabited with a person who was HIV-positive.

Explanation 2.—For the removal of doubts, it is hereby clarified that adoption of medically advised safeguards and precautions to minimize the risk of infection shall not amount to discrimination. [Human Immunodeficiency Virus and Acquired Immune Deficiency Syndrome (Prevention and Control) Act (16 of 2017), S. 29(d)].

Discrimination against women. The term "discrimination against women" shall mean any distinction, exclusion or restriction made on the basis of sex which has the effect or purpose of impairing or nullifying the recognition, enjoyment or exercise by women, irrespective of their marital status, on a basis of equality of men and women, of human rights and fundamental freedoms in the political, economic, social, cultural, civil or any other field. Article 1 of convention on Political Rights of Women as cited in *S. Lalitha Sundari* v. *R. Kethar Nathan*, AIR 2002 Mad 17, 22.

Discrimination with reasons. "Discrimination with reasons" means rational classification for differential treatment having nexus to the constitutionally permissible object. *State of Kerala* v. *N.M. Thomas*, AIR 1976 SC 490.

Discuss. Exchange or compare opinions; expound the various views; held on any subject. To exchange views or information.

Disease. A condition of the body, or some part or organ of the body, in which its functions are disturbed, or deranged. [Mica Mines Labour Welfare Fund Act (22 of 1946), S. 3(2)(a)(i)].

In this Act, unless there is anything repugnant in the subject or context, "DISEASED" means affected with glanders or farcy or any other dangerous epidemic disease among horses which the State Government may, by notification in the Official Gazette, specify in this behalf. [Glanders and Farcy Act (13 of 1899), S. 2]

'Disease' means an impairment of the normal state of the living animal that interrupts or modifies the performance of the vital functions being a response to environmental factors (as malnutrition, industrial hazards or climate) or to specific infective agents (as worms, bacteria or viruses) or to inherent defects of the organism (as various genetic anomalies) or to combinations of these factors. *State of Goa* v. *Colfax Laboratories Ltd.*, (2004) 9 SCC 83, 92, para 8.

Disentailment. The barring of an entailed interest.

Disentitle. To deprive of title. [Indian Evidence Act (1 of 1872), S. 5, *Explanation*].

Disfigure. To mar the figure or appearance of; to deform.

Disfranchise. To deprive of citizenship.

Disgorged amount. The disgorged amount refers to the amount received through disgorgement or disposal of securities. [Companies Act (18 of 2013), section 125(3), *Expln.*]

Disgrace. Loss of grace or honour. [Navy Act (62 of 1957), S. 2(2)(b)].

The term "disgrace" signifies loss of honor, respect, or reputation, same or bring disfavour or discredit [*Ravi Yashwant Bhoir* v. *District Collector, Raigad*, (2012) 4 SCC 407, para 15].

Disgraceful. Shameful; having a stigma. [Indian Evidence Act (1 of 1872), S. 9, ill. (b)]; [Air Force Act (45 of 1950), S. 46(a)].

'Disgraceful' means giving offence to moral sensibilities and injurious to reputation or conduct or character deserving or bringing disgrace or shame. [*Ravi Shankar Bhoir* v. *District Collector, Raigad*, (2012) 4 SCC 407, para 15].

Disgraceful conduct. Shameful behaviour. [Indian Evidence Act (1 of 1872), S. 9, ill. (b)]; [Air Force Act (45 of 1950), S. 46(a)].

Disguise. Garb used to conceal identity.

Dishonest. Wanting in honesty.

Dishonest act. fraudulent act, "fraudulent act" being a conduct involving bad faith, dishonesty, a lack of integrity or moral turpitude. [Black's Law Dictionary (8th Edn.) as cited in *Executive Engineer, Southern Electricity Supply Company of Orissa Limited (SOUTHCO)* v. *Sri Seetaram Rice Mills*, (2012) 2 SCC 108, para 21].

Dishonest concealment of fact. Dishonest concealment of fact is a deception. Dishonest depends upon the state of mind at the time of concealment or the intention behind it. *Bauwarilal* v. *State,* AIR 1956 All 341, 346, 347. [IPC (45 of 1860), S. 415]

Dishonest intention. A person can be said to have dishonest intention if in taking the property it is his intention to cause gain, by unlawful means, of the property to which the person so gaining is not legally entitled or to cause loss, by wrongful means, of property to which the person so losing is legally entitled. *K.N. Mehra* v. *State of Rajasthan*, AIR 1957 SC 369, 372. [IPC (45 of 1860), S. 378]

'Dishonest intention' means taking the property with the intention to cause gain, by unlawful means, of the property to which the person so gaining is not legally entitled or to cause loss, by wrongful means, of property to which the person so losing is legally entitled. [*Executive Engineer, Southern Electricity Supply Company of Orissa Limited (SOUTHCO)* v. *Sri Seetaram Rice Mill*, (2012) 2 SCC 108, para 19].

Dishonest misappropriation of property. See IPC (45 of 1860), S. 403.

Dishonestly. Whoever does anything with the intention of causing wrongful gain to one person or wrongful loss to another person, is said to do that thing "dishonestly". [IPC (45 of 1860), S. 24] [Now (w.e.f. 1-7-2024) repealed & replaced by Bharatiya Nyaya Sanhita, 2023 (45 of 2023)]

"Dishonestly" means doing anything with the intention of causing wrongful gain to one person or wrongful loss to another person. [(w.e.f. 1-7-2024) Bharatiya Nyaya Sanhita, 2023 (45 of 2023), section 2(7)]

The word "dishonestly" in S. 24, IPC (45 of 1860), has a technical meaning which is at variance with its popular sense as implying deviation from probity. It is used in connection with *property* and has nothing to do with *probity*. If a person causes wrongful gain or wrongful loss by unlawful means in respect of property to which he is not legally entitled, he acts "dishonestly" within the meaning of S. 24, though he may act from laudable motives. The word "dishonestly" does not necessarily imply wrongful gain to accused himself.

S. 24, IPC, is not an exhaustive definition of the word "dishonestly". The section does not say that the word is applicable only when there is an intention of causing wrongful gain to one person or wrongful loss to another but properly construed means that of intention of causing such wrongful gain or loss is to be considered as coming within the wider class of dishonest actions.

With a dishonest act.

Dishonestly receiving stolen property. Whoever dishonestly receives or retains any stolen property knowing or having reason to believe the same to be stolen property shall be punished with imprisonment of either description for a term which may extend to three years or with fine or with both. [IPC (45 of 1860), S. 411]

Dishonesty. Lack of probity; disposition to deceive; a dishonest act.

'Dishonesty' is a state of mind which has to be shown to exist before a person can be punished under a provision. [*Executive Engineer, Southern Electricity Supply Company of Orissa Limited (SOUTHCO)* v. *Sri Seetaram Rice Mill*, (2012) 2 SCC 108, para 18].

'Dishonesty' and 'fraud'. 'Dishonesty' and 'fraud' have distinct meanings in law in contradistinction to their meanings in the ordinary English parlance. Dishonesty requires an intention to cause wrongful loss or wrongful gain of property, but it does not require deception or concealment as a constitute element. On the other hand, fraud does not require an intention as there can be fraud even where there is no intention to cause pecuniary loss or damage to the person deceived. Fraud, however, does require concealment or deception. The element of deception is an essential ingredient of fraud and it is not necessary for dishonesty. In the words of SUBBA RAO J:

"...the expression 'defraud' involves two elements, namely, deceit and injury to the person deceived. Injury is something other than economic loss, *i.e.*, deprivation of property, whether movable or immovable, or of money and it will include any harm whatever caused to any person in body, mind, reputation or such others. In short, it is a non-economic or non-pecuniary loss. A benefit or advantage to the deceiver will almost always cause loss or detriment to the deceived. Even in those rare cases where there is a benefit or advantage to the deceiver, but no corresponding loss to the deceived, the second condition is satisfied." *Vimla* v. *Delhi Administration*, AIR 1963 SC 1572, 1576-77.

Dishonour. (*In Mercantile Law and usage*) The refusal or neglect to accept a bill of exchange or other negotiable instrument on presentation for acceptance, or to pay it at maturity.

The reverse of honour [IPC (45 of 1860), S. 355]; to refuse to honour a bill of exchange. [Negotiable Instruments Act (26 of 1881), S. 91].

Dishonour of cheque. Return of cheque with the endorsement 'exceeds arrangements' would amount to 'dishonour of cheque' under Section 138 of the Act. [*Bimal Kumar Nopani* v. *State of U.P.,* AIR 2006 (NOC) 945 (All) : 2006 (3) ALJ 619] [Negotiable Instruments Act (26 of 1881), S. 138]

Dishonour of woman. This term involves the idea of violation of chastity or modesty.

Dishonoured bill of exchange. A bill of exchange not honoured or accepted.

Dishonoured by non-acceptance. "A bill of exchange is said to be dishonoured by nonacceptance when the drawee or one of several drawees, not being partners, makes default in acceptance upon being duly required to accept the bill, or where presentment is excused and the bill is not accepted." [Negotiable Instruments Acts (26 of 1881), S.91]

Dishonoured by non-payment. "A promisory note, bill of exchange or cheque is said to be dishonoured by non-payment when the maker of the note, acceptor of the bill or drawee of the cheque makes default in payment upon being required to pay the same." [Negotiable Instruments Act (26 of 1881), S.92]

Disjecta membra. Scattered members; disjoined portion or parts.

Disk. A thin, flexible magnetic disk, enclosed in a rather stiff protective jacket. Depending on your system, it will be 5-1/4 inches in diameter or 8 inches in diameter. Some newer mini-systems are appearing with disks that are 3 inches in diameter. Documents and software programs are stored on disks. The amount of data that can be placed on a disk is not directly related to its diameter, but rather to the density of its formatting. (Often disks are called "diskettes."). (*Computer*)

A circular plate coated with a substance that can be magnetized to store data. *Floppy disks,* or *diskettes,* are made of a flexible material. *Hard disks* are made of a rigid material. (*Computer*)

Disk name. The name you assign a disk. It may be an actual name, an abbreviation, or an alphanumeric code. This name will thereafter be used in the system to gain access to the contents of the disk. You can change a disk name at any time. (*Computer*)

Disk space. Disk space is the amount of storage space you're allocated to use on the server, also server space and Web space. The more disk space you have, the bigger your Web site can be. It's used to store everything related to your Web site such as your regular html files, images, multimedia files, anonymous ftp files, POP mail messages, CGI scripts, and any other files that make up your Web site.

Dislocation. Displacement, especially displacement of a bone from its natural position in the joint. [Motor Transport Workers Act (27 of 1961), S. 13, *second Prov.*].

Disloyalty. The quality of being disloyal; now especially violation of allegiance or duty to one's State or Government. [IPC (45 of 1860), S. 124A, *Expln.* 1].

Dismiss. To let go; to relieve from a duty.

To send away or remove from office, employment or position; to reject.

TO DISMISS, DISCHARGE, DISCARD, *Dismiss* is applicable to persons of all stations, but used more particularly for the higher orders : *discharge* on the other hand is confined to those in a subordinate station. A clerk is *dismissed;* a menial servant is *discharged* : an officer is *dismissed;* a soldier is *discharged.* Neither *dismiss* nor *discharge* define the motive of the action; they are used indifferently for that which is voluntary, or the contrary : *discard,* on the contrary always marks a dismissal that is not agreeable to the party discarded. A person may request to be *dismissed* or *discharged,* but never to be *discarded.* The *dismissal* or *discharge* frees a person from the obligation or necessity of performing a certain duty; the *discarding* throws him out of a desirable rank or station. A minister desires to be *dismissed* when his views are not accepted by the Governor; a military commander asks for a *discharge* when the Government is not prepared to give effect to his plans; a husband *discards* an unchaste wife.

Dismissal. The action of dismissing; deprivation of office, dignity or position; the fact or state of being dismissed; rejection.

'Dismissal' may or may not be a final decision on merits of the rights in controversy, but the dismissal puts an end to the suit or terminates the suit by disposing of. *Premier Enterprises* v. *State of Meghalaya,* AIR 1992 Gau 98, 100. [CPC (5 of 1908), S. 80(3); O. VII, R. 10, 11(d)]

In ordinary parlance, it means nothing more or less than termination of a person's office. Dismissal is the ultimate and most drastic disciplinary sanction which may be inflicted by an employer for an act of misconduct against an industrial workman. If termination of service therefore, which is not by way of punishment would not tantamount to dismissal. *Moti Ram Deka* v. *General Manger, North East Frontier Rly,* (1964) 2 LLJ 467, 493 (SC), per Gajendragadkar.

Dismissal and Removal. Dismissal from service disqualifies a civil servant from future employment, whereas removal from service ordinarily does not. *Tribhuwan Nath* v. *State of Bihar,* AIR 1960 Pat 116, 123. [Civil Services (Classification, Control and Appeal) Rules, R. 55]

The words 'dismiss' and 'remove' mean nothing more or less than the termination of the person's office. The effect of dismissal or removal of one from his office is to discharge him from that office. In that sense, the said words comprehend the very termination of the services of a Government servant. *Moti Ram Deka* v. *N.E. Frontier Railway,* AIR 1964 SC 600, 621. [Constitution of India, Art. 311]

Dismissal for default. The expression "dismissal for default" does not include a dismissal for non-payment of deficit court-fee. [AIR 1942 Cal 539] [CPC (5 of 1908], S. 2(2)]

Dismissal from service. A phrase used in law relating to Government servants which means a termination of service for default, as opposed to a termination *simpliciter.* In service law, a person cannot be dismissed without holding an inquiry into his conduct, and certain other formalities have to be complied with. Any termination which casts a stigma on the employee is regarded as a dismissal for this purpose.

Dismissal of action. The termination of a civil action in favour of the defendant.

Dismissal or **removal.** 'Dismissal' or 'removal' includes every kind of termination of service. The effect of 'dismissal' or 'removal' of one person from his office is to discharge him from that office. [*Moti Ram* v. *General Manager, N.E.F. Railways Maligaon, Pandu,* AIR 1964 SC 600]

Dismissal, or removal, or reduction in rank. Any and every termination of service is not a dismissal, removal or reduction in rank. A termination of service brought about by the exercise of a contractual right is not *per se* dismissal or removal, as has been held by Supreme Court, in *Satish Chandre Anand* v. *Union of India*, AIR 1953 SC 250. If the termination of service is founded on the right flowing from contract or the services rules then, *prima facie*, the termination is not a punishment and carries with it no evil consequences and so Article 311 is not attracted. . . . A reduction in rank like wise may be by way of punishment or it may be an innocuous thing.... *Parshotam Lal Dhingra* v. *Union of India*, AIR 1958 SC 36. [Constitution of India, Art. 311]

The three expression *i.e.* "Dismissal", "Removal" and "Reduction in Rank" used in Art. 311 are technical expressions and they denote a punishment and do not include either simple termination or merely sending back a servant to his substantive post. *N. Ramanatha Pillai* v. *State of Kerala,* AIR 1973 SC 2641. [Constitution of India, Art. 311]

Dismissed. The word "dismissed" has been stated to be a word of very ambiguous meaning and that it is merely a convenient expression for the termination of an employment whatever its nature may be. The word dismissal has to be understood in the context in which it occurs and that it denotes the termination of an employment as a penalty is a matter of recent development. *Workers Employed in Hirakud Dam* v. *State of Orissa,* AIR 1971 SC 2242. [Constitution of India, Art. 311]

Dismissal of SLP by the Supreme Court by simply saying 'dismissed', means dismissal without going into its merits and the Court did not consider it fit to exercise its powers. *V.M. Salgaocar & Bros Pvt. Ltd.* v. *CIT*, (2000) 5 SCC 373, para 8. [Constitution of India, Art. 136]

'Dismissed' and 'Appeal is dismissed'. When SLP is dismissed by simply saying 'dismissed' it means that Supreme does not consider it to be a fit case for exercise of its jurisdiction under Article 136. On the other hand when it dismissed an appeal by saying 'appeal is dismissed' then Supreme Court upholds the decision of the High Court or of the tribunal from which appeal is provided. *V.M. Salgaokar & Bros. Pvt. Ltd.* v. *CIT*, (2000) 5 SCC 373, para 8 : AIR 2000 SC 1623. [Constitution of India Arts. 133(3), 136]

Dismissed and removed. In their ordinary parlance, the words 'dismissed' and 'removed' mean nothing more or less than the termination of a person's office. The effect of dismissal or removal of one from his office is to discharge him from that office. In that sense, the said words comprehend every termination of the services of a Government servant. *Moti Ram Deka* v. *G.M., North East Frontier Railway,* MLJ : QD (1961-1965) Vol. II C1025 : AIR 1964 SC 600 : (1964) 2 Lab LJ 467. [Constitution of India, Art. 311]

Disobedience. The action of disobeying; the fact of being disobedient.

Disobey. To refuse or neglect to obey; to transgress or violate the commands or orders of.

Disorder. Wrong order; disturbance; an ailment; disease (usually weaker than disease and not implying structural change).

Disorder is described as being a public disturbance, riot, civil disorder. 'Disorderly conduct' is defined as a behavior that tends to disturb public peace, undermines public safety or causes an offence to public morals. [Black's Law Dictionary as cited in M.I.D.C. and Ors. vs. Murar Ramchandra Ghatge 2017(2)LLN640(Bom.), para 8]

The Oxford Dictionary defines 'disorder' as being a violent behavior and outbreak of rioting or public disorder. [Oxford Dictionary as cited in *M.I.D.C. and Ors. vs. Murar Ramchandra Ghatge* 2017(2)LLN640(Bom.), para 8]

Disorderly. Not regulated by the restraints of morality; not complying with the restraints of law or social order; confused or out of order; 'lawless' or contrary to good morals; as, disorderly behaviour.

Disorderly conduct. In its broad sense the term *disorderly conduct* "embraces certain minor offences which are usually defined by statute and consist of disturbance of the peace and quiet of the public or communities, or families or a class of persons, or conduct which tends to cause or provoke a breach of the peace or corrupt public morals."

Disorderly house. A bawdy house or brothel.

Disown. Deny ownership or authorship or connection with or responsibility for a thing; repudiate; disclaim.

To refuse to recognise.

Disparage. To bring reproach or discredit.

Disparage/Disparagement means "to speak of slightingly undervalue, to bring discredit or dishonor upon, the act of deprecating, derogation, a condition of low estimation or valuation, a reproach, an unjust classing or comparison with that which is of less worth, and degradation. [International Websters' Comprehensive *Dictionary as cited in Godrej Sara Lee Ltd. vs. AVM Production Pvt. Ltd. and Ors. 2017(70)PTC282(Mad), para 25]*

"To bring dis-credit on, slightingly of and depreciate." [Oxford Dictionary as cited in Godrej Sara Lee Ltd. vs. AVM Production Pvt. Ltd. and Ors. 2017(70)PTC282(Mad), para 25]

Disparagement. Matter which is intended by its publisher to be understood or which is reasonably understood to cast doubt upon the existence or extent of anothers' property or upon its quality. If it disparaged also his reputation direclty or indirectly then an action for defamation will also lie.

Disparagement means matter which is intended by its publisher to be understood or which is reasonably understood to cast doubt upon the existence or extent of another's property, whether tangible or intangible, or upon its quality. It is a falsehood that tends to denigrate the goods or services of another party. Similarly, disparagement of goods is a statement about a competitor's goods which is untrue or misleading and is made to influence or tends to influence the public not to buy. [V.K. Ahuja, *Intellectual Property Rights in India*, 2015, LexisNexis Butterworths at p. 567].

The settled law on the subject appears to be that a manufacturer is entitled to make a statement that his goods are the best and also make some statements for puffing of his goods and the same will not give a cause of action to other traders or manufacturers of similar goods to institute proceedings as there is no disparagement or defamation to the goods of the manufacturer so doing. However, a manufacturer is not entitled to say that his competitor's goods are bad so as to puff and promote his goods. It, therefore, appears that if an action lies for defamation an injunction may be granted. *Reckitt & Colman of India Ltd* v. *Kiwi TTK Ltd.* (1996) 63 DLT 29.

Disparate impact. Discrimination caused by employment policies unrelated to job qualifications, but without the intent to discriminate.

Disparate treatment. International discrimination by employers.

Dispel. To clear away; to banish.

Dispensary. A place where medicines are dispensed. [IPC (45 of 1860), S. 275].

Dispense. Deal out (as, dispensing justice); prepare and issue (as, dispensing medicine); grant exemption from and obligation; not insist upon (as, dispensing with one's services).

Dispense with. To exempt, excuse from doing something; to relax or set aside the obligation. (*Black*)

Disperse. Break up from an assembled state (as, dispersing an unlawful assembly by use of force).

To scatter in all directions; to go different ways; to scatter; to break up from an assembled state.

Displace. Shift from a position previously occupied; oust; as, displacement of a servant.

Displaced. Ousted or removed from its place or position.

Displaced bank. Means a banking company which before the 15th of August, 1947, carried on the business of banking, whether wholly or partly, in any area now forming part of West Pakistan and is declared to be a displaced bank within the meaning of this Act by the Central Government by notification in the Official Gazette. [Displaced Persons (Debt Adjustment) Act (70 of 1951), S. 2(7)]

Displaced creditor. Means a displaced person to whom a debt is due from any other person, whether a displaced person or not. [Displaced Persons (Debts Adjustment) Act (70 of 1951), S. 2(8)] [Now repealed by Act 4 of 2018]

Displaced debtor. 'DISPLACED DEBTOR' means a displaced person from whom a debt is due or is being claimed. [Displaced Persons (Debts Adjustment) Act (70 of 1951) S. 2(9)] [Now repealed by Act 4 of 2018]

Displaced family. Means any family, who on account of acquisition of land has to be relocated and resettled from the affected area to the resettlement area. [S. 3(k) of the Right to Fair Compensation & Transparency in Land Acquisition, Rehabilitation & Resettlement Act, 2013 (30 of 2013)]

Displaced person. "DISPLACED PERSON" means—

(i) a person who, being placed from any area now forming part of Pakistan on account of civil disturbances or fear of such disturbances, has settled and is engaged or intends to engage in any business or industry in India, or

(ii) a person in India who, having had his business, industry or property, wholly or partially, such business, industry or property on account of civil disturbances or the fear of such disturbances, and who is engaged, or intends to engage in any business or Industry in India. [Rehabilitation Finance Administration Act (12 of 1948), S. 2(d)]

"DISPLACED PERSON" means any person who, on account of the setting up of the Dominions of India and Pakistan, or on account of civil disturbances or the fear of such disturbances in any area now forming part of West Pakistan, has, after the 1st day of March, 1947, left, or been displaced from, his place of residence in such area and who has been subsequently residing in India, and includes any person who is resident in any place now forming part of India and who for that reason is unable or has been rendered unable to manage, supervise or control any immovable property belonging to him in West Pakistan, but does not include a banking company. [Displaced Person (Debt Adjustment) Act (70 of 1951), S. 2(10)] [Now repealed by Act 4 of 2018]

"DISPLACED PERSON" means any person who on account of the setting up of the Dominions of India and Pakistan or on account of civil disturbances in any area now forming part of Pakistan, has, on or after the 1st day of March, 1947, left, or been displaced from, his place of residence in such area and who has been subsequently residing in India. [Transfer of Evacuee Deposit Act (15 of 1954), S. 2(c)].

Definition of 'displaced person' refers not only to natural person but also to artificial person such as

Corporation. *Steels and General Mills Ltd.* v. *General Accident Fire and Life Assurance Corporation Ltd.,* AIR 1952 Punj 229. [Displaced Persons (Institution of suits) Act 1948, S. 3]

Defines 'Displaced person'— as a person who has left or been displaced from his place of residence in any area now forming part of Pakistan and includes any person who is a resident in any place now forming part of India and who is unable to manage his property in Pakistan. *Mardas Singh* v. *Ram Prasad,* AIR 1954 Pepsu 110. [Displaced Persons (Debts Adjustment) Act (70 of 1951), S. 2(10)] [Now repealed by Act 4 of 2018]

Display. An opening or unfolding, exhibition, manifestation ostentations show, exhibition for effect, parade. *20th Century Lites* v. *Goodman*, 64 Cal App. 2d Supp. 938, 149 p. 2d 88, 91.

Display right. An exclusive right of a copyright holder to exhibit the copy of protected work publicly, whether directly or by means of technology.

Displeasure. The fact or feeling of being displeased or offended.

Disposal. "DISPOSAL" means deposit, treatment, storage and recovery of any hazardous wastes. [Hazardous Waste (Management and Handling) Rules, 1989, R. 3(q)]

"DISPOSAL" means final disposal of municipal solid wastes in terms of the specified measures to prevent contamination of groundwater, surface water and ambient air quality. [Municipal Solid Wastes (Management and Handling) Rules, 2000, R. 2(viii)]

"Disposal" is frequently, used in the sense of regulating, ordering, conducting, a thing or business.

The action of disposing of *i.e.*, settling or definitely dealing with (a case); being disposed of; the action of disposing of *i.e.*, transferring into new hands or getting done with. [Constitution of India, Art. 49].

The expression 'Disposal' appearing in entry 41 is wide enough to cover the extinguishment of a mortgage. Entry 41 relates to custody, management and disposal of property. S. Rg. [Constitution of India, Sch. 7, List III, Entry 41]

The word 'disposal' is of wide import and would include all acts or process of disposal in the sense of regulating, ordering, conducting or conditioning of something or business and also putting in a particular place or location, anything. *Tata Engineering & Locomotive Co. Ltd.* v. *State of Bihar*, (2000) 5 SCC 346, para 17.

"DISPOSAL means transfer of title in the goods to any other person, and therefore, it would not include mere dispatch to own, self or to its agents or to its branch offices or depots". *Goodyear India Ltd.* v. *State of Haryana,* 1990 (27) ECR 5 (SC).

Dispose. Arrange or group with regard to relative position of things; generally used in connection with the preposition "of," and means to determine the fate of; to exercise the power of control over; to fix the condition, application, employment, *etc.*, of; to direct or assign for a use; to exercise finally one's powers of control over; to pass over into the control of another.

To transfer into new hands or by settling [CrPC 1973 (2 of 1974), S. 133(l)]; to get done with; to settle a matter finally or definitely; to arrange a mater.

Dispose of. The words 'dispose of' merely mean put an end to the appeals by any of the recognized methods including disposal for default, by compromise *etc. Dr. K.R.K. Talwar* v. *Union of India*, AIR 1977 Delhi 189, 192. [Public Premises (Eviction of Unauthorized Occupants) Act (40 of 1971), S. 9(4)]

Disposing power. Power to dispose of [CPC (5 of 1908), S. 50(1)]; [Provincial Insolvency Act (5 of 1920), S. 2(1)(d)].

Disposition. "DISPOSITION" includes any trust, covenant, agreement or arrangement. [Estate Duty Act (34 of 1953), S. 16(c)]

Disposal; plan or arrangement for the disposal; distribution of something; definite settlement with regard to some matter.

The term 'disposition' has been defined in *Stroud's Judicial Dictionary* as a devise 'intended to comprehend a mode by which property can pass, whether by act of parties or by an act of the law' and 'includes transfer and change of property'. *Madras Refinaries* v. *Board of Revenue, Madras*, AIR 1977 SC 500, 504. [Indian Stamp Act (2 of 1899), S. 4(1)]

The word 'disposition' means giving away or giving up by a person of something which was his own. *Collector of Estate Duty, Andhra Pradesh Hyderabad* v. *Kancharla Kesava Rao*, AIR 1973 SC 2484, 2485. [Estate Duty Act (34 of 1953), S. 24]

It is not a term of law. It has no precise meaning. Its meaning has to be gathered from the context in which it is used. In Section 2(xxiv) of the Gift tax Act (18 of 1958) it refers to a bilateral or a multi-lateral act and it does not refer to a unilateral act. *Goli Eswariah* v. *Gift Tax Commissioner*, AIR 1970 SC 1722 at 1726.

The action of disposing of [Indian Evidence Act (1 of 1872), S. 91, *Expln.* 1]; the complex of attitudes, proclivities and responses conditioning conduct. [Indian Evidence Act (1 of 1872), S. 55, *Expln.*].

Disposition of property. A gift deed under Mohamedan Law does not create 'disposition of property'. *Jubeda Khatoon* v. *Moksed Ali*, AIR 1973 Gauhati 105, 106. [Indian Evidence Act (1 of 1872), S. 91]

Disposition, Prior. A disposition earlier in time or higher in order of preference. [T.P. Act (4 of 1882), S. 27].

Dispossess. Oust or dislodge person from possession of property.

To put out of possession [Specific Relief Act (47 of 1963), S. 6(2)(a)]; to be put out of possession.

Dispossessed. The word 'dispossessed' in the second proviso means to be out of possession, removed from the premises, ousted, ejected or excluded. *R.H. Bhutani* v. *Mani j. Desai*, AIR 1968 SC 1444, 1449. [CrPC, 1973 (2 of 1974), S. 145(4), 2nd Proviso and 6]

The action of dispossessing; the state of being dispossessed.

Disproportion. The condition of being out of proportion. [Indian Evidence Act (1 of 1872), S. 148(3)].

Disprove. To prove to be false or erroneous. [Indian Evidence Act (1 of 1872), S. 4].

Disproved. Not proved; want of proper proof.

Disproved fact. A fact is said to be *disproved* when, after considering the matters before it, the Court either believes that it does not exist, or considers its non-existence so probable that a prudent man ought, under the circumstances of the particular case, to act upon the supposition that it does not exist. [Indian Evidence Act (1 of 1872), Ss. 3, 4] [Now (w.e.f. 1-7-2024) repealed & replaced by Bharatiya Sakshya Adhiniyam, 2023 (47 of 2023), section 2(1)(c)]

Dispute. A conflict or contest; sometimes used in the sense of controversy.

The meaning of the word "dispute" is, "a controversy having both positive and negative aspects. It postulates the assertion of a claim by one party and its denial by the other." *Canara Bank* v. *National Thermal Power Corporation,* 2001 (1) SCC 43.

'DISPUTE' means claim of ascertained money valued at Rupees. 50,000 or more relating to any difference arising out of the execution or non-execution of a works contract or part thereof. [M.P. Madhyastham Adhikaram Adhiniyam 29 of 1983, s. 2(d) as cited in M.P. Rural Road Development Authority v. L.G. Chaudhary Engineers and Contractors, (2012) 3 SCC 495, para 6].

The expression "dispute or difference" means a controversy fairly definite and of real substance, connected with the employment or non-employment or with the terms of employment or the conditions of labour of any person, and is one in which the contesting parties are directly interested in maintaining the respective contentions. [*Prabhakar* v. *Joint Director, Sericulture Department*, (2015) 15 SCC 1, para 31].

To argue about, to contend for, to oppose by argument, to call in question-to argue or debate (with, about or over)—a contest with words; an argument; a debate, a quarrel. [*Prabhakar* v. *Joint Director, Sericulture Department*, (2015) 15 SCC 1, para 32]

"DISPUTE" includes a suit or arbitration proceedings relating to—

(a) the existence of the amount of debt;

(b) the quality of goods or service; or

(c) the breach of a representation or warranty. [Insolvency and Bankruptcy Code (31 of 2016), S. 5(6)].

"DISPUTE" means any matter touching the business, constitution, establishments or management of a society capable of being the subject of litigation and includes a claim in respect of any sum payable to or by a society, whether such claim be admitted or not. [Kerala Co-operative Societies Act (21 of 1969), S. 2(i) **as cited in** *K.A. Annamma* v. *Secretary, Cochi Co-operative Hospital Society Limited,* (2018) 2 SCC 729, para 30

Dispute, Matter in. Something which is the subject matter of some controversy. [CPC (5 of 1908), O. XIV, R. 6(c)].

Dispute prevention. Initiatives which persons and organisations take to structure their operations to minimise the risk of disputes and/or structuring relationships by contract to avoid litigation of those operations to minimise violations. (*Arbitration*)

Dispute touching the business of the society. A dispute as to the validity of the election of the Chairman of the Board of Directors is not a dispute touching the business of the society. [Co-operative Societies Act (2 of 1912), S. 43(2)]

Disputed fee. Means the fee determined under the provisions of the Income-tax Act, 1961 (43 of 1961) in respect of which appeal has been filed by the appellant. [Direct Tax Vivad se Vishwas Act, 2020 (3 of 2020), section 2(1)(f)]

Disputed income. In relation to an assessment year, means the whole or so much of the total income as is relatable to the disputed tax. [Finance (No. 2) Act (21 of 1998), S. 87(e)]

"Disputed income", in relation to an assessment year, means the whole or so much of the total income as is relatable to the disputed tax. [Direct Tax Vivad se Vishwas Act, 2020 (3 of 2020), section 2(1)(g)]

Disputed penalty. Means the penalty determined in any case under the provisions of the Income-tax Act, 1961, where—

(i) such penalty is not levied or leviable in respect of disputed income or disputed tax, as the case may be;

(ii) an appeal has been filed by the appellant in respect of such penalty. [Direct Tax Vivad se Vishwas Act, 2020 (3 of 2020), section 2(1)(i)]

Disputed tax. Means the total tax determined and payable, in respect of an assessment year under any direct tax enactment but which remains unpaid as on the date of making the declaration under Section 88. [Finance (No. 2) Act (21 of 1998), S. 87(f)]

Disputed value of gift. In relation to an assessment year, means the whole or so much of the value of gift as is relatable to the disputed tax. [Finance (No. 2) Act (21 of 1998), S. 87(i)]

Disputed wealth. In relation to an assessment year, means the whole or so much of the net wealth as is relatable to the disputed tax. [Finance (No. 2) Act (21 of 1998), S. 87(g)]

Disputes arising out of or in relation to contracts. The words of the Bye-law "arising out of or in relation to contracts" are sufficiently wide to comprehend matters, which can legitimately arise under Section 20. *Dhanrajamal Gobindram* v. *Shamji Kalidas and Co.,* AIR 1961 SC 1285. [Arbitration Act (10 of 1940), S. 20] [Now repealed & replaced by Act 26 of 1996]

Disqualification. That which disqualifies or incapacitates.

Disqualification or disability. A recommendation for deportation by a Court under Aliens Order, 1953, is not to be regarded as either a disqualification or a disability imposed on a person. R. v. *Akan,* (1972) 3 All ER 285, 288 (CA). [Criminal Justice Act 1946, S. 12(2)]

Disqualified. "DISQUALIFIED" means disqualified for being chosen as, and for being, a member of either House of Parliament or of the Legislative Assembly or Legislative Council of a State. [Representation of the People Act (43 of 1951), S. 7(b)]

Rendered unqualified or unfit.

Disqualified by or under any law made by Parliament. A disqualification would be imposed "by" a law made by Parliament when the Parliamentary statute directly enacts the disqualification or imposes a prohibition upon certain persons to stand for election. The words "under a law" would signify those cases where the disqualification is not to be found in the Parliamentary statute itself but is imposed by virtue of powers enabling this to be done; in other words where it is imposed by a law made by a subordinate law making authority. *G. Narayanaswami Naidu* v. *Krishnamurthy,* AIR 1958 Mad 343, 360. [Constitution of India, Art. 191(1)(e)]

Disqualify. In its natural and ordinary sense to incapacitate; to disable; to divest or deprive of the qualities or properties necessary for any purpose; to render unfit; to incapacitate; to deprive of legal capacity.

Disregard. Neglect; treating as something of unimportance; to pay no attention to.

Disrupt. To break apart; preventing normal continuance of.

Disruptive. "Disruptive" means producing or resulting from or attending disruption. *State of Punjab* v. *Sukhpal Singh,* AIR 1990 SC 231.

Disruptive activities. Demand of Khalistan by making provocative speeches comes within the ambit of 'disruptive activities' under Section 4 of the Act. *Esher Singh* v. *State of A.P.*, AIR 2004 SC 3030. [TADA Act (28 of 1987), S. 4]

Disruptive activity. Means any action taken, whether by act or by speech or through any other media or in any other manner whatsoever,—

(i) which questions, disrupts or is intended to disrupt, whether directly or indirectly, the sovereignty and territorial integrity of India; or

(ii) which is intended to bring about or support any claim, whether directly or indirectly, for the cession of any part of India or the cession of any part of the India from the Union. [Terrorist and Disruptive Activities (Prevention) Act (28 of 1987), S. 4(2)]

Disseisin. (*Or Disseizin*) A species of injury by ouster to the estate of another. A wrongful putting out of him that is seised of the freehold. (1 Inst. 277). As where a person enters into lands or tenements, and his entry is not lawful, and keeps him that hath the estate from the possession thereof. (*Bract. lib.* 4, c. 3; *Tomlin*). It is a tortious ouster; an ouster of the rightful owner of the *seizin*; the wrongful ouster of the rightful tenant from the possession and an usurpation of the freehold; a privation of *seizin*, the act of wrongfully depriving a person of the *seizin* of land; putting a man out of possession; the term also applies to an estate gained by wrong and injury.

Disseminate. To sow or scatter abroad; to propagate; to diffuse. [CrPC 1973 (2 of 1974), S. 108(1)(i)].

Disseminated. For the purposes of sub-sections (3) and (4), "DISSEMINATED" means making known or communicated the information to the public through notice boards, newspapers, public announcements, media broadcasts, the internet or any other means, including inspection of offices of any public authority. [Right to Information Act (22 of 2005), S. 4(4), *Expln.*]

Disseminates. [CrPC 1973 (2 of 1974), S. 108]. The word does not refer to the number of acts performed or to something in the nature of it. A simple act is enough, if there is something to show that a repetition of the act is probable.

Dissemination. The action of disseminating or scattering widely.

"Dissemination of knowledge" would mean spreading of knowledge widely or disbursement of knowledge widely. Therefore, the said set of expressions on their own, would only mean any attempt for spreading of knowledge or disbursement of knowledge. [*Maharishi Mahesh Yogi Vedic Vishwavidyalaya* v. *State of M.P.*, (2013) 15 SCC 677, para 50].

The expression "dissemination of knowledge" is the spreading of knowledge over wide frontiers. "Dissemination of knowledge" would mean spreading of knowledge widely or disbursement of knowledge widely. *[Maharishi Mahash Yogi Vedic Vishwavidyalaya* v. *State of M.P.*, (2013) 15 SCC 677, para 50]

Dissent. Contrariety of opinion; refusal to agree with something already stated or adjudged or to an act previously performed (as) a dissenting judgment.

Disagreement with an opinion; to disagree with or object to an action.

Dissentiente. Delivering a dissenting judgment.

Dissenting opinion or **Dissenting Judgment.** The opinion or judgment in which a judge announces his dissent from the conclusion held by the majority of the COURT, and expounds his own views.

Dissenting shareholder. For the purposes of section 235 of Act 18 of 2013, 'dissenting shareholder' includes a shareholder who has not assented to the scheme or contract and any shareholder who has failed or refused to transfer his shares to the transferee company in accordance with the scheme or contract. [*Explanation* to section 235 of the Companies Act, 2013 (18 of 2013)]

Disservice. The rendering of an ill service or ill turn, injury or detriment.

Dissesin. The wrongful putting out a man that is actually seised of a free hold.

Dissociate. To separate from society or associaton of any kind. [Trade Unions Act (16 of 1926), S. 4(2)]

Dissolute. Unrestrained; loose in morals and conduct.

Dissolution. In general, a dissolving; a break up; destroying.

The relaxation of any tie, bond or binding power; the breaking up of any constituted body of persons.

Ending of a Parliament with a view to have fresh election. In India, only the House of People, the lower house of Parliament, may be dissolved.

AS APPLIED TO CONTRACTS, the annulling of a contract by relieving the parties of its provisions.

AS APPLIED TO CORPORATIONS, the extinguishment of its existence in the manner prescribed by law.

AS APPLIED TO MARRIAGES, a divorce.

IN COURT PRACTICE, rendering a legal proceeding null, abrogating or revoking it; unlosing its binding force.

Dissolution and **divorce.** The word 'dissolution' relates to the marriage, bond itself, whereas the word 'divorce' relates to the parties to the marriage bond; and it is apt to refer to 'divorce' when speaking of parties and 'dissolution' when speaking of the bond. *Deacock* v. *Deacock*, (1958) 2 All ER 633, 635 (CA). [Matrimonial Causes Act, 1950, Ss. 16, 19]

Dissolution and **prorogation.** Constitution of India, Arts. 107(3), 174(2)(*a*) & (*b*), 196.

Dissolution of Parliament is invariably proceeded by prorogation, and what is true about the result of prorogation, is, it is said, a *fortiori* true about the result of dissolution. Dissolution of Parliament is sometimes described as "a civil death of Parliament." Ilbert, in his work on 'Parliament', has observed that 'Prorogation means the end of a session (not of Parliament)"; and adds that 'like dissolution, it kills all bills which have not yet passed." He also describes dissolution as an "end of a Parliament (not merely of a session) by royal proclamation", and observes that" it wipes the state clean of all uncompleted bills or other proceedings." *Purushothaman Nambudiri* v. *State of Kerala*, AIR 1962 SC 694, 698.

"It relates to the personnel or the incumbent of an office whereas the term "abolition" pertains to the very existence of the post or the institution itself. Whenever the legislature of a State is dissolved, the incumbents who are the members of the legislature cease to be so but the institution of legislature is not abolished by the dissolution. Where a tribunal is dissolved with proposals to reconstitute it, it is only dissolution and not abolition. *Gurdit Singh* v. *State*, AIR 1970 P&H 491 at 501 (FB).

Dissolution and **reconstitution.** 'Dissolution' and 'reconstitution' are two distinct legal concepts, for, a dissolution brings the partnership to an end while a reconstitution means the continuation of the partnership under altered circumstances. *Commissioner of Income Tax, West Bengal III,* v. *Pigot Champan & Company.* (1982) 2 SCC 330. [Indian Partnership Act (9 of 1932), S. 39].

Dissolution by agreement. A firm may be dissolved with the consent of all the partners or in accordance with a contract between partners. [Indian Partnership Act (9 of 1932), S. 40]

Dissolution of a firm. The dissolution of partnership between all the partners of a firm is called the dissolution of the firm. [Indian Partnership Act (9 of 1932), S. 39]

Dissolution, prorogation and adjournment. Dissolution puts an end to the life of the House of People or the Legislative Assembly and general elections are required to reconstitute them. Prorogation means simply an end of the session of the legislature. Adjournment only suspends the sitting of a House. [Constitution of India, Art. 85, 107, 174 and 196]

Distance education system. Means the system of imparting education through any means of communication, such as broadcasting, telecasting, correspondence courses, seminars, contact programmes or the combination of any two or more such means. [Mizoram University Act (8 of 2000), S. 2(h); Maulana Azad National Urdu University Act, 1996 (2 of 1997), S. 2(g)]; [Mahatma Gandhi Antarrashtriya Hindi Vishwavidyalaya Act, 1996 (3 of 1997), S. 2(g) and Baba Saheb Bhimrao Ambedkar University Act (58 of 1994), S. 2(h) and Tezpur University Act (45 of 1993), S. 2(h)]

"DISTANCE EDUCATION SYSTEM" means the system of imparting education through any means of communication, such as broadcasting, telecasting, internet, correspondence courses, seminars, contact programmes, e-learning or the combination of such means. [S. 2(k) of the Rajiv Gandhi National Aviation University Act, 2013 (26 of 2013)]

Distillation. The conversion of any substance into vapour in a vessel so arranged that the vapours are condensed and collected against in a separate vessel.

Distilled. Obtained or produced by distillation.

Distillery. A place or building where alcoholic liquors are distilled or manufactured; distilling establishment.

Works where distilling is carried on.

Distinct. Not confounded with each other or with something else; possessing differentiating characteristics; different in quality or kind not like.

The only meaning that the word 'distinct' can have is to indicate that there should be no connection between the various acts which give rise to criminal liability. *Chummoo* v. *State,* AIR 1954 All 795, 797. [CrPC 1973 (2 of 1974), S. 218]

The most imperative requisite of the word 'distinctive' when used in relation to the goods in respect of which a trade mark is registered, is that the trade mark should be adopted to distinguish the goods of the proprietor from the goods of the other persons. *Mohd. Rafiq* v. *Modi Sugar Mills Ltd.,* AIR 1972 Del 46, 48. [Trade and Merchandise Marks Act (43 of 1958), S. 9(3)]

Distinct matter. The agreement to refer any dispute whatever arising out of the contract to arbitration contained in a written contract is a part of the contract itself and not a "*distinct matter*" within the meaning of the S. 5 of the Indian Stamp Act (2 of 1899).

In its popular sense, the expression "distinct matters" would connote something different form distinct "categories". Two transactions might be of the same description, but all the same they might be distinct. *Board of Revenue* v. *A.P. Benthall,* AIR 1956 SC 35, 38.

Distinct offence. By "distinct offence", it is meant that it must be an offence entirely unconnected with a former offence charged.

Distinct subjects. The expression 'distinct subjects' clearly means subjects which are quite independent of each other and do not arise out of or relate to the same act of facts or circumstances. *D.M. Kaushik* v. *Gradnate Gas Service,* AIR 1978 P&H 213, 216.

The terms "distinct subjects" in S. 17 of the Court Fees Act (7 of 1870) are equivalent to "distinct causes of action".

'Subject' in S. 17 of the Court Fees Act means 'cause of action' and 'cause of action' means the whole of the facts on which, taken together, the right to relief is based. It is clear that there may be a series of events or facts of which some only are necessary as a foundation for a particular claim, whereas the same facts with others subsequently arising or disclosed may form the foundation of another and further claim. Separate claims to relief preferred by separate claimants are generally separate and "distinct subjects" within the meaning of S. 17 of the Court Fees Act (7 of 1870).

The word "subject" in S. 17, (Court Fees Act) is not the same as "cause of action". On the one hand it is difficult to see how distinct causes of action can ever be one subject while on the other hand it is possible for a suit based on one cause of action to embrace more than one subject. Separate claims to relief are ordinarily to be considered as separate and distinct subjects even though they are based on one cause of action.

Distinction. The mark or indication of special honour or regard; special honour or regard; worthiness or fitness for special honour or recognition; [Institutes of Technology Act (59 of 1961), S. 6(1)(i)]; the act of distinguishing; a difference [Geneva Conventions Act (6 of 1960), 3rd Sch, Art 16].

Distinctive. "DISTINCTIVE" in relation to the goods in respect of which a trade mark is proposed to be registered, means adopted to distinguish goods with which the proprietor of the trademark is or may be connected in the course of trade from goods in case of which no such connection subsists, either generally or, where the trade mark is proposed to be registered subject to limitations, in relation to use within the extent of the registration. [Trade and Mechandise Marks Act (43 of 1958), S. 9(3)] [Now repealed & replaced by Act 47 of 1999]

Serving as a mark or token by which something may be known from others of its kind.

Distinctive device or mark. In the Trade Mark Law a *distinctive device or Mark* is "a Mark or Device of such kind as, in case of infringement it shall be clear what it is that is being infringed, and that the mark is something distinct from all other marks used in the same class of goods".

A device or mark is none the less distinctive because it is a pictorial representation of the article; but colour alone will not make a device "distinctive".

Distinctive number. In relation to a high denomination bank note means the number including the alphabetical and numerical prefixes appearing on the face of the note. [High Denomination Bank Notes (Demonetisation) Act (11 of 1978), S. 2(c)]

Distinctiveness. An essential element of a device claimed to be a trademark is that it identifies the goods of a particular merchant and distinguishes them from the goods of others. A word, symbol, shape, or colour serving this purpose is said to be distinctive. Certain marks are inherently distinctive while others only acquire distinctiveness over time. A distinctive mark may lose its distinctiveness over time and become generic.

As "distinctiveness" includes inherent adaptability to distinguish, and also the effect of other circumstances in particular of user, the evidence required to establish distinctiveness may vary with the nature of the mark. In cases of low inherent adaptability such evidence must place the matter beyond reasonable doubt, and stronger evidence is required than in a passing off case as registration asserts a title against the world. The consideration of future possibilities as well as present circumstances is clearly relevant. HALSBURY, 4th Edn., Vol. 48, para 52, p. 41.

Distinctly. Clearly; explicitly; definitely; precisely; unmistakably. In a distinct manner.

The word "distinctly" means "directly", indubitably "strictly", "unmistakably". *Mohd. Inayatullah* v. *State of Maharashtra*, AIR 1976 SC 483, 485. [Indian Evidence Act (1 of 1872), S. 27]

Distinctly relates to the fact thereby discovered. The phrase 'distinctly relates to the fact thereby discovered' occurring in Section 27 of the Act is the linchpin of the provision. This phrase refers to that part of the information supplied by the accused which is the direct and immediate cause of the discovery. [*State (NCT of Delhi)* v. *Navjot Sandhu*, AIR 2005 SC 3820 : (2005) 11 SCC 600, 710, para 143] [Indian Evidence Act (1 of 1872), S. 27]

Distinguenda sunt tempora; aliud est facere aliud perficere. (*Maxim*) Times are to be distinguished; it is one thing to do, another to complete.

Distinguenda sunt tempora distingue tempora et concordabis leces. (*Maxim*) Times are to be distinguished; distinguish times and you will make laws agree. (*Latin for Lawyers*).

Distinguish. (*Distinguishing cases*) To point out an essential difference; to prove a case cited as applicable to be really inapplicable.

DISTINGUISH, DISCRIMINATE. We *distinguish* by the eye or the mental perception; we *discriminate* by the judgment alone. We *distinguish* broadly; we *discriminate* nicely. (*Smith Syn. Dis.*)

Distinguished. Differentiated from other; individually distinct; noted; eminent. [Aligarh Muslim University Act (40 of 1920), Sch., Item 24(1)].

Distinguished name. A set of data that identifies a real-world entity, such as a person in a computer-based context. (*Information Technology*).

Distinguishing mark. A birth mark, scar, or other like feature which distinguishes a person.

Distracted. Disordered in intellect; deranged; mad; absentminded.

Distrain. To seize goods and chattel as security for the payment of any obligation for which such action is made lawful.

To seize by force. [Court Fees Act (7 of 1870), S. 19(xiii)].

Distraint. The action of distraining; distress.

Distress. Anguish or affliction affecting the body, spirit or community; the legal seizure and detention of chattel to satisfy out of the proceeds of its sale, some debt or claim, especially unpaid rent.

The term 'distress' primarily connotes a summary remedy by which a person is entitled without legal process to take into his possession the personal chattels of another person, to be held as a pledge to compel the performance of a duty, or the satisfaction of a debt or demand. By almost universal sanction the term "distress" is now used to designate both the process of taking; and the chattels taken, though originally it applied only to the taking. HALSBURY, 4th Edn., Vol. 13, para 201, p. 107.

Distress damage feasant. This is an ancient form of extra-judicial redress. The phrase means the distraint of things doing damage. This right can be exercised by an occupier of land with reference to cattle or other things which go on his land and cause damage there. He can distrain and keep them as security or pledge for payment of compensation for the injury done by them. The distraint is usually of cattle but is not confined to them and extends to all the chattels animate and inanimate.

Distressed seaman. Means a seaman engaged under this Act who, by reason of having been discharged or left behind from, or shipwrecked in, any ship at a place outside India, is in distress at that place. [Merchant Shipping Act (44 of 1958), S. 3(9)]

Distributable union duties of excise. Means forty seven and a half per cent of the net proceeds of the union duties of excise levied and collected under the Central Excises and Salt Act (1 of 1944), and any other law for the levy and collection of such duty unless the law earmarks the proceeds of the duty for any special purpose. [Union Duties of Excise (Distribution) Act (24 of 1979), S. 2]

Distributable union duties of excise on electricity. Means the net proceeds of union duties of excise on electricity levied and collected, other than in union territories, under the Central Excises and Salt Act (1 of 1944) and any other law for the levy and collection of such duty, unless the law earmarks proceeds of the duty for the special purpose. [Union Duties of Excise (Electricity) Distribution Act (14 of 1980), S. 2]

Distribute. To deal out or bestow in portions or shares among many; give each a share; arrange in sets.

Distributed income. Means the consideration paid by the company on buy-back of shares as reduced by the amount which was received by the company for issue of such shares. [(w.e.f. 1-6-2013) *Explanation* (*ii*) to section 115QA(1) of the Income-tax Act, 1961 (43 of 1961)]

Distributing licensee. Means, the licensee authorized by his license to supply energy to other licensees for distribution by them. [Indian Electricity Act (9 of 1910), Sch., cl. IX] Act (9 of 1910) repealed and replaced by Act (36 of 2003).

Distributing main. Means the portion of any main with which a service line is, or is intended to be, immediately connected. [Indian Electricity Act (9 of 1910), S. 2(e)] Act (9 of 1910) repealed and replaced by Act (36 of 2003).

Distribution. "DISTRIBUTION" includes distribution by way of samples, whether free or otherwise. [Cigarettes and Other Tobacco Products (Prohibition of Advertisement and Regulation of Trade and Commerce, Production, Supply and Distribution) Act (34 of 2003), S. 3(c) and Indecent

Representation of Women (Prohibition) Act (60 of 1986), S. 2(b)]

'Distribution' has broad contours and cannot be limited to meaning only one method i.e. auction. It envisages all such methods available for distribution/allocation of natural resources which ultimately sub serve the "common good". [*Natural Resources Allocation, Re*, (2012) 10 SCC 1, para 112].

The word 'distribution' used in Article 39(b) must be broadly construed so that a Court may give full and comprehensive effect to the statutory intent continued in Article 39(b). It should not be construed in a purely literal sense so as to mean only division of a particular kind or to particular persons. The words, apportionment, allotment, allocation, classification, clearly fall within the broad sweep of the word 'distribution'. So construed, the word 'distribution' as used in Article 39(b) will include various facets, aspects, methods and terminology of a broad-based concept of distribution. Therefore, the word 'distribution' does not merely mean that property of one should be taken over and distributed to others like land reforms where the lands from the big landlords are taken away and given to landless labourers or for that matter the various urban and rural ceiling Acts. That is only one of the modes of distribution but not the only mode. *State of Tamil Nadu* v. *L. Abu Kavur Bai,* AIR 1984 SC 326. [Constitution of India, Art. 39(b)]

The action of distributing.

'DISTRIBUTION' (*in the Law of Succession*) in its technical sense, denotes the division of personal assets of an intestate, after administration and the payment of all debts against the estates and expenses of the administration, among the persons entitled as heirs or next of kin. The term distribution is sometimes applied to the division among the heirs or next of kin of the residue of both real and personal estate. In general the term *distribution*, when applied to the estate of a deceased person, refers to the ultimate division of the estate among the next of kin, in case of intestacy, or among the beneficiaries under a will after the estate is free from debt, and does not include the payment of debt against the estate by the executor or the administrator.

The word "distribution" means allotment or apportionment of the surplus amongst the shareholders, as soon as the capital stands reduced. *Punjab Distilling Industries* v. *I.T. Commissioner*, AIR 1965 SC 1862, 1869.

Distribution main. A "distribution main" has been defined by clause (e) of Section 2 to mean the portion of any main with which a service line is or is intended to be, immediately connected. *State of U.P.* v. *Hindustan Aluminium Corpn.* AIR 1979 SC 1459. [Uttar Pradesh Electricity (Regulation of Supply, Distribution, Consumption and Use) Order, 1977 and Indian Electricity Act (9 of 1910), S. 2(e)]

Distribution right. A copyright holder's exclusive right to sell, lease, or otherwise transfer copies of the protected work to the public. (*Copyright*)

Berne Convention does not provide for author's right of distribution of copies of a work but Article 6 of the World Intellectual Property Organization (WIPO) Treaty grants such a right to authors and WIPO Performances and Phonograms Treaty grants it to performers and phonogram producers respectively. (*Copyright*)

Distributive justice. Justice as expressed in the distribution of rights, privileges, duties, and liabilities among classes and members of the community.

District. "DISTRICT" means local limits of the jurisdiction of a principal Civil Court of original jurisdiction, and includes the local limits of the ordinary original civil jurisdiction of a High Court. [CPC (5 of 1908), S. 2(4)]

'DISTRICT' means a district in a State. [Constitution of India, Arts. 243(a) and 243 P(b)]

"District ADR Centre" means the District Alternative Dispute Resolution Centre established with the funds of the 13th Finance Commission and includes any other similar facilities like Nyayaseva Sadans at the district level. [National Legal Services Authority (Legal Aid Clinics) Regulations, 2011, Regn. 2(b)] as substituted by National Legal Service Authority (Legal Aid Clinics) Amendment Regulations, 2014, S. 3(i)].

District Court. "DISTRICT COURT" means, in the case of any petition under this Act, the Court of the District Judge within the local limits of whose ordinary jurisdiction, or of whose jurisdiction under this Act, the husband and wife reside or last resided together. [Indian Divorce Act (4 of 1869), S. 3(3)]

"DISTRICT COURT" means a principal Civil Court of original jurisdiction, and includes a High Court having ordinary original civil jurisdiction. [Indian Tramways Act (11 of 1886), S. 3(13)]

"DISTRICT COURT" means, in any area for which there is a city civil Court, that Court, and in any other area the principal civil Court of original jurisdiction, and includes any other civil Court which the State Government may, by notification, specify as the Court competent to deal with all or any of the matters specified in this Act. [Mental Health Act (14 of 1987), S. 2(b)]

"DISTRICT COURT" has the meaning assigned to that expression in the Code of Civil Procedure, and includes, a High Court in the exercise of its ordinary original civil jurisdiction. [Guardians and Wards Act (8 of 1890), S. 4(4)]

"DISTRICT" means the local limits of the jurisdiction of a principal civil Court of original jurisdiction (hereinafter called a "District Court"), and includes the local limits of the ordinary original civil jurisdiction of a High Court. [CPC (5 of 1908), S. 2(4)].

"DISTRICT COURT" includes the High Court in its ordinary original civil jurisdiction. [Registration Act (16 of 1908), S. 2(4)]

"DISTRICT COURT" means the principal Civil Court of original jurisdiction in any area outside the local limits for the time being of the Presidency-towns. [Lunacy Act (4 of 1912), S. 3]

"DISTRICT COURT" means the principal Civil Court of original jurisdiction in a district, but does not include a High Court in the exercise of its ordinary original civil jurisdiction. [Companies Act (1 of 1956), S. 2(14)]

District Child Protection Unit. Means a Child protection Unit for a District, established by the State Government under section 106, which shall function under the supervision of the District Magistrate to ensure the implementation of this Act and other child protection measures in the district. [Juvenile Justice (Care and Protection of Children) Act, 2015 (2 of 2016), section 2(26)]

District Election Officer. Means an officer designated or nominated by the State Election Commission. [Kerala Municipality Act, Kerala Act No. 20 of 1994, S. 2(13)]

District forum. "DISTRICT FORUM" means a Consumer Disputes Redressal Forum established under clause (a) of Section 9. [Consumer Protection Act (68 of 1986), S. 2(h)]

District Judge. Shall mean the Judge of a "principal Civil Court of original jurisdiction, but shall not include a High Court in the exercise of its ordinary or extraordinary original civil jurisdiction. [General Clauses Act (10 of 1897), S. 3(17)]

"DISTRICT JUDGE" means a Judge of a principal Civil Court of original jurisdiction however designated. [Indian Divorce Act (4 of 1869), S. 3(2)]

The expression "district judge" includes Judge of a city civil Court, Additional district judge, Joint district judge, Assistant district judge, Chief judge of a small cause Court, Chief presidency magistrate, Additional chief presidency magistrate, Sessions judge, Additional sessions judge and Assistant sessions judge. [Constitution of India, Art. 236(a)]

"DISTRICT JUDGE" the inclusive definition of the expression 'district judge' in article 236(a) of the Constitution of India has been very widely construed to include hierarchy of specialized Civil Courts, *viz.*, Labour Courts and Industrial Courts which are not expressly included in the definition. *Associated Indem Mechanical (P.) Ltd.* v. *West Bengal S.S.I.D.C. Ltd.*, AIR 2007 SC 788 : 2007 AIR SCW 489. Also see, *State of Maharashtra* v. *Labour Law Practitioners' Association*, AIR 1998 SC 1233.

District Magistrate. The words "DISTRICT MAGISTRATE" shall mean the chief officer charged with the executive administration of a district in criminal matters by whatsoever designation such officer is called. [Ben Act VI of 1870 (Village Chaukidari), S. 1]

"DISTRICT MAGISTRATE", in relation to any area for which a Commissioner of Police has been appointed, means the Commissioner of Police thereof and includes—

(a) any such Deputy Commissioner of Police, exercising jurisdiction over the whole or any part of such area, as may be specified by the State Government in this behalf in relation to such area or part; and

(b) an Additional District Magistrate. [Explosives Act (4 of 1884), S. 4(c)]

"DISTRICT MAGISTRATE" shall include a Chief Presidency Magistrate. [Reformatory Schools Act (8 of 1897), S. 4]

"DISTRICT MAGISTRATE" means, in the case of a Presidency-town or the town of Rangoon, the Commissioner of Police. [Criminal Tribes Act (6 of 1924), S. 2]

"DISTRICT MAGISTRATE", in relation to any area for which a Commissioner of Police has been appointed, means the Commissioner of Police thereof and includes any such Deputy Commissioner of Police, exercising jurisdiction over the whole or any part of such area, as may be specified by the State Government in this behalf in relation to such area or part. [Arms Act (54 of 1959), S. 2(d)]

"DISTRICT MAGISTRATE" means the District Magistrate and includes the Additional District Magistrate or any such Magistrate as may be appointed in this behalf by the Government, having territorial jurisdiction over the Municipality. [Manipur Municipalities Act (43 of 1994), S. 2(13)]

The term 'DISTRICT MAGISTRATE' occurring in Rule 4, of U.P. Kshettra Panchayats and Zila Panchats (Removal of Pramukhaya, UP-Pramukhs, Adhyakshas and Upadhyakshas) Enquiry Rules, 1977, does not include 'Additional District Magistrate'. *State of U.P.* v. *Janki Denipal*, (2003) 3 SCC 117, para 7 : AIR 2003 SC 1825.

District Superintendent. The words "DISTRICT SUPERINTENDENT" and "DISTRICT SUPER-INTENDENT OF POLICE" shall include any Assistant District Superintendent or other person appointed by general or special order of the State Government to perform all or any of the duties of a District Superintendent of Police under this Act in any District. [Police Act (5 of 1861), S. 1]

Distrust. Want of trust of confidence.

Disturb. To agitate and destroy (quiet *etc.*).

Disturb the public tranquility. Disturbing the calmness or serenity concerning the people as a whole. [CrPC 1973 (2 of 1974); S. 153A(1)(b), IPC (45 of 1860), S. 107(1)].

Disturbance. Any act which causes annoyance to another or disturbs the work of another which is carried on in a peaceful or calm atmosphere.

The interruption of tranquillity or of a regular proceeding or of a settled condition; public commotion; violent agitation in the body politic.

Disturbed area. The expression 'disturbed area' occurring in Section 2(b) read with Section 3 of the Act would mean that there must exist a grave situation of law and order on the basis of which the Governor/Administrator of the State/Union Territory or the Central Government can form an opinion that the use of armed forces in aid of the civil power is necessary. *Naga People's Movement of Human Rights* v. *Union of India*, AIR 1998 SC 431. [Armed Forces (Special Powers) Act (28 of 1958), Ss. 2(b) and 3]

Diversion. The turning aside (of any person or thing), from any course, object or occupation; a turning aside of one's course or attention; deviation; deflexion [CPC (5 of 1908), Sch I, App. A, Form No. 27(4)]; the act or an instance of diverting from one course or use to another. [Industries (Development and Regulation) Act (65 of 1951), S. 18AA(l)(a)]

Divert. To turn aside from its direction or course; to deviate.

Divest. To take away (property *etc.* vested in any one). [Religious Endowments Act (20 of 1963), Preamble].

Divide. To separate into parts; to distribute among a number.

Dividend. In general something to be divided; a fund to be divided; a sum to be divided into equal parts; or an amount to be distributed proportionately. A portion of the principal or profits divided among several owners; an equitable share of surplus; the share of one of the individuals among whom a sum is to be divided; a share or part allotted in division; the interest paid on to public funds.

"DIVIDEND" includes—

(a) any distribution by a company of accumulated profits, whether capitalised or not, if such distribution entails the release by the company; to its shareholders or all or any part of the assets of the company;

(b) any distribution to its shareholders by a company of debentures, debenture-stock, or deposit certificates in any form, whether with or without interest, and any distribution to its preference shareholders of shares by way of bonus, to the extent to which the company possesses accumulated profits, whether capitalised or not;

(c) any distribution made to the shareholders of a company on its liquidation, to the extent to which the distribution is attributable to the accumulated profits of the company immediately before its liquidation, whether capitalised or not;

(d) any distribution to its shareholders by a company on the reduction of its capital, to the extent to which the company possesses accumulated profits which arose after the end of the previous year ending next before the 1st day of April, 1933, whether such accumulated profits have been capitalised or not;

(e) any payment by a company, not being a company in which the public are substantially interested, of any sum (whether as representing a part of the assets of the company or otherwise) made after the 31st day of May, 1987, by way of advance or loan to a shareholder, being a person who is the beneficial owner of shares (not being shares entitled to a fixed rate of dividend whether with or without a right to participate in profits) holding not less than ten per cent of the voting power, or to any concern in which such shareholder is a member or a partner and in which he has a substantial interest (hereafter in this clause referred to as the said concern) or any payment by any such company on behalf, or for the individual benefit, of any such shareholder, to the extent to which the company in either case possesses accumulated profits;

but "DIVIDEND" does not include—

(i) a distribution made in accordance with sub-clause (*c*) or sub-clause (*d*) in respect of any share issued for full cash consideration, where the holder of the share is not entitled in the event of liquidation to participate in the surplus assets;

(*i-a*) a distribution made in accordance with sub-clause (*c*) or sub-clause (*d*) in so far as such distribution is attributable to the capitalised profits of the company representing bonus shares allotted to its equity shareholders after the 31st day of March, 1964, and before the 1st day of April, 1965;

(ii) any advance or loan made to a shareholder or the said concern by a company in the ordinary course of its business, where the lending of money is a substantial part of the business of the company;

(iii) any dividend paid by a company which is set off by the company against the whole or any part of any sum previously paid by it and treated as a dividend within the meaning of sub-clause (*e*), to the extent to which it is so set off.

(iv) any payment made by a company on purchase of its own shares from a shareholder in accordance with the provisions of section 77A of the Companies Act, 1956 (1 of 1956);

(v) any distribution of shares pursuant to a demerger by the resulting company to the shareholders of the demerged company (whether or not there is a reduction of capital in the demerged company).

Explanation 1.—The expression "accumulated profits", wherever it occurs in this clause, shall not include capital gains arising before the 1st day of

April, 1946, or after the 31st day of March, 1948, and before the 1st day of April, 1956;

Explanation 2.—The expression "accumulated profits" in sub-clauses (*a*), (*b*), (d) and (*e*), shall include all profits of the company up to the date of distribution or payment referred to in those sub-Clauses, and in sub-clause (*c*) shall include all profits of the company up to the date of liquidation, but shall not, where the liquidation is consequent on the compulsory acquisition of its undertaking by the Government or a corporation owned or controlled by the Government under any law for the time being in force, include any profits of the company prior to three successive previous years immediately preceding the previous year in which such acquisition took place. [Income-tax Act (43 of 1961), S. 2(22)]

"DIVIDEND" means the share of the subscriber in the amount of discount available under the chit agreement for rateable distribution among the subscribers at each instalment of the chit. [Chit Funds Act (40 of 1982), S. 2(h)]

"DIVIDEND" includes bonus. [Imperial Bank of India (47 of 1920), S. 2(c)]

"DIVIDEND" includes any interim dividend. [Companies Act (1 of 1956), S. 2(14A)]

A share or portion of any sum of money, especially profit of a joint stock company, to be divided amongst a number of persons, the shareholders; [Presidency-towns Insolvency Act (3 of 1909), Ss. 69, 71 and 72]

"DIVIDEND" in its ordinary connotation means the sum paid to or received by a shareholder proportionate to his shareholding in a company out of the total sum distributed. *Commissioner of Income-Tax Calcutta* v. *Nalin Behari Lal Singha,* AIR 1970 SC 388.

"DIVIDEND" includes any interim dividend. [S. 2(35) of the Companies Act, 2013 (18 of 2013)]

Dividend warrants. Written orders to a banker authorising the payment of dividends; an order representing a stock-holder's dividend.

Dividends. In section 115BBD of Act 43 of 1961, 'dividends' shall have the same meaning as is given to 'dividend' in section 2(22) of Act 43 of 1961 but shall not include section 2(22)(e) thereof. [S. 115BBD(3)(i) of the Income-tax Act, 1961 (43 of 1961) as inserted (w.e.f. 1-4-2012) by the Finance Act, 2011 (8 of 2011)]

Divine displeasure. Displeasure of or pertaining to god, goddess or diety.

Division. The action of dividing or state of being divided into parts; a portion; a portion of a country as marked for some political, administrative or other purpose.

A mode of arriving at a decision on a proposed measure or question by recording votes for or against it. Division is ordered by the Chair when his opinion on the question just decided by voice vote is challenged by members who demand a division.

Division Bench. A Court comprised of two or more judges and which is not a full bench.

Divisional application. Means—

(i) an application containing a request for the division of goods or services in a class for the registration of a trade mark; or

(ii) a divided application made by the division of a single application for the registration of a trade mark for separate classes of goods or services. [trade Marks Rules, 2017, R. 2(1)(h)].

Division Court. A Court composed of two or more judges of the High Court and sitting generally in special cases. The expression "Division Court" in S. 39, Letters Patent, does not apply only to a Division Court sitting on the Original Side. (32 C. 963 : 9 ICWN 566) Division Court must consist of at least two judges. [AIR 1922 Pat 13 (1)]

Divorce. Divorce is nothing more nor less than another name for dissolution of marriage, whether the same results from act of parties or is a consequence of proceedings at law and it would be wrong to regard the two terms as not being synonymous with each other unless the legislature makes a direction to the contrary. *Zohara Khatoon* v. *Mohd. Ibrahim*, AIR 1981 SC 1243, 1251. [Dissolution of Muslim Marriages Act (8 of 1939), S. 2]

Divorce a mensa et thoro. 1. A judicial decree which terminates the obligation and right of cohabitation but does not affect the status of the parties as married persons or dissolve the marriage. 24 Am J2d Div & S § 1. A limited, partial or qualified divorce which suspends the marriage relation and modifies the duties and obligations but leaves the marriage bond in full force,—a judicial separation. 2. A final judgment for divorce, if the divorce granted is an absolute divorce, dissolves the marriage bond and changes the status of the parties; if the divorce is limited, or, as sometimes called, a decree of separation from bed and board, it merely relieves the parties from their obligations and rights as to cohabitation, support, and property interests. *Givens* v. *Givens* 121 Fla 271, 63 So 574; *People* v. *John* 181 Misc 921, 44 NYS2d 806. *(Ballantine's Law Dictionary, 3rd Edn.)*

Divorced woman. Means a Muslim woman who was married according to Muslim law, and has been divorced by, or has obtained divorce from her husband in accordance with Muslim law. [Muslim Women (Protection of Rights on Divorce) Act (25 of 1986), S. 2(a)]

Divulge. To disclose to other person or persons a subject matter which was considered to be a secret one.

To disclose; to reveal. [Indian Criminal Law Amendment Act (14 of 1908), S. 17E(11)].

Divulgation right. In the approach of the author's right system, one of the four principal moral rights, namely the right to decide when and in what way the work will be divulged. (*Jal Sterling, Sweet and Maxwell*) (*Copyright*)

Diwan. A royal Court; a council of state; tribunal of revenue or justice. A minister; a chief officer of state; an honorary title; civil officer of a district under the later Muhammadan administration.

Diwani. The civil administration; office of Diwan, as opposed to the Nizamat or Faujdari, the military and criminal administration. Of or relating to a Diwan, civil as opposed to criminal. The office, jurisdiction, emoluments *etc.*, of a Diwan. The right to receive the collections of Bengal, Bihar and Orissa, conferred on the East India Company by the Titular Moghul.

DNA. De-oxy-ribonucleic acid, the nucleoprotein of chromosomes.

The double-helix structure in cell nuclei that carries the genetic information of most living organisms.

An organic substance found in the nucleus of living cells that provides the genetic Code that determines a person's individual characteristics. (*Criminal*)

The material in a cell that makes up the genes and controls the cell. (*Biological Term*)

DNA Fingerprinting (genetic fingerprinting). A method of identification specially for evidentiary purposes by analyzing and comparing the DNA from samples of tissue.

DNA Profiling. The process in which the body samples are examined so as to reveal and assess the composition of the human genetic coding material, allowing deductions as to whether or not two or more samples have come from the same person.

DNS. (*Abbr.*) Domain Name System. The Domain Name System is the system that translates Internet *domain names* into *IP numbers*. A "DNS Server" is a *server* that performs this kind of translation. (*Matisse Enzer-Glossary of Internet Terms*)

Dock. "DOCK" (in Port Trust Act) shall include all basins, cuts, quays, wharves, warehouses, tramways, and other works and things appertaining to any dock. [Ben Act (3 of 1890), S. 3(3).

"Dock" includes all basins, locks, cuts, entrances, graving docks, graving blocks, inclined planes, slipways, gridirons, moorings, transit-sheds, warehouses, tramways, railways and other works and things appertaining to any dock, and also the portion of the sea enclosed or protected by the arms or groynes of a harbour. [Major Port Authorities Act, 2021 (1 of 2021), section 2(1)(f)]

A space or waterway between two piers or wharves, as for receiving a ship while in port.

(*In Court practice*) the place or cage in a Court of criminal law in which a prisoner is placed during his trial.

A dock is an artificial inclosure, connected with a harbour or a river, provided for the reception of vessels, and is generally shut off from the harbour or river by gates for regulating the inflow and outflow of water. It may be a dry or graving dock, used for the inspection and repair of vessels, or a wet dock, used for their loading and discharge. A dock may include a lock leading from it to a river. (*36 Halsbury's Laws (4th Edn.) para 401*)

Dock receipt. An interim certificate which is issued by a maritime shipping company for the delivery of goods at the dock and entitling the designated person to receive a bill of lading. Also called as *Dock warrant*.

Dock work. "DOCK WORK" means any work in or within the vicinity of any port in connection with, or required for, or incidental to the loading, unloading, movement or storage of cargoes into or from ship or other vessel, port, dock, storage place or landing place, and includes—

(i) work in connection with the preparation of ships or other vessels for receipt or discharge of cargoes or leaving port; and

(ii) chipping, painting or cleaning of any hold, tank, structure or lifting machinery or any other storage area in board the ship or in the docks. [Dock Workers (Safety Health and Welfare) Act (54 of 1986), S. 2(d)]

"Dock work" means any work in or within the vicinity of any port in connection with, or required for, or incidental to, the loading, unloading, movement or storage of cargoes into or from ship or other vessel, port, dock, storage place or landing place, and includes—

(i) work in connection with the preparation of ships or other vessels for receipt or discharge of cargoes or leaving port;

(ii) all repairing and maintenance processes connected with any hold, tank structure or lifting machinery or any other storage area on board the ship or in the docks; and

(iii) chipping, painting or cleaning of any hold, tank, structure or lifting machinery or any other storage area in board the ship or in the docks. [Code on Social Security, 2020 (36 of 2020), section 2(25)] [Occupational Safety, Healthy & Working Conditions Code, 2020 (37 of 2020), section 2(1)(s)]

Dock worker. Means a person employed or to be employed directly or by or through any agency (including a contractor) with or without knowledge of the principal employer, whether for remuneration or not, on dock work. [Dock Workers Safety Health and Welfare Act (54 of 1986), S. 2(e)]

Docket. A brief writing on a small piece of paper or parchment, containing the effect of a greater writing; a register; endorsement on paper showing its subject or contents.

Dockyard. A storage place for naval stores or timber for ship building with facilities for building or reparing ships.

Doctrine. A principle, specially a legal principle, that is widely adhered to.

Doctrine of implied powers. It is well established rule of construction that a power to do something essential for the proper and effectual performance of the work which the statute has in contemplation may be implied. *Assistant Collector of Central Excise* v. *National Tobacco Co. of India Ltd.*, AIR 1972 SC 2563.

Doctrine of basic structure. The "doctrine of basic structure" was nothing more than a set of obvious inferences relating to the interests of the Constitution makers arrived at by applying the established cannons of construction rather broadly as they should be so far as an organic constitutional document meant to govern fate of the nation is concerned. *State of Karnataka* v. *Union of India,* AIR 1978 SC 68.

Doctrine of colourable legislation. If the Constitution of a State distribute the legislative powers amongst different bodies which have to act within their respective spheres marked out by specific legislative entries, or if there are limitation on the legislative authority in the shape of fundamental rights, questions do arise as to whether the Legislature in a particular case has or has not, in respect to the subject-matter of the statute or in the method of enacting it, transgressed the limits of its constitutional powers. Such transgression may be patent, manifest or direct, but it may also be disguised, covert and indirect and it is to this latter class of cases that the expression "colourable legislation" has been applied in certain judicial pronouncements. *Gajapati Narayan Deo* v. *State of Orissa*, AIR 1953 SC 375.

The doctrine of eclipse can be invoked only in the case of pre constitutional law made validly. But it has no application to post constitutional laws infringing the fundamental rights as they would be void *ab initio in toto* or to the extent of the contravention of the fundamental rights. *Deep Chand* v. *State of U.P.,* AIR 1959 SC 648, 659, 660.

Doctrine of cy pres. *Cy pres.* A principle of equity construction substituting the nearest feasible condition or purpose of a trust for an impossible one.

Doctrine of double jeopardy. A driver of State Roadways bus caused an accident resulting in death of one person and injury to another. The Motor Accidents Claims Tribunal awarded a huge amount as a compensation against. The State Roadways for the said accident, following which the State Roadways imposed a penalty of reduction of pay upon the driver. Subsequently the said bus driver was convicted under Section 304-A of the Code following which the penalty upon the driver was enhanced to termination of his service from State Roadways by the Department. It was held that there is no question of applicability of principle of double jeopardy under Article 20(2) of the Constitution in such a case. [*State of Haryana* v. *Balwant Singh*, AIR 2003 SC 1253 : (2003) 3 SCC 362, 364-65, paras 4 to 6, relying on *Union of India* v. *P.D. Yadav*, (2002) 1 SCC 405, 425, para 25] [Constitution of India, Art. 20(2); IPC (45 of 1860), S. 304A]

Doctrine of eclipse. This doctrine, flowing from the prospective nature of Art. 13(1) of the Constitution of India, was evolved by the Supreme Court in *Bhikaji* v. *State of M.P.*, AIR 1955 SC 781, meaning thereby that a valid pre-constitutional law violating a fundamental right becomes inoperative treating it as having been eclipsed by the relevant fundamental right. If this fundamental is amended and the shadow is removed, the law will revive and operate. However, the law subsists for pre-constitutional rights and liabilities.

An existing law inconsistent with a fundamental right though becomes inoperative from the date of the commencement of the Constitution is not dead altogether.

Doctrine of election. The same principle is stated in *White and Tudor's Leading Cases in Equity*, Vol. (*sic*) 18th Edn. at p. 444 as follows: 'Election is the obligation imposed upon a party by Courts of equity to choose between two inconsistent or alternative rights or claims in cases where there is clear intention of the person from whom he derives one that he should not enjoy both... That he who accepts a benefit under a deed or Will must adopt the whole contents of the instrument.' [**As referred in** *National Insurance Co. Ltd.* v. *Mastan*, AIR 2006 SC 577 : (2006) 2 SCC 641, 649, p. 25]

Doctrine of eminent domain. Art. 300-A embodies the 'doctrine of eminent domain' which comprises two parts, (*i*) acquisition of property in public interests and (*ii*) payment of reasonable compensation therefor. [*State of Bihar* v. *Project Uchcha Vidya Sikshak Sangh*, (2006) 2 SCC 545, 573, p. 65] [Constitution of India, Art. 300-A]

Doctrine of equal pay for equal work. For the purpose of invoking the 'doctrine of equal pay for equal work', the nature of work and responsibility attached to the post are some of the factors which are bound to be taken into consideration. [*Mahendra L. Jain* v. *Indore Development Authority,* AIR 2005 SC 1252 : JT (2004) 10 SC 1]

Doctrine of equality. A person not qualified for appointment cannot claim such right on the basis of his fundamental rights and by invoking the 'doctrine of equality' under Art. 14 of the Constitution of India. [*State of Punjab* v. *Tara Singh Shahi*, (1996) 8 SCC 448]

The 'doctrine of equality' cannot be invoked by an employee of a corporation with that of other corporation as each public sector undertaking is an independent entity and free to have its own service conditions as per law. On the basis of this doctrine, Board of Directors of the Corporation who themselves forms a different class cannot be equated with other employees in regard to conditions of service applicable to them. [*Suresh Chandra Singh* v. *Fertilizer Corpn. of India Ltd.*, (2004) 1 SCC 592, 594, para 7]

Doctrine of estoppel. To invoke the doctrine of estoppel embodied in Section 115, three conditions must be satisfied : (1) representation by a person to another; (2) the other shall have acted upon the said representation; and (3) such action shall have been detrimental to the interests of the person to whom the representation has been made. Where the first two conditions are satisfied but the third is not, there is no scope to invoke the doctrine of estoppel. *Gyarsi Bai* v. *Dhansukh Lal,* MLJ : QD (1961-1965) Vol III C564 : (1965) 2 SCJ 783 : AIR 1965 SC 1055 [Evidence Act (1 of 1872), S. 115]

Doctrine of fairness or the duty to act fairly and reasonably. "..... Doctrine of fairness or the duty to act fairly and reasonably is a doctrine developed in the administrative law field to ensure the rule of law and to prevent failure of justice where the action is administrative in nature. Just as principles of natural justice ensure fair decision where the function is *quasi* judicial, the doctrine of fairness is certainly not be invoked to amend, alter or vary the express terms of the contract between the parties. This is so, even if the contract is governed by statutory provisions, *i.e.* where it is a statutory contract—or rather more so. It is one thing to say that a contract—every contract—must be construed reasonably having regard to its language. But this is not what the licensees say. They seek to create an obligation on the other party to the contract, just because it happens to be the State. They are not prepared to apply the very same rule in converse case, *i.e.* where the State has abundant supplies and wants the licensees to lift all the stocks. The licensees will undertake no obligation to lift all those stocks even if the State suffers loss. This one sided obligation in modification of express terms of the contract, in the name of duty to act fairly, is what we are unable to appreciate..." *Assistant Excise Commissioner* v. *Issac Peter*, 1994 AIR SCW 2616, 2636, as **referred to** in *Oil and National Gas Corporation Ltd.* v. *Streamline shipping Co. Pvt. Ltd*, AIR 2002 Bom 420, 422.

Doctrine of feeding the estoppel. The doctrine of feeding the estoppel envisages that where grantor has purported to grant an interest in land which he did not at the time possess, but subsequently acquires, the benefit of his subsequent acquisition, goes automatically to the earlier grantee, or as is usually expressed feeds the estoppel. [*Hardev Singh* v. *Gurmail Singh,* AIR 2007 SC 1058, 1060, para 14]

Doctrine of flexibility. While interpreting the constitution, the constitutional Courts are not only required to take into consideration their own experience over the time, the international treaties and covenants but also keeping the doctrine of flexibility in mind. [*Union of India* v. *Naveen Jindal,* AIR 2004 SC 1559 : (2004) 2 SCC 510, 539, para 40]

Doctrine of harmonious construction. A law should be so interpreted as to give effect to all its parts and the presumption should be that no conflict or repugnancy was intended between the various provisions of the statute.

Doctrine of issue estoppel. The statement of law made by the Supreme Court in *State of U.P.* v. *Nawab Hussain*, AIR 1977 SC 1680, is to the following effect (Paras 3 and 4) :

"The principle of estoppel per *rem judicatum* is a rule of evidence. It may be said to be "the broader rule of evidence which prohibits the reassertion of a cause of action." This doctrine is based on two theories; (i) the finality and conclusiveness of judicial decisions for the final termination of disputes in the general interest of the community as a matter of public policy, and (ii) the interest of the individual that he should be protected from multiplication of litigation." as cited in *P.N. Govindan* v. *Abdul Kari Subaida Beevi*, AIR 1998 Ker 50, 57.

Doctrine of legitimate expectation. The 'doctrine of legitimate expectation' is only an aspect of Article 14 of the constitution dealing with the citizens in a non-arbitrary manner and thus, by itself, does not give rise to an enforceable right but in testing the action taken by the Government authority whether arbitrary or otherwise, it would be relevant. [*State of W.B.* v. *Niranjan Singha,* (2001) 2 SCC 326, 329, para 4]

A person may have a 'legitimate expectation' of being treated in a certain way by an administrative authority even though he has no legal right in private law to receive such treatment. This doctrine has an important place in developing law of judicial review. It can provide a sufficient interest to enable one who cannot point to existence of a substantive right to obtain leave of Court to apply for judicial review. Doctrine of legitimate expectation is to be confined mostly to right of a fair hearing before a decision which results in negativing a promise or withdrawing an undertaking. It does not give scope to claim a relief straightaway from administrative authorities. [*Bannari Amman Sugars Ltd.* v. *Commercial Tax Officer,* (2004) 9 SCALE 604]

(Doctrine of) lifting the veil. The doctrine of lifting the veil has been applied in the words of Palmer, in five categories of cases : where companies are in relationship of holding and subsidiary (or subsubsidiary) companies; where a share-holder has lost the privilege of limited liability and has become directly liable to certain creditors of the company on the ground that, with his knowledge, the company continued to carry on business six months after the number of its members was reduced below the legal minimum; in certain matters pertaining to the law of taxes, death duty and stamps, particularly where the question of the 'controlling interest' is in issue; in the law relating to exchange control, and in the law relating to trading with the enemy where the test of control is adopted. [*P.C. Agarwala* v. *Payment of Wages Inspector,* (2005) 8 SCC 104, 121, para 22] [See also PLAMER'S *Company Law*, 20th Edn., p. 136, now p. 215, 24th Edn.1987]

Doctrine of lis pendens. The principle of *lis pendens* enforced in England both by Courts of law and equity is embodied in S 52. The section does not declare that all the transfers made *pendente lite* are null and void but what is provided for is that such transfers will be subject to the decree or order passed or made in the suit. In other words the transfer will be subservient to the decree or order. (1946) 2 MLJ 35 : AIR 1947 Mad 18 : (1937) 2 MLJ 286 : AIR 1937 PC 251 and AIR 1943 Cal. 577, **Relied on.** If the decree or order does not create a right in any party in respect of any specific property transferred no question of *lis pendens* can possibly arise. Where the property covered by the transfer was not affected by the partition decree passed in a suit pending at the time of the transfer and no part of the property allotted to the plaintiff was from and out of the properties covered by the transfer, and no charge for *mesne profits* was created in the partition decree, the decree for *mesne profits*, is nothing more than a simple decree for money and is not enforceable against the judgment-debtors personally and against their other properties. It is not specifically enforceable against properties covered by the transfer, and there is no question of the decree prevailing over the transfer. *Ahmed Ali Khan* v. *Banguluru Veeralla,* MLJ : QD (1956-1960) Vol. IV C2582 : (1958) Andh LT 938 : (1959) 1 An WR 72 : AIR 1959 AP 280. [Transfer of Property Act (4 of 1882), S. 52]

Doctrine of merger. 'Doctrine of merger' is a common law doctrine founded on the principle of propriety in the hierarchy of justice delivery system. The purpose of the doctrine is that there cannot be more than one decree or operative order governing the same subject-matter at a given point of time. It is the decree or order of the superior Court, tribunal or authority which is the final, binding and operative decree or order wherein merges the decree or order passed by the Court below. [*Kunhayammed* v. *State of Kerala,* AIR 2000 SC 2587 : (2000) 245 ITR 360 (SC)]

Doctrine of natural justice. The concept of 'natural justice' cannot be put into a straitjacket. It is futile, therefore, to look for definitions or standards of natural justice from various decisions and then try to apply them to the facts of any given case. The only essential point has to be kept in mind in all cases that the person concerned should have a reasonable opportunity of presenting his case and that the administrative authority concerned should act fairly, impartially and reasonably. [*Keshav Mill Co. Ltd.* v. *Union of India,* (1973) 1 SCC para 8. See also *Kumaon Mandal Vikas Nigam Ltd.* v. *Girja Shankar Pant and Ors.*, (2001) 1 SCC (LCS) 189, para 1]

Doctrine of necessity. 'Doctrine of necessity' was held to be not applicable where Council of Ministers refused to grant sanction for prosecution and the Governor on his discretion sanctioned for the prosecution of Ministers contrary to the advice of the Council of Ministers. [*M.P. Special Police Establishment* v. *State of M.P.,* (2004) 8 SCC 788, 806, para 33]

Doctrine of *noscitur a sociis*. The principle underlying *noscitur a sociis* is that two or more words which are susceptible of analogous meaning when are coupled together are to be understood as used in their cognate sense, taking, as it were their colour from each other, that is, the more general is to be restricted to a sense analogous to the less general. [*Municipal Corpn. of Greater Bombay* v. *Bharat Petroleum Corpn. Ltd.,* (2002) 4 SCC 219, 225-26, para 7]

Doctrine of occupied field. Pre-empted field.

Doctrine of parens patriae. The expression *parens patriae* appears in Volume 31 page 99 of the Words and Phrases in *American Constitution Law* by Laurance B. Tribe (1978) Edition at paragraph 324. It is stated that in its capacity as proprietor a State may satisfy the requirement of injury to its own interest by an assertion of harm to the State as such. It was further stated that the State may sue for wrongs suffered by it and also for public institutions. In its *quasi* sovereign capacity the State has an interest independent of and behind the title of the citizens in all the earth and air within its domain. It was emphasised that as *parens patriae* on behalf of the citizens where State's capacity as *parens patriae* is not located by the Federal Structure, the protection of the General Health comfort and welfare of State inhabitants have been held to give the State itself a sufficient interest. The doctrine was upheld in *Charan Lal Sahu* v. *U.O.I.*, AIR 1990 SC 1480, para 63 while upholding the validity of the Bhopal Gas (Disaster Processing of Claims) Act, 1985.

Doctrine of pari delicto. The "doctrine of pari delicto" is not designed to reward the 'wrongdoer' or to penalize the 'wronged', by denying to the victim of exploitation access to justice. The doctrine is attracted only when none of the parties is a victim of such exploitation and both parties have voluntarily and by their free will joined hands to flout the law for their mutual gain. *Mohd. Salimuddin* v. *Misri Lal,* AIR 1986 SC 1019.

Doctrine of pith and substance. It means examining the true nature and character of the law in order to know whether it comes within the purview of the Union List or the State List *e.g.* the State law will be invalid even if it incidentally touches the Union List unless it goes into that List so far that its substance falls within that List.

Doctrine of pleasure. Under the Indian Constitution a public servant though works at the pleasure of the President or the Governor as the case may be, does not work, at his mercy.

Doctrine of presumption of innocence. In view of the prevalent criminal jurisprudential system in the country, the doctrine of 'presumption of innocence' in favour of the accused makes the justice itself a victim which ultimately weakens the criminal justice dispensation system. Be that as it may, an onerous duty is cast upon the criminal Courts in the country to ensure that no innocent person is convicted and deprived of his personal liberties. [*Bijoy Singh* v. *State of Bihar,* AIR 2002 SC 1949]

Doctrine of promissory estoppel. The doctrine of promissory estoppel has been evolved by equity to avoid injustice. Its object is to interpose equity share of its form to mitigate the rigour of strict law. Purpose of this doctrine is to avoid or prevent a detriment to party asserting the estoppel by compelling opposite party to adhere to assumption upon which the former acted or abstained from acting. [*Bannari Amman Sugars Ltd.* v. *Commercial Tax Officer,* (2004) 9 Scale 604]

The 'doctrine of promissory estoppel' is not based on the principle of estoppel. It is a doctrine evolved by equity in order to prevent injustice. Where a party by his words or conduct makes a promise to another person in unequivocal and clear terms intending to create legal relations knowing or intending that it would be acted upon by the other party, the promise would be binding by the other party to whom the promise is made and it is so acted upon on the party making it. [*Banglore Development Authority and ors.* v. *R. Hanumaiah and ors.,* (2005) 12 SCC 508, 525, para 28]

Doctrine of proportionality. The doctrine of proportionality originated as far back as in the 19th century in Russia and was later adopted by Germany, France and other European Countries. Since 1952, this principle has been applied vigorously to legislative and administrative action in India. The administrative action in our country has to be tested on the principle of proportionality, just as it is done in the case of main legislation. [*Teri Oat Estates (P.) Ltd.* v. *U.T. Chandigarh and ors.,* (2004) 2 SCC 130, 145, 146, para 45, 49. See also *Om Kumar* v. *Union of India,* (2001) 2 SCC 386]

The principle of 'proportionality' means that the question whether while regulating exercise of fundamental rights, the appropriate or least restrictive choice of measures has been made by the legislature or the administrator so as to achieve the object of legislations or the purpose of administrative order as the case may be. Under this principle the Court will see that the legislature and administrative authority maintain a proper balance between the adverse effects which the legislation or the administrative order may have on the rights, liberties or interests of persons keeping in mind the purpose which they were intended to serve. [*Teri Oat Estates (P.) Ltd.* v. *U.T. Chandigarh and ors.,* (2004) 2 SCC 130, 145, para 46]

Doctrine of proprietary estoppel. "The overwhelming weight of authority shows that detriment is required. But the authorities also show that it is not a narrow or technical concept. The detriment need not consist of the expenditure of money or other quantifiable financial detriment, so long as it is something substantial. The requirement must be approached as part of a broad inquiry as to whether repudiation of an assurance is or is not unconscionable in all the circumstances." [*Gillett* v. *Holt,* (2000) 2 All ER 289, 308 : (2000) 3 WLR 815 (CA); *See also Jai Narain Parasrampuria and ors.* v. *Pushpa Devi Saraf and ors.*, (2006) 7 SCC 756, 777-78, p. 38]

Doctrine of prospective overruling. The sum and substance of the doctrine of prospective overruling is that when the Court finds or lays down the correct law in the process of which the prevalent understanding of the law undergoes a change, the Court, on consideration of justice and fair deal, restricts the operation of the new-found law to the future so that its impact does not fall on the past transaction. [*Golak Nath* v. *State of Punjab,* AIR 1967 SC 1643. See also *Kailash Chand Sharma* v. *State of Rajasthan,* (2002) 6 SCC 562, 589]

For the first time the Apex Court in *Golak Nath* v. *State of Punjab* accepted the doctrine of 'prospective overruling' and laid down following propositions : (1) The doctrine of prospective overruling can be invoked only in matters arising under our Constitution; (2) it can be applied only by the highest Court of the country *i.e.* the Supreme Court as it has the constitutional jurisdiction to declare law binding on all the Courts in India; (3) the scope of the retrospective operation of the law declared by the Supreme Court superseding its 'earlier decisions' is left to its discretion to be moulded in accordance with the justice of the cause or matter before it. [AIR 1967 SC 1643, 1669. See also *Sarwan Kumar and ors.* v. *Madan Lal Aggarwal,* (2003) 4 SCC 147, 157, para 15]

Doctrine of public trust. The 'doctrine of public trust' though in existence from Roman times, is enunciated in its modern form by US Supreme Court in *Illinois Central Railroad Co.* v. *People of the State of Illinois*, where the Court held:

'The bed or soil of navigable waters is held by the people of the State in their character as sovereign in trust for public use for which they are adapted... The State holds title to the bed of navigable waters upon a public trust and no alienation or disposition of such property by the State which does not recognise and not in execution of this trust, is permissible.' [146 US 387 : 36 L Ed 1018 (1892). As **relied in** *Intellectuals Forums, Tirupathi* v. *State of A.P.*, (2006) 3 SCC 549, 574, para 74]

Doctrine of repugnancy. Repugnancy arises when two enactment's, both within the competence of the two legislatures collide and when the Constitution expressly or by necessary implication provides that the enactment of one legislature has superiority over the other then to the extent of the repugnancy the one supersedes the other. The test of two legislations containing contradictory provisions is not, however the only criterion of repugnancy, for if a competent legislature with a superior efficacy or expressly or impliedly evinces by its legislation an intention to cover the whole field, the enactments of the other legislature whether passed before or after would be over borne on the ground of the 'doctrine repugnancy'. [*State of Orissa* v. *M.A. Tulloch & Co.,* AIR 1964 SC 1284 : (1964) 4 SCR 461, 477.

Doctrine of *res gestae*. The essence of the doctrine of *res gestae* in evidence is that the facts which though are not in issue are so connected with the fact in issue as to form part of the same transaction and thereby become relevant like fact in issue. *Babulal Choukhani* v. *Western India Theatres, Ltd.,* MLJ : QD (1956-1960) Vol. II C2490 : (S) AIR 1957 Cal 709 : (1958) 28 Com Cas 565. [Evidence Act (1 of 1872), S. 6]

Doctrine of *res ipsa liquitur*. The doctrine of *res ipsa loquitur* only means that an accident by its nature be more consistent with its being caused by negligence for which the defendant is responsible than by other causes, and in such a case the mere fact of the accident would be *prima facie* evidence of such negligence. [*MPSRT Corpn* v. *Sudhakar*, AIR 1968 MP 47 (*Cole* v. *De Trafford,* 1918 2 KB 523)]

Doctrine of *res judicata*. Where substitution application filed by the legal heirs of the deceased-appellant was rejected as not maintainable on the ground that separate applications were not filed for substitution, setting aside abatement of appeal and condonation of delay and thereafter separate applications were filed, it was held that the subsequent application for substitution would not be hit by doctrine of '*res judicata.*' [*Ganeshprasad Badrinarayan Lahoti* v. *Sanjeevprasad Jamna Prasad Chourasiya,* (2004) 7 SCC 482, 486, para 10]

Doctrine of restitution. The principle of the 'doctrine of restitution' is that on the reversal of the decree' the law imposes an obligation on the party to the suit who received the benefit of the erroneous decree to make restitution to the other party for what he has lost. This obligation arises automatically on the restitution on the reversal or modification of the decree and necessarily carries with it the right to restitution of all that has been done under the erroneous decree, and the Court is bound in making the restitution to the same position they were in of the time of passing an erroneous decree. [*Padanathil Rugmini Amma* v. *P.K. Abdulla*, (1996) 7 SCC 668, 673, p. 12], **relying on** *Binayak Swain* v. *Ramesh Chandra Panigraahi*, AIR 1966 SC 948]

The principle of the doctrine of restitution is that on the reversal of a judgment the law raises an obligation on the party to the record who received the benefit of the erroneous judgment to make restitution to the other party for what he had lost and that it is the duty of the court to enforce that obligation unless it is shown that restitution would be clearly contrary to the real justice of the case. [*Lal Bhagwant Singh* v. *Sri Kishen Das*, AIR 1953 SC 136, Para 4, as cited in *State of Gujrat* v. *Essar Oil Limited*, (2012) 3 SCC 522, para 61].

Doctrine of separation of powers. The doctrine advocating the three compartments of government namely the executive, the legislature and the judiciary to be coordinate (equally important) and independent in their respective functions.

The Indian Constitution has not indeed recognised the doctrine of separation of powers in its absolute rigidity, but the functions of the different parts of branches of the Government (Legislature, Executive and Judiciary) have been sufficiently differentiated and consequently it can very well be said that Indian Constitution does not contemplate assumption, by one organ or part of the state of functions that essentially belong to another. The executive indeed can exercise the powers of departmental or subordinate legislation when such powers are delegated to it by the legislature. *Ram Jawaya Kapur* v. *State of Punjab,* AIR 1955 SC 549, 556.

Doctrine of severability. It means that, if a law is violative of fundamental rights of the Constitution, it will be inoperative only to the extent of inconsistency. The law minus the inoperative portion will stand. If the inoperative part is not severable, the whole law will be inoperative. It is the intention of the legislature which is decisive in determining whether the operative portion of the statute is severable from the inoperative portion or not.

The doctrine of severability is applicable only if it is possible to separate the legal from the unconstitutional portion of the provision. If it is not possible to do so, the entire provision has to be struck down as unconstitutional. *State of Madhya Pradesh* v. *Banajirao Shinde,* AIR 1968 SC 1053, 1056.

A rule of interpretation; it means that where some particular provision of statue offends against a constitutional limitation, but that provision is severable from the rest of the statue, only that offending provision will be declared void by the Court and not the entire statute. The main tests to determine severability are (i) whether the part pronounced valid can stand alone and be enforceable; (ii) whether the effect is to substitute for the law intended by the Legislature one they may never have been willing. (*Constitutional and Parliamentary Term*)

Doctrine of *stare decisis*. Under the '*stare decisis*' rule, a principle of law which has become settled by a series of decisions generally is binding on the

Courts and should be followed in similar cases. This rule is based on expediency and public policy, and although generally it should be strictly adhered to by the Courts, it is not universally applicable. [Corpus Juris Secundum, **as referred in** *Maktul* v. *Manbhari,* AIR 1958 SC 918. See also *Saurashtra Cement & Chemical Industries Ltd.* v. *Union of India,* (2001) 1 SCC 91, 116, para 32]

Doctrine of strict liability. There are seven exceptions formulated by case-laws to the doctrine of strict liability. One of such exceptions is 'act of stranger' *i.e.* if the escape was caused by the unforeseeable act of a stranger, the rule of strict liability does not apply. [WINFIELD on Tort, 15th Edn., page 535 **as referred in** *M.P.E.B* v. *Shail Kumari,* (2002) 2 SCC 162, 165, para 10]

Doctrine of subrogation. Doctrine of 'subrogation' confers upon the insurer the right to receive the benefit of such rights and remedies as the assured has against third parties in regard to the loss to the extent that the insurer has indemnified the loss and made it good. [*Oberai Forwarding Agency* v. *New India Assurance Co. Ltd.,* AIR 2000 SC 855 : (2000) 2 SCC 407, para 17]

Doctrine of suppression of mischief rule. 'Parliament intends that an enactment shall remedy a particular mischief and it is therefore presumed that Parliament intends that the Court, when considering, in relation to the facts of the instant case, which of the opposing constructions of the enactment corresponds to its legal meaning, should find a construction which applies the remedy provided by it in such a way as to suppress that mischief. The doctrine originates in Heydon's case. [(1584) 3 Co Rep 7a : 76 ER 637] where Barons of the Exchequer resolved that for the sure and true interpretation of all statutes in general four things are to be discerned and considered :

1. What was the common law before the making of the Act;
2. What was the mischief and defect for which the common law did not provide;
3. What remedy Parliament has resolved and appointed to cure the disease of the common wealth; and
4. the reason of the remedy,

and then the office of all the judges is always to make such construction as shall :

(a) suppress the mischief and advance the remedy; and

(b) suppress subtle inventions and evasions for the continuance of the mischief *pro privato commodo* (for private benefit); and

(c) add force and life to the cure and remedy according to the true intent of the makers of the Act *pro publico* (for the public good). [HALSBURY'S *Laws of England,* Vol. 44(1), 4th Edn. **as referred in** *National Insurance Co. Ltd.* v. *Baljit Kaur and ors.,* (2004) 2 SCC 1, 6, para 15 : AIR 2004 SC 1340]

Doctrine of *ultra vires*. The order may be a nullity or void but these terms have no absolute sense : their meaning is relative. If this principle of illegal relativity is borne in mind, the law can be made to operate justly and reasonably in cases where doctrine of *ultra vires*, rigidly applied, would produce unacceptable results. [*Rafique Bibi* v. *Sayed Waliuddin,* (2004) 1 SCC 287, 291, para 7]

Doctrine of unjust enrichment. The 'doctrine of unjust enrichment' is that no person can be allowed to enrich inequitably at the expense of another. A right of recovery under the 'doctrine of unjust enrichment' arises where a retention of benefit is considered contrary to justice or against equity. This doctrine is bases on equity and it can be invoked to deny the benefit to which a person is not otherwise entitled. Section 11-B of the Act merely gives a legislative recognition of this doctrine. [*Sahkari Khand Udyog Mandal Ltd.* v. *CCE,* (2005) 3 SCC 738, 748, paras 32 & 45] [Central Excise Act (1 of 1944), S. 11-B] [Now repealed by Act 12 of 2017]On the basis of the 'doctrine of unjust enrichment' it was held that when the very collection of a tax was held to be without authority of law, the claim of the such tax payers for refund could not be denied merely on the ground that the petitioners had passed on the money to the State Government and in turn the money was sent to the Central Government and latter the Central Government appropriated the same by passing it back to the various State Pollution Control Boards. [*U.P. Pollution Control Board* v. *Kanoria Industrial Ltd.,* (2001) 2 SCC 549, 561, para 26]

Doctrines. What is taught; the teachings of a person, sect or religion; dogma; tenet.

DOCTRINE, DOGMA, TENET. A *doctrine* rests on the authority of the individual by whom it is framed; the *dogma* on the authority of the body by whom it is maintained; a *tenet* rests on its own intrinsic merits.

Document. "DOCUMENTS" shall include any matter written, expressed or described upon any substance by means of letters, figures or marks, or by more than one of those means which is intended to be is used, or which may be used, for the purpose of recording that matter. [General Clauses Act (10 of 1897), S. 3(18)]

"DOCUMENT" includes summons, notice, requisition, order, other legal process, and registers, whether issued, sent or kept in pursuance of this or any other Act, other otherwise. [Companies Act (1 of 1956), S. 2(15)]

"Document" includes summons, notice, requisition, order, declaration, form and register, whether issued, sent or kept in pursuance of this Act or under any other law for the time being in force or otherwise, maintained on paper or in electronic form. [Companies Act, (18 of 2013), s. 2(36)].

"DOCUMENT" shall include any matter written, expressed or described upon any substance by means of letters, figures or marks, or by more than one of those means in printed or electronic version, which is intended to be used, or which may be used, by the Interim Pension Fund Regulatory and Development Authority, or Authority or an intermediary or any other entity connected with the National Pension System, for the purpose of recording that matter. [Pension Fund Regulatory and Development Authority Act (23 of 2013), s. 2(d)].

"DOCUMENT" means any record or information, preserved in any,—

(i) handmade form such as writing, drawing, painting, with any implement on any surface, directly or indirectly;

(ii) photographic form such as microfilm, microfiche, prints, slides, negatives, videotapes, motion pictures, photocopies or digital storage;

(iii) mechanical form such as writing, pressing, printing or typing;

(iv) computerized, electrical, electronic or magnetic form such as tape recordings, cassettes, compact discs or any information on an electronic or magnetic storage device, such as hand disks, portable memory cards, sticks or diskettes, or smart cards, backup tapes, personal digital devices, CD or DVD discs, optical discs, printer buffers, ZIP drives, pen drives, thump drives or electronic notebooks, as well as printouts or readouts from any magnetic storage device, including information preserved in files and have been "deleted" from electronic, magnetic, optical storage devices or facilities, and includes anything in which such information, is found or recoverable. [Securities and Exchange Board of India (Procedure for Search and Seizure Regulations, 2014, Regn. 2(1)(e)].

"DOCUMENT" includes an electronic record as defined in clause (t) of sub-section (l) of Section 2 of the Information Technology Act, 2000. [Income-tax Act (43 of 1961), S. 2(22AA)]

"DOCUMENT" includes any painting, drawing, photograph, or other visible representation. [Indian States [(Protection against Disaffection) Act, 1923, S. 2]

"DOCUMENT" includes part of a document. [Official Secrets Act (19 of 1923), S. 2(3)]

This word is also used in collection with other words (as) forged document; making a false document; private document; public document.

An instrument on which is recorded matter which may be used as evidence.

"The word "document" denotes any matter expressed or described upon any substance by means of letters, figures or marks, or by more than one of those means, intended to be used, or which may be used, as evidence of that matter." [IPC (45 of 1860), S. 29; Indian Evidence Act (1 of 1872), S. 3; General Clauses Act (10 of 1897), S. 3(18)]

Letters imprinted on the trees and intended to be evidence, that the trees had been passed by the Forest Ranger, and so could be removed from the place where they were lying in the forest are a 'document' within the meaning of S. 29, Indian Forest Act (16 of 1927).

The word 'document' in S. 50 of the Registration Act (16 of 1908) means a document which is legally enforceable.

The meaning of the "document" or of a particular part of it is to be sought for in the document itself That is, undoubtedly the primary rule of construction to which Section 90 to 94 of the Indian Evidence Act give statutory recognition and effect, with certain exceptions contained in Sections 95 to 98 of the Act. Of course, "the document" means "the document" read as a whole and not piecemeal. *Delhi Development Authority* v. *Durga Chand Kaushish,* AIR 1973 SC 2609.

"DOCUMENT" includes summons, notice, requisition, order, declaration, form and register, whether issued, sent or kept in pursuance of this Act or under any other law for the time being in force or otherwise, maintained on paper or in electronic form. [S. 2(36) of the Companies Act, 2013 (18 of 2013)]

"DOCUMENT" shall include any matter written, expressed or described upon any substance by means of letters, figures or marks, or by more than one of those means, in printed or in electronic version, which is intended to be used, or which may be used, by the Interim Pension Fund Regulatory and Development Authority, or Authority or an intermediary or any other entity connected with the National Pension System, for the purpose of recording that matter. [S. 2(1)(d) of the Pension Fund Regulatory & Development Authority Act, 2013 (23 of 2013)]

"Document" means any matter expressed or described or otherwise recorded upon any substance by means of letters, figures or marks or any other means or by more than one of those means, intended to be used, or which may be used, for the purpose of recording that matter and includes electronic and digital records. . [(w.e.f. 1-7-2024) Bharatiya Sakshya Adhiniyam, 2023 (47 of 2023), section 2(1)(d)]

"Document" includes any painting, drawing or photograph, or other visible representation. [(w.e.f. 1-7-2024) Bharatiya Nagarik Suraksha Sanhita, 2023 (46 of 2023), section 98(2)(b)]

Document of title. A document which confers a title.

Document of title to goods, includes "bill of lading, dock warrant, warehouse-keeper's certificate, and warrant or order for the delivery of goods, and any other document used in the ordinary course of business as proof of the possession or control of goods, or authorising or purporting to authorise, either by endorsement or by delivery, the possessor of the document to transfer or to receive goods thereby represented." [Sale of Goods Act (3 of 1930), S. 2]

Documentary. A dramatically structured film of an actual event or of a play giving the impression of an actual event.

Documentary evidence. Evidence found recorded in a document as opposed to oral evidence.

All documents which could, in law, be considered as evidence by the Court [Indian Evidence Act (1 of 1872), S. 3].

Does. The word "does" in S. 70 of the Indian Contract Act (9 of 1872) includes payment of money.

Does not appear and is absent. The words 'does not appear' govern cases where there is some sort of wilful act on the part of the complainant or at least a culpable negligence in keeping himself away from the Court on the date fixed for the hearing. *Ali Dar* v. *Mohd. Shariff,* AIR 1966 J&K 60, 62. [CrPC, 1973 (2 of 1974), S. 256]

Doli capax. Capable of crime. Having sufficient understanding to distinguish between right and wrong.

Doli incapax. Incapable of crime. (*Latin for Lawyers*)

This conclusive presumption has been adopted for children under seven years of age. [IPC (45 of 1860), S. 82].

Dolo facit qui petit quod redditurus est. (*Lat.*) It is fraudulent to claim what you must restore.

Dolo malo pactum se non servabit/servaturum. (*Lat.*) (D 2, 14, 7). A pact made with malicious intent will not be upheld.

Dolum ex indiciis perspicuis probari convenit. Fraud should be proved by clear proofs.

Dolus auctoris non nocet successori. The fraud of a predecessor does not prejudice the successor.

Dolus auctoris non nocet successori, nisi in causa lucrativa. (*Lat.*) The fraud of the author does not affect the successor (except) when he acquires by a lucrative title (gratuitously).

Dolus circuitu non purgatur. (*Lat.*) Fraud is not purged by circuity. [*Bax. Max. Reg. I*]

Dolus dans locum contractui. Fraud giving rise to the contract.

Dolus et fraus nemini patrocinentur (patrocinari debent). Deceit and fraud should excuse or benefit no one (they themselves require some excuse).

Dolus et fraus una in parte sanari debent. (Noy, Max 45) Deceit and fraud should always be remedied.

Dolus est machinatio, cum aliud dissimulat aliud agit. Deceit is a trickery for it pretends to one thing and does another.

Domain. Lands as held or ruled over; an estate; a realm.

A part of the Internet name that specifies certain details about the **host** such as its location and whether it is part of a commercial, governmental, or educational entity. The address is written as a series of names separated by full stops. (*Information Technology*)

Part of a web or e-mail address. Separated from the rest of the address by dots.

Domain name. Name for identifying an organisation or a person *etc.* in a series of characters which may include letters, numbers or marks as an address on the internet. (*Copyright*)

The unique name that identifies an Internet site. Domain Names always have 2 or more parts, separated by dots. The part on the left is the most specific, and the part on the right is the most general. A given machine may have more than one Domain Name but a given Domain Name points to only one machine. For example, the domain names :

matisse.net

mail.matisse.net

workshop.matisse.net

preconcept.org

preconcept.biz

can all refer to the same machine, but each domain name can refer to no more than one machine.

Usually, all of the machines on a given Network will have the same thing as the righthand portion of their Domain Names (matisse.net in the examples above). It is also possible for a Domain Name to exist but not be connected to an actual machine. This is often done so that a group or business can have an Internet e-mail address without having to establish a real Internet site. In these cases, some real Internet machine must handle the mail on behalf of the listed Domain Name. (*Matisse Enzer-Glossary of Internet Terms*)

Domain Name System (DNS). A text name matched to the Internet protocol that makes it easier for users to access sites. (*Cyber Law*)

Domestic. One who lives in the family of another as a hired household assistant; a house servant.

Domestic animals, includes any pet bird, and also birds kept in captivity and trained as decoy birds.

"DOMESTIC ANIMAL" means any animal which is tamed or which has been or is being sufficiently tamed to serve some purpose for the use of man or which, although it neither has been nor is being or is intended to be so tamed, is or has become in fact wholly or partly tamed. [Prevention of Cruelty to Animals Act (59 of 1960), S. 2(d)]

Domestic arbitration. An arbitration which usually takes place between the citizens or residents of the same State and the law applicable to determine the dispute between them is the law of the State. All arbitrations, which take place in India under Part I of the Indian Arbitration and Conciliation Act (26 of 1996) and which turn out domestic awards, are called domestic arbitrations. In a domestic arbitration, the arbitral tribunal shall decide the dispute submitted to arbitration in accordance with the substantive law for the time being in force in India. *(Arbitration)*

Domestic arbitration agreement. An arbitration agreement which does not provide, expressly or by implication, for arbitration in a State other than the United Kingdom and to which neither — (a) an individual who is a national of, or habitually resident in, any State other than the United Kingdom; nor (b) a body corporate which is incorporated in, or whose central management and control is exercised in, any State other than the United Kingdom. (*Arbitration*)

Domestic award. An arbitral award made under Part I of the Arbitration and Conciliation Act (26 of 1996) shall be considered as a domestic award. In other words, the award which would result from such arbitration taking place in India would be domestic award.

Domestic building. "DOMESTIC BUILDING" "includes a dwelling-house, and any other building not being a public building or of the Warehouse class." [Land Buildings Act, 1894, S. 5, cl. 26]

"DOMESTIC BUILDING" includes a dwelling-house and any other masonry building which is neither a building of the warehouse class nor a public building as defined in this section nor a place exclusively used for private worship. [Calcutta Municipal Corporation Act, 1980, S. 2(28)]

Domestic company. Means an Indian company, or any other company which, in respect of its income liable to tax under the Income-tax Act has made the prescribed arrangements for the declaration and payment within India of the dividends (including dividends on preference shares) payable out of such income. [Income-tax Act (43 of 1961), S. 2(22A)]

"DOMESTIC COMPANY" means an Indian company or any other company which in respect of its income liable to income-tax under the Income-tax Act for the assessment year commencing on the 1st day of April, 2005, has made the prescribed arrangements for the declaration and payment within India of the dividends (including dividends on preference shares) payable out of such income. [Finance Act (18 of 2005), S. 2(12)(a)]

Domestic Custodian Bank. In this scheme, unless the context otherwise requires :—

"DOMESTIC CUSTODIAN BANK" means a banking company which acts as a custodian for the ordinary shares or foreign currency convertible bonds of an Indian company which are issued by it against global depositary receipts or certificates; [Issue of Foreign Currency Convertible Bonds and Ordinary Shares (Through Depositary Receipt Mechanism) Scheme, 1993, S. 2(a)]

Domestic Depository. For the purposes of Rule 13 of the Companies (Registration of Foreign Companies) Rules, 2014, 'Domestic Depository' means custodian of securities registered with the Securities and Exchange Board of India and authorized by the issuing company to issue IDRs. [*Explanation* (*i*) to Rule 13(3) of the Companies (Registration of Foreign Companies) Rules, 2014]

Domestic incident report. Means a report made in the prescribed form on receipt of a complaint of domestic violence from an aggrieved person. [S. 2(e) of the Protection of Women from Domestic Violence Act, 2005 (43 of 2005)]

Domestic industry. "DOMESTIC INDUSTRY" means the producers—

(i) as a whole of the like article or a directly competitive article in India; or

(ii) whose collective output of the like article or a directly competitive article in India constitutes a major share of the total production of the said article in India. [Customs Tariff Act (51 of 1975), S. 8C(7)(a) *as inserted by Finance Act (20 of 2002), S. 129*]

"DOMESTIC INDUSTRY" means the domestic producers as a whole engaged in the manufacture of the like article and any activity connected therewith or those whose collective output of the said article constitutes a major proportion of the total domestic production of that article except when such producers are related to the exporters or importers of the alleged dumped article or are themselves importers thereof in which case (such producers may be deemed) not to form part of domestic industry :

Provided that in exceptional circumstances referred to in sub-rule (3) of Rule 11, the domestic industry in relation to the article in question shall be deemed to comprise two or more competitive markets and the producers within each of such market a separate industry, if—

(i) the producers within such a market sell all or almost all of their production of the article in question in that market, and

(ii) the demand in the market is not in any substantial degree supplied by producers of the said article located elsewhere in the territory;

Explanation—For the purposes of this clause,—

(i) producers shall be deemed to be related to exporters or importers only if,—

(a) one of them directly or indirectly controls the other; or

(b) both of them are directly or indirectly control a third person; or

(c) together they directly or indirectly controlled by a third person subject to the condition that are grounds for believing or suspecting that the effect of the relationship is such as to cause the producers to behave differently from non-related producers.

(ii) a producer shall be deemed to control another producer when the former is legally or operationally in a position to exercise restraint or direction over the latter. [Customs Tariff (Identification, Assessment And Collection of Anti-Dumping Duty on Dumped Articles And For Determination of Injury) Rules, 1995, R. 2(b)]

Domestic relationship. Means a relationship between two persons who live or have, at any point of time, lived together in a shared household, when they are related by consanguinity, marriage, or through a relationship in the nature of marriage, adoption or are family members living together as a joint family. [S. 2(f) of the Protection of Women from Domestic Violence Act, 2005 (43 of 2005)]

Domestic servant. Is a servant who sleeps in the dwelling-house of his master; in other words, an indoor servant. The expression "domestic servant" would not be confined to the servants who actually worked in the house, but would include other persons who ordinarily form part of an Indian establishment, such as coachmen, syces, *malis*, palkibearers, and gardeners.

Domestic servants are those employees who, forming part of the employer's residential establishment, are engaged upon work of such a character that it brings them into the close personal proximity of the employer and is mainly concerned with the household. HALSBURY, 4th Edn., Vol. 16, para 508, p. 318.

Domestic Tariff Area. Means area except special economic zone, export-oriented undertakings, Software Technology Park unit and Electronic Hardware Technology Park unit. [Customs Tariff Act (51 of 1975), Gen. Exemption No. 42, 13 (13) *Expln.* (ii)]

"DOMESTIC TARIFF AREA" means the whole of India (including the territorial waters and continental shelf) but does not include the areas of the Special Economic Zones. [Special Economic Zones Act (28 of 2005), S. 2(i)]

Domestic tribunal. "It refers to committees or associations like trade unions, social clubs, professional ladies who have a right to adjudicate upon the rights or disputes between their members". When created by statute they should be called "Statutory Tribunals" and not domestic tribunals.

Domestic violence. Violence committed by one family or household member against another.

"DOMESTIC VIOLENCE" for the purposes of Act 43 of 2005, the expression 'domestic violence' means any act, omission or commission or conduct of the respondent shall constitute domestic violence in case it—

(a) harms or injures or endangers the health, safety, life, limb or well-being, whether mental or physical, of the aggrieved person or tends to do so and includes causing physical abuse, sexual abuse, verbal and emotional abuse and economic abuse; or

(b) harasses, harms, injures or endangers the aggrieved person with a view to coerce her or any other person related to her to meet any unlawful demand for any dowry or other property or valuable security; or

(c) has the effect of threatening the aggrieved person or any person related to her by any conduct mentioned in clause (a) or clause (b); or

(d) otherwise injures or causes harm, whether physical or mental, to the aggrieved person.

Explanation I.—For the purposes of this section,—

(i) "physical abuse" means any act or conduct which is of such a nature as to cause bodily pain, harm, or danger to life, limb, or health or impair the health or development of the aggrieved person and includes assault, criminal intimidation and criminal force;

(ii) "sexual abuse" includes any conduct of a sexual nature that abuses, humiliates, degrades or otherwise violates the dignity of woman;

(iii) "verbal and emotional abuse" includes—

(a) insults, ridicule, humiliation, name calling and insults or ridicule specially with regard to not having a child or a male child; and

(b) repeated threats to cause physical pain to any person in whom the aggrieved person is interested;

(iv) "economic abuse" includes—

(a) deprivation of all or any economic or financial resources to which the aggrieved person is entitled under any law or custom whether payable under an order of a court or otherwise or which the aggrieved person requires out of necessity including, but not limited to, household necessities for the aggrieved person and her children, if any, stridhan, property, jointly or separately owned by the aggrieved person, payment of rental related to the shared household and maintenance;

(b) disposal of household effects, any alienation of assets whether movable or immovable, valuables, shares, securities, bonds and the like or other property in which the aggrieved person has an interest or is entitled to use by virtue of the domestic relationship or which may be reasonably required by the aggrieved person or her children or her stridhan or any other property jointly or separately held by the aggrieved person; and

(c) prohibition or restriction to continued access to resources or facilities which the aggrieved person is entitled to use or enjoy by virtue of the domestic relationship including access to the shared household.

Explanation II.—For the purpose of determining whether any act, omission, commission or conduct of the respondent constitutes "domestic violence" under this section, the overall facts and circumstances of the case shall be taken into consideration. [S. 3 of the Protection of Women from Domestic Violence Act, 2005 (43 of 2005). Also see S. 2(g) of the Protection of Women from Domestic Violence Act, 2005 (43 of 2005)]

Domestic worker. Means a woman who is employed to do the household work in any household for remuneration whether in cash or kind, either directly or through any agency on a temporary, permanent, part time or full time basis, but does not include any member of the family of the employer. [S. 2(e) of the Sexual Harassment of Women at Workplace (Prevention, Prohibition & Redressal) Act, 2013 (14 of 2013)]

Domesticated or cultivated species. Means species in which the evolutionary process has been influenced by humans to meet their needs. [United Nations Conference on Environment and Development : Convention on biological diversity, ILM (1992), Art. (2)]

Domicile. The place where one has permanent residence to which, if absent, he has the intention of returning. [Constitution of India, Art 5].

Domicile relates to the place where a person or his parents reside. [Constitution of India, Art. 15]

An intention to reside forever in a country where one has taken up his residence is an essential constituent element for existent of the domicile in country. *Louis De Raedt.* v. *Union of India,* AIR 1991 SC 1886.

By "domicile" is meant a permanent home. Domicile means the place which a person has fixed as a habitation of himself and his family not for a mere special and temporary purpose, but with a present intention of making it his permanent home. Domicile denotes connection with the territorial system of law. Mere residence is not domicile. *Abdus Samad* v. *State of West Bengal,* AIR 1973 SC 505.

The word 'domicile' used in the rules regulating admissions to medical colleges framed by some of the States may be interpreted in the loose sense of permanent residence in the State in which the medical college is situated and not in the technical sense in which it is used in private international law. *Pradeep Jain* v. *Union of India,* AIR 1984 SC 1420.

Domicile and nationality. Domicile is different from citizenship. A person may have one nationality or citizenship and a different domicile or he may have a domicile but no nationality. Ordinarily, domicile has not the effect of altering a previous nationality. In a State, a person may be a member of civil society alone as distinguished from political society. Membership of the political society determines his political status or nationality on which depends his permanent allegiance or personal association to his sovereign. This membership of civil society, that is his domicile, determines his civil status. Domicile implies connection with territory, not membership or community which is at the root of the notion of citizenship or nationality. A person with a domicile may be stateless, *i.e* without any nationality. *Abdur Rahman* v. *State,* MLJ : QD (1961-1965) Vol I C2278 : 1964 (2) CrLJ 327 : AIR 1964 Pat 384. [Constitution of India (1950), Art. 5]

Domicile of origin. The term 'domicile of origin' constitutes the domicile of an infant and continued until abandoned, or until the acquisition of a new domicile in a different place. *Laxami Narayan* v. *State of Jharkhand*, AIR 2002 Jhar 104, para, 10.

Domiciled. As applied to a bill of exchange means that it is payable at a particular place.

Having domicile.

Domiciliary. "Domiciliary" means of a dwelling place. A domiciliary visit is a visit of officials to search or inspect a private house. *Kharak Singh* v. *State of U.P.,* AIR 1963 SC 1295.

Domiciliary Hospitalisation Benefit. Means Medical treatment for a period exceeding three days for such illness/disease/injury which in the normal course would require care and treatment at a hospital/nursing home/clinic but actually taken whilst confined at home in India under any of the following circumstances, namely :—

(i) The condition of the patient is such that he/she cannot be removed to the hospital/nursing home/clinic; or

(ii) The patient cannot be removed to hospital/ nursing home/clinic for lack of accommodation therein; or

(iii) The patient prefers to be confined at home for treatment with the approval of the attending medical practitioner subject however that domicialiary hospitalisation benefits shall not cover :

i. expenses incurred for pre and post-hospital treatment, and

ii. expenses incurred for treatment for any of the following diseases :

1. Asthma
2. Bronchitis
3. Chronic Nephritis and Nephritic Syndrome
4. Diarrhoea and all types of Dysenteries including Gas-troenteritis
5. Diabetes Mellitus and Insi-pids
6. Epilepsy
7. Hypertension

8. Influenza, Cough and Cold
9. All Psychiatric or Psychosomatic Disorders
10. Viral Fever of duration for less than 10 days
11. Tonsilitis and Upper Respiratory Tract Infection including Laryngitis and Phyringitis
12. Pyrexia of Unknown Origin. [Scheme of Hospitalisation and Domiciliary Hospitalisation Benefit Policy, specified for the purpose of section 80D of the Income-tax Act (43 of 1961)]

Domiciliary visit. The expression 'domiciliary visit' means that the police authorities are authorised to enter the premises of the suspect, knock at the door and have it opened and search it for the purpose of ascertaining his presence in the house. *Kharak Singh* v. *State of U.P.*, AIR 1963 SC 1295, 1300. [V.P. Police Regulations, Reg. 236(*b*)]

Dominant heritage. "The land for the beneficial enjoyment of which the right exists is called the dominant heritage." [Indian Easements Act (5 of 1882), S. 4]

Dominant owner. 'The owner and the occupier of (dominant heritage) is called the dominant owner." [Indian Easement Act (5 of 1882), S. 4]

Dominant tenant. The person who holds a dominant estate and hence benefits from an easement.

Dominant tenement. A term used in the constitution of servitudes, and means the tenement or subject in favour of which the service is constituted.

Dominion. A self-governing autonomous State within the British Commonwealth; the power or right of governing and controlling; lands or domain subject to sovereignty or control.

Dominium a possessione cepisse dicitur. (*Lat.*) Right is said to have its beginning from possession.

Domus sua cuique est tutissimum refugium. A maxim meaning "Every man's house is his refuge."

To every one his house in his surest refuge.

Domus tutissimum cuique refugium atque receptaculum sit. A man's house should be his safest refuge and shelter. (*Black*)

Dona clandestina sunt semper suspiciosa. (*Lat.*) (3 Rep. 81) Clandestine gifts are always open to suspicion.

Donate. To give generally for a specific object; to bestow freely; to grant; to give gratuitously, or without any consideration—especially for a fund or institution.

Donatio mortis causa. (*Lat.*) A gift of personal property in anticipation of death.

Donatio non praesumitur. (*Maxim*) A gift is not presumed, *i.e.* the general presumption is against a gift.

Donationum alia perfecta alia incepta, et non perfecta; ut si donatio lecta fuit et concessa ac traditio mondum fuerit subsecuta. Some gifts are perfect, others incipient and not perfect; as if a gift were ready and agreed to but delivery had not been followed.

Donatio perficitur possessione accipientis. (*Lat.*) (*Jenk. Cent.* 109). A gift is perfected by the possession of the receiver. (*Broom. Leg. Max.*)

Donatio propter nuptias. (*Lat.*) A gift in consideration of marriage.

Donation. The action of donating or giving, presentation; gratuitous transfer of property from one to another; that which is presented; a gift.

When a person who is the owner of a thing, voluntarily transfers the title and possession of the same from himself to another, without any consideration, it is donation. *E.T. Commissioner* v. *P.V.G. Raju*, AIR 1976 SC 140, 142.

Donator nunquam desinit possidere antequam donatarius incipiat possidere. (*Lat.*) (Dyer, 281) He that gives never ceases to possess until he that receives begins to possess.

Done or intended to be done. The words "done or intended to be done" in S. 4 of the Epidemic Diseases Act (3 of 1897), do not include omissions.

Donee. "DONEE" means any person who acquires any property under a gift, and where a gift is made to a trustee for the benefit of another person, includes both the trustee and the beneficiary. [Gift-tax Act (18 of 1958), S. 2(viii)]

DONEE is the person whom a certain existing movable or immovable property is, voluntarily and without consideration, gifted. [Transfer of Property Act (4 of 1882), S. 122]

One to whom a gift is made; one who takes without valuable consideration. *Donee* is a person to whom property is given.

Donor. "DONOR" means any person, not less than eighteen years of age, who voluntarily authorises the removal of any of his human organs for therapeutic purposes under sub-section (1) or sub-section (2) of Section 3. [Transplantation of Human Organs Act (42 of 1994), S. 2(f)]

"DONOR" means the donor of semen, in the case of a male and of ovum, in the case of a female. [Delhi Artificial Insemination (Human) Act, 1995 (12 of 1996), S. 2(b)]

"DONOR" means any person who makes a gift. [Gift-tax Act (18 of 1958), S. 2(ix)]

Transferor of certain existing movable or immovable property voluntarily and without consideration is called the donor. [Transfer of Property Act (4 of 1882), S. 122]

A giver; a grantor; one who makes a gift. (*Tomlin*)

Donor is he who gives lands or tenements to another. It also means a party conferring a power.

Donum. In the civil law, a gift; a free gift.

Doordarshan. Means the offices, *kendras* and other establishments, by whatever name called, which immediately before the appointed day, formed part of or were under the Directorate-General. Doordarshan of the Union Ministry of Information and Broadcasting. [Prasar Bharti (Broadcasting Corporation of India) Act (25 of 1990), S. 2(h)]

Dope testing laboratory. Means a laboratory established or recognised under section 26. [National Anti-Doping Act, 2022 (15 of 2022), section 2(m)]

Doping. An international term in sport for improvement of competitor's dexterity by psychological stimuli (encouragement) or chemical (narcotics); the latter fought by the International Olympic Committee and other international sports institutions.

Doping Control. Includes all steps and processes from test distribution planning up to the disposal of any appeal and enforcement of consequences, including all steps and processes in between, including but not limited to, testing, investigation, whereabouts, Therapeutic Use Exemptions, sample collection and handling, laboratory analysis, Results Management, hearings and appeals, and investigations or proceedings relating to an Anti-Doping Rule Violation. [National Anti-Doping Act, 2022 (15 of 2022), section 2(n)]

Doping in sport. Means the occurrence of any Anti-Doping Rule Violations specified in section 4. [National Anti-Doping Act, 2022 (15 of 2022), section 2(o)]

Dormant. Silent.

Dormant claim. A claim in abeyance.

Dormant company. A company which does not enter into any significant accounting transaction.

Dormant partner. A partner unknown as such to those doing business with the firm.

Dormitory. A room, suite of rooms, or building used to sleep in; a bed-room with a number of beds; sleeping quarters or sleeping house; a lodging house.

Dormiunt aliquando leges, nunquam moriuntur. (*Maxim*) The laws sometimes sleep, they never die.

DOS. (*abbr.*) Disk Operating System. Usually used as an abbreviation for MS-DOS, a microcomputer operating system developed by Microsoft.

Dos dower. (*Roman Law*). The property which is contributed by a wife, or anyone else on her behalf to her husband, to enable him to support the expenses of the marriage.

Doti lex favet; praemium pudoris est' ideo parcatur. (*Maxim*) The law favours dower; it is the reward of chastity, therefore let it be preserved. (*Latin for Lawyers*)

Double (Dual) citizenship. Citizenship of two countries such as the people of the U.S.A. are the citizens of the U.S.A. (the federation) as well as that of the State, they belong.

Double-density disk. A disk that is initialized in such a way as to take considerably more data than a single-density disk. The amount varies from nearly double to over three times as much, depending on your system. (*Computer*)

Double entry. (*In the law of accounts*) A term among merchants to signify that books of account are kept in such a manner that they present the debit and credit of every transaction. It is used in contradistinction to single entry.

Double insurance. Where a person, being insured by one policy, effects another on the same subject with other insurers, he may recover the amount of his actual loss against either set of insurers.

Double insurance is over insurance of an interest by two or more policies. As marine insurance is a contract of indemnity, there is no need to or advantage in insuring for an amount in excess of the value of the subject matter of insurance in one or more policies. For, in any event, the assured cannot recover more than an indemnity provided by the Act. [Marine Insurance Act (11 of 1963), S. 34(1)]

If the insurance policy is taken from more than one underwriter where period of insurance, subject matter of insurance and sum insured are same, then this is called double insurance.

Double jeopardy. A second prosecution after a first trial for the same offence.

The fifth amendment of the American Constitution provides *inter alia* "Nor shall any person be subjected for the same offence to be put twice in jeopardy of life and limb".

No person shall be prosecuted or punished for the same offence more than once. *Mohinder Pratap Singh* v. *Director Health Services,* AIR 1956 Punj 81, 82. [Constitution of India, Art. 20(2)]

Double patenting. The rule that an invention cannot receive both a utility patent and a design patent. (*Cyber Law*)

Double plea. A pleading is double, when it contains more claims, charges or defences than one.

Double taxation. Courts always look with disfavour upon double taxation, and statutes will be construed, if possible, so as to avoid double taxes.

Double taxation in the strict legal sense means taxing the same property or subject-matter twice, for the same purpose, for the same period and in the same territory. *Sri Krishna Das* v. *Twon Area Committee*, (1990) 183 ITR 401, 410 (SC). [Income-tax Act (43 of 1961), S. 4]

Double-taxation agreement. Agreement between two countries that the income of non-residents should not be taxed both in their country of origin and in the country in which they live. (*Business Term*)

Doubt. The (subjective) state of uncertainty as to the truth or reality of anything; a feeling of uncertainty as to something; apprehension.

DOUBT (benefit of). To give one the benefit of doubt is to suppose him innocent rather than guilty.

"Doubt" means 'uncertainty of mind; the absence of a settled opinion or conviction; the attitude of mind towards the acceptance of or belief in a proposition, theory, or statement, in which the judgment is not at rest but inclines alternately to either side'. [Black's Law Dictionary as cited in *Natural Resources Allocation, In Re*, Special Reference No. 1 of 2012, (2012) 10 SCC 1, para 27].

Doubtful asset. "DOUBTFUL ASSET" means (*a*) a term loan, or (*b*) a lease assets, or (*c*) a hire purchase asset, or (*d*) any other asset which remains a sub-standard asset for a period exceeding two years. [Non-Banking Financial Companies Prudential Norms (Reserve Bank) Directions, 1998, Para 2(1)(iv)]

"DOUBTFUL ASSET" means a term loan, or a leased asset, or a hire purchase asset, or any other asset, which remains a sub-standard asset for a period exceeding two years; [Housing Finance Companies (NHB) Directions, 2001, Direction. 2(h)]

"DOUBTFUL ASSET" means a borrowal account which has remained a non-performing asset for more than two years but less than three years. [R. 3(1)(b) of the Nidhi Rules, 2014]

Doubtful integrity. There must be preponderance of probability for the reasonable man to entertain doubt regarding possibility to justify to ram an officer with the label 'doubtful integrity'. *M.S. Bindra* v. *Union of India*, (1998) 7 SCC 310, para 13 : AIR 1998 SC 3058.

Dower. (*in English law*) The portion which a widow hath of the lands of her husband at his decease, for the sustenance of herself, and education of her children. (*Tomlin*)

(*in Mahomedan Law*) Money paid or agreed to be paid by intended husband to wife at the time of marriage and in consideration of marriage. It is either *prompt* dower or *deferred* dower.

Down. Not operating. Used to describe a computer that has been shut down for maintenance or is not running because of a failure in its hardware or software. (*Computer*)

Download. The transfer of a file from one computer to another.

Transferring data (usually a file) from a another computer to the computer you are using. The opposite of *upload.* (*Matisse Enzer-Glossary of Internet Terms*)

To transfer the data whether in graphics or text form, from the Internet to the permanent storage area *i.e.* the hard disk on computer. (*Internet*)

Dowry. "In this Act, 'DOWRY' means any property or valuable security given or agreed to be given either directly or indirectly :

(a) by one party to a marriage to the other party to the marriage; or

(b) by the parents of either party to a marriage or by any other person, to either party to the marriage or to any other person;

at or before or any time after the marriage in connection with the marriage of the said parties, but does not include dower or *mahr* in the case of persons to whom the Muslim Personal Law (Shariat) applies."

Explanation.—The expression "valuable security" has the same meaning as in Section 30 of the Indian Penal Code. [Dowry Prohibition Act (28 of 1961), S. 2] [Also see S. 2(h) of the Protection of Women from Domestic Violence Act, 2005 (43 of 2005)]

For the purposes of this sub-section, "dowry" shall have the same meaning as in section 2 of the Dowry Prohibition Act, 1961 (28 of 1961). [(w.e.f. 1-7-2024) Bharatiya Nayaya Sanhita, 2023 (45 of 2023), section 80(1), Explanation]

There are three occasions related to dowry. One is before the marriage, second is at the time of marriage and the third is "at any time" after the marriage. The third occasion may appear to be an unending period. But the crucial words are "in connection with the marriage of the said parties." This means that giving or agreeing to give any property or valuable security on any of the above three stages should have been in connection with the marriage of the parties. There can be many other instances for payment of money or giving property as between the spouses. For example, some customary payments in connection with birth of a child or other ceremonies are prevalent in different societies. Such payments are not enveloped within the ambit of "dowry". *Satvir Singh* v. *State of Punjab,* AIR 2001 SC 2828.

The word 'dowry' includes the demands made subsequent to the marriage. *State of A.P.* v. *Raj Gopal Asama*, (2004) 4 SCC 470, 476, para 8. [Dowry Prohibition Act (28 of 1961), S. 2]

The word 'dowry' under Section 2 of the Act would include any demand of money, property or valuable security made from the bride or her parents or other relatives by the bridegroom or his parents or other relatives or *vice versa* where such demand is not properly referable to any legally recognized claim and is relatable only to the consideration of marriage. *Reema Aggarwal* v. *Anupam*, (2004) 3 SCC 199, 209, para 16. [Dowry Prohibition Act (28 of 1961), S. 2]

The meaning of 'dowry' confining and limiting the same to the time at or before marriage got enlarged, under Dowry Prohibition Act (43 of 1986) and extended even to the period after the marriage and that there be no need to also show any agreement for the payment of such dowry to make it punishable as an offence. *Vidha Devi* v. *State of Haryana*, (2004) 9 SCC 476, 480, para 7.

"DOWRY". 'Dowry' is a fairly well known social custom or practice in India. Any property or valuable security should be given or agreed to be given either directly or indirectly at or before or any time after the marriage and in connection with the marriage of the parties. Therefore, the giving or taking of property or valuable security must have some connection with the marriage of the parties and a correlation between the giving or taking of property or valuable security with the marriage of the parties is essential. *Appasaheb* v. *State of Maharashtra*, AIR 2007 SC 763 : 2007 AIR SCW 456.

"DOWRY". A demand for money on account of some financial stringency or for meeting some urgent domestic expenses or for purchasing manure cannot be termed as a demand for 'dowry' as the said word is normally understood.[*Appasaheb* v. *State of Maharashtra*, (2007) 9 SCC 721 : (2007) 3 SCC (Cri) 468, para 9 as cited in *Rohtash* v. *State of Haryana*, (2012) 6 SCC 589, para 12].

Dowry death. Where the death of a woman is caused by any burns or bodily injury or occurs otherwise than under normal circumstances within seven years of her marriage and it is shown that soon before her death she was subjected to cruelty or harassment by her husband or any relative of her husband for, or in connection with, any demand for dowry, such death shall be called "dowry death", and such husband or relative shall be deemed to have caused her death. [Indian Penal Code 1860, S. 304B(1)] [(w.e.f. 1-7-2024) repealed and replaced by Bharatiya Nyaya Sanhita, 2023 (45 of 2023), section 80(1)]

For the purposes of this section, "dowry death" shall have the same meaning as in section 80 of the Bharatiya Nyaya Sanhita, 2023. [(w.e.f. 1-7-2024) Bharatiya Sakshya Adhiniyam, 2023 (47 of 2023), section 118, *Explanation*]

Dowry demand. Demanding of share of wife in the ancestral property would not amount to a 'dowry demand'. [*Baldev Singh* v. *State of Punjab*, (2008) 13 SCC 233, 241, para 19] [IPC (45 of 1860), S. 304-B, Evidence Act (1 of 1872), S. 113-B; Dowry Prohibition Act (28 of 1961), S. 2]

Dowry or Dote. (*Dos Mulieries*) Was in ancient times applied to that which the wife brings her husband in marriage; otherwise called, *maritagium* or marriage goods; but these are termed more properly, goods given in marriage, and the marriage portion. (*Tomlin*)

An amount paid by a Mohammadan in connection with the marriage of his daughter to the prospective bridegroom for the purchase of property in the joint names of his daughter and the would be son-in-law, the marriage not having taken place, cannot be construed as the amount paid or agreed to be paid at or before or after the marriage as consideration for the marriage of the parties, and the amount paid is not dowry. *V.N. Sreedharan* v. *Bhaskaran,* AIR 1986 Ker 48, 49. [Dowry Prohibition Act (28 of 1961), Ss. 2 and 3]

Draconian. Harsh; severe; derived from Draco, the ancient Athenian law giver.

Draft. A rought sketch of a writing or document, from which the final or fair copy is made; the depth to which a ship sinks in waters; an order for payment of money.

Draftsman. One who draws or frames a document (as) a will, conveyance, *etc.*

Dragoman. An interpreter.

One who draws pleadings or other writings; one who draws plans and sketches.

Drain. "DRAIN" includes a sewer, a house-drain, a drain of any other description, a tunnel, a culvert, a ditch, a channel and any other device for carrying off sullage, sewage, offensive matter, polluted water, waste water, rain water or subsoil water. [Manipur Municipalities Act (43 of 1994), S. 2(14) and New Delhi Municipal Council Act (44 of 1994), S. 2(12)]

"DRAIN" includes a sewer, pipe, ditch, channel and any other device for carrying off sewage, offensive matter, polluted water, sullage, waste water, rain water or subsoil water, and any ejectors, compressed air mains, sealed sewage mains and special machinery or apparatus for raising, collecting, expelling or removing sewage or offensive matter to the sewage outfall. [Bom Act III of 1888 (City Bom Municipal), S. 3(*u*)]

Drainage-work. "DRAINAGE-WORK" includes escape-channels from a canal, dams, weirs, embankments, sluices, groins and other works for the protection of lands from flood or from erosion, formed or maintained by the State Government under the provisions of Part VII of this Act, but does not include works for the removal of sewage from towns. [Northern India Canal Drainage Act (8 of 1873), S. 3(3)]

"DRAINAGE-WORK" means any work in connection with a system of irrigation which has been or may hereafter be made or improved by the Government for the purposes of the drainage of the country, and includes escape-channels from a canal, dams, weirs, embankments, sluices, groins and other works connected therewith, but does not include works for the removal of sewage form towns. [Ben Act III of 1876 (*Irrigation*), S. 3]

A "*drainage-work*", as defined in S. 3(4) of the Irrigation Regulation includes a natural or artificial channel for the discharge of waste or surplus water; a *trench* or drain carrying surplus water from a place higher up and conveying it to a place lower down is a drainage work and therefore an irrigation work within the meaning of Ss. 3 and 46(*ii*) of the Regulation. (15 Mys LJ 51)

Drained weight. In relation to a solid commodity contained in a free flowing liquid, means the weight of such solid commodity after the liquid has been drained for a period of two minutes. [Standards of Weights and measures (Pack Comm.) R. 1977), R. 2(e)]

Dramatic work. Includes any piece for recitation, choreographic work or entertainment in dumb show, the scenic arrangement or acting, form of which is fixed in writing or otherwise but does not include a cinematography film. [Copyright Act (14 of 1957), S. 2(h)]

Draught. The depth to which a ship sinks in water; drawing or pulling.

Draught cattle. 'Draught cattle' means the cattle which have an inherent potential for draught purpose like pulling, traction of loads *etc.* [*State of Gujarat* v. *Mirzapur Moti Kureshi Kassab Jamat,* (2005) 8 SCC 534]

"DRAUGHT CATTLE" A 'draught cattle' may lose its utility on account of injury or sickness and may be rendered useless as a draught cattle during that period. This would not mean that if a draught cattle ceases to be of utility for a short period on account of sickness or injury, it is excluded from the definition of the expression 'draught cattle' and deprived of the benefit of Article 48 of the Constitution of India. *State of Gujarat* v. *Mirzapur Moti Kureshi Kassab Jamat*, AIR 2006 SC 212 : 2005 AIR SCW 5723.

Draw. "DRAW" means the manner specified in the chit agreement for the purpose of ascertaining the prized subscriber at any instalment of the chit. [Chit Funds Act (40 of 1982), S. 2(i)]

To write in due form; to prepare a draft of, (as) to draw a deed of sale; to draw a plaint or petition; act of drawing (as), drawing of lots; drawn game.

Draw inference. To infer.

Drawal. "DRAWAL" mean drawal of foreign exchange from an authorised person and includes opening of Letter of Credit or use of International Credit Card or International Debit Card or ATM Card or any other thing by whatever name called which has the effect of creating foreign exchange liability. [Foreign Exchange Management (Current Account Transactions) R., 2000, Rule. 2(b) and Foreign Exchange Management (Permissible Capital Account Transactions) Reg, 2000, Reg. 2(b)]

Drawback. An allowance upon the duties due on imported merchandise when the importer, instead of selling it, re-exports it; or the refund of such duties if already paid [Customs Act (52 of 1962), S. 74(1)]; a defect.

"Drawback" in relation to any goods manufactured in India and exported, means the rebate of duty, tax or cess chargeable on any imported inputs or on any domestic inputs or input services used in the manufacture of such goods [The Central Goods and Services Tax Act, 2017 (12 of 2017), S. 2(42)]

"DRAWBACK" means the repayment of duties or taxes previously charged on commodities, from which they are relieved on exportation. *State of U. P.* v. *Delhi Cloth Mills*, AIR 1991 SC 735.

Drawee. The person on whom an order or bill of exchange is drawn. [Negotiable Instruments Act (26 of 1881), S. 7].

Drawee in case of need. When in the bill or in any indorsement thereon the name of any person is given in addition to drawee to be resorted to in any case of need, such person is called a "drawee in case of need." [Negotiable Instruments Act (26 of 1881), S. 7].

Drawer. The maker of a bill of exchange or cheque is called the "*drawer*"; the person thereby directed to pay is called the "*drawee.*" [Negotiable Instruments Act (26 of 1881), S. 7].

An authorised signatory of a company becomes a drawer as he has been authorised to do so in respect of the account maintained by the company. [*Aneeta Hada* v. *Godfather Travels and Tours Private Limited*, (2012) 5 SCC 661, para 14] [Negotiable Instruments Act, 1881, s. 7]

The word 'drawer' as used in cl. (d) of S. 76 of the Negotiable Instrument Act (26 of 1881) does not include the 'maker' of a pronote.

Drawing. A representation on a plane surface, by means of lines and shades; act or fact of drawing; the drawing of lots in a lottery.

A representation by lines; writing out.

Dredge. *As a noun*, in its original meaning, a net or drag for taking oysters; it is now called a machine for cleansing canals and rivers; but sometimes applied to a dredger. *As a verb*, to gather or take with a dredge; to remove sand, mud and filth from the beds of rivers, harbours and canals with a dredging machine.

Dredger. For the purpose of Notification No. 262/58-customs, dredger is a ocean-going vessel. *Collector* v. *Dredging Corpn. of India,* 1991 (55) ELT A33 (SC).

Dredging. "DREDGING" includes removal of material including, silt, sediments, rocks, sand, refuse, debris, plant or animal matter in any excavating, cleaning, deepening, widening or lengthening, either permanently or temporarily, of any river, port, harbour back-water or estuary. [Finance Act (32 of 1994), S. 65(36a) *as inserted by Finance Act (18 of 2005), S. 88(a)(ix)* (now repealed by Goods and Services Tax Act, 2017)]

Scooping up or removing earth from the bottom of a river, bay *etc.* [Mines Act (35 of 1952), S. 2(1)(ii)]

Driftway. A common way for driving cattle.

Drink and driving. Is an offence to be in charge of a motor vehicle when under the influence of drink or drugs to such an extent as to be incapable of having proper control of the vehicle.

Drive-in-cinema. Means a Cinema with an open air theatre premises into which admission may be given to persons desiring to view the Cinema while sitting in motor cars only. Admission of persons other than those desiring to view the Cinema while sitting in motor cars shall not be allowed in a 'drive-in-

Cinema' premises. [Andhra Pradesh Cinemas (Regulation) 1970, Reg. 2(dd)]

'DRIVE-IN-CINEMA' means a cinema with an open-air-theatre premises into which admission may be given normally to persons desiring to view the cinema while sitting in motor cars. However, where an auditorium is also provided in a 'drive-in-cinema' premises, persons other than those desiring to view the cinema while sitting in motor cars can also be admitted. Such drive-in-cinemas may have a capacity to accommodate not more than one thousand cars. [Karnatka Cinema (Regulations) Rules, 1971, R. 111-A]

Driver. "DRIVER", includes, in relation to a motor vehicle which is drawn by another motor vehicle, the person who acts as a steersman of drawing vehicle. [Motor Vehicle Act (59 of 1988), S. 2(9)]

Driving licence. Means the licence issued by a competent authority under chapter II authorising the person specified therein to drive, otherwise than a learner, a motor vehicle or a motor vehicle of any specified class or description. [Motor Vehicle Act (59 of 1988), S. 2(10)]

Driving under the influence. The offence in which one operates a motor vehicle in a physically or mentally impaired condition, specially after consuming alcohol or drugs.

Driving without insurance. An offence which is committed by a driver of a motor vehicle who uses or allows someone else to use a motor vehicle on a road without valid third-party insurance.

Driving without a licence. An offence which is committed by the driver of motor vehicle on a public road without a driving licence or provisional driving licence valid for the vehicle he is driving.

Droit Administratif. "*Droit administratif* or 'administrative law' has been defined by French authorities in general terms as 'the body of rules which regulate the relations of the administration or of the administrative authority towards private citizens". A.V. DICCY'S *Introduction to the Study of the Law of the Constitution,* 10th ed. p. 332.

Droit ne done pluis que soit demaunde. Justice gives no more than is demanded.

Drought. Means the naturally occurring phenomenon that exists when precipitation has been significantly below normal recorded levels, causing serious hydrological imbalances that adversely affect land resource production systems; [United Nations Convention to Combat Desertification in Those Countries Experiencing Serious Drought and/or Desertification, particularly in Africa, June (17, 1994), Art. 1(c)] ILM (1994)

Drug. A simple substance used alone or as an ingredient in medicine; a substance used in the composition of medicines; a substance or commodity used as a remedy for decease; any mineral substance used in chemical operations.

"DRUGS" includes—

(i) all medicines for internal or external use of human beings or animals and all substances intended to be used for or in the diagnosis, treatment, mitigation or prevention of any disease or disorder in human beings or animals, including preparations applied on human body for the purpose of repelling insects (like mosquitoes);

(ii) such substances (other than food) intended to affect the structure or any function of the human body or intended to be used for the destruction of vermin or insects which cause disease in human beings or animals, as may be specified from time to time by the Central Government by notification in the Official Gazette;

(iii) all substances intended for use as components of a drug including empty gelatin capsules; and

(iv) such devices intended for internal or external use in the diagnosis, treatment, mitigation or prevention of diseases or disorder in human beings or animals, as may be specified from time to time by the Central Government by notification in the Official Gazette, after consultation with the Board. [Drugs and Cosmetics Act (23 of 1940), S. 3(b)]

"DRUG" includes—

(i) a medicine for the internal or external use of human beings or animals;

(ii) any substance intended to be used for or in the diagnosis, cure, mitigation, treatment or prevention of disease in human beings or animals;

(iii) any article, other than food, intended to affect or influence in any way the structure or any organic function of the body of human beings or animals;

(iv) any article intended for use as a component of any medicine, substance or article, referred to in sub-clauses (i), (ii) and (iii). [Drugs and Magic Remedies (Objectionable Advertisements) Act (21 of 1954), S. 2(b)]

The definition of "drugs", is comprehensive enough in taking in not only medicines but also substances intended to be used for or in the treatment of diseases of human beings or animals. *Tulsi Ram* v. *State of U.P.*, AIR 1963 SC 665, 666.

'DRUG' includes "all medicines for internal or external use of human beings or animals and all substances intended to be used for or in the diagnosis, treatment, mitigation or prevention of disease in human beings or animals." *S.K. Amir* v. *State of Maharashtra,* AIR 1974 SC 469.

Any article, other than food, which is intended to affect or influence in any way any organic function of the body of a human being is a drug. *Zaffar Mohammad* v. *State of W.B.*, AIR 1976 SC 171,

172. [Drugs and Magic Remedies (Objectionable Advertisements) Act (21 of 1954), S. 2(*b*)(*iii*)]

The term 'drug' includes medicinal or other preparations for internal or external use of human beings or animals *etc. Bhagwan Singh* v. *State of Punjab*, (1999) 9 SCC 573 para 8. [Drugs and Cosmetics Act (23 of 1940), S. 3(b) and Drugs and Cosmetic Rules, 1945, R. 50 A(1)(ii)]

Drug trafficking. Doing or being concerned in producing or supplying a controlled drug.

Druggist. Is one who deals in drugs and medicines; dealer in drugs. The term is synonymous with "pharmacist" or "chemist." It is not essential that a druggist should compound or manufacture medicines in order to constitute him as such. It is said that the term druggist properly means one whose occupation is to buy and sell drugs without compounding or preparation; but in its usual acceptation it means one who deals either in medicines or in materials that are used in compounding medicines.

Drums and containers. An electric torch case is a receptacle in which the torch batteries are kept and it is therefore a container— within the meaning of item 24. *Regional Provident Fund Commission U.P.* v. *Great Eastern Electroplates Ltd.,* AIR 1959 All 133, 134. [Employees' Provident Funds Act (19 of 1952), Sch. I., Expl., Item (24)]

Drunk. Overcome by alcoholic liquor.

Drunkard. A drunken person; a person under intoxication; person who is often found in a drunken state or condition.

Drunken person. An intoxicated person.

Drunkenness. The state of being drunk; intoxication.

Dry cleaner. "Dry cleaner" means any commercial concern providing service in relation to dry cleaning. [Finance Act (32 of 1994), S. 65(38) (now repealed by Goods and Services Tax Act, 2017)]

Dry cleaning. Includes dry cleaning of apparels, garments or other textile, fur or leather articles. [Finance Act (32 of 1994), S. 65(37) (now repealed by Goods and Services Tax Act, 2017)]

Dry latrine. Means a latrine other than a water-seal latrine. [Employment of Manual Scavengers and Constructions of Dry Latrines (Prohibition) Act (46 of 1993), S. 2(c)]

DSL (Digital Subscriber Line). A technical standard for high-speed communications over the same twisted-pair wires used for common telephone connections. There are several forms, including SDSL (symmetric digital subscriber line) and ADSL (asymmetric digital subscriber line).

DSL. (*Abbr.*) Digital Subscriber Line. A method for moving data over regular phone lines. A DSL circuit is much faster than a regular phone connection, and the wires coming into the subscriber's premises are the same (copper) wires used for regular phone service. A DSL circuit must be configured to connect two specific locations, similar to a leased line (however a DSL circuit is not a *leased line.*

A common configuration of DSL allows downloads at speeds of up to 1.544 megabits (not megabytes) per second, and uploads at speeds of 128 kilobits per second. This arrangement is called *ADSL* : Asymmetric Digital Subscriber Line.

In theory ADSL allows download speeds of up to 9 megabits per second and upload speeds of up to 640 kilobits per second.

DSL is now a popular alternative to Leased Lines and ISDN, being faster than ISDN and less costly than traditional Leased Lines. (*Matisse Enzer-Glossary of Internet Terms*)

Due. *As a noun*, an existing obligation; an indebtedness; a simple indebtedness without reference to the time of payment : a debt ascertained and fixed though payable in future; *As an adjective*, capable of being justly demanded; claimed as of right; owing and unpaid; remaining unpaid; payable; regular; formal; according to rule or form.

so covered by the expression 'due'. [*Modern Industries* v. *SAIL*, (2010) 5 SCC 44 : (2010) 2 SCC (Civ) 280, para 42 as cited in *Purbanchal Cables and Conductors Private Limited* v. *Assam State Electricity Board*, (2012) 7 SCC 462, para 16].

The term 'due' is defined by Webster to mean that which is owed; that which custom, statute or law requires to be paid and by Worcester, that which anyone has a right to demand, claim or possess; that which can justly be required. A debt or other obligation is due when it is legally enforceable, *i.e.*, when the creditor has a right to demand payment and to enforce collection. *Custodian General of Evacuee Property* v. *Harnan Singh,* AIR 1957 Punj 58, 59. [Administration of Evacuee Property Act (31 of 1950), S. 48(1)]

The words 'payable', 'due' and 'recoverable' have been used in the Act, synonymously and therefore any sums recoverable or payable under the Act would be sums due under the Act. *Hazara Singh Gauda Singh* v. *State of Punjab,* AIR 1961 Punj 34, 40 (FB). [Displaced Persons (Compensation and Rehabilitation) Act (44 of 1954), S. 30(1)]

The word 'due' means all moneys owed or payable, even though their recovery may be barred by the Law of Limitation. *Bharat B & D Mfg. Co.* v. *Bombay Municipality,* AIR 1978 Bom 369, 365. [Indian Electricity Act (9 of 1910), S. 24(1)]

Due means "payable" without reference to any time and is not limited to rent *etc.* falling due in future, and therefore the section enables the government to recover any sum due under a mining lease as an arrear of land revenue irrespective of whether the sum became due or the mining lease was executed prior to or after coming into force of the Act. *Gwalior Red Chalk Corporation* v. *Tehsildar,* AIR 1969 MP 48 at 49. [Mines and Minerals (Regulation and Development) Act (67 of 1957), S. 25]

Where there is no question of enforcing payment, the word 'due' used in S. 60 means, due for payment by the mortgagor on expiry of the time during which he authorised detention by the mortgagee of possession and enjoyment of usufruct or rent and profits of the property. *Nandvana Jatashankar Dasabhai* v. *Sorathia Jiva Vasan*, AIR 1953 Kutch 4. [Transfer of Property Act (4 of 1882), S. 60]

That which is owing or payable as a debt; that which is due to anyone legally or morally [CPC (5 of 1908); fitting; proper; appropriate. [CPC (5 of 1908), O. VIII, R. 6, iii. (f), O. V, R 17].

"DUE" the word 'due' has variety of meanings, in different context it may have different meanings. In its narrowest meaning, the word 'due' may import a fixed and settled obligation or liability. In a wider context, the amount can be said to be 'due', which may be recovered by action. The amount that can be claimed as 'due' and recoverable by an action may sometimes be also covered by the expression 'due'. *Modern Industries* v. *Steel Authority of India Ltd.*,(2010) 5 SCC 44 : (2010) 2 SCC (Civ) 280,, para 42 as cited in *Purbanchal Cables and Conductors Private Limited* v. *Assam State Electricity Board*, (2012) 7 SCC 462, para 16].

Due care. Just, proper, and sufficient care, so far as the circumstances demand; the absence of negligence. That degree of care that a reasonable person can be expected to exercise to avoid harm reasonably foreseeable if such care is not taken. That care which an ordinarily prudent person would have exercised under the same or similar circumstances. (*Black*)

Such care as is requisite.

Due consideration. To give such weight or significance to a particular factor as under the circumstances it seems to merit, and this involves discretion. Such care as is requisite. (*Black*)

Due course. The word is also used in conjunction with other words as in the terms, holder in *due course*; payment in due course. The prescribed, normal or logical course of events.

Due course of justice. The expression 'due course of justice' would cover all the three classes of cases in S. 2(*c*)—(*i*) scandalising the authority of any Court. (*ii*) prejudices or interferes or tends to interfere with the due course of any judicial proceeding. (*iii*) interferes or tends to interfere with or obstructs or tends to obstruct, the administration of justice. *Registrar of the Orissa High Court* v. *Baradakanta Misra,* AIR 1973 Ori 244, 279. [Contempt of Courts Act (70 of 1971), S. 13]

If the act complained scandalizes the judicial officer in regard to the discharge of his judicial functions it thereby substantially interferes or tends to interfere with the "due course of justice" which is a facet of the "administration of justice". *R. Subba Rao* v. *Advocate General Andhra Pradesh*, AIR 1981 SC 755, 759.

Due course of law. This phrase is synonymous with "due process of law", or "the law of the land," and the general definition thereof is "law in its regular course of administration through Courts of justice". (*Black*)

Due date. Date on which payment of interest or principal becomes due and payable.

For the purposes of this clause "DUE DATE" means the date by which the assessee is required as an employer to credit an employee's contribution to the employee's account in the relevant fund under any Act, rule, order or notification issued thereunder or under any standing order, award, contract of service or otherwise. [Income-tax Act (43 of 1961), S. 36(1)(va). *Expln*]

In this sub-section, "DUE DATE" means,—

(a) where the employer is—
   (i) a company; or
   (ii) a person (other than a company) whose accounts are required to be audited under this Act or under any other law for the time being in force, the 31st day of October of the assessment year;

(b) in the case of any other employer, the 31st day of July of the assessment year. [Income-tax Act (43 of 1961), S. 115WD(1) *Expln. as inserted by Finance Act (18 of 2005), S. 37.*

Due diligence. Such watchful caution and foresight as the circumstances of the particular case demand.

'Due diligence' is the idea that reasonable investigation is necessary before certain kinds of relief are requested. [*J. Samuel* v. *Gattu Mahesh*, (2012) 2 SCC 300, para 13].

'Due diligence' means reasonable diligence. It means such diligence as a prudent man would exercise in the conduct of his own affairs. [*Chander Kanta Bansal* v. *Rajinder Singh Anand,* AIR 2008 SC 2234, 2237-38, para 10]

Due notice. Public or personal notice ordered by the Judge in his discretion; such notice as is prescribed by law.

No fixed rule can be recognised as to what shall constitute '*due notice*'. Due is a relative term, and must be applied to each case in the exercise of the discretion of the Court in view of the particular circumstances.

Due-on-sale clause. A mortgage provision which gives the lender an option to accelerate the debt if the borrower transfers or conveys any part of the mortgaged real estate to someone without the consent of the lender.

Due performance of a contract. Performance of a contract in a requisite manner. [Indian Stamp Act (2 of 1899), Sch 1, item 57].

Due process of law. The application of the law as it exists in the fair and regular course of administrative procedure.

'Due process of law' means that nobody ought to be condemned unheard. The due process of law means a person in settled possession will not be dispossessed except by the due process of law. Due process means an opportunity for the defendant to file pleadings including written statement and documents before the court of law. It does not mean the whole trial. Due process of law is satisfied the moment rights of the parties ore adjudicated upon by a competent court. [*Maria Margarida Sequeira Fernandes* v. *Erasmo Jack De Sequeira*, (2012) 5 SCC 370, para 81].

In India the concept of due process of law has not been accepted; the Constitution of India adopted the expression; 'procedure established by law' does not guarantee the right to any particular procedure to deprive a person of his life or liberty; the legislature is left free to lay down any procedure; this accepts the English principles of supremacy of law. (*Constitutional and Parliamentary Term*)

The best description of the expression 'due process of law' would be to say that it means in each particular case such an exercise of the powers of the Government as the settled maxims of law permit and sanction and under such safeguards for the protection of the individual rights as those maxims prescribe for the class of cases to which the one in question belongs. *A.K. Gopalan* v. *State of Madras*, AIR 1950 SC 27, 99.

Due proclamation. Official formal public announcement in a requsite, appropriate or prescribed manner.

Due regard. The expression 'due regard' means that the licensing authority must pay proper attention to several circumstances in balancing the considerations for grant, or refusal of a permit. *T.P. Sunderlingam* v. *State of Madras,* AIR 1971 Mad 245, 249. [Rice Milling Industry (Regulation) Act (21 of 1958), S. 5(*a*)]

Due service. Service made in proper time, and in proper manner; as ordained by law.

Service (of a process) in a prescribed manner. [CrPC 1973 (2 of 1974), S. 66(2)].

Due to. It refers those assessees who maintain their accounts according to the mercantile system of accountancy. *Commissioner of Income Tax, Bombay* v. *Chunnilal* v. *Mehta & Sons P. Ltd.*, AIR 1972 SC 268, 272. [Income-tax Act (43 of 1961), S. 10(5)]

Dues. "DUES" means any dues payable by any person to the Reconstruction Bank in relation to any assistance given by, or any bond or debenture issued to, the Reconstruction Bank, and includes interest, rent, costs, charges and commission payable in relation thereto. [Industrial Reconstruction Bank of India Act (62 of 1984), S. 2(h)]

"DUES" means any liability which is claimed as due from any person by an approved institution and includes interest, costs, charges and other amount payable in relation thereto. [National Housing Bank Act (53 of 1987), S. 36 C(e)]

A word of general significance, and includes all contractual obligations.

The word "dues" in Art. 13 of the Provincial Small Cause Courts Act (9 of 1887), must be taken to comprise only dues similar in kind to those specifically mentioned therein. also applies to shares in even what has been paid voluntarily to a religious association.

Duly. Regularly; fitly; in a due, fit, suitable, or becoming manner; in due manner; when or as due; in due time or proper manner, order, form *etc.*; in accordance with what is right, required or suitable; according to law or some rule of law; legally on proper authority.

'Duly' excludes any arbitrary exercise of power. *H.L. Trehan* v. *Union of India*, AIR 1989 SC 568, 571. [Caltex (Acquisition of Shares of Caltex Coil Refining (India) Ltd. and of the Undertakings in India of Caltex (India) Ltd. Act (17 of 1977), S. 11(1)]

The word 'duly' means properly. *State of Orissa* v. *Kaushalya Dei*, AIR 1965 ORI 38, 42. [CrPC 1973 (2 of 1974), Ss. 292(1) & 293(1)]

The word "duly" means properly, regularly or in due manner. *L.I.C. of India* v. *Dj. Bahadur*, AIR 1988 SC 2181, 2216. [Life Insurance Corporation Act (31 of 1956), S. 11]

Duly account for. To render accounts in a due manner. [CPC (5 of 1908), Sch. I, App. F, Form No. 10].

Duly appointed. Means appointed in accordance with the provisions of this Act or with the rules or regulations made thereunder. [Employee's State Insurance Act (34 of 1948), S. 2(7)]

Duly authorised person. The words "duly authorised" would include duly authorised either by the action of the party indebted or by force of law or order of the Court. *Md. Kamgarh Shah* v. *Jagdish Chandra*, AIR 1960 SC 953, 960. [Limitation Act (36 of 1963), S. 19]

Duly authorized. Implies that all things have been done which are requisite to confer legal authority.

The words "duly authorised" in Order VI, Rule 14, need not be restricted to mean authorised by proper written authority or by power of attorney. [CPC (5 of 1908), O. VI, R. 14]

Duly served. Served in a manner prescribed by law, as applied to the service of summons.

Due service can only be service effected in the manner prescribed by the code. *K.A. Desai & Co.* v. *Vijasinhji Bhimsinhji,* AIR 1954 Sau 84. [CPC (5 of 1908), S. 27]

Substituted service may or may not be due service according to the circumstances of the case. It is open to the dependent to establish that he never avoided service and that, in any case, notice of the claim had not been brought home to him. *G. Shanmukhi* v. *Utakur Venkataswamy Reddy,* AIR 1957 AP 1, 4. [CPC (5 of 1908), O. 5, R. 20]

Duly stamped. "DULY STAMPED" as applied to an instrument, means that the instrument bears an adhesive or impressed stamp of not less than the proper amount and that such stamp has been affixed or used in accordance with the law for the time being in force in India." [Indian Stamp Act (2 of 1899), S. 2(11)]

If an instrument after becoming liable to duty in one State on execution becomes liable to duty also in another State on receipt there, it must first be stamped in accordance with the law of the first State and it will not require to be further stamped in accordance with the law of the second State and where the rate in the second State is higher, it will require to be stamped only with the law and the rules in force in the second State. *New Central Jute Mills* v. *State of West Bengal,* AIR 1963 SC 1307, 1312. [Indian Stamp Act (2 of 1899), S. 3]

A document bearing a stamp of proper description and exceeding in value the amount of duty prescribed, is a duly stamped document. *Anoop Chand* v. *Nathal,* AIR 1965 Raj 114, 115. [Indian Stamp Act (2 of 1899), S. 35]

Duly sworn. A swearing according to law; lawfully sworn. A term which imports the administration of an oath according to the formula prescribed by law.

Dum bene se gasserit. During good behaviour.

Dum casta vixerit. (*Lat.*) So long as she shall remain chaste.

Dumb witness. A witness who is mute or incapable of speaking on expressing himself in words.

Dumping. "DUMPING" means :

(i) any deliberate disposal of wastes or other matter from vessles, aircraft, platforms or other man-made structures at sea;

(ii) any deliberate disposal of vessels, aircraft, platforms or other man-made structures at sea;

"DUMPING" does not include :

(i) the disposal of wastes or other matter incidental to, or derived from the normal operations of vessels, aircraft, platforms or other man-made structures at sea and their equipment, other than wastes or other matter transported by or to vessels, aircraft, platforms or other man-made structures at sea, operating for the purpose of disposal of such matter or derived from the treatment of such wastes or other matter on such vessels, aircraft, platforms or structures;

(ii) placement of matter for a purpose other than the mere disposal thereof, provided that such placement is not contrary to the aims of this Convention. [UN Convention on the Law of Sea, Art. 1(5)(a)]

Sending superfluous goods for sale at low price abroad with a view to maintaining home price and capturing foreign trade.

Duo non possunt in solido unam rem possidere. (*Lat.*) (Co. Litt. 368a) Ownership or possession in entirety cannot be in two persons of the same thing.

Duplicate. A copy of the original; the double of anything; a counterpart.

A second copy of a letter or official document; a second copy of a bill drawn in two parts; consisting of or existing in two corresponding or identical parts or examples; a copy or transcript. [Indian Museum Act (10 of 1910), S. 7(c)].

Duplicate originals. When the counterparts, of a document are made and delivered by each party to the other they are commonly spoken of as 'duplicate originals.'

Duplicate will. A will which is executed in duplicate, one copy of the will is kept with the testator and the other is to be deposited with someone else.

Duplicating equipment. Means any mechanical contrivance or device used or intended to be used for making copies of any work. [Copyright Act (14 of 1957), 2(hh)]

Duplicity. Double dealing; bad faith.

Duplicating process. 'DUPLICATING PROCESS' means any process involving the use of an appliance for producing multiple copies. [(English) Copyright Act, 1956, S. 41(7)]

Dura lex sed lex. 'Dura lex sed lex' means "the law is hard but it is the law". [*Popat Bahiru Govardhane* v. *Special Land Acquisition Officer*, (2013) 10 SCC 765, para 13].

Durante absentia. (*Lat.*) During absence.

Durante bene placito. During the pleasure of the grantor.

Duration. Extent, limit, or time; during which a thing lasts; the power of enduring.

The meaning assigned to expression 'duration' on the marginal notes of Articles 83 and 172 of the Constitution cannot be assigned to the expression 'duration' occurring in proviso to Art. 243-ZF. So the expression 'duration' occurring in proviso to Art. 243-ZF when read in reference to the context does not include the extended term of the municipality. *Surendra Kr. Gupta* v. *State,* AIR 1994 All 349, 355. [Constitution of India, Arts. 243-ZF, 83, 172]

A portion of time which is measurable, or during which exists, lasts or is in progress. [Arms Act (54 of 1959), S. 21(i)].

Duress. Standing alone it means any intimidation, or restraint on action or anything tending to restrain free and voluntary action. In its more extended sense, the word means 'that degree of severity, either threatened and impending, or actually inflicted, which is sufficient to overcome the mind and will of a person of ordinary firmness.'

Generally speaking, duress may be said to exist whenever one, by the unlawful act of another, is induced to make a contract or to perform some other act under circumstances which deprive him of the exercise of free will.

Durgah. Means the institution known as the Durgah Khawaja Saheb Ajmer, and includes the premises called the Durgah Sharif with all buildings contained therein, together with all additions thereto or all alterations thereof which may hereafter be made from time to time. [Durgah Khwaja Saheb Act (36 of 1955), S. 2(c)]

Durgah Endowment. Includes—

(i) the Durgah Khawaja Saheb, Ajmer;

(ii) all buildings and movable property within the boundaries of Durgah Sharif;

(iii) Durgah Jagir, including all land, houses and shops and all immovable property wherever situated belonging to the Durgah Sharif;

(iv) all other property and all income derived from any source whatsoever dedicated to the Durgah or placed for any religious, pious or charitable purposes under the Durgah Administration, including the Jagirdari villages of Hokran and Kishanpur in Ajmer; and

(v) all such nazars or offerings as are received on behalf of the Durgah by the Nazim or any person authorised by him. [Durgah Khwaja Saheb Act (36 of 1955), S. 2(d)]

During. In the time of; in the course of. Throughout the whole continuance of.

During (in) the course of employment. When a person is on leave, he is not at all in the course of his employment. He is not supposed to do any work for the employer. *Divisional Superindent Northern Railway* v. *Umrao,* AIR 1960 All 283, 285. [Workmen's Compensation Act (8 of 1923), S. 3]

During the currency of lease. The phrase 'during the currency of lease' means subsistence of lease and it is not confined to the term as agreed to between the parties. *Changayya* v. *Sub-Collector,* AIR 1966 AP 4, 8. [Andhra Tenancy Act (18 of 1956), Ss. 11 and 13]

During the pleasure of. So long as (a particular person) pleases.

During the pleasure of the Governor. "The Ministers shall hold office during the pleasure of the Governor." [Constitution of India, Art. 164(1)]

During the pleasure of the President. "The Ministers shall hold office during the pleasure of the President." [Constitution of India, Art. 74(2)]

Dutch auction. Starting the auction sale of an article at a price above its value, and gradually lowering it to an amount at which a sale is effected or the article withdrawn.

Dutiable goods. "DUTIABLE GOODS" means any article on which a duty of land customs is leviable by virtue of a notification issued under S. 5 of the Indian Tariff Act, 1894. [Act (29 of 1924) Land Custom, S. 2, cl. (*d*)]

'DUTIABLE GOODS' means the medicinal and toilet preparations specified in the schedule as being subject to the duties of excise levied under this Act. [Medicinal and Toilet Preparations (Excise Duties) Act (16 of 1955), S. 2(c)]

'DUTIABLE GOODS' means any goods which are chargeable to duty and on which duty has not been paid. [Customs Act (52 of 1962), S. 2(14)]

Duties. Imports or customs taxes; taxes and charges levied upon goods, chattels, commodities or manufactures.

Duties of excise and taxes on sale of goods. *Governor-General in Council* v. *Province of Madras*, AIR 1945 PC 98 Quoted—A duty of excise is under the Indian Constitution a duty on production levied on a product and grounded on the fact of production, while a sales tax is a tax levied on a dealer on the occasion of a sale. *Ram Raj Tobacco Trading Co.* v. *Asst. Commercial Tax Officer,* AIR 1957 Mad 325, 329. [Constitution of India, Sch. 7, List I, Entry 84]

Duty. Action, or an act, that is due by moral or legal obligation; that which one ought or is bound to do; official function; a levy; work; period of duty.

A legal obligation that is owed or due to another and that needs to be satisfied; an obligation for which somebody else has a corresponding right. [Black's Law Dictionary as cited in *Urmila Devi* v. *Yudhvir Singh*, (2013) 15 SCC 624, para 55].

The expression "duty" means an amount which shall be collected as a condition for granting the permission to possess, transport, import/export or sell opium. *Organon (India) Ltd.* v. *Collector of Excise*, AIR 1994 SC 2489, 2501 [Opium Act (1 of 1878), S. 5]

'Duty' is an obligation recognized by law to avoid conduct brought with unreasonable risk of damage to another. *Rajkot Municipal Corpn.* v. *Manjulben Jayantilal Nakem*, (1997) 9 SCC 552, para 14.

The word "duty" means an indirect tax imposed on the importation or consumption of goods. [*Union of India* v. *Nitdip Taxtile Processors Private Limited*, (2012) 1 SCC 226, para 26].

DUTY, OBLIGATION, Law and conscience dictate to a man what is his *duty*, and the neglect of it is a violation of right or virtue. *Obligation* is more practical, and is dictated rather by usage and propriety. *Obligation* has also very often the sense of the power that binds while *duty* is the thing enforced. A *duty* never can be against reason; an *obligation* may be even absurd, as depending upon custom, *Obligation* is defined by the extent of the power which obliges; *duty* by the ability of the subject who performs. (*Smith Syn. Dis.*)

Duty and discretion. A statutory discretion is not, however necessarily or, indeed, usually, absolute; it may be qualified by express and implied legal duties to comply with substantive and procedural requirements before a decision is taken whether to act and how to act. Moreover there/may be a discretion whether to exercise a power, but no discretion as to the mode of its exercise; or a duty to act when certain conditions are present, but a discretion how to act. Discretion may thus be coupled with duties. [*Halsbury's Laws of England,* 4th Edition, Vol. I para 28 as cited in *National Insurance Co. Ltd.* v. *Keshav Bahadur*, AIR 2004 SC 1581, 1583, para 8]

Duty and misconduct. It would be anomalous to say that a public servant has misconducted himself in the discharge of his duty. "Duty" and "misconduct" go ill-together. If a person has misconducted himself as a public servant, it would not ordinarily be in the discharge of his duty, but the reverse of it. *Dhaneshwar* v. *Delhi Administration*, AIR 1962 SC 195, 198.

Duty of care. A duty to use due care toward others in order to protect them from unnecessary risk of harm.

Duty of excise. A duty of excise is a tax-levy on home-produced goods of a specified class or description, the duty being calculated according to the quantity or value of the goods and which is levied because of the mere fact of the goods having been produced or manufactured and unrelated to and not dependent on any commercial transaction in them. *Chhotabhai* v. *Union of India*, AIR 1962 SC 1006, 1018. [Constitution of India, Sch. 7, List I, entry 84]

The expression "duty of excise" means excise duty payable under the Central Excises and Salt Act (1 of 1944). It cannot bear an extended meaning, so as to include special excise duty and auxiliary excise duty. *Union of India* v. *Modi Ruber Ltd.*, AIR 1986 SC 1882, 1887. [Central Excise Rules (1944), R. 8(1)]

Duty to act. The obligation to take some action so as to prevent harm to another, and failure of which may be liable, depending on the relationship of the parties and the circumstances.

Duty to exercise due care. The duty to use reasonable care in one's actions; the failure to use due care may result in negligence.

Duzargan. *Duzargan* is a Persian word. It does not only mean predecessors or ancestors, but also the elders who may or may not be directly related who may form either near or distant relatives. *State of Bihar* v. *Sri Radha Krishna Singh*, AIR 1983 SC 684, 701. [Indian Evidence Act (1 of 1872), S. 13 and 32(5)]

DVB. (*Abbr.*) Digital Video Broadcasting. A technique developed and standardised by an international DVB project group, for digital transmission of TV signals. (*Telecommunication*)

Dwell. To inhabit; to reside; to remain; to be domiciled; to live in a place; to have a habitation; to have a fixed place of residence; to abide as a permanent resident; or to inhabit for a time; to live in a place; to have a habitation for some time or permanence.

Dwelling-house. Is defined as the house or the building in which a person lives or which is inhabited by man; an inhabited house; the house of his personal abode; a place of habitation; a place of residence; habitation; a house occupied or intended to be occupied as a residence.

Dwelling place is a flexible expression primarily the expression means residence, abode, or home, where an individual is supposed usually to live and sleep. In other words it must be a house or a portion thereof which could be regarded as an abode or home of the assessee in the taxable territories. *C.I.T. Madras* v. *K.S. Ratnaswamy*, AIR 1980 SC 525, 529.

Dwelling place. This expression "dwelling place" in a taxing statute means a house or a portion thereof which could be regarded as an abode or home of the assessee in the taxable territories. *CIT, Madras* v. *K.S. Ratnaswamy,* AIR 1980 SC 525.

Dwelling unit. 'DWELLING UNIT' means a building or part thereof which is used or is intended to be used by a family for habitation. [Delhi Development Authority (Management and Disposal of Housing Estates) Regulations 1968, Regn. 2(15)]

Dye. A natural or synthetic colouring.

Dying declaration. Dying declarations are statements made by a dying person as to the injuries which culminated in his death or the circumstances under which the injuries were inflicted. Statements made by a deceased long prior to the occurrence resulting in death are not dying declarations and not admissible under the Indian Evidence Act (1 of 1872), S. 32. The necessity of recording a dying declaration arises only when the hopes of life of the man are given up.

A statement by a person as to the cause of his death or as to any of the circumstances of the transaction which resulted in his death; this is a statement that comes within the scope of Section 32(1) of the Indian Evidence Act (1 of 1872)].

Statements made by a person who is lying at the point of death, and is conscious of his approaching death, in reference to the manner in which he received the injuries of which he is dying, or other immediate cause of his death, and in reference to the person who inflicted such injuries or the connection with such injuries of a person who is charged or suspected of having committed them; which statements are admissible in evidence in a trial for homicide (and occasionally, at least in some jurisdictions, in other case) where the killing of the declarant is the crime charged to the defendant. [Black's Law Dictionary (5th Edn.) as cited in *Ramakant Mishra* v. *State of U.P.*, (2015) 8 SCC 299, para 9].

The dying declaration is a statement by person as to the cause of his death or as to any of the circumstances of the transaction which resulted in his death and it becomes relevant under Section 32(1) of the Indian Evidence Act in a case in which the cause of that person's death comes into question. *Tapinder Singh* v. *State of Punjab,* AIR 1970 SC 1566. Also see *Bhayani Luhana Radhabai* v. *State of Gujarat,* (1977) 1 SCC 762. [Indian Evidence Act (1 of 1872), S. 32(1)]

Dying intestate. It would be noticed that the Privy Council interpreted the words "dying intestate" as merely meaning "in the case of intestacy of a Hindu male." *Daya Singh* v. *Dhan Kaur,* AIR 1974 SC 665.

It covers both situations of dying either without having made any will or having made an invalid will. *Manshan* v. *Tej Ram,* AIR 1980 SC 558.

Dyspnoea. Shortness or difficulty of breathing, associated with syncope, and disease of the heart, lungs, larynx, or windpipe.

E

e-commerce. Means buying and selling of goods through the internet on an e-commerce platform, the payment for which shall be done through international credit or debit cards and as specified by the Reserve Bank of India from time to time. [Export by Post Regulations, 2018, Regn. 3(1)(b)].

"E-COMMERCE" means buying and selling of goods and services including digital products over digital and electronic network. [Legal Metrology (Packaged Commodities) Rules, 2011, R. 2(bd)].

Means buying or selling of goods or services including digital products over digital or electronic network. [Consumer Protection Act, 2019 (35 of 2019), section 2(16)]

e-commerce entity. Means a company incorporated under the Companies Act, 1956 or the Companies Act, 2013, or a foreign company covered under clause (42) of Section 2 of the Companies Act, 2013, or an office, branch or agency in India covered under sub-clause (*ii*) of clause (*v*) of Section 2 of the Foreign Exchange Management Act, 1999 (42 of 1999) owned or controlled by a person resident outside India and conducting e-commerce business. [Legal Metrology (Packaged Commodities) Rules, 2011, R. 2(be)].

e-governance. Includes use of information and communication technology to promote efficient and cost-efficient services to the public. [Dadra and Nagar Haveli Excise Regulation (1 of 2012), S. 2(23); Andaman and Nicobar Islands Excise Regulation (3 of 2012), S. 2(18)].

e-Form. §§ See under *'FORM'* or *'E-FORM.'*

"e-Insurance Account" or **"eIA".** Is an electronic account opened by a person with an insurance repository wherein the portfolios of insurance policies of a policyholder are held in an electronic form. [Insurance Regulatory and Development Authority of India (Insurance of e-Insurance Policies) Regulations, 2016, Regn. 2(iii)].

"e-insurance policy" or **"electronic insurance policy".** Shall mean a policy document which is an evidence of insurance contract issued by an insurer and digitally signed in accordance with the applicable provisions prescribed by law and issued in an electronic form either directly to the policyholder by the insurer or through the platform of registered Insurance repository. [Insurance Regulatory and Development Authority of India (Insurance of e-Insurance Policies) Regulations, 2016, Regn. 2(vii)].

e-KYC authentication facility. Means a type of authentication facility in which the biometric information and/or OTP and Aadhaar number securely submitted with the consent of the Aadhaar number holder through a requesting entity, is matched against the data available in CIDR, and the Authority returns a digitally signed response containing e-KYC data along with other technical details related to the authentication transaction. [Aadhaar (Authentication) Regulations, 2016, Regn. 2(1)(j)].

e-KYC data. Means demographic information and photograph of an Aadhaar number holder. [Aadhaar (Authentication) Regulations, 2016, Regn. 2(1)(k)].

"e-KYC User Agency" or **"KUA".** Shall mean a requesting entity which, in addition to being an AUA, uses e-KYC authentication facility provided by the Authority. [Aadhaar (Authentication) Regulations, 2016, Regn. 2(1)(l)].

"e-proposal" or **"electronic proposal".** Mean a proposal form for an insurance policy filed in electronic form by the prospect with his electronic signature. [Insurance Regulatory and Development Authority of India (Insurance of e-Insurance Policies) Regulations, 2016, Regn. 2(vi)].

Ea est accipienda interpretatio, quae vitio caret. (*Maxim*) That interpretation is to be received which is free from fault.

Each. Every one of any number separately considered, or every one of several. The word is understood to mean every one of the two or more individuals composing the whole, considered separately from the rest.

Everyone. [CPC (5 of 1908), O. XXI, R. 77(1)].

Ear-witness. A witness who testifies about something that he heard but did not see.

Earliest opportunity. The period connoted by the phrase "earliest opportunity" begins to run from the time the person detained expresses his desire or intention to make a representation. *State of Bombay* v. *Atma Ram*, AIR 1951 SC 157, 173. [Constitution of India, Art. 22(5)]

The expression 'earliest opportunity' occurring in Art. 22(5) of the Constitution would mean that there should not be any delay in affording an adequate opportunity to the detenue of making a representation against the order of detention. *Sophia Gulam Mohd. Bham* v. *State of Maharashtra*, AIR 1999 SC 3051. [Constitution of India, Art. 22(5)].

The word "earliest" in Section 13 which qualifies "opportunity" must equally qualify the corresponding obligation of the State to deal with the representation, if and when made, as expeditiously as possible. The 'opportunity' contemplated by the section is the opportunity to make a representation against the detention order to the Government. *Vijay Kumar* v. *State of Jammu & Kashmir,* AIR 1982 SC 1023. [Jammu & Kashmir Public Safety Act, 1978, S. 13]

Early. Pertaining to the first part or period of some division of time, or of some course in time; in advance of the usual or appointed time (early crops; early fruits; early spring).

Early neutral evaluation. The use of a neutral to give his opinion on a matter often of the potential outcome of the dispute.

Earmark. A mark put upon a thing to distinguish it from another. A mark of identity or ownership.

Earn. To receive as return for work done or services rendered; to obtain or deserve as the reward of labour.

Earned. In order that the income can be said to have accrued to or earned by the assessee it is not only necessary that the assessee must have contributed to its accruing or arising by rendering services or otherwise but he must have created a debt in his favour. *E.D. Sassoon & Co. Ltd.* v. *I.T. Commissioner, Bom,* AIR 1954 SC 470, 482.

Earned income. Income which arises in respect of remuneration for any office or employment.

Earned leave. The concept of 'earned leave' is rooted in the principle inherent in Rule 4 of the All India Services (Leave) Rules *i.e.*, the performance of duty is the basis of earning leave. Although the expression 'earned leave' is not employed in the High Court Judges (Conditions of Service) Act (28 of 1954), the fundamental premise for the grant of leave to a Judge is that he has earned it by virtue of the time spent by him on actual service. *Union of India* v. *Gurnam Singh,* AIR 1982 SC 1265.

Where a person was compulsorily retired and he was not given the earned leave which had accumulated in the course of his service it was held that no grievance can be made of this fact. *Horace Ross* v. *State of M.P.,* 1962 MP 252.

Earned surplus. The earned surplus represents 'reserves'. The accumulated profits of the assessee company according to the system of accounting at the end of the year were not carried forward into the account of the next year as they could not be, according to the system of accounting prevalent in the United States. They had to be allocated to some account, and they were allocated to "Earned Surplus" which was intended for and was used in subsequent years for the purpose of the business of the assessee company. *I.T. Commissioner (Central) Calcutta* v. *Standard Vacuum Oil Co.*, AIR 1966 SC 1393, 1401. [Profits Tax Act (1947), Sch. II 12, 2(11)]

Earnest. A token act or a nominal payment done before hand by the buyer as a pledge or sign of good faith especially as a partial purchase price to bind the seller.

A part payment of the purchase price of goods. A coin or some other thing of value given by a buyer to signify the conclusion of a bargain between him and the seller. The buyer loses the earnest if he fails to perform his part of the contract. Also means a fixed determination; a pledge or payment given as an assurance of earnest or serious purpose to fulfil a promise or discharge an engagement.

Earnest money. Money paid as earnest to bind a bargain or ratify a sale being done by way of earnest. (*Tomlin*)

Earnest money is the sum of money paid by the buyer of property under a contract for sale in order to bind the seller to the terms of the agreement of sale. In other words it is a guarantee for the performance of a contract. *Puttu Lal Govind Dass* v. *Achchey Lal Nandu Lal,* AIR 1956 VP 42, 43. [Transfer of Property Act (4 of 1882), S. 55]

Earnest money is part of the purchase price when the transaction goes forward: it is forfeited when the transaction falls through, by reason of fault or failure of the vendee [sic: vendee]. [*Kunwar Chiranjit Singh* v. *Har Swarup,* AIR 1926 PC 1 as cited in *Maula Bux* v. *Union of India*, (1969) 2 SCC 554 : AIR 1970 SC 1955]. See also *Airports Authority of India* v. *R.K. Singhal*, AIR 2012 Del 51, para 5.

Something given for the purpose of binding a contract which is forfeited if the contract do not go off and adjusted in price if the contract goes through. *In the matter of; HUDA* v. *Kewal Krishan Geol,* AIR 1996 SC 1981.

A nominal sum given by the vendee to the vendor in a contract of sale or the like as a token that the parties are in earnest and have made up their minds; the vendee will lose his money, if he fails to perform his part. [TP Act (4 of 1882), S. 55(6)(b)].

PRINCIPLES OF DEPOSIT AND FORFEITURE OF EARNEST MONEY AS PROPOUND BY THE SUPREME COURT:—

(1) It must be given at the moment at which the contract is concluded.

(2) It represents a guarantee that the contract will be fulfilled or, in other words, 'earnest' is given to bind the contract.

(3) It is part of the purchase price when the transaction is carried out.

(4) It is forfeited when the transaction falls through by reason of the default or failure of the purchaser.

(5) Unless there is anything to the contrary in the terms of the contract in default committed by the buyer, the seller is entitled to forfeit the earnest. *Delhi Development Authority* v. *Grihsthapana Cooperative Group Housing Society Ltd.,* AIR 1995 SC 1176 : AIR 1995 SC 1312.

Earnest money and **penalty—distinction.** Earnest money is a payment actually made by the vendee whereas the penalty is the compensation sought for the breach and yet to be recovered. *Amar Nath Nikkuram* v. *Mohan Singh,* AIR 1954 MB 134, 135. [Indian Contract Act (9 of 1972), S. 74].

Earning capacity. A person's ability or power to earn money, given the person's talent, skills, training, and experience. Value of an employee's services to a company.

Earning value. Earning value means the value of an equity share computed by taking the average of profits after tax as reduced by the preference dividend and adjusted for extraordinary and non-recurring items, for the immediately preceding three years and further dividend by the number of equity shares of the investee company and capitalised at the following rates :

- Predominantly manufacturing company : 8%
- Predominantly trading company : 10%
- Any other company, including an NBFC : 12%

If an investee company is a loss making company the earning value will be taken at *Zero.* [Non-Banking Financial Companies Prudential Norms (Reserve Bank) Directions, 1998, S. 2(1)(v)].

Earnings. That which is earned; reward; that which is gained or merited by labour; the reward for personal services, whether in money or other goods; the price of services performed; gains derived form service or labour without the aid of capital. Sometimes the term means more than the wages of labour.

Earth. The habitation of man.

The ground as a mere surface; land.

Easement. A service or convenience which one neighbour hath of another, by grant or prescription, without profit; as, a way through his land.

"An easement is a right which the owner or occupier of certain land possesses, as such, for the beneficial enjoyment of that land, to do and continue to do something, or to prevent and continue to prevent something being done, in or upon, or in respect of, certain other land not his own." [Indian Easements Act (5 of 1882), S. 4].

"EASEMENT" includes a right not arising from contract, by which one person is entitled to remove and appropriate for his own profit any part of the soil belonging to another or anything growing in, or attached to or subsisting upon, the land of another. [Limitation Act (36 of 1963), S. 2(f)]

Easement impliedly released. "An EASEMENT is IMPLIEDLY RELEASED :

(a) where the dominant owner expressly authorises an act of a permanent nature to be done on the servient heritage, the necessary consequence of which is to prevent his future enjoyment of the easement, and such act is done in pursuance of such authority,

(b) where any permanent alteration is made in the dominant heritage of such a nature as to show that the dominant owner intended to cease to enjoy the easement in future.

Explanation.—Mere non-user of an easement is not an implied release within the meaning of this section." [Indian Easements Act (5 of 1882), 38, Expl. 1 and 2.]

Easement of necessity. Where one person transfers or bequeaths immovable property to another,—

(a) if an easement in other immovable property of the transferor or testator is necessary for enjoying the subject of the transfer or bequest, the transferee or legatee shall be entitled to such easement; or

(b) * * * *

(c) if an easement in the subject of the transfer or bequest is necessary, for enjoying other immovable property of the transferor or testator, the transferor or the legal representative of the testator, shall be entitled to such easement; or

(d) * * * * *

(e) if an easement over the share of one of them is necessary for enjoying the share of another of them, the latter shall be entitled to such easement.

(f) * * * *

The easement mentioned in this section, clause (a), (c) and (e), are called the EASEMENT OF NECESSITY. [Indian Easement Act (5 of 1882), S. 13]

One in which the easement is indispensable to the enjoyment of the dominant estate. Such arises by operation of law when land conveyed is completely shut off from access to any road by land retained by granter or by land of grantor and that of a stranger. (*Black*)

Easement of support. An easement of support of a building by another's land or building may be acquired by grant or prescription.

Eat inde sine die. (*Lat.*) Let him go without a day, the word signify that matter be dismissed without further judicial proceeding against the criminal.

Eating-house. "EATING-HOUSE" includes a hotel; restaurant or any other place where any eatable is served on payment, whether or not such payment is separately made for such eatable or is included in the amount charged for boarding and lodging. [Wild Life Protection Act (53 of 1972), S. 44(1) *Expln.*]

'Eating house' means any premises to which the public are admitted and where any kind of food is prepared or supplied for consumption on the premises for the profit or gain of any person owing or having an interest in or managing such premises. [Bombay Municipal Corporate Act, 1888 (3 of 1888), S. 3(ff) as cited in *Brihanmumbai Mahanagarpalika* v. *Willingdon Sports Club*, (2013) 16 SCC 260, para 12].

A public place where food is sold to casual guests to be eaten upon the premises; and may include on oyster-stall.

Eaves dropping. Knowingly and without lawful authority listen surreptitiously, to private conversation; offence of listening under walls, windows or caves of a house.

Ecclesiastic. A person in holy orders; a clergyman; a priest; one consecrated to the service of the church.

Ecclesiastical. Denotes something belonging to, or set apart for the church; as distinguished from civil or secular, with regard to the world. (*Tomlin*)

Ecclesiastical Court. In England, a Court having jurisdiction over matters concerning the Church of England as well as the duties and rights of the people serving it, but whose modern jurisdiction is limited to matters of ecclesiastical discipline and church property.

Ecclesiastical jurisdiction. Jurisdiction over ecclesiastical cases and controversies; such that exercised by the ecclesiastical Courts.

Ecclesiastical law. The law administered in the ecclesiastical Courts.

ECMS. Electronic Copyright Management System which permits identification and recording of use of protected material by digital identification signals which are incorporated in the film and sound recording etc. (*Copyright*)

'Ecocentrism' supports the protection of all life forms, not just those which are of value to humans or their needs and underlines the fact that humans are just one among the various life forms on earth. [Environmental Ethics, Stanford Encyclopedias of Philosophy, 2002; Revised Edn. 2088 as cited in *T.N. Godavarman Thirumulpad* v. *Union of India*, (2012) 4 SCC 362, para 32].

Ecological. It does not mean 'pertaining to ecology' but 'good for the environment'.

Ecology. An international term for biological science on the management, structure and functioning of nature, object of organized international co-operation, especially developed under UN patronage in the field of human ecology. Environmental protection.

The science which deals with inter-relationships between the various organisms living in an area and also their relationship with the physical environment.

Ecology Party. The Green Party was given this name.

A broad term describing business activities with associated technical data that are conducted electronically. (*Cyber Law*)

General term that encompasses any commercial transaction involving the exchange of goods, services, or information over the Internet. (*Cyber Law*)

E-commerce. The practice of buying and selling goods and services through online consumer services on the Internet.

E-contracts. Also known as electronic contracts. These are made by parties using computers and Internet wherein offer, acceptance and consideration and all essential elements of formation of contract are fulfilled online. [Karnika Seth, *Computers Internet and New Technology Laws*, 2021, LexisNexis, Glossary of Legal Terms].

Economic. Pertaining to wealth. [Constitution of India, Preamble].

Economic abuse. For the purposes of section 3 of Act 43 of 2005, 'economic abuse' includes—(a) deprivation of all or any economic or financial resources to which the aggrieved person is entitled under any law or custom whether payable under an order of a court or otherwise or which the aggrieved person requires out of necessity including, but not limited to, household necessities for the aggrieved person and her children, if any, stridhan, property, jointly or separately owned by the aggrieved person, payment of rental related to the shared household and maintenance; (b) disposal of household effects, any alienation of assets whether movable or immovable, valuables, shares, securities, bonds and the like or other property in which the aggrieved person has an interest or is entitled to use by virtue of the domestic relationship or which may be reasonably required by the aggrieved person or her children or her stridhan or any other property jointly or separately held by the aggrieved person; and (c) prohibition or restriction to continued access to resources or facilities which the aggrieved person is entitled to use or enjoy by virtue of the domestic relationship including access to the shared household. [*Explanation* I (iv) to S. 3 of the Protection of Women from Domestic Violence Act, 2005 (43 of 2005)]

Economic activity. As is generally understood, refers to any activity consisting of offering products in a market regardless of whether the activities are intended to earn profit. [*Competition Commission of India* v. *Coordination Committee of Artistes and Technicians of West Bengal Film and Television*, (2017) 5 SCC 17, para 44].

Economic boycott. means—

(i) a refusal to deal with, work for hire or do business with other person; or

(ii) to deny opportunities including access to services or contractual opportunities for rendering service for consideration; or

(iii) to refuse to do anything on the terms on which things would be commonly done in the ordinary course of business; or

(iv) to abstain from the professional or business relations that one would maintain with other person. [Scheduled Castes and the Scheduled Tribes (Prevention of Atrocities) Act (33 of 1989, S. 2(1)(bc) as inserted by Amending Economic Duress Act (1 of 2016)].

Economic duress. An unlawful coercion to perform an act by threatening financial injury at a time when one cannot exercise free will.

Economic indicator. A statistical measure used to describe the state of the economy or to predict its direction.

Economic interests of a nation. 'Economic interests of a nation' are the goals which a nation wants to attain to fulfill its national objectives. It is the part of our national interest, meaning thereby national interest cannot be seen with the spectacles (glasses) devoid of economic interest. It includes in its ambit a wide range of economic transactions or economics activities necessary and beneficial to attain the goals of a nation, which definitely includes as an objective economic empowerment of its citizens. [*Reserve Bank of India* v. *Jayantilal N. Mistry*, (2016) 3 SCC 525, para 74].

Economic justice. Economic justice means that every man will get just reward for his labour according to his ability irrespective of his colour, caste, creed or other social position. It also means that people are not to be discriminated on account of economic conditions. *Express newspaper* v. *Union of India,* AIR 1958 SC 578.

Economic life. The duration of the profitability of an asset which is usually shorter than its physical life.

Economic offence. Includes criminal breach of trust, forgery, counterfeiting of currency-notes, bank-notes and Government stamps, *hawala* transaction, mass-marketing fraud or running any scheme to defraud several persons or doing any act in any manner with a view to defraud any bank or financial institution or any other institution or organisation for obtaining monetary benefits in any form. [(w.e.f. 1-7-2024) Bharatiya Nyaya Sanhita, 2023 (45 of 2023), section 111(1), *Explanation* (iii)]

Economic rent. Rent which yields a fair return and capital expenses.

Economic security. Includes financial, monetary and fiscal stability security of means of production and distribution, food security, livelihood security, energy security, ecological and environmental security. [S. 2(ea) of the Unlawful Activities (Prevention) Act, 1967 (37 of 1967) as inserted by the Unlawful Activities (Prevention) Amendment Act, 2012 (3 of 2013)]

Economic sanctions. Enforcement of international obligations by means of economic and financial pressure.

Economic significance. The expression "economic significance" cannot mean more profit to the inventor that is something which would follow from any new product (which may even not be a new invention). The expression "economic significance" must mean economic significance to the society for example if an invention leads to significance reduction in costs or significant reduction in the consumption of imported components thereby saving foreign exchange, it may be considered an invention of economic significance. [*Novartis AG* v. *Union of India*, (2013) 6 SCC 1, para 8].

Economic union. An economic community that requires member nations to adopt a common currency and to integrate their economic policies.

Economically vulnerable or backward classes. Means persons who live below the poverty line. [Insurance Regulatory and Development Authority (Obligations and Insurers to Rural or Social Sectors) Regulations, 2000, Reg. 2(f)].

Economically weaker sections. For the purposes of this article and article 16, "economically weaker sections" shall be such as may be notified by the State from time to time on the basis of family income and other indicators of economic disadvantage. [Constitution of India, Article 15, *Explanation*]

Means such weaker sections as are referred to in *Explanation* to clause (6) of article 15 of the Constitution. [Central Educational Institutions (Reservation in Teachers' Cadre) Act, 2019 (10 of 2019), section 2(e)]

Economiser. Means any part of a feed-pipe that is wholly or partially exposed to the action of flue gases for the purposes of recovery of waste heat. [Indian Boilers Act (5 of 1923), S. 2(cc)]

Economy. Thrifty management; frugality; economy of a country.

Economy of scale. A decline in the per-unit cost production of a product resulting from increased output, due to increased production facilities.

Ecosystem. Means a dynamic complex of plant, animal and micro-organism communities and their non-living environment interacting as a functional unit. [United Nations Conference on Environment and Development : Convention on Biological Diversity, Art. 2 (June 5, 1992)]

Edict. An ordinance or command.

Edit keys. The functional keys that allow you to instruct the system directly to perform functions relating to editing. Moving the cursor, going to a page or word, searching or finding, replacing, filing or ending, inserting required page ends, calling up view mode, are all typical functions performed directly by pressing edit keys. (*Cyber Law*)

Edition. As applied to a publication, the total number of copies issued or published at once; a republication, sometimes with a revision and correction; any publication of a book previously published.

Editor. "EDITOR" means the person who controls the selection of the matter that is published in a newspaper. [Press and Registration of Books Act (25 of 1867), S. 1(1)]

A person who edits, especially a person who prepares, suprintends, revises or corrects a book, magazine or newspaper for publication.

Educated, unemployed youth. Educated unemployed youth in legal connotation denotes a class of citizens who after completing their education are faced with unemployment. When a person is still pursuing his course of studies in a university, he is not 'educated unemployed youth'. *Bishnu Ram Borah* v. *Parag Saikia*, AIR 1984 SC 898, 899.

Education. Is the bringing up; the process of developing and training the powers and capabilities of human beings. In its broadest sense, the word comprehends not merely the instruction received at school, or college but the whole course of training moral, intellectual and physical; is not limited to the ordinary instruction of the child in the pursuits of literature.

"Education" means "a debt due from present to future generations". [George Peabody as cited in *Maharishi Mahesh Yogi Vedic Vishwavidyalaya* v. *State of Madhya Pradesh*, (2013) 15 SCC 677, para 24].

"Education" means the "transmission of civilization". [Mr.Will Durrant as cited in *Maharishi Mahesh Yogi Vedic Vishwavidyalaya* v. *State of Madhya Pradesh*, (2013) 15 SCC 677, para 24].

"Education" means 'bringing up or training;... strengthening of the powers of body or mind; culture'. [Chambers Dictionary as cited in *Maharishi Mahesh Yogi Vedic Vishwavidyalaya* v. *State of Madhya Pradesh*, (2013) 15 SCC 677, para 44].

Education is a process which engages many different actors: the one who provides education (the teacher, the owner of an educational institution, the parents), the one who receives education (the child, the pupil) and the one who is legally responsible for the one who receives education (the parents, the legal guardians, society and the state.) The actors influence the right to education. [*Society for Unaided Private Schools of Rajasthan* v. *Union of India*, (2012) 6 SCC 1, para 5].

Education means not only learning how to read and write alphabets or get mere information but it means to acquire knowledge and wisdom so that one may lead a better life and become a better citizen to serve the nation in a better way. [*Bhartiya Seva Samaj Trust* v. *Yogeshbhai Ambalal Patel*, (2012) 9 SCC 310, para 21].

"Education is the most powerful weapon which you can use to change the word". [By Nelson Mandela as cited in *Maharishi Mahesh Yogi Vedic Vishwavidyalaya* v. *State of M.P.*, (2013) 15 SCC 677, para 23].

Act or process of providing with knowledge. [Constitution of India, Art. 41].

The sense in which the word "education" has been used is the systematic instruction, schooling or training given to the young in preparation for the work of life. It also connotes the whole course of scholastic instructions which a person has received. What education connotes is the process of training and developing the knowledge, skill, mind and character of students by formal schooling. *Loka Shikshana Trust* v. *I. T. Commissioner, Mysore*, AIR 1976 SC 10,14.

Education department. Of or relating to education [Representation of the People Act (43 of 1950), S. 27(3)(b)]; [Trade Unions Act (16 of 1926), S. 15(h)].

Educational institution. Means a school, seminary, college university, professional academies, training institutes or other educational establishment, not necessarily a chartered institution and includes not only buildings, but also all grounds necessary for the accomplishment of the full scope of educational instruction, including those things essential to mental, moral and physical development. [Noise Pollution (Regulation and Control) Rules, 2000, R. 2(e)].

The words "educational institutions" are of very wide import and would include a University also. *S. Azeez Basha* v. *Union of India*, AIR 1968 SC 662, 670. [Constitution of India, Art. 30 (1)]

Educationist. A specialist in the theory and methods of education. [University Grants Commission Act (3 of 1956), S. 5(3)(c)]

Efface. To remove any written or printed thing.

To obliterate; more widely, to cause to disappear. [IPC (45 of 1860), S. 261].

Effect. "Wherever the causing of a certain effect, or an attempt to cause that effect, by an act or by an omission, is an offence, it is to be understood that the causing of that effect partly by an act and partly by an omission is the same offence." [IPC (45 of 1860), S. 36]

(*Noun*) A result which follows a given act; consequence; event and sometimes used as synonymous with weight (as) effect of evidence. The "Effect" of a cause, is anything which would not have happened but for that cause; and it is none the less an effect of such a cause, because it has been developed or accelerated by something supervening.

The word 'effect' in Ss. 32 and 33 means 'scope, tenor and drift'. *National Aluminium Co. Ltd.* v. *Panda Engineering Works (P.) Ltd.*, AIR 1991 Ori 297, 301. [Arbitration Act (10 of 1940) (*repealed*), S. 32, 33]

Something caused or produced; a result, consequence [Indian Evidence Act (1 of 1872), S. 136, ill. (d)]; the operative influence; the state or fact of being operative; the impression produced on the mind. [Indian Contract Act (9 of 1872), S. 12, ill. (b)].

(*Verb.*) To produce; to bring to pass; to cause to be.

Effect, to that. Having that influence; having the purport or tenor. [CrPC 1973 (2 of 1974), S. 329(1)].

Effective. In operation; capable of bringing about an effect; productive of result; actual.

Effective capital. For the purposes of Section II of Part II of Schedule V of Act 18 of 2013, 'effective capital' means the aggregate of the paid-up share capital (excluding share application money or advances against shares); amount, if any, for the time being standing to the credit of share premium account; reserves and surplus (excluding revaluation reserve); long-term loans and deposits repayable after one year (excluding working capital loans, over drafts, interest due on loans unless funded, bank guarantee, etc., and other short-term arrangements) as reduced by the aggregate of any investments (except in case of investment by an investment company whose principal business is acquisition of shares, stock, debentures or other securities), accumulated losses and preliminary expenses not written off. [*Explanation I* to section IV of Part II of Schedule V of the Companies Act, 2013 (18 of 2013)]

Effective date. 'EFFECTIVE DATE' means 30th June, 1996 which shall cover all eligible loans disbursed upto and outstanding as on 30th June 96. [Debt Relief Scheme for borrowers in State of J and K, para 2(e) issued under J and K Debtor's Relief Act (15 of 1976), S. 4].

Effective driving licence. The expression 'effective driving licence' occurring in Section 3(1) of the Act would mean a valid driving licence both as regards the period and type of the vehicle. *Ashok Gangadhar Maratha* v. *Oriental Insurance Co. Ltd.,* (1999) 6 SCC 620, para 5. [Motor Vehicles Act (59 of 1988), S. 3(1)].

Effective implementation. An implementation which is productive of the desired effect. [Unit Trust of India Act (52 of 1963), S. 21(k)].

Effective licence. The words 'effective licence' used in Section 3 cannot be imported for 149(2) of the Act for the words 'duly licenced'. *National Insurance Co. Ltd.* v. *Swaran Singh,* (2004) 3 SCC 297, 324, para 44. [M.V. Act (59 of 1988), Ss. 3, 149(2)]

Effective representation. If a procedure under Art. 21 has to be reasonable fair and just, that the word "effective representation" appearing in Art. 22(5) must be construed so as to provide a real and meaningful opportunity to the person detained to explain his case to the detaining authority in his representation. *Kamla* v. *State of Maharashtra,* AIR 1981 SC 814, 816. [Constitution of India, Art. 22(5)]

Effects. "EFFECTS" in relation to a seaman includes clothes and documents. [Merchant Shipping Act (44 of 1958), S. 3(10)]

"EFFECTS" mean any direct or indirect—immediate on delayed adverse consequences caused by an industrial accident or, *inter alia*;

(i) human beings, flora and fauna,

(ii) soil, water, air and landscape

(iii) the interaction between the factors in (i) and (ii)

(iv) material assets and cultural heritage, including historical monuments. [UN : Convention on the Transboundary Effects of Industrial Accidents (March 17, 1992), Art. 1(c)]

Goods and chattels; movable property.

Effectual. Characterized by adequate power to produce an intended effect.

Effectual cancellation. The question whether the cancellation of a stamp on an instrument amounts to effectual cancellation as required by S. 12, Indian Stamp Act (2 of 1899), depends on the particular circumstances of each case. The true test to be applied is, if, the stamp became detached from the document to which it had been affixed and came to the possession of an ordinary normal person, whether he could conscientiously use that stamp again.

Effectually. So as to answer the purpose. [Income-tax Act (43 of 1961), S. 297(2)(e)].

Efficacious. Able to produce the intended result.

That which produces or is certain to produce the intended effect. [Specific Relief Act (47 of 1963), S. 41(h)].

Efficacy. Effectiveness. [IPC (45 of 1860), S. 275].

"Efficacy" means "the ability to produce a desired or intended result". [New Oxford Dictionary of English, Edn. 1998 as cited in *Novartis AG* v. *Union of India,* (2013) 6 SCC 1, para 157].

Efficiency. Power to produce the result intended; skilfulness.

The expression "efficiency" includes all relevant matters necessary for one's discharging duties efficiently and satisfactorily. *State of U.P.* v. *K.U. Ansari,* (2002) 1 SCC 616 (620, 621).

Efficiency bar. The crossing of the efficiency bar in the substantive rank by an employee would at the most prove his efficiency in that rank. That fact cannot be taken as displaying his merit, ability and efficiency entitling him to promotion. *B.C. Tewari* v. *M.P. State,* AIR 1960 MP 216, 217. [Constitution of India, Arts. 311]

Efficient. Causing effects; producing results; actively operative.

Adequately skilled and active. [Industrial Finance Corporation Act (15 of 1948) (*Repealed by Act 23 of 1993*), S. 15].

Efficient cause. The working cause or the cause which produces the effects or results.

Effigy. A figure or representation of a person. If made with intent to make the subject an object of ridicule, it is a libel.

Effluent. [Damodar Valley Corporation Act (14 of 1948), S. 22(2)(iii)]; [Factories Act (63 of 1948), S. 12(1) & 18(2)].

Effluvia. Unpleasant exhalation or smell. [Beedi and Cigar Workers (Conditions of Employment) Act (32 of 1966), S. 8].

Efflux. Running of time; expiration by lapse of time.

Efflux of time. When this phrase is used in leases, conveyances, and other like deeds, it indicates the expiration of an agreed term of years *etc.* specified in the deed or writing.

The lapse or expiry of time. [T.P. Act (4 of 1882), S. 111(a)]; [Companies Act (1 of 1956), S. 294(4)].

Effort. An exertion of strength or power, whether physical or mental; strenuous endeavour; laborious attempt; struggle directed to the accomplishment of an object; an effort to excel.

E-form. Means the form in the schedule to the Companies (Authorised to Registered) Rules, 2014, which shall be used for the matter to which it relates. [R. 2(1)(d) of the Companies (Authorised to Registered) Rules, 2014]

Egress. The path or opening by which a person goes out; exit.

Ei incumbit probatio qui dicit non qui negat. The burden of proof lies upon him who affirms, not upon him who denies. (*Latin for Lawyers*)

Ei incumbit probatio qui dicit non qui negat; cum per rerum naturam factum negantis probatio nulla sit. (*Maxim*) The burden of proof lies upon him who affirms, not upon him who denies : since by the nature of things he who denies a fact cannot produce any proof.

Ei qui affirmat, non ei qui negat, incumbit probatio. The burden of proof lies on him who affirms a fact, not on him who denies it.

Either. One or the other of two, taken indifferently as the case requires. (*Ame. Cyc.*)

The word 'either' means each of the two. *Sudruddin Suleman* v. *J.H. Patwardlen,* AIR 1965 Bom 224, 260. [Land Acquisition Act (1 of 1894), S. 17(3)] [Now repealed & replaced by Act 30 of 2013].

'Either', 'Or'. The words 'either' and 'or' are indicative of two separate sets of circumstance. *Govindram Ramprasad* v. *Assessing Authority (Sales Tax)*, AIR 1958 MP 16, 19. [M.B. Sales Tax Act (30 of 1950), S. 2(q)].

Either party. The one or the other of the two parties.

The words "either party" would also cover the legal heirs who have stepped into the shoes of the spouses under the law and such persons would also be competent to ask for variation & modification of the order for maintenance. That term would also include the holders of the estate with lawful title for the time being. *Aruna Basu* v. *Dorothea Mitra*, AIR 1983 SC 916, 920. [Special Marriage Act (63 of 1954), S. 37(2)].

Eject. To send away; to thrust out. As applied to a person to compel him against his desire to leave a place.

To evict from property [T.P. Act (4 of 1882), Ss. 112, prov. and 114]; to throw out. [IPC (45 of 1860), S. 443].

Ejection. A turning out of possession by action of law or by physical force or the threat of it.

Ejectment. An action to recover immediate possession of real property; an action to try the right of possession to the land in controversy; a possessory action. '*Ejectment*' is designed to protect and enforce the right of possession derived from ownership of title.'

Ejus est interpretari cujus est condere. (*Lat.*) (*Maxim*) It belongs to him to interpret (or explain) who enacts; the right of interpreting belongs to him who enacts. (*Trayner*)

Ejus est nolle, qui potest velle. (*Lat.*) He who can will (exercise volition) has a right to refuse to will (to withhold consent).

He may be unwilling who can be willing—*i.e.,* he who can consent may object.

Ejus est periculum cujus est dominium aut commodum. He who has the dominion or advantage has the risk. It is the risk to whom the property belongs, or who reaps the advantage.

Ejus nulla culpa est cui parere necesse sit. (*Maxim*) He is not guilty for fault who necessarily obeys; that is, no one incurs fault or blame through, the performance of an act which he is under the necessity of performing.

He who is bound to obey is in no fault as where the proper officer executes a criminal, or where an officer of justice, in the legal exercise of a particular duty, kills a person who resists. (*Latin for Lawyers*)

Ejusdem generis. "Of the same kind or species." A well known maxim of construction. The phrase "*ejusdem generis*" means "of the same kind" and is more restricted than the word 'analogous.'

"Ejusdem generis: [Latin] "of the same kind or class"](17c) 1. A canon of construction holding that when a general word or phrase follows a list of specifics, the general word or phrase will be interpreted to include only items of the same class as those listed. [Black's Law Dictionary as cited in *Sebastian T. Joseph* v. *Kerala State Commission for Protection of Child Rights*, LNIND 2017 KER 18141. para 20]

The principle of "ejusdem generis" means "where a law lists specific classes of persons or things and then refers to them in general, the general statements only apply to the same kind of persons or things specifically listed". [*Manga* v. *State of Uttarakhand*, (2013) 7 SCC 629, para 46].

The phrase '*ejusdem generis*' is a mere rule of constitution and not a rule of substantive law and is not applicable where the intention of the legislature is otherwise clear.

The rule of '*ejusdem generis*' should never be invoked where its application appears to defeat the general intent of the instrument to be construed.

Of the same kind or nature. Where a list of specific items is followed by general concluding clause, this is deemed to be limited to things of the same kind as those specified.

The *ejusdem generis* rule strives to reconcile the incompatibility between specific and general words. This doctrine applies when :

(i) the statute contains an enumeration of specific words;

(ii) the subjects or enumeration constitute a class or category;

(iii) that class or category is not exhausted by the enumeration;

(iv) the general term follows the enumeration;

(v) there is no indication of a different legislative intent. *Amar Chandra Chakraborty* v. *Collector of Excise*, AIR 1972 SC 1863, 1868;

ACCE v. *Ramdev Tobacco Co.*, 1991 (51) ELT 631 (SC).

Ejusdem generis applies only when the provision enumerates specific words, such enumeration constitutes a class, that the enumeration or the class is not exhaustive, general terms follow the enumeration and that there is no different legislative intent. If the enumerated items belong to a complete genus, the principle that the meaning of general words should be confined to those of narrower genus does not apply. *Grasim Industries Ltd. C.C*, 2002 (141) ELT 593 (SC).

Ejusdem generis and analogous. The expression, "any other sufficient cause" found in O. XLVII, R. 1(c) of the Code must be interpreted to mean a reason sufficient or ground at least analogous to those specified immediately before. It must be *ejusdem generis* to the reasons previously stated. There is a distinction between the words, '*ejusdem generis*' and 'atleast analogous'. The Latin phrase '*ejusdem generis*' according to Chamber's Twentieth Century Dictionary means, 'of the same kind'. The word analogous means bearing same; corresponds with or resembles to, similar in certain circumstances or relation". So, the phrase '*ejusdem generis*' is more restricted than the word, 'analogous'. The popular meaning for the word, *ejusdem generis* is, it is a rule of legal construction that general words following enumeration of particulars are to have their generality limited by reference to the preceding particular enumeration and to be construed as including only all other articles of the like nature and quality. *Shanmugam Servai* v. *P. Periyakaruppan Servai,* AIR 1996 Mad 411, 414.

Ejusdem generis rule. The '*edjusdem generis* rule' is often useful or convenient, but it is merely a rule of construction, not a rule of law. [*N.A.L.G.O.* v. *Bolton Corpn.*, (1943) AC 166. *See also Manglore Electric Supply Co.* v. *CIT (West Bengal)*, (1978) 3 SCC 248, 254, 55, para 9]

Elapse. To slip away; to expire. [T.P. Act (4 of 1882), S. 17(1)(b) and Constitution of India, Art. 108 (1)].

Elderly. Somewhat old; bordering on old age (as, elderly people).

Eldest. The *prima facie* meaning of "eldest" is the first born" as, the eldest son or daughter.

Eldest male line. The male line which has existed the greatest number of years.

Eldest male lineal descendant. First male lineal descendant.

Elect. To choose; to pick out; to select from a number or to make a choice of. And the term is also used as meaning to prefer; to take by preference, *etc.* 'Sometimes the word is used in the sense of 'appoint'.

To cast vote for the purpose of selecting members of any legislative, municipal or other authority, of whatever character, the method of selection which is, by or under any law prescribed, as by election; to select by election; to choose which of two courses a person who has the opportunity and right to elect, will take. [CPC (5 of 1908), O. XXXII, R. 12(2)].

Electa una via non datur recursus ad alteram. (*Maxim*) He who has chosen one way cannot have recourse to another.

Elected. Chosen by a popular vote (as *elected* member of legislative assembly as opposed to a *nominated* member).

Electio semel facta, et placitu testatum non patitur regressum. (*Maxim*) Election once made, and plea witnessed, suffers not a recall.

Electio semel facta non-petitur regressum. (*Maxim*) Election once made cannot be recalled.

Election. "ELECTION" means an election to fill any vacancy in any of the words of any municipality. [Kerala Municipality Act, 1994, Ker Act (No. 20 of 1994), S. 2(14) as amended by Kerala Act (N. 8 of 1995)]

The word "ELECTION" denotes an election for the purpose of selecting members of any legislative, municipal or other public authority, of whatever character, the method of selection to which is by or under, any law prescribed by election. [IPC (45 of 1860), S. 21, *Expln.* 3]

"ELECTION" means an election to fill a seat or seats in either House of Parliament or in the House or either House of the Legislature of a State other than the State of Jammu and Kashmir. [Representation of People Act (43 of 1951), S. 2(1) (d)].

"ELECTION" means any election, by whatever means held under any law for the purpose of selecting members of Parliament or of any Legislature, local authority or other public authority. [Prevention of Corruption Act (49 of 1988), S. 2(a)].

Election in law is when a man is left to his own free will to take or do one thing or another, which he pleases (*Jacob*); it is more frequently applied to the choosing between two rights by a person who derives one of them under an instrument in which an intention appears that he should not enjoy both; this word is also commonly applied to the choosing of representatives. [Eleventh, IPC (45 of 1860), S. 21; T.P. Act (4 of 1882), S. 35 and CPC (5 of 1908), O. I, R. 2].

In the narrow sense the word "election" is used to mean the final selection of a candidate. In the wide sense, the word is used to connote the entire process culminating in a candidate being declared elected.

The term 'election' in Art. 329(b), Constitution of India has been used in its comprehensive sense, embracing the whole procedure whereby an elected member is returned. *Narayan Bhaskar Khare* v. *Election Commission of India*, AIR 1957 SC 649, 697.

The issue of notifications under S. 151 and 39(2) of the Representation of the People Act (43 of 1951) is a part of the process of 'election' within the meaning of Art. 329(b) of the Constitution of India. *Amin Ahmad* v. *Nand Lal Sinha,* AIR 1953 Pat 293, 295.

In the narrow sense it is used to mean the final selection of a candidate which may embrace the result of the poll when there is polling, or a particular candidate being returned unopposed when there is no poll. In the wide, sense the word 'election' connotes the entire "process culminating in a candidate being declared elected". *Election Commission of India* v. *Shivaji*, AIR 1988 SC 61, 64. [Representation of the People Act (43 of 1951), S. 2(a)].

The word 'election' as occurring in Art. 329 of the Constitution includes the entire process from the issue of notification under Section 14 of the Act to the declaration of the result under Section 66 of the Act. *Election Commission of India* v. *Ashok Kumar,* (2000) 8 SCC 216, para 14 : AIR 2000 SC 2979. [Constitution of India, Art. 329 and Representation of the People Act (43 of 1951), Ss. 14 and 66].

The word 'election' includes the rejection of a nomination paper with which the process of election begins.

GENERAL ELECTION. A general election is an election held to select an officer after the expiration of the full term of the former officer.

Election agent. An agent appointed by a candidate to look after his interest at and to represent him at an election. [Representation of the People Act (43 of 1951).

Election Commission. 'ELECTION COMMISSION' means the Election Commission appointed by the President under Article 324. [Representation of the People Act (43 of 1950), S. 2(d); Presidential and Vice-Presidential Elections Act (31 of 1952), S. 2(c).]

A constitutional body in India created for the purpose of holding elections to Parliament, State Legislatures and offices of President and Vice-President.

Election in the case of Prime Minister. Means an election to either House of Parliament of a person who holds the office of Prime Minister at the time of such election or is appointed as Prime Minister after such election. [Disputed Elections (Prime Minister and Speaker) Act (16 of 1977), S. 2(e)]

Election in the case of Speaker. Means an election to the House of people of a person who holds the office of speaker at the time of such election or is chosen as the speaker for the for that House after such election. [Disputed Elections (Prime Minister and Speaker Act (16 of 1977), S. 2(f)]

Election of remedies. Broadly speaking, an election of remedies is the choice by a party to an action of one of two or more co-existing remedial rights, where several such rights arise out of the same facts; but the term has been generally limited to a choice by a party between inconsistent remedial rights. (*Bouvier*).

Election petition. Petition for enquiry in the validity of elections. [Representation of the People Act (43 of 1951), S. 83(1) and Manipur (Hill Areas) District Councils Act (76 of 1971), S. 17].

Election process. The process of framing electoral rolls is not part of the election process. *Inderjit Barua* v. *Election Commission*, AIR 1986 SC 103. [Representation of People Act (43 of 1951), S. 80]

Electiones fiant rite et libere sine interruptione aliqua. Let elections be just and free without interruption.

Elector. One who elects, or one who has the right of choice. Also one who exercises the right of election.

Elector means a person who is entered in the electoral rolls in force at the time of election.

'Elector' in relation to a constituency means a person whose name is entered in the electoral roll of that constituency for the time being in force and who is not subject to any of the disqualifications mentioned in Section 16 of the Representation of the People Act (43 of 1950). *Hari Prasad Mulshankar Trivedi* v. *V.B. Raju,* AIR 1973 SC 2602 : (1974) 3 SCC 415. Dt. 28-08-1973. [Representation of the People Act (43 of 1951, S. 2(e)]

In this sub-section, ELECTOR means a person who was entitled to vote at the election to which the election petition relates, whether he has voted at such election or not. [Representation of the People Act (43 of 1951), S. 81(1) *Expln.*.]

'ELECTOR' in relation to a Presidential election means a member of the electoral college referred to in Article 54, and in relation to a Vice-President election means a member of the electoral college referred to in Art. 66. [Presidential and Vice-Presidential Elections Act (31 of 1952), S. 2(d)]

An 'elector' is a person whose name is included in the voters' list for the time being in force and who is not subject to any disqualification referred to under Section 74. Kerala Municipalities Act (20 of 1994), S. 2(15) as **referred to** in *M.A. Vaheed* v. *Jobai Silva*, AIR 1998 Ker 318, 321, para 10.

Electoral College. A body of persons entitled to vote at an election, but not constituted on the basis of a territorial constituency. [Representation of the People Act (43 of 1951), S. 39(1) and Constitution of India, Art. 54 and Art. 66(1)].

The President shall be elected by the members of an electoral college consisting of—

(a) the elected members of both Houses of Parliament; and

(b) the elected members of the Legislative Assemblies of the States.

Expln.—In Article 54 and in Article 55, "State" includes the National Capital Territory of Delhi and the Union Territory of Pondicherry. [Constitution of India, Art. 54]

Electoral right. "ELECTORAL RIGHT" means the right of a person either to stand or not to stand as a candidate or to withdraw or not to withdraw his candidature or to vote in an election. [Kerala Municipality Act (Kerala Act No. 20 of 1994), S. 2(16), as amended by Kerala Act No. 8 of 1995]

"Electoral right" means the right of a person to stand, or not to stand as, or to withdraw from being, a candidate or to vote or refrain from voting at an election. [(w.e.f. 1-7-2024) Bharatiya Nyaya Sanhita, 2023 (45 of 2023), section 169(b)]

The right of a person to stand or not to stand as, or to withdraw from being a candidate or to vote or refrain from voting at an election. [IPC (45 of 1860), S. 171B and Representation of the People Act (43 of 1951), S. 79(d)].

Electoral roll. An official list of voters at an election [Representation of the People Act (43 of 1950), S. 13B].

Electorate. The whole body of those entitled to vote at an election. Representation of the People Act (43 of 1951), [S. 10(2)(a)].

Electric supply line. Means a wire, conductor or other means used for conveying, transmitting or distributing energy (whether by overhead line or underground cable), together with any casing, coasting, covering, tube, pipe or insulator enclosing, surrounding or supporting the same or any part thereof, or any apparatus connected therewith for the purpose of so conveying, transmitting or distributing such energy and includes any support, cross-arm, stay, strut or safety device erected or set up for that purpose. [Indian Electricity Act (9 of 1910), S. 2(f)] Act (9 of 1910) repealed and replaced by Act (36 of 2003).

"Electric supply line" and "works". An electric supply line means a wire, conductor or other means used for conveying, transmitting or distributing energy.

Works includes electric supply line and any building, plant, machinery, apparatus and any other thing of whatever description required to supply energy to the public. *Upper Ganges Valley Electricity Supply Co. Ltd.* v. *U.P. Electricity Board,* AIR 1973 SC 683. [Indian Electricity Act (9 of 1910), S. 2(n)] Act (9 of 1910) repealed and replaced by Act (36 of 2003).

Electrical and mechanical products. The scope of the words 'electrical and mechanical products' is not to cover all products which are made by means of mechanical or electrical process but it means products which are utilised for purposes of producing electricity or implements and other apparatus and machinery or goods like fans, radios and battery shells. *Great Eastern Electroplaters Ltd.* v. *Regional Provident Fund Commission,* AIR 1966 All 495, 497. [Employees' Provident Funds Act (19 of 1952), Schedule I, *Explanation*]

Electrical goods. Only such articles, the use of which cannot be had except with the application of electrical energy, can be termed electrical goods or appliances.

Electrical, mechanical or general engineering product. The expression 'general engineering' does not include electrical or mechanical engineering and also other branches of engineering known by specific or special titles. *Regional P.F. Commissioner* v. *Shibu Metal Works*, AIR 1965 SC 1076, 1081. [Employees' Provident Funds Act (19 of 1952), Sch.I]

Electromagnetic intrusion. The intentional insertion of electromagnetic energy into transmission paths in any manner, with the objective of deceiving operators or causing confusion. (*Cyber Law*)

Electromagnetic radiation-Waves-Frequencies-Spectrum. "Electromagnetic (EM) radiation is a phenomenon which occurs in the universe. Sunlight is a familiar example of EM radiation. So is the light from the stars. EM radiation travels in waves at different frequencies. Frequency of a wave and its length are inversely proportional. Generally, EM radiation is classified on the basis of wavelength into radio wave, microwave, terahertz (or sub-millimeter) radiation, infrared, the visible region is perceived as light, ultraviolet, x-rays and gamma rays. Waves with frequencies ranging from 300 GHz to 3 kHz (corresponding wavelength ranging from 1 millimeter to 100 kilometers) are called radio waves. Radio waves have the longest wavelengths in the electromagnetic spectrum. The entire range of frequencies in EM radiation is called EM spectrum.

EM radiation interacts with matter in different ways across the spectrum. These types of interaction are so different that historically different names have been applied to different parts of the spectrum, as though these were different types of radiation. Thus, although these "different kinds" of EM radiation form a quantitatively continuous spectrum and wavelengths, the spectrum remains divided for practical reasons related to these qualitative interaction differences. [*Bharti Airtel Limited* v. *Union of India*, (2015) 12 SCC 1, para 5].

Electronic agent. Computer program, or electronic or other automated means, used by a person to initiate an action or to respond to electronic messages or performances, on the person's behalf, without review or action by another individual. (*Cyber Law*)

Electronic bill payment and presentment (EBPP). Analog or digital electronic means—telephone, fax, e-mail, third-party electronic bill payment service, and the like—to transmit billing and payment information. (*Cyber Law*)

Electronic business centre (EBC). A group of electronic transaction-processing systems in the Patent and Trademark Office, including patent searches. (*Cyber Law*)

Electronic cigarette. Means an electronic device that heats a substance, with or without nicotine and flavours, to create an aerosol for inhalation and includes all forms of Electronic Nicotine Delivery Systems, Heat Not Burn Products, e-Hookah and the like devices, by whatever name called and whatever shape, size or form it may have, but does not include any product licensed under the Drugs and Cosmetics Act, 1940 (23 of 1940).

Explanation.—For the purposes of this clause, the expression "substance" includes any natural or artificial substance or other matter, whether it is in a solid state or in liquid form or in the form of gas or vapour. [Prohibition of Electronic Cigarettes (Production, Manufacture, Import, Export, Transport, Sale, Distribution, Storage & Advertisement) Act, 2019 (42 of 2019), section 3(d)]

Electronic Commerce. "Electronic commerce" means the supply of goods or services or both, including digital products over digital or electronic network [The Central Goods and Services Tax Act, 2017 (12 of 2017), S. 2(44)]

Electronic commerce operator. "Electronic commerce operator" means any person who owns, operates or manages digital or electronic facility or platform for electronic commerce [The Central Goods and Services Tax Act, 2017 (12 of 2017), S. 2(45)]

Electronic communication means the communication of any written, verbal, pictorial information or video content transmitted or transferred (whether from one person to another or from one device to another or from a person to a device or from a device to a person) by means of an electronic device including a telephone, mobile phone, or other wireless telecommunication device, or a computer, or audio-video player or camera or any other electronic device or electronic form as may be specified by notification, by the Central Government. [(w.e.f. 1-7-2024) Bharatiya Nagarik Suraksha Sanhita, 2023 (46 of 2023), section 2(1)(i)]

Electronic Communication Networks (ECN). Electronic bulletin boards that communicate availability and price of securities. (*Cyber Law*)

Electronic communications. Transfer of signs, signals, writing, images, sounds, data, or intelligence of any nature transmitted in whole or part by wire, radio, electromagnetic, photoelectric, or photo-optical system. (*Cyber Law*)

"ELECTRONIC COMMUNICATION" means any transmission of signs, signals, writings, images, sounds, data or intelligence of any nature transmitted in whole or in part by a wire, radio, electromagnetic, photo electronic or photo optical system that affects inland or foreign commerce but does not include—

(i) the radio portion of a cordless telephone communication that is transmitted between the wireless telephone hand-set and the base unit; or

(ii) any wire or oral communication; or

(iii) any communication made through a tone only paging device; or

(iv) any communication from a tracking device. [Prevention of Terrorism Act (15 of 2002), S. 36(a)]

Electronic Communications Privacy Act (ECPA). Federal law that expanded the provisions of wiretapping law to cellular phones, voice mail, Internet downloads, and e-mail. (*Cyber Law*)

Electronic Communications Privacy Act (ECPA) of 1986. This act outlaws the unauthorized interception, access, and disclosure of wire or electronic communications. (*Cyber Law*)

Electronic Data Gathering Analysis and Retrieval (EDGAR). SEC system for posting corporate filings and disclosures on line. (*Cyber Law*)

Electronic data interchange. The use of electronic-data transmission networks to exchange informations.

Transactions using a system of interconnected computers that exchange data among merchant buyers, sellers, banks, carriers, warehouses, and other parties on a regular basis. (*Cyber Law*)

Transfer of electronic data between companies. (*Cyber Law*)

Electronic dissemination right. The right authorizing the inclusion of material in an electronic dissemination service, includes cabling, interactive services, wireless broadcasting etc. (*Copyright*)

Electronic dissemination service. Any service making available material consisting of items of authors' works, sound recordings, films, photographs etc. by wire or wireless means; such a service may be confined to private use or made available to the public. (*Copyright*)

Electronic form. With reference to information means any information generated, sent, received or stored in media, magnetic, optical, computer memory, micro film, computer generated micro fiche or similar device. [Information Technology Act (21 of 2000), S. 2(1)(r)]

A computer-based version of a paper record. (*Internet and E-commerce*)

Electronic form evidence. For the purposes of this section, 'electronic form evidence' means any information of probative value that is either stored or transmitted in electronic form and includes computer evidence, digital audio, digital video, cell phones, digital fax machines. [Information Technology Act (21 of 2000), S. 79-A, *Expln.* as inserted by Act (10 of 2009), S. 79-A, *Expln.*]

Electronic Freedom of Information Act (EFOIA). Federal act extending the provisions of the *Freedom of Information Act* to electronic files (*Cyber Law*)

Electronic Funds Transfer Act (EFTA). This act outlaws the giving of inaccurate or insufficient information in an EFT, or transactions involving counterfeit, stolen, or fictitious debit instruments. (*Cyber Law*)

Electronic Gazette. Means the Official Gazette published in the electronic form. [Information Technology Act (21 of 2000), S. 2(1)(s)]

Electronic Governance or E-Governance. Use of internet and computers to facilitate government functioning and for efficient administration and delivery of services to citizens. For example, e-government initiatives include automating online process of registration of companies with Registrar of Companies through MCA21 project, online filing of licenses and permissions and certificates for birth and death. [Karnika Seth, *Computers Internet and New Technology Laws*, 2021, LexisNexis, Glossary of Legal Terms].

Electronic Hardware Technology Park (EHTP). Means any park set up in accordance with the Electronic Hardware Technology Park (EHTP) Scheme notified by the Government of India in the Ministry of Commerce and Industry. [Income Tax Act (43 of 1961), S. 10A, *Expln.* 2(iii)]

Electronic mail (E-mail). For the purposes of this section, terms 'electronic mail' and 'electronic mail message' means a message or information created or transmitted or received on a computer, computer system, computer resource or communication device including attachments in text, image, audio, video and any other electronic record, which may be transmitted with the message. [Information Technology Act (21 of 2000), S. 66A, *Expln.* as substituted by Act (10 of 2009), S. 32]

'Electronic mail (E-mail)' means message sent, received or forwarded in digital form via a computer based communication mechanism. [Limited Liability Partnership Rules, 2009, R. 2(ix)]

Messages sent, received or forwarded in digital form via a computer-based communication mechanism. (*Information Technology*)

Service provided by a number of organizations (notably Prestel in the UK and Internet worldwide) that allows two computer users linked by *modem* to deposit messages on each other's machines. (*Insurance*)

Messages, such as memos or correspondence, transmitted between people by means of computers and computer networks. (*Computer*)

"ELECTRONIC MAIL" means message sent, received or forwarded in digital form using any electronic communication mechanism such that the message so sent, received or forwarded is storable and retrievable. [R. 2(1)(h) of the Companies (Registration Offices and Fees) Rules, 2014; R. 2(1)(g) of the Companies (Specification of Definitions Details) Rules, 2014]

Electronic means. Means an authorised and secured computer programme which is capable of producing confirmation of sending communication to the participant entitled to receive such communication at the last electronic mail address provided by such participant and keeping record of such communication. [Insolvency and Bankruptcy Board of India (Insolvency Resolution Process for Corporate Persons) Regulations, 2016, Regn. 2(1)(h); Insolvency and Bankruptcy Board of India (Liquidation Process) Regulations, 2016, Regn. 2(1)(d)].

Electronic media. Includes radio and any other broadcasting media notified by the Central Government in the Official Gazette. [Representation of the People Act (43 of 1951), S. 39A *Expln.* (a)]

Electronic mode. For the purpose of Rule 18 of the Companies (Management & Administration) Rules, 2014, the expression 'electronic mode' shall mean any communication sent by a company through its authorized and secured computer programme which is capable of producing confirmation and keeping record of such communication addressed to the person entitled to receive such communication at the last electronic mail address provided by the member. [*Explanation* to Rule 18(1) of the Companies (Management & Administration) Rules, 2014]

"ELECTRONIC MODE" for the purposes of Rule 3 of the Companies (Accounts) Rules, 2014, the expression 'electronic mode' includes "electronic form" as defined in section 2(1)(r) of Information Technology Act, 2000 (21 of 2000) and also includes an "electronic record" as defined in section 2(1)(t) of the Information Technology Act, 2000 (21 of 2000) and "books of account" shall have the meaning assigned to it under Act 18 of 2013. [*Explanation* to Rule 3 of the Companies (Accounts) Rules, 2014]

"ELECTRONIC MODE" for the purposes of section 2(42) of Act 18 of 2013, means carrying out electronically based, whether main server is installed in India or not, including, but not limited to—

(i) business to business and business to consumer transactions, data interchange and other digital supply transactions;

(ii) offering to accept deposits or inviting deposits or accepting deposits or subscriptions in securities, in India or from citizens of India;

(iii) financial settlements, web based marketing, advisory and transactional services, database services and products, supply chain management;

(iv) online services such as telemarketing, telecommuting, telemedicine, education and information research; and

(v) all related data communication services, whether conducted by e-mail, mobile devices, social media, cloud computing, document management, voice or data transmission or otherwise.

Explanation.—For the purposes of this clause, electronic based offering of securities, subscription thereof or listing of securities in the International Financial Services Centres set up under section 18 of the Special Economic Zones Act, 2005 (28 of 2005) shall not be construed as 'electronic mode' for the purpose of clause (42) of section 2 of the Act.

[R. 2(1)(h) of the Companies (Specification of Definitions Details) Rules, 2014; R. 2(1)(c) of the Companies (Registration of Foreign Companies) Rules, 2014]

Electronic publishing. The act which makes works and other productions available to the public by electronic means; sometimes embraces publication in the form of CD-ROM. (*Copyright*)

Electronic record. For the purposes of this section and section 93 'electronic records' are said to be in proper custody if they are in the place in which, and looked after by the person with whom such document is required to be kept; but no custody is improper if it is proved to have had a legitimate origin, or the circumstances of the particular case are such as to render that origin probable. [(w.e.f. 1-7-2024) Bharatiya Sakshya Adhiniyam, 2023 (47 of 2023), section 81, Explanation]

Means data, record or data generated, image or sound stored, received or sent in an electronic form or micro film or computer generated micro fiche. [Information Technology Act (21 of 2000), S. 2(1)(t)] [Also see R. 2(1)(f) of the Companies (Registration Offices and Fees) Rules, 2014; R. 2(1)(i) of the Companies (Specification of Definitions Details) Rules, 2014]

Record that is created, generated, sent, communicated, or received by electronic means; UETA and federal E-SIGN make equivalent to written documents for most purposes under law. (*Cyber Law*)

A computer-based version of a paper form. (*Internet and E-commerce*).

Electronic registry. 'Electronic registry' means an electronic repository or storage system in which the information or documents are received, stored, protected and preserved in electronic form. [Limited Liability Partnership Rules, 2009, R. 2(viii)]

"ELECTRONIC REGISTRY" means an electronic repository or storage system of the Central Government in which the information or documents are received, stored, protected and preserved in electronic form. [R. 2(1)(g) of the Companies (Registration Offices and Fees) Rules, 2014; R. 2(1)(j) of the Companies (Specification of Definitions Details) Rules, 2014]

Electronic roadshow. A management presentation to qualified investors following delivery of prospectuses. Content is limited to materials in the prospectus but it is (usually) good publicity. (*Cyber Law*)

Electronic self-help. Under UCITA, right of licensor to disable software or information availability on the licensee's system, such as when the licensee's access to programs or databases is refused by the licensor's server or software use is not reauthorized. (*Cyber Law*)

Electronic service provider. Means a person who provides technologies or processes to enable a product seller to engage in advertising or selling goods or services to a consumer and includes any online market place or online auction sites. [Consumer Protection Act, 2019 (35 of 2019), section 2(17)]

Electronic signature. 'Electronic signature' means authentication of any electronic record by a subscriber by means of the electronic technique specified in the Second Schedule and includes digital signature. [Information Technology Act (21 of 2001) S. 2(ta) as inserted by amending Act (10 of 2009), S. 4E]

An electronic symbol or process attached to or logically associated with a record, used with the intent to sign the record. (*Cyber Law*)

An electronic sound, symbol or process attached to or logically associated with a contract or other record and executed or adopted by a person with the intent to sign the record. Not associated with any particular technology. (*Internet and E-commerce*)

Electronic Signatures in Global and National Commerce Act. Federal legislation on electronic signatures. (*Cyber Law*)

Electronic surveillance. The use of telephone tapping, hidden microphones (bugging) or cameras, or similar means to obtain evidence.

Electronic transmission. Means a communication—

(a) delivered by—

(i) facsimile telecommunication or electronic mail when directed to the facsimile number or electronic mail address, respectively, which the company or the officer has provided from time to time for sending communications to the company or the officer respectively;

(ii) posting of an electronic message board or network that the company or the officer has designated for such communications, and which transmission shall be validly delivered upon the posting; or

(iii) other means of electronic communication, in respect of which the company or the officer has put in place reasonable systems to verify that the sender is the person purporting to send the transmission; and

(b) that creates a record that is capable of retention, retrieval and review, and which may thereafter be rendered into clearly legible tangible form. [R. 35(2) of the Companies (Incorporation) Rules, 2014; R. 35(4) of the Companies (Incorporation) Rules, 2014]

Electronic voting system. For the purposes of Rule 20 of the Companies (Management & Administration) Rules, 2014, the expression 'electronic voting system' means a 'secured system' based process of display of electronic ballots, recording of votes of the members and the number of votes polled in favour or against, such that the entire voting exercised by way of electronic means gets registered and counted in an electronic registry in a centralized server with adequate 'cyber security'. [*Explanation* (*i*) to Rule 20(2) of the Companies (Management & Administration) Rules, 2014 as it stood prior to substitution by Companies (Management and Administration) Amendment Rules, 2016]

Electronic warfare. Any military action involving the use of electromagnetic and directed energy to control the electromagnetic spectrum or attack the enemy. Also called EW. (*Cyber Law*)

Electronics intelligence (ELINT). Technical and geolocation intelligence derived from foreign non-communications, electromagnetic radiations emanating from sources other than nuclear detonations or radioactive sources. (*Cyber Law*)

Electronics security. The protection resulting from all measures designed to deny unauthorized persons information of value that might be derived from their interception and study of non-communications electromagnetic radiations (radar). This term is also (more loosely) used to connote the topical area or task specialization focusing on achieving this type of protection. (*Cyber Law*)

Elementary education. Means education in such subject and upto such standard as may be prescribed. [Tamil Nadu Compulsory Elementary Education Act (TN Act No. 33 of 1995), S. 2(3)]

'Elementary education' means the education from first class to eighth class. [Right of Children to Free and Compulsory Education Act (35 of 2009), S. 2(f)]

Elementary school. Means a school recognised as an elementary school by the competent authority and includes any elementary school in existence on the date of commencement of this Act which has been recognised as such by the Director of Elementary Education or by any authority of the Education Department. [Tamil Nadu Compulsory Elementary Education Act (TN Act No. 33 of 1994), S. 2(4)]

Eligibility. The quality of being eligible.

"Eligibility": qualification. The eligibility for the post may at times be misunderstood to mean qualification. In fact, eligibility connotes the minimum criteria for selection, that may be laid down by the executive authority/legislature by way of any statue or rules, while the term "qualification", may connote any additional norms laid down by the authorities. [*State of Gujarat* v. *Arvindkumar T. Tiwari*, (2012) 9 SCC 545, para 6].

Eligible. Worthy of choice; desirable; that may be selected, or elected; worthy of choice or adoption; suitable. (*Standard Dict.*); the quality of being eligible.

Applied to the selection of persons, the word has two meanings *i.e.* "legally qualified," or "fit to be chosen."

Eligible articles or things. Means all handmade articles or things, which are of artistic value and which requires the use of wood as the main raw material. [Taxation Laws (Amendment) Ordinance (2 of 2003), S. 3, *Expln.* 7(b)]

Eligible assessee. For the purposes of section 54GB of Act 43 of 1961, 'eligible assessee' means an individual or a Hindu undivided family. [S. 54GB(6)(a) of the Income-tax Act, 1961 (43 of 1961) as inserted (w.e.f. 1-4-2013) by the Finance Act, 2012 (23 of 2012)]

Eligible borrower. Means the energy service company, empanelled by the Bureau or joint venture of energy service companies to whom credit facility has been provided by the participating financial institution, referred to Rule 5. [Energy Conservations (Partial Risk Guarantee Fund for Energy Efficiency) Rules, 2016, R. 2(1)(e)].

Eligible duties. For the purposes of sub-sections (3), (4) and (6), the expression "eligible duties" means—

(*i*) the additional duty of excise leviable under section 3 of the Additional Duties of Excise (Goods of Special Importance) Act, 1957 (58 of 1957);

(*ii*) the additional duty leviable under sub-section (1) of section 3 of the Customs Tariff Act, 1975 (51 of 1975);

(*iii*) the additional duty leviable under sub-section (5) of section 3 of the Customs Tariff Act, 1975 (51 of 1975);

(*iv*) the additional duty of excise leviable under section 3 of the Additional Duties of Excise (Textile and Textile Articles) Act, 1978 (40 of 1978);

(*v*) the duty of excise specified in the First Schedule to the Central Excise Tariff Act, 1985 (5 of 1986);

(*vi*) the duty of excise specified in the Second Schedule to the Central Excise Tariff Act, 1985 (5 of 1986); and

(*vii*) the National Calamity Contingent Duty leviable under section 136 of the Finance Act, 2001 (14 of 2001),

in respect of inputs held in stock and inputs contained in semi-finished or finished goods held in stock on the appointed day. [Central Goods and Service Tax Act (12 of 2017), s. 140(10), *Explanation 1*].

Eligible duties and taxes. For the purposes of sub-section (5), the expression "eligible duties and taxes" means—

(*i*) the additional duty of excise leviable under section 3 of the Additional Duties of Excise (Goods of Special Importance) Act, 1957 (58 of 1957);

(*ii*) the additional duty leviable under sub-section (1) of section 3 of the Customs Tariff Act, 1975 (51 of 1975);

(*iii*) the additional duty leviable under sub-section (5) of section 3 of the Customs Tariff Act, 1975 (51 of 1975);

(*iv*) the additional duty of excise leviable under section 3 of the Additional Duties of Excise (Textile and Textile Articles) Act, 1978 (40 of 1978);

(*v*) the duty of excise specified in the First Schedule to the Central Excise Tariff Act, 1985 (5 of 1986);

(*vi*) the duty of excise specified in the Second Schedule to the Central Excise Tariff Act, 1985 (5 of 1986);

(*vii*) the National Calamity Contingent Duty leviable under section 136 of the Finance Act, 2001 (14 of 2001); and

(*viii*) the service tax leviable under section 66B of the Finance Act, 1994 (32 of 1994),

in respect of inputs and input services received on or after the appointed day. [Central Goods and Service Tax Act (12 of 2017), S. 140(10), *Explanation 2*].

For removal of doubts, it is hereby clarified that the expression "ELIGIBLE DUTIES AND TAXES" excludes any cess which has not been specified in *Explanation 1* or *Explanation 2* and any cess which is collected as additional duty of customs under sub-section (1) of section 3 of the Customs Tariff Act, 1975 (51 of 1975). [Central Goods and Services Tax Act (12 of 2017), S. 140, *Explanation 3*].

Eligible company. For the purposes of section 54GB of Act 43 of 1961, 'eligible company' means a company which fulfils the following conditions, namely:—

(i) it is a company incorporated in India during the period from the 1st day of April of the previous year relevant to the assessment year in which the capital gain arises to the due date of furnishing of return of income under section 139(1) by the assessee;

(ii) it is engaged in the business of manufacture of an article or a thing;

(iii) it is a company in which the assessee has more than fifty per cent share capital or more than fifty per cent voting rights after the subscription in shares by the assessee; and

(iv) it is a company which qualifies to be a small or medium enterprise under the Micro, Small and Medium Enterprises Act, 2006 (27 of 2006). [S. 54GB(6)(b) of the Income-tax Act, 1961 (43 of 1961) as inserted (w.e.f. 1-4-2013) by the Finance Act, 2012 (23 of 2012)]

"ELIGIBLE COMPANY" means a public company as referred to in section 76(1) of Act 18 of 2013, having a net worth of not less than one hundred crore rupees or a turnover of not less than five hundred crore rupees and which has obtained the prior consent of the company in general meeting by means of a special resolution and also filed the said resolution with the Registrar of Companies before making any invitation to the Public for acceptance of deposits: *Provided* that an eligible company, which is accepting deposits within the limits specified under section 180(1)(c) of Act 18 of 2013, may accept deposits by means of an ordinary resolution. [R. 2(1)(e) of the Companies (Acceptance of Deposits) Rules, 2014]

Eligible co-operative bank. Means a cooperative bank the law for the time being governing which provides that—

(i) an order for the winding up, or an order sanctioning a scheme of compromise or arrangement or of amalgamation or reconstruction, of the bank may be made only with the previous sanction in writing of the Reserve Bank;

(ii) an order for the winding up of the bank shall be made if also required by the Reserve bank in circumstances referred to in Section 13D;

(iii) if so required by the Reserve Bank in public interest or for preventing the affairs of the bank being conducted in a manner detrimental to the interests of the depositors or for securing the proper management of the bank, an order shall be made for the supersession of the committee of management or other managing body (by whatever name called) of the bank and the appointment of an administrator therefor for such period or periods not exceeding 5 years in the aggregate as may from time to time be specified by the Reserve Bank;

(iv) an order for the winding up of the bank or an order sanctioning a scheme of compromise or arrangement or of amalgamation or reconstruction or an order for the supersession of the committee of management or other managing body (by whatever name called) of the bank and the appointment of an administrator therefore made with the previous sanction in writing or on the requisition of the Reserve Bank shall not be liable to be called in question in any manner; and

(v) the liquidator or the insured bank or the transferee bank, as the case may be, shall be under an obligation to repay the Corporation in the circumstances to the extent and in the manner referred to in Section 21. [Deposit Insurance and Credit Guarantee Corporation Act (47 of 1961), S. 2(gg)]

Eligible equity share. "ELIGIBLE EQUITY SHARE" means,—

(i) any equity share in a company being a constituent of BSE-500 Index of the Stock Exchange, Mumbai as on the 1st day of March, 2003 and the transactions of purchase and sale of such equity share are entered into on a recognised stock exchange in India;

(ii) any equity share in a company allotted through a public issue on or after the 1st day of March, 2003 and listed in a recognised stock exchange in India before the 1st day of

March, 2004 and the transaction of sale of such share is entered into on a recognised stock exchange in India. [Income-tax Act (43 of 1961), S. 10(36), *Expln.*]

Eligible fixed capital investment. "Eligible fixed capital investment" (EFCI) means investment made in land, new buildings, new plant and machinery and imported second hand machinery from outside the country and installation expenditure capitalized for plant and machinery and installation capitalised for plant and machinery's capitalized interest during construction not exceeding 5% of the total fixed capital investment; and technical know-how fees or drawing fees paid in lump sum to foreign collaborators or foreign suppliers as approved by the Government of India or paid to laboratories recognized by the State Government or Central Government and rail sidings, rolling stock, racks and railway engines, owned by the unit. [Rajasthan Sales Tax New Incentive Scheme for Industries, 1989, Clause 2(e) as cited in *Commercial Tax Officer, Rajasthan* v. *Binani Cements Limited,* (2014) 8 SCC 319, para 11].

Eligible households. Means households covered under the priority households and the Antyodaya Anna Yojana referred to in section 3(1) of Act 20 of 2013. [S. 2(3) of the National Food Security Act, 2013 (20 of 2013)]

Eligible industrial unit. 'Eligible industrial unit' means—

(i) a new industrial unit or expansion or diversification of the existing unit, which—

- (i) has obtained certificate of registration under the Act;
- (ii) is not a public sector undertaking where the Central Government held 51% or more shares;
- (iii) is not availing incentive of interest-free loan from the Industries Department for investment after the 1st day of April, 1988;
- (iv) is not included in Schedule III appended to these Rules except the tiny units set up in a rural area on or after 1-4-1992, in which capital investment in plant and machinery including market price of plant and machinery taken on base or otherwise, does not exceed rupees five lacks, shall not form part of Schedule III;
- (v) is not availing or has not availed the incentive of exemption under section 13 of the Act.

(ii) a sick industrial unit recommended by the High-Powered Committee for the grant of fiscal relief either in the form of exemption from the payment of sales tax or purchase tax or both or deferment of tax. [Haryana General Sales Tax Rules, 1975, R. 28-A. (2)(f) as cited in *State of Haryana* v. *Bharti Teletech Limited,* (2014) 3 SCC 556, para 18].

Eligible officer. Means an officer eligible to be considered for promotion to these posts of Principal Director, Director, Joint Director, Deputy Director, Section Officer or Assistant Section Officer, as the case may be, in accordance with Rules 7 and 8 of these rules, as per the instructions issued by the Government from time to time. [Armed Forces Headquarters Civil Service Rules, 2018, R. 2(e)].

Eligible start-up. For the purposes of this section, "ELIGIBLE START-UP" means a company or a limited liability partnership engaged in eligible business which fulfils the following conditions, namely:—

(*a*) it is incorporated on or after the 1st day of April, 2016 but before the 1st day of April, 2019;

(*b*) the total turnover of its business does not exceed twenty-five crore rupees in any of the previous year beginning on or after the 1st day of April, 2016 and ending on the 31st day of March, 2021;

(*c*) it holds a certificate of eligible business from the Inter-Ministerial Board of Certification as notified in the Official Gazette by the Central Government. [Income-tax Act (43 of 1961), S. 80-IAC, *Explanation (ii)*].

Eligible project or scheme. Means such project or scheme for promoting the social and economic welfare of, or the uplift of, the public as the Central Government may, by notification in the Official Gazette, specify in this behalf on the recommendations of the National Committee. [Income-tax Act (43 of 1961), S. 35 AC (6), *Expln.* (b)]

Eligible transaction. 'ELIGIBLE TRANSACTION' means any transaction—

(A) carried out electronically on screenbased systems through a stock broker or sub-broker or such other intermediary registered under Section 12 of the Securities and Exchange Board of India Act, 1992 in accordance with the provisions of the Securities Contracts (Regulation) Act, 1956 or the Securities and Exchange Board of India Act, 1992 or the Depositories Act, 1996 and the rules, regulations or bye-laws made on directions issued under those Acts or by banks or mutual funds on a recognised stock exchange; and

(B) which is supported by a time stamped contract note issued by such stock broker or sub-broker or such other intermediary to every client indicating in the contract note the unique client identity number allotted under any Act referred to in sub-clause (*A*) and permanent account number allotted under this Act. [Income-tax Act (43 of 1961), S. 43(5)(e), *Expln.*1(i)]

"ELIGIBLE TRANSACTION" for the purposes of proviso (e) to section 43(5) of Act 43 of 1961, the expression 'eligible transaction' means any transaction,—

(A) carried out electronically on screen-based systems through member or an intermediary, registered under the bye-laws, rules and regulations of the recognised association for trading in commodity derivative in accordance with the provisions of the Forward Contracts (Regulation) Act, 1952 (74 of 1952) and the rules, regulations or bye-laws made or directions issued under that Act on a recognised association; and

(B) which is supported by a time stamped contract note issued by such member or intermediary to every client indicating in the contract note, the unique client identity number allotted under the Act, rules, regulations or bye-laws referred to in sub-clause (A), unique trade number and permanent account number allotted under the Act 43 of 1961. [(w.e.f. 1-4-2014) *Explanation 2(ii)* to section 43(5) of the Income-tax Act, 1961 (43 of 1961)]

Elope. To run away, escape privately, especially used of a woman, either married or unmarried, who runs away with a lover.

"ELOPE" is never used in any other sense than criminally.

Else. Besides; except that mentioned other than the person, thing, place *etc.* mentioned.

Elsewhere. In another place; in any other place. (*Burril*)

Elucidate. Rendering lucid; explaining. [CPC (5 of 1908), O. XXVI, R. 9].

Elude. To avoid by artifice; to evade; to baffle; to remain undiscovered (as), to elude deduction; to elude an officer.

E-mail. E-mail is a way of sending messages electronically to other people from your P.C. (*Information Technology*)

E-MAIL. Also called electronic mail, refers to messages sent over the Internet. E-mail can be sent and received via newer types of wireless phones, but you generally need to have a specific e-mail account. (*Telecommunication*)

E-MAIL. (Electronic Mail). Messages, usually text, sent from one person to another via computer. E-mail can also be sent automatically to a large number of addresses. (*Matisse Enzer-Glossary of Internet Terms*)

E-mail accounts (POP3). These are your email boxes on a server that can be accessed directly to retrieve your mail using such programs as Outlook Express and Netscape Mail. Each POP3 has its own password to ensure privacy, so each of your employees could have their own e-mail address. (*Cyber Law*)

E-mail address. The unique private Internet address to which your e-mail is sent. Takes the form of user@host. (*Information Technology*)

E-mail aliases. Your main POP account for your domain allows the system to capture any name that may be sent to your domain name. This means as long as the @yourdomain.com is proper, any name in front of it will be delivered to your main POP account. Each alias can be forwarded or redirected to any other address of your choice. (*Cyber Law*)

E-mail forwarding. Any e-mail address at your domain may be configured to forward to any other real internet e-mail address. For example, sales @yourname.com can forward to you@aol.com if you like. (*Cyber Law*)

E-mail mini mailing lists. Use it to send your customers news and updates about your product or services without e-mailing each one separately. Visitors can add themselves to your list or take themselves off automatically. You send one e-mail and it goes to every e-mail address on the list. The system is capable of multiple lists, each of which can handle up to 1,000 e-mail addresses and outgoing messages up to 75K each. (*Cyber Law*)

Emancipation. An act by which a person who was once in the power or under the control of another is rendered free (*Burril*); setting free from subjection, dependence or control; the state of freedom, liberation.

Emasculation. The action of depriving of virility. [IPC (45 of 1860), S. 320].

Embankment. "EMBANKMENT" includes— every bank, dam, wall and dyke made or used for excluding water from, or for retaining water upon, any land; every sluice, spur groyne, training-wall or other work annexed to, or portion of, any such embankment; every bank, dam, dyke, wall, groyne or spur made or erected for the protection of any such embankment or of any land from erosion or overflow by or of rivers, tides, waves or waters; and also all buildings intended for purposes of inspection and supervision. [Ben Act II of 1882 (*Embankment*), S. 3]

"EMBANKMENT" means any embankment constructed for the purpose of excluding, regulating or retaining water, and includes all earthen walls, dams, canals, drains, piers, groins, sluices, buildings, water gauges, benchmarks and other works subsidiary to any such embankment; Bur. Act IV of 1909 (*Embankment*), S. 3, cl. 1.

A structure raised to hold water back. [Salt Cess Act (49 of 1953), S. 2(c) (i)]; [Indian Railways Act (9 of 1890), S. 7(1)].

A structure raised to hold water, back [Salt Cess Act (49 of 1953), S. 2(c) (i)]; [Indian Railways Act (24 of 1989), S. 11(a)].

Embargo. Prohibition to sail; a restrain and detention by public authority; an order of the government prohibiting the departure of ships or goods from the ports of the country; a detention of vessels in port. *Embargo* is a prohibition upon shipping, not to go out of any part on a war breaking out, & c.

An embargo may be measure of public utility, hostility, or defence; and sometimes, like reprisal, retortion and pacific blockade, is resorted to as a mode of putting stress upon a weaker State.

Embarrass. To hinder through perplexity; to entangle; to render intricate "Embarrass" applied to pleadings means that matter is introduced in pleading that a party is not entitled to make use of. [*per* JESSEL, *M.R., Heugh* v. *Chamberlian*, 25 WR 742. A Defence is not "embarrassing" merely because in consistent statements of facts are alleged. (Re *Morgan*, 35 Ch D 492)

Embarrassed, Become. To tall into difficulties [Indian Contract Act (9 of 1872), S. 133, ill. (d)]; to be placed in perplexity.

Embarrassment. Perplexity, confusion or constraint. [CPC (5 of 1908), O. I, R. 2].

Embezzle. Divert funds fraudulently to one's own use.

Embezzlement. Dishonest misappropriation of property by a person, who comes in possession thereof lawfully. [Indian Evidence Act (1 of 1872), S. 126, *Expln*., ill. (c)].

Emblem. "EMBLEM" means any emblem, seal, flag, insignia, coat-of-arms or pictorial representation specified in the schedule. [Emblems and Names (Prevention of Improper Use) Act (12 of 1950), S. 2(a)]

Symbol; heraldic device.

Embodied. Incorporated in [T.P. Act (4 of 1882), S. 58(c)]; included in a body [Army Act (46 of 1950), S. 2(1)(e)]; became a limb of.

Embossed. Prefaced, ornamented or finished by embossing. [Indian Post Office Act (6 of 1898), S. 2(g)].

Embryo. Means a developing human organism after fertilisation till the end of eight weeks (fifty-six days). [Pre-Natal Diagnostic Techniques (Regulation and Prevention of Misuse) Act (57 of 1994), S. 2(bb)]"Embryo" means a developing or developed organism after fertilisation till the end of fifty-six days from the day of fertilisation. [Assisted Reproductive Technology (Regulation) Act, 2021 (42 of 2021), section 2(1)(f)]

"Embryo" means a developing or developed organism after fertilisation till the end of fifty-six days. [Surrogacy (Regulation) Act, 2021 (47 of 2021), section 2(1)(j)]

Embryologist means a person who possesses any post-graduate medical qualification or doctoral degree in the field of embryology or clinical embryology from a recognised university with not less than two years of clinical experience. [Surrogacy (Regulation) Act, 2021 (47 of 2021), section 2(1)(k)]

Emergency. Any event or occasional combination of circumstances which call for immediate action or remedy; pressing necessity; exigency; a sudden or unexpected happening; an unforeseen occurrence or condition.

An unforeseen combination of circumstances or the resulting state that calls for immediate action.

The expression "emergency" even if understood in its common parlance would mean an exigent situation. Black's Law Dictionary, 12th Edn. as cited in *Ramlila Maidan Incident, In re*, (2012) 5 SCC 1, para 133].

A serious, unexpected, and potentially dangerous situation requiring immediate action. [Concise Oxford Dictionary, 11th Edn. as cited in *Ramlila Maidan Incident, In re*, (2012) 5 SCC 1, para 133].

Emergency provision. A provision to meet the exigencies of a particular emergency.

For Emergency Provisions in India, See, The Constitution of India, Part XVIII.

Emergency risks. 'EMERGENCY RISKS' means such risks arising from—

(i) action taken by an enemy or action taken in combating an enemy or in repelling an imagined attack by an enemy.;

(ii) any explosion or fire which involves any explosives or munition or other dangerous things required for the purposes of defence against any action of the enemy and which happens, or is caused by, through, or in connection with, the manufacture, storage or transportation of any such explosives, munition or other dangerous things;

(iii) measures taken under proper authority to avoid the spreading of, or otherwise to mitigate, the consequences of damage occurring (whether accidentally or not) as the direct result of any such action as is described in subclause (i) of any such explosion or fire as is described in sub-clause (ii);

(iv) precautionary or preparatory measures taken under proper authority with a view to preventing or hindering the carrying out of any attack by an enemy, being measures involving risk to property;

(v) precautionary or preparatory measures involving the doing of work on land and taken under proper authority in any way in anticipation of enemy action being measures involving risk to property;

(vi) precautionary or preparatory measures taken under proper authority with a view to denying facilities to an enemy, being measures involving damage to or diminution of the value of property. [Emergency Risks (Factories) Insurance Act (63 of 1962), S. 2(l); Emergency Risks (Goods) Insurance Act (62 of 1962), S. 2(f)]

Emeritus is used with a professional title to indicate that the person bearing it has retired but keeps the title as an honour.

Emigrant. "EMIGRANT" means any person who emigrates or has emigrated or who has been registered as an emigrant under the Emigration Act, and includes any dependent of an emigrant, but does not include—(i) any person emigrating to a country in which he has resided for not less than five years or the wife or child of such person, or (ii) the wife or child of any person who has lawfully emigrated when such wife or child departs for the purpose of joining such person. (Act 7 of 1922, S. 2)

"EMIGRANT" means any citizen of India who intends to emigrate or emigrates, or has emigrated but does not include—

(i) a dependent of an emigrant, whether such dependent accompanies the emigrant or departs subsequently for the purpose of joining the emigrant in the country to which that emigrant has lawfully emigrated.

(ii) any person who has resided outside India at any time after attaining the age of eighteen years, for not less than three years or the spouse or child of such person. [Emigration Act (31 of 1983), S. 2(d)]

A person leaving a country for permanent residence elsewhere. [Emigration Act (7 of 1922), S. 2(1)(aa)].

Emigrant conveyance. Means any conveyance specially chartered for conveyance of emigrants or for conveying emigrants exceeding such number as may be prescribed :

Provided that the Central Government may by notification, declare that any conveyance conveying emigrants to such place as may be specified in the notification shall not be deemed to be an emigrant conveyance. [Emigration Act (31 of 1983), S. 2(e)]

Emigrant labourer. A person who has last entered Assam as an assistant emigrant and is employed on a tea estate. This term does not include a person who, having accompanied an assistant emigrant to Assam as a child dependent on him, has become an adult and is so employed. [Tea Districts Emigrant Act (22 of 1932), S. 2(h) (*The Act stands repealed by the Act 50 of 1970*)

Emigrant ship. Any ship specially chartered for the conveyance of emigrants or conveying emigrants exceeding a prescribed number. [Indian Emigration Act (7 of 1922), S. 2(cc) (*Repealed by Act No. 31 of 1983, S. 45*)]

Emigrate is to remove from one country or state to another, for the purpose of residence, employment or labour.

"EMIGRATE" and "EMIGRATION" mean the departure by sea out of British India of—(i) any person who departs under an agreement to work for hire in any country beyond the limits of India, and (ii) any person who is assisted to depart, otherwise than by a relative, if he departs, for the purpose or with the intention of working for hire or engaging in agriculture in any country beyond the limits of India. [Emigration Act (7 of 1922), S. 2]

Emigration. "EMIGRATION" means the departure out of India of any person with a view to taking up any employment (whether or not an agreement or other arrangement to take up such employment and whether with or without the assistance of a recruiting agent or employer) in any country or place outside India. [Emigration Act (31 of 1983), S. 2(f)]

The act of changing one's domicile from one country or state to another.

Leaving one's country to take up permanent residence in other country.

Eminent. The word 'eminent' means, rising above others, conspicuous, distinguished. *Midhuna Nathan* v. *State of T.N.,* AIR 1996 Mad 178, 188.

Eminent domain. The inherent power of a governmental entity to take privately owned property, especially land, and convert it to public use, subject to reasonable compensation for the taking.

The right of the State or the Sovereign to its or his own property is absolute while that of the Subject or citizen to his property is only paramount, the citizen holds his property subject always to the right of the sovereign to take it for a public purpose. This right is called "eminent domain".

This expression refers to the power of the sovereign to take property for public use without the owner's consent upon making just compensation. *Coffee Board* v. *Commissioner of Commercial Taxes*, AIR 1988 SC 1487, 1498.

Emissary. Person sent usually on an odious or underhand mission; one sent on some secret state business.

Emission. "EMISSION" means any solid or liquid or gaseous substance coming out of any chimney, duct or flue or any other outlet. [Air (Prevention and Control of Pollution) Act (14 of 1981), S. 2(j)]

"EMISSIONS" means the release of green house gases and/or their precursors into the atmosphere over a specified area and period of time. [United Nations Conference on Environment and Development—Frame Work Convention on Climate Change, May 9, 1992]

An act or instance of emitting. [Indian Wireless Telegraphy Act (17 of 1933), S. 2(1)].

Emolument. Salary; profits from an office or employment.

Profits or perquisites from office, employment or labour [Employees' Provident Funds and Miscellaneous Provisions Act (19 of 1952), S. 2(b); 112(3)(a), Constitution of India, Art. 59(3)]

'EMOLUMENTS' means and includes—

(i) pay, other than special pay granted in view of his personal qualifications, which has been sanctioned for a post held by him substantively or in an officiating capacity (including temporary capacity under emergency provisions) or to which he is entitled by reason of his position in a cadre:

(ii) special pay, dearness pay and personal pay; and

(iii) any other remuneration which may be specially claused as emoluments by the Government. Tamil Nadu Pension Rules, (1978), R. 30(1) as cited in *Kallakkurichi Taluk Retired Officials Association, Tamil Nadu* v. *State of T.N.*, (2013) 2 SCC 772, para 16].

The word 'emoluments' for the purpose of R. 31 of the Pension Rules relating to Government servant would mean the pay which he is drawing as defined in R. 9 (21)(9)(i) of the Fundamental Rules. *Govt. of AP* v. *Syed Yousuddin Ahmed*, (1997) 7 SCC 24, para 8 : AIR 1997 SC 3439. [A.P. Revised Pension Rules, 1980, R. 31]

The 'Suspension allowance' comes within definition of 'emoluments' under Rule 49 of the Rules. *R.P. Kapur* v. *Union of India*, (1999) 8 SCC 110, para 25 : AIR 1999 SCC 3589. [Railway Services (Pension) Rules, 1993, R. 49]

"EMOLUMENT" the term 'emolument' is a wider term than basic pay. It generally refers to the salary or profits from employment or office. But the term 'emolument' is not used in the general sense in the service Rules relating to pension. The word 'emolument' is defined for purposes of pension. In fact, all rules governing pension, define the word 'emolument' by giving a special or specific meaning, for purposes of pension calculation. Where a word is defined, there can be no reference or reliance on any general meaning. *N. D. P. Namboodripad* v. *UOI*, AIR 2007 SC 1782 : 2007 AIR SCW 2972.

For the purposes of this section, "EMOLUMENTS" means any sum paid or payable to an employee in lieu of his employment by whatever name called, but does not include—

(*a*) any contribution paid or payable by the employer to any pension fund or provident fund or any other fund for the benefit of the employee under any law for the time being in force; and

(*b*) any lump-sum payment paid or payable to an employee at the time of termination of his service or superannuation or voluntary retirement, such as gratuity, severance pay, leave encashment, voluntary retrenchment benefits, commutation of pension and the like. [Income-tax Act (4 of 1961), S. 80JJAA, *Explanation (iii)*].

Emolument Emergency treatment. For the purposes of this section "EMERGENCY TREATMENT" includes transportation of the person with mental illness to a nearest mental health establishment for assessment. [Mental Healthcare Act (10 of 2017), S. 94, *Explanation*].

Emergent year. The epoch or date whence any people begin to compute their time.

Emerging area of knowledge. In the context of De-Novo Institutions means such specialized/niche areas of knowledge which are considered desirable and useful and not usually imparted in the country. [UGC (Institutions Deemed to be Universities) Regulations, 2019, Regn. 2(2.08)]

Emotional distress (mental distress). Pain or suffering effecting the mind often caused by physical injury, may be actionable as a ground for divorce or recoverable as damages.

Employ. To engage or use the services of (a person). To keep (a person) in service; to make use of [IPC (45 of 1860), S. 14 and CrPC 1973 (2 of 1974), S. 197(1)(a)]; to apply to a purpose. [Indian Trusts Act (2 of 1882), S. 4(b)].

Employed. The expression 'employed' in S. 1(3), Employees, Provident Fund Act (10 of 1952) taken in the context of the Act as a whole would imply subject to the statutory definition in S. 2(f), the existence of the relationship of master and servant between an employer and worker. It would certainly exclude a contractor from the scope of the definition of an employee in S. 2(f). *Annamalai Mudaliar & Bros.* v. *Regional Provident Fund Commissioner,* AIR 1955 Mad 387, 391.

The word 'employed' does not only connote employed on wages but also being occupied or engaged in some form of activity. *State Govt. Madhya Pradesh* v. *Jiwa Bhai Nathabai,* AIR 1953 Nag 172. [Factories Act (63 of 1948), S. 66(1)(b)].

The word 'employed' has got two meanings : (1) They are engaged to do a particular work on a piece rate basis. (2) There is a contract of service between the employer and the worker.

The test to be applied in deciding whether the relationship of master and servant was present is whether the time of the person who worked was at the disposal of the master. *K. Kesava Reddiar* v. *Labour Appellate, Tribunal,* AIR 1957 Mad 632, 634.

The word 'employed' connotes that there is a relationship brought about by express or implied contract of service. The employee renders service for which he is engaged by the employer and the employer pays the employee in cash or paid as agreed between them or statutorily prescribed. *Workman Food Corporation of India*, v. *Food Corporation of India*, AIR 1985 SC 670, 674.

Employed for payment. Though Section 77 does not indicate by whom the extra persons were employed for payment to bring it under the term 'corrupt practice' by reading Sec. 77 with Rules 117, 118 it is clear that the employment for payment must be by the candidate in the election or his agent. *Rananjaya Singh* v. *Baijnath Singh*, AIR 1954 SC 749, 751. [Representation of the People Act (43 of 1951), Ss. 77, 123(7) and Rules 117, 118]

An employee who is engaged in any work or operation which is incidentally connected with the main industry of the employer would be a workman provided the other requirements of S. 2(3) are satisfied. *J.K. Cotton Spinning and Weaving Mills*

Co. Ltd. v. *Labour Appellate Tribunal*, AIR 1964 SC 737, 740. [Workmen's Compensation Act (8 of 1923), S. 2(3)]

Employed person. Includes the legal representative of a deceased employed person. [Payment of Wages Act (4 of 1936), S. 2(i)]

Employed to work. See, [Constitution of India, Art. 24].

Employee. "Employee" means, any person (other than an apprentice engaged under the Apprentices Act, 1961 (52 of 1961), employed on wages by an establishment to do any skilled, semi-skilled or unskilled, manual, operational, supervisory, managerial, administrative, technical or clerical work for hire or reward, whether the terms of employment be express or implied, and also includes a person declared to be an employee by the appropriate Government, but does not include any member of the Armed Forces of the Union. [Code on Wages, 2019 (29 of 2019), section 2(k)]

"Employee" means any person (other than an apprentice engaged under the Apprentices Act, 1961) employed on wages by an establishment, either directly or through a contractor, to do any skilled, semi-skilled or unskilled, manual, operational, supervisory, managerial, administrative, technical, clerical or any other work, whether the terms of employment be express or implied, and also includes a person declared to be an employee by the appropriate Government, but does not include any member of the Armed Forces of the Union (52 of 1961) [Code on Social Security, 2020 (36 of 2020), section 2(26) and its proviso]

"Employee" means any person (other than an apprentice engaged under the Apprentices Act, 1961 (52 of 1961)) employed by an industrial establishment to do any skilled, semi-skilled or unskilled, manual, operational, supervisory, managerial, administrative, technical or clerical work for hire or reward, whether the terms of employment be express or implied, and also includes a person declared to be an employee by the appropriate Government, but does not include any member of the Armed Forces of the Union. [Industrial Relations Code, 2020 (35 of 2020), section 2(l)]

"Employee" means,--

(i) in respect of an establishment, a person (other than an apprentice engaged under the Apprentices Act, 1961 (52 of 1961)) employed on wages by an establishment to do any skilled, semi-skilled, unskilled, manual, operational, supervisory, managerial, administrative, technical, clerical or any other work, whether the terms of employment be express or implied; and

(ii) a person declared to be an employee by the appropriate Government, but does not include any member of the Armed Forces of the Union. [Occupational Safety, Healthy & Working Conditions Code, 2020 (37 of 2020), section 2(1)(t) and its proviso]

Means any person who is employed for hire or reward to do any work, skilled or unskilled manual or clerical, in a scheduled employment in respect of which minimum rates of wages have been fixed; and includes an outworker to whom any articles or materials are given out by another person to be made up, cleaned, washed, altered, ornamented, finished, repaired, adapted or otherwise processed for sale for the purposes of the trade or business of that other person where the process is to be carried out either in the home of the out worker or in some other premises not being premises under the control and management of that other person; and also includes an employee declared to be an employee by the appropriate Government, but does not include any member of the Armed Forces of the Union. [Minimum Wages Act (11 of 1948), S. 2(i)]

"Employee" means a person employed at a workplace for any work on regular, temporary, *ad hoc* or daily wage basis, either directly or through an agent including a contractor, with or without the knowledge of the principal employer whether for remuneration or not, or working on a voluntary basis or otherwise, whether the terms of employment are express or implied and includes co-worker, a contract worker, probationer, trainee, apprentice or called by any other such name. [Sexual Harassment of Women at Workplace (Prevention, Prohibition and Redressal) Act (14 of 2013), S. 2(f)].

'EMPLOYEE' means any member of the teaching and nonteaching staff of a recognized school and includes Shikshan Sevak. [Maharashtra Employees of Private Schools (Conditions of Service) Regulation Act, 1977 (3 of 1978), S. 2(7) as cited in *Deepali Gundu Surwase* v. *Kranti Junior Adhyapak Mahavidyalaya*, (2013) 10 SC 324, para 19].

"EMPLOYEE" means any person who is employed for wages in any kind of work, manual or otherwise, in or in connection with a coal mine, and who gets his wages directly or indirectly from the employer, and includes—

(1) any person employed by or through a contractor in or in connection with a coal mine, and

(2) for the purposes of Coal Mines Provident Fund Scheme, also

  (i) any other person who is employed as sanitary worker, mali, teacher, or domestic servant in or in connection with a coal mine and who receives wages directly from the employer, and

  (ii) Any apprentice or trainee who receives stipend or other remuneration from the employer. [Coal Mines Provident Fund and Misc. Provisions Act (46 of 1948), S. 2(d)]

"EMPLOYEE" means any person who is employed for wages in any kind of work, manual or otherwise, in or in connection with the work of an establishment, and who gets his wages directly or indirectly from the employer, and includes any person—

(i) employed by or through a contractor in or in connection with the work of the establishment;

(ii) engaged as an apprentice, being an apprentice engaged under Apprentices Act, 1961, or under the standing orders of the establishment. [Employees' Provident Fund Act (19 of 1952), S. 2(f)]

"EMPLOYEE" means any person (other than apprentice) employed on a salary or wage not exceeding three thousand and five hundred rupees per mensem in any industry to do any skilled or unskilled manual, supervisory, managerial, administrative, technical or clerical work for hire or reward, whether the terms of employment be express or implied. [Payment of Bonus Act (21 of 1965), S. 2(13)]

"EMPLOYEE" means an employee participating in a provident fund, but does not include a personal or domestic servant. [Income Tax Act (43 of 1961), Sch. IV, Part A, R. 2(b)]

For the purposes of these guidelines—'EMPLOYEE' means :

(a) a permanent employee of the company,

(b) 'director' of a company, whether whole time or not, [Employees' Stock Option Plan or Scheme, 2001, S. 7, *Expln.* (i)]

"EMPLOYEE" means:—

(a) a permanent employee of the company working in India or out of India; or

(b) a director of the company, employed as a whole time director or executive director of a company. [Unlisted Companies (Issue of Sweat Equity Shares), Rules, 2003, R. 2(ii)]

"EMPLOYEE" means any person appointed by the University and includes teachers and other staff of the University. [University of Allahabad Act (26 of 2005), S. 3(k)] [Also see S. 2(l) of the Rajiv Gandhi National Aviation University Act, 2013 (26 of 2013); S. 3(j) of the Rani Lakshmi Bai Central Agricultural University Act, 2014 (10 of 2014)]

One who works for an employer; one who is employed; one who works for wages or salary or who is engaged in the service of another; one whose time and skill are occupied in the business of his employer; one who works for another for hire.

The term 'employee' will not include an ex employee or part employee. *State* v. *Giridharilal Bajaj,* AIR 1962 Bom 130, 32. [Companies Act (1 of 1956), S. 419].

The definition of the term 'employee' in S. 2(f) includes a person employed directly by employer, one employed through a contractor and also one employed in a factory or one employed in connection with the work of the factory and as such a home worker, by virtue of his rolling beedies thus involving in the activity connected with the work of the factory is employee. *P.M. Patel & Sons* v. *Union of India*, AIR 1987 SC 447, 450. [Employees' Provident Funds and Miscellaneous Provisions Act (19 of 1952), S. 2(f)].

"Employees" include workmen and nonworkmen. *All India Bank Officers' Confederation* v. *Union of India*, AIR 1989 SC 2049, 2045. [Banking Companies (Acquisition and Transfer of Undertakings) Act (5 of 1970), S. 9]

"Employee" means any person employed for wages in or in connection with the work of a factory or establishment and (1) who is directly employed by the principal employer on any work of, or incidental or preliminary to or connected with the work of the factory or establishment, whether such work is done by the employee in the factory or establishment or elsewhere; or (2) who is employed by or through an immediate employer on the premises of the factory or establishment or under supervision of the principal employer or his agent or work which is ordinarily part of the work of the factory or establishment or which is preliminary to the work carried on in or incidental to the purpose of the factory or establishment." *B.M. Lakshmanamurthy* v. *The Employees' State Insurance Corporation, Bangalore,* AIR 1974 SC 759.

It includes the contract labour employed by the Contractor. *Regional Director, Employees' State Insurance Corporation* v. *Kerala State Drugs and Pharmaceuticals Ltd.,* 1995 Supp. (3) SCC 148.

It includes ex-employee who is no more in the employment. *Pali Devi* v. *Chairman Managing Committee,* AIR 1996 SC 1589.

A teacher employed in a school and not doing the work of any skilled or unskilled or of a manual or clerical nature is not an employee under the Act. *Haryana Unrecognised Schools Association* v. *State of Haryana,* AIR 1996 SC 2108. [Minimum Wages Act (11 of 1948), S. 2(*i*)]

The word 'employee' under Section 2(e) of the Act does not include teachers employed in schools as they do not fall under category of skilled, semi-skilled, or unskilled, manual, supervisory, technical or clerical employees. They are also not employed in managerial or administrative capacity. *Ahmedabad Pvt. P.T. Association* v. *Administrative Officer*, AIR 2004 SC 1426, 1432, paras 22, 23. [Payment of Gratuity Act (39 of 1972), S. 2(e)]

The 'trainee' particularly whose services were confirmed later, would come within the ambit of 'employee'. *B.R. Chowdhury* v. *Indian Oil Corpn. Ltd.,* (2004) 2 SCC 177, 184, para 11.

The word 'employees' does not include apprentices, as ordinarily understood. *Employees S.I. Corporation* v. *Tata E. Co.,* AIR 1966 Pat 445, 447. [National Cadet Corps Act (31 of 1948), S. 6].

"EMPLOYEE" for the purposes of section 62(1)(b) of Act 18 of 2013 and rule 12 of the Companies (Share Capital & Debentures) Rules, 2014, 'employee' means—

(a) a permanent employee of the company who has been working in India or outside India; or

(b) a director of the company, whether a whole time director or not but excluding an independent director; or

(c) an employee as defined in clauses (a) or (b) of a subsidiary, in India or outside India, or of a holding company of the company or of an associate company but does not include—

(i) an employee who is a promoter or a person belonging to the promoter group; or

(ii) a director who either himself or through his relative or through any body corporate, directly or indirectly, holds more than ten percent of the outstanding equity shares of the company. [*Explanation* to rule 12(1) of the Companies (Share Capital & Debentures) Rules, 2014]

"EMPLOYEE" for the purposes of Rule 8 of the Companies (Share Capital & Debentures) Rules, 2014, the expression 'employee' means—

(a) a permanent employee of the company who has been working in India or outside India, for at least last one year; or

(b) a director of the company, whether a whole time director or not; or

(c) an employee or a director as defined in sub-clauses (a) or (b) above of a subsidiary, in India or outside India, or of a holding company of the company. [*Explanation* (*i*) to Rule 8(1) of the Companies (Share Capital & Debentures) Rules, 2014]

"EMPLOYEE" for the purposes of section 327 of Act 18 of 2013, the expression 'employee' does not include a workman. [*Explanation* (*b*) to section 327 of the Companies Act, 2013 (18 of 2013)]

"EMPLOYEE" means any person (other than an apprentice) who is employed for wages, whether the terms of such employment are express or implied, in any kind of work, manual or otherwise, in or in connection with the work of a factory, mine, oilfield, plantation, port, railway company, shop or other establishment to which this Act applies, but does not include any such person who holds a post under the Central Government or a State Government and is governed by any other Act or by any rules providing for payment of gratuity. [Payment of Gratuity Act, 1972 (39 of 1972), S. 2(e)]

"EMPLOYEE" the teachers are clearly not intended to be covered by the definition of the term 'employee' for the purpose of Payment of Gratuity Act 1972. *Ahmedabad Pvt. Primary Teachers' Association* v. *Administrative Officer*, AIR 2004 SC 1426 : 2004 AIR SCW 356.

"EMPLOYEE" means a person employed at a workplace for any work on regular, temporary, *ad hoc* or daily wage basis, either directly or through an agent, including a contractor, with or, without the knowledge of the principal employer, whether for remuneration or not, or working on a voluntary basis or otherwise, whether the terms of employment are express or implied and includes a co-worker, a contract worker, probationer, trainee, apprentice or called by any other such name. [S. 2(f) of the Sexual Harassment of Women at Workplace (Prevention, Prohibition & Redressal) Act, 2013 (14 of 2013)]

Employees stock option. Means the option given to the whole-time directors, officers or employees of a company, which gives such directors, officers or employees the benefit or right to purchase or subscribe at a future date, the securities offered by the company at a pre-determined price. [Companies Act (1 of 1956), S. 2(15A)]

"Employees' stock option" means the option given to the directors, officers or employees of a company or of its holding company or subsidiary company or companies, if any, which gives such directors, officers or employees, the benefit or right to purchase, or to subscribe for, the shares of the company at a future date at a pre-determined price. [Companies Act (18 of 2013), S. 2(37)].

"EMPLOYEES STOCK OPTION" means the option given to the directors, officers or employees of a company or of its holding company or subsidiary company or companies, if any, which gives such directors, officers or employees, the benefit or right to purchase, or to subscribe for, the shares of the company at a future date at a pre-determined price. [S. 2(37) of the Companies Act, 2013 (18 of 2013)]

Employer. One who employs; one who engages or keeps men in service; one who uses or engages the services of other persons for pay or salary.

"Employer" means a person who employs, whether directly or through any person, or on his behalf or on behalf of any person, one or more employees in his establishment and where the establishment is carried on by any department of the Central Government or the State Government, the authority specified, by the head of such department, in this behalf or where no authority, is so specified the head of the department and in relation to an establishment carried on by a local authority, the chief executive of that authority. [Code on Wages, 2019 (29 of 2019), section 2(l) with its inclusions]

"Employer" means a person who employs, whether directly or through any person, or on his behalf, or on behalf of any person, one or more employees in his establishment and where the establishment is carried on by any department of the Central Government or the State Government, the authority specified, by the head of such department, in this behalf or where no authority is so specified, the head of the department and in relation to an establishment carried on by a local authority, the chief executive of that authority. [Code on Social Security, 2020 (36 of 2020), section 2(27) with its inclusions]

"Employer" means a person who employs, whether directly or through any person, or on his behalf or on behalf of any person, one or more employee or worker in his establishment and where the establishment is carried on by any department of the Central Government or the State Government, the authority specified by the head of the department in this behalf or where no authority is so specified, the head of the department, and in relation to an establishment carried on by a local authority, the chief executive of that authority. [Industrial Relations Code, 2020 (35 of 2020), section 2(m) with its inclusions]

"Employer" means a person who employs, whether directly or through any person, or on his behalf, or on behalf of any person, one or more employees in his establishment and where the establishment is carried on by any Department of the Central Government or the State Government, the authority specified, by the head of such Department, in this behalf or where no authority, is so specified, the head of the Department and in relation to an establishment carried on by a local authority, the Chief Executive of that authority. [Occupational Safety, Healthy & Working Conditions Code, 2020 (37 of 2020), section 2(1)(u) with its inclusions]

"Employer" means—

(i) in relation to any department, organization, undertaking, establishment, enterprise, institution, office, branch or unit of the appropriate Government or a local authority, the head of that department, organisation, undertaking, establishment, enterprise, institution, office, breach or unit or such other officer as the appropriate Government or the local authority, as the case may be, may by an order specify in this behalf;

(ii) in any workplace not covered under sub-clause (i), any person responsible for the management, supervision and control of the workplace;

Explanation.—For the purposes of this sub-clause "management" includes the person or board or committee responsible for the formulation and administration of policies for such organization;

(iii) in relation to workplace covered under sub-clause (i) and (ii), the person discharging contracted obligations with respect to his or her employees;

(iv) in relation to a dwelling place or house, a person or a household who employs or benefits from the employment of domestic worker, irrespective of the number, time period or type of such worker employed, or the nature of the employment or activities performed by the domestic worker. [Sexual Harassment of Women at Workplace (Prevention, Prohibition and Redressal) Act (14 of 2013), S. 2(g)].

'EMPLOYER', in relation to any unprotected workers engaged by or through contractor, means the principal employer and in relation to any other unprotected worker, the person who has ultimate control over the affairs of such establishment are entrusted, whether such person is called an agent, manager or is called by any other name prevailing in the scheduled employment. [Maharashtra Mathadi Hamal and Other Manual Workers (Regulation and Employment and Welfare) Act (30 of 1969), S. 2(3) as cited in *Pepsico India Holding Private Limited* v. *Grocery Market and Shops Board*, (2016) 4 SCC 493, para 8].

"EMPLOYER" includes any body of persons, whether incorporated or not and any managing agent of an employer and the legal representative of a deceased employer, and, when the services of a workman are temporarily lent or let on hire to another person by the person with whom the workman has entered into contract of service or apprenticeship, means such other person while the workman is working for him. [Workmen's Compensation Act (8 of 1923), S. 2(1)(e)]

"EMPLOYER" means any person who employs, whether directly or through another person, or whether on behalf of himself or any other person, one or more employees in any scheduled employment in respect of which minimum rates of wages have been fixed under this Act, and includes, except in sub-section (3) of Section 26,—

(i) in a factory where there is carried on any scheduled employment in respect of which minimum rates of wages have been fixed under this Act, any person named under clause (f) of sub-section of Section 7 of the Factories Act, 1948 as manager of the factory;

(ii) in any scheduled employment under the control of any Government in India in respect of which minimum rates of wages have been fixed under this Act, the person or authority appointed by such Government for the supervision and control of employees or where no person or authority is so appointed, the head of the department;

(iii) in any schedule employment under any local authority in respect of which minimum rates of wages have been fixed under this Act, the person appointed by such authority for the supervision and control of employees or where no person is so appointed the chief executive officer of the local authority;

(iv) in any other case where there is carried on any scheduled employment in respect of which minimum rates of wages have been fixed under this Act, any person responsible to the owner for the supervision and control of the employees or for the payment of wages. [Minimum Wages Act (11 of 1948), S. 2(e)]

"EMPLOYER", when used in relation to a coal mine, means any person who is the immediate proprietor or lessee or occupier of the coal mine or of any part thereof and in the case of coal mine the business whereof is being carried on by a liquidator or receiver, such liquidator or receiver and in the case of a coal mine owned by a company the business whereof is being carried on by a managing agent, such managing agent; but does not include a person who merely receives a loyalty, rent or fine, from the coal mine, or is merely the proprietor of the coal mine, subject to any lease, grant or licence for the working thereof, or is merely the owner of the soil and not interested in the coal of the coal mine; but any contractor for the working of a coal mine or any part thereof shall be subject to this Act, in like a manner as if he were an employer, but not so as to exempt the employer from any liability. [Coal Mines Provident Fund and Misc. Provisions Act (46 of 1948), S. 2(e)]

"EMPLOYER", when used in relation to a plantation, means the person who has the ultimate control over the affairs of the plantation, and where the affairs of any plantation are entrusted to any other person (whether called a managing agent, manager, superintendent or by any other name) such other person shall be deemed to be the employer in relation to that plantation. [Plantations Labour Act (69 of 1951), S. 2(e)]

"EMPLOYER" means any person who employs one or more other persons to do any work in an establishment for remuneration and includes any person entrusted with the supervision and control of employees in such establishment. [Apprentices Act (52 of 1961), S. 2(f)]

"EMPLOYER" means any person who maintains a provident fund for the benefit of his or its employees, being—

(i) a Hindu undivided family, company, firm or other association of persons, or

(ii) an individual engaged in a business or profession the profits and gains whereof are assessable to income-tax under the head "Profits and gains of business or profession. [Income Tax Act (43 of 1961), Sch. IV, Part A, R. 2(a)]

'EMPLOYER' means,—

(i) a company;

(ii) a firm;

(iii) an association of persons or a body of individuals, whether incorporated or not,

(iv) a local authority; and

(v) every artificial juridical person, not falling within any of the preceding subclauses.

[Income-tax Act (43 of 1961), S. 115W(a), *as inserted by Finance Act (18 of 2005), S. 37*]

"EMPLOYER" means—

(i) in relation to an establishment which is under the control of the government, a person or authority appointed by the government for the supervision and control of employees or where no person or authority is so appointed, the head of the department;

(ii) in relation to an establishment under any local authority, the person appointed by such authority for the supervision and control of employees or where no person is so appointed, the chief executive of the local authority;

(iii) in any other case, the person who, or the authority which, has the ultimate control over the affairs of the establishment and where the said affairs are entrusted to any other person whether called a manager, managing director, managing agent or by any other name, such person. [Maternity Benefit Act (53 of 1961), S. 3(d)]

"EMPLOYER" means—

(i) in relation to an establishment which is a factory, the owner or occupier of the factory, including the agent of such owner or occupier, the legal representative of a deceased owner or occupier and, where a person has been named as a manager of the factory under clause (f) of sub-section (1) of Section 7 of the Factories Act, 1948, the person so named; and

(ii) in relation to any other establishment, the person who, or the authority which, has ultimate control over the affairs of establishment, and where the said affairs are entrusted to a manager, managing director or managing agent, such manager, managing director or managing agent. [Factories Act (63 of 1948), S. 2(e) and Payment of Bonus Act (21 of 1965), S. 2(14)]

"EMPLOYER" means any person providing or offering to provide, employment in any country or place outside India. [Emigration Act (31 of 1983), S. 2(1)(g)]

"EMPLOYER" in relation to a dock worker means the person by whom he is employed or is to be employed on dock work, whether for remuneration or not. [Dock Worker (Safety Health and Welfare) Act (54 of 1986), S. 2(f)]

"EMPLOYER" means,—

(i) in relation to a Government, the authority notified by the Head of the Department in this behalf or where no such authority is notified, the Head of the Department; and

(ii) in relation to an establishment, the chief executive officer of that establishment. [Persons with Disabilities (Equal Opportunities, Protection of Rights and full participation) Act, 1995 (1 of 1996), S. 2(j)]

"EMPLOYER", in relation to an establishment, means the owner thereof, and includes,—

(i) in relation to a building or other construction work carried on by or under the authority of any department of the Government, directly without any contractor, the authority specified in this behalf, or where no authority is specified, the head of the department;

(ii) in relation to a building or other construction work carried on by or on behalf of a local authority or other establishment, directly without any contractor, the chief executive officer of that authority or establishment;

(iii) in relation to a building or other construction work carried on by or through a contractor, or by the employment of building workers supplied by a contractor, the contractor; [Building and other Construction workers (Regulation of Employment and conditions of service) Act (27 of 1996), S. 2(1)(i)]

The expression 'employer' means the owner of a coal mine as defined in clause (g) of S. 3 of the Indian Mines Act 1923. *State of Bihar* v. *S.K. Roy*, AIR 1966 SC 1995, 1996. [Coal Mines Provident Fund and Misc. Provisions Act (46 of 1948), S. 2(e)].

The word 'employer' does not include the intermediary persons who employed the workers for the conduct of the business for the principal employer. *Joseph Joseph* v. *State of Kerala*, (2002) 3 SCC 8, para 7 : AIR 2002 SC 1117. [Kerala Toddy Workers Fund Act (22 of 1969), S. 2(c)]

"EMPLOYER". Means—

(i) in relation to any department, organisation, undertaking, establishment, enterprise, institution, office, branch or unit of the appropriate Government or a local authority, the head of that department, organisation, undertaking, establishment, enterprise, institution, office, branch or unit or such other officer as the appropriate Government or the local authority, as the case may be, may by an order specify in this behalf;

(ii) in any workplace not covered under sub-clause (i), any person responsible for the management, supervision and control of the workplace.

Explanation.—For the purpose of this sub-clause, management includes the person or board or committee responsible for formulation and administration of policies for such organisation;

(iii) in relation to workplace covered under sub-clauses (i) and (ii), the person discharging contractual obligations with respect to his or her employees;

(iv) in relation to a dwelling place or house, a person or a household who employs or benefits from the employment of domestic worker, irrespective of the number, time period or type of such worker employed, or the nature of the employment or activities performed by the domestic worker. [S. 2(g) of the Sexual Harassment of Women at Workplace (Prevention, Prohibition & Redressal) Act, 2013 (14 of 2013)]

An "employer" is a person who employs another person under a contract of employment, express or implied, to perform work for the employer. [*ITC Limited, Gurgaon* v. *Commissioner of Income Tax (TDS), Delhi,* (2016) 6 SCC 652, para 17].

Employer's liability. The "law of employers' liability" has by usage become the expression employed to express the liability imposed by law upon certain employers of labour to make pecuniary compensation to their workmen in respect of personal injury suffered in the course of their employment.

Employers' liability insurance. Is the general designation of a certain kind of branch of the insurance business, which provides indemnity to employers against liability for accidents to employees. It is a recent form of accident insurance and is the outgrowth of a demand for indemnity to employers against the liability of their employees for injuries occurring in the prosecution of business or industrial enterprises. (*Ame Cyc.*) This has become familiar since the passing of employers' liability Acts. It insures an employer against claim for compensation for damage on the part of an employee for injuries suffered.

Employment. "EMPLOYMENT" means any service, occupation or engagement (not being service), occupation or engagement under the Central Government or a State Government), in any kind of work within the meaning of clause (o), for wages or for reward, and all its grammatical variations and cognate expressions shall be construed accordingly. [Emigration Act (31 of 1983), S. 2(1)(h)]

The act of employing; the state of being employed; business; calling; commission; occupation; office; profession; service; vocation; that which engages the head or hands; object of industry; appointment; engagement.

The action of employing; the state of being employed. [Industrial Disputes Act (14 of 1947), S. 2(q) and Constitution of India, Art. 16(1)].

The matters relating to employment include all matters in relation to employment both prior and subsequent to the employment which are incidental to the employment and form part of the terms and conditions of such employment. *Jaisinghari* v. *Union of India*, AIR 1967 SC 1427, 1431. [Constitution of India, Art. 16].

The Governor is not under the employment of the Government of India. *Har Govind Pant Chancellor, University of Rajasthan,* AIR 1978 Raj 72. [Constitution of India, Article 319(d) 157].

The word 'employment' in Article 319(d) is understood to mean the relationship of employer and employee does not include the office of Governor because the Governor is the head of the State and holds a high constitutional office which carries with it important constitutional functions and duties. Appointment of the Governor by the President does not make the Governor an employee or servant of the Government of India. *Hargovind Pant* v. *Raghukul Tilak,* (1979) 3 SCC 458. [Constitution of India, Art. 319(d)]

The word employment used in the entry was used in its most general sense of "the action of employing or the state of being employed" and not with reference to any particular trade, business or occupations. *Madhya Pradesh Mineral Industry Association* v. *Regional Labour Commissioner (Central) Civil Lines,* AIR 1958 Bom 332, 334. [Minimum Wages Act (11 of 1948), Sch. A., Part-I, Entry No. 8].

A contract of employment may be in respect of either piece-work or time-work; but it does not follow from the fact that the contract is for piece work that it must be a contract of employment. *Harish Chandra Bajpai* v. *Triloki Singh*, AIR 1957 SC 444, 457. [Representation of the People Act (43 of 1951), S. 123(7)].

"Employment" means an act of employing. *Central Board of Direct Taxes* v. *Aditya V. Birla,* AIR 1988 SC 420.

The word 'employment' takes within its fold, the aspect of promotions to posts above the stage of initial level of recruitment. *Ajit Singh (II)* v. *State of Punjab,* (1999) 7 SCC 209, para 22 : AIR 1999 SC 3471. [Constitution of India, Art. 16(1)]

Employment and appointment. The words 'employment' and 'appointment' connote two different conceptions. "Appointment" obviously refers to appointment to an office. The term "appointment" therefore implies the conception of tenure, duration, emolument & duties and obligations fixed by law or by some rule having the forces of law. It is obvious that these elements are absent in the case of a public employment which is a contract for a temporary purpose. *Sukhnandam Thakur* v. *State of Bihar*, AIR 1957 Pat 617, 632. [Constitution of India, Art. 16].

"Employment" and **"regularization of service"—distinction.** There lies a distinction between the expression "employment" and "regularization of service". The expression "employment" signifies a fresh employment to fill the vacancies whereas the expression "regularisation of service" signifies that the employee, who is already in service, his services are regularised as per service regulations. [*Management of the Barara Cooperative Marketing-cum-Processin Society Limited* v. *Workman Pratap Singh,* (2019) 2 SCC 743, para 20].

Employment exchange. EMPLOYMENT EXCHANGE means any office or place established and maintained by the Government for the collection and furnishing of information, either by the keeping of registers or otherwise, respecting—

(i) persons who seek to engage employees;

(ii) persons who seek employment; and

(iii) vacancies to which persons seeking employment, may be appointed. [Employment Exchange (Compulsory) Notification of Vacancies Act (31 of 1959), S. 2(d)]

Employment injury. "EMPLOYMENT INJURY" means a personal injury to an employee caused by accident or an occupational disease arise out of and in the course of his employment, being an insurable employment, whether the accident occurs or the occupational disease is contracted within or outside the territorial limits of India. [Employees' State Insurance Act (34 of 1948), S. 2(8)]

"Employment injury" means a personal injury to an employee, caused by accident or an occupational disease, as the case may be, arising out of and in the course of his employment,—

(i) for the purposes of Chapter IV, if the employee is an insured or insurable employee under section 28 whether such accident occurs or the occupational disease is contracted within or outside the territorial limits of India; and

(ii) for the purposes of Chapter VII, whether such accident occurs or the occupational disease is contracted within or outside the territorial limits of India. [Code on Social Security, 2020 (36 of 2020), section 2(28)]

The injury suffered by the workman while going to the place of work, is not an employment injury. *Regional Director, ESI Corporation* v. *Francis De Costa,* 1996(6) SCC 1.

Empower. To invest legally or formally with power; to authorise. [IPC (45 of 1860), Ss. 19 and 20].

Empowered to place or keep any person in confinement. The expression "empowered to place or keep any person in confinement" comprehends police and prison authorities or those under an obligation bylaw or by virtue of office to take into custody and keep in confinement any person. *R.S. Nayak* v. *A.R. Antulay,* AIR 1984 SC 684.

En banc. The practice of a Court, in which cases are normally tried before panels of judges, to collectively sit and hear a case with the full complement of judges present. [CRAIG R. DUCAT—*Constitutional Interpretation*].

An informal meeting held by the Commission to hear presentations on specific topics by diverse parties. The Commissioners, or other officials, question presenters and use their comments in considering FCC rules and policies on the subject matter under consideration. (*Telecommunication*)

En masse. In a mass; in a large group all at once; all together.

En route. On the way; in the course of transportation.

En ventre sa mere. Child in womb.

Enable. To render able.

Enable it to pronounce judgement. The appellate Court must require the additional evidence to enable it to pronounce judgment. The true test is whether the appellate Court is able to pronounce judgment on the materials before it without taking into consideration the additional evidence sought to be adduced. *Arjun Singh* v. *Kartar Singh*, AIR 1951 SC 193, 195. [CPC (5 of 1908), O. XLI, R. 27(1)]

Enabling clause. That portion of a statute or constitution which gives to governmental officials the power and authority to put it into effect and to enforce.

Enabling statute. A statute which makes it lawful to do something which would not otherwise be lawful. Such statutes or Acts are passed for a variety of purposes; for instance, to authorise the taking of land compulsorily to carry out some public work, or to legalise what would otherwise be a public or private nuisance.

Enact. To ordain; to establish by law; to perform or effect; to decree.

To make into an Act. [Constitution of India, Preamble and Art. 123 (3)].

Enacting words. Introductory part of a statute, stating the authority which enacted it.

Enactment. Shall include a Regulation and any Regulation of the Bengal, Madras or Bombay Code and shall also include any provision contained in any Act or in any such Regulation as aforesaid. [General Clauses Act (10 of 1897), S. 3(19)].

That which is enacted; a statute; one of the provisions of a law. [General Clauses Act (10 of 1897), S. 3(19)].

The word 'enactment' does not mean the same thing as 'Act', Act means the whole Act, whereas a section or part of a section may be an 'enactment'. *Prabodh Verma* v. *State of U.P.*, AIR 1985 SC 167.

The expression 'enactment' applies not only to a complete Act but also to the various provisions in an Act.

Encashment. The action of encashing or converting into cash.

Encircle, To. To surround. [Geneva Conventions Act (6 of 1960), 1st Sch., Art. 15].

Enclosure. An enclosed space. [Factories Act (63 of 1948), S. 28(1)(b)]; [CPC (5 of 1908), O. XXI, R. 35 (3)].

Encourage. To embolden; to incite to anything; to give courage; to inspirit; to raise confidence.

Encroach. To intrude usurpingly; make gain upon, occupy, or use the land, right, or authority of another; to gain unlawfully lands, property or authority of another.

Encroacher. Means any person or institution, public or private, occupying waqf property, in whole or part, without the authority of law and includes a person whose tenancy, lease or licence has expired or has been terminated by mutawalli or the Board. [S. 3(ee) of the Waqf Act, 1995 (43 of 1995) as inserted by the Wakf (Amendment) Act, 2013 (27 of 2013)]

Encroachment. The action of encroaching *i.e.* intruding usurpingly (on others' territory, rights *etc.*). [T.P. Act (4 of 1882), S. 108(n)].

An infringement of another's right or intrusion on another's property.

"Encroachment" means unauthorised occupation of Government land or public land other than streets, lanes, footpath and parks, by way of putting temporary, semi permanent or permanent structure for residential use or commercial use or any other use. [National Capital Territory of Delhi Laws (Special Provisions) Second Act (20 of 2011), S. 3(c)].

"ENCROACHMENT" means unauthorised occupation of Government land or public land by way of putting temporary, semi-permanent or permanent structure for residential use or commercial use or any other use. [S. 2(1)(c) of the National Capital Territory of Delhi Laws (Special Provisions) Act, 2011 (5 of 2011)]

'ENCROACHMENT' means any unauthorized occupation of any highway or part thereof, and includes an unauthorized—

(*i*) erection of a building or any other structure, balconies, porches, projections on or over or overhanging the highway;

(*ii*) occupation of a highway beyond the prescribed period, if any, for stacking building materials or goods of any description, for exhibiting articles for sale, for erecting poles, ownings, tents, pandals, hoardings and other similar erections or for parking vehicles or staffing animals or for any other purpose; and

(*iii*) excavation or dumps of any sort made or extended on any highway or underneath such highway. [Bombay Highways Act (40 of 1955), S. 2(f) **as cited in** *Sayyed Ratanbhai Sayeed* v. *Shirdi Nagar Panchayat,* (2016) 4 SCC 631, para 48].

Encrypted. In respect of a signal of cable television network, means the changing of such signal in a systematic way so that the signal would be unintelligible without a suitable receiving equipment and the expression "unencrypted" shall be construed accordingly. [Cable Television Network (Regulation) Act (7 of 1995), S. 4A Expl. (c)]

For the purposes of this section, "Encrypted", in respect of a signal of cable television network, means the changing of such signal in a systematic way so that the signal would be unintelligible without use of addressable system and the expression "Unencrypted" shall be construed accordingly. [Cable Television Networks (Regulation) Act (7 of 1995), S. 4A, *Explanation* (c) as substituted by Amending Act 21 of 2011].

Encryption. The first step in cryptography, whereby plaintex data is encoded by use of a mathematical algorithm to create cipher text stored in a different format known as ciphertext. (*Cyber Law*].

The mathematical processing of securing text or data by making it unintelligible to all but the intended recipient. Encryption is based on two components—a Cryptographic algorithm and a key. (*Information Technology*)

These scramble data and so keep them private from those who want to sneak a peek or drop an eave (eavesdroppers). (*Cyber Law*)

A technology that scrambles digital information according to a code that allows authorised users to unscramble the data later. (*Internet and E-commerce*).

Transformation of data by the use of cryptography to produce unintelligible data (encrypted data) to ensure its confidentiality. [Organization for Economic Cooperation and Development Guidelines for Cryptography Policy 1997].

Encrypted program-carrying satellite signal. "A program-carrying satellite signal that is transmitted in a form whereby the aural or visual characteristics, or both, are modified or altered for the purpose of presenting the unauthorised reception by persons without the authorised equipment that is designed to eliminate the effects of such modification or alteration, of a program carried in that signal." [NAFTA, Article 1721] (*Copyright*)

Encryption. The encoding of signals for the purpose of controlling access to or modification or verification of transmitted data.

Encumber. To burden with a claim.

The word 'encumber' means burden of legal liability on property. *State of H.P.* v. *Tarsem Singh,* (2001) 8 SCC 104, para 7.

Encumbrance. Burden or property; impediment; mortgage or other claim on property.

The word 'encumbrances' shall not include a right of easement. *Ratanchand* v. *Kasim Khaleeli,* AIR 1964 Mad 209, 216. [Displaced persons (Compensation and Rehabilitation) Act (44 of 1954), S. 12]

(1) A burden or impediment. (2) Law—a mortgage or other claim on property or assets. [Concise Oxford English Dictionary (10th Edn., Revised) as cited in *Saraswati Devi* v. *Delhi Development Authority*, (2013) 3 SCC 571, para 35].

(1) That which encumbers. (2) Law—any lien or liability attached to real property. (3) One's wife, child or dependent. Also spelled incumbrance. [Webster's Comprehensive Dictionary (International Edition, Vol. I) as cited in *Saraswati Devi* v. *Delhi Development Authority*, (2013) 3 SCC 571, para 36].

Any right existing in another to use the land or whereby the use by the owner is restricted. The word "encumbrance" imports within itself every right or interest in the land, which may subsist in a person other than the owner, if it anything which places the burden of a legal liability upon property. The word "encumbrance" in law has to be understood in the context of the provision under consideration but ordinarily its ambit and scope is wide. [*Saraswati Devi* v. *Delhi Development Authority*, (2013) 3 SCC 571, para 40].

The word "encumbrance", according to its ordinary significance, means any right existing in another to use the land or whereby the use by the owner is restricted. The word "encumbrance" imports within itself every right or interest in the land, which may subsist in a person other than the owner; it is anything which places the burden of a legal liability upon property. The word "encumbrance" in law has to be understood in the context of the provision under consideration but ordinarily its ambit and scope is wide. Seen thus, it is difficult to see why a binding contract entered into between an auction-purchaser and the Government on approval of the highest bid relating to sale of property, which is part of compensation to the auction purchaser, should come within the purview of the word "encumbrance." [*Saraswati Devi* v. *Delhi Development Authority*, (2013) 3 SCC 571, para 40]

The word "encumbrance" can only mean interests in respect of which a compensation was made under section 11 or could have been claimed. It cannot include the right of the Government to levy assessment on the lands. *Collector of Bombay* v. *Nusserwanji*, AIR 1955 SC 298, 305. [Land Acquisition Act (1 of 1894), S. 16] [Now repealed & replaced by Act 30 of 2013]

A claim, lien, liability attached to property, as mortgage *etc.* [CPC (5 of 1908), S. 73(1), prov. (c)].

Encumbrancer. One who has a legal claim on an estate. [T.P. Act (4 of 1882), S. 60A(2)].

A trespasser or unauthrorised occupant does not come within the meaning of 'encumbrancer' under Section 26 of E.P. Holdings (Consolidation and Prevention of Fragmentation) Act, 1948. *Mange Ram* v. *Financial Commissioner*, (2003) 2 SCC 1, para 2 : AIR 2003 SC 807.

End entity signature. "End entity signature" means authentication of any electronic by an end entity by means of a digital signature, electronic method or procedure in accordance with the provision of section 3 or 3A the Act. [Digital Signature (End Entity) Rules, 2015, R. 2(1)(h)] [Information Technology Act (21 of 2000), Ss. 3 or 3A].

Endanger. To put in peril. [IPC (45 of 1860), Ss. 279 and 280].

"Endanger" or "endangerment" means the act or an instance of putting someone or something in danger; exposure to peril or such situation which would hurt the concept of life as understood in its wider sense. [Black's Law Dictionary, (8th Edn.) as cited in *Bihar Public Service Commission* v. *Saiyad Hussain Abbas Rizwi*, (2012) 13 SCC 61, para 27]. 'Endangered species'

Endangered species. 'Endangered species' are these "in danger of extinction throughout all or a significant portion of their range." [*T.N. Godavarman Thirumulpad* v. *Union of India*, (2012) 4 SCC 362, para 48].

Endeavour. To exert physical and intellectual strength toward the attainment of an object. (*Black*)

The effort directed to attain an object; strenuous. [Constitution of India, Art. 51A (j)]

Endorse (indorse). Means 'putting the personal signature and not putting a facsimile or lithographic signature'. *Kamala Bala Dassi* v. *State of West Bengal,* AIR 1962 Cal 269, 272. [West Bengal Land Acquisition and Requisition Rules (1948) R. 3 (1)].

To make an endorsement on. [Constitution of India, Art 110 (4)].

Endorsee (indorsee). "ENDORSEE" means the person in whose favour an endorsement is made, and in the case of successive endorsements, the person in whose favour the last endorsement is made. [Railways Act, 1989 (24 of 1989), S. 2(12) and Multimodal Transportation of Goods Act, 1993 (28 of 1993), S. 2(g)]

The person to whom a bill of exchange or promissory note is transferred by endorsement.

A person in whose favour an endorsement is made.

Endorsement (indorsement). "Endorsement" and "*endorsed*" include and apply to an entry in writing by a registering officer on a rider or covering slip to any document tendered for registration under the Registration Act. [Registration Act (16 of 1908), S. 2(5)].

"Endorsement", in relation to an advertisement, means—

(i) any message, verbal statement, demonstration; or

(ii) depiction of the name, signature, likeness or other identifiable personal characteristics of an individual; or

(iii) depiction of the name or seal of any institution or organisation,

which makes the consumer to believe that it reflects the opinion, finding or experience of the person making such endorsement. [Consumer Protection Act, 2019 (35 of 2019), section 2(18)]

"ENDORSEMENT" means the signing by the consignee or the endorsee after adding a direction on a railway receipt to pass the property in the goods mentioned in such receipt to a specified person. [Railways Act (24 of 1989). S. 2(13)]

"ENDORSEMENT" means the signing by the consignee or the endorsee after adding a direction on a negotiable multimodal transport document to pass the property in the goods mentioned in such document to a specified person. [Multimodal Transportation of Goods Act (27 of 1993), S. 2(h)]

'When the maker or holder of a negotiable instrument signs the same, otherwise than as such maker, for the purpose of negotiation, on the back or face thereof or on a slip of paper annexed thereto, or so signs for the purpose a stamped paper intended to be completed as a negotiable instrument, he is said to indorse the same, and is called the "indorser". [Negotiable Instruments Act (26 of 1881), S. 15].

The signing of one's name on the back of a bill or note; an act which transfers the right in it to the endorsee.

A writing on the back of a document; this will include an endorsement on a negotiable instrument and also the writing in evidence of payment of any amount or portion of amount due on a document.

Endorsement in blank. Endorsement in blank means writing one's name merely on the back of a railway receipt without specifying any restrictions as to payee, manner of payment, *etc.*, which details may be filled in by the holder thereof, in that, when the consignor endorsed in blank and handed over the railway receipt to him, the consignor thereby authorised the holder thereof, to fill up the blank in whatever manner he liked; and therefore, an endorsement in blank was as good and effective as full and complete endorsement. *State of Bihar* v. *Union of India,* AIR 1959 Pat 438, 440.

An endorsement where the endorser signs his name only. [Negotiable Instruments Act (26 of 1881), S. 16(1)].

Endorser (indorser). The person who transfers a negotiable instrument to another by endorsement.

A person who endorses any document. See, Endorsement.

Endow. To bestow upon; to give; to bestow; to bequeath; to invest with; to furnish with a portion of goods or estates; to settle on as a permanent possession; to furnish with a permanent fund or property; to make provisions for the support of a corporation or institutions.

Endowment. Property or money bestowed as a permanent fund; property held in trust for any charity. (*Oxford*)

A permanent provision for any institution or person; all property belonging to or given or endowed for religious and charitable purposes. [CPC (5 of 1908), S. 92(2)].

'Endowment' means property or pecuniary means bestowed as a permanent fund, as endowment of a college, hospital or library, and is understood in common acceptance as a fund fielding income for support of an institution. [*Words and Phrases, Permanent* Edn., Vol. 14-A, 167, as cited in *Shiromani Gurudwara Prabandhak Committee* v. *Somnath Dass,* (2000) 4 SCC 146 para 36.

Endowment is dedication of property for purposes of religion or charity having both the subject and object certain and capable of ascertainment. *Pratap Singhji* v. *Charity Commissioner Charity,* AIR 1987 SC 2064, 2069.

ENDOWMENT, GIFT, PRESENT, BENEFACTION. In their simplest signification the distinction between these is obvious. An *Endowment* is a gift in perpetuity, of which the usufruct is continually accruing; as to give a sum of money, of which the interest may serve to endow a public institution.

A *gift* is usually from one who is in some sense a superior, and intended to benefit the person to whom it is given.

A *present* is commonly from an equal or an inferior, as a mark of affection or respect, or from a desire to please or to gain favour.

A *benefaction* is a gift sufficiently important to be of lasting value, but not like endowment, amounting to a maintenance of the institution or the individual on which it is conferred. (*Smith Syn. Dis.*)

Endowment policy. A policy payable at a certain time at all events, or sooner if the party should die sooner; an insurance into which enters the element of life. In one respect it is a contract payable in the event of a continuance of life; in another in the event of death before the period specified. (15 (*Ame Cyc.* 1046)

Ends of justice. The objectives of justice. "Ends of justice are solemn words and not mere polite expression in juristic methodology and justice is the pursuit and end of all law. But these words do no mean vague and indeterminate notions of justice according to statutes and laws of the land. *Debendranath* v. *Satya Bala Dass,* AIR 1950 Cal 217, 233. [CPC (5 of1908), S. 151].

"Ends of justice" refers to justice to all the parties. This phrase refers to the best interest of the public within the four corners of the statute. In fact, it means preservation of proper balance between the Constitutional/Statutory rights of an individual and rights of the people at large to have the law enforced. [*Yakub Abdul Razak Memon* v. *State of Maharashtra*, (2013) 13 SCC 1, para 1551].

By "ends of justice" is meant not only justice to the parties but also to witnesses and other who may be inconvenienced. *Sangram Singh* v. *Election Tribunal Kotah,* AIR 1955 SC 425.

Enemy. Hostile person; opponent; member of a hostile army or nation; hostile force.

"ENEMY" includes all armed mutineers, armed rebels, armed rioters pirates and any person in arms against whom it is the duty of any person subject to military law to act. [Army Act (46 of 1950), S. 3(x); Air Force Act (45 of 1950), S. 4(xviii)].

"ENEMY" includes all armed rebels, armed mutineers, armed rioters and pirates and any person in arms against whom it is the duty of any person subject to naval law to act. [Navy Act (62 of 1957), S. 3(7)]

"ENEMY" includes all armed mutineers, armed rebels, armed rioters, pirates and any person in arms against whom it is the duty of any person subject to this Act to take action. [Indo-Tibetan Border Police Force Act (35 of 1992), S. 2(1)(i) and Border Security Force Act (47 of 1968), S. 2(j)]

"ENEMY" means—

(i) any person or country committing external aggression against India;

(ii) any person belonging to a country committing such aggression;

(iii) such other country as may be declared by the Central Government to be assisting the country committing such aggression;

(iv) any person belonging to such other country. [Personal Injuries (Emergency Provisions) Act (59 of 1962), S. 2(3); Emergency Risks (Goods) Insurance Act (62 of 1962), S. 2(a) and Emergency Risks (factories) Insurance Act (63 of 1962), S. 2(b)]

One that hates and wishes or seeks to injure another. [Army Act (46 of 1950), S. 3(x) and Air Force Act (45 of 1950), S. 4(xviii)].

The term 'enemy' includes any unfriendly state. *Kuthuddin* v. *State of Rajasthan,* AIR 1967 Raj 257, 258. [Official Secrets Act (19 of 1923), S. 3]

ENEMY, FOE. An *enemy* is not so formidable as a foe; the former may be reconciled, but the latter always retains a deadly hate. Any *enemy* may be so in spirit, in action, or in relation; a *foe* is always so in spirit, if not in action likewise; a man may be an *enemy* to himself, though not a *foe*. Those who are national or political *enemies* are often private friends, but a *foe* is never anything but a foe. A single act may create an *enemy*, but continued warfare crates a *foe*.

"Enemy" or "enemy subject" or "enemy firm". Means a person or country who or which was an enemy, an enemy subject or an enemy firm, as the case may be under, Defence of India Act, 1962 and the Defence of India Rules, 1962, or the Defence of India Act, 1971 and the Defence of India Rules, 1971, but does not include a citizen of India. [Enemy Property Act (34 of 1968), S. 2(b)]

Enemy property. "ENEMY PROPERTY" means any property for the time being belonging to or held or managed on behalf of an enemy, an enemy subject or an enemy firm; Provided that where an individual enemy subject dies in the territories to which this Act extends, any property which immediately before his death, belonged to or was held by him or was managed on his behalf, may, notwithstanding his death, continue to be regarded as enemy property for the purposes of this Act. [Enemy Property Act (34 of 1968), S. 2(c)]

Property belonging to an enemy of the country. For the purposes of this clause, it is hereby clarified that "ENEMY PROPERTY" shall, notwithstanding that the enemy or the enemy subject or the enemy firm has ceased to be an enemy due to death, extinction, winding up of business or change of nationality or that the legal heir and successor is a citizen of India or the citizen of a country which is not an enemy, continue and always be deemed to be continued as an enemy property. [Enemy Property Act (34 of 1968), S. 2(c), *Explanation 1*].

For the purposes of this clause, the expression "ENEMY PROPERTY" shall mean and include and shall be deemed to have always meant and included all rights, titles and interests in, or any benefit arising out of, such property. [Enemy Property Act (34 of 1968), S. 3(c), *Explanation 2*].

For the purposes of this clause, the expression "ENEMY PROPERTY" shall mean and include and shall be deemed to have always meant and included all rights, titles and interests in, or any benefit arising out of, such property. [Enemy Property Act (3 of 1968), s. 2(c), *Explanation 2*].

Enemy territory. This means—

(i) any area which is under the sovereignty of an enemy;

(ii) any area which the Central Government may declare to be enemy territory. [Defence of India Act (51 of 1962), S. 2(d)]

Energy. Means electrical energy—

(i) generated, transmitted or supplied for any purpose; or

(ii) used for any purpose except the transmission of a message. [Indian Electricity Act (9 of 1910), S. 2(g)] Act (9 of 1910) repealed and replaced by Act (36 of 2003).

"ENERGY" means any form of energy derived from fossil fuels or non-fossilsources orrenewable sources. [Energy Conservation Act (52 of 2001), S. 2(h)]

Energy audit. Means the verification, monitoring and analysis of use of energy including submission of technical report containing recommendations for improving energy efficiency with cost benefit analysis and an action plan to reduce energy consumption. [Energy Conservation Act (52 of 2001), S. 2(i)]

Energy auditor means any individual possessing the qualifications prescribed under clause (m) of section 14. [Energy Conservation Act (52 of 2001), section 2(ia)]

Energy charter declaration or Declaration. Means a non binding instrument, the negotiation of which is authorised and the text of which & approved by the charter conference, which is entered into by two or more contracting parties to complement or supplement the provisions of this treaty. [Energy Charter treaty. (12 Dec. 1994), I.L.M. (1995)]

Energy conservation and sustainable building code means the code which provides norms and standards for energy efficiency and its conservation, use of renewable energy and other green building requirements for a building. [Energy Conservation Act (52 of 2001), section 2(j)]

Energy consumption standards. Means the norms for process and energy consumption standards specified under clause (a) of Section 14. [Energy Conservation Act (52 of 2001), S. 2(k)]

Energy conservation measures. Mean the measures incorporated in the building design for saving energy, or enhancing comfort in peak electrical or thermal demand, or reducing cooling or heating load covering any element of a component with any other element of the same or other component of the Code and includes any such measure incorporated in the said building design of the proposed or existing building. [Energy Conservation Building Code Rules, 2018, R. 2(1)(m)].

Energy Conservation Rules. Means the Energy Conservation (Energy Consumption Norms and Standards for Designated Consumers, Form, Time within which, and Manner of Preparation and Implementation of Scheme, Procedure for Issue of Energy Savings Certificate and Value of Per Metric Ton of Oil Equivalent of Energy Consumed) Rules, 2012 and as amended from time to time. [Central Electricity Regulatory Commission (Terms and Conditions for Dealing in Energy Savings Certificate) Regulations, 2016, Regn. 2(1)(j)].

Energy performance index. Means annual energy consumption of a building in kilo Watt-hours per square meter of the area of the building which shall be calculated as per the following formula:

$$\text{Energy performance Index} = \frac{\text{Annual energy consumption in kwh}}{\text{Total builtup area (excluding storage area and the parking in the basement in m}}$$

[Energy Conservation Building Code Rules, 2018, R. 2(1)(n)].

Energy performance index ratio. Means the ratio of the energy performance index of the proposed building to the energy performance index of the standard baseline building. [Energy Conservation Building Code Rules, 2018, R. 2(1)(o)].

Energy recovery. Means energy recovery from waste that is conversion of waste material into usable hear, electricity or fuel through a variety of processes including combustion, gasification, pyrolisation, anaerobic digestion and land fill gas recovery. [Plastic Waste Management Rules, 2016, R. 3 (ab)].

Energy savings performance contract. Means a contract entered into the beneficiary and the borrower under which payments to the borrower are based on the meeting specified performance guarantees related to the implementation of energy efficiency project under Fund. [Energy Conservation (Partial Risk Guarantee Fund for Energy Efficiency) Rules, 2016, R. 2(1)(g)].

Energy service company. Means a company or set-up for implementing energy efficiency projects, which is empanelled with the Bureau. [Energy Conservation (Partial Risk Guarantee Fund for Energy Efficiency) Rules, 2016, R. 2(1)(h)].

Enface. To write or stamp on the face.

Energy cycle. Means the more energy chain, including activities related to prospecting for, exploration, production, conversion, storage, transport, distribution and consumption of the various forms of energy, and the treatment and disposal of wastes, as well as the decommissioning, cessation or closure of these activities, minimizing harmful environmental impacts. [Energy Charter Protocol on Energy Efficiency and Related Environmental Aspects, Art. 1(4)]

Energy Management Centre. Means the Energy Management Centre set up under the Resolution of the Government of India in the erstwhile Ministry of Energy, Department of Power No. 7(2)/87-EP (Vol. IV), dated the 5th July, 1989 and registered under the Societies Registration Act, 1860. [Energy Conservation Act (52 of 2001), S. 2(l)]

Enforce. To put in execution; to cause to take effect; to urge (as, to *enforce* an argument); to impose (as, to *enforce* a course of conduct or action on a person) As *applied* to *process*, the term implies execution of process.

To compel the observance of; to put in execution. [IPC (45 of 1860), S. 141 (fourth)]; [T.P. Act (4 of 1882), S. 11].

'Enforce' means the taking of such action on the part of the creditor which compels the debtor to effect repayment of the loan such as the institution of a suit, attachment of sale of the latter's properties, *etc.* Making a demand from the debtor to repay the loan would not amount to enforcing repayment. *Totalal* v. *State,* AIR 1963 Raj 6, 8. [Companies Act (1 of 1956), S. 295(3)]

Enforce a partition. To bring about a partition. [T.P. Act (4 of 1882), S. 44].

Enforceability. The quality or state of being enforceable.

Enforceable. Capable of being enforced. [CPC (5 of 1908), S. 64].

Enforcement. In the case of contracts, doing something to make the opposite party perform his part of the contract.

The action of enforcing. [Indian Contract Act (9 of 1872), S. 33].

It means to impose or compel obedience to law or to compel observance of law. *S.M.D. Kiran Pasha* v. *Govt. of A.P.,* (1990) 1 SCC 328.

Enforcing the liability of any surety. 'Surety' in the expression 'enforcing the liability of any surety' means a person who stood surety for the principal debtor the furnished property as security. *M.S.F.C.* v. *Jaycee Drugs and Pharmaceutical (P.) Ltd.,* AIR 1991 Bom 96, 103. [State Financial Corporation Act (63 of 1950), Ss. 31 and 32]

Enfranchise. To set free; invest with electoral franchise; to render a holding free from some obligation (as, enfranchisement of *inams*)

Engage. To bind by promise [Emigration Act (31 of 1983), S. 16(1)]; to pledge oneself to do; to hire (servant *etc.*); to employ oneself in; to enter into conflict [Navy Act (62 of 1957), S. 34(a)]; to employ. [Constitution of India, Art. 124].

If an employer is alleged to be engaged in discharging any employee then even before the actual order of discharge is passed he can be said to be engaged in such discharge if it is shown that an attempt is made towards such a discharge with an intention to ultimately discharge the employee. *Hindustan Lever* v. *Ashok V Kate*, AIR 1996 SC 285, 294. [Maharashtra Recognition of Trade Unions and Prevention of Unfair Labour Practices Act (1971), S. 28, Sch. 4, Item l]

Engaged in any industry. The expression "engaged in any industry" specified in Schedule I should be interpreted to mean "mainly engaged in any industry specified in Schedule I". If a factory is engaged in two industrial activities one of which is its primary, principal or dominant activity and the other is purely a subsidiary, incidental, minor or feeding activity, then it is the primary or dominant activity which should determine the character of the factory under Section 1(3)(a). *Regional P.F. Commissioner* v. *S.K.M. Manufacturing Co*., AIR 1962 SC 1536, 1542. [Employees Provident Funds Act (19 of 1952), S. 1(3)(a)]

Engaged in business. Occupied in doing business. [Indian Partnership Act (9 of 1932), S. 6, *Expln.* 2(a)].

Engagement. Engagement means some sort of undertaking or contractual obligation.

Any formal promise, agreement or undertaking. [Constitution of India, Art. 131, prov.].

Engineer. *As applied to civil matters*, the term refers to a person employed in the construction of fixed public works, or to the designing and construction of public works.

As applied to Mechanical operations, one who manages an engine; a person who has charge of an engine and its connected machinery.

As used in connection with railways, the party in charge of the locomotive.

A person versed in design, construction and use of engines or machines or in any of the various branches of engineering. [Inland Vessels Act (11 of 1917), S. 20].

"The Engineer" means the Engineer in charge of the public embankments of the district, or any part thereof, or any Engineer specially appointed by the Lieutenant-Governor of Bengal to perform the functions of an Engineer in respect of any tract of country or of any works. Ben. Act II of 1882 (Embankment), S. 4.

Engineering. The activity or the functions of an engineer; the science by which the properties of matter and the sources of energy in nature are made useful to man in structures, machines and products; relating to engineering.

The work done by or the occupation of, an engineer, the application of the science for directly useful purposes as, construction, propulsion, communication or manufacture. The action of working artfully to bring something about. A field of study or activity concerned with deliberate alteration or modification in some particular area. [The New Shorter Oxford English Dictionary as cited in *Association of Management of Private Colleges* v. *All India Council for Technical Education*, (2013) 8 SCC 271, para 62.6].

Engineering in the broader sense, is that branch of human endeavour by which the forces of nature are brought under human control and the properties of matter made useful in structures and machines. [Webster's Comprehensive Dictionary as cited in *Association of Management of Private Colleges* v. *All India Council for Technical Education*, (2013) 8 SCC 271, para 62.6]. 'Engineering operations'

'Engineering operations' means formation or laying out of means of a access to road. [Bangalore Development Authority Act 12 of 1976, S. 2(k) as cited in *Bangalore Development Authority* v. *Aircraft Employees' Co-operative Society Limited*, (2012) 3 SCC 442, para 9].

Engineering operations. Include the formation or laying out of a street or means of access to a road or laying out of means of water supply, drainage, electricity, gas or other utility service. [Maharashtra Regional and Town Planning Act (37 of 1996)]

"ENGINEERING OPERATIONS" include the formation or laying out of means of access to a road or the laying out of means of water supply, drainage, sewerage or of electricity cables or lines or of telephone lines or any other communication lines of cables. [Punjab Regional and Town Planning and Development Act (Punjab Act No. 11 of 1995), S. 2(p)]

English mortgage. A mortgage in which the mortgagor binds himself to repay the mortgaged money on a certain date and transfers the mortgaged property absolutely to the mortgagee subject to its retransfer on payment. [T.P. Act (4 of 1882), S. 58(e) and (g)].

Where the mortgager binds himself to repay the mortgage-money on a certain date and transfers the mortgaged property absolutely to the mortgagee, but subjects to a proviso that he will retransfer it to the mortgager upon payment of the mortgage-money as agreed, the transaction is called an English mortgage. [Transfer of Property Act (4 of 1882), S. 58(e)]

Engrave. To carve. [IPC (45 of 1860), S. 502].

Engraving. "ENGRAVINGS" include etchings, lithographs, woodcuts, prints, and other similar works, not being photographs. [Copyright Act (14 of 1957), S. 2(i)]

The act or art of producing upon hard material incised or raised patterns, characters, lines and the like; an engraved plate; a print.

Engross. To make a fair copy; to write or copy in a bold clear hand; to copy the rude draft of an instrument in a fair, large hand.

Enhance. To raise; to increase. [IPC (45 of 1860), S. 75].

Enjoin. To command; to require with earnestness; to prescribe; to order or direct with urgency; to admonish or instruct or direct with authority.

To command (A person to do) [CrPC 1973 (2 of 1974), 2nd Sch., Form No. 24]; to forbid by injunction. [IPC (45 of 1860), S. 291].

Enjoy. To have the benefit of; to have the advantage of using; take delight in.

A person can be said to 'ENJOY' a benefit within the meaning of S. 70 of the Indian Contract Act (9 of 1872), only by accepting a benefit when he has the option of declining or accepting it.

Enjoyment. The action or state of enjoying. [T.P. Act (4 of 1882), S. 44].

Enjoys the benefit. In S. 70, Indian Contract Act (9 of 1972) means "accepts and enjoys" the benefit.

The use of the word 'enjoy' in S. 105 Transfer of Property Act (4 of 1882) instead of the word 'possess' does not mean that the section contemplated the exclusion of possession. *G.G. in Council* v. *Indar Mani,* AIR 1950 East Punj 296.

Enlarge. To extend; to widen; to increase.

Enmity. State or condition of being an enemy.

ENMITY, ANIMOSITY, HOSTILITY. *Enmity* lies in the heart; it is deep and malignant. *Animosity*, a spirit, lies in the passions; it is fierce and vindictive. *Hostility* lies in the action; it is mischievous and destructive.

Enquiry. "An official process to find out the cause of something or to find out information about something; a request for information about somebody/something; a question about somebody/something; the act of asking questions or collecting information about somebody/something." [Oxford Advanced Learner's Dictionary as cited in *Kathiroor Service Cooperative Bank Limited* v. *Commissioner of Income Tax* (CIT), (2014) 14 SCC 352, para 14.3].

An act of asking for information and also consideration of some evidence, may be documentary. *Ashwani Kumar Saxena* v. *State of M.P.*, (2012) 9 SCC 750, para 27].

An enquiry under the CrPC does not merely mean an enquiry into an offence; its meaning is considerably wider and extends to enquiries into matters which are not offences. Proceedings under S. 145(7) of the CrPC, 1973 (2 of 1974) are enquiries.

The use of the word 'enquiry' in C1. 7, Sch. IV should ordinarily connote an inquiry which approximates to a judicial enquiry where parties are called upon and are given an opportunity to lead evidence and they do lead evidence in support of their respective claims. *British Medical Stores* v. *L. Bhagirath Mal,* AIR 1955 Punj 5, 11. [Delhi and Ajmer-Merwara Rent Control Act (19 of 1947), Sch. IV, C1. 7]

When a Member of Legislative Assembly tendered his resignation, the Speaker put necessary questions and elicited answers from him. The procedure adopted by the Speaker constitutes "enquiry". *Vikram Singh* v. *Shri Ram Ballabhji Kasat,* AIR 1995 MP 140, 147. [Constitution of India, Art. 190(3)(b) *Prov.*]

Enquiry officer. Means an officer of the Authority or any person specifically appointed by it to conduct an enquiry for purposes of these regulations. [Insurance Regulatory and Development Authority (Registration of Indian Insurance Companies) Regulations, Reg. 2(d)]

Enrol. The act of inserting names in an orderly manner into any book.

Enrolled person. Means an under-officer or other person enrolled under this Act. [Indo-Tibetan Border Police Force Act (35 of 1992), S. 2(1)(j)] [Border Security Force Act, 1968, s. 2(1)(k)]

Enrolled workman. Means a workman (whether Badli workman or permanent or temporary workmen) whose name is borne on the muster roll, or as the case may be in Badli Register of a Factory on the first day of a specified period. [Gujarat Payment of Unemployment Allowance to Workmen in Factories Act (20 of 1981), S. 2(b)]

Ensure. To secure; to make sure, certain or safe.

Entail. To involve; to make necessary. An estate settled with regard to the rule of its descent.

Entailment. A word sometimes used in the same sense as devise; settlement of succession of landed estate so that it cannot be bequeathed at pleasure; inalienable inheritance.

Entangle. To become entangled or involved in difficulty.

Enter. To inscribe upon records [T.P. Act (4 of 1882), S. 3, *Expln.* 1, prov. (a)]; to go or come into; to join or engage in; to begin; to admit.

Entered. The reasonable interpretation of the words, "entered in the electoral roll" contained in S. 2(1)(e) of the Act, should be, "included in the electoral roll." *Chandra Shekhar Prasad Singh* v. *Jai Prakash Singh,* AIR 1959 Pat 450, 453. [Representation of the People Act (43 of 1951), S. 2(1)(e)].

Entering. One word 'entering' clearly indicates that the conveyance to be liable to the toll must enter the Municipality from places outside it. A vehicle which is already in the limits of the Municipality, when it plies for hire cannot be held to have entered the municipal limits. *Mainpuri Municipality* v. *Kanhaiya Lal,* AIR 1960 SC 184, 185 [U.P. Municipalities Act (2 of 1916), S. 128(VII)].

Entering upon reference. The arbitrators enter upon reference when they take upon themselves the office of arbitrators and exercise some functions as arbitrators. If they need and determine the date of hearing and issue directions as to pleadings they exercise the functions of arbitrators. *Bajranglal Laduram* v. *Ganesh Commercial Co.,* AIR 1951 Cal 78. [Arbitration Act (10 of 1940) (*repealed*), S. 9]

An arbitrator enters upon a reference when, after having accepted the reference, he applies, his mind and does something in furtherance and execution of the work of arbitration. *Soneylal Thakur* v. *Laxminarain Thakur,* AIR 1957 Pat 395, 397. [Arbitration Act (10 of 1940) (*repealed*), S.11(1)].

When the sole arbitrator held the meetings and gave directions to the parties as to the future progress of the arbitration, he entered upon the reference. (Arbitration Act (10 of 1940) (*repealed*), Sch. I, R. 3).

The Arbitrator should do some judicial act for the progress of the reference like ordering that the university should file a statement and then only it can be inferred that he has entered the reference.

Enterpreneur. One who undertakes an enterprise. [Industrial Finance Corporation Act (15 of 1948) (*Repealed by Act 23 of 1993*), S. 32B(3)(c)].

Enterprise. "ENTERPRISE" means a person (including a permanent establishment of such person) who is, or has been, or is proposed to be, engaged in any activity, relating to the production, storage, supply, distribution, acquisition or control of articles or goods, or know-how, patents, copyrights, trade-marks, licences, franchises or any other business or commercial rights of similar nature, or any data, documentation, drawing or specification relating to any patent, invention, model, design, secret formula or process, of which the other enterprise is the owner or in respect of which the other enterprise has exclusive rights, or the provision of services of any kind, or in investment, or providing loan or in the business of acquiring, holding, underwriting or dealing with shares, debentures or other securities of any other body corporate, whether such activity or business is carried on, directly or through one or more of its units or divisions or subsidiaries, or whether such unit or division or subsidiary is located at the same place where the enterprise is located or at a different place or places. [Income-tax Act (43 of 1961), S. 92F(iii)]

"ENTERPRISE" means a person or a department of the Government, who or which is, or has been, engaged in any activity, relating to the production, storage, supply, distribution, acquisition or control of articles or goods, or the provision of services, of any kind, or in investment, or in the business of acquiring, holding, underwriting or dealing with shares, debentures or other securities of any other body corporate, either directly or through one or more of its units or divisions or subsidiaries, whether such unit or division or subsidiary is located at the same place where the enterprise is located or at a different place or at different places, but does not include any activity of the Government relatable to the sovereign functions of the Government including all activities carried on by the departments of the Central Government dealing with atomic energy, currency, defence and space. [Competition Act, 2002 (12 of 2003), S. 2(h)]

Business concern.

Entertain. To admit in order to deal with [T.P. Act (4 of 1882, S. 109, prov.]; to cherish.

The expression "entertain" means to "admit a thing for consideration" and when a suit or proceeding is not thrown out *in limine* but the Court receives it for consideration and disposal according to law it must be regarded as entertaining the suit or proceeding, no matter whatever the ultimate decision might be.

The word 'entertain' in the proviso means not 'receive' or 'accept' but "to proceed to consider on merits" or "adjudicate upon". *Haji Rahim Bux & Sons* v. *Firm Samiullah and Sons,* AIR 1963 All 320, 330. [CPC (5 of 1988), O. XXI, R. 90, *Proviso* 2]

"ENTERTAIN" means "file or received by the High Court" and it has no reference to the actual hearing of the application for leave to appeal, otherwise the result would be that in many cases applications for leave to appeal would be barred because the applications have not been put up for hearing before the High Court within 60 days of the order of acquittal. *Lala Ram* v. *Hari Ram,* AIR 1970 SC 1093.

The expression "entertain" as meaning 'adjudicate upon' or 'proceed to consider on merits'. *Hindusthan Commercial Bank Ltd.* v. *Punnu Sahu (Dead) Through LRs,* AIR 1970 SC 1384.

Entertainment. The act of furnishing accommodation, refreshment, good cheer or diversion; mental enjoyment, instruction or amusement afforded by anything seen or heard, as, a play, *etc.*, the act of providing gratification or diversion; the act of receiving a host; hospitable reception; hospitable provision for the wants of a guest; a formal or elegant meal, *etc.*; a hospitable report; a banquet; a public reception; the receiving and accommodating guests, either with or without reward.

A diverting performance, specifically a public performance, as a concert, drama, or the like; a source or means of amusement; instruction or amusement afforded by anything seen or heard, as a spectacle, a play, etc.; mental enjoyment, or that which amuses or diverts; that which serves for amusement; also the act of providing gratification or diversion. The term has been held to include recreational activities, such as games, sports, plays and dancing. [Corpus Juris Secundum, Vol. XXX as cited in *Bangalore Turf Club Limited* v. *Regional Director, Employees' State Insurance Corporation,* (2014) 9 SCC 657, para 43.4].

The action of providing or being provided with amusement or enjoyment. As event or performance designed to entertain. [Concise Oxford English Dictionary, 11 Edn. (Revised) as cited in *Bangalore Turf Club Limited* v. *Regional Director, Employees' State Insurance Corporation*, (2014) 9 SCC 657, para 43.1]

"ENTERTAINMENT" includes any exhibition, performance, amusement, game or sport to which persons are ordinarily admitted on payment. [DMC Act, 1957 (66 of 1957), S. 2(16) incorporating DMC Amendment Act, 1993 (67 of 1993) and New Delhi Municipal Council Act (44 of 1994), S. 2(13)]

ENTERTAINMENT with all its grammatical variations and cognate expressions means :

(i) a horse race to which persons are admitted on payment.

(ii) Cinematograph show including video shows to which persons are admitted on payment or exhibition of films or moving pictures which are viewed and heard on the television receiving set, with the aid of any type of antennae with the cable net work attached to it or cable television for which persons are required to make payment by way of contribution or subscription or installation and connection charges or any other charges collected in any manner whatsoever :

(iii) Any amusement or recreation or any entertainment, provided by a multi system operator or exhibition or performance or pageant or a game or sport whether held indoor or outdoor to which persons are admitted on payment.

Explanation:—Recognised game or sport shall mean Cricket, Hockey, Foot Ball, Basket Ball, Tennis, Golf, Volley Ball, Badminton, Kabbadi, Swimming, Athletics, Base-Ball, Weight Lifting, and any other sport or game the Government may notify." [Karnataka Entertainment Tax Act (30 of 1958), S. 2(e)(iii)].

'ENTERTAINMENT' includes any exhibition, performance, amusement, game, sport or race to which persons are admitted for payment but does not include any magic performance. [Kerala (Local Authorities) Entertainment Tax Act. (20 of 1961), S. 2(4)].

One word "entertainment" includes theatres, dramatic performances, cinemas, sports and the like. *Y.V. Srinivasamurthy* v. *State of Mysore*, AIR 1959 SC 894, 896. [Constitution of India, Sch. VII, List II, Entry 62].

"ENTERTAINMENT" includes any exhibitional performance, amusement, game or sport to which persons are admitted for payment. *Geeta Enterprises* v. *State of U.P.,* AIR 1983 SC 1098. [UP Entertainment and Betting Tax Act, 1937, S. 2(3)]

Ordinarily, "entertainment" connotes something which may be beneficial for the mental or physical well being but is not essential or indispensable for human existence. A bare necessity, like ordinary meal, is essential or indispensable and, therefore, is not 'entertainment'. If such a bare necessity is offered by another, it is hospitality but not entertainment. Unless the definition of 'entertainment' includes hospitality, the ordinary meaning of 'entertainment' cannot include hospitality. *CIT* v. *Patel Bros. & Co., Ltd.,* AIR 1995 SC 1829.

That which affords interest or amusement [Emigration Act (31 of 1983), S. 2(o)(vi) and Protection of Civil Rights Act (22 of 1955), S. 2(c)]; hospitable reception.

Entertainment expenditure. ENTERTAINMENT EXPENDITURE includes all expenditure incurred in connection with business on the entertainment of customers and or constituents. The entertainment may consist of providing refreshment or other sorts of entertainment. [Income Tax Act (43 of 1961), S. 37(2A) omitted by Finance Act, 1997]

Entertainment event. "Entertainment event" means an event or a performance which is intended to provide recreation, pastime, fun or enjoyment, by way of exhibition of cinematographic film, circus, concerts, sporting event, pageants, award functions, dance, musical or theatrical performances including drama, ballets or any such event or programme. [Finance Act (32 of 1994), S. 65B(24)] (omitted by Finance Act, 2015) (now repealed by Goods and Services Tax Act, 2017)]

Entice. To allure; to attract; to seduce; to coax. A word which may import an initial, active, and wrongful effort; (as) enticing away a married woman.

The word 'entice' occurring in Section 361 of IPC (45 of 1860) seems to involve idea of inducement or allurement by giving rise to hope or desire in the other. This can take many forms. This may work immediately or it may create continuous and gradual but imperctible impression culminating after sometime, in achieving its ultimate purposes of successful inducement. *Thakorlal D. Vadgama* v. *State of Gujarat,* AIR 1973 SC 2313. Also See *Prakash* v. *State of Haryana,* AIR 2004 SC 227, 230, para 8. [IPC (45 of 1860), S. 361]

ENTICE, ALLURE, DECOY, SEDUCE, TEMPT. *Entice* is to draw on or instigate by means of a feeling internal to one's self, as hope or desire, *Allure* is to do the same thing by means of something external to one's self, as prospect of gain. *Decoy is* to lead on quietly into the snare, as opposed to violent and noisy modes of capture, as "to *decoy* troops into an ambush." To *seduce* is to draw aside from the path of duty, integrity, or chastity by false or alluring representations. To *tempt* is to bring an influence, commonly no creditable one; to bear upon another to induce him to do something. (*Smith Syn. Dis.*)

Entice (away). To allure; to attract by hope of pleasure or profit. [IPC (45 of 1860), S. 498].

Enticed. The two expressions "taking" and "enticing" evidently have two different connotations. In order to mean the accused "enticed" away the girl, it is necessary to have some evidence to the effect that the accused had given her some temptation or promise or assurance or allurement which had the effect of an irresistible force upon the girl. [*Larance Kannan Das* v. *State,* MLJ : Digest (1984), p. 483 : CrLJ 1819 Bom]. [IPC (45 of 1860), S. 361 and 363]

Enticement. The action of enticing. [IPC (45 of 1860), S. 498].

A promise of marriage made to a minor girl by the accused amounts to enticement of a minor under Section 361 of the Code. *Moniram Hazarika* v. *State of Assam,* (2004) 5 SCC 120, 123, para 5 [IPC (45 of 1860), S. 361]

"Entices" and "takes". The expression used in S. 361, IPC (45 of 1860) is "Whoever takes or entices any minor." The words 'takes' does not necessarily connote taking by force and it is not confined to use of force, actual or constructive. These words merely mean "to cause to go" "to escort" or "to get into possession." The word "entice" seems to involve the idea of the inducement or allurement by giving rise to hope or desire in the other. The two words 'takes' and 'entices' are intended to be read together so that each takes to some extent its colour and content from the other. *Thakorlal D. Vadgama* v. *State of Gujarat,* (1973) 2 SCC 413, 421. [IPC (45 of 1860), S. 361]

Entire. Undivided, unmingled, complete in all its parts; whole.

Entire amount admitted by him to be due. 'Entire amount admitted by him to be due'. The expression 'entire amount admitted by him to be due' means the entire gross amount, whether as rent or compensation for use and occupation, calculated at the admitted rate of rent for the admitted period of arrears after making no other deduction except the taxes, if any, paid to a local authority in respect of the building on lessor's account and the amount, if any, deposited in any court under section 30 of the U.P. Urban Buildings (Regulation of Letting, Rent and Eviction) Act, 1972. [C.P.C., 1908, Order 15, Rule 5(2), *Explanation* 2, as amended in U.P. as cited in *Satya Kumari Kamthan* v. *Noor Ahmad,* (2013) 9 SCC 177, para 6].

Entire amount of rent due. The expression 'entire amount of rent due' would include rent which has become time-barred. *K.G.V. Trust* v. *Shri Ram Chadurvedi*, AIR 1978 SC 287, 289.

Entirely. Denotes the whole, in contradistinction to "moiety" which denotes the half part. It means completeness, total sum.

Entirety. The whole; completeness. [Companies Act (1 of 1956), Sch. I, table A. 6].

Entitle. To give a claim, right, or title to; to give a right to demand or receive; to furnish with grounds for claiming.

Entitled. Having a title to.

Entitled as of right. Having a title as a matter of his right.

Entitled as of right to practice. The phrase 'entitled as of right to practice' is an emphatic affirmation of a right to plead and to act independently of the will or discretion of any other person. *Asvini Kumar Ghuse* v. *Arabinda Bose*, AIR 1952 SC 369, 377.

[Supreme Court Advocates (Practice in High Court) Act (18 of 1951), S. 2].

Entitled consumer. "ENTITLED CONSUMER" means a person in a cantonment who is paid from the Defence Services Estimates and is authorised by general or special order of the Central Government to receive a supply of water for domestic purposes from the Military Engineer Services or the Public Works Department on such terms and conditions as may be specified in the order. [Cantonments Act (2 of 1924), S. 2(xi-c)]

Entitled to. The expression 'entitled to' occurring in clause of partnership deed that 'heirs or representative of deceased partner shall be 'entitled to' be partners in firm' cannot be construed to mean in place of deceased partner. [*Usha Gopirathnam* v. *P.S. Ranganathan,* AIR 2008 (NOC) 2137 (Kar) : 2008(3) AIR Kar R 291]

Entitled to act. The following persons shall be deemed persons "ENTITLED TO ACT" as and to the extent hereinafter provided (that is to say)—

trustees for other persons beneficially interested shall be deemed the persons entitled to act with reference to any such case, and that to the same extent as the persons beneficially interested could have acted it free from disability :

a married woman, in cases to which the English law is applicable, shall be deemed to the person so entitled to act and whether of full age or not, to the same extent as if she were unmarried and of full age; and

the guardians of minors and the committees or managers of lunatics or idiots shall be deemed respectively the persons so entitled to act, to the same extent as the minors, lunatics or idiots themselves, if free from disability, could have acted :

Provided that—

(i) no person shall be deemed "entitled to act" whose interest in the subject-matter shall be shown to the satisfaction of the Collector or Court to be adverse to the interest of the person interested for whom he would otherwise be entitled to act;

(ii) in every such case the person interested may appear by a next friend or, in default of his appearance by a next friend, the Collector or Court, as the case may be, shall appoint a guardian for the case to act on his behalf in the conduct thereof;

(iii) the provisions of Order XXXII of the Schedule to the Code of Civil Procedure, 1908 shall, mutatis mutandis, apply in the case of persons interested appearing before a Collector or Court by a next friend, or by a guardian for the case, in proceedings under this Act; and

(iv) no person "entitled to act" shall be competent to receive the compensation money payable to the person for whom he is entitled to act unless he would have been competent to alienate the land and receive and give a good discharge for the purchase money on a voluntary sale. [Land Acquisition Act (1 of 1894), S. 3(g)]

Entitled to avoid. Having a title to avoid *i.e.* to make null. [Indian Contract Act (9 of 1872), S. 19A].

Entitled to possession. The expression "entitled to possession" means that in the case of stolen property the person who originally lost it is entitled to possession of the same. The person who purchased it in good faith for value is only entitled to be compensated. *Roshan Lal* v. *State,* AIR 1957 Punj 297, 299. [CrPC 1973 (2 of 1974), Ss. 452 (1)&(2) and 453]

Entitled to retain. Having a title to hold or continue to hold in possession or use. [Indian Contract Act (9 of 1872), S. 170, ill. (a)]; [Sale of Goods Act (3 of 1930), S. 47(1)].

Entitled to share in rateable distribution of assets. The words "entitled to share in rateable distribution of assets, in R. 90 of O. XXI, CPC (5 of 1908) refer to decree-holders who are entitled to a rateable distribution under S. 73 of the CPC (5 of 1908). The right to receive dividend before the Official Receiver is not contemplated by the rule.

Entity. Something that has a real existence. [Asian Development Bank Act (18 of 1966), Sch., Art. 50 (2)].

Entity includes person, estate, trust, governmental unit.

Entrapment. The deliberate planting of apparent flaws in a system for the purpose of detecting attempted penetrations. (*Cyber Law*)

Entries in the Lists. The Entries in the Lists are not powers but are only fields of legislation and widest import and significance must be given to the language used by Parliament in the various entries. *Balaji* v. *Income Tax Officer*, AIR 1962 SC 123, 125. [Government of India Act, 1935, Sch. VII, List I, Entry 54]

Entrust. To charge or invest with a trust; to commit to another with a certain confidence regarding his care.

Entrusted. The expression 'entrusted' in Section 409 is used in a wide sense and includes all cases in which property is voluntarily handed over for a specific purpose and is dishonestly disposed of contrary to the terms on which possession has been handed over. *Som Nath Puri* v. *State of Rajasthan,* AIR 1972 SC 1490. [IPC (45 of 1860), S. 409]

Entrustment. The term 'entrustment' carries with it the implication that the person handing over any property or on whose behalf that property is handed over to another, continues to be its owner. Further the person handing over the property must have confidence in the person taking the property so as to create a fiduciary relationship between them. *State of Gujrat* v. *Jaswantlal Nathalal*, AIR 1968 SC 700, 701. [IPC (45 of 1860), S. 405]

The term 'entrustment' is not necessarily a term of law. It may have different implications in different contexts. In its most general signification all it imports is the handing over possession for some purpose which may not imply the conferring of any proprietary right at all. [*Ram Narayan Popli* v. *CBI*, (2003) 3 SCC 641, para 363 : 2003 SC (Cri) 869 as cited in *Robert John D'Souza* v. *Stephen V. Gomes*, (2015) 9 SCC 96, para 9].

The term 'entrustment' carries with it the implication that the person handing over any property or on whose behalf the property is handed over to another, continues to be its owner. 'Entrustment' is not necessarily a term of law. It may have different implications in different contexts. In its most general significance, all its imports is handing over the possession for some purpose which may not imply the conferment of any proprietary right therein. *Rashmi Kumar* v. *Mahesh Kumar Bhada,* (1997) 2 SCC 397. [IPC (45 of 1860), Ss. 405 & 406] *See also Ram Narain Popli* v. *CBI*, (2003) 3 SCC 641, para 363 : AIR 2003 SC 2748.

Entry. "ENTRY" in relation to goods means an entry made in a bill of entry shipping bill or bill of export and includes in the case of goods imported or to be exported by post, the entry referred to in S. 82 or the entry made under the regulation made under S. 84. [Customs Act (52 of 1962), S. 2(16)]

"ENTRY" means entry by water, land or air. [Passport (Entry into India) Act (34 of 1920), S. 2]

"ENTRY" includes landing at any port in British India during the period the ship's stay on her way to a destination outside British India. [Immigration into India (3 of 1924), S. 2(*b*)]

The act of recording or enrolling.

AS APPLIED TO A BUILDING, a passage leading into a house or other building or a room; coming or going is the mere putting of a hand into a hole in. The wall without putting it through the hole is not an entry into the house.

AS APPLIED TO WRITINGS, that which is written in words or figures.

AS APPLIED TO BOOKS OF ACCOUNT. Setting down items of account in writing; the act of setting down or causing to be set down transactions in writing; recording or causing to be recorded; in due form; the act of making a record of a fact or transaction (as, ledger entry); the act of setting down the particulars of a sale or other transaction in a merchant's or tradesman's account books.

AS APPLIED TO JUDICIAL PROCEEDINGS, recording in due form and order a thing done in Court.

AS APPLIED TO REAL ESTATE, the act of going on land with the intention of asserting a right in such land; taking possession of land by the legal owner; act by which an individual acquires an inceptive right to a portion of vacant land or the unappropriated soil of the country.

AS APPLIED TO WAREHOUSING. An entry made at the Custom House giving particulars of dutiable goods to be stored on import in a bonded warehouse, such goods are not liable to duty until taken out for consumption.

Entry into India is not synonymous with remaining in India. *Chhanga Khan* v. *State,* AIR 1956 All 69. [Passport (Entry into India) Act (34 of 1920), S. 3]

That which is entered (in a record) [Customs Act (52 of 1962), S. 2(16)]; the action of entering or going in. [Reciprocity Act (9 of 1943), S. 2(b)].

Entry of goods. With all its grammatical variations and cognate expressions, means, entry of goods:

(*i*) into a local area from any place outside such area,

(*ii*) into a local area from any place outside the State,

(*iii*) into a local area from any place outside the territory of India, for consumption, use or sale therein:

Provided that in case of such goods which are liable to tax under Section 12(1) of the Bihar Finance Act, 1981, entry of goods shall mean entry of goods into local area from any place outside the State for consumption, use or sale therein.

Explanation.—Entry of goods into a local area for consumption, use or sale therein from any place outside the territory of India shall also be deemed to be any entry of goods for the purpose of this Act.

Entry into possession. The act of going upon land to assert some right over it.

Enumerate. To designate, or specifically mention; to count to mention in detail, or reckon up singly; to recount; to relate.

To narrate one after another. [Industrial Finance Corporation Act (15 of 1948) (*Repealed by Act 23 of 1993*), S. 5A].

Enumerated. Means expressly or specifically mentioned.

Enunciate. To state publicly; to announce or proclaim.

Enure. To operate; to take effect.

Environment. A surrounding. [Delhi Urban Art Commission Act (1 of 1974), S. 11(1) and Constitution of India, Art. 48A].

"ENVIRONMENT" includes water, air and land and the interrelationship which exists among and between water, air and land, and human beings, other living creatures, plants, microorganism and property. [National Environment Tribunal Act (27 of 1995), S. 2(d) and Employment of Manual Scavengers and Construction of Dry Latrines (Prohibition), Act (46 of 1993), S. 2(d) and Section 2(a) of The Environment (Protection) Act (29 of 1986), S. 2(d). *See also* National Environment Appellate Authority (Appeal) Rules, 1997, R. 2(d)]

The word 'Environment' is a broad spectrum which brings within its sweep hygienic atmosphere and ecological balance. *Virender Gaur* v. *State of Haryana,* (1995) 2 SCC 577.

Environmental impact. Means any effect caused by a given activity on the environment, including human health and safety, flora, fauna, soil, air, water, climate, landscape and historical monuments or other physical structures or the interactions among these factors : it also includes effects on cultural heritage or socio economic conditions resulting from alterations to those factors. [Energy Charter Protocol on Energy Efficiency and Related Environmental Aspects, Art. 1(7)]

Environmental impact assessment. Means a national procedure for evaluating the likely impact of a proposed activity on the environment. [UN Convention on Environmental Impact Assessment in a Transboundary Context (25 Feb. 1991), Art. 1(vi)]

Environmental pollutant. Means any solid, liquid or gaseous substance present in such concentration as may be, or tend to be, injurious to environment. [Employment of Manual Scavengers and Construction of Dry Latrines (Prohibition) Act (46 of 1993), S. 2(e); Environment (Protection) Act (29 of 1986), 2(b)].

Environmental pollution. Means the presence in the environment of any environmental pollutant. [Employment of Manual Scavengers and Construction of Dry Latrines (Prohibition) Act (46 of 1993), S. 2(f)]

Environmental services. "Environmental services" includes—

(i) provision of goods such as wood, non-timber forest products, fuel, folder, water and provision of services such as grazing, tourism, wildlife protection and life support;

(ii) regulating services such as flood moderation, carbon sequestration and heath of soil, air and water regimes;

(iii) supporting such other services necessary for the production of ecosystem services, biodiversity, nutrient cycling and primary production including pollination and seed dispersal. [Compensatory Afforestation Fund Act (38 of 2016), S. 2(e)].

Environmentally sound management of hazardous wastes. Means taking all steps to ensure that the hazardous wastes are managed in a manner which will protect human health and the environment against the adverse effects which may result form such wastes. [Hazardous Waste (Management and Handling) Rules, 1989, R. 3(x)]

Envoy. A high ranking diplomat.

A public minister sent by one sovereign government to another for transacting diplomatic business. [CPC (5 of 1908), S. 83]

Eodem modo quo oritur, eodem modo dessolvitur. In the same way in which anything is constituted, it may be destroyed.

Epileptic psychosis. 'Epilepsy usually occurs from early infancy, though it may occur at any period of life. Individuals, who have had epileptic fits for years, do not necessarily show any mental aberration, but quite a few of them suffer from mental deterioration. Religiousity is marked feature in the commencement, but the feeling is only superficial. Such patients are peevish, impulsive and suspicious, and are easily provoked to anger on the slightest cause.

'The disease is generally characterised by short transitory fits of uncontrollable mania followed by complete recovery. The attacks, however, become more frequent. There is a general impairment of the mental faculties, with loss of memory and self-control. At the same time, hallucinations of sight and hearing occur and are followed by delusions of a persecuting nature. They are deprived of all moral sensibility, are given to the lowest forms of vice and sexual excesses, and are sometimes dangerous to themselves as well as to others. In many long-standing cases, there is a progressive dementia or mental deficiency.

'True epileptic psychosis is that which is associated with epileptic fits. This may occur before or after the fits, or may replace them, and is known as pre-epileptic, post-epileptic and masked or psychic phases (psychomotor epilepsy).' [Medical Jurisprudence and Toxicology by Modi, 24th Edn., 2011 as cited in *State of Rajasthan* v. *Shera Ram,* (2012) 1 SCC 602, para 20]

Equal opportunity. Freedom from discrimination (as in employment) on the basis of race, colour, religion, national origin, sex, disability, age, or sometimes sexual orientation.

Equal pay. It means that men and women in the same employment must be paid at the same rate for like work or work rated as equivalent or of equal value.

Equal pay for equal work. The equal pay directive makes clear that equal work embraces work of equal value as well as work which is the same.

Article 39(d) proclaims 'equal pay for equal work for both men and women' as a Directive Principle of State Policy. 'Equal pay for equal work for both men and women' as a Directive Principle of State Policy. 'Equal pay for equal work for both men and women' means equal pay for equal work for everyone and as between the sexes. *Randhir Singh* v. *Union of India,* AIR 1982 SC 879 (para 8) [Constitution of India, Art. 39(d)]

Equal pay for equal work, Doctrine of. Though doctrine of 'equal pay for equal work' is considered to be a concomitant of Article 14 as much as equal pay for unequal work will also be a negation of that right, equal pay would depend upon not only the nature or the volume of work, but also on the qualitative difference as regards reliability and responsibility as well and though the functions may be the same, but the responsibilities do make a real and substantial difference. [*State of Orissa* v. *Balram Sahu,* (2003) 1 SCC 250, 256, para 11]

Equal protection. The guarantee of the 'equal protection' of the laws means the protection of equal laws. It forbids class legislation, but does not forbid classification which rests upon reasonable grounds of distinction. *Charanjit Lal Chowdhury* v. *Union of India,* AIR 1951 SC 41. [Constitution of India, Art. 14]

Equal protection of the laws. What the equal protection clause means is simply this that the same law should govern those similarly circumstanced, it cannot and does not prohibit different laws for those differently circumstanced. *Deodat Rai* v. *State,* AIR 1951 All 718, 731. [Constitution of India, Art. 14]

The phrase 'equal protection of the laws' means in essence the right to equal treatment in similar circumstances. The right is equally observed if the law makes all prosecutions for a particular offence subject to the sanction of a prescribed authority or if it provides that no such sanction is necessary. It is violated if, without reasonable grounds, it provides that sanction shall be necessary in some cases and not in others. *Bhai Singh* v. *State*, MLJ : QD (1956-1960) Vol. I C2187 : 1960 All LJ 68 : 1960 All WR (HC) 37 : 1960 All CrR 50 : 1960 CrLJ 776 : AIR 1960 All 369 (FB). [Constitution of India, Art. 14]

Equal protection must mean that there will not be arbitrary discrimination made by the laws themselves in their administration.

It merely requires that all persons subjected to such legislation shall be treated alike under like circumstances and conditions both in the privileges conferred and in the liabilities imposed. *Charanjit Lal Chaoudhury* v. *Union of India*, AIR 1951 SC 41 **Rel. on.** *Kameshwar Singh* v. *State of Bihar*, AIR 1951 Pat 91.

Equality. Likeness in possessing the same rights and privileges, and immunities, and being liable to the same duties. A word which conveys the idea of identity in size and form.

The word 'equality' means equality among equals and it does not provide an absolute equality of all in all circumstances. *Desu Naidu* v. *A.P. Public Service, Commission,* AIR 1967 AP 353, 357. [Constitution of India, Art. 14]

"EQUALITY" under Article 16 could not have a different content from equality under Article 14. Equality of opportunity for unequals can only mean aggravation of inequality. Equality of opportunity admits discrimination with reason and prohibits discrimination without reason. *State of Kerala* v. *N.M. Thomas,* AIR 1976 SC 490. [Constitution of India, Art. 14]

"Equality before law" and "equal protection of laws". The two expressions 'equality before law' or 'the equal protection of laws' within the territory of India do not mean the same thing even if there may be much in common. The word 'law' in the former expression is used in a generic sense—a philosophical sense—whereas the word 'laws' in the latter expression denotes specific laws in force. *Sri Srinivasa Theatre* v. *Govt. of T.N.,* AIR 1992 SC 999. [Constitution of India, Art. 14]

Equality before the law. The expression 'equality before the law' does not imply that the same law should apply to all persons in the same state. It does not refuse to take note of differentiations in economic and social functions or for the need for special types of *quasi*-judicial tribunals, due to the growing tendency towards the enlargement of State intervention in the economic and social life of the country. *Asiatic Engineering Co.* v. *Achhru Ram,* AIR 1951 All 746, 770. [Constitution of India, Art. 14]

"Equality before the law" does not mean absolute equality of men but it postulates that there shall not be any special privilege by reason of birth or creed or the like in favour of an individual. *Raja Kulkarni* v. *State of Bombay,* AIR 1951 Bom 105, 120.

The words mean substantial equality of treatment. Identical treatment under equal circumstances. *Abdur Rahim* v. *Joseph A. Pinta,* AIR 1951 Hyd 11 (FB).

Reasonable classification is permissible. What is prohibited is arbitrary selections or discrimination within the class. *Kamal Mal Singh* v. *Helu Ram,* AIR 1952 Raj 17.

Equality of opportunity. Equality of opportunity in matters of promotion, must mean equality as between members of the same class of employees, and not equality between members of separate independent classes. *A.I.S. Ms And Asst. S. Ms. Assu.* v. *G.M. Central Railway*, AIR 1960 SC 384, 386. [Constitution of India, Art. 16]

Equality of opportunity for all citizens. Clause (1) of Article 16 clearly provides for equality of opportunity to all citizens in the services under the State. It is important to note that the Constitution uses the words "equality of opportunity for all citizens." This inherently implies that the opportunity must be given not only to a particular section of the society or a particular class of citizens but to all citizens of India. *State of Kerala* v. *N.M. Thomas,* AIR 1976 SC 490. [Constitution of India, Art. 16]

Equalisation levy. In this chapter, unless the context otherwise requires, "EQUALISATION LEVY" means the tax leviable on consideration received or receivable for any specified service under the provisions of this Chapter. [Finance Act (32 of 1994), S. 164(d)].

Equality of opportunity in matters of promotion. "Equality of opportunity in matters of promotion" must mean equality as between members of the same class of employees and not equality between members of separate, independent classes. *All India Station Masters and Assistant Station Masters Association, Delhi* v. *General Manager, Central Railway,* AIR 1960 SC 384.

Equally divided in opinion. The 'opinion' contemplated by S. 392, CrPC 1973 (2 of 1974) is nothing more or nothing less than the decision as to the operative order to be passed in the case. It is not merely what may be called the inclination of the judge as to the view to be taken on the questions arising in the case. It is only where there is any difference as to the disposal of the case, that it can be said that the Judges are divided in opinion. *State of Orissa* v. *Minaketan Patnaik,* AIR 1953 Ori 160.

Equipment. 'EQUIPMENT', in relation to a ship, includes boats, tackle, pumps, apparel, furniture, life-saving appliances of every description, spars, masts, rigging and sails, fog signals, lights, shapes and signals of distress, medicines and medical and surgical stores and appliances, charts, radio installations, appliances for preventing, detecting or extinguishing fire, buckets, compasses, axes lanterns, loading and discharging gears and appliances of all kinds and all other stores of articles belonging to or to be used in connection with or necessary for the navigation and safety of the ship. [Merchant Shipping Act (44 of 1958), S. 3(11)]

"EQUIPMENT" as referred to in the definition of chemical weapons production facility in Article II comprises specialized equipment and standard equipment. [Chemical Weapons Convention Act (34 of 2000), (Verification Annex) 5]

The implements used in an operation or activity; apparatus. [Mines Act (35 of 1952), S. 38(1) and Army Act (46 of 1950), S. 54(a)].

Equipment leasing company. Any company which is a financial institution carrying on as its principal business, the activity of leasing of equipment. [Non-Banking Financial Companies Acceptance of Public Deposits (Reserve Bank) Directions, 1998, Para 2(1)(ii)]

Equitable. Marked by a due consideration for what is fair, unbiased or impartial; according to natural justice; untrammelled by technical niceties of the law.

Equitable assets. The assets which a creditor could, under the old practice, reach only through a Court of equity.

Equitable charge. Any agreement in writing and properly signed, however informal, by which any property, real or personal, is to be security for a sum of money, is a charge, and amounts to an equitable mortgage. [*See* T.P. Act (4 of 1882), Ss. 58-59].

Equitable estoppel. The doctrine of part performance is clearly one of equitable estoppel and a party who is not privy to the transaction on which the estoppel rests can take no advantage of it. (4 OWN 913 : AIR 1927 Oudh 482).

Equitable lease. An agreement for the grant of an interest in land on terms that correspond to a legal lease but do not comply with a necessary formal requirements of legal lease.

Equitable mortgage. A mortgage which is recognised in equity but not in law.

Equitable rights. A right which is cognizable within a Court of equity.

Equitably. Fairly; justly; impartially; in an equitable manner (as), the laws should be *equitably* administered.

Equitas est aequalitas. Equality is equity, or, as it is sometimes expressed, "equity delights in equality."

Equitas sequitur legem. (*Lat.*) Equity follows the law.

Equities. Alternative term for *ordinary shares.* Equities entitle their holder to share in the issuing company's profits.

Equity, is defined to be a correction, or qualification of the law, generally made in that part wherein it faileth, or is too severe. In other words "the correction of that wherein the law, by reason of its universality, is deficient." (*Tomlin*)

'Equity' usually means 'an equitable interest in property'. [*M.P. Mathur* v. *DTC*, (2006) 13 SCC 706, para 14 as cited in *Monnet Ispat and Energy Limited* v. *Union of India*, (2012) 11 SCC 1, para 181].

'Equity' means 'floating equity' a term which may be used to describe the interest of a beneficiary under a will.' [*M.P. Mathur* v. *DTC*, (2006) 13 SCC 706, para 14 as cited in *Monnet Ispat and Energy Limited* v. *Union of India*, (2012) 11 SCC 1, para 181].

Sometimes, it means 'a mere equity', which is a procedural right ancillary to some right of property, for example, an equitable right to have a conveyance rectified. [*M.P. Mathur* v. *DTC*, (2006) 13 SCC 706, para 14 as cited in *Monnet Ispat and Energy Limited* v. *Union of India*, (2012) 11 SCC 1, para 181].

'Equity' means 'the right to obtain an injunction or other equitable remedy'. [*M.P. Mathur* v. *DTC*, (2006) 13 SCC 706, para 14 as cited in *Monnet Ispat and Energy Limited* v. *Union of India*, (2012) 11 SCC 1, para 181].

Equity is the system of law which, prior to the fusion of law and equity effected by the Supreme Court of Judicature Acts 1873 (of England) and 1875, was administered by the Court of Chancery. These Acts emphasised, rather than diminished, the importance of the principles which made up the former system of equity jurisprudence, and it will be necessary, for the purpose of understanding these principles, to make frequent reference to the practice of the Court of Chancery and from time to time to make some mention of the history of the system. HALSBURY 4th Edn., Vol. 16, para 1201, p. 807.

Body of legal rules and remedies developed by the Court of Chancery parallel to but separate from the common law; that which is fair and right; the recourse to general principles of justice to correct and supplement the ordinary law.

For the purposes of sub-section (11), the expression "equity" means in terms of fair allocation of resources taking into account the health social and economic burden of mental illness on individuals, their families and caregivers. [Mental Healthcare Act (10 of 2017), S. 18(11), *Explanation (iii)*].

Equity acts in personam. Equity grants relief in the form of personal decrees as contrasted with law which awards money damages.

Equity and law. Equity is no part of the law, but a moral virtue, which qualifies, moderates, and reforms the rigour, hardness and edge of the law, and is a universal truth. It does also assist the law, where it is defective and weak in the constitution (which is the life of the law), and defends the law from crafty evasions, delusions and mere subtleties, invented and contrived to evade and elude the common law, whereby such as have undoubted right are made remediless.

Equity capital. Ordinary capital. [Esso (Acquisition of Undertakings in India) Act (4 of 1974), S. 4(2)(a)].

Equity follows the law. The mistakes remained in the documents of bid due to gross negligence in not checking the same before the submission of bid by the bidder and the rectification or correction in documents were not sought by him within time. Considering the maxim 'equity follows the law' it was held that the bidder was not entitled to rectification of mistakes for being considered along with the other bidders. *W.B. State Electricity Board* v. *Patel Engg. Co.,* (2001) 2 SCC 451, para 28.

Equity of redemption. Incident to every mortgage is the right of the mortgagor to redeem, a right which is called his equity of redemption, and which continues notwithstanding that he fails to pay the debt in accordance with the proviso for redemption. HALSBURY, 4th Edn., Vol. 32, para 407, p. 190.

Equity of statute. The sound interpretation of a statute, taking into consideration its reason and spirit.

The judicial rule of law for interpreting statutes applies the grammatical approach, thereby to bring out the value judgment incorporated in the statute itself. Sometimes it is called the 'equity of the statute'. *Authorised Officer, Thanjavur* v. *S. Naganatha Ayyar,* AIR 1979 SC 1192.

Equity oriented fund. For the purposes of this clause, "EQUITY ORIENTED FUND" means a fund—

(i) where the investible funds are invested by way of equity shares in domestic companies to the extent of more than fifty percent of the total proceed of such fund; and

(ii) which has been set up under a scheme of a Mutual Fund specified under clause (23D);

Provided that percentage equity share holding of the fund shall be computed with reference to the annual average of the monthly averages of the opening and closure figures. [Income-tax Act (43 of 1961), S. 10(38) *Expln.* (*Inserted by Finance (No. 2) Act (23 of 2004), S. 5*]

"EQUITY ORIENTED FUND" for the purposes of section 80CCG of Act 43 of 1961, 'equity oriented fund' shall have the meaning assigned to it in the *Explanation* to section 10(38). [(w.e.f. 1-4-2014) *Explanation* to section 80CCG of the Income-tax Act, 1961 (43 of 1961)]

Equity share capital. All share capital of a company which is not preferential capital. [Companies Act (1 of 1956), S. 85(2)].

"EQUITY SHARE CAPITAL" for the purposes of section 43 of Act 18 of 2013, the expression 'equity share capital', with reference to any company limited by shares, means all share capital which is not preference share capital. [*Explanation (i)* to section 43 of the Companies Act, 2013 (18 of 2013)]

Equity will not suffer a wrong to be without a remedy. The maxim upon which the enforcement of uses and trusts was founded by the Court of Chancery. A wrong will not go unredressed if the Courts are able to remedy it.

Equivalent. Equal in value, measure, force, effect *etc.*

By using the expression "equivalent" one means that there are some degrees of flexibility or adjustment which do not lower the stated requirement. [*Chandrakala Trivedi* v. *State of Rajasthan*, (2012) 3 SCC 129, para 8].

Eradicate. To destroy to the roots; to root out.

Eradication. The act or process of pulling up by the roots.

Erasure. A scraping, scratching, or rubbing out; removal of a word or part of a word from a writing by any means; obliteration.

The action of erasing; an instance of erasing. [Registration Act (16 of 1908), S. 20(1)]; [Trade and Merchandise Marks Act (43 of 1958), S. 106(1)].

Erect. To erect is to build; to construct; to raise and set up in an upright or perpendicular position; to set up; raise up; to set up or found or establish or institute.

To put up by the fitting together of materials or parts. [Indian Contract Act (9 of 1872), S. 73, ill. (1)]; [Indian Railways Act (9 of 1890), S. 7(1)(d)].

Erect a building. The expression 'to erect a building' means—

(a) to erect a new building or any site, whether previously built upon or not.

(b) to re-erect—

(i) any building of which more than one-half of the cubical contents above the level of plinth have been pulled down, burnt or destroyed, or

(ii) any building of which more than one-half of the superficial area of the external wall above the level of plinth has been pulled down, or

(iii) any frame-building of which more than half of the number of posts or beams in the external walls have been pulled down;

(c) to convert into a dwelling house any building or any part of a building not originally constructed for human habitation, subsequently appropriated for any other purpose;

(d) to convert into more than one dwelling house a building originally constructed as one dwelling house only;

(e) to convert into a place of religious worship or a sacred building any place or building not originally constructed for such purpose;

(f) to roof or cover an open space between walls or buildings to the extent of the structure formed by the roofing or covering of such space;

(g) to convert two or more tenements in a building into a greater or lesser number of such tenements;

(h) to convert into a stall, shop, office, warehouse or godown, workshop, factory or garage any building not originally constructed for use as such, or to convert any building constructed for such purpose by sub-division or addition, in greater or lesser number of such stalls, shops, offices, warehouses or godowns, workshops, factories or garages;

(i) to convert a building, which, when originally constructed, was legally exempt from the operation of any building regulation contained in any other law for the time being in force, into a building which, had it been originally erected in its converted form, would have been subject to such building regulations;

(j) to convert into, or use as a dwelling house, any building which has been discontinued as, or appropriated for any purpose other than, a dwelling house;

(k) to make any addition to a building;

(l) to close permanently any door or window in any external wall;

(m) to remove or reconstruct the principal staircase or to alter its position. [Bengal Municipal Act, 1993, S. 197(1)].

Erect or re-erect. "ERECT OR RE-ERECT" any building includes:—

(i) any material alteration or enlargement of any building.

(ii) the conversion, by structural alteration, into place for human habitation of any building not originally constructed for human habitation;

(iii) the conversion into more than one place for human habitation of a building originally constructed as one such place;

(iv) the conversion of two or more places of human habitation into a greater number of such places;

(v) such alterations of a building as affect an alteration of its drainage or sanitary arrangements or materially effect its security.

(vi) the addition of any rooms, buildings out houses, or other structures to any building and

(vii) the Construction, in a wall adjoining any street or land not belonging to the owner of the wall, of a door opening on to such street or land. [Punjab Regional and Town Planning and Development Act, Punjab Act No. (11 of 1995), S. 2(Q)]

Erect or re-erect any building. The expression "erect or re-erect any building" includes: (*a*) any material alteration or - enlargement of any building; (*b*) the conversion by structural alteration into a place for human habitation of any building not originally constructed for human habitation; (c) such alterations in a building as materially affect its drainage or security; and (*d*) the addition of any rooms, buildings, outhouses or other structures to any building. [U.P. Act (1 of 1900), (Municipalities), S. 3, cl. 9].

Erection. "ERECTION" in relation to a building includes extension, alteration or re-erection. [Slum Areas (Improvement and Clearance) Act (96 of 1956), S. 2(d)]

"ERECTION, commissioning or installation" means any service provided by a commissioning and installation agency in relation to,—

(i) erection, commissioning or installation of plant, machinery or equipment; or

(ii) installation of—

(a) electrical and electronic devices, including wirings or fittings therefor; or

(b) plumbing, drain laying or other installations for transport of fluids; or

(c) heating, ventilation or air-conditioning including related pipe work, duct work and sheet metal work; or

(d) thermal insulation, sound insulation, fire proofing or water proofing; or

(e) lift and escalator, fire escape staircases or travelators; or

(f) such other similar services. [Finance Act (32 of 1994), S. 65(39a) *as substituted by Finance Act (18 of 2005), S. 88(a)(x)* (now repealed by Goods and Services Tax Act, 2017)]

ERMES. European Radio Message System / Enhanced Radio Message System. Radio message system with better performance than the POCSAG. (*Telecommunication*)

Erosion. A gradual eating away of the soil by the operation of the currents of tides.

Erroneous. Deviating from the law; inequitable; incorrect; unlawful.

"Erroneous" means 'wrong; incorrect'. [Oxford English Dictionary as cited in *Murugesan* v. *State*, (2012) 10 SCC 383, para 33].

Erroneously. By error. [CrPC 1973 (2 of 1974), S. 460]

Erroneously refunded. The expression erroneously refunded means refunded by means of an order which is erroneously made. *G.F. Industries* v. *Union of India*, AIR 1977 SC 456, 458. [Customs Act (52 of 1962), S. 27].

Error. A mistake of law or of fact in the judgment of a Court; mistake of any kind.

"A mistake in judgment or deviation from the truth in matters of fact, and from the law in matters of judgment; mis-statement or misdescription erroneously and not willfully introduced; unintentional misdescription; excess." (*Ame Cyc.*)

Something incorrectly done through ignorance or inadvertence. [CPC (5 of 1908), S. 99, CrPC 1973 (2 of 1974), S. 215].

ERROR, MISTAKE, BLUNDER, HALLUCINATION. An *error* is any deviation from the standard or course of right, truth, justice, or accuracy, which is not intentional. A *mistake* is an error committed under a misapprehension or misconception of the nature of a case. An *error* may be from the absence of knowledge; a *mistake* is from insufficient or false observation. *Blunder* is a practical *error* of a peculiarly gross or awkward kind, committed through glaring ignorance, heedlessness, or awkwardness. *Hallucination* is an illusion of the perception, a phantasm of the imagination. (*Smith Syn. Dis.*)

Error apparent on the fact of record. *See* C.P. Code (5 of 1908), O. XLVII, R. 1.

Error apparent on face of record will be, only when the reasons given by the arbitrator in his award are opposed to any statutory requirements or the reasons are legally erroneous. *Baldev Singh* v. *Union of India,* AIR 1965 J&K 28, 30. [Arbitration Act (10 of 1940) (*repealed*), S. 14).

The meaning of this expression is well settled and the error of law envisaged should be so patent that a bare perusal of the judgment and the record on which it is based would show that there was error. *Dholpur Co.-op. Transport and Multi-purpose Union Ltd.* v. *Appellate Authority,* AIR 1955 Raj 19, 26. [Constitution of India, Art. 226]

The High Court, in the exercise of its jurisdiction under Art. 226, interferes when there is error of law apparent on the face of the record, and not where there is only an error of fact however apparent and however gross. *Rajinder Prasad* v. *Punjab State,* AIR 1966 Punj 185, 200 (FB).

Error claculi. (*Lat.*) A mistake or error in the calculation.

Error, defect or irregularity. In S. 105, CPC (5 of 1908), means error, defect or irregularity affecting the decision of the case on the merits.

Error juris nocet. A mistake of law injures (the party labouring under the mistake). As a rule, a mistake of law being an erroneous opinion as to what the law is on a point, is not a ground for granting rescission of a contract.

Error message. A brief message that may appear on your screen to tell you that you cannot perform a function the way you are trying to perform it. The message will usually prompt you to help you perform the function in a way that works in the system. (*Computer*)

Error of fact. That *error* which proceeds either from ignorance of that which clearly exists, or from a mistaken belief in the existence of that which has none. (*Ame Cyc.*)

Error of law. The term includes the ignorance of legal consequences of the known existence or non-existence of facts. (*Ame Cyc.*)

Error of law on the face of award. An error of law on the face of the award means you can find in the award of a document actually incorporated thereto as for instance a note appended by the arbitrator stating the reasons for his judgment some legal proposition which is the basis of the award and which you can then say is erroneous. But this rule does not apply where questions of law are specifically referred to the arbitrator for his decision. *Union of India* v. *Ballia Ram*, AIR 1963 SC 1685, 1691. [Arbitration Act (10 of 1940) (*repealed*), S. 30]

Error of law or fact. It is settled law that where a Court has jurisdiction to determine a question and it determines that question, it cannot be said that it has acted illegally or with material irregularity because it has come to an erroneous decision on a question of fact or even of law. *Jai Hirji Tara Poravala* v. *K.A. Hamid (Dr.),* MLJ : QD (1956-1960) Vol. I C1061 : AIR 1956 Bom 323. [CPC (5 of 1908), S. 115]

Error on the face of the record. *Certiorari* will not issue to correct a mere error of law or fact. The distinction between a mere error and an error apparent on the face of the record has not been defined, but the decision must be left to be determined judicially on the facts of each case : (1955) 1 Mad LJ (SC) 157 : 1955 SCJ 267 : (S) AIR 1955 SC 233 and AIR 1956 All 603, **Followed**. *Haji Abdul Shakoor* v. *Rent Control & Eviction Officer,* MLJ : QD (1956-1960) Vol. II C54 : AIR 1959 All 440. [Constitution of India, Art. 226]

Error or mistake apparent on face of record. It is well settled that the mistake or error justifying a review under O. XLVII, R. 1, CPC (5 of 1908) is most often an error of fact and may in certain cases be one of law also. But in all cases it should be an error of inadvertence; in the case of an error of law it should not have been arrived at by a process of conscious reasoning. The test in such matters is whether the Court itself would have made the correction if it was award of the particular fact or circumstance while writing the judgment. In other words, whether it is an inadvertent mistake or error or a conscious application of mind leading to a result which one party may consider to be erroneous or a mistake. *Ramaswami Padayachi* v. *Shanmugha*

Padayachi, MLJ : QD (1956-1960) Vol. I C1864 : (1959) 2 Mad LJ 201.

Error placitandi aequitatem non tollit. (*Maxim*) A clerical error does not take away equity.

Error qui non resistitur, approbatur. (*Maxim*) An error which is not resisted is approved. (*Latin for Lawyers*)

Escalating annuity. A type of annuity whose payments grow stepwise each year.

Escalation clause. An 'escalation clause' according to its accepted legal connotation means a clause which takes care of the rise and fall of prices in the market. *DCG Mills Co. Ltd.* v. *Raj State Electricity Board,* AIR 1986 SC 1126.

Escape. To effect one's flight from [Children Act (60 of 1960) (*repealed*), S. 49]; [CrPC 1973 (2 of 1974), S. 37(a)].

ESCAPE, ELUDE, EVADE. *Escape* involves the idea of successful effort to avoid danger, or the power, coercion, or even observation of another. To *Elude* is to escape by artifice, vigilance, or dexterity, and implies some person or force at work, from which we escape. To *Evade* is to go out of the way or reach of a thing or person.

Escaped assessment. The wrong allowance of inadmissible personal expenses of the assessee in computing the taxable income in the original assessment constitutes escapement of income, profits or gains liable to assessment.

The expression 'escaped assessment' includes that of a turnover which has not been assessed at all, because for one reason or other no assessment proceedings were initiated and therefore no assessment was made in respect thereof. *Anandji Haridas & Co. (P) Ltd.* v. *S.P. Kasturi*, AIR 1968 SC 565, 572.

Escaping assessment. The words "escaping assessment" apply equally to cases where a notice was received by the assessee but resulted in no assessment at all and to cases where due to any reason no notice was issued to the assessee and therefore there was no assessment of his income. *Commissioner of Income-tax* v. *Narsee Nagsee and Co.*, AIR 1960 SC 1232, 1235. [Business Profits Tax Act, 1947, S. 14].

Escaped convict. A convict, who has run away from lawful custody. [Cr PC 1973 (2 of 1974), Ss. 40(1)(b) and 73(1)].

Escheat. The lapsing of property to the sovereign or State on the death of the owner intestate and without heir [Hindu Succession Act (30 of 1956), S. 29]; property falling by escheat to the State. [Laws Local Extent Act (15 of 1874), Second Sch.].

The term now signifies a falling of a deceased's estate into the general property of the state upon his death intestate and without lawful heirs, and is applied indifferently to all rights of property of whatever nature. The property itself which reverts to the state is also termed an *escheat.*

Escort. A body of armed men to guard a person or goods on a journey. [Army Act (46 of 1950), S. 42(c)].

Escrow. A written instrument, which by its terms imports a legal obligation deposited by the grantor, promisor, or obligor, or his agent with a stranger or third person.

Escrow account. A bank account set up in hard currency in the joint names of the buyer and seller and in which the various monies involved in any export sale in general and in a counter trade agreement in particular (usually a forward purchase) are held in trust. (*Trade Finance*)

Escrow agents. The 'escrow agents', normally, are persons who are trusted by the parties of contract under an escrow arrangement to act fairly and without bias notwithstanding their relationship with the respective parties. [*Siddhivinayak Realties (P) Ltd.* v. *Tulip Hospitality Services Ltd.,* (2007) 4 SCC 612, 626, para 37]

Escrow arrangement. An 'escrow arrangement' is normally arrived at in order to safeguard the interest of the parties for the purpose of a contract. [*Siddhivanayak Realities (P) Ltd.* v. *Tulip Hospitality Services Ltd.,* (2007) 4 SCC 612, 626, para 37]

E-Sign. Act giving electronic signatures and contracts the same validity as traditional hand-written and copy signatures. (*Cyber Law*)

Especially within the knowledge of the accused. The word 'especially' means facts that are pre-eminently or exceptionally within the knowledge of the accused. *Shambhur Nath* v. *State of Ajmer*, AIR 1956 SC 404, 406. [Indian Evidence Act (1 of 1872), S. 106]

Espionage. The practice of using spies to collect information about what another country government or company is doing or plans to do.

Involves the act of spying or monitoring, and includes the theft or misappropriation of secrets by computer or other means. (*Cyber Law*)

Essence. A basis underlying or constituting entity. [Indian Contract Act (9 of 1872), S. 55 and Sale of Goods Act (3 of 1930), S. 11].

Essence of the contract. Any condition or stipulation in a contract which is mutually understood and agreed by the parties to be of such vital importance that a sufficient performance of the contract cannot be had without exact compliance with it is said to be 'of the essence of the contract'.

Constituted substance of contract. [Indian Contract Act (9 of 1872), S. 55 and Sale of Goods Act (3 of 1930), S. 11].

Essential. Indispensably necessary; important in the highest degree; requisite that which is required for the continued existence of a thing.

Indispensably requisite [Representation of the People Act(43 of 1951), S. 8(4)(a)(i)]; constituting or forming part of the essence. [Specific Relief Act (47 of 1963), S. 16(b) and Indian Contract Act (9 of 1872), S. 20].

Essential character. "ESSENTIAL CHARACTERISTICS" means such heritable traits of a plant variety which are determined by the expression of one or more genes of other heritable determinants that contribute to the principal features, performance or value of the plant variety. [Protection of Plant Varieties and Farmers' Right Act (53 of 2001), S. 2(h)]

Essential commodities. 'ESSENTIAL COMMODITIES' means any of the following commodities—

(i) cattle fodder, including oilcakes and other commodities;

(ii) coal including coke and other derivatives;

(iii) component parts and other accessories of automobiles;

(iv) cotton and woollen textiles;

(v) drugs;

Explanation : In this sub-clause, "drug" has the meaning assigned to it in clause (b) of S. 3 of the Drugs and Cosmetics Act, 1940 (23 of 1940),

(vi) foodstuffs, including edible oilseeds and oils;

(vii) iron and steel, including manufactured products of iron and steel;

(viii) paper including newsprint, paper board and straw board;

(ix) petroleum and petroleum products;

(x) raw cotton, whether ginned or unginned and cotton seed;

(xi) raw jute;

(xii) any other class of commodity which the Central Government may, by notified order declare to be an essential commodity for the purposes of this Act, being a commodity with respect to which Parliament has power to make laws by virtue of Entry 33 in List III in the Seventh Schedule to the Constitution. [Essential Commodities Act (10 of 1955), S. 2(a)]

Essential elements of friendly information. Key questions likely to be asked by adversary officials and intelligence systems about specific friendly intentions, capabilities, and activities, so they can obtain answers critical to their operational effectiveness. (*Cyber Law*)

Essential supply or service. "ESSENTIAL SUPPLY OR SERVICE" includes supply of water, electricity, lights in passages and on staircases, conservancy and sanitary services. [Delhi Rent Act (33 of 1995), S. 21 *Expl.* 1]

Essentially derived variety. In respect of a variety (the initial variety), shall be said to be essentially derived from such initial variety when it —

(i) is predominantly derived from such initial variety, or from a variety that itself is predominantly derived from such initial variety, while retaining the expression of the essential characteristics that result from the genotype or combination of genotypes of such initial variety;

(ii) is clearly distinguishable from such initial variety; and

(iii) conforms (except for the differences which result from the act of derivation) to such initial variety in the expression of the essential characteristics that result from the genotype or combination of genotype of such initial variety. [Protection of Plant Varieties and Farmers' Right Act (53 of 2001), S. 2(i)]

Essentials of a family arrangement. The essentials of a family arrangement are :—

(1) There must be an agreement amongst the various members of the family intended to be generally and reasonably for the benefit of the family.

(2) The agreement should be with the object either of compromising doubtful or disputed rights, or for preserving the family property, or the peace and security of the family by avoiding litigation, or for saving its honour.

(3) Being an agreement, there is consideration for the same, the consideration being the expectation that such an agreement or settlement will result in establishing or ensuring amity and goodwill amongst the relations. (*Mathuri Pullaiah* v. *Mathuri Narasimha*, AIR 1966 SC 1836 as referred in *M.N. Aryamurthi* v. *M.L. Subbaraya Setty,* AIR 1972 SC 1279, 1285).

Esso. Means Esso Eastern Inc., a foreign company within the meaning of Section 591 of the Companies Act, 1956, incorporated under the laws of State of Delaware in the United States of America, and having its principal office at 2401 South Gessner City of Housten, State of Texas, in the United States of America. [Esso (Acquisition of Undertakings in India) Act (4 of 1974), S. 2(b)]

Esso Standard. Means Esso Standard Refining Company of India Limited, being a company as defined in the Companies Act, 1956, and having its registered office at Administration Building, Mahul, Bombay 400074. [Esso (Acquisition of Undertaking in India) Act (4 of 1974), S. 2(c)]

Establish. To set up; to find; to prove; to place beyond doubt [Indian Evidence Act (1 of 1872), S. 9]; [Unlawful Activites (Prevention) Act (37 of 1967), S. 7(4)]; to make a convention [Geneva Conventions Act (6 of 1960), 1st sch., Art. 55]; to prepare (a list) [(general provisions), Art. 127, Geneva Conventions Act (6 of 1960), IVth Sch, pt. I].

For the purpose of Art. 30 (1) the word 'establish' means "to bring into existence". *S. Azeez Basha* v. *Union of India*, AIR 1968 SC 662, 672. [Constitution of India, Art. 30(1)].

Established. Unless a manufacturing process was carried on in any part of the factory, it cannot be said that the factory had been established even if the factory may have been registered (earlier); *i.e.* in the Year 1949. *Great Eastern Electroplaters Ltd.* v. *Regional Provident Fund Commissioner,* AIR 1956 All 495, 498. [Employee's Provident Funds Act (19 of 1952), S. 16]

Establishment. "Establishment" means any place where any industry, trade, business, manufacture or occupation is carried on and includes Government establishment. [Code on Wages, 2019 (29 of 2019), section 2(m)]

"Establishment" includes an advertising agency, commission agent, manufacturing, trading or any other commercial agency which carries on any business, trade or profession or any work in connection with or incidental or ancillary to any commercial activity, trade or profession, or such other class or classes of persons including public utility entities in the manner as may be prescribed. [Consumer Protection Act, 2019 (35 of 2019), section 2(19)]

"Establishment" means—

(a) a place where any industry, trade, business, manufacture or occupation is carried on; or

(b) a factory, motor transport undertaking, newspaper establishment, audiovisual production, building and other construction work or plantation; or

(c) a mine, port or vicinity of port where dock work is carried out.

[Code on Social Security, 2020 (36 of 2020), section 2(29) and explanation]

"Establishment" means—

(i) any body or authority established by or under a Central Act or a State Act or an authority or a body owned or controlled or aided by the Government or a local authority, or a Government company as defined in section 2 of the Companies Act, 2013 (18 of 2013), and includes a Department of the Government; or

(ii) any company or body corporate or association or body of individuals, firm, cooperative or other society, association, trust, agency, institution. [Transgender Persons (Protection of Rights) Act, 2019 (40 of 2019), section 2(b)]

"Establishment" means—

(i) a place where any industry, trade, business, manufacturing or occupation is carried on in which ten or more workers are employed; or

(ii) motor transport undertaking, newspaper establishment, audio-video production, building and other construction work or plantation, in which ten or more workers are employed; or

(iii) factory, for the purpose of Chapter II, in which ten or more workers are employed, notwithstanding the threshold of workers provided in clause (*w*); or

(iv) a mine or port or vicinity of port where dock work is carried out. [Occupational Safety, Healthy & Working Conditions Code, 2020 (37 of 2020), section 2(1)(v) and proviso]

"Establishment" means—

(i) a factory;

(ii) a mine;

(iii) a plantation;

(iv) an establishment wherein persons are employed for the exhibition of equestrian, acrobatic and other performances;

(iva) a shop or establishment; or

(v) an establishment to which the provisions of this Act have been declared under sub-sec (1) of Section 2 to be applicable. [Maternity Benefit Act (53 of 1961), S. 3(e)]

"ESTABLISHMENT" means—

(i) any office, or

(ii) any place where any industry, trade, business or occupation is carried on, and includes any technical institution or training centre. [National Service Act (28 of 1972), S. 2(b)]

"ESTABLISHMENT" means—

(i) any office or department of the Government or a local authority; or

(ii) any place where any industry, trade business manufacture or occupation is carried on. [Inter-State Migrant Workman (Regn. *etc.*) Act (30 of 1979), S. 2(d)]

An establishment means a permanent commercial organization or a manufacturing establishment. [Words and Phrases, Permanent Edn., Vol. 15 as cited in *Bangalore Turf Club Limited* v. *Regional Director, Employees' State Insurance Corporation,* (2014) 9 SCC 657, para 34.2].

An establishment is the place where one is permanently fixed for residence or business such as on office or place of business with its fixtures. [Words and Phrases, Permanent Edn., Vol. 15 as cited in *Lorenzetti* v. *American Trust Co.*, 45F Supp. 128, p.139 (ND Cal 1942). See also *Bangalore Turf Club Limited* v. *Regional Director, Employees' State Insurance Corporation*, (2014) 9 SCC 657, para 34.2].

An institution or a place of business. [Black's Law Dictionary, 7th Edn. (1999) as cited in *Bangalore Turf Club Limited* v. *Regional Director, Employees' State Insurance Corporation*, (2014) 9 SCC 657, para 34.1].

'Establishment' means any places or premises, including the precincts thereof, in which or in any part of which any scheduled employment is being or is ordinarily carried on [Maharashtra Mathadi, Hamal and Other Manual Workers (Regulation of Employment and Welfare) Act 30 of 1969) S.2(4) as cited in *Pepsico India Holding Private Limited* v. *Grocery Market and Shops Board*, (2016) 4 SCC 493, para 8].

'Establishment' would not only include any place or premises in which manufacture of petrochemicals is being carried on, but would also include the precincts thereof, which would include transportation made beyond the factory gate but within the precincts of the factory. [Pepsico *India Holding Private Limited* v. *Grocery Market and Shops Board,* (2016) 4 SCC 493, para 16] [Maharashtra Mathadi, Hamal and Other Manual Workers (Regulations of Employment and Welfare) Act (30 of 1969) S. 2(4)].

"ESTABLISHMENT" means any place or premises, including the precinets thereof, in which or in any part of which any scheduled employment is ordinarily carried on. [W.B. Mazdoor, Tindal, Loader, Godownman and Other Workers (Regulation of Employment and Welfare) (51 of 1981), S. 2(5)]

"ESTABLISHMENT" includes a shop, commercial establishment, work-shop, farm, residential hotel, restaurant, eating house, theatre or other place of public amusement or entertainment. [Child Labour (Prohibition and Regulation) (61 of 1986), S. 2(iv)]

"ESTABLISHMENT" means a corporation established by or under a Central, Provincial or State Act, or an authority or a body owned or controlled or aided by the Government or a local authority or a Government company as defined in Section 617 of the Companies Act, 1956, and includes Departments of a Government. [Persons with Disabilities (Equal Opportunities, Protection of Rights and full Participation) Act, 1995 (1 of 1996), S. 2(k)]

"ESTABLISHMENT" means any establishment belonging to, or under the control of, Government, any body corporate or firm, an individual or association or other body of individuals which or who employs building workers in any building or other construction work; and includes an establishment belonging to a contractor, but does not include an individual who employs such workers in any building or construction work in relation to his own residence the total cost of such construction not being more than rupees ten lakhs. [Building and other Construction Workers (Regulation of Employment and Conditions of Service) Act (27 of 1996), S. 2(1)(j)]

"ESTABLISHMENT" includes any place where any industry is carried on. [Apprentices Act (52 of 1961), S. 2(g)]

Establishment means the bringing into being of an institution and it must be by a minority community. *State of Kerala* v. *Mother Provincial*, AIR 1970 SC 2079, 2082. [Constitution of India, Art. 30(1)].

"Establishment" means bringing into being of an institution and it must be by a minority community. It matters not if a single philanthropic individual, with his own means, founds the institution or the community at large contributes the funds. *State of West Bengal* v. *Guru Nanak Education Trust,* AIR 1987 Cal 232, 237. [Constitution of India, Art. 30]

Establishment means an organisation which employs persons, between whom and the establishment, the relationship of employee and employer comes to exist. *V. Transport (P) Ltd.* v. *R.P.F. Commr.,* AIR 1965 Mad 466, 467. [Employees Provident Fund Act (19 of 1952), S. 16] [(*As amended in 1960*)]

From the use of the expression 'establishment' in the Act it is clear that the establishment must exist in some definite and identifiable form. Webster's International dictionary defines it to mean "the place where one is permanently fixed for residence or business, residence, including grounds, furniture equipage, retinue, *etc.*, with which one is fitted out; also, an institution or place of business, with its fixtures and organised staff, as, large establishment, a manufacturing establishment". *Christopher Pinenta* v. *Life Insurance Corporation of India,* AIR 1958 Bom 451, 456. [Industrial Dispute Act (14 of 1947), S. 18(3)(c)].

An Establishment which carries on any business trade, or profession or any work in connection with or incidental and ancillary to, any business trade or profession. *Ram Kumar Misra* v. *State of Bihar*, AIR 1984 SC 537, 539.

"ESTABLISHMENT" means a business or other organization, or the place where an organization operates and includes a Government establishment and private establishment. [Energy Conservation Building Code Rules, 2018, R. 2(1)(p)].

"ESTABLISHMENT" includes a government establishment and private establishment. [Rights of persons with Disabilities Act (49 of 2016), S. 2(i) **as cited in** *Disabled Rights Group* v. *Union of India,* (2018) 2 SCC 397, para 11].

"ESTABLISHMENT" means a body corporate or cooperative society or any organisation or institution or two or more persons jointly carrying out a systematic activity for a period of twelve months or more at one or more places for consideration or otherwise, for the production, supply or distribution of goods or services. [Human Immunodeficiency Virus and Acquired Immune Deficiency Syndrome (Prevention and Control) Act (16 of 2017), S. 2(f)].

Something that is established; an organised staff of employees or servants, including or occasionally limited to, the building in which they are located. [Contract Labour (Regulation and Abolition) Act (37 of 1970), S. 2(2)(e) and Arms Act (54 of 1959), S. 21(1), *Expln.*]; to establish.

Establishment in private sector. Means an establishment which is not an establishment in public sector. [Apprentices Act (52 of 1961), S. 2(h)]

"ESTABLISHMENT IN PRIVATE SECTOR" means establishment which is not an establishment in public sector and where ordinarily twenty five or more persons are employed to work for remuneration. [Employment Exchanges (Compulsory Notification of Vacancies) Act (31 of 1959), S. 2(g)]

Establishment in public sector. Means an establishment owned, controlled or managed by—

(1) the Government or a department of the Government;

(2) a Government company as defined in Section 617 of the Companies Act, 1956;

(3) a corporation (including a co-operative society) established by or under a Central, Provincial or State Act, which is owned, controlled or managed by the Government;

(4) a local authority. [Apprentices Act (52 of 1961), S. 2(i)]

"ESTABLISHMENT IN PUBLIC SECTOR" means an establishment owned, controlled or managed by—

(a) Government company as defined in Section 617 of the Companies Act, 1956;

(b) a corporation in which not less than forty percent of its capital is held (whether singly or taken together) by—

(i) the Government; or

(ii) the Reserve Bank of India; or

(iii) a corporation owned by the Government or the Reserve Bank of India. [Payment of Bonus Act (21 of 1965), S. 2(16)]

Estate. The expression "estate", shall, in relation to any local area, have the same meaning as that expression or its local equivalent has in the existing law relating to land tenures in force in that area and shall also include—

(i) any *jagir, inam* or *muafi* or other similar grant and in the States of Tamil Nadu and Kerala, any *janmam* right;

(ii) any land held under *ryotwary* settlement;

(iii) any land held or let for purposes of agriculture or for purposes ancillary thereto, including waste land, forest land, land for pasture or sites of buildings and other, structures occupied by cultivators of land, agricultural labourers and village artisans. [Constitution of India, Art. 31A(2)(a)]

"ESTATE" means any area administered as one unit which contain land planted with rubber plants. [Rubber Act (24 of 1947), S. 3(c)]

"ESTATE" means any interest in lands and the aggregate of such interests vested in a person or aggregate of persons capable of holding the same : Bom Act V of 1879 (Land Revenue Code), S. 3, cl (5)]

"ESTATE" means the area administered as one unit which contains land planted with cardamon plants. [Spices Board Act (10 of 1986), S. 2(f)]

"ESTATE" (*in Revenue Law*) means any area-(a) for which a separate record-of-rights has been made; or (*b*) which has been separately assessed to land-revenue, or would have been so assessed if the land-revenue had not been released, compounded for or redeemed; or (*c*) which the Local Government may, by general rule or special order, declare to be an estate. [Pun Act (17 of 1887) (Land-Revenue), S. 3, cl. (1)]

"ESTATE" means all lands which are borne on the revenue-roll of a Collector as liable for the payment of one and the same demand of land revenue. [Ben. Act V of 1897 (Estates Partition), S. 3. cl. (9)]

'ESTATE' means any land and several fishery and ferry rights included under one entry in any of the general registers of revenue— paying lands and revenue-free lands, prepared and maintained under the law for the time being in force by the Collector of a district, and includes revenue-free land and several fishery and ferry rights not entered into any register and share in or of an estate. [Bihar Land Reforms Act (30 of 1950), S. 2(i)].

The word 'estate' has undoubtedly in law a diversity of meaning and a variety of signification. It may mean the property of a living man or that of a deceased person which passes to his administrator. Generally speaking, this word may mean the property of every character but ordinarily it is applied to the property of a deceased person or a ward or a lunatic or a bankrupt *etc.* according to which meaning it conveys an idea of property which is administered by administrators or executors or in Courts. *Jal Kaur* v. *Pala Singh,* AIR 1961 SC 391, 394. [Hindu Succession Act (30 of 1956), S. 8]

The Pandarawaka Verumpattoru can be regarded as a local equivalent of an estate under C1 (2)(a) of Art. 31A. *Purushothaman Nambudiri* v. *State of Kerala,* AIR 1962 SC 694, 709. [Constitution of India, Art. 31A(2)].

The 'estate' of a deceased person is a bundle of rights, powers, immunities and liabilitites which survive him. With reference to a living person, 'estate' means the interest he has in lands and other subjects of property; it designates property, real or personal, in which he has a right or interest. *B. Rajeevi R. Hegde* v. *Addl. Agni, I.T.O.,* (1981) 27 ITR 855, 858 (Ker). [Income Tax Act (43 of 1961), S. 159(4)].

The interest which anyone has in lands, tenements or other effects; property in which one has a right or interest; a landed property. [Constitution of India, Art. 31A, margin].

Estate agent. Means a person who negotiates or acts on behalf of one person in a transaction of transfer of his property, whether by way of sale, lease, licence mortgage or otherwise, with another person and receives remuneration for his services in the form of commission, and includes also a person who introduces to each other for negotiation such persons or their agents;

Explanation.—The person who acts as described in clause (a) shall be deemed to be an estate agent, even if he styles himself as a land or housing agent, property or real estate consultant, property dealer, realtor or by any other name. [Punjab Apartment and Property Regulation Act, 1995 (Punjab Act No. 14 of 1995), S. 2(o)]

Estate duty. "ESTATE DUTY" means a duty to be assessed on or by reference to the principal value, as certained in accordance with such rules as may be prescribed by or under laws made by Parliament or the Legislature of a State relating to the duty, of all property passing upon death or deemed, under the provisions of the said laws, so to pass. [Constitution of India, Art. 366(9)]

Duty payable on the value of property of which any person may die possessed.

Estimate. *As a noun*, a valuing or rating by the mind, without actually measuring, weighing, or the like : rough or approximate calculation; an approximate judgment or opinion as a rough or an accurate calculation, or measurement. *As a verb,* to judge and form an opinion of the value, from imperfect data; (to fix the worth of) roughly or in a general way; to form an opinion of, as to amount, number, *etc.*, from imperfect data, comparison or experience; to make an estimate of; to rate; to calculate roughly; to assess. (*Ame Cyc.*)

Valuation; to fix a notion of quantities, numbers, magnitudes, *etc.* without active enumeration or measurements. [Indian Contract Act (9 of 1872), S. 73, *Expln.*].

Estoppel. An estoppel is an admission, or something which the law treats as an equivalent to an admission, of so high and conclusive a nature that any one who is affected by it is not permitted to contradict it. (*Tomlin*)

"Estoppel" cometh of the French word 'estoupe', from where the English word stopped; and it is called an estoppel or conclusion, because the man's own act or acceptance stoppeth or closeth up his mouth to allege or plead the truth. (Co Litt. 352 a) [Lord Edward Coke, Chief Justice of the King's Bench and 17th Century English Jurist as cited in *Kamaljit Singh* v. *Sarabjit Singh*, (2014) 16 SCC 472, para 11].

"A bar that prevents one from asserting a claim or right that contradicts what one has said or done before or what has been legally established as true." [Black's Law Dictionary (9th Edn., p. 629) as cited in *Kamaljit Singh* v. *Sarabjit Singh*, (2014) 16 SCC 472, para 13].

There is said to be an estoppel where a party is not allowed to say that certain statement of fact is untrue, whether in reality it is true or not. Estoppel, or 'conclusion' as it is frequently called by older authorities, may, therefore, be defined as a disability whereby a party is precluded from alleging or proving in legal proceedings that a fact is otherwise than it has been made to appear by the matter giving rise to that disability. Estoppel is often described as a rule of evidence, but the whole concept is more correctly viewed as a substantive rule of law. HALSBURY, 4th Edn., Vol. 16, para 1501, p. 1008.

"On the principle that a person may not approbate and reprobate a special species of estoppel has arisen. The principle that a person may not approbate and reprobate express two propositions :

(1) That the person in question, having a choice between two courses of conduct is to be treated as having made an election from which he cannot resile.

(2) That he will be regarded, in general at any rate, as having so elected unless he has taken a benefit under or arising out of the course of conduct, which he has first pursued and with which his subsequent conduct is inconsistent." [HALSBURY'S *Law of England*, 4th Edn. Vol. 16 (Reissue) para 957 at page 844 as cited in C. 8 *MD, NTPC Ltd.* v. *R.C. Builders*, AIR 2004 SC 1330, 1339, para 36].

In the broad sense of the term "estoppel" is a bar which precludes a person from denying the truth of a fact which has in contemplation of law become settled by the acts and proceedings of judicial or legislative officers, or by the act of the party himself, either by conventional writing or by representations, express or implied, in pais.

When one person has, by his declaration, act or omission, intentionally caused or permitted another person to believe a thing to be true and to act upon such belief, neither he nor his representative shall be allowed in any suit or proceeding between himself and such person or his representative, to deny the truth of that thing. [Indian Evidence Act (1 of 1872), S. 115] [(w.e.f. 1-7-2024) repealed and replaced by Bharatiya Sakshya Adhiniyam, 2023 (47 of 2023), section 121].

ESTOPPEL is a rule of equity which forbids truth being pleaded or representation, on which faith another has acted to his detriment, being retracted. A promise which the promisor knows, or reasonably should know, will be relied upon by the promisee, shall be enforceable if the promisee has altered his position to his detriment in reliance on the promise. The soul of estoppel is equity, not facility for inequity. Nor is estoppel against statute permissible because public policy animating a statutory provision may then become the casualty. *Commissioner of Income Tax (Central)* v. *B.N. Bhattacharjee,* AIR 1979 SC 1725.

Estoppel against statute. What is meant by there being no estoppel against a statute is that a person is not estopped by a previous statement as to the existence of a statutory provision from contending that the converse is the statutory provision. The only rule to which estoppels are subject is that they cannot override the law of the land. The question of clash between the law of the land and an estoppel arises only when the statement on which the estoppel is founded is about the state of the law of the land, *i.e.* a statement of law. *Jai Ram* v. *Lakshmi Devi,* MLJ : QD (1961-1965) Vol III C662 : ILR (1963) 2 All 976 : 1963 All LJ 832 [Evidence Act (1 of 1872), S. 115]

Estoppel and res judicata. Estoppel by record amounts to *res judicata.* [*Sunderbai* v. *Devaji Despande,* AIR 1954 SC 82]

"Estoppel" and "Waiver". *Waiver* is distinct from *estoppel,* in *waiver* the essential element is actual intent to abandon or surrender right, while in *estoppel* such intent is immaterial. *Provash*

Chandra Dalui v. *Biswanath Banerjee,* AIR 1989 SC 1834.

Estoppel by acceptance of benefits. "As a general principle, one who knowingly accepts the benefits of a contract or conveyance is estopped to deny the validity or binding effect on him of such contract or conveyance." American jurisprudence, 2nd Edn. Vol. 28, 1966, pages 677, 680 as cited in *C & MD, NTPC Ltd.* v. *R.C. Builders and Contractors*, AIR 2004 SC 1330, 1339, para 37.

Estoppel by acquiescence. Acquiescence implies that a person who is said to have acquiesced did so with knowledge of his rights and other person acted in the *bona fide* belief that he was acting within his rights. The absence of either of these elements makes the doctrine inapplicable.

Estoppel by contract. A party is bound by the terms of his own contract until set aside or annulled for fraud, accident or mistake.

Estoppel by deed. Estoppel by one's own deed; not permitted to aver against the deed.

Where there is a statement of facts in a deed made between parties and verified by their seals, an estoppel results, and is called "estoppel by deed". If upon the true construction of the deed the statement is that of both or all the parties, the estoppel is binding on each party; if otherwise, it is only binding on the party making it. It seems that an estoppel also arises upon a deed poll, the mode of its execution being equally solemn with that of a deed made *inter partes.* HALSBURY, 4th Edn., Vol. 16, para 1594, p. 1009.

Estoppel by election. The intentional exercise of a choice between inconsistent alternatives that bars the person making the choice from the benefits of the one not selected.

Estoppel by judgment. A bar which precludes the parties to an action to relitigate, after final judgment, the same cause of action or ground of defence, or any fact determined by the judgment; *res judicata.*

Estoppel by laches. A neglect to do something which one should do or to seek to enforce a right at a proper time has been termed, (with questionable propriety), "estoppel by laches." (*Ame Cyc.*)

Estoppel by negligence. Is where a man is "estopped by another's misrepresentation, if, in breach of some duty to the person deceived, he has supplied the person making the representation with that which was necessary to make it credible." (16 *Ame Cyc.* 681).

Estoppel by record. A judgment not only creates a right, it works as estoppel. A judgment creating a charge on immovable property binds not only the parties to the suit but also their privies. The term "privy" is a term of the law meaning a partaker who is not a party, that is, in this connection, it includes all who derive title to the land, the subject of the charge from one who was a party to the suit by the decree in which the land was charged. It follows, therefore, that the charge is effective against a *bona fide* purchaser of the land for value without notice by reason of the law of estoppel by record.

Estoppel by silence. Arises where a person who is under a duty to another to speak "refrains from doing so, and thereby leads the other to believe in the existence of a state of facts in reliance upon which he acts to his prejudice."

Estoppel by verdict. Precludes the parties to an action from re-litigating a fact which had been determined in a previous action between them.

Estoppel by warranty. Is based on the principle of "giving effect to the manifest intention of the grantor appearing on the deed, as to the lands or estate to be conveyed, and of preventing the grantor from derogating from or destroying his own grant by any subsequent act."

Estoppel in pais. "Estoppel in pais" includes all forms of estoppel not arising from a record, from a deed, or from a written contract.

"TITLE BY ESTOPPEL" OR "RIGHT OF ESTOPPEL" is said to arise also where one person makes to another a statement which is afterwards acted upon, since in any action brought afterwards upon faith of that statement by the person to whom it was made, the person making it, is not allowed to deny that the facts were what he represented them to be, although in truth they were different. (16 *Ame Cyc.* 683). A tenant cannot dispute his landlord's title.

Estoppel of record. Estoppel of record or *quasi* of record also known as estoppel per *rem judicatam* arises (1) where an issue of fact has been judicially determined in a final manner between the parties by a tribunal having jurisdiction, concurrent or exclusive, in the matter, and the same issue comes directly in question in subsequent proceedings between the same parties; (2) where the first determination was by a Court having exclusive jurisdiction and the same issue comes incidentally in question in subsequent proceedings between same parties; (3) in some cases where an issue of fact affecting the status of a person or thing has been necessarily determined in a final manner as a substantive part of a judgment *in rem* of a tribunal having jurisdiction to determine that status, and the same issue comes directly in question in subsequent civil or criminal proceedings between any parties whatever. Where the earlier decision is that of a Court of record, the resulting estoppel is said to be 'of record'; where it is that of any other tribunal, whether constituted by agreement of the parties or otherwise, the estoppel is said to be '*quasi* of record'. HALSBURY, 4th Edn., Vol. 16, para 1503, p. 1009.

Estoppel of tenant. No tenant of immovable property, or person claiming through such tenant, shall, during the continuance of the tenancy, be permitted to deny that the landlord of such tenant had, at the beginning of the tenancy, a title to such immovable property. [Indian Evidence Act (1 of 1872), S. 116]

Estoppel per rem judicatam. "Estoppel per rem judicatam" is a generic term which in modern law includes two species. The first species, 'cause of action estoppel', is that which prevents a party to an action from asserting or denying, as against the other party, the existence of a particular cause of action, the non-existence or existence of which has been determined by a Court of competent jurisdiction in previous litigation between the same parties. If the cause of action was determined to exist, *i.e.*, judgment was given on it, it is said to be merged in the judgment, or for those who prefer Latin, transit in *rem judicatam*. If it was determined not to exist, the unsuccessful plaintiff can no longer assert that it does; he is estopped per *rem judicatam*. This is simply an application of the rule of public policy expressed in the Latin maxim, '*nemo debet bis vexari pro una at eadem causa*'. In this application of the maxim, *causa* bears its literal Latin meaning. The second species, 'issue estoppel', is an extension of the same rule of public policy. There are many causes of action which can only be established by proving that two or more different conditions are fulfilled. Such causes of action involve as many separate issues between the parties as there as conditions to be fulfilled by the plaintiff in order to establish his cause of action; and there may be cases where the fulfilment of an identical condition is a requirement common to two or more different causes of action. If in litigation on one such cause of action any of such separate issues whether a particular condition has been fulfilled is determined by a Court of competent jurisdiction, either on evidence or on admission by a party to the litigation, neither party can, in subsequent litigation between them on any cause of action which depends on the fulfilment of the identical condition, assert that the condition was fulfilled if the Court has in the first litigation determined that it was not, or deny that it was fulfilled if the Court in the first litigation determined that it was." [*Thoday* v. *Thoday*, (1964) 1 All ER 341, 352 B. See also *Bhanu Kumar Jain* v. *Archana Kumar,* (2005) 1 SCC 787, 798, para 31]

Estoppel, promissory. That which arises when there is a promise which promisor should reasonably expect to induce action or forbearance of a definite and substantial character on the part of promisee, and which does induce such action or forbearance and such promise is binding if injustice can be avoided only by enforcement of promise.

Estuary. Is the tidal part of a river.

Et cetera (Etc.). And so forth; and so on; and the rest; and others; others of the like kind.

The word '*etc.*' does not share the character of an inclusive definition and cannot therefore enlarge the scope of the expression 'institution'. *K.V. Mathew* v. *District Manager, Telephones Ernakulam,* AIR 1984 Ker, 40, 42. [Telegraph Act (13 of 1885), S. 7].

Ethernet. A type of network designed to interconnect computers over a limited area, such as an office building. (*Computer*)

There is more than one type of Ethernet. By 2001 the standard type was "100-Base T" which can handle up to about 100,000,000 bits-per-second and can be used with almost any kind of computer. (*Matisse Enzer-Glossary of Internet Terms*)

A very common method of networking computers in a LAN. Ethernet will handle about 10,000,000 bits-per-second and can be used with almost any kind of computer. (*Internet and E-commerce*).

Ethical. Moral obligations which one person owes to another.

Etiquette (*Parliamentary*)**.** Conventional rules of personal behaviour and courtesy observed between members of the same profession, beside the rules which the members of a legislature are required to observe while the House is sitting.

The rules and conventions with regard to the conduct of Members in the House called rules of parliamentary etiquette as laid down and followed in the Indian Parliament are as under:—

While the House is sitting, a Member—

(a) shall not read any book, newspaper or letter except in connection with the business of the House;

(b) shall not interrupt any member while speaking by disorderly manner;

(c) shall bow to the Chair while entering or leaving the House and also when taking or leaving his seat;

(d) shall not pass between the Chair and any member who is speaking;

(e) shall not leave the House when the Speaker is addressing the House;

(f) shall always address the Chair;

(g) shall keep to his usual seat while addressing the House;

(h) shall maintain silence when not speaking in the House;

(i) shall not obstruct proceedings, hiss or interrupt and shall avoid making running commentaries when speeches are being made in the House;

(j) shall not applaud when a stranger enters any of the galleries or the special box;

(k) shall not, while speaking, make any reference to the strangers in any of the galleries.

European community. The European Economic community came into operation on January 1, 1958, based on the treaty of Rome, with six participating member states (France, Italy, the Federal Republic of Germany, Belgium, the Netherlands and Luxembourg).

European Convention on Human Rights. A convention, originally formulated in 1950, aimed at protecting the human rights of all people in the member states of the Council of Europe.

European Council. A body which consists of the heads of government of the member states of the European Union.

European Court. The Court of justice of European Community.

European Economic Community (EEC). Association of some twelve European nations that were joined by a customs union and committed to the promotion of free trade within the boundaries of the community.

European Union (EU). An association of European nations, with the purpose of achieving full economic unity (and eventual political union) by agreeing to eliminate barriers to the free movement of capital, goods, and labour among the member nations.

Euthanasia. (or mercy killing). The causing or hastening of death, particularly of incurable or terminally ill patients, and at their own request. Generally it is treated as illegal and not distinguishable from murder.

A painless putting to death of persons having an incurable disease; an easy death. Also mercy killing. [New Webster's Dictionary (Deluxe Encyclopedic Edn.) **as cited in** *Common Cause (A Registered Society)* v. *Union of India,* (2018) 5 SCC 1, para 597].

The painless killing of a patient suffering from an incurable and painful disease or in an irreversible comma. [Oxford English Dictionary **as cited in** *Common Cause (A Registered Society)* v. *Union of India,* (2018) 5 SCC 1, para 598].

A deliberate act undertaken by one person with the intention of either painlessly putting to death or failing to prevent death from natural causes in cases of terminal illness or irreversible coma of another person. [World Health Organisation **as cited in** *Common Cause (A Registered Society)* v. *Union of India,* (2018) 5 SCC J, para 598].

Euthanasia as the meaning of word suggests is an act which leads to a good death. Some positive act is necessary to characterize the action as euthanasia. Euthanasia is also commonly called "assisted suicide" due to the above reasons. [*Common Cause (A Registered Society)* v. *Union of India,* (2018) 5 SCC 1, para 629.6].

(i) INVOLUNTARY EUTHANASIA refers to the termination of life against the will of the person killed; (ii) NON-VOLUNTARY EUTHANASIA refers to the termination of life without the consent or opposition of the person killed; (iii) VOLUNTARY EUTHANASIA refers to termination of life at the request of the person killed; (iv) ACTIVE EUTHANASIA refers to a positive contribution to the acceleration of deaths; (v) PASSIVE EUTHANASIA refers to the omission of steps which might otherwise sustain life. [Common Cause (A Registered Society) v. Union of India, (2018) 5 SCC 1, para 384].

Evacuation. Any organised withdrawal or removal from an area.

Evacuee. "EVACUEE" means any person—

(i) who, on account of the setting up of the Dominions of India and Pakistan or on account of civil disturbances or the fear of such disturbances, leaves or has, on or after the 1st day of March 1947, left, any place in a State for any place outside the territories now forming part of India, or

(ii) who is resident in any place now forming part of Pakistan and who for that reason is unable to occupy, supervise or manage in person his property in any part of the territories to which this Act extends, or whose property in any part of the said territories has ceased to be occupied, supervised or managed by any person or is being occupied, supervised or managed by an unauthorised person, or

(iii) who has, after the 14th day of August 1947, obtained, otherwise than by way of purchase or exchange, any right to, interest in or benefit from any property which is treated as evacuee or abandoned property under any law for the time being in force in Pakistan, or

(iv) who has, after the 18th day of October 1949, transferred to Pakistan, without the previous approval of the Custodian, his assets or any part of his assets situated in any part of the territories to which this Act extends; or

(v) who has, after the 18th day of October 1949, acquired, if the acqutisition has been made in person, by way of purchase or exchange, or, if the acquisition has been made by or through a member of his family, in any manner whatsoever, any right to, interest in, or benefit from, any property which is treated as evacuee or abandoned property under any law for the time being in force in Pakistan;

Explanation I.—For the purposes of sub-clause (iii), the acquisition of any right to, interest in or benefit from any such property as is referred to in that sub-clause by a firm, private limited company or trust of which any person or any member of the family of such person wholly dependent on him for the ordinary necessaries of life is a partner, member of beneficiary, as the case may be, shall be deemed to be an acquisition by that person within the meaning of that sub-clause.

Explanation II.—For the purposes of sub-clause (iv), the transfer to Pakistan by any person of any reasonable sum of money in accordance with the rules made in this behalf by the Central Government for the purpose of financing any transaction in the ordinary course of his trade or for the maintenance of any member of the family of such person shall not be deemed to be a transfer of his assets within the meaning of that sub-clause.

Explanation III.—For the purposes of sub-clause (v), the acquisition of any right to, interest in, or benefit from any such property as is referred to in that sub-clause by a firm, private limited company or trust of which any person is a partner, member or beneficiary, as the case may be, shall be deemed to be an acquisition by that person of such right, interest or benefit within the meaning of that sub-clause. [Administration of Evacuee Property Act (31 of 1950), S. 2(d)]

"EVACUEE" means any person who, on account of the setting up of the Dominions of India and Pakistan or on account of civil disturbance or the fear of such disturbances, has, on or after the 1st day of March, 1947, left any place in the territories to which this Act extends and who is now residing in any place forming part of Pakistan. [Transfer of Evacuee Deposits Act (15 of 1954), S. 2(d)]

The word, 'evacuee' includes person in whom right, title and interest of evacuee rests at the time of acquisition. *Union of India* v. *Syed Kharuddin,* AIR 1974 All 98, 99. [Displaced Persons (Compensation and Rehabilitation Act (44 of 1954), S. 18]

A person removed from his home in the time of war or pressing danger.

Evacuee and custodian. The evacuee could neither take possession of his property, nor lease, nor sell it without the custodian's consent, nor mortgage it, nor realise its income; whereas the custodian could take its possession, realise its income, alienate and in certain circumstances demolish it. All the rights that the evacuee had in the property he left in Pakistan were exercisable by the Custodian excepting that he could not appropriate the proceeds for his own use. The evacuee could not exercise any rights in that property except with the consent of the Custodian. He merely had some beneficial interest in that property. No doubt that residual interest in a sense is ownership. *R.B. Jodha Mal Kuthiala* v. *Commissioner of Income-Tax Punjab, Jammu & Kashmir, Himachal Pradesh and Patiala,* AIR 1972 SC 126.

Evacuee interest. In relation to a composite property means the right, title and interest of an evacuee in that property. *Azimunnissa* v. *Deputy Custodian, Evacuee Properties, District Deoria,* AIR 1961 SC 365. [Evacuee Interest (Separation) Act (64 of 1951), S. 2(e)]

Evacuee property. 'EVACUEE PROPERTY' means any property of an evacuee (whether held by him as an owner or as a trustee or as a beneficiary or as a tenant or in any other capacity), and includes any property which has been obtained by any person from an evacuee after the 14th day of August 1947, by any mode of transfer which is not effective by reason of the provisions contained in Section 40 of the Administration of Evacuee Property Act, 1950; but does not include—

(i) any ornament and any wearing apparel, cooking vessels or other household effects in the immediate possession of an evacuee;

(ii) any property belonging to a joint stock company, the registered office of which was situated before the 15th day of August 1947 in any place now forming part of Pakistan and continues to be so situated after the said date. [Administration of Property Act (31 of 1950), S. 2(f)]

"EVACUEE PROPERTY" means any property which has been declared or is deemed to have been declared as "evacuee property" under the Administration of Evacuee Property Act, 1950. [Displaced Persons (Compensation and Rehabilitation) Act (44 of 1954), S. 2(c)]

The phrase "evacuee property" includes the interest of an evacuee in any property held as a trustee or beneficiary. The phrase also includes *wakf* property and interest therein. *State of Bihar* v. *Amar Singh,* AIR 1955 SC 282, 287.

Evade. To avoid by some dexterity; by some device or stratagem; to elude; to escape (as) to evade a blow; to evade punishment; to evade the force of an argument.

To avoid. [IPC (45 of 1860), S. 52A]; to elude. [Indian Trusts Act (2 of 1882), S. 96].

The word 'evade' in the context means defeating the provision of law of paying duty. *Tamil Nadu Housing Board* v. *CCE,* 1995 Suppl (1) SCC 50.

Evaluation. Act or process of evaluating or ascertaining the value. [North-Eastern Hill University Act (24 of 1973), S. 5(17) and Dakshina Bharat Hindi Prachar Sabha Act (14 of 1964), S. 7(4)].

Evaporation. The change by which any substance is converted from a liquid state into and carried off in vapours; the process of evaporating, concentrating by conversion of a part into vapours. [Central Excises and Salt Act (1 of 1944), S. 2(j)(1)] [Now repealed by Act 12 of 2017].

Evasion. The action of evading or escaping as by artifice or contrivance. [Indian Trusts Act (2 of 1882), S. 96 and Income-tax Act (43 of 1961), S. 291(1)].

Evasion of tax. Evasion of tax means illegal non-payment of tax which is due.

Evasive answer. An answer that neither directly admits nor denie a question; in pleadings this is considered to be a failure to answer.

Evasive denial. A denial conducted in a vague and ambiguous language which avoids direct and clear answer to the question. [CPC (5 of 1908), O. VIII, R. 4].

Evasively. By evasion of subterfuge; in a manner to avoid direct reply. Pleading "evasively", is the converse of answering to the point, or replying directly.

In an evasive manner. [CPC (5 of 1908), O. VIII, R. 4].

Event. Something that happens [Indian Partnership Act (9 of 1932), S. 41(b)]; case. [Industrial Development Bank of India Act (18 of 1964), S. 6(5)].

Event management. Means any service provided in relation to planning, promotion, organising or presentation of any arts, entertainment, business, sports or any other event and includes any consultation provided in this regard. [Finance Act (32 of 1994), S. 65(40) (now repealed by Goods and Services Tax Act, 2017)]

Event manager. Means any person who is engaged in providing any service in relation to event management in any manner. [Finance Act (32 of 1994), S. 65(41) (now repealed by Goods and Services Tax Act, 2017)]

Event of, in the. In case of. [CrPC 1973 (2 of 1974), S. 349]

Eventual adjustment. Ultimate adjustment. [Personal Injuries (Compensation Insurance) Act (37 of 1963), S. 8(5)(h)].

Eventual remedy. Ultimate or resulting remedy. [Indian Contract Act (9 of 1872), S. 139].

Eventually. Finally; ultimately.

Every. Each; all things; each one and all, the whole number, but each separately considered; all the separate individuals which constitute the whole, regarded one by one. By the context this word may be restrained in its meaning, and it may be used as the equivalent of any. (16 *Ame Cyc.* 819).

All taken one by one. [Navy Act (62 of 1957), S. 29(1)].

EVERY DISTINCT OFFENCE. 'Distinct' means 'not identical'. It stresses characteristics that distinguish. Two offences would be distinct if they be not in any way inter-related. *Banwarilal Jhunjhunwala* v. *Union of India*, AIR 1993 SC 1620, 1624. [CrPC 1973 (2 of 1974), S. 218(1)]

Every one. Every person, including a corporation; each (as), *every one* of them is right.

Every person. The plain meaning of the phrase 'every person' is that it comprehends all persons without limitation and irrespective of nationality, allegiance, rank, status, caste, colour or creed. *Mobarik Ali Ahmed* v. *State of Bombay*, AIR 1957 SC 857, 870. [IPC (45 of 1860), S. 2]

Every question relating to valuation. The expression "EVERY QUESTION RELATING TO VALUATION", in S. 12(i) of the Court-Fees Act (7 of 1870), is of a comprehensive nature and cannot be construed in the restricted sense of a question relating to appraisement of Court-fee as distinguished from the question of category. [ILR 1937 Mad 275 : 166 IC 615 (2) : 1936 MWN 1392 : 44 LW 845 : AIR 1937 Mad 81 : (1937) 1 MLJ 1(FB)].

Evict. To eject. [T.P. Act (4 of 1882), S. 51].

Eviction. A recovery of land, *etc.* by force of law. (*Tomlin*)

In its original and technical meaning it is an expulsion by the assertion of a paramount title, and by process of law; a recovery of land, etc, by force of law; a lawful dispossession by judgment of law; an ouster. Act of the landlord with the intention and having the effect of depriving the tenant of the enjoyment of the demised premises; the term is now popularly applied to every class of expulsion.

The words "eviction" and "vacation" do not mean mere physical removal of the occupant. It means that on eviction land has to be restored to the original position so as to be used for the purpose for which it was given to the occupant. *State of Bombay* v. *Fakir Umar Dhouse*, AIR 1961 SC 722, 724, 725.

The action which deprives the tenant of the enjoyment of the premises and the rent is therefore suspended and the right of the landlord to recover it is gone, the tenant, in the eyes of the law, is evicted.

"Eviction" and "vacation". The word "eviction" and "vacation" mean that on eviction the land has to be restored to the original position so as to be used for the purpose for which it was given to the occupant. *State of Bombay* v. *Fakir Umar Dhanse,* AIR 1961 SC 722.

Evidence. "EVIDENCE" means and includes—

(1) all statements which the Court permits or requires to be made before it by witnesses, in relation to matters of fact under inquiry; such statements are called *oral evidence*; (2) all documents produced for the inspection of the Court; such documents are called *documentary evidence*. [Indian Evidence Act (1 of 1872), S. 3]] [Now (w.e.f. 1-7-2024) repealed & replaced by Bharatiya Sakshya Adhiniyam, 2023 (47 of 2023)]

"Evidence" means and includes—

(i) all statements including statements given electronically which the Court permits or requires to be made before it by witnesses in relation to matters of fact under inquiry and such statements are called oral evidence;

(ii) all documents including electronic or digital records produced for the inspection of the Court and such documents are called documentary evidence. [(w.e.f. 1-7-2024) Bharatiya Sakshya Adhiniyam, 2023 (47 of 2023), section 2(1)(e)]

"Evidence" means "any matter of fact, the effect, tendency or design of which presented to mind, is to produce in the mind a persuasion concerning the existence of some other matter of fact—a persuasion either affirmative or disaffirmative of its existence. Of the tax facts so connected, the latter may be distinguished as the principal fact, and the former as the evidentiary fact." [Bentham as cited in *Hardeep Singh* v. *State of Punjab*, (2014) 3 SCC 92, para 61].

"Any knowable fact or group of facts, not a legal or a logical principle, considered with a view to its being offered before a legal tribunal for the purpose of producing a persuasion, positive or negative, on the part of the tribunal, to the truth of a proposition, not of law, or of logic, on which the determination of the tribunal is to be asked." [Wigmore on Evidence as cited in *Hardeep Singh* v. *State of Punjab*,(2014) 3 SCC 92, para 62].

The word 'evidence' is used in common parlance in three different senses: (a) as equivalent to relevant, (b) as equivalent to proof, and (c) as equivalent to the material, on the basis of which courts come to a conclusion about the existence or non-existence of disputed facts. [*Kalyan Kumar Gogoi* v. *Ashutosh Agnihotri*, (2011) 2 SCC 532, para 33 : (2011) 1 SCC (Civ) 513 : (2011) 1 SCC (Cri) 741 : AIR 2011 SC 760 as cited in *Hardeep Singh* v. *State of Punjab*, (2014) 3 SCC 92, para 66].

"The word *'evidence'* signifies in its original sense, the state of being evident; *i.e.*, plain, apparent, or notorious. But by an almost peculiar inflexion of our language, it is applied to that which tends to render evident or to generate proof. This is the sense in which it is commonly used in our law books. Evidence, thus understood, has been well-defined, any matter of fact, the effect, tendency, or design of which is, to produce in the mind a persuasion, affirmative or disaffirmative, of the existence of some other matter of fact." (Best Ev. 11).

"Evidence is that which makes a matter in dispute clear, evident".

Evidence is the means from which an inference may logically be drawn as to the existence of a fact. It consists of proof by testimony of witnesses, on oath; or by writings or records. (*Tomlin*)

Evidence is the usual means of proving or disproving a fact or matter in issue. The law of evidence indicates what may properly be introduced by a party, (that is, what is admissible), and also what standard of proof is necessary (that is, the quality or quantity of evidence necessary in any particular case). In short, the law of evidence governs the means and manner in which a party may substantiate his own case, or refute that of his opponent. HALSBURY, 4th Edn., Vol. 17, para 1, p. 4.

The word "evidence" signifies only the instruments by means of which relevant facts are brought before the Court, *viz*, witnesses and documents, and by means of which the Court is convinced of these facts.

The word "evidence" in S. 322(1) of the CrPC 1973 (2 of 1974) means all facts and statements which have been disclosed by enquiry and is not restricted to depositions recorded by the Magistrate.

The word 'evidence' means all statements which the Court permits or requires to be made before it by witnesses. The statements of witnesses include statements made by them in cross-examination and re-examination. *Banwari Lal* v. *State,* AIR 1956 All 385, 390. [CrPC 1973 (2 of 1974), S. 244]

That which, a Court of justice is permitted by law to take into consideration for making clear or ascertaining the truth of the fact or point in issue. [Indian Evidence Act (1 of 1872), S. 3].

'Evidence' includes electronic records, and video conferencing. *State of Maharashtra* v. *Praful B. Desai,* (2003) 4 SCC 601, para 12 : AIR 2003 SC 2053. [Indian Evidence Act (1 of 1872), S. 3]

DIRECT AND CIRCUMSTANTIAL EVIDENCE. Direct and circumstantial evidence differ merely in their logical relation to the fact in issue; evidence as to the existence of the fact is direct, while circumstantial evidence relates to the existence of facts which raise a logical inference as to the existence of the fact in issue.

PRIMARY AND SECONDARY EVIDENCE. Best *evidence* or primary evidence is that particular means of proof which is indicated by the nature of the fact under investigation as the most natural and satisfactory; the best evidence the nature of the case admits; such evidence as may be called for in the first instance upon the principle that its non-production gives rise to a reasonable suspicion that, if produced, it would tend against the fact alleged. (*Abbott*)

All evidence which shows upon its face that better remains behind, is secondary. "Evidence which carries on its face no indication that better remains behind is not secondary, but primary. And *evidence* which is originally secondary may become primary by the loss of that which was originally primary.

Evidence, documentary. All documents which could, in law, be considered as evidence by the Court.

Evidence of accomplice. Taylor, in his treatise has observed that 'accomplice' are usually interested and always infamous witnesses, and whose testimony is admitted from necessity, it being often impossible, without having recourse to such evidence, to bring the principal offender to justice (Taylor in 'A Treatise on the Law of Evidence' (1931) vol. 1, para 967, as referred in *K. Hasim* v. *State of T.N.*, AIR 2005 SC 128, 133, para 30.

Evidence, oral. Oral statements which the Court permits or requires to be made before it by witness, in relation to matters of fact under enquiry.

Evidence, primary. The best evidence as opposed to secondary evidence, *e.g.*, original document itself. [Indian Evidence Act (1 of 1872), S. 62].

Evidence, secondary. That species of proof which is admitted in the absence of primary evidence *e.g.* admissible copy of document. [Indian Evidence Act (1 of 1872), S. 63].

Evil. Anything that causes harm or mischief. [Indian Evidence Act (1 of 1872), S. 24].

Evolution. The theory that human beings did not originally appear in their present form, but are descended from earlier animal lifeforms and gradually developed their present characteristics over a long period of time.

Ex abundanti cautela. (*Maxim*) From or out of abundance of caution.

Ex cadre post. A post outside the cadre of posts comprised in a Service. It would be anomalous to treat a post in the Service as an ex cadre post merely for the reason that the post is temporary. Therefore, all posts in the service, whether permanent or temporary are generally regarded as cadre posts. *O.P. Singla* v. *Union of India,* AIR 1984 SC 1595.

Ex-cadre transfer. The expression 'ex-cadre transfer' occurring in Regn. 2(e) stipulates that 'ex-cadre transfer' means transfer of an employee from one cadre to another or in respect of an employee not being a member of an cadre, his transfer from one post to another. *Maharashtra State Electricity Board* v. *Rama Rajaramji Wadekar*, (2002) 10 SCC 254, para 4. [Maharashtra State Electricity Board Employees' Seniority Regulations, 1961, Regn. 2(e)].

The transfer of Sub-Engineers from one circle to the other is an 'ex-cadre transfer' under Regn. 2(e) of the Regulations. *Maharashtra State Electricity Board* v. *Rama Rajaramji Wadekar,* (2002) 10 SCC 254, para 6. [Maharashtra State Electricity Board Employees' Seniority Regulations, 1961, Regn. 2(e)].

Ex-communication from any caste or community. (*Maxim*) The action of excluding an offender from the privilege and sacraments of caste or community [Representation of the People Act (43 of 1951), S. 123(2)(a)(i)].

Ex debitio justitiae. (*Maxim*) As a matter of right. The phrase refers to remedies to which a person is entitled as a matter of right as opposed to a remedy which is discretionary.

It is designed to promote justice. [*Rajasthan State Industrial Development and Investment Corporation* v. *Diamond & Gem Development Corporation Limited*, (2013) 5 SCC 470, para 21].

Ex diuturnitate temporis omnia proesumun-tur. (*Maxim*) Elapse of long time leads to a presumption that all things have been properly done.

Ex dolo malo non oritur actio. (*Maxim*) A right of action cannot rise out of fraud. (*Broom*)

Ex dolo malo non oritur actio or ex turpi causa non oritur actio. (*Maxim*) The right of action cannot arise out of fraud or out of transgression of law. *Immani Appa Rao* v. *G. Ramalingamurthi*, AIR 1962 SC 370 at p. 375.

Ex-facie. In the light of what is apparent.

Ex facto jus oritur. (*Lat.*) The law (arises) depends on the fact.

Ex fictione juris. (*Lat.*) By a fiction of law.

Ex gratia. (*Lat.*) By favour.

Out of grace; as a matter of grace, favour, or indulgence; gratuitous. A term applied to anything accorded as a favour; as distinguished from that which may be demanded *ex debito*, as a matter of right.

Ex gratia is an act of gratis and has no connection with the liability of the State in Law. The very nature of the relief and its dispensation by the State cannot be government by directions in the nature of mandamus unless of course there is an apparent discrimination in the manner of grant of such relief. [*Sudesh Dogra* v. *Union of India*, (2014) 6 SCC 486, para 22].

As a matter of grace or favour.

Ex gratia payment. Payment made by one who recognizes no legal obligation to pay but who makes payment to avoid greater expense as in the case of a settlement by an insurance company to avoid costs of suit. A payment without legal consideration. (*Black*)

Ex malis moribus bonae leges natae sunt. Good laws arise from evil morals, *i.e.* are necessitated by the evil behaviours of men.

Ex-necessiate rei. From the necessity of the case.

Ex nudo pacto non oritur actio. From a bare agreement (parol and without consideration) no action arises.

Ex-officio. By virtue or because of an office or offices. [General Clauses Act (10 of 1897), S. 15, Constitution of India, Art. 64 and Art. 89(1)].

Ex officio member. Means a member who is appointed to be a member by virtue of his office, and for the purpose of Gaon Panchayat or Anchalik Panchayat—or Zila Parishad and may include local members of Parliament local members of Legislative Assemblies, State government officials, Representative of local co-operative societies and representative of local scheduled or non scheduled banks. [Assam Panchayat Act (Assam Act No. 18 of 1994), S. 2(12)]

Ex pacto illicito non oritur actio. No action arises on an illegal agreement.

Ex parte. From, of, or by one side, or one party; hence partial, done for or by one party. From one side. O. IX, R. 6(a), CPC (5 of 1908), lays down when the Court may proceed *ex parte* but there appears to be no explanation in the Code what *ex parte* procedure is.

Expression used to signify something done or said by one person not in the presence of his opponent.

Of the one part; from one party. This term is applied in law to a proceeding by one party in the absence of, and without notice to, the other. On or from one side only.

A person who obtains an *ex parte* decree is responsible for slips in the decree.

Even giving to the expression '*ex parte*' its plain natural meaning, the expression '*ex parte*' does carry with it the connotation that a Court or a Judge or a Tribunal has proceeded in the absence of other party when it could have had the other party before it or when it was not prevented by law from having the other party before it. *P.N. Fibrus Ltd.* v. *Overseas Films Corporation Ltd.,* AIR 1958 Bom 10, 12. [CPC (5 of 1908), O. IX, R. 13]

Ex-parte decree. A decree passed by trial Court disposing of suit on the basis of plaintiff's evidence only due to non-appearance of contesting defendant at subsequent stages in the suit and on his failure to lead his evidence comes within the ambit of '*ex parte* decree' and it is not a decree on merits. *Ansari Sakeenabi* v. *Maligi Moideensab,* AIR 1997 Kant 339, 340, para 8. [CPC (5 of 1908), O. IX, R. 13].

Ex parte injunction. A preliminary injunction issued after the Court has heard from only the moving party.

Ex parte proceeding. A proceeding at the instance and for the benefit of one party only and without notice to or contestation by any person adversely interested.

Ex post facto. By matter happening afterwards; from a later act or event.

By subsequent act; by virtue of a thing done after some particular event; done after another thing and operating retrospectively.

Ex post facto law. A law that makes something a crime that was not illegal at the time the act was done or that increases the penalty after a crime was committed. [Craig R. Ducat —*Constitutional Interpretation*].

An act or statute changing the law as to previous events or contracts.

Ex post facto legislation. 'Ex post facto legislation' means a law which acts or operates as from a date anterior to its promulgation. Such a legislation may either take among the rights created by previous transaction or validate what was in its inception invalid. *Govindarajan* v. *State of Mysore,* AIR 1963 Mys 265, 274. [Constitution of India, Art. 245]

Ex procedentibus et consequentibus est optima interpretatio. (1 Rol. Rep. 375). The best interpretation is made from that which precedes and follows.

Ex proprio vigore. Of their own force.

Ex-Situ Conservation. Means the conservation of components of biological diversity outside their natural habits. [United Nations Conference on Environment and Development Convention on Biological Diversity (June 5, 1992), Art. 2]

Ex tempore. By lapse of time; without preparation.

Ex total materia emergat resolutio. (*Maxim*) The explanation, construction or resolution should arise out of the whole subject-matter."

Ex-turpi causa. (*Lat.*) From an immoral consideration.

Ex turpi causa non oritur actio. (*Maxim*) A petitioner who comes into Court founding his cause of action on an illegality, will not get any assistance from the Court.

The maxim '*Ex turpi causa non oritur actio*' means that no right of action arises from an immoral or illegal cause. The suit to receive any money advanced by way of capital is not maintainable. *Babulal Swaruphand Shah* v. *South Satara (Fixed Delivery) Merchants' Association Ltd.,* AIR 1960 Bom 548, 550. [Indian Contract Act (9 of 1872), S. 23].

Ex turpi contractu non oritur actio. (*Maxim*) No action arises on an immoral contract. (*Bouvier*)

Ex vi termini. The interpretation of a term by virtue of its own essential meaning, and not by extrinsic evidence, whether the term is used in a philological or legal sense.

Ex visceribus actus. It means construction of the Act as a whole. [*Executive Engineer, Southern Electricity Supply Company of Orissa Limited (SOUTHCO)* v. *Sri Seetaram Rice Mill,* (2012) 2 SCC 108, para 17].

Exact. *As an adjective*, precisely accurate, rigorous. *As a verb*, demand; enforce payment; insist upon; demand urgently.

Precise [IPC (45 of 1860), S. 28, *Expln.*1]; to force or compel the payment.

Exact nature. The precise nature. [Limitation Act (36 of 1963), S. 18, *Expln.* (a)].

Exact period. A period which is not vague or uncertain. [T.P. Act (4 of 1882), S. 24].

Exaction. The act of demanding and receiving; illegal or exorbitant demand; extortion; arbitrary impost. (*Tomlin*)

The act or process of exacting.

Examination. "EXAMINATION" in relation to any goods, includes measurement and weighment thereof. [Customs Act (52 of 1962), S. 2(17]

A weighing; balancing; search; minute inspection; investigation; inquiry; an investigation made in order to form a judgment.

In this section and sections 53A and 54,— "examination" shall include the examination of blood, blood stains, semen, swabs in case of sexual offences, sputum and sweat, hair samples and finger nail clippings by the use of modern and scientific techniques including DNA profiling and such other tests which the registered medical practitioner thinks necessary in a particular case. [Cr PC, 1973 (2 of 1974), section 53, *Expln.* As substituted by CrPC (Amendment) Act (25 of 2005), section 8] [Now (w.e.f. 1-7-2024) repealed & replaced by Bharatiya Nagarik Suraksha Sanhita, 2023 (46 of 2023)]

In this section and sections 52 and 53,-- "Examination" shall include the examination of blood, blood stains, semen, swabs in case of sexual offences, sputum and sweat, hair samples and finger nail clippings by the use of modern and scientific techniques including DNA profiling and such other tests which the registered medical practitioner thinks necessary in a particular case. [(w.e.f. 1-7-

2024) Bharatiya Nagarik Suraksha Sanhita, 2023 (46 of 2023), section 51, *Explanation* (a) & section 184, *Explanation*]

Examination-in-chief. "The examination of a witness by the party who calls him is called his examination-in-chief." [Indian Evidence Act (1 of 1872), S. 137] [(w.e.f. 1-7-2024) repealed and replaced by Bharatiya Sakshya Adhiniyam, 2023 (47 of 2023), section 142(1)]

Examination of a witness. The phrase 'examination of a witness' does not necessarily mean examination and cross-examination of that witness. What type of examination of a witness is contemplated would depend upon the object and purpose of that particular provision. [*Ranadhir Basu* v. *State of W.B.*, (2000) 3 SCC 161, 168, para 7]

Examination room. Means a room where film is examined, repaired, cleaned, waxed or rewound. [Cinematograph Film Rules, 1948, R. 2(f)]

Examine. To formally interrogate a witness or an accused person; to test critically. [Indian Contract Act (9 of 1872), S. 19, ill. (b)].

Examining body. Means a University, agency or authority to which an institution is affiliated for conducting examinations in teacher education qualifications. [National Council for Teachers Education Act (73 of 1993), S. 2(d)]

Examining Court. A term applied to a Court or Magistrate when sitting for the purpose of enquiring into a criminal accusation against a person. (*Ame Cyc.*)

Excavate. The term 'excavate' would include digging of land for the purpose of making 'bore' with a view to fetching water.

Excavation. An uncovered cutting in the earth, as distinguished from a covered cutting or tunnel. (*Webster*)

A cavity formed by digging; the action of excavating. [Workmen's Compensation Act (8 of 1923), Sch. II, item XVI].

The term. 'excavation' means 'hole', 'hollow' or 'cavity' made by digging out. *Tarkeshwar Sio Thakar Jin* v. *B.D. Dey & Co.*,AIR 1979 SC 1669,1671.

Excess money. For the purposes of this section, "EXCESS MONEY" means the difference between the arm's length price determined in primary adjustment and the price at which the international transaction has actually been undertaken;

"primary adjustment" to a transfer price, means the determination of transfer price in accordance with the arm's length principle resulting in an increase in the total income or reduction in the loss, as the case may be, of the assesse;

"secondary adjustment" means an adjustment in the books of account of the assesse and its associated enterprise to reflect that the actual allocation of profits between the assesse and its associated enterprise are consistent with the transfer price determined as a result of primary adjustment, thereby removing the imbalance between cash amount and actual profit of the assesse. [Income-tax Act (43 of 1961), S. 92-CE, *Explanation (i)*].

Exceed. To go beyond. [T.P. Act (4 of 1882), S. 65A(2)(e)].

Except. Not including; unless. The word has also been construed to mean "until".

To leave or take out: exclude; omit; save; not including; unless. The word has also been construed to mean until. [Armed Forces (Jammu and Kashmir) Special Powers Act, 1990 (21 of 1990), S. 7(i) as cited in \, (2012) 6 SCC 228, para 67].

Excepted. Made an exception of.

Excepted expenses. In relation to repatriation expenses, means repatriation, expenses incurred in cases where the cause of the seaman being left behind is desertion, or absence without leave or imprisonment for misconduct or discharge from his ship by a Marine Board on the ground of misconduct. [Merchant Shipping Act (44 of 1958), S. 3(36)(b)]

Excepted matters. The clause, recording that the decision of the senior officer, being the adjudicator, shall be final and binding between the parties, is popularly known as 'excepted matters' in a Government or governmental agencies' contract. *Food Corpn. of India* v. *Sreekanth Transport,* (1999) 4 SCC 491, para 2 : AIR 1999 SC 2184.

Excepted temple. Means

(a) a temple which before 1801 was and since 1963 has continued to be, under the sole management of a trustee whose nomination did not vest in, nor was exercised by, the Government nor was subject to the confirmation of the Government or of any public officer, or

(b) a temple founded since 1842, the right of succession to the office of trustee whereof is hereditary or specially provided for by the founder. [T.N. Hindu Religious Endowment Act, 1926 (2 of 1927), S. 9(5)].

Exceptio probat regulam de rebus non exceptis. An exception proves the rule concerning things not excepted. (*Bouvier*)

Exception. Act of excepting or excluding from a number designated or from a description; that which is excepted or separated from others in a general rule of description; a person, thing, or case specified as distinct or not included; an act of excepting, omitting from mention or leaving out of consideration. (*Black*) [Armed Forces (Jammu & Kashmir) Special Powers Act, 1990 (21 of 1990), S. 7(i) as cited in *General Officer Commanding, Rashtriya Rifles* v. *CBI*, (2012) 6 SCC 228, para 67].

Something that is excepted; a person, thing or case to which the general rule is not applicable; exclusion of anything or person. [IPC (45 of 1860), S. 6]; an objection. [CPC (5 of 1908), O. XI, R. 10].

Exceptional. Of the nature of forming an exception; unusual.

Exceptional depravity and Exceptional hardship. Adultery plus desertion or cruelty constitutes exceptional hardships to the wife. Adultery with another matrimonial offence may cause exceptional hardship, *e.g.* when a wife has a child by her adultery. If a husband commits adultery within a few weeks of his marriage or promiscuously or with his wife's sister or a servant in the home, that may be held to be exceptional depravity. Cruelty coupled with drunkenness and neglect may be exceptional hardship or if coupled with perverted lust exceptional depravity. *Meganatha Nayagar* v. *Shrimathi Susheela,* AIR 1957 Mad 423, 427. [Hindu Marriage Act (25 of 1955), S. 14(1), *Prov.*].

Excess. Overstepping due limits. The quality or state of exceeding the proper or reasonable limit or measure. (*Webster*)

The amount or degree by which one thing exceeds another [Taxation Laws (Continuation and Validation of Recovery Proceedings) Act (11 of 1964)]; more than or above the usual or specified amount [Unit Trust of India Act (52 of 1963), S. 4(3)]; [Constitution of India, Art. 115(1)(b)].

Excess of jurisdiction. A phrase used to describe an order of a subordinate tribunal which it did not have jurisdiction to pass. The phrase is also used if an executive authority does something which the statute does not authorise it to do.

Excess realisation. 'EXCESS REALISATION', in relation to each grade of levy-sugar, (i) means the price realised by any producer, on the sale of levy sugar of such grade, in excess of (a) the controlled price, or (b) where any fair price has been fixed by a Court for levy sugar of such grade, such fair price and (ii) includes any realisation representing the difference between the controlled price and the price allowed by the Court by an interim order, if such interim order is set aside, whether by the Court which made the order or in appeal or revision.

Expln.—For the removal of doubt, it is hereby declared that where in relation to levy sugar of any grade sold by any producer, the producer has realised towards duties of excise with respect to such sugar any amount in excess of amount payable by way of such duties, such excess shall also be deemed to be excess realisation within the meaning of this clause. [Levy Sugar Price Equalisation Fund Act (31 of 1976), S. 2(b)]

Excessive. Tending to or marked by excess; more than reasonable or necessary.

Characterised by or exhibiting excess. [IPC (45 of 1860), S. 63].

Exchange. When two persons mutually transfer the ownership of one thing for the ownership of another, neither the thing nor both things being money only, the transaction is called an "EXCHANGE". [T.P. ACT (4 of 1882), S. 118]

A mutual grant of equal interests, the one in consideration of the other [T.P. Act (4 of 1882), Ss. 46 (a) and 118]; centre.

An exchange involves the transfer of property by one person to another and reciprocally the transfer of property by that other to the first person. There must be a mutual transfer of ownership of one thing for the ownership of another. *I.T. Commissioner Bombay* v. *Rasiklal Moneklal*, AIR 1989 SC 1333, 1335.

(*In Commercial Law*). A negotiation by which one person transfers to another goods or funds which he has in a certain place, either for other goods, or at a price agreed upon, or at a price which is fixed by commercial usage.

Exchange and sale. (Distinction). The definition of 'exchange' given in Section 118 of the Transfer of Property Act (4 of 1882) is not limited to immovable property. It applies not only to an exchange of land but also barter of goods. Barter, though in most respect analogous to sale, is certainly not *identical* with it, because one of the essential elements of sale is the element of price which must be money paid or promised, according as the agreement may be for a cash or credit sale. If the consideration given be something other than money it is not a sale. If goods be given in exchange for goods, it is a barter, If no valuable consideration be given for the transfer, it is a gift and not a sale. It is not every transaction involving a transfer of property and payment that constitutes sale; the payment may be the motive for making a gift, or for giving some benefit by agreement or otherwise. A sale should always be for a price, but in the case of exchange the transfer of the ownership of one thing is not for any price paid or promised, but for transfer of another thing in return. Having regard to the essential distinction between the concept of a sale and exchange it cannot be held that an exchange is identical with sale within the meaning of the Madras Food grains Control Order, 1950. *Balaramaiah* v. *Narapareddy,* MLJ : QD (1956-1960) Vol. III C2302 : 1958 Andh LT 350. [Madras Food Grains Control Order (1950)]

"Exchange" and "Transfer". An exchange involves the transfer of property by one person to another and reciprocally the transfer of property by that other to the first person. There must be a mutual transfer of ownership of one thing for the ownership of another. *CIT.* v. *Rasiklal Maneklal,* AIR 1989 SC 1333.

Exchange broker. A person who negotiates money or merchandise transactions for other.

Exchange rate. The price (or rate) at which one currency is exchanged for another currency, for gold, or for Special Drawing rights (SDR's).

Exchange risk premium. "EXCHANGE RISK PREMIUM" means a premium paid by a person borrowing foreign currency from a public financial institution to cover the risk which may be borne by such institution on account of fluctuations in exchange rate of foreign currencies borrowed by such institution. [Income-tax Act (43 of 1961), S. 10(13A), *Expln.* (ii)]

Exchange value. The price or value for which a thing can be exchanged.

STOCK EXCHANGE. A building or room in which Stock-brokers meet to transact their business of purchasing and selling stocks.

Exchequer. A term connected with the revenues of the department of public service charged with receipt and custody of State revenues : royal or national treasury. An ancient Court of record wherein all causes touching the revenue and rights of the crown were heard and determined. (*Tomlin*)

Exchequer Chamber. Formerly an English court for the correction and prevention of errors of law in the three superior common law courts. It consisted of the judges of two of the courts sitting together to decide questions appealed from the other. Questions of unusual difficulty and importance were reserved for the decision of the full court, consisting of all the judges of the three courts, and sometimes the Lord Chancellor. By the Judicature Act, 1873, this court was abolished, and its jurisdiction transferred to the Court of Appeal. (*The Law Dictionary*)

Excisable. A finding that the goods are marketable is a pre-requisite or *sine qua non* for the levy of duty. The article should be capable of being sold to consumers in the market, as it is, without anything more. 'Manufacture' by itself will not justify levy of duty. *Union Carbide* v. *U.O.I.*, 1986 (24) ELT 169 (SC).

Excisable goods. Means goods specified in the schedule to the Central Excise Tarrif Act, 1985, as being subject to a duty of excise and includes salt. [Central Excises and Salt Act (1 of 1944), S. 2(d)]

Installation or erection of turbo alternator on platform constructed on land would be immovable property and cannot be 'excisable goods' for it has neither mobility nor marketability as understood in the Excise Law. *Triveni Engineering and Industries Ltd.* v. *Commissioner of Central Excise,* AIR 2000 SC 2896 p. 2901.

Excise. A duty charged on home goods, either in the process of their manufacture or before their sale to the home consumers. [Sale of Goods Act (3 of 1930), S. 64A(2)(a)]; matters relating to intoxication *etc.*

Excise duties. Are taxes imposed on articles of home product for home consumption or on their manufacture or sale.

"Excise duty" is a tax on articles produced or manufactured in the taxing country. Generally speaking, the tax is on the manufacturer or the producer, yet laws are to be found which impose a duty of excise at stages subsequent to the manufacture or production. *A.B. Abdul Kadir* v. *State of Kerala,* AIR 1976 SC 182.

Excise duty is in essence a tax on manufacture or production of goods and excise duty can be levied only on such goods as are manufactured or produced within the State. *Shroff and Co.* v. *Municipal Corporation of Greater Bombay,* (1989) Supp. 1 SCC 347.

'Excise duty' and **'countervailing duty'.** 'Excise duty' is a duty on manufacture of goods, whereas 'countervailing duty' is a duty imposed on excisable articles imported into the State in order to counterbalance the excise duty. (In this case Indian-made foreign liquor was imported into the State of Orissa). *S.K. Patnaik* v. *State of Orissa,* (2000) 1 SCC 413, para 4 : AIR 2000 SC 612. [Bihar and Orissa Excise Act (2 of 1915), Ss. 27, 28]

Excise-officer. "EXCISE OFFICER" means any officer of the Excise Department of any State and includes any person empowered by the collecting Government to exercise all or any of the powers of an excise officer under this Act. [Medicinal and Toilet Preparation (Excise Duties) Act (16 of 1955), S. 2(d)]

Excision. The act of removing by cutting out or as if by cutting out. [Cinematograph Act (37 of 1952), S. 4(1)(iii)].

Excite. To stir up; to incite; to rouse up. [IPC (45 of 1860), S. 300, *Excep.* I., ill. (a)].

Excited utterance. A statement which concerns a startling event (as a physical assault) and which is made by a person while under stress caused by the event.

Exclude. To shut out, whether by thrusting out or by preventing admission; to debar; to reject; to prohibit; to expel; to eject; to dispossess; to except.

To shut out from place, society, privilege *etc.* [Employers' Liability Act (24 of 1938), S. 3A].

Excluded from possession. In case of co-owners, the possession of one is in law possession of all. It is not necessary that the co-owner should be in actual possession nor it is necessary that he should be getting a share or income from the property. Unless ouster or exclusion is proved, he is not excluded from possession. *Neelavathi* v. *N. Natarajan*, AIR 1980 SC 691, 692, 695.

Excluded assets. For the purposes of this part includes—

(a) unencumbered tools, books, vehicles and other equipment as are necessary to the debtor or bankrupt for his personal use or for the purpose of his employment, business or vocation;

(b) unencumbered furniture, household equipment and provisions as are necessary for satisfying the basic domestic needs of the bankrupt and his immediate family;

(c) any unencumbered personal ornaments of such value, as may be prescribed, of the debtor or his immediate family which cannot be parted with, in accordance with religious usage;

(d) any unencumbered life insurance policy or pension plan taken in the name of debtor or his immediate family; and

(e) an unencumbered single dwelling unit owned by the debtor of such value as may be prescribed. [Insolvency and Bankruptcy Code (31 of 2016), S. 79(14)].

Excluded debt. Means—

(a) liability to pay fine imposed by a court or tribunal;

(b) liability to pay damages for negligence, nuisance or breach of a statutory, contractual or other legal obligation;

(c) liability to pay maintenance to any person under any law for the time being in force;

(d) liability in relation to a student loan; and

(e) any other debt as may be prescribed. [Insolvency and Bankruptcy Code (31 of 2016), S. 79(15)].

Exclusion. The act or an instance of excluding. [IPC (45 of 1860), S. 91; and Constitution of India, Art. 19 (6)(ii)].

Exclusive. Possessed and enjoyed to the exclusion of others; debarred from a participation or enjoyment; undivided, sole (as exclusive possession; exclusive privilege); not including, admitting or pertaining to any other; opposed to inclusive; not to be taken into account.

Exclusive distribution agreement. Includes any agreement to limit, restrict or withhold the output or supply of any goods or allocate any area or market for the disposal or sale of the goods. [Competition Act, 2002 (12 of 2003), S. 3(4) *Expl.*(c)]

Exclusive Economic Zone of India. Means the exclusive zone of India in accordance with the provisions of Section 7 of Territorial waters, Continental Shelf, Exclusive Economic Zone and other Maritime Zones Act, 1976. [Maritime Zones of India (Regulation of Fishing by Foreign Vessels) Act (42 of 1981), S. 2(a)]

Exclusive evidence. The only facts that have any probative force at all on a particular matter in issue.

Exclusive jurisdiction. A Court's power to adjudicate an action or class of actions to the exclusion of all other Courts.

Exclusive licence. Means a licence which confers on the licencee or on the licencee and persons authorised by him, to the exclusion of all other person (including the owner of the copyright), any right compromised in the copyright in a work, and "exclusive licencee" shall be construed accordingly. [Copyright Act (14 of 1957), S. 2(j)]

'EXCLUSIVE LICENCE' means a licence from a patentee which confers on the licensee of on the licensee and persons authorised by him to the exclusion of all other persons (including the patentee) any right in respect of the patented invention, and "exclusive licensee" shall be construed accordingly. [Patents Act (39 of 1970), S. 2(f)]

Exclusive occupation. Means exclusive occupation as a residence, and this is not reduced merely because the landlord reserves a right of entry from time to time.

Exclusive possession. Exclusive possession by adverse possessor means that adverse possessor must show an exclusive dominion over the land and an appropriation of it to his own use and benefit, and not for another.

Exclusive supply agreements. Includes any agreement restricting in any manner the purchaser in the course of his trade from acquiring or otherwise dealing in any goods other than those of the seller or any other person. [Competition Act, 2002 (12 of 2003), S. 3(4) *Expl.* (b)]

Exclusively. To the exclusion of all others; without admission of any others to participation. In an exclusive manner; solely.

Excommunicatio. Excommengement or ex-communication. It is a sentence pronounced by an ecclesiastical Court depriving the person on whom it is passed of the spiritual benefits of the sacrament. For the more heinous ecclesiastical offences, the sentence could also be one of excluding the accused from the company of all Christians.

Excommunication. In religious order, excommunication is a sentence of censure pronounced by one of the spiritual Courts for offences falling under ecclesiastical consequence. Its consequences are that the person concerned is either excluded from the secretariat or even from the company of all persons of same order. *P.M. A. Metropolitan* v. *Moran Mar Marthoma,* AIR 1995 SC 2001.

Excommunication and fine. Distinctions are supposed to exist between ex-communication and fine and also between payment of a fine and giving a caste dinner. The fine imposed for transgressions of caste regulations may be a fixed sum of money or the price of a dinner, but it is a fine in both cases. And the excommunication is merely the only means available for enforcing the payment of the fine. Every such disciplinary decision of a caste can be regarded either as a sentence of excommunication which can be set aside on payment of a fine or as a sentence of fine with excommunication in default of payment. (76 IC 314 : AIR 1924 Nag 157).

Excommunication from caste. To put out of caste.

The decision of the "*Jamait*" or Council of the Khoja community ex-communicating a person is within the scope of its authority if arrived at in a manner consonant with the ordinary principles of justice, but if it is not so arrived at, the Court would have jurisdiction to interfere.

Exculpate. To clear from the charge of a fault or crime.

Exculpatory. Clearing or tending to clear from alleged fault or guilt; excusing.

Exculpatory clause. A contract clause which releases one of the parties from liability for his or her wrongful acts. A provision in a document which protects a party from liability arising, in the main, from negligence; such clause is common in leases, contracts and trusts. Such clause in favour of a trustee in will implies that trustee has power which he purports to execute, and it exculpates him where this power is exercised in good faith.

Exculpatory statement or evidence. A statement or other evidence which tends to justify, excuse or clear the defendant from alleged fault or guilt.

Excusable. That which may be excused; admitting of palliation. [IPC (45 of 1860), S. 80, ill.].

Excusable homicide. "Excusable homicide" is that committed by one doing a lawful act without intention to hurt, as by accident or misadventure, or a homicide committed in self-defense. (*26 Am Jur 226*)

Excuse. The act of excusing, exculpating or pardoning.

That which is offered as reason for being excused; that which serves to excuse or to extenuate (a fault or offence); to accept a plea in exculpation of; to free from a task, obligation *etc.*

Executable. A binary file containing a program in machine language that is ready to be executed (run). MS-DOS and Windows machines use the filename extention "exe" for these files. (*Cyber Law*)

Applied to programs, "executable" means a program that can be performed by the computer rather than a source program that must be assembled or compiled before it can be executed. An executable program is usually called an "object" program. (*Computer*)

Executant. That person, who executes or makes a document.

Execute. To go through the formalities necessary for the validity of; hence to sign, seal *etc.* (a document); to carry into effect; to put to death in pursuance of a sentence.

Carry into effect (as, to execute a plan or command; to execute a decree or order of a Court; to execute a judicial sentence); to make a legal instrument valid (as, to execute a deed is to give it validity by signing or signing and sealing as required by law; to discharge functions (as, execute an office); inflict capital punishment or (as, the execution of a prisoner on whom sentence of death has been pronounced.

The word 'execute' means 'to complete as a legal instrument; to perform what is required to give validity to.' [Words and Phrases (Permanent Edn.) as cited in *Rajendra Pratap Singh* v. *Rameshwar Prasad,* (1998) 7 SCC 602, para 11 : AIR 1999 SC 37].

Executed within the jurisdiction of the Court. Carried out legally according to its terms within the limits of territory over which the Court exercises its powers. [CPC (5 of 1908), S. 43].

Executio est finis et fructus legis. (*Maxim*) An execution is the end and the fruit of law.

Executio juris non habet injuriam. (*Maxim*) The execution of the process of law does no injury.

Execution. The accomplishment of a thing; the completion of an act or instrument; the fulfilment of an undertaking (as) execution of a contract or deed.

"Execution" with reference to an instrument means "signed" and "signature". [Stamp Act, 1899, as amended by West Bengal, S. 2(12) as cited in *Additional District Sub-Registrar, Siliguri* v. *Pawan Kumar Verma*, (2013) 7 SCC 537, para 6].

The action of executing (a document) or for carrying into effect; the action of executing a death sentence; the infliction of capital punishment. [Geneva Conventions Act (6 of 1960), 1st Sch., Art. 3(d)].

The word 'execution' stands derived from the Latin *ex sequi,* meaning, to follow out, follow to the end, or perform, and equivalent to the French *executer,* so that, when used in their proper sense, all three convey the meaning of carrying out some act or course of conduct to completion. [Corpus Juris Secundum, Vol. 33, as cited in *Hameed Joharan* v. *Abdul Salam,* (2001) 7 SCC 573, para 1].

In criminal law "execution" means the putting to death of a criminal under such a sentence of Court.

In reference to the act of the executor in carrying out the provisions of a will, the terms "execution" and "executed" mean the settlement of the estate under the provisions of law.

Execution of a deed or other instrument. Thus when the terms are applied to a written instrument they include the performance of all acts which may be necessary to render it complete as a deed or an instrument importing the intended obligation, of every act required to give the instrument validity, or to carry it into effect or to give it the forms required to render it valid. (*Webster*)

The term execution of document consists in signing a document, written out, read over and understood and does not consist of merely signing a blank paper. *Birbal Singh* v. *Harphool Khan,* AIR 1976 All 23 at 24. [Negotiable Instruments Act (26 of 1881), S. 118].

Execution of a document is not mere signing of it. It is a solemn act of the executant who must own up the recitals in the instrument and there must be clear evidence that he put his signature in a document after knowing fully its contents. *Bhuthani Nath* v. *Kamleshwari Nath,* AIR 1972 Assam & Nagaland, 15, 17. [Registration Act (16 of 1908), S. 60(2)].

Execution of decree or order. Execution signifies in law the obtaining of actual possession of any thing acquired by judgment of law. EXECUTION signifies the last performance of an act as of a judgment &c. It is the obtaining possession of any thing recovered by judgment of law. (*Tomlin*)

This *execution*, or putting the law in force, is performed in the different manners, according to the nature of the action upon which it is founded, and of the judgment which is had or recovered. (*Tomlin*)

EXECUTION in the usual legal sense of the word, is a judicial writ grounded on the judgment of the Court from whence it issues; and is supposed to be granted by the Court at the request of the party at whose suit it is issued, to give him satisfaction on the judgment which he hath obtained. (*Tomlin*)

When there still remains something substantial to be done under a decree before it can become thoroughly effectual, that decree has to be 'executed' within the meaning of Civil Procedure Code (5 of 1908). As to execution of decrees and orders of Courts, *See* Civil Procedure Code (5 of 1908), O. XXI.

Execution of writ. Issuing out of Court, directed to an officer thereof, and running against the body or goods of a party.

Execution proceedings. *Execution* is a separate proceeding from the previous steps in the suit. The term "proceedings" in S. 6 of the General Clauses Act (10 of 1897) does not include proceedings in execution after decree.

Proceedings for the execution of decree or order.

Execution sale. A sale in execution of a decree.

Execution, stay of. The stopping for a limited period (as when an appeal is pending) an execution of a judgment decree or order that is, of the judgment creditor's right to issue execution. This is called a stay of execution.

Execution, writ of. The purpose of a *writ of an execution* is to authorize the officer to whom it is directed, and delivered, to seize and hold the property of the debtor for the satisfaction of the amount ordered to be made by such writ. [See Civil Procedure Code (5 of 1908), O. XXI]. A *writ of execution* has been defined as the final process and the end of the law; the end and fruit of the law; the act of carrying into effect the judgment of decree of a Court; the final judgment of a Court, or other jurisdiction, and the writ which authorises the officer so to carry into effect such judgment; a judicial writ issuing from the Court where the judgment is rendered.

Executioner. One who puts another to death in satisfaction of a death sentence.

Executive. "EXECUTIVE" in relation to a trade union, means the body by whatever name called to which the management of the affairs of the trade union is entrusted. [Industrial Disputes Act (14 of 1947), S. 2(gg)]

"Executive", in relation to a Trade Union, means the body by whatever name called, to which the management of the affairs of a Trade Union is entrusted. [Industrial Relations Code, 2020 (35 of 2020), section 2(n)]

Pertaining to the execution of the laws. (*Webster*)

That branch of the government which is entrusted with the enforcement of laws as distinguished from the legislative and judicial branches; having the function of executing.

Executive action. The expression 'executive action' in Art. 166 is comprehensive enough and apt to include even orders which emerge after, and embody the results of a judicial or *quasi*-judicial disposal by Government. [Constitution of India, Art. 166]

Executive Council. Means the Executive Council of the University. [S. 2(m) of the Rajiv Gandhi National Aviation University Act, 2013 (26 of 2013)]

Executive Director. Means a whole time director as defined in section 2(94) of Act 18 of 2013. [R. 2(1)(k) of the Companies (Specification of Definitions Details) Rules, 2014]

Executive officer means such officer of the appropriate Government as may be notified by that Government for the purposes of Chapter XIII or an officer authorised in writing by such executive officer to discharge his duties under that Chapter. [Code on Social Security, 2020 (36 of 2020), section 2(30)]

Executive power. Power of executing. [IPC (45 of 1860), S. 55A(a)].

Executor. "EXECUTOR" means a person to whom the execution of the last will of a deceased person is, by the testator's appointment, confided. [Indian Succession Act (39 of 1925), S. 2(*c*)].

"EXECUTOR" means the executor or administrator of a deceased person. [Estate Duty Act (34 of 1953), S. 2(8) and Gift Tax Act (18 of 1958), S. 2(x) and Wealth Tax Act (27 of 1957), S. 2(i)]

One who executes or carries out; a person appointed by a testator to execute or give effect to his will after his decease. [Wealth Tax Act (27 of 1957), S. 2(i); Gift-tax Act (18 of 1958), S. 2(x) and CPC (5 of 1908), O. VIII, R. 6(3), ill. (a)].

The word "executor" in its widest sense signifies the enforcement of or giving effect to the judgment or orders of the court of justice. In a narrower sense, it means the enforcement of those judgments or orders by a public officer under the writs of *fieri facias,* possession, delivery, sequestration, *fieri facias de bonis ecclesiasticis,* etc. [*Meenakshi Saxena* v. *ECGC Limited,* (2018) 7 SCC 479, para 15].

Executor de son tort. (*or Executor of his own wrong*) is he that takes upon him the office of an Executor by intrusion, not being so constituted by the testator".

A person who intermeddles with the estate of the deceased, or does any other act which belongs to the office of the executor, while there is no rightful executor or administrator in existence, thereby makes himself an executor of his own wrong. [Indian Succession Act (39 of 1925), S. 303]

Executor of will. A person appointed by the testator to carry out the provisions of the will as the legal personal representative of the deceased. [CPC (5 of 1908), 1st Sch., App. A, form No. 9].

Executory. That which remains to be carried into effect.

Exemplary. Such as may serve for a warning to others; such as may deter from wrong doing.

Exemplary damages. Damages on an increased scale, awarded to plaintiff over and above actual or ordinary damages, where wrong done to plaintiff was aggravated by circumstances of violence, oppression, malice, fraud, or wanton and wicked conduct on part of defendant. *Goines* v. *Pennsylvania R. R.*, 208 Misc. 103, 143 N.Y.S. 2d 576, 583.

Exemplary manner. A manner deserving imitation. [Navy Act (62 of 1957), S. 79 and Army Act (46 of 1950), S. 122(4)].

Exempli gratia. (*Lat.*) As; for an example; e.g.

Exempt. To give immunity from a liability, obligation, penalty, law or authority. [Indian Evidence Act (1 of 1872), S. 23, *Expln.*].

The word 'exempt' shows that a person is put beyond the application of law. *Dhanrajamal Gobindram* v. *Shamji Kalidas and Co*, AIR 1961 SC 1285, 1290. [Foreign Exchange Regulation Act, 1947, S. 5].

Exempt supply. "Exempt supply'' means supply of any goods or services or both which attracts nil rate of tax or which may be exempt from tax under S. 8, or under S. 6 of the Integrated Goods and Services Tax Act, and includes non-taxable supply [The Union Territory Goods and Services Tax Act, 2017 (14 of 2017), S. 2(4)]

Exempted. That which has been granted exemption.

The expression "exempted" in clause (o) does not only mean full exemption from duty because under S. 25 of the Act power has been conferred to grant exemption from the whole or any part of the duty of customs leviable on the goods specified in the notification. This means that clause (o) would also cover cases where partial exemption from duty has been granted in respect of the goods in question. *Jacsons Thevara* v. *CCE,* AIR 1991 SC 647. [Customs Act (52 of 1962), S. 111(o)]

Exempted goods. "Exempted goods" means any goods exempted from tax in accordance with the provisions of the Act. [Rajasthan Value Added Tax Act (4 of 2003), S. 2(13) as cited in *Commercial Taxes Officer* v. *A Infrastructure Limited*, (2015) 15 SCC 98, para 13].

Exempted employee. Means an employee who is not liable under this Act to pay the employee's contribution. [Employees' State Insurance Act (34 of 1948), S. 2(10)]

"EXEMPTED EMPLOYEE" means an employee to whom a Scheme or the Insurance Scheme, as the case may be, would, but for the exemption granted under Section 17, have applied. [Employees' Provident Funds Act (19 of 1952), S. 2(ff)]

"Exempted employee" for the purposes of Chapter III, means an employee to whom any of the schemes referred to in section 15, but for the exemption granted under this Code, would have applied and for the purposes of Chapter I V, means an employee, whose wage is specified in the notification by the Central Government and who is not liable to pay employee's contribution. [Code on Social Security, 2020 (36 of 2020), section 2(31)]

Exempted establishment. Means an establishment in respect of which an exemption has been granted under S. 17 from the operation of all or any of the provisions of any Scheme or the Insurance Scheme, as the case may be, whether such exemption has been granted to the establishment or such to any person or class of persons employed therein. [Employees' Provident Act (19 of 1952), S. 2(fff)]

Exempted goods. Means goods which are exempt from the whole of the duty of excise leviable thereon, and includes goods which are chargeable to "Nil" rate of duty. [CENVAT Credit Rules, 2002, R. 2(d)]

Exempted person. An Indian Christian, a Hindu, a Mohammedan, a Parsi or a Buddhist or a person exempted under S. 352 of the Indian Succession Act, 39 of 1925 are exempted from the operation of that Act. [Administrator-General's Act (3 of 1913), S. 2(2) (The Act repealed by the Act (45 of 1963)]

Exemption. "EXEMPTION", in relation to any duty of excise, means exemption from the whole or any part of such duty. [Central Excise Laws (Amendment and Validation) Act (58 of 1982), S. 2(c)]

An exemption is freedom from any liability, payment of tax or duty. It may assume different application in a growing economy such as provisioning for tax holiday to new units, concessional rate of tax to goods or persons for a limited period under specific conditions. [*State of Jharkhand* v. *La Opala R.G-Limited*, (2014) 15 SCC 136, para 16].

The action of exempting; the state of being exempted; immunity from a liablity, obligation, penalty, law or authority. [Income-tax Act (43 of 1961), S. 119(2)(b)].

Freedom from liability, tax or duty like any exception. *Union of India* v. *Wood Papers Ltd.,* AIR 1991 SC 2049.

Exercisable. Capable of being exercised. [Estate Duty Act (34 of 1953), S. 2(9); CPC (5 of 1908), O. XLI, R. 8 and Constitution of India, Art. 73(1)(b)].

Exercise. For the purposes of these guidelines—

'EXERCISE' means an application by the employee to the company for issue of shares against the option vested in him in pursuance of such plan or scheme, as the case may be. [Employees' Stock Option Plan or Scheme, 2001, S-7, *Expln.* (ii)]

Regular or repeated appropriate use of a faculty, power or body organ [Army Act (46 of 1950), S. 39(d)]; to bring into play; to realize in action [T.P. Act (4 of 1882), S. 57(e)]; [Prevention of

Cruelty to Animals Act (59 of 1960, S. 11(1)(g)]; [Constitution of India, Art. 19(3)].

Exertion. The active exercise of any power or faculty. [Hindu Succession Act (30 of 1956), S. 14(1), *Expln.*]; [Navy Act (62 of 1957), S. 43(e)].

Exhaust. To use up completely [T.P. Act (4 of 1882), S. 68(2) and Indian Trusts Act (2 of 1882), S. 83(c)]; an arrangement (as of fans) for withdrawing undesirable fumes, dusts or odours from an enclosure (as a factory, room or kitchen).

Exhaustion of remedies. The doctrine that, if an administrative remedy is provided by statute, a claimant must seek relief first from the administrative body before judicial relief is available.

The doctrine that where an administrative remedy is provided, relief must be sought exhausting such remedy before the courts will act. *(Ballentine's Law Dictionary, 3rd Edn.)*

Exhaustion of right. When the right to distribute a particular copy of a work is once exercised, then it is said that the right regarding that copy has been exhausted. (*Copyright*)

Exhibit. "EXHIBIT" means exhibit at any entertainment to which the public are admitted through sale of tickets. [Prevention of Cruelty to Animals Act (59 of 1960), S. 21]

Anything exhibited; any document which, in the course of a judicial proceeding, is produced and put in Court to form part of the record and to give information to arrive at a decision; to expose to view.

The action of exhibiting or showing publicly; a public display (of works of art *etc.*); the place of the display an allowance given to a student [Jawaharlal Nehru University Act (53 of 1966), S. 5(8) and Aligarh Muslim University Act (40 of 1920), S. 5(8)].

AS APPLIED TO A COMPLAINT, OR INFORMATION, in a criminal case, the word means "to present the same to a public officer".

'Exhibit' means a document exhibited for the purpose of being taken into consideration in deciding some question or other in respect of the proceeding in which it is filed. *Rakhaldas Pramanick* v. *Shantilata Ghose,* AIR 1956 Cal 619. [Court Fees Act (7 of 1870), S. 4].

Exhibition. The action of exhibiting or showing publicly; a public display (of works of art *etc.*); the place of the display; an allowance given to a student [Jawaharlal Nehru University Act (53 of 1966), S. 5(8) and Aligarh Muslim University Act (40 of 1920), S. 5(8)].

'Exhibition by means of video' means any exhibition in public, on payment for admission, of moving pictures or series of pictures by playing or replaying a pre-recorded cassette by means of video cassette player whether on the screen of a television set or video or otherwise." [U.P. Cinemas (Regulation) Act, 1955 (3 of 1956) (as adopted by State of Uttarakhand), S. 2(aa) as cited in *District Magistrate, Haridwar* v. *Harish Malhotra*, (2015) 11 SCC 513, para 3].

Exhort. To preach, to urge, to persuade.

Exhumations. The removal from the earth of something buried, especially a human corpse; disinterment.

Disinterment. [Geneva Conventions Act (6 of 1960), Art. 17].

Exigency, Emergency. The *exigency* is more common, but less pressing; the *emergency* is imperious when it comes, but comes less frequently; a prudent traveler will never carry more money with him than what will supply the *exigencies* of his journey; and in case of an *emergency* will rather borrow from his friends than risk his property.

Such need or necessity as belongs to the occasion. [Army Act (46 of 1950), S. 112(e)].

Exim Bank. The Export-Import Bank of India established under the Export-Import Bank of India Act, 1981. [Foreign Exchange Management (Export of Goods and Services) Regulations, 2000, Reg. 2(iii)]

Exist. To have existence; to live. To be in being.

Existence. Being; the fact or state of existing. [T.P. Act (4 of 1882), Ss. 13 and 14; Army Act (46 of 1950), S. 37(d) and Constitution of India, Art. 131]

"Existence : a) Reality, as opp to appearance. b) The fact or state of existing; actual possession of being. Continued being as a living creature, life, esp. under adverse conditions. Something that exists; an entity, a being. All that exists. (Page 894 - Oxford English Dictionary) [The Shorter Oxford English Dictionary as cited in *Mobilox Innovations Private Limited* v. *Kirusa Software Private Limited* AIR 2017 SC 4532, para 36]

Existence of public right. An entity or life or continuance in being of the rights pertaining to the people, State or community. [CrPC 1973 (2 of 1974), S. 137(1)].

Existence or extent of a legal right. The expression "existence or extent of a legal right" is meant to establish one's claim in a suit. *State of Karnataka* v. *Union of India,* AIR 1978 SC 68.

Existent. At present existing. [T.P. Act (4 of 1882), S. 3(c)]; [Mines Act (35 of 1952), S. 8, prov.].

Existing academy. Means the Academy of Scientific and Innovative Research established in pursuance of the resolution of the Government of India in the Ministry of Science and Technology, Department of Scientific and Industrial Research, Council of Scientific and Industrial Research, *vide* No. 6/1/CSIR-AcSIR/2010-PPD, dated 1-7-2010. [(w.e.f. 3-4-2012) S. 2(h) of the Academy of Scientific & Innovative Research Act, 2011 (13 of 2012)]

Existing bank. "EXISTING BANK" means any of the following banks, namely:—

(i) Bank of Bikaner, Limited

(ii) Bank of Indore, Limited omitted by Act 7 of 2011

(iii) *** omitted by Act 56 of 1962

(iv) Bank of Mysore, Limited

(v) Bank of Patiala

(vi) Travancore Bank, Limited. [State Bank of India (Subsidiary Banks) Act (38 of 1959), S. 2(d)]

"EXISTING BANK" means a banking company specified in column 1 of the First Schedule, being a company the deposits of which, as shown in the return as on the last Friday in June 1969, furnished to the Reserve Bank of India under Section 27 of the Banking Regulation Act, 1949 (10 of 1949) were not less than rupees fifty crores. [Banking Companies (Acquisition and Transfer of Undertakings) Act (5 of 1970), S. 2(f)]

"EXISTING BANK" means a banking company specified in column 1 of the First Schedule, being a company the total of the demand and time liabilities in India of which, as shown in the return as on the 14th day of March, 1980, furnished to the Reserve Bank under Section 42 of the Reserve Bank of India Act, 1934 amounts to not less than rupees two hundred crores. [Banking Companies (Acquisition & Transfer of Undertakings) Act (40 of 1980), S. 2(d)]

Existing banking company. 'EXISTING BANKING COMPANY' means a banking company carrying on business of banking at the commencement of this Act which either holds a licence at such commencement under Section 22 of the Banking Companies Act, 1949 or having applied for such licence has not been informed by notice in writing by the Reserve Bank that a licence cannot be granted to it and includes the State Bank and a subsidiary bank, but does not include a defunct banking company. [Deposit Insurance and Credit Guarantee Corporation Act (47 of 1961), S. 2(h)]

Existing company. In the Companies Act, 1913, means a company formed and registered under the Indian Companies Act, 1866, or under any Act or Acts repealed thereby, or under the Indian Companies Act, 1882; Act VII of 1913 (Companies), S. 2, cl. 7.

Existing co-operative bank. Means a cooperative bank carrying on the business of banking at the commencement of the Deposit Insurance Corporation (Amendment) Act, 1968, which either holds a licence at such commencement under Section 22 of the Banking Regulation Act, 1949, or having applied for such licence has not been informed by notice in writing by the Reserve Bank that a licence cannot be granted to it but does not include a defunct co-operative bank. [Deposit Insurance and Credit Guarantee Corporation Act (47 of 1961), S. 2(hh)]

Existing Council. Means the Indian Council of World Affairs, a society registered under the Societies Registration Act, 1860, and functioning as such immediately before the appointed day. [Indian Council of World Affairs Act (29 of 2001), S. 3(e)]

Existing Government Company. Means a Government company which is carrying on business on the appointed day. [National Company Limited (Acquisition And Transfer of Undertakings) Act (42 of 1980), S. 2(d)]

Existing industrial undertaking. Means—

(a) in the case of an industrial undertaking pertaining to any of the industries specified in the First Schedule as originally enacted, an industrial undertaking which was in existence on the commencement of this Act or for the establishment of which effective steps had been taken before such commencement; and

(b) in the case of an industrial undertaking pertaining to any of the industries added to the First Schedule by an amendment thereof, an industrial undertaking which is in existence on the coming into force of such amendment or for the establishment of which effective steps had been taken before the coming into force of such amendment. [Industries (Development and Regulation) Act (65 of 1951), S. 3(bb)]

Existing insurer. Means every insurer the management of whose undertaking has vested in the Central Government under Section 3 of the General Insurance (Emergency Provisions) Act 1971, and includes the undertaking of the Life Insurance Corporation in so far as it relates to the general insurance business carried on by it. [General Insurance Business (Nationalisation) Act (52 of 1972), S. 3(e)]

Existing law. "EXISTING LAW" means any law, Ordinance, order, bye-law, rule or regulation passed or made before the commencement of this Constitution by any Legislature, authority or person having power to make such a law, Ordinance, order, bye-law, rule or regulation. [Constitution of India, Art. 366(10)].

The words 'existing law' in Art. 19(5), Constitution of India include not only the law made by a statute but also any personal law, custom or usage having the force of law.

To have the status of an existing law, the law should have been made by a legislature having power to make such law. *Jeejeebhoy* v. *Asst. Collector, Thana*, AIR 1965 SC 1096, 1101.

A law passed by a Legislature would not come within the definition of an 'existing Indian Law' unless such Legislature had power to make the law in question.

The word 'existing law' means any law, Ordinance, Order, bye-law, rule or regulation. It is obvious that 'existing law' refers to statutes. It was the statutory law that was meant, for, in order to be existing law it must be any law, ordinance, order *etc.* passed or made by the Legislature or other competent authority. It does not include, for instance, the personal laws of the Hindus or Muslims nor would it embrace within its scope customs or usages which had acquired the force of law.

The expression 'existing law' would include only laws passed by a competent authority as well as rules, bye-laws and regulations made by virtue of statutory power. It would not include administrative orders which are traceable not to any law made by the Legislature but derive their force from executive authority and made either for the convenience of the administration or for the benefit of individual. *State of Gujarat* v. *Vora Piddali*, AIR 1964 SC 1043, 1064.

"EXISTING LAW" means any law, notification, order, rule or regulation relating to levy and collection of duty or tax on goods or services or both passed or made before the commencement of this Act by Parliament or any Authority or person having the power to make such law, notification, order, rule or regulation. [Central Goods and Services Tax Act (12 of 2017), S. 2(48); Union Territory Goods and Services Tax Act (14 of 2017), S. 2(5)]

Existing law and **law in force.** The expressions 'existing law' and 'law in force' used in the constitution denote two distinct subject matters. When the constitution intends to refer to a law which is in force at the time of the constitution, it uses the expression 'law in force'. 'Existing law' means law enacted before the Constitution, though it may not have been brought into operation in whole or in part. *P.P. Kutti Keya* v. *State of Madras,* AIR 1954 Mad 621.

Existing liability. For the removal of doubts, it is hereby declared that the 'existing liability' does not include advance tax payable in accordance with the provisions of Part C of Chapter XVII of Act 43 of 1961. [(w.e.f. 1-6-2013) *Explanation 2* to section 132B of the Income-tax Act, 1961 (43 of 1961)]

Existing Securities and Exchange Board. Means the Securities and Exchange Board of India constituted under the Resolution of the Government of India in the Department of Economic Affairs No. 1(44) SE/86, dated the 12th day of April, 1988. [Securities and Exchange Board of India Act (15 of 1992), S. 2(1)(c)]

"Existing State of Jammu and Kashmir". Means the State of Jammu and Kashmir as existing immediately before the appointed day, comprising the territory which immediately before the commencement of the Constitution of India in the Indian State of Jammu and Kashmir. [Jammu & Kashmir Reorganisation Act, 2019 (34 of 2019), section 2(e)]

Exit. Means a passage, channel or means of egress from any building, storey or floor area to street or other open space of safety. [Delhi Cinematograph (Exhibition of film by VCR) Rules, 1986, R. 2(ix)].

Exonerate. To free a person from blame or a duty imposed on him.

To release a person or property from liability. [Food Corporation Act (37 of 1964), S. 9(1)(b)].

TO EXONERATE, EXCULPATE. We *exonerate* him upon whom a charge has lain, or who has the load of guilt; we *exculpate* ourselves when there is any danger of being blamed; circumstances may sometimes tend to *exonerate;* the explanation of some person is requisite to *exculpate.*

Expansion. The word 'expansion' is derived from the word 'expand' which means 'to become greater or bigger in size, to spread out.' *State of Gujarat* v. *Saurashtra Cement & Chemical Industries Ltd.,* (2003) 2 SCC 394, para 9 : AIR 2003 SC 1132.

Setting up a new unit to increase the production in addition to the two existing units shall come within the meaning of the word 'expansion' of existing units. *State of Gujarat* v. *Saurashtra Cement & Chemical Industries Ltd.,* (2003) 2 SCC 394, para 10 : AIR 2003 SC 1132.

'Expansion/diversification of industrial unit' means a capacity set up or installed during the operative period which creates additional productions / manufacturing / facilities for manufacture of the same product/products as of the existing unit (expansion) or different products (diversification) at the same or new location—

(i) in which the additional fixed capital investment made during the operative period exceeds 25% of the fixed capital investment of the existing unit; and

(ii) which results into increase in annual production by 25% of the installed capacity of the existing unit in case of expansion. [Haryana General Sales Tax Rules, 1975, R. 28A(2)(d) as cited in *State of Haryana* v. *Bharti Teletech Limited*, (2014) 3 SCC 556, para 19].

Expansion card. An integrated circuit card that plugs into an expansion slot on a motherboard to provide access to additional peripherals or features not built into the motherboard. (*Cyber Law*)

Expatriate. To quit one's country, renouncing citizenship in and allegiance to that country and taking residence in and becoming a citizen of another country. 3 Am J2d Aliens § 120. Noun: One who has expatriated himself. *(Ballentine's Law Dictionary, 3rd Edn.)*

Expatriate staff. Means a person whose provident/superannuation/pension fund is maintained outside India by his principal employer outside India. [Foreign Exchange Management (Remittance of Assets) Regulations, 2000, Reg. 5, *Expln.* (a)]

Expatriation. Renunciation of allegiance to one's native country.

Expectancy. That which is expected or hoped for. The condition of being deferred to a future time, or of dependence upon an expected event. With respect to the time of their enjoyment, estates may either be in possession or in expectancy; and of expectancies there are two sorts, one created by the act of the parties, called a "remainder", the other by act of law, called a "reversion".

Expectancy of succession. The expression 'expectancy of succession', usually called 'spec. successions', means that the property does not vest *in presenti* and consequently a person having such expectancy of succession has no property which could be attached or sold. *Basant Lal* v. *Dwarka Prasad,* AIR 1978 All 436, 438. [CPC (5 of 1908), 60 (1), Prov. (m)]

Expectancy of succession by survivorship. Anticipation to succeed a person to the exclusion of his heirs by virtue of being a joint tenant with him and surviving him. [CPC (5 of 1908), S. 60(1), prov. (m)].

Expectation. The action of mentally looking for something to take place; anticipation [; when the expectation is of an unhappy thing [Indian Evidence Act (1 of 1872), S. 32(1)].

Expectation of death. Death being expected. [Indian Evidence Act (1 of 1872), S. 32(1)].

Expectation of life. The number of years which, in the ordinary course, a particular person might have expected to survive.

Expedient. Advantageous; fit; proper; suitable to the circumstances of the case.

"Expedient" means 'Characterised by suitability, practicality, and efficiency in achieving a particular end; fit, proper or advantageous under the circumstances.' [Webster's Third New International Dictionary as cited in *Union of India* v. *Major S.P. Sharma*, (2014) 6 SCC 351, para 68].

'Advantageous; fit, proper, or suitable to the circumstances of the case'. [Shorter Oxford English Dictionary (3rd Edn.) as cited in *Union of India* v. *Major S.P. Sharma*, (2014) 6 SCC 351, para 68].

In one sense, "expedient" (adj) means "apt and suitable to the end in view", "practical and efficient," "polite", "profitable", "advisable," "fit, proper and suitable to the circumstances of the case". In another shade, it means a device "characterised by mere utility rather than principle, conducive to special advantage rather than to what is universally right." *State of Gujarat* v. *Jamuadad*, AIR 1974 SC 2233, 2238.

Expedit reipublicae ut sit finis litium. (*Lat.*) It is in the interest of the public that there is an end of litigation.

Expedit republicae ne sua re quis male utatur. (*Maxim*) It is for the public good that no one should use his property badly.

Expedition. An excursion undertaken for a specific purpose.

Expeditious disposal. The 'expeditious disposal' of any representation only means that which could be expeditiously disposed of by the authority concerned without any unexplained delay or delay through carelessness. *Ahmad Nassar* v. *State of T.N.,* (1999) 8 SCC 473, para 8.

Expel. To eject; to dislodge. [Indian Partnership Act (9 of 1932), S. 33(1)].

Expelled partner. Dislodged partner. [Indian Partnership Act (9 of 1932), S. 33(2)].

Expend. To spend. [CPC (5 of 1908), S. 2(17)(g)].

Expend; Expenditure. 'To expend is to spend; expenditure is spending money or amount expended.

Payments made for purchases of stock-in-trade would be covered by the term expenditure. *Attar Singh Gurmukh Singh* v. *I.T.O. Ludhiana* AIR 1991 SC 2109, 2113 [Income Tax Act (43 of 1961), S. 40A].

The term 'expenditure' denotes 'spending' or paying out or away. It does not necessarily involve actual delivery of a parting with money or property. If there are cross claims and as a result of the accounting the balance due is only paid, the amount which is debited against the settlement of the accounts may appropriately be termed 'expenditure'. *C.I.T.* v. *Nainital Bank Ltd*, (1966) 62 ITR 638, 641 (SC) [Income-tax Act (43 of 1961), S. 37(1)].

'EXPENDITURE' is not necessarily confined to the money which has been actually paid out. It covers a liability which has accrued or which has been incurred although it may have to be discharged at a future date. However, a contingent liability which may have to be discharged in future cannot be considered as expenditure. *Madras Industrial Investment Corpn. Ltd. v. CIT,* AIR 1997 SC 2063.

Disbursement; the action or practice of expending; the amount expended. [Constitution of India, Art. 112(2)].

Expenditure in connection with election incurred or authorised. All money laid out having to do with election but not money liable to be refunded to the candidate, is contemplated. *Vidya Sagar Joshi* v. *Surinder Nath Gautam*, AIR 1969 SC 288 at 291. [Representation of the People Act (43 of 1951), S. 123(6) and S. 77, *Expln.*(1)].

Expenditure on goods. "EXPENDITURE ON GOODS" means the cost to the manufacturer of the goods at the factory or works including containers. [Customs Tariff (Determination of Origin of Goods Under The Bangkok Agreement) Rules, 1976, Sch. (1) *Expln.*]

Expenditure on material. Means the cost to the manufacturer of the material at the factory or works, including containers. [Customs Tariff (Determination of Origin of the U.A.R. and Yugoslavia) Rules, 1976, Sch., R. 2, *Expln.*]

"EXPENDITURE ON MATERIAL" means the cost of the manufacture of the material at the factory or works, including containers but excluding royalities. [Customs Tariff (Determination of Origin of Other Preferential Areas) Rules, 1977 and Notification Issued Thereunder, R. 3(c)]

Expense of, At the. At the sacrifice of; to the detriment of. [T.P. Act (4 of 1882), S. 63].

Expenses of commission. The expression 'expenses of the commission' in O. XXVI, R. 15, CPC (5 of 1908) does not include the expenses of the opposite party and includes only the commissioner's fee and the expenses incurred by the commissioner in connection with the execution of the commission. *Asepand Nanakchand Agarwal* v. *C. A. Ayyatburai,* AIR 1956 TC 260, 262.

Expense. Expenses. For the purposes of this regulation, "EXPENSES" include the fee to be paid to the interim resolution professional, fee to be paid to insolvency professional entity, if any, and fee to be paid to professionals, if any, and other expenses to be incurred by the interim resolution professional. [Insolvency and Bankruptcy Board of India (Insolvency Resolution Process for Corporate Persons) Regulations, 2016, Regn. 33, *Explanation*].

For the purposes of this regulation, "EXPENSES" include the fee to be paid to the resolution professional, fee to be paid to insolvency professional entity, if any, and fee to be paid to professionals, if any, and other expenses to be incurred by the resolution professional. [Insolvency and Bankruptcy Board of India (Insolvency Resolution process for Corporate Persons) Regulations, 2016, Regn. 34].

Experience. Knowledge or practical wisdom gained from what one has observed, ecountered or undergone.

Experientia docet. Experience teacheth.

Experientia per varios actus legem facit.

Experience by various acts makes law.

Experience is the mistress of things.

Experiment. "EXPERIMENT" means any experiment performed any living animal including on operation for the purpose of discovering something unknown or testing some hypothesis or establishing or illustrating some truth. [Experiments on Animals (Control and Supervision) R. 1968, Rules 2(c)]

An action or operation undertaken in order to discover something unknown.

Expert. "When the Court has to form an opinion upon a point of foreign law, or of science, or art, or as to identity of handwriting or finger impressions, the opinions upon that point of persons specially skilled in such foreign law, science or art, or in questions as to identity of handwriting or finger impressions are relevant facts. Such persons are called experts." [Indian Evidence Act (1 of 1872), S. 45] [Now (w.e.f. 1-7-2024) repealed & replaced by Bharatiya Sakshya Adhiniyam, 2023 (47 of 2023)]

When the Court has to form an opinion upon a point of foreign law or of science or art, or any other field, or as to identity of handwriting or finger impressions, the opinions upon that point of persons specially skilled in such foreign law, science or art or any other field, or in questions as to identity of handwriting or finger impressions are relevant facts and such persons are called experts. [(w.e.f. 1-7-2024) Bharatiya Sakshya Adhiniyam, 2023 (47 of 2023), section 39(1)]

For the purposes of this sub-section, an Examiner of Electronic Evidence shall be an "expert". [(w.e.f. 1-7-2024) Bharatiya Sakshya Adhiniyam, 2023 (47 of 2023), section 39(2), Explanation]

"EXPERT" means a person who holds post graduate degree, and has a working experience of at least ten years in the line and has held responsible positions in the Government or private sector. [Punjab Health Systems Corporation Act (Punj Act No. 6 of 1996), S. 2(d)]

"EXPERT" means a person trained in mental health, medicine and child development or other related discipline, who may be required to facilitate communication with a child whose ability to communicate has been affected by trauma, disability or any other vulnerability. [Protection of Children from Sexual Offences Rules, 2012, R. 2(c)].

In a general sense, an expert is a person of peculiar knowledge or skill; one who has peculiar knowledge or skill as to some particular subject, such as any art or science, or particular trade, or profession, or any special branch of learning; and is professionally or peculiarly acquainted with its practices and

usages; a person who has technical and peculiar knowledge in relation to matters with which the mass of mankind are supposed not to be acquainted; he who has some special, particular or practical knowledge in relation to some special department of the affairs of men as would qualify him to stand as an expert, skilled enough to teach others. (*Ame Cyc.*)

The term "expert" includes "anyone who holds himself out to the public as specially qualified in any line by knowledge or skill." Palmer Company Precidents 16 Edn., Page 23 [Companies Act (1 of 1956), S. 60(1)(a)].

A person who has made special study of the subject or acquired special experience therein.

"EXPERT" includes an engineer, a valuer, a chartered accountant, a company secretary, a cost accountant and any other person who has the power or authority to issue a certificate in pursuance of any law for the time being in force. [S. 2(38) of the Companies Act, 2013 (18 of 2013)]

Expert arbitrator. An arbitrator selected by the parties because he has a special and professional knowledge and skills of the subject under dispute. An 'expert arbitrator' is justified in deciding the dispute on his expert knowledge without taking any evidence.

Expert Committee. Means a Committee consisting of academics or other experts in the relevant fields of knowledge or practice to be nominated by

Chairman of the Commission and include representatives of the Statutory bodies; and there may be as many Expert Committees as the Commission may determine for different purposes. [UGC (Institutions Deemed to be Universities) Regulations, 2019, Regn. 2(2.09)].

Expert opinion. The testimony of an expert stating his opinion on a given subject.

Expert testimony. Testimony by an expert witness.

If scientific, technology, or other specialized knowledge will assist the trier of fact to understand the evidence or to determine a fact in issue, a witness qualified as an expert by knowledge, skill, experience, training, or education, may testify thereto in the form of an opinion or otherwise.

Opinion evidence of some person who possesses special skill or knowledge in some science, profession or business which is not common to the average man and which is possessed by the expert by reason of his special study or experience.

Expert witness. One who by reason of education or specialized experience possesses superior knowledge respecting a subject about which persons having no particular training are incapable of forming an accurate opinion or deducing correct conclusions.

Experto crede. Means an expert should be believed.

Expiration. The coming to an end. [T.P. Act (4 of 1882), S. 14 and Indian Contract Act (9 of 1872), S. 35].

Expire. The word 'expire' means to come to an end or to put an end to, or to terminate or to become void, or to become extinct. *Pradip Kumar Das*, v. *State of W.B.*, AIR 1974 SC 2151, 2153. [Maintenance of Internal Security Act (26 of 1971) (*repealed*), S. 14]

Expiry. The termination of a time or period fixed by law, contract or agreement. [Indian Partnership Act (9 of 1832), S. 17(b)].

Explain. Make known in detail.

To make plain or intelligible; to account for; to make oneself understood. [CrPC 1973 (2 of 1974), S. 164(2)].

Explanation. That which explains. [Constitution of India, Art. 25(2)(b), *Expln.* (1)].

An explanation merely widens the scope of the main section. It does not carve out a particular exception to the contents of the main section. *Sonia Bhatia* v. *State of U.P.,* AIR 1981 SC 1274.

Explanatory. Serving to explain; containing an explanation; having the function of explaining. [Indian Evidence Act (1 of 1872), S. 9, ill. (d)].

Explicit. Not obscure or ambiguous, having no disguised meaning or reservation. Clear in understanding.

Exploit. To exploit means to turn to industrial account. If not only includes extraction of ore but also includes turning of the ore to industrial account. *Metal Corporation of India* v. *Union of India*, AIR 1970 Cal 15, 20.

Exploitation. Utilization or working of a natural resource; the action of exploiting *i.e.*, making use of meanly or unjustly for one's own advantage. *Timblo Lunaos Ltd. Margo* v. *Jorge Anibal Motor Sequeira,* AIR 1977 SC 734. [Children Act (60 of 1960) (*repealed*), S. 9(3); Constitution of India, Art. 39(f) and Art. 46].

"EXPLOITATION" the expression 'exploitation' shall include any act of physical exploitation or any form of sexual exploitation, slavery or practices similar to slavery, servitude, or the forced removal of organs. [*Explanation* 1 to section 370 of IPC, 1860 (45 of 1860), as substituted by the Criminal Laws (Amendment) Act, 2013 (13 of 2013)]

The expression "exploitation" shall include any act of physical exploitation or any form of sexual exploitation, slavery or practices similar to slavery, servitude, beggary or forced removal of organs. [Now (w.e.f. 1-7-2024) repealed & replaced by Bharatiya Nyaya Sanhita, 2023 (45 of 2023), section 143(1), *Explanation* 1]

Exploration. The action of exploring. [Oil and Natural Gas Commission Act (43 of 1959), S. 14(2)(a)].

Exploration operation. Means any operation undertaken for the purpose of exploring, locating or proving the mineral deposits. [Offshore Areas Minerals (Development and Regulation] Act, 2002 (17 of 2003), S. 4(e)]

Explore. To search through or into; to investigate unknown regions.

Explosion. The action of going off with a loud noise or of bursting under the influence of suddenly developed internal enrgy.

Explosive. "EXPLOSIVE" (*a*) means gunpowder, nitro-glycerine, dynamite, guncotton, blasting powders, fulminate of mercury or of other metals, coloured fires and every other substance, whether similar to those above mentioned or not, used or manufactured with a view to produce a practical effect by explosion or a pyrotechnic effect; (*b*) includes fog signals, fire-works, fuses, rockets, percussion-caps, detonators, cartridges, ammunition of all descriptions, and every adaptation or preparation of an explosive as above defined. [Explosive Act (4 of 1884), S. 4(d)].

Relating to, characterised or operated by, or suited to cause explosion. [Constitution of India, 7 Sch., List 1; Item 5].

Explosive substance. The expression "EXPLOSIVE SUBSTANCE" shall be deemed to include any materials for making any explosive substance also any apparatus, machine, implement or material used, or intended to be used, or adapted for causing, or aiding in causing, any explosion in or with any explosive substance; also any part of any such apparatus, machine or implement. [Explosive Substances Act (6 of 1908), S. 2].

The expression 'explosive substances' under Section 5 means type of bombs and dynamites. *State of T.N.* v. *Sivarasan,* (1997) 1 SCC 682, para 26. [TADA Act (28 of 1987), S. 5]

Export. That which is exported [Constitution of India, Art. 49]; the action of exporting; to send out commodities from one country to another.

"EXPORT" means to take out of the territories administered by any Government to sea, or to any foreign territory, or to any territory administered by another Government. [Opium Act (1 of 1878), S. 3].

"EXPORT" means to take out of India by land, sea or air to any place outside India other than a country or territory notified in this behalf by the Central Government by notification in the Official Gazette. [Tea Act (29 of 1953), S. 3(f)]

"Export" means taking out of India to a place outside India. [Antiquities and Art Treasures Act (52 of 1972), S. 2(c)]

"EXPORT" means export from India of products or services of any industrial concern in small scale sector. [Small Industries Development Bank of India, Act (39 of 1989), S. 2(f)]

"EXPORT", with its grammatical variations and cognate expressions, means—

(i) the taking out of India to a place outside India any goods,

(ii) provision of services from India to any person outside India. [Foreign Exchange Management Act (42 of 1999), S. 2(l)]

"EXPORT" with its grammatical variations and cognate expressions, means taking out of India to a place outside India. [Standards of Weights and Measures Act (60 of 1976), S. 2(e) and Customs Act (52 of 1962), S. 2(18); Cigarettes and Other Tobacco Products (Prohibition of Advertisement and Regulation of Trade and Commerce, Production, Supply and Distribution) Act (34 of 2003), S. 3(d); Cigarettes (Regulation ofProduction, *etc.*) Act (49 of 1975), S. 2(d)] *See also* Rule 2(e) of the Hazardous Waste (Management and Handling) Rules, 1989; Rule 2(c) the Manufacture, Storage and Import of Hazardous Chemicals Rules, 1989.

For the purpose of this Rule, the explanation 'EXPORT' means a sale in the course of inter State trade or commerce or in the course of export of the goods out of territory of India, where such sale occasions movement of the goods from the State. [Bombay Sales Tax Rules (1959), R. 41-E, *Expln.*]

"Export" includes the taking or sending out of goods by land, sea or air, on consignment or by way of sale, lease, hire-purchase, or under any other arrangement by whatever name called, and in the case of software, also includes transmission through any electronic media. [Foreign Exchange Management (Export of Goods and Services) Regulations, 2000, Reg. 2(iv)]

"EXPORT" means—

(i) taking goods, or providing services, out of India, from a Special Economic Zone, by land, sea or air or by any other mode, whether physical or otherwise; or

(ii) supplying goods, or providing services, from the Domestic Tariff Area to a Unit or Developer; or

(iii) supplying goods, or providing services, from one Unit to another Unit or Developer, in the same or different Special Economic Zone. [Special Economic Zones Act (28 of 2005), S. 2(m)]

That which is exported [Constitution of India, Art. 49]; the action of exporting; to send out commodities from one country to another.

Goods and services produced in one country and sold in other countries in exchange for goods and services, gold, foreign exchange or settlement of debt. [*Anti-Dumping Law*]

The word "export" has reference to taking out of goods which had become part and parcel of the mass of the property of the local area and will not apply to goods in transit *i.e.*, brought into the area for the purpose of being transported out of it. *Central India Spinning and Weaving and Manufacturing. Co Ltd., Empress Mills* v. *Municipal Committee Wardha*, AIR 1958 SC 341, 347.

While all exports involve a taking out of the country, all goods taken out of the country cannot be said to be exported. The test is that the goods must have a foreign destination where they can be said to be imported. *Burmah S. C. S. & D. & D. Co.* v. *Commercial Tax Officer*, AIR 1961 SC 315, 324. [Constitution of India, Art. 286(1)(b)].

Export, in the course of. Every sale or purchase preceding the export is not necessarily to be regarded as within the course of export. It must be inextricably bound up with the export, and a sale or purchase unconnected with the ultimate export as an integral part thereof is not within the exemption under the sales tax law. *Burmah S.O.S. & D. Co.* v. *Commercial Tax Officer*, AIR 1961 SC 315, 323. [Constitution of India, Art. 286 (1) (b)]

Export allotment. 'EXPORT ALLOTMENT' means the total quantity of tea which may be exported during any one financial year. [Tea Act (29 of 1953), S. 3(g)]

Export and import. "EXPORT" AND "IMPORT", means respectively taking out of, and bringing into India by sea, land or air. [Rubber Act (24 of 1947), S. 3(d)]

"EXPORT" AND "IMPORT" means, respectively, export from or import into India or any other country of goods or services, or both. [Export-Import Bank of India Act (28 of 1981), S. 2(d)]

Export and Import Policy. Means Export and Import Policy, 1 April 2002-31 March 2007, published by the Government of India in the

Ministry of Commerce and Industry vide notification No. 1(Re-2003)/2002-07, dated 31st March, 2003, as amended from time to time. [Customs Tariff Act (51 of 1975), Gen. Exemption No. 42, 13(13) *Expln* (iii)]

Export from India. To take out of India by land, sea or air across any of the Customs frontiers defined by the Central Government. [Dangerous Drugs Act (2 of 1930) (*now repealed*), S. 2(k)]

Export goods. 'EXPORT GOODS' means any goods which are to be taken out of India to a place outside India. [Customs Act (52 of 1962), S. 2(19)]

Export of services. Means the supply of any service when,—

(i) the supplier of service is located in India;

(ii) the recipient of service is located outside India;

(iii) the place of supply of service is outside India;

(iv) the payment for such service has been received by the supplier of service in convertible foreign exchange; and

(v) the supplier of service and the recipient of service are not merely establishments of a distinct person in accordance with *Explanation* 1 in Section 8. [Integrated Goods and Services Tax Act (13 of 2017), S. 2(6)].

"Export House Certificate" or "Trading House Certificate". Means a valid Export House Certificate or Trading House Certificate, as the case may be, issued by the Chief Controller of Imports and Exports, Government of India. [Income-tax Act (43 of 1961), S. 80 HHC (4C) *Expln.* (c)]

Export in relation to the Special Economic Zones. "EXPORT IN RELATION TO THE SPECIAL ECONOMIC ZONES" means taking goods or providing services out of India from a Special Economic Zone by land, sea, air, or by any other mode, whether physical or otherwise. [Income-tax Act (43 of 1961), S. 10AA, *Expln. (ii) as inserted by Special Economic Zones Act (28 of 2005), Second Schedule (c)*]

Export of goods. "export of goods" with its grammatical variations and cognate expressions, means taking goods out of India to a place outside India [The Integrated Goods and Services Tax Act, 2017 (13 of 2017), S. 2(5)]

Export out of. While all exports involve a taking out of the country, all goods taken out of the country cannot be said to be exported. The test is that the goods must have a foreign destination where they can be said to be imported. *Burmah S. O. C. & D Co.* v. *Commercial Tax Officers*, AIR 1961 SC 315, 324. [Constitution of India, Art. 286(1)(b)]

Export out of India. Shall not include any transaction by way of sale or otherwise, in a shop, emporium or any other establishment situate in India, not involving clearance at any customs station as defined in the Customs Act, 1962. [Income-Tax Act (43 of 1961), S. 80 HHC (4), *Expl.* (aa)] and [Taxation Laws (Amendment) Ordinance (2 of 2003), S. 3, *Expln.* 7(d)]

Export price. In relation to an article, means the price of the article exported from the exporting country or territory and in cases where there is no export price or where the export price is unreliable because of association or a compensatory arrangement between the exporter and the importer or a third party, the export price may be constructed on the basis of the price at which the imported articles are first resold to an independent buyer or if the article is not resold to an independent buyer, or not resold in the condition as imported, on such reasonable basis as may be determined in accordance with the rules made under sub-section (6). [Custom Tariff Act (51 of 1975), S. 9 *Expl.* (b)]

Export sale. An 'export sale' is one in which the assessee figures as an exporter, privity having been established between him and foreign buyer, either through direct negotiation or dealing, or through the local representatives of the latter, as sale will occasion an export or there will be an export sale only where the sale is to a foreign buyer with whom the local seller has privity and when as a direct result of such sale the goods are transported across the frontier. *Gandhi Sons Ltd.* v. *State of Madras,* AIR 1955 Mad 722. [Constitution of India, Art. 286(1)(B)].

Export turnover. Means the consideration in respect of export of articles or things or computer software received in, or brought into, India by the assessee in convertible foreign exchange in accordance with subsection (3), but does not include freight, telecommunication charges or insurance attributable to the delivery of the articles or things or computer software outside India or expenses, if any, incurred in foreign exchange in providing the technical services outside India. [Income-tax Act (43 of 1961), S. 10A, *Expl.* 2(iv)]

"EXPORT TURNOVER"; means the consideration in respect of export by the undertaking, being the Unit of articles or things or services received in, or brought into, India by the assessee but does not include freight, telecommunication charges or insurance attributable to the delivery of the articles or things outside India or expenses, if any, incurred in foreign exchange in rendering of services (including computer software) outside India. [Income-tax Act (43 of 1961), S. 10AA, *Expln. 1(i), as inserted by Special Economic Zones Act (28 of 2005), Second Schedule (c)*]

"EXPORT TURNOVER" means the consideration in respect of computer software received in, or brought into, India by the assessee in converitable foreign exchange in accordance with sub-section (2), but does not include freight, telecommunication charges or insurance attributable to the delivery of the computer software outside India or expenses, if any, incurred in foreign exchange in providing the technical service outside India. [Income-Tax Act (43 of 1961), S. 80HHE, *Expln.* (c)]

"EXPORT TURNOVER" means the consideration in respect of the software or software rights specified in clauses (d), (e), (g), (h) and (i), received in, or brought into, India by the assessee in convertible foreign exchange in accordance with sub-section. (2), but does not include fright, telecommunication charge or insurance attributable to the delivery of such software outside India or expenses, if any, incurred in foreign exchange in providing the technical service outside India. [Income Tax Act (43 of 1961), S. 80HHF, *Expln.* (c)]

"EXPORT TURNOVER" means the consideration in respect of export by the undertaking of eligible articles or things received in, or brought into, India by the assessee in convertible foreign exchange in accordance with sub-section (3), but does not include freight, telecommunication charges or insurance attributable to the delivery of the articles or things outside India. [Taxation Laws (Amendment) Ordinance (2 of 2003), S. 3, *Expln.* 7(c)]

Export value. In relation to export by way of lease or hire-purchase or under any other similar arrangement, includes the charges, by whatever name called, payable in respect of such lease or hire-purchase or any other similar arrangement. [Foreign Exchange Management (Export of Goods and Services) Regulation, 2000, Reg. 2(v)]

Exportation. The shipping or carrying out the native commodities of a state or country for other countries. (*Tomlin*)

Exporter. In relation to any goods at any time between their entry for export and the time when they are exported, includes any owner or any person holding himself out to be the exporter. [Customs Act (52 of 1962), S. 2(20)]

"EXPORTER" means any person under the jurisdiction of the exporting country and includes the exporting country, who exports hazardous chemical. [Manufacture, Storage and Import of Hazardous Chemicals Rules, 1989, R. 2(d)].

"EXPORTER" means any person under the jurisdiction of the exporting country who exports hazardous wastes and the exporting country itself, who exports hazardous wastes. [Hazardous Wastes (Management and Handling) R, 1989, R. 3 (g)]

Expose. To remove from shelter; to leave unprotected, especially form weather; to place in a situation to be affected or acted on. (*Webster*)

To exhibit openly [IPC (45 of 1860), S. 275]; to leave without shelter or defence [IPC (45 of 1860), S. 307, ill. (b)]; to lay open to (danger *etc.*) [Emigration Act (31 of 1983), S. 11(1)]; to disclose a shameful showing up.

Expositio, quae ex visceribus causae nascitur, est aptissima et fortissima in lege. (*Maxim*) An exposition, which springs from the vitals of a cause, is the fittest and most powerful in law.

Exposure. The state of being exposed; openness to danger; accessibility to anything that may affect, especially detrimentally.

As to EXPOSURE AND ABANDONMENT OF CHILD by parent or person having care of it. (*See* IPC (45 of 1860), S. 317].

Expound. To lay open the meaning of; to make clear; to interpret; to remove an obscurity (as) expounding a law.

Express. Given in direct terms; definite; explicit; manifest; opposite of dubious; not implied or left to inference; made unambiguous; stated or declared; that which is made known and not left to implication. (*Bouvier*)

Expressed and not merely implied; explicit; to give expression to.

Express authority. "An authority is said to be express when it is given by words spoken or written." [Indian Contract Act (9 of 1872), S. 187].

Express bus. Means a *omnibus* plying under a contract-carriage permit or under a stage carrier permit or special stage carrier permit with a limited or selected number of stages commonly known as Express Bux or Limited Service bus. [West Bengal Additional Tax and One Time Tax on Motor Vehicles Act, 1989, S. 2(d)]

Express condition. The expression 'express condition' occurring in S. 111(g) means that the condition must be clear, manifest, explicit and unambiguous. *Raghuram Rao* v. *Eric P. Mathias*, (2002) 2 SCC 624, para 22 : AIR 2002 SC 797 [T.P. Act (4 of 1882), S. 111(g)].

Express consent. Express consent means positive consent, not an acquiscence in the form of an implied consent.

Express contract. An 'express contract' means the reciprocal promises contained in the words of the contract or resulting from a true construction of them and excludes stipulations which may arise out of any usage or custom or which may be inferred from the conduct or course of dealings between the parties. *Alapaty Ramamoorthy* v. *Polisetti Satyanaryanan,* AIR 1958 AP 550, 554. [Sale of Goods Act (3 of 1930), S. 35].

Express delivery. Means delivery by a special messenger or conveyance. [Indian Post Office Act (6 of 1898), S. 8 *Expln.*].

Express leave. A permission granted manifestly. [CPC (5 of 1908), S. 147].

Express promise. "In so far as the proposal or acceptance of any promise is made in words, the promise is said to be express." [Indian Contract Act (9 of 1872), S. 9]

EXPRESS PROMISE, is the express stipulation of the party making it to do or not to do a particular thing; the term is distinguished from "implied" promise.

Express provision. To be an 'express provision' with regard to something it is not necessary that the thing should be specially mentioned; it is sufficient that it is directly covered by the language, however broad the language may be which covers it, so long as the applicability arises directly from the language used and not by inference therefrom. *Needle Industries* (*India*) *Ltd.* v. *Needle Industries Newey* (*India*) *Holding Ltd.*, AIR 1981 SC 1298.

Express revocation. (*Of a will*). An act performed when the change of mind or intention of the testator to revoke is declared by a subsequent will or codicil.

Express trust. A trust created by express words, as distinguished from an implied trust. [CPC (5 of 1908), S. 92(1)].

Express warranty. A warranty created by the overt words or actions of the seller. [See also Marine Insurance Act (11 of 1963), S. 35]

"Express warranty" means any material statement, affirmation of fact, promise or description relating to a product or service warranting that it conforms to such material statement, affirmation, promise or description and includes any sample or model of a product warranting that the whole of such product conforms to such sample or model. [Consumer Protection Act, 2019 (35 of 2019), section 2(20)]

Expressa nocent, non expressa non nocent. (*Maxim*) Things expressed are (may be) prejudicial; things not expressed are not."

Things expressed harm, things not expressed do not. (*Latin for Lawyers*)

Expressed. One of the meanings of 'expressed' is to make known the opinions or the feelings of a particular person and when a secretary to Government apprehends a man and tells him in the order that this is being done under the orders of the Governor, he is in substance saying that he is acting in the name of the Governor. *State of Bombay* v. *Purushottam Jog Naik*, AIR 1952 SC 317, 318. [Constitution of India, Art. 166(1)]

The word 'expressed' in S. 15-B(2) does not mean that it should be expressed in writing and it can be oral. *Thangaswami* v. *I.T. Commissioner,* AIR 1966 Mad 103, 111.

EXPRESSED means stated or declared in direct terms; set forth in words; not left to inference or implication.

Expressio unius alterius exclusio. (*Maxim*) The express mention of one person or thing is the exclusion of another. (*Latin for Lawyers*)

(*Maxim*) Express mention of one thing implies the exclusion of another.

This is a maxim for ascertaining the intention of the legislature. Where the statutory language is plain and the meaning clear, there is no scope for applying the rule. *Parbhani Transport Co-operative Society Ltd.* v. *Regional Transport Authority*, AIR 1960 SC 801, 804.

The maxim '*expressio unius (est) expressio alterius*' or its synonym '*expressure facit cassare tacitum*' should be allowed to get the upperhand in the matter of interpretation of the particular statute before the Court and, if the Court finds some reasonable explanation for the provision which may fit in with the *ex abundanti cautela* theory and exclude application of the maxim expressio *unius (est) expressio alterius*, the Court may refuse to apply the said maxim and proceed to hold that the particular insertion was by way of greater caution.

Expressio unius est exclusion alterius. 'Expressio unius est exclusion alterius' means, if a statute provides for a thing to be done in a particular way, then it has to be done in that manner and in no other manner and following any other course is not permissible. [*J. Jayalalithaa* v. *State of Karnataka*, (2014) 2 SCC 401, para 34].

Expression. A word, phrase or form of speech; the act of manifesting by action or language. [Preamble, Constitution of India]

Expressly. Explictly.

In an express, clear or distinct, direct or pointed manner; plainly; with a distinct purpose; in direct term (*i.e.*) not by implication. In its primary meaning the term denotes precision of statement, as opposed to ambiguity, implication, or inference, and is equivalent to "in an express manner, or in direct terms." It is also commonly used to designate purpose, and as equivalent to especially, or particularly, or for a distinct purpose or object.

The term 'expressly' in the context does not mean that there should be anything in writing as evidence of entrustment. The word 'expressly' is often times used in antithesis to the word 'impliedly'. The word 'expressly' has been used only to mean 'clearly'. *State of Madras* v. *K. Ramaswamy,* AIR 1958 Mad 585, 586. [Payment of Wages Act (4 of 1936), S. 7(2)(c)].

EXPRESSLY BARRED. In S. 9, CPC (5 of 1908), means barred by any enactment for the time being in force.

Expressly excluded. The expression "expressly excluded" signifies exclusion by words and does not mean exclusion by a process of construction or reasoning. *Harbir Singh* v. *Alihasan*, AIR 1966 All 161, 162.

The word 'expressly' occurring in Section 193 of CrPC 1973 (2 of 1974) denotes those exceptions which are indicative of the legislative mandate that a Court of Session can depart from the interdict contained in the Section only if it is provided differently in clear and unambiguous terms. *Vidyadharan* v. *State of Kerala,* (2004) 1 SCC 215, 222, para 18.

Expressum facit cessare tacitum. (*Maxim*) Expression precludes implication.

"A thing expressed puts an end to tacit implication." (*Trayner*).

The legislature should be deemed to have borne in mind the principle that "expressum *Facit cessare tacitum*" (What is expressed makes what is silent to cease). *Bhai Mohan Singh* v. *Hind Iran Bank Limited,* AIR 1959 Punj 225, 228. [Displaced Persons (Debts Adjustment) Act (70 of 1951), Ss. 19 and 20].

Exprocedentibus et consequent ibus optima fit interpretatio. The best interpretation is made from things preceding and following, *i.e.*, the context.

Expropriation. A taking, as of privately owned property, by government under eminent domain.

A voluntary surrender of rights of claims; the act of divesting oneself of that which was previously claimed as one's own, or renouncing it. In this sense it is the opposite of "appropriation".

The action of the State in taking or modifying the property rights of an individual *etc.* in the exercise of its sovereignty. [Asian Development Bank Act (18 of 1966), Sch., Art. 51].

Expulsion. Bring out; taking away the privileges enjoyed in an institution or society.

An action of expelling [Indian Partnership Act (9 of 1932), S. 72(a)]; the fact or state of being expelled. [Employees' State Insurance Act (34 of 1948), S. 2(14B)].

Expunction. The act of expunging : the state of being expunged.

Expunge. To strike out from a record.

Expunging remarks. The power to expunge remarks is extraordinary and is exercisable when a clear case is made out—question to be considered is whether judge in making the remarks acted with impropriety. S. v. *Ranga,* AIR 1967 SC 903.

Adverse remarks against a subordinate judicial officer unless necessary to decide an issue involved in the case, shall be expunged. *In the matter of 'K' a Judicial Officer*, AIR 2001 SC 972 (975).

Extend. To prolong; to continue or continue in any direction; stretch out; to stretch out of reach; to expand; to enlarge or lengthen the bounds or dimensions of; lengthen. And it is sometimes used as equivalent to the word "exceed" (as) to extend the bounds of jurisdiction.

To have a certain area, range or scope; to enlarge in area, range or scope.

Whether the term is understood in the etymological sense to stretch or draw out or in the ordinary sense to enlarge, to expand or to amplify the term lends itself to a variety of meanings. *National Industrial Corporation Ltd.* v. *Registrar of Companies,* AIR 1963 Punj 239, 241. [Companies Act (1 of 1956), S. 18(4)].

'Extend', according to the New International Dictionary, means "increase the size of, enlarge, to increase the scope, meaning or application of. What is non-existent cannot be extended. *Lekh Raj* v. *4th Addl. District Judge, Meerut,* AIR 1982 All 265, 271. [Cantonments (Extension of Rent Control Laws) Act (46 of 1957), S 3].

Extend to and include. The words "shall extend to and include" often used in an interpretation clause are wider and go further than the words "shall mean"; and denote that, in addition to the popular meaning given to a word or phrase, such word or phrase shall also have the meanings given to it by the Interpretation Clause.

Extended area. "EXTENDED AREA" means any area or route to which the operation of any road transport service of a Corporation has been extended in the manner provided in Section 20. [Road Transport Corporation Act (64 of 1950), S. 2(c)]

Extensible Business Reporting Language. For the purposes of Rule 12(2) of the Companies (Accounts) Rules, 2014, the term 'Extensible Business Reporting Language' means a standardised language for communication in electronic form to express, report or file financial information by companies under Rule 12 of the Companies (Accounts) Rules, 2014. [*Explanation* to Rule 12(2) of the Companies (Accounts) Rules, 2014]

Extension. The act of extending or stretching out; enlargement in any direction, in length, breadth, or circumference; the continuance of an existing thing; (as) extension of the term of Parliament.

The word 'extention' when used in its proper and usual sense in connection with a lease means a prolongation of the lease. *Provash Chandra Dalvi* v. *Biswanath Banerjee*, AIR 1989 SC 1834, 1839. [Calcutta Thika Tenancy Act (2 of 1949), S. 2(5)].

IN COMMERCIAL LAW : Extension is an indulgence by giving time to pay a debt, or perform an obligation; an agreement made between a debtor and his creditors, by which the latter in order to enable the former embarrassed in his circumstances, to retrieve his standing, agree to wait for a definite length of time after their several claims should become due and payable, before they will demand payment. (*Bouvier*)

Extension education. Means the educational activities concerned with the training of orchardists, farmers and other groups serving agriculture, horticulture, fisheries and improved practices related thereto and the various phases of scientific technology related to agriculture and agricultural production including post harvest technology and marketing. [Central Agricultural University Act (40 of 1992), S. 2(j)]

"EXTENSION EDUCATION" means the educational activities concerned with the training of orchardists, farmers and other groups serving agriculture, horticulture, fisheries and improved practices related thereto and the various phases of scientific technology related to agriculture and agricultural production including post harvest technology and marketing. [S. 3(k) of the Rani Lakshmi Bai Central Agricultural University Act, 2014 (10 of 2014)]

Extent. Space, degree or time to which anything is extended [Constitution of India, Art. 131]; dimensions.

Extent of interest. (in the Land Registration Act) Means the share or interest in an estate or revenue free property of which the person with respect to whom the words are used is in possession as proprietor or manager [Bengal Act 7 of 1876 (Land Registration), S. 3, cl. (3)].

Extant variety. M

eans a variety available in India which is—

(i) notified under Section 5 of the Seeds Act, 1966; or

(ii) Farmers variety or

(iii) a variety about which there is common knowledge or

(iv) any other variety which is public domain. [Protection of Plant Varieties and Farmers Right Act (53 of 2001), S. 2(j)]

Extenuate. To lessen the gravity of a thing by partial excuse.

Extenuating. That tends to diminish culpability. [CrPC 1973 (2 of 1974), S. 360(3)].

Extenuating circumstances. Such as render a delict or crime less aggravated, heinous, or reprehensible than it would otherwise be, or tend to palliate or lessen its guilt. Such circumstances may ordinarily be shown in order to reduce the punishment or damages. In contract law, unusual or extraordinary events that prevent performance within specified time (*e.g.*, Strike by workers or suppliers). (*Black*)

External aids. The dictionary meaning of word, as an external aid, cannot be looked at where that word has been statutorily defined or judicially interpreted. But in otherwise situation the Court may take the aid of dictionaries to ascertain the meaning of a word in common parlance, bearing in mind that a word is used in different senses according to its context and a dictionary gives all the meanings of a word, and the Court has, therefore, to select the particular meaning which is relevant to the context in which it has to interpret that word. *State of Orissa* v. *Titaghur Paper Mills Company Limited,* AIR 1985 SC 1293.

External assignment. Means the temporary posting to another organization, including secondment, tour of duty and staff exchange programme, wherein the accrual and disbursement of remuneration including pay, allowances and perquisites would be borne by the Board. [Securities and Exchange Board of India (Employees' Service) Regulations, 2001, Regn. 3(1)(ga)].

External Commercial Borrowings (ECB). Means borrowing by an eligible resident entity from outside India in accordance with framework decided by the Reserve Bank in consultation with the Government of India. [Foreign Exchange Management (Borrowing and Landing) Regulations, 2018, Regn. 2(iv)].

External Commercial Lending (ECL). Means lending by a person resident in India to a borrower outside India in accordance with framework decided by the Reserve Bank in consultation with the Government of India. [Foreign Exchange Management (Borrow and Lending) Regulations, 2018, Reng. 2(v)].

External debt. Refers to outstanding contractual liabilities of residents of a country to non-residents in gross terms, involving payment of interest with or without principal or payment of principal with or without interest. [*M L Tannan, Banking Law & Practice in India*, 2021, LexisNexis, Dictionary of Banking Terminology].

External development works. Mean roads, foot-paths, water-supply, sewers, drains, tree planting, street lighting, provision for community building and for treatment and disposal of sewage and sullage water, or any other work in a colony necessary for its proper development. [Punjab Development and Property Regulation Act, 1995 (Punjab Act No. 14 of 1995), S. 2(p)]

'External development works' include water supply, sewerage, drains, necessary provisions of treatment and disposal of sewage, sullage and storm water, roads, electrical works, solid waste management and disposal, slaughter houses, colleges, hospitals, stadium/sports complex, fire stations, grid sub-stations, etc. and any other work which the Director may specify to be executed in the periphery of or outside the colony/area for the benefit of the colony/area. [Haryana Development and Regulation of Urban Areas Act (8 of 1975), S. 2(g) as cited in *DLF Limited* v. *Manmohan Lowe*, (2014) 12 SCC 231, para 24].

'EXTERNAL DEVELOPMENT WORKS' include sewerage, drains, roads and electrical works which may have to be executed in the periphery of, or outside, a colony for the joint benefit of two or more colonies. [Haryana Development and Regulation of Urban Areas Act (8 of 1975), S. 2(g)]

Extinct. To destroy; or put out.

Extinction. The complete wiping out; annihilation. [Indian Trusts Act (2 of 1882), S. 77].

Extinguish. The words "extinguish," "extinguished", "extinguishment" when used in their exact sense express the idea of a complete wiping out, destruction, or annihilation, and not a mere suspension. It is in this sense that the terms are properly applied to contracts, rights, titles, interests, or a debt; or other obligation whether the effect produced is by the act of God, or by operation of law; or by the act of party.

To put a total end to [T.P.Act (4 of 1882), S. 60]; to put out. [Indian Electricity Act (9 of 1910), S. 45] [Now repealed & replaced by Act 36 of 2003].

Extinguishment. The extinction or annihilation, of a right, estate, etc, by means of its being merged in, or consolidated with another, generally a greater or more extensive, right or estate. This *Extinguishment* is of various natures, as applied to various rights;

viz. estates, debts, liberties, services and ways. (*Tomlin*)

The action of extinguishing. [Constitution of India, Art. 31 A (1) (a)].

Extinguishment and modification. While extinguishment indicates a total annihilation of the right whether it be in respect of the entire estate or a part of it, modification covers a case where a right in the estate is abridged or impaired short of extinguishment to the prejudice of the person in whom the right resides. *Saut Singh* v. *State of J&K*, AIR 1959 J&K 35, 42 (FB). [Constitution of India, Art. 31-A]

Extort. To obtain possessions or knowledge by force or compulsion *etc.*; to wrest from another by force, menace, duress; to obtain money or other valuable thing either by compulsion, by actual force, or by the force of motives applied to the will, and often more overpowering and irresistible than physical force. This term which necessarily implies the adoption of illegal means.

To practise extortion. [Indian Evidence Act (1 of 1872), S. 8, *Expln.* 2, ill. (a)].

Extortion. 'Whoever intentionally puts any person in fear of any injury to that person, or to any other, and thereby dishonestly induces the person so put in fear to deliver to any person any property or valuable security, or anything signed or sealed, which may be converted into a valuable security, commits 'EXTORTION.' [IPC (45 of 1860), S. 383] [(w.e.f. 1-7-2024) repealed and replaced by Bharatiya Nyaya Sanhita, 2023 (45 of 2023), section 308].

The action or practice of extorting or wresting anything, especially money, from a person by force or by undue exercise of authority or power; an act of illegal exaction; getting money *etc.* by violence, threats, misuse of authority *etc.* [CrPC 1973 (2 of 1974), S. 211, ill. (c)].

(*Extorsio*) In its widest sense means any oppression under pretence or colour of right. In a popular sense it is used as equivalent to black mailing or obtaining money by threats. But its ordinary and proper legal meaning is the taking of money or any valuable thing by any public officer by colour of his office, and otherwise than in good faith or a mistake as to the law, where none or less is due; or before it is due.

Extortion is robbery if the offender, at the time of committing the extortion, is in the presence of the person put in fear, and commits the extortion by putting that person in fear of instant death, of instant hurt, or of instant wrongful restraint to that person or to some other person, and, by so putting in fear, induces the person so put in fear then and there to deliver up the thing extorted. The offender is said to be present if he is sufficiently near to put the other person in fear of instant death, of instant hurt, or of instant wrongful restraint. [(w.e.f. 1-7-2024) Bharatiya Nyaya Sanhita, 2023 (45 of 2023), section 309(3)]

Extra. A Latin preposition, occurring in many legal phrases meaning, without, or outside of, beyond, except.

Extra cursum curial. This expression means authorising that particular judge (before whom a suit or proceeding is pending) to give whatever decision he thought fit without following the strict and rigid rule of practice and procedure of the Court.

Extra-judicial. (Out-of-Court) Something which is done without judicial proceedings. Thus we speak of *extra-judicial* evidence, or that a distress is an extra-judicial remedy. Something which is said by a Judge or judicial officer in a judicial proceeding, but beyond its scope.

Extra-judicial statement. Any utterance, written or oral, made outside of Court. It is governed by the hearsay rule and its exceptions when offered in Court as evidence.

Extra-legal. Outside of the law.

Extra legem positus est civiliter mortuus. (*Maxim*) One who is put out of the law (*i.e.*, outlawed) is civilly dead.

Extra-ordinary. Beyond or out of the common order or rule; not usual, regular or of a customary kind; not ordinary. The word does not mean what has never been previously heard of, or within former experience, but only what is beyond the ordinary, usual or common experience.

Outside the usual or ordinary. [T.P. Act (4 of 1882), S. 57(e)].

Extra-ordinary circumstances. Factors of time, place, *etc.*, which are not usually associated with a particular thing or event; out of the ordinary factors.

Extra-ordinary original civil jurisdiction. The authority or power (of a High Court) to entertain and decide any original civil (not criminal, appellate or revisional) proceeding about matters such as matrimonial, admiralty *etc.* which are different from ordinary civil matters. [CPC (5 of 1908), O. XLIX, R. 3].

Extra-ordinary remedies. The writs of *mandamus, quo warranto, habeas corpus*, and some others are often classified or termed "extra-ordinary remedies," in contradistinction to the ordinary remedy by action.

Extra-ordinary risk. A risk lying outside of the sphere of the normal, arising out of conditions not usual in the business. It is one which is not normally and necessarily incident to the employment, and is one which may be obviated by the exercise of reasonable care by the employer.

Extra premium. Means a charge for any risk not provided for in the minimum contract premium. [Insurance Regulatory and Development Authority (Actuarial Report and Abstract) Regulation, 2000, Reg. 2(c); Insurance Act (4 of 1938), Sch. IV, Part I (5)].

Extra territorial jurisdiction. Beyond the geographical limits of a particular jurisdiction.

Extra-territorial offence. An offence committed beyond the territory of the State. [IPC (45 of 1860), S. 4].

Extra-territorial operation. The words "extra-territorial operation" are used in two different senses as connoting firstly, law in respect of acts or events, which take place inside the state but have operation outside, and secondly, laws with reference to the nationals of a state in respect of their acts outside. *Bengal Immunity Co. Ltd.* v. *State of Bihar*, AIR 1955 SC 661, 750. [Constitution of India, Art. 245]

Extra territorium jus dicenti impune non paretur. (*Maxim*) The sentence of one adjudicating beyond his jurisdiction cannot be obeyed with impunity.

Extra vires. Beyond powers.

Extract. Excerpt; quotation; a portion or fragment of any writing [Indian Evidence Act (1 of 1872), S. 78(3)]; to draw anything from a substance by heat; distillation; solvents. [Oil Industry (Development) Act (47 of 1974), S. 2(e)].

Extracting. "Extracting", means drawing out or obtaining. A tooth is 'extracted' as much as is fruit juice and as much as a mineral. *Bhagwan Dass* v. *State of U.P.,* AIR 1976 SC 1393.

Extradition. International extradition is the surrender by one nation to another, for trial and punishment, of a person accused or convicted of an offence within the jurisdiction of the latter. "Extradition is the surrender by one State to another of a person desired to be dealt with for crimes of which he has been accused or convicted and which are justiciable in the Courts of the other State". *State of West Bengal* v. *Jugal Kishore More*, AIR 1969 SC 1171 at 1175.

The term 'EXTRADITION' denotes the process whereby under a concluded treaty one State surrenders to any other State at its request, a person accused or convicted of a criminal offence committed against the laws of the requesting State, such requesting State being competent to try the alleged offender. *Rosiline George* v. *Union of India,* (1994) 2 SCC 80, 91, 92.

Extradition throughout the history of the practice, has remained a system consisting of several processes whereby one sovereign surrenders to another sovereign a person sought after as an accused criminal or a fugitive offender. This delivery of individuals to a requesting sovereign is usually based on treaties or bilateral agreements but sometimes & it also occurs by reciprocity and comity as a matter of courtesy and goodwill between sovereigns as in this case. Therefore, "world public order" is the recurring theme based on which the extradition is practiced by the states. [*Abu Salem Abdul Qayyum Ansari* v. *Central Bureau of Investigation*, (2013) 12 SCC 1, para 32].

The action of giving up a fugitive criminal to the authorities of the State in which the crime was committed. [IPC (45 of 1860), S. 216 and Constitution of India, VII Sch., list I, item 18].

Extradition offence. "EXTRADITION OFFENCE" means—

(i) in relation to a foreign State, being a treaty State, an offence provided for in the extradition treaty with that State;

(ii) in relation to a foreign State, other than a treaty State, an offence punishable with imprisonment for a term which shall not be less than one year under the laws of India or of a foreign State and includes a composite offence. [Extradiction Act (34 of 1962), S. 2(c)]

Extradition treaty. A treaty between two or more nations which provides for the extradition from each of the countries to any of the others of persons charged with specified offences. [Extradition Act (34 of 1962), S. 2(c)(i)].

"EXTRADITION TREATY" means a treaty or agreement made by India with a foreign State relating to the extradition of fugitive criminals; and includes any treaty agreement or arrangement relating to the extradition of fugitive criminals made before the 15th day of August, 1947 which extends to, and is binding on, India [Extradiction Act (34 of 1962), S. 2(d)]

Extramural powers. Powers exercised by a municipality outside its corporate limits.

Extraneous matter. Means any matter contained in an article of food which may be carried from the raw materials, packaging materials or process systems used for its manufacture or which is added to it, but such matter does not render such article of food unsafe. [S. 3(1)(i) of the Food Safety & Standards Act, 2006 (34 of 2006)]

Extravagant. Passing the bounds of reason; wild; absurd; exorbitant.

Wildly excessive. [Land Acquisition Act (1 of 1894), S. 27(2)].

Extreme. The best of worst; a thing of the superlative degree; most urgent; greatest; highest; immoderate; excessive; most violent.

Extremely difficult. Difficult to the utmost degree. [Specific Relief Act (47 of 1963), S. 8(c)].

Extremis probatis praesumuntur media. (*Maxim*) Extremes being proved, those things which fall within or between them are presumed.

Extrinsic evidence. Evidence not legitimate before the tribunal in which the determination of a case is tried; such facts or circumstances outside, or not referred into, a written document, which serve to explain or vary its meaning and sometimes to contradict it.

Extrinsic evidence is evidence from a source outside a document by means of which it is sought to interpret the document. Instances of it are previous quarrels, ill-feeling, repetition of the libels, unnecessary publicity. The untruth of the statement is by itself no evidence of malice.

Extrinsic words. Words not forming part of the document in question. [Legal Tender (Inscribed Notes) Act (28 of 1964), S. 2].

Extrusion. The forcing of solid metal through a suitably shaped orifice under compressive forces. Extrusion is somewhat analogous to squeezing tooth paste through a tube, although some cold extrusion processes more nearly resemble forging, which also deforms metals by application of compressive forces. Most metals can be extruded, although the process may not be economically feasible for high strength alloys. [The Textbook McGraw-Hill Encyclopedia of Science and Technology as cited in *Commissioner of Customs, New Delhi* v. *Caryaire Equipment India Private Limited*, (2012) 4 SCC 645, para 15].

Eye-witness. One who saw the act, fact, or transaction to which he testifies.

Eyre. "A judicial visitation of the counties by justices appointed for the purpose of bearing all pleas." [*See* Pollock and Maitland, History of English Law].

F

Fabric. Things put together; structure; building; woven material. A term which includes elastic cords and braids manufactured of silk and India rubber.

"Fabric is a cloth of a particular kind".

Fabric: Tyre Cord fabric. By and large a tyre cord fabric is regarded as textile fabric. *Delhi Cloth and General Mills Co. Ltd.* v. *State of Rajasthan*, AIR 1980 SC 1552.

Fabricare. To make. Used in old English law of a lawful coining, and also of an unlawful making or counterfeiting of coin. Used in an indictment for forging a bill of lading. (*Black*)

Fabricate. To make a false evidence in order to deceive the Court. *In criminal law*, a word which has been said to import a criminal intention—a *mens rea,* a wrongful act, an act done with a *mens rea*, fraud or falsehood, a false or fraudulent concoction, knowing it to be wrong and contrary to law (as) fabricating false evidence.

To forge. [IPC (45 of 1860), S. 193]

Fabricated evidence. Evidence manufactured or arranged after the fact, and either wholly false or else warped and discoloured by artifice and contrivance with a deceitful intent.

Fabricating false evidence. Whoever causes any circumstance to exist, or makes any false entry in any book or record, or makes any document containing a false statement, intending that such circumstance, false entry or false statement may appear in evidence in a judicial proceeding, or in a proceeding taken by law before a public servant as such, or before an arbitrator, and that such circumstance, false entry or false statement, so appearing in evidence, may cause any person who in such proceeding is to form an opinion upon the evidence, to entertain an erroneous opinion touching any point material to the result of such proceeding, is said "to fabricate false evidence." [IPC (45 of 1860), S. 192] [(w.e.f. 1-7-2024) repealed and replaced by Bharatiya Nyaya Sanhita, 2023 (45 of 2023), section 228]

Fabrication. To manufacture.

To construct or manufacture an industrial product. [Oxford Dictionary as citied in *Voltas Limited* v. *State of Gujarat*, (2015) 7 SCC 527, para 20].

Face. *In commercial law*, the word is used in its apparent or obvious meaning; (as) face value. As applied to an instrument that which is shown by the mere language or evidence (*Black*) as, 'on the face of the document'. The principal sum which it expresses to be due or payable, without any additions in the way of interest or costs. (*Black*)

Face of an instrument is that which it shows without extrinsic evidence.

Face of record. The entire record of a case in court up to the point at which reference is made to it. *State* v. *Haines*, 51 La Ann 731, 25 So 372. (*Ballentine's Law Dictionary, 3rd Edn.)*

Face value. As applied to commercial paper, the value expressed on the face of the writing.

ON THE FACE OF IT. Judging by appearances; as, a document false and fabricated on the *face* of it.

The value indicated on the face of the instrument; nominal value written or printed on the face of bonds, notes, debentures or other documents indicating their par value. [Industrial Finance Corporation Act (15 of 1948) (*Repealed by Act 23 of 1993*), S. 4A(1)(a)]

Facies. The face or countenance; the exterior appearance or view; hence, contemplation of study of a thing on its external or apparent side. Thus, *prima facie* means at the first inspection, on a preliminary or exterior scrutiny. When we speak of a "*prima facie* case", we mean one which, on its own showing, on a first examination, or without investigating any alleged defences, is apparently good and maintainable. (*Black*)

Facilis est lapsus juventutis. Youth is very liable to err. (*Morgan Leg. Max.*) It is on this and similar other maxims that the laws for the protection of infants, and expectant heirs of young age from the artifice of moneylenders are founded.

Facilitate. To render easier. [IPC (45 of 1860), S. 107, *Expln*. 2].

Facility. "FACILITY" in the context of Article VI means any of the industrial sites as defined below ("plant site", "plant" and "unit"). [Chemical Weapons Convention Act (34 of 2000), (Verification Annex), 6]

"FACILITY" means any location wherein the processes, incidental to the waste generation, collection, reception, treatment, storage and disposal are carried out. [Hazardous Wastes Management and Handling) Rules, 1989, R. 3(12), as amended in May' 2003].

"FACILITY" means any of the four facilities offered by the European Economic Community under its International Institutional Partners Scheme, as given in the annexure to this Scheme. [European Economic Community International Institutional Partners (ECIIP) Scheme, 1993, Para. 2(c)].

The quality of being easily performed; absence of difficulty; dexterity; ease in performance; that which promotes the ease of any action.

"FACILITY" means any establishment wherein the solid waste management processes namely segregation, recovery, storage, collection, recycling, processing, treatment of safe disposal are carried out. [Solid Waste Management Rules, 2016, R. 3(1)(22)].

Facility agreement. Means an agreement or arrangement between a State Party and the Organisation relating to a specific facility subject to on-site verification pursuant to Articles IV, V and

VI. [Chemical Weapons Convention Act (34 of 2000), (Verification Annex), 7]

Facinus quos inquinat a equat. Guilt makes equal those whom it stains.

Facsimile. Exact copy of a writing or picture, *etc.*; FAX.

An exact copy; counterpart or representation [IPC (45 of 1860), S. 263A(3)]; [Life Insurance Corporation Act (31 of 1956), S. 32]

"FACSIMILE (FAX)" means a form of telecommunication by which fixed graphic images, such as printed texts and pictures are scanned and the information converted into electrical signals for transmission over the telecommunication system. [Finance Act (32 of 1994), S. 65(1)(36)]

Fact. "FACT" means and includes—(1) anything, state of things, or relation of things capable of being perceived by the senses; (2) any mental condition of which any person is conscious. [Indian Evidence Act (1 of 1872), S. 3][Now (w.e.f. 1-7-2024) repealed & replaced by Bharatiya Sakshya Adhiniyam, 2023 (47 of 2023)]

"fact" means and includes—

(i) any thing, state of things, or relation of things, capable of being perceived by the senses;

(ii) any mental condition of which any person is conscious. [(w.e.f. 1-7-2024) Bharatiya Sakshya Adhiniyam, 2023 (47 of 2023), section 2(1)(f) and illustrations]

FACT is a term having a variety of meanings; thus it may signify either a state of things, that is, an existence or a motion, that is, an event; an act action or deed; a thing done (*Bouvier*); an effect produced; or achieved (*Webster*); something fixed unchangeable; a reality as distinguished from supposition or opinion (*Walker*); a truth as distinguished from fiction or error; a circumstance; an occurrence or event; an incident; an event or incident. (*Ame. Cyc.*).

The definition of fact does not restrict a fact to something which can be exhibited as a material object. Statements of prisoners while in police custody leading to discovery of material object held to be admissible as leading to discovery of relevant fact. A statement is included in the definition of "fact". The word 'fact,' in S. 157 of the Indian Evidence Act (1 of 1872) is not used in the limited sense of 'event' but also includes a continuing fact, such as possession. Possession is a fact within S. 3 of the Act.

Section 11 makes the existence of facts admissible and not statements as to such existence, unless of course the fact of making that statement is itself a matter in issue. In other words recitals in a document are not 'facts' as mentioned in Section 11 unless the existence of those recitals is itself a matter in issue. *Rayjappa* v. *Nilakanta Rao,* AIR 1962 Mys 53, 59. [Indian Evidence Act (1 of 1872), S. 11]

An occurrence, quality or relation, the reality of which is manifested in experience or may be inferred with certainty. [T.P. Act (4 of 1882), S. 3, *Expln.* III and Constitution of India, Art. 22 (6)].

Fact discovered. The words 'fact discovered' in S. 27 are not merely descriptive of the physical object produced but embrace the place from which the object is produced, the knowledge of the accused as to this and the information given must relate distinctly to this fact. *Mohd. Inayatulla* v. *State of Maharashtra*, AIR 1976 SC 483, 485. [Indian Evidence Act (1 of 1872), S. 27]

Fact-finding. The process of taking evidence to determine the truth about a disputed point.

Fact in issue. The expression "FACTS IN ISSUE" means and includes—

Any fact from which either by itself or in connection with other facts, the existence, non-existence, nature or extent or any right, liability, or disability, asserted or denied in any suit or proceeding, necessarily follows.

Explanation.—Whenever, under the provisions of the law for the time being in force relating to Civil Procedure (5 of 1908), any Court records an issue of fact, the fact to be asserted or denied in the answer to such issue is a fact in issue. [Indian Evidence Act (1 of 1872), S. 3 *Expln.*].

Fact or law, question of. The circumstances which govern the distinction between the powers of Judge and jury (in English law) are frequently of a complicated nature, and though the general principle may be laid down that it is for the Judge to determine the law and the jury the facts in any given case, it is often extremely difficult to draw any sharp line of division. (1 Co. Litt. 155-b. Hargrave's edition, and Taylor on Evidence. 1900 ed., Vol. I. pp. 23 *et. seq.*)

Fact or matter in issue. A fact or matter on which the plaintiff proceeds by his action and which the defendant controverts in his pleadings.

Facta probanda. (*Lat.*) Facts which must be proved; facts in issue.

Facta probantia. (*Lat.*) Facts given in evidence to prove facta probanda; evidentiary facts.

Facta sunt potentiora verbis. (*Maxim*) Facts are more powerful than words. (*Bouvier*).

Facta tenent multa quae fieri prohibentur. (*Lat.*) (12 Rep. 125) Deeds contain many things which are prohibited to be done.

Factfinder. One that tries to determine the facts of a case, situation, or relationship.

Faction. Self-interested or unscrupulous party, especially in politics.

FACTION, PARTY. The term *party* has of itself nothing odious, that of *faction* is always so. One may have a *party* for one's merit, from the number and ardour of one's friends; but a *faction* is raised by busy and turbulent spirits for their own purposes. *Faction* is the demon of discord, armed with the power to do endless mischief, and intent alone on destroying whatever opposes its progress; woe to that state into which it has found an entrance; *party* spirit may show itself in noisy debate; but while it keeps within the legitimate bounds of opposition, it is an evil that must be endured.

Facto. In fact; as where anything is actually done, *etc.* (*Tomlin*)

Facto ad jus non datur consequentia. (*Maxim*) Inference from the fact to the law is not allowed.

Factor. A factor is a mercantile agent who, in the customary course of his business as such agent, is entrusted with the possession or control of goods, wares, or merchandise for sale on commission. An agent employed to sell goods or merchandise consigned or delivered to him, by or for his principal, for a compensation commonly called "factorage" or "commission."

One who acts for another; an agent entrusted with the possession of goods for the purpose of sale [IPC (45 of 1860), S. 409]; something (as an element, circumstance or influence) that contributes for the production of a result. [Press Council Act (37 of 1978)].

"FACTOR" means a non-banking financial company as defined in section 45-I(*f*) of the Reserve Bank of India Act, 1934 (2 of 1934) which has been granted a certificate of registration under sub-section (1) of section 3 or any body corporate established under an Act of Parliament or any State Legislature or any Bank or any company registered under the Companies Act, 1956 (1 of 1956) engaged in the factoring business. [S. 2(i) of the Factoring Regulation Act, 2011 (12 of 2012)]

FACTOR, AGENT. The *factor* only buys and sells on the account of others; the *agent* transacts every sort of business in general; merchants and manufacturers employ *factors* abroad to dispose of goods transmitted; lawyers are frequently employed as *agents* for the receipt and payment of money, the transfer of estates, and various other pecuniary concerns.

FACTOR AND BROKER DISTINGUISHED. "The difference between a factor and a broker is that a factor is intrusted with the possession of the goods which he is authorised to sell, and has a special property in and lien upon them, whereas a broker is a mere negotiator and is not, as a general rule, intrusted with the possession of the goods, and therefore has no such special property or lien."

Factoring business. Means the business of acquisition of receivables of assignor by accepting assignment of such receivable or financing, whether by way of making loans or advances or otherwise against the security interest over any receivable but does not include—

(i) credit facilities provided by a bank in its ordinary course of business against security of receivables;

(ii) any activity as commission agent or otherwise for sale of agricultural produce or goods of any kind whatsoever or any activity relating to the production, storage, supply, distribution, acquisition or control of such produce or goods or provision of any services.

Explanation.—For the purposes of this clause—

(i) the expression "agricultural produce" shall have the meaning assigned to it under clause (a) of Section 2 of the Agricultural Produce (Grading and Marking) Act, 1937 (1 of 1937); and

(ii) the expression "goods" and "commission agent" shall have the meanings assigned to them respectively under clause (d) and *Explanation* (ii) of clause (i) of section 2 of the Forward Contracts (Regulation) Act, 1952 (74 of 1952). [Factory Regulation Act, 2011 (12 of 2012), S. 2(j)].

Factory. "FACTORY" means any premises (including the precincts thereof) wherein twenty or more workers are working or were working on any day of the preceding twelve months and in any part of which any manufacturing process connected with the production of sugar is being carried on or is ordinarily carried on with the aid of power. [Sugarcane Act (15 of 1934), S. 2(2)].

"FACTORY" means any premises, including the precincts thereof, wherein or in any part of which excisable goods other than salt are manufactured, or wherein or in any part of which any manufacturing process connected with the production of these goods is being carried on or is ordinarily carried on. [Central Excise Act (1 of 1944), S. 2(e)] [Now repealed by Act 12 of 2017].

"Factory" means a factory as defined in clause (*m*) of section 2 of the Factories Act, 1948 (63 of 1948). [Code on Wages, 2019 (29 of 2019), section 2(n)]

"Factory" means any premises including the precincts thereof—

(a) whereon ten or more employees are working, or were working on any day of the preceding twelve months, and in any part of which a manufacturing process is being carried on with the aid of power, or is ordinarily so carried on, or

(b) whereon twenty or more employees are working, or were working on any day of the preceding twelve months, and in any part of which a manufacturing process is being carried on without the aid of power, or is ordinarily so carried on,

but does not include a mine, or a mobile unit belonging to the Armed Forces of the Union, railways running shed or a hotel, restaurant or eating place. [Code on Social Security, 2020 (36 of 2020), section 2(32) and explanations]

"Factory" means any premises including the precincts thereof—

(i) whereon twenty or more workers are working, or were working on any day of the preceding twelve months, and in any part of which a manufacturing process is being carried on with the aid of power, or is ordinarily so carried on; or

(ii) whereon forty or more workers are working, or were working on any day of the preceding twelve months, and in any part of which a manufacturing process is being carried on without the aid of power, or is ordinarily so carried on,

but does not include a mobile unit belonging to the armed forces of the Union, railways running shed or a hotel, restaurant or eating place. . [Occupational Safety, Healthy & Working Conditions Code, 2020 (37 of 2020), section 2(1)(w) and its proviso and explanations.]

"FACTORY" means any premises including the precincts thereof—

(a) whereon ten or more persons are employed for wages on any day of the preceding twelve months, and in any part of which a manufacturing process is being carried on without aid thereof power or is ordinarily so carried on; or

(b) whereon twenty or more persons are employed or were employed for wages on any day of preceding twelve month, and in any part of which a manufacturing process is being carried on without the aid of power or is ordinarily so carried on, but does not includes Mines Act, 1952 or a railway running shed. [Employee's State Insurance Act (34 of 1948), S. 2(12)]

FACTORY means any premises including the precincts thereof—

(i) whereon ten or more workers are working, or were working on any day of the preceding twelve month, and any part of which a manufacturing process is being carried on with aid of power, or is ordinarily so carried on, or,

(ii) whereon twenty or more workers are working, or were working on any day of the preceding twelve months, and in any part of which manufacturing process is being carried on without the aid of power, or is ordinarily so carried on,—

but does not include a mine subject to the operation of the Mines Act (35 of 1952), or a mobile unit belonging to the armed forces of the Union, a railway running shed or hotel, restaurant or eating place.

Expln. I—For computing the number of workers for the purposes of this clauses all the workers in different groups and relays in a day shall be taken into account;

Expln. II—For the purposes of this clause, the mere fact that an Electronic Data Processing Unit or a Computer Unit is installed in any premises or part thereof, shall not be construed to make it a factory if no manufacturing process is being carried on in such premises or part thereof. [Factories Act (63 of 1948), S. 2(m)]

"FACTORY" means any premises, including the precincts thereof, in any part of which a manufacturing process is being carried on.

(i) with the aid of power, provided that fifty or more workers are working or were working thereon on any day of the preceding twelve months; or

(ii) without the aid of power, provided that one hundred or more workers are working on were working thereon on any day of the preceding twelve months and provided further that in no part of such premises any manufacturing process is being carried on with the aid of power. [Industries (Development and Regulation) Act (65 of 1951), S. 3(c)]

"FACTORY" means any premises, including the precincts thereof, in any part of which a manufacturing process is being carried on or is ordinarily so carried on, whether with the aid of power or without the aid of power. [Employee's Provident Funds and Miscellaneous Provisions Act (19 of 1952), S. 2(g)]

"FACTORY" means any premises (including the precincts thereof) wherein sugar is being produced by the vacuum pan process. [Sugar Export Promotion Act (30 of 1958), S. 2(g)].

"FACTORY" means any premises (including the precincts thereof), where or in any part of which sugar is being manufactured by the vacuum pan process, or, wherein or in any part of which, any manufacturing process connected with the production of sugar by the vacuum pan process is being carried on or is ordinarily carried on. [Sugar (Regulation of Production) Act (55 of 1961), S. 2(b)].

A building or buildings with plant for the manufacture of goods. [Indian Contract Act (9 of 1872), S. 19, ill. (a)].

"FACTORY" means any premises, including the precincts thereof, in any part of which a manufacturing process is carried on. The expression 'premises, including the precincts thereof' takes within its connotation not merely the building but the open area or the compound about that particular building. *S.T. Trading Co.* v. *UOI,* AIR 1966 Guj 116, 112. [Employees Provident Funds Act (19 of 1952), S. 2(g)]

The Department of Publications and Press of the Andhra University is a 'factory', as the printing of text books, journals, registers, forms and various items of stationery constitute 'manufacture' and there are more than 20 persons employed in the concerned establishment. *Andhra University* v. *R.P.F. Commissioner of A.P.*, AIR 1986 SC 463, 466.

The essential requisites of a factory under the Act are (1) a premises, a geographical area within a certain boundary (2) in a part of which at least manufacturing process should be carried on with the aid of power and (3) twenty or more persons should be working in the premises. It is not necessary that all the twenty persons should be working in the same section or department. *Employees State Insurance Corporation* v. *S.M. Sriramulu Naidu,* AIR 1960 Mad 248, 251. [Employees State Insurance Act (34 of 1948), S. 2(12)]

"FACTORY" means any premises including the precincts thereof whereon twenty or more persons are employed or were employed for wages on any day of the preceding twelve months, and in any part of which a manufacturing process is being carried on with the aid of power or is ordinarily so carried on but does not include a mine subject to the operation of the Mines Act, 1952 or a railway running shed. *B.M. Lakshmanamurthy* v. *Employees' State Insurance Corporation, Bangalore,* AIR 1974 SC 759.

The construction of a railway line to be laid over several kms. of land would necessarily imply fixed sites and premises on which such construction activity gets carried on in a phased manner, every part of the said land would consist of a 'factory' at a given point of time. Once the work is finished and construction activity comes to an end, the premises thereof may cease to be a factory. *Lal Mohammad* v. *Indian Railway Construction Co. Ltd.,* (1999) 1 SCC 596, para 17: AIR 1999 SC 355. [Factories Act (63 of 1948), S. 2(m)]

FACTORY means any premises including the precincts thereof in any part of which sugar is manufactured by vacuum pan process and at its own option, ethanol from molasses or B-heavy molasses. [Sugarcane (Control) Order, 1966, Clause 2(c) as substituted by Amending Order, 2016

Factory is that establishment where manufacturing process is carried on with or without the aid of power. Carrying on this manufacturing process or manufacturing activity is thus a prerequisite. It is equally pertinent to note that it covers only those workers who are engaged in the said manufacturing process. [*Lanco Anpara Power Limited* v. *State of U.P.*, (2016) 10 SCC 329, para 34].

Factory and workshop. Every place in which any manual labour is exercised by way of trade or for purposes of gain in or incidental to the making of any article, or part of any article or altering, repairing, ornamenting, or finishing it, or otherwise adapting it for sale is *prima facie* a "factory" or a "workshop." If the employer of those who work there has the right of access to the place or has control over it. If any machinery moved or worked by steam, water, or other mechanical power is used in such manufacture, or in aid of such manual labour, the place is a "factory". If no machinery moved or worked by any mechanical power is used there the place is, generally speaking, "workshop"; but to this rule there are some exceptions.

Factory buildings. 'FACTORY BUILDINGS' include all buildings comprised in the factory, and such other buildings (including residential buildings for staff and workmen, hospitals and welfare centres) within a radius of two miles from the main factory building as are in the same ownership and occupation as the factory and are used for the purposes of the factory. [Emergency Risks (Factories) Insurance Act, 1962, S. 2(d) now repealed by Act 4 of 2018]

Factory or works cost. Means the cost of production to the manufacturer at the factory or works and shall include the value of containers and other forms of interior packing ordinarily sold with an article when it is sold in retail, but shall not include the manufacturer's or exporter's profit or the cost of exterior packing, carriage to port and other charges incidental to the export of the article subsequent to its manufacture. [Customs Tariff, Customs Tariff (Determination of Origin of Other Preferential Areas) Rules 1977 and Notification Issued Thereunder, R. 3(d)]

Factory prices. The prices at which goods may be bought, bought-at-factories, as distinguished from the prices of those bought in the market, after they have passed into the hands of third parties or shopkeepers.

Facts. The word 'facts' in Section 12-A(6)(a) may be taken to have been used in the sense in which it is used in the law of evidence, that is to say as including the factum probandum or the principal fact to be proved and the factum probans or the evidentiary fact from which the principal fact follows immediately or by inference. *State of Andhra* v. *Sri Arisetty Sriramulu*, AIR 1957 AP 130, 132 (FB). [Madras General Sales Tax Act 9 of 1939. S. 12-A(6)(a)]

Facts in issue. "FACTS IN ISSUE" means and includes—

Any fact from which either by itself or in connection with other facts, the existence, non-existence, nature or extent or any right, liability, or disability, asserted or denied in any suit or proceeding, necessarily follows.

Explanation.—Whenever, under the provisions of the law for the time being in force relating to Civil Procedure (5 of 1908) any Court records an issue of fact, the fact to be asserted or denied in the answer to such issue is a fact in issue. [Indian Evidence Act (1 of 1872), S. 3]] [Now (w.e.f. 1-7-2024) repealed & replaced by Bharatiya Sakshya Adhiniyam, 2023 (47 of 2023)]

"Facts in issue" means and includes any fact from which, either by itself or in connection with other facts, the existence, non-existence, nature or extent of any right, liability or disability, asserted or denied in any suit or proceeding, necessarily follows.

Explanation.—Whenever, under the provisions of the law for the time being in force relating to Civil

Procedure, any Court records an issue of fact, the fact to be asserted or denied in the answer to such issue is a fact in issue. [(w.e.f. 1-7-2024) Bharatiya Sakshya Adhiniyam, 2023 (47 of 2023), section 2(1)(g) and illustrations]

The "*facts in issue*" are facts out of which some legal right, liability or disability, involved in the enquiry, necessarily arises, and upon which, accordingly, a decision must be arrived at. Matters which are affirmed by one party to a suit and denied by the other may be denominated facts in issue; what facts are in issue in particular cases, is a question to be determined by the substantive law or in some cases by that branch of the law of procedure which regulates the law of pleadings, civil or criminal. [*Introduction to the Indian Evidence Act, Stephen, pp. 12, 13*]

Facts of which courts take judicial notice. **See Indian Evidence Act (1 of 1872), S. 57.**

Factum a judice quod ad ejus officium non spectat non ratum est. (*Lat.*) (10 Rep. 76) An act of a judge which does not pertain to his office is of no force.

Factum a judice quod ad officium ejus non pertinet ratum non est. (*Lat.*) Anything done by a judge which does not belong to his office (that is, does not fall within his official authority) is not valid.

Factum cuique suum, non adversario nocere debet. A man's actions should injure himself, not his adversary.

Factum imprestabile. (*Lat.*). An act that cannot be performed : an impossibility.

Factum infectum fieri aequit. (*Maxim*) "What is done cannot be undone." (*Bouvier*).

Factum juridicum. (*Lat.*). A juridical fact.

Factum probanda. Facts which require to be proved.

Factum probandum. Facts that are in issue, that are to be proved.

Factum probans. A probative or evidentiary fact; a subsidiary or connected fact tending to prove the principal fact in issue; a piece of circumstantial evidence.

Factum probantia. Facts which are given in evidence to prove other facts in issue.

Factum unius alteri nocere non debet. The deed of one should not hurt another.

Facultas probationum non est angustanda. (*Lat.*) (4 Inst. 279) The facility of proofs is not to be narrowed.

Facultative. "FACULTATIVE" means the reinsurance of a part or all of a single policy in which cession is negotiated separately and that the reinsurer and the insurer have the option of accepting or declining each individual submission. [Insurance Regulatory and Development Authority (General Insurance-Reinsurance) Regulations, 2000, Reg. 2(d)].

Faculty. A department of learning at a university, or the professors constituting it [Aligarh Muslim University Act (40 of 1920), S. 2(g)]; right, authority or privilege to act. [Geneva Conventions Act (6 of 1960), Art. 43].

Faculty. "The Oxford Universal Dictionary provides for the meaning of faculty as follows:

'I. The power of doing anything. An ability or aptitude, whether natural or acquired, for any special kind of action; formerly also, ability in general. A power or capacity. A physical capacity or function. One of the powers of the mind e.g. the will, the reason, memory.

II. A department of knowledge. One of the department of learning at a University. An art, trade, occupation, profession. The whole body of Masters, Doctors in any one of the studies. The members of a profession regarded as one body.

III. Power, liberty, or right of doing something conferred by law or favour. A dispensation, licence granted by an eccl. Superior to someone to do something which otherwise he could not legally do.'

Webster's New Twentieth Century Dictionary provides for the meaning of faculty as follows:

'1. That power of the mind or intellect which enables it to receive, revive or modify perceptions; as, the faculty of seeing, of hearing, of imagining, of remembering.

2. Facility of performance; the peculiar skill derived from practice, or practice aided by nature; habitual skill or ability; dexterity; adroitness; knack; as, one has remarkable faculty of telling a story.

3. Power; authority.

4. In the Roman Catholic church, a privilege; a right or power granted to a person by favour or indulgence, to do what by law he may not do; specifically, an authorization by a superior bestowing ecclesiastical rights upon a subordinate; often used in the plural.

5. The individuals constituting a scientific profession, or a branch of one, taken collectively; especially, the medical profession.

6. Collectively, the masters and professors of the several departments of a university, or any one of the departments; as the faculty of arts, of theology, of medicine, or of law.'

According to Stroud's Judicial Dictionary of Words and Phrases Faculty means: 'Faculty signifies a privilege or special dispensation, granted unto a man by favour and indulgence to do that which by the law he cannot do.'

According to Black's Law Dictionary faculty means: Ability; power; capability. Teaching staff of school.

[As cited in *Ashutosh Kumar Singh and Ors.* v. *Union of India*, 2017 (11) ADJ 103 (ALLHC)]

"FACULTY" means Faculty of the University. [S. 3(l) of the Rani Lakshmi Bai Central Agricultural University Act, 2014 (10 of 2014)]

"Faculty" means the faculty of a Central Educational Institution. [Central Educational Institutions (Reservation in Teachers' Cadre) Act, 2019 (10 of 2019), section 2(f)]

Faculty of the Academy. Means Academy professors, professors of eminence, distinguished professors, outstanding professors, senior professors, emeritus professors, professors, associate professors, assistant professors, visiting faculty, and such other persons as may be appointed for imparting instruction or conducting research in the Academy or institutions maintained by the Academy and includes the scientists of Council of Scientific and Industrial Research assigned for imparting instruction or conducting research. [(w.e.f. 3-4-2012) S. 2(i) of the Academy of Scientific & Innovative Research Act, 2011 (13 of 2012)]

Fail. To leave unperformed; to omit; to neglect; as distinguished from refuse, which latter involves an act of the will, while the former may be an act of inevitable necessity. (*Bouvier*).

To fall short in performance or attainment [T.P. Act (4 of 1882), S. 58(b)]; to be unavailing; to be or become non-existent; to become insolvent (used for a business man) [Indian Contract Act (9 of 1872), S. 50, ill. (a)].

Failed to provide. The words "failed to provide" do imply a duty to provide. If there is no such duty to provide, it cannot be said that the husband has failed to provide maintenance to his wife. *Ahmed Abdul Quder* v. *Raffat,* AIR 1978 AP 417, 419. [Dissolution of Muslim Marriages Act (8 of 1939), S. 2(ii)]

Failure. The fact of failing. *Failure* is opposed to success.

The word 'failure' contemplated in R. 2, O. IX of the CPC (5 of 1908), includes not only absolute failure to pay but also failure to pay within a certain time fixed by the Court therefor.

Failure of consideration. Consideration, originally existing and good, becoming worthless, non-existent or barred. [T.P. Act (4 of 1882), S. 126].

Failure of justice. The defeat of a particular right, or the failure of preparation for a particular wrong, from the lack or inadequacy of a legal remedy for the enforcement of the one or the redress of the other. The term is also colloquially applied to the miscarriage of justice which occurs when the result of a trial is so palpably wrong as to shock the moral sense. (*Black*).

Deduction of rental amount for the occupation of the company's quarters occupied by the wife the employee from out of the maintenance payable by the husband cannot be said to occasion any failure of justice. *In the matter of B.H.P. & V. Ltd., Visakhapatnam,* AIR 1985 AP 207, 211. [CPC (5 of 1908), S. 115, *Proviso*, (as added by 1976 amendment)]

Non-administration of proper justice or-miscarriage of justice due to non-compliance with procedure, disregard of law or like causes. [CrPC, 1973 (2 of 1974), S. 465(1)].

Failure to exercise jurisdiction. CPC (5 of 1908), Section 115, cl. (b). If a *bona fide* application (under Order XIX, Rule 2 of CPC (5 of 1908)) for summoning deponent for cross-examination is rejected erroneously there is a failure to exercise jurisdiction.

Failure to maintain. The failure of either spouse to provide reasonable maintenance for the other or to make a proper contribution towards the maintenance of any children of the family during the subsistence of the marriage.

Fair. *As an adjective*, in common usage, the word conveys some idea of justice or equity; impartial; free from suspicion of bias; equitable (*Webster*); reasonable; honest; upright; and as applied to the weather, a fair weather is one free from clouds; not obscure.

A periodical gathering of buyers and sellers in a place and at a time ordained by law or custom [Indian Evidence Act (1 of 1872), S. 7, ill. (a)]; free from blemish or disfigurement; free from irregularities. [CrPC, 1973 (2 of 1974), S. 407(1)(a)].

The words 'fair and equitable' both mean 'just and unbiased'. The words mean fair and equitable in fact, and not what the lessor subjectively considered to be fair and equitable. *U.T. Mangalmurti* v. *State of Bombay*, AIR 1959 SC 639, 642.

Fair and equitable benefit sharing. Means sharing of benefits as determined by the National Biodiversity Authority under Section 21. [Biological Diversity Act, 2002 (18 of 2003), S. 2(g)]

Fair comment. A *'fair comment'* (excusing what would otherwise be a libel) is a comment which is either true, or which, if false, expresses the real opinion of its author (as to the existence of a matter of fact, or otherwise), such opinion having been formed with a reasonable degree of care and on reasonable grounds.

The defence of fair comment may be raised in answer to a criminal prosecution for libel. It seems that if the defence is to be raised it must be raised by formal plea and must presumably state the matter of public interest and the facts and matters relied on to support the comment, as in civil actions. HALSBURY, 4th Edn., Vol. 28, para 285, p. 141.

The accusing of Courts of 'harassing' would not come within ambit of expression 'fair comment' under criminal contempt. *J.R. Parashar* v. *Prasant Bhushan,* (2001) 6 SCC 735, para 38.

Fair competition. Open, equitable, just competition, which is fair as between competitors and as between any of them and his customers. See Antitrust acts, Clayton Act; Price-fixing; Sherman Antitrust Act.

Fair consideration fixed in good faith. *Prima facie* the market value is the fair consideration and it is for the party alleging that it is not so to plead and prove that there are circumstances to suggest that it is not the fair consideration. If the consideration of the sale deed is in excess of the market value, it must be presumed that the consideration was not fixed in good faith.

Fair criticism. A 'fair criticism' is that which, while criticising the act of a Judge, does not impute any ulterior motive to him. *Padmahasini* v. *C.R. Srinivas,* (1999) 8 SCC 711, para 5 : AIR 2000 SC 68.

Fair dealing. Good faith. (*Ballentine's Law Dictionary, 3rd Edn.)*

Fair dismissal. Dismissal of an employee when a tribunal decides that an employer has acted reasonably in dismissing the employee and that the dismissal was for a lawful reason, *i.e.* on the grounds of the employee's capability, qualifications, or conduct; redundancy; the fact that it would be illegal to continue employing the employee; or some other sufficient and substantial reason.

Fair, just, equitable, reasonable, moderate. All these terms are applicable to persons, their conduct, and their demands.

"FAIR" denotes an estimate in detail of what is reciprocally just; a *fair* price for an article is that which seems right considering the circumstances of buyer and seller and sale. A *fair* man is he who is ready to look at other's interests as well as his own, and to view matters without partiality, prejudice, or selfseeking.

"JUST" is more comprehensive, and implies the application of principles of retributive justice, where it is due. There is a dignity and sternness about the term *Just* which does not belong to *fair,* So prizes are said to be *fairly* won and *justly* awarded.

"EQUITABLE" is according to equity, and so has the force of the noun itself, which is not mere fairness, but such as may serve to supplement the imperfection of law or rule.

"REASONABLE" denotes what is fair under another aspect. As the *fair* is the right between man and man, the *reasonable* is the right in itself, as it would commend itself not only to the just but to the wise man. The reasonable, however, extends beyond the matters of intercourse between man and man, to the essential nature of things which are in accordance with common sense or common experience.

"MODERATE" as commonly employed, denotes a marked absence of excess in demand; this may or may not flow from justice or fairness—the term states nothing but the fact. "I purchased the article at a moderate price" indicates nothing as to the intentions of the seller. Moderate measures may be and very often are, the expressions of justice, but they may also originate in prudence or be dictated by necessity. (*Smith. Syn. Dis.*)

The words 'Fair and equitable' both mean 'just and unbiased.' The words mean fair and equitable in fact, and not what the lessor subjectively considered to be fair and equitable. *D.T. Mangalmurti* v. *State of Bombay*, AIR 1959 SC 639, 642.

Fair market price. Price of an arm's length transaction between a willing seller and a willing buyer, each acting in his or her own self-interest.

Fair market value. "FAIR MARKET VALUE", in relation to a capital asset, means—

(i) the price that the capital asset would ordinarily fetch on sale in the open market on the relevant date; and

(ii) where the price referred to in subclause (i) is not ascertainable, such price as may be determined in accordance with the rules made under this Act. [Income Tax Act (43 of 1961), S. 2(22B)]

In this Chapter, unless the context otherwise requires—

"FAIR MARKET VALUE",

(i) In relation to any immovable property transferred by way of sale or exchange, being immovable property of the nature referred to in sub-clause (*i*) of clause (*e*), means the price that the immovable property would ordinarily fetch on sale in the open market on the date of execution of the instrument of transfer of such property;

(ii) In relation to any immovable property transferred by way of lease, being immovable property of the nature referred to in sub-clause (*i*) of clause (*e*), means the premium that such transfer would ordinarily fetch in the open market on the date of execution of the instrument of transfer of such property, if the consideration for such transfer had been by way of premium only;

(iii) In relation to any immovable property transferred, being immovable property of the nature referred to in sub-clause (*ii*) of clause (*e*), means the consideration in the form of money that such transfer would ordinarily fetch in the open market on the date of the transfer, if such transfer had been made only for consideration in money. [Income tax Act (43 of 1961), S. 269A(2)(d)].

Fair market value of the shares. For the purposes of section 56(2)(viib) of Act 43 of 1961, the 'fair market value of the shares' shall be the value—

(i) as may be determined in accordance with such method as may be prescribed; or

(ii) as may be substantiated by the company to the satisfaction of the Assessing Officer, based on the value, on the date of issue of shares, of its assets, including intangible assets being goodwill, know-how, patents, copyrights, trademarks, licences, franchises or any other business or commercial rights of similar nature, whichever is higher. [*Explanation* (*a*) to section 56(2)(viib) of the Income-tax Act, 1961 (43 of 1961) as inserted (w.e.f. 1-4-2013) by the Finance Act, 2012]

Fair play. Equal opportunities; just treatment.

Fair practice. The term describing the parameters of the making and extent of quotations from works in such circumstances not infringing the author's rights. [Berne Convention, Article 10(1)]

The term describing exceptions by way of illustrations in broadcasts, publications, visual or sound recordings for teaching. [Berne Convention, Article 10(2)] (*Copyright*)

Fair price. 'FAIR PRICE', in relation to levy sugar, means the price fixed by the Court in excess of the controlled price and where an interim price, fixed by the Court, is superseded by a price which is finally fixed by the Court, the price so finally fixed. [Levy Sugar Price Equalization Fund Act (31 of 1976), S. 2(c)].

"Fair price" has to be determined in respect of the entire produce ensuring to the industry a reasonable return on the capital employed in the business of manufacturing sugar. *Anakapalle Co-op. Agrl. and Industrial Society Ltd.* v. *Union of India,* AIR 1973 SC 734.

Fair price shop. Means a shop which has been licensed to distribute essential commodities by an order issued under section 3 of the Essential Commodities Act, 1955 (10 of 1955), to the ration card holders under the Targeted Public Distribution System. [S. 2(4) of the National Food Security Act, 2013 (20 of 2013)]

Fair procedure. Fair procedure would mean that the candidates taking part in the examination must be capable of competing with each other by fair means. One cannot have an advantage either by copying or by having a foreknowledge of the question paper or otherwise. *B. Ramanjini* v. *State of Andhra Pradesh*, AIR 2000 SC 2023.

Fair rate. Means the fair rate fixed under Section 39 and includes the rate as revised under Section 40. [Delhi Rent Act (33 of 1995), S. 2(c)]

Fair rent. There are three guidelines in the calculation of the fair rent. The first is to have regard to fair market rents for similar properties. The second is to compare registered rents for other, similar protected tenancy properties. The third is to ascertain what would be a fair return to the landlord on the capital value of his house. *Western Heritable Investment Co. Ltd.* v. *Husband*, (1983) 3 All ER 65, 69 (HL). [Rent (Scotland) Act, 1971, S. 42(2)]

Fair trial. A trial in which law has been administered with fairness, without prejudice to any of the parties. [CPC (5 of 1908), O. VI, R. 16(b)].

'Fair trial' means a trial in which bias or prejudice for or against the accused, the witnesses, or the cause which is being tried, is eliminated. 'Fair trial' obviously would mean a trial before an impartial judge, a fair prosecutor and atmosphere of judicial calm. If the witnesses get threatened or are forced to give false evidence that also would not result in a 'fair trial'. The failure to hear material witness is certainly denial of 'fair trial'. *Zahira Habibulla H. Sheikh* v. *State of Gujarat*, (2004) 4 SCC 158, 184, para 36.

Fair use. (1) An exemption from copyright infringement that permits reasonable use in research, teaching, news reporting, criticism, or parody, (2) The right of others to use the descriptive and suggestive words in a trademark, such as geographical terms or surnames, or to use the trademark in news reporting or parody.

"FAIR USE" a defence taken against allegation of infringement of Copyright; for example, that the article was copied for personal research and study and not for commercial use. [Karnika Seth, *Computers Internet and New Technology Laws*, 2021, LexisNexis, Glossary of Legal Terms].

Fair value. "FAIR VALUE" in relation to immovable property in disturbed areas means such value of the property as approximate the market value of such property. [Gujarat Prohibition of Transfer of Immovable Property and Provision for Protection of Tenants from Eviction from Premises in Disturbed Area Act (Gujarat Act No. 12 of 1991), S. 2(b)]

FAIR VALUE means the 'mean' of the earning value and break up value. [Non-Banking Financial Companies Prudential Norms (Reserve Bank) Directions, 1998, Para 2(1)(vi)].

Fair wage. Fair wage must be sufficiently high to provide a standard family with food, shelter, clothing, medical care and education of children appropriate to the workman but not at a rate exceeding his wage earning capacity in the class of establishment to which he belongs. *Kamani Metals & Alloys Ltd.* v. *Workmen*, AIR 1967 SC 1175, 477. [Industrial Disputes Act (14 of 1947), 3rd Sch., item 1]

Fair wear and tear. Means not only wear and tear through natural agencies or fair use by the occupier, but also further disrepair resulting from the failure to make good such wear and tear.

Fairly. An agreement to do a work 'fairly' or 'diligently' and 'regularly,' or 'uninterruptedly' or 'efficiently'. (*Stroud*)

Properly; rightfully. [CPC (5 of 1908), O. XI, R. 18(1)]; [CPC (5 of 1908), O. XXI, R. 66(2)].

Fairness. Characterized by justness and equity.

Fait. A fact; a deed; an act; an act done. (*Ballentine's Law Dictionary, 3rd Edn.)*

Fait accompli. Fact or deed accomplished, presumably irreversible. An accomplished act.

Fait enrolle. (*Lat.*) An enrolled deed of a sale of a freehold estate.

Fait justitia ruat caelum. (*Lat.*) Let right be done, though the heavens should fall.

Faith. Confidence; credit; trust; belief in divine truth; reliance; credence; purpose; intent; sincerity (as, good faith).

GOOD FAITH. Fairness; loyalty; fidelity; sincerity.

BAD FAITH. Insincerity intent to deceive.

Faith, in bad. *Mala fide.* [Industrial Finance Corporation Act (15 of 1948) (*Repealed by Act 23 of 1993*), S. 30C(2)].

Faithful. Observant of compacts, treaties, contracts, vows, or other engagements; loyal; sincere; true to one's word. (*Cent.*)

True and constant in affection or allegiance; loyal. [Indian Partnership Act (9 of 1932), S. 9].

Faithfully. Diligently, without unnecessary delay; it is also a usual formula in closing a letter; (as, yours *faithfully*).

Dutifully; conscientiously; loyally. [Navy Act (62 of 1957), S. 13].

Fall back. Retreat.

Fall due. To become due (as, a debt falling due on a particular date).

Fallow. Means uncultivated; barren; ploughed, but left uncropped for the year.

Falsa demonstratio. (*Lat.*) False designation; erroneous description of a person or thing. 'Where the deed of settlement fixed boundaries of the land but wrongly mentioned the extent of land, the incorrectly described quantity has to be rejected as it is *falsa demonstratio*'. *Tranglaobi Pisciculture Cooperative Society Ltd.* v. *Chief Commissioner,* AIR 1969 Manipur 84 at 87. [T.P. Act (4 of 1882), S. 8]

Falsa demonstratio non nocet. (*Lat.*) Erroneous description does not vitiate a deed. 'A false description does not render a deed or other writing inoperative.' The maxim *falsa demonstratio non nocet* means that if there be a sufficient and adequate description to create a certainty of what was meant, subsequent erroneous additions will not vitiate a description otherwise accurate.

Falsa demonstratio non nocet ae corpore constat. A false description does not vitiate a document.

Falsa demonstratio non nocet cum de corpore (persona) constat. (*Lat.*) The maxim, means that misdescription has no effect, when the thing or person meant is otherwise indicated clearly. The maxim is meant only to cure defects arising out of unintentional misdescription and not to change the nature proceedings by alterations in the document. *State of A.P.* v. *Prem Prakash*, AIR 1966 All 504, 507. [CrPC, 1973 (2 of 1974), S. 417(3)]

Falsa demonstratione legatum non-pere-mitur. (*Maxim*) A legacy is not destroyed by an incorrect description. (*Bouvier*)

Falsa grammatica non vitiat concessionem. (*Lat.*) False or bad grammar does not vitiate a grant when the intent of the parties plainly appears.

Falsa orthographia non vitiat chartam. (*Lat.*) False spelling does not vitiate a deed.

False. Erroneous; untrue; the opposite of correct, or true.

'False' is in essence incorrect, or purposefully untrue, deceitful etc. Thus, the word "false" is used to cover only unlawful falsehood. It means something that is dishonest, untrue and deceitful, and implies an intention to perpetrate some treachery or fraud. In jurisprudence, the word "false" is used to characterise a wrongful or criminal act, done intentionally and knowingly, with knowledge actual or constructive. The word "false" may also be used in a wide or narrower sense. When used in its wider sense, it means something that is untrue whether or not stated intentionally or knowingly, but when used in its narrower sense, it may cover only such falsehoods, which are intentional. [*Ravinder Singh* v. *Sukhbir Singh*, (2013) 9 SCC 245, para 18].

Deceitful. [S. 205, IPC (45 of 1860)]; deceptive [IPC (45 of 1860), S. 281]; artificial; sham [IPC (45 of 1860), S. 415, ill. (c)]; not corresponding to truth [IPC (45 of 1860), S. 182]; counterfeit; spurious. [IPC (45 of 1860), S. 267].

It will include only such falsehoods which are intentional. Thus where a dealer who honestly though incorrectly represented that a particular article falls within the description of goods specified in his certificate he lacks '*mens rea*' and cannot be penalised under the Section. *Commissioner of Sales Tax* v. *Bombay General Stores,* AIR 1969 MP 213 at 215. [Central Sales Tax Act (74 of 1956), S. 10(b)]

False charge. An accusation made to a person who has nothing to do under the law with setting the Criminal Law in motion would not amount to a charge within the meaning of S. 211, IPC (45 of 1860). But allegations of an offence made to a competent authority or other person with a statutory standing in the matter for the purpose of obtaining sanction to prosecute while not amounting to institution of criminal proceedings, amount to making of a charge within the meaning of S. 211.

Untrue allegation of a wrong or offence. [IPC (45 of 1860), S. 211].

False claim. Undue assertion of a right to something. [IPC (45 of 1860), S. 209].

False defence. An untrue defence. [CPC (5 of 1908), S. 35A(4)].

False demonstratio non nocet cum de corpore constant. A false description does not vitiate a document when the thing is described with certainty.

'False document' defined. *See* Making a false document; Indian Penal Code (45 of 1860), S. 464.

A document deliberately drawn up incorrectly or intentionally falsified. [IPC (45 of 1860), S. 464].

A bail order written in the handwriting of a stenographer of the High Court without his signature even though it was not passed by the High Court was held to be a 'false document'. [*State of U.P.* v. *Ranjit Singh*, AIR 1999 SC 1201 : (1999) 2 SCC 617]

False document (Forgery), essentials. To constitute an offence of forgery, the document must be purported to have been signed, made or sealed by a person who did not in fact do it. It is of the essence of making a false document that the signature, seal or the date of it should be false. The fact that a document contains false recitals or statements which induce a person so deceived to part with or deliver property would not make it an offence of forgery. *Public Prosecutor* v. *Thall Gangadharudu*, MLJ : QD 56-60 Vol. IV C999 : 1956 ALT 678 : 1956 Andh WR 805. [IPC (45 of 1860), Ss. 463, 464]

False entry. An entry which is either totally fictitious, or fictitious to some extent; an untrue or incorrect entry in contra-distinction to 'correct' entry. An entry would be a false entry or a statement in a record or document would be a false entry, if it does either by reason of some false additions or of some material omissions misrepresent the truth.

A matter falsely entered in any record or register, account book *etc.* [Indian Evidence Act (1 of 1872), S. 15, ill. (b)].

False evidence. 'Whoever being legally bound by an oath or by any express provision of law to state the truth, or being bound by law to make a declaration upon any subject, makes any statement which is false, and which he either knows or believes to be false, or does not believe to be true is said to give false evidence.

Explanation 1. A statement is within the meaning of this section whether it is made verbally or otherwise.

Explanation 2. A false statement as to the belief of the person attesting is within the meaning of this section, and a person, may be guilty of giving false evidence by stating that he believes a thing which he does not believe, as well as by stating that he knows a thing which he does not know. [IPC (45 of 1860), S. 191] [(w.e.f. 1-7-2024) repealed and replaced by Bharatiya Nyaya Sanhita, 2023 (45 of 2023), section 227]

Untrue evidence. [Indian Evidence Act (1 of 1872), S. 153].

False imprisonment is a trespass committed against a person, by arresting and imprisoning him without just cause, contrary to law; or where a man is unlawfully detained without legal process. To constitute the injury of false imprisonment two points are necessary, the detention of the person and the unlawfulness of such detention. (*Tomlin*)

False information. Untrue information. [IPC (45 of 1860), S. 177].

False instrument. An instrument or weight, *etc.* which is not genuine or does not conform to the prescribed standard. [IPC (45 of 1860), S. 267].

False measure. Wrong measure.

A spurious instrument for measuring. [IPC (45 of 1860), S. 267].

False package. Means any package which does not conform to the provision of this Act or any rule or order made thereunder in relation to such package. [Standards of Weights and Measures Act (60 of 1976), S. 2(f)]

False personation. The offence of falsely representing some other person and acting in the character.

Falsely pretending to be some other person. [IPC (45 of 1860), S. 205].

False plea. A statement of case that is obviously frivolous or absurd and is made only for the purpose of vexation or delay.

False representation. A representation to be considered as false may be affirmative or failure to disclose a known fact which the person who knows it has a duty to disclose.

An incorrect statement made or account given with a view to influencing the opinion or action of the person to whom such statement is made or account is given. [IPC (45 of 1860), S. 118].

False sample. A sham sample. [IPC (45 of 1860), S. 415, ill. (c)].

False seal. A seal which is not genuine. [CrPC, 1973 (2 of 1974), S. 94(2)(e)].

False signals or **False light.** It is a felony for any person unlawfully to mark, alter, or remove any light or signal, or unlawfully to exhibit any false light or signal with intent to bring any ship, vessel, or boat into or unlawfully and maliciously to do anything tending to, the immediate loss or destruction of any ship, vessel, or boat.

False statement. Statement knowingly false, or made recklessly without honest belief in its truth, and with purpose to mislead or deceive. (*Black*)

Untrue statement. [IPC (45 of 1860), S. 181].

False swearing (*Perjury*). In its ordinary sense, swearing to what the deponent knows to be untrue; swearing corruptly; swearing which is morally, wilfully false, not merely mistaken; is the act of knowingly and intentionally stating upon oath what is not true.

False trade-description. A trade description which is false or misleading in a material respect as regards the goods to which it is applied. [Trade and Merchandise Marks Act (43 of 1958), S. 2(f)].

An inaccurate or incomplete description of a commodity is not a 'false trade description'.

"FALSE TRADE DESCRIPTION" means—

(i) a trade description which is untrue or misleading in a material respect as regards the goods to which it is applied; or

(ii) any alteration of a trade description as regards the goods to which it is applied whether by way of addition effacement or otherwise where that alteration makes the description untrue or misleading in a material respect; or

(iii) any trade description which denotes or implies that there are contained, as regards the goods to which it is applied, more yards or meters than there are contained therein standard yards or standard meters; or

(iv) any marks or arrangement or combination thereof applied to goods in such manner as to be likely to lead persons to believe that the goods are the manufacture or merchandise of some person other than the person whose merchandise or manufacture they really are; or

(v) any false name or initials of a person applied to goods in such manner as if such name or initials were a trade description in any case where the name or initials—

(a) is or are not a trade mark or part of a trade mark; and

(b) is or are identical with or decepively similar to the name or initials of a person carrying on business in connection with goods of the same description and who has not authorised the use of such name or initials; and

(c) is or are either the name or initials of a fictitious person or of some person not *bona-fide* carrying on business in connection with such goods, and the fact that a trade description is a trade mark or a part of trade mark shall not prevent such trade description being a false trade description within the meaning of this Act. [Trade and Merchandise Marks Act (43 of 1958), S. 2(f)] [Now repealed & replaced by Act 47 of 1999]

"FALSE TRADE DESCRIPTION" means—

(I) a trade description which is untrue or misleading in a material respect as regards the goods or services to which it is applied; or

(II) any alteration of a trade description as regards the goods or services to which it is applied, whether by way of addition, effacement or otherwise, where that alteration makes the description untrue or misleading in a material respect; or

(III) any trade description which denotes or implies that there are contained, as regards the goods to which it is applied, more yards or metres than there are contained therein standard yards or standard metres; or

(IV) any marks or arrangement or combination thereof when applied—

(a) to goods in such a manner as to be likely to lead persons to believe that the goods are the manufacture or merchandise of same person other than the person whose merchandise or manufacture they really are;

(b) in relation to services in such a manner as to be likely to lead persons to believe that the services are provided or rendered by same person other than the person whose services they really are; or

(V) any false name or initials of a person applied to goods or services in such manner as if such name or initials were a trade description in any case where the name or initials—

(a) is or are not a trade mark or part of a trade mark; and

(b) is, or are identical with or deceptively similar to the name or initials of a person carrying on business in connection with goods or services of the same description or both and who has not authorised the use of such name or initials; and

(c) is or are either the name or initials of a fictitious person or some person not *bona fide* carrying on business in connection with such goods or services, and the fact that a trade description is a trade mark or part of a trade mark shall not prevent such trade description being a false trade description within the meaning of this Act. [Trade Marks Act (47 of 1999), S. 2(1)(i)]

False trade-mark. 'False trade mark' means mark in any goods, package or other receptacle containing goods in a manner reasonably calculated to cause it to be believed that the goods so marked, or any goods contained in any such receptacle so marked had a connection in the course of trade with a person, with whom they had not such connection. *Kundanlal* v. *State,* AIR 1958 All 643, 644. [IPC (45 of 1860), S. 482]

False weight. Wrong weight.

A spurious weight which is not what it appears on its face or is represented to be. [IPC (45 of 1860), S. 265].

False weight or measure. Means any weight or measure which does not conform to the standards established by or under this Act in relation to that weight or measure. [Standards of Weight and Measures Act (60 of 1976), S. 2(g)]

Falsely charges. The meaning of the expression 'falsely charges' is simply 'falsely accuses'. *Dasrathi Mondal* v. *Haridas,* AIR 1959 Cal 293. [IPC (45 of 1860), S. 211]

The expression 'falsely charges' cannot mean giving false evidence, as a prosecution witness against an accused person during the course of a criminal trial. 'Falsely charges' must refer to the criminal accusation, pulling or seeking to put in motion the machinery of criminal investigation and not when seeking to prove the false charge by making deposition in support of the charge framed in that trial. *Santokh Singh* v. *Izhar Hussain*, AIR 1973 SC 2190, 2194. [IPC (45 of 1860), S. 211]

Falsification. The action of making (something) false; fraudulent alteration; perversion (of facts). [CrPC 1973 (2 of 1974), S. 220(2)].

Falsification of account. Falsifying an account by destroying, altering or mutilating any book or writing with intent to defraud. [IPC (45 of 1860), S. 477A].

Falsify. To prove false; to avoid or defeat; *Falsify* is to give a false appearance to anything to reverse or avoid, as a verdict, or judgment (*Burrill*); to prove a thing to be false (*Bouvier*). In criminal law, to forge or counterfeit; to make false; (as, false coin; false document) To make false mutilation or addition. [Navy Act (62 of 1957), S. 60].

Falsus. (*Lat.*) False, fraudulent; erroneous; deceitful; mistaken. In the sense of 'deceiving' or 'fraudulent', it is applied to persons in respect to their acts and conduct, as well as to things; and in the sense of 'erroneous', it is applied to persons on the question of personal identity.

Falsus in uno, falsus in omnibus. (*Maxim*) False in one thing, false in all.

This maxim has not received general acceptance in different jurisdictions in India nor has this maxim come to occupy the status of a rule of law. It is merely a rule of caution. All that it amounts to is that in such cases the testimony may be disregarded and not that it must be disregarded. *Nisar Ali* v. *State of Uttar Pradesh*, AIR 1957 SC 366, 368.

The maxim is neither a sound rule of law nor a rule of practice. Hardly one comes across a witness whose evidence does not contain a grain of untruth or at any rate exaggerations, embroidaries or embellishments. *Ugar Ahir* v. *State of Bihar*, AIR 1965 SC 277, 279.

The maxim does not apply to India. Indian Court can reject a part of the evidence of witness and can accept the other part of the evidence. *Rambir* v. *State of Punjab*, AIR 1973 SC 1409, 1412.

The Courts in India have been reluctant to act on the maxim yet the disregard of the maxim cannot be pushed too far. The whole statement should be scruitinised and if found unsatisfactory, it must be rejected. *State of M.P.* v. *Banshilal Behari,* AIR 1958 MP 13, 15. [Indian Evidence Act (1 of 1872), S. 118]

If after considering the whole mass of evidence, a residue of acceptable truth is established by the prosecution beyond reasonable doubt the Courts are bound to give effect to the result flowing from it, and not throw it over-board on purely hypothetical and conjectural grounds. *The State of Punjab* v. *Hari Singh*, AIR 1974 SC 1168, 1173. [Indian Evidence Act (1 of 1872), S. 3; IPC (45 of 1860), S. 300]

The maxim is not applicable in India and witnesses cannot be branded as liars. Even if a major portion of evidence is found to be deficient, in case residue is sufficient to prove guilt of an accused, notwithstanding acquittal of a number of other co-accused persons, his conviction can be maintained. *Krishna Mochi* v. *State of Bihar,* (2002) 6 SCC 81, para 51: AIR 2002 SC 1965.

The maxim is merely a rule of caution. It cannot be said that when a portion of the prosecution evidence is discarded as unworthy of credence, there cannot be any conviction. *Narain* v. *State of M.P.*, (2004) 2 SCC 455, 457, para 8.

Family. No definite number of persons is necessary to constitute a family when the term is used in its primary sense, except that there must be at least two persons, for it is obvious that a collection of persons must consist of more than one person; a husband and wife living together without children, servants or any one at all may constitute a family. The word is frequently used in common speech without reference to any established household, but merely for the purpose of indicating the individuals related, as husband, wife or parents and children.

"Family" means all or any of the following relatives of an employee or an unorganised worker, as the case may be, namely:—

(a) a spouse;

(b) a minor legitimate or adopted child dependent upon the employee or an unorganised worker, as the case may be;

(c) a child who is wholly dependent on the earnings of the employee or an unorganised worker, as the case may be, and who is—

  (i) receiving education, till he attains the age of twenty-one years; and

  (ii) an unmarried daughter;

(d) a child who is infirm by reason of any physical or mental abnormality or injury and is wholly dependent on the earnings of the employee or an unorganised worker, as the case may be, so long as the infirmity continues;

(e) dependent parents (including father-in-law and mother-in-law of a woman employee), whose income from all sources does not exceed such income as may be prescribed by the Central Government;

(f) in case the employee or an unorganised worker, as the case may be, is unmarried and his parents are not alive, a minor brother or sister wholly dependent upon the earnings of the Insured Person. [Code on Social Security, 2020 (36 of 2020), section 2(33)]

"Family" means a group of people related by blood or marriage or by adoption made in accordance with law. [Transgender Persons (Protection of Rights) Act, 2019 (40 of 2019), section 2(c)]

"Family", when used in relation to a worker, means—

(i) spouse;

(ii) children including adopted children of the worker who are dependent upon him and have not completed the age of eighteen years; and

(iii) parents, grand-parents, widowed daughter and widowed sister dependent upon such worker.

Explanation.—For the purposes of this clause, such dependents shall not be included who are, for the time being, getting such income from such sources, as may be prescribed by the appropriate Government. [Occupational Safety, Healthy & Working Conditions Code, 2020 (37 of 2020), section 2(1)(x)]

"Family" means,—

(i) the spouse and children of the person, and

(ii) the parents, grand-parents, brothers and sisters of the person if they are wholly or mainly dependent on the said person [The Central Goods and Services Tax Act, 2017 (12 of 2017), S. 2(49)]

For the purpose of this sub-clause 'FAMILY' means husband, wife, sons and unmarried daughters living jointly with him. [Madhya Pradesh Lokayukta Evam Uplokyakta Act, 1981 (37 of 1981), S. 2(b)(iv) *Explanation* as cited in *Lokayukta, Justice Ripusudan Dayal* v. *State of Madhya Pradesh*, (2014) 4 SCC 473, para 17].

For the purposes of this section, the expression 'FAMILY' shall mean the transferee, his or her wife or husband (as the case may be) and minor children, and where the transferee is a minor also his or her parents. [U.P. Zamindari Abolition and Land Reforms Act, 1950 (1 of 1951), S. 154(2), *Explanation* as cited in *State of Uttarakhand* v. *Guru Ram Das Educational Trust*, (2012) 10 SCC 648, para 5].

"FAMILY" means all or any of the following relatives of an insured person, namely:—

(i) a spouse;

(ii) a minor legitimate or adopted child dependent upon the insured person;

(iii) a child who is wholly dependent on the earnings of the insured person who is—

(a) receiving education, till he or she attains the age of twenty-one years,

(b) an unmarried daughter;

(iv) a child who is infirm by reason of any physical or mental abnormality or injury and is wholly dependent on the earnings of the insured person, so long as the infirmity continues.

(v) dependent parents. [Employees' State Insurance Act (34 of 1948), S. 2(11)]

'Family', when used in relation to a worker, means—

(i) his or her spouse, and

(ii) the legitimate and adopted children of the worker dependant upon him or her, who have not completed their eighteenth year, and includes, parents and widow sister, dependent upon him or her. [Plantation Labour Act (69 of 1951), S. 2(ee) as amended by Act No. 17 of 2010]

'FAMILY' means—

(i) in the case of male, his wife, his children whether married or unmarried, his dependent parents and his deceased son's widow and children;

Provided that if a person proves that his wife has ceased under the personal law governing him or the customary law of the community to which the spouses belong to be entitled to maintenance, she shall no longer be deemed to be a part of such person's family for the purpose of this Act unless such person subsequently intimates by express notice in writing, to the Central Government that she shall continue to be so regarded; and

(ii) in the case of female, her husband, her children, whether married or unmarried, her dependent parents, her husband's dependent parents and her deceased son's widow and children:

Provided that if a person by notice in writing to the Central Government expresses her desire to exclude her husband from the family, the husband and his dependent parents shall no longer be deemed to be a part of such person's family for the purpose of this Act, unless such person subsequently cancels in writing any such notice.

Explanation.—in either of the above two cases if the child or, as the case may be, the child of a deceased son, of a person has been adopted by another person and if under the personal law of the adopter adoption is legally recognised such a child shall be considered as excluded from the family of the first mentioned person. [Merchant Shipping Act (44 of 1958), S. 11A]

'FAMILY' in relation to an employee, shall be deemed to consist of—

(i) in the case of a male employee, himself, his wife, his children, whether married or unmarried, his dependant parents and dependant parents of his wife and the widow and children of his predeceased son, if any,

(ii) in the case of a female employee, herself, her husband, her children, whether married or unmarried, her dependant parents, and dependant parents of her husband, and the widow and children of her predeceased son, if any.

Explanation.—Where the personal law of an employee permits, the adoption by him of a child, any child lawfully adopted by him shall be deemed to be included in his family, and where a child of an employee has been adopted by another person and such adoption is, under the personal law of the person making such adoption, lawful, such child shall be deemed to be excluded from the family of the employee. [Payment of Gratuity Act (39 of 1972), S. 2(h)]

'Family', in relation to a person, includes the ascendant and descendant of such person. [Bonded

Labour System (Abolition) Act (19 of 1976), S. 2(h)]

'Family,' in relation to an operator, means his wife and dependent children and includes his dependent parents. [Dangerous Machines (Regulation) Act (35 of 1983), S. 3(g)]

'Family', in relation to an occupier, means the individual, the wife, or husband, as the case may be, of such individual, and their children, brother or sister of such individual. [Child Labour (Prohibition & Regulation) Act (61 of 1986), S. 2(v)]

For the purposes of this clause and clause (r), "FAMILY" means parents, spouse, dependent sons and daughters or such other relatives as are ordinarily living with the tenant and are dependent upon him. [Delhi Rent Act (33 of 1995), S. 22 *Expl.* II]

'Family' in relation to a person means the person, the wife or husband, as the case may be, of such person and his or her—

(i) minor sons and unmarried daughters, and

(ii) minor grandsons and unmarried granddaughters in the male line, whose father and mother are dead. [Tamil Nadu Land Reforms (Fixation of Ceiling on Land) Act (58 of 1961), S. 3(14)]

"Family", in relation to a landlord or tenant of a building, means, his or her—

(i) spouse,

(ii) male lineal descendants,

(iii) such parents, grandparents and any unmarried or widowed or divorced or judicially separated daughter or daughter of a male lineal descendant, as may have been normally residing with him or her, and includes, in relation to a landlord, any female having a legal 'right of residence in that building." [U.P. Urban Buildings (Regulation of Letting, Rent and Eviction) Act, 1972, S. 3(g)]

"Family" means the employee's spouse, legitimate children, step-children, deceased son's widow, deceased son's legitimate children, deceased son's step-children, dependent parents, sisters, minor brothers and the dependent parents of the employee's spouse. [Income-tax Rules, 1962, R. 101A(6), *Expln.*]

'Family' includes the Freedom Fighter and his/her spouse and minor dependant children. [Chandigarh Allotment of Built-up Houses/ Flats on Leasehold Hire Purchase Basis Freedom Fighters scheme (1988), Cl. 1(c) under Capital of Punjab (Development and Regulation) Act (27 of 1952), S. 3]

For the purpose of this sub-clause 'family' means such relations of the landlord as ordinarily live with him and are dependent upon him. [Haryana Urban (Control of Rent & Eviction) Act (11 of 1973), S. 13(v), *Expln.*]

"The father, the mother, and the children, ordinarily constitute a "family". A family constitutes all who live in one house under one head". (Page 303). "The word "family" is narrowed or enlarged in some instances, to include near kindred in others heirs or to embrace relations by marriage." (Page 305). *Words and Phrases. Permanent Edition*, Volume 16. Pp. 303, 305) as cited in *Payal Sawhney* v. *Meenakshi Suri,* (FB) AIR 1995 J&K 36, 43.

Hindu law—The word 'family' in its popular sense means children. *Devki Nandan* v. *Murlidar*, AIR 1957 SC 133, 139.

The word 'family' does not mean a group of persons who are recognised in law as having a right of succession or having a claim to a share in the property in dispute. *Ram Chavan* v. *Girija Nandini*, AIR 1966 SC 323, 329.

The word *family* in a will held to mean 'the testator's descendants and their wives living at the time of his death'.

Even if members of a joint Hindu Family live in different places because of their being employed in offices or carrying on other avocations the tie is strong enough to include them within the term 'family'.

'Family' means a primary social group consisting of parents and their offsprings and as such the land-holder, his wife and his offsprings consisting of three minor sons and three minor daughters constitute a family. *State of Gujarat* v. *Jat Laxmanji Talsji*, AIR 1988 SC 825, 828.

"FAMILY" for the purposes of Schedule V of Act 18 of 2013, 'family' means the spouse, dependent children and dependent parents of the managerial person. [*Explanation III* to section IV of Part II of Schedule V of the Companies Act, 2013 (18 of 2013)]

"FAMILY" includes a person, his or her spouse, minor children, minor brothers and minor sisters dependent on him:

Provided that widows, divorcees, and women deserted by families shall be considered separate families.

Explanation.—An adult of either gender with or without spouse or children or dependants shall be considered as a separate family for the purposes of Act 30 of 2013. [S. 3(m) of the Right to Fair Compensation & Transparency in Land Acquisition, Rehabilitation & Resettlement Act, 2013 (30 of 2013)]

Family agreement, arrangement, or, settlement. An agreement or arrangement made between a father and his son or children, or between brothers, and other members of a family to dispose of property in a different manner from what would otherwise take place.

Family arrangement. *Bona fides* is of the essence of the validity of a family arrangement, and a family arrangement must be concluded with the object of setting *bona fide* a dispute arising out of conflicting claims to property, which was either existing at the time or was likely to arise in future.

An arrangement entered into between the members of one family for the benefit of the family as a whole.

A family arrangement is an agreement between members of the same family intended to be generally and reasonably for the benefit of the family either by compromise of doubtful or disputed rights or by pressuring the family property or the peace and security of the family by avoiding litigation or by saving its honour. The agreement may be implied from a long course of dealings, but it is more usual to embody or to effectuate the agreement in a deed to which the term 'family arrangement' is applied. *Halsbury's Laws of England,* Third Edition Vol 17 Pages 215-216.

A family arrangement, as a matter of law, be inferred from a long course of dealings between the parties. *Sahu Madho Das* v. *Pandit Mukand Ram,* AIR 1955 SC 481.

A family arrangement is intended to bring about harmony in the family and the Courts should lean strongly in favour of such a family arrangement. *Krishna Beharilal* v. *Gulabchand,* AIR 1971 SC 1041. (*Hindu Law*)

Family Court. A Court which has jurisdiction over matters involving divorce, child custody and support, paternity, domestic violence, and other family-law issues.

Family debt. (*In Hindu Law*) No *debt* can be strictly a family debt, that is a debt binding on the family, unless it is borrowed for legal necessity or for the benefit of the estate or for any obligatory religious purposes. The test of a family debt is the purpose of the debt, not merely its antecedency.

Family in relation to a landlord or tenant of a building. FAMILY IN RELATION TO A LANDLORD OR TENANT OF A BUILDING, means : "his or her—

(i) spouse,

(ii) male lineal descendants,

(iii) such parents, grandparents and any unmarried or widowed or divorced or judicially separated daughter or daughter of a male lineal descendant, as may have been normally residing with him or her.

and includes, in relation to a landlord, any female having a legal right of residence in that building. [Uttar Pradesh Urban Building (Regulation of Letting, Rent and Eviction) Act (13 of 1972), S. 3(g)]

Family law. An area of law dealing with family relations including divorce, adoption, paternity, custody, and support.

Family mansion. A large house belonging to the family. [CPC (5 of 1908), O. XXI, R. 32, ill.].

Family member. A conceived child could not be considered as member of the family while determining ceiling area.

Family pedigree. A geneological table of the family. [Indian Evidence Act (1 of 1872), S. 32(6)].

Family pension. For the purposes of this clause "FAMILY PENSION" means a regular monthly amount payable by the employer to a person belonging to the family of an employee in the event of his death. [Income-tax Act (43 of 1961), S. 57(iia), *Expln.*]

Family Pension Fund. 'FAMILY PENSION FUND' means the 'Family Pension Fund' established under the Coal Mines Family Pension Scheme formed under sub-section (1) of Section 3E. [Coal Mines Provident Fund and Misc. Provisions Act (46 of 1948), S. 2(ee) now omitted by Act 23 of 1996, sec. 3 (w.e.f. 31-3-1998)]

Family settlement. "Family settlement" is a recognition of pre-existing rights though it may operate in the future. Such mutual recognition of rights cannot amount to a transfer. Thus there is no bar to the arrangements being effected to under the local law. [*Sriram* v. *Giridharilal,* MLJ : YD (1983), para 999 : 1982 All WC 865]. [*Hindu Law*]

Family tree. Geneological chart.

Family Unit. Family Unit means an individual, his spouse, or spouses, minor sons, unmarried minor daughters.

A seperated minor son is as much a member of the family unit as a joint son with his father. *B. Bapi Raju* v. *State of A.P.*, AIR 1983 SC 1073, 1078.

Family use. Such use as is appropriate to the individual needs of the members of a household, and to the needs of the members collectively.

Family way, In the means, with child.

Famine and scarcity affected area. Shall mean an area affected by famine or scarcity in respect of which a declaration has been made by State Government under an appropriate law by a notification in the official Gazette. [Rajasthan Bovine Animal (Prohibition of Slaughter and Regulation of Temporary Migration of Export) Act, 1995, S. 2(k)]

Famosus libellus. (*Lat.*) A scandalous libel.

False package. Means package the container of which has a fancy trade value of its own in addition to the value of the commodity contained in such package. [Standards of Weights and Measures (Pack Comm.) Rules, 1977, R. 2(f)]

Farce. A short dramatic entertainment, in which ludicrous qualities are greatly exaggerated for the purpose of exciting laughter; a short play of low comic character; dramatic piece meant merely to excite laughter; an absurdly futile proceeding.

Fare. A rate of charge for the carriage of passengers; cost of passenger's conveyance; food provided (as, bill of fare).

The price of conveyance or passage.

'FARE', means the total amount of all charges of whatever nature (including charges, if any, for provision of food or accommodation) payable to the carrier by or on behalf of a passenger in respect of his international journey. [Finance (No. 2) Act (32 of 1971), S. 44(d)]

'FARE' means money paid for a passage by land or water. This includes sums payable for season tickets or in respect of the hire of a contract carriage. [Motor Vehicles Act (4 of 1939), S. 2(6)] The Act of 1939 stands repealed by Motor Vehicles Act (59 of 1988) whose Section 2(12) says "FARES" includes sums payable for a season ticket or in respect of the hire of a contract carriage.

'FARE' means the total amount of all charges of whatever nature (including charges, if any, for provisions of food or accommodation) payable to the carrier by or on behalf of a passenger in respect of his inland journey.

(i) fuel surcharge, if any, payable and

(ii) fee, if any payable for the amenities given to the passengers and visitors at any aerodrome. [Finance Act (13 of 1989), S. 41(d)]

"FARE" means the charge levied for the carriage of passengers. [Railways Act (24 of 1989), S. 2(14)]

"FARE" means the charge levied for the carriage of passengers. [Delhi Metro Railway (Operation and Maintenance) Act (60 of 2002), S. 2(1)(e)]

Farm building. Means a structure erected on land asscried or held for the purpose of agriculture for all or any of the following purposes connected with such land or any other land belonging to or cultivated by the holder thereof, namely:—

(a) for storage of agricultural implements, manure or fodder;

(b) for the storage of agricultural produce;

(c) for sheltering cattle;

(d) for residence of members of family servants or tenants of the holder, or

(e) for any other purpose which is an integral part of his cultivating arrangement. [Maharashtra Land Revenue Code (41 of 1966), S. 2(9)]

Farm house. Dwelling place on a farm.

If the 'dwelling house' is situated in the midst of a farm or is a part of the farm, it shall be called a 'farm house'. *Municipal Corporation of Delhi* v. *Naresh Kumar,* (1997) 4 SCC 766, para 4 : AIR 1997 SC 3629.

The dwelling house on agricultural land can be construed to be a 'farm house'. *L. Kuppuswamy* v. *Superintending Engineer, T.N.E.B., Villupuram,* AIR 1998 Mad 142, 143, para 6. [Indian Electricity Act (9 of 1910), Sch. Cls. 5 & 6]

Farm product. A term applicable to an article which is produced by the soil, either under cultivation, or by nature, by labour or otherwise, and of spontaneous growth. Under some circumstances the term will embrace animals as horses, swine, sheep *etc.* And it has even been said to embrace meat, manure, and cord-wood.

Farm yard. Yard of a farm house.

Farmer. 'FARMER' means any person who—

(i) cultivates crops by cultivating the land himself; or

(ii) cultivates crops by directly supervising the cultivation of land through any other person; or

(iii) conserves and preserves, severally or jointly, with any other person any wild species or traditional varieties or adds value to such wild species or traditional varieties through selection and identification of their useful properties. [Protection of Plant Varieties and Farmers Rights Act (53 of 2001), S. 2(k)]

A person engaged in the tillage of the soil; an agriculturist; a husbandman; a man who cultivates a considerable tract of land.

One who undertakes the collection of revenue *etc.* paying a fixed sum for the proceeds. [T.P. Act (4 of 1882), S. 6(i)]; cultivator.

Farmer is one who cultivates land, whether as the freehold proprietor or tenant, for any purpose connected with agriculture.

Husbandman is one who performs manual labour in tillage, whether on his own account or as a hired servant.

Agriculturist admits the idea of scientific or theoretical farming, and farther still, the science of farming with or without the practice of it. (*Smith Syn. Dis.*)

Farmers' variety. 'FARMERS' VARIETY', means a variety which—

(i) has been traditionally cultivated and evolved by the farmers in their fields; or

(ii) is a wild relative or land race of a variety about which the farmers possess the common knowledge. [Protection of Plant Varieties and Farmers' Rights Act (53 of 2001), S. 2(l)]

Farming. The occupation of a farmer. The practice of agriculture.

Farming stock. The stock appertaining to cultivation such as harvested crops *etc.* [CPC (5 of 1908), Sch. 1, App. A, Form No. 24 (4)].

'FARMING STOCK' means crops or horticultural produce, whether growing or severed from the land, and after severance whether subjected to any treatment or process of manufacture or not; live stock, including poultry or bees and the produce and progeny thereof; and any agricultural or horticultural produce whether subjected to any treatment or process of manufacture or not; seeds and manures; agricultural vehicles, machinery, and other plant; agricultural tenants' fixtures and other agricultural fixtures which a tenant is by law authorised to remove. [(English) Agricultural Credits Act, 1928, S. 5]

Farmstead. Farm with buildings.

Farrier. "FARRIER" means a person who carries on the business of shoeing cattle. [Prevention of Cruelty to Animals (Licencing of Farriers) Rules 1965, R. 2(b)]

A farrier is defined by Johnson as (1) 'a shoer of horses,' and (2) "one who professes the medicine of horses." According to the same authority, *farriery* "is the practice of trimming the feet and cutting the diseases of horses."

Farriery. 'FARRIERY' means any work in connection with the preparation or treatment of the foot of a horse for the immediate reception of a shoe thereon, the fitting by nailing or otherwise of a shoe to the foot or the finishing off of such work to the foot. [(English) Farriers (Registration) Act, 1975, S. 18]

Fashion designer. Means any person engaged in providing service in relation to fashion designing. [Finance Act (32 of 1994), S. 65(44) now repealed by the Central Goods and Services Tax Act, 2017]

Fashion designing. Includes any activity relating to conceptualising, outlining, creating the designs and preparing patterns for costumes, apparels, garments, clothing accessories, jewellery or any other articles intended to be worn by human beings and any other service incidental thereto. [Finance Act (32 of 1994), S. 65(43) now repealed by the Central Goods and Services Tax Act, 2017]

Fast. Abstinence from food. [Indian Evidence Act (1 of 1872), S. 57(9)]; quick; rapid.

Fast dye. A fast dye need not necessarily be a deep dye. Fast colour means a colour which cannot be removed by water or possibly by sun. The colour itself may be light or deep. *State* v. *Munnilal,* AIR 1953 Punj 204.

Fastened. Attached firmly. [General Clauses Act (10 of 1897), S. 3(26) and Registration Act (16 of 1908), S. 2(6)].

Fatal. Deadly; resulting in death. [IPC (45 of 1860), S. 92, ill. (c)].

Fatal injury. A term embracing injuries resulting in death, which as used in accident and disability insurance policies is distinguished from 'disability', which embraces injuries preventing the insured from performing the work in which he is usually employed, but not resulting in death. (*Black*)

Fatawa *(Arabic)***.** A collection or digest of judicial decisions. The best known is the *fatawa Alamgiri*, compiled by order of Aurangzeb. [*P. Ramanath Aiyar's, The Law Lexicon*, 2017, LexisNexis].

Father. The male parent; a male who has begotten a child, also an adopted father, or a male ancestor more remote than a parent.

'FATHER' in the case of any one whose personal law permits adoption, includes an adoptive father. [General Clauses Act (10 of 1897), S. 3(20)]

The expression 'father' in Art. 109 includes a grandfather and even a great grand father or paternal uncle or grand uncle. *Sudarshan Prasad* v. *Radhakishan Ram,* AIR 1982 All 218, 224. [Limitation Act (36 of 1963), Art. 109]

Fatigue duty. Manual or menial work often assigned as a punishment by a member of one of the military services other than Navy. [Railway Protection Force Act (23 of 1957), S. 9(1)(ii)(b)].

Fatstock. 'FATSTOCK' means fat cattle, fat sheep and fat pigs and the carcases of those animals. [(English) Agriculture Act, 1967, S. 25]

Faujdari-Adalat. A criminal Court. Under the Muhammadan Government this was the title of a district criminal Court, sub-ordinate to the central one, called the Nizamat adalat.

Fault. 'FAULT' means wrongful act or default. [Sale of Goods Act (3 of 1930), S. 2(5)]

A slip, error or mistake [Indian Contract Act (9 of 1872), S. 150]; a default. [IPC (45 of 1860), S. 81, ill. (a)].

Favorabilia in lege sunt fiscus, dos, vita, libertas. (*Maxim*) Things favourably considered in law are the treasury, dower, life, liberty.

Favorabiliores rei potius quam actores habenter. (*Lat.*) (D. 50, 17, 125) Defenders are held to be in a more favourable position than pursuers.'

Favoritism. Showing favour in the matter of selection on circumstances other than merit.

Favour. Partiality; bias; good will; approval; affection (*Burrill*); support; help (as, cheque drawn in one's *favour;* an argument in *favour* of homerule).

"Favour" means "approval or liking; unfair preferential treatment, inclination, prejudice, predilection." [Concise Oxford English Dictionary, 11th Edn., Revised and Black's Law Dictionary, 8th Edn.) as cited in *Secretary, Ministry of Health and Welfare, Government of Maharashtra,*(2012) 13 SCC 118, para 31].

Exceptional kindness [IPC (45 of 1860), S. 109, ill. (a)]; partiality [Navy Act (62 of 1957), S. 104(1)].

Favouritism. According to *Oxford English Dictionary*, "favouritism" means—a deposition to show, or the practice of showing favour or partiality to an individual or class, to the neglect of others having equal or superior claims; under preference. Similarly, "partiality" means the quality or character of being partial, unequal state of judgment and favour of one above the other, without just reason, prejudicial or undue favouring of one person or party: or one side of a question; prejudge, unfairness, bias. [**As referred in** *CEAT Ltd.* v. *Anand Abasaheb Hawaldar*, (2006) 3 SCC 56, 61, para 12]

FAX. 'A machine that scans documents electronically and transmits a photographic image of the contents to a receiving machine by telephonic line' or a document received by such a machine. [Chambers 21st Century Dictionary, Allied publishers Ltd. (1996), **relied in** *Great Offshore Ltd.* v. *Iraniam Offshore Engg. & Construction Co.,* (2008) 14 SCC 240, 256, para 57]

Facsimile; a method of transmitting an exact copy of writing/printing over telephone lines.

FDISK. The disk-partitioning program used in DOS and several other operating systems to create the master boot record and allocate partitions for the operating system's use. (*Cyber Law*)

Fealty. In feudal law, the obligation of fidelity which the tenant owed to his lord'; fidelity. The oath taken at the admittance of every tenant, to be true to the lord of whom he holds his land; and he that holds land by the oath of fealty, has it in the freest manner. (*Tomlin*)

Fear. The emotion of pain or uneasiness caused by the sense of impending danger. [IPC (45 of 1860), S. 90].

"Fear" means "an unpleasant emotion caused by threat of danger, pain or harm; a feeling of anxiety regarding the likelihood of something unwelcome happening". [Concise Oxford English Dictionary, 11th Edn., Revised as cited in *Secretary, Ministry of Health and Welfare, Government of Maharashtra* v. *S.C. Malte*, (2012) 13 SCC 118, para 31].

Feasance. The doing or execution of an act, condition or obligation; performance.

Feasibility. Practicability; possibility.

Feasible. Capable of being done, performed, or effected; that may be accomplished or carried out; practically possible. (*Cent.*; *Webs. Dic.*)

Feature file. Means fictionalised story film exceeding 2,000 metres in length in 35 mm or corresponding length in other gauges or in video. [Cinematograph (Certification) Rules, 1983, R. 2(ix)]

Feature film. Means a full length cinematograph film produced wholly or partly in India with a format and a story woven around a number of characters where the plot is revealed mainly through dialogues and not wholly through narration, animation or cartoon depiction and does not include an advertisement film. [Cine-Workers Welfare Fund Act (33 of 1981), S. 2(c); Cine-Workers of Cinema Theatre Workers (Regulation of Employment Act (50 of 1981), S. 2(f); Cine-Workers Welfare Cess Act (30 of 1981)]

Feature writer. One who writes a feature *i.e.* a column, appearing regularly in a newspaper or magazine. [Working Journalists and Other Newspaper Employees (Conditions of Service) and Miscellaneous Provisions Act (45 of 1955), S. 2(f)].

Federal. Concerning a political society in which several states form a unity, but remain independent in internal affairs.

Federal co-operative. Means a federation of co-operative societies registered under this Act and whose membership is available only to a co-operative society or a multi-State co-operative society. [Multi-State Co-operative Societies Act (39 of 2002), S. 2(k)]

Federal purposes. The expression means the 'purposes of the Central Government'. *Abdullabhai M. Bhagat* v. *ITO*, AIR 1961 SC 1389 : (1961) 42 ITR 711.

Federalism. Federal principles of government.

Federating States. Federating States—it is a union of States, either by treaty or by legislation by the concerned states. [Constitution of India, Art. 1]

Federation. Government based on federal principles; group of states for political purposes; federated society.

A union of societies or organisations; a political unit with a central government and consisting of several States each of which claims control of its internal affairs. [Trade Unions Act (16 of 1926), S. 2(h)].

Fee, and Fee-simple. Tenant in fee-simple, is he who has lands or tenements to hold to him and his heirs for ever. (*Tomlin*)

Fee, Fees. FEES, are a charge or emolument, or compensation for particular acts or services; reward or compensation for services rendered or to be rendered,—a payment in money for official or professional services, whether the amount be optional or fixed by custom; compensation paid to professional men, as an attorney or physician; the reward or compensation allowed by law to an officer for specific services performed by him in the discharge of his official duties; frequently for services rendered in the progress of a cause, to be paid by the parties obtaining the benefit of the acts, or receiving the services, at whose instances they were performed. Sometimes the term may mean charges, and is often used interchangeably with the term 'costs'.

A 'fee' is generally defined to be a charge for special service rendered to individuals by some governmental agency. The amount of fee levied is supposed to be based on the expenses incurred by the Government in rendering the service though in many cases the costs are arbitrarily assessed. *Commissioner H.R.E.* v. *Sri Lakshmindra Thirtha Swamiar Sri Shirur Mutt,* AIR 1954 SC 282, 295.

A levy by a public authority in return for certain functions performed by it; professional or other remuneration.

"FEE" means the amount payable in pursuance of the provisions of the Act and these rules for any petition or application or interlocutory application or a document or for certified copy of document or order of the Tribunal or such other paper as may be specified in Schedule of Fees to these rules and includes any modifications as may be made thereto or any fee as prescribed for filing of documents to the Tribunal by these rules. [National Company Law Tribunal Rules, 2016, R. 2(12)].

Fee simple. An estate of inheritance; estate in absolute ownership.

Fee-tail. Free-hold property entailed in a certain line of descent.

Feeble minded. Person of severe sub-normality.

Feed end. The point from where material is furnished. [Factories Act (63 of 1948), S. 27, prov.].

Feed-oats. Feed-oats come under the category of grain in item 42 of the schedule. *Collector of Customs* v. *K. Ganga Setty*, AIR 1963 SC 1319, 1321. [Import Trade Control Schedule.]

Feed-pipe. "FEED-PIPE" means any pipe or connected fitting wholly or partly under pressure through which feed-water passes directly to a boiler and which does not form an integral part thereof. [Indian Boilers Act (5 of 1923), S. 2(ccc)]

Feeding bottle. Means any bottle or receptacle used for the purpose of feeding infant milk substitutes, and includes a teat and a valve attached or capable of being attached to such bottle or receptacle. [Infant Milk Substitutes, Feeding Bottles and Infant Foods (Regulation of Production, Supply and Distribution) Act (41 of 1992), S. 2(c)]

Feeding the estoppel. The doctrine of 'feeding the estoppel' can apply only where the alienor, vendor, or mortgagor, makes a fraudulent or erroneous representation that he was authorised to transfer interest in the property by virtue of an absolute title possessed by him. It is only in such case the subsequent enlargement of the interest of the alienor or transferor will benefit the transferee; in such a case, an heir or a person claiming under the alienor may be equally estopped. [Hindu Succession Act (30 of 1956), S. 14]

Feeling. Organic sensation; consciousness by touch etc; bodily consciousness; [Indian Evidence Act (1 of 1872), S. 14]; emotion.

Fees. Means the fees as specified in the Companies (Registration Offices and Fees) Rules, 2014. [R. 2(1)(c) of the Companies (Authorised to Registered) Rules, 2014]

Fees and **Taxes.** Fees taken in Court cannot be equated to taxes. *The Secretary Govt. of Madras, Home Department* v. *Zenith Lamps And Electricals Ltd.*, AIR 1973 SC 724, 729. [Constitution of India, Sch 7, List 2, Entry 3]

Feign. To give a sham appearance of. [Army Act (46 of 1950), S. 46(b)].

Fellowship. A sum of money granted for advanced study or research; the stipend of a fellow of an educational institution; the state of being a member of a university.

Felo de se. Self murderer. A man of the age of discretion, and *compos mentis*, who voluntarily kills himself, by stabbing, poison, or any other way. One who deliberately puts an end to his own existence, or commits an unlawful, malicious act, the consequence of which is his own death.

One who feloniously commits suicide. [Coroners Act (4 of 1871), S. 30].

Felon. One who has committed felony; one convicted of felony.

Felonia implicatur in qualibet proditione. (*Lat.*) (3 Inst. 15) Felony is implied in every treason.

Felony. Crime of any kind,—legally graver than misdemeanour.

Female line. The line of ascent or descent through woman. [Hindu Succession Act (30 of 1956), S. 3(1)(h)(b)].

Fence. A barrier intended to prevent intrusion; to put such barrier. [CrPC, 1973 (2 of 1974), S. 133(1)(e)]; to practise the art of attack and defence with sword and the like.

Feoffment. The historical method of granting a freehold estate in land by actual delivery of possession orig. by livery of seisin.

Ferae naturae. Beasts and birds of a wild disposition, such as deer, hares, pheasants, partridges & c. as distinguished from those *domitac naturae*, or tame, such as horses, sheep, poultry, & co. (*Wharton*)

Fermented liquor. A 'FERMENTED LIQUOR' means malt liquor, wine, pachwai and fermented tari, and shall, if the Local Government, subject to the control of the Governor-General in Council, so directs include any other fermented liquor, and also tari, though it may not have perceptibly begun to ferment. [Excise Act (12 of 1896), S. 3, repealed by the Excise Act, 1896 S. 2 and Schedule.].

Ferocious. Fierce; savage. [Indian Evidence Act (1 of 1872), S. 14, ill. (c)].

Ferry. Includes a bridge of boats, pontoons or rafts, a swing bridge, a flying bridge and a temporary bridge, and the approaches to, and landing-places of, a ferry and "Punjab" and "Ajmer" mean the territories which, immediately before the 1st November, 1956, were comprised in the State of Punjab and Ajmer, respectively. [Northern India Ferries Act (17 of 1878), S. 3]

"FERRY" includes a bridge of boats, pontoons or rafts a swing bridge, a fly-bridge and a temporary bridge and the approaches to and landing places of a ferry. [Indian Railways Act, 1989 (24 of 1989), S. 2(15)]

A ferry is a franchise or exclusive right of carrying passengers, animals or goods across a river or other body of water at a particular place, and taking a toll for so doing, which is called ferriage.

Fertilisation means the penetration of the ovum by the spermatozoan and fusion of genetic materials resulting in the development of a zygote. [Surrogacy (Regulation) Act, 2021 (47 of 2021), section 2(1)(l)]

Fertilizer. 'FERTILISERS' means such oil-based chemical compounds which when employed in agriculture provide either single or multiple plant nutrients in any one or more of the forms of nitrogen, phosphorus and potash. [Oil Industry (Development) Act (47 of 1974), S. 2(f)]

A substance used to fertilize the soil *e.g.* a chemical manure.

Festinatio justitiae est noverca infortunii. (*Maxim*) Hasty justice is the step-mother of misfortune. (*Black*)

Festival. Festal day; merry making.

A time of festive celebration. [Indian Evidence Act (1 of 1872), S. 57(9)].

Festive occasion. For the purposes of this sub-rule, the expressions "festive occasion" shall include any National function or State function as notified by the Central Government or State Government. [Noise Pollution (Regulation and Control) Rules, 2000, R. 5(3), *Explanation* (*i*)].

Fete. Festival; great entertainment.

Feticide. Abortion has been defined authoritatively as 'feticide'—the intentional destruction of the fetus (foetus) in the womb or any untimely delivery brought about with the intent to cause the death of the fetus (foetus). [Butterworth's *Medico-Legal Encyclopaedia*]

Fetish. A symbol arousing sexual excitation; the substituting of a part of an article for the sexual object.

Fettering. The act of shackling or placing manacles on another.

Feuda ad instar patrimoniorum sunt redacta. (*Maxim*) Lands held in fee are reduced to the character of a patrimony or succession. (*Trayner*)

Feudal law. The law of feuds or feudal estates; the system of law by which the creation, enjoyment and transmission of feudal estates were regulated, and the rights and duties growing out of the relation of lord and vassal defined and enforced.

Feudal system. The system of feuds. "A political and social system which prevailed throughout Europe during the eleventh, twelfth and thirteenth centuries." Medieval European polity based on relation of vassel and superior arising from holding of lands in feud; the system of feuds or fiefs; a system of tenure, the origin of which is traced to the peculiar policy and usages of the northern nations who overturned the Roman empire and settled in its province.

Fiat jus, ruat justitia. (*Lat.*) Let law prevail, though Justice fail.

Fiat justitia. (*Lat.*) Let justice be done.

Fiat justitia, ruat coelum. Let justice be done, though heavens fall.

Fictio cedit veritati; fictio juris non est ubi veritas. (*Lat.*) (11 Rep. 51) Fiction yields to truth; where there is truth, fiction of law exists not.

Fictio est contra veritatem, sed pro veritate habetur. Fiction is against the truth, but it is to be esteemed truth.

Fictio juris non est ubi veritas. Where truth is, fiction of law does not exist.

Fictio legis inique operatur alicui damnum vel injuriam. (*Lat.*) (3 Rep. 36) A legal fiction does not properly work loss or injury.

Fictio legis neminem laedit. (*Maxim*) A fiction of law injures no one. (*Bouvier*)

Fictio legis non operatur damnum vel injuriam. A legal fiction does not work loss or injustice.

Fiction. (*in law.*) A false averment on the part of the plaintiff which the defendant is not allowed to traverse, the object being to give the Court jurisdiction. (*Main. Anc. Law*)

Fiction of law. A supposition of law that a thing is bad without inquiring whether it be so or not that it may have the effect of truth so far as is consistent with justice *e.g.* ejectnent, fine, trover *etc.*

Fictitious. Feigned, assumed, imaginary, not real, counterfeit, false, not genuine; regarded as a legal fiction.

Fictitious entry. A fabricated entry is obviously a fictitious entry. *Bachan* v. *Kankar*, AIR 1972 SC 2151, 2160.

Fictitious person. An imaginary person. [IPC (45 of 1860), S. 464, *Expln.* 2].

Fictitious stamp. "FICTITIOUS STAMP" means any stamp falsely purporting to be issued by government for the purpose of denoting a rate of postage or any facsimile on imitation or representation, whether on paper or otherwise, of any stamp issued by government for that purpose. [IPC (45 of 1860), S. 263A(3)] [Now (w.e.f. 1-7-2024) repealed & replaced by Bharatiya Nyaya Sanhita, 2023 (45 of 2023), section 186(3), same definition in new Sanhita]

A spurious stamp.

Fidelity. Loyalty; faithfulness; conformity to fact and truth; honesty.

The quality of being faithful; faithfulness; loyalty to a person, party *etc.* [Indian Contract Act (9 of 1872), S. 139, ill. (c)].

In insurance terminology, the word 'fidelity' is understood as assurance to indemnify against loss consequent upon the dishonesty or default. *Food Corporation of India* v. *New India Assurance Co. Ltd.*, AIR 1994 SC 1889, 1894. [Indian Contract Act (9 of 1872), Ss. 28, 23]

Fidelity bond. A bond for faithfulness.

Fides servanda. (*Maxim*) Good faith must be observed. (*Bouvier*)

Fiducial relation. "Fiducial relation : confidential relation." There is a technical distinction between a 'fiducial relation' which is more correctly applicable to legal relationship between parties, such as guardian and ward, administrator and heirs, and other similar relationships, and 'confidential relation' which includes the legal relationships, and also every other relationship wherein confidence is rightly reposed and is exercised. [Words and Phrases, Permanent Edn. (Vol. 16-A, p. 41) as cited in *Marcel Martins* v. *M. Printer*, (2012) 5 SCC 342, para 33].

Fiduciary. *As a noun,* a trustee, a person holding the character of a trustee, or a character analogous to that of a trustee. *As an adjective,* in the nature of a trust; having the characteristics of a trust; analogous to a trust; relating to or founded upon a trust or confidence.

Generally, the term 'fiduciary' applies to any person who occupies a position of peculiar confidence towards another. It refers to integrity and fidelity. It contemplates fair dealing and good faith, rather than legal obligation, as the basis of the transaction. The term includes those informal relations which exist whenever one party trusts and relies upon another, as well as technical fiduciary relations. [Words and Phrases, Permanent Edn. (Vol. 16-A, p. 41) as cited in *Marcel Martins* v. *M. Printer*, (2012) 5 SCC 342, para 33].

"What constitutes a fiduciary relationship is often a subject of controversy. It has been held to apply to all persons who occupy a position of peculiar confidence towards others, such as a trustee, executor, or administrator, director of a corporation or society, medical or religious advisor, husband and wife, an agent who appropriates money put into his hands for a specific purpose of investment, collector of city taxes who retains money officially collected, one who receives a note or other security for collection. In the following cases debt has been held to be not a fiduciary one: a factor who retains the money of his principal, an agent under an agreement to account and pay over monthly, one with whom a general deposit of money is made." [Bouvier's Law Dictionary as cited in *Marcel Martins* v. *M. Printer*, (2012) 5 SCC 342, para 36].

"Fiduciary capacity' implies a relationship that is analogous to the relationship between a trustee and the beneficiaries of the trust. The expression is in fact wider in its import for it extends to all such situation as place the parties in positions that are founded on confidence and trust on the one part and good faith on the other. [*Marcel Martins* v. *M. Printer*, (2012) 5 SCC 342, para 37].

Of or pertaining to, or of the nature of, trust or reliance. [T.P. Act (4 of 1882), S. 55(2), prov.].

Fiduciary capacity. One is said to act in a "fiduciary capacity" or receive money or contract a debt in a "fiduciary capacity," when the business which he transacts, or the money or property which he handles, is not his own or for his own benefit, but for the benefit of another person as to whom he stands in a relation implying and necessitating great confidence and trust on the one part and a high degree of good faith on the other part. The term is not restricted to technical or express trusts, but includes also such offices or relations as those of all attorney at law, a guardian, executor, or broker, a director of a corporation, and a public officer. (*Black*)

Position or character founded in trust or confidence. [CPC (5 of 1908), S. 51, prov. (c)].

Fiduciary contract. An agreement by which a person delivers a thing to another on the condition that he will restore it to him; a contract based on mutual trust and confidence.

Fiduciary duty. The duty of loyalty that requires confidentiality and prohibits conflict of interest.

Fiduciary position. A position of trust or confidence. If a person occupies a fiduciary position towards another, it is his duty, like a trustee, to protect the interests of such person, and he cannot use such position to benefit himself.

Fiduciary relationship. "Fiduciary relationship" is a relationship in which one person is under a duty to act for the benefit of the other on matters within the scope of the relationship. Fiduciary relationship—such as trustee-beneficiary, guardian-ward, agent-principal, and attorney-client require the highest duty of care. Fiduciary relationships usually arise in one of four situations: (1) When one person places trust in the faithful integrity of another, who as a result gains superiority or influence over the first, (2) when one person assumes control and responsibility over another, (3) when one person has a duty to act for or give advice to another on matters falling within the scope of the relationship, or (4) when there is a specific relationship that has traditionally been recognized as involving fiduciary duties, as with a lawyer and a client or a stockbroker and a customer. [Black's Law Dictionary (7th Edn., p. 640) as cited in *Marcel Martins* v. *M. Printer*, (2012) 5 SCC 342, para 34].

Fief. A charge for labour or services, specially professional services.

Field. A place where battle is fought; an area of active military operation; [Air Force Act (45 of 1950), S. 77]; a piece of ground enclosed for tillage or pasture.

Field firing. In this chapter, 'FIELD FIRING' includes air armament practice. [Manoeuvres, Field Firing and Artillery Practice Act (5 of 1938), S. 8(a)]

Field of selection. Means the list of eligible officers, arranged in the order of their seniority, from which selections shall be made for inclusion in the Select List. [Armed Forces Headquarters Civil Service Rules, 2018, R. 2(f)].

Field notes. A record of the measurements made by a surveyor or of the observations made by a searcher in the field. [Mines Act (35 of 1952), S. 57(u)].

Field Officer. A military officer above the rank of Captain and below the rank of General. [Army Act (46 of 1950), S. 83].

Field punishment. A kind of penal servitude for offence. [Army Act (46 of 1950), S. 75, omitted by the Army Amendment Act of 1992, S.2, w.e.f 06-09-1992].

Field Strength. Means Electric field strength (dbμA/m) of the radio sign' [Use of Very Low Power Radio Frequency Devices or Equipments for Inductive Applications (Exemption from Licensing Requirement) Rules, 2015, R. 3(d)].

Fifteen clear days. When so many clear days or so many days 'at least' are given to do an act or 'not less than' so many days are to intervene both the terminal days are excluded from the computation. *Satyanarayana Agarwal* v. *Baidyanath Mandal,* AIR 1972 Pat 29, 32. [Arbitration Act (10 of 1940) (*repealed*), S. 9(b)]

Fifteen days notice. If a notice gives at least 15 days to the tenant and if it expires with the end of the month of tenancy it is a good notice to determine the lease. The period should not be less than 15 days but there is no outside limit; the notice can be given several months before the date on which the landlord desires to determine the lease. *Motilal Pannalal* v. *Kailash Narain, MLJ : QD* 56-60 Vol. IV C 2741 : 1960 MPC 365 : 1960 MPLJ 87 : 1960 Jab LJ 190 : AIR 1960 MP 134. [T.P. Act (4 of 1882), S. 106]

Fight. To strike or contend for victory, in the battle or in single combat; to attempt to defeat, subdue, or destroy an enemy, either by blows or weapons. (*Webster.)*

Verbal abuses are not fight as it is well settled that at least two persons are needed to fight. [*State of Orissa* v. *Khaga,* (2013) 14 SCC 649, para 10].

The word 'fight' occurring in Section 300 Excep. IPC postulates a bilateral transaction in which blows are exchanged between the parties. *Sikander* v. *State,* (1999) 3 SCC 569, para 5 : AIR 1999 SC 1406. [IPC (45 of 1860), S. 300, Excep. 4]

A fight is a combat between two or more persons with or without weapons. *Dhirajbhai Gorakhbhai Nayak* v. *State of Gujarat,* (2003) 9 SCC 322, para 11. [IPC (45 of 1860), S. 300, Excep. 4]

The word 'fight' occurring in Section 300, Exception 4, means a combat between two and more persons whether with or without weapons. *Ghappoo Yadav* v. *State of M.P.,* (2003) 3 SCC 528, para 10 : AIR 2003 SC 1620. [IPC (45 of 1860), S. 300, Exception 4]

More than a verbal quarrel; should not have been pre-arranged; not a *per se* palliating circumstance. [IPC (45 of 1860), S. 300, Exception 4]

Figure. A character or symbol representing a number [Indian Evidence Act (1 of 1872), Ss. 3 and 73]; form; shape [IPC (45 of 1860), S. 29(a)].

The numerical characters by which numbers are denoted, expressed or written.

Figure head. The head in the figure; a nominal head.

Filature. The realing of silk [Central Silk Board Act (61 of 1948), S. 4(3)(d)].

Filature raw silk. Means a raw silk reeled from silk work cocoons with the help of any instrument worked by power. [Central Silk Board Act (61 of 1948), S. 3(c)]

File. A collection of data grouped into one unit on a disk. (*Cyber Law*)

To place on file; to deliver as a legal paper or instrument after complying with any conditions precedent (as the payment of the fee) to the proper officer.

File allocation table. (FAT or FAT32) DOS uses the FAT to manage the disk data area. The FAT tells DOS which portions of the disk belong to each file. The FAT links together all of the clusters belonging to each file, no matter where they are on disk. The FAT is a critical file: You should be sure to back it up regularly. FAT32 is a newer type of FAT, which was designed to handle large hard disks. The older FAT (FAT16) can only support partitions up to two gigabytes in size. FAT32 can handle partitions that are thousands of gigabytes. (*Cyber Law*)

File name. The name or alphanumeric code you have given the system to identify a particular document (*Computer*)

File slack. File slack potentially contains randomly selected bytes of data from computer memory. This happens because DOS/Windows normally writes in 512 bytes blocks called "sectors." Clusters are made up of blocks of sectors. If there is not enough data in the file to fill the last sector in a file, DOS/Windows makes up the difference by padding the remaining space with data from the memory buffers of the operating system. This randomly selected data from memory is called "RAM Slack" because it comes from the memory of the computer. RAM Slack can contain any information that may have been created, viewed, modified, downloaded, or copied during work sessions that have occurred since the computer was last booted. Thus, if the computer has not been shut down for several days, the data stored in the file slack can come from work sessions that occurred in the past. (*Cyber Law*)

File system. The word 'file' according to the Law Lexicon means to deposit with the proper custodian for keeping; to place in the official custody of the clerk; to put upon the files of among the records of a Court. *Gopalkrishnan Iyer* v. *Padmanabhan,* AIR 1972 Ker 96, 97. [Provincial Insolvency Act (5 of 1920), S. 10(2)]

A system for organizing directories and files, generally in terms of how it is implemented in the disk-operating system. (*Cyber Law*)

File Transfer Protocol (FTP). An application protocol that offers file system access from the Internet suite of protocols. (*Information Technology*)

System that moves files from one computer to another. (*Cyber Law*)

Filer. "Filer" means an authorized representative of that person or any party to the proceeding who files any document with the Tribunal in relation to a case filed under the Act, or any rules thereunder. [National Company Law Tribunal Rules, 2016, R. 2(13)] [Companies Act, (18 of 2013)].

Filleting. Cutting into pieces or slices of fish. [Marine Products Export Development Authority Act (13 of 1973), S. 3(l)].

Film. Means motion picture or sound recording film having a nitrocelluloe base whether in the form of exposed or unexposed film, positives, negatives, scraped or used film. [Cinematograph Film Rules, 1948, R. 3(g)]

'FILM' means a cinematograph film. [Cinematograph Act (37 of 1952), S. 2(dd)]

Film artist. Means any person engaged in his professional capacity in the production of a cinematograph film whether produced by him or by any other person, as—

(i) an actor;

(ii) a cameraman;

(iii) a director, including an assistant director;

(iv) a music director, including an assistant music director;

(v) an art director, including an assistant art director;

(vi) a dance director, including an assistant dance director;

(vii) an editor;

(viii) a singer;

(ix) a lyricist;

(x) a story writer;

(xi) a screen-play writer;

(xii) a dialogue writer; and

(xiii) a dress designer. [Income-tax Rules, 1962, R. 6F(2), *Expln.* (c)]

Film cement. Means any compound of collodian, amylacetate or similarly combustible cements used for repairing film. [Cinematograph Film Rules, 1948, R. 3(h)]

Film software. Means a copy of a cinematograph film made by any process analogous to cinematography on acetate polyester or celluloid film positive, magnetic tape, digital media or other optical or magnetic devices and certified by the Board of film certification constituted by the Central Government under Section 3 of the Cinematograph Act, 1952 (37 of 1952). [Income-tax Act (43 of 1961), S. 80HHF, *Expln.* (d)]

Filter. To purify; to make a liquid flow down through a porus substance, so as to keep off the dross and send down the pure matter.

Filtering. The word 'filtering' is not synonym of the word purifying under Heading 84.21 of the Act. It is one method of purification. *A.P. Industrial Components Ltd.* v. *CCE,* (2000) 10 SCC 5, para 1. [Central Excise Tariff Act, 1985 (5 of 1986), Heading 84.21]

Filth. "FILTH" includes offensive matter and sewage. [New Delhi Municipal Council Act (44 of 1994), S. 2(15]

"FILTH" includes sewage, excreta, dung, putrid and putrifying substances and all other substances causing danger to public health, if not removed. [Kerala Municipality Act, (Kerala Act No. 20 of 1994), S. 2(18) as amended by Kerala Act No. 8 of 1995]

Filthy. Dirty, vulgar, indecent, obscene, lewd, offensive to the moral sense, morally depriving, debasing.

Filtration. Separation of a software program's unprotected ideas from protected expression. (*Cyber Law*)

Filum. An imaginary thread or line passing through the middle of a stream or road.

Filum aquae. The middle line of a stream or body of water.

Final. In its ordinary signification, last; that which absolutely ends or concludes a matter (as, final decision) precluding further controversy on the question passed upon; that which terminates or ends a matter or proceeding not absolutely, however sometimes it may mean conclusive.

"The expression 'final' prima facie connotes that an order passed on appeal under the Act is conclusive and no further appeal lies against it." [*South Asia Industries (P.) Ltd.* v. *S.B. Sarup Singh*, AIR 1965 SC 1442, para 17 : (1965) 2 SCR 756 as cited in *Presiding Officer, Court of Inquiry* v. *Sunil Issar*, (2013) 11 SCC 695, para 24]. [Delhi Rent Control Act, 1958, S. 43].

Ultimate; conclusive. [Indian Partnership Act (9 of 1932), S. 37 and Constitution of India, Art. 108(4), prov.]

Final and binding. Clause in Section 35 of the Arbitration and Conciliation Act, 1996 does not mean final for all intents and purposes. The finality is subject to any recourse that an aggrieved party might have under a statute or an agreement providing for arbitration in the second instance. The award is binding in a limited context. [*Centrotrade Minerals and Metal Inc.* v. *Hindustan Copper Limited*, (2017) 2 SCC 228, para 36].

Final and **conclusive.** A person gives a *final* judgment; but in order to make it *conclusive* it must be satisfactory to all parties (*i.e.*) not be taken in appeal by any dissatisfied party.

Use of words 'final' or 'final and conclusive' in a statute does not prevent judicial review altogether of orders of Sub-ordinate Courts or Tribunals or interference by the superior Courts in the exercise of the superior courts of supervisory and *certiorari* jurisdiction. *Union of India* v. *P.M. Paul,* AIR 1985 Ker 206, 213. [Arbitration Act (10 of 1940) (*repealed*), Ss. 5, 12. 39]

Final decision. A decision *obiter* of any question not necessary to the disposal of the suit is not a final decision.

A preliminary decree in a mortgage suit or a partition suit must in so far as the matters dealt with by it are concerned, be regarded as conclusive. The finality of a decree does not necessarily depend upon its being executable. *Venkata Reddy* v. *Pethi Reddy*, AIR 1963 SC 992, 995 [Provincial Insolvency Act (5 of 1920) as amended in 1948. S. 28-A].

Final decree does not mean last decree, but decree determining rights finally.

A decree which concludes the proceedings of a case.

Final hearing. The stage of proceedings relating to the determination of a subject matter upon its merits.

Final judgment. A judgment which is not subject to appeal.

Final Offer Arbitration. Is wherein parties to the dispute present their claims before a panel that decides to grant or reject a claim which is valid and enforceable. [Karnika Seth, *Computers Internet and New Technology Laws*, 2021, LexisNexis, Glossary of Legal Terms].

Final order. The term "final order" in S. 109 of the Code of Civil Procedure, denotes an order which finally decides any matter directly at issue in the case in respect of the right of the parties.

The test of finality is whether the order in question finally disposes of the rights of the parties and the court is not concerned with the question whether the cardinal points in the suit had been determined.

"FINAL ORDER" in Indian Stamp Act (2 of 1899), Art. 45(C) refers to the final order of the lowest Court of original jurisdiction empowered to give an order for effecting a partition at the time it is passed.

For the purposes of this article, the expression "FINAL ORDER" includes an order deciding an issue which, if decided in favour of the appellant, would be sufficient for the final disposal of the case. [Constitution of India, Article 132, *Explanation*

Final order passed on appeal. An order passed by the High Court in the exercise of its revisional jurisdiction, under S. 115 of the Code of Civil Procedure (5 of 1908).

Where the order of the single Judge sought to be appealed from is made merely for appointment of an arbitrator, it having decided no question of right, is not a final order.

An order directing the appointment of a receiver was not a final order.

In order to constitute a final order it is necessary that the order should be one by which the suit or the proceeding is finally disposed of whichever way the decision went. The decision of an important or vital issue which may ultimately affect the fate of the proceeding is by itself not enough.

An order is final if it accounts to a final decision relating to the rights of the parties in dispute in a civil proceeding. If after the order, the civil proceeding still remains to be tried and the rights in dispute between the parties have to be determined, the order is not a final order. *Jethanand & Sons* v. *State of U.P.*, AIR 1961 SC 794, 796.

Order of High Court rejecting application for condonation of delay in filing appeal is not final order since there was no adjudication of the rights of the parties.

Final perimeter. Means the final inspection site perimeter as agreed in negotiations between the inspection team and the inspected State Party, in accordance with Part X, paragraphs 16 to 21, of this Annex: [Chemical Weapons Convention Act (34 of 2000), (Verification Annex) 21(c)]

Final place of destination. Means a place in a country in which the goods are ultimately imported and cleared through Customs of that country. [Foreign Exchange Management (Transfer or Issue of any Foreign Security) Regulations, 2000, Reg. 7]

Final products. Means excisable goods, manufactured or produced from inputs, except matches. [CENVAT Credit Rules, 2002, R. 2(e)]

Final withdrawal. The expression 'final withdrawal' occurring in R. 3(3) of the Rules would mean the final withdrawals made by an employee while continuing in service for the purposes mentioned in clause 5-C (2) of the Regulations. *Hari Ram Gupta* v. *State of U.P.,* AIR 1998 SC 2483. [U.P Palika (Contralised) Service Retirement Benefits Rules, 1981, R. 3(3) and Pension and General Provident Fund Regulations, cl. 5-C (2)]

Finality of order. An order under S. 23, Provincial Small Cause Courts Act (9 of 1887) returning a plaint to be presented to the regular Courts, is final, and confers jurisdiction on the latter.

Finally. At the end or conclusion; ultimately; at last; lastly. Conclusively; so as to make an end. (*Cent.*)

Finally decided. A matter cannot be considered to be finally decided, unless in point of fact it was actually decided by all the tribunals before which that particular matter came for decision. [CPC (5 of 1908), S. 11]

An issue cannot be said to be finally decided, unless the decree is based on the finding thereon, and unless the party affected thereby has had an opportunity of appealing against it.

Prior applications should have been decided on merits. *Revathi* v. *Venkataraman,* AIR 1951 Mad 745. [CPC (5 of 1908), S. 10]

Finally heard and decided. No Court shall try any suit or issue in which the matter directly and substantially in issue has been directly and substantially in issue in a former suit between the same parties, or between parties under whom they or any of them claim, litigating under the same title, in a Court competent to try such subsequent suit or the suit in which such issue has been subsequently raised and has been heard and finally decided by such Court. [CPC (5 of 1908), S. 11]

Finance. Pecuniary resources of the state (termed public finance), a company or person; science of revenue.

The pecuniary resources of a government or a company; to provide with necessary funds.

Financial accommodation. Something done to oblige, usually spoken of a loan of money or commercial paper. [Reserve Bank of India Act (2 of

1934), S. 2(biii), omitted by the Act 61 of 1981, S. 61 and Schedule 11, w.e.f 12-07-1982.].

Financial asset. "FINANCIAL ASSET" means debt or receivables and includes—

(i) a claim to any debt or receivables or part thereof, whether secured or unsecured; or

(ii) any debt or receivables secured by, mortgage of, or charge on, immovable property; or

(iii) a mortgage, charge, hypothecation or pledge of movable property; or

(iv) any right or interest in the security, whether full or part underlying such debt or receivables; or

(v) any beneficial interest in property, whether movable or immovable, or in such debt, receivables, whether such interest is existing, future, accruing, conditional or contingent; or

(va) any beneficial right, title or interest in any tangible asset given on hire or financial lease or conditional sale or under any other contract which secures the obligation to pay any unpaid portion of the purchase price of such asset or an obligation incurred or credit otherwise provided to enable the borrower to acquire such tangible asset; or

(vb) any right, title or interest on any intangible asset or licence or assignment of such intangible asset, which secures the obligation to pay any unpaid portion of the purchase price of such intangible asset or an obligation incurred or credit otherwise extended to enable the borrower to acquire such intangible asset or obtain licence of the intangible asset; or;

(vi) any financial assistance. [Securitisation and Reconstruction of Financial Assets and Enforcement of Security Interest Act (54 of 2002), S. 2(1)(l) amended by Act 44 of 2016, (w.e.f. 1-9-2016]

Any asset that is cash or will yield or can be converted to cash.

Financial assistance. Means any loan or advance granted or any debentures or bonds subscribed or any guarantees given or letters of credit established or any other credit facility extended by any bank or financial institution. [Securitisation and Reconstruction of Financial Assets and Enforcement of Security Interest Act (54 of 2002), S. 2(1)(k)]

"FINANCIAL ASSISTANCE" means any kind of financial assistance given—

(i) for establishing, expanding, modernising, renovating or running any industrial undertaking; or

(ii) for the purpose of vocational training; or

(iii) for the development, of agriculture or agro industry; or

(iv) for the purpose of any other kind of planned development recognised by the State Govt.; or

(v) for relief against distress caused by fire or serious drought, flood or other natural calamities; or

(vi) for the purpose of carrying out any state sponsored scheme;

(vii) for any other prescribed purpose. [Gujarat Public Money (Recovery of Dues) Act (17 of 1979), S. 2(d)].

Financial business. The business of the House Parliament/Legislature which relates directly either to expenditure or taxation and is transacted under specially devised forms in Committees and the House. Financial business includes any business which the Speaker/ Chairman holds as coming within this category under the Constitution; the procedure in relation to financial business in the House is to be regulated by law.

Financial commitment. Means the amount of direct investment by way of contribution to equity and loan and 50 per cent of the amount of guarantees issued by an Indian. [Foreign Exchange Management (Transfer or Issue of any Foreign Security) Regulations, 2000, Reg. 2(f)]

Financial company. "FINANCIAL COMPANY" means a company, other than a company referred to in sub-clause (i), (ii) or (iii) of clause (5A), being—

(i) a hire-purchase finance company, that is to say, a company which carries on, as its principal business, hire-purchase transactions or the financing of such transactions;

(ii) an investment company, that is to say, a company which carries on, as its principal business, the acquisition of shares, stock, bonds, debentures, debenture stock or securities issued by the Government or a local authority, or other marketable securities of a like nature;

(iii) a housing finance company, that is to say, a company which carries on, as its principal business, the business of financing of acquisition or construction of houses, including acquisition or development of land in connection therewith;

(iv) a loan company, that is to say, a company [not being a company referred to in sub-clauses (i) to (iii)] which carries on, as its principal business, the business of providing finance, whether by making loans or advances or otherwise;

(v) a mutual benefit finance company, that is to say, a company which carries on, as its principal business; the business of acceptance of deposits from its members and which is declared by the Central Government under Section 620 A of the Companies Act, 1956, to be a Nidhi or Mutual Benefit Society;

(vi) a residuary non-banking company other than a financial company referred to in sub-clause (i), (ii), (iii), (iv) or (v), that is to say, a company which receives any deposit under any scheme or arrangement, by whatever name called, in one lump sum or in installments by way of contributions or subscriptions or by sale of units or certificates or other instruments or in any other manner;

(vii) a miscellaneous finance company, that is to say, a company which carries on exclusively, or almost exclusively, two or more classes of business referred to in the preceding sub-clauses. [Interest-tax Act (45 of 1974), S. 2(7)].

Financial contract. Means any spot, forward, future, option or swap transaction involving interest rates, commodities, currencies, shares, bonds, debentures or any other financial instrument, any repurchase of securities and lending transaction or any other similar transaction or combination of such transactions entered into in the financial markets. [S. 2(k) of the Factoring Regulation Act, 2011 (12 of 2012)]

Financial corporation. A corporate body formed with the object of financing industrial undertakings.

'FINANCIAL CORPORATION' means a financial corporation established under Section 3 and includes a joint financial corporation established under Section 3A [State Financial Corporation Act (63 of 1951), S. 2(b)]

Financial establishment. "Financial establishment" means "any person or group of individuals or a firm carrying on business of accepting deposits under any scheme or arrangement or any other manner but does not include a corporation or a cooperative society owned or controlled by any State Government or the Central Government, or a banking company as defined under section 5 of the Banking Regulation Act, 1949." [Pondicherry Protection of Interests of Depositors in Financial Establishment Act, 2004 (1 of 2005), S. 2(d) as cited in *New Horizon Sugar Mills Limited* v. *Government of Pondicherry*, (2012) 10 SCC 575, para 20].

Financial institution. Means—

(*a*) a scheduled bank;

(*b*) financial institution as defined in Section 45-I of the Reserve Bank of India Act, 1934 (2 of 1934);

(*c*) public financial institution as defined in clause (72) of Section 2 of the Companies Act, 2013 (18 of 2013); and

(*d*) such other institution as the Central Government may by notification specify as a financial institution. [Insolvency and Bankruptcy Code (31 of 2016), S. 3(14)].

"FINANCIAL INSTITUTION" means any non-banking institution which carries on as its business or part of its business any of the following activities, namely:—

(i) the financing, whether by way of making loans or advances or otherwise, of any activity other than its own;

(ii) the acquisition of shares, stock, bonds, debentures or securities issued by a Government or local authority or other marketable securities of a like nature;

(iii) letting or delivering of any goods to a hirer under a hire purchase agreement as defined in clause (c) of Section 2 of Hire Purchase Act, 1972;

(iv) the carrying on of any class of insurance business;

(v) managing, conducting or supervising, as foreman, agent or in any other capacity, of chits or kuries as defined in any law which is for the time being in force in any State, or any business which is similar thereto;

(vi) collecting, for any purposes or under any scheme or arrangement by whatever name called, monies in lump sum or otherwise, by way of subscriptions or by sale of units, or other instruments or in any other manner and awarding prizes or gifts, whether in cash or kind, or disbursing monies in any other way, to person from whom monies are collected or to any other person, but does not include any institution, which carries on as its principal business,—

(a) agricultural operations; or

(aa) industrial activity; or

Explanation.—for the purposes of this clause, "industrial activity" means any activity specified in sub-classes (i) to (xviii) of clause (c) of Section 2 of the Industrial Development Bank of India Act, 1964;

(b) the purchase or sale of any goods (other than securities) or the providing of any services; or

(c) the purchase, construction or sale of immoveable property, so however that no portion of income of the institution is derived from the financing of purchases, constructions or sales of immoveable property, by other person. [R.B.I. Act (2 of 1934), S. 45-I(c)]

"FINANCIAL INSTITUTION" means a banking company to which the Banking Regulation Act, 1949 (10 of 1949), applies (including any bank or banking institution referred to in Section 51 of that Act); or any other financial institution which the Central Government may, by notification in the Official Gazette, specify in this behalf. [Income-tax Act (43 of 1961), S. 80E(3)(b)].

FINANCIAL INSTITUTION means—

(i) a public financial institution specified in or under Section 4A of the Companies Act, 1956;

(ii) a State financial, Industrial or Investment corporation;

(iii) the State Bank of India or a subsidiary bank as defined in the State Bank of India (Subsidiary Banks) Act,1959;

(iv) a nationalised bank, that is to says a corresponding new bank as defined in Section 2 of—

(a) the Banking Companies (Acquisition and Transfer of Undertakings) Act, 1970; or

(b) Banking Companies (Acquisition and Transfer of Undertakings) Act, 1980;

(v) the General Insurance Corporation of India established in pursuance of the provisions of Section 9 of the General Insurance Business (Nationalisation) Act, 1972;

(vi) the Industrial Reconstruction Corporation of India, or

(vii) any other institution which the Central Government may, by notification, specify in this behalf. [Monopolies and Restrictive Trade Practices Act (54 of 1969), S. 2(da) (now repealed by Competition Act, 2002)].

"FINANCIAL INSTITUTION" means—

(i) a public financial institution within the meaning of Section 4A of the Companies Act, 1956;

(ia) the securitisation company or reconstruction company which has obtained a certificate of registration under sub-section (4) of section 3 of the Securitisation and Reconstruction of Financial Assets and Enforcement of Security Interest Act, 2002 (54 of 2002);

(ib) a debenture trustee registered with the Board and appointed for secured debt securities;

(ii) such other institution as the Central Government may, having regard to its business activity and the area of its operation in India, by notification, specify. [Recovery of Debts Due to Banks and Financial Institutions Act (51 of 1993), S. 2(h) as amended by Act 44 of 2016 (w.e.f 1-9-2016]

"FINANCIAL INSTITUTION" means—

(i) a public financial institution within the meaning of Section 4A of the Companies Act, 1956;

(ii) any institution specified by the Central Government under sub-clause (*ii*) of clause (*h*) of Section 2 of Recovery of Debts Due to Banks and Financial Institutions Act, 1993;

(iii) the International Finance Corporation established under the International Finance Corporation (Status, Immunities and Privileges) Act, 1958;

(iiia) a debenture trustee registered with the Board and appointed for secured debt securities;

(iiib) asset reconstruction company, whether acting as such or managing a trust created for the purpose of securitisation or asset reconstruction, as the case may be;

(iv) any other institution or non-banking financial company as defined in clause (*f*) of Section 45-I of the Reserve Bank of India Act, 1934, which the Central Government may, by notification, specify as financial institution for the purposes of this Act. [Securitisation and Reconstruction of Financial Assets and Enforcement of Security Interest Act (54 of 2002), S. 2(1)(m) as amended by Act 44 of 2016 (w.e.f 1-9-2016)]

"FINANCIAL INSTITUTION" means a financial institution as defined in clause (c) of Section 45-1 of the Reserve Bank of India Act, 1934 and includes a chit fund company, a co-operative bank, a housing finance institution and non-banking financial company. [Prevention of Money Laundering Act (15 of 2003), S. 2(1)(l)]

"FINANCIAL INSTITUTION" means a financial institution as defined in section 45-I(c) of the Reserve Bank of India Act, 1934 (2 of 1934) and includes a chit fund company, a housing finance institution, an authorized person, a payment system operator, a non-banking financial company and the department of posts in the Government of India. [S. 2(1)(*l*) of the Prevention of Money-Laundering Act, 2002 (15 of 2003) as substituted by the Prevention of Money-Laundering (Amendment) Act, 2012 (2 of 2013)]

"FINANCIAL INSTITUTION" for the purposes of section 80EE of Act 43 of 1961, 'financial institution' means a banking company to which the Banking Regulation Act, 1949 (10 of 1949) applies including any bank or banking institution referred to in section 51 of that Act or a housing finance company. [(w.e.f. 1-4-2014) S. 80EE(5)(*a*) of the Income-tax Act, 1961 (43 of 1961)]

"FINANCIAL INSTITUTION" includes a scheduled bank, and any other financial institution defined or notified under the Reserve Bank of India Act, 1934 (2 of 1934). [S. 2(39) of the Companies Act, 2013 (18 of 2013)]

Financial institution means a unit set up in an International Financial Services Centre and which is engaged in rendering financial services in respect of any financial product. [International Financial Services Centres Authority Act, 2019 (50 of 2019), section 3(1)(c)]

Financially literate. For the purpose of this regulation, "financially literate" shall mean a person who has the ability to read and understand basic financial statements i.e. balance sheet, profit and loss account, and statement of cash flows. [Securities and Exchange Board of India (Prohibition of Insider Trading) Regulations, 2015, Regn. 2(1)(*c*), *Explanation*]

Financial lease. "Financial lease" means a lease under any lease agreement of tangible asset, other than negotiable instrument or negotiable document, for transfer of lessor's right therein to the lessee for a certain time in consideration of payment of agreed amount periodically and where lessee becomes the owner of the such assets at the expiry of the term of lease or on payment of the agreed residual amount, as the case may be. [Recovery of Debts due to Banks and Financial Institutions Act (51 of 1993), S. 2(ha) as inserted by Amending Act (44 of 2016)].

"FINANCIAL LEASE" means a lease under a lease agreement of tangible asset, other than negotiable instrument or negotiable document, for transfer of lessor's right therein to the lessee for a certain time in consideration of payment of agreed amount periodically and where lessee becomes the owner of the such assets at the expiry of the term of lease or on payment of the agreed residual amount, as the case may be. [Recovery of Debts Due to Banks and Financial Institutions Act (51 of 1993), S. 2(ha)].

"FINANCIAL LEASE" means a lease under any lease agreement of tangible asset, other than negotiable instrument or negotiable document, for transfer of lessor's right therein to the lessee for a certain time in consideration of payment of agreed amount periodically and where the lessee becomes the owner of the such assets at the expiry of the term of lease or on payment of the agreed residual amount, as the case may be. [Securitisation and Reconstruction of Financial Assets and Enforcement of Security Interest Act (54 of 2002), S. 2(1)(ma)].

Financial Memorandum. A memorandum required to accompany all bills to be introduced in Parliament involving expenditure. (*Constitutional and Parliamentary Term*)

Financial obligation. An obligation to pay money under a contract or for breach thereof is in a sense a 'financial obligation'. But in the context of the above order, if the expression be construed '*ejusdem generis*' it implies an obligation in the nature of an obligation in respect of loans and guarantees, incurred or undertaken by the State. *State of West Bengal* v. *Serajuddin Batley*, AIR 1954 SC 193, 194.

Financial product. Means securities, contracts of insurance, deposits, credit arrangements including loans and advances by banks and financial institutions, retirement benefit plans, small savings instruments, foreign currency contracts other than contracts to exchange one currency (whether Indian or not) for another which are to be settled immediately, or any other instrument as may be prescribed. [Insolvency and Bankruptcy Code (31 of 2016), S. 3(15)].

"Financial product" means—

(*i*) *securities;*

(*ii*) *contracts of insurance;*

(*iii*) *deposits;*

(*iv*) *credit arrangements;*

(*v*) foreign currency contracts other than contracts to exchange one currency for another that are to be settled immediately; and

(*vi*) any other product or instrument that may be notified by the Central Government from time to time. *[International Financial Services Centres Authority Act, 2019 (50 of 2019), section 3(1)(d)]*

Financial statement. A balance sheet, income statement, or annual report that summarizes an individual's or organization's financial condition on a specified date or for a specified period by reporting assets and liabilities.

"FINANCIAL STATEMENT" for the purposes of section 129 of Act 18 of 2013, except where the context otherwise requires, any reference to the 'financial statement' shall include any notes annexed to or forming part of such financial statement, giving information required to be given and allowed to be given in the form of such notes under the Companies Act, 2013 (18 of 2013). [*Explanation* to section 129 of the Companies Act, 2013 (18 of 2013)]

"FINANCIAL STATEMENT" in relation to a company, includes—

(*i*) a balance sheet as at the end of the financial year;

(*ii*) a profit and loss account, or in the case of a company carrying on any activity not for profit, an income and expenditure account for the financial year;

(*iii*) cash flow statement for the financial year;

(*iv*) a statement of changes in equity, if applicable; and

(*v*) any explanatory note annexed to, or forming part of, any document referred to in sub-clause (*i*) to sub-clause (*iv*):

Provided that the financial statement, with respect to One Person Company, small company and dormant company, may not include the cash flow statement. [S. 2(40) of the Companies Act, 2013 (18 of 2013)]

"Financial statement", in relation to the Corporation, includes—

(i) a balance-sheet as at the end of the financial year;

(ii) a profit and loss account for the financial year;

(iii) cash flow statement for the financial year;

(iv) a statement of changes in equity, if applicable; and

(v) any explanatory note annexed to, or forming part of, any document referred to in sub-clause (i) to sub-clause (iv). [Life Insurance Corporation Act, 1956 (31 of 1956), section 2(4b)]

Financial service. Includes any of the following services, namely—

(*a*) accepting of deposits;

(*b*) safeguarding and administering assets consisting of financial products, belonging to another person, or agreeing to do so;

(*c*) effecting contracts of insurance;

(*d*) offering, managing or agreeing to manage assets consisting of financial products belonging to another person;

(*e*) rendering or agreeing, for consideration, to render advice on or soliciting for the purposes of—

(*i*) buying, selling, or subscribing to, a financial product;

(*ii*) availing a financial service; or

(*iii*) exercising any right associated with a financial product or financial service;

(*f*) establishing or operating an investment scheme;

(*g*) maintaining or transferring records of ownership of a financial product;

(*h*) underwriting the issuance or subscription of a financial product; or

(*i*) selling, providing, or issuing stored value or payment instruments or providing payment services. [Insolvency and Bankruptcy Code (31 of 2016), S. 3(16)]. *"Financial service" means—*

(*i*) buying, selling, or subscribing to a financial product or agreeing to do so;

(*ii*) *acceptance of deposits;*

(*iii*) Safeguarding and administering assets consisting of financial products, belonging to another person, or agreeing to do so;

(*iv*) effecting contracts of insurance;

(*v*) offering, managing or agreeing to manage assets consisting of financial products belonging to another person;

(*vi*) exercising any right associated with a financial product or financial service;

(*vii*) establishing or operating an investment scheme;

(*viii*) maintaining or transferring records of ownership of a financial product;

(*ix*) underwriting the issuance or subscription of a financial product;

(*x*) providing information about a person's financial standing or creditworthiness;

(*xi*) selling, providing, or issuing stored value or payment instruments or providing payment services;

(*xii*) making arrangements for carrying on any of the services in sub-clauses (*i*) to (*xi*);

(*xiii*) rendering or agreeing to render advice on or soliciting for the purposes of—

(*A*) buying, selling, or subscribing to, a financial product; or

(*B*) availing any of the services in sub-clauses (*i*) to (*xi*); or

(*C*) exercising any right associated with a financial product or any of the services in clauses (*i*) to (*xi*);

(xiv) any other service that may be notified by the Central Government from time to time. *[International Financial Services Centres Authority Act, 2019 (50 of 2019), section 3(1)(e)]*

Financial year. The year commencing on the first day of April. [General Clauses Act (10 of 1897), S. 3(21)]

The year by or for which accounts are reckoned. [Companies Act (1 of 1956), S. 2(17) and Constitution of India, Art. 115(1)].

"FINANCIAL YEAR" (in the Life Assurance Companies Act) means each period of twelve months at the end of which the balance of the accounts of the Life Assurance Company is struck, or, if no such balance is struck, then the calendar year. [Act 6 of 1912 (Life Assurance Companies Act), S. 2(4). *See also* Pro. Soc. Act, S. 2].

"FINANCIAL YEAR" means, in relation to any body corporate, the period in respect of which any profit and loss account of the body corporate laid before it in annual general meeting is made up, whether that period is a year or not :

Provided that, in relation to an insurance company, "financial year" shall mean the calendar year referred to in sub-sec. (1) of S. 11 of the Insurance Act (4 of 1938). [Companies Act (1 of 1956), S. 2(17)]

Year of account for financial purposes, often not coinciding with the calendar year. For example, in India the financial year (or fiscal year) runs from April 1 to March 31 of the following year. In the United States, the fiscal year runs from July 1 to June 30.

Period of twelve months, beginning at any time in the calendar year, used for company accounting purposes. Or, for purposes of corporation tax, it is the period of twelve months beginning on 1 April to which the tax applies.

"FINANCIAL YEAR" in relation to any company or body corporate, means the period ending on the 31st day of March every year, and where it has been incorporated on or after the 1st day of January of a year, the period ending on the 31st day of March of the following year, in respect whereof financial statement of the company or body corporate is made up:

Provided that on an application made by a company or body corporate, which is a holding company or a subsidiary of a company incorporated outside India and is required to follow a different financial year for consolidation of its accounts outside India, the Tribunal may, if it is satisfied, allow any period as its financial year, whether or not that period is a year:

Provided further that any application pending before the Tribunal as on the date of commencement of the Companies (Amendment) Act, 2019, shall be disposed of by the Tribunal in accordance with the provisions applicable to it before such commencement:

Provided also that a company or body corporate, existing on the commencement of this Act, shall, within a period of two years from such commencement, align its financial year as per the provisions of this clause. [S. 2(41) of the Companies Act, 2013 (18 of 2013)]

"Financial year", in relation to any multi-State co-operative society or class of such societies, means the year ending on the 31st day of March of the year and where the accounts of such society or class of such societies are, with the previous sanction of the Central Registrar, balanced on any other day, the year ending on such day. [Multi-State Co-operative Societies Act, 2002 (39 of 2002), section 3(ka)]

Financing. The act or process of raising or providing funds.

Find. In its primary meaning to come to; obtain; to meet, and hence to reach; to attain to; to arrive at; to discover; to determine; to declare (as, to find a person guilty or innocent). In law, to ascertain by judicial inquiry to determine a controversy in favour of one of the parties, as to "find for the plaintiff," "find true bill."

To determine a fact in dispute by verdict or decision. [Black's Law Dictionary as cited in *Anand Brothers Private Limited* v. *Union of India*, (2014) 9 SCC 212, para 12.2].

To arrive at a conclusion; to come to a finding [CrPC, 1973 (2 of 1974), S. 308(5)]; to obtain or come to have something desirable, as if without effort [Indian Contract Act (9 of 1872), S. 71].

Finder. Even though the actual finder is in the employment of another person and in the course of execution of works under such employment certain treasure is found, the person who actually discovers the treasure must be held to be the finder and not the person who employs the actual finder. *Isaac Judson* v. *Govt. of Pondicherry,* AIR 1982 Mad 1, 2. [Indian Treasure Trove Act (6 of 1878), S. 4]

Finder of goods. A finder of goods is in the position of a bailee. He has no right to sue the owner for compensation for the trouble and expenses incurred by him to preserve the goods and find out the owner, but he may retain the goods until he receives the compensation; and where the owner has offered a specific reward for the return of goods lost, the finder may sue for such reward, and may retain the goods until he receives it. Under certain circumstances, he may sell the goods found. [Indian Contract Act (9 of 1872), Ss. 168 and 169]

Finding. The conclusion of a judicial proceeding in respect of an issue, action or a trial; judicial verdict; the result of a judicial inquiry; the result of the deliberations of a jury or a court. [CPC (5 of 1908), O. XIV, R. 7(c)].

"The conclusion reached by judicial or other inquiry." [Oxford Dictionary as cited in *Anand Brothers Private Limited* v. *Union of India*, (2014) 9 SCC 212, para 12.1].

"The act of finding; that which is found; discovery; (2) Law/A conclusion arrived at before an official or a court; (3) Support; expense." [Webster's Comprehensive Dictionary as cited in *Anand Brothers Private Limited* v. *Union of India*, (2014) 9 SCC 212, para 12.3].

A 'finding' could only be that which was necessary for the disposal of an appeal in respect of an assessment of a particular year. *Bhanji Bhagwandas* v. *Commissioner of Income Tax*, AIR 1968 SC 139, 141; *Daffadar Bhagat Singh and Sons* v. *I.T.R A Ward Ferozepure*, AIR 1969 SC 340 at 342.

Finding is a decision on an issue framed in a suit. *C.I.T. Andhra Pradesh* v. *Vadde Pulliah & Co.*, AIR 1973 SC 2434, 2436.

A finding given in appeal, revision, or reference arising out of an assessment but must be a finding necessary for the disposal of the particular case, in respect of particular assessee and in relation to the particular assessment year. *Rajinder Nath Etc.* v. *Commissioner of Income Tax Delhi*, AIR 1979 SC 1933, 1934. [Income-tax Act (43 of 1961), S. 153(3)(ii)]

Finding in the affirmative. Finding which answers the question in the affirmative. [CPC (5 of 1908), O. XIV, R. 6].

Finding lost goods. *[Finding of lost goods*— See Indian Treasure Trove Act (6 of 1878)] By the general rule of the common law one who finds and appropriates a lost article not buried in or attached to the soil acquires the title thereto and the right to possession thereof against all the world except the true owner.

Finding of fact. A determination by a judge, or administrative agency of a fact supported by the evidence in the record, usually presented at the trial or hearing.

A determination by a Judge, jury, or administrative agency of a fact supported by the evidence in the record, usually presented at the trial or hearing. [Black's Law Dictionary as cited in *Anand Brothers Private Limited* v. *Union of India*, (2014) 9 SCC 212, para 12.2].

A finding that a person is a 'workman' is a 'finding of fact'. [*New India Motors* v. *K.T. Morri,* AIR 1960 SC 875]

Mala fide dismissal of a workman is a 'finding of fact'. [*Central India Coal fields Ltd.* v. *Ram Bilas,* AIR 1961 SC 1189]

Findings. Allowing claims by an Arbitrator without giving any reasons in support thereof by only using cryptic expressions like 'claim sustained', 'partly sustained' and 'not sustained' would not amount to 'findings.' [*Union of India* v. *Wazir Chand Bhalia,* AIR 2008 (NOC) 2219] [J&K Arbitration Act (2 of 2002), S. 30]

Fine. A pecuniary punishment for an offence. [IPC (45 of 1860), S. 40]; a money payment by a tenant to his landlord on a particular occasion. [Mines Act (35 of 1952), S. 2(1)(i)].

Finger impression. The impression left upon a surface where a finger has touched it.

Finger print. Impression of finger on paper used for indentification of persons—especially used in the criminal intelligence department.

Finis finem litibus imponit. The fine puts an end to litigations. (*Latin for Lawyers*)

Fishing vessel. Means a ship or boat fitted with mechanical means of propulsion which is exclusively engaged in sea-fishing for profit. [Marine Products Export Development Authority (13 of 1972), S. 3(g)]

F.I.R. First Information Report. It is the earliest and the first information of a cognizable offence recorded by an officer in charge of a police station. *T.T. Antony* v. *State of Kerala*, AIR 2001 SC 2637. [CrPC, 1973 (2 of 1974), S. 154]

Fire. To propel from, as if from gun; the phenomenon of combustion as manifested in light flames and heat and in heating, destroying and altering effects.

Fire insurance business. Means the business of effecting, otherwise than incidentally to some other class of insurance business, contracts of insurance against loss by or incidental to fire, or other occurrence customarily included among the risks insured against in fire insurance policies. [Insurance Act (4 of 1938), S. 2(6A)]

Fire prevention and fire safety measures. Mean such measures as are necessary in accordance with the building bye-laws for the prevention, control and fighting of fire and for ensuring the safety of life and property in case of fire. [Delhi Fire Prevention and Fire Safety Act (56 of 1986), S. 2(g)]

Fire-proof. Proof against fire; incombustible.

Fire resisting material. Means any material which has certain degree of fire resistance. [Delhi Cinematograph (Exhibition of Film by V.C.R.), Rules, 1986, R. 2(xi)]

Firearm. A weapon from which the shot is discharged by gun. [Arms Act (54 of 1959), S. 2(1)(b)].

"FIREARMS" means arms of any description designed or adapted to discharge a projectile or projectiles of any kind of the action of any explosive or other forms of energy, and includes,—

(i) artillery, hand-grandes, riot-pistols or weapons of any kind designed or adapted for the discharge of any noxious liquid, gas or other such thing,

(ii) accessories for any such firearms designed or adapted to diminish the noise or flash caused by fire thereof,

(iii) parts of, and machinery for manufacturing firearms, and

(iv) carriages, platforms and appliances for mounting, transporting and serving artillery. [Arms Act (54 of 1959), S. 2(1)(e)]

This term includes all kinds of canons, rifles, shotguns, and pistols, whatever the compound used for propelling the missile or bullet.

Firewall. A collection of hardware and/or software components or a system that sits between the Internet and a network through which all traffic from inside to outside, and *vice-versa,* must pass through and which ensures that only authorised traffic, as defined by the local security policy, is allowed to pass through it. The firewall itself has to be immune to penetration. (*Information Technology*)

A metaphorical label for a set of hardware and software components protecting system resources (servers, LANs) from exogenous attack via a network (from Internet users) by intercepting and checking network traffic. The "mix" of hardware and software accomplishing firewall operations can vary. For LAN installations of any size, the typical approach is to install one or more computers "positioned" at critical junctures (gateways) and dedicated to the firewall functions. It is typically the case that such installations are configured such that all external connections (modems, ports) are "outside" the firewall (with respect to its domain of protection), or at least "abut" it on its "external face." The firewall's own "internal" connection into the protected domain is typically the focus of monitoring functions. A system or combination of systems that enforces a boundary between two or more networks. Gateway that limits access between networks in accordance with local security policy. The typical firewall is an inexpensive micro-based Unix box kept clean of critical data, with a bunch of modems and public network ports on it but just one carefully watched connection back to the rest of the cluster. (*Information Technology*)

A computer between the networked computers and the network, that secures this system from unauthorized access. (*Cyber Law*)

Firewall/Double Firewall. One of several types of intelligent devices (such as routers or gateways) used to isolate networks. Firewalls make it difficult for attackers to jump from network to network. A double firewall is two firewalls connected together. Double firewalls are used to minimise risk if one firewall gets compromised or provide address translation functions. (*Information Technology*)

Firewall machine. A specific computer dedicated to effecting a firewall.

Firm. Persons who have entered into partnership with one another are called individually "partners" and collectively a "FIRM". [Indian Partnership Act (9 of 1932), S. 4].

"It is not a legal entity and is a collective term for partners who have entered into partnership with one another". *Bharat Sarvodaya Mills Co. Ltd.* v. *Mohatta Brothers,* AIR 1969 Guj 178 at 182. [Indian Partnership Act (9 of 1932), S. 4]

The expression 'firm' is a compendious term which describes the association of several persons who are interested in a business. The general law 'knows nothing of the term as a body'. But the judicature enables partners of a firm to sue or be sued in the name of their firm. With that end in view, the legislature formulated O. XXX of the Civil Procedure Code. *Narain Das Mangal Sen* v. *Anand Behari Misra,* AIR 1958 MP 408. [CPC (5 of 1908), O. XXX, R. 1]

A business unit or enterprise [Indian Partnership Act (9 of 1932), S. 4]; not weak, wavering or uncertain.

"FIRM" for the purposes of Chapter X of Act 18 of 2013, the word 'firm' shall include a limited liability partnership incorporated under the Limited Liability Partnership Act, 2008 (6 of 2009). [*Explanation* to section 139(4) of the Companies Act, 2013 (18 of 2013)]

"Firm" shall have the meaning assigned to it in section 4 of the Indian Partnership Act, 1932 (9 of 1932), and includes,—

(i) the limited liability partnership as defined in clause (*n*) of sub-section (1) of section 2 of the Limited Liability Partnership Act, 2008 (6 of 2009); or

(ii) the sole proprietorship,

registered with the Institute. [Chartered Accountants Act, 1949 (38 of 1949), section 2(1)(ca)]

Firm name. The name, title or style under which a commercial house transacts business. [Indian Partnership Act (9 of 1932), S. 4].

Firm's name. The word 'firm' or 'firm's name' is merely a compendious description of all the partners collectively. *Purushottam & Co* v. *Manilal & Sons*, AIR 1961 SC 325, 328 [Indian Partnership Act (9 of 1932), S. 4]

Firman (of Former Ruler). The '*Firmans*' were expressions of the sovereign will of the *Nizam* and they were binding in the same way as any other law; nay, they would override all other laws which were in conflict with them. So long as a particular '*Firman*' held the field, that alonewould govern or regulate the rights of the parties concerned, though it could be annulled or modified by a later '*Firman*' at any time the *Nizam* willed. *Ameer-Un-Nissa Begam* v. *Mahbood Begum*, AIR 1955 SC 352, 359.

Firmware. Software contained in a read-only memory (ROM) device. (*Cyber Law*)

First assured career progression scale. 'First assured career progression scale' with reference to—

(i) government servant means the revised scale as mentioned in Column 3 of Part 1 of Schedule I against the name of post(s) in Column 2 of part 1 of Schedule I, on which the government servant was recruited as a direct recruited fresh entrant in the Government service,

(ii) all other government servants not covered in subclause (i) above but on whom these Rules apply, the pay scale mentioned in Column 3 of Part II of Schedule I against the pay scale mentioned in Column 2 of Part II of Schedule I, as the corresponding existing scale prescribed for the past against which such government servant was recruited as a direct recruited fresh entrant in the Government service:

Provided that the First Assured Career Progression scale may also be referred to as first ACP scale or ACP I scale. [Haryana Civil Services (Assured Career Progression) Rules, 1998, R. 3(e) as cited in *State of Haryana* v. *Sita Ram*, (2013) 16 SCC 677, para 4].

First charge. A charge which will have priority over all others. [CPC (5 of 1908), O. XXXIII, R. 10].

First-class. Of the best quality; first-rate; superior quality.

A term often used in describing goods in a contract of sale and implying that they are such as correspond with the best of their kind in general use, not merely with the best of a single manufacturer, unless, indeed, the two superlatives coincide. *Munshi Ram* v. *Union of India,* (1972) 3 SCC 866.

First day of hearing. The words 'First day of hearing' do not mean the day for the return of the summons or the returnable day but the day when the Court applies its mind to the case. *Sham Lal* v. *Atma Nand Jain Sabha, Dal Bazar*, AIR 1987 SC 197, 201. [East Punjab Urban Rent Restriction Act (3 of 1949), S. 13(2) Proviso (1)]

First degree. The grade given to the most serious forms of crimes (burglary in the *first degree*).

First hearing. The expression "first hearing" in O. XXXV, R. 4, CPC (5 of 1908), means the date on which the Court goes into the pleadings in order to understand the contentions of the parties.

The expression 'FIRST HEARING' means the date for filing written statement or for hearing mentioned in the summons or where more than one of such dates are mentioned, the last of the dates mentioned. [CPC (5 of 1908), O. XV, R 5, *Expln.* 1 (as applicable in Punjab, Haryana and Chandigarh) as cited in *Mangat Singh Trilochan Singh* v. *Stapal*, AIR 2003 SC 4300, 4301, para 7]

By the expression 'first hearing' of the suit, the day for the appearance of defendant fixed under the rule is meant and in a case where summons has been issued for settlement of issues only, the date mentioned in the summons is the first date of hearing of the suit. *Abdul Hai* v. *Rahatullah Mian,* AIR 1974 Pat 244. [CPC (5 of 1908), O. V, R. 5]

The 'first hearing' means the day on which the court goes into the pleadings in order to understand the contention of the parties and in suits in which issues are to be framed, the first hearing would be the day on which such issues are framed in as much as on that day the Court goes into the pleadings with a view to understand the contentions of the parties, and where summons are issued for the final disposal of the case, the first day of appearance would be the first hearing. *Hasanukharai Govindji* v. *Patel Mavji Jesam,* AIR 1953 San 106, 107. [CPC (5 of 1908), O. VIII, R. 1]

First information report (F.I.R.). First report of the alleged offence lodged with the police.

First instance. First instance means from the very beginning. The Court has to take recourse to the provision for reconciliation in the first instance *i.e* from the very beginning. *Sushma Kumar* v. *Om Prakash,* AIR 1993 Pat 156, 160. [Hindu Marriage Act (25 of 1955), S. 23(2)]

First instance, Court of. A Court of original jurisdiction in which legal proceedings may be instituted. [Suits Valuation Act (7 of 1887), S. 11(1)(a)].

First offence. For the purposes of section 441 of Act 18 of 2013, any second or subsequent offence committed after the expiry of a period of three years from the date on which the offence was previously compounded, shall be deemed to be a 'first offence'. [*Explanation* (*a*) to section 441(2) of the Companies Act, 2013 (18 of 2013)]

First stage dealer. Means a dealer who purchases the goods directly from,—

(i) the manufacturer under the cover of an invoice issued in terms of the provisions of Central Excise Rules, 2002 or from the depot of the said manufacturer, or from premises of the consignment agent of the said manufacturer or from any other premises from where the goods are sold by or on behalf of the said manufacturer, under cover of an invoice; or

(ii) an importer or from the depot of an importer or from the premises of the consignment agent of the importer, under cover of an invoice. [CENVAT Credit Rules, 2002, R. 2(f)]

First unit scheme. 'FIRST UNIT SCHEME' means the unit scheme made before commencement of the Unit Trust of India (Amendment) Act, 1966. [Unit Trust of India Act (52 of 1963), S. 2(cb)]

Fiscal. Of or pertaining to the treasury or public revenue or finance. (*English*)

Fiscal deficit. "FISCAL DEFICIT" means the excess of total disbursements, from the Consolidated Fund of India, excluding repayment of debt, over total receipts into the Fund (excluding the debt receipts), during a financial year. [Fiscal Responsibility and Budget Management Act (39 of 2003), S. 2(a)]

Fiscal deficit means net borrowings of all kinds by a government. These borrowings are from (a) the public under various small saving schemes, (b) commercial banks, and other financial institutions, and (c) Central Bank. Fiscal deficit makes no distinction between one type of borrowing and the other although the implication of borrowings from central bank is different from borrowings from other sources.

Fiscal indicators. Means the measures such as numerical ceilings and proportions to gross domestic product, as may be prescribed, for evaluation of the fiscal position of the Central Government. [Fiscal Responsibility and Budget Management Act (39 of 2003), S. 2(b)]

Fiscal Statutes. (*Interpretation of Statutes*). In construing fiscal statutes and in determining the liability of a subject to tax one must have regard to the strict letter of the law and not merely to the spirit of the statute or the substance of the law. *A. V. Fernandez* v. *State of Kerala*, AIR 1957 SC 657, 661.

Fiscal year. The financial year.

Fish. "FISH" defined. Bur. Act 3, 1905, S. 3(3); Reg. 3, 1889, S. 32(1)(*b*).

"FISH" includes, besides other fish, turtle, estuary tortoises, seaslugs (beche-de-mer), shell-fish and mother-of-pearl shells. [Bur. Act (3 of 1905) (Burma Fisheries) S. 3, Cl. (1); Ben. Act (2 of 1889), S. 2]

"FISH" includes shellfish. [Indian Fisheries Act (4 of 1897), S. 3(1)]

'FISH' means any aquatic animal, whether piscine or not and includes shellfish, crustacean, molluscs, turtle (chelonia), aquatic mammal (the young, fry, eggs and spawn thereof), holothurians, coelenterates, sea weed, coral (porifera) and any other aquatic life. [Maritime Zones of India (Regulation of Fishing by Foreign Vessels) Act (42 of 1981), S. 2(b)]

The fish whether in raw or processed form is known as fish. According to WEBSTER'S Comprehensive Dic., fish means *inter alia* "the flesh of a fish used as food." A fish after cleaning cutting of head and tail or deshelling remains fish. Fish may be processed at more than one stage but that does not result in bringing out a different commodity. *Regional Executive Kerala Fisherman' Welfare Fund Board* v. *Fancy Food,* AIR 1995 SC 1620.

A vertebrate cold blooded animal with gills and fins living wholly in water. *I.T.C. Ltd.* v. *Person Incharge, AMC, Kakinada*, AIR 2004 SC 1796, 1799, para 6.

Fish Group. 'FISH GROUP' includes—

1. Live fish including fish with or without life in any form.
2. Dry fish.

3. Live prawn including prawn with or without life in any form.
4. Dry prawn. [Notification issued under Section 3 of A.P. (Agricultural Produce & Liv stock) Markets Act (16 of 1966).

Fishery. Any collection of water, running or still, tidal or not-tidal, which is of itself of a permanent nature or is or has recently been connected with any waters of a permanent nature, in which fish may be found; and it includes the sea and the sandbanks on which turtle and estuary tortoises habitually lay their eggs.

The occupation or industry of catching fish; a collection of water in which fish may be found. [CrPC 1973 (2 of 1974), S. 145(2)]; fishing establishment; a legal right to take fish at a certain place or in a particular water.

Fishing. To catch fish.

"FISHING" means catching, taking, killing, attracting or pursuing fish by any method and includes the processing, preserving, transferring, receiving and transporting of fish. [Maritime Zones of India (Regulation of Fishing by Foreign Vessel) Act (42 of 1981), S. 2(c)]

Fishing vessel. Means a ship fitted with mechanical means of propulsion which is exclusively engaged in sea fishing for profit. [Merchant Shipping Act (44 of 1958), S. 3(12)]

'FISHING VESSEL' means a ship or boat fitted with mechanical means of propulsion which is exclusively engaged in sea-fishing for profit. [Marine Products Export Development Authority Act (13 of 1972), S. 3(g)]

"FISHING VESSEL" means a boat or ship, whether or not fitted with mechanical means of propulsion, which is engaged in sea fishing for profit and includes

(i) a Country Craft, and

(ii) a Canoe

engaged in sea fishing for profit. [Maharashtra Marine Fishing Regulation Act (54 of 1981), S. 2(d)]

"Fishing vessel" means a vessel fitted with mechanical mode of propulsion, which is exclusively engaged in fishing for profit, within inland waters. [Inland Vessels Act, 2021 (24 of 2021), section 3(o)]

Fishing weir. 'FISHING WEIR' means any erection, structure, or obstruction fixed to the soil either temporarily or permanently across, or partly across, a river or branch of a river, and used for the exclusive purpose of taking or facilitating the taking of fish. [(English) Salmon and Freshwater Fisheries Act, 1975, S. 41(1)]

Fissile material. Means uranium 233, uranium 235, plutonium or any material containing these substances or any other material that may be declared as such by notification by the Central Government. [Atomic Energy Act (33 of 1962), S. 2(b)]

Fit. To be in harmony with; be of right measure shape, etc; adaptation; adjustment.

Suited to the circumstances of the case; answering the purpose; proper or appropriate. [CPC (5 of 1908), O. XLV, R. 3(1)].

'Fit' means 'a person to be appointed shall be legally eligible'. *Union of India* v. *Lt. General, Rajendra Singh Kadyan*, (2000) 6 SCC 698, Para 20.

Fit facility. "Fit facility" means a facility being run by a government organization or a registered voluntary or non-governmental organization, prepared to temporarily own the responsibility of a particular child for a specific purpose, and such facility is recognized as fit for the said purpose, by the Committee, as the case may be, or the Board, under sub-section (1) of section 51. [Juvenile Justice (Care and Protection of Children) Act, 2015 (2 of 2016), S. 2(27)].

Fit for habitation. A statutory implied covenant applied to certain tenancies at a very low rent. Premises are regarded as not reasonably fit for habitation if they are defective in one or more of the following: repair, stability, freedom from damp, natural lighting, ventilation, water supply, drainage and sanitary conveniences, facilities for cooking and for storage and preparation of food, and disposal of waste water. A landlord normally has no obligation to see that premises are fit for habitation when the statutory provisions do not apply.

Fit institution. Means a governmental or a registered non-governmental organisation or a voluntary organisation prepared to own the responsibility of a child and such organisation is found fit by the competent authority. [Juvenile Justice (Care and Protection of Children) Act (56 of 2000), S. 2(h) now repealed by Act 2 of 2016]

Fit one for appeal to the Supreme Court. A mere ground of delay in giving a judgment does not fall within the words 'fit one for appeal to the Supreme Court' even if it is felt by the High Court that the delay might have led to omission to consider arguments on question of fact and law. *Achyet Adhicary* v. *State of West Bengal*, AIR 1963 SC 1039, 1040. [Constitution of India Act, Art. 136]

Fit person. Means a person, being a social worker or any other person, who is prepared to own the responsibility of a child and is found fit by the competent authority to receive and take care of the child. [Juvenile Justice (Care and Protection of Children) Act (56 of 2000), S. 2(i) now repealed by Act 2 of 2016]

"Fit person" means any person, prepared to own the responsibility of a child, for a specific purpose, and such person is identified after inquiry made in this behalf and recognized as fit for the said purpose, by the Committee or, as the case may be, the Board, to receive and take care of the child. [Juvenile Justice (Care and Protection of Children) Act, 2015 (2 of 2016), S. 2(28)].

"FIT PERSON" OR "FIT INSTITUTION" means any person or institution (not being a police station or jail) found fit by the competent authority to receive and take care of a Juvenile entrusted to his or its care and protection on the terms and conditions specified by the competent authority. [Juvenile Justice Act (53 of 1986), S. 2(f); Children Act (60 of 1960), S. 2(jj)]

Fitting. Anything supplied as a part, equipment *etc.*; fixture *etc.*

Fitting out. To supply things fit and necessary. [Geneva Conventions Act (6 of 1960), 2nd Sch., Art. 24].

Fix. To make firm, stable, or fast; to set or place permanently; to fasten immovably; to settle; (as, to fix the price) to settle permanently. Sometimes used in the sense of "allow."

To appoint [Hindu Succession Act (30 of 1956), S. 4(2), omitted by Act 39 of 2005 w.e.f. 09-09-2005]; to make or keep permanent; to determine; to decide.

Fixation of ceiling. Fixing the maximum limit.

Fixation of rates of wages. The fixation of rates of wages depends on the capacity of the industry which in turn is to be considered on an industry-cum-region basis after taking a fair cross section of the industry. The capacity of the industry depends on the elasticity of demand for the product, the possibility of tightening up the organisation *etc. Express Newspapers Ltd.* v. *Union of India*, AIR 1958 SC 578, 605. [Industrial Disputes Act (14 of 1947), S. 2(rr)]

Fixed. Definite and settled; appointed.

Fixed assets. 'Fixed assets' in general comprise those assets which are held for the purpose of conducting a business, in contradistinction to those assets which the proprietor holds for the purpose of converting into cash and they include real estate, building, machinery, staff car of technical adviser of the company, *etc.*, *Union of India* v. *United Collieries Ltd.*, AIR 1985 SC 192, 195. [Coal Mines (Nationalization) Act (26 of 1973), S. 2(h)(xii)]

Tangible property used in operating a business which will not be consumed or converted into cash or its equivalent during the current accounting priod; *e.g.* plant, machinery, land, buildings, fixtures. Contrasted with liquid assets. *e.g.* cash, securities. (*Black*)

Tangible assets (as land, buildings or machinery) of a permanent or long term nature.

"Fixed capital" and **"circulating capital".** Fixed capital is something which the owner keeps in his possession but turns to profit: *circulating capital* however, is turned over in the process of profit-making. *Karanpura Development Co. Ltd.* v. *C.I.T.*, AIR 1962 SC 429. Also see *Sutlej Cotton Mills Ltd.* v. *Commissioner of Income Tax, Calcutta*, AIR 1979 SC 5.

Fixed capital investment. Includes investment in plant and machinery and land and building of an industry. [Khadi and Village Industries Commission Act (61 of 1956), S. 2(cc)]

"FIXED CAPITAL INVESTMENT". Apart from the actual investment in or cost of the specific items of land, building, plant, machinery, equipment apparatus, components moulds dyes, jigs and fixtures, no other item of expense is includible under the head of 'fixed capital investment' for the purposes of *Explanation 4* to section 4A of the U.P. Trade Tax Act 15 of 1948. *Commissioner of Trade Tax* v. *Kajaria Ceramics Ltd.*, AIR 2005 SC 2968 : 2005 AIR SCW 3450.

Fixed capitals. Money invested in land, buildings and other property of a more or less permanent nature.

Fixed charge. A charge on specific property.

Fixed cumulative dividends. Fixed dividends added, if not paid when due, to the next payment or a future payment. [Companies Act (1 of 1956), Sch. VI, pt. I].

Fixed day. The appointed day. [Indian Contract Act (9 of 1872), S. 73, ill. (k)].

Fixed establishment. "Fixed establishment" means a place (other than the registered place of business) which is characterised by a sufficient degree of permanence and suitable structure in terms of human and technical resources to supply services, or to receive and use services for its own needs [The Central Goods and Services Tax Act, 2017 (12 of 2017), S. 2(50)]; [The Integrated Goods and Services Tax Act, 2017 (13 of 2017), S. 2(7)]

Fixed fee or licence fee. The term 'licence fee' or 'fixed fee' used in the context of U.P. Excise Act, the ordinance read with preamble and the Excise (Amendment) Rules, are the amount of consideration receivable by the State Government for parting with the exclusive privilege of vending foreign liquor in favour of a private party under a licence. *State of U.P.* v. *Sheopat Rai*, AIR 1994 SC 813, 819. [U.P. Excise Act (4 of 1910), S. 24-A]

Fixed platform. Means an artificial island, installation or structure permanently attached to the seabed for the purpose of exploration for, or exploitation of resources or for other economic purposes. [Suppression of Unlawful Acts Against Safety of Maritime Navigation and fixed Platform on Continental Shelf Act (69 of 2002), S. 2(e)]

Fixed rate. 'FIXED RATE' in relation to dividends on share capital, other than ordinary share capital, includes a rate fluctuating in accordance with the maximum rate of income-tax. [Business Profit Tax Act (21 of 1947), S. 2(11)]

Fixed term. A tenancy or lease for a fixed period.

"Fixed term employment" means the engagement of an employee on the basis of a written contract of employment for a fixed period:

Provided that—

(a) his hours of work, wages, allowances and other benefits shall not be less than that of a permanent employee doing the same work or work of a similar nature; and

(b) he shall be eligible for all benefits, under any law for the time being in force, available to a permanent employee proportionately according to the period of service rendered by him even if his period of employment does not extend to the required qualifying period of employment. [Code on Social Security, 2020 (36 of 2020), section 2(34)]

"Fixed term employment" means the engagement of a worker on the basis of a written contract of employment for a fixed period:

Provided that—

(a) his hours of work, wages, allowances and other benefits shall not be less than that of a permanent worker doing the same work or work of similar nature;

(b) he shall be eligible for all statutory benefits available to a permanent worker proportionately according to the period of service rendered by him even if his period of employment does not extend to the qualifying period of employment required in the statute; and

(c) he shall be eligible for gratuity if he renders service under the contract for a period of one year. [Industrial Relations Code, 2020 (35 of 2020), section 2(o)]

Fixture. Something usually and permanently attached or appended; movable chattel (as a machine) which by reason of annexation to real property and adaptation to continuing use in connection with the realty is considered a part of the realty. [Workmen's Compensation Act (8 of 1923), Sch., II, item (ix)].

Fixtures. Moveable additions to a building or land securely fastened to it.

Flag. Piece of hunting *etc.,* usually oblong or square attached to staff, as stand or ensign. Each country has its own special flag.

YELLOW FLAG. Flag of ship with infectious disease; hospital ship; ship in quarantine.

WHITE FLAG. Flag hoisted as a sign of surrender or as a flag of truce.

Flag of truce. White flag indicating desire for peace.

A white flag displayed as an invitation to the enemy to confer or carried on as sign of peaceful intention by one sent to deal with the enemy. [Army Act (46 of 1950), S. 34(f)].

Flag officer. "FLAG OFFICER" means an officer of the rank of Admiral of the Fleet, Admiral, Vice-Admiral or Rear-Admiral. [Navy Act (62 of 1957), S. 3(8)]

Flagrant. If a partner brings himself within the penalties of the criminal law. *e.g.* gets convicted of a shabby fraud in travelling on a railway without a ticket, he is guilty of a "flagrant breach" of the duties of a partner, within a clause in his partnership articles authorizing his expulsion, and such conduct is "detrimental" to the partnership business (*Carmichael* v. *Evans*, [1904] 1 Ch. 486); but mere immorality, *e.g.* adultery, is not to the "discredit or injury" of the partnership, within such a clause, unless it affects the partnership itself, *e.g.* immorality of a medical man towards some of the patients of his firm (*per* ROMILLY M.R., *Snow* v. *Milford*, 18 LT 142). See further *Green* v. *Howell*, [1910] 1 Ch. 495.

Flagrant abuse. The expression 'flagrant abuse' occurring in Section 16(1)(e) of the Act means must be 'glaring, notorious, enormous, scandalous or wicked'. *State of Punjab* v. *Bhajan Singh*, (2001) 3 SCC 565, para 14 : AIR 2001 SC 1098. [Punjab Municipal Act (3 of 1911), S. 16(1)(e)]

Flagrant necessity. A case of urgency rendering lawful an otherwise illegal act, as an assault to remove a man from impending danger.

Flagrantly. The expression "flagrantly" means glaringly, notoriously, scandalously. *Bhagat Ram* v. *State of Punjab*, AIR 1972 SC 1571, 1577.

Flagrantly abused his position. The clause means that a member of a committee in disregard of his duty, does any act or acts which shock a reasonable mind. It does not mean that the abuse of the position must have occurred over a long period of time. *Joginder Singh* v. *State of Punjab*, AIR 1963 Pun 280, 288. [Punjab Municipal Act (3 of 1911), S. 16(1)(e)]

Mere act of an elected President of Municipal Council of entering upon his office as President before approval and publication of his name in Official Gazette on account of wilful omission of State Govt. would not come within the ambit of the expression 'flagrantly abused his position' under Section 16(1)(e) of the Act. *State of Punjab* v. *Bhajan Singh*, (2001) 3 SCC 565, para 14 : AIR 2001 SC 1098. [Punjab Municipal Act (3 of 1911), S. 16(1)(e)]

Flame. An e-mail that is abusive or argumenative. Usually includes the words "You are a . . ." somewhere in the message. (*Cyber Law*)

FLAME. Originally, "flame" meant to carry forth in a passionate manner in the spirit of honorable debate. Flames most often involved the use of flowery language and flaming well was an art form. More recently flame has come to refer to any kind of derogatory comment no matter how witless or crude. (*Matisse Enzer-Glossary of Internet Terms*)

Flame-mail. An inflammatory, aggressive, abusive or deliberately antisocial e-mail. (*Information Technology*)

Flame war. When an online discussion degenerates into a series of personal attacks against the debators, rather than discussion of their positions. A heated exchange. (*Matisse Enzer-Glossary of Internet Terms*)

Flash. A sudden burst of bright light.

Flash/Flashing point. "FLASH-POINT" of any petroleum means the lowest temperature at which it yields a vapour which will give a momentary flash when ignited, determined in accordance with provisions of Chapter II and the rules made thereunder. [Petroleum Act (30 of 1934), S. 2(c)]

The lowest temperature at which a vapour gives off from a liquid with flash or ignite.

Flat. As an *adjective*, having an even and horizontal surface, or nearly so, without marked prominences or depressions. (*Webster : Int. Dict.*).

A level part; plain; a storey of floor of a house especially one, or part of one, used as separate residence.

'Flat' means a part of any property, intended to be used for residential purposes, including one or more rooms with enclosed spaces located on one or more floors; with direct exit to a public street or road or to a common area leading to such streets or roads and includes any garage or room whether or not adjacent to the building in which such flat is located provided by the colonizer/owner of such property for use by the owner of such flat for parking any vehicle or for residence of any person employed in such flat, as the case may be. [Haryana Development and Regulation of Urban Areas Act (8 of 1975), S. 2(gg) as cited in *DLF Limited* v. *Manmohan Lowe*, (2014) 12 SCC 231, para 25].

'FLAT' means a portion of building, which can be delineated with definite outline on plan and which can be definitely marked on site, and which is a dwelling unit. [Delhi Development Authority (Management and Disposal of Housing Estates) Regulations, 1968, Regulation 2(17)].

Flavoured Milk. By whatever name called, may contain nuts (whole, fragmented or ground) chocolate, coffee or any other edible flavor, edible food colours and cane sugar. Flavoured milk shall be pasteurised, sterilized and boiled. The type of milk shall be mentioned on the label. [Food Safety and Standards (Food Safety and Standards (Food Products, Standards and Food Additives) Regulations, 2011, Regn. 1.2.5 **as cited in** *Swami Achyntanand Tirth* v. *Union of India,* (2016) 9 SCC 699, para 43].

Flat rate system. Means a system of charging on telephones under which a subscriber is required to pay fixed annual rental for the line connecting his telephone to any exchange within the exchange system, but not any call fees for local calls from his telephones. [Indian Telegraph Rules, 1951, R. 2(o)]

Flaying. To strip off the skin from. [Khadi and Village Industries Commission Act (61 of 1956), Sch., item 5].

Fleet. Naval armament; number of warships under one commander-in-chief; number of ships or boats sailing in company.

Flexible. Capable of being bent: yielding to pressure; capable of modification or adaptation.

Flight. 'FLIGHT' means a journey by air beginning when the aircraft takes off and ending when the aircraft next alights thereafter. [Civil Aviation (Licensing) Act, 1960, S. 10, Civil Aviation Act, 1982, S. 105(13)].

For the purposes of this Act the period during which an aircraft is in FLIGHT shall be deemed to include any period from the moment when all its external doors are closed following embarkation until the moment when any such door is opened for disembarkation, and, in the case of a forced landing, any period until the competent authorities take over responsibility for the aircraft and for persons and property on board. [Aviation Security Act, 1982, S. 38(3)(A)]

Flip flop arbitration. In Flip flop arbitration, each party makes a final settlement offer and the arbitrator chooses that one which he considers most reasonable; both sides come under pressure to submit a reasonable offer; also called 'pendulum arbitration', 'baseball arbitration'. *(Alternative Dispute Redressal)*

Float. Issue and offer for sale. [Industrial Development Bank of India Act (18 of 1964), S. 9(1)(f)(i)].

Floating capital. Capital which a trader or banker reserves for ordinary business operations and does not appropriate for fixed or permanent investment.

Floating charge. A continuing charge on the assets of the company creating it; but permitting the company to deal freely with the property in the usual course of business until the security holder shall intervene to enforce his claim. [Companies Act (1 of 1956), S. 123(1)].

While a specific charge is one which, without more, fastens on ascertained and definite property or property capable of being ascertained or defined, a floating charge moves with the property which it is intended to affect until some event occurs or some act is done which causes it to settle and fasten on the subject of the charge within its reach and grasp. It is of the essence of a floating charge that it remains dormant until the undertaking charged ceases to be a going concern or until the person in whose favour the charge is created intervenes. HALSBURY, 4th Edn, Vol. 7 para 824, p. 489.

Floating charge or security. A floating charge is a special charge which is recognised by the Indian Companies Act. A floating charge is created by making the assets of the undertaking or the company, a security for the payment of debts into which a company enters. Such a charge might cover properties which may be specified or unspecified in the document creating the charge. *Krishna Deva Bharagara* v. *Official Liquidator U.P. Oil Industries Ltd.,* AIR 1962 All 101, 103. [Companies Act (1 of 1956), S. 125]

It is a charge over all the fixed assets of a company as well as the goods in the process of manufacture and unsold manufactured goods, so long in the custody of the company and without any hindrance the company can use its fixed assets and machinery and sell, its manufactured goods with the charge holder having the power to take possession of fixed assets and all available movable and immovable properties as soon as the company committed default, stopped working or went into liquidation, at that point the floating charge becomes fixed. *Bank of Maharashtra Limited* v. *Official Liquidator*, AIR 1969 Mys 280 at 291 and 292. [Companies Act (1 of 1956), S. 293]

Floating-point arithmetic. The arithmetic operations performed in a computer in which the position of the binary point in a number is specified by a point position indicator associated with each number. (*Computer*)

Floating policy. (*In Marine Insurance*) Policy that covers certain specified goods without naming the ship by which they are to be conveyed.

FLOATING POLICY is a policy which describes the insurance in general terms, and leaves the name or names of the ship or ships and other particulars to be defined by subsequent declaration. [Marine Insurance Act (11 of 1963), S. 31(1)]

Floating security. Security on the property of a company as a going concern; used in regard to the security of a limited company, and forming a charge on its assets, but not enforceable unless there is default in payment.

An equitable charge on the assets for the time being of a going concern. [Estate Duty Act (34 of 1953), S. 19(5)].

Floating zone. A zone that is to be used for a designated purpose and that is approved as to particular characteristics (as size and type of buildings) but whose location is to be determined in the future.

Flog. To beat or strike, lash. [Air Force Act (45 of 1950), S. 77(2)].

Flood warning system. 'FLOOD WARNING SYSTEM' means any system whereby, for the purpose of providing warning of any danger of flooding, information with respect to—

(a) rainfall, as measured at a particular place within a particular period, or

(b) the level or flow of any inland water, or part of an inland water, at a particular time, or

(c) other matters appearing to the authority providing the system to be relevant for that purpose is obtained and transmitted whether automatically or otherwise, with or without provision for carrying out calculations based on such information and for transmitting the results of those calculations. [(English) Land Drainage Act, 1976, S. 32(5) Repealed by Water Consolidation (Consequential Provisions) Act 1991, (w.e.f. 1.12.1991)]

Flooding. Become full with fluid, especially to excess. [Mines Act (35 of 1952), S. 22(2)].

Floor crossing. Changing one's allegiance from one party to another. (*Constitutional and Parliamentary Term*)

Floor of the House. That part of the legislative Chamber which is technically 'within the House', *i.e.* between the Bar of the House and the Speaker's Chair. Debate may not take place outside these limits and a Member may only address the House from the Floor. (*Constitutional and Parliamentary Term*)

Flotsam. Floating wrecklessly. A term applied to a ship which is sunk or otherwise perished, and the goods float upon the sea, or to goods that are found floating on the waves; goods lost at sea and found floating on the water.

Goods floating upon the sea which belong to the State, unless claimed by the true owners thereof. [Customs Act (52 of 1962), S. 21].

Fluctuate. Move up and down; irregular rise and fall (as) a fluctuating market; fluctuation of prices of commodities.

Fluctuation. Rise and fall (of prices, rates etc.) [Industrial Finance Corporation Act (15 of 1948) (*Repealed by Act 23 of 1993*), S. 27(4)(b)(i)].

Flue. A channel in a chimney for conveying flame or smoke to the outer air. [Emergency Risks (Undertakings) Insurance Act (51 of 1971), S. 2(a)]; [Factories Act (63 of 1948), S. 36(1)].

Fly. See, [Cotton Ginning and Pressing Factories Act (12 of 1925), S. 2(e)]; to move through the air especially on wings or in aircraft; to move swiftly.

Foetal death. 'FOETAL DEATH' means absence of all evidence of life prior to the complete expulsion or extraction from its mother of a product of conception irrespective of duration of pregnancy. [Registration of Births and Deaths Act (18 of 1969), S. 2(c)]

Foeticide. The killing of a foetus.

Foetus. Fully developed embryo in womb. [Maternity Benefit Act (53 of 1961), S. 4(3)].

"FOETUS" means a human organism during the period of its development beginning on the fifty-seventh day following fertilisation or creation (excluding any time in which its development has been suspended) and ending at the birth. [Pre-Natal, Diagnostic Techniques (Regulation and Prevention of Misuse) Act (57 of 1994), S. 2(be)]

"Foetus" means a human organism during the period of its development beginning on the fifty-seventh day following fertilisation or creation (excluding any time in which its development has been suspended) and ending at the birth. [Surrogacy (Regulation) Act, 2021 (47 of 2021), section 2(1)(m)]

Follow. To go or come after; to move behind in the same path or direction. (*Webster : Int. Dect.*)

In the construction of statutes the word generally means next after, unless the context requires a different construction.

To go or come after; to conform to. [Constitution of India, Art. 51A(b)].

Follow trust property. The doctrine which allows a benficiary to claim the trust property, however it may be charged or allotted in its nature or character subject to the requirement that the property is capable of being identified as acquired with or shown to represent the original estate; to trace. [Indian Trusts Act (2 of 1882), S. 63].

Food. Has been defined as "what is eaten for nourishment to organic bodies; nutriment; aliment; victuals; provisions." (*Cent. Dict.*)

"A substance that promotes the growth of animal or vegetable life." "Every article used for food or drink by man."

"Food" means "what one takes into the system to maintain life and growth". [The Shorter Oxford English Dictionary (Third Edn.) as cited in *Gulati and Company* v. *Commissioner of Sales Tax, U.P., Lucknow,* (2014) 14 SCC 286, para 15].

"Food" means—

"material consisting of carbohydrates, fats, proteins and supplementary substances.... that is taken or absorbed into the body of an [Organism] in order to sustain growth, repair, and all vital processes and to furnish energy for all activity of the origanism... something that nourishes or develops or sustains". [Webster's Third New International Dictionary as cited in *Gulati and Company* v. *Commissioner of Sales Tax, U.P., Lucknow*, (2014) 14 SCC 286, para 15].

"FOOD" means any article used as food or drink for human consumption other than drugs and water. The term includes,—

(a) any article which ordinarily enters into or is used in the composition or preparation of human food, and

(b) any flavouring matter or condiments, and

(c) any other article which the Central Government, having regard to its use, nature, substance or quality, declare, by notification in the Official Gazette, as food for the purposes of this Act. [Prevention of Food Adulteration Act (37 of 1954), S. 2(V)]. Also see *State of Tamil Nadu* v. *R. Krishnamurthy*, AIR 1980 SC 538.

"FOOD" means any article of nourishment for human consumption and also includes any substance intended for the use of infants, invalids or convalescents as an article of food or drink. [Patents Act (39 of 1970), S. 2(g)]

"FOOD" includes every article used for food or drink by man other than drugs or water, and any article which ordinarily enters into or used in the composition or preparation of human food and also includes confectionery, flavouring and colouring matter, spices and condiments. [Manipur Municipality Act (43 of 1994), S. 2(18)]

Ice is 'food' under the Essential Commodities Act. *New India Industrial Corporation* v. *Union of India,* AIR 1980 Del 277, 280. [Essential Commodities Act (10 of 1955), S. 3]

Linseed oil is comprehended by the definition of 'food'. *Municipal Board, Kanpur* v. *Janki Prasad,* AIR 1963 All 433, 436 (FB).

Kesari Dal is an article of food. *State of U.P.* v. *Babu Lal,* AIR 1977 All 339, 344 (FB) [Prevention of Food Adulteration Act (37 of 1954), S. 2(v)(a)]

An article generally or commonly used for human consumption or in the preparation of human food is 'food'. Gingelly oil, mixed or not with groundnut oil, whether described or exhibited as an article of food for human consumption or as an article of internal use only is 'food' within the meaning of S. 2(v). *State of Tamil Nadu* v. *Rs. Krishnamurthy*, AIR 1980 SC 538, 539, 540.

"FOOD" means any substance, whether processed, partially processed or unprocessed, which is intended for human consumption and includes primary food to the extent defined in section 3(1)(zk) of Act 34 of 2006, genetically modified or engineered food or food containing such ingredients, infant food, packaged drinking water, alcoholic drink, chewing gum, and any substance, including water used into the food during its manufacture, preparation or treatment but does not include any animal feed, live animals unless they are prepared or processed for placing on the market for human consumption, plants, prior to harvesting, drugs and medicinal products, cosmetics, narcotic or psychotropic substances:

Provided that the Central Government may declare, by notification in the Official Gazette, any other article as food for the purposes of this Act having regards to its use, nature, substance or quality. [S. 3(1)(j) of the Food Safety & Standards Act, 2006 (34 of 2006)]

Food additive. Means any substance not normally consumed as a food by itself or used as a typical ingredient of the food, whether or not it has nutritive value, the intentional addition of which to food for a technological (including organoleptic) purpose in the manufacture, processing, preparation, treatment, packing, packaging, transport or holding of such food results, or may be reasonably expected to result (directly or indirectly), in it or its by-products becoming a component of or otherwise affecting the characteristics of such food but does not include "contaminants" or substances added to food for maintaining or improving nutritional qualities. [S. 3(1)(k) of the Food Safety & Standards Act, 2006 (34 of 2006)]

Food & foodstuff. A thing may be a food or a food stuff even if not directly consumed and has no nutritive value but is only used for culinary purposes in the preparation of food. Wheat & Wheat products are food even if they are not consumed as they are but have to be cooked or have to undergo some mechanical process before the same are ready for consumption. *Nathuni Lal Gupta* v. *State*, AIR 1964 Cal 279, 282. [Defence of India Rules (1962), R. 35(5)]

Food stuff has no special meaning of its own. It merely carries in back to the definition of 'food' because food stuff is anything which is used as food. *Collector of Central Excise, Bombay* v. *Parle Exports (P) Ltd.*, AIR 1989 SC 644.

Food Analyst. Means an analyst appointed under section 45 of Act 34 of 2006. [S. 3(1)(*l*) of the Food Safety & Standards Act, 2006 (34 of 2006)]

Food Authority. Means the Food Safety and Standards Authority of India established under section 4 of Act 34 of 2006. [S. 3(1)(m) of the Food Safety & Standards Act, 2006 (34 of 2006)]

Food business. Means any undertaking, whether for profit or not and whether public or private, carrying out any of the activities related to any stage of manufacture, processing, packaging, storage, transportation, distribution of food, import and includes food services, catering services, sale of food or food ingredients. [S. 3(1)(n) of the Food Safety & Standards Act, 2006 (34 of 2006)]

Food business operator. In relation to food business means a person by whom the business is carried on or owned and is responsible for ensuring the compliance of this Act, Rules and Regulations made thereunder. [S. 3(1)(o) of the Food Safety & Standards Act, 2006 (34 of 2006)]

Food colours and syrup essences. Food colours and syrup essences are edible goods whereas 'dyes and colours' are compositions thereof. *Commissioner of Sales Tax U.P.* v. *S.N. Brothers, Kanpur*, AIR 1973 SC 78, 82.

Food crops. Include crop of sugar-cane. [Essential Commodities Act (10 of 1955), S. 2(b)]

Food grains. Grains useful for human consumption.

Food grade. Means material made of substances which are safe and suitable for their intended use, and shall not endanger human health or result in unacceptable change in the composition of the food or organoleptic characteristics. [Food Safety and Standards (Packaging) Regulations, 2018, Regn. 2(1)(b)].

Food (Health) Authority. Means the Director of Medical and Health Services or the Chief Officer in charge of Health Administration in a State, by whatever designation he is known, and includes any officer empowered by the Central Government or the State Government, by notification in the official Gazette, to exercise the powers and perform the duties of the Food (Health) Authority under this Act with respect to such local area as may be specified in the notification. [Prevention of Food Adulteration Act (37 of 1954), S. 2(vi)]

Food Importer. Means a Food Business Operator importing or desirous of importing article of food into Indian Territory, who is duly licensed as importer under the Food Safety and Standards (Licensing and Registration of Food Business) Regulations, 2011 made under the Act. [Food Safety and Standards (Import) Regulations, 2017, Regn. 2(1)(l)].

Food laboratory. Means any food laboratory or institute established by the Central or a State Government or any other agency and accredited by National Accreditation Board for Testing and Calibration Laboratories or an equivalent accreditation agency and recognised by the Food Authority under section 43 of Act 34 of 2006. [S. 3(1)(p) of the Food Safety & Standards Act, 2006 (34 of 2006)]

Food safety. Means assurance that food is acceptable for human consumption according to its intended use. [S. 3(1)(*q*) of the Food Safety & Standards Act, 2006 (34 of 2006)]

Food safety audit. Means a systematic and functionally independent examination of food safety measures adopted by manufacturing units to determine whether such measures and related results meet with objectives of food safety and the claims made in that behalf. [S. 3(1)(r) of the Food Safety & Standards Act, 2006 (34 of 2006)]

Food Safety Management System. Means the adoption of Good Manufacturing Practices, Good Hygienic Practices, Hazard Analysis and Critical Control Point and such other practices as may be specified by regulation, for the food business. [S. 3(1)(s) of the Food Safety & Standards Act, 2006 (34 of 2006)]

Food Safety Officer. Means an officer appointed under section 37 of Act 34 of 2006. [S. 3(1)(t) of the Food Safety & Standards Act, 2006 (34 of 2006)]

Foods for special dietary uses or functional foods or nutraceuticals or health supplements. Means:

(a) foods which are specially processed or formulated to satisfy particular dietary requirements which exist because of a particular physical or physiological condition or specific diseases and disorders and which are presented as such, wherein the composition of these foodstuffs must differ significantly from the composition of ordinary foods of comparable nature, if such ordinary foods exist, and may contain one or more of the following ingredients, namely:—

 (i) plants or botanicals or their parts in the form of powder, concentrate or extract in water, ethyl alcohol or hydro alcoholic extract, single or in combination;

(ii) minerals or vitamins or proteins or metals or their compounds or amino acids (in amounts not exceeding the Recommended Daily Allowance for Indians) or enzymes (within permissible limits);

(iii) substances from animal origin;

(iv) a dietary substance for use by human beings to supplement the diet by increasing the total dietary intake;

(b) (i) a product that is labelled as a "Food for special dietary uses or functional foods or nutraceuticals or health supplements or similar such foods" which is not represented for use as a conventional food and whereby such products may be formulated in the form of powders, granules, tablets, capsules, liquids, jelly and other dosage forms but not parenterals, and are meant for oral administration;

(ii) such product does not include a drug as defined in clause (b) and ayurvedic, sidha and unani drugs as defined in clauses (a) and (h) of section 3 of the Drugs and Cosmetics Act, 1940 (23 of 1940) and rules made thereunder;

(iii) does not claim to cure or mitigate any specific disease, disorder or condition (except for certain health benefit or such promotion claims) as may be permitted by the regulations made under this Act;

(iv) does not include a narcotic drug or a psychotropic substance as defined in the Schedule of the Narcotic Drugs and Psychotropic Substances Act, 1985 (61 of 1985) and rules made thereunder and substances listed in Schedules E and EI of the Drugs and Cosmetics Rules, 1945. [*Explanation* (1) to S. 22 of the Food Safety & Standards Act, 2006 (34 of 2006)]

Food security. Means the supply of the entitled quantity of foodgrains and meal specified under Chapter II of Act 20 of 2013. [S. 2(6) of the National Food Security Act, 2013 (20 of 2013)]

Food security allowance. Means the amount of money to be paid by the concerned State Government to the entitled persons under section 8 of Act 20 of 2013. [S. 2(7) of the National Food Security Act, 2013 (20 of 2013)]

Foodgrains. Means rice, wheat or coarse grains or any combination thereof conforming to such quality norms as may be determined, by order, by the Central Government from time to time. [S. 2(5) of the National Food Security Act, 2013 (20 of 2013)]

Foodstuff. A substance used as food.

"Foodstuff" means "a substance suitable for consumption as food". [Oxford Advanced Learner's Dictionary as cited in *Gulati and Company* v. *Commissioner of Sales Tax, U.P. Lucknow*, (2014) 14 SCC 286, para 14(a)]. "foodstuff" "foodstuff" means "any material, substance, etc. that can be used as food". [Collins English Dictionary as cited in *Gulati and Company* v. *Commissioner of Sales Tax, U.P., Lucknow*, (2014) 14 SCC 286, para 14(6)].

Milk and milk products fall within the definition of 'food stuff'. *Kanwaljit Singh* v. *UOI,* 1995 (Supp) 1 SCC 273. [Essential Commodities Act (10 of 1955), Sec 2(a)(v)].

"Foodstuff" would refer to anything with a nutritive value which is consumed for growth or sustaining one's life. [*Gulati and Company* v. *Commissioner of Sales Tax, Uttar Pradesh, Lucknow,* (2014) 14 SCC 286, para 16].

"FOODSTUFFS", include—

(i) coconuts and areca nuts;

(ii) eggs and egg products;

(iii) fish, whether fresh, frozen, dried or preserved;

(iv) fruit, whether fresh, dried or dehydrated;

(v) honey;

(vi) meat, whether fresh, frozen or preserved;

(vii) milk and milk products;

(viii) vegetables; [National Co-operative Development Corporation Act (26 of 1962), S.2 (da)]

"FOODSTUFFS" means ready-to-eat food and food products, fast food, processed and cooked food in liquid, powder, solid or semi-solid form. [Recycled Plastic Manufacture and Usage Rules, 1999, R. 2(b)]

Turmeric is foodstuff. *State of Bombay* v. *Virkumar Gulabchand Shah*, AIR 1952 SC 335, 339.

A stuff which is commonly used as food by the generality of living being is foodstuff. It is not legitimate to restrict the meaning of that word to things which are used as food by human beings. Cattle feed and poultry feed are food to the cattle and the poultry and therefore they are foodstuffs. Rice bran is a foodstuff. *Sat Pal Gupta* v. *State of Haryana*, AIR 1982 SC 798, 799. [Essential Commodities Act (10 of 1955), S. 2(a)(v) & 3]

The expression "foodstuffs" must include cooked food also. *Welcome Hotel* v. *State of A.P.*, AIR 1983 SC 1015, 1018.

Foodstuff applies to all what is eaten for the nourishment of the body, not only of human but also for animals, and as such cattle feed, is foodstuff. *Surinder Pal* v. *State of Punjab,* AIR 1989 P&H 49, 50, 51. [Essential Commodities Act (10 of 1955), S. 2(a)]

The expression 'foodstuffs' include '*Ghee*'. *State Govt. of M.P.* v. *Seth Parasmal,* AIR 1952 Nag 10.

Tea does not come within the ambit of 'foodstuff'. S. *Samuel* v. *Union of India*, AIR 2004 SC 218, 226, paras 25 to 27]

"FOODSTUFF". According to the *Chambers Dictionary*, the term 'foodstuff' means a substance used as food. According to *Words and Phrases*, Permanent Edition, Vol. 17, page 313, the word 'foodstuffs' means food which has been subjected to "canning" or similar "preparation". The *New Oxford Encyclopedic Dictionary* defines the term 'foodstuff' as material for food and the term 'foodstuffs' as articles of food in bulk. S. *Samuel, M. D., Harrisons Malayalam* v. *UOI*, (2004) 1 SCC 256.

Foot print. Impression left by the foot.

Footer. Text placed automatically at the bottom of each page, such as a document name, page number, date, or author's name. (*Computer*)

Footing. Firm position; established place; relative condition.

For all purposes. The expression "for all purposes" indicates that when an assessment is made for a particular assessment year it is good for all purposes as far as that assessment is concerned, *i.e.*, for all purposes for imposing tax liability determining the quantum of the liability and for recovering it. *HL Sud, I.T.O. Companies Circle 1(1), Bombay* v. *Tata Engineering and Locomotive Co. Ltd.*, AIR 1969 SC 319 at 322.

'For all purposes' and 'all the ties'. The word 'ties' is a very wide and comprehensive word and would include all types of bonds, social, religious, cultural or any other that bound the adoptee to his natural family. *Khazan Singh* v. *Union of India,* AIR 1980 Del 60, 66. [Hindu Adoption and Maintenance Act (78 of 1956), S. 12]

For any other purpose. The words mean for the enforcement of any legal right and the performance of any legal duty. *Bhagaram Tuloule* v. *State of Bihar,* AIR 1950 Pat 387 (FB).

Property leased for running a cinema house falls under 'for any other purpose'. *Sushila Narendraji Singh* v. *State of U.P.,* AIR 1972 All 427, 428. [Transfer of Property Act (4 of 1882), S. 106.]

The expression 'for any other purpose' in Article 226 means for any purpose other than the enforcement of fundamental rights. [*A.D.M., Jabalpur* v. *Shivakant Shukla*, (1976) 2 SCC 521, 586, para 109] [Constitution of India, Art. 226]

For any other reason. The words "for any other reason" occurring in Rules 12 and 13 have to be read as pertaining to reasons causing a defect in the record analogous to the defect caused by the death of a party or change of status of a party, as, for example, when there is a devolution of interest by assignment or operation of law. [Supreme Court Rules 1950, O. 16, R. 12 and 13]

For any other sufficient reason. The words 'for any other sufficient reason' cannot be given a very wide meaning and must be given the meaning in the context of this special reason, namely that the reasons are analogous to those preceding these words. *Controller Amanat Rai Mazhabi* v. *Wahid Ali Khan*, AIR 1956 Bhopal 48. [CPC (5 of 1908), O. XLVII, R. 1(1)(c)]

The expression 'for any other sufficient reason' means a reason sufficient on grounds at least analogous to those specified immediately previously. [CPC (5 of 1908), O. XLVII, R. 1(1)(c)]

For any purpose. For any purpose includes collateral purpose. *Sanjeeva Reddi* v. *Johanputra,* AIR 1972 AP 373, 375. [Indian Stamp Act (2 of 1899), S. 35]

For any sufficient reason. The words *"for any other sufficient reason"* in S. 623, CPC, (1882) do not apply and cannot apply to something which came into existence after the decree was made, and the discovery of new and important matter or evidence must also be in existence at the time of the decree. [24 M. 1 at p. 10 (PC) *foll.*) 14 CWN 244 : 11 CLJ 26 : 5 IC 182]

For any unlawful purpose. The purpose contemplated by S. 552 CrPC, must be in itself unlawful and must not be construed so as to make it include purposes which though not unlawful in themselves might only become so when entertained towards a child in opposition to the wishes of its guardian. *The State* v. *Billi*, AIR 1953 Nag 128, 130. [Criminal Procedure Code (5 of 1898), S. 552, now S. 98 of 1974 Code]

For anything done or ordered to be done. The non-compliance with the provisions of the statute by omitting to do what the act enjoins will be anything done or ordered to be done under the Act. *Public Prosecutor, Madras* v. *R. Raju*, AIR 1972 SC 2504, 2509. [Central Excise and Salt Act (1 of 1944), S. 40(2)]

For consideration. In return of some consideration. [T.P. Act (4 of 1882), S. 45].

For money. (*In Stock Exchange*) A sale "for money" involves immediate delivery of the securities purchased and payment of receipt.

For payment to the decree-holder. The words "for payment to the decree holder" in CPC (5 of 1908), O. XXI, R. 89(1)(b)) mean that he is the person solely entitled to the money which has been paid into Court.

For that end. The words 'for that end' means for the purpose of committing theft or for the purpose of removing any article of theft. *Titiv* v. *State of Bihar,* AIR 1966 Pat 453, 457. [IPC (45 of 1860), S. 390]

For that purpose. The expression 'FOR THAT PURPOSE' occurring in Art. 256 refers to the requirement of compliance with the laws made by Parliament. *Sharma Transport* v. *Govt. of A.P.*, (2002) 2 SCC 188, para 9 : AIR 2002 SC 322. [Constitution of India, Art. 256]

For the account. (*In Stock Exchange*) Business transactions included in current account for settlement on the next settling day.

For the benefit of. The expression 'for the benefit of' means that the holder of the property is the legal owner himself. *Kripashanker* v. *Commissioner of Wealth Tax,* AIR 1966 Pat 371, 372. [Wealth Tax Act (27 of 1957), S. 21(1)]

For the benefit of wife and children. The words of S. 6 of Married Women's Property Act (3 of 1874) "for the benefit of his wife, or of his wife and children, or any of them" should be construed as "for the benefit of his wife or of his children, or of his wife and children, or any of them.'

For the purpose of. The words 'for the purpose of' indicate that the scope of the inquiry (by the commission) is not necessarily limited to the particular or specific matters enumerated in any of the entries in the list concerned but may extend to inquiries into collateral matters which may be necessary for the purpose legislative or otherwise, of those particular matters. *Ramakrishna Dalmia* v. *Justice Tendolkar*, AIR 1958 SC 538, 545. [Constitution of India, Art. 246; Sch. 7, List I, Entry 94; List III, Entry 45]

For the purpose of consumption in the state. The expression "for the purpose of consumption in that state" must be understood as having reference not merely to the individual importer or purchaser but as contemplating distribution eventually to consumers in general within the State. *State of Bombay* v. *United Motors Ltd.*, AIR 1953 SC 252, 258. [Constitution of India, Art. 286(1)(*a*)]

For the purpose of growing tea. The word 'for the purpose of growing tea' would mean growing tea plants, no matter whether for the purpose of collecting leaves or for the purpose of collecting seeds. *Banwarilal Chokham* v. *A.M. Deshmukhya,* AIR 1958 Ass 155, 156. [Minimum Wages Act (11 of 1948), Sch., Item No. 4]

For the purpose of the business. The expression "for the purpose of the business" is essentially wider than the expression "for the purpose of earning profits". It covers not only the running of the business or its administration but also measures for the preservation of the business, protection of its assets and property. It may legitimately comprehend many other acts incidental to the carrying on of the business. *Gift Tax Commissioner, Kerala* v. *P.G.T. Timbers*, AIR 1972 SC 23, 28. [Gift Tax Act (18 of 1958), S. 5(1)(*xiv*)]

For the purpose of this Act. The expression 'for the purpose of this Act', unless the content otherwise requires would mean 'all the purposes' thereof. *Ashok Leyland* v. *State of T.N.*, (2004) 3 SCC 1, 37, para 87.

For the purposes of execution. The words "for the purposes of execution of the decree" in S. 28 of the Presidency Small Cause Courts Act (15 of 1882) only mean that, as between the judgment-debtor and the judgment-creditor, property of this particular class (*i.e.*, tiled huts) shall, for the purposes of execution, be deemed to be moveable.

For the purposes of the Act. "For the purposes of the Act" surely means for the purposes of all and not only some of the provisions of the Act. *M.K. Kochu Devassy* v. *State of Kerala*, AIR 1979 SC 358.

For the same offence. Expression "for the same offence" means under the same section of law. [Indian Evidence Act (1 of 1872), S. 30]

For the time being. At that time. [Income-tax Act (43 of 1961), S. 2(19) and Constitution of India, Art. 22(3)(a)].

"FOR THE TIME BEING" means at the moment or existing position. *Jivendra Nath Kaul* v. *Collector/ District Magistrate,* (1992) 3 SCC 576, 580.

The expression 'for the time being' occurring in Section 2(b) would imply that the declaration as disturbed area under Section 3 of the Act cannot operate indefinitely. *Naga People's Movement of Human Rights* v. *Union of India*, AIR 1998 SC 431. [Armed Forces (Special Powers) Act (28 of 1958), S. 2(b)]

For the time being in force. The expression 'for the time being in force' denotes time indefinite and refers to indefinite state of facts which will arise in future and which may vary from time to time.

The words "for the time being in force" are inserted only for determining the forum of an appeal and for regulating the procedure. *Lallubhai Keshavaram Joshi* v. *Nirmalaben Lallularam Joshi,* AIR 1972 Guj 174, 177. [Hindu Marriage Act (25 of 1955), Ss. 24, 28]

For value received. Generally the expression "for value received" used in a pronote imports a consideration.

For value, transferee. A person, who has passed a valuable consideration for the property transferred to him. [Specific Relief Act (47 of 1963), S. 19(b)].

Foras. During the 18th century the East India Company started reclaiming Foras lands which are salt batty lands reclaimed from the sea, and invited the inhabitants to cultivate them, at first without payment of any assessment and subsequently on favourable rates. These payments were called "Foras". *Collector of Bombay* v. *Nussewa Nii*, AIR 1955 SC 298, 302.

Forbear. Abstain; refrain from; be patient. When unqualified by terms of restriction, in reference to a debt, in the popular sense, a term which is equivalent to "wait," without any adjunct whatever, and has regard to a general forbearance.

To abstain or desist from. [Indian Contract Act (9 of 1872), S. 127, ill. (b)].

Forbearance. The action of forbearing [Indian Contract Act (9 of 1872), S. 137]; [Presidency-towns Insolvency Act (3 of 1909), S. 45(1)(c)].

Forbid. To command, not to allow a thing to happen.

To command against; to prohibit [Indian Evidence Act (1 of 1872), S. 151 and Indian Contract Act (9 of 1872), S. 63, ill. (a)]; [Constitution of India, Art. 17].

TO FORBID, PROHIBIT, INTERDICT. *Forbid*, is the ordinary term; *prohibit* is the judicial term; *interdict* the moral term.

Forbidden degrees. The degrees of relationship within which marriage is forbidden and no sexual relations can be had.

Force. "A person is said to use force to another if he causes motion, change of motion, or cessation of motion to that other or if he causes to any substance such motion, or change of motion, or cessation of motion as brings that substance into contact, with any part of that other's body, or with anything which that other is wearing or carrying, or with anything so situated that such contact affects that other's sense of feeling :

Provided that the person causing the motion or change of motion, or cessation of motion, causes that motion, change of motion, or cessation of motion in one of the three ways hereinafter described :

First—By his own bodily power.

Secondly—By disposing any substance in such a manner that the motion or change or cessation of motion takes place without any further act on his part, or on the part of any other person.

Thirdly—By inducing any animal to move, to change its motion, or to cease to move. [IPC (45 of 1860), S. 349] [(w.e.f. 1-7-2024) repealed and replaced by Bharatiya Nyaya Sanhita, 2023 (45 of 2023), section 128]

General Reserve Engineer Force of the Border Roads Organisation is a civilian construction force and they are an integral part of the Armed Forces. *R. Viswan* v. *Union of India*, AIR 1983 SC 658, 673. [Constitution of India, Art. 33]

A group of men collected together, as for instance, police force [IPC (45 of 1860), S. 349]; to constrain or compel by physical moral or intellectual means or by the exigencies of circumstances.

Force custody. Means an officer, a subordinate officer, an under-officer or other enrolled person. [Border Security Force Act (47 of 1968), S. 2(m)]

"FORCE CUSTODY" means the arrest or confinement of a member of the Force according to rules. [Indo-Tibetan Border Police Force Act (35 of 1992), S. 2(1)(m)]

Force majeure. Irresistible force or compulsion; circumstance beyond one's control.

The expression 'force *majeure*' is not a mere French version of the Latin expression "*vis major*". It is a term of wider import. Strikes, breakdown of machinery, which, though normally not included in "*vis major*" are included in "force *majeure*", the intention is to save the performing party from the consequences of anything over which he has no control. *Dhanrajamal Gobindram* v. *Shamji Kalidas and Co.*, AIR 1961 SC 1285, 1291. [Indian Contract Act (9 of 1872), S. 29]

FORCE MAJEURE means act of God, war, insurrection, riot, civil commotion, strike, earthquake, tide, storm, tidal wave, flood, lightning, explosion, fire and any other happening which the lessee could not reasonably prevent or control. *Mohd. Serajuddin* v. *State of Orissa,* AIR 1969 Ori 152 at 162. [Indian Contract Act (9 of 1872), S. 56]

Superior power. [Commercial Documents Evidence Act (30 of 1939, Sch., pt. II, item 17].

Force majeure clause. A clause in a contract specifying events such as strikes, *etc.*, which would excuse the non-performance of a contractual obligation.

Force or **violence.** While the word 'force' has been defined in S. 349, the word 'violence' has not been defined in the code. 'Violence' must therefore be understood in its ordinary sense. 'Violence' is a word of wider import than 'force' and includes force used against inanimate objects also. *Sunder Singh* v. *State,* AIR 1955 All 232 (FB). [IPC (45 of 1860), S. 146]

Forced. The word 'forced' in S. 366, IPC (45 of 1860) can also be taken to be used in the ordinary dictionary sense as including forced by stress of circumstances.

Forced labour. Any factor which deprives a person of a choice of alternatives and compels him to adopt one particular course of action may properly be regarded as 'force' and if labour or service is compelled as a result of such 'force' it would be 'forced labour'. *People's Union for Democratic Rights* v. *Union of India*, AIR 1982 SC 1473, 1490. [Constitution of India, Art. 23(1)]

Where a person provides labour or service to another for remuneration which is less than the minimum wage, the labour or service provided by him clearly falls within the scope and ambit of the words "forced labour" under Article 23, Constitution of India. *Sanjit Roy* v. *State of Rajasthan*, AIR 1983 SC 328, 332.

Where a prisoner in a jail provides labour or service to another for remuneration which is less than the minimum wage, the labour or service provided by him clearly falls within the scope and ambit of the words 'forced labour'. *In the Matter of 'Prison Reforms' Enhancement of Wages of Prisoners*, AIR 1983 Ker 261, 271.

Compelled or imposed labour. [Constitution of India, Art. 23(1)].

The words 'forced labour' occurring in Art. 23 of the Constitution would mean involuntary and compulsory service by a person irrespective of the Act that he is paid remuneration either minimum or even higher. Imposition of hard labour on the convicted prisoners is not included within the concept of it. *State of Gujarat* v. *Hon'ble High Court of Gujarat*, AIR 1998 SC 3164. [Constitution of India, Art. 23]

Forced resignation. It means a resignation not voluntarily given by the employee but is brought about by force, duress, or any other manner by the employer. It is by the act of the employer. In substance the contract of service comes to end by the action on the part of employer and amounts to termination of service by the employer. [*Shriram Swami Shikshan Sanstha, Nagpur* v. *Education Officer Zilla Parisad Nagpur,* MLJ : Digest (1984), p. 283 : 1984 Lab IC. 100 : 1984 Mah LJ 31]. [Maharashtra Employees of Private Schools (Conditions of Service) Regulation Act (III of 1978), Ss. 8 & 9]

Forces. Means regular Army, Navy and Air Force or any part of any one or more of them. [Air Force Act (45 of 1950), S. 4(xix) and Army Act (46 of 1950), S. 3(xi)]

Forecast. Foresight; conjectural estimate of something future.

Forcible. Effected by force or threat of force against opposition or resistance.

Forcible detainer. A forcible holding possession of any lands or tenements, whereby the lawful entry of justices, or others having a right to enter, is barred or hindered

Forcible rape. Aggravated form of statutory rape.

Sexual intercourse against a person's will by use of threat or force. (*Criminal*)

Forcibly. By force.

Forcibly and wrongfully. It is not necessary that actual force or violence should have been used to some person or persons before a dispossession can be said to be 'forcible'. When the dispossession is effected by a show of criminal force sufficient to intimidate those in possession and to deter them from resistance, the latter are said to have been forcibly dispossessed. *S.M. Dokhan* v. *Madholala,* AIR 1953 Ajmer 74, 76. [CrPC, 1973 (2 of 1974), S. 145(6)(a)]

Foreclose. To debar a mortgagor from his right to redeem a mortgage.

Foreclosed. Shut out or excluded; as the barring of the equity of redemption on mortgages, *etc.* (*Tomlin*)

Foreclosure. Foreclosure in theory, at least, is merely a decree determining the equitable right of a mortgagor to redeem after the mortgagee's estate has become absolute at law.

The action of foreclosing. [T.P. Act (4 of 1882), S. 67].

Forefather. Those from whom one's father or mother is descended; the earlier generations of a family or race; ancestor.

Foreign arbitral award. An arbitration award which is made in one country and enforced in another country. *(Alternative Dispute Redressal)*

Foreign company. Means a company which is not a domestic company. [Income-tax Act (43 of 1961), S. 2(23A)] [Also see *Explanation* to section 24 of the Pension Fund Regulatory & Development Authority Act, 2013 (23 of 2013)]

'FOREIGN COMPANY' means a body corporate incorporated outside India, and includes a firm or other association of individuals. [Foreign Exchange Management (Establishment in India of Branch or Office or other Place of Business) Regulations, 2000, Reg. 2(b)]

"FOREIGN COMPANY" for the purposes of section 234(2), the expression 'foreign company' means any company or body corporate incorporated outside India whether having a place of business in India or not. [*Explanation* to section 234(2) of the Companies Act, 2013 (18 of 2013)]

"FOREIGN COMPANY" means any company or body corporate incorporated outside India which—

(*a*) has a place of business in India whether by itself or through an agent, physically or through electronic mode; and

(*b*) conducts any business activity in India in any other manner. [S. 2(42) of the Companies Act, 2013 (18 of 2013)]

Foreign country. "FOREIGN COUNTRY" means any country other than India. [Limitation Act (36 of 1963), S. 2(g)]

"FOREIGN COUNTRY" means a country or place outside, and includes a ship which is for the time being in the territorial waters of such a country or place. [Foreign Marriage Act (33 of 1969), S. 2(c)]

When used in relation to countries in political sense, the term "foreign" refers to the jurisdiction of government of the country.

Any country, state or kingdom not one's own. [CPC (5 of 1908), S. 83, *Expln.* and Constitution of India, VII sch., list I, item 14].

Foreign Court. "FOREIGN COURT" means a Court situate outside India and not established or continued by the authority of the Central Government. [CPC (5 of 1908), S. 2(5)]

Foreign currency. "FOREIGN CURRENCY" means any currency other than Indian currency. [Foreign Exchange Regulation Act (46 of 1973), S. 2(g)] [Now repealed & replaced by FEMA, 1999 (42 of 1999)]

"Foreign currency" shall have the meaning assigned to it in clause (*m*) of section 2 of the Foreign Exchange Management Act, 1999 (42 of 1999). [International Financial Services Centres Authority Act, 2019 (50 of 2019), section 3(1)(f)]

[Also see *Explanation* (a) to section 194LC of the Income-tax Act, 1961 (43 of 1961) as inserted (w.e.f. 1-7-2012) by the Finance Act, 2012]

Foreign currency account. Means an account held or maintained in currency other than the currency of India or Nepal or Bhutan. [Foreign Exchange Management (Foreign Currency Accounts by a Person Resident in India) Regulations, 2000, Reg. 2(iii)]

Foreign currency and **Indian currency.** The expression "foreign currency" means 'any currency other than Indian currency' Section 2(*G*) of the Foreign Exchange Regulation Act (46 of 1973). According to Section 2(*k*) of that Act, 'Indian currency' means 'currency which is expressed or drawn in Indian Rupee but does not include special bank notes and special one-rupee notes issued under Section 28-A of the Reserve Bank of India Act (2 of 1934).

Foreign currency convertible bond (FCCB). Means a bond issued by an Indian company expressed in foreign currency, and the principal and interest in respect of which is payable in foreign currency. [Foreign Exchange Management (Transfer or Issue of any Foreign Security) Regulations, 2000, Reg. 2(g)]

In this scheme, unless the context otherwise requires—

"FOREIGN CURRENCY CONVERTIBLE BONDS" means bonds issued in accordance with this scheme and subscribed by a nonresident in foreign currency and convertible into ordinary shares of the issuing company in any manner, either in whole, or in part, on the basis of any equity related warrants attached to debt instruments; [Issue of Foreign Currency Convertible Bonds and Ordinary Shares (Through Depositary Receipt Mechanism) Scheme, 1993, S. 2(b)]

Foreign direct investment (FDI). Investment by a foreign firm that gives it at least a 10% ownership in the local firm. FOREIGN DIRECT INVESTMENT' (FDI) means investment through capital instruments by a person resident outside India in an unlisted Indian company; or in 10 per cent or more of the post issue paid-up equity capital on a fully diluted basis of a listed Indian company;

Note.—In case an existing investment by a person resident outside India in capital instruments of a listed Indian company falls to a level below 10 per cent of the post issue paid-up equity capital on a fully diluted basis, the investment shall continue to be treated as FDI.

Explanation.—Fully diluted basis means the total number of shares that would be outstanding if all possible sources of conversion are exercised. [Foreign Exchange Management (Transfer or Issue of Security by a Person Resident outside India) Regulations, 2017, Regn. 2(xvii)].

Foreign Educational Institutions. Means—(*i*) an Institution duly established or incorporated in its home country and offering educational programmes at the undergraduate and higher levels in its home country and (*ii*) which offers or proposes to offer programme(s) of study leading to the award of degree(s) through conventional face to face mode, but excluding distance mode, in a twinning arrangement with any Indian Educational Institutions. [University Grants Commission (Promotion and Maintenance of Standards of Academic Collaboration between Indian and Foreign Educational Institutions) Regulations, 2016, Regn. 2(h)].

Foreign enterprise. "Foreign enterprise" will include a foreign company. A foreign company is a company incorporated under the law of the foreign country concerned. A branch unit or establishment of Indian Company doing business in a foreign country or situated in a foreign country is not "foreign enterprise". *Petron Engg. Construction (P) Ltd.* v. *Central Board of Direct Taxes*, AIR 1989 SC 501, 505. [Income Tax Act (43 of 1961), S. 80-O]

For the purposes of this clause, the expression "foreign enterprise" means a person who is a non-resident. [Income-tax Act (43 of 1961), S. 10(15A) *Expl.*]

Foreign exchange (F/X). Foreign currency includes all deposits, credits, drafts, bills of exchange *etc.*, in foreign currency. [Foreign Exchange Regulation Act (46 of 1973), S. 2(g) and Industrial Finance Corporation Act (15 of 1948) (*Repealed by Act (23 of 1993)*, S. 27(1)].

"FOREIGN EXCHANGE" means foreign currency and includes—

(i) all deposits, credits and balances payable in any foreign currency, and any drafts, traveller's cheques, letters of credit and bills of exchange, expressed or drawn in Indian currency but payable in any foreign currency;

(ii) any instrument payable, at the option of the drawee or holder thereof or any other party thereto, either in Indian currency or foreign currency or partly in one and partly in another. [Foreign Exchange Regulation Act (46 of 1973), S. 2(h) and Finance Act (11 of 1987), S. 99(d)]

"FOREIGN EXCHANGE" means foreign currency and includes,—

(i) deposits, credits and balances payable in any foreign currency,

(ii) drafts, travellers cheques, letters of credit or bills of exchange, expressed or drawn in Indian currency but payable in any foreign currency,

(iii) drafts, travellers cheques, letters of credit or bills of exchange drawn by banks, institutions or persons outside India, but payable in Indian currency. [Foreign Exchange Management Act (42 of 1999), S. 2(n)]

Foreign exchange asset. In this chapter, unless the context otherwise requires, —

"FOREIGN EXCHANGE ASSET" means any specified asset which the assessee has acquired or purchased with, or subscribed to in, convertible foreign exchange. [Income-tax Act (43 of 1961), S. 115 C(b)]

Foreign exchange bonds. Means the Bonds, issued by the State Bank of India constituted under the State Bank of India Act, 1955 in accordance with such scheme as the Reserve

Bank of India may, by notification in the Official Gazette, specify in this behalf, the investment wherein is made on or after the date of commencement of this Act but before the specified date.

Explanation.—For the purpose of this clause, "specified date" means the 1st day of December, 1991 or such other later date as the Central Government may, by notification in the Official Gazette, specify in this behalf. [Remittance of Foreign Exchange and Investment on Foreign Exchange Bonds (Immunities and Exemptions) Act (41 of 1991), S. 5(1)(a).

Foreign exchange derivative contract. Means a financial transaction or an arrangement in whatever form and by whatever name called, whose value is derived from price movement in one or more underlying assets, and includes,

(a) a transaction which involves at least one foreign currency other than currency of Nepal or Bhutan, or

(b) a transaction which involves at least one interest rate applicable to a foreign currency not being a currency of Nepal or Bhutan, or

(c) a forward contract,

but does not include foreign exchange transaction for Cash or Tom or Spot deliveries. [Foreign Exchange Management (Foreign Exchange Derivative Contracts) Regulations, 2000, Reg. 2(v)]

Foreign exchange due. Means the amount which a person has a right to receive or claim in foreign exchange. [Foreign Exchange Management (Realisation, Repatriation and Surrender of Foreign Exchange) Regulations, 2000, Reg. 2(iii)]

Foreign exchange rate. The price at which the currency of one country can be bought with the currency of another country.

Foreign-going ship. 'FOREIGN-GOING SHIP' means a ship not being a home-trade ship, employed in trading between any port or place in India and any other port or place, or between ports or places, outside India or between ports or places, outside India. [Merchant Shipping Act (44 of 1858), S. 3(13)]. See also *Karan Vaswani (Capt.)* v. *Union of India*, (2000) 3 SCC 602 para 6 : AIR 2000 SC 1446.

A vessel weighing more than 3000 tons gross would come within the definition of 'foreigngoing ship' under Section 3(13) of the Act, even if it plies between a port and place in India to another port and place in India. *National Union of Seafarers of India* v. *D.G. of Shipping, Mumbai*, AIR 2000 Bom 333, 337, para 6. [Merchant Shipping Act (44 of 1958), S. 3(13)]

Foreign-going vessel or aircraft. Means any vessel or aircraft for the time being engaged in the carriage of goods or passengers between any port of airport in India and any port or airport outside India, whether touching any intermediate port or airport in India or not. It includes—

(i) any naval vessel of a foreign Government taking part in any naval exercises;

(ii) any vessel engaged in fishing or any other operations outside the territorial waters of India, and

(iii) any vessel or aircraft proceeding to a place outside India for any purpose whatsoever. [Customs Act (52 of 1962), S. 2(21)]

Foreign hospitality. Means any offer, not being a purely casual one, made by a foreign source for providing a person with the costs of travel to any foreign country or territory or with free board, lodging, transport of medical treatment. [Foreign Contribution (Regulation) Act (49 of 1976), S. 2(d)]

Foreign Institutional Investor. For the purposes of this section, —

(a) the expression "foreign institutional investor" means such investor as the Central Government may, by notification in the Official Gazette, specify in this behalf. [Income-tax Act 1961, *Explanation* (a) to S. 115AD. Also see (w.e.f. 1-6-2013) *Explanation* (*a*) to section 194LD of the Income-tax Act, 1961 (43 of 1961)]

Foreign instrument. Any instrument, not drawn, made or made payable like "Inland instrument" (S. 11 of Act 26, 1881) shall be deemed to be a foreign instrument. [Negotiable Instruments Act (26 of 1881), S. 12]

Foreign insurer. "FOREIGN INSURER" means an existing insurer incorporated under the law of any country outside India. [General Insurance Business (Nationalisation) Act (57 of 1972), S. 3(f)]

Foreign judgment. The judgment of a foreign Court. [CPC (5 of 1908), S. 2(6)]

The expression 'foreign judgment' must be understood to mean 'an adjudication by a foreign Court' upon the matter before it and it would be quite impracticable to hold that a foreign judgment means a statement by a foreign Judge of the reasons for his order. *Abdul Wazid* v. *Vishwanathan,* AIR 1953 Mad 261. [CPC (5 of 1908), S. 13]

Foreign jurisdiction. "FOREIGN JURISDICTION" means any jurisdiction which by treaty, agreement, grant, usage, sufferance or other lawful means, the Central Government has for the time being in or in relation to any area outside India. [Foreign Jurisdiction Act (47 of 1947), S. 2(a)]

Such jurisdiction as a State has with regard to its subjects when they are, or with regard to acts done, outside its boundaries. [Constitution of India, Art. 260].

Foreign language. Means a language which is neither an Indian language nor the English language. [Cigarettes (Regulation of Production, Supply and Distribution) Act (49 of 1975), S. 2(e) and Cigarettes and Other Tobacco Products

(Prohibition of Advertisement and Regulation of Trade and Commerce, Production, Supply and Distribution) Act (34 of 2003), S. 3(e)]

Foreign liquor. "FOREIGN LIQUOR" includes every liquor imported into India, other than Indian liquor. [Andhra Pradesh Prohibition Act (AP Act No. 17 of 1995), S. 2(4)]

The words 'foreign liquor' in S. 24-A includes denatured spirit. The words can not be given a restricted meaning for, the word consumption cannot be confined to consumption of beverage alone. *State of U.P.* v. *Synthetics & Chemicals Ltd.*, AIR 1980 SC 614. [U.P. Excise Act, 1910, S. 24-A and R. 12]

"Foreign liquor" and **"denatured spirit".** Foreign liquor was defined as including specially denatured spirit. Specially denatured spirit means spirit rendered unfit for human consumption in such manner as may be prescribed by the Excise Commissioner by notification in this behalf and does not include ordinary denatured spirit for general use. *State of Uttar Pradesh* v. *Synthetics and Chemicals Ltd.*, AIR 1980 SC 614.

Foreign matter. 'FOREIGN MATTER' means any extraneous matter other than foodgrain and shall comprise organic or inorganic matter. [T.N. Scheduled Articles (Prescription of Standards) Order, 1977, S. 2(d) issued under S. 3 of E.C. Act (10 of 1955)]

Foreign power. On a correct interpretation of the meaning of the words "the relations of India with foreign powers" there is no doubt that Pakistan must be regarded as a foreign power, although that country may be a part of the commonwealth as India is. *Jagan Nath Sathu* v. *Union of India*, AIR 1960 SC 625, 628. [Preventive Detention Act (4 of 1950), S. 3]

Foreign project. "FOREIGN PROJECT" means a project for—

(i) the construction of any building, road, dam, bridge or other structure outside India;

(ii) the assembly or installation of any machinery or plant outside India;

(iii) the execution of such other work (of whatever nature) as may be prescribed. [Income-tax Act (43 of 1961), S. 80 HHB (2)(b)]

Foreign security. Means any security created or issued elsewhere than in India, and any security the principal of or interest on which is payable in any foreign currency or elsewhere than in India. [Foreign Exchange Regulation Act (46 of 1973), S. 2(i)]

"FOREIGN SECURITY" means any security, in the form of shares, stocks, bonds, debentures or any other instrument denominated or expressed in foreign currency and includes securities expressed in foreign currency, but where redemption or any form of return such as interest or dividends is payable in Indian currency. [Foreign Exchange Management (42 of 1999), S. 2(o)]

Foreign service. Extraneous service; service in another country than one's own.

Foreign state. "FOREIGN STATE" includes any persons or person exercising or assuming to exercise the powers of Government in or over any country, colony, province or people, beyond the limits of India. [Foreign Recruiting Act (4 of 1874), S. 2]

"FOREIGN STATE" means any State outside India which has been recognised by the Central Government. [CPC (5 of 1908), S. 87A(a)]

"FOREIGN STATE" means any State outside India and includes every constituent part, colony or dependency of such state. [Extradition Act (34 of 1962), S. 2(e)]

A company of foreign origin having all its shares owned by a foreign Government, is a 'foreign state' under Section 86 of the Code. *Kenya Airways* v. *Jinibai B. Kheshmala*, AIR 1998 Bom 287, 301, para 34. [CPC (5 of 1908), S. 86]

For the purposes of this Constitution 'foreign State' means any State other than India:

Provided that, subject to the provisions of any law made by Parliament, the President may by order declare any State not to be foreign State for such purposes as may be specified in the order. [Constitution of India, Article 367(3)]

Foreign travel. Means a travel, the whole or any part of which is outside India. [Finance Act (11 of 1987), S. 99(e)]

Foreigner. The word "FOREIGNER" shall denote a person, (*a*) who is not a natural born British subject as defined in sub-Ss. (1) and (2) of S. 1 of the British Nationality and Status of Aliens Act, 1914, or (*b*) who has not been granted a certificate of naturalisation as a British subject under any law for the time being in force in British India : provided that any British subject who, under any law for the time being in force in British India, ceases to be a British subject shall thereupon be deemed to be a foreigner, [Foreigners Act (3 of 1864), S. 1].

"FOREIGNER" means a person who is not a citizen of India. [Foreigners Act (31 of 1946), S. 2]

A person who is not a citizen of India is a foreigner. [Foreigners Act (31 of 1946), S. 2]

In a general sense, this is applied to a person belonging to another nation or country.

A person, who has after the first day of March 1947, migrated from the territory of India to the territory included in Pakistan shall not be deemed to be a citizen of India and he is only a foreigner. *State of Assam* v. *Tilkedar Ali*, AIR 1972 SC 2166, 2168. [Foreigners Act (31 of 1946), S. 2(1)]

Forejudge. To judge or determine before hearing evidence.

Forensic medicine. Forensic medicine is the science which deals with the application of every branch of medical knowledge to the purposes of the law. "*Legal medicine*" "*State medicine*," and "*Medical Jurisprudence*" are practically synonymous.

Forensics. Pertaining to or belonging to the courts. In the field of public discussion or debate. (*Ballentine's Law Dictionary, 3rd Edn.*)

Foreshore. "FORESHORE" in relation to a port, means the area between the high water mark and the low water mark relating to that Major Port. [Major Port Authorities Act (1 of 2021), S. 2(1)(g)]

'FORESHORE' includes the shore and bed of the sea and of every channel, creek, bay, estuary and navigable river as far up it as the tide flows, [Salmon and Fresh-water Fisheries Act, 1975, S. 41].

'FORESHORE' means the shore and bed of the sea and of any tidal water, below the line of the medium high tide between the spring tides and the neap tides. [Limitation Act (9 of 1908), Sch 1, para 11(3)]

The part of the shore which remains covered with water at the High Tide and gets uncovered at the Low Tide. S. *Jagannath* v. *Union of India*, (1997) 2 SCC 87, para 23 : AIR 1997 SC 811.

Foresight. A capacity which is frequently notionally postulated of a hypothetical 'reasonable man' when a Court is seeking to determine whether a particular defendant should or should not be held liable for a particular happening.

Forest. The word 'forest' bears extended meaning of a tract of land covered with trees, shrubs, vegetation and undergrowth intermingled with trees and pastures, be it of natural growth or man-made forestation. *Samatha* v. *State of A.P.*, AIR 1997 SC 3297.

"FOREST" means a tract of land covered with trees (whether standing, felled, found or otherwise), shrubs, bushes, or woody, vegetation, whether of natural growth or planted by human agency and existing or being maintained with or without human effort, or such tract of land on which such growth is likely to have an effect on the supply of timber, fuel, forest produce, or grazing facilities, or on climate, stream flow, protection of land from erosion, or other such matters and includes—

(i) land covered with stumps of trees of forest;

(ii) land which is part of a forest or lies within it or was part of a forest or was lying within a forest on the 30th day of August, 1975;

(iii) such pasture land, water-logged or cultivable or noncultivable land, lying within or linked to a forest, as may declared to be forest by the State Government;

(iv) forest land held or let for purpose of agriculture or for any purposes ancillary thereto;

(v) all the forest produce therein, whether standing, felled, found or otherwise. [Maharashtra Private Forests (Acquisition) Act, 1975, S. 2(c-i) as cited in *Godrej and Boyce Manufacturing Company Limited* v. *State of Maharashtra*, (2014) 3 SCC 430, para 18].

The word 'forest' means a parcel of land on which trees have been grown. The rubber plantation containing rubber trees would be regarded as private 'forest' within the ambit of Section 2(a) of the Act. *State of Kerala* v. *Pullangode Rubber and Produce Co. Ltd.*, (1999) 6 SCC 99, paras 5 & 6 : AIR 1999 SC 2522. [Madras Preservation of Private Forest Act (27 of 1949), S. 2(a)]

Forest shall include all statutory recognised forests, whether designated as reserved, protected or otherwise. [*State of Uttarakhand* v. *Kumaon Stone Crusher*, (2018) 14 SCC 537, para 126].

Forest Land. "FOREST LAND" includes any wasteland containing shrubs and trees and any other class of land declared to be forest land by a notification of the State Government. [Orissa Communal, Forest and Private Lands (Prohibition of Alienation) Act, (1 of 1948), S. 2(c) as cited in *Chandradhoja Sahoo* v. *State of Orissa*, (2012) 12 SCC 419, para 14].

Forest offence. 'FOREST OFFENCE' means an offence punishable under this Act or under any rule made thereunder. [Indian Forest Act (16 of 1927), S. 2(3)]

"FOREST OFFENCE" means an offence punishable under this Act or any Rule made thereunder. [Kerala Forest Act, 1961 (4 of 1962), S. 2(e) as cited in *State of Kerala* v. *P.V. Mathew*, (2012) 4 SCC 457, para 14].

Forest Officer. 'FOREST OFFICER' means any person whom the State Government or any officer empowered by the State Government in this behalf, may appoint to carry out all or any of the purposes of this Act or to do anything required by this Act or any rule made thereunder to be done by a Forest Officer. [Indian Forest Act (16 of 1927), S. 2(2)]

Forest produce. Includes (*a*) the following when found in, or brought from a reserved forest or public forest-land, that is to say—(*i*) trees and leaves, flowers and fruits, and all other parts or produce not hereinafter mentioned of trees; (*ii*) plants not being trees (including grass, creepers, reeds and moss), and all parts of produce of such plants; (*iii*) wild animals and skins, tusks, horns, bones, silk cocoons, honey and wax, edible birds' nests, bats' guano, and all other parts or produce of animals; and (*iv*) peat, surface-soil, rock and minerals (including lime-stone laterite, mineral oils and all products of mines or quarries); and (*b*) the following whether found in, or brought from, any such forest or forest-land, or not, that is to say— timber, charcoal, caoutchouc, catechu, woodoil, resin, natural varnish, bark, lac, *mahua* flowers and myrabolams. [Burma Forests Act (4 of 1902), S. 3(6)]

'FOREST PRODUCE' includes—

(i) the following whether found in, or brought from a forest or not, that is to say— Timber, charcoal, wood oil, gum, resin, natural varnish, bark lac, fibres and roots of sandalwood and rosewood; and

(ii) the following when found in, or brought from, a forest, that is to say—

(a) trees and leaves, flowers and fruits, and all other parts or produce not hereinbefore mentioned, of trees;

(b) plants not being trees (including grass, creepers, reeds and moss) and all parts of produced of such plant; and

(c) silk cocoons, honey and wax;

(d) peat, surface oil, rock and minerals (including limestone, laterite, mineral oils and all products of mines or quarries). [Wildlife Protection Act, 1972, S. 2(f) as cited in *State of Kerala* v. *P.V. Mathew*, (2012) 4 SCC 457, para 14].

'FOREST PRODUCE' includes—

(a) the following whether found in, or brought from, a forest or not, that is to say:—

Timber, charcoal, caoutchouc, catechu, wood-oil, resin, natural varnish, bark, lac, *mahua* flowers, *mahua* seeds, kuth and myrabolams; and

(b) the following when found in or brought from a forest, that is to say :—

(i) trees and leaves, flowers and fruits, and all other parts or produce, not herein before mentioned, of trees,

(ii) plants not being trees (including grass, creepers, reeds and moss), and all parts or produce of such plants,

(iii) wild animals and skins, tusks, horns, silk, cocoons, honey and wax, and all other parts or produce of animals, and

(iv) peat, surface soil, rock and minerals (including limestone, laterite, mineral oils and all products of mines or quarries). [Indian Forest Act (16 of 1927), S. 2(4)]

Forestry. Science or art creating, managing and improving forests.

The science of planting and taking care of forests.

Foreword. Preface; introductory remarks (as) Foreword of a book.

Forfeit. To lose the right, or to render oneself liable to be deprived of something in consequence of an offence or breach of a condition or the like [T.P. Act (4 of 1882), S. 35, ill.]; to lose the right *etc.* [Bonded Labour System (Abolition) Act (19 of 1976), S. 2(g)(3)]; to subject to forfeiture [CPC (5 of 1908), O. XXI, R. 86].

Forfeiture. Forfeiture is the divestiture of specific property without compensation in consequence of some default or act forbidden by law.

The word 'forfeiture' is used in S. 114 in a technical sense and is incurred in case the lessee breaks an express condition which provides that on breach thereof the lessor may re-enter and even in such a case the lessor has to give notice in writing to the lessee of his intention to determine the lease. *Bhagwant Rambhae Khere* v. *Ramachandra Kesho Pathak,* AIR 1953 Bom 129, 133. [TP Act (4 of 1882), S. 114]

The action of forfeiting or the fact of being forfeited. [T.P. Act (4 of 1882) and Art. 34, Constitution of India]

Forge. To make in the likeness of something else (*Webster*); to fabricate by false imitation; to make or fabricate a thing in imitation of another with a view to deceive and defraud; to make falsely; to counterfeit.

To do the act of forgery; to fabricate. [IPC (45 of 1860), Ss. 466, 467 and 471]; to form by heating and hammering.

Forged. Made by forgery. [Indian Evidence Act (1 of 1872), S. 126, ill. (b)].

Forged document. A false document made wholly or in part by forgery is designated "a forged document." [IPC (45 of 1860), S. 470].

Document brought into existence by forgery. [CrPC 1973 (2 of 1974), S. 94(2)(d)].

Forger. One who commits forgery. [CrPC, 1973 (2 of 1974), S. 110(a)].

Forgery. "Whoever makes any false document or part of a document, with intent to cause damage or injury to the public or to any person, or to support any claim or title, or to cause any person to part with property, or to enter into any express or implied contract, or with intent to commit fraud or that fraud may be committed, commits forgery". [IPC (45 of 1860), S. 463, *Expln.*] [(w.e.f. 1-7-2024) repealed and replaced by Bharatiya Nyaya Sanhita, 2023 (45 of 2023), section 336(1)].

"A man's signature of his own may amount to forgery". [IPC (45 of 1860), S. 464, *Expln.*] [(w.e.f. 1-7-2024) repealed and replaced by Bharatiya Nyaya Sanhita, 2023 (45 of 2023), section 335, *Expln. 1*]

The making of a false document in the name of a fictitious person, intending it to be believed that the document was made by a real person, or in the name of a deceased person, intending it to be believed that the document was made by the person in his lifetime, may amount to forgery. [(w.e.f. 1-7-2024) Bharatiya Nyaya Sanhita, 2023 (45 of 2023), section 335, *Expln. 2*]

Forgings. [Income-tax Act (43 of 1961), 5th sch., item 11].

Forgive. To pardon; remit fine, debt, *etc.*

Form. In these rules, unless the context otherwise requires—

"FORM" means a form appended to these rules and also includes forms as prescribed by the Department of Posts. [National Savings Certificate (VIII Issue) Rules, 1989, S. 2(viii)]

"FORM" means the Form of the Cost Audit Report and includes auditor's observations and suggestions, Annexure and Proforma to the Cost Audit Report; [Cost Audit Report Rules, 2001, R. 2(c)]

Manner; method; way of doing anything; formal procedure; the visible aspect of a thing; proforma.

"FORM" means the form in the schedule to the Companies (Authorised to Registered) Rules, 2014, which shall be used for the matter to which it relates. [R. 2(1)(d) of the Companies (Authorised to Registered) Rules, 2014]

'Form' means "the particular way in which something appears or exists or a shape of someone or something". [Macmillan Dictionary as cited in *State of Jharkhand* v. *La Opala R.G. Limited,* (2014) 15 SCC 136, para 22].

"Form" means "visible shape or configuration of something" or the "style, design, and arrangement in an artistic work as distinct from its content". [Oxford Dictionary as cited in *State of Jharkhand* v. *La Opala R.G. Limited,* (2014) 15 SCC 136, para 22]

Form of procedure. Fixed or formal way or the mode in which successive steps in litigation are taken. [CPC (5 of 1908), S. 4(1)].

Form of return. [Industrial Development Bank of India Act (18 of 1964), S. 37(2)(h)].

Form of security. Shape and structure of anything that makes the money more assured in its payment or more readily recoverable. [CPC (5 of 1908), O. XLV, R. 7(1)(a), prov.].

Form or method. For the purposes of this sub-section, the term "FORM OR METHOD", in relation to a rate of duty of excise, means the basis, including valuation, weight, number, length, area, volume or any other measure, on which the duty may be levied. [Central Excise Act (1 of 1944), S. 3-B(b), *Explanation*]

Forma legalis forma essentialis. (*Maxim*) Legal form is an essential form. (*Bouvier; Latin for Lawyers*)

Forma non observata infertur adnullatio actus. Form not being observed, a nullity of the act is inferred. (*Latin for Lawyers*)

Forma pauperis. A suit may be instituted by a pauper who is a person, not possessed of sufficient means to enable him to pay the fee prescribed by law for the plaint in such suit. [CPC (5 of 1908), O. XXXIII]

Formal. Done in due form, or with solemnity; according to regular method. (*Webster*)

Formal defect. A 'formal defect' would seem to connote every kind of defect which does not affect the merits of the case. It cannot be said that the defect of non-inclusion of certain necessary parties is a 'formal defect'.

The defect which was likely to arise in the way of the plaintiff succeeding, was in the nature of a formal defect for there was a form which had to be adhered to in the matter of giving evidence in regard to the proof of the will. *Sheo Kumar Devedi* v. *Thekurji Maharaj Brijman,* AIR 1959 All 463, 465. [CPC (5 of 1908), O. XXIII, R. 1(3)(a)]

Formal document. A document following or according with established form, custom or rule and not deviating from what is usual or generally acceptable. [CPC (5 of 1908), O. XLV, R. 7(1)(b)(i)].

Formal expression. An expression following a prescribed form. [CPC (5 of 1908), S. 2(2)].

Formal order. Where the order of the commissioner required the Income Tax Officer to look into the books of account of the assessee and make an estimate in the light of the material based on those books and directed him to substitute his estimate for the income already assessed and modify the assessment accordingly and in pursuance of the order of the Income Tax Officer, by his order substituted his estimate, the final order is that of the Income Tax Officer and not of the commissioner. *Kishanlal Harichand* v. *Income Tax Officer, Nizamabad,* AIR 1973 SC 1010, 1011.

Formal parties. Parties who have no interest in the controversy between the real litigants, but have an interest in the subject-matter, which may be conveniently settled in the suit, and thereby prevent further litigation. (*Chadbourne* v. *Coe,* 51 Fed 479, 480).

Formal party. A person who is named in the pleadings as a party to an action who is not a necessary or indispensable party, but who is a merely nominal party to the action. (*Minnis* v. *Southern Pacific Co.* (C.C.A. Cal) 98 Fed. (2d) 913).

Formal warning. "A FORMAL WARNING shall mean a warning personally addressed to a prisoner by the Superintendent and recorded in the punishment-book and on the prisoner's history ticket." [Prisons Act (9 of 1894), S. 46(1), *Expln.*]

Formality. An established order; a rule of proceeding; a formal mode or method. (*Cent. Dict.*)

That which pertains to outward form; a formal act or observance; something being required to be done for form's sake. [Indian Evidence Act (1 of 1872), S. 92, prov. (2)].

Format. General arrangement of plan; to give a form. [Cine Workers Welfare Fund Act (33 of 1981), S. 2(c)].

Formation. The manner in which a thing is formed; structure; construction; conformation.

The action or process of forming. [Mines Act (35 of 1952), S. 58(v)].

Former. Preceding or going before in a series; antecedent in order of action, *etc.* (*Cent. Dict.*)

Earlier in time; pertaining to a period anterior to that in question; the first mentioned; occuring in the past.

Former Court. The Court in which the matter under consideration was dealt with earlier; the Court mentioned earlier.

Former French Establishments. Means the territories which immediately before the appointed day were comprised in the French Establishment in India known as Pondicherry, Karikal, Mahe and Yanam. [Pondicherry (Administration) Act (49 of 1962), S. 2(c)]

Former Indian High Court. Means the High Court at Rangoon, the High Court at Lahore, the Chief Court of Sind or the Judicial Commissioner's Court of North West Frontier Province. [High Court Judges (Conditions of Service) (28 of 1954), S. 2(1)(e)]

Former suit. The expression 'former suit' under Section 11, CPC (5 of 1908), means a previously decided suit. *Prabha Singh Surjit Singh* v. *Sanka Narasimha Rao,* AIR 1957 AP 992, 993. [CPC (5 of 1908), S. 11]

The expression 'former suit' shall denote a suit which has been decided prior to the suit in question whether or not it was instituted prior thereto. [*Sri Gangai Vinayagar Temple* v. *Meenakshi Ammal*, (2015) 3 SCC 624, para 23] [CPC (5 of 1908), S. 11, *Explanation* I].

To raise the bar of *res judicata*, the expression 'former suit'; in Section 11, CPC (5 of 1908), denotes the suit which has been decided prior to the suit in question whether or not it was instituted prior thereto. *Tulison Traders Delhi* v. *Gurdit Singh,* AIR 1974 Del 190, 195.

The suit that was instituted and in some cases decided also before the suit under consideration. [CPC (5 of 1908), S. 11, *Expln*. I].

Formula. A conventional statement intended to express some fundamental truth or principle. [Payment of Bonus Act (21 of 1965), S. 34(3)]; [Drugs and Cosmetics Act (23 of 1940), S. 18(a)(iii)].

Fornication. Voluntary sexual intercourse between two unmarried persons.

Forsake. To abandon; give up; desert.

To renounce or surrender. [Navy Act (62 of 1957), S. 35(c)].

Forswear. Abjure; renounce; perjure oneself.

Fortified food. Means a food, as specified under the Food Safety and Standards (Food Products Standards and Food Additives) Regulations, 2011, that has undergone the process of fortification as per the provisions of these regulations. [Food Safety and Standards (Fortification of Foods) Regulations, 2018, Regn. 2(1)(d)].

Fortes fortuna juvat. Fortune favours the brave.

Forthwith. The term 'forthwith' means within a reasonable time. *Samsnath* v. *Bhagwat Nath,* AIR 1966 All 615, 616. [CPC (5 of 1908), O. XVII, R. 3 as amended by Allahabad High Court]

The word 'forthwith' cannot be taken to mean a mandate to decide the suit the same day as a penalty for default. *Kurilal Rangta* v. *Banarsi Devi,* AIR 1986 All 94, 104. [CPC (5 of 1908), O. XVII, R. 3]

Forthwith means immediately or without delay. [CPC (5 of 1908), O. XXI, R. 84]

Forthwith means "as soon as possible; without any delay". *Gopal Mondal* v. *State of West Bengal*, AIR 1975 SC 1807. [Maintenance of Internal Security Act (26 of 1971), S. 3(3)]

Maxwell in Interpretation of Statutes (11th Edition) at p. 341 observes as follows:—When a statute requires that something shall be done 'forthwith' it should be probably understood as allowing a reasonable time for doing it. *Bidya Deb Barma etc.* v. *District Magistrate, Tripura, Agartala*, AIR 1969 SC 323 at 325. [Preventive Detention Act (4 of 1950), S. 3(3)]

An Act which is to be done forthwith must be held to have been so done, when it is done with all reasonable despatch and without avoidable delay. The term 'forthwith' in S. 3(3) cannot mean the same thing as 'as soon as may be' in S. 7, and the former is more peremptory than the latter. *Kesha Nilkanth Joglakar* v. *Commissioner of Police*, AIR 1957 SC 28, 31, 32. [Preventive Detention Act (4 of 1950), Ss. 3(3) and 7]

"Forthwith in the section means immediately after the expiry of the time fixed for withdrawal of nomination papers". *K.K. Husenkhan* v. *Nijalingappa,* AIR 1968 Mys 18 at 25. [Representation of the People Act (43 of 1951), S. 53(2)]

It means with all reasonable quickness and reasonable prompt time. *Rao Mahmood Ahmed Khan* v. *Ranbir Singh,* AIR 1995 SC 2195.

Fortnight. Means a fortnight ending on the 15th day or on the last day of a month according to Gregorian Calendar.

"Fortnight" shall mean the period from Saturday to the second following Friday, both days inclusive. [Banking Regulation Act (10 of 1949), section 18(1), *Explanation (b)*]

Fortuitous. If the post is created to meet a situation which has suddenly arisen on account of happening of some event of temporary nature, such appointment to such a post can aptly be described as 'fortuitous'. *Rudra Kumar Sain* v. *Union of India*, (2000) 8 SCC 25, para 19 : AIR 2000 SC 2808.

Forum. A place of jurisdiction; the place where a remedy is sought; jurisdiction; a Court of justice; a Court; a place where legal redress is sought.

Forum non conveniens. The principle that a case should be heard in a Court of the place where parties, witnesses, and evidence are primarily located.

Forum originis. The forum or Court of nativity; place of a person's birth, considered as a place of jurisdiction.

Forum rei. (*Lat.*) [Forum of the thing] The Court of the country in which the subject of a dispute is situated.

Forward. In the forepart; transmit to transport or to carry.

To send towards the place of destination; to send forward.

Forward contract. A contract providing for performance on a future date.

'FORWARD CONTRACT' means a transaction involving delivery, other than cash or Tom or Spot delivery, of foreign exchange. [Foreign Exchange Management (Foreign Exchange Derivative Contracts) Regulations, 2000, Reg. 2 (iv)]

'FORWARD CONTRACT' means a contract of sale under which the date on which the cereals to which the contract relates are required to be delivered cannot fall within the month in which the contract is made or within the month immediately following that month. [(English) Cereals Marketing Act, 1965, S. 24 now repealed by the Agriculture and Horticulture Development Board Order, 2008 (1-4-2008)].

A forward contract is a contract for the sale or purchase of goods which postpones the delivery of goods and the payment of price therefor for a period exceeding eleven days. *Raymon & Co. (India) Pvt. Ltd.* v. *Waverley Jute Mills Co. Ltd.*, AIR 1959 Cal 89, 91. [Forward Contracts (Regulation) Act (74 of 1952), S. 2(*c*)]

The term 'forward contracts' includes speculative contracts ostensibly for delivery of goods. *Shivanarayan* v. *State of Madras*, AIR 1967 SC 986, 989.

A contract providing for performance on a future date.

Forward trading. Trading in goods or shares for delivery in the future. Such transactions are regulated or prohibited in India. For example, in specified areas, shares can only be sold in the Stock Exchange (whose rules require delivery in a specified period) or for ready delivery.

Foster. To nourish. [Jawaharlal Nehru University Act (53 of 1966), Sch. I, item (i)].

Foster care. "Foster care" means placement of a child, by the Committee for the purpose of alternate care in the domestic environment of a family, other than the child's biological family, that has been selected, qualified, approved and supervised for providing such care. [Juvenile Justice (Care and Protection of Children) Act, 2015 (2 of 2016), S. 2(29)].

Foster home. A household in which care is provided to a child who has been orphaned or removed from the home of his or her natural parents (as for reasons of abuse, neglect, or delinquency)

Foster parent. A person looking after a foster child. Foster parents have no legal rights over the children they foster, who may be removed from their care by their parents or legal guardian.

Foster son. A 'foster son' is a son who is not the real son or direct descendant of a person after his marriage. A 'foster child' need not be the real legitimate child of the person who brings him up. He is essentially the child of another person but is nursed, reared and brought up by another person as his own son. *K.V. Muthu* v. *Angamuthu Ammal*, AIR 1997 SC 628.

Fostering. Caring for a child by a person who is neither a parent by blood nor by adoption.

Foujadarry Court. A Court for administering the criminal law. (*Fifth Report*)

The *Foujdary* Court was simply a Police Court, and so far dealt with the possession that it prevented the occupation being disturbed by violence.

Fouling. Rendering filthy or dirty. [IPC (45 of 1860), S. 277].

Found undesirable to be retained. When the order refers to the fact that the appellant was found undesirable to be retained in the Government service it expressly casts a stigma on the appellant and in that sense, must be held to be on order of dismissal and meant that the Government did not think it desirable or necessary to continue the appellant in its employment. *Jagdish Mitter* v. *Union of India*, AIR 1964 SC 449.

Founded on facts. Based on facts. [Presidency Towns Insolvency Act (3 of 1909), S. 14(2)].

Foundling. A deserted or exposed infant; a child found without a parent or guardian, its relatives being unknown. (*Black*; *Ame. Cyc.*)

An unclaimed infant; a child deserted by unknown parents. [Indian Trusts Act (2 of 1882), S. 4, ill. (a)].

Four corners. The whole of an instrument.

Four corners rule. A rule holding that if a document (as a contract, deed, or will) appears on its face to be complete no outside evidence may be used to challenge it.

Fourth degree. A grade given to less serious forms of crimes.

Fowl. *As a noun* any bird; especially any large eatable bird. (*Webster Int. Bird.*) *As a verb*, to catch or kill wild fowl, for game or food, as by shooting, or by decoys, nets, *etc.*, (*Ame. Cyc.*)

'FOWL' includes any cock, hen, chicken, capon, turkey, goose, gander, duck, drake, guineafowl, peacock, peahen, swan, or pigeon. [(English) Protection of Animals Act, 1911, S. 15]

Fraction. A fragment; a separate portion; a disconnected part; a fragment or broken part; a portion of a thing less than the whole.

Any part or a unit. [Companies Act (1 of 1956), S. 287(2)]; a fragment or small piece [Gift Tax Act (18 of 1958), S. 46(2) (ee)].

Fractionem diei non recipit lex. Fraction of a day, the law takes no notice of. (*Bouvier*)

Fracture. The primary meaning of the word "fracture" is "breaking" though it is not necessary in the case of fracture of the skull bone that it be divided into two separate parts because it may consist merely of a crack; but if it is a crack it must be a crack which extends from the outer surface of the skull to the inner surface.

The breakage or rupture of a bone.

A fracture should affect a break in the bones, that is, there should be a rupture or fissure in them. *Centre of Legal Research* v. *State of Kerala*, AIR 1936 SC 2192, 2195. [IPC (45 of 1860), Ss. 320, 324 and 326]

Fragmentation. The action or process of breaking into fragments.

The state of having a file scattered around a disk in pieces rather than existing in one contiguous area of the disk. Fragmented files are slower to read than unfragmented files. (*Cyber Law*)

Frame. Construction; structure; constitution; to shape; to give shape; to make.

Frame issues. To draft or draw up the point or points in question arising out of pleadings containing statements of facts or law which one party affirms and the other denies. [CPC (5 of 1908), O. XIV, R. 3 and 4]; settling of issues.

Frame of suit. The form in which the suit has been instituted. [CPC (5 of 1908), O. L, R. 1(b)].

Frame the issue. The words 'frame the issue' mean only that a separate issue should be framed, but it is not necessary for the purpose of that section that the issues relating to these questions alone need be framed and those relating to the merits postponed. All the issues may be framed at the same time, but while deciding the Court should apply its mind at first to the questions mentioned in Section 7(a); and follow it up, by the decision on the other issues. By choosing therefore to proceed to hear all the issues together, the trial Court commits no violation either of Section 7(a) of the Madhya Pradesh Act or Section 13(a) of the Madhya Bharat Act. *Ranjitsingh Raisinghji Thakur* v. *Bapuniyan Sardarkhan,* MLJ : QD (1961-1965) Vol. II C2809 : 1962 MPLJ 951 : 1962 MPC 292 : 1962 Jab LJ 1020. [M.P. (C.P. and Berar) Money-Lenders Act (13 of 1934), S. 7(a) and Madhya Pradesh (CP and Berar) Money Lenders Act (13 of 1934), S. 13(a)]

Framing. An act of fraudulent display of contents of one website within another person's website with the purpose of making the user believe that he is actually viewing the former's website. Third party content is used intentionally within the frames of the web site. Aparna Viswanathan, *Cyber Law: Indian & International Perspectives*, 2012, LexisNexis Butterworths at p. 274.

Franchise. "FRANCHISE" means an agreement by which the franchisee is granted representational right to sell or manufacture goods or to provide service or undertake any process identified with franchisor, whether or not a trade mark, service mark, trade name or logo or any such symbol, as the case may be, is involved. [Finance Act (32 of 1994), S. 65(47) *as substituted by Finance Act (18 of 2005), S. 88(a)(xi)*]

The right of voting; voting qualification; privilege or exemption by privilege or grant.

Franchisee. Independent operator of a business who buys a franchise and operates under control of the franchisor. (*Cyber Law*)

Frater consanguineus. A brother by the father's side.

Frater uterinus. A brother or half-brother having the same mother.

Fraternal. Brotherly.

Fraternity. Brotherliness; guild; company with common interests; a religious body; a set of men of the same class.

Fraternity means brotherhood and common interest. [*Subramanian Swamy* v. *Union of India,* (2016) 7 SCC 221, para 157].

Fraud. "FRAUD" means and includes any of the following acts committed by a party to a contract, or with his connivance, or by his agent, with intent to deceive another party thereto or his agent, or to induce him to enter into the contract: (1) the suggestion, as to a fact, of that which is not true by one who does not believe it to be true; (2) the active concealment of a fact by one having knowledge or belief of the fact; (3) a promise made without any intention of performing it; (4) any other act fitted to deceive; (5) any such act or omission as the law specially declares to be fraudulent.

Explanation.—Mere silence as to facts likely to affect the willingness of a person to enter into a contract is not fraud, unless the circumstances of the case are such that, regard being had to them, it is the duty of the person keeping silence to speak, or unless his silence is in itself, equivalent to speech. [Indian Contract Act (9 of 1872), S. 17]

'Fraud' includes any act, expression, omission or concealment committed whether in a deceitful manner or not by a person or by any other person with his connivance or by his agent while dealing in securities in order to include another person as his agent to deal in securities, whether or not there is any wrongful gain or avoidance of any loss, and shall also include—

(1) a knowing misrepresentation of the truth or concealment of material fact in order that another person may act to his detriment;

(2) a suggestion as to a fact which is not true by one who does not believe it to true;

(3) an active concealment of a fact by a person having knowledge or belief of the fact;

(4) a promise made without any intention of performing it;

(5) a representation made in a reckless and careless manner whether it be true or false;

(6) any such act or omission as any other law specifically declares to be fraudulent;

(7) deceptive behaviour by a person depriving another of informed consent or full participation;

(8) a false statement made without reasonable ground for believing it to be true;

(9) the act of an issuer of securities giving out misinformation that affects the market price of the security, resulting in investors being effectively misled even though they did not rely on the statement itself or anything derived from it other than the market price. And 'fraudulent' shall be construed accordingly.

Nothing contained in this clause shall apply to any general comments made in good faith in regard to—

(a) the economic policy of the Government

(b) the economic situation of the country

(c) trends in the securities market; or

(d) any other matter of a like nature

Whether such comments are made in public or in private; [SEBI (Prohibition of Fraudulent and Unfair Trade Practices relating to Securities Market) Regulation, 2003 S. 2(c) as cited in *Securities and Exchange Board of India* v. *Pan Asia Advisors Limited*, (2015) 14 SCC 71, para 74].

Criminal deception; the using of false representations to obtain an unjust advantage or to injure the rights or interests of another.

The word "fraud" *as used in the Penal Code* is used in its ordinary and popular acceptation; a man who deliberately makes a false document with false signatures in order to shield and conceal an already perpetrated fraud is himself acting with intent to commit fraud within the S. 463, IPC (45 of 1860).

A person who freely consents to the solemnisation of the marriage after seeing the girl cannot object to the validity of the marriage on the ground of fraud. *Srikantaradhya* v. *Kamalamma,* AIR 1984 Karn 236, 239. [Hindu Marriage Act (25 of 1955), S. 12(1)(*c*)]

The word, does not include cases of misrepresentation or active concealment even of material facts inducing consent of a party. A wife knew that she was suffering from venereal disease, which fact she concealed from the husband. That is not a fraud under Section 12(1)(*c*). *Madhusudan* v. *Chandrika,* AIR 1975 MP 174, 179. [Hindu Marriage Act (25 of 1955), S 12(1)(c)]

Whenever fraud is alleged two elements are at least essential, viz., first deceit or intention to deceive or, in some cases a mere secrecy: and secondly, either actual injury or possible injury or an intention to expose some person either to actual injury or to a risk of possible injury by means of deceit or secrecy.

It is well settled that misrepresentation itself amounts to fraud. *Ram Chandra Singh* v. *Savitri Devi,* (2003) 8 SCC 319, para 17.

CONSTRUCTIVE FRAUD. A constructive fraud has been said to be "an act which the law declares to be fraudulent, without inquiring into its motive; not because arbitrary rules on this subject have been laid down but because certain acts carry in themselves an irresistible evidence of fraud."

"FRAUD" for the purposes of section 447 of Act 18 of 2013, 'fraud' in relation to affairs of a company or any body corporate, includes any act, omission, concealment of any fact or abuse of position committed by any person or any other person with the connivance in any manner, with intent to deceive, to gain undue advantage from, or to injure the interests of, the company or its shareholders or its creditors or any other person, whether or not there is any wrongful gain or wrongful loss. [*Explanation* (*i*) to section 447 of the Companies Act, 2013 (18 of 2013)]

Fraud feasor. One who has committed fraud.

Fraud in fact. Actual fraud.

Fraud in law. Fraud that is presumed to have occurred in light of the circumstances irrespective of intent to deceive.

Fraud or force. The words "fraud or force" contemplate some act of violence or deceit at the incident of an interested party, whereby the decree holder is prevented from executing his decree and do not contemplate a mere judicial order restraining that execution. To hold it otherwise would be doing violence to the plain English of the section. [MLJ : FYD (01-50), V. 2, p. 2924 : AIR (Vol. 32) 1945 Mad 70]. [CPC (5 of 1908), S. 48]

Fraud unravels everything. The maxim 'fraud unravels everything' was not applied where question of fraud and collusion become purely academic on the facts of the case. [*Biswanath Poddar* v. *Archana Poddar,* AIR 2001 SC 2849 : (2001) 8 SCC 187, 196, paras 16 & 17]

Fraud vitiates all. The principle 'fraud vitiates all' cannot be extended to rejection of plaint. [*Kapildeo Prasad* v. *Ramanand Prasad,* AIR 2007 Pat 1, 3, para 7]

Fraudulent. Deceitful; serving the purpose of, or accomplished by fraud. [IPC (45 of 1860), Ss. 171 and 496 and Indian Contract Act (9 of 1872), S. 17(5)].

Fraudulent alienation. In a general sense, the transfer of property with an intent to defraud creditors, lienors, or others. In a particular sense, the act of an administrator who wastes the assets of the estate by giving them away or selling at a gross undervalue.

Fraudulent breach of trust. [Presidency-towns Insolvency Act (3 of 1909), S. 39(2)(j)].

Fraudulent claim. A claim characterised by, or of the nature of fraud. [Indian Evidence Act (1 of 1872), S. 153., ill. (a)].

Fraudulent conversion. Receiving into possession money or property of another and fraudulently withholding, converting, or applying the same to or for one's own use and benefit, or to the use and benefit of any person other than the one to whom the money or property belongs. (*Black*)

Fraudulent intention. An intention to defraud. [CPC (5 of 1908), O. VI, R. 10].

Fraudulent means. For the purposes of rule 11(b) of the Companies (Appointment and Qualification of Directors) Rules, 2014, the expression 'fraudulent means' means if the DIN is obtained with an intent to deceive any other person or any authority including the Central Government. [*Explanation* (*ii*) to rule 11 of the Companies (Appointment & Qualification of Directors) Rules, 2014]

Fraudulent misrepresentation. "A misrepresentation is fraudulent if the maker intends his assertion to induce a party to manifest his assent and the maker (a) knows or believes that the assertion is not in accord with the facts, or (b) does not have the confidence that he states or implies in the truth of the assertion, or (c) knows that he does not have the basis that he states or implies for the assertion." [Restatement (Second) of Contracts, S. 162(a)]

A false statement as to material fact, made with intent that another rely thereon, which is believed by other party and on which he relies and by which he is induced to act and does act to his injury, and statement is fraudulent if speaker knows statement to be false or if it is made with utter disregard to its truth or falsity. *Cormack* v. *American Underwriters Corp.*, 288 NW 2d 634. As basis for civil action, establishment of representation, falsity, scienter, deception, and injury, are generally required.

Fraudulent preference. Every conveyance or transfer of property or charge thereon made, every payment made, every obligation incurred and every judicial proceedings taken or suffered by any person unable to pay his debts as they become due from his own money in favour of any creditor with a view to giving one creditor a preference over other creditors is fraudulent and void as against the trustee in bankruptcy, if the debtor became bankrupt within three months. [Presidency-towns Insolvency Act (3 of 1909), S. 34(2)].

Fraudulent proceeding. A proceeding is fraudulent if the claim made therein is untrue, but that the claimant has managed to obtain the verdict of the Court in his favour by practising fraud on the Court. In a fraudulent suit the combat between the parties is real and earnest. *Nagnbai* v. *B. Shama Rao*, AIR 1956 SC 593, 599. [Transfer of Property Act (4 of 1882), S. 52]

Fraudulent purchaser. A purchaser, who has obtained the sale to himself by fraud.

Fraudulent representation. A false representation is made fraudulent if made—

(a) knowingly

(b) without belief in its truth, or

(c) recklessly without care whether it be true or false. *Derry* v. *Peek*, (1889) 14 App Cas. 337.

Fraudulent trading. Carrying on business with the intention of defrauding creditors or for any other fraudulent purpose.

Fraudulently. The word "*fraudulently*" in S. 206, IPC (45 of 1860), cannot be interpreted as meaning nothing more than "dishonestly." The two words do not mean exactly the same thing. A dishonest act is not necessarily a fraudulent act. The elements which make an act fraudulent are, first deceit or an intention to deceive and in some cases mere secrecy. Where there is neither an intention to deceive, not secrecy, the act, though dishonest is not fraudulent.

The term "fraudulently" in S. 471, IPC (45 of 1860), does not necessarily connote deceit and injury to the person deceived. It may, but it need not, do so.

"A person is said to do a thing fraudulently if he does that thing with intent to defraud, but not otherwise." [IPC (45 of 1860), S. 25]] [Now (w.e.f. 1-7-2024) repealed & replaced by Bharatiya Nyaya Sanhita, 2023 (45 of 2023)]

"Fraudulently" means doing anything with the intention to defraud but not otherwise. [(w.e.f. 1-7-2024) Bharatiya Nyaya Sanhita, 2023 (45 of 2023), section 2(9)]

In a deceitful manner. [IPC (45 of 1860), S. 25].

Fraus est celare fraudem. It is a fraud to conceal a fraud. (*Latin for Lawyers*)

Fraus et dolus nemini patrocinari debent. (*Lat.*) (3 Rep. 78b) Fraud and deceit ought not to benefit anyone.

Fraus et jus nunquam cohabitant. Fraud and justice never dwell together. (*Latin for Lawyers*)

Fraus omnia vitiat. Fraud vitiates everything.

Free. To set at liberty; relieve.

Not bound or confined; not obstructed or impeded; not subject to any other authority or control; without compulsion; not costing anything.

The word "free" in the long title to the 2009 Act stands for removal by the State of any financial barrier that prevents a child from completing 8 years of schooling. [*Society for Unaided Private Schools of Rajasthan* v. *Union of India*, (2012) 6 SCC 1, para 7] [Right of Children to Free and Compulsory Education Act (35 of 2009), Title].

Free alongside ship (FAS). Means that the price includes all costs of transportation and delivery of the goods alongside of the ship.

Free and fair elections. The right to vote in 'free and fair elections' in always in terms of an electoral system prescribed by national legislation. The right to vote derives its colour from the right to 'free and fair elections'. Right to vote is not an ingredient of the 'free and fair elections'. [*Kuldip Nayar* v. *Union of India*, AIR 2006 SC 3127 : (2006) 7 SCC 1, 147, para 48]

Free beer claim. Free beer claim is a claim which covers all the possible ways of achieving a certain result. (*Patents*)

Free-board. "FREEBOARD" means the distance measured vertically downwards, amidships from the upper edge of deck line to the upper edge of the related load line. [Merchant Shipping Act (44 of 1958), S. 3(14)]

Free consent. Consent (in Contract Act) is said to be free when it is not caused by—(1) coercion, (2) undue influence, (3) fraud, (4) misrepresentation, (5) mistake. [Indian Contract Act (9 of 1872), S. 14]

Consent without any control or compulsion, of free will. [Indian Contract Act (9 of 1872), S. 14].

Free days. Free days means only Sundays and holidays. *Board of Trustees of the Port of Bombay* v. *Indian Goods Supplying Co.*, AIR 1977 SC 1622, 1626.

Free entry. A customs entry for free goods.

Free from average. A marine insurance term denoting that no claim for partial loss or average but only in respect of total loss, can be entertained. [Marine Insurance Act (11 of 1963), Sch., Memorandum].

Free of charge. Without payment.

Free passage. [Indian Easements Act (5 of 1882), S. 17(b)]; unimpeached passage; to allow to pass without constraints [Geneva conventions Act (6 of 1960), IVth sch., pt. 1 (general provisions), Art. 23].

Free reserve. For the purposes of this clause, "FREE RESERVES" means all reserves created out of the profits and share premium account but does not include reserves created out of revaluation of assets, write back of depreciation provisions and amalgamation. [Companies Act (1 of 1956), S. 2(29A) *Expl.*, inserted by Companied (Second Amendment) Act, 2002 w.e.f. 01-04-2003 and Sick Industrial Companies (Special Provisions) Act (1 of 1986), S. 3(1)(ca) *Expl.*]

"Free reserves: means such reserves which, as per the latest audited balance sheet of a company, are available for distribution as dividend:

Provided that—

(i) any amount representing unrealised gains, notional gains or revaluation of assets, whether shown as a reserve or otherwise, or

(ii) any change in carrying amount of an asset or of a liability recognised in equity, including surplus in profit and loss account on measurement of the asset or the liability at fair value, shall not be treated as free reserves. [Companies Act, (18 of 2013), S. 2(43)].

The aggregate of the balance in the share premium account, capital and debenture redemption reserves and any other reserve shown or published in the balance sheet of a company and created through an allocation of profits, not being a reserve created for repayment of any future liability or for depreciation in assets or for bad debts or a reserve created by revaluation of the assets of the company. [Non-Banking Financial Companies Acceptance of Public Deposits (Reserve Bank) Directions, 1998, para 2(1)(iii)]

Free reserves. For the purposes of section 68 of Act 18 of 2013, 'free reserves' includes securities premium account. [*Explanation II* to section 68 of the Companies Act, 2013 (18 of 2013)]

"FREE RESERVES" means such reserves which, as per the latest audited balance sheet of a company, are available for distribution as dividend:

Provided that—

(*i*) any amount representing unrealised gains, notional gains or revaluation of assets, whether shown as a reserve or otherwise, or

(*ii*) any change in carrying amount of an asset or of a liability recognized in equity, including surplus in profit and loss account on measurement of the asset or the liability at fair value,

shall not be treated as free reserves. [S. 2(43) of the Companies Act, 2013 (18 of 2013)]

Free time. A trader is invariably allowed a reasonable time to enable him to load or unload his wagon or to deliver his goods at or remove them from the station; this is known as 'free time', and no charge is made for it. *Puttulal* v. *N.E. Railway,* AIR 1960 All 438, 444. [Indian Railways Act (9 of 1890), S. 3(14), 46-C(*h*)]

Free-to-air channel. In respect of a cable television network, means a channel, the reception of which would not require the use of any addressable system, to be attached with the receiver set of a subscriber. [Cable Television Networks (Regulation) Act (7 of 1995), S. 4A, *Expla.* (e)]

Free Trade and Warehousing Zone. "FREE TRADE AND WAREHOUSING ZONE" means a Special Economic Zone wherein mainly trading and warehousing and other activities related thereto are carried on. [Special Economic Zones Act (28 of 2005), S. 2(n)]

Free trade throughout the territory of India. The words "free trade throughout the territory of India" contemplated in Art. 301 would be one with no tariff and no restrictions or disadvantages of any kind of importing or exporting from the different States. Free trade means complete freedom of inter-State trade. *State of Bihar* v. *Harihar Prasad*, AIR 1989 SC 1119. [Constitution of India, Art. 301]

Free trade zone (FTZ). "FREE TRADE ZONE" means the Kandla Free Trade Zone and the Saning Electronics Export Processing Zone and includes any other free trade zone which the Central Government may, by notification in the Official Gazette, specify for the purposes of this section. [Income Tax Act (43 of 1961), S. 10-A *Expl*-2(v)]

Alternative name for a *freeport.*

Freedom. Personal liberty; civil liberty; independence; liberty of action (as) freedom of contract.

Freedom fighter. If a person who has been sentenced to imprisonment for six months or more for freedom struggle, comes out within a month or so, for whatever reason, without serving his sentence, he is not a 'freedom fighter' within the meaning of Scheme. *Union of India* v. *Manohar Lal Azad*, 2002 (10) SCC 568. [Swantara Sainik Samman Pension Scheme, 1980, Para 4(a) & *Expln.* 2]

Freedom from arrest. Liberty from apprehension by legal authority. (*Constitutional and Parliamentary Term*)

Freedom of Assembly. A fundamental right given to citizens under the Indian Constitution. [Art. 19(1)(b)]

Freedom of association. The right to join others in a common undertaking that would be lawful if perused individually.

A guaranteed fundamental right to citizens for any lawful purpose; the right to form in an association does not include any guaranteed right to strike; nor does it include the right to obtain recognition by the Government. [Art. 19(1)(c)]

Freedom of communication. One of the fundamental liberties of individuals to have freedom to communicate information and comments orally, in newspapers and books, on radio and television, and to receive information and comments from others by the same means.

Freedom of conscience. "Freedom of conscience involves freedom of thought, opinion and religion and includes the right to manifest a chosen religion." 8 HALSBURY'S *Laws*, 4th ed. Para 835.

Freedom of expression/speech. Freedom of expression has four broad social purposes to serve; (i) it helps an individual to attain self fulfilment, (ii) it assists in the discovery of truth, (iii) it strengthens the capacity of an individual in participating in decision-making and (iv) it provides a mechanism by which it would be possible to establish a reasonable balance between stability and social change. All members of society should be able to form their own beliefs and communicate them freely to others. *Indian Express Newspapers (Bombay) Private Ltd.* v. *Union of India*, AIR 1986 SC 515. [Constitution of India, Art. 19]

"Freedom of expression" necessarily connotes that what one has a right to express may be communicated to others; and that includes right to freedom of circulation of ideas. [*All-India Bank Employees' Assn.* v. *National Industrial Tribunal*, (1962) 3 SCR 269 : AIR 1962 SC 171 as cited in *Subramanian Swamy* v. *Union of India*, (2016) 7 SCC 221, para 105].

The freedom of speech under Article 19(1)(a) means the right to express one's opinion by words of mouth, writing, printing, picture or in any other manner. S. *Rangarajan* v. *P. Jagajivan Ram*, 1989 (2) SCC 574 : JT 1989 (2) SC 70 : 1989 (2) SCR 204 : 1989 (1) Scale 812. [Constitution of India, Art. 19(1)(a)]

"Freedom of speech" means freedom to speak so as to be heard by others, and, therefore, to convey one's idea to others. [*All-India Bank Employees' Assn.* v. *National Industrial Tribunal*, (1962) 3 SCR 269 : AIR 1962 SC 171 as cited in *Subramanian Swamy* v. *Union of India,* (2016) 7 SCC 221, para 105].

The expression 'freedom of speech and expression' includes right to acquire information and to disseminate it. It is necessary for self-fulfilment. It enables people to contribute to debate on social and moral issues. It is the only vehicle of political discourse so essential to democracy. It plays an important role in facilitating artistic and scholarly endeavours of all sorts. *Secretary, Ministry of Information and Broadcasting Govt. of India* v. *Cricket Association of Bengal*, 1995 (2) SCC 161 : AIR 1995 SC 1236, as referred in *People's Union for Civil Liberties* v. *Union of India*, AIR 2004 SC 1242,1254, para 52. [Constitution of India Art. 19(1)(9)]

'Freedom of expression' includes the right to not express. *National Bank of Canada* v. *R.C.U.*, 1984 (1) SCR 269, p. 377 text, and *Irwin Toy* v. *Quebec (Attorney General)*, 1989 (1) SCR 927 as referred in *Union of India* v. *Naveen Jindal*, AIR 2004 SC 1559, 1569, para 47.

Freedom of expression. 'Freedom of expression' is an essential process of advancing knowledge and discovering truth. The values and functions of the freedom of expression in democratic polity are obvious. 'Freedom of expression' is essentially as a means of assuring individual self-fulfilment. The proper end of man is the realisation of his character and potentialities as a human being. For the achievement of this self-realisation the mind must be free. [*American Law by* THOMAS EMERSON **as referred in** *Maneka Gandhi* v. *Union of India*, AIR 1978 SC 597 : (1978) 1 SCC 248, 346, para 104]

Freedom of information. Means the right to obtain information from any public authority by means of.—

(i) inspection, taking of extracts and notes;

(ii) certified copies of any records of such public authority;

(iii) diskettes, floppies or in any other electronic mode or through printouts where such information is stored in a computer or in any other device. [Freedom of Information Act (5 of 2003), S. 2(c) now repealed by the Right to Information Act, 2005 (22 of 2005)]

Freedom of movement. The fundamental right to move freely throughout the territory of India without any discriminatory barriers; it has three aspects : (i) the right to move from any part of the country to any other part; (ii) the right to move out of the country; (iii) the right to return to the country from abroad. [Art. 19(1)(d)]

Freedom of press. Liberty of press as now understood and enjoyed is of recent origin. The term itself means only the liberty of publication without the previous permission of the Government, *i.e.*, neither Courts of Justice, nor any other Judges whatever are authorised to take notice of writings intended for the press, but are confined to those which are actually printed. *In Re G. Alavandar,* AIR 1957 Mad 427, 430. [Constitution of India, Art. 19(1)(*a*)]

The expression 'freedom of the press' has not been used in Article 19 but it is comprehended within Article 19(1)(a). This expression means freedom from interference from authority which would have the effect of interference with the content and circulation of newspapers. There cannot be any interference with that freedom in the name of public interest by publishing facts and opinions without which a democratic electorate cannot make responsible judgments. Freedom of the press is the heart of social and political intercourse. The press has now assumed the role of the public educator making formal and non-formal education possible in a large scale particularly in the developing world, where television and other kinds of modern communication are not still available for all sections of society. *Indian Express Newspapers (Bombay) Private Ltd.* v. *Union of India,* AIR 1986 SC 515. [Constitution of India, Art. 19(1)(a)]

Right to print and publish material without governmental intervention or restrictions.

Freedom of the press means principally the right to publish without any previous licence or censorship.

Freedom of profession, occupation or business. A fundamental right of the citizens of India.

All citizens have the right to choose their own employment or to take up any trade or calling subject to the restrictions imposed by the State in the interest of public welfare such as, prescription of professional or technical qualifications necessary for practising any profession or occupation and carrying on any business or trade by the State or a State-owned corporation to the complete or partial exclusion of citizens. The restriction should be 'reasonable' and the Court has the competence to examine the reasonableness. [Art. 19(1)(g)]

Freedom of religion. Right to believe or not to belive in any form of religion; right to practise and exercise one's religious beliefs.

It includes freedom of performance of necessary rituals which are integral part of religion—The question as to what constitute essential part of religion, has to be decided by Court. *Pannalal Banshilal Pitti* v. *State of Andhra Pradesh,* AIR 1996 SC 1023.

Freedom of residence. A fundamental constitutional right guaranteed to all citizens of India enabling them to reside and settle in any part of the territory of India; the object being to remove the internal barriers within India or between any of its parts. [Art. 19(1)(e)]

Freedom of speech and expression. Right to express one's thoughts and opinions, of course under certain reasonable restrictions.

Freedom of speech does not mean that a person is at liberty to say what he pleases at all times and under all circumstances, for it has been held repeatedly that the right of freedom of speech cannot have been and obviously was not intended to give immunity for every possible use of language. This right may sometimes become a wrong if, for example, a person were to indulge in the use of language which is so defamatory, insulting, inciting or provocative as to be reasonably likely to cause disorder and violence. *Vivendra* v. *State of Punjab,* AIR 1957 Punj 1, 4. [Constitution of India, Art. 19(1)(*a*)]

A fundamental constitutional right guaranteed to every citizen to express his convictions and opinions freely by word of mouth, writing, printing, picture or by any visible representation; includes the right to propagate or publish views of others, freedom to such information and ideas and freedom of discussion. [Art. 19(1)(a)]

Freehold. That land or tenement which a man holds in fee-simple, fee tail, or for term of life. (*Tomlin*)

An estate to be a freehold must possess these two qualities; immobility, *i.e.* the property must be either land or some interest issuing out of or annexed to land; and for indeterminate duration, if the utmost period of time to which an estate can endure be fixed and determined, it cannot be a freehold. (*Wharton*)

Land or building that are owned freehold are owned absolutely by the freeholder.

Freely convertible currency. Means a currency which is widely traded in international foreign exchange markets and widely used in international transactions. [Energy Charter Treaty, Art. 1(14) (12 Dec 1994)]

Freeze-out. Situation in which a company successfully out-competes its competitors, causing a new ice-age for them and thus freezing them out of the market.

Freezing. Means temporarily prohibiting the transfer, conversion, disposition or movement of property by an order issued under Section 58F. [Wild Life (Protection) Act (53 of 1972), S. 58B(e)]

"Freezing" or "Seizure". Means temporarily prohibiting the transfer, conversion, disposition or movement of property or temporarily assuming custody or control of property on the basis of an order issued by a Court or a competent authority. [U.N. Convention against Illicit Traffic in Narcotic Drugs and Psychotropic Substances, 1988, Art. 1(l)] (*Vienna*)

Freight. "FREIGHT" includes the profit derivable by a ship-owner from the employment of his ship to carry his own goods or other movables, as well as freight payable by a third party, but does not include passage money. [Marine Insurance Act (11 of 1963), S. 2(b)]

"FREIGHT" means the charge levied for the carriage of goods including transhipment charges if any. [Indian Railways Act (24 of 1989), S. 2(17)]

Hire for transportation of goods. [Indian Contract Act (9 of 1872), S. 54, ill.(a); Inland Vessels Act (1 of 1917), S. 54-A(1)(b)].

The money paid for carriage of goods by sea; or in a larger sense, it is taken for the price paid for the use of ship to transport goods; and for the cargo, or burthen of the ship.

"Freight" and "handling charges". Where a dealer transports goods from his factory to his place of business and sells them at a price which is arrived at after taking into account "freight and handling charges" incurred by him in transporting the goods, the amount of 'freight and handling charges' included in the price would be part of the 'sale price'. *Hindustan Sugar Mills* v. *State of Rajasthan*, AIR 1978 SC 1496.

French settlements. French colony. [Indian Succession Act (39 of 1925), S. 10, ill. (vi)].

Frequent. To visit often; occurring often.

Frequenting. Visiting often.

Fresh evidence. 'FRESH EVIDENCE' must have the quality of newness, or the feature of having become newly available and obtainable. *R.* v. *Medical Appeal Tribunal*, (1959) 3 All ER 40, 47 (CA). [National Insurance (Industrial Injuries) Act, 1946, S. 40(1)]

Fresh facts. If the fresh facts cannot form the basis for a conclusion on which the detention order can be made then those facts are not fresh facts which will justify the detaining authority to make an order of detention. *Har Jas Dev Singh* v. *State of Punjab*, AIR 1973 SC 2469, 2463. [Maintenance of Internal Security Act (26 of 1971), Ss. 3 and 14(2)]

Fresh pursuit. The right of a person to use reasonable force so as to retake property which has just been taken.

"Friend" or "agent". A 'friend' who, in truth and substance, is a friend of the detenu may appear for the detenu but if such a "friend" also happens to be a legal practitioner, he cannot as of right, appear before the Advisory Board on behalf of the detenu. But a 'friend' or an 'agent' of the detenu who is essentially a comrade in the profession of the detenu for which he is detained, such a 'friend' or 'agent' will also be barred from appearance on behalf of the detenu. *Devji Vallabhbhai Tandel* v. *Administrator of Goa, Daman & Diu*, AIR 1982 SC 1029.

Friendly suit. A suit brought not in a hostile manner, the object being to settle some point of law, or do some act which cannot safely be done except with the sanction of a Court of justice.

Fringe benefits. For the purposes of this Chapter, "FRINGE BENEFITS" means any consideration for employment provided by way of—

(a) any privilege, service, facility or amenity, directly or indirectly, provided by an employer, whether by way of reimbursement or otherwise, to his employees (including former employee or employees);

(b) any free or concessional ticket provided by the employer for private journeys of his employees or their family members; and

(c) any contribution by the employer to an approved superannuation fund for employees. [Income-tax Act (43 of 1961), S. 115WB(1) as inserted by Finance Act (18 of 2005), S. 37]

Fringe benefits is a term embracing a variety of employees' benefits, paid by the employers and supplementing the workers' basic wage or salary. [*International Encyclopaedia of Social Science, Vol. 16, p. 424*]

Frisk. To run the hand rapidly over the outer clothing of (a suspect) for the purpose of finding concealed weapons. The purpose of frisking a suspect is to insure the safety of an officer making an investigation against concealed weapons, not to uncover evidence. The officer must be justified in his or her encounter of the suspect and must have a reasonable suspicion that the suspect is armed. The scope of the frisk must be limited to the discovery of weapons.

Frivolous. Of little or no weight or importance; not with serious attention; manifestly futile.

Frivolous suit. A lawsuit which has no legal basis, often filed to harass or extort money from the defendant.

Frivolously. In a frivolous manner. [Industrial Disputes Act (14 of 1947), S. 10(1), 2nd prov.].

From. It is a well-settled principle that the word 'from' is akin to "after" and that the word "from" if used for the purpose of and in reference to the computation of time, as for example, from a stated date, that stated date is *prima facie* excluded from computation. *Srinivisa Silk Mills* v. *State of Mysore,* AIR 1962 Mys 117, 123. [General Clauses Act (10 of 1897), S. 9(1)]

The use of word 'from' in Section 81(1) of the Act would mean that the first day for computing the period of limitation should be excluded for the convenience of the parties. *Quarry Owner's Assn.* v. *State of Bihar*, (2000) 8 SCC 649, para 14 : AIR 2000 SC 2870. [Representation of the People Act (43 of 1951), S. 81(1)]

From the bar. The expression 'from the bar' occurring in R. 7 of the Rules, would only mean from the class or group of advocates practising in Courts of law. *Sushma Suri* v. *Govt. of National Capital Territory of Delhi*, (1999) 1 SCC 330 para 11. [Constitution of India, Art. 233(2) and Delhi Higher Judicial Service Rules, 1970, R. 7]

'From' and **'up to'.** The word "from" is the indicator of starting point, the expression "up to" signifies the terminating point, putting an end to the transport journey. [*Commissioner of Central Excise and Service Tax* v. *Ultra Tech Cement Limited*, (2018) 2 SCC 721, para 9] [Cenvant Credit Rules, 2004, R. 2(I)]

From time to time. Now and again. [Industrial Disputes Act (14 of 1947), S. 2(n), prov. and Constitution of India, Art. 75(6)].

'From time to time' means 'occasionally'. [Century Dictionary as cited in *State of Rajasthan* v. *Basant Agrotech (India) Limited*, (2013) 15 SCC 1, para 19].

"The phrase 'from time to time' means an occasion may arise, at intervals, now and then occasionally. [Words and Phrases, Vol. 17-A, 1974 as cited in *Flory* v. *Meeker*, 240 P2d 1177, page 1190 : 940 Or 257 (1952)] See also *State of Rajasthan* v. *Basant Agrotech (India) Limited*, (2013) 15 SCC 1, para 49.

'From time to time' means, 'at intervals; now and then' [Universal Dictionary as cited in *State of Rajasthan* v. *Basant Agrotech (India) Limited*, (2013) 15 SCC 1, para 49].

In constitutional amendment, authorizing, legislature to alter salaries of named county officers 'from time to time', the quoted phrase does not mean from 'term to term' [*Almon* v. *Margan County*, 16 So 2d 511, p. 114 : 245 Ala 241 (1944) as cited in *State of Rajasthan* v. *Basant Agrotech (India) Limited*, (2013) 15 SCC 1, para 49].

'From time to time' means occasionally; that is, as the occasion requires, and thereof the words cannot be held to mean that the legislature may not decrease the number of Judges after an increase thereof. [State v. Mc Bride, 70P 25, p. 27 : 29 Wash 335 (1902) as cited in *State of Rajasthan* v. *Basant Agrotech (India) Limited*, (2013) 15 SCC 1, para 49].

Front. The word 'front' in respect of a building means the entrance side.

Front page extensions. FrontPage is Microsoft's simple Web-page editor designed for nonprogrammers. It includes many of its own scripts and special effects, but to use them, you have to install the FrontPage "extensions" on your Web site. You should either plan to use CGI-based applications or FrontPage. FrontPage does not provide the ability to edit or maintain files in your home directory and does not upload in true ascii. (*Cyber Law*)

Frontage. Land abutting on street or water; land between front of building and road.

The extent of land along a highway or street. The frontage is often used as a means of determining taxation or assessments.

Frontager. A person owning or occupying land that abuts a highway, river, seashore, or the like.

Frontier worker. Refers to a migrant worker who retains his or her habitual residence in a neighbouring state to which he or she normally returns every day or at least once a weak. [International Convention on the Protection of the Rights of All Migrant Workers and Members of Their Families (25 Feb. 1991), Art. 2(a)]

Fronting. Abutting or adjoining.

"FRONTING" merely means that the article should face or have its front toward, opposite or over against the house or the street. It is not a term of art but one that signifies its meaning according to common notions. *Links Advertisers and Business Promoters* v. *Commissioner, Corporation of the City of Bangalore*, AIR 1977 SC 1646.

Frozen account. An account on which funds may not be withdrawn until a lien is satisfied and a court order or other legal process makes the account available for withdrawal (*e.g.*, the account of a deceased person is frozen pending a court order distributing the funds to the new lawful owners. [*ML Tannan Banking Law & Practice in India*, Vol. 2, 2021, LexisNexis, Dictionary of Banking Terminology].

Frozen assets. An asset that is difficult to convert into cash because of Court order or other legal process.

Assets which cannot be traded because they are mortgaged in favour of some class of creditors, *e.g.*, debenture holders.

Frozen deposits. Bank deposits that cannot be withdrawn because, as when the financial institution is insolvent.

Fructus naturales. (*Lat.*) Natural fruits those fruits or profits of land, or other thing, which are produced solely by the powers of nature.

Fruits of a crime. The material objects which are acquired by the means and in consequence of the commission of a crime.

Frustra legis auxilium quaerit qui in legem committit. (*Lat.*) (2 Hale P.C. 386) Vainly does he who offends against the law seek the help of the law.

Frustration. "Frustration may be defined as the premature determination, owing to the occurrence of an intervening event of change of circumstances so fundamental as to be regarded by the law both as striking at the root of the agreement and as entirely beyond what was contemplated by the parties when they entered into the agreement. If, therefore, the intervening circumstance is one which the law would not regard as so fundamental as to destroy the basis of the agreement, there is no frustration. Equally if the terms of the agreement show that the parties contemplated the possibility of such an intervening circumstances arising, frustration does not occur. Neither does it arise when one of the parties had deliberately brought about the supervening event by his own choice. But where it does not arise frustration operates to bring the agreement to an end as regards both parties forthwith and quite apart from volition." *Kalyani*

Spinning Mills Ltd. v. *Sudha Shashikant Shroff*, AIR 1995 Cal 48, 61, para 29.

Fuel oil. Means heavy distillates or residues from crude oil or blends of such materials intended for use as a fuel for the production of heat or power of a quality equivalent to the 'American Society for Testing and Materials' Specification for Number Four Fuel Oil (Designation D 396-69)', or heavier. [Merchant Shipping Act (44 of 1958), S. 352 S-a, *Expl.* (ii)]

Fugitive. A person who flees or escapes; a refugee; A criminal suspect who flees, evades, or escapes arrest, prosecution, or imprisonment, especially by fleeing the jurisdiction or by hiding.

Fugitive criminal. Means a person who is accused or convicted of an extradition offence within the jurisdiction of a foreign State and includes a person who, while in India, conspires, attempts to commit or incites or participates as an accomplice in the commission of an extradition offence in a foreign State. [Extradition Act (34 of 1962), S. 2(f)]

Fugitive economic offender. Means any individual against whom a warrant for arrest in relation to a Scheduled Offence has been issued by any Court in India, who

(*i*) has left India so as to avoid criminal prosecution; or

(*ii*) being abroad, refuses to return to India to face criminal prosecution. [Fugitive Economic Offenders Act (17 of 2018), S. 2(1)(f)].

Fugitive criminal of a foreign state. A criminal who is fleeing. [Extradition Act (34 of 1962), Preamble].

Fulfil. To fulfil a promisee is to perform it according to the engagement.

To complete; to accomplish.

Full age. The age at which persons come to the rights of adults under the law.

Full Bench. The full body or assembly of Judges.

A Full Bench is frequently five or seven judges or even more, but is not necessarily literally the full body of judges of the High Court.

Full blood. A term of relation denoting descent from the same couple.

"Two persons are said to be related to each other by full blood when they are descended from a common ancestor by the same wife." [Special Marriage Act (43 of 1954), S. 2, *Expln.* II].

Full brother, sister. Born of the same father and mother.

Full Court. A Court sitting in banc, implying strictly, the presence of all the judges.

Full disclosure. Term used in variety of legal contexts *e.g.* a fiduciary who participates in a transaction for his own benefit is required to fully reveal the details of such. In consumer law, the obligation to reveal all details of a transaction to the consumer. (*Black*)

Full faith and credit clause. Constitutional provision that requires each state to recognize the laws and legal proceedings of all other states.

Full hearing. Embraces not only the right to present evidence, but also a reasonable opportunity to know the claims of the opposite party, and to meet them. Give full opportunity to the parties to lead evidence and address arguments.

Full settlement. Adjusting all matters in dispute between the parties and releasing the opposite parties of all obligations.

Full time. The expression 'total full time earnings' can only mean the earnings he earns in a day by working full time on that day, the full time to be in accordance with the period of time given in the notice displayed in the factory for a particular day. This is further apparent from the fact that any payment for overtime or for bonus is not included in computing the total full time earnings. *Shankar Balaji Waje* v. *State of Maharashtra*, AIR 1962 SC 517, 523. [Factories Act (63 of 1948), S. 80(1)]

Full time earnings. The expression "total full time earnings" means the earnings a workman earns in a day by working full time on that day, the full time to be in accordance with the period of time given in the notice displayed in the factory for a particular day. *Shankar Balaji* v. *State of Maharashtra*, AIR 1962 SC 517, 523. [Factories Act (63 of 1948), S. 80(1)]

Full wages last drawn. The words 'full wages last drawn' occurring in Section 17-B of the Act indicate that the wages that were actually paid and not the amount that would be payable or are required to be paid. *Dena Bank* v. *Kirti Kumar T. Patel*, (1999) 2 SCC 106, para 22 : AIR 1998 SC 511. [Industrial Disputes Act (14 of 1947), S. 17-B]

The words 'full wages last drawn' occurring in S. 17-B of the Act mean which would have been drawn by the workman if he had continued in service if the order terminating his services had not been passed. *Dena Bank* v. *Kiriti Kumar T. Patel*, (1999) 2 SCC 106, para 21 : AIR 1998 SC 511. [Industrial Disputes Act (14 of 1947), S. 17-B]

Fully. The word 'fully' means 'thoroughly', 'completely', 'entirely', so as not to leave any trace of the impression created by the torture of fear. *Bhagirath* v. *State of M.P.*, AIR 1959 MP 17, 19. [Indian Evidence Act (1 of 1872), S. 28]

Fully diluted basis. Shall mean, in relation to the percentage holding of the Central Government on such basis, the total number of shares held by the Central Government expressed as a percentage of the total number of shares of the Corporation that would be outstanding if all possible sources of conversion are exercised. [Life Insurance Corporation Act, 1956 (31 of 1956), section 2(4c)]

Fully paid up shares. Shares whose value has been paid in full [Companies Act (1 of 1956), S. 77(2)(c)].

Function. "FUNCTION", in relation to a computer, includes logic, control, arithmetical process, deletion, storage and retrieval and communication or telecommunication from or within a computer. [Information Technology Act (21 of 2000), S. 2(1)(u)]

Employment; discharge of office. (*Wharton*)

The kind of action proper to a person as belonging to a class, especially to the holder of any office; official duties [Wealth-tax Act (27 of 1957), S. 11A]; to perform one's part [Representation of the People Act (43 of 1951), S. 73, prov., (b)]; [Official Languages Act (19 of 1963), S. 3(4)]; [Delhi High Court Act (26 of 1966), S. 17(2)].

Functional pay scale. 'Functional pay scale' in relation to a government servant means the pay scale which is prescribed for the post held by the government servant. It does not mean any other pay scale in which the government servant is drawing his pay as a personal measure to him with any other justification like based on length of service, or on higher/additional qualification or on upgradation of pay scale due to any other reason. [Haryana Civil Services (Assured Career Progession) Rules, 1998, R. 3(d) as cited in *State of Haryana* v. *Sita Ram*, (2013) 16 SCC 677, para 4].

Functional plan. Means a plan prepared to elaborate one or more elements of the regional plan. [National Capital Region Planning Board Act (2 of 1985), S. 2(d)]

Functus officio. A term applied to something which once has had a life and power, but which has become of no virtue whatsoever. Thus, when an agent has completed the business with which he was entrusted his agency is *functus officio*. If a bill of exchange be sent to the drawee, and he passes it to the credit of the holder, it is *functus officio* and cannot be further negotiated; when arbitrators cannot agree and choose an umpire they are said to be *functus officio*.

As soon as a registration officer registered a document presented to him for registration, the function in the performance of which the document was produced before him is over and thereafter he becomes *functus officio*, having no power under Section 38 to impound the document. *Komalchand* v. *State of M.P.*, AIR 1966 MP 20, 22 (FB). [Indian Stamp Act (2 of 1899), S. 33(1)]

One who has fulfilled his office or is out of office; an authority who has performed the act authorised so that the authority is exhausted.

Fund. An account usually of the nature of a *reserve* or a *provision* which is represented by specifically earmarked *assets*.

"FUND" means the International Oil Pollution Compensation Fund established by the Fund Convention. [Merchant Shipping Act (44 of 1958), S. 352S(c); (*Inserted by Merchant Shipping (Amendment) Act, 2002*)]

"Fund" includes—

(a) any cash;

(b) cash equivalents; and

(c) any right, or obligation, to receive or pay, the cash or cash equivalent. [Income-tax Act (43 of 1961), Chap. XA, S. 102(5) as inserted by Finance Act, (17 of 2013)].

"Fund" means the Environmental Protection Fund established under section 16. [Environment (Protection) Act, 1986 (29 of 1986), section 2(ca)]

"FUND" means the African Development Fund established under the agreement. [African Development Fund Act (1 of 1982), S. 2(b)]

"FUND" means the Public Liability Insurance Fund established and maintained by an owner in accordance with provision to subsection (3) of Section 4 of the Act. [Public Liability Insurance Rules, 1991, R. 2(d) and Public Liability Insurance Act (4 of 1991), S. 4(3)]

The word 'fund' may mean actual cash resources of a particular kind (*e.g.* money in a drawer or a bank), or it may be a mere accountancy expression used to describe a particular category which a person uses in making up his accounts. *R.K. Dalmia* v. *Delhi Administration*, AIR 1962 SC 1821, 1834. [IPC (45 of 1860), S. 405, Explanations]

Fund is a systematic accumulation of cash or any separation of assets to meet future tax liability. Only an accounting entry of an exact sum being earmarked for payment of tax liability arising at the end of the current accounting year is not a fund. *Commissioner of Income Tax* v. *Duncan Brothers and Co. Ltd.,* (1996) 8 SCC 31, paras 13 and 14.

A stock or sum of money, especially one set apart for a particular purpose. [Countess of Dufferin's Fund Act (63 of 1957), Preamble].

"FUND" includes—(a) any cash; (b) cash equivalents; and (c) any right, or obligation, to receive or pay, the cash or cash equivalent. [(w.e.f. 1-4-2016) S. 102(5) of the Income-tax Act, 1961 (43 of 1961); (still-born) Section 102(6) of the Income-tax Act, 1961 (43 of 1961) as inserted (w.e.f. 1-4-2014) by the Finance Act, 2012 and omitted (w.e.f. 1-4-2014) by the Finance Act, 2013]

Fund convention. Means the International Convention on the Establishment of an International Fund for Compensation for Oil Pollution Damage, 1992 as amended from time to time. [Merchant Shipping Act (44 of 1958), S. 352 S(d)]

Fund convention country. Means a country in which the Fund Convention is for the time being in force. [Merchant Shipping Act (44 of 1958), S. 352 S(e)]

Fundamental law. The basic, organic law which determines the governing principles of a state; the constitutional law.

Fundamental rights. Those rights which have their source, and are explicitly or implicitly guaranteed, in the Constitution, See, Chapter III of The Constitution of India.

Fundamental rights are those rights which the State enforces against itself. *Golak Nath* v. *State of Punjab,* AIR 1967 SC 1643, 1708. Per HIDAYATULLAH, J. [Constitution of India, Part III]

Funding. Process whereby a floating debt is converted into stock. The term "funding" has been sometimes applied to the process of collecting together a variety of outstanding debts against corporations, the principal of which was payable at short periods, and borrowing money upon the bonds or stocks of the corporation to pay them off.

Funding a debt. The pledging of a specific fund to keep down the interest, and ultimately discharge the principal. When the extinguishment of the debt is contemplated, it is called a "sinking fund".

Funds. "FUNDS", used with reference to any local authority, includes any local or municipal fund to the control or management of which such authority is legally entitled, and any cess, rate, duty or tax which such authority is legally entitled to impose, and any property vested in such authority. [Local Authorities Loans Act (9 of 1914), S. 2]

Funeral. Burial of the dead with ceremonial observances.

Disposal of the dead, with any ceremonies or observances connected therewith. [Indian Trusts Act (2 of 1882), S. 41].

Funeral and testamentary expenses. The expenses necessary to meet the cost of last ceremony of the testator and other expenses incidental to the proper performance of the duty of an executor. [CPC (5 of 1908), Sch. I, app. D, form No. 17, item 4].

Funeral expenses. Money expended in procuring the internment, cremation, or other disposition of a corpse, including suitable monument, perpetual care of burial lot and entertainment of those participating in wake. (*Black*)

Funeral rite. A formal procedure or act in a religious or other solemn observance, pertaining to the burial or cremation of the dead.

Furiosi nulla voluntas est. (*Lat.*) A mad man has no will. (*Broom; Cyc. Law Dic.*)

Furiosus nullum negotium contrahere potest. A lunatic cannot make a contract.

Furlough. (*of person in military service*) Leave of absence from duty granted to soldiers; the length of time and conditions being stated on the furlough paper. The soldier remains under orders, and if without leave he quits the place to which he has permission to go, or if he disguises or conceals himself so that orders cannot reach him. or otherwise so acts as to furnish proof of an intention not to return to duty (though on furlough at the time), he may be tried for desertion.

The term 'furloughs' are variously known as temporary leaves, home visits or temporary community release. For decades, prisons have occassionally granted short furloughs to inmates who were suddenly faced with a severe family crisis such as a death or grave illness in the immediate family. Furloughs of that type are treated as special circumstances, and often the inmate must be accompanied by an officer as part of the terms of the temporary release. [*Dictionary of American Penology* by VERGIL L. WILLIAMS as cited in *State of Haryana* v. *Mohinder Singh*, (2000) 3 SCC 394 para 11 : AIR 2000 SC 890.

Furnish. To supply, provide, or equip, for accomplishment of a particular purpose. (*Black*)

Furniture. All articles of convenience or decoration used for the purpose of furnishing a place of business or an office are articles of furniture. *Chandan Mela Products (P.) Ltd.* v. *State of Gujarat,* (1969) 23 STC 29 (Guj). [Income-tax Act (43 of 1961), S. 32]

Movable articles (such as chairs, tables *etc.*) for use or ornament in a house, office or the like.

Further. At a greater distance in time; additional; more; going beyond; to promote or advance.

Further enquiry. The expression 'further enquiry' includes reconsideration of the same materials and also taking further evidence, if necessary, the entire matter having been left to the Magistrate. *Banchhanidhi* v. *Srinibass,* AIR 1967 Ori 62, 65. [CrPC, 1973 (2 of 1974), S. 398]

The expression 'further enquiry' has come to have a technical meaning and it simply means reconsideration of the matter. *Shyamlal Rula* v. *State*, AIR 1954 Pat 441. [CrPC 1973 (2 of 1974), S. 398]

Further evidence. The term 'further evidence' used in the sub-section means 'evidence which is not already on record'. That evidence may be of various kinds, the only restriction being that that evidence should not already be on the record of the case. *Hanuman Prasad* v. *State,* MLJ : QD (1961-1965) Vol. II C1836 : 1961 All LJ 82 : 1962 All WR (HC) 107 : 1961 All CrR 52 : 1962 (1) CrLJ 632. [CrPC (5 of 1898), S. 146(1-A).]

Further inquiry. It cannot be accepted that on ordering a 'further inquiry' under Section 398, the entire evidence already recorded is wiped off. When 'further inquiry' is ordered in the case by a superior Court, the Magistrate has to reappraise that very evidence which was examined prior to the passing of the order which was set aside in the revision or any other evidence cited in the complaint but not examined earlier, but examined after the remand. [*Gurdial Singh* v. *Kartar Singh,* MLJ : YD (1981), para 48 : 1980 CrLJ 955 (P&H)]. [CrPC (2 of 1974), S. 398]

Further investigation. The expression 'further investigation' occurring in Section 173(8) of the Code does not mean 'fresh investigation' or 're-investigation'. *K. Chandrashekhar* v. *State of Kerala*, (1998) 5 SCC 223, para 24 : AIR 1998 SC 2001. [CrPC 1973 (2 of 1974), S. 173(8)]

Further investigation. "Further investigation" is where the investigation officer obtains further oral or documentary evidence after the final report has been filed before the court in terms of Section 173(8). This power is vested with the executive. It is the continuation of previous investigation and, therefore, is understood and described as "further investigation". The scope of such investigation is restricted to the discovery of further oral and documentary evidence. Its purpose is to bring the true facts before the court even if they are discovered at a subsequent stage to the primary investigation. It is commonly described as "supplementary report". "Supplementary report" would be the correct expression as the subsequent investigation is meant and intended to supplement the primary investigation conducted by the empowered police officer. Another significant feature of further investigation is that it does not have the effect of wiping out directly or impliedly the initial investigation conducted by the investigating agency. This is a kind of continuation of the previous investigation. The basis is discovery of fresh evidence and in continuation of the same offence and chain of events relating to the same occurrence incidental thereto. In other words, it has to be understood in complete contradistinction to a "reinvestigation", "fresh" or "de novo" investigation. [*Vinay Tyagi* v. *Irshad Ali*, (2013) 5 SCC 762, para 22] [Criminal Procedure Code, 1973 (2 of 1974), S. 173(8)].

Further or other relief. The words 'further or other relief' in S. 92(*h*) mean relief of the same nature as those contemplated in S. 92(*a*) to (*g*). [CPC (5 of 1908), S. 92(*h*)]

Further relief. The expression 'further relief' means a relief which is inherent in the original declaration claimed, a relief without which the declaratory relief claimed would be ineffective, infructuous and unworkable.

Further working. The expression 'further working' means some process or activity which is to be undertaken after surface working on the material. *Speed way Rubber Co.* v. *CCE*, (2002) 5 SCC 527, para 23 : AIR 2002 SC 2108. [Central Excise Tariff Act, 1985 (5 of 1986), Sub-Headings 4008.21, Chapter 40, Note 9 prior 1990 Amendment]

Furtherance. Act of furthering, helping forward, promotion, advancement, or progress. (*Black*)

Furtum conceptum. Received theft; the offence of receiving stolen goods.

Furtum est contrectatio rei alienae fraudulenta cum animo furandi invito illo domino cujus res illa fuerat. Theft, is the fraudulent handling of another's property, with an intention of stealing, against the will of the proprietor, whose property it was. (*Black*)

Furtum non est ubi initium habet detentionis per dominum rei. It is not theft where the commencement of the detention arises through the owner of the thing. (*Broom; Cyc. Law Dic.*)

Fuse. A tube, cord or the like filled or saturated with combustible matter for igniting an explosive. [Explosives Act (45 of 1884), S. 4(1)(d)].

Fushk. The word *fushk* means annulment or abrogation. It comes from a root which means 'to annul' or to 'rescind'. Hence it refers to the power of a Muslim *qazi* to annul a marriage on the application of the wife. [A AAFyzee, *Outlines of Muhammedan Law*, Oxford University Press, New Delhi, 4th edn. 1974 at 168, **quoted in** Dr Kauser Edappagath, *Divorce and Gender Equity in Muslim Personal Law of India*, 2014, LexisNexis at p. 115]

Future advance. Advance or loan to be given in future.

Future and contingent liabilities. Liabilities that may or may not be owed in future; dependent on the outcome of a contingency. [CPC (5 of 1908), O. XX, R. 13(2)].

Future day. Day that is to come. [CPC (5 of 1908), O. XLI, R. 30].

Future estate. An estate to which a person is entitled in future; an estate in expectancy.

Future goods. "FUTURE GOODS" means goods to be manufactured or produced or acquired by the seller after making of the contract of sale. [Sale of Goods Act (3 of 1930), S. 2(6)].

Goods which do not exist or which could not be identified at the time of contract to sell such goods.

Future interest. The interest accruing due after the date of the order till the date of recovery. [CPC (5 of 1908), S. 32]

Future maintenance. Means of future sustenance. [T.P. Act (4 of 1882), S. 6(dd)].

Futures contract. A legal agreement between a buyer/seller and an established exchange or its clearing house in which the buyer/seller agrees to take/make delivery of something at a specified price at the end of a designated period.

Futures market. Market that deals in futures and options on bonds, commodities, foreign currencies are shares.

Futures option. The right of a buyer to buy from or sell to a writer a designated futures contract at a designated price at any time during the period stated.

G

Gage. "Signifies a Pawn or Pledge". The same word has now been changed into Wage. (Cowell).

Gain. Something obtained or acquired.

'Gain' means—

(i) a gain in property or supply of services, whether temporary or permanent; or

(ii) an opportunity to earn remuneration or greater remuneration or to gain a financial advantage otherwise than by way of legitimate remuneration. [Digital Personal Data Protection Act, 2023 (22 of 2023), section 2(o)]

"Gain" means that which is acquired or comes as a benefit. [Words and Phrases, Permanent Edition, Vol. 18 as cited in *Thorn* v. *De Breteuil*, 83 NY Supp 849, 856 : 86 App Div 405 (1903)]. See also *Brihanmumbai Mahanagarpalika* v. *Willingdon Sports Club*, (2013) 16 SCC 260, para 22.

"Gain" means something wanted or valued that is gotten; something that is gained; especially: money gotten through some activity or process, something that is helpful : advantage or benefit; an increase in amount, size, or number. [Merriam Webster Dictionary as cited in *Brihanmumbai Mahanagarpalika* v. *Willingdon Sports Club*, (2013) 16 SCC 260, para 21].

"Gain" means increase or addition to what one has of that which is of profit, advantage, or benefit; resources or advantage acquired, profit, opposed to laws; act of gaining something; specially, the obtaining or amassing of profit or valuable possessions; acquisition; accumulation. [Breuer's Income Tax, In re 190 SW2d 248, 249: 354 Mo 578 (1945) as cited in *Brihanmumbai Mahanagarpalika* v. *Willingdon Sports Club*, (2013) 16 SCC 260, para 22].

Gainfully occupied person means a person who is engaged in any trade, business, profession, office, employment or vocation and is wholly or substantially dependent thereon for livelihood, or a person, though temporarily unemployed, is normally so engaged and dependent. [Personal Injuries (Emergency Provisions) Act (59 of 1962), S. 2(4)]

Gaining wrongfully. "A person is said to gain wrongfully when such person retains wrongfully, as well as when such person acquires wrongfully". [IPC (45 of 1860), S. 23] [Now (w.e.f. 1-7-2024) repealed & replaced by Bharatiya Nayaya Sanhita, 2023 (45 of 2023), section 2(38), same definition in new Sanhita]

Gains of learning. Means all acquisitions of property made substantially by means of learning, whether such acquisitions be made before or after the commencement of this Act and whether such acquisitions be the ordinary or the extraordinary result of such learning. [Hindu Gains of Learning Act (30 of 1930), S. 2(b)]

Gallantry. Splendid appearance; show magnificance; bravery; courage; heroism (as, the troops attacked the fort with great gallantry.

Gallows. Structure on which criminals are hanged; punishment of hanging.

Gamble. Play game of chance for money.

Gambling. To play or game for money or other stake.

Gambling according to the common use and understanding of that word is a generic term, and includes within its meaning every act, game, and contrivance by which one intentionally exposes money or other thing of value to the risk or hazard of loss by chance.

A prize competition for which a solution was prepared before hand is clearly a gambling prize competition. *State of Bombay* v. *R.M.D. Chamarbaugwala*, AIR 1957 SC 699, 707.

If we come across any activity or undertaking whose determination is controlled or influenced by chance or accident and which undertaking is undertaken or activity entered into with consciousness of risk, then the definition of 'gambling' would be satisfied. *State of Bombay* v. *R.M.D. Chamarbaugwala,* AIR 1956 Bom 1, 6. [Constitution of India, Sch. VII, list II, Entries 34 & 62]

Prize Competitions which do not require substantial skill ought to be considered as gambling transactions. *J.N. Gupta* v. *State of West Bengal,* AIR 1959 Cal 141, 145.

Game. Signifies animals pursued and taken by sportsmen.

It includes physical contents, whether of man or beast, when practised for the purpose of deciding wagers, or for the purpose of diversion, as well as games of hazard or skill by means of instruments or devices.

GAME, PLAY, GAMBLING. Boys are at *play* when they amuse themselves in a random manner. When they go to cricket they begin a *game*. But in regard to the verbs, to *play* a *game* is the phrase used because to game is restricted to playing at games of chance or gambling. (*Smith Syn. Dis.)*

Game officer. Means any officer, warden or servant appointed or authorised for any of the purposes of this Act. [Goa, Daman & Diu Wild Animals and Wild Birds Protection Act (21 of 1965), S. 2(d)]

Gamete. Means sperm and oocyte. [Surrogacy (Regulation) Act, 2021 (47 of 2021), section 2(1)(n)] [Assisted Reproductive Technology (Regulation) Act, 2021 (42 of 2021), section 2(1)(g)]

Gamete donor. Means a person who provides sperm or oocyte with the objective of enabling an infertile couple or woman to have a child. [Assisted Reproductive Technology (Regulation) Act, 2021 (42 of 2021), section 2(1)(h)]

Gaming. "Gaming" which is substantially the same in meaning as "gambling," has been defined to be a contract between two or more persons by which they agree to play by certain rules at cards, dice, or other contrivance and that one shall be the loser and the other the winner. Where in a certain game, certain operations are to be performed to enable the gamester to play the game, the persons taking part in such operations must be deemed to be "gaming" within the provisions of the Gaming Act as they actually assist in the gaming. [*Mahomed Hassan* v. *Emperor*, 31 SLR 44 : 169 IC 35 : 38 Cr LJ 668 : 9 RS 255 : AIR 1937 Sind 99].

Gaming and playing. The words "gaming" and 'playing" with their grammatical variations and cognate expressions, include taking part in the game of *ti* or in any other game or pretended game of a like nature. [Bur. Act 1 of 1899 (Gambling), S. 3, cl. 2].

Gaming house. Any place such as house, room, tent, enclosure, space vehicle, vessel or any place whatsoever in which gaming takes place or in which instruments of gaming are kept or used for gaming. *Kishan Chander* v. *State of Madhya Pradesh,* AIR 1965 SC 307.

Gang. A number of people closely associated; a set of persons working together in a squad or shift; a company of persons working together for anti-social purposes.

The word 'gang' is derived from the Anglo Saxon word 'gangan' to go, and its dictionary meaning is "a number going in company, hence a company or number of persons associated for a particular purpose." The expression 'belong to a gang of persons' in S. 401, I.P.C. (45 of 1860), means the same thing as, to be one of a gang of persons.' A person who receives stolen property from them cannot be said to belong to their gang. [99 IC 851 : 28 Cr LJ 179 : 28 Punj LR 19 : AIR 1927 Lah 524]

"Gang" means a group of persons, who acting either singly or collectively, by violence, or threat or show of violence, or intimidation, or coercion or otherwise with the object of disturbing public order or of gaining any undue temporal, pecuniary, material or other advantage for himself or any other person, indulge in anti-social activities…." [U.P. Gangster and Anti-Social Activities (Prevention) Act (7 of 1986), S. 2(b) as cited in *Dharmendra Kirthal* v. *State of U.P.*, (2013) 8 SCC 368, para 16].

The essence of the word is, that the persons should act in concert and therefore two or more persons can constitute a gang. *Sharaf Shah Khan* v. *State of A.P.,* AIR 1963 AP 314, 322. [IPC (45 of 1860), S. 400]

Gang rape. Where a woman is raped by one or more persons constituting a group or acting in furtherance of a common intention, each of those persons shall be deemed to have committed the offence of rape [(w.e.f. 1-7-2024) Bharatiya Nyaya Sanhita, 2023 (45 of 2023), section 70(1)]

Where a woman is raped by one or more persons constituting a group or acting in furtherance of a common intention, each of those persons shall be deemed to have committed the offence of rape and shall be punished with rigorous imprisonment for a term which shall not be less than twenty years, but which may extend to life which shall mean imprisonment for the remainder of that person's natural life, and with fine:

Provided that such fine shall be just and reasonable to meet the medical expenses and rehabilitation of the victim:

Provided further that any fine imposed under this section shall be paid to the victim. [Indian Penal Code 1860, S. 376D, as substituted by the Criminal Law (Amendment) Act 2013].

"Gangster" means a member or leader or organizer of a gang and includes any person who abets or assists in the activities of a gang enumerated in clause (b), whether before or after the commission of such activities or harbours any person who has indulged in such activities. [U.P. Gangsters and Anti-Social Activities (Prevention) Act (7 of 1986), S. 2(c) as cited in *Dharmendra Kirthal* v. *State of U.P.*, (2013) 8 SCC 368, para 17].

Gangway. Gangway means a way over which one goes and a plank placed across a duct for the purpose of people crossing it is a 'gangway'.

A passage way. [Factories Act (63 of 1948), S. 32(a)]; [Workmen's Compensation Act (8 of 1923), Sch. II (vii)(f)].

Ganja. '*Ganja*' that, is the flowering or fruiting tops of the cannabis plant (excluding the seeds and leaves when not accompanied by the tops), by whatever name they may be known or designated. [NDPS Act (61 of 1985), S. 2(iii)(b)] (H) Intoxicating drug, used for smoking. From this a drink called *bhang* is also made.

Gaol. Signifies a Cage for Birds; but, metaphorically is used for Prison. And from thence the keeper of the prison is called *Gaoler,* or *Gayler"*. (*Termes de la Ley; Jacob*)

Gaoler. Is the master of a prison; one that hath the custody of the place where prisoners are kept. (*Tomlin*)

A person incharge of gaol. [Navy Act (62 of 1957), S. 156].

Garb. Dress. [IPC (45 of 1860), S. 140].

Garbling. The process of garbling consists of washing, drying and winnowing with a view to cleaning it by removing all dust and dirt. It is a manufacturing process. *V.M. Patel* v. *Inspector of Factories,* AIR 1958 Ker 237, 239. [Factories Act (63 of 1948), S. 2(k)(1)]

Garnish. To warn; act of extracting money from prisoners.

Garnishee. A person in whose hands a debt is attached *i.e.* who is warned not to pay money which he owes to another person when the latter is indebted to the person warning or giving notice.

Garnishee order. Order of Court to attach money or goods belonging to a judgment debtor in the hands of a third person.

An order served upon a garnishee requiring him not to pay or deliver the money or property of the debtor (defendant) to him and/or requiring him to appear in Court and answer to the suit of the plaintiff to the extent of his liability to the defendant. [CPC (5 of 1908), S. 128(2)(d)].

Garnishment. Process of attachment of money in respect of which a garnishee order has been obtained.

Garnishment is proceeding by which plaintiff in an action seeks to reach the rights and effects of defendant by calling into Court some third party, who has such effects in his possession or who is indebted to defendant.

Garrison. Troops stationed in fortress, town *etc.* to defend it. Troops or soldiers engaged on garrison duty *(i.e.)* in defence.

A place in which troops are quartered. [Army Act (46 of 1950), S. 34(a)].

Garrotting. The criminal choking or strangling of a person, with intent to commit an indictable offence.

Gas. 'GAS' means a matter in gaseous state which predominantly consists of methane. [Gujarat Gas (Regulation of Transmission, Supply and Distribution) Act, 2001, S. 2(h)]

Gasoline. Liquid got from petroleum etc used for heating purposes.

"Gas cylinder" or **"cylinder".** Means any closed metal container having a volume exceeding 500 ml but not exceeding 1000 liters intended for the storage and transport of compressed gas, including any liquefied petroleum gas (LPG) container of liquefied natural gas (LNG) container or compressed natural gas (CNG) cylinder fitted to motor vehicle as its fuel tank but not including any other such container fitted to a special transport or undercarriage and includes a composite cylinder and cryogenic container, however, the water capacity of cylinder used for storage of CNG, nitrogen or compressed air may exceed 1000 liters up to 3000 liters provided the diameter of such cylinder does not exceed 60 cm. [Gas Cylinder Rules, 2016, R. 2(1)(xxviii)].

Gather. Cause to assemble; collect; amass; infer; deduce.

Gatwall or Ghatwal. An officer who has charge of a pass in the mountains or a landing place on a river. (*Fifth Report*).

Gauge. Standard measure to which things must conform (as) measure of capacity; contents of barrel; diameter of bullet; thickness of sheet iron or other metallic sheet. As used in Railway Law, the terms broad gauge, narrow gauge, and meter gauge occurs.

Gay. Men who are attracted to men, although this term is sometimes also used generically for all same sex attracted persons. [Michall Kirby, former Judge of the High Court of Austrial **as cited in** *Navtej Singh Johar* v. *Union of India,* (2018) 10 SCC 1, para 151].

Gazette. "Official Gazette" or "Gazette" shall mean the Gazette of India or the official Gazette of a State. [General Clauses Act (10 of 1897), S. 3(39)]

It is a publication of an official character which contains government notifications, lists of public appointments and honours, legal notices, *etc.*

The OFFICIAL GAZETTER is a Government book, publication or newspaper, which appears on a fixed day or days in every week and is the official organ for the publication of government orders and regulations, government circulars, rules, and bye-laws, and other public notices.

An official newspaper containing lists of government appointments, legal notices, despatches *etc.* [General Clauses Act (10 of 1897), S. 3(39) and Constitution of India, art. 366(19)]

Gazetted. Published in the (official) gazette; whose appointment has to be published in the official gazette.

Gazetted officer. An officer who holds a gazetted post. [CPC (5 of 1908), S. 2(17)(c)].

Gazetteer. The geographical dictionary, or the historic account, or the general description of any place, district or province.

GB (Gigabyte). A unit of storage capacity equal to 1,073,741,824 bytes. (*Computer*)

Gelding. A castrated animal. [Indian Forest Act (16 of 1927), S. 71].

Gender. In all Acts "unless the contrary intention appears, words importing the Masculine Gender shall include Females.

"The pronoun he and its derivatives are used of any person whether male or female." [IPC (45 of 1860), S. 8] [Now (w.e.f. 1-7-2024) repealed & replaced by Bharatiya Nyaya Sanhita, 2023 (45 of 2023)]

"Gender".—The pronoun "he" and its derivatives are used of any person, whether male, female or transgender.

Explanation.—"Transgender" shall have the meaning assigned to it in clause (*k*) of section 2 of the Transgender Persons (Protection of Rights) Act, 2019 (40 of 2019). [(w.e.f. 1-7-2024) Bharatiya Nyaya Sanhita, 2023 (45 of 2023), section 2(10)]

Gender and number. In any Act, unless the contrary intention appears—

(a) words importing the masculine gender include the feminine;

(b) words importing the feminine gender include the masculine;

(c) words in the singular include the plural and words in the plural include the singular. [(English) Interpretation Act, 1978, S. 6]

General. Pertaining to all or most of the parts of a whole; pertaining in common to various persons or things; prevalent; usual; applicable to a whole class of objects, cases or occasions. [CrPC 1973 (2 of 1974), S. 15(1) and Constitution of India, Art. 12, main heading]; holding superior rank [Cardamom Act (42 of 1965), S. 19(1)]; [CPC (5 of 1908), S. 80(b)]; public; inclusive and manifesting or characterised by scope, diversity or variety; a military officer of a high rank.

GENERAL, UNIVERSAL. The general rule admits of many exceptions; the universal rule admits of none.

General is opposed to particular, and universal to individual.

General agent. A person who is authorised by his principal to execute all deeds, sign all contracts, or purchase all goods required in a particular trade, business, or employment.

General annuity business. Means the business of effecting contracts to pay annuities on human life but does not include contracts under pension business. [Insurance Regulatory and Development Authority (Registration of Indian Insurance Companies) Regulations, 2000, Reg. 2(e) as it stood prior to substitution by Seventh Amendment Regulation of 2016]

General assembly. The supreme deliberative body of the United Nations.

General assets. Of a company means, the funds available for payment of the general creditors.

General assumpsit. "General assumpsit is brought for breach of a fictitious or implied promise raised by law from a debt founded upon an executed consideration. The basis of the action is the promise implied by law from the performance of the consideration, or from a debt or legal duty resting upon the defendant." Benjamin J. Shipman, *Handbook of Common-Law Pleading, S.* 59, at 153 (Henry Winthrop Ballantine ed., 3d ed. 1923).

General average. A contribution made by the proprietors in general of a ship or cargo towards the loss sustained by any individual of their number whose property has been voluntarily sacrificed for the common safety.

General average act. A sacrifice or expenditure, extraordinary in nature, voluntarily and reasonably incurred, in time of peril, for the common safety of the maritime adventure.

General average contribution. Is defined to be a contribution by all the parties in a sea adventure to make the loss sustained by one of their number on account of sacrifices voluntarily made of part of the ship or cargo to save the residue and the lives of those on board from an impending peril, or for extraordinary expense necessarily incurred by one or more of the parties for the general benefit of all the interests embarked in the enterprise. "The object of general average contribution is to indemnify the person making the general Average Sacrifice against so much of the loss caused directly thereby as does not fall to his own proportionate share."

General average loss. The loss resulting from throwing away the cargo into the sea to save the ship and it is shared by the owner of the ship and the owner of the cargo.

A loss caused by or directly consequential on a general average act.

General average sacrifice. A contribution by all parties in a sea adventure to make good the loss sustained in a general average act.

General balance of accounts. A balance determined after taking into consideration all the concerned accounts of parties. [Indian Contract Act (9 of 1872), S. 171].

General character. The estimation in which a person is held in the community where he lives.

General clause. A clause of general application or containing a general provision. [Indian Evidence Act (1 of 1872), S. 86].

General Commission Agent. Means a trader who *bona fide* buys or sells or offers to buy or sell for an agreed commission, any agricultural produce on behalf of another person and does or offers to do anything necessary for completing and carrying out the transactions of such sale or purchase. [Gujarat Agricultural Produce Markets Act, 1963 (Guj Act No. 20 of 1964), S. 2(vii)]

General Count. A count which states in a general way the plaintiff's claim.

General custom or right. A custom or right common to any considerable class of persons. [Indian Evidence Act (1 of 1872), S. 48, *Expln.*] [Now (w.e.f. 1-7-2024) repealed & replaced by Bharatiya Sakshya Adhiniyam, 2023 (47 of 2023)]

The expression "general custom or right" includes customs or rights common to any considerable class of persons.

Illustration

The right of the villagers of a particular village to use the water of a particular well is a general right within the meaning of this section. [(w.e.f. 1-7-2024) Bharatiya Sakshya Adhiniyam, 2023 (47 of 2023), section 42, *Explanation*]

General damages. Such damages as necessarily result from the injury complained of as contrasted with special damages.

General deposit. A general deposit is one in which the identical subject-matter need not be returned and as distinguished from a deposit for safekeeping, this form of deposit has been termed a deposit for exchange, that is, one in which the depository is only bound to return a thing corresponding in kind to that which is deposited. In determining whether or not a deposit is special, the character of the business of the depository is entitled to considerable weight, but is not controlling. [*Corpus Juris Secundum*, Vol. 26-A, as referred in *Siddheshwar Sahakari Sakhar Karkhana Ltd.* v. *CIT,* (2004) 12 SCC 1, 20, para 33]

General disposition. A general bent of mind; general inclination.

General education. Means every branch of education other than religious, professional, medical, technical or special education. [Karnataka Education Act, 1983, S. 2(16)]

General election. Means the election held under this Act for the Constitution on reconstitution of a Panchayat after the expiry of its term or otherwise. [Kerala Panchayat Raj Act (Ker Act No. 13 of 1994), S. 2(xvii)]

A general election means an election in all the wards of the municipality for all the seats, and one in which all the voters eligible to vote in the municipality are given an opportunity of exercising their franchise. *Provat Chandra Sircar* v. *R.C. Sen*, AIR 1955 Cal 83.

General exception. An exception of a general nature.

General Government debt. Means the sum total of the debt of the Central Government and the State Governments, excluding inter-Governmental liabilities. [Fiscal Responsibility and Budget Management Act (39 of 3003), S. 2(bb) as substituted by Finance Act (13 of 2018)].

General guardian. : Special guardian. A general guardian is one who has the general care and control of the person and estate of his ward; while a special guardian is one who has special or limited powers and duties with respect to his ward e.g., a guardian who has the custody of the estate but not of the person, or vice versa, or a guardian ad litem. [Black's Law Dictionary, 5th Edn. as cited in *Roxann Sharma* v. *Arun Sharma*, (2015) 8 SCC 318, para 5].

General information. Information of the people in general. [Trade Unions Act (16 of 1926), S. 30(2)].

General insurance business. Means fire, marine or miscellaneous insurance business, whether carried on singly or in combination with one or more of them. [Insurance Act (4 of 1938), S. 2(6B)]

"GENERAL INSURANCE BUSINESS" means fire, marine or miscellaneous insurance business, whether carried on singly or in combination with one or more of them but does not include capital redemption business and annuity certain business. [General Insurance Business (Nationalisation) Act (57 of 1972), S. 3(g)]

General intent. Common or collective intention.

General legacy. A pecuniary legacy payable out of the general assets of a testator.

General lien. The right which the bailee of a chattel has to retain possession of it from the owner, under certain circumstances.

General manager. A person having general control on all matters of a company or corporation or of any particular department of a company or corporation.

The top executive officer of a company or institution having the management of the whole affairs thereof. [Industrial Finance Corporation Act (15 of 1948), (*Repealed by Act 23 of 1993*), S. 16].

General meeting. "GENERAL MEETING" in the Imperial Bank Act means the annual meeting of the shareholders of the Bank Act. [Imperial Bank of India Act (47 of 1920), S. 2(d)].

"GENERAL MEETING" means a meeting of the general body of a multi-State co-operative society and includes special general meeting. [Multi State Cooperative Societies Act (39 of 2002), S. 3(m)]

"GENERAL MEETING" means a meeting of the general body of a Co-operative Society. [A.P. Mutually Aided Co-operative Societies Act (AP Act No. 30 of 1995), S. 2(n)]

General Officer. A General, Lieutenant General or Major General [Army Act (46 of 1950), S. 102(2)].

General Officer Commanding the district. The expression 'GENERAL OFFICER COMMANDING THE DISTRICT' means the officer for the time being in command of the forces in a District. [Works of Defence Act (7 of 1903), S. 2(d)]

General pardon. A pardon which is extended by the government to a group or class of persons, usually for a political offence.

General police district. The words "GENERAL POLICE DISTRICT" shall embrace any Presidency, State or place, or any part of any Presidency, State or place, in which the Police Act shall be ordered to take effect. [Police Act (5 of 1861), Interpretation Clause]

General power. "GENERAL POWER" includes every power or authority enabling the donee or holder thereof to appoint or dispose of property as he thinks fit, whether exercisable by instrument *inter vivos* or by will or both, but exclusive of any power exercisable in a fiduciary capacity under a disposition not made by himself or exercisable as mortgagee. [Estate Duty Act (34 of 1953), S. 2(9) now repealed by Act 20 of 2000]

General power of attorney. A power of attorney which authorises the attorney to do all acts of a certain class from time to time, such as to carry on business, collect debts, *etc.* is called a general power as opposed to a special or particular power. [Companies Act (1 of 1956), S. 337(iii) now replaced by Companies Act, 2013].

General power of transfer. The power of the Court to transfer any suit, appeal or other proceedings to a subordinate Court generally. [CPC (5 of 1908), S. 24].

General practice. A practice observed in business generally.

General public. The expression 'general public' in Art. 19(5) of the Constitution of India is wide enough to include a section of the public and the removal of the grievances of a particular section is very often in the interests of the public generally. *Jamath Mosque* v. *Vakhan Joseph,* AIR 1955 TC 227 (FB).

The interest of a section of the members of the public is included in the term 'general public'. *Jugal Kishore Bhadri* v. *Labour Commissioner,* AIR 1958 Pat 442, 444.

General purposes. Include such identified purposes for which no specific amount is allocated or any amount so specified towards general purpose or any such purpose by whatever name called, in the offer document filed with the Board:

Provided that any issue related expenses shall not be considered as a part of general purpose merely because no specific amount has been allocated for such expenses in the offer document filed with the Board. [Securities and Exchange Board of India (Real Estate Investment Trusts) Regulations, 2014, Regn. 2(1)(pa)].

General purposes committee. Constituted by the Speaker to consider and advise on such matters concerning the affairs of the House as may be referred to it by him from time to time.

General reputation. The general reputation of a man is that which he bears among his fellow townsmen, or in the neighbourhood in which he lives.

Mere suspicion of complicity in this or that isolated offence is not evidence of general reputation. A person cannot be put upon security merely upon the ground that he was suspected by the Police six times of having committed various burglaries.

General rules of construction. The general rules of determining the sense, real meaning or proper explanation of obscure or ambiguous terms or provisions in a statute, written instrument or oral agreement.

General ship. A ship in which the owners and master contract with various consignors to ship their goods, normally under bills of lading as contrasted with a ship chartered to one or more persons under a charter-party for the carriage of their goods only. (*Walker*)

Generale tantum valet in generalibus quantum singulare in singulis. (*Lat.*) When words are general they are to be taken in a general sense, just as words relating to a particular thing are to be taken as referring only to that thing.

General will. A concept of Rousseau, to the effect that a community has a collective good which is not the same thing as the private interests of its members. In accordance with the analogy of an organism, it may be said to have a will of its own, the general will (*volonte generale*).

General words of abuse may not be defamatory, but to speak of a person that he is a beast and a pig in his conduct is defamatory.

Generale dictum generaliter est interpretandum. (*Maxim*) A general expression is to be interpreted generally.

Generalia specialibus non derogant. General things do not derogate from special. [*Patna Improvement Trust* v. *Lakshmi Devi*, AIR 1963 SC 1077 (1081-82).

The maxim means that if a special provision has been made on a certain matter, that matter is excluded from the general provisions. [*Subramanian Swamy* v. *Manmohan Singh*, (2012) 3 SCC 64, para 65].

General law yields to special law, should they operate in the same field on same subject. [*Commercial Tax Officer, Rajasthan* v. *Binani Cements Limited*, (2014) 8 SCC 319, para 34].

It means special law will always prevail over the general law. [*Anvar P.V.* v. *P.K. Basheer*, (2014) 10 SCC 473, para 22].

Special Acts are not repealed by general Acts unless there be some express reference to the previous legislation, or a necessary inconsistency in the two Acts standing together, which prevents the maxim from being applied.

A general provision relating to meetings and the formalities to be served in connection therewith does not become inapplicable *in toto* to a particular meeting mentioned in another section, simply because some of the language of the general section is not appropriate to a meeting of the later description.

This maxim will apply to a case of conflict between two Statutes—the prior enactment being special and the subsequent enactment being general. Meaning—the special enactment would prevail over the general enactment.

Generalia sunt praeponenda singularibus. (*Maxim*) General things are to be put before particular things.

Generalia verba sunt generaliter intelligenda. (*Maxim*) General words are to be understood generally.

Generalibus specialia derogant. (*Lat.*) (H. 51). Special things derogate from general.

Considering the maxim the Apex Court observed that if the intention of the rule making authority was to establish a rule of universal application to all the services in the State of Kerala for which the Special Rules are made then the Special Rule will give way to the General Rules enacted for that purpose. If the language is clear and unqualified, the subsequent General Rule would prevail despite repugnancy. *S. Prakash* v. *K.M. Kurian,* (1999) 5 SCC 624, Para 14 : AIR 1999 SC 2094.

Generalis clausula non porrigitur ad ea quae antea specialiter sunt comprehensa. (*Lat.*) (8 Rep. 154). A general clause does not extend to those things which are before specially provided for.

On the basis of maxim the Apex Court observed that when provisions relating to resolving disputes between society and its employees are given in

Societies Act, a Special Act, the provisions of Industrial Disputes Act (14 of 1947) a general Act are not applicable. *R.C. Tiwari* v. *M.P. State Coop. Marketing Federation Ltd.,* (1997) 5 SCC, paras 4 & 5. [M.P. Cooperative Societies Act, 1960 (17 of 1961), S. 64]

Generalis regula generaliter est intelligenda. (*Maxim*) General rules must be generally understood.

Generality. Total applicability. [Epidemic Diseases Act (3 of 1897), S. 2(2) and Constitution of India, Art. 31B]

Generally : Ordinarily. The word 'generally' means as a general rule, whereas the word 'ordinarily' means 'in the large majority of cases but not invariably. *Padmanabhacharya* v. *State of Mysore*, AIR 1968 Mys 280, 285.

Generate. Means to produce electricity from a generating station for the purpose of giving supply to any premises or enabling a supply to be so given. [Electricity Act (36 of 2003), S. 2(29)]

Generating company. Means any company or body corporate or association or body of individuals, whether incorporated or not, or artificial juridical person, which owns or operates or maintains a generating station. [Electricity Act (36 of 2003), S. 2(28)]

"GENERATING COMPANY" means a company registered under the Companies Act, 1956 and which has among its objects the establishment, operation and maintenance of generating stations. [Electricity (Supply) Act (54 of 1948), S. 2(4A) now repealed by Act 36 of 2003 (w.e.f. 10-6-2003)]

'Bharat Hydro Power Corporation Ltd.' is a 'Generating company' within the meaning of Section 2(4-A) of the Act. *Bharat Hydro Power Corpn. Ltd., Guwahati* v. *State of Assam,* AIR 1998 Gau 49, 72, para 59. [Electricity (Supply) Act (54 of 1948), S. 2(4-A)]

"Generating station" or "station". Means any station for generating electricity, including any building and plant with step-up transformer, switch-gear, switch yard, cables or other appurtenant equipment, if any, used for that purpose and the site thereof; a site intended to be used for a generating station, and any building used for housing the operating staff of a generating station, and where electricity is generated by water-power, includes penstocks, head and tail works, main and regulating reservoirs, dams and other hydraulic works, but does not in any case include any sub-station. [Electricity Act (36 of 2003), S. 2(30) and Electricity (Supply) Act (54 of 1948), S. 2(5)] [Now repealed by Act 36 of 2003]

Generation. A whole body of persons living, average time at which children are ready to replace parents, reckoned at 30 years.

Offspring of the same parent regarded as a step in the line of descent from an ancestor. [Hindu Marriage Act (25 of 1955), S. 3(f)(i)]; production; [Income-tax Act (43 of 1961), S. 2(18), *Expln.* 2]; [Mines Act (35 of 1952), S. 57(p)].

Generation to generation. The expression "generation to generation" shows that a heritable estate is given.

Generator of wastes. Means persons or establishments generating municipal solid wastes. [Municipal Solid Wastes (Management and Handling) Rules, 2000, R. 3(x)].

Generic claim. A generic claim, usually found in patent specifications relating to chemical compounds, covers a number of compounds having common structural features. (*Patents*)

Generic name. 'GENERIC NAME' in relation to a commodity means the name of the genus of the commodity, for example, in the case of common salt, sodium chloride is the generic name. [Standard of Weights and Measures (Packaged Commodities) Rules, 1977, R. 6(1)(b) *Expln.*]

Genericide means loss or cancellation of a trademark that no longer distinguishes the owner's product from others' products. It occurs when a trade-mark becomes such a household name that the consuming public begins to think of the mark not as a brand name but as a synonym for the product itself.

Genetic Clinic. Means a clinic, institute, hospital, nursing home or any place, by whatever name called which is used for conducting pre-natal diagnostic procedures. [Pre-Natal Diagnostic Techniques (Regulation and Prevention of Misuse) Act (57 of 1994), S. 2(d)]

"GENETIC CLINIC" includes a vehicle, where ultrasound machine or imaging machine or scanner or other equipment capable of determining sex of the foetus or a portable equipment which has the potential for detection of sex during pregnancy or selection of sex before conception, is used. [Pre-conception and Pre-natal Diagnostic Techniques (Prohibition of Sex Selection) Act, 1994, S. 2(d) *Expl.*]

Genetic Counselling Centre. Means an institute, hospital, nursing home or any place, by whatever name called, which provides for genetic counselling to patients. [Pre-Natal Diagnostic Techniques (Regulation and Prevention of Misuse) Act (57 of 1994), S. 2(c)]

Genetic engineering. "GENETIC ENGINEERING" means the technique by which heritable material, which does not usually occur or will not occur naturally in the organism or cell concerned, generated outside the organism or the cell is inserted into said cell or organism. It shall also mean the formation of the new combinations of genetic material by incorporation of a cell into a host cell, where they occur naturally (self cloning) as well as modification of an organism or in a cell by deletion and removal of parts of the heritable material. [Rules for the Manufacture, Use, Import,

Export and Storage of Hazardous Micro Organisms Genetically Engineered Organisms or Cells, Rules 1989, R. 3(iv)]

The alteration of genes, which control hereditary characteristics, by human intervention.

Genetic Laboratory. Means a laboratory and includes a place where facilities are provided for conducting analysis or tests of samples received from genetic clinic for pre-natal diagnostic test. [Pre-Natal Diagnostic Techniques (Regulation and Prevention of Misuse) Act (57 of 1994), S. 2(e)]

"GENETIC LABORATORY" includes a place where ultrasound machine or imaging machine or scanner or other equipment capable of determining sex of the foetus or a portable equipment which has the potential for detection of sex during pregnancy or selection of sex before conception, is used. [Pre-Natal Diagnostic Techniques (Regulation and Prevention of Misuse) Act (57 of 1994), S. 2(e) *Expl.*]

Genetically engineered or modified food. Means food and food ingredients composed of or containing genetically modified or engineered organisms obtained through modern biotechnology, or food and food ingredients produced from but not containing genetically modified or engineered organisms obtained through modern biotechnology. [*Explanation* (2) to S. 22 of the Food Safety & Standards Act, 2006 (34 of 2006)]

Geneva Conventions. A series of international agreements establishing proper treatment of prisoners of war and of persons injured or killed in battle; the first of which was drafted in 1864. It has been adopted by most of the nations in revised forms.

Genocide. An act committed with the intent to destroy, in whole or part, a national, ethnic, racial, or religious group.

Gentlemen's agreement. Generally an unsigned and unenforceable agreement made between parties who expect its performance because of good faith. (*Black*)

Genuine. Natural, not spurious or counterfeit. [Constitution of India, Art. 101(3), prov.]

Geographical division. Division according to geography. [Indian Evidence Act (1 of 1872), S. 57(9)].

Geographical indication. In relation to goods, means an indication which identifies such goods as agricultural goods, natural goods or manufactured goods as originating, or manufactured in the territory of a country, or a region or locality in that territory, where a given quality, reputation or other characteristic of such goods is essentially attributable to its geographical origin and in case where such goods are manufactured goods one of the activities of either the production or of processing or preparation of the goods concerned takes place in such territory, region or locality, as the case may be. [The Geographical Indications of Goods (Registration and Protection) Act, 1999, S. 2(1)(e)]

It is, however, clarified that any name which is not the name of country, region or locality of that country shall also be considered as the geographical indication if it relates to a specific geographical area and is used upon or in relation to particular goods originating from that country, region or locality, as the case may be. V K Ahuja, *Intellectual Property Rights in India,* 2015, LexisNexis Butterworths.

Explanation.—For the purposes of this clause, any name which is not the name of a country, region or locality of that country shall also be considered as the geographical indication if it relates to a specific geographical area and is used upon or in relation to particular goods originating from that country, region or locality, as the case may be. [Geographical Indications of Goods (Registration and Protection) Act (48 of 1999), S. 2(1)(e)]

Germane. Closely or significantly related; relevant; pertinent; appropriate; relative.

Germane to the business. Appropriate to the business; in close relationship to the business.

Gerrymandering. The practice of dividing a geographical area into electoral districts, often of highly irregular shape, to give one political party an unfair advantage by diluting the opposition's voting strength.

Gestation. Period (usually 266 days) from conception to birth, during which the baby develops in the mother's womb.

Gestation period. The period from the alleged date of last coitus between the couple and birth of the child. The period of pregnancy.

Gesture. A posture or movement of the body; an action expressive of the sentiment or passion or intended to show inclination or disposition. [IPC (45 of 1860), Ss. 298 and 509].

Getting in. To take charge, possession or control of.

Ghastly; Grim. *Ghastly* is the same word as ghostly; hence the predominant idea is that of a supernatural or deathlike pallor, from which the signification has been extended to denote simply deadly, horrible; as, "ghastly wounds." *Grim* is, on the other hand, essentially connected with life and the expression of the countenance of man or beast. Surliness, ferocity, and gravity, combined into a fixed and rigid expression, would constitute *grimness* (as) a "grim fight'. (*Smith Syn. Dic.)*

Gherao. The word '*gherao*' means a physical blockade of a target, either by encirclement or forcible occupation.

Gift. "GIFT" is the transfer of certain existing moveable or immovable property made voluntarily and without consideration, by one person, called the donor, to another, called the donee and accepted by or on behalf of the donee. [Transfer of Property Act (4 of 1882), S. 122].

"The voluntary transfer of property to another without compensation." [Black's Law Dictionary as cited in *Nusli N. Wadia* v. *The Commissioner of Income Tax, Central II* [2017] 394 ITR 638(Bom), para 13]

The plain dictionary meaning of 'Gift' as given in the Oxford Dictionary is:- "A thing given willingly to someone without payment." [Oxford Dictionary as cited in *Nusli N. Wadia* v. *The Commissioner of Income Tax, Central II* [2017] 394 ITR 638 (Bom), para 13]

"GIFT" means the transfer by one person to another of any existing movable or immovable property voluntarily and without consideration in money or money's worth, and includes the transfer or conversion of any property referred to in Section 4 deemed to be a gift under that section.

Expln. A transfer of any building or part there of referred to in clause (iii), clause (iiia) or clause (iiib) of the Section 27 of Income-tax Act by the person who is deemed under the said clause to be the owner thereof made voluntarily and without consideration in money or money's worth, shall be deemed to be a gift made of by such person. [Gift-tax Act (18 of 1958), S. 2(xii)]

The act of a Manager of joint Hindu family throwing his self acquired property into the common stock of the family without any consideration, is transfer of property and is gift. *Commissioner Gift Tax* v. *Satyanarayana Murthi,* AIR 1965 AP 95, 98. [Gift-tax Act (18 of 1958), S. 2(xii)]

A Gift is a transfer which does not contain any element of consideration in any shape or form. Love, affection, spiritual benefit and many other factors may enter in the intention of the donor to make a gift but these filial considerations cannot be called or held to be legal considerations as understood by law. *Sonia Bhatia* v. *State of U.P. and others*, AIR 1981 SC 1274, 1280. [Transfer of Property Act (4 of 1882), S. 122]

AN ORAL GIFT of moveable property must be "accompanied by delivery of possession." There must be a giving and taking."

Gift and will. One of the tests to be applied, for the purpose of seeing whether the document is a will or not, is whether it is revocable. If the document is revocable, it must be construed as a will.

A transfer by one person to another of any existing movable or immovable property made voluntarily or without consideration of money or money's worth. [Gift-tax Act (18 of 1958), S. 2(xii)].

GIFT, PRESENT, DONATION. The *gift* is an act of generosity or condescension; the *present* is an act of kindness, courtesy, or respect. The *gift* passes from the rich to the poor, from the high to the law, and creates an obligation; the *present* passes either between equals, or from the inferior to the superior. The *gift* is private, and benefits the individual; the *donation* is public, and serves some general purpose : what is given to relieve the necessities of any poor person is a *gift*; what s given to support an institution is a *donation*.

Gift in contemplation of death. A gift of personal property made in anticipation of death on specific condition that the donor dies as anticipated.

Gift tax. A gift tax is not a tax on lands and buildings but is a levy upon a particular use, which is transmission of title by gift. *Second G.T. Officer* v. *D.H. Hazareth*, AIR 1970 SC 999, 1002.

Gifts before the nuptial fire. Under the Hindu law, "gifts before the nuptial fire" is only a term to signify all gifts during the continuance of the marriage ceremonies. Such gifts made to the bride constitute her *stridhanam* property.

Gig worker means a person who performs work or participates in a work arrangement and earns from such activities outside of traditional employer-employee relationship. [Code on Social Security, 2020 (36 of 2020), section 2(35)]

Gilda mercatoria. (*Lat.*) A guild merchant; an assembly or meeting of merchants.

Gin. Machine for separating cotton from its seeds; also used to denote spirit distilled from grain or malt.

Ginned. (Cotton) cleared of its seeds. [Central Sales Tax Act (74 of 1956), S. 14(ii)].

Ginning and pressing cotton is a manufacturing process.

Gipsy. The word 'gipsy' means a person leading a nomadic life with no, or no fixed, employment and with no fixed abode.

Girasdar. 'GIRASDAR' means any talukdar, bhagdar, bhayat, cadet or mulgirasia and includes any person whom the Government may, by notification in the Official Gazette, declare to be a Girasdar for the purposes of this Act. [Saurashtra Act 25 of 1951, S. 2(15) as cited in *State of Gujarat* v. *Manoharsinhji Pradyumansinhji Jadeja*, (2013) 2 SCC 300, para 36].

Girl. A female who has not completed the age of twenty-one years. [Suppression of Immoral Traffic in Women and Girls Act (104 of 1956), S. 2(b)]

The word "girl" is not limited to mean only the unmarried female. Acts apply whether the female in question is married or unmarried and the whole matters on the status of the female from the point of view of the marriage or no marriage but on the question of age. [MLJ : FYD (01-50), V. 2, p. 823 : AIR 1929 Cal 99]. [Calcutta Suppression of Immoral Traffic Act (XIII of 1923), S. 4]

A female generally under the age of 16 years. *R.* v. *Prince,* LR 2 C.C.R. 154.

Gist. The ground or essence of a legal action.

Give and bequeath. (*Will-Construction*) The use of the words 'give and bequeath' shows that the testator intended to give his wife a benefit under his will apart from and quite regardless of any contractual obligation he might be under any covenant.

Give in adoption. To give a child to another for being adopted by him as his issue. [Hindu Adoptions and Maintenance Act (78 of 1956), S. 9].

Given a notice. The giving of the notice is not complete unless and until it reaches the person concerned or its actual tender to him. Merely despatching of the notice to the address of the person does not complete the giving of the notice. *Ambalal Morarji Soni* v. *Union of India*, AIR 1972 Guj 126, 130. [Gold Control Act (45 of 1968), S. 69 (*Repealed*)]

Gives information. The expression "gives information" in S. 203, IPC (45 of 1860) means "volunteers information".

Giving a notice. The expression 'giving a notice' occurring in Section 138(b) of the Act, would mean that the payee has to perform the process by sending the notice to the drawer of the cheque at his correct address. *K. Bhaskaran* v. *Sankaran Vaidhyam Balau,* (1999) 7 SCC 510, para 18 : AIR 1999 SC 3762. [Negotiable Instruments Act (26 of 1881), S. 138(b)]

The 'giving of notice' is distinguished from 'receiving of the notice'. It provides that a person notifies or gives notice to another by taking such steps as may be reasonably required to inform the other in the ordinary course, whether or not such person actually comes to know of it. 'A person 'receives' a notice when it is duly delivered to him or at the place of his business. [Black's Law Dictionary as cited in *Devendra Singh vs. State of U.P. and Ors.* Writ No. 51900 of 2017, decided on 21-11-2017 para 38]

Giving false evidence. "Whoever, being legally bound by an oath or by an express provision of law to state the truth, or being bound by law to make declaration upon any subject, makes any statement which is false, and which he either knows or believes to be false or does not believe to be true, is said to give false evidence." [IPC (45 of 1860), S. 191]

Glaring. Conspicuous; patent.

Glassware. The term 'glassware' includes lenses and object glasses.

'Glassware' would include crockery such as drinking vessels (drinkware) and tableware and general glass items such as vases, pots. etc. [New Oxford Dictionary, Merriam-Webster Dictionary and Macmillan Dictionary as cited in *State of Jharkhand* v. *La Opala R.G. Limited*, (2014) 15 SCC 136, para 23].

'Glassware' the term glassware would generally encompass ornaments, objects and articles made from glass. [*State of Jharkhand* v. *La Opala R.G. Limited*, (2014) 15 SCC 136, para 23].

Clinical syringes cannot be considered as 'glassware'. *Indo International Industries* v. *S.T. Commissioner U.P.*, AIR 1981 SC 1079, 1082.

Global Depository Receipt (GDR). Means a security issued by a bank or a depository outside India against underlying rupee shares of a company incorporated in India. [Foreign Exchange Management (Transfer or Issue of any Foreign Security) Regulations, 2000, Reg. 2(i)]

In this scheme, unless the context otherwise requires—

"GLOBAL DEPOSITARY RECEIPTS" means any instrument in the form of a depositary receipt or certificate (by whatever name it is called) created by the Overseas Depositary Bank outside India and issued to non-resident investors against the issue of ordinary shares or Foreign Currency Convertible Bonds or issuing company. [Issue of Foreign Currency Convertible Bonds and Ordinary Shares (Through Depositary Receipt Mechanism) Scheme, 1993, S. 2(c)]

"GLOBAL DEPOSITORY RECEIPT" means any instrument in the form of a depository receipt, by whatever name called, created by a foreign depository outside India and authorised by a company making an issue of such depository receipts. [S. 2(44) of the Companies Act, 2013 (18 of 2013)]

Global information environment. All individuals, organizations, or systems, most of which are outside the control of the military or national command authorities, that collect, process, and disseminate information to national and international audiences. (*Cyber Law*)

Global Positioning System (GPS). A US satellite system that lets those on the ground, on the water or in the air determine their position with extreme accuracy using GPS receivers. (*Telecommunication*)

Global search and replace. A feature that automatically searches out every instance of a string of characters in a document and replaces them with a different string of characters. You have told the system which word or phrase to search and which word or Phrase to use as the replacement. The word "global" indicates this process occurs throughout the entire document without stopping, rather than moving from one instance to the next individually on your command. (*Computer*)

Globalization. The trend of bringing major financial markets across the world closer together through technological innovations in communications.

"GLOBALIZATION". This term connotes a process by which the national economy moves towards a single borderless world economy with open market. It implies expansion of markets for goods, services, labour and capital beyond national boundaries. Independence of countries, competition and dominance of market and private sector characterize the globalization process. [*ML Tannan Banking Law & Practice in India*, Vol. 2, 2021, LexisNexis, Dictionary of Banking Terminology]

Increasing internationalization of all markets, industries and commerce. [*P. Ramanath Aiyar's, The Law Lexicon*, 2017, LexisNexis].

Glorification. In relation to *Sati,* whether such *Sati* has been committed before or after the commencement of this Act, includes among other things,—

(i) the observance of any ceremony or the taking out of a procession in connection with the commission of *Sati;* or

(ii) the supporting, justifying or propagating the practice of *Sati* in any manner; or

(iii) the arranging of any function to eulogise the person who has committed *Sati;* or

(iv) the creation of a trust, or the collection of funds, or the construction of a temple or other structure or the carrying on of any form of worship or the performance of any ceremony thereat, with a view to perpetuate the honour of, or to preserve the memory of a person who has committed *Sati.* [Commission of Sati (Prevention) Act, 1987 (3 of 1988), S. 2(b)]

'GLORIFICATION', in relation to *sati*, includes, among other things, the observance of any ceremony or the taking out of a procession in connection with the *sati* or the creation of a trust or the collection of funds or the construction of a temple with a view to perpetuating the honour of, or to preserve the memory of the person committing *sati.* [Rajasthan Sati (Prevention) Act (40 of 1987), S. 2(b)]

Glorification in any manner. The expression 'glorification in any manner' occurring in Section 6(2) of Rajasthan *Sati* (Prevention) Act (40 of 1987) means the Acts towards commission of *sati* or glorification of *Sati. State of Rajasthan* v. *Hat Singh,* (2003) 2 SCC 152, para 12 : AIR 2003 SC 791.

Glossa. A gloss; an explanation or interpretation. A note inserted between the lines or in the margins of a text to explain difficult words.

Glossary. Explanations of abstruse or obsolete or technical terms; a partial dictionary.

Gnati. The term 'gnati' means agnates only and does not include cognates. *Chandrappa* v. *Gynammma*, AIR. 1953 Hyd 275, 276 (FB)

"Literally interpreted in Sanskrit it means a brother also. The word 'Gnati' will not mean "illegitimate sons". *Krishna* v. *Sarvagna Krishna*, AIR 1970 SC 1795 at 1810.

Go slow strike. A planned slowing down of industrial production on the part of labour until certain demands are met.

Goa. Means the area comprised in the assembly constituencies of the Union territory other than the area comprised in the Daman assembly constituency and the Diu assembly constituency. [Goa, Daman and Diu (opinion poll) Act (38 of 1966), S. 2(f)]

God's penny. Earnest money.

Godown. Storage, warehouse for goods.

"Godown" means any warehouse or other place, by whatever name called, used for the storage of any article or substance required for any manufacturing process which means any process for, or incidental to, making, finishing or packing or otherwise treating any article or substance with a view to its use, sale, transport, delivery or disposal as finished products. [Occupational Safety, Healthy & Working Conditions Code, 2020 (37 of 2020), section 2(1)(y)]

Going armed. If a person carries a gun not in his hand but tied to his bicycle in the manner of a piece of luggage, he must be said to be going armed.

A person carrying a revolver with four live cartridges in a bag "goes armed" and is not merely in possession of a weapon.

Gold. "GOLD" includes gold in the form of coin, whether legal tender or not or in the form of bullion or ingot, whether refined or not. [Banking Regulation Act (10 of 1949), S. 5(g)]

A precious yellow metal. [Gold (Control) Act (45 of 1968) (*Repealed*), S. 2(b)].

"Gold," does not always mean pure gold, but merely what in common parlance is called gold.

The word 'gold' includes ornaments. It also include its alloy, whether virgin, melted, remelted, wrought, or unwrought, in any shape or form of a purity of not less than nine carats and includes any gold coin, any ornament and any other article of gold. *Collector of Customs & Central Excise, Cochin* v. *Kesava Reddiar*, AIR 1972 Ker 120, 121.

Gold bullion. Means gold in lumps or bars.

Gold certificate. In this Scheme unless the context otherwise requires—"GOLD CERTIFICATE" means the final receipt issued to a subscriber of the Scheme after the gold tendered by him has been assayed and accepted as deposit by a designated bank. [Gold Deposit Scheme, 1999, S. 2(ii)]

Gold coin. Means gold coin of any country which has not been demonetised.

Gold value. [Indian Carriage of Goods by Sea Act (26 of 1925), Sch., Art. 9].

Golden hour. Means the time period lasting one hour following a traumatic injury during which there is highest likelihood of preventing death by providing prompt medical care. [Motor Vehicles Act, 1988 (59 of 1988), section 2(12A)]

Golden opportunity. An opportunity characterized by a high degree of excellence or a condition of great happiness and prosperity; exceptionally valuable, well disposed and timely opportunity.

Golden rule. (*Law of interpretation*) The principle that the statutes and instruments be construed in their grammatical and ordinary sense of words unless it leads to some manifest absurdity.

Golden share. A share which enables the holder, usually the government, to outvote all other shareholders on certain types of company resolution.

Good. Valid; sufficient in law; effectual; unobjectionable; responsible; solvent; able to pay an amount specified; of a value corresponding with its terms; collectible; commendable; worthy; morally excellent; having the right qualities; satisfactory.

Adequate; effective; valid; morally excellent; right; sound; well founded; agreeable.

"GOOD" means material or product. [Goods Agreement (Safeguard Measures) Rules, 2016, R. 2(1)(e)].

"GOOD" means any merchandise, product, article or material. [India-Japan Comprehensive Economic Partnership Agreement (Bilateral Safeguard Measures) Rules, 2017, R. 2(1)(d)].

Good and bad. If the bad is not separable from the good the whole is bad.

Good and sufficient cause. For delay in taking certain legal steps would include the lunacy of the applicant.

Good and sufficient reason. Not obeying a legitimate order of his superior by a member of the Police Force has to be regarded as an act of indiscipline and would certainly provide a good and sufficient reason for initiating a disciplinary proceeding. *Secretary to Government* v. *ACJ Britto,* AIR 1997 SC 1393, 1396. [T.N. Police Subordinate Services (D&A) Rules, 1955, R. 2].

Good and tenantable repairs. "GOOD AND TENANTABLE REPAIRS" under this section and Section 20 shall mean such repairs as shall keep the premises in the same condition in which it was let out except for the normal wear and tear. [Delhi Rent Act (33 of 1995), S. 19(1) *Expln.*]

Good behaviour. An orderly conduct of a prisoner which allows him to reduce the term of his sentence; a standard by which judges are considered fit to continue their term of office; sureties for good behaviour may be ordered to be furnished by a person charged with an offence.

Surety for the good behaviour is surety for the peace, or good behaviour of a subject towards the King and the people. (See CrPC 1973 (2 of 1974), S. 108). The term signifies the exact carriage or behaviour of a subject to a King and his Leige People to which men sometimes, for their loose demeanor, are bound; and he that is bound to this is more strictly bound than to the peace, for the peace is not broken without an actual Affray, Battery &c; but this may be forfeited by the number of a man's company or his weapons. (*Termes de la Ley*)

Good cause. Reason which is found to be adequate or proper and justified by a Court or a competent authority dealing with the matter.

The expression 'good cause' requires lesser degree of proof than that of 'sufficient cause'. *Madan Lal* v. *Shyamlal,* (2002) 1 SCC 535, para 5. [CPC (5 of 1908), O. XIII, R. 2]

Failure on the part of the counsel or his clerk or the party's representative to see the order of Court actually recorded, does not constitute 'good cause' for the purpose of extending the time. Due care and attention should be a condition precedent for sustaining the plea of 'good cause'. *Muti Ram* v. *UOI,* AIR 1967 Del 58, 60.

Good character. Good general reputation for those qualities of mind or morals impressed on a person by nature or habit, and distinguishing him from other persons; as, reputation for chastity, veracity, peaceableness, *etc.*

A character that is morally praise-worthy. [Indian Evidence Act (1 of 1872), Ss. 53 and 54].

Good Conduct and **good behaviour.** We speak of a man's good behaviour in the social circle, of his *good conduct* in his family, as a citizen, or in life. *Good conduct* is meritorious and virtuous. *Good behaviour* may be natural or artificial. The conduct has relation to the station of men's lives, or the circumstances in which they are placed. *Good conduct* will include right behaviour as a part of it, and a proper demeanour will flow necessarily out of it. (*Smith. Syn. Dic.*)

Good consideration. A consideration of blood, or of natural love and affection (as compared with valuable consideration)

A consideration that will legally sustain transaction. [Indian Evidence Act (1 of 1872), S. 114, ill. (c)].

Good credit. Sound reputation entitling one to be trusted with money or goods advanced. [Indian Contract Act (9 of 1872), S. 195, ill. (b)].

Good delivery. (*Stock Exchange term*) This term indicates that a security is in proper form and condition.

Good faith. "Nothing is said to be done or believed in "good faith" which is done or believed without due care and attention." [IPC (45 of 1860), S. 52] [Now (w.e.f. 1-7-2024) repealed & replaced by Bharatiya Nyaya Sanhita, 2023 (45 of 2023), section 2(11), same definition in new Sanhita].

"Good faith" means a thing which is, in fact, done honestly, whether it is done negligently or not. Anything done with due care and attention, which is not mala fide, is presumed to have been done in good faith. There should not be personal ill will or malice, no intention to malign and scandalise. [*Army Headquarters* v. *CBI,* (2012) 6 SCC 228, para 70 : (2012) 3 SCC (Cri) 88 : AIR 2012 SC 1890 as cited in *Rajasthan State Industrial Development and Investment Corporation* v. *Subhash Sindhi Cooperative Housing Society, Jaipur,* (2013) 5 SCC 427, para 25].

"Good faith" means that which is founded on genuine belief and commands a loyal performance. The act which proceeds on reliable authority and accepted as truthful is said to be in good faith. It is the opposite of the intention to deceive. A duty performed in good faith is to fulfill a trust reposed in an official and which bears an allegiance to the superior authority. Such a duty should be honest in intention, and sincere in professional execution. It is on the basis of such an assessment that an act can be presumed to be in good faith for which while judging a case the entire material on record has to be assessed. [*General Officer Commanding, Rashtriya Rifles* v. *Central Bureau of Investigation*, (2012) 6 SCC 228, para 74 (General Clauses Act (10 of 1897), S. 3(22))].

"A thing shall be deemed to be done in "good faith" where it is in fact done honestly, whether it is done negligently or not." [General Clauses Act (10 of 1897), S. 3(22)]

"Nothing shall be deemed to be done in good faith which is not done with due care and attention." [Limitation Act (36 of 1963), S. 2(h)]

Honesty; absence of fraud, collusion or deceit. A state of mind indicating honesty and lawfulness of purpose. [IPC (45 of 1860), S. 52 and

General Clauses Act (10 of 1897), S. 3(22)].

Good faith imports the exercise of due care and attention. The standard of care required is that of reasonably prudent man acting with care and caution. *Kedarnath* v. *State of U.P.*, AIR 1965 All 233, 236. [IPC (45 of 1860), S. 405]

Good faith requires care and caution and prudence in the background of context and circumstances. *Chaman Lal* v. *State of Punjab*, AIR 1970 SC 1372, 1375.

When in spite of objection about the misjoinder of the Government as a party, the party plaintiff proceeded with the suit in the trial Court and revising Court, to avoid issue of a notice to the Government under S. 80, CPC (5 of 1908), he cannot be considered to have prosecuted that litigation in good faith. *Rabindra Nath Samuel Dawson* v. *Sivakami and others*, AIR 1972 SC 730, 732.

Ignorance of the advocate about the elementary matter as to in which Court an appeal should be filed cannot be considered to be good faith. *Brij Bhushan* v. *Madan Mohan Lal,* AIR 1973 Punj 269, 271.

Defective valuation and improper computation of court-fees does not mean lack of good faith. *Vijay Kumar Rampal* v. *Diwan Devi*, AIR 1985 SC 1669, 1670.

The words 'good faith' relate to whether the officer believed in good faith that he has got jurisdiction to deal with the question. *M. Chayamma* v. *G. Veerabhadrarao,* AIR 1979 AP 253, 255. [Judicial Officers' Protection Act (18 of 1850), S. 1A (as amended by AP Act (23 of 1958)]

The expression 'good faith' does not postulate due enquiry. The requirements of S. 19(b) are that the transferee has paid money in good faith and he has done so without notice of the original contract. *Ram Lakhan* v. *Ram Govind,* AIR 1977 All 328, 330. [Specific Relief Act (47 of 1963), S. 19(b)]

The word 'GOOD FAITH' includes a due enquiry. *Bimal Chandra Das* v. *Mammatha Nath Das,* AIR 1954 Cal 345. [Transfer of Property Act (4 of 1882), S. 51]

A transfer in good faith is a *bona fide* transfer, whereby the tenure-holder genuinely and irrevocably transfers all right, title, and interest in the land in favour of transferee, in the ordinary course of management of his affairs and which is but a collusive arrangement, or device of subterfuge to enable the tenureholder to continue to hold the surplus. *Brijendra Singh* v. *State of U.P.*, AIR 1981 SC 636, 639.

BELIEF IN GOOD FAITH. Where a man consciously avoided making an enquiry on any matter, he may nevertheless be said to have a belief on that matter but that belief would in such a case not be a belief in good faith.

Good-faith purchaser. A person who buys something for value without notice of another's claim to the item or of any defects in the title of a seller.

Good reason. Sound reason. [CrPC 1973 (2 of 1974), Sch. II, form No. 9; Companies Act (1 of 1956), S. 248(1) now replaced by Companies Act, 2013].

Good repair. A repair satisfying the respectable occupant who uses the premises fairly.

Good Samaritan defense (defence). A defense (defence) against the Communications Decency Act protecting an online service provider or user of an interactive computer service from civil liability as a publisher or speaker of any information provided by another content provider. (*Cyber Law*)

Good service. A service (of process) which is effective in law; good performance of a duty or function. [Army Act (46 of 1950), S. 3(xiv)].

Good time. The credit awarded to a prisoner for good conduct, which can reduce the duration of the prisoner's sentence.

Good title. A perfect title, free and clear from any legal exception or charge or encumbrance thereon.

In a contract of sale of real property, means such a title as will be passed on to purchaser in an action for specific performance, and as would be answered to in an action of ejectment by any claimant. [Sale of Goods Act (3 of 1930), S. 29].

Goods. "GOODS" includes all materials, commodities, and articles. [Constitution of India, Art. 366(12)]

"Goods" means all kinds of movable property, whether tangible or intangible, other than newspapers, money, actionable claims, stocks, shares and securities, and includes materials, articles and commodities used in any form in the execution of works contract, livestock and all other things attached to or forming part of the land which is agreed to be served before sale or under the contract of sale". Rajasthan Value Added Tax Act (4 of 2003), S. 2(15) as cited in *Commercial Taxes*

Officer v. *A Infrastructure Limited*, (2015) 15 SCC 98, para 13].

"Goods" means every kind of movable property other than money and securities but includes actionable claim, growing crops, grass and things attached to or forming part of the land which are agreed to be severed before supply or under a contract of supply [The Central Goods and Services Tax Act, 2017 (12 of 2017), S. 2(52)]

For the purposes of this section, "goods" means every kind of movable property, other than actionable claims, stocks, shares, moneys, bullion and specie, and all instruments referred to in clause (*a*) of sub-section (1) of section 6. [Banking Regulation Act (10 of 1949), section 8, *Expln.*]

"GOODS" includes inanimate things of every kind. [Indian Railways Act (9 of 1890), S. 3, cl. 9]

They should be known to the market as materials, commodities and articles that are capable of being sold. [*Escorts Limited* v. *Commissioner of Central Excise, Faridabad*, (2015) 9 SCC 109, para 10].

"GOODS" includes also bullion, wares and merchandise. [Imperial Bank of India Act (47 of 1920), S. 2(e)]

"GOODS" includes goods, wares, merchandises, and articles of every kind whatsoever, except live animals and cargo which by the contract of carriage is stated as being carried on deck and is so carried. [Carriage of Goods by Sea Act (26 of 1925), Sch, Art. 1(c)]

"GOODS" means every kind of moveable property other than actionable claims and money; and includes stock and shares, growing crops, grass, and things attached to or forming part of the land which are agreed to be severed before sale or under the contract of sale. [Sale of Goods Act (3 of 1930), S. 2(7)]

"GOODS" means every kind of movable property other than actionable claims, money and securities. [Forward Contracts (Regulation) Act (74 of 1952), S. 2(d)]

"Goods" means—

(i) petroleum crude;

(ii) high speed diesel;

(iii) motor spirit (commonly known as petrol);

(iv) natural gas;

(v) aviation turbine fuel; and

(vi) alcoholic liquor for human consumption.

[Central Sales Tax Act (74 of 1956), S. 2(d) as amended by Act 18 of 2017 (w.e.f 1-7-2017)]

"GOODS" includes—

(a) vessels, aircrafts, and vehicles;

(b) stores;

(c) baggage;

(d) currency and negotiable instruments; and

(e) any other kind of moveable property. [Customs Act (52 of 1962), S. 2(22)]

"GOODS" includes livestock and every kind of movable property. [Major Port Trust Act (38 of 1963), S. 2(h)] [Now repealed by s. 75(1) of Act 1 of 2021]

"GOODS" means goods as defined in Sales of Goods Act (3 of 1930), and includes—

(i) products manufactured, processed or mined in India;

(ii) shares and stocks including issue of shares before allotment;

(iii) in relation to goods, supplied; distributed or controlled in India, goods imported into India. [Monopolies and Restrictive Trade Practices Act (54 of 1969), S. 2(e) now repealed by Act 12 of 2003 (w.e.f. 1-9-2009)]

"GOODS" includes all such things as may be subject to adjudication as prize, but in the case of a naval prize does not include any aircraft or boat unless the aircraft or boat is a part of cargo of a ship. [Naval and Aircraft Prize Act (59 of 1971), S. 2(d)]

"GOODS" includes all materials, commodities and articles in a solid, liquid or gaseous state and all forms of energy. [Export-Import Bank of India (28 of 1981), S. 2(e)]

"Goods" means every kind of movable property and includes "food" as defined in clause (*j*) of sub-section (1) of section 3 of the Food Safety and Standards Act, 2006 (34 of 2006). [Consumer Protection Act, 2019 (35 of 2019), section 2(21)]

"GOODS" includes live-stocks and anything (other than equipment ordinarily used with the vehicle) carried by a vehicle except. driving persons, but does not include luggage or personal effects carried in a motor car or in a trailer attached to a motor car or the personal luggage of passengers travelling in the vehicle. [Motor Vehicles Act (59 of 1988), S. 2(13)]

"GOODS" includes—

(i) containers, pallets or similar articles of transport used to consolidate goods; and

(ii) live animals. [Multimodal Transportation of Goods Act (28 of 1993), S. 2(i)]

"GOODS" means any property including live animals, containers, pallets or such other articles of transport or packaging supplied by the consignor, irrespective of whether such property is to be or is carried on or under the deck. [Multimodal Transportation of Goods Act (28 of 1993), S. 2(i) (*as amended*)]

"GOODS" means every kind of movable property other than actionable claims and money. [Interest on Delayed Payments to small scale and Ancillary Industrial Undertakings Act (32 of 1993), S. 2, *Expln.*, (ii)(d)]

"GOODS" includes animals. [New Delhi Municipal Council Act (44 of 1994), S. 2(16)]

"GOODS" means anything which is the subject of trade or manufacture. [Trade Marks Act (47 of 1999), S. 2(i)(j)]

"GOODS" means any agricultural, natural or manufactured goods or any goods of handicraft or of industry and includes food stuff. [Geographical Indications of Goods (Registration and Protection) Act (48 of 1999), S. 2(f)]

"GOODS", in relation to Toxic Chemicals, Precursors or Discrete Organic Chemicals including those Discrete Organic Chemicals containing elements of phosphorous, sulphur or fluorine, means any material, commodity, article or compound consisting of such Toxic Chemicals, Precursors or Discrete Organic Chemicals including those Discrete Organic Chemicals containing elements of phosphorous, sulphur or fluorine and includes materials, commodities, articles, compounds or apparatus used in the production, processing or storing of Toxic Chemicals, Precursors or Discrete Organic Chemicals including those Discrete Organic Chemicals containing elements of phosphorous, sulphur or fluorine. [Chemical Weapons Convention Act (34 of 2000), S. 2(e)]

"GOODS" means goods as defined in the Sale of Goods Act, 1930 and includes—

(A) products manufactured, processed or mined;

(B) debentures, stocks and shares after allotment;

(C) in relation to goods supplied, distributed or controlled in India, goods imported into India. [Competition Act, 2002 (12 of 2003), S. 2(i)]

"GOODS" means every kind of property whether in goods or in some other form involved in the execution of a works contract. [Maharashtra Sales Tax on The Transfer of Property in Goods Involved in The Execution of Works Contracts (Re-enacted) Act No. 36 of 1989, S. 2(f)]

"GOODS" includes live animals; where the goods are consolidated in a container, pallet or similar article of transport or where they are packed, "goods" includes such article of transport or packaging if supplied by the shipper. [Hamburg Rules, Art. 1, R. (5)]

'GOODS' include any container pallet or similar article of transport or packaging if supplied by the consignor. [U.N. Convention on International Multimodal Transport of Goods, Geneva May 24, 1980, Art. 1(7)]

The term "GOODS" includes goods, wares, merchandise, and articles of every kind whatsoever, except live animals and cargo which by the contract of carriage is stated as being carried on deck and is so carried. [United States Carriage of Goods by Sea Act, 1936, S. 1(c)]

"GOODS" includes goods or burden of any description. [HALSBURY, 4th, Edn, Vol. 40, para 730, p. 554.]

"GOODS" includes goods, wares, merchandises, and articles of every kind whatsoever, except live animals and cargo which by the contract of carriage is stated as being carried on deck and is so carried. [Hague Visby Rules, Art. 1, R. (c)]

Goods does not include newspaper. *Newspaper Commissioner of Sales Tax* v. *Express Printing Press,* AIR 1983 Bom 190, 121.

To become goods an article must be something which can ordinarily come to the market to be bought and sold. *Union of India* v. *Delhi Cloth and General Mills*, AIR 1963 SC 791, 795; *South Bihar Sugar Mills Ltd.* v. *Union of India*, AIR 1968 SC 922, 928.

The term 'goods' which includes all materials, commodities and articles carries with it, the implication that the materials, commodities *etc.*, are for purposes of trade. Goods have essentially commercial character. The expression would not include in its ambit 'luggage' and 'personal effects'. Stated shortly 'goods' whatever the expression may include, would mean trade goods or goods of a commercial character. *H.P. Barua* v. *State of Assam,* AIR 1955 Ass 249, 260. [Constitution of India, Sch. VII, List II, Entry 56 and Art. 366(12)]

The word 'goods' would include a vessel. *Chowgule & Co. Pvt. Ltd.* v. *Union of India*, AIR 1987 SC 1176, 1183. [Customs Act (52 of 1962), Ss. 2(22) and 46(1)]

Electric energy is moveable property and covers the term 'goods'. *Harda Municipality* v. *H. Electric Supply Co.,* AIR 1964 MP 101, 108.

The stationery sold by the assessee to his customers is goods and when the assessee brings into existence printed stationery to the order of the individual customer, he produced a commercial commodity which is capable of being sold or supplied. *Sardar Printing Works* v. *Sales Tax Commissioner,* AIR 1958 MP 30, 31.

Shares in a company are "goods." Movable property, merchandise; wares.

Goods and chattels. The term "goods" is not so wide as "chattels" for it applies to inanimate objects, and does not include animals or chattels real, as a lease for years of house or land, which "chattels" does include. It has however been held that "Goods" and "Chattels" are synonymous expressions.

The words 'goods and chattels' in the Provincial Small Cause Courts Act (9 of 1887) do not include fixtures.

Goods and services tax. "Goods and services tax" means any tax on supply of goods, or services or both except taxes on the supply of the alcoholic liquor for human consumption. [Constitution of India, Article 366(12A)]

Goods bailed. The litigation papers and case files do not come within the ambit of the expression 'goods bailed' under Ss. 171 and 148 of the Act. *R.D. Saxena* v. *Balram Prasad Sharma,* (2000) 7 SCC 264, paras 8 and 9 : AIR 2000 SC 2912. [Indian Contract Act (9 of 1872), Ss. 171 and 148]

Goods carriage. Means any vehicle constructed or adapted for use solely for the carriage of goods, or any motor vehicle not so constructed or adapted when used for the carriage of goods. [Motor Vehicles Act (59 of 1988), S. 2(14)]

Goods, Future. Goods to be manufactured or produced or acquired by the seller after the making of the contract for sale. [Sale of Goods Act (3 of 1930), S. 2(6)].

Goods identified. Specific goods and agreed upon at the time a contract of sale is made. [Sale of Goods Act (3 of 1930), S. 2(14)].

Goods manufactured. The nature and extent of the process to which the crude oil is subjected to make it refined oil, brings it within meaning of the expression 'goods manufactured' under Section 3(3)(b)(iii) of the Act. *B.P. Oil Mills Ltd.* v. *Sales Tax Tribunal,* (1998) 6 SCC 577, para 7 : AIR 1998 SC 3055. [U.P. Trade Tax Act (15 of 1948), S. 3(3)(b)(iii)]

Goods sold and delivered. A phrase used to indicate the action brought when the sale and delivery of goods furnish the cause.

Goods transport agency. Means any person who which provides service in relation to transport of goods by road and issues consignment note, by whatever name called. [Finance Act (32 of 1994), S. 65(50)(50b) (*Inserted by Finance Act (23 of 2004), S. 90*) now repealed by Central Goods and Service Tax Act, 2017]

Goods, Unascertained. Goods which have not been specified.

Goods vehicle. Means any motor vehicle, constructed or adapted for use for the carriage of goods or any motor vehicle not so constructed or adapted but used for carriage of goods solely or in addition to passengers and includes a trailer when attached to such vehicle. [West Bengal Motor Vehicles Taxation of Goods and Passengers Act (4 of 1985), S. 2(2)]

'GOODS VEHICLE' means a motor vehicle constructed or adapted for use for the carriage of goods, or a trailer so constructed or adapted. [(English) Road Traffic Act, 1972, S. 196(1) and of [(English) Road Traffic (Foreign Vehicles) Act, 1972, S. 7(1)]

'GOODS VEHICLE' means a motor vehicle constructed or adopted for the carriage of goods or burden of any description, on a trailer as constructed or adapted. [Road Traffic Regulation Act, 1984, S. 138(1)]

"GOOD VEHICLE" means a motor vehicle constructed or adapted for use for the carriage of goods, or a trailer so constructed or adapted. [HALSBURY 4th Edn., Vol., 40, para 730, p. 554]

Goodwill. The state of wishing well to a person [Indian Evidence Act (1 of 1872), S. 14]; the possession of a ready-made connection of customers, considered as a separate element in the saleable value of a business. [Indian Partnership Act (9 of 1932), Ss. 14 and 55(3)].

The benefit which arises from the establishment of particular trades or occupations. Intrinsic value of the good repute and custom of an established trade or business.

The term 'goodwill' signifies the value of the business in the hands of a successor, so far as increased by the continuity of the undertaking being preserved in the shape of the right to use the old name and otherwise. It means every affirmative advantage, as contrasted with negative advantage that has been acquired in carrying on the business, whether connected with the premises of the business or its name or style and everything connected with or carrying with it the benefit of the business. *Ramnik Vallabhdas Madhvani* v. *Taraben Pravin Lal Madhvani,* (2004) 1 SCC 497, 523, para 68.

It includes reputation, connections of the firm or the owner which induces customers to deal with a particular firm or concern. It is treated as part of the assets of the firm. *State* v. *Bundi Electric Supply Co.,* AIR 1970 Raj 36 at 41. [Partnership Act (9 of 1932), S. 14]

Every positive advantage that has been acquired by the old firm in carrying on the business whether connected with the premises in which the business was carried on or with the name or any other matter, carrying with it the benefit of the business. It is the connection thus formed together with the circumstances whether of habit or otherwise which tend to make it permanent that constitute the goodwill.

"It is the value of the attraction to customers arising from the name, and reputation for skill, integrity, efficient business management, or efficient service." *R.C. Cooper* v. *Union of India*, AIR 1970 SC 564 at 611. [Banking Companies (Acquisition and Transfer of Undertaking) Act (22 of 1969), S. 4]

The goodwill of a business is the intangible value to it independent of its visible assets by reason of the business being a well established one having a good reputation. *K.A. Subramanium* v. *Controller of Estate Duty,* AIR 1962 Mad 315, 318. [Estate Duty Act (34 of 1953), S. 36]

The goodwill of a business depends upon a variety of circumstances or a combination of them. The location, the service, the standing of the business, the honesty of those who run it, and the lack of competition and many other factors go individually or together to make up the goodwill, though locality always plays a considerable part. *SC Cambatta and Co. (P) Ltd.* v. *Commissioner of Excess Profits Tax*, AIR 1961 SC 1010, 1012.

Goodwill bonus. "Goodwill bonus" is a bonus which is given by the employer out of his free consent in order that there may be goodwill between him and his workmen, but there can be no question of imposing a goodwill bonus by industrial Courts, as imposition of such a bonus is a contradiction of its very concept. *New Maneck Chowk Spinning Weaving Co. Ltd.* v. *Textile Labour Association,* AIR 1961 SC 867.

Goonda. Means a person who either by himself or as a member of or leader of a gang, habitually commits or attempts to commit or abets the commission of offences punishable under Chapter VIII, Chapter XV, Chapter XVI, Chapter XVII or Chapter XXII of the Indian Penal Code (Central Act XLV of 1860). [Karnataka Prevention of Dangerous Activities of Bootleggers *etc.* Act (12 of 1985), S. 2(g), amended by Act 16 of 2001 (w.e.f 08.05.2001)]

Goshala. Means a charitable institution established for the purpose of keeping, breeding, rearing and maintaining cattle, or for the purpose of reception, protection and treatment of infirm "aged or diseased" cattle and includes a "pinjrapole" where such cattles are kept." [Bihar Goshala Act (28 of 1950), S. 2(d)]

Gounti-riyati lands. Means land recorded as such in the settlement papers in the merged territories of the former State of Burma. [Orissa Merged Territories (Village Offices Abolition) Act (10 of 1963), S. 2(g)]

Govern. To rule with authority; to regulate; to manage.

Govern, Rule, Regulate. *Govern* is to exercise power or authority with judgment and knowledge; hence govern is never taken by itself in a bad sense. *Rule* denotes no more than control and direction by superior authority or power, however exercised. *Rule* is exercised over the wills and actions of men only. The despot *rules*, the constitutional monarch *governs*. *Govern* implies a subject of some importance. *Rule* is applicable to trivial things as well. *Regulate* denotes the exercise of a controlling power over force already in action or progress; as, to *regulate* finances. It denotes less dignity and authority than *rule* or *govern*, but closer care and management, and the exercise of judgment and address. The wise man will *govern* his passions, while he *rules* his conduct and carefully *regulates* his expenditure and his affairs. (*Smith Syn. Dis.*)

TO GOVERN, RULE, REGULATE. The exercise of authority enters more or less into the signification of these terms, but to *govern* implies the exercise like wise of judgment and knowledge. To *rule* implies rather the unqualified exercise of power, the making the will the rule; a king *governs* his people by means of wise laws and an upright administration; a *despot* rules over a nation according to his arbitrary decision; if he have no principle his *rule* becomes an oppressive tyranny. These terms are applied either to persons or things : persons govern or rule others; or they govern, rule, or *regulate* things.

Regulate is a species of governing simply by judgment; the word is applicable to things of minor moment. Where the force of authority is not so requisite : one governs the affairs of a nation, we *regulate* the concerns of an individual. We govern our passions, but we regulate our affections.

Governing body of a Society. Means the Governors Council, Directors, Committee, Trustees or other body by whatever name called, to whom by the regulations of the society management or its affairs is entrusted. [Madhya Pradesh Society Registration Adhiniyam Act (44 of 1973), S. 3(d)]

Governing Law. Also known as the choice of law, proper law or substantive law, it is the law that applies to decide a dispute between two parties, usually used in context where two individuals may belong to different jurisdictions with differing laws but expressly or impliedly choose the law that will prevail on terms of an agreement in case a dispute arises from that relationship or agreement. In case where no express or implied choice is made by parties as to governing law, conflict of law principles decide which country's governing law shall prevail or apply to a dispute between the parties to a contract. [Karnika Seth, *Computers Internet and New Technology Laws*, 2021, LexisNexis, Glossary of Legal Terms].

Government. "The word "GOVERNMENT" denotes the Central Government or the Government of a State." [IPC (45 of 1860), S. 17]

"GOVERNMENT" means the Central Government or a State Government [(w.e.f. 1-7-2024) Bharatiya Nyaya Sanhita, 2023 (45 of 2023), section 2(12)]

In this section and also in sections 178 to 181 (both inclusive), and sections 183 to 185 (both inclusive) the word "Government", when used in connection with, or in reference to any stamp issued for the purpose of denoting a rate of postage, shall, notwithstanding anything in clause (12) of section 2, be deemed to include the person or persons authorised by law to administer executive Government in any part of India or in any foreign country. [(w.e.f. 1-7-2024) Bharatiya Nyaya Sanhita, 2023 (45 of 2023), section 186(4)]

The established system of political rule; the governing power of the country consisting of the executive and the legislature or the executive only [IPC (45 of 1860), S. 17; General Clauses Act (10 of 1897), S. 3(23) and Constitution of India, Art. 317(4) and Art. 320(3)]; the action of governing.

GOVERNMENT, ADMINISTRATION. *Government* has a more extensive meaning than *administration;* the former includes every exercise of authority; while *administration* implies only that exercise of authority which consists in putting the laws or will of another in force. When we speak of the *Government*, as it respects the persons, it implies the whole body of constituted authorities; and the administration, only that part which puts in execution the intentions of the whole : the *government* of a country therefore may remain unaltered, while the *administration* undergoes many changes : it is the business of the *government* to make treaties of peace and war; and without a *government* it is impossible for any people to negotiate : it is the business of the *administration* to administer justice, to regulate the finances and to direct all the complicated concerns of a nation;

without an *administration* all public business would be at a stand.

From the legal point of view, government may be described as the exercise of certain powers and the performance of certain duties by public authorities or officers, together with certain private persons or corporations exercising public functions. The structure of the machinery of government, and the regulation of the powers and duties which belong to different parts of this structure, are defined by the law, which also prescribes, to some extent, the mode in which these powers are to be exercised or those duties are to be performed. Government generally connotes three estates, namely, the Legislature, the Executive and the Judiciary. In a narrow sense it connotes executive only. HALSBURY, 3rd Edn., Vol. 7, p. 187.

State Electricity Board is not Government. *V.P. Nair* v. *K.S.E. Board,* AIR 1989 Ker 86, 88, 89.

The expression 'government' will not include the Food Corporation of India.

The Collector is not Government and the letter of the Collector cannot be treated as or equated to a binding directive or order of the Government. *Subhash Kumar* v. *Special Officer, Hyderabad Municipal Corporation,* AIR 1985 AP 352, 361.

'Government' referred to in the definition of the expression 'appropriate Government' is the Government exercising administrative or executive authority and not the Government exercising its powers as an employer in an industry. *Superintending Engineering Mackhund* v. *Workmen of Mackhund Hydro Electric Project,* AIR 1960 Ori 205, 209. [Industrial Disputes Act (14 of 1947), S. 2(a)]

The word, includes Central as well as State Government. *Basti Sugar Mills Co. Ltd. Basti* v. *UOI,* AIR 1974 All 125, 126. [Indian Stamp Act (2 of 1899), S. 3, *Prov.*]

"GOVERNMENT" means the Central Government. [S. 2(d) of the Coinage Act, 2011 (11 of 2011)]

Government analyst. "GOVERNMENT ANALYST" means—

(i) in relation to Ayurvedic, Siddha or Unani drug, a Government Analyst appointed by the Central Government or a State Government under Section 33-F; and

(ii) in relation to any other drug or cosmetic, a Government analyst appointed by the Central Government or a State Government under Section 20. [Drugs and Cosmetics Act (23 of 1940), S. 3(c)]

The term "Government Analyst" would include all analysts appointed by the State Government as well as by the Central Government. *Ram Shankar Misra* v. *State of U.P.,* AIR 1979 SC 727.

"Government" and "an officer of the Government". The word 'Government' in Art. 102(1)(a) and in Art. 191(1)(a) of the Constitution and the word 'Government' in the expression 'an officer of Government' in Section 21 of the Act should be interpreted liberally so as to include within its scope the Legislature, the Executive and the Judiciary. There is no watertight compartment between the three major organs of the State. An officer of the State Legislature, though belongs under Art. 187 to the staff of the State Legislature, is still an 'officer of Government' in the sense the expression 'Government' is used in Art. 102(1)(a) and 191(1)(a). *Pashupati Nath Sukul* v. *Nem Chandra Jain,* AIR 1984 SC 399. [Constitution of India, Arts. 102(1)(a), 191(1)(a) and 187 and Representation of People Act (43 of 1951), S. 21]

Government and State—Distinction. The State, to use the term employed in political science, is the body politic. The Government is merely the aggregate of the instrumentalities employed by such body in performing its functions. *Ram Kirpal* v. *UOI,* AIR 1955 All 468, 472.

Government assurances. Assurances, promises, undertakings given by Ministers from time to time on the Floor of the House.

Government Assurances Committee. A Committee to ensure timely implementation of assurances given by Ministers on the Floor of the House, constituted for the first time by the Speaker, Lok Sabha on December 1, 1953; consists of not more than 15 members who are nominated by the Speaker.

Government Bill. A Bill moved by a minister.

Government business. In the Indian Parliament, Government Business means items of business initiated by the Government. (*Constitutional and Parliamentary Term*)

Government company. For the purposes of this Act, 'GOVERNMENT COMPANY' means any company in which not less than 51 per cent of the paid-up share capital is held by the Central Government, or by any State Government or Governments, or partly by the Central Government and partly by one or more State Governments and includes a company which is a subsidiary of a Government company as thus defined. [Companies Act (1 of 1956), S. 617 now replaced by Companies Act, 2013]

"GOVERNMENT COMPANY" means a company in which not less than fifty-one percent of the paid up share capital is held by the Central Government. [Atomic Energy Act (33 of 1962), S. 2(1)(bb), inserted by Atomic Energy (Amendment) Act, 1987 Act No. 29 of 1987 w.e.f 08.09.1987.]

"GOVERNMENT COMPANY" for the purposes of section 23(2) of Act 23 of 2013, the expression 'Government company' shall have the meaning assigned to it in section 617 of the Companies Act, 1956 (1 of 1956). [*Explanation* to section 23(2) of the Pension Fund Regulatory & Development Authority Act, 2013 (23 of 2013)]

"GOVERNMENT COMPANY" means any company in which not less than fifty-one per cent of the paid-up share capital is held by the Central Government, or by any State Government or Governments, or partly by the Central Government and partly by one or more State Governments, and includes a company which is a subsidiary company of such a Government company. [S. 2(45) of the Companies Act, 2013 (18 of 2013)]

Government circulars. Documents which are circulated by Government departments on behalf of the ministers, setting out principles and practices for the exercise of ministerial powers delegated to others.

Government department. The Improvement Trust works as an agent or instrumentality of the State Government and as such the Improvement Trust is a State Govt. Department. *Urban Improvement Trust* v. *Padmnand,* AIR 1980 Raj 176, 181. [Rajasthan Land Acquisition Act (24 of 1953), S. 11]

Government dues, in relation to any scheduled Act means any tax, duty, penalty, fine, interest, annuity deposit or any other sum payable to the Government by an assessee under that Act. [Taxation Laws (Continuation and Validation of Recovery Proceedings) Act (11 of 1964), S. 2(b)]

Government employees. Government employees are civil servants and not workmen. *Sub-Divisional Inspector of Post, Vaikam* v. *Theyyam Joseph*, AIR 1996 SC 1271.

Government establishment. Means a corporation established by or under a Central Act or State Act or an authority or a body owned or controlled or aided by the Government or a local authority or a Government company as defined in Section 2 of the Companies Act, 2013 (18 of 2013) and includes a Department of the Government. [Rights of Persons with Disabilities Act (49 of 2016), S. 2(k)].

"Government establishment" means any office or department of the Government or a local authority. [Code on Wages, 2019 (29 of 2019), section 2(o)]

Government funded programme. Means any programme, policy, scheme or other provision under which food is sold, distributed or otherwise made available to the public by the central or State Government. [Food Safety and Standards (Fortification of Foods) Regulations, 2018, Regn. 2(1)(e)].

Government gazette. The official gazette of the government. [Indian Evidence Act (1 of 1872), S. 37].

Government guidelines. Govt. guidelines cannot be resorted to, to interpret the statute. *Bhim Singhji* v. *Union of India,* AIR 1981 SC 234.

Government hospital. Includes a departmental dispensary whether full-time or part-time established and run by a Department of the Government for the medical attendance and treatment of a class or classes of Government servants and members of their families, a hospital maintained by a local authority and any other hospital with which arrangements have been made by the Government for the treatment of Government servants. [Income-tax Act (43 of 1961), S. 80 DDB *Expln.* (ii)]

"GOVERNMENT HOSPITAL" includes a military hospital, any railway hospital notified in this behalf by the Central Government, a hospital maintained by a local authority and any other hospital with which arrangements have been made by the Government for the treatment of its officers. [All India Services (Medical Attendance) Rules, 1954, R. 2(e)]

Government interested. In relation to a Board, means the Governments of those States which in the opinion of the Central Government, are likely to be interested in, or affected by, the functions of the Board under this Act. [River Boards Act (49 of 1956), S. 3(b) and S. 4.]

Government land. The term 'Government land' in Section 35 of the Survey Act (Bom 1 of 1865), means land belonging to Government, *i.e.*, land of which Government is the proprietor, and does not include land in which the proprietary rights in the soil vest in a private individual, whether or not it be subject to payment of assessment to Government. [Survey Act (Bom 1 of 1865), S. 35]

Government marker. Government Marker means the persons employed by the Government for making the requisite marking on the goods. *Union of India* v. *P.W. & G. Mills,* AIR 1967 Punj 497, 500. [Indian Railways Act (9 of 1890), S. 72]

Government notification. A notice which is published by the authority of the government [Indian Evidence Act (1 of 1872), S. 37].

Government of the State. For the purposes of this article, the Government of the State means the person for the time being recognised by the President as the Maharaja of Jammu and Kashmir acting on the advice of the Council of Ministers for the time being in office under the Maharaja's Proclamation dated the fifth day of March, 1948. [Constitution of India, Article 370(1)(b), *Explanation*]

Government pleader. "GOVERNMENT PLEADER" includes any officer appointed by the State Government to perform all or any of the functions expressly imposed by the Civil Procedure Code on the Government Pleader and also any pleader acting under the directions of the Government Pleader. [CPC (5 of 1908), S. 2(7)]

A pleader retained by or acting for the government.

Government premises. Means any premises belonging to, or taken on lease or requisitioned by the State Government. [Bihar Govt. Premises (Rent Recovery and Eviction) Act (20 of 1956), S. 2(c)].

Government promissory note. A promissory note issued by the government. [CrPC 1973 (2 of 1974), S. 445].

Government Provident Fund. Means a Provident Fund, other than a Railway Provident Fund, constituted by the authority of the Government for any class or classes of its employees or of persons employed in educational institutions or employed by bodies existing solely for educational purposes. [Provident Funds Act (39 of 1925), S. 2(d)] S. 2(*d*) of the Provident Funds Act (19 of 1925) requires that the "fund" should be constituted by the authority of the Government. The mere fact that the Provident Fund Rules framed by a private body have been approved by the Government, is not sufficient to show that the fund to which the rules relate was constituted by the Government in the absence of proof that the Government made any rules requiring the private body to maintain the Provident Fund.

Government Resolutions. Resolutions moved by ministers.

Government revenue. All public money which the State collects and receives from whatever source and in whatever manner.

Government Savings Bank. Means—

(i) a Post Office Savings Bank; or

(ii) a banking company, or any other company or institution, as the Central Government may, by notification in the Official Gazette, specify, for the purposes of this Act. [Government Savings Bank (5 of 1873), S. 3, *substituted by Finance Act (23 of 2004), S. 116)*]

Government security. "GOVERNMENT SECURITIES" shall mean securities of the Central Government or of any State Government, but in any Act or regulation made before the commencement of the Constitution shall not include securities of the government of any Part B State. [General Clauses Act (10 of 1897), S. 3(24)]

"GOVERNMENT SECURITY" means promissory notes (including treasury bills), stock-certificates, bearer bonds and all other securities issued by the Central Government at any time or by the Government of any Part A state before the 1st November, 1956, or by a State Government on or after that date any loan contracted either before or after the passing this Act, but does not include a currency note. [Indian Securities Act (10 of 1920), S. 2(a)]

"GOVERNMENT SECURITY" means—

(a) a security, created and issued, by the Government for the purpose of raising a public loan, and having one of the following forms, namely :—

(i) stock transferable by registration in the books of the Bank; or

(ii) a promissory note payable to bearer; or

(iii) a bearer bond payable to bearer; or

(iv) a form prescribed in this behalf;

(b) any other security created or issued by the Government in such form and for such of the purposes of this Act as may be prescribed. [Public Debt Act (18 of 1944), S. 2(2) and Insurance Act (4 of 1938), S. 2(7)]

"GOVERNMENT SECURITY" means a security created and issued, whether before or after the commencement of this Act, by the Central Government or a State Government for the purpose of raising a public loan and having one of the forms specified in clause (2) of Section 2 of the Public Debt Act, 1944. [Securities Contracts (Regulations) Act (42 of 1956), S. 2(b)]

A security issued or guaranteed by the government. [General Clauses Act (10 of 1897), S. 3(24)].

"GOVERNMENT SECURITY" for the purpose of section 194LD of Act 43 of 1961, 'Government security' shall have the meaning assigned to it in section 2(*b*) of the Securities Contracts (Regulation) Act, 1956 (42 of 1956). [(w.e.f. 1-6-2013) *Explanation* (*b*) to section 194LD of the Income-tax Act, 1961 (43 of 1961), inserted w.e.f 01.06.2013.]

Government servant. A 'Government servant' is certainly one appointed by the Government. A *serpanch* is not a Government servant. But a person in the service of Government includes a person elected to an office but performing Governmental functions and removable from service by the Government. *Raghunath* v. *Kishore Chandra,* AIR 1958 Ori 260, 279. [Representation of the People Act (43 of 1951), S. 123(7)]

A Government servant remains a Government servant even when he is sent on deputation to foreign service and therefore the definition of the term Government servant will not have the same meaning in the context of a Government servant sent on deputation. *Jai Jai Ram* v. *U.P. State Road Transport Corporation,* AIR 1996 SC 2289.

Government-Servant in permanent employment. Means an officer who hold substantively or provisionally a permanent post or who holds a lien on permanent post or who would have held a lien on permanent post had the lien not been suspended. [CCS (Leave) Rules, 1972, R. 3(j)]

Government undertaking. 'GOVERNMENT UNDERTAKING' means any Industrial undertaking carried on—

(i) by a department of the Government, or

(ii) by a corporation established by a Central, Provincial or State Act, which is owned or controlled by the Government, or

(iii) by a Government company as defined in section 617 of the Companies Act, 1956, or

(iv) by an institution wholly or substantially financed by the Government.

Government ward. Shall mean any person of whose property or of whose person and property, the Court of wards may, for the time being, have the superintendence under this Act. [Gujarat Court of Wards Act, 1963 (37 of 1963), S. 2(a)]

Government work. Means a work which is made or published by or under the direction or control of—

(i) The government or any department of the government;

(ii) any Legislature in India;

(iii) any Court, Tribunal or other judicial authority in India. [Copyright Act (14 of 1957), S. 2(k)]

Governmental enterprise. A project or undertaking by the government of a more or less permanent nature. (*Black*)

Governmental instrumentality. Any agency constitutionally or legislatively created that is immune from taxation. A governmental instrumentality is that which performs an important governmental function. (*Black*)

Governor. "GOVERNOR" means the Governor or any person discharging the functions of the Governor of any State or of two or more States. [Governor's (Emoluments Allowances and Privileges) Act (43 of 1982), S. 2(a)]

The executive head of each constituent State of the Union of India. [CrPC, 1973 (2 of 1974), S. 284(1), prov. and Constitution of India, Art. 200].

Grab. The word 'grab' means to seize, grasp, or snatch forcibly or suddenly with the hand, hence to take possession of suddenly, violently, or dishonestly. *Smith* v. *Pure Oil Co.,* 128 SW 2d 931, 933 : 278 Ky 430, as cited in *Konda Lakshmana Bapuji* v. *Govt. of AP,* (2002) 3 SCC 258, para 34 : AIR 2002 SC 1012.

Grace. Signifies concession not claimable as of right.

GRACE, FAVOUR. *Grace* denotes a benefit gratuitously conferred or a service gratuitously rendered. *Favour* has in it more of personal affection and interest, the sign of desire for the well being of the person favoured. *Grace* excludes right and strict merit *Favour* is preference of persons for any cause. *Grace* is removed from justice, and *favour* from impartiality. *Grace* excludes equivalent, but does not exclude partial deserving. *Favour* supposes no merit beyond pleasing. One may grant *grace* to an enemy, one shows *favour*, or confers *favours* only on those one loves. (*Smith. Syn. Dis.*)

Grace marks. The expression 'grace marks' means 'marks granted' other than marks 'obtained'. The grant of grace marks is a matter of concession. *Maharashtra State Board of Secondary & Higher Secondary Education* v. *Amit,* (2002) 6 SCC 153, para 13 : AIR 2002 SC 2686. [Maharashtra Regulation 52, (3)(a), Note 1-(2)(d) and Note 2(3)]

Grade. A degree in the scale of rank, dignity, proficiency, *etc.* [CPC (5 of 1908), S. 15].

The dictionary meaning of 'grade' is rank, positive in scale, a class or position in a class according to the value. *Hari Nandan* v. *S.N. dikshit*, AIR 1970 SC 40 at 41.

The word 'grade' having various shades of meaning in the service jurisprudence, is sometimes used to denote a pay-scale and sometimes a cadre. A cadre may consist only of permanent posts or sometimes, as is quite common these days, also of temporary posts. *A.K. Subramaniam* v. *Union of India*; *S.S. Ojha* v. *Union of India,* AIR 1975 SC 483.

Grade designation. Means a designation prescribed as indicative of the quality of any scheduled article. [Agricultural Produce (Grading and Marketing) Act (1 of 1937), S. 2(d)]

Grade designation mark. Means a mark prescribed as representing a particular grade designation. [Agricultural Produce (Grading and Marketing) Act (1 of 1937), S. 2(e)]

Grade of a Court. depends on the pecuniary or other limitations of the jurisdiction of the particular Court.

"Graduate or technical apprentice" means an apprentice who holds, or is undergoing training in order that he may hold a degree diploma in engineering or non-engineering or technology or equivalent qualification granted by any institution recognised by the Government and undergoes apprenticeship training in any designated trade. [Apprentices Act (52 of 1961), S. 2(1)(j) as substituted by Amending Act 29 of 2014

Graduate. To obtain a degree from a university or college. [North-Eastern Hill University Act (24 of 1973), S. 7]; one who has taken a degree in a college or university [Aligarh Muslim University Act (40 of 1920), Sch., Statute 43, *Expln.*].

Those not having taken any degree are called undergraduates. (*Tomlin*)

Graduate or apprentice. Means an apprentice who holds, or is undergoing training in order that he may hold a degree or diploma in engineering or non-engineering or technology or equivalent qualification granted by any institution recognised by the Government, and undergoes apprenticeship training in any such subject field in engineering or technology as may be prescribed. [Apprentices Act (52 of 1961), S. 2(j) amended by Act 29 of 2014 (w.e.f 05.12.2014)].

Gram Nyayalaya. 'Gram Nyalayaya' means a Court established under sub-section (1) of Section 3. [Gram Nyayalaya Act, 2008 (4 of 2009) S. 2(a)]

Gram Panchayat. 'Gram Panchayat' means an institution (by whatever name called) of self government constituted, at the village level, under Article 243-B of the Constitution for the rural areas. [Gram Nyayalayas Act, 2008, (4 of 2009), S. 2(b)]

'*Gram Panchayat'* under A.P. Panchayat Raj Act (13 of 1994) is 'Self Government' having both constitutional and Statutory status, to itself as well as its people within its territory. *Velpur Gram Panchayat* v. *Asstt. Director of Marketing, Guntur,*

AIR 1998 AP 142, 153, 154, paras 17 & 18. [Constitution of India, Art. 243(d)]

Gram Sabha. Means a body consisting of persons registered in the electoral rolls relating to a village comprised within the area of Panchayat at the village level. [Const., Art. 243(b) and Manipur Panchayat Raj Act (26 of 1994), S. 2(h)] Also see *State of Uttar Pradesh* v. *Pradhan Sangh Kshettra Samiti,* AIR 1995 SC 1512.

"*Gram Sabha*" means a village assembly which shall consist of all adult members of a village and in case of States having no *Panchayats*, *Padas*, *Tolas* and other traditional village institutions and elected village committees, with full and unrestricted participation of women. [Scheduled Tribes and other Traditional Forest Dewellers (Recognition of Forest Rights) Act, 2006 (2 of 2007), S. 2(g)]

Gramdan. Means a voluntary donation of land in a village for the purposes of this Act and in accordance with the provisions thereof. [Madhya Pradesh Gramdan Adhiniam, 1971 (1 of 1972), S. 2(a)]

Gramdan Kisan. Means a person who holds land as such under this Act and includes his heirs and successors-in-interest. [Madhya Pradesh Gramdan Adhiniam, 1971 (1 of 1972), S. 2(b)]

Grammatica falsa non vitiat chartam. (*Lat.*) Grammatical error does not vitiate a writing. Applied in *Whirlpool Corpn.* v. *Registrar of Trade Marks,* (1998) 8 SCC 1, para 12 : AIR 1999 SC 22.

Grammatical variation. An expression which is another grammatical form of expression. [General Clauses Act (10 of 1897), S. 3(1)]; [Emigration Act (7 of 1922), S. 2(1)(e)].

Grandchildren. "The word "GRANDCHILDREN" applies only to lineal descendants in the second degree of the person whose grandchildren" are spoken of". [Indian Succession Act (39 of 1925), S. 99(*b*)].

Granite. "GRANITE" includes all mines, minerals, ore, coal, limestone and slate. *State of Mysore* v. *Swamy Satyanand Saraswati, Religious Preacher, Raichur,* AIR 1971 SC 1569.

Grant. For the purposes of these guidelines—'GRANT' means the issue of options under such plan or scheme of the company. [Employees' Stock Option Plan or Scheme, 2001, S. 7, *Expln.* (iii)]

An operative word of conveyance, particularly appropriate to deeds of grant, properly so called, but used in other conveyances also, such as deeds of bargain and sale, and leases.

The action of granting or bestowing; an authoritative bestowal or conferring of a right; a gift or assignment of money *etc.* out of a fund [Industrial Development Bank of India Act (18 of 1964), S. 13]; the thing granted or bestowed; to bestow by a formal act [Companies (Profits) Surtax Act (7 of 1964), S. 24A(a) and Plantations Labour Act (69 of 1951), S. 42, prov.]; to accede to [Cr PC 1973 (2 of 1974), S. 432(2)].

Although the word "grant" is used in Art. 337 the word "aid" is used in Arts. 29(2) and 30(2), but there can be no question that the word "aid" in these two articles will cover the "grant" under Art. 337. *Kerala Education Bill 1957, Re,* AIR 1958 SC 956, 980. [Constitution of India, Art. 337]

In the widest sense, 'grant' may comprehend everything that is granted or passed from one to another by deed. But commonly, the term is applied to rights created or transferred by the Crown, *e.g.,* grants of pensions, patents, charters, franchise. *Mohsin Ali* v. *State of Madhya Pradesh,* AIR 1975 SC 1518.

The word 'grant' used in the Act includes within it everything granted by the Government to any person including a licence granted by virtue of an agreement. *Haji S.V.M. Mohamed Jamaludeen Bros. & Co.* v. *Govt. of T.N.,* (1997) 3 SCC 466, para 17 : AIR 1997 SC 1368. [Government Grants Act (15 of 1895), Ss. 2 and 3]

Graphical representation. Means the representation of a trade mark for goods or services represented or capable of being represented in paper form and includes representation in digitized form. [Trade Marks Rules, 2017, R. 2(1)(k)].

Grant-Back Clause. Grant-Back clause grants the licensor the rights in the improvements made by the licensee in the licenced invention in a licence agreement. (*Patents*)

Grant of administration. The authority received by an administration from a competent Court to administer the estate of a deceased person. [Indian Succession Act (39 of 1925), S. 2(f)].

Grant of lease. Conveyance of real estate on lease; to pass by deed of lease.

Grant of probate. Giving of the officially verified copy of a will together with the certificate of its having been proved. [Court-fees Act (7 of 1870), S. 19C].

"Grant" or **"Grant in aid".** Means any sum of money paid as aid out of the State funds to any educational institution. [Karnataka Education Act, 1983 (Ker. Act No. 1 of 1995), S. 2(18)]

Grantee. 'GRANTEE' means a person to whom pension, grant or scholarship has been sanctioned under this Act. [T.N. Payment of Pension to Tamil Scholars and Miscellaneous Provisions Act (23 of 1983), S. 2(c)].

Granting line of credit. Line of credit signifies a limit of credit extended by bank to its customer to the full extent of which the customer may avail itself in his dealing with the bank but which the customer may not exceed. It most frequently covers a series of transactions in which case when the customer's line of credit is nearly exhausted or not replenished, the customer is expected to reduce its indebtedness by payments to the bank before making additional use thereof. [Export-Import Bank of India Act (28 of 1981), S. 10(g)].

Grantor. A person who gives, bestows, or concedes a thing; the proper and customary word to designate the party who conveys by deed, and in legal parlance is understood to be the party who makes and executes a deed or conveyance; the most common and comprehensive word used to mean one who transfers, by any mode of conveyance, property in houses or lands.

One who makes a grant. [Estate Duty Act (34 of 1953), S. 26(1)].

Gratification. The word "gratification" is not restricted to pecuniary gratifications, or to gratifications estimable in money. [IPC (45 of 1860), S. 161 (*Repealed by the Prevention of Corruption Act, 1988, S. 31 w.e.f 09.09.1988*)]

A person who offers, or agrees to give, or offers or attempts to procure, a gratification shall be deemed to give a gratification. A person who obtains or agrees to accept or attempts to obtain a gratification shall be deemed to accept a gratification, and a person who accepts a gratification as a motive for doing what he does not intend to do, or as a reward for doing what he has not done, shall be deemed to have accepted the gratification as a reward. [(w.e.f. 1-7-2024) Bharatiya Nyaya Sanhita, 2023 (45 of 2023), sections 170(2) & 170(3)]

Prima facie, therefore, voluntary acceptance of an amount of money or a valuable thing by a public servant will amount to acceptance of gratification. *State* v. *Punadlik Bhikaji Ahire,* AIR 1959 Bom 543, 547.

In its literal dictionary meaning, the word 'gratification', means satisfaction of appetite or desire, and it could not be construed to mean money paid by way of a bribe. *Sailendranath Bose* v. *State or Bihar*, AIR 1968 SC 1292, 1296.

The word 'gratification' cannot be confined only to payment of money. It means anything received other than legal remuneration. *C.I. Emden* v. *State of U.P.*, AIR 1960 SC 548, 551.

If a candidate withdraws from the election on an assurance that in respect of his brother's candidature in another constituency, the opposite party will support him, this assurance is a gratification. *Abolchand* v. *Ralia Ram Panna Lal,* AIR 1963 Punj 516, 520. [Representation of the People Act (43 of 1951), S. 123(1)(B)]

The word 'gratification' is used in Section 4(1) to denote acceptance of something to the pleasure or satisfaction of the recipient. *State of A.P.* v. *V. Vasudeva Rao*, (2004) 9 SCC 319, 329, para 24. [Prevention of Corruption Act (2 of 1947), S. 4(1)]

"GRATIFICATION" does not include offers and acceptances of mere promises, but requires an officer and acceptance relating to a thing of some value, though not necessarily estimable in terms of money. A mere offer to help in getting employment is not such offer of gratification within the meaning of Section 123(1)(B) as to constitute it a corrupt practice. *Mohan Singh* v. *Bhanwarlal,* AIR 1964 SC 1366. [Representation of Act (43 of 1951), S. 123(1)(B)]

A reward, recompense, gratuity. [*epealed*), IPC (45 of 1860), S. 161]

Gratuitous. Without valuable or legal consideration. [Transfer of Property Act (4 of 1882), S.35]

A term applied to voluntary deeds of conveyance.

Gratuitously. In a gratuitous manner [Indian Contract Act (9 of 1872), S. 70]; [Indian Railways Act (9 of 1890), S. 3(15)].

Gratuity. A lump sum paid (in addition to pension) to a retiring employee, specially under civil service. [Coir Industry Act (45 of 1953), S. 27(1)].

Gratuity is a payment in the nature of a gift and the donar cannot be compelled to make a gift. Gratuity is not synonymous with compensation. A gratuity is something given freely or without recompense and it cannot be demanded as of right, as it does not involve a return of consideration, where payment is made as a part of contemplated compensation for services rendered by an employee according to the rules of service, the claim for payment in a Court of Law cannot be rejected on the ground that it has been styled as gratuity. *Raja Sir Harinder Singh* v. *S. Bhag Singh,* AIR 1961 Punj 443, 444, 445.

'Gratuity' in its etyomological sense means a gift especially for services rendered or return for favours received. A claim for gratuity is a legitimate claim which the workmen may make and which in appropriate cases may give rise to an industrial dispute. *Delhi Cloth and General Mills Co. Ltd.* v. *Their workmen*, AIR 1970 SC 919, 930. [Income-tax Act (43 of 1961), S. 17(1)(iii)]

"Gratuity" and "pension". Gratuity is a lump sum payment while pension is a periodic payment of a stated sum. They are both "efficiency devices" and are considered necessary for an "orderly and humane elimination" from industry of superannuated or disabled employees who, but for such retiring benefits, would continue in employment even though they function inefficiently. *Burhanpur Tapti Mills* v. *Mazdoor Singh,* AIR 1965 SC 830.

Gratuity, gift. *Gift*, being simply a thing given, *gratuity* is a certain kind of gift. It is commonly expected as due, but could not be enforced as a legal term. (*Smith Syn. Dis.*)

Gravamen. The substance of a complaint or accusation.

Gravamen of the charge. The portion of the indictment which weighs most heavily against the accused.

Grave implies seriousness, importance, weight *etc.* "Grave misconduct" makes the character or conduct serious or very serious.

The expression "grave" indicates that provocation be of such a nature so as to give cause for alarm to the appellant. [*Sukhlal Sarkar* v. *Union of India*, (2012) 5 SCC 703, para 9] [Indian Penal Code (45 of 1860), S. 300, Exception I]. The term grave only adds an element of virulent intensity to what is otherwise likely to provoke retaliation. [*B.D. Khunte* v. *Union of India*, (2015) 1 SCC 286, para 15].

Grave and sudden provocation. Intensely stirring up a person to such a pitch of anger or hatred abruptly that he instantly loses control over himself and is led to do what he would not do if he could weigh or contemplate the nature or significance of his act. [IPC (45 of 1860), S. 300, except. 1]; [Cr PC 1973 (2 of 1974), S. 222, ill. (b)].

'Grave and sudden provocation' would normally mean that a person placed in such circumstances could lose self-control but only temporarily and that too, in proximity to the time of provocation. [*Budhi Singh* v. *State of Himachal Pradesh*, (2012) 13 SCC 663, para 18].

Grave emergency. Means a condition as determined by the Central Government wherein the Board is unable to discharge its duties appropriately and includes acts of sedition, non-performance, unlawful and illegal actions, negligence and financial misappropriation. [Major Port Authorities Act, 2021 (1 of 2021), section 2(1)(i)]

Article 352(1) makes no distinction between the threat to the security of India by war or external aggression on one hand and threat to the security of India by internal disturbance on the other. In fact, both situations are covered by the expression 'grave emergency' in Article 352(1). *Additional District Magistrate, Jabalpur* v. *Shivakant Shukla,* AIR 1976 SC 1207. [Constitution of India, Art. 352(1)]

Grave misconduct. Intentional serious dereliction of duty and misappropriation of funds by the Headmaster of the institution would amount to 'grave misconduct' as the conduct of a Headmaster must be a role model. [*Om Prakash Mann* v. *Director of Education, (Basic)*, (2006) 7 SCC 558, 560, p. 10] (*Service Law*).

A wrong statement made by the applicant in application form about his previous prosecution would not be deemed to be a grave misconduct' so as to impose extreme punishment of termination from service. [*Regional Manager, Bank of Baroda* v. *Presiding Officer, Central Govt. Industrial Tribunal*, AIR 1999 SC 912 : (1999) 2 SCC 247] (*Service Law*)

Gravity. (a) 'Gravity' in relation to any liquid, means the ratio of the weight of a volume of the liquid to the weight of an equal volume of distilled water, the volume of each liquid being computed as at 20°C;

(b) where the gravity of any liquid is expressed as a number of degrees that number shall be the said ratio multiplied by 1,000; and

(c) 'original gravity' in relation to any liquid in which fermentation has taken place means its gravity before fermentation.

Seriousness of harm, an offence, *etc.* as judged from an objective, legal standpoint.

Great grand-daughter. Daughter of a son's son. [Hindu Adoptions and Maintenance Act (78 of 1956), S. 21(v)].

Great grand-son. Son of a son's son. [Hindu Adoptions and Maintenance Act (78 of 1956), S. 21(iv)].

Great seal. Signifies the great seal of the United Kingdom.

Green house gases. Means those gaseous constituents of the atmosphere, both natural and anthropogenic that absorb and re-emit infrared radiation.

Greenwich Mean Time. The standard time observed in Britain. [Mines Act (35 of 1952), S. 4].

Grid. Means the high voltage backbone system of inter-connected transmission lines, sub-station and generating plants. [Electricity Act (36 of 2003), S. 2(32)]

Grievance. Means a claim by a person that he sustained injustice or undue hardship in consequence of mal-administration. [Maharashtra Lokayukta and Upa-Lokayuktas Act (66 of 1971), S. 2(d)]

Grievous. The following kinds of hurt only are designated as "grievous", namely:—

(a) Emasculation.

(b) Permanent privation of the sight of either eye.

(c) Permanent privation of the hearing of either ear.

(d) Privation of any member or joint.

(e) Destruction or permanent impairing of the powers of any member or joint.

(f) Permanent disfiguration of the head or face.

(g) Fracture or dislocation of a bone or tooth.

(h) Any hurt which endangers life or which causes the sufferer to be during the space of fifteen days in severe bodily pain, or unable to follow his ordinary pursuits. [(w.e.f. 1-7-2024) Bharatiya Nyaya Sanhita, 2023 (45 of 2023), section 116]

Grievous bodily harm. Serious physical injury.

Grievous hurt. The following kinds of hurt only are designated as "grievous".

First.—Emasculation.

Secondly.—Permanent privation of the sight of either eye.

Thirdly.—Permanent privation of the hearing of either ear.

Fourthly—Privation of any member of joint.

Fifthly.—Destruction or permanent impairing of the powers of any member or joint.

Sixthly.—Permanent disfiguration of the head or face.

Seventhly.—Fracture or dislocation of a bone or tooth.

Eighthly.—Any hurt which endangers life or which causes the sufferer to be, during the space of twenty days, in severe bodily pain, or unable to follow his ordinary pursuits. [IPC (45 of 1860), S. 320] [Now (w.e.f. 1-7-2024) repealed & replaced by Bharatiya Nyaya Sanhita, 2023 (45 of 2023), section 116]

"GRIEVOUS HURT" means—

(a) emasculation;

(b) permanent privation of the sight or either eye;

(c) permanent privation of the hearing of either ear;

(d) privation of any member or joint;

(e) destruction or permanent impairing of the powers of any members or joint;

(f) permanent disfiguration of the head or face; or

(g) any hurt which endangers life. [Parsi Marriage and Divorce Act (3 of 1939), S. 2(4)]

Grievous injury. To be a grievous injury it is not necessary that a bone should be cut through and through or that the crack must extend from the outer to the inner surface or that there should be displacement of any fragment of the bone. If there is a break by cutting or splintering of the bone or there is a rupture or fissure in it, it would amount to a fracture. *Hori Lal* v. *State of U.P.*, AIR 1970 SC 1969, 1971. [IPC (45 of 1860), S. 320]

Gross. Whole; entire; total; without deduction; taking in the whole; having no deduction or abatement.

Flagrant. [T.P. Act (4 of 1882), S. 78]; whole; total [Indian Partnership Act (9 of 1932), S. 6, *Expln.* I]; entire (as distinguished from net).

Gross amount. Whole or total amount. [T.P. Act (4 of 1882), S. 69A(6)].

Gross domestic product (GDP). Is a measure of the total value of final goods and services produced within a country during a given year. [*ML Tannan Banking Law & Practice in India*, Vol. 2, 2021, LexisNexis, Dictionary of Banking Terminology]

Gross income. Total income without taking out permissible deduction. [Trade Unions Act (16 of 1926), S. 15(j)]

Gross indecency. A sexual act that is more than ordinary indecency but falls short of actual intercourse. It may include masturbation and indecent physical contact.

Gross misconduct. Misconduct of a flagrant nature. [Maternity Benefit Act (53 of 1961), S. 12(2) (a), prov.].

Gross mismanagement. [Companies Act (1 of 1956), S. 338 now replaced by Companies Act, 2013].

Gross National Product (GNP). The value in current prices of all final goods and services produced by the economic system over a time period, usually one calendar year. It is the best known and most widely used single measure of the performance of a nation's economy. It includes personal consumption expenditures for goods and services, gross private domestic investment, government purchases of goods and services, and the net export of goods and services.

Gross neglect. Gross negligence. [T.P. Act (4 of 1882), S. 78].

The term "gross neglect" means and involves a failure on the part of a person to take such reasonable precautions against the risk of an innocent person being deceived in the circumstances of the particular case.

Gross negligence. Negligence marked by total or nearly total disregard for the rights of others and by total or nearly total indifference to the consequences of an act. [Indian Trusts Act (2 of 1882), S. 3].

"Gross negligence" is a term of relative import. Its true meaning can be judged only with reference to the duties which a person is obliged to perform. An act or omission may gross negligence and amount to misconduct for one small class of persons while it may not be so for some other class of persons and simply be termed as mere negligence or an act of inadvertence or oversight. [*Council of Institute of Chartered Accountants of India, New Delhi* v. *Satish Chand Jain*, AIR 2013 All 170, para 11

"Gross negligence," "sometimes called 'wilful blindness" is the same thing as 'negligence', with the addition of a vituperative epithet" (*per* ROLFE, B. *Wilson* v. *Brett*, 11 MW 115, 116).

Gross profit. Gross profit means the excess of the sales (less returns) over the cost of the goods sold including the expenses directly attributable to putting the goods in a saleable condition. The expenses will not include selling commission. *Ganesan* v. *A.K. Joscelyne,* AIR 1957 Cal 33, 42.

Gross rent. "Gross rent" is the annual rent which a tenant might reasonably be expected to pay for an hereditament if the landlord undertook to bear the expenses necessary to maintain the hereditament in a state to command that rent.

Gross settlement system. 'Gross settlement system' means a payment system in which each settlement of funds or securities occurs on the basis of separate or individual instructions. [Payment and Settlement Systems Act (51 of 2007), S. 2(1)(d)]

Gross; Total. The gross implies that from which nothing has been taken : the total signifies that to which nothing need be added. The gross weight in trade is applicable to any article, the whole of which good or bad, pure or dross, is included in opposition to the net weight; the total amount supposes all to be included which ought to form a part, in opposition to any smaller amounts or subdivisions.

Gross total income. "GROSS TOTAL INCOME" means the total income computed in accordance with the provisions of the Act without making any deduction under chapter IV A. [Income-tax Act (43 of 1961), S. 80 B(5)]

The amount of compensation received by the appellant on compulsory acquisition of agricultural land which did not come within the ambit of 'income' under Section 2(24)(vi) could not have formed part of 'gross total income' within the meaning of clause (iv) of S. 109 of Income-tax Act (43 of 1961). *Delhi Farming & Construction (P.) Ltd.* v. *CIT,* (2003) 5 SCC 36, para 15 : AIR 2003 SC 1316.

Gross value. "GROSS VALUE" means the wholesale price, or, if there be no such price, the estimated value, with, in either case, freight, landing charges, and duty paid beforehand; provided that, in the case of goods or merchandise customarily sold in bond, the bonded price is deemed to be the gross value. "Gross proceeds" means the actual price obtained at a sale where all charges on sale are paid by the sellers. [Marine Insurance Act (11 of 1963), S. 71(4)]

Gross vehicle weight. Means in respect of any vehicle the total weight of the vehicle and load certified and registered by the registering authority as permissible for that vehicle. [Motor Vehicles Act (59 of 1988), S. 2(15)]

Gross weight. The whole weight of goods and merchandise, including the dust and dross, and also the chest or bag, upon which tare and trett are allowed.

Ground. Basis; foundation. [Constitution of India, Art. 122(1)]

Ground lease. A long term (usually 99 year) lease of land only; this kind of lease typically involves commercial property, and any improvement built by the lessee revert to the lessor.

Grounds of detention. The 'grounds of detention' are the "basic facts" on which conclusions are founded and these are different from subsidiary facts or further particulars of these basic facts. Each "basic fact" would constitute a ground and particulars in support thereof or the details would be subsidiary facts or further particulars of the said basic facts which will be integral part of the "ground" [*Gautam Jain* v. *Union of India,* (2017) 3 SCC 133, para 22].

Groundless. Destitute of foundation, authority or support; having no real cause or reason; unfounded.

The term 'groundless' means that the material furnished by the records is such that no reasonable basis or foundation, whatever, can be found to support the accusation made against the accused. *State of Mysore* v. *Gundappa,* AIR 1966 Mys 78, 80. [CrPC, 1973 (2 of 1974), S. 239]

Grounds. The term 'grounds' means not only the conclusions of fact but also all the basic facts on which the conclusions were founded. *Prakashchandra Mehta* v. *Commissioner Secretarty Government of Kerala,* AIR 1986 SC 687, 699. [Conservation of Foreign Exchange and Prevention of Smuggling Activities Act (52 of 1974), S. 3(3); Constitution of India, Art. 22(5)]

The grounds will generally indicate the conclusions drawn by the appropriate authority with respect to the suspected activities of any particular person and those grounds when communicated, will enable the detenu to make a representation. *State of Bombay* v. *Atma Ram,* AIR 1951 SC 157, 172. [Preventive Detention Act (4 of 1950), S. 3.]

Grounds of appeal. Grounds on which an appeal is preferred. [CrPC 1973 (2 of 1974), S. 385(3)].

Grounds of arrest. Per DESAI, J.,—The words "grounds for such arrest" occurring in Art. 22(1) should be interpreted in the light of the reasons for the provisions. If a person is arrested on a warrant the grounds or reasons for the arrest are the warrant. If he is arrested without a warrant, he must be told why he has been arrested. If he is arrested for committing an offence, he must be told that he has committed a certain offence for which he would be placed on trial. Informing him merely of the law applicable to that act would not be enough. *Vimal Kishore* v. *State of U.P.,* MLJ : QD (1956-1960) Vol. I C2433 : (S) AIR 1956 All 56 : 1956 CrLJ 13 : ILR (1956) 2 All 527. [Constitution of India, Art. 22(1)]

Grounds of objection. The expression does not include the reasons given to sustain grounds of objection.

Grounds on which the order has been made. The scope and intendment of the expression "the grounds on which the order has been made" in Sections 3(3) and 7 of the Act are quite different and it is not essential that the grounds which are furnished to the detenu must have been before the State Government before it approves of the order. *Shamrao Vishnu Parulekar* v. *District Magistrate, Thana,* AIR 1957 SC 23. [Preventive Detention Act, 1950, Ss. 3(3) and 7]

Groundwater. Means water existing in an acquifiar below the surface of the ground at any particular location of the local area regardless of the geological structure in which it is stationary or moving and includes all ground water reservoirs. [A.P. Ground Water (Regulation for Drinking Water Purposes) Act (A.P. Act (7 of 1996), S. 2(4)]

Group. "GROUP" means a group of—

(i) two or more individuals, association of individuals, firms, trusts, trustees or bodies corporate (excluding financial institution), or any combination thereof, which exercises or is established to be in a position to exercise control, directly or indirectly, over any body corporate, firm or trust, or

(ii) associated person.

Expln. For the purposes of this clause :

(I) a group of person who are able, directly or indirectly, to control the policy of body corporate, firm or trust, without having a controlling interest in that body corporate, firm or trust, shall also be deemed to be in position to exercise control over it;

(II) "associated person"

(a) in relation to a director of a body corporate means—
   (i) a relative of such director, and includes a firm in which such director or his relative is a partner;
   (ii) any trust of which any such director or his relative is a trustee;
   (iii) any company of which such director, whether independently or together with his relatives, constitutes one-fourth of its Board of Directors;
   (iv) any other body corporate are appointed or controlled by the director of the first mentioned body corporate or his relative, whether acting singly or jointly;

(b) in relation to the partner of a firm, means a relative of such partner and includes any other partner of such firm; and

(c) in relation to the trustee of trust, means any other trustee of such trust.

(III) Where any person is an associated person in relation to another the latter shall also be deemed to be an associated person in relation to the former. [Monopolies and Restrictive Trade Practices Act (54 of 1969), S. 2(ef) now repealed by Act 12 of 2003 (w.e.f. 1-9-2009)]]

Group annuity. An annuity which is payable to members of a group, specially employees, who are covered by a single annuity contract.

Group libel. Libel which defames the class of persons, specially because of their race, sex, religion, national origin.

Group litigation. A set of lawsuits, instituted on behalf of or against numerous persons recognised as one litigating entity.

"Group foster care" means a family like care facility for children in need of care and protection who are without parental care, aiming on providing personalized care and fostering a sense of belonging and identity, through family like and community base solutions. [Juvenile Justice (Care and Protection of Children) Act, 2015 (2 of 2016), S. 2(32)].

'Group housing' means a building designed and developed in the form of flats for residential purpose or any ancillary or appurtenant building including community facilities, public amenities and public utility as may be prescribed. [Haryana Development and Regulation of Urban Areas Act (8 of 1975), S. 2(hh) as cited in *DLF Limited* v. *Manmohan Lowe*, (2014) 12 SCC 231, para 26].

Grove. The word 'grove' conveys compactness or at any rate substantial compactness to be recognised as a unit by itself which must consist of group of trees in sufficient number to preclude the land on which they stand from being primarily used for a purpose, such as cultivation, other than as a grove land. *Sardar Chandrojirao Angre* v. *State of Madhya Pradesh*, AIR 1968 SC 494, 496. Character of 117 IC 616 : 1929 A. 557. [Madhya Bharat Abolition of Jagirs Act (28 of 1951), S. 5(b)(iv)]

Grove is a cluster of trees sufficient in number specially planted by human agency to prevent its use for any other purpose, but not large enough to constitute forest. *Radhika Prasad* v. *State of M.P. Bhopal*, AIR 1972 M.P. 124, 125.

Grower. "GROWER" means a person who grows any minor forest produce in the land in his possession, whether as an occupant, tenant or in any other capacity and includes in relation to such produce grass in any unoccupied land or any forest land or forest land comprised in any reserved or protected forest constituted under the Indian Forest Act 1927 (XVI of 1927):—

(a) where such land is leased—the lessee, and

(b) where such land is not leased—the State Government. [Gujarat Minor Forest Produce Trade Nationalisation Act (7 of 1979), S. 2(7)]

Growing crops. A crop which exists in contemplation of law from the time the seed is deposited in the ground until after it is harvested; an interest in land. As used in reference to levy of execution on any growing crop it imports that the crop is not come to maturity, but is green or not made.

A "growing crop" necessarily means a crop which is in existence and which is in the process of coming to fruition. (171 IC 553 : AIR 1937 Nag 289.)

Moveable property includes growing crops and growing crops will not *ipso facto* pass to the purchaser of the land, unless the growing crops are specifically sold along with it. *Chhatradhrilal* v. *Shyamabai,* AIR 1966 MP 67, 70. [CPC (5 of 1908), O. XXI, R. 94]

The expression 'growing crop' might appropriately comprehend *tendu* leaves, but would not include '*Adjat* timber', bamboos, nor even *tendu* plants. *Mahadeo* v. *State of Bombay*, AIR 1959 SC 735, 740. [M.P. (Abolition of Proprietary Rights (Estates, Mahals and Alienated Lands Act (1 of 1951), Ss. 3, 4]

GSM. (*abbr.*) Global System for Mobile communications. Digital cellular radio technology. Operates in the 900 MHz waveband. (*Telecommunication*)

GSM Base Transceiver Station (BTS). The term base transceiver station describes the radio installation (according to the GSM standard), antenna and other equipment permanently installed at a specified location and which provides coverage in one or more radio cells. (*Telecommunication*)

GSM jammers. Systems designed to prevent the use of GSM mobile telephone terminals (mobile handsets in particular) by interfering with the signal.

Restaurants and concert halls owners are increasingly critical about the use of GSM mobile phones in their premises, so much, that they are beginning to think about using "jammers". However, to disrupt communications is opposed to the principle of liberalisation of telecommunications and constitutes an offence. It is thus forbidden to sell, install and use this type of equipment.

It is a fact that jammers can have negative, even serious consequences for users of mobile phones (for example in case of emergencies). Moreover, the propagation characteristics of radio waves make it impossible to limit the action range of a jammer to the room where it is installed. As a result, jammers can also disrupt other communications in the area.

The real problem is not GSM communications themselves, but the inadequate use of the equipment. Surely anybody would be irritated by the untimely ringing of a mobile phone right in the middle of a concert or a movie. Thus, instead of setting up jammers, it would be wiser to encourage users to be more respectful of other people when using their mobile phones. One possibility could be to use detectors indicating when mobile phones are switched on.

By prohibiting this kind of installations on its territory, Switzerland supports the position of the member states of the European Union. (*Telecommunication*)

Guarantee. Includes any obligation undertaken before the commencement of this Constitution to make payments in the event of the profits of an undertaking falling short of a specified amount. [Constitution of India, Art. 366(13)]

A guarantee is an accessory contract, by which the promisor undertakes to be answerable to the promisee for the debt, default or mis-carriage of another person, whose primary liability to the promisee must exist or be contemplated. HALSBURY, 4th Edn, Vol. 20, para 101, p. 49.

A collateral contract by which a third party promises to pay a debtor's debt; one of the situations requiring a written contract under the statute of frauds. (*Cyber Law*)

Guarantee claim. Is the amount of risk coverage which the participating financial institution opts to claim from the Bureau under Partial Risk Guarantee Fund for Energy Efficiency. [Energy Conservation (Partial Risk Guarantee Fund for Energy Efficiency) Rules, 2016, R. 2(1)(k)].

Guarantee facility. Means guarantee provided by Partial Risk Guarantee Fund for Energy Efficiency based on certain pre-defined criterion, to any loan extended by the participating financial institution to an eligible borrower. [Energy Conservation (Partial Risk Guarantee Fund for Energy Efficiency) Rules, 2016, R. 2(1)(l)].

Guarantee fund. Reserve fund set apart to meet possible losses.

Guarantee : Guaranty. "A guarantee is a collateral engagement to answer for the debt, default, or miscarriage, of another person."

The action of securing or guaranteeing security. [Constitution of India, Art. 110 (b)]; [Constitution of India, Art. 32 (1)]

Guarantee insurance is a guarantee against loss in cases a person named shall make a designated default or be guilty of specified conduct.

Guaranteed stock. Stock, the interest on which, or the principal, or both, is guaranteed.

Guarantees. "GUARANTEES" means the terms in regard to benefits or premiums or charges, which may not be altered during the currency of the policy. [Insurance Regulatory and Development Authority (Actuarial Report and Abstract) Regulation, 2000, Reg. 2(e)]

Guarantor. "GUARANTOR" means any person providing insurance or other financial security to cover the owner's liability. [Merchant Shipping Act (44 of 1958), S. 352 S(f)]

One who gives a guarantee; a surety. [Gold (Control) Act (45 of 1968) (*repealed*), S. 2(h), *Expln.* (a)(iii)].

Guard. Protector; escort; official in charge of a train (railway guard); soldiers protecting place or person; a separate portion of an army (as advance guard; rear guard; mount guard *etc.*).

A person or group of persons that guards. [Air Force Act (45 of 1950), S. 82(c) and Army Act (46 of 1950), S. 34(a)]; to stand over [CrPC, 1973 (2 of 1974), S. 94(1)(d)]; to protect from danger or attack; to escort; to ward, watch or take care of.

Guardian. "GUARDIAN" means a person having the care of the person of a minor or of his property, or of both his person and property. [Guardians and Wards Act (8 of 1890), S. 4(2)]

"GUARDIAN" includes any person having legal custody of or control over a child. [Children (Pledging of Labour) Act (2 of 1933), S. 2]

Any person to whom the care, nature or custody of any child falls by law, or by natural right or recognized usage, or who has accepted or assumed the case, nature or custody of any child, or to whom the care, nature or custody of any child has been entrusted by any lawful authority. [Tamil Nadu Elementary Education Act (8 of 1920), S. 3(viii) as cited in *Roxann Sharma* v. *Arun Sharma*, (2015) 8 SCC 318, para 7].

A person lawfully invested with the power, and charged with the duty, of taking care of the person and managing the property and rights of another person, who, for defect of age, understanding, or self-control, is considered incapable of administering his own affairs. One who legally has the care and management of the person, or the estate, or both, of a child during its minority." [Black's Law Dictionary, 5th Edn. as cited in *Roxann Sharma* v. *Arun Sharma*, (2015) 8 SCC 318, para 5].

"GUARDIAN" means a person having the care of the person of a minor or of his property or of both his person and property and includes—

(i) a natural guardian,

(ii) a guardian appointed by the will of the minor's father or mother,

(iii) a guardian appointed or declared by a Court, and

(iv) a person empowered to act as such by or under any enactment relating to any Court of wards. [Hindu Minority and Guardianship Act (32 of 1956), S. 4(b)]

"GUARDIAN" in relation to a child, includes any person who, in the opinion of the competent authority having cognizance of any proceedings in relation to a child, has, for the time being, the actual charge of, or control over, that child. [Children Act (60 of 1960), S. 2(k)] Also see *Chandra Prabhuji Jain Temple* v. *Harikrishna,* AIR 1973 SC 2565.

"GUARDIAN" means a person having the care of the person of a minor or a lunatic. [Medical Termination of Pregnancy Act (34 of 1971), S. 2(a)]

"GUARDIAN" includes any person who has accepted or assumed the care or custody of any child. [Vaccination Act (13 of 1880), S. 2(3)].

"GUARDIAN" in relation to a Juvenile, includes any person who in the opinion of the competent authority, having cognizance of any proceedings in relation to a Juvenile, has, for the time being, the actual charge of, or Control over, that Juvenile. [Juvenile Justice Act (53 of 1986), S. 2(g)]

"GUARDIAN" in relation to a child, means his natural guardian or any other person having the actual charge or control over the child and recognised by the competent authority as a guardian in course of proceedings before that authority. [Juvenile Justice (Care and Protection of Children) Act, 2000, S. 2(31)]

"GUARDIAN" means any person whom the care, nurture or custody of any child falls by law or by natural right or by recognised usage or who has accepted or assumed to care, nurture or custody of any child or to whom the care, nurture or custody of any child has been entrusted by any lawful authority. [Tamil Nadu Elementory Education Act, 1994, (TN Act No. 33 of 1995), S. 2(6)]

"One who has or is entitled to the custody of the person or property (or both) of a minor or an idiot, or other person legally incapable of managing his own affairs. [Children Act (60 of 1960) (*repealed*), S. 2(k) and Constitution of India, Art. 28(3)]

"GUARDIAN" in relation to a child, means a person having the care and custody of that child and includes a natural guardian or guardian appointed or declared by a court or a statute. [Right of Children to Free and Compulsory Education Act 2009 (35 of 2009), S. 2(g)].

Guardian ad litem. A guardian of a party appointed to look after the interest of that party in that suit. [T.P. Act (4 of 1882), S. 103]; [CPC (5 of 1908), O. XXXII, R. 4].

Guardian, Natural. "The natural guardians of a Hindu minor, in respect of the minor's person as wells as in respect of the minor's property (excluding his or her undivided interest in joint family property), are—

(a) in the case of a boy or an unmarried girl—the father, and after him, the mother; provided that the custody of a minor who has not completed the age of five years shall ordinarily be with the mother;

(b) in the case of an illegitimate boy or an illegitimate unmarried girl—the mother, and after her, the father;

(c) in the case of a married girl—the husband.

Provided that no person shall be entitled to act as the natural guardian of a minor under the provisions of this section—

(a) if he has ceased to be a Hindu, or

(b) if he has completely and finally renounced the world by becoming a hermit (*vanaprastha*) or an ascetic (*yati* or *Sanyasi*)

Explanation—In this section the expression "father" and "mother" do not include a stepfather and a step-mother." [Hindu Minority and Guardianship Act (32 of 1950), Ss. 4 (c) and 6].

Guardian of the person. A person who guards the body of another person who is a minor. [Guardians and Wards Act (8 of 1890), S. 24].

Guardian of the property. A person having the care of the property of a minor.

Guardian, Testamentary. A guardian appointed by the last will of a father for the person and real and personal estate of his child until the latter arrives at full age. [Hindu Minority and Guardianship Act (32 of 1956, S. 9].

Guardianship. The condition or fact of being a guardian. [Hindu Minority and Guardianship Act (32 of 1956), Ss. 6 and 7].

Guess. Guesstimate : Conjecture. 'Guess' as understood in its common parlance is an estimate without any specific information while 'calculations' are always made with reference to specific data. 'Guesstimate' is an estimate based on a mixture of guesswork and calculations and it is a process in itself. At the same time 'guess' cannot be treated synonymous to 'conjecture'. 'Guess' by itself may be a statement or result based on unknown factors while 'conjecture' is made with a very slight amount of knowledge, which is just sufficient to incline the scale of probability. 'Guesstimate' is with higher certainty than mere 'guess' or a 'conjecture' per se. [*Kamta Prasad Singh* v. *State of Bihar*, (1976) 3 SCC 772 : AIR 1976 SC 2219 as cited in *Bhule Ram* v. *Union of India*, (2014) 11 SCC 307, para 9]

GUI. (*abbr.*) Graphical User Interface. A method of driving software through the use of windows, icons, menus, buttons and other graphical devices. (*Cyber Law*)

Guidance. The action of guiding or leading. [Indian Trusts Act (2 of 1882), S. 57].

Guide. Directing principle; standard.

To lead, conduct or direct [Jawaharlal Nehru University Act (53 of 1966), S. 5(9)]; he who or that which guides.

Guillotine. A specially drastic rule or closure motion for shortening discussion; the most drastic method of curtailing debate in a legislature.

Guilt. Culpability; Having committed the offence in question.

The act of having committed, or of being guilty of some specified or implied offence; guiltiness.

Guilt or Fault Theory of Divorce. According to this theory a marriage can be dissolved only if one of the parties to the marriage has, after the solemnization of marriage, committed some matrimonial offence. The offence must be one that is recognized as a ground for divorce. [Dr Kauser Edappagath, *Divorce and Gender Equity in Muslim Personal Law of India*, 2014, LexisNexis]

Guiltless. Innocent of the offence charged.

Guilty. Culpable; criminal; having committed an offence. There is no difference between the expressions "found guilty" and convict."

That has incurred guilt; deserving punishment and moral reprobation [IPC (45 of 1860), S. 6, ill. (b)]; involving guilt; culpable. [IPC (45 of 1860), S. 108, *Expln.* 3, ill. (a)].

Guilty knowledge. That has incurred guilt; deserving punishment and moral reprobation involving guilt; culpable.

Guilty mind. The state of mind which the prosecution must prove a defendant to have had at the time of committing a crime in order to secure a conviction.

Gun-cotton. Cotton steeped in nitric or sulphuric acid, used for blasting.

An explosive prepared by saturating cotton with nitric and sulphuric acids. [Explosives Act (4 of 1884), S. 4(1)(a)].

Gynaecologist. Means a person who possesses a post-graduate qualification in gynaecology and obstetrics. [Pre-Natal Diagnostic Techniques (Regulation and Prevention of Misuse) Act (57 of 1994), S. 2(f)]

H

Habeas corpus means 'have the body'. A writ issued to bring a person before a court, to ensure that his imprisonment is not illegal.

A writ or order requiring that a prisoner be brought before a court at a stated time and place to decide the legality of his detention or imprisonment; commands the judge of the inferior court to produce the body of the defendant with a statement of the cause of his detention, to do and to receive whatever the higher court shall decree; the right of *habeas corpus* safeguards one against illegal detention or imprisonment. (*Constitutional and Parliamentary Term*)

A writ to a jailor to produce a prisoner in person before the court and to state the reasons for detention. [Constitution of India, Art. 32(2)].

See also under writ.

Habemus optimum testem confitentem reum. (*Maxim*) We have the best witness in an accused who confesses the charge.

Habit. Settled tendency or practice; mental constitution. The word 'habit' implies a tendency or capacity resulting from the frequent repetition of the same acts. The words '*habit*' and '*habitually*' imply frequent practice or use. These words are used in S. 110, CrPC, 1973 (2 of 1974), in the sense of depravity of character as evidenced by the frequent repetition or commission of offences mentioned in the section.

"Habit is the disposition of a person toward a certain thing". It need not be the uniform or unvarying rule, but, to be a habit, it must be the ordinary course of conduct the general rule or custom.

The word "habit" has a clear, well-understood meaning, being nearly the same as "custom", and cannot be applied to a single act.

A settled disposition or tendency to act in a certain way especially one acquired by frequent repetition of the same act. [Indian Evidence Act (1 of 1872), S. 7, ill. (c)].

Habitability. The condition of a building where the inhabitants can live free of serious defects which might harm health and safety.

Habitable. That can be inhabited; 'habitable', applied to a room, means, "a room constructed or adapted to be inhabited."

HABITABLE, is, what is reasonably fit for the occupation of a tenant of the class which occupies it.

Habital. Means any area in the range of a migratory species which contains suitable living conditions for that species. [Convention on the Conservation of Migratory Species of Wild Animals (1980), Art. 1(g)]

Habitancy. The term "habitancy" expresses the fact of residence at a place with the intent to regard and make it a home.

The word "habitancy" is more comprehensive than "domicile." In some respects, "habitancy" includes "domicile" and embraces citizenship and municipal relations.

Habitat. Includes land, water or vegetation which is the natural home of any wild animals. [Wild Life (Protection) Act (53 of 1972), S. 2(15)]

Habitation. Place of abode.

Where one stops for a long time in a place for the management of his business affairs, while he resided with his family at another place, he has simply a habitation at the former place, and not a domicile.

HABITATION, ABODE, DOMICILE. *Habitation* is a place which one inhabits, not necessarily a house or tenement of any kind. *Abode* has the same sense, but with a less direct reference to the constant passing of one's life there. *Habitation* is the natural or habitual place of abode. *Domicile* adds to the idea of habitation and abode a relationship to society and civil government, and is consequently a term rather technical than conversational. An *abode* is pleasant or unpleasant, convenient or inconvenient. A *habitation* is suitable or unsuitable, healthy or unhealthy, commodious or otherwise. *Habitation* points more directly than abode to furnishing necessary shelter and protection. The woods are the *abodes* of birds, their nests are their *habitations*. The legal force of the term *domicile* is a residence at a particular place, with positive or presumptive proof of an intention to remain there. (*Smith Syn. Dis.*)

Habitual. Constant; customary; addicted to a specified habit.

Doing by force of habit or constantly or repeatedly. [CrPC, 1973 (2 of 1974), S. 110].

"HABITUAL" means formed or acquired by or resulting from habit; frequent use or custom; formed by repeated impressions.

Habitual carnal intercourse. In the phrase "habitual carnal intercourse", the word "habitual" should be understood in its common acceptation.

Habitual criminal. The term "habitual criminal" may be applied to any one who has been previously more than twice convicted of crime, sentenced, and committed to prison.

Habitual cruel and inhuman treatment. If the treatment is persistently cruel and inhuman, and is occasionally characterized by personal violence, so as to beget the apprehension that it is liable to occur again at any time, it is sufficient to constitute "habitual cruel and inhuman treatment."

Habitual dealing in slaves. A person who habitually imports, exports, removes, buys, sells, traffics, or deals in slaves, is said to be habitually dealing in slaves. [IPC (45 of 1860), S. 371]

Habitual drunkard. An habitual drunkard is one who makes it a habit, or who habitually becomes intoxicated by the voluntary use of intoxicating liqours.

Habitual drunkenness or intoxication. The terms "habitual drunkenness," "habitual intemperance," "habitual intoxication, and continued habits of intoxication" are equivalent and capable of the same definition, and are defined as the fixed and irresistible habit of getting drunk.

Habitual ill-treatment. If within the first twenty days of the wife, living with her husband, she is assaulted by him shut up in a room and ill-treated in other manners, it is a case of habitual ill-treatment. *Khacheru* v. *Mt. Khairunnisa,* AIR 1952 All 638, 639. [Dissolution of Muslim Marriages Act (8 of 1939), S. 2(VIII)(a)]

Habitual insanity. Habitual insanity is such insanity as is, in its nature, continuous and chronic.

Habitual intemperance. The phrase 'habitual intemperance' means the custom or habit of getting drunk; the constant indulgence in such stimulants as wine, brandy, and whisky, whereby intoxication is produced; not the ordinary use, but the habitual use, of them. The habit should be actual or confirmed. It may be intermittent. It need not be continuous, or even of daily occurrence.

Habitual offender. A person who is persistently leading a dishonest and criminal life. [CrPC, 1973 (2 of 1974), S. 110]

Habitual repair. To put premises in "habitual repair" means to improve the state of repair, and render the premises reasonably fit for an ordinary occupier of such premises. *Mohd. Mohideen Rowther* v. *D. Mohideen Rowther,* AIR 1960 Mad 24, 26. [T.P. Act (4 of 1882), Ss. 72(b), 63-A(2), 76 (d)]

Habitual residence. The place or country where a person has his home.

"Habitual Respondent" is a person against whom a previous complaint of sexual harassment has been received by the GSICC on earlier occasion, irrespective of whether the matter with or without an inquiry and except where the Respondent has been exonerated in the previous complaint. [Gender Sensitisation and Sexual Harassment of Women in the Supreme Court of India (Prevention, Prohibition and Redressal) Regulations, 2013, Regn. 2(e)].

Habitual thief. Habit has to be proved by an aggregate of acts and it would strain the provision of S. 110, CrPC, 1973 (2 of 1974) if it were to be held that a man being suspected mainly by the police in four thefts after he had been acquitted on a charge of theft amounted to sufficient evidence of habit.

Habitually. The term "*habitually*" means, "usually," "generally," or according to custom. It does not refer to the frequency of the occasions but rather to the invariability of the practice.

Habitually negligent. By habit negligent; persistently negligent. [Indian Evidence Act (1 of 1872), S. 14, ill. (n)].

Hacker. The person intentionally/purposely gaining or trying to gain unauthorised access to material stored in a database or any other computerised format.

Someone who is enthusiastically knowledgeable in the field of computers or one who spends his or her time breaking into other people's computer systems with the objective of stealing data. (*Cyber Law*)

Hacking. The process of gaining access to computers or sites where no access was intended—this may be a crime in some jurisdictions. (*Cyber Law*)

The word 'hacking' is used to refer to all forms of unauthorized access to computer program, whether by insiders or outsiders.

Gaining unauthorized access to a computer system. This is a summary offence under the Computer Misuse Act, 1990. Under this Act it is also an offence, triable summarily or on indictment, to engage in hacking with the intention of committing another offence (*e.g.* theft, diverting funds), or to destroy, corrupt, or modify computer-stored information or programs while hacking. This offence can be committed either through using one computer to gain access to another computer or simply by gaining access to one computer only. Copyright protection applies. (*England*) (*Oxford Law Dictionary, 5th Edn., 2003*)

Gaining of unauthorized access to the data stored in computer systems. Hacking is an intentional act of breaking into a computer system with the objective of stealing data that can be used for purposes of identity theft or other fraud. (Aparna Viswanathan, *Cyber Law: Indian & International Perspectives,* 2012, LexisNexis Butterworths at p. 14.)

Hackney-carriage. "HACKNEY-CARRIAGE" means any wheeled vehicle drawn by animals and used for the conveyance of passengers which is kept, or offered, or plied, for hire." [Hackney Carriage Act (14 of 1879), S. 2].

It is a carriage exposed for hire to the public, whether standing in the public street, or exposed for public use in a private gateway. The test is whether the carriage is held out for the general accommodation of the public or not.

Hacktivism. Hacktivism is a term which combines the concepts of 'hacking' and 'activism' which means the hacking into the computer system of another for a social or a political purpose. Aparna Viswanathan, *Cyber Law: Indian & International Perspectives,* 2012, LexisNexis Butterworths at p. 13.

Haeredes successores que sui cuique liberi. (*Maxim*) Every man's children are his heirs and successors.

Haereditas. An inheritance; an estate by descent or succession.

Haereditas est successio in universum jusquod defunctus habuerat. (*Maxim*) Inheritance is the succession to every right which was possessed by the late possessor.

Haereditas nihil aliud est, quam successio in universum jus quod defunctus habuerit. The right of inheritance is nothing else than the faculty of succeeding to all the rights of the deceased. (*Latin for Lawyers*)

Haeres de facto. Heir from fact; an heir from the deed or act of the ancestor.

Haeres legitimus est quem nuptiae demonstrant. (*Maxim*) The lawful heir is he whom wedlock shows so to be. (*Latin for Lawyers*)

Hague Convention. Means the Convention for the Suppression of Unlawful Seizure of Aircraft signed at the Hague on the 16th day of December, 1970. [Anti-Hijacking Act (65 of 1982), S. 2(d)] [Now repealed by Act 30 of 2016]

Half a year. In leasing a fixed term which begins on a quarter day and ends on the next but one quarter day.

Half-an-hour discussion. On matters arising out of questions already answered, half-an-hour discussion can be held in the Lok Sabha during the last half-an-hour of the sitting on Mondays, Wednesdays and Fridays and in the Rajya Sabha from 5 p.m. to 5.30 p.m. on any day allotted by the Chairman, after three days' advance notice by the member wishing to raise the discussion. The Speaker/Chairman decides in each case whether the matter needs elucidation and is of sufficient public importance.

Half-blood. The children of the same mother, but who have different fathers, are no less brothers and sisters of the half blood than are the children of a common father, but who have different mothers.

"Two persons are said to be related to each other by half blood when they are descended from a common ancestor but by different wives." [Hindu Succession Act (30 of 1956), S. 3(1)(e) and Special Marriage Act (43 of 1954), S. 2, *Expln.* II].

Half-blooded. Born of different races.

Half brother (or sister). Brother (or sister) by one parent only.

Half-holiday (*in a factory*) means a day in which the latter half is allowed as a holiday.

Half-mast high. (*of flag*) Lowered to half height of mast as a mark of respect to the illustrious dead.

Half way homes. Means a transitional living facility for persons with mental illness who are discharged as impatient from a mental health establishment, but are not fully ready to live independently on their own or with the family. [Mental Health Care (Rights of Persons with Mental Illness) Rules, 2018, R. 2(1)(c)].

Half year. "HALF-YEAR" means a half-year commencing on the 1st day of April or the 1st day of October, or such other date as the State Government may, by notification, appoint. [Manipur Municipalities Act (43 of 1994), S. 2(20)]

Half-yearly rests. Rests for every half year. [Indian Trusts Act (2 of 1882), S. 23(f)].

Hall. A large building in a university meant mainly for the residence of students. [University of Hyderabad Act (39 of 1974), S. 2(j)].

"HALL" means a unit of residence for the students of the University or of a College or an Institution maintained by the University. [S. 2(o) of the Rajiv Gandhi National Aviation University Act, 2013 (26 of 2013)]

Hallucination. "The word 'hallucination' is defined according to lexicographers, as, an error; a blunder; a mistake; a fallacy; and, when used in describing the condition of a person, does not necessarily carry an imputation of insanity."

"Hallucinations" are also used in respect of certain errors of eyesight, hearing, and the like, as where the patient imagines that he sees an object when there is none, or hears a voice when no sound strikes his ear.

"Voices" are the most common type of hallucination in schizophrenia. Hallucinations include seeing people or objects that are not there, smelling odors that no one else detects, and feeling things like invisible fingers touching their bodies when no one is near. [*Veer Pal Singh* v. *Secretary, Ministry of Defence*, (2013) 8 SCC 83, para 14.1].

Hamlet. "Hamlet" and "vill" are in common acceptation used as synonymous terms; a small village, generally attached to another and sometimes larger village.

Hanafi Mussalman. Means a follower of the *Mussalman* faith who conforms to the tenets and doctrines of the Hanafi School of Mussalman law. [Mussalman Wakf Validating Act (6 of 1913), S. 2, cl. 2]

Hand. A person's signature (as), a document under one's hand and seal, a style of writing (as), a legible hand.

Terminal part of human arm beyond wrist [Personal Injuries (Compensation Insurance) Act (37 of 1963), Sch.]; a person employed; employed worker [Workmen's Compensation Act (8 of 1923), S. 15(2)].

Hand bill. Printed notices (as, of advertisement of sale by public auction) circulated by hand.

The word "handbill," in its usual acceptance is synonymous with the words "printed circular".

A small printed bill or announcement usually for distribution by hand. [Representation of the People Act (43 of 1951), S. 127A(3)(b)].

Hand cuffs. Pair of metal rings, generally made of iron, joined by short chain, for securing prisoner's hands.

Hand grenade. A grenade to be thrown by hand. [Arms Act (54 of 1959), S. 2(1)(e)(i)].

Hand writing. Writing with the hand, specially of a particular person.

The term "handwriting" includes generally whatever a party has written with his hand, and not merely his common and usual style of chirography.

The cast or form of writing peculiar to each hand or person; something written by hand. [Indian Evidence Act (1 of 1872), S. 67].

What was understood by handwriting must now in the present times after more than a century of the enactment of that provision, be necessarily understood to include typewriting as well, since typing has become more common than handwriting. *State* v. *S. J. Choudhary*, AIR 1996 SC 1491, 1496. [Indian Evidence Act (1 of 1872), S. 45]

Handbook of Procedures Volume-I. Means the Handbook of Procedures Volume-I, 2002-2007 published by the Government of India in the Ministry of Commerce and Industry *vide* Public Notice No. 1/2002-2007, dated the 31st March,

2002. [Customs Tariff Act (51 of 1975), General Exemption No. 43, iii (a) *Expln.* (ii)]

Handicapped. "HANDICAPPED" means a person—

(i) visually handicapped;

(ii) hearing handicapped;

(iii) suffering from locomotor disability; or

(iv) suffering from mental retardation. [Rehabilitation Council of India Act (34 of 1992), S. 2(1)(c)]

A person with physical disability that limits the capacity to work and puts him to disadvantage. [Medical Termination of Pregnancy Act (34 of 1971), S. 3(2)(ii)].

Handicapped dependant. Shall mean a person who—

(i) is a relative of the individual or, as the case may be, is a member of the Hindu undivided family and is not dependant on any person other than such individual or Hindu undivided family for his support or maintenance; and

(ii) is suffering from a permanent physical disability (including blindness) or is subject to mental retardation, being a permanent physical disability or mental retardation specified in the rules made by the Board for the purposes of Section 80DD, which is certified by a physician, a surgeon, an oculist or a psychiatrist, as the case may be, working in a Government hospital, and which has the effect of reducing considerably such person's capacity for normal work or engaging in a gainful employment or occupation. [Income-tax Act (43 of 1961), S. 80DDA (4)(b)]

Handicapped person. For the purposes of this section, "HANDICAPPED PERSON" shall mean a person who is as if being an assessee entitled for the time being to the benefits of deduction under Section 80U of the Income-tax Act, 1961. [Delhi Rent Act (33 of 1995), S. 26 *Expl.* I]

Handicraft. Manual skill; manual art or trade. Goods produced by hand, *e.g.*, certain pottery, woven goods, embroidery, basket work, *etc.*

Only a very small portion of required work was done by hand. The main part of the manufacture of *agarbatis*, *etc.* was done with the aid of power. It was the machine that produced predominantly the end product. In that view of the matter, agarbatis were not handicrafts. (Para 10). *Padmini Products* v. *Collector of Central Excise,* AIR 1989 SC 2278.

Tests for determination of handicrafts, laid down:

"(1) It must be predominantly made by hand. It does not matter if some machinery is also used in the process. (2) It must be graced with visual appeal in the nature of ornamentation or in-lay work or some similar work lending it an element of artistic improvement. Such ornamentation must be of a substantial nature and not a mere pretence." *Collector of Central Excise* v. *Louis Shoppe,* 1996 (3) SCC 445.

Furniture does not qualify as "handicraft, because to be called handicraft, it must be predominantly made by hand, it must be graced with visual appeal in the nature of ornamentation or inlay work or some similar work lending it an element of artistic improvement. Such ornamentation must be of substantial nature and not mere pretence. *CCE* v. *Louis Shoppe,* 1996 (65) ECR 246 (SC) : 1996 (82) ELT 13 (SC).

Handicraft goods. For the purposes of this rule, the expression "handicraft goods" has the meaning as assigned to it in the Government of India, Ministry of Finance, notification No. 32/2017-Central Tax dated the 15th September, 2017 published in the Gazette of India, Extraordinary, Part II, Section 3, sub-section (i), vide number GSR 1158(E), dated the 15th September, 2017 as amended from time to time. [Central Goods and Services Tax Rules, 2017, R. 138, *Explanation 1*].

Handle. To touch; feel; to manage in using with the hands (as a spade or a weapon); to manage; to cope with, control or direct (staff or a company); to deal with; dispose of (work etc.); to trade in; to engage in buying and selling; to move, carry, store or arrange (material); to deal with (as in case of money or cash); to operate by hand (a machine or instrument).

"TO HANDLE A COMMODITY" means to buy and sell such commodity; and the power to HANDLE A FUND implies the power to use it in making purchases and to sell the thing, *etc.*, for the purpose of changing the investment.

Handling. In relation to any hazardous substance, means the manufacture, processing, treatment, package, storage, transportation by vehicle, use, collection, destruction, conversion, offering for sale, transfer or the like of such hazardous substance. [National Environmental Tribunal Act (27 of 1995), S. 2(c); and Public Liability Insurance Act (6 of 1991), S. 2(c); and Environment (Protection) Act (29 of 1986), S. 2(d)]

Handling stolen goods. Dishonestly receiving goods that one knows or believes to be stolen or undertaking, arranging, or assisting someone to retain, remove, or dispose of stolen goods.

Handloom. Means any loom, other than powerloom. [Handlooms (Reservation of Articles For Production) Act (22 of 1985), S. 2(b)]

Handsale. A sale of chattels concluded by the shaking of hands.

Hang. To remain undetermined; to be in suspense. The word is also used to denote the infliction of capital punishment by suspension (as) to hang a murderer.

Hanging. Pending; during the pendency. Hanging is a form of death, produced by suspending the body, with a ligature round the neck, the constricting force being the weight of the body or a part of the body weight. Another words, the hanging is the ligature compression of the neck by the weight of one's body due to suspension. [*State of Rajasthan* v. *Ramesh*, (2015) 17 SCC 673, para 16].

Hank. The word 'hank' without the aid of any explanation whatsoever, means in the cotton trade a coil of definite length of 840 yards. *C.S. & W. Mills*

v. *Collector of Customs,* AIR 1967 Ker 62. [Central Excises and Salt Act (1 of 1944), S. 3]

Hank means "a coil of yarn". *Cannanore Spinning and Weaving Mills* v. *Customs Collector*, AIR 1970 SC 1950 at 1952. [Central Excise Rules (1944), R 8].

Happen. Come to pass by chance or otherwise. To occur. [Indian Evidence Act (1 of 1872), S. 92, ill. (j)].

The word "happen" is defined by the words to fall out, to befall, to come unexpectedly.

Harass. "Injure" and "injury" are words having numerous and comprehensive popular meanings, as well as having a legal import. A line may be drawn between these words and the word "harass" excluding the latter from being comprehended within the word "injure" or "injury". The synonyms of "harass" are: to weary, tire, perplex, distress, tease, vex, molest, trouble, disturb. They all have relation to mental annoyance, and a troubling of the spirit.

Harassment. The subjection of a person to aggressive pressure or intimidation through unwanted sexual advances.

The term "harassment" in its connotative expense includes torment and vexation. [*Mehmood Nayyar Azam* v. *State of Chhattisgarh*, (2012) 8 SCC 1, para 22].

Harbour. "The word "HARBOUR" includes the supplying a person with shelter, food, drink, money, clothes, arms, ammunition or means of conveyance, or the assisting a person by any means, whether of the same kind as those enumerated in this section or not, to evade apprehension." [IPC (45 of 1860), S. 52A].

A place of shelter for ships, specially where they may lie sheltered by the shore or by works extended from it [Indian Evidence Act (1 of 1872), S. 32, ill. (d)]; to give shelter to. [IPC (45 of 1860), S. 52A].

"Harbour" includes supplying a person with shelter, food, drink, money, clothes, arms, ammunition or means of conveyance, or the assisting a person by any means, whether of the same kind as those enumerated in this clause or not, to evade apprehension. [(w.e.f. 1-7-2024) Bharatiya Nyaya Sanhita, 2023 (45 of 2023), section 2(13)]

Harbour Master. Means a person lawfully appointed and licensed as such by the Board (Board of Trade, UK) to perform such duties as may from time to time, be assigned to him by the Deputy Conservator. [New Mangalore Port (Authorisation of Power) Regulations, 1980, as cited in *Karan Vaswani* v. *Union of India*, (2000) 3 SCC 602, para 5 : AIR 2000 SC 1446]

Harbouring offenders. To "harbour" used in respect of harbouring offenders means, to give such persons shelter, or to permit them to congregate, even though it be only to take part in a "friendly lead" for the purpose of raising a legitimate subscription.

"Whenever an offence has been committed, whoever harbours or conceals a person whom he knows or has reason to believe to be the offender, with the intention of screening him from legal punishment is said to harbour such offender." [IPC (45 of 1860), S. 212]

Hard cases. Cases in which the application by the Court of a precise, unmodified legal rule would almost certainly produce injustice.

Hard copy. A copy of computer output that is printed on paper in a visually readable form. (*Information Technology*)

Hard disk. A device containing one or more inflexible platters coated with material in which data can be recorded magnetically, together with their read/ write heads, the head-positioning mechanism, and the spindly motor in a sealed case that protects against outside contaminants. The protected environment allows the head to fly 10 to 25 millionths of an inch above the surface of a platter rotating typically at 3600 to 7200 rpm; therefore, much more data can be stored and accessed much more quickly than on a floppy disk. Most hard disks contain from two to eight platters. Also called : hard disk drive. [Computer Dictionary by Micro-soft, 5th Edn., 246 **as referred in** *Commr. of Customs* v. *Hewlett Packard India Sales (P) Ltd.*, (2007) 8 SCC 404, 409, para 16]

Hard labour. As used in sentencing convicted persons; ordinary industry at some mechanical trade.

A sentence condemning a prisoner to hard labour in the penitentiary does not signify that the labour shall be of unusual severity, but means no more than that it is compulsory and continuous during the term of imprisonment. It does not subject the person to any other than legal punishment, or to labour of any other kind or degree than must have been endured if the word "hard" had been omitted; the penitentiary, being not a mere place for improvement but involving subjection to involuntary or compulsory labour during the continuance of the sentence.

Hard bodily labour (imposed upon certain class of criminals during their terms of imprisonment). [(fourthly), IPC (45 of 1860), S. 53].

Hard money. Hard money is a coin of the precious metals, of a certain weight and fineness, with the government's stamp thereon, denoting its value as a medium of exchange or currency.

Hard return. A return caused by pressing the return key rather than an automatic return (soft return) created by the system when a line turns over. The hard return will function wherever it appears, even though the document rearranges itself when text is added or deleted. (*Computer*)

Hardship. Suffering; privation. [Specific Relief Act (47 of 1963), S. 20(2)(b)].

Hardware. The word "hardware", in octroi rates of municipality does not include electric fans. It comes much more nearly under the terms of machinery.

The physical equipment parts of a word processing system. Printers and keyboards are hardware. (*Computer*)

The physical components of a computer system. They typically include the mother board, disk drives, display, keyboard, and the CPU (central processing unit). (*Computer*)

Hardware weapons. These include radio frequency or electromagnetic pulse weapons that knock out a system's electronic equipment.

Hare system. Single transferable vote system. Under this system candidates are not elected by their obtaining majority or plurality of the votes cost, but by their obtaining a quota of designated number of votes or a certain proportion of the entire vote in which electors are permitted to express second, third or additional choices. *Lalit Mohan Pandey* v. *Pooran Singh*, AIR 2004 SC 2303. [U.P. Zila Panchayats (Election of Adhyaksha and U.P Adhyaksha and Settlement of Election Disputes) Rules, 1994, Rules 26, 33 to 35]

Harijan. It is well-known that the word '*Harijan*' applies to untouchables. *State* v. *Puranchand*, AIR 1958 MP 352, 353. [Untouchability (Offences) Act, 1955, S. 3]

Harm. "harm", in relation to a product liability, includes—

(i) damage to any property, other than the product itself;

(ii) personal injury, illness or death;

(iii) mental agony or emotional distress attendant to personal injury or illness or damage to property; or

(iv) any loss of consortium or services or other loss resulting from a harm referred to in sub-clause (*i*) or sub-clause (*ii*) or sub-clause (*iii*),

but shall not include any harm caused to a product itself or any damage to the property on account of breach of warranty conditions or any commercial or economic loss, including any direct, incidental or consequential loss relating thereto. [Consumer Protection Act, 2019 (35 of 2019), section 2(22)]

The expression 'harm' means also physical injury. *Veeda Manezes* v. *Yusuf Khan*, AIR 1966 SC 1773, 1775. [IPC (45 of 1860), Ss. 81, 87, 88, 89, 91 to 93, 95, 100, 104, 106, 415, 469 and 499]

Evil (Physical or otherwise) as done or suffered. [IPC (45 of 1860), S. 81].

Harmful. That which causes harm; damaging.

Harmful publication. "HARMFUL PUBLICATION" means any book, magazine, pamphlet, leaflet, newspaper or other like publication which consists of stories told with the aid of pictures or without the aid of pictures or wholly in pictures, being stories portraying wholly or mainly—

(i) the commission of offences; or

(ii) acts of violence or cruelty; or

(iii) incidents of repulsive or horrible nature; in such a way that the publication as a whole would tend to corrupt a young person into whose hands it might fall, whether by inciting or encouraging him to commit offences or acts of violence or cruelty or in any other manner whatsoever. [Young Persons (Harmful Publication) Act (93 of 1956), S. 2(a)]

Harmful substance. Means any hazardous, noxious, or other substance, the introduction of which into the marine environment would result in pollution or adversely affect the biological processes due to its toxity and/or persistence and/or bioaceumulation characteristics. [Convention on the Protection of the Black Sea against Pollution, 21-22 April 1992, Art. II(4)]

'HARMFUL SUBSTANCE' means any hazardous, noxious, or other substance which if introduced into the sea is liable to cause pollution. [Convention on the Protection of the Marine Environment of the Beltic Sea Area Helsinki, March 22, 1974, Art. 1(b)]

Harmonious construction. (*Interpretation of Statutes*) It is a recognised rule of interpretation of statutes that the expression used therein should ordinarily be understood in a sense in which they best harmonise with the object of the statute, and which effectuate the object of the legislature. If an expression is susceptible of a narrow or technical meaning, as well as a popular meaning, the court would be justified in assuming that the legislature used the expression in the sense which would carry out its object and reject that which rendors the exercise of its powers invalid. *New India Sugar Mills Ltd.* v. *Commissioner, Sales Tax*, AIR 1963 SC 1207, 1213.

Harmonised System. "Harmonised System" means the nomenclature of the Harmonised Commodity Description and Coding System defined in the International Convention on the Harmonised Commodity Description and Coding System including all legal notes thereto, as adopted and implemented by the respective countries under their respective tariff laws. [Customs Tariff (Determination of Origin of Products under the Duty Free Preference Scheme for Least Developed Countries) Rules, 2015, R. 2(k)].

Harmonization. The process of making procedures measures applied by different countries—especially those affecting international trade—more compatible, as by effecting simultaneous tariff cuts applied by different countries so as to make their tariff structures more uniform.

Harmonization of laws. The process by which member states of the EU make changes in their national laws, in accordance with Community legislation, to produce uniformity, particularly relating to commercial matters of common interest.

Has been. "When not followed by a participle is the present perfect tense of "to be" and accordingly indicates that the state of thing has existed and may be (but not necessarily is) continuing and therefore even advocates who are not actively practising on the date of appointment are eligible to be appointed as judge provided he is qualified." *Chandra Mohan* v. *State of U.P.*, AIR 1969 All 230 at 234. [Constitution of India, Art. 233(2)]

Whether the expression 'has been' denotes transaction prior to the enactment of the statute in question or a transaction after the coming into force of the statute, has to be gathered from the provision, in which the expression 'has been' occurs or from the other provisions of the statute. *Secretary R.T.A. Bangalore* v. *D.P. Sarma*, AIR 1989 SC 509, 513.

Has been constructed. The expression "has been constructed" obviously cannot include within its sweep a building which is not fully constructed or in the process of construction. [*Giridhar G. Yadalam* v. *Commissioner of Wealth Tax,* (2015) 17 SCC 664, para 16].

Has been referred. These words cannot be isolated from the context. The said expressions may have different connotations when they are used in different contexts. *Workmen* v. *Firestone Tyre & Rubber Co. of India, (Pvt.) Ltd.,* AIR 1973 SC 1227. [Industrial Disputes Act (14 of 1947), S. 2-A]

Has for at least ten years been advocate of High Court. The expression 'has for at least ten years been advocate of High Court' does not mean that the advocate should actually practice for ten years in High Court. *V.G. Row* v. *N. Krishnaswamy,* AIR 1967 Mad 345, 346. [Constitution of India, Art. 217(2)(*b*)]

Has notice. The words "has notice," mean has knowledge or information "and not has received a formal notice.

Has reason to believe. The expression "reason to believe" in S. 34 does not mean purely subjective satisfaction on the part of the Income Tax Officer. The belief must be held in good faith. It cannot be merely a pretence. *Madhya Pradesh Industries Ltd.* v. *ITO,* AIR 1970 SC 1011. [Income-tax Act (11 of 1922), S. 34]

Has served on the committee. 'Has served' means that the act of serving has already been completed or it was done and may be (but not necessarily is) continuing. *Harbhajan Singh* v. *State of Punjab,* AIR 1973 P&H 31, 33.

Hash. An algorithm that maps or translates one set of bits into another (generally smaller) set in such a way that it gives the same result, everytime the algorithm is executed using the same message as input. (*Information Technology*)

Hash function. For the purposes of this sub-section, "HASH FUNCTION" means an algorithm mapping or translation of one sequence of bits into another, generally smaller, set known as "hash result" such that an electronic record yields the same hash result every time the algorithm is executed with the same electronic record as its input making it computationally infeasible—

(a) to derive or reconstruct the original electronic record from the hash result produced by the algorithm;

(b) that two electronic records can produce the same hash result using the algorithm.

(c) Any person by the use of a public key of the subscriber can verify the electronic record.

(d) The private key and the public key are unique to the subscriber and constitute a functioning key pair. [Information Technology Act (21 of 2000), S. 3(2) *Expl.*, S. 3(3) and 3(4)]

A hash function is a one-way mathematical function that takes a variable-length input string (sometimes called a pre-image) and outputs a fixed-length string (called a hash, hash value, hash word or message digest). The iterative process that computes a hash from a pre-image is termed hashing. Hashing is used in proving that electronic commerce messages have not been modified, corrupted or altered. (*Information Technology*)

A hash function is an algorithm which converts a large amount of data into a smaller amount of data which are called keys. Aparna Viswanathan, *Cyber Law: Indian & International Perspectives,* 2012, LexisNexis Butterworths at p. 61.

Hassle. A disagreement or argument; a fight.

Hasten. Cause haste; accelerate; make haste.

Hatch. The covering of a hatchway; a small gate. [Commercial Documents Evidence Act (30 of 1939), Sch., pt. 11, item 1(iii)].

Hatch covering. An arrangement for covering and protecting hatchway or other deck covering. [Indian Dock Labourers Act (19 of 1934), S. 5(1)(g)].

Hate speech. Speech that carries no meaning other than the expression of hatred for some group, such as a particular race, especially in circumstances in which the communication is likely to provoke violence. [Black's Law Dictionary, 9th Edn. as cited in *Pravasi Bhalai Sangathan* v. *Union of India*, (2014) 11 SCC 477, para 9].

'Hate Speech' is an effort to marginalize individuals based on their membership in a group. Using expression that exposes the group to hatred, hate speech seeks to delegitimise group members in the eyes of the majority, reducing their social standing and acceptance within society. Hate speech, therefore, rises beyond causing distress to individual group members. It can have a societal impact. Hate speech lays the groundwork for later, broad attacks on vulnerable that can range from discrimination, to ostracism, segregation, deportation, violence and, in the most extreme cases, to genocide. Hate speech also impacts a protected group's ability to respond to the substantive ideas under debate, thereby placing a serious barrier to their full participation in our democracy. [*Pravasi Bhalai Sangthan* v. *Union of India*, (2014) 11 SCC 477, para 8].

Haulage. Charges for the use of trucks, wagons, or carriages, from one point to another.

Haulage road. A passage in a coal mine along which coal is transported. [Mines Act (35 of 1952), S. 57(q)].

Hauling. The words "handling" and "hauling" are not synonymous words. Hauling is a transportation, while handling involves touching, holding, moving, or managing with the hand.

Have been acting as such. The words "have been acting as such" in S. 109 of the Indian Evidence Act (1 of 1872) would be applicable even when there is only one single instance proved. This would therefore be sufficient to bring about the relationship of landlord and tenant so as to throw the onus of proving the contrary on the other party.

Have not been able to live together. The expression "have not been able to live together" indicates the concept of broken down marriage and it would not be possible to reconcile themselves. *Sureshta Devi* v. *Om Prakash*, AIR 1992 SC 1904, 1907. [Hindu Marriage Act (25 of 1955), S. 13-B]

Have regard to. The phrase "have regard to" has generally directory effect and not a binding effect. *New Orissa Transport Company (P) Ltd.* v. *Regional Transport Authority,* AIR 1957 Ori 121, 124.

The expression 'have regard to' only directs the Govt. to consider as relevant data material to which it must have regard. *Saraswati Industrial Syndicate Ltd.* v. *Union of India*, AIR 1975 SC 460, 462.

Having an interest in the trust. The "interest" of the parties here contemplated in S. 92(1), CPC (5 of 1908), must be the "interest" that is threatened or infringed.

Having been nominated. The expression 'having been nominated', means that the candidate, either in person or through his proposer, has delivered to the Returning Officer, in the manner and within the time prescribed, a nomination paper completed in the prescribed form and signed by the candidate and by an elector of the constituency as proposer. *Hariram Singh* v. *Kanta Prasad,* AIR 1966 MP 255, 260. [Constitution of India, Sch 3, Form VII-A (as amended in 1963 by 10th Amendment)]

Having regard to. The words 'having regard to' in a statutory provisions do not mean that there must be very strict compliance with the statutory provision, but that the provision should be taken for guidance only.

The expression 'having regard to' means that great weight and dominant regard must be attached to the provisions of the statute where such words appear. *Teknarayan Mahesh Prasad* v. *State of Bihar,* AIR 1972 Pat 230, 235.

Having the force of law. The expression 'having the force of law' means that a particular set of rules or a particular notification, although may not strictly be called law, may still have the force of a law which means that it would be enforced in a court of justice. *C. Shirappa* v. *G. Murigappa,* AIR 1958 Mys 184, 187. [States Reorganisation Act (37 of 1956), S. 169]

Hawker. One who carries goods from place to place for sale.

Hazard. Danger; peril, risk or probability of loss or injury.

To engage in a wager of any kind is a hazard; subjecting to fine one who shall engage in any hazard or game on which money is bet, won, or lost.

The word "hazard", in its ordinary sense, means chance, luck or accident, rather than mere uncertainty or contingency.

The mutual "hazards" assumed by parties when they enter into a partnership relation, and which qualify the terms of partnership agreements, includes sickness, which is the act of God, temporary absence or death, or other casualties.

"HAZARD" means a biological, chemical or physical agent in, or condition of, food with the potential to cause an adverse health effect. [S. 3(1)(u) of the Food Safety & Standards Act, 2006 (34 of 2006)]

Hazardous. "Hazardous," is used in an Act authorising a board of health to abate nuisances, sources of foulness, or causes of sickness *Hazardous* to the public health, means simply dangerous or perilous.

"Hazardous" means involving danger or potential danger. [Occupational Safety, Healthy & Working Conditions Code, 2020 (37 of 2020), section 2(1)(z)]

The terms "hazardous" and "extra-hazardous," as used in an insurance policy authorizing the insured premises to be used for hazardous and extra-hazardous purposes, have no technical meaning, and must be taken in their ordinary and popular meaning, of dangerous and extra-dangerous.

Fraught with hazard of risk; perilous. [Workmen's Compensation Act (8 of 1923), S. 2(3)].

Hazardous cleaning. By an employee, in relation to a sewer or septic tank, means its manual cleaning by such employee without the employer fulfilling his obligations to provide protective gear and other cleaning devices and ensuring observance of safety precautions, as may be prescribed or provided in any other law, for the time being in force or rules made thereunder. [S. 2(1)(d) of the Prohibition of Employment as Manual Scavengers & Their Rehabilitation Act, 2013 (25 of 2013)]

Hazardous employment. High risk and extra perilous work. When used in context of workers' compensation, it refers to employment which requires employer to carry workers' compensation coverage or its equivalent regardless of the number of employees. (*Black*)

Hazardous process. Means any process or activity in relation to an industry specified in the First Schedule where, unless special care is taken, raw materials used therein or the intermediate or finished products, by-products, wastes or effluents thereof would—

(i) cause material impairment to the health of the persons engaged in or connected therewith, or

(ii) result in the pollution of the general environment;

Provided that the State Government may, by notification in the Official Gazette, amend the First Schedule by way of addition, omission or variation of any industry specified in the said Schedule. [Factories Act (63 of 1948), S. 2(cb)]

"Hazardous process" means any process or activity in relation to an industry or plantation specified in the First Schedule where, unless special care is taken, raw materials used therein or the intermediate or finished products, bye-products, hazardous substances, wastes or effluents thereof or spraying of any pesticides, insecticides or chemicals used therein, as the case may be, would—

(i) cause material impairment to the health of the persons engaged in or connected therewith, or

(ii) result in the pollution of the general environment. [Occupational Safety, Healthy & Working Conditions Code, 2020 (37 of 2020), section 2(1)(za)]

Hazardous substance. "HAZARDOUS SUBSTANCE" means any substance or preparation which by reason of its chemical or physiochemical properties or handling is liable to cause harm to human beings, other living creatures, plants, microorganism, property or the environment. [Environment (Protection) Act, 1986 (29 of 1985), S. 2(e)]

"Hazardous substance" means any substance or such quantity of the substance as may be prescribed by the appropriate Government or preparation of which by reason of its chemical or physio-chemical properties or handling is liable to cause physical or health hazards to human being or may cause harm to other living creatures, plants, micro-organisms, property or the environment. [Occupational Safety, Healthy & Working Conditions Code, 2020 (37 of 2020), section 2(1)(zb)]

Hazardous to life. Any disturbance of the basic environment elements, namely air, water and soil, which are necessary for life, would be 'hazardous to life' within the meaning of Article 21 of the Constitution. [*M.C. Mehta* v. *Kamal Nath,* AIR 2000 SC 1997 : (2000) 6 SCC 213, 219, para 8]

Hazardous waste. Means a substance which—

(a) falls under this Chapter; and

(b) is defined or specified in the Export and Import Policy of the Central Government issued from time to time, and includes even waste oils and discarded containers specified in the Schedules to the Hazardous Wastes (Management and Handling) Rules, 1989. [Customs Tariff Act (51 of 1975), I Sch. Import Tariff, S. VI, Chap. 38, Note 6, Supplementary Note (2)]

Hazardous wastes site. Means a place for collection, reception, treatment, storage and disposal of hazardous wastes which has been duly approved by the competent authority. [Hazardous Wastes (Management and Handling) Rules, 1989, R. 3(15), as amended in 20-5-2003.]

He. The pronoun "he" when used in any Code, includes a female as well as a male, unless there is some express declaration to the contrary.

The word "he," when used in the revenue act, includes male, female, company, corporation, firm, society, singular or plural number.

The word 'he' occurring in O. IX, R. 13 of CPC would include the person who has stepped into the shoes of the defendant for moving an application for setting aside the *ex parte* decree. *Raj Kumar* v. *Sardari Lal,* (2004) 2 SCC 601, 607, para 13. [CPC (5 of 1908), O. IX, R. 13]

He who comes to equity must come with clean hands. Considering the maxim the Apex Court held that the question of dismissal of writ petition on the ground of unclean hands cannot subserve the ends of justice and the matter ought to have been dealt with on its merits with proper appreciation of the facts. The petition cannot be dismissed *in limine* on the ground of unclean hands. *Municipal Corpn. of Delhi* v. *Nirmal Sachdeva,* (2001) 10 SCC 364, paras 8, 9 & 10.

He who seeks equity must do equity. Specific performance is an equitable relief and 'he who seeks equity can be put on terms to ensure that equity is done to the opposite party over while granting the relief. [*K. Kalpana Saraswathi* v. *P.S.S. Somasundaram Chettiar,* AIR 1980 SC 512 : (1980) 1 SCC 630, 633, para 4]

Head. Chief; leading: principal; the upper part or principal source of a stream.

A main division of a writing; a topic [CrPC 1973 (2 of 1974), S. 2(b)]; a chief or principal; the uppermost or foremost part of an animal's body.

Head lease. The execution of the original document by the owner of free-hold land on the first granting of a lease to the leaseholder.

Head money. Money paid for killing or capturing a person (as an outlaw); bounty. [Navy Act (62 of 1957), S. 49(2)].

Head of delegation. Means the delegate changed by the sanding State with the duty of acting in that Capacity. [Vienna Convention on the Representation of States in their Relations with International Organisations of a Universal Character, 1975, March 14, Art. I (24)]

Head of Department. Heads of Departments may be taken to mean members of the Cabinet; or chief officers of departments of Government.

Head of the Department is one who was directly working under a Secretariat Department without intervention of any high officer and who was declared as appointing authority. *V.S. Murthy and others* v. *Deputy Chief Accounts Officer and others*, AIR 1983 SC 403, 407.

The expression 'Head of Department' has two distinct meanings. It may be limited to Heads of the various Departments of the Secretariat, namely the Secretaries of the Departments, or else it may also include Heads of Departments of attached offices either under the Union Government or under the State Government. National Saving Commissioner and the Collector of a District are not Heads of Departments. *UOI* v. *Sudhir Kumar Roy,* AIR 1963 Ori 111, 113, 114. [Indian Evidence Act (1 of 1872), S. 123]

Head of household. The primary income-provider of a family.

Head of school. Means the principal academic officer, by whatever name called, of a recognised school. [Delhi School Education Act (18 of 1973), S. 2(k)]

'Head of a School', or 'Head' means the person, by whatever name called in charge of the academic and administrative duties and functions of a school conducted by any Management and recognised or deemed to be recognized under this Act, and includes a Principal, Vice-Principal, Headmaster,

Headmistress, Assistant Headmaster, Assistant Headmistress or Superintendent thereof. [Maharashtra Employees of Private Schools (Conditions of Service) Regulation Act, 1977, S. 2(9) as cited in *Viman Vaman Awale* v. *Gangadhar Makhriya Charitable Trust*, (2014) 13 SCC 219, para 12].

Head of the department, Officer at the. One having the chief command of the department. [Indian Evidence Act (1 of 1872), S. 123].

Head of the mission. Is the person charged by the sending State with the duty of acting in that capacity. [Diplomatic Relations (Vienna Convention) Act (43 of 1972), Sch. Article 1(a)]

"HEAD OF MISSION" means as the case may be, the permanent representative or the permanent observer. [Vienna Convention on the Representation of States in their Relations with International Organisations of a Universal Character, 1975, March, 14, Art. I(17)]

Head of the Archives. Means a person holding the charge of the Archives of the Union territory Administration. [Public Records Act (69 of 1993), S. 2(c)]

Head of the office. For the purpose of exercising the powers as appointing, disciplinary, appellate or reviewing authority means the authority declared to be head of the office under the general financial rules. [CCS (CCA) Rules, 1965, R. 2(i)]

Head office expenditure. Means executive and general administration expenditure incurred by the assessee outside India, including expenditure incurred in respect of—

(a) rent, rates, taxes, repairs or insurance of any premises outside India used for the purposes of the business or profession;

(b) salary, wages, annuity, pension, fees, bonus, commission, gratuity, perquisites or profits in *lieu of* or in addition to salary, whether paid or allowed to any employee or other person employed in, or managing the affairs of, any office outside India;

(c) travelling by any employee or other person employed in, or managing the affairs of, any office outside India; and

(d) such other matters connected with executive and general administration as may be prescribed. [Income-tax Act (43 of 1961), S. 44C, *Expln.* (iv)]

Head works. A structure for controlling the quantity of water. [Punjab Re-organisation Act (31 of 1966), S. 79(i)(c)].

Header. Text placed automatically at the top of each page, such as a document name, page number, date, or author's name. (*Computer*)

Heading. Words placed at the head of a chapter, paragraph etc. [Punjab Legislative Council (Abolition) Act (46 of 1969), S. 5(b)]; the front or top of anything [Trade and Merchandise Marks Act (43 of 1958), S. 2(1)(j)].

Headnote. A brief summary of a legal rule or significant facts in a case, which, among other headnotes applicable to the case, precedes the printed opinion in reports. A syllabus to a reported case; a summary of the points decided in the case, which is placed at the head of beginning of the opinion. (*Black*)

Concise statement of the legal principles contained in a law report at the beginning.

Headrace and tail race. The race or flume which brings water to a mill-wheel and the part of the mill-race below the wheel. [Factories Act (63 of 1948), S. 21(1)(ii)].

Health. Freedom from sickness or suffering; a right to the enjoyment of which is one of the absolute rights of persons. (*Kenny.*)

Soundness of the body. [CrPC 1973 (2 of 1974), S. 144(1) and Constitution of India, Art. 25(1)].

The term health implies more than an absence of sickness. Health is thus a state of complete physical, mental and social well being and not merely the absence of disease or infirmity. *CESC Ltd.* v. *Subhash Chandra Bose,* AIR 1992 SC 573.

The state of complete physical, mental and social well being is health. It is a fundamental human right of the workmen. *Kirloskar Brothers Ltd.* v. *Employees' State Insurance Corporation*, AIR 1996 SC 3261.

Health and fitness service. Means service for physical well-being such as, sauna and steam bath, turkish bath, solarium, spas, reducing or slimming salons, gymnasium, *yoga*, meditation, massage (excluding therapeutic massage) or any other like service. [Finance Act (32 of 1994), S. 65(42) now repealed by Central Goods and Services Tax Act, 2017]

Health care system. Means an institution or organisation engaged either directly or indirectly, in health care for mothers, infants or pregnant women, and includes a health worker in private practice, but does not include a pharmacy or drug store. [Infant Milk Substitutes, Feeding Bottles and Infant Foods Regulation of Production Supply and Distribution Act (41 of 1992), S. 2(d)]

Health club and fitness centre. Means any establishment, including a hotel or resort, providing health and fitness service. [Finance Act (32 of 1994), S. 65(43) now repealed by Central Goods Service Tax Act, 2017]

Health Government Scheme. For the purpose of these regulations, Health Government scheme shall include any scheme launched by the Government to cover health risk including personal accident of public at large such as Rashtriya Swasthya Bima Yojana, etc. [Insurance Regulatory and Development Authority of India (Expenses of Management of Insurers Transaction General or Health Insurance Business) Regulations, 2016, Regn. 2(1)(vii)].

Health Group. Shall include any health including personal accident policy/travel policy issued to group/body corporate to cover the health risk of members of group. [Insurance Regulatory and Development Authority of India (Expenses of

Management of Insurers Transaction General or Health Insurance Business) Regulations, 2016, Regn. 2(1)(vi)].

"Health insurance business" or "health cover". Means the effecting of contracts which provide sickness benefits or medical, surgical or hospital expense benefits, whether in-patient or out-patient, on an indemnity, reimbursement, service, prepaid, hospital or other plans basis, including assured benefits and long-term care. [Insurance Regulatory and Development Authority (Registration of Indian Insurance Companies) Regulations, 2000, Reg. 2(f)]

"Health insurance business" means the effecting of contracts which provide for sickness benefits or medical, surgical or hospital expense benefits, when in-patient or out-patient travel cover and personal accident cover. [Insurance Act (4 of 1938), S. 2 (6C) as inserted by Act (5 of 2015)].

Health Officer. Means the senior executive medical officer in military employ on duty in a cantonment. [Cantonment Act (2 of 1924), S. 2(xiv)]

Health visitor. Means a person who has obtained the health visitor's certificate from any Health School, institution or examining body recognised in this behalf by the Council. [Rajasthan Nurses Midwives Health Visitors and Auxiliary Nursing— Midwives Registration Act (9 of 1964), S. 2(c)]

Health worker. Means a person engaged in health care for mothers, infants or pregnant women. [Infant Milk substitutes, Feeding Bottles and Infant Foods (Regulation of Production, Supply and Distribution) Act (40 of 1992), S. 2(e)]

Healthcare provider, Means any individual whose vocation or profession is directly or indirectly related to the maintenance of the health of another individual and includes any physician, nurse, paramedic, psychologist, counselor or other individual providing medical, nursing, psychological or other healthcare services including HIV prevention and treatment services. [Human Immunodeficiency Virus and Acquire Immune Deficiency Syndrome (Prevention and Control) Act (16 of 2017), S. 2(h)].

Healthcare service personnel. Means a person who while carrying out his duties in relation to epidemic related responsibilities, may come in direct contact with affected patients and thereby is at the risk of being impacted by such disease, and includes—

(i) any public and clinical healthcare provider such as doctor, nurse, paramedical worker and community health worker;

(ii) any other person empowered under the Act to take measures to prevent the outbreak of the disease or spread thereof; and

(iii) any person declared as such by the State Government, by notification in the Official Gazette. [Epidemic Diseases Act, 1897 (3 of 1897), section 1A(b)]

Health Retail. Shall include health insurance policies including personal accident/Travel policy issued to individual to cover the health risk of individual or his family. [Insurance Regulatory and Development Authority of India (Expenses of Management of Insurers Transaction General or Health Insurance Business) Regulations, 2016, Regn. 2(1)(viii)].

Heap. Means any unit of a commodity for sale where such sale is intended to be made without any weighment or measurement or, where the sale is made by number, without counting the number. [Standards of Weights and Measures (Enforcement) Act (54 of 1985),S. 3(e)]

Hear. The hearing of the suit would be on a date to which it may have been adjourned to be taken up by the court for applying its mind to it. [CPC (5 of 1908), O. XVII, R. 2]

Hear and determine. The words "hear and determine" refer to judicial determination after the hearing and weighing of testimony on both sides, and do not generally include an *ex parte* proceeding.

Authority to hear and determine a cause is jurisdiction to try and decide all the questions involved in the controversy.

The power to hear and determine is an essential ingredient of original jurisdiction, and the authority to examine and correct errors is the distinguishing characteristic of appellate power. To hear and determine a criminal case is to proceed to try the case and pass sentence.

TO HEAR, HEARKEN, OVERHEAR. We *hear* sounds; we *hearken* for the sense; we *over-hear* the words: a quick ear *hears* the smallest sound; a willing mind *hearkens* to what is said, a prying curiosity leads to *over-hearing*.

Hear the parties. The phrase 'hear the parties' only means that arguments should be heard and does not include oral examination of the parties and their witnesses. [CrPC 1973 (2 of 1974), S. 145(4)]

Heard and finally decided. To support a plea of *res judicata*, it is not enough that the parties are the same, and that the same matter is in issue. The matter must have been "heard and finally decided." [CPC (5 of 1908), S. 11]

Where an appellate Court confirms the decree of the first Court on the strength of the oath of a party to the suit on a question of fact, the decree of the appellate Court is none the less a final adjudication.

Heard from. "Heard from" as used when saying that one person has not heard from another, refers to some direct personal communication by letter or otherwise.

In an action for divorce under an Act which declares that absence for three years without being heard of is a ground for divorce, proof that the party had not been "*heard from*" is not equivalent to proof that the party had not been "*heard of*."

Hearing. A judicial session held for the purpose of deciding issues of fact or that of law; in administrative law, presentment of argument by the affected individual to the decision-making authority.

The trial of a suit is called a "hearing" and, technically considered, this includes not only the introduction of the evidence and arguments of the counsels, but the pronouncing of the decree by the Presiding Officer.

A term, properly applied to the argument and consideration of the case at the several stages of its orderly progress, and, when applied to that upon which the case is absolutely determined, it is qualified by the word "final".

The hearing of a complainant and of the parties does not necessarily mean their examination. It merely amounts to a granting of audience.

"Hearing" includes communication of data and documents through electronic mode. [Income-tax Act (43 of 1961), section 2(23C)]

"Hearing" as used in the CPC, does not mean the 'hearing of arguments' only. It refers to all the stages of the trial of a suit, namely, the settling of issues, taking of evidence and hearing of arguments or other proceedings tending to a final adjudication of the suit." *Kanaran Nambiar* v. *Ramunni Nambiar,* AIR 1961 Ker 290, 292. [CPC (5 of 1908), O. XXII, R. 6]

Listening to pleadings, evidence and arguments especially in a court of law; the trial of a cause [T.P. Act (4 of 1882), S. 69-A(10) and CPC (5 of 1908), O. XVII, R. 2]; audition [CrPC 1973 (2 of 1974), S. 164(4)]; the faculty or sense by which sound is perceived [Workmen's Compensation Act (8 of 1923), S. 10-B, *Expln.*].

Hearing aid. 'Hearing aid' means an instrument intended for use by a person suffering from impaired hearing to assist that person to hear better.

Hearing de novo. Generally, a new hearing or a hearing for the second time, contemplating an entire trial in same manner in which matter was originally heard and a review of previous hearing. Trying matter anew the same as if it had not been heard before and as if no decision had been previously rendered. *Ray* v. *Illinois Racing Bd.,*1 Dist., 133 Ill. App. 3d 510 : 69 Ill. Dec. 451, 454, 447 N.E. 2d 886, 889. On hearing "*de novo*" Court hears matter as Court of original and not appellate jurisdiction. *Collier & Wallis* v. *Astor,* 9 Cal. 2d 202 : 70 P.2d 171, 173.

Hearing handicap. Means deafness with hearing impairment of 70 decibels and above, in the better ear, or total loss of hearing in both ears. [Rehabilitation Council of India Act (34 of 1992), S. 2(11)(d)]

Hearing impairment. Means loss of sixty decibels or more in the better year in the conversational range of frequencies. [Persons with Disabilities (Equal Opportunities, Protection of Rights and Full Participation) Act, 1995 (1 of 1996), S. 2(l)]

Hearing, Personal. Hearing in person.

Hearsay. What one hears (but does not know that to be true); gossip. "In its legal sense 'Hearsay' Evidence is all evidence which does not derive its value solely from the credit given to the witness himself but which rests also, in part, on the veracity and competence of some other person." (*Taylor on Evidence*, 9th Ed., 368)

The word 'hearsay' is used in various senses. Sometimes it means whatever a person is heard to say; sometimes it means whatever a person declares on information given by someone else. *J.D. Jain* v. *Management, State Bank of India,* AIR 1982 SC 673, 676.

Hearsay evidence. Evidence consisting of what the witness has heard others say of what is commonly said.

Hearsay rule. "The great hearsay rule . . . . is a fundamental rule of safety, but one overenforced and abused,—the spoiled child of the family,—proudest scion of our jury-trial rules of evidence, but so petted and indulged that it has become a nuisance and an obstruction to speedy and efficient trials." JOHN H. WIGMORE, *A Students' Textbook of the Law of Evidence,* 238 (1935).

Heat of passion. Passion or anger suddenly aroused at the time by some immediate and reasonable provocation, by words or acts. It has no application to passion or anger which comes from an old grudge where there is no immediate cause or provocation.

The term "heat of passion," used to characterize murder in the second degree, is not used in its technical sense, but as a condition of mind, contradistinguished from a cool state of blood.

By "heat of passion" is meant passion or anger suddenly aroused at the time, by some immediate reasonable provocation by words or acts of deceased at the time.

The heat of passion that will take away the malice from an act manifestly dangerous to human life, and reduce homicide to manslaughter, must be caused by lawful provocation.

The expression 'heat of passion' occurring in Section 300, Exception 4 of IPC (45 of 1860), requires that there must no time for the passions to cool down, and which clouds men's sober reason and urges them to deeds which they would not otherwise do. *Ghappoo Yadav* v. *State of M.P.,* (2003) 3 SCC 528, para 10.

Heavy goods vehicle. Means any goods carriage the gross vehicle weight of which or a tractor or a road-roller the unladen weight of either of which, exceeds 12000 kilograms. [Motor Vehicles Act (59 of 1988), S. 2(16)]

Heavy package. 'HEAVY PACKAGE' means a package or other object weighing not less than one metric ton, which is equal to one thousand kilogrammes or 1204.6 standard pounds or 26.8 standard maunds. [Marking of Heavy Packages Act (39 of 1951), S. 2(a)]

Heavy passenger motor vehicle. Means any public service vehicle or private service vehicle or educational institution bus or omnibus the gross vehicle weight of any of which, or a motor car the unladen weight of which, exceeds 12,000 kilograms. [Motor Vehicles Act (59 of 1988), S. 2(17)]

Hedge. Protection against current or anticipated risk exposure, usually through the purchase of a derivative.

Hedge fund. An investment fund that seeks high returns, usually by taking high risks such as investing in new financial instruments. (*Investment; Trade Finance*)

Heifer. Means a female of the age of three years and below belonging to the species of bovine animal. [Rajasthan Bovine Animal (Prohibition of Slaughter and Regulation of Temporary Migration or Export) Act (23 of 1995), S. 2(l)]

Heinous. (Of a crime or its perpetrator) that is shockingly atrocious or odious.

Heinous offence. Crime which is wicked in a high degree. [Long title, Forfeiture Act (9 of 1859)]

Heir. A person who inherits or may by law inherit. [T.P. Act (4 of 1882), S. 38, ill.].

An heir is one who takes by descent.

The word "heir" must be construed in a broad and general sense so as to include all those on whom the estate of the deceased devolves whether on intestacy or by means of testamentary instrument like a will. *Gulzara Singh Nanta Singh* v. *Tej Kaur,* AIR 1961 Punj 288, 291. [Hindu Adoptions and Maintenance Act (78 of 1956), S. 22(1)]

The word "heirs" as used in a will giving property to the heirs of testator's children, should be construed as descriptive of a class of beneficiaries.

In a will written in English, the word "heirs" would naturally include heirs as at the date of the testator's death, subject always to a contrary intention declared in the will.

The word "heirs" cannot normally be limited to issues only. It must mean all persons who are entitled to the property of another under the law of inheritance. *Augurbala* v. *Debabrata,* AIR 1951 SC 293, 300; *N. Krishnammal* v. *R. Ekambaram,* AIR 1979 SC 1298, 1301.

Heir apparent. A person whose right of inheritance is indefeasible, provided he outlives the ancestor. [T.P. Act (4 of 1882), S. 6(a)].

Heir-at-law. A legal heir; an heir in whom intestate's real property as distinguished from his personal estate is vested by operation of law and not by will. [Estate Duty Act (34 of 1953), S. 53(2)].

Heir presumptive. An heir, whose right to an inheritance may be defeated by a birth of nearer relative.

Heir, Right. The heir at common law as opposed to the heirs by special local customs. [Indian Succession Act (39 of 1925), S. 93].

Heirloom. The term is used to denote personal property that has been in the family for generations.

Held. As a technical term, 'held' embraces two ideas that of actual possession of some subject of dominion or property, and that of being invested with legal title or right to hold or claim such possession.

Held connotes both ownership as well as possession. It is not possible to interpret only in sense of possession. It obviously means that an owner who is not in actual possession will also be taken to be a holder of land. A transferee under unregistered sale deed pursuant to an agreement for sale, is a holder although he is not in possession. *State of A.P.* v. *Mohd. Ashrafuddin,* AIR 1982 SC 913, 915.

The word 'held' connotes the existence of a right or title in the holder.

"The word 'held' means lawfully held, to possess by legal title." *Budhan Singh* v. *Babi Bux,* AIR 1970 SC 1880 at 1884.

Had the ownership or use of, as one's own; in reference to the decision of a court decided.

"Held" or "occupied". The words "held" or "occupied" carry the same meaning and there is no manner of doubt that if the land is in the lawful possession of the factory and was being used for the purpose of the factory, the land vested in the Government as per Section 3 of the 1971 Act. [*Gaurav Aseem Avtej* v. *Sugar Corporation Limited,* (2018) 6 SCC 518, para 19] [U.P. Undertaking (Acquisition) Act (23 of 1971), S. 3].

Held benami. The word "held" has to be understood as "possessed or occupied". If a property stood in the name of A in the city survey record, it was occupied by B. In such a case, it cannot be said the property was held by A either benami or otherwise. *Laxman Sakha Ram Salvi* v. *Baldrishna Balvant Ghatage,* AIR 1995 Bom 190, 193. [Benami Transactions (Prevention) Act (45 of 1988), S. 4]

Heliport. Means an area, either at ground level or elevated on a structure, used or intended to be used for the landing and take-off of helicopters and includes any area for parking helicopters and all buildings and structures thereon or appertaining thereto. [Airports Authority of India Act (55 of 1994), S. 2(j) and National Airport Authority Act (64 of 1985), S. 2(e)]

Helper. One who helps; a labourer, who renders assistance to a senior artisan.

Hemp. Means any variety of the hemp plant from which intoxicating drugs can be produced. [Excise Act (12 of 1896), S. 3]

'HEMP' means—

(i) the leaves, small stalks and flowering and fruiting tops of the Indian hemp plant (*Cannabis sativa L.*) including all forms known as *bhang, siddi or ganja;*

(ii) *charas,* that is, resin obtained from the Indian hemp plant, which has not been submitted to any manipulations other than those necessary for packing and transport; and

(iii) any mixture, with or without neutral materials, any of the above forms of hemp or any drink prepared therefrom. [Dangerous Drugs Act (2 of 1930), S. 2(c)]

Herbal remedy. Means a medicinal product consisting of a substance produced by subjecting a plant or plants to drying, crushing or any other process, or of a mixture whose sole ingredients are two or more substances so produced, or of a mixture whose sole ingredients are one or more substances so produced and water or some other inert substance.

Henceforth. From now on.

Hereafter. Later in this document.

Hereby. The word 'hereby' used in business and legal correspondence does not connote the point of time. It always means 'through'.

When it is said that the tenancy is hereby terminated it will mean that the tenancy is terminated through notice. *Laxmi Devi* v. *Chandramani Devi,* AIR 1971 All 506, 511.

By this act or document. [T.P. Act (4 of 1882), S. 2(a)].

Hereditaments. Hereditament is the largest word of all in that kind; for whatsoever may be inherited is an hereditament, be it corporeal or incorporeal, real or personal, or mixt.

Hereditary. Descended or capable of descending from an ancestor to a descendent. [Registration Act (16 of 1908), S. 2(6)].

Hereditary office. "HEREDITARY OFFICE" means every office held hereditarily for the performance of duties connected with the administration or collection of the public revenue or with the village-police, or with the settlement of boundaries, or other matters of civil administration: the expression includes such office even where the services originally appertaining to it have ceased to be demanded. [Bom Act 3 of 1874 (Hereditary offices), S. 4].

Hereditary patelship. Means every village office of a revenue or police patel held hereditarily under the existing water law for the performance of duties connected with the administration or collection of the public revenue of a village or with the village police or with the settlement of boundaries or other matters of civil administration of a village and includes such office even where the services originally appertaining to it have ceased to be demanded. [Gujarat Patel Watans Abolition Act (48 of 1961), S. 2(7)]

Hereditary trustee. 'HEREDITARY TRUSTEE' means the trustee of a religious institution, the succession to whose office devolves by hereditary right or is regulated by usage or is specifically provided for by the founder, so long as such scheme of succession is in force. [Tamil Nadu Religious and Charitable Endowments Act (22 of 1959), S. 6(11).]

'HEREDITARY TRUSTEE' means the trustee of a religious endowment, succession to whose office devolves by hereditary right or by nomination by the trustee for the time being, or is otherwise regulated by usage or is specially provided for by the founder, so long as such scheme of succession is in force. [T.N. Hindu Religious Endowment Act, 1926 (2 of 1927), S. 6(11))]

Herein. The words of S. 2 of the T.P. Act (4 of 1882) "Nothing herein contained shall be deemed to affect any transfer in execution of a decree" only mean nothing contained in S. 2 and not nothing contained in the Transfer of Property Act shall affect execution sale.

The meaning of the word "herein" as used in legal phraseology, is to be determined by the context. It may refer to the section, the chapter, or the entire enactment in which it is used; and this rule is applicable to the construction of a document as well as of the statute.

The authority to 'herein' determine the cause is jurisdiction to try and decide all of the cases involved in the controversy.

Herein : hereinafter. "Where a testator, by his will, charges his lands with the payment of the legacies "hereinafter" bequeathed, the charge does not extend to legacies bequeathed by a codicil".

"HEREIN", "HEREBY", AND "HEREINAFTER" are synonyms confining the thing spoken of to the matter on hand.

HEREIN PROVIDED FOR. The phrase "herein provided for," as used in Statutes, generally, if not always refers to the act, chapter, or title, but not to the section of the act in which it is found.

Hereinafter. "Hereinafter," as used in a general denial of every allegation of the complaint not 'hereinafter' specifically admitted, is to be construed as embracing "all that follows, and authorizes the plaintiffs to avail themselves of any admissions therein contained."

Hereinafter named. As used in a will to describe executors as hereinafter named, refers to those finally named by operative words.

Subsequent to the clause or covenant in which the word is used and in the same statue or document.

Hereinafter provided. Provided after this in this document.

Hereinbefore. Before, in this document.

Hereof. Of this thing.

Heretofore. Before this time. **Hereunder.** Later in this document. **Herewith.** With or in this document.

Heritable rights. Rights of the heir; rights to land or whatever may be intimately connected with land or other immovable property.

Heritage. (*In Hindu Law*) The term 'heritage' (signifies that wealth which becomes the property of another, solely by reason of relation to the owner.

Heritage, Dominant. The property for the beneficial enjoyment of which a right of easement exists. Thus an estate, the owner of which has, by virtue of his ownership, a right of way over another man's lands is called the 'dominant heritage' in respect thereof; and the land over which the right of way exists is called the 'servient heritage' [Indian Easements Act (5 of 1882), S. 4]; [T.P. Act (4 of 1882), S. 6(c)].

Hermeneutics. The art of interpreting texts, especially as a technique used in critical legal studies.

Hertzian waves. Electro-magnetic waves of frequencies lower than 3,000 gigacycles per second propagated in space without artificial guide. [Wireless Telegraphy Act (17 of 1933), S. 2(1); and Indian Telegraph Act (13 of 1885), S. 2(1), *Expln.* Repealed by Repealing Act of 1938]

Heuristic. Of or relating to a method of learning or problem-solving by using trial-and-error and other experimental techniques.

Hexadecimal numbering system. A system in which four binary digits are read as a decimal digit, 0 through 9, and six letters, usually A through F. Counting progresses 1,2,3,4,5, 6,7,8, 9, A,B,C,D,E, F. A total of sixteen combinations are used; therefore the name hexadecimal is given to this system. (*Computer*)

Hiba. (In *Mohammedan Law*) A gift in law; a perfect gift, one accompanied by delivery and acceptance. A gift on a death-bed is considered a bequest. (*Wil. Gloss*)

Hibanamah. (In *Mohammedan Law*) A deed of gift.

Hide. To conceal from view; to keep secret.

Hide of land. A certain quantity of land, such as might be ploughed with one plough in a year.

Hides and skin. Hides and skin are termed 'leather' even as soon as the process of tanning is over and the danger of their putrefaction is put an end to S. 14(1)(iii) of the CST Act includes within its scope hides and skins until they are 'dressed' This represents the stage when they undergo the process of finishing and assume a form in which they can be readily utilised for manufacture of various commercial articles. In this view, it is hardly material that coloured leather may be a form of leather or may even be said to represent a different commercial commodity. *State of T.N.* v. *Mahi Traders,* AIR 1989 SC 1167. [Central Sales Tax Act (74 of 1956), S. 14(1)(iii)]

The finished product *i.e.* 'tanned leather' even though it may have changed in physical appearance or chemical combination and even though it may commercially be a different item still remains a 'hide' or a 'skin'. *Park Leather Industry (P.) Ltd.* v. *State of U.P.,* (2001) 3 SCC 135 para 21 : AIR 2001 SC 931. [U.P. Krishi Utpadan Mandi Adhiniyam (25 of 1964), S. 2(a) & Sch. Part G Entry 11]

Hierarchy. A body of persons or things, ranked in grades, order or classes, one above another. [Constitution of India, Art. 323B(3)(a)].

High and low water mark. Between "high and low water-mark" means medium high and low water-mark *i.e.,* half way between the spring tide and neap tide high and low water-marks respectively (*Webber* v. *Richards*, 10 LJQB 203 : 1 G. & D. 114).

High Commissioner. A representative of the government of one British Commonwealth country in the capital of another, with representational functions broadly similar to those of an ambassador. [CPC (5 of 1908), S. 86(4)(b)].

High Court. In section 280A(1) of Act 43 of 1961, 'High Court' means the High Court of the State in which a Magistrate of first class designated as Special Court was functioning immediately before such designation. [*Explanation* to section 280A(1) of the Income-tax Act, 1961 (43 of 1961) as inserted (w.e.f. 1-7-2012) by the Finance Act, 2012 (23 of 2012)]

"HIGH COURT" for the purposes of section 74 of Act 30 of 2013, "High Court" means the High Court within the jurisdiction of which the land acquired or proposed to be acquired is situated. [*Explanation* to S. 74 of the Right to Fair Compensation & Transparency in Land Acquisition, Rehabilitation & Resettlement Act, 2013 (30 of 2013)]

High Court decisions. A Court which is subordinate to a High Court is bound to follow the decision in law of a Bench of that Court unless the decision of the Bench has been overruled by a decision of a Full Bench of that Court or unless the law has been altered by a subsequent Act of the legislature.

High Court or **High Court of Justice** or **High Court of Judicature.** In this clause "High Court" means a High Court which exercises, or which at any time before the commencement of this Constitution exercised, jurisdiction in any part of the territory of India. [Constitution of India, Article 124(3), *Explanation I*]

"HIGH COURT" means any Court which is deemed for the purposes of this Constitution to be a High Court for any State and includes—

(a) any Court in the territory of India constituted or reconstituted under this Constitution as a High Court, and

(b) any other Court in the territory of India which may be may be declared by Parliament by law to be a High Court for all or any of the purposes of this Constitution. [Constitution of India, Art. 366(14)]

The highest court of a State. [Constitution of India, Part VI, Chapter V].

In this Part and in Part IIIA, "High Court", in relation to a banking company, means the High Court exercising jurisdiction in the place where the registered office of the banking company is situated or, in the case of a banking company incorporated outside India, where its principal place of business in India is situated. [Banking Regulation Act (10 of 1949), section 36B]

The expression "High Court" means the High Court having jurisdiction in relation to the place at which the registered office of the company concerned is situate. *Stridewell Leathers (P) Ltd.* v. *Bhankerpur Bimbhaoli Beverages (P) LTD.*, AIR 1994 SC 158, 165. [Companies Act (1 of 1956), S. 10(1)(a)]

The term "High Court" in Ss. 117 and 120, CPC (5 of 1908), includes a single Judge of the High Court exercising the functions of that Court.

'High Court' is a Court of record under Art. 215 of the Constitution meaning thereby that all the original records of the Court are preserved by it and it has all the powers of such a superior Court of record including the power to punish for contempt of itself as well as to determine the question about its own jurisdiction. *High Court of Judicature at Allahabad* v. *Raj Kishore Yadav,* (1997) 3 SCC 11, para 10 : AIR 1997 SC 1186. [Constitution of India, Art. 215]

The High Court of justice. [General Clauses Act (10 of 1897), S. 3(25) and Constitution of India, Art. 112(3)(d)(iii)].

High Definition Television (HDTV). An improved television system which provides approximately twice the vertical and horizontal resolution of existing television standards. It also provides audio quality approaching that of compact discs. (*Telecommunication*)

High denomination bank note. Means a bank note of the denominational value of one thousand rupees, five thousand rupees or ten thousand rupees, issued by the Reserve Bank. [High Denomination Bank Notes (Demonetisation) Act (11 of 1978), S. 2(d)]

High public or political office. The term "high public or political office" used in the Act contemplates only a special class of officers or politicians who may be categorised as follows—(1) Officials wielding extraordinary powers entitling them to take major policy decisions and holding positions of trust and answerable and accountable for their wrongs, (2) persons responsible for giving to the State a clean, stable and honest administration, (3) persons occupying a very elevated status in whose hands lie the destiny of the nation. *V.C. Shukla* v. *State*, AIR 1980 SC 1382, 1411.

High Seas. Seas that are open to all, and represent the entire sea-space beyond the three miles limit of the shore. The expression includes all oceans, seas, bays, channels, rivers, creeks and waters below low watermark, and where great ships could go, with the exception only of such parts of such oceans, &c. as were within the body of some country.

In other matters than crimes connected with admiralty jurisdiction it may be important at times to discriminate between the sea and the high sea, but in crimes the seas or the high seas or the ocean means much the same.

"High seas" denotes all parts of the seas not included in the territorial sea and internal waters of any state. The high seas are *res communis* and are open to all nations, so that no State may validly purport to subject any part of them to its sovereignty. Freedom of the high seas comprises *inter alia*, both for coastal and non-coastal States, freedom to navigation, freedom of fishing, freedom of lay submarine cables and pipelines, and freedom to fly over the high seas. HALSBURY, 4th Edn., Vol. 18, para 1478, p. 758.

In International law 'high seas' means all parts of the sea not included in the territorial sea and internal waters of any state. (49 Halsbury, 4th edn., para 284).

The sea or ocean lying outside the territorial waters or maritime belts of a country. [Extradition Act (34 of 1962), S. 23].

High second class marks. 'High second class marks' is one where the marks face a little short of first class marks and the candidate narrowly misses first class. *J.P. Kulshrestha* v. *Allahabad University*, AIR 1980 SC 2141, 2145. [Allahabad University Act (3 of 1921), S. 32(2)(*f*)]

High-Security Zone. An area to which access is controlled through an entry point and limited to authorized, appropriately screened personnel and properly escorted visitors. High-Security Zones should be accessible only from Security-Zones, and are separated from Security-Zones and operations zones by a perimeter. High-Security Zones are monitered 24 hours a day a week by security staff, other personnel or electronic means.

High speed diesel (HSD). Means any hydrocarbon oil conforming to the Indian Standards Specification of Bureau of Indian Standards IS: 1460:2000. [Customs Tariff Act (51 of 1975), I Sch., Import Tariff, S. V, Chap. 27, Note 3, Supplementary Note (e)]

High support. Means an intensive support, physical, psychological and otherwise, which may be required by a person with benchmark disability for daily activities, to take independent and informed decision to access facilities and participating in all areas of life including education, employment, family and community life and treatment and therapy. [Rights of Persons with Disabilities Act (49 of 2016), S. 2(l)].

High water and low water. *High Water*, is the line marked by the periodical flow of the Tide, excluding the advance of waters above that line by winds or storms or freshets or floods; *Low Water*, is the further receding point of Ebb.

High water mark. "High-water mark", in relation to a Major Port, means a line drawn through the highest points reached by ordinary spring-tides at any season of the year at that Major Port. [Major Port Authorities Act, 2021 (1 of 2021), section 2(1)(j)]

High-water mark in a river or stream is the point to which the water usually rises in an ordinary season of high water.

Higher education. "HIGHER EDUCATION" means full-time studies for any graduate or post-graduate course in engineering, medicine, management or for post-graduate course in applied sciences or pure sciences including mathematics and statistics. [Income-tax Act (43 of 1961), S. 80E(3)(e) as substituted by Finance Act (18 of 2005), S. 25]

Higher Educational Institution (HEI). Means a university recognized under Section 2(f) of the UGC Act, 1956 or an institution deemed to be university under Section 3 of the UGC Act, 1956 or an affiliating college/institution or a constituent unit of a university. [University Grants Commission (Promotion of Academic Integrity and Prevention of Plagiarism in Higher Educational Institutions) Regulations, 2018, Regn. 2(h)].

Higher Secondary Course. Means course immediately following the High School Certificate Course and covering a period of two academic years which is provided for either in a College or a Higher Secondary School and includes Art, Science, Commerce and vocational Courses. [Orissa Higher Secondary Education Act (19 of 1982), S. 2(i)]

'Higher Secondary School' means a school which with or without lower classes maintains Classes IX and X and/or XI and XII and prepares students for the High School and/or Intermediate Examinations of the Intermediate Board or a University. [Educational Code of Uttar Pradesh (Revised 1958 Edn.), Para 1 (xxvi)(d) as cited in *State of U.P.* v. *Pawan Kumar Divedi*, (2014) 9 SCC 692, para 22].

Highest degree of care and diligence. Is an expression to measure the care and diligence which a very prudent man would exert in that business under all circumstances.

Highly belated. Inordinate highly delayed normally connotes inordinate delay—Delay of a few days is not inordinate delay. *Improvement Trust, Hoshiarpur* v. *Land Acquisition Tribunal,* 1995 Supp (3) SCC 652.

Highly improbable. Very improbable. [Indian Evidence Act (1 of 1872), S. 114, ill. (b)].

Highly probable. Very probable. [Indian Evidence Act (1 of 1872), S. 11(2)].

Highway. "HIGHWAY" means a National Highway declared as such under Section 2 of the National Highways Act, 1956 and includes any Expressway or Express Highway vested in the Central Government, whether surfaced or unsurfaced, and also includes—

(i) all lands appurtenant to the Highway, whether demarcated or not, acquired for the purpose of the Highway or transferred for such purpose by the State Government to the Central Government;

(ii) all bridges, culverts, tunnels, cause-ways, carriageways and other structures constructed on or across such Highway; and

(iii) all trees, railings, fences, posts, signs, signals, kilometre stone and other Highway accessories and materials on such Highways. [Control of National Highways and Land Traffic Act, 2002 (13 of 2003), S. 2(e)]

A public road open to all passengers; the ordinary or main route by land or water. [IPC (45 of 1860), S. 392].

If a bridge spans a stream at the crossing of a highway, and within the limits of the highway, it is to be regarded as a part of the highway.

A bridge which is constantly travelled by pedestrians and used by families and others, and crossed by people daily, is a public highway.

Bridges are but streets or highways over water.

A road or canal constructed by the public or a corporation is a public highway for the public benefit. If the public have a right to passage thereon by paying a reasonable stipulated uniform toll, its exaction does not make its use private.

Public highways include turnpikes, railroads, and bridges used as thoroughfares, and the charge of a toll over them in no way affects their character as public highways. They are public because of the right of the public to use them.

A stream which, in its natural condition, is capable of being used for immediate purpose of navigation, must also be regarded as a public highway.

A highway is a passage over which members of the public are entitled to pass and repass. The essential characteristic of a highway is that every person should have the right to use it for the appropriate kind of traffic. [Indian Easements Act (5 of 1882), S. 28]

Highway man. One who robs on highway.

Highway robbery. Robbery being the forcibly and dishonestly taking from the person of another of goods or money of any value by violence or putting him in fear, to make it highway robbery it is only necessary further to prove that it was committed on or near a highway.

Hijacking. To steal something in transit. [Anti-hijacking Act (65 of 1982), S. 3(1)].

Hilly area. For the purposes of this Section "HILLY AREA" means any area located at a height of one thousand metres or more above the sea level. [Income-tax Act (43 of 1961), S. 80IA (12)(aa)]

Hindi. 'HINDI' means Hindi in Devanagari script. [Official Languages Act (19 of 1963), S. 2(b)]

Hindrance. Obstacle. [Navy Act (62 of 1957), S. 41(d)].

Hindu. The term "Hindu" with regard to the application of Hindu Law includes not only those who are Hindu by religion but also those who are commonly known as such.

Hindu Law. The Hindu Law to be administered by the Courts consists of *shastras* which claim divine sanction and are followed by the *Brahmins* generally, and also of the usages or approved habitual practices of those communities whose caste status depends upon the degree of conformity of their usages to *shastras*.

Hindu Law (*Sources of*). "The whole *Veda* is the (first) source of the sacred law; next the tradition and the virtuous conduct of those who know the (*Veda*); also the customs of holy men; and (finally) self-satisfaction. But by *Sruti* (revelation) is meant the *Veda*, and by *Smriti* (tradition), the Institutes of the sacred law; these two must not be called into question in any matter, since from these two the sacred law shone forth.

Hindu undivided family. Hindu undivided family is neither a firm nor an association of persons. It is a separate entity by itself. *I.T.O. Gorakhpur* v. *Ram Prasad*, AIR 1974 SC 454, 457. [Excess Profits Tax Act (15 of 1940), S. 14]

Hindu undivided family includes 'Jain Undivided Family'. *Commissioner of Wealth Tax* v. *Champa Kumar Singh*, AIR 1972 SC 2119, 2124. [Wealth Tax Act (27 of 1957), S. 3]

'Hinduism' as a religion, incorporates all forms of belief without mandating the selection or elimination of any one single belief. It is a single belief that has no single founder; no single scripture and no single set of teachings. It has been described as Sanatan Dharma, namely, eternal faith, as it is the collective wisdom and inspiration of the centuries that Hinduism seeks to preach and propagate. [*Adi Saiva Sivachariyargal Nala Sangam* v. *Government of Tamil Nadu*, (2016) 2 SCC 725, para 1].

Hindutva. Ordinarily Hindutva is understood as a way of life or a state of mind and it is not equated with or understood as religious Hindu fundamentalism. The word 'Hindutva' is used and understood as a synonym of 'Indianisation' *i.e.* development of uniform culture by obliterating the differences between all the cultures co-existing in the country. *R.V. Prabhoo* v. *P.K. Kunte*, AIR 1996 SC 1113. 1130.

Hire. "HIRE" means the sum payable periodically by the hirer under a hire-purchase agreement. [Hire Purchase Act (26 of 1972), S. 2(a)] [Now repealed by Act 31 of 2005]

To hire is to engage in service for a stipulated reward, as to a hire a servant, or to hire labourers by the day or month; to engage a man for temporary service of wages.

The word "hiring" implies a request and a contract for a compensation, and has but this one meaning when used in the ordinary affairs and business of life.

Payment contracted to be made for the temporary use of anything [IPC (45 of 1860), S. 157]; to take on hire [Indian Contract Act (9 of 1872), S. 73, ill. (b)].

Hire purchase. A system by which goods are obtained on hire. This becomes the absolute property of the hirer on paying the last of the installments stipulated to be paid by him, but until then he cannot deal with the goods, having no ownership in them.

A system by which a hired article becomes the property of the hirer after a stipulated number of payments [Hire-Purchase Act (26 of 1972), S. 3] [Now repealed by Act 31 of 2005]

; to take on hire purchase system.

Hire purchase agreement. "HIRE-PURCHASE AGREEMENT" means an agreement under which goods are let on hire and under which the hirer has an option to purchase them in accordance with the terms of the agreement and includes an agreement under which—

(i) possession of goods is delivered by the owner thereof to a person on condition that such person pays the agreed amount in periodical installments, and

(ii) the property in the goods is to pass to such person on the payment of the last such installments, and

(iii) such person has a right to terminate the agreement at any time before the property so passes. [Hire Purchase Act (26 of 1972), S. 2(c)] [Now repealed by Act 31 of 2005].

A hire purchase agreement is not an agreement of sale until the condition specified therein is fulfilled.

Hire purchase price. "HIRE PURCHASE PRICE" means the total sum payable by the hirer under a hire-purchase agreement in order to complete the purchase of or the acquisition of property in the goods to which the agreement relates; and includes any sum so payable by hirer under the hire-purchase agreement by way of a deposit or other initial payment, or credited or to be credited to him under such agreement on account of any such deposit or payment, whether that sum is to be or has been paid to the owner or to any other person or is to be or has been discharged by payment or money or by transfer or delivery of goods or by any other means; but does not include any sum payable as a penalty or as a compensation or damages for a breach of agreement. [Hire Purchase Act (26 of 1972), S. 2(d)] [Now repealed by Act 31 of 2005]

Hire workmen. To engage workmen for wages. [Indian Contract Act (9 of 1872), S. 188, ill. (b)].

Hirer. "HIRER" means the person who obtains or has obtained possession of goods from a owner under a hire-purchase agreement, and includes a person to whom hirer's rights or liabilities under the agreement have passed by assignment or operation of law. [Hire Purchase Act (26 of 1972), S. 2(e)] [Now repealed by Act 31 of 2005]

Hiring agreement and **Hire purchase agreement.** A *hiring agreement* relating to moveable property is an arrangement (often embodied in a document) between two parties, the one the hirer, the other the owner (or lessor) whereby the owner agrees to lend and the hirer to hire certain chattels in return for a consideration, usually money, payable by installments at fixed dates, the goods to be returned on demand at a specified time. A *hire-purchase agreement* is a development of this. It usually provides that on the due payment of all the installments the property shall become the property of the hirer and the agreement shall then terminate; but that so long as any of the installments remain unpaid the chattels shall remain the property of the owner.

His. "His," as used in a suit against several persons, charging that "defendant did keep in his possession," etc., refers to each of the defendants, notwithstanding one of them was a woman. "His" includes "her".

The pronoun 'his' as used in cl. (*d*) of S. 125(1) includes both a male and a female. In other words, the parents will be entitled to claim maintenance against their daughter. *Vijaya* v. *Kashi Rao*, AIR 1987 SC 1100, 1102. [CrPC, 1973 (2 of 1974), S. 125(1)(*d*)]

His income. The words 'his income' must include every item of income which goes to make up his total income assessable under the Act. *Income Tax Commissioner*, *Kerala* v. *P.K. Kochammu Amma*, AIR 1980 SC 2114, 2116. [Income-tax Act (43 of 1961), S. 139(1)]

His property. The expression 'his property' in Ss. 2(*h*) and 59, means not only the properties owned by the testator on the date of the will, but also those which he may acquire after that date and before his death. *Guneshwar Chutic* v. *Haren Chutic,* AIR 1974 Gau 73, 78. [Indian Succession Act (39 of 1925), S. 2(*h*) and S. 59]

History-sheet. "History sheet" is a continuous methodical record of public events or a whole trail of events connected with a person or a thing. It will refer to aggregate of past events or course of human affairs. *Nagabhushanam* v. *Ankam Ankaiah,* AIR 1968 AP 74 at 82.

History-ticket (*in respect of a prisoner*). Means the ticket exhibiting such information as is required in respect of each prisoner by the Prisoners Act or the rules thereunder. [Prisons Act (9 of 1894), S. 3(6)]

Hit. "Hits" are often used as a very rough measure of load on a server, *e.g.* "Our server has been getting 300,000 hits per month." Because each "hit" can represent anything from a request for a tiny document (or even a request for a missing document) all the way to a request that requires some significant extra processing (such as a complex search request), the actual load on a machine from 1 hit is almost impossible to define. [Internet E-Commerce]

As used in reference to the World Wide Web, 'hit' means a single request from a web *browser* for a single item from a web *server;* thus in order for a web browser to display a page that contains 3 graphics, 4 ?hits? would occur at the server : 1 for the *HTML* page, and one for each of the 3 graphics. (*Matisse Enzer-Glossary of Internet Terms*)

Hit and run motor accident. The expression 'hit and run motor accident' means an accident arising out of the use of a motor vehicle whose identity cannot be ascertained in spite of reasonable efforts for the purpose. *Theethi* v. *MACT, Palakkad,* AIR 1996 Ker 237.

HIV-affected person. Means an individual who is HIV-positive or whose partner (with whom such individual normally resides) is HIV-positive or has lost a partner (with whom such individual resided) due to AIDS. [Human Immunodeficiency Virus and Acquired Immune Deficiency Syndrome (Prevention and Control) Act (16 of 2017), S. 2(j)].

HIV-positive person. Means a person whose HIV test has been confirmed positive. [Human Immunodeficiency Virus and Acquired Immune Deficiency Syndrome (Prevention and Control) Act (16 of 2017), S. 2(k)].

HIV-related information. Means any information relating to the HIV status of a person and includes—

(*i*) information relating to the undertaking performing the HIV test or result of and HIV test;

(*ii*) information relating to the care, support or treatment of that person;

(*iii*) information which may identify that person; and

(*iv*) any other information concerning that person, which is collected, received, accessed or recorded in connection with an HIV test, HIV treatment or HIV-related research or the HIV status of that person. [[Human Immunodeficiency Virus and Acquired Immune Deficiency Syndrome (Prevention and Control) Act (16 of 2017), S. 2(l)].

HIV test. Means a test to determine the presence of an antibody or antigen of HIV. [Human Immunodeficiency Virus and Acquired Immune Deficiency Syndrome (Prevention and Control) Act (16 of 2017), S. 2(m)].

Hoard. To amass and deposit in secret; to store in excess [CrPC, 1973 (2 of 1974), S. 110(f)(ii)]; a screen or board for display of bill, advertisements *etc.* [Delhi Urban Art Commission Act (1 of 1974), S. 11(2)(f)].

The word 'hoard' in the context means to amass and deposit in secret. *Kamal Prasad* v. *District Magistrate, Saran*, AIR 1975 SC 726, 727, 728. [Maintenance of Internal Security Act (26 of 1971), S. 3(2)]

Hoc quidem perquam durum es sed ita lex scripta est. Hard may be the law, yet it should be given effect to.

Hodgepodge. An unorganized mixture.

Hoist. An elevator, lift etc. [Factories Act (63 of 1948), S. 28(1)(a)].

Hoist or Lift. The words "hoist or lift" do not include a fork lift truck. [Factories Act (63 of 1948), S. 28, margin].

Hold. To have or keep as one's own; to own as property; to be in possession or enjoyment of; to occupy an office [CrPC, 1973 (2 of 1974), S. 13]; the interior cavity in a ship or vessel (or lower deck) where the cargo is stored [Indian Dock Labourers Act (19 of 1934), S. 5(1)(d)].

"Hold" means "to possess by a lawful title". [Black's Law Dictionary (8th Edn.) as cited in *Union of India* v. *Robert Zomawia Street*, (2014) 6 SCC 707, para 10].

"Hold" means, to possess, to be owner or holder or tenant of. [Oxford English Dictionary as cited in *Union of India* v. *Robert Zomawia Street*, (2014) 6 SCC 707, para 11].

"Hold" means "to have the ownership or use of; keep as one's own". [The Random House Dictionary of the English Language (Unabridged Edition) as cited in *Union of India* v. *Robert Zomawia Street*, (2014) 6 SCC 707, para 11].

Hold Court. When a Judge holds Court, he directs, controls, and governs it as the chief officer, and this is also the meaning of the word "preside."

Hold elections. In its wide connotation the phrase will include all steps such as the delimitation of constituencies, the compilation of electoral rolls, etc., which are a necessary preliminary to the actual conduct of elections. In the restricted sense, this phrase would cover only the actual holding of elections. *State of Gujarat* v. *Jamnadas*, AIR 1974 SC 2233, 2238.

Hold out. To represent. [Indian Partnership Act (9 of 1932), S. 28(1)]; [Chartered Accountants Act (38 of 1949), S. 2(2)(ii)].

Hold over. The holding over constitutes merely an enlargement of the term, and the lease is applied thereto with the same force as though it had been re-executed.

Hold the post. There is nothing in the language of Art. 311 to indicate that the Constitution makers intended to make any distinction between persons who hold permanent civil posts and those who officiate in permanent and temporary posts. It is not correct to say that the persons who merely officiate in such posts cannot be said to 'hold' the post on the allegation that they only perform the duties of such posts. *P.L. Dhingra* v. *Union of India*, AIR 1958 SC 36, 43. [Constitution of India, Art. 311]

Hold them both liable. The words "hold them both liable" mean that the party dealing with agent can join both the agent and the principal in one suit. [Indian Contract Act (9 of 1872), S. 233]

Hold up. "Holding up," when used in relation to an attack on a train, is distinctly and universally understood to mean the forcible detention of a train, with intent to commit a robbery or some other felony.

Holder. "HOLDER", in relation to any operating right, means the lessee, licensee or permittee, as the case may be, in respect of such operating right. [Offshore Areas Minerals (Development and Regulation) Act, 2002 (17 of 2003), S. 4(f)]

"HOLDER", in relation to a savings certificate, means—

(i) a person who holds the savings certificate issued in accordance with the provisions of this Act and of any rules made thereunder at any time before the date on which the Finance Bill, 2005 receives the assent of the President; and

(ii) an individual who holds the savings certificate issued in accordance with the provisions of this Act and of any rules made thereunder at any time on or after the date on which the Finance Bill, 2005 receives the assent of the President. [Government Saving Certificates Act (46 of 1959), S. 2(a) *as substituted by Finance Act (18 of 2005), S. 117*]

One who holds; a tenant, occupier, possessor or owner. [Negotiable Instruments Act (26 of 1881), S. 8]; [Constitution of India, Art. 102(1)(a)].

The term "holder" as used in the negotiable instrument law, means the payee or indorsee of a bill or note, who is in possession of it, or the bearer thereof.

The term 'holder' will not include a person who, though in possession of the instrument, has not right to recover the amount due thereon from the parties, such as the finders of a lost instrument payable to bearer or a thief in possession of such an instrument, or even the payee himself, if he is prohibited by an order of court from receiving the amount due on the instrument. *Anjannith* v. *Nagappa,* AIR 1967 AP 61, 63. [Negotiable Instruments Act (26 of 1881), S. 8]

"HOLDER" is a word of similar import to "bearer," and by either of these words a note may be made negotiable by delivery.

The word "holder" in a policy of insurance providing that the same may be converted into cash, "at the option of the holder, at any time after the expiration of 5 years from the date herein," etc., means the person to whom the policy is by its terms payable the owner thereof.

Holder for value. "Every Indorsee of a Bill has his own title and that of each intermediate party; and if he or any of such parties gave value for the bill, without fraud, he is a Holder for Value".

It is also well settled that a pledgee or mortgagee of property is a holder for value.

Holder in due course. "HOLDER IN DUE COURSE" means any person who for consideration became the possessor of a promissory note, bill of exchange or cheque if payable to bearer or the payee or indorsee thereof, if payable to order before the amount mentioned in it became payable, and without having sufficient cause to believe that any defect existed in the title of the person from whom he derived his title. [Negotiable Instruments Act (26 of 1881), S. 9]

A holder in due course is one who holds the instrument free from any defect of the title of prior parties.

One who has taken a bill of exchange complete and regular on the face of it, before it was overdue and who took it in good faith and for value without notice of any defect in it. [Negotiable Instruments Act (26 of 1881), S. 9].

The Indian definition of 'holder in due course' in Negotiable Instruments Act imposes a more stringent condition on the holder than the English definition and it is based on the law laid down in an old English case, *Gill* v. *Cubitt,* (1824) 3 B & C 466. Under the Indian law, a holder, to be a holder in due course, must not only have acquired the bill, note or cheque for valid consideration but should have acquired the cheque without having sufficient cause to believe that any defect existed in the title of the person from whom he derived his title. *U. Ponnappa Moothan Sons* v. *Catholic Syrian Bank Ltd.,* AIR 1991 SC 441.

Holder of a note or bill of exchange. One to whom a note or bill of exchange has been made over (*i.e.*) who is the endorsee or payee of it and who has lawful possession of it for the time being.

"Holder" of a promissory note, bill of exchange or cheque. Means any person entitled in his own name to the possession thereof and to receive or recover the amount due thereon from the parties thereto. Where the note, bill or cheque is lost or destroyed, its holder is the person so entitled at the time of such loss or destruction. [Negotiable Instruments Act (26 of 1881), S. 8]

Holder of a share. The words "holder of a share" denote, in so far as the company is concerned, only a person who as a share-holder, has the claim entered on the register of members. *Howrah Trading Co.* v. *I.T. Commissioner*, AIR 1959 SC 775, 779.

Holder of agricultural land. A holder of agricultural land not exceeding eight hectare of unirrigated land or four hectares of irrigated land within the State as an occupancy tenant or a Government lessee is a holder of agriculture land. *Namdeo* v. *Collector; East Neemar, Khandwa,* AIR 1996 SC 973.

Holders of equity shares. The term "holders of equity shares" means persons whose names are entered in the register of members. *Balakrishnan Gupta* v. *Swadeshi Polytex Ltd.*, AIR 1985 SC 520. [Companies Act (1 of 1956), S. 81(1)(a)]

Holding. "HOLDING" means a share or portion of an estate held by one landowner or jointly by two or more landowners. [Punjab Land Revenue Act (17 of 1887), S. 3(3)].

"Holding" means a parcel or parcels of land held by a raiyat and forming the subject of a separate tenancy. [Orissa Tenancy Act (11 of 1913), S. 3(8) as cited in *State of Orissa* v. *Harapriya Bisoi*, (2009) 12 SCC 378, para 26 : (2009) 4 SCC (Civ) 719] See also *State of Orissa* v. *Fakir Charan Sethi*, (2015) 1 SCC 466, para 14.

"HOLDING" means the total land held by a person as an occupant or tenant, or as both. [Maharashtra Project Affected Persons Rehabilitation Act (32 of 1989), S. 2(8)]

"HOLDING" means land held under one title or agreement and surrounded by one set of boundaries. [Manipur Municipalities Act (43 of 1994), S. 2(21)]

'HOLDING' means the land or land held by a person as a *Bhumidhar, Sirdar, Asami* or *Gaon Sabha* or an *Asami* mentioned in Section 11 of the Uttar Pradesh Zamindari Abolition and Land Reforms Act, 1950, or as a tenant under the U.P. Tenancy Act, 1939, other than a sub-tenant or as a Government lessee, or as a sub-lessee of a Government lessee, where the period of sub-lease is co-extensive with the period of the lease. [U.P. Imposition of Ceiling on Land Holding Act, 1960 (1 of 1961), S. 3(9).

"HOLDING" means a parcel or parcels of land held under a single transaction by a tenant from a landlord and shall include any portion of holding as above defined which the landlord and the tenant have agreed or are bound to treat as a separate holding. [Kerala Land Reforms Act, 1964, S. 2(17)]

The expression as used in the provision means the land held by an intermediary as owner— It is not necessary that such intermediary should have conducted a *hat* or *bazar* on it. *Mosammat Bibi Sayeeda* v. *State of Bihar,* AIR 1996 SC 1936.

"HOLDING" means land held under one title or agreement and surrounded by one set of boundaries. Provided that where two or more adjoining holdings form part and parcel of the site or premises of a dwelling house, manufactory, warehouse or place of trade or business, such holdings shall be deemed to be one holding. [Ben Act (3 of 1884), Municipal, S. 6, cl. 3].

As a parcel or parcels of land held under a single engagement by a tenant as a *kanam* from a *jenmi* and shall include any portion of a holding which the *jenmi* and *kanam* tenant have agreed to treat as a separate holding. *Cochin Devaswom Board, Trichur* v. *Vamana Setti,* AIR 1966 SC 1980.

The land which is held by a person.

'To hold land' means "to be lawfully in actual possession of land as owner or tenant." *Bhikoba Shanker* v. *Mohanlal Punchand*, AIR 1982 SC 865, 870.

Holding a judicial office. The expression "holding a judicial office" signifies more than the discharge of judicial functions while holding some other office. The phrase postulates that there is an office and that the office is primarily judicial. *Statemen (P) Ltd.* v. *H.R. Deb*, AIR 1968 SC 1495, 1500. [Industrial Disputes Act (14 of 1947), S. 7(3)(*d*)]

Holding capacity. Means the maximum number of street vendors who can be accommodated in any vending zone and has been determined as such by the local authority on the recommendations of the Town Vending Committee. [S. 2(1)(b) of the Street Vendors (Protection of Livelihood and Regulation of Street Vending) Act, 2014 (7 of 2014)]

Holding charge. A criminal charge of some minor offence filed to keep the accused in custody while prosecutors take time to build a bigger case and prepare more serious charges.

Holding company. In relation to one or more other companies, means a company of which such companies are subsidiary companies. *Explanation.*—For the purposes of this clause, the expression "company" includes any body corporate [S. 2(46) of the Companies Act, 2013 (18 of 2013)]

Holding in stock. It is wide enough to include cases requiring the millers or the wholesale dealers to sell to the Govt. When he is holding in stock any quantity of rice not on his own account but on account of third party whose paddy has been dehusked by the miller or has been stocked by the miller as Commission Agent provided the liability to sell on such third person. *Teknarayan Mahesh Prasad* v. *State of Bihar,* AIR 1972 Pat 250, 257. [Essential Commodities Act (10 of 1955), S. 3(2)(*f*)]

Holding of an office of profit. For determining whether a person holds an office of profit under a Govt. is the amount of control which the Govt. exercises over that officer. *D.R. Gurushanthappa* v. *Abdul Khuddus Anwar,* AIR 1969 SC 744.

Holding of investments. The expression 'holding of investments' covers not only the Companies whose principal business is the acquisition and holding of shares, debentures, stocks or other securities but also companies whose primary or principal source of income is house property or capital gains as well. *Nawn Estates (P) Ltd.* v. *C.I.T. West Bengal*, AIR 1977 SC 153, 157.

Holding of land. Means the total land held by a person as an owner, occupant or tenant or otherwise. [S. 3(n) of the Right to Fair Compensation & Transparency in Land Acquisition, Rehabilitation & Resettlement Act, 2013 (30 of 2013)]

Holding out. By "holding out a woman to be the wife of another" is meant that the purported husband by language and conduct leads the world to believe that the parties are living, and associating themselves together as husband and wife.

Holding over. The continuance after the termination of the lease of the relation of landlord and tenant with the assent of both parties and the overt act, by which the relation might be continued, may be either the receipt of rent by the landlord, or his assent to the continuance of the tenancy by other act or words. [T.P. Act (4 of 1882), S. 116].

Holds. The expression 'holds' includes a two fold idea of the actual possession of a thing and also of being invested with a legal title. *Handique* v.

Agricultural I.T. Board, Assam, AIR 1966 SC 1191, 1192.

Holds office during the pleasure. Article 310 makes it clear beyond doubt that except as expressly provided by the Constitution, every servant of the Union of India holds office during the pleasure of the President. *Om Prakash* v. *Superintendent of Post Offices,* AIR 1960 J&K 97, 101. [Constitution of India, Arts. 310, 311]

Holiday. A day of exemption or cessation from work (generally does not include Sunday). [Indian Evidence Act (1 of 1872), S. 57(9)].

Holograph. A document, like a will or deed, which is entirely handwritten by its author.

Holograph/Holographic will. Where the entire will is in the handwriting of the testator and has been corrected in various places and the corrections have been initialled by the testator, such a 'holograph will' require very little evidence to prove due execution and attestation of the Will. [*Shashi Kumar Banerjee* v. *Subodh Kumar Banerjee*, AIR 1964 SC 529]

Holography. An authentification technology involving the use of images incorporated into a photopolymer process.

Home. "HOME" means an institution, whether called an orphanage, a home for neglected women or children, a widow's home or by any other name, maintained or intended to be maintained for the reception, care, protection or welfare of women or children. [Orphanages and Other Charitable Homes (Suppression and Control) Act (10 of 1960), S. 2(d)]

The home is the place where men permanently reside, and to which they intend to return when away from it.

A person's home may be in his own house or his hired lodgings.

Residence of one's family. [Emigration Act (7 of 1922), S. 24(2)(i)].

Home-based worker. Means a person engaged in, the production of goods or services for an employer in his home or other premises of his choice other than the workplace of the employer, for remuneration, irrespective of whether or not the employer provides the equipment, materials or other inputs. [Code on Social Security, 2020 (36 of 2020), section 2(36)]

Home consumption. The term denotes goods consumed in the country of their production, or imported goods stored in a bonded warehouse until duty is paid.

The expression "goods imported for home consumption" preclude one from giving an interpretation that the imported goods cannot be at all exported and incline one to hold that, it is only used in contrast to the expression "for warehousing". *M.J. Export Ltd.* v. *C.E. & Gold (Control) Appellate Tribunal*, AIR 1992 SC 2014, 2020. [Customs Act (52 of 1962), S. 68]

Home page. Either the first page loaded by your **browser** at start-up, or the main Web document for a particular group, organisation, or person. (*Information Technology*)

Home Page (or Homepage). Several meanings. Originally, the web page that your browser is set to use when it starts up. The more common meaning refers to the main web page for a business, organization, person or simply the main page out of a collection of web pages, *e.g.* "Check out so-and-so's new Home Page." Usually, the web page automatically loaded when a user starts the web browser which, in modern business can be set by the user. Another sloppier use of the term refers to practically any web page as a "homepage," *e.g.* "that website has 65 homepages and none of them are interesting". (*Internet and E-commerce*).

Homeless person. One who has no living accommodation that he is entitled to occupy or is unlawfully excluded from his own living accommodation, or whose accommodation is mobile and cannot be placed in a location where he is permitted to reside in it.

Homeopathy. Means the system of medicine founded by Dr. Hahnemann and includes the Biochemic system of medicine founded by Dr. Schussler and the expression 'Homeopathic' shall be construed accordingly. [W.B. Homeopathic System of Medicine Act (33 of 1963), S. 2(3)]

Homestead. Any tank appurtenant to the dwelling house. Any dwelling house which is situated in an agricultural or horticultural land, which is intended for the dwelling of persons is a 'homestead' and is included in the definition of land. *K.N. Farms Industries (Pvt.) Ltd.* v. *State of Bihar*, AIR 2009 SC 3031.

"HOMESTEAD" means, unless the context otherwise requires any dwelling house erected by the person permitted to have the use and occupation of any land for the purpose of such erection, and includes any such dwelling house reconstructed by the Kudikidappukaran in accordance with the provisions of Section 79. [Kerala Land Reforms Act, 1963 (1 of 1964), S. 2(25), *Explanation* II(b) as cited in *Madhavi Amma* v. *S. Prasannakumari*, (2013) 4 SCC 77, para 12].

Homestead land. The housestead land is *prima facie* the land where the home of the agriculturist is situated and in which he resides. *Achaibar Missir* v. *Sohan Teli,* AIR 1951 Pat 215.

Homesteads. A homestead is the dwelling-house constituting the family residence, together with the land upon which it is situated and the appurtenances connected therewith.

The term "homestead" includes dwelling-houses in which families reside, with the usual and customary appurtenances, including different buildings of every kind necessary or convenient for family use, and lands for the purpose thereof. If situated in the country, it may include a garden or farm. If situated in town, it may include one or more lots, or one or more blocks. In either case it is limited by extent, merely.

A house with its dependent buildings and offices. [CrPC 1973 (2 of 1974), S. 65].

Homicide. The killing of a human being by another human being. [IPC (45 of 1860), S. 299].

Homicide by misadventure. "Homicide by misadventure" is a term used to denote the accidental killing of another where the slayer is doing a lawful act, unaccompanied by any criminally careless or reckless conduct.

Homicide in self-defence. Homicide in self-defence is homicide committed in the defence of one's own life or that of his family, relatives, or dependents, where the law permits such defence.

Homologue. That which is of the same essential nature. [Workmen's Compensation Act (8 of 1923), Sch. II, pt. B]; [Factories Act (63 of 1948), Sch. II, Entry 9].

Homosexual. People of either gender who are attracted, sexually, emotionally and in relationship, to persons of the same sex. [Michael Kirby, former Judge of the High Court of Australia **as cited in** *Navtej Singh Johar* v. *Union of India,* (2018) 10 SCC 1, para 151].

Homosexual conduct. Sexual behaviour between persons of the same sex.

Honourably Acquitted. 'The expression "honourably acquitted" is one which is unknown to courts of justice. Apparently it is a form of order used in courts martial and other extra-judicial tribunals. We said in our judgment that we accepted the explanation given by the appellant, believed it to be true and considered that it ought to have been accepted by the government authorities and by the Magistrate. Further, we decided that the appellant had not misappropriated the monies referred to in the charge. It is thus clear that the effect of our judgment was that the appellant was acquitted as fully and completely as it was possible for him to be acquitted. Presumably, this is equivalent to what government authorities term "honourably acquitted"'. [*State of Assam* v. *Raghava Rajgopalachari*, 1972 SLR 44 (SC), para 8 as cited in *Deputy Inspector General of Police* v. *S. Samuthiram*, (2013) 1 SCC 598, para 25].

The expression "honourably acquitted" is one which is unknown to Courts of justice. Apparently it is a form of order used in Courts-martial and other extra judicial tribunals. Where on a prosecution for alleged misappropriation, the Court accepted the explanation of the accused and decided that he was not guilty of any misappropriation, the acquittal is full and complete and presumably in the language of the Government authorities, "honourable", (61 Cal 168).

Honorarium. A voluntary fee paid especially to a professional man for his services. [Khadi and Village Industries Commission Act (61 of 1956), S. 14(2), prov.].

Honour. To accept and comply with the terms of (a bill of exchange) [Sale of Goods Act (3 of 1930), S. 25(3)]; respect; high estimation; to accept and pay when due.

Hope. The word "hope", as used in a will, in a clause stating that the testator *hopes* a legatee will make a certain disposition of the fund bequeathed, is a word of intention, which the Court will carry into effect, as if the testator had used an absolute word of devise in trust.

"Hope" is a wishful feeling floating on nebulous foams projected into the unknown future. Deep hidden in "hope" dwells a lingering doubt, a speck of suspicion, that what is desired and expected may not turn out true. Not unoften, in the mind of the person hoping, there lurks subconscious fear that the "hope" may turn out a "dupe". *Channdran* v. *State of Madras*, AIR 1978 SC 1574, 1581.

"Hope" and **"believe".** The word "hope" suggests a lingering doubt that what is desired and expected may not turn out to be true whereas the word "believe", in the sense in which it is used in Section 164(2), has logical confidence or rational conviction as its essential element. *Chandran* v. *The State of Madras,* AIR 1978 SC 1574. [CrPC, 1973 (2 of 1974), S. 164(2)]

Hornbook. A book explaining the basics of a given subject; a textbook containing the rudimentary principles of an area of law.

Horoscope. A horoscope prepared by a person who is dead and who had special means of knowledge and whose handwriting is proved is admissible in evidence under S. 32(5) of the Indian Evidence Act (1 of 1872). (*Nani Gopal* v. *Trustees for the Improvement of Calcutta,* AIR 1938 Cal 43).

Hors de combat. Unfit to fight, disabled. [Geneva Convention Act (6 of 1960), Ist Sch., Art. 3]

Horse. "HORSE" includes ponies, mules, donkeys, asses, other equine animal of both sexes and their young ones. [Madhya Pradesh Horse Sickness Act, 1960, S. 2(a)]

"HORSE includes a Mule"; and applies to any beast of whatever description used for burden or draught, or for carrying persons. [Army Act, 1881, S. 190) and Tolls (Army and Air Force Act (11 of 1901), S. 2(e)].

Horse race. "HORSE RACE" means a horse race upon which wagering or betting may be lawfully made. [Income-tax Act (43 of 1961), S. 74A(3) *Expln.* (b)]

Horticulture. Includes any activity undertaken in respect of obtaining horticulture produce. [Maharashtra Horticulture Development Corporation Act (25 of 1988), S. 2(l)]

It means the cultivation of the garden. *Kasturi* v. *Gaon Sabha,* (1989) 4 SCC 55. [Delhi Land Reforms Act, 1954, S. 3(13)]

Horticulture produce. Includes—

(i) fruit, including fresh, dried or frozen fruits, or by-product of any of them;

(ii) vegetables of any kind grown for human consumption

(iii) spices, nuts *etc.*;

(iv) flowers;

(v) herbs, medicinal plants,

(vi) seeds, plants, trees and other planting material in respect of any of the produce described in sub-clause (i) to (v). [Maharashtra

Horticulture Development Corporation Act, 1988, S. 2(m)]

Hospital. "HOSPITAL" includes family welfare centre, child welfare centre, maternity centre and health centre. [Cantonments Act (2 of 1924), S. 2(xv)]

"HOSPITAL" includes a nursing home, clinic, medical centre, medical or teaching institution for therapeutic purposes and other like institution. [Transplantation of Human Organs Act (42 of 1994), S. 2(g)]

"HOSPITAL" means any premises including a maternity home, nursing home, hospital or any other place not established or maintained by Government Funds, used or intended to be used for storage, supply or artificial insemination of semen. [Delhi Artificial Insemination (Human) Act, 1995 (12 of 1996), S. 2(e)]

"HOSPITAL" means any premises used for the reception of the sick and their treatment as Indoor patient. [Orissa Clinical Establishments (Control and Regulation) Act, 1990 (4 of 1992), S. 2(d)]

"HOSPITAL" means an institution for the reception and care of sick, wounded, infirm or aged persons, and includes government or private hospitals, nursing homes and clinics. [Noise Pollution (Regulation and Control) Rules, 2000, R. 2(f)]

Hospital/Nursing Home/Clinic shall be deemed to mean any institution in India operated for the care and treatment of sickness and injuries and which has been registered either as a Hospital or Nursing Home or Clinic with the local authorities and is under the supervision of a registered and qualified Doctor.

The term "Hospital" shall not include an establishment which is a place of rest, a place for the aged, a place for drug addicts, a place of alcoholics or a hotel. [Scheme of Hospitalisation and Domiciliary Hospitalisation Benefit Policy, Specified for the purpose of section 80D of the Income-tax Act (43 of 1961)]

"HOSPITAL" means the precincts of the hospital and includes the precincts of any institution for the reception and treatment of persons during convalescence or of persons requiring medical attention or rehabilitation. [*Explanation* (b) to S. 376(2) of IPC, 1860 (45 of 1860), as substituted by the Criminal Laws (Amendment) Act, 2013 (13 of 2013). Also see *Explanation* 4 to S. 376C of IPC, 1860 (45 of 1860), as substituted by the Criminal Laws (Amendment) Act, 2013 (13 of 2013)] [Now (w.e.f. 1-7-2024) repealed & replaced by Bharatiya Nayaya Sanhita, 2023 (45 of 2023), section 64(2), *Explanation* (b), same definition in new Sanhita]

Hospital project. Means a project for constructing a hospital with at least one hundred beds for patients. [Income-tax Act (43 of 1961), S. 10(23G), *Expln.* 1(h)]

Host. A remote computer used by the Internet Service Provider to connect the user to the Internet. (*Internet*)

Your host is the computer you contact to get on to the Net. (*Information Technology*)

Any computer on a *network* that is a repository for services available to other computers on the *network.* it is quite common to have one host machine provide several services, such as *SMTP* (email) and *HTTP* (web). (*Matisse Enzer-Glossary of Internet Terms*)

Any computer on a network that is a repository for services available to other computers on the network. It is quite common to have one host machine provide several services, such as WWW and USENET. (*Internet and E-commerce*)

Host country. Means the country in which the foreign entity receiving the direct investment from an Indian party is registered or incorporated. [Foreign Exchange Management (Transfer of Issue of any Foreign Security) Regulations, 2000, Reg. 2(j)]

Host bank. Means the financial institution hosting the repayment account. [Insolvency and Bankruptcy Board of India (Information Utilities) Regulations, 2017, Regn. 2(1)(f)].

Hostage. A person given up to an enemy as a security for the due performance of a contract between belligerent powers.

"HOSTAGE" means a passenger or a crew member of an aircraft or any security personnel on board the aircraft or a ground support staff involved in the maintenance of the aircraft, who is unlawfully seized or detained without his consent, or with his consent obtained by fraud or duress, by an individual or by a group of persons, during the transit of an aircraft or when it is stationed at an airport, with an intention to secure any demand or fulfillment of any condition made by such individual or such group of persons. [Anti-Hijacking Act (30 of 2016), S. 2(f)].

Hosticide. A person who kills an enemy; the killing of an enemy.

Hostile. In order to obtain leave to cross-examine, all that is necessary is that the witness's testimony should have been adverse to the party calling him and that the value of the witness's testimony is to be judged in the light of the results of such cross-examination. It is unreasonable that the good or bad faith of a witness instead of being judged by the test of cross-examination should be held to be prejudged by the mere fact that cross-examination is permitted.

Hostile attack. 'HOSTILE ATTACK' means any attack by any person or body of persons, whether during any war, external aggression, internal disturbance or otherwise which endangers the security of any life, property, place or thing in India or any part of the territory thereof. [Civil Defence Act (27 of 1968), S. 2(c)]

Hostile environment sexual harassment. Sexual harassment that has the effect of unreasonably interfering with a victim's work performance or creating an intimidating, hostile, or offensive working environment that affects the victim's psychological well-being.

Hostile possession. Possession which is asserted against the claims of all others, including the record owner.

Hostile takeover. Attempt to purchase control of a company that is unwelcome to some of the target's shareholders and directors.

Hostile witness. The witness who makes statements adverse to the party calling and examining him, and who may, with the permission of the Court, be cross-examined by that party.

A hostile witness is a witness who, from the manner in which he gives his evidence, shows that he is not desirous of telling the truth to the Court.

Hostility. Act of warfare; war [Naval and Aircraft Prize Act (59 of 1971), S. 2(c); Indian Soldiers (Litigation) Act (4 of 1925), S. 3(b) and Indian Evidence Act (1 of 1872), S. 57(11)].

Hot spot. The only place on earth where a certain endangered specie is found.

Hot state. Means a state in whose territory a United Nations operation is conducted. [U.N. Convention on the Safety of United Nations and Associated Personnel GA 49/59, 17 Feb 1995, Art. 1(d)]

Hotch pot. Blending and mixing of property belonging to different persons in order to divide it.

Hotch-potch. A commixture of property in order to secure an equable division amongst children; in Hindu Law joint property of the Hindu undivided family.

Hotel. Includes a refreshment room, a boarding house, a lodging house, a coffee house and a café. [Protection of Civil Rights Act (22 of 1955), S. 2(aa)]

"HOTEL" includes a building or part of a building where residential accommodation is, by way of business, provided for a monetary consideration. [Hotel Receipts tax Act (54 of 1980), S. 2(6) and Expenditure tax Act (35 of 1987), S. 2(6)]

Hotel or lodging house. Means a building or a part of a building where lodging, with or without board or other services, is provided for a monetary consideration. [Delhi Rent Act (33 of 1995), S. 2(d)]

Hotel project. Means a project for constructing a hotel of not less than three-star category as classified by the Central Government. [Income-tax Act (43 of 1961), S. 10(23G), *Expln.* 1(g) Now omitted by the Finance Act, 2006 (w.e.f. 1-4-2007)]

Hotelier. Means the owner of the hotel and includes the person who for the time being is in charge of the management of the hotel. [Maharashtra Tax on Luxuries (in hotels and Lodging Houses) Act (41 of 1987), S. 2(f)]

Hours of darkness. The time between half an hour after sunset and half an hour before sunrise.

Hours of work. Means the time during which a motor transport worker is at the disposal of the employer or of any other person entitled to claim his services and includes—

(i) the time spent in work done during the running time of the transport vehicle;

(ii) the time spent in subsidiary work; and

(iii) periods of mere attendance at terminals of less than fifteen minutes.

Note:—The phrases "running time" "subsidiary work" and "period of mere attendance" explained under the heading *Explanation* to this section, have been incorporated under respective alphabets. [Motor Transport Workers Act (27 of 1961), S. 2(f)]

House. A place of dwelling or habitation. [CrPC 1973 (2 of 1974), S. 65].

"HOUSE" includes schools; also factories and other buildings in which persons are employed. [Bur. Act XIX of 1884 (Rangoon Water Works), S. 2, cl. 4].

"HOUSE" includes any hut, shop, warehouse or building. [Ben Act (3 of 1884) (Municipal), S. 6, cl. 4]

'HOUSE' means either House of Parliament or the Legislative Assembly or, as the case may be, either House of the Legislature of a State. [Constitution of India, Tenth Schedule, 1(a)]

"HOUSE" means a house suitable for occupation by a Military Officer or a military mess. The term includes the land and buildings appurtenant to a house. [Cantonment (House Accommodation) Act (6 of 1923), S. 2(f)]

'HOUSE' includes any building or part of a building with its appurtenances and outhouses used for any purpose whatsoever. [Orissa House Rent Control Act, 1967 (4 of 1968), S. 2(3)]

"HOUSE" means any hut, shop, warehouse, workshop, masonry or framed. [Manipur Municipalities Act (43 of 1994), S. 2(22)]

The word 'house' clearly means a building in the ordinary sense of the word, and such building need not necessarily be always for the habitation of man or beast.

The term 'house' in the statute in reference to gambling houses, includes a boat equipped to carry on gambling business.

The word 'house' is sometimes used as an equivalent expression for the word 'firm'.

Generally "house" is a structure of permanent character. It is structurally severable from other tenements and it includes a house used for business. *Tata E and L Co.* v. *Gram Panchayat Pimpri*, AIR 1976 SC 2463, 2467.

Each of the rooms in a building does not constitute independent building, even though it has an independent access. *Bijay Singh Suvana* v. *Land Acquisition, Collector of Calcutta,* AIR 1990 Cal 246, 252. [Land Acquisition Act (1 of 1894), S. 49]

House arrest. 1. Electronic Monitoring Surveillance. Sentence imposed on a convicted criminal ordering that person to remain in the individual's home for a specified period of time instead of going to prison. 2. Involuntary confinement of anti-government political activists to their private residences in dictatorial and communist countries to reduce contacts with their associates and the media. (*Ballentine's Law Dictionary, 3rd Edn.*)

Cofining a person accused or convicted of crime to his home.

House-breaking. "A person is said to commit "house-breaking" who commits house trespass if he effects his entrance into the house or any part of it in any of the six ways herein after described; or if, being in the house or any part of it for the purpose of committing an offence, or having committed an offence therein, he quits the house or any part of it in any of the six ways, that is to say:—

First.—If he enters or quits through a passage made by himself, or by any abettor of the house-trespass, in order to the committing of the house trespass.

Secondly.—If he enters or quits through any passage not intended by any person, other than himself or an abettor of the offence, for human entrance; or through any passage to which he has obtained access by scaling or climbing over any wall or building.

Thirdly.—If he enters or quits through any passage which he or any abettor of the house-trespass has opened, in order to committing of the house-trespass by any means by which that passage was not intended by the occupier of the house to be opened.

Fourthly.—If he enters or quits by opening any lock in order to the committing of the house trespass, or in order to the quitting of the house after a house-trespass.

Fifthly.—If he effects his entrance or departure by using criminal force or committing an assault, or by threatening any person with assault.

Sixthly.—If he enters or quits by any passage which he knows to have been fastened against such entrance or departure, and to have been unfastened by himself or by an abettor of the house-trespass.

Explanation.—Any out-house or building occupied with a house, and between which and such house there is an immediate internal communication, is the part of the house within the meaning of this section." [IPC (45 of 1860), S. 445] [(w.e.f. 1-7-2024) repealed and replaced by Bharatiya Nyaya Sanhita, 2023 (45 of 2023), section 330(2)].

House-breaking by night. Whoever commits house-breaking after sunset and before sunrise, is said to commit "house-breaking by night." [IPC (45 of 1860), S. 446].

House Committee. A committee of a legislature which deals with the accommodation of its members; it also supervises other facilities such as medical aid, food *etc.* provided to the members; it is an advisory committee.

House drain. Means any drain of, and used for the drainage of, one or more buildings or premises and made merely for the purpose of communicating therefrom with a municipal drain. [Maharashtra Municipalities Act (11 of 1965), 2(17)]

"House-gully" or "service passage". "HOUSE-GULLY" means a passage or strip of land constructed, set apart or utilized for the purpose of serving as a drain or of affording access to a privy, urinal, cesspool or other receptacle for filthy or polluted matter, to municipal servants or to person employed in the cleansing thereof or in the removal of such matter therefrom. [Bom Act 3 of 1888 (City Bom Municipal), S. 3, cl. (v)]

"HOUSE-GULLY" means a passage or strip of land constructed, set apart or utilised for the purpose of serving as or carrying a drain or affording access to a latrine, urinal, cesspool or other receptacle for filth or other polluted matter, by municipal employee or other person employed in the cleansing thereof or in the removal of such matter therefrom. [New Delhi Municipal Council Act (44 of 1994), S. 2(18)]

"HOUSE-GULLY" or "SERVICE PASSAGE" means a passage or strip of land constructed, set apart or utilised, for the purpose of serving as or carrying a drain or affording access to a latrine, privy, urinal, cesspool or other receptacle of filthy or polluted matter by municipal employees or other persons employed in the cleansing thereof or in the removal of such matter therefrom, and includes the air-space above such passage or land. [Manipur Municipalities Act (43 of 1994), S. 2(23)]

House-keeper. One who keeps or occupies a house, as distinguished from a mere boarder or lodger.

House of Assembly. By the provisions of the Government of India Act, 1935, it has been indicated that the Legislature at the Centre was 'bi-cameral'. The Lower Chamber was called 'House of Assembly'. The Upper Chamber was called 'Council of States'. *Kuldip Nayar* v. *UOI*, AIR 2006 SC 3127 : 2006 AIR SCW 4394.

House of Commons. The Lower House of the English Parliament.

House of Lords. The Upper House of the English Parliament.

House of the People. The Lower House of the Indian Parliament. [Constitution of India, Art. 79].

House property. 'House Property' means not only the house and the site on which the house stands but also the site appurtenant to the house and which is necessary for its enjoyment. It includes garden, compound and yard, which are enjoyed as part of the house. *Subbarayulu* v. *Venkataramanamma,* AIR 1953 Mad 540.

House rent. Includes shop rent.

House-trespass. Whoever commits criminal trespass by entering into or remaining in any building, tent or vessel used as a human dwelling or any building used as a place of worship, or as a place for custody of property, is said to commit "house trespass."

Explanation.—The introduction of any part of the criminal trespasser's body is entering sufficient to constitute house-trespass. [IPC (45 of 1860), S. 442] [(w.e.f. 1-7-2024) repealed and replaced by Bharatiya Nyaya Sanhita, 2023 (45 of 2023), section 329(2)].

Household goods. Household goods "mean every article of a permanent nature which is not consumed in its enjoyment".

Householder. "HOUSE HOLDER" means a person who occupies any premises as his dwelling. [Maharashtra Keeping and Movement of Cattle in Urban Areas (Control) Act (45 of 1976), S. 2(c)]

Master or chief of a family; one who keeps house with his family.

The word 'house-keeper' will generally be understood to have reference to a person who performs services in the taking care of a house in connection with the inmates residing therein.

Householder will not include a lodger or temporary inmate.

Houses and other buildings. The words "houses and other buildings" in S. 60(1)(*c*), CPC (5 of 1908), mean not only the residential house lived in by the agriculturist but also the other buildings occupied by him.

'Houses', 'both Houses', either House and 'House. The expressions 'Houses', both 'Houses', 'either Houses' and 'the House' in the context of Arts. 79, 83, 85 of the Constitution are used synonymously with the institutions known as the Council of States and House of the People and are interchangeable expression. *Election Commission, in Re spl. Reference No.* 1-2002 *Gujarat Election Matter,* (2002) 8 SCC 237, para 62. [Constitution of India, Arts. 79, 83, 85, 143]

Housing estate. 'HOUSING ESTATE' means a group of houses built by the authority for dwelling purposes and may comprise all or any of the following namely:

(a) a dwelling unit;

(b) land under and appurtenant to such dwelling unit.

(c) roads and paths, sewers, storm water drains, street lighting and other similar amenities;

(d) open spaces intended for recreations and ventilations.

(e) convenient shopping, schools, community halls or other amenity for common use. [Delhi Development Authority (Management and Disposal of Housing Estates) Regulations, 1968, Regn. 2(23)]

Housing finance company. For the purposes of section 80EE of Act 43 of 1961, 'housing finance company' means a public company formed or registered in India with the main object of carrying on the business of providing long-term finance for construction or purchase of houses in India for residential purposes. [(w.e.f. 1-4-2014) S. 80EE(5)(*b*) of the Income-tax Act, 1961 (43 of 1961)]

Housing finance institution. Includes every institution, whether incorporated or not, which primarily transacts or has as its principal object, the transacting of the business of providing finance for housing whether directly or indirectly. [National Housing Bank Act (53 of 1987), S. 2(d)]

Housing project. Means a project for—

(i) the construction of any building, road, bridge or other structure in any part of India;

(ii) the execution of such other work (of whatever nature) as may be prescribed. [Income-tax Act (43 of 1961), S. 80HHBA (2), *Expln.* (a)]

Housing society. Means a society, the object of which is to provide its members with open plots for housing, dwelling houses or flats, or if open plots, the dwelling houses or flats are already acquired, to provide its members common ameneties and services. [Maharashtra Co-operative Societies (Second Amendment) Act, 1985 (20 of 1986), S. 2(16)]

Hovercraft. A vehicle which is designed to be supported when in motion wholly or partly by air expelled from the vehicle to form a cushion of air of which the boundaries include the ground, water or other surface beneath the vehicle.

Hoverport. Any area, whether on land or elsewhere, which is designed, equipped, set apart or commonly used for affording facilities for the arrival and departure of hovercraft.

Housing trust. A trust set up to provide housing, or whose funds are devoted to charitable purposes.

However. The word 'however' in a deed or will indicates an alternative intention, a contrast with the previous clause, and a modification of it under certain circumstances.

HSCSD. (*abbr.*) High Speed Circuit Switched Data. Circuit-switched data service, unlike GPRS, which is packet-switched. It is therefore suitable even for time-critical applications. Data transfer rates up to 57.6 kbit/s per user are possible. (*Telecommunication*)

HTML. Hypertext mark-up language. The language used to create documents on the www. (*Information Technology*)

Hypertext Markup Language is the encoding scheme used to create and format a web document. A user need not be an expert programmer to make use of HTML to create hypertext documents that can be put on the Internet. [NIIT] (*Internet*)

(*abbr.*) Hyper Text Markup Language. The coding language used to create *Hypertext* documents for use on the *World Wide Web.* HTML looks a lot like old-fashioned typesetting code, where you surround a block of text with codes that indicate how it should appear additionally; in HTML you can specify that a block of text, or a word, is linked to another file on the Internet. HTML files are meant to be viewed using a World Wide Web Client Program, such as Netscape or Mosaic. *See also* Client, Server, WWW. (*Internet and E-commerce*)

The "hyper" in Hypertext comes from the fact that in HTML you can specify that a block of test, or an image, is linked to another file on the Internet. HTML files are meant to be viewed using a "Web Browser".

HTML is loosely based on a more comprehensive system for markup called SGML. (*Matisse Enzer-Glossary of Internet Terms*)

HTTP. Hypertext Transfer Protocol is state-less, *i.e.* there is no continuous connection between the server and the client computers. The server simply receives a request from the browser, at which time a connection is established, and sends back the requested data, after which the connection is severed. If the browser wants more data, a new connection is established. This is a one transaction and out delivery mechanism. Hence, every time a browser requests data a new session is established between the browser and the server. [NIIT] (*Internet*)

Hyper Text Transfer Protocol. The protocol for moving *hypertext* files across the *Internet.* Requires a HTTP *client* program on one end, and an HTTP *server* program on the other end. HTTP is the most important protocol used in the *World Wide Web (WWW).* (*Matisse Enzer-Glossary of Internet Terms*)

Hukamnama. *Hukamnama* which a *jagirdar* has to pay to the government under Section 190(1) of the Marwar Land Revenue Act, 1949, upon recognition being according to his succession to the *jagir* is not a tribute within the meaning of Section 2(r) of the Rajasthan Land Reforms and Resumption of Jagirs Act, 1952). *Thakur Bahadur Singh* v. *State of Rajasthan,* AIR 1961 SC 1338.

Human dwelling. The determining factor to find out whether a place is a human dwelling or not within the meaning of S. 442, IPC (45 of 1860), is not the existence of the shutters or the fact that the door was shut or open at the time of entry by the accused but the nature of the structure as a whole and the purpose for which it was intended to be and was being used.

Human law. Human laws, as distinguished from divine laws, are those having man for their author.

Human organ. Means any part of a human body consisting of a structured arrangement of tissues which, if wholly, removed, cannot be replicated by the body. [Transplantation of Human Organs Act (42 of 1994), S. 2(h)]

Human right. Right to acquire property is a 'human right'. *Chandigarh Housing Board* v. *Devinder Singh,* AIR 2007 SC 1723 : 2007 AIR SCW 2724.

Human rights. "HUMAN RIGHTS" means the right relating to life, liberty, equality and dignity of the individual guaranteed by the Constitution or embodied in the International Covenants and enforceable by Courts in India. [Protection of Human Rights Act, 1993 (10 of 1994), S. 2(d)]

Humanities. The branches of learning regarded as having primarily a cultural character and usually including languages, literature, history, mathematics and philosophy. [Institutes of Technology Act (59 of 1961), S. 14(d)].

Humidity. Moisture; a moderate degree of wetness. [Factories Act (63 of 1948), S. 15(1)].

Hundi. A bill of exchange.

Hundred per cent export oriented undertaking. For the purposes of this sub-section "HUNDRED PER CENT EXPORT ORIENTED UNDERTAKING" means an undertaking which has been approved as a hundred per cent export oriented undertaking by the board appointed in this behalf by the Central Government in exercise of the powers conferred by Section 14 of the Industries (Development and Regulation) Act, 1951 (65 of 1951), and the rules made under that Act. [Central Excise Act (1 of 1944), S. 3, *Explanation 2*].

Hung Parliament. Parliament wherein no Party has won a working majority. (*Constitutional and Parliamentary Term*)

Hunt. "HUNT" means to hunt, kill or capture any animal or bird by any method and includes every attempt to kill or capture it, or to take or destroy any part of its body or eggs or nest, or to disturb its eggs or nest. [Gujarat Wild Animals and Wild Birds Protection Act (32 of 1963), S. 2(e)] See also *Chief Forest Conservator* v. *Nisar Khan,* (2003) 4, SCC 595 para 13 : AIR 2003 SC 1805.

Hunting. With its grammatical variations and cognate expressions, includes,

(a) capturing, killing, poisoning, snaring and trapping of any wild animal and every attempt to do so;

(b) driving any wild animal for any of the purposes specified in sub-clauses (a);

(c) injuring or destroying or taking any part of the body of any such animal or, in the case of wild birds or reptiles, damaging the eggs of such birds or reptiles, or disturbing the eggs or nests of such birds or reptiles. [Wild Life (Protection) Act (53 of 1972), S. 2(16)]

Hurt. "Whoever causes bodily pain, disease or infirmity to any person is said to cause hurt." [IPC (45 of 1860), S. 319].

The word 'hurt' includes both physical and mental pain.

To cause pain to; to damage; a bodily injury. [IPC (45 of 1860), S. 319] [(w.e.f. 1-7-2024) repealed and replaced by Bharatiya Nyaya Sanhita, 2023 (45 of 2023), section 114].

Husband. "HUSBAND" shall mean a married man domiciled in India, who shall have completed the age of sixteen years, and shall not be a Christian, a Muhammadan nor a Jew. [Converts' Marriage Dissolution Act (21 of 1866), S. 3(a)]

A man joined to a woman by marriage. [Indian Evidence Act (1 of 1872), S. 120].

'Husband', as used in the will of a woman who had obtained a void divorce from a legal husband, and who afterwards went through a form of marriage with another man, with whom she lived, the will reciting that the testatrix was the wife of the person with whom she had thus lived, and providing as follows: "I give and bequeath to my husband one-half of my personal property," is construed to mean the person with whom the testatrix has been living up to the time of her death and not her legal husband.

It would be appropriate to construe the expression 'husband' to cover a person who enters into marital relationship and under colour of such proclaimed or feigned status of husband subjects the woman concerned to cruelty or coerces her in any manner or for any of the purposes enumerated in Ss. 304-B, 498 of IPC (45 of 1860). *Reema Aggarwal* v. *Anupam,* (2004) SCC 199, 210, para 18.

Husband and Wife are made so by marriage, and being thus joined, are accounted but one person in law.

The word 'wife' or 'husband' is clearly indicative of a marital relationship. The relationship of husband and wife must subsist at the time of the accrual of the income. *P.J.P. Thomas* v. *I.T. Commissioner*, AIR 1964 SC 587, 592.

The word "access" between husband and wife means no more than opportunity of intercourse and does not imply actual co-habitation.

"HUSBAND AND WIFE" the bare fact that man and woman live as 'husband and wife' it does not at any rate normally give them the status of husband and wife even though they may hold themselves before the society as husband and wife and the society treats them as husband and wife. *Surjit Kaur* v. *Garja Singh*, AIR 1994 SC 135. Also see, *Koppisetti Subbharao alias Subramaniam* v. *State of A.P.*, AIR 2009 SC 2684.

HUSBAND, SPOUSE. The *husband* designates the physical quality, the *spouse* answers to the spouse as one party to another, the *spouse* the social connection. The *husband* answers to the wife, as the man to the woman. The *spouse* is the higher, more spiritual term, the *husband* is the head of the wife, over whom he has legal rights. The *spouse* is the partner of the wife in moral as well as natural union. (*Smith Syn. Dis.*)

Husbandry. The business of a farmer; tillage.

Hush money. A money paid to induce a person to stifle a prosecution, or to refrain from giving evidence or information.

Hut. HUT means any building, no material portion of which above the plinth level is constructed of masonry or of squared timber framing or of iron framing. [Cantonments Act (2 of 1924), S. 2(xvi)]

'Hut' means dwelling house constructed by a person other than the person permitted to occupy it—

(i) at a cost at the time of construction, not exceeding seven hundred and fifty rupees; or

(ii) which could have at the time of construction yielded a monthly rent not exceeding five rupees, and includes any such dwelling house reconstructed by the Kudikidappukaran in accordance with the provisions of section 79. [Kerala Land Reforms Act, 1963 (1 of 1964), S. 2(25) *Explanation* II(a) as cited in *Madhavi Amma* v. *S. Prasannakumari*, (2013) 4 SCC 77, para 12].

"HUT" means any building which is constructed principally of wood, mud, leaves, grass or thatch and includes any temporary structure of whatever size or any small building of whatever materials made which a village Panchayat may declare to be a hut for the purposes of this Act. [Kerala Panchayat Raj Act (13 of 1994), S. 2(xx)]

"HUT" means any building which is constructed principally of wood, bamboo, mud, leaves, grass, cloth or thatch and includes any structure of whatever material made which the Council may declare to be a hut for the purposes of this Act. [New Delhi Municipal Council Act (44 of 1994), S. 2(19)]

"HUT" means any building, which is constructed principally of wood, bamboo, mud, leaves, grass or thatch and includes any temporary structure of whatever size or any small building of whatever material made. [Manipur Municipalities Act (43 of 1994), S. 2(24)]

The expression 'hut' cannot be restricted only to huts or cottages intended to be lived in. It will also take in any shed, hut or other crude or third class construction consisting of an enclosure made of mud or by poles supporting a tin or asbestos roof that can be put to use for any purpose—residential or non-residential, in the same manner as any other first class construction. The Tamil word 'kaichalai' denotes a structure or a roof put up by hand. *Suryakumar Govindjee* v. *Krishnammal,* (1990) 4 SCC 343, 350. [T.N. Buildings (Lease and Rent Control) Act, 1960, S. 2(2)]

Hybrid. Means any security which has the character of more than one type of security, including their derivatives. [Companies Act (1 of 1956), S. 2(19A) now replaced by the Companies Act, 2013]

Hybrid award. Award in the instant case by arbitrator have to be described as hybrid which are partly speaking and partly non-speaking awards. *Bharat Coking Coal Ltd.* v. *L.K. Ahuja and Co.*, AIR 2001 SC 1179. [Arbitration Act (10 of 1940), S. 14, 30 and 33]

Hybrid bill. A hybrid bill is a Bill before Parliament which is general in application and, accordingly, a public Bill, but which in its application particularly affects private or local interests and which is accordingly referred to the Examiners of Private Bills, and is treated in its intermediate stages generally in the same way as a Private Bill but ultimately becomes a public Act. (*Walker*) (*U.K.*)

Hybrid cloud. A hybrid cloud is a composition of two or more clouds (private or public) that remain separate cloud entities but share certain technology which permits interoperability. [Saurabh Srivastava, 'Cloud Computing is a game changer for Indian Businesses,' Financial Express, September 20, 2010].

Hybrid debt capital instruments. In this category, fall a number of capital instruments, which combine certain characteristics of equity and certain characteristics of debt. Each has a particular feature, which can be considered to affect its quality as capital. [*ML Tannan Banking Law & Practice in India*, Vol. 2, 2021, LexisNexis, Dictionary of Banking Terminology].

Hybrid security. 'Hybrid security' means 'A security with features of a debt instrument (such as a bond) and an equity interest (such as share or stock).' [Black's Law Dictionary (8th Edn.) as cited in *Sahara India Real Estate Corporation Limited* v. *Securities and Exchange Board of India*, (2013) 1 SCC 1, para 184].

Hydrants. A connection for attaching a hose to a water-main or a fire-plug. [Cantonments Act (2 of 1924), S. 2(xxxix)].

Hydrocarbon. Means very large group of chemical compounds composed of carbon and hydrogen. [Offshore Areas Minerals (Development and Regulation) Act, 2002 (17 of 2003), S. 4(g)]

Hydrological drought. "Hydrological drought" is deficiencies in surface and subsurface water supplies leading to a lack of water for normal and specific needs. Such conditions arise, even in times of average (or above average) precipitation when increased usage of water diminishes the reserves. [*Swaraj Abhiyan* v. *Union of India*, (2016) 7 SCC 498, para 36].

Hypertext. Transfer protocol is the standard method of transferring HTML documents between browsers and web servers. (*Information Technology*)

Hypothecate. A contract by which specified property is hypothecated for the performance of an act, signifies that possession is not an incident of the mortgage, and the fact of possession is entirely distinct from the contract of hypothecation.

Hypothecation. "HYPOTHECATION" means a charge in or upon any movable property, existing or future, created by a borrower in favour of a secured creditor without delivery of possession of the movable property to such creditor, as a security for financial assistance and includes floating charge and crystallization of such charge into fixed charge on movable property. [Securitisation and Reconstruction of Financial Assets and Enforcement of Security Interest Act (54 of 2002), S. 2(1)(n)]

Hypothecation is defined as "a right which a creditor has over a thing belonging to another, and which consists in the power to cause it to be sold in order to be paid his claim out of the proceeds."

Pledging or pawning; a lien on property. [T.P. Act (4 of 1882), and S. 4(3)(b), Coking Coal Mines (Emergency Provisions) Act (64 of 1971), S. 3(c)].

Hypothesis. Pledging or pawning; a lien on property [T.P. Act (4 of 1882), S. 3(c) and Coking Coal Mines (Emergency Provisions) Act (64 of 1971), S. 4(3)(b)].

Hypothetical dispute. Issues based on mere supposition.

Hypothetical question. A trial which solicits an expert witness's opinion based on assumptions treated as facts established by evidence.

Hypothecation. Hypothecation : Pledge. In case of a pledge, the security is in possession of the pledge, but in the case of hypothecation, the possession remains with the owner i.e., the pawnor. Though such a distinction exists, yet it is an accepted legal principle the hypothecation is treated as a sub-species of pledge and virtually, has the same legal effect. [*Infrastructure Leasing and Financial Services Limited* v. *BPL Limited*, (2015) 3 SCC 363, para 51].

I

Ibid. *Ibidem*; in the same place. In the same book or passage.

Ibidem. Frequency abbreviated as *ibid*, meaning in the same place, book or page.

Id certum est quod certum reddi potest; sed id magis certum est quod de semet ipso est certum. That is certain which can be made certain, but that is most certain which is certain on the face of it. (*Latin for Lawyers*)

Id idem. The same.

Id, quod nostrum est, sine facto nostro ad alium transferri non potest. What belongs to us cannot be transferred to another without our consent.

Iddat. A free woman married by a valid contract should keep *iddat* for the death of her husband during four months and ten days when she is not pregnant, whatever be her age, whether she is a child or full grown, and whether her husband had arrived at maturity or not. ...... If she is pregnant, the *iddat* is the largest of the two periods, that is, it is prolonged to delivery, if that should not occur till after the expiration of four months and ten days from her husband's death, whereas if she is delivered before the expiration of that time she is to wait for its completion.

Iddat period. Means, in the case of a divorced woman,—

(i) three menstrual courses after the date of divorce, if she is subject to menstruation,

(ii) three lunar months after her divorce if she is not subject to menstruation, and

(iii) if she is enceinte at the time of her divorce, the period between the divorce and the delivery of her child or the termination of her pregnancy, whichever is earlier. [Muslim Women's (Protection of Rights on Divorce) Act (25 of 1986), S. 2(b)]

Idea. An object of the mind existing in apprehension, thought or conception.

IDEA, NOTION, CONCEPTION, PERCEPTION, SENSATION. The perceiving of something external by the mind through the senses is called a *sensation*; the image as it exists in the mind as a matter of reflexion is an *idea*. When two or more ideas are combined so that the expression of them would take the form of an affirmation, this is a *notion*. *Conception* is a conscious act of the understanding, assimilating objects or impressions.

Sensation is physical, and *perception* that operation of the mind in regard to external things which follows and is based upon sensation. (*Smith Syn. Dis.*)

Idem est facere et nolle prohibere cum possis. It is the same thing to do a thing as not to prohibit it when in your power.

Idem est nihil dicere et insufficienter dicere. (*Lat.*) It is the same thing to say nothing and not to say enough.

Idem est non probari et non esse : non deficit jus sed probatio. What is not proved and what does not exist, are the same; it is not a defect of the law, but of proof.

Idem sonans. (*Lat.*) "Of the same sound," or sounding the same".

Identical. The very same; expressing or resulting in identity. Exactly similar for all practical purposes.

Identifiable constituent. If the component is capable of identification by a chemical or other test as a component of a finished product falling within the schedule, it would be an identifiable constituent within the meaning of S. 3(3) Explanation. *State of Madras* v *H.R. K. Naidu*, AIR 1970 SC 1027, 1028. [Tamil Nadu General Sales Tax Act (1 of 1959), S. 3(3), *Explanation*].

Identification. Proof in a legal proceeding that a person, document, or other thing is that which it is alleged to be. Establishment of identity.

Evidence of identity; to identify a person or thing is to show that he or it is the person or thing in question. [CPC (5 of 1908), O. VII, R. 17 (2)].

Identification number. Means the limited liability partnership identification number or the corporate identity number, as the case may be, of the corporate person. [Insolvency and Bankruptcy (Application to Adjudicating Authority) Rules, 2016, R. 3(1)(f)].

Identification parade. A parade conducted in order to test if a witness is able to identify the accused.

Identified goods. The goods of which the identity has been established. [Sale of Goods Act (3 of 1930), S. 2(14)].

Identify. To determine the identity of.

Identifying. Includes establishment of a proof that the property was derived from, or used in, the commission of an offence. [CrPC, 1973 (2 of 1974), S. 105A(b)] [Now (w.e.f. 1-7-2024) repealed & replaced by Bharatiya Nagarik Suraksha Sanhita, 2023 (46 of 2023)]

In this Chapter, unless the context otherwise requires "identifying" includes establishment of a proof that the property was derived from, or used in, the commission of an offence. [(w.e.f. 1-7-2024) Bharatiya Nagarik Suraksha Sanhita, 2023 (46 of 2023), section 111(b)]

"IDENTIFYING" includes establishment of proof that the property was derived from, or used in, the illegal hunting and trade of wild life and its products. [Wild life (Protection) Act (53 of 1972), S. 58B(f)]

Identity. (*In Patent Law*). Such sameness between two designs, invention or combinations as will constitute the one an infringement of the patent granted to the other.

In the law of evidence, the authenticity of a person or thing.

The quality or condition of being the same; absolute or essential sameness; oneness.

Identity card. A card which establishes the identity of the holder. [Representation of the People Act (43 of 1951), S. 61(b)].

Identity change. Merely because the steel tube is galvanised it does not mean that it ceases to be a steel tube. *Gujarat Steel Tubes* v. *State of Kerala,* AIR 1990 SC 1779.

Identity of interests. In civil procedure, it is a relationship between two parties who are so close that suing one serves as notice to another, so that the other party may be joined in the suit.

Identity of parties. In civil procedure, it is a relationship between two parties who are so close to each other that a judgment against one prevents action against the other party because of *res judicata.*

Identity theft. Occurs when personal identifiable information (PII) such as an account number or Social Security number is stolen and used to obtain financial services. (*Cyber Law*)

Idiot. A person so mentally deficient by birth as to be incapable of ordinary reasoning or rational conduct. [Registration Act (16 of 1908), S. 2(10].

Idol. Image of deity as object of worship; object of great reverence and devotion (as) idol of the people.

Idolater. Worshipper of idols; devout admirer.

If. The word 'if' in S. 79(2) is obviously a mistake and must be read as "as if" because the word 'if' standing by itself makes no sense at all. *Municipal Corporation* v. *Rai Bahadur Seth Hiralal*, AIR 1968 SC 642, 646. [M.B. Municipalities Act (1 of 1954), S. 79(2)]

If he has failed for any 3 years to pay rent within the period specified in Section 14. If the tenant makes only part payments of rent for any three years, he would be a persistent defaulter even if the aggregate of the amount in arrears does not exceed the total rent of two years, for the purpose of the sub-section. *Dhan Singh Ramakrishna Chauduri* v. *Laxminarayan Ramakrishnan*, AIR 1974 SC 1613, 1616, 1617. [Bomay Tenancy and Agricultural Lands Act (67 of 1948), S. 25(2)]

If it appears. In one sense the word 'appear', may refer to that which is seen by the eye, but it is also used in its broad sense as signifying that which is made clear by evidence or is clear to the comprehension when applied to matters of reasoning or opinion. *Abdoola Hasoon & Co.* v. *Corporation of Calcutta,* AIR 1950 Cal 36, 43.

If it is so prescribed. The effect of the expression "if it is so prescribed" is that when the rules prescribed the circumstances in which temporary injuction can be issued, ordinarily the Court is not to use its inherent powers to make the necessary orders in the interests of justice, but is merely to see whether the circumstances of the case bring it within the prescribed rule. *Manohar Lal* v. *Seth Hira Lal*, AIR 1962 SC 527, 532. [CPC (5 of 1908), S. 94]

If satisfied. The grounds on which the Central Government or the State Government was satisfied, based on which the detention order is issued, must be such as a rational human being can consider connected in some manner with the objects which were to be prevented from being attained. *State of Bombay* v. *Atma Ram*, AIR 1951 SC 157, 160. [Preventive Detention Act (4 of 1950), S. 3]

If sold in the open market. The words 'if sold in the open market' do not contemplate actual sale or the actual state of the market, but only enjoins that it should be assumed that there is an open market and the property can be sold in such a market and on that basis, the value has to be found out. *Ahmed Ariff* v. *Wealth Tax Commissioner Calcutta*, AIR 1971 SC 1691, 1696. [Wealth Tax Act (27 of 1957), S. 7(1)]

Ignominy. 'Ignominy' is defined to be public disgrace, infamy, reproach, or dishonour.

Ignorance. Ignorance of a particular fact—that is, want of knowledge of that fact—consists in this : that the mind, though sound, and capable of receiving an impression, has never acted upon that subject, because that subject has never been brought to the notice of the perceptive faculties.

Want of knowledge.

The terms 'IGNORANCE' AND 'MISTAKE', in legal contemplation, do not import the same significance, and should not be confounded. Ignorance implies a total want of knowledge in reference to the subject-matter; mistake admits a knowledge, but implies a wrong conclusion.

Ignorance (of Law). Want of knowledge of the law shall not excuse any man from the penalty of it. Every person is bound at his peril to take notice of what the law of the realm is and ignorance of it, though it be invincible, where a man affirms that he hath done all that in him lies to know the law, will not excuse him. (*Tomlin*)

IGNORANCE OF LAW, within the meaning of the rule that ignorance of law will not excuse is to be construed as meaning ignorance of the laws of one's own country or state. Ignorance of the law is ordinarily very much of an excuse as leads to a reduction of the sentence though it cannot lead to an acquittal.

Ignorance of law is no excuse. The maxim "ignorance of law is no excuse" cannot be carried to the extent of saying that every person must be persumed to know that a piece of legislation enacted by a legislature of competent jurisdiction must be held to be invalid, in case it prescribes differential treatment, and he must, therefore, refuse to submit to it or incur the peril of the bar of waiver being raised against him. *Basheshar Nath* v. *Commissioner of Income Tax*, AIR 1959 SC 149, 172.

Ignorantia eorum quae quis scire tenetur non excusat. Ignorance of those things which everyone is bound to know excuses not. (*Latin for Lawyers*)

Ignorantia facti excusat ; ignorantia juris non-excusat. Ignorance of the fact excuses; ignorance of the law excuses not.

Ignorantia judicis est calamitas innocentis. The ignorance of the judge is the misfortune of the innocent. (*Latin for Lawyers*)

Ignorantia juris non-excusat. (*Lat.*) Ignorance of law is no excuse.

The principle laid down in the *maxim* '*Ignorantia juris non excusat*' was found not applicable in a case where a litigant was an illiterate farmer and his counsel failed to take appropriate steps to bring the legal representatives of the deceased on record in time, on proper advice. *Rama Ravalu Gavade* v. *Sataba Gavadu Gavade,* (1997) 1 SCC 261, para 6. [CPC (5 of 1908), O. XXII, Rr. 9 & 10-A]

Applying the *maxim* the Apex Court held that one cannot be heard taking shelter behind one's own convenient ignorance. *Karnataka Rare Earth* v. *Senior Geologist, Deptt. of Mines & Geology,* (2004) 2 SCC 783, 790, para 9.

Ignorantia juris, quod quisque scire tenetur, neminem excusat. Ignorance of the law which every one is bound to know excuses no one.

Ignorantia legis juris neminem excusat. Ignorance of law is no excuse. *Basheshwar Nath* v. *Commissioners of Income-tax, Delhi and Rajasthan,* AIR 1959 SC 149.

Ignorantia praesumitur ubi scientia non probatur. Ignorance is presumed where knowledge is not proved.

Ignore. To reject as false or ungrounded; refuse to take notice of reject. To willfully disregard; to set aside.

Ignoscitur ei qui sanguinem suum qualiter redemptum voluit. He is justified who has acted in pure defence of his own life or limb.

Ijma. An assemblage, a Court; a dogmatic opinion delivered by a council of doctors. [*P. Ramanatha Aiyar's, The Law Lexicon*, 2017, LexisNexis].

Ila. In *ila* the husbands swear by God not to have sexual intercourse with his wife for a period of not less than four months and abstains therefrom during the said period. After the expiry of the period of four months, in Hanafi law, the marriage is dissolved without legal process, but in Ithna Ashari and Sahfi law, legal proceedings are necessary. [Tahir Mahmood, *The Muslim Law of India*, LexisNexis, 3rd edn., 2002 at 101 **quoted in** Dr Kauser Edappagath, *Divorce and Gender Equity in Muslim Personal Law of India*, 2014, LexisNexis at p.119]

Ilium. (*In Med. Jur.*) The last portion of the small intestines, hence also illac region.

Ill treat. Treat badly or with cruelty. To deal with badly. [Stage-Carriages Act (16 of 1861), S. 9].

Illatom. (*Hindu law*) Illatom is the affiliation of a son-in-law in consideration of assistance in the management of family property. A specific agreement to that effect is necessary. *Pthari Venkateshswarulu* v. *Damacharla Chinna Raghavulu,* AIR 1957 AP 604, 605.

Illatom adoption. Where a person is taken into a family *illatom* with a view to marrying him to the daughter of the taker, the *illatom* is not rendered invalid by the mere fact that the marriage is celebrated after the death of the taker.

Illatom son-in-law in Andhra. (*Hindu Law*) In Andhra an illatom son-in-law is a boy incorporated into the family with a view to give a daughter in marriage and is customarily recognised as an heir in the absence of a natural-born son. *P. Lakshmi Reddi* v. *L. Lakshmi Reddy*, AIR 1957 SC 314, 317.

Illegal. "The word "illegal" is applicable to everything which is an offence or which is prohibited by law, or which furnishes ground for a civil action : and a person is said to be "legally bound to do" whatever it is illegal in him to omit." [IPC (45 of 1860), S. 43] [Now (w.e.f. 1-7-2024) repealed & replaced by Bharatiya Nyaya Sanhita, 2023 (45 of 2023)]

The word "illegal" is applicable to everything which is an offence or which is prohibited by law, or which furnishes ground for a civil action. [(w.e.f. 1-7-2024) Bharatiya Nyaya Sanhita, 2023 (45 of 2023), section 2(15)].

Contrary to law. [IPC (45 of 1860), S. 32 and Constitution of India, Art. 326].

Illegal contract. There is a wide distinction between that class of contracts which are unlawful in the sense that the law will not enforce them, and which we usually term 'void' contracts, and that other class which are designated as 'illegal' contracts. Money paid in furtherance of an illegal contract cannot be recovered back, but it is otherwise as to money paid in furtherance of a contract which by statute is void, but not illegal, as in the case of contracts void under the statutes of frauds.

Illegal entrant. A person unlawfully entering or seeking to enter in breach of a deportation order or of the immigration laws.

Illegal migrant. Means a person in respect of whom each of the following conditions is satisfied, namely:—

(i) he has entered into India on or after the 25th day of March, 1971;

(ii) he is a foreigner;

(iii) he has entered into India without being in possession of a valid passport or other travel document or any other lawful authority in that behalf. [Illegal Migrants Determination by Tribunals Act (39 of 1983), S. 3(c)]

Illegal, or Irregular order. An order is illegal if it is opposed to any enactment or any rule having the force of law. It is irregular if the procedure followed is in violation of the principles of natural justice and fair play. *Kesava Rao* v. *Subba Raju*, AIR 1957 AP 55, 57. [Constitution of India, Art. 226]

Illegal strikes. Strikes that involve violence, discrimination against certain employees, violations of a cooling-off period, or attempts to coerce recognition of a noncertified union.

An "illegal strike" cannot by definition be "authorised absence." *U.P. State Bridge Corporation* v. *U.P. Rajya Setu Nigam*, (2004) 4 SCC 268, 279, para 21.

Illegal : Unlawful. The word "illegal" has been given a very wide meaning and it has the same meaning as "unlawful".

Illegality. Illegality signifies that which is contrary to the principles of law, and denotes a complete defect in the proceedings.

The quality of being illegal. [Indian Evidence Act (1 of 1872), S. 92, *Prov.* (1)].

Illegality and irregularity. An 'irregularity' is a want of adherence to some prescribed rule or mode of proceeding, and consists in omitting to do something that is necessary for the due and orderly conducting of a suit, or doing it in an unreasonable time or improper manner. An "illegality," on the other hand, is properly predicable of radical defects only, and signifies that which is contrary to the principles of law as distinguished from mere rules of procedure. It denotes a complete defect in jurisdiction or proceedings.

If in the proceedings any principle of natural justice has been violated and if it has resulted in substantial failure of justice, it would be an illegality. *Govt. of India* v. *National Tobacco Co.,* AIR 1977 AP 250, 261 (FB). [Constitution of India, Art. 226(1), Sub Cl. (c)]

Illegally. In an illegal manner.

Illegally acquired property. In relation to any person to whom this Chapter applies, means,—

(i) any property acquired by such person, wholly or partly out of or by means of any income, earnings or assets derived or obtained from or attributable to illegal hunting and trade of wild life and its products and derivatives;

(ii) any property acquired by such person, for a consideration or by any means, wholly or partly traceable to any property referred to in sub-clause (i) or the income or earning from such property, and includes—

(A) any property held by such person which would have been, in relation to any previous holder thereof, illegally acquired property under this clause if such previous holder had not ceased to hold it, unless such person or any other person who held the property at any time after such previous holder or, where there are two or more such previous holders, the last of such previous holders is or was a transferee in good faith for adequate consideration;

(B) any property acquired by such person, for a consideration, or by any means, wholly or partly traceable to any property falling under Item (A), or the income or earnings therefrom. [Wild Life (Protection) Act (53 of 1972), S. 58B(g)]

"ILLEGALLY ACQUIRED PROPERTY", in relation to any person to whom this Act applies, means—

(i) any property acquired by such person whether before or after the commencement of this Act, wholly or partly out of or by means of any income, earnings or assets derived or obtained from or attributable to any activity prohibited by or under any law for the time being in force relating to any matter in respect of which Parliament has power to make laws; or

(ii) any property acquired by such person, whether before or after the commencement of this Act, wholly or partly out of or by means of any income, earnings or assets in respect of which any such law has been contravened; or

(iii) any property acquired by such person, whether before or after the commencement of this Act, wholly or partly out of or by means of any income, earnings or assets the source of which cannot be proved and which cannot be shown to be attributable to any act or things done in respect of any matter in relation to which Parliament has no power to make laws, or

(iv) any property acquired by such person, whether before or after the commencement of this Act, for a consideration, or by any means, wholly or partly traceable to any property referred to in sub-clauses (i) to (iii) or and includes—

(A) any property held by such person which would have been, in relation to any previous holder thereof, illegally acquired property under this clause if such previous holder had not ceased to hold it, unless such person or any other person who held the property at any time after such previous holder or, where there are two or more such previous holders, the last of such previous holders is or was a transferee in good faith for adequate consideration;

(B) any property acquired by such person, whether before or after the commencement of this Act, for a consideration, or by any means, wholly or partly traceable to any property falling under item (A), or the income or earnings therefrom. [Smugglers & Foreign Exchange Manipulators Act (13 of 1976), S. 3(c)]

Illegible. Unreadable. [Indian Evidence Act (1 of 1872), S. 98].

Illegitimacy. The status of a child born not in lawful wedlock. [Children Act (60 of 1960) (*repealed*), S. 50(3)].

Illegitimate. Not born in lawful wedlock. [IPC (45 of 1860), S. 361, *Excep.*].

Not legitimate; bastard.

Illegitimate blood. [Special Marriage Act (43 of 1954), S. 2(b), *Expln.* (b)].

Illegitimate child. It is impossible to treat the illegitimate sons born of a Christian father and a Hindu woman living in adultery with him as the sons of a *Sudra* father.

Illegitimation. Act of illegitimating; bastardizing.

Illicit. Prohibited by law; unlawful; illegal; contrary to morals or public order.

Not authorized or allowed; improper, irregular; not sanctioned by law, rule or custom; without proper licence or authority. [IPC (45 of 1860), S. 366].

Illicit cohabitation. Illicit means unlawful or forbidden, and co-habitation means the living together as man and wife.

It is a state of living together in which illicit sexual intercourse is inferable.

Illicit connection. 'Illicit connection', as used in the statute defining seduction, is equivalent to "sexual intercourse".

Illicit intercourse. For the purposes of this section 'ILLICIT INTERCOURSE' means sexual intercourse between persons not united by marriage or by any union or tie which, though not amounting to a marriage, is recognised by the personal law or custom of the community to which they belong or, where they belong to different communities, of both such communities, as constituting between them a *quasi*-marital relation. [IPC (45 of 1860), S. 372, *Explanation* II] [Now (w.e.f. 1-7-2024) repealed & replaced by Bharatiya Nayaya Sanhita, 2023 (45 of 2023)]

Unlawful intercourse. [IPC (45 of 1860), S. 366] [Now (w.e.f. 1-7-2024) repealed & replaced by Bharatiya Nayaya Sanhita, 2023 (45 of 2023)]

For the purposes of this section "illicit intercourse" means sexual intercourse between persons not united by marriage or by any union or tie which, though not amounting to a marriage, is recognised by the personal law or custom of the community to which they belong or, where they belong to different communities, of both such communities, as constituting between them a *quasi*-marital relation. [(w.e.f. 1-7-2024) Bharatiya Nayaya Sanhita, 2023 (45 of 2023), section 98, *Explanation* 2 & section 99, *Explanation* 2].

Illicit relations. Any form of unlawful sexual intercourse such as fornication or adultery.

Illicit traffic. In relation to narcotic drugs and psychotropic substances, means—

(i) cultivating any coca plant or gathering any portion of coca plant;

(ii) cultivating the opium poppy or any cannabis plant;

(iii) engaging in the production, manufacture, possession, sale, purchase, transportation, warehousing, concealment, use or consumption, import inter-State, export inter-State, import into India, export from India or transhipment, of narcotic drugs or psychotropic substances;

(iv) dealing in any activities in narcotic drugs or psychotropic substances other than those provided in sub-clauses (i) to (iii); or

(v) handling or letting any premises for the carrying on of any of the activities referred to in sub-clauses (i) to (iv), other than those permitted under the Narcotic Drugs and Psychotropic Substances Act, 1985, or any rule or order made, or any condition of any licence, term or authorisation issued thereunder and includes—

(1) financing, directly or indirectly, any of the aforementioned activities;

(2) abetting or conspiring in the furtherance of or in support of doing any of the aforementioned activities; and

(3) harbouring persons engaged in any of the aforementioned activities. [Prevention of Illicit Traffic in NDPS Act (46 of 1988), S. 2(e)]

Illiquid asset. An asset which is difficult to convert into cash.

Illiteracy. The quality or condition of being illiterate.

Illiterate. Not literate. [Workmen's Compensation Act (8 of 1923), S. 22(3)].

Illness. 'Illness" as used in an application for a life insurance policy requiring the applicant to give full particulars of any illness which he had since childhood, means a disease or ailment of such a character as to affect the general soundness and healthfulness of the system seriously, and not a mere temporary indisposition, which does not tend to undermine or weaken the constitution of the insured.

Illuminant. That which illuminates. [Central Excises and Salt Act (1 of 1944), Sch. 1, Item No. 7].

Illusion. Deceptive appearance.

Distorted or misinterpreted sensory impression which, in contrast to hallucinations, arises from an actual stimulus, *i.e.*, shadow is taken to be a man, specks on window are seen as a swarm of mosquitos. Prevalent in delirious states. The misinterpretation of a real, external, sensory experience.

An image or impression in the mind, excited by some external object addressing itself to one or more of the senses, but which, instead of corresponding with the reality, is perverted, distorted, or wholly mistaken, the error being attributable to the imagination of the observer, not to any defect in the organs of sense. (*Black*)

Illusory. Deceiving by false appearances; fallacious; illusive.

Relating to, or marked by illusion; based on or producing illusion.

Illusory promise. A promise which appears on its face to be so insubstantial as to impose no obligation on the promisor.

Illustrate. Make clear by examples, drawings, *etc.*

Illustration. An illustration is defined as a pictorial or other representation placed in a book or other publication to elucidate the text. Illustrations to sections of an Act are examples of the application of the principle of the sections to concrete cases.

That which illustrates; example.

Illustrative. By way of illustration. [Ancient Monuments and Archaeological Sites and Remains Act (24 of 1958), S. 2(b)(iii)].

Image. A sculptured figure.

Imbargo. A stop, stay, arrest upon ships or merchandise, by public authority. This arrest of shipping is commonly of the ships of foreigners in time of war and differences with States to whom they are belonging. (*Tomlin*).

Imbecile. An imbecile is one destitute of strength, either of body or mind; weak; feeble; impotent; decrepit.

Imbecility. (*In Med. Jur.*) A form of mental disease consisting in mental deficiency.

IMBECILITY is defined as the quality of being imbecile; feebleness of mind; feebleness of body or mind. Absolute imbecility implies a total want of reason and a total loss of memory.

Imbedded in the earth. Fixed in the earth. [T.P. Act (4 of 1882), S. 3(b)].

Imbezzle. To steal, pilfer, or purloin; or where a person entrusted with goods, wastes and diminishes them. (*Tomlin*)

IMHO. (*abbr.*) (In My Humble Opinion) A shorthand appended to a comment written in an online forum, IMHO indicates that the writer is aware that they are expressing a debatable view, probably on a subject already under discussion. One of many such shorthands in common use online, especially in discussion forums. (*Matisse Enzer-Glossary of Internet Terms*)

Imitation. The making of one thing in the similitude or likeness of another; as, counterfeit coin is said to be made "in imitation" of the genuine. That which is made or produced as a copy; an artificial likeness; a counterfeit; simulating something superior.

An imitation of a trademark is that which so far resembles the genuine trade mark as to be likely to induce the belief that it is genuine, whether by the use of words or letters similar in appearance or in sound, or by any sign, device, or other means. The test of "colourable imitation" is, not whether a difference may be recognized between the names of two competing articles when placed side by side, but whether the difference will be recognized by the purchaser with no opportunity for comparison. *The Best Foods* v. *Hemphill Packing Co.*, D.C.Del., 5 F.2d 355, 357. (*Black*)

The action or product of imitating; an artificial likeness.

Imitation of trade mark. An imitated trade mark resembles the genuine trade mark which induces one to believe that it is a genuine trade mark.

Immaterial. Not material, essential or necessary; not important or pertinent; not decisive.

Having little substance. [Indian Evidence Act (1 of 1872), S. 126, *Prov.* 2].

Immaterial allegation or **averment.** An immaterial averment is one alleging with needless particularity or unnecessary circumstances what is immaterial and unnecessary, and which might properly have been stated more generally and without such circumstances or particulars, or, in other words, it is a statement of unnecessary particulars in connection with, and as descriptive of, what is material.

An 'immaterial allegation', as the term is used with reference to pleadings, is an averment which may be stricken from the pleadings, without leaving it insufficient.

Immaterial averment. An allegation which may be stricken from a pleading. A statement of unnecessary particulars in connection with and descriptive of what is material.

Immaterial evidence. Evidence which lacks in probative value.

Immaterial issue. An issue made by the pleadings joined on a point which is not decisive of the rights of the parties in the cause. An issue taken upon some collateral matter, the decision of which will not settle the question in dispute between the parties in action.

An immaterial issue is where a material allegation in the pleadings is not reversed, but an issue is taken on some other point, which, though decided by the Court will not determine, the merits of the cause.

Immaterial variance. A variance which is too slight to mislead or prejudice the defendant.

Immediate. Direct, as opposed to consequential. Acting with nothing interposed or between or without the intervention of another object as a cause.

Not separated from its object by any medium : directly related; nearest.

Occurring, acting or accomplished without loss of time; made or done at once; instant [Sale of Goods Act (3 of 1930), S. 5(1)]; [Inland Vessels Act (1 of 1917), S. 63(b)]; acting or being without the intervention of another object, cause or agency [Specific Relief Act (47 of 1963), S. 8]; characterised by contiguity;

existing without intervening space or substance; being near at hand; direct; with nothing in between. [Indian Evidence Act (1 of 1872), S. 26].

Immediate cause. The term 'immediate cause', in speaking of the contributory negligence of a plaintiff as being the immediate cause of his injury, is synonymous with the phrase 'proximate cause'.

Immediate death ; Instantaneous death. If an injury severs some of the principal blood vessels and causes the person injured to bleed to death, his death may be regarded as immediate, though not instantaneous. When it is said that the death must be immediate, it is not meant that it must follow the injury within a period of time too brief to be perceptible. If a blow upon the head produces unconsciousness and renders the person injured incapable of intelligent thought or speech or action, and he so remains for several minutes, and then dies, his death may very properly be considered as immediate, though not instantaneous. The words 'instantaneous' and 'immediate', as used in reference to such death, do not mean precisely the same thing, but the word 'immediate' is more comprehensive and elastic in its meaning. Of course, an instantaneous death is an immediate death, but an immediate death is not necessarily and in all cases an instantaneous death.

Immediate employer. If a particular work in two places has an intimate correlation and is a piece of an integrated whole and the said work by the contractors through their labour is ordinarily part of the work of the principal factory, the contractors are 'immediate employer' of the principal employer. *B.M. Laxmanamurthy* v. *Employees' State Insurance Corporation, Bangalore*, AIR 1974 SC 759, 763. [Employees' State Insurance Act (34 of 1948), S. 2(13)]

Immediate export. The words 'immediate export' mean that the goods should be exported within the reasonable time. A reasonable time depends upon the factors like the quantity of goods, the time reasonably necessary for unloading, sorting and reloading them, the availability of trucks for export etc. *Delhi Municipality* v. *Man Mohan Tuli,* AIR 1979 Del 144, 152. [Delhi Municipal Corporation Act (66 of 1957), S. 178(1)]

Immediate notice. 'Immediate' is defined as without any time intervening; without any delay. It is often used, like similar expressions, with less strictness than the literal meaning requires, as 'an immediate answer'. Thus, in a bond requiring immediate notice of an accident, it is evident that the word was not used in its literal sense.

As used in an indemnity bond requiring immediate notice of any defalcation, a delay of six or eight days, where no prejudice resulted, is not, as a matter of law, other than immediate notice. In a case of such a character some time may elapse after a well-grounded suspicion before a person ought, in prudence, to make any charge of fraud or dishonesty. Mere laches is not enough. Knowledge of a defalcation frequently depends upon a long train of events, or the examination of extended accounts. Unjust inferences and false accusations are always to be avoided. It is only of acts which may create a loss for which the surety is responsible—that is, a loss arising from fraud or dishonesty—that immediate notice is exacted.

Immediate possession. The words 'immediate possession' convey the sense of urgency with which the whole thing has to be accomplished. *B.N. Setia* v. *P.C. Tondon,* AIR 1980 Del 68, 71.

Direct possession, as opposed to mediate possession. [Specific Relief Act (47 of 1963), S. 8; CPC (5 of 1908), O. XXXIX, R. 9].

Immediately. It has two meanings-one indicating the relation of cause and effect, and the other the absence of time between two events. In the former sense, it means proximately, as opposed to "mediately;" without intervention of anything. In the latter sense, it means at once; in an instant; instantaneously. Instantly.

Instantly; proximately; opposed to mediately. The term 'immediately' means within a reasonable time.

The term has two meanings. One, indicating the relation of cause and effect the other, the absence of time between two events. In the former sense, it means proximately, without intervention of anything, as opposed to 'immediately'. In the latter sense, it means instantaneously. [*Rosali V.* v. *Taico Bank,* (2009) 17 SCC 690, para 31 : (2011) 2 SCC (Civ) 626 : AIR 2007 SC 998 as cited in *Ram Karan Gupta* v. *J.S. Exim Limited,* (2012) 13 SCC 568, para 15]. Order XXI, Rule 84, CPC.

The word immediately has been used in the Article 134-A to convey a sense of urgency. If an oral application is made before the judgment, decree or order or sentence such application must have been made immediately. *Kesarva S. Jankhandi* v. *Ramchandra S. Jamkhand,* AIR 1981 Kar 97, [Constitution of India, Art. 134-A]

The word "immediately" in a will means 'without the intervention of any other estate or interest'.

The word 'immediately' connotes proximity in time to comply and proximity in taking steps to re-sell on failure to comply the requirement of deposit as first condition that is to take place within relatively short interval of time and without any other intervening recurrence. *Rao Mahmood Ahmed Khan* v. *Ranbir Singh*, AIR 1995 SC 2195, 2198.

Immemorial. From a time whereof the memory of man runs not to the contrary. Ancient; beyond memory of living men.

Immemorial usage. A practice which existed from the time out of mind.

Immemorial user. A phenomenon is said to be happening from time immemorial when the date of its commencement is not within the memory of man or the date of its commencement is shrouded in the mists of antiquity. *Rudrayya* v. *Venthayya*, AIR 1961 SC 1821, 1823.

Immigrant. One who immigrates (*i.e*) comes into the country as settler therein.

Immigrate. The word 'immigrate' means 'migrate into a country'. The word 'migrate' may have in some contexts the wider meaning "come or removed to a place without an intention to reside permanently" and in some context the narrower meaning "come or removed to a place with the intention of residing there permanently". *Shanno Devi* v. *Mangal Sain*, AIR 1961 SC 58, 62. [Constitution of India, Art. 6]

Immigration. The flow of foreigners into a country as settlers as permitted by law.

Imminent. Immediate; about to happen; on the instant.

Impending; threatening; coming on shortly. [Constitution of India, Art. 352(1), *Expln.*].

Imminent danger. 'Imminent danger,' sufficient to justify the taking of life in self-defence, means such an overt, actual demonstration as makes killing necessary to self-preservation, though it is not necessary that danger should in fact exist. There must be such danger as might appear to defendant's comprehension, as a reasonable man, to require the taking of life. The apprehension of danger by the accused must be on grounds sufficient to satisfy a reasonable man that his life or limbs were in peril, or that great bodily harm was about to be inflicted on him.

Immoral. Contrary to public welfare; against public morals; morally wrong or evil; dissolute.

The case law both in England and India confines the operation of the word to sexual immorality. *Charnlal Parakh* v. *Mahadeadas*, AIR 1959 SC 781, 797. [Indian Contract Act (9 of 1972), S. 23]

Against public morals; dissolute. [Indian Contract Act (9 of 1872), S. 23, ill. (k)]; [IPC (45 of 1860), S. 361, *Excep.*].

Immoral conduct. A conduct which is wilful, flagrant or shameless in the opinion of respectable people.

Immoral contract. A contract founded upon immoral consideration.

Immoral or opposed to public policy. The term " as immoral, or opposed to public policy" in S. 23 of the Indian Contract Act is of restrictive nature. Immorality contemplated has reference to the sexual immorality and not to general deviations of any or all types. Unless there is clear evidence to show that the consideration of the gift was to secure immoral purposes or was in any manner, unlawful or prohibited by law, it cannot be rightly presumed, only because the female companion was not married to the donor that the consideration itself be treated as one having nexus to sexual relations between man and woman. [*Susila Bhihu Shindey* v. *Sulochana Baburao Bhoj,* MLJ : YD (1982), p. 383 : (1981) Bom LR 267] [Indian Contract Act (9 of 1872), Ss. 23, 25]

Immoral purpose. The expression 'immoral purpose' occurring in Section 11(i)(c) of the Act would cover within its meaning prostitution as well as living of a woman as a one man's mistress. [*Kanchanmala Dassi* v. *Lilabati Debi*, AIR 1951 Cal 164 : 87 CLJ 332] [W.B. Premises Rent Control Act (1948), S. 11(1)(c)]

Immoral purposes. The words "immoral purposes" connote in a wide and general sense all purposes involving conduct which has the property of being wrong rather than right in the judgment of the majority of contemporary fellow citizens.

Immoral traffic offender. Means a person who commits or abets the commission of any offence under the Suppression of Immoral Traffic in Women and Girls Act, 1956. [A.P. Prevention of Dangerous Activities of Bootleggers Act (1 of 1986), S. 2(i)]

Immorality. In the law of contracts, a contract with an immoral object or purpose, is void.

Immovable. Fixed; not liable to be removed; permanent.

Immovable property. "IMMOVEABLE PROPERTY" shall extend to and include messuages, tenements, and hereditaments, corporeal and incorporeal, of every tenure or description, whatever may be the estate or interest therein. [Trustees Act (27 of 1866), S. 2].

"IMMOVEABLE PROPERTY" shall include land, benefits to arise out of land, and things attached to the earth, or permanently fastened to anything attached to the earth. [General Clauses Act (10 of 1897), S. 3(26)].

"IMMOVEABLE PROPERTY" does not include any machinery or plant (other than machinery or plant installed in a building for the convenient occupation of the building) even though attached to, or permanently fastened to anything attached to, the earth. [Income-tax Act (43 of 1961), S. 11(5)(x), *Expln.*]

"Immovable property" means landed property and may include structures embedded in the earth such as walls or buildings for the permanent beneficial enjoyment. [*Shaha Ratansi Khimji and Sons* v. *Kumbhar Sons Hotel Private Limited*, (2014) 14 SCC 1, para 17].

"Immovable property" means,—

(i) any land or any building or part of a building, and includes, where any land or any building or part of a building is transferred together with any machinery, plant, furniture, fittings or other things, such machinery, plant, furniture, fittings or other things also.

Explanation.—For the purposes of this sub-clause, land, building, part of a building, machinery, plant, furniture, fittings and other things include any rights therein;

(ii) any rights of the nature referred to in clause (b) of sub-section (1) of Section 269AB. [Income-tax Act (43 of 1961),S. 269A(e)]

It does not include standing timber, growing crops or grass. [T.P. Act (4 of 1882), S. 3]

"Immovable property" includes wharfage-rights and all other rights exercisable on, over, or in respect of, any land, wharf, dock or pier. [Major Port Authorities Act, 2021 (1 of 2021), section 2(1)(k)]

"IMMOVEABLE PROPERTY" includes land, buildings, hereditary allowances, rights to ways, lights, ferries, fisheries or any other benefit to arise out of land, and things attached to the earth or permanently fastened to anything which is attached to the earth but not standing timber, growing crops or grass. [Government Management of Private Estate Act (10 of 1892), S. 2(1); Registration Act (16 of 1908), S. 2(6)]

Real or immoveable property consists of (1) land; (2) that which is affixed to land; (3) that which is incidental or appurtenant to land; (4) that which is immovable by law.

The right to enter on a land coupled with a right to catch and carry away the fish is a 'profit *a prendre*' which is a benefit arising out of land and so it is immovable property. *Ananda Behera* v. *State of Orissa*, AIR 1956 SC 17, 19.

Under the Civil Procedure Code and Limitation Act standing crops have repeatedly been held to be immoveable property. So long as the crops are on the ground, they must be regarded as immoveable property. When these are severed from the land they become moveable property.

Immovable property shall include land, benefits to arise out of land, and things attached to the earth, or permanently fastened to anything attached to the earth. Unless there is something repugnant in the subject or context, immovable property does not include standing timber, growing crops or grass. *Board of Revenue* v. *A.M. Ansari*, AIR 1976 SC 1813.

The plant and machinery which are permanently embedded in earth with an intention of running a fertilizer factory, were held to be immovable properties. *Duncans Industries Ltd.* v. *State of U.P.*, (2000) 1 SCC 633, para 8 : AIR 2000 SC 355.

Installation or erection of turbo alternator on the platform constructed on the land would be 'immovable property'. *Triveni Engineering & Industries Ltd.* v. *CCE*, (2000) 7 SCC 29, para 23 : AIR 2000 SC 2896.

The 'immovable property', referred to in para 3 of the Regulations would obviously include a holding as well. *Amrendra Pratap Singh* v. *Tej Bahadur Prajapati*, AIR 2004 SC 3782, 3789, para 13. [Orissa Scheduled Areas Transfer of Immovable Property (By Scheduled Tribes) Regulations, 1956, para 3].

The words "immoveable property" mentioned in S. 58, T.P. Act (4 of 1882), denote not only the property itself as distinguished from any equity of redemption which the mortgagor might at the time possess in the said property, but include the rights of the mortgagor in the property mortgaged at the time of the second mortgage or, in other words, his equity of redemption in such property. The equity of redemption in mortgaged property is immoveable property.

Where a plant equipped with the necessary machinery to draw water from the well and to supply water to other fields connected with the lease-hold interest in the lands whereon some supper-structures are constructed in the subject of mortgage, such equipment is the immoveable property. *Mahijibhai Patel* v. *Dolatram Chanhammal,* AIR 1972 Guj 166, 171. [Limitation Act (36 of 1963), Art. 62]

The interest of the mortgagee in the mortgaged property is manifestly a "benefit to arise out of land," and is therefore itself immovable property.

"IMMOVABLE PROPERTY" for the purposes of section 194-IA of Act 43 of 1961, 'immovable property' means any land (other than agricultural land) or any building or part of a building. [(w.e.f. 1-6-2013) *Explanation* (b) to Section 194-IA of the Income-tax Act, 1961 (43 of 1961)]

Immunity. A personal favour granted by law contrary to the general rule.

An immunity is a right peculiar to some individual or body; an exemption from some general duty or burden; a personal benefit or favour granted by law contrary to the general rule.

Freedom from liability; exemption conferred by any law, from a general rule. [Constitution of India, Art. 65(3) and Art. 105(3)].

Immunity from prosecution. The object of Section 64, (NDPS Act) being the same as Section 307 CrPC 1973 (2 of 1974), it should logically follow that it may be exercised at any time during the course of the trial. It is true that the words "immunity from prosecution" have been used, but the phrase does not mean anything more than the power to withdraw from prosecution. That can be exercised at any time in the course of the trial, but before the judgment is delivered. The definition of the word "immunity" in the context of Section 64 is : "Freedom or exemptions from penalty, burden or duty." *Jasbir Singh* v. *Vipin Kumar Jaggi,* AIR 2001 SC 2734. [NDPS Act (61 of 1985), S. 64 and CrPC, 1973 (2 of 1974), S. 307]

Impact. Means any effect caused by a proposed activity on the environment including human health and safety, flora, fauna, soil, air, water, climate, landscapes and historical monuments or other physical structures or the integration among these factors. It also includes effects on cultural heritage or socio-economic conditions resulting from alterations to those factors. [UN Convention on

Environmental Impact Assessment in a Transboundary Context, Feb. 25, 1991, Art. I (vii)]

The word 'impact' occurring in insurance policy would cover the damage caused to the building and machinery on account of the bulldozer moving closely on the road. *United India Insurance Co. Ltd.* v. *Pushpalaya Printers,* AIR 2004 SC 1700 : (2004) 3 SCC 694, 699, para 6.

Impair. To diminish in quality, value, excellence or strength of a thing.

The word 'impair' means to make worse; to weaken; to enfeeble. To make or become worse or less; to lessen, reduce or diminish the quantity or quality.

When a construction is alleged to materially impair the value or utility of building, the construction should be of such a nature as to substantially diminish the value of the building either from the commercial and monetary point of view or from the utilitarian aspect of the building. *Om Pal* v. *Anand Swarup*, 1988 (4) SCC 545.

Impaired capital. Capital which is worth less than the par value of the issued stock.

Impairing the morals of a minor. The offence of an adult's engaging in sex-related acts, short of intercourse, with a minor *e.g.* fondling, taking obscene photographs, and showing pornographic materials.

Impairment. 'IMPAIRMENT' means—

(a) total or partial loss of a bodily function;

(b) total or partial loss of a part of the body;

(c) malfunction of a part of the body; and

(d) malformation or disfigurement of a part of the body—

and includes, in relation to a person with a past or present impairment an impairment which presently exists or existed in the past but has now ceased to exist. [Equal Opportunity Act, 1984, S. 4]

Impartial. Free from bias; indifferent between the parties.

Impartiality. The quality of being impartial. [Indian Evidence Act (1 of 1872), S. 153, *Except*. 2].

Impartible. Indivisible.

Impassable. That cannot be passed along, through or across. [Indian Easements Act (5 of 1882), S. 24, ill. (d)].

Impawn. To put in pawn; pledge.

Impeach. To challenge to call in question; to attack [Indian Evidence Act (1 of 1872), S. 153, *Exception* 2]; to bring to a charge against.

Impeach, Impeachment. To impeach, as applied to a person, is to accuse, to blame, to censure him. It includes the imputation of wrong doing. To impeach his official report or conduct is to show that it was occasioned by some partiality, bias, prejudice, inattention to or unfaithfulness in the discharge of that duty, or that it was based on such error that the existence of such influence may be justly inferred from the extraordinary character or grossness of the error.

For impeachment of the President of India, See, Art. 56(b) and 61, the Constitution of India.

Impeach or confirm the credit. To attack or corroborate a person's credibility. [Indian Evidence Act (1 of 1872), S. 158].

Impeachable. Liable for impeachment. [TP Act (4 of 1882), S. 69(3)].

Impeachable waste. Waste which results in liability on the part of the person committing it.

Impeachment of witness. Accusation of a witness of want of veracity.

The word "impeach," when used in reference to a witness, signifies to discredit, or to show or prove that he is unreliable or unworthy of belief. "Where he has been successfully impeached, and his evidence has not been, either in whole or in part, corroborated by other credible testimony in the cause, it is within the province of the Court trying the issue to entirely disregard his testimony."

'Impeachment,' as applied to the impeachment of a witness in a legal proceeding, means an attack on the person's credibility as a witness, a mere conflict between a witness's testimony and the testimony of another witness in regard to some fact is not an impeachment of the former.

Impede. 'Impede' is not synonymous with 'obstruct'. An obstacle, which renders access to an inclosure inconvenient, impedes the entrance thereto, but does not obstruct it, if sufficient room be left to pass in and out. 'Obstruct' means 'to prevent, to close up.'

To get in the way of the progress of. [Collection of Statistics Act (32 of 1953), S. 8(b)].

Impediment. The word 'impediment' must mean an impediment in law and such impediments are well known, *e.g.* minority, unsoundness of mind, apostacy, *etc.* The mere fact that two persons are rival claimants for the office, cannot be described as an 'impediment' to the appointment of a *mutawalli. Hazrat Syed Shah Mustarshid Ali Al Quadari* v. *Commissioner of Wakfs,* AIR 1954 Cal 436, 440.

Disabilities, or hindrances to the making of contracts such as infancy, want of reason, *etc.*

Impediments in law. Legal disabilities; persons under impediments are those within age, *non-compos mentis*, in prison. beyond sea. *etc.* by whom by a saving in several laws, have time to claim and prosecute their rights, after the impediments are removed. (*Tomlin*) *See also* Limitation Act (36 of 1963), S. 6.

Impending. 'Impending' denotes something that hangs suspended over us, and may remain so indefinitely.

Imperative. Mandatory, commanding.

Obligatory. [Indian Trusts Act (2 of 1882), S. 38, ill. (a)].

Imperfect. Not perfect; not complete in all its parts; wanting a part; defective; deficient.

Imperfect self-defense (defence). A defence based on self-defence that does not shield the defendant from all liability but reduces the liability specially because the defendant actually but unreasonably believed that he or she was in imminent danger of death or great bodily injury.

Imperial. The primary signification of 'imperial' was 'pertaining to supreme authority; royal; sovereign; supreme.'

Of or relating to Britain as an imperial State. [Indian Partnership Act (9 of 1932), S. 58(3)].

Imperitia culpae adnumeratur. (*Lat.*) Want of skill is reckoned as a fault.

Impermissible avoidance arrangement. An 'impermissible avoidance arrangement' means an arrangement, the main purpose of which is to obtain a tax benefit, and it—

(a) creates rights, or obligations, which are not ordinarily created between persons dealing at arm's length;

(b) results, directly or indirectly, in the misuse, or abuse, of the provisions of this Act;

(c) lacks commercial substance or is deemed to lack commercial substance under section 97, in whole or in part; or

(d) is entered into, or carried out, by means, or in a manner, which are not ordinarily employed for *bona fide* purposes. [(w.e.f. 1-4-2016) S. 96(1) of the Income-tax Act, 1961 (43 of 1961)]

Impersonation. False impersonation is representing oneself to be a public officer or employee or a person licensed to practice or engage in any profession or vocation for which a licence is required by state law with knowledge that such representation is false.

The act of impersonating or the state of being impersonated. [Workmen's compensation Act (8 of 1923), S. 8(9)].

Impertinence. The introduction of immaterial or unnecessary allegations into a pleading which may be struck out on the order of the Court or Judge.

Impertinent. That which is not relevant or pertinent.

Impervious. Not allowing entrance or passage through. [Factories Act (63 of 1948), S. 11(1)(d)(ii)].

Impinge. To encroach or infringe (*on* or *upon*) (impinge on the defendant's rights).

Implantation. Means the attachment and subsequent penetration by the zona-free blastocyst, which starts five to seven days following fertilisation. [Surrogacy (Regulation) Act, 2021 (47 of 2021), section 2(1)(p)]

Implead. To make one a party to an action or suit.

To sue or prosecute a person by course of law [Drugs and Cosmetics Act (23 of 1940), S. 32A]; to make a party. [Trade and Merchandise Marks Act (43 of 1958), S. 114].

Impleader. A procedure to bring a third party into a law suit, especially through a defendent's third party action.

Implement. A tool forming part of an equipment for work [Wealth-tax Act (27 of 1957), S. 5(1)(ix)]; to give effect to. [long title, Asian Development Bank Act (18 of 1966)].

Implementation. Giving practical effect to. [Unit Trust of India Act (52 of 1963), S. 21(k)].

Implementing agency. Includes any Department of the State Government, the Zila Parishad, any other Local authority or State Government-undertaking, which is entrusted by the State Government with the task of implementing any works taken up under the scheme. [Maharashtra Employment Guarantee Act, 1977 (20 of 1978), S. 2(d)]

Implementing of treaties and agreements with other countries. The phrase "implementing of treaties and agreements with other countries" mean that the legislature has power not merely to make rules as to the mode in which treaties and agreements with foreign countries should be regulated but also to make laws on the subject matters of the treaties and agreements so that they may be given effect to in India. *Bimla Devi* v. *Chaturvedi*, AIR 1953 All 613, 615.

Implementing officer. Means the highest officer of the implementing agency in the District or any officer subordinate to him to whom any of the powers or duties of the agency have been entrusted. [Maharashtra Employment Guarantee Act, 1977 (20 of 1978), S. 2(e)]

Implements. Things necessary in any trade, without which the work cannot be performed. (*Tomlin*)

Implicate. Involve; entangle (as) to implicate a person in a charge or crime.

To bring into intimate or incriminating connection; to involve. [Indian Evidence Act (1 of 1872), S. 114, ill. (b)].

TO IMPLICATE, INVOLVE. People are said to be *implicated* who have taken ever so small a share in a transaction; but they are *involved* only when they are deeply concerned : the former is likewise especially applied to criminal transactions, the latter to those things which are in themselves troublesome : thus a man is *implicated* in the guilt of robbery who should stand by and see it done, without interfering for its prevention.

Implication. The implication or inference which may arise in the construction of statutes is of something not expressly declared, but arise out of that which is directly or expressly declared therein.

IMPLICATION is such a strong probability that an intention to the contrary can not be supposed.

(*Necessary implication*). A necessary inference of something not directly declared, between parties in deeds, agreements, &c., arising from what is admitted or expressed. When the law giveth anything to a man, it giveth, implicitly (or rather impliedly) whatsoever is necessary for enjoying the same. (*Tomlin*).

It is a maxim of law that an heir at law can only be disinherited by express devise or necessary implication, and that implication has been defined to be such a strong probability that an intention to the contrary cannot be supposed.

The fact of being implied without being expressed.

Implication of law. By 'grants or reservations by implication of law' is meant such as the law implies from the circumstances, and which are not found by construction in a contract. The familiar instance of a reservation by implication of law is a way of necessity.

Implied. It means indicated not in express words but by logical inference for association or necessary consequence. [Indian Partnership Act (9 of 1932), S. 11(1)].

Implied abrogation. The repeal of a statute by a new one which is quite to the contrary.

Implied acceptance. An 'implied acceptance,' as the term is used in speaking of the implied acceptance of a street or highway, arises in cases where the public authorities have done acts recognizing the existence of a public high way, and treated it as one of the public ways of a locality. When control of a way is assumed by the authorities representing a public corporation, the acceptance will be implied.

(*Of bill of exchange*) is an acceptance by the drawee of a bill of exchange which the law implies from his conduct.

Implied agreement. The agreement though not fully expressed in words, is nevertheless a genuine agreement of the parties. It is implied only in this : that it is to be inferred from the acts or conduct of the parties, instead of from their spoken words. The engagement is signified by conduct, instead of words.

Implied assumpsit. "Implied assumpsit" is an undertaking presumed in law to have been made by a party by his conduct, though he has not made an express promise. The law implies a promise or contract to do that which a party is legally bound to perform, and where by law a duty is imposed a promise will be implied.

Implied authority. "An authority is said to be implied when it is to be inferred from the circumstances of the case; and things spoken or written, or the ordinary course of dealing, may be accounted circumstances of the case." [Indian Contract Act (9 of 1872), S. 187].

Implied condition. One not expressed but implied by law.

Implied confession. A confession in which the person does not plead of being guilty, but asks for mercy and light sentence from the Court.

Implied consent. 'Implied consent' is defined to be that manifested by signs, actions, or facts, or by inaction, silence, or other conduct which raises a presumption that the consent has been given.

Implied contract. Such a contract as the law presumes a man to have promised to perform.

The word "implied" may be more appropriate to contracts implied by law, but it is sometimes used to designate what may be called tacit contracts, that is, contracts where the proposal or the acceptance or both are signified, not by words, but by acts or conduct. But before there can be such a tacit or implied contract, the acts or the conduct relied upon must be of such nature that it can only give rise to the inference that there must have been an implied offer and acceptance. *Umedsingh Hamira Singh* v. *Marsden Mills Ltd.*, AIR 1959 Bom 143, 147.

IMPLIED CONTRACT AND EXPRESS CONTRACT. An express contract is one to which the minds of the parties have assented, while implied contracts are those implied by law from the facts and circumstances of the transaction, although they are even against the consent of the party to be bound. The distinction between an express contract and an implied one is that in one the liability arises directly from the contract, while in the other the contract is implied, or arises from the liability.

Implied easement. An implied easement is an casement resting upon the principle that, where the owner of two or more adjacent plots sells a part thereof, he grants by implication to the grantee all those apparent and visible easements which are necessary for the reasonable use of the property granted, which at the time of the grant are used by the owner of the entirety for the benefit of the part granted.

Implied in fact. Inferable from the facts of the case.

Implied malice. Malice inferred from the conduct of a person.

Implied notice. Implied notice may be knowledge imputed impliedly by collateral facts of such a nature as to cast on the party the legal duty of not being wilfully or negligently ignorant of all proper inferences to be drawn from such facts.

Notice is of two kinds, actual and constructive. Actual notice may be either express or implied, in the one, it is established by direct evidence; in the other, by proof of circumstances from which it is inferable as a fact.

Implied powers. Implied powers are such as are necessary to carry into effect those which are expressly granted, and which must therefore be presumed to have been within the intention of the grant.

Implied promise. "In so far as such proposal or acceptance is made otherwise than in words, the promise is said to be implied." [Indian Contract Act (9 of 1872), S. 9].

The law recognises two kinds of promises : express and implied. The first is the express stipulation of the party making it to do or not to do a particular thing. The second, the law presumes from some benefit received by the party against whom it is raised.

Implied ratification. An implied ratification frequently arises from the acceptance of benefits which are the result of the authorised acts; for, when one with full knowledge receives the profits or benefits, he may be presumed to have ratified and accepted the conditions by which they are effected.

The authorities all agree that, although ratification by a principal of an agent's authorised acts may be implied, as well as expressed, nevertheless there can be no ratification binding on the principal which was not made with the full knowledge of all the material circumstances of the case.

Implied release. "Mere non-user of an easement is not an implied release within the meaning of this section." [Indian Easements Act (5 of 1882), S. 38, *Expln.* II]

Implied repeal. On a question under Art. 254(1) where an Act of Parliament prevails against a law of the State, no question of repeal arises; but the principle of implied repeal rests, namely, that if the subject-matter of the later legislation is identical with that of the earlier, so that they cannot both stand together, then the earlier, is repealed by the later enactment, will be equally applicable to a question where the further legislation by Parliament is in respect of the same matter as that of the state law. *Zaveribhai* v. *State of Bombay*, AIR 1954 SC 752, 758. [Constitution of India Art. 254.]

Implied revocation. The revocation of a will is implied when the existence of the intention of the testator to revoke is presumed and inferred from some subsequent act or event.

Implied tenancy. Tenancy presumed from the payment and acceptance of a sum in the nature of the rent.

Implied trust. IMPLIED TRUSTS are those that arise when trusts are not directly or expressly declared in terms, but Courts from the whole transaction and the words used, imply or infer that is was the intention of the parties to create a trust.

Implied use. A use which arose when legal ownership was transferred, but the transferor did not state for whose benefit the property was to be; the benefit of the property therefore still belonged to the transferor.

Implied waiver. A waiver is implied whenever it may be reasonably and fairly inferred from the act or omission or silence of the party who has the power of waiving.

Implied warranty. A warranty which is presumed by law.

EVERY warranty in a sale of goods is a promise that the article is so and when this promise may be implied by the contract of the vendor, or may result from the nature and circumstances of the sale, it is then called a "implied warranty."

A warranty that the articles sold are merchantable and fit for the purpose for which they are intended. [Sale of Goods Act (3 of 1930), S. 16(3)].

Impliedly. Implicity; by implication.

Imply. To enfold; to involve or comprise.

Import. "IMPORT" means to bring into the territories administered by any Local Government from sea, or from foreign territory, or from a territory administered by any other Local Government. [Opium Act (1 of 1878), S. 3]

"IMPORT" means the bringing or taking by sea and or air across any customs frontier as defined by the Central Government. [Destructive Insects and Pests Act (2 of 1914), S. 2(b)]

"IMPORT" means bringing to India. [Aircraft Act (22 of 1934), S. 2(3)]

"IMPORT" means bringing into India from a place outside India. [Seeds Act (54 of 1966), S. 2(7)]

"IMPORT" means bringing into any place within the territories to which this Act extends from a place outside those territories. [Insecticides Act (46 of 1968), S. 3(d)]

"IMPORT", with its grammatical variations and cognate expressions, means bringing into India from a place outside India. [Cigarettes and other Tobacco Products (Prohibition of Advertisement and Regulation of Trade and Commerce, Production, Supply and Distribution) Act (34 of 2003), S. 3(f) and Cigarettes (Regulation of Production, *etc.*) Act (49 of 1975), S. 2(f); Customs Act (52 of 1962), S. 2(23)]

"IMPORT", in relation to any technology, means the bringing into India, of such technology from a place outside India. [Research & Development Cess Act (32 of 1986), S. 2(d)]

"IMPORT" means import into India of services or goods including all materials, commodities and articles in a solid, liquid or gaseous state and all forms of energy for the use of any industrial concern in the smallscale sector. [Small Industries Development Bank of India Act (39 of 1989), S. 2(g)].

"IMPORT", with its grammatical variations and cognate expressions, means bringing into India any goods or services [Foreign Exchange Management Act (42 of 1999), S. 2(p)].

"IMPORT" means—

(i) bringing goods or receiving services, in a Special Economic Zone, by a Unit or Developer from a place outside India by land, sea or air or by any other mode, whether physical or otherwise; or

(ii) receiving goods, or services by a Unit or Developer from another Unit or Developer of the same Special Economic Zone or a different Special Economic Zone. [Special Economic Zones Act (28 of 2005), S. 2(o)]

A thing brought in from a foreign country; to convey as meaning; to signify; to be of importance or consequence to; something contained as signification or intention.

The term "import" means to bring into a country merchandise from abroad, and is the direct converse of the term "export" which means to carry from a state or country, as wares in commerce.

Goods brought into the country from abroad. The importation of certain goods, as authorised reprints of copyright books, false coin, and indecent or obscene prints, is expressly forbidden and with regard to certain other goods, such as wine, spirits, and tobacco, restrictions are imposed as to the place and manner of their importation.

"Import" is not merely the bringing into but comprises something more *i.e.*, "incorporating and mixing up of the goods imported with the mass of the property" in the local area. *Central India Spinning And Weaving And Manufacturing Co. Ltd. The Express Mills.* v. *Municipal Committee, Wardha*, AIR 1958 SC 341, 347.

The word 'import' means 'bringing into India from outside India' that it is not limited to importation for commerce only but includes importation for transit across the country. *Gramophone Co. of India Ltd* v. *Birendra Bahadur Pandey*, AIR 1984 SC 667, 680 [Copyright Act (14 of 1957), S. 51, 53].

"IMPORT" means bringing into India any article of food by land, sea or air. [S. 3(1)(v) of the Food Safety & Standards Act, 2006 (34 of 2006)]

"Import" and "export". Means respectively bringing into, or taking out of, India any goods by land, sea or air. [Foreign Trade (Development and Regulation) Act (22 of 1992), S. 2(e)]

Import into and Export out of. The words 'export out of' and 'import into' mean the exportation out of the country and importation into the country respectively. *State of Travancore-Cochin* v. *Shanmugha Vilas Cashewnut Factory*, AIR 1953 SC 333. [Constitution of India., Art. 286(1)(b)]

Import of Goods. "import of goods" with its grammatical variations and cognate expressions, means bringing goods into India from a place outside India [The Integrated Goods and Services Tax Act, 2017 (13 of 2017), S. 2(10)]

Import of goods into India. The 'import of goods into India' would commence when the same cross into her territorial waters but continues and is completed when the goods become part of the mass of goods within the country. *Garden Silk Mills Ltd.* v. *Union of India,* (1999) 8 SCC 744, para 18. [Customs Act (52 of 1962), S. 2(23)]

Import of services. "Import of services" means the supply of any service, where—

(i) the supplier of service is located outside India;

(ii) the recipient of service is located in India; and

(iii) the place of supply of service is in India [The Integrated Goods and Services Tax Act, 2017 (13 of 2017), S. 2(11)]

Import quota. Amount of a particular goods that a government allows to be imported.

Importation of girl or boy from foreign country. Whoever imports into India from any country outside India any girl under the age of twenty-one years or any boy under the age of eighteen years with intent that girl or boy may be, or knowing it to be likely that girl or boy will be, forced or seduced to illicit intercourse with another person, shall be punishable with imprisonment which may extend to ten years and shall also be liable to fine. [(w.e.f. 1-7-2024) Bharatiya Nyaya Sanhita, 2023 (45 of 2023), section 141]

Imported goods. Means any goods brought into India from a place outside India but does not include goods which have been cleared for home consumption. [Customs Act (52 of 1962), S. 2(25)]

Import of services. Means the supply of any service, where—

(i) the supplier of service is located outside India;

(ii) the recipient of service is located in India; and

(iii) the place of supply of service is in India. [Integrated Goods and Services Tax Act (13 of 2017), S. 2(11)].

Imported into municipal limits. The expression "imported into municipal limits" has to be interpreted as meaning "imported into the municipal limits for the purposes of consumption, use or sale" only. *Indian Oil Corporation* v. *Municipal Corporation Jullunder*, AIR 1993 SC 844, 848.

Importer. "IMPORTER" in relation to any goods at any time between their importation and the time when they are cleared for home consumption, includes any owner or any person holding himself out to be importer. [Customs Act (52 of 1962), S. 2(26)].

"IMPORTER" means an occupier or any person who imports hazardous wastes. [Hazardous Waste (Management and Handling) Rules, 1989, Rule 2(l)]

"IMPORTER" means a person who brings a motor vehicle into a local area from any place outside the state for use or sale therein or who owns the vehicle at the time of its entry into the local area. [Andhra Pradesh for an Entry of Motor Vehicles into Local Areas Act (26 of 1996), S. 2(g)]

One who causes imports to be brought in.

The term "importer" does not include a person who purchases goods from an importer after they have been brought within the boundaries and jurisdiction.

The term "importer" does not include one who receives from an importer.

The word 'importer' occurring in S. 2(26) of the Act includes owner of the goods. *Associated Cement Companies Ltd.* v. *Commr. of Customs,* (2001) 4

SCC 593, para 66 : AIR 2001 SC 593. [Customs Act (52 of 1962), S. 2(26)]

Importing. That imports or signifies. [IPC (45 of 1860), S. 9]; [General Clauses Act (10 of 1897), S. 13(1)].

Imports. Articles imported from foreign countries. They are the articles themselves which are brought into the country.

Importuning. Soliciting. [Cantonments Act (2 of 1924), S. 236].

Impose. "Imposed by a law" is equivalent to the expression "imposed under a law."

The word 'impose' in S. 59 means the actual levy of the tax after authority to levy it has been acquired by rules duly made and sanctioned, and it is such imposition that is made subject to the general or special orders of the Government. *Municipality of Anand* v. *State of Bombay*, AIR 1962 SC 988, 991.

To levy or exact (a tax or duty). [Black's Law Dictionary (10th Edn.) as cited in *Fortis Hospital Limited* v. *Commissioner of Customs, Import*, (2015) 12 SCC 715, para 13].

A levy or exact which has become payable and has to be paid. [*Fortis Hospital Limited* v. *Commissioner of Customs, Import*, (2015) 12 SCC 715, para 13].

Lay or inflict (a tax, duty, charge, obligation, etc.) (on or upon), especially forcibly; compel compliance with; force (oneself) on or upon the attention, etc. of. [*Fortis Hospital Limited* v. *Commissioner of Customs, Import*, (2015) 12 SCC 715, para 13].

To put, place, to place authoritatively; to levy. [Court-fees Act (7 of 1870), S. 29 and Constitution of India, Art. 19(2)].

Imposed in accordance with the provisions of the act. The expression "imposed in accordance with the provisions of the act" means "imposed in accordance with the procedure provided under the Act". *Raichur Municipality* v. *B.A. Prasanna*, AIR 1968 SC 255, 258.

Imposition. The term "imposition" is generally used for the levy of a tax or duty by legislative provisions indicating the subject-matter of the tax and the rates at which it has to be taxed. *Assistant Collector of Central Excise, Calcutta Division* v. *National Tobacco Co. of India Ltd.*, AIR 1972 SC 2563.

Imposition and collection. The expression 'imposition and collection' occurring in preamble of the Act would mean imposition already made or collection already made under state laws. *District Mining Officer* v. *Tata Iron and Steel Co.*, (2001) 7 SCC 358.

Impossibility. A thing which is impossible in law, is all one with a thing impossible in nature : and if any thing in a bond or deed is impossible to be done, such deed, *etc.* is void. (*Tomlin*).

The quality of being impossible. [Indian Contract Act (9 of 1972), S. 30].

Impossibilium nulla obligatio est. (*Lat.*) There is no obligation to perform impossible things.

Impossible. The word 'impossible' has not been used here in the sense of physical or literal impossibility. If it is impracticable and useless from the point of view of the object and purpose which the parties had in view; and if an untoward event or change of circumstances totally upsets the very foundation upon which the parties rested their bargain, it can very well be said that the promisor finds it impossible to do the acts which he promised to do. *Satyabrata Ghose* v. *Mugneeram Bangeer & Co.*, AIR 1954 SC 44, 46. [Indian Contract Act (9 of 1872), S. 56]

The word 'impossible' should be construed in a liberal sense so as to embrace within its purview acts which become impracticable or extremely hazardous and cannot be said to have been used, in a physical or literal sense. It is sufficient for the act to be impossible that it becomes impracticable or useless from the view of the object and purpose which the parties had in view. *Hari Singh* v. *Dewani Vidyawati,* AIR 1960 J&K 91, 94.

Not possible. [Indian Evidence Act (1 of 1872), S. 11, ill. (a)].

Impossible contract. One in which a party undertakes the performance of an act impossible in its nature.

Impossible events, Contingent on. [Indian Contract Act (9 of 1872), S. 36].

Impost. A tax, duty, imposition or tribute. [Companies Act (1 of 1956), S. 537(2)].(Replaced by Act 2013)

Impostor. One who pretends to be some one else in order to deceive others.

Impotence. Potency in the case of males means power of erection of the male organ plus discharge of healthy semen containing living spermatozoa and in case of females, menses. *Venkasteswara Rao* v. *Nagamani,* AIR 1962 AP 151, 152. [Hindu Marriage Act (25 of 1955), S. 12(1)(a)]

Impotence simply means inability to perform the sexual act. It may be pathological or psychological, permanent or temporary, complete or partial.

Impotency. 'Impotency,' as a cause for divorce, means an incurable defect, and not every temporary or occasional incapacity, but permanent and lasting inability for copulation and procreation.

The word 'barrenness' is in no sense the synonym of impotency.

Incapacity for sexual intercourse is an essential ingredient of impotency. Such an inability may arise from a variety of causes including the mental and moral disability. *Jagdish Kumar* v. *Sita Devi,* AIR 1963 Punj 114, 115. [Hindu Marriage Act (25 of 1955), S. 12(1)(a)]

Impotent. Powerless; decrepit; without power of sexual intercourse.

Impotency is the lack of ability to perform full and complete sexual intercourse. Impotent and partial intercourse would not amount to consummation of marriage, and if the husband was incapable of performing the sexual intercourse fully he would be in law deemed to be impotent. *Rita Nighawan* v. *Shri Balkrishnan,* AIR 1973 Del 200, 207. [Hindu Marriage Act (25 of 1955), S. 12(1)(a)]

A party is impotent if his or her mental or physical condition makes consummation of the marriage a practical impossibility. *Dig Vijay Singh* v. *Pratap Kumari*, AIR 1970 SC 137, 138.

Impotentia excusat legem. (*Maxim*) 'Impotency excuses the law'.

The impossibility of doing what is required by the law excuses from the performance.

Where the law creates a duty or charge and the party is disabled to perform it, without any default in him, and he has no remedy, there the law will in general excuse him. *In Re Presidential Elections* 1974 *in Special Reference No.* 1 of 1974, AIR 1974 SC 1682, 1683. [Indian Evidence Act (1 of 1872), S. 3]

Impound. To keep in the custody of the law.

Impound as relating to the 'impounding' of cattle implies an inclosed space.

To shut up in or as in a pound; to take possession of (a document or the like) for being held in custody in accordance with law.

"IMPOUND" the word 'impound' means to take possession of a document or thing for being held in custody in accordance with law. *Suresh Nanda* v. *CBI*, AIR 2008 SC 1414.

Impounding cattle. Keeping cattle under the charge of pound-keeper who will not return the same to the owner except on payment of a penalty.

Impounding goods. Placing goods in the possession of a distrainer or officer of Court.

Impounding of document. A Court has no power to impound a document under the Stamp Act after it has become *functus officio.* The "impounding" of a document should be held to take place not when a verbal order is given by the Court but when it is carried out, that is, when the document is taken into custody by the Court and an endorsement is made thereon.

According to the Oxford Dictionary "impound" means "to take legal or formal possession of" and impounding of a document cannot be made after the disposal of the suit. *Varghese* v. *State of Kerala,* AIR 1989 Ker 248, 249, 250. [Indian Stamp Act (2 of 1899), S. 33]

To place or keep a document in the custody of a Court which is done if it is a forged one or if it is one that has not the adequate stamp affixed to it or if it otherwise appears to be a suspicious document. [CPC (5 of 1908), S. 30(a)].

Impracticability. A fact which excuses a party from performing an act, specially a contractual duty.

Impracticable. 'Impracticable' is defined as incapable of being effected from lack of adequate means; impossible of performance; not feasible.

The word 'impracticable' must be understood to be impracticable from the business point of view. It must not be held impracticable on the slightest excuse. *Bengal and Assam Investors Ltd.* v. *J.K. Eastern Industries Private Ltd.,* AIR 1956 Cal 658, 661. [Companies Act (1 of 1956), S. 186(1)]

'Impracticable' presupposes that the action is 'possible' but owing to certain practical difficulties or other reason it is incapable of being performed. *Major Radha Krishan* v. *Union of India*, AIR 1996 SC 3091.

Not practicable. [Indian Trusts Act (2 of 1882), S. 11].

Imprescriptible rights. Rights unattainable by prescription.

Impressed. Imprinted; produced by pressure. [IPC (45 of 1860), Ss. 263 and 486].

Impressed stamp. "IMPRESSED STAMP" includes,—

(a) labels affixed and impressed by the proper officer; and

(b) stamps embossed or engraved on stamped paper. [Indian Stamp Act (2 of 1899), S. 2(13)].

Impression. An image fixed on the mind; a belief; act of impressing or making a mark by force or pressure applied (as) impression produced on wax by a seal.

The effect produced by external force or influence on the senses or the mind [Indian Evidence Act (1 of 1872), S. 28]; belief, generally ill-founded.

Impressment. Forcibly taking for the public service. [(18), Defence and Internal Security of India Act (42 of 1971), S. 3(2)].

Imprest. A loan or advance of money. [Companies Act (1 of 1956)(Replaced by Act 2013) and Art. 267(2), Constitution of India, S. 369(2), *Expln.*].

Imprison. Put into Prison.

'IMPRISON' means 'to confine; to incarcerate; to shut up or restrain one of his liberty.'

Imprisonment. "IMPRISONMENT" is defined as the deprivation of the liberty of another without his consent.

'Imprisonment,' as used in criminal statutes, alone and unqualified, does not mean imprisonment with hard labour, but means any other confinement than the latter.

"Imprisonment" shall mean imprisonment of either description as defined in the IPC (45 of 1860), S. 53, and General Clauses Act (10 of 1897), S. 3(27).

In case of life means imprisonment for life/imprisonment for the remainder of the convict's life. [*Duryodhan Rout* v. *State of Orissa*, (2015) 2 SCC 783, para 18] [General Clauses Act (of 1897), S. 3(27)].

The fact or condition of being imprisoned *i.e.* confined in prison. As a punishment it consists in the detention of an offender in prison. [General Clauses Act (10 of 1897), S. 3(27) and Constitution of India, Art. 361(3)].

Imprisonment for debt is the imprisonment upon process in civil actions, the object and the sole purpose of which is the collection of debts.

Imprisonment for life. In calculating fractions of terms of punishment, imprisonment for life shall be reckoned as equivalent to imprisonment for twenty years unless otherwise provided. [(w.e.f. 1-7-2024) Bharatiya Nyaya Sanhita, 2023 (45 of 2023), section 6]

Improbable. Not probable. [Indian Evidence Act (1 of 1872), S. 11(2)].

Improper. Means "wrongful". Not proper.

Improper acceptance. It would have been an improper acceptance, if the want of qualification was apparent on the electoral roll itself or on the face of the nomination paper and the Returning Officer overlooked that defect or if any objection was raised and enquiry made as to the absence of qualification in the candidate and the Returning Officer came to wrong conclusions on the materials placed before him. *Durga Shankar Mehta* v. *Raguraj Singh*, AIR 1954 SC 520, 524. [Representation of People Act (43 of 1951), S. 100(1)(c)]

Improper admission of evidence. Receiving of evidence which was not capable or worthy of being admitted. [Indian Evidence Act (1 of 1872), S. 167].

Improperly. Not in accordance with propriety, modesty, good taste or good manners. [TP Act (4 of 1882), S. 69(3)].

Improve. The charter of a corporation, declaring that its object is to improve, sell, lease or otherwise dispose of real estate, means 'the performance of any act, whether on or off the land, the direct and proximate tendency of which is to benefit the property or enhance its value."

To enhance in value or quality. [TP Act (4 of 1882), S. 63A(1)].

Improved value. In real estate appraisal, it is the land value plus the improvement value.

Improvement. "IMPROVEMENT" means any work which adds to the letting value of land, and includes the following, namely,—

(a) the construction of wells, tanks and other works for the storage, supply or distribution of water for the purposes of agricultural, or for the use of men and cattle employed in the agriculture;

(b) the preparation of land for irrigation;

(c) the drainage, reclamation from rivers or other waters, or protection from floods or from erosion or other damage by water, of land used for-agricultural purposes or wasteland which is culturable;

(d) the reclamation, clearance, enclosure or permanent improvement of land for agricultural purposes;

(e) the renewal or reconstruction of any of the foregoings works or alterations therein or; additions thereto, and

(f) such other works as the State Government may, from time to time, by notification in the Official Gazette, declare to be improvements for the purposes of this Act. [Land Improvement Loans Act (19 of 1983), S. 4(2)]

Betterment; enhancement or augmentation of value or quality; [Indian Trusts Act (2 of 1882), S. 20(d)]; a permanent addition to or betterment of real property that enhances its capital value and that involves the expenditure of capital or money and is designed to make the property more useful or valuable as distinguished from ordinary repairs. [TP Act (4 of 1882), S. 63A(1) and CPC (5 of 1908), S. 2(12)]; [Land Improvement Loans Act (19 of 1883), S. 4(2)].

The word 'improvement' connotes an idea of permanance, namely, some permanent benefit which would accrue to the reversioner or remainderman. *Bimal Chandra Das* v. *Mammatha Nath Das,* AIR 1954 Cal 345, 347. [Transfer of Property Act (4 of 1882), S. 51]

Improvement notice. Means a notice issued under section 32 of Act 34 of 2006. [S. 3(1)(w) of the Food Safety & Standards Act, 2006 (34 of 2006)]

Improvident. Unforeseeing [Specific Relief Act (47 of 1963), S. 20, *Expln.* 1].

Imprudence. Want of prudence. [Army Act (46 of 1950), S. 91(d)].

Impugn. To call into question; to challenge (the truth of a statement).

Impunity. An exemption or protection from punishment.

Imputation. Something imputed against (someone). [Indian Evidence Act (1 of 1872), S. 14, ill. (e)].

Imputation of unchastity. A statement imputing unchastity or adultery to a woman or girl, which is defamatory and actionable whether or not it has caused actual financial or material loss.

Imputation of unfitness or incompetence. A statement calculated to disparage someone in his office, profession, calling, trade, or business, which is defamatory and actionable whether or not it has caused actual financial or material loss.

Impute. To attribute or assign to [Hindu Widows' Remarriage Act (15 of 1856), Preamble]; to ascribe usually evil.

Imputed income. Income calculated from the supposed value of intangible or non-cash sources.

Imputed knowledge. This phrase is sometimes used as equivalent to "implied notice," *i.e.*, knowledge attributed or charged to a person because the facts in question were open to his discovery and it was his duty to inform himself as to them. In law of agency, notice of facts brought to the attention of an agent within the scope of his authority or employment is chargeable to his principal in most cases.

An understanding that is attributed to a person who had a duty to learn the facts, whether or not that person actually knew them.

In a summary way. Summarily [CrPC 1973 (2 of 1974), S. 260(1)].

In accordance with. The words 'in accordance' in S. 47-A mean 'in conformity' or 'as provided for'. *Mahesh Chandra* v. *Tara Chand Modi*, AIR 1958 All 374, 386 (FB) [U.P. Municipalities Act (2 of 1916), S. 47A(1)]

In aequali jure melior est conditio possidentis. (*Lat.*) In equal rights the condition of the possessor is the better; or where the rights of the parties are equal, the claim of the actual possessor shall prevail.

In all. The limiting of the liability to twenty thousand rupees in all must be read as referring to each claimant separately and it can't be restricted to the total claim of the several persons injured in one accident. *Motor Burners' Insurance Co Ltd.* v. *Jadavji Keshavji*, AIR 1981 SC 2059.

In ambiguis orationibus maxime sententia spectanda est ejus, qui eas protulisset. In ambiguous expressions the intention of him who used them should especially be regarded.

In any case. In S. 167, Indian Evidence Act (1 of 1872) also includes criminal trials.

"IN ANY CASE" the phrase 'in any case' in section 378(1) of CrPC, 1974, without hesitation, means 'in all cases', but the opening words in the said section put fetters on the State Government in directing appeal to be filed in two types of cases mentioned in section 378(2). *Lalu Prasad Yadav* v. *State of Bihar*, AIR 2010 SC 1561.

In any other manner whatsoever. It is wide enough to include property acquired under an award or a decree. *Bapusaheb Bharu Saheb Patel* v. *Gangabai,* AIR 1972 Bom 16, 22. [Hindu Succession Act (30 of 1956), S. 14(1), *Expln.*]

In any proceeding under this Act. Revision application under S. 115, CPC (5 of 1908) is also a proceeding under the Act. *Surendra Kumar Asthana* v. *Kamlesh Asthana,* AIR 1974 All 110, 112. [Hindu Marriage Act (25 of 1955), S. 24]

The expression "in any proceedings under this Act" connotes the proceedings before the Court in which an award has been passed. *Tayarai Gowda* v. *Sul. L.A. Officer,* AIR 1965 Mys 93, 94. [Land Acquisition Act (1 of 1894), S. 54 (*as amended by Mysore Act (17 of 1961)*)]

In any reference. In the context of S. 31(4), it is reasonable to think that the phase 'in any reference' means 'in the matter of a reference'. The word 'reference' having been defined in the Act as 'reference to arbitration', the phrase 'in a reference' would mean 'in the matter of a reference to arbitration'. "The phrase 'in a reference' is therefore, comprehensive enough to cover also an application first made after the arbitration is completed and a final reward is made. *Kumbha Mawji* v. *Dominion of India*, AIR 1953 SC 313, 318. [Arbitration Act (10 of 1940) (*repealed*), S. 31(4)].

In arbitrio judicis. At the discretion of the judge.

In arbitrium (arbitio) judicis. At the pleasure (descretion) of the judge.

In articulo mortis. At the point of death.

In atrocioribus delictis punitur affectus licet non sequatur effectus. In more atrocious crimes, the intent is punished though the effect does not follow.

In attendance. Present. [CrPC 1973 (2 of 1974), S. 309(1)].

In autre droit. In another's right, that is, in a representative capacity. An executor who sues for a debt due to his testator is said to sue in *autre droit.*

In being. Held to include a child *in utero*.

An unborn child after conception, if it was subsequently born alive, and so far advanced to maturity as to be capable of living, is considered as 'in case' from the time of its conception, where it is for the benefit of the child that it should be so considered.

In camera. In chambers; in private; in the judge's private room; not in open Court.

When the Court proceedings are held in the private chamber of a judge or when it is held in Court hall after excluding all spectators, the proceeding are said to be held in camera.

In private; in chamber (as opposed to 'in open Court'). [Contempt of Courts Act (70 of 1971), S. 7(1)].

In camera inspection. A trial judge's private consideration of evidence.

In capita. By heads; per capita.

In case. In the event of contingency.

In casu extremae necessitatis omnia sunt communia. In cases of extreme necessity, everything is common.

In charging. The word "in charging" mean "in demanding a price at the present time for services to be rendered". *U.D.S. Mills* v. *S.S.L. Railway*, AIR 1963 SC 21, 220 [Indian Railways Act (9 of 1890), S. 41(1)(b)(c)].

In common. Jointly.

That is shared, experienced or possessed together or equally. [Indian Railways Act (9 of 1890), S. 48].

In-competition Testing. Means collection of sample for testing from an athlete who is participating in a competition where such collection is made at any time during the period commencing at 11:59 p.m. on the day before the competition in which such athlete is scheduled to participate till the end of such competition and the sample collection process related to such competition. [National Anti-Doping Act, 2022 (15 of 2022), section 2(q)]

In conformity with. So as to be in harmony with. [Constitution of India, Art. 145(3), *Prov.*].

In consideration of marriage. In considering whether a settlement was made in consideration of marriage there are three tests: (1) It must be made on the occasion of marriage; (2) It must be conditioned only to take effect on the marriage taking place; (3) It must be made by a person for the purpose of or with a view of encouraging or facilitating the marriage.

In consimili casu, consimile debet esse remedium. (*Lat.*) In similar cases, the remedy should be similar.

In consuetudinibus non diuturnitas temporis sed soliditas raionis est consideranda. (*Lat.*) In customs, not the length of the time but the reason should be considered.

In consultation with. 'In consultation with' means to obtain the view of the person or body to be consulted in order to arrive at some conclusion in respect of the matter on which the advice is sought. *Akhil Bhartiya Grahak Panchayat (Bombay Branch* v. *State of Maharashtra,* AIR 1985 Bom 14, 25.

In contemplation of death. In taxation and property law, a transaction, commonly a transfer or gift of property, made by the donor with a view towards his death.

In contractibus, benigna, in testamentis, benignior ; in restitutionibus, benignissima interpretatio facienda est. (*Lat.*) In contracts, the interpretation or construction should be liberal; in wills more liberal; in restitutions most liberal.

In contractibus, rei veritas potius quam scriptura perspici debet. In contracts, the truth of the matter ought to be regarded rather than the writing.

In contractibus tacite insunt quae sunt moris et consuetudinis. In contracts, those things which are of custom and usage are tacitly implied.

In contractis tacite insunt quae sunt moris et consuetudinis. The clauses which are in accordance with custom and usage are an implied part of every contract.

In contrahenda venditione, ambiguum pactum contra venditorem interpretandum est. In negotiating a sale, an ambiguous agreement is to be interpreted against the seller.

In contravention of. In violation of. [CrPC 1973 (2 of 1974), S. 94(2)(b) and Constitution of India, Art. 13(2)].

In conventionibus contrahentium voluntas potius quam verba spectari placuit. In agreement the rule is to regard the intention of the contracting parties rather than their words.

In-Country Escort. Means individuals specified by the inspected State Party and, if appropriate, by the Host State, if they so wish, to accompany and assist the inspection team during the in-country period. [Chemical Weapons Convention Act (34 of 2000), (Verification Annex), 9]

In-country period. Means the period from the arrival of the inspection team at a point of entry until its departure from the State at a point of entry. [Chemical Weapons Convention Act (34 of 2000), (Verification Annex), 10]

In criminalibus, probationes debent esse luce clariores. In criminal cases, the proof must be clearer than light. (*Latin for Lawyers*)

In curia. (*Lat.*) In Court.

In custodia legis. In the custody of the law; under the control of the Court.

In derogation of. In partial abrogation or repeal (of a law); detracting from; in impairment of.

In abrogation or repeal of. [*KSL and Industries Limited* v. *Arihant Threads Limited*, (2015) 1 SCC 166, para 36].

In diem. (*Lat.*) For a day.

In discharge of his duty. The words "in the discharge of his duty as such public servant" mean "in the discharge of duty imposed by law on such public servant in the particular case and do not cover an act done by him in good faith under colour of his office." *Narsayya* v. *State,* AIR 1953 Nag 292, 295. [IPC (45 of 1860), S. 332]

In disjunctivis sufficit alteram partem esse veram. In disjunctives, it is sufficient if either part be true.

In dobio, pro lege fori. In a doubtful case, the law of the forum is to be preferred.

In dubiis benigniora praeferenda sunt. In doubtful matters, the more favourable are to be preferred.

In dubiis non praesumitur pro testamento. In doubtful cases, there is no presumption in favour of the will.

In dubio haec legis constructio quam verba ostendunt. In a doubtful case, that is the construction of the law which the words indicate.

In due course. In the prescribed, normal or logical course of events.

In due course of law. Means under some rule or enactment in force.

In effect. In force or operation.

In eo quod plus sit semper inest et minus. **The less is always included in the greater.**

In esse. In existence.

In expositione instrumentorum, mala grammatica, quod fieri potest, vitanda est. In the construction of instruments, bad grammar is to be avoided as much as possible.

In favour of. On the side of; to the advantage of; out of a preference for; so as to be payable to. [Constitution of India, Art. 16(4)].

In fictione juris semper aequitas existit. Equity is the life of a legal fiction. (*Latin for Lawyers*).

In force. In effect.

Operative. [T.P. Act (4 of 1882), S. 2(b)].

In forma pauperis. As a pauper, *i.e.* relieved of the payment of Court costs. As a poor person unable to pay Court fees.

In the character of a pauper.

In furtherance of common intention. Before it could be said that an act was done in furtherance of a common intention, there must have been a pre-arranged plan or common design to commit the act prior to its commission. *In the Basappa,* AIR 1951 Mys 1, 4. [IPC (45 of 1860), Ss. 34 and 149]

In good faith. Mere knowledge of an impending execution against a transferor is not sufficient to make the transferee a transferee otherwise than *in good faith*, when he does not share the intention of the transferor to defeat or delay his creditors.

'In good faith' means 'honestly, without fraud, collusion, or deceit; really, actually, without pretence and without intent to assist or act in furtherance of a fraudulent or otherwise unlawful scheme'. [Words and Phrases, Permanent Edn., Vol. 18-A, p. 91 as cited in *Brijendra Singh* v. *State of U.P.*, (1981) 1 SCC 597 : AIR 1981 SC 636, para 18]. See also *General Officer Commanding, Rashtriya Rifles* v. *CBI*, (2012) 6 SCC 228, para 71.

If a purchaser acts honestly he is acting 'in good faith'.

Having good faith. [IPC (45 of 1860), S. 52].

In hand. In one's possession or control. [Limitation Act (36 of 1963), S. 10].

In his absence. The words "in his absence" in S. 198(1) & (2) of the CrPC 1973 (2 of 1974), refer to the original entrustment and not to the time of the complaint, and the restriction is not intended to afford immunity to an offender but to prevent a person unconnected with the woman from giving publicity to a matter which neither the husband not the guardian is willing to agitate.

In his enim quae sunt favorabilia animae quamvis sunt damnosa rebus, fiat aliquando extentio statuti. In things that are favourable to the spirit, though injurious to property, an extension of the statute should sometimes be made.

'In his name' and 'let out by him'. The expression 'in his name' and 'let out by him' clearly convey the idea that the premises must be owned by him directly which is the case where he, as heir, steps into his father's shoes who owned the building in his own name and let it out himself. *Kanta Goel* v. *B.P. Pathak*, AIR 1977 SC 1599, 1601.

In his opinion. The words 'in his opinion' does not mean that the opinion of the custodian can be unrelated to the facts and circumstances placed before him at the inquiry. It cannot mean that the conclusion can be arbitrary or entirely subjective. *Dhiraj Lal* v. *Dy. Custodian of Evacuee Property,* AIR 1955 Mad 75, 77. [Administration of Evacuee Property Act (31 of 1950), S. 40(4)]

In his view. The words "in his view" mean "in the presence of" or "within the sight of."

In issue. In dispute. [Indian Evidence Act (1 of 1872), S. 21(2)].

In judiciis minori aetati succurritur. In judicial proceedings infancy is favoured.

In judicio non creditur nisi juratis. (*Lat.*) In law, no one is credited unless he is sworn.

In jure non remota causa, sed proxima, spectatur. (*Lat.*) In law the proximate, and not the remote, cause is to be regarded. (*Black*)

In kind. In the form of goods or property as distinguished from money.

In law. Implied by law; presumed by law.

In lieu of. In place of; instead of. [CrPC 1973 (2 of 1974), S. 87].

In lieu of dower. If land is given as dower prompt, no registration is necessary. But if a dower is fixed in cash and instead of paying it, the land is given, it will be *in lieu of* dower and it should be a registered document.

In lieu of payment. The expression '*in lieu of* payment' connotes that payment is outstanding (ie) that there is subsisting obligation on the Income-tax Officer to pay. *Hindustan Construction Co.* v. *V.S. Gaitende*, AIR 1965 SC 1316, 1319.

In like manner. The words 'in like manner' do not mean anything more in the context than 'similarly'.

In the same (similar) way. [T.P. Act (4 of 1882), S. 65A(3)]; [Constitution of India, Art. 148(1)].

In limine. (*Lat.*) At the outset; preliminarily; on the threshold.

In litem. (*Lat.*) In or during the litigation.

In loco. (*Lat.*) In the place.

In loco parentis. In the place of a parent.

The proper definition of a "person in *loco parentis*" to a child, is a person who means to put himself in the situation of a lawful father to the child, with reference to the office and duty of making provision for the child.

In maleficiis voluntas non exitus spectatur. In offences, the intention is regarded, not the event.

In matters of religion. Introduces, even though as a temporary measure, some more designated Sikh Members into the Interim Gurdwara Board by means of an indirect method. This is not a matter of religion. *Sardar Sarup Singh* v. *State of Punjab*, AIR 1959 SC 860, 866. [Constitution of India, Art. 26 (b)].

In my possession. The use of the phrase 'in my possession' in a bequest of 'stock in my possession,' is sufficient to render the bequest specific, and to show that testator intended to devise the specific property, and not a quantity or species of the thing bequeathed.

In novo casu novum remedium apponendum est. (*Lat.*) In a new state of facts a new legal remedy must be applied.

In obscuris quod minimum est sequimur. In obscure cases, we follow that which is least so.

In obtaining the licence. The expression "in obtaining the licence" does not mean in "obtaining the original licence only and it will include the expenditure incurred in taking a licence by assignment, *etc.*" *Union of India* v. *Karanpura Development Co. Ltd.*, AIR 1976 Pat 121, 123. [Coal Bearing Area (Acquisition and Development) Act (20 of 1957), S. 13(1)(i)]

In odium spoliatoris omnia praesumuntur. All things are presumed against a wrong doer. (*Latin for Lawyers*).

In omni actione ubi duae concurrunt districtiones videlicet in rem et in personam illa districtio tenenda est quae magis timetur et magis ligat. In every action where two distresses concur, that is *in rem* and in personam, that is to be chosen which is most dreaded, and which binds most firmly.

In omnibus. In all things.

In omnibus obligationibus, in quibus dies non ponitur, praesenti die debetur. In all obligations, when no time is fixed for the performance, the thing is due immediately.

In omnibus poenalibus judiciis, et aetati et imprudentiae succurritur. (*Lat.*) In all trials for penal offences, allowance is made for youth and lack of discretion.

In operation. An ordinance which has been pronounced a nullity by a Court of competent jurisdiction, and the proceedings under it set aside as illegal, cannot be said to be in operation.

In operation, Defunct Companies. Though a company is in the course of being wound up and not carrying on any business, yet so long as it remains undissolved, it will be considered to be in operation.

In order. The words "in order to" or "in order that," are used to intensify "with intent".

The words 'in order' can fairly, and should be construed as 'substantially in order' rather than 'in perfect order'.

In paenalibus causis benignius interpretandum est. In penal cases, the more favourable interpretation is to be made.

In pais. Out of Court; outside Court or legal proceedings; without legal proceedings or documents.

In pari causa. (*Lat.*) In a similar case; under like conditions.

In pari causa possessor potior haberi debet. (*Lat.*) Where the causes are equal, the persons in possession should be preferred.

In pari causa potior est conditio possidentis. When two parties have equal rights, the advantage is in favour of the one having possession.

In pari delicto. In equal fault; equally culpable or criminal; in a case of equal fault or guilt. A person who is *in pari delicto* with anoher differs from *a paricepes criminis* in this, that the former term always includes the latter, but the latter does not always include he former. (*Black*)

When both parties are equally in fault. [*Surasailbalini Debi* v. *Phanidra Mohan Majumdar*, AIR 1965 SC 1364].

In pari delicto potior est conditio defendentis (et possidentis). Where both parties are equally in fault, the condition of the defendant is preferable.

Where both parties do not show that there was any conspiracy to defraud a third person or to commit any other illegal act, the maxim, *in pari delicto etc.*, can hardly be made applicable. *Kedar Nath Motani* v. *Prahlad Rai*, AIR 1960 SC 213, 216. [Indian Contract Act (9 of 1872), S. 23; [Transfer of Property Act (4 of 1882), S. 53]

The maxim *In pari delicto potior est conditio possidentis* (where both the parties are equally in the wrong, the condition of the possessor is better), is not applicable to a case where both the parties are not the party to the fraud.

This maxim must not be understood as meaning that where a transaction is vitiated by illegality the person left in possession of goods after its completion is always and of necessity entitled to keep them. *Waman Shriniwas Kini* v. *Ratilal Bhagwandas and Co.*, AIR 1959 SC 689, 693.

Trusts Act (2 of 1822) constitutes an exception to the doctrine embodied in the maxim, *in pari delicto potior est conditio possidentis.* The maxim has no application to cases falling under S. 65 of the Indian Contract Act (9 of 1872) but only to cases falling under S. 84, Indian Trusts Act (2 of 1882). The maxim only protects a party in actual possession of an advantage; it cannot be the foundation of an enforceable right. *Appana Radha Sri Krishna Rao* v. *V.K.M. Kodandarama Chetti*, AIR 1960 AP 190, 193. [Indian Trusts Act (2 of 1882), S. 84 and Indian Contract Act (9 of 1872), S. 65 and S. 84]

In pari materia. Upon the same matter or subject or in an analogous case.

Statutes are *in pari materia* which relate to the same person or thing, or to the same class of persons or things.

"The phrase 'statutes *in pari materia*' is applicable to private statutes or general laws made at different times, but in reference to the same subject.

Statutes that are *in pari materia* are to be construed as though they had originally constituted one enactment.

In pari passu. On equal footing.

In particular. The words "in particular" indicate that restrictions imposed on the fundamental rights guaranteed by Art. 19(1)(g) which are reasonable and which are in the interests of the general public are saved by Art. 19 (6) as it originally stood, the subject-matter covered by the said provision being justiciable. *Akadasi* v. *State of Orissa*, AIR 1963 SC 1047, 1054. [Constitution of India, Art. 19(1)(g)]

Particularly. [Constitution of India, Art. 38(2)].

In patient. A patient in a hospital or infirmary who received lodgings and food as well as treatment—distinguished from out patient. [Employees' State Insurance Act (34 of 1948), S. 56(2)].

In payment of. A receipt on the foot of an account, reciting that certain notes are received 'in payment of the above account.' construed not to mean that the notes were taken in absolute payment thereof, but only to mean that the proceeds of the notes would be applied on the account when collected.

In pendente. In suspense.

In person. Without counsel in the conduct of one's action or defence.

In personam. Against person.

Proceedings in personam 'are proceedings which seek the recovery of a personal judgment.'

In personam actio est, qua cum eo agimus qui obligatus est nobis ad faciendum aliquid vel dandum. The action *in personam* is that by which we sue him who is under obligation to us to do something or give something.

In personem. In respect of a person; proceeding *in personem* is one directed or with reference to a specific person.

In plino lumine. In full light; in day time.

In poenalibus causis benignius in terpre-tandum est. (*Lat.*) In penal causes, law should be interpreted with leniency. (*Latin for Lawyers*)

In possession or power. The word 'possession' or 'power' implies that the document is in actual and physical possession or control of the concerned person. [CPC (5 of 1908), O. XIII, R.1]

In present or **in future.** The words in future have no reference to interest on principal amount that may accrue in future. [Registration Act (16 of 1908), S. 17(1)(b)]

In praesenti. At present; to take effect at once.

At the present time; at once; immediately effective.

In praesentia majoris potestatis, minor potestas cessat. In the presence of the superior power, the minor power ceases.

In pretio emptionis et venditionis naturaliter licet contrahentibus se circumvenire. In the price of buying and selling, it is naturally allowed to the contracting parties to overreach each other.

In proportion to. 'In proportion to its value' in an Act requiring that all property shall be taxed in proportion to its value, only means that no species of property, from which tax may be collected shall be taxed higher than any other species of property, and does not operate to preclude the Legislature from exempting certain property from taxation.

In propria causa nemo judex. No one can be a judge in his own cause.

In pursuance of. In carrying out; in exercise of the power granted by.

The words 'in pursuance of' used in a notification do not mean what would be conveyed by "in exercise of power conferred by". The words "in pursuance of" have several meanings. It may appropriately in a particular case mean 'confirmable to' or 'in accordance with'.

In quarters. In living accommodation. [Assam Rifles Act (5 of 1941) (*repealed*), S. 7(b)].

In question. In dispute; at issue. [Indian Evidence Act (1 of 1872), S. 14, *Expln*]

In re. In the matter; in the transaction.

In re dubia benigniorem interpretationem sequi, non minus justius est, quam tutius. In a doubtful case, to follow the milder interpretation is not less the more just than it is the safer course.

In re dubia magis inficiatio quam affirmatio intelligenda. (*Lat.*) In a doubtful matter, the negative is to be understood rather than the affirmative.

This is because the burden of proof is upon him who affirms rather than upon him who denies, a negative being more difficult of proof than an affirmative. (*Latin for Lawyers*).

In re lupanri, testes lupanares admittentur. In a matter concerning brothel, prostitutes are admitted as witnesses.

In re propria iniquum admodum est alicui licentiam tribuere sententiae. It is extremely unjust that any one should be a judge in his own cause.

In rebus manifestis errat qui actoritates legum allegat ; quia perspicua vera non sunt probanda. He errs who alleges the authorities of law in things manifest, because obvious truths need not be proved.

In receipt. The expression "in receipt" of the rents and 'profits of any land' or estate when used in an Act in conjunction with the words 'in possession of the land,' denote, not the receipt of rent from a tenant but, the receipt of the actual proceeds of the land.

In regard to. In the context in which they occur in S. 115(5), the words "in regard to" mean "for" or "for the purpose of". *M.A. Jaleel* v. *State of Mysore,* AIR 1961 Mys 210, 216. [States Reorganisation Act (37 of 1956), S. 115(5)]

In relation to. The words 'in relation to' do not mean that the offence must have been committed after the proceeding has started. Even if the offence was committed prior to the proceeding, it can be said to be in relation to the proceeding. If a proceeding is related to an offence, the offence itself is related to the proceeding. *Harikesh Neg* v. *State of Tripura,* AIR 1965 Tri 13, 14. [CrPC 1973 (2 of 1974), S. 195(1)(b)]

The expression 'in relation to' means to bring into association or connection with. 'In relation to' is equivalent to or synonymous with as to 'conerning with' and 'pertaining to'. *Doypack Systems (P) Ltd.* v. *Union of India,* AIR 1988 SC 782, 800. [Swadeshi Cotton Mills Co. Ltd. (Acquisition and Transfer of Undertakings), Act (30 of 1986), S. 3]

In relation to in that State. The expression "in relation to in that State" does not mean that the scheduled castes so specified are deemed to be or considered to be scheduled castes for that state alone. The entire caste, race, or tribe, or a part of or group within caste, race or tribe could be specified to be scheduled caste in relation to a State. *Manju Singh* v. *Dean, B.J. Medical College,* AIR 1986 Guj 175, 179. [Constitution of India, Art. 341(1)]

In rem. Against the property, not against a person.

A proceeding *in rem* is a proceeding instituted against a thing, and not against a person.

A proceeding *in rem*, in a strict sense, is one taken directly against property, and has for its object the disposition of the property, without reference to the title of individual claimants but in a larger and more general sense the term 'proceeding *in rem*' is applied to actions between parties where the direct object is to reach and dispose of property owned by them, or of some interest therein.

A judgement *in rem* is generally said to be a judgment declaratory of the status of some subject matter, whether this be a person, or a thing. Thus the probate of a will fixes the status of the document as a will; so a decree establishing or dissolving a marriage is a judgment in *rem*, because it fixes the status of the person. A judgment or forfeiture against specified articles of goods for violation of the revenue laws is a judgment *in rem*. In such case the judgment is conclusive against all the world, and, if the expression 'strictly in rem' may be applied to any class of cases, it should be confined to such as these.

An act or proceeding is *in rem* when it is done or directed with reference to no specific person and consequently against or with reference to all whom it might concern, or 'all the world'.

In rem; In personam. A judgment *in rem* settles the destiny of the *res* itself and binds all persons claiming an interest in the property inconsistent with the judgment even though pronounced in their absence; a judgment *in personam*, although it may concern a res, merely determines the rights of the litigants *inter se* to the *res*. *Viswanathan* v. *Abdul Wajid,* AIR 1963 SC 1, 15.

In render. Such as the tenant had to yield to the landlord, *e. g.*, rent.

In respect of. Giving the words 'in respect of' their widest meaning viz. 'relating to' or 'with reference to' it is plain that this relationship must be predicated of the grant, renewal or continuance of a lease and a lease must come into existence simultaneously or nearabout the time that the money is received. *Tularam Relumlal* v. *State of Bombay,* AIR 1954 SC 496.

The words 'in respect of' include even a document which was prepared before the proceedings started in a Court of law but was produced or given evidence in that proceeding. *Har Prasad* v. *Hansram,* AIR 1966 All 124, 127. [CrPC 1973 (2 of 1974), S. 195(1)(b)(ii)]

The words "in respect of" are wide enough to permit charges being made as terminals so long as any of these things, viz., stations, sidings, wharves, depots, warehouses, cranes and other similar matters have been proved and are being maintained. The words "in respect of" used in S. 3 (14) mean "for the provision of" and not "for the user of". *Sahadasa Saharanpur Light Railway Co. Ltd.* v. *Upper Doab Sugar Mills Ltd.,* AIR 1960 SC 695, 701, 702. [Indian Railways Act (9 of 1890), S. 3 (14)] Seeing that; as regards.

"In respect of" and "In". The phrase 'in respect of' has a wider connotation than the word 'in' and so long as the Speaker's action is relatable to any of the provisions dealing with his powers for regulating the procedure and conduct of business in the Legislature the Court's jurisdiction would be ousted. An authority who is conferred jurisdiction to decide a question, has jurisdiction to decide it either rightly or wrongly and so long as he is acting within his jurisdiction, he is immune from interference by a Court of justice. *Godavaris Misra* v. *Nandakishore,* AIR 1953 Ori 111, 116.

In respect of any employment. The words "in respect of any employment" used in Art. 16 (2) must include all, matters relating to employment as specified in Art. 16 (1). *General Manager Southern Railway* v. *Rangachari,* AIR 1962 SC 36, 41. [Constitution of India, Art. 16(2)]

In respect of the goods. The expression "in respect of goods" in Rule 5(1)(i) of the Rules means only "on the goods" and cannot take in the raw materials out of which the goods were made. *State of Madras* v. *Swastik Tobacco Factory,* AIR 1966 SC 1000. [Madras Gen. Sales Tax Turnover and Assessment Rules, 1939, R. 5(1)(i)]

In respect of the same matter. If the later legislation deals not with the matters which formed the subject of the earlier legislation but with other and distinct matters though of a cognate and allied character, then there is no question of the later legislation being enacted in respect of the same matter as contemplated under Art. 254(2). *Zaverbhai* v. *State Of Bombay,* AIR 1954 SC 752, 757. [Constitution of India, Art. 254(2)]

In restitutionibus benignissima interpretatio facienda est. The most favourable construction is to be made in restitutions.

In satisfaction of claim arising under the charge. CPC (5 of 1908), O. XXXIV, R. 14, where the charge is created by the decree itself, it cannot be said that the decree has been obtained for the payment of money in satisfaction of a claim arising under the charge. *Jagdamba Misir* v. *Ram Jit Singh,* AIR 1953 All 253, 254.

In-service candidates. 'In-service candidates' within the meaning of R. 19(2) is one who has put in a minimum of two years' service in respective fields in the rural areas and is selected against the reserve quota and not others. *Government of AP* v. *V. Nagaraju,* (1998) 8 SCC 66, para 8. [Andhra Pradesh Rules for Admission to Post Graduate Courses in the Medical Colleges, R. 19(1)]

In service training. The language of Schedule Column (10) of Himachal Pradesh Forest Service (Class II) Recruitment, Promotion and certain conditions of Service Rules, 1966 as amended by the Third Amendment Rules of 1986 is clear and unambiguous and unequivocally indicates that the period of training shall be treated as "in service." There is no prohibition or restrictions in the statutory rules prohibiting the "in service" period for being counted for the purpose of seniority. *State of U.P.* v. *J.L. Sharma,* AIR 1998 SC 378. [Himachal Pradesh Forest Service (Class II) Recruitment, Promotion and certain conditions of Service Rules, 1966, Col. 10]

In similar circumstances. The phrase "in similar circumstances" occurring in Section 4(2)(a) qualifies and governs both expressions, namely, "same" and "similar accommodation". *Miran Devi* v. *Birbal Dass,* AIR 1977 SC 2191. [East Punjab Urban Rent Restriction Act, 1949, S. 4(2)(a)]

In situ conservation. Means the conservation of ecosystems and natural habitats of and the maintenance and recovery of viable populations of species in their natural surroundings and, in the case of domesticated or cultivated species in the surroundings where they have developed their distinctive properties. [UN Convention on Environment and Development; Convention on Biological Diversity, Rio de Janeiro June 5, 1992, (Art. 2)]

In so doing. The phrase 'in so doing,' as used in an indictment that the defendant committed an assault with the intent in so doing of committing murder, is equivalent to the words 'then and there,' and means that the defendant then and there made an assault with the intent to commit murder.

In statu quo. In the same state; without change. Status quo.

'In statu quo' means being placed in the same position in which the party was at the time of the inception of a contract which is sought to be rescinded.

In such case. The words 'in such case' with which S. 74 of Registration Act (16 of 1908) opens, are equivalent to saying, "when, under the last preceding under S. 73, an application has been presented to the Registrar within thirty days after the making of the order of refusal by the Sub-Registrar."

In suit. Which is in issue in the suit.

In terrorem populi. To the terror of the people.

In testamentis plenius testatoris intentionem scrutamur. In testaments, we should seek diligently the will of the testator. (*Trayner*)

The paramount principle in construing wills is the intention of the testator. (*Latin for Lawyers*)

In testamentis plenius voluntates testantium interpretantur. In testaments, the will of the testator should be liberally construed.

In the absence of a contract to the contrary. In S. 82 of the Transfer of Property (4 of 1882) Act do not necessarily refer to a contract to the contrary executed at the time of the mortgage.

In the absence of such Court. The words 'in the absence of such Court' mean in the absence of a city civil Court, having jurisdiction in the matter. *West Bengal Financial Corporation* v. *Ghed Series Pvt. Ltd.,* AIR 1973 Cal 268, 276. [State Financial Corporation Act (63 of 1951), S. 32(11)]

In the course of. 'In the course of' means 'during' the winding up. *Jaddnath Roy* v. *Bank of Calcutta Ltd.,* AIR 1952 Cal 506. [Banking Companies Act, 1949, S. 45 A & S. 45-B]

The word 'course' conveys the idea of a gradual and continuous flow, an advance, a journey, a passage or progress from one place to another. Etymologically, it means and implies motion, a forward movement. *State of Travancore Cochin* v. *Shanmugha Vilas Cashewnut Factory,* AIR 1953 SC 333, 346. [Constitution of India, Art. 286 (1)(b)]

The expression "in the course of" in Art. 286 (1) (b) postulates that the transaction of sale must be an integral part of the activity of exporting the goods out of the country. *Madhadrao Ram Bali Ram* v. *State of Bihar,* AIR 1959 Pat 30.

The words 'in the course of' in the context of this section import that the statement must be made as a step in a pending investigation to be used in that investigation. *Sube Chaudhary* v. *King,* AIR 1950 Pat 44, 46. [CrPC 1973 (2 of 1974), S. 162]

In the course of business. The expression "in the course of business" in S. 32(2) of the Indian Evidence Act (1 of 1872), means in the way that business (which may be of a purely private or even trivial nature) is conducted. It has no connection with a course of business, which suggests a series of acts of business; the section would therefore apply to an act or of acts of a simple and private nature.

In the course of carrying on of business. The expression 'in the course of carrying on of business' means that the gift should have some relationship with the carrying on of the business. There must be some integral connection or relation between the making of the gift and the carrying on of the business. *Gift Tax Commissioner, Kerala* v. *P.G.T.*

Timbers, AIR 1972 SC 23, 27. [Gift Tax Act (18 of 1958), S. 5(1)(xiv)]

In the course of employment. An accident cannot be said to arise out of and in the Course of employment if it takes place on a public road in the absence of any circumstances showing that the nature of the employment of the workman required him to be there. The proximity of the place of accident to the place of work is irrelevant for this purpose. *Commissioners for the Port of Calcutta* v. *Kaniz Fatema*, AIR 1961 Cal 310, 313. [Workmen's Compensation Act (8 of 1923), S. 3(1)]

If a man (sailor) detests the seafaring life and jumps out deliberately off the deck and off the rails into the sea, he is certainly not doing it in the course of employment. *Mackinnon Mackenzie & Co. Ltd.* v. *Velma Williams*, AIR 1964 Cal 94, 98.

In the course of export. The expression "in the course of export" implies not only a period of time during which the movement is in progress but postulates a connected relation, sales in the course of export out of the territory of India means sales taking place not only during the activities directed to the end of exportation of the goods out of the country but also as part of or connected with such activities. *Mohd. Serajuddin* v. *State of Orissa*, AIR 1975 SC 1564, 1576. [Central Sales Tax Act (74 of 1956), S. 5(1)]

The words 'in the course of export' in Art. 286 (1)(b), Constitution of India cannot bear the same meaning as 'for the purposes of export'. The former would have a more restricted meaning than the latter. These words may mean the period when the goods exported begin their international journey and it will end when that journey ceases. *C. Govindarajulu Naidu & Co.* v. *State of Madras*, AIR 1953 Mad 116.

The concept of export in Art. 286, Constitution of India postulates, just as the word import, the existence of two termini as those between which the goods are intended to move or between which they are intended to be transported, and not a mere movement of goods out of the country without any intention of their being landed in specie in some foreign port. *State of Kerala* v. *Cochin Coal Company Ltd.*, AIR 1961 SC 408, 410.

The sale which actually occasions the export or import would fall within Art. 286(1)(b), Constitution of India. The sale under which the report is made that is protected by Art. 286(1)(b) and a purchase which precedes, such a sale does not fall within its purview though it is made for the purpose of or with a view to export. *East India Tobacco Co.* v. *State of Andhra pradesh*, AIR 1962 SC 1733, 1736, 1737.

In the course of export of the goods outside the territory of India. Aviation spirit and/or aviation turbine fuel sold to foreign going air-crafts for consumption during flight cannot be held to be sales of goods in the course of the export of the goods out of the territory of India, as mentioned in Art. 286(1)(b). *Burmah Shell Oil Storage and Distribution Company of India* v. *State of Bombay,* AIR 1962 Bom 295, 296, 301. [Constitution of India, Art. 286 (1) (b)]

In the course of inter-state trade. The sale by a trader in one State to a user in another state would be a sale 'in the course of inter-state trade' and there is no reason for imposting the restriction that the transaction should be one between two traders only. *State of Bombay* v *United Motors Ltd.*, AIR 1953 SC 252, 258. [Constitution of India, Art. 286(2)]

In the course of inter-state trade or commerce. If under the terms of the contracts of sale, the purchasers were required to remove the goods from the State of Bihar to other states, such sales must be held to be sales in the course of inter-state trade or commerce. *State of Bihar* v. *Tata Engineering & Locomotive Co. Ltd.*, AIR 1971 SC 477, 481. [Constitution of India, Art. 286 (2)]

In the course of the same transaction. No general rule can be laid down as to when different offences can be said to have been committed in the course of the same transaction and the question must be decided on the facts of each particular case. When the accusation against all the accused persons is that they carried out a single scheme by successive acts done at intervals and there was a complete unity of project and the whole series of acts were so linked together by one motive and design as to constitute one transaction, a joint trial is not only valid but desirable. AIR 1938 PC 130 : (1938) 1 Mad LJ 647, **Rel. on.** *Abdul Hamid* v. *The State of Tripura*, MLJ : QD (1956-1960) Vol. II C1561, 1958 CrLJ 97 : AIR 1958 Tripura 1. [CrPC (5 of 1898), S. 235]

The words "in the course of the same transaction" only mean during the period when the first act forming the series was committed and the commission of the last act ended. *State* v. *Mangtu Ram,* AIR 1962 Raj 155, 156. [CrPC 1973 (2 of 1974), S. 223(d)]

In the course of transmission by post. Until an article despatched by post is delivered or can be said to be delivered, it will be deemed to be in the course of transmission. *Radha Kishan* v. *State of U.P.*, AIR 1963 SC 822, 825. [Post Office Act (6 of 1898), S. 3(a)]

In the course of winding up. Once a petition for winding up has been presented everything thereafter is in the course of winding up of a company, although it does not necessarily follow that a winding up order will be made at the end of the day.

In the custody of any Court. The words 'in the custody' of any Court imply actual custody.

In the discharge of his duties. It is descriptive of the offence and not forming an ingredient of the offence. *Manshankar* v. *State,* AIR 1970 Guj 97 at 105. [Prevention of Corruption Act (2 of 1947), S. 5(1)(d)]

In the event. 'In the event, however,' as used in a will bequeathing a sum of money to the children of testator's sister, providing that 'in the event, however,' of the death of such children, refers to a future, not a past, event.

In the exercise of. Making use of; putting in operation of.

In the exercise of any power exercisable thereunder. The words "in the exercise of any power exercisable there under" appear to mean simply 'under that Act'. *Adarsh Bhundar* v. *Sales Tax Officer,* AIR 1957 All 475, 482 (FB).

In the first instance. As the first step in proceeding; in the first place.

In the form. A statutory permission that a thing or matter shall be "in the form" or to the "effect" or "to the like effect" prescribed means that the form must be strictly and literally followed.

In the hands of a person. The words 'in the hands' can and must only mean held by, owned by, and cannot mean physical holding of a property. *Raichand Gulabchand* v. *Dattatrya Shankar Mote,* AIR 1964 Bom 1, 4. [Transfer of Property Act (4 of 1882), S. 100]

In the interests of. Article 19(2) protects a law imposing reasonable restrictions on the exercise of the right to freedom of speech and the expression "in the interest of" public order, which is much wider than "for maintenance of" public order. If certain activities have a tendency to cause public disorder, a law penalising such activities as an offence cannot but be held to be a law imposing reasonable restriction "in the interests of" public order although in some cases those activities may not actually cause a breach of public order. *Ramji Lal Modi* v. *State of U.P.,* AIR 1957 SC 620; *Supt. Central Prison* v. *(Dr.) Lohia,* AIR 1960 SC 633, 639. [Constitution of India, Article 19(2)]

The expression "in the interests of" makes the ambit of protection (by the law) very wide. A law may not have been designed to directly maintain public order and yet it may have been enacted in the interests of public order. *Ramji Lal Modi* v. *State of U.P.*, AIR 1957 SC 620, 622 as referred in *Supt. Central Prison* v. *Lohia*, AIR 1960 SC 633, 639, para 12. [Constitution of India, Art. 19(2)]

In the interest of justice. Any Court may take cognizance of an offence after the expiry of the period of limitation, if it is satisfied on the facts and in the circumstances of the case that the delay has been properly explained or that it is necessary to do so in the interests of justice. [Code of Criminal Procedure, 1973 (2 of 1974), S. 473]

In the interest of public. The words in the interest of public as used in Ss. 2 and 3 of the Punjab Special Powers Press Act, 1956 are of great amplitude and are of much wider connotation than the words for the maintenance of. The expression in the interest of makes the ambit of the protection very wide for a law may not have been designed to directly maintain public order or to directly protect the general public against any particular evil and yet it may have been brought on a statute book in the interests of public order. *Virendra* v. *State of Punjab,* AIR 1957 SC 896.

In the interest of the general public. The expression 'general public' is wide enough to include a section of the public. Interest of the general public amounts to be deemed to be synonymous with the interests of the public of the whole of the country. All that this phrase means is, that a legislation passed in the interests of a limited class of persons, or for a territorially limited area, might well be a legislation in the public interests, despite the fact, that the public in other parts of the country might not be affected by such a legislation. *Kishori Lal* v. *State,* AIR 1957 Punj 244, 248. [Constitution of India, Art. 19(5)]

The expression "interests of the general public" is a wide expression which covers within its broad sweep all kinds of interests of the general public including interests of the sovereignty and integrity of India, security of India and friendly relations of India with foreign States. *Maneka Gandhi* v. *Union of India*, AIR 1978 SC 597, 645 [Passports Act (15 of 1967), S. 10(3)(c)].

The expression "in the interest of general public" embraces public security, public order and public morality.

In the interest of the security of State. The expressions "security of State" and "in the interest of the security of State" have different connotations. The expressions used under proviso (c) to cl. (2) of Art. 311 is the expression "in the interest of the security of State and not "for the security of the State", the meaning of the words "in the interest of" are wider than simply the expression "security of the State". The expression "in the interest of" includes everything that even indirectly helps the security of the State. *State of W.B.* v. *Narendra Narayan Das*, MLJ : YD 1977 Suppl to Oct C 732 : (1977) Lab IC 856. [Constitution of India, Art. 311(2)(c)]

In the interests of public order. The words 'in the interests of public order' are wider than 'for maintenance of' only in this sense that they include anything that even indirectly helps the maintenance of public order. If by 'for maintenance of' one understands anything that helps directly or indirectly or remotely the maintenance of public order, there is hardly any distinction between 'in the interests of public order' and 'for maintenance of public order. *Ram Nanden* v. *State,* AIR 1959 All 101, 104 (FB). [Constitution of India, Art. 19(2)]

The words must mean and include any measure or direction or order which assists in or is conducive to the maintenance and preservation of public order. *Indulal K. Yagnik* v. *State,* AIR 1960 Bom 399, 403.

In the manufacture of goods. When we speak of goods being required in the manufacturing process, we talk of goods which have gone to the making of it. Such goods may not be directly contained in the finished goods but it must be actually required, to transform the raw material into the finished goods by that particular process. *Bhartiya Electric Steel Co. Ltd.* v. *Commercial Tax Officer,* AIR 1956 Cal 299, 302. [Bengal Finance (Sales Tax) Act (6 of 1941), S. 5(2)(9)(ii)]

The expression 'in the manufacture of goods' should normally encompasses the entire process carried on by the dealer of converting raw materials into finished goods where any particular process is so integrally connected with the ultimate production of goods that but for that process, manufacture or processing of goods would be commercially inexpedient, goods required in that process would fall within the expression "in the manufacture of goods". *J.K. Cotton Spg. & Wog Mills* v. *Sales Tax Officer*, AIR 1965 SC 1310, 1313. [Central Sales Tax Act (74 of 1956), S. 8(3)(b)]

In the opinion of. The words 'in the opinion of' do not always lead to the construction that the process of entertaining 'the opinion' is an altogether subjective process not lending itself even to a limited scrutiny by the Court that such an opinion was not formed on relevant facts or within the limits. *Barium Chemicals Ltd.* v. *Company Law Board*, AIR 1967 SC 295, 324 [Companies Act (1 of 1956), S. 237(b)]

Ordinarily when the term "in its Opinion" is used in conferring powers on an administrative authority the conclusion reached by such authority is reached by it on its subjective satisfaction or consideration and not objectively. *Sahela Ram* v. *State,* AIR 1968 Punj 127 at 132.

In the opinion of Income-tax Officer. As observed in *Commissioner of Income Tax* v. *Macmillar and Co.*, AIR 1958 SC 207 the expression "in the opinion of the Incomes Tax Officer" does not confer a mere discretionary power. In the context it imposes a statutory duty on the Income-tax Officer to examine in every case the method of accounting employed by the assessee and to see whether or not it has been regularly employed and to determine whether the income, profits and gains of the assessee could properly be deducted therefrom. *Commissioner of Income Tax* v. *A. Krishnasekaran Mudalir*, AIR 1964 SC 1843, 1847.

In the opinion of the custodian. The use of the expression, 'in the opinion of the custodian' was not intended to invest the custodian with arbitrary authority. In forming his opinion, he was bound to act judicially. *Custodian Evacuee Property* v. *Rabia Bai*, AIR 1976 SC 2557, 2565. [Administration of Evacuee Property Act (31 of 1950), S. 10(2)(n)]

In the ordinary course of business in S. 32(2) of the Indian Evidence Act (1 of 1872) indicates the current routine of the business which was usually followed by the person whose declaration it is sought to introduce.

This phrase indicates the current routine of business which was usually followed by the person whose declaration it is sought to introduce and does not apply to any particular transaction of an exceptional kind such as the execution of a deed of mortgage but to the business or professional employment in which the declarant was ordinarily or habitually engaged.

The expression 'in the ordinary course of business' is susceptible of one meaning viz., that there should be a series of transactions as distinguished from one transaction. A stray transaction may not be said to constitute an ordinary course of business. *Peddi Virayya* v. *Doppalpudi Subba Rao,* AIR 1959 AP 647, 648. [Central Excises and Salt Act (1 of 1944), S. 2(a)]

In the pay of. The word "pay" must be construed in the context to mean wages or money given for service. The term "in the pay of" means "in the employment of". *Manshankar* v. *State,* AIR 1970 Guj 97 at 103. [IPC (45 of 1860), S. 21, Twelfth]

In the performance of functions. The expression 'any instrument chargeable, in his opinion, with duty, is produced or comes in the performance of his functions' necessarily implies that the power to empower under 33 (1) can be exercised only so long as the function is not performed or completed and not afterwards. *Komalchand* v. *State of M.P.*, AIR 1966 MP 2022 (FB). [Indian Stamp Act (2 of 1899), S. 33(1)]

In the possession or power. In one's possession or within one's control.

In the prescribed manner. The phrase 'with prescribed manner' in S. 8(4) confers power on the rule making authority to prescribe a rule stating the particulars to be mentioned in the prescribed form, the nature and value of the goods sold, the parties to whom they are sold and to which authority the form is to be furnished but the phrase does not authorise the rule making authority to prescribe timelimit within which declaration is to be filed by registered dealer. *S.T. Officer, Ponkunnam* v. *K.I. Abraham*, AIR 1967 SC 1823, 1825. [Central Sales Tax Act (74 of 1956), S. 8]

In the presence of. In the sight of.

In the second instance. Where an indorser indorsed a note, 'to be liable in the second instance,' such words should be construed to make sure against the maker of the note a condition precedent to the indorser's liability.

In the time of. During the life time of. [Legal Representatives Suits Act (12 of 1855), S. 1].

In the trade. The words "in the trade" refer not only to the trades people but also to the public. *Corn Products Refining Co.* v. *Shangrila Food Products Ltd.*, AIR 1960 SC 142, 144.

In the way of his business as agent. The expression "in the way of his business" means that the property is entrusted to him in the ordinary course of his duty or habitual occupation or profession or trade. *R.K. Dalmia* v. *Delhi Administration*, AIR 1962 SC 1821, 1840. [IPC (45 of 1860), S. 409]

In the whole. The expression "in the whole" means taking all the items of maintenance together, not all the members of the family put together. *Ramesh Chander* v. *Veena Kaushal*, AIR 1978 SC 1807, 1811. [CrPC 1973 (2 of 1974), S. 125]

In the winding up. The words "in the winding up" must relate to a point of time subsequent to the making of the order of winding up, although it may be that the appointment order is contained in the same order by which winding up is made. *Vishal Pal Sharma* v. *Sukh Sanchara, K. Co. (P.) Ltd.*, AIR 1962 All 88, 90.

In toto. (*Lat.*) Altogether; wholly; entirely.

In toto et pars continetur. A part is included in the whole. (*Bouvier*).

In transit/transitu. (*Lat.*) Goods are 'in transit' so long as they are on their passage, and until they come into the actual or constructive possession of the vendee, or of some person acting for him.

"IN TRANSIT", in relation to the carriage of goods by railway, means the period between the commencement and the termination of transit of such goods, and unless otherwise previously determined—

(a) transit commences as soon as the railway receipt is issued or the consignment is loaded, whichever is earlier;

(b) transit terminates on the expiry of the free time allowed for unloading of consignment from any rolling stock and where such unloading has been completed within such free time, transit terminates on the expiry of the free time allowed, for the removal of the goods from the railway premises. [Railway Act (24 of 1989), S. 2(21)]

Opium which is being carried about from place to place in a boat is no doubt "in transit" although the boat may be temporarily anchored or otherwise fastened.

The expression 'in transit' has been used to indicate the responsibility of the Railway in respect of the period upto the termination of transit. *Punjab National Bank* v. *Beniprasad*, AIR 1981 MP 95, 100. [Indian Railways Act (9 of 1890), Ss. 73 and 77]

In trust. The use of the term 'in trust' in a will rebuts the idea that an absolute estate was intended to be granted to the person mentioned.

In use. This phrase sometimes connotes an accustomed use, something generally and habitually done.

In utero matris. In the mother's womb.

In ventre sa mere. In the mother's womb. A child *in ventre sa mere* is to be considered as born. [10 Lah 713 : 116 IC 545 : 1929 L. 254 (2)]

In view of. 'In view of all the circumstances,' as used in a definition of ordinary care as that degree of care which ought reasonably to be expected from a person of ordinary prudence *in view of all the circumstances*, is not substantially different from 'under like circumstances.

In virtue of. Through the force of; by authority of. [CrPC 1973 (2 of 1974), S. 32(1)].

Inability. Inability is defined as the state of being unable, physically, mentally or morally; want of ability; lack of power, capacity, or means.

The term 'inability,' as is used a contract for the employment of a teacher, providing that, if by his inability or negligence, the interests of the school suffer, the school board may annul the contract, means the same as 'incompetency.'

Inability to maintain itself. The *inability to maintain itself* relates to the absence of sufficient maturity of physical and mental development in the child rendering it in consequence unable to earn its living by its own efforts and does not refer to inability through poverty or absence of means.

'Inability to pay' and **'insolvency'.** Are synonymous, but solvency does not mean ability to pay at all times, under all circumstances, and everywhere on demand, nor does it require that a person should have in his possession the amount of money necessary to pay all claims against him. Difficulty in paying particular demands is not insolvency.

Inaccessible. Whether or not a witness beyond the jurisdiction of the state is 'inaccessible,' in the sense in which that word is used in Acts relating to the procuring of his evidence is, in each particular case, a question for determination by the trial Judge in the exercise of a sound discretion.

Inactive company. For the purposes of section 455 of Act 18 of 2013, 'inactive company' means a company which has not been carrying on any business or operation, or has not made any significant accounting transaction during the last two financial years, or has not filed financial statements and annual returns during the last two financial years. [*Explanation* (*i*) to section 455(1) of the Companies Act, 2013 (18 of 2013)]

Inadequacy. Inadequacy of remedy at law, to entitle a party to equitable relief, exists where the case made demands preventive relief, as, for instance, the prevention of multiplicity of suits, or the prevention of irreparable injury. The mere assertion that the apprehended acts will inflict irreparable injury is not enough, but facts must be alleged from which the Court may reasonably infer that such would be the result.

The expression 'inadequacy of remedy by damages' means that the damages obtainable at law are not such compensation as will in effect, though not *in specie*, place the parties in the position in which they formerly stood.

Damages are called inadequate within the definition of irreparable injury, when those which can be obtained at law are not such as will compensate and place the parties in a position in which they formerly stood.

Inadequacy of price. 'Inadequate price', is a term applied to indicate a want of sufficient consideration for a thing sold, or such a price as under ordinary circumstances would be insufficient. (*Bouvier*).

The 'inadequacy of price,' which of itself will justify a Court in setting aside a transfer of realty is defined as an inequality so strong, gross, and manifest that it must be impossible to state it to a man of common sense without producing an exclamation at the inequality of it.

Inadmissible. Not receivable as evidence.

Not admissible; not to be admitted or entertained [IPC (45 of 1860), S. 200, *Expln.* and Constitution of India, Art. 114(2)]; [Income-tax Act (43 of 1961), S. 143(1)(a), Prov. (iii)].

Inadvertence. 'Inadvertence' is lack of heed, fullness or attention.

Inalienable. Not transferable.

Inam. A grant by government, often revenue free. [Constitution of India, Art. 31A(2)(i)].

Inam proceedings. The *Inam* proceedings are primarily concerned with the fixation of the quit rent of the *inam* lands with a view to offer to the *inamdar* the enfranchisement thereof on condition of paying the quit rent in perpetuity. *Harihar* v. *Hari,* AIR 1950 Ori 257, 259.

Inamdar. 'INAMDAR' means the religious or charitable institution for which a Devasthan inam is held, whether such inam is actually entered in the relevant revenue record in the name of such institution or of any person in charge of such institutions or having the management thereof. [Gujarat Devasthan Inams Abolition Act (16 of 1969), S. 2(10)].

Holder of any thing as a favour; the holder of an *inam.* A person in the possession of rent free, or favourably rented lands : or in the enjoyment, under the assignment thereof, of the Government dues of a particular portion of land, granted for charity, *etc.*

Inamdar means a person holding an *inam* or a share therein either for his own benefit or in trust and includes the successor-in-interest of an *inamadar*. *Mohd. Shaukat Hussain Khan* v. *State of Andhra Pradesh*, AIR 1974 SC 1480, 1485.

Inanimate things. Things which are not endowed with life or spirit. [Indian Railways Act (9 of 1890), S. 3(a)].

Incapable. The phrases 'incompetent,' 'mentally incompetent,' and 'incapable,' as used in the chapter relating to guardians of insane and incompetent persons, shall be construed to mean any person who, though not insane, is by reason of old age, disease, weakness of mind, or from any other cause, unable unassisted to properly manage and take care of himself or his property, and by reason thereof would be likely to be deceived or imposed upon by artful or designing persons.

Wanting in capacity or ability.

Incapable : Incompetent. *Incapable* is an absolute term, denoting inadequate mental, or physical, or moral power, or general unfitness or insusceptibility. *Incompetent* denotes a specific and relative incapacity as to a given task, duty, office, or undertaking. An incompetent person; an incapable subject. (*Smith Syn. Dis.*).

Incapable of giving evidence. The incapacity to give evidence mentioned in S. 33 of the Indian Evidence Act (1 of 1872) need not be a permanent one; something short of permanent incapacity might satisfy the words of the section "incapable of giving evidence."

Incapable of remaining before the Court. The words "incapable of remaining" refer to an accused's physical incapacity to remain before the Court and not where he is only inconvenienced. *Chimanlal* v. *Parashar Singh,* AIR 1957 Nag 101, 102.

Incapable of work. One who cannot work by reason of some specific disease or bodily or mental disablement, or deemed in accordance with regulations to be so incapable.

Incapacitated person. Any person, impaired by reason of mental illness, mental deficiency, physical illness or disability, advanced age, chronic use of drugs, chronic intoxication, or other cause (except minority) to the extent that he lacks sufficient understanding or capacity to make or communicate responsible decisions concerning his person.

Incapacitation. The action of depriving or disabling of legal capacity; the state of being disabled or lacking legal capacity.

Incapacity. Want of legal. physical, or intellectual capacity; want of power or ability to take or dispose; want of legal ability; to act inefficiently; incompetency; lack of adequate power.

Want of capacity; inability; powerlessness; legal disqualification. [Constitution of India, Art. 124(4)].

Incapacity to contract, either wholly or in part, may arise from a variety of causes. These are political or professional status; (2) infancy; (3) artificiality of construction, as in the case of corporations; (4) lunacy or drunkenness.

Incarceration. The act or process of confining someone.

Incentive. Something that arouses feeling or incites to action.

Incentive bonus. Economically speaking the clerical staff and the subordinate staff also take part in the production and there is no reason for excluding them altogether from the scheme of incentive bonus. *Burn & Co.* v. *Their Employees*, AIR 1960 SC 896, 897.

Inception. Initial stage.

An inception of a note is when it was first given or when it first became the evidence of the existing contract. It has no legal inception until it is delivered to some person as evidence of a subsisting debt. Merely writing and signing a note, and retaining it in the hands of the drawer, forms no contract.

Incerta persona. (*Lat.*) Uncertain person.

Incest. Sexual intercourse between persons who are within the prohibited degrees of affinity or consanguinity. Incest may be defined as sexual commerce, either habitual or in a single instance, and either under a form of marriage or without it, between persons too nearly related in consanguinity or affinity to be entitled to inter-marry.

Incestuous adultery. "INCESTUOUS ADULTERY" means adultery committed by a husband with a woman with whom, if his wife were dead, he could not lawfully contract marriage by reason of her being within the prohibited degrees of consanguinity (whether natural or legal) or affinity. [Indian Divorce Act (4 of 1869), S. 3(6)]

Adultery constituting or involving sexual intercourse or interbreeding between closely related or regarded as related in degrees in which marriage is prohibited [Indian Divorce Act (4 of 1869), S. 3(6)].

Incharge. One having the care, custody or superintendence. [IPC (45 of 1860), S. 137].

Inchoate. Imperfect; incipient; not completely formed; incomplete; unfinished (as) inchoate instrument, inchoate contract.

Begun but not completed. [Negotiable Instruments Act (26 of 1881), S. 20].

Inchoate bill. A bill of exchange wanting in some material particular.

Inchoate instrument. Instruments required by law to be registered or recorded are said to be "inchoate" prior to registration, in that they are then good only between the parties and privies and as to persons having notice.

Inchoate interest. An inchoate interest in real estate is not a persent interest therein, and therefore is not the subject of grant or conveyance.

Incidence. Falling on or contract with a thing (as) incidence of taxation.

An act or the fact or manner of falling upon or affecting; a happening.

Incidence of such duty. The expression 'incidence of such duty' means 'the burden of duty'. *Union of India* v. *Solar Pesticides Pvt. Ltd.,* (2000) 2 SCC 705, para 17 : AIR 2000 SC 862. [Customs Act (52 of 1962), S. 27(2), Proviso (a)]

Incident. "INCIDENT" means any occurrence, or series of occurrences having the same origin, which causes pollution damage or creates a grave and imminent threat of causing such damage. [Merchant Shipping Act (44 of 1958), S. 352 H(a) *Inserted by Amending Act (63 of 2002), S. 23*].

"Incident" means an occurrence, other than an accident, associated with the operation of an aircraft which affects or could affect the safety of operation. [Aircraft (Investigation of Accidents and Incidents) Rules, 2012, R. 2(p)].

"INCIDENT" means an event involving the actual or probable discharge into the sea of harmful substance or effluents containing such a substance. [Helsinki Convention on the Protection of the Marine Environment of the Baltic Sea (1974), Art. 2(7)].

That which follows the principal things. '*Incident*' is a thing necessarily depending upon, appertaining to, or following another that is more worthy or principal. Thus timber trees are incident to the freehold, and so is a right of way.

Something dependent upon, appertaining or subordinate to or accompanying something else of greater or principal importance; something arising or resulting from something else of greater or principal importance. [TP Act (4 of 1882), S. 2(b)].

Incident power. A power which, although not expressly granted, must exist, it being necessary to the accomplishment of an express purpose.

Incidental. A thing is deemed to be incidental or appurtenant to land when it is by right used with the land for its benefit, as in the case of a way, or water course, or of a passage for light, air, or heat, from or across the land of another.

The word "incidental" does not merely refer to a matter of casual nature. The procedure for disposal of an appeal includes as a necessary incidental matter the filling of an appeal on a proper fee. *State of Orissa* v. *Chakobai Ghelabhai And Co*, AIR 1961 SC 284, 287.

A thing is incidental to another if it merely appertains to something else as primary. A store run by the owner of a textile undertaking for sale of provisions, to the workmen employees of the factory is incidental to the business of manufacture of textiles. *State of Tamil Nadu* v. *Binny Ltd.*, AIR 1980 SC 2038, 2040.

Occurring or likely to occur in fortuitous or subordinate conjunction with something else. [Constitution of India, Art. 4(1) and Art. 169(2)].

Incidental authority. An authority which is needed to carry out actual or apparent authority.

Incidental business. The necessary and incidental business referred to in the articles of association of a corporation, which state that its business shall be the manufacture of clothing of every description, and the sale of clothing so manufactured, and the transaction and sale of all other business necessary and incidental to such manufacture and sale of clothing, does not include a purely mercantile business, such as the buying and selling of ready-made clothing.

Incidental damages. Losses which are reasonably associated with or related to actual damages.

Incidental expenses. The adjective 'incidental,' as used in appropriation bills to qualify the word "expenses," has a technical and well-understood meaning. It is usual for administrative or executive body to enumerate the principal classes of expenditure which they authorize, such as hire, fuel, light, postage, telegram, *etc.*, and then to make a small appropriation for the minor disbursements incidental to any great business, which cannot well be foreseen, and which it would be useless to specify more accurately. For such disbursements a round sum is appropriated under the head of 'incidental expenses.'

The phrase 'incidental expenses,' when used in an appropriation bill includes expenses of postage, printing, and stationery.

Incineration. Means an engineered process involving burning or combustion of solid waste to thermally degrade waste materials at high temperatures. [Solid Waste Management Rules, R. 3(1)(27)].

Incise. Make a cut into (as) incised wound.

Incite. Stir or urge to do an act. To spur on.

Incitement. The act of persuading another person to commit a crime.

Incivile est, nisi tota lege prospecta, una aliqua particula eius proposita judicare vel respondere. It is improper, unless the whole law has been examined, to give judgment or advice upon a view of a single clause of it.

Incivile est, nisi tota sententia inspecta, de aliqua parte judicare. It is improper to pass an opinion on any part of a passage without examining the whole.

Include. The word 'include' is very generally used in interpretation clauses in order to enlarge the meaning of the words or phrases occurring in the body of the statute; and when it is so used those words or phrases must be construed as comprehending, not only such things, as they signify according to their natural import, but also those things which the interpretation clause declared that they shall include. [Principles of Statutory Interpretation (12th Edn., 2010), p. 181 by justice G.P. Singh as cited in *Mamta Surgical Cotton Industries, Rajasthan* v. *Assistant Commissioner (Anti-Evasion), Bhilwara, Rajasthan*, (2014) 4 SCC 87, para 51].

It goes without saying that interpretation of a word or expression must depend on the text and the context. The resort to the word 'includes' by the legislature often shows the intention of the legislature that it is wanted to give extensive and enlarged meaning to such expression. Sometimes, however, the context may suggest that word 'includes' may have been designed to mean 'means'. The setting, context and object of an enactment may provide sufficient guidance for interpretation of the word 'includes' for the purposes of such enactment. [Karnataka Power Transmission Corporation v. Ashok Iron Works (P) Ltd., (2009) 3 SCC 240, para 17 : (2009) 1 SCC (Civ) 802 as cited in *Mamta Surgical Cotton Industries, Rajasthan* v. *Assistant Commissioner (Anti-Evasion), Bhilwara, Rajasthan*, (2014) 4 SCC 87, para 53].

Include or shall be deemed to include. The word 'include' or 'shall be deemed to include' is very generally used in interpretation clauses in order to enlarge the meaning of words or phrases occurring in the body of the statute or where it is intended that while the term defined should retain its ordinary meaning, its scope should be widened by specific enumeration of certain matters which its ordinary meaning may or may not comprise so as to make the definition enumerative and not exhaustive and when it is so used, these words or phrases must be considered as comprehending not only such things as they signify according to their natural import, but also those things which the interpretation clause declares that they shall include. *Chandra Mohan Saha* v. *UOI,* AIR 1953 Ass 193, 195.

Includes. The word "includes' is a phrase of extension and not of restrictive definition. It is not equivalent to "means". "Include" is very generally used in interpretation clauses in order to enlarge the meaning of the words or phrases occurring in the body of the statute; and when it is so used these words or phrases must be construed as comprehending not only such things as they signify according to their natural import, but also those things which the interpretation clause declares that they shall include.

The word "includes" in S. 3(a) of the Land Acquisition Act (1 of 1894) shows that the legislature intended to lump together in one single expression "land" several things or particulars such as, the soil, the buildings on it, any charges on it, and other interests in it, all which have a separate existence and are capable of being dealt with either in a mass or separately as the exigencies of each case arising under the Act may require.

Where the term 'include' is used in interpretation clauses there the words or phrases occurring in the body of the statute must be construed as comprehending, not only such things as they signify according to their nature and import but also those things which the interpretation clause declares that they shall include. *Taj Mahal Hotel* v. *C.I.T., Hyderabad,* AIR 1969 AP 84 at 86.

Wherever a definition uses the word 'includes' it must be understood as comprising something used in interpretation clauses in order to enlarge the meaning of words or phrases occurring in the body of the statute. *Dilworth* v. *Commissioner of Stamps,* 1899 AC 99, 105.

The word used in an inclusive definition denotes extension and cannot be restricted in any sense.

State of Bombay v. *Hospital Mazdoor Sabha*, AIR 1960 SC 610, 614.

In the context of S. 4, the word 'includes' is used only to enumerate the different classes of persons coming within the definition of guardian. *Ramchandra* v. *Annapoorni Ammal,* AIR 1964 Ker 269, 271. [Hindu Minority and Guardianship Act (32 of 1956), S. 4(b)]

The word 'include' is very generally used in interpretation clauses in order to enlarge the meaning of words or phrases occurring in the body of the statute; and when it is so used these words or phrases must be construed as comprchending not only such things as they signify according to their natural import but also those things which the interpretation clause declares that they shall include. *Regl. Director ESIC* v. *High Land Coffee Works*, AIR 1992 SC 129, 131.

Including. 'Including' is a term of extension. It imports addition. It adds to the subject matter already comprised in the definition. *A.C. Patel* v. *Vishwanath Chada,* AIR 1954 Bom 204.

Inclusio unius est exclusio alterius. The inclusion of one is the exclusion of another.

Inclusion. Comprising as a part.

Inclusive. Embracing; comprehensive.

Inclusive education. Means a system of education wherein students with and without disability learn together and the system of teaching and learning is suitably adapted to meet the learning needs of different types of students with disabilities. [Rights of Persons with Disabilities Act (49 of 2016), S. 2(m)].

"Inclusive education" means a system of education wherein transgender students learn together with other students without fear of discrimination, neglect, harassment or intimidation and the system of teaching and learning is suitably adapted to meet the learning needs of such students. [Transgender Persons (Protection of Rights) Act, 2019 (40 of 2019), section 2(d)]

Income. "INCOME" includes—

(i) profits and gains;

(ii) dividend;

(iia) voluntary contributions received by a trust created wholly or partly for charitable or religious purposes or by an institution established wholly or partly for such purposes or by an association or institution referred to in sub-clause (*iv*) or sub-clause (*v*) or by any university or other educational institution referred to in sub-clause (*iiiad*) or sub-clause (*vi*) or by any hospital or other institution referred to in sub-clause (*iiiae*) or sub-clause (*via*) of clause (*23C*) of section 10 or by an electoral trust;

Explanation.—For the purposes of this sub-clause, 'trust' includes any other legal obligation;

(iii) the value of any perquisite or profit *in lieu* of salary taxable under clauses (2) and (3) of Section 17;

(*iiia*) any special allowance or benefit, other than perquisite included under sub-clause (*iii*), specifically granted to the assessee to meet expenses wholly, necessarily and exclusively for the performance of the duties of an office or employment of profit;

(*iiib*) any allowance granted to the assessee either to meet his personal expenses at the place where the duties of his office or employment of profit are ordinarily performed by him or at a place where he ordinarily resides or to compensate him for the increased cost of living;

(iv) the value of any benefit or perquisite, whether convertible into money or not, obtained from a company either by a director or by a person who has a substantial interest in the company, or by a relative of the director or such person, and any sum paid by any such company in respect of any obligation which, but for such payment, would have been payable by the director or other person aforesaid;

(*iva*) the value of any benefit or perquisite, whether convertible into money or not, obtained by any representative assessee mentioned in clause (*iii*) or clause (*iv*) of sub-section (1) of Section 160 or by any person on whose behalf or for whose benefit any income is receivable by the representative assessee (such person being hereafter in this sub-clause referred to as the "beneficiary") and any sum paid by the representative assessee in respect of any obligation which, but for such payment, would have been payable by the beneficiary;

(v) any sum chargeable to income-tax under clauses (*ii*) and (*iii*) of Section 28 or Section 41 or Section 59;

(*va*) any sum chargeable to income-tax under clause (*iiia*) of Section 28;

(*vb*) any sum chargeable to income-tax under clause (*iiib*) of Section 28;

(*vc*) any sum chargeable to income-tax under clause (*iiic*) of Section 28;

(*vd*) the value of any benefit or perquisite taxable under clause (*iv*) of Section 28;

(*ve*) any sum chargeable to income-tax under clause (*v*) of Section 28;

(vi) any capital gains chargeable under Section 45;

(vii) the profits and gains of any business of insurance carried on by a mutual insurance company or by a co-operative society, computed in accordance with Section 44 or any surplus taken to be such profits and gains by virtue of provisions contained in the First Schedule;

(viia) The profits and gains of any business of banking (including providing credit facilities) carried on by a co-operative society with its members;

(viii) *****]

(ix) any winnings from lotteries, crossword puzzles, races including horse races, card games and other games of any sort; or from gambling or betting of any form or nature whatsoever;

Explanation.—For the purposes of this sub-clause,—

(i) 'lottery' includes winnings from prizes awarded to any person by draw of lots or by chance or in any other manner whatsoever, under any scheme or arrangement by whatever name called;

(ii) 'card game and other game of any sort' includes any game show, an entertainment programme on television or electronic mode, in which people compete to win prizes or any other similar game;

(x) any sum received by the assessee from his employees as contributions to any provident fund or superannuation fund or any fund set up under the provisions of the Employees' State Insurance Act, 1948 (34 of 1948), or any other fund for the welfare of such employees;

(xi) any sum received under a Keyman insurance policy including the sum allocated by way of bonus on such policy.

Explanation.—For the purposes of this clause, the expression "Keyman insurance policy" shall have the meaning assigned to it in the *Explanation* to clause (10D) of Section 10.

(xii) any sum referred to in clause (*va*) of section 28;

(xiii) any sum referred to in clause (*v*) of sub-section (2) of section 56;

(xiv) any sum referred to in clause (*vi*) of sub-section (2) of section 56;

(xv) any sum of money or value of property referred to in clause (*vii*) or clause (*viia*) of sub-section (2) of section 56;

(xvi) any consideration received for issue of shares as exceeds the fair market value of the shares referred to in clause (*viib*) of sub-section (2) of section 56.

(xvii) any sum of money referred to in clause (*ix*) of sub-section (2) of section 56;

(xviia) any sum of money or value of property referred to in clause (*x*) of sub-section (2) of section 56;

(xviib) any compensation or other payment referred to in clause (*xi*) of sub-section (2) of section 56;

(xviic) any sum referred to in clause (xii) of sub-section (2) of section 56;

(xviid) any sum referred to in clause (xiii) of sub-section (2) of section 56;

(xviii) assistance in the form of a subsidy or grant or cash incentive or duty drawback or waiver or concession or reimbursement (by whatever name called) by the Central Government or a State Government or any authority or body or agency in cash or kind to the assessee other than,—

(a) the subsidy or grant or reimbursement which is taken into account for determination of the actual cost of the asset in accordance with the provisions of *Explanation 10* to clause (*1*) of section 43; or

(b) the subsidy or grant by the Central Government for the purpose of the corpus of a trust or institution established by the Central Government or a State Government, as the case may be. [Income-tax Act (43 of 1961) S. 2(24)]

'INCOME' means—

(i) profits and gains;

(ii) dividends and interests;

(iii) the value of any benefit or perquisite whether convertible into money or not, obtained from a company either by a director or a person who has substantial interest in the company, and any sum paid by such company in respect of any obligation, which but for such payment would have been payable by the director or other person aforesaid, occurring or arising to a person within the State from any profession, trade or calling other than agriculture. [M.P. Vriti Kar Adhiniyam (16 of 1995), S. 2(e)]

'Income is defined as that gain which proceeds from labour, business, or property of any kind; the profits of commerce or business.

"INCOME" IN THE INCOME-TAX Act connotes a periodical monetary return coming in with some sort of regularity from definite sources. The source is not necessarily one which is expected to be continuously productive but it must be one whose object is the production of a definite return, excluding anything in the nature of a mere windfall.

Income means that which comes in as the periodical produce of one's work, business, lands or investments; annual or periodical receipts accruing to a person or corporation.

The income by sale of forest trees is income and is taxable.

The prize money in a motor rally received by the winner is income. *Commissioner of Income Tax* v. *G.R. Karthikeyan*, AIR 1993 SC 1671, 1675. [Income-tax Act (43 of 1961), S. 2(24)]

The expression 'income' includes not merely what is received or what comes in by exploiting the use of a property but also what one saves by using it oneself. *Bhagwandas* v. *Union of India*, AIR 1981 SC 907, 911. [Constitution of India, Seventh Schedule, List I, Entry 82].

'*Balali*' And '*Shagirdi*' which the assessees get from persons to whom goods are sold are payments which have to be included in the income of the firm from which profits are to be determined. *Daya Chand Hardial* v. *C.I.T.*, AIR 1954 Punj 52. [Excess Profits Tax Act (15 of 1940), S. 2(13)]

The term "income" is wide in its import and elastic in its ambit. The amount received by the petitioner from the Trust Fund is "income" within the meaning of the proviso to S. 3(1). *Walashan Prince Nawab Muazzam Jah Bahadur* v. *Expenditure Tax Officer*, AIR 1961 AP 374, 377. [Expenditure-tax Act (35 of 1987), S. 3(1), Proviso]

The expression 'income' cannot take within its sweep the capital assets like lands and hereditaments and can only include the return accruing from those assets. *Gita* v. *Prohat Kumar,* AIR 1988 Cal 83, 84. [Hindu Marriage Act (25 of 1955), S. 24]

The expression 'income' does not mean mere production of receipt of a commodity which may be converted into money. Income arises when the commodity is disposed of by sale, comsumption or use in the manufacture or other processes carried on by the assessee of that commodity. *Rajalinga Raja* v. *State of Madras*, AIR 1967 SC 814, 815.

Income and Capital. In popular and also in legal parlance "capital" is understood as the source of income and "income" as the fruit of capital. *CIT* v. *Shamlal Narula,* AIR 1963 Punj 411, 414. [Land Acquisition Act (1 of 1894) S. 34.

'Income' and 'profits'. 'Income and 'profits' are not synonymous in all cases. In ordinary economic sense the expression 'income' includes not only what is received or what comes in by exploiting the use of property but also what one saves by using it one self and in this sense the word 'income' and 'profits' are to be treated differently. [*Mahila Vikas Mandal Colaba* v. *State of Maharashtra,* (2005) 6 SCC 184]

Income as returned means income as disclosed or shown in the return filed. *Mansukhlal* v. *C. Bombay City II, Bombay*, AIR 1966 SC 835 at 839.

Income assessed in a foreign country. The expression "income assessed in a foreign country" would clearly mean subject to tax in the foreign country. *CIT, West Bengal, Calcutta* v. *Clive Insurance Co. Ltd.*, AIR 1978 SC 1290.

Income by way of stake money. Means the gross amount of prize money received on a race horse or race horses by the owner thereof on account of the horse or horses or any one or more of the horses winning or being placed second or in any lower position in horse races. [Income-tax Act (43 of 1961), S. 74A(3) *Expln.* (c)]

Income derived from voluntary contribution. The expression 'income derived from voluntary contribution' occurring in S. 12(1) of the Act refers to income in the form of voluntary contributions received by the recipient religious or charitable trust. *R.B. Shreeram Religious & Charitable Trust* v. *CIT,* (1998) 5 SCC 730, para 8 : AIR 1998 SC 2419. [Income-tax Act (43 of 1961), S. 12(1)]

Income from investment. The rent derived from the building may be income from investment. *Commissioner, City Corporation* v. *Harihara Iyer*, AIR 1961 Ker 62, 66.

Income from other sources. The residuary head of income can be resorted to only if none of the specific heads is applicable to the income in question. It comes into operation only after the preceeding heads are excluded. *S.G. Mercantile Corporation P. Ltd.* v. *Commissioner of Income Tax, Calcutta*, AIR 1972 SC 732, 736.

Income or Profit. Profit or income can mean only the balance after deducting charges and losses and not mere gross receipts.

Income profits or gains have escaped assessment. The expression "income profits or gains have escaped assessment" is to be interpreted as including cases where part of the income has escaped assessment.

Income sufficient for support. The word 'sufficient' connotes that the income of the applicant must be such which would be sufficient for a normal person for his or her sustenance as well as to meet the necessary expenses of the proceeding. *Krishnapriya* v. *Birakishore,* AIR 1987 Ori 65, 67. [Hindu Marriage Act (25 of 1955); Ss. 24 and 13]

Income-tax. "Income-tax" is a tax on income. It is not meant to be a tax on anything else. It is one tax, not a collection of taxes essentially distinct.

Income-tax has always been regarded as a typical example of a direct tax. There is a marked distinction between a tax on gross income and a tax on income which for taxation purposes means gains and profits. There may be considerable gross revenues but no income taxable by an Income-tax in the accepted sense.

Income tax authority. Means a Commissioner, a Joint Commissioner, a Director, a Joint Director, an Assistant Director, Deputy Director or an Assessing Officer and for the purposes of clause (i) of sub-section (1), clause (i) of sub-section (3) and sub-section (5), includes an Inspector of Income-tax if so authorised by any such authority. [Income-tax Act (43 of 1961), S. 133A(6) *Expln.* (a)]

The term 'Income-tax authority' includes the Income-tax Officer, Assistant Appellate Commissioner and others and not Income-tax Appellate Tribunal. *I.T. Commissioner, Calcutta* v. *B.N. Bhattacharjee*, AIR 1979 SC 1725, 1730. [Income-tax Act (43 of 1961), Ss. 245-A (1)(d), 245-C (1-B)(iii)]

Incommodum non solvit argumentum. (*Lat.*) An inconvenience does not settle an argument.

Incommunicado. A person accused of a crime who does not have the right of communicating with other than the ones in charge of his custody or the one investigating the crime.

Incompatibility. Incapability of existing or being exercised together. As ground for divorce, refers to such deep and irreconcilable conflict in personalities or temperaments of parties as makes it impossible for them to continue normal marital relationship. Such conflict of personalities and dispositions must be so deep as to be irreconcilable and irremediable. (*Black*)

Incompetency. The state of being incompetent; inadmissibility as evidence.

The quality of being incompetent; incapacity or disqualification. [Constitution of India, Art. 369(b)].

Incompetent. Unqualified; ineligible; unfit; inadmissible as evidence.

Not competent; not having the requisite capacity or qualification. [Indian Evidence Act (1 of 1872), S. 118, *Expln.* and TP Act (4 of 1882), S. 103].

Incompetent : Incompetency. One is incompetent who is wanting in the requisite qualifications for the business intrusted to him.

Inconclusive. Not conclusive; subject to disproof.

Inconclusive proof. Proof that does not bring to an end a doubt.

Inconsistent. When an Act says that its provisions are to be observed except so far as they may be "inconsistent" with another or a previous statute, the inconsistency connoted must be one "so at variance with the machinery and procedure indicated by the previous Act that, if that obligation were added, the machinery of the previous Act would not work".

Now, "Inconsistent", according to Black's Legal Dictionary, means "mutually repugnant or contradictory; contrary, the one to the other so that both cannot stand, but the acceptance or establishment of the one implies the abrogation or abandonment of the other". [Black's Legal Dictionary as cited in *Deepjyoti Gas Agency, Pandu Guwahati and Ors.* v. *State of Assam and Ors.* Criminal Petition No. 384/2014, decided on 13-12-2017].

If the provisions in the two legislations relate to the same subject matter, to the same situation and both substantially overap and are co-extensive and at the same time so contrary and repugnant in their terms and impact that one must perish wholly if the other were to prevail at all, then, only then, are they inconsistent. *Basti Sugar Mills* v. *State of U.P.*, AIR 1979 SC 262, 269. [Payment of Bonus Act (21 of 1965), S. 34]

Not consistent; not agreeing in substance, spirit or form; contrary to one another. [Constitution of India, Art. 140].

Inconsistent : Inconsistency. Things are said to be inconsistent when they are contrary to one another, so that one infers the negation, destruction or falsity of the other.

'Inconsistency' implies opposition; antagonism; repugnance.

Inconsistently. In an inconsistent manner.

Inconvenience. A discomfort; something that gives trouble.

"Inconvenience means" (1) the state of quality of being inconvenient, (2) something inconvenient; a hindrance, trouble, or difficulty. [Collin's dictionary as cited in *Shreya Singhal* v. *Union of India*, (2015) 5 SCC 1, para 54].

Inconvertible paper currency. Paper money which cannot be exchanged on demand for cash to its full nominal value. Such currency is generally at a discount in the market.

Incorporate. To form or unite into a corporation either by character or by statute.

An Act which is repealed and in part re-enacted by a subsequent and consolidating Act is thereby "incorporated" with the latter Act.

To unite or combine with something else so as to form one body. [long title, Jawaharlal Nehru University Act (53 of 1966)]; [Forward Contracts Act (74 of 1952), S. 6(2)(b)].

Incorporated. Constituted as a body corporate legally authorised to act as a single person [Income-tax Act (43 of 1961), S. 2(17)(ii) and Constitution of India, Art. 317(4)]; [Trade and Merchandise Marks Act (43 of 1958), S. 7(2)].

A will consists of more than one document; to the original will duly executed may be attached one or more codicils, also duly executed, and the original will and the codicils must be read together. The codicils are said to be incorporated with the will.

Incorporated company. The term 'incorporated company' is defined as a corporation formed for the purpose of carrying on a business for profit; and, while it is true that an incorporated city or town is a corporation, yet it is not a company in any sense, so that a municipal corporation is not an incorporated company.

"INCORPORATED COMPANY" An 'incorporated company' does not owe its existence to the Companies Act. An 'incorporated company' is formed by the act of any seven or more persons (or two or more persons for a private company) associated for any lawful purpose subscribing their names to a Memorandum of Association and by complying with the requirements of the Companies Act in respect of registration. *Dalco Engineering*

Private Ltd. v. *Shree Satish Prabhakar Padhye* v. *UOI*, AIR 2010 SC 1576.

Incorporated town. An incorporated town is not a village, city, or township, within the meaning of a statute authorizing villages, cities, and townships to issue bonds in aid of a railroad.

The word 'town' is sometimes employed to designate a township; but the term 'incorporated town' is seldom, if ever, employed to embrace such a body.

The action of forming into a body corporate legally authorised to act as a single person; the merging of one thing in another so that the two form a single whole. [Citizenship Act (57 of 1955), S. 7].

Incorporation. The act of incorporating.

A right having no material existence in itself, but attaching as a right or profit to some actual thing. [IPC (45 of 1860), S. 141, Fourth].

Incorporation of company. The act or process of forming or creating a company.

Incorporeal. Intangible; without substance, as a right. Without body; not of a material nature; the opposite of corporeal.

Incorporeal chattel. An 'incorporeal chattel' means an interest arising out of personal property, as an incorporeal hereditament is an interest or right issuing out of land.

Incorporeal hereditament. 'Incorporeal hereditaments' are not the object of sensation, can neither be seen nor handled, are creatures of the mind, and exist only in contemplation. A species of incorporeal hereditaments is that of ways, or the right of going over another man's ground.

Incorporeal property. Intangible property; choses in action.

Incorporeal real property. Incorporeal real property is defined to be the right issuing out of or annexed to a thing corporeal, and consists of the right to have some part only of the produce or benefit or the corporeal property, or to exercise a right or have an easement or privilege or advantage over or out of it.

Incorporeal rights. A right having no material existence in itself, but attaching as a right or profit to some actual thing.

Incorporeal thing. Incorporeal things are such as are not manifest to the senses, and which are conceived only by understanding such as the rights of inheritance, servitudes, and obligations.

Incorrect view. An incorrect conception. [CPC (5 of 1908), S. 13(c)].

Incorrigible. Incapable of being corrected, reformed, amended, or improved.

Increase. Growth; enlargement; multiplication.

Increase of hazard. Some alteration or change in the situation or condition of insured property which tends to increase the risk.

Increased quantity. Includes increase in imports whether in absolute terms or relative to domestic production. [Customs Tariff (Identification and Assessment of Safeguard Duty) Rules, 1997, R. 2(c)]

Increment. Increase; profit. A unit of increase in quantity or value.

'Increment' has a definite concept in service law jurisprudence. It is an increase or addition on a fixed scale, it is an increase in salary on such a scale. [*State of Punjab* v. *Jaswant Singh Kanwar*, (2014) 13 SCC 622, para 12].

A promotion from a lower grade to a higher grade though both the grades may be in the same cadre is not an increment or increments by way of special promotions. *State Bank of India* v. *Presiding Officer, Central Government Labour Court, Dhanbad*, AIR 1972 SC 2189.

"INCREMENT" the term 'increment' has a definite concept in service laws. It is conceptually different from revision of pay scale. 'Increment' is an increase or addition on a fixed scale; it is a regular increase in salary on such a scale. *State of Kerala* v. *P. V. Neelakandan Nair*, AIR 2005 SC 3066 : 2005 AIR SCW 3489.

Incriminate. To charge with crime.

To involve in an accusation or charge. [Payment of Wages Act (4 of 1936), S. 14(4)(f)].

Incriminating circumstance. One which tends to show that a crime has been committed or that some particular person committed it.

Incriminatory. Tending to show that a crime has been committed.

Incroachment (enchroachment). An unlawful gaining upon the right or possession of another man. As where a man sets his hedge or wall too far into the ground of his neighbour, that lies next to him, he is said to make encroachment upon him. (*Tomlin*).

Inculpate. To incriminate; to accuse of crime or fault.

Inculpatory. Incriminatory; accusing.

Incumbent. One authorised by law to discharge the duties of an office. One who holds an official or political post.

Incumbrance or Encumbrance. is a burdensome and troublesome load; a burden, obstruction, an impediment; anything that impedes motion or action, or renders it difficult or laborious; clog; hindrance; check; a word used as synonymous with "obstruction"; a burden or charge upon property; a legal claim or lien upon an estate which may diminish its value; a liability resting upon an estate; anything that impairs the use or transfer of property; an embarrassment of an estate or property so that it cannot be disposed of without being subject to it. As applied to an estate in land, it may fairly include whatever charges, burdens, obstructs, or impairs its use, or prevents or impedes its transfer.

"INCUMBRANCES" includes any liability which may be recovered or satisfied from the assets of the tea undertaking or, as the case may be, tea unit or the person owning the tea undertaking or tea unit. [Tea Act (29 of 1953), S. 16E(1) *Expln.*]

"INCUMBRANCES" includes mortgages and terminable charges. [Estate Duty Act (34 of 1953), S. 2(10)]

The term "INCUMBRANCES" used with reference to a tenancy, means any lien, sub-tenancy, easement or other right or interest created by the tenant on his tenure or holding or in limitation of his own interest therein. [Ben. Act 8 of 1885 (Tenancy), S. 161]

"INCUMBRANCES" means a charge upon or claim against land arising out of a private grant or contract. [Pun Act 17 of 1887 (Land Revenue), S. 3, cl. 16]

"INCUMBRANCES" includes a mortgage, charge, usufructuary grant and any interest other than that of an ordinary tenant or of an alienee or *taluqdar*, and "incumbrancer" means a person in whom an incumbrance vests; [Bom. Act 6 of 1888 (Guzarat Taluqdars) S. 2, cl. (*e*)].

A claim, lien or liability attached to property, *e.g.* a mortgage, charge or usufruct. [TP Act (4 of 1882), S. 55(1)(g)].

Incur. To entail; to become liable or subject to.

Incurred. The word "incur" is used in the sense of meeting with, of being exposed to, of being liable to.

Incurred or Authorised. Authorisation means acceptance of the responsibility. Authorisation must precede the expenditure. Authorisation means reimbursement by the candidate or election agent of the person who has been authorised by the candidate or by the election agent of the candidate to spend or incur. *Indira Nehru Gandhi* v. *Raj Narain*, AIR 1975 SC 2299, 2329 [Representation of the People Act (43 of 1951), S. 77, 83(1)(b) and 123(6)].

Indebted. Being in debt. [Indian Evidence Act (1 of 1872), S. 34, ill.].

Indebtedness. The state or condition of being in debt.

Indecency. An act against good behaviour and just delicacy.

Indecent. Not decent; unfit to be heard or seen.

Indecent assault. The crime of making an assault or an actual physical contact with a person involving an element of sexual affront or harm, *e.g.* by exposing the male organ to a woman, or by a person attempting to touch, or touching, the sexual organs of another without that other's consent and against the other's will.

Indecent conduct. Act of gross indecency with children or inciting them to commit such act.

Indecent exposure. An exhibition of one's private parts.

The phrase 'indecent exposure of the person,' in its well-settled and accepted signification, means the exhibition of such parts of the person as modesty or a sense of self respect requires to be kept usually covered.

Indecent liberties. 'Indecent and improper liberties with the person of a child' means such liberties as the common sense of society would regard as indecent and improper, and to constitute the offence the liberties taken with the person of the child need not have been with her private parts.

Indecent representation of women. Means the depiction in any manner of the figure of a woman, her form or body or any part thereof in such a way as to have the effect of being indecent or derogatory to or denigrating, woman, or is likely to deprave, corrupt or injure the public morality or morals; [Indecent Representation of Women (Prohibition) Act (60 of 1986), S. 2(c)]

Indefeasible. Not subject to being defeated or avoided.

Not liable to be defeated or done away with; that cannot be made void. [Limitation Act (36 of 1963), S. 25(1)].

Indemnification. The right of a party ordered to pay a judgment to receive reimbursement from the ultimately responsible party.

Indemnify. To make good a loss which one person has suffered in consequence of the act or default of another. [Companies Act (1 of 1956), S. 244(2)(Replaced by Act 2013) and Constitution of India, Art. 34].

Indemnity. A legal obligation to cover the liability of another.

Formal legal acceptance of responsibility against damage or loss.

Indemnity springs from contract express or implied.

Security or protection against hurt, loss or damage [Working Journalists and Other Newspaper Employees (Conditions of Service) and Miscellaneous Provisions Act (45 of 1955), S. 19]; exemption from incurred penalties or liabilities; something that indemnifies or is by way of reimbursement for incurred liabilities [Indian Contract Act (9 of 1872), S. 124]; [All India Service Regulation (Indemnity) Act (19 of 1975), S. 1(1)].

Indemnity and guarantee. Indemnity is a contract, express or implied, "to keep a person who has entered, or is about to enter, into a contract of liability indemnified against the liability independently of the question whether a third person makes default or not; it differs from a guarantee which is a promise to pay the creditor if the principal debtor makes default in payment."

Indemnity bond. An undertaking given by an obligor to reimburse an obligee for any loss suffered due to the conduct of the obligor or a third person. *State Street Bank* v. *U.S. Fid. & Guar.*, 181 Ill. App. 3d 1081 : 132 Ill Dec. 216 : 539 N.E. 2d 779, 780.

Indenture. A deed or elaborate contract signed by two or more parties.

Independence. The right of a nation to manage all its affairs, whether internal or external, without control from other nations.

Independence of judiciary. Impartiality, independence, fairness and reasonableness in decision making are the hallmarks of the judiciary. If

'Impartiality' is the soul of the judiciary, 'Independence' is the lifeblood of the judiciary. Without independence, impartiality cannot thrive. Independence is not the freedom for Judges to do what they like. It is the independence of judicial thought. It is the freedom from interference and pressures which provides the judicial atmosphere where he can work with absolute commitment to the cause of justice and constitutional values. [*Union of India* v. *Madras Bar Association*, (2010) 11 SCC 1, para 46 as cited in *Secretary, Ministry of Health and Welfare, Government of Maharashtra* v. *S.C. Malta*, (2012) 13 SCC 118, para 27]. *Union of India* v. *R. Gandhi, President, Madras Bar Association*, (2010) 11 SCC 1, para 46

Independence of the Indian judiciary. The independence of the Indian judiciary is one of the most significant features of the Constitution. Any policy or decision of the Government which would undermine or destroy the independence of the judiciary would not only be opposed to public policy but would also impinge upon the basic structure of the Constitution. It has to be clearly understood that the State policies should neither defeat nor cause impediment in discharge of judicial junctions. To preserve the doctrine of separation of powers, it is necessary that the provisions falling in the domain of judicial field are discharged by the judiciary and that too, effectively. [*Brij Mohan Lal* v. *Union of India*, (2012) 6 SCC 502 : (2012) 2 SCC (L&S) 117, para 105 as cited in *Secretary, Ministry of Health and Welfare, government of Maharashtra* v. *S.C. Malta*, (2012) 13 SCC 118, para 28].

Independent. A politician who is independent of any party. Sometimes these independents themselves form a separate party.

The expression 'independent' used in S. 9 means a person other than those who are employers and employees in relation to the scheduled employment in respect of which the minimum wages are sought to be fixed. *Bengal Motion Pictures Employees' Union (P.) Ltd.* v. *Kohinoor Pictures,* AIR 1964 Cal 519, 525. [Minimum Wages Act (11 of 1948), S. 9]

Being or acting free of the influence of something; not in a subordinate position. [Industrial Disputes Act (14 of 1947), S. 2(i)].

Independent contract. One, the enforcement of which does not depend upon the performance of any other contract.

Independent contractor. One who, exercising an independent employment, contracts to do a piece of work according to his own methods, and without being subject to his employer's control, except as to the result of the work.

An independent contractor is one who undertakes to produce a given result but so that in the execution of the work he is not under the order or control, of the person for whom he does it, and may use his own discretion in things not specified beforehand. *Shivandan* v. *Punjab National Bank*, AIR 1955 SC 404, 409.

Whether person is independent contractor or not is a question of fact. Independent contractor is not the same thing as ordinary servant. *Harish Chander* v. *Triloki Nath,* AIR 1956 SC 444.

Independent corroboration. Independent evidence must not only make it safe to believe that the crime was committed but must in some way reasonably connect or tend to connect the accused with it by confirming in some material particular the testimony of the accomplice or complainant that the accused committed the crime. The corroboration must come from independent sources. *Rameshwar Kalyan Singh* v *State of Rajasthan*, AIR 1952 SC 54, 57, 58. [Indian Evidence Act (1 of 1872), S. 133]

Independent director. Means an independent director referred to in sub-section (6) of section 149. [S. 2(47) of the Companies Act, 2013 (18 of 2013)]

An "independent director" in relation to a company, means a director other than a managing director or a whole-time director or a nominee director,—

(a) who, in the opinion of the Board, is a person of integrity and possesses relevant expertise and experience;

(b) (i) who is or was not a promoter of the company or its holding, subsidiary or associate company;

(ii) who is not related to promoters or directors in the company, its holding, subsidiary or associate company;

(c) who has or had no pecuniary relationship, other than remuneration as such director or having transaction not exceeding ten per cent of his total income or such amount as may be prescribed, with the company, its holding, subsidiary or associate company, or their promoters, or directors, during the two immediately preceding financial years or during the current financial year;

(d) none of whose relatives—

(i) is holding any security of or interest in the company, its holding, subsidiary or associate company during the two immediately preceding financial years or during the current financial year. [Companies Act (18 of 2013), section 149(6) and proviso]

Independent evidence. Evidence from outside; evidence; which is not biased. [Indian Evidence Act (1 of 1872), S. 156, ill.].

Independent of contract. This phrase in the definition of a tort means virtually, other than wrongs which are regarded as breach of contract and serves to indicate the actual content of these phrases in the modern law.

Independent persons. Persons in the service or employment of the government are also independent persons. *State of Andhra Pradesh* v. *Narayana Velur Beedi Manufacturing Factory*, AIR 1973 SC 1307, 1311. [Minimum Wages Act (11 of 1948), S. 9]

Independent persons are not persons belonging to the category of employers or to category of employees. *Ministry of Labour and Rehabilitation* v. *Tiffin's B.A. & P. Ltd*, AIR 1985 SC 1391, 1392.

Independent witness. A witness normally to be considered 'independent witness' unless he or she springs from sources which likely to be tainted and that usually means unless the witness has cause, such as enmity against the accused, to wish to implicate him falsely. [*Dalip Singh* v. *State of Punjab*, AIR 1953 SC 364 **followed in** *S. Sudershan Reddy* v. *State of A.P.*, (2006) 10 SCC 163, 168, paras 13 & 14; *Guli Chand* v. *State of Rajasthan*, (1974) 4 SCC 698] See also *Kartik Malhar* v. *State of Bihar,* (1996) 1 SCC 614, 622, para 16.

If a person happened to be a prosecution witness in other instances, it cannot be said that he is not an 'independent witness'. [*Joseph Fernandez* v. *State of Goa,* AIR 2000 SC 3502 : (2000) 1 SCC 707, 708]

'Consolidation officer' who was a witness to the search and seizure of the accused and recovery of currency notes from his pocket in a trap was held to be an 'independent witness' in as much as he was in no way concerned with the success of the trap that was laid by raiding party. [*Ram Ishwar Choudhary* v. *State of Bihar,* (2000) 10 SCC 157, 158]

Indeterminate. Uncertain; not fixed.

Indeterminate sentence. An uncertain or indefinite sentence for crime. A criminal sentence in which the term of imprisonment is left uncertain except so far as the minimum or maximum are concerned. After the minimum term has elapsed, the penal authorities, often a board of parole, fix the exact term. This is based on the modern doctrine of penology that the punishment should be individualized.

Index. An alphabetical list, usually at the end of a book, of the names, subjects, *etc.* occurring in it, with indications of the places where they occur. [TP Act (4 of 1882), S. 3, *Expln.* 1, Prov. (3)].

Indexation. An international term for a system proposed in the UN by the developing countries to link the prices of their exports to the prices of manufactured goods imported from developing countries.

Indexed cost of acquisition. Means an amount which bears to the cost of acquisition the same proportion as Cost Inflation Index for the year in which the asset is transferred bears to the Cost Inflation Index for the first year in which the asset was held by the assessee or for the year beginning on the 1st day of April, 1981, whichever is later. [Income-tax Act (43 of 1961), S. 48, *Expln.*(i)]

Indexed cost of any improvement. Means an amount which bears to the cost of improvement the same proportion as Cost Inflation Index for the year in which the asset is transferred bears to the Cost Inflation Index for the year in which the improvement to the asset took place. [Income-tax Act (43 of 1961), S. 48, *Expln.*(iv)]

India. "INDIA" shall mean,—

(a) as respects any period before the establishment of the Dominion of India, British India together with all territories under the suzerainty of such as Indian Ruler, and the tribal areas;

(b) as respects any period after the establishment of the Dominion of India and before the commencement of the Constitution, all territories for the time being included in that Dominion and,

(c) as respects any period after commencement of the Constitution, all territories for the time being comprised in the territory of India. [General Clauses Act (10 of 1897), S. 3(28), (*as this clause still stands.*)]

"India" means the territory of India as referred to in article 1 of the Constitution, its territorial waters, seabed and sub-soil underlying such waters, continental shelf, exclusive economic zone or any other maritime zone as referred to in the Territorial Waters, Continental Shelf, Exclusive Economic Zone and other Maritime Zones Act, 1976, and the air space above its territory and territorial waters [The Central Goods and Services Tax Act, 2017 (12 of 2017), S. 2(56)]

"India" means the territory of India as referred to in article 1 of the Constitution, its territorial waters, seabed and subsoil underlying such waters, continental shelf, exclusive economic zone or any other maritime zone as referred to in the Territorial Waters, Continental Shelf, Exclusive Economic Zone and other Maritime Zones Act, 1976 (80 of 1976), and the air space above its territory and territorial waters; [Income-tax Act (43 of 1961), S. 2(25A) substituted by the Finance Act, 2007, w.r.e.f. 25-8-1976].

"INDIA" includes the territorial waters of India. [Customs Act (52 of 1962), S. 2(27)]

"India" means the territory of India as referred to in Article 1 of the Constitution, its territorial waters, seabed and sub-soil underlying such waters, continental shelf, exclusive economic zone or any other maritime zone as referred to in the Territorial

Waters, Continental Shelf, Exclusive Economic Zone and Other Maritime Zones Act, 1976, (80 of 1976), and the air space above its territory [Biological Diversity Act, 2002 (18 of 2003), section 2(gb)]

India-Bangladesh Agreement. "India-Bangla-desh Agreement" means the agreement between the Government of the Republic of India and the Government of the People's Republic of Bangladesh concerning the Demarcation of the Land Boundary between India and Bangladesh and Related Matters dated the 16th day of May, 1974, Exchange of Letters dated the 26th day of December, 1974, the 30th day of December, 1974, the 7th day of October, 1982, the 26th day of March, 1992 and protocol to the said agreement dated the 6th day of September, 2011, entered into between the Government of India and Bangladesh, the relevant extracts of which are set out in the Third Schedule [Constitution (One Hundredth Amendment) Act, 2015, S. 2(c)].

Indian Christian. "INDIAN CHRISTIAN" means a native of India who is, or in good faith claims to be, of unmixed Asiatic descent and who professes any form of the Christian religion. [Indian Succession Act (39 of 1925), S. 2(d); Administrator General Act (3 of 1913), S. 4(4)]

Indian coin. Indian coin is metal stamped and issued by the authority of the Government of India in order to be issued as money and metal which has been so stamped and issued shall continue to be Indian Coin for the purpose of this Chapter, notwithstanding that it may have ceased to be used as money. [IPC (45 of 1860), S. 230]

Indian company. Means a company formed and registered under the Companies Act, 1956 (1 of 1956), and includes—

(i) a company formed and registered under any law relating to companies formerly in force in any part of India (other than the State of Jammu and Kashmir and the Union territories specified in sub-clause (iii) of this clause);

(ia) a corporation established by or under a Central, State or Provincial Act;

(ib) any institution, association or body which is declared by the Board to be a company under clause (17);

(ii) in the case of the State of Jammu and Kashmir, a company formed and registered under any law for the time being in force in that State;

(iii) in the case of any of the Union territories of Dadra and Nagar Haveli, Goa, Daman and Diu, and Pondicherry, a company formed and registered under any law for the time being in force in that Union territory :

Provided that the registered or, as the case may be, principal office of the company, corporation, institution, association or body in all cases is in India. [Income-tax Act (43 of 1961), S. 2(26)]

"INDIAN COMPANY" means a company incorporated in India. [Foreign Exchange Management (Transfer or Issue of Security by a person Resident Outside India) Regulations, 2000, Regn. 2(v)]

Indian Computer Emergency Response Team (CERT-In). The IT Amendment Act, 2008 has established CERT-In as a statutory authority under newly inserted s. 70B of Information Technology Act read with notification published in Part II, s. 3, sub-s. (ii) of the Gazette of India, Extraordinary, dated October 27, 2009.

Section 70B (4) of the Information Technology Act, states that CERT-In has been designated to serve as the national agency to perform the following functions in the area of cyber security for the following functions, (i) collection, analysis and dissemination of information on cyber incidents; (ii) forecast and alerts of cyber security incidents; (iii) emergency measures for handling cyber security incidents; (iv) coordination of cyber incidents response activities; (v) issue guidelines, advisories, vulnerability notes and whitepaper relating to information security practices, procedures, prevention, response and reporting of cyber incidents; (vi) such other functions relating to cyber security as may be prescribed. Apar Gupta, *Commentary on Information Technology Act,* LexisNexis Butterworths Wadhwa Nagpur, 3rd Edn. 2016.

Indian Consular Officer. 'INDIAN CONSULAR OFFICER' means the Consul General, Counsel, Vice-Consul. Consular agent and Proconsul appointed as such by the Central Government, and includes any person authorised by the Central Government to perform the functions of Consul-General, Consul. Vice-Consul, Consular agent or Pro-Consul. [Merchant Shipping Act (44 of 1958), S. 3(17)]

Indian Consulate. Means the office of a Consular Officer of the Government of India where a register of births is kept or where there is no such office, such office as may be prescribed. [Citizenship Act (57 of 1955), S. 2(d)]

Indian currency. Means currency which is expressed or drawn in Indian rupees but does not include special bank notes and special one rupee notes issued under Section 28A of the Reserve Bank of India Act, 1934. [Foreign Exchange Management Act (42 of 1999), S. 2(q) and Foreign Exchange Regulation Act (46 of 1973), S. 2(k)]

Indian Depository Receipt. Means any instrument in the form of a depository receipt created by a domestic depository in India and authorised by a company incorporated outside India making an issue of such depository receipts. [S. 2(48) of the Companies Act, 2013 (18 of 2013). Also see *Explanation* to Rule 13(1) of the Companies (Registration of Foreign Companies) Rules, 2014]

Indian entity. Means a company or a body corporate or a firm in India. [Foreign Exchange Management (Borrowing or Lending in Foreign Exchange) Regulations, 2000, R. 2(e)]

Indian-fishing boat. For the purposes of this Part, "INDIAN FISHING BOAT"—

(a) every fishing vessel, as defined in clause (12) of Section 3;

(b) every sailing vessel, whether or not fitted with mechanical means of propulsion, solely engaged in fishing for profit;

(c) every boat or craft of any other type used solely for fishing which the Central Government may, by notification in the Official Gazette, specify to be a fishing boat for the purposes of this section, which is owned wholly by persons to each of whom any of the descriptions specified in clause (*a*) or in clause (*b*) or in clause (*c*), as the case may be, of Section 21 applies or which satisfies such other requirements as the Central Government may, by notification in the Official Gazette, specify. [Merchant Shipping Act (44 of 1958), S. 435 B]

Indian hemp. Means—

(i) the leaves, small stalks and flowering or fruiting tops of the Indian hemp plant (*Cannabis sativa L.*), including all forms known as *bhang*, *siddhi*, or *ganja*;

(ii) charas, that is, the resin obtained from the Indian hemp plant, which has not been submitted to any manipulations other than those necessary for packing and transport;

(iii) any mixture, with or without neutral materials, of any of the above forms of Indian hemp or any drink prepared therefrom; and

(iv) any extract or tincture of any of the above forms of Indian hemp. [Medicinal and Toilet Preparations *etc.* Act (16 of 1955), S. 2(e)]

Indian Insurer. For the purpose of these regulations means an Indian Insurance Company who has been granted certificate of registration by the Authority under the Insurance Regulatory and Development Authority (Registration of Indian Insurance Companies) Regulations, 2000 notified from time to time to carry out general insurance business or health insurance business. [Insurance Regulatory and Development Authority of India (General Insurance-Reinsurance) Regulations, 2016, Regn. 2(k)].

Indian Income-tax. The expression "INDIAN INCOME-TAX" means Income-tax and Super-tax charged in accordance with the provisions of the Income-tax Act. [Income-tax Act (11 of 1922), S. 49(2)(a)]

Indian insurance company. Means any insurer, being a company which is limited by shares, and,—

(a) which is formed and registered under the Companies Act, 2013 (18 of 2013) as a public company or is converted into such a company within one year of the commencement of the Insurance Laws (Amendment) Act, 2015 (5 of 2015);

(b) in which the aggregate holdings of equity shares by foreign investors, including portfolio investors, do not exceed forty-nine per cent. of the paid up equity capital of such Indian insurance company, which is Indian owned and controlled, in such manner as may be prescribed.

Explanation.—For the purposes of this sub-clause, the expression "control" shall include the right to appoint a majority of the directors or to

control the management or policy decisions including by virtue of their shareholding or management rights or shareholders agreements or voting agreements;

(c) whose sole purpose is to carry on life insurance business or general insurance business or re-insurance business or health insurance business. [Insurance Act (4 of 1938), S. 2(7A)]

Indian language. "INDIAN LANGUAGE" means a language specified in the Eighth Schedule to the Constitution, and includes any dialect of such language. [Cigarettes and other Tobacco Products (Prohibition of Advertisement and Regulation of Trade and Commerce, Production, Supply and Distribution) Act (34 of 2003), S. 3(g) & Cigarettes (Regulation of Production *etc.*) Act (49 of 1975), S. 2(g)]

Indian law. "INDIAN LAW" shall mean any Act, Ordinance, Regulation, Order, Bye-law or other instrument which before the commencement of the Constitution had the force of law in any Province of India, or part thereof, or thereafter has the force of law in any Part A state or Part C state or part thereof, but does not include any Act of Parliament of the United Kingdom or any Order in Council, rule or other instrument made under such Act. [General Clauses Act (10 of 1897), S. 3(29)].

Indian medicine. Means the system of Indian medicine commonly known as Ashtang Ayurveda, Siddha or Unani Tibb or Sowa-Rigpa whether supplemented or not by such modern advances as the Central Council may declare by notification from time to time. [Indian Medicine Central Council Act (48 of 1970), S. 2(e)]

Indian national. Means a citizen of India and includes a firm or other association, if all the members of the firm or, as the case may be, the members of the association, are citizens of India. [Offshore Areas Minerals (Development and Regulation) Act, 2002 (17 of 2003), S. 4(h)]

"Indian Ownership" of an Indian Insurance Company means more than 50 per cent of the equity capital in it is owned by resident Indian citizens or Indian companies, which are owned and controlled by resident Indian citizens. [Indian Insurance Companies (Foreign Investment) Rules, 2015, R. 2(l)].

Indian party. Means a company incorporated in India or body created under an Act of Parliament, making investment in Joint Venture or Wholly Owned Subsidiary abroad, and includes any other entity in India as may be notified by Reserve Bank :

Provided that when more than one such company incorporated or bodies under an Act of Parliament, makes a direct investment in the foreign entity, all such companies or bodies together shall constitute the 'Indian party.' [Foreign Exchange Management (Transfer or Issue of any Foreign Security) Regulations, 2000, Reg. 2(k)]

Indian promoter. Means and includes—

(i) a company formed under the Companies Act, 1956 (1 of 1956), which is not a subsidiary as defined in Section 4 of that Act;

(ii) a banking company as defined in sub-section (4A) of Section 2 of the Act but does not include a foreign bank or branch thereof functioning in India;

(iii) a Public financial institution as defined in Section 4A of the Companies Act, 1956 (1 of 1956);

(iv) a co-operative society registered under any relevant law for the time being in force;

(v) a person, who is an Indian citizen or a combination of persons who are Indian citizens. [Insurance Regulatory and Development Authority (Registration of Insurance Companies) Regulations, 2000, Regn. 2(g)]

Indian Rate of Tax. The expression "INDIAN RATE OF TAX" means the rate determined by dividing the amount of Indian income-tax after deduction of any relief due under the provisions of this Act but before deduction of any relief due under this Chapter by the total income. [Income-tax Act (43 of 1961), S. 91(3), *Expln.* (ii)]

Indian re-insurer. "INDIAN RE-INSURER" means an insurer who carries on exclusively reinsurance business and is approved in this behalf by the Central Government. [Insurance Regulatory and Development Authority (General Insurance-Reinsurance) Regulations, 2000, Reg. 2(*e*)]

Indian Reserve Forces. The expression "INDIAN RESERVE FORCES" means the forces constituted by the India Reserve Forces Act, 1888 and includes officers belonging to the Army in India Reserve of Officers or to the Regular Reserve of Officers and members of the Indian Air Force Volunteer Reserve when subject to military or air force law, as the case may be. [Tolls (Army and Air Force) Act (8 of 1888), S. 2(g)]

Indian standard. The standard, including any tentative or provisional standard, established and published by the Indian Standards Institution, in relation to any article or process. The term includes any standard recognised by the Indian Standards Institution. [Indian Standards Institutions (Certification Marks) Act (36 of 1952), S. 2(c)]

"INDIAN STANDARD" means the standard (including any tentative or provisional standard) established and published by the Bureau, in relation to any article or process indicative of the quality and specification of such article or process and includes—

(i) any standard recognised by the Bureau under clause (b) of Section 10; and

(ii) any standard established and published, or recognised, by the Indian Standards Institution and which is in force immediately before the date of establishment of the Bureau. [Bureau of Indian Standards Act (63 of 1986), S. 2(g)]

Indian Standards Institution. Means the Indian Standards Institution set up under the Resolution of the Government of India in the late Department of Industries and Supplies No. 1 Std. (4)/45, dated the 3rd day of September, 1946, and registered under the Societies Registration Act, 1860. [Bureau of Indian Standards Act (63 of 1986), S. 2(h)]

Indian State. "INDIAN STATE" means any territory recognised before the commencement of this Constitution by His Majesty or the Government of the Dominion of India as being such a State. [Constitution of India, Article 363(2)(a)]

"INDIAN STATE" means any territory which the Government of the Dominion of India recognised as such a State. [Constitution of India, Art. 366 (15)]

"INDIAN STATE" shall mean any territory which the Central Government recognised as such a State before the commencement of the Constitution, whether described as a State, an Estate, a Jagir or otherwise. [General Clauses Act (10 of 1897), S. 3(30)]

Indian Venture Capital Undertaking. Means a company incorporated in India whose shares are not listed on a recognized stock exchange in India and which is not engaged in an activity under the negative list specified by SEBI. [Foreign Exchange Management (Transfer or Issue of Security by a Person Resident Outside India) Regulations, 2000, Reg. 2(va)]

Indian vessel. Means—

(I) a vessel owned by Government or by a corporation established by a Central Act or a Provincial or State Act, or

(II) a vessel—

(i) which is owned wholly by persons to each of whom any of the following descriptions applies :—

(1) a citizen of India;

(2) a company in which not less than sixty per cent of the share capital is held by citizens of India;

(3) a registered co-operative society every member whereof is a citizen of India or where any other co-operative society is a member thereof, every individual who is a member of such other co-operative society is a citizen of India; and

(ii) which is registered under the Merchant Shipping Act, 1958, or under any other Central Act or any Provincial or State Act.

Explanation.—For the purposes of this clause, "registered co-operative society" means a society registered or deemed to be registered under the Co-operative Societies Act, 1912, or any other law relating to co-operative societies for the time being in force in any State. [Maritime Zones of India (Regulation *etc.*) Act (42 of 1981), S. 2(e)]

Indian waters. "INDIAN WATERS," for the purposes of Sections 31, 97 and 99, means the seas extending from the shores of India to such limits as may be prescribed. [Navy Act (62 of 1957), S. 3(11)]

Indian work. Means a literary, dramatic or musical work,—

(i) the author of which is a citizen of India, or
(ii) which is first published in India, or
(iii) the author of which, in case of an unpublished work, is at the time of the making of the work, a citizen of India. [Copyright Act (14 of 1957), S. 2(l)]

Indicate. To point out.

Indication. Includes any name, geographical or figurative representation or any combination of them conveying or suggesting the geographical origin of goods to which it applies. [Geographical Indications of Goods (Registration and Protection) Act (48 of 1999), S. 2(1)(g)]

Indict. To charge one with crime by indictment or information. To accuse before a Court for some offence.

Indictee. One against whom an indictment has been found.

Indictment. An indictment is a brief narrative of the offence charged, which must contain a certain description of the crime and the facts necessary to constitute it.

An indictment is a written accusation, preferred before the Crown Court, signed by the proper officer of that Court and charging one or more persons with the commission of one or of a number of offences. HALSBURY, 4th Edn., Vol. 11, para 193, p. 118.

A written accusation that an offence has been committed by one or more persons.

INDICTMENT is a general remedy for the redress of public injuries, and may be field in all cases where an offence is created and punishment imposed, authorizing in such cases penal actions.

Indifferent. Neutral as to the parties or subject matter concerned in a controversy.

Indigenous films. The words "indigenous films" in S. 12(4) are general and unqualified in their contents, and must include in their ordinary and accepted sense cultural as well as other films. *Chief Commr.* v. *Brijniwas Das,* AIR 1963 SC 408. [Cinematograph Act (37 of 1952), S. 12(4)]

Indigenous medicine. 'INDIGENOUS MEDICINE' means one or all of the three of medicine that is Ayurvedic, Siddha and Unani System of medicine. [Karnataka Ayurvedic & Unani Practitioners Registration and Medical Practitioner's Miscellaneous Provisions Act, 1961, Section 2(e) *Expl.*]

Indigenous peoples. People whose ancestors inhabited a place or country when persons from another culture or ethnic background arrived on the scene and dominated them through conquest, settlement, or other means and who today live more in conformity with their own social, economic, and cultural customs and traditions than with those of the country of which they now form a part (also : "native peoples" or "tribal peoples"). (*Biodiversity*)

People who are original or natural inhabitants of a country.

Indigent. A person is an indigent person,—

(a) if he is not possessed of sufficient means (other than property exempt from attachment in execution of a decree and the subject-matter of the suit) to enable him to pay the fee prescribed by law for the plaint in such suit, or
(b) where no such fee is prescribed, if he is not entitled to property worth one thousand rupees other than the property exempt from attachment in execution of a decree, and the subject-matter of the suit. [CPC (5 of 1908), O. XXXIII, R. 1, *Expl. I*].

Needy; poor; destitute of means of decent or comfortable existence.

Indigent defendant. A person who is not in the position to hire a lawyer, and who upon indictment, becomes eligible to receive attorney appointed by the Court.

Indirect. Not direct.

Indirect confession. The term, 'indirect confessions' is used in the criminal law to designate confessions inferred from the conduct, *etc.*, of the accused.

Indirect contempt. Indirect contempt of Court occurs where the alleged contempt is not committed in the presence of the Court.

Indirect cost. "INDIRECT COSTS" means costs, not being direct costs, allocated in the ratio of the export turnover in respect of trading goods to the total turnover. [Income-tax Act (43 of 1961), S. 80 HHC (3) *Expl.* (e)]

Indirect evidence. Circumstantial evidence.

Indirect tax. Ordinarily all taxes paid primarily by persons who can shift the burden upon some one else, or who are under no legal compulsion to pay them, are considered indirect taxes.

It is tax levied on commodities; a tax indirectly paid by the consumer.

All taxes are usually divided into two classes—those which are direct, and those which are indirect; that under the former denomination are included taxes on land or real property, and under the latter taxes on consumption.

All taxes on expenses or consumption are indirect taxes.

Indirect tax dispute. In this Scheme, unless the context otherwise requires, "INDIRECT TAX DISPUTE" means a dispute in respect of any of the provisions of the Act which is pending before the Commissioners (Appeals) as an appeal against the impugned order as on the 1st day of March, 2016. [Indirect Tax Dispute Resolution Scheme, 2016, S. 213(1)(g), Finance Act (2 of 2016)].

Indirect tax enactment. Means the Customs Act, 1962 or the Central Excise Act, 1944 or the Customs Tariff Act, 1975 or the Central Excise Tariff Act, 1985 or the relevant Act and includes the rules or regulations made under such enactment. [Finance Act (21 of 1998), S. 87(j)]

Indirect transfer. Refers to income arising from the transfer of shares between foreign companies of underlying assets in India. [Parthasarthi Shome, *Taxation Principles and Applications – A compendium*, 2014, LexisNexis, at p. 544]

Indirectly. Not directly aimed at or attained; not immediately resulting from an action or cause.

Indispensable evidence. Evidence without which a certain fact cannot be proved.

Indispensable party. Indispensable parties are those who not only have an interest in the subject-matter of the controversy, but an interest of such nature that a final decree cannot be made without affecting their interest.

It is a general rule that, where a party is directly affected by a decree, he is an indispensable party to the suit.

Indissolubility of marriage (Doctrine of). The Christian concept of marriage has been that marriage, being obligatory for every human being (except a church man), is a sacrament, having been ordained by Goa, and an indissoluble solemn union entered into by the parties with their full and free volition for life so as to prevent fornication (moral sin) and with a view to providing safeguard against depopulation. [Paras Diwan, *Law of Marriage and Divorce*, 1988, Wadhwa and Company **quoted in** Dr Kauser Edappagath, *Divorce and Gender Equity in Muslim Personal Law of India*, 2014, LexisNexis]

Individual. For the purposes of this clause, the expression "INDIVIDUAL" shall also include,—

(i) his legal heirs; or

(ii) where a partition has taken place among the members of the Hindu undivided family, every member of such family having a share in the Gold Bonds. [Gold Bonds (Immunities and Exemptions) Act (25 of 1993), S. 2(b), *Expl. n*]

The word 'individual' occurring in Entry 86 of List-I covers a HUF which comprises of several individuals. The expression 'individuals' cannot merely mean individual human beings but is wide enough to comprehend individuals forming units like a HUF. The use of the word "individuals" in plural is not of special significance because under Section 13(2) of the General Clauses Act (10 of 1897), words in singular shall include the plural and *vice-versa*. *Banarasi Dass* v. *Wealth Tax Officer,* AIR 1965 SC 1387, 1392. [Constitution of India, Sch. VII, List I, Entry 86]

The expression 'individual' occurring in Section 64(1) does not include the *'Karta'* of the Hindu undivided family. *CIT* v. *Om Prakash,* (1999) 6 SCC 349, para 22 : AIR 1999 SC 2534. [Income-tax Act (43 of 1961), S. 64(1)(i) and (ii)]

A single human being [T.P. Act (4 of 1882), S. 5]; characteristic of an individual [Specific Relief Act (47 of 1963), S. 4]; [Constitution of India, Art. 43].

Individual business. Means individual insurance contracts issued on single/joint lives. [Insurance Regulatory and Development Authority (Actuarial Report and Abstract), Regulations 2000, Regn. 2(f)]

Individual pension account. Means an account of a subscriber, executed by a contract setting out the terms and conditions under the National Pension System. [S. 2(1)(e) of the Pension Fund Regulatory & Development Authority Act, 2013 (23 of 2013)]

Individually. The word "individually" in O. XXX, R. 6, CPC (5 of 1908) is not synonymous with "in person".

In an individual manner, singly. [Indian Partnership Act (9 of 1932), S. 4]; [Seeds Act (54 of 1966), S. 2(8)].

Individuals. The word 'individual' will not include a dead human-being or non-existing group of persons or corporations (at the time of commencement of the Act).

The word 'individual' does not mean only human being and it includes juristic person like a Hindu Idol. *Jogendra Nath Naskar* v. *Calcutta*, AIR 1969 SC 1089 at 1093; *Official Trustee Of West Bengal, for the Trust of Chitra Dassi* v. *C.I.T. West Bengal, Calcutta*, AIR 1974 SC 1355, 1357.

Constitution of India, Sch. VII, List I, Entry 86. *Commissioner of Income Tax* v *Sodra Devi*, AIR 1957 SC 832 Relied on. The expression 'individuals' includes a body of individuals like a Hindu Undivided Family. *L. Jugal Kishore* v. *Wealth Tax Officer,* AIR 1961 All 487, 491 (FB). [Wealth Tax Act (27 of 1957), S. 3]

Indivisible. Incapable of division.

Indoors. Means inside buildings or places in which the shielding will typically provide the necessary attenuation to protect wireless telegraphy against undue interference. [Use of Very Low Power Ultra-wideband Devices (Exemption from Licensing Requirements) Rules, 2018, R. 2(l)]..

Indo-Pakistan agreements. Mean the Agreements dated the 10th day of September, 1958, the 23rd day of October, 1959 and the 11th day of January, 1960 entered into between the Governments of India and Pakistan, the relevant extracts of which are set out in the Second Schedule. [Acquired Territories (Merger) Act (64 of 1960), S. 2(d)]

Indorse. The legal meaning of the term 'indorse' is 'putting a name on the back of any instrument or paper'.

Indorsee. If the indorser of a negotiable instrument adds a direction to pay the amount mentioned in the instrument to a specified person, the person so specified is called the "INDORSEE" of the instrument. [Negotiable Instruments Act (26 of 1881), S. 16(1)]

One to whom a negotiable instrument is indorsed.

The person in whose favour a note or bill is endorsed. [Negotiable Instruments Act (26 of 1881), S. 9].

Indorsee in due course. One who in good faith in the ordinary course of business, for value, before its apparent maturity or presumptive dishonour, and without knowledge of its actual dishonour, acquires a negotiable instrument indorsed to him, generally, or payable to bearer.

Indorsement. When the maker or holder of a negotiable instrument signs the same, otherwise than as such maker, for the purpose of negotiation, on the back or face thereof or on a slip of paper annexed thereto, or so signs for the same purpose a stamped paper intended to be completed as a negotiable instrument, he is said to indorse the same, and is called the "indorser". [Negotiable Instruments Act (26 of 1881), S. 15]

"INDORSEMENT" (endorsement) include and apply to an entry in writing by a registering officer on a rider or covering slip to any document tendered for registration under this Act. [Registration Act (16 of 1908), S. 2(5)]

Indorsement in blank. An indorsement in blank is made by the mere writing of the indorser's name on the back of the bill, without the mention of the name of any person in whose favour the indorsement is made.

An indorsement written on the back of a bill. [Negotiable Instruments Act (26 of 1881), S. 13(1), *Expln.* (ii)].

INDORSEMENT "IN BLANK" AND "IN FULL", AND "ENDORSEE." If the indorser (of a bill of exchange or promissory note signs his name only, the indorcement is said to be "in blank," and if he adds a direction to pay the amount mentioned in the instrument to, or to the order of a specified person, the indorsement is said to be "in full" and the person so specified is called the "indorsee" of the instrument. The provisions of the Negotiable Instruments Act relating to a payee shall apply with the necessary modifications to an indorsee. [Negotiable Instruments Act (26 of 1881), S. 16].

Indorsement in full. An indorsement which mentions the name of the person in whose favour it is made is called an 'indorsement in full.' [Negotiable Instruments Act (26 of 1881), S. 16]

Indorsement without recourse. An indorsement of a negotiable instrument with the words "without recourse" after the indorsee's name, thus rendering him not liable as an indorser.

Indorser. One who indorses a negotiable instrument.

An indorser is one who by his signature transfers the legal interest in a note.

Under the commercial law an indorser is the payee, who, acquiring from the maker, indorses the note to convey title to another, the indorsee; and the indorsee becomes indorser when he in turn places his name on the note to transfer it.

One who indorses, *i.e.* being the payee or holder, writes his name on the back of a bill of exchange *etc.* [Negotiable Instruments Act (26 of 1881), S. 7].

Indubitable proof. 'Indubitable proof' means evidence that is not only found credible, but of such weight and directness as to make out the facts alleged beyond a doubt.

Induce. To prevail on; to bring about; to pursuade. (*Tomlin*).

To inspire, call forth or bring about by influence or stimulation. [IPC (45 of 1860), S. 366].

Inducement. (*In pleadings*) A pleading often contains some prefatory averments which are necessary to introduce and explain the material facts alleged. These are called "matters of inducement". Such are averments stating who the parties are, how they are connected, and other surrounding circumstances leading up to the matters in dispute.

'Inducement' is defined as "a motive or consideration that leads one to action or to additional or more effective actions. [Merriam Webster Dictionary as cited in *Securities and Exchange Board of India and Ors.* v. *Kanaiyalal Baldevbhai Patel,* 2017 (11) SCALE 600, para 51]

Mere payment of any gratification to a third person for securing or procuring some votes in favour of a particular candidate without the establishment of any nexus between the money and the inducement to the voter will not be sufficient to prove that the voter is indirectly induced on account of the payment of gratification to the third person. *Kalya Singh* v. *Genda Lal*, AIR 1975 SC 1634, 1637 [Representation of the People Act (43 of 1951), S. 123(1)(A)(a) and (b)].

That which induces; something attractive by which a person is led on or persuaded to action.

Induction. The act or process of initiating; or that of reasoning from specific instances to general propositions.

Indulgence. The act of indulging or the state of being indulgent.

Industrial. Of or pertaining to an industry.

Industrial activity. "INDUSTRIAL ACTIVITY" means—

(i) an operation or process carried out in an industrial installation referred to in schedule 4 involving or likely to involve one or more hazardous chemicals and includes on-site storage or on-site transport which is associated with that operation or process as the case may be; or

(ii) isolated storage; or

(iii) pipeline. [Manufacture, Storage and Import of Hazardous Chemicals Rules, 1989, R. 2(h)]

"INDUSTRIAL ACTIVITY" includes an operation or process,—

(i) carried out in an industrial installation referred to in Schedule – 4 involving or likely to involve one or more hazardous chemicals;

(ii) on-site storage or on-site transport which is associated with that operation or process as the case may be;

(iii) isolated storage. [Chemical Accidents (Emergency Planning, Preparedness, and Response) Rules, 1996, R. 2(c)]

Industrial adjudication. In the case of industrial adjudication, the claims of the employer based on the freedom of contract have to be adjusted into with the claims of the industrial employees for social justice. In order that industrial adjudication should be completely free from the tyranny of dogmas or the sub-conscious pressure of pre-conceived notions, it is of utmost importance that the temptation to lay down broad principles should be avoided. *R.B. Diwan* v. *Industrial Tribunal*, AIR 1963 SC 630, 634.

Industrial company. "INDUSTRIAL COMPANY" means a company which owns one or more industrial undertakings. [Companies Act (1 of 1956), S. 2(19AA)](replaced by Act 2013)

According to Section 2(7)(c) of the Finance Act, 1981, an "INDUSTRIAL COMPANY" means a company which is mainly engaged in the business of generation or distribution of electricity or any other form of power or in the construction of ships or in the manufacture or processing of goods or in mining.

"INDUSTRIAL COMPANY" means a company which is mainly engaged in the business of generation or distribution of electricity or any other form of power or in the carriage, by road or inland waterways, of passengers or goods or in the construction of ships or in the execution of projects or in the manufacture or processing of goods or in mining.

Explanation—For the purposes of this clause,—

(i) a company shall be deemed to be mainly engaged in the business of generation or distribution of electricity or any other form of power or in the carriage, by road or inland water ways, of passengers or goods or in the construction of ships or in the execution of projects or in the manufacture or processing of goods or in mining, if the income attributable to any one or more of the aforesaid activities included in its total income of the previous year (as computed before making any deduction under Chapter VIA of the Income-tax Act) is not less than fiftyone per cent of such total income.

(ii) "project" means a project for the construction of a building, road, bridge or otherwise structure or assembly or installation of any machinery or plant. [Finance Act (32 of 1985), S. 8(c)]

A company running a cold storage is not an "industrial company". *Delhi Cold Storage Ltd.* v. *Commissioner of Income-Tax*, AIR 1991 SC 2125. [Finance Act (1973), S. 2(7)(c)]

According to Section 2(7) (c) of the Finance Act, 1981, an "industrial Company" means a company which is mainly engaged in the business of generation or distribution of electricity or any other form of power or in the construction of ships or in the manufacture or processing of goods or in mining.

Industrial concern. "INDUSTRIAL CONCERN" means any concern engaged or to be engaged in—

(i) the manufacture, preservation or processing of goods;

(ii) mining or development of mines;

(iii) the hotel industry;

(iv) the transport of passengers or goods by road or by water or by air or by rope-way or by lift;

(v) the generation or distribution of electricity or any other form of power;

(vi) the maintenance, repair, testing or servicing of machinery of any description, or vehicles or vessels or motor boats or trailers or tractors;

(vii) assembling, repairing or packing any article with the aid of machinery or power;

(viii) the setting up or development of an industrial area or industrial estate;

(ix) fishing or providing shore facilities for fishing or maintenance thereof;

(x) providing special or technical knowledge or other services for the promotion of industrial growth;

(xi) providing weigh bridge facilities;

(xii) the research and development of any process or product in relation to any of the matters aforesaid; or

(xiii) such other activity as may be approved by the Development Bank,

Explanation 1.—The expression "processing of goods" includes any art or process for producing, preparing or making an article by subjecting any material to a manual, mechanical, chemical, electrical or any other like operation.

Explanation 2.—If any doubt arises as to whether a concern is an industrial concern or not, the same shall be referred to the Development Bank for its decision and the decision of the Development Bank thereon shall be final. [State Financial Corporation Act (63 of 1951), S. 2(c)]

"INDUSTRIAL CONCERN" means a public limited company or a co-operative society or a firm or any other person or body of persons engaged in the manufacture, assembling, packing, preservation or processing of goods or in mining or in the generation or distribution of electricity or any other form of power. [Collection of Statistics Act (32 of 1953), S. 2(d)]

"INDUSTRIAL CONCERN" means any concern engaged or to be engaged in,—

(i) the manufacture, preservation or processing of goods;

(ii) shipping.

(iii) mining including development of mines;

(iv) the hotel industry;

(v) the transport of passengers or goods by road or by water or by air or by rope-way or by lift;

(vi) the generation, storage or distribution of electricity or any other form of energy;

(vii) the maintenance, repair, testing or servicing of machinery or equipment of any description or vehicles or vessels or motor boats or trailers or tractors.

(viii) assembling, repairing or packing any article with the aid of machinery or power;

(ix) the setting up of or development of, an industrial area or an industrial estate;

(x) fishing or providing shore facilities for fishing or maintenance thereof;

(xi) providing special or technical knowledge or other services for the promotion of industrial growth; or

(xii) providing engineering, technical, financial, management, marketing or other services or facilities for industry.

(xiii) service industry such as altering, ornamenting, polishing, finishing, oiling, washing, cleaning or otherwise treating or adapting any article or substance with a view to its use, sale, transport, delivery or disposal;

(xiv) providing medical, health or other allied services;

(xv) providing services relating to information technology, telecommunication or electronics;

(xvi) leasing, sub-leasing or giving on hire or hire-purchase of industrial plants, equipments, machinery or other assets including vehicles, ships and aircraft;

(xvii) such other activity as the Central Government may, having regard to the objects of this Act, by notification in the Official Gazette, specify in this behalf; or

(xviii) the research and development of any concept, technology, design, process or product whether in relation to any of the matters aforesaid, including any activities specified under sub-clause (xvii), or any other matter.

Explanation.—The expression "processing of goods" includes any art or process for producing, preparing or making an article by subjecting any material to a manual, mechanical, chemical, electrical or any other like operation. [Industrial Development Bank of India (18 of 1964), S. 2(c)].

"INDUSTRIAL CONCERN"—(1) means any concern engaged, or to be engaged, in—

(i) the manufacture, preservation or processing of goods;

(ii) shipping;

(iii) mining;

(iv) the hotel industry;

(v) the transport of passengers or goods by road or by water or by air or by rope-way or by lift;

(vi) the generation or distribution of electricity or any other form of power;

(vii) the maintenance, repair, testing or servicing of machinery of any description or vehicles or vessels or motor boats or trailers or tractors;

(viii) assembling, repairing or packing any article with the aid of machinery or power;

(ix) the development of any contiguous area of land as an industrial estate;

(x) fishing or providing shore facilities for fishing or maintenance thereof;

(xi) providing special or technical knowledge or other services for the promotion of industrial growth; or

(xii) the research and development of any process or product in relation to any of the matters aforesaid,

(2) and includes—

(i) an undertaking owned, controlled or managed by a company, firm or other body corporate, which is, or is to be, so engaged.

(ii) such other concern as the Central Government may, by notification in the Official Gazette, specify in this behalf.

Explanation.—The expression "processing of goods" includes any art or process for producing, preparing or making an article by subjecting any material to manual, mechanical, chemical, electrical or any other like operation. [Industrial Reconstruction Bank of India Act (62 of 1984), S. 2(i)]

"INDUSTRIAL CONCERN" has the meaning assigned to it in clause (c) of Section 2 of the Industrial Development Bank of India Act, 1964, and includes any other person in whose favour a foreign collaboration involving this import of technology is approved or automatically approved or automatically approved in accordance with the Industrial Policy of the Government of India in force from time to time. [Research & Development Cess Act (32 of 1986), S. 2(e)]

A business established for an industrial purpose. [Industrial Finance Corporation Act (15 of 1948) (*Repealed by Act 23 of 1993*), S. 2(c)].

Industrial co-operative society. "INDUSTRIAL COOPERATIVE SOCIETY" means a cooperative society, the object of which includes manufacture and marketing of goods by or with the help of its members and providing supplies and services to them and to small producers and entrepreneurs and includes a cooperative society established with the object of facilitating the operation of such society. [West Bengal Cooperative Societies Act, 1983, Section 2(25)]

Industrial democracy. Participation of employees in company management.

Industrial disease benefits. Benefits payable to employees in respect of injuries and prescribed diseases arising from the employment.

Industrial dispute. "INDUSTRIAL DISPUTE means any dispute or difference between employees and employers, or between employers and workmen, or between workmen and workmen, which is connected with employment or non-employment or the terms of employment or with the conditions of labour, of any person. [Industrial Disputes Act (14 of 1947), S. 2(k)].

"Industrial dispute" includes also disputes that might arise between municipalities and their employees in branches of work that can be said to be analogous to the carrying out of a trade or business. *D.N. Banerji* v. *P.R. Mukherjee*, AIR 1953 SC 58, 63. [Industrial Disputes Act (14 of 1947), S. 2(k)]

"Industrial dispute" means,—

(i) any dispute or difference between employers and employers, or between employers and workers or between workers and workers which is connected with the employment or non-employment or the terms of employment or with the conditions of labour, of any person; and

(ii) any dispute or difference between an individual worker and an employer connected with, or arising out of, discharge, dismissal, retrenchment or termination of such worker. [Code on Wages, 2019 (29 of 2019), section 2(q)]

"Industrial dispute" means any dispute or difference between employers and employers or between employers and workers or between workers and workers which is connected with the employment or non-employment or the terms of employment or with the conditions of labour, of any person and includes any dispute or difference between an individual worker and an employer connected with, or arising out of discharge, dismissal, retrenchment or termination of such worker. **[Industrial Relations Code, 2020 (35 of 2020), section 2(q)]**

The 'industrial dispute' referred to and defined in S. 2(k) must be construed to mean not a dispute between an individual workman and the management but a dispute which though it may originate in an action with regard to an individual workman, has developed into a dispute in which the majority of the workmen in the establishment are interested. *New India Assurance Co. Ltd.* v. *Central Government Industrial Tribunal,* AIR 1953 Pat 321. **Relied on** *South Bihar Sugar Mills Ltd.* v. *State of Bihar,* AIR 1956 Pat 274, 276.

The expression 'industrial dispute' as ordinarily understood and construed conveys a dispute between an employer on the one hand and the workmen acting collectively on the other. This definition cannot be widened by a statutory rule or regulation promulgated under the statute or by executive fiat. *Newspapers Ltd.* v. *State Industrial Tribunal*, AIR 1957 SC 533, 537.

An individual grievance, at the time the reference, made by the Government, assumes the character of an industrial dispute. *Workman* v. *Rangavilas Motors, (P) Ltd.*, AIR 1967 SC 1040, 1043.

The term 'dispute' is not restricted merely to a dispute between an employer and recognized majority union but takes within its wide sweep any dispute or difference between employer and workman, including a minority union of workman. *Tata Chemicals* v. *Workman, Tata Chemicals*, AIR 1978 SC 828, 833.

A dispute between an employer and an employee who has been dismissed and who makes a claim for reinstatement and compensation, would be an 'industrial dispute' within the meaning of Sec. 2(12) of the Act. *Central Provinces Transport Service Ltd.* v. *Raghunath Gopal Patwardhan*, AIR 1957 SC 104. [Industrial Disputes Act (14 of 1947), S. 2(12)]

The dispute in the present case which was in respect of a person who was not a workman and belonged to a different category altogether, could not be said to be a dispute within the meaning of Sec. 2(k). *Workmen of Dimakuchi Tea Estate* v. *Management of Dimakuchi Tea Estate*, AIR 1958 SC 353. [Industrial Disputes Act (14 of 1947), S. 2(k)]

The definition of "Industrial dispute" in Section 2(k) requires three things, namely (i) There should be a dispute or difference. (ii) The dispute or difference should be between employers and employers, or between employers or workmen or between workmen and workmen. (iii) The dispute or difference must be connected with the employment or non-employment or the terms of employment or with the conditions of labour of any person. *Standard-Vacuum Refining Co. of India* v. *Their Workmen*, AIR 1960 SC 948. [Industrial Disputes Act (14 of 1947), S. 2(k)]

A workman was dismissed after proper disciplinary proceedings and an appeal against dismissal was also rejected. Hence any dispute raised by the said workman after lapse of seven years cannot be an 'industrial dispute'. *Nedungadi Bank Ltd.* v. *K.P. Madhavan Kutty,* (2000) 2 SCC 455, para 7 : AIR 2000 SC 839. [Industrial Disputes Act (14 of 1947), Ss. 10, 2 (k)]

The definition of industrial dispute in Section 2(k) shows that before any dispute raised by any person can be said to be industrial dispute, it must be shown that it is connected with the employment or non-employment of that person. *Dharam Pal Prem Chand* v. *Dharampal Premchand*, AIR 1966 SC 182. [Industrial Disputes Act (14 of 1947), S. 2(k)]

The definition of "industrial dispute" in Section 3(17) is so wide and comprehensive, that, even if an award is subsisting between the parties, if a difference arises between them, the said difference would amount to an industrial dispute for the purpose of Sec. 73 and a notice of change need not be given, either by the employer or by the employee. *Ahmedabad Mill Owner's, Association* v. *Textile Labour Association,* AIR 1966 SC 497. [Bombay Industrial Relations Act, 1947, Ss. 3(17) and 73]

The term "industrial dispute" connotes a real and substantial difference having some element of persistency and contiguity till resolved and likely if not adjusted to endanger the industrial peace of the undertaking or the community. When parties are at variance and the dispute or difference is connected with the employment, or non-employment or the terms of employment or with the conditions of labour there comes into existence an industrial dispute. *Shambu Nath Goyal* v. *Bank of Baroda*, AIR 1978 SC 1088.

Industrial employees. The expression "industrial employees" is not limited to the class of employees who are employed directly or indirectly for the purpose of manufacturing process carried on by the factory. *Cotton Spinning And Weaving Mills Co. Ltd.* v. *Labour Appellate Tribunal*, AIR 1964 SC 737, 742.

Industrial establishment. 'INDUSTRIAL ESTABLISHMENT' means—

(i) an industrial establishment as defined in clause (ii) of Section 2 of the Payment of Wages Act, 1936 (IV of 1936), or

(ii) a factory as defined in clause (m) of Section 2 of the Factories Act, 1948 (63 of 1948), or

(iii) a railway as defined in clause (4) of Section 2 of the Indian Railways Act, 1890 (9 of 1890), or

(iv) the establishment of a person who, for the purpose of fulfilling a contract with the owner of any industrial establishment, employs workmen. [Industrial Employment (Standing Orders) Act (20 of 1946), S. 2(e)]

The expression 'industrial establishment' may be interpreted as (1) an industry, (2) an industrial concern within an industry (3) an industrial establishment which may itself be the whole of the industrial concern or which may be part of a larger industrial concern, (4) a section of an industrial establishment and (5) categories of workman in an industrial establishment or in a section thereof. *India Type and Rubber Co.* v. *Workers of I.T.R.G.*, AIR 1958 Mad 205, 208. [Industrial Disputes Act (14 of 1947), S. 256]

Industrial establishment or undertaking. Means an establishment or undertaking in which any industry is carried on:

Provided that where several activities are carried on in an establishment or undertaking and only one or some of such activities is or are an industry or industries, then,—

(i) if any unit of such establishment or undertaking carrying on any activity, being an industry, is severable from the other unit or units of such establishment or undertaking which is not carrying on or aiding the carrying on of any such activity, such unit shall be deemed to be a separate industrial establishment or undertaking;

(ii) if the predominant activity or each of the predominant activities carried on in such establishment or undertaking or any unit thereof is an industry and the other activity or each of the other activities carried on in such establishment or undertaking or unit thereof is not severable from and is, for the purpose of carrying on, or aiding the carrying on of, such predominant activity or activities, the entire establishment or undertaking or, as the case may be, unit thereof shall be deemed to be an industrial establishment or undertaking. **[Industrial Relations Code, 2020 (35 of 2020), section 2(r)]**

Means an establishment undertaking in which any industry is carried on;

Provided that where several activities are carried on in an establishment or undertaking and only one or some of such activities is or are an Industry or industries, then,

(a) if any unit of such establishment or undertaking carrying on any activity, being an industry, is severable from the other unit or units of such establishment or undertaking, such unit shall be deemed to be a separate industrial establishment or undertaking;

(b) if the predominant activity or each of the predominant activities carried on in such establishment or undertaking or any unit thereof is an industry and the other activity or each of the other activities carried on in such establishment or undertaking or unit thereof is not severable from and is, for the purpose of carrying on, or aiding the carrying on of, such predominant activity or activities, the entire establishment or undertaking or, as the case may be, unit thereof shall be deemed to be an industrial establishment or undertaking. [Industrial Disputes Act (14 of 1947), S. 2(ka)]

"INDUSTRIAL ESTABLISHMENT OR UNDERTAKING" means an establishment or undertaking in which any industry is carried on. [Industrial Disputes Act (14 of 1947), S. 2(ka)].

Industrial goods. Means the products of industrial co-operatives or cottage and village industries or products of allied industries in the rural area and includes any handicrafts or rural crafts. [National Co-operative Development Corporation Act (26 of 1962), S. 2(dba)]

Industrial in the tiny and decentralised sector. Means industrial concerns in the tiny and decentralised sector and "industrial concern in the tiny and decentralised sector" means an industrial concern in which the investment in machinery and plant is not in excess of rupees two lakhs or such higher amount as the Central Government may specify by notification in this behalf having regard to trends in industrial development and other relevant factor. [National Bank for Agriculture and Rural Development Act (61 of 1981), S. 2(i)]

Industrial injuries. Injuries sustained by persons at work, arising out of and in the course of their employment. Compensation is payable by way of industrial injury benefit and if tortious liability can be established, damages may also be recoverable at common law or for breach of statutory duty.

Industrial maintenance. A system by which each industry should provide for its own unemployees.

Industrial matter. A dispute as to whether three persons or two persons should work a calender Machine is a matter relating to work and is therefore covered by the term industrial matter as used in C.P. and Berar Industrial Disputes Settlement Act, 1947. *Model Mills, Manager* v. *Dharam Dass,* AIR 1958 SC 311.

Industrial model town. Means industrial area developed by the State Government or its agencies or private developers as integrated township with provision of social infrastructure such as residential, communication, educational, medical, recreational, commercial and other appropriate facilities. [Rajasthan Industrial Area Development Authority Act (Raj Act No. 7 of 1996), S. 2(f)]

Industrial or other establishment. Means any—

(a) tramway service, or motor transport service engaged in carrying passengers or goods or both by road, for hire or reward;

(aa) air transport service other than such service belonging to, or exclusively employed in the military, naval or air forces of the Union or the Civil Aviation Department of the Government of India;

(b) dock, wharf or jetty;

(c) inland vessel, mechanically propelled;

(d) mine, quarry or oilfield;

(e) plantation;

(f) workshop or other establishment in which articles are produced, adapted or manufactured with a view to their use, transport or sale;

(g) establishment in which any work relating to the construction, development or maintenance of buildings, roads, bridges or canals, or relating to operations connected with navigation, irrigation or the supply of water, or relating to the generation, transmission and distribution of electricity or any other form of power is being on;

(h) any other establishment or class of establishments which the Central Government or a State Government may, having regard to the nature thereof, the need for protection of persons employed therein and other relevant circumstances, specify, by notification in the Official Gazette. [Payment of Wages Act (4 of 1936), S 2(ii)]

Industrial plant. Means any plant used for any industrial or trade purposes and emitting any air pollutant into the atmosphere. [Air (Prevention and Control of Pollution) Act (14 of 1981), S. 2(k)]

Industrial pocket. Means any industrial zone ear marked by the Industrial Development Corporation of the State Government or by the State Government. [Chemical Accidents (Emergency Planning, Preparedness, and Response) Rules, 1996, R. 2(d)]

Industrial premises. 'INDUSTRIAL PREMISES' means any place or premises (not being a private dwelling house) including the precincts thereof, in which or in any part of which any industry or manufacturing process connected with the making of *beedi* or *cigar* or both is being or is ordinarily carried on with or without the aid of power. [Beedi and Cigar Workers (Conditions of Employment) Act (32 of 1966), S. 2(i)]

"Industrial premises" means any place or premises (not being a private dwelling house), including the precincts thereof, in which or in any part of which any industry, trade, business, occupation or manufacturing is being ordinarily carried on with or without the aid of power and includes a godown attached thereto. [Occupational Safety, Healthy &

Working Conditions Code, 2020 (37 of 2020), section 2(1)(zc)]

Industrial property. "Patents, utility models, industrial designs, trade marks, service marks, trade names, indications of service or appellations of origin and the repression of unfair competition." [Article 1(2), Paris Convention for the Protection of Industrial Property Act, 1967]

Industrial pursuit. Industrial pursuit includes a mercantile business for the sale of goods, mining supplies, *etc.* The term 'industrial pursuit' is a very broad expression.

Industrial purpose. 'INDUSTRIAL PURPOSE' means any purpose connected with an industrial undertaking where the process of manufacturing any article is carried on with the aid of power and includes a purpose connected with excavation, underground or otherwise where any operation for the purpose of searching for, or obtaining a mineral has been or is being carried on. [A.P. Non-Agricultural Land Assessment Act (14 of 1963), S. 2(d)]

Industrial rationalization. Means the transfer of all or a portion of the calculated level of production of one party to another, for the purpose of achieving economic efficiencies or responding to anticipated short-falls in supply as a result of plant enclosures. [Montreal Protocol on substances that deplete the Ozone Layer, 1987, Art. I(8)]

Industrial school. School where children are taught any trade, business, or other avocation.

Industrial undertaking. "INDUSTRIAL UNDERTAKING" means any undertaking pertaining to a scheduled industry carried on in one or more factories by any person or authority including Government. [Industries (Development and Regulation) Act (65 of 1951), S. 3(d)]

"INDUSTRIAL UNDERTAKING" means any undertaking, pertaining to any industry carried on in one or more factories or units by any company, as defined in clause (aa) of Section 3 of the Industries (Development and Regulation) Act, 1951 but does not include a small-scale industrial undertaking as defined in clause (j) of the section. [Companies Act (1 of 1956), S. 2(19AB)]

"INDUSTRIAL UNDERTAKING" means any undertaking which is mainly engaged in the business of generation or distribution of electricity or any other form of power or in the construction of ships or in the manufacture or processing of goods or in mining. [Income-tax Act (43 of 1961), S. 33B, *Expln.*]

"INDUSTRIAL UNDERTAKING" means any undertaking which is engaged in—

(i) the manufacture or processing of goods; or

(ii) the manufacture of computer software; or

(iii) the business of generation or distribution of electricity or any other form of power; or

(iiia) the business of providing telecommunication services, whether basic or cellular, including radio paging, domestic satellite service, network of trunking, broad band network and internet services; or

(iv) mining; or

(v) the construction of ships, aircraft or rail systems. [Income-tax Act (43 of 1961), S. 72A(7) (aa)]

"INDUSTRIAL UNDERTAKING" means any undertaking pertaining to a scheduled industry and includes an undertaking engaged in any other industry, or in any trade, business or service which may be regulated by Parliament by law. [Central Industrial Security Force Act (50 of 1968), S. 2(b)]

"INDUSTRIAL UNDERTAKING" includes any undertaking for the manufacture, preservation, storage or processing of goods, or mining or the hotel industry, or the transport of passengers or goods, or the generation or distribution of electricity or any other form of energy or for the development of any contiguous area of land as an industrial estate.

Explanation.—The expression "processing of goods" includes any art or process for producing, preparing or making an article by subjecting any material to a manual, chemical, electrical or any other like operation. [Gujarat Public Moneys (Recovery of Dues) Act (17 of 1979), S. 2(g)]

"INDUSTRIAL UNDERTAKING" means any undertaking pertaining to a scheduled industry carried on in one or more factories by any company but does include—

(i) an ancillary industrial undertaking as defined in clause (aa) of Section 3 of the Industries (Development & Regulation) Act, 1951; and

(ii) a small scale industrial undertaking as defined in clause (j) of the aforesaid Section 3. [Sick Industrial Companies (Special Provisions) Act (1 of 1986), S. 3(f)]

An establishment to fall within the definition of an undertaking, it must be a factory *i.e.* an establishment carrying on manufacturing process by 50 or more workmen with aid of power. *Ramnarayan Satyanarayan Agarwal Distilleries Pvt. Ltd.* v. *Associated Alcohols & Breweries Ltd.*, AIR 1995 SC 1686.

To be an industrial undertaking, the work of manufacture or production should be carried on in one or more factories by person or authority including Government.

Business of a hotel or chain of hotels is not an 'industrial undertaking' under S. 80-J of the Act. *Indian Hotels Co. Ltd.* v. *Income Tax Officer,* (2000) 7 SCC 39, para 12 : AIR 2000 SC 2645. [Income-tax Act (43 of 1961), S. 80-J]

Industrial undertaking in public sector. Means an industrial undertaking owned, controlled or managed by—

(i) a Government company as defined in S. 617 of the Companies Act, 1956 (1 of 1956);

(ii) a corporation established by or under a Central, Provincial or State Act, which is controlled or managed by the Government. [Central Industrial Security Force Act (50 of 1968), S. 2(c)]

Industrial use. Includes the use of any land or building or part thereof for the purpose of industry. [W. Bengal Town and Country (Planning and Development) Act (13 of 1979), S. 2(11)]

Industrialist. One owning or engaged in the management of an especially large scale industry. [Institutes of Technology Act (59 of 1961), S. 11(c)].

Industry. INDUSTRY means any systematic activity carried on by co-operation between an employer and his workmen (whether such workmen are employed by such employer directly or by or through any agency, including a contractor) for the production, supply or distribution of goods or services with a view to satisfy human wants or wishes (not being wants or wishes which are merely spiritual or religious in nature), whether or not,—

(i) any capital has been invested for the purpose of carrying on such activity; or

(ii) such activity is carried on with a motive to make any gain or profit, and includes—

(a) any activity of the Dock Labour Board established under Section 5A of the Dock Workers (Regulation of Employment) Act, 1948;

(b) any activity relating to the promotion of sales or business or both carried on by an establishment,

but does not include—

(1) any agricultural operation except where such agricultural operation is carried on in an integrated manner with any other activity (being any such activity as is referred to in the foregoing provisions of this clause) and such other activity is the predominant one,

Explanation.—For the purposes of this sub-clause, "agricultural operation" does not include any activity carried on in a plantation as defined in clause (f) of Section 2 of the Plantations Labour Act, 1951; or

(2) hospitals or dispensaries; or

(3) educational, scientific, research or training institutions; or

(4) institutions owned or managed by organisation wholly or substantially engaged in any charitable, social or philanthropic service; or

(5) khadi or village industries; or

(6) any activity of the Government relatable to the sovereign functions of the Government including all the activities carried on by the departments of the Central Government dealing with defence research, atomic energy and space;

(7) any domestic service; or

(8) any activity, being a profession practised by an individual or body of individuals, if the number of persons employed by the individual or body of individuals in relation to such profession is less than ten; or

(9) any activity, being an activity carried on by a co-operative society or a club or any other like body of individuals, if the number of persons employed by the co-operative society, club or other like body of individuals in relation to such activity is less than ten. [Industrial Disputes Act (14 of 1947), S. 2(j)]

"Industry" means any systematic activity carried on by co-operation between an employer and worker (whether such worker is employed by such employer directly or by or through any agency, including a contractor) for the production, supply or distribution of goods or services with a view to satisfy human wants or wishes (not being wants or wishes which are merely spiritual or religious in nature), whether or not,—

(i) any capital has been invested for the purpose of carrying on such activity; or

(ii) such activity is carried on with a motive to make any gain or profit, but does not include—

(i) institutions owned or managed by organisations wholly or substantially engaged in any charitable, social or philanthropic service; or

(ii) any activity of the appropriate Government relatable to the sovereign functions of the appropriate Government including all the activities carried on by the departments of the Central Government dealing with defence research, atomic energy and space; or

(iii) any domestic service; or

(iv) any other activity as may be notified by the Central Government. **[Industrial Relations Code, 2020 (35 of 2020), section 2(p)]**

"Industry" means any systematic activity carried on by co-operation between an employer and worker (whether such worker is employed by such employer directly or by or through any agency, including a contractor) for the production, supply or distribution of goods or services with a view to satisfy human wants or wishes (not being wants or wishes which are merely spiritual or religious in nature), whether or not,—

(i) any capital has been invested for the purpose of carrying on such activity; or

(ii) such activity is carried on with a motive to make any gain or profit, but does not include—

(a) institutions owned or managed by organisations wholly or substantially engaged in any charitable, social or philanthropic services; or

(b) any activity of the appropriate Government relatable to the sovereign functions of the appropriate Government including all the activities carried on by the Departments of the Central Government dealing with defence research, atomic energy and space; or

(c) any domestic service; or

(d) any other activity as may be notified by the Central Government. [Occupational Safety, Healthy & Working Conditions Code, 2020 (37 of 2020), section 2(1)(zd)]

"INDUSTRY" means any industry or business in which any trade, occupation or subject fied in engineering or technology or any vocational course may be specified as a designated trade. [Apprentices Act (52 of 1961), S. 2(k)]

"industry" means any industry or business in which any trade, occupation or subject field in engineering or non-engineering or technology or any vocational course may be specified as a designated trade or optional trade or both;. [Water (Prevention and Control of Pollution) Cess Act (36 of 1977), S. 2(c) substituted by Act 19 of 2003 (w.e.f. 6-5-2003)]

'Industry' is defined by lexicographers to be habitual diligence in any employment, either bodily or mentally, and is as applicable to the sale of goods, which is the chief business of a merchant as to the transportation of goods, which is the chief business of an express carrier.

The word 'industry' means only the place where the process of manufacture or production of goods is carried on and it cannot in any event include 'hospitals, dispensaries or nursing homes. *Msco. Pvt. Ltd.* v. *Union of India*, AIR 1985 SC 76, 79. [Customs Act (52 of 1962), S. 11N-Notification Dt. 15-7-1977]

The definition of industry is in two parts. In its first part it means any business, trade, undertaking, manufacture or calling of employers. This is with reference to occupation of employers in respect of certain activities, By the second part of the definition any calling, service, employment, handicraft or industrial occupation or avocation of workmen is included in the concept of industry. *Madras Gymkhana Club Employees' Union.* v. *Management of Gymkhana Club*, AIR 1968 SC 554, 561.

The linch-pin of the definition of industry is to ascertain the systematic activity which the organisation is discharging namely whether it partakes the nature of a business or trade or is an undertaking or manufacture or calling of employers. If it is that and there is co-operation of the employer and the employee resulting in the production of material services, it is an industry notwithstanding that its objects are charitable or that it does not make profit or even where profits are made, they are not distributed among the members. *Management of Federation of Chamber Of Commerce And Industry* v. *Their Workmen R.K.Mittal*, AIR 1972 SC 763, 777.

Swaraj Ashram is 'industry'. *Swaraj Ashram* v. *Industrial Tribunal U.P.*, AIR 1979 SC 1210.

By applying the dominant nature test, viz., the existence of predominant nature of the services and integrated nature of the department, in the absence of employers not carrying on any business, trade, undertaking, manufacture or calling of employers, irrigation department of State is an industry. Des Raj v. State of Punjab, AIR 1988 SC 1182, 1193.

An educational institution is 'industry'. *A. Sundarambal* v. *Govt. of Goa, Daman & Diu*, AIR 1988 SC 1700, 1702.

Khadi and Village Industries Board is an 'industry' as the board engages itself in selling the blankets prepared out of the wool supplied by the Board and not from the various societies. *Gopal* v. *Administrative Officer, M.P.K. & V.I. Board*, AIR 1986 SC 504, 508.

Industry involves essentially the manufacture of commodities.

Systematic economic activity or any branch thereof; a trade or manufacture. [Constitution of India, Art. 19(6)(ii)].

Industry carried on under the authority of the central government. For an industry to be carried on under the authority of the Central Government, it must be an industry belonging to the Central Government, that is to say, its own undertaking. A controlled industry is not necessarily an industry carried on by or under the authority of the Central Government. *Bharat Glass Works* v. *State of West Bengal,* AIR 1957 Cal 347, 349. [Industrial Disputes Act (14 of 1947), S. 2(a)(1) and 10]

Industry or Business. In the ordinary and non-technical sense, industry or business means an undertaking where capital and labour co-operate with each other for the purpose of producing wealth in the shape of goods, machines, tools etc and for making profits. The concept of industry applies even to agriculture, horticulture, pisciculture and so on and so forth. *D.N. Banerjee* v. *P.R. Mukherjee*, AIR 1953 SC 58, 60. [Industrial Disputes Act (14 of 1947), S. 2(j), (k) & (s)]

Industry partner. "industry partner" means an individual, or a trust established under the Indian Trusts Act, 1882, or a company established under the Companies Act, 2013, or society formed and registered under the Societies Registration Act, 1860, or a financial institution or a combination of one or more of such industry partners [The Indian

Institutes of Information Technology (Public Private Partnership) Act, 2017 (23 of 2017), S. 3(g)]

Ineffectual. Not producing the proper or usual effect. [Indian Easements Act (5 of 1882), S. 38, ill.(b)].

Inefficiency. The word "inefficiency" used in respect of a Police Officer, is sufficiently broad to include the inability of the officer to read or write the English language or the language of the District.

Ineligibility. Disqualification or legal incapacity to be elected to an office or appointed to a particular position. Thus, an alien or naturalized citizen is ineligible to be elected President of the United States. This incapacity arises from various causes, and a person may be incapable of being elected to one office who may be elected to another; the incapacity may also be perpetual or temporary.

Ineligible. Not qualified to hold office.

The word "ineligible" means not eligible; disqualifying; not qualified to be chosen to an office.

Not eligible. [Representation of the People Act (43 of 1951), S. 52, 2nd *Prov.* and Constitution of India, Art. 16(2)].

Inescapable peril. A danger which one cannot avoid without another's help.

Inevitable accident is synonymous with act of God.

An inevitable accident is an event which happens not only without the concurrence of the will of man, but in spite of all efforts on his part to prevent it.

An "inevitable accident" is a catastrophe occurring without any intervention of man.

The plea of *inevitable accident* is good defence to actions for negligence and trespass, but if relied on it must be specially pleaded.

An accident which happens without the slightest degree of negligence or which could not have been avoided in spite of due care. [TP Act (4 of 1882), S. 55(3)].

Infamous conduct. Conduct causing or bringing infamy. [Indian Medicine Central Council Act (48 of 1970), S. 26(2)].

Infamy. Ill fame; bad conduct; vile nature. Loss of reputation or position as a result of a person's being convicted of an infamous crime.

Infancy. The state of an infant.

The state or period of being an infant; early childhood. [Ancient Monuments and Archaeological Sites and Remains Act (24 of 1958), S. 7(1)].

Infant food. Means any food (by whatever name called) being marketed or otherwise represented as a complement to mother's milk to meet the growing nutritional needs of the infant after the age of four months. [Infant Milk Substitutes Etc. Act (41 of 1992), S. 2(f)]

"INFANT FOOD" shall have the meaning assigned to it in section 2(1)(f) of the Infant Milk Substitutes, Feeding Bottles and Infant Foods (Regulation of Production, Supply and Distribution) Act, 1992 (41 of 1992). [S. 3(1)(x) of the Food Safety & Standards Act, 2006 (34 of 2006)]

Infant milk substitute. Means any food being marketed or otherwise represented as a partial or total replacement for mother's milk, whether or not it is suitable for such replacement. [Infant Milk Substitutes Etc. Act (41 of 1992), S. 2(g)]

"INFANT MILK SUBSTITUTE" shall have the meaning assigned to it in section 2(1)(g) of the Infant Milk Substitutes, Feeding Bottles and Infant Foods (Regulation of Production, Supply and Distribution) Act, 1992 (41 of 1992). [S. 3(1)(x) of the Food Safety & Standards Act, 2006 (34 of 2006)]

Infantiae proximus. (*Lat.*) Next to infancy.

Infanticide is murder of new born child especially with the consent of the mother.

Infantry. Foot soldiers.

Infection. "INFECTION" means infection by any insect, fungus, or other pest injurious to a crop. [Destructive Insects and Pests Act (2 of 1914), S. 2(c)]

"Infection" is the subtle or virulent matter proceeding from diseased bodies and imparting the same to others.

An infective agent. [Destructive Insects and Pests Act (2 of 1914), S. 2(c)].

Infectious. A person infected with a pathogen, capable of transmitting it to another person.

Infectious disease. An "infectious" disease is one originating from a cause acting by hidden influences or through the pollution of water or the atmosphere or from the various rejections from animals as distinguished from a "contagious" disease, which is communicated by contract or bodily exhalation.

A disease which is apt to be communicated by infection. [Cantonments Act (2 of 1924), S. 175(2)].

Infectious or contagious disease. Means cholera, plague, small-pox, chicken-pox, kala-azar, tuberculosis, diphtheria and typhoid or enteric fever or such other dangerous disease as the Government may notify in this behalf. [Manipur Municipalities Act (43 of 1994), S. 2(25)]

"INFECTIOUS OR CONTAGIOUS DISEASES" means cholera, leprosy, enteric fever, small pox, tuberculosis, diphtheria, plague and any other epidemic, endemic or infectious disease which the Central Government may, by notification in the Official Gazette, declare to be an infectious or contagious disease for the purposes of this Act. [Cantonments Act (2 of 1924), S. 2(xvii)] [Now repealed & replaced by Act 41 of 2006]

Infectious or contagious disorders. The expression "INFECTIOUS OR CONTAGIOUS DISORDERS" include tick-pest, anthrax, glanders, farcy, scabies and any other disease or disorder which may be specified by the Central Government by notification in the

Official Gazette. [Livestock Importation Act (9 of 1898), S. 2(a)]

Infective animal. Is one which is affected with a scheduled disease or has recently been in contact with or in close proximity to an animal so infected. [Orissa Animal Contagious Diseases Act (8 of 1949), S. 3(b)]

Infer. To derive by reasoning or implication; to guess.

Inference. A deduction or conclusion from known facts; a permissible deduction from the evidence. A process by which a conclusion is reached by considering the facts and deducing a logical consequence from them.

Inferential. Deducible or inferable from proved facts.

Inferential fact. An 'inferential fact' is an inference or conclusion from evidence. It is true such conclusions are not conclusions of law, but they are inferences or conclusions of fact.

Inferior Court. A general term for a Court of lower rank than another, or other Courts, the jurisdiction of which is frequently limited, the decisions of which are normally subject to appeal to a superior Court, and which is subject to the control of a superior Court.

Inferior holder. "INFERIOR HOLDER" means a person who is in possession of an alienated land whether by inheritance or succession or valid transfer under the tenancy law or otherwise and holds such land not on payment of rent but on payment of assessment in cash or kind to the alienee or jiwaidar. [Gujarat Surviving Alienations Abolition Act (33 of 1963), S. 2(15)]

Inferred agreement. An agreement in which, the intention of the parties is the matter of inference from their conduct.

Infertility. Means the inability to conceive after one year of unprotected coitus or other proven medical condition preventing a couple from conception. [Assisted Reproductive Technology (Regulation) Act, 2021 (42 of 2021), section 2(1)(j)]

Infirm. The idea of being aged or infirm is closely connected with the ability of a person to earn his or her livelihood. Parents are aged vis-a-vis their sons, or daughters and if they are unable to make their own living, they may as well be called infirm. *Munni Devi* v. *Chhoti,* AIR 1983 All 444, 448. [Hindu Adoptions and Maintenance Act (78 of 1956), S. 20]

Infirmity. Feebleness of body resulting from some disease (now mostly old age). [IPC 1973 (45 of 1860), S. 319].

Inflate. Raise prices artificially.

Inflation. A condition in which the volume of purchasing power is constantly running ahead of the output of goods and services, with the result that as incomes and prices rise the value of money falls.

"Inflation" means the year wise in monthly Consumer Price Index expressed in terms of percentage. [Reserve Bank of India Act (2 of 1934), S. 2(c-i) as inserted by Finance Act (28 of 2016), S. 221(ii)].

Inflict. Deal; deliver forcibly; (as) to inflict a blow, pain, or penalty.

Influence. The power or capacity of causing an effect in indirect or intangible ways. [CrPC 1973 (2 of 1974), S. 316].

Inform. To give information, especially in accusation.

To impart knowledge of some particular fact or occurrence to. [Constitution of India, Art. 38(1)].

Informal. Lacking in due form.

Conducted or carried out with formal; regularly prescribed or ceremonious procedure.

Informality. Absence of or non-observance of due or prescribed form.

The quality or fact of being informal *i.e.* not done or made according to form or not observing form. [IPC (45 of 1860), S. 200, *Expln.*].

Informant. Is the giver of information.

A person who informs a police officer or magistrate of the commission of a cognizable offence. [CrPC 1973 (2 of 1974), S. 154(1)].

INFORMANT, INFORMER. These two epithets, from the verb to inform, have acquired by their application an important distinction. The *informant* being he who informs for the benefit of others, and the *informer* to the molestation of others. What the *informant* communicates is for the benefit of the individual, and what the *informer* communicates is for the benefit of the whole. The *informant* is thanked for his civility in making the communication; the *informer* undergoes a great deal of odium, but is thanked by not one, not even by those who employ him.

Information. "INFORMATION" includes data, text, images, sound, voice, codes, computer programmes, software and data bases or micro film or computer generated micro fiche. [Information Technology Act (21 of 2000), S. 2(1)(v)]

"INFORMATION" means any material in any form relating to the administration, operations or decisions of a public authority. [Freedom of Information Act (5 of 2003), S. 2(d)]

"INFORMATION" means any material in any form, including records, documents, memos, e-mails, opinions, advices, press releases, circulars, orders, logbooks, contracts, reports, papers, samples, models, data material held in any electronic form and information relating to any private body which can be accessed by a public authority under any other law for the time being in force. [Right to Information Act (22 of 2005), S. 2(f)]

An information is a written accusation of crime preferred by the public prosecuting officer.

That of which one is apprised of or told [Payment of Wages Act (4 of 1936), S. 20(3)]; an initiatory step in proceedings of a criminal nature in the form of a complaint. [IPC (45 of 1860), Ss. 176 and 177].

"Information" as used in a public advertisement offering a reward to any person who would give such information as would lead to the conviction of a party who had robbed certain premises, comprehends every mode by which information can be conveyed that might have the effect of discovering and convicting the guilty person.

The words "information with respect to its affairs which they may reasonably expect" shows that the information sought for must be about the affairs of the company and something which could reasonably be expected to be supplied. *Kumaranunni* v. *Mathrubhumi Printing and Publishing Co.,* (1983) 54 Com Cases 370, 384 (Ker). [Companies Act (1 of 1956), S. 237]

A mere expression of opinion by the Central Board of Revenue does not amount to information. *Asst. Controller of Estate Duty* v. *Mir Usman Ali Khan,* AIR 1965 AP 132, 136. [Estate Duty Act (34 of 1953), S. 59]

The expression 'information' means instruction or knowledge derived from an external source concerning facts or particulars, or as to law relating to a matter bearing on the assessment. *Commissioner of Income tax* v. *A. Raman and Co.*, AIR 1968 SC 49, 51. [Income-tax Act (43 of 1961), S. 147(1)(*b*)]

The opinion of an internal audit party of the Income-tax Department on a point of law cannot be regarded as "information". *Indian and Eastern Newspapers Society, New Delhi* v. *Commissioner of Income Tax, New Delhi*, AIR 1979 SC 1960, 1967. [Income-tax Act (43 of 1961), S. 147(b)]

The knowledge of the fact that the appellants had not submitted their quarterly returns as well as the treasury challans, constituted an information to the assessing authority. *Anandji Haridas and Co. (P) Ltd.* v. *S.R. Kasture*, AIR 1968 SC 565, 573.

A statement by the referee as to the truth or otherwise regarding a question in a dispute, when the Court needs information on such question, is information. *Hirachand Kothari* v. *State of Rajasthan*, AIR 1985 SC 998, 1001. [Indian Evidence Act (1 of 1872), S. 20]

"INFORMATION" the term 'information' although is of wide import, must be read in the context of which it has been used. 'Information' may include statement which falls short of confession as well as statement which amounts to confession. *R.* v. *Babulal*, ILR 6 All 509, 537. Also see, *Sarabjit Rick Singh* v. *UOI*, AIR 2008 SC (Supp) 368.

Information agency. Means a press, broadcasting, film, television or facsimile organisation, public or private, regularly engaged in the collection and dissemination of news material, created and organised under the laws and regulation of contracting state in which the central organization is domiciled and which, in each contracting State where it operates, functions under the laws and regulations of that State. [Convention on the International Right of Correction 16 Dec. 1952, Art. 1(2)].

Information and belief. Allegations of a verified pleading are made on information and belief when positive knowledge is wanting.

An averment upon "*information and belief*" is sufficient as to a fact within the defendant's knowledge and not within the plaintiff's.

Information assets. All information resources used in the course of any organisation's business including application software, hardware, system software and computer networks. (*Information Technology*)

Information attack. Directly corrupting information without visibly changing the physical entity within which it resides. In the wake of an information attack, an information function is indistinguishable from its original state except through inspecting its data or instructions. (*Cyber Law*)

Information-based warfare (IBW). Synonym for information warfare. An approach to armed conflict focusing on managing and using information in all its forms and at all levels to achieve a decisive military advantage, specially in the joint and combined environment. (*Cyber Law*)

Information collection. That aspect of IW activities concerned with the acquisition of data. An organization needs a variety of information to support its operations. Information collection includes the entry points for information into an organization from both internal and external sources. Issues include quantity (completeness), quality (accuracy), and timelines of this information. Business examples of collection systems include point-of-sale (POS) systems, market surveys, government statistics, and internal management data. Military examples of collection systems include tactical radars and other sensors. (*Cyber Law*)

Information compromise. That class or type of IW threat that involves a competitor gaining access to an organization's proprietary data. (*Cyber Law*)

Information denial. Measures beyond normal protection to specifically target an adversary's collection systems. There are two types of denial; direct attacks on the adversary's information systems, and providing misinformation to its systems to deceive and induce the adversary to take actions that are not to its advantage. For the military, direct attacks include electronic warfare (jamming) of sensors and radio links. Besides direct attacks, there are safer ways to corrupt an adversary's databases. These rely on providing false information to the targeted competitor's collection systems to induce this organization to make bad decisions based on this faulty information. (*Cyber Law*)

Information destruction. That class or type of IW threat to one's data assets that involves the loss of these data (or loss of access to these data) as the result of a hostile attack by an adversary. (*Cyber Law*)

Information dominance. In warfare, an operational advantage obtained through superior effectiveness of informational activity (acquisition and processing of data, information, and/or knowledge), to the extent that this advantage is demonstrated in practice through superior effectiveness of instrumental activity. (*Cyber Law*)

Information dominance warfare (IDW). The subcategory of information warfare (IW) aimed at leveraging data, information, and knowledge to tactical and strategic advantage, as opposed to leveraging the media, channels, and vehicles of information transfer and/or processing. The goal of IDW is to achieve information dominance. (*Cyber Law*)

Information is property. The principle that trade secrets have commercial value and should be treated like property. (*Cyber Law*)

Information memorandum. "INFORMATION MEMORANDUM" means a process undertaken prior to the filing of a prospectus by which a demand for the securities proposed to be issued by a company is elicited, and the price and the terms of issue for such securities is assessed, by means of a notice, circular, advertisement or document. [Companies Act (1 of 1956), S. 2(19B)](Replaced by Act 2013)

Information security (INFOSEC). The protection of unauthorized access to or modification of information, whether in storage, processing, or transit, and against the denial of service to authorized users or the provision of service to unauthorized users, including those measures necessary to detect, document, and counter such threats. (*Cyber Law*)

Information Security Management System. Means a set of policies, processes and procedures to establish, implement, operate, monitor, review, maintain and continually improve information security and minimise the risks by development, maintaining, implementing and reviewing the adequate and appropriate security controls. [Information Technology (Information Security Practices and Procedures for Protected System) Rules, 2018, R. 2(1)(f)].

Information Security Steering Committee. Means the committee comprising higher management officials of the organization, responsible for continuously improving and strengthening the cyber security posture of the protected system and also plan, develop, review remedial actions to mitigate and recover from malicious cyber incidents. [Information Technology (Information Security Practices and Procedures for Protected System) Rules, 2018, R. 2(1)(g)].

Information society. The term "information society" describes the form of society being created in the "information age", based mainly on the increasingly interactive acquisition, storage, processing, transmission, distribution and use of information and knowledge, in which a productive relationship between information resources and knowledge-intensive production play a major role. It is characterised in particular by the convergence of three sectors : information technology, telecommunications and content. (*Telecommunication*)

Information system(s). "INFORMATION SYSTEM" means a system for generating sending, receiving, storing or otherwise processing data messages. [UNCITRAL Model Law on Electronic Commerce, Dec. 16, 1996, Art. 2(f)]

Information technology. "INFORMATION TECHNOLOGY" means any service in relation to designing, developing or maintaining of computer software, or computerised data processing or system networking, or any other service primarily in relation to operation of computer systems. [Finance Act (32 of 1994), S. 65(19), *Expln.* (b) *as substituted by Finance Act (18 of 2005), S. 88a(v) now repealed by Goods and Services Tax Act, 2017*]

Information Technology Security. All aspects related to defining, archieving, maintaining confidentiality, integrity, availability, accountability, authencity and reliability. (*Information Technology*)

Information Technology Security Policy. Rules, directives and practices that govern how information assets, including sensitive information are managed, protected and distributed within an organization and its Information Technology systems. (*Information Technology*)

Information technology service. Means any service which results from the use of any information technology software over a system of information technology products for realising value addition. [Income-tax Act (43 of 1961), S. 115 ACA (3); *Expln.* (b)]

Information technology software. Means any representation of instructions, data, sound or image, including source code and object code, recorded in a machine readable form and capable of being manipulated or providing inter-activity to a user, by means of an automatic data processing machine falling under heading information technology products but does not include non-information technology products. [Income-tax Act (43 of 1961), S. 115 ACA (3), *Expln.* (c)]

"Information technology software" means an representation of instructions, data, sound or image, including source code and object code, recorded in a machine readable form, and capable of being manipulated or providing interactivity to a user, by means of computer or an automatic data processing machine or any other device or equipment. [Finance

Act (32 of 1994), S. 65B(28) *now repealed by Goods and Services Tax Act, 2017*].

Information technology software and information technology services. In this scheme, unless the context otherwise requires—

'INFORMATION TECHNOLOGY SOFTWARE AND INFORMATION TECHNOLOGY SERVICES' means the companies which deal with such activities as defined in recommendation No. 19(*a*) and (*b*) of the notification dated 25th July, 1998, issued by the Planning Commission. [Issue of Foreign Currency Convertible Bonds and Ordinary Shares (Through Depository Receipt Mechanism) Scheme, 1993, S. 2(h)]

Informed consent. A person's agreement to allow something to happen, made with full knowledge of the risks involved and the alternatives.

"Informed consent" means consent given for a specific intervention, without any force, undue influence, fraud, threat, mistake or misrepresentation, and obtained after disclosing to a person adequate information including risks and benefits of, and alternatives to, the specific intervention in a language and manner understood by the person [The Mental Healthcare Act, 2017 (10 of 2017), S. 2(1)(i)]

Informer. One who furnishes information for the prosecution of a crime.

Infortunium. Misfortune; misadventure; accident.

Infra. Below; within : beneath; under; later in this text.

Infraction. A breach or violation of a duty.

Infrastructure. "INFRASTRUCTURE" includes structures such as docks, wharves, jetties, landing stages, locks, buoys, inland ports, cargo handling equipment, road and rail access and cargo storage spaces, and the expression "infrastructural facilities" shall be construed accordingly. [Inland Waterways Authority of India Act (82 of 1985), S. 2(f)]

Infrastructure capital company. Means such company which makes investments by way of acquiring shares or providing long-term finance to any enterprise or undertaking wholly engaged in the business referred to in sub-section (4) of section 80-IA or sub-section (1) of section 80-IAB or an undertaking developing and building a housing project referred to in sub-section (10) of section 80-IB or a project for constructing a hotel of not less than three-star category as classified by the Central Government or a project for constructing a hospital with at least one hundred beds for patients. . [Income-tax Act (43 of 1961), S. 2(26A)

Infrastructure capital fund. Means such fund operating under a trust deed registered under the provisions of the Registration Act, 1908 (16 of 1908) established to raise monies by the trustees for investment by way of acquiring shares or providing long-term finance to any enterprise or undertaking wholly engaged in the business referred to in sub-section (4) of section 80-IA or sub-section (1) of section 80-IAB or an undertaking developing and building a housing project referred to in sub-section (10) of section 80-IB or a project for constructing a hotel of not less than three-star category as classified by the Central Government or a project for constructing a hospital with at least one hundred beds for patients.[Income-tax Act (43 of 1961), S.2(26B)]

Infrastructure debt fund scheme. Means a mutual fund scheme that invests primarily (minimum 90% of scheme assets) in the debt securities or securitized debt instrument of infrastructure companies or infrastructure capital companies or infrastructure projects or special purpose vehicles which are created for the purpose of facilitating or promoting investment in infrastructure, and other permissible assets in accordance with these regulations or bank loans in respect of completed and revenue generating projects of infrastructure companies or projects or special purpose vehicles. [Securities Exchange Board of India (Mutual Funds) Regulation 1996, Regulation 49(L)(1). Also see (w.e.f. 1-6-2013) *Explanation (ii)* to section 115R(2) of the Income-tax Act, 1961 (43 of 1961)]

Infrastructure development. In this Scheme, unless the context otherwise requires,—

"INFRASTRUCTURE DEVELOPMENT" includes, roads (including approach roads), water supply and sewerage, common effluent treatment facility, telecom network, generation and distribution of power, air-conditioning and such other facilities as are used for common purpose of the units therein. [Industrial Park Scheme, 1999, S. 2(f)]

Infrastructure facilities. "INFRASTRUCTURE FACILITIES" means industrial, commercial or social infrastructure or other facilities necessary for the development of a Special Economic Zone or such other facilities which may be prescribed. [Special Economic Zones Act (28 of 2005), S. 2(p)

"INFRASTRUCTURE FACILITIES" for the purposes of section 186 of Act 18 of 2013, the expression 'infrastructure facilities' means the facilities specified in Schedule VI of Act 18 of 2013. [*Explanation* (*b*) to section 186 of the Companies Act, 2013 (18 of 2013)]

Infrastructure facility. "INFRASTRUCTURE FACILITY" means,—

(a) a road including toll road, a bridge or a rail system.

(b) a highway project including housing or other activities being an integral part of the highway project;

(c) a water supply project, water treatment system, irrigation project, sanitation and sewerage system or solid waste management system;

(d) a port, airport, inland waterway or inland port. [Income-tax Act (43 of 1961), S. 81-1A(b), *Expln.*]

"INFRASTRUCTURE FACILITY" means—

(i) a road, highway, bridge, airport, port, Railways including BOLT, road transport system, a water supply project, irrigation project, industrial parks, water treatment system, solid waste management system, sanitation and sewerage system;

(ii) generation or distribution or transmission of power;

(iii) telecommunication;

(iv) project for housing;

(v) any other public facility of a similar nature as may be notified by the Authority in this behalf in the Official Gazette. [Insurance Regulatory and Development Authority (Registration of Indian Insurance Companies) Regulations, Reg. 2(h)]

Infrastructure projects. For the purposes of section 55(2) of Act 18 of 2013, the expression 'infrastructure projects' means the infrastructure projects specified in Schedule VI of the Companies Act, 2013 (18 of 2013). [*Explanation* to section 55 of the Companies Act, 2013 (18 of 2013)]

Infringe. To commit a breach of.

Infringement. The unlawful sale or use of a patented invention; or copyright. The act of infringing; an unlawful trespass on a right or privilege.

Breach of a law or violation of a right.

Infringing copy. A copy of any work usually made without the authority of the owner of the reproduction right in the work. (*Copyright*)

"Infringing copy" shall have the same meaning as assigned to it in sub-clause (ii) of clause (m) of section 2 of the Copyright Act, 1957. [Cinematograph Act, 1952 (37 of 1952), section 2(ddd)]

"INFRINGING COPY" means,—

(i) in relation to a literary, dramatic, musical or artistic work, a reproduction thereof otherwise than in the form of a cinematographic film;

(ii) in relation to a cinematographic film, a copy of the film made on any medium by any means;

(iii) in relation to a sound recording, any other recording embodying the same sound recording, made by any means;

(iv) in relation to a programme or performance in which such a broadcast reproduction right or a performer's right subsists under the provisions of this Act, the sound recording or a cinematographic film of such programme or performance, if such reproduction, copy or sound recording is made or imported in contravention of the provisions of this Act. [Copyright Act (14 of 1957), S. 2(m)]

Ingot. A mass of cast metal. [Gold (Control) Act (45 of 1968) (*repealed*), S. 2(r)]; [Telegraph Wires (Unlawful Possession) Act (74 of 1950), S. 41].

Ingots. Ingots or billets of steel are the steel bars when taken from the moulds of a steel manufactory, the words being applied to the finished product as it is ready for shipping.

Ingredient. The material (*ghee* or fat) used for cooking a sweetmeat such as *jangiri*, is not an ingredient of it. The ingredients are blackgram, rice and sugar, and these have to be cooked together by frying in *ghee* in order to make the sweetmeat. No doubt some of the cooking material does penerate into the sweetmeat, but that does not make it an ingredient.

The term 'ingredient' in R. 24 cannot and will not include the volume content. *Bharat Pulverising Mills Ltd.* v. *Joint Director of Agriculture*, AIR 1993 Mad 74, 77. [Insecticides Rules 1971, R. 24]

A component part; a constituent unit [Central Excises and Salt Act (1 of 1944), S. 6(a)]; [Arms Act (54 of 1959), S. 2(1)(b)(vii)].

"INGREDIENT" Means any substance, including a food additive used in the manufacture or preparation of food and present in the final product, possibly in a modified form. [S. 3(1)(y) of the Food Safety & Standards Act, 2006 (34 of 2006)]

Ingress. Right of entrance. A grant of a right of "ingress, egress, and regress" is a grant of a right of way from the *locus a quo* to the *locus ad quem*, and from the *locus ad quem* forth to any other spot to which the grantee may lawfully go or back to the *locus a quo*.

Entering on. [Factories Act (63 of 1948), S. 36(2)].

INGRESS, EGRESS AND REGRESS. These words mean "entering on", "going out" and "coming back", respectively and are used in leases to permit the lessee to enter on the land and, when the lease has expired to remove the fixtures or emblements.

Inhabit. Dwell in; occupy.

Inhabitant. "INHABITANT", in relation to a cantonment, or local area, any person ordinarily residing or carrying on business, or owning or occupying immovable property therein, and in case of a dispute, means any person declared by the District Magistrate to be an inhabitant. [Cantonments Act (2 of 1924), S. 2(xviii)]

"INHABITANT" used with reference to a local area means any person ordinarily residing or carrying on business or owning or occupying immovable property therein. [Manipur Municipalities Act (43 of 1994), S. 2(26)]

"INHABITANT", in relation to the municipal area of New Delhi includes any person ordinarily residing or carrying on business or owning or occupying immovable property therein and in case of a dispute, means any person or persons declared by the Chairperson to be an inhabitant. [New Delhi Municipal Council Act (44 of 1994), S. 2(20)]

"INHABITANT" used with reference to any local area includes any person ordinarily residing or carrying on business or owing or occupying immoveable property therein. [U.P. Act (1 of 1900), (Municipalities), S. 3, cl. 5.]

A person residing or domiciled in a particular place.

Inherent. Forming an essential or intrinsic element of; existing inseparably within an object or person; innate. (*New Webster's Dictionary of the English Language*)

Inherent power. Power which, while not expressly granted will nevertheless be deemed to exist or be inherent in a Court, or a corporate or governmental body. [CPC (5 of 1908), S. 151].

Inherent right. The Bill of Rights of one of the States of U.S., provides : "All men are created equally free and independent, and have certain inherent and inalienable rights amongst which are those of enjoying life and liberty, of acquiring possession and protecting property and reputation, and of pursuing their own happiness. To secure these rights Governments are instituted among men, deriving their just powers from the consent of the Government". The term "inherent and inalienable rights" as used in the said Bill of Rights, undoubtedly includes the right to purchase, lease and cultivate lands, and to perform honest labour for wages with which to support one's self and family.

Inherent vice. An inherent defect in certain goods which makes them liable to damage.

Inherit. To receive property as heir. "Inherit" means, succession by descent. To take by inheritance. To take, or to have; to become possessed of; to take as heir at law by descent or distribution; to descend.

Inheritance. Succession by descent; it also includes which descends to the heir on the death of the owner intestate.

Inhibition. A prohibition of proceeding in a cause or matter.

Inhuman treatment. In family law, so severe a physical or mental cruelty that it endangers life or health which may be a ground for divorce.

Iniquum est aliquem rei sui esse judicem. It is improper for a person to be a Judge in his own cause.—*Ballentine.*

Initial. To make a mark or sign a document, *etc.* with initials or the initial letter of the person's name.

To put one's initials on [CPC (5 of 1908), O. XIII, R. 4(1)(d)]; existing at or constituting at the beginning.

Initial assessment year. For the purposes of this section, "INITIAL ASSESSMENT YEAR" means the assessment year relevant to the previous year, in which the industrial undertaking begins to manufacture or produce articles or things, or to operate its cold storage plant or plants or the ship is first brought into use or the business of the hotel starts functioning. [Income-tax Act (43 of 1961), S. 80IA (12)(e)]

For the purposes of this section, "INITIAL ASSESSMENT YEAR"—

(i) in the case of an industrial undertaking or cold storage plant or ship or hotel, means the assessment year relevant to the previous year in which the industrial undertaking begins to manufacture or produce articles or things, or to operate its cold storage plant or plants or the cold chain facility or the ship is first brought into use or the business of the hotel starts functioning;

(ii) in the case of a company carrying on scientific and industrial research and development, means the assessment year relevant to the previous year in which the company is approved by the prescribed authority for the purposes of sub-section (8);

(iii) in the case of an undertaking engaged in the business of commercial production or refining of mineral oil referred to in sub-section (9), means the assessment year relevant to the previous year in which the undertaking commences the commercial production or refining of mineral oil. [Income-tax Act (43 of 1961), S. 801B (14)(c)]

"INITIAL ASSESSMENT YEAR" means the assessment year relevant to the previous year in which the undertaking or the enterprise begins to manufacture or produce articles or things, or commences operation or completes substantial expansion. [Income-tax Act (43 of 1961), S. 80 IC (8)(V)]

"INITIAL ASSESSMENT YEAR" means the assessment year relevant to the previous year in which the assessee starts paying interest on the loan. [Income-tax Act (43 of 1961), S. 80E(3)(d) *as substituted by Finance Act (18 of 2005), S. 25*]

Initial Investigation. The "initial investigation" is the one which the empowered police officer shall conduct in furtherance of registration of an FIR. Such investigation itself can lead to filing of a final report under section 173(2) of the code and shall take within its ambit the investigation which the empowered officer shall conduct in furtherance of an order for investigation passed by the court of competent jurisdiction in terms of section 156(3) of the Code. [*Vinay Tyagi* v. *Irshad Ali*, (2013) 5 SCC 762, para 21]. [Criminal Procedure Code, 1973 (2 of 1974), Ss. 173(2) and 156(3)].

Initialize. To prepare a disk to receive data. The data may be a software program or documents. The preparation may be for single- or double-density use, depending on your needs and the capabilities of your system. (*Computer*)

Initials. The initial letters of an individual's name and surname, organisation, state or other entity. [Trade and Merchandise Marks Act (43 of 1958), S. 2(1)(f)(v)] [Now repealed & replaced by Act 47 of 1999]

Initial offer. Means the first offer of units of an REIT to the public for subscription and includes an offer for sale of REIT units by an existing unit holder to the public. [Securities and Exchange Board of India (Real Estate Investment Trusts) Regulations, 2014, Regn. 2(1)(qb)].

Initial period. Means the period of three years reckoned from the date on which the provisions of section 130 of the Finance Act, 2021 shall come into force. [Life Insurance Corporation Act, 1956 (31 of 1956), section 2(4e)]

Initiation date. Means the date on which a financial creditor, corporate applicant or operational creditor, as the case may be, makes an application to the Adjudicating Authority for initiating corporate insolvency resolution process or the pre-packaged insolvency resolution process, as the case may be. [Insolvency and Bankruptcy Code (31 of 2016), S. 5(11)].

Initiate. Organize; set on foot; to admit a person into the mysteries of a science or secret society with rites and forms.

Initiates any disciplinary proceedings. The expression 'initiates any disciplinary proceedings', does not refer to the stage when the authorities apply their minds to the initiation of the proceedings. *Tark Nath* v. *Govt. of India,* AIR 1967 Pat 81, 84. [All India Services (Discipline and Appeal) Rules (1955), R. 7(1)]

Initiative. The prerogative of submitting proposed laws.

Injunction. An order or judgment by which a party to an action is required to do or refrain from doing a particular thing. [CrPC 1973 (2 of 1974), S. 142(1)].

Injunction, Interim. Injunction granted until the hearing of the case by a Court subject to its further orders.

Injunction, Mandatory. Injunction ordering a person to do a thing.

Injunction pendente lite. A temporary injunction to operate pending a hearing on the merits, or until the final decree is rendered.

Injunction, Perpetual. Injunction which forms part of the judgment or order and is not restricted as to time.

Injunction, Prohibitory. Injunction restraining a person from doing a thing.

Injure. To injure means to do harm to; inflict damage or detriment upon; impair or deteriorate in any way; to do wrong; harm; impair.

Injuria. (*Lat.*) By '*injuria*' is meant a tortious act. It need not be wilful and malicious; for, though it be accidental, if it be tortious, an action will lie.

A legal wrong.

Injuria non excusat injuriam. A wrong does not excuse a wrong.

Injuria propria non cadet beneficium facientis. No one shall profit by his own wrong.

Injuria servi dominum pertingit. The master is liable for injury done by his servant.

Injuria sine damno. Injury without damage; an infringement of a right without causing damage.

Injuria sine damnum and damnum obsque injuria. Injury without a damage and a damage without wrongful act.

Injurious. Anything that is hurtful, disturbs happiness, impairs rights, or prevents the enjoyment of them is 'injurious,' and, if it causes displeasure or gives pain or unpleasant sensations, it is offensive.

Tending to cause injury. [CrPC 1973 (2 of 1974), S. 133(1)(b)].

Injurious falsehood. The name "injurious falsehood" is used as a convenient title for wrongs which consist in causing damage to a person by making false statements or representations to other, while deceit consists in causing damage by making a representation to the party suffering the damage. These wrongs are (a) slander of title or of goods (b) passing off goods, (c) imitation of the name of another's business.

Injury. "The word "INJURY" denotes any harm whatever illegally caused to any person, in body, mind, reputation or property." [IPC (45 of 1860), S. 44] [Now (w.e.f. 1-7-2024) repealed & replaced by Bharatiya Nyaya Sanhita, 2023 (45 of 2023)]

"Injury" means any harm whatever illegally caused to any person, in body, mind, reputation or property. [(w.e.f. 1-7-2024) Bharatiya Nyaya Sanhita, 2023 (45 of 2023), section 2(14)]

"INJURY" includes permanent total or permanent partial disability or sickness resulting out of an accident. [Public Liability Insurance Act (6 of 1991), S. 2(ii) and National Environment Tribunal Act (27 of 1995), S. 3 *Expl.* (ii)]

"Injury" means any harm whatever illegally caused to any person, in body, mind or property. [Consumer Protection Act, 2019 (35 of 2019), section 2(23)]

"Injury" in S. 189 of the IPC (45 of 1860) implies an illegal harm. The mere threat to bring a legal complaint either before a Court or before the Police constable's superiors for the constable's action in stopping a motor car is no "injury".

The word 'injury' in S. 95. includes also injury to reputation and mental pain. *Parikh Jhvan Manilal* v. *Shah Chatilal Chemilal,* AIR 1960 Bom 326, 328. [CPC (5 of 1908), S. 95]

It could have relation only to acts of a party which are wrongful and not to legitimate acts of persons who pursue the remedies allowed to them by law. *Narayan Rao Maroti Rao Pimpalkar* v. *Woman Natheji Wamkhade,* AIR 1974 Bom 319, 320. [CPC (5 of 1908), O. XXXIX, R. 1(C)]

Where Plaintiff in possession of agricultural land files a suit for declaration of title and injunction, the apprehension that the defendant by executing the order of Revenue Tribunal would take possession of the agricultural land, is not injury within the meaning of O. XXXIX, R. 1 (*c*), CPC (5 of 1908). *Prabhakar* v. *Dayaram,* AIR 1980 MP 125, 128.

The word 'injury' is a word of large import and cannot be restricted to mean monetary injury only. It would include loss of the society of the deceased. *Abdulkhadar Ebrahim Sura* v. *Kasinath Moreshwar Chandani,* AIR 1968 Bom 267, 270. [Fatal Accident Act (13 of 1855), S. 1-A]

Injuries, in the sense of wrongful invasions of a right, may be considered as of two kinds : (1) Pecuniary and (2) non-pecuniary. Pecuniary injuries are such as can be, and usually are, without difficulty estimated by a money standard. Loss of real or personal property, or of its use, loss of time, and loss of services are examples of those kinds of injuries. Non-pecuniary injuries are those for the measurement of which no money standard is or can be applicable.

An infringement of the rights of another, in his person, reputation or property for which an action lies at law. [IPC (45 of 1860), S. 44 and CrPC 1973 (2 of 1974), S. 37(c)].

"INJURY" includes any impairment, whether permanent or temporary, and 'injurious to health' shall be construed accordingly. [*Explanation* to S. 48 of the Food Safety & Standards Act, 2006 (34 of 2006)]

Injury and Damages. There is a material distinction between 'damages' and injury'. Injury is the wrongful act or tort which causes loss or harm to another. Damages are allowed as an indemnity to the person who suffers loss or harm from the injury. The word 'injury' denotes the illegal act. The term 'damages' means the sum recoverable as amends for the wrong. The words are sometimes used as synonymous terms, but they are in strictness words of widely different meaning.

Injury causing death. If an employee but for an injury would not have died at the time at which and in the way in which he did die, the accident though it merely hastened a deep— scated disorder, is regarded as resulting in an 'injury causing death' within the Workmen's Compensation Act. [*Words & Phrases*, Permanent Edition, Vol. 21 at page 448].

Injustice. Unjust act; unfairness.

Unjust action. [CPC (5 of 1908), O. XV, R. 3(1)].

Injustum est, nisi tota lege inspecta, de una aliqua ejus particula proposita judicare vel respondere. (*Maxim*) It is unjust to give judgment or advice concerning any particular clause of a law without having examined the whole law.

Inkjet printer. A computer output device that produces text or images, usually on paper, by ejecting fine drops of ink onto the paper in precise patterns. The ink is ejected through an assembly of minute nozzles held a close distance away from the surface of the paper. (*Information Technology*)

Inland. The expression "INLAND", used in relation to a postal article means—

(i) posted in India and addressed to any place in India or to any place for which a post office is established by the Central Government beyond the limits of India or;

(ii) posted at any post office established by the Central Government beyond the limits of India and addressed to any place for which any such post office is established or to any place in India.

Provided that the expression "inland" shall not apply to any class of postal articles which may be specified in this behalf by the Central Government by notification in the Official Gazette when posted in or at or addressed to any places or post offices which may be described in such notification. [Post Office Act (6 of 1898), S. 2(b)]

Of or pertaining to the interior part of a country. [Agricultural Refinance Corporation Act (10 of 1963), S. 2(a)].

Inland bill of exchange. An *inland bill* of exchange is a bill which is, or on its face purports to be, both drawn and payable within the state. Any other bill is a *foreign bill.*

Inland instrument. "A promissory note, bill of exchange or cheque drawn or made in India, and made payable in, or drawn upon any person resident in India, shall be deemed to be an inland instrument". [Negotiable Instruments Act (26 of 1881), S. 11]

Inland journey. INLAND JOURNEY in relation to a passenger means—

(i) his journey from any place within the territories to which this Act extends to any other place within the said territories; or

(ii) if his journey is from or to any place in the territories to which this Act extends to or from a place in the State of Jammu and Kashmir, so much of his journey as falls within the said territories,

but does not include, in either case, a journey which is performed on a through international ticket and which precedes or forms part of a series of journeys preceding, or follows, or forms part of a series of journeys following, a journey to or from a place outside India on the same ticket.

Explanation. For the purpose of determining the portion of journey referred to in sub-clause (ii) falling within the territories to which this Act extends, the journey referred to therein shall be deemed to terminate at or, as the case may be, commence from Amritsar irrespective of whether the aircraft by which the passenger is travelling overflies or halts at Amritsar. [Inland Air Travel Tax Act, 1971, S. 2(d)]

"INLAND JOURNEY", in relation to a passenger, means his journey from aerodrome on board any aircraft to another aerodrome. [Finance Act (13 of 1989), S. 41(e)]

Inland vessel. Means a vessel not ordinarily plying outside the limits of the territorial waters surrounding India. [Emergency Risks (Undertaking) Insurance Act (51 of 1971), S. 2(g)]

Inland water. "INLAND WATER," means any canal, river, lake or navigable water in India. [Indian Railways Act (9 of 1890), S. 3(3)]

"INLAND WATER" means any canal, river, lake or other navigable water. [Inland Vessels Act (1 of 1917), S. 2(b)]

Any of the waters within the territory of a State as contrasted with open seas or marginal waters bordering another State. [Obstructions in Fairways Act (16 of 1881), S. 13].

Inland waterway. Means any canal, river, lake or other navigable water in India. [Marking of Heavy Packages Act (39 of 1951), S. 2(b)]

Inmate. Occupant of house, *etc.* (*Termes de la Ley*)

One who lives in the same house or apartment with another. [IPC (45 of 1860), S. 111, ill. (c)]; [Reformatory Schools Act (8 of 1897), S. 6(a)].

Inn. An inn is a place resorted to by travellers for lodging and accommodation; a place provided for the lodging and entertainment of travellers.

Innavigability. Unseaworthiness of a ship.

Innavigable. Incapable of floating ships.

Innocence. Freedom from guilt. The absence of guilt. The law presumes in favour of innocence. (*Black*)

The fact of not being guilty of that with which one is charged; guiltlessness; the condition of being innocent. [CrPC 1973 (2 of 1974), S. 367(1)].

Innocent agent. A person whose act on behalf of a principal is unlawful but does not merit prosecution as he or she had no knowledge of the principal's illegal purpose.

Innocent infringement. In Copyright law, infringement in which a person, unintentionally and unconsciously borrows a protected work.

Innocent infringer. Innocent infringer means a person committing infringement on account of absence of knowledge of existence of a patent is an innocent infringer. All the more, an innocent infringer could not have reasonably been expected to have knowledge of the same. *(Patents)*

Innocent junior user. A person who, without any actual or constructive knowledge, uses a trademark which has been previously used in a geographically distant market, and who may continue to use the trademark in a limited geographic area as long as the senior user does not use the mark there.

Innocent misrepresentation. A misrepresentation which is made in the honest but mistaken belief that it was correct and with no intention to deceive or defraud.

Innocent passage. The right of a foreign ship to pass through a country's territorial waters, specially waters connecting two open seas; the right of a foreign vessel to travel through a country's maritime belt without paying a toll. Passage is considered innocent as long as it is not prejudicial to the peace, good order, and security of the coastal country.

Innocent purchaser. One, who by an honest agreement purchases property or acquires an interest therein without knowledge or means of knowledge sufficient to charge him in law with knowledge of any infirmity in law in the title of the seller. [CrPC 1973 (2 of 1974), S. 453].

Innocent trespass. A trespass committed either unintentionally or in good faith.

Innocent woman. An innocent woman is one whose character is unsullied; that is, undefiled, not stained with moral turpitude.

An innocent woman is one who has never had illicit intercourse with any man, and who is chaste, or pure, and it is not necessary that she has a mind free from lustful and lascivious desires.

Innovation. An exchange of one obligation for another, so as to make the second come in the place of the first.

Innuendo. Allusive; depreciatory remark or hint.

The office of the innuendo is merely to interpret the meaning of the language used. Indeed, the word 'meaning' is a synonym of the word 'innuendo,' and so is the phrase 'that is to say.'

The purpose of an innuendo is to define the defamatory meaning which the plaintiff attaches to the words and to show how they came to have that meaning and how they relate to the plaintiff.

The word innuendo is applied to signify, in a proceeding for the defamation, the averment of a particular meaning in a passage *prima facie* innocent, which if proved, would establish its defamatory character. If a statement does not convey any defamatory imputation in its natural meaning, it may be because the words are innocent, or true or have two or more meanings some of which are innocent or have no well-known meaning as in the case of slang, provincialisms, local or technical term not in common use. In all such cases the plaintiff should set forth, by a statement in the plaint known as the innuendo, the special or secondary meaning of a defamatory character, which the words complained of conveyed to the persons to whom they were published.

Inoculation. "INOCULATION" means any operation performed with the object of producing the disease of small-pox in any person by means of variolous matter. [Vaccination Act (13 of 1880), S. 2(5)]

Inofficious testament. A will which is made contrary to the natural duty of the testator and without proper regard to the claims of his relatives.

Inoperative. The word 'inoperative' is used when the existence of the law is recognised but its operation is stopped during the time, a law of superior origin is prevailing. *Abdulkhader* v. *State of Mysore,* AIR 1951 Mys 72, 97 (FB). [Constitution of India, Art. 251]

Without practical force.

The word 'inoperative can be said to cover these cases where the arbitration agreement has ceased to have effect, such as revocation by the parties. [The New York Convention, 1958—An Overview", Article II (3) by Albert Jan Van Den Berg as cited in *World Sport Group (Mauritius) Limited* v. *MSM Satellite (Singapore) PTE, Limited,* (2014) 11 SCC 639, para 34].

Input. "INPUT" means all goods, except high speed diesel oil and motor spirit, commonly known as petrol, used in or in relation to the manufacture of final products whether directly or indirectly and whether contained in the final product or not, and includes lubricating oils, greases, cutting oils, coolants, accessories of the final products cleared along with the final product, goods used as paint, or as packing material, or as fuel, or for generation of electricity or steam used for manufacture of final products or for any other purpose, within the factory of production.

Explanation 1.—The high speed diesel oil or motor spirit, commonly known as petrol, shall not be treated as an input for any purpose whatsoever.

Explanation 2.—Inputs include goods used in the manufacture of capital goods which are further used in the factory of the manufacturer. [CENVAT Credit Rules, 2002, R. 2(g)]

"Input" means any goods other than capital goods used or intended to be used by a supplier in the course or furtherance of business [The Central Goods and Services Tax Act, 2017 (12 of 2017), S. 2(59)]

'INPUTS' means all goods or services intended for use by the client. [Finance Act (32 of 1994), S. 65(19) *Expln. (as inserted by Finance Act (18 of 2005), S. 88(a)(v)* now repealed by Goods and Service Tax Act, 2017]

Input service. "Input service" means any service used or intended to be used by a supplier in the course or furtherance of business [The Central Goods and Services Tax Act, 2017 (12 of 2017), S. 2(60)]

Input tax. In the UK value added tax system, the tax that is collected from the seller of goods by the Customs and Excise.

"Input tax" in relation to a registered person, means the central tax, State tax, integrated tax or Union territory tax charged on any supply of goods or services or both made to him and includes—

(a) the integrated goods and services tax charged on import of goods;

(b) the tax payable under the provisions of sub-S.(3) and (4) of S. 9;

(c) the tax payable under the provisions of sub-S.(3) and (4) of S. 5 of the Integrated Goods and Services Tax Act;

(d) the tax payable under the provisions of sub-S.(3) and (4) of S. 9 of the respective State Goods and Services Tax Act; or

(e) the tax payable under the provisions of sub-S.(3) and (4) of S. 7 of the Union Territory Goods and Services Tax Act, but does not include the tax paid under the composition levy [The Central Goods and Services Tax Act, 2017 (12 of 2017), S. 2(62)]

Inquest. Legal or judicial inquiry into a matter of fact. (*Termes de la Ley.*)

An inquiry under the law as to the death of a person who has died under suspicious circumstances. [Coroners Act (4 of 1871), S. 10].

Inquire. To seek knowledge by putting a question; to ask; to make investigation or inquisition. [TP Act (4 of 1882) and Art. 263(a), Constitution of India, S. 69A(5)]

Inquiring authority. "INQUIRY AUTHORITY" means an officer or authority appointed by the Central Government or by any officer or authority subordinate to that Government to hold a departmental inquiry and includes any officer or authority who is empowered by or under any law or rule for the time being in force to hold such inquiry. [Departmental Enquiries (Enforcement of Attendance of Witnesses and Production of Documents) Act (18 of 1972), S. 3(b)]

A person or body having the authority to make an inquiry. [Departmental Inquiries (Enforcement of Attendance of Witnesses and Production of Documents) Act (18 of 1972), S. 3(b)].

Inquiry. "INQUIRY" means every inquiry, other than a trial, conducted under this Code by a Magistrate or Court. [CrPC 1973 (2 of 1974), S. 2(g)] [Now (w.e.f. 1-7-2024) repealed & replaced by Bharatiya Nagarik Suraksha Sanhita, 2023 (46 of 2023)]

"Inquiry" means every inquiry, other than a trial, conducted under this Sanhita by a Magistrate or Court. [(w.e.f. 1-7-2024) Bharatiya Nagarik Suraksha Sanhita, 2023 (46 of 2023), section 2(1)(k)]

Even where facts are admitted, the Court cannot admit a fact in issue unless the fact in issue is gone into and enquired which is prerequisite to the exercise of jurisdiction or power of the Court, when the Court sits for giving relief. *Ram Nagine Singh* v. *S.V. Sohni,* AIR 1976 Pat 36, 46. [Constitution of India, Art. 163(3)]

'Inquiry' means every inquiry, other than a trial, conducted under this code by a Magistrate or court. [Criminal Procedure Code, 1972 (2 of 1974), S. 2(g) as cited in *Vijay Dhanuka* v. *Najima Mamtaj*, (2014) 14 SCC 638, para 14].

"Inquiry" means "a request for information, either procedural or substantive" [Black's Law Dictionary, 9th Edn., 2009, p. 864 as cited in *Kathiroor Service Co-operative Bank Limited* v. *Commissioner Income Tax (CIB)*, (2014) 14 SCC 352, para 14.4].

'Inquiry' means: 'in search for knowledge; investigation; a question'. [Chambers 20th Century Dictionary as cited in *Kathiroor Service Co-operative Bank Limited* v. *Commissioner of Income Tax (CIB)*, (2014) 14 SCC 352, para 14.5].

"Inquiry or enquiry" means "question" or "the process of asking a question". [Cambridge Advanced Learner's Dictionary & Thesaurus as cited in *Kathiroor Service Cooperative Bank Limited* v. *Commissioner of Income Tax (CIB)*, (2014) 14 SCC 352, para 14.3].

"Inquiry or enquiry""Inquiry or enquiry" connote: "(1) examination into facts or principles; (2) a request for information; (3) a systematic investigation often of a matter of public interest". [Merriam-Webster Unabridged Dictionary as cited in *Kathiroor Service Co-operative Bank Limited* v. *Commmissioner of Income Tax (CIB)*, (2014) 14 SCC 352, para 14.2].

The term includes a proceeding under S. 145, CrPC 1973 (2 of 1974).

The word 'inquiry' does not always mean a judicial inquiry. Whether it does or does not depend on the context in which it is used. *Mohammed Umar* v. *Inspector General Police, V.P.*, AIR 1967 All 767, 769.

The act of inquiring. [CrPC 1973 (2 of 1974), S. 2(g) and Indian Evidence Act (1 of 1872), S. 151].

Inquiry in camera. (In the chamber) An enquiry where the public are excluded from the Courts; an enquiry in a judge's chamber as opposed to the one in open Court. [Insurance Act (4 of 1938), S. 52M(2) now repealed by Act 5 of 2015].

Inquisitio post mortem. An inquest after death.

Inquisition. Official or judicial inquiry; investigation.

Insane. Mad; senseless.

Affected with insanity. [IPC (45 of 1860), S. 89]; [Limitation Act (36 of 1963), S. 6(1)].

Insane delusion. Belief of facts which no reasonable person would have believed.

'Insane delusion' is that diseased state or condition of mind which 'gives to airy nothing a local habitation and a name.'

An insane delusion is not only one which is an error, but one in favour of the truth of which there is no evidence, but the clearest evidence often to the contrary. It must be a delusion of such character that no evidence or argument would have the slightest effect to remove.

Insanitary latrine. Means a latrine which requires human excreta to be cleaned or otherwise handled manually, either *in situ*, or in an open drain or pit into which the excreta is discharged or flushed out, before the excreta fully decomposes in such manner as may be prescribed:

Provided that a water flush latrine in a railway passenger coach, when cleaned by an employee with the help of such devices and using such protective gear, as the Central Government may notify in this behalf, shall not be deemed to be an insanitary latrine. [S. 2(1)(e) of the Prohibition of Employment as Manual Scavengers & their Rehabilitation Act, 2013 (25 of 2013)]

Insanity. Unsoundness of mind as a consequence of brain disease; madness; mental derangement. [Indian Contract Act (9 of 1872), S. 6(4)]; [Companies Act (1 of 1956),(Replaced bt Act 2013) Sch. 1, table A, interpretation 63].

Insanity defence. An affirmative defence which alleges that a mental disorder caused the accused to commit the crime.

Inscribe. To write or mark or trace words, names or figures on paper, wood, metal, or stone, *etc.*

Inscribed note. A note which has something written in it (after it being printed). [Legal Tender (Inscribed Notes) Act (28 of 1964), S. 1].

Inscribed stock. Stock for which a certificate of ownership is not issued.

Inscription. Words, names or figures written, marked or traced on paper, wood, metal or stone *etc.* [Indian Evidence Act (1 of 1872), S. 3, ill. (3)]; the insertion of word or words between the lines of a writing. [Registration Act (16 of 1908), S. 43(1)].

Insect infested. It means that the article so abounds in insects dead or living, that it is rendered unfit for human consumption. *Municipal Corporation of Delhi* v. *Kacheroo Mal*, AIR 1976 SC 394, 396. [Prevention of Food Adulteration Act (37 of 1954), S. 2(*i*)(*f*)].

Insecticide. Means—

(i) any substance specified in the Schedule; or

(ii) such other substance (including fungicides and weedicides) as the Central Government may, after consultation with the Board, by notification in the official Gazette, include in the Schedule from time to time; or

(iii) any preparation containing any one or more of such substances. [Insecticides Act (46 of 1968), S. 2(e)]

Insensible. Unintelligible.

Incapable or bereft of feeling or sensation. [IPC (45 of 1860), S. 92 ill. (a)]; [Prevention of Cruelty to Animals Act (59 of 1960), S. 17(2)(c)].

Inseparable. One that is not separable from another. [Income-tax Act (43 of 1961), S. 56(2)(iii)]

Insert. To place text into a document between characters that are already in the document. The system will rearrange existing text around the new, inserted text. (*Computer*)

Insert in. To set or put in.

"Insert" means place, fit, thrust. [Concise Oxford dictionary as cited in *Suresh Kumar Koushal* v. *Naz Foundation*, (2014) 1 SCC 1, para 59.6].

Inside information. An information about a financial or market situation of a company which is obtained not from public disclosure but from a source within the company or a source which owes the company a duty to keep the information confidential.

Inside the State. Inter-district and intra-district transport of *Mahua flowers* are both within 'inside the State' under R. 11. *State of Orissa* v. *Sanjay Kumar Gadodia,* (1997) 11 SCC 119, para 4. [Orissa Excise (Mahua Flower) Rules, 1976, R. 11]

Insider. Person such as a corporate officer or director with access to privileged company information.

Person with special knowledge derived from holding a privileged position within a group or company. It is illegal for the person to use that information in dealing on the stock exchange.

"INSIDER" means any person who—

(i) is or was connected with the company or is deemed to have been connected with the company and is reasonably expected to have access to unpublished price sensitive information in respect of securities or a company, or

(ii) has received or had access to such unpublished price sensitive information. [SEBI (Prohibition of Insider Trading) Regulations, 1992, Regn. 2(e) **as cited in** *Chintalapati Srinivasa Raju* v. *Securities and Exchange Board of India,* (2018) 7 SCC 443, para 13.2].

"INSIDER" means any person who is:

(i) a connected person; or

(ii) in possession of or having access to unpublished price sensitive information. [Definition as replaced by SEBI (Prohibition of Insider Trading) Regulations, 2015, Regn. 2(g) **as cited in** *Chintalapati Srinivasa Raju* v. *Securities and Exchange Board of India,* (2018) 7 SCC 443, para 14].

Insider dealing. The use of material, non public information in trading the shares of a company by a corporate insider or other person who owes a fiduciary duty to the company.

Insider trading. For the purposes of section 195 of Act 18 of 2013, 'insider trading' means—

(*i*) an act of subscribing, buying, selling, dealing or agreeing to subscribe, buy, sell or deal in any securities by any director or key managerial personnel or any other officer of a company either as principal or agent if such director or key managerial personnel or any other officer of the company is reasonably expected to have access to any non-public price sensitive information in respect of securities of company; or

(*ii*) an act of counselling about procuring or communicating directly or indirectly any non-public price-sensitive information to any person. [*Explanation (a)* to section 195(1) of the Companies Act, 2013 (18 of 2013)]

Insitu conditions. Means conditions where genetic resources exist within ecosystems and natural habitats and in the case of domesticated or cultivated species, in the surroundings where they have developed their distinctive properties. [UN Convention on Environment and Development : Convention on Biological Diversity, Rio de Janeiro, June 5, 1992, Art. 2]

Insolence. Overbearing; insulting; rude. [Assam Rifles Act (5 of 1941), S. 7(g)].

Insolvency. The state of one who has not property sufficient for the full payments of his debts; the condition of being insolvent. [Indian Evidence Act (1 of 1872), S. 41 and Constitution of India, VII Sch., list III, item 9].

Insolvency practitioner. A person who is appointed to officiate in the winding up of a company or in bankruptcy proceeding.

Insolvent. A person is INSOLVENT who has ceased to pay his debts in the usual course of business, or who is incapable of paying them. [Indian Contract Act (9 of 1872), S. 96 (*Repealed by Act 3, 1930*)]

'A person is said to be INSOLVENT who ceased to pay his debts in the ordinary course of business, or cannot pay his debts as become due, whether he has committed an act of insolvency or not'. [Sale of Goods Act (3 of 1930), S. 2(8)]

"An "insolvent" is a person who cannot pay his debts in full." The term "insolvent" may be employed to designate (1) a debtor whose assets are not sufficient to pay his debts; (2) a debtor who is not able to pay all his debts from his own means, or whose property is not in such a situation that all his debts may be collected out of it by legal process; or, as is more frequently the case, (3) a debtor who is not able to pay his debts in the usual course of business or meet his pecuniary engagements. So too the term may be used as referring only to one who has been judicially declared to be insolvent.

One whose assets at their present fair valuation are insufficient to pay debts. [Constitution of India, Art. 102(1)(c)].

Insolvent circumstances. By being in "insolvent circumstances" is meant that the whole property and credits are not equal in amount, at a fair appraisement, to the debts due by the party.

Insolvent debtor. A debtor, who is not able to pay his debts in the usual course of business or to meet his pecuniary engagement. [Indian Contract Act (9 of 1872), S. 201].

Insolvency commencement date. Means the date of admission of an application for initiating corporate insolvency resolution process by the adjudicating authority under Sections 7, 9 or section 10, as the case may be. [Insolvency and Bankruptcy Code, 2016, S. 5(12) **as cited in** *Innoventive Industries Limited* v. *ICICI Bank,* (2018) 1 SCC 407, para 19].

Insolvency professional. Means a person enrolled under Section 206 with an insolvency professional agency as its member and registered with the Board as an insolvency professional under Section 207. [Insolvency and Bankruptcy Code (31 of 2016), S. 3(19)].

Insolvency resolution process costs. Means—

(a) the amount of any interim finance and the costs incurred in raising such finance;

(b) the fees payable to any person acting as a resolution professional;

(c) any costs incurred by the resolution professional in running the business of the corporate debtor as a going concern;

(d) any costs incurred at the expense of the Government to facilitate the insolvency resolution process; and

(e) any other costs as may be specified by the Board. [Insolvency and Bankruptcy Code [31 of 2016), S. 5(13)].

Insolvency resolution process period. Means the period of one hundred and eighty days beginning from the insolvency commencement date and ending on one hundred and eightieth day. [Insolvency and Bankruptcy Code (31 of 2016), S. 5(14)].

Inspect. Power to 'inspect' documents, includes, generally, a right to take copies. Examine officially; look closely into.

The word 'inspect' includes the meter reading. *K.S. Upadhya* v. *State Electricity Board U.P.*, AIR 1977 All 185, 189. [Indian Electricity Act (9 of 1910), S. 20(1)(*a*)]

View closely and critically; to examine; to investigate or oversee officially. [Indian Partnership Act (9 of 1932), S. 12(d)].

Inspect means 'to look; to view or oversee for the purpose of examination; to look into; to view and examine for the purpose of ascertaining the quality or condition of the thing; to view and examine for the purpose of discovering and correcting errors.

Inspected State Party. Means the State Party on whose territory or in any other place under its jurisdiction or control an inspection pursuant to this Convention takes place, or the State Party whose facility or area on the territory of a Host State is subject to such an inspection; it does not, however, include the State Party specified in Part II, paragraph 21 of this Annex. [Chemical Weapons Conventions Act (34 of 2000), (Verification Annex), 12]

Inspecting Authority. Means an officer or a term of officers of the Board, which has been directed by the Board, to conduct the inspection of a service provider. [Insolvency and Bankruptcy Board of India (Inspection and Investigation) Regulations, 2017, Regn. 2(1)(f)].

Inspecting officer. Means a person authorised by the State Government or by the licensing authority to inspect any psychiatric hospital or psychiatric nursing home. [Mental Health Act (14 of 1987), S. 2(c)]

"INSPECTING OFFICER" means any officer of the fisheries department not below the rank of an inspector of fisheries as may be authorised by the Director to exercise the powers conferred on and discharge the duties imposed upon, the inspecting officer under this Act, for such area as may be specified by the Director. [Tamil Nadu Aquaculture (Regulation) Act (T.N. Act 6 of 1995), S. 2(h)]

Inspection. "INSPECTION", in relation to a commodity, means the process of determining whether a batch of goods in that commodity complies with the standard specifications applicable to it or any other specifications stipulated in the export contract generally by inspecting either the whole batch or a selected sample or samples which purport to represent the whole batch. [Export (Quality Control and Inspection) Act (22 of 1963), S. 2(c)]

The right of public officials to examine articles which are subject to regulation, or to examine conditions in housing, industry or public utilities to see whether statutory rules are being enforced; right of buyers to examine goods sold under the implied conditions permitting such examination; the right of a party to an action to examine and copy documents in the possession of the other party, when such documents are relied in the trial of the case. [CPC (5 of 1908), S. 30(a)].

Inspection Assistant. Means an individual designated by the Technical Secretariat as set forth in Part II, Section A, of this Annex to assist inspectors in an inspection or visit, such as medical, security and administrative personnel and interpreters. [Chemical Convention Act (34 of 2000), (Verification Annex), 13]

Inspection laws. The object of inspection laws is to improve the quality of articles produced by the labour of the country, and fit them for exportation, or, it may be, for domestic use. They act upon the subject before it becomes an article of foreign commerce or of inter provincial commerce and prepare it for that purpose.

The office of inspection laws is to certify the quantity and quality of the articles inspected, whether imports or exports, for the protection of buyers and consumers.

Inspection manual. Means the compilation of additional procedures for the conduct of inspections developed by the Technical Secretariat. [Chemical Weapons Convention Act (34 of 2000), (Verification Annex), 15]

Inspection of documents. The preliminary examination of documents by the party opposing him who offers them in evidence.

Inspection right. The legal entitlement in certain circumstances so as to examine articles or documents, like, a consumer's right to inspect goods before paying for them.

Inspector. "INSPECTOR" means an Inspector of Railways appointed under the Railways Act. [Indian Railways Act (9 of 1890), S. 3(8)].

"An Inspector" should be read as any Inspector and the singular would include the plural. [Companies Act (1 of 1956), S. 249(1)(*a*)](Replaced by Act 2013)

Inspectorship deed. A deed defining the position or status of an inspector. [Indian Stamp Act (2 of 1899), Sch., item 34].

Installation. The act of giving a person possession of an office, rank, or order with the customary ceremonial services. The ceremony of investing one with a public office.

The action of setting up or fixing in position for service or use; a mechanical apparatus set-up or put in position for use. [Central Industrial Security Force Act (50 of 1968), S. 10(b)]; [Damodar Valley Corporation Act (14 of 1948), Ss. 17 and 29].

Installation State. In relation to a nuclear installation, means the contracting party in whose territory that installation is situated or if it is not situated within the territory of any state the contracting party by which or under the authority of which the nuclear installation is operated. [Vienna Convention on Civil Liability for Nuclear Damage, 21 May, 1963, Art. 1(d)]

Installed. The expression 'installed' did not necessarily mean 'fixed in position' but was also used in the sense of 'intended or introduced'. Installed would certainly mean 'to place an apparatus in a position for service or use'. When an engine is fixed in a vehicle it is installed within the meaning of the expression. *Commissioner of Income-tax* v. *Mir Mohammad Ali*, AIR 1964 SC 1693, 1697. [Income-tax Act (43 of 1961), S. 33]

If the plant in combination with other appliances in the business effectuates and perpetuates the trade of commerce, then, in relation to such plant, 'installed' means such induction or introduction whereby the plant may be placed in a position for service or use in the business. *Sundaram Motors (P.) Ltd.* v. *C.I.T.*, (1969) 71 ITR 587, 593 (Mad) [Income-tax Act (43 of 1961), S. 33]

Installed capacity. For the purposes of this rule,—

"INSTALLED CAPACITY" means the capacity of production existing on the date of amalgamation. [Income-tax Rules, 1962, R. 9C *Expln.* (a)]

Instalment, Installment. Any of the successive parts in which a sum is to be paid.

Each of several parts into which a sum payable is divided in order to be paid at different fixed times; one of several parts presented at intervals.

Instance. A precedent; instigation; solicitation.

The word 'instance' as a verb means 'to urge, entreat urgently, importune'. 'Instance' does not imply the same degree of obligation to obey as does 'command'. *State of Karnataka Adimurthy*, AIR 1983 SC 822, 823. [Indian Electricity Act (9 of 1910), S. 50]

Instance, Court of first. Original or trial Court.

Instance of, At the. On the motion or request of.

Instant. Precise moment; very short time (as) in an instant.

Instant death. 'Instant death,' as used in a special finding, in an action for damages for death, that the death was of that nature commonly known as 'instant death,' may be applied to a death caused by an injury necessarily fatal, where death results in a few moments from it.

Instantaneous. Means done or occurring in an instant, or without the intervention of any perceptible portion of time.

Instantly. At once; immediately; directly.

Instead. The ordinary and popular meaning of the word 'instead,' and the phrase 'in its stead,' is in the room of, *in lieu* of, in the place of. They are expressions of substitution of one thing for another of equivalence.

Instigate. "A person who, by wilful misrepresentation, or by wilful concealment of a material fact which he is bound to disclose, voluntarily causes or procures, or attempts to cause or procure, a thing to be done, is said to instigate the doing of that thing". [IPC (45 of 1860), S. 107, *Expln.* 1]

To 'instigate' means to stimulate or goad to an action, especially a bad action. One of its synonyms is 'abet', which means in law to aid, promote, or encourage the commission of an offence.

The word 'instigate' means urge to do some drastic or inadvisable action or stimulate or incite. *Sanju* v. *State of M.P.*, (2002) 5 SCC 371, para 12 : AIR 2002 SC 1998. [IPC (45 of 1860), S. 107]

To urge to something (mostly to evil).

Instigates and incites. The words 'instigates' and 'incites' should be read to signify something deeper than a mere asking of a person to do a particular act. There must be something in the nature of solicitation to constitute instigation or incitement under S. 27. The words 'instigates' and 'incites' appear to be synonymous. *State of Bihar* v. *Ramen Nath*, AIR 1958 Pat 259, 261. [Industrial Disputes Act (14 of 1947), S. 27]

Instigation. Inciting; bringing about.

A word uttered in the fit of anger or emotion without intending the consequences to actually follow cannot be said to be 'instigation' in the context of S. 107 of IPC. *Ramesh Kumar* v. *State of Chhatisgarh*, (2001) 9 SCC 618, para 20. [IPC (45 of 1860), S. 107*, first*]

'Instigation' is to goad, urge forward, provoke, incite or encourage to do 'an act'. [*Chitresh Kumar*

Chopra v. *State (Govt. of NCT of Delhi)*, (2009) 16 SCC 605, para 16 : (2010) 3 SCC (Cri) 367 : AIR 2010 SC 1446 as cited in *Praveen Pradhan* v. *State of Uttaranchal*, (2012) 9 SCC 734, para 15].

The words uttered in a fit of anger or omission without any intention cannot be termed as instigation. [*Praveen Pradhan* v. *State of Uttaranchal*, (2012) 9 SCC 734, para 17].

Instigation and incitement. The words 'instigates' and 'incites' should be read to signify something deeper than a mere asking of a person to do a particular act. There must be something in the nature of solicitation to constitute instigation or incitement under S. 27 of the Industrial Disputes Act. The words seem to convey the meaning 'to goad or urge forward or to provoke or encourage the doing of an act.' The words 'instigates' and 'incites' appear to be synonymous and there must be something tangible evidence to show that the persons responsible for such action were deliberately trying to stir up other persons to bring about a certain object. *State of Bihar* v. *Ramen Nath,* MLJ : QD (1956-1960) Vol. III C1427 : 1957 BLJR 629 : AIR 1958 Pat 259. [Industrial Disputes Act (14 of 1947), S. 27]

Institute. Set on foot; commence. "Instituted," in respect of legal proceedings means, "commenced". To begin an action; to accuse; to appoint an heir by will.

Criminal proceedings cannot be said to be 'instituted' until a formal charge is openly made against the accused by complaint before a magistrate.

An institution; initiate; start.

Instituted. *Also means*, established *e.g.*, a society instituted for the purposes of science, & c.

The word 'instituted' in S. 3(5) can therefore be taken as meaning 'settling on foot an enquiry' and is more than a mere filing of a claim. S. *Suppiah Chettiar* v. *V. Chimathurai*, AIR 1957 Mad 216, 220. [Workmen's compensation Act (8 of 1923), S. 3(5)]

Instituted upon a complaint. In case of competition between two parallel proceedings, one based upon private complaint and other on a police report, the former loses its identity and merges in the latter. Such a case cannot be termed as one instituted upon a complaint. *Sudhakar* v. *Dayanadhi,* AIR 1965 Ori 114, 117. [CrPC 1973 (2 of 1974), S. 378(4)]

Institution. An establishment of a public character; a place where the business of a society is carried on; the organisation itself.

"Institution" does not mean filing; presenting or initiating the proceedings, rather it means taking cognizance as per the provisions contained in CrPc. [*General Officer Commanding, Rashtriya Rifles* v. *Central Bureau of Investigation*, (2012) 6 SCC 228, para 41].

Institution is one whose cause is not personal, but public, and which does not carry on business making profits; and whose profit be not made in private account. *K.V. Mathew* v. *District Manager, Telephones, Ernakulam,* AIR 1984 Ker 40, 41. [Indian Telegraph Act (13 of 1885), S. 2]

"Institution" means a recognized intermediate college, higher secondary school or high school, and includes, where the context so requires, a part of an institution. [U.P. Intermediate Education Act, 1921, as amended in 1975 as cited in *State of U.P.* v. *Pawan Kumar Divedi*, (2014) 9 SCC 692, para 21].

"Institution" means recognized institution for the time being receiving maintenance grant from the State Government and includes a Sanskrit Mahavidyalaya or a Sanskrit Vidyalaya receiving maintenance grant from the State Government. [Uttar Pradesh High Schools and Intermediate colleges (Payment of Salaries of Teachers and other Employees) Act, 1971, S. 2(b) as cited in *State of U.P.* v. *Pawan Kumar Divedi*, (2014) 9 SCC 692, para 23].

'Institution' means a recognized Junior High School for the time being receiving maintenance grant from the State Government. [Uttar Pradesh Junior High Schools (Payment of Salaries of Teachers and Other Employees) Act, 1978, S. 2(e) as cited in *State of U.P.* v. *Pawan Kumar Divedi,* (2014) 9 SCC 692, para 28].

The fact of being instituted [TP Act (4 of 1882), S. 52 *Expln.*]; an establishment; organisation or association instituted for the promotion of some object, specially one of public utility [Dakshina Bharat Hindu Prachar Sabha Act (14 of 1964), preamble]; a custom that is usually widely sanctioned or tolerated and that in some degree contributes to group welfare. [Punjab Laws Act (4 of 1872), S. 5].

Institution of a case. The expression may mean filing/presentation or received or entertained by the court. [Central Officer Commanding, Rasthriya Rifles v. Central Bureau of Investigation, (2012) 6 SCC 228, para 34].

"INSTITUTION" means an institution, school, college or centre of studies maintained by or admitted to the privileges of the University for imparting education, training and research in aviation studies or in its associated disciplines. [S. 2(p) of the Rajiv Gandhi National Aviation University Act, 2013 (26 of 2013)]

Institution, Contributing. An institution that makes a contribution. [Unit Trust of India Act (52 of 1963), S. 2(b)].

Institution for persons with disabilities. Means an institution for the reception, care, protection, education, training, rehabilitation or any other service of persons with disabilities. [Persons with Disabilities (Equal Opportunities Protection of Rights and Full Participation) Act, 1995 (1 of 1996), S. 2(m)]

Institution of criminal proceedings. A person who sets the criminal law in motion by making a false charge to the police of a cognizable offence institutes criminal proceedings within the meaning of S. 211, IPC (45 of 1860).

Institutional arbitration. An arbitration conducted under the rules of a body or an institution, which may be national or international and to which the parties agreed to refer their disputes for settlement. (*Arbitration*)

Institutional lender. A business, specially a bank, which routinely loans money to the general public.

Institutional mediation means mediation conducted under the aegis of a mediation service provider. [Mediation Act, 2023 (32 of 2023), section 3(f)]

Instruct. To give instructions; to direct; to advise.

To declare or make known to an agent the acts which he may do on the authority of his principal. [Indian Contract Act (9 of 1872), S. 195, ill. (a)].

Instruction. Something that is imparted in order to instruct [IPC (45 of 1860), Ill. to *Expln.* 1 of S. 29]; the action of instructing or teaching; the imparting of knowledge or skill; education. [Trade Unions Act (16 of 1926), S. 2(h), *Prov.* (iii)].

Instructions. The information given to a counsel or solicitor, to enable him to conduct the client's case in Court.

Instrument. (a) every document, by which any right or liability is, or purports to be, created, transferred, limited, extended, extinguished or recorded;

(b) a document, electronic or otherwise, created for a transaction in a stock exchange or depository by which any right or liability is, or purports to be, created, transferred, limited, extended, extinguished or recorded; and

(c) any other document mentioned in Schedule I,

but does not include such instruments as may be specified by the Government, by notification in the Official Gazette. [Indian Stamp Act (2 of 1899), S. 2(14)]

"INSTRUMENT" includes every document by which any right or liability is, or purports to be, created, transferred, modified, limited, extended, suspended, extinguished or recorded. [Notaries Act (53 of 1952), S. 2(b)]

'INSTRUMENT' includes affidavits. *Sambasivaraju* v. *Chadrayya,* AIR 1967 AP 87, 89. [Indian Stamp Act (2 of 1899), S. 2(14)]

Where a document does not itself create, transfer, limit, extend, or record any right of liability but only recites the details of an already completed transaction it does not fall within the definition of 'instrument'. *Bhagwan Singh* v. *Hardial Singh,* AIR 1975 P&H 256, 257.

Instrument means an instrument chargeable with duty, irrespective of whether such instrument falls or does not fall within the definition thereof. *Ramashankar Pathak* v. *Collector, Central Excise, Allahabad,* AIR 1971 All 287, 289.

The word "instrument" used in S. 39 of Act (8 of 1890), Guardian and Wards Act should be confined to instruments *ejusdem generis* with a Will, and a decree passed by a Civil Court is not an instrument within the contemplation of the section.

Instrument in T.P. Act means a non-testamentary instrument. [T.P. Act (4 of 1882), S. 3].

The proceedings recorded in Court which are signed by the parties can also be termed as an instrument in writing. *Krishna Mohan Singh* v. *Shri Chand Gupta,* AIR 1993 Del 365, 366. [CPC (5 of 1908), O. XXIII, R. 3, *Expln.* (Allahabad High Court Amendments)]

The word 'instrument' means a legal document. *Udai Pratap Gir* v. *Shanta Devi,* AIR 1956 All 492, 493.

Instrument means a writing usually importing a document of a formal legal kind, but it does not include Acts of Parliament unless there is statutory definition to that effect in any Act. *Vishnu Pratap Sungar Works Ltd.* v. *Chief Inspector of Stamps,* AIR 1968 SC 102, 104.

The expression "instrument" in S. 8 includes reference to the Order made by the President in exercise of his constitutional powers. *Mohan Chowdhury* v. *Chief Commissioner, Union Territory of Tripura,* AIR 1964 SC 173, 179. [General Clauses Act (10 of 1897), S. 8(1)]

The word 'instrument' would include awards made by Industrial Courts of competent jurisdiction. *Purshotham* v. *V.B. Potdar,* AIR 1966 SC 856, 859. [Payment of Wages Act (4 of 1936), S. 2(*vi*)(*d*), (Maharashtra Amendment)]

A tool; implement; weapon; a formal legal document whereby a right is created or confirmed or a fact recorded; a formal writing of any kind, as an agreement deed, charter or record, drawn up and executed in technical form; a formal written document having legal effect, either as creating liability or as affording evidence of it. [Constitution of India, Art. 77(2)].

Instrument of accession. A legal document under which Rules of the Indian Princely States joined the Union of India. [Foreign Awards (Recognition and Enforcement) Act (45 of 1961), Art. IX(2)]; [Constitution of India, Art. 370(1)(b)].

Instrument of gaming. The expression "INSTRUMENTS OF GAMING" means and includes—(*a*) any cards, dice, counters, coins, gaming-tables, gaming-cloths, gaming-boards or other articles devised or actually used for the purpose of gaming; (*b*) any boxes, receptacles, lists, papers, tickets or forms used for the purpose of the game of *ti* or any other game or pretended game of a like nature. [Bur. Act 1 of 1899 (Gambling) S. 3, cl. 3]

"INSTRUMENT OF GAMING" includes any article used or intended to be used as a means or appurtenance of, or for the purpose of carrying on or facilitating gaming. (West Bengal Gambling and Prize Compensation Act, 1957) [West Bengal Act (33 of 1957), S. 2(1)(c)]

Instrument of partition. "INSTRUMENT OF PARTITION" means any instrument whereby co-owners of any property divide or agree to divide such property in severalty, and also includes,—

(i) a final order for effecting a partition passed by any revenue authority or any Civil Court;

(ii) an award by an arbitrator directing a partition; and

(iii) when any partition is effected without executing any such instrument, any instrument or instruments signed by the co-owners and recording, whether by way of declaration of such partition or otherwise, the terms of such partition amongst the co-owners. [Indian Stamp Act (2 of 1899), S. 2(15)]

A decree for a partition is an instrument of partition [*vide*. S. 2(15) of the Indian Stamp Act (2 of 1899)] and as such has got to be engrossed on stamp paper. An "*instrument of partition*" includes in its definition award by an arbitrator directing a partition. AIR 1922 All 283.

To constitute instrument of partition, the document must be one which is executed by co-owners and the partition must have been effected by that instrument. *Siya Ram* v. *State of U.P.*, AIR 1972 All 518, 519.

Instrument of trust. The instrument, if any, by which the trust is declared, is called the "INSTRUMENT OF TRUST". [Indian Trusts Act (2 of 1882), S. 3]

Instruments payable on demand. "A promissory note or bill of exchange, in which no time for payment is specified, and a cheque are payable on demand". [Negotiable Instrument Act (26 of 1881), S. 19].

Instrumental. Serviceable, helpful.

Instrumentality. Something by which an end is achieved, means. [Asian Development Bank of India Act (18 of 1966), Sch., Art. 50 (2)]; something that serves as an intermediary or agent through which one or more functions of a controlling force are carried out; agency or instrumentality of the Government.

Instruments, Ambiguous. "Where an instrument may be construed either, as a promissory note or bill of exchange, the holder may at his election treat it as either, and the instrument shall be thenceforward treated accordingly". [Negotiable Instruments Act (26 of 1881), S. 17]

Insubordinate language. Language showing disobedience to authority [Army Act (46 of 1950), S. 40(c) and Navy Act (62 of 1957), S. 47(c)]; [Lok Sahayak Sena Act (53 of 1956), S. 8(1)(11)(b)].

Insubordination. 'Insubordination' means a refusal to subordinate oneself to authority, and it does not follow that a mere failure to obey an order amounts to insubordination.

The quality or state of being insubordinate; defiance of authority; disobedience of superior authority. [IPC (45 of 1860), S. 138].

Insufficiency. Lack of form or substance in a pleading.

Insufficient. Not sufficient; deficient in force, quality or amount; inadequate. [Constitution of India, Art. 115 (1)(a)].

Insufficient grounds. The words 'insufficient grounds' mean without reasonable or probable cause.

Insufficient security. 'A security is insufficient within the meaning of this section unless the value of the mortgaged property exceeds by one third, or, if consisting of buildings, exceeds by one-half, the amount for the time being due on the mortgage. [Transfer of Property Act (4 of 1882), S. 66, Expln. and Indian Easements Acts (5 of 1882), S. 10, Expln.]

Insufficient Stamp. The words "insufficient stamp" in CPC (5 of 1908), O. VII, R. 11(*c*), do not refer to nor include a wholly unstamped paper.

Insult. Affront; scornful abuse.

A gross indignity offered to another whether by act or by word; to offer indignity to someone.

(1) To treat, mention, or speak to rudely; offend; affront; (2) to assault; attack; (3) an offensive or contemptuous remark or action; affront; slight; (4) a person or thing producing the effect of an affront; (5) an injury or trauma. [Collin's Dictionary as cited in *Shreya Singhal* v. *Union of India*, (2015) 5 SCC 1, para 54].

Insurable interest is a financial or legal interest which an insured must have in the person, object or activity covered by an insurance policy.

Insurable, Nature of an. Of such nature that it may be insured. [TP Act (4 of 1882), S. 69A(7)].

Insurable property. Means any ship, goods or other movables which are exposed to maritime perils. [Marine Insurance Act (11 of 1963), S. 2(c)]

Insurance. "INSURANCE" shall include—

(a) a policy of insurance on the life of an individual or the spouse or the child of such individual or a member of a Hindu undivided family securing the payment of specified sum on the stipulated date of maturity, if such person is alive on such date notwithstanding that the policy of insurance provides only for the return of premiums paid (with or without any interest thereon) in the event of such person dying before the said stipulated date;

(b) a policy of insurance effected by an individual or a member of a Hindu undivided family for the benefit of a minor with the object of enabling the minor, after he has attained majority to secure insurance on his own life by adopting the policy and on his being alive on a date (after such adoption) specified in the policy in this behalf. [Income-tax Act (43 of 1961), S. 80C(8)(iii), *as inserted by Finance Act (18 of 2005), S. 21*]

"Insurance" means an arrangement by which a company, individual or intending couple undertake to provide a guarantee of compensation for medical expenses, health issues, specified loss, damage, illness or death of surrogate mother and such other prescribed expenses incurred on such surrogate mother during the process of surrogacy. [Surrogacy (Regulation) Act, 2021 (47 of 2021), section 2(1)(q)]

Insurance advertisement. Means and includes any communication directly or indirectly related to a policy and intended to result in the eventual sale or solicitation of a policy from the members of the public, and shall include all forms of printed and published materials or any material using the print and/or electronic medium for public communication such as :

(i) newspapers, magazines and sales talks;
(ii) billboards, hoardings, panels;
(iii) radio, television, website, e-mail, portals;
(iv) representations by intermediaries;
(v) leaflets;
(vi) descriptive literature/circulars;
(vii) sales aids flyers;
(viii) illustrations form letters;
(ix) telephone solicitations;
(x) business cards;
(xi) videos;
(xii) faxes; or
(xiii) any other communication with a prospect or a policyholder that urges him to purchase, renew, increase, retain or modify a policy of insurance.

Explanation.—The following materials shall not be considered to be an advertisement provided they are not used to induce the purchase, increase, modification or retention of a policy of insurance:—

(i) materials used by an insurance company within its own organisation and not meant for distribution to the public;
(ii) communications with policy holders other than materials urging them to purchase, increase, modify, surrender or retain a policy;
(iii) materials used solely for the training, recruitment and education of an insurer's personnel, intermediaries, counsellors and solicitors, provided they are not used to induce the public to purchase, increase, modify or retain a policy of insurance;
(iv) any general announcement sent by a group policyholder to members of the eligible group that a policy has been written or arranged. [Insurance Regulatory and Development Authority (Insurance and Advertisements and Disclosure) Regulations, 2000, Reg. 2(b)]

Insurance agent. "INSURANCE AGENT" means an insurance agent licensed under Sec. 42 who receives or agrees to receive payment by way of commission or other remuneration in consideration of his soliciting or procuring insurance business relating to the continuance, renewal or revival of policies of insurance. [Insurance Act (4 of 1938), S. 2(10)]

Anyone who in any manner aids in the transaction of an insurance company's business.

The term 'insurance agent' includes any acknowledged agent, surveyor, broker, or any other person who aids in any manner in transacting business.

Insurance auxiliary service. Means any service provided by an actuary, an intermediary or insurance intermediary or an insurance agent in relation to general insurance business or life insurance business and includes risk assessment, claim settlement, survey and loss assessment. [Finance Act (32 of 1994), S. 65(1)(46) now repealed by Goods and Services Tax Act, 2017]

Insurance broker. A broker who procures insurance and negotiates between the insurer and the insured. [Indian Contract Act (9 of 1872), S. 212, ill. (c)].

Insurance business transacted in India. Includes insurance business, wherever effected, relating to any property situate in India or to any vessel or aircraft registered in India. [Insurance Act (4 of 1938), S. 40C(2) *Expln.* (c) as it stood prior to amendment by Act 5 of 2015, sec. 47 (w.r.e.f. 26-12-2014)].

Insurance commission. Means any remuneration or reward, whether by way of commission or otherwise, for soliciting or procuring insurance business (including business relating to the continuance, renewal or revival of policies of insurance). [Finance Act (18 of 2005), S. 2(12)(b)]

Insurance company. "INSURANCE COMPANY" means a company that carries on the business of insurance either solely or in common with any other business or businesses. [Companies Act (7 of 1913), S. 2(8)]

"Insurance company" means a company as defined in section 2 of the Insurance Act, 1938 (4 of 1938). [Industrial Relations Code, 2020 (35 of 2020), section 2(s)]

An 'insurance company' is an institution which undertakes to pay a sum of money on the death of the assured, or at another fixed time, in consideration of premiums, assessments, or payments made in any other way.

Insurance contract. A contract of insurance, like other contracts, is concluded by offer and acceptance. If there is a stipulation that the liability will attach itself under the contract only if premium is paid that will be a condition precedent to the policy taking effect.

Insurance Council. Will consist of Life Insurance Corporation of India, General Insurance Corporation of India and its four subsidiaries and other Insurance Companies which will be permitted to do insurance business in future. [Redressal of Public Grievances Rules, 1998, R. 2(f)]

Insurance cover. Risks covered by an insurance; protection afforded by an insurance. [Insurance Act (4 of 1938), S. 2(9)(c)].

Insurance Fund. Means the Deposit-Linked Insurance Fund established under clause (*c*) of sub-section (*1*) of section 16. [Code on Social Security, 2020 (36 of 2020), section 2(38)]

Insurance office. An office that carries on the business of insurance. [Indian Evidence Act (1 of 1872), S. 15, ill. (a)].

Insurance or Assurance. "A contract, by which a person, (who thence is termed the insurer, or, from the form of the instrument, which is signed by him alone, the Underwriter) in consideration of a sum of money, technically called the premium, becomes bound to secure a party against the risk of loss happening from certain events marked out by the contract. The party deriving security from the contract is called the insured, or more commonly assured, and the contract itself is termed a Policy of Insurance."

Insurance Scheme. Means the Deposit-Linked Insurance Scheme framed under clause (*c*) of sub-section (*1*) of section 15. [Code on Social Security, 2020 (36 of 2020), section 2(40)]

Insurance segments. For the purpose of these regulations, shall mean the following—

(i) Fire;

(ii) Marine;

(iii) Health (including Personal Accident and Travel);

(iv) Motor;

(v) Miscellaneous;

(vi) Any other segment (under miscellaneous segment) which contributes more than 10 per cent of the Gross Written Premium of the Miscellaneous segment of business;

(vii) Any other segment as may be specified by the Authority from time to time. [Insurance Regulatory and Development Authority of India (General Insurance—Reinsurance) Regulations, 2016, Regn. 2(l)].

Insurance Web Aggregator. For the purpose of these regulations is a person registered by the Authority under these regulations. [Insurance Regulatory and Development Authority of India (Insurance Web Aggregators) Regulations, 2017, Regn. 2(o)].

Insurance policy. Document effecting insurance issued by the insurer to the insured.

A document containing an undertaking in consideration of a premium or premiums, to pay a specified amount or part thereof in the event of a specified contingency.

Insure. To make an insurance.

To secure the payment of a sum of money in the event of loss of or of damage to property or of death or physical injury to a person in consideration of the payment of a premium and observance of certain conditions. [CPC (5 of 1908), O. VIII, R. 6(3), ill. (c)]; [Administrators General Act (45 of 1963), S. 41(2)].

Insured. That in respect of which insurance has been obtained; the person indemnified by his contract of insurance [TP Act (4 of 1882), S. 49]; a policy holder.

Insured person. Means a person who is or was an employee in respect of whom contributions are or were payable under this Act and who is, by reason thereof, entitled to any of the benefits provided by this Act. [Employees' State Insurance Act (34 of 1948), S. 2(14)]

"Insured Person" means the Insured Person referred to in section 28. [Code on Social Security, 2020 (36 of 2020), section 2(39)]

"INSURED PERSON" means an individual by whom or on whose behalf an insurance policy has been taken on personal lines. [Redressal of Public Grievances Rules, 1998, R. 2(i)]

Insurer. "INSURER" means—

(a) any individual or unincorporated body of individuals or body corporate incorporated under the law of any country other than India, carrying on insurance business (not being a person specified in sub-clause (c) of this clause) which—

(i) carries on that business in India, or

(ii) has his or its principal place of business or is domiciled in India, or

(iii) with the object of obtaining insurance business, employs a representative, or maintains a place of business, in India.

(b) any body corporate (not being a person specified in sub-clause (c) of this clause) carrying on the business of insurance which is a body corporate incorporated under any law for the time being in force in India, or stands to any such body corporate in the relation of a subsidiary company within the meaning of Indian Companies Act, 1913, as defined by sub-sec. (2) of Sec. 2 of that Act, and

(c) any person who in India has a standing contract with underwriters who are members of the Society of Lloyd's whereby such person is authorised within the terms of such contracts to issue protection notes, cover notes, or other documents granting insurance cover to others on behalf of the underwriters, but does not include principle agent, chief agent, special agent, or an insurance agent or a provident society in Part III. [Insurance Act (4 of 1938), S. 9 repealed by Act 5 of 2015 *(w.r.e.f. 26-12-2014)*]

'Insurer' includes a person intending to carry on a business or a person who has ceased to carry on a business. [*Vanguard Fire and General Insurance Company Limited* v. *Fraser and Ross* AIR 1960 SC

971 as cited in *National Insurance Company Limited* v. *Kirpal Singh*, (2014) 5 SCC 189, para 12].

"INSURER" means an insurer, as defined in the Insurance Act, who carries on general insurance business in India, and includes an insurer whose registration under that act has not remained wholly cancelled for a period of six months immediately before the appointed day, but does not include the Life Insurance Corporation of India established under the Life Insurance Corporation Act, 1956, or any State Government which carries on general insurance business. [General Insurance (Emergency Provisions) Act (17 of 1971), S. 2(e)]

"INSURER" means any person carrying on the general insurance business or life insurance business in India. [Finance Act (32 of 1994), S. 65(1)(48) now repealed by Central Goods and Services Tax Act, 2017]

The word 'insurer' is used in the Act to include (*a*) persons actually carrying on insurance business; (*b*) persons about to commence insurance business; and (*c*) persons who have stopped insurance business but against whom claims or liabilities might be outstanding. *V.F. & G. Insurance Co.* v. *Fraser and Ross*, AIR 1960 SC 971, 976. [Insurance Act (4 of 1938), S. 2(*d*)]

The person assuring against loss. [Life Insurance Corporation Act (31 of 1956), S. 2(6)].

Insurgent. Rebels in arms against the Government of their country who have not been recognized by other countries as belligerents; one engaging in an insurrection; partaking of an insurrection.

Insurrection. Mutiny; open and active opposition to the execution of law. A rebellion of citizens or subjects of a country, or state against its government.

Insurrection, Armed. The action of rising in arms or open resistance (with arms) against established authority or governmental restraint; an incipient or limited rebellion. [Indian Evidence Act (1 of 1872), S. 6, ill. (b)].

Intact. Unimpaired; whole; undiminished. [Seeds Act (54 of 1966), S. 16(2)].

Intangible. Not tangible; not cognizable by the sense of touch.

Intangible asset. Means—

under writer's commission and such preliminary and promotional expenditure shown as a debit in the capital account of the undertaking as has fairly arisen in promoting the business of electricity supply excluding any amount paid on account of goodwill. [Electricity (Supply) Act (54 of 1948), Sch. 6, para 17(4) repealed by Act 36 of 2003 (w.e.f. 10-6-2003)]

Intangible property. As used chiefly in the law of taxation, this term means such property as has no intrinsic and marketable value, but is merely the representative or evidence of value, such as certificates of stock, bonds, promissory notes, copyrights, and franchises.

The expression "INTANGIBLE PROPERTY" shall include—

(a) marketing related intangible assets, such as, trademarks, trade names, brand names, logos (b) technology related intangible assets, such as, process patents, patent applications, technical documentation such as laboratory note books, technical know-how;

(c) artistic related intangible assets, such as, literary works and copy rights, musical compositions, copyrights, maps, engravings;

(d) data processing related intangible assets, such as, proprietary computer software, software copyrights, automated databases, and integrated circuit marks and masters;

(e) engineering related intangible assets, such as, industrial design, product patents, trade secrets, engineering drawing and schematics, blue prints, proprietary documentation;

(f) customer related intangible assets, such as, customer lists, customer contracts, customer relationship, open purchase orders;

(g) contract related intangible assets, such as, favourable supplier, contracts, licence agreements, franchise agreements, non-compete agreements;

(h) human capital related intangible assets, such as, trained and organized work force, employment agreements, union contracts.

(i) Location related intangible assets, such as, lease hold interest, mineral exploitation rights, easements, air rights, water rights;

(j) goodwill related intangible assets, such as, institutional goodwill, professional practice goodwill, personal goodwill of professional celebrity goodwill, general business going concern value;

(k) methods, programmes, systems, procedures, campaigns, surveys, studies, forecasts, estimates, customer lists, or technical data;

(l) any other similar item that derives its value from its intellectual content rather than its physical attributes. [Income-tax Act (43 of 1961), S. 92B(2), *Explanation* (ii)].

There are numerous examples of such property. They share only one common feature, *viz*, that it is a kind of property which cannot be physically touched. It can, however, have considerable value.

One of the oldest forms of intangible property is the 'goodwill' attached to a business. Goodwill can arise from the location of a business but its most important feature is the reputation and good name attaching to it. Such goodwill can be sold.

Intellectual property is also intangible property.

Actionable claims are a valuable kind of intangible property.

"INTANGIBLE PROPERTY" for the removal of doubts, it is hereby clarified that the expression 'intangible property' shall include—

(a) marketing related intangible assets, such as, trademarks, trade names, brand names, logos;

(b) technology related intangible assets, such as, process patents, patent applications, technical documentation such as laboratory notebooks, technical know-how;

(c) artistic related intangible assets, such as, literary works and copyrights, musical compositions, copyrights, maps, engravings;

(d) data processing related intangible assets, such as, proprietary computer software, software copyrights, automated databases, and integrated circuit masks and masters;

(e) engineering related intangible assets, such as, industrial design, product patents, trade secrets, engineering drawing and schematics, blueprints, proprietary documentation;

(f) customer related intangible assets, such as, customer lists, customer contracts, customer relationship, open purchase orders;

(g) contract related intangible assets, such as, favourable supplier, contracts, licence agreements, franchise agreements, non-compete agreements;

(h) human capital related intangible assets, such as, trained and organised work force, employment agreements, union contracts;

(i) location related intangible assets, such as, leasehold interest, mineral exploitation rights, easements, air rights, water rights;

(j) goodwill related intangible assets, such as, institutional goodwill, professional practice goodwill, personal goodwill of professional, celebrity goodwill, general business going concern value;

(k) methods, programmes, systems, procedures, campaigns, surveys, studies, forecasts, estimates, customer lists, or technical data;

(l) any other similar item that derives its value from its intellectual content rather than its physical attributes. [*Explanation* (*ii*) to section 92B of the Income-tax Act, 1961 (43 of 1961) as inserted (w.r.e.f. 1-4-2002) by the Finance Act, 2012 (23 of 2012)]

Integral. Ordinarily speaking "integral means" of a whole or necessary to the completeness of a whole and as "forming a whole." (*Raghunatharao Ganpatrao* v. *Union of India,* 1994 (Supp.) I SCC 191, 219).

Integral multiple. A quantity which contains another quantity some number of times without remainders, pertaining to a whole, not fractional. [Delimitation Commission Act (76 of 1972), S. 8(b) *Prov.*].

Integrated activities. A purchase for export is not an activity so integrated with the exportation so that the former could be regarded as done in the course of the latter. *State of Travancore, Cochin* v. *S.V.C. Factory*, AIR 1953 SC 333, 336. [Constitution of India, Art. 286 (1)(*b*)]

'Integrated commercial complex' means building containing apartments sharing common services and facilities and having their undivided share in the land and meant to be used for office or for practicing of any profession or for carrying on any occupation, trade, business or such other type of independent use, as may be prescribed. [Haryana Development and Regulation of Urban Areas Act (8 of 1975), S. 2(hhh) as cited in *DLF Limited* v. *Manmohan Lowe*, (2014) 12 SCC 231, para 27].

Integrated contract. A contract which expresses the full and complete intent of the parties. It is also called as *Integrated writing.*

Integration. Process of bringing together several sections or people following different faiths as equals.

Integrity. An unimpaired or unmarred condition. [Constitution of India, Art. 19(2)]; uprightness; honesty.

Moral uprightness; honesty. [Oxford Dictionary as cited in *Union of India* v. *P. Gunasekaran*, (2015) 2 SCC 610, para 20].

'Integrity' means soundness of moral principle of character, fidelity, honesty, free from every biasing or corrupting influence or motive and a character of uncorrupted virtue. It is synonymous with probity, purity, uprightness, rectitude, sinlessness, sincerity. The charge of negligence, inadvertence or unintentional act would not culminate into the case of doubtful integrity. [*Vijay Singh* v. *State of U.P.*, (2012) 5 SCC 242, para 18].

It takes in its sweep, probity, innocence, truthfulness, openness, sincerity, blamelessness, immaculacy, rectitude, uprightness, virtuousness, righteousness, goodness, cleanness, decency, honour, reputation, nobility, irreproachability, purity, respectability, genuineness, moral excellence, etc. In short, it depicts sterling character with firm adherence to a code of moral values. [*Union of India* v. *P. Gunasekaran*, (2015) 2 SCC 610, para 20].

Intellectual property. Classification of intangible property rights based on ideas, expression, and inventions.

The legal rights which result from intellectual activity in the literary, artistic, industrial and scientific fields. (*Information Technology*)

"INTELLECTUAL PROPERTY" includes copyrights and related rights, trademarks, geographical indications, industrial designs, patents, layout designs of integrated circuits and the protection of undisclosed information. [Energy Charter Treaty, 12 Dec. 1994, Art. I(12)]

Intellectual Property Rights. "INTELLECTUAL PROPERTY RIGHT" means any right to intangible property, namely, trade marks, designs, patents or any other similar intangible property, under any law for the time being in force, but doe not include copyright. [Finance Act (32 of 1994), S. 65(55a) (*Inserted by Finance Act (23 of 2004), S. 90*) now repealed by Central Goods and Services Tax Act, 2017]

Article 1721 of North American Free Trade Agreement (NAFTA) provides that it 'refers to copyright and other related rights, trade mark rights, patent rights, rights in layout designs of semi conductor integrated circuits, trade secret rights, plant breeders' rights, rights in geographical indications and industrial design rights'. (*Copyright*)

Intellectual property service. Means,—

(a) transferring, whether permanently or otherwise; or

(b) permitting the use or enjoyment of, any intellectual property right. [Finance Act (32 of 1994), S. 65(55)(55b) (Inserted by Finance Act (23 of 2004), S. 90) now repealed by Central Goods and Services Tax Act, 2017]

Intelligence. Understanding as a quality admitting of degree; secret information. [Army Act (46 of 1950), S. 34(d)].

Intelligible. Capable of being understood; comprehensible. [Indian Evidence Act (1 of 1872), Ss. 98 and 119].

Intend. To 'intend' must be understood to mean the same with 'design' or 'contemplate.'

"Intention" connotes an ability to carry it into effect. A man cannot properly be said to "intend" to do a work of reconstruction when he has not the means to carry it out. He may hope to do so; he will not have the intention to do so.

Intended. Designed or contemplated; intentional.

Intended use. Means the use for which the medical device is intended according to the data supplied by the manufacturer on the labeling or in the document containing instructions for use of such device or in promotional material relating to such device, which is as per approval obtained from the Central Licensing Authority. [Medical Devices Rules, 2017, R. 3(v)].

Intending couple. Means a couple who have a medical indication necessitating gestational surrogacy and who intend to become parents through surrogacy. [Surrogacy (Regulation) Act, 2021 (47 of 2021), section 2(1)(r)]

Intending woman. Means an Indian woman who is a widow or divorcee between the age of 35 to 45 years and who intends to avail the surrogacy. [Surrogacy (Regulation) Act, 2021 (47 of 2021), section 2(1)(s)]

Intendment. Intendment of the law is the understanding or intelligence of the law that which the law intends or presumes.

It is an *intendment of law* that every man is innocent until proved guilty; that every officer acts in his office with fidelity; that the children of a married woman born during wedlock are the children of her husband.

Interpretation; construction.

Intendment of law (*intellectus legis*). The understanding, intention, and true meaning of law. The judges ought to judge according to the common intendment of law. (*Tomlin*)

Intent. "The phrase 'with intent to,' or its equivalents, may mean any one of at least four different things:—(1) That the intent referred to must be the sole or exclusive intent; (2) that it is sufficient if it is one of several concurrent intents; (3) that it must be the chief or dominant intent, any others being subordinate or incidental; (4) that it must be a determining intent, that is to say, an intent in the absence of which the act would not have been done, the remaining purposes being insufficient motives by themselves. It is a question of construction which of those meanings is the true one in the particular case." JOHN SALMOND, *Jurisprudence* 383-84 (GLANVILLE L. WILLIAMS ED., 10th ed. 1947).

"Intent" is something aimed at or wished as a goal; it is something that one resolves to do; it is a will to achieve as an end; it is a direction as one's course; it is planning towards something to be brought about; it is something that an individual fixes the mind upon; it is a design for a particular purpose. [*Sahara India Real Estate Corporation Limited* v. *Securities and Exchange Board of India*, (2013) 1 SCC 1, para 292].

Intent ; Intention. In criminal law, as general rule, to involve guilt, the accused must have done or omitted some thing contrary to law. It would revolutionise criminal law to say that criminal responsibility for conduct never depends on intention. The mere existence of the intention without commission of the act or the commission of the act without the intent, does not, as general rule, constitute crime. In the case of civil wrongs, on the contrary, the general rule is that the motive of the defendant in breaking a contract or committing a tort, is immaterial on the question of legal liability.

Every sane person of the age of discretion is presumed to intend the natural and probable consequences of his own acts. Every actual consequence is a natural and probable consequence unless and until the contrary is affirmatively shown.

Intention is the result of working of the brain, and can be gathered from judging the act and the circumstances under which it was done.

Intention must be gathered from words used by the accused. If the natural and inevitable consequence of such words is hatred or disaffection the intention must be presumed.

The word "intention" means that the act intended is in the future and the law makes relevant statements made by a conspirator with reference to the future.

The words 'in reference to their common intention' mean in reference to what at the time of the statement was intended in the future.

"The general presumption is that the parties have expressed every material term which they intended should govern their agreement, whether oral or in writing. But it is well recognised that there may be cases where obviously some term must be implied if the intention of the parties is not to be defeated. The implications must arise inevitably to give effect to the intention of the parties.

Purpose; design, meaning; import. [IPC (45 of 1860), S. 35 and Constitution of India, Art. 90, *Prov.*].

Intent to defraud. The term "intent to defraud" contains two elements, deceit and injury. A person is said to deceive another if by suggestion false or *suppressio veri* or by both intentionally induces another to believe a thing to be true. S. *Harnam Singh* v. *State*, AIR 1976 SC 2140, 2145. [IPC (45 of 1860), S. 477-A]

Intentio inservire debet legibus, non leges intentioni. Intentions ought to be subservient to the laws, not the laws to intentions. (*Latin for Lawyers*).

Intention and **knowledge.** Knowledge as contrasted with intention would more properly signify a state of mental realisation in which the mind is a passive recipient of certain ideas and impressions arising in it or passing before it. It would refer to a bare state of conscious awareness of certain facts in which human mind might itself remain supine or inactive. On the other hand, intention connotes a conscious state in which mental faculties are roused into activity and summoned into action for the deliberate purpose of being directed towards a particular end specified and which the human mind conceives and perceives before itself. *Faquira* v. *State,* AIR 1955 All 321, 325. [IPC (45 of 1860), S. 300]

Intention and **motive.** Intention has been defined as the fixed direction of the mind to a particular object, or a determination to act in a particular manner, and it is distinguishable from 'motive' that which incites or stimulates action. S. *Raghbir Singh Sandhawalla* v. *C.I.T.,* AIR 1958 Punj 250, 253.

Intention and Volition. Intention in the usual sense of design includes and implies the presence of volition, or the capacity to exercise one's will to do or not to do an act. It is sometimes used as synonymous with volition as when it is said that a child or a lunatic can have no intention to injure.

Intention of a document. The sense of a document, which is derived from perusal and comprehension of its content.

Intention of the legislature. Is a common but very slippery phrase; which, popularly understood, may signify anything from intention embodied in positive enactment to speculative opinion as to what the legislature probably would have meant, although there has been an omission to enact it. In a Court of law what the legislature intended to be done or not to be done can only be legitimately ascertained from that which it has chosen to enact, either in express words or by reasonable and necessary implication.

Intention to abandon. The intention has a positive as well as a negative aspect. The negative aspect implies that the person who abandons will cease to have all connections with the property. The positive aspect of the intention must be that the property is to go back to the person who would be entitled to it in the absence of the person who abandons. *Lala Shri Ram* v. *Nand Kishore,* AIR 1958 All 107, 108.

Intentional. Done by or with intention; intended.

Intentional tort. A tort which is committed by someone acting with general or specific intent.

Intentionally. A person who, by his declaration, act, or omission, had caused another to believe a thing to be true and to act upon that belief, must be held to have done so "intentionally" within the meaning of the statute, if a reasonable man would take the representation to be true, and believe it was meant that he should act upon it.

The word "intentionally" in S. 115 does not mean that the conduct of the person making the representation should have been fraudulent or that it should not have been made under a mistake or misapprehension. The motive or state of knowledge of the representer is immaterial. *Harbans Lal Arora* v. *Divisional Suptd. Central Railway,* AIR 1960 All 164, 174. [Indian Evidence Act (1 of 1872), S. 115]

A person becomes homeless intentionally if he deliberately has done or failed to do anything in consequence of which he has ceased to occupy accommodation which was available for his occupation and which it would have been reasonable for him to continue to occupy.

Done on purpose. [CrPC 1973 (2 of 1974), S. 108(1)(i)].

Inter. Between; among; in; to bury.

Inter alia. Among other things.

Inter arma leges silent. (*Lat.*) Between armies the law is silent.

Inter-connected undertaking.

"Inter-connected undertaking" means two or more undertakings which are interconnected with each other in any of the following manners, namely—

(A) if one owns or controls the other;

(B) where the undertakings are owned by firms, if such firms have one or more common partners;

(C) where the undertakings are owned by bodies corporate,—

(i) if one body corporate manages the other body corporate; or

(ii) if one body corporate is a subsidiary of the other body corporate; or

(iii) if the bodies corporate are under the same management; or

(iv) if one body corporate exercises control over the other body corporate in any other manner;

(D) where one undertaking is owned by a body corporate and the other is owned by a firm, if one or more partners of the firm,—

(i) hold directly or indirectly, not less than fifty per cent of the shares, whether preference or equity, of the body corporate; or

(ii) exercise control, directly or indirectly, whether as director or otherwise, over the body corporate;

(E) if one is owned by a body corporate and the other is owned by a firm having bodies corporate as its partners, if such bodies corporate are under the same management;

(F) if the undertakings are owned or controlled by the same person or by the same group; (G) if one is connected with the other either directly or through any number of undertakings which are inter connected undertakings within the meaning of one or more of the foregoing sub-clauses.

(G) if one is connected with the other either directly or through any number of undertakings which are inter-connected undertakings within the meaning of one or more of the foregoing sub-clauses.

Explanation I.—For the purposes of this clause, two bodies corporate shall be deemed to be under the same management—

(i) if one of such body corporate exercises control over the other or both are under the control of the same group or any of the constituents of the same group; or

(ii) if the Managing Director or manager of such body corporate is the Managing Director or manager of the other; or

(iii) if one such body corporate holds not less than one-fourth of the equity shares in the other or controls the composition of not less than onefourth of the total membership of the Board of Directors of the other; or

(iv) if one or more directors of such body corporate constitute, or at any time within a period of six months immediately preceding the day when the question arises as to whether such bodies corporate are under the same management, constituted (whether independently or together with relatives of such directors or employees of the first mentioned body corporate) one-fourth of the directors of the other; or

(v) if the same individual or individuals belonging to a group, while holding (whether by themselves or together with their relatives) not less than one-fourth of the equity shares in one such body corporate also holds (whether by themselves or together with their relatives) not less than one-fourth of the equity shares in the other; or

(vi) if the same body corporate or bodies corporate belonging to a group holding, whether independently or alongwith its or their subsidiary or subsidiaries, not less than one-fourth of the equity shares in one body corporate, also hold not less than one fourth of the equity shares in the other; or

(vii) if not less than one-fourth of the total voting power in relation to each of the two bodies corporate is exercised or controlled by the same individual (whether independently or together with his relatives) or the same body corporate (whether independently or together with his subsidiaries) or

(viii) if not less than one-fourth of the total voting power in relation to each of the two bodies corporate is exercised or controlled by the same individuals belonging to a group or by the same bodies corporate belonging to a group or jointly by such individual or individuals and one or more of such bodies corporate; or

(ix) if the directors of one such body corporate are accustomed to act in accordance with the directions or instructions of one or more of the directors of the other, or if the directors of both the bodies corporate are accustomed to act in accordance with the directions or instructions of an individual, whether belonging to one group or not.

Explanation II.—If a group exercises control over a body corporate, that body corporate and every other body corporate, which is constituent of, or controlled by, the group shall be deemed to be under the same management.

Explanation III.—If two or more bodies corporate under the same management hold in the aggregate, not less than onefourth equity share capital in any other body corporate, such other body corporate shall be deemed to be under the same management as the first mentioned bodies corporate.

Explanation IV.—In determining whether or not two or more bodies corporate are under the same management, the shares held by financial institutions in such bodies corporate shall not be taken into account.

Illustration

Undertaking B is inter-connected with undertaking A and undertaking C is inter-connected with undertaking B.

Undertaking C is inter-connected with undertaking A; if undertaking D is inter-connected with undertaking C, undertaking D will be inter-connected with undertaking B and consequently with undertaking A; and so on.

Explanation V.—For the purposes of this clause, "group" means a group—

(i) two or more individuals, associations of individuals, firms, trust, trustees or bodies corporate (excluding financial institutions), any combination thereof, which exercises or is established to be in a position to exercise, control, directly or indirectly, over any body corporate, firm or trust; or (ii) "associated persons."

Explanation VI.—For the purposes of this clause—

(I) a group of persons who are able, directly or indirectly to control the policy of a body corporate, firm or trust, without having a controlling interest in that body corporate, firm or trust, shall also be deemed to be in a position to exercise control over it;

(II) associated persons—

(a) in relation to a director of a body corporate, means—

(i) a relative of such director, and includes a firm in which such director or his relative is a partner;

(ii) any trust of which any such director, or his relative is a trustee;

(iii) any company of which such director, whether independently or together with his relatives, constitutes onefourth of its Board of Directors;

(iv) any other body corporate, at any general meeting of which not less than one-fourth of the total number of directors of such other body corporate are appointed or controlled by the director of the first mentioned body corporate or his relative, whether acting singly or jointly;

(b) in relation to the partner of a firm, means a relative of such partner and includes any other partner of such firm; and

(c) in relation to the trustee of a trust, means any other, trustee of such trust; (III) Where any person is an associated person in relation to another, the latter shall be deemed to be an associated person in relation to the former. [Central Excise Act (10 of 1944), S. 4(3)(b), *Explanation* (i) now repealed by Central Goods and Services Tax Act, 2017].

Means two or more undertakings which are inter-connected with each other in any of the following manner, namely :—

(i) if one owns or controls the other,

(ii) where the undertakings are owned by firms, if such firms have one or more common partners,

(iii) where the undertakings are owned by bodies corporate.

(a) if one body corporate manages the other body corporate, or

(b) if one body corporate is a subsidiary of the other body corporate, or

(c) if the bodies corporate are under the same management, or

(d) if one body corporate exercises control over the other body corporate in any other manner;

(iv) where one undertaking is owned by a body corporate and the other is owned by a firm, if one or more partners of the firm—

(a) hold, directly or indirectly, not less than fifty per cent of the shares, whether preference or equity, of the body corporate, or

(b) exercise control, directly or indirectly, whether as director or otherwise, over the body corporate,

(v) if one is owned by a body corporate and the other is owned by a firm having bodies corporate as its partners, if such bodies corporate are under the same management,

(vi) if the undertakings are owned or controlled by the same person or by the same group,

(vii) if one is connected with the other either directly or through any number of undertakings which are inter-connected undertakings within the meaning of one or more of the foregoing sub-clauses.

Explanation I.—For the purposes of this Act, two bodies corporate, shall be deemed to be under the same management,—

(i) if one such body corporate exercises control over the other or both are under the control of the same group or any of the constituents of the same group; or

(ii) if the managing director or manager of one such body corporate is the managing director or manager of the other; or

(iii) if one such body corporate holds not less than one-fourth of the equity shares in the other or controls the composition of not less than one-fourth of the total membership of the Board of directors of the other; or

(iv) if one or more directors of one such body corporate constitute, or at any time within a period of six months immediately preceding the day when the question arises as to whether such bodies corporate are under the same management, constituted (whether independently or together with the relatives of such directors or the employees of the first mentioned body corporate) one-fourth of the directors of the other; or

(v) if the same individual or individuals belonging to a group, while holding (whether by themselves or together with their relatives) not less than one-fourth of the equity shares in one such body corporate also hold (whether by themselves or together with their relatives) not less than one-fourth of the equity shares in the other; or

(vi) if the same body corporate or bodies corporate belonging to a group holding, whether independently or along with its or their subsidiary or subsidiaries, not less than one-fourth of the equity shares in one body corporate, also hold not less than one-fourth of the equity shares in the other; or

(vii) if not less than one-fourth of the total voting power in relation to each of the two bodies corporate is exercised or controlled by the same individual (whether independently or together with his relatives) or the same body corporate (whether independently or together with its subsidiaries); or

(viii) if not less than one-fourth of the total voting power in relation to each of the two bodies corporate is exercised or controlled by the same individuals belonging to a group or by the same bodies corporate belonging to a group, or jointly by such individual or individuals and one or more of such bodies corporate; or

(ix) if the directors of the one such body corporate are accustomed to act in accordance with the directions or instructions of one or more of the directors of the other, or if the directors of both the bodies corporate are accustomed to act in accordance with the directions or instructions of an individual, whether belonging to a group or not.

Explanation II.—If a group exercises control over a body corporate, that body corporate and every other body corporate, which is a constituent of or controlled by, the group shall be deemed to be under the same management.

Explanation III.—If two or more bodies corporate under the same management hold, in the aggregate, not less than one-fourth equity share capital in any other body corporate, such other body corporate shall be deemed to be under the same management as the first-mentioned bodies corporate.

Explanation IV.—In determining whether or not two or more bodies corporate are under the same management, the shares held by financial institutions in such bodies corporate shall not be taken into account. [Monopolies and Restrictive Trade Practices Act (54 of 1969), S. 2(g)] Act 54 of 1969, repealed by Act 12 of 2003.

Inter-Parliamentary Union. A world-wide organization of Parliamentarians united in common action to secure and maintain the full participation of their respective State in the firm establishment and development of representative institutions and promotion of international peace and cooperation, particularly by supporting the objectives of the United Nations. Members of the parliaments of different countries constitute different National Groups of this Union.

Inter partes. Between two or more parties.

Inter se or Inter sese. Between or among themselves.

Inter-state. Between different states belonging to some central authority (as) interstate commerce.

Inter-State co-operative society. Means a multi-State co-operative society as defined in clause (p) of Section 3 of the Multi-State Co-operative Societies Act, 2002 and includes any co-operative society registered under any other law for the time being in force, which has, subsequent to its formation, extended any of its objects to more than one State by enlisting the participation of persons or by extending any of its activities outside the State, whether directly or indirectly or through an institution of which it is a constituent. [Companies Act (1 of 1956), S. 581A(e)](replaced by Act 2013)] [Companies Act (18 of 2013), section 378A(c)]

Inter-State corporation. Means any body corporate constituted under any of the Acts specified in the Schedule and functioning in two or more States by virtue of Section 109 of the States Re-organisation Act, 1956, or of any other enactment relating to reorganisation of States. [Inter-State Corporation Act (38 of 1957), S. 2]

Inter-state council. A Constitutional body for effecting co-ordination between States.

Inter-State migrant worker. Means a person who is employed in an establishment and who—

(i) has been recruited directly by the employer or indirectly through contractor in one State for employment in such establishment situated in another State; or

(ii) has come on his own from one State and obtained employment in an establishment of another State (hereinafter called destination State) or has subsequently changed the establishment within the destination State,

under an agreement or other arrangement for such employment and drawing wages not exceeding eighteen thousand rupees per month or such higher amount as may be notified by the Central Government from time to time. [Code on Social Security, 2020 (36 of 2020), section 2(41)] [Occupational Safety, Healthy & Working Conditions Code, 2020 (37 of 2020), section 2(1)(zf)]

Inter-State migrant workman. Means any person who is recruited by or through a contractor in one state under an agreement or other arrangement for employment in an establishment in another state, whether with or without the knowledge of the principal employer in relation to such establishment. [Inter-State Migrant Workmen (Regulation of Employment and Conditions of Service) Act (30 of 1979), S. 2(e)]

Inter State river valley authority. Means an authority established by or under any law in force immediately before the commencement of the Constitution of India or any law made by Parliament for regulating or developing any inter State river valley or river. [W.B. Duty on Inter-State River Valley Authority Electricity Act (7 of 1973), S. 2(c)]

Inter-State sale or purchase. A sale or purchase of goods shall be deemed to take place in the course of inter-State trade or commerce if the sale or purchase—

(a) occasions the movement of goods from one State to another; or

(b) is effected by a transfer of documents of title to the goods during their movement from one State to another. [Central Sales Tax Act (74 of 1956), S. 3)]

Inter-State transmission. Includes—

(i) the conveyance of energy by means of a main transmission line from the territory of one State to the territory of another State;

(ii) the conveyance of energy across the territory of an intervening State as well as conveyance within the State which is incidental to such inter-State transmission of energy;

(iii) the transmission of energy within the territory on a system built, owned, operated, maintained or controlled by a central transmission utility or by any person under the supervision and control of a central transmission utility. [Electricity Regulatory Commission Act (14 of 1998), S. 2(e)]

Inter-State transmission system. Includes—

(i) any system for the conveyance of electricity by means of main transmission line from the territory of one State to another State;

(ii) the conveyance of electricity across the territory of an intervening State as well as conveyance within the State which is incidental to such inter-State transmission of electricity;

(iii) the transmission of electricity within the territory of a State on a system built, owned, operated, maintained or controlled by a Central Transmission Utility. [Electricity Act (36 of 2003), S. 2(36)]

Inter-valuation period. "INTER-VALUATION PERIOD" means, as respects any valuation, the period to the valuation date of that valuation from the valuation date of the last preceding valuation in connection with which an abstract was prepared under this Act or under the enactments repealed by thus Act, or, in a case where no such valuation has been made in respect of the class of business in question, from the date on which the insurer began to carry on that class of business. [Insurance Act (4 of 1938), Sch. (4) part I(5) Now Schedule 4 has been omitted by Act 42 of 2002 (w.e.f. 23-9-2002)].

Inter vivos. Between living persons. [Income-tax Act (43 of 1961), Ist Sch., 2(1)(b) and Estate Duty Act (34 of 1953), S. 9(1)]; [Hindu Adoptions and Maintenance Act (78 of 1956), S. 13]; [Hindu Disposition of Property Act (15 of 1916), S. 3(a)].

From one living person to another. [Hindu Adoptions; Maintenance Act (78 of 1956), S. 13].

Intercept. "INTERCEPT" means the aural or other acquisition of the contents by wire, electronic or oral communication through the use of any electronic, mechanical or other device. [Prevention of Terrorism Act (15 of 2002), S. 36(b)]

Seize, catch or stop (letter *etc.*) in transmit (as) interceptions of suspicious letters by Post Office.

To take, seize or stop by the way or before arrival at the destination. [Indian Telegraph Act (13 of 1885), S. 5(1)(b)].

Interception. The act of listening in and recording communications, intended for another party for the purpose of obtaining intelligence; the act of engaging an enemy force on its way towards its objective.

"INTERCEPTION" to monitor and intervene mobile/internet connection for lawful surveillance or other law enforcement purposes. [Karnika Seth, *Computers Internet and New Technology Laws*, 2021, LexisNexis, Glossary of Legal Terms].

Interconnection. Linking telecommunications equipment and services allowing their functional integration thanks to logic systems and telecommunications techniques, and opening up access to third party services. (*Telecommunication*)

Intercourse. Social communication between individuals.

'Intercourse' means 'sexual connection' [Concise Oxford Dictionary as cited in *Suresh Kumar Koushal* v. *Naz Foundation*, (2014) 1 SCC 1, para 59.6].

Sexual intercourse; dealings or connections (as in common affairs, civilities or business) between persons, organisations or nations.

INTERCOURSE, COMMUNICATION, CONNECTION, COMMERCE. *Intercourse* and *commerce* subsist only between persons; *communication* and *connection* between persons and things. An *intercourse* with persons may be carried on in various forms; either by an *interchange* of civilities, which is a friendly intercourse; an *exchange* of commodities, which is a commercial intercourse; or an *exchange* of words, is a verbal and partial intercourse : a *communication* in this sense is a species of intercourse; namely, that which consists of a permanent intercourse; since one who has a regular intercourse for purposes of trade with another is said to have a *connection* with him, or to stand in *connection* with him. There may, therefore, be a partial *intercourse* or *communication* where there is no *connection*, nothing to bind or link the parties to each other : but there cannot be a *connection* which is not kept up by continual *intercourse*.

'Intercourse' under S. 375 of the Code means sexual connection. *Koppulla Venkat Rao* v. *State of A.P.*, (2004) 3 SCC 602, 606, para 12. [IPC (45 of 1860), S. 375]

Interdict. To forbid or restrain.

Interest. "INTEREST" means rate of interest and includes the return to be made over and above what was actually lent, whether the same is charged or sought to be recovered specifically by way of interest or otherwise. [Usurious Loans Act (10 of 1918), S. 2(1)]

"INTEREST" means interest payable in any manner in respect of any moneys borrowed or debt incurred (including a deposit, claim or other similar right or obligation) and includes any service fee or other charge in respect of the moneys borrowed or debt incurred or in respect of any credit facility which has not been utilised. [Income-tax Act (43 of 1961), S. 2(28A)]

For the purposes of this sub-clause, the expression "INTEREST" shall not include interest paid on delayed payment of loan or on default. [Income-tax Act (43 of 1961), S. 10(15)(iv) *Expln.* 1A]

Interest is the compensation allowed by law, or fixed by the parties for the use or forbearance of money, or as damages for its detention. [Corpus Juris Secundum, Vol. 47 as cited in *Hyder Consulting (UK) Limited* v. *State of Orissa*, (2015) 2 SCC 189, para 74.4].

Interest is compensation paid by the borrower to the lender for deprivation of the use of his money [Stroud's Judicial Dictionary, 7th Edn., 2008, Vol. 2, p. 1385 as cited in *Hyder Consulting (UK) Limited* v. *State of Orissa*, (2015) 2 SCC 189, para 74.5].

The price paid for borrowing money generally expressed as a percentage of the amount borrowed paid in one year. [Webster's Third New International Dictionary, Vol. 3 as cited in *Hyder Consulting (UK) Limited* v. *State of Orissa*, (2015) 2 SCC 189, para 74.3].

"INTEREST" means interest on loans and advances made in India and includes—

(a) commitment charges unutilised portion of any credit sanctioned for being availed of in India; and

(b) discount on promissory notes and bill of exchange drawn or made in India,

but does not include—

(i) interest referred to in sub-section (1B) of Section 42 of the Reserve Bank of India Act, 1934;

(ii) discount on treasury bills. [Interest-tax Act (45 of 1974), S. 2(7)]

"INTEREST" means the time value of the funds or money involved, which, unless otherwise agreed, is calculated at the rate and on the basis customarily accepted by the banking community for the funds of money involved. [UN Commission on International Trade Law : Model Law on International Credit Transfers (Nov 25. 1992), Art. 2(m)]

'Interest' means concern; advantage; good; share; portion; part or participation.

A person interested is one having an interest; *i.e.*, a right of property, or in the nature of property, less than title.

"Interest" would be the return or compensation for the use or retention by one person of a sum of money belonging to or owed to another. It may be understood to mean the amount which one has contracted to pay for the use of borrowed money. It is a consideration paid either for the use of money or for forbearance in demanding it, after it has fallen due, and thus, it could be said to be a charge for the use or forbearance of a particular amount of money. In this sense, it is a compensation allowed in law for use of money belonging to another or for the delay in paying the said money after it has become payable. [*Hyder Consulting (UK) Limited* v. *Governor, State of Orissa*, (2015) 2 SCC 189, para 75].

The word "interest" has a basic meaning of participation in advantage, profit and responsibility. "Interest" is a right, title or share in a thing [*Zelia M. Xavier Fernandes E. Gonsolves* v. *Joana Rodrigues*, (2012) 3 SCC 188, para 17].

On a consideration of various provisions of various Acts dealing with evacuees and evacuee property it appears that the word "interest" was used in the definition to mean interest not derived from a right or title in the property but existing independently of it. *Azizum Nisa* v. *Asst. Custodian,* AIR 1957 All 561, 571. [Administration of Evacuee Property Act (31 of 1950), S. 2(*f*)]

The term "interest" in S. 91(*a*) of the Transfer of Property Act (4 of 1882) means present interest.

The term "interests" in S. 21 of the Land Acquisition Act (1 of 1894) means admitted interests.

Interest is a consideration paid either for use of money or for forbearance in demanding it, after it has fallen due. It is a compensation allowed by law or fixed by parties, or permitted by custom or usage for use of money, belonging to another, or for the delay in paying the money after it has become payable. *C.I.T.* v. *Sham Lal Narula,* AIR 1963 Punj 411, 414. [Land Acquisition Act ((1 of 1894), S. 34]

Under O. XXI, R. 89(1), CPC (5 of 1908) the only person in whose favour sale can be set aside is a person who owned the property or has an interest therein by virtue of a title acquired before the sale.

The word 'interest' in O. XXI, R. 89, has got a very wide import and should be construed very liberally so that any inchoate right which a party may have over a property may be sufficient "interest" to enable him to apply under O. XXI, R. 89, CPC (5 of

1908). *Radharaman Choudhary* v. *Gulab Thakur,*AIR 1959 Pat 50, 52.

The word "interest" means interest in the property *i.e.* the subject matter of the suit and the interest is the interest of the person who was the party to the suit. *Rikhu Dev* v. *Som Dass*, AIR 1975 SC 2159, 2160. [CPC (5 of 1908), O. XXII, R. 10(2)]

The term "interest" is not limited to financial interest only and may include interest arising out of fiduciary duties or closeness of relationship such as that of father and son or daughter, or husband and wife. *Firestone Tyre and Rubber Co.* v. *Synthetics and Chemicals Ltd.*, (1970) 2 Com LJ 200 (Bom). [Companies Act (1 of 1956), S. 300]

A person is said to have interest in a matter when he has rights, advantages, duties, liabilities or the like whether present or future connected with it [Constitution of India, Art. 19(5) and Art. 22(6)]; money paid for the use of money lent (the principal) or for forbearance of debt, according to a fixed rate [Constitution of India, Art. 112(3)(c) and Art. 202(3)(c)]; a feeling of intentness, concern or curiosity about something.

Interest-based bargaining. A sophisticated bargaining technique employed by the mediators in the mediation process to bring about settlement agreement between the disputing parties by exploring the interests of the parties beyond their legal positions. These interests provide potential resources for settlement that tap the additional dimensions of relationships and provide the basis for settling conflicts in the interest and according to the determinations of the parties. (*Arbitration*)

Interest-based dispute resolution. Interest-based dispute resolution defines disputes in terms of interests (not positions) and works to reconcile the interests to obtain a mutually-satisfactory solution. Interest-based dispute resolution looks to future, focuses on maintaining cordial relationships, furthers the restructuring of relationships between disputants, announces results as accommodative resolutions, acts as a custom-and-tailor-made process and affords a role for parties too, hence is branded as interest-based system. Interest-based dispute resolution systems include conciliation, mediation negotiation and partnering. (*Arbitration*)

Interest-based mediation. In the interest-based mediation, the mediator focuses on the interests or needs of the parties. Interest-based mediation is also known as *Process Centred Mediation (PCM)*. (*Arbitration*)

Interest, Compound. Interest upon interest.

Interest in expectancy. 'INTEREST IN EXPECTANCY' includes an estate in remainder or reversion and every other future interest whether vested or contingent, but does not include reversions expectant upon the determination of leases. [Estate Duty Act (34 of 1953), S. 2(11)]

Interest of justice. The phrase "interest of justice" as used under the clause (c) of section 437(3) means "good administration of justice" or "advancing the trial process" and inclusion of broader meaning should be shunned because of purposive interpretation. [*Kunal Kumar Tiwari* v. *State of Bihar,* (2018) 16 SCC 744, para 9].

Interest in the estate of the deceased. The true meaning of the expression "interest in the estate of the deceased, "occurring in 283(1)(*c*) of the Act, is, that an interest, however slight or the base possibility of an interest or even an interest dependent upon remote contingencies is sufficient to, entitle a person to oppose a will. A person, who claims independently and outside of a will and disputes the right of the testator to dispose of the property, or a person who claims paramount title adversely, against the testator, has no such interest within the meaning of S. 283(1)(c) of the Act. The interest in the estate of the deceased, must be an interest under the deceased. *Mutukdhari Singh* v. *Prem Debi*, AIR 1959 Pat 570, 576. [Indian Succession Act (39 of 1925), S. 283(1)(c)]

Interest in the trust. The words 'interest in the trust' in S. 92 of CPC (5 of 1908) must be interpreted to mean some such interest which is affected by mismanagement so that the person is interested in having the affairs of the trust set right by Court. *Farruan Ali Khan* v. *Mohd. Raza Khan,* AIR 1950 All 62, 65.

Interest of general public. The expression 'interest of general public', must have nexus or relation to the objects of the Act namely registration and better protection of trade marks and for the prevention of the use of fraudulent marks on merchandise. *Colgate Palmolive* v. *K.V. Swaminathan,* AIR 1991 Bom 111, 116. [Trade and Merchandise Marks Act (43 of 1958), S. 49(3)]

"Interest of General Public" is a comprehensive expression comprising several issues which affect public welfare, public convenience, public order, health, morality safety, etc., all intended to achieve the socio-economic justice for people. [*Amarnath Shrine, In Re* v. *Union of India*, (2013) 3 SCC 247, para 13] [Constitution of India, Art. 21].

Interest of public order. Any restriction that helps to maintain public order or prevents an apprehension of public disorder is in the interests of public order. A restriction that has nothing to do with the maintenance of public order, *i.e.* one that does not help the maintenance of public order or does not avert a threat to public order cannot be said to be in the interests of public order. *Ram Nandan* v. *State,* AIR 1959 All 101, 104 (FB). [Constitution of India, Art. 19(2)]

Interest of Security of India. For the purposes of this section, the expression "INTEREST OF THE SECURITY OF INDIA" means any action necessary for the security of India which relates to the use of a layout-design or a semiconductor integrated circuit incorporating a layout-design or an article incorporating such semiconductor integrated circuit and which—

(a) relates to fissionable materials or the materials from which they are derived; or

(b) relates to the traffic in arms, ammunition and implements of war and to such traffic in other goods and materials as is carried on directly or indirectly for the purpose of supplying a military establishment; or

(c) is taken in time of war or other emergency in international relations. [Semiconductor Integrated Circuit Layout-Design Act (37 of 2000), S. 68, *Expln.*]

Interest of the public. The 'interests of the public' cannot include matters which have nothing to do with the interests of the public which was going to use the Motor Vehicles in question or such as are wholly unconnected with the user of the roads or the transport system which was under consideration of the Road Transport Authority. *Onkarmal* v. *R.T. Authority*, AIR 1956 Cal 490, 495. [Motor Vehicles Act (4 of 1939), S. 55(*a*)]

Interest of the public generally. The words 'the interest of the public generally' in S. 47, Motor Vehicles Act, are designedly general words, and so unnecessary, narrow and technical construction should be applied. Whether nationalisation of transport is ultimately or primarily in the interest of the general public may be a debatable point, but is always and certainly a question which can lawfully be considered under the expression 'interest of the public generally' and its consideration is therefore not excluded. Similarly, congestion is also a matter which not only comes within the expression 'the interest of the public generally' but also within the other expression 'the condition of the roads included in the proposed route or area' in S. 47 of the Act. Both these considerations are not only germane but very relevant in considering any application for a stage carriage permit. The amendment in Art. 19(6)(ii) of the Constitution of India clearly recognises the nationalisation of the State Transport and for State permits. Further when power is given to the Regional Transport Authority under S. 47(3) to limit the number of carriages, it is in order to avoid congestion. *Naib Transport (Private) Ltd.* v. *S.N. Mukherjee,* MLJ : QD (1956-1960) Vol. IV C41 : 62 Cal WN 414 : AIR 1958 Cal 652. [Motor Vehicles Act (4 of 1939), S. 47]

Interest on money. The legal profit or recompense, on loans of money, to be taken from the borrower by the lender. (*Tomlin*)

Interest is payments stipulated to be made for the loan or use of money.

Interest on securities. Means,—

(i) interest on any security of the Central Government or a State Government;

(ii) interest on debentures or other securities for money issued by or on behalf of a local authority or a company or a corporation established by a Central, State or Provincial Act. [Income-tax Act (43 of 1961), S. 2(28B)]

Interest reipublicae ne maleficia remaneant impunita. (*Maxim*) It concerns the commonwealth that crimes do not remain unpunished.

Interest reipublicae ne sua re quis male utatur. (*Maxim*) It concerns the State that no one should make a wrongful use of his property.

Interest reipublicae suprema hominum testamenta rata haberi. (*Maxim*) It concerns the commonwealth that men's last wills be sustained.

Interest reipublicae ut sit finis litium. (*Maxim*) It is in the interest of the State that there should be an end of law-suit.

It is for the general welfare that a period be put to litigation. [*Maniben Devraj Shah* v. *Municipal Corporation of Brihan Mumbai*, (2012) 5 SCC 157, para 18].

It concerns the state that there be an end to law suits. [Roman Jurisprudence as cited in *Dr. Subramanian Swamy* v. *State of T.N.*, (2014) 5 SCC 75, para 39].

Interest, Simple. Interest computed solely upon the principal.

Interest upon interest. The expression "interest on upon interest" means compound interest.

Interested. Having interest. [IPC (45 of 1860), S. 189].

Interested and affected. The union which sponsors the cause of an individual workman is interested in the dispute; but the workmen who are members of the union are not necessarily affected by the dispute. *Workman* v. *Rangavilas Motors (P) Ltd.*, AIR 1967 SC 1040, 1043. [Industrial Disputes Act ((14 of 1947), S. 10(1)(d)]

Interested director. Means a director who is in any way, whether by himself or through any of his relatives or firm, body corporate or other association of individuals in which he or any of his relatives is a partner, director or a member, interested in a contract or arrangement, or proposed contract or arrangement, entered into or to be entered into by or on behalf of a company. [Omitted S. 2(49) of the Companies Act, 2013 (18 of 2013)]

Interested evidence. Interested evidence is that sort of evidence, the source of which is likely to be tainted. *Binami Properties (P.) Ltd.* v. *G.A. Hussain & Co.,* AIR 1967 Cal 390, 401. [Indian Evidence Act (1 of 1972), S. 120]

Interested in the payment of money. The words "interested in the payment of money" used in S. 69 of the Indian Contract Act (9 of 1872) do not mean that the interest should be such as would stand the test of a judicial trial. It is sufficient if the person who makes the payment honestly believes that his own interest requires that it should be made, even though that belief is not quite sound in law.

Interested in the payment of money which another is bound by law to pay in S. 69 of the Indian Contract Act (9 of 1872), may include the apprehension of any kind of loss or inconvenience and not merely the actual detriment capable of assessment in money.

Interested in the result of the appeal. A party to the suit against whom the right of appeal has been barred by limitation so far as he is concerned is not a person "interested in the result of the appeal" within the meaning of O. XLI, R. 20(1), CPC (5 of 1908).

It cannot be laid down as an inflexible rule of interpretation that a party against whom a suit has been dismissed and as against whom the right of appeal has become barred is "interested in the result of the appeal" filed by the plaintiff within the meaning of O. XLI, R. 20(1), C.P. Code (5 of 1908).

Interested party. Includes—

(i) an exporter or a foreign producer or the importer of an article subject to investigation for being dumped in India, or a trader or business association a majority of the members of which are producers, exporters or importers of such an article;

(ii) the government of the exporting country; and

(iii) a producer of the like article in India or a trade and business association a majority of the members of which produce the like article in India. [Customs Tariff (Identification, Assessment and Collection of Anti-Dumping Duty on Dumped Articles and for Determination of Injury) Rules, 1995, R. 2(c)]

"INTERESTED PARTY" includes—

(i) an exporter or foreign producer or the importer of an article subject to investigation for being subsidised or a trade or business association a majority of the members of which are producers, exporters or importers of such an article; and

(ii) a producer of the like article in India or a trade and business association a majority of the members of which produce the like article in India. [Customs Tariff (Identification, Assessment and Collection of Countervailing Duty on Subsidized Articles and for Determination of injury) Rules, 1995, R. 2(c)].

"INTERESTED PARTY" includes—

(i) any exporter of foreign producer or the importer of an article subjected to investigation for purposes of imposition of safeguard duty or a trade or business association, majority of the members of which are producers, exporters or importers of such an article;

(ii) the government of the exporting country; and

(iii) a producer of the like article or directly competitive article in India or a trade or business association, a majority of members of which produce or trade the like article or directly competitive article in India; [Customs Tariff (Identification And Assessment of Safeguard Duty) Rules, 1997, R. 2(d)]

Interested person. The expression 'interested person' is defined as including a person claiming an interest in the compensation. *Kako Bai* v. *Land Acquisition Collector,* AIR 1956 Punj 231, 232. [Land Acquisition Act (1 of 1894), Ss. 3(b) and 18]

Interested witness. A close relative who is a very natural witness cannot be regarded as an interested witness. The term "interested" postulates that the person concerned must have some direct interest in seeing that the accused person is somehow or the other convicted either because he had some *animus* with the accused or for some other reason. *Dalbir Kaur* v. *State of Punjab,* AIR 1977 SC 472.

In the expression 'interested witness' the term 'interested' postulates that the witness must have some direct interest in having the accused somehow or the other convicted for some *animus* or for some other reason. A close relative who is a natural witness cannot be regarded as 'interested witness'. [*Kartik Malhar* v. *State of Bihar,* (1996) 1 SCC 614, 621, para 15. See also *Namdeo* v. *State of Maharashtra,* (2007), 14 SCC 150, 161, para 29; *Ashok Kumar Choudhary* v. *State of Bihar,* (2008) 12 SCC 173, 177, para 8.

Where there is nothing on record to show that any enmity or motive on the part of witnesses to speak against the accused, the witnessses cannot be termed as interested witnesses merely because three of them were advocates and the fourth was the driver of the deceased especially when undoubtedly all of them were in the same car by which the deceased went to the Court and all of them were present at the scene of occurrence. [*Nisar Ahmad Fajmohmed Kaji* v. *State of Gujarat,* (1998) 9 SCC 23]

Interests of general public. The fact that the acquisition is for a company does not necessarily imply that the purpose for which it is acquired is not one for the benefit of the entire public. *R.L. Aurora Ram Ditta Mal* v. *State of Uttar Pradesh,* MLJ : QD (1956-1960) Vol. I C2393 : AIR 1958 All 126. [Constitution of India, Art. 19(6)]

Interests of justice. The provision of limitation has been enacted in the Code of 1973, with the obvious purpose of preventing abuse of the process of the Court by filing belated and stale prosecutions. Such statutory purpose should not be allowed to be defeated by taking recourse to the magic words of "interests of justice" unless there is manifestation of compelling or justifiable reason in the complaints and in the order of taking cognizance to do so. [*S.K. Bajaj* v. *D.K. Bhattacharya,* MLJ : YD (1982), p. 419 : 1982 CrLJ 210]. [CrPC (2 of 1974), S. 473]

Interests of public generally. The words "interests of the public" which are found in the Act relate to the interests of the travelling public for whose convenience and need stage carriages are provided. The interests of the public as mentioned in the Act can not include matters which have nothing to do with the interests of the public which was going to use the Motor Vehicles in question, or such as are wholly unconnected with the user of the roads or the transport system which was under consideration of the R.T.A. in the given case. In considering whether to grant permits or not in a particular route the R.T.A. cannot be permitted to take into consideration matters which are totally unconnected with the particular subject-matter which is under consideration. The interests of a public who uses a particular route could not be served by preferring refugees or political sufferers, who are most likely to lack resources, or by granting permits to scheduled tribes or backward hillmen, who would be most likely to lack in efficiency. It would not be permissible to import wider considerations of politics or philanthropy and the like, which, while highly commendable from other points of view, have nothing to do with the efficient running of such services. AIR 1948 Mad 400 : (1948) 1 MLJ 85, **Rel. on.** *Onkarmal Mistri* v. *Regional Transport Authority Darjeeling,* MLJ : QD (1956-1960) Vol. III C56 : 60 Cal WN 13 : AIR 1956 Cal 490. [Motor Vehicles Act (4 of 1939), S. 55(1)(a)]

Interface. 'Interface' is a device or connection or program that joins one device or system to another. [Oxford Advanced Learner's Dictionary as cited in *People's University* v. *State of M.P.*, (2012) 9 SCC 714, para 12].

Interfere. Meddle; intervene, with person or things.

To enter into or take part in the concerns of others; to intermeddle.

Interference. The action or fact of interfering or intermeddling. [TP Act (4 of 1882), S. 108(n)].

"INTERFERENCE" means the effect of unwanted energy due to one or a combination of emissions, radiations or induction upon reception in a radio communication system, manifested by any performance degradation, misinterpretation, or loss of information which could be extracted in the absence of such unwanted energy. [Use of Very Low Power Ultra-wideband Devices (Exemption from Licensing Requirements) Rules, 2018, R. 2(o)].

Interfering with witnesses. Attempting to prevent a witness from giving evidence or to influence the evidence he gives.

Interim. Meanwhile; in the meantime (as) interim receiver.

Interim appeal (interlocutory appeal). An appeal against an order made during the pre-trial stage of civil litigation.

Interim injunction. Interim injunction is a discretionary remedy and the discretion can hardly be interfered with in revision if it is neither arbitrary nor capricious. The plaintiff seeking temporary injunction must satisfy that he has a *prima facie* case that the right which he seeks to protect in fact exists. In other words he must show that there is a serious question to be tried and there is a fair chance of its being decided in his favour. The High Court can in revision set aside the order of the lower Court granting injunction, where the plaintiff could not make out *prima facie* case and the order was not called for in view of the balance of convenience and absence of possibility of irreparable loss to plaintiff. [T S MISRA, J] *Nabi Bux* v. *Madan Gopal,* MLJ : YD (1978) C 304 : 1978 All LJ 301. [CPC (5 of 1908), O XXXIX, R. 1]

Injunction granted until the hearing of the case by a Court subject to its further orders.

Interim order. A temporary Court order; some order in the course of proceedings, not being a final order *e.g.*, preliminary injunction.

Interim Order, is an order made by the Court to have effect only for a time.

Interim Pension Fund Regulatory and Development Authority. Means the Interim Pension Fund Regulatory and Development Authority set up by the Central Government through Resolutions No. F. No. 5/7/2003-ECB&PR, dated 10-10-2003, and F. No. 1(6)/2007-PR, dated 14-11-2008. [S. 2(1)(f) of the Pension Fund Regulatory & Development Authority Act, 2013 (23 of 2013)]

Interim relief. Relief granted by a Court pending the final determination of the suit; such relief is granted to the plaintiff to protect his rights if he makes out a *prima facie* case, and after considering the balance of convenience, *i.e.* the inconvenience to the plaintiff if relief is refused, and the inconvenience to the defendant if it is granted.

Interim statement. A periodic financial report of a company issued during a fiscal year to indicate the performance of a company.

Interior decorator. Means any person engaged, whether directly or indirectly, in the business of providing by way of advice, consultancy, technical assistance or in any other manner, services related to planning, design or beautification of spaces, whether man-made or otherwise and includes a landscape designer. [Finance Act (32 of 1994), S. 65(1)(49) now repealed by Goods and Services Tax Act, 2017]

Interlineation. The insertion of a word or words between the lines of a writing. [Registration Act (16 of 1908), S. 20(1)]

Interlocking. Locking or clasping with each other. [Factories Act (63 of 1948), S. 28(1)(e)]

Interlocutory. 'Interlocutory,' in law, means, not that which decides the cause, but that which only settles some intervening matter relating to the cause.

Interlocutory application. An application made in the course of an action; an application made for keeping things in *status quo* till the rights can be decided or for the purpose of obtaining some *interim* direction of the Court. [Presidency Small Cause Courts Act (15 of 1882), S. 9(aa)].

Interlocutory costs. Costs awarded to a party by the Court before judgment, during the progress of a cause.

Interlocutory decree. One made pending the cause, and before final hearing on the merits.

An 'interlocutory decree' is generally applied to decrees in which some matter either of law or of fact is directed preparatory to a final decision.

Interlocutory injunction. Injunction *pendente lite*.

Interlocutory judgment. An order of Court made in the progress of cause, requiring something to be done or observed, but not determining the controversy.

An interlocutory judgment is one which determines some preliminary or sub-ordinate point or plea, or settles some special question or default arising in the progress of the cause, but does not adjudge the ultimate rights of the parties, or finally put the case out of Court.

Interlocutory order. An interlocutory order is one which is made pending the cause and before a final hearing on the merits.

An interlocutory order is made to secure some end and purpose necessary and essential to the progress of the suit, and generally collateral to the issues formed by the pleadings and not connected with the final judgment.

The term 'interlocutory order' merely denotes orders of a purely *interim* or temporary, nature which do not decide or touch the important rights or the liabilities of the parties. *Amar Nath* v. *State of Haryana*, AIR 1977 SC 2185, 2189. [CrPC 1973 (2 of 1974), S. 397(2)]

The order taking cognizance of an offence by a Court, whether it is so done illegally or without jurisdiction, will be an interlocutory order. *Madhu Limayee* v. *State of Maharashtra*, AIR 1978 SC 47, 53.

INTERLOCUTORY ORDER has to be construed in contradiction to or in contrast with Final Order. It means not a final order, but an intermediate order. It is made between the commencement of an action and the entry of the judgment. *V.C. Shukla* v. *State through CBI*, AIR 1980 SC 962, 976. [Special Courts Act (22 of 1979), S. 11; CrPC 1973 (2 of 1974), S. 397(2)]

Interlocutory proceeding. Proceeding taken during the course of an action and incident to the principal object of the action, namely, the judgment.

Interloper. Person who intercepts the trade of a company of merchants.

Intermeddle. To interfere with or meddle with the concerns or business of others.

To meddle with the affairs or property of another [CPC (5 of 1908), S. 2(11)].

Intermeddler. A person who meddles with the affair of others in which one has no concern.

Intermediary "intermediary", with respect to any particular electronic records, means any person who on behalf of another person receives, stores or transmits that record or provides any service with respect to that record and includes telecom service providers, network service providers, internet service providers, web-hosting service providers, search engines, online payment sites, online-auction sites, online-market places and cyber cafes; [Information Technology Act (21 of 2000), S. 2(1)(w) as amended by Act 10 of 2009 (w.e.f 27-10-2009)]

"Intermediary" includes pension fund, central record-keeping agency, National Pension System Trust, pension fund adviser, point of presence and such other person or entity connected with collection, management, record-keeping and distribution of accumulations. [Pension Fund Regulatory and Development. Authority Act (23 of 2013), S. 2(g)].

"Intermediary" means a broker, an agent or any other person, by whatever name called, who arranges or facilitates the supply of goods or services or both, or securities, between two or more persons, but does not include a person who supplies such goods or services or both or securities on his own account [The Integrated Goods and Services Tax Act, 2017 (13 of 2017), S. 2(13)]

"INTERMEDIARY" means

(i) a stock-broker, sub-broker share transfer agent, banker to an issue, trustee to a trust deed, registrar to an issue, merchant banker, underwriter, portfolio manager, investment adviser or any other intermediary associated with securities market and registered under section 12 of the Securities and Exchange Board of India Act, 1992 (15 of 1992); or

(ii) an association recognised or registered under the Forward Contracts (Regulation) Act, 1952 (74 of 1952) or any member of such association; or

(iii) intermediary registered by the Pension Fund Regulatory and Development Authority; or

(iv) a recognised stock exchange referred to in clause (f) of section 2 of the Securities Contracts (Regulation) Act, 1956 (42 of 1956);. [Prevention of Money-laundering Act (15 of 2003), S. 2(1)(n) as amended by Act 2 of 2013 (w.e.f 15-2-2013)]

"INTERMEDIARY" with respect to a particular data message, means a person who, on behalf of another person, sends, receives or stores that data message or provides other services with respect to that data message. [UNCITRAL Model Law in Electronic Commerce, Dec. 16, 1996, Art. 2(e)]

'INTERMEDIARY' means a member of the association and includes a collateral Manager, a clearing house or such other person who is associated with the commodity derivatives market and is specified as such by the Central Government for the purposes of the Act. [Forward Contacts (Regulations) Act, 1952 (74 of 1952), S. 2(ea) as inserted by Amending Ordinance (No. 3 of 08), S. 3(v)]

"INTERMEDIARY" means,—

(i) a stock-broker, sub-broker, share transfer agent, banker to an issue, trustee to a trust deed, registrar to an issue, merchant banker, underwriter, portfolio manager, investment advisor or any other intermediary associated with securities market and registered under section 12 of the SEBI Act, 1992 (15 of 1992); or

(ii) an association recognised or registered under the Forward Contracts (Regulation) Act, 1952 (74 of 1952) or any member of such association; or

(iii) intermediary registered by the Pension Fund Regulatory & Development Authority; or

(iv) a recognised stock exchange referred to in section 2(f) of the Securities Contracts (Regulation) Act, 1956 (42 of 1956). [S. 2(1)(n) of the Prevention of Money-Laundering Act, 2002 (15 of 2003) as substituted by the Prevention of Money-Laundering (Amendment) Act, 2012 (2 of 2013)]

"INTERMEDIARY" includes pension fund, central recordkeeping agency, National Pension System Trust, pension fund adviser, retirement adviser, point of presence and such other person or entity connected with collection, management, recordkeeping and distribution of accumulations. [S. 2(1)(g) of the Pension Fund Regulatory & Development Authority Act, 2013 (23 of 2013)]

Intermediary and proprietor. The expression 'intermediary' is defined in Section 3(12) as, "intermediary", with reference to an estate means a "proprietor", under-proprietor, *etc.* Section 3(21) defines a proprietor to mean, as respects an estate, a person owning the estate and includes the heirs and successors in interest of the proprietor. *Rani Ratnesh Kumari* v. *State of U.P.,* AIR 1978 SC 1450. [U.P. Zamindari and Land Reforms Act, 1950, S. 3(12)&(21)]

Intermediary bank. Means any receiving bank other than the originator's bank and the beneficiary's bank. [U.N. Commission on International Trade Law : Model Law on International Credit Transfers, Nov. 25, 1992, Art. 2(g)]

Intermediary interest. Means an estate or any rights or interest therein held or owned by or vested in an intermediary and any reference to 'estate' in this Act shall be construed as including a reference to 'intermediary interest' also. [Orissa Estates Abolition Act, 1951 (1 of 1952), S. 2(hh) **as cited in** *Jagannath Temple Managing Committee* v. *Siddha Math,* (2015) 16 SCC 542, para 58.1].

Intermediary or insurance intermediary. Includes insurance brokers, re-insurance brokers, insurance consultants, surveyors and loss assessors. [Insurance Regulatory and Development Authority Act (41 of 1999), S. 2(f)]

"INTERMEDIARY OR INSURANCE INTERMEDIARY" includes insurance brokers, reinsurance brokers, insurance consultants, surveyors and loss assessors, or any other person representing or assisting an insurer in one or more of the following:

(i) soliciting, negotiating, procuring or effectuating an insurance contract or a renewal of an insurance contract;

(ii) disseminating information relating to coverage or rates;

(iii) forwarding an insurance application;

(iv) servicing and delivering an insurance policy or contract;

(v) inspecting a risk;

(vi) setting a rate;

(vii) investigating or assessing a claim or loss;

(viii) transacting a matter after the effectuation of a contract; or

(ix) representing or assisting an insurance or other person in any other manner in the transaction of insurance with respect to a subject of insurance resident, located or to be performed in India;

(x) servicing a policy or contract. [Insurance Regulatory and Development Authority (Insurance Advertisements and Disclosure) Regulations, 2000, Regn. 2(c)]

Intermediate. Lying or being in the middle place or degree; of the intervening period; one that acts as agent; a chemical compound formed as an intermediate step between the starting material and the final product (as a dye intermediate) [Employees' Provident Funds and Miscellaneous Provisions Act (19 of 1952), Sch. I (viii)].

Intermediate disposition. The act or power of disposing in the intervening period. [Estate Duty Act (34 of 1953), S. 16(2)(a)].

Intermediate dividends. Dividends for the intervening period. [Indian Trusts Act (2 of 1882), S. 23, ill. (d)].

Intermediate fact. Intervening fact. [Indian Evidence Act (1 of 1872), S. 136, ill. (d)].

Intermediate level. Means a level between the village and districts levels specified by the Governor of a state by public notification to be the intermediate level for the purpose of this Act. [Constitution (Seventy-third Amendment) Act 1992, Art. 243(C)]

Intermix. To mix together. [Drugs and Cosmetics Act (23 of 1940), S. 19(2)(b)].

Intern. To hold one as a political prisoner; the detention of ships, sailors, soldiers or property of a belligerent by a neutral nation, during hostilities.

Internal check and internal audit. The internal check is most often carried out by the employees or directors of the company and it consists in checking the day to day transactions which operate continuously as part of the routine system. The internal audit is conducted by a qualified auditor who is generally in the employment of the company. *Council of the Institute of Chartered Accountants of India* v. *Rajaram,* AIR 1960 Mad 122, 123. [Chartered Accountants Act (38 of 1949), S. 21]

Internal Complaints Committee (ICC). Means Internal Complaints Committee to be constituted by an TI under sub-regulation (1) of Regulation 4 of these regulations and shall include any duly constituted Body already functioning with the same objective (like the Gender Sensitization Committee Against Sexual Harassment (GSCASH)); Provided that in the latter case the TI shall ensure that the constitution of such a Body is as required for ICC under these regulations. Provided further that such a Body shall be bound by the provisions of these regulations. [All India Council for Technical Education (Gender Sensitization, Prevention and Prohibition of Sexual Harassment of Women Employees and Students and Redressal of Grievances in Technical Educational Institutions) Regulations, 2016, Regn. 2(i)].

Internal development works. Means roads, foot-paths, water supply, sewers, drains, tree planting, street lighting, provision for community building and for treatment and disposal of sewage and sullage water, or any other work in a colony necessary for its proper development.

"Internal Development works" means—

(i) metalling of roads and paving of footpaths;

(ii) turfing and plantation with trees of open spaces;

(iii) street lighting;

(iv) adequate and wholesome water supply;

(v) sewers and drains both from storm and sullage water and necessary provision for their treatment and disposal; and

(vi) any other work that the Director may think necessary in the interest of proper development of a colony. [Haryana Development and Regulation of Urban Areas Act (8 of 1975), S. 2(i) as cited in *DLF Limited* v. *Manmohan Lowe*, (2014) 12 SCC 231, para 28].

Internal disturbance. What is meant by 'internal disturbance' is a rebellion or insurrection and not an ordinary breach of the public peace. *Ram Nandan* v. *State,* AIR 1959 All 101, 111 (FB). [Constitution of India, Arts. 19(2) and 352]

Internal sale quota. Means that portion, stated in terms of bulk or weight, of the whole of the coffee produced by the estate in the year, which a registered estate is permitted under this Act to sell in the Indian market. [Coffee Act (7 of 1942), S. 3(h)]

Internal waters. Any natural or artificial body or stream of water within the territorial limits of a country, such as a bay, gulf, river mouth, creek, harbour, port, lake, or canal.

International commercial arbitration. Means an arbitration relating to disputes arising out of legal relationships, whether contractual or not, considered as commercial under the law in force in India and where at least one of the parties is—

(i) an individual who is a national of, or habitually resident in, any country other than India; or

(ii) a body corporate which is incorporated in any country other than India; or

(iii) a company or an association or a body of individuals whose central management and control is exercised in any country other than India; or

(iv) the Government of a foreign country. [Arbitration and Conciliation Act (26 of 1996), S. 2(1)(f)]

"INTERNATIONAL COMMERCIAL ARBITRATION". Where both parties have Indian nationalities, then the arbitration between such parties cannot be said to be an international commercial arbitration. *TDM Infrastructure Pvt. Ltd.* v. *UE Development India Pvt. Ltd.*, AIR 2008 SC (Supp) 1143.

International commercial conciliation. 'International commercial conciliation' shall have the same meaning as the expression 'international commercial arbitration' in clause (f) of sub-section (l) of Section 2, subject to the modification that for the word 'arbitration' occurring therein, the word 'conciliation' shall be substituted. [Arbitration and Conciliation Act (26 of 1996), S. 1(2) *Expln.*]

International convention. Means an international agreement concluded among States in written form and governed by International Law. [United Nations Convention on International Multi-Modal Transport of Goods, Geneva, May 24, 1980, Art. 1(8)]

"INTERNATIONAL CONVENTION" means—

(a) the Single Convention on Narcotic Drugs, 1961 adopted by the United Nations Conference at New York in March, 1961;

(b) the Protocol, amending the Convention mentioned in sub-clause (a), adopted by the United Nations Conference at Geneva in March, 1972;

(c) the convention on Psychotropic Substances, 1971 adopted by the United Nations Conference at Vienna in February, 1971; and

(d) any other international convention, or protocol or other instrument amending an international convention, relating to narcotic drugs or psychotropic substances which may be ratified or acceded to by India after the commencement of this Act. [Narcotic Drugs and Psychotropic Substances Act (61 of 1985), S. 2(ix)]

International Court of Justice. The United Nations Tribunal consisting of 15 members to adjudicate disputes between countries that voluntarily submit cases for decision. It primarily sits at Hague and Netherlands.

International Covenants. Means the International Covenant on Civil and Political Rights and the International Covenant on Economic, Social and Cultural Rights adopted by the General Assembly of the United Nations on the 16th December, 1966. [Protection of Human Rights Act, 1993 (10 of 1994), S. 2(1)(f)]

International event. Means an event or competition where the International Olympic Committee, the International Paralympic Committee, an International Federation, a major event organisation or another international sport organisation is the governing body for such event or appoints the technical officials for the event. [National Anti-Doping Act, 2022 (15 of 2022), section 2(r)]

International Federation. Means the international governing body for a particular sport. [National Anti-Doping Act, 2022 (15 of 2022), section 2(s)]

International journey in relation to a passenger, means—

(i) his journey from the last customs port or customs airport of departure of the ship or aircraft in the territories to which this Chapter extends to a place outside India, and includes further journeys by such passenger outside India by the same or different carriers;

(ii) his journey from a place outside India to the first customs port or customs airport of arrival of the ship or aircraft in the territories, irrespective of whether the journey commences or terminates at such customs port or customs airport. [Finance Act (32 of 1971), S. 44(e)]

International Law. The term, *International Law*, is in modern times generally understood as denoting the system of customary and conventional rules which regulate the conduct and intercourse of civilised States, and which are accepted by such States as of international obligation.

The body of rules regulating the relations of nations, interest and resolving the conflict between laws of different nations when applicable to particular matters or transactions. [CPC (5 of 1908) and Art. 51, Const, S. 13(c)].

International mediation means mediation undertaken under this Act and relates to a commercial dispute arising out of a legal relationship, contractual or otherwise, under any law for the time being in force in India, and where at least one of the parties, is—

(i) an individual who is a national of, or habitually resides in, any country other than India; or

(ii) a body corporate including a Limited Liability Partnership of any nature, with its place of business outside India; or

(iii) an association or body of individuals whose place of business is outside India; or

(iv) the Government of a foreign country. **[Mediation Act, 2023 (32 of 2023), section 3(g)]**

International multimodal transport. Means the carriage of goods by at least two different modes of transport on the basis of a multimodal transport contract from a place in one country at which the goods are taken in charge by the multimodal transport operator to a place designed for delivery situated in a different country. The operations of pick up and delivery of goods carried out in the performance of a unimodal transport contract, as defined in such contract, shall not be considered as international transport. [United Nations Convention on International Multimodal Transport of Goods, Geneva, May 24, 1980, Art. I(d)]

International prototype of the kilogram. Means the prototype sanctioned by the First General Conference on Weights and Measures held in Paris in 1889, and deposited at the International Bureau of Weights and Measures. [Standards of Weights and Measures Act (60 of 1976), S. 2(l)]

International transaction.

The expression "International Transaction" shall include—

(a) the purchase, sale, transfer, lease or use of tangible property including building, transportation vehicle, machinery equipment, tools, plant, furniture, commodity or any other article, product or thing;

(b) the purchase, sale, transfer, lease or use of tangible property, including the transfer of ownership or the provision of use of rights regarding land use, copyrights, patents, trademarks, licences franchises, customer list, marketing channel, brand, commercial secret, know-how, industrial property right, exterior design or practical and new design or any other business or commercial rights of similar nature;

(c) capital financing, including any type of long-term or short-term borrowing, lending or guarantee, purchase or sale of marketable securities or any type of advance, payments or deferred payment or receivable or any other debt arising during the course of business;

(d) provision of services, including provision of market research, market development, marketing management, administration, technical service,

(e) a transaction of business restructuring or reorganization, entered into by an enterprise with an associated enterprise, irrespective of the fact that it has bearing on the profit, income, losses or assets of such enterprises at the time of the transaction or at any future date. [Income-tax Act (43 of 1961), S. 92- B, *Explanation* (i)].

For the removal of doubts, it is hereby clarified that the expression 'international transaction' shall include—

(a) the purchase, sale, transfer, lease or use of tangible property including building, transportation vehicle, machinery, equipment, tools, plant, furniture, commodity or any other article, product or thing;

(b) the purchase, sale, transfer, lease or use of intangible property, including the transfer of ownership or the provision of use of rights regarding land use, copyrights, patents, trademarks, licences, franchises, customer list, marketing channel, brand, commercial secret, know-how, industrial property right, exterior design or practical and new design or any other business or commercial rights of similar nature;

(c) capital financing, including any type of long-term or short-term borrowing, lending or guarantee, purchase or sale of marketable securities or any type of advance, payments or deferred payment or receivable or any other debt arising during the course of business;

(d) provision of services, including provision of market research, market development, marketing management, administration, technical service, repairs, design, consultation, agency, scientific research, legal or accounting service;

(e) a transaction of business restructuring or reorganisation, entered into by an enterprise with an associated enterprise, irrespective of the fact that it has bearing on the profit, income, losses or assets of such enterprises at the time of the transaction or at any future date. [*Explanation* (*i*) to section 92B of the Income-tax Act, 1961 (43 of 1961) as inserted (w.r.e.f. 1-4-2002) by the Finance Act, 2012 (23 of 2012)]

International voyage. Means a voyage from or to a port or place in India to or from a port or place outside India. [Merchant Shipping Act (44 of 1958), S. 3(18A)]

"International voyage" means a voyage by a ship entitled to fly the flag of one State to or from a part, shipyard, or offshore terminal under the jurisdiction of another State. [Merchant Shipping Act (44 of 1958), part XI-B, S. 356(f) as inserted by amending Act (31 of 2014)].

"INTERNATIONAL VOYAGE" means a voyage from a country to which the present Convention applies to a port outside such country, or conversely. [International Conference of Safety of Life at Sea, 1974, Chap. 1, Part A, Regn. 2(d)]

International water course. Means a water course parts of which are situated in different states. [UN Convention on the Law of the Non-navigational Uses of International Water Courses, May 21, 1997, Art. 2(b)]

Internee. An interned person; a man, who has been restricted or confined within prescribed limits as enemy, alien or combat troop who takes refugee in a neutral country. [margin, Foreigners Act (31 of 1946), S. 4(1)].

Internet. "Internet" means a global information system which is locally linked together by a globally unique address, based on Internet Protocol or its subsequent enhancements or upgradations and is able to support communications using the Transmission Control Protocol or Internet Protocol suite or its subsequent enhancements or upgradations and all other Internet Protocol compatible protocols. [Finance Act (32 of 1994), S. 65(56b) as inserted by Finance Act (21 of 2006), S. 68(15) now repealed by Goods and Services Tax Act, 2017]

The vast collection of inter-connected networks that are connected using the *TCP/IP* protocols and that evolved from the *ARPANET* of the late 60's and early 70's.

A co-operatively run global collection of computer networks with a common addressing scheme : the TCP/IP protocols. (*Information Technology*)

The Internet connects tens of thousands of independent networks into a vast global *internet* and is probably the largest *Wide Area Network* in the world. (*Matisse Enzer-Glossary of Internet Terms*)

Any time you connect 2 or more *networks* together, you have an internet, as in international or inter-state. (*Matisse Enzer-Glossary of Internet Terms*)

Internet Corporation for Assigned Names and Numbers (ICANN). A nonprofit public-benefit non government organization with an international board of directors. Its mission is to create new top-level domain names. Selected by the U.S. Government to manage the domain name system.

Internet Explorer. It is the most popular browser which comes in-built with the world's most popular operating system called "Windows" from Microsoft. (*Internet*)

Internet Protocol (IP). A unique computer address that consists of four series of three numbers allowing communication between computers. (*Cyber Law*)

Internet-protocol address. The ten-digit identification tag used by computers to locate specific websites.

Internet Protocol television service. 'Internet Protocol television service ' or IPTV service' means delivery of multi-channel television programmes in adderssable mode by using Internet Protocol over a closed network of one or more service providers. [Register of Interconnect Agreements (Broadcasting and Cable Services) Regulation, 2004 as inserted by Fourth Amendment Regn., 2009); Telecommunication (Broadcasting and Cable Services) Interconnection Regulation (13 of 2004), Regn. 2(la) (inserted by fifth Amendment Regulations, 2009); Standards of Quality Service (Broadcasting and Cable Services) (Cable Television-Non-CAS Areas) Regulations, 2009, Regn. 2(o)

Internet Service Provider (ISP). Means Internet Service Provider licensed by DoT to provide internet service throughout India. [Flight and Maritime Connectivity Rules, 2018, R. 2(1)(i)].

Internet Tax Freedom Act (ITFA). Federal law that placed a temporary moratorium on new taxes or new application of existing taxes on Internet transactions. (*U.S.A.*) (*Cyber Law*)

Internet telephony. 'Internet telephony' means telecommunication service through internet and includes fax, audio conferencing and video conferencing. [Finance Act (32 of 1994), S. 65(57a) as inserted by Finance Act (21 of 2006), S. 68(16) now repealed by Goods and Services Tax Act, 2017]

Internment. The confinement of prisoners of war in the interior of a country.

Interpleader. A remedy available to a person who is under liability for any debt, money, goods, or chattels in which he claims no interest, and for or in respect of which he is or expects to be sued by two or more parties making adverse claims thereto. The cause of the interpleader being that a defendant shall not be charged to two severally where no default is in him.

A proceeding devised to enable a person, if the same debt, duty or thing is claimed adversely by two or more parties, to compel them to litigate the right or title between themselves and thereby to relieve himself from the suits which they might otherwise bring against him.

Interpleader suit is defined to be "one where two or more persons severally claim the same debt, duty, or thing from the complainant under different titles or in separate interests : and he, not claiming any title or interest therein himself, and not knowing to which of the claimants he ought of right to render the debt or duty or deliver the property, is either molested by an action, brought against him or fears that he may be compelled to interplead and state their several claims so that the Court may adjudge to whom the matter or thing in controversy belongs".

Interpolate. Make insertions (generally misleading) in a book *etc.*; interject a remark in a talk or discourse or debate.

Interpolation. Insertion of words in a complete document, often extraneous or false ones to change its meaning.

Interpose. In a strictly narrow sense, to 'interpose a defence' in an action is to plead it or set it up by answer.

To place between, in space or time, often with implication of obstruction or delay. [CrPC 1973 (2 of 1974), S. 149].

Interposition. The act of submitting something as a defence to an opponent's claim.

Interpret. To explain/to translate into intelligible language. [Coroners Act (4 of 1871), S. 19].

Interpret truthfully. To translate correctly.

Interpretare et concordare leges legibus est optimus interpretandi modus. (*Lat.*) (*Maxim*) To interpret and reconcile laws so that they harmonize is the best mode of interpretation. (*Bouvier*).

Interpretatio chartarum benigne facienda est ut res magis valeat quam pereat. (*Lat.*) The construction of deed is to be made liberally, that the thing may rather avail than perish.

Interpretation. The determination of the meaning of a writing; the art of finding out the true sense of any form of words, that is the sense in which their author intended to convey, and of enabling others to derive from them the same idea which the author intended to convey; the art of finding out or collecting the intention of a writer, either from his words, or from other conjecture, or from both; the use of some other signs or marks, besides the words of the speaker or writer, in order to collect his meaning; the mere finding of the true sense of the special form of words used. (*Ame. Cyc.*)

"Interpretation" means the action of explaining the meaning of something. [*Sudevanand* v. *State Through CBI*, (2012) 3 SCC 387, para 28.1]

Process of ascertaining the meaning of a given text [Indian Evidence Act (1 of 1872), S. 3 and Constitution of India, Art. 145(3)]; translation. [CrPC 1973 (2 of 1974), S. 279]; [IPC (45 of 1860), S. 191, *Expln.* 2, ill. (e)].

Interpreter. One who translates orally the words of persons speaking different languages in their presence; a person sworn by a Court to interpret the testimony of a witness, when given in a language other than commonly used by the Court. [CrPC 1973 (2 of 1974), S. 282]; a translator.

Interpritivism. A doctrine of constitutional interpretation which holds that Judges must follow norms of values expressly stated or implied in the language of the constitution.

Interregnum. Interval when state has no normal ruler, specially an interval of pause between two successive reigns.

Interrogation. In criminal law, the process of questions propounded by police to person arrested or suspected to seek solution of crime. Such person is entitled to be informed of his rights, including right to have counsel present, and the consequences of his answers. If the police fail or neglect to give these warnings, the questions and answers are not admissible in evidence at the trial or hearing of the arrested person.

Custodial interrogation. Questioning initiated by law enforcement officers after a person has been taken into custody. (*Black*)

Interrogatories are particular questions in writing, demanded of witnesses or parties brought in to be examined in a case. These interrogatories must be exhibited by the parties in the suit on each side; which are either direct for the party that produces them, or counter on behalf of the adverse party; and generally both plaintiff and defendant may exhibit *direct and counter, or cross Interrogatories.* (*Tomlin*)

Where a man speaks upon a subject of his own accord, he naturally tells the whole of what he knows; but where he is examined on interrogatories formally administered to him, his answers are naturally confined to the particulars to which he is so interrogated; and as the examining party generally knows beforehand the scope of the witness's evidence, he has an opportunity of so shaping his questions as that they may elicit everything in his favour with which the witness is acquainted, and keep back everything of a contrary tendency.

Written questions addressed on behalf of one party to a suit before the trial thereof to the party, who is bound to answer them in writing upon oath. [CPC (5 of 1908), S. 30(a)].

Interrupt. To stop or hinder by breaking in or upon; to prevent from proceeding; to disturb. (*Worcester*)

Interruption. Nothing is an interruption within the meaning of this section unless where there is an actual cessation of the enjoyment by reason of an obstruction by the act of some other than the claimant, and unless such obstruction is submitted to or acquiesced in for one year after the claimant has notice thereof, and of the person making or authorizing the same to be made. [Indian Easements Act (5 of 1882), S. 15, *Expln.* II]

Adverse obstruction. [CrPC 1973 (2 of 1974), S. 345(3)]; [Indian Easements Act (5 of 1882), S. 6].

The occurrence of some act or fact, during the period of prescription, which is sufficient to arrest the running of the statute of limitations.

Lawyer appealing to Magistrate during pendency of proceedings against rude behaviour of *chaprasi* is no interruption of the Court proceedings.

The term "interruption" refers to an adverse obstruction and not a mere discontinuance of user.

Where the tenants of a village having a customary right to graze their cattle in certain uncultivable land, for ten specified months in every year; the fact that a custom has grown up by which the proprietors of the land exclude the cattle for the remaining two months does not constitute an "interruption" of the customary right, but only limits its duration.

The word "interruption" in cl. (*c*) of Section 108 of T.P. Act (4 of 1882) includes disturbance of possession by a person with a paramount title.

Intersect. To cross; literally, to cut into or between; a word which imports the intersection of one line with another.

Interstate. Pertaining to the mutual relations of the states; existing between or including, different states. (*Webster*)

Interstate agreement. An agreement between two states.

Inter state commerce. Interstate commerce is commerce between two or more states of a federal union.

INTERSTATE COMMERCE means the interchange of commodities between citizens of the different states.

'Interstate commerce' is not business done within a state, but is business done between two or more states, or business commenced in one state and ended in another.

The term 'interstate commerce' may be applied to the transportation of merchandise from a place in one state to a place in another.

Intersex. Persons who are born with a chromosomal pattern or physical characteristics that do not clearly fall on one side or the other of a binary male female live. [Michael Kirby, former Judge of the High Court of Australia **as cited in** *Navtej Singh Johar* v. *Union of India,* (2018) 10 SCC 1, para 151].

Interstate law. The rule and principles used to determine controversies between resident of different states.

Interstate sales. When the contract itself involved the movement of goods from the factory situated in one state to the purchaser in another state across the border it is an interstate sale. *Cement Marketing Co.* v. *State of Mysore*, AIR 1963 SC 980, 983. [Constitution of India, Art. 286(2)]

Interstate trade, commerce and intercourse. It means trade, commerce and intercourse throughout the territory of India which, subject to certain restrictions, shall be free. [Constitution of India, Arts. 301-304].

Interstate trade or **commerce.** "INTER STATE TRADE OR COMMERCE", in relation to any weight or measure or other goods which are bought sold, supplied, distributed or delivered by weight, measure or number, means the purchase, sale, supply; distribution or delivery which—

(i) occasions the movement of such weight, measure or other goods from one State to another, or

(ii) is effected by a transfer of document of title to such weight, measure or other goods during its movement from one State to another.

Explanation I—Where any such weight or measure is, or other goods are, delivered to a carrier or other bailee for transmission, the movement of such weight, measure or other goods shall, for the purposes of sub-clause (ii), be deemed to commence at the time of such delivery and terminate at the time when delivery is taken from such carrier or bailee.

Explanation II—Where the movement of any such weight, measure or other goods commences and terminates in the same State, it shall not be deemed to be a movement of such weight, measure or other goods from one State to another merely by reason of the fact that in the course of such movement it passes through the territory of any other State. [Standards of Weights and Measures Act (60 of 1976), S. 2(m)]

The expression "interstate trade or commerce" is not confined to mean trade or commerce between the states as such between a seller state and a purchaser state. It is interstate trade where goods sold or purchased under contracts of sale move from one State to another. Trade movement of goods from one State to another is the insignia of inter-state trade though the trade is very often between individuals, firms, companies and corporations. *Dhiraj Lal* v. *Commissioner of Commercial Taxes,* AIR 1963 Cal 442, 450. [Constitution of India Art, 286]

Interval. Any dividing tract in space of time. Where an "interval" of so many days has to elapse between two events the days are clear days, and have to be reckoned exclusive of both the days between which the interval is to elapse.

A space of time between the recurrence of similar conditions or states; a space between things.

Intervening. Coming between; occurring in the meantime; interfere; modify the course of events.

Intervening act. An unanticipated event which comes between the initial event in a sequence and the end result, as a consequence natural course of events are altered which might have connected a wrongful act to an injury.

Intervening cause. An action which intervenes between the original wrongful act and the ultimate injury loss or damages so that the original wrong doer is not responsible for the injury, loss or damages.

Intervention. The action of intervening; stepping in, or interfering in any affair, so as to affect its course or issue. [TP Act (4 of 1882), S. 69(1)].

Interview. Meeting of persons for purpose of discussion; meeting by a journalist of person whose views he wishes to ascertain for publication in the journal.

Question or converse with especially in order to obtain information or ascertain personal qualities. [Aligarh Muslim University Act (40 of 1920), S. 29(2)(a)].

Intestacy. Condition of a person possessed of property dying without having made a will.

The quality or state of being or dying intestate. [Constitution of India, VII Sch., list, III, Item. 5].

Intestate. A person who dies without making a will; the condition of dying without having made any will. "*Intestate*", means and includes, "every person deceased who has left undisposed of by will the whole, or any portion, of the estate on which he might (if not subject to incapacity) have tested."

Without leaving will. [CPC (5 of 1908), O. VIII, R. 6(3), ill. (b)]; [Hindu Succession Act (30 of 1956), S. 3(1)(g)].

Intestate law. The relevant enactment which governs succession to estates of those who die without a valid will.

Intestate succession. Means and includes, "succession in cases of partial, as well as of total, intestacy."

Intestatus decedit, qui aut omnio testamentum non facit aut non jure fecit, aut id quod fecerat ruptum irritumve factum est ; aut nemo ex eo haeres existit. (*Maxim*) He dies intestate who either has made no will at all or has not made it legally, or whose will which he had made has been annulled or become ineffectual, or to whom there is no living heir. (*Bouvier*)

Intimacy. A term which means nothing more than close and familiar acquaintance. In its ordinary signification, and as generally applied to persons, the word 'intimacy' would be understood to mean a proper friendly relation of the parties; but as employed in a special sense it conveys the idea of an improper relation, an intimacy at least disreputable and degrading.

Intimate. Close in friendship or acquaintance; familiar; confidential. (*Webster*)

To make known; formally to notify [Sale of Goods Act (3 of 1930), S. 43]; close in acquaintance or association; very familiar.

Intimation. Making known; hinting; implying. A formal notification. [CPC (5 of 1908), 1st Sch., App. E, No. 22].

Intimidation. INTIMIDATION is putting a man in fear with a view of inducing him to enter into a contract or to pay money, or to do or abstain from doing some other act. The act of making one timid or fearful, by a declaration of an intention or determination to injure another by the commission of some unlawful act. *Intimidation* includes, any words or acts, intended and calculated to put any person in fear of any injury or danger to himself or to any member of his family or to any person in his employment, or in fear of any injury to or loss of property, business, employment, or means of living.

Intoxicant. Rectified spirit is an intoxicant. *Vijendrajit* v. *State of Bombay*, AIR 1953 SC 247, 248.

Intoxicants is a word used as synonymous with intoxicating liquors.

Intoxicate. Make drunk; elate. This word relates generally to the use of strong drink.

Intoxicated; Intoxication. 'Intoxication' is a word nearly synonymous with 'inebriety,' or 'inebriation,' and is expressive of that state or condition which inevitably follows from taking into the body, by swallowing or drinking, excessive quantities of intoxicating liquors.

The state of being intoxicated. [IPC (45 of 1860), S. 85].

Merely smelling of alcohol does not amount to being in a State of intoxication. Something more is necessary and that is the accused must be in a State of drunkenness. *Connabatula Satya Rao* v. *State,* AIR 1954 Andhra 4.

Intoxicating. Producing or fitted to produce intoxication.

Intoxicating drug. "INTOXICATING DRUG" means *opium, ganja, bhang, charas* and any preparation or admixture thereof, and includes any other intoxicating substance or liquid which the Central Government may, by notification in the Official Gazette declare to be an intoxicating drug for the purposes of this Act. [Cantonments Act (2 of 1924), S. 2(xix)]

Intoxicating liquor. The power to legislate relating to intoxicating liquor comprises of liquor which contains alcohol whether it is potable or not. *State of U.P.* v. *Synthetics & Chemicals Ltd.*, AIR 1980 SC 614, 620. [Constitution of India, Sch. 7, List II, Entry 8]

Intoxication. A defense based on a lack of *criminal intent* associated with intoxication, especially if it is involuntary.

Intoxication, State of. The quality or state of being drunk. [CrPC 1973 (2 of 1974), Sch. 2, Form 32(7)]; [IPC (45 of 1860), S. 510].

Intra-state commerce. Commerce wholly within a state.

Intra-State transmission system. Means any system for transmission of electricity other than an inter-State transmission system. [Electricity Act (36 of 2003), S. 2(37)]

Intra vires. Within the powers; within the authority given by law.

Intranet. An in-house electronic communication system.

The deployment of Internet technology inside an organisation which uses the Internet protocols. An intranet needs no connection to the global public Internet. (*Information Technoloy*)

Internal links between a company's computers that provide similar function to the *Internet* but in house. (*Business Term*)

A private *network* inside a company or organization that uses the same kinds of software that you would find on the public *Internet*, but that is only for internal use. Compare with *extranet.* (*Matisse Enzer-Glossary of Internet Terms*)

A private network inside a company or organization that uses the same kinds of software that you would find on the public Internet, but that is only for internal use. As the Internet has become more popular many of the tools used on the Internet are being used in private networks, for example, many companies have web servers that are available only to employees. Note that an Intranet may not actually be an internet—it may simply be a network. (*Internet and E-commerce*).

(Upper case I) The vast collection of interconnected networks that all use the TCP/IP protocols and that evolved from the ARPANET of the late 60's and early 70's. (*Internet and E-commerce*).

(Lower case i) Any time you connect 2 or more networks together, you have an internet as in international or inter-state. (*Internet and E-commerce*).

Intrastate. Within the boundaries of a state, as distinguished from across state boundaries, which would make something inter- state. (CRAIG R. DUCAT—*Constitutional Interpretation*)

Intrinsic. Internal; relating to some essential nature of something.

Intrinsic ambiguity. An ambiguity which clearly appears on the face of a document, arising from the language itself.

Intrinsic fraud. That fraud which occurs within framework of actual conduct of trial and pertains to and affects determination of issues presented therein, and it may be accomplished by perjury, or by use of false or forged instruments, or by concealment or misrepresentation of evidence. Fraud is "intrinsic fraud" where judgment is founded on fraudulent instruments or perjured evidence or the fraudulent actions pertain to an issue involved in original action and litigated therein.

Intrinsic value. The 'intrinsic value' of a thing is its true, inherent, and essential value, not depending on accident, place, or persons, but the same every where and to every one.

Introduce. To present formally; to bring a bill or measure before the legislature; [Constitution of India, Art. 3, *Prov.* and Art. 109(1)]; to usher or bring a person into a society or body [Indian Partnership Act (9 of 1932), S. 31(2)]; to make known personally

Introduction. (*to a book or writing*) That part of it in which are detailed those facts which elucidate the subject.

The act or process of introducing *i.e.* bringing into; the act of presenting a Bill *etc.* formally; a preliminary, preparatory or initial explaining; the action of making known personally.

Introduction from the Sea. Means transportation into a State of specimens of any species which were taken in the marine enforcement not under the jurisdiction of any State. [Convention on International Trade in Endangered Species of Wild Fauna and Flora (Cites), Art. 1(e)]

Introductory. Serving to introduce something; prefatory; preliminary.

INTRODUCTORY, PRELIMINARY, PREPARATORY. In the case of the *Introductory* the proceeding commonly has a reference to thought and understanding while *preliminary* relates to matters of action. *Preparatory* relates to the purpose rather than the object, or the doer rather than the deed. (*Smith Syn. Dis.*)

Intrude. To enter uninvited; an act of encroachment. [IPC (45 of 1860), S. 509]

Invalid. The word 'invalid' has precisely the same meaning as the two words 'not valid'.

Of no force; without legal force; void. (Art. 255, Constitution of India].

Invalid carriage. "INVALID CARRIAGE" means a motor vehicle specially designed and constructed, and not merely adopted, for the use of a person suffering some physical defect or disability, and used solely by or for such a person. [Motor Vehicles Act (59 of 1988), S. 2(18)]

Invalid will. A will which fails to make an effective dispossession of property.

Invalidate. To render invalid. [Constitution of India, Art. 71(2)]; to render of no force or effect, especially to deprive of legal efficacy.

Invalidation. The action of rendering invalid.

Invalidity. The lack of binding legal force. [TP Act (4 of 1882), S. 30].

Invasion. Hostile inroad into another country; assailing; encroaching on other's rights.

"Invasive alien species". Means a species of animal or plant which is not native to India and whose introduction or spread may threaten or adversely impact wild life or its habitat. [Wild Life (Protection) Act (53 of 1972), section 2(16A)]

Invasive device. Means a device which, in whole or part, penetrates inside the body, either through a body orifice or through the surface of the body. [Medical Devices Rules, 2017, R. 3(w)].

Inveigle. To decoy, to beguile; to entice; to seduce; to wheedle; to persuade to something bad by deceptive arts or flattery, or by any artful or seductive means.

Invention. "INVENTION" means any manner of new manufacture, and includes an improvement and an alleged invention. [Indian Patents and Design Act (2 of 1911), S. 2(8)]

"INVENTION" means a new product or process involving an inventive step and capable of industrial application. [Patents Act (39 of 1970), S. 2(j), (*as amended by Act 38 of 2002, w.e.f. 20.5.2003*)]

Inventive step. Means a feature of an invention that involves technical advance as compared to the existing knowledge or having economic significance or both and that makes the invention not obvious to a person skilled in the art. [Patents Act (39 of 1970), S. 2(1)(ja) *as substituted by Patents (Amendment) Act) (15 of 2005), S. 2(f)*]

Inventory. An itemised written list of all the chattels in a particular place or belonging to a particular estate, such as the estate of an intestate or a bankrupt. [CPC (5 of 1908), O. XXI, R. 12].

Invest—Investment. To invest is to employ for some profitable use; convert into some other form of wealth, usually of a more or less permanent nature; to surround with or place in; to place so that it will be safe and yield a profit. As used in connection with money or capital, to give money for some other property.

To establish in the possession of any office, position, property *etc.*; to endow with power, authority or privilege; to employ money in the purchase of anything from which interest or profit is expected. [IPC (45 of 1860), S. 405, ill. (c)].

Investigate. To inquire into (generally used for inquiry by police). [Indian Evidence Act (1 of 1872), S. 157 and Constitution of India, Art. 61(4)]

Investigating officer. The officer who makes the investigation.

Investigation. "Investigation" includes all the proceedings under this Sanhita for the collection of evidence conducted by a police officer or by any person (other than a Magistrate) who is authorised by a Magistrate in this behalf.

Explanation.—Where any of the provisions of a special Act are inconsistent with the provisions of this Sanhita, the provisions of the special Act shall prevail. [(w.e.f. 1-7-2024) Bharatiya Nagarik Suraksha Sanhita, 2023 (46 of 2023), section 2(1)(l)]

The dictionary meaning is "an examination for the purpose of discovering information about something". [New Lexicon Webster's Dictionary of the English Language as cited *Atul Sharma vs. State of U.P. and Ors.*, 2017 (2) ACR 1801 in para 29]

Investigation is "an official examination of the facts about a situation, crime, etc". It means "to carefully examine the facts of a situation, an event, a crime etc. to find out the truth about it or how it happened." [Oxford Advanced Learner's Dictionary of Current English as cited in *Atul Sharma vs. State of U.P. and Ors.*, 2017 (2) ACR 1801, para 30, 31]

"INVESTIGATION" includes all the proceedings under this Code for the collection of evidence conducted by a police-officer or by any person (other than a Magistrate) who is authorized by a Magistrate in this behalf." [CrPC 1973 (2 of 1974), S. 2(h) and Constitution of India, Art. 142(2)] [Also see S. 2(1)](g) of the Lokpal & Lokayuktas Act, 2013 (1 of 2014)]

Investigating Authority. Means an officer or a team of officers of the Board, which has been directed by the Board, to conduct the investigation of a service provider. [Insolvency and Bankruptcy Board of

India (Inspection and Investigation) Regulations, 2017, Regn. 2(1)(e)].

Investigator. Means a person appointed by the Aircraft Accident Investigation Bureau to investigate an accident o a serious incident as Investigator-in-Charge under Rule 11, or by the Central Government for Formal Investigation under Rule 12, or authorized by Bureau to conduct preliminary investigation under sub-rule (1) of Rule 9 or sub-rule (2) of Rule 7; or an Investigator-in-Charge appointed by DG, CA under Rule 13. [Aircraft (Investigation of Accidents and Incidents) Rules, 2017, R. 2(20)].

Investigator-in-Charge. Means a person charged, on the basis of his or her qualifications, with the responsibility for the organization, conduct and control of an investigation;

Note: Nothing in this clause shall preclude the functions of an Investigator-in-Charge being assigned to the Court referred to in Rule 12 or other body. [Aircraft (Investigation of Accidents and Incidents) Rules, 2017, R. 2(21)].

Investing company. For the purpose of this clause, "the investing company or the venture of a company" means a body corporate whose investment in the company would result in the company becoming an associate company of the body corporate. [Companies Act (18 of 2013), S. 2(76)(viii), *Explanation* as substituted by Amending Act 1 of 2018].

Investiture. Induction of a person to an office or dignity.

Investment. An expenditure of money for income or profit; capital outlay; the sum invested.

The word "Investment" is not a word of art but has to be interpreted in a popular sense. It is not capable of legal definition but a word of current vernacular. The words "invest" and "investment" are to be taken in the business sense of laying out of money for interest or profit. [Companies Act (1 of 1956), S. 292(3)] (Replaced by Company Act 2013)

Investment banker. Means an Investment banker registered with the Securities and Exchange Commission in USA, or the Financial Services Authority in UK, or appropriate regulatory authority in Germany, France, Singapore or Japan. [Foreign Exchange Management (Transfer or Issue of any Foreign Security) Regulations, 2000, Reg. 2(l)]

Investment business. Method of dealing in, arranging deals in, managing and advising on investments.

Investment company. Investment company is a financial institution, like a mutual fund invests its capital in other companies by purchasing shares or otherwise.

"INVESTMENT COMPANY" means a company whose principal business is the acquisition of shares, stocks, debentures or other securities. [Insurance Act (4 of 1938), S. 2(10A)]

"INVESTMENT COMPANY" mean a company whose gross total income (as defined in Section 80B of the Income-tax Act) consists mainly of income which is chargeable under the heads "Income from house property", "Capital gains" and "Income from other sources" or of income by way of interest on securities. [Finance Act (49 of 1991), S. 9(d)]

"INVESTMENT COMPANY" for the purposes of section 186 of Act 18 of 2013, the expression 'investment company' means a company whose principal business is the acquisition of shares, debentures or other securities and a company will be deemed to be principally engaged in the business of acquisition of shares, debentures or other securities, if its assets in the form of investment in shares, debentures or other securities constitute not less than fifty per cent of its total assets, or if its income derived from investment business constitutes not less than fifty per cent as a proportion of its gross income. [*Explanation* (a) to section 186 of the Companies Act, 2013 (18 of 2013)]

Investment depreciation reserve. Money reserved to protect a concern against the fall in value of the investment.

Investment exchange. An organisation which offers to deal in securities with a subscriber whose identity is not revealed to other subscribers and which records and confirms acceptance of its offers.

Investment in securities. The word 'investment' in itself literally, means nothing more or less than to lay out money; and, therefore, where a person purchases securities whether as his stock-in-trade or by way of capital investment, he is in either case investing in securities.

Investment on repatriation basis. Means an investment the sale proceeds of which are, net of taxes, eligible to be repatriated out of India, and the expression 'Investment on non-repatriation basis', shall be construed accordingly. [Foreign Exchange Management (Transfer or Issue of Security by a Person Resident Outside India) Regulations, 2000, Reg. 2(vi)]

Investor. For the purposes of Chapter XII-EA of Act 43 of 1961, 'investor' means a person who is holder of any securitised debt instrument or securities issued by the securitisation trust. [(w.e.f. 1-6-2013) *Explanation* (*a*) to section 115TC of the Income-tax Act, 1961 (43 of 1961). Also see (w.e.f. 1-4-2014) *Explanation* to section 10(35A) of the Income-tax Act, 1961 (43 of 1961)]

Invitat culpam qui peccatum praeterit. (*Maxim*) He encourages a fault who overlooks a transgression. (*Peloubet*)

Invitation. A mere permission on licence by a railraod company to cross its road is not an invitation to do so.

Safety gates at a railroad crossing, which should be closed in case of danger, if standing open, may amount to an invitation to the traveller on the high way to cross.

Invitation to treat. It is advertising of goods and services that invite an offer from a customer to buy a product or service. It is different from an Offer made by a seller or service provider. Here a customer picks up a product and makes an offer to purchase and seller accepts it forming a legal contract. [Karnika Seth, *Computers Internet and New Technology Laws*, 2021, LexisNexis, Glossary of Legal Terms].

Invito beneficium non datur. (*Lat.*) No benefit is given to one unwilling.

Invoice. An invoice is written account of particulars of goods delivered to a purchaser, and of their prices, and the charges concerning them.

A list of the particular items of goods shipped or sent to a factor, consignee or purchaser with their value or price and charges. [Trade and Merchandise Marks Act (43 of 1958)

Invitee. "INVITEE" means a subject matter expert, who may be invited to share his knowledge on the subject and ceases to continue his association with the Scientific Committee or Scientific Panel on completion of the limited purpose of such invitation. [Food Safety and Standards Authority of India (Transaction of Business and Procedures for the Scientific Committee and Scientific Panels) Regulations, 2016, Regn. 2(1)(e)].

Invoke. To resort to. [Art. V(1), Foreign Awards (Recognition and Enforcement) Act (45 of 1961), S. 76(1)(c)].

Involuntary. Not voluntary or willing; contrary or opposed to will or desire; independent of volition or consenting action of mind; unwilling; unintentional; not accidental. (Century Dic.)

Not done willingly or by choice. [Indian Trusts Act (2 of 1882), S. 30].

Involuntary conduct. A conduct which cannot be controlled because one is suffering from a physical or mental condition or is acting under duress.

Involve. To comprise, to contain, to include by rational or logical construction; to connect with something as a natural or logical consequence or effect; to include necessarily; to imply; (*Webster*)

To entangle, implicate in charge or crime.

Involves. A case cannot be said to involve a question unless its decision is necessary for the purpose of the case.

The term 'involves' implies a considerable degree of necessity. The mere circumstance that a question of law is raised in a case would not justify the inference that the proposed appeal 'involves' a question of law as envisaged under Art. 133 unless it is necessary to decide the question of law for a proper decision of the case. *Israr Ahmad* v. *State of U.P.*, AIR 1993 All 87, 89. [Constitution of India, Art. 133 (1)(*a*)]

Inward supply. "inward supply" in relation to a person, shall mean receipt of goods or services or both whether by purchase, acquisition or any other means with or without consideration [The Central Goods and Services Tax Act, 2017 (12 of 2017), S. 2(67)]

I.P. member of the Indian Police Service. Means a person who was appointed to the Police Service of the Crown in India known as the Indian Police and who on the appointed day is a member of the Indian Police Service. [Former Secretary of State Service Officers (Conditions of Service) Act (59 of 1972), S. 2(d)]

Ipse dixit. (*Lat.*) He said it to himself.

Ipsissima verba. (*Lat.*) In the very same words.

Ipso facto. By the fact itself; by the very act itself (*Rapalje & L.L. Dict.*); by the mere fact automatically. (*Tomlin*)

IPv4. Internet Protocol, version 4. The most widely used version of the Internet Protocol (the "IP" part of *TCP/IP*).

IPv4 allows for a theoretical maximum of approximately four billion *IP Numbers* (technically 2^{32}), but the actual number is far less due to inefficiencies in the way blocks of numbers are handled by networks. The gradual adoption of IPv6 will solve this problem. (Matisse Enzer-Glossary of Internet Terms)

IRC. (abbr.) Internet Relay Chat. Basically a huge multi-user live chat facility. There are a number of major IRC servers around the world which are linked to each other. Anyone can create a channel and anything that anyone types in a given channel is seen by all others in the channel. Private channels can (and are) created for multi-person conference calls. (Matisse Enzer-Glossary of Internet Terms)

Iron and steel. The expression "iron and steel" means not only 'iron and steel' in the original condition but also 'iron and steel' in the shape of bars, flats and plates. *State of M.B.* v. *Hiralal*, AIR 1966 SC 1546, 1547.

Irrational. Unreasonable; illogical; insane; not endowed with reason.

Irreconcilable. That which cannot be reconciled; incompatible.

Irrecoverable. That which cannot be recovered or remedied.

Irredeemable. That which cannot be redeemed; irreclaimable; hopeless.

Irrefragable. Unanswerable; not to be controverted; impossible to refute.

Irregular. Not according to rule; improper or insufficient, by reason of departure form the prescribed course. Not regular; contrary to rule.

Irregular Corps. The expression "IRREGULAR CORPS" means any force other than the Regular Forces or the Territorial Army or the National Cadet Corps raised and maintained in India under the authority of the Central Government or any other force which may be notified in this behalf by order published in the Official Gazette. [(Indian) Tolls (Army and Air Force) Act (11 of 1901), S. 2(f)]

Irregularity. An irregularity is defined to be the want of adherence to some prescribed rule or mode of proceeding; and it consists either in omitting to do something that is necessary for the due and orderly conducting of a suit, or doing it in an unreasonable time or improper manner.

The quality or state of being irregular. [CrPC 1973 (2 of 1974), S. 461 and Constitution of India, Art. 122(1)].

The word 'irregularity' covers any case that has not been done in the manner laid down by the statute in respect of what that matter might be. The word does not cover a case of procedural irregularity only. *Martin Burn Ltd.* v. *Calcutta Corporation*, AIR 1966 SC 529, 534.

'Irregularity' and 'illegality'. An appointment which was made throwing all constitutional obligations and statutory rules to the winds would render the same illegal whereas 'irregularity' presupposes substantial compliance with the rules. [*State of U.P.* v. *Desh Raj*, (2007) 1 SCC 257, 260, para 10. **relying on** *State of Mysore* v. *S.V. Narayanappa,* AIR 1967 SC 1071; *R.N. Najundappa* v. *T. Thimmiah*, (1972) 1 SCC 409; *B.N. Nagarajan* v. *State of Karnataka*, (1979) 4 SCC 507]

Irregularity in publishing the sale. The irregular preparation of the actual proclamation definitely announcing that a sale will be held and giving particulars regarding the property to be sold is an "irregularity in publishing the sale" within the O. XXI, R. 90 of CPC (5 of 1908).

Irregularly. Not regularly; not inconformity with rule or principle. [TP Act (4 of 1882), S. 69(3)].

Irrelevancy. (*in the Law of Pleadings*) An answer is said to be 'irrelevant' when the matter which it sets forth has no bearing on the question in dispute, does not affect the subject-matter of the controversy, and can in no way affect or assist the decision of the Court.

Irrelevant. Not pertinent; without relation to the matter in issue; redundant; a term which has the signification of not applicable.

In the law of evidence, means not relevant; not relating to or applicable to the matter in issue; not supporting the issue. (*Black*)

Not relevant. [Indian Evidence Act (1 of 1872), S. 24].

Irrelevant evidence. Facts not in issue or not tending to prove facts in issue.

Irreparable. That which cannot be repaired, restored, or adequately compensated for in money, or where the compensation cannot be safely measured; that which cannot be repaired, retrieved, put back again, or atoned for.

Irreparable injury. A term which means that the injury must be a grievous one, a material one, and not adequately reparable in damages. That which cannot be measured by any known pecuniary standard. The basic principle on which injunctions should be issued is that the plaintiff must show that an injunction is necessary to protect him from irreparable injury and that mere inconvenience is not enough. By the term "irreparable injury" is meant injury which is substantial and could never be remedied or adequately remedied or atoned for by damages.

By the term 'irreparable injury' is not meant that there must not be any physical possibility of repairing the injury. All that is meant is that the injury would be a grievous one, and at least a material one and not adequately reportable in damages.

Irrepleviable or Irreplevisable. That which can not be replevied or set at large on sureties.

Irresistible force. Force that cannot be controlled or resisted. [TP Act (4 of 1882), S. 108(m)]; [Requisitioning and Acquisition of Immovable Property Act (30 of 1952), S. 6(1)].

Irresistible impulse. The absence of sufficient mental power to choose between right and wrong.

A person acts under an 'irresistible impulse' when, by reason of duress or mental disease, he has lost the power to choose between right and wrong, to avoid doing the act in question; his free agency being at the time destroyed.

'IRRESISTIBLE IMPULSE' in criminal law, is that uncontrollable impulse produced by disease of the mind, which is sufficient to override the reason and judgment, and obliterate the sense of right as to the act done, and deprive the accused of the power to choose between them. This impulse is born of the disease, and when it exists capacity to know the nature of the act is gone.

Irrespective of. Without respect or regard to; independent or regardless of. [TP Act (4 of 1882), S. 51].

Irretrievable breakdown. A broad ground for divorce which is predicated on the development of incompatibility between marriage partners and that is used in many States as a sole ground for no fault divorce.

Irrevocable. That which cannot be revoked.

Irrevocable offer. An offer with which an offerror makes a binding promise not to withdraw the offer.

Irrevocable transfer. "IRREVOCABLE TRANSFER" includes a transfer of assets which, by the terms of the instrument effecting it is not revocable for a period exceeding six years or during the lifetime of the transferee, and under which the transferor derives no direct or indirect benefit but does not include a transfer of assets if such instrument—

(i) contain any provision for the re-transfer, directly or indirectly, of the whole or any part of the assets or income therefrom to the transferor, or

(ii) in any way gives the transferor a right to re-assume power, directly or indirectly, over the whole or any part of the assets or income therefrom. [Wealth-tax Act (27 of 1957), S. 4(b)]

A transfer that cannot be revoked, repealed or annulled. [Welath-tax Act (27 of 1957), S. 4(5)].

Irrevocable trust. A trust which cannot be terminated by the settlor once it is created.

Irrigated land. Means land irrigated by flow irrigation by canal constructed or maintained, improved or controlled by the Central or the State Government or by a body corporate constituted under any law but does not include water logged or sand-cast lands. [Orissa Land Reforms (Amendment) Act (13 of 1965), S. 2(13)]

Irrigation project. Means the planning, construction, maintenance and management of,

(i) major irrigation project having irrigable command area of more than 10,000 hectares,

(ii) medium irrigation project having irrigable command area of more than 2000 hectares and upto 10,000 hectares.

(iii) minor irrigation project having irrigable command area of more than 250 hectares and upto 2,000 hectares, and shall include command area development, flood control and other allied activities. [Maharashtra Krishna Valley Development Corporation Act (Mah. Act 15 of 1996), S. 2(d)]

Irrigation-work. "IRRIGATION WORKS" means a work or system of works, natural or artificial, not being a minor irrigation work as defined in Section 2 of the Rajasthan Minor Irrigation Works Acts, 1953, and includes—

(a) any canal, channel, pipe or reservoir constructed, maintained or controlled by the State Government for the supply or storage of water.

(b) any work, embankment, structure or supply and escape-channel connected with such canal, channel, pipe or reservoir.

(c) any water course.

(e) any part of a river, stream, lake or natural collection of water or natural drainage channel to which the State Government applies the provisions of Part II of this Act. [Irrigation and Drainage Act 1954, Section 3(1)(ii)]

Irrigation. The action of supplying land with water by artificial means. [IPC (45 of 1860), S. 430].

Irrigation by percolation. The words "irrigation by percolation" cover cases where sub-soil water derived by percolation from a river or channel belonging to Government is taken by percolation to the roots of trees.

Irruption. The action of bursting or breaking in. [Mines Act (35 of 1952), S. 23(1)(b)].

Is. The word 'is' although normally referring to the present often has a future meaning. It may also have a past signification as in the sense of 'has been'. *F.S. Gandhi* v. *Commissioner of Wealth-tax*, AIR 1991 SC 1866, 1869. [Wealth Tax Act (27 of 1957), S. 2(*b*) (2)(*iii*)]

Is being carried on. The expression 'is being carried on' occurring in sub-sec. (7) relates to the state of affairs at the time the representation to the Registrar is made and not to something which is a matter of past history. *Coimbatore Spinning and Weaving Co. Ltd.* v. *M.S. Srinivasan,* AIR 1959 Mad 229, 232. [Companies Act (1 of 1956), S. 234(7)]

Is damnum dat qui jubet dare ejus vero nulla culpa est cui parere necesses est. (*Maxim*) He occasions a loss who gives orders to cause it; but no blame attaches to him who is under the necessity of obeying. (Morgan)

Is living in adultery. Living in adultery means, continuous course of adulterous life as distinguished from one or two lapses from virtue.

Is otherwise invalid. The words 'is otherwise invalid' are perfectly general and intended to be so. They cover all forms of invalidity, including invalidities which amount to nullities. *Saha & Co.* v. *Ishar Singh Kripal,* AIR 1956 Cal 321, 326 (FB). [Arbitration Act (10 of 1940) (*repealed*), S. 30(*c*)]

The non-existence or invalidity of an arbitration agreement of reference are neither contemplated by nor included in the words 'or is otherwise invalid'. [Arbitration Act (10 of 1940) (*repealed*), S. 30(c)]

'Is', 'resides', 'last resided'. The expression 'is' cannot be given the same meaning as the word 'resides' or the expression 'last resided' under Section 126(1) of the Code. It is wider in its concept than the word resides and what matters is his physical presence at the particular point of time. It cannot be construed to be a fleeting presence, though it may not necessarily be for considerable length of time as the expression 'resides' may 'require'. *Vijay Kumar Prasad* v. *State of Bihar*, AIR 2004 SC 2123 : (2004) 5 SCC 196, 200, para 15. [CrPC, 1973 (2 of 1974), S. 126(1)]

ISDN. (*abbr.*) Integrated Services Digital Network. A digital telephone network, ISDN can dramatically speed up transfer of information over the Internet or over a remote LAN connection, especially rich media like graphics, audio or video or applications. Out-of-band signalling is used to communicate information simultaneously, over fewer channels than would otherwise be needed. Typically an domestic ISDN line runs 128 kb per second although far higher speeds are possible with commercial links. (*Information Technology*)

Basically a way to move more data over existing regular phone lines. ISDN is available to much of the USA and in most markets it is priced very comparably to standard analog phone circuits. It can provide speeds of roughly 128,000 bits-per-second over regular phone lines. In practice, most people will be limited to 56,000 or 64,000 bits-per-second.

Unlike *DSL, ISDN* can be used to connected to many different locations, one at a time, just like a regular telephone call, as long the other location also has ISDN. (*Matisse Enzer-Glossary of Internet Terms*)

Isolated. Placed or standing apart or alone; solitary.

Isolation. The separation from other things or persons. [Mines Act (35 of 1952), S. 22(2)].

Issuable plea. A plea which raises a defence on the merits of the case, and on which a plaintiff may take issue and go to trial.

Issue. The word 'issue' includes offspring of both sexes.

An adopted son does not fall within the meaning of the term 'issue.'

"Issue" is a general name, including all, even to the remotest, descendants.

The word 'issue' is a general term, which, if not qualified or explained, may be construed to include grandchildren as well as children.

The word 'issues' ordinarily means descendants of all degress.

Son's son would be issue how-low-soever. *Kunju Kesavan* v. *M.M. Philip*, AIR 1964 SC 164, 166.

All the copies of a periodical or newspaper printed for a specific day or month, produced and made available at once or on a certain date; an offspring [TP Act (4 of 1882), S. 17(2)(ii)]; a point arising for decision out of the allegation of the plaintiff and the defendant in a cause [Constitution of India, Art. 132(3), expln.]; the action of sending or giving out officially or publicly; to cause to become available by officially putting forth or distributing or granting or proclaiming or promulgating.

"ISSUE" means to put a coin into circulation for use as money. [S. 2(e) of the Coinage Act, 2011 (11 of 2011)]

"Issues: charges". "Issues" are not the same as charges. They are not framed prior to the commencement of trial. They are only "identified" at the time of writing the judgement. [*Vinubhai Ranchhodbhai Patel* v. *Rajivbhai Dudabhai Patel*, (2018) 7 SCC 743, para 36].

Issue, In. In controversy.

Issue joined means an issue of fact reached by the parties, as distinguished from cases where the defendant does not plead or appear, and thus no issue is raised.

The words 'after issue joined' were construed to mean after the end of the pleadings.

By the '*matter in issue*' is to be understood that matter upon which the plaintiff proceeds by his action, and which the defendant controverts by his pleadings.

Issue notice. Does not always mean mere posting of notice. It refers sometimes to actual service of notice.

Issue of capital. Means the issuing or creation of any securities, whether for cash or otherwise and includes the capitalisation of profits or reserves for the purpose of converting partly paid-up shares into fully paid-up shares or increasing the par value of shares already issued. [Capital Issues (Control) Act (29 of 1947), S. 2(b)]

Issue of fact. An issue of fact arises when the allegations in an indictment are denied by the defendant, or the allegations of any subsequent pleading are controverted.

Issue of law. Is an issue upon a matter of law or consisting of matter of law. (*Burril*)

Issue of process. Going out of the hands of the clerk, expressed or implied, to be delivered to the process server for service. A writ or notice is *issued* when it is put in proper form and placed in an officer's hands for service, at the time it becomes a perfected process.

Issued. An execution is "*issued*" only when it is properly attested by a clerk, and delivered to the process server to be executed by him.

Any process may be considered 'issued' if made out and placed in the hands of a person authorised to serve it, and with a *bona fide* intent to have it served.

DISCIPLINARY PROCEEDINGS. The word 'issued' (in the context of issue of a charge-sheet) means that the decision to initiate disciplinary proceedings is taken and translated into action by despatch of the charge-sheet leaving no doubt that the decision had been taken. *Delhi Development Authority* v. *H.C. Khurana*, AIR 1993 SC 1488, 1493.

The word 'issued' means and implies that the voluntary submission of the returns by the assessee has been done before such notice was served on the assessee. *C.N.T.* v. *Kundan Lal Behari Lal* (1975) 99 ITR 581 (SC). [Income-tax Act (43 of 1961), S. 273-A]

Issued capital. Means such capital as the company issues from time to time for subscription. [S. 2(50) of the Companies Act, 2013 (18 of 2013)]

Issued generally. Means, in relation to a prospectus, issued to persons irrespective of their being existing members or debenture-holders of the body corporate to which the prospectus relates. [Companies Act (1 of 1956), S. 2(22)]

Issuer. Means any person making an issue of securities. [Depositories Act (22 of 1996), S. 2(f)] [Indian Stamp Act (2 of 1899), section 2(15A)]

Issuing company. Means an Indian Company permitted to issue Foreign Currency Convertible Bonds or ordinary shares of that company against Global Depository Receipts. [Issue of Foreign

Currency Convertible Bonds And Ordinary Shares (Through Depository Receipt Mechanism) Scheme, 1993, S. 2(d)]

It is taking palce. The use of the present progressive tense is to denote some thing which is taking palce at present. What has already taken place cannot be described by saying that it is taking place. *U.D.S. Mills* v. *S.S.L. Railways*, AIR 1963 SC 217, 220. [Indian Railways Act (9 of 1890), S. 41(1)(*b*)(*c*)]

Ita utere tuo ut alienum non laedas. (*Maxim*) Use your own property so as not to injure your neighbour's.

Item. An 'item' is a separate particular of an account.

An 'item,' as used with reference to an itemized account, means an article, a separate particular in an account.

An entry in an account; a clause of a document.

Itenerate. To travel on a circuit for the purpose of holding Court.

J

Jaggery. "Jaggery" or *gur* means any product obtained by boiling or processing juice pressed out of sugarcane. *Shakkar* being so obtained would be comprehended within the definition given in Para A. 07.05. *Mohammed Yamin* v. *State of Uttar Pradesh,* AIR 1973 SC 484. [Prevention of Food Adulteration Act, 1954, Rules, Appendix B, para A. .07.05]

Jagir. A tenure common under the Mohammadan government, in which the public revenues of a given tract of land were made over to a servant of the state together with the powers requisite to enable him to collect and appropriate such revenue, and administer the general government of the district. The assignment was either conditional or unconditional; in the former case, some public service, as the levy and maintenance of troops, or other specified duty, was engaged for; the latter was left to the entire disposal of the grantee. The assignment was either for stated term, or, more usually, for the life time of the holder, lapsing on his death, to the state, although not unusually renewed to his heir, on payment of a *nazarana*, or fine, and sometimes specified to be a hereditary assignment.

Both in its popular sense and legislative practice, the word '*Jagir*' is used as connoting State grants which conferred on the grantees rights 'in respect of land revenue'. *Thakur Amar Singhji* v. *State of Rajasthan*, AIR 1955 SC 504, 521.

The expression '*Jagir*' is apposite only in the context of alienation of land revenue recoverable from the tillers. *Dhiraj Himmatsinghji* v. *State of Rajasthan*, AIR 1987 SC 82, 86.

Jagir land. "JAGIR LAND" includes also a share held hereditarily of the revenues of a Government village, but does not include *siri* or *mamul* or garden grants. [Bom. Act XX of 1896 (Incumbered Estates (Sindh) S. 2, Cl. 1].

"JAGIR LANDS" in relation to any office of Village Police means lands by whatever name described or locally known whether or not recorded as such in the settlement papers, held as emolument in respect of such office. [Orissa Offices of Village Police (Abolition) Act (3 of 1964), S. 2(e)]

Jagirdar. One who holds a *jagir*.

Jail. A jail is a house or building used for the purpose of a public prison, or where persons under arrest are kept. The word 'jail' means any place of confinement used for detaining a prisoner.

A place or building for the confinement of persons committed by process of law. [CrPC 1973 (2 of 1974), Sch. II, form 15].

Jail delivery, Commission of. One of the commissions issued to judges of assize in England to try all accused persons held in jail until the arrival of the judges at the circuit town, and to deliver, *i.e.* discharge, those who were acquitted.

Jailer. One who has charge of a jail or prison and prisoners.

Java. A programming language that allows small programmes to be sent over a network and can run on any machine. (*Penelope Lawrence*) (*Internet*)

Universal computer language run by a program built into browsers. (*Cyber Law*)

A computer language developed by Sun Microsystems. Java was designed to meet the challenges of application development in the context of heterogeneous, network-wide distributed environments. Paramount among these challenges is secure delivery of applications that consume the minimum of system resources, can run on any hardware and software platform, and can be extended dynamically. (*Information Technology*)

Java is a network-oriented programming language invented by Sun Microsystems that is specifically designed for writing programs that can be safely downloaded to your computer through the Internet and immediately run without fear of viruses or other harm to your computer or files. Using small Java programs (called "Applets"); Web pages can include functions such as animations, calculators, and other fancy tricks.

We can expect to see a huge variety of features added to the Web using Java, since you can write a Java program to do almost anything a regular computer program can do, and then include that Java program in a Web page. (*Internet and E-commerce*)

Java is a network-friendly programming language invented by Sun Microsystems.

Java is often used to build large, complex systems that involve several different computers interacting across networks, for example transaction processing systems.

Java is also becoming popular for creating programs that run in small electronic devicws, such as mobile telephone.

A very common use of Java is to create programs that can be safely downloaded to your computer through the Internet and immediately run without fear of viruses or other harm to your computer or files. Using small Java programs (called "*Applets*"), Web pages can include functions such as animations, calculators, and other fancy tricks. (*Matisse Enzer-Glossary of Internet Terms*)

Java applet. A small program written in Java which is embedded within another application—usually a web Browser—and which can run on any system that runs the other application. (*Information Technology*)

Java chat rooms. Real-time chat via a Java applet that allows visitors to your Web site to engage in live discussion with you or with each other. You can provide it just for fun, or use it to interact with your customers in realtime. (*Cyber Law*)

JavaScript. JavaScript is a programming language that is mostly used in web pages, usually to add features that make the web page more interactive. When JavaScript is included in an *HTML* file it relies upon the browser to interpret the JavaScript. When JavaScript is combined with *Cascading Style Sheets* (CSS), and later versions of HTML (4.0 and later) the result is often called *DHTML*. (*Matisse Enzer-Glossary of Internet Terms*)

JavaScript was invented by Netscape and was going to be called "LiveScript", but the name was changed to JavaScript to cash in on the popularity of Java. JavaScript and Java are two different programming languages. (*Internet and E-commerce*).

JDK. (*abbr.*) Java Development Kit. A software development package from Sun Microsystems that implements the basic set of tools needed to write, test and debug *Java* applications and *applets*. (*Matisse Enzer-Glossary of Internet Terms*)

Jeopardy. Hazard; danger; peril. The risk of conviction and punishment.

Jeopardy, Double. Protection from such jeopardy has been provided in English common law '*nemo debet Vexari*' (meaning that a man may not be put twice in peril for the same offence) and in the Fifth Amendment to U.S. Constitution. In India, no person can be prosecuted and punished for the same offence more than once, the ambit and content of this guarantee are narrower than the American doctrine of 'double jeopardy'. Article 20(2) bars a second prosecution only where the accused has been both prosecuted and punished for the same offence previously;

American principle is that there may be jeopardy even though the person was not actually punished in the previous proceeding.

Jetsam, jettison, and jetson. Anything thrown out of a ship, being in danger of wreck, and by the waves driven to the shore. (*Tomlin*)

Cargo thrown into the sea and goods which have been voluntarily cast over-board from a vessel in a storm or other contingency to lighten the ship.

The throwing overboard of goods from necessity to lighten the vessel in a storm, or to prevent capture or for any other cause. [Marine Insurance Act (11 of 1963), S. 2(e)].

A carrier by water may, when, in case of extreme peril, (it is necessary for the safety of the ship or cargo), throw overboard or otherwise sacrifice any or all the cargo or appurtenances of the ship. Throwing property therefrom for such purpose is called 'jettison,' and the loss incurred thereby is called a 'general average loss.'

Jetty. A projection; a kind of pier.

A "jetty" is an approach to a steamer and a landing place for the passengers travelling on such steamer. So a 'jetty' is a part of a 'steamer', which is included within the word 'railway' within the meaning of Sec. 82-A(1) of the Act. *Mohd. Khaliludin* v. *UOI*, AIR 1962 Pat 109, 112. [Indian Railways Act (9 of 1890), Ss. 3(2) and 82A(1)]

Jewel. A precious stone; a gem; a valuable stone set and prepared for wear; an ornament of dress, usually made of a precious metal, having precious stones as a part of its design.

An ornament of precious metal often set with stones or finished with enamel work [IPC (45 of 1860), S. 511, ill (a)]; a precious stone.

"Jewel" and "Jewellery." "JEWELLERY" includes—

(i) ornaments made of gold, silver, platinum or any other precious metal or any alloy containing one or more of such precious metals, whether or not containing any precious or semi-precious stones, and whether or not worked or sewn into any wearing apparel;

(ii) precious or semi-precious stones, whether or not set in any furniture, utensils or other article or worked or sewn into any wearing apparel. [Wealth-tax Act (27 of 1957), S. 5, *Expln.* (a)]

The terms "jewel" and "jewellery", refer to articles of value for adornment, especially those made from gold, silver or precious stones. The terms are, therefore, wide enough to cover not merely precious stones or articles of adornment made with the use of precious stones, but also other articles of value made from gold, silver, platinum or precious metals. Ordinarily speaking, when a person talks about jewelry, he includes ornaments which are made of gold, silver or any other precious metal also irrespective of whether these articles have precious stones embedded in them or not. *Commissioner of Wealth Tax* v. *Binapani Chakravarty,* AIR 1995 SC 1380.

Jiwai land. Means land held by a cadet of the alienee's family for the purpose of maintenance. [Gujarat Surviving Alienations Abolition Act (33 of 1963), S. 2(16)]

Jiwaidar. Means a cadet of the alienee's family holding *Jiwai* land for his maintenance. [Gujarat Surviving Alienations Abolition Act, 1963 (33 of 1963), S. 2(17)]

Job. A particular piece of work; something to be done; any undertaking of a defined or restricted character. (*Century*)

Job work.."Job work" means any treatment or process undertaken by a person on goods belonging to another registered person and the expression "job worker" shall be construed accordingly [The Central Goods and Services Tax Act, 2017 (12 of 2017), S. 2(68)]

Jobber. A merchant who purchases goods from importers or manufacturers and sells to retailers (*Webster*); a person who sells to any one who comes to him at a fraction above the market price, and buys of any one at a fraction below the market price.

Jobbing. The practice of a middleman or stock jobber. [Income-tax Act (43 of 1961), S. 43(5)(c)].

Join. To unite; act together; to connect; to join in the execution of an instrument.

To bring together; to combine; to enter into or to take upon employment.

The word 'join,' as used in a statute requiring the husband and wife to join in the conveyance of the wife's separate property means must unite—that is, act together—in the execution of the deed.

Joinder. A joining of parties as plaintiffs or defendants; a joining of causes of actions or defence. (*Webster*)

The act of joining.

Joinder of causes of action. Joining together two or more causes of action in the same suit or proceeding. [CPC (5 of 1908), O. II, R. 3(1)].

Joinder of charges. The entire tenor of the provisions of S. 239 indicates that several persons could be tried together for several offences committed in the circumstances mentioned therein. Under S. 239(b) (now S. 223 of CrPC 1973 (2 of 1974) persons accused of several offences and persons accused of abetment thereof could be tried together at one trial. *K. Satwant Singh* v. *State of Punjab,* AIR 1960 SC 266.

Section 239(b) (now S. 223 of CrPC, 1973) does not permit the trial of a principal offender and a person accused of abetment unless the trial relates to only one offence. (*Bakshish Singh* v. *State,* AIR 1959 P&H 448).

Joinder of parties. The joining of several parties as plaintiffs or defendants in the same suit or action.

The joining of all or any of those persons as plaintiffs or defendants in whom the right to any relief is alleged to exist, or who is alleged to possess any interest in the subject-matter of litigation or who in the view of the Court, is a proper or necessary party for the adjudication. [CPC (5 of 1908), O. I, R. 6].

Joining together. A case of two or more political parties agreeing to form a new political party while retaining their separate identity. *Ramashanker Kaushik* v. *Election Commission of India,* AIR 1974 SC 445, 452. [Election Symbol (Reservation and Allotment) Order (1968), Para 16(1)(2)]

Joint. Joined; combined; involving the united activity of two or more. [CPC (5 of 1908), S. 135A(1)(c)].

'Joint' is defined as united; combined; done by or between two or more unitedly; shared by or between two or more.

Joint action. Action brought by two or more as plaintiffs or against two or more as defendants; an action in which two or more unite, or are united as parties.

Joint and several. Constituting or relating to rights which two or more persons entitled thereto may assert either together or separately or to duties or liabilities of two or more persons for which they may be held liable either together or separately.

Joint and several liability. A liability is said to be joint and several when the creditor may sue one or more of the parties to such liability separately or all of them together at his option.

Joint and several promissory note. A pronote in which the executants are jointly as well as severally liable. [Indian Contract Act (9 of 1872), S. 132, ill].

Joint authorship. As to literary work, when several persons contribute to the execution of a common design, each can claim joining authorship. A person cannot claim joint authorship by merely making alterations, additions and the like.

Joint-body. Means any bilateral or multilateral commission or other appropriate institutional arrangements for cooperation between the riparian parties. [U.N. Convention on the Protection and Use of Transboundary Watercourses and International Lakes, March 17, 1992, Art. 1(4)]

Joint bond. A joint bond is one executed and delivered by two or more persons jointly.

Joint cadre.—

(a) in relation to the Indian Administrative Service, has the meaning assigned to it in the Indian Administrative Service (Cadre) Rules, 1954;

(b) in relation to the Indian Police Service, has the meaning assigned to it in the Indian Police Service (Cadre) Rules, 1954; and

(c) in relation to the Indian Forest Service, has the meaning assigned to it in the Indian Forest Service (Cadre) Rules, 1966. [North-Eastern Areas (Reorganisation) Act (81 of 1971), S. 61(1)]

Joint committee. A committee appointed by both Houses of a Legislature for the purpose of considering joint action or resolving differences between the two Houses. [CPC (5 of 1908), S. 135A(1)(c)].

Joint Commissioner. 'Joint Commissioner' means a person appointed to be a Joint Commissioner or an Additional Commissioner under sub-section (1) of section 117. [Income-tax Act (43 of 1961), section 2(28C)]

Joint Commissioner (Appeals). "Joint Commissioner (Appeals)" means a person appointed to be a Joint Commissioner of Income-tax (Appeals) or an Additional Commissioner of Income-tax (Appeals) under sub-section (1) of section 117. [Income-tax Act (43 of 1961), section 2(28CA)]

Joint contract. One in which the contacting parties are jointly bound to perform the promise or obligation or receive the benefit of the same.

Joint contractors. Those who contract jointly.

Joint custody. Custody of children awarded jointly to the parents so that they share the legal responsibility for their upbringing.

Joint decree. A decree in favour of or against more than one person jointly. [CPC (5 of 1908), O. XXI, R. 18(4), ill. (d)].

Joint decree-holder. Persons who jointly hold a decree against another. [CPC (5 of 1908),

O. XXI, R. 15(1)].

Joint Degree. A "Joint Degree", for the purposes of these regulations, means a single degree jointly awarded by the Indian Educational Institution and the collaborating Foreign Educational Institute. [University Grants Commission (Promotion and Maintenance of Standards of Academic Collaboration between Indian and Foreign Educational Institutions) Regulations, 2016, Regn. 2(j)].

Joint enterprize. *In criminal law*, two or more persons setting out to commit a conspired offence.

Joint family. "JOINT FAMILY" means a family of which the members live together, have a common mess and are descendants from a common ancestor and shall include wives or husbands, as the case may be, of its members, but shall exclude married daughters and their children. [Manipur Municipalities Act (43 of 1994), S. 2(27)]

"JOINT FAMILY" means an undivided Hindu family and in the case of other persons, a group or unit the members of which by custom or usage are jointly in estate or residence. [Gujarat Agricultural Lands Ceiling Act, 1960 (27 of 1961), S. 2(16)]

"JOINT FAMILY" means on undivided Hindu family and in the case of other persons, a group or unit the members of which are by custom joint in possession or residence. [Gujarat Ownership of Flats Act (13 of 1973), S. 2(m)]

In a case where property is jointly held by the members of a family, in order to prove separation it is not sufficient to show that there has been separation in mess only; there must be proof of separation in estate as well. 20 IC 28 (29), *per* MOOKERJEA and BEACHCROFT, *JJ.*

An undivided Hindu family; a consanguineal family unit consisting of descendants of a common ancestor who generally maintain a common residence and are subject to common social, economic and religious regulations. [Companies Act (1 of 1956), S. 11(3)].(Replaced by Act 2013)

Joint family property. The words *"Joint family property,"* mean the property of joint family, and not the joint property of the family. Thus the article would not apply where the property is joint, but the family is not.

Property held by the members of a family as joint tenants with rights of survivorship. [Limitation Act (36 of 1963), S. 7, *Expln.* 2].

Joint Farming Society. Means a Joint Farming Society (registered or deemed to be registered as such, under any law for the time being in force relating to the registration of Co-operative Societies) the members of which cultivate jointly the land held by the members or by the Societies. [Maharashtra Agricultural Lands (Ceiling on Holdings) (27 of 1961), S. 2(15)]

'JOINT FARMING SOCIETY' means a Co-operative Society in which with the object of increasing agricultural production land is acquired from outside in the name of the Co-operative Society and is collectively and Jointly cultivated by the members themselves on behalf of a Co-operative Society. [Delhi Co-operative Societies Rules, 1973, R. 4(g)]

Joint indictment. An indictment brought against two or more offenders charging them jointly.

Joint interest. Interest of two or more persons together.

Joint judgement debtors. When one of the joint judgment debtors pays off the decretal debt, he has a right to contribution from his co-judgment debtor to what extent and in what proportion may depend upon the circumstances of each case. *Nami Lal* v. *Tirthalal,* AIR 1953 Cal 513, 514. [Indian Contract Act (9 of 1872), S. 43]

Joint liability. The special liability of a Hindu son to pay his father's debts on the pious obligation theory is not a 'joint' liability with the father. 35 IC 918 : 31 MLJ 386.

Joint meeting. A meeting at which members of more than one body meet together. [CPC (5 of 1908), S. 135A(1)(c)].

Joint member. "JOINT MEMBER" shall mean any one of two persons admitted jointly to the membership of a co-operative society under sub-section (4) of Section 69, and shall include either of the following persons so admitted—(i) husband and wife, (ii) father and son or unmarried daughter, and (iii) mother and son or unmarried daughter. [West Bengal Co-operative Societies Act, 1983, S. 2(28), Explanation]

Joint obligation. An obligation undertaken by two or more persons who may be sued together or released from the obligation together.

Joint occupation. Occupation jointly by two or more persons. [Arms Act (54 of 1959), S. 35].

Joint possession. Possession held by two or more persons or parties in conjunction. [T.P. Act (4 of 1882), S. 44]

Joint promise. A promise jointly made by two or more persons. [Indian Contract Act (9 of 1872), S. 42]

Joint promisee. One to whom along with another or others a promise has been made. [Indian Contract Act (9 of 1872), S. 38(3)]

Joint promisor. A person who makes a promise jointly with another or others. [Indian Contract Act (9 of 1872), S. 43].

Joint property. A term which may be employed as meaning partnership property. (*Ame Cyc.*)

Joint return. A return filed together by spouses.

Joint session. Used in relation to a legislature, the word implies the meeting together and commingling of the two Houses, which, when so met and commingled, act as one body.

Joint sitting. Sitting of two or more bodies together. [CPC (5 of 1908), S. 135A(1)(c) and Constitution of India, Art. 108(1)]

Joint stock. Stock or capital held in company; capital held as a common stock or fund.

Joint stock bank. Joint Stock Company for the purpose of banking.

Joint-stock-company. An association of individuals possessing a common capital divided into shares of which each member possesses one or more. [T.P. Act (4 of 1882), S. 127, ill (a)].

The company in which shares of the member are transferable and the death and bankruptcy of a member does not dissolve the company. The business is administered, not by members but by their agents.

Joint tenancy. A joint tenancy exists where a single estate in property, real or personal, is owned by two or more persons under one instrument or act of the parties.

Joint-tenants. Those who hold an estate by or in joint tenancy. [Hindu Succession Act (30 of 1956), S. 19(b)].

Joint tort-feasors. Two or more persons acting in concert in commission of a tort.

Joint trial. A trial of more persons than one held in the absence of the accused who has absconded or who fails to comply with a proclamation issued under section 84 of the Bharatiya Nagarik Suraksha Sanhita, 2023 shall be deemed to be a joint trial for the purpose of this section. [(w. e. f. 1-7-2024) Bharatiya Sakshya Adhiniyam, 2023 (47 of 2023), section 24, Explanation II]

Joint undivided estate. "JOINT UNDIVIDED ESTATE" means an estate of which two or more persons are proprietors. [Ben. Act 5 of 1897 (Estates Partition), S. 3, cl. 10].

Joint undivided family. (*In Hindu Mithakshara Law*) Members of the same family holding property in common, as joint tenants, with rights of survivorship.

Joint venture. "JOINT VENTURE (JV)" means a foreign entity formed, registered or incorporated in accordance with the laws and regulations of the host country in which the Indian party makes a direct investment. [Foreign Exchange Management (Transfer or Issue of any Foreign Security) Regulations, 2000, Reg. 2(m); Foreign Exchange Management (Transfer or Issue of Security by a person Resident Outside India) Regulations, 2000, Reg. 2(vii)]

The expression "joint venture" is more frequently used in the United States. It connotes a legal entity in the nature of a partnership engaged in the joint undertaking of a particular transaction for mutual profit or an association of persons or companies jointly undertaking some commercial enterprise whether in all contribute assets and share risks. It requires a community of interest in the performance of the subject matter, a right to direct and govern the policy in connection therewith, and duly, which may be altered by agreement, to share both in profit and losses. *New Horizons Ltd.* v. *Union of India,* (1995) 1 SCC 478.

A business undertaking by two or more persons, engaged in a single project.

Joint venture abroad. Means a foreign concern formed, registered or incorporated in a foreign country in accordance with the laws and regulations of that country and in which investment has been made by an Indian entity. [Foreign Exchange Management (Borrowing or Lending in Foreign Exchange) Regulations, 2000), Reg. 2(f)]

Joint will. A joint will is a will made by two or more testators contained in a single document, duly executed by each testator, disposing either of their separate properties or of their joint properties. It is not, however, recognised in English law as a single will. It operates on the death of each testator as his will disposing of his own separate property, and is in effect two or more wills. *K. Gobindan* v. *T.T. Lakshmi Amma,* AIR 1959 SC 71, quoting HALSBURY, 2nd Edn., Vol. 34. p. 17.

Persons may make joint wills which are revocable at any time by either of them or by the survivor. A joint will is looked upon as the will of each testator, and may be proved on the death of the one. But the survivor will e treated in equity as a trustee of the joint property if the equitable doctrine of mutual will applies. Under this doctrine there must be an agreement for the survivor to be bound by the arrangement between them; but the mere fact of the execution of a joint will is not sufficient to establish such an agreement for the survivor to be bound. If this doctrine applies, a legacy to a legatee who survived the first testator, but predeceased the second, does not lapse. where a joint will is followed by a separate will which is conditional on a condition that fails, the joint will is not revoked even though the subsequent separate will contains a revocation clause. [Theobald on Wills, 19th Edn. (Sweet & Maxwell), para 1-011 **as cited in** *K.S. Palanisami* v. *Hindu Community in General and Citizens of Gopichettipalayam,* (2017) 13 SCC 15, para 30].

Joint work. A work prepared by two or more authors with the intention that their contributions will be merged into interdependent or inseparable parts of a unitary whole. [U.S. Copyright Act, 1976, S.10] (*Copyright*)

Jointly. In a joint manner.

Jointly and severally. Persons who bind themselves jointly and severally in a bond or note may all be sued together or any one or more of them at the option of promisee.

Jointly concerned. Concerned together. [IPC (45 of 1860), Ss. 394 and 460].

Jointly designate. To name in a joint manner. [T.P. Act (4 of 1882), S. 37].

Jointly tried. Tried together. [Indian Evidence Act (1 of 1872), S. 30, ill. (a)].

Jointure. "A competent livelihood for the wife of lands and tenements, to take effect in profit or possession presently after the death of the husband, for the life of the wife at least." (*Bouvier*)

Joridara/Joridari System. It was a custom with mixture of both polygamy and polyandry. Under this system the eldest brother amongst the brothers was the pivot and the woman who was brought into the house in a marriage ceremony became the wife of all brothers who joined him or associated with him. It was not necessary for all the brothers to join the joridari but when two or more brothers join together in this common marriage, the wife became the common wife of these brothers. If over a period of time the brothers wanted to marry another woman and bring her into the family, she also became the joint wife of all the brothers. [*Baan Singh v. Devi Ram*, AIR 2012 HP 57, para 8].

Journal. Is a day-book or diary of transactions used in many cases, as by merchants and tradesmen in their accounts; by mariners in observations at sea, &c. (*Tomlin*)

JOURNAL also means the official record of what is done and passed in the legislative assembly.

A periodical publication containing news in any particular sphere [Indian Evidence Act (1 of 1872), S. 81]; a daily record of commercial transactions entered as they occur in order to the keeping of accounts [Bankers' Books Evidence Act (18 of 1891), S. 3].

Journey. In its original signification meant a day's travel, but in use it has attained a broader though less definite meaning, and it is now applied to a travel by land from place to place without restriction of time.

Travel. [CrPC 1973 (2 of 1974), S. 57].

Joyriding. Driving of someone else's automobile or other conveyance illegally without his permission but without any intention of depriving the owner of it permanently.

Judex. The judicial power which examines the truth of the fact, the law arising upon it, and if an injury has been done, applies the remedy. (*In old English Law*) A judge,—one who declares the law, or administers justice between contending parties.

Judex bonus nihil ex arbitrio suo faciat, nec propositione domesticae voluntatis, sed juxta leges et jura pronunciet. (*Maxim*) A good judge should do nothing of his own arbitrary will nor on the dictate of his personal inclination but should decide according to law and justice. (*Burrill*)

A good judge does nothing from his own judgment, or from a dictate of private will; but he will pronounce according to law and justice. (*Latin for Lawyers*)

Judex damnatur cum nocens absolvitur. (*Maxim*) The judge is condemned, when a guilty person escapes punishment. (*Wharton*)

Judex debet judicare secundum allegata et probata. (*Maxim*) The judge ought to decide according to the allegations and the proofs. (*Black*)

Judex est lex loquens. (*Maxim*) The judge is the speaking law. (*Bouvier; Latin for Lawyers.*)

Judex habere debet duos sales; salem sapientiae, ne sit insipidus, et salem conscientiae, ne sit diabolus. (*Maxim*) A judge should have two salts,—the salt of wisdom, lest he be insipid; and the salt of conscience, lest he be devilish. (*Latin for Lawyers*)

Judex non potest esse testis in propria causa. (*Maxim*) A judge cannot be a witness to his own cause. (*Wharton*)

Judex non potest injuriam sibi datam punire. (*Maxim*) A judge cannot punish an injury (a wrong) done to himself. (*Wharton*; *Latin for Lawyers*; *Black*)

Judge. One invested with authority to determine any cause or question in a Court of judicature. [IPC (45 of 1860), S. 19; Bankers' Books Evidence Act (18 of 1891), S. 2(6) and Constitution of India, Art. 124(2A)].

A judge is a public officer, who by virtue of his office is clothed with judicial authority.

"JUDGE" means the presiding judicial officer in every Civil and Criminal Court, by whatever title he is designated. [Legal Practitioner Act (18 of 1879), S. 3].

The word "JUDGE" denotes not only every person who is officially designated as a Judge, but also every person.—

Who is empowered by law to give, in any legal proceeding, civil or criminal, a definitive judgment, or a judgment, which, if not appealed against, would be definitive, or a judgment which, if confirmed by some other authority, would be definitive, or

Who is one of a body of persons, which body of persons is empowered by law to give such a judgment. (IPC (45 of 1860), S. 19] [Now (w. e. f. 1-7-2024) repealed & replaced by Bharatiya Nyaya Sanhita, 2023 (45 of 2023)]

"Judge" means a person who is officially designated as a Judge and includes a person,—

(i) who is empowered by law to give, in any legal proceeding, civil or criminal, a definitive judgment, or a judgment which, if not appealed against, would be definitive, or a judgment which, if confirmed by some other authority, would be definitive; or

(ii) who is one of a body or persons, which body of persons is empowe-red by law to give such a judgment.

Illustration

A Magistrate exercising jurisdiction in respect of a charge on which he has power to sentence to fine or imprisonment, with or without appeal, is a Judge. [(w. e. f. 1-7-2024) Bharatiya Nyaya Sanhita, 2023 (45 of 2023), section 2(16)]

In this article, the expression "Judge" does not include an acting Judge or an additional Judge. [Constitution of India, Article 376(3)

"JUDGE" means not only every person who is officially designated as a Judge, but also every person—

(a) who is empowered by law to give in any legal proceeding a definitive judgment, or a judgment which, if not appealed against would be definitive, or a judgment which, if confirmed by some other authority, would be definitive; or

(b) who is one of a body of persons which body of persons is empowered by law to give such a judgment as is referred to in cl. (a). [Judge (Protection) Act (59 of 1985), S. 2]

A returning officer scrutinizing the nomination papers of the contesting candidates in the election for the managing committee of a co-operative society is not a judge. *Data Ram* v. *Ved Prakash Chopra,* AIR 1970 P&H 21 at 22. [IPC (45 of 1860), S. 19]

A judge has been defined as a public officer lawfully appointed to decide litigated questions according to law; an officer, so named who presides in some Court (*Bouvier*).

He must not only be impartial, but he must pay a blind obedience to the law. Whether good or bad, he is bound to declare what the law is, and not to make it. He is not an arbitrator, but an interpreter of the law. "It is his duty to be patient in the investigation of the case, learned in considering it, and firm in his judgment."

TO JUDGE. "To Judge" of a matter, means, to come to a conclusion on it.

Judge advocate. An officer of a Court-martial, who combines the character of adviser to the Court with that of public prosecutor.

Judge Attorney-General. "Additional Judge Attorney-General", "Deputy Judge Attorney" General" and "Judge Attorney" mean, respectively, the Judge Attorney-General, an Additional Judge Attorney-General, a Deputy Judge Attorney-General and a Judge Attorney of the Security Guard appointed in the appropriate rank by the Central Government. [National Security Guard Act (47 of 1986), S. 2(m)]

"Additional Judge Attorney-General" "Deputy Judge Attorney-General" and "Judge Attorney" mean respectively the Judge Attorney-General, an Additional Judge Attorney-General, a Deputy Judge Attorney-General and a Judge Attorney of the Force appointed in the appropriate rank by the Central Government. [Indo-Tibetan Border Police Force Act (35 of 1992), S. 2(o)]

Judge de facto. One who holds and exercises the office of a judge under color of lawful authority and by a title valid on its face, though he has not full right to the office, as where he was appointed under an unconstitutional statute, or by an usurper of the appointing power, or has not taken the oath of office.

Judge in chamber. A judge who passes orders while sitting in his chamber.

Judge-made law. Used in the sense of judicial decisions which construe away the meaning of Acts and Statutes or find the meanings in them the legislature never intended. It is also sometimes used as meaning simply the law established by judicial precedent. (*Cooley Const. Lim.* 70)

Judge of a Court of Small Causes. The expression, "The judge of the Court of Small Causes" in cl. (8) of Sch. II, Provincial Small Cause Courts Act (9 of 1887) must be taken to apply either to a Court of Small Causes constituted under the act or to a Court invested with the jurisdiction of a Court of Small Causes.

Judge's summons. 'Judge's summons' means a summons returnable before the Judge in Chambers or in Court. [Companies (Court) Rules, 1959, R. 2(9) **as referred in** *Chembra Orchard Produce Ltd.* v. *Regional Director of Company Affairs*, (2009) 2 SCC 547, 549, para 2]

Judgment. "JUDGMENT" means the statement given by the Judge on the grounds of decree or order. [CPC. (5 of 1908), S. 2(9)].

Judgment is the determination of a Court declaring the rights to be recognised and the remedies to be awarded between the parties upon facts found by the Court or admitted by the parties or upon their default in the course of proceedings instituted for the redress of a legal injury. (*Ency. of the Laws of England*)

A judgment is the determination or sentence of law, pronounced by a competent judge or Court; as the result of an action or proceeding instituted in or before such Court or judge, affirming that upon the matters submitted for its decision, a legal duty or liability does or does not exist. (*Black*)

'Judgment' includes decree, order, sentence or determination of any court, tribunal, Judge or judicial officer. [The Supreme Court Rules, 2013, Order I, Rule 2(1)(k) as cited in *Yakub Abdul Razak Memon v. State of Maharashtra*, (2015) 9 SCC 552, para 17].

"Judgment" is a formal intimation of the decision and its contents formally declared in a judicial way in open court. In other words, it is a declaration of the mind of the court at the time of pronouncement. [*Yakub Abdul Razak Memon v. State of Maharashtra*, (2013) 13 SCC 1, para 97].

Proudly, a judgment is a document, which incorporates, (a) brief statement of the plaint and written statement, (b) gist of the evidence adduced by the parties; (c) discussion on issues involved; (d) consideration of the arguments advanced by the parties; (e) reference to the relevant provisions of law; (f) the opinion of the judge/judges and (g) the royal seal. [*Taste Hotels Pvt. Ltd. v. Medisetty Jayasri*, AIR 2012 AP 4, para 15].

A judicial decision or order in Court; the statement given by the judge of the grounds of his decree or order [CPC (5 of 1908), S. 2(9) and Constitution of India, Art 136(1)]; the capacity for judging; discretion; disternment.

JUDGMENT DISTINGUISHED FROM DECREE. The term "judgment" is properly restricted to proceedings at law, while a "decree" is the determination, sentence, or adjudication of a competent Court upon the controversy submitted for its decision.

An Interlocutory Order which decides matters of moment or affects vital and valuable rights of the parties and which works serious injustice to the party concerned is a judgment.

The word 'judgment' in Art. 133 has been used in the sense of a decision finally determining the rights of the parties in the proceeding and not as defined in the Code of Civil Procedure. *Inda Devi* v. *Board of Revenue,* AIR 1957 All 116, 117. [Constitution of India Art. 133]

An order under Sec. 145(6) CrPC, 1973 (2 of 1974) whether passed *ex parte* or after hearing the parties is not a Judgment within the meaning of Section 362 [CrPC 1973 (2 of 1974)].

The Criminal Procedure Code, unlike the Civil Procedure Code, does not define 'judgment'. A 'judgment' means the expression of the opinion of the Court arrived at after a due consideration of the evidence and all the arguments. *Ramantar Thakur* v. *Date of Bihar*, AIR 1957 Pat 33, 35. [CrPC 1973 (2 of 1974) S. 354]

The word 'judgment' is a word of general import and means only 'judicial determination or decision of a Court'. Even if 'judgment' is to be understood in a limited sense, it does not follow that an application during preliminary enquiry—which is necessarily prior to judgment in the trial—is excluded. *State of Bihar* v. *Ram Naresh*, AIR 1957 SC 389, 395. [CrPC 1973 (2 of 1974), S. 321].

Judgment is of the affirmation by the law of the legal consequences attending a proved or admitted state of affairs or facts. Its recording gives an official certification to a pre-existing retention or establishes a new one or pre-existing grounds. *Gundir Sagar* v. *State of Punjab*, AIR 1974 SC 1791, 1794.

A mere refusal to give interim relief in a litigation, where ultimately the relief claimed may be granted, would not amount to a judgment.

An order refusing appointment of a receiver and grant of an *ad interim* injunction is a judgment. *Shah Bahulal Khimji* v. *Jayaban*, AIR 1981 SC 1786, 1818.

The order of the High Court dismissing an application for restoration of suit which was dismissed for default earlier is a judgment.

Judgment and decree. The expression 'judgment and decree' merely states that a decree shall follow the judgment and that it does not preclude the High Court from making a rule to the effect that in suits for money no decree need be drawn up if neither party has to recover anything unless the Judge otherwise directs. AIR 1934 Pat 266 (DB). [CPC (5 of 1908), S. 33]

Judgment and order. An order is a decision made during the progress of the cause, either prior or subsequent to final judgment, settling some point of practice or some point collateral to the main issue presented by the pleadings, and necessary to be disposed of before such issue can be passed upon by the Court, or necessary to be determined in carrying into execution of the final judgment. (23 *Ame. Cyc.* 667)

Judgment by consent. Voluntary settlement of an action.

Judgment-creditor. A creditor having a legal right to enforce execution of a judgment for a sum of money. [Limitation Act (36 of 1963), S. 17(2)].

Judgment-debt. A legal obligation to pay a debt or damages evidenced by a judgment entered in a Court of record and enforceable by execution or other judicial process. [Presidency-towns Insolvency Act (3 of 1909), S. 2(b) and Provincial Insolvency Act (5 of 1920), S. 2(1)(a)].

Judgment-debtor. "JUDGMENT-DEBTOR" means any person against whom a decree has been passed or an order capable of execution has been made. [CPC (5 of 1908) S. 2(10)].

One whose obligation to pay a judgment debt remains unsatisfied; a person against whom a judgment directing to pay a sum of money is still executable [CPC (5 of 1908), S. 2(10) and Provincial Insolvency Act (5 of 1920), S. 2(1)(a)].

The word 'judgment-debtor' does not include legal representatives. *Yogesh Sharma* v. *Devidayal*, AIR 1977 Del 270, 271. [CPC. (5 of 1908), S. 60 (1)]

State is in position of Judgment-debtor, in land acquisition cases, when decree is passed. *R.N. Dey* v. *Bhagyabati Pramanik,* (2000) 4 SCC 400, para 7. [CPC (5 of 1908), S. 2(10)]

The term "*judgment-debtor*" includes only a person against whom a decree has been passed or an order capable of execution has been made, and no one else.

Judgment, Decree or final order. In order that a decision should fall within the definition of the word 'judgment' or final order (1) it must finally decide the rights of the parties and the word 'judgment' means a final judgment and not an interlocutory judgment, and by which right to the relief claimed is decided with regard to all matters in issue, and (2) an order is final if it finally disposes of the rights of the parties and if it does not, it is not final even though it may decide a vital issue in the case. *Sardar Kapur Singh* v. *UOI,* AIR 1957 Punj 173, 186 (FB). [Constitution of India, Art. 133].

Judgment, Definitive. A judgment that finally decides the controversy. [IPC (45 of 1860), S. 19].

Judgment, Dissenting. A justice's judgment with or without an accompanying opinion of non-concurrence with a decision of the majority of justices of the Court.

Judgment in personam. A 'Judgment *in personam*' is, in form as well as in substance, between the parties claiming the right, and that it so *inter partes* appears by the record itself.

Judgment in rem. Is one pronounced upon the status of some particular person or thing and which binds all persons.

The judgment entered in the probate Court upon the probate of a will is a judgment *in rem*.

Judgment inter partes or Judgment in personam. Is one which operates only upon those who have been duly made parties and then privies, being against the person merely, and not settling the status of any person or thing.

Judgment on the merits. The expression 'judgment on the merits' implies that it must have been passed after contest and after evidence has been let in by both sides. *Chintamani* v. *Paika Samal,* AIR 1956 Ori 136, 142. [CPC. (5 of 1908), Sec. 13(*b*)]

Judgment of conviction. Without pronouncement of a judgment in the open court, signed and dated, it is difficult to treat it as a judgment of conviction. *Athipalayan, In re,* 1960 SCC Online Mad 33 : AIR 1960 Mad 507]. See also *Ajay Singh v. State of Chhattisgarh,* (2017) 3 SCC 330, para 18.

Judgment-proof. Uninsured, insolvent, or otherwise unable to pay a judgment.

Judgment with costs. Means only such costs as have been incurred through the adversary's act.

Judicandum est legibus, non exemplis. (*Maxim*) Judgment is to be given according to the laws, not according to examples or precedents. (*Black*)

Judicature. A judge's office, function or authority; action of administering justice through Courts.

A Court, or rather a power which distributes justice. Power of dispensing justice; jurisdiction; a tribunal.

'JUDICATURE' is defined to be a Court, or rather a power which distributes justice.

'Judicature' is used to designate with clearness that department of government which it was intended should interpret and administer the law.

Judicature, Court of civil. A Court of justice of a civil nature. [CPC (5 of 1908), preamble].

Judici officium suum exedenti non paretur. Effect is not given to the decision of a judge delivered in excess of his jurisdiction.

Judicia officium suum excedenti non paretur. To a judge exceeding his office there is no obedience. (*Jenk.*)

Judicia posteriora sunt in lege fortiora. The latter decisions are the stronger in law.

Judicial. Belonging to a cause, trial or judgment; belonging to or emanating from a judge as such; the authority vested in a judge (*Bouvier*); of, or belonging to a Court of justice; of or pertaining to a judge; pertaining to the administration of justice; proper to a Court of law.

The term 'judicial' extends to the acts and orders of a competent authority which has power to impose a liability or to give a decision which determines the rights or property of the affected parties. The term 'judicial' embraces even the acts of special tribunals which though administrative in character perform functions resembling those of Courts. *Bhailal Jagdish* v. *Addl. Dy. Commissioner,* AIR 1953 Nag 89 (FB).

A statutory authority, making a decision, after investigation and deliberation, which binds, concludes and imposes obligations upon and affects the rights of individuals, acts judicially. *Subramaniam* v. *T.R. of Co-op. Societies,* AIR 1965 AP 69, 72, 73.

Belonging to judgment in a Court of law or to a judge in relation to his function; pertaining to the administration of justice; proper to a legal tribunal, regulating from or fixed by a judgment in Court; having the function of judgement [Cr PC 1973 (2 of 1974), S. 338(1); IPC (45 of 1860), S. 193 and Constitution of India, Art. 144].

Judicial activism. A philosophy of administering justice whereby judges allow their personal views about public policy, ignoring precedents.

Innovative, dynamic and law making role of the Court with a forward looking attitude discording reliance on old cases and also mechanical, conservative and static view.

Progressive judicial thinking, developing the law for handling constructively the contemporary problems of society.

A creative thought process through which the Court displays vigour, enterprise, initiative pulsating with the urge of creating new and refined principles of law.

A sort of judicial creativity.

Judicial admission. A voluntary admission made in Court or before a magistrate.

Judicial authority. Authority pertaining to the office of a judge. Such authority relates to hearing and determining questions in controversy. A judicial authority exercising judicial power of the State is an authority having its own hierarchy of superior and inferior court, the law of procedure according to which it would dispose of mattes coming before it depending upon the nature of jurisdiction exercised by acting in judicial manner. [*Thakur Das* v. *State of M.P.,* (1978) 1 SCC 27, para 7 **as cited in** *Life Insurance Corporation of India v. Nandini J. Shah,* (2018) 15 SCC 356, para 24].

Judicial Commissioner. Means the Judicial Commissioner of any Province. [*See* Pun Regn. 7 of 1901 (N.W.F.P. Law and justice), S. 2(1), cl. (*a*)]

JURISDICTIONAL COMMISSIONER. For the purposes of this sub-rule, the expressions, "jurisdictional Commissioner" means the Commissioner having jurisdiction over the place declared as address in the application for enrolment as the GST Practitioner in FORM GST PCT-1. It shall refer to the Commissioner of Central Tax if the enrolling authority in FORM GST PCT-1 has been selected as Centre, or the Commissioner of State Tax if the enrolling authority in FORM GST PCT-1 has been selected as State. [Central Goods and Service Tax Rules, 2017, R. 83-A(13), *Explanation (a)*]

Judicial and administrative function. The "judicial function" entrusted to a Judge is inalienable and differs from an administrative or ministerial function, which can be delegated or permanence whereof may be secured through authorisation. The 'judicial function' consists in the interpretation of law and its application by Rule or discretion to the facts of particular cases. [*Jamal Uddin Ahmad* v. *Abu Saleh Najmuddin*, (2003) 4 SCC 257]

Judicial and Ministerial acts. The acts of justices of the peace may be either judicial or ministerial. If justices in dealing with a particular matter have to exercise their discretion in arriving at a decision, they are acting judicially; if on the other hand, they are merely required to do a particular act and are precluded from entering into the merits of the matter, they are said to be acting ministerially. The duty of a magistrate, for instance, in respect to admitting a person to bail is a judicial act, as it involves inquiries on which discretion must be exercised.

'Judicial' function consists in interpretation of law and its application by rule or discretion to facts of particular cases by the judge entrusted and it is inalienable. On the other hand 'ministerial acts' can be delegated or performance whereof can be secured through authorization and in it nothing is left to discretion. *Jamal Uddin Ahmad* v. *Abu Saleh Najmuddin*, AIR 2003 SC 1917 : 2003 (4) SCC 257. [Representation of the People Act (43 of 1951), S. 81]

'Judicial' and 'quasi judicial'. 'Judicial' and *'quasi-*judicial' by GREER LJ in the case of *Cooper* v. *Wilson* in the following words defined as :

A true judicial decision presupposes an existing dispute between two or more parties, and then involves four requisites: (1) The presentation not necessary orally of their case by the parties to the dispute; (2) if the dispute between them is a question of fact, the ascertainment of the fact by means of evidence adduced by the parties to the dispute and often with the assistance of argument by or on behalf of the parties on the evidence; (3) if the dispute between them is question of law, the submission of legal argument by the parties, and (4) a decision which disposes of the whole matter by a finding upon the facts in dispute and application of the law of the land to the facts so found, including, where required a ruling upon any disputed question of law. A *quasi*-judicial decision equally presupposes an existing dispute between two or more parties and involves (1) and (2), but does not necessarily involve (3) and never involves (4). The place of (4) is in fact taken by administrative action, the character of which is determined by the minister's free choice. (1937) 2 KB 309, 340, per GREER L.J. and SCOTT, cited with approval in *Bharat Bank Ltd.* v. *Employees of Bharat Bank Ltd.*, 1950 LLJ 921, 930.

Judicial and Quasi-Judicial order. An order of judicial or *quasi*-judicial nature does not mean that it should have been passed by a Court of Law. It includes orders by tribunals or authorities other than regular Courts of Justice.

To constitute a *quasi*-judicial order or judicial order, the authority passing the order should be under an obligation to hear the parties, to make an enquiry, to weigh the evidence and to base its conclusion thereon. Its decision should be based on the result of the enquiry and not on its own discretion.

Judicial approach. The expression 'Judicial approach' postulates (*a*) that the authority in arriving at the decision or taking action must be found to act fairly and justly, and not be merely expected to do so, and (*b*) that it does so on the basis to which objective test can be applied, limited by the consideration of the facts and circumstances of the case and the evidence led by the parties and the application of law to the facts and circumstances. When this test is testified, it becomes obvious that the act or decision is judicial and not administrative done or made in the wake of expediency or policy. *Parduman Singh* v. *State of Punjab*, AIR 1958 Punj 63, 70.

Judicial authority. Authority pertaining to the office of a judge. Such authority relates to hearing and determining questions in controversy.

Judicial bond. A bond which is required by Courts to secure costs of appeal, attachment and injunction of a party.

Judicial cognizance. Cognizance of a case taken by a judge or magistrate.

Judicial committee. An offshoot of the Privy Council forming the highest Court of appeal.

Judicial Committee of the Privy Council. A tribunal composed of members of the Privy Council established in 1833. It used to be the Court of final appeal from the Ecclesiastical Courts, from the Courts in India, the colonies, the Channel Islands and the Isle of Man.

Judicial comity. "Judicial comity" is the principle in accordance with which the courts of one state or jurisdiction will give effect to the laws and judicial decisions of another, not as a matter of obligation, but out of deference and respect. [Black's Law Dictionary, 5th Edn., Judicial Comity as cited in *World Sport Group (Mauritius) Limited v. MSM Satellite (Singapore) PTE. Limited*, (2014) 11 SCC 639, para 22].

Judicial confession. A confession of guilt, made by a prisoner before a magistrate, or in Court, in the due course of legal proceedings.

Judicial creativity. Apparent power of judges to modify the scope and pattern of existing offences and to create new offences.

Judicial custody. An accused can be in custody not merely when the police arrests him, produces him before a Court and gets a remand to judicial or other custody but he can be in 'judicial custody' when he surrenders before the Court and submits to its directions. [*Nirnajan Singh* v. *Prabhakar Rajaram Kharote*, (1980) 2 SCC 559, 563, p. 9]

Judicial decision. Opinions, or determinations, or the sentiments of the Judges delivered in a cause in Court before them, and which form the decree or judgment of the Court. (*Tomlin*)

JUDICIAL DECISION is the application by a Court of competent jurisdiction of the law to a state of facts proved or admitted to be true, and a declaration of the consequences which follow. The "judicial decision" must be a decision pronounced by an officer competent to deal with the matter.

A judicial decision is merely a decision which is in fact exercised by the Courts in accordance with strict legal procedure, whereas a *quasi*-judicial decision is given by an administrator or an administrative Court entitled to follow its own procedure provided only that the rules of natural justice are observed. [CPC. (5 of 1908), S. 24].

Judicial decision or act. The requisites of a judicial decision or act are: If (*a*) a competent authority not being Court in the ordinary sense, (*b*) has power to give a binding and authoritative decision, (*c*) after hearing evidence and upon consideration of facts and circumstances, and (*d*) imposing liability or affecting the rights of the parties, there is a duty to act judicially. *Parduman Singh* v. *State of Punjab,* AIR 1958 Punj 63, 69. [Constitution of India, Art. 226]

Judicial dictum. (*Lat.*) A remark in passing.

Judicial discretion means sound discretion guided by law. It must be governed by rule, not humour. It must not be arbitrary, vague, or fanciful, but legal and regular.

Judicial discretion is a discretion in discerning the course prescribed by the law; a perceiving by, through or according to the law of what would be just.

Judicial discretion is the option which a judge may exercise either to do or not to do that which is proposed to him that he shall do; that discretion which is not, and cannot be, governed by any fixed principles or rules; a discretion to be guided by the spirit principles, and analogies of the law; such an exercise of authority in the mode of proceeding for the enforcement of rights or the redress of wrongs as is reasonably designed to promote substantial justice.

A judicial discretion presupposes that power has been confided to a tribunal to act or refrain from acting in a particular way in certain proved or admitted circumstances. Some of the instances are the discretion regarding payment of costs, appointment of receiver, granting of injunction, cases under O. IX, R. 9 or O. XLI, R. 19, CPC. (5 of 1908).

Judicial documents. Proceedings relating to litigation. The term includes inquisitions, examinations, depositions, affidavits, and other written papers, when they have become proofs of its proceedings and are found remaining on the files of a judicial Court. (*Ame Cyc.*)

Judicial error. An error growing out of a mistaken application of the law to the facts.

Judicial evidence. Judicial evidence is evidence of mutable phenomena, through human agency addressed to human tribunal.

Judicial experience. "Judicial experience" would mean the knowledge or skill gained by a person by actually working as a judge in a Court of law. In other words it denotes the experience which a Judge obtains by regular application of his unbiased and unprejudiced mind to the determination of disputes between two or more parties adjudicating upon their legal rights or liabilities. *Badridass Kanhaiyalal* v. *Appellate Tribunal of State Transport Authority,* AIR 1960 Raj 105, 114.

Judicial fact. Fact which is taken by the Court as proved without hearing evidence.

Judicial function. The exercise of a judicial function is the doing of something in the nature of or in the course of an action in Court.

The 'judicial functions' are those which are to be discharged by the Judges as per the rules of the Court and cannot be delegated. *Jamaluddin Ahmad* v. *Abu Saleh Najmuddin,* (2003) 4 SCC 257, para 13 : AIR 2003 SC 1917.

Judicial immunity. The exemption of a judge or magistrate from personal actions for damages arising from the exercise of his judicial office.

Judicial impropriety. When a position, in law, is well settled as a result of judicial pronouncement of the Court, it would amount to judicial impropriety to say the test, for the subordinate Courts including the High Courts, is to ignore the settled decisions and then to pass a judicial order, which is clearly contrary to the settled legal position. [*K.S. Paripoornan, K. Venkatawasamu and B.N. Kirpal, JJ.* v. *Dwarikesh Sugar Industrial Limited,* (1997) 5 Supreme 29]

Judicial independence. It has many dimensions, namely, fearlessness of other power centres, economic or political, and freedom from prejudices, acquired and nourished, by the class to which the Judge belongs. The heart of judicial independence is judicial individualism. [*High Court of Judicature at Bombay through its Registrar* v. *Shirish kumar Rangarao Patil and another,* (1997) 6 SCC 339]

Judicial : Judicial act. The term "judicial" does not necessarily mean acts of a Judge or legal tribunal sitting for the determination of matters of law, but a judicial act may be an act done by competent authority upon a consideration of facts and circumstances and imposing liability or affecting the rights of others. The authority must "exercise some right or duty to decide" before its act can be called 'judicial.' The act of the presiding member of a municipal council in declaring the result of a poll is a purely ministerial or administrative act—and not judicial.

A judicial act seems to be an act done by a competent authority upon a consideration of facts and circumstances and imposing liability or affecting the rights of others. Thus it must be that of a person or persons who have legal authority to determine questions affecting the rights of parties and in a judicial manner. *Kalavagunta Srirama Rao* v. *Kalavagunta Suryanarayana Murthy,* AIR 1954 Mad 340, 343.

An act involving the exercise of judicial power. [Indian Evidence Act (1 of 1872), S. 114, ill. (e)].

The duties of the Election Officer certainly fit it with the definition of 'judicial acts'. He has legal authority to decide on the objection raised by the candidate. The question decided by him affects the rights of the parties and in deciding the objections raised he hears the parties and may also make an enquiry and therefore he has a duty to act judicially. *Bandi Visweswara Rao* v. *Deputy Panchayat Officer,* AIR 1957 AP 539, 542.

Judicial legislation. The words 'judicial legislation' mean judicial pronouncements giving interpretation to several statutes, which the legislature never intended.

Judicial Member. In Chapter XXVII of Act 18 of 2013, unless the context otherwise requires, "Judicial Member" means a member of the Tribunal or the Appellate Tribunal appointed as such and includes the President or the Chairperson, as the case may be. [S. 407(b) of the Companies Act, 2013 (18 of 2013)]

"JUDICIAL MEMBER" means a Judicial Member of the Lokpal. [S. 2(1)(h) of the Lokpal & Lokayuktas Act, 2013 (1 of 2014)]

Judicial misconduct. That the failure to consider material document amounted to judicial misconduct and the award was liable to set aside irrespective of whether it was a speaking award or not and irrespective of whether there was proof of prejudice or not. [*Bhai Sardar Singh and Sons, New Delhi* v. *New Delhi Municipal Committee,* MLJ : YD (1982), p. 587 : AIR 1981 Delhi 374]. [Arbitration Act (10 of 1940), S. 30]

Judicial notice. The notice which a judge will take of a fact without proof. Acceptance by Court for the purpose of a case, of the truth of certain notorious facts without requiring proof.

For the purposes of convenience and without a party's proof, a Court's acceptance of a well-known and indisputable fact; the power of the Court to accept such a fact.

The recognition by a Court for the purposes of a case of the existence or truth of certain facts as being self-evident or common knowledge (no evidence being required to prove those facts). [CPC (5 of 1908), S. 87-A(2)].

Judicial office. An office which relates to the administration of justice; includes the legal capacity and obligation of the incumbent to render judicial service, by holding one or more Courts of justice.

The expression 'judicial office' is used in the proviso in the sense in which the term judicial is used in Ss. 253 to 256, 'a person holding judicial office being a member of the judicial service or in short a judicial officer'. *In The Matter of Enrolment of Sri H.P. Chaudhari,* AIR 1959 All 472. [Bar Councils Act (38 of 1926), S. 9, Rule 1, Proviso]

Judicial officer. The term "judicial officers" includes judges and justices of all Courts and all persons exercising judicial powers by virtue of their office.

The words "Judicial Officer" mean a subsisting office with a substantive position which has an existence independent from its holder. *Kumar Padma Prasad* v. *Union of India,* AIR 1992 SC 1213, 1231. [Constitution of India, Art. 217(2)(*a*)]

Judicial opinion. The direct solemn and deliberate decision of the Court upon the issue raised by the record and presented in the argument. The term is sometimes used as importing a judgment or decree.

Judicial orders. The order passed by the Chief Commissioner is a judicial order as it seeks to maintain the rights of the respondents within a political community by means of the physical force of the state. *Oinam Ibomcha Singh* v. *Nithonjam Mangi Singh,* AIR 1957 Mani 18, 21. [Constitution of India, Art. 226]

Judicial power. The authority to determine the rights of persons or property by arbitrating between adversaries in specific controversies at the instance of a party thereto; the authority vested in some Court, officer, or person to hear and determine when the rights of persons or property or the propriety of doing an act is the subject-matter of adjudication.

If a body which has power to give a binding and authoritative decision, is able to take action so as to enforce that decision, then but only by them, all the attributes of judicial power are plainly present. [Words and Phrases Legal Defined by John B. Saunders, Vol. 3 at p. 113 as cited in *Jawahar Singh v. United Bank of India*, AIR 2015 Cal. 306, para 70].

A Judge exercises 'judicial powers' not only when he is deciding suits, but also when he exercises disciplinary powers which are properly appurtenant to the office of a Judge. [A.G. of Gambia v. N'Jie, 1961 AC 617 as cited in *Jawahar Singh v. United Bank of India,* AIR 2015 Cal 306, Para 70].

'Judicial Process' includes compelling a respondent to appear before it. [*Surya Baksh Singh v. State of U.P.*, (2014) 14 SCC 222, para 7].

Power which the state exercises to restore the *virculun juris* which is disturbed when there is an infringement or invasion of a legal right. Power to examine questions submitted for determination with a view to the pronouncement of an authoritative decision as to rights and liabilities of one or more parties. *Firm S. Mohammad Ali* v. *V.V. Madhavarao,* AIR 1964 AP 132, 135. [CPC. (5 of 1908), S. 24].

The Legislatures in India cannot exercise a power which can be described as essentially judicial and not legislative. Where the Legislature on finding that there has been a lacuna in creating jurisdiction applies it, it acts within the legislative field. Where, however, the Legislature goes further than this and compels the determination of a case at the hands of a Court taking it completely out of the reach of the Court to make a contrary decision, the matter is one under judicial and not legislative power. *Biharilal* v. *Ramacharan,* AIR 1957 MP 165, 167. [Constitution of India, Art. 245]

Judicial power and discretionary power. The terms "discretionary power" and "judicial power" are often used interchangeably; but there are many acts requiring the exercise of discretion which may fairly be considered of a judicial nature, and yet they do not in any proper sense come within the judicial power, as applicable to the Courts. (*Ame Cyc.*)

Judicial proceeding. "*Explanation 1.*—A trial before a Court-martial is a judicial proceeding. *Explanation 2.*—An investigation directed by law preliminary to a proceeding before a Court of justice, is a stage of a judicial proceeding, though that investigation may not take place before a Court of justice". [IPC (45 of 1860), S. 193, *Explns. 1 & 2*]] [(w. e. f. 1-7-2024) repealed and replaced by Bharatiya Nyaya Sanhita, 2023 (45 of 2023), section 229, *Explanations 1 & 2*]

An investigation directed by a Court according to law, and conducted under the authority of a Court, is a stage of a judicial proceeding, though that investigation may not take place before a Court [(w. e. f. 1-7-2024) Bharatiya Nyaya Sanhita, 2023 (45 of 2023), section 229, *Explanation 3*]

"JUDICIAL PROCEEDING" includes any proceeding in the course of which evidence is or may be legally taken on oath. [CrPC 1973 (2 of 1974), S. 2(i); [Now (w. e. f. 1-7-2024) repealed & replaced by Bharatiya Nagarik Suraksha Sanhita, 2023 (46 of 2023), section 2(1)(m), same definition in new Sanhita]

A general term for proceeding in Courts; for the course authorized to be taken in various cases to secure the determination of controversy; to obtain the enforcement of a right or the redress or prevention of a wrong. (*Abbott*)

The term includes an execution proceeding.

An application to leave to sue is a stage in a judicial proceeding.

The investigation made by the Junior Inspector of Mines was not a judicial proceeding. [Indian Evidence Act (1 of 1872), S. 33]

Every investigation of proceeding under Sec. 40 is deemed to be a judicial proceeding by a legal fiction embodied in sub-sec. (4) though the proceedings are neither in nor before any Court at that stage. But there is no such deeming provision under Sec. 39 bringing every investigation or proceeding in its ambit as "a judicial proceeding" within the meaning of S. 193 and 228 of the IPC (45 of 1860). *K.T.M.S. Mohammad* v. *Union of India*, AIR 1992 SC 1831, 1838. [Foreign Exchange Regulation Act (46 of 1973), S. 39, 40]

The proceedings before the Income Tax Officer are judicial proceedings and all the incidents of such judicial proceedings have to be observed before the result is arrived at. The assessee would have a right to inspect the record and all relevant documents before he is called upon to lead evidence in rebuttal in proceedings. *Smaj Mall Mohta & Co.* v. *A.V. Viswanatha Sastri*, AIR 1954 SC 545, 553.

Proceedings to be judicial, should relate in some way to the administration of justice or to the ascertainment of any right or liability. In that view, demarcation of the boundaries of land is not judicial proceeding. *Dhani Ram* v. *Sub-divisional Judge Theog,* AIR 1965 HP 25, 27. [IPC (45 of 1860), S. 228]

Judicial process. In its largest sense, the term comprehends all the acts of the Court from the beginning of its proceedings to the end.

In a narrower sense it is the means of compelling the defendant to appear in Court for suing out the original writ in civil, and after indictment in criminal cases. (*Bouvier*)

Judicial question. A question, where the validity of certain acts are involved, the determination of which is entrusted to the judiciary, when such question is raised by a person who has suffered or is threatened with some special injury which he seeks to redress or prevent. (*Ame Cyc.*)

Judicial record. A precise history of a suit from its commencement to its termination, including the conclusions of law thereon, drawn by the proper officer for the purpose of perpetuating the exact state of facts.

Record of proceedings in a Court of law. [Indian Evidence Act (1 of 1872), S. 86].

Judicial reference. Reference made to a superior Court by proper parties or authorized officers on points of law arising on a given statement of facts.

Judicial remedies. Such remedies as are administered by the Courts of justice, or by judicial officers legally empowered for that purpose.

Judicial restraint. A philosophy of judicial decision making whereby the Courts avoid indulging their personal views about the public good and instead merely try to interpret the law as legislated and according to precedents.

Judicial review. The power of the Courts to review the legislative and executive action and determine their validity.

Broadly speaking, judicial review in India comprises three aspects : Judicial review of legislative action, judicial review of judicial decisions and judicial review of administrative action *L. Chandra Kumar* v. *Union of India.* (1997) 228 ITR 725, 758 (SC).

Judicial sales. A judicial sale is one made, under the process of a Court having competent authority to order it, by an officer legally appointed and commissioned to sell : one made by a Court of competent jurisdiction, in a pending cause through its authorized agent.

A sale under an order or decree of Court is a judicial act. The Court is the vendor, and the officer conducting the sale is the mere agent of the Court. The sale is a transaction between the Court and the purchaser. A sale is not a judicial sale, properly speaking, unless it is one made on an order of the Court and subject to confirmation by the Court. Proceedings for judicial sales are ordinarily *in rem.* (*Ame Cyc.*)

Judicial separation. A lesser form of divorce, See Indian Divorce Act (4 of 1869), Ss. 22-25.

A separation of husband and wife under orders of Court which puts an end to cohabitation but not to the marriage itself. [Hindu Marriage Act (25 of 1955), S. 10(1)].

Judicial service. The expression "JUDICIAL SERVICE" means a service consisting exclusively of persons intended to fill the post of district judge and other civil judicial posts inferior to the post of district judge. [Constitution of India, Art. 236(b)]

Judicial Settlement Conference. An Alternative Dispute Resolution procedure used in United States' state and federal Courts in which the judge convenes a meeting in his or her chambers to see whether the parties can find a basis for settlement by agreement with a trial. (*ADR : Brown & Marriat*)

Judicial trial. A fair trial, the purpose of which is to truly ascertain the material facts in issue.

Judicial tribunal. A Court. A board of arbitrators is not a "Court" or "judicial tribunal" in any proper sense of those terms. It has none of the powers that appertain to Courts to regulate their proceedings or enforce their decisions.

Judicial trustee. A trustee appointed by a Court to execute a trust.

Judicially. Exercising judicial functions. [IPC (45 of 1860), S. 20].

Judiciary. A term applied to a co-ordinate department of the government, which construes and applies the laws; relating to that department of the government that has to do with the expounding and administering of the law; the officers of that department of government that expounds and administers the law; the judges taken collectively. Pertaining to Courts of law. The laws of a free government are construed and applied by the judiciary, or judicial department. This department has distinct and independent powers, designed to operate as a check upon those of the legislative and executive departments. It is confined to its own functions, and can neither encroach upon nor be made subordinate to those of another.

The judiciary is a co-ordinate department of the government, and is not a mere sub-ordinate branch, dependent for existence and power on the legislative will.

Judiciis posterioribus fides est adhibenda. (*Maxim*) Credit is to be given to the latest decisions.

Judicious. According to sound judgment. Well-considered; discreet.

Judiciously. To act skilfully with discretion or wisdom prudently.

Judicis est jus dicere, non dare. (*Maxim*) It is the province of a judge to declare the law, not to give it.

Judicis (nostrum) est judicare secundum allegata et probata. (*Maxim*) It is the duty of a judge to determine according to what is alleged and proved.

Judicis officium est opus diei in die suo perficere. (*Maxim*) It is the duty of a judge to finish the work of each day within that day.

Judicium a non suo judice datum nullius est momenti. (*Maxim*) A judgment given by one who is not the proper judge is of no force.

Judicium non debet esse illusorium; suum effectum habere debet. (*Maxim*) A judgment ought not to be illusory; it ought to have its proper effect.

Judicium semper pro veritate accipitur. (*Maxim*) A judgment is always accepted as true. (*Trayner*)

Jump bail. Failure of the accused to appear in the Court at the appointed time even after furnishing a bail-bond and promising to appear.

Junction. In the ordinary acceptation as applied to railroads a term which is frequently employed to designate the point or locality where two or more lines of railway meet.

Juncture. A union; a joining; a critical or important point of time.

Junior. A word meaning younger; later born; later in office or rank; an addition or description used to designate the individual referred to; and addition to distinguish between two or more persons of the same name; a character used to distinguish a man from an elder man of the same name and place.

The addition of 'junior' is no part of a person's name, but it is used as merely descriptive of the person, and is assumed, applied, and discarded at will. This addition to a name is at the best but presumptive evidence that of two persons bearing the same name the person thus designated is the younger.

A person holding a position of lesser standing in a hierarchy of ranks. [CrPC 1973 (2 of 1974), S. 132(3)(b)].

'Junior Basic School' means a school teaching children generally between 6 and 11 years of age in class I to V (i.e., primary section). [Educational Code of Uttar Pradesh (Revised 1958 edn.), Para 1 (xxvi) (b) as cited in *State of U.P. v. Pawan Kumar Divedi*, (2014) 9 SCC 692, para 22].

"Junior Basic School" means an institution other than the High Schools or Intermediate colleges imparting education up to Class V. [Uttar Pradesh Recognised Basic Schools (Recruitment and Conditions of Service of Teachers and other Conditions) Rules, 1975, R. 2(e) as cited in *State of U.P. v. Pawan Kumar Divedi*, (2014) 9 SCC 692, para 26].

Junior College of Education. Means a School imparting teacher education to persons for being appointed as teachers in preschool centres or primary schools. [Maharashtra Employees of Private Schools

(Conditions of Service) Regulation Act (3 of 1977), S. 2(10)]

Junior Commissioned Officer. Means a person commissioned, gazetted or in pay as a junior commissioned officer in the regular Army or the Indian Reserve Forces, and includes a person holding a junior commission in the Indian Supplementary Reserve Forces or the Territorial Army, who is, for the time being, subject to this Act. [Army Act (46 of 1950), S. 3(xii)]

'Junior High School' means an institution other than high school or intermediate college imparting education to boys or girls or both from Class V to VIII (inclusive). [Uttar Pradesh Recognised Basic Schools (Junior High Schools) (Recruitment and Conditions of service of Teachers) Rules, 1978, R. 2(e) as cited in *State of U.P. v. Pawan Kumar Divedi*, (2014) 9 SCC 692, para 27].

Junior management grade. In relation to a public sector bank, means the lowest grade of officers in that bank. [Banking Service Commission Act (44 of 1984), S. 2(e)]

Junior partner. A partner whose participation is limited with respect to both profits and management.

Jura eodem modo destituuntur quo constitu-untur. (*Lat.*) (2 Dwarr. Stat. 672) Laws are abrogated by the same means which they are made" (*Wharton L. Lex.*; *Latin for Lawyers*).

Jura in a re-aliena or servitudes. A charge or burden resting upon one estate for the benefit or advantage of another; a species of incorporeal rights. An easement is a right of a person in possession of land to do and to continue to do something, or to prevent something being done, on another's land, *e.g.* a right of way, right to light. It belongs to the class of rights known in the Roman Law as *jura in re aliena* or servitudes.

Jura in personam. Rights primarily available against specific persons. A right to enforce a particular person's obligation to another.

Jura in rem. Rights which are available only against the world at large.

Jura non-remota causa sed proxima spectatur. In law the immediate or proximate not the remote cause of any event is regarded.

Jura publica anteferenda privatis. (*Maxim*) Public rights are to be preferred to private. (*Coke Litt.* 130)

Jural. Pertaining to law or jurisprudence; legal; pertaining to rights and obligations.

Juramentum est indivisible, et non est admittendum in parte verum et in parte falsum. (*Maxim*) An oath is indivisible; it is not to be held partly true and partly false.

Jurat. A term which means that the affiant swore before the officer taking the affidavit; a certificate of the officer who administered the oath that the affiant had subscribed and sworn before him; that part of an affidavit where the officer certifies that it was sworn before him. (*Bouvier*; *Ame Cyc.*)

Juratores sunt judices facti. Juries are the judges of fact. In a trial by jury, while a judge decides questions of law and instructs the jury on matters of law, the facts in issue are solely within the province of the jury. (*Latin for Lawyers*)

Juri sanguinis nunquam praescribitur. (*Maxim*) No prescription runs against a right by blood. (*Trayner*)

Juridical. Relating to the dispensation of justice; belonging to the office of a judge. Pertaining to or relating to law; legal. (*Burrill.*)

Legal; juristic. [Estate Duty Act (34 of 1953), S. 2(19)].

Juridical evidence. Evidence through human agency addressed to a human tribunal.

Juridical personality. A body of persons, a corporation, a partnership or other legal entity that is recognised by law as a subject of rights and duties; artificial persons. [Asian Development Bank Act (18 of 1966), Sch., Art. 49].

Juridical possession. A tenant's occupation after termination of lease is as tenant by sufference and his possession cannot be considered as unauthorised. The possession of a tenant by sufference is a juridical possession. *Mogilipuvvu Annapurniah* v. *Malampati Narasimha Rao,* AIR 1982 AP 253, 255. [Transfer of Property (4 of 1882), Sec. 108]

The phrase 'juridical possession' has been used to mean possession as distinguished from occupation or custody; exclusive and effective possession as distinguished from the intrusion which is not acquiesced in by the opponent.

Jurimetrics. The use of scientific or empirical methods which includes measurements, in the study or analysis of legal matters.

Juris effectus in executione consistit. The effect of law depends upon execution. (*Latin for Lawyers*)

Juris praecepta sunt haec, honeste vivere, alterum non laedere suum cuique tribuere. (Inst. Lib. 1). These are the precepts of the law; to live honourably; to injure nobody; and to render every man his due.

Juris quidem ignorantiam cuique nocere, facti verum ignorantiam non nocere. (*Maxim*) Ignorance of fact prejudices no one, ignorance of law does. (*Bouvier*)

Jurisdiction. "JURISDICTION" includes rights, power and authority. [Foreign Jurisdiction Act (47 of 1947), S. 2(b)]

An authority or power, which a man hath to do justice in causes of complaint brought before him (*Tomlin*).

By 'jurisdiction, is meant the authority which a court has to decide matters that are litigated before it or to take cognizance of matters presented in a formal way for its decision. The limits of this authority are imposed by the statute, charter or commission under which the court is constituted, and may be extended or restricted by similar means. [Halsbury's Laws of England 4th Edn., Vol. 10, para 715 as cited in *Foreshore Co-operative Housing Society Limited v. Praveen D. Desai*, (2015) 6 SCC 412, para 45].

'Jurisdiction' is the authority to decide a given case one way or the other. Without jurisdiction, a court cannot proceed at all in any case; jurisdiction is the power to declare law, and when it ceases to exist, the only function remaining to a court is that of announcing the fact and dismissing the cause. [American Jurisprudence, Vol. 32-A, para 581 as cited in *Foreshore Co-operative Housing Society Limited v. Praveen D. Desai*, (2015) 6 SCC 412, para 46].

The power to hear and determine the particular case involved; the power of a Court or a judge to entertain an action, petition, or other proceeding; the legal power of hearing and determining controversies. As applied to a particular claim or controversy, jurisdiction is the power to hear and determine that controversy. The term imports authority to expound or apply the laws, and excludes the idea of power to make the laws; means (1)

The right to adjudicate on a given point. (2) The local extent within which the Court can and does exercise the right when ascertained. The term "jurisdiction" means authority or power to act in a matter, and not authority or power to do an act in a particular manner.

By jurisdiction is meant the authority on which a Court has to decide matters that are litigated before it or to take cognizance of matters presented in a formal way for its decision. HALSBURY, 4th Edn., Vol. 10, para 715, p. 323.

Power or authority in general; legal authority or power; the authority or power of a Court to entertain and decide on any judicial proceedings; the area over which the power of the Court extends. [CrPC 1973 (2 of 1974), S. 14 and Constitution of India, Art. 32(3)].

Jurisdiction may be local, pecuniary, personal or with reference to the subject-matter of the suit.

The term "jurisdiction" in respect of *res judicata* appears to mean essential jurisdiction, *viz.*, competency to entertain the suit with reference to its subject-matter and to the powers of the Court.

The rule for jurisdiction is, that nothing shall be intended to be out of the jurisdiction of the superior Court, but that which specially appears to be so; and on the contrary, nothing shall be intended to be within the jurisdiction of an inferior Court but that which is so expressly alleged.

The word 'jurisdiction' really signifies the initial jurisdiction to take cognizance of a case. It refers to the shape at which proceedings are instigated in a Court and not to the jurisdiction of the ordinary criminal Court and the Court to decide the case on merits. *Delhi Special Police Establishment, New Delhi* v. *Lt. Col. S.K. Loraiya*, AIR 1972 SC 2548, 2551.

Jurisdiction means the authority which a Court has to decide matters that are litigated before it or to take cognizance of matters are presented in a formal way for its decision. *Kunheema Umma* v. *P. Balakrishnan,* AIR 1967 Ker 97, 99. [CPC. (5 of 1908), S. 9]

The word meant the entitlement "to enter upon the enquiry in question". *M.L. Sethi* v. *R.P. Kapur*, AIR 1972 SC 2379, 2384. [CPC. (5 of 1908), Sec. 115]

The expression 'jurisdiction' does not mean the power to do or order the act impugned, but generally the authority of the Judicial Officer to act in the matter. *Anower Hussain* v. *Ajoy Kumar*, AIR 1965 SC 1651, 1654. [Judicial Officers' Protection Act (18 of 1850), S. 1]

Before a Court can be held to have jurisdiction to decide a particular matter it must not only have jurisdiction to try the suit brought but must also have the authority to pass the orders sought for. It is not sufficient that it has some jurisdiction in relation to the subject-matter of the suit. Its jurisdiction must include the power to hear and decide the questions at issue, the authority to hear and decide the particular controversy that has arisen between the parties. *Official Trustee West Bengal* v. *Sachindra*, AIR 1969 SC 823, 828. [Indian Trusts Act (2 of 1882), Sec. 34]

CIVIL JURISDICTION is that which is possessed when the subject-matter is not of criminal nature.

CRIMINAL JURISDICTION is that which exists for the punishment of offences.

EXCLUSIVE JURISDICTION is that which gives to one tribunal sole power to try a case.

ORIGINAL JURISDICTION. The phrase *Original Jurisdiction* does not mean exclusive jurisdiction, and two or more Courts may have original jurisdiction; and it may be of the same actions.

ORIGINAL AND APPELLATE JURISDICTION. Original Jurisdiction is jurisdiction conferred upon, or inherent in, a Court in the first instance. Appellate jurisdiction is the power and authority conferred upon a superior Court to rehear and determine causes which have been tried in inferior Courts.

PECUNIARY JURISDICTION. Jurisdiction is limited by the extent or value of the subject-matter of suit.

Where the jurisdiction of a Court is limited by the amount or value of the property in litigation it is called the pecuniary jurisdiction.

TERRITORIAL JURISDICTION. Territorial jurisdiction is the power of the tribunal considered with reference to the territory within which it is to be exercised.

Jurisdiction and power. There is a distinction between 'jurisdiction' and 'power', in that jurisdiction has reference to the exercise of power and the extent and the limits within which such power is exercisable for the administration of justice. But jurisdiction is defined in terms of power. It is the power of the Court to hear and determine a cause, to adjudicate and to exercise any judicial power in relation to it and to award the remedies provided by law upon a state of facts proved or admitted and presented to the Court in a formal way for its decision. The concept of jurisdiction embraces the power to grant the remedies provided by law. *Dayabhai Poonambhai Patel* v. *Regional Transport Authority,* AIR 1951 MB 124, 140 (FB).

Jurisdiction clause. That part of a plaint which sets forth, or is intended to give, the facts that confers on the Court, jurisdiction in the suit.

Jurisdiction of a Collector. Means the district to which such Collector is appointed, or throughout which any officer vested with the powers of a Collector is authorised to exercise such powers. [Ben Act (7 of 1868), (Land Revenue Sales), S. 1]

Jurisdiction of Court. There can be justification in saying that a Court has 'jurisdiction in any dispute', only when it is authorised to decide it finally. Jurisdiction of a Court may be limited either locally or personally, or as to amount, or as to the character of the questions to be determined. *Dalmia Dadri Cement Co. Ltd.* v. *CIT,* AIR 1955 Pepsu 3, 8. [Constitution of India, Art. 363]

Jurisdiction of suspicion. Provision for preventive detention, in itself, is a departure from ordinary norms. It is generally resorted to either in times of war or of apprehended internal disorders and disturbances of a serious nature. Its object is to prevent a greater danger to national security and integrity than any claim which could be based upon a right, moral or legal, to individual liberty. It has been aptly described as a "jurisdiction of suspicion." *Additional District Magistrate, Jabalpur* v. *Shivakant Shukla,* AIR 1976 SC 1207.

Jurisdiction of the cause. Is the power over the subject-matter conferred by law.

Jurisdiction of the subject-matter. 'Jurisdiction of the subject matter' is the power to hear and determine cases of the general class to which the proceeding in question belongs.

Jurisdictional facts. Facts, the existence of which is necessary to the validity of the proceeding, and without which the act of the Court is a mere nullity.

"COURT OF JURISDICTION COMPETENT TO TRY." The terms "the Court of jurisdiction competent to try" in S. 13, CPC. (5 of 1908) must be taken to mean a Court having jurisdiction not only as to the nature but also as to the amount of the suit.

Jurisdictional limits. The physical boundaries or the constitutional or statutory limits within which authority of a Court may be exercised.

Jurisdictional plea. A plea which asserts that the Court lacks jurisdiction either over the defendant or over the subject matter of the case.

Jurisprudence is the science of law. The term, which is now properly employed only in this technical sense, has also been employed in various other senses, respectively suggested by etymology, by historical accident, or by the pursuit of euphony, Etymologically, "*jurisprudentia,*" like "*juris scient in,*" originally denoted merely such a knowledge of the laws of his country as was possessed by a practising lawyer at Rome. By historical accident, "jurisprudence" has come to mean in France the decisions of the Courts. But the use of the term in a specific and technical sense is indispensable. As so used, it is the name of the science which defines legal conceptions, and classifies them in accordance with their observed affinities. The province of jurisprudence is therefore to determine what is meant by "law", what are its sources and species, and what are the objects which it serves. (*Ency. of the Laws of England*)

ANALYTICAL JURISPRUDENCE deals with speculations as to such ideas as Duty, Intent, Ownership, Possession *etc.*

COMPARATIVE JURISPRUDENCE deals with the ground work and typical conceptions which are common to all legal systems or to all that have made any considerable way towards completeness.

ETHICAL JURISPRUDENCE is a term sometimes applied to positive law or law, which would in itself be best fitted for a nation in certain given circumstances. (*Bouvier Pollock Oxford Lectures*)

INTERNATIONAL JURISPRUDENCE. The science and theory of International Law.

Jurisprudentia. Jurisprudence. It is the science of law which treats the principles of positive and substantive law and legal relations. Its function is to ascertain the principles on which legal rules are based, to classify them in their proper order and show the relation in which they stand to one another. It is not merely a history of law; its function is to separate the essential elements of legal principles from its historical accidents on a comparative study of the legal institutions of various countries. It has no direct concern with questions of moral or political policy, but when a new and doubtful case arises to which two different rules seem, when taken literally, to be equally applicable, it may be, and often is, the function of jurisprudence to consider the ultimate effect which would be produced if each rule were applied to an indefinite number of similar cases, and to choose that rule, when so applied, as will produce the greatest advantage to the community.

Jurist. One who is versed or skilled in law; now commonly a person eminent mainly for knowledge of the theoretic side of the law.

Juristic. Pertaining to jurisprudence, law or jurist.

Juristic act. An act intended to have a legal effect.

Juristic development. Legal evolution; development of law owing to jurists.

Juristic person. A body of persons; a corporation; a partnership or other legal entity that is recognised by law as the subject of rights and duties, called also artificial person.

A legal entity other then a natural person such as corporations, associations, offices, estates, funds, deities, idols *etc.*

It is well-settled that a trust is not a juristic person or a corporate person. [Income Tax Act (43 of 1961), Sec. 2(35)]

'GURU GRANTH SAHIB' is a 'juristic person'. *Shiromani Gurudwara Prabandhak Committee, Amritsar* v.

Somnath Dass, (2000) 4 SCC 146, para 42 : AIR 2000 SC 1421.

Juror. Jurors are men qualified and sworn to try a cause according to the evidence.

A member of the jury. [Oaths Act (44 of 1969), S. 4(1)(c)].

Jury. A certain number of men sworn to inquire of, and try, a matter of fact, and declare the truth, upon such evidence as shall be delivered them in a cause; and they are sworn judges upon evidence in matter of fact. (*Tomlin*)

Body of laymen selected by lot to ascertain, under the guidance of a judge, the truth in question of fact arising in sessions cases. [IPC (45 of 1860), S. 229].

GRAND JURY. A jury of not less than twelve, nor generally, more than twenty-three, whose duty it was to examine into accusations against persons charged with crime, and if they saw just cause, then to find bills of indictment against them to be presented to the Court. (*Wharton; Bouvier*)

Jury-man. A juror.

Jus. Right, justice; law; power or authority.

JUS is a term with two meanings: (1) Law considered in the abstract, or law taken as a system, an aggregate, a whole, or some one particular system or body of particular laws; and (2) a right in general or in the abstract.

Jus ad rem. A right to a thing; a right to a thing without possession.

Jus commune. The common law; common right.

The common and natural rule of right.

Jus constitui oportet in his quae ut plurimum accidunt non quae ex inopinato. (*Maxim*) Laws ought to be made with a view to those cases which happen most frequently, and not to those which are of rare or accidental occurrence. (*Latin for Lawyers*)

Jus est norma recti : et quicquid est contra normam recti est injuria. (*Maxim*) Law is a rule of right; and whatever is contrary to the rule of right is an injury. (*Latin for Lawyers*)

Jus et fraus nunquam cohabitant. (*Maxim*) Right and fraud never dwell together.

Jus ex (es) injuria non oritur. (*Maxim*) A right does not arise out of an injury. (*Latin for Lawyers*)

Jus gentium. The Law of Nations. The law by which kingdoms and societies in general are governed. (*Tomlin*)

Of which the term "Law of Nations" and *"Droit des gens"* are translations, is a term in Roman Law. The *jus gentium*, when opposed to the *jus civile*, means the institutions of Roman law, admitted by all civilised peoples of antiquity. The *jus gentium* was not international law, nor was it, so to speak, philosophical or ideal law, which is a product of ethical reasoning though the two notions were often confounded; for the rules of law in question were founded on reasons, and were therefore also called *jus naturale* or *Jus naturae*. (*Ency. of the Laws of England*)

Jus haereditatis. The right of inheritance.

Jus in personam, (*Lat.*) is a right against a person: a right which gives its possessor a power to oblige another person to give or procure, to do or not to do, something.

Jus in re aliena. (*Lat.*) A right in another's property such as an easement.

Jus in re propria. A right of a person in his own property.

Jus in rem. *'Jus in rem'* is a right in respect of a thing. A right *in rem* postulates a duty imposed upon all persons generally. A right *in rem* is protected against the world at large. Where the intervention of the Court is sought for the adjudication of a right or title to property, not merely as between the parties but against all persons generally, the action is *in rem*. *Viswanathan* v. *Abdul Wajid*, AIR 1963 SC 1, 15.

Jus jurandi forma verbis differt, re convenit; hunc enim sensum habere debet: ut deus invocetur. (*Lat.*) Oaths differ in pattern of their words but come to the same conclusion; every oath must call on their deity to witness.

Jus legitimum. A legal right.

Jus naturae. The law of nature.

Jus naturae proprie est dictamen rectaeration is quo scimus quid turpe quid honestum quid faciendum quid fugiendum. (*Maxim*) The law of nature is properly the dictate of right reason by which we know what is dishonourable and what is honourable; what should be done and what should be avoided.

Jus non scriptum. The unwritten law. "The unwritten law declared by the tacit consent and customs of the people."

Jus privatum. (*Lat.*) The municipal or civil law.

Jus publicum privatorum pactis mutari non potest. (*Maxim*) A public right cannot be altered by the agreements of private persons.

Jus respicit aequitatem. (*Lat.*) (Co. Litt. 24b) The law regards equity.

Jus sanguinis. The right of blood, particularly in relation to nationality.

Jus soli. The law of the place of one's birth.

Jus strictum. (*Lat.*) Strict law.

Jus tertii. The right or interest of a third person. When a person is sued in respect of certain property he may sometimes set up as a defence that the title to such property is not in the plaintiff but in some third person.

In an action for ejectment, the plaintiff is entitled to succeed solely on the strength of his prior possession and the defendant is not entitled to set up the right of a third party unless he claims under him and makes good that claim.

The right of a third party.

Jus triplex est; proprietatis, possessionis, et possibilitatis. Right is threefold; of property, of possession, of possibility.

Jus vendit quod usus approbavit. (*Lat.*) The law dispenses with what use has approved.

Just. *As an adjective*, fair; adequate; reasonable; probable; right in accordance with law and justice; right in law or ethics; rightful; legitimate; well founded; conformable to laws; conforming to the requirements of right or positive law; conformed to rules or principle of justice. *As an adverb of time*, the word "Just" is equivalent to "at this moment"; of the least possible time since. (*Ame Cyc.*)

Being in conformity with justice. [IPC (45 of 1860), S. 191, *Expln.*, 2, ill. (a) and Constitution of India, Art 42]; fair.

The word 'just' as its nomenclature, denotes equitability, fairness and reasonableness having a large peripheral field. The largeness is, of course, not arbitrary; it is restricted by the conscience which is fair, reasonable and equitable, if it exceeds; it is termed as unfair, unreasonable, unequitable, not just. [*Helen C. Rebello v. Maharashtra SRTC*, (1999) 1 SCC 90, para 28 : 1999 SCC (Cri) 197 : AIR 1998 SC 3191 as cited in *K. Suresh v. New India Assurance Company Limited*, (2012) 12 SCC 274, para 9].

Just and convenient. In ascertaining what is a "*just or convenient*" regard should be had to what is "just" according to settled legal principles, as well as to what is "convenient" (*See* CPC. (5 of 1908), O. XXXIX, R. 1). In ascertaining what is "just," regard must be had to what is "convenient."

The words 'just and convenient' have been construed as meaning that 'it is practicable and the interests of justice require it'. *Madhu Lal* v. *Ramji Daschironji Lal,* AIR 1953 MB 85. [CPC. (5 of 1908), O. XL, R. 1]

Just and equitable. The words 'just and equitable' in the enactment specifying the grounds for winding up by the Court are not to be read as being '*ejusdem generis'* with the preceding words of the enactment. *Rajahmundry Electric Supply Corporation Ltd.* v. *A. Nageshwara Rao*, AIR 1956 SC 213, 216.

Just and fair. The words 'just and fair' apply to the moral qualities of acts, dealings, and transactions and cannot be properly construed as having reference to formal legal proceedings.

Just and reasonable. Pragmatism and common sense approach need not be outlawed in favour of unduly sophisticated, unduly refined, disingenuous approach, if two views are possible and what is reasonable, as also accords with reason, prevails over what is unreasonable, but may also accord with reason. "just and reasonable" may well prevail instead of "just and unreasonable" when both the sides are equally able to provide good reasons in support of their respective pleas. [*Prabhat Silk and Cotton Mills Co. Ltd, Surat* v. *Union of India,* MLJ : YD (1983), p. 690 : (1982) 23 GLR 557]. [Constitution of India, Art. 226]

Just and true account. The 'just and true account' requiring a person to render a just and true account, means an account honestly stated. It does not require the statement of the exact account which a Court may find to be due.

Just cause. 'Just cause' to be shown for a Court to do anything, does not add much weight, though it may add a little. It means, some substantial reason must be shown.

The words 'just cause' in S. 263 are exhaustive and not merely illustrative. Merely the failure to file an inventory or the account within the specified time is not sufficient. It must be established that the person to whom the grant has been made wilfully and without reasonable cause omitted to exhibit them. *In Re. T. Arumuga Mudaliar,* AIR 1955 Mad 622.

[Indian Succession Act (39 of 1925), S. 263, *Explanation*]

Just compensation. 'Just and reasonable compensation' as used in an agreement that solicitors should have a just and reasonable compensation for their services, means neither more nor less than the fees or compensation allowed to them by law for the services.

The term 'just compensation,' in an Act prohibiting the taking of property for public use without just compensation, does not mean that the property so taken shall be valued and its price paid in money, but that the individual who claims to be a sufferer in consequence of the exercise of the right of eminent domain over his property shall be recompensed for the actual injury which he may have sustained, all circumstances considered, by the measure of which he complains. In ascertaining the question of the injury, undoubtedly an estimation of the value of the property taken at the time of the taking is a necessary step; but if the benefits, real and substantial, resulting to the complainant, are equal in pecuniary value to the value of that of which the public has deprived him, they constitute a just compensation for the deprivation to which he has been subjected.

'JUST COMPENSATION,' in an Act providing that private property shall not be taken for public use without just compensation, means 'a full and perfect' equivalent, for the property taken. The noun 'compensation,' standing by itself, carries the idea of an equivalent, so that if the adjective 'just' had been omitted, and the provision was simply that the property should not be taken without 'compensation,' the natural import of the language would be that the compensation should be equivalent to the property, and this is made emphatic by the adjective 'just.'

'Just compensation,' in an Act forbidding the taking of private property without just compensation, means 'that the equivalent to be rendered for the property taken shall be real, substantial, full, and ample.

'Just compensation,' as used in an Act, requiring a just compensation to be paid for property seized means an equivalent, a recompense in value for the property taken; what the article would sell for in the market quality and quantity considered, and not the price which the owner might demand, or which some person for especial reason might be willing to give.

Just debts. Where a clause in a will directed that all the just debts of testator be paid, the phrase 'after all my just debts are paid' should be construed as used by the testator in compliance with the universal custom, having its origin in the solemnity which attends a final disposition of earthly concerns, and does not mean that any debt barred by the statute of limitation is to be revived.

A will requiring that the executor shall 'pay the just debts' of the accused out of the estate should not be construed to force the payment of a just debt held by a person who neglected the legal proof of his demand until more than three years had elapsed after the issuance of letters testamentary, and until after the estate has been finally settled according to law, and the administration closed. The words will not strip the estate of just defence.

Where a testator directed that his just debts should be paid, it was held that the expression 'just debts' only included debts for which the testator was legally liable.

(*in Hindu Law*). In the absence of any proof of wanton waste and reckless extravagance, the money actually borrowed in the ordinary course of dealings whether from the alienee or from a third person is a "just debt". The mere fact that it seems to have swollen in a short time does not make any difference.

The word 'just' has reference to the nature of the debt and not to the person who has advanced the money.

Just, fair and reasonable procedure. The fiat of Article 21, is that any procedure which deprives a person of his life or liberty must be just fair and reasonable. 'Just, fair and reasonable procedure' implies a right to free legal services where he cannot avail them. It implies a right to a speedy trial. It implies human conditions of detention, preventive or punitive. [*T.V. Vatheesawran* v. *State of T.N.,* (1983) 2 SCC 68, 78, p. 20] [Constitution of India, Art. 21]

Just ground. The word 'just' has various meanings, but the connection in which it is used in an instruction in relation to justifiable homicide, where the circumstances were such as to afford the accused 'just and reasonable grounds for believing himself to be in danger of death,' seems to be based upon the definition 'rightful, legitimate, well founded'. When so construed, just ground for believing must necessarily be reasonable ground.

Just provocation. In order to reduce what could otherwise be murder in the first degree to manslaughter, there should be a 'lawful' or 'reasonable' provocation, as, for example, a blow; but in order to reduce what would otherwise be murder in the first degree, in order to eliminate from it the element of deliberation and bring it down to murder in the second degree, grievous and degrading words of reproach would amount to 'just provocation,' as contradistinguished from 'lawful and reasonable provocation.'

Just valuation. The word 'just' in an act requiring a local authority to provide such regulation as shall secure a just valuation for taxation of all property, real and personal, is used as the equivalent of 'correct,' 'honest,' and 'true'. Its use requires the valuation of all property of the same kind in the same taxing district by a uniform and equal standard.

Just value. The 'just value' at which an Act shall appraise taxable property is the market value of the property.

Justa causa. A term meaning lawful ground; often used as synonymous with reasonable cause.

Justice. In its common acceptation, the rendering of every man his due; the constant and perpetual desire to render every one his due; the dictate of right according to the consent of mankind generally, or of that portion of mankind who may be associated in one government, or who may be governed by the same principles and morals.

"Justice" encompasses not just the rights of the convict, but also of the victims of the crime as well as of the law abiding section of society who look towards the Courts as vital instruments for preservation of peace and the curtailment or containment of crime by punishing those who transgress the law. [*Surya Baksh Singh v. State of U.P.*, (2014) 14 SCC 222, para 7].

As applied to the judiciary, a judicial officer; a person duly commissioned to hold Courts or to try and decide controversies and administer the laws; a term often used interchangeably with judge, and is broad enough to include the judge of any Court in state.

Justice is the basis of a state; a sure bond of all commerce. Human society, far from being an intercourse of assistance and good offices, would be no longer anything but a vast scene of robbery, if there were no respect of this virtue, which secures to every one his own. It is still more necessary between nations than between individuals, because injustice produces more dreadful consequences in the quarrels of these powerful bodies politic, and it is still more difficult to obtain redress.

'Justice,' the establishment and enforcement of which is the object of all law, is a comprehensive term, in which are included the three great objects—the security of life, liberty, and the pursuit of happiness.

In a judicial sense, justice is nothing more or less than exact conformity to some obligatory law; and all human actions are either just or unjust as they are in conformity to or in opposition to law.

The exercise of authority or power in maintenance of right; vindication of right by assignment of reward or punishment; the administration of law or the form and processes attending it; the principle of just dealing; just conduct [CPC (45 of 1860), O. XXXV,

R. 4(1)(b) and Constitution of India, preamble.]; a judge of High Court or the Supreme Court; the quality of being morally just or righteous [IPC (45 of 1860), S. 191, *Expln.* 2, ill. (a)].

The word 'justice' is used interchangeably with 'judge'.

"Justice" in S. 151. CPC. means that standard of justice which the CPC. (5 of 1908) is designed to achieve.

Justice according to law, Administer. Administration of justice according to law is administration according to authoritative precepts or norms (patterns) or guides developed and applied by an authoritative technique, which individuals may ascertain in advance of controversy and by which all are reasonably assured of receiving like treatment. [Navy Act (62 of 1957), S. 104(1)].

Justice, equity. Justice is a written or prescribed law, to which one is bound to conform and make it the rule of one's decisions : equity is a law in our hearts; it conforms to no rule but to circumstances, and decides by the consciousness of right and wrong. Justice is exclusive, it assigns to every one his own; it preserves the subsisting inequality between men; equity is communicative; it seeks to equalise the condition of men by a fair distribution. Justice forbids us doing wrong to any one; and requires us to repair the wrongs we have done to others; equity forbids us doing to others what we would not have them do to us; it requires us to do to others what in similar circumstances we would expect from them. The obligations to justice are imperative; the observance of its laws is enforced by the civil power, and the breach of them is exposed to punishment; the obligations to equity are altogether moral; we are impelled to it by the dictates of conscience. Justice is inflexible, it follows one invariable rule, which can seldom be deviated from consistently with the general good; equity, on the other hand, varies with the circumstances of the case, and is guided by discretion; justice may, therefore, sometimes run counter to equity, when the interests of the individual must be sacrificed to those of the community; and equity sometimes tempers the rigour of justice by admitting of reasonable deviations from the literal interpretations of its laws.

Justice, equity and good conscience. The words "justice, equity, and good conscience," with reference to India practically mean cases, principles and rules of English law, if found applicable to Indian society and circumstances.

The decision of a case according to the principles of justice, equity and good conscience has generally meant decision according to the principles of English Law applicable to a similar state of circumstances.

Justice of the peace. A justice of the peace is a judicial officer of inferior rank, holding a Court, and having usually civil jurisdiction of a limited nature, for the trial of minor cases, to an extent prescribed by special or general statutes, and for the conservation of the peace and the preliminary hearing of criminal complaints and the commitment of offenders; a judicial officer of special and limited jurisdiction, both civil and criminal. In English law justices of the peace are judges of record appointed by the Crown to be justices within a certain district for the conservation of the peace, and for the execution of the diverse things, comprehended within their commission and within diverse statutes, committed to their charge.

A Magistrate appointed to keep the peace within a given jurisdiction. [Presidency-towns Insolvency Act (3 of 1909), S. 117(c)].

Justices in eyre. Itinerant or travelling justices.

Justice is blind. The expression that justice is blind means that the Court shall merely regard litigants as they appear from their claims put forward in the Courts and not as individuals having any personal characteristics. It cannot be considered to mean that the Courts are to act so blindly that they do not even see the course they are pursuing.

Justices' election. "JUSTICES' ELECTION" and "fellows' election' mean, respectively, an election of a councillor by justices or by fellows. [Bom Act III of 1888 City Bom Municipal), S. 3, Cl (*j*)]

Justices of Assise. (*In Old English Law*) A particular kind of justices in *eyre* appointed or commissioned to determine certain actions called *assises*, or take verdicts in such actions.

Justices of gaol delivery. Justice in eyre, who acted under a special commission to deliver the gaols of persons confined in them.

JUSTICE OF GAOL DELIVERY are those who are sent with commission, to hear and determine all causes appertaining to such, who for any offence are cast into gaol.

Justices of oyer and terminer. Justices deputed upon some special occasion, to hear and determine some peculiar causes, such as cases of riotous assembly.

Justiciability. The character of a dispute being in the proper form to be considered by a Court. (CRAIG R. DUCAT — *Constitutional Interpretation*)

The quality or state of being appropriate or suitable for review by a Court.

Justiciable. Proper to be examined in Courts of justice; subject to action of Court of justice.

Justiciar, or Justicier. A Judge; Justice. (*Tomlin*)

Justifiable. Rightful; warranted or sanctioned by law; that which can be shown to be sustained by law; excusable.

Justifiable homicide. The killing of a human creature without fault or blame, as by command of the law.

JUSTIFIABLE HOMICIDE is the killing of a human being in necessary self-defence, or in the defence of habitation, property, or person against one who manifestly intends or endeavours, by violence or surprise, to commit a known felony upon either person or property, or against any person or persons who manifestly intend to endeavour in a violent, riotous, or tumultuous manner to enter the habitation of another for the purpose of assaulting or offering personal violence to any person dwelling or being therein.

Justification. A maintaining or showing good reason in Court why one did such a thing which he is called to answer. (*Tomlin*)

The showing in Court of a sufficient lawful reason why a party charged or accused did that for which he is called to answer.

Justified. Done on adequate reasons, sufficiently supported by credible evidence, when weighted by unprejudiced mind, guided by common sense and by correct rules of law. [*Raj Kapoor* v. *Laxman*, (1980) 2 SCC 175, 178, p. 6]

Justified by law. An act is justified by law, if it is warranted, validated and made blameless by law. *Raj Kapoor* v. *Laxman*, AIR 1980 SC 605, 607. [IPC (45 of 1860), S. 79]

Justified by necessity. In deciding a question as to whether a mortgage by the *mahant* of an *asthal* is "justified by necessity" the matter should be approached not from an absolute standard of necessity, but from the point of view of what considerations would weigh in the mind of a prudent manager. "Necessity and benefit of estate" are general and elastic terms. To a religious institution like a *Math* or *asthal*, its prestige and influence are of vital importance. Preservation of its prestige and influence is no less necessary than preservation of its property. Where there is evidence showing that an elephant was being maintained in an *asthal* from a very early time and that an elephant was necessary for use during festivals in the *asthal*, a mortgage by the mahant to purchase an elephant would be justified by necessity in the absence of anything to show that he did not act as a prudent manager. 1941 PWN 75 : 22 Pat LT 239 : AIR 1941 Pat 354.

Justify. To make out, or establish according to law, particularly the sufficiency of bail.

To prove or show to be just, desirable, warranted or useful [IPC (45 of 1860), S. 79].

Justifying bail. Demonstrating to a Court granting bail that one is capable of meeting the surety specified in the bail (for example, disclosing one's financial resources).

Justinian. Flavius Justinianus from 527-565 A.D., the Roman Emperor who codified the Roman law and published it. It superseded all the previous Roman law.

Justitia. Statute law; ordinance.

Justitia debet esse libera, quia nihil iniquius venali justitia; plena, quia justitia non debet claudicare; et celeris, quia dilatio est quaedam negatio. Justice ought to be free, because nothing is more iniquitous than venal justice; full, because justice ought not to halt; and speedy, because delay is a kind of denial. (*Latin for Lawyers*)

Justitia est constans et perpetua voluntas jus suum cuique tribuendi. Justice is the constant and perpetual disposition or will of giving to every man his right.

Justitia est duplex : viz severe puniens, et vere praeveniens. Justice is two fold, viz: severely punishing, and really or efficiently preventing.

Justitia est virtus excelleus et Altissimo complaceus. Justice is an excellent virtue and pleasing to the most high.

Justitia nec differenda nec neganda est : Justitia non est neganda, non differenda. Justice is not to be denied or delayed.

Justitia non novit patrem nec matrem; solam veritatem spectat justitia. Justice knows not father nor mother; justice looks at truth alone.

Justly. The term 'justly' as used in the consideration of what a plaintiff in attachment is 'justly entitled to recover,' includes not only what in good faith to the debtor he is entitled to recover, but also what he is entitled to recover in good faith and justice to other creditors.

Jute. An Indian bast fibre, white jute (Corchorus Capsularis) and tossa jute (Corchorus Olitorius) which is used for the manufacture of coarse sacking and bags (gunny sack). Old gunny and sacking are used as raw material in papermaking. [Indian Standard Glossary of Terms used in Paper Trade and Industry IS 4661 : 1999 as cited in *Coastal Paper Limited v. Commissioner of Central Excise, Visakhapatnam*, (2015) 10 SCC 664, para 30].

Jute manufacture. Means any articles specified in the Schedule which contains more than fifty per cent of jute (including Bimilipatam Jute or mesta fibre of any sort) by weight of the total fibre content and in the production of which any process is ordinarily carried on with the aid of power.

Explanation—"Power" means electrical energy any other form of energy which is mechanically transmitted and is not generated by any human or animal agency. [Jute Manufactures Cess Act (28 of 1983), S. 2(a)]

Jute packaging material. Means Jute, Jute Yarn, Jute twine, Jute sacking cloth, hessian cloth, Jute bags or any other packaging material containing not less than seventy-five per cent by weight of jute. [Jute Packaging Materials (Compulsory Use in Packing Commodities) Act (10 of 1987), S. 2(c)]

Juvenile. "JUVENILE" means a boy who has not attained the age of sixteen years or a girl who has not attained the age of eighteen years. [Juvenile Justice Act (53 of 1986), S. 2(h)]

Young; pertaining to youth; a young person. A person, not reached the age at which he should be treated as an adult by the criminal justice system.

Juvenile Courts. Courts having special jurisdiction, of a paternal nature, over delinquent and neglected children.

Juvenile delinquency. A status in a juvenile characterised by anti-social behaviour, waywardness, incorrigibility; an offence committed by a person who is under 16 years of age.

Juvenile offenders. Persons of young age who have committed crimes; persons sent to reformatory schools.

Children who have committed an indictable offence.

"Juvenile" or "child". Means a person who has not completed eighteenth year of age. [Juvenile Justice (Care and Protection of Children) Act (56 of 2000), S. 2(k)]

Juxta conventionem. According to the convenant.

Juxta formam statuti. According to the form of the statute.

Juxtaposition. A placing or being placed in nearness or contiguity; or side by side; as a juxtaposition of words. (*Black*)

K

Kalakshetra. Means the institution known as Kalakshetra founded by the late Thirumathi Rukmini Devi Arundale, situated at Adyar, Madras, and includes its constituent units. [Kalakshetra Foundation Act, 1993 (6 of 1994), S. 3(j)]

Karaoke. Term applicable to recorded pro ductions enabling the viewers to hear the music, seeing the video images and the lyrics at the same time; literally means 'empty orchestra' in Japanese. (*Copyright*)

"Karta" and "Manager". The two expressions i.e. karta and Manager may be understood to be not synonymous and the expression "manager" may be understood as denoting a role distinct from the karta. [*Shreya Vidyarthi* v. *Ashok Vidyarthi,* (2015) 16 SCC 46, para 22].

Katra. The primary meaning of the word "*Katra*" is enclosure and the secondary meaning is market. Generally, a *Katra* would be a residential locality though there might be purely residential *Katras*. Even purely residential *katras* would consist of a large number of houses to which a large number of people will resort. *Bhau Ram* v. *Baij Nath Singh*, AIR 1962 SC 1476, 1484. [Punjab Pre-emption Act (1 of 1913), S. 5]

(*Oudh*), a 'street' or hamlet, *i.e.* a line of houses for families and their dependents : (*Pad. Pow.* ii 241).

Kazi. A Judge, civil, criminal, and ecclesiastical, among the Mahomedans. (*Mac. Mah. Law.*) Under the Muhammadan Empire, the Kazi was a civil and criminal Judge. Under British rule he became an adviser to the Courts on points of Muhammadan law. He still holds a high place in Musalman communities, and leads the public prayers on great festivities. He is also registrar of marriages and divorces for which he receives fees; he has also usually some endowment.

Kazin. Means any small bank or ridge surrounding or dividing a field. [Bur. Act IV of 1909 (Embankment), S. 3 cl. 2]

Keel. A ship's bottom; the chief foundation timber, reaching from stem to stem holding the whole frame together.

In an iron or steel ship, the term signifies the plates that correspond to the keel timbers of a wooden ship.

A flat bottomed ship.

Keep. To hold; to retain in one's power or possession; not to lose or part with; to preserve; to retain; to preserve in the same state or tenor; to maintain or carry on; conduct or manage; to have the control and management, as for example, to have the control and management of places where liquors are sold, of bawdy-houses, of gambling establishments *etc.*; to have in possession, use care or custody, hence to use and enjoy; to maintain; support as in a prison, or asylum; so also as applied to animals, to tend to feed to pasture; to supply with necessaries of life. As an intransitive verb, to remain sound, sweet, fresh or the like; (*as*) meat will keep for two days.

Keep a man. A charge that a married woman 'keeps' a man not her husband would be understood by the ordinary hearer as imputing the crime of adultery.

Keep a mistress. The word 'kept' has many significations, according to the subjects to which it is applied. But it is a common and well-established sense of it, when used in reference to connections between the sexes, to denote habitual and criminal carnal conversation amounting to cohabitation. Every one knows at once what is meant by the terms 'kept mistress,' or what is laid to the charge of a man who is said 'to keep a mistress.' It is not the meritorious act of providing for or maintaining a virtuous lady in her innocence, but it is the vicious one of having a wanton at his command for carnal gratification, and of keeping her for sexual uses. This is the natural import of the words in themselves, as the people in the country would universally understand them. To say that a man 'kept' a woman amounts to a charge of incontinency against her.

Keep a woman. Where, in an action for defamation, it appeared that defendant said that the plaintiff was keeping a woman not his wife, the Court said : 'It is difficult to conceive how the charge that the plaintiff was keeping Mrs. B., when taken in connection with the other words spoken, or considered by themselves, could have been understood by the hearers in any other sense than that the plaintiff was guilty of criminal intercourse with her. If they did not mean that, what did they mean? The words 'keep' and 'keeping' have no doubt several meanings, but their signification in a particular case depends upon the context, the words with which or the circumstances under which they are used. But when it is said, in reference to a woman, that a man is 'keeping a woman,' the ordinary and popular construction of that language is that the relation between the parties is one which involves criminal intercourse.'

Keep for the benefit of. To 'keep' is to retain in one's power and possession, and to 'keep for the benefit of' is to keep for the use, enjoyment, and support; and the term 'to be kept' for the benefit of a legatee's children means to be kept for the use and support and enjoyment of such children, and creates a trust in their behalf.

Keep house of ill-fame. Frequenting, 'keeping, or maintaining' houses reputed to be houses of bawdy and ill-fame, imply much more than to live in such a house, as to 'keep' a hotel implies more than to live in one. The controlling head of the hotel 'keeps', it, while the individuals who take their meals and lodge in such hotel, and have no other domicile, 'live' therein; so the controlling head of a house of ill-fame, or a house reputed to be a house of ill-fame 'keeps' such house.

Keep in good repair. A devise of a house, conditioned that the devisee should 'keep it in good repair', requires a rebuilding of the house if destroyed by fire.

'To keep in good repair' means that during the whole term the premises shall be in good repair.

Keep in possession. The expression 'keeping' in possession of contraband liquors, involves the idea of continuity or habit, the words meaning to have habitually in possession, the word 'keeping' being defined as to maintain habitually, to have habitually in stock or for sale, and implies more than the mere having in temporary possession.

Keep in repair. A covenant in a lease to 'repair, uphold, and support,' or 'to keep in repair and have as found,' or 'to repair and keep in repair,' or 'to keep in good repair, natural wear and tear excepted', all impose upon the covenantor the duty of rebuilding or restoring the premises destroyed or injured by the elements.

Keep; Observe; Fulfil. To *keep* marks simply perseverance or continuance in a thing; a man *keeps* his word if he does not depart from it; to *observe* marks fidelity and consideration : we *observe* a rule when we are careful to be guided by it : to *fulfill* marks the perfection and consummation of that which one has kept; we *fulfill* a promise by acting in strict conformity to it.

Keep on the premises. The word 'kept' as used in fire insurance policy providing that it shall be void if certain substances are kept on the premises, implies a use of the premises, as a place of deposit for the prohibited articles for a considerable period of time.

Keep; Preserve; Save. Things are *kept* at all times, and under all circumstances; they are *preserved* in circumstances of peculiar difficulty and danger; they are *saved* in the moment in which they are threatened with destruction; things are *kept* at pleasure; they are *preserved* by an exertion of power; they are *saved* by the use of extraordinary means; the shepherd *keeps* his flock by simply watching over them; children are sometimes wonderfully *preserved* in the midst of the greatest dangers; things are frequently *saved* in the midst of fire by the exertions of those present.

Keep record. When it is said that the clerk of a Court shall keep a record, or that a record shall be kept by such clerk, reference is not made to the mere possession and control of the book in which matters are recorded but rather to the work itself in writing up the record.

The term 'to keep a record,' as used in reference to legislative proceedings, means to make a permanent record of the whole proceedings.

Keeper. The word 'keeper' is defined to be one who has the care, custody, or superintending of anything, as the 'keeper' of a park.

Keeper of a sarai. "KEEPER OF A SARAI" includes the owner and any person having or acting in the care or management thereof. [Sarais Act (22 of 1867), S. 2]

Keeper of disorderly house. In a penal statute, means the proprietor, and not prostitutes who occupy rooms in such house.

Keeper of the Great Seal is a lord by his office, styled Lord Keeper of the Great Seal of England, and is of the King's Privy Council; through his hands pass all charters, commissions and grants of the King, under the Great Seal; without which seal many of those grants and commissions are of no force in law; for the King is by interpretation of law a corporation, and passeth nothing but by the Great Seal, which is, as the public faith of the kingdom, in the high esteem and reputation justly attributed thereto. The Great Seal consists of two impressions, one being the very seal itself with the effigies of the King stamped on it; the other has an impression of the King's arms in the figures of a target, for matters of a smaller moment, as certificates, *etc.* And anciently, when the King travelled into France or other foreign kingdoms, there were two Great Seals; one went with the King, and another was left with the Custos Regni, or the Chancellor. &c. If the Great Seal be altered, the same is notified in the Court of Chancery, and public proclamations made thereof by the Sheriffs, *etc.* (*Tomlin*)

Keeper of the King's conscience. The Lord High Chancellor.

Keeper of the Privy Seal. That officer, through whose hands all charters, pardons, *etc.*, pass, signed by the King, before theycome to the Great Seal; and something which do not pass the seal at all. (*Tomlin*)

Keeping. The word *'keeping'* in the IPC (45 of 1860), S. 361, connotes the fact that it is compatible with independence of action and movement in the object kept. It implies neither apprehension nor detention, but rather maintenance, protection and control, manifested, not by continual action but as available on necessity arising.

KEEPING, CUSTODY. The *keeping* amounts to little more than having purposely in one's possession; but *custody* is a particular kind of keeping, for the purpose of preventing an escape; inanimate objects may be in one's *keeping*; but a prisoner, or that which is in danger of getting away, is placed in *custody*. A person has in his *keeping* that which he values as the property of an absent friend; the officers of justice get into their *custody* those who have offended against the laws, or such property as has been stolen. (*Crobb.*)

Keeping is simple and generic. *Custody* is a specific *keeping*, involving responsibility, and is for the sake of obviating escape in the case of persons, and loss in the case of inanimate objects; as the *custody* of prisoners, of documents. (*Smith. Sys. Dis.*)

"Keeping" is not confined to storing of materials for subsequent use, and there is a "keeping" of materials even when they are waste materials.

Keeping a brothel. The expression 'keeping a brothel' means a place being used as brothel and a person in charge so keeping it. It is not necessary that there should be repeated visits by persons to the place for the purpose of prostitution. *Krishnamurithy* v. *Public Prosecutor, Madras*. AIR 1967 SC 567, 568. [Suppression of Immoral Traffic in Women and Girls Act (104 of 1956), S. 3 (1)]

Keeping or Keeping for use. The words 'keeping' and 'keeping for use' do not mean the same thing. An owner may 'keep' a motor vehicle in his garage and yet he may not keep it for use. *State* v. *Jujar Singh,* AIR 1959 Raj 80.

Keeping out of keeping of lawful guardian. Regarding the interpretation of the word 'keeping', it is not the physical presence in the precincts of the father's house that matters, but whether the girl was in fact under her father's guardianship. Whether she left the house as the result of a pre-arranged plan between her and the accused or whether she went out to answer the calls of nature, it cannot make any difference. *In Re. Khalandar Sahib,* AIR 1955 AP 59, 60. [IPC (45 of 1860), S. 361]

Keeping silence. The expression "keeping silence" implies intentional concealment as distinguished from mere non-disclosure; the withholding must be fraudulent, as necessarily is the case when a material circumstance is intentionally concealed.

Keeping the peace. Avoiding a breach of peace; dissuading or preventing others from breaking the peace. [CrPC 1973 (2 of 1974), S. 106(1)].

Keeps. The word 'keeps' means some continuous process; not a mere isolated moment.

A mere state of running through or even halting of the vehicle in the course of the journey through the State of Mysore for its outside destination, will not be sufficient to constitute 'keeping of that' vehicle in the State. *State of Mysore* v. *Sundaram Motors (P.) Ltd,* AIR 1980 SC 148, 150.

To 'keep' is to 'maintain, carry on, conduct, or manage.' (as) to keep a lodging house.

KEEP implies habitual, and not mere occasional, use for the purpose prohibited by a statute.

Kendra. Means any telecasting centre with studios or transmitters or both and includes a relay station. [Prasar Bharti (Broadcasting Corporation of India) Act (25 of 1990), S. 2(k)]

Kentlege. Permanent ship-ballast, and generally consisting of pigs of iron.

Kept. In association with the use of the vehicle, the word 'kept' has an element of stationariness. It is something more than mere stoppage or halt for rest, food *etc.* in course of transit. *State of Mysore* v. *Sundaram Motors Pvt. Ltd,* AIR 1980 SC 148, 149.

Kept in regular course of business. A daybook, which has been entered after four months from the happening of an event and the rough notes of which are not available is not a document which can be held to have been kept in the regular course of business. These remarks apply *a fortiori* to a ledger which is prepared from such a day-book.

Kept woman. Mistress.

Kerb crawling. The offence committed by a man for soliciting a woman for prostitution in a street or public place either from a motor vehicle or having just alighted from one, when the soliciting is persistent or likely to cause annoyance to the woman or nuisance to other people in the vicinity.

Kernel. An essential part of the operating system, responsible for resource allocation, low-level hardware interfaces, security, and more. (*Cyber Law*)

Key. An instrument for fastening and opening a lock. The delivery of the key of a warehouse is symbolical delivery of the goods stored therein.

KEYS are also implements of housebreaking. Though commonly used for lawful purposes, they are capable of being employed for purposes of housebreaking. (*Bouvier*)

Key Component of Binary or Multi-component Chemical Systems. (Hereinafter referred to as "key component") means : The Precursor which plays the most important role in determining the toxic properties of the final product and reacts rapidly with other chemicals in the binary or multi-component system. [Chemical Weapons Convention Act (34 of 2000), Art. II (4)]

Key escrowing/Key archiving. A set of policies, procedures, and mechanisms that provides backup access to cryptographic keys necessary to decrypt data outside of a normal application. Key escrow in particular carries connotation of key storage with a third party, whereby law enforcement agencies might be able to acquire keys used to decrypt messages from suspected criminals. Key archiving more generally refers to the topic of key storage for the purpose of recovering encrypted data when the original decryption key is lost, stolen, or needed for some other purpose. (*Information Technology*)

Key generation. The creation of a key or a distinct pair of Public and Private keys. (*Information Technology*)

Key length. Encryption strength is a function both of the algorithm and the key length used with the algorithm. As a rule, the longer the key length, the greater the security. (*Information Technology*)

Key logger system/Magic lantern. Keystroke recording software that may, among other features, read users' passwords as they enter them and has the ability to secretly record all computer activity. (*Cyber Law*)

Key Loggers. A software program or a device designed to secretly monitor and log all keystrokes. Key-logging devices are small devices that can be fixed to the keyboard, or placed within a cable or the computer itself. Key-logging software is made up of programs dedicated to tracking and logging keystrokes. Aparna Viswanathan, *Cyber Law: Indian & International Perspectives,* 2012, LexisNexis Butterworths at p. 15.

Key management. The generation, storage, distribution, deletion, archiving, and application of keys in accordance with an established security policy. (*Information Technology*)

Key management personnel. "Key managerial personnel", in relation to a company, means—

(*i*) the Chief Executive Officer or the managing director or the manager;

(*ii*) the company secretary;

(*iii*) the whole-time director;

(*iv*) the Chief Financial officer;

(*v*) such other officer, not more than one level below the directors who is in whole-time employment, designated as key managerial personnel by the Board; and

(*vi*) such other officer as may be prescribed. [Companies Act (18 of 2013), section 2(51)].

Key pair. In an asymmetric crypto system, means a private key and its mathematically related public key, which are so related that the public key can verify a digital signature created by the private key. [Information Technology Act (21 of 2000), S. 2(1)(x)]

Key-person insurance. Insurance designed to protect a business firm against the loss of income resulting from the death or disability of a key employee.

Keyboard. The hardware part that has keys for entering characters and commands. It is either part of the terminal or is connected to the terminal by a flexible cable. (*Computer*)

Keyman insurance policy. "KEYMAN INSURANCE POLICY" means a life insurance policy taken by a person on the life of another person who is or was the employee of the first mentioned person or is or was connected in any manner whatsoever with the business of the first mentioned person. [Income-tax Act (43 of 1961), S. 10 (10D), *Expln.*]

Keystroke. One press of any key on the keyboard, including spaces, returns, and any command keys. (*Computer*)

Keystroke monitoring. A form of user surveillance in which the actual character-by character traffic (that user's keystrokes) are monitored, analyzed, and/or logged for future reference. A specialized form of audit trail software, or a specially designed device, that records every key struck by a user and every character of the response that the host computer returns to the user.

Keystroke save. A feature on some systems that allows you to put a certain number of characters into a temporary memory and play them back on command for any number of times until you replace them with a new set of characters. On other systems, this feature can be used with the cut-and-paste feature. (*Computer*)

Khala. Dissolution of the marriage at the suit of the wife, in which she agrees to make her husband compensation for her loss by relinquishing to him an adequate portion of her peculiar property, and by foregoing claim for dower; also disinheriting a son; turning him out of doors.

Khandsari. "KHANDSARI SUGAR", that is to say, sugar in the manufacture of which neither a vacuum pan nor a vacuum evaporator is employed. [Sugar (Regulation of Production) Act (55 of 1961), S. 2(f)(i)]

Khar land. Means such tidal land as is made cultivable by protecting it by means of on embankment from the sea or tidal river and includes all such land in whatever manner described, whether as *Khar Khajan Kharepat-gazni* or otherwise. [Gujarat Khar Lands Act, 1963 (17 of 1964), S. 2(d)]

Kharif. The autumn harvest.

Kharif crop. The autumn harvest; crops sown at the beginning of the rains and reaped from October to December : Rice, Juar, Tur, Cotton.

Khas possession. *Khas* possession is actual possession, that is, a foothold on the land, an actual entry, a possession in fact, a standing upon it, and occupation of it, as a real, administrative act done. *Gurucharan Singh* v. *Kamala Singh*, AIR 1977 SC 5, 15.

Khas possession means actual possession. When lands are in possession of tenant-at-will the landlord cannot be said to be in *khas* possession. *Ramesh Bejoy Sharma* v. *Pasupati Rai*, AIR 1979 SC 1769, 1777, 1776.

Khasra. *Khasra* is a register recording the incidents of a tenure and is a historical record. *Khasra* would serve the purpose of a deed of title, when there is no other title deed. The interpretation of *Khasra* would necessarily be a question of law. *Changa* v. *Bhagwan Dei,* AIR 1949 All 493, 496.

A *Khasra* is normally a field book containing a list of the tenants in occupation of agricultural land and it is not one of the registers which are included in the record of rights which carries with it a presumption that the statements made in it are true. *Din Mohammad* v. *Secretary of State,* 1942 ALJ 422.

'Khasra' refers to the "field book" or village register recording the possession or tenure of agricultural land. [*Sarjeet Singh v Hari Singh*, (2015) 1 SCC 760, para 6].

'Khasra' means annual village register showing the possession of the land as a cultivator. *Kasturchand* v. *Harbilash,* (2000) 7 SCC 611, para 8 : AIR 2000 SC 3137. [M.B Zamindari Abolition Act (13 of 1951), S. 4(2)]

Khasra girdawari. Crop inspection register; a government record.

Khasra girdwari is the crop or harvest inspection record pertaining to the land. [*Sarjeet Singh v. Hari Singh*, (2015) 1 SCC 760, para 6].

The mere entry of *khudkasht* in *khasra girdawaris* of a certain village in the name of a person is not conclusive that the person resides in that village for purposes of cultivation as *khudkasht* does not only mean cultivation by the person himself but also includes cultivation through his servants and associates.

Khata. The ultimate or individual (family holding in co-sharing village).

An account book, a day book, a journal or ledger, also an account; account current-one kept with an individual, or of a particular concern with respect to the receipts and outlay upon it; an account of real or personal property; also the paper or book in which such accounts are kept.

Khatadar or khetedar. Holding of a lot : *i.e.*, to distinguish a holder of a share in the whole estate, as such from anyone not a co-sharer who might be a tenant or *milkmaqbuza*, or an *arazidar*, or a plot or sub-proprietor and not a *khatadar*.

Khatauni. (*a*) Village statement showing demand and collections of sums paid in by headmen. (*b*) A statement of the demand on a holding.

An entry in the *khatauni* of a settlement is to be accepted unless its incorrectness is demonstrated in a convincing manner.

'Khatauni' and 'khasras.' Unless instruments of title are involved, findings of fact arrived at by a Court of first appeal cannot be questioned in second appeal, although documentary evidence has to be considered. "*Khataunis*" and "*Khasras*" cannot always be regarded as instruments of title. Where the entries in the "*Khatauni*" and the "*Khasras*" are relied on by the parties with reference to the question whether a certain plot was occupied by the plaintiff alone or by him and the defendant jointly, such entries are mere items of evidence and cannot be regarded as instruments of title.

Khevat. The term *'Khevat'* in the phrase '*Hasab rasad Khevat*' may mean proprietary land or the land revenue assessed on the land.

Khewat. One of the old survey records, a list of co-sharers and proprietors in the village with their interests and share of revenue payable.

Khewat is the register maintained under the U.P. Land Revenue Act, 1901, mentioning all the proprietors in the *mahal* including the proprietors of specific areas specifying the nature and extent of the interest of each.

Khiraj. The land revenue.

Khot. Includes (*a*) a mortgagee lawfully in possession of *khotki*, (*b*) all co-sharers in a khotki [Bom. Act I of 1880 (*Khoti* Settlement), S. 3, cl. 2]

Khoti. Means the aggregate of the rights and interests vested in a *khot* as such. [Bom. Act I of 1880 (*Khoti* Settlement), S. 3, cl. 3.]

Khoti-land. "KHOTI-LAND" means land in respect of which a *khot* has, as such, any right or interest and which is not *dhara* land. [Bom. Act I of 1880 (Khoti Settlement) S. 3, cl. 10]

Khud-kasht. Land cultivated by a proprietor (for himself) in a co-sharing village estate.

KHUD-KASHT is a resident cultivator, one cultivating his own hereditary lands.

'Khud-kasht' denotes a proprietor of land who is cultivating it himself. [*Sarjeet Singh v. Hari Singh*, (2015) 1 SCC 760, para 10].

The word '*Khudhast*' means personal cultivation and that is a neutral expression, which might include both private lands and *bakasht* lands, that is to say, *raiyati* lands, which had come into the possession of the propreitor by surrender, abandonment or otherwise. *Harihar Prasad Singh*, v. *Deonarain Prasad*, AIR 1956 SC 305, 308.

Literally speaking the word "*khudkasht*" means personal cultivation. The definition of this expression contained in S. 5(23) of the Rajasthan Tenancy Act, which is in two parts, indicates that it has been used in the same sense in the Act. The expression '*khudkasht*' as defined in S. 5(23) of the Tenancy Act would not include land in possession of and cultivated by a tenant or mortgagee. *Budha* v. *Amilal,* AIR 1991 SC 663.

Khudkasht, kamat and sir. The word '*Khudkasht*' in a deed of transfer of property means personal cultivation, and that is a neutral expression, which might include both private lands and *bakasht* lands, that is to say, *raiyati* lands, which had come into the possession of the proprietor by surrender, abandonment or otherwise. But the word '*kamat*' has a definite connotation, and means private lands. The word '*sir*' is synonymous with '*kamat*' and '*zirat*' and means private lands of the proprietor. *Harihar Prasad* v. *Deonarain,* MLJ : QD (1956-1960) Vol. IV C2168 : (1956) SCJ 279 :1956 SCA 316 : 1956 BLJR 306 : ILR 35 Pat 221 : 1956 SCC 124 : 1956 SCR 1 : (S) AIR 1956 SC 305 (SC). [Bihar Tenancy Act (1885), S. 116]

Khudkasht land. '*Khudkasht land*' means land cultivated by *zamindar* himself. *Mishrilal* v. *Dhirendra Nath,* AIR 1999 SC 2286. [Madhya Bharat Zamindari Abolition Act (13 of 1951), S. 2(c)]

Khula. Sub-section (2) of Section 319 of the Mohammedan Law deals with divorce by khula which is a divorce at the instance of the wife, in which she gives or agrees to give a consideration to the husband for her release from the marriage tie. In such a case, the terms of the bargain are matters, of arrangement between the husband and the wife and the wife, as the consideration, may release her dyn-mahr (dower) and other rights, or make any other agreement for the benefit of the husband. Khula is effected by an offer from the wife to compensate the husband, if he releases her from her marital ties, and acceptance by the husband of the offer. *Shihabudheen* v. *Shybi* 2009 (4) KLT 96.

Kickback. Payoff; returning a portion of a monetary sum received, especially as a result of coercion or a secret agreement.

Kidnapping. An act of stealing, abducting or carrying away a person by force or fraud. [IPC (45 of 1860), Ss. 359, 360 and 361].

KIDNAPPING is of two kinds; kidnapping from India, and kidnapping from lawful guardianship. [IPC (45 of 1860), S. 359.]

KIDNAPPING is of two kinds: kidnapping from India, and kidnapping from lawful guardianship—(a) whoever conveys any person beyond the limits of India without the consent of that person, or of some person legally authorised to consent on behalf of that person, is said to kidnap that person from India; (b) whoever takes or entices any child or any person of unsound mind, out of the keeping of the lawful guardian of such child or person of unsound mind, without the consent of such guardian, is said to kidnap such child or person from lawful guardianship.

Explanation.—The words "lawful guardian" in this clause include any person lawfully entrusted with the care or custody of such child or other person.

Exception.—This clause does not extend to the act of any person who in good faith believes himself to be the father of an illegitimate child, or who in good faith believes himself to be entitled to the lawful custody of such child, unless such act is committed for an immoral or unlawful purpose. [(w. e. f. 1-7-2024) Bharatiya Nyaya Sanhita, 2023 (45 of 2023), section 137]

Kidnapping for begging. Where any person, not being the lawful guardian of a child employs or uses such child for the purposes of begging, it shall be presumed, unless the contrary is proved, that he kidnapped or otherwise obtained the custody of such child in order that such child might be employed or used for the purposes of begging. [(w. e. f. 1-7-2024) Bharatiya Nyaya Sanhita, 2023 (45 of 2023), section 139(3)]

Kidnapping for ransom. "Whoever kidnaps or abducts any person or keeps a person in detention after such kidnapping or abduction, and threatens to cause death or hurt to such person, or by his conduct gives rise to a reasonable apprehension that such person may be put to death or hurt, or causes hurt or death to such person in order to compel the Government or any foreign State or international inter-Governmental organization or any other person to do or abstain from doing any act or to pay a ransom, shall be punishable with death, or imprisonment for life, and shall also be liable to fine." (Indian Penal Code, 1860) *Malleshi* v. *State of Karnataka*, (2004) 8 SCC 95, 98 (SC). [(w. e. f. 1-7-2024) Bharatiya Nyaya Sanhita, 2023 (45 of 2023), section 140]

Kidnapping from India. "Whoever conveys any person beyond the limits of India without the consent of that person, or of some person legally authorized to consent on behalf of that person is said to kidnap that person from India." [IPC (45 of 1860), S. 360] [(w. e. f. 1-7-2024) repealed and replaced by Bharatiya Nyaya Sanhita, 2023 (45 of 2023), section 137]

Kidnapping from lawful guardianship. "Whoever takes or entices any minor under sixteen year of age if a male, or under eighteen years of age if a female, or any person of unsound mind, out of the keeping of the lawful guardian of such minor or person of unsound mind without the consent of such guardian, is said to kidnap such minor or person from lawful guardianship." [IPC (45 of 1860), S. 361] [(w. e. f. 1-7-2024) repealed and replaced by Bharatiya Nyaya Sanhita, 2023 (45 of 2023), section 137]

Kill; Killing. "Killing is causing the death, of a person by an act or omission but for which the person killed would not have died when he did, and which is directly and immediately connected with the death. The question whether a given act or omission is directly and immediately connected with the death of any person, is a question of degree dependent upon the circumstances of each particular case.

A charge of "killing" a human being signifies a voluntary and unlawful killing.

TO KILL, MURDER, ASSASSINATE, SLAY, OR SLAUGHTER. To *kill* is the general and the indefinite term signifying simply to take away life; to *murder* is to kill with open violence and injustice; to *assassinate* is to murder by surprise, or by means of lying in wait : to *slay* is to kill in battle; to *kill* is applicable to men, animals, and also vegetables; to *murder* and *assassinate* to men only : to *slay* mostly to men, but sometimes to animals; to *slaughter* only to animals in the proper sense, but it may be applied to men in the improper sense, when they are killed like brutes, either as to the numbers or to the manner of killing them.

Kiln. The term "kiln" conveys the idea of an outer structure of a permanent nature within which bricks are burnt.

Kin—Nearest of kin. Primarily the words "nearest of kin" indicate the nearest degree of consanguinity, and they are perhaps more frequently used in this sense than in any other.

The words "nearest of kin," as used in a residuary clause of will, mean nearest blood relation, when the context does not imply the contrary.

Kinship; blood relationship; legal relationship by blood. [Guardians and Wards Act (8 of 1890), S. 17(2)].

Kind. Means one or more related species or sub-species of crop plants each individually or collectively known by one common name such as cabbage, maize, paddy and wheat. [Seeds Act (54 of 1966), S. 2(8)]

A specific variety [Seeds Act (54 of 1966), S. 2(8)]; a class of things [Army Act (46 of 1950), S. 108].

Kindred. A term employed to designate a relation by birth or consanguinity. *Kindred*, are a certain body of persons of kin or related to each other. There are three degrees of kindred in law; one in the right line descending, another in the right line ascending, and the third in the collateral line. (*Tomlin*)

Kindred or **consanguinity.** Kindred or consanguinity is the connexion or relation or persons descended from the same stock or common ancestor. [Indian Succession Act (39 of 1925), S. 24]

Kinematograph includes a moving picture machine or other similar apparatus.

King can do no wrong. This is a maxim of English law. It means that the king is not legally responsible for anything he may be pleased to do or for any omission.

KINGLY, ROYAL, REGAL. *Kingly* means like a king; *Royal* belonging to the person of a king; *Regal* belonging to the attributes of a king. A *kingly* form; a *royal* residence; *regal* magnificence. (*Smith. Sys. Dis.*)

King's Bench/Queen's Bench. The Supreme Court of Common Law in England. The Court of King's Bench is so called because the King used formerly to sit in Court in person. During the reign of a queen it is called the Queen's Bench; and under the usurpation in Cromwell's time, it was styled the Upper Bench. (*Tomlin*)

Kinsman. One of the same kin, and so related by blood. [T.P. Act (4 of 1882), S. 6(a)].

KINSMAN, RELATIVE. *Kinsman* is one of the same kin, and so related by blood. *Relative* is one connected either by blood or by affinity.

Kith: Kith and Kin. Acquaintance and kins-folk.

Kleptomania is a form of mania manifesting itself in a propensity to commit theft.

Knacker's yard. Any premises which is used in connection with the business of slaughtering, flaying or cutting up animals the flesh of which is not intended for human consumption.

Knew. The word "knew" in S. 149, IPC indicates a state of mind at the time of the commission of the offence and not knowledge acquired in the light of subsequent events. *Sidhu Gope* v. *Emperor,* AIR 1946 Pat 84. [IPC (45 of 1860), S. 149].

Any member of an unlawful assembly guilty of an offence committed by another member of the unlawful assembly must have known that such offence might be committed in prosecution of the common object of the assembly. The word "knew" indicates a state of mind at the time of the commission of the offence, subsequent acts cannot affect that knowledge.

Knock-and-announce rule. The requirement that the police knock at the door and announce their identity, authority, and purpose before entering a residence to execute an arrest or search warrant.

Knock down. Striking on the ground by auctioneer in assigning lot to bidder by tap of hammer.

In common parlance and in the language of the auction room property is understood to be "knocked down" or "struck off" when the auctioneer, by the fall of his hammer or by any other adequate or visible announcement, signifies to the bidder that he is entitled to the property on paying the amount of his bid according to the terms of the sale.

Knock-for-knock agreement. An agreement between insurers whereby each will pay the claim of its insured without claiming against the other party's insurance.

Knock-out agreement. An agreement by dealers not to bid against each other at an auction. Such an agreement is illegal.

Knockoff. An unauthorized copy or imitation of another's product, usually for sale at a substantially lower price than the original.

Know-how. Practical knowledge, technique and skill to achieve some practical end especially in the field of industry or technology; it is considered to be an intangible property in which rights may be bought and sold.

Know Your Customer complaint bank account. For the purposes of this section, the expression "Know Your Customer complaint bank account" means the account which complies with the conditions specified in the regulations made by the Reserve Bank under the Banking Regulation Act, 1949 (10 of 1949). [Specified Bank Notes (Cessation of Liabilities) Act (2 of 2017), S. 4, *Explanation*].

Knowing the nature of the act. The words "knowing the nature of the act" in the S. 84, of the IPC (45 of 1860), have nothing to do with the appreciation of the moral quality or the forming a correct estimate as to its legal consequence.

Knowingly. The primary definition of the word "knowingly" is with "knowledge."

"Knowingly." as used in laws authorizing the bringing of actions to recover certain penalties against whoever shall knowingly sell, supply, *etc.*, milk in an improper condition specified, should be construed to mean actual personal knowledge.

With knowledge. [IPC (45 of 1860), S. 151]. Crimes are in the present day much more accurately defined by statute or otherwise than they formerly were. The mental element of most crimes by one of the words 'Maliciously,' 'Fraudulently', 'Negligently,' 'Knowingly' (or "willfully") is defined; but it is the general, practice of the legislature to leave unexpressed some of the mental elements of crime.

The term 'knowingly' signifies knowledge of the facts on which the contravention of the provisions for allotment of shares takes place. *Burton* v. *Bevan,* (1908) 2 Ch. 240. [Companies Act (1 of 1956), S. 72 (4)]

An individual acts "knowingly" when he acts with awareness of the nature of his conduct.

A person acts knowingly with respect to a material element of an offence when : (*i*) if the element involves the nature of his conduct or the attendant circumstances, he is aware that his conduct is of that nature or that such circumstances exist; and (*ii*) if the element involves a result of his conduct, he is aware that it is practically certain that his conduct will cause such a result.

Knowingly and unlawfully. Where a statute provides that, to constitute an offence, the act must be done knowingly, an indictment charging the act as done unlawfully is insufficient, in as much as the word "unlawfully" neither comprehends nor is equivalent in meaning to the word "knowingly."

Knowingly and wilfully. "Knowingly", in an indictment that a person "willfully, knowingly, maliciously and falsely" said, deposed, and swore on oath, is equivalent to saying that he corruptly swore : for the words used necessarily involve "corruptly."

A statute providing that every person who knowingly and willfully obstructs, resists or opposes any officer in serving or attempting to serve or execute any process or warrant shall be punishable, *etc.*, implies knowledge of the issuance of the writ or other process and an evil intent to resist the officer in the execution thereof.

Where the president of a corporation did not know of the obstruction of a public road, and had no part therein, he is not guilty of willfully or knowingly obstructing such road.

This phrase, in reference to violation of a statute, means consciously and intentionally. (*Black*)

Knowingly permits. An Act providing for the punishment of the owner of a building or tenement who "knowingly permits" it to be used for the keeping and sale of intoxicating liquors for tippling purposes, implies permission or consent, as well as knowledge.

Knowledge. The certain perception of truth; belief which amounts to or results in moral certainty; indubitable apprehension; information, intelligence, implying truth, proof and conviction; the act or state of knowing; clear perception of fact; that which is or may be known; acquaintance with things ascertainable; specific information; settled belief; reasonable conviction; anything which may be the subject of human instruction. (*Ame Cyc.*)

The fact of knowing [Indian Contract Act (9 of 1872), S. 132, ill.]; the sum total of what is known [Indian Evidence Act (1 of 1872), S. 14].

The word "notice" is not synonym for the word 'knowledge'. 'Notice' is a word which involves that knowledge may be imparted by notice.

CONSTRUCTIVE KNOWLEDGE. Knowledge imputed to a person who, through exercise of reasonable care or because of skill, should have been in the know of the fact.

PERSONAL KNOWLEDGE. Knowledge acquired directly through one's own senses; first hand information.

"Knowledge" and "actual knowledge". Have sometimes been held to be synonymous.

The "knowledge," as used in a contract by which company bound itself to make good to a bank such pecuniary loss as the latter might sustain by reason of the fraud or dishonesty of a named employee in connection with his duties, providing that the contract would be void if the bank continued in its service an employee of whose untrustworthiness they had knowledge, means actual knowledge, and not constructive.

Knowledge and Belief. "Knowledge" is nothing more than men's firm belief, and is distinguished from "belief" in that the latter includes things which do not make a very deep impression on the memory. The difference is ordinarily merely in degree.

"Believe" is to exercise trust or confidence; to exercise belief in; to be persuaded upon evidence, arguments, and deductions, or by other circumstances other than personal knowledge. "Knowledge," is the act or state of knowing; clear perception of fact; that which is or may be known. It means acquaintance with things ascertained or ascertainable; specific information.

Knowledge and Notice. "Knowledge" is not synonymous with notice, but when a person is spoken of as having actual or constructive notice it means no more than that under the indicated circumstances the man is legally chargeable with knowledge.

The terms "knowledge" and "notice" are not synonymous or interchangeable, and should not, therefore be confounded the one with the other. That which clearly does not amount to positive knowledge may often, in a legal sense, constitute actual notice.

"Knowledge" and "notice" are not synonymous, although the effects produced by notice are the same, in many cases, as result from actual knowledge.

Knowledge and reason to believe. The two words 'knowledge' and 'reason to believe' are more or less *ejusdem generis* though 'knowledge' will be on a slightly higher plane than 'reason to believe'. *Hamid Ali* v. *State,* AIR 1961 Tri 46, 48. [IPC (45 of 1860), Ss. 489-B, 489-C]

Knowledge, Information and belief. The verification of a petition praying a discovery and the appointment of a receiver by the petitioner as being true to the best of his knowledge, information, and belief, is insufficient, as the words "knowledge, information, and belief", upon the construction most favourable to the competition means that the affiant has knowledge that some of averments of the petition are true; that while he does not know, he has been informed and believes that others of the averments are true; and that as to yet other averments he has neither knowledge or information, but, without knowing the facts or ever having been informed of their truth, he believes them to be true.

Knowledge of decree. The words 'knowledge of decree' means that the applicant must have knowledge not merely that a decree had been passed against him, but that a particular decree has been passed against him in a particular Court in favour of a particular man for a particular sum.

The expression 'knowledge of the decree' means knowledge of the particular decree sought to be set aside. *Panna Lal* v. *Murari Lal*, AIR 1967 SC 1384, 1386.

Knowledge of the law. The knowledge of the law with which every man is charged includes a knowledge of the constituent facts which make the law. That the legislature enacted a certain law is a fact, but a knowledge of the law imputed to every man comprises a knowledge of that fact. That a certain law is valid or void is another fact, but every man is presumed to know whether it is valid or void, else he could not know the law.

Known sources of income. *Swamy* v. *State*, AIR 1960 SC 7. Quoted—The expression 'known sources of income' must have reference to sources known to the prosecution on a thorough investigation of the case and not sources known to the accused. *Sajjan Singh* v. *State of Punjab*, AIR 1964 SC 464, 470. [Prevention of Corruption Act (2 of 1947), S. 5(3)]

Receipt by way of share in the partition of ancestral property or bequest under a will or advances from close relations would come within the expression "known sources of income" provided the second condition stands fulfilled that is to say, such receipts were duly intimated to the authorities as prescribed. [*Kedari Lal v. State of Madhya Pradesh*, (2015) 14 SCC 505, para 10].

'Known Sources of Income' means income received from any lawful source and such receipt has been intimated in accordance with the provisions of any law, rules or orders for the time being applicable to a public servant. [Prevention of Corruption Act, 1988 S. 13(1)(e) Explanation as cited in *Yougendra Kumar Jaiswal v. State of Bihar*, (2016) 3 SCC 183, para 120].

Kohat salt. "KOHAT SALT" means salt produced in the district of Kohat in the Punjab. [Salt Act (12 of 1882), S. 3]

Konkan coast. Means that part of the western coast of India which is commonly known as the "KONKAN COAST". [Konkan Passenger Ships Acquisition Act (62 of 1973), S. 2(d)]

Kosangas company. Means the partnership firm registered under the Indian Partnership Act, 1932, with head office at 53/57, Lakshmi Insurance Building, Sir Phizozshah Mehta Road, Bombay-1 as it existed immediately before its dissolution on the 5th September, 1977. [Kosangas Company (Acquisition of Undertaking) Act (28 of 1979) S. 2(c)]

Krishak. 'KRISHAK' means the son/daughter of a *bona fide* agriculturist, resident of the State of Madhya Pradesh whose principal/ main livelihood is dependent on agriculture and not on other occupation or service. [M.P. Professional Examination Board Rules for Conduct of Pre-Engineering test, Pre-Medical Test and Pre-Agriculture Test, Examination, 1995, Ch. I.R. 1.7.4]

L

La ley faovur la vie d'un home. *(Maxim)* The law favours a man's life.

Label. "LABEL" means any written, printed or graphic matter on the immediate package and on every other covering in which the package is placed or packed and includes any written, printed or graphic matter accompanying the insecticide. [Insecticides Act (46 of 1968), S. 3(h)]

"LABEL" means any written, marked, stamped, printed, or graphic matter affixed to, or appearing upon, any commodity or package containing any commodity. [Standards of Weights and Measures Act (60 of 1976), S. 2(n)]

"LABEL" means a display osf written marked, stamped, printed or graphic matter affixed to, or appearing upon, any container. [Infant Milk Substitute, Feedings Bottles and Infant Foods (Regulation of Production, Supply, and Distribution) Act (41 of 1992), S. 2(h)]

"LABEL" means any written, marked, stamped, printed or graphic matter, affixed to, or appearing upon, any package. [Cigarettes and other Tobacco Products (Prohibition of Advertisement and Regulation of Trade and Commerce, Production, Supply and Distribution) Act (34 of 2003), S. 3(h); Indecent Representation of Women (Prohibition) Act (60 of 1986), S. 2(d)].

A placard or slip attached to an object to denote its contents, destination or ownership.

"LABEL" means any tag, brand, mark, pictorial or other descriptive matter, written, printed, stenciled, marked, embossed, graphic, perforated, stamped or impressed on or attached to container, cover, lid or crown of any food package and includes a product insert. [S. 3(1)(z) of the Food Safety & Standards Act, 2006 (34 of 2006)

Labelled or **Sealed.** Neither the word "labelled" nor the word "sealed" necessarily means that it should contain the name of manufacturer.

Labour. "LABOUR" includes labourers, cattle and appliances necessary for the execution of the work for which labour is to be supplied. [Pun. Act III of 1905 (Minor Canals), S. 3, cl. 9]

Manual, servile work, manual exertion of a toilsome nature; physical toil or bodily exertion; the act of doing what requires a painful exertion of strength; work to be done; child birth, travail; hard muscular effort directed to some useful end, as agriculture, manufactures, and the like; intellectual exertion and mental effort.

The general body of labourers and operatives who take part in production or construction; a general and collective name for all workmen whether organised or unorganised [Cardamom Act (42 of 1965), S. 4(3)(e)(iv)]; bodily or mental toil [Collection of Statistics Act (32 of 1953), S. 3(c)(xi)]; the pains of child birth [Employees' State Insurance Act (34 of 1948), S. 2(3)].

"Labour" and **"skill".** "Skill", means *inter alia*, "the familiar knowledge of any science, art, or handicraft, as shown by dexterity in execution or performance; technical ability". "Labour" means *inter alia* : "physical or mental exertion, particular for some useful or desired end". *Chandrakant Manilal Shah* v. *CIT.,* AIR 1992 SC 66.

Labour contract. An agreement between an employer and a union which governs working conditions, wages, benefits and grievances.

Labour Court. The expression 'Labour Court' in section 33C(2) of the Industrial Disputes Act, 1947 (14 of 1947), has to be given an extended meaning so as to include court constituted under any law relating to investigation and settlement of industrial disputes in force in any State. *Vijaya Bank* v. *Shyamal Kumar Lodh*, AIR 2010 SC 3563.

Labour dispute. A controversy between an employer and employees regarding their conditions of employment.

Labour organization. An organization of workers' which is formed to collectively negotiate with employers about such issues as salary, benefits, hours and working conditions.

Labour union. Trade union. It is an association of workmen, usually but not necessarily, employed in the same trade, for the purpose of combined action in securing the most favourable wages and conditions of labour.

Labourer. The word "LABOURER" includes persons who exercise any handicraft specified in rules to be made in that behalf by the State Government. [Northern India C. & D. Act (8 of 1873), S. 63]

One who performs physical labour as a service or for livelihood. [CPC (5 of 1908), S. 60(1), *Prov.* (h)].

A person who does spinning and a person who does weaving can be regarded as labourer. [CPC (5 of 1908), S. 60(1)]

A draughtsman is not a 'labourer'.

Lac. 'LAC' includes any form of manufactured or unmanufactured lac other than refuse lac. [Produce Cess Act (15 of 1966), S. 2(e)]

Laches. Slackness or negligence, or not doing.

Laziness or lack of promptitude in pursuing a legal remedy. [Court-fees Act (7 of 1870), S. 14].

Laches to bar the plaintiff's right must amount to waiver, abandonment, or acquiescence and to raise a presumption of any of these, the evidence of conduct must be plain and unambiguous.

Lacuna. Defect; flaw in a written instrument.

Laden weight. In respect of any motor vehicle, means the registered laden weight recorded in the certificate of registration and, in cases where the vehicle is not registered or the laden weight is not recorded in the certificate of registration the laden weight determined by the registering authority in such manner as it may deem fit. [Kerala Motor Vehicles Taxation Act, 1976 (19 of 1976), S. 2(b)]

Lagan. Goods which are abandoned at sea but attached to a buoy so that they may be recovered.

Laggard. A share that does not keep up with the average price of comparable shares.

Laid down. Expounded or stated positively. [Beedi and Cigar Workers (Conditions of Employment) Act (32 of 1966), S. 26(2)].

Laissez faire. Government abstention from interference with individual action, especially in commerce.

Lame duck. A can't term in the Stock Exchange for a person unable to meet his engagements.

A speculator in stock who has overbought and can not meet his commitments. An elected officeholder who is to be succeeded by another, between the time of the election and the date that his successor is to take office.

Lame duck session. Legislative session conducted after election of new members but before they are installed and hence the session in which participants are voting for the last time as elected officials because of their failure to get re-elected or retiring voluntarily.

Lanced poppy heads. Means the capsules of the poppy plant whatever in the original form, cut, crushed or powdered from which the juice has been extracted. [Rajasthan Narcotic Drugs and Psychotropic Substances Rules, 1985, R. (2)(r)]

Land. "LAND" includes a revenue-free estate, a revenue-paying estate, and a permanent transferable tenure, whether such estate or tenure be subject to incumbrances or not. [Ancient Monuments Preservation Act (7 of 1904), S. 2(5)]

"LAND" includes the bed of the sea or river below high-water mark, and also things attached to the earth or permanently fastened to anything attached to the earth. [Major Port Trusts Act (38 of 1963), S. 2(k)]

"Land" includes the bed of the sea or river below high-water mark, and also things attached to the earth or permanently fastened to anything attached to the earth. [Major Port Authorities Act, 2021 (1 of 2021), section 2(1)(n)]

"Land" means—

(i) in relation to any period prior to the specified date, land which is used or capable of being used for agricultural purpose and includes the sites of form buildings appurtenant to such land.

(ii) in relation to any other period, land which is used or capable of being used for agricultural purposes, and includes—

(a) the sites of form buildings appurtenant to such land;

(b) the land on which grass grows naturally;

(c) the bid lands held by the Girasdars or Barkhalidars under the Saurashtra Land Reforms Act, 1951 (Saurashtra Act 25 of 1951), the Saurashtra Barkhali Abolition Act, 1951 (Saurashtra Act 26 of 1951) or the Saurashtra Estates Acquisition Act, 1952 (Saurashtra Act 3 of 1952), as the case may be;

(d) such bid lands as are held by a person who, before the commencement of the Constitution (26th Amendment) Act, 1971 was a ruler of an Indian State Comprised in the Saurashtra area of the State of Gujrat, as his private property in pursuance of the covenant entered into by the Ruler of such State. [Gujrat Agricultural Lands Ceiling Act, 1960 (After the Amendment),S. 2(17) as cited in *State of Gujrat* v. *Manoharsinghji Pradyumansinhji Jadeja*, (2013) 2 SCC 300, para 34].

"Land" means land held or occupied for purposes connected with agriculture horticulture or animal husbandry which includes pisciculture and poultry farming. [U.P. Zamindari Abolition and Land Reform Act (10 of 1951), S. 3(14) as cited in *Hari Sagar Educational Trust* v. *Uttaranchal Gramin Bank*, AIR 2012 Utr 8, para 15].

"Land" means any agricultural land, bid land or cultivable waste. [Saurashtra Act (25 of 1951), S. 2(18) as cited in [*State of Gujrat* v. *Manoharsinghji Pradyumansinhji Jadeja*, (2013) S SCC 300, para 36].

"LAND" means land of any description whatsoever and includes benefits arising out of land and things attached to the earth, or permanently fastened to anything attached to the earth. Saurashtra Act, (3 of 1952), S. 2(l) as cited in *State of Gujarat* v. *Manoharshinji Pradyumansinhji Jadeja*, (2013) 2 SCC 300, para 35].

The expression "LAND" includes immovable property of every description and any rights in or over such property. [Assam Reorganisation (Meghalaya) Act (55 of 1969), Sch. III(2) *Expln.*]

"LAND" includes canals, creeks and other water channels, reservoirs, rivers, streams and lakes whether artificial or natural, marshes and wet lands and also includes boulders and rocks. [Wild Life (Protection) Act (53 and 1972), S. 2(17)]

"LAND" includes benefits arising out of land and things attached to the earth or permanently fastened to anything attached to the earth. [Control of National Highways (Land and Traffic) Act, 2002 (13 of 2003), S. 2(h) and National Highways Act (48 of 1956), S. 3(b)]

'LAND' means land which is used or capable of being used for agriculture or horticulture and includes land which is an orchard, *Kharhur* or pasturage or forest land or even land perennially submerged under water or the homestead of a land-holder. [Bihar Land

Reforms (Fixation of Ceiling Area and Acquisition of Surplus Land) Act (12 of 1962)]

"LAND" includes benefits to arise out of land and things attached to the earth or permanently fastened to any thing attached to the earth. [Punjab Regional and Town Planning and Development Act (Punjab Act (11 of 1995), S. 2(5) and Slum Areas (Improvement and Clearance Act (96 of 1956), S. 2(a)]

"LAND" means a portion of the surface of the earth comprising the ground or soil and every thing under it or over it, and things which are attached to the earth (such as buildings, structures and trees), things which are permanently fastened to the earth, easements, rights and appruntences belonging to them and benefits arising out of them and includes the sites of villages towns and cities. [Punjab Apartment Ownership Act (Punjab Act, 13 of 1995), S. 2(p)]

"LAND" includes any right or interest in any land. [Delhi Metro Railway (Operation and Maintenance) Act (60 of 2002), S. 2(1)(g)]

'LAND' means land which was occupied or was let, for agricultural purposes or for purposes subservient to agriculture or for posture in *kharif,* 1971 and includes

(a) structure on such land used for purposes connected with agriculture;

(b) areas covered by, or fields floating over water;

(c) forest land and wooded wastes;

(d) trees standing on land; and

(e) (omitted)

(but does not include an orchard or) site of a building or a structure within municipal area notified area or village *abadi* or any land appurtenant to such building or structure. [J&K Agrarian Reforms Act (17 of 1976), S. 2(9)]

"LAND" includes benefits to arise out of land, things attached to the earth or permanently fastened to anything attached to the earth and rights created by law over any street. [New Delhi Municipal Council Act (44 of 1994), S. 2(21)]

"LAND" includes benefits arising out of land, houses and things attached to the earth or permanently fastened to anything attached to the earth and also land covered by water. [Manipur Municipalities Act (43 of 1994), S. 2(28)]

The word "LAND" shall extend to messuages, and all other hereditaments, whether corporal, or incorporal and whether freehold or of any other tenure, and to money to be laid out in the purchase of land, and to chattels and other personal property transmissible to heirs, and also to any share of the same hereditaments and properties or any of them, and to any estate of inheritance or estate for any life or lives, or other estate transmissible to heirs, and to any possibility, right or title of entry or action, and any other interest capable of being inherited, and whether the same estates, possibilities, rights, titles and interests, or any of them, shall be in possession, reversion, remainder or contingency. [Act XXX of 1839 (Inheritance), S. 1].

"LAND" includes benefits to arise out of land, and things attached to the earth, or permanently fastened to anything attached to the earth, and also shares in, or charges on, the revenue or rent of villages, or other defined portions of territory. [Bom Act V of 1879 (Land Revenue Code), S. 3, cl. 4].

"LAND" includes the bed of the sea below high-water mark. [Bom Act VI of 1879 (Port Trust Aden (Bom.), S. 3, cl. 6].

"LAND" includes the bed of the sea below high-water mark, and also things attached to the earth or permanently fastened to anything attached to the earth. [Bom Act VI of 1886 (Port Trust (Karachi)), S. 2, cl. 4].

"LAND" includes houses and buildings and corporeal hereditaments and tenements of any tenure, unless where there are words to exclude houses and buildings or to restrict the meaning to tenements of some particular tenure. [Ben Act I of 1889 (General Clauses), S. 5(1)].

"LAND" shall include land which is built, upon or covered with water. [Bom Act III of 1901 (District Manual), S. 3, Cl. 6].

"LAND" includes the sites of villages, towns and cities; it also includes trees, growing crops and grass, fruits upon, and juice in trees, rights-of-way, ferries, fisheries and all other benefits to arise out of land, and things attached to the earth or permanently fastened to things attached to the earth. [Bom. Revenue Jurisdiction Act (10 of 1876), S. 3]

'LAND' includes benefits to arise out of land, and anything attached to the earth, or permanently fastened to anything attached to the earth, and also shares in, or charges on, the revenue or rent of villages or other defined areas. [Karnataka Land Revenue Act, 1964, S. 2(14)]

It includes anything fixed to the land; and growing trees and crops, except those which, broadly speaking, are produced in the year by the labour of the year. HALSBURY, 3rd Edn., Vol. 32, p. 249.

In the Land Acquisition Act, the expression "land" includes benefits to arise out of land, and things attached to the earth or permanently fastened to anything attached to the earth. [Land Acquisition Act (1 of 1894), S. 3(*a*) repealed]

Though the term 'land' in Section 3 (*a*) of the Land Acquisition Act (1 of 1894) (repealed) is defined as including things attached to the earth, the Act does not contemplate the acquisition of things attached to the land without the land itself. It is only the land including the rights which arise out of it, and not merely some subsidiary right, which is capable of acquisition under the Act.

According to the definition in sec. 3 (1) of the Act the word 'land' includes standing trees. *Socklatings Tea Co.* v. *Collector, Sibsagar,* AIR 1977 Gau 61, 65. [Land Acquisition Act (1 of 1894), S. 3(1) repealed]

The word "land," in the ordinary legal sense, comprehends everything of a fixed and permanent nature and therefore embraces growing trees.

The word "land" includes the water into the earth, which is the result of natural and ordinary percolation through the soil, such water being a part of the land itself.

"Land" includes the bed of the sea below high-water mark.

The word "land" in O. XXI., R. 54 (2), CPC (5 of 1908) is used by the legislature in a restricted sense, and does not include buildings and other constructions thereon.

The definition of "land" in S. 145(2) of CrPC, 1973 (2 of 1974) cannot include the movable property such as the stock of medicines in a shop.

The expression 'land' in the legal sense is a comprehensive expression which is wide enough to include structures, if any, raised thereon. *P. Rami Reddy* v. *State of A.P.*, AIR 1988 SC 1626, 1635. [Constitution of India, Sch. 5, Para 5, (2)(*a*)]

The word "lands" is wide enough to include all lands, whether agricultural or not, and it would be plainly unreasonable to assume that it includes non-agricultural lands but does not include agricultural lands. *Raja Jagannath Baksh Singh* v. *State of Uttar Pradesh*, AIR 1962 SC 1563, 1568. [Constitution of India, Sch. 7, List II, Entry 49]

The word 'land' includes not only the face of the earth, but also everything under or over it, and has in its legal signification an indefinite extent upward or downward giving rise to the maxim, *cujus est solum ejus est usque ad coelum*. *Anant Mills* v. *State of Gujarat*, AIR 1975 SC 1234, 1250.

Land does not mean only agricultural land. *Begum Shah Hussain* v. *Attar Singh,* AIR 1960 J&K 110, 112. [Court-Fees Act (7 of 1870), S. 7(*v*)(*b*)]

It does not include urban land situated within urban areas though used for growing crops or fruits. *Ramji Sharma* v. *State of Bihar*, 1996 (10) SCC 671.

Land includes the land on the surface as well as below the surface. (*State of Bihar* v. *Indian Aluminium Co.*, AIR 1997 SC 3592).

Land in S. 145, CrPC, 1973 (2 of 1974) is used, synonymous with immovable property which includes things attached to earth. Mill, therefore, which is attached to the earth will fall within the scope of immovable property or land.

"LAND" includes benefits to arise out of land, and things attached to the earth or permanently fastened to anything attached to the earth. [S. 3(p) of the Right to Fair Compensation & Transparency in Land Acquisition, Rehabilitation & Resettlement Act, 2013 (30 of 2013)]

"LAND". It is no doubt true that the word 'land' would not have included a tank, in the normal sense, but for its definition specifically including even land perennially submerged under water. If a tank appurtenant to the dwelling house is land, it follows that any tank appurtenant to agricultural/horticultural land used to irrigate or water such agricultural/horticultural land, will also be 'land'. *K. N. Farms Industries (Pvt.) Ltd.* v. *State of Bihar*, AIR 2009 SC 3031.

"LAND" the term 'land' as occurring in Entry 49 of List II of the Constitution of India has a wide connotation. Land remains land though it may be subjected to different user. The nature of user of the land would not enable a piece of land being taken out of the meaning of land itself. *State of W. B.* v. *Kesoram Industries Ltd.,* AIR 2005 SC 1646.

Land appurtenant. In relation to any building means—

(i) in an area where there are building regulations, the minimum extent of land required under such regulations to be kept as open space for the enjoyment of such building, which in no case shall exceed five hundred square meters, or

(ii) in an area where there are no building regulations, an extent of five hundred square meters contiguous to the land occupied by such building, and includes in the case of any building constructed before the appointed day with a dwelling unit therein, an additional extent not exceeding five hundred square meters of land, if any, contiguous to the minimum extent referred to in sub-clause (i) or the extent referred to in sub-clause (ii), as the case may be. [Urban Land (Ceiling and Regulation) Act (33 of 1976), S. 2(g)]

The expression 'land appurtenant' as defined in S. 2(g) and used in S. 4(9) means not a land contiguous to some other land but the very land which is a part of the same plot or area which contains the building or dwelling house. *State of U.P.* v. *L.J. Johnson,* AIR 1983 SC 1303. [Urban Land (Ceiling and Regulation) Act, 1976, S. 2(g)]

Land, Arable. Fit for tillage.

Land bank. For the purposes of section 101 of Act 30 of 2013, "Land Bank" means a governmental entity that focuses on the conversion of Government owned vacant, abandoned, unutilised acquired lands and tax-delinquent properties into productive use. [*Explanation* to S. 101 of the Right to Fair Compensation & Transparency in Land Acquisition, Rehabilitation & Resettlement Act, 2013 (30 of 2013)]

Land based pollution. Means pollution of the sea caused by discharges from land reaching the sea waterborne, air borne or directly from the coast including outfalls from pipelines. [Convention on the Protection of the Marine Environment of the Beltic Sea Area, Helsinki, Mar 22, 1974, Art. 2(2)]

Land cultivated personally. "LAND CULTIVATED PERSONALLY" means land cultivated on one's own account—

(a) by one's own labour; or

(b) by the labour of any member of one's family; or

(c) by servants on wages payable in cash or kind (but not in share of the crops) or by hired labour under one's personal supervision or the personal supervision of any member of one's family;

Provided that in the case of a person who is a widow or a minor or is subject to any physical or mental disability or who is in service as a member of the armed forces of the Union, land shall be deemed to be cultivated personally even without such personal cultivation. M.P. Abolition of Jagirs Act (28 of 1951), S. 2(viii)]

Land customs area. Means any area adjoining a foreign frontier for which a Collector of Land Customs has been appointed. [Land Customs Act (19 of 1924), S. 2(g)]

Land Development Bank. 'LAND DEVELOPMENT BANK' or 'Co-operative land development Bank' means a co-operative society registered under Co-operative Societies Act for the time being in force in Uttar Pradesh, admitted as a member of the State Land Development Bank, and having as its main object the advancement of loans to its members on the mortgage of or charge on immovable property, or against unconditional guarantee of the State Government generally for improvement of land and other productive purposes connected with agriculture. [U.P. Co-operative Land Development Banks Act, 1964, S. 2(e)]

Land drainage. The drainage of land and the provision of flood warning systems.

Land filling. Means disposal of residual solid wastes on land in a facility designed with protective measures against pollution of ground water, surface water and air fugitive dust, wind-blown litter, bad odour, fire hazard, bird menace, pets or rodents, greenhouse gas emissions, slope instability and erosion. [Municipal Solid Wastes (Management and Handling) Rules, 2000, Rule 3 (xi)]

Land forces. In a certain and general sense, the terms 'army' and 'land forces' do embrace militia in actual service. The militia do serve on land, and therefore, in a popular sense, are a part of the land forces.

Armed forces that operate on land as distinguished from those that operate on the sea or in the air. [CrPC, 1973 (2 of 1974), S. 132(3)(a)].

Land grabber. Means a person illegally tapes possession of any land (whether belonging to Govt., local authority or any other person) or enters into or creates illegal tenancies or leave and licence agreements or any other agreement in respect of such lands, or who constructs unauthorised structures thereon for sale or hire, or give such lands to any person on rental or lease and licence basis or for construction or use and occupation of unauthorised structures or he knowingly gives financial aid to any person for taking illegal possession of such lands, or for construction of unauthorised structures thereon or who collects or attempts to collect from any occupier of such lands, rent, compensation or other charged by criminal intimidation or who evicts or attempts to evict any such occupier by force without resorting to the lawful procedures, or who abets in any manner the doing of any of the abovementioned things. [A.P. Prevention of Dangerous Activities of Boot-leggers *etc.* Act, 1996, S. 2(j)]

'LAND GRABBER' means a person or a group of persons who commits land grabbing and includes any person who gives financial aid to any person for taking illegal possession of lands or for construction of unauthorised structures thereon, or who collects or attempts to collect from any occupiers of such lands rent, compensation or other charges by criminal intimidation or who abets the doing of any of the above mentioned acts; and also includes the successors in interest. [A.P. Land Grabbing (Prohibition) Act (12 of 1982), S. 2(d)]

The word 'land grabber' means a person who has taken, unauthorisedly, unfairly, greedily, snatched forcibly, violently, unscrupulously, any land belonging to the Government or a local authority, a religious or charitable institution or endowment, including a *wakf*, or any other private person without any lawful entitlement with a view to take illegal possession of such lands. *Konda Lakshmana Bapuji* v. *Govt. of A.P.*, (2002) 3 SCC 258, para 38. [Andhra Pradesh Land Grabbing (Prohibition) Act (12 of 1982), S. 2(d)]

A person who knowingly enters into possession of land illegally and without any lawful entitlement would come within the ambit of the expression 'land-grabber' under Section 2(d) of the Act. *Gauni Satya Reddy* v. *Govt. of A.P.*, AIR 2004 SC 3661, 3664, para 8. [A.P. Land Grabbing (Prohibition) Act (12 of 1982), S. 2(d)]

Land grabbing. 'LAND GRABBING' means every activity of grabbing of any land (whether belonging to the Government, a local authority, a religious or charitable institution or endowment, including a *wakf* or any other private person) by a person or a group of persons, without any lawful entitlement and with a view to illegally taking possession of such lands, or enter into or create illegal tenancies or lease and licences, agreements, or any other illegal agreements in respect of such lands or to construct unauthorised structures thereon for sale or hire, or give such lands to any person on rental lease and licence basis for construction, or use and occupation, of unauthorised structures; and the term 'to grab land' shall be construed accordingly. [A.P. Land Grabbing (Prohibition) Act (12 of 1982), S. 2(e)]

The grabbing of any land without any lawful entitlement and with a view to take possession of such lands illegally would come within the ambit of 'land grabbing' under Section 2(e) of the Act. *Gauni Satya Reddi* v. *Govt. of A.P.*, AIR 2004 SC 3661, 3664, para 8. [A.P. Land Grabbing (Prohibition) Act (12 of 1982), S. 2(e)]

Land held. The words 'land held' occurring in S. 3(42) of the Act would mean that the female must be in possession of the land as owner or with some element of title on the date of commencement of the Act. *A.G. Varadarajulu* v. *State of T.N.,* (1998) 4 SCC 231, para 27. [T.N. Land Reforms (Fixation of Ceiling on Land) Act (58 of 1961), S. 3(42)]

Land held by a person under the personal cultivation. The essence of "personal cultivation" seems to be by or on behalf of the owner of the land. When he grows the crop he grows it in his own right and not on behalf of any person. *Chandra Sekhar Singh Bhedi* v. *State of Orissa,* AIR 1972 SC 486, 491. [Constitution of India, Article 31A(1)]

Land holder. "LAND-HOLDER" means any person responsible for the payment of the land-revenue, if any assessed on land. It also includes the proprietor of land the land revenue of which has been wholly, or in part, released, compounded for, redeemed or assigned. [Pun. District Board Act (20 of 1883), S. 3(3)]

"LAND-HOLDER" means a person under whom a tenant holds land and to whom the tenant is, or but for a special contract would be, liable to pay rent for the land. [Delhi (Urban Area) Tenants Relief Act (30 of 1961), S. 2(c)]

Proprietor or a superior tenant of land.

Holder of land; a tenant or proprietor of land; a person to whom rent is payable in respect of the land; proprietor of the land responsible for the payment of the revenue. [CPC (5 of 1908), S. 4(2)].

Land holding. Means the total land in the State in possession of a person whether as owner mortgagee lessee, tenant or in any other lawful capacity and if such a person held land jointly with others, his share in such holding. [H.P. Abolition of Land Revenue on Uneconomic Holdings Act, 1977 (2 of 1978), S 2(a)]

Land in its natural condition. "Land is in its natural condition when it is not excavated and not subjected to artificial pressure." [Indian Easements Act (5 of 1882), S. 7, illustration (e), *Explanation*]

Land laws. Laws relating to landed property.

Land or water. For the purposes of this section, the expression "land or water" includes buildings, markets, fisheries, crops or other produce of land, and the rents or profits of any such property. [(w. e. f. 1-7-2024) Bharatiya Nagarik Suraksha Sanhita, 2023 (46 of 2023), section 164(2) & section 166(1), Explanation]

The expression land or water in section 145(2) is wide enough to include standing trees and therefore a dispute about the actual possession of standing trees would come within the scope of section 145. If crops or other produce of land could be deemed to be immovable property for the purpose of section 145, much more so should be the case of trees growing on land. 11 Cal WN 198 : 24 Cal WN 1039 and AIR 1934 Nag 112, **relied on.** *Moopil Nayar v M.C. Chandy,* Mad LJ : QD (1956-1960) Vol. II C1313 : 1957 Ker LJ 466 : 1957 Ker LT 537 : (1957) Mad LJ (Cri) 436 : ILR (1957) Kerala 646. [CrPC (5 of 1898), section 145]

Land owner. Means—

(i) in relation to a land personally cultivated, the owner of such land;

(ii) in relation to a land hold by a cultivating tenant such cultivating tenant;

(iii) in any other case, the person in actual possession of the land and includes his heirs, assignees and legal representatives. [Kerala Agricultural Workers Act (18 of 1974), S. 2]

"LAND OWNER" does not include a tenant or an assignee of land-revenue, but does include a person to whom a holding has been transferred, or an estate or holding has been transferred, or an estate or holding has been let in farm, under Land Revenue Act for the recovery of an arrear of land-revenue or of a sum recoverable as such an arrear, and every other person not hereinbefore in this clause mentioned who is in possession of an estate or any share or portion thereof, or in the enjoyment of any part of the profits of an estate. [Pun. Act XVII of 1887, (Land Revenue), S. 3, cl. 2]

"LAND OWNER" includes any person,—

(i) whose name is recorded as the owner of the land or building or part thereof, in the records of the authority concerned; or

(ii) any person who is granted forest rights under the Scheduled Tribes and Other Traditional Forest Dwellers (Recognition of Forest Rights) Act, 2006 (2 of 2007) or under any other law for the time being in force; or

(iii) who is entitled to be granted Patta rights on the land under any law of the State including assigned lands; or

(iv) any person who has been declared as such by an order of the court or Authority. [S. 3(r) of the Right to Fair Compensation & Transparency in Land Acquisition, Rehabilitation & Resettlement Act, 2013 (30 of 2013)]

Landrace. Means primitive cultivar that was grown by ancient farmers and their successors [Biological Diversity Act, 2002 (18 of 2003), section 2(gc)]

Land record. "LAND RECORDS" means records maintained under the provisions of, or for the purpose of, this Code and includes a copy of maps and plans of a final town planning scheme improvement scheme or a scheme of consolidation of holdings which has come into force in any area; under any law in force in the State and forwarded to any revenue or survey officer under such law or otherwise. [Maharashtra Land Revenue Code (41 of 1966), S. 2(18)]

Official records kept in respect of each plot of revenue paying lands, public as well as private lands.

Land-revenue. "LAND-REVENUE" means all sums and payments, in money or in kind, received or claimable by or on behalf of Government from any person on account of any land held by or vested in him, and any cess or rate authorized by Government under the provisions of any law for the time being in force. [Bom Act of 1876 (Revenue Jurisdiction), S. 3]

"LAND-REVENUE" means revenue assessed upon land under the provisions of the Land and Revenue Act. [Bur. Act II of 1880 (District Cesses and Rural Police), S. 2].

The words "LAND-REVENUE" signify any sum of money legally claimable by Government from any person on account of any land, or interest in or right exercisable over, land held by or vested in him, under whatever designation such sum may be payable. [Bom Act II of 1876 (Bom City Land Revenue), S. 3, cl. 2

"LAND-REVENUE" includes *trini* or grazing dues levied for grazing on Government lands. [Punjab Act XX of 1883 (Dist. Board), S. 3, cl. 2].

The revenue derived by the State by taxation of lands and of profits on land. [TP Act (4 of 1882), S. 69A(8), (1)].

Land-suit. "LAND-SUIT" means a suit relating to immoveable property. or to any right or interest in immoveable property. [Bur Act VI of 1900. (LB Courts), S. 2, cl. (*b*)].

Land tax. Tax on land; one of the chief sources of revenue to the Government.

Land tenure. It connotes various types of holdings of land, involving the King or the government, the *zamindar,* the *inamdar* and various other types of landholders, lessors sub lessors, lessees and sub-lessees under or through them and evolved at various stages of Indian history by various rulers, *nawabs* and chieftains—Hindu, Muslim and British—differently in different parts of the country. *Accountant and Secretarial Services Pvt. Ltd.* v. *Union of India,* AIR 1988 SC 1708.

Land-use planning. The deliberate, careful development of real estates through methods, like, zoning and environmental impact studies.

Landed estate. The phrase "landed estate" embraces not only the land, but all houses, fixtures, and improvements of every kind thereon, and all machinery, neat, cattle, horses, and mules, when attached to and used on a plantation or farm. The ordinary meaning of the words "landed estate" seems to be an interest in and pertaining to lands. Thus we say a "landed proprietor", and mean thereby any person having an estate in lands, whether highly improved or not.

Landed property. Real estate, whether in fee simple or leasehold, and whether improved or unimproved.

Property in the form of land. [Indian Evidence Act (1 of 1872), S. 90, ill(a)].

Landing charges. The phrase 'landing charges' means the expenditure incurred by an importer for bringing goods on board ship to land. *Coromandal Fertilizers Ltd.* v. *Collector of Customs,* (2000) 1 SCC 448, para 7.

Landing place. LANDING PLACE includes a pier, wharf, quay, jetty and a stage, whether fixed or floating. [Indian Tolls (Army & Air force) Act (2 of 1901), S. 2(h)]

Landless. Means such persons or class of persons who may be,—(i) considered or specified as such under any State law for the time being in force; or (ii) in a case of landless not being specified under sub-clause (i), as may be specified by the appropriate Government. [S. 3(q) of the Right to Fair Compensation & Transparency in Land Acquisition, Rehabilitation & Resettlement Act, 2013 (30 of 2013)]

Landless labourer. Means a person who does not hold any agricultural land and whose principal means of livelihood is manual labour. [Kerala Debtors (Temporary Relief Act (30 of 1975), S. 2(a)]

Landless persons. Means a person who does not hold any land for purposes of agriculture and earns his livelihood principally by manual labour on agricultural land, and intends to take to agriculture. [Maharashtra Agricultural Lands (Ceiling on Holdings) Act, 1981, S. 2(17)]

Landless persons mean those landless labourers who are versed in agriculture, want to take to it, and have no other means of subsistence. *U.P. Bhoodan Yagno Samiti* v. *Braj Kishore*, AIR 1988 SC 2239, 2244.

Landless poor person. For the purpose of this sub-section "LANDLESS POOR PERSON" means a person whose total extent of land held by him either as owner or as cultivating tenant or as both does not exceed 1.011715 hectares (two-and-half acres) of wetland or 2.023430 hectares (five acres) of dry land and whose monthly income other than from such lands does not exceed thousand rupees per mensem or twelve thousand rupees per annum. However, those of the tenants who own residential property exceeding two hundred square yards in Urban Area shall not be considered as landless poor for the purpose of purchase of endowments property. [A.P. Charitable and Hindu Religious Institutions & Endowments Act (30 of 1987), S. 82(2), *Explanation* **as cited in** *Dokiseela Ramulu* v. *Sri Sangameswara Swamy Varu,* (2017) 2 SCC 69, para 13].

Landlord. "LANDLORD" means a person immediately under whom a tenant holds, and includes the Government. [Ben Act VIII of 1885 (Tenancy), S. 3(4).]

For the purpose of this Section,

The expression 'landlord' does not include a tenant or sub-tenant who has given premises on licence. [Bombay Rents, Hotel and Lodging House Rates Control Act (57 of 1947), S. 13-A2, *Expl.* (a)]

'LANDLORD' means a person from whom a tenant holds land on lease. [Goa, Daman and Diu Agricultural Tenancy Act (7 of 1964), S. 2(12)].

'Landlord' means any person who is, for the time being receiving or entitled to receive rent in respect of any house whether on his own account, or on account, or on behalf, or for the benefit of any other person, or as a trustee, guardian or receiver for any other person and includes in respect of his sub-tenant, a tenant who has sub-let any house and includes every person not being a tenant who from time to time derives title under a landlord. [Assam Urban Areas Rent Control Act, (17 of 1972), S. 2(c) as cited in *Ambica Prasad* v. *Mohd. Alam*, (2015) 13 SCC 13, para 10].

"LANDLORD" includes the person who is receiving or is entitled to receive the rent of a building, whether on his own account or on behalf of another or on behalf of himself and others or as an agent, trustees, executor, administrator, receiver or guardian or who would so receive the rent or be entitled to receive the rent, if the building were let to a tenant. [Kerala Buildings (Lease and Rent Control) Act (2 of 1965), S. 2(3)]

"LANDLORD" means a person who, for the time being is receiving, or is entitled to receive, the rent of any premises, whether on his own account or on account of or on behalf of, or for the benefit of, any other person or as a trustee, guardian or receiver for any other person or who would so receive the rent or be entitled to receive the rent, if the premises were let to a tenant. [Delhi Rent Act (33 of 1995), S. 2(e) and Requisitioning and Acquisition of Immovable Property Act (30 of 1952), S. 2(c)]

'LANDLORD' means a person, who for the time being is receiving, or is entitled to receive, the rent of any accommodation, whether on his own account or on account of or on behalf of or for the benefit of, any other person or as a trustee guardian or receiver for any other person or who would so receive the rent or be entitled to receive the rent, if the accommodation were let to a tenant and includes every person not being a tenant who from time to time derives title under a landlord. [M.P. Accommodation Control Act (41 of 1961), S. 2(b)]

'Landlord' means the landlord of a tenant of the first degree. [West Bengal Premises Rent Control (Temporary Provisions) Act (17 of 1950), S. 13 *Expln.* (a)]

The definition of "landlord" under S. 2 of the W.B. Premises Tenancy Act, 1956 shows that even if the rent is received by a person not on his own account but on account of any other person, such as his principal or his ward, he is for the purpose of the Act a landlord. *Swadesh Ranjan Sinha* v. *Haradeb Banerjee*, AIR 1992 SC 1590.

He of whom lands are holden. (*Tomlin*)

The word generally implies not the mere lordship or ownership of the soil, but, the relationship to a tenant.

Not only the owner but also any person receiving rent, whether on his own account or on behalf of or for the benefit of any other person or as a trustee, guardian, or receiver for any other person, is also the landlord. [*Ambica Prasad* v. *Mohd. Alam*, (2015) 13 SCC 13, para 12].

The person letting the land is called the "landlord", and the party to whom the lease is made is called the "tenant."

"Landlord" means a person immediately under whom a tenant holds, and includes the Government.

The expression 'landlord' includes an usufructuray mortgage where the tenanted premises is the subject of usufructuary mortgage. *Narpatchand A. Bhandari* v. *Shantilal Moolshankar Jani*, AIR 1993 SC 1712, 1718.

The expression 'landlord' means whosoever is the landlord at the time of efflux of tenancy. *Pukh Raj Jain* v. *Padma Kashyapm*, AIR 1990, SC 1133, 1136.

The proprietor of land; a person who demises lands or tenements to a tenant. [Requisitioning and Acquisition of Immovable Property Act (30 of 1952), S. 2(c)].

The expression 'Landlord' means whosoever is the land lord at the time of efflux of tenancy. *Pukhraj Jain* v. *Padma Kashyap*, AIR 1990 SC 1133, 1136. [Delhi Rent Control Act (59 of 1958), S. 2(*e*)]

The expression "landlord" is not limited to denote the owner of the house but it has to be understood in the wide sense to include a person to whom the rent is payable as also his agent. *Vasudha Srivastava* v. *Kamla Chauhan*, AIR 1992 SC 1454, 1455. [U.P. Urban Buildings (Regulation of Letting, Rent and Eviction Act (13 of 1972), S. 3(*i*)]

Landmark. Boundary mark; marking a stage on crisis in history.

A mark for designating the boundary of land. [IPC (45 of 1860), S. 434].

Landmark decision. A judicial decision, significantly changing the existing law.

Language. The 'language' is a tool of communication between human beings, and hence that meaning should be given to a word which helps communication between people. *U.P. State Agro Industrial Corporation Ltd.* v. *Kisan Upbhokta Parishad*, AIR 2008 SC 777.

Lapse. (*In testamentary law*) The failure of a devise or bequest by the death of the devisee or legatee in the lifetime of the testator is called a lapse.

To run its course; to fall or pass from one proprietor to another by omission, negligence or failure [Constitution of India, Art. 107(3)]; fault; error.

Lapse of offer. An offer is considered to have lapsed where no acceptance has been made within a reasonable time or specified time.

Lapsed devise and **void devise.** There is a distinction between a "lapsed" and a "void" devise in the former case the devisee dies in the intermediate time between the making of the will and the death of the testator, but in the latter case the devise is void from the beginning, as if the devisee be dead when the will was made.

Lapsed legacy. A "lapsed legacy" is one which has never vested or taken effect. It has been defined as one which, originally valid, afterwards fails because the capacity or willingness of the donee to take has ceased to exist before he obtained a vested interest in the gift.

Laptop/Laptop computer. A small computer designed for portability. Laptop computers typically use a full-sized or nearly full-sized keyboard, liquid-crystal displays (LCD's), and high-capacity batteries. (*Computer*)

"A laptop computer, or simply laptop (also notebook computer or notebook), is a small mobile computer, which usually weighs 2.2.- 18 pounds (1-6 kilograms), depending on size, materials, and other factors.

Laptops are usually run on a single main battery or from an external AC/DC adapter which can charge the battery while also supplying power to the computer itself. Many computers also have a 3 volt cell to run the clock and other processes in the event of a power failure.

As personal computers, laptops are capable of the same tasks as a desktop computer, although they are typically less powerful for the same price. They contain components that are similar to their desktop counterparts and perform the same functions, but are miniaturised and optimised for mobile use and efficient power consumption. Laptops usually have liquid crystal displays and most of them use different memory modules for their random access memory (RAM), for instance, SO-DIMM in lieu of the larger DIMMs. In addition to a built-in keyboard, they may utilise a touchpad (also known as a trackpad) or a pointing stick for input, though an external keyboard or mouse can usually be attached." [Wikipedia **as referred in** *Commr. of Customs* v. *Acer India (P) Ltd.*, (2008) 1 SCC 382, 388, para 13]

Larboard. A nautical term meaning board.

Larceny. Larceny is the taking and carrying away of the mere personal goods of another with intent to steal the goods.

The word 'larceny' in English law contemplates permanent gain or loss and is different from 'theft' under the Indian Penal Code (45 of 1860), S. 378. *K.N. Mehra* v. *State of Rajasthan*, AIR 1957 SC 369, 372.

Largesse. Charitable or generous giving; a present; gift, or donation given unselfishly.

Lascivious. That which tends to excite lust; as in the phrase lascivious behaviour; loose; wanton; lewd; lustful; tending to produce voluptuous or lewd emotions, as in the phrase lascivious work or publication.

Lascivious behaviour. In an Act making "gross lewdness and lascivious behaviour" punishable by imprisonment, *etc.*, includes an indecent exposure of the person of a man to a woman, with a view to excite unchaste desires on her part and to induce her to yield.

Last come, first go. Principle of last come first go is the normal principle on the application of which a reversion on account of exigencies of public service should stand regulated. *J.K. Iron and Steel Co.* v. *Its Workmen,* AIR 1960 SC 1288 (1291).

Last date for making nominations. The 'last date for making nominations' must mean the last hour of the last date during which presentation of nomination papers is permitted under Section 33 of the (43 of 1951) Act". *Narendra Madivalapa Kheni* v. *Manikrao Patil,* AIR 1977 SC 2171, p. 2180. [Representation of People Act (43 of 1951), S. 33]

Last illness. The term "last illness," includes any sickness for which a physician is called, which continues until the death of the patient. It is not necessary that the sickness should in the first instance confine the patient to her room.

Last preceding. Immediately preceding [Indian Evidence Act (1 of 1872), S. 21, ill. (e)]; [TP Act (4 of 1882), S. 29].

Last-proximate-act test. In criminal law, a test based on whether the accused does the final act necessary to commit an offence.

Last resided. The expression "last resided" means the place where the person had his last temporary residence. *Jagir Kaur* v. *Jaswant Singh*, AIR 1963 SC 1521, 1524. [CrPC, 1973 (2 of 1974), S. 126(1)(c)]

The expression 'reside' is not confined to permanent residence alone. It is wide enough to cover temporary as well as permanent residence. *Tulsiram Dewaji* v. *Narbadbai,* AIR 1958 MP 255, 256.

Last resided together. The permanent or temporary nature of the residence of the husband and wife is not material. But there must an intention on the part of the two to reside together for some length of time, even though it might be short. *Ashok* v. *Vishwa Bharti,* AIR 1978 All 18, 19. [Hindu Marriage Act (25 of 1956), S. 19 (iii)]

Last resort. The Court from which no appeal lies to the higher Court in the same jurisdiction.

Last will and testament. "A last will and testament" may be defined as the disposition of one's property to take effect after death."

Lata culpa dolo aequiparatur. (*Maxim*) Gross negligence is tantamount to fraud.

Latens. Latent; hidden; not apparent.

Late fee. Means a fee payable in addition to the prescribed call charges for a local or trunk call, made from or to a public call office outside its regular working hours. [Indian Telegraph Rules, 1951, R. 2(u)]

Latent. Not manifest; hidden; concealed; not visible or apparent.

Latent ambiguity. An ambiguity not evident; not on the surface.

LATENT AMBIGUITY arises where the words of a written instrument are not plain and intelligible, but by reason of extraneous facts a certain and definite application of those words is found impossible.

That species of uncertainty or ambiguity in an instrument which is not apparent from a reading of it but which is revealed when the terms of the instrument are applied or made operative; *e.g.* in a bill of lading goods are to be delivered at "Essex Railroad Wharf", and there are two such wharfs with the same name. (*Black*)

Latent dangers. Dangers not seen, or perceptible to the senses by their presence.

Latent defects. "Latent defect" means a defect which is not obvious to the eye and is not apparently noticeable.

A defect which is not apparently noticeable by ordinary examination. [Indian Railways Act (9 of 1890), S. 73(h)].

Later created right. A right created at a later time. [TP Act (4 of 1882), S. 48].

Lateral. Proceeding from the side (as) lateral motion; lateral support. (*Webster*)

Lateral support. The right of lateral and subjacent support is the right to have land supported by the adjoining land or the soil beneath. The right of a landowner to the natural support of his land by adjoining land. The adjoining owner has the duty not to change his land (such as lowering it) so as to cause this support to be weakened or removed.

Latest census figures. Mean the census figures with respect to Meghalaya ascertainable from the latest census of which the finally published figures are available. [Assam Reorganisation (Meghalaya) Act (55 of 1969), S. 12(6), *Expln.*]

Latrine. "LATRINE" means a place set apart for defecation together with the structure comprising such place, the receptacle therein for collection of human excreta and the fittings and apparatus, if any connected therewith. [Employment of Manual Scavengers and Construction of Dry Latrines (Prohibition) Act (46 of 1993), S. 2(i)]

"LATRINE" means a place set apart for defecating or urinating or both and includes a closet of the dry or water borne type and urinal. [Kerala Municipality Act (Ker Act, 20 of 1994), S. 2(20)]

Latrocinium. The prerogative of adjudging and executing thieves; also larceny; theft; a thing stolen.

Latter. Later; more recent. (*Century*)

That has been mentioned second of the two. [TP Act (4 of 1882), S. 21].

Launching state. Means (i) a State which launches or procures the launching of a space object. (ii) A State from whose territory or facility a space object is launched. [1972 Convention on International Liability for Damage Caused by Space Objects, Art. I(c) Adopted by GA Resolution 2777 XXVI dated 29 Nov. 1971]

Launder. To transfer (money or instruments deriving from illegal activity) so as to conceal the true nature and source.

Laundering. Term used to describe investment or other transfer of money flowing from racketeering, drug transactions, and other illegal sources into legitimate channels so that its original source cannot be traced.

Laundering money. The processing through an apparently legal channel of money obtained illegally, so that its original sources cannot be traced.

Law. The system of authoritative materials for grounding or guiding judicial and administrative action recognised or established in a politically organised society. [Scheduled Areas (Assimilation of Laws) Act (16 of 1953), S. 2(b) and Constitution of India, Art. 13(3)(a)].

"LAW" includes any ordinance, order, bye-law, rule, regulation, notification, custom or usage having in the territory of India the force of law. [Constitution of India, Art. 13(3)(a)]

"LAW" includes any enactment, ordinance, regulation, order, bye-law, rule, scheme, notification or other instrument having, immediately before the appointed day, the force of law in the whole or in any part of the existing State of Jammu and Kashmir. [Jammu & Kashmir Reorganisation Act, 2019 (34 of 2019), section 2(f)]

Law is a rule prescribed by society for the government of human conduct; a rule of action or of civil conduct prescribed by competent authority, by the law making power of the state, by the proper law-making authority, by the supreme authority for the government of human action, by the sovereign power, an established or permanent rule, established by the supreme power, or the power having the legislative control of the particular subject; an act, enactment, ordinance, or statute, prescribed by the legislative power; the declared will of the legislature; a rule ordained and made known by the legislature, for the government of the people in the state, which they are bound to obey.

Circulars issued by the Union of India relating to payment of service charges to local bodies in respect of Central Govt. properties are not mere administrative instructions but are executive orders having the force of law. *Food Corporation of India* v. *Allepy Municipality,* AIR 1996 Ker 241, 255. [Constitution of India, Art. 73(a)]

An agreement of the Ruler expressed in the shape of a contract cannot be regarded as a law. A law must follow the customary forms of laws making and must be expressed as a binding rule of conduct. It is not every indication of the will of the Ruler, however expressed, which amounts to a law. An indication of the will meant to bind as a rule of conduct and enacted with some formality either traditionally or specially devised for the occasion, results in a law but not an agreement to which there are two parties, one of which is the Ruler. *Bengal Nagpur Cotton Mills Ltd.* v. *Board of Revenue*, AIR 1964 SC 888, 891.

If the word 'law' includes not only enacted statute but also common law, it would also include industrial law as it has been evolved by industrial decisions. *Provincial Transport Services* v. *State Industrial Court*, AIR 1963 SC 114, 117.

A law generally is a body of rules which have been laid down for determining legal rights and legal obligations which are recognised by Courts. Law in the case of an absolute monarch is his command which has to be obeyed by the citizens whether they agree with it or not. *Raj Kumar Nursing Pratap Singh Deo* v. *State of Orissa*, AIR 1964 SC 1793, 1797.

A mere executive order cannot possibly come under 'existing law' or 'law in force' as defined in the Constitution, Art. 13(1). *K.O. John* v. *State,* AIR 1956 TC 117, 118.

A notification or an executive direction issued by the State Government against the provisions of the statute will come within the definition of the expression 'law' referred to in Art. 13 of the Constitution. AIR 1958 SC 538.

Law does not include constitutional amendments. *His Holiness Kesavananda Bharati Sripanda-galvan* v. *State of Kerala*, AIR 1973 SC 1461, 1648.

The word "law" is used in the expression "equality before law" in a generic sense—a philosophical sense—whereas in the expressions "the equal protection of laws" it is used denoting specific laws in force. *Sri Srinivasa Theatre* v. *Government of Tamilnadu*, AIR 1992 SC 999, 1004. [Constitution of India, Art. 14]

A law existing at the time when the constitution came into effect would be a law. *State* v. *Banwari,* AIR 1951 All 615. [Constitution of India, Art. 17]

The 'law' means a law passed by a competent Legislature in regard to the administration of the property belonging to the denomination. [Constitution of India, Art. 26(*d*)]

The expression 'law' embraces within its ambit statutory rules. [Constitution of India, Art. 226(3), (as substituted by 42nd Amendment Act); 13(2) and Art. 309]

The expression 'Law' includes the Act of Legislature, as also the rules validly made thereunder. *H.G.E. Corporation* v. *Superindent of Orissa Excise.* AIR 1966 Pat 248, 252. [Constitution of India, Art. 265]

'Law' means any law enacted either by legislature itself or by its delegate, and the notification issued by the U.P. Government being in the exercise of the legislative power, is law. *Video Electronical (P) Ltd.* v. *State of Punjab*, AIR 1990 SC 820, 835. [Constitution of India, Arts. 304, 366]

By the publication of an order in the Gazette of India, it is to be treated as law made under Art. 327. *Meghraj* v. *Delimitation Commission*, AIR 1967 SC 669, 674. [Constitution of India, Art. 327]

The term 'law' is not limited to legislative enactments. All forms of delegated legislation and conditional legislation amount to law. All orders and notification made and issued under statutory powers and which are legislative in nature amount to law. *State of M.P.* v. *Ramachandran,* AIR 1977 MP 68, 73 (FB). [Indian Evidence Act (1 of 1872), Ss. 57 and 78.

Law includes not only legislative enactments but also judicial precedents. An authoritative judgment of the courts including higher judiciary is also law. [*Viredra Kumar Dixit* v. *State of U.P.,* 2014 SCC Online All 16476 : (2014) 9 ADJ 1596]. See also *Bhargavi Constructions v. Kothakapu Muthyam Reddy,* (2018) 13 SCC 480, paras 28 to 32].

Law abiding. Obedient to the laws of the land.

Law and order. The normal state of a civilized society.

The expression "law and order" is a comprehensive expression which may include not merely "public order" but also matters such as "public peace", public tranquility "and" orderliness in a locality or a local area and perhaps some other matters of public concern too. "Public order" is something distinct from order or orderliness in a local area. [*Ramlila Maidan Incident, In Re*, (2012) 5 SCC 1, para 49].

Law and order and **public order.** The true distinction between the areas of 'law & order' and 'Public Order' is one of the degree and extent of the reach of the act in question upon society. AIR 1970 SC 1228 Quoted. *Babul Mitra* v. *State of West Bengal*, AIR 1973 SC 197, 199. [Maintenance of Internal Security Act (21 of 1978) (*repealed*), S. 3(1)(*a*)(*ii*)]

While the expression 'law and order' is wider in scope in as much as contravention of law always affects order, while 'public order' has a narrower ambit and public order would be affected by only such contravention which affects the community or the public at large. *Victoria Persuadars* v. *Lalmal Saima*, AIR 1992 SC 687, 689. [National Security Act (65 of 1980), S. 3(2)]

Law declared by the Supreme Court. "The law declared" referred to in Art. 141 is the Law to be gathered from any judgment in a case decided by the Supreme Court, whether it is the judgment of a Judge forming the majority or of a Judge is a minority and dissenting. *Mahendra Bhawanji Thakar* v. *S.P. Parde,* AIR 1964 Bom 170, 176. [Constitution of India, Art. 141]

A decision which is not express and is not founded on reasons nor it proceeds on consideration of issue cannot be deemed to be a law declared to have a binding effect as is contemplated by Art. 141. That which escapes in the judgment without any occasion is not *ratio decidendi.* Any declaration or conclusion arrived without application of mind or preceded without any reason cannot be deemed to be declaration of law or authority of a general nature binding as a precedent. *State of U.P.* v. *Synthetics and Chemicals Ltd.*, (1991) 4 SCC 139. [Constitution of India, Art. 141]

Law for the time being in force. "The law for the time being in force" concerning any particular matter, whether it be the collection of the revenue or anything else, is a comprehensive expression which includes, not one particular statute but the whole body of law, whether in one or more statutes or outside a statute altogether, which for the time being governs the particular matter. *Shiromani Sugar Mills Ltd.* v. *Governor General in Council,* (1945) 15 Comp Cases 153.

A law cannot be said to be in force unless it is brought into operation by legislative enactment, or by the exercise of authority by a delegate empowered to bring it into operation. *Orissa State* v. *Chandrasekhar*, AIR 1970 SC 398, 401.

The words "any law for the time being in force" in sub-section (2) of Section 4 must be given their natural meaning and the natural meaning of these words would be any law which was in force at the time, when the Hindu Succession Act was enacted. The intention of the Legislature was to save that law, *i.e.* the law regarding devolution of tenancy rights, which was in force before the coming into force of the Hindu Succession Act. *Sitabai* v. *Kothulal Bandhu Lodhi,* AIR 1959 Bom 78, 81. [Hindu Succession Act (30 of 1956), S. 4(2)]

Law operative at the time in question. [Provincial Small Cause Courts Act (9 of 1887), S. 3(b)].

Law graduate. Means a person who has obtained a bachelor's degree in law from any University established by law in India. [Advocate Act (25 of 1961), S. 2(h)]

Law imposing taxation. The expression 'laws imposing taxation' occurring in our constitution should receive a limited construction. A law dealing with taxation is not necessarily a 'law imposing taxation'. A law which prescribes the conditions on which the tax liability should arise can properly be described as part of the law imposing the tax. *Palaniappa Chettiar and Co.* v. *Deputy Commercial Tax Officer,* AIR 1959 Mad 317, 322. [Constitution of India, Art. 286(3)]

Law in force. "LAW IN FORCE" includes laws passed or made by Legislature or other competent authority in the territory of India before the commencement of this constitution and not previously repealed, notwithstanding that any such law or any part thereof may not be then in operation either at all or in particular areas. [Constitution of India, Arts. 13(3)(b) and 372, *Expln.* I]

The words 'law in force' should not receive any technical meaning but should be understood in a sense which gives them a fair measure of amplitude.

The phrase 'law in force' as used in Art. 20, Constitution of India must be understood in its natural sense as being the law in fact in existence and in operation at the time of the commission of the offence as distinct from the law 'deemed' to have become operative by virtue of the power of legislature to pass retrospective laws. *Rao Shiv Bahadur Singh* v. *State of Vindya Pradesh*, AIR 1953 SC 394, 399.

The words 'law in force' as used in Art. 372 Constitution of India are wide enough to include not merely a legislative enactment but also any regulation or order which has the force of the law. *Edward Mills Co. Ltd.* v. *State of Ajmer*, AIR 1955 SC 25.

It is not possible to hold that a mere rule of construction adopted by English Courts and also by some of the Indian Courts to ascertain the intention of the Legislature was a law in force within the meaning of this term. There is an essential distinction between a law and a canon of construction. So a rule of construction is not a 'law in force'. *Superintendent and Remembrancer of Legal Affairs, W.B.* v. *Corporation of Calcutta*, AIR 1967 SC 997, 1007. [Constitution of India, Art. 372]

Law knowing person. Means either a law graduate or a person having some elementary knowledge or experience in legal matters. [Madhya Pradesh Gram Nyayalaya Adhiniyam, 1996 (M.P. 26 of 1997), S. 2(i)]

Law merchant. The Law Merchant is neither more nor less than the usages of merchants and traders in the different departments of trade ratified by the decisions of Courts of Law, which, upon such usages being proved before them, have adopted them as settled law, with a view to the interests of trade and the public convenience, the Courts proceedings therein on the well-known principle of law that, with reference to transactions in the different departments of trade, Courts of law, in giving effect to the contracts and dealings of the parties, will assume that the latter have dealt with one another on the footing of any custom or usage prevailing generally in the particular department. By this process, what before was usage, only unsanctioned by legal decision, has become engrafted upon, or incorporated into, the Common Law and may thus be said to be part of it.

THE LAW MERCHANT is not a rigidly fixed body of law, but is constantly expanding.

The legal rules formerly applied to cases arising in commercial transactions especially by Courts. [Marine Insurance Act (11 of 1963), S. 91].

Law of a State. The law of a State signifies, in its ordinary acceptation, whatever is an expression of the legislative, as distinguished from the executive or judicial power of a state. Under Art. 213, the Governor is authorised, subject to the conditions laid down therein, to issue ordinances which have the force of law, and these ordinances are clearly laws of the state. Under Art. 252, it is open to Parliament action on resolutions of the Legislatures of two or more States, to enact laws on subjects which are within the exclusive competence of the States. They are no doubt the laws of the States concerned. *M.P.V. Sundararamiers & Co.* v. *State of Andhra Pradesh*, AIR 1958 SC 468, 487. [Constitution of India, Art. 286(2)]

Law of a State in force. The expression "law of a State in force" in this clause shall include a law of a State passed or made before the commencement of this Constitution and not previously repealed, notwithstanding that it or parts of it may not be then in operation either at all or in particular areas. [Constitution of India, Article 288(1), *Explanation*]

Law of evidence. The law of evidence is a collection of general rules established by law (1) for declaring what is to be taken as true without proof; (2) for declaring the presumptions of law, both those which are disputable and those which are conclusive; (3)for the production of legal evidence; (4)for the exclusion of whatever is not legal; (5)for determining in certain cases the value and effect of evidence.

Law dealing with the receiving and judging of evidence. [CPC (5 of 1908), O. XIII, R. 10(3)].

Law of insolvency. Law dealing with the estate of one who has not property sufficient for the full payment of his debts [Companies Act (1 of 1956), S. 528 now replaced by Companies Act, 2013].

Law of limitation. Law dealing with limitation. [CPC (5 of 1908), O. VII, R. 6].

Law of nations. A system of rules and principles established among nations, for the regulation of their intercourse; the *jus gentium*. International Law.

Law of nature. The law of nature is that which God at the time of creation of the nature of man infused into his heart, for his preservation and direction; and this is *lex-aeterna*, the moral law, called also the law of nature. And by this law, written with the finger of God in the heart of man, where the people of God a long time governed, before the law was written by Moses, who was the first reporter or writer of law in the world."—(Lord COKE, *Calvin's Case* (1608), 4 Co. 21.).

Law of prior decision. A rule of law based on decisions of Courts in contrasts to rules of law based on legislative enactment.

Law of the land. The general law of the state. LAW OF THE LAND means due process of law. (*Kenney*)

Law of the Road. Rule of the Road; navigation rules.

Law Officer. A public functionary employed in the administration of law or to advise a government in legal matters. [CPC (5 of 1908), O. XXVI, R. 20(b)].

Law relating to state monopoly. The expression "law relating to state monopoly" means the law relating to the monopoly in its absolutely essential features. In such cases the Court should enquire what are the provisions of the said law which are basically and essentially necessary for creating the State monopoly. *Akadasi* v. *State of Orissa*, AIR 1963 SC 1047, 1054. [Constitution of India, Art. 19(6)(ii) and Art. 305]

Law Reports. A general term, for the published volumes narrating and recording the decisions of the Courts. (*Abbott*)

Law, Retrospective. "Retrospective laws are *prima facie*, of questionable policy, and contrary to the general principle that legislation by which the conduct of mankind is to be regulated ought, when introduced for the first time, to deal with future acts, and ought not to change the character of past transactions carried on upon the faith of the then existing law." *Willis J. Phillips* v. *Eyre* (1870) LR 6 QB 23.

Law review. A journal containing articles and commentary on legal topics by the scholars of law.

Law, Rule and notification. 'Law' is one thing and an act done or order issued under the law is another thing. When we speak of 'law' we mean something which is enforceable and which is not capable of being rejected by the Courts as uncertain, unreasonable or as repugnant to the law of the lands. Where a statute under the authority of which rules are promulgated itself declares that they shall have the same effect as if enacted in the statute, the validity of the rules cannot be canvassed by Courts of law. Nor can any Court reject them as uncertain and unenforceable. But where the statute does not so provide their validity can be canvassed and the Court can reject them as unenforceable on the ground of unreasonableness or uncertainty. They do not constitute 'law.' The essence of the law is that it is enforceable as law, and though the Courts may construe it they cannot reject or quash it. A power to regulate does not involve a power to prohibit. A notification issued in exercise of a power conferred by Statute is as much a part of the law as if it had been incorporated in the statute. The command is, in every sense a command by the appropriate Legislative authority.

Law school. An institution for formal legal education and training.

Law suit. Suit instituted in a law Court. An action at law; litigation.

Law, Validity of. Even the tax law must satisfy two tests before it can be a valid law, namely (1) that the appropriate legislature has competency to make the law; (2) that it does not take away or abridge any of the fundamental rights. *Balaji* v. *Income Tax Officer*, AIR 1962 SC 123, 128. [Constitution of India, Art. 19].

Lawful. That which in its substance is sanctioned or justified by law; (as) opposed to unlawful or illegal; peaceable, as lawful citizen.

By lawful, it means not contrary to law, public policy or void *ab initio*, or unlawful. But the term 'lawful' cannot include grounds like fraud, undue influence and coercion by which the decree can be avoided, treating it as voidable. Till it is avoided and displaced, it can be treated as lawful for the limited purpose of O. XXIII, R. 3, CPC *S.G. Thimappa* v. *T. Anantha,* AIR 1986 Kar 1 at 4. [CPC (5 of 1908), O. XXIII, R. 3 and 3-A]

The term 'lawful' has a wider meaning than the term 'legal'. 'Legal' is what is in conformity with the letter or rules of the law as administered in the Court. 'Lawful' is what is in conformity with the principles or spirit of the law whether moral or judicial. *Motilal* v. *Badrilal,* AIR 1957 MB 183, 184

According to or not contrary to law; permitted by law; appointed, sanctioned or recognised by law; legally qualified or entitled. [CrPC 1973 (2 of 1974), S. 220, ill(e)].

Lawful act. A lawful act is one not forbidden by the penal law.

Act which is according to law. [Indian Contract Act (9 of 1872), S. 222].

Lawful adventure. A lawful undertaking, enterprise or venture involving financial risk or speculation. [Indian Partnership Act (9 of 1932), S. 41(b)].

Lawful age, means age of majority.

Lawful agreement. Lawful Agreement means an agreement enforceable by law.

The word 'lawful' occurring in O. XXIII, R. 3, CPC (5 of 1908) means an agreement which is legally enforceable. A contract to pay future rent for a period beyond three years from the date of decree is perfectly lawful. *Krishnan Krishnan* v. *Kandan Velu,* AIR 1955 TC 233.

Lawful and Legal. The meaning of the expression lawful is wider than legal. Legal is associated with Act, Rules *etc.* and lawful means that which is not illegal, against law or impermissible. [*Bhupad Prasad R.V.* v. *State of A.P.,* (1995) 2 CTC 342 : AIR 1996 SC 140]

Lawful guardian. 'The words "lawful guardian" in this section include any person lawfully entrusted with the care or custody of a minor or other person'. [IPC (45 of 1860), S. 361, *Explanation*] [Now (w. e. f. 1-7-2024) repealed & replaced by Bharatiya Nyaya Sanhita, 2023 (45 of 2023)]

Exception.—This clause does not extend to the act of any person who in good faith believes himself to be the father of an illegitimate child, or who in good faith believes himself to be entitled to the lawful custody of such child, unless such act is committed for an immoral or unlawful purpose. [(w. e. f. 1-7-2024) Bharatiya Nyaya Sanhita, 2023 (45 of 2023), S. 137(1), *Explanation*]

The words "lawful guardian" in S. 361, IPC, include not only the parents or relations in whose house the minor lives and is brought up, but also any other person with whom the minor resides by the consent, express or implied, of those who have the higher legal right. The term does not include a person who has himself gained possession of the minor by an offence under Section 361, IPC (45 of 1860). [Now (w. e. f. 1-7-2024) repealed & replaced by Bharatiya Nyaya Sanhita, 2023 (45 of 2023)] IC 97 (98).

A person who is legally entitled or is legally appointed to the care and management of the person or property of another person, such as a minor or a person of unsound mind or otherwise incapable under the law to do the same. [IPC (45 of 1860), S. 361, *Expln*].

The expression "Lawful guardian" in S. 361, IPC (45 of 1860) includes a *de facto* guardian. 22 Pat 263 : AIR 1943 Pat 212.

A *de facto* guardian of a minor who takes upon himself the management of the minor's property without being the legal guardian under Hindu Law or a guardian duly appointed by authority is not a lawful guardian within the meaning of S. 20, Limitation Act (36 of 1963), so as to entitle him to keep alive a debt which would otherwise become barred.

The words 'lawful guardian' are of wider connotation than the words 'legal guardian'. The word 'lawful' in that section has been deliberately used in its wider connotation and that word would mean that wherever the relationship of a guardian and a ward is established by means which are lawful and legitimate that relationship is intended to be included within the meaning of the words 'lawful guardian' as used in this section. *State* v. *Ramji Vitual Chandhari,* AIR 1958 Bom 381, 384.

Lawful guardianship. The test of lawful guardianship is that the infant or minor should be in a position to apply to his guardian for protection. 1929 Cr C 543 : AIR 1929 Sind 249(2).

Lawful heirs : Heirs. The words "heirs." or "lawful heirs" used in a will, must be construed in their legal and ordinary sense, unless other provisions of the will show that the testator meant other persons than those who would be heirs in the legal sense.

Where property was devised for life, with remainder to the testator's "lawful heirs," the words "lawful heirs" were held to have reference to those persons who were the lawful heirs of the testator at the time of his death.

Lawful holder. In speaking of the 'lawful holder' of negotiable paper, that term may include one who holds the paper merely as trustee for the real owner, for the purpose of collecting the same in his own name for the benefit of such real owner.

Lawful increase. Means an increase in rent permitted under the provisions of this Act. [Delhi Rent Act, 1995 (33 of 1995), 2(f)]

Lawful Interception. Legally sanctioned official access to private communications such as telephone calls and e-mail messages. Aparna Viswanathan, *Cyber Law: Indian & International Perspectives,* 2012, LexisNexis Butterworths at p. 167.

Lawful issue. The words "lawful issue," when used in a will, ordinarily and generally mean descendants.

Lawful orders. "Lawful order," as used in a statute defining contempt of Court to be the disobedience or resistance of a lawful order of a Court or judge, does not mean an order which is not erroneous; but an erroneous order or judgment, though unlawful and liable to be reversed on appeal, is obligatory until reversed, and disobedience of it is contempt.

Lawful possession. The term "lawful possession" is not convertible with "innocent possession," in legal terminology. Intent does not enter into whether an act is unlawful or tortious, though it does as to whether it is innocent or criminal.

Lawful possession is not litigious possession and must have some foundation in a legal right to possess the property which cannot be equated with a temporary right to enforce recovery of the property in case a person is wrongfully or forcibly dispossessed from it. *M.C. Chockalingam* v. *V. Manickavasagam*, AIR 1974 SC 104, 110.

Lawful process. "Lawful process" in any action or proceeding manifestly refers to process emanating from Court, and cannot be understood to refer to such acts or notices between private parties as derive no authority from a Court, but simply serve to create a right to action.

Lawfully. A person should be regarded in the eye of law as having been lawfully entrusted with the care and custody of a minor, if he has acquired control over the minor lawfully and in such circumstances as would imply trust, even though he may not have been formally entrusted with the care and custody of the minor by a third person.

The word "lawfully" in S. 70 of the Indian Contract Act (9 of 1872) is not merely a surplusage. In using that word, the Legislature had in contemplation cases in which a person holds such relation to another as either directly to create or reasonably to justify the inference that by some act done for another person, the doer was entitled to look for compensation to the person benefitted. S. 70 of the Indian Contract Act (9 of 1872) ought not to be so read as to justify the officious interference of any one with the affairs or properties of another, or to impose an obligation in respect of services which the person sought to be charged with did not wish to have rendered.

The word "lawfully" as used in S. 70 of the Indian Contract Act (9 of 1872) is of the very essence of the section, and in every case we have to find out whether, the person making a payment of money had any lawful interest in making it at the time when the payment was made. If a person holding a charge on a property makes a payment in order to save it from being sold *bona fide* believing that it is necessary to do so in order that it may remain intact for satisfaction for his debt, the payment is made "lawfully" within the meaning of the section.

The word "lawfully" in the context indicates that after something is delivered or something is done by one person for another and that thing is accepted and enjoyed by the latter, a lawful relationship is born between the two which under the provisions of S. 70 gives rise to a claim for compensation. *State of West Bengal* v. *B.K. Mondal*, AIR 1962 SC 779, 788. [Indian Contract Act (9 of 1872), S.70]

In a lawful manner. [IPC (45 of 1860), S. 151].

Lawgiver. A judge with power of interpreting law.

Lawmaker. The branch of Government which is responsible for the making of statutory laws.

Laws, Law in force and existing law. "Laws in force" includes laws passed or made by a Legislature or other competent authority in the territory of India before the commencement of this Constitution and not previously repealed, notwithstanding that any such law or any part thereof may not be then in operation either at all or in particular areas. [Constitution of India, Article 13(3)(b)]

The order passed by the Magistrate under this section are 'laws' within the meaning of Arts. 13 and 19(2) & (6). The provisions of S. 144 were also an 'existing law' within the meaning of Art. 19(2) to (6) and 'law in force' within the meaning of Art. 13 (1). *Rajnarain Singh* v. *District Magistrate,* AIR 1956 All 481, 444. [Constitution of India, Arts. 13 and 19; Section 144, CrPC, 1973 (2 of 1974)]

Laws of Oleron. The laws of Oleron were introduced into England by King Richard, the crusader, and are to a large extent the basis of the maritime law of that country.

Lawyer. A counsellor or one learned in the law. (*Tomlin*)

One who pursues the profession of law; a legal expert.

Lay days. Number of days allowed for the loading and unloading of a ship. For any days taken in excess of the agreed number "demurrage" becomes payable.

Lay down. Relinquish (as) office.

Lay down ones arms. Cease fighting; surrender.

Lay down the law. Declare the law.

Lay judges. Persons not legally qualified or trained who exercise judicial functions, or participate with trained judges in exercising judicial functions.

Lay-off. "Lay-off" (with its grammatical variations and cognate expressions) means the failure, refusal or inability of an employer on account of shortage of coal, power or raw material or the accumulation of stocks or the break down of machinery or natural calamity or for any other connected reason to give employment to a workman whose name is borne on the mustor-rolls or his industrial establishment and who has not been retrenched;

Explanation.—Every workman whose name is borne on the muster-rolls of the industrial establishment and who presents himself for work at the establishment at the time appointed for the purpose during normal working hours on any day and is not given employment by the employer within two hours of his so presenting himself, shall be deemed to have been laid off for that day within the meaning of this clause:

Provided that if the workman, instead of being given employment at the commencement of any shift for any day is asked to present himself for the purpose during the second half of the shift for the day and is given employment then, he shall be deemed to have been laid off only for one half of that day.

Provided further that if he is not given any such employment even after so presenting himself, he shall not be deemed to have been laid off for the second half of the shift for the day and shall be entitled to full basic wages and dearness allowance for that part of the day. [Industrial Disputes Act (14 of 1947), S. 2(kkk)]

"Lay-off" (with its grammatical variations and cognate expressions) means the failure, refusal or inability of an employer on account of shortage of coal, power or raw materials or the accumulation of stocks or the break-down of machinery or natural calamity or for any other connected reason, to give employment to a worker whose name is borne on the muster rolls of his industrial establishment and who has not been retrenched.

Explanation.— Every worker whose name is borne on the muster rolls of the industrial establishment and who presents himself for work at the establishment at the time appointed for the purpose during normal working hours on any day and is not given employment by the employer within two hours of his so presenting himself shall be deemed to have been laid-off for that day within the meaning of this clause:

Provided that if the worker, instead of being given employment at the commencement of any shift for any day is asked to present himself for the purpose during the second half of the shift for the day and is given employment then, he shall be deemed to have been laid-off only for one-half of that day:

Provided further that if he is not given any such employment even after so presenting himself, he shall not be deemed to have been laid-off for the second half of the shift for the day and shall be entitled to full basic wages and dearness allowance for that part of the day. [Industrial Relations Code, 2020 (35 of 2020), section 2(t)]

The very term 'lay-off' assumes and implies that the employer is not under a condition to offer employment to his employee. *Nutan Mills* v. *Employees State Insurance Corporation,* AIR 1956 Bom 336, 340.

Lay-off only means that the employee is temporarily unemployed and would not be entitled to wages, (According to the Standing Orders) a person 'laid off' would be entitled to preference when the working of the factory is resumed. *Upper India Cauper Mills Co. Ltd.* v. *J.C. Mathur,* AIR 1959 All 664, 669.

A period during which a workman is temporarily discharged. [Industrial Disputes Act (14 of 1947), S. 2(kkk)].

Lay out. The act or process of laying out or planning in detail.

Lay witness. A witness who does not testify as an expert and hence who may give only opinions or make inferences which are based on first hand knowledge and helpful in understanding the testimony or in determining facts.

Layer. For the Purposes of Section 2(87) of the Act 18 of 2013 'layer' in relation to a holding company means its subsidiary or subsidiaries. [*Explanation (d)* to section 2(87) of the Companies Act, 2013 (18 of 2013)]

Layout-design. Means a layout of transistors and other circuitry elements and includes lead wires connecting such elements and expressed in any manner in a semiconductor integrated circuit. [Semi-conductor Integrated Circuit Layout Design Act (37 of 2000), S. 2(h)]

"LCNG". Means CNG produced at the fueling station from LNG by pumping and vaporisation. [Static and Mobile Pressure Vessels (Unfired) Rules, 2016, R. 2(xxx-b)].

LCD and LED. "The two principal method of forming numbers and letters on instruments such as calculators and digital watches. A basic pattern of seven bars is used to form the digits of 0 to 9 and several letters. To form other letters and symbols, more than seven bars are required.

"In the LED (light emitting diode), the bars are made of a substance that permits an electric current to flow through in one direction only. A substance used in this way is called a diode. As the current flows, the diode gives off red, blue, yellow, or other coloured light, depending on the compound of which it is made. For example, gallium phosphide (GaP) emits a green glow. Electric circuits in the instrument selectively turn on the current to the bars to form the various numbers and letters.

"In the LCD (liquid crystal display), the bars are made of liquid crystals. These are a kind of hybrid material, not quite a liquid and not quite a solid. They can't be poured readily, as with liquids, nor are their molecules locked in place, as with true solids. But the molecules can be rotated slightly by an electric current. When no current flows, the bars are not noticeable, because they reflect light to the same extent as the rest of display surface. But when current flows through a bar, its molecules rotate and its ability to reflect light is reduced. The bar appears darker than the area around it and forms part of a number or letter". [Blooms Dictionary of "Science for Everyone" as cited in *Secure Meters Limited* v. *Commissioner of Customs, New Delhi*, (2015) 14 SCC 239, para 16].

Leachate. "LEACHATE" means liquid that seeps through solid wastes or other medium and has extracts of dissolved or suspended material from it. [Municipal Solid Wastes (Management and Handling) Rules, 2000, Rule 2(xii)]

Lead. (*Noun*) "One of the useful metals remarkable for its softness and durability." (*Verb*). To guide; to show the method of attaining; to draw : to go first and show the way.

A heavy soft bluish-grey metal. [Mines and Minerals (Regulation and Development) Act (67 of 1957), Sch I, item 10]; to guide on a way; to be first or foremost in some respect.

"LEAD" for the purpose of these regulations means information pertaining to a person who has accessed the website of an Insurance Web Aggregator and has submitted contact information of any kind, for obtaining information on prices or features or benefits of insurance products. [Insurance Regulatory and Development Authority of India (Insurance Web Aggregators) Regulations, 2017, Regn. 2(g)].

Lead Generation. For the purpose of these regulations, is the process of collecting the details of the prospects to ascertain their intention of purchase Insurance Policy, before proceeding with solicitation of insurance products. [Insurance Regulatory and Development Authority of India (Insurance Web Aggregators) Regulations, 2017, Regn. 2(h)].

Lead Management System. (LMS) for the purpose of these regulations refers to the software implemented by the Insurance Web Aggregator for recording filtering, validating, grading, distribution, follow up and closure of leads from the enquiries received on the website of the website of the Insurance Web Aggregator. [Insurance Regulatory and Development Authority of India (Insurance Web Aggregators) Regulations, 2017, Regn. 2(i)].

Leaders of a political party. For the purposes of clause (a) of *Explanation 1,* the expression "leaders of a political party", in respect of any election, means—

(i) where such political party is a recognised political party, such persons not exceeding forty in number, and

(ii) where such political party is other than a recognised political party, such persons not exceeding twenty in number,

whose names have been communicated to the Election Commission and the Chief Electoral Officers of the states by the political party to be leaders for the purpose of such election, within a period of seven days from the date of the notification for such election published in the Gazette of India or Official Gazette of the State, as the case may be, under this Act. [Representation of the People Act (43 of 1951), S. 77, *Explanation 2*].

Leader. One who leads; one of the main editorials or articles in a newspaper. [section 2(f), Working Journalists and Other Newspaper Employees (Conditions of Service) and Miscellaneous Provisions Act (45 of 1955)].

"Leader" means the Head of a Department or the Head of an Institute or organization. [National Dental Commission Act, 2023 (21 of 2023), section 2(o)]

'LEADER' in relation to a legislature party, means a member of the party chosen by it as its leader and includes any other member of the party authorised by the party to act, in the absence of the leader as, or discharge the functions of, the leader of the party for the purpose of these rules. [Members of the Kerala Legislative assembly (Disqualification on ground of defection) Rules, 1986, R. 2(f)]

The chief person in a party who is followed by the other persons belonging to that party.

Leader of the Council. Means the Prime Minister, if he is a member of the Council or a Minister who is a member of the Council and is nominated by the Prime Minister to function as the leader of the Council. [Rules of Procedure and Conduct of Business in the Council of States (Rajya Sabha), R. 2(1)]

Leader of the House. A member of the Government appointed by the Prime Minister to control the arrangement of business in the House; the Prime Minister himself. *(Constitutional and Parliamentary Term)*

Leader of the opposition. "LEADER OF THE OPPOSITION", in relation to either House of Parliament, means that member of the Council of States or the House of the People, as the case may be, who is, for the time being, the Leader in the House of the party in opposition to the Government having the greatest numerical strength and recognised as such by the chairman of the Council of States or the Speaker of house of the People, as the case may be.

Explanation—Where there are two or more parties in opposition to the Government, in the Council of States or in the House of the People having the same numerical strength, the Chairman of the Council of States or the Speaker of the House of the People, as the case may be, shall, having regard to the status of the parties, recognise any one of the leaders of such parties as the leader of the Opposition for the purposes of this section and such recognition shall be final and conclusive. [Salary & Allowances of Leaders of Opposition in Parliament Act (33 of 1977), S. 2]

"Leader of the opposition" means the member of the Assembly who is for the time being recognised as such by the Speaker of the Assembly. [Haryana Legislative Assembly (Allowances and Pension of Members) Act (2 of 1975), S. 2(b)]

Leader of the largest minority Party in a legislature; an office recognized under the Rules of the House. (*Constitutional and Parliamentary Term*)

Leading. Settling or determining (as) leading case. (*Burrill*)

Leading case. Legal decision used as an important precedent. A reported case considered as settling any particular point of law and which is looked upon and followed as a guide for subsequent cases.

Leading marks are the signs placed on crates for the purpose of easily identifying the goods contained in them.

Leading principle of construction. The only principle of construction which is applicable without qualification to all wills and overrides every other rule of construction, is that the testator's intention is collected from a consideration of the whole will taken in connection with any evidence properly admissible, and the meaning of the will and of every part of it is determined according to that intention. [Halsbury's Laws of England, 4th Edn., Vol 50, p. 239, para 408 as cited in *Mathai Samuel v. Eapen Eapen*, (2012) 13 SCC 80, para 22].

Leading question. "Any question suggesting the answer which the person putting it wishes or expects to receive is called a leading question." [Indian Evidence Act (1 of 1872), S. 141] [(w. e. f. 1-7-2024) repealed and replaced by Bharatiya Sakshya Adhiniyam, 2023 (47 of 2023), S, 146(1)]

League of Nations. A Conventional Assembly set up in 1920 with a membership of 58 States. The covenant of 26 articles was its charter, pledging these States to promote international cooperation and achieve peace and security by accepting obligations not to go to war and to respect treaties. It has been replaced by the United Nations Organisation. And the Charter of the United Nations was signed on 26 June, 1945, after the Second World War II (1939-1945).

Leapfrog attack. Any form of intrusion or attack accomplished by exploitation of data or information obtained on a site or server other than the attack's target. (*Cyber Law*)

Learner's licence. "LEARNER'S LICENCE" means the licence issued by a competent authority under Chapter II authorising the person specified therein to drive as a learner, a motor vehicle or a motor vehicle of any specified class or description. [Motor Vehicles Act (29 of 1988), S. 2(19)]

Learner Support Centre. Means a centre established, maintained or recognised by the Higher Educational Institution for advising, counseling, providing interface between the teacher and the learners, and rendering any academic and any other related service and assistance required by the learners. [University Grants Commission (Open and Distance Learning) Regulations, 2017, Regn. 2(k)].

Learner Support Services. Means and includes such services as are a provided by a Higher Educational Institution in order to facilitate the acquisition of teaching-learning experiences by the learner to the level prescribed by or on behalf of the Commission in respect of a programme of study. [University Grants Commission (Open and Distance Learning) Regulations, 2017, Regn. 2(l)].

Learning. "LEARNING" means education, whether elementary, technical or scientific, special or general, and training of every kind which is usually intended to enable a person to pursue any trade, industry, profession or avocation of life. [Hindu Gains of Learning Act (30 of 1930), S. 2(c)]

The definition of the term "learning" is very wide and almost encompasses within its sweep every acquired capacity which enables the acquirer of the capacity "to pursue any trade, industry, profession or avocation in life". *Chandrakant Manilal Shah* v. *CIT*, AIR 1992 SC 66. [Hindu Gains of Learning Act (30 of 1930), S. 2(c)]

Lease. "A lease of immoveable property is a transfer of a right to enjoy such property, made for a certain time, express or implied, or in perpetuity, in consideration of a price paid or promised, or of money, a share of crops, service or any other thing of value, to be rendered periodically or on specified occasions to the transferor by the transferee, who accepts the transfer on such terms. The transferor is called the *lessor*, the transferee is called the *lessee,* the price is called the *premium,* and the money, share, service or other thing to be so rendered is called the *rent*". [T.P. ACT (4 of 1882), S. 105].

"LEASE" means a lease of immoveable property, and includes also - (*a*) a patta, (*b*) a *kabuliyat* or other undertaking in writing, not being a counterpart of a lease, to cultivate, occupy or pay or deliver rent for immoveable property; (*c*) any instrument by which tolls of any description are let; (*d*) any writing on an application for a lease intended to signify that the application is granted. [Indian Stamp Act (2 of 1899), S. 2(16)]

"LEASE" includes a counterpart, *kabuliyat,* an undertaking to cultivate or occupy, and an agreement to lease. [Registration Act (16 of 1908), S. 2(7)].

'LEASE' means any agreement or arrangement whereby the right to use any goods for any purpose is transferred by one person to another whether or not for specified period for cash, deferred payment or other valuable consideration without the transfer of ownership, and includes a sub-lease but does not include any transfer on hire-purchase or any system of payment by instalments. [Rajasthan Sales Tax Act, 1954, S. 2(23)]

'LEASE' means a transfer of a right to enjoy land, made orally in writing, for specified, or unspecified period, and in consideration of rent. [Goa, Daman and Diu Agricultural Tenancy Act (7 of 1964), S. 2(13)]

A lease is a conveyance by the owner of an estate to another of a portion of his interest therein for a term less than his own, in consideration of a certain annual or stated or other recompense.

Lease and **Licence.** The crucial test in each case is whether the instrument is intended to create or not to create an instrument in the property the subject-matter of the agreement. If it is in fact intended to create an interest in the property it is a lease, if it does not, it is a licence. In determining whether the agreement creates a lease or a licence the test of exclusive possession, though not decisive, is of significance. *Sohan Lal Naraindas* v. *Laxmidas Raghunath Gadit*, (1971) 1 SCC 276, 279-80. [Transfer of Property Act (4 of 1882), S. 52]

Lease-back. A long-term lease of real estate or equipment that has been sold to an independent agent and is then taken back under the lease agreement by the original seller.

Lease for agricultural purposes. A lease of a coffee garden is not an agricultural lease within the meaning of S.117, Transfer of Property Act (4 of 1882).

A lease of land for the cultivation of betel is an agricultural lease.

Where a certain land is given for "cultivation and building tenant's house", held that the lease was for a mixed purpose, agricultural and non-agricultural, for a lump rent.

Lease for years. A contract by which one conveys lands, tenements or hereditaments for life, for a term of years, or at will or for any less interest than that of the lessor usually for a specified rent or compensation. [Indian Succession Act (39 of 1925), S. 111, ill (ii)].

"Lease from month to month" and "Lease from year to year". "In the absence of a contract or local law or usage to the contrary, a lease of immoveable property for agricultural or manufacturing purposes shall be deemed to be a lease from year to year, terminable, on the part of either lessor or lessee, by six months' notice expiring with the end of the year of the tenancy; and a lease of immoveable property for any other purpose shall be deemed to be a lease from month to month, terminable, on the part of either lessor or lessee, by fifteen days' notice expiring with the end of a month of the tenancy." [T.P. ACT (4 of 1882), S. 106]

Lease in perpetuity. 'Lease in perpetuity' in private law cannot be used to construe agreements between two sovereign States, where neither of them is bound by private law of the other. *Union of India* v. *Sukumar Sengupta,* AIR 1990 SC 1692.

Lease of the buildings. The expression 'lease of buildings' includes the landed area appurtenant thereto. *K. Bhagirathi G. Shenoy*v. *K.P. Ballakuraya*, (1999) 4 SCC 135, para 23. [Kerala Land Reforms Act, 1963 (1 of 1964), S. 3(1)(ii)]

Leased circuit. Means a dedicated link provided between two fixed locations for exclusive use of the subscriber and includes a speech circuit, a data circuit or a telegraph circuit. [Finance Act (32 of 1994), S. 65(1)(50) now repealed by Central Goods and Services Tax Act, 2017]

Leasehold. An estate in land for a term of years.

A tenure by way of lease; land held on lease. [TP Act (4 of 1882), S. 72(e)].

Leasehold house. A house held on lease. [Indian Trusts Act (2 of 1882), S. 16, ill. (b)].

Leasehold mortgage. A mortgage which is secured by the leasehold interest of the lessee.

Leasehold ownership. Ownership of property under a lease. The period of ownership depends on the term of the lease.

Leases only of the buildings with the land if any appurtenant thereto. The expression 'leases only other buildings with the land if any, appurtenant thereto' occurring in Section 3(1)(ii) of the Act, would mean the 'leases of the building which has landed areas as adjunct or appendage or incident to the building'. *K. Bhagirath G. Shenoy* v. *K.P. Ballakuraya*, (1999) 4 SCC 135, para 7. [Kerala Land Reforms Act, 1963 (1 of 1964), S. 3(i)(ii)]

Least Restrictive Alternative. "Least restrictive alternative" or "least restrictive environment" or "less restrictive option" means offering an option for treatment or a setting for treatment which—

(i) meets the person's treatment needs; and

(ii) imposes the least restriction on the person's rights [The Mental Healthcare Act, 2017 (10 of 2017), S. 2(1)(j)]

Leave. For the purposes of this chapter LEAVE shall not include weekly days of rest or holidays or festivals or other similar occasions, whether occurring during or at either end of the period of leave. [Mines Act (35 of 1952), S. 50, Chap. VII]

'LEAVE' includes earned leave, half pay leave, commuted leave, leave not due, extraordinary leave, study leave, special disability leave, maternity leave or any other authorised leave of absence. [All India Services (leave) Rules, 1955, R. 2(k)]

As a noun, permission. *As a verb*, according to the context or the intent with which it is employed, the word may mean to abscond; to deliver; to depart; to get off; to give; to go away from; to quit; to remove from; to resign; to submit; to suffer to remain; to withdraw from. (*Ame Cyc.*)

Plain grammatical meaning of the word 'leave' in relation to an employee is 'voluntarily leaving of the service by him' and would not include a case where he is discharged or dismissed or his services are terminated by his employee. *Superintendence Co. of India (P) Ltd.*, v. *Krishnan Murgai*, AIR 1980 SC 1717, 1721.

Permission to do something; an authorised absence from duty or employment. [CrPC 1973 (2 of 1974), S. 198(1)(b)]; to quit or depart from.

Leave of absence. Permission to be absent from duty [CrPC 1973 (2 of 1974), S. 198(1)(b) and Constitution of India, Art. 125(2)]; [Companies Act (1 of 1956), S. 283(1)(g) now replaced by Companies Act, 2013].

In India, if a member of either House of parliament remains absent from all sittings of the House for a period of sixty days without permission of the House, his seat may be declared vacant, the period of sixty days is a single unbroken period, a member who has not made and subscribed the oath or affirmation is also entitled to ask for leave of absence from the sittings of the House.

Leave of Court. Permission granted by the Court to do something which, without such permission, would not be allowable. (*Bouvier*)

Permission from the Court. [CrPC 1973 (2 of 1974), S. 198(2), *Prov.*].

Leave of the House. The formal approval given by the House of a Legislature to a member to move a motion or withdraw the same. The member can seek the leave of the House only after he has been permitted to do so by the Speaker; he then rises in his place and asks for leave. After the leave is granted, the member cannot withdraw his motion without the permission of the House.

Leave salary. Means the monthly amount admissible to a member of the services who has been granted leave under these rules. [All India Services (Leave) Rules, 1955, R. 2(e)]

Leave with allowances. Means leave other than extraordinary leave. [All India Services (Death-Cum-retirement Benefits) Rules, 1958, R. 2(e)]

Lecture. "LECTURE" includes address, speech and sermon. [Copyright Act (14 of 1957), S. 2(n)]

Ledger. A book of accounts in which a trader enters the names of all persons with whom he has dealings, and also enters the nature of the dealings.

A book containing accounts to which debits and credits resulting from business transactions are posted from books of original entry. [Bankers' Books Evidence Act (18 of 1891), S. 2(3)].

Legacy. Something received by will [TP Act (4 of 1882), S. 6(a)]; bequest.

Legal. Of or relating to law; founded upon law; conforming to or permitted by law; recognised by law. [CPC (5 of 1908), S. 2 (11); Constitution of India, Art. 39 A and Art. 131].

Legal adviser. One who advises regarding the matters relating to law and legal proceedings. [Indian Evidence Act (1 of 1872), S. 129].

Legal aid. Free legal services provided to those who can not afford it.

Legal Aid Centre. Means a place designated by the Committee under these rules for the purpose of extending legal assistance to the needy persons through the Advocates or retired Judge. [Maharashtra State Legal Aid Centre Rules, 1989, R. 2(v)]

Legal and lawful. Legal and lawful normally, convey same sense and are usually interchangeable. What is legal is lawful. But what is lawful may be so without being formally legal. "The principal distinction between the terms 'lawful' and 'legal' is that former contemplates the substance of law, the latter the form of law. "Lawful possession" means a legal possession which is also rightful or at least excusable. Thus that which is not *stricto legalo* may yet be lawful. It should not be forbidden by law. Legal is associated with provisions in the Act, rules *etc.* whereas lawful visualises all that is not illegal against law or even permissible. Lawful is wider in connotation than legal. *Krishna Kishore Firm* v. *Government of A.P.*, AIR 1990 SC 2292.

Legal looks mere to the letter and lawful to the spirit of the law. Legal is more appropriate for conformity to positive rules of law, lawful for accord with ethical principles. [Advocates Act (25 of 1961), S. 30(ii)]

Legal assets. "Money arising from the sale of the property of a deceased person are called 'legal assets' in the hands of an executor or administrator, out of which the creditors of the estate are paid.

Legal character. The legal word 'character' in S. 41 means status, it is something more than a mere right. *Radha Bai* v. *Kadar Ali,* AIR 1957 MB 159, 160. [Indian Evidence Act (1 of 1872), S. 41]

A character or position as recognised by law. [Specific Relief Act (47 of 1963), S. 34]; [Air Force Act (45 of 1950), S. 4(xi)].

'Legal character' and **'civil nature'.** The words 'legal character' and 'civil nature' mean various legal rights, immunities, privileges and power of a person. Declaration of date of birth is not merely a declaration of an event but a declaration of a legal status. *State of Karnataka* v. *T. Srinivas,* AIR 1988 Kant 67, 75. [CPC (5 of 1908), S. 9]

Legal cruelty. Any conduct of the husband which causes disgrace to the wife or subjects her to a course of annoyance and indignity amounts to legal cruelty. *Kamala Devi* v. *Amarnath,* AIR 1961 J&K 33, 34. [Indian Divorce Act (4 of 1869), S. 10]

Legal curator. Legal guardian. [TP Act (4 of 1882), S. 103].

Legal custody. A custody authorised by law. [Indian Evidence Act (1 of 1872), S. 78(6)].

Legal death of living person means brain death *i.e.* when a person's body does not respond to an external stimuli; legal death of a corporation *i.e.* its civil death means the state of a corporation which has formally dissolved or become bankrupt, leaving an estate to be administered for the benefit of the shareholders and creditors.

Legal defect. Defect of a legal nature. [IPC (45 of 1860), S. 21, *Expln* (2)].

Legal disability. Disability which can be enforced by law [Workmen's Compensation Act (9 of 1923), S. 8(1)].

Legal discretion. A discretion to be exercised with the limits which the law fixes; a discretion to be exercised according to the rules of law.

Legal entity and **legal person.** A legal entity means only a thing recognised by the law real in itself and distinct from its qualities and attributes. While every legal person is necessarily a legal entity, the converse is not true.

Legal entity identifier. "Legal entity identifier" means a unique identity code assigned to a person by an issuer for the purpose of identifying that person in such derivatives or financial transactions, as may be specified by the Reserve Bank from time to time. [Payment and Settlement Systems Act (51 of 2007), S. 2 (db) as inserted by Amending Act, (18 of 2015)].

Legal ethics. That branch of moral science which treats of the duties which a member of the legal profession owes to the public, to the Court, to his professional brethren and to his client.

Legal evidence. Legal evidence is admissible evidence; if not legal, it is not admissible.

LEGAL EVIDENCE is not confined to the human voice or oral testimony but includes every tangible object capable of making a truthful statement; such evidence being roughly classified as "documentary evidence." In oral evidence the witness is the man who speaks; in documentary evidence the witness is the thing that speaks.

Legal fact. A fact which triggers a particular legal consequence.

Legal fees. Lawful charges or charges according to law. [Indian Evidence Act (1 of 1872), S. 76].

Legal fiction. A legal fiction presupposes the correctness of the state of facts on which it is based and all the consequences which flow from that state of facts have got to be worked out to their logical extent. If the purpose of legal fiction is for a specified purpose, one cannot travel beyond the scope of that purpose. *Bengal Immunity Co.* v. *State of Bihar*, AIR 1955 SC 661, 709.

Legal formalism. The theory which states that law is a set of rules and principles independent of other political and social institutions.

Legal heir. One who, under the laws of intestacy, is entitled to receive an intestate descendant's property, specially real property.

'Legal heirs' and **'legal representatives'.** Legal heirs may be legal representatives but not always legal heirs are persons entitled to inherit the surviving estate of the deceased. Legal representatives as defined in S. 2(11) of CPC (5 of 1908) are persons who in law represent the estate of deceased person, and includes any person who intermeddles with the estate of the deceased and where a party sues or is sued in a legal representative character the person on whom the estate devolves on the death of the party so suing or sued. *Mercy* v. *Aisha Damal,* 1987 (2) KLT 166 of 167.

Legal heirs or representatives. The 'legal heirs or representatives' of the erstwhile employee comes within the meaning of expression 'officer or employee of a company' under Section 630 of the Act but it does not include other family members of such employee, living with him. *J.K. (Bombay) Ltd.* v. *Bharti Matha Mishra*, AIR 2001 SC 649 : (2001) 2 SCC 700, 706, para 8. [Companies Act (1 of 1956), S. 630 now replaced by Companies Act, 2013]

Legal impossibility. An impossibility which occurs due to the fact that, what the defendant intended to do, is not prohibited by law.

Legal incidents. The incidents that follow or go together as a matter of law. [TP Act (4 of 1882), S. 8].

Legal insanity. Any mental disorder severe enough to prevent one from having legal capacity and also excuses one from criminal or civil responsibility.

It is only legal insanity which furnishes a ground for exception and there can be no legal insanity unless the cognitive faculties of the accused are, as a result of unsoundness completely impaired, incapable of knowing the nature of the act or not being able to distinguish right from wrong. [*Lala Sk.* v. *State,* MLJ : Digest (1984), p. 338 : (1983) 87 Cal WN 556]. [IPC (45 of 1860), S. 84]

Legal investments. Approved classes of investments to which savings banks, trust funds and insurance reserves are limited by law, as being within the prudent and safe range.

Legal lease. A contract or grant that creates an estate in land for a term of years absolute.

Legal liability. Any liability imposed on a person by a Court of law.

"Legal Malice" or "malice in law" means something done without lawful excuse'. In other words, 'it is an act done wrongfully and willfully without reasonable or probable cause, and not necessarily an act done from ill feeling and spite'. It is a deliberate act in disregard of the rights of other. [Words and Phrases Legally Defines, 3rd Edn., 1989 as cited in HMT Ltd. v. Mudappa, JT (2007) (3) SC 112 : AIR 2007 SC 1106, para 18. See also *Vimla Tiwari* v. *State of U.P.*, AIR 2012 All 142, para 41.

Malice in its legal sense means malice such as may be assumed from the doing of a wrongful act intentionally but without just cause of excuse, or for want of reasonable or probable cause. [*S.R. Venkataraman* v. *Union of India*, (1979) 2 SCC 491, para 5 : 1979 SCC (L&S) 216 : AIR 1979 SC 49 as cited in *J. Jayalalithaa* v. *State of Karnataka*, (2014) 2 SCC 401, para 25].

'Legal malice' or 'malice in law' means 'something done without lawful excuse'. In other words, it is an act done wrongfully and willfully without reasonable or probable cause, and not necessarily an act done from ill feeling and spite. It is a deliberate act in disregard of the rights of others'. [Words and Phrases Legally Defined, 3rd Edn., London Butterworths, 1989 as cited in *State of A.P.* v. *Govardhanlal Pitti*, (2003) 4 SCC 739, para 12 as cited in *G. Jayalal* v. *Union of India*, (2013) 7 SCC 150, para 17].

"Legal malice" or "malice in law" means something done without lawful excuse. It is a deliberate act in disregard to the rights of others. It is an act which is taken with an oblique or indirect object. It is an act done wrongfully and willfully reasonable or probable cause, and not necessarily an act done from ill feeling and spite. [*Ravi Yashwant Bhoir* v. *District Collector, Raigad*, (2012) 4 SCC 407, para 47].

Legal maxims. 'Legal maxims' means fundamentals or the first principles of law. They are manifestly founded in reason, public convenience and necessity and they are the basis of law and may be either directly applied, or qualified or limited, according to the exigencies of the particular case and novelty of the circumstances which present themselves. *Jamaluddin Ahmad* v. *Abu Saleh Najmuddin*, (2003) 4 SCC 257, para 21.

Legal misconduct. Misconduct not amounting to moral turpitude is called legal misconduct. Legal misconduct means misconduct in the judicial sense arising from some honest, though erroneous, breach and neglect of duty and responsibility on the part of the arbitrator causing miscarriage of justice. *Indian Minerals Co.* v. *N.I.L.M. Association,* AIR 1958 All 692, 697. [Arbitration Act (10 of 1940) (*repealed*), S. 30 (a)]

Legal mortgage. A mortgage which is created by operation of law; a first mortgage.

Legal notice. A "legal notice", means, a notice provided by law, as distinguished from one prescribed by contract. It is notice given as and in the manner prescribed by law.

LEGAL NOTICE means something more than bare knowledge of the given facts. It is knowledge brought home to a party in a prescribed form. When its terms are so unambiguous that the meaning cannot without negligence or intention be misunderstood the notice is sufficient. Defects in form, by which a party is not misled to his injury, do not render a notice invalid; but a notice giving wrong information or being silent as to material information which the statute requires, cannot be regarded as legal notice.

Legal owner. One recognized by law as the owner of something; especially, one who holds legal title to property for the benefit of another.

Legal person. A legal person is any subject matter other than a human being to which the law attributes personality. *Som Prakash Rekhi* v. *UOI,* AIR 1981 SC 212.

Salmond on Jurisprudence-10th Edition, Chap 15, S. 116 A legal person is any subject matter other than a human being to which the law attributes-personality. Legal persons, being the arbitrary creations of the law, may be of as many kinds as the law pleases. There are two such classes, namely, corporations and trade unions. *Mohd Ishaq* v. *I.T. Commissioner*, AIR 1951 All 512, 513, 514. [Income-tax Act (11 of 1922), S. 16(3)(b)]

Legal personality is the sum total of a person's legal rights and duties.

Legal possession. 'Legal possession' may mean that possession which is recognised and protected as such by law. It is ordinarily associated with *de facto* possession. It may exist without *de facto* possession. [*Gangadhar B.* v. *B.G. Rajanalingam,* (1996) 1 CTC 271 : AIR 1995 SC 780]

Legal possession and **De facto possession.** The possession which is recognised and protected as such by law. Legal possession is ordinarily associated with *de facto* possession; but legal possession may exist without *de facto* possession and *de facto* possession is not always regarded as possession in law. A person who, although having no *de facto* possession, is deemed to have possession in law is sometimes said to have constructive possession. *B. Gangadhar* v. *B.G. Rajalingam,* AIR 1996 SC 780.

Legal practice. Representing the employer in a Court or tribunal would not amount to 'legal practice' at the bar. *Sunil Kumar Goyal* v. *Rajasthan Public Service Commission*, (2003) 6 SCC 171, para 9.

Legal practitioner. "LEGAL PRACTITIONER" means an advocate, vakil or attorney of any High Court, a pleader, mukhtar or revenue agent. [Legal Practitioners Act (18 of 1879), S. 3]

"LEGAL PRACTITIONER" means any advocate or agent of the Supreme Court or any advocate, vakil or attorney of any High Court or any pleader authorized under any law for the time being in force to practise in any Court of law. [Notaries Act (53 of 1952), S. 2(c)]

'LEGAL PRACTITIONER' means an advocate, vakil or attorney of any High Court, and includes a pleader in practice. [Estate Duty Act (34 of 1953), S. 83 *Expln.* (b)]

"LEGAL PRACTITIONER" means an advocate or *vakil* of any High Court, a pleader *mukhtar* or revenue agent. [Advocates Act (25 of 1961), S. 2(i)]

One who is engaged in the exercise or employment of legal profession; a person who practises law, such as an advocate, *vakil* or attorney of any High Court, a pleader, *mukhtiyar* or revenue agent. [Notaries Act (53 of 1952), S. 2(c); Legal Practitioners' Act (18 of 1879), S. 3 and Constitution of India, Art. 22(1)].

"LEGAL PRACTITIONER" the expression 'legal practitioner' is a well defined and explained term. It, by any stretch of imagination, cannot include a serving Judge who might have been appointed as a presenting officer in the departmental proceedings. *Dinesh Chandra Pandey* v. *High Court of Madhya Pradesh*, AIR 2010 SC 3055.

Legal presumption. A legal assumption made by the Court to ascertain facts which are established and no contradictory evidence is produced.

Legal procedure. The course of procedure in a legal action or in a suit in litigation.

Legal proceeding. "LEGAL PROCEEDING" means,—

(i) any proceedings or inquiry in which evidence is or may be given.

(ii) an arbitration; and

(iii) any investigation or inquiry under the CrPC, 1973 (2 of 1974), or under any other law for the time being in force for the collection of evidence, conducted by a police officer or by any other person (not being a magistrate) authorised in this behalf by a magistrate or by any law for the time being in force. [Banker's Books Evidence Act (18 of 1891), S. 2(4)]

"Any proceedings in court of justice...By which property of debtor is seized and diverted from his general creditors...This turn includes all proceedings authorised or sanctioned by law, and brought or instituted in a court of justice or legal tribunal, for the acquiring of a right or the enforcement of a remedy." [Black's Law Dictionary (4th Edn.) as cited in *Maharashtra Tubes Limited* v. *State Industrial & Investment Corpn.*, (1993) 2 SCC 144]. See also

General Officer Commanding, Rashtriya Rifles v. *C.B.I.*, (2012) 6 SCC 228, para 31).

The phrase "legal proceedings" connotes a term which means the proceedings in a court of justice to get a remedy which the law permits to the person aggrieved. It includes any formal steps or measures employed therein. It is not synonymous with the term 'judicial proceedings'. Every judicial proceeding is a legal proceeding but not vice versa, for the reason that there may be a 'legal proceeding" which may not be judicial at all. [*General Officer Commanding, Rashtriya Rifles* v. *Central Bureau of Investigation*, (2012) 6 SCC 228, para 29].

"Legal proceedings" means proceedings regulated or prescribed by law in which a judicial decision may be given; it means proceedings in a court of justice by which a party pursues a remedy which a law provides, but does not include administrative and departmental proceedings. [*General Officer Commanding, Rashtriya Rifles* v. *Central Bureau of Investigation*, (2012) 6 SCC 228, para 32].

'LEGAL PROCEEDING' means any proceeding under any law before any Court, tribunal, officer, authority, arbitrator, started on a plaint, petition of appeal, application, reference, or otherwise. [Rajasthan Relief Undertakings (Special Provision) Act (9 of 1961), S. 4 (1)(b) *Expln.*]

Legal proceeding means a proceeding regulated or prescribed by law in which a judicial decision may or must be given.

Legal proceeding mean any proceedings authorised by law for redressal of a legal grievance or for violation of a legal right.

Legal process. The words "legal process" mean all the proceedings in an action or proceeding.

Process, whether by a writ or by warrant, is legal whenever it is not defective in the frame of it and is issued in the ordinary course of justice from a Court or Magistrate having jurisdiction of the subject-matter, though there have been error or irregularity in the proceedings previous to the issuance of the process.

The legal procedure [Indian Contract Act (9 of 1872), S. 188, ill. (a)]; a process (summons *etc.*) issued by a Court of law (or other competent authority).

Legal professional adviser. A person whose profession is to give legal advice [Indian Evidence Act (1 of 1872), S. 129].

Legal proof. Given evidence on the record which is admissible and excluding from consideration any that may have been wrongly admitted.

Legal question. A question, which is decided by the Judge, related to the application or interpretation of law.

Legal realism. The theory which states that law is based, not on formal rules or principles, but instead on judicial decisions that should derive from social interests and public policy.

Legal remedy. A remedy at law; a suit or proceeding in a Court of justice.

Legal remuneration. The words, "legal remuneration" are not restricted to remuneration which a public servant can lawfully demand, but includes all remuneration which he is permitted by the Government, which he serves, to accept. [IPC (45 of 1860), S. 161, *Expln. as stood prior to it being omitted by Act, 49 of 1988*]

Legal representative. "LEGAL REPRESENTATIVE" means a person who in law represents the estate of a deceased person, and includes any person who intermeddles with the estate of the deceased and, where a party sues or is sued, in a representative character, the person on whom the estate devolves on the death of the party so suing or sued [CPC (5 of 1908), S. 2(11)].

The term "legal representative" ordinarily means the executor or administrator, though sometimes, when required by the context and surrounding circumstances, it is held to mean *next-of-kin* and, under rare and peculiar facts, may mean heirs, who themselves, in a broad sense, are often regarded as the legal representatives of the decedent.

Legal representative is one who suffers on account of the death of a person due to a motor vehicles accident and need not necessarily be a wife, husband, parent and child. *O.S.R.T. Corporation Ahmedabad* v. *Ramnbhai*, AIR 1987 SC 1690, 1699.

The definition contained in Section 2(11) of CPC (5 of 1908) is inclusive in character and its scope is wide, it is not confined to legal heirs only instead it stipulates a person who may or may not be heir, competent to inherit the property of the deceased but he should represent the estate of the deceased person. It includes heirs as well as persons who represent the estate even without title either as executors or administrators in possession of the estate of the deceased. All such persons would be covered by the expression "legal representative". If there are many heirs, those in possession *bona fide*, without there being any fraud or collusion, are also entitled to represent the estate of the deceased. *Custodian of Branches of BANCO National Ultramarino* v. *Nalini Bai Naique*, AIR 1989 SC 1589, 1591.

One who, lawfully represents another in any matter whatsoever. [CPC (5 of 1908), S. 2(11)].

For the purposes of the section, "LEGAL REPRESENTATIVE" means a person who in law represents the estate of a deceased person, and includes any person who intermeddles with the estate of the deceased and where a party sues or its sued in a representative character, the person on whom the estate devolves on the death of the party so suing or sued. [Securities Contracts (Regulation) Act (42 of 1956), S. 23-JC, *Explanation*].

For the purposes of this section "LEGAL REPRESENTATIVE" means a person who in law represents the estate o a deceased person, and includes any person who intermeddles with the estate of the deceased and where a party sues or is sued in a representative character, the person on whom the estate devolves on the death of the party so suing or sued. [Depositories Act (22 of 1996), S. 19-IC, *Explanation*].

Legal right. A capacity residing in one man of controlling with the assistance of the state, the action of others; a right that may be enforced in a civil action.

Legal service. Includes the rendering of any service in the conduct of any case or other legal proceedings before any Court or other authority or tribunal and the giving of advice on any legal matter. [Legal Services Authorities Act (39 of 1987), S. 2(c)]

Legal tender. The act of tendering (in the performance of a contract or satisfaction of a claim) such payment or service and at such time and place as the law prescribes or permits [Constitution of India, VIIth Sch., list I, item 36]; currency prescribed by law as that in which payment may be made [Legal Tender (Inscribed Notes) Act (28 of 1964), S. 2 and Reserve Bank of India Act (2 of 1934), S. 2(d)].

Legal tender note. Currency note; a genuine and current note issued by the Government or other competent authority.

Legal theory (or theory of law or theory of legal science). Phrases sometimes used as generally equivalent to jurisprudence (q.v.) in its narrower sense, or to legal philosophy (q.v.) or philosophy of law, but sometimes distinguished from legal philosophy as being more concerned with structure, classification, and organization of bodies of law in various societies than with the more philosophic problems of law. (*Walker*)

Legal title. A title which evidences apparent ownership but not necessarily signifies full and complete title or a beneficial interest.

Legal year. The period made up, in any year, of the four Court sittings.(*England*)

Legalism. The ethical attitude that holds moral conduct to be a matter of rule following, and moral relationships to consist of duties and rights determined by rules."

Legality. Lawfulness. The state or character of being legal; in conformity with law. The quality of being legal. [CrPC 1973 (2 of 1974), S. 397(1)].

"Legality" is lawfulness. It refers to strict adherence to law, prescription, or doctrine; the equality of being legal. [*Hindustan Petroleum Corporation Limited* v. *Dilbahar Singh*, (2014) 9 SCC 78, para 29.1].

Legalize. To make legal or lawful. [Indian Contract Act (9 of 1872), S. 30].

Legally. In a legal manner [TP Act (4 of 1882), S. 44]; by law.

Legally and justly due. The expression "legally and justly due", clearly indicates that the first and initial duty of the claims officer is to find out whether any principal amount is at all due to the creditor which he is entitled to recover either in law or justly. *I. & G.I. Trust, London* v. *P. Chandra*, AIR 1967 SC 1251, 1256.

Legally assisted person. A person who receives free legal advice, assistance or representation provided by the State.

Legally authorised. The phrase 'legally authorised' denotes that the tribunal or person has been authorised by a statute or statutory rules. [Advocates Act (25 of 1961), S. 30(ii)]

Legally bound to do. "A person is said to be "legally bound to do" whatever it is illegal in him to omit". [IPC (45 of 1860), section 43] [Now (w. e. f. 1-7-2024) repealed & replaced by Bharatiya Nyaya Sanhita, 2023 (45 of 2023), S. 2(15), same definition in new Sanhita]

Legally competent. Competent according to law. [Indian Evidence Act (1 of 1872), S. 157].

Legally married. United in wedlock lawfully or according to law. [Indian Evidence Act (1 of 1872), S. 32, ill. (f)].

Legally qualified. Enabled by law; having the qualifications prescribed by law. [CPC (5 of 1908), Sch I, App E, Form 29, No. 3].

Legally recoverable. The words "legally recoverable" have no reference to the ability of the debtor to pay the demand in full, and a sum is legally recoverable though in the result the creditor, must be satisfied with a dividend.

Obtainable by judgment or trial. [CPC (5 of 1908), O. VIII, R. 6(1)].

Legatarius. (*Lat.*) One to whom property is bequeathed; a legatee or legatary, a legate, messenger, or envoy.

Legatee. The person to whom a legacy is given. (*Burrill*)

A person designated to receive any property under a will. [Wealth-tax Act (27 of 1957), S. 19(6)].

"Legatee" means a person to whom there has been or is bequeathed an estate.

Legatee and his descendants. The words 'legatee and his heirs' or 'legatee and the heirs of his body' or 'legatee and the children born of his loins' *etc.* only indicate the intention of the testator to confer an absolute estate on the legatee. *T. Kunhikkalavan* v. *E. Kochuraman,* AIR 1952 Mad 685, 686. [Indian Succession Act (39 of 1925), S.97]

Legatee, Residuary. A legatee inheriting a testator's residuary estate. [Indian Succession Act (39 of 1925), S. 232].

Legatee, Universal. A legatee inheriting a legacy under civil law by which a testator gives to one or more persons all his estate subject to the duty of paying particular legacies and debts and carrying out fidel commissary bequests. [Indian Succession Act (39 of 1925), S. 232].

Legation. A diplomatic mission in a foreign country headed by a minister. [Diplomatic and Consular Officers (Oaths and Fees) Act (41 of 1948), S. 2(b)].

Legatos violare contra jus gentium est. (*Maxim*) It is contrary to the law of nations to injure ambassadors. (*Black*)

Legatum morte testatoris tantum confirmatur, sicut donatio inter vivos traditione sola. A legacy is confirmed by the death of a testator, in the same manner as a gift from a living person is by delivery alone.

Legatum nominis. (*Lat.*) Legacy of a debt.

Legatum partitionis. A legacy where the legatee divide the inheritance with the heir.

Legatum poenae nomine. A legacy by way of penalty, to constrain their heir to do or not to do something.

Leges figendi et refigendi consuetudo periculo sissima est. The practice of fixing and refixing (making and remaking) the laws is a most dangerous one.

Leges naturae perfectissimae et immutabiles; humani vero juris conditio semper in infinitum decurrit, et nihil est in eo quod perpetuo stare possit. (7 *Rep.* 25): The laws of nature are most firm and immutable : human law has always a tendency to multiply to infinity; there is nothing therein that will continue perpetually. (*Principia legis.*; *Latin for Lawyers*)

Leges posteriores priores contrarias abrogant. (*Maxim*) (*Lat.*) Later laws repeal earlier laws inconsistent therewith. (*Broom*)

Leges suum vigilantibus non dormientibus subveniunt. Laws aid the vigilant, not the negligent.

Legible. Capable of being read or deciphered. [Indian Carriage of Goods by Sea Act (26 of 1925), Sch I, Article III, R. 3(a)]; [Registration Act (16 of 1908), S. 43(1)].

Legislate. To make or enact laws. (*Abbott*)

Legislation. The act of making, giving or enacting laws. (*Wharton*)

The enactments of a legislator or a legislative body. [Constitution of India, Art. 35].

Legislative. That makes or enacts laws; law making; making, giving, or enacting laws; relating or pertaining to the passing of laws; of, or pertaining to legislation. (*Worcester*)

"LEGISLATIVE", as the word is used in speaking of the legislative department of the government, means the organ or organs of the government which make the law.

Having the power or performing the function of legislating; of or relating to a legislature. [Indian Evidence Act (1 of 1872), S. 74(1)(iii)]; [Constitution of India, Art. 55(2) and Art. 168(2)].

Legislative act. An act which prescribes what the law shall be in future cases arising under it; an act of the legislative department of the government, by which the law, to be applied in future cases under particular states of fact, is established in the form of a statute, ordinance, or other written form. (*Ame Cyc.*)

Legislative and Judicial functions. The judicial functions consists in the Court deciding the rights of parties who appear before it, but the rights are to be determined and decided according to law. The legislative function is for the legislature to lay down the law which will govern parties and transactions and direct the Court to give effect to that law. *Gulabrao* v. *Pandurang,* AIR 1957 Bom 266, 268. [Constitution of India, Art. 245].

Adjudication of the rights of the parties according to law enacted by the legislature is a judicial function. In the performance of this function, the Court interprets and gives effect to the intent and mandate of the legislature as embodied in the statute. On the other hand, it is for the legislature to lay down the law, prescribing norms of conduct which will govern parties and transactions and to require the Court to give effect to that law. (*I.N. Saksena* v. *State of Madhya Pradesh*, AIR 1976 SC 2250).

Legislative Assembly. The lower house of the State Legislature where the legislature is bicameral (Bihar, Maharashtra, Karnataka; UP) and where the State Legislature is unicameral it is called legislative assembly. [Constitution of India, Art. 168(2)]

Law-making body generally composed of elected representatives.

House of State Legislature; where the legislature is bicameral, it is applied to the Lower House; composed of members chosen by direct elections; seats to be reserved for Scheduled Castes and Scheduled Tribes in proportion to total number of seats in Assembly and their total population in the State; Governor may nominate members of Anglo-Indian community if it is not adequately represented in the Assembly; total membership not more than 500 and not less than Sixty; normal duration five years but may be dissolved earlier by the Governor. (*Constitutional and Parliamentary Term*)

Legislative competence. The legal capacity, power or jurisdiction of a legislative body to make law.

Legislative Council. The upper house of the State Legislature where the house is bicameral. [Constitution of India, Art. 168 (2)].

Legislative immunity. An immunity of a legislator from civil liability which arises from the performance of legislative duties.

Legislative intention. "By legislative intent", as that term is used with relation to the interpretation of statutes, is meant the intent as gathered from the Act itself, and sometimes viewed in the light of the knowledge of the Court, in common with the public at large, of well known conditions which may seem to have led up to the Act under construction. But such consideration of extraneous facts is not resorted to defeat the Act, but to aid in its interpretation.

Legislative law. The body of law which is derived from statutes instead of Constitution or judicial decisions.

Legislative power. The law making power; the power to make laws; that power in a state which gives and makes laws for the people; a power to enact laws or to declare what the law shall be; the power to enact new rules for the regulation of future conduct, rights, and controversies.

"Legislative power" and "judicial power". Legislature makes new law which becomes binding on all persons over whom the Legislature exercises legislative power : the Judicature applies already existing law in the resolution of disputes between particular parties; and judges may not deviate from this duty. *Indira Nehru Gandhi* v. *Raj Narain,* AIR 1975 SC 2299.

Legislative relations means a relation between Union of India and the States in the field of law making which can be summed up like this. The Parliament has exclusive power to make laws on the subjects mentioned in the Union List; the State Legislature can make laws on the subjects of the State list.

Both Parliament and the State Legislature has power to make laws on the subjects of concurrent list, but in case of conflicts in their laws, the law made by Parliament prevails; Parliament can make laws on the subjects of State lists during the proclamation of emergency, in national interest if a resolution is passed to that effect by the Council of States, and on request by two or more State Legislatures Residuary subjects lie with the Parliament.

Legislator. One who makes laws within a given jurisdiction; a member of a legislative body.

Legislature. A body of persons invested with power of making the laws of a country or state. [Estate Duty Act (34 of 1953), S. 5(2) and Constitution of India, Art. 3, *Prov.*].

The term 'Legislature' means the House or the Houses of Legislature, as the case may be and it does not include the Governor. *Union of India* v. *V. Basvaih*, AIR 1979 SC 1415, 1422. [Constitution of India, Art. 252, 168]

Legislature party. In relation to a member of a House belonging to any political party in accordance with the provisions of paragraph 2 or paragraph 3 or, as the case may be, paragraph 4, means the group consisting of all the members of that House for the time being belonging to that political party in accordance with the said provisions. [Constitution of India, Tenth Schedule. 1(b)]

Legitimacy. The quality of being a legitimate child. [Indian Evidence Act (1 of 1872), S. 112].

LEGITIMACY, as the word imports, requires that the child be born in a manner approved by law.

Legitimacy of child. A child born in wedlock.

Legitimate. Lawfully begotten; born in wedlock. [CrPC 1973 (2 of 1974), S. 125(1)(b)]; in accordance with law or propriety [Indian Evidence Act (1 of 1872), S. 90, *Expln*].

Legitimate child. A legitimate child is one born in lawful wedlock, or born before the marriage of its parents, who afterwards marry and which receives the recognition of its father; and one of such children is just as legitimate before the law as the other.

Legitimate expectation. The "expectation" which shall be protected must be "legitimate" though it may not amount to a right in the conventional sense. But the hope or desire of a person to obtain a favourable order, notwithstanding that he had not complied with the necessary requirements may not amount to a legitimate expectation. *Govt. of A.P.* v. *Heh The Nizam VIII of Hyderabad,* AIR 1993 AP 76, 89. [Constitution of India, Art. 14].

"A person may have a legitimate expectation of being treated in a certain way of an administrative authority even though he has no legal right in private law to receive such treatment. The expectation may arise either from a representation or promise made by the authority, including an implied representation, or from consistent past practice." [Halsbury's Laws of England, Fourth Edn., Vol-1(1)151]

Legitimate purpose. For the purpose of illustration, the term "legitimate purpose" shall include sharing of unpublished price sensitive information in the ordinary course of business by an insider with partners, collaborators, lenders, customers, suppliers, merchant bankers, legal advisors, auditors, insolvency professionals or other advisors or consultants, provided that such sharing has not been carried out to evade or circumvent the prohibition of these regulation. [Securities and Exchange Board of India (Prohibition of Insider Trading) Regulations, 2015, Regn. 3(2A), *Explanation*].

Legitimate origin. An origin which is in accordance with law. [Indian Evidence Act (1 of 1872), S. 90, *Expln*].

Legitimate son. Lawful son; a son conceived or born of parents legally married to each other. [Workmen's Compensation Act (8 of 1923), S. 2(1)(d)(i)].

Legitime imperanti parere necesse est. (*Lat.*) It is necessary to obey one legitimately commanding. (*Latin for Lawyers*)

Legumes whole and legumes split. Legume is edible pod of leguminous, plant; vegetable used for food. A split legume is obtained by a manufacturing process of whole grain of legumes. '*saboot*' '*dal*' *i.e.* the whole grain split into two folds in its processed form. It was held that '*dal*', is an agricultural produce also, and legume, the whole grain, including its split form '*dal*', in the legal provisions in question. *Krishi Utpadan Mandi Samiti* v. *Ganga Dal Mill*, AIR 1984 SC 1870.

Lend. To grant temporary possession of (a thing) on condition of the return of the same or its equivalent; to let out (money *etc.*) at interest. [Indian Evidence Act (1 of 1872), S. 8, ill. (g)].

Lend and loan. The word 'lend' means to deliver to another a thing for use on condition that the thing lent shall be returned with or without compensation for the use made of it, by the person to whom it was lent.

A loan contracted creates a debt. A debt can also be created without contracting a loan. The relationship between of banker and a customer *qua* moneys deposited in the Bank is that of debtor and creditor. *Ram Ratan* v. *Director of Enforcement*, AIR 1966 SC 495, 496. [Foreign Exchange Regulation Act (7 of 1947) (*Repealed*), S. 4(1)]

Lender. In this scheme, unless the context otherwise requires,—

"LENDER" means a person who deposits the securities registered in his name or in the name of any other person duly authorised on his behalf with an approved intermediary for the purpose of lending under the scheme. [Securities Lending Scheme, 1997, S. 3(e)]

One from whom a loan is taken.

Lender of money. A person who lends money. [Indian Partnership Act (9 of 1932), S. 6, *Expln* 2(a)]. For the purpose of this sub-regulation, "lenders" shall mean all scheduled commercial banks (excluding Regional Rural Banks) and All India Financial Institutions. [Securities and Exchange Board of India (Issue of Capital and Disclosure Requirements) Regulations, 2018, Regn. 158(6), *Explanation*].

Lending Public Financial Institution. LENDING PUBLIC FINANCIAL INSTITUTION means—

(a) a public financial institution specified in or under Section 4A of the Companies Act (1 of 1956);

(b) a State Financial, Industrial or Investment Corporation;

(c) a scheduled commercial bank;

(d) the General Insurance Corporation of India;

(e) any other institution which the RBI may, by notification, specify in this behalf. [Non-Banking Financial Companies Acceptance of Public Deposits (Reserve Bank) Directions, 1998, para 2(1)(vii)]

Lenity. The quality or condition of being lenient; mercy or clemency.

Leonina societas. (*Lat.*) A leonine partnership—*i.e.*, a partnership in which one of the partners bears all the loss, while another receives all the profit.

Leper asylum. The State Government may, by notification in the official Gazette, appoint any place to be a leper asylum if it is satisfied that adequate arrangements have been made or will be made for the accommodation and medical treatment of lepers therein, and may, by a like notification, specify the local areas from which lepers may be sent to such asylum. [Lepers Act, 1898 (3 of 1898), S. 3]

Leper Asylum Board. The State Government shall constitute for every leper asylum appointed under Section 3 Board consisting of not less than three member, one of whom at least shall be a Medical officer of the Government. [Lepers Act, 1898 (3 of 1898), S. 5]

Leprosy-cured person. Means any person who has been cured of leprosy but is suffering from—

(i) loss of sensation in hands or feet as well as loss of sensation and paresis in the eye and eye-lid but with no manifest deformity;

(ii) manifest deformity and paresis but having sufficient mobility in their hands and feet to enable them to engage in normal economic activity;

(iii) extreme physical deformity as well as advanced age which prevents him from undertaking any gainful occupation, and the expression "leprosy cured" shall be construed accordingly. [Persons with Disabilities (Equal Opportunities, Protection of Rights and Full Participation) Act, 1995 (1 of 1996), S. 2(i)]

Les fictions naissent de la loi, et non la loi des fictions. Fictions arise from the law, and not law from fictions.

Les lois ne se chargent de punir que les actions exterieures. The law delights in equity; it covets perfection; it is a rule of right.

Lesbian. A female whose major source of sexual gratification is by contact with other females. Lesbianism is homosexuality in the female.

Lese majesty. [Law French "injured majesty"]

Lessee. "LESSEE" means a person to whom a lease has been granted of the right of user of a tramway and of demanding and taking the authorized tolls. [Tramways Act (11 of 1886), S. 3(11)]

"LESSEE" means the person in whose name the production lease is granted. [Offshore Areas Minerals (Development and Regulation) Act, 2002 (17 of 2003), S. 4(i)]

A person to whom a lease is made; he is an owner *pro tanto*, of the estate which is leased to him.

A person cannot be a lessee unless he has enjoyment of the property which is the subject of the lease.

A person to whom a lease is made. [TP Act (4 of 1882), S. 105].

Lessor. A person by whom a lease is made. [TP Act (4 of 1882), S. 105].

Let. To lease or grant the use and possession of a thing for hire. [TP Act (4 of 1882), S. 25, ill. (a)].

Let or to be let separately for residential or non-residential purposes. The words 'let or to be let separately for residential or nonresidential purposes' occurring in Section 2(iii) of the Act, would mean that when both a residential portion and a non-residential portion of a building are let under a composite lease the whole building would come within term "building". *Boddu Narayanamma* v. *Sri Venkatarama Aluminium Co.*, (1999) 7 SCC 589, para 10. [Andhra Pradesh Buildings (Lease, Rent and Eviction) Control Act (15 of 1960), S. 2(iii)]

Let separately. The word "separately" in S. 2(2) is intended to emphasise that, for purposes of the Act, a building means any unit comprising the whole or part of a building that is separately let out. It does not mean and it cannot mean that composite leases of land and building would not be covered by it. *Suryakumar Govindjee* v. *Krishnammal,* (1990) 4 SCC 343, 355, 356. [T.N. Buildings (Lease and Rent Control) Act, 1960, S. 2(2)]

Let to hire. To give on hire [Indian Contract Act (9 of 1872), S. 23, ill. (k)]; to give on hire (when used with reference to a hire purchase transaction).

Lethal. Deadly.

Letter. A message in writing; an epistle. [CrPC 1973 (2 of 1974), S. 91(3)(b)]; a character representing one of the elementary sounds used in speech; an alphabetic symbol. [Trade and Merchandise Marks Act (43 of 1958), S. 2(1)(f)].

Letter of attornment. A grantor's letter to a tenant, stating that the leased property has been sold and directing the tenant to pay rent to the new owner.

Letter of credence. A written instrument given to an ambassador, envoy or minister accredited to a sovereign and addressed to the sovereign or state to which the minister is delegated.

Letter of credit. A written instrument, addressed by one person to another, requesting the latter to give credit to the person in whose favor it is drawn.

A letter of credit is in principle an undertaking by a banker to meet drafts drawn under the credit by the beneficiary of the credit in accordance with the conditions laid down therein. HALSBURY, 4th Edn., Vol. 3, para 131, p. 99.

A letter written by one person to another requesting to advance money or entrust goods to a particular person for which the writer's credit is pledged [Indian Stamp Act (2 of 1899), S. 2(3)(c)].

Letter of Exchange. Bill of Exchange.

Letter of indemnity. Letter undertaking to be responsible for any loss or damage sustained under certain specified circumstances.

Letter of request. A document issued to a foreign Court requesting a judge to take evidence from a specific person within the jurisdiction of that Court.

Letter press. The process of printing direct from an inked raised surface upon which the paper is impressed. [Factories Act (63 of 1948), S. 2(k)(iv)].

Letters of administration. "LETTERS OF ADMINISTRATION" includes any letter of administration whether general or with a copy of the will annexed or limited in time or otherwise. [Administrators-General Act (45 of 1963), S. 2(b)]

Where a person possessed of property dies intestate, or without an executor, a Court having probate jurisdiction will grant to a proper person an authority called letters of administration by which the grantee, the administrator, becomes clothed with powers and duties similar to those of an executor. [Limitation Act (36 of 1963), S. 9 *Prov.*].

Letters of guardianship. A document which a Court issues in appointing a guardian to care for a minor's or an incapacitated adult's well being, property and affairs.

Letters of mart. Letters of mart (or marque) were commissions issued by governments in time of war entitling privately-owned vessels to cruise in search for, and to attack, the shipping of a hostile power without being guilty of piracy. Such cruising amounted to a deviation. The Declaration of Paris respecting Maritime Law of 1856 prohibited privateering and letters of mart have long since ceased to be issued. (25 HALSBURY'S Laws (4th edn) para 164).

Letters patent. Writings of the sovereign duly sealed whereby a person or a company is enabled to do acts or enjoy privileges which he or it could not do or enjoy without such authority. [Indian Stamp Act (2 of 1899), Sch. I, Item 30].

A document that grants some right or privilege and is issued under the government seal but is open to public inspection.

Letters rogatory. It is a formal Communication in writing sent by a Court in which action is pending to a foreign Court or Judge requesting the testimony of a witness residing within the Jurisdiction of that foreign Court may be formally taken thereon under its direction and transmitted to the issuing Court making such request for use in a pending legal contest or action. (*Union of India* v. *W.N. Chadha,* AIR 1993 SC 1082).

Letters testamentary. The instrument by which a probate Court approves the appointment of an executor under a will and authorizes the executor to administer the estate.

Letting. The word 'letting' has nowhere been defined but in common parlance it means 'leasing.' According to the definition of lease in the T.P. Act (4 of 1882), S. 105, the essential ingredients are that the land should be transferred for a certain time or in perpetuity and that it should be transferred in consideration of a price or a periodical payment.

All the houses which are put for commercial use or are used by outsiders as lessees or licensees for money consideration will come within the meaning of the word "letting". *Patna Municipality* v. *Kailash Behari,* AIR 1965 Pat 288, 291.

Level crossing. 'LEVEL CROSSING' means an intersection of a road with lines of rails at the same level. [Indian Railways Act (24 of 1989), S. 2(22)]

Leverage. The ability to finance an investment with a small amount of one's own funds, such as a down payment, with the balance consisting of borrowed funds.

Leverage ratio. The ratio of the amount of debt of a firm to the value of the assets of a firm.

Leveraged recapitalization. Recapitalization in which the corporation substitutes debt for equity in the capital structure, usually to make the corporation less attractive as a target for hostile takeover.

Levy. The imposition or collection of an assessment tax, tribute or fine [long title, Central Sales Tax Act (74 of 1956)]; to impose or collect a tax. [CPC (5 of 1908), O. XVI, R. 4(2); Taxation Laws (Continuation and Validation of Recovery Proceedings) Act (11 of 1964), S. 4].

The word "levied" means "charged" as well as "assessed". *Ujagar Prints* v. *Union of India*, AIR 1989 SC 516, 538. [Additional Duties of Excise (Goods of Special Importance) Act (58 of 1957), S. 3]

Levy means to raise for the purposes of collecting the fine or to enforce an execution for a certain sum. [IPC (45 of 1860), S. 70]

Levy a tax. To levy a tax means "to impose or assess" or "to impose, assess or collect under the authority of law". It is a unilateral act of superior legislative power to declare the subjects and rates of taxation and to authorise the collector to proceed to collect the tax. *Firm L. Hazari Mal Kuthila* v. *I.T.O.*, AIR 1957 Punj 5, 10. [Constitution of India, Art. 265]

Levy and imposition. There is a distinction between imposition and levy *i.e.* assessment and collection of a tax. The imposition of tax is by an Act of the competent legislature and is purely legislative act. The levy and the collection of a tax is a process subsequent to the imposition of the tax by the statute. *Ramprasad* v. *War Profits Tax Officer,* AIR 1953 MB 20, 25. [Constitution of India, Art. 265 and 277]

Lewd and lascivious cohabitation. The act of a man and woman living together openly without being married to each other.

"Lewdness" and **"Prostitution."** "Prostitution," and "lewdness" when used distinctly in a penal statute applying to both sexes are not synonymous words. If a man and woman resort to a house of ill fame for the purpose of sexual relations, her purpose is "prostitution," and his, "lewdness."

Lex. Literally "Law; a law : the law."

Lex causae. (*Lat.*) The applicable law.

Lex citius tolerare vult privatum damnum quam publicum malum. (*Maxim*) The law will more readily tolerate a private loss than a public evil.

Lex contra id quod praesumit, probationem non receipit. (*Maxim*) The law admits no proof against that which it presumes.

Lex deficere non potest in justitia exhibenda. (*Lat.*) The law cannot be wanting in dispensing justice. (*Latin for Lawyers*)

Lex dilationes semper exhorret. The law always abhors delays. (*Latin for Lawyers*)

Lex est dictamen rationis. (*Maxim*) Law is the dictate of reason. (*Latin for Lawyers*)

Lex est exercitus judicium tutissimus ductor. (*Maxim*) (*Lat.*) The law is the safest leader of the army of judges.

Lex est ratio, summa, quae jubet quae sunt utilia et necessaria et contraria prohibet. (*Lat.*) (Co. Litt. 319b) Law is the highest reason, which commands those things which are useful and necessary, and forbids what is contrary thereto. (*Latin for Lawyers*)

Lex est sanctio sancta, jubens honesta et prohibens contraria. (*Lat.*) (2 Inst. 587) Law is a sacred sanction, commanding what is right and prohibiting the contrary. (*Burrill*)

Lex est summa ratio insita a natura quae jubet ea, quae facienda sunt, prohibetque contraria. (1 *Bl. Comm.* 44): Law is the perfection of reason implanted in us by nature, which enjoins what should be done, and forbids what we should not do.

Lex est tutissima cassis sub clypeo legis nemo decipitur. (*Lat.*) (2 Inst. 56) Law is the safest helmet; under the shield of the law no one is deceived.

Lex fori. The law of the forum of Court.

Lex injusta non est lex. (*Maxim*) An unjust law is not a law. (*Peloubet*)

Lex intendit vicinum vicini facta scire. (*Lat.*) (Co. Litt. 78) The law intends (or presumes) that one neighbour knows what another neighbour does.

Lex judicat de rebus necessario faciendis, quasi re ipsa factis. The law judges of things that must necessarily be done, as if they were in fact done. (*Burrill*).

Lex Loci. (*Lat.*) The law of the place; local law.

Lex loci actus. (*Lat.*) The law of the place where the act was done.

Lex loci delcitus (delicti). (*Lat.*) The law of the place where the crime took place.

Lex Mercatoria. *(Lat.)* The lexmercatoria, or law merchant, is a body of legal principles founded on the customs of merchants in dealings with each other, and though at first distinct from the common law, afterwards became incorporated into it. Though part of the general law of England, it is distinguished by a separate name, because it applies to particular subjects, and is based on principles more or less different from those which the common law recognizes in other matters, and also because these principles were engrafted into the municipal law by gradual adoption from the lexmercatoria or general body of European usages, in matters relating to commerce. [(See *Smith Mercantile Law (1905); Mitchell, The Law Merchant Ency. of the Laws of England*) quoted in *P Ramanatha Aiyar's The Law Lexicon*, 2012].

Lex necessitatis est lex temporis, scilicet instantis. (*Lat.*) (Hob. 159) The law of necessity is the law of the time, that is, of the instant, or present moment.

Lex neminem cogit ad vana seu inutilia peragenda. (*Lat.*) The law compels no man to do that which is futile or fruitless.

Lex neminem cogit ostendere quod nescire praesumitur. (*Lat.*) (Lofft, 569) The law compels no one to make unknown that which he is presumed not to know.

Lex nemini facit injurium. (*Lat.*) The law does injury to no one.

Lex nemini operatur iniquum. (*Lat.*) The law works injustice to no one.

Lex nemini operatur iniquum, nemini facit injuriam (*Jenk, Cent.* 22): The operation of the law never results in injury or in a wrong.

Lex nil facit frustra, nil jubet frustra. (*Lat.*) The law does nothing in vain and commands nothing in vain.

Lex nil frustra facit. (*Lat.*) (Jenk. Cent. 17) The law does nothing in vain.

The courts/tribunal will not exercise jurisdiction in futility. The law will not itself attempt to do an act which would be vain. [*Executive Engineer, Southern Electricity Supply Company of Orissa Limited (South Co)* v. *Sri Seetaram Rice Mill*, (2012) 2 SCC 108, para 82].

Lex nil frustra jubet. (*Lat.*) The law commands nothing vainly.

Lex non a rege est violanda. (*Lat.*) (Jenk. Cent. 7) (*Maxim*) The law is not to be violated by the king.

Lex non cogit ad impossibilia. (*Maxim*) "The law does not compel the doing of impossibilities."

The maxim was applied where the last day for preferring a petition was a public holiday and the next day was Sunday. The petition could be filed on Monday. *Manohar Joshi* v. *Nitin Bahurao Patil*, AIR 1996 SC 706 and where the lifting of tendu leaves as per tender condition became impossible due to stay order of the Court. *State of Rajasthan* v. *Anil Kumar Sunil Kumar & Party*, (2000) 4 SCC 342, para 7 : AIR 2000 SC 1441.

Lex non consilia nuda, sed actus apertos Respicit. (*Lat.*) The law regards not mere intentions, but open acts.

Lex non curat de minimis. (*Lat.*) The law does not regard small matters.

Lex non debet deficere conquerentibus in justitia exhibenda. (*Lat.*) The law ought not to fail in dispensing justice to those with a serious grievance. (*Latin for Lawyers*)

Lex non deficit in justitia exhibenda. (*Lat.*) The law does not fail in showing justice. (*Burrill*).

Lex non exacte definit, sed arbitrio boni viri permittit. (*Lat.*) The law does not define exactly, but trusts in the judgment of a good man.

Lex non intendit aliquid impossibilia. (*Maxim*) The law does not intend anything impossible. (*Burrill*)

Lex non novit patrem, nec matrem; solam veritatem. The law knows neither father nor mother; only the truth. (*Latin for Lawyers*)

Lex non oritur ex injuria. (*Lat.*) The law does not arise from an unlawful act.

Lex non patitur fractiones et divisiones statuum. (*Lat.*) The law does not suffer fractions and divisions of statutes.

Lex non requirit verificari quod apparet curiae. (*Maxim*) (*Lat.*) The law does not require that to be verified (or proved) which is apparent to the Court. (*Burrill*)

Lex nostra neminem absentem damnat. (*Lat.*) Our law condemns no one in his absence.

Lex orbis, insanis et pauperibus pro tutore atque parente est. (*Lat.*) The law is the guardian and father of orphans, the insane, and the poor.

Lex plus laudatur quando ratione probatur. The law is most worthy of approval when it is consonant to reason. (*Latin for Lawyers*)

Lex posterior derogat priori. (*Maxim*) (*Lat.*) A later statute takes away the effect of a prior one.

Lex punit mendacium. (*Lat.*) The law punishes falsehood.

Lex pure poenalis, obligat tantum ad Poe-Ro nam, non item ad culpam; lex poenalis mixta, et ad culpam obligat, et ad poenam. (*Lat.*) The law, merely penal, binds only as to penalty, not as to fault; the mixed penal law binds both to fault and penalty. (*Tayler L. Gloss.*)

Lex rejicit superflua, pugnantia, incongrua. (*Lat.*) (*Jenk. Cent.* 133, 140, 176) The law rejects superfluous, contradictory, and incongruous things.

Lex reprobat moram. (*Maxim*) The law dislikes delay. (*Latin for Lawyers*)

Lex respicit aequitatem. (*Lat.*) The law pays regard to equity.

Lex semper dabit remedium. (*Lat.*) The law will always give a remedy.

Lex semper intendit quod convenit rationi. (*Lat.*) (*Co. Litt.* 78, *b*). The law always intends what is agreeable to reason.

Lex situs. (*Lat.*) Means a country of dispute resolution either agreed by parties to a contract or decided by the arbitrator or forum for dispute resolution such as the Seat of arbitration designating place of forum. [Karnika Seth, *Computers Internet and New Technology Laws*, 2021, LexisNexis, Glossary of Legal Terms].

Lex spectat ad proximam non ad remotam causam. (*Maxim*) The law looks to the proximate not to the remote cause.

Lex spectat naturae ordinem. (*Lat.*) (*Maxim*) The law regards the order and course of nature. (*Broom*)

Lex succurrit ignoranti. (*Lat.*) The law assists the ignorant.

Lex succurrit minoribus. (*Lat.*) The law aids minors.

Lex talionis. (*Lat.*) The law of retaliation (as) an eye for an eye, a tooth for a tooth

Lex uno ore omnes alloquitur. (*Maxim*) The law addresses all with one (the same) mouth or voice. (*Burril*)

Lex vigilantibus, non dormientibus, subvenit. (*Lat.*) Law assists the wakeful, not the sleeping.

LGBT or **LGBTIQ.** Lesbian, Gay, Bisexual, Transsexual, Intersex and Queer minorities. The word 'Queer' is sometimes used generically, usually by younger people, to include the members of all the sexual minorities. The court usually avoided this expression because of its pejorative overtones within an audience unfamiliar with the expression. However, it is spreading and, among the young, is often seen as an instance of taking possession of a pejorative word in order to remove its sting. [Michael Kirby, former Judge of the High Court of Australia **as cited in** *Navtej Singh Johar v. Union of India,* (2018) 10 SCC 1, para 151]

Liabilities in India. Shall not include the paid-up capital or the reserves or any credit balance in the profit or loss account of the banking company. [Banking Regulation Act (10 of 1949), S. 25(3)(b)]

Liability. The condition of one who is subject to a duty which may be judicially enforced; that for which one is liable. [Indian Partnership Act (9 of 1932), S. 30(7)(a) and Constitution of India, Art. 15(2)].

The express 'LIABILITY' shall include all liabilities in respect of expenditure contracted for and all disputed or contingent liabilities [Companies Act (1 of 1956), Part III, (7)(1), Schedule VI now replaced by Companies Act, 2013]

"LIABILITY", in relation to owner of a vessel, includes liability of the vessel herself. [Merchant Shipping Act (44 of 1958), S. 352(d)]

"LIABILITY" includes liability in respect of any civil deposit, local fund deposit, charitable or other endowment, provident fund account, pension or actionable wrong. [State of Himachal Pradesh Act (53 of 1970), S. 37(4)(C) *Expln.* (a) and North-Eastern Areas (Reorganisation) Act (81 of 1971), S. 50(4)(b) *Expln.* (a)]

"Liability", as a legal term, signifies that condition of affairs which gives rise to an obligation to do a particular thing to be enforced by action; as we say an executor is liable for the debts of his testator or a principal is liable for the acts of his agent.

"Liability" is responsibility; the state of one who is bound in law and justice to do something which may be enforced by action. This liability may arise from contracts, either express or implied, or in consequence of torts committed.

In criminal law, this term covers every form of punishment to which a man subjects himself by violating the law of the land.

The word 'liability' in its widest import means an obligation or duty to do something or to refrain from doing something. Parliament intended to include in the word 'liability' not only a financial obligation but also obligations of every other kind, including one of reinstating a government servant wrongly dismissed. *W.W. Joshi* v. *State of Bombay,* AIR 1959 Bom 363, 365. [States Reorganisation Act (37 of 1956), Ss. 87, 88]

Liability, Civil. Accountability and responsibility to another enforceable by legal civil sanctions. [Companies Act (1 of 1956), S. 62 now replaced by Companies Act, 2013].

Liability, Criminal. Accountability and responsibility to another enforceable by legal criminal sanctions. [CrPC 1973 (2 of 1974), S. 250(5)].

Liability incurred. The words "liability incurred" are very general and comprehensive and ordinarily take in both civil and criminal liability. *Kapur Chand* v. *State of Bombay*, AIR 1958 SC 993, 995.

Liability limit. The maximum coverage which an insurance company provides in an insurance policy.

Liability, Vicarious. A principal is liable for acts of his agent within the scope of his authority. A person may become liable for a prosecution instituted by his agent under his authority, express or implied. In such a case the malice of his agent will be imputed to him. It is on this principle that a corporation is liable for his tort, though it has no mind and cannot be guilty of malice.

Liability without fault. Liability which does not depend on actual negligence or intent to harm, but which is based on the breach of an absolute duty to make anything safe.

Liabilities in India. In this section, and in section 24, "liabilities in India" shall not include—

(i) the paid-up capital or the reserves or any credit balance in the profit and loss account of the banking company;

(ii) any advance taken from the Reserve Bank or from the Exim Bank or from the Reconstruction Bank or from the National Housing Bank or from the National Bank, or from the Small Industries Bank, or from the National Bank for Financing Infrastructure and Development or from the other development financial institution by the banking company;

(iii) in the case of a Regional Rural Bank, also any loan taken by such bank from its Sponsor Bank. [Banking Regulation Act (10 of 1949), section 18(1), *Explanation (a)*]

It shall not include the paid-up capital or the reserves or any credit balance in the profit or loss account of the banking company. [Banking Regulation Act (10 of 1949), section 25(3)(b)]

In this section and in section 24, "liabilities in India" shall not include—

(i) the paid-up capital or the reserves or any credit balance in the profit and loss account of the co-operative bank;

(ii) any advance taken from a State Government, the Reserve Bank, the Exim Bank, the Reconstruction Bank, the National Housing Bank, the National Bank, the Small Industries Bank, or from the National Co-operative Development Corporation established under section 3 of the National Co-operative Development Corporation Act, 1962 (26 of 1962) by the co-operative bank;

(iii) in the case of a State or Central co-operative bank, also any deposit of money with it representing the reserve fund or any part thereof maintained with it by any other co-operative society within its area of operation, and in the case of a Central co-operative bank, also an advance taken by it from the Co-operative Bank of the State concerned;

(iv) in the case of a primary co-operative bank, also any advance taken by it from the Co-operative Bank of the State concerned or the Central co-operative bank of the district concerned;

(v) in the case of any co-operative bank, which has granted an advance against any balance maintained with it, such balance to the extent of the amount outstanding in respect of such advance; and

(vi) in the case of any co-operative bank, the amount of any advance or other credit arrangement drawn and availed of against approved securities. [Banking Regulation Act (10 of 1949), sections 18(1), *Explanation (a)* and 56(j)]

Liable. Bound or obliged by law; compellable to make satisfaction of a claim or debt. Exposed to a certain contingency or casualty more or less probable; financially responsible; to be obliged to pay, at least, upon a contingency. According to the context the word may mean bound or obliged; likely or probable.

Subject to an obligation. [IPC (45 of 1860), S. 112]; responsible. [CrPC 1973 (2 of 1974), S. 429(1)].

The word "liable" denotes : (1) Legally subject or amenable to; (2) Exposed or subject to or likely to suffer from (something prejudicial); (3) Subject to the possibility of (doing or undergoing something undesirable). The word "liable" occurring in many statutes, has been held as not conveying the sense of an absolute obligation or penalty but merely importing a possibility of attracting such obligation or penalty, even where this word is used along with the words "shall be". *Superintendent and Remembrance of Legal Affairs* v. *Abani Maity*, AIR 1979 SC 1029, 1032.

The word 'liable' means a future possibility or probability happening which may or may not actually occur. *State* v. *Amin Tulsi Ram,* AIR 1957 Punj 55, 56. [IPC (45 of 1860), S. 381]

"Liable to tax". In relation to a person and with reference to a country, means that there is an income-tax liability on such person under the law of that country for the time being in force and shall include a person who has subsequently been exempted from such liability under the law of that country. [Income-tax Act (43 of 1961), S. 2(29A)]

Liaise. To maintain contact between units of the same organisation; to ensure concerted action; a close connection. [Tobacco Board Act (4 of 1975), S. 8(4)].

Lian. In *lian*, it is the imputation of adultery of the wife, made by the husband, which entitles her to file a suit for dissolution of marriage and get decree for divorce, if she proves the charge of adultery to be false. [S A Khader, *Muslim Law of Marriage and Succession*, EBC, Calcutta, 1998 at 43 **quoted in**

Dr Kauser Edappagath, *Divorce and Gender Equity in Muslim Personal Law of India*, 2014, LexisNexis at p. 120]

Libel. Any published statement in writing damaging to the reputation of a person. [Indian Evidence Act (1 of 1872), S. 6, ill. (c)].

A defamatory statement especially in writing but it includes also pictures, signs, or electronic broadcast.

"Libel" and **"Slander."** False defamatory words, if written and published Constitute a libel, if spoken a slander.

Libelant. A person who publisher's a written defamatory statement.

Libellee. The suitor defendant against whom libel has been filed.

Libellous character. Constituting or containing a libel; defamatory. [Indian Evidence Act (1 of 1872), S. 32, ill. (n)].

Liberal. Free in bestowal or concession; generously inclined. (*Century*)

Liberal economy. Is that which is regulated by the market forces (that is why it is also termed as market economy). Prices of goods and services in such an economy are determined in a free price system set up by supply and demand. This is often contrasted with planned economy in which a Central Government determines the price of goods and services using a fixed price system. It is also contrasted with mixed economy where the price system is entirely free, but under some government control or heavily regulated. [*Modern Dental College and Research Centre* v. *State of M.P.,* (2016) 7 SCC 353, para 88].

Liberal construction or Liberal interpretation. Does not mean that the words shall be forced out of their natural meaning, but simply that the words should receive a fair and reasonable interpretation, so as to attain the object for which the instrument is designed and the purpose to which it is applied.

LIBERAL CONSTRUCTION does not mean enlargement or restriction of any plain provision of law. If a statutory provision is plain and unambiguous, it is the duty of the Court to enforce it as it is written. If it is ambiguous or doubtful, or susceptible of different construction or interpretations, then such liberality of construction may be indulged in as, within the fair interpretation of its language, will effect its apparent object and promote justice.

Libertas est naturalis facultas ejus quod cuique facere libet, nisi qudo de jure aut vi prohibetur. (*Maxim*) (*Lat.*) Liberty is that natural faculty which permits every one to do anything he pleases except that which is restrained by law in force.

Libertas est res inestimabilis. (*Lat.*) Liberty is an inestimable thing.

Libertas omnibus rebus favorabilior est. Liberty is more favored than all things (anything).

Liberty. Freedom; individual freedom; personal freedom. Freedom from restraint under conditions essential or equal enjoyment of the same right by others; freedom from all restraints but such as are justly imposed by law; or regulated by law. It means the enjoyment of the rights which belong to us as individuals.

Liberty, At. Free. [CrPC 1973 (2 of 1974), S. 281(4)].

Liberty of speech. The right to state facts and express opinions.

Liberty of the press. The liberty of the press consists in the right to publish with impunity the truth, with good motives and for justifiable ends, whether it respects governments or individuals; the right freely to publish whatever the citizen may please, and to be protected against any responsibility for so doing, except in so far as such publications, from their blasphemy, or scandalous character, may be a public offence, or as by their falsehood and malice they may injuriously affect the standing and reputation, or pecuniary interests, of individuals.

Liberum corpus nullam recipit aestimatio-nem. The body of a freeman does not admit of valuation : the life of a freeman is above all valuation. (*Burrill*).

Liberum est cuique apud se explorare an expediat sibi consilium. It is free for every one to weigh the matter in his own mind; or to have resort to counsel. (*Tayler L. Gloss.*)

Everyone is free to ascertain for himself whether a recommendation is advantageous to him.

Libre recherché scientifique. 'Libre recherché scientifique' means "free scientific research". [*Badshah* v. *Urmila Badshah Godse*, (2014) 1 SCC 188, para 18].

Licence. "Where one person grants to another, or to a definite number of other persons a right to do, or continue to do, in or upon the immoveable property of the grantor, something which would, in the absence of such right, be unlawful, and such right does not amount to an easement or an interest in the property, the right is called a LICENCE." [Indian Easements Act (5 of 1882), S. 52]

"LICENCE" Means a licence issued in accordance with the provisions of this Act and rules made thereunder and includes a licence issued in the electronic form [Arms Act, 1959 (54 of 1959)]

An authority to do something which would otherwise be inoperative, wrongful or illegal; a formal permission from a constituted authority to do something. [Indian Easements Act (5 of 1882), S. 52].

"Licence" means a licence to practice dentistry granted under sub-section (1) of section 31. [National Dental Commission Act, 2023 (21 of 2023), section 2(p)]

Licence and **Permit.** A licence is not necessarily a permit. A licence is intended to regulate business while a permit would be one without which a business can ever be started so that a permit may amount to a prohibition of the business in regard to persons who are unable to obtain the same. *Sajjan Bank* v. *Reserve Bank of India,* AIR 1961 Mad 8, 12. [Constitution of India, Art. 19 (1)(g), (19)(6)]

Licensed chemist. Means a person who has obtained a licence under these rules for the sale on prescription of narcotic drugs and for the manufacture of narcotic drugs from materials which he is lawfully entitled possess. [Bihar Narcotic Drugs and Psychotropic Substances Rules, 1985, R. 2(e)]

Licensed dealer. Means a person who has obtained licence under these rules for the sale of narcotic drug and psychotropic substances otherwise than on prescription and for manufacture of narcotic drugs from materials which he is lawfully entitled to possess. [Bihar Narcotic Drugs and Psychotropic Substances Rules, 1985, R. 2(m)]

Licensee. A person to whom licence has been granted or who holds a licence. [Indian Electricity Act (9 of 1910), S. 2(h)]; [Damodar Valley Corporation Act (14 of 1948), S. 19(i)].

"A person who has a privilege to enter upon land arising from the permission or consent, express or implied, of the possessor of land but who goes on the land for his own purpose rather than for any purpose or interest of the possessor." [Black's Law Dictionary, 6th Edn. as cited in *Prabhudas Damodar Kotecha* v. *Manhabala Jeram Damodar*, (2013) 15 SCC 358, para 51].

A licensee is a person who has permission to do an act which without such permission would be unlawful. [Stroud's Judicial Dictionary of Words and Phrases, 6th Edn., Vol. 2 as cited in *Prabhudas Damodar Kotecha* v. *Manhabala Jeram Damodar*, (2013) 15 SCC 358, para 52].

Licensing State. Means the Contracting State which operates or which has authorised the operation of a nuclear ship under its flag. [Convention on the Liability of Operators of Nuclear Ships, Brussels, May 25, 1962, Art. 1(2)]

Licensor. The person who gives a licence.

A person with authority to grant licences, or who grants licences. [Indian Evidence Act (1 of 1872), S. 117].

Lie detector/Lie detecting machine. Any device which records involuntary bodily responses associated with conscious lying.

Lien. It signifies an obligation, tie, or claim annexed to, or attaching upon, any property without satisfying which such property cannot be demanded by its owner. (*Tomlin*)

A right by which a person in possession of the property holds and retains it against the other in satisfaction of a demand due to the party retaining it [CPC (5 of 1908), O. VIII, R. 6(2) and Sales Goods Act (3 of 1930), S. 47, margin].

"The word 'lien' is a generic term and, standing alone, it includes lien acquired by way of contract, or by operation of law." [*State of M.P.* v. *Sandhya Tomar*, (2013) 11 SCC 357, para 10].

"Lien" connotes the civil right to a Government servant to hold the post "to which he is appointed substantively". [*State of Madhya Pradesh* v. *Sandhya Tomar*, (2013) 11 SCC 357, para 10].

'A lien- (without effecting a transference of the property in a thing)-is the right to retain possession of a thing until a claim be satisfied; as it is either particular or general. [*Bombay Stock Exchange* v. *V.K. Kandalgaonkar*, (2015) 2 SCC 1, para 31].

'Lien' connotes the right of a civil servant to hold the post substantially to which he is appointed. When a person with a lien against a post is appointed substantially to another post, he acquires a lien against the latter post. Then the lien against his previous post automatically disappears. *Ramlal Khunrana* v. *State of Punjab*, AIR 1989 SC 1985, 1987. [Constitution of India, Art. 309]

Lien creditor. A creditor whose claim is secured by a lien on a particular piece of property of a debtor.

Lien holder. A holder having or owning a lien.

Lieu there of, In. Instead of or in place of it.

Lieutenant-Governor. The administrator of the union territory of Delhi, appointed under Art. 239 shall be designated as the Lieutenant Governor. [Constitution of India, Art. 239 - AA(1)].

Life. "The word "LIFE" denotes the life of a human being, unless the contrary appears from the context". [IPC (45 of 1860), S. 45(1)] [Now (w. e. f. 1-7-2024) repealed & replaced by Bharatiya Nyaya Sanhita, 2023 (45 of 2023), S. 2(17), same definition in new Sanhita

The word "life" in Art. 21, means not merely the right to the continuance of a person's animal existence but a right to the possession of each of his organs—his arms and legs *etc. Kharak Singh* v. *State of U.P.*, AIR 1963 SC 1295, 1302. [Constitution of India, Art. 21]

"Life" includes reputation of an individual as well as the right to live with freedom [*Bihar Public Service Commission* v. *Saiyed Hussain Abbas Rizwi*, (2012) 13 SCC 61, para 27].

By the term 'life' as here (Article 21) used something more is meant than mere animal existence. The inhibition against its deprivation extends to all these limbs and faculties by which life is enjoyed. [*Field, J. in Munn* v. *Illinois*, 24 L ED 77 : 94 US 113 (1876) as cited in *Kharak Singh* v. *State of U.P.*, AIR 1963 SC 1295 : (1963) 2 Cri LJ 329 : (1964) 1 SCR 332, para 15]. See also *Mahmood Nayyar Azam* v. *State of Chhatisgarh*, (2012) 8 SCC 1, para 26].

'LIFE' includes not merely physical existence but also the use of any faculty or limb as also the right to live with human dignity. *Bachan Singh* v. *State of Punjab*, AIR 1982 SC 1325.

'LIFE' does not include livelihood. *A.V. Nachane* v. *Union of India*, AIR 1982 SC 1126.

The period from birth to death; animate existence [IPC (45 of 1860), S. 45]; living beings, especially the living things of a particular kind, quality or environment. [Title, Wild Life (Protection) Act (53 of 1972)].

Life assurance business. Means the issue of, or the undertaking of liability under, policies of assurance upon human life, or the granting of annuities upon human life. [Life Insurance Act (6 of 1912), S. 2(5)]

Life boat. Boat for saving shipwrecked persons. [Geneva Conventions Act (6 of 1960), IInd sch, Art. 26].

Life buoy. [Workmen's Compensation Act (8 of 1923), Sch II, item (vii)(f)].

Life-care contract. An agreement where one party is assured of care and maintenance for life in exchange for a transfer of property to the other.

Life convict. One who is convicted with a sentence of imprisonment for life. [IPC (45 of 1860), S. 307].

Life estate. An estate for life is defined to be a freehold interest in lands, the duration of which is confined to the life, or lives of some particular person or persons, or to the happening or not happening of some uncertain event.

Life expectancy. The period for which a man of a given age and sex is expected to live, taking into account his individual characteristics.

Life imprisonment. The expression 'life imprisonment' means an imprisonment for the whole of a convict's natural life and does not automatically expire on his serving sentence of 14 years and 20 years, unless of course, the sentence is remitted or committed by the Government in accordance with law. There is no provision in law that the life imprisonment expires on serving out the sentence for 14 years or 20 years. *Mahak Singh* v. *State of U.P.*, AIR 1999 All 274 (P. 283).

Life insurance. LIFE INSURANCE in a broader sense comprises any contract in which one party agrees to pay a given sum upon happening of a particular event contingent upon the duration of human life, in consideration of the immediate payment of a smaller sum or certain equivalent periodical payments by another. *Chandulal Harjivandas* v. *CIT*, AIR 1967 SC 816, 818.

Life insurance business. "LIFE INSURANCE BUSINESS" means the business of effecting contracts of insurance upon human life, including any contract whereby the payment of money is assured on death (except death by accident only) or the happening of any contingency dependent on human life, and any contract which is subject to payment of premium for a term dependent on human life and shall be deemed to include—

(a) granting of disability and double and triple indemnity accident benefits, if so provided in the contract of assurance,

(b) the granting of annuities upon human life and

(c) The granting of superannuation allowances and annuities payable out of any fund applicable solely to the relief and maintenance of persons engaged or who have been engaged in any particular profession, trade or employment or of the dependants of such persons. [Insurance Act (4 of 1938), S. 2(11)]

Life interest. An interest or estate which determines on the termination of life [TP Act (4 of 1882), S. 46, ill. (b)]; [Indian Easements Act (5 of 1882), S. 8, ill. (b)].

"Life interest" means an interest which determines on the termination of life. It is incapable of being transferred by such person to others being personal in nature. Such person, therefore, could enjoy the "life interest" only during his/her lifetime which is extinguished on his/her death. [*Ranvir Dewan* v. *Rashmi Khanna,* (2018) 12 SCC 1, para 42.6].

Life, Liberty, and Property. The term "life, liberty and property" is a representative term, and is intended to cover every right to which a member of the body politic in a free country is entitled under the law. This term includes the right of self-defence, freedom of speech, religious and political freedom, exemption from arbitrary arrest, and the right freely to buy and sell as others may. Indeed, it embraces all our liberties, personal, civil and political, including the rights to labour, to contract, to terminate contracts, and to acquire property.

Life-sustaining procedure. A medical procedure in which mechanical or artificial means are used to sustain, restore or substitute for a vital function and which serves only or primarily to postpone death.

Life tenant. A person who holds property beneficially during his life-time. [Estate Duty Act (34 of 1953), S. 21(1)(ii)].

Life time. Duration of a person's life.

Duration of one's whole life [TP Act (4 of 1882), S. 14].

Lifetime disability benefit. Disability benefit which is payable for the life of the insured so long he is totally disabled.

Ligan. Good which are sunk in the sea but tied to a buoy so as to be found later.

Ligeantia est quasi legis essentia; est vinculum fidei. Allegiance is, as it were. the essence of law; it is the chain of faith.

Ligeantia est vinculum fidei; ligeantia est legis essentia. (*Lat.*) Allegiance is the bond of fealty, and the essence of law.

Ligeantia naturalis nullis claustris coercetur, nullis metis refraenatur nullis finibus premitur. (*Lat.*) Natural allegiance is restrained by no barriers, reined by no bounds, stopped by no limits.

Light. A window or opening in a wall or roof for the admission of light; opposite of darkness. [Registration Act (16 of 1908), S. 2(6)]; [Industrial Disputes Act (14 of 1947), S. 2(n)(iv)]; [Inland Vessels Act (1 of 1917, S. 52(2)(e)].

Light commercial vehicle. The expression 'Light commercial vehicle' means only a 'light motor vehicle' that was intended to be used for commercial purpose and does not exceed 4000 Kgs in weight. *Asstt. Commr.* v. *Swaraj Mazda Ltd.,* (2001) 9 SCC 404, para 1.

Light dues. Charges levied on ships for the maintenance of light-house, beacons, *etc.*, around the coasts.

Light motor vehicle. Means a transport vehicle or omnibus the gross vehicle weight of either of which or a motor car or tractor or road-roller the unladen weight of any of which, does not exceed 7,500 kilograms. [Motor Vehicles Act (59 of 1988), S. 2(21)]

The expression 'light motor vehicle' as occurring in S. 2(21) of the Act and R. 2(e) would mean 'a motor vehicle which is not a transport vehicle'. *Ashok Gangadhar Maratha* v. *Oriental Insurance Co. Ltd.,* (1999) SCC 620, para 6. [Motor Vehicles Act (59 of 1988), S. 2(21) and Central Motor Vehicles Rules, 1989, R. 2(e)]

Lighthouse. "LIGHTHOUSE" includes any lightvessel, fog-signal, buoy, beacon or any mark, sign or apparatus exhibited or used for the guidance of ships. [Indian Light House Act (17 of 1927), S. 2(d)]

A tower or other building equipped to guide navigators by means of a powerful light that gives a continuous or interrupted signal. [Lighthouse Act (17 of 1927), S. 2(d)].

Lights are those openings which are made rather for the admission of light than to look out of.

RIGHT TO LIGHT. Light like air and water, is provision of nature, for general use of man-kind, and essential to man's very existence. Like air and water, it flows over the land of one person to that of another for the use of both, and, to secure the due use and enjoyment of light by both, the law recognizes mutual rights and obligations on the part of both, that each may be restrained from infringing the rights of the other and depriving him of them unjustly. It is obvious that the right of a land owner to unobstructed light across his neighbour's land must, if unrestricted and unlimited, at once come into conflict with the right of that neighbour's to build near the extremity of his land, in such a way as to obstruct the light. The two rights could not co-exist if unrestricted, and the law has therefore stepped in to define and determine the respective rights and obligations of neighbours.

Like. While the context often determines its signification the term is generally defined to mean analogous; resembling; having resemblance; similar; equal; same in quantity, amount, or extent; having the same, or nearly the same, appearance, qualities, or characteristics; resembling; similar to; equal in quantity, quality, or degree; exactly corresponding. (*Webster*)

The word 'like' means only 'similar' and not same. [Indian Electricity Act (9 of 1910), S. 22]

Like article. "LIKE ARTICLE" means an article which is identical or alike in all respects to the article under investigation for being dumped in India or in the absence of such an article, another article which although not alike in all respects, has characteristics closely resembling those of the articles under investigation. [Customs Tariff (Identification, Assessment and Collection of AntiDumping Duty on Dumped Article and for Determination of Injury) Rules, 1995, R. 2(d)]

"LIKE ARTICLE" means an article which is identical or alike in all respects to the article under investigation. [Customs Tariff (Identification and Assessment of Safeguard Duty) Rules, 1997, R. 2(e)]

Like manner : Like conditions. "Like manner" and subjection to "like conditions" to mean similar and not identical manner and conditions. (*Ram Bali Rajbhar* v. *State of West Bengal*, AIR 1975 SC 623).

Likely to disturb communal harmony. It envisages the result of engenderment of feelings of enmity and hatred. *A.J. Faridi* v. *Union of India,* AIR 1970 All 383 at 389. [Defence of India Rules (1962), R. 35(6)(g)]

Likely to promote feelings of enmity and hatred. Likely to promote feelings of enmity and hatred is not the same thing as "likely to disturb communal harmony", but a stronger word which signifies creation of feelings of enmity and hatred". *A.J. Faridi* v. *Union of India,* AIR 1970 All 383 at 389. [Defence of India Rules (1962), R. 35(6)(g)].

Likely to result in lack of communal harmony. "Lack of harmony signifies cessation of feelings of friendship." *A.J. Faridi* v. *Union of India,* AIR 1970 All 383 at 389. [Defence of India Rules (1962), R. 35(6)(g)].

Limbs of Government. Neither the Council of Ministers nor an individual Minister can attend to the numerous matters that come up before the Government. Those matters have to be attended to and decisions taken by various officials at various levels. When those officials discharge the functions allotted to them, they are doing so as limbs of the Government and not as persons to whom the power of the Government had been delegated. (*Sanjeevi Naidu* v. *State of Madras,* AIR 1970 SC 1102.

Limeshell. 'Limeshell' is in the nature of a deposit of lime, which might be derived from marine animal shells upon further processing and after admixture with other inorganic elements. *V.P. Pithupitchai* v. *Special Secretary, Govt. of T.N.,* (2003) 9 SCC 534, para 18.

Limestone. Include minerals like lime-shell, calcareous sand and sea sand essentially composed of lime shell, marl, kankar or lime kankar. [Limestone and Dolamite Mines Labour Welfare Funds Act (62 of 1972), S. 2(bb)]

Limine, In. On the threshold; in the beginning itself.

Limit. A boundary line or territorial point; a boundary; abound beyond which something ceases to be possible or allowable [CrPC 1973 (2 of 1974), S. 7(2)]; limitation; term; duration [IPC (45 of 1860), S. 65].

Limitation. "LIMITATION" (with its grammatical variations) means any limitations of the exclusive rights to the use of a trade mark given by the registration of a person as proprietor thereof, including limitations of that right as to mode of use as to use in relation to goods to be sold or otherwise traded in within India, or as to use in relation to goods to be exported to any market outside India. [Trade and Merchandise Marks Act (43 of 1948), S. 2(i)]

"LIMITATION" (with its grammatical variations) means any limitation of the exclusive right to the use of a trade mark given by the registration of a person as proprietor thereof, including limitations of that right as to mode or area of use within India or outside India. [Trade Marks Act (47 of 1999), S. 2(1)(l)]

In its ordinary sense, restriction or circumspection; in its ordinary legal and popular sense, the word refers to the time within which an action may be brought, or some act done, to preserve a right.

The statutory specification of a period, or the period specified by statutes within which an action must be brought [Income-tax Act (43 of 1961), S. 249]; restriction [Jayanti Shipping Company (Taking Over of Management) Act (24 of 1966) (*Repealed*), S. 14; the limiting or marking out of the bounds of an estate in property. [TP Act (4 of 1882), Ss. 10 and 12].

Limitation and **Condition.** The principal difference between a condition and a limitation is that a condition does not defeat the estate, when broken, until it is avoided by the act of the grantor, but a limitation marks the period which is to determine the estate, without entry of claim.

Limitation of liability. The imposition of a maximum amount of liability for loss of damage.

Limitation period. A statutory period after which a lawsuit or prosecution cannot be brought in Court.

Limited. Narrow, restricted; circumscribed; construed; controlled and governed; not absolute.

Confined within limits; restricted in extent, number or duration. [Indian Contract Act (9 of 1872), S. 179].

Limited appeal. An appeal from only certain portions of a decision, these portions of decision includes only the adverse or unfavourable portions.

Limited guardianship. For the purposes of this sub0section "LIMITED GUARDIANSHIP" means a system of joint decision which operates on mutual understanding and trust between the guardian and the person with disability, which shall be limited to a specific period and for specific decision and situation and shall operate in accordance to the will of the person with disability. [Rights of Persons with Disabilities Act (49 of 2016), S. 14(1), *Explanation*].

Limited by law. The term "limited by law" when used in a statute, is to be construed as meaning limited by the statutes law, and not to mean limited by the general common law.

Limited common areas and facilities. Means there common areas and facilities designated in the deed of apartment as reserved for the use of certain apartment as apartments to the exclusion of the other apartments. [Tamil Nadu Apartment Ownership Act, 1994 (TN Act 7 of 1995), S. 3(o)]

"LIMITED COMMON AREAS AND FACILITIES" means those common areas and facilities which are designated in writing by the promoter before the allotment, sale or other transfer of any apartment as reserved for use of certain apartment or apartments to the exclusion of the other apartments. [Delhi Apartment Ownership Act (58 of 1986), S. 2(q) and Punjab Apartment Ownership Act, 1995 (Punjab Act) (13 of 1995), S. 2]

Limited company. "LIMITED COMPANY" means a company limited by shares or by guarantee. [Companies Act (1 of 1956) replaced by Companies Act, 2013, S. 2(23)]

A joint-stock company the liability of the members of which for the debts of the company is limited by statute.

Limited estate. The expression 'limited estate' has been used in several places and by necessary implication it can only mean the limited estate of a woman according to the Hindu Mitakshara Law. *Ningapuma* v. *Patel Linge Gowde,* AIR 1954 Mys 179.

Wife in possession of land from her husband *in lieu of* maintenance from him becomes absolute owner of the land, by virtue of her right to maintenance. *Gulwant Kaur* v. *Mohinder Singh*, AIR 1987 SC 2251, 2254. [Hindu Succession Act (30 of 1956), S. 14 (1) and (2)]

Limited interest. A duration or extent of property less than that of absolute property. [Indian Contract Act (9 of 1872), S. 179].

Limited liability. In regard to companies, means that the liability of shareholders does not extend beyond the paying in of the amount represented by their respective shareholding.

Limited liability partnership. Partnership form that limits malpractice liability for partners who are not directly involved in an incident.

"LIMITED LIABILITY PARTNERSHIP" means a partnership formed and registered under Limited Liability Partnership Act, 2008 (6 of 2009). [Limited Liability Partnership Act, 2008 (6 of 2009), S. 2(1)(n). Also see S. 115JF(c) of the Income-tax Act, 1961 (43 of 1961) as inserted (w.e.f. 1-4-2012) by the Finance Act, 2011]

Limited liability partnership agreement. 'Limited liability partnership agreement' means any written agreement between the partners of the limited liability partnership or between the limited liability partnership and its partners which determines the mutual rights and duties of the partners and their rights and duties in relation to that limited liability partnership. [Limited Liability Partnership Act, 2008 (6 of 2009), S. 2(o)]

Limited owner. A person having an ownership that is not absolute or perfect *i.e.* one for a limited period. [Limitation Act (36 of 1963), S. 20(3)(a)].

Limited ownership. Ownership, in the fullest sense, is a sum-total of all the rights which may possibly flow from title to the property, while limited ownership, in its very nature, must be a bundle of rights constituting in their totality not full ownership but something less. A widow has the occupation, control and usufruct of the property to the exclusion of all others and such relation to the property falls squarely within the meaning of the expression limited owner's in S. 14 (1). *Vajia* v. *Jhakorbhai*, AIR 1979 SC 993, 996, 1002. [Hindu Succession Act (30 of 1956), S. 14 (1) (2)]

Limited partnership. A partnership in which there are special partners who contribute special sums as capital, and who are not liable for the debts of the partnership beyond the fund so contributed.

Limited return. Means the maximum dividend as may be specified by the articles. [Companies Act (1 of 1956), S. 581A(c) now replaced by Companies Act, 2013]

Limited time. Time, the extent or duration of which has been defined. [CPC (5 of 1908), O. VI, R. 18].

Limited warranty. A warranty which does not cover full labour and material for repairs.

Line. "LINE" means any wire, cable, tube, pipe, insulator, conductor or other similar thing (including its casing or coating) which is designed or adapted for use in carrying electricity and includes any line which surrounds or supports, or is surrounded or supported by or is installed in close proximity to, or is supported, carried or suspended in association with, any such line. [Electricity Act (36 of 2003), S. 2(40)]

A wire or a pair of wires connecting one telegraph or telephone station with another; a succession of ancestors or descendants of an individual; a narrow elongated mark drawn or projected.

The word "line" in the expression telegraph line does not connote the existence of a defined channel of communication which has got a physical existence. *Senior Electric Inspector* v. *Laxminarayan Chopra*, AIR 1962 SC 159.

Line clear. What is meant by line-clear is not that the lines in the station yard are clear for reception of the train but that there is no obstruction on the track beyond the outer most signals on the down side of the station which the train has to enter. *Awadh Bahari Sharma* v. *State of Madhya Pradesh*, AIR 1956 SC 738, 742.

Line Ministry. Means a Ministry in the Government of India, which has been so nominated with respect to a project, by the Government of India, in the Ministry of Finance (Department of Economic Affairs). [Customs Tariff Act (51 of 1975), General Exemption No. 2(iii), *Expln.* (b)]

Line of credit. The maximum amount of credit which is extended to a borrower by a given lender.

Line of navigation. The words "LINE OF NAVIGATION" shall mean any navigable channel subject to the provisions of the Canals Act. [Ben. Act V of 1864 (Canals), S. 1.]

Linea recta semper praefertur transversali. (*Maxim*) The right line is always preferred to the collateral.

Lineage. Heirs, race, progeny, descendants in a common line from a common progenitor. (*Webster*)

Lineal. That which comes in a direct line.

Lineal ascendant. An ancestor in the direct line of ascent. [Income-tax Act (43 of 1961), S. 2(41)].

Lineal consanguinity. "LINEAL CONSANGUINITY" is that which subsists between two persons, one of whom is descended in a direct line from the other, as between a man and his father, grandfather and great-grand-father, and so upwards in the direct ascending line; or between a man and his son, grandson, great-grandson and so downwards in the direct descending line. Every generation constitutes a degree, either ascending or descending. A person's father is related to him in the first degree, and so likewise is his son, his grandfather and grandson in the second degree; his great-grandfather and great-grandson in the third degree, and so on." [Indian Succession Act (39 of 1925), S. 25].

Lineal descendant. A descendant in the direct line of descent. [Estate Duty Act (34 of 1953), S. 17(4)(ii)(c)(iii), *Expln.* (a)].

The connection or relation between two persons, one of whom is descended in a direct line from the other, as between a man and his father, grandfather, and so upwards in the direct ascending line; or between a man and his son, grandson, great grandson and so downwards in the direct descending line. [Indian Succession Act (39 of 1925), S. 25]

An 'adopted son' of an Indian Christian of Hindu Origin will come within the ambit of 'Lineal descendant' under S. 37 of the Act. *Ajit Datt* v. *Ethel Walters,* AIR 2001 All 109, 133, para 65. [Indian Succession Act (39 of 1925), S. 37]

A son or a grandson can be said to be a lineal descendant of his mother or grand-mother respectively.

The term "lineal descendants" includes all the descendants and is not restricted to male descendants line.

"LINEAL DESCENDANT" providing that lineal descendants shall take from their ancestor, *etc.*, includes a legally adopted child.

Lineal heir. One who is either an ancestor or a descendant of the descendant, *e.g.*; a parent or child.

Link. A unit in a connected series; anything which serves to connect or bind together the things which precede and follow it. *As a verb*, to couple, or join together.

A uniform resource locator [URL] that is embedded in a web page. (*Internet and E-commerce*)

A connection between two items of hypertext. (*Information Technology*)

Linked business. Means life insurance contracts or health insurance contracts under which benefits are wholly or partly to be determined by reference to the value of underlying assets or any approved index. [Insurance Regulatory and Development Authority (Registration of Indian Insurance Companies) Regulations, 2000, Rgn. 2(i)]

Linked site. The website to which another website provides a hypertext link. (*Cyber Law*)

Linked transaction. A transaction which is linked to, but not part of, a regulated agreement and is entered into by a debtor or hirer with any other person.

Linking. Providing a hypertext link from one website to another. (*Cyber Law*)

Linking occurs where the Uniform Resource Locator (URL), that is, the website address provided connects to a specific page on a website rather than the home page. Aparna Viswanathan, *Cyber Law: Indian & International Perspectives,* 2012, LexisNexis Butterworths at p. 273.

Linking site. The website that provides a link to another website. (*Cyber Law*)

Linux. A widely used Open Source Unix-like operating system. Linux was first released by its inventor Linus Torvalds in 1991. There are versions of Linux for almost every available type of computer hardware from desktop machines to IBM mainframes. The inner workings of Linux are open and available for anyone to examine and change as long as they make their changes available to the public. This has resulted in thousands of people working on various aspects of Linux and adaptation of Linux for a huge variety of purposes, from servers to TV- recording boxes. (*Matisse Enzer-Glossary of Internet Terms*)

Liquid. Able to flow like water; capable of being readily converted into cash.

Liquid assets. Readily realisable property, such as coins, notes, and other high class securities. Assets that are readily convertible into cash.

Liquidate. To adjust; to settle; to ascertain or reduce to precision in amount; to ascertain the balance due, to whom due and to whom payable; to clear away, to lessen a debt; to clear up; to clear from obscurity; to pay; to satisfy. (*Webster*)

To settle the debt by payment or other adjustment; to ascertain and set out clearly the liabilities of a company or a firm; to get rid of by force or violence.

Liquidated amount. A figure which is readily computed, based on an agreement's terms.

Liquidated claim. A claim concerning an amount which has been agreed on by the parties or which can be precisely determined by operation of law or by the terms of the agreement of parties.

Liquidated damages. An amount which is contractually stipulated as a reasonable estimation of actual damages to be recovered by one party if the other party breaches.

Liquidated damages : Penalty. Where a contract provides a forfeiture for the purpose of securing the payment of a sum of money or the performance of an act which may be compensated in damages, the sum forfeited may be deemed a penalty and not liquidated damages.

Liquidated demand. A liquidated demand is a claim for a specific sum of money payable under a contract expressed or implied not being in the nature of a penalty, or of unliquidated damages; or a claim for a specific sum recoverable by action for an amount due under a judgment or order of the Court, brought by the person entitled against the person liable to pay; or a claim for a sum of money whether or not in the nature of damages or penalty, recoverable under a statute which contains an express provision that the sum sued for may be recovered as a liquidated demand, or as liquidated damages. (*Ency. of the Laws of England*)

A demand of a specific amount which has already been fixed by law or parties. [CPC (5 of 1908), S. 128(2)(f)(i)].

Liquidated sum. Liquidated sum means the sum which was ascertainable after simple arithmetical calculation by the parties or the Court. [Provincial Insolvency Act (5 of 1920), S. 9 (1) (b)]

Liquidating distribution. A distribution of trade or business assets by dissolving partnership or corporation.

Liquidating partner. The person who is appointed to settle the accounts collect the assets, adjust the claims, and pay the debts of dissolving on insolvent firm.

Liquidation. The action or operation of winding up the affairs of a firm or company; determination of liabilities and apportionment of assets towards discharging the indebtedness [Indian Contract Act (9 of 1872), S. 143, ill. (b)]; ascertainment and setting out clearly the liabilities of a company or a firm.

The act of determining the exact amount of something such as debt, damage *etc.* that before was uncertain; the act of setting a debt by payment or other satisfaction; the act of converting assets into cash for setting debts.

Liquidation of debt. The settling of a debt by payment or other adjustment. [Indian Contract Act (9 of 1872), S. 143, ill. (b)].

Liquidation price. A price which is paid for sold property to liquidate a debt.

Liquidation value. The value of business or an asset which is sold outside the ordinary course of business.

Liquidator. Where a partnership is manually dissolved, and one of the members of the firm is made the liquidator the position which he occupies is one of agency. He becomes the sole authorizing agent of the partnership for the single purpose of winding up and settling its affairs He represents creditors on the one hand, and all of the partners on the other, and for this reason he is sometimes spoken of as a trustee; but he is not accurately so described, inasmuch as he has in his possession no more property or power after being appointed liquidator than he had before.

A person appointed to carry out the winding up of a company or firm. [Coal Mines Provident Fund and Miscellaneous Provisions Act (46 of 1948), S. 2(e)].

Liquefied natural gas. Means a fluid in the cryogenic liquid state composed predominantly of methane. [Static and Mobile Pressure Vessels (Unfired) Rules, 2016, R. 2(xxxi-a); Gas Cylinder Rules, 2016, R. 2(1)(xxxviii-a)].

Liquor. "LIQUOR" includes—

(a) Spirits of wine, denatured spirits, methylated spirits, rectified spirits, wine, beer and every liquid consisting of or containing alcohol; and

(b) any other intoxicating substance which the Government may, by notification declare to be liquor for the purposes of this Act, but does not include toddy. [Andhra Pradesh Prohibition Act, 1995 (AP Act, 17 of 1995), S. 2(6)]

The word 'liquors', as commonly used, includes all that are spirituous, vinous, or inferior fermented, including malt.

The word 'liquor' covers not only those alcoholic liquids which are generally used for beverage purposes and produce intoxication, but also all liquids containing alcohol. *State of Bombay* v. *F. N. Balsara*, AIR 1951 SC 318, 325.

"LIQUOR" includes spirits of wine, methylated spirits, spirits, wine, toddy, beer, and all liquid consisting of or containing alcohol. (*Southern Pharmaceuticals and Chemicals, Trichur* v. *State of Kerala*, (1981) 4 SCC 391).

Lis. A suit, action, controversy, or dispute.

A controversy or dispute, a suit or action at law. There is a lis where there is an affirmation by one party and denial by another. *Kihoto Hollohan* v. *Zachillhu*, JT 1992 (1) SC 600.

"Lis" means "a piece of litigation; a controversy or dispute". [Black's Law Dictionary (8th Edn.) as cited in *Namit Sharma* v. *Union of India*, (2013) 1 SCC 745, para 78.1].

Lis alibi pendens. (*Lat.*) An action or suit pending elsewhere.

Lis pendens. (*Lat.*) A pending suit.

Lis means a suit, action controversy, or dispute, and *lis pendens* means a pending suit. The doctrine denotes those principles and rules of law which define and limit the operation of the common-law maxim *pendente lite nihil innovetur*, that is, pending the suit nothing should be changed.

The rule of "*lis pendens*" is statutory and imposes two conditions : (*i*) the existence of a contentious suit, and (*ii*) that the transfer should be during its active prosecution in a Court of the kind described in S. 52, Transfer of Property Act (4 of 1882).

List. A roll; a roster [Naval and Aircraft Prize Act (5 of 1971), S. 2(b)]; to prepare a list; to enter in a list.

List of auqaf. Means the list of auqaf published under section 5(2) or contained in the register of auqaf maintained under section 37 of Act 43 of 1995. [S. 3(g) of the Wakf Act, 1995 (43 of 1995) as substituted by the Wakf (Amendment) Act, 2013 (27 of 2013)]

Listed company. Means a company which has any of its securities listed on any recognised stock exchange. [S. 2(52) of the Companies Act, 2013 (18 of 2013)]

Listed Indian Company. Means an Indian company which has any of its capital instruments listed on a recognized stock exchange in India and the expression 'Unlisted Indian Company' shall be construed accordingly. [Foreign Exchange Board (Transfer or Issue of Security by a Person Resident outside India) Regulations, 2017, Regn. 2(xxxi)].

Listed public companies. Means a public company which has any of its securities listed in any recognised stock exchange. [Companies Act (1 of 1956), S. 2(23A) now replaced by Companies Act, 2013]

Listed securities. For the purposes of section 112(1) of Act 43 of 1961, 'listed securities' means the securities which are listed on any recognised stock exchange in India. [*Explanation (aa)* to section 112(1) of the Income-tax Act, 1961 (43 of 1961) as introduced (w.e.f. 1-4-2013) by the Finance Act, 2012 (23 of 2012)]

Listed security. A security which is accepted for trading on a securities exchange.

Listing. Listing means the admission of the securities of a company to trading privileges on a Stock Exchange. *Raymond Synthetics Ltd.* v. *Union of India*, AIR 1992 SC 847.

Lists. Means lists prepared by the Government of India from time to time for purposes of making provision for the reservation of appointments or posts in favour of backward classes of citizens which, in the opinion of that Government, are not adequately represented in the services under the Government of India and any local or other authority within the territory of India or under the control of the Government of India. [National Commission for Backward Classes Act (27 of 1993), S. 2(c)]

Lite pendente. (*Lat.*) While the action is pending.

Litera scripta manet vox emissa volat. Lasting is the written thing, spoken things speed away.

Literal construction or interpretation. Strict construction.

A term applied where we collect the intention of a deed, will, or statute from the words used only.

The "literal interpretation" of a statute, is finding out the true sense by making the statute its own expositor. If the true sense can thus be discovered. There is no resort to construction. It is, beyond question, the duty of Courts, in construing statutes, to give effect to the intent of the law-making power, and seek for that intent in every legitimate way, but first of all in the words and language employed.

Literal method. A method for the construction of a statute by the Courts.

Literary. Concerning the writing, study, or content of literature, especially of the kind valued for quality of form. [Oxford English Dictionary as cited in *Krishika Lulla* v. *Shyam Vithalrao Devkatta*, (2016) 2 SCC 521, para 11].

Literary and artistic work, in the International Copyrights Act, 1886, "unless the context otherwise requires, means every book, print, lithograph, article of sculpture, dramatic piece, musical composition, painting, drawing, photograph, and other work of literature and art.

Literary property. The physical property in which an intellectual production is embodied, like book, screenplay or lecture.

Literary work. "LITERARY WORK" includes computer programmes, tables and compilations including computer data basis. [Copyright Act (14 of 1957), S. 2(o)]

Something intended to afford either information and instruction, or pleasure, in the form of literary enjoyment.

"Literary work" includes maps, charts, plans, tables, and compilations.

"Literary works" are works, other than audio- visual works, expressed in words, numbers, or other verbal or numerical symbols or indicia, regardless of the nature of the material objects, such as books, periodicals, manuscripts, phono records, film, tapes, disks, or cards in which they are embodied.

Lithograph. A print from a drawing on stone or other substance.

Lithography. The art or process of producing a figure or image on a flat specially prepared stone or plate in such a way that it will absorb and print with special ink. [Delivery of Books and Newspapers (Public Libraries) Act (27 of 1954), S.2(a)].

Litigable. Able to be contested or disputed in Court.

Litigant. A party to a lawsuit.

Litigate. To dispute or contend in form of law; to carry on a suit. (*Burril*)

Litigating under the same title. *See* CPC (5 of 1908), S. 11.

Words mean in the same right, as the adopted son of Shankar though that claim of his was sought to be based on a later adoption than one in the former suit. *Sundarabai* v. *Devaji Shankar Deshpande*, AIR 1954 SC 82, 84.

The crucial test for determining whether the parties are litigating in a suit under the same title as in the previous suit is of the capacity in which they sued or were sued. *Syed Hafiz Mir* v. *Abdul Nayeen Khan*, AIR 1960 MP 250, 251.

Litigation. A judicial controversy; a contest in a Court of Law; a judicial proceeding for the purpose of enforcing a right. Law suit; process of carrying on a law suit.

The action of carrying on a suit in law; legal proceedings. [CPC (5 of 1908), O. XXIV, R. 4(2)].

Litigation friend. An adult responsible for the conduct and cost of legal proceedings instituted on behalf of, or against, a child or a mentally disordered person.

Litigosa ignorantia juris est potius quam scientia. Ignorance of the law, rather than familiarity with it, is the most frequent cause of law suits.

Litis nomen omnem actionem significat, sive in rem, sive in personam sit. (*Lat.*) A law suit signifies every action, whether it be *in rem* or *in personam*.

Littleman. An association of persons, registered or unregistered, can file a petition under Article 226, Constitution of India for enforcement of the rights and in case of members of such an association are themselves unable to approach the Court by reason of poverty, disability or socially, economically disadvantaged position. *Umesh Chand Vinod Kumar* v. *Krishi Utpadan Mandi Samiti, Bharathana,* AIR 1984 All 46, 50.

Littleton. An English Judge of the reign of Edward IV; who wrote a treatise on tenures, on which Coke wrote a commentary.

Littoral. A word used in describing the rights of the upland owners along the seashore and tide lands.

Live-birth. Means the complete expulsion or extraction from its mother of a product of conception, irrespective of the duration of pregnancy, which, after such expulsion or extraction, breathes or shows any other evidence of life, and each product of such birth is considered live born. [Registration of Birth & Death Act (18 of 1969); S. 2(d)]

Live-stock. All cattle, horses, mules, sheep, asses, any hogs are deemed live-stock; domestic animals kept for farm purposes especially marketable animals, as cattle, horses and sheep.

"LIVESTOCK" includes horses, kine, camels, sheep and any other animal which may be specified by the Central Government by notification in the Official Gazette. [Livestock Importation Act (9 of 1898), S. 2(b)]

"LIVESTOCK" includes all animals to be raised for milk, meat, fleece skin, wool and other by-products. [National Co-operative Development Corporation Act (26 of 1962), S. 2(dbb)]

"LIVESTOCK" means farm animals and includes buffaloes, bulls, bullocks, camels, cows, donkeys, goats, sheep, horses, mules, yaks, pigs, ducks, geese, poultry and their young but does not include any animal specified in Schedules I to V. [Wild Life (Protection) Act (53 of 1972), S. 2(18A)]

'Livestock' means cows, buffaloes, bullocks, bulls, goats and sheep, and includes poultry, fish and such other animals as may be declared by the Government by notification to be livestock for the purpose of this Act. [A.P. (Agricultural Produce & Livestock) Markets Act (16 of 1966), S. 2 (v)]

Animals kept or dealt in for use or profit. [CPC (5 of 1908), S. 128(2)(b)]; S. 80P(2)(a)(iv), Income-tax Act (43 of 1961)].

'Prawn' comes within the ambit of the expression 'livestock' under S. 2(v) of the Act. *I.T.C. Ltd.* v. *Person Incharge, A.M.C., Kakinada,* AIR 2004 SC 1796, 1799, para 6. [Andhra Pradesh (Agricultural Produce & Livestock) Markets Act (16 of 1966), S. 2(v)]

LIVESTOCK is, ordinarily speaking, not confined to domestic animals. The word 'live- stock takes in 'animals' of any description. (*Royal Hatcheries (P.) Ltd.* v. *State of A.P.*, 1994 (Supp) I SCC 429, 432).

'Fishes' are not domestic animals and are not included within the meaning of the term 'livestock'. *Maheshwari Fish Seed Farm* v. *T.N. Electricity Board,* (2004) 4 SCC 705, 713, para 15.

Livelihood. Subsistence.

Means of living. [CPC (5 of 1908), S. 60(1), *Prov.* (b)].

Living. Abiding; having a domicile; having one's home; residing; sojourning; being; subsisting; subsistence.

Continuing alive. [TP Act (4 of 1882), S. 5].

The term 'any other wife living' means any other wife living with the husband. *A. Annamalad* v. *Perumayee Ammal,* AIR 1965 Mad 139, 142. [Hindu Adoptions and Maintenance Act (78 of 1956), S. 18(2) (d)]

Living child. A child *en ventre sa mere* at its father's death is deemed living, and entitled to participate in a devise to children living at their father's death.

Living in adultery. A state or condition of repeated adulterous intercourse as distinguished from a single or occasional act of adultery. [CrPC 1973 (2 of 1974), S. 125(4)].

A single or occasional act of criminal intercourse, without having co-habited, is not a "living together in adultery".

Living in adultery and committing adultery (Distinction). There is a distinction between "committing adultery" and "living in adultery". Living in adultery means, following a course of adulterous conduct more or less continuous; a single act of adultery cannot be considered as living in adultery. *Mahalingam Pillai* v. *Amsavalli,* MLJ : QD (1956-1960) Vol. III C436 : (1956) 2 Mad LJ 289. [Hindu Marriage Act (25 of 1955), S. 13(1)(i)]

Living in brothel. Residence in a brothel for about four days before rescue comes within the meaning of the words "lives in".

Living memory. The period over which the recollection of living people extends.

Living on immoral earnings. Using money obtained from prostitution for one's livelihood or upkeep.

Living person. Includes a company or association or body of individuals, whether incorporated or not, but nothing herein contain shall affect any law for the time being in force relating to transfer of property to or by companies, associations or bodies of individuals. [T.P. Act (4 of 1882), S. 5]

The expression 'living person' occurring in S. 5 of the Act includes 'juristic person' also. *Hindustan Lever* v. *State of Maharashtra,* AIR 2004 SC 326, 341, para 45. [T.P. Act (4 of 1882), S. 5]

Living separately. The expression 'living separately' connotes not living like husband and wife. The parties may live under the same roof by force of circumstances, and yet they may not be living as husband and wife. The parties may be living in different houses and yet they could live as husband and wife. *Sureshta Devi* v. *Om Prakash*, AIR 1992 SC 1904, 1907. [Hindu Marriage Act (25 of 1955), sec. 13-B(1)]

Living separately by mutual consent. All that has been agreed upon is, that the husband is willing to pay a certain amount specified in the agreement. This cannot amount to living separately by mutual consent. *Rao Saheb* v. *Prayag Bai,* AIR 1956 Hyd 189, 190. [CrPC 1973 (2 of 1974), S. 125(5)]

Living trust. A voluntary trust or a trust *inter vivos*; the one created by the trustor in his life-time, as distinguished from a testamentary trust.

Living will. A document, signed with the formalities which are necessary for a will, by which a person states the intention to refuse medical treatment and to release health care providers from all liability if the person becomes both terminally ill and unable to communicate such a refusal.

LLU. (*abbr.*) Local Loop Unbundling. Possibility provided by the dominant provider to other providers of using the line linking the subscriber to the local exchange, exclusively or on a shared basis. (*Telecommunication*)

Loan. "LOAN" means a loan whether of money or in kind, and includes any transaction which is in the opinion of the Court, in substance, a loan. [Usurious Loans Act (10 of 1918), S. 2(2)].

"LOAN" means a sum of money advanced by the Administration—

(i) to a displaced person for the purpose of any business or industry in which he is engaged or intends to engage himself, or

(ii) in respect of any business or industry, a substantial portion of which is owned by displaced person. [Rehabilitation Finance Administration Act (12 of 1948), S. 2(e)]

Lending. [Usurious Loans Act (10 of 1918), S. 2(2)].

A contract of loan of money is a contract whereby one person lends or agrees to lend a sum of money to another, in consideration of a premise express or implied to repay that sum on demand, or at a fixed or determinable future time, or conditionally upon an event which is bound to happen, with or without interest." [Chitty on Contracts, Vol. II, 30th Edn., p. 909 as cited in *Keshavlal Khemchand and Sons Private Limited v. Union of India*, (2015) 4 SCC 770, para 29]

The word 'loan' includes not only an actual advance, whether of money or in kind, but also a transaction on a bond bearing interest executed in respect of past liability. *Jiwa nlal* v. *Rameshwarlal*, AIR 1967 SC 1118, 1120. [Bihar Money-Lenders (Regulation of Transactions), Act (7 of 1939), S. 2(f)]

Advancing of money by one person to another under an agreement by which the recipient of money agrees to repay the amount on such agreed terms with regard to the time of repayment and the liability to pay interest. [*Keshavlal Khemchand and Sons Private Limited* v. *Union of India*, (2015) 4 SCC 770, para 29].

Loan and **debt.** A loan is something quite different from a debt. A loan contracted creates a debt, but there may be a debt contracted without contracting a loan.

Loan capital. Money which is raised by company issuing debentures.

Loan certificate. A certificate which is issued by the clearing house to a borrowing bank in an amount equal to a specified percentage of the value of the borrowing bank's collateral on deposit with the clearing house's loan committee.

Loan for consumption. An agreement in which a given quantity of goods is delivered to a borrower who consumes them and who is obligated to return not those very goods, but goods of the same quantity, type and quality.

Loan participation. A method of transfer of a fraction of loans originated by a bank by issuing a participation certificate in favour of another bank, whereby the other bank becomes a fractional investor in and beneficiary of the loan.

Loan to value ratio. For the purposes of rule 20 of the Nidhi Rules, 2014, the term 'loan to value ratio' means the ratio between the amount of loan given and the value of gold or jewellery against which such loan is given. [*Explanation* to rule 20(6)(d) of the Nidhi Rules, 2014]

Loan value. The maximum amount which can be safely lent on life insurance or property without any damage to the lender's right to protection if the borrower fails to repay.

Loans or advances. Shall not include any transaction which the Reserve Bank may, having regard to the nature of the transaction, the period within which, and the manner and circumstances in which, any amount due on account of the transaction is likely to be realised, the interest of the depositors and other relevant considerations, specify by the general or special order as not being a loan or advance for the purpose of this section. [Banking Regulation Act (10 of 1949), S. 20, *Expln.* (a)]

Loansharking. The act of lending money at high interest rates and threatening or using extortion to enforce repayment.

Lobby. "LOBBY" means the covered corridor immediately adjoining the Chamber and co-terminus with it. [Rules of Procedure and Conduct of Business in the Council of States (Rajya Sabha), R. 2(1)]

Lobbying. Seeking by bribery or other dishonest means to influence the vote of a member of legislature.

"Lobbying" signifies to address or solicit members of a legislative body, in the lobby or elsewhere, with the purpose of influencing their votes, and a contract for lobbying is void as against public policy.

Local. Relating to a particular place; belonging or confined to a particular place; distinguished from general, personal, or transitory; pertaining to a place, or to fixed or limited portion of space; limited or confined to spot, place, or definite district; fixedness in a place. (*Bouvier*)

The term 'local' is frequently applied to an area smaller than an entire estate or country as a whole.

Pertaining to a locality or place [CPC (5 of 1908), S. 60(1)(g), *Prov*. and Constitution of India, Art. 31A(2)].

Local Act. An Act having application in a locality only as distinguished from one having application throughout the country.

Local and personal Act. Act of Parliament with restricted, local or personal application, enacted on petition from local or formal sponsor. [Indian Evidence Act (1 of 1872), S. 57(2)].

Local area. "LOCAL AREA" means the area within five kilometers radial distance from a telephone exchange or where the telegraph authority has declared any area served by an exchange system to be a local area for the purpose of telephone connection, such area. [India Telegraph Rules, 1951, R. 2(w)]

"LOCAL AREA" means any area, whether urban or rural, declared by the Central Government by notification in the Official Gazette, to a local area for the purposes of this Act. [Prevention of Food Adulteration Act (37 of 1954), S. 2(vii)]

The proper meaning to be attached to the words 'local area' in Entry 52 of the constitution, is an area administered by a local body like a municipality, a district board, a local board, a union board, *panchayat* or the like. The premises of a factory is therefore not a 'local area.' *Diamond Sugar Mills Ltd.*, v. *State of Uttar Pradesh*, AIR 1961 SC 652, 658. [Constitution of India, Seventh Schedule, State List, Entry 52]

The Constitutional intention of using the word "local area" was to understand it in the sense of any area which is administered by a local body that may be a corporation, Municipal Board or a district board. Such an interpretation is derived from the use of this phrase in various other Articles of the Constitution such as Articles 3(b), 12, 245(1), 246 and so on. *Shantikumar M. Sancheti* v. *State of Maharashtra*, (1995) 1 SCC 351, 355.

An area under the administration of a local authority; an area smaller than the entire state or country. [Constitution of India, Art. 31A(2)].

"LOCAL AREA" means any area, whether urban or rural, notified by the Commissioner of Food Safety, to be a local area for the purposes of Act 34 of 2006. [S. 3(1)(zb) of the Food Safety & Standards Act, 2006 (34 of 2006)]

Local Area Network (LAN). Local Area Network (LAN) is a computer network that is confined to a building or a cluster of buildings. A 'LAN' is a network that is typically personal to an organization and is installed for the exclusive use of a particular office or factory of a given organization. (*Information Technology*)

Local assessments. A tax to pay for improvements (such as sewers and sidewalks) in a designated area, levied on property owners who will benefit from the improvements.

Local authority. "Local authority" means—

(a) a "Panchayat" as defined in clause (d) of Article 243 of the Constitution;

(b) a "Municipality" as defined in clause (e) of Article 243P of the Constitution;

(c) a Municipal Committee, a Zilla Parishad, a District Board, and any other authority legally entitled to, or entrusted by the Central Government or any State Government with the control or management of a municipal or local fund;

(d) a Cantonment Board as defined in S. 3 of the Cantonments Act, 2006;

(e) a Regional Council or a District Council constituted under the Sixth Schedule to the Constitution;

(f) a Development Board constituted under article 371 of the Constitution; or

(g) a Regional Council constituted under Article 371A of the Constitution [The Central Goods and Services Tax Act, 2017 (12 of 2017), S. 2(69)]

Means any body of persons for the time being invested by law with the control and administration of any matters within a specified local area. [Cattel Trespass Act (1 of 1871), S. 3]

"LOCAL AUTHORITY" includes a town planning authority (by whatever name called) set up under any law for the time being in force. [Land Acquisition Act (1 of 1894), S. 3(aa) repealed]

"LOCAL AUTHORITY" means any person legally entitled to the control or management of any local or municipal fund, or legally entitled to impose any cess, rate, duty or tax within any local area. [Local Authorities Loans Act (9 of 1914), S. 2]

"LOCAL AUTHORITY" shall mean a municipal committee, district board, body of port commissioners or other authority legally entitled to, or entrusted by the Government with the control or management of a municipal or local fund. [General Clauses Act (10 of 1897), S. 3 (31)].

"LOCAL AUTHORITY" means in the case of—

(1) a local area which is—

(a) a municipality, the municipal board or municipal corporation;

(b) a cantonment, the cantonment authority;

(c) a notified area, the notified area committee;

(2) any other local area, such authority as may be prescribed by the Central Government or the State Government under this Act [Prevention of Food Adulteration Act (37 of 1954), S. 2(viii)]

"LOCAL AUTHORITY" means a Municipal Committee, District Board or other authority for the time being invested by law with the control and administration of any matters within a specified local area. [Prevention of Cruelty to Animals Act (59 of 1960), S. 2(e)]

"Local authority means an authority legally entitled to or entrusted by the Government with the control or Management of a local fund". "The Dock Labour board is local authority." *Bhikari Behara* v. *Dhanapatia,* AIR 1970 Cal 176 at 178. [CPC (5 of 1908), O. XXI, R. 48 (1)]

An authority in order to be a local authority must be of like nature and character of a Municipal committee; District Board, a Body of Port Commissioners, possessing of the distinctive attributes and characteristic of Municipal Committees but possessing one essential feature that it is legally entitled to or entrusted by the Government with control and management of a municipal or local fund. *Union of India* v. *R. C. Jain*, AIR 1981 SC 951, 952. [Payment of Bonus Act (21 of 1965), S. 32 (iv); General Clauses Act (10 of 1897), S. 3 (31)]

"LOCAL AUTHORITY" includes a town planning authority (by whatever name called) set up under any law for the time being in force, a Panchayat as defined in article 243 and a Municipality as defined in article 243P, of the Constitution. [S. 3(s) of the Right to Fair Compensation & Transparency in Land Acquisition, Rehabilitation & Resettlement Act, 2013 (30 of 2013)]

"LOCAL AUTHORITY" includes Panchayat, municipality, district board, cantonment board, town planning authority and in the States of Assam, Manipur, Meghalaya, Mizoram, Nagaland and Tripura where Panchayats do not exist, the village council or committee or any other body, by whatever name called, which is authorised under the Constitution or any law for the time being in force for self-governance or any other authority or body vested with the control and management of civic services, within a specified local area. [S. 2(8) of the National Food Security Act, 2013 (20 of 2013)]

"LOCAL AUTHORITY". It ordinarily would be a statutory authority. *Deewan Singh* v. *Rajendra Pd. Ardevi*, AIR 2007 SC 767 : 2007 AIR SCW 461.

"LOCAL AUTHORITY" means a Municipal Corporation or a Municipal Council or a Nagar Panchayat, by whatever name called, or the Cantonment Board, or as the case may be, a civil area committee appointed under section 47 of the Cantonment Act, 2006 (41 of 2006), or such other body entitled to function as a local authority in any city or town to provide civic services and regulate street vending and includes the "planning authority" which regulates the land use in that city or town. [Street Vendors (Protection of Livelihood and Regulation of Street Vending) Act, 2014 (7 of 2014), S. 2(1)(c)]

"LOCAL AUTHORITY" means the Delhi Municipal Corporation established under the Delhi Municipal Corporation Act, 1957 (66 of 1957), or the New Delhi Municipal Council established under the New Delhi Municipal Council Act, 1994 (44 of 1994) or the Delhi Development Authority established under the Delhi Development Act, 1957 (61 of 1957), legally entitled to exercise control in respect of the areas under their respective jurisdiction. [S. 2(1)(d) of the National Capital Territory of Delhi Laws (Special Provisions) Act, 2011 (5 of 2011). See also S. 2(1)(d) of the National Capital Territory of Delhi Laws (Special Provision) Second Act, 2011 (20 of 2011)]

"LOCAL AUTHORITY". Means,—(*i*) a Municipality or a Panchayat, as defined in clause (*e*) and clause (*f*) of article 243P of the Constitution, which is responsible for sanitation in its area of jurisdiction; (*ii*) a Cantonment Board constituted under section 10 of the Cantonments Act, 2006; and (*iii*) a railway authority. [S. 2(1)(f) of the Prohibition of Employment as Manual Scavengers & Their Rehabilitation Act, 2013 (25 of 2013)]

Local bodies. Means Panchayats and Municipalities, by whatever name called, within the meaning of clause (1) of Article 243B and clause (1) of Article 243Q of the Constitution and in the absence of any Panchayats or Municipalities, institutions of self-government constituted under any other provision of the Constitution or any Central Act or State Act. [Biological Diversity Act, 2002 (18 of 2003), S. 2(h)]

Local Body Tax. Means a tax on the entry of goods into the limits of the city, for consumption, use or sale therein, levied in accordance with the provisions of Chapter XIB, but does not include cess as defined in clause (6-A) and Octroi as defined in clause (42). [Maharashtra Municipal Corporation Act (59 of 1949), S. 2(31-A) **as cited in** *Sodexo SVC India Private Limited* v. *State of Maharashtra,* (2015) 6 SCC 479, para 8].

Local call. Mean a call from the subscriber's line to another line on any exchange within the same exchange system. [Indian Telegraph Rules, 1951, R. 2(x)]

Local candidate. This rule defines a local candidate as meaning a temporary Government servant not appointed regularly in accordance with the Rules of Recruitment of that service. *State of Mysore* v. *Narayanappa*, AIR 1967 SC 1071, 1072.

Local Courts. Courts, whose jurisdiction is limited to particular territories or districts.

Local division. "LOCAL DIVISION" means a sub-division, *pargana, thana*, police division or jurisdiction, or other division according to which the *mauzawar* register of the district is arranged. Ben. Act 111 of 1876 (Land Registration), S. 3, cl. 5.]

Local expression. An expression peculiar to a particular locality. [Indian Evidence Act (1 of 1872), S. 98].

Local fund. "LOCAL FUND" means any fund under the control or management of a local authority. [Cattle Trespass Act (1 of 1871), S. 3].

Local funds administered by Government. Means the fund administered by a body which, by law or rule having the force of law, comes under the control of the Government and over whose expenditure the Government retains complete and direct control. [Central Civil Services (Pension) Rules, 1972 R. 2(m)]

Local Government. A government at a lower level than the state government such as at a city level (corporation).

Local (Health) Authority. In relation to a local area, means the officer appointed by the Central Government, by notification in the Official Gazette, to be in charge of Health administration in such area with such designation as may be specified therein. [Prevention of Food Adulteration Act (37 of 1954), S. 2(viiia)]

Local inquiry. An inquiry made at the spot. [CrPC 1973 (2 of 1974), S. 148(1)].

Local inspection. An inspection of the locality *i.e* the place of occurrence or other relevant place. [CrPC 1973 (2 of 1974), S. 310(1)].

Local investigation. Inspection of locality.

An investigation made at the spot. [CPC (5 of 1908), S. 75(b)].

Local investigation report. Report of the officer making a local investigation.

Local jurisdiction. "LOCAL JURISDICTION", in relation to a Court or Magistrate, means the local area within which the Court of Magistrate may exercise all or any of its or his powers under this Code and such local area may comprise the whole of the State, or any part of the State, as the State Government may by notification specify. [CrPC, 1973 (2 of 1974), S. 2(j)] [Now (w. e. f. 1-7-2024) repealed & replaced by Bharatiya Nagarik Suraksha Sanhita, 2023 (46 of 2023)]

Territorial jurisdiction; jurisdiction over the locality; local limits of jurisdiction. [section 187(1), CrPC 1973 (2 of 1974)] [Now (w. e. f. 1-7-2024) repealed & replaced by Bharatiya Nagarik Suraksha Sanhita, 2023 (46 of 2023)]

"Local jurisdiction", in relation to a Court or Magistrate, means the local area within which the Court or Magistrate may exercise all or any of its or his powers under this Sanhita and such local area may comprise the whole of the State, or any part of the State, as the State Government may, by notification, specify. [(w. e. f. 1-7-2024) Bharatiya Nagarik Suraksha Sanhita, 2023 (46 of 2023), S. 2(1)(n)]

Local Law. "LOCAL LAW" is a law applicable only to a particular part of India [IPC (45 of 1860), S. 42]] [Now (w. e. f. 1-7-2024) repealed & replaced by Bharatiya Nyaya Sanhita, 2023 (45 of 2023), S. 2(18), same definition in new Sanhita]

Law applicable to a particular locality or area. [section 42, IPC (45 of 1860)] [Now (w. e. f. 1-7-2024) repealed & replaced by Bharatiya Nyaya Sanhita, 2023 (45 of 2023)]

As regards the Union Territory of Pondicherry, the law of limitation embedded in the French Code Civil would be a local law. *Justinimo* v. *Antomin*, AIR 1979 SC 984. [Limitation Act (36 of 1963), S. 29(2) and (3)]

Local lighthouse. Means any light house which is not a general light house. [Lighthouse Act (17 of 1927), S. 2(e)]

Local lighthouse authority. Means a State Government, local authority or other person having the superintendence and management of a local light house. [Lighthouse Act (17 of 1927), S. 2(f)]

Local limit. A limit in relation to locality or area. [Indian Contract Act (9 of 1872), S. 27, *Expln.* and Constitution of India, Art. 32(3)].

Local Line Convention. Means the International Convention on Load Lines signed in London on the 5th day of April, 1966, as amended from time to time. [Merchant Shipping Act (44 of 1958), S. 3(20)]

Local manager. The manager posted at the particular place. [CrPC 1973 (2 of 1974), S. 63].

Local meeting. Means the annual meeting of the shareholders whose names are registered in a branch register. [Imperial Bank of India (47 of 1920), S. 2(f)]

Local newspaper. A newspaper published from a particular locality; a newspaper having circulation in the locality. [CPC (5 of 1908), O. XXI, R. 67(2)].

"LOCAL NEWSPAPER" in relation to any area within the Jurisdiction of a Regional Planning Board, Planning Authority or of a Development Authority means any newspaper published or circulating within that area. [Maharashtra Regional and Town Planning Act (37 of 1966), S. 2(16)]

Local novelty. A patent can be invalidated by prior publication only if the publication was in the country granting the patent. *(Patents)*

Local option. An option which allows a municipality or other governmental unit to determine a particular course of action without the specific approval of state officials.

Local or other authority. The words 'local or other authority' must be construed '*ejusdem generis*' with Government or Legislature and so construed can only mean authorities exercising governmental functions. The University of Madras does not come within the scope of Art. 12, Constitution of India. *University of Madras* v. *Shantha Bai,* AIR 1954 Mad 67.

The words 'local or other Authority' mean authorities exercising Government functions and will not include persons, natural or public, who cannot be regarded as instrumentalities of the Government. The Punjab University is not a local or other authority falling within the definition of State. *Krishan Gopal* v. *Punjab University,* AIR 1966 Punj 34.

A municipal committee, district board, body of port commissioners or other authority legally entitled to or entrusted by the Government with the management or control of a municipal or local fund. [General Clauses Act (10 of 1897), S. 3(31) and Constitution of India, Art. 110(2)].

Local rule. A rule which is based on physical conditions of a state, and the customs, beliefs and character of its people; a rule through which an individual Court supplements the procedural rules applying generally to all Courts within its jurisdiction.

Local self-government. The principle of local self-government is regarded as fundamental in all democratic political institutions. It means that local affairs shall be decided upon and regulated by local authorities, and that the citizens of particular districts have the right to determine upon their own public concerns and select their own local officials without being controlled by the general public or the state at large.

Locality. The word "locality" signifies a particular district; confined to a limited region; opposed to "general"; limited by boundaries, large or small. (*Anderson*)

The word "*locality*" in S. 100(4) of CrPC 1973 (2 of 1974) does not mean the same quarter of the town as the place which is searched.

"Locality is a place with an area which is sufficiently small and compact, so that naming it amounts to a notice to all inhabitants of that area." *Hazari* v. *State,* AIR 1976 MP 76, 82. [Land Acquisition Act (1 of 1894), S. 4(1) repealed]

Locality risk. The risk of exposure to a sudden variation in temperature from a low temperature to a high temperature by reason of the workman having to move from a low temperature area to a high temperature area, is a 'locality risk'. *S. Fernandes* v. *B.P. (India) Ltd.,* AIR 1957 Bom 52, 54. [Workmen's Compensation Act (8 of 1923), S. 3]

Location. Position [Plantations Labour Act (69 of 1951), S. 12(3)]; an area or tract of land; a position or site occupied or available for occupancy or marked by some distinguishing feature [Factories Act (63 of 1948), S. 48(3)(a)].

Location Data. Data which provides the geographic position of the mobile phone user. Aparna Viswanathan, *Cyber Law: Indian & International Perspectives,* 2012, LexisNexis Butterworths at p. 236.

Location of the recipient. "location of the recipient of services" means,—

(a) where a supply is received at a place of business for which the registration has been obtained, the location of such place of business;

(b) where a supply is received at a place other than the place of business for which registration has been obtained (a fixed establishment elsewhere), the location of such fixed establishment;

(c) where a supply is received at more than one establishment, whether the place of business or fixed establishment, the location of the establishment most directly concerned with the receipt of the supply; and

(d) in absence of such places, the location of the usual place of residence of the recipient [The Integrated Goods and Services Tax Act, 2017 (13 of 2017), S. 2(14)]

Location of the recipient of services.

"Location of the recipient of services" means,—

(a) where a supply is received at a place of business for which the registration has been obtained, the location of such place of business;

(b) where a supply is received at a place other than the place of business for which registration has been obtained (a fixed establishment elsewhere), the location of such fixed establishment;

(c) where a supply is received at more than one establishment, whether the place of business or fixed establishment, the location of the establishment most directly concerned with the receipt of the supply; and

(d) in absence of such places, the location of the usual place of residence of the recipient [The Central Goods and Services Tax Act, 2017 (12 of 2017), S. 2(70)]

Location of the supplier of services. "Location of the supplier of services" means,—

(a) where a supply is made from a place of business for which the registration has been obtained, the location of such place of business;

(b) where a supply is made from a place other than the place of business for which registration has been obtained (a fixed establishment elsewhere), the location of such fixed establishment;

(c) where a supply is made from more than one establishment, whether the place of business or fixed establishment, the location of the establishment most directly concerned with the provision of the supply; and

(d) in absence of such places, the location of the usual place of residence of the supplier [The Integrated Goods and Services Tax Act, 2017 (13 of 2017), S. 2(15)]; [The Central Goods and Services Tax Act, 2017 (12 of 2017), S. 2(71)]

Lock. A barrier on a river which can be opened and closed at will [Workmen's Compensation Act (8 of 1923), Sch II, item (vii)(b)].

Lock-out. "LOCK-OUT" means the temporary closing of a place of employment or the suspension of work, or the refusal by an employer to continue to employ any number of persons employed by him. [Industrial Disputes Act (14 of 1947), S. 2(l)]

"Lock-out" means the temporary closing of a place of employment, or the suspension of work, or the refusal by an employer to continue to employ any number of persons employed by him. [Industrial Relations Code, 2020 (35 of 2020), section 2(u)]

A lock-out has been defined to be the closing of a factory or workshop by an employer, usually to bring the workmen to satisfactory terms by a suspension of wages.

'Lock out' and **'closure'.** In order to determine whether the employer has imposed lock-out, or closed the establishment, it is not necessary to approach the matter from the angle that the closure has to be irrevocable, final and permanent and that lock out is necessarily temporary or for a period. Closing down an industrial establishment may be on eventualities such as suffering continuous loss, no possibility of revival of business, or inability for various other reasons to continue to industrial activity. [*General Labour Union (Red Flag) Bombay* v. *B.V. Chaman,* AIR 1985 SC 297 : (1985) I LLJ 82 (SC)]

Lock-up. A place for temporary detention of the persons under arrest.

Lockdown. The confinement of prisoners to their cells for a temporary period as a security measure.

Lockout and lay off (Distinction). 'Lock-out' can be described as the antithesis of a 'strike'. Just as a strike is a weapon available to the employees for enforcing their industrial demands, a lock-out is a weapon available to the employer to persuade, by a coercive process, the employees to see his point of view and to accept his demands. The use of both the weapons by the respective parties must, however, be subject to the relevant provisions of the Act. 1952 Lab AC 62 (Lati), **relied on**. Stated broadly, lay-off generally occurs in a continuing business, whereas a lock-out is the closure of the business. In the case of lay-off, owing to the reasons specified in S. 2(kkk), the employer is unable to give employment to one or more workmen. In the case of a lock-out, the employer closes the business and locks out the whole body of workmen for reasons which have no relevance to causes specified in S. 2(kkk). The nature of the two concepts is entirely different and so are their consequences. In the case of a lay-off, the employer may be liable to pay compensation as provided by S. 25(C), (D) and (E) of the Act; but this liability cannot be invoked in the case of lock-out. The liability of the employer in cases of lock-out would depend upon whether the lock out was justified and legal or not; but whatever the liability, the provisions applicable to the payment of layoff compensation cannot be applied to the cases of lock-out. Where the closure of business amounts to a lock-out under S. (2)(1), it does not come within definition of 'lay-off' so as to entitle workers to claim lay-off, compensation. *Kairbetta Estate, Kotagiri P.O.* v. *Raja Manickam,* MLJ : QD (1956-1960) Vol. III C1296 : (1960-61) 18 FJR 241 : AIR 1960 SC 893 : (1960) 2 Lab LJ 275 : (1960) 3 SCR 371 : (1961) 1 SCJ 103. [Industrial Disputes Act (14 of 1947), Ss. 2(kkk), 25(C), (D) and (E)]

Loco parentis. By the expression a person '*in loco parentis*' is meant a person who puts himself in the situation of a lawful father of the child, with reference to the father's office and duty of making provision for the child.

Locomotor disability. Means disability of the bones, joints or muscles leading to substantial restriction of the movement of the limbs or any form of cerebral palsy. [Persons with Disabilities (Equal Opportunities, Protection of Rights and Full Participation) Act, 1995 (repealed)(1 of 1996), S. 2(o)]

"LOCOMOTOR DISABILITY" means a person's inability to execute distinctive activities associated with moving, both himself and objects, from place to place, and such inability resulting from affliction of either bones, joints, muscles or nerves. [Rehabilitation Council of India Act (34 of 1992), S. 2(1)(e)]

Locus delicti. The place where an offence takes place.

Locus in quo. The place in which the cause of action arose, or where anything is alleged, in pleadings, to have been done. (*Black*)

Locus regit actum. (*Lat.*) The act is governed by the law of the place where it is done.

Locus standi. A place of standing, a right of appearance in a Court of justice.

A person must have a sufficiency of interest to sustain his standing to sue.

The right or capacity to bring an action or to appear in a court. [Concise Oxford English Dictionary as cited in *Amanullah* v. *State of Bihar*, (2016) 6 SCC 699, para 19].

"Locus standi" is a Latin term, the general meaning of which is "place of standing." [*Amanullah* v. *State of Bihar*, (2012) 6 SCC 699, para 19].

The person who is aggrieved or affected has the standing before the court that is to say he only has a right to move the court for seeking justice. [*Amanullah* v. *State of Bihar*, (2016) 6 SCC 699, para 19].

LOCUS STANDI signifies a right to bring an action and to be heard.

Lodging-house. Means a building or part of a building which is let in lodgings or occupied to any extent in common by members of more than one family. [Bur. Act 3 of 1898 (Municipalities), S. 2, cl. (6).]

"LODGING HOUSE" means a house in which visitors or other persons are lodged on hire for a night or more. [Manipur Municipalities Act (43 of 1994), S. 2(31)]

Logging. The action of hewing timber into logs. [Workmen's Compensation Act (8 of 1923), Sch II, item (xxiii)].

Logical interpretation. Interpretation of a document in accordance with formal and, apparently, logical, criteria of reasoning.

Lok Adalat. Camp Courts, initiated in 1980 by Mr. P.N. Bhagwati, the then C.J., held in various parts of the country with their main characteristics such as deciding cases on the basis of agreement between the parties, no legal counsels allowed, and covering mainly the areas of marriage, family and social disputes and disputes relating to rent, eviction, challans of vehicles and insurance *etc.*

The word '*Lok adalat*' means people's Court. It is one of the components of Alternative Dispute Resolution System based on Gandhian principles. The object behind *Lok Adalats* is to provide alternative resolution or devise for expeditious and inexpensive justice. [*P.T. Thomas* v. *Thomas Job*, AIR 2005 SC 3575 : (2005) 6 SCC 478]

Lok Sabha. House of the People (Lower House of Indian Parliament).

Lok Sabha Secretariat. Means and includes the Lok Sabha Secretariat at Delhi and any camp office set up outside Delhi for the time being for, or under the authority of, the speaker. [Rules of Procedure and Conduct of Business in Lok Sabha Edn., 7, R. 2(1)]

Lokpal. Means the body established under section 3 of Act 1 of 2014. [S. 2(1)(i) of the Lokpal & Lokayuktas Act, 2013 (1 of 2014)]

Long Distance Charging Area (LDCA). Means one of the several areas, into which the country is divided and declared as such for the purpose of charging for trunk calls. [Flight and Maritime Connectivity Rules, 2018, R. 2(1)(j)].

Long-term appointment. Means appointment for an indefinite period as distinguished from a purely temporary, or ad hoc appointment like appointment against leave or other local vacancies or unfilled direct recruitment quota vacancies of a duration not exceeding one year. [*Armed Forces Headquarters Civil Service Rules,* 2018, R. 2(i)]

Long film. Is a film with a length exceeding 2000 metres in 35 mm or corresponding length in other gauges or on video. [Cinematograph (Certification) Rules, 1983, R. 2(xi)]

Long range transboundary air pollution. Means air pollution whose physical origin is situated wholly or in part within the area under the national jurisdiction of one state and which has adverse effects in the area under the jurisdiction of another state at such a distance that it is not generally possible to distinguish the contribution of individual emission sources or group of sources. [Convention on Long Range Transboundary Air Pollution (1979), Art. I(b)]

Long-term borrowings. Means—

(i) any moneys borrowed by the company from Government or the Industrial Finance Corporation of India or the Industrial Credit and Investment Corporation of India or any other financial institution which is eligible for deduction under clause (*viii*) of subsection (1) of Section 36 or any banking institution (not being a financial institution referred to above), or

(ii) any moneys borrowed or debt incurred by it in a foreign country in respect of the purchase outside India of capital plant and machinery, where the terms under which such moneys are borrowed or the debt is incurred provide for the repayment thereof during a period of not less than seven years. [Income-tax Act (43 of 1961), S. 35D, *Expln.* (c)]

Long-term business. Insurance business that includes ordinary and industrial life assurance annuities and pensions.

Long-term capital asset. Means a capital asset which is not a short-term capital asset. [Income tax Act (43 of 1961), S. 2(29A)]

Long-term capital gain. Means capital gain arising from the transfer of a long-term capital asset. [Income tax Act (43 of 1961), S. 2(29B)]

In this Chapter, unless the context otherwise requires,—

"LONG-TERM CAPITAL GAINS" means income chargeable under the head "Capital gains" relating to a capital asset, being a foreign exchange asset which is not a short-term capital asset. [Income-tax Act (43 of 1961), S. 115 C(d)]

Long-term finance. Means any loan or advance where the terms under which moneys are loaned or advanced provide for repayment along with interest thereof during a period of not less than five years. [Income- tax Act (43 of 1961), S. 11(5)(ixa), *Expln.* (a)]

Long-term specified asset. Means any bond redeemable after three years issued, on or after the 1st day of April, 2000, by the National Bank for Agriculture and Rural Development established under Section 3 of the National Bank for Agriculture and Rural Development Act, 1981 or by the National Highways Authority of India constituted under Section 3 of the National Highways Authority of India Act, 1988. [Income Tax Act (43 of 1961, S. 54 EC, *Expln.* (b)]

Loophole. An ambiguity, omission or exception especially in statutes and documents which helps to avoid a rule without violating its literal sense. In taxation, a provision in the tax code by which a taxpayer may legally avoid or reduce his income taxes.

Loose sheets of account papers. Loose sheets of account papers have not the probative force of a book of account regularly kept. *Ganesh Prasad* v. *Narendra Nath*, AIR 1953 SC 431, 432. [Indian Evidence Act (1 of 1872), Ss. 34 and 90]

Lose. Be deprived of; cease to have; casually and involuntarily to part with the possession, so that the mind has no impress of, and can have no recourse to, the event.

"Losing wrongfully" defined. Act 45, 1860, section 23.

A person is said to lose wrongfully when such person is kept out of any property, as well as when such person is wrongfully deprived of property. [IPC (45 of 1860), section 23] [Now (w. e. f. 1-7-2024) repealed & replaced by Bharatiya Nayaya Sanhita, 2023 (45 of 2023), S. 2(38), same definition in new Sanhita]

To miss from one's possession. [TP Act (4 of 1882), S. 31, ill. (a)].

Loss. In its most general sense the word 'loss' means any deprivation. In some instances it may mean that which can never be recovered, and in others that of which a party is dispossessed.

"Loss" means—

(i) a loss in property or interruption in supply of services, whether temporary or permanent; or

(ii) a loss of opportunity to earn remuneration or greater remuneration or to gain a financial advantage otherwise than by way of legitimate remuneration. [Digital Personal Data Protection Act, 2023 (22 of 2023), S. 2(p)]

The act or fact of losing; the harm or privation resulting from losing; the thing lost; an amount by which the cost exceeds the selling price; opposed to profit. [TP Act (4 of 1882), S. 72(e)].

LOSS, DAMAGE, DETRIMENT. Whatever is gone from us which we wish to retain is a *loss*; hence we may sustain a loss in our property, in our reputation, in our influence, in our intellect, and every other object of possession : whatever renders an object less serviceable or valuable, by any external violence, is a *damage*, as a vessel suffers a damage in a storm : whatever is calculated to cross a man's purpose is a *detriment*; the bare want of a good name may be a *detriment* to a young tradesman.

The word "loss" in S. 75 of the Indian Railways Act (9 of 1890) includes loss caused by theft or wilful neglect of the servants of the railway administration.

There is no warrant for giving a restricted interpretation to the word 'loss' in S. 77. Loss would include loss to the owner on account of non-delivery or misdelivery as well, Loss may be occasioned by non- delivery on account of the tortuous conduct of the Railway or its servants or by the conversion of the goods or by the goods being lost in transit. *Darjeeling Himalayan Railway Co. Ltd.* v. *Jetmull Bhojraj,* AIR 1958 Cal 390, 393. [Indian Railways Act (9 ot 1890), S. 77]

Loss asset. 'LOSS ASSET' means—

(a) an asset which has been identified as loss asset by the NBFC or its internal or external auditor or by the RBI during the inspection of the NBFC, to the extent it is not written off by the NBFC; and

(b) an asset which is adversely affected by a potential threat of non-recoverability due to either erosion in the value of security or non-availability of security or due to any fraudulent act or omission on the part of the borrower. [Non- Banking Financial Companies Prudential Norms (Reserve Bank) Directions, 1998, Para 2(1)(viii)]

"LOSS ASSET" means a borrowal account which has remained a non-performing asset for more than three years or where in the opinion of the Board, a shortfall in the recovery of the loan account is expected because the documents executed may become invalid if subjected to legal process or for any other reason.

[R. 3(1)(c) of the Nidhi Rules, 2014]

Loss leader. Product or service offered for sale at a substantial loss in order to attract customers.

Loss of amenity. Loss or reduction of a claimant's mental or physical capacity to do the things he used to do, suffered as a result of personal injuries.

Loss of consortium. Loss of society, affection, assistance and conjugal fellowship and includes loss or impairment of sexual relations.

Loss or damage. The expression 'loss or damage' includes any loss or damage caused to shipper or consignee in respect of which he makes a grievance and claims compensation from the shipping company. *Goverdhandas* v. *New Dholera Steamship Ltd.,* AIR 1965 Ker 51, 55.

The word 'loss' is intended to mean and includes every kind of loss to the owner of the goods whether it is the whole of the consignment which is not delivered or part of the consignment which is not delivered. *American Export Isbrandstan Liues Ine* v. *Joc Lopez*, AIR 1972 SC 1405, 1407.

Loss reserve. The amount set up as the estimated cost of a claim.

Lost property. A property which is no longer in the possession of the owner due to accident, negligence, or carelessness and which cannot be located by an ordinary diligent search.

Lot. That which causes, falls, or happens; chance; fortune; hazard; anything used in determining a question by chance, or without a man's choice or will; a share.

An object used as one of the counters in determining a question by chance; the unit offered at one time (for sale *etc.*). [Indian Trusts Act (2 of 1882), S. 37].

Lottery. "LOTTERY" includes winnings from prizes awarded to any person by draw of lots or by chance or in any other manner whatsoever, under any scheme or arrangement by whatever name called. [Income-tax Act (43 of 1961), S. 2(24)(ix) *Expl.* (i)]

"LOTTERY" means a scheme, in whatever form and by whatever name called, for distribution of prizes by lot or chance to those persons participating in the chances of a prize by purchasing tickets. [Lotteries (Regulation) Act (17 of 1998), S. 2(b)]

Scheme for the disposal or distribution of property by chance. The term "lottery" has not technical meaning in the law distinct from its popular signification. A lottery is a scheme for the distribution of prizes by chance.

A game of chance or a distribution of money or prize by chance without the application of choice or skill. [IPC (45 of 1860), S. 294A].

Loudspeaker. "LOUD SPEAKER" or "SOUND AMPLIFIER" means an instrument whereby soft sounds whether vocal, instrumental or recorded are augmented. [Rajasthan Noises Control Act (12 of 1963), S. 2(i)]

A device for amplifying sound [Representation of the People Act (43 of 1951), S. 131(1)(a)]; [Unlawful Activities (Prevention) Act (37 of 1967), S. 3(4)(c)].

Low Power FM Radio (LPFM). A broadcast service that permits the licensing of 50-100 watt FM radio stations within a service radius of up to 3.5 miles and 1-10 watt FM radio stations within a service radius of 1 to 2 miles. (*Telecommunication*)

Low Power Television (LPTV). A broadcast service that permits program origination, subscription service or both via low powered television translators. LPTV service includes the existing translator service and operates on a secondary basis to regular television stations. Transmitter output is limited to 1,000 watts for normal VHF stations and 100 watts when a VHF operation is on an allocated channel. (*Telecommunication*)

Low-sensitive. Applies to information that, if compromised, could reasonably be expected to cause injury outside the national interest, for example, disclosure of an exact salary figure. (*Information Technology*)

Low water. A term only predicable of those parts of rivers within the ebb and flow of tides, to distinguish the water line at spring or neap tides.

Low water mark. "LAW-WATER MARK" means the lowest point reached by ordinary ebb springtides at any season of the year. Bur. Act IV of 1905 (Burma Port), S. 4, Cl. 5; Bom Act VI of 1886, S. 2.

LAW-WATER MARK in relation to a port, means a line drawn through the lowest points reached by ordinary, springtides at any season of the year at that port. [Major Port Trusts Act (38 of 1963), S. 2(l)]

The "low-water mark" of a fresh-water river is the point to which the river recedes at its lowest stage.

Lower Court. A trial Court or intermediate appellate Court from which an appeal lies; district Courts; subordinate Courts.

Lower grade employee. Means daftry, peon, bhisti, mali, lamp-lighter, chowkidar, mazdoor of safaiwala or any other employee declared by Central Government to be a lower grade employee for the purposes of this Act. [Cantonments Act (2 of 1924), S. 2(xixa)]

Lowest grade. Lowest degree of quality or value. [CPC (5 of 1908), S. 15].

Loyalty. Faithfulness to the existing government; being true to allegiance; being devoted to the legitimate sovereign.

LRIC. (*abbr.*) (Prospective) Long Run Incremental Cost. The cost borne by a provider to cope with the increase in production due to interconnection. The increase in means of production (network capacity) is possible only in the long term. The cost factors which enter into the composition of the model are for the most part valued at their current value and efficiency (Forward Looking) rather than their historical value and efficiency. The aim of this approach is to base the interconnection price as realistically as possible on the costs attributable to it. (*Telecommunication*)

Lucid interval. "Lucid interval" doe not mean a perfect restoration to reason, but a restoration so far as to be able beyond doubt to comprehend and do an act with such reason, memory and judgment as to make it legal.

The term "*lucid interval*" means not an apparent tranquility or seeming repose, not a simple diminution or remission of the disease, but a temporary cure; an intermission so clearly marked that it perfectly resembles a return of health and must be continued for a length of time sufficient to give certainty to the temporary restoration of reason.

An interval of reason enjoyed by an insane person, or lunatic; as used in speaking of lucid intervals of insane persons, not merely a cessation of the violent symptoms of the disorder, but a restoration of the faculties of the mind sufficiently to enable the party soundly to judge of the act.

Lugano Convention. An international convention on jurisdiction and the enforcement of judgments in civil and commercial matters opened for signature at lugano on 16th September 1988.

It has been brought into force by the Civil jurisdiction and Judgments Act 1991.

Lump sum. "LUMP SUM", in regard to royalties or copyright fees, includes an advance payment on account of such royalties or copyright fees which is not returnable. [Income-tax Act (43 of 1961), S. 80 QQB, *Expln.* (d)]

"LUMP SUM" includes an advance payment on account of such royalties which is not returnable. [Income-tax Act (43 of 1961), S. 80RRB, *Expln.* (b)]

Lump-sum alimony. Alimony which is in the form of a single and definite sum not subject to modification.

Lump sum rate. Means the rate mutually agreed upon between a railway administration and a consignor for the carriage of goods and for any service in relation to such carriage. [Railway Act (24 of 1989), S. 2(24)]

Lunacy. Unsoundness of mind [CrPC (2 of 1974), S. 335(2)].

Lunatic. Affected with lunacy or of unsound mind. [Indian Evidence Act (1 of 1872), S. 118, *Expln.*]; [CPC (5 of 1908), O. XXXII, R. 16].

"LUNATIC" shall mean any person who shall have been found by due course of law to be of unsound mind and incapable of managing his affairs. [Act XXVII of 1866 (Trustees), S. 2]

"A Lunatic is one who hath had understanding but, by disease, grief or other accident, hath lost the use of his reason. He is, indeed properly one that hath lucid intervals, sometimes enjoying his senses and sometimes not; and that, frequently depending upon the change of the Moon." (*Jacob.*)

"Lunatic" means an idiot or person of unsound mind. [Indian Lunacy Act (4 of 1912) (*repealed*), S. (3) 5].

Lunatic means a person suffering from unsoundeness of mind or insanity which may be either intermittent or permanent. *Kartrix Chandra Banerjee* v. *Manjurani Banerjee,* AIR 1973 Cal 545, 548. [Hindu Marriage Act (25 of 1955), S. 13 (iii)]

Lunatic asylum. A place where lunatics are kept and treated. [CrPC 1973 (2 of 1974), S. 335(2)].

Lurking house-trespass. Whoever commits house-trespass, having taken precautions to conceal such house-trespass from some person who has a right to exclude or eject the trespasser from the building, tent, or vessel which is the subject of the trespass, is said to commit "lurking house-trespass". [IPC (45 of 1860), S. 443] [(w. e. f. 1-7-2024) repealed and replaced by Bharatiya Nyaya Sanhita, 2023 (45 of 2023), S. 330(1)]

Lurking house trespass means that the accused took some active means to conceal their presence. The accused would take some steps to escape notice. *Nasiruddin* v. *State of Assam*, AIR 1971 SC 1254, 1255. [IPC (45 of 1860), S. 457]

Lurking house-trespass by night. Whoever commits lurking house-trespass after sunset and before sunrise, is said to commit "lurking house-trespass by night". [IPC (45 of 1860), S. 444]] [(w. e. f. 1-7-2024) repealed and replaced by Bharatiya Nyaya Sanhita, 2023 (45 of 2023), S. 331]

Lust. Sexual desire especially of a violent self-indulgent character. [fourthly, IPC (45 of 1860), S. 100].

Lustful. Lascivious.

Luxury. The connotation of the word "luxury" is something which conduces enjoyment over and above the necessaries of life. It denotes something which is superfluous and not indispensable and to which we take with a view to enjoy, amuse or entertain ourselves. *A.B. Abdul Kadir* v. *State of Kerala*, AIR 1976 SC 182, 190 [Constitution of India, Sch. 7, List II, Entry 62].

Things in which there is element of extravagance or indulgence, are also 'luxuries' and they do not confine to goods and articles alone. There can be the element of extravagance or indulgence in the quality of services and activities. *Express Hotels (P) Ltd.* v. *State of Gujarat*, AIR 1989 SC 1949, 1957.

Luxury provided in hotel. 'LUXURY PROVIDED IN HOTEL' means,—

(i) accommodation for lodging provided in hotel, the rate of charges for which (including charges for air-conditioning, telephone, television, radio, music, extra beds and other amenities; for which charges are compulsorily payable, but excluding charges for food and drinks) is not less than one hundred and fifty rupees per room per day.

(ii) provision in hotels, whether to resident or others of such facility as health club, beauty parlour, swimming pools, conference hall and the like for which charges are separately made. [Karnataka Tax on Luxuries Act (22 of 1979), S. 2(5)]

Lying in wait. Waiting and watching in ambush with intent to kill. In criminal law, hiding in ambush or concealment; being in ambush for the purpose of injuring or murdering another. (*Bouvier L. Dict.*)

Lying by. Neglecting to assert rights, or allowing persons to deal with land or other property as if one had no interest in it.

Lysimeter. Is a device used to measure rate of movement of water through or from a soil layer or is used to collect percolated water for quality analysis. [Rule 3(xiii), Municipal Solid Wastes (Management and Handling) Rules 2000]

M

Machine. "MACHINE" includes prime movers, transmission machinery and all other appliances whereby power is generated, transferred, transmitted or applied to a dangerous machine. [Dangerous Machines (Regulation) Act (35 of 1983), S. 3(i)]

Appliance and apparatus for applying mechanical power consisting of a number of parts each having a definite function. [Indian Contract Act (9 of 1872), S. 73, ill. (i)]; [Indian Evidence Act (1 of 1872), S. 63, ill. (b)].

Machinery. "MACHINERY" includes prime movers, transmission machinery and all other appliances whereby power is generated, transformed, transmitted or applied. [Factories Act (63 of 1948), S. 2 (j)]

"Machinery" means any article or combination of articles assembled, arranged or connected and which is used or intended to be used for converting any form of energy to perform work, or which is used or intended to be used, whether incidental thereto or not, for developing, receiving, storing, containing, confining, transforming, transmitting, transferring or controlling any form of energy. [Occupational Safety, Healthy & Working Conditions Code, 2020 (37 of 2020), section 2(1)(zg)]

Machines or their parts taken collectively. [T.P. Act (4 of 1882), S. 8 and Companies Act (1 of 1956), S. 383]; the system of instrumentalities and organised activities by means of which an organisation functions or a social or other process is carried on.

'MACHINERY', implies the application of mechanical means to the attainment of some particular end by the help of natural forces.

For ascertaining the meaning of the expression 'machinery' what appears to be essential is that there must be some mechanical contrivances which by themselves or the combination with one or more other mechanical contrivances, by the combined movement and interdependent operation of their respective parts generate power or evoke, modify, apply or direct natural forces. *India Leaf Spring Mfg. Co. (P.) Ltd.* v. *C.I.T.,* (1989) 175 ITR 639, 643 (AP). [Income Tax Act (43 of 1961), S. 32]

The word 'machinery' when used in ordinary language *prima facie* means some mechanical continuances which, by themselves or in combination with one or more, other mechanical continuances, by the combined movement and inter-dependent operation of their respective parts, generate power, or evoke, modify, apply or direct natural forces with the object in each case of effecting so definite and specific a result. *CIT* v. *Mir Mohammad Ali*, AIR 1964 SC 1693, 1696.

Made. The word 'made' in this rule might refer to the proclamation of sale as well as the announcement of the sale, as it says that it shall be made and published in the manner provided by the Rule 54(2). The word 'made' cannot be taken to include the preparation of proclamation of sale. *Seshatiri Aiyar* v. *Valambal Ammal,* AIR 1952 Mad 377, 381. [CPC, (5 of 1908), O. XXI, R. 54]

Made over or assign. Where the words "made over" or the word "assign" are used, the intention of parties has to be looked into and that is whether the parties wanted to have an endorsement of the promissory note and not an assignment. If an endorsement contains words equivalent to a direction to pay though there may not be the actual words connoting the direction it would amount to a direction to pay within the meaning of Section 16. *P.K. Murugan* v. *Vallabhan Kantan,* AIR 1955 Mad 53, 56. [Negotiable Instruments Act (26 of 1881), S. 16]

Mafi. Remitted; free : applied to lands exempt from the payment of revenue. An assignment of land revenue—the smaller grants and those not made to ex-rulers, or men of much local influence, or on account of distinguished political or military services are usually called *m'afis*.

Magazine. A receptacle in which anything is stored; a storehouse; a warehouse.

A supply chamber; a military store for explosives. [Navy Act (62 of 1957), S. 59]; a periodical that usually contains a miscellaneous collection of articles, stories, poems and pictures and is directed at the general reading public.

Magic. The use of means that are believed to have supernatural power, to cause a supernatural being to produce or prevent a particular result; the art of producing surprising phenomena resembling the result of magic. [Indian Contract Act (9 of 1872), S. 56, ill.(a)].

Magic remedy. Includes a talisman, mantra, Kavacha and any other charm of any kind which is alleged to possess miraculous powers for or in the diagnosis, cure, mitigation, treatment or prevention of any disease in human beings or animals or for affecting or influencing in any way the structure or any organic function of the body of human beings or animals. [Drugs and Magic Remedies Act (21 of 1954), S. 2(c)]

Magis de bono quam de malo lex intendit. (*Maxim*) The law favours a good rather than a bad construction.

Magisterial. Pertaining or suitable to a magistrate; of the rank of a magistrate; authoritative; proud; dignified.

Magisterial functions. The functions of a magistrate.

Magistrate. "MAGISTRATE" shall include every person exercising all or any of the powers of a Magistrate under the Code of Criminal Procedure for the time being in force. [General Clauses Act (10 of 1897), S. 3(32)]

In this Code,—

(a) any reference, without any qualifying words, to a magistrate, shall be construed, unless the Context otherwise requires,—

(i) in relation to an area outside a metropolitan area, as a reference to a Judicial Magistrate;

(ii) in relation to a metropolitan area, as reference to a Metropolitan Magistrate. [CrPC 1973 (2 of 1974), S. 3(1)(a)]

Unless the context otherwise requires, any reference in any law, to a MAGISTRATE without any qualifying words, MAGISTRATE of the first class or a MAGISTRATE of the second class shall, in relation to any area, be construed as a reference to a Judicial Magistrate of the first class or Judicial Magistrate of the second class, as the case may be, exercising jurisdiction in such area. [(w. e. f. 1-7-2024) Bharatiya Nagarik Suraksha Sanhita, 2023 (46 of 2023), section 3(1)]

"Magistrate" means a Judicial Magistrate of the first class exercising jurisdiction under the Code of Criminal Procedure, 1973 (2 of 1974), in the area where the married Muslim woman resides. [Muslim Women (Protection of Rights on Marriage) Act, 2019 (20 of 2019), section 2(b)]

"Magistrate" means,—

(i) in relation to a metropolitan area, the Metropolitan Magistrate;

(ii) in relation to any other area, the Judicial Magistrate of the first class; or

(iii) in relation to ordering someone to give security for his good behaviour or maintaining peace, the Executive Magistrate. [Criminal Procedure (Identification) Act, 2022 (11 of 2022), section 2(1)(a)]

A public officer, invested with some part of the executive or judicial power of the state. He exercises criminal jurisdiction.

A civil officer charged with the administration of the laws and having criminal jurisdiction of the first instance; a public officer invested with judicial powers in criminal jurisdiction. [General Clauses Act (10 of 1897), S. 3(32) and Constitution of India, Art. 22(2)].

"MAGISTRATE" means the Judicial Magistrate of the first class, or as the case may be, the Metropolitan Magistrate, exercising jurisdiction under the Code of Criminal Procedure, 1973 (2 of 1974), in the area where the aggrieved person resides temporarily or otherwise or the respondent resides or the domestic violence is alleged to have taken place. [S. 2(i) of the Protection of Women from Domestic Violence Act, 2005 (43 of 2005)]

Magistrate having jurisdiction in the case. The expression 'a Magistrate having jurisdiction in the case' in S. 60, Criminal Procedure Code (5 of 1898), clearly means the Magistrate having jurisdiction to try the case. There is no distinction between 'a Magistrate having jurisdiction in the case' and 'a Magistrate having jurisdiction to try the case'. The section only refers to the power of the police to grant bail. *Gulam Mohd. Azimuddin* v. *State*, MLJ : QD (1956-1960) Vol. II C1220 : 1959 MPC 128 : 1959 CrLJ 600 : 1959 MPLJ 322 : 1959 Jab LJ 227 : AIR 1959 MP 147.

Magistrate may take cognizance of any cognizable offence. The words 'the Magistrate may take cognizance of any cognizable offence' in Section 190(1)(b) of the CrPC 1973 (2 of 1974) have been construed to mean "must take cognizance" leaving no discretion to the Magistrate. *Shri A.C. Agarwal, Sub-Divl. Magistrate, Delhi* v. *Ram Kali*, AIR 1968 SC 1, p. 5.

Magistrate of the district. The words "MAGISTRATE OF THE DISTRICT" shall mean the chief officer charged with the executive administration of a district and exercising the powers of a Magistrate, by whatever designation the chief officer charged with such executive administration is styled. [Police Act (5 of 1861), S. 1]

A judge of an inferior Court with limited jurisdiction in criminal and sometimes in civil matters.

Magistrates in session. Magistrates sitting for the trial and disposal of a case.

Magna Carta (Magna Charta). Is the Charter of Liberties granted in the ninth year of King Henry III. It is called, either for the excellency of the laws therein contained, or because there was another Charter called the Charter of the Forest, established with it, which was the less of the two; or in regard of the great troubles in obtaining it, and the remarkable solemnity in denouncing excommunication and anathemas against the brakers thereof. (*Tomlin*)

The name usually given to the charter originally granted by King John, and afterwards re-enacted and confirmed by Parliament (more than thirty times. The Charter now in force is the statute 9 Hen. III. It contained provisions to protect the subjects from the abuse of royal prerogative in the matter of arbitrary arrest and imprisonment, and from amercements, purveyance and other extortions. (*Ame Cyc.*)

The circumstances leading up to the acceptance of the terms of the barons, and the promulgation of these in Magna Carta belong to the region of the history of constitutional law. The statute was originally promulgated in 1215, was re-issued in 1216 and 1217, and in the shape which it finally took, in 1225. Since that date, it has been confirmed thirty four times, the last monarch who thus expressly recognised it being Henry VI.

Magna culpa dolus est. (*Maxim*) Great neglect is equivalent to fraud. (*Cyclopedic; Ame Cyc.*)

Magna est dilictum seipsum interficere quam alium. It is as great a crime to kill one's self as to kill another.

Magna negligentia culpa est, magna culpa dolus est. Gross negligence is a fault, gross fault is a fraud.

Magnetic storage device. Includes wax blanks, discs or blanks, strips or films for the purpose of original sound recording. [Finance Act (32 of 1994), S. 65(1)(63) now repealed by Goods and Services Tax Act, 2017]

Magna est veritas, et praevalebit. Truth is great, and shall prevail.

Mahant. The head of a religious establishment of the medicant order of the Hindus. (*Wil Gloss.* 317)

Mahomedan Law. The expression rules of Mahomedan Law is not the same as 'the laws of the koran.' [8 Pat 690 : 115 IC 546 : 1929 Pat 81 (FB)]

Mahr. A marriage settlement of property on the wife; it is a necessary concomitant of a contract of marriage among Mahomedans; a marriage portion or gift settled on a wife before marriage. Dower.

MAHR is dower or marriage-gift among Mahomedans settled upon a wife before marriage : it may be either *Muajil*, prompt, immediate; or *muwajil*, deferred to some specified time. If no amount of dower is agreed upon at the time of marriage, the wife is entitled to a customary provision, *Mahr-i-misl*, or one suited to her condition. The written contract of dower or marriage settlement. (*Wil Gloss.* 320)

Maiden speech. First speech.

M.P's first speech in Parliament. By courtesy he is not interrupted and it is customary to give precedence to him and for the following member to compliment him. (*Constitutional and Parliamentary Term*)

Mail. The term 'mail' means a bag, valise, or portmanteau used in the conveyance of letters, papers, and packages by any person acting under the authority of the Post Master General from one post office to another. Each bag so used is a 'mail' of which there may be several in the same vehicle as the "way mail", the "general mail", the "letter mail", or the "newspaper mail".

Mail agent. A type of intelligent agent that performs many activities related to an e-mail program, such as generating autoresponse messages and selectively forwarding incoming messages. (*Cyber Law*)

Mail and wire fraud statutes. These statutes make it a crime to use the mails, interstate, or foreign communications to fraudulently obtain money or property. (*Cyber Law*)

Mail bag. The expression "MAIL BAG" includes a bag, box, parcel or any other envelope or covering in which postal articles in course of transmission by post are conveyed, whether it does or does not contain any such article. [Indian Post Office Act (6 of 1898), S. 2(c)].

Mail bomb/mailbomb. Unlike logic bomb (a thing), mail bomb is a verb used to connote deliberately deluging a target system or host with e-mail messages for purposes of harassment, degradation of service, or even denial of service. (*Cyber Law*)

Mail cover. Transactional information on the outside of a mailing envelope or in headers of an e-mail message. (*Cyber Law*)

Mail gateway. A system which translates e-mail between different systems, for example, between Internet mail and your own Microsoft office mail. (*Cyber Law*)

Mail server. A type of server configured to allow users to send, receive, and store e- mails. (*Cyber Law*)

Mail ship. The expression "MAIL SHIP" means a ship employed for carrying mails, pursuant to contract or continuing arrangement, by the Central Government or Her Majesty's Government or the Government of any British possession or foreign country. [Indian Post Office Act (6 of 1898), S. 2(d)]

Mail storm/mailstorm. What the target system or users see when being mail bombed. Any large amount of incoming e-mail sufficient to disrupt or bog down normal local operations. What often happens when a machine with an Internet connection and active users reconnects after extended downtime—a flood of incoming mail that brings the machine to its knees. (*Cyber Law*)

Mailing list compilation and mailing. "MAILING LIST COMPILATION AND MAILING" means any service in relation to—

(i) compiling and providing list of name, address and any other information from any source; or

(ii) sending document, information, goods or any other material in a packet, by whatever name called, by addressing, stuffing, sealing, metering or mailing,

for, or on behalf of, the client. [Finance Act (32 of 1994), S. 65(63a) *as inserted by Finance Act (18 of 2005), S. 88(a)(xiii)* now repealed by Goods and Services Tax Act, 2017]

Maim. To inflict some permanent injury; to cripple; to multilate. To maim is to wilfully and maliciously cut off or otherwise deprive a person of a hand, arm, finger, toe, foot, leg, nose, or ear, to put out an eye, or in any way to deprive the person of any other member of his body.

Main. "MAIN" means any electric supply-line through which electricity is, or is intended to be, supplied. [Electricity Act (36 of 2003), S. 2(42)]

"MAIN" means a pipe laid by Authority for the purpose of giving a general supply of water as distinct from a supply of an individual consumer, and includes any apparatus used in connection with such a pipe. [Kerala Water and Sewerage Act (14 of 1986), S. 2(xiii)]

Main residential house. The term 'main residential house' does not mean the entire building as an integral whole but means only that part of it which is in the occupation of the person himself. *UDF Bhan* v. *Kapoor Chand,* AIR 1967 Punj 52, 56 (FB). [CPC (5 of 1908), S. 60(1), (*ccc*) (State amendments, Punjab & Haryana)].

Main transmission lines. Means all high pressure cables and overhead lines (not being an essential part of the distribution system of licence) transmitting electricity from a generating station to another generating station or to a sub-station, together with any step-up and step-down transformers, switch-gear and other works necessary to and used for the control of such cables or overhead line, and such buildings or part thereof as may be required to accommodate such transformers, switch-gear and other works and the operating staff thereof. [Electricity (Supply) Act (54 of 1948), S. (5)(b)]

Maintain. To keep in a state, repair and do other acts to prevent a decline from existing state or condition; to keep in existence; to sustain against opposition or danger; to bring action; to keep; to provide for; to bear the expenses of [Constitution of India, Art. 26 (a)]; to supply necessaries such as food, lodging, clothing *etc.* or money in lieu there- of to persons in a position of dependence; to uphold in argument; assert or affirm.

"MAINTAIN", with its grammatical variations and cognate expressions, does not, when used in relation to a house or other construction, include the doing of any act necessary for keeping such house or construction, until the making of the award referred to in Section 12 or until the exercise, prior to the making of the award, of the powers of demolition conferred, in case of emergency, by Section 6, sub-sections (1) and (3), in the state in which it was at the time of the publication of the notice referred to in Section 3, sub-section (2). [Works of Defence Act (7 of 1903), S. 2(h)]

"MAINTAIN" with its grammatical variations and cognate expressions, includes the fencing, covering in, repairing, restoring and cleansing of a protected monument, and the doing of any act which may be necessary for the purpose of preserving a protected monument or of securing convenient access thereto. [Ancient Monuments and Archeological Sites and Remains Act (24 of 1958), S. 2(f)]

Maintainable. Capable or fit to be maintained. [CPC (5 of 1908), O. VIII, R. 2].

Maintainable profits. The "maintainable profits" would be a certain percentage (say 80%) of the net profits of the company, after deduction of taxes payable by it and this would be a measure of potential yield per share. *Commissioner of Wealth Tax* v. *Mahadeo Jalan and Mahabir Prasad Jalan,* AIR 1973 SC 1023.

Maintenance. MAINTENANCE includes—

(i) in all cases, provision for food, clothing, residence, education and medical attendance and treatment;

(ii) in the case of an unmarried daughter, also the reasonable expenses of an incident to her marriage. [Hindu Adoptions and Maintenance Act (78 of 1956), S. 3 (b)]

"MAINTENANCE" include(s) the fencing, covering in, repairing, restoring and cleansing of a protected monument, and the doing of any act which may be necessary for the purpose of maintaining a protected monument or of securing convenient access thereto. [Ancient Monuments Preservation Act (7 of 1904), S. 2(4)]

"MAINTENANCE,"—

(i) in relation to official residence, include the provision of electricity, gas and water,

(ii) in relation to motor vehicle, includes the pay and allowances of chauffeurs and the provision of oil and petrol or other fuel. [Governors (Emoluments, Allowances & Privileges) Act (43 of 1982), S. 2(b)]

'MAINTENANCE' means execution of such works on the irrigation system as are necessary to ensure that the physical system designed to the standards operates for proper distribution of water to the landholders in the area of operation. [Andhra Pradesh Farmers Management of Irrigation Systems Act (AP Act 11 of 1997), S. 2(r)]

On a petition for divorce, nullity of marriage or judicial separation, the Court may make an order for maintenance pending suit, that is to say, an order requiring either party to the marriage to make to the other such periodical payments for his or her maintenance and for such term, being a term beginning not earlier that the date of the presentation of the petition and ending with the date of the determination of the suit, as the Court thinks reasonable An application for such an order may be made, in accordance with rules of Court, by a petitioner or by a respondent. HALSBURY, 4th Edn., Vol. 13, para 791, pp. 376-377.

Maintenance, necessarily must encompass a provision for residence. Maintenance is given so that the lady can live in the manner, more or less, to which she was accustomed. The concept of maintenance must, therefore, include provision for food and clothing and the like and take into account the basic need of a roof over the head. *Mangat Mal* v. *Punni Devi,* (1995) 6 SCC 88. [Hindu Succession Act (30 of 1956), S. 14(1)]

Officious interference in another's suit; a legal term signifying the interference in a suit by some one having no direct interest in it.

MAINTENANCE also means of subsistence, supply of necessaries and conveniences; aid, support, assistance; the support which one person who is bound by law to do so, gives to another for his living. (*Bouvier*)

'Right of maintenance' generally includes 'right of residence' also.

Maintenance includes the cost of education till the child is old enough to earn his living and thus relieve the father of the burden of his maintenance.

Maintenance must vary according to the position and status of a person. It does not only mean food and raiment. *Maharani Esarkunverba* v. *I.T. Commissioner*, AIR 1960 SC 1343, 1346.

In the statute relating to bastardy, and providing that the father should be liable for the maintenance of the child, maintenance includes the expenses of lying-in or childbed expenses, such as board, wages, and other charges attendant on nursing the child, and necessary expenditures at the birth of the child.

Within the meaning of a statute giving the Court jurisdiction to charge a man with the maintenance of his illegitimate child, the term "maintenance" includes the reasonable cost of supporting the child and the necessary expenses incident to its birth and burial; but does not include the value of services rendered by an attorney for the mother in the bastardy proceedings.

The word 'maintenance' means and includes provision for food, shelter, clothing, *etc*. *Adiveppa* v. *Tanjewwa,* AIR 1975 Kar 198, 199. [T.P. Act (4 of 1882), S. 39]

'Maintenance' and 'repair'. The distinction between words 'maintenance' and 'repair', in the context of construction is virtually with- out any difference. For maintaining a bridge one would have to keep it in good repair and by repairing it, it is also maintained. *State of U.P.* v. *Devidayal Singh*, (2000) 3 SCC 5, para 24 : AIR 2000 SC 561.

Maintenance and support. Maintenance is an act of maintaining, that is, to support with money. Support means to provide money for a person to live on. *Pradeep Kumar Kapoor* v. *Shailija Kapoor,* AIR 1989 Del 10, 12. [Hindu Marriage Act (25 of 1955), S. 24]

Maintenance-effect on divorce. If there is no specific provision to the contrary, nothing that is there in the code of criminal procedure will affect any special provision in force or in other words there being nothing to the contrary the provisions of Section 125 criminal procedure code will have no effect on Section 44 of the Indian Divorce Act. *James Fredrick Rowland* v. *Raynah Rowland,* AIR 1959 Cal 703, 704. [CrPC 1973 (2 of 1974), S. 125; Indian Divorce Act (4 of 1869), S. 44]

Maintenance of a prisoner includes the expenses of inquiring into the mental state of a prisoner who becomes insane, and of removing him to a lunatic asylum, and maintaining him there during the currency of his sentence.

MAINTENANCE OF A PRISONER from public funds "includes all such necessary expenses incurred in respect of a prisoner for food, clothing custody, safe conduct, and removal from one place of confinement to another or otherwise," from the time the order of committal is made out until his death or discharge; and includes, the cost of his conveyance from where he is committed to his place of confinement, and the cost of his food, *etc.* when in a lunatic asylum during the term of his imprisonment". (*Stroud*)

Maintenance of public order. By the expression "maintenance of public order" what is intended is the prevention of grave public disorder. It is not the same as maintenance of law and order. "Maintenance of law and order" means the prevention of disorders of comparatively lesser gravity and of local significance. *B. Sundar Rao* v. *State of Orissa,* AIR 1972 SC 739.

Maintenance or repair. "MAINTENANCE OR REPAIR" means any service provided by—

(i) any person under a contract or an agreement; or

(ii) a manufacturer or any person authorised by him,

in relation to,—

(a) maintenance or repair including reconditioning or restoration, or servicing of any goods or equipment, excluding motor vehicle; or

(b) maintenance or management of immovable property.

[Finance Act (32 of 1994), S. 65(64) *as substituted by Finance Act (18 of 2005), S. 88(a)(xiv)* now repealed by Goods and Services Tax Act, 2017]

Maintenance order. Means a decree or order, other than an order of affiliation, made by a Court in the exercise of civil or criminal jurisdiction for the periodical payment of sums of money towards the maintenance of the wife or other dependents of the person against whom the order is made. [Maintenance Orders Enforcement Act (18 of 1921), S. 2]

Maintenance pending suit. An order of a Court for temporary periodical payments during the hearing of a petition for divorce, nullity or judicial separation.

Major. "MAJOR" means a person who has completed the age of eighteen years. [Immoral Traffic (Prevention) Act (104 of 1956), S. 2(ca)]

One who has attained the age of majority *i.e.* an age at which he becomes legally capable of conducting his own affairs (generally) 18 years); an officer of the army.

Major accident. Means, an incident involving loss of life inside or outside the installation, or ten or more injuries inside and/or one or more injuries outside or release of toxic chemicals or explosion or fire or Public Interest Litigation large of hazardous chemicals resulting in on-site or off-site emergencies or damage to equipment leading to stoppage of process or adverse effects to the environment. [Manufacture, Storage and Import of Hazardous Chemicals Rules, 1989, R. 2(j)]

Major Accident Hazardous (MAH) installations. Means, isolated storage and industrial activity at a site handling (including transport through carrier or pipe-line) of hazardous chemicals equal to or, in excess of the threshold quantities specified in, Column 3 of schedule 2 and 3 respectively. [Manufacture, Storage and Import of Hazardous Chemicals Rules, 1989, R. 2(ja)]

Major continet in se minus. (*Maxim*) The greater includes the less.

Major haereditas venit unicuique nostrum a jure et legibus quam a parentibus. (*Lat.*) A greater inheritance comes to every one of us from right and the laws than from parents.

Major district roads. Means the important roads within a district of a State notified as such by the State Government. [Motor Vehicles (Driving) Regulations, 2017, Regn. 2(1)(g)].

Major numerus in se continet minorem. (*Maxim*) The greater number contains in itself the less.

Major port. "MAJOR PORT" means a port declared to be a major port by or under any law made by Parliament or any existing law and includes all areas for the time being included within the limits of such port. [Constitution of India, Art. 364 (2)(a)]

"Major port" means a major port as defined in clause (*8*) of section 3 of the Indian Ports Act, 1908 (15 of 1908). [Industrial Relations Code, 2020 (35 of 2020), section 2(v)]

Any port which the Central Government may be notification in the Official Gazette declare or may under any law for the time being in force have declared to be a MAJOR PORT. [Indian Ports Act (15 of 1908), S. 3(8)].

"Major road". Means the highway, road or street designated as such by any highway authority or local authority within its jurisdiction. [Motor Vehicles (Driving) Regulations, 2017, Regn. 2(1)(h)].

Major repair or improvement. In respect of a building means a repair or improvement as a result of which the capital value of the building is increased by more than fifteen thousand rupees. [Building Tax Ordinance, 1974 (10 of 1974), S. 2(h)]

Major Surgical and/or Major Disease. Means treatment taken in the hospital for the following diseases. Benefits under this extension are payable in addition to the benefits payable under Benefit 1(B) of Table of Benefits.

(i) Renal Diseases

(ii) Cerebral or Vascular Strokes

(iii) Open and closed heart Surgery

(iv) Kidney Transplantation and Dialysis

(v) Malignancy

(vi) T.B. which includes Pulmonary T.B.

(vii) Encephalitis (Viral)

(viii) Neuro-surgery

(ix) Total replacement of joints. [Scheme of Hospitalisation and Domiciliary Hospitalization Benefit Policy, specified for the purpose of S. 80D of the Income- tax Act (43 of 1961)]

Majority. More than half; the age at which, by law, a person is entitled to the management of his own affairs and to the enjoyment of civic rights.

The word is usually referred to the only method of determining the acts of many, by a majority in numbers. The major part of members of parliament enact laws, and the majority of electors choose members of parliament; the act of the major part of any corporation in accounted the act of the corporation; and where the majority is, there, by the law, is the whole." (*Tomlin*)

The age at which by law, a person is entitled to the management of his own affairs and to the enjoyment of civil rights; more than half of any number of items. [Navy Act (62 of 1957), S. 96(1), prov.]; more than half of the votes cast at any type of election [Army Act (46 of 1950), S. 132(1) and Constitution of India, Art. 61(2)(b)].

Majority is a term signifying the greater number. In legislative and deliberative assemblies, it is usual to decide questions by a majority of those present and voting. This is sometimes expressed as a "simple" majority, which means that a motion is carried out by the mere fact that more votes are cast for than against, as distinct from a "special" majority where the size of the majority is critical. [Shackleton on the Law and practice of Meetings, 11th Edn., paras 7-30 **as cited in** *State of M.P.* v. *Mahendra Gupta,* (2018) 3 SCC 635, para 16].

Majority, Age of. A person attains his majority at 12 O'clock at night of the day preceding his 18th or 21st birthday as the case may be. [Indian Majority Act (9 of 1875), Ss. 2, 3 & 4]

Majority or majority of apartment owners. Means the apartment owners with fifty one per cent or more of votes in accordance with the percentages assigned in the declaration of the apartments for voting purposes. [Kerala Apartment Ownership Act (5 of 1984), S. 3(q), almost to the similar effect Punjab Apartment Ownership Act (Punjab Act (13 of 1995), S. 3(s)]

Majority rule. The foundation of the republican system of government. (*Ballentine's Law Dictionary, 3rd Edn.*)

Rule by the choice of the majority of those who actually vote, irrespective of whether a majority of those entitled participate. *N.L.R.B.* v. *Standard Lime & Stone Co.,* CCA Va., 149 F.2d 435, 437.

"Majority stake". Means—

(*i*) holding more than one-half of the equity share capital in the body corporate; or

(*ii*) holding more than one-half of the voting rights in the body corporate; or

(*iii*) having the right to receive or participate in more than one-half of the distributable dividend or any other distribution by the body corporate. [Companies (Significant Beneficial Owners) Rules, 2018, R. 2(1)(d)].

Make. To bring into being; to cause to exist; to create; to construct; to frame; to fashion.

'Make' means 'cause to exist', 'to bring about' or 'to produce'. [Collins English Dictionary, p. 889 as cited in *Pt. Rishikesh v. Salma Begum*, (1995) 4 SCC 718, para 17]. See also *State of Kerala v. Mar Apparaem Kuri Company Limited*, (2012) 7 SCC 149, para 5].

The word "MAKE" includes also the power to amend, alter or rescind. [Securities Contracts (Regulation) Act (42 of 1956), S. 10(1)]

Make an application. The words "he shall not be entitled to make an application under this section" in O. XXI, R. 89 (2), CPC (5 of 1908), cannot mean merely "he shall not be entitled to present an application" under the section, but the word "make" must mean "carry on" or "prosecute".

Make an award. To 'make an award' is to form and publish a judgment on the facts.

Make apology. To make an acknowledgement intended as an atonement for some improper or injurious act, accompanied by an expression of regret. [CrPC 1973 (2 of 1974), S. 348].

Make award. To give an award in the arbitration proceeding. [Land Acquisition Act (1 of 1894), S. 49(3)].

Make away with. Words charging the plaintiff with being the father of a bastard child by his sister-in-law, of which she was pregnant, and that he wished the defendant to "make away with it", are actionable *per se*, as importing a wish that the defendant should destroy the child as soon as born. They import that the plaintiff applied to defendant to commit murder.

The word "make away with", in a charge that a person made away with some of another's logs, do not of themselves import a charge of larceny, and therefore are not slanderous *per se*.

Make composition. To make mutual settlement or agreement.

Make good. To "make good" damage to property means to restore things to the condition in which they were before.

Make good the loss. To make up the deficiency. [Indian Partnership Act (9 of 1932), S. 27].

Make over. To hand over.

Make public. To make known to public.

Maker. The creator; executant. [Negotiable Instruments Act (26 of 1881), S. 15].

Maker and Drawer. Throughout the Negotiable Instruments Act, a clear distinction has been made between the words "*maker*" and "*drawer*", the former word being used in a more general sense as applying to promissory notes, negotiable instruments and cheques, while the word "drawer" is restricted to bills of exchange or cheques only, and is nowhere used in connection with promissory notes.

Maker and endorser. The difference between a maker of a note and an indorser or a guarantor is that the contract of the first, by its terms, imports an unconditional obligation to pay money, and that of the last, by its terms, imports a conditional obligation.

Makes any order admitting any instrument in evidence. The order contemplated by S. 61 is an order about the sufficiency or insufficiency of the stamp with reference to a document which has been admitted in evidence. The expression does not mean an order formally admitting a documents in evidence. *H.H. Sir Syed Ali Raza Khan* v. *Saranbehari Mathur,* AIR 1960 All 359, 360. [Indian Stamp Act (2 of 1899), S. 61(1)]

Making a false document. "A person is said to make a false document—

First.—Who dishonesty or fraudulently makes, signs, seals or executes a document or part of a document, or makes any mark denoting the execution of a document, with the intention of causing it to be behaved that such document or part of document was made, signed, sealed or executed by or by the authority of a person by whom or by whose authority he knows that it was not made, signed, sealed or executed, or at a time at which he knows that it was not made, signed, sealed or executed; or

Secondly.—Who, without lawful authority, dishonestly or fraudulently, by cancellation or otherwise, alters a document in any material part thereof, after it has been made or executed either by himself or by any other person, whether such person be living or dead at the time of such alteration; or

Thirdly.—Who dishonestly or fraudulently causes any person to sign, seal, execute or alter a document, knowing that such person by reason of unsoundness of mind or intoxication can not, or that by reason of deception practised upon him, he does not know the contents of the document or the nature of the alteration." [IPC (45 of 1860), S. 464] [(w. e. f. 1-7-2024) repealed and replaced by Bharatiya Nyaya Sanhita, 2023 (45 of 2023), S. 335]

Making of the order. An order may be taken to be made on the date it came into existence, if the nature of the order is such that it is not necessary to communicate it to anyone. If an order is made which affects the rights of a person, then the order must be communicated to such person in order to be complete and effective. An order which affects the interests of a person cannot be said to be effectively made until it has been brought to his notice. *Nripendra N. Majumdar* v. *N.M. Bardhan,* AIR 1959 Cal 219, 221.

"MAKING OF THE ORDER" an 'order' ordinarily would be presumed to have been made when it is signed. Once it is signed and an entry in that regard is made in the requisite register kept and maintained in terms of the provisions of a statute, the same cannot be changed or altered. It, subject to the other provisions contained in the Act, attains finality. Where, however, communication of an order is a necessary ingredient for bringing an end result to a status or to provide a person an opportunity to take recourse of law if he is aggrieved thereby; the order is required to be communicated. *M.C.D.* v. *Qimat Rai Gupta*, AIR 2007 SC 2742 : 2007 AIR SCW 4952.

Making promissory note payable to bearer on demand. A payee endorsing a promissory note in blank cannot be said to have "made a promissory note payable to bearer on demand." When a promissory note is drawn up, signed and delivered to the payee; it is 'made' once and for all and a subsequent endorsement is no part of the "making".

Making the law and Commencement of the Act. Distinction. Commencement of the Act is distinct from making the law. As soon as assent is given by the President to the law passed by Parliament it becomes law. Commencement of the Act may be expressed in the Act itself, namely, from the moment the assent was given by the President and published in the Gazette, it becomes operative. *Rishikesh* v. *Salma Begum*, JT 1995 (4) SC 401, 412.

Making up of accounts. 'Making up of accounts' means ascertaining the profits and loss accruing during the particular period. Merely closing of ledger at the end of a year and carrying forward balances of the year to the beginning of the next year would not amount to making up of accounts. *Bhailal Tribhovandas and Co.* v. *C.I.T.*, (1968) 68 ITR 136, 139 (Guj). [Income Tax Act (43 of 1961), S. 3]

Mala fide. In bad faith.

MALA FIDE means want of good faith, personal bias, grudge, oblique or improper motive or ulterior purpose. An act done honestly is deemed to have been done in good faith, *State of Bihar* v. *P.P. Sharma*, AIR 1991 SC 1260.

In acquisition of land, if the object is the illegitimate one in taking away the land of a person to vent the hostility of another person, the acquisition of land is *mala fide*. *State of Punjab* v. *Gurdial Singh*, AIR 1980 SC 319, 321.

A *mala fide possessor* of real estate is one who is in possession knowing that the title is contested by a third person claiming a better right to it.

The taking of an estate after notice of a prior right makes one a *mala fide purchaser*.

Mala fide exercise. A "*mala fide* exercise" of power does not necessarily imply any moral turpitude and may only mean that the statutory power is exercised for purpose other than those for which the power was intended by law to be exercised. *Additional District Magistrate, Jabalpur* v. *Shivakant Shukla*, AIR 1976 SC 1207.

Mala fide exercise of power. The right of an officer to get rid of an obstruction during an investigation then and there might be mistaken. It could not be said that such action was necessarily *mala fide* and so entirely divorced from or unconnected with the discharge of their duty that it was an independent act maliciously done or perpetrated. *Matajog Dobey* v. *H.C. Bhari*, AIR 1956 SC 44, 50.

"Mala fide in fact" and "Mala fide in law". *Mala fide* has been divided into two types of malice which strike any action at the root or is generally *mala fide in fact* the other is called *mala fide in law*. Allegations which stem from malice. And when examined on the basis of admitted facts and materials show that they are bordering concoction of a story to make out a care for investigation, may fall in either of the two categories of *mala fide*. (*Association for Protection of Public Rights and Interest through its Secretary* v. *State of Bihar*, 1991 (1) BLJR 161 at 196).

Mala fides. Bad Faith. The opposite of *bona fides*.

Mala in se. Acts bad or wrong in themselves. Acts are said to be *mala in se* which are contrary to the law of nature or rules of morality; such, for example, are murder, theft, robbery, and other crimes.

Mala prohibita. Acts *mala prohibita* are acts forbidden by law but not otherwise wrong.

Acts which are wrong because they are prohibited by law.

Mala (Male) res se habet cum quo virtute effici debeat a tenatur pecunia. That is a bad case wherein one attempts to accomplish with money that which ought to be prompted by virtue.

Maladministration. "MALADMINISTRATION" means action taken or purporting to have been taken in the exercise of administrative functions in any case—

(i) Where such action or the administrative procedure or practice governing such action is unreasonable, unjust, oppressive or improperly discriminatory; or

(ii) Where there has been negligence or undue delay in taking such action, or the administrative procedure or practice governing such action involves undue delay. [Maharashtra Lokayukta and Up-Lokayukta Act (46 of 1971), S. 2(g)]

Malapportionment. The combined effect of legislative districts whose boundaries are improperly drawn.

Male. Of the sex that begets offspring. [IPC (45 of 1860), S. 10]; [CrPC 1973 (2 of 1974), S. 64].

Male diction. Evil speaking; curse; calling down of evil to a person.

Male issue. The whole class of male descendants, whether descended through or from males or females.

Male-factors. Evil doers; criminals.

Maledicta expositio quae corrumpit textum. (*Lat.*) It is a bad exposition which corrupts the text.

Maleficia non debent remanere impunita, et impunitas affectum continuum tribuit delinquenti. (*Lat.*) Evil deeds ought not to remain unpunished, and impunity affords continual incitement to the delinquent. (*Morgan*; *Latin for Lawyers*)

Malfeasance. Evil doing; ill conduct; the doing of what one ought not to do; the commission of some act which is positively unlawful; the doing of an act which is wholly wrongful; the unjust performance of some act which the party had no right to do, or which he had contracted not to do. (*Ame Cyc.*)

Malfeasance : Misfeasance : Non-feasance. The words 'malfeasance', 'misfeasance' and 'non-feasance' cover a vide range of cases. Malfeasance would apply to a case where an act prohibited in law is done by a person. Non-feasance would apply to a case where a person omits to do some act prescribed by law, and misfeasance would apply to a case where a lawful act is done in an improper manner. *Kharul Bashar* v. *Thaum Lal,* AIR 1957 All 553, 556.

Malguzari. (*H.*) Revenue assessment, or land capable of paying assessment. Paying revenue, assessed.

The word "*malguzari*" ordinarily means revenue, and not rent, much less actual rent. (AIR 1925 Pat 421, *Reversed.*) 106 IC 571 : 54 IA 432 : 26 ALJ 19 : 8 PLT 813 : 32 CWN 260 : 47 CLJ 90 : AIR 1927 PC 250 : 54 MLJ 293 (PC); *see also* 4 OLJ 148 : 40 IC 42.

Malice. Unlawful intent. (Craig R. Ducat — *Constitutional Interpretation*)

"MALICE", in common acceptation, means, ill will against a person; but in its legal sense, it means, a wrongful act done intentionally without just cause or excuse". *Chairman & M.D. BPL Ltd.* v. *S.P. Gururaja,* AIR 2003 SC 4536.

The legal meaning of malice is "ill-will or spite towards a party and any indirect or improper motive in taking an action". This is sometimes described as "malice in fact." [Words and Phrases Legally Defined, 3rd Edn., 1989 as cited in *HMT Ltd. v. Mudappa*, JT 2007 (3) SC 112 : AIR 2007 SC 1106, para 18]. See also *Vimla Tiwari v. State of U.P.*, AIR 2012 All 142, para 41.

Malice signifies the presence of some improper and wrongful motive that is to say, an intent to use the legal process in question for some other than its legally appointed and appropriate purpose.

'Malice' consists in a conscious violation of the law to the prejudice of another and certainly has different meanings with respect to responsibility for civil wrongs and responsibility for crime. [*W.B. SEB v. Dilip Kumar Ray*, (2007) 14 SCC 568, para 15 : (2009) 1 SCC (L&S) 860 : AIR 2007 SC 976 as cited in *Ravinder Singh v. Sukhbir Singh*, (2013) 9 SCC 245, para 22].

It means exercise of statutory power for 'purposes foreign to those for which it is in law intended.' It means conscious violation of the law to the prejudice of another, a depraved inclination on the part of the authority to disregard the rights of others, where intent is manifested by its injurious acts. Passing an order for unauthorized purpose constitutes malic in law. [*Ravi Yashwant Bhoir v. Collector*, (2012) 4 SCC 407, para 48 : AIR 2012 SC 1339 as cited in *J. Jayalalitha v. State of Karnataka*, (2014) 2 SCC 401, para 26].

'Malice in the legal sense imports (1) the absence of all elements of justification, excuse or recognised mitigation, and (2) the presence of either (a) an actual intent to cause the particular harm which is produced or harm of the same general nature, or (b) the wanton and wilful doing of an act with awareness of a plain and strong likelihood that such harm may result....' [*W.B. SEB v. Dilip Kumar Ray*, (2007) 14 SCC 568, para 15 : (2009) 1 SCC (L&S) 860 : AIR 2007 SC 976 as cited in *Ravinder Singh v. Sukhbir Singh*, (2013) 9 SCC 245, para 22].

It signifies an intentional doing of a wrongful act without just cause or excuse or an action determined by an improper motive. [CPC (5 of 1908), O. VI, R. 10].

Malice aforethought. Is the term used in law to designate the wicked and mischievous intent with which a man wilfully does a wrongful act, and is to be inferred from acts committed or words spoken.

"MALICE AFORETHOUGHT" is a condition of the mind which shows a heart regardless of duty and fatally bent on mischief, the existence of which is inferred from acts committed or words spoken.

Malice in fact. "Malice in fact" means express malice.

MALICE IN FACT OR ACTUAL MALICE, relates to the actual state or condition of the mind of the person who did the act.

Malice in fact is where the malice is not established by legal presumption or proof of certain facts, but is to be found from the evidence in the case.

Malice in fact implies a desire or intention to injure, while malice in law is not necessarily inconsistent with an honest purpose.

Malice in law. 'Malice in law" means implied malice.

Mala fide action or "malice in law" are not to be easily presumed. The mere non-adherence to the strict procedure followed by a judicial tribunal does not amount to either acting *mala fide* or acting contrary to natural justice. *Bireshwar Chakravarti* v. *L.N. Kaula,* AIR 1957 All 671, 677. [Indian Evidence Act (1 of 1872), S. 114]

Malice in law denotes absence of legal excuse. *N.C. Jute Mills* v. *Finance Ministry,* AIR 1966 Cal 151, 159.

Malice in its legal sense means malice such as may be assumed from the doing of a wrongful act intentionally but without just cause or excuse, or for want of reasonable or probable cause. *S.R. Venkataraman* v. *Union of India*, AIR 1979 SC 49, 51.

Malicious. "MALICIOUS" means with a fixed hate, or done with evil intention or motive; not the result of sudden passion.

Given to malice; characterised by malice. [IPC (45 of 1860), S. 295A].

In order to establish malice as contemplated by this section, it is not necessary for the prosecution to prove that, the applicant bore ill-will or enmity against specific persons. If the injurious act was done voluntarily without a lawful excuse, malice may be presumed. *Baba Khalil Ahmad* v. *State,* AIR 1960 All 715, 719. [IPC (45 of 1860), S. 295 A]

Malicious abuse of legal process. A malicious abuse of legal process consists in the malicious misuse or misapplication of process to accomplish a purpose not warranted or commanded by order of Court; the malicious perversion of a regularly issued process, whereby an improper result is secured.

Malicious abuse of process. Wilfully misapplying Court process to obtain object not intended by law. The wilful misuse or misapplication of process to accomplish a purpose not warranted or commanded by the writ. An action for malicious abuse of process lies in the following cases. A malicious petition or proceeding to adjudicate a person an insolvent, to declare a person lunatic or to wind up a company, to make action against legal practioner under the Legal Practitioners Act, maliciously procuring arrest or attachment in execution of a decree or before judgment, order or injunction or apointment of receiver, arrest of a ship, search of the plaintiff's premises, arrest of a person by police.

Malicious arrest. Arrest without reasonable and probable cause.

Malicious criminal prosecution. In an action for a malicious criminal prosecution, the plaintiff must prove the following points : (a) that the plaintiff was prosecuted by the defendant; (b) that the prosecution ended in plaintiff's favour, (c) that the defendant acted without reasonable and probable cause, (d) that the defendant was actuated by malice. It is then for the defendant to make out a defence recognised by law.

Malicious falsehood. A right of action exists where one person has, orally or in writing, with actual malice communicated an untrue statement disparaging the plaintiff's title, goods, or other property and calculated, in the ordinary course, to produce and, in fact, producing actual damage. (*Walker*)

Malicious intention. As used in an Act relating to libels, and providing that the truth of the matter contained in the publication is a sufficient justification, unless malicious intention is proved, means an actual malicious intention, or, in other words, express malice.

Malicious mischief. "Malicious mischief, or damage is an injury done either out of a spirit of wanton cruelty, or black, diabolical revenge." (*Blackstone Com.*)

Malicious prosecution. "A judicial proceeding instituted by one person against another, from wrongful or improper motive and with- out probable cause to sustain it."

"A prosecution begun in malice, without probable cause to believe that it can succeed and which finally ends in failure."

A prosecution on some charge of crime which is wilful, wanton, or reckless, or against the prosecutor's sense of duty and right, or for ends he knows or its bound to know are wrong and against the dictates of public policy.

Malicious prosecution and maintenance. The wrong known as malicious prosecution and maintenance consists causing damage by means of an abuse of the process of Courts of law.

Malicious publication. A publication, qualified or privileged, in malicious in the law of slander and liable, if it is not made in good faith. If not made for the reason which renders it privileged, but from a wrongful, indirect, and ulterior motive, and it is false, it is malicious.

Malicious trespass. The act of one who maliciously or mischievously injures or causes to be injured any property of another or any public property.

Maliciously. With deliberate intention to injure; with ill-will, malevolence, grudge, spite, or enmity; wilfully.

In a malicious manner; out of malice. [Explosive Substances Act (6 of 1908), S. 3]; [IPC (45 of 1860), S. 219].

"MALICIOUSLY," as used in criminal statutes, means nothing more than that the act should be done voluntarily, unlawfully, and without excuse or justification.

Malignantly. Feeling or showing intense ill- will. [IPC (45 of 1860), S. 270].

Malignantly implies a sort of general malice and very strong evidence is necessary to prove malignantly or wantonly. *State of Orissa* v. *R.C. Chowala,* AIR 1966 Ori 192, 194. [IPC (45 of 1860), S. 153]

Malik. The word "*malik*" is of very common use in many parts of India and it cannot certainly be regarded as a technical term of conveyancing. *Ram Gopal* v. *Nandlal*, AIR 1951 SC 139, 141.

A bequest to a woman as '*malik*' imports a full proprietary right, unless there is something in the context to qualify it. *Ram Bharosey* v. *Lachmandas,* AIR 1954 All 715.

The expression '*malik*' has been consistently understood by Courts as conveying the idea of absolute ownership. *Pearey Lal* v. *Rameshwar Das*, AIR 1963 SC 1703, 1705.

Malik mustakil. "The under words "malik mustakil" are strong, clear and unambiguous and signify that the estate given is an absolute one, unless qualified by the other words and circumstances appearing in the same document." AIR 1952 SC 145 **Quoted**. *Krishna Beharilal* v. *Gulabchand*, AIR 1971 SC 1041, 1043; *S. Harnam Singh* v. *State*, AIR 1976 SC 2140, 2145.

Malinger. To pretend illness or to produce or protract disease in order to escape duty (especially of soldiers and sailors). [Army Act (46 of 1950), S. 46(b)].

Malingering. "Malingering" has been defined as a deception practised by any body, from which they try to make out that they are sick when they are not sick.

Malitia est acida, est mali animi affectus. Malice is sour, it is the quality of a bad mind.

Malpractice. Evil practice in a professional capacity and a resort to methods and practices unsanctioned and prohibited by law; misbehaviour; practice contrary to established rules (*Century*); improper or immoral conduct; objectionable practice (*Standard*); evil practice; illegal conduct.

Maltreatment. This would include improper or unskillful treatment by a surgeon of his patient, which may result from ignorance, neglect or wilfulness, not necessarily implying that the conduct of the surgeon in the treatment of the patient's wounds was either wilfully or grossly careless.

Maltreatment of children. Emotional, physical and sexual abuse of children. Emotional abuse includes acts or failures to act by parents or guardians that have caused or could cause, serious behavioral, cognitive, emotional, or mental disorders and neglect is the failure to provide for the child's basic needs; it may be physical, educational, or emotional. Physical abuse is the inflicting of physical injury on a child. Sexual abuse is inappropriate sexual behaviour with a child. It also includes child prostitution or their trafficking for such purposes. (*Human Rights*)

Malum in se. Literally "a wrong in itself." An act involving illegality from the very nature of the transaction.

Malum non habet efficientem, sed deficientum, causam. Evil has not an efficient, but a deficient, cause.

Malum non praesumitur. (*Lat.*) Wickedness is not presumed.

Malum quo communius, eo pejus. The more common an evil is, the worse it is.

Malus usus est abolendus. (*Lat.*) An evil custom ought to be abolished.

Malware. Any-harmful software or hardware, including viruses, worms, logic bombs, and so on. (*Cyber Law*)

Man. The word "MAN" denotes a male human being of any age. [IPC (45 of 1860), S. 10] [Now (w. e. f. 1-7-2024) repealed & replaced by **Bharatiya Nyaya Sanhita, 2023 (45 of 2023)**, section 2(19), same definition in new Sanhita]

An adult male human being [IPC (45 of 1860), S. 10]; a human being [Indian Contract Act (9 of 1872), Ss. 12, ill. (b) and 195]; to employ.

"Man" and "Woman". Means male and female human beings, respectively, of any age. [Equal Remuneration Act (25 of 1976), S. 2(d)]

Man-made fabrics. The fabric containing 33% polyester, 32% viscose and 35% cotton comes within the ambit the expression 'manmade fabrics' under Item 22, as it is known in the trade. *C.C.E.* v. *Gaekwar Mills Ltd.*, (1997) 2 SCC 213, para 6. [Central Excise and Salt Act (1 of 1944), Item 22]

Man of ordinary prudence. A person having usual kind of sound judgment in practical-affairs. [Indian Contract Act (9 of 1872), Ss. 151 and 195].

Manage. To control according to law; to direct; govern; administer; to conduct; carry on; to direct the concerns of; to have under control and direction.

The words "*manage*" and "*control*" are held to be synonymous.

In the context of business, 'manage' means 'to control, to guide, to administer, to conduct or direct affairs; carry on business'. *R. Dalmia* v. *I.T. Commissioner, New Delhi*, AIR 1977 SC 988, 991.

Management. Management is defined as government, control, superintendence, physical or manual handling or guidance, the act of managing by direction or regulation, or administration.

The action of managing [CrPC, 1973 (2 of 1974), S. 144(1)]; a governing body *i.e.* a Board of Directors, a Board of Governors *etc.* [Companies Act (1 of 1956), Sch. 6, Pt. 1, note (i) now replaced by the Companies Act, 2013].

"Management, maintenance or repair". Means any service provided by—

(*i*) any person under a contract or an agreement; or

(*ii*) a manufacturer or any person authorised by him, in relatives to—

(*a*) management of properties, whether immovable or not;

(*b*) maintenance or repair of properties, whether immovable or not; or

(*c*) maintenance or repair including reconditioning or restoration, or servicing of any goods, excluding motor vehicle. [Finance Act, 1994, S. 65(64) **as cited in** *Safety Retreading Company Private Limited* v. *Commissioner of Central Excise, Salem,* (2017) 3 SCC 640, para 3].

Management consultant. Means any person who is engaged in providing any service, either directly or indirectly, in connection with the management of any organisation or business in any manner and includes any person who renders any advice, consultancy or technical assistance, in relation to financial management, human resources management, marketing management, production management, logistics management, procurement and management of information technology resources or other similar areas of management. [Finance Act (32 of 1994), S. 65(1)(63) now repealed by Goods and Services Tax Act, 2017]

Management of Digital Signature Certificate. Management of Digital Signature Certificate includes, but only limits to distribution, storage, accounting, public compromise, dissemination, revocation, recovery, suspension and administration of Digital Signature Certificate. (*Information Technology*)

Manager. "MANAGER" means the manager of an encumbered estate appointed under any law for the time being in force relating to encumbered estates. [Transfer of Evacuee Deposits Act (15 of 1954), S. 2(e)]

"MANAGER" means an individual (not being the managing agent) who, subject to the superintendence, control and direction of the board of directors, has the management of the whole, or substantially the whole, of the affairs of a company, and includes a director or any other person occupying the position of a manager, by whatever name called, and whether under a contract of service or not." [Companies Act (1 of 1956), S. 2(24)]

The word, 'Manager' in relation to religious or charitable endowment is not a term of art. The said word denotes the person who is in charge of the administration of the endowment or manages the property or supervises the performance of the charity and the word is one of very wide and general import. *State Wakf Board, Madras* v. *Subramaniam,* AIR 1977 Mad 79, 82. [Limitation Act (36 of 1963), Art. 96].

One who manages [Constitution of India, Art. 31A(1)(d)]; manager of a Hindu undivided family.

"MANAGER" means an individual who, subject to the superintendence, control and direction of the Board of Directors, has the management of the whole, or substantially the whole, of the affairs of a company, and includes a director or any other person occupying the position of a manager, by whatever name called, whether under a contract of service or not. [S. 2(53) of the Companies Act, 2013 (18 of 2013)]

Manager of a hotel. Includes any person in charge of the management of the hotel. [Delhi Rent Act (33 of 1995), S. 2(g)]

Manager of College. Means a person or body of persons in charge or control of the management of a College and recognised by the University to which such college is affiliated. [Gujarat Affiliated Colleges Services Tribunal Ordinance, 1981, S. 2(e)]

Managerial, Administrative and Supervisory capacity. A supervisor need not be a manager or an administrator. A supervisor can be a workman so long as he does not exceed the wage limit of Rs. 500/- p.m. A supervisor, irrespective of his salary, is not a workman who has to discharge functions mainly of managerial nature by reason of the duties attached to his office or of the powers vested in him. *Mcleod and Co.* v. *Sixth Industrial Tribunal,* AIR 1958 Cal 273, 280. [Industrial Disputes Act 14 of 1947), S. 2(s)]

Managing agent. "MANAGING AGENT" means any person appointed or acting as the representative of another person for the purpose of carrying on such other person's trade or business, but does not include an individual manager subordinate to an employer. [Employee's Compensation Act (8 of 1923), S. 2(f); Employees' State Insurance Act (34 of 1948), S. 2(14-A)]

"MANAGING AGENT" includes

(i) Secretaries and treasures;

(ii) Where the managing agent is a company any director of such company and any member thereof who holds substantial interest in such company.

(iii) Where the managing agent is a firm, any partner of such firm. [Banking Regulation Act (10 of 1949), S. 5 (gg)]

Managing committee. Means the individual or the body of individuals entrusted or charged with the management and administration of a private educational institution and where a society, trust, or an association manages more than one such institution includes the managing committee of each such institution. [Karnataka Education Act, 1983 (1 of 1995), S. 2(19)]

Managing contractor. Means the person or body of persons, who with the previous consent in writing of the State Government, has entered into an arrangement, contract or understanding, with the owner of a coking coal mine or coke oven plant under which the operations of the coking coal mine or coke oven plant are substantially controlled by such person or body of persons. [Coking Coal Mines (Nationalisation) Act (36 of 1972), S. 3(i)]

"MANAGING CONTRACTOR" means the person, or body of persons, who, with the previous consent, in writing, of the State Government has entered into an arrangement, contract or understanding, with the owner of a coal mine under which the operations of the coal mine are substantially controlled by such person or body of persons. [Coal Mines (Nationalisation) Act (26 of 1973), S. 2(g)]

Managing director. "MANAGING DIRECTOR", in relation to a banking company means a director who, by virtue of an agreement with the banking company or of a resolution passed by the banking company in general meeting or by its Board of Directors or, by virtue of its memorandum or articles of association, is entrusted with the management of the whole, or substantially the whole, of the affairs of the company and includes a director occupying the position of a managing director, by whatever name called;

Provided that the managing director shall exercise his power subject to the superintendence, control and director of the Board of Directors. [Banking Regulation Act (10 of 1949), S. 5(h)]

"MANAGING DIRECTOR" means a director who, by virtue of an agreement with the company or of a resolution passed by the company in general meeting or by its Board of directors or by virtue of its memorandum or article of association, is entrusted with substantial powers of management which would not otherwise be exercisable by him, and includes a director occupying the position of a managing director, by whatever name called:

Provided that the power to do administrative acts of a routine nature when so authorised by the Board such as the power to affix the common seal of the company to any document or to draw and endorse and cheque on the account of the company in any bank or to draw and endorse any negotiable instrument or to sign any certificate of share or to direct registration of transfer of any share, shall not be deemed to be included within substantial power of management.

Provided further that a managing director of a company shall exercise his power subject to the superintendence, control and direction of its Board of directors. [Companies Act (1 of 1956), S. 2(26)]

'MANAGING DIRECTOR', in relation to an industrial undertaking, means a person (whether called a managing agent, general manager, manager, chief executive officer or by any other name) who exercises control over the affairs of that undertaking. [Central Industrial Security Force Act (50 of 1968), S. 2(e)]

"MANAGING DIRECTOR" means a director who, by virtue of the articles of a company or an agreement with the company or a resolution passed in its general meeting, or by its Board of Directors, is entrusted with substantial powers of management of the affairs of the company and includes a director occupying the position of managing director, by whatever name called.

Explanation.—For the purposes of this clause, the power to do administrative acts of a routine nature when so authorised by the Board such as the power to affix the common seal of the company to any document or to draw and endorse any cheque on the account of the company in any bank or to draw and endorse any negotiable instrument or to sign any certificate of share or to direct registration of transfer of any share, shall not be deemed to be included within the substantial powers of management. [S. 2(54) of the Companies Act, 2013 (18 of 2013)]

Mandamus. A writ issued by the Supreme Court or a High Court to compel a judicial or *quasi*-judicial, governmental or semi-governmental bodies, public authorities, governmental instrumentalities and even private bodies performing public functions to perform their mandatory duties.

A command. The order of *mandamus* is an order of a most extensive remedial nature, and is, in form, a command issuing from the High Court of Justice, directed to any person, corporation or inferior tribunal, requiring him or them to do some particular thing therein specified which appertains to his or their office and is in the nature of a public duty. Its purpose is to remedy defects of justice; and accordingly it will issue, to the end that justice may be done, in all cases where there is a specific legal right and no specific legal remedy for enforcing that right; and it may issue in cases where, although there is an alternative legal remedy, yet that mode of redress is less convenient, beneficial and effectual. HALSBURY, 4th Edn., Vol. 1, para 89, p. 111.

A prerogative order issued in certain cases to compel the performance of duty of a public or *quasi*-public nature. [Constitution of India, Art. 32(2)].

Mandap. Means any immovable property as defined in Section 3 of the Transfer of Property Act (4 of 1882) and includes any furniture, fixtures, light fittings and floor coverings therein let out for a consideration for organising any official, social or business function. [Finance Act (32 of 1994), S. 65(66) now repealed by Goods and Services Tax Act, 2017]

Mandap keeper. Means a person who allows temporary occupation of a *mandap* for a consideration for organising any official, social or business function. [Finance Act (32 of 1994), S. 65(67) now repealed by Goods and Services Tax Act, 2017]

Mandatarius terminos sibi positos transgredi non potest. (*Lat.*) A mandatory cannot exceed the bounds of his authority

Mandate. A command from a superior official or judge to an inferior, ordering him how to act.

A *mandate* is a contract by which a lawful business is committed to the management of another, and by him undertaken to be performed without reward.

A MANDATE, PROCURATION, OR LETTER OF ATTORNEY is an act by which one person gives power to another to transact for him, and in his name, one or several affairs.

A 'MANDATE' is a writ, process, or other written direction issued pursuant to law out of a Court, or made, pursuant to law, by a Court or judge thereof, commanding a person to do, or to refrain from doing, an act therein specified.

AN INJUNCTION ORDER is a mandate.

Mandatory. A "mandatory" provision in a statute is one which must be observed, as distinguished from a "directory" provision, which is one which leaves it optional with the department or officer to which it is addressed to obey it or not, as he may see fit.

The directions in a statute which are not of the essence of the thing to be done, but which are given with a view to the orderly and prompt conduct of the business, and by a failure to do which the rights of those interested will not be prejudiced, are not commonly to be regarded as mandatory.

Mandatory and directory. The question whether a statutory provision is absolute or merely directory has to be determined not only on the language of the provision but also on the relation of that provision to the general object intended to be secured by it. *S.C. Barat* v. *H.V. Pataskar,* AIR 1962 MP 180, 184.

Mandatory enactment. There is no universal rule to aid in determining whether mandatory enactments shall be considered directory only or obligatory with an implied nullification for disobedience. It is the duty of the Court to try to get at the real intention of the legislature by carefully attending to the whole scope of the statute to be construed. *H.N. Rishbud* v. *State of Delhi*, AIR 1955 SC 196, 200.

Mandatory injunction. A "mandatory injunction" is one which commands the defendant to do some positive act.

"MANDATORY INJUNCTIONS" are those which require of a party the performance of some act.

An injunction ordering a person to do a thing. [Specific Relief Act (47 of 1963), S. 39].

Mandatory national law. Means any statutory law concerning carriage of goods the provisions of which cannot be departed from by contractual stipulation to the detriment of the consignor. [UN

Convention on International Multimodal Transport of Goods, Geneva, 24 May 1980, Art. I(9)]

Mandatory penalty. A sentence which is set by law with no discretion for the judge to individualize punishment.

Mandatory presumption. A presumption which cannot be overcome by any additional evidence or argument.

Mandatory rule. A rule containing a command. [Income-tax Act (43 of 1961), S. 13(1)(c), prov.].

Mandatory statute. A statute which requires a course of action as opposed to merely permitting it.

Mandatory term. A term which is imperative. [Income-tax Act (43 of 1961), S. 13(1)(c), prov.].

Mandatum nisi gratuitum nullum est. (*Lat.*) Unless a mandate is gratuitous, it is not a mandate.

Mandi or Mundy. (*H.*) A market, a special market, one for any particular article : perhaps the original of the word Mondovy, called, the mart at Mirzapur. (Reg. ix. 1810, S. 43). A whole sale shop. (*Wil. Gloss.*)

Manganese ore. Includes ferrogenous manganese ore or ferro-manganese ore. [Iron Ore Mines (Manganese Ore Mines and Chrome Ore Mines) Labour Welfare Found Act (61 of 1976), S. 2(f)]

Manifest. Obvious; apparent; plain; needing no evidence to make it more clear; that which is open, palpable, uncontrovertible.

A *manifest* is a declaration of the entire cargo; a "*bill of lading*" is a declaration of a specific part of the cargo. A manifest is essentially a summary of all the bills of lading.

A list of goods of a merchant vessel making up her cargo with the names of shippers [Naval and Aircraft Prize Act (59 of 1971), S. 2(b)]; to indicate [Indian Easements Act (5 of 1882), S. 38; ill. (d)].

Manifest error on record. The original I.T.O., in deciding to allow the full amount of development rebate agreed to the request of the assessee that the revised balance-sheet subsequently forwarded should be considered adequate, although the original balance- sheet filed alongwith the return was perhaps technically defective. *Held,* that the successor I.T.O., had no jurisdiction to add back the development rebate under S. 154 on the ground that it was erroneously granted. If the original I.T.O., was of the view that the revised balance-sheet satisfied the requirements of law to claim development rebate, this view which was the possible view cannot be subsequently rectified under S. 154 on the basis of manifest error on record. [Chandurkar and Desai, JJ] *The Commissioner of Income-tax* v. *Chunial Bhagwandas Mehta,* MLJ : YD (1978) Suppl C 1493 : 1978 Tax LR 818 : (1978) 2 ITJ 331 : 113 ITR 436 (Bom). [Income-tax Act (43 of 1961), S. 154]

Manifest injustice. As a ground for withdrawing a plea of guilty; something more than the expectation of a sentence less severe than that actually imposed. Injustice from conduct improperly inducing accused to expect lenient punishment or from the accused's misunderstanding, reasonably entertained, of the trial judge's remarks, regarding the severity of the sentence that might be imposed. (*Ballentine's Law Dictionary, 3rd Edn.*)

Manifesta probatione non indigent. (*Maxim*) Manifest things require no proof.

Manifestation. The act of revealing or declaring. [Employee's Compensation Act (8 of 1923), Sch. III, Pt. B].

Manifesto. A public written declaration of the intentions, opinions or motives of a leader, party or body.

Manifolding. Term applied to a fraudulent trick with half-notes. A man cuts a bank-note in two, sending one half to one tradesman with an order for goods, and the other half in the same way to another getting credit from both for prompt despatching of goods.

Manipulate. To work with the hands; to handle or manage; to turn to one's own purpose or advantage.

Manipulation. Handling of apparatus. [Employee's Compensation Act (8 of 1923), Sch. II, item xxvii].

Mankind. The race or species of human beings, in law, females as well as males.

Human species. [T.P. Act (4 of 1882), S. 18].

Manner. Mode of action, way of performing or effecting anything; method; style; the way of managing; the way of doing a thing; the method or procedure; general method.

A way, mode, method of doing anything or mode of proceeding in any case or situation. [T.P. Act (4 of 1882), S. 3, prov. (1)]; [CrPC, 1973 (2 of 1974), Ss. 68(1) and 108(1)(i)].

Manner and **condition.** The word 'manner' refers to the procedure to be followed in the matter of institution and hearing of the appeal. The word 'condition' has reference to the nature, quality, qualifications of the order or decision itself against which an appeal is proposed to be filed and the other circumstances touching the right of appeal. *Rama Shankar* v. *Official Liquidator,* AIR 1956 All 222, 223.

Manner and form. The expression "manner and form", as used in a plea covers matters of both substance and form.

The expression "in such manner," as used in a corporation bye-law providing that shares of stock shall be transferable "in such manner" as the company shall direct, is not synonymous with "in such form". By the word 'form' is meant the mode, or external appearance, of the thing. The word "manner", although it includes the form, is much more comprehensive. It is synonymous with 'method' or 'peculiar way', and hence he who is authorized to prescribe the 'manner' has authority to direct the peculiar way in which anything is to be done.

Manor. A manor has been defined as "a certain circuit of ground granted by the King to some baron or man of worth as an inheritance for him or his heirs, with the exercise of such jurisdiction within the said compass as the King saw fit to grant and subject to the performance of such services and yearly rents as were by the grant required."

Manpower. Power available from or supplied by the physical effort of man, strength expressed in terms of available persons.

Manpower recruitment agency. Means any commercial concern engaged in providing any service, directly or indirectly, in any manner for recruitment of manpower, to a client. [Finance Act (32 of 1994), S. 65(1)(68) now repealed by Goods and Services Tax Act, 2017]

Manpower recruitment or supply agency. "MANPOWER RECRUITMENT OR SUPPLY AGENCY" means any commercial concern engaged in providing any service, directly or indirectly, in any manner for recruitment or supply of manpower, temporarily or otherwise, to a client. [Finance Act (32 of 1994), S. 65(68) *as substituted by Finance Act (18 of 2005), S. 88(a)(xv)* now repealed by Goods and Services Tax Act, 2017]

Mansion or Mansion house. A "mansion house", not only includes the mansion or dwelling house, but also such houses as are appurtenant thereto, as the kitchen, laundry, smokehouse, or dairy.

Large house. [CPC (5 of 1908), O. XXI, R. 32, ill.].

Manslaughter. Manslaughter is voluntary homicide, committed under the influence of sudden passion arising from an adequate cause but neither justified nor excused by law.

Mansuetae naturae. Of a tame nature.

Tamed and domisticated animals. A distinction has been made between two species of animals, tame animals or animals *mansuetae naturae* as they are called *e.g.* a dog or horse and ferocious animals.

Manual signifies what is employed or used by the hand and whereof a present profit may be made; a thing is said to be in the manual occupation of one, where it is actually used or employed by him. (*Tomlin*)

Requiring or involving physical skill or energy [Industrial Finance Corporation Act (15 of 1948) (*Repealed by Act 23 of 1993*), S. 2(c), *Expln.*]; a book containing in concise form the principles, rules and directions needed for the mastery of art.

Manual rating insurance. An insurance whereby the premium is set, using a book which classifies certain risks on a general basis, instead of evaluating each individual case.

Manual scavenger. Means a person engaged in or employed for manually carrying human excreta and the expression "manual scavenging" shall be construed accordingly. [Employment of Manual Scavengers and Construction of Dry Latrines (Prohibition) Act (46 of 1993), S. 2(j)]

"MANUAL SCAVENGER" means a person engaged or employed, at the commencement of this Act or at any time thereafter, by an individual or a local authority or an agency or a contractor, for manually cleaning, carrying, disposing of, or otherwise handling in any manner, human excreta in an insanitary latrine or in an open drain or pit into which the human excreta from the insanitary latrines is disposed of, or on a railway track or in such other spaces or premises, as the Central Government or a State Government may notify, before the excreta fully decomposes in such manner as may be prescribed, and the expression "manual scavenging" shall be construed accordingly.

Explanation.—For the purpose of this clause,—

(*a*) "engaged or employed" means being engaged or employed on a regular or contract basis;

(*b*) a person engaged or employed to clean excreta with the help of such devices and using such protective gear, as the Central Government may notify in this behalf, shall not be deemed to be a 'manual scavenger'. [S. 2(1)(g) of the Prohibition of Employment as Manual Scavengers & Their Rehabilitation Act, 2013 (25 of 2013)]

Manufactory. A manufactory is a house or place where anything is manufactured.

A place where manufacturing process goes on. [Indian Railways Act (9 of 1890), S. 3(4)(c)].

It is something more than a building. It includes not only the building, but the machinery necessary to produce the particular goods manufactured, and the engines and other powers required to propel such machinery.

The word 'manufactory' used in the Schedule 12 has for the purposes of the Minimum Wages Act (11 of 1948) to be construed in such a manner as to include within its scope processes of *Bidi* making carried on by the employees at their respective houses. *Loknath Nathulal* v. *State of M.P.,* AIR 1960 MP 181, 183. [Minimum Wages Act (11 of 1948), Sch. 12]

Manufacture. "MANUFACTURE" or "MANUFACTURING PROCESS" means any process for making, altering, repairing, ornamenting, finishing, packing, oiling, washing, cleaning, breaking up, demolishing or otherwise treating or adapting any article or substance with a view to its use, sale, transport, delivery or disposal. [Employees Provident Funds & Misc. Provisions Act (19 of 1952), S. 2(i-c)]

"MANUFACTURE" in relation to an explosive includes the process of—

(1) dividing the explosive into its component parts or otherwise breaking up or unmaking the explosive, or making fit for use any damaged explosive; and

(2) remaking, altering or repairing the explosive. [Explosive Act (4 of 1884), S. 4(h)]

"MANUFACTURE" includes any art, process or manner of producing, preparing or making an article, and also any article prepared or produced by manufacture. [Patents and Designs Act (2 of 1911), S. 2(10)].

"MANUFACTURE" in relation to any drug (or cosmetic) includes any process or part of a process for making, altering, ornamenting, finishing, packing, labelling, breaking up or otherwise treating or adopting any drug (or cosmetic) with a view to its sale and distribution but does not include the compounding or dispensing (of any drug, or the packing of any drug or cosmetic), in the ordinary course of retail business; and "to manufacture" shall be construed accordingly. [Drugs and cosmetics Act (23 of 1940), S. 3(f)]

"MANUFACTURE" includes any process,—

(i) incidental or ancillary to the completion of a manufactured product; and

(ii) which is specified in relation to any goods in the Section or Chapter notes of the Fourth Schedule as amounting to manufacture or;

(iii) which in relation to the goods specified in the Third Schedule, involves packing or repacking of such goods in a unit container or labelling or re-labelling of containers including the declaration or alteration of retail sale price on it or adoption of any other treatment on the goods to render the product marketable to the consumer;

and the word manufacture shall be construed accordingly and shall include not only a person who employs hired labour in the production or manufacture of excisable goods, but also any person who engages in their production or manufacture on his own account; [Central Excise Act (1 of 1944), S. 2(f) amended by Act 32 of 2003 now repealed by Goods and Services Tax Act, 2017]

The expression "MANUFACTURE" does not include the construction of the complete unit of a motor vehicle except for purposes of experiment or research. [Road Transport Corporation Act (64 of 1950), S. 19(2) *Expln.*]

"MANUFACTURE" includes any process incidental or ancillary to the completion of the manufacture of any dutiable goods. [Medicinal & Toilet Preparation (Excise Duties) Act (16 of 1955), S. 2(f)]

"MANUFACTURE", in relation to any insecticide, includes—

(i) any process or part of a process for making, altering finishing, packing, labelling, breaking up or otherwise treating or adopting any insecticide with a view to its sale, distribution or use but does not include the packing or breaking up of any insecticide in the ordinary course of retail business; and

(ii) any process by which a preparation containing an insecticide is formulated. [Insecticides Act (46 of 1968), S. 3(j)]

"MANUFACTURE" means a manufacture of animal articles. [Wild Life (Protection) Act (53 of 1972), S. 2(19)]

"MANUFACTURE", in relation to narcotic drug or psychotropic substances, includes—

(1) all processes other than production by which such drugs or substances may be obtained;

(2) refining of such drugs or substances;

(3) transformation of such drugs or substances; and

(4) making of preparation (otherwise than in a pharmacy on prescription) with or containing such drugs or substances. [Narcotic Drugs and Psychotropic Substances Act (61 of 1985), S. 2(x)]

"MANUFACTURE" in the relation to any ozone depleting substance includes—

(i) any process or part of a process for making, altering finishing, packing, labelling, blending or otherwise treating or any ozone depleting substance with a view to sell, distribute or use but does not include the repacking or breaking up of any ozone depleting substance in the ordinary course of retail business; and

(ii) any process in which a preparation containing ozone depleting substance is formulated. [Ozone Depleting Substances (Regulation and Control) Rules, 2000, R. 2(h)]

"MANUFACTURE" means to make, produce , fabricate, assemble, process or bring into existence, by hand or by machine, a new product having a distinctive name, character or use and shall include processes such as refrigeration, cutting, polishing, blending, repair, remarking, re-engineering and includes agriculture, aquaculture, animal husbandry, floriculture, horticulture, pisciculture, poultry, sericulture, viticulture and mining. [Special Economic Zones Act (28 of 2005), S. 2(r)]

Producing by labour [Income-tax Act (43 of 1961), S. 2(13)]; the making of materials or articles (now on a large scale) by physical labour or mechanical power; to do, produce or make [Indian Contract Act (9 of 1872), S. 73, ill. (q)].

As a noun, manufacture is defined as : (1) the process of making anything by art, or reducing materials into a form fit for use, by the hand or by machinery (*Worcestor*); (2) anything made or manufactured by hand, or manual dexterity, or by machinery. *As a verb*, the word is defined as meaning to form by manufacture, or workmanship, by the hand or machinery; to make by art and labour. (*Ame. Cyc.*)

Manufacture is : (1) The application, to material, of labour or skill, whereby the original article is changed to a new, different, and useful article, provided the process is of a kind popularly regarded as manufacture, or (2) the product of such process.

Reintroducing the electrolyte into the battery and recharging it if it is necessary will not come under the definition of "manufacture". *State of Maharashtra* v. *Shiv Dutt and Sons*, AIR 1992 SC 692, 696.

When a person who manufactures kerosine and yarn gets acid sludge and cotton waste regularly, the latter subsidiary items must also be considered as manufactured. *Commission of Sales Tax, Bombay*, v. *Bharat Petroleum Corporation Ltd.*, AIR 1992 SC 959, 965.

The word 'manufacture' means the transformation of the goods into a new commodity commercially known as a distinct and separate commodity having its own character, use and name, whether it be the result of one process or the several processes. *Gramophone Co. of India Ltd.* v. *Collector of Customs*, (2000) 1 SCC 549, para 13.

The expression 'manufacture' occurring in Sections 32 A(1) & 2(b)(iii) of the Act includes the conversion of the raw berry into coffee beans after undergoing the required nine processes. *Aspin Wall & Co. Ltd.* v. *CIT*, (2001) 7 SCC 525, paras 15 & 16. [Income-tax Act (43 of 1961), Ss. 32A(1) & 2(b)(iii)]

'Manufacture implies a change, but every change is not manufacture and yet every change of an article is the result of treatment, labour and manipulation. But something more is necessary and there must be transformation; a new and different article must emerge having a distinctive name, character or use.' [Permanent Edn. of Words and Phrases, Vol. 26, American Judgment as cited in *Union of India v. Delhi Cloth & General Mills Co. Ltd.*, AIR 1963 SC 791 : (1977) 1 LET J 199, para 14]. See also *Commissioner of Central Excise, Bangalore-II v. Osnar Chemical Private Limited*, (2012) 2 SCC 282, para 32.

If power is used for any of the numerous processes that are required to turn the raw material into a finished article known to the market the clause will be applicable. *Union of India* v. *Delhi Cloth and General Mills*, AIR 1963 SC 791, 795. [Central Excise and Salt Act (1 of 1944) as amended by Act, 38 of 1960, S. 2(*f*)]

Manufacture implies a change and there must be transaction, a new and different article emerging with a distinctive name, character or use. Grey fabric, after undergoing various processes of bleaching, dyeing, signing, printing, finishing *etc.* emerges as a commercially different commodity with its own price structure, custom and other commercial incidents, involving 'manufacture'. *Ujagar Prints* v. *Union of India*, AIR 1989 SC 516, 527, 528; *Empire Industries Ltd.* v. *Union of India*, AIR 1986 SC 662, 673; *South Bihar Sugar Mills Ltd.* v. *Union of India*, AIR 1968, SC 922, 928.

In the light of the above connotation of 'manufacture' sawn timber does not come under manufactures. *Collector, C.E. Madras* v. *Kutty F.D. & F. Co. (P) Ltd.*, AIR 1988 SC 1164, 116.

The ironing of newly stitched clothes is an essential part and for that power was used and it is part of manufacturing process. *Regional Director, E.S.I. Corporation* v. *Ram Chander*, AIR 1986 SC 113, 115.

'Manufacture' means to bring into existence a new substance and does not mean merely to produce some change in a substance. So the process of cutting running length fibre (low) into short length fibre (stable fibre) is not manufacture. *Collector of Central Excise* v. *Kiran Spinning Mills*, AIR 1988 SC 871, 872. [Central Excise and Salt Act (1 of 1944), S. 35 L (*b*)]

What is to be determined is whether there has been the manufacture of a new product which has a separate commercially current name in the market. The mere giving a new name by the seller to what is really same product is not the manufacture of a new product. *State of Maharashtra* v. *Central Provinces Manganese Ore. Co. Ltd.*, AIR 1977 SC 879, 888. [Constitution of India, Article 286, 245, 246]

Manufacture—Manufacturing process—is that as a result of undergoing the process a distinct commercial commodity different from the raw material comes into existence. *Municipal Council, Demoh* v. *Firm Prabhudas Kishoredas*, AIR 1982 SC 844, 848.

The several types of processes that are included in the expression "manufacture" should be applied to the basic article or substance so that the use, sale, transport delivery or disposal of the article as such could be achieved. *Kamlakar* v. *Central Board of Trustees,* AIR 1967 Bom 259, 262. [Employees' Provident Funds Act (19 of 1952), S. 2 (i-c)]

'Manufacture' means such transformation that brings about a new and different article with a distinctive name and character for use. *T.P. Sundarlingam* v. *State of Madras,* AIR 1971 Mad 245, 252. [Rice Milling Industry (Regulation) Act (21 of 1958)]

'Manufacture' implies something more of a change of material. To constitute 'manufacture' there must be such transformation in the change out of which a new and different article must emerge having a distinctive name, character or use. Coffee powder from coffee seeds is not manufacture. *Meghraj* v. *B. Sheshagiri Rao,* AIR 1977 Kar 163, 164. [T.P. Act (4 of 1882), S. 106]

Retreating old tyres does not bring into being a commercially distinct or different entity and so is not manufacturing process. *P.C. Cheriyan* v. *Barfi Devi*, AIR 1980 SC 86, 89.

When a mixture of different drugs is prepared by the medical practitioner or by his employees specially for the use of a patient and it is normally incapable of being passed from hand to hand as a commercial commodity, the mixture cannot be said to be manufactured. *C.S.T., U.P.* v. *Sukh Deo*, AIR 1969 SC 499 at 501.

The offence of manufacture of an excisable article necessarily includes that of possession and the two offences cannot be called "distinct" for the purposes of S. 31 of the CrPC, 1973 (2 of 1974).

The expression 'manufacture' has in ordinary acceptance a wide connotation, it means making of articles, or material commercially different from the basic components, by physical labour or mechanical process, and a manufacturer is a person by whom or under whose directing or control the articles or materials are made. *C.S.T.* v. *Sukh Deo*, (1969) 23 S.T.C. 385, 387 (SC).

"MANUFACTURE" means a process or adoption or any treatment for conversion of ingredients into an article of food, which includes any sub-process, incidental or ancillary to the manufacture of an article of food. [S. 3(1)(zc) of the Food Safety & Standards Act, 2006 (34 of 2006)]

"MANUFACTURE" the term 'manufacture' has not been defined in the Income-tax Act, 1961 (43 of 1961). In the absence of a definition of such term, it has to be given a meaning as is understood in common parlance. It is to be understood as meaning the production of articles for use from raw or prepared materials by giving such materials new forms, qualities or combinations whether by hand labour or machines. If the change made in the article results in a new and different article then it would amount to a manufacturing activity. *Aspinwall & Co. Ltd.* v. *CIT*, AIR 2001 SC 3708 : 2001 AIR SCW 3444.

"Manufacture" and "Assemble". Dictionary meaning of the word *manufacture* is to make. Originally it was by hand but now done by machine on large scale. It also means to produce in quantity. Expression manufacture is the very mixture of French and Latin words 'Manufacture' under which 'manu' means 'by hand' and 'facture' means 'making' and jointly, manufacture means to make. Thus it becomes clear that manufacture means to make something or to produce something. Insofar as expression 'assemble' is concerned, the dictionary meaning is to put together the parts of. *Shakti Auto Garage Gors.* v. *Asstt Regional Transport Officer, Jamnagar,* AIR 1996 Guj 54, 66.

Manufacture and manufacturing process. It will depend upon the circumstance of each case whether a particular business carried on comes within the definition of "manufacturing process". To constitute a manufacture there must be a transformation. Mere labour bestowed on an article even if the labour is applied through machinery, will not make it a manufacture, unless it has progressed so far that transformation ensues, and the article becomes commercially known as another and different article from that which begins its existence. *Chinnish A.M. In re,* MLJ : QD (1956-1960) Vol. III C1/2 : 1957 CrLJ 1418 : (1957) 1 Lab LJ 280 : 1957 All WR (Sup) 28 : (1957) Mad LJ (Cri) 67 : (1957) 1 MLJ 155 : AIR 1957 Mad 755. [Factories Act (25 of 1934), S. 2(k)]

'Manufacture' and 'produce'. The expressions 'manufacture' and 'produce' are normally associated with movables articles and goods, big and small, but they are never employed in denote the construction activity of the nature involved in the construction of a dam or for that matter a bridge, a road or a building.

Manufacture and semi-manufacture. Manufacture of gold ornaments falls within the expression "semi-manufactures or manufactures" in item (1)(*B*)(2). *Harakchand* v. *Union of India*, AIR 1970 SC 1453, 1462. [Industries (Development and Regulations) Act (65 of 1951), Sch. I., Item (1)(*B*)(2)]

Manufacture of salt. "MANUFACTURE OF SALT" includes the separation or purification of salt obtained in the manufacture of saltpetre, the separation of salt from earth or other substance so as to produce alimentary salt, and the excavation or removal of natural saline deposits or efflorescence. [Salt Act (12 of 1882), S. 3.]

Manufacture or produce. For the purposes of this section, "MANUFACTURE OR PRODUCE" shall include the cutting and polishing of precious and semi-precious stones. [Income tax Act (43 of 1961), S. 10 B, *Expln.* 4]

Manufactured articles. The application of labour to an article, either by hand or mechanism, does not make the article necessarily a "manufactured article", within the meaning of that term as used in the tariff laws. They are not manufactured articles until they have been manufactured into new or different articles, having a distinctive name, character, or use.

Manufacturer. A 'manufacturer' is defined to be one who is engaged in the business of working raw materials into wares suitable for use; who gives new shapes, new qualities, new combinations to matter which has already gone through some artificial process. A manufacturer prepares the original substance for use in different forms. He makes to sell, and stands between the original producer and the dealer and first consumer, depending for his profit and on the labour which he bestows on the raw materials.

"MANUFACTURER" means any person engaged in the manufacture of any article in the making of which rubber is used. [Rubber Act (24 of 1947), S. 3(e)]

"MANUFACTURER" means a person who manufactures articles from any animal or plant specified in Schedules I, II and VIII, as the case may be. [Wild Life (Protection) Act (53 of 1972), S. 2(19)]

MANUFACTURER in relation to any weight or measure, means a person who or a firm or a Hindu undivided family which—

(i) makes or manufactures such weight or measures,

(ii) makes or manufactures one or parts, claims the end product to be a weight or measure manufactured by himself or itself as the case may be,

(iii) does not make or manufacture any part of such weight or measure but assembles parts thereof made or manufactured by others and claims the end products to be a weight or measure manufactured by himself or itself as the case may be,

(iv) puts, or causes to be put, his own mark on any complete weight or measure made or manufactured by himself or itself, as the case may be.

Expln.—Where any manufacture despatches any weight or measure or any part thereof to any branch office maintained by him, or if such branch office shall not be deemed to be a manufacturer even though the parts despatched to it one assembled at such branch office. [Standard of Weights and Measures Act (60 of 1976), S. 2(o)]

"MANUFACTURER" means a manufacturer of species. [Spices Board Act (10 of 1986), S. 2(h)]

"MANUFACTURER", in relation to any dangerous machine or any part thereof, means a person who, or a firm or a Hindu undivided family which,—

(i) makes or manufactures such dangerous machine or part thereof,

(ii) makes or manufactures one or more parts and acquires the other parts of such dangerous machine and, after assembling those parts, claims the end product to be a product manufactured by himself, or itself, as the case may be,

(iii) does not make or manufacture any part of such dangerous machine but assembles parts thereof made or manufactured by other and claims the end product to be a product manufactured by himself, or itself, as the case may be,

(iv) puts, or cause to be put, his or its own mark on any complete dangerous machine made or manufactured by any other person and claims such product to be a product made or manufactured by himself, or itself, as the case may be. [Dangerous Machine (Regulation) Act (35 of 1983), S. 3(j)]

"MANUFACTURER" means the manufacturer of any article or process. [Bureau of India Standard Act (63 of 1986), S. 2(k)]

"MANUFACTURER" means a person who—

(i) makes any goods or parts thereof; or

(ii) assembles any goods or parts thereof made by others; or

(iii) puts or causes to be put his own mark on any goods made by any other person. [Consumer Protection Act, 2019 (35 of 2019), section 2(24)]

"MANUFACTURER" means a person who is engaged in the manufacture of motor vehicles. [Motor Vehicles Act (59 of 1988), S. 2(21A)]

"MANUFACTURER" in relation to any factory manufacturing lead acid batteries or components thereof means a person or Chief Executive Officer (CEO) of the company who has control over the affairs of the factory on the premises for the sale and collection of lead acid batteries or components thereof. [Batteries Management and Handling Rules, 2001, R. 3(l)]

The owner or operator of a manufactory; the producer of goods by labour. [Tea Act (29 of 1953), S. 3(i)].

A person who is engaged in the work of printing and dyeing textiles purchased by him and in the business of selling or supplying the printed and dyed material, is a manufacturer. *Hirala Jatmal* v. *Commissioner of Sales Tax,* AIR 1957 MP 37, 38.

"MANUFACTURER" means a person engaged in the business of manufacturing any article of food for sale and includes any person who obtains such article from another person and packs and labels it for sale or only labels it for such purposes. [S. 3(1)(zd) of the Food Safety & Standards Act, 2006 (34 of 2006)]

Manufacturing "establishments". Includes all the usual and necessary appliances for storing, manufacturing, weighing, packing, and delivering the manufactured articles after the process of manufacture is completed. In order that a particular article or class of articles should constitute a part of an "establishment", it is not essential that they be actually employed in the process of manufacture.

Manufacturing process. "MANUFACTURING PROCESS" means process for—

(i) making, altering, repairing, ornamenting, finishing, packing, oiling, washing, cleaning, breaking up, demolishing, or otherwise treating or adapting any article or substance with a view to its use, sale, transport, delivery or disposal, or

(ii) pumping oil, water, sewage or any other substance, or

(iii) generating, transforming or transmitting power, or

(iv) composing types for printing, printing by letter press, lithography, photogravure or other similar process or book binding; or

(v) constructing, reconstructing, repairing, refitting, finishing or breaking up ships or vessels; or

(vi) preserving or storing any article in cold storage. [Factories Act (63 of 1948), S. 2 (k)]

"MANUFACTURING PROCESS" means any process for—

(i) making, altering, repairing, ornamenting, finishing, oiling, washing, cleaning, breaking up, demolishing, refining, or otherwise treating or adapting any article or substance with a view to its use, sale, transport, delivery or disposal; or

(ii) pumping oil, water, sewage or any other substance; or

(iii) generating, transforming or transmitting power; or

(iv) composing, offset printing, printing by letter press, lithography, photogravure screen printing, three or four dimensional printing, prototyping, flexography or other types of printing process or book binding; or

(v) constructing, reconstructing, repairing, refitting, finishing or breaking up ships or vessels; or

(vi) preserving or storing any article in cold storage; or

(vii) such other activities as the Central Government may notify. [Code on Social Security, 2020 (36 of 2020), section 2(42)] [Occupational Safety,

Healthy & Working Conditions Code, 2020 (37 of 2020), section 2(1)(zi)]

"MANUFACTURE" or "MANUFACTURING PROCESS" means any process for making, altering, repairing, ornamenting, finishing, packing, oiling, washing, cleaning, breaking up, demolishing or otherwise treating or adapting any article or substance with a view to its use, sale, transport, delivery or disposal. [Employees Provident Funds & Misc. Provisions Act (19 of 1952), S. 2(ic)]

'Manufacturing' means bringing into existence a new substance. 'process' means merely bringing out some changes in the substances. The pumping of brine in salt pans with the aid of diesel pump for the purpose of manufacturing sodium sulphate and lifting raw materials to the platform at the head of kiln by aid of power for manufacture of lime from coke and lime stone are activities carried on with the aid of power in the manufacturing process. *Collector of Central Excise* v. *Rajasthan State Chemical Works*, AIR 1991 SC 2222, 2229.

'Manufacture' means 'bringing into existence a new substance' and does not mean merely 'to produce some change in a substance', however minor in consequence the change may be. [*Union of India v. Delhi Cloth & General Co. Ltd.*, AIR 1963 SC 791 : (1977) 1 ELTJ 199, para 14 as cited in *Commissioner of Central Excise, Bangalore-II v. Osnar Chemical Private Limited*, (2012) 2 SCC 282, para 32].

"Manufacture" takes place when the raw material undergo a series of changes and transformation that result in the formation of a commercially distinct commodity having a different name, character and use. It is equally well settled that physical presence of an input in the final finished excisable goods is not a prerequisite for claiming MODVAT credit under Rule 57A of Central Excise Rules, 1944. It may very well be indirectly related to manufacture and still be necessary for the completion of the manufacture of the final product. It needs little emphasis that the process of manufacture is complete only when the product is rendered marketable. Thus, manufacture is intrinsically integrated with marketability. [*Flex Engineering Limited v. Commissioner of Central Excise, Uttar Pradesh*, (2012) 5 SCC 609, para 23].

'Manufacture' with all its grammatical variations and cognate expressions means producing, making, extracting, altering, ornamenting, finishing or otherwise processing, treating, adapting any goods but does not include such manufacture or manufacturing process as may be prescribed. [*Steel India v. State of Jharkhand*, (2015) 13 SCC 390, para 16] [Bihar Finance Act (5 of 1981), S. 7(3)(b)].

The process of converting see water into salt comes within the definition of manufacturing process. *Ardeshir* v. *Bombay State*, AIR 1962 SC 20, 35. [Factories Act (63 of 1948), S. 2(k)]

Drying of husk cannot be said to be manufacturing process. *Mewa Lal* v. *Tara Rani,* AIR 1973 All 165. [Transfer of Property Act (4 of 1882), S. 106]

That it must be proved that a certain commodity was produced; that the processes of production must involve either labour or machinery; that the end of product comes into existence after the manufacturing process is complete, should have a different name and should be put to a different use. The commodity should be so transformed as to lose, its original character. *Idanandas* v. *Anant Ramachandra Phadke (Dead) By L. R.s* AIR 1982 SC 127. [Transfer of Property Act (4 of 1882), S. 106]

Manufacture involves series of processes. Process in manufacture implies not only the production but the various stages through which raw material is subjected to change by different operations. It is the cumulative effect of the various processes to which the raw material is subjected that the manufactured product emerges. Therefore, each step towards such production would be a process in relation to the manufacture. Where any particular process is so integrally connected with the ultimate production of goods that, but for that process manufacture of processing of goods, would be impossible or commercially inexpedient that process is one in relation to the manufacture. *Collector of Central Excise, Jaipur* v. *Rajasthan State Chemical Works, Deedwana, Rajasthan,* AIR 1991 SC 2222]

'MANUFACTURE' includes every processing of goods which brings into existence a commercially different and distinct commodity but shall not include such processing as may be notified by the State Government. [Rajasthan Sales Tax Act, 1994 (22 of 1995), S. 2(27) as cited in *Mamta Surgical Cotton Industries, Rajasthan v. Assistant Commissioner (Anti-Evasion), Bhilwara, Rajasthan*, (2014) 4 SCC 87, para 13].

'MANUFACTURE' means producing, making, mining, collecting, extracting, altering, ornamenting, finishing or otherwise processing, treating or adopting any goods; but does not include such manufactures or manufacturing processes as may be prescribed. [U.P. Trade Tax Act, 1948, S. 2(e-1) as cited in *State of U.P. v. Jaiprakash Associates Limited*, (2014) 4 SCC 720, para 22].

The expression 'manufacturing process' may include the process of repairing, washing, or cleaning of any article with a view to use it, under Section 2(14-AA) of the Act. *E.S.I. Corpn.* v. *Triplex Dry Cleaners,* (1998) 1 SCC 196, para 6. [Employee's State Insurance Act (34 of 1948), S. 2(14-AA)]

The activity of running of a petrol diesel pump is not covered by the definition of 'manufacturing process', while the process activities of 'cleaning', 'oiling', 'washing', 'lubricating', or 'repairing' of the vehicles at the service station are covered by the definition. *Ravi Shankar* v. *State of Rajasthan,* AIR 1993 Raj 117, 126. [Factories Act (63 of 1948), S. 2 (*k*)]

"MANUFACTURING PROCESS" pumping oil is also a 'manufacturing process'. *Qazi Noorul H.H.H. Petrol Pump* v. *Dy. Director*, ESI Corporation, AIR 2009 SC (Supp) 1729.

Manufacturing process without aid of power. If any of the processes is carried on with the aid of power though outside the factory, the exemption under Tariff Item 68 cannot be claimed. *Standard Fire Works Industries, Sivakasi* v. *Collector of Central Excise, Madura*, AIR 1987 SC 829, 831. [Central Excises and Salt Act (1 of 1944), First Schedule, Tariff item No. 68]

Manufacturing purpose. 'MANUFACTURING PURPOSE' means the making of articles of trade and commerce by means of machinery. *Uma Rao Mal* v. *Heera Lal,* AIR 1973 Raj 337, 341. [Transfer of Property Act (4 of 1982), S. 106]

The purpose of manufacture. [T.P. Act (4 of 1882), S. 106].

Manuscript. Something written with the hand; a book or paper written with the hand, or a writing of any kind, in contradistinction to a printed document (*Webster*); books written with the hand.

A written or typewritten document as distinguished from a printed copy. [Ancient Monuments and Archaeological Sites and Remains Act (24 of 1958), S. 2(b)(i)].

Map. A drawing upon a plain surface, representing a part of the earth's surface and the relative position of objects thereon.

A representation of the earth's surface or a part of it, its physical and political features *etc.* or of the heavens, delineated on a flat surface of paper *etc.* according to a definite scale or projection. [Indian Evidence Act (1 of 1872), S. 36].

Marauder. One who, while employed in the army as a soldier, commits larceny or robbery in the neighbourhood of the camp, or while wandering away from the army. (*Bouvier*)

***Mareva* injunction.** There is a particular form of interlocutory injunction which is known as *Mareva* injunction, the purpose of which is to restrain the defendant from disposing of assets which may be required to satisfy the plaintiff's claim or removing them from the jurisdiction of the court. V K Ahuja, *Intellectual Property Rights in India,* 2015, LexisNexis Butterworths.

Margin. A vertical blank column to the left or right of an area occupied or to be occupied by the main body of the printed or written text; difference.

Margin account. A brokerage account in securities transaction, which allows an investor to buy or sell securities on credit, with the securities serving as collateral for broker's loan.

Margin call. Demand from a stockbroker to a client to deposit fresh securities or cash to maintain the requirements of a minimum margin initially agreed upon.

Margin money. Means the money required as the share of the beneficiary for granting financial assistance by the financial banking institutions and other organisations. [Himachal Pradesh Antodaya Corporation Act (17 of 1979), S. 2(k)]

Margin of dumping. In relation to an article, means the difference between its export price and its normal value. [Customs Tariff Act (51 of 1975), S. 9, *Expln.* (a)]

Margin transaction. A securities or commodities transaction which is made through a broker on a margin account.

Marginal cost. Cost incurred in raising the level of output by one unit of production beyond the original target.

Marginal farmer. Means a farmer who own's land measuring not more than one acre of irrigated land or two acres of unirrigated land:

Provided that for a marginal farmer belonging to any of the Scheduled Tribes, the maximum area of land to be owned and cultivated for the purposes of this Act will be four acres of irrigated land or eight acres of unirrigated land. [Bihar Debt Relief Act, 1976 (10 of 1977), S. 2(d)]

"MARGINAL FARMER" means a cultivator with an unirrigated land holding up to one hectare or irrigated land holding up to one-half hectare. [S. 3(t) of the Right to Fair Compensation & Transparency in Land Acquisition, Rehabilitation & Resettlement Act, 2013 (30 of 2013)]

Marginal note. The notes printed at the side of sections of an Act. Though they are not parts of the Act, yet they may be considered to ascertain the objectives of the Act.

Marginal profit. The difference between the selling price and the cost of the marginal unit of output.

Marine insurance. Marine Insurance is a contract whereby one party, for a stipulated sum, undertakes to indemnify the other against loss arising from marine perils.

Insurance against loss by damage or destruction of cargo, freight or merchandise or the means or instruments of transportation or communication whether on land, sea or air. [Commercial Documents Evidence Act (30 of 1939), Sch., Pt. 1, item 9].

Marine products. 'MARINE PRODUCTS' include all varieties of fishery products known commercially as shrimp, prawn, lobster, crab, fish, shell-fish, or other aquatic animals or plants or part thereof and any other products which the authority may by notification in the *Gazette of India,* declare to be marine products for the purposes of this Act. [Marine Products Export Development Authority Act (13 of 1972), S. 3(h)]

"MARINE PRODUCTS" includes fish and shell fish grown or cultured and caught from any inland waters. [Fisherman Welfare Societies Act, 1980 (Kerala Act 7 of 1981), S. 2(i)]

Maris et foeminae conjunctio est de jure naturae. The union of male and female is founded on the law of nature.

Marital. Relating to, or connected with, the status of marriage pertaining to a husband.

Marital agreement. Any agreement between spouses concerning the division and ownership of marital property.

Marital-communication privilege. The privilege which allows a spouse not to testify about confidential communications made with the other spouse during the marriage.

Marital intercourse. Intercourse between persons married to each other. [Hindu Marriage Act (25 of 1955), S. 12(2)(b)(iii)].

Marital property. Property which is acquired from the time when a marriage begins until one spouse files for divorce.

Marital rape. The act of having sexual intercourse with a wife by her husband without the consent of his wife.

"Marital relationship" means the legally protected marital interest of one spouse to another which include marital obligation to another like companionship, living under same roof, sexual relation and the exclusive enjoyment to them, to have children, their upbringing, services in the home, support, affection, love, liking and so on. [*Pinakin Mahipatray Rawal v. State of Gujarat*, (2013) 10 SCC 48, para 19].

Maritime. Pertaining to the sea or ocean or the navigation thereof.

Maritime jurisdiction. Jurisdiction relating to sea, or commerce and navigation of the sea. [Indian Evidence Act (1 of 1872), S. 57(6)].

Maritime law. Law relating to harbours, ship and seaman; an important branch of the commercial law of maritime nations.

Maritime perils. "MARITIME PERIL" means the perils consequent on, or incidental to, the navigation of the sea, that is to say, perils of the seas, fire, war perils, pirates, rovers, thieves, captures, seizures, restraints and detainments of princes and people, jettisons, barratry and any other perils which are either of the like kind or may be designated by the policy. [Marine Insurance Act (11 of 1963), S. 2(e)]

Maritime zones of India. Means the territorial waters, the contiguous zone, the continental shelf, the exclusive economic zone or any other maritime zone of India. [Coast Guard Act (30 of 1978), S. 2(m)]

"MARITIME ZONES OF INDIA" means the territorial water of India or the exclusive economic zone of India. [Maritime Zone of India (Regulation of Fishing by Foreign Vessels) Act (42 of 1981), S. 2(g)]

Mark. Sign; indication; character; to make a mark on; to indicate.

'MARK' includes a device, brand, heading, label, ticket, pictorial representation, name, signature, word, letter or numeral or any combination thereof. [Indian Standards Institution (Certification Marks) Act (36 of 1952), S. 2(g); Bureau of India Standards Act (63 of 1986), S. 2(l)]

'MARK' includes a device, brand, heading, label, ticket, name, signature, word, letter or numeral or any combination thereof. [Trade and Merchandise Marks Act (43 of 1958), S. 2(j)]

"MARK" includes a device, brand, heading, label, ticket, name, signature, word, letter, numeral, shape of goods, packaging or combination of colours or any combination thereof. [Trade Marks Act (47 of 1999), S. 2(1)(m)]

Marked copy of the electoral roll. Means the copy of the electoral roll set apart for the purpose of making the name of electors to whom ballot papers are issued at an election. [Darjeeling Gorkha Hill Council (Elections) Rules, 1988, R. 2(d)]

Market. "MARKET" includes any place where persons assemble for the sale or for the purpose of exposing for sale, meat, fish, fruits, vegetables, animals intended for human food or any other article of human food whatsoever, with or without the consent of the owner of such place notwithstanding that there may be no common regulation for the concourse of buyers and sellers and whether or not any control is exercised over the business of, or the persons frequenting, the market by the owners of the place or by any other person, but shall not include a single shop or group of shops not being more than six in number and shops within units lines. [Cantonments Act (2 of 1924), S. 2(xx)]

A public place for buying and selling.

The expression 'market' is used in the Act as meaning either the market proper or the market yards or both. *Lakhan Lal* v. *State of Bihar*, AIR 1968 SC 1408, 1411.

'Market' means business as well as the place where business is carried on. *Naverly Jute Mills* v. *Haymon & Mco*, AIR 1963 SC 90, 95.

An open space or covered building in which cattle, provision *etc.* are exposed for sale. [Indian Evidence Act (1 of 1872), S. 32, ill. (j)]; [Minimum Wages Act (11 of 1948), Sch., Pt. II].

'Market abuse' refers to the use of manipulative and deceptive devices, giving out incorrect or misleading information, so as to encourage investors to jump into conclusions, on wrong premises, which is known to be wrong to the abusers. [*N. Narayanan v. Adjudicating Officer, Securities and Exchange Board of India*, (2013) 12 SCC 152, para 33].

"Any use, intended or otherwise, of depository receipts or market of depository receipts in a manner, which has potential to cause or has caused abuse of the securities market in India, is market abuse and shall be dealt with accordingly." [Depository Receipts Scheme, 2014, para 10(1) as cited in *Securities and Exchange Board of India v. Pan Asia Advisors Limited*, (2015) 14 SCC 71, para 95].

'Market definition'. Is a tool to identify and define the boundaries of competition between films. It serves to establish the framework within which competition policy is applied by the Commission. [*Competition*

Commission of India v. *Coordination Committee of Artistes and Technicians of West Bengal Film and Television*, (2017) 5 SCC 17, para 34].

Market functionary includes a broker, a commission agent, an exporter, an importer, a ginner, a presser, a processor, a stockist, a trader, a weighman, warehouse man, hammal, surveyor & such other person as may be declared under the rules or the byelaws. [M.P. Krishi Upaj Mandi Act, S. 2(f)].

Market manipulation. Market manipulation is normally regarded as the 'unwarranted' interference in the operation of ordinary market forces of supply and demand and thus undermines the 'integrity' and efficiency of the market. [Palmer's Company Law, 25th Edn. (2010), Vol. 2, p. 11097 as cited in *N. Narayanan v. Adjudicating Officer, Securities and Exchange Board of India*, (2013) 12 SCC 152, para 21].

Market overt. In open market, *i.e.*, a place sanctioned by law or custom for selling and buying and open to the public; a place, market, or shop for the public sale of goods.

"Marketplace based model of e-commerce". Means providing of an information technology platform by an e-commerce entity on a digital and electronic network to act as a facilitator between buyer and seller. [Legal Metrology (Packaged Commodities) Rules, 2011, R. 2(bf)].

Market price. MARKET PRICE in relation to any goods means the wholesale price of the goods in the ordinary course of trade in India. [Customs Act (52 of 1862), S. 2(30)]

The price at which a seller is ready and willing to sell and a buyer ready and willing to buy in the ordinary course of trade. The price actually given in current market dealings; price established by public sales or sales in the way of ordinary business. The actual price at which a given stock or commodity is currently sold, or has recently been sold in open market, that is, not at forced sale, but in the usual and ordinary course of trade and competition between sellers and buyers equally free to bargain, as established by records of late sales. In the case of a security, market price is usually considered the last reported price at which the stock or bond is sold.

Market price is synonymous with market value, and means the price actually given in current market dealings, or the price at which the supply and demand are equal. (*Black*)

The price usually given in current market dealings. [Indian Contract Act (9 of 1872), S. 73, ill. (o)].

Market proper. Means any area including all lands with the building thereon, within such distance of the principal market or submarket yard, as may be notified in the Official Gazette by the State Government, to be a market proper. [Punjab Agricultural Produce Markets Act (23 of 1961), S. 2(k)]

Market research agency. Means any commercial concern engaged in conducting market research in any manner, in relation to any product, service or utility, including all types of customised and syndicated research services. [Finance Act (32 of 1994), S. 65(1)(69) now repealed by Goods and Services Tax Act, 2017]

Market value. The market value is not determined by theoretical considerations, what has to be seen is the value in the market and not the value calculated in an abstract manner by applying a multiplier to some unknown earlier sale. *C.I.T.* v. *Arun Mehra,* (1986) 157 ITR 308, 318 (Del). [Income-Tax Act (43 of 1961), S. 269-A]

"Market value" shall mean the full amount which a recipient of a supply is required to pay in order to obtain the goods or services or both of like kind and quality at or about the same time and at the same commercial level where the recipient and the supplier are not related [The Central Goods and Services Tax Act, 2017 (12 of 2017), S. 2(73)]

"MARKET VALUE", in relation to an instrument through which—

(a) any security is traded in a stock exchange, means the price at which it is so traded;

(b) any security which is transferred through a depository but not traded in the stock exchange, means the price or the consideration mentioned in such instrument;

(c) any security is dealt otherwise than in the stock exchange or depository, means the price or consideration mentioned in such instrument. [Indian Stamp Act (2 of 1899), section 2(16B)]

'Market Value' means, in relation to any property which is the subject-matter of an instrument, the price which such property would have fetched or would fetch if sold in open market on the date of execution of such instrument as determined in such manner and by such authority as may be prescribed by rules made under this Act or the consideration stated in the instrument, whichever is higher. [Stamp Act (2 of 1899), as amended by West Bengal, S. 2(16-B) as cited in *Additional District Sub-Registrar, Siliguri v. Pawan Kumar Verma*, (2013) 7 SCC 537, para 5].

Market value means the price that a willing purchaser would pay to a willing seller for a property, having regard to its existing condition, with all its existing advantages and its potential possibilities when laid out in its most advantageous manner excluding any advantage due to the carrying out of the scheme for the purposes for which the property is compulsorily acquired. *Raghubans Narain* v. *Govt. of U.P.*, AIR 1967 SC 465, 467. [Land Acquisition Act (1 of 1894), S. 23]

"Market value" means what a willing purchaser would pay a willing seller for the property, having regard to the advantages available to the land and the development activities which may be going on in the vicinity and potentiality of the land and as such, an offer of sale of land to an industrialist on concessional rates with a view to induce him to set up industry in a particular area is not market value. *Mahibir Prasad* v. *Collector, Cuttack*, AIR 1987 SC 720, 721 [Now repealed & replaced by Act 30 of 2013].

The term 'market value' means, the price which a willing purchaser of the land is ready to offer as consideration therefor to the seller. *Dayal Singh* v. *Union of India,* (2003) 2 SCC 593, para 19 : AIR 2003 SC 1140. [Requisition and Acquisition of Immovable Property Act (30 of 1952), S. 8(3)]

A price at which both buyers and sellers are willing to do business; the market or current price. [Court-fees Act (7 of 1870), S. 7(iii)].

"MARKET VALUE" means the value of land determined in accordance with section 26 of Act 30 of 2013. [S. 3(u) of the Right to Fair Compensation & Transparency in Land Acquisition, Rehabilitation & Resettlement Act, 2013 (30 of 2013)]

"MARKET VALUE" for the purposes of section 80-IA(8) of Act 43 of 1961, 'market value', in relation to any goods or services, means—

(i) the price that such goods or services would ordinarily fetch in the open market; or

(ii) the arm's length price as defined in section 92F(ii) of Act 43 of 1961, where the transfer of such goods or services is a specified domestic transaction referred to in section 92BA of Act 43 of 1961. [*Explanation* to section 80-IA(8) of the Income-tax Act, 1961 (43 of 1961) as substituted (w.e.f. 1-4-2013) by the Finance Act, 2012 (23 of 2012)]

Marketability. Salability; the probability of selling property, goods, securities, or services at specified times, prices, and terms.

Marketable. Such things as may be sold; such for which a buyer may be found.

Marketable means saleable or suitable for sale. *Indian Cable Co. Ltd., Calcutta* v. *Collector of Central Excise*, AIR 1995 SC 64, 69. [Central Excise and Salt Act (1 of 1944), S. 3] [Now repealed by Act 12 of 2017]

Saleable. Such things as may be sold in the market; those for which a buyer may be found; merchantable. [Black's Law Dictionary (6th Edn.) as cited in *Bhagwati Developers Private Limited v. Peerless General Finance and Investment Company Limited*, (2013) 9 SCC 584, para 21.1].

"(1) Capable of being marketed that may or can be bought or sold; suitable for the market; that finds a ready market; that is in demand, saleable.

(2) Of or pertaining to buying or selling; concerned with trade; of price, value, that may be obtained in buying or selling." [Oxford English Dictionary, Vol. 1, p. 1728 as cited in *Bhagwati Developers Private Limited v. Peerless General Finance and Investment Company Limited*, (2013) 9 SCC 584, para 21.2].

Marketable security. "MARKETABLE SECURITY" means a security of such a description as to be capable of being sold in any stock market in India. [Indian Stamp Act (2 of 1899), S. 2(16-A)].

Marketed. The term 'marketed' includes the entire process commencing from storage till delivery including display of article for sale. *Chaware Oil Industries, Karanja* v. *State of Maharashtra,* AIR 1985 Bom 160, 165.

The action of selling or buying in market. [Cardamom Act (42 of 1965), S. 7(4), prov.; Income-tax Act (43 of 1961), S. 80P(2)(vii)].

Marketing. "MARKETING" includes all activities in connection with the transport, grading, pooling, marketing and sale of industrial produce, whether in the primary form or in semi-processed or processed form. [W.B. Backward Classes Development and Finance Corporation Act (9 of 1995), S. 2(c)]

Marketing does not mean selling only through an auction and that too, to the highest bidder. *Coffee Board* v. *Famous Coffee & Tea Works,* AIR 1965 Mad 14, 20. [Coffee Act (7 of 1942), S. 25]

The word 'marketing' is an expression of wide import. It involves exchange functions such as buying and selling, physical functions such as storage, transportation, processing and other commercial activities such as standardisation, financing, marketing intelligence *etc. Kerala State Cooperative Marketing Federation Ltd.* v. *CIT,* (1998) 5 SCC 48, para 7 : AIR 1998 SC 2303.

Marketing of crops. Includes the processing of crops prior to marketing by any agricultural producers or any organisation of such producers. [National Bank for Agricultural and Rural Development Act (61 of 1981), S. 2(k)]

Marriage. "MARRIAGE" means a marriage between Parsis whether contracted before or after the commencement of this Act. [Parsi Marriage and Divorce Act (3 of 1936), S. 2(6)]

MARRIAGE includes a purported marriage which was void *ab initio* and "husband" and "wife" shall be construed accordingly. [Matrimonial Causes (War Marriages) Act (40 of 1948), S. 2(b)]

That act of marrying, the ceremony by which two persons are made husband and wife; particular matrimonial unions. [Indian Evidence Act (1 of 1872), S. 112 and Indian Majority Act (9 of 1875), S. 2(a)].

Marriage is a civil and religious contract, whereby a man is joined and united to a woman, for the purposes of civilized society. (*Tomlin*)

'Marriage' is often described as one of the basic civil rights of man/woman, which is voluntarily undertaken by the parties in public in a formal way, and once concluded, recognizes the parties as husband and wife. [*Indra Sharma v. V.K.V. Sarma*, (2013) 15 SCC 755, para 24].

"INVALID MARRIAGE". Where a marriage is accepted as valid by relations, friends and others for a long time it cannot be declared as 'invalid marriage'. *Koppisetti Subbharao alias Subramaniam* v. *State of A. P.*, AIR 2009 SC 2684.

Marriage ceremony. Religious or civil proceeding to solemnize a marriage.

Marriage certificate. A certificate issued as an evidence of marriage.

Marriage settlement. A deed executed and making a settlement of property in consideration of a marriage about to take place.

Marriage with another woman. "MARRIAGE WITH ANOTHER WOMAN" means marriage of any person, being married, to any other person during the life of the former wife, whether the second marriage shall have taken place within India or elsewhere. [Indian Divorce Act (4 of 1869), S. 3(8)].

Marry. To constitute as husband and wife according to the laws and customs of a nation. [Indian Contract Act (9 of 1872), S. 65, ill. (a)].

"Material sensing device". Means a radio determination device designed to detect the location of objects within a structure or to determine the physical properties of a material. [Use of Very Low Power Ultra-wideband Device (Exemption from Licensing requirements) Rules, 2018, R. 2(r)].

"Materials recovery facility" (MRF). Means a facility where non-compostable solid waste can be temporarily stored by the local body or any other entity mentioned in Rule 2 or any person or agency authorised by any of them to facilitate segregation, sorting and recovery of recyclables from various components of waste by authorised informal sector of waste pickers, informal recyclers or any other work force engaged by the local body or entity mentioned in Rule 2 for the purpose before the waste is delivered or taken up for its processing or disposal. [Solid Waste Management Rules, 2016, R. 3(1)(31)].

Martial. Pertaining to or suited for war.

Martial law. It originally meant the law administered by the Court-martial which dealt with "the offences and miscarriages of soldiers contrary to the laws and rules of the army."

Martial law, in the most usual sense of the term, meaning "the suppression of ordinary law, and the temporary Government of a country or parts of it by military tribunals".

Martyr. 'MARTYR' means a person, who has evinced remarkable enthusiasm for Tamil language and Tamil culture and while striving to uphold his enthusiasm for Tamil language or in his zeal to preserve the growth of Tamil language or to preserve the Tamil culture, has lost his life. [T.N. Payment of Pension to Tamil Scholars and Miscellaneous Provisions Act (23 of 1983), S. 2(d)]

Masking. In critical legal studies, the act or an instance of concealing something's true nature.

Masonry building. MASONRY BUILDING means any building other than a hut and includes any structure, a substantial part of which is made of masonry, reinforced concrete, steel, iron or other metal. [Calcutta Municipal Corporation Act, 1980, S. 2(51)]

Mass customization. Mass production of products customized to customer order, promising the quality control and efficiency advantages of mass production but with made-to-order customization; it would reduce inventory costs and shorten production delays; *e.g.*, manufacturing to order in on-line ordering and configuration of personal computers. (*Cyber Law*)

Mass media. A medium of communication (as the newspapers, radio, motion pictures, television) that is designed to reach the mass of the people and that tends to set the standards, ideas and aims of the masses. [Water (Prevention and Control of Pollution) Act (6 of 1974), S. 16(2)(e)].

Mass migration area. The expression "MASS MIGRATION AREA" means the territories which immediately before the 1st November, 1956, were comprised in the following states or areas, namely:—

(i) the State of Punjab;

(ii) the State of Patiala and East Punjab States Union;

(iii) the State of Ajmer;

(iv) the State of Delhi;

(v) the State of Himachal Pradesh;

(vi) the district of Alwar, Bharatpur and Bikaner in the State of Rajasthan and the districts of Saharanpur, Dehra Dun, Meerut and Muzaffarnagar in the State of Uttar Pradesh. [Transfer of Evacuee Deposit Act (15 of 1954), S. 4(2), *Expln.*]

Master. "MASTER",—

(a) in relation to any vessel or aircraft means any person, other than a pilot, harbour master, assistant harbour master or berthing master, having for the time being the charge or control of such vessel or aircraft, as the case may be; and

(b) in relation to any boat belonging to ship, means the master of that ship. [Explosives Act (4 of 1884), S. 4(g)]

"MASTER", in relation to any vessel or any aircraft making use of any Major Port, means any person having for the time being the charge or control of such vessel or such aircraft, as the case may be, except a pilot, harbour master, assistant harbour master, dock master or berthing master of the Major Port. [Major Port Authorities Act, 2021 (1 of 2021), section 2(1)(r)]

With reference to a ship means any person (except a pilot or harbour master) having for the time being control or charge of the ship [General Clauses Act (10 of 1897), S. 3(33)]; an individual having control, authority or predominance over another. [IPC (45 of 1860), S. 381].

Master agreement. In labour law, it is an agreement between a union and industry leaders, whose terms serve as a model for agreements between the union and individual companies within the industry.

Master and Servant. He is to be deemed a master who has the superior choice, control, and direction of the servant, and whose will the servant represents, not merely in the ultimate result of the work, but in the details. (*Ame Cyc.*)

One who exercises personal authority over another, is the master and that other is his servant.

"A person employed by another to render personal services to the employer" is a servant.

A master is one who not only prescribes to the workman the end of his work, but directs or at any moment may direct the means also or as it has been put retains the power of controlling the work. A servant is a person subject to the command of his master as to the manner in which he shall do his work. *Shaffi* v. *Commissioner E&P. Tax,* AIR 1960 SC 1269.

Master of ship. The person entrusted with the care and navigation of a ship.

Master of the ship. "MASTER," used with reference to a ship, shall mean any person (except a pilot or harbour-master) having for the time being control or charge of the ship. [General Clauses Act (10 of 1897), S. 3(33)].

Master plan. "MASTER PLAN" in relation to an area within an urban agglomeration or any part thereof, means the plan (by whatever name called) prepared under any law for the time being in force or in pursuance of an order made by the State Government for the development of such area or part thereof and providing for the stages by which such development shall be carried out. [Urban Land (Ceiling and Regulation) Act (33 of 1976), S. 2(h)]

A municipal plan for housing, industry and recreation facilities *etc.*

"MASTER PLAN" means the Master Plan for Delhi with the perspective for the year 2021, notified *vide* Notification No. S.O. 141(E), dated 7-2-2007 under the Delhi Development Act, 1957 (61 of 1957). [S. 2(1)(e) of the National Capital Territory of Delhi Laws (Special Provisions) Act, 2011 (5 of 2011)]

Material. Of such consequences, importance or significance as to be likely to influence the determination of a cause; to alter the character of an instrument, *etc.*; corporeal; of or consisting of matter [Industrial Disputes Act (14 of 1947), S. 11(3)(b)]; the matter from which anything is made [IPC (45 of 1860), Ss. 475 and 476]; that out of which anything is or may be made. [Arms Act (54 of 1959), S. 2(1)(b)(iii)].

Material date. For the purposes of sub-section "MATERIAL DATE"—

(i) in relation to an Indian ship, means the 21st July 1968;

(ii) in relation to a foreign ship belonging to a country to which the Load Line Convention applies, means the date as from which it is declared under Section 283 that the Government of such country has accepted the Load Line Convention or, as the case may be, that the said Convention has been applied to such country. [Merchant Shipping Act (44 of 1958), S. 283A(2)]

Material discrepancies. In evidence, 'material discrepancies' are those which are not normal and not expected of a normal man. 'Material discrepancies' corrode the credibility of a party's case. *Gangadhar Behera* v. *State of Orissa*, (2002) 8 SCC 381, 392, para 15. See also *Bhargavan* v. *State of Kerala*, JT 2003 (9) SC 513 : 2003 (7) SLT 228; *Syed Ibrahim* v. *State of A.P.*, (2006) 10 SCC 601, 605-06, para 10.

Material evidence. The word 'Material' used in the phrase 'material evidence' makes no difference in the meaning of the expression.

Material fact. The word 'material' means necessary for the purpose of formulating a complete cause of action; and if anyone 'material' fact is omitted, the statement of claim is bad. *Hari Vishnu Kamath* v. *Election Tribunal,* AIR 1958 MP 168, 171. [Representation of the People Act (43 of 1951), S. 83(1)(a)]

The expression 'material facts' means such facts as would afford a basis for the allegation made in the petition and would constitute the cause of action. *Hari Shanker Jain* v. *Sonia Gandhi,* (2001) 8 SCC 233, para 23.

Material facts and material particulars. All those facts which are essential to clothe the petitioner with a complete cause of action, are "material facts" which must be pleaded, and failure to plead even a single material fact amounts to disobedience of the mandate of Section 83(1)(a). "Particulars", on the other hand, are "the details of the case set up by the party". "Material particulars" within the contemplation of clause (b) of Section 83(1) would therefore mean all the details which are necessary to amplify, refine and embellish the material facts already pleaded in the petition in compliance with the requirements of clause (a). *Shri Udhav Singh* v. *Madhav Rao Scindia,* AIR 1976 SC 744. [Representation of People Act (43 of 1951), S. 83(1)(a) & (b)]

The facts which are essential to disclose a complete cause of action are material facts and the details of the case and pleas to amplify, refine, or explain material facts, are 'material particulars'. *Mahendra Pal* v. *Ram Dass Malanger,* (2000) 1 SCC 261, para 7 : AIR 2000 SC 16.

There is distinction between material facts and particulars. Material facts are primary or basic facts which must be pleaded by the party in support of the case set up by him either to prove his cause of action or defence. Particulars, on the other hand, are details in support of material facts pleaded by the party. They amplify, refine and emblish material facts by giving finishing touch to the basic contours of a picture already drawn so as to make if full, more clear and more informative. Particulars ensure conduct of fair trial and would not take the opposite party by surprise. *Mahadeorao Sukaji Shivankar* v. *Ramaratan Bapu*, (2004) 7 SCC 181, 185, para 7.

Material form. The words 'material form' are used only to emphasize that reproduction of an artistic work should take a tangible form and such material forms are the canvas, marble and bronze or similar substance in three dimensions, when the artistic work is a sculpture. *D.C. Bureau* v. *United Concern,* AIR 1967 Mad 381, 387. [Copyright Act (14 of 1957), S. 14(c)(i)]

Material irregularity. Omission to mention a certain thing required by the statute is material irregularity. The non-inclusion of municipal taxes in the sale proclamation in respect of a house sold in execution of a decree is not material irregularity.

Material issue of law. Question of law of importance likely to influence the determination of a cause.

Material particulars. The illustration (b) to S. 114, Indian Evidence Act (I of 1872) uses the words "in material particulars", but what are material particulars must depend upon the facts of the particular case.

Material propositions. "MATERIAL PROPOSITIONS" are those propositions of law or fact which a plaintiff must allege in order to show right to sue or a defendant must allege in order to constitute his defence. [CPC (5 of 1908), O. XIV, R. 1(2)].

Material question. Substantial question. [CPC (5 of 1908), O. V, R. 1(2)(b)].

Material resource of the community. The expression "material resource of the community" does not mean that the ownership of the resources must already vest in the State. The distribution envisaged by Article 39(b) necessarily includes transformation of wealth from private ownership into public ownership by nationalisation. Hence the expression 'material resources of the community' is not confined to natural resources; it is not confined to resources owned by the public; it means and includes all resources, natural and man-made, public and private-owned. *Sanjeev Coke Manufacturing Company* v. *Bharat Cocking Coal Limited,* AIR 1983 SC 239. [Constitution of India, Art. 39(b)]

The term material resources of the community would embrace all things which are capable to produce wealth for community. *Assam Sillimanite Ltd* v. *Union of India,* AIR 1992 SC 938.

Material resources. The term 'material resources' cover not only natural or physical resources but also movable or immovable properties. *State of Tamilnadu* v. *Labu Kavur Bai*, AIR 1984 SC 326, 343. [Constitution of India, Art. 39(b)]

Electrical energy generated and distributed by various undertakings also falls under the term material resources. *Tinsukhia Elect. Supply Co.* v. *State of Assam,* AIR 1990 SC 123.

Material services. Material Services in Art. 19(1)(g) involve an activity carried on through co-operation between employers and employees to provide the community with the use of something such as electric power, water, transportation, mail delivery, telephone and the like. *Safdargunj Hospital* v. *K.S. Sethi*, AIR 1970 SC 1407.

Material thing. A thing consisting of matters. [Indian Evidence Act (1 of 1872), S. 60, prov.].

Material witness. The test whether a witness is material is not whether he would have given evidence in support of the defence. The test is whether he is a witness "essential to the unfolding of the narrative on which the prosecution is based". *Narain* v. *State of Punjab*, AIR 1959 SC 484, 487.

Materiality. In *Law of Evidence*, the bearing of facts on a disputed issue. In *Pleadings*, the bearing of allegations on the issues in the case.

Materially. Substantially; essentially; in "an important degree".

To a significant extent or degree. [Indian Contract Act (9 of 1872), Ss. 150, and 133, ill. (b)].

Materially affected. The words "the result of the election has been materially affected" indicate that the result should not be judged by the mere increase or decrease in the total number of votes secured by the candidate but by proof of the fact that the wasted votes would have been distributed in such a manner between the contesting candidates as would have brought about the defeat of the returned candidate. *Vashist Narain* v. *Dev Chandra*, AIR 1954 SC 513, 515. [Representation of the People Act (43 of 1951), S. 100(1)(d)]

If the party challenging the declaration comes forward with the delegations of malpractice and such other acts, the burden of proof is on that person and unless he proves that had it not been for the malpractice, he would have secured more votes, he would not have succeeded and it could have been then said that the result of the election was not materially affected. *Dippala Suri Dora* v. *V.V. Giri*, AIR 1958 AP 724, 733. [Representation of the People Act (43 of 1951), S. 100(1)(d)]

Materially altered. 'Materially altered, means a substantial change in the character, form and structure of the building without destroying its identity. *Om Prakash* v. *Amar Singh*, AIR 1987 SC 617, 619.

Materials. The substance or matter from which anything is made [Indian Contract Act (9 of 1872), S. 188, ill. (b)]; the whole or a notable part of the elements or constituents of something physical (when used with reference to dismantled or broken material). [CPC (5 of 1908), S. 60(2)].

The matter of which a thing is or may be made; the constituent parts of something. [Shorter Oxford English Dictionary as cited in *Escorts Limited v. Commissioner of Central Excise, Faridabad*, (2015) 9 SCC 109, para 9]

"Maternity benefit", in respect of Chapter VI, means the payment referred to in sub-section (*1*) of section 60. [Code on Social Security, 2020 (36 of 2020), section 2(43)].

Maternity home. Means an establishment where women are usually received or accommodated for the purpose of antenatal and postnatal care in connection with child birth. [Orissa Clinical Establishments (Control and Regulation) Act, 1990 (4 of 1992), S. 2(e)]

Maternity leave. A leave during the period of pregnancy.

Mate's receipt. Receipt given by the mate of a ship when goods are brought alongside for loading.

Math. 'MATH' means a Hindu religious institution with properties attached thereto and presided over by a person, the succession to whose office devolves in accordance with the direction of the founder of the institution or is regulated by usage and—

(i) whose duty it is to engage himself in imparting religious instruction or rendering spiritual service; or

(ii) who exercises or claims to exercise spiritual headship over a body of disciples; and includes places of religious worship or instruction which are appurtenant to the institution;

Explanation : Where the headquarters of a math are outside the State but the math has properties situated within the State, control shall be exercised over the math in accordance with the provisions of this Act, in so far as the properties of the math situated within the State are concerned". [Tamil Nadu Hindu Religion and Endowment Act (22 of 1959), S. 6(13)]

Matricide. The act of killing one's own mother.

Matrimonial. Of or pertaining to marriage. [Indian Evidence Act (1 of 1872), S. 41].

Matrimonial home. It is not necessarily the house of husband or the house of his parents. Both wife and husband go in fully employed at different places decided to book ownership flat at Bombay. Husband contributing initial amount and wife paying the remaining amount. Held the flat at Bombay was matrimonial home of the parties. *Alka Bhaskar Bakre* v. *Bhaskar Satchidand Bakre,* AIR 1991 Bom 164 at 175. [Hindu Marriage Act (25 of 1955), S. 13(1)(ia)]

The house where husband and wife live together.

Matrimonial jurisdiction. The jurisdiction for suits for the redress of injuries respecting rights on marriage. [Indian Evidence Act (1 of 1872), S. 41].

Matrimonial offence. An offence against the vows of marriage. The vows of marriage are well known. Desertion is certainly one offence, and cruelty as defined by the law is another. *Richardson* v. *Richardson,* (1949) 2 All ER 330 at 332. CA, per BUCKNILL LJ, (1950) P 16.

Misbehaviour which includes adultery, desertion, or cruelty, by a party to a marriage.

Matrimonial proceedings (matrimonial causes). Proceedings for divorce, judicial separation, or nullity of marriage.

Matrimonium subsequens legitimos facit. (*Maxim*) A subsequent marriage makes the children legitimate. (*Peloubet*)

Matrimonium subsequens tollit peccatum praecedens. Subsequent marriages cure precedent criminality.

Matrimony. The act or state of being married.

Matter. "MATTER" means an article, news-item, news-report, or any other matter which is published by a newspaper or transmitted by a news agency by any means whatsoever and includes a cartoon, picture, photograph, strip or advertisement which is published in a newspaper. [Press Council (Procedure for Inquiry) Regulations 1979, Regn. 2(e)]

Some substance or essential thing, opposed to form. (*Bouvier*)

In law, a fact or facts constituting a whole or a part of a ground of action or defence.

A subject (as a fact, an event or course of events, or a circumstance, situation or question) of interest or relevance; an object of thought or consideration [CPC (5 of 1908), O. XI, R. 2]; [CPC (5 of 1908), O. XI, R. 1, prov.]; [Metal Corporation of India (Acquisition of Undertakings) Act (36 of 1966), S. 10(1)(b)]; physical substance [Army Act (46 of 1950), S. 142(7)].

The 'matter' to which Art. 133 applies is the appellate jurisdiction of the Supreme Court in appeals from High Courts in regard to civil matters, and does not include the requirements or conditions with regard to which the Court must be satisfied before it issues a certificate. *Ram Sahai* v. *Ram Sevak*, AIR 1956 All 321, 322 [Constitution of India, Art. 135, 133].

The word 'matter' is of wider import than particulars, and would also comprehend the grounds on which the election is sought to be set aside. *Harish Chandra Bajpai* v. *Triloki Singh*, AIR 1957 SC 444, 452.

Matter directly and substantially in issue. The word "substantially" signifies "in effect" though not "in express terms." and the word "directly" is used in contra-distinction to the words "incidentally" and "collaterally".

Matter en (in) ley ne serra mise en (in) bouche (boutche) del jurors. Matter of law shall not be put into the mouths of jurors.

Matter in difference. The subject on which there is difference between the parties. [Guardians and Wards Act (8 of 1890), S. 47(i)]; [Religious Endowments Act (20 of 1863), S. 16].

Matter in dispute. Matter over which proceedings are started in a Court of law.

Something which is the subject-matter of some controversy. [Indian Evidence Act (1 of 1872), S. 20]; [CPC (5 of 1908), O. XIV, R. 6(c)].

Matter in issue. It is the "matter in issue," not the subject-matter of the suit, that forms the essential test of *res judicata*. *Vijay Kumar* v. *Manohar Lal,* AIR 1979 Del 1, 6.

The words 'matter in issue' mean the right litigated between the parties.

Matter in suit means entire matter in controversy and not one of the several issues in the case.

Matter incidental thereto. If question of reinstatement and/or compensation is referred to a Tribunal for adjudication, the question of granting interim relief till the decision of the Tribunal with respect to the same matter would be a matter incidental thereto and need be specifically referred in terms to the Tribunal. *Hotel Imperial* v. *Hotel Workers Union*, AIR 1959 SC 1342, 1348. [Industrial Disputes Act (14 of 1947), S. 10(4)]

Matter of fact. A matter that is or is demonstrable as a fact; matter involving primarily proof of evidence (distinguished from matter of law). [CPC (5 of 1908), O. VI, R. 8].

Matter of law. Matter in dispute which has got to be resolved by the application of statutory rules and procedures as well as legal precedents in contra-distinction to matter of fact.

A matter which pertains to or concerns law.

Matter of mixed law and fact. Matter depending for solution on questions of both law and fact.

Matter of policy. [Unit Trust of India Act (52 of 1963), S. 30]; [National Cadet Corps Act (31 of 1948), S. 12(1)].

Matter of public interest. Anything which affects the interest of, or in which are interested the public at large. [Indian Evidence Act (1 of 1872), S. 32(4)].

Matters and causes testamentary. These words comprehend "all matters and causes relating to the grant and revocation of Probate of Wills, or of Administration."

Matters in controversy. The expression "matters in controversy" in S. 2, sub-section 2 of the CPC (5 of 1908) cannot be pressed so as to exclude matters which, though as it happened they were common ground, must have been actually decided, if any question had arisen, and were the foundation of the whole determination.

Matters in controversy in the suit. Are not merely matters which arise on the face of the plaint as at first presented. They may include matters which are of vital importance between the parties but which may come to arise and in respect of which the parties may be at controversy at a subsequent stage of a suit and the question as to whether a suit survives or not in such a matter.

Matters incidental thereto. The words, 'matters incidental thereto' should not be interpreted so as to give vague and indeterminate jurisdiction to the Tribunals especially over independent matters. The intention of the Government as expressed by the plain language of the order of reference cannot be permitted to be ignored. Matters which require independent consideration or treatment and have their own importance, cannot be considered 'incidental'. *Jaipur Spinning & Weaving Mills, Ltd. Jaipur* v. *President, Jaipur Spinning & Weaving Mills, Ltd. Mazdoor Union, Jaipur,* MLJ : QD (1961-1965) Vol III C2834 : (1959) 2 Lab LJ 656 : ILR (1960) 10 Raj 17) [Industrial Disputes Act (14 of 1947), S. 10(1)(c), 10(4)]

Matters of religion. The expression 'matters of religion' embraced not merely matters of doctrine and belief pertaining to the religion but also the practice of it or to put it in terms of Hindu theology, not merely its *Gnana* but also its *Bhakti* and *Karma Kandas*. *Sri Venkataramana Devaru* v. *State of Mysore*, AIR 1958 SC 255, 264. [Constitution of India, Art. 26(b)]

Matters relating to employment. The expression "matters relating to employment" includes not only the initial stage of employment but also the stage of promotion. *Madhusudan* v. *State of Kerala*, AIR 1961 Ker 203, 206. [Constitution of India, Art. 16(1)]

Matters sub judice. Matters awaiting judicial decision which are not referred to in debate as a general principle of parliamentary procedure.

Maturity. "The maturity of a promissory note or bill of exchange is the date at which it falls due. Every promissory note or bill of exchange which is not expressed to be payable on demand, at sight or on presentment is at maturity on the third day after the day on which it is expressed to be payable." [Negotiable Instruments Act (26 of 1881), S. 22]

Payability (of a bill); the quality or state of being mature; full development [Industrial Finance Corporation Act (15 of 1948) (*Repealed by Act 23 of 1993*), S. 21(3)(b)].

The amount that is due and payable on the date of maturity.

Applied to commercial paper, the time when the paper becomes due and demandable. (*Bouvier*)

Maturity date. "MATURITY DATE" means a fixed date on which benefit may become payable either absolutely or contingently. [Insurance Regulatory and Development Authority (Actuarial Report and Abstract) Regulations, 2000, Rgn. 2(h)]

Maturity value. The amount an investor receives when a security is redeemed at maturity not including any periodic interest payments.

Maund. Means a weight of three thousand two hundred tolas, each tola being a weight of one hundred and eighty grains troy. [Indian Railways Act (9 of 1890), S. 3(17)]

Maxicab. Means any motor vehicle constructed or adapted to carry more than six passengers, but not more than twelve passengers, excluding the driver, for hire or reward. [Motor Vehicles Act (59 of 1988), S. 2(22)]

Maxima illecebra est peccandi impunitatis spes. (*Maxim*) The greatest incitement to guilt is the hope of sinning with impunity. (*Peloubet*)

Maxime paci sunt contraria vis et injuria. The greatest enemies to peace are force and wrong.

Maxims. A proposition (especially in aphoristic or sententious form) expressing some general truth of science or experience. [Indian Evidence Act (1 of 1872), S. 114, ill; (i)].

MAXIMS are the foundations of the law, and conclusions of reason; therefore ought not to be impugned, but always to be admitted; but they may by reason be conferred and compared the one with the other, though they do not vary.

MAXIM, PRECEPT, RULE, LAW. Maxim is a moral truth that carries its own weight with itself. Precept, Rule and Law, signify the thing specifically chosen or marked out, all borrow their weight from some external circumstances : the precept derives its authority from the individual delivering it; the rule acquires a worth from its fitness for guiding us in our proceeding : the law, which is a species of rule, derives its weight from the sanction of power.

Maxims and **precedents** are not to be mechanically applied : they are of assistance insofar as they furnish guidance by compendiously summing up principles based on rules of common sense and logic. *Rohit Pulp & Paper Mills* v. *Collector,* AIR 1991 SC 754.

Maximum demand. In relation to any period shall, unless otherwise provided in any general or special order of the State Government, mean twice the largest number of kilowatt- hours or kilo-volt ampere-hours supplied and taken during any consecutive thirty minutes in that period. [Electricity (Supply) Act (54 of 1948), S. 2(8)]

"MAXIMUM DEMAND" as defined in Section 2(8) of the Act has always reference to a past period and there can be no maximum demand in relation to a future period. The phrase should not be given two meanings, one for the licensee and the other for the consumer asking for the maximum demand. *Sihor Electricity Works Ltd.* v. *Gujarat Electricity Board,* AIR 1969 SC 770. [Electricity Supply Act (54 of 1948), S. 2(8)]

"Maximum power spectral density". Means the maximum power within the specified measurement bandwidth, within the device operating band; measurements in the 5 725-5 875 MHz band are made over a bandwidth of 500 KHz; measurements in the 5 150-5 250 MHz, 5 250-5 350 MHz, and 5 470-5 725 MHz bands are made over a bandwidth of 1 MHz or 26 dB emission bandwidth of the device, whichever is less. [Use of Wireless Access System including Radio Local Area Network in 5GHz (Exemption from Licensing Requirement) Rules, 2018, R. 2(g)].

Maximum marginal rate. Means the rate of income-tax (including surcharge or income-tax, if any,) applicable in relation to the highest slab of income in the case of an individual, association of persons or, as the case may be, body of individuals as specified in the Finance Act of the relevant year. [Income Tax Act (43 of 1961), S. 2(29C)]

May. Is generally permissive not mandatory. In general, 'may' is an auxiliary verb qualifying the meaning of another verb by expressing ability, contingency, possibility, or probability. (*Webster*)

Even though the section uses the word 'may' keeping in view the objective of the Act and the context in which it has been used, it should be read as "shall". Otherwise it would frustrate the objective of the sub-section. *N. Nagendra Rao & Co.* v. *State of A.P.*, AIR 1994 SC 2663, 2671. [Essential Commodities Act (10 of 1955), S. 6-A(2)]

The word "may" introduces an element of discretion which has to be exercised by the court of competent jurisdiction in accordance with law. [*Shyamal Ghosh v. State of West Bengal*, (2012) 7 SCC 646, para 71].

May and shall, *"May"* may sometimes mean "shall."

The word "may" is sometimes used' to give a discretion to Courts but it is also sometimes used merely to show that the Courts are given the jurisdiction to exercise a power and not to give them a discretion to decline to exercise the jurisdiction granted to them. Enabling words are always compulsory where they are words to effectuate a legal right.

When the word "may" is used, the ordinary rule of interpretation is that the requisite condition being fulfilled the Court will and ought to exercise the powers it may exercise, and the word "may" though primarily permissive is in certain circumstances treated as mandatory.

The use of the word 'may' does not necessarily indicate that the whole of clause (5) is an unabling provision leaving it to the parliament to decide whether to enact a law even for the investigation and proof of the misbehaviour or incapacity or not. *Sub-committee of Judicial Accountability* v. *Union of India*, AIR 1992 SC 320, 352. [Constitution of India, Art. 124(5)]

The word 'may' must be construed as to mean 'shall' and is mandatory. *Keshav Chandra Joshi* v. *Union of India*, AIR 1991 SC 284, 294. [Constitution of India, Art. 309]

The word 'may' is capable of meaning 'must' or 'shall' in the light of the context where a discretion is conferred upon public authority, coupled with an obligation, the word 'may' denoting discretion should be construed to mean a command. AIR 1963 SC 1618 Quoted. *Textile Commissioner* v. *Sagar Textile Mills*, AIR 1977 SC 1516, 1517.

The word "may" in S. 31, CrPC 1973 (2 of 1974), not only confers a power but also imposes a duty of putting it in use. The word "may" in that section should be read as meaning "shall."

Where a statute directs the doing of a thing for the sake of justice or public good, the word 'may' has the same force as the word 'shall'.

The words 'may take cognizance' in the context means 'must taken cognizance'. *Sub-Divisional Magistrate* v. *Ram Kali*, AIR 1968 SC 1, 5. [CrPC 1973 (2 of 1974), S. 190(1)]

The word "may" in S. 44 of the CPC (5 of 1908) has the same force as the word "shall."

It signifies discretionary power of the Court. The Court has the power to make an *ex parte* order appointing a commissioner. *Subba Gounder* v. *Palanathal*, AIR 1969 Mad 204 at 207. [CPC (5 of 1908), O. XXXIX, R. 6]

The word 'may' means 'must' and it is obligatory on the Court to strike out the defence. *Sohan Lal* v. *Hodal Singh,* AIR 1979 All 230, 232. [CPC (5 of 1908) (U.P. Amendment), O. XV, R. 5]

The word 'may' confers a discretionary power on the Textile Commissioner. *Ramappa Bhimappa* v. *UOI,* AIR 1977 Kant 100, 106. [Essential Commodities Act (10 of 1955), S. 3]

The expression 'may' does not confer a discretion but conveys almost a mandate. *Tarun Ranjan Majumdar* v. *Siddhardha Datta,* AIR 1991 Cal 76, 77. [Guardians and Wards Act (8 of 1890), S. 25(1)]

The expression 'may' refers to a duty imposed upon Government. In that sense, 'may' has the implication of an obligation. *Firestone Tyre and Rubber Co. of India Ltd.* v. *K.P. Krishnan,* AIR 1956 Bom 273, 274. [Industrial Disputes Act (14 of 1947), S. 12(5)]

The expression 'may' in S. 17(2) means 'must'. *State (Delhi Admn.)* v. *I.K.Nangia*, AIR 1979 SC 1977, 1980. [Prevention of Food Adulteration Act (37 of 1951), S. 17(2), *Expln.*]

Though the word 'may' might connote merely an enabling or permissive power in the sense of the usual phrase "it shall be lawful", it is also capable of being construed as referring to a compellable duty, particularly when it refers to a power conferred on a Court or other judicial authority. *Ramji Missar* v. *State of Bihar*, AIR 1963 SC 1088, 1092. [Probation of Offenders Act (20 of 1958), S. 11(1)]

The word 'may' in Rule 13 means that a promissory note can be stamped with either adhesive stamps or engrossed on a stamp papers of proper value. *M. Gopal Pandithar* v. *D.M. Cum Collector Chingleput,* AIR 1978 Mad 412, 413. [Indian Stamp Act (2 of 1899), Ss. 11 and 74]

The word 'may' in this context has the same force as 'shall'. *Sensmal* v. *State of Rajasthan,* AIR 1957 Raj 211, 213. [Indian Stamp Act (2 of 1899), S. 42(2)]

Having regard to the context, the expression 'may' used in a statute has varying significance. In some contexts it is purely permissive, in others, it may confer a power to exercise it as laid down. *Societe De Traction Etc.* v. *Kamani Engineering Co. Ltd.*, AIR 1964 SC 558, 562.

In construing a power the Court will read the word 'may' as 'must' when the exercise of the power will be in furtherance of the interest of a third person for securing which the power was given. Enabling words are always potential and never in themselves significant of any objection. *Province of Bombay* v. *Khushaldas*, AIR 1950 SC. 222, 262.

INTERPRETATION OF STATUTES. The word 'may' generally does not mean 'must' or 'shall'. It is well-settled that the word 'may' is capable of meaning 'must' or 'shall' in the light of the context. It is clear that where a discretion is conferred on a public authority coupled with an obligation, the word, 'may' which devotes discretion should be construed to mean a command. Sometimes, the Legislature uses the word 'may' out of deference to the high status of the authority on whom the power and the obligations are intended to be conferred and imposed. *State of Uttar Pradesh* v. *Jogendra Singh*, AIR 1963 SC 1618, 1620.

May be allowed to appeal. The words "may be allowed to appeal" in O. XLIV, R. 1, CPC (5 of 1908), implies that a discretion is vested in the judge to allow or disallow the petition.

May by law provide. The words 'may by law provide' do not necessarily exclude delegation and it will have to be seen in each case how far the intention of the constitution was that the entire provision should be made by law without recourse to any rules framed under the power of delegation. *D.S. Garewala* v. *State of Punjab*, AIR 1559 SC 512. [Constitution of India, Art. 312]

May by order direct. The expression 'may by order direct' implies that the Court has got a discretion whether or not to direct an inquisition for the purpose of ascertaining whether a person is of unsound mind and incapable of managing himself and his affairs. *V. Rangacharyulu* v. *Gopal Krishnamaccharyulu,* AIR 1962 AP 110, 112. [Indian Lunacy Act (4 of 1912) (*repealed*), S. 62]

May enquire. See also "May proceed to enquire".

May have been allowed to officiate continuously. It means actual and continuous officiation and not a fortuitous or fictional officiation. *State of Bihar* v. *Madan Mohan Prasad*, AIR 1976 SC 404, 409.

May make such order in the matter as it thinks fit. The words "may make such order in the matter as it thinks fit" should be fairly construed to empower a Court to permit the suit instituted by or on behalf of a minor to be continued after taking steps to see that a next friend of the minor is named and brought on record to conduct the suit on behalf of the minor. *Bachh Rai* v. *Sunder Mal,* AIR 1963 Raj 119, 122. [CPC (5 of 1908), O. XXXII, R 2(2)]

May presume. Whenever it is provided by this Adhiniyam that the Court may presume a fact, it may either regard such fact as proved, unless and until it is disproved or may call for proof of it. [(w. e. f. 1-7-2024) Bharatiya Sakshya Adhiniyam, 2023 (47 of 2023), section 2(1)(h)]

The expression 'may presume' is defined in Section 4 of the Act. The presumptions falling in this category are compendiously known as factual presumptions or discretionary presumptions. [*T. Shankar Prasad* v. *State of A.P.,* (2004) 3 SCC 753, 760, para 9] [Indian Evidence Act (1 of 1872), S. 4]

"Whenever it is provided by this Act that the Court *may presume* a fact, it may either regard such fact as proved, unless and until it is disproved, or may call for proof of it." [Indian Evidence Act (1 of 1872), S. 4].

The expression 'may prove' means that the trial Court has a discretion either to presume a fact or to call for proof of it. *Rangu* v. *Rambha,* AIR 1967 Bom 382, 386. [Indian Evidence Act (1 of 1872), S. 90]

The expression 'may presume', occurring in S. 4 of the Act, refers to the 'factual presumptions' or discretionary presumptions. *M. Narsinga Rao* v. *State of A.P.,* (2001) 1 SCC 691, para 13 : AIR 2001 SC 318. [Indian Evidence Act (1 of 1872), S. 4]

May proceed to enquire. 'May proceed to enquire' and 'may enquire'. For the purpose of this section the expressions 'may proceed to enquire' and 'may enquire' include investigation by the police agency put at the disposal of Lokayukta and Uplokayukta in pursuance of sub-section 3 of section 3. [M.P. Lokayukta and UP-Lokayukta Act (37 of 1981), S. 7(ii) Explanation as cited in *Lokayukta, Justice Ripusudan Dayal v. State of M.P.*, (2014) 4 SCC 473, para 19].

May seize any cattle trespassing on such land. The expression "may seize any cattle trespassing on such land and doing damage thereto" does not connote that the seizure must be effected in the process of trespass and causation of damage on the land. The expression "trespassing on such land and doing damage thereto" means that the owner or occupier of the field damaged should proceed to seize the cattle when they had trespassed and were causing damage. *Lokanath Gope* v. *State,* AIR 1960 Pat 385, 386. [Cattle Trespass Act (1 of 1871), S. 10]

Mayhem. The crime of maliciously injuring a person's body, especially to impair or destroy the victim's capacity for self-defence.

Mayor's Court. An old Court established in some cities, in which the mayor sat with the powers of a police judge or committing magistrate in respect to offences committed within the city, and sometimes with civil jurisdiction in small causes. (*Black*)

MCL. Means the extent to which a cooperative society may receive deposits, loans and advances from non-members. [Delhi Cooperative Societies Rule, 1973, R. 2 (XV)]

McNaghten rule. A test for defence on insanity ground, holding person not criminally responsible for an act when his mental disability prevented him to know the nature and quality of his act or whether his act was right or wrong.

Meal. Means hot cooked or pre-cooked and heated before its service meal or take home ration, as may be prescribed by the Central Government. [S. 2(9) of the National Food Security Act, 2013 (20 of 2013)]

'Meal' means hot cooked or pre-cooked and heated before its service meal or take home ration, as may be prescribed by the Central Government. [National Food Security Act (20 of 2013), S. 2(9)].

Mean. *As a noun*, the middle between two extremes; and that either in time or dignity (*Jacob*).

As a verb, to have in mind, view, or contemplation; to intend. (*Century*)

Mean and include. The expression "mean and include" affords an exhaustive explanation of the meaning which, must invariably be attached to these words or expressions. *Mahalakshmi Oil Mills* v. *State of A.P.*, AIR 1989 SC 335, 339. [Central Excise and Salt Act (1 of 1944), Sch. I, item 4]

Mean high tide. Average of all high tides.

Means. Has the meaning [T.P. Act (4 of 1882), S. 3]; something with the help of which desired end is attained or made most likely [IPC (45 of 1860), S. 29].

The expression "*means*" in S. 125(1), CrPC 1973 (2 of 1974), does not signify only visible means such as real property or definite employment. If a man is healthy and able bodied he must be taken to have the means to support his wife. *Dhani Ram* v. *Ral Del,* AIR 1955 All 320.

The expression 'means' in Section 51, *Expln.* only connotes realisable assets. *Mohd. Ibrahim* v. *State Bank of Travancore,* AIR 1964 Mad 233, 234.

The word 'means' referred in Cl (b) of O. XXXIII, R. 9, CPC (5 of 1908) must be the 'means' that should have been acquired by or otherwise come to the possession of the plaintiff after adjudication of the petition for leave under O. XXXIII, R. 7.

The expression "the means" can generally be equated with the resources at the disposal of a tenant or what he is getting or can fairly be assumed likely to get, irrespective of his source. *Abdul Haq* v. *Hafiz Abdul Rashid Khan,* AIR 1975 Del 13, 15. [Slum Areas (Improvement and Clearance) Act (96 of 1956), S. 19(4)(a)]

When the word 'means' is employed in a definition it shows that the definition is a hard and fast definition and that no other meaning can be assigned to the word or the expression defined than is put down in the definition.

Means and includes. The word 'means' is a term of restriction, while the word 'includes' is a term of enlargement. When both the words 'means' and 'includes' are used together to define a thing, the intention of the legislature is to supply restricted meaning to the term. The term 'includes' can be given a slightly enlarged meaning, if the definition of the term in the Act does not violate it. *Lachcho* v. *Damon Mal,* AIR 1986 All 303, 305. [Indian Evidence Act (1 of 1872), S. 63]

The words 'means and includes' indicate 'an exhaustive explanation of the meaning which for the purposes of the Act, must invariably be attached to these words or expressions'. *P. Kasilingam* v. *P.S.G. College of Technology*, AIR 1995 SC 1395, 1400. [T.N. Private Colleges (Regulation) Rules (1976), R. 2(b)]

Means of access. Means any permanent means of access, whether private or public, for vehicles of any kind. [Control of National Highways (Land and Traffic) Act, 2002 (13 of 2003), S. 2(i)]

"Means of access" includes any means of access whether private or public, for vehicles or for foot passengers, and includes a road. [Bangalore Development Authority Act 12 of 1976, S. 2(o) as cited in *Bangalore Development Authority v. Aircraft Employees' Cooperative Society Limited*, (2012) 3 SCC 442, para 9].

Means of living. Resources for livelihood.

Means of support. In its general sense, all those resources from which the necessaries and comforts of life are or may be supplied, such as lands, goods, salaries, wages, or other sources of income.

Meantime. The intervening time.

"IN THE MEANTIME" are words of relation, and refer not only to a time that is to begin, but to a time which is also to end.

Measure. An instrument for measuring [IPC (45 of 1860), Ss. 265 and 267]; a quantity [Indian Contract Act (9 of 1872), S. 73, ill. (e)]; means to an end [Industrial Finance Corporation Act (15 of 1948) (*Repealed by Act 23 of 1993*), S. 34(4); Constitution of India, Art. 257(3)]; a legislative enactment proposed or adopted.

Measure of damages. In action for injuries damages would primarily represent compensation for loss of service and consequential damage *e.g.* cost of hiring another servant, payment of salary or pension to a disabled servant.

Measurement. Includes finger impressions and foot-print impressions. [Identification of Prisoners Act (33 of 1920), S. 2]

"Measurement" is the act or process of measuring. [*Ritesh Sinha v. State of U.P.*, (2013) 2 SCC 357, para 38].

"Measurements" includes finger-impressions, palm-print impressions, foot-print impressions, photographs, iris and retina scan, physical, biological samples and their analysis, behavioural attributes including signatures, handwriting or any other examination referred to in section 53 or section 53A of the Code of Criminal Procedure, 1973 (2 of 1974). [Criminal Procedure (Identification) Act, 2022 (11 of 2022), section 2(1)(b)]

Measuring frequency and intensity of the speech sound waves falls within the ambit of inclusive definition of the term "measurements". [*Ritesh Sinha v. State of U.P.*, (2013) 2 SCC 357, para 39]

"Measurement and verification". Means the mutually agreed procedures, between the borrower and the beneficiary, for measurement and verification of energy savings achieved periodically after the commissioning of the energy efficiency projects. [Energy Conservation (Partial Risk Guarantee Fund for Energy Efficiency) Rules, 2016, R. 2(1)(q)].

"Measurement and verification agency". Means an empanelled measurement and verification agency of the Bureau under Partial Risk Guarantee Fund for Energy Efficiency. [Energy Conservation (Partial Risk Guarantee Fund for Energy Efficiency) Rules, 2016, R. 2(1)(o)].

Measurer. Means a person whose business is to measure a consignment of agricultural produce for sale. [Bihar Agricultural Produce Markets Act (16 of 1960), S. 2(l)]

Measuring instrument. Any instrument of length, capacity, volume, temperature, pressure or gravity, or for the measurement and determination of quantities of any substance.

Meat. "MEAT" includes blood, bones, sinew, eggs, shell or carapace, fat and flesh with or without skin, whether raw or cooked, of any wild animal or captive animal, other than a vermin. [Wild Life (Protection) Act (53 of 1972), S. 2(20)]

A term which applies not only to the flesh of all animals used for food, but, in a general sense, to all kinds of provisions fit for the sustenance of man.

Meat on hoof. 'Meat on hoof' becomes meat proper as soon as the goat is slaughtered and the skin is pulled off. *Niranjit Lal* v. *State of Assam*, AIR 1985 SC 1387, 1390.

Mechanical power. Power produced by machines.

Mechanical process. A process involving the use of machine. [Indian Evidence Act (1 of 1872), S. 63(2)].

Mechanical products. Mere manufacture of wooden toys like rocking horses will not amount to manufacture of mechanical products. *M.V. Gopalan* v. *State of Madras,* AIR 1963 Mad 134, 136. [Employees Provident Funds Act (19 of 1952), Sch. 1]

Mechanical royalty. The payment to which a songwriter is entitled each time a mechanical-right holder reproduces a song on a phonorecord. (*Copyright*)

Mechanically propelled vessel. Means every description of vessel propelled wholly or in part by electricity, steam or other mechanical power. [Inland Vessel Act (1 of 1917), S. 2(c)]

Med-Arb. In Med-Arb initially conciliation/mediation is adopted and if efforts fail, it leads to arbitration. [Karnika Seth, *Computers Internet and New Technology Laws*, 2021, LexisNexis, Glossary of Legal Terms].

Medal. A piece of metal bearing devices and inscriptions, struck or cast to commemorate a person, an institution, or an event, or as an appreciation of special merit or skill.

Median. For the purposes of rule 5 of the Companies (Appointment & Remuneration of Managerial Personnel) Rules, 2014, the expression 'median' means the numerical value separating the higher half of a population from the lower half and the median of a finite list of numbers may be found by arranging all the observations from lowest value to highest value and picking the middle one. [*Explanation* (*i*) to rule 5(1) of the Companies (Appointment & Remuneration of Managerial Personnel) Rules, 2014]

"MEDIAN" for the purposes of rule 5 of the Companies (Appointment & Remuneration of Managerial Personnel) Rules, 2014, if there is an even number of observations, the 'median' shall be the average of the two middle values. [*Explanation* (*ii*) to rule 5(1) of the Companies (Appointment & Remuneration of Managerial Personnel) Rules, 2014]

"Mediated settlement agreement". Means mediated settlement agreement referred to in sub-section (1) of section 19. [Mediation Act, 2023 (32 of 2023), section 3(n)]

Mediation. A form of alternative dispute resolution in which a third party, usually professionally trained, helps the parties to resolve their differences.

"Mediation" includes a process, whether referred to by the expression mediation, pre-litigation mediation, online mediation, community mediation, conciliation or an expression of similar import, whereby parties attempt to reach an amicable settlement of their dispute with the assistance of a third person referred to as mediator, who does not have the authority to impose a settlement upon the parties to the dispute. [Mediation Act, 2023 (32 of 2023), section 3(h)]

Mediation agreement. An agreement by the parties to submit to mediation all or certain disputes which have arisen or which may arise between them; a mediation agreement may be in the form of a mediation clause in a contract or in the form of a separate contract.

"Mediation agreement" means a mediation agreement referred to in sub-section (1) of section 4. [Mediation Act, 2023 (32 of 2023), section 3(j)]

Mediator. One who mediates or interposes between the parties at variance for the purpose of reconciling them.

"Mediator" means a person who is appointed to be a mediator, by the parties or by a mediation service provider, to undertake mediation, and includes a person registered as mediator with the Council.

Explanation.—Where more than one mediator is appointed for a mediation, reference to a mediator under this Act shall be a reference to all the mediators. [Mediation Act, 2023 (32 of 2023), section 3(i)]

Medical. Of or pertaining to or having to do with the art of healing a disease, or the science of medicine; containing medicine; used in medicine.

Of, relating to, or concerned with physicians, as distinguished from surgery [IPC (45 of 1860), S. 275]; pertaining to the healing art. [Mines Act (35 of 1952), S. 21(1)].

Medical Authority. For the purposes of this section,—

"MEDICAL AUTHORITY" means the medical authority as referred to in clause (*p*) of Section 2 of the Persons With Disabilities (Equal Opportunities, Protection of Rights and Full Participation) Act, 1995, or such other medical authority as may, by notification, be specified by the Central Government for certifying "autism", "cerebral palsy", "multiple disabilities", "person with disability" and "severe disability" referred to in clauses (*a*), (*c*), (*h*), (*j*) and (*o*) of Section 2 of the National Trust for Welfare of Persons with Autism, Cerebral Palsy, Mental Retardation and Multiple Disabilities Act, 1999. [Income-tax Act (43 of 1961), S. 80U, *Expln.* (b) (*Substituted by Finance (No. 2) Act (23 of 2004), S. 19 Expln. (b)*)]

Medical examination. Of the person of the accused may be made with his consent which need not 'necessarily be in writing.'

Medical examiner. A public officer who determines the necessity of and conducts autopsies to find the cause of death.

Medical facility. Means such facility as may be notified by the State Government to be a medical facility for the purposes of Act 43 of 2005. [S. 2(j) of the Protection of Women from Domestic Violence Act, 2005 (43 of 2005)]

Medical geneticist. Means a person who possesses a degree or diploma or certificate in medical genetics in the field of pre-natal diagnostic techniques or has experience of not less than two years in such held after obtaining—

(i) any one of the medical qualifications recognised under the Indian Medical Council Act, 1956; or

(ii) a post-graduate degree in biological sciences. [Pre-Natal Diagnostic Techniques (Regulation and Prevention of Misuse) Act (57 of 1994), S. 2(g)].

Medical institution. Means any institution, within or without India, which grants degree, diplomas or licences in medicine. [Medical Council Act (102 of 1956), S. 2(e)]

"MEDICAL INSTITUTION" means any institution, within or without India, which grants degree, diplomas or licences in Homoeopathy. [Homoeopathy Central Council Act (59 of 1973), S. 2(e)]

"MEDICAL INSTITUTION" means any institution within or outside India which grants degrees, diplomas or licences in medicine and include affiliated colleges and deemed to be Universities. [National Medical Commission Act, 2019 (30 of 2019), section 2(i)]

Medical jurisprudence. Sometimes called Forensic or Legal Medicine, is described in Dr. Taylor's standard work on the subject as a branch of medicine, and he defines it as "the science which teaches the application of every branch of medical knowledge to the purposes of the law."

That part or branch of the science of medicine which relates to law.

"Medical management" means treatment and other necessary activities for providing the medical care to complement the treatment. [New Drugs and Clinical Trials Rules, 2019, R. 2(1)(u)].

Medical officer. Means a gazetted medical officer of Government, and includes a medical practitioner declared by general or special order of the Local

Government to be a medical officer. [Indian Lunacy Act (4 of 1912), S. 3(7)]

Medical officer in charge. In relation to any psychiatric hospital or psychiatric nursing home means the medical officer who, for the time being is in charge of that hospital or nursing home. [Mental Health Act (14 of 1987), S. 2(j)] [Indian Lunacy Act (*repealed*) (4 of 1912), S. 3(7)]

"Medical officer in charge" in relation to any mental health establishment means the psychiatrist or medical practitioner who, for the time being, is in charge of that mental health establishment [The Mental Healthcare Act, 2017 (10 of 2017), S. 2(1)(m)]

Medical practitioner. Means a holder of a qualification to practise medicine and surgery which can be registered in the United Kingdom in accordance with the law for the time being in force for the registration of medical practitioners, and includes any person declared by general or special order of the Local Government to be a medical practitioner. [Indian Lunacy Act (4 of 1912), S. 3]

Medical practitioner or practitioner. Means a person who is engaged in the practice of modern scientific medicine in any of its branches including surgery and obstetrics, but not including veterinary medicine or surgery or the Ayurvedic, Unani, Homeopathic or Biochemic system of medicine. [Maharashtra Medical Council Act (46 of 1965), S. 2(d)]

Medical Subordinate. "MEDICAL SUBORDINATE" means an Assistant Surgeon, apothecary or qualified Hospital Assistant. [Prisons Act (9 of 1894), S. 3 (8).]

"Medical termination of pregnancy" means the termination of pregnancy permissible under the provisions of the Medical Termination of Pregnancy Act, 1971 (34 of 1971). [Code on Social Security, 2020 (36 of 2020), S. 2(45)]

Medicaments. The term 'medicaments' has been defined as products comprising two or more constituents which have been mixed or compounded together for therapeutic or prophylactic uses or unmixed products suitable for such uses. *CCE* v. *Shree Baidyanath Ayurwed Bhawan Ltd*., AIR 2009 SC (Supp) 1090.

Medicaments. 'Medicaments' means good (other than food or beverages such as dietetic, diabetic or fortified foods, tonic beverages) not falling within Heading 30.02 or 30.04 which are either—

(a) products comprising two or more constituents which have been mixed or compounded together for therapeutic or prophylactic uses; or

(b) unmixed products suitable for such uses put up in measured doses or in packings for retail sale or for use in hospitals." [*Commissioner of Central Excise v. Wockhardt Life Sciences Limited*, (2012) 5 SCC 585, para 18] [Central Excise Tariff Act, 1985 (5 of 1986) Ch. 30, Ch. Note 2(i)].

The products, comprising two or more constituents which have been compounded together either for therapeutic or prophylactic uses, would fall within the meaning of the expression "medicaments". [*Commissioner of Central Excise v. Wockhardt Life Sciences Limited*, (2012) 5 SCC 585, para 18].

Medicinal. Having healing properties, attributes, relating or pertaining to the science and art concerned with the cure, alleviation and prevention of disease and with restoration and preservation of health. [IPC (45 of 1860), S. 275].

Medicinal preparation. 'MEDICINAL PREPARATION' includes all drugs which are a remedy or prescription prepared for internal or external use of human beings or animals and all substances intended to be used for or in the treatment, mitigation or prevention of disease in human beings or animals. [Medicinal and Toilet Preparations (Excise Duties) Act (16 of 1955), S. 2(g)]

Medicinal purposes. The words 'Medicinal purposes' in Art. 47 seem to contemplate the user of liquor for making medicinal preparations and do not contemplate the free use of intoxicating drinks as medicine. *Sarish Majumdar* v. *State of Tamil Nadu,* AIR 1979 Mad 246, 254 (FB). [Constitution of India, Art. 47]

Medicine. Means modern scientific medicine in all its branches and includes surgery and obstetrics, but does not include veterinary medicine and surgery. [Medical Council Act (102 of 1956), S. 2(f)]

A substance or preparation used in treating disease [Drugs and Cosmetics Act (23 of 1940), S. 3(h)]; modern scientific medicine in all its branches and includes surgery and obstetrics but does not include veterinary medicine and surgery. [Indian Medical Councils Act (102 of 1956), S. 2(f)].

Medicine or drug. Includes—

(i) all medicines for internal or external use of human beings or animals,

(ii) all substances intended to be used for or in the diagnosis, treatment, mitigation or prevention of diseases in human beings or animals,

(iii) all substances intended to be used for or in the maintenance of public health, or the prevention or control of any epidemic disease among human beings or animals,

(iv) insecticides, germicides, fungicides, weedicides and all other substances intended to be used for the protection or preservation of plants;

(v) all chemical substances which are ordinarily used as intermediates in the preparation or manufacture of any of the medicines or substances above referred to. [Patents Act (39 of 1970), S. 2(1)(*l*) substituted by Act 15 of 2005 and now replaced by a definition for the word 'new invention']

Medicine or drug includes insecticides, germicides, fungicides, weedicides and all other substances intended to be used for the protection or preservation of plants. And all chemical substances which are originally used as intermediates in the preparation or manufacture of any medicines. *Bayer Aktiengesellschaft of Lever-kusen Federal Republic of Germany* v. *Controller of Patents Govt. of India,* AIR 1982 Cal 30, 32. [Patents Act (39 of 1970), S. 2(1)(*l*)].

"Medicine" means modern scientific medicine in all its branches and includes surgery and obstetrics, but does not include veterinary medicine and surgery. [National Medical Commission Act, 2019 (30 of 2019), section 2(j)]

Mediclaim. A policy providing reimbursement of medical expenses incurred in India as an inpatient or at home as a result of accident or illness in certain situations. (*Insurance*)

Mediclaim benefits. Certain benefits in a mediclaim policy payable as a result of disability caused by illness which is covered under the policy. (*Insurance*)

Medicolegal. Requiring involvement of medical science to law.

Medium goods vehicle. "MEDIUM GOODS VEHICLE" means any goods carriage other than a light motor vehicle or a heavy goods vehicle. [Motor Vehicles Act (59 of 1988), S. 2(23)]

Medium irrigation protect. Means an irrigation protect capable of irrigating an area below ten thousand hectares and above two thousand hectares. [Kerala Command Areas Development Act (37 of 1986), S. 2(17)]

Medola. Involves settlement using mediation where a neutral third party selects between the finally negotiated offers which are binding on the parties. [Karnika Seth, *Computers Internet and New Technology Laws*, 2021, LexisNexis, Glossary of Legal Terms].

Meeting. "The term "meeting" connotes coming together of persons for certain purposes. It is a gathering of persons with a specific object in view".

Assembling of a number of persons for discussions and acting upon some matter of common interest; sitting on a particular session [Food Corporations Act (37 of 1964), S. 9(2)(b)]; [Representation of the People Act (43 of 1951), S. 126(1)]; [Industrial Finance Corporation Act (15 of 1948), S. 14(5) (*Repealed by Act of 1993*); Constitution of India, Art. 101(4)].

For a meeting there must be at least two persons. The word '*prima facie*' connotes coming together of persons for certain purpose.

MEETING, INTERVIEW. A meeting is an ordinary concern, and its purpose familiar; meetings are daily taking place between friends : an interview is extra-ordinary and formal; its object is commonly business.

ADJOURNED MEETING is a continuation of the original meeting.

Meeting of the minds. Concurrence or mutual consent of the parties or persons on some point or object.

Melior est conditio possidentis, et rei quam actoris. (*Maxim*) The condition of the party in possession is the better one, and that of a defendant is better than that of a plaintiff. (*Burrill*)

Melius est in tempore occurrere, quam post causam vulneratum remedium quaerere. It is better to meet a thing in time, than after an injury is inflicted, to seek a remedy.

Melior est justitia vere praeveniens quam severe puniens. (*Maxim*) That justice which absolutely prevents (a crime) is better than that which severely punishes it. (*Burril*)

Melius est jus deficiens quam jus incertum. (*Maxim*) Law that is deficient is better than law that is uncertain.

Melius est omnia mala pati quam malo concentire. (*Maxim*) It is better to suffer all wrongs, than to consent to wrong. (*Burril*)

Melius est petere fontes quam sectari rivulos. (*Maxim*) It is better to go to the fountain head than to follow little streamlets. (*Wharton*)

Melius est recurrere quam male currere. It is better to run back than to run badly.

Melius est ut decem noxii evadant quam ut unus innocens pereat. (*Maxim*) It is better that ten guilty persons escape than that one innocent person perish. (*Morgan*)

Member. "MEMBER" includes a person joining in the application for the registration of a society and a person admitted to membership after registration in accordance with the by-laws and any rules. [Co-operative Societies Act (2 of 1912), S. 2(*c*)].

A person considered in relation to any aggregate of individuals to which he belongs; particularly one who has united with or has been formally chosen as a corporate part of an association or public body of any kind.

In anatomy, a limb.

"MEMBER". In Chapter XXVII of Act 18 of 2013, unless the context otherwise requires, 'Member' means a member, whether Judicial or Technical of the Tribunal or the Appellate Tribunal and includes the President or the Chairperson, as the case may be. [S. 407(*c*) of the Companies Act, 2013 (18 of 2013)]

"MEMBER". In relation to a company, means—

(*i*) the subscriber to the memorandum of the company who shall be deemed to have agreed to become member of the company, and on its registration, shall be entered as member in its register of members;

(*ii*) every other person who agrees in writing to become a member of the company and whose name is entered in the register of members of the company;

(*iii*) every person holding shares of the company and whose name is entered as a beneficial owner in the records of a depository. [S. 2(55) of the Companies Act, 2013 (18 of 2013)]

In this section and in the preceding sections of this Chapter,-- "member", in relation to the armed forces, means a person in the armed forces other than an officer. [(w. e. f. 1-7-2024) Bharatiya Nagarik Suraksha Sanhita, 2023 (46 of 2023), S. 151(3)(c)]

"MEMBER" means a member of the Authority and includes its Chairperson. [S. 2(1)(f) of the Pension Fund Regulatory & Development Authority Act, 2013 (23 of 2013)]

"MEMBER" means a Member of the Lokpal. [S. 2(1)(j) of the Lokpal & Lokayuktas Act, 2013 (1 of 2014)]

Member co-operative. Means a co-operative society or a multi-State co-operative society which is member of a federal co-operative. [Multi State Cooperative Societies Act (39 of 2002), S. 2(o)]

Member in charge of the Bill. Means in the case of a Government Bill any Minister and in any other case the Member who has introduced the Bill. [Rules of Procedure and Conduct of Business in the Council of States (Rajya Sabha), R. 2(1)]

Member : Independent. In India, an elected member of a legislature who has been elected as such otherwise than as a candidate set up by any political party; an independent member loses his membership of the House if he joins any political party after his election to the House; groups formed by independent members are recognized as such by the Speaker.

Member of a family. In the sub-section, the expression "MEMBER OF A FAMILY", means wife or husband, parent, step-parent, grand-parent, brother, sister, half-brother, half-sister, child, step-child and grand-child :

Provided that in deducing any such relationship as aforesaid any illegitimate person and any adopted person shall be treated as being or as having been the legitimate child of his mother and reputed father or, as the case may be, of his adopters. [Carriage by Air Act, 1972, S. 5(2) *Expln.*]

Member of a Legislative Assembly. A member of a Legislative Assembly is not a public servant within the meaning of Section 21, twelfth (a) of the Code. [*R.S. Nayak* v. *A.R. Antulay,* (1984) 2 SCC 183, 243, p. 71] [IPC (45 of 1860), S. 21, twelfth (a)]

Member of prisoner's family. Means the husband, wife, son, daughter, father, mother, brother or sister of the prisoner. [Haryana Good Conduct Prisoner's (Temporary Release Act) (28 of 1988), S. 2(b)]

Member of scheduled castes. Means a member of such races or tribes or parts of or groups within castes, races or tribes specified as scheduled castes with respect to State of Madhya Pradesh under Art 341 of the Constitution of India. [Madhya Pradesh Gramin Rin Vimukti Adhiniyam, 1982 (5 of 1983), S. 2(h)]

Member of scheduled tribes. Means a member of such tribes or tribal communities or parts of or groups within such tribes or tribal communities specified as such with respect to the State of Madhya Pradesh under Art. 342 of the Constitution of India. [Madhya Pradesh Gramin Rin Vimukh Adhiniyam, 1982 (5 of 1983), S. 2(i)]

Member of such family. Wife of one of the members of the joint family owning the dwelling house is a member of such family within the meaning of S. 4. *Makhan Lall Bose* v. *Sam Sushma Rani Bose,* AIR 1953 Cal 164. [Partition Act (4 of 1893), S. 4]

Member of the bar. The expression 'member of the bar' occurring in relevant Rule would mean only that a particular class of persons who are actually practising in Courts of law as pleaders or advocates. *Sushma Suri* v. *Govt. of National Capital Territory of Delhi,* (1999) 1 SCC 330, para 9. [Delhi Higher Judicial Services Rules, 1970, R. 7]

Member of the Coast Guard. Means an officer, a subordinate officer, a sailor or other enrolled person. [Coast Guard Act (30 of 1978), S. 2(n)]

Member of the diplomatic staff. Are the members of the staff of the mission having diplomatic rank. [Diplomatic Relations (Vienna Convention) Act (43 of 1972), Sch., Article 1(d)]

Member of the family. Means any member of the family of any person who is wholly dependent upon the earnings of such person for the provisions of the ordinary necessaries of life or who shares with such person in the ordinary expenses of the household to which they jointly belong or who owns property or carries on business jointly with such person. [Administration of Evacuee Property (31 of 1950), S. 2(g)]

"MEMBER OF THE FAMILY", in relation to a Governor, means the [spouse and the dependent children and dependent parents] of the Governor. [Governors (Emoluments, Allowances and Privileges) (43 of 1982), S. 2(c)]

Member of the Force. "MEMBER OF THE FORCE" means a person who has been appointed to the Force by the Commandant, whether before or after the commencement of this Act, and in Sections 1,3,6,7,16,17,18 and 19, includes also a person appointed to the Force by the Central Government, whether before or after such commencement. [Central Reserve Police Force Act (66 of 1949), S. 2(d)]

"MEMBER OF THE FORCE" means a person appointed to the Force other than a superior officer. [Railway Property (Unlawful Possession) Act (29 of 1966), S. 2(b)]

'MEMBER OF THE FORCE' means an officer, a subordinate officer, an under-officer or other enrolled persons. [Border Security Force Act (47 of 1968), S. 2(1)(o)]

"MEMBER OF THE FORCE" means an officer, a subordinate officer, an under-officer or other enrolled person. [Indo-Tibetan Baroda Police Force Act (35 of 1992), S. 2(1)(p)]

Member of the Fund. Means an advocate admitted to the benefits of the Fund and who continues to be a member thereof under the provisions of this Act. [Advocates' Welfare Fund Act (45 of 2001), S. 2(i)]

'Member of the fund' means an advocate admitted to the benefits of the Fund and continuing to be a member thereof under the provisions of this Act. [Tamil Nadu Advocates, Welfare Fund Act (49 of 1987), S. 2(i) as cited in *S. Seshachalam v. Bar Council of T.N.*, (2014) 16 SCC 72, para 12].

Member of the Indian Administrative Service. Means a person who was initially appointed to the Civil Service of the Crown in India known as the Indian Civil Service and who subsequently became a member of the Indian Administrative Service. [All India Services (PF) Rules, 1955, R. 2(gg)]

Member of the Indian Police Service. Means a person who has initially been appointed to the Police Service of the Crown in India known as the Indian Police and who subsequently became a member of Indian Police Service. [Indian Police Service (Raj) Rules 1954, R. 2(cc)]

Member of the press council. Every member of the press council and every officer or other employee appointed by the council shall be deemed to be a public servant within the meaning of Section 21 of the Indian Penal Code (45 of 1960). [Press Council of India Act (37 of 1978), S. 24]

Member of the security guard. Means an officer, an Assistant Commander, a Ranger or a combatised tradesman. [National Security Guard Act (47 of 1986), S. 2(n)]

Member of the service staff. Are the member of the staff of the mission in the domestic service of the mission. [Diplomatic Relations (Vienna Convention) Act (43 of 1972), Sch. Art. 1(g)]

Member of the staff of the mission. Are the members of the diplomatic staff, of the administrative and technical staff and of the service staff of the mission. [Diplomatic Relations (Vienna Convention) Act (43 of 1972), Sch. Article 1(c)]

Member of unlawful assembly. Every person who knows that an offence was likely to be committed by the unlawful assembly in persecution of common object and continues to be its members, is a MEMBER OF THAT UNLAWFUL ASSEMBLY. [IPC (45 of 1860), S. 149]

Whoever, being aware of facts which render any assembly an unlawful assembly, intentionally joins that assembly, or continues in it, is said to be a MEMBER OF UNLAWFUL ASSEMBLY. [IPC (45 of 1860), S. 142]

Member State. Means the country which has ratified the Bangkok Agreement. [Customs Tariff (Determination of Origin of Goods Under The Bangkok Agreement) Rules, 1976, R. 3(c)]

Members of family. A person can be properly regarded as being the member of his wife's family and not merely of his father's family. *Sudalimuthu* v. *Palaniyandavan*, AIR 1966 SC 469, 470.

Members of his family. A daughter, her husband and children may or may not be covered by the words 'members of the family' but certainly an adopted daughter and her husband cannot be included in this phrase. *B.N. Gupta* v. *Satyawadi,* AIR 1954 Punj 41.

A married daughter is also a member of the family. *P.V. Parthasarathy Chettiar* v. *State of Tamil Nadu,* AIR 1984 Mad 32, 34.

The brother's son of the petitioner brought up by the petitioner-landlord will be a member of the family. *Angamuthammal* v. *K.V. Muthu,* AIR 1984 Mad 179, 185.

Members of immediate family. Means wife, husband, children and parents. [Special Protection Group Act (34 of 1988), S. 2(e)]

Members of Parliament. The members of the House of People (Lok Sabha) and that of the Council of States (Rajya Sabha).

Members of the administrative and technical staff. Are the member of the staff of the mission employed in the administrative and technical service of the mission. [Diplomatic Relations (Vienna Convention) Act (43 of 1972), Sch. Article 1(f)]

Members of the Group. Means a person who has been appointed to the Group by the prescribed authority whether before or after the commencement of this Act. [Special Protection Group Act (34 of 1988), S. 2(d)]

Memorandum. A note to help the memory; a brief note in writing of some transaction, or an outline of some intended instrument; an instrument drawn up in brief and compendious form.

"MEMORANDUM" means the memorandum of association of a company as originally framed or as altered from time to time in pursuance of any previous companies law or of this Act. [Companies Act (1 of 1956), S. 2(28)]

"MEMORANDUM" means the memorandum of the Institute filed with the Registrar of Joint-Stock companies under the Societies Registration Act, 1860. [Statistical Institute Act (57 of 1959), S. 2(b)]

"MEMORANDUM" means the memorandum of association of a company as originally framed or as altered from time to time in pursuance of any previous company law or of the Companies Act, 2013 (18 of 2013). [S. 2(56) of the Companies Act, 2013 (18 of 2013)]

Memorandum of association. The document which contains particulars of the specific objects for which a company is established, and covering the whole scope of operations, beyond which it is not legal to go.

"Memorandum of understanding". Means a formal agreement between the Bureau and the participating financial institution empanelled with the Bureau. [Energy Conservation (Partial Risk Guarantee Fund for Energy Efficiency) Rules, 2016, R. 2(1)(p)].

Memorial. Means the Jallianwala Bagh National Memorial to perpetuate the memory of these killed or wounded on the 13th day of April, 1919, on the site known as the Jallianwala Bagh Amritsar. [Jalianwala Bagh National Memorial Act (25 of 1951), S. 2(a)]

In Law, a short note, abstract, memorandum, or rough draft of the orders of the Court, from which the records thereof may at any time be fully made. (*Ame Cyc.*)

Memorials or petitions. According to the strict construction of the words of Art. 320(3)(c) an application for review would be covered by the words 'memorials or petitions'. *State of U.P.* v. *Manbodhan Lal Srivastava*, AIR 1957 SC 912, 916. [Constitution of India, Art. 320 (3)(c)]

Menace. A menace is a threat to injure whether it be to reputation person or property.

(1) to threaten with violence, danger, etc.; (2) a threat of the act of threatening; (3) something meaning; a source of danger; (4) a nuisance. [Collin's Dictionary as cited in *Shreya Singhal v. Union of India*, (2015) 5 SCC 1, para 54].

Mens rea. A guilty mind.

Mens rea is a state of mind. Under the Criminal Law, '*mens rea*' is considered as the 'guilty intention' and unless it is found that the accused had the guilty intention to commit the 'crime' he cannot be guilty of committing the crime. *Director of Enforcement* v. *M.C.T.M. Corpn. Pvt. Ltd.*, AIR 1996 SC 1100, 1103.

'Mens rea' and **'negligence'.** *Mens rea* and 'negligence' are both fault elements, which provide a basis for imposition of liability in criminal cases. *Mens rea* focuses on the mental state of the accused and requires proof of a positive state of mind such as intent, recklessness or wilful blindness and 'negligence' on the other hand measures the conduct of the accused on the basis of an objective standard, irrespective of the accused's subjective mental state. *Asstt. Commr.* v. *Velliappa Textiles Ltd.,* (2003) 11 SCC 405, 436, para 56

Mens testatoris in testamentis spectanda est. (*Maxim*) The intention of the testator is to be regarded in wills. (*Black*)

Mensa et thoro. From bed and board.

Mental anguish. Pain or suffering which affect the mind often as a result of physical injury.

Mental cruelty. "Mental cruelty as a course of unprovoked conduct toward one's spouse which causes embarrassment, humiliation, and anguish so as to render the spouse's life miserable and unendurable. The plaintiff must show a course of conduct on the part of the defendant which so endangers the physical or mental health of the plaintiff as to render continued cohabitation unsafe or improper, although the plaintiff need not establish actual instances of physical abuse." [24 *American Jurisprudence* 2d, **as referred in** *Samar Ghosh* v. *Jaya Ghosh*, (2007) 4 SCC 511, 530, para 42]

Mental cruelty. 'The quality of being cruel; disposition of inflicting suffering; delight in or indifference to another's pain; mercilessness; hard-heartedness'. The term "mental cruelty" has been defined in the Black's Law Dictionary [8th Edition, 2004] as under: "Mental Cruelty - As a ground for divorce, one spouse's course of conduct (not involving actual violence) that creates such anguish that it endangers the life, physical health, or mental health of the other spouse." [Shorter Oxford Dictionary as cited in *Gurpreet Kaur vs. Rajeev Singh* (18.12.2017 - ALL HC) : First Appeal Defective Nos. 6, 4 and 5 of 2011, decided on 18-12-2017 (All HC), para 13]

Mental disorder. The expression "MENTAL DISORDER" means mental illness, arrested or incomplete development of mind, psychopathic disorder or any other disorder or disability of mind and includes schizophrenia. [Parsi Marriage and Divorce Act (3 of 1936), S. 32., *Expln.* (a)]

The expression 'MENTAL DISORDER' means mental illness, arrested or incomplete development of mind, psychopathic disorder or any other disorder or disability of mind and includes schizophrenia. [Hindu Marriage Act (25 of 1955), S. 13(1)(iii) *Expln.* (a)]

Mental health. The definition of health advanced by the Word Health Organisation is that it is "the state of complete, mental, physical and social well-being, and not merely an absence of disease infirmity. [*See* GLANVILLE WILLIAMS : Criminal Law, 2nd Edn., c. 13, S. 13.6, p. 300]

Mental healthcare. "Mental healthcare" includes analysis and diagnosis of a person's mental condition and treatment as well as care and rehabilitation of such person for his mental illness or suspected mental illness [The Mental Healthcare Act, 2017 (10 of 2017), S. 2(1)(o)]

Mental health establishment. "Mental health establishment" means any health establishment, including Ayurveda, Yoga and Naturopathy, Unani, Siddha and Homoeopathy establishment, by whatever name called, either wholly or partly, meant for the care of persons with mental illness, established, owned, controlled or maintained by the appropriate Government, local authority, trust, whether private or public, corporation, co-operative society, organisation or any other entity or person, where persons with mental illness are admitted and reside at, or kept in, for care, treatment, convalescence and rehabilitation, either temporarily or otherwise; and includes any general hospital or general nursing home established or maintained by the appropriate Government, local authority, trust, whether private or public, corporation, co-operative society, organization or any other entity or person; but does not include a family residential place where a person with mental illness resides with his relatives or friends [The Mental Healthcare Act, 2017 (10 of 2017), S. 2(1)(p)]

"Mental health nurse". Means a person with a diploma or degree in general nursing or diploma or degree in psychiatric nursing recognized by the Nursing Council of India established under the Nursing Council of India Act, 1947 (38 of 1947) and registered as such with the relevant nursing council in the State. [Mental Healthcare Act (10 of 2017), S. 2(1)(q)].

"Mental health professional". Means—

(*i*) a psychiatrist as defined in clause (*x*); or

(*ii*) a professional registered with the concerned State Authority under Section 55; or

(*iii*) a professional having a postgraduate degree (Ayurveda) in Mano Vigyan Avum Manas Roga or a postgraduate degree (Homoeopathy) in Psychiatry or a postgraduate degree (Unani) in Moalijat (Nafasiyatt) or a postgraduate degree (Siddha) in Sirappu Maruthuvam. [Mental Healthcare Act (10 of 2017), S. 2(1)(r)].

Mental illness. "Mental illness" means a substantial disorder of thinking, mood, perception, orientation or memory that grossly impairs judgment, behaviour, capacity to recognize reality or ability to meet the ordinary demands of life, mental conditions associated with the abuse of alcohol and drugs, but does not include mental retardation which is a condition of arrested or incomplete development of mind of a person, specially characterised by subnormality of intelligence [The Mental Healthcare Act, 2017 (10 of 2017), S. 2(1)(s)]

Means any mental disorder other than mental retardation. [Persons with Disabilities (Equal Opportunities, Protection of Rights and full Participation) Act, 1995 (1 of 1996), S. 2(q)]

Mental or physical disability. Means mental or physical disability by reason of which the person subject to such disability is incapable of cultivating land by person, labour or supervision. [Bihar Land Reforms (Fixation of Ceiling Area and Acquisition of Surplus Land) Act, 1961 (12 of 1962), S. 2(h)]

Mental retardation. Means a condition of arrested or incomplete development of mind of a person which is specially, characterised by sub-normality of intelligence. [Rehabilitation Council of India Act (34 of 1992), S. 2(1)(h); Persons with Disabilities (Equal Opportunities Protection of Rights and Full Participation) Act, 1995 (1 of 1996), S. 2(r) and National Trust for Welfare of Persons with Autism, Cerebral Palsy, Mental Retardation and Multiple Disabilities Act (44 of 1999), S. 2(g)]

Mentally ill person. Means a person who is in need of treatment by reason of any mental disorder other than mental retardation. [Medical Termination of Pregnancy Act (31 of 1971), S. 2(b); Mental Health Act (14 of 1987), S. 2(l)]

Mentally ill prisoner. Means a mentally ill person for whose detention in, or removal to, a psychiatric hospital, psychiatric nursing home, jail or other place of safe custody, an order referred to in Section 27 has been made. [Mental Health Act (14 of 1987), S. 2(m)]

Mention. To direct attention to; to speak briefly of; to name casually or incidentally; to refer to.

Mercantile. Pertaining to merchants or the business of merchants; having to do with trade or the buying and selling of commodities; having to do with trade or commerce.

MERCANTILE, COMMERCIAL. *Mercantile* respects the actual transaction of business or a transfer of merchandise by sale or purchase; *Commercial* comprehends the theory and practice of commerce hence we speak in a peculiar manner of a *mercantile* house, a *mercantile* town a *mercantile* situation, and the like; but of a *commercial* education, a *commercial* people, *commercial* speculations, and the like.

Mercantile agent. "MERCANTILE AGENT" means mercantile agent having in the customary course of business as such agent authority either to sell goods, or to consign goods for the purpose of sale, or to buy goods or to raise money on the security of goods. [Sale of Goods Act (3 of 1930), S. 2(9)]

Mercantile document of title to goods. The expression "MERCANTILE DOCUMENT OF TITLE TO GOODS" includes a bill of lading, dock-warrant, ware house-keeper's certificate, railway receipt, warrant or order for the delivery of goods, and any other document used in the ordinary course of business as proof of the possession or control of goods, or authorising or purporting to authorise, either by endorsement or by delivery, the possession of the document to transfer or receive goods thereby represented. [T.P. Act (4 of 1882), S. 137, *Expln.*]

Mercantile law. The law of commercial transactions derived from the law merchant which includes, among other things, commercial paper, insurance and certain types of agency.

Mercenary. A professional soldier hired by someone other than his or her own government to fight in a foreign country.

Merchandise. A term of a very extended meaning, covering all articles of commerce; the objects of commerce; the subjects of commerce and traffic; any article which is the object of commerce, or which may be bought or sold in trade; all kinds of personal property which is bought and sold in the market.

Merchant Banker. Means any person who is engaged in the business of issue management either by making arrangements regarding selling, buying or subscribing to securities or acting as manager, consultant, adviser or rendering corporate advisory service in relation to such issue management. [Securities and Exchange Board of India (Merchant Bankers) Regulations 1992, regulation 2(*cb*). Also see *Explanation* (*ii*) to rule 13(3) of the Companies (Registration of Foreign Companies) Rules, 2014.]

Merchant-exporter. Means a person engaged in trading activity and exporting goods. [Customs Tariff Act (51 of 1975), Gen. Exemption No. 42, 13(13) *Expln* (viia)]

Merchantable. *In the law of sales*, the saleable quality of an article at the average market price; marketable.

Salable, and fit for the market; sound and undamaged; such as is generally sold in the market; vendible in market.

Merchantable quality. The word 'merchantable' can only mean commercially saleable. *Trustees, Port of*

Calcutta v. *Bengal Corporation,* AIR 1979 Cal 142, 146. [Sale of Goods Act (3 of 1930), S. 16, *Exceptions* (1) and (2)]

The Act does not give any definition yet the word has by long use become a term of art in commercial law. Merchantable quality means that the goods comply with the description in the contract so that to a purchaser buying goods of that description the goods would be good tender. *Sorabji Hormusha Jobhi and Co.* v. *M. Ismail,* AIR 1960 Mad 520, 524.

The mere fact that a motor car needed repairs more expensive than was thought at the time of sale did not necessarily mean that it was not of "merchantable quality".

Mere. Only; only this; nothing else; simple; bare.

Mere equity. A right which affects property that is less significant than an equitable right or a legal right; it does not affect anyone except the parties to the transaction in which it is contained. An example is the right to rectify a document.

Merely. Is a term which is to be given a reasonable construction according to the subject-matter.

The words "MERELY ON THE GROUNDS THAT NO CHARGE WAS FRAMED" in S. 464 of the CrPC 1973 (2 of 1974) mean a case where the offence being a petty one and the evidence being fairly taken, the Court framed no charge at all. But where the Court frames a charge, then it cannot be said that the conviction is invalid merely on the ground that no charge was framed. Such a case does not come under S. 465(1) of the CrPC 1973 (2 of 1974).

S. 460, CrPC 1973 (2 of 1974) makes it quite clear that the proceedings mentioned therein shall not be set aside 'merely' on the ground of the magistrate not being empowered by law. Where there are other grounds on which the proceedings are questioned S. 460, cannot be availed. *Tulsibala Rakhit* v. *N.N. Khosal,* AIR 1953 Cal 109.

Merged territory. Shall mean the territories which by virtue of an order made under S. 290A of the Government of India Act, 1935, were immediately before the commencement of the Constitution being administered as if they formed part of a Governor's Province or as if they were a Chief Commissioner's Province. [General Clauses Act (10 of 1897), S. 3(34)]

Merger. Extinguishment of a right, estate, contract, company, action *etc.* by absorption in another. [T.P. Act (4 of 1882), S. 101].

Merit. A term which may be, but is not necessarily, synonymous with "fitness".

Merit consists of a high degree of intelligence coupled with a keen and incisive mind, sound knowledge of the basic subjects and infinite capacity for hard work and also calls for a sense of social commitment and dedication to the cause of the poor. *Pradeep Jain* v. *Union of India,* AIR 1984 SC 1420.

Merito beneficium legis amittit, qui legem ipsam subvertere intendit. (*Lat.*) (2 *Inst* 53). He justly loses the benefit of law who purposes to overturn the law itself.

Meritorious consideration. One founded upon some moral obligation.

Merits. The real or substantial grounds of an action or defence in contra-distinction to some technical or collateral matter raised in the course of the case. [Presidency Small Causes Courts Act (15 of 1882), S. 69]

Mesne. A term which signifies merely intervening, middle; intermediate.

Mesne mortgagee. A person in whose favour a mortgage is executed on a date intermediate between the dates of other mortgages of the same property. [T.P. Act (4 of 1882), S. 94].

Mesne profits of property means those profits which the person in wrongful possession of such property actually received or might with ordinary diligence have received therefrom, together with interest on such profits, but shall not include profits due to improvements made by the person in wrongful possession. [CPC (5 of 1908), S. 2, cl. 12]

Message. "MESSAGE" means any communication sent by telegraph, or given to a telegraph officer to be sent by telegraph or to be delivered. [Indian Telegraph Act (13 of 1885), S. 3(3)]

Meta-tags. A meta tag is an encoded statement in the Hypertext Markup Language (HTML) that provides information regarding some of the content of a web page. The meta tag is placed near the top of the HTML in a Web page as part of the heading. Based on the information fed into a meta tag by the net surfer, search engines index the pages which could be of interest to an internet user. Aparna Viswanathan, *Cyber Law: Indian & International Perspectives,* 2012, LexisNexis Butterworths at p. 272.

The embedding of key words or identifiers into the HTML, script of a site, in order to generate as many visitors or 'hits' on a site, is called key metatagging. The result is that any user of a browser or search engine inputting a key word or phrase that is the same or similar to the key word or phrase in the HTML script on your site, will be led to your site. (*Cyber Law*)

Metal. Means any metal, base metal, alloy, gold, silver or any other material which may be described by the Government for the purpose of any coin. [S. 2(f) of the Coinage Act, 2011 (11 of 2011)]

Metallurgical factory. 'METALLURGICAL FACTORY' means—

(i) a factory in which iron or steel is being processed or manufactured;

(ii) any other factory, being a factory in which iron ore is used for any purpose, which the Central Government may, by notification in the Official Gazette, declare to be a metallurgical factory for the purpose of this Act. [Iron Ore Mines Labour Welfare Cess Act, 1961, S. 1A(c)]

Meteorological drought. "Meteorological drought" means the deficiency of precipitation from expected or normal levels over an extended period of time. Meteorological drought usually precedes other kinds of drought and is said to occur when the seasonal rainfall received over an area is less than 25% of its long-term average value. It is further classified as moderate drought if the rainfall deficit is 26-50% and severe drought when the deficit exceeds 50% of the normal. [*Swaraj Abhiyan v. Union of India*, (2016) 7 SCC 498, para 36].

Metes and Bounds. Ascertained by measurements and boundaries.

Metre. The distance, at zero degree centigrade and under normal atmospheric pressure, between the axis of the two medium lines traced on the platinum-iridium bar deposited at the International Bureau of Weights and Measures and declared international prototype of the metre by the First General Conference of Weights and Measures. [Standards of Weights and Measures Act (89 of 1956), S. 2(d)]

Metro alignment, in relation to any metropolitan city, means such alignment of the metro railway as is specified in the Schedule under that city and includes the metro railway. [Metro Railways (Construction of Works) Act (33 of 1978), S. 2(h)]

Metro railway administration. In relation to any metro railway, means the General Manager of that metro railway. [Metro Railways (Construction of Works) Act (33 of 1978), S. 2(j)]

"METRO RAILWAY ADMINISTRATION" in relation to—

(i) a Government metro railway means the General Manager of that railway; or

(ii) a non-Government metro railway means the person who is the owner or lessee of that metro railway or the person working that metro railway under an arrangement with the owner or lessee of that metro railway. [Delhi Metro Railway (Operation and Maintenance) Act (60 of 2002), S. 2(1)(j)]

Metro railway official. Means any person employed by the Central Government or by a metro railway administration in connection with the services of a metro railway. [Delhi Metro Railway (Operation and Maintenance) Act (60 of 2002), S. 2(1)(k)]

Metro railways. Means a metro railway or any portion thereof for the public carriage of passengers, animals or goods and includes—

(a) all land within the boundary marks indicating the limits of the land appurtenant to a metro railway;

(b) all lines of rails, sidings, yards or branches worked over for the purposes of, or in connection with, a metro railway;

(c) all stations, offices, ventilation shafts and ducts, warehouses, workshops, manufactories, fixed plants and machineries, sheds, depots and other works constructed for the purpose of, or in connection with, a metro railway. [Metro Railways (Construction of Works) Act (33 of 1978), S. 2(i)]

"Metro railway" means the metro railway as defined in sub-clause (*i*) of clause (*1*) of section 2 of the Metro Railways (Operation and Maintenance) Act, 2002 (60 of 2002). [Industrial Relations Code, 2020 (35 of 2020), section 2(w)]

Metropolitan area. Means an area having a population of ten lakhs or more, comprised in one or more districts and consisting of two or more Municipalities or Panchayats or other contiguous areas, specified by the Governor by public notification to be a Metropolitan area for the purposes of this Part. [Constitution of India, Art. 243 P(c)]

The State Government may, by notification, declare that, as from such date as may be specified in the notification, any area in the State comprising a city or town whose population exceeds one million, shall be a metropolitan area for the purposes of this Code. [CrPC, 1973 (2 of 1974), S. 8]

Metropolitan area network (MAN). A type of network designed to deliver data, video, and digital voice to all organizations within a metropolitan area. (*Cyber Law*)

Metropolitan city. Means the Metropolitan city of Bombay, Calcutta, Delhi or Madras. [Metro Railways (Construction of Works) Act (33 of 1978), S. 2(k)]

Metropolitan city of Delhi. shall have the meaning assigned to it in clause (c) of article 243P of the Constitution.[Subsituted by Metro Railways (Amendment) Act, 2009]..

Metus quen agnoscunt leges in excusationem criminis est talis qui cadere possit in constantem virum. The fear which the law acknowledges in the excuse of a crime is such as can fall upon a steady man.

Mica works. "Mica works" is a general term of widest possible import and includes all kinds of works in relation to mica including mining. *N.K. Jain* v. *Labour Commissioner,* AIR 1957 Raj 35, 36. [Minimum Wages Act (11 of 1948), Sch, Part I, Item 10]

Micro-organisms. Shall include all the bacteria, viruses, fungi, mycoplasma, cells lines, algae, protodones and nematotes indicated in the schedule and those that have not been presently known to exist in the country or not have been discovered so far. [Rules for the Manufacture, Use, Import, Export and Storage of Hazardous Micro Organisms, Genetically Engineered Organisms or Cells Rules, 1989, R. 3(v)]

Midwife. MIDWIFE means a person who holds a certificate in midwifery granted by any authority recognised in this behalf by the Council. [Rajasthan Nurses, Midwives; Health Visitors and Auxilliary, Nurse Midwives Registration Act (9 of 1964), S. 2(d)]

Middleman. An agent who acts as an intermediary between two parties, and upon whom does not devolve the duty of negotiating for either, and who may contract for and receive commissions from both.

Might. Is equivalent to "had power" or "was possible."

Might and ought. In deciding the question, of *res judicata*, as to whether any matter might and ought to have been made a ground of defence or attack in a previous suit, one important test is, whether the matters in the two suits are so dissimilar that their union might lead to confusion.

Might maintain. The words 'might maintain' mean 'has the power or is entitled to maintain' and for this one has to turn to the provisions of S. 59 Provincial Insolvency Act (5 of 1920); [CPC (5 of 1908), O. XXII, R. 8(1)]

Migrans jura amittatac privilegia et immunitates domicilii prioris. One who emigrates will lose the rights, privileges, and immunities of his former domicile.

Migrated. The word 'migration' definitely suggests an element of permanent change of residence and not merely movement from one place to another. *S.M. Zaki* v. *State of Bihar,* AIR 1953 Pat 112. [Constitution of India, Art. 7]

Migrated means going from one territory to the other, the movement being voluntary and not being for a specific purpose and for a short and limited period. *Kulathil Mammu* v. *State of Kerala*, AIR 1966 SC 1614, 1618.

Migration. The expression 'migration' in Art. 7 of the Constitution of India embraces in its scope two conceptions; (1) going from one place to another and (2) the intention to make the destination a place of abode or residence in future. *Badruzzumman* v. *State,* AIR 1951 All 16.

The act of moving from one place to another. [Constitution of India, VII Sch., List I, item 81]

Migration is changing one's abode, quitting one's place of abode and settling permanently at another place. *Vimla Bai* v. *Hiralal Gupta,* 1990 (2) SCC 22.

Migration used in Article 7 of the Constitution of India embraces two conceptions : (1) going from one place to another, and (2) the intention to make the destination a place of abode or residence in future; It has the notion of transference of allegiance from the country of departure to the country of adoption; migration means coming to India with the intention of residing here permanently.

Milch cattle. Include all cattle breeds which have an inherent potential for milk production. *State of Gujarat* v. *Mirzapur Moti Kureshi Kassab Jamat*, AIR 2006 SC 212 : 2005 AIR SCW 5723.

Mile. "MILE" means a nautical mile of 1.852 meters. [Merchant Shipping Act (44 of 1958), S. 356B(h)]

Mileage. An allowance for travelling expenses at a certain rate per mile; total miles travelled in a day or other period of time.

Military. Army [CrPC 1973 (2 of 1974), S. 132 (3)(a)]; relating to army [Army Act (46 of 1950), S. 3(xiv)].

Military aircraft. Means any aircraft belonging to the Armed Forces and includes any armed aircraft in the service of the Armed Forces and any other aircraft used as a transport or auxiliary or in any other way for the purpose of prosecuting or aiding hostilities. [Naval and Aircraft Prize Act (59 of 1971), S. 2(g)]

Military custody. "MILITARY CUSTODY" means the arrest or confinement of a person according to the usages of the service and includes air force custody. [Indian Army Act (7 of 1911), S. 7(14) and Army Act (46 of 1950), S. 3(xiii)]

Military law. The law relating to and administered by military Courts, it is concerned with the trial and punishment of offences committed by military officers, soldiers and the like. [Army Act (46 of 1950), S. 7]

It is a branch of law as valid as any other, and it differs from the general law of the land in authority only in this : that it applies to officers and soldiers of the army, but not to other members of the body politic, and that it is limited to breaches of military duty.

Military men. Members of the army; army men. [heading, CPC (5 of 1908), O. XXVIII].

Military, naval or air force. Army, navy or air force. [CrPC 1973 (2 of 1974), S. 475(1)].

Military officer. "MILITARY OFFICER" means a commissioned or warrant officer of the Indian military or air forces on military or air force duty in a cantonment, an officer of the Cantonments Department and any person in Army departmental employment whom the officer commanding the District may at any time, by an order in writing, place on the same footing as a military officer for the purposes of this Act. [Cantonments (Home Accommodation) Act (6 of 1923), S. 2(g)]

"MILITARY OFFICER" means a person who being an officer within the meaning of the Army Act, 1950, the Navy Act, 1957 or the Air Force Act, 1950, is commissioned, gazetted or in pay as an officer doing army, naval or air force duty with the army, navy or air force, or is an officer doing such duty in any army, branch or part of any of those forces. [Cantonments Act (2 of 1924), S. 2(xxi)]

Military police-officer. There shall be six classes of *Military police-officers* namely:—

(i) subahdars,

(ii) jamadars,

(iii) havildars,

(iv) naiks,

(v) lance-naiks,

(vi) sepoys,

and such grades in each class as the Local Government may direct. [Bur. Act XV of 1887 (Military Police), S. 5, cl. 1.]

Military reward. "MILITARY REWARD" includes any gratuity or annuity for long service or good conduct, any good conduct pay, good service pay or pension and any other military pecuniary reward. [Indian Army Act, 1911 (7 of 1911), S. 7(15)]

"MILITARY REWARD" includes any gratuity or annuity for long service or good conduct, good service pay or pension, and any other military pecuniary reward. [Army Act (46 of 1950), S. 3(xiv)]

Military service. 'MILITARY SERVICE' means enrolled or commissioned service in any of the three wings of the Indian Armed Forces (including service as a warrant officer) rendered by a person during the period of operation of the Proclamation or Emergency made by the President under Article 352 of the Constitution on 26.10.1962 or such other service as may hereafter be declared as military service for the purposes of these rules. Any period of military training followed by military service shall also be reckoned as military service. [Punjab Government National Emergency (Concession) Rules, 1965]

Milk. Includes cream, skimmed milk, separated milk and condensed, sterlized, desiccated or toned milk. [Maharashtra Municipalities Act (40 of 1965), S. 2(23)]

Addition of water to milk also amounts to adulteration within the meaning of Section 2(i) ((ia) after amendment by Act 34 of 1976) (b), (c) or (d). While 'milk', is a generic term, the identity of the article of food is dependent on the source. 'Cow's milk', 'buffalo's milk', 'goat's milk', 'camel's milk', 'horse's milk', 'donkey's milk' are all different from each other and are consumed by different sections of people, sometimes for ailment, sometimes for improving health and, in the case of 'horse's milk, for exhilaration and nourishment. Shortly put, they are different articles of food and the name of one cannot be appropriated for the other by a seller without being tracked down by Section 2(ix)(c). *Kisan Trimbak Kothuda* v. *State of Maharashtra,* (1977) I SCC 300. [Prevention of Food Adulteration Act (37 of 1954), S. 2(ix)(c)]

Milk product. 'MILK PRODUCT' means any article of food or drink wholly or partly manufactured or derived from milk. [Agricultural Marketing Act, 1958, S. 42(1)]

"MILK PRODUCT" means—

(i) sterilised standardised, recombined, toned, double-toned, skimmed, flavoured or acidified milk;

(ii) ice-cream;

(iii) cream;

(iv) cheese;

(v) butter;

(vi) milk powders;

(vii) weaning foods with milk and infant milk foods;

(viii) malted milk foods with or without cocoa powder;

(ix) ghee;

(x) anhydrous milk fat and butter oil;

(xi) casein;

(xii) any other product containing milk or any of the milk products specified above which the Central Government may by notification in the Official Gazette, specify in this behalf. [National Dairy Development Board Act (37 of 1987), S. 3(h)]

Milk products means the product obtained from milk such as cream, malai, curd, skimmed milk curd, chhanna, cheese, processed cheese, ice cream, condensed milk sweetened and unsweetened, condensed skimmed milk sweetened and unsweetened, milk powder, skimmed milk powder, partly skimmed milk powder, khoa, infant milk food, table butter and deshi butter. *Kishan Chand* v. *Delhi Administration,* AIR 1979 SC 1128.

Mill. "MILL" means any contrivance whereby the waterpower of any canal is used for grinding, sawing or pressing, or for driving or working machinery or for any other similar purpose, and includes all subsidiary works and structures connected with any such contrivance except the canal itself. [Punjab Act III of 1905 (Minor Canals), S. 3, cl. x.]

A building or a collection of buildings with machinery by which the process of manufacturing is carried on.

Milling. "Milling" has been held to be synonymous with "manufacturing."

Milling rice. In order to come within the definition of the expression 'milling rice', paddy must be subjected to a milling process and the yield may be either rice or a rice product like 'beaten rice' or rice flakes. *Narayana Kamath* v. *Director of Food Supplies,* AIR 1967 Mys 1, 2. [Rice Milling Industry (Regulation) Act (21 of 1958), S. 6]

MIME. (*abbr.*) Multi-purpose Internet Mail Extensions. This enables you to attach files to e-mail. (*Cyber Law*)

A method of encoding or decoding programs so that they can be sent as normal text e-mail messages. (*Cyber Law*)

Originally a standard for defining the types of files attached to standard Internet mail messages. The MIME standard has come to be used in many situations where one computer programs needs to communicate with another program about what kind of file is being sent.

For example, *HTML* files have a MIME-type of test/html, *JPEG* files are image/jpeg, *etc.* (*Matisse Enzer-Glossary of Internet Terms*)

The standard for attaching non-text files to standard Internet mail messages. Non-text files include graphics, spreadsheets, formatted word-processor documents, sound files, *etc.*

An email program is said to be MIME Compliant if it can both send and receive files using the MIME standard.

When non-text files are sent using the MIME standard they are converted (encoded) into text-although the resulting text is not really readable.

Generally speaking the MIME standard is a way of specifying both the type of file being sent (*e.g.* a Quicktime video file), and the method that should be used to turn it back into its original form.

Besides email software, the MIME standard is also universally used by Web Servers to identify the files they are sending to Web Clients, in this way new file formats can be accommodated simply by updating the Browsers' list of pairs of MIME-Types and appropriate software for handling each type. (*Internet and E-commerce*).

Minatur innocentibus qui parcit nocentibus. (*Lat.*) (4 Rep 45) He threatens the innocent who spares the guilty.

Mind. In its legal sense, a term meaning the ability to will, to direct, to permit, or to assent; a word sometimes used as convertible with the word memory.

Mine. "MINE" means any excavation where any operation for the purpose of searching for or obtaining minerals has been or is being carried on and includes—

(i) all borings, bore holes, oil wells and accessory crude conditioning plants, including the pipe conveying mineral oil within the oilfields;

(ii) all shafts, in or adjacent to and belonging to a mine, whether in the course of being sunk or not;

(iii) all levels and inclined planes in the course of being driven;

(iv) all open cast workings;

(v) all conveyors or aerial ropeways provided for the bringing into or removal from a mine of minerals or other articles or for the removal of refuse therefrom;

(vi) all adits, levels, planes, machinery, works, railways, tramways and sidings in or adjacent to and belonging to a mine;

(vii) all protective works being carried out in or adjacent to a mine;

(viii) all workshops and stores situated within the precincts of a mine and under the same management and used primarily for the purposes connected with that mine or a number of mines under the same management;

(ix) all power stations, transformer sub-stations, convertor stations, rectifier stations and accumulator storage stations for supplying electricity solely or mainly for the purpose of working the mine or a number of mines under the same management;

(x) any premises for the time being used for depositing sand or other material for use in a mine or for depositing refuse from a mine or in which any operations in connection with such, sand, refuse or other material is being carried on, being premises exclusively occupied by the owner of the mine;

(xi) any premises in or adjacent to and belonging to a mine on which any process ancillary to the getting, dressing or preparation for sale of minerals or of coke is being carried on. [Mines Act (35 of 1952), S. 2(1)(j)]

"MINE" means any excavation where any operation for the purpose of searching for or obtaining minerals has been or is being carried on, and includes—

(i) all borings and bore holes;

(ii) all shafts adjacent to, and belonging to or in, a mine, whether in the course of being sunk or not;

(iii) all levels and inclined planes in the course of being driven;

(iv) all open cast working;

(v) all conveyors or aerial ropeways provided for bringing into or removal from a mine of minerals or other articles or for the removal of refuse therefrom;

(vi) all lands, buildings, wors, adits, levels, planes, machinery and equipment, vehicles, railways, tramways and siding belonging to, or in, or about, a mine;

(vii) all workshops belonging to, or in, a mine including buildings, machinery, instruments, stores, equipment of such workshops and the lands on which such workshops stand;

(viii) all coal in stock or in transit or under production and other stores, stocks and instruments belonging to, or in, a mine;

(ix) all power stations belonging to, or in, a mine or operated for supplying electricity for the purpose of working the mine or a number of mines;

(x) all lands, buildings and equipment belonging to, or in, a mine where the washing of coal or manufacture of coke is carried on;

(xi) all other fixed assets, movable or immovable, and current assets, belonging to a mine, whether within its premises or outside.

Explanation.—The expression "current assets" does not include,—

(a) dues representing the sale of coal and coal products effected at any time before the appointed day and outstanding immediately before the said day;

(b) dues from the Coal Board, established under Section 4 of the Coal Mines (Conservation, Safety and Development) Act, 1952, prior to the repeal of the said Act, with respect to any period before the appointed day;

(c) dues from sundry debtors, loans and advances to other parties and investments not being investments in the coking coal mine;

(d) security deposits made by the owners with the Coal Controller appointed by the Central Government or with the Railways for the fulfilment of contracts or with a State Electricity Board for the payment of bills;

(e) earnest money deposited by the owners with the Railways for obtaining contracts. [Coking Coal Mines (Nationalisation) Act (36 of 1972), S. 3(j)]

"MINE" means any place in the offshore area wherein any exploration or production operation is carried on, together with any vessel, erection, appliance, artificial island or platform and premises in the offshore area used for the purposes of exploration, winning, treating or preparing minerals, obtaining or extracting any mineral or metal by any mode or method, and includes any area covered by an exploration licence or production lease where exploration or production operation has been, or is being, or may be, carried on under the provisions of this Act. [Offshore Areas Minerals (Development and Regulation) Act, 2002 (17 of 2003), S. 4(k)]

An excavation made in the earth for the purpose of digging metallic ores or coal, salt, precious stones, *etc.* [Mines Act (35 of 1952), S. 2(1)(i) and Contract Labour (Regulation and Abolition) Act (37 of 1970), S. 2(g)(iii)].

Under the definition of 'mine' in S. 2(h), fixed asset, moveable or immovable', belonging to the owner of a mine is also 'mine'. As the staff car of the Technical Advisor is fixed asset, it is 'mine', though the Technical Advisor has put the staff car to his personal use. *Union of India* v. *United Colleries Ltd.*, AIR 1985 SC 192, 195. [Coal Mines (Nationalisation) Act (26 of 1973), S. 2(h)(xii)]

Land adjacent to a mine and used for carrying on the mining operations and also, for the purposes of mine, for carrying on mining operations in respect of the part of the seam lying immediately below the surface, comes under the term 'mine'. *Kali Prasad* v. *Bharat Coaking Coal Ltd.*, AIR 1989 SC 1530, 1533. [Coal Mines (Nationalisation) Act (26 of 1973), S. 2(L)(iv),(vi)]

Coal mine includes coke oven plant. *Sanjeev Coke Manufacturing Company* v. *Bharat Coking Coal Ltd.*, AIR 1983 SC 239, 244. [Coking Coal Mines (Nationalisation) Act (36 of 1972), S. 3(j)]

'Mine' and 'obtain'. The expression 'mine', according to clause (b) of S. 3, means any excavation for the purpose of searching for or obtaining minerals. Here the word 'obtain' is used to cover the various processes necessary to get the mineral and would include the processes covered by the expressions 'winning', 'working', 'getting', *etc. Gujarat Pottery Works Private Ltd.* v. *B.P. Sood,* AIR 1967 SC 964. [Mines and Minerals (Regulation and Development) Act, 1948, S. 3(b)]

Mine infrastructure. "Mine infrastructure" includes mining infrastructure such as tangible assets used for coal mining operations, being civil works, workshops, immovable coal mining equipment, foundations, embankments, pavements, electrical systems, communication systems, relief centres, site administrative offices, fixed installations, coal handling arrangements, crushing and conveying systems, railway sidings, pits, shafts, inclines, underground transport systems, hauling systems (except movable equipment unless the same is embedded in land for permanent beneficial enjoyment thereof), land demarcated for afforestation and land for rehabilitation and resettlement of persons affected by coal mining operations under the relevant law. [Coal Mines (Special Provisions) Act (11 of 2015), S. 3(1)(j)].

Mineral. "MINERALS" includes all minerals except mineral oils. [Mines & Minerals (R&D) Act (67 of 1957), S. 3(d)]

"Mineral" means all substances which can be obtained from the earth by mining, digging, drilling, dredging, hydraulicing, quarrying or by any other operation and includes mineral oils (which in turn include natural gas and petroleum). [Mines Act (35 of 1952), S. 2(jj)]

"MINERALS" include all substances obtained or obtainable from the soil including (alluvium or rocks) by underground or surface working. [Atomic Energy Act (33 of 1962), S. 2(c)]

"MINERAL" includes all minerals except mineral oil and hydrocarbon resources relating thereto. [Offshore Areas Minerals (Development and Regulation) Act, 2002 (17 of 2003), S. 4(l)]

Any thing that grows in mines, and contains metals. (*Tomlin*)

The term "minerals" includes all such bodies of mineral substances, lying together in seams, beds, or strata as are commonly worked for profit and have a value independent of the surface of the land, whether extracted from a mine or a quarry or even occurring as an outcrop.

Minerals include granite, clay, limestone, freestone and the stone used.

Brick-earth or clay is a mineral. *Laddenmal* v. *State of Bihar,* AIR 1965 Pat 491, 499. [Constitution of India, Sch. 7, List I, item 54]

The word 'mineral' includes salt no matter that in certain cases it is not produced out of the mines but by natural processes or surface workings. The word 'mineral' cannot necessarily be restricted to something which is dug out of a mine or pit or from inside the bowls of the earth. *Bhoorchand* v. *State of Rajasthan,* AIR 1957 Raj 213, 216.

The word 'minerals' includes water under Section 2(ba) of the Act. *Ichchapur Industrial Coop. Society Ltd.* v. *Competent Authy., ONGC,* (1997) 2 SCC 42, paras 15 & 17 : AIR 1997 SC 42. [Petroleum and Minerals Pipelines (Acquisition of Right of User in Land) Act (50 of 1962), S. 2(ba).

The word 'minerals' occurring in Section 80-HHC 2b(ii) includes all minerals extracted from the earth including granite. *Stonecraft Enterprises* v. *CIT,* (1999) 3 SCC 343, para 7 : AIR 1999 SC 1638. [Income-tax Act (43 of 1961), S. 80-HHC 2(b)(ii)]

A mineral as judicially defined would mean an inorganic substance found either on or in the earth which may be garnered and exploited for profit. *V.P. Pithupitchai* v. *Special Secretary, Govt. of T.N.*, (2003) 9 SCC 534, para 13 : AIR 2003 SC 2455.

Mineral—any substance that is neither animal non vegetable. In narrow sense, no more than precious metals like gold and silver. It is also meant substances obtained from underneath the surface of the earth by digging or quarrying. Brick earth is a mineral. *Banersi Das Chandha and Bros.* v. *Lt. Governor, Delhi Administration*, AIR 1978 SC 1587, 1588. [Mines and Minerals (Regulations and Development) Act (67 of 1957), S. 3(e)]

Mineral Concession Rules. Means the Mineral Concession Rules, for the time being in force, made by the Central Government under the Mines and Minerals (Regulation and Development) Act, 1957. [Metal Corporation (Nationalisation and Miscellaneous Provisions) Act (100 of 1976), S. 2(d)]

Mineral development. Scientific exploitation of minerals without waste is undoubtedly part of mineral development. *Premium Granites* v. *State of Tamil Nadu*, AIR 1994 SC 2233, 2248. [Mines and Minerals (Regulation and Development Act (67 of 1957), S. 15)]

Mineral oils. MINERAL OILS include natural gas and petroleum. [Oilfields (Regulation and Development) Act (53 of 1948); S. 3(e) and Mines and Minerals (Regulation and Development) Act (67 of 1957), S. 3(b)]

"MINERAL OILS" include casing head condensate natural gas and petroleum. [Gujarat Rural Development Cess Act (4 of 1984), S. 2(c) and Oil Industry (Development) Act (97 of 1974), S. 2(h); Income-tax Act (43 of 1961), S. 293A *Expln.* (a) and Offshore Areas Minerals (Development and Protection) Act, 2002 (17 of 2003), S. 4(m)]

Mineral resources. Means all non-living natural non-renewable resources, including fossils fuels metallic and non-metallic metals. [Convention on the Regulation of Antartic Mineral Resource Activities (1988), Art. I(6)]

Minerals. There are no words of restriction which qualify the word 'minerals' and it would be reasonable to assume that in the absence of any such limitation, the word must be read to include all kinds of minerals in all its forms, *i.e.*, whether subject to any process or not as long as it continued to retain the characteristics of the mineral. *Gem Granites* v. *CIT*, AIR 2005 SC 1455.

Mines and minerals. The words 'mines and minerals' include all substances capable of being worked for profit below the top surface of the land. They include sand and gravel and clay but not peat.

Minima poena corporalis est major qualibet pecuniaria. (*Maxim*) The smallest corporal punishment is greater than any pecuniary one.

Minime mutanda sunt quae certam habuerunt interpretationem. (*Lat.*) (Co. Litt. 365a) Things which have had a certain interpretation (Whose interpretation has been settled, as by common opinion) are not to be altered.

Minimum. "MINIMUM" must mean in each as much as minimum in aggregate. (*D.G. Telecommunication* v. *T.N. Peetambaram*, AIR 1987 SC 162).

Minimum. Black's Law Dictionary defines 'minimum,' an adjective: of, relating to, or constituting the smallest acceptable or possible quantity in a given case. The Oxford English Dictionary defines 'minimum,' a noun, as the least or smallest amount or quantity possible, attainable, or required. [As cited in *Bindu Radhakrishnan vs. Employees State Insurance Corporation,*2017 (4) SCT 760 (Kerala), para 44]

Minimum support price. Means the assured price announced by the Central Government at which foodgrains are procured from farmers by the Central Government and the State Governments and their agencies, for the central pool. [S. 2(10) of the National Food Security Act, 2013 (20 of 2013)]

Minimum wage. Minimum wages can be termed as living wages which ensure not only bare physical subsistence but also the maintenance of health and decency. *Bijoy Cotton Mills* v. *State of Ajmer*, AIR 1955 SC 33, 35. [Minimum Wages Act (11 of 1948), Ss. 3,4 & 25]

Minimum Wage : Living Wage. The bare subsistence minimum wage is a wage which would be sufficient to cover the bare physical needs of a worker and his family that is, a rate which has got to be paid to the worker irrespective of the capacity of the industry to pay. The statutory minimum wage is the minimum prescribed by the statute and it will provide for some measure of education, medical requirements and amenities. The living wage should enable the male earner to provide for himself and his family not merely the bare essentials of food, clothing and shelter but a measure of frugal comfort including education for children, protection against ill-health and misfortunes including old age. *Express Newspapers Ltd.* v. *UOI*, AIR 1958 SC 578, 602, 601.

Mining. The process or business of making or working of mines [Mines Act (35 of 1952), S. 12(1)(e)]; an encased explosive anchored or floating in water or placed on or under the earth that may be detonated by contract, the passage of time, magnetic force, sound waves or controlled means designed to destroy or damage. [Arms Act (54 of 1959), S. 2(1)(b)(ii)].

Mining lease. "MINING LEASE" means a lease granted for the purpose of searching for, winning; working, getting, making merchantable, carrying away or disposing of mineral oils or for purposes connected therewith, and includes an exploring or a prospecting licence. [Oilfields (Regulation and Development) Act (53 of 1948), S. 3(d)].

'MINING LEASE' means a lease granted for the purpose of undertaking mining operations, and includes a sub-lease granted for such purpose. [Mines and Minerals (Regulation and Development) Act (67 of 1957), S. 3(c)]

The term "mining lease" includes a contract between the mining company and miner, whereby the former promises the latter to dig for mineral on certain of its property for a stipulated royalty, although there is no determinate term fixed.

Where the sludge or slurry deposited in a river bed does not convert the river bed into a mine, the lease to collect such sludge or slurry is not a mining lease. *Industrial Final Marketing Co.* v. *UOI,* AIR 1985 Cal 143, 146. [Mines and Minerals (Regulation and Development) Act (67 of 1957), S. 3(c) and (d)]

Mining operations. Means any operations undertaken for the purpose of winning any mineral. [Mines and Minerals (Regulation and Development) Act (67 of 1957), S. 3(d)]

"Mining operations" and "winning of minerals." The expression "winning of minerals" in the definition of 'mining operations' is spacious enough to comprehend every activity by which the mineral is extracted or obtained from the earth irrespective of whether such activity is carried out on the surface or in the bowels of the earth. It is wrong to assume that mines and minerals must always be sub-soil and that there can be no minerals on the surface of the earth. *Tarkeshwar Sio Thakur Jiu* v. *Dar Dass Dey & Co.,* AIR 1979 SC 1669. [Mines and Minerals (Regulation and Development) Act (67 of 1957), S. 3(d)]

Minister. The administrative head of a department of state; one to whom the management of the affairs are entrusted.

"MINISTER" means a member of the Council of Ministers, a Minister of State, a Deputy Minister, or a Parliamentary Secretary. [Rules of Procedure and Conduct of Business in the Council of States (Rajya Sabha), R. 2(1)]

"MINISTER" means a Union Minister but does not include the Prime Minister. [S. 2(1)(k) of the Lokpal & Lokayuktas Act, 2013 (1 of 2014)]

'Minister-in-charge'. Means the Minister or Minister of State, if appointed to hold independent charge as the case may be, appointed by the Governor to be in charge of the department of the Government to which the relevant case belongs.

Explanation.—A case shall be deemed to belong to the department to which under the schedule to these rules, the subject-matters thereof pertains or its mainly related. [Rules framed under Article 166(2) & (3), Constitution of India, R. 2(f) **as cited in** *Lalaram* v. *Jaipur Development Authority,* (2016) 11 SCC 31, para 59].

'Minister of State'. Means a Minister of State appointed by the Governor to hold independent charge of a department or to assist a Minister in the discharge of his responsibilities or both. [Rules framed under Articles 166(2) & (3) of the Constitution of India, R. 2(f) **as cited in** *Lalaram* v. *Jaipur Development Authority,* (2016) 11 SCC 31, para 59]

Ministerial. Acting at the commands of another, or acting as the agent for another or under superior authority; clerical, of or pertaining to ministry or service; a term sometimes used as synonymous with the word administrative.

Of or relating to an act that involves obedience to instructions or laws instead of discretion, judgment, or skill the court clerk's ministerial duties include recording judgments on the docket. [Black's Law Dictionary as cited in *State of Maharashtra v. Saeed Sohail Sheikh,* (2012) 13 SCC 192, para 26].

"Ministerial" as a technical legal term has no single fixed meaning. It may describe any duty the discharge whereof requires no element of discretion or independent judgment. It may often be used more narrowly to describe the issue of a formal instruction, in consequence of a prior determination which may or may not be of a judicial character. [*State of Maharashtra v. Saeed Sohail Sheikh,* (2012) 13 SCC 192, para 27].

Ministerial act. A ministerial act may be defined to be one which a person performs in a given state of facts, in a prescribed manner, in obedience to the mandate of a legal authority, without regard to, or the exercise of, his own judgment upon the property of the act done.

Official action, the result of performing a certain and specific duty arising from designated facts, is a ministerial act.

The administration of an oath is a ministerial act.

'An act performed without the independent exercise of discretion or judgment. If the act is mandatory, it is also termed a ministerial duty.' [Black's Law Dictionary as cited in *State of Maharashtra v. Saeed Sohail Sheikh,* (2012) 13 SCC 192, para 26].

Ministerial act or duty. The expression 'ministerial act or duty' means the administrative functions of a High Court which may be delegated to the ministerial and administrative staff of the High Court, to aid the Judges in discharge of their judicial functioning. *Jamaluddin Ahmad* v. *Abu Saleh Najmuddin,* (2003) 4 SCC 257, para 23 : AIR 2003 SC 1917.

Ministerial duty. A duty in which nothing is left to discretion; a duty performed by one acting under superior authority, or not with unlimited control; a simple, definite duty, arising under conditions admitted or proved to exist, and imposed by law.

'A duty that requires neither the exercise of official discretion nor judgment.' [Black's Law Dictionary as cited in *State of Maharashtra v. Saeed Sohail Sheikh,* (2012) 13 SCC 192, para 26].

The sale of property of insolvent by the receiver is not ministerial duty. [Provincial Insolvency Act (5 of 1920), S. 59]

Ministerial office. 'An office that does not include authority to exercise judgment, only to carry and orders given by a superior office, or to perform duties or acts required by rules, statutes, or regulations. [Black's Law Dictionary as cited in *State of Maharashtra v. Saeed Sohail Sheikh*, (2012) 13 SCC 192, para 26].

Ministry. The body of ministers of the state. The term Ministry is wider than Cabinet, and includes all the holders of political office who come in and go out with the Prime Minister.

Minor. "MINOR" means a person who has not attained the age of eighteen years. [Citizenship Act (57 of 1955), S. 2(e)]

"MINOR" means any person subject to the Indian Majority Act (9 of 1875), S. 3, who has not attained his majority within the meaning of that Act, and any other person who has not completed the age of eighteen years, and "minority" means the status of any such person [Indian Succession Act (39 of 1925), S. 2(e)]

"MINOR" means a person who is not deemed to have attained his majority under S. 3 of the Indian Majority Act (9 of 1875); [Government Savings Bank Act (5 of 1873), S. 3].

"MINOR" means a person who has not completed the age of twenty-one years and who is not a widower or a widow. [Christian Marriage Act (15 of 1872), S. 3]

A person who has not attained majority [Citizenship Act (57 of 1955), S. 2(e)]; [Child Marriage Restraint Act (19 of 1929), S. 2(d) and Constitution of India, Art. 28(3)]; inferior in importance; small.

"MINOR" means a person who has not attained the age of eighteen years. [Code on Social Security, 2020 (36 of 2020), section 2(47)]

Minor ante tempus agere non potest in casu proprietatis, nec etiam convenire. A minor before majority cannot act in a case of property, nor even agree.

Minor children. "MINOR CHILDREN" means, in the case of sons of Native fathers, boys who have not completed the age of sixteen years, and, in the case of daughters of Native fathers, girls who have not completed the age of thirteen years; in other cases it means unmarried children who have not completed the age of eighteen years. [Indian Divorce Act (4 of 1869), S. 3(5)].

Minor discrepancies. 'Minor discrepancies', which do not materially affect the prosecution case would not create any infirmities. [*State of A.P.* v. S. *Rayappa,* (2006) 4 SCC 512, 516, p. 9]

Minor girl, Taking or enticing of. Where a girl under sixteen leaves the guardianship of husband of her own free will and stays with the accused, there is no taking or enticing of her under the Penal Code. [IPC (45 of 1860), S. 361].

Minor mineral. This expression means "building stone, boulder shingle, gravel, lime-stone and *kankar* used for lime burning, murrum, brickearth, ordinary clay, ordinary sand and road metal". *Bhagwandas Gangasahai* v. *Union of India*, AIR 1956 SC 175, 176.

Earth or clay used for making bricks would be a minor mineral. *Ramlal* v. *H.G. Dange*, AIR 1963 Bom 117, 120. [Mines and Minerals (Regulation and Development) Act (67 of 1957), S. 3(3)]

Minor minorem custodire non debet, allios enim praesumitur male regere qui seipsum regere nescit. (*Maxim*) A minor ought not to be guardian to a minor, for he who knows not how to govern himself, is presumed to be unfit to govern others.

Minor offence. An offence of less importance. [CrPC 1973 (2 of 1974), S. 222(1)].

Minorities. Means the minorities based on religion such as Muslims, Christians, Sikhs, Buddhists, Zorestians (Parsis), Jains and Jews and such minorities within the preview of Article 29 of the Constitution of India as the State Government may, by notification specify from time to time. [West Bengal Minorities Development and Finance Corporation Act (18 of 1995), S. 2(b)]

Minority. The state or condition of a minor; infancy; a personal privilege allowed to an infant, by operation of law; *also*, a legal disability; also the smaller number of votes of a deliberative assembly; opposed to majority.

The word 'minority' occurring in Article 30 is not defined in the Constitution but literally it means 'a non-dominant' group. It is a relative term and is referred to represent the smaller two numbers, sections or group called 'majority'. In that sense, there may be political minority, religious minority, linguistic minority *etc. T.M.A. Pai Foundation* v. *State of Karnataka,* (2002) 8 SCC 481, para 244. [Constitution of India, Article 30]

The word 'minority' is not defined in the Constitution. In common parlance it should be referred to any community which is numerically less than 50% of the population of the State concerned. *M. David* v. *Convenor, EAMCET-2000, Hyderabad,* AIR 2001 AP 278, 282 para 14. [Constitution of India, Art. 29 and 30]

Minority community. Any community, religious or linguistic, numerically less than fifty percent of the population of the State, is a minority community. [Constitution of India, Art. 30(1)].

A minority community can effectively conserve its language, script or culture by and through educational institutions. Education being a State subject the existence of a minority community should in all circumstances and for purposes of all laws of that State be determined on the population of the whole State. *In re Kerala Education Bill*, 1957, AIR 1958 SC 956, 976, 977. [Constitution of India, Arts. 29, 30]

Minority Educational Institution. Means a college or institution (other than a University) established or maintained by a person or group of persons from amongst the minorities. [National Commission for Minority Institution Act, 2004 (2 of 2005), S. 2(g)]

Minority elementary school. Means a school administered by a linguistic or religious minority as envisaged in clause (1) of Art. 31 of the Constitution and which has been in receipt of Govt. grant prior to its being taken by the State Government. [Bihar Non-Government Elementary Schools (Taking over of control) Act (30 of 1976), S. 2(b)]

Minority institution. Where an institution was established by prominent citizens which included not only Muslims but also several Hindus and the institution was established for the spread and promotion of the education in general and not merely for the benefit of any particular community, it cannot be called a minority institution. *Badrul Hasan Qadiri* v. *State of U.P.*, AIR 1992 All 220, 223. [Constitution of India, Art. 30(i)]

Minority occupation. Means a traditional occupation followed by the minorities. [WB Minorities Development and Finance Corporation Act (18 of 1995), S. 2(c)]

Mint. A place where money is coined under public authority. [IPC (45 of 1860), S. 244]. "MINT" in the Coinage Act includes the Mints now existing and any which may hereafter be established. [Coinage Act (3 of 1906), S. 2(*b*)]

"MINT" means the Security Printing and Minting Corporation of India Limited formed and incorporated under the Companies Act, 1956 (1 of 1956), or any other organisation established by or under the authority of the Government to make a coin by stamping metal. [S. 2(g) of the Coinage Act, 2011 (11 of 2011)]

Minute. The 60th part of an hour; a official memorandum drafted usually to authorise or recommend a course of action; note; very small in size, tiny.

Minutes. In practice, memoranda of what takes place in Court made by authority of the Court. In business law, memoranda of notes of a transaction or proceeding.

THE MINUTES OF A COURT are the memoranda of what takes place in Court and made by authority of the Court.

The record of proceedings of a meeting of an assembly, committee *etc.*, a brief summary of events or transactions [Industrial Finance Corporation Act (15 of 1948) (*Repealed by Act 23 of 1993*), S. 14(5)].

Minutes of a meeting. The minutes of a meeting are *prima facie* evidence of what happened at the meeting.

Miranda rights. [From *Miranda* v. *Arizona,* the 1966 U.S. Supreme Court ruling establishing such rights] : the rights (as the right to remain silent, to have an attorney present, and to have an attorney appointed if indigent) of which an arresting officer must advise the person being arrested. A reading of the Miranda rights usually includes a warning that anything said could be used as evidence. No statements made by an arrested person or evidence obtained therefrom may be introduced at trial unless the person was advised of or validly waived these rights. A fresh reading of the Miranda rights. A fresh reading of the Miranda rights may be required by the passage of time after the initial reading, as for example if a previously silent person begins to speak or police interrogate a person more than once. (*Merriam Webster*)

Miranda Warning. A warning that informs suspects of their right to remain silent, to have counsel present and to have the state appoint and pay for counsel if the suspects cannot afford one. It also warns suspects that anything they say can be used against them in Court. (*Criminal*)

Mirror. Generally speaking, "to mirror" is to maintain an exact copy of something. Probably the most common use of the term on the Internet refers to "mirror sites" which are *web* sites, or *FTP* sites that maintain copies of material originated at another location, usually in order to provide more widespread access to the resource. For example, one site might create a library of software, and 5 other sites might maintain mirrors of that library. (*Matisse Enzer-Glossary of Internet Terms*)

Generally speaking, "to mirror" is to maintain an exact copy of something. Probably the most common use of the term on the Internet refers to "mirror sites" which are web sites, or FTP sites that maintain exact copies of material originated at another location, usually in order to provide more widespread access to the resource.

Another common use of the term "mirror" refers to an arrangement where information is written to more than one hard disk simultaneously, so that if one disk fails, the computer keeps on working without losing anything. (*Internet and E-commerce*)

Mirror sites. Heavily used sites, particularly FTP ones, are often replicated at other locations to relieve the load. These are mirror sites. (*Cyber Law*)

Misadventure. Mischance; misfortune; ill luck.

A misadventure is an accident by which injury results to another. When applied to homicide, misadventure is the act of a man who, in the performance of a lawful act, without any intention to do harm, and after using proper precaution to prevent danger, unfortunately kills another person.

Misapplication. Improper, illegal, wrongful, or corrupt use or application of funds, property, *etc.*; a term which does not of itself import wilfulness.

The action of misapplying; improper, illegal, *etc.* [Charitable Endowments Act (6 of 1890), S. 14].

The word 'misapplication' means a wrong or incorrect application not necessarily a wrongful application, and there can be a perfectly innocent misapplication. *Palaicentral Bank* v. *Joseph Augusti,* AIR 1966 Ker 121, 135. [Companies Act (1 of 1956), S. 543]

Misapply. To apply improperly (some money or property). [Indian Trusts Act (2 of 1882), S. 15, ill. (h)].

Misappropriate. The wrongful conversion of or dealing with anything by the person to whom it has been entrusted.

Appropriating to wrong use. [IPC (45 of 1860), S. 403].

Misappropriation. A term which does not necessarily means speculation, although it may mean that.

Misappropriation, Criminal. Dishonestly misappropriating or converting to one's own use any immovable property. [IPC (45 of 1860), S. 403] [(w. e. f. 1-7-2024) repealed and replaced by Bharatiya Nyaya Sanhita, 2023 (45 of 2023), S. 314].

Misappropriation of property. "A dishonest misappropriation for a time only is a misappropriation within the meaning of this section." [IPC (45 of 1860), S. 403, *Expln.* 1]

A dishonest misappropriation for a time only is a misappropriation within the meaning of this section. [(w. e. f. 1-7-2024) Bharatiya Nyaya Sanhita, 2023 (45 of 2023), S. 314, *Explanation 1*]

Misbehaviour. Ill conduct; improper or unlawful behaviour.

Misbranded. "MISBRANDED"—an article of food shall be deemed to be misbranded—

(a) if it is an imitation of, or is a substitute for, or resembles in a manner likely to deceive another article of food under the name of which it is sold, and is not plainly and conspicuously labelled so as to indicate the true character;

(b) if it is falsely stated to be the product of any place or country;

(c) if it is sold by a name which belongs to another article of food;

(d) if it is so coloured, flavoured or coated, powdered or published that the fact that the article is damaged is concealed or if the article is made to appear better or of greater value than it really is;

(e) if false claims are made for it upon the label or otherwise;

(f) if, when sold in packages which have been sealed or prepared by or at the instances of the manufacturer or producer and which bear his name and address, the contents of each package are not conspicuously and correctly stated on the outside thereof within the limits of variability prescribed under this Act;

(g) if the package containing it, or the label on the package bears any statement, design or device regarding the ingredients or the substances contained therein, which is false or misleading in any material particular; or if the package is otherwise deceptive with respect to its content;

(h) if the package containing it or the label on the package bears the name of a fictitious individual or company as the manufacturer or producer of the article;

(i) if it purports to be, or is represented as being, for special dietary uses, unless its label bears such information as may be prescribed concerning its vitamin, mineral, or other dietary properties in order sufficiently to inform its purchaser as to its value for such uses;

(j) if it contains any artificial flavouring, artificial colouring or chemical preservative, without a declaratory label stating that fact or in contravention of the requirements of this Act or rulers made thereunder;

(k) if it is not labelled in accordance with the requirements of this Act or rules made thereunder. [Prevention of Food Adulteration Act (37 of 1954), S. 2(ix)]

Branded falsely or in a misleading way. [Prevention of Food Adulteration Act (37 of 1954), S. 2(ix)].

Misbranded food. Means an article of food—

(A) if it is purported, or is represented to be, or is being—

(i) offered or promoted for sale with false, misleading or deceptive claims either;

(a) upon the label of the package, or

(b) through advertisement, or

(ii) sold by a name which belongs to another article of food; or

(iii) offered or promoted for sale under the name of a fictitious individual or company as the manufacturer or producer of the article as borne on the package or containing the article or the label on such package; or

(B) if the article is sold in packages which have been sealed or prepared by or at the instance of the manufacturer or producer bearing his name and address but—

(i) the article is an imitation of, or is a substitute for, or resembles in a manner likely to deceive, another article of food under the name of which it is sold, and is not plainly and conspicuously labelled so as to indicate its true character; or

(ii) the package containing the article or the label on the package bears any statement, design or device regarding the ingredients or the substances contained therein, which is false or misleading in any material particular, or if the package is otherwise deceptive with respect to its contents; or

(iii) the article is offered for sale as the product of any place or country which is false; or

(C) if the article contained in the package—

(i) contains any artificial flavouring, colouring or chemical preservative and the package is without a declaratory label stating that fact or is not labelled in accordance with the requirements of this Act or regulations made thereunder or is in contravention thereof; or

(ii) is offered for sale for special dietary uses, unless its label bears such information as may be specified by regulation, concerning its vitamins, minerals or other dietary properties in order sufficiently to inform its purchaser as to its value for such use; or

(iii) is not conspicuously or correctly stated on the outside thereof within the limits of variability laid down under this Act. [S. 3(1)(zf) of the Food Safety & Standards Act, 2006 (34 of 2006)]

Miscarriage. "MISCARRIAGE" means expulsion of the contents of uterus at any period prior to or during the twenty-sixth week of pregnancy but does not include any miscarriage, the causing of which is punishable in the IPC (45 of 1860). [Maternity Benefit Act (53 of 1961), S. 3(j); Employee's State Insurance Act (34 of 1948), S. 2(14-B)]

"Miscarriage" (In Medical Jurisprudence) is, technically speaking, the expulsion of the ovum or embryo from a female within the first six weeks after conception.

"Miscarriage" means expulsion of the contents of a pregnant uterus at any period prior to or during the twenty-sixth week of pregnancy, but does not include any miscarriage, the causing of which is punishable under the Indian Penal Code (45 of 1860). [Code on Social Security, 2020 (36 of 2020), S. 2(48)]

Miscarriage means the expulsion of the product of conception before the 28th week of conception and a child born out of miscarriage could not survive even with special care. *Mahendra* v. *Sushila*, AIR 1965 SC 364, 391. [Indian Evidence Act (1 of 1872), S. 112]

Miscarriage of justice. Prejudicial to substantial rights of a party.

Miscellaneous. Of various kinds; of mixed composition or character.

Miscellaneous insurance business. "MISCELLANEOUS INSURANCE BUSINESS" means the business of effecting contracts of insurance which is not principally or wholly or any kind included in clauses (6A), (11) and (13A). [Insurance Act (4 of 1938), S. 2(13B)]

Miscellaneous petition. Means any application to the Tribunal in any appeal or revision petition instituted in the Tribunal for any direction or order of interim nature. [State Transport Appellate Tribunal Rules 1988, R. 2(d)]

"Miscellaneous-Corporate/Group". For the purpose of these regulations, miscellaneous Corporate/Group shall include—

(*a*) Workmen's Compensation/Employers' Liability,

(*b*) Product Liability,

(*c*) Engineering,

(*d*) Aviation,

(*e*) Public Liability Insurance policies issued to Group/Body Corporate, and

(*f*) Any other segments which may be specified by the Authority from time to time. [Insurance Regulatory and Development Authority of India (Expenses of Management of Insurers Transacting General and Health Insurance Business) Regulations, 2016, Regn. 2(i)(x)].

"Miscellaneous Retail". For the purpose of these regulations, miscellaneous retail shall include insurance policies issued to an individual/family in the following segments—

(*a*) Public Liability; and

(*b*) Any other segments which may be specified by the Authority from time to time. [Insurance Regulatory and Development Authority of India (Expenses of Management of Insurers Transacting General or Health Insurance Business) Regulations, 2016, Regn. 2(i)(x)].

Mischief. "Whoever, with intent to cause, or knowing that he is likely to cause, wrongful loss or damage to the public or to any person, causes the destruction of any property or any such change in any property or in the situation thereof as destroys or diminishes its value or utility, or affects it injuriously, commits "mischief".

Explanation 1. It is not essential to the offence of mischief that the offender should intend to cause loss or damage to the owner of the property injured or destroyed. It is sufficient if he intends to cause, or knows that he is likely to cause, wrongful loss or damage to any person by injuring any property, whether it belongs to that person or not.

Explanation 2. "Mischief may be committed by an act affecting property belonging to the person who commits the act, or to that person and others jointly". [IPC (45 of 1860), S. 425] [(w. e. f. 1-7-2024) repealed and replaced by Bharatiya Nyaya Sanhita, 2023 (45 of 2023), S. 324(1)].

Mischief of the statute. The wrongs which are intended to be redressed by a statute.

Mischief rule. The rule of interpretation in which the interpretation is done in such a way so as to suppress the mischief intended to be remedied by the statute. It is also termed as *rule in Heydon's case*.

Misconceived. Misconceived means that an application, though not maintainable, has been moved. *Ram Pratap* v. *Mohan Lal,* AIR 1967 All 161, 162. [CPC (5 of 1908), S. 115]

Misconception. The action of misconceiving; a notion resulting from misconceiving. [IPC (45 of 1860), S. 90].

Misconception of Court. The misconception by the Court as to the concession made by the learned advocate appearing before it or of the attitude taken up by the party must be regarded as sufficient reason analogous to an error on the face of the record. *M.M.B. Catholicas* v. *M.P. Athanrasius*, AIR 1954 SC 526, 543. [CPC (5 of 1908), O. XLVII, R. 1]

Misconduct. The term "misconduct" implies a wrongful intention, and not a mere error of judgment.

Malfeasance; improper conduct. [Aligarh Muslim University Act (40 of 1920), S. 40(3)(a)].

MISCONDUCT is not necessarily the same thing as conduct involving moral turpitude.

The term 'misconduct' in its general parlance denotes something unbecoming of the person in doing or abstaining from doing which is reasonably expected of him. It is a relative term, the gravity of which may differ from person to person or from case to case, depending upon the facts and circumstances. It is not something which can be kept or analysed in water-tight compartment or within the hold of a specified parameters. [*State of Kerala v. G. Sreedharan Nair*, AIR 2013 Ker 1, para 19].

The word "misconduct" is a relative term, and has to be construed with reference to the subject-matter and the context wherein the term occurs, having regard to the scope of the Act or statute which is being, construed. "Misconduct" literally means wrong conduct or improper conduct.

"A transgression of some established and definite rule of action, a forbidden act, a dereliction of duty, unlawful behavior, wilful in character, improper or wrong behavior, its synonyms are misdemeanor, misdeed, misbehavior, delinquency, impropriety, mismanagement offence, but not negligence or carelessness". [Black's Law Dictionary, 6th Edn. as cited in *Ravi Yashwant Bhoir v. District Collector, Raigad*, (2012) 4 SCC 407, para 11].

Mere error of judgment resulting in doing of negligent act does not amount to misconduct. However, in exceptional circumstances, not working diligently may be a misconduct. An action which is detrimental to the prestige of the institution may also amount to misconduct. When the office bearer is expected to act with absolute integrity and honesty in handling the work, any misappropriation, even temporary, of the funds, etc. constitutes a serious misconduct, inviting severe punishment. [*Disciplinary Authority-cum-Reg. Manager v. Nikunja Bihari Patnaik*, (1996) 9 SCC 69 : 1996 SCC (L&S) 1194 as cited in *Ravi Shankar Bhoir v. District Collector, Raigad*, (2012) 4 SCC 407, para 13].

The expression "misconduct" has to be understood as a transgression of some established and definite rule of action, a forbidden act, unlawful behavior, wilful in character. It may be synonymous as misdemeanor impropriety and mismanagement. In a particular case, negligence or carelessness may also be a misconduct for example, when a watchman leaves his duty and goes to watch cinema, though there may be no theft or loss to the institution but leaving the place of duty itself amounts to misconduct. It may be more serious in case of disciplinary forces. [*Ravi Yashvant Bhoir v. District Collector, Raigad*, (2012) 4 SCC 407, para 18].

The expression 'misconduct" has to be construed and understood in reference to the subject-matter and context wherein it occurs taking into consideration the scope and object of the statute which is being construed. Misconduct is to be measured in the terms of the nature of misconduct and it should be viewed with the consequences of misconduct as to whether it has been detrimental to the public interest. [*Ravi Yashwant Bhoir v. District Collector, Raigad*, (2012) 4 SCC 407, para 19].

Misconduct literally means wrong or improper conduct *i.e.* conduct in violation of a definite rule of action. It ordinarily means failure to do what is required of a person to be done. An omission to do what is required of a person to do may therefore constitute misconduct even though the person has not acted wilfully or maliciously. *Shaikh Mohammad* v. *G.G. In Council,* AIR 1954 Nag 337. [Indian Railways Act (9 of 1890), S. 72]

Misconduct does not necessarily mean moral turpitude, dishonesty or any action which would be unethical or immoral but misconduct for the purpose of the Arbitration Act should be legal misconduct. *Mohinder Singh & Co.* v. *Union of India,* AIR 1972 J&K 63, 71. [Arbitration Act (10 of 1940) (*repealed*), S. 11]

In the absence of statutory definition the word has to be understood, in its ordinary dictionary meaning as improper conduct. *V. Dakshinamoorthy* v. *Commissioner of Inquiry,* AIR 1980 Mad 89, 85 (FB). [Commission of Inquiry Act (60 of 1952), Ss. 3 and 83(a); Advocates Act (25 of 1961), S. 35].

Misconduct of promoters or directors as understood in the Companies Act means not misconduct of every kind but such as has produced pecuniary loss to the company by misapplication of its assets or other act. *Barium Chemicals Ltd* v. *Company Law Board*, AIR 1967 SC 295, 327. [Companies Act (1 of 1956), S. 237(b)(ii)]

The term 'misconduct' may involve moral turpitude, it must be improper or wrong behaviour, wilful in character; forbidden act, a transgression of established and definite rule of action or code of conduct but not mere error of judgment, carelessness or negligence in performance of the duty; the act complained of bears forbidden quality or character. *State of Punjab* v. *Ram Singh*, AIR 1992 SC 2188, 2191. [Constitution of India, Arts. 309, 311].

Misconduct, inter alia, envisages breach of discipline, although it would not be possible to lay down exhaustively as to what would constitute conduct and discipline, which, however, is wide enough to include wrongful omission or commission whether done or omitted to be done intentionally or unintentionally. It means "improper behavior, intentional wrong doing or deliberate violation of a rule of standard or behaviour. [*Prabodh Kumar Bhowmik v. University of Calcutta*, (1994) 2 Cal LJ 456, para 14 as cited in

Council of Institutes of Chartered Accountants of India, New Delhi v. Satish Chand Jain, AIR 2013 All 170, para 11].

The expression 'misconduct' means, wrong or improper misconduct, unlawful behaviour, misfeasance, wrong conduct, misdemeanour *etc. Baldev Singh Gandhi* v. *State of Punjab,* (2002) 3 SCC 667, para 9 : AIR 2002 SC 1124.

'Misconduct', *inter alia,* envisages breach of discipline. It is wide enough to include wrongful omission or commission whether done or omitted to be done intentionally or unintentionally. It means, improper behaviour, intentional wrongdoing or deliberate violation of a rule or standard of behaviour. It is a violation of a definite law. *Noratanmal Chaurasia* v. *M.R. Murli*, (2004) 5 SCC 689, 693, paras 7 & 8.

Gross or habitual negligence in performance of duty may not involve *mens rea* but may still constitute misconduct for disciplinary proceedings. *Union of India* v. *J. Ahmed*, AIR 1979 SC 1022, 1027. [Indian Services Death-cum-Retirement Benefits (1958), R. 16(2)]

"It is a charge of positive act or a conduct which would be quite incompatible with the express and implied norms, of the relationship of the employee to the employer in such an organisation, there must be material in support of such a serious charge". *Management of Presidency Talkies* v. *N.S. Natarajan,* AIR 1969 Mad 121 at 123. [Industrial Disputes Act (14 of 1947), S. 33(2)(b)]

Clause 10 of Standing Order 22 quoted as follows : Drunkenness, fighting, indecent or disorderly behaviour, use of abusive language, wrongfully interferring with the work of other employees or conduct likely to cause a break of the peace or conduct endangering the life or safety of any other person, assault & threat of assault, any act subversive of discipline and efficiency and any act involving moral turpitude committed within the premises of the establishment or in the vicinity thereof. *Glaxo Laboratories (P) Ltd.* v. *Presiding Officer, Labour Court Meerut*, AIR 1984 SC 505, 508. [Industrial Employment (Standing Orders) Act (20 of 1946), Pre. S. 13-A]

Misconduct in office. "Misconduct in office" may be defined as unlawful behaviour or neglect by a public officer, by which the rights of a party have been affected.

Any unlawful behavior by a public officer in relation to the duties of his office, wilful in character. Term embraces acts which the office-holder had no right to perform, acts performed improperly, and failure to act in the face of an affirmative duty to act." [Black's Law Dictionary, 6th Edn. as cited in *Ravi Yashwant Bhoir v. District Collector, Raigad*, (2012) 4 SCC 407, para 11].

"Misconduct or conduct unbecoming of an Advocate-on-record" : For the purpose of these rules, 'MISCONDUCT OR CONDUCT UNBECOMING OF AN ADVOCATE-ON-RECORD' shall include—

(a) mere name lending by an Advocate-on-Record without any further participation in the proceedings of the case,

(b) absence of the Advocate-on-Record from the Court without any justifiable cause when the case is taken up for hearing; and

(c) failure to submit appearance slip duly signed by the Advocate-on-Record of actual appearance in the court. [Supreme Court Rules, 2013, Order IV, R. 10, Explanation].

Misconstrue. To construe wrongly; to interpret erroneously.

Misdelivery. The word 'misdelivery' is restricted to a wrong delivery involving some form of mistake or inadvertence. *Eswara Iyer & Sons* v. *M.B. Transport Co.,* AIR 1964 Mad 516, 517. [Carriers Act (3 of 1865), S. 2]

Misdemeanor or Misdemeanour. A crime less than felony. The term 'misdemeanour' is generally used in contra-distinction to felony, and comprehends all indictable offence which do not amount to felony; as perjury, libels, assaults *etc.* An offence lower than felony.

Misdescription. An error or falsity in the description of the subject-matter of a contract which deceives one of the parties to his injury, or is misleading in a material or substantial point.

Misdirection. Misdirection is something which a judge in his charge tells the jury and is wrong or in a wrong manner tending to mislead them. Even an omission to mention matters which are essential to the prosecution or the defence case in order to help the jury to come to a correct verdict may also in certain circumstance amount to a misdirection. *K.M. Nanavati* v. *State of Maharashtra*, AIR 1962 SC 605, 616.

Wrong direction, the error of judge in charging a jury, the action of misdirecting.

Misera est servitus ubi jus est vagum, aut incertum. (*Lat.*) Miserable must be the condition of those people where the administration of the law is capricious and uncertain.

Misfeasance. The improper doing of an act which a person might lawfully do; a wrongful and injurious exercise of lawful authority, or the doing of the lawful act in an unlawful manner.

The improper performance of a lawful act. [Presidency-towns Insolvency Act (3 of 1909), S. 82].

Misfeasance is said to cover every misconduct by an officer of a company, as such, for which he might have been sued.

The mere fact that a few debts due to the company had been allowed to become barred by time does not amount to misfeasance on the part of the Directors. *Faridabad Rubber Soles (P.) Ltd.* v. *S.L. Chopra,* AIR 1995 P&H 180, 182. [Companies Act (1 of 1956), S. 543]

Misfeasance and **Non-feasance.** Misfeasance is the improper doing of an act which a person might lawfully do. Nonfeasance is the omission of an act which a person ought to do.

Misfeasance in public office. Malicious abuse of power, deliberate maladministration and unlawful acts causing injury by public officer. *Common Cause, A Registered Society* v. *Union of India,* AIR 1999 SC 2979.

Misfortune. Ill luck; ill fortune; calamity; adverse fortune; an unlucky accident; mishap, or mischance.

Bad fortune; adversity; mishap [Presidency towns Insolvency Act (3 of 1909), S. 103A(2)(b)].

Misjoinder. The improper joining together of parties to a suit as plaintiffs or defendants, or of different causes of action.

Improper joining. [CrPC 1973 (2 of 1974); O. I, R. 9, CPC (5 of 1908), S. 464(1)].

The joinder in one action of defendants against whom there is no common cause of action, but that against one is totally disconnected with that against the other, except in so far as it is historically connected as one matter in a transaction, is a misjoinder. The word "misjoinder" in S. 99, CPC (5 of 1908), includes "non-joinder."

Misjoinder of charges. Improper joinder of different charges against one or more accused. [CrPC 1973 (2 of 1974), S. 464(1)].

Misjoinder of parties. Wrongful joining of persons as plaintiffs or defendants in a cause. [CPC 1973 (5 of 1908), O. I, R. 13].

Mislead. To lead into error; to lead in a wrong direction; to lead astray. [IPC (45 of 1860), Ss. 118, ill. and 281].

"Misleading advertisement" in relation to any product or service, means an advertisement, which—

(i) falsely describes such product or service; or

(ii) gives a false guarantee to, or is likely to mislead the consumers as to the nature, substance, quantity or quality of such product or service; or

(iii) conveys an express or implied representation which, if made by the manufacturer or seller or service provider thereof, would constitute an unfair trade practice; or

(iv) deliberately conceals important information. [Consumer Protection Act, 2019 (35 of 2019), section 2(28)]

Misnomer. The using one name for another; a misnaming (*Tomlin*); mistake in a name; the giving an incorrect name to a person in a pleading, deed, will or other document.

Wrong name. [Representation of the People Act (43 of 1951), S. 33(4), prov.].

Misnomer means giving an incorrect or wrong name to a person even in a legal document. *Masood* v. *Bikran Singh,* AIR 1975 All 402, 403. [Representation of the People Act (43 of 1951), Ss. 33 (4), Proviso and 100(1)(c)]

Mispleading. According to its etymology and natural meaning, pleading amiss, or pleading wrongly.

Misprision. Misapprehension, misconception, mistake.

Misrecital. Making incorrect statement of a factual matter in a contract, deed, pleading or other instrument.

Misrepresentation. "MISREPRESENTATION" means and includes—

(1) the positive assertion, in a manner not warranted by the information of the person making it, of that which is not true, though he believes it to be true;

(2) any breach of duty which, without an intent to deceive, gains an advantage to the person committing it, or any one claiming under him, by misleading another to his prejudice or to the prejudice of any one claiming under him;

(3) causing, however innocently, a party to an agreement to make a mistake as to the substance of the thing which is the subject of the agreement. [Indian Contract Act (9 of 1872), S. 18]

Statement or conduct which conveys a false or wrong impression. [Indian Contract Act (9 of 1872), S. 18].

Mis-selling. For the purpose of this clause, "mis-selling" means sale of securities or services relating to securities market by any person, directly or indirectly, by—

(*i*) knowingly making a false or misleading statement, or

(*ii*) knowingly concealing or omitting material facts, or

(*iii*) knowingly concealing the associated risk, or

(*iv*) not taking reasonable care to ensure suitability of the securities or service to the buyer. [Securities and Exchange Board of India (Prohibition of Fraudulent and Unfair Trade Practice relating to Securities Market) Regulations, 2003, Regn. 4(2)(*s*)]

Mistake. An unconscious ignorance or forgetfulness of a fact, past or present, material to the contract, or a belief in the present existence of a thing material to the contract, which does not exist; some intentional act, omission, or error arising from ignorance, surprise, imposition, or misplaced confidence; in a legal sense, the doing of an act under an erroneous conviction, which act, but for such conviction would not have been done.

Misapprehension as to the existence of a thing, arising either from ignorance or from a false belief on the point. [Indian Contract Act (9 of 1872), S. 21].

The word 'mistake' in S. 72 of the Indian Contract Act includes a mistake of law and money paid under a mistake of law could be recovered. Payment 'by mistake' in S. 72 must refer to a payment which was not legally due and which could not have been enforced : the mistake is in thinking that the money paid was due when in fact it was not due. *Steel and Wire Products Ltd.* v. *Superintendent of Commercial taxes,* AIR 1957 Pat 112, 115. [Indian Contract Act (9 of 1872), S. 72]

Mistake apparent from the record. Non consideration of a decision of jurisdictional High Court or of the Supreme Court can be said to be a 'mistake apparent from the record' for the purpose of Section 254(2) of the Act. [*Assistant Commissioner Income Tax* v. *Saurashtra Kutch Stock Exchange Ltd.*, (2008) 14 SCC 171, 183-84, para 33] [Income-tax Act (43 of 1961), S. 254(2)]

Mistake apparent on the face of the record. A mistake which is obvious, manifest and patent and about which there can be no two opinions.

The words 'mistake or error apparent on the face of record' include an apparent mistake on question of law on which there can be no two opinions. *Kifayatullah* v. *Executive Officer Municipal Board,* AIR 1956 Bhopal 7, 8.

Mistake apparent on the record. A "mistake apparent on the record" must be an obvious and patent mistake and not something which can be established by a long drawn process of reasoning on points on which there may conceivably be two opinions. A decision on a debatable point of law is not a mistake apparent from the record. *T.S. Balaram, Income Tax Officer, Company Circle IV, Bombay* v. *Volkart Brothers, Bombay,* (1971) 2 SCC 526.

Mistake in fact or law. Mistake of fact or mistake of law. [prov. 1, Indian Evidence Act (1 of 1872), S. 92].

Mistake of fact. A mistake which takes place when some fact which really exists is unknown; or some fact is supposed to exist which really does not exist. Mistake of foreign laws is a mistake of fact.

A mistake as to any matter of fact not being mistake of law. [IPC (45 of 1860), S. 76 and Indian Contract Act (9 of 1872), S. 21].

Mistake of law. A mistake of law occurs when a person having full knowledge of facts comes to an erroneous conclusion as to their legal effect.

Mistake of law ordinarily means mistake as to existence or otherwise of any law or a relevant subject as well as mistake as to what the law is. *The King* v. *Tustipada Mandal,* AIR 1951 Ori 284. [Indian Penal Code (45 of 1860), S. 79]

A mistake as to the legal consequences or significance of an act, transaction or state of affairs or mistake on point of law. [IPC (45 of 1860), Ss. 76 and 79].

MISTAKE OR INADVERTENCE. The words "mistake or inadvertence' in Section 28 of the Court-fees Act (7 of 1870) mean mistake or inadvertence on the part of the Court or its officers, and not that on the part of an appellant or his advisers.

Mistress. A woman who illicitly occupies the place of a wife. (*Century*)

Concubine. [CrPC 1973 (2 of 1974), S. 125(3), *expln.*].

Misuse. To use amiss; to use wrongfully. Wrong or improper use. [Factories Act (63 of 1948), S. 111(1)(a)].

Misuse of power or misapplication of power. "Misuse of Power" or "misapplication of power" or a "Detournement do Puvior" (as it is called in French Administrative Law), are terms correctly employed to describe the use of a power in this illegal fashion. The exercise of every power, whatever its nature, lodged in Government authorities, is controlled by the need to confine it to the ambit within which it could justly and reasonably be expected to take place. A power used under the misapprehension that it was needed for effectuating a purpose, which was really outside the law or the proper scope of the power, could be said to be an exercise for an extraneous of collateral purpose. *State of Mysore* v. *P.R. Kulkarni,* AIR 1972 SC 2170.

Misuser. An abuser of any liberty or benefit; abuse of an office or franchise (*Black*); unlawful use of a right.

Mitakshara. Of all commentaries that by Vijnaneshwar called the *Mitakshara* on the institutes of Yagnayavalkya has obtained the foremost place in Hindu Law and is now acknowledged to be the most authoritative record of the Laws of the Hindus. All over India its supreme authority is acknowledged, though in Bengal and Bombay its authority is only next to that of *Dayabhaga* and *Mayuka.*

Mitakshara law. The law as laid down in the commentary of Vijnavalkaya *smrti* named *'Mitakshra'* written by Vijnaneshwara in the eleventh century. [Limitation Act (36 of 1963), S. 7, *Expln. 2*].

Mitakshara School of Hindu law. The branch of Hindu law which follows the tenets laid down in Mitakshara. [Companies Act (1 of 1956), S. 430(3)].

Mitigate. To reduce in amount or degree (as) to mitigate the damage caused by a wrongful act.

Mitigating circumstances are those which tend to disprove malice.

To make less severe, violent, cruel, intense, painful; to lessen. [IPC (45 of 1860), S. 352, *Expln.*]; [Army Act (46 of 1950), S. 179(b)].

Mitigating circumstances are those which, though not proving the truth of the charge, yet tend in some appreciable degree towards such proof, and thus permit of an inference that defendant was not actuated by malice in his charge. They may be of such a nature as to show that defendant, if mistaken, believed the charge to be true when it was made.

MITIGATING CIRCUMSTANCES are such as do not amount to a justification or excuse of the offence or act in question but may properly be considered in mitigation of the punishment or damages.

Mitigation. Diminution in degree, amount, or severity; moderation; a reduction in punishment or penalty. (*English*)

The action of mitigating; abatement of anything penal or of damages. [Air Force Act (45 of 1950), S. 187]; [Drugs and Cosmetics Act (23 of 1940), S. 3(a)].

Mitiores pdenae nobis semper placuere. (*Maxim*) It is more pleasing to the law to inflict a light than a severe punishment. (*Morgan*)

Mitius imperanti melius paretur. The more mildly one commands, the better is he obeyed.

Mix. To blend; to mingle.

Mixed action. A form of Court action which combines a claim relating to real property with a claim for damages.

Mixed fund. A fund of money which is derived from the sale of both real and personal property.

Mixed novelty. A patent can be invalidated by prior printed publication anywhere in the world but the prior use should only be in the country granting the patent. *(Patents)*

Mixed property. Property which has some of the attributes of both real and personal property. Emblements are an example.

Mixed Supply. "Mixed supply" means two or more individual supplies of goods or services, or any combination thereof, made in conjunction with each other by a taxable person for a single price where such supply does not constitute a composite supply.

Illustration.— A supply of a package consisting of canned foods, sweets, chocolates, cakes, dry fruits, aerated drinks and fruit juices when supplied for a single price is a mixed supply. Each of these items can be supplied separately and is not dependent on any other. It shall not be a mixed supply if these items are supplied separately [The Central Goods and Services Tax Act, 2017 (12 of 2017), S. 2(74)]

Mixture. That which is mixed or mingled; a mass or compound consisting of different ingredients blended together; that which results from mixing; a compound or combination of different ingredients, parts or principles. (*Century*)

The produce of mixing. [Indian Contract Act (9 of 1872), S. 155].

Mob. A tumultuous crowd. [IPC (45 of 1860), S. 106, ill.].

Mobile vendors. Means street vendors who carry out vending activities in designated area by moving from one place to another place vending their goods and services. [S. 2(1)(d) of the Street Vendors (Protection of Livelihood and Regulation of Street Vending) Act, 2014 (7 of 2014)]

"Mobile tower". Means a temporary or permanent structure, equipment or instrument erected or installed on land or upon any part of the building or premises for providing telecommunication services. [Gujarat Provincial Municipal Corporation Act (59 of 1949), S. 2(34-AA) **as cited in** *Ahmedabad Municipal Corporation* v. *GTL Infrastructure Limited,* (2017) 3 SCC 545, para 6].

A mobile tower is certainly not a building. [*Ahmedabad Municipal Corporation* v. *GTL Infrastructure Limited,* (2017) 3 SCC 545, para 32].

Mobilia personam sequuntur, immobilia situm. Movable things follow the person, immovable their site or locality.

Mobilia sequntur personam. Moveables follow the person (*i.e.*) the law of the person.

Movables follow the person. A person's powers of dealing with his moveable estate and its devolution on his death are governed by the law of his domicile.

Mobilia situm non habent. (*Lat.*) Moveables have no locality; that is, they are not regarded as having any locality of their own different from that of the domicile of their owner.

Mock. To divide; to laugh at; to ridicule; to treat with scorn and a contempt.

Mock trial. A fictitious trial organised for students of law or sometimes for lawyer to practise the techniques of advocacy.

Mockingbird. A computer program or process that mimics the legitimate behavior of a normal system feature (or other apparently useful function) but performs malicious activities once invoked by the user. (*Cyber Law*)

Mockup. A false demonstration designed to improve the appearance or effect of an ad. (*Cyber Law*)

Mode. "Mode" means the customary manner; prevailing style; the manner in which a thing is done.

Way or manner of doing or being; a method or procedure; a form [CrPC, 1973 (2 of 1974) S. 298]; [Inland Vessels Act (1 of 1917), S. 29(2)(a)].

Mode of exercising power. *Interpretation of Statutes. Nazir Ahmed's case*-AIR 1936 P.C. 253 quoted-when a statutory power is conferred for the first time upon a Court, and the mode of exercising it is pointed out, it means that no other mode is to be adopted. *Parbhani Transport Corp. Society Ltd.* v. *Regional Transport Authority*, AIR 1960 SC 801, 804.

Mode of life. Way of living. [Indian Evidence Act (1 of 1872), S. 149, ill. (d)].

Mode of recovery. A manner of recovering money *etc.* [State Agricultural Credit Corporations Act (60 of 1968), S. 28]; [Wealth-tax Act (27 of 1957), S. 32].

Mode of transport. Means carriage of goods by road, rail, inland waterways or sea. [Multimodal Transportation of Goods Act (28 of 1993), S. 2(j)]

Model. "MODEL" includes design, pattern and specimen. [Official Secrets Act (19 of 1923), S. 2(4)]

Object or figure made in clay, wax *etc.* and intended to be reproduced in more durable materials [Income-tax Act (43 of 1961), S. 80-O]; something to be copied [Copyright Act (14 of 1957), S. 2(za)]; an imitation of something on a smaller scale; preparing a model.

A copy or imitation of the thing to be represented; a facsimile in three dimensions, a reproduction in miniature of objects under consideration.

Model Agreement. Means a document specifying the general form and content for an agreement concluded between a State Party and the Organization for fulfilling the verification provisions specified in this

Annex. [Chemical Weapons Convention Act (34 of 2000), (Verification Annex), 19]

Model bye-laws. Means a set of bye-laws approved and proposed by Registrar for general adoption by a class of cooperative society. [Delhi Cooperative Societies Rules, 1973, R. 2(xvi)]

Model EDI Trading Partner Agreement. Standard terms for use in electronic data interchange transactions. (*Cyber Law*)

Modelling tools. Instruments for preparing models. [Indian Evidence Act (1 of 1872), S. 98, ill.].

Modem. Modulator/DEModulator. The device that takes signals from your computer and translates them into a suitable form for the telephone system. The reverse procedure takes place at a modem on the host computer. The faster the speed of a modem, the better the response when transferring large amounts of information.

A device that connects a computer to a phone line. A telephone for a computer. A modem allows a computer to talk to other computers through the phone system. Basically, modems do for computers what a telephone does for humans. (*Matisse Enzer-Glossary of Internet Terms*)

(Modulator, DEModulator)—A device that you connect to your computer and to a phone line, that allows the computer to talk to other computers through the phone system. Basically, modems do for computers what a telephone does for humans. (*Internet and Ecommerce*)

Moderate. To make temperate or reasonable. [Aligarh Muslim University Act (40 of 1920), S. 33(3)].

Moderate limits. Reasonable limits.

Moderator. One who moderates a question paper. [Aligarh Muslim University Act (40 of 1920), S. 29(1)(g)].

Modern advances. The expression 'MODERN ADVANCES' means advances made in various branches of modern scientific medicine, clinical, non-clinical biosciences, also technological innovations made from time to time and notify that the courses and curriculum conducted and recognised by the Central Council of Indian Medicine are supplemented by such modern advances. *Mukhtar Chand (Dr.)* v. *State of Punjab,* (1998) 7 SCC 579, para 46 : AIR 1999 SC 468.

Modern medicine. 'MODERN MEDICINE' means modern scientific medicine including surgery and obstetrics. [Karnataka Ayurvedic & Unani Practitioners' Registration and Medical Practitioners' Miscellaneous Provisions Act, 1961, S. 2(e) expln.]

Modesty. The word 'modesty' is not to be interpreted with reference to the particular victim of the act, but as an attribute associated with female human beings as a class. It is a virtue which attaches to a female on account of her sex. *Major Singh Lachhaman Singh* v. *State,* AIR 1963 Punj 443, 445. [Indian Penal Code (45 of 1860), S. 354]

The ultimate test for ascertaining whether the modesty of a woman has been outraged, assaulted or insulted is that the action of the offender should be such that it may be perceived as one which is capable of shocking the sense of decency of a woman. A person slapping on the posterior of a woman in full public glare would amount to outraging her modesty for it was not only an affront to the normal sense of feminine decency but also an affront to the dignity of the lady. *Rupan Deol Bajaj* v. *Kanwar Pal Singh,* AIR 1996 SC 309.

Modesty is defined as the quality of being modest; and in relation to a woman, 'womanly propriety of behaviour; scrupulous chastity of thought, speech and conduct'. *Raju Pandurang Mahale* v. *State of Maharashtra*, (2004) 4 SCC 371, 372, para 13.

The quality of being modest; womanly propriety of behaviour. [IPC (45 of 1860), S. 509].

Modification. A change; an alteration which introduces new elements into the details, or cancels some of them, but leaves the general purpose and effect of the subject-matter intact.

A change or alteration which introduces new elements into the details of some of them, but leaves the general purpose and effect of the subject matter intact [Indian Evidence Act (1 of 1872), S. 73 and Constitution of India, Art. 35(b)]; [Constitution of India, Art. 31A(1)(a)].

The term 'modification' would include the making of additions and omissions. In the context of S. 392, 'modification' would mean additions to the scheme of compromise and/or arrangement or omission therefrom solely for the purpose of making it workable. *S.K. Gupta* v. *K.P. Jain*, AIR 1979 SC 734, 744. [Companies Act (1 of 1956), Ss. 392(1)(b) and 2(29)]

That word in the context of the Article only means a modification of the proprietary right of a citizen like an extinguishment of that right and cannot include within its ambit a mere suspension of the right of management of estate for a time, definite or indefinite. *Raghubir Singh* v. *Court of Wards*, AIR 1953 SC 373, 375. [Constitution of India, Art. 31-A]

Modification in Art. 370(1)(d) must be given the widest meaning in the context of a constitution and in that sense it includes an amendment and it cannot be limited to such modifications as do not make any radical transformation. *Kesavananda Bharati* v. *State of Kerala,* AIR 1973 SC 1461, per RAY, J.). [Constitution of India, Art. 370(1)(d)]

The word 'modification' also means addition. The power to extend an enactment subject to modifications will comprehend the power to add certain provisions to that enactment and extend to the area concerned the enactment so added to. *Sant Singh* v. *State of J&K,* AIR 1959 J&K 35, 40 (FB). [Constitution of India, Art. 370(1)(d)]

The word 'modify' in Art. 392(1), Constitution of India conveys the sense of a partial change and not a complete change. *Anand Bihari Mishra* v. *Ram Sahay,* AIR 1952 MB 31.

Modification means maintenance of the order with slight change. This would not include an attempt at validation of the order which was illegal at its inception. *Vinraomal* v. *State of Rajasthan,* AIR 1955 Raj 6, 11. [Preventive Detention Act (4 of 1950), S. 13]

Modify. To change, or vary, to qualify or reduce.

To make a modification; to alter without radical transformation. [Indian Evidence Act (1 of 1872), S. 92, prov. (4)]

The word 'modify' has been introduced in the section with some purpose and the purpose could only have been to use an expression of wider connotation so as to include not only reduction but also other kinds of alteration. *Western India Theatres Ltd.* v. *Municipal Corporation of The City of Poona,* AIR 1959 SC 586, 589.

The power of enhancement of sentence cannot be included in the term 'modify'.

"Modify" and "Modification". Shall include the making of additions and omissions. [Companies Act (1 of 1956), S. 2(29)]

Modus debt esse certus, rationabilis, et perantiquus. (*Maxim*) A custom ought to be reasonable, certain, and very ancient. (*Morgan*)

Modus et conventio vincunt legem. (*Maxim*) The form of agreement and the convention of parties overrule the law. (*Broom*)

Modus operandi. The manner of doing the business.

Mode of operation; the way in which a thing, cause *etc.* operates; the way in which a person goes to work; a distinct pattern or method of procedure thought to be characteristic of an individual criminal and habitually followed by him.

Modus transferrendi. The manner of conveying or transferring.

MODVAT. 'MODVAT' is basically a duty collecting procedure which provides relief to manufacturer on duty element borne by him in respect of inputs used by him. Under 'MODVAT', excisable finished product made out of duly-paid inputs, are given relief of excise duty to extent of duty paid on inputs. [*Dharmpal Satyapal v. Commissioner of Contract Excise,* (2005) 4 SCC 337, 348, para 25].

Mofussil. Separated, particularised, distinguished, divided into distinct parts, detailed. The sub-ordinate divisions of a district in contra-distinction to the term 'saddur' which implies the chief seat of Government; also the country as opposed to town; the interior of the country.

Mofussil dewanny adawlut. The Ancient Provincial Court of Civil Justice.

Mohammedan law. The Personal Law of the Mahammadans that is administered to them in India.

Moiety. Means, generally, half part. (*Jacob*)

Molasses. Means the final residual by-product of factories manufacturing sugar from cane, or by refining *gur*, by means of vacuum pans, but does not include convertible malasses which are the final residual by-product of factories operating on the open pan system. [West Bengal Molasses Control Act, 1973 (6 of 1973), S. 2(a)]

'MOLASSES' means heavy, dark coloured viscous liquid produced in the final stage of manufacture of sugar by vacuum pan from sugarcane or gur, when the liquid as such or in any form of admixture contains sugar. [U.P. Sheera Niyantran Adhiniyam, 1964, S. 2(d)]

Molest. The word "molest" carries with it some suggestion of interference or restraint or obstruction. Where a person who is served with a demand notice by the bill-collector of a *Panchayat* Board abuses not the bill-collector but some unnamed person inimically disposed forwards him who had given information leading to an exaggerated assessment he cannot be said to have "molested" any person in the performance of his duty. 1941 Mad 834 : (1941) 2 MLJ 356.

To annoy a person constituting a criminal offence.

To cause trouble, grief or vexation; to annoy. [Protection of Civil Rights Act (22 of 1955), S. 7(1)(b)].

Molestation. Behaviour which has the effect or intention of annoying or pestering one's spouse (or cohabitant) or children. Such an act need not involve violence or physical assault; harassment (for example by threatening letters or telephone calls) may constitute molestation.

Molesting. The word molesting does not imply necessarily either violence or threats of violence. It can apply to any conduct which can properly be regarded as such a degree of harassment.

Molten. Melted; in a state of fusion or solution; made or produced by means of melting.

Moment. A very short time. [Indian Majority Act (9 of 1875), S. 4, ill. (a)].

Momentum. The quantity of motion in a moving body. In the civil law, an instant; an indivisible portion of time. (*Black*)

Monarchy. A form of government with the supreme power in the hands of a single person who inherits it.

Monastery. A house of religious retirement or of seclusion from the world for persons under religious vows.

Monetary equivalent. Equivalent in money. [Companies Act (1 of 1956), S. 314(2) (a)].

Monetary relief. Means the compensation which the Magistrate may order the respondent to pay to the aggrieved person, at any stage during the hearing of an application seeking any relief under this Act, to meet the expenses incurred and the losses suffered by the aggrieved person as a result of the domestic violence. [S. 2(k) of the Protection of Women from Domestic Violence Act, 2005 (43 of 2005)]

Money. "Money" means legal tender, cheque, promissory note, bill of exchange, letter of credit, draft, pay order, traveler cheque, money order, postal or electronic remittances or any such similar instrument but shall not include any currency that is held for its numismatic value. [Finance Act (32 of 1994), S. 65-B(33) now repealed by Goods and Services Tax Act, 2017].

"MONEY" includes a cheque, postal order or money-order. [Prize Competitions Act (42 of 1955), S. 2(b)]

The word 'money' would not be interpreted as 'money's worth'. *CIT* v. *Kasturi & Sons Ltd.*, (1999) 3 SCC 346, para 11 : AIR 1999 SC 1275.

Money bill. A bill for raising revenue was technically called a "money bill". It is a bill levying a tax on all or some of the persons, property, or business of the country for a public purpose.

For the purposes of this Chapter, a Bill shall be deemed to be a MONEY BILL if it contains only provisions dealing with all or any of the following matters, namely :—

(a) the imposition, abolition, remission, alteration or regulation of any tax;

(b) the regulation of the borrowing of money or the giving of any guarantee by the Government of India, or the amendment of the law with respect to any financial obligations undertaken or to be undertaken by the Government of India;

(c) the custody of the Consolidated Fund or the Contingency Fund of India, the payment of moneys into or the withdrawal of moneys from any such Fund;

(d) the appropriation of moneys out of the Consolidated Fund of India;

(e) the declaring of any expenditure to be expenditure charged on the Consolidated Fund of India or the increasing of the amount of any such expenditure;

(f) the receipt of money on account of the Consolidated Fund of India or the public account of India or the custody or issue of such money or the audit of the accounts of the Union or of a State; or

(g) any matter incidental to any of the matters specified in sub-clauses (a) to (f). [Constitution of India, Arts. 110(1), 199(1)]

A bill which in the opinion of the Speaker of the Lok Sabha contains only provisions dealing with matters contained in the Art. 110 of the Constitution and that of the Speaker of the Vidhan Sabha with the matters contained in the Art. 199.

Money, Cash. Money is applied to everything which serves as a circulating medium; cash is, in strict sense, put for coin only; bank notes are money; guineas and shillings are cash : all cash is therefore money, but all money is not cash.

Money changer. One whose occupation is the exchanging of kinds of denominations of currency. [Foreign Exchange Regulation Act (7 of 1947), S. 2(m)].

Money circulation scheme. Means any scheme, by whatever name called, for the making of quick or easy money, or for the receipt of any money or valuable thing as the consideration for a promise to pay money, on any event or contingency relative or applicable to the enrolment of members into the scheme, whether or not such money or thing is derived from the entrance money of the members of such money or thing is derived from the entrance money of the members of such scheme or periodical subscriptions. [Prize Chit and Money Circulation Schemes (Bonning) Act (43 of 1978), S. 2(c)]

Money consideration. A consideration in the form of money [Sale of Goods Act (3 of 1930), S. 2(10)].

Money due or to become due on account of pension. The words "money due or to become due on account of pension" occurring in Section 11 of the Pensions Act, 1871 includes the commuted portion of the pension payable to an employee after his retirement. *Union of India* v. *Wing Commander R.R. Hingorani (Retd.),* AIR 1987 SC 808. [Pensions Act (23 of 1871), S. 11]

Money, Head. Money paid for killing or capturing a person (as an outlaw) [Navy Act (62 of 1957), S. 49(2)].

Money laundering. Whosoever directly or indirectly attempts to indulge or knowingly assists or knowingly is a party or is actually involved in any process or activity connected with the proceeds of crime and projecting it as untainted property shall be guilty of offence of MONEY LAUNDERING. [Prevention of Money-Laundering Act (15 of 2003), S. 3]

Money lender. Means

(i) an individual or

(ii) an undivided Hindu family, or

(iii) a company (not being a banking company as defined in Section 5 of Banking Regulation Act, 1949), body or institution other than such of them as may, by notification in the Official Gazette, be exempted from the provisions of this Act by the State Govt. on being satisfied that it is necessary or expedient so to do in public interest;

(iv) or an un-incorporated body of individuals, who or which,—

(a) carries on the business of money-lending in the State; or

(b) supplies, as a trader or dealer, goods other than agricultural goods on credit, on condition of payment of interest by the buyer at a rate higher than that prescribed in Section 29 in case the payment of sale price is not made within the stipulated period; or

(c) has his or its principal place of such business in the State. [Rajasthan Money-Lenders Act 1963 (15 of 1964), S. 2(10)]

Money lending. The act or occupation of lending money at interest.

Money market. A financial centre, where institutions comprising the money market are well developed; the lenders and borrowers of short term funds and the intermediaries, who bring them together [Reserve Bank of India Act (2 of 1934), S. 45L(3)]; [Indian Contract Act (9 of 1872), S. 16, Ill (d)].

Money overpaid. Money paid more than is due. [CPC (5 of 1908), App. A, form No. 2].

Money suit. A process instituted in a Court of justice for recovery of money. [CPC (5 of 1908), O. VII, R. 2].

Moneys. The word 'moneys' used in Section 41(2) of the Act has to be interpreted only as actual 'money' or cash not as any other thing or benefit which could be evaluated in terms of 'money'. *CIT* v. *Kasturi & Sons Ltd.,* (1999) 3 SCC 346, para 11 : AIR 1999 SC 1275. [Income-tax Act (43 of 1961), S. 41(2)]

Money's worth. Anything recognised as equivalent to money [Presidency-towns Insolvency Act (3 of 1903), S. 46, *Expln.*].

Moneylender. One whose business is lending money at interest. [Indian Contract Act (9 of 1872), S. 16, ill. (c)].

A person who does a few disconnected and isolated transactions is not a money lender. *K. Icilda Walling* v. *V. Lokendra Sriram*, AIR 1987 SC 2047, 2048.

Monism. The theory in which national and international law form part of one legal structure, in which international law is supreme.

Monition. A monition, or admonition, means 'warning' or 'caution', generally given by Courts to young offenders.

Monitoring. To check and adjust to test; to watch; to observe; to keep track of; regulate *etc.*

Monitoring operation. Means the operations for collecting observing and interpreting the data relating to the environment of the protected area and the changes thereto. [Silent Valley Protected Area (Protection of Geological Balance) Act (14 of 1979), S. 2(e)]

Monogamy. The fact of being married to only one spouse.

Monolith. A mountain or a large hill apparently composed of one kind of rock; a column of soil several feet deep removed as a unit; a single block of stone especially one shaped into a pillar or monument. [Ancient Monuments and Archaeological Sites and Remains Act (24 of 1958), S. 2(a)].

Monopolistic trade practice. Means a trade practice which has, or is likely to have, the effect of—

(i) maintaining the prices of goods or charges for the services at an unreasonable level by limiting, reducing or otherwise controlling the production, supply or distribution of goods of any description or the supply of any services or in any other manner;

(ii) unreasonably preventing or lessening competition in the production, supply or distribution of any goods or in the supply of any services;

(iii) timing technical development or capital investment to the common detriment or allowing the quality of any goods produced, supplied or distributed, or any service rendered, in India to deteriorate;

(iv) increasing unreasonably,—

(a) the cost of production of any goods, or

(b) charges for the provision, or maintenance, of any services;

(v) increasing unreasonably,—

(a) the prices at which goods are, or may be, sold or resold, or the charges at which the services are, or may be, provided, or

(b) the profits which are, or may be, derived by the production, supply or distribution (including the sale of purchase) of any goods or by the provision of any services;

(vi) preventing or lessening competition in the production, supply or distribution of any goods; or in the provision or maintenance of any services by the adoption of unfair methods or unfair or deceptive practices. [Monopolies and Restrictive Trade Practices Act (54 of 1969), S. 2(i)]

Monopoly. A "monopoly" is defined as an exclusive right granted to a few of something which was before of common right.

A monopoly is a special privilege conferred on one or more persons to the absolute exclusion of the others.

A literal meaning of the word 'monopoly' is 'exclusive possession of a trade in some commodity' and this is generally confessed as a privilege by the state. In certain circumstances monopoly in a particular kind of trade or business may be in the interests of the public but in other circumstances, it may have a contrary effect and may be destructive of individual enterprise. *Sri Rama Vilas Service (P.) Ltd.* v. *Raman and Raman (Private) Ltd.,* AIR 1935 Mad 492, 495. [Constitution of India, Art. 19(1)(g)]

Month. "MONTH" shall mean a month reckoned according to the British calendar [General Clauses Act (10 of 1897), S. 3(35)].

Any one of the twelve portions into which conventional year is divided. [General Clauses Act (10 of 1897), S. 3(35)].

"When the period prescribed is a calendar month, running from any arbitrary date, the period expires with the day in the succeeding month immediately preceding the day corresponding to the date upon which the period starts running save that if the period starts at the end of a calendar month which contains more days than the next succeeding month, the period expires at the end of the latter month." *Halsbury's Laws of England,* 3rd Edition, Vol. 37 page 142.

Six months will mean Six British Calendar months and not 180 days. *Tomal Labiri* v. *Kumar P.N. Tagore*, AIR 1978 SC 1811, 1813.

Monthly allowance. A limited portion of sum especially of money payable every month. [CrPC, 1973 (2 of 1974), S. 125(1) and CPC (5 of 1908), S. 57].

Monthly rate. A rate calculated by the month [CrPC, 1973 (2 of 1974), S. 125(1)].

Monthly wages. The expression "MONTHLY WAGES" means the amount of wages deemed to be payable for a month's service (whether the wages are payable by the month or by whatever other period or at piece rates) and calculated as follows, namely :—

(a) where the employee[1] has, during a continuous period of not less than twelve month immediately preceding the accident, been in the service of the employer who is liable to pay compensation the monthly wages of the workman shall be one-twelfth of the total wages which have fallen due for payment to him by the employer in the last twelve month of that period;

(b) where the whole of the continuous period of service immediately preceding the accident during which the employee was in the service of the employer who is liable to pay the compensation was less than one month, the monthly wages of the employee shall be the average monthly amount which, during the twelve months immediately preceding the accident, was being earned by an employee employed on the same work by the same employer, or, if there was no workman so employed, by a workman employed on similar work in the same locality;

(c) in other cases including cases in which it is not possible for want of necessary information to calculate the monthly wages under clause (b), the monthly wages shall be thirty times the total wages earned in respect of the last continuous period of service immediately preceding the accident from the employer who is liable to pay compensation, divided by the number of days comprising such period.

Explanation—A period of service shall, for the purposes of this section be deemed to be continuous which has not been interrupted by a period of absence from work exceeding fourteen days. [Employee's Compensation Act (8 of 1923), S. 5]

1. Subs. by Act 45 of 2009 w.e.f. 18-1-2010.

Moor. In navigation, to fix or secure a vessel in a particular place by casting anchor, or by fastening with cables or chains; to tie or fasten a vessel to the shore or to a buoy or some other stationary object.

Moored. Secured (in case of ship, boat *etc.*) in a particular place by means of chains or ropes either fastened to the shore or to anchor. [IPC (45 of 1860), S. 350, ill.(a)].

Moot Court. A fictitious Court held usually in law schools to argue hypothetical or moot cases, specially at appellate level.

Moral. Of or pertaining to the rules of right conduct; concerning the distinction of right from wrong. (*Century*)

Of or relating to principles or consideration of right and wrong action or good or bad character.

Moral absolutism. The view which states that a person's action can always properly be seen as right or wrong, regardless of the situation or the consequences.

Moral obligation. A moral obligation, in law, is defined as one which cannot be enforced by action, but which is binding on the party who incurs it, in conscience and according to natural justice.

A legal liability suspended or barred in some technical way short of substantial satisfaction.

Moral turpitude. The morally culpable quality held to be present in some criminal offences as distinguished from others. [Companies Act (1 of 1956), S. 385(1)(c)].

Anything done contrary to justice, honesty, principle or good morals; an act of baseness, vileness or deprivity in the private and social duties which a man owes to his fellowmen or society in general; contrary to the accepted and customary rule of right and duty between man and man. (*American Encyclopaedia of Law*) [Companies Act (1 of 1956), S. 267]

A conviction of a person under S. 16 of the Act does not mean that he has committed an offence involving moral turpitude, unless the facts on which the conviction is based are known. *Prem Kumar* v. *State of H.P.,* AIR 1980 HP 45, 46. [Prevention of Food Adulteration Act (37 of 1954), S. 16]

Morality. The quality or fact of conforming to or deriving from right, ideals of human conduct. [Customs Act (52 of 1962), S. 11(2)(b)]; [Constitution of India, Art. 19(2)].

'Morality' means the ideas about right and wrong which are accepted by the right thinking members of the society as a whole of the country. *Brir Gopal* v. *State of M.P.,* AIR 1979 MP 173, 181.

Moratorium. A legal authorisation to a debtor to postpone payment for a certain time. [Asian Development Bank Act (18 of 1966), Sch., Art. 53].

More or less. A limited deviation.

Morphing. Digitally changing an image gradually into a different image. (*Cyber Law*)

Mors dicitur ultimum supplicium. (*Lat.*) (3 Inst. 212) Death is called the 'last punishment,' the "extremity of punishment.

Mors ultima linea rerum est. Death is the closing limit of human transactions.

Mortal wound. The term "mortal wound" may apparently be used to designate a wound calculated and adequate to produce death, as well as one which is necessarily mortal. One inflicting such wound cannot exonerate himself by showing that some conduct of the deceased or his agencies after the wound was inflicted lessened the chances of his recovery, and thus caused death.

A wound that causes death. [IPC (45 of 1860), S. 92, ill. (b)].

Mortality. An actuarial table based upon statistical records of mortality over a number of years giving the rate of death for hundred. [Life Insurance Corporation Act (31 of 1956), Sch. 1, Pt. B, para 4(b)(i)].

Mortally injured. [Prevention of Cruelty to Animals Act (59 of 1960), S. 13(3)].

Mortgage. "The transfer of an interest in specific immoveable property for the purpose of securing the payment of money advanced or to be advanced by way of loan, an existing or future debt, or the performance of an engagement which may give rise to pecuniary liability". [T.P. Act (4 of 1882), S. 58(a)].

To make a mortgage.

A mortgage is the conveyance of an estate by way of pledge for the security of a debt.

Mortgage, Anomalous. A mortgage which is not a simple mortgage, a mortgage by conditional sale, usufructuary mortgage, an English mortgage or a mortgage by deposit of title deeds. [T.P. Act (4 of 1882), S. 58(g)].

Mortgage by conditional sale. Where the mortgagor ostensibly sells the mortgaged property—

on condition that on default of payment of the mortgage money on a certain date the sale shall become absolute, or

on condition that on such payment being made the sale shall become void, or

on condition that on such payment being made the buyer shall transfer the property to the seller, the transaction is called a mortgage by conditional sale and mortgagee a mortgagee by conditional sale :

Provided that no such transaction shall be deemed to be a mortgage, unless the condition is embodied in the document which effects or purports to effect the sale. [T.P. ACT (4 of 1882), S. 58(c)]

A mortgage where the mortgagor ostensibly sells the property on certain conditions. [T.P. Act (4 of 1882), S. 58(c)].

Mortgage by deposit of title-deeds. A mortgage in Presidency-towns or other towns specified in this behalf in which documents of title to immovable property are deposited with a creditor to create a security. [T.P. Act (4 of 1882), S. 58(f)].

Mortgage commitment. A written agreement of a lender with a borrower, stating the terms on which it will lend money for the purchase of specified real property, usually with a limitation of time.

Mortgage debt. "MORTGAGE DEBT" means any liability in respect of a property due under any form of mortgage (including any usufructuary mortgage or mortgage by conditional sale) whether such liability is payable presently or in future or under any decree or order of a Court or otherwise, or whether ascertained or not, which—

(i) in any case where it is incurred by an evacuee, is secured by the mortgage of the interest of such person in the property in favour of a person, not being an evacuee;

(ii) in any case where it is incurred by a person not being an evacuee, is secured by the mortgage of the interest of such person in the property in favour of an evacuee;

but does not include any such liability of an evacuee arising out of any transaction entered into or after the 14th day of August, 1947 unless such transaction has been confirmed by the Custodian under the Administration of Evacuee Property Act, 1950. [Evacuee Interest Separation Act (64 of 1951), S. 2(f)]

The debt which is secured by a mortgage. [Indian Easements Act (5 of 1882), S. 37, ill. (d)].

Mortgage deed. The instrument of mortgage by which the transfer of interest in immovable property is effected. [T.P. Act (4 of 1882), S. 58 (a)].

"MORTGAGE DEED" includes every instrument whereby for the purpose of securing money advanced, or to be advanced, by way of loan, or an existing or future debt, or the performance of an engagement, one person transfers, or creates to, or in favour of, another, a right over or in respect of specified property. [Indian Stamp Act (2 of 1899), S. 2(17)]

Mortgage, English. A mortgage in which the mortgagor binds himself to repay the mortgage money on a certain date and transfers the mortgaged property absolutely to the mortgagee subject to its retransfer on payment. [T.P. Act (4 of 1882), S. 58(e)].

Mortgage, instrument of. A deed by which a mortgage is effected.

Mortgage, intermediate. Intervening mortgage.

The amount to secure which a mortgage is executed [T.P. Act (4 of 1882), S. 58(a)].

Mortgage-money. The principal money and interest of which payment is secured in a mortgage for the time being, are called the mortgage money. [T.P. Act (4 of 1882), S. 58(a)]

Mortgage security. Property conveyed as mortgage in order to secure loan [R. 4(3), CPC (5 of 1908), O. XXXIV].

Mortgagee. "MORTGAGEE" shall be taken to include every person to whom or in whose favour any mortgage pledge or charge is made or transferred.

[Trustees and Mortgagees Powers Act (28 of 1866), S. 1]

The transferee of a mortgaged property [T.P. Act (4 of 1882), S. 58(a)].

MORTGAGEE, is one that takes or receives a mortgage.

Mortgagee in possession. One who takes possession of the mortgaged land by virtue of an agreement between him and the mortgagor.

A mortgagee having possession of mortgaged property. [T.P. Act (4 of 1882), S. 72].

Mortgagium scuto magis quam gladio est. A mortgage is used as a shield rather than a sword.

Mortgagor. "MORTGAGOR" shall be taken to include every person by whom any mortgagee pledge or charge shall be made. [Trustees and Mortgagees Powers Act (28 of 1866), S. 1]

One who transfers an interest in specific immovable property by creating a mortgage. [T.P. Act (4 of 1882), S. 58(a)].

Mortis causa. By reason of or in contemplation of death.

Mortis causa, Donation. Donation made in contemplation of death. [T.P. Act (4 of 1882), S. 129].

Mortis causam tribuerunt. (*Lat.*) They did that which occasioned the death.

Mortis momentum est ultimum vitae momentum. The moment of death is the last moment of life.

Mortuary. A place in which dead bodies are kept until burial. [Cantonments Act (41 of 2006), S. 177(a)].

Mos retinendus est fidelissimae vetustatis. A custom of the truest antiquity is to be retained.

Most favoured nation. There are two forms of the most-favoured-nation clause in treaties, the unconditional and the conditional. In its unconditional or general form this clause binds one party to a treaty to grant to the other party all favours and privileges it has similarly granted in the past or will grant in the future to any third State. In its conditional form it provides that all favours or privileges granted by one party to a third State specifically in exchange for certain favours or privileges shall accrue to the other party only upon fulfilment of like conditions.

Most favoured nation (MFN) principle. MFN is the "normal," non-discriminatory tariff charged on imports of a good. In commercial diplomacy, exporters seek MFN treatment that is, the promise that they will be treated as well as the most favoured exporter. Called normal trade relations in the United States. (*WTO*)

Mother. Inherently distinct; mother means only natural mother who has given birth to the child, not the one who is the wife of one's father by another marriage. *Kirti KantD. Vadodaria* v. *State of Gujarat,* (1996) 4 SCC 479.

Motherboard or **system board.** The main printed circuit board in a microcomputer. It contains various integrated circuits (including the microprocessor and RAM chips) and slots (receptacles) for expansion cards. (*Computer*)

Motion. A motion is a method of making, an application to the Court where in the course of the proceedings it is necessary to invoke its assistance in any matter requiring to be speedily dealt with.

Use of word "motion" to indicate the process of investigation and proof in the Judges (Inquiry) Act, 1968 because the allegations have to be presented to the 'Speaker' does not make it 'motion in the House' notwithstanding use of that expression in S. 6. Otherwise, S. 6 would not say that no further step is to be taken in case of a finding of 'not guilty'. It only means that when the allegation is not proved, the Speaker need not commence the process under clause (4) which is started only in case it is proved. *Sub-Committee on Judicial Accountability* v. *Union of India,* (1991) 4 SCC 699. [Judges (Inquiry) Act (51 of 1968), Ss. 3 & 6]

Movement [IPC (45 of 1860), S. 349]; a formal proposal made in deliberative assembly; motion in Court [CrPC 1973 (2 of 1974), S. 407(3) and Constitution of India, Art. 121].

Broadly speaking a 'motion' is a proposal brought by a member before a House of the Parliament or State Legislature for eliciting decision or expressing the opinion of the House on a matter of public importance. No discussion can take place in a House except on a motion made with the consent of the Speaker or the Chairman of the House, as the case may be.

Motion of thanks. A formal resolution adopted by both Houses of Parliament expressing thanks to the Head of the State for his address to the Houses assembled together. (*Constitutional and Parliamentary Term*)

Motion to strike. In pleading, it is a request that either insufficient defences or immaterial, redundant, impertinent, or scandalous statement to be deleted from the pleading of an opponent.

Motive. Motive is that which stimulates or incites an action; the mainspring of human action; some cause or reason that moves the will and induces action; the moving power which impels to action for a definite result.

Cause and reason that moves the will and induces action; an inducement or that which leads or tempts the mind to indulge in a criminal act.

Motor cab. Means any motor vehicle constructed or adapted to carry not more than six passengers excluding the driver for hire or reward. [Motor Vehicles Act (59 of 1988), S. 2(25)]

Motor car. "MOTOR CAR" means any motor vehicle other than a transport vehicle, omnibus, road-roller, tractor, motor cycle or adapted vehicle. [Motor Vehicle Act (59 of 1988), S. 2(26)

Motor cycle. A two wheeled motor vehicle, inclusive of any detachable side-car having an extra wheel, attached to the motor vehicle. [Motor Vehicles Act (59 of 1988), S. 2(27)]

Motor transport undertaking. Means a motor transport undertaking engaged in carrying passengers or goods or both by road for hire or reward and includes a private carrier. [Motor Transport Workers Act (27 of 1961), S. 2(g) and Kerala Motor Transport Workers Welfare Fund Act (21 of 1985), S. 2(h)]

Motor vehicle. "MOTOR VEHICLE" or "vehicle" means any mechanically propelled vehicle adapted for use upon roads whether the power of propulsion is transmitted thereto from an external or internal source and includes a chassis to which a body has not been attached and a trailer, but does not include a vehicle running upon fixed rails or a vehicle of a special type adapted for use only in a factory or in any other enclosed premises or a vehicle having less than four wheels fitted with engine whose capacity is not exceeding twenty five cubic metres. [Motor Vehicles Act (59 of 1988), S. 2(28)]

Movable. (*Moveable*) A movable is something substantive which has locality and may move or be moved, including money and bonds for money, but not a debt merely as such.

Movable dwelling. Any tent, any van or other conveyance whether on wheels or not, and, subject as hereinafter provided, any shed or similar structure, being a tent, conveyance or structure which is used regularly, or at certain seasons only, or intermittently, for human habitation.

Movable property. "The words "MOVABLE PROPERTY" are intended to include corporeal property of every description, except land and things attached to the earth or permanently fastened to anything which is attached to the earth". [IPC (45 of 1860), S. 22] [Now (w. e. f. 1-7-2024) repealed & replaced by Bharatiya Nyaya Sanhita, 2023 (45 of 2023)]

"Movable property" includes property of every description, except land and things attached to the earth or permanently fastened to anything which is attached to the earth. [Now (w. e. f. 1-7-2024) repealed & replaced by Bharatiya Nyaya Sanhita, 2023 (45 of 2023), S, 2(21)].

"MOVABLE PROPERTY" includes growing crops. [CPC (5 of 1908), S. 2(13)]

"MOVABLE PROPERTY" includes standing timber, growing crops and grass, fruits upon and juice in trees, and property of every other description, except immovable property. [Registration Act (16 of 1908), S. 2(29)].

"MOVABLE PROPERTY" shall mean property of every description, except immovable property. [General Clauses Act (10 of 1897), S. 3(36)]

Electricity is moveable property. *Harda Municipality* v. *Harda Electric Supply Co.,* AIR 1964 MP 101, 107.

The words 'movable property' in S. 421 (1) CrPC, 1973 (2 of 1974) refer to tangible movable property which can be seized and which must be belonging to the offender.

Insurance policies are moveable property coming under S. 17. *Bulchand Chandiram* v. *Bank of India Ltd.*, AIR 1968 SC 1475, 1480. [Displaced Persons (Debts Adjustment) Act (70 of 1951), S. 17]

Movable property includes money.

Huts are not immovable property. The word "movable" does not comprehend everything which a judgment debtor has a right to remove, but means property which is capable of being moved in an existent state.

Movables. "MOVABLES" means any movable tangible property, other than the stip, and includes money, valuable securities and other documents. [Marine Insurance Act (11 of 1963), S. 2(f)]

Move. To shift, remove [IPC (45 of 1860), S. 378, *Expln.*]; to change position or posture or otherwise exhibit outward activity [IPC (45 of 1860), S. 378, ill. (c)]; to move the Court; to propose.

Movement. The action or process of moving. [Food Corporation Act (37 of 1964), S. 13(1)]; [Gift-tax Act (18 of 1958), S. 5(xv)].

Movement disorders.'Movement disorders' may appear as agitated body movements. A person with a movement disorder may repeat certain motions over and over. In the other extreme, a person may become catatonic. Catatonia is a state in which a person does not move and does not respond to others. Catatonia is rare today, but it was more common when treatment for schizophrenia was not available. [*Veer Pal Singh v. Secretary, Ministry of Defence*, (2013) 8 SCC 83, para 14.1].

Moving papers. The papers which constitute or support a motion in Court proceeding.

MSQL database. A database engine used for accessing individual records. (*Cyber Law*)

MUD. Multi-User Dungeon or Dimension. A (usually text-based) multi-user simulation environment. Some are purely for fun and flirting, others are used for serious software development, or education purposes and all that lies in between. A significant feature of most MUDs is that users can create things that stay after they leave and which other users can interact within their absence, thus allowing a world to be built gradually and collectively. (*Matisse Enzer-Glossary of Internet Terms; Internet and E-commerce*)

Muhammadan registrar. "MUHAMMADAN REGISTRAR" means any person who is duly authorized to register marriages and divorces among Mohammadans. [Ben. Act 1 of 1876 (Mohammadan Marriage and Divorce Registration), S. 2]

Mukhia. A *Mukhia* is a village headman or in any event a village officer and so the action of the candidate in utilising his services for the purpose of canvassing is a corrupt practice. *Hari Shanker* v. *Sibban Lal Saksena*, AIR 1956 SC 314, 315. [Representation of the People Act (43 of 1951), Ss. 123, 83 and 100(2)(b)]

Mukhtar. An agent, a steward; a representative. (*Mac. Moh. Law.*)

A legal practitioner on the criminal and revenue side only; agent; a representative; one holding a power of attorney. [Indian Contract Act (9 of 1872), S. 23(j) and CPC (5 of 1908), S. 135(2)].

A *mukhtar* is an attorney whether appointed specially or generally or certificated as a legal practitioner; and a *mukhtar nama* is a document which empowers him to act for the person by or on whose behalf the document is to be executed.

The institution of proceedings against a *mukhtar* or other legal practitioner for professional misconduct under the Legal Practitioners Act amounts to "prosecution" of such legal practitioner. The proceedings though not criminal, are akin to criminal proceedings.

Mulct. A mulct is a fine imposed for an offence; a penalty.

To impose a fine or penalty. [Navy Act (62 of 1957), Ss. 51 and 81(1)(k)].

Mulier amissa pudicitia haud alia abnuerit. When a woman has lost her chastity she may be suspected of not refusing any thing else of a crime.

Mulier puisne : Bastard eigne. When a man had a bastard son, and afterwards marries the mother, and by her has also a legitimate son, the elder son is *bastard eigne* and the younger son is *mulier puisne.*

Multa impediunt matrimonium contrahendum, quæ non dirimunt contractum. (*Lat.*) Many things hinder the contraction of a marriage, which do not detract from its validity when contracted.

Multa in jure communi contra rationem disputandi, pro communi utilitate introducta sunt. (*Lat.*) (Co. Litt. 70) (*Maxim*) Many things have been introduced into the common law with a view to the public good, which are inconsistent with sound reason.

Multa multo exercitatione facilius quam regulis percipies. (*Lat.*) (4 Inst. 50) You will perceive many things much more easily by practice than by rules.

Multa non vetat lex, quae tamen tacite damnavit. (*Lat.*) The law forbids not many things which yet it has silently condemned.

Multa transeunt cum universitate, quae non per se transeunt. Many things pass with the whole, which do not pass separately.

"Multilayer/composite food packaging". Means a food packaging material composed of two or more layers of same or different types of packaging materials specified under these regulations. [Food Safety and Standards (Packaging) Regulations, 2018, Regn. 2(1)(c)].

Multi-dwelling building. Includes any building consisting either of asingle self contained unit having built up area of more than 100 square meters, or more than one independent unit used for domestic, commercial or office premises but does not include building constructed for educational institutions, industrial enterprises or by any other non-profitable organisations and suchother organisations as may be notified by the Government in public interest.. [Goa Tax on Infrastructure Act (12 of 1997), S. 2(6)] substituted by Amendment Act, 1997 (Goa Act 2 of 1998).

Multi multa nemo omnia novit. Many men have known many things; no man has known everything.

Multi-purpose dam. Means a dam which is constructed for purposes of flood control and for other purposes. [Brahmaputra Board Act (46 of 1980), S. 13 *Expln.*]

Multi-State co-operative bank. Means a multi-State co-operative society which is a primary co-operative bank. [Banking Regulation Act (10 of 1949), S. 56 (cciia) (Inserted by Banking Regulation (Amendment) and Miscellaneous Provisions Act (24 of 2004), S. 2(1)(B))].

Multi-State co-operative society. Multi-State co-operative society. In this part, unless context otherwise requires, "Multi-State Co-Operative Society" means a society with objects not confined to one State or registered or deemed to be registered under any law for the time being in force relating to such co-operatives. [Constitution of India, Part IXB, Article 243ZH(d)].

Means a multi-State co-operative society registered as such under any Central Act for the time being in force relating to the multi-State co-operative societies but does not include a national co-operative society and a federal co-operative. [Banking Regulation Act (10 of 1949), sections 5(cciiib) and 56(c)(i)]

Multi-State co-operative society with limited liability. Means a society having the liability of its members limited by its bye-laws to the amount, if any, unpaid on the shares respectively, held by them or to such amount as they may, respectively, thereby undertake to contribute to the assets of the society, in the event of its being wound up. [Multi State Cooperative Societies Act, 1984 (51 of 1984), S. 3(l); Multi-State Cooperative Societies Act (39 of 2002), S. 2(q)]

Multi-storeyed building. Means a building constructed on any land, containing four or more apartments, or two or more buildings in any area designated as a block, pocket or otherwise, each containing two or more apartments, with a total of four or more apartments in all such buildings and includes a building containing two or three apartments in respect of which a declaration has been made under the proviso to Section 2. [Delhi Apartments Ownership Act (58 of 1956), S. 3(s)]

Multifarious suits. The marginal note to S. 17 of the Court Fees Act, 'multifarious suits' does not limit the general terms of the section. The dictionary meaning of 'multifarious' is 'many' or various'. *Firm of Koppula Venkataswamy and Son* v. *Rayalaseema Bank Ltd.,* AIR 1957 AP 1019, 1021. [Court Fees Act (7 of 1870), S. 17]

Multifariousness. By "multifariousness" in pleading means the improperly joining distinct and independent matters, and thereby confounding them.

Multilateral. Having many sides; many sided. [Foreign Awards (Recognition and Enforcement) Act (45 of 1961), Art. VII(1)].

Involving more than two parties.

Multilevel marketing scheme. For the purposes of this section "Multilevel Marketing Scheme" means any scheme or programme or arrangement or plan (by whatever name called) for the purpose of soliciting and procuring insurance business through persons not authorized the said purpose with or without consideration of whole or part of commission or remuneration earned through such solicitation and procurement and includes enrolment of persons into a multi-level chain for the said purpose either directly or indirectly. [Insurance Act (4 of 1938), S. 42-A, Explanation as substituted by Amending Act (5 of 2015)].

Multimedia. Combinations of various types of content, which can include text, audio, graphics, and video. (*Cyber Law*)

The presentation of information and entertainment with some combination of text, graphics (pictures), sound, video, and animation. (*Computer*)

Multimodal transport contract. Means a contract under which a multimodal transport operator undertakes to perform or procure the performance of multimodal transportation against payment of freight. [Multimodal Transportation of Goods Act (28 of 1993), S. 2(l)]

"MULTIMODAL TRANSPORT CONTRACT" means a Contract whereby a multimodal transport operator undertakes, against payment of freight, to perform or to procure the performance of International Multimodal Transport. [U.N. Convention on International Multimodal Transport of Goods, Geneva May 24 (1980), Art. I(3)]

Multimodal transport document. Means a document which evidences a multimodal transport contract, the taking in charge of the goods by the multimodal transport-contractor, and an undertaking by him to deliver the goods in accordance with the terms of that contract. [UN Convention on International Multimodal Transport of Goods Geneva May 24 (1980), Art. I(4)]

"MULTIMODAL TRANSPORT DOCUMENT" means a negotiable or non-negotiable document evidencing a multimodal transport contract and which can be replaced by electronic data interchange messages permitted by applicable law. [Multimodal Transportation of Goods Act (28 of 1993), S. 2(la)]

Multimodal transport operator. Means any person who—

(i) concludes a multimodal transport contract on his own behalf or through another person acting on his behalf;

(ii) acts as principal, and not as an agent either of the consignor or of the carrier participating in the multimodal transportation, and who assumes responsibility for the performance of the said contract; and

(iii) is registered under sub-section (3) of Section 4. [Multimodal Transportation of Goods Act, 1993 (28 of 1993), S. 2(m)]

"MULTIMODAL TRANSPORT OPERATOR" means any person who on his behalf through another person acting on his behalf concludes a multimodal transport contract and who acts as a principal, not as an agent or on behalf of the consignor or of the carriers participating in the multimodal transport operations, and who assumes responsibility for the performance of the contract. [U.N. Convention on International Multimodel Transport of Goods Geneva May 24 (1980)]

Multimodal transportation. Means carriage of goods by two or more modes of transport from the place of acceptance of the goods in India to a place of delivery of the goods outside India. [Multimodal Transportation of Goods Act, 1993 (28 of 1993), S. 2(k)]

Multiplex et indistinctum parit confusionem; et quaestiones, quo simpliciores, eo lucidiores. (*Hob.* 335) : Multiplicity and vagueness result in confusion; and questions, the more simple they are, the more lucid.

Multiplex theatre. Means a building of a prescribed area, comprising of two or more cinema theatres and commercial shops of such size and number and having such other facilities and amenities as may be prescribed. [Income-tax Act (43 of 1961), S. 8IB(14)(da)]

"Multiplex Theatre Complex". Means an entertainment-cum-cultural centre which provides—

(*i*) within the limits of Municipal Corporation of Brihan Mumbai not less than four theatres in a complex with minimum total seating capacity of 1250; and

(*ii*) any where else in the state, not less than three theatres in a complex with minimum total seating capacity of 1000,

and such other incidental and connected matters and facilities and multi-entertainment activities and other facilities as specified by the Government in this behalf, by notification in the Official Gazette. [Bombay Entertainments Duty (Amendment) Act, 2001 (Mah. 2 of 2002), S. 2(fa) **as cited in** *Commissioner of Income Tax-I, Kolhapur* v. *Chaphalkar Brothers, Pune,* (2018) 13 SCC 358, para 2].

Multiplicity. The quality or state of being multiple, manifold or various. [Specific Relief Act (47 of 1963), S. 41(a)].

Multiplicity of proceedings. A state of affairs where several distinct actions are brought on the same issue. [Specific Relief Act (47 of 1963), S. 41(a)].

The expressions "multiplicity of proceedings" or "multiplicity of actions", according to Black's Law Dictionary, is the existence of two or more law suits litigating the same issue against the same defendant. [Black's Law Dictionary as cited in *Khaleel v. Aranjikkal Jamal Muhammed* ILR 2017(4) Kerala 920, para 33]

Multiplicity of suits. "Multiplicity of suits" is a phrase descriptive of a state of affairs where several different actions are brought on the same issue. The law abhors multiplicity of suits, and will not admit trivial distinctions. If two actions are brought for the same cause against the same person, the Court will interfere and relieve.

Multiplicity transgressione crescat poenae inflictio. As transgression is multiplied, the infliction of punishment should increase.

Multitude. A "multitude of people, must be ten or more."

MULTITUDE is an assemblage of many people.

Municipal. Relating to the local-self government or the corporate government of city or town [Indian Evidence Act (1 of 1872), S. 78(5)]; [Government Building Act (4 of 1899), preamble].

Municipal area. "MUNICIPAL AREA" means any municipal area with a population of twenty thousand or more the control or management of which is entrusted to a municipal committee, a town area committee, a town committee or any other authority. [National Highways Act (48 of 1956), S. 3]

Municipal authority. The expression "MUNICIPAL AUTHORITY" includes a municipal corporation or a body of municipal commissioners constituted by, or under the provisions of, any law or enactment for the time being in force. [Government Buildings Act (4 of 1899), S. 2].

"MUNICIPAL AUTHORITY" means Municipal Corporation, Municipality, Nagar Palika, Nagar Nigam, Nagar Panchayat, Municipal Council including notified area committee (NAC) or any other local body constituted under the relevant statutes and, where the management and handling of municipal solid waste is entrusted to such agency. [Municipal Solid Wastes (Management and Handling) Rules, 2000, R. 2(xiv)]

Municipal body. A body of persons in a town having the powers of acting as one person, of holding and transmitting property, and of regulating the government of the town. [Indian Evidence Act (1 of 1872), S. 78(5)].

Municipal Commissioner. An elected (or in some cases nominated) representative to a municipality to represent a particular ward; the chief officer of a municipal corporation. [IPC (45 of 1860), S. 21, ill.].

The expression "MUNICIPAL COMMISSIONERS" means a body of municipal commissioners or a municipal committee constituted under the provisions of any enactment for the time being in force. [Vaccination Act (13 of 1880), S. 2]

Municipal corporation. A municipal corporation is an investing of the people of the place with the local government thereof.

A public corporation created by law to act, as an agency of administration and local self-government. [Income-tax Act (43 of 1961), S. 2(1-A)(c)(ii)(A)].

A municipal corporation is commonly called a "municipality."

Municipal district. "MUNICIPAL DISTRICT" shall mean any local area which is at present a municipal district, and any local area which may hereafter be constituted a municipal district. [Bom Act III of 1901 (District Municipality), S. 3, cl. (5)].

Municipal drain. "Municipal drain" means a drain belonging to the municipal authority or under its direction, management and control. [U.P. Act III of 1894 (Sewerage and Drainage), S. 3, cl. (8)]

Municipal law. The term municipal law, as now understood, has no reference to the law of municipalities or of local government, but is employed as signifying national or territorial law or the law of a country or state, as distinguished from international law or usage; i.e. it refers to the law which belongs to men as linked to others in some political society, and determines all questions of public and private right within the national jurisdiction.

Municipal market. "Municipal market" means a market vested in or managed by the Council. [New Delhi Municipal Council Act (44 of 1994), S. 2(25)]

Municipal slaughter-house. "Municipal slaughter house" means a slaughter house vested in or managed by the corporation. [Delhi Municipal Corporation Act (66 of 1957), S. 2(30)]

Municipal solid waste. Includes commercial and residential wastes generated in a municipal or notified areas in either solid or semisolid form excluding industrial hazardous waste but including treated bio-medical wastes. [Municipal solid Wastes (Management and Handling) Rules, 2000, R. 2(xv)]

Municipality. Means any local area declared to be a municipality.

Municipality in State. A Corporation or a Municipal Council or Nagar Panchayat is constituted on the strength of population and the area or place where it is constituted namely rural or urban. But all the three are deemed to be municipality. *Cantonment Board Secunderabad* v. *G. Venketram Reddy*, AIR 1995 SC 1210, 1211 [Cantonment Act (2 of 1924), S. 60].

Muniments of title. A general expression for all means of evidence, by which an owner, corporate or individual, may defend title to real property.

Munitions of war. Includes the whole or any part of any ship, submarine, aircraft, tank or similar engine, arms and ammunition, torpedo, or mine intended or adapted for use in war, and any other article, material, or device, whether actual or proposed, intended for such use. [Official Secrets Act (19 of 1923), S. 2].

Ammunition and all supplies for direct military action; material used in war for defence or attack [Official Secrets Act (9 of 1923), S. 2(5)].

Murder. Except in the cases hereinafter excepted, culpable homicide is murder, if the act by which the death is caused is done with the intention of causing death, or—

2ndly.—If it is done with the intention of causing such bodily injury as the offender knows to be likely to cause the death of the person to whom the harm is caused, or—

3rdly.—If it is done with the intention of causing bodily injury to any person and the bodily injury intended to be inflicted is sufficient in the ordinary course of nature to cause death, or—

4thly.—If the person committing the act knows that it is so imminently dangerous that it must, in all probability, cause death or such bodily injury as is likely to cause death, and commits such act without any excuse for incurring the risk of causing death or such injury as aforesaid.

Exception 1. When culpable homicide is not murder.—Culpable homicide is not murder if the offender, whilst deprived of the power of self-control by grave and sudden provocation, causes the death of the person who gave the provocation or causes the death of any other person by mistake or accident.

The above exception is subject to the following provisos :—

First.—That the provocation is not sought or voluntarily provoked by the offender as an excuse for killing or doing harm to any person.

Secondly.—That the provocation is not given by anything done in obedience to the law, or by a public servant in the lawful exercise of the powers of such public servant.

Thirdly.—That the provocation is not given by anything done in the lawful exercise of the right of private defence.

Explanation.—Whether the provocation was grave and sudden enough to prevent the offence from amounting to murder is a question of fact.

Exception 2.—Culpable homicide is not murder if the offender, in the exercise in good faith of the right of private defence of person or property, exceeds the power given to him by law and causes the death of the person against whom he is exercising such right of defence without premeditation, and without any intention of doing more harm than is necessary for the purpose of such defence.

Exception 3.—Culpable homicide is not murder if the offender, being a public servant or aiding a public servant acting for the advancement of public justice, exceeds the powers given to him by law, and causes death by doing an act which he, in good faith, believes to be lawful and necessary for the due discharge of his duty, as such public servant and without ill-will towards the person whose death is caused.

Exception 4.—Culpable homicide is not murder if it is committed without premeditation in a sudden fight in the heat of passion upon a sudden quarrel and without the offender's having taken undue advantage or acted in a cruel or unusual manner.

Explanation.—It is immaterial in such cases which party offers the provocation or commits the first assault.

Exception 5.—Culpable homicide is not murder when the person whose death is caused, being above the age of eighteen years, suffers death or takes the risk of death with his own consent. [IPC (45 of 1860), S. 300]

Except in the cases hereinafter excepted, culpable homicide is murder,—

(a) if the act by which the death is caused is done with the intention of causing death; or

(b) if the act by which the death is caused is done with the intention of causing such bodily injury as the offender knows to be likely to cause the death of the person to whom the harm is caused; or

(c) if the act by which the death is caused is done with the intention of causing bodily injury to any person and the bodily injury intended to be inflicted is sufficient in the ordinary course of nature to cause death; or

(d) if the person committing the act by which the death is caused, knows that it is so imminently dangerous that it must, in all probability, cause death, or such bodily injury as is likely to cause death, and commits such act without any excuse for incurring the risk of causing death or such injury as aforesaid.

Exception 1.—Culpable homicide is not murder if the offender, whilst deprived of the power of self-control by grave and sudden provocation, causes the death of the person who gave the provocation or causes the death of any other person by mistake or accident:

Provided that the provocation is not,—

(a) sought or voluntarily provoked by the offender as an excuse for killing or doing harm to any person;

(b) given by anything done in obedience to the law, or by a public servant in the lawful exercise of the powers of such public servant;

(c) given by anything done in the lawful exercise of the right of private defence.

Explanation.—Whether the provocation was grave and sudden enough to prevent the offence from amounting to murder is a question of fact.

Exception 2.—Culpable homicide is not murder if the offender in the exercise in good faith of the right of private defence of person or property, exceeds the power given to him by law and causes the death of the person against whom he is exercising such right of defence without premeditation, and without any intention of doing more harm than is necessary for the purpose of such defence.

Exception 3.—Culpable homicide is not murder if the offender, being a public servant or aiding a public servant acting for the advancement of public justice, exceeds the powers given to him by law, and causes death by doing an act which he, in good faith, believes to be lawful and necessary for the due discharge of his duty as such public servant and without ill-will towards the person whose death is caused.

Exception 4.—Culpable homicide is not murder if it is committed without premeditation in a sudden fight in the heat of passion upon a sudden quarrel and without the offender's having taken undue advantage or acted in a cruel or unusual manner.

Explanation.—It is immaterial in such cases which party offers the provocation or commits the first assault.

Exception 5.—Culpable homicide is not murder when the person whose death is caused, being above the age of eighteen years, suffers death or takes the risk of death with his own consent. [(w. e. f. 1-7-2024) Bharatiya Nyaya Sanhita, 2023 (45 of 2023), section 101]

The crime of killing a person under circumstances previously defined by statute. [IPC (45 of 1860), S. 300].

Murder is when one is slain with a man's will, and with malice prepended or forethought.

The word 'murder' in S. 25 means unlawful homicide or unlawful killing of a human being and not in the technical sense as defined inS. 300 IPC. [Hindu Succession Act (30 of 1956), S. 25]

Murder and Culpable Homicide (Distinction). Section 299 of the IPC (45 of 1860) which defines culpable homicide deals with a genus. Murder is a species of culpable homicide and has been defined in S. 300, IPC. It is the gravest form of culpable homicide. S. 304 of the IPC deals with culpable homicide not amounting to murder. It is in two parts. The first part of S. 304 deals with culpable homicide not amounting to murder which is an offence of a lesser degree than murder as defined in Section 300. The second part of Section 304 deals with a less aggravated form of culpable homicide not amounting to murder. The controversy in most cases arises in cases falling under clause 'thirdly' of S. 300 and cases falling outside the ambit of the said clause and yet covered by the words of Section 299. In order to bring a case within the mischief of clause 'thirdly' of S. 300, a bodily injury should be intended and such bodily injury should be sufficient in the ordinary course of nature to cause death. In determining the aforesaid factors, sometimes the nature of the weapon used and sometimes the part of the body on which the injury is caused and sometimes both are relevant. [J.M.L. Sinha and S.J. Hyder, JJ.] *Ram Jatan* v. *State,* MLJ : YD (1979) Suppl. to Feb. p. 714 : 1979 A Cr R 105 (All).

Murder simplicitor : Accidental murder. If the dominant intention of the act of felony is to kill any particular person then such killing is not an accidental murder but is a murder simpliciter, while if the cause of murder or act of murder was originally not intended and the same was caused in furtherance of any other felonious Act then such murder is an accidental murder. *Rita Devi* v. *New India Assurance Co. Ltd.,* (2000) 5 SCC 113, para 10 : AIR 2000 SC 1930.

Murderer. One who commits a murder. [Hindu Succession Act (30 of 1956), S. 25].

Museum. Any place permanently used for the exhibition of sculpture, casts, models, or other similar objects.

Music software. "MUSIC SOFTWARE" includes series of sounds or music recorded on magnetic tape, cassette, compact discs and digital media which can be played or reproduced on any appropriate apparatus. [Income-tax Act (43 of 1961), S. 80HHF, *Expln. (e)*]

Music video. A video recording having moving image aspect closely associated with music performance of certain type. (*Copyright*)

Musical work. 'Musical work' means a work consisting of music and includes any graphical notation of such work but does not include any words or any action intended to be sung, spoken or performed with the music. [The Copyright Act, 1957, S. 2 (p)].

Even a song is sung which has music, it will not become a 'musical work' within the meaning of Section 2(p) of the Act. [*Saregama India Ltd.* v. *Suresh Jindal,* AIR 2006 Cal 340, 347, para 46) [Copyright Act (47 of 1957), S. 2(p)]

"MUSICAL WORK" means any combination of melody and harmony or either of them, printed, reduced to writing or otherwise graphically produced or reproduced. [Copyright Act (14 of 1957), S. 2(p)]

Muslim personal law. "Muslim Personal Law" may have two meanings depending upon context of its use. Such phrase in commonly understood sense may mean religious or Divine law of Muslim by which they believe to be governed as a matter of faith. The phrase in the second sense may mean all special statutory laws applying only to Muslim as distinct from general law applying to all cases of people in general. *Fed. of Pak.* v. *Farishta;* PLD 1981 SC 120. (*Pak.*) (*Legal Terms & Phrases*—ILYAS KHAN)

Muster. *As a noun*, a term sometimes applied to a troop of soldiers already enrolled, armed, and trained. *As a verb*, to call together a military force; to accept or approve the troops collected.

Muster roll. Roster; a register of all workmen of the industrial establishment. [Industrial Disputes Act (14 of 1947), S. 2(kkk)].

Muta. (*Arabic*) Temporary marriage; gift to a divorced wife, see mut'at al-talaq.

"Muta'' is a very vague and unsatisfactory form of contract for personal relations. There must be definite time during which the relationship is to last and definite sum or thing specified dower. 117 IC 561 : AIR 1929 R 35.

Mutah. A temporary marriage; a left-handed marriage; allowed by the Shiahs, but considered illegal by the Sunnis.

Mutation. A significant basic alteration; substitution of the name of a person by the name of another in relation to property in the record showing right or title to the property. [Sonthal Parganas Act (37 of 1855), S. 1, prov.].

Mutatis mutandis. With the necessary changes in points of detail. (*Wharton*)

With such change as may be necessary. [Registration Act (16 of 1908), S. 39].

'With the necessary changes in points of detail, meaning that matters or things are generally the same, but to be altered when necessary, as to names, offices, and the like.' [Black's Law Dictionary (Revised 4th Edn. 1968) as cited in *Rajasthan State Industrial Development and Investment Corporation* v. *Diamond & Gem Development Corporation Limited*, (2013) 5 SCC 470, para 17].

The expression '*mutatis mutandis*' itself implies applicability of any provision with necessary changes in points of detail. The rules which are adopted make the principles embodied in the rules applicable and not the details pertaining to particular authority or things of that nature. *Prahlad Sharma* v. *State of U.P.*, (2004) 4 SCC 113, 120, para 11.

Mutawalli. The Superintendent or Treasurer of a mosque. An administrator or procurator of any religious or charitable foundation. (*Mac. Moh. Law*)

The warden of a mosque or of an endowment.

MUTTAWALLI means any person appointed either verbally or under any deed or instrument by which a *wakf* has been created or by a competent authority to be the *mutwalli* of a *wakf*, and includes any person who is a *mutawalli* of a *wakf* by virtue of any custom or who is a *naib-mutawalli*, *khandim*, *mujawar*, *Sajjadanashin*, *amin* or other person appointed by a *mutawalli* to perform the duties of a *mutawalli* and save as otherwise provided in this Act, any person, committee, or corporation for the time being managing or administering any *wakf* or *wakf* property : Provided that no member of a committee or corporation shall be deemed to be a *mutawalli* unless such member is an office bearer of such committee or corporation. [Wakf Act (43 of 1995), S. 3 (i)].

A "*Mutawalli*" is more like a manager than a trustee and so far as the *wakf* property is concerned, has to see that the beneficiaries get the advantage of the usufruct. *Bibi Saddiqa Fatima* v. *Saiyed Mohammad Mahmood Hasan,* AIR 1978 SC 1362.

Mutilate. To cut off a limb or an essential part of the body (*Webster*); to deprive of some essential part; to render imperfect.

To render imperfect by cutting off or destroying a part [IPC (45 of 1860), S. 477A and Companies Act (1 of 1956), 234A(1)].

Mutilated note. In order to be mutilated a part of the currency note must be missing. When two parts of the same note are pasted together, it cannot be said that any part is missing. *Reserve Bank of India* v. *Ram Kumar Varshney,* AIR 1963 All 574, 578. [Reserve Bank of India Act (2 of 1934), S. 28; Reserve Bank of India (Note Refund) Rules, 1935 (R. 2 (2)]

Mutilation. The depriving a man of any member, or limb; cutting off or destroying a part of a document.

Mutineer. One that mutinises [Army Act (46 of 1950), S. 3(x)].

Mutiny. Open revolt against constituted authority; specially revolt of soldiers, sailors against their officers. [IPC (45 of 1860), Ss. 5 and 131].

Mutt. A *Mutt* dedicated for the use of ascetics generally or for the ascetic of a particular sect or cult is a public institution. A private *Mutt,* where the property is given to the head of a *Mutt* for his personal benefit only, is also recognised. *Bihar State Board Religious Trust, Patna* v. *Mahant Sri Biswshwar Das,* (1971) 1 SCC 574.

Mutt and temple (Distinction). The primary distinction between temple and *mutt* is that the central part of the temple is the idol while in the *mutt* the presiding element is not the deity but the ascetic or religious teacher who with his disciples form a spiritual brotherhood. In the case of a temple the idol is the grantee of the endowment and is the owner in an ideal sense. In the case of a *Math* the ownership is vested in the entire institution represented by the *Mahant* or religious head. The deity of a temple is a juristic person. Under Hindu Law, *Maths*, choultries and similar institutions are a class of foundations raised to the status of a juristic person and can become the bearer of rights and duties. *Jagannath Mahaparu* v. *Kumar Bimal Chandra Singh,* MLJ : QD (1961-1965) Vol III C1173 : 25 Cut LT 345.

Mutual. Reciprocally acting or related, reciprocally receiving; reciprocally giving and receiving; a word which denotes a common interest.

Reciprocal; belonging to each respectively. [T.P. Act (4 of 1882), S. 111(e)].

Mutual accounts. 'Mutual accounts', by which are meant not where one only of two parties has received money and made payments on account of the other, but where each of two parties has received and paid on account of the other.

Mutual agreement. A reciprocal agreement. [T.P. Act (4 of 1882), S. 111(e)].

Mutual benefit company. "MUTUAL BENEFIT COMPANY" means a company not notified under Section 620A of the Companies Act (1 of 1956) and carrying on the business a non-banking financial institution,—

(a)* on 9th January, 1997; and

(b) having the aggregate of net owned funds and preferential share capital of not less than ten lakhs of rupees; and

(c) has applied for issue of certificate of registration to the Bank on or before 9th July, 1997; and

(d) is complying with the requirements contained in the relevant provisions of the Directions issued under Section 637A of the Companies Act (1 of 1956) to Nidhi Companies by the Central Government. [Non-Banking Financial Companies Acceptance of Public Deposits (Reserve Bank) Directions, 1998, para 2(1)(ixa)]

Mutual benefit society. A society formed for the common benefit of all the members composing the same [Income-tax Act (43 of 1961), S. 36(1), *Expln.*].

Mutual consent. 'Mutual consent' as used in S. 125 (4) and (5), CrPC 1973 (2 of 1974), means a consent on the part of the husband and wife to live apart no matter what the circumstances may be. *Gurdian Kaur* v. *Jang Singh,* AIR 1959 Punj 185, 189.

The words 'mutual consent' imply that the desire to live apart should emanate from both parties and that none of them should be forced to take recourse to separate living and ultimately submit to it only as a result of circumstances brought about by one of the parties. *Sn. Chameli* v. *Gajaraj Bahadur Gupta,* AIR 1954 All 33, 34.

Mutual dealing. Mutual credit or mutual dealings simply mean reciprocal demands which must be naturally terminated in a debt. When there are reciprocal demands available by one party against the other in the same capacity, it is a clear case in which a set-off is a matter of course. *H. Naiku* v. *Panchanan Das,* AIR 1954 Ori 7. [Provincial Insolvency Act (5 of 1920), S. 46]

Mutual desertion. Result of each spouse, independently and without just cause leaving each other.

Mutual fund. Means a fund established in the form of a trust to raise monies through the sale of units to the public or a section of the public under one or more schemes for investing in securities including money market instruments or gold or gold related instruments or real estate assets. [Securities and Exchange Board of India (Mutual Funds) Regulations 1996, regulation 2(q)].

Mutual promises. The promises which are reciprocally exchanged and become consideration for each other, so that a contract is created by them.

Mutual trading operations. "For this doctrine to apply it is essential that all the contributors to the common fund are entitled to participate in the surplus and that all the participators in the surplus are contributors, so that there is complete identity between contributors and participators.

This means identity as a class, so that at any given moment of time the persons who are contributing are identical with the persons entitled to participate; it does not matter that the class may be diminished by persons going out of the scheme or increased by other coming in." [British Tax Encyclopedia (1), 1962 Edn. (edited by G.S.A. Wheatcroft), p. 1201 as cited in *Bangalore Club v. Commissioner of Income Tax,* (2013) 5 SCC 509, para 19].

Mutual will. A will is mutual when two testators confer upon each other reciprocal benefits, as by either of them constituting the other his legatee; that is to say, when the executants fill the roles of both testator and legatee towards each other, *K. Govindan* v. *T. T. Lakshmi Amma,* AIR 1959 SC 71, 75. [Indian Succession Act (39 of 1925), S. 74]

Mutuality of contract. The doctrine of mutuality means that the contract must be mutually enforceable by each party against the other. Mutuality does not mean equality and exact arithmetical correspondence. It means each party to the contract must have the freedom to enforce his rights under the contract against the other. *Dasarath Gyen* v. *Satyanarayan Ghosh,* AIR 1963 Cal 325, 327.

Mutuality of obligation. An agreement between both parties to a contract to be bound in some way.

Mutually indebted. Indebted to each other. [Indian Contract Act (9 of 1872), S. 50, ill. (b)].

My heirs. The expression 'my heirs' has to be construed as equivalent to 'my legal heirs'. (The words 'my heirs' in the will mean that in the event of the beneficiary's death, without any male issue, the devolution of the estate given to him for life will be regulated in favour of the testator's heirs in accordance with the Hindu Law of intestate succession). *N. Krishnammal* v. *Ekambaram,* AIR 1979 SC 1298, 1301. [Indian Succession Act (39 of 1925), Ss. 74 and 93].

N

Naga Hills Tuensang Area. Means the Naga Hills Tuensang Area specified in Part-B of the Table appended to paragraph 20 of the Sixth Schedule to the Constitution comprising the areas which at the commencement of the Constitution were known as Naga Hills District and the Naga Tribal Area. [State of Nagaland Act (27 of 1962), S. 2(e)]

Naked. Describing a security, particularly a derivative, that is not covered or hedged against various risks.

Naked authority. The authority which is granted by a principal to an agent, without involving any obligations between them.

Naked confession is one that is not sufficient to lay a basis for conviction, it being a confession which relates no circumstances proven to have existed.

Naked contract. Contract devoid of consideration. No contract at all.

Naked promise. A promise without consideration whereon therefore, no action can be founded.

Nallus commodum capere potest de injuria sua propria. (*Maxim*) 'No man can take advantage of his own wrong'. He who prevents a thing from being done shall not avail himself of the non-performance he has occasioned. The maxim applies to the class of cases in which fraud has been committed by one party to a transaction, and is relied upon as a defence by the other. *Rathnavelusami* v. *Manickavelu,* AIR 1951 Mad 542, 546.

Nam debes melioris conditionis esse quam actor meus a quo jus in me transit. (*Maxim*) One should not be placed in a better condition than the person to whose rights he succeeds.

Name. "NAME" includes any abbreviation of a name. [Emblems and Names (Prevention of Improper Use), Act (12 of 1950), S. 2(c) and Merchandise Marks Act (4 of 1889), S. 2(5) (Repealed); Trade Marks Act (47 of 1999), S. 2(1)(o) and Geographical Indications of Goods (Registration and Protection) Act (48 of 1999), S. 2(1)(h)]

Named. Mentioned or specified by name; described by name; [TP Act (4 of 1882), S. 69A(2)]; mentioned; stated.

"ABOVE-NAMED" means "above mentioned".

Namely. A term which imports interpretation, that is it indicates what is included in the previous term.

The word "namely" imports enumeration of what is comprised in the preceding clause. It ordinarily serves the purpose of equating what follows with the clause described before. *State of Bombay* v. *Bombay Education Society*, AIR 1954 SC 561, 565.

That is to say. [Indian Partnership Act (9 of 1932), S. 44].

Narco analysis. The term 'narco analysis' is derived from the Greek word 'narke' meaning 'numbness' and is used as a psychotherapeutic that uses barbiturates drugs or truth serums to induce a state of unconsciousness in which secrets come to the surface since the person testifying is not in control of what he/she says. [As published in The Times of India, Lucknow, A daily news papers dated 8th January 2007, para 7]

Process whereby a subject is put to sleep, or into a semi-somnolent state by means of chemical injections and then interrogated while in this dream-like state.

Narcosis. Insensible state.

Narcotic. (*Med.*) Inducing drowsiness or sleep; a drug having such influence.

A substance which when swallowed, inhaled or injected into the system, induces drowsiness, sleep *etc.*

Narcotic drug. "NARCOTIC DRUG" means coca leaf, cannabis (hemp), opium, poppy straw and includes all manufactured drugs. [Narcotic Drugs and Psychotropic Substances Act (61 of 1985), S. 2(xiv)]

"NARCOTIC DRUG" or "NARCOTIC" means a substance which is cocoleaf, or coca derivative, or opium, or Indian hemp and shall include any other substance capable of causing or producing in human beings dependence, tolerance and withdrawal syndromes and which the Central Government may, by notification by the Official Gazette, declare to be narcotic drug or narcotic. [Medicinal and Toilet Preparations (Excise Duties) Act (16 of 1955), S. 2(h)]

Drugs having the effect of inducing stuper, sleep or insensibility.

Narcotic drug and narcotics. Narcotic is a substance which relieves pain, induces sleep and in large doses brings on stuper, coma and even death, as opium, hemlock, alchohol *etc.*Chloral hydrate is a narcotic or a narcotic drug., *Indian C & P. Works* v. *State of Andhra Pradesh*, AIR 1966 SC 713, 718. [Constitution of India, Sch. VII, List II, Entry 51]

"Narcotic drug" and "psychotropic substance". Shall have the meanings respectively assigned to them in the Narcotic Drugs and Psychotropic Substances Act, 1985. [Juvenile Justice (Care and Protection of Children) Act (56 of 2000), S. 2(n)]

Narcotic substance. [Extradition Act (34 of 1962), 2nd Sch., Item 16].

Narcotics. A substance which when swallowed, inhaled or injected into the system, induces drowsiness, sleep *etc.*

Narrative. An account or narration. [CrPC 1973 (2 of 1974), S. 275(3)].

Naslan bad naslan. The expression '*naslan bad naslan*' means 'heritable and heritable only by the lineal male descendants'. It also means 'heritable and alienable estate'. *Bajrang Bahadur Singh* v. *Bhaktraj Kher*, AIR 1953 SC 7.

Natal. Of birth.

Nation. A body politic; a society of men united together for the purpose of promoting their mutual safety and advantage by the joint efforts of their combined strength. The inhabitants of a territory united under the same Government, and possessing as a whole an independent status. The word is generally but inaccurately used as a synonym of State.

National. Common to or characteristic of a whole nation.

One that owes permanent allegiance to a nation without regard to place of residence or to possession of a more formal status [Trade and Merchandise Marks Act (43 of 1958), S. 132]; of or relating to a nation.

National bank bills. The term "national bank bills" is used to designate "a kind or part of the national currency."

National Blood Transfusion Council. Means a society registered under the Societies Registration Act, 1860 and has an officer not below the rank of an Additional Secretary to the Government of India dealing with the AIDS Control Project as its Chairman, by whatever name called. [Income-tax Act (43 of 1961), S. 80G (2)(a)(iiih), *Expln.* (a)]

National Capital Region. Means the areas specified in the Schedule : Provided that the Central Government with the consent of the Government of the concerned participating State and in consultation with the Board, may; by notification in the Official Gazette add any area to the Schedule or exclude any are a therefrom. [National Capital Region Planning Board Act (2 of 1985), S. 2(f)]

National colours. National flag, ensign or standard. [Geneva Conventions Act (6 of 1960), IInd Sch., Art. 35].

National Commission for Safai Karmacharis. Means the National Commission for Safai Karamcharis constituted under section 3 of the National Commission for Safai Karmacharis Act, 1993 (64 of 1993), and continued by Resolution of the Government of India in the Ministry of Social Justice and Empowerment *vide* No. 17015/18/2003-SCD-VI, dated 24th February, 2004 and as amended from time to time. [S. 2(1)(h) of the Prohibition of Employment as Manual Scavengers & Their Rehabilitation Act, 2013 (25 of 2013)]

National Committee. Means the Committee constituted by the Central Government, from amongst persons of eminence in public life, in accordance with the rules made under this Act. [Income-tax Act (43 of 1961), S. 35AC (6), *Expln.* (a)]

National council. Means the National Council for Training in Vocational Trades established by the resolution of the Government of India in the Ministry of Labour (Directorate General of Resettlement and Employment) No TR/E P-24/56, dated the 21st August, 1956 and re-named as the National Council for Vocational Training by the resolution of Government of India in the Ministry of Labour. (Directorate General of Employment and Training) No. DGET/12/ 21/80TC, dated the 30th September, 1981. [Apprentices Act (52 of 1961), S. 2(l)]

National defence. A generic concept that refers to the military and naval establishments and the related activities of national preparedness and includes all matters directly and reasonably connected with the defense of the nation against its enemies.

National Do Not Call Registry. National Do Not Call Registry means a portal consisting of telephone numbers of subscribers who do not want to receive unsolicited commercial communication. [Telecom Unsolicited Commercial Communication Regulations, 2007, Reg. 6, Chapter II]

National flag. A flag serving as distinctive emblem of a particular nation. [Indian Evidence Act (1 of 1872), S. 57(8) and Constitution of India, Art. 51A(a)].

National function or State function. For the purposes of this sub-rule, "NATIONAL FUNCTION OR STATE FUNCTION" shall include—

(A) Republic Day;

(B) Independence Day;

(C) State Day; or

(D) such other day as notified by the Central Government or the State Government. [Noise Pollution (Regulation and Control) Rules, 2000, R. 5(3), *Explanation (ii)*].

National Holiday. For the purposes of section 96(2) of Act 18 of 2013, 'National Holiday' means and includes a day declared as National Holiday by the Central Government. [*Explanation* to section 96(2) of the Companies Act, 2013 (18 of 2013)]

National income. The value in a country's money of the total production of goods and services in that country for one year.

National Information Infrastructure (NII). A general label for the composite network of data or information systems and connectivity channels that serve as the foundation for U.S. economic, political, and military operations. (*Cyber Law*)

National laboratory. Means a scientific laboratory functioning at the national level under the aegis of the Indian Council of Agricultural Research, the Indian Council of Medical Research, the Council of Scientific and Industrial Research, the Defence Research and Development Organisation, the Department of Electronics, the Department of Bio Technology or the Department of Atomic Energy. [Central Excise Tariff Act 1985 (5 of 1986), Gen Exemption No. 20 (1)(c)(vi) *Expln.* (a)]

National Level Expert Committee for Road Safety. Means the Committee constituted by the Central Government for the purpose of review and recommendations of the proposals for Road Safety Works submitted by the State Government. [Central Road Fund (State Roads) Rules, 2014, R. 2(1)(ga)].

National Long Distance (NLD) service. Refers to the provision of telegraph service over the national long distance network of the licensee between SDCAs of two licensed service areas. [Flight and Maritime Connectivity Rules, 2018, R. 2(1)(r)]..

National Pension System. Means the contributory pension system referred to in section 20 of Act 23 of 2013 whereby contributions from a subscriber are collected and accumulated in an individual pension account using a system of points of presence, a central recordkeeping agency and pension funds as may be specified by regulations. [S. 2(1)(i) of the Pension Fund Regulatory & Development Authority Act, 2013 (23 of 2013)]

National Pension System Trust. Means the Board of Trustees who hold the assets of subscribers for their benefit. [S. 2(1)(j) of the Pension Fund Regulatory & Development Authority Act, 2013 (23 of 2013)]

National Register. Means the National Register for Dentists or the National Register for Dental Auxiliaries, as the case may be, maintained by the Ethics and Dental Registration Board under section 30. [National Dental Commission Act, 2023 (21 of 2023), S. 2(r)]

National security. The term as authorizing summary dismissal of government employee in the interest of 'national security' will apply only to those activities which are directly concerned with the nation's safety as distinguished from the general welfare. (*Cole* v. *Young,* 100 L ed. 1396 : 351 US 536).

National Social Security Board. Means the National Social Security Board for Unorganised Workers constituted under sub-section (*1*) of section 6. [Code on Social Security, 2020 (36 of 2020), S. 2(49)]

National symbol. The national flag became a national symbol by a resolution of the constituent assembly. There are four other possibilities by which a symbol may become a national symbol. They are(1) by law passed by the Parliament, (2) a declaration by the Government of India either under powers granted by law or in exercise of their executive powers (3) by international recognition and (4) by recognition by the nation as a whole, the recognition being either express or implied. *Karan Singh* v. *Jamma Singh,* AIR 1959 All 427, 430. [Representation of the People Act (43 of 1951), S. 123(3)].

National treatment (Principle of). This principle means that a state must grant same or equal rights to foreigners/foreign goods as it grants to its own citizens or goods produced in their own country. The TRIPS Agreement incorporates this principle akin GATT and GATS. [Karnika Seth, *Computers Internet and New Technology Laws*, 2021, LexisNexis, Glossary of Legal Terms].

Nationalisation. The expression "nationalisation" means 'the acquisition and control of privately-owned business by government'. *Maharashtra State Electricity Board* v. *Thana Electric Supply Co.,* AIR 1990 SC 153.

Nationalisation or **expropriation.** The word 'nationalisation' is limited to property actually taken over by the State. The addition of the word 'expropriation' covers a case where the property is not directly taken over by the State but is brought under the control of the State by means of sequestration followed by sale., *Benin* v. *Whimster*, (1975) 3 All ER 706, 714 (CA). [Foreign Compensation (Egypt) Order 1971, Art. 2(2).]

Nationalised bank. Means a corresponding new bank specified in the First Schedule to the Banking Companies (Acquisition and Transfer of Undertakings) Act, 1970 or a corresponding new bank specified in the First Schedule to the Banking Companies (Acquisition and Transfer of Undertakings) Act, 1980). Industrial Development Bank of India (18 of 1964), S. 2(da) and National Co-operative Development Corporation Act (26 of 1962), S. 2(dd)]

Nationalised text-book. Means any book prescribed for class I to V of any school which is published under the authority of the State Government and declared as such by notification issued by the State Government. [West Bengal Nationalised Text-books Act, 1977 (18 of 1977), S. 2(c)]

Nationalism. Favouring or striving after the unity, independence, interests or domination of a nation.

Nationality. Distinctive national qualities; membership of a nation; race forming part of one or more political nations.

NATIONALITY is the condition or status of belonging to a Nation or State, either by birth or naturalisation.

Nationality and **citizenship.** 'Nationality' has reference to the jural relationship which may arise for consideration under international law; 'citizenship' has reference to the jural relationship under municipal law. Nationality determines, the civil rights of a person, natural or artificial, particularly with reference to international law, whereas citizenship is intimately connected with civil rights under municipal law., *State Trading Corporation of India Ltd.* v. *Commercial Tax Officer*, AIR 1963 SC 1811, 1819.

Nationalization. Government takeover of the ownership and management of a private firm with payment of compensation.

Nationalize. To bring under the control of government; to give the status of a citizen.

Native. Belonging to a place by birth [Indian Succession Act (39 of 1925), S. 2(d)]; used by the British to denote Indians in legislation *etc.*

Native Christian. The expression "NATIVE CHRISTIANS" includes the Christian descendants of Natives of India converted to Christianity, as well as such converts. [Christian Marriage Act (15 of 1872), S. 3]

Native husband. "NATIVE HUSBAND" shall mean a married man domiciled in British India, who shall have completed the age of sixteen years, and shall not be a Christian, a Muhammadan nor a Jew.

[Native Convert's Marriage Dissolution Act (21 of 1866), S. 3]

Native law. Shall mean any law, or custom having the force of law, of any persons domiciled in British India other than Christians, Muhammadans and Jews. [Native Convert's Marriage Dissolution Act (21 of 1866), S. 3)]

Native State. "NATIVE STATE" means the territories of any Native Prince or State in alliance with Her Majesty. [Christian Marriage Act (15 of 1872), S. 3]

"NATIVE STATE" means any State in India which is under the protection or political control of Her Majesty or of which the Government shall have acknowledged the supremacy. [Native Coinage Act (9 of 1876), S. 2]

Native wife. "NATIVE WIFE" shall mean a married woman domiciled in British India, who shall have completed the age of thirteen years, and shall not be a Christian, a muhammadan nor a Jewess. [Native Convert's Marriage Dissolution Act (21 of 1866), S. 3]

Nativity. The dictionary meaning of the word 'nativity' is birth. *P. Rajendran* v. *State of Madras*, AIR 1968 SC 1012, 1015. [Constitution of India, Art. 15(1)]

Natura non facit saltum, ita nec lex. (*Lat.*) (Co. Litt. 238b) Nature makes no leap, nor does the law.

Natura non facit vacuum; nec lex supervacuum. (*Lat.*) (Co. Litt. 79a) Nature makes no vacuum; the law nothing purposeless.

Natural. The term 'natural' means proceeding from physical causes or conditions or based upon moral considerations as distinguished from legal causes or legal considerations.

Innate; based upon the innate moral feelings of mankind [CPC (5 of 1908), S. 13(d)]; taking place in accordance with the ordinary course of nature. [Indian Evidence Act (1 of 1872), S. 114].

Natural affection. The affection which a husband, a father, a brother, or other near relative naturally feels towards those who are so nearly allied to him. It sometimes supplies the place of a valuable consideration in contracts, and natural affection is a good consideration in a deed.

Natural and probable consequences. Consequences which can be anticipated from an action by an ordinary prudent man.

Natural-born citizen. Every person born within the territories of a state, whether the parents are citizens or aliens, is a natural born citizen of that state.

Natural child. "Natural child" is a phrase generally employed to designate children born out of lawful wedlock.

The law denominates as "natural children" illegitimate children who have been acknowledged by their father.

Natural consequences. Damages which are the natural consequences of an act, to be the basis of legal redress, must not only be the natural sequence of the wrongful act or omission, but must flow directly from it in observance of some well-understood and recognized material force.

Natural decay, Subject to. Liable to deterioration which takes place in accordance with the ordinary course of nature. [CrPC 1973 (2 of 1974), S. 85(2)].

Natural gas. "NATURAL GAS" means gas consisting primarily of hydrocarbons obtained from oil wells or gas wells. [Oil Industry (Development) Act (47 of 1974), S. 2(i)]

Natural gasoline liquid (NGL). Is a lowboiling liquid petroleum product extracted from Natural Gas. [Customs Tariff Act (51 of 1975), I Sch. Import Tariff, S. V, Chap. 27, Note 3, Supplementary Note (b)]

Natural guardian. The expression 'natural guardian' as defined in S. 6 of the Act means father, mother and in case of married girl, the husband. *Githa Hariharan* v. *Reserve Bank of India,* AIR 1999 SC 1149 : (1999) 1 SCC 228, para 44. [Hindu Minority and Guardianship Act (32 of 1956), S. 6]

Natural justice. By "natural justice" we mean that which is founded in equity, in honesty, and right.

Justice based upon the innate moral feeling of mankind. [CPC (5 of 1908), S. 13(d)].

'Natural justice' is an expression of English Common Law. Natural justice is not a single theory – it is a family of views. In one sense administering justice itself is treated as natural virtue and, therefore, a part of natural justice. It is also called the "naturist," approach to the phase "natural justice" and is related to "moral naturalism." Moral naturalism captures the essence of commonsense morality – that good and evil, right and wrong, are the real features of the natural world that human reason can comprehend. In this sense, it may comprehend virtue ethics and virtue jurisprudence in relation to justice as all these are attributes of natural justice. [*Dharampal Satyapal Limited v. Deputy Commissioner of Central Excise, Guwahati*, (2015) 8 SCC 519, para 18].

Natural justice would mean the natural sense of what is right and wrong. [*Dharampal Satyapal Limited v. Deputy Commissioner of Central Excise, Gauhati*, (2015) 8 SCC 519, para 22].

"Indeed, natural justice is a pervasive facet of secular law where a spiritual touch enlivens legislation, administrative and adjudication, to make fairness a creed of life. It has many colours and shades, many forms and shapes and, save where valid law excludes it, applies when people are affected by acts of Authority. It is the bone of healthy government, recognized from earliest times and not a mystic testament of Judge-made law. Indeed, from the legendary days of Adam—and of Kautilya's Arthasastra —the rule of law has had this stamp of natural justice which makes it social justice. We need not go into these deeps for the present except to indicate that the roots of natural justice and its foliage are noble and not newfangled. Today its application must be sustained by current legislation, case law or other extant principle, not the hoary chords or legend and history Our jurisprudence has sanctioned its prevalence even like the Anglo-American system." *Mohinder Singh Gill* v. *Chief Election Commissioner*, AIR 1998 SC 851.

The phrase 'natural justice' means a fair crack of the whip, per Lord RUSSEL of Killowen, in *Fairmount Investments Ltd.* v. *Secy. of State for Environment,* 1976 (1) WLR 1255, as cited in *Canara Bank* v. *Debasis Das,* (2003) 4 SCC 557, para 20 : AIR 2003 SC 2041.

The phrase 'natural justice' means universal justice. *Drew* v. *Drew and Lebura* (Macq at p. 8, per Lord GRANWORTH, as cited in *Canara Bank* v. *Debasis Das,* (2003) 4 SCC 557, para 20 : AIR 2003 SC 2041.

The expression "natural justice" may not be capable of precise definition. But the basic and fundamental requirements of "natural justice" are well known and have been repeatedly affirmed by Courts of highest authority. Particular forms of legal procedure may not be necessary, but it is of the very essence of an enquiry and a decision that the person enquiring must be one without bias and should render the decision in a judicial spirit and in accordance with the principles of substantial justice. *Andhra Scientific Co. Ltd.* v. *A. Seshagiri Rao,* AIR 1960 526, 533. [Industrial Disputes Act (14 of 1947), S. 10(1)]

'Natural justice' and 'Legal justice'. The expressions 'natural justice' and 'legal justice' are the substance of justice which is to be secured by both and whenever 'legal justice' fails to achieve this solemn purpose, 'natural justice' is called in aid of 'legal justice'. *Canara Bank* v. *Debasis Das,* (2003) 4 SCC 557, para 14 : AIR 2003 SC 2041.

Natural law. NATURAL LAW is defined as "a law which so necessarily agrees with the nature and state of man that without observing its maxims, the peace and happiness of society can never be preserved," and is so called "because a knowledge of them may be attained merely by the light of reason, from the fact of their essential agreeableness with the constitution of human nature."

Natural liberty. The power of acting as one think fit, without any restraint or control, unless by the law of nature.

Natural market. Means a market where sellers and buyers have traditionally congregated for the sale and purchase of products or services and has been determined as such by the local authority on the recommendations of the Town Vending Committee. [S. 2(1)(e) of the Street Vendors (Protection of Livelihood and Regulation of Street Vending) Act, 2014 (7 of 2014)]

Natural person. A human being as distinguished in law from an artificial or juristic person. [Estate Duty Act (34 of 1953), S. 2(19)].

Natural presumptions. (*In evidence*) Presumptions of fact; those which depend upon their own form and efficacy in generating belief or conviction in the mind, as derived from those connections which are pointed out by experience.

Natural resources. Natural resources are generally understood as elements having intrinsic utility to mankind. They may be renewable or non-renewable. They are thought of as the individual elements of the natural environment that provide economic and social services to human society and are considered valuable in their relatively unmodified, natural form. A natural resource's value rests in the amount of the material available and the demand for it. The latter is determined by its usefulness to production. Natural resources belong to the people but the State legally owns them on behalf of its people and from that point of view natural resources are considered as national assets, more so because that State benefits immensely from their value. [*Centre for Public Interest Litigation v. Union of India*, (2012) 3 SCC 1, para 63].

Natural witness. Witnesses who were staying in a house just opposite to the house of the accused, and entered the house by breaking open the compound gate and witnessed the occurrence of murder which took place in the house, were natural witnesses. *Om Parkash* v. *State of Punjab*, AIR 1993 SC 138.

When the incident of murder occurred in the property of deceased himself, the presence of kith and kin of deceased is natural and such persons would be the most 'natural witnesses' as their presence in their own property normally cannot be doubted. *Chavda Jivanji Chelaji* v. *State of Gujarat,* JT (2001) 3 SC 551 : 2001 (2) SLT 547. [Evidence Act (1 of 1872), S. 3]

If murder is committed in a dwelling house, the inmates of the house are natural witnesses. If murder is committed in a brothel, prostitutes and paramours are natural witnesses. If murder is committed on a street., only passersby will be witnesses. [*Rana Pratap v. State of Haryana,* (1983) 3 SCC 327, para 3 **as cited in** *Vijendra Singh v. State of U.P.,* (2017) 11 SCC 129, para 32].

Naturalisation. "Naturalisation" is the act of adopting a foreigner, and clothing him with the privileges of a native citizen.

The act or process of naturalising. [Citizenship Act (57 of 1955), S. 6; Constitution of India, VIIth Sch, list 1, Item No. 17].

Naturalised citizen. One who being born an alien, has lawfully become a citizen of the State under the state laws.

Naturally. By natural or inherent character. [Indian Evidence Act (1 of 1872), S. 16].

Nature. General characteristics and feelings of mankind (as) human nature.

The material world; the creative and regulative physical power which is conceived as operating in the physical world and is the immediate course of all its phenomenon; the inherent power or force by which the physical and mental activities of man are sustained; the inherent and inseparable combination of properties essentially pertaining to anything and giving it its fundamental character [CPC (5 of 1908), S. 18(1), *Prov.*]; kind; order [S. 96(1)(f), Employees' State Insurance Act (34 of 1948); character [Central Sales Tax Act (74 of 1956), S. 13(4)(g)].

AGAINST NATURE. Unnatural; immoral; irrational.

STATE OF NATURE. Unregenerate condition; condition of man before society was organized.

Nature and value of the suit. Character and monetary worth of the action. [prov., CPC (5 of 1908), S. 18(1)].

Nature, Civil. Of a civil character as opposed to criminal character.

Nature conservation. 'NATURE CONSERVATION' means the conservation of flora, fauna or geological or physiographical features. [(English) Nature Conservancy Council Act, 1973, S. 1(2)]

Nature, Law of. Justinian's Institutes describe the *jus naturale* as that taught by nature to all animal creation, including the humanrace. Blackstone, defines the law of nature as the "will of man's Maker." "For as God", says he, "when He created matter and endued it with a principle of mobility, established certain rules for the perpetual direction of that motion; so, when He created man and endued him with freewill to conduct himself in all parts of life, He laid down certain immutable laws of human nature whereby that freewill is in some degree regulated and restrained and gave him also the faculty of reason to discover the purport of those laws" (Commentaries, 4th ed., 1770, bk.i.p. 39.)

Nature reserve. In this Part (Part III : nature conservation) of this Act the expression 'nature reserve' means land managed for the purpose—

(a) of providing, under suitable conditions and control, special opportunities for the study of, and research into, matters relating to the fauna and flora of Great Britain and the physical conditions in which they live, and for the study of geological and physiographical features of special interest in the area, or

(b) of preserving flora, fauna or geological or physiographical features of special interest in the area,

or for both those purposes. [(English) National Parks and Access to the Countryside Act, 1949, S. 15]

Nature vis maxima. (*Lat.*) (Noy Max. 26) The greatest force is that of nature.

Nauseous or **offensive trade.** A deed prohibiting the grantee from maintaining any "nauseous or offensive trade" on the lot, will not be construed to include a grocery or provision store.

Nautical. Pertaining to ships or to navigation.

Nautical mile. 1. A marine mile; a linear measure of distance on the sea, equivalent to approximately 6,080 feet, the name being taken from the knots in a ship's log line. 2. The International Nautical Mile is 1.150779 statute miles. (*Ballentine's Law Dictionary, 3rd Edn.*)

Naval. Pertaining to the navy or ships or warships. Of or pertaining to, connected with, characteristic of or used in, the navy.

Naval custody. Means the arrest or confinement of a person in the prescribed manner or in accordance with the usages of the naval service, and includes military or air force custody. [Navy Act (62 of 1957), S. 3(12)]

Naval establishment. Means an establishment belonging to, or under the control of, the India Navy whether within or without India. [Navy Act (62 of 1957), S. 3(12A)]

Naval forces. Those which constitute the navy of the state. Navy. [CrPC 1973 (2 of 1974), S. 132(3)(a)].

Naval men. Members of naval forces. [heading, CPC (5 of 1908), O. XXVIII].

Naval tribunal. Means a Court-martial constituted under S. 97 and includes a disciplinary Court constituted under S. 96, a commanding officer or other officer or authority exercising powers of punishment under this Act. [Navy Act (62 of 1957), S. 3(15)]

Naval usages. The usages referred to are usages in regard to the mode and manner of arrest and confinement and not usages under which a person can be kept in custody or confinement. *State* v. *Kawas Manekshaw Nanavati,* AIR 1960 Bom 502, 510. [Navy Act (62 of 1957), S. 3(12)]

Navigable. Affording passage for ships. Admitting of being navigated; affording passage for ships or boats. [IPC (45 of 1860), S. 431].

Navigable channel. Means a channel navigable during the whole or a part of the year. [Inland Waterways Authority of India Act (82 of 1985), S.2(i)]

Navigation. The science or art of conducting ships or aircraft from one place to another; the method of determining position, course and distance travelled over the surface of the earth by the principles of geometry and astronomy and other devices. [Inland Vessels Act (1 of 1917), S. 52(2)(j)].

Navigational tools. Allow the user to surf the Web. Microsoft Internet Explorer and Netscape Navigator are two popular examples. (*Cyber Law*)

Navy. A regularly organised and maintained naval force. [Indian Evidence Act (1 of 1872), S. 57(3)].

Nazul and Milkiyat Sarkar. 'Nazul' and 'Milkiyat Sarkar' means land which is the property of Government and which—

(a) is not included in a holding in a village;

(b) is not recorded as banjar, scrub jungle, hills and rocks, rivers, village forest or Government forest;

(c) is not recorded as village roads, gothan, grazing land, abadi and pastures;

(d) is not reserved for any communal purpose for the nistar of village; and

(e) is not service land; falls under two classes viz. 'nazul' and 'milkiyat sarkar'. Nazul includes such government land as is used either for building purposes or purposes of public convenience such as markets, or recreation grounds or which is likely to be used for such purposes in future. Government land in the occupation or on the books of a department of the State Government or of the Central Government are not to be excluded from the classification and will be recorded as 'nazul' or 'milkiyat sarkar', as the case may be. In brief, it may be stated that 'nazul' is that land which has a site value as opposed to an agricultural value. [M.P. Land Revenue Circular, Part IV as cited in *Collector, District Gwalior v. Cine Exhibitors Private Limited,* (2012) 4 SCC 441, para 18].

Ne curia deficeret in justitia exhibenda. Nor should the Court be deficient in showing justice.

Ne dominia rerum sint incerta, neve lites sint perpetuae. (*Lat.*) Lest the ownership of things should remain uncertain, or lawsuits never come to an end.

Ne fictio plus valeat in casu ficto quam veritas in casu vero. (*Lat.*) A fiction is of no more value in a fictitious case than truth in a real case.

Ne quaere litem cum licet figere. Seek not a law suit when you can escape it.

Ne quid in loco publico vel itinere fiat. Nothing shall be done (put or erected) in a public place or way.

Ne seipsum praecipites in discriminem. (*Max-im*) Judge not too hastily.

Near. In close proximity; at a short distance. [CrPC 1973 (2 of 1974), S. 40(1)(e)].

Near relative. Means spouse, son, daughter, father, mother, brother or sister. [Transplantation of Human-Organs Act (42 of 1994), S. 2(i)]

In this section, "near relative" means a parent, spouse, lineal descendant, brother or sister. [(w. e. f. 1-7-2024) Bharatiya Nagarik Suraksha Sanhita, 2023 (46 of 2023), S. 435, *Explanation*]

Nec vi, nec clam, nec precario. It means, peaceful, open and continuous. [*Tribhuvanshankar v. Amrutlal,* (2014) 2 SCC 788, para 27].

Necessaries. Items that cannot be done without.

Those necessaries which a husband is bound to furnish his wife are described in general as such articles of food or apparel or medicine, or such medical attendance and nursing, or such private means of locomotion or private habitation of furniture, or such provision for or protection in society, and the like, as a husband, considering his ability and standing, ought to furnish the wife for her sustenance and the preservation of her health and comfort.

Things which are indispensable to living, such as food, shelter and clothing.

Necessary. Indispensable, requisite; indispensably requisite, useful, incidental or conducive; essential; unavoidable; impossible to be otherwise; not to be avoided; inevitable; (*Ame. Cyc.; Webster Cen. Dic.*)

That cannot be done without.

Necessary and Expedient. "Necessary" and "Expedient". The term "necessary" means what is indispensable, needful, essential. The term has a precise meaning and connotation and there is nothing vague or nebulous about it. The term "expedient" has no doubt a wide ambit and gives large scope to the exercise of power. But this expression has also a recognized connotation in the eye of law. The dictionary meaning of the term "expedient" that would in the context in which it is used and which a most fitting is "useful for effecting a desired result; fit or suitable for the purpose", *Jayantilal Parshottamdas Kapali* v. *State of Gujarat,* (1970) 11 Guj LR 403 **as referred to** in *R.P. Kapoor* v. *Charity Commissioner, Maharashtra State,* AIR 1989 Bom 274, 280.

Necessary easement. One which is necessary for the enjoyment of the property as it stood at the time when such property was acquired under the title in virtue of which the easement is claimed. [Indian Easements Act (5 of 1882), S. 13].

Necessary expenses. The term "necessary expenses", in a statute providing that a town may raise and expend money for the support of schools, and for all necessary expenses arising in the town, includes the expense of a suit against the agents or servants of a town, in which its interests are directly involved.

Necessary for disposal of suit. The use of this language in this Article can only mean that the question involved must be such that it is not possible to dispose of the suit without determining the constitutional question raised. *Faqir Chand Agarwal* v. *Bhagwanti,* AIR 1958 Punj 287, 288. [Constitution of India, Art. 228]

Necessary implication. "Necessary implication" is that which leaves no room to doubt. It is not an implication upon conjecture.

The requisite process of involving or fact of being in some condition *etc.* [CPC (5 of 1908), O. VIII, R. 5(1)].

The phrase "necessary implication" as applied in the law of statutory construction, means an implication that is absolutely necessary and unavoidable.

Necessary means. "Means necessary to the end," signifies any means calculated to produce the end, and is not confined to those single means without which the end would be entirely unobtainable.

Necessary parties. "Necessary parties" are parties whose presence is essential and in whose absence no effective decree can at all be passed. *U.P.* v. *Atiga,* AIR 1941 FC 16. [CPC (5 of 1908), O. I, R. 9]

Necessary party. To an action is one without whose presence a substantial decree cannot be made.

A necessary party is the person who ought to be joined as party to the suit and in whose absence an effective decree cannot be passed by the court. [*Vidur Impex and Traders Private Limited v. Tosh Apartment Private Limited*, (2012) 8 SCC 384, para 36.2].

A party without impleading whom a claim cannot be legally settled by Court. [CPC (5 of 1908), O. XXXII, R. 13(1)].

Where two persons were parties in proceedings before Commissioner as well as the Board of Revenue and they succeeded in the said proceedings and the orders of the said tribunal were in their favour, it would be against all principles of natural justice to make an order adverse to them behind their back, and any order so made could not be an effective one. They were, therefore, necessary parties before the High Court. *Udit Narain Singh Malpaharia* v. *Addl. Member, Board of Revenue, Bihar,* AIR 1963 SC 786, 790).

A party without whose presence no effective or complete adjudication of the dispute can be made and no relief can be granted, is a necessary party. (*Aliji Momonji & Co.* v. *Lalji Mavji,* AIR 1997 SC 64. [CPC (5 of 1908), O. I, R. 10]

Necessary party and proper party. (Distinction) A failure to join any party does not on that account alone entail the dismissal of a suit by virtue of O.I, R. 9. There is a distinction between the non-joinder of a necessary party and that of a proper party. A party is necessary for the purposes of a litigation when in his absence the Court cannot pass an effective decree at all and a party is proper whose presence would assist the Court in adjudication of the controversy. *Dhan Singh Yadav* v. *Badri Prasad,* MLJ : QD (1961-1965) Vol I C1218 : ILR (1963) 13 Raj 668 : AIR 1963 Raj 198 [CPC (5 of 1908), O.I, Rr. 9 and 10]

Necessary repair. Such repairs by a lessee as are necessary for the use of the leased premises by the tenant for the purposes for which they were leased. (*Ballentine's Law Dictionary, 3rd Edn.*)

Necessitas excusat aut extenuat delictum in capitalibus, quod non operatur idem in civilibus. (*Lat.*) (Bacon Max. Reg. 25) Necessity excuses or extenuates delinquency in capital cases, which could not operate the same in civil cases.

Necessitas facit licitum quod alias non est licitum. (*Maxim*) Necessity makes that lawful which otherwise is not lawful. (*Morgan*)

Necessitas inducit privilegium. (*Lat.*) Necessity introduces privilege; or necessity brings the privilege into play.

Necessitas non habet legem. (*Maxim*) Necessity knows no law.

Necessitas publica major est quam privata. (*Maxim*) Public necessity is greater than private.

Necessitas quod cogit defendit. (*Lat.*) (Hale P.C. 54) Necessity defends what it compels.

Necessitas sub lege non continetur quia quod alias non est licitum necessitas facit licitum. Necessity is not restrained by law; since what otherwise is not lawful necessity makes lawful.

Necessitate precepti; sed non necessitate medii. (*Lat.*) Consent is necessary in the case of a contract executory, as an act of obedience to the law; but not essential to the validity of an executed contract.

Necessities, necessaries. *Necessity* is the mode or state of circumstances or the thing which circumstances render necessary; the *necessary* is that which is absolutely and unconditionally necessary.

Necessities of life. Things that are indispensable to the living (an infant's necessities include food, shelter, and clothing).

Necessity. Irresistible force; inevitable consequence; that which is essentially requisite; great or urgent public convenience.

Necessity may be an excuse for committing what otherwise would be a criminal offence.

'Need' and **'require'.** Both denote a certain degree of want with a thrust within demanding fulfilment. *Shanti Sarup Gupta* v. *Mahesh Chand Gupta,* AIR 1999 SC 2507.

Needlessly. Without necessity; unnecessarily; wantonly; used in a statute with reference to mutilating or killing an animal, the term has been construed to mean without any useful motive without serving any useful purpose. Without any necessity. [Indian Evidence Act (1 of 1872), S. 152].

Needs. The word 'needs' suggests that there has to be a necessity for a decision by the Supreme Court on the question, and such a necessity can be said to exist when, for instance, two views are possible regarding the question and the High Court takes one of the said views. Such a necessity can also be said to exist when a different view has been expressed by another High Court. (*State Bank of India* v. *Shri N. Sundara Money,* AIR 1976 SC 1111).

Nefarium est per formulas legis laqueos innectere innocentibus. It is infamous to lay snares for the innocent through forms of law.

Negatio destruit negationem, et ambo faciunt affirmativum. (*Lat.*) (Co. Litt. 146b) A negative destroys a negative, and both make an affirmative.

Negatio duplex est affirmatio. A double negative is an affirmative.

Negatio non potest probari. (*Maxim*) Denial cannot be proved. (*Morgan*)

Negative. *As an adjective*, a word implying denial, negation, or difference. *As a noun*, a term used in photography to designate the original plate, made sensitive by chemicals, which is printed under the sunlight or other suitable artificial light by the camera.

That expresses or implies or contains negation [CPC (5 of 1908), O. XIV, R. 6]; to refuse to accept; to demonstrate the falsity of; to contradict [Sale of

Goods Act (3 of 1930), S. 62]; photographic image that reproduces the bright parts of the photographed subject as dark areas and the dark parts as light areas, that is usually on a transparent material on which this image is produced. [Copyright Act (14 of 1957), S. 2(t)].

Negative averment. (*In pleading*) An agreement in some of the pleadings in a case in which a negative is asserted.

Negative covenant. The term "negative covenant", and not the word "condition", is correctly used to designate a provision in a deed that the premises thereby conveyed are not to be used for saloon purposes

Negative effective capital. For the purposes of Schedule V of Companies Act of 2013, 'negative effective capital' means the effective capital which is calculated in accordance with the provisions contained in *Explanation I* to section IV of Part II of Schedule V of the Companies Act, 2013 (18 of 2013) is less than zero. [*Explanation V* to section IV of Part II of Schedule V of the Companies Act, 2013 (18 of 2013)]

Negative pregnant. A negative pregnant is such a form of negative expression as may imply or carry with it an affirmative. A negative pregnant involves and admits of an affirmative implication at least an implication of some kind favourable to the adverse party.

Neglect. A failure to do what is required; omission; forbearance to do anything that can be done or that requires to be done; the omission to do or perform some work, duty or act; the omission or disregard of some duty; the omission from carelessness to do something that can be done and that ought to be done; negligence. Neglect to do a thing means to omit to do a duty which the party is able to do.

The word 'neglects' is wide enough to cover erosion of the kind indulged in by the petitioner. (It certainly cannot mean that a person on whom a notice has been served can only be prosecuted if he fails to any reply at all and that any sort of reply to the notice, however inadequate or evasive, is sufficient to avert the prosecution for failure to comply with the terms of the notice). *Pirthi Raj* v. *State,* AIR 1958 Punj 396, 397. [Cantonments Act (2 of 1924), S. 103(2)].

To disregard; to pay little or no attention to; to fail to perform, render, discharge (a duty); to take (a precaution). [TP Act (4 of 1882), S. 27, ill.(a)].

Neglected child. "NEGLECTED CHILD" means a child who—

(i) is found begging; or

(ii) is found without having any home or settled place of abode or any ostensible means of subsistence or is found destitute, whether he is an orphan or not; or

(iii) has a parent or guardian who is unfit or unable to exercise or does not exercise proper care and control over the child; or

(iv) lives in a brothel or with a prostitute or frequently goes to any place used for the purpose of prostitution, or is found to associate with any prostitute or any other person who leads an immoral, drunken or depraved life. [Children Act (60 of 1960), S. 2(l)]

The words "neglected child" has been defined to mean any child who for any reason is destitute or homeless or abandoned, or dependent upon the public for support, or has not proper parental care or guardianship, or who habitually begs or receives alms, or who is found living in any house of ill-fame or with any vicious or disreputable persons, or whose home by reason of neglect, cruelty, or depravity on the part of its parents, guardian, or other person, in whose care it may be, is an unfit place for such child.

Neglected juvenile. The expression 'neglected juvenile' occurring in S. 2(1) of the Act would include 'child prostitutes' or 'children of prostitutes'. *Gaurav Jain* v. *Union of India,* AIR 1997 SC 3021. [Juvenile Justice Act (53 of 1986), S. 2(1)]

Neglects or refuses to maintain. The mere fact of a second marriage cannot *ipso facto* establish 'such neglect or refusal' within the meaning of sub-sec. (1) of S. 125 CrPC 1973 (2 of 1974) for a man may marry a second time and still not refuse to maintain his first wife. *S. Belarani Chatterjee* v. *Bhupal Chandra Chatterjee,* AIR 1956 Cal 134, 135. [CrPC 1973 (2 of 1974), S. 125(1)]

Neglects to pay. The expression "neglects to pay the sum demanded" in Section 434 (1)(a) is not equivalent to the word "omitted". Neglect to pay a debt on demand is omission to pay without reasonable cause. When a debt is *bona fidely* disputed by the debtor, there is no neglect to pay. *Yashodan Chit Fund Pvt. Ltd., In re,* (1980) 50 Com Cases 356 (Bom). [Companies Act (1 of 1956), S. 434(1)(a)].

Negligence. Negligence in law signifies a coming short of the performance of duty.

Want of attention to what ought to be done or looked after; lack of proper care in doing something; omission to do something which a reasonable man, guided upon the considerations which ordinarily regulate the conduct of human affairs, would do, or doing something which a prudent and reasonable man would not do. [IPC (45 of 1860), S. 81, ill.(a)].

Duties owned to patient. A person who holds himself out as ready to give medical advice or treatment impliedly undertakes that he is possessed of skill and knowledge for the purpose. Such a person, whether he is a registered medical practitioner or not, who is consulted by a patient, owes him certain duties, namely, a duty of care in deciding whether to undertake the case; a duty of care in deciding what treatment to give; and a duty of care in his administration of that treatment. A breach of any of these duties will support an action for negligence by the patient. [Halsbury's Laws of England, 4th Edn., Vol. 26, pages 17- 18 as cited in *P.B. Desai v. State of Maharashtra*, (2013) 15 SCC 481, para 41].

Negligence would mean careless conduct in commission or omission of an act connoting duty, breach and damage suffered by a person to whom the plaintiff owes a duty of care, is crucial to understand the nature and scope of tort of negligence. (*Rajkot Municipal Corporation* v. *Manjulben Jayantilal Nakum,* 1997 (9) SCC 552 : JT 1997 (1) SC 580).

The expression 'negligence' means breach of a legal duty to care. *Pramod kumar Rasikbhai Jhaveri* v. *Karmasey Kunvargi Tak,* (2002) 6 SCC 455, para 8 : AIR 2002 SC 2864.

The authors give there meanings to negligence in forensic speech viz. (i) in referring to a state of mind, when it is distinguished in particular from intention; (ii) in describing conduct of a careless type; and (iii) as the breach of a duty to take care imposed by either common law or statute. The three meanings are then explained thus:

The first meaning: Negligence as a state of mind can be contrasted with intention. An act is intentional when is purposeful and done with the desire or object of producing a particular result. In contrast, negligence in the present sense arises where someone either fails to consider a risk of particular action, or having considered it, fails to give the risk appropriate weight.

The second meaning: Negligence can also be used as a way to characterize conduct, although such a use may lead to imprecision when considering negligence as a tort. Careless conduct does not necessarily give rise to breach of a duty of care, the defining characteristic to the tort of negligence. The extent of a duty of care and the standard of care required in performance of that duty are both relevant in considering whether, on any given facts conduct which can be characterized as careless, it actionable in law.

The Third meaning: The third meaning of negligence, and the one with which this volume is principally concerned, is conduct which, objectively considered, amounts to breach of a duty to take care. [Charlsworth and Percy on Negligence (12th Edn.) as cited in *Sushil Ansal v. State*, (2014) 6 SCC 173, para 52].

The authors set out the following four separate requirements of the tort of negligence:

"(1) the existence in law of a duty of care situation i.e., one in which the laws attaches liability to carelessness. There has to be recognition by law that the careless infliction of the kind of damages in suit on the class of person to which the claimant belongs by the class of person to which the defendant belongs is actionable;

(2) breach of the duty of care by the defendant i.e., that it failed to measure up to the standard set by law;

(3) a casual connection between the defendant's careless conduct and the damage;

(4) that the particular kind of damage to the particular claimant is not so unforeseeable as to be too remote." [Clerk & Lindsell on Torts (18th Edn.) as cited in *Sushil Ansal v. State*, (2014) 6 SCC 173, para 53].

'Negligence' means either subjectively a careless state of mind, or objectively careless conduct. It is not an absolute term but is a relative one; it is rather a comparative term. In determining whether negligence exists in a particular case, all the attending and surrounding facts and circumstances have to be taken into account. *Municipal Corpn. of Greater Bombay* v. *Laxman Iyer,* (2003) 8 SCC 731, para 6.

A negligence could be composite or contributory. "Negligence" does not always mean absolute carelessness, but want of such a degree of care as is required in particular circumstances. "Negligence" is failure to observe, for the protection of the interests of another person, the degree of care , precaution and vigilance which the circumstances justly demand, whereby such other person suffers injury. [*Ramlila Maidan Incident, In Re*, (2012) 5 SCC 1, para 229].

Negligence is "the absence of proper care, caution and diligence; of such care, caution and diligence, as under the circumstances reasonable and ordinary prudence would require to be exercised."

"Negligence" means omission to do something which a reasonable and prudent person guided by the consideration which ordinarily regulate human affairs would do or doing something which a prudent and reasonable person guided by similar consideration would not do. Negligence is not an absolute term but is a relative one; it is rather a comparative term. [*Ravi Kapoor v. State of Rajasthan*, (2012) 9 SCC 284, para 11].

Negligence, Actionable. The act or omission amounting to want of ordinary care on the part of the complaining party which concurring with defendant's negligence, is proximate cause of injury.

CONTRIBUTORY NEGLIGENCE. "Negligence by itself affects no one with liability. Where negligence produces no damage to others it is not actionable. A man has a right to be as negligent as he pleases, provided only that in being negligent he does not interfere with the rights of other people. The corollary of this is that if one man sees another guilty of negligence he cannot stand upon his abstract rights, and, having sustained damage through ignoring the manifest consequences of the other's action fix the consequences of his persistency on him. He is bound, so far as he can, to avoid the probability of damage brought into being by the negligent act of the other. If he does not do what he can in this direction, he is guilty of *contributory negligence,* and must himself bear the consequences of his want of care. *Contributory negligence,* then, is negligence in not avoiding the consequences arising from the negligence of some other persons, when means and opportunity are afforded to do so." (See *per* COLERIDGE, J., *Clayards* v. *Dethick,* (1848) 12 QB 439, at 445; 76 RR 305.)

Negligence and gross negligence. The expression 'negligence and gross negligence' in the context of

Order XXXII, R. 7 of the Code have to be appreciated in the context of diligence and non diligence of the guardian. [*Alaparthi Satyasi* v. *Alaparthi Subba Rao,* AIR 2007 (NOC) 1926 (AP)]. [CPC (5 of 1908), O. XXXII, R. 7]

"Negligence" and "rashness". There is a clear distinction between "negligence" and "rashness" (and that distinction is contemplated even by S. 279, IPC (45 of 1860). In the case of negligence, "the party does not do an act which he was bound to do because he adverts not to do it." In the case of rashness, the party does an act and breaks a positive duty. He thinks of the provable mischief, but in consequence of a missupposition begotten by insufficient advertence, he assumes that the mischief will not ensue in the given instance or case. The radical idea denoted is always this. The "party runs a risk of which he is conscious". Even in ordinary parlance, "negligence" connotes want of proper care and "rashness", conveys the idea of recklessness or the doing of an act without due consideration. Where the charge against the accused is not of negligent driving but of rash driving, all that is to be determined is whether the accused was proceeding at a reckless speed and if so whether that speed was such as to endanger human life or to be likely to cause hurt or injury to any other person.

One of the ingredients is that there must be a duty to take care. The standard of care that the law enjoins is governed by the knowledge and skill that the office or occupation requires, by the magnitude of the task and by gravity of the consequences that are likely to ensue if the requisite degree of care is not exercised. *Kedarnath* v. *State of U.P.,* AIR 1965 All 233, 236. [IPC (45 of 1860), S. 405]

NEGLIGENCE AND CONTRIBUTORY NEGLIGENCE. A clear distinction exists between negligence and contributory negligence. Negligence is contributory when and only when, it directly and proximately induces the injury in whole or in part.

Negligence by railway. There is an obligation on the part of the railway company or administration to ensure that whenever the railway passes over a thoroughfare adequate warning should be given to the public of the passing of the trains at the time they pass so that accidents may be avoided. This duty need not necessarily be a statutory duty. It is implied and inherent in the functions to be discharged by the Railway Administration in the matter of running their railways. If such a warning or notice is not given, it is considered as negligence by Railway. *Swarnalata* v. *UOI,* AIR 1963 Ass 117, 122.

Negligence per se. The omission to do what the law requires, or the failure to do anything in a manner prescribed by law, is negligence *per se*.

Negligent. Careless, heedless, want of attention.

The term "negligent" imports a want of such attention to the nature or probable consequences of the act or omission as a prudent man ordinarily bestows in acting in his own concerns.

Negligent entrustment. Entrusting dangerous article to another whom lender knows, or should know, is likely to use it in a manner involving unreasonable risk of harm to others.

Negligent escape. An escape occurring without the consent of but through the carelessness of, the custodian.

Negligent homicide. Homicide which results from the careless performance of a legal or illegal act in which the danger of death is apparent.

Negligently. Without exercising the degree of care which a person of ordinary sense and prudence, under like circumstances, and in the performance of a like act, would have exercised.

In a negligent manner. [General Clauses Act (10 of 1897, S. 3(22)].

Negotiability. "Negotiability" is a technical term, derived from the usage of merchants and bankers in transferring, primarily, bills of exchange, and afterwards promissory notes.

Negotiable. Capable of being transferred by assignment, sale indorsement, or delivery; capable of being passed by assignment or endorsement.

Capable of being negotiated, transferable or assignable in the course of business from one person to another. [TP Act (4 of 1882), S. 137].

Negotiable air way bill. Any written securities which may be transferred by indorsement and delivery or by delivery merely, so as to vest in the indorsee the legal title and thus enable him to sue thereon in his own name. [Indian Carriage by Air Act (69 of 1972), Item 15(3), 2nd Sch.].

Negotiable instrument. (1) "A 'negotiable instrument' means a promissory note, bills of exchange or cheque payable either to order or to bearer.

Explanation (*I*)—A promissory note, bill of exchange or cheque is payable to order which is expressed to be so payable or which is expressed to be payable to a particular person, and does not contain words prohibiting transfer or indicating an intention that it shall not be transferable.

Explanation (*II*).—A promissory note, bill of exchange or cheque is payable to bearer which is expressed to be so payable or on which the only or last indorsement is an indorsement in blank.

Explanation (*III*),—Where a promissory note, bill of exchange or cheque, either originally or by indorsement, is expressed to be payable to the order of a specified person, and not to him or his order, it is nevertheless payable to him or his order at his option.

(2) A negotiable instrument may be made payable to two or more payees jointly, or it may be made payable in the alternative to one of two, or one or some of several payees." [Negotiable Instruments Act (26 of 1881), S. 13]

Where an Instrument, is by the custom of the trade, transferable, like cash, by delivery, and is also capable of being sued upon by the person holding it *pro tempore*, there it is entitled to the name of a Negotiable Instrument, and the property in it passes to a *bona fide* transferee for value.

Negotiable multimodal transport document. Means a multi-modal transport document which is—

(i) made out to order or to bearer; or

(ii) made out to order and is transferable by endorsement; or

(iii) made out to bearer and is transferable without endorsement. [Multi-modal Transportation of Goods Act (28 of 1993), S. 2(n)]

Negotiate. To effect something; to conclude by bargain, treaty, or agreement; to sell, to pass; to transfer for a valuable consideration.

To transfer for value by delivery or indorsement. [IPC (45 of 1860), S. 464, *Expln.* 1, ill.(b)]; to hold intercourse; to bargain or trade; to conduct communications or conferences.

Negotiating State. Means a state which took part in the drawing up and adoption of the text of the treaty. [Vienna Convention on the Law of Treaties, 1969, Art. 2(e)]

Negotiation. "When a promissory note, bill of exchange or cheque is transferred to any person, so as to constitute that person the holder thereof, the instrument is said to be negotiated." [Negotiable Instruments Act (26 of 1881), S. 14].

A business transaction; the action of negotiating; the process of being negotiated. [Negotiable Instruments Act (26 of 1881), S. 48].

Negotiation of a bill. The transfer of a bill of exchange from one person to another so that the transferee becomes the holder.

Neighbouring residential area. Means a neighbouring area declared as such by the management of the Pre-School Centre. [Maharashtra Pre-School (Regulation of Admission) Act, 1996 (29 of 1997), S. 2(e)]

Nullus commodum capere potest de injuria sua propria. (*Lat.*) No man can take advantage of his own, wrong is one of the salient tenets of equity.

Nemine contra dicente. No one dissenting. The phrase is used to denote the unanimous decision of a Court or a deliberative body.

Neminem laedit qui jure suo utitur. (*Maxim*) He who stands on his own rights injures no one.

Neminem oportet esse sapientiorem legibus. (*Lat.*) (Co. Litt. 97b) No man need be wise than the laws.

Nemini in alium plus quam licet concessum est legibus. More is allowed to no one against another, than is conceded by the laws.

Nemo. No one; nobody.

Nemo admittendus est inhabilitare seipsum. (*Lat.*) Nobody is to be admitted to incapacity himself.

Nemo agit in seipsum. (*Lat.*) (Jenk. Cent. 40) No man acts against himself.

Nemo aliquam partem recte intelligre potest antequam totum perlegit. No one can properly understand a part until he has read the whole.

Nemo allegans suam turpitudinem audiendus est. (*Maxim*) No one alleging his own baseness is to be heard.

Father made a gift in favour of his minor son. During the donee's lifetime the donor did or said nothing to suggest that the gift was fictitious. On the contrary, all his acts and statements tended to show that he intended to make a real gift. But when the minor donee died, it became convenient to the donor to ignore the gift and to claim that he remained all along owner of the estate and that the gift was meant only to enable the Court of Wards to take charge of the property. He also got a deed of relinquishment executed by the widow of the donee in his favour reciting that the gift in her husband's favour was fictitious. *Held*, that the maxim *nemo allegans turpitudinem suam est audiendus* would be applicable, and the donor or his representatives cannot be allowed to take advantage of his own wrong-doing and deny that the gift was fictitious.

When the Plaintiff entered into an illegal contract and he had no knowledge of the illegality of the contract, when he entered into the contract, relief cannot be denied to the plaintiff on the basis of the maxim—'*Nemo allegan sturpitudinam suam est andiendus*'.

Nemo allegans turpitudinam quam audiendus est. The maxim '*Nemo allegans turpitudinam quan andiendus est*' (a person who has polluted his hands by being a party or privy to a fraudulent transaction shall not be allowed to approach the fountain of justice with his own infamy on his lips and obtain relief on the strength of such a transaction), does not apply to a transaction which is based on fraud committed by the plaintiff.

Nemo bis punitur pro eodem delicto. (*Maxim*) No man is punished twice for the same offence.

Nemo bis vexari debet pro eadem causa. No man should be harassed twice for the same offence.

Nemo cogitationis poenam patitur. (*Maxim*) No one suffers punishment on account of his thoughts.

Nemo cogitur rem suam vendere etiam justo pretio. (*Maxim*) No man is compelled to sell his own property, even for a just price.

Nemo commodum capere potest de injuria sua propria. No one can take an advantage from his own injury. (*Latin for Lawyers*)

Nemo condemnari debet inauditus nec summonitus. (*Maxim*) No one should be condemned unheard, or unsummoned.

Nemo contra factum suum venire potest. (*Maxim*) No one can come against his own deed.

This is the doctrine of estoppel as applied to matter contained in a valid sealed instrument. Where a fact is stated in a deed in such a way as to make it the statement of a party to the deed that party will be precluded from afterwards denying, in an action brought upon that instrument, the fact so recited. (*Latin for Lawyers*)

Nemo damnum facit nisi qui id fecit quod facere jus non habet. (*Maxim*) No one does damage, unless he is doing what he has no right to do.

Nemo dat quid non habet. (*Maxim*) No one can give who does not possess.

No man can transfer better title than he himself has.

No one gives what he has not got. [*State of A.P. v. Star Bone Mills and Fertiliser Company*, (2013) 9 SCC 319, para 7].

The principle of this maxim is contained in S. 27, Sale of Goods Act (3 of 1930). *Rameshwar* v. *Tara Singh*, AIR 1958 Raj 269, 273.

Applying the maxim the Apex Court held that the vendee could not acquire a valid title on the basis of sale deed executed by the vendor, who acquired a citizenship of Pakistan who had no right, title or interest in the land to obtain *bhumidhari* right on demise of his mother due to losing citizenship of India. *Sewa Ram* v. *Union of India,* (1997) 5 SCC 166, para 3 : AIR 1997 SC 2620.

Nemo de domo sua extrahi debet. No one can be forcibly taken from his own house.

Nemo debet aliena jactura locupletari. (*Maxim*) No one ought to gain by anothers loss.

Nemo debet bis puniri pro uno delicto. No one should be punished twice for one fault.

'No one ought to be punished twice for one offence'. [Maqbool Hussain v. State of Bombay, AIR 1953 SC 325 : 1953 Cri LJ 1432 as cited in *Sangeetaben Mahendrabhai Patel v. State of Gujrat*, (2012) 7 SCC 621, para 14].

Nemo debet bis vexari pro eadem causa. No person should be twice vexed for the same offence.

The principle based on this maxim is provided in Section 300 of the code and applying the same the Apex Court held that a second trial against the same accused on the same facts even for a different offence if a different charge against him for such offence could have been made under Section 221(1) of the code or he could have been convicted for such other offence under Section 221(2) of the code, is debarred. *State* v. *Nalini,* (1999) 5 SCC 253, para 236 : AIR 1999 SC 2640. [CrPC, 1973 (2 of 1974), Ss. 300, 221(1) & (2)]

No one ought to be vexed twice if it appears to the court that it is for one and the same cause. [Union of India v. P.D. Yadav, (2002) 1 SCC 405 : (2002) SCC (L&S) 149, para 25 as cited in *Sangeetaben Mahendrabhai Patel v. State of Gujarat*, (2012) 7 SCC 621, para 21].

No man shall be put in jeopardy twice for one and the same offence. [*State (NCT of Delhi) v. Sanjay*, (2014) 9 SCC 772, para 50].

Nemo debet bis vexari, si constat curiae quod sit pro una et eadem causa. (*Lat.*) (5 Rep. 61) No one should be twice punished, if it appear to the Court that it is for one and the same cause." (*Peloubet's Leg. Max.*; 5 Coke 61; *Broom Leg. Max.* 294)

Nemo debet esse judex in causa propria sua. HALSBURY says : This principle "*nemo debet esse judex in causa propria sua*" precludes a justice, who is interested in the subject matter of a dispute, from acting as a justice therein. (Halsbury's Laws of England, Vol. XXI, p. 535, para 952).

This principle applies to all tribunals and bodies which are given jurisdiction to determine judicially the rights of parties. *Manak Lal* v. *Prem Chand Singhvi*, AIR 1957 SC 425, 429.

Nemo debet esse judex in propria causa. No one should be a judge in his own cause.

The maxim is not applicable to a case where Deputy Registrar of Society passes an order superseding the Committee of Management even though he is a member of the committee in his capacity as the Director of the Co-operative Society.

Nemo debet esse testis in sua propria causa. (*Maxim*) No one ought to be a witness in his own cause.

Nemo debet essee judex in propria causa . No one should be a judge in his own cause.

This principle precludes a justice, who is interested in the subject matter of a dispute, from acting as a justice therein.

This principle applies to all tribunals and bodies which are given jurisdiction to determine judicially the rights of parties. *Manak Lal* v. *Prem Chand Singhvi*, AIR 1957 SC 425, 429.

This is the underlying principle in S. 479 of CrPC 1973 (2 of 1974).

Nemo debet rem suam sine facto aut defectu suo amittere. No one should lose his property without his own act or negligence.

Nemo est cogendus quis ad substituendum. No one is compelled to substitute another in his own place.

Nemo est haeres viventis. No one is an heir to the living.

Nemo ex alterius facto praegravari debet. (*Lat.*) No man is to be burdened in consequence of another's act.

Nemo ex proprio dolo consequitur actionem. (*Lat.*) No one acquires a right of action from his own wrong.

Nemo ex suo delicto meliorem suam conditionem facere potest. (*Lat.*) No one can improve his condition by his own wrong.

Nemo firut repente turpissimus. 'No one becomes dishonest all of a sudden'. The maxim is not unexceptional but still it is a salutary guideline to judge human conduct, particularly in the field of administrative law. On the basis of maxim it was observed that the authority should not altogether ignore the reputation in which the officer was held till recently, while evaluating the materials for compulsory retirement of an employee. *M.S. Bindra*

v. *Union of India,* (1998) 7 SCC 310, para 13 : AIR 1998 SC 3058.

Nemo inauditus nec insummonitus condemnari debet, si non sit contumax. (*Lat.*) (Jenk Cent 8) No man should be condemned unheard and unsummoned, unless for contumacy.

Nemo judex in causa sua. No one should be a judge in his own cause.

Nemo jus sibi dicere potest. (*Lat.*) No one can declare the law of himself.

Nemo me impune lacessit. No one attacks me with impunity.

Nemo moriturus praesumitur mentire. No one at the point of death is presumed to lie.

A man will not meet his Maker with a lie in his mouth. [*Bhajju v. State of M.P.*, (2012) 4 SCC 327, para 11]

Applying the maxim the Apex Court observed that the dying declarations are admitted in evidence upon consideration that such declarations are made in extremity, when the maker is at the point of death and when every hope of this world is gone, when every motive to falsehood is silenced and the mind induced by the most powerful consideration to speak the truth. *Uka Ram* v. *State of Rajasthan,* (2001) 5 SCC 254, para 6 : AIR 2001 SC 1814. [Indian Evidence Act (1 of 1872), S. 32]

'Nemo plus juris tribuit quam ipse habet.' No one can bestow or grant a greater right, or a better title than he has himself. [*State of Andhra Pradesh v. Star Bone Mills and Fertiliser Company*, (2013) 9 SCC 319, para 7].

Nemo potest esse simul actor et judex. No one can be both the plaintiff and the judge at the same time.—*Ballentine.*

Nemo potest esse simul actor et judex. No one can be at once suitor and judge.

Nemo potest gladii potestam sibi vel cujus alterius coercitionis ad alium transferre. No one to whom is delegated a power of coercion can himself transfer it to another.

Nemo potest habere duas militias nec duas dignitates. No man can fill two offices or two dignities.

Nemo potest immittere in alienum. (*Lat.*) No one can throw or place anything into another's field.

Nemo potest mutare consilium suum in alterius injuriam. (*Lat.*) (D. 50, 17, 15). No one is allowed to change his own mind to the injury of another.

Nemo potest nisi quod de jure potest. (*Lat.*) No man can do anything except what he can do lawfully; or, that is not considered to be within the power of any one which he cannot lawfully perform.

Nemo potest plus juris ad alium transferre quam ipse habet. (*Co. Lit.* 309; *Wing. Max.* 56). No one can transfer a greater right to another than he himself has.

Nemo praesumitur esse immemor suae aeternae salutatis; et maxime in articulo mortis. (*Lat.*) (6 Rep. 76) No one is presumed to be forgetful of his own eternal welfare, and more particularly in the point of death.

Nemo praesumitur malus. (*Lat.*) No one is presumed to be bad.

Nemo prudens punit ut praeterita revocentur sed ut futura praeveniantur. No wise man punishes that things done, may be revoked, but that future wrongs may be prevented.

Nemo punitur pro alieno delicto. (*Lat.*) No one is to be punished for the crime of another.

Nemo repente turpissimus. No one becomes bad in an instant.

Nemo sibi esse judex vel suis jus dicere debet. (*Lat.*) No one ought to be his own judge, or the tribunal in his own affairs.

Nemo praesumitur malus. (*Maxim*) No one is presumed bad.

Nemo tenetur ad impossibilia. (*Lat.*) No one is bound to do an impossibility.

Nemo tenetur armare adversarium contra se. (*Lat.*) (Wing. 665) No one is bound to arm his adversary against himself.

Nemo tenetur divinare. (*Lat.*) (4 Rep. 28) No one is bound to know a thing before it happens.

Nemo tenetur edere instrumenta contra se. (*Lat.*) No man is bound to produce writings against himself.

Nemo tenetur informare qui nescit sed quisquis scire quod informat. No one who is ignorant of a thing is bound to give information of it, but every one is bound to know that which he gives information of.

Nemo tenetur jurare in suam turpitudinem. (*Lat.*) No one is bound to testify to his own baseness.

Nemo tenetur prodere seipsum. (*Lat.*) No one is bound to swear to the fact of his own criminality.

Nemo tenetur seipsum accusare. (*Lat.*) No man can be compelled to criminate himself.

Nemo tenetur seipsum infortunios et periculis exponere. No one is bound to expose himself to misfortunes and dangers.

Nemo unquam judicet in se. No one can ever be a judge in his own cause.

Nemo videtur fraudare eos qui sciunt et consentiunt. No one is considered as defrauding those who know and consent.

Neonatology. The branch of medicine dealing with the development of newborn children, as well as various disorders of early infancy.

Nephew. The son of a brother or sister or brother-in-law or sister-in-law. [margin, Indian Succession Act (39 of 1925), S. 46].

The words "nephews" and "nieces" apply only to children of brothers or sisters. [Indian Succession Act (39 of 1925), S. 99(*c*)].

Nephew, Great. A grandson of one's brother or sister. [Indian Succession Act (39 of 1925), S. 28, ill. (ii)].

Nervous shock. An action lies for nervous shock and bodily illness or disorder supervening on it, though the shock was caused not by the application of physical force to the body of the sufferer by the works or acts calculated to cause emotional disturbances like fear, sorrow or distress to him. Injury to health due to nervous shock is a form of bodily harm for which damages may be claimed. But for the defendant to be liable he must owe a duty to the plaintiff to take care with respect to him and the fact that the plaintiff would suffer injury from nervous shock as a result of the defendant's act must have been reasonably foreseen by him, and the plaintiff must have been within the area of potential danger.

Net. Free from all charges and deductions. "NET" is a term used among merchants to designate the quantity, amount, or value of an article or commodity after all fare and charges are deducted.

Internet, the Web. (*Cyber Law*)

After expenses, or short for the internet. (*Cyber Law*)

Net agricultural income. In relation to a person, means the total amount of agricultural income, from whatever source derived, of that person computed in accordance with the rules contained in Part IV of the First Schedule. [Finance Act (18 of 2005), S. 2(12)(c)]

Net annual income. 'NET ANNUAL INCOME' in relation to a *wakf* means the gross income thereof from all sources in a year excluding only—

(i) land revenue, cess, rates and taxes payable to the Government or any local authority; and

(ii) donations given or offerings made with a specific direction that they shall form part of the corpus of the *wakf*:

Provided that the interest or income, if any, accruing from such donations or offerings shall be taken into account in calculating the gross annual income. [Wakf Act (29 of 1954), S. 3(g)]

For the purposes of this Act, "NET ANNUAL INCOME" shall mean the gross income of the wakf from all sources, including nazars and offerings which do not amount to contributions to the corpus of the wakfs, in a year after deducting therefrom the following, namely :—

(i) the land revenue paid by it to the Government;

(ii) the rates, cesses, taxes and licence fees, paid by it to the Government or any local authority;

(iii) expenditure incurred for all or any of the following purposes, namely : —

(a) maintenance of, or repairs to, irrigation works, which shall not include the capital cost of irrigation;

(b) seeds or seedlings;

(c) manure;

(d) purchase and maintenance of agricultural implements;

(e) purchase and maintenance of cattle for cultivation;

(f) wages for ploughing, watering, sowing, transplanting, harvesting, threshing and other agricultural operations :

Provided that the total deduction in respect of an expenditure incurred under this clause shall not exceed ten per cent. of the income derived from lands belonging to the *wakf;*

(iv) expenditure on sundry repairs to rented buildings, not exceeding five per cent. of the annual rent derived therefrom, or the actual expenditure, whichever is less;

(v) sale proceeds of immovable properties or rights relating to, or arising out of immovable properties, if such proceeds are reinvested to earn income for the *wakf.* [Waqf Act (43 of 1995), S. 72(1) *Expln.*]

Net asset value. Value of a company's shares determined by dividing its net assets by the number of issued shares.

Net balance in current accounts. Shall, in relation to a banking company, mean the excess, if any, of the aggregate of the credit balances in current account maintained by that banking company with the State Bank of India or a subsidiary bank or a corresponding new bank over the aggregate of the credit balance in current account held by the said banks with such banking company. [Banking Regulation (10 of 1949), S. 18(1) *Expln.* (c)]

Net Book Value. Means—

(a) in the case of hire purchase asset, the aggregate of over-due and future instalments receivable, as reduced by the balance of unmatured finance charges, and further reduced by the provisions made as per paragraph 8(2)(i) of the RBI Directions relating to Prudential Norms;

(b) in the case of leased asset, aggregate of capital portion of overdue lease rentals accounted as receivable and depreciated book value of the lease asset as adjusted by the balance of lease adjustment account. [Non-Banking Financial Companies Prudential Norms (Reserve Bank) Directions, 1998, para 2(1)(xi)]

Net consideration. "NET CONSIDERATION" means the full value of the consideration received or accruing as a result of the transfer of the capital asset as reduced by any expenditure incurred wholly and exclusively in connection with such transfer. [Income-tax Act (43 of 1961), S. 11 (1A) *Expln.* (III)]

For the purpose of this action; "NET CONSIDERATION", in relation to the transfer of a capital asset, means the full value of the consideration received or accruing as a result of the transfer of the capital asset as reduced by the expenditure incurred wholly and exclusively in connection with such transfer. [Income-tax Act (43 of 1961), S. 54EA(3) *Expln.* (b)] [Also see Income-tax Act 1961 *Explanation* to S. 54F and S. 54GB(6)(c) of the Income-tax Act, 1961 (43 of 1961) as inserted (w.e.f. 1-4-2013) by the Finance Act, 2012]

Net cost. The cost of an item, arrived at by subtracting any financial gain from the total cost.

Net deposit. Means sixty per cent. of the amount of deposit made by any person with the National Housing Bank in accordance with the scheme. [Voluntary Deposits (Immunities and Exemptions) Act (47 of 1991), S. 2(e)]

Net income. Income of a business deducting the expense only. Profits or income of a business after deducting all necessary charges and expenses.

"NET INCOME," as used when speaking of the net income of an estate, is equivalent to rents, profits, or income.

"NET INCOME" in the Indian Divorce Act (4 of 1869), S. 36, has its ordinary meaning—the amount of income minus deductions on account of income-tax, charges for pension fund and the like.

Net income from property. Net income is what remains out of gross income after deducting all ordinary and necessary expenditure incurred in earning it and keeping the same.

Net lease rentals. 'NET LEASE RENTALS' mean gross lease rentals as adjusted by the lease adjustment account debited/credited to the profit and loss account and as reduced by depreciation at the rate applicable under Schedule XIV of the companies Act, 1956 (1 of 1956). [Non-Banking Financial Companies Prudential Norms (Reserve Bank) Directions, 1998, para 3]

Net loss is the excess of all expenses and losses over all revenues and gains.

Net owned fund. Means—

the aggregate of the paid-up equity capital and free reserves as disclosed in the latest balance-sheet of the housing finance institution after deducting therefrom—

(i) accumulated balance of loss;

(ii) deferred revenue expenditure; and

(iii) other intangible assets. [National Housing Bank Act (53 of 1987), S. 29A *Expln.* (1)]

Net owned funds. Means the aggregate of paid up equity share capital and free reserves as reduced by accumulated losses and intangible assets appearing in the last audited balance sheet: *Provided* that the amount representing the proceeds of issue of preference shares shall not be included for calculating Net Owned Funds. [R. 3(1)(d) of the Nidhi Rules, 2014]

Net premium. "NET PREMIUMS" means the premiums taken credit for in the valuation in connection with which any statement is prepared. [Insurance Act (4 of 1938), Sch. Fifth, Part I(5) Now Schedule 5 has been omitted by Act 42 of 2002 (w.e.f. 23-9-2002)].

"NET PREMIUMS" means as respects any valuation the premium taken credit for in the valuation. [Insurance Act (4 of 1938), Sch. Fourth, Part I, (5) Now Schedule 5 has been omitted by Act 42 of 2002 (w.e.f. 23-9-2002)].

Net premium income. Means the amount of premium received as reduced by the amount of reinsurance premium paid during the relevant previous year. [Income-tax Rules, 1962, R. 6E *Expln. (a)*]

Net present value. Net present value means the real value of a receipt or payment in future, which will be deflated because of interest.

Net price. The correct price after deducting all discounts.

Net proceeds. The sum actually received after making all deductions; what remains of the gross proceeds after all expense and loss incurred in realizing them are deducted.

The net proceeds of a sale of land is what remains of the gross proceeds after paying the expenses of the sale.

Proceeds free from all charges and deductions. [O. XXXIV, rule 6, CPC (5 of 1908)

Net profits. In computing the net profits of a company in any financial year for the purpose of section 197,—(a) credit shall be given for the sums specified in sub-section (2), and credit shall not be given for those specified in sub-section (3); and (b) the sums specified in sub-section (4) shall be deducted, and those specified in sub-section (5) shall not be deducted. [Companies Act (18 of 2013), section 198(1)]

Profits after all charges and expenses have been deducted; the gain that accrues on an investment after deducting the loss and expenses of the business; the gain which accrues on an investment after deducting expenses and losses.

"Net profits" mean the divisible profits and are to be ascertained after deduction of excess profits tax which is payable by the assessee. *I.T. Commissioner* v. *Delhi Flour Mills Co. Ltd.*, AIR 1959 SC 185, 188. [Excess Profits Tax Act (15 of 1940), S. 4]

Net wealth. "NET WEALTH" mean the amount by which the aggregate value computed in accordance with the provisions of this Act of all assets, where ever located, belonging to the assessee on the valuation date, including assets required in his net wealth as on that date under this Act, is in excess of the aggregate value of all debts owed by the assessee on the valuation date which have been incurred in relation to the said assets. [Wealth-tax Act (27 of 1957), S. 2(m)]

Net wealth is the difference on the valuation date between the aggregate value computed in accordance with the provision of the act of the assets belonging to the assessee and the aggregate value of all the debts owed by the assessee. *Standard Mills* v. *Commissioner of Wealth Tax*, AIR 1967 SC 595, 597. [Wealth Tax Act (27 of 1957), S. 2(*m*)]

A coparcenrary has unity of possession but not unity of ownership on the property. In pursuance to a decree for partition each coparcener takes a defined share and that share is his "net wealth". *Commissioner of Wealth Tax, W.B.* v. *Bishwanath Chatterjee*, AIR 1976 SC 1492, 1496. [Wealth Tax Act (27 of 1957), S. 2 (*m*)]

Net weight. The weight of an article after deducting from the gross weight *i.e.* deducting the weight of the boxes, casks, *etc.*, containing the same.

Net worth. "NET WORTH" means the sum total of the paid-up capital and free reserves after deducting the provisions or expenses as may be prescribed. [Companies Act (1 of 1956), S. 2(29A)]

"NET WORTH" means the sum total of the paid up capital and free reserves. [Sick Industrial Companies (Special Provisions) (1 of 1986), S. 3(1)(ga)]

"NET WORTH" means the aggregate value of the paid-up share capital and all reserves created out of the profits and securities premium account and debit or credit balance of profit and loss account, after deducting the aggregate value of the accumulated losses, deferred expenditure and miscellaneous expenditure not written off, as per the audited balance sheet, but does not include reserves created out of revaluation of assets, write-back of depreciation and amalgamation. [S. 2(57) of the Companies Act, 2013 (18 of 2013)]

Net value of taxable supplies. For the purposes of this sub-section, the expression "net value of taxable supplies" shall mean the aggregate value of taxable supplies of goods or services or both, other than services notified under sub-section (5) of Section 9, made during any month by all registered persons through the operator reduced by the aggregate value of taxable suppliers returned to the suppliers during the said month. [Central Goods and Services Tax Act (12 of 2017), s. 52(1), *Explanation*].

'Net worth' and 'current worth'. The concept of 'Net Worth' always denotes the excess of the book value of all assets over liabilities and market value of the assets is never taken into consideration; in fact the market value of assets which gives the 'current worth' becomes a relevant factor when in liquidation the question has to be considered whether the company possesses assets which would be sufficient to meet all its creditors or not. (*CIT, Bombay* v. *Mahindra and Mahindra Ltd.*, AIR 1984 SC 1182).

Netiquette. An unofficial attempt at self-regulation by businesses engaged in cyber-space; a kind of ethical code that requires courtesy online and respect for bandwidth capacity. (*Cyber Law*)

Basic Standards of behaviour expected from Internet users. (*Penelope Lawrence*) (*Internet*)

The supposed etiquette of the Internet community—for example avoiding the use of quoting, spamming and SHOUTING — use of capitals is taken as being the equivalent of shouting in real life. (*Cyber Law*)

The enquette on the Internet. (*Internet and E-commerce*)

Netizen. Derived from the term citizen, referring to a citizen of the *Internet*, or someone who uses networked resources. The term connotes civic responsibility and participation. (*Matisse Enzer-Glossary of Internet Terms; Internet and E-commerce*)

Netscape. The most popular browser—claims 70% plus of the market. (*Cyber Law*)

A *WWW Browser* and the name of a company. The Netscape (tm) browser was originally based on the *Mosaic* program developed at the National Center for Supercomputing Applications (NCSA).

Netscape has grown in features rapidly and is widely recognized as the best and most popular web browser. Netscape corporation also produces web server software.

Netscape provided major improvements in speed and interface over other browsers, and has also engendered debate by creating new elements for the HTML language used by Web pages—but the Netscape extensions to HTML are not universally supported.

The main author of Netscape, Mark Andreessen, was hired away from the NCSA by Jim Clark, and they founded a company called Mosaic Communications and soon changed the name to Netscape Communications Corporation. (*Internet and E-commerce*) (NCSA).

Netting agreement. Means any agreement among the system participants for the purpose of determination by the system provider of the amount of money or securities due or payable or deliverable as a result of setting off or adjusting the payment obligations or delivery obligations among the system participants, including the claims and obligations arising out of the termination by the system provider, on the insolvency or dissolution or winding up of any system participant or such circumstances as the system provider, may specify in its rules or regulations or bye-laws (by whatever name called), of the transactions admitted for settlement at a future date so that only a net claim be demanded or a net obligation be owned. [S. 2(l) of the Factoring Regulation Act, 2011 (12 of 2012)]

Netwar. A synonym for cyberwar. (*Cyber Law*)

Network. It is a communication system where a group of computers and other devices like printers are connected by cables and other hardware. The data is shared between the computers. A network, besides facilitating data communication, allows resources to be shared among all the systems connected to the network. (*Information Technology*)

A system of interconnected computers, typically connected by electrical cables or twisted wire pairs. Networking computers allows individual users to send communications to others users., share computer files, or work simultaneously on a single computer database. Some networks are set up so that most of the shared files and computer resources are concentrated on one or more computers called *servers*, which make these resources available to other computers called *clients*. In a *peer-to-peer network,* each computer on the network can operate independently. (*Computer*)

Any connection of two or more computers that enables them to communicate. Networks may include transmission devices, servers, cables, routers and satellites. The phone network is the total infrastructure for transmitting phone messages. (*Telecommunication*)

Any time you connect 2 or more computers together so that they can share resources, you have a computer network. Connect 2 or more networks together and you have an *internet.* (*Matisse Enzer—Glossary of Internet Terms; Internet and E-commerce*)

Network administrator. The person at a computer network installation who designs, controls, and manages the use of the computer network. (*Information Technology*)

Network service provider. Means an intermediary. [Information Technology Act (21 of 2000), S. 79 *Expln.*]

Network Service Operator. Means the operator defined under the Unified Licence (Virtual Network Operator) which owns the telecom core network and provides core network service to the Virtual Network Operator to connet different parts of the access network and gateway to other networks. [Telecommunication Mobile Number Portability Regulations, 2009, Regn. 2(je)].

Network software. 'Network software' is a software which enables the group of computers to communicate. [*Commr. Of Customs* v. *Hewlett Packard India Sales (P) Ltd.*, (2007) 8 SCC 404, 410, para 17]

Network Solutions, Inc. (NSI). A private company that, until recently, held a monopoly on second-level domain name registration. (*Cyber Law*)

Network spoofing. In network spoofing, a system presents itself to the network as though it were a different system (system A impersonates system B by sending B's address instead of its own). The reason for doing this is that systems tend to operate within a group of other "trusted" systems. Trust is imparted in a one-to-one fashion; system A trusts system B (this does not imply that system B trusts system A). Implied with this trust is that the system administrator of the trusted system is performing his or her job properly and maintaining an appropriate level of security for his or her system. Network spoofing occurs in the following manner : if system A trusts system B and system C spoofs (impersonates) system B, then system C can gain otherwise denied access to system A. (*Cyber Law*)

Network worm. A worm that migrates across platforms over a network by copying itself from one system to another by exploiting common network facilities, resulting in execution of the (replicated) worm on that system and potentially others. (*Cyber Law*)

Neurasthenia. Neurosis manifested chiefly by exhaustion, mental and physical fatigue, irritability and poorly localized symptoms without any underlying physical disorder.

Neutrality. Neutrality in international law indicates the condition of a State which is not a party in a dispute between other States. Strictly speaking, neutrality consists in the abstinence from any participation in a public, private, or civil war and impartial conduct towards both parties.

Nevertheless. This word has been used as equivalent in meaning to "notwithstanding."

In spite of that; yet.

New. Having existed or having been made but a short time ago; having originated or occurred lately; of late origin; recent; fresh; modern.

A set of things which is different from that immediately proceeding it may well be called new. A situation which once existed and then ceased to exist (disappeared) may properly attract the word 'new' on reappearance. *P. Venkaiah* v. *G. Krishna Rao*, AIR 1981 SC 1910, 1914.

New asset. For the purposes of section 32AC of Act 43 of 1961, 'new asset' means any new plant or machinery (other than ship or aircraft) but does not include—

(i) any plant or machinery which before its installation by the assessee was used either within or outside India by any other person;

(ii) any plant or machinery installed in any office premises or any residential accommodation, including accommodation in the nature of a guest house;

(iii) any office appliances including computers or computer software;

(iv) any vehicle; or

(v) any plant or machinery, the whole of the actual cost of which is allowed as deduction (whether by way of depreciation or otherwise) in computing the income chargeable under the head 'Profits and gains of business or profession' of any previous year. [(w.e.f. 1-4-2014) S. 32AC(4) of the Income-tax Act, 1961 (43 of 1961)]

"NEW ASSET" for the purposes of section 54GB of Act 43 of 1961, 'new asset' means new plant and machinery but does not include—

(i) any machinery or plant which, before its installation by the assessee, was used either within or outside India by any other person;

(ii) any machinery or plant installed in any office premises or any residential accommodation, including accommodation in the nature of a guest-house;

(iii) any office appliances including computers or computer software;

(iv) any vehicle; or

(v) any machinery or plant, the whole of the actual cost of which is allowed as a deduction (whether by way of depreciation or otherwise) in computing the income chargeable under the head 'Profits and gains of business or profession' of any previous year. [S. 54GB(6)(d) of the Income-tax Act, 1961 (43 of 1961) as inserted (w.e.f. 1-4-2013) by the Finance Act, 2012]

New co-operative bank. Means a cooperative bank which begins to transact the business of banking after the commencement of the Deposit Insurance Corporation (Amendment) Act, 1968, under a licence granted to it under section 22 of the Banking Regulation Act, 1949, and includes a primary credit society becoming a primary co-operative bank after such commencement. [Deposit Insurance and Credit Guarantee Corporation Act (47 of 1961), S. 2(kk)]

New cultivation. Means cultivation of land which remained uncultivated for three consecutive years. [Kerala Preservation of Trees and Regulation of Cultivation in Hill Areas Ordinance 1983, S. 2(e)]

New Government company. Means a Government company formed and registered on or after the appointed day. [Hooghly Docking And Engineering Company Limited (Acquisition and Transfer of Undertakings Act (55 of 1984), S. 2(e); Inchek Tyres Limited And National Rubber Manufacturers Limited (Nationalisation) Act (17 of 1984), S. 2(d); National Company Limited (Acquisition and Transfer of Undertaking) Act (42 of 1980), S. 2(e)]

New industrial undertaking. Means an undertaking which is not formed,—

(a) by the splitting up, or the reconstruction, of a business already in existence; or

(b) by the transfer to a new business of machinery or plant previously used for any purpose. [Income-tax Act (43 of 1961), S. 32(iia) *Expln.* (1)]

New industrial unit. "New industrial unit" means an industrial unit which commences commercial production during the operative period of the Scheme. The definition provides an exclusion of certain industries from the purview of new industrial unit. They are industrial units established by transferring or shifting or dismantling an existing industry and an industrial unit established on the site of an existing unit manufacturing similar goods. [Rajasthan Sales Tax New Incentive Scheme for Industries, 1989, Clause 2(a) as cited in *Commercial Tax officer, Rajasthan v. Binani Cements Limited*, (2014) 8 SCC 319, para 5].

New invention. "NEW INVENTION" means any invention or technology which has not been anticipated by publication in any document or used in the country or elsewhere in the world before the date of filing of patent application with complete specification, *i.e.,* the subject matter has not fallen in public domain or that it does not form part of the state of the art. [Patents Act (39 of 1970), S. 2(1)(l) *as substituted by Patents (Amendment) Act (15 of 2005), S. 2(g).*

New in vitro diagnostic medical device. Means any medical device as referred to in sub-clause (A) of clause (zb) used for in vitro diagnosis that has not been approved for manufacture for sale or for import by the Central Licensing Authority and is being tested to establish its performance for relevant analyte or other parameter related thereto including details of technology and procedure required. [Medical Devices Rules, 2017, R. 3(zh)]

New issue. Shares of a company offered to the public, through a public issue, for the first time to be listed on the Stock Exchange.

New machinery. The word 'new' may have different meanings, but when, used with reference to a machine, its meaning is 'new made or brought into existence for the first time'. *Cochin Company* v. *C.I.T.*, (1968) 67 ITR 199, 202 (SC). [Income Tax Act (43 of 1961), S. 33]

New point. The expression 'new point' means the point not argued before the High Court and absence of any decision on the point by the High Court. *State of Orissa* v. *Durga Bharan Das*, AIR 1966 SC 1547, 1551. [Constitution of India, Art. 133]

"New ship" or "new vessel". Means a ship or vessel whose keel is laid or which is at a similar stage of construction on or after the material date as defined in sub-section (2). [Merchant Shipping Act (44 of 1958), S. 283A(b)]

For the purposes of this section, "NEW SHIP" includes a qualifying ship which, before the date of acquisition by the qualifying company was used by any other person, if it was not at any time previous to the date of such acquisition owned by any person resident in India. [Income-tax Act (43 of 1961), Chapter XII G, S. 115 VT *Expln.* (Inserted by Finance Act (23 of 2004), S. 30)]

"NEW SHIP" means a ship the keel of which is laid or which is at a similar stage of construction on or after the date of coming into force of the present Convention. [International Conference on Safety of Life at Sea, 1974, Chap. 1, Part A, Reg. 2(k)]

New trial. A *new trial* is a re-trial in the same Court.

A new trial is a re-examination in the same Court of an issue of fact after a verdict by a jury, report of a referee, or decision by the Court.

Trial afresh. [CrPC 1973 (2 of 1974), S. 464(2)(b)].

Newly discovered evidence. Proof of some new and material fact in the case, which has come to light since the verdict or judgment.

Newly independent State. Means a successor state the territory of which immediately before the date of the succession of States was a dependant territory for the international relations of which the predecessor state was responsible. [Vienna Convention on Succession of States in Respect of Treaties, 1978, Art. 2(f)]

News. Tidings; fresh events reported.

Court decisions may be news, especially in cases in which some questions of public importance are involved or which by nature of the dispute rouse public interest. *All India Reporter Ltd.* v. *State of Maharashtra,* AIR 1983 Bom 201, 205. [Working journalists and other Newspaper Employees (conditions of service) and Miscellaneous Provisions Act (45 of 1955), S. 2(*b*)]

Information about recent decisions of Courts of record could be news in which the public are interested. *All India Reporter Karmachari Sangh* v. *AIR (Ltd.)*, AIR 1988 SC 1325, 1330.

News sheet. Means any document other than a newspaper containing public news or comments on public news. [Prevention of Publication of Objectionable Matter Act (27 of 1976), S. 2(f)]

Newspaper. A periodical publication containing intelligence of passing events. [Indian Evidence Act (1 of 1872), S. 81].

"NEWSPAPER" includes a news agency report containing material for publication in a newspaper. [Constitution of India, Art. 361(A)(2) *Expln.*]

"NEWSPAPER" means any printed periodical work containing public news or comments or public news. [Press and Registration of Books Act (25 of 1867), S. 1(g)]

"NEWSPAPER" means any printed periodical work containing public news or comments on public news published in conformity with the provisions of Section 5 of the Press and Registration of Book Act, 1867. [Delivery of Books & Newspapers (Public Libraries) Act (27 of 1954), S. 2(aa)]

"NEWSPAPER" means any printed periodical work containing public news or comments on public news and includes such other class of printed periodical work as may, from time to time, be notified in this behalf by the Central Government in the Official Gazette. [Working Journalists and other Newspaper Employees (Conditions of Service) and Miscellaneous Provisions Act (45 of 1955), S. 2(b)]

"NEWSPAPER" means any printed periodical work containing public news or comments on public news appearing at intervals of not more than a week. [Newspaper (Price and Page) Act (45 of 1956), S. 2(b)]

"NEWSPAPER" means any periodical work containing public news or comments on public news. [Prevention of Publication of Objectionable Matter Act (27 of 1976), S. 2(e)]

"NEWSPAPER" means any printed periodical work containing public news or comments on public news, and includes a news-agency supplying material for publication in a newspaper. [Parliament Proceedings (Protection of Publication) Act (15 of 1977), S. 2]

Periodical—especially publication with the news, advertisement *etc.*

A newspaper in the ordinary acceptation of the term is a publication in sheet form, intended for general circulation, published regularly at short intervals and containing intelligence of current events of general interest. It follows from this definition that if a publication contains the general current news of the day, it is none the less a newspaper because it is devoted primarily to special interests, such as legal, religious, political, mercantile, or sporting.

Pamphlets giving predictions of lucky figures, number or dates and only stray news items cannot be considered as a newspaper. In the absence of any significant news contents in these publications, the mere fact that the publications are brought out daily, has no relevancy in deciding that they are newspaper.

The essential pre-requisite of a periodical, in order to make it a 'newspaper', is that it must contain mainly public news or comments on public news. *P.S.V. Iyer* v. *Commissioner of Sales Tax,* AIR 1960 Ori 221, 223.

Newspaper employee. Means any working journalist, and includes any other person employed to do any work in, or in relation to, any newspaper establishment. [Working Journalists and Other Newspaper Employees (Conditions of Service) and Miscellaneous Provisions Act (45 of 1955), S. 2(c)]

Newspaper establishment. Means under the control of any person or body of persons, whether incorporated or not, for the production or publication of one or more newspapers or for conducting any news agency or syndicate and includes newspaper establishments specified as one establishment under the Schedule.

Explanation—For the purpose of this clause,—

(a) different departments, branches and centers of newspaper establishments shall be treated as parts thereof;

(b) a printing press shall be deemed to be a newspaper establishment if the principal business thereof is to print newspaper. [Working Journalists and Other Newspaper Employees (Conditions of Service) and Miscellaneous Provisions Act (45 of 1955), S. 2(d)]

Next. The word "next" means nearest.

Coming directly after another [Indain Partnership Act (9 of 1932), S. 48(a)]; the nearest [Army Act (46 of 1950), S. 137(5); [Representation of the People Act (43 of 1951), S. 30(a)]; immediately following in order [CrPC 1973 (2 of 1974), S. 246(4)].

A reference to the next or following section or other division of a statute means the section or other division immediately following.

Next available preference. The expression 'next available preference' means the second or subsequent preference recorded in consecutive numerical order for continuing candidate, preferences for candidates already excluded being ignored. [U.P. Zila Panchayats (Election of Adhyaksha and Upadhyaksha and Settlement of Election Disputes) Rules, 1994, Sch. II, clause (3)]

Next day. "Next day", in a legal sense, means the next business day.

The next day on which notice of default in payment should be made after presentment and protest means the next business day.

Hence, where the protest was made on Saturday, the notice was properly mailed on the next Monday, leaving the intermediate Sunday out of the computation.

Next following. Immediately following [TP Act (4 of 1882), Ss. 55 and 108]; [S. 14(5), Industrial Finance Corporation Act (15 of 1948); (*Repealed by Act (23 of 1993)*); Copyright Act (14 of 1957), S. 23(1)].

Next friend. *Prochein ami* or next friend is said to be any person who will undertake the infant's cause. It is not limited to any particular relative.

A person who is admitted or appointed by a Court as a special guardian to act for the benefit of a minor or any person not *sui juris*; the guardian of a plaintiff in a case. [CPC (5 of 1908), O. XXXII, R 1].

The Court may control a next friend, as well as a guardian *ad litem*, and should permit or direct what is most for the interest of the infant. In reason, there can be no difference between the power of a next friend and of a guardian *ad litem*. The one is permitted by the Court to prosecute on behalf and in the name of an infant, and the other is appointed by the Court to defend the suit of an infant.

Next friend of the minor. The person who takes steps in the suit on behalf of the minor automatically constitutes himself the next friend of the minor. AIR 1972 All 81 (82). [CPC (5 of 1908), O. XXXII, R. 1]

Next of kin. "NEXT OF KIN" includes a widower or widow of a deceased person or any other person who by law would be entitled to letters of administration in preference to a creditor or legatee or the deceased. [Administrators General Act (45 of 1963), S. 2(c)]

Nexus. (*Lat.*) Bond of connection.

NIC. (*abbr.*) Network Information Center. Generally, any office that handles information for a network. The most famous of these on the Internet was the Inter NIC, which was where most new domain names were registered until that process was decentralized to a number of private companies. Also means "Network Interface card", which is the card in a computer that you plug a network cable into. (*Matisse Enzer Glossary of Internet Terms*)

NIC also refers to Network Interface Card which plugs into a computer and adapts the network interface to the appropriate standard. ISA, PCI, and PCMCIA cards are all examples of NICs.

In India: Also the National Informatics Centre. (*Internet and E-commerce*)

Nidhi. In this section, "Nidhi" means a company which the Central Government may, by notification in the Official Gazette, declare to be a Nidhi or Mutual Benefit Society, as the case may be. [Companies Act (18 of 2013), section 406(1)]

For the purpose of this sub-rule, "NIDHI" means a company which has been incorporated as a Nidhi with the object of cultivating the habit of thrift and savings amongst its members, receiving deposits from and lending to, its members only, for their mutual benefit, and which complies with such rules as are prescribed by the Central Government for regulation of such class of companies. [Companies (Management and Administration) Rules, 2014, R. 20(2), *Explanation*].

Niece. Brother's daughter; sister's daughter; a daughter of one's brother or sister or brother-in-law or sister-in-law. [margin, Indian Succession Act (39 of 1925), S. 46].

Nigrum nunquam excedere debet rubrum. (*Lat.*) The black should never go beyond the red (*i.e.*) the text of a statute should never be read in a sense more comprehensive than the rubric, or title.

Nihil cuiquam expedit quod per leges non licet. That which is contrary to law cannot be profitable to any one.

Nihil facit error nominis cum de corpore constat. (*Maxim*) An error of name is nothing when there is certainty as to the person. (*Peloubet*)

Nihil habet forum ex scena. (*Maxim*) The Court has nothing to do with what is not before it. (*Latin for Lawyers*)

Nihil honestum amico est opportuno amicus. Nothing can be honest which is destitute of justice.

Nihil in lege intolerabilius est eandem rem diverso jure censeri. (*Lat.*) (4 *Rep.* 93*a*) Nothing is more intolerable in law than that the same thing be judged by different rules.

Nihil infra regnum subditos magis conservat in tranquillitate et concordia quam debita legum administratio. (*Lat.*) (2 Inst. 158) Nothing preserves in tranquillity and concord those who are subjected to the same government better than a proper administration of the laws.

Nihil iniquius quam acquitatem nimis intendere. Nothing is so unjust as to extend equity too far.

Nihil interest ipso jurequis actionem non habeat an per exceptionem infirmetur. The law does not concern itself as to who may not have the right to an action, or who may be injured by an exception.

Nihil magis justum est quam quod necessarium est. Nothing is more just than that which is necessary.

Nihil nequam est praesumedum. Nothing wicked is to be presumed.

Nihil perfectum est dum aliquid restat agendum. (*Lat.*) (9 *Rep.* 9*b*). Nothing is perfect while something remains to be done.

Nihil possumus contra veritatem. We can do nothing against truth.

Nihil quod est contra rationem est licitum. (*Lat.*) (Co. Litt. 97b) Nothing that is against reason is lawful. Nothing is permitted which is contrary to reason.

Nihil quod est contra rationem est licitum. (*Maxim*) Nothing is permitted which is contrary to reason. (*Latin for Lawyers*)

Nihil tam conveniens est naturali aequitati quam voluntatem domini rem suam in alium transferre retum haberi. (*Lat.*) (1 Rep. 100) Nothing is so consonant to natural equity as to regard the wish of the owner in transferring his own property to another.

Nil consensui tam contrarium est quam vis atque metus. (*Maxim*) There can be no consent when under duress of force or fear. (*Morgan*)

Nil facit error nominis cum de corpore vel persona constat. (*Lat.*) A mistake in the name does not matter when the body or person is manifest.

Nil sine prudenti fecit ratione vetustas. Antiquity did nothing without a good reason.

Nil tam proprium imperii ac libertatis quam legibus vivere. Nothing is so becoming to authority as to live according to the law.

Nil utile aut honestum quod legibus contrarium. Nothing is useful or honorable that is contrary to law.

Nisi. (*Lat.*) "The word "*nisi*" is often affixed, as a kind of elliptical expression, to the words 'rule', 'order', 'decree', 'judgment', or 'confirmation', to indicate that the adjudication spoken of is one which is to stand as valid and operative unless the party affected by it shall appear and show cause against it, or take some other appropriate step to avoid it or procure its revocation." A decree or judgment *Nisi*, is one that is conditional and requires something more to be done to make it absolute.

Not final or absolute; unless.

Nisi prius. (*Lat.*) Unless before.

Unless the word is often affixed, as a kind of elliptical expression, to the words, "rule", "order", "decree", "judgment", or "confirmation", to indicate that the adjudication spoken of is one which is to stand as valid and operative unless the party affected by it shall appear and show cause against it, or take some other appropriate step to avoid it or procure its revocation. Thus a "decree *nisi*" is one which will definitely conclude the defendant's rights unless; within the prescribed time, he shows cause to set it aride to successfully appeals. The word in this sence, is opposed to "absolute." And when a rule *nisi* is finally confirmed, for the defendant's failure to show cause against it, it is said to be "made absolute."

Nizam. Administration; also an administrator.

Nizamat. The Office of Nizam. As an adjective Nizamat means criminal, as opposed to diwani or civil as the Nizam or Governor exercised the highest criminal authority leaving the adjudication of civil causes to his Diwan.

Nizamat-Adalat. A criminal Court. Under the Muhammadan Government the highest criminal Court was so called and district criminal Court was called the Faujdari Adalat.

NNTP. (*abbr.*) Network News Transfer Protocol. The internal protocol used between news servers to exchange articles. (*Cyber Law*)

The protocol used by *client* and *server* software to carry *USENET* postings back and forth over a *TCP/IP network.* If you are using any of the more common software such as *Netscape,* Nuntius, Internet Explorer, *etc.*, to participate in *newsgroups* then you are benefiting from an NNTP connection. (*Matisse Enzer-Glossary of Internet Terms; Internet and E-commerce*)

'No' and **'shall'.** The word 'no' and 'shall' as used in Section 197 of the Code would mean that the bar on the exercise of power to take cognizance of any offence is absolute and complete. *State of Orissa* v. *Ganesh Chandra Jew,* AIR 2004 SC 2179, 2184, para 11. [CrPC 1973 (2 of 1974), S. 197]

No appeal has been preferred. The phrase 'No appeal has been preferred' would also mean a situation where SLP was not allowed. *Kunhayammad* v. *State of Kerala,* (2000) 6 SCC 359, para 38 : AIR 2000 SC 2587. [CPC (5 of 1908), O. XL, R.1(1)]

No confidence motion. The motion to ascertain whether the Council of Ministers enjoys the confidence of the Lok Sabha or not.

A motion expressing want of confidence in Government; it is moved by a member or leader of Opposition. (*Constitutional and Parliamentary Term*)

No-confidence vote. A constitutional method by which the legislature by a majority of vote forces the cabinet or ministry to resign.

No contest clause. In a 'no-contest clause' in a licensing agreement of a patent the licensee agrees that he will not attack the validity of the patent licenced in any proceeding. (*Patents*)

No-day-yet-named motion. A motion admitted by the Speaker and for discussion of which no date has been fixed.

No Electronic Theft Act (NET Act) of 1997. Amending the Copyright Infringement Act establishing that there is infringement, even without economic gain to the user, when the copyrighted material has a total retail value of more than $2,500. (*Cyber Law*)

Federal law prohibiting willful infringement of copyrighted material online, even if no profit is made. (*U.S.*) (*Cyber Law*)

No estoppel against statute. The arbitrator had no jurisdiction to make an award after expiry of specified time of four months in the absence of any order of extension. Parties are not estopped by their conduct from challenging validity of an award on the ground that it was made beyond time, merely because they participated in the arbitration proceedings before arbitrator after expiry of the prescribed period as the established principle is that there can be no estoppel against a statute. *Inder Sain Mittal* v. *Housing Board,* (2002) 3 SCC 175, para 11 : AIR 2002 SC 1157.

No sufficient ground for proceeding. Unless the evidence led is self-contradictory, or intrinsically untrustworthy, one cannot say that there is no sufficient ground for proceeding. *Nirmaljit Singh*

Hoon v. *State of W.B.*, AIR 1972 SC 2639, 2646. [CrPC 1973 (2 of 1974), S. 203]

No work, no pay. Where an employee of a bank was promoted with retrospective effect and her pay was fixed in the relevant payscale notionally from the date of Apex Court's decision, but she claimed the arrears of salary from the retrospective date of promotion, it was held that the Apex Court's order granting relief of promotion was as a gesture of *gratis* and not by way of right hence she was not entitled to arrears of pay on the principle of 'no work, no pay'. [*A.K. Soumini* v. *State Bank of Travancore,* (2003) 7 SCC 238, 243, para 9]

Where a Government servant had willfully been absent from the office for a period of more than three years, applying the principle 'no work no pay' it was held that he had no right to receive the monetary/retiral benefits during the period in question. [*State of Rajasthan* v. *Mohd. Ayub Naz,* (2006) 1 SCC 589, 596, p. 18]

Node. Any device connected to the Internet, with an IP address, is a node. (*Cyber Law*)

In a network, a point at which one or more functional units connect channels or data circuits. (*Information Technology*)

Any single computer connected to a network. (*Internet and E-commerce*)

Noil. Short fibre removed during the combing of a textile fibre and spun into yarn for cloth. [Central Silk Board Act (41 of 1948), S. 3(f)].

Noise. "NOISE" means sound from any source whatever of such character as causes or is likely to cause mental or physical discomfort to a man of ordinary sensibility or susceptibility or causes or is likely to cause disturbance in the study. [Madhya Pradesh Kolahal Niyantran Adhiniyam 1985 (1 of 1986), S. 2(c)]

Nolle prosequi. To be unwilling to prosecute. Withdrawal by the Public Prosecutor of a criminal proceeding against an accused.

Nolo contendere. A plea which does not admit guilt but submits to the decision of Court.

Nominal. Existing in name only as distinguished from real or actual; of the nature of, consisting in, pertaining or relating to, a name or names (as opposed to things); stated or expressed.

Nominal asset. An asset whose value is difficult to asset, *e.g.*; Judgment or claim.

Nominal capital. The legal measure of the share capital with which the company is initially formed or as subsequently increased and upto which the company can issue shares.

"NOMINAL CAPITAL" means such capital as is authorized by the memorandum of a company to be the maximum amount of share capital of the company. [S. 2(8) of the Companies Act, 2013 (18 of 2013)]

Nominal consideration. "Nominal consideration" when used in reference to the value of property as a consideration for an exchange of property, means the inflated or trade value of the property.

Nominal damage. 'Nominal damages' is a technical phrase which means that the Court has negatived anything like real damage, but is affirming by nominal damages that there is an infraction of a legal right, which, though it gives the plaintiff no right to any real damages at all, yet gives him a right to the verdict or judgment because his legal right has been infringed. *S.K. CC Bank* v. *Subramanyam,* AIR 1963 AP 250, 251. [Negotiable Instruments Act (26 of 1881), S. 31]

Nominal partner. A person who holds himself out as having an interest in a business.

Nominal wages. In relation to any labour means a wage which is less than;

(a) the minimum wages fixed by the Government, in relation to the same or similar labour, under any law for the time being in force, and

(b) where no such minimum wage has been fixed in relation to any form of labour, the wages that are normally paid, for the same or similar labour, to the labourers working in the same locality. [Bonded Labour System (Abolition) Act (19 of 1976), S. 2(i)]

Nominate. To select a candidate to be voted for a public office; or as a member of a legislative or representative assembly; to name or to recommend for confirmation.

To name or designate a person for some position or office.

Nominated authority. Means an officer not below the rank of a Station Officer nominated by the Chief Fire Officer, and includes an officer nominated by a local authority or a railway administration as a nominated authority for the purposes of this Act. [Delhi Fire Prevention and Fire Safety Act (56 of 1986), S. 2(i)]

Nominated website. A website designated by the Certifying Authority for display of information such as fee schedule, Certification Practice Statement, Certificate Policy *etc.* (*Information Technology*)

Nomination. Appointment; a resolution submitted to the electors that the party named is a candidate for their suffrage for an office named.

The action, process or instance of nominating; the act, process or an instrument of nominating; an act or right of designating for an office or duty.

Nominee. "NOMINEE" means nominee appointed by a member of the fund to receive the benefits arising from such membership in the event of his death. [Rajasthan Advocates Welfare Fund Act (15 of 1987), S. 2(g)]

"NOMINEE" means a person nominated in the prescribed manner by a member of the Fund to receive the amount, which may be due to the member, from the Fund in the event of his death before the amount is paid to him. [Goa Advocates

Welfare Fund Act, 1995 (Goa Act (2 of 1997), S. 2(k)]

A person selected as a candidate for office; a person who has been selected by a party as its candidate for a public office.

A person named for any office, duty or position. [Companies Act (1 of 1956), S. 4(3)(b)(i)].

The term 'nominee' apparently means a holder of shares, having no beneficial interest in the shares, the whole beneficial interest remaining in one or more other persons. *Ramaiya's Companies Act*, 12th Edition, p. 262. [Companies Act (1 of 1956), S. 42(4)]

Nominee director. For the purposes of section 149 of Act 18 of 2013, 'nominee director' means a director nominated by any financial institution in pursuance of the provisions of any law for the time being in force, or of any agreement, or appointed by any Government, or any other person to represent its interests. [*Explanation* to section 149(7) of the Companies Act, 2013 (18 of 2013)]

"Nominee" under policy of insurance. A nominee under a policy of Insurance in the Official or Public Branch of the Government Life Assurance Department is not the beneficial owner under the rules governing the Insurance unless the wording of the nomination has that effect. Where the nomination merely authorises the Insurance Company to pay the amount to the "nominee", it does not amount to a bequest in favour of the nominee; nor does it create any right in the nominee except the right to collect it. The "nominee" is not in the position of a *cesti que trust*, but, is merely authorised to receive payment.

Non-acceptance. Failure or refusal to accept [Negotiable Instruments Act (26 of 1881), S. 7]; [Constitution of India, Art. 323(1)].

Non-access. (*In Matrimonial Law*) absence of opportunities for sexual intercourse between husband and wife; the absence of such intercourse.

Non-assessee online recipient. Means Government, a local authority, a governmental authority or an individual receiving online information and database access or retrieval services in relation to any purpose other than commerce, industry or any other business or profession, located in taxable territory;

Explanation.—For the purposes of this clause, "governmental authority" means an authority or a board or any other body:

(*i*) set up by an Act of Parliament or a State legislature; or

(*ii*) established by Government,

with 90% or more participation by way of equity or control, to carry out any function entrusted to a municipality under Article 243-W of the Constitution. [Service Tax Rules, 1994, R. 2(1)(ccba)].

Non accipi debent verba in demonstrationem falsam quae competunt in limitationem veram. (*Lat.*) (Bac. Max. Reg. 3) Words ought not to be accepted to import a false description, which may have effect by way of true limitation.

Non-age. Being under age; minority.

The condition of being under twenty one years and consequently not of age to manage one's property and affairs [Indian Majority Act (9 of 1875), preamble].

Non-agricultural holding. Means all forest land hold by a *Bhumiswami* within the State. [M.P. Akrishik Jot Vchehatam Seema Adhyadish (3 of 1981), S. 2(d)]

Non-agricultural land. 'Non-agricultural land' means land other than the land used exclusively for purpose of agriculture, but does not include the land used exclusively for—

(i) Cattle sheds,

(ii) Hay-ricks. [A.P. Non-Agricultural Land Assessment Act (14 of 1963), S. 2(g)]

Non alienat qui dumtaxat omittit possessionem. He does not alienate who merely gives up possession." (*Peloubet Leg. Max.*)

Non-Aligned Movement (NAM). A loose coalition of developing countries that meets at the head of states level every few years in an attempt to coordinate positions on international political and economic issues.

Non-Alignment. The political attitude of a state which does not associate, or identify itself with the political ideology or objective espoused by other states, groups of states, or international causes, or with the foreign policies stemming therefrom. It does not preclude involvement, but express the attitude of no precommitment to a particular state (or bloc) or policy before a situation arises.

Non aliter a significatione verborum recedi oportet quam cum manifestum est aliud sensisse testatorem. We must never depart from the signification of words, unless it is evident that they are not conformable to the will of the testator. (*Bouvier*)

Non-apparent easement. "A non-apparent easement is one that has no such sign" (some permanent sign which upon careful inspection by a competent person, would be visible to him). [Indian Easements Act (5 of 1882), S. 5]

Non-apparent servitude. "Non-apparent servitudes" are such as have no exterior signs of their existence.

Non-appearance. Failure to appear. [CrPC (2 of 1974), S. 256(1)].

Non assumpsit. He did not promise.

Non-bailable. Not admitting of bail as a matter of right [CrPC (2 of 1974), S. 43(1)].

"Non-banking financial company" means—

(i) a financial institution which is a company;

(ii) a non-banking institution which is a company and which has as its principal business the receiving of deposits, under any scheme or arrangement or in any other manner, or lending in any manner;

(iii) such other non-banking institution or class of such institutions, as the Bank may, with the previous approval of the Central Government and by notification in the Official Gazette, specify. [Reserve Bank of India Act (2 of 1934), S. 45-I(f)]

"Non-Banking Financial Company" means a Non-Banking Financial Company as defined in clause (f) of section 45-I of the Reserve Bank of India Act, 1934 and includes Housing Finance Companies, Merchant Banking companies, Micro Finance Companies, Mutual Benefit Companies, Venture Capital Fund Companies, Stock Broker or Sub-Broker Companies, Nidhi Companies, Chit Companies, Securitisation and Reconstruction Companies, Mortgage Guarantee Companies, Pension Fund Companies, Asset Management Companies and Core Investment Companies. [Companies (Indian Accounting Standards) Rules, 2015, R. 2(1)(g)]

Non-banking financial company engaged in factoring business. For the removal of doubts it is hereby clarified that a 'non-banking financial company engaged in factoring business' shall be treated as engaged in factoring business as its "principal business" if it fulfils the following conditions, namely:—

(*a*) if its financial assets in the factoring business are more than fifty per cent. of its total assets or such per cent. as may be stipulated by the Reserve Bank; and

(*b*) if its income from factoring business is more than fifty per cent. of the gross income or such per cent as may be stipulated by the Reserve Bank. [*Explanation* to section 3 of the Factoring Regulation Act, 2011 (12 of 2012)]

Non-Banking Institutions. "NON-BANKING INSTITUTION" means a company, corporation, or co-operative society. [RBI Act (2 of 1934), S. 45-I(c)]

Non-belligerent. A party or person not recognised as waging war. [Geneva Conventions Act (6 of 1960), IIIrd Sch., Art. 4].

Non-biodegradable garbage. Means the waste garbage or material which is not biodegradable garbage and includes polyethylene, nylon and other plastic goods such as PVC polypropylane and polystyrene, which are not capable of being destroyed by an action of living beings and are more specifically included in the schedule to this Act. [H.P. Non-biodegradable Garbage (Central) Act, 1995 (15 of 1995), S. 2(e) and Goa Non-biodegradable Garbage (Central) Act 1996 (Goa Act No. 5 of 1997), S. 2(e)]

Non bis in idem. Not twice for the same [Geneva Conventions Act (6 of 1960), IIIrd Sch., Art. 86].

The maxim relates to the principle that no man may be tried for the same offence twice. (*Latin for Lawyers*)

Non capitur qui jus publicum sequitur. He is not snared who follows public right.

Non-cognizable offence. "NON-COGNIZABLE OFFENCE" means an offence for, and "non-cognizable case" means a case in, which a police officer has no authority to arrest without warrant. [CrPC 1973 (2 of 1974), S. 3(l)].

Means an offence for which, and "non-cognizable case" means a case in which, a police officer has no authority to arrest without warrant. [(w. e. f. 1-7-2024) Bharatiya Nagarik Suraksha Sanhita, 2023 (46 of 2023), S. 2(1)(o)]

Non combustible material. Means the material which neither burns nor gives off inflammable vapour in sufficient quantity to ignite a pilot flame. [Delhi Cinematograph Rules, 1981, R. 2(xiv)]

Non-commissioned officer. An officer in the military, naval or air force, who does not hold a commission. [CrPC 1973 (2 of 1974), S. 132(3)(b)].

"NON-COMMISSIONED OFFICER" means a person holding a non-commissioned rank in the Territorial Army, and includes an acting non-commissioned officer. [Territorial Army Act (56 of 1948), S. 2(c)]

"NON-COMMISSIONED OFFICER" means a person holding a non-commissioned rank or an acting non-commissioned rank in the Air Force, and includes any person holding a non-commissioned rank or an acting non-commissioned rank in any Air Force Reserve or the Auxiliary Air Force when subject to this Act. [Air Force Act (45 of 1950), S. 4(xx)]

"NON-COMMISSIONED OFFICER" means a person holding a non-commissioned rank or an acting non-commissioned rank in the regular. Army or the Indian Reserve Forces and includes a non-commissioned officer or acting non-commissioned officer of the Indian Supplementary Reserve Forces or the Territorial Army, who is for the time being subject to this Act. [Army Act (46 of 1950), 3(xv)]

Non-compliance. Failure or refusal to comply. (*Tomlin*)

Non-compliance with the provisions of the constitution. The expression 'non-compliance with the provisions of the constitution' is sufficiently wide to cover such cases where the question is not one of improper acceptance or rejection of the nomination by the Returning Officer but there is a fundamental disability in the candidate to stand for election at all. *Durga Shankar Mehta* v. *Raghuraj Singh*, AIR 1954 SC 520, 524.

Non compos mentis. One not of sound mind, memory, and understanding. Insane.

"NON COMPOS MENTIS" is a generic term, and includes all species of madness, whether it arises on idiocy, sickness, lunacy, or drunkenness.

Non-conformance report. Means a report issued to the customs authorities and the food importer by the Authorised Officer, or any other officer specifically authorised for this purpose, by the food authority, for non-compliance of the provisions of the Act and the rules and regulations made thereunder, of the consignment o the Food Importer. [Food Safety and Standards (Import) Regulations, 2017, Regn. 2(1)(n)].

Non crimen per se neqe privatum demnum sed publicum malum, leges spectant. The law regards a crime as working public evil; not merely as a wrong by itself or as a private loss.

Non culpabilis. (*Lat.*) The plea of 'not guilty'.

Non deberet alii nocere quod inter alios actum esset. No one ought to be injured by that which has taken place between other parties.

Non debet actori licere quod reo non permittitur. A plaintiff ought to be allowed what is not permitted to a defendant.

Non debet adduci exceptio ejusdem rei cujus petitur dissolutio. (*Lat.*) An exception of the thing whose abolition is sought ought not to be adduced.

Non debet cui plus licet, quod minus est, non licere. (*Lat.*) (D. 50, 17, 21) He who is permitted to do the greater may with greater reason do the less.

Non debet melioris conditionis esse quam auctor meus a quo jus in me transit. One cannot be in a better condition as to his title than the grantor whose title he takes.

Non definitur in jure quid sit conatus. (*Lat.*) (6 Rep. 42) What an attempt is, is not defined in law.

Non-delivery. Neglect or failure to deliver.

Non-delivery of goods. Neglect, failure or refusal to deliver the goods by a carrier.

Non-discriminatory. For the purpose of this clause, the term "NON-DISCRIMINATORY" means lack of discrimination on the grounds of religion, caste, gender or place of birth and such other grounds as may be specified. [Insolvency and Bankruptcy Code (31 of 2016), S. 196(2)(c), *Explanation*

Non efficit affectus nisi sequatur effectus. (*Lat.*) The intention amounts to nothing unless some effect follows.

Non enim tam auctoritatis in disputando, rationis momenta quaerenda sunt. In every argument, more respect is to be had to reason than to authority.

Non-est. Non-existent.

Non est arctius vinculum inter homines quam jusjurandum. (*Lat.*) (Jenk. Cent. 126) There is no stronger link among men than an oath.

Non est certandum de regulis juris. There is no disputing about rules of law.

Non est factum. (*Lat.*) It is not his deed.

Non est lex sed servitus, adea teneri quebus non consenseris. It is not law but servitude to be held by what we have not consented to.

Non est recedandum a communi observantia. (*Lat.*) (2 Rep. 74) There is no departure from a common observance.

Non est regula quin fallit. There is no rule without an exception. (*Latin for Lawyers*; *Black*)

Non est reus nisi mens sit rea. One is not guilty unless his intention be guilty.

Non-explosive. Not explosive. [Factories Act (63 of 1948), S. 37(4)].

Non-forest purpose. "NON-FOREST PURPOSE" means the breaking up or clearing of any forest land or portion thereof for—

(a) the cultivation of tea, coffee, spices, rubber plants, oil bearing plants, horticulture crops or medicinal plants;

(b) any purpose other than reafforestation, but does not include any work relating or ancillary to conservation, development and management of forests and wild-life, namely, the establishment of check-posts, fire line, wireless communications and construction of fencing, bridges and culverts, dams, water holes, trench marks, boundary marks, pipelines or other like purposes. [Forest (Conservation) Act (69 of 1980), S. 2(iv) *Expln.*]

Non-formal education Means the education of a person upon fifteen years of age who has not attended any educational institution at any time before or as the case may be, who is a drop out from an educational institution at any level of his studies therein to enable him to enter the formal educational system at an appropriate level. [Karnataka Education Act, 1983 (1 of 1995), S. 2(22)]

Non-fulfilment. Non-accomplishment [TP Act (4 of 1882), S. 34]; non-performance [Indian Contract Act (9 of 1872), S. 75].

Non-Government metro railway. Means a metro railway other than a Government metro railway. [Delhi Metro Railway (Operation and Maintenance) Act (60 of 2002), S. 2(l)]

Non-Government railway. Means a railway other than a Government railway. [Railways Act (24 of 1989), S. 2(25)]

Non-gratuitous act. An act which is not gratuitous. [Indian Contract Act (9 of 1872), S. 70].

Non-hereditary trustee. Means a trustee who is not a hereditary trustee. [H.P. Hindu Public Religious Institutions and Charitable Endowments Act (18 of 1984), S. 2(h)]

Non impedit clausula derogatoria, quo minus ab eadem potestate res dissolvantur a qua constituuntur. (*Lat.*) (Bac. Max. Reg.19)A derogatory clause does not prevent acts from being dissolved by the same power which constituted them.

Non in legendo sed in intelligendo leges consistunt. (*Lat.*) (8 Rep. 167) The laws consist, not in being read, but in being understood.

Non in tobulis est jus. (*Lat.*) The law is not in the books.

Non-joinder. The omission to join some person as party to a suit, whether as plaintiff or defendant, who ought to have been so joined, according to law.

Omission to join (as a party to a suit).

Non Journalist newspaper employee. Means a person employed to do any work in, or in relation to any newspaper establishment but does not include any such person who —

(i) is a working journalist, or

(ii) is employed mainly in a managerial or administrative capacity, or,

(iii) being employed in supervisory capacity, performs, either by the nature of duties attached to his offices or by reason of the powers vested in him, functions mainly of a managerial nature. [Working Journalists and Other Newspaper Employees (Conditions of Service) and Miscellaneous Provisions Act (45 of 1955), S. 2(dd)]

Non-judicial. Other than judicial. [CPC (5 of 1908), S. 128(2)(i)].

Non-judicial oath. There is an essential difference between a judicial and a "non-judicial oath". A judicial oath is one taken before an officer is open Court, and a non-judicial oath is one taken before an officer *ex parte*, or out of Court.

Non jus ex regula, sed regula ex jure. (*Lat.*) The law does not arise from the rule, but the rule from the law.

Non-liability. The absence of liability [Negotiable Instruments Act (26 of 1881), S. 131].

Non-lapsable fund. Means the Fund created from the commercial revenues of *Akashvani* and *Doordarshan* to meet expenditure on certain schemes. [Prasar Bharti (Broadcasting Corporation of India) (25 of 1990), S. 2(p)]

Non-linked business. Means life insurance contracts or health insurance contracts which are not linked business. [Insurance Regulatory and Development Authority (Registration of Indian Insurance Companies) Regulations, Regn. 2(j)]

Non-municipal area. Means an area in the State, which is not a municipal area and includes any area which is declared to be a cantonment under the [Cantonments Act, 1924 (2 of 1924)]. [Maharashtra Luxury cum-Entertainment and Amusement Tax on Holders of the Television Sets Act (19 of 1982), S. 2(e)]

Non-observance. Failure to observe [TP Act (4 of 1882), S. 65(d)].

Non observata forma, infertur adnullatio actus. (*Lat.*) (5 Co. Eccl. 1.98) When the form is not observed, it is inferred that the act is annulled.

Non obstante. (*Lat.*) Notwithstanding : or not opposing.

Non obstante clause. A non obstante clause is a legislative device which is usually employed to give overriding effect to certain provisions over some contrary provisions that may be found either in the same enactment or some other enactment that is to say, to avoid the operation and defect of all contrary provisions. *Sebastian M. Hongrary* v. *Union of India*, AIR 1984 SC 1022, 1026.

A clause used in public and private instruments intended to preclude, in advance, any interpretation contrary to certain declared objects or purposes.

Nonwithstanding; an overriding clause.

Non officit affectus nisi sequatur effectus. Sed in actrocioribus delictis punitur affectus, licet non sequatur effectus. The intention is not hurtful unless an effect follow. But in the most atrocious crimes the intention is punished, although no effect follow. (*Latin for Lawyers*)

Non officit conatus nisi sequatur effectus. An attempt does not harm unless a consequence follows.

Non omne damnum iducit injuriam. It is not every loss that produces an injury.

Non-omne licitum honestum. (*Lat.*) Not every lawful thing is honorable.

Non omne quod licet honestum est. (*Maxim*) Not everything which is permitted by law is honourable. (*Peloubet*)

Non-par policies. Or "policies without participation in profits" means policies which are not entitled for any share in surplus (profits) during the term of the policy. [Insurance Regulatory and Development Authority (Actuarial Report and Abstract) Regulations, 2000, Rgn. 2(i)]

Non-payment. Failure or neglect to pay; the condition of not being paid. [CPC (5 of 1908), O. XXXVII, R. 6].

Non-performance. Neglect or failure to perform [TP Act (4 of 1882), S. 65(d)]; [Indian Easements Act (5 of 1882), S. 6].

Non-performing asset. Means an asset or account of a borrower, which has been classified by a bank or financial institution as sub-standard, doubtful or loss asset, in accordance with the directions or under guidelines relating to asset classifications issued by the Reserve Bank. [Securitisation and Reconstruction of Financial Assets and Enforcement of Security Interest Act (54 of 2002), S. 2(1)(o)]

NON-PERFORMING ASSET means—

(a) an asset, in respect of which, interest has remained overdue for a period of six months or more;

(b) a term loan inclusive of unpaid interest, when the instalment is overdue for a period of six months or more or on which interest amount remained overdue for a period of six months or more;

(c) a demand or call loan, which remained overdue for a period of six months or more from the date of demand or call or on which interest amount remained overdue for a period of six months or more;

(d) a bill which remains overdue for a period of six months or more;

(e) the interest in respect of a debt or the income on receivables under the head 'Other current assets' in the nature of short term loans/advances, which facility remained overdue for a period of six months or more;

(f) any dues on account of sale of assets or services rendered or reimbursement of expenses incurred, which remainded overdue for a period of six months or more;

(g) the lease rental and hire purchase instalment, which has become overdue for a period of twelve months or more;

(h) in respect of loans, advances and other credit facilities (including bills purchased and discounted), the balance outstanding under the credit facilities (including accrued interest) made available to the same borrower/beneficiary when any of the above credit facilities becomes non-performing asset;

In the case of lease and hire purchase transactions, an NBFC may classify each such account on the basis of its record of recovery. [Non-Banking Financial Companies Prudential Norms (Reserve Bank) Directions, 1998, para 2(1)(xii)]

"NON-PERFORMING ASSET" means an asset in respect of which

(a) interest or principal (or instalment thereof) is overdue for a period of more than 180 days;

(b) interest for principal is overdue for a period of more than 180 days from the expiry of planning period, wherever applicable;

(c) any other receivable, if it is overdue for a period of more than 180 days. [Securitisation Companies/Reconstruction Companies Prudential Norms (Reserve Bank) Directions, 2002, S. 2(ii)]

"NON-PERFORMING ASSET" means a borrowal account in respect of which interest income or instalment of loan towards repayment of principal amount has remained unrealised for twelve months. [R. 3(1)(e) of the Nidhi Rules, 2014]

Non pertinet ad judicem secularem cognoscere de iis quae sunt mere spiritualia annexa. (*Lat.*) (2 Inst. 488) It pertains not to the secular judge to take cognizance of things purely spiritual.

Non possessori incumbit necessitas probandi possessiones ad se pertinere. (*Maxim*) A person in possession is not bound to prove that the possession belongs to him. (*Latin for Lawyers*)

Non potest adduci exceptio ejusdem rei cujus petitur dissolutio. (*Lat.*) (Bac. Max.22) A matter, the validity of which is at issue in legal proceedings, cannot be set up as a bar thereto.

Non potest probari quod probatum non relevat. (*Lat.*) That cannot be proved which, if proved, would be immaterial.

Non potest rex subditum renitentem onerare impositionibus. The king cannot load a subject with imposition against his consent.

Non potest videri desisse habere, qui nunquam habuit. He cannot be considered as having ceased to have a thing, who never had it.

Non-practising allowance. Allowance paid *in lieu* of the condition of not being allowed to practise.

Non praestat impedimentum quod de jure non sortitur effectum. An impediment which does not by law produce a consequence avails nothing.

Non præscribi protest rebus meræ facultatis. (*Lat.*) There is no prescription against those rights which consist in the power of doing or not doing a certain thing.

Non-prized subscriber. Does not include a defaulting subscriber. [Chit Fund Act 1982 (40 of 1982), S. 2(k)]

Non-production. Not producing; not offering for inspection or consideration [Indian Evidence Act (1 of 1872), S. 159].

Non quod voluit testator, sed quod dixit in testamento inspicitur. Not what the testator wished, but what he said, is condidered in construing a will.

Non-receipt of notice. The fact of not getting the notice [Companies Act (1 of 1956), S. 172(3)].

Non-reciprocating country. A country which does not reciprocate [Estate Duty Act (34 of 1953), S. 49].

Non-recovery. The fact of not getting or obtaining. [CrPC 1973 (2 of 1974), S. 424(2)].

Non-recurring expenditure. Means expenditure other than recurring expenditure. [General Financial Rules, 1963, R. 2(xx)]

Non recusat ad minora dimittere lex. The law does not refuse to descend to the smallest details.

Non refert an quis assensum suum praefert verbis, an rebus ipsis et factis. (*Lat.*) (10 Rep. 52) It matters not whether a man gives his assent by his words or by his acts and deeds.

Non refert an quis assensum suum praefert verbis, au rebus ipsis et factis. It matters not whether a man gives his assent by his words or by his acts and deeds. (*Latin for Lawyers*)

Non refert quid notum sit judici, si noium non sit in forma judicii. No judge should import his private knowledge of the facts into a case." "It matters not what is known to the judge, if it is not known to him judicially. (*Bouvier*)

Non-registration. The absence of registration [Registration Act (16 of 1908), S. 49].

Non-resident. Not residing at the place in question [Income-tax Act (43 of 1961), S. 2(30)].

One who does not reside in, or is not a resident of, a particular place; one who has his abode in another state; one who resides out of the state.

Non-resident alien. One who is neither a citizen of the State nor resident of the state; an alien not residing in the state.

Non-resident dealer. Means a dealer who effects purchases or sales of any goods in the State, but who has no fixed place of business or residence in the State. [Maharashtra Sales Tax (17 of 1979), S. 2(19)]

Non-resident defendant. The defendant, who at the time of the commencement of the suit does not actually reside or carry on business within the local limits of the jurisdiction of the Court. [CPC (5 of 1908), S. 20, ill. (b)].

Non-resident Indian. Means an individual, being a citizen of India or a person of Indian origin who is resident outside India.

Explanation 1.—A person shall be deemed to be of Indian origin if—

(i) he, or either of his parents or any of his grand-parents, was a citizen of India by virtue of the Constitution or the Citizenship Act, 1955; or

(ii) he at any time held an Indian passport:

Provided that nationals of Pakistan or Bangladesh shall not be deemed to be of Indian origin.

Explanation 2.—A spouse (not being a national of Pakistan or Bangladesh) of a person of Indian origin shall also be deemed to be of Indian origin. [Remittances of Foreign Exchange and Investment in Foreign Exchange Bonds (Immunities and Exemptions) Act (41 of 1991), S. 5(1)(b)]

"NON-RESIDENT INDIAN" means an individual, being a citizen of India or a person of Indian origin who is not a "resident". *Explanation*—A person shall be deemed to be of Indian origin if he, or either of his parents or any of his grand-parents, was born in undivided India. [Income-tax Act (43 of 1961), S. 115 C(e)]

Non-residential building. The expression 'non-residential building' occurring in Section 2(d) includes expression 'shop-cumflat'. *Shabbir Ahmad* v. *Shamlal,* (2002) 3 SCC 118, para 16 : AIR 2002 SC 1036. [East Punjab Urban Rent Restriction Act (3 of 1949) S. 2(d) as extended to Chandigarh in 1974]

Non-satisfaction. The absence of satisfaction. [CPC (5 of 1908), app. E, form No. 3].

Non-resident taxable person. "non-resident taxable person" means any person who occasionally undertakes transactions involving supply of goods or services or both, whether as principal or agent or in any other capacity, but who has no fixed place of business or residence in India [The Central Goods and Services Tax Act, 2017 (12 of 2017), S. 2(77)]

Non-taxable online recipient. "Non-taxable online recipient" means any Government, local authority, governmental authority, an individual or any other person not registered and receiving online information and database access or retrieval services in relation to any purpose other than commerce, industry or any other business or profession, located in taxable territory

Explanation.—For the purposes of this clause, the expression "governmental authority" means an authority or a board or any other body,—

(i) set up by an Act of Parliament or a State Legislature; or

(ii) established by any Government, with ninety per cent. or more participation by way of equity or control, to carry out any function entrusted to a municipality under article 243W of the Constitution [The Integrated Goods and Services Tax Act, 2017 (13 of 2017), S. 2(16)]

Non solum quid licet, sed quid est conveniens, considerandum; quia nihil quod est inconveniens est licitum. Not only what is permitted but what is proper is to be considered, because nothing improper is lawful.

Non-state actor. "NON-STATE ACTOR" is a person or entity not acting under the lawful authority of any country. [Weapons of Mass Destruction and Their Delivery Systems Prohibition of Unlawful Activities) Act (21 of 2005), S. 4(g)]

Non-statutory body. A body not established by a statute [Parliament (Prevention of Disqualification) Act (10 of 1959), S. 3(i)].

Non suit. A renunciation of a suit by the plaintiff most common upon the discovery of some error or defect, when the matter is so far proceeded in that the Court is ready to deliver their verdict. (*Cowell. Tomlin*)

Non sum doctus nec instructus, nec curo de victoria, modo ministretur justitia. *Testis*, *i.e.*, a witness, should be able to say from his heart, I am neither taught nor instructed what to say, I am indifferent as to the event of the cause; I am only anxious that justice be administered.

Non teaching Staff. Means

(i) in relation to the university, the non teaching staff, not holding any teaching staff, not holding only teaching post (including part time teaching post) appointed or recognised as such by the university and

(ii) in relation to an affiliated College, the non teaching staff, not holding any teaching post (including part time teaching post), appointed or recognised by the university or appointed by such college, but does not include an officer or a librarian. [Burdwan University Act (W.B. Act, 23 of 1981), S. 2(13)]

Non-testamentary. Otherwise than by a will; other than by a will.

Non-transferable specific delivery contract. "NOT-TRANSFERABLE SPECIFIC DELIVER CONTRACT" means a specific delivery contract, the rights or liabilities under which or under any delivery order, railway receipt, bill of lading, warehouse receipt or any other document of title relating thereto are not transferable. [Forward Contracts (Regulation) Act (74 of 1952), S. 2(f)]. [Securities Contract (Regulation) Act (45 of 1965), S. 2(ca) as inserted by Finance Act (20 of 2015), S. 133].

Non-tribal transferee. The expression "non-tribal transferee" as defined includes his successors-in-interest; and if he or his successor had, on or after March 15, 1971, transferred land in favour of any person whether a tribal or a non-tribal, includes also such a person. *Lingappa Pochanna Appelwar* v. *State of Maharashtra,* AIR 1985 SC 389.

Non-user. Literally "neglect to use" a neglect to exercise an office.

Non valet donatio nisi subsequatur traditio. A gift is not valid unless accompanied by possession. This, of course, refers only to gifts *inter vivos* and not to testamentary gifts. (*Latin for Lawyers*)

Non verbis sed ipsis rebus leges imponimus. Not upon words, but upon affairs, themselves do we impose laws.

Non videtur consensum retinuisse si quis ex praes cripto minantis aliquod immutavit. (*Lat.*) If a person has changed anything at the demand of a party threatening, he is not considered to have maintained his consent.

Non videtur perfecte cujusque id esse quod ex casu auferri potest. That does not truly belong to any one which can be taken from him upon occasion. (*Bouvier*)

Nonassertive conduct. In evidence law, it is the nonverbal behaviour which is not intended to be a statement, such as fainting while being questioned as a suspect by a police officer.

Noncallable security. A security which cannot be redeemed, or bought back at the option of the issuer.

Nonconsent. Lack of voluntary agreement.

Noncumulative dividend. A dividend that does not accrue for the benefit of a preferred shareholder if there is a passed dividend in a particular year or period.

Noncumulative voting. A voting system in a corporation in which a shareholder is limited in board elections to vote no more than the number of shares he or she owns for a single candidate as a result the majority of shareholders elect the entire Board of Directors.

Nonfeasance. The omission of a duty cast by law; the omission of an act which a person ought to do; neglect of duty. (*Tomlin*)

Nongovernmental organisation (NGO). Any scientific, professional, public interest or business organisation which is neither affiliated with nor under the direction of the Government.

Noninterpretivism. In constitutional interpretation; the doctrine holding that judges are not confined to the Constitution's text or preratification history but may instead look to evolving social norms and values as the basis for constitutional judgments.

Nonintervention will. A will which authorizes the executor to settle and distribute the estate without the supervision of the Court.

Nonresident parent. A parent who is not living with his or her child and who may be liable to pay child support maintenance.

Nonsuit. A judgment given against a plaintiff who neglects to prosecute, fails to show a legal cause of action, or to present sufficient evidence.

Norm. An ideal standard binding upon the members of a group and serving to guide, control or regulate proper and acceptable behaviour.

Normal discrepancies. In evidence 'normal discrepancies' are those which are due to normal errors of observation, normal errors of memory, due to lapse of time, due to mental disposition such as shock and horror at the time of occurrence. They do not corrode the creditability of a party's case. *Bhargavan* v. *State of Kerala*, AIR 2004 SC 1058 : JT 2003 (9) SC 515.

Normal discrepancies in evidence. 'Normal discrepancies' in evidence are those which are due to normal errors of observation, normal errors of memory due to lapse of time, due to mental disposition such as shock and horror at the time of occurrence and those are always there however honest and truthful a witness may be. 'Normal discrepancies' do not corrode the credibility of a party's case. *Gangadhar Behera* v. *State of Orissa*, AIR 2002 SC 3633 : (2002) 8 SCC 381 : JT 2002 (8) SC 135.

Normal labour or Normal delivery. Normal Labour or Normal delivery means series of processes by which the nature or almost nature products of conception are expelled from the mother's body and during which no artificial means are used. *Mahendra* v. *Sushila*, AIR 1965 SC 364, 388. [Indian Evidence Act (1 of 1872), S. 112]

"Non-transferable specific delivery contract" means a specific delivery contract, the rights or liabilities under which or under any delivery order, railway receipt, bill of lading, warehouse receipt or any other documents of title relating thereto are not transferable. [Securities Contract (Regulation) Act (45 of 1965), S. 2(ca) as inserted by Finance Act (20 of 2015), S. 133].

Normal price. The price at which goods are ordinarily sold by the assessee to a buyer in the course of wholesale trade. Where the goods are sold at different prices to different classes of buyers, each such price shall be deemed to be the normal price. [*Commissioner of Customs and Central Excise, Nagpur v. Ispat Industries Limited*, (2016) 1 SCC 631 15] [Central Excise Act (1 of 1944), S. 4 (as amended in 1973)] [Now repealed by Act 12 of 2017].

Normal value. "Normal value" is, where excise duty is chargeable on any excisable goods with reference to value, such value shall be deemed to be price at which such goods are ordinarily sold by the assesse to a buyer in the course of wholesale trade for delivery at the time and place of removal and where the assesse and the buyer had no interest directly or indirectly in the business of each other and the price is the sole consideration of the sale. Normal price, therefore, is the amount paid by the buyer for the purchase of goods. [*Commissioner of Central Excise, Mumbai v. Fiat India Private Limited*, (2012) 9 SCC 332, para 43].

North-eastern area. Means the area comprising the States of Arunachal Pradesh, Assam, Manipur, Meghalaya, Mizoram, Nagaland and Tripura. [North-Eastern Council Act (84 of 1971), S. 2(b)]

North-Eastern region. Means the North-Eastern region of India comprising the States of Arunachal Pradesh, Manipur, Meghalaya, Mizoram, Sikkim and Tripura. [Central Agricultural University Act (40 of 1992), S. 2(e); Income Tax Act (43 of 1961), S. 10C *Expln.* (iii) and S. 80 1B (14)(d)]

"NORTH-EASTERN REGION" means the North-Eastern region of India comprising the State of Meghalaya and the Union Territories of Arunachal Pradesh and Mizoram. [North-Eastern Hill University Act (24 of 1973), S. 2(l)]

North-Eastern States. Means the States of Arunachal Pradesh, Assam, Manipur, Meghalaya, Mizoram, Nagaland and Tripura. [Income-tax Act (43 of 1961), S. 80 IC(8)(vii)]

Noscitur a sociis. (*Lat.*) (*3T.R. 87*) The meaning of a doubtful word may be ascertained by reference to the meaning of the words associated with it."

Noscuntur a sociis is a rule of construction which means that when two or more words which are susceptible of analogous meaning are coupled together they are understood to be used in their cognate sense. They take as it were their colour from each other, that is, the more general is restricted to a sense analogous to a less general. *State of Bombay* v. *Hospital Mazdoor Sabha*, AIR 1960 SC 610, 613.

The maxim means—All the associated words will take colour from each other. *Rainbow Steels Ltd.* v. *Sales Tax Commissioner, U.P.*, AIR 1981 SC 2101, 2104.

It is not a sound principle in interpretation of statutes to lay emphasis on one word disjuncted from its preceding and succeeding word. A word in a statutory provision is to be read in collocation with its companion words. The pristine principle has much relevance in understanding the import of words in a statutory provision. *K. Bhagirathi G. Shenoy* v. *K.P. Ballakuraya,* (1999) 4 SCC 135, para 6 : AIR 1999 SC 2143.

Noscitur ex socio qui non cognoscitur ex se. He who cannot be known from himself may be known from his associates. (*Morgan Leg. Max.*)

Not. A word expressing negation, denial, or refusal.

To read the words "or not" as joined to each other, and to substitute them by "nor" would be to change the structure of the whole sentence and therefore its meaning. An interpretation which so radically alters the meaning of the clause, cannot be accepted. *Ranchhoddas Atmaram* v. *Union of India,* AIR 1961 SC 935.

Not according to law. Ignoring the weight of evidence, proceeding on a wrong premise of law or deriving such conclusion from the established facts as betray a lack of reason and/or objectivity would render the finding of Rent Controller 'not according to law' under Section 25-B(8) proviso of the Act. *Shiv Sarup Gupta* v. *Mahesh Chand Gupta (Dr.),* (1999) 6 SCC 222, para 11 : AIR 1999 SC 2507. [Delhi Rent Control Act (59 of 1958), S. 25B(8) proviso]

Not being the High Court. The use of expression 'not being the High Court' in Rule 11(4) could not be construed to stop or prevent the High Court from supporting summary dismissal order in appeals by reasons. *Dhanroop* v. *Purushottamdas Purohit,* AIR 2000 MP 118, 120, paras 9 & 10. [CPC (5 of 1908), O. XLI, R. 11(4)]

Not earlier than thirty days. "Not earlier than thirty days" would include the 30th day but not the 29th day because 29th day must be regarded as earlier than thirty days. *Jai Charan Lal* v. *State of U.P.*, AIR 1968 SC 5, 8.

Not essential. Specific performance of a contract cannot be enforced in favour of a person who fails to aver and prove that he has performed or has always been ready and willing to perform the essential terms of the contract which are to be performed by him and where a contract involves the payment of money, it is 'not essential' for the plaintiff to actually tender to the defendant or to deposit in Court any money except when so directed by the Court. [Specific Relief Act (47 of 1963), S. 16(c), Expln. (1)]

The expression 'not essential' occurring in Section 16(c) *Expln.* (i) means 'need not do', but does not mean 'one cannot do so'. *Syed Dastagir* v. *T.R. Gopalkrishna Setty,* (1999) 6 SCC 337, para 11 : AIR 1999 SC 3029. [Specific Relief Act (47 of 1963), S. 16(c), *Expln.* (i)]

Not exceeding. Not more than [IPC 45 of 1860, S. 154]; [TP Act (4 of 1882), S. 57(a)(2)].

Not found. Where the notice sent by the landlord to the tenant on the correct address is returned with the endorsement 'NOT FOUND', such service will be presumed to be good. *A.E.K. Kaliappa Nadar* v. *Sv.K.R. Amirtha Unlavendammal,* AIR 1973 Mad 255, 256. [T.P. Act (4 of 1882), S. 106]

Not guilty. The general issue of plea of the defendant in any criminal action or prosecution. (*Tomlin*)

A denial of the charges by an accused person in Court.

Not inconsistent with the provisions of this act. These words in S. 1 of the Indian Contract Act (9 of 1872) apply to "any usage or custom of trade" or "any incident of any contract."

Not later than. The expression 'not later than' means 'within a period of'. *Harinder Singh* v. S. *Karnail Singh*, AIR 1957 SC 271.

Not later than fourteen days. The words 'not later than fourteen days' must be held to mean the same thing as 'within a period of fourteen days'. *Harinder Singh* v. *S. Karnail Singh*, AIR 1957 SC 271, 273.

Not negotiable. The words which are marked on a cross cheque indicating that a transferee for value of the cheque gets no better title to it than his transferor had.

Not ordinarily resident. If an assessee resides in the taxable territories for more than two years, then he is not 'not ordinarily resident' in the taxable territories, or in other words, if an assessee does not reside in the taxable territories for more than two years he is entitled to the exemption which 'not ordinarily resident' gives to him. *Manibhai S. Patel* v. *I.T. Commissioner,* AIR 1953 Bom 258, 259.

Not otherwise provided. The words 'not otherwise provided for in this Act' should not be understood to refer to anything except a provision for the actual fee leviable. It does not refer to the provision for computation of values. *In re Rajmannar,* AIR 1953 Mad 746, 749. [Court Fees Act (7 of 1870), Sch. I, Art. 1]

Not-permanently resident. Means a person resident in India for employment of a specified duration (irrespective of length thereof) or for a specific job or assignment, the duration of which does not exceed three years. [Foreign Exchange Management (Possession and Retention of Foreign Currency) Regulations, 2000 Reg. 4 and Foreign Exchange Management (Remittance of Assets) Regulations, 2000 Reg. 5]

Not proceeding from true source. "Not proceeding from true source" only means that the thing is not what it pretends to be, which only means that it is not genuine or legitimate. *Chaitanya Kumar* v. *Sushila,* AIR 1975 SC 1718, 1721.

Not proved, fact. A fact is said not to be proved when it is neither proved nor disproved. [Indian Evidence Act (1 of 1872), S. 3] [Now (w. e. f. 1-7-2024) repealed & replaced by Bharatiya Sakshya Adhiniyam, 2023 (47 of 2023).

The expression 'not proved' does not mean 'false' under Section 3 of this Act. *A. Abdul Rashid Khan* v. *P.A.K.A. Shahul Hamid,* (2000) 10 SCC 636, para 11. [Indian Evidence Act (1 of 1872), S. 3]

Not strictly justified by law. The words "not strictly justified by law" in S. 99, IPC (45 of 1860), apply to cases in which there is an excess of jurisdiction as distinct from a complete absence of jurisdiction.

Notary. Person with authority to draw up deeds and perform other legal formalities.

A person publicly authorised to draw up or attest contracts or similar documents, to protest bills of exchange etc and discharge other duties of a formal character. [Notaries Act (53 of 1952), S. 2(d)].

Notary public. A person publicly authorised to draw up or attest contracts or similar documents to protest bills of exchange, *etc.* and discharge other formal duties; a public officer whose function it is to certify signatures and documents on oath. [Indian Evidence Act (1 of 1872), S. 57(6)].

Notation. The process of making a memorandum of some special circumstance on a probate or letters of administration.

Note. Only a trier of fact (someone with the authority to resolve disputes) can make an ultimate determination of non-repudiation. By way of illustration, a digital signature verified pursuant to this certification practice statement can provide proof in support of a determination of non-repudiation by a trier of fact, but does not by itself constitute non-repudiation. (*Information Technology*)

A brief statement of particulars of some fact. [CPC (5 of 1908), O. XI, R. 1]; a bank note or other form of paper that is current money [IPC (45 of 1860), S. 489A]; to record a note.

Note, Accommodation. A bill, draft or note made, drawn, accepted, or endorsed by one person for another without consideration to enable that other to raise money or obtain credit thereby. [Negotiable Instruments Act (26 of 1881), S. 59, prov]

Note at the foot. A brief record at the bottom of the text. [CPC (5 of 1908), O. XI, R. 1].

Note of authority. A letter of authority to act *etc.* [CPC (5 of 1908), O. XXVII, R. 8(1)].

Notice. Intimation; a writing; placard, board, etc, conveying an intimation or warning [IPC (45 of 1860), S. 154 and Constitution of India, Art. 61(2)(a)]; knowledge or cognizance. [Indian Evidence Act (1 of 1872), S. 56].

NOTICE, in its legal sense, may be defined as "information concerning a fact actually communicated to a party by an authorised person, or actually derived by him from a proper source, or else presumed by law to have been acquired by him, which information is regarded as equivalent to knowledge in its legal consequences." [T.P. Act (4 of 1882), S. 3; Indian Trust Act (2 of 1882), S. 3]

Subsequent transferee obtaining transfer deed in respect of the property found to be in possession of the first transferee in whose favour transfer was effected by a registered deed, could not be said to be transferee without notice of the previous transfer. *Annapurna* v. *Munshi,* AIR 1967 All 531, 532. [T.P. ACT (4 of 1882), Ss. 43 and 3]

Notice, Giving in writing. The notice transmitted by fax would fall within the ambit of expression 'giving notice in writing' under Section 138 prov. (b) of the Act. *Sil Import* v. *Exim Aides Silk Exporters,* (1999) 4 SCC 567, para 18. [Negotiable Instruments Act (26 of 1881), S. 138, prov. (b)]

Notice in writing. The word 'notice' denotes merely an intimation to the party concerned of a particular fact. It cannot be limited to a letter. Notice may take several forms. It must, to be sufficient, be in writing and must intimate quite clearly that the award has been made and signed. *Parasramka Commercial Co. Ltd.* v. *Union of India*, AIR 1970 SC 1654, 1656. [Arbitration Act (10 of 1940) (*repealed*), S. 14(1)]

Notice : Knowledge. The word 'notice' is of wider import than the word 'knowledge'. A person may not have actual knowledge of a fact but he may have notice of it. *Ram Niwas* v. *Bano,* (2000) 6, 685 para 18 : AIR 2001 SC 2921. [T.P. ACT (4 of 1882), S. 3, *Expln.* II]

Notice of dishonour. Notice given by the holder of a bill of exchange to the drawer when the bill is refused or payment delayed.

Notice of the appeal. The expression 'notice of the appeal' means notice of the day fixed for hearing and disposal of the appeal and not merely notice to the respondent that an appeal has been filed.

Notice to government. The object of a notice under S. 80, CPC (5 of 1908) is to inform Government, or the public officers concerned, generally of the nature of the suit which is intended to be filed against them. The notice need not set out all the facts and details of the case which the plaintiff intended to prove.

Notice to quit. A "NOTICE TO QUIT" is a notice which, on its expiry does, of itself or in accordance with a subsisting contract, puts an end to a relationship of Landlord and Tenant. [T.P. Act (4 of 1882), S. 113].

Notices. "When a quasi-judicial body embarks on determining disputes between the parties it must adhere to the rule "*Audo Alterum Partem*" which says no one should be condemned unheard. Notice is the first limb of this rule, it must be precise and unambiguous, it must apprise the party determinatively the case he has to meet, adequate time for his representation must be given. In the absence of notice of the kind and such reasonable opportunity the order passed against the person in absentia becomes wholly vitiated.

Notifiable disease. Any disease, which is required by law to be reported to Official Health Authorities [heading, Factories Act (63 of 1948), Sch III].

Notification. A written or printed matter that gives notice. [CrPC 1973 (2 of 1974), S. 1(2), *Prov* and Constitution of India, Art. 13(3)(a)].

"NOTIFICATION" means a notification published in the Official Gazette of the appropriate Government and the expression "notified" shall be construed accordingly. [Advocates' Welfare Fund Act (45 of 2001) S. 2(j)]

Formal declaration, proclamation and publication of an order either generally or in the manner prescribed. [Land Acquisition Act (1 of 1894), S. 4(1)]

Notification of succession. Means in relation to a multilateral treaty any notification, however phrased or named, made by a successor state expressing its consent to be considered as bound by the treaty. [Vienna Convention on Succession in Respect of Treaties, 1978, Art. 2(g)]

Notifications, orders, rules and bye-laws. The words "NOTIFICATIONS, ORDERS, RULES AND BYE-LAWS" have no reference to judicial orders, the passing and cancellation whereof is subject to and regulated by the procedural law of the land. Obviously the word 'orders' refer to non-judicial orders. [General Clauses Act (10 of 1897), S. 21]

Notified is used as implying a 'notice given' by some person whose duty it was to give it, in some manner prescribed, and to some person entitled to receive it. An election petition will be competent only after the election or selection is notified and not before.

Notified commodity. Means any commodity other than agricultural produce and foodstuffs which the Central Government may, by notification in the official Gazette, declare to be a notified commodity for the purposes of this Act, being a commodity with respect to which Parliament has power to make laws by virtue of Entry 33 in List III in the Seventh Schedule to the Constitution. [National Co-operative Development Corporation Act (26 of 1962), S. 2(e)]

"NOTIFIED COMMODITY" means any commodity other than agricultural produce which the Central Government may, by notification in the official Gazette, declare to be a notified commodity for the purposes of this Act, being a commodity with respect to which Parliament has power to make laws by virtue of Entry 33 III in the Seventh Schedule to the Constitution. [Warehousing Corporation Act (58 of 1962), S. 2(e)]

Notified date. In relation to goods of any description means the date on which the notification in relation to such goods is issued under Section 11-B. [Customs Act (52 of 1962), S. 11-A(c)]

Notified order. The term 'notified order' means an order notified in the official gazette and it will cover special as well as general orders relating to the matters specified. *Santosh Kumar* v. *State*, AIR 1951 SC 201, 202.

Notified place. Means a place of pilgrimage or a place where a fair, mela or exhibition is being or is likely to be held, which the Central Government has, by notification in the official Gazette, declared to be a notified place for the purposes of this Act. [Terminal Tax on Railway Passengers Act (69 of 1956), S. 2(c)]

Notify. To inform; to make known; to give notice to; to inform by words or writings, or by any signs which are understood. (*Webster*)

"NOTIFY" means to notify in the Official Gazette and the expression "notification" shall be construed accordingly. [Foreign Exchange Management Act (42 of 1999), S. 2(t)]

To give notice of [CrPC 1973 (2 of 1974), S. 75]; to make a notification of.

Notify means to declare or to give notice and is to be contrasted with a mere intent of a cloistered order which means something which has been published to the citizenary at large. *Kashmiri Lal* v. *State of Punjab,* AIR 1984 P&H 87, 89. [Land Acquisition Act (1 of 1894), S. 4 (1)] [Now repealed & replaced by Act 30 of 2013]

Notional sales tax liability. Means—

(*i*) amount of tax payable on the sales of finished products of the eligible industrial unit under the local sales tax law but for an exemption computed at the maximum rates specified under the local sales tax law as applicable from time to time; and

Explanation.—The sales made on consignment basis within the State of Haryana or branch transfer within the State of Haryana shall also be deemed to be sales made within the State and liable to tax;

(*ii*) amount of tax payable under the General Sales Tax Act, 1956, on the sale of finished products of the eligible industrial unit made in the course of inter-State trade or commence computed at the rate of tax applicable to such sales as if these were made against certificate in Form C on the basis that the sales are eligible to tax under the said Act.

Explanation.—The branch transfers or consignment sales outside the State of Haryana shall be deemed to be sale in the course of inter-State trade or commerce.

Note.—The expression and terms, if any, appearing in this Rule not defined above shall unless context otherwise requires carry the same meaning as assigned to them under the Act and Rules made thereunder. [Haryana General Sales Tax Rules, 1975, R. 28-A(2)(n)] [Haryana General Sales Tax Act (20 of 1973)].

Noting for non-acceptance. The making of a memorandum on a bill of exchange by a notary which states that the bill has been presented for payment or acceptance and that it has been dishonoured [CPC (5 of 1908), O. XXXVII, R. 6].

Notorious. Well known; talked of much; unfavourably known; Generally or commonly known acknowledged or spoken of; publicly known and spoken of; generally known and talked of by the public.

Notorious facts. Matters of common knowledge of which, generally, judicially notice will be taken.

Notorious possession. Possession or control which is evident to others.

Notwithstanding. In spite of. [Indian Evidence Act (1 of 1872), S. 162].

Notwithstanding anything contained in law for.... in force. Sub-section (1) of Section 4 contains the words "notwithstanding anything contained in law for the time in force". The above *non obstante* clause points to the conclusions that the provisions of Section 4 would have over-riding effect and shall prevail if the other conditions prescribed are fulfilled. (*Ishar Das* v. *State of Punjab,* AIR 1972 SC 1295). [Probation of Offenders Act (20 of 1958), S. 4(1)]

Notwithstanding clause. A clause to prevail over other clauses.

Nova constitutio futuris formam imponere debet, non praeteritis. (Lat.) A new law ought to regulate what is to follow, not the past. [Principles of Statutory Interpretation by Justice G.P. Singh, 9th Edn., 2004, p. 438 as cited in *Zile Singh v. State of Haryana,* (2004) 8 SCC 1, para 13]. See also *Purbanchal Cables and Conductors Private Limited v. Assam State Electricity Board,* (2012) 7 SCC 462, para 65.

Novation. Novation is the substitution by mutual agreement of one debtor or of one creditor for another whereby the old debt is extinguished, or the substitution of a new debt or obligation for an existing one, which is thereby extinguished.

Substitution of a new debtor, creditor, contract, *etc.* in place of an old one [Indian Contract Act (9 of 1872), S. 62].

In every novation there are four essential requisites; (1) A previous valid obligation; (2) the agreement of all the parties to the new contract; (3) the extinguishment of the old contract; and (4) the validity of the new one. A novation is new contractual relation. It is based upon a new contract by all the parties interested.

In order to operate as a novation under S. 62 of the Indian Contract Act (9 of 1872), the new contract must involve present suppression or extinguishment of the liability arising under the old contract. A mere agreement between the parties to effect such a supersession or extinguishment at a future date cannot constitute novation. A contract for sale between the parties amounts to such an agreement. *Vishram Arjun* v. *Irukalla Shakariah,* AIR 1957 AP 784, 787.

The word 'novation' means the extinguishment of the terms of an earlier contract and the creation of another between new persons, at least one of who is a stranger to the original contract and there must be the mutual consent of all parties concerned. *Appukuttan* v. *Attappa,* AIR 1966 Ker 303, 305. [Indian Contract Act (9 of 1872), S. 62]

Noxious. Injurious; unwholesome [273 and 278, IPC (45 of 1860), Ss. 272].

"NOXIOUS" not only means hurtful and offensive to the smell, but it is also the translation of the very technical term 'nocivus'; it is not necessary that the smell should be unwholesome, it is enough if it renders the enjoyment of life and property uncomfortable.

Noxious liquid substance. Means any substance which has been designated as such by rules made under this Part. [Merchant Shipping Act (44 of 1958), S. 356B(g) (*Substituted by Merchant Shipping (Amendment) Act, 2003*)]

Noxious matter. An injurious or unwholesome matter. [CPC (5 of 1908), App. A, No. 24, para 2].

NPA. NPA is an asset which ceases to generate income for the creditors (Banks or financial institution) i.e., a loan or advance made by the banks on which interest and/or installment of principal amount is overdue for a specified period depending upon the nature of the loan or advance –whether the loan or advance is a term loan or agricultural loan, money advanced on bill discounting, etc. [*Keshavlal Khemchand and Sons Private Limited v. Union of India,* (2015) 4 SCC 770, para 37].

Nuclear installation area. In relation to a nuclear installation means the exclusion area and the sterilized area in relation to such installation. [UP Regulation of Buildings and Use of Land (Nuclear Installation Area) Act, 1988 (19 of 1992), S. 2(5)]

Nuclear reactor. 'NUCLEAR REACTOR' means any plant (including any machinery, equipment or appliance, whether affixed to land or not) designed or adapted for the production of atomic energy by a fission process in which a controlled chain reaction can be maintained without an additional source of neutrons. [(English) Nuclear Installations Act, 1965, S. 26]

Nuclear ship. Means a ship provided with a nuclear power plant. [Merchant Shipping Act (44 of 1958), S. 3(22)A]

Nuclear weapon or other nuclear explosive device. "NUCLEAR WEAPON OR OTHER NUCLEAR EXPLOSIVE DEVICE" means any nuclear weapon or other nuclear explosive device as may be determined by the Central Government, whose determination in the matter shall be final. [Weapons of Mass Destruction and Their Delivery Systems (Prohibition of Unlawful activities (21 of 2005) Act, S. 4(h)]

Nudi consensus obligatio contrario consensu dissolvitur. (*Lat.*) The binding force of a contract made with no consideration is dissolved by an agreement to the contrary.

Nudum pactum. Literally, "A nude pact." A promise that cannot be enforced, either at law or in equity; an executory contract without a consideration, or a naked promise; a voluntary promise, without any other consideration than mere good-will or natural affection.

No contract at all.

Nuisance. "NUISANCE" includes any act, omission, place or thing which causes or is likely to cause injury, danger, annoyance or offence to the sense or sight, smelling or hearing or disturbance to rest or sleep or which is or may be, dangerous to life or injurious to health or property. [Manipur Municipalities Act (43 of 1994), S. 2(37) and New Delhi Municipal Council Act (44 of 1994), S. 2(28) and Cantonment Act (2 of 1924), S. 2(xxii)]

An inconvenience materially interfering with ordinary comforts of human existence; anything injurious or obnoxious to the community or to an individual as a member of it, for which some legal remedy may be found. [IPC (45 of 1860), S. 268].

Nuisance is an inconvenience materially interferes with the ordinary physical comfort of human existence. It is not capable of precise definition. It may be public or private nuisance. As defined in Section 268 IPC (45 of 1860), public nuisance is an offence against public either by doing a thing which tends to the annoyance of the whole community in general or by neglect to do anything which the common good requires. It is an act or omission which causes any common injury, danger or annoyance to the public or to the people in general who dwell or occupy the property in the vicinity. On the alternative it causes injury, obstruction, danger or annoyance to persons who may have occasion to use public right. It is the quantum of annoyance or discomfort in contra distinction to private nuisance which affects an individual is the decisive factor. (*Vasant Manoj Nikumba* v. *Baburao Bhikanna Naidu,* 1995 Supp(4) SCC 54).

A tea stall, causing hindrance in the free flow of traffic on road, comes within ambit of 'nuisance' *A.L. Ranjana* v. *Ravindra Ishwardas Sethna,* (2003) 1 SCC 379, para 6.

Nuisance ordinarily means that which annoys or hurts or that which is offensive. If persons indulge in the act of beating on a railway platform it is found to cause annoyance to other persons who happen to be there at that time. *Durga Prasad* v. *State,* AIR 1962 Raj 92, 93. [Indian Railways Act (9 of 1890), S. 120(*b*)]

"Nuisance" and "annoyance". All nuisance may be annoyance but all acts of annoyance may not amount to nuisance. (*Laxmiben Mavjibhai* v. *Shankarbhai Mulubhai,* 1995 (2) Guj LR 1320 at 1332).

Anything done which unwarrantably affects the rights of others, endangers life, or health, give offence to the senses, violates the laws of decency or obstructs the comfortable and reasonable use of property, may amount to nuisance Annoyance also, more or less, means the same thing as nuisance. What is nuisance or annoyance is a question of fact depending on the facts and circumstances of each case. (Patil J.) *Gopal Vaman* v. *Krishnaji Tatyarao,* MLJ : YD (1979) Supp to Feb. p. 519 : (1979) 2 Ren CR 10 : 1979 (2) Rent LR 573 : (1979) 1 Kant LJ 319. [Karnataka Rent Control Act (1961), S. 21 (1) (d)]

Nul charter, nul vente, ne nul done vault perpetualment, si le adonor n'est seise al temps de contracts de deux droits, sc. del droit de possession et del droit de properite. No grant, no sale, no gift, is valid forever unless the donor, at the time of the contract, is seised of two rights, namely, the right of possession, and the right of property.

Nul ne doit s'enrichir aux depens des autres. No one ought to enrich himself at the expense of others.

Nul prendra advantage de son tort demesne. No one shall take advantage of his own wrong.

Null. Of no legal force or effect; void; of no binding force or validity, of no efficacy; invalid; nugatory; useless.

Naught; of no validity or effect. [Hindu Marriage Act (25 of 1955), Ss. 11 and 16].

Null and void. This is a term which according to the context may sometimes mean void, and sometimes voidable. (*Ame. Cyc.*)

"The words 'null and void' may be interpreted as referring to those cases where the arbitration agreement is affected by some invalidity right from the beginning, such as lack of consent due to misrepresentation, duress, fraud or under influence. ["The New York Convention, 1958 – An Overview," Article II(3) by Albert Jan Van Den Berg as cited in *World Sport Group (Mauritius) Limited v. MSM Satellite (Singapore) PTE, Limited*, (2014) 11 SCC 639, para 27].

Of no legal effect; a nullity.

Nulla bona. No goods.

Nulla impossibilia aut inhonesta sunt praesumenda; vera autem et honesta et possibilia. (*Lat.*) (Co. Litt. 78b) No things that are impossible or dishonorable are to be presumed; but things that are true and honorable and possible.

Nulla lex nulla iniura. (*Lat.*) "If there is no law, there is no wrongdoing."

Nulla pactione effici potest ne dolus praestetur. (*Lat.*) It cannot be effected by any agreement, that there is no accountability for fraud"

Nulla poena capitis nulla quae hominum remve ejus destraut esse potest nisi legibus praefinita. There can be no capital punishment, or form of punishment destructive either to the individual or his property, which is not established by law before the fact.

Nulla poena sine lege. (*Lat.*) There ought to be no penalty without legal authority.

It means that a person should not be made to suffer penalty except for a clear breach or existing law. [*Vijay Singh v. State of U.P.*, (2012) 5 SCC 242, para 21].

Nulla res vehementius rempublicam continet quam fides. Nothing binds the republic more closely than the fidelity of its citizens.

Nulla unquam de morte hominis cunctatio longa est. There should be no long delay in matters involving human life.

Nulle regle sans faute. There is no rule without a fault.

Nulli differemus justitiam. To no one should we delay justice.

Nulli res sua servit jure servitutis. (*Lat.*) No man's property is under burden of a servitude to himself : no one can have a right of servitude over his own subject.

Nulli vendemus, nulli negabimus aut differemus justitiam vel rectum. Justice and right shall be sold, denied, or delayed to no one.

Nullification. To make something void.

Nullity. A thing which is null and void; an error in litigation which is incurable (*Wharton*); a proceeding that is taken without any foundation for it, or that is essentially defective, or that is expressly declared to be "nullity" by a statute.

The state or fact of being legally null and void. [Hindu Marriage Act (25 of 1955), S. 16].

Nullity, Decree of. A decree declaring (a marriage) null and void [Hindu Marriage Act (25 of 1955), S. 11].

Nullity of marriage. There are two classes of cases in which marriages are, or may be, declared null and void; marriages which are void *ab initio*, and marriages which are only voidable at the suit of one of the contracting parties. The former class may itself be subdivided into two heads, namely, the case of marriages which are, *ex-necessitate rei*, no marriages at all; and marriages which are only rendered absolutely null and void by statute. To put the most extreme case, a ceremony of marriage performed between two persons of the same sex would, by the law of nature, and by all laws human and divine, be nothing but a mockery and absolute nullity.

A defect in marriage that would render it void or voidable in an action to annul the marriage.

'Nullity' or 'without jurisdiction'. The expressions 'nullity' or 'without jurisdiction' are relative terms and depending upon the particular situation. Unless the executing Court is absolutely confident, it cannot be said that a decree is a 'nullity' or 'without jurisdiction' and thereby inexecutable. [*Chanda Engineers (India) Ltd.* v. *U.C.O. Bank*, AIR 2005 Cal 28, 45, p. 37]

Nullity suit. Nullity suit (*or suit for Nullity of marriage.*) A term used in reference to a suit to annul a pretended marriage, which has for its purpose a decree that a marriage that is void or voidable shall be judicially declared to be void. (*See* Ind. Divorce Act.) It differs essentially from a "divorce suit"—A divorce suit is for the purpose of dissolving a marriage which the parties thereto had legal capacity to enter into.

Nullius filius. (*Lat.*) Son of no one.

Nullum crimen majus est inobedientia. (*Lat.*) (Jenk. Cent. 77) No crime is greater than disobedience.

Nullum crimen nulla poena sine lege. There is no crime nor punishment except in accordance with law.

Nullum crimen patitur is qui non prohibet cum prohibet non potest. He who fails to prevent that it is not possible for him to prevent is guilty of no crime.

Nullum crimen sine lege. (*Lat.*) There should be no crime except according to predetermined, fixed law.

Nullum crimen sine poena. (*Lat.*) There should be no crime without a penalty.

Nullum iniquum est praesumendum in jure. (*Lat.*) (7 Rep. 71) No inequity is to be presumed in law.

Nullus commodum capere potest de injuria sua propria. (Lat.) "Persons violating the law cannot be permitted to urge that their offence cannot be subjected to inquiry, trial or investigation." [*Devendra Kumar v. State of Uttaranchal*, (2013) 9 SCC 363, para 25].

No one can take advantage of his own wrong. [*Hardeep Singh v. State of Punjab*, (2014) 3 SCC 92, para 33].

Nullus idoneus testis in re sua intelligitur. (*Maxim*) No person is understood to be a competent witness in his own cause.

Nullus liber homo capiatur, vel imprisonetur aut exulet, aut aliquo modo destruatur, nisi per legale judicium parium, suorum, ve per legem terrae. No freeman shall be taken, imprisoned, or exiled or in any other manner destroyed, save by the lawful judgment of his peers, or by the law of the land.

Nullus liber homo disseisietur de libero tenemento suo, nisi per legale judicium perium suorum vel per legem tere. No freeman shall be dispossessed of his freehold, save by the lawful judgment of his peers, or by the law of the land.

Nullus Tempus aut locus occurit regi (Lat.). It means that a crime never dies. [*Sarah Mathew v. Institute of Cardiovascular Diseases*, (2014) 2 SCC 62, para 15].

'Nullus Tempus aut locus occurit regi' means that a crime never dies. [*Sarah Mathew v. Institute of Cardiovascular Diseases*, (2014) 2 SCC 62, para 12 and 30].

Nullus videtur dolo facere qui suo jure utitur. (*Lat.*) (D. 50, 17, 55) No man is to be esteemed a wrongdoer merely who avails himself of his legal right.

Number. A collection of units.

Mark or symbol having arithmetical value. [IPC (45 of 1860), S. 294A]; a number [General Clauses Act (10 of 1897), S. 17(1)].

"Unless the contrary appears from the context, words importing the singular number include the plural number, and words importing the plural number include the singular number". [Indian Penal Code (45 of 1860), S. 9] [Now (w. e. f. 1-7-2024) repealed & replaced by Bharatiya Nyaya Sanhita, 2023 (45 of 2023), S. 2(22), same definition in new Sanhita]

The singular includes the plural. 227 IC 228.

Numbered. Bearing a number. [CPC (5 of 1908), O. IV, R. 2].

Numerator. The part of a fraction that is above the line and signifies the number of parts of the denomination taken; one that numbers. [Income-tax Act (43 of 1961), S. 35A(1)(ii)].

Numerous. The word 'numerous' in O. X, R. 8 CPC (5 of 1908) is by no means a term of art. It has an ordinary meaning implying a group of persons, such as would make it inconvenient to implead all of them individually. The word is not synonymous with 'numberless' or Innumerable'. *Kailash Pat* v. *Brij Gopal*, AIR 1950 All 405, 406.

Nunquam crescit ex post facto praeteriti delicti aestimatio. (*Lat.*) (Bac. Max. Reg. 8) The quality of a past offence is never aggravated by that which happens subsequently.

Nuptial. Pertaining to or connected with a marriage contract.

Nuptias non concubitus sed consensus facit. (*Maxim*) Not cohabitation but consent makes marriage. (*Latin for Lawyers*)

Nurse. "NURSE" means a qualified nurse holding a certificate or a diploma recognised by the Chief Administrative Officer of the State or a registered nurse in a State in which there is statutory provision for the registration of nurses. [All India Services (Medical Attendance) Rules, 1954, R. 2(h)]

To nurse, used with reference to an adult, conveys the idea that the object of care is sick or is an invalid.

Nurse dai. Means a trained *dai* who has passed the examination in nursing prescribed by the Punjab Nurses Registration Council or one who has been registered with the said Council and has been taken over from the said council in transferred territories merged in Himachal Pradesh under Section 5 of the Punjab Reorganisation Act, 1966. [Himachal Pradesh Nurses Registration Act, 1977 (15 of 1978), S. 2(h)]

Nursery. "NURSERY" means any fruit, and/or ornamental plant nursery or tissue culture unit in Goa where fruit and/or ornamental plants are in regular course of business, propagated and sold for transplantation or cultivation but does not include such a nursery belonging to or managed by the Government. [Goa Fruit and Ornamental Plant Nurseries (Regulation) Act, 1995 (Goa Act No. 13 of 1997), S. 2(g)]

A place where young trees are propagated, for the purpose of being transplanted into orchards, plantations, *etc.*

A place designed for the care or training of children; an area where trees, shrubs or plants are grown for transplanting for use as stocks for budding and grafting.

Nursery-man. Means any person engaged in the production and sale of fruit or ornamental plants. [Goa Fruit and Ornamental Plant Nurseries (Regulation) Act, 1995 (Goa Act No. (13 of 1997), S. 2(h)]

Nursery school. "Nursery school" means, a school where children of pre-basic stage i.e., from about three to six years of age are taught. [Educational Code of U.P. (Revised 1958 Edn.), Para 1 (xxvi)(a) as cited in *State of U.P. v. Pawan Kumar Divedi*, (2014) 9 SCC 692, para 22].

Nursing home. "NURSING HOME" means an establishment or premises used or intended to be used for the reception of and providing medical care including nursing care in any form to persons suffering from sickness, injury or infirmity. [Orissa Clinical Establishments (Control and Regulation) Act, 1990 (4 of 1992), S. 2(f)]

A premises having medical facilities for indoor and outdoor patients having upto 30 beds in a nursing home and would be managed by a doctor on commercial basis. [*Chairman and Chief Executive Officer, Noida Authority v. Mange Ram Sharma*, (2012) 7 SCC 65, para 6] [Noida Master Plan, 2031, Ch. 7.30, Serial No. 87 (5.22)].

A private hospital; a private home or other place where maintenance and personal or nursing care are provided for three or more persons, who are unable to care for themselves properly. [Income-tax Act (43 of 1961), S. 80D(2)(i)].

Nurture. To educate; to train; to bring up. Fostering care; bringing up.

Nourishing. [Indian Trusts Act (2 of 1882), S. 4, ill. (a)].

Nutrition. Food; nourishing.

Supplying or receiving of nourishment, food. [Mica Mines Labour Welfare Fund Act (22 of 1946), S. 3(2)(a)(iv)].

O

Oath. The word "OATH" includes a solemn affirmation substituted by law for an oath, and any declaration required or authorized by law to be made before a public servant or to be used for the purpose of proof, whether in a Court of Justice or not. [IPC (45 of 1860), S. 51] [Now (w. e. f. 1-7-2024) repealed & replaced by Bharatiya Nyaya Sanhita, 2023 (45 of 2023)]

"Oath" includes a solemn affirmation substituted by law for an oath, and any declaration required or authorised by law to be made before a public servant or to be used for the purpose of proof, whether in a Court or not. [(w. e. f. 1-7-2024) Bharatiya Nyaya Sanhita, 2023 (45 of 2023), S. 2(23)]

"OATH" shall include affirmation and declaration in the case of persons by law allowed to affirm or declare instead of swearing. [General Clauses Act (10 of 1897), S. 3(37)].

A solemn appeal to God (or to something sacred) in witness that a statement is true or a promise binding; an act or swearing; the form of words in which such a statement or promise is made. [IPC (45 of 1860), S. 51; General Clauses Act (10 of 1897), S. 3(37) and Constitution of India, Art. 60].

The real purpose of the oath is that the person concerned must give an undertaking to bear true faith and allegiance to the constitution and uphold the sovereignty and integrity of India. *V. R. Sutaria* v. *N. P. Bhanvadia*, AIR 1970 SC 765, 767 [Constitution of India, Art. 173 (a), Schedule 3, Form 7 A].

A solemn statement in the name of God made by the member of a Legislature before he takes his seat in the House affirming his allegiance to the Constitution and his resolve to uphold the sovereignty and integrity of the country. (*Constitutional and Parliamentary Term*)

Oath Commissioner. Commissioner or other person so authorised to administer oaths.

Oath of office. The oath to be taken before assuming a public office.

Obedience. The action or practice of obeying. [CrPC 1973 (2 of 1974), S. 132(2)(d) and S. 350].

Obedientia est legis essentia. Obedience is the essence of the law.

Obiter. By the way; in passing; incidentally; collaterally.

It is an expression of opinion (formed) by a judge on a question immaterial to the *ratio decidendi*, and unnecessary for the decision of the particular case. It is in no way binding on any Court, but may receive attention as being an opinion of high authority.

Obiter dicta or **dicta.** (*Lat.*) An opinion of law not necessary to the decision.

The expression "obiter dicta" means "by the way"; "in passing"; "incidentally." Obiter dicta is the expression of opinion stated in the judgment by a Judge which is unnecessary of a particular case. Obiter dicta is an observation which is either not necessary for the decision of the case or does not relate to the material facts in issue. [*Odisha Power Generation Corporation Ltd. v. State of Odisha*, AIR 2015 Ori 128, para 34].

The phrase '*obiter dictum*' means an observation by the Court on a legal question suggested in a case before it but not arising in such manner as to require a decision. *Director of Settlements A.P.* v. *M.R. Apparao,* (2002) 4 SCC 638, para 7 : AIR 2002 SC 1598. [Constitution of India, Art. 141]

"Dicta are opinion of a Judge which do not embody the resolution or determination of the court, and made without argument or full consideration of the point, are not the professed deliberate determinations of the Judge himself; obitor dicta are opinions uttered by the way, not upon the point or question pending, as if turning aside for the time from the main topic of the case to collateral subjects; it is mere observation by a Judge on a legal question suggested by the case before him, but not arising in such a manner as to require decision by him; 'obitor dictum' is made as argument or illustration, as pertinent to other cases as to the one on hand, and which may enlighten or convince, but which is no sense are a part of the judgment in the particular issue, not binding as a precedent, but entitled to receive the respect due to the opinion of the Judge who utters them; discussion in an opinion of principles of law which are not pertinent, relevant, or essential to determination of issue before court is 'obitor dictum'." [Words and Phrases, Permanent Edn., Vol. 29 as cited in *Arun Kumar Aggarawal v. State of M.P.*, (2014) 13 SCC 707, para 25].

A Judicial comment made while delivering a judicial opinion, but one that is unnecessary to the decision in the case and therefore not precedential (although it may be considered persuasive).—Often shortened to dictum or, less commonly, obitor…

Strictly speaking an "obitor dictum" is a remark made or opinion expressed by a judge, in his decision upon a cause, "by the way"—that is, incidentally or collaterally, and not directly upon the question before the court; or it is an statement of law enunciated by the Judge or court merely by way of illustration, argument, analogy, or suggestion…. In the common speech of lawyers, all such extrajudicial expression of legal opinion are referred to as "dicta" or "obitor dicta", these two terms being used interchangeably.'" [Black's Law Dictionary, (9th Edn., 2009) as cited in *Arun Kumar Aggarwal v. State of M.P.*, (2014) 13 SCC 707, para 24].

In the course of a suit many incidental questions arise indirectly connected with the main question for consideration, the observations in such questions, whether casual or of collateral relevance are known as "*obiter dicta*" or simply "*dicta*". *Marta Silva* v. *Piedade Cardozo,* AIR 1969 Goa 94 at 101.

Object. Something on which the purposes are fixed as the end of an action or effort [IPC (45 of 1860), Ss. 141 and 146 and Constitution of India, Art. 356(1)(c)]; something visible or tangible [Indian Evidence Act (1 of 1872), S. 3, ill. (a)]; [IPC (45 of 1860), S. 293]; to make an objection [Income-tax Act (43 of 1961), S. 246(a)]; something that arouses feeling (as of pity, amusement or disgust) in an observer. [Margin, Indian Succession Act (39 of 1925), S. 76].

The word "object" in S. 23, Indian Contract Act (9 of 1872) is not used in the same sense as "consideration." It means purpose or design.

The word 'object' would mean the purpose and design which is the object of the contract. If it is opposed to public policy which tends to defeat any provision of law or purpose of law, it becomes unlawful and thereby it is void under S. 23. (*Gurmukh Singh* v. *Amar Singh,* (1991) 3 SCC 79). [Indian Contract Act (9 of 1872), S. 23]

The word 'object' occurring in Section 149 of IPC means the purpose or design. *State of Maharashtra* v. *Kashirao,* (2003) 10 SCC 434, 441, para 12. [IPC (45 of 1860), S. 149]

"OBJECT" the word 'object' means the purpose or design and, in order to make it 'common', it must be shared by all. *Shivjee Singh* v. *State of Bihar*, AIR 2009 SC 417.

Object code. Computer code, derived by a computer or assembler program, from source code, into a form understandable by machine rather than human forms-also called executable and/or machine code. (*Cyber Law*)

Object, Common. An object shared by all concerned. [IPC (45 of 1860), S. 141].

Object held sacred. The word 'object' has to be interpreted '*ejusdem generis*' with a place of worship. Interpreted like that, it would mean that the section would apply only to cases where an idol in a temple is sought to be destroyed, damaged or defiled. The word "any object held sacred by any class of persons" even otherwise will apply only to idols in a temple or when they are carried out in processions as festival occasions. *A. Veerabhadran Chettiar* v. *E.V. Ramaswamy Naicker,* AIR 1955 Mad 550. [IPC (45 of 1860), S. 295]

Any object however trivial or destitute or real value in itself, if regarded as sacred by any class of persons would come within the meaning of the expression 'object held sacred'. *Veerabadran Chettiar* v. *Ramaswami Naicker*, AIR 1958 SC 1032, 1035. [IPC (45 of 1860), S. 295]

Object of general public utility. An object beneficial to a section of the public is an object of general public utility. To serve a charitable purpose it is not necessary that the object should be to benefit the whole of mankind or all persons in a particular country or State. It is sufficient if the intention to benefit a section of the public as distinguished from a specified individual is present. *Ahmedabad Rana Caste Association* v. *CIT, Gujarat,* AIR 1972 SC 273.

Object-Oriented Program. A type of programming language well-suited for use with a graphical user interface; typically uses computer code that is attached to such objects as windows and buttons that are displayed for the user. (*Computer*)

Objection. The action of stating something in opposition to a person or thing; an adverse reason, argument or contention.

Objectionable matter. The ordinary grammatical meaning of the words is that words which are grossly indecent are within the definition; words which are scurrilous are within the definition; words which are obscene are within the definition; and the words which are intended for blackmail are within the definition of 'objectionable matter'. *S. Jeelani* v. *State,* AIR 1954 Cal 488, 489.

Objective. Pertaining or considered in relation to its object constituting or belonging to an object of action, thought or feeling; denoting the object or point to which the operations are directed.

Objective assessment. An 'objective assessment' (here for the purpose of affiliation of a dental college) would be one which is based on the information gathered from the entire record pertaining to the relevant period and not just one stray lapse or mistake. [*Shri Gangajali Education Society v. Union of India,* (2017) 16 SCC 656, para 14].

Objector. The person who objects or makes an objection to something. [Income-tax Act (43 of 1961), 2nd Sch., Item 11(3)].

Obligatio mandati consensu contrahentium consistit. The authority of an agent to contract for his principal rests on the consent of his principal.

Obligation. "OBLIGATION" includes every duty enforceable by law. [Specific Relief Act (47 of 1963), S. 2(a)]

A duty; the bond of legal necessity which binds together two or more determinate individuals. [Constitution of India, Art. 49].

Obligation and **duty.** "Duty and obligation, though the terms, in one of the sense of the latter, are often used interchangeably, are not the same thing. 'Obligation', says Lord COKE, 'is a word of large extent', although it sometimes means only duty, and always includes this meaning it often imports something more." [*Wood* v. *Wood*, 14 Rich. (SC) 148, 156; *Ame Cyc.*]

Obligee. One towards whom another is under an obligation.

Obligor. "OBLIGOR" means a person liable to the originator, whether under a contract or otherwise, to pay a financial asset or to discharge any obligation in respect of a financial asset, whether existing, future, conditional or contingent and includes the borrower. [Securitisation and Reconstruction of

Financial Assets and Enforcement of Security Interest Act (54 of 2002), S. 2(1)(q)]

One who binds himself to another by contract; one who places himself under a legal obligation. [Indian Evidence Act (1 of 1872), S. 114, ill. (i)].

Obliterate. To deface, efface, to blot out, to destroy. Pasting over a piece of paper would constitute an "obliteration" in law; so also strong black line drawn over and along the whole name is said to obliterate it. obliteration denotes covering over by some means words originally written so as to render them no longer legible; complete cancellation of such words.

Obloquy. Blame; reprehension; censure; reproach. To expose one to 'obloquy' is to expose him to censure and reproach.

Obnoxious. Offensive, odious, hateful.

Obscene. For the purposes of this Act an article shall be deemed to be OBSCENE if its effect or (where the article comprises two or more distinct items) the effect of any one of its items is, if taken as a whole, such as to tend to deprave and corrupt persons who are likely, having regard to all relevant circumstances, to read, see or hear the matter contained or embodied in it. [Obscene Publications Act, 1959, S. 1(1)]

Extremely offensive under contemporary community standards of morality and decency; grossly repugnant to the generally accepted notions of what is appropriate. [Black's Law Dictionary as citied in *Devidas Ramachandra Tuljapurkar v. State of Maharashtra*, (2015) 6 SCC 1, para 8].

'Obscene' means disgusting to the senses usually because of some filthy, grotesque or unnatural quality, grossly repugnant to the generally accepted notions of what is appropriate. [Webster's New International Dictionary as cited in *Devidas Ramachandra Tuljapurkar v. State of Maharashtra*, (2015) 6 SCC 1, para 9].

An article is deemed to be obscene, if its effects, or where the article two or more distinct items, the effect of any one of its items if taken as a whole, is to tend to deprave and corrupt persons, who are likely having regard to all the relevant circumstances to read, to see or hear matters contained or embodied in it. [Jowitts' Dictionary of English Law as cited in *Devidas Ramachandra Tuljapurkar v. State of Maharashtra*, (2015) 6 SCC 1, para 9].

The tendency of which is to deprave those whose minds are open to immoral influence and into whose hands the matter is likely to fall; offensive to modesty or decency. [IPC (45 of 1860), S. 293].

The meaning of the word 'obscene' is repulsive, filthy, loathsome, indecent and lewd. But every indecent or repulsive or filthy article will not come under the definition. *Public Prosecutor* v. *A.D. Sabapathy,* AIR 1958 Mad 210.

If the words addressed were clearly offensive to the chastity and modesty of the girls and they are likely to express and personate something which delicacy and purity and decency forbade to be expressed, it is an obscene act. *Zafar Ahmad Khan* v. *State,* AIR 1963 All 105, 107. [IPC (45 of 1860), S. 294]

Obscene and indecent exhibition of the person. The words 'obscene and indecent exhibition of the person,' mean 'an exposure of those parts of the person which are commonly considered as private, and which custom and decency require should be covered and kept concealed from public sight. They do not mean or include obscene or indecent prints, pictures placed on the clothes worn on the person.

Obscene exhibition of person. By an "obscene exhibition of the person" is meant any offensive, disgusting, and indelicate presenting to view, show, or display of the person.

Obscene object. Anything tangible or visible which is offensive to good taste or which tends to corrupt the morals or to lower the standards of right and wrong especially as to sexual relationship. [CrPC 1973 (2 of 1974), S. 94(2)(f)].

Obscene publications. A book, pamphlet, paper, writing, drawing, painting, representation, figure or any other object, including display of any content in electronic form shall be deemed to be obscene if it is lascivious or appeals to the prurient interest or if its effect, or (where it comprises two or more distinct items) the effect of any one of its items, is, if taken as a whole, such as to tend to deprave and corrupt persons who are likely, having regard to all relevant circumstances, to read, see or hear the matter contained or embodied in it. [(w. e. f. 1-7-2024) Bharatiya Nyaya Sanhita, 2023 (45 of 2023), section 294(1)]

Obscenity. Lewdness; impurity; indecency; calculated to shock the moral sense of man by a disregard of chastity or modesty".

The concept of obscenity is moulded to a very great extent by the social outlook of the people who are generally expected to read the book. It usually differs from country to country depending on the standards of morality of contemporary society in different countries. Even the outlook of a Judge may differ from another Judge on the question of obscenity inasmuch as even in the matter of objective assessment the subjective attitude of the Judge hearing the matter is likely to influence, though unconsciously, his mind and his decision on the question. (*Samaresh Bose* v. *Amal Mitra,* (1985) 4 SCC 289, 313, 314, 316).

'Obscenity' means character or quality of being obscene, conduct, tending to corrupt the public merely by its indecency or lewdness. [Black's Law Dictionary as cited in *Devidas Ramachandra Tuljapurkar v. State of Maharashtra*, (2015) 6 SCC 1, para 9].

The tendency of which is to deprave those whose minds are open to immoral influence and into whose hands the matter is likely to fall; offensive to modesty or decency. [IPC (45 of 1860), S. 293]

"Obscenity" and "pornography". The word, as the dictionaries tell us, denotes the quality of being obscene which means offensive to modesty or decency; lewd, filthy and repulsive. It cannot be denied that it is an important interest of society to suppress obscenity. There is, of course, some difference between obscenity and pornography in that the latter denotes writings, pictures, *etc.*, intended to arouse sexual desire while the former may include writings *etc.* not intended to do so but which have that tendency. Both, of course, offend against public decency and morals but pornography is obscenity in a more aggravated form. The books on medical science with intimate illustrations and photographs, though in a sense immodest, are not considered to be obscene but the same illustrations and photographs collected in book form without the medical text would certainly be considered to be obscene. *Ranjit D. Udeshi* v. *State of Maharashtra,* AIR 1965 SC 881. [IPC (45 of 1860), S. 292]

Obscuritas pacti nocet ei qui apertius loqui poruit. Ambiguity in a contract (treaty) works against the party who could have expressed himself more clearly.

Observance. Keeping a promise; performance of an obligation legal or moral; perceiving; watching; taking notice of.

Observation. View, reflection; remark; statement; observed truth or facts; remarks in speech or writing in reference to something observed. [Indian Evidence Act (1 of 1872), S. 21, ill. (b)].

Observation home. "OBSERVATION HOME" means a home established by a State Government or by a voluntary organisation and certified by that State Government under Section 8 as an observation home for the juvenile in conflict with law. [Juvenile Justice (Care and Protection of Children) Act (56 of 2000), S. 2(q) now repealed by Act 2 of 2016]

Observe. To adhere to; to follow [T.P. Act (4 of 1882), S. 65(d)]; to see [Indian Evidence Act (1 of 1872), S. 126, ill. (c)]; to perceive; to watch.

Observer. For the purposes of sub-section (2) and sub-section (3), "OBSERVER" shall include a Regional Commissioner or any such officer of the Election Commission as has been assigned under this section the duty of watching the conduct of election or elections in a constituency or group of constituencies by the Commission. [Representation of the People Act (43 of 1951), S. 20B (*Expl.*)]

"OBSERVER" means a representative of a requesting State Party or a third State Party to observe a challenge inspection. [Chemical Weapons Convention Act (34 of 2000), (verification Annex.), 20]

Observer delegate. "OBSERVER DELEGATE" means any person designated by a state to attend as an observer the proceeding of an organ or of a conference. [Vienna Convention on the Representation of States in their Relations with International Organizations of a Universal Character, 1975, Art. 2(25)]

Observer delegation. "OBSERVER DELEGATION" means, as the case may be the observer delegation to an organ or the observer delegation to a conference. [Vienna Convention on representation of State in their relations with International Organizations of a Universal Character 1975, Art. 1(12)]

Obsolete. Unrepealed, but not enforced.

That is no longer practised or used; out of date, said of a law or practice which has ceased to be enforced or be in use by reason of change of manners and circumstances [Indian Evidence Act (1 of 1872), S. 98]; [Air Corporations Act (27 of 1953), Sch., part. II, (f)]; no longer functional; a product gone out of date.

Obstruct. To hinder or prevent from progress; to check; to stop; to retard the progress of. [Cardamom Act (42 of 1965), S. 24(a)]; [CrPC 1973 (2 of 1974), S. 41(1)(e)].

To obstruct a highway means to stop up and wholly prevent travel upon a road, or render it unfit for travel.

(1) to block (a road, a passageway, etc.) with an obstacle; (2) to make (progress or activity) difficult; (3) to impede or block a clear view of. [Collin's Dictionary as cited in *Shreya Singhal v. Union of India*, (2015) 5 SCC 1, para 51].

Obstructing justice means impeding or obstructing those who seek justice in Courts, or those who have duties or powers of administering justice therein.

Obstruction. The word 'obstruction' in S. 186 connotes some overt act in the nature of violence or show of violence. It cannot be said that a man obstructed another if that man runs away from arrest or if he does not actually submit to the arrest. *Phudki* v. *State,* AIR 1955 All 104. [IPC (45 of 1860), S. 186]

A person or a thing that obstructs. [Collin's Dictionary as cited in *Shreya Singhal v. Union of India*, (2015) 5 SCC 1, para 51].

"Obstruction" has a wider meaning than mere physical obstruction and it includes tangible obstruction and even a protest is obstructing. *E. Aswathappa* v. *Karnataka Electricity Board,* AIR 1987 Kant 282, 284. [Indian Telegraph Act (13 of 1885), S. 16]

Obstruction of a highway. A public nuisance may arise by reason of a fence across a highway or a trench in it, or by some other interference with free and convenient passage, *i.e.*, collecting crowds at a theatre or a public meeting, near a highway.

Obstruction of a highway refers to something which permanently or temporarily removes the whole or part of the highway from public use altogether.

Obstruction of justice. Interference with the orderly administration of law and justice.

The offense of intentionally hindering or obstructing the arrest, conviction, and punishment of accused persons, including all proper and necessary proceedings for administering justice. Often defined by various state statutes. (*The Law Dictionary*)

Obstruction of officer. "To obstruct an officer" means to oppose that officer. It does not mean to oppose or impede the process with which the officer is armed, or to defeat its execution, but that the officer himself shall be obstructed. It is opposition to the officer, and the words 'obstruct, resist, or oppose' have, in this connection, nearly the same meaning.

Obtain maintenance from. The word 'obtain' as used in the proviso is significant. It does not merely mean that the widow is somehow managing to live with or is being maintained by her father or mother or that her father or mother are somehow managing to save their widowed daughter from starvation, for if this were to be the meaning placed on the word 'obtain', then, apparently, the basic and main purpose and object of the Hindu Adoptions and Maintenance Act would be thwarted rather than advanced. *Jal Kaur* v. *Pala Singh,* AIR 1961 Punj 391, 395. [Hindu Adoptions and Maintenance Act (78 of 1956), S. 19, proviso]

Obtainable. Something which can be obtained; capable of being obtained; liable to be obtained. [Specific Relief Act (47 of 1963), S. 10, *Expln.* (ii)(a)].

Obtained. The word 'obtained' may well be used in the sense of 'procured with effort' and would certainly describe correctly a situation where something is achieved by a person through his exertion in spite of opposition from others. *Zohara Khatoon* v. *Mohd. Ibrahim,* AIR 1981 SC 1243, 1252. [CrPC 1973 (2 of 1974), S. 125(1)].

Obtaining. The expression 'obtaining' connotes an element of effort on the part of the suitor or applicant. *State of Bihar* v. *Mohd. Ismail,* AIR 1966 Pat 1, 6 (FB). [Limitation Act (36 of 1963), S. 12, *Expln*]

The word obtain 'in S. 123(7) connotes 'purpose' or 'effort' behind the action of the candidate. It has not been used in the sense of a passing receipt of assistance without the candidate being even conscious of the fact that the assistance has been rendered. *Motilal* v. *Mangla Prasad,* AIR 1958 All 794, 797. [Representation of the People Act (43 of 1951) (as amended in 1956), S. 123(7)]

Obtaining minerals. The word 'obtain' covers the various process necessary to set the mineral and would include the processes covered by the expressions 'winning', 'working', 'getting' *etc.* *Gujaraj Potter Works* v. *B. P. Sood*, AIR 1967 SC 964, 967. [Mines and Minerals (Regulation and Development) Act (58 of 1968), S. 2(b)]

Obtaining or attempting to obtain. The words 'obtaining' or 'attempting to obtain' can certainly include threat. [IPC (45 of 1860), S. 161]

Obtains. The word 'obtains' does not eliminate the idea of acceptance of what is given or offered to be given, though it connotes also an element of effort on the part of the receiver. *Ram Kishan* v. *Delhi State,* AIR 1956 SC 476. [Prevention of Corruption Act (2 of 1947), S. 5(1)(d)]

"Obtains" or **"accepts"** or **"attempts to obtain".** For the purposes of this section, the expressions "OBTAINS" of "ACCEPTS" or "ATTEMPTS TO OBTAIN" shall cover cases where a person being a public servant, obtains or "accepts" or attempts to obtain, any undue advantage for himself or for another person, by abusing his position as a public servant or by using his personal influence over another public servant or by any other corrupt or illegal means. [Prevention of Corruption Act (49 of 1988), S. 7, *Explanation 2* as substituted by Amending Act (6 of 2018)].

Obtaining a certificate copy by reporting entity. Shall mean comparing the copy of officially valid document so produced by the client with the original and recording the same on the copy by the authorised officer of the reporting entity in a manner prescribed by the regulator. [Prevention of Money-laundering (Maintenance of Records) Rules, 2005, R. 9(4), *Explanation*].

Obtemperandum est consuetudini rationabili tanquam legi. (*Maxim*) A reasonable custom is to be obeyed as law. (*Peloubet*; *Wharton*)

Obviate. To prevent by anticipatory measures; to do away with. [CrPC 1973 (2 of 1974), S. 142(1)].

Obvious. Readily perceived by the eye, or intellect; seen or realized at the first glance; apparent in the exercise of ordinary observation and which is disclosed by the use of the eyes and other senses; patent; easily seen.

Obvious imitation. 'Obvious imitation' means something which strikes one at once as being so like the original design, the registered design, as to be almost unmistakable. *Britannia Industries Ltd.* v. *Sara Lee Bakery,* AIR 2000 Mad 497, 503, para 39.

Occasion. An opportunity; the time at which something happens; a particular time marked by some occurrence or by its special character [Indian Contract Act (9 of 1872), S. 56, ill. (e)]; something that produces an effect or brings about an event.

Occasional. Occurring at times, but not constant regular or systematic (*Webster*); happening now and then; incidental.

OCCASIONAL, CASUAL. These are both opposed to what is fixed or stated; but occasional carries with it more than the idea of un-frequency, and casual that of un-fixedness, or the absence of all design.

Occasions. Occasions does not necessarily mean to cause or to be immediate cause—it means in a wider sense to bring about especially in a incidental or subsidiary manner. *Coffee Board, Bangalore* v. *Joint Commercial Tax Officer, Madras*, AIR 1971 SC 870, 882.

The expression 'occasions' means the immediate and direct cause. *Mohd. Serajuddin* v. *State of Orissa*, AIR 1975 SC 1564, 1573. [Central Sales Tax Act (74 of 1956), S. 5 (1)]

Occasions export. Where the sale was not directly and substantially connected with export, and where between the seller and ultimate buyers intermediaries were involved, such a sale would not occasion any export. *Manganese Ore (India)* v. *Regional Assistant Commissioner of Sales Tax, Jabalpur*, AIR 1976, SC 410, 412. [Central Sales Tax Act (74 of 1956), S. 5 (1)]

Occultatio thesauri inventi. (*Lat.*) The concealment of found treasure.

Occultatio thesauri inventi fraudulosa. (*Lat.*) (3 Inst. 133) The concealment of discovered treasure is fraudulent.

Occupancy. The act of occupying. [Registration Act (16 of 1908), S. 21(2)].

Possession; the act of taking or holding possession; the taking possession of things corporeal, which are without an owner, with the intention of appropriating them to one's own use; the taking possession of those things which before belonged to nobody. Applied to land, possession; actual possession; possession as owner. Of beasts *feroe naturae*, the actual, corporal possession of them.

Occupancy right. The term commonly used in reference to cultivators who have higher rights in the land they cultivate than mere tenants-at-will.

Occupancy tenant. An 'OCCUPANCY TENANT' means tenant or a *raiyat* having occupancy right in his holding under the tenancy laws continued in force in the merged states. [Orissa Merged State's Laws Act, 1950, S. 7, *Expln.* (i)]

'OCCUPANCY TENANT' means a tenant who, immediately before the commencement of this Act, is recorded as an occupancy tenant in the revenue records and includes a tenant who, after such commencement, obtains a right of occupancy in respect of the land held by him whether by agreement with the landlord or through a court of competent jurisdiction or otherwise, and includes also the predecessors and successors-in-interest of an occupancy tenant. [Punjab Occupancy Tenants (Vesting of Proprietary Rights) Act, 1952 (98 of 1953), S. 2(f) as cited in *Tara Chand v. Gram Panchayat, Jhupa Khurd*, (2012) 13 SCC 269, para 5].

Occupant. "OCCUPANT" in the Tenancy Act includes every *zamindar*, tenure-holder, farmer and other person entitled to receive rents in respect of land, or holding land on a claim that he is so entitled, and every *raiyat* in occupation of land. [Ben Act V of 1875 (Survey), S. 2].

A person occupying or holding or in actual possession; an occupier [Presidency Small Cause Courts Act (15 of 1882), S. 41, para 3]; one who holds possession under title, lease or tenancy at will; one who occupies a particular place or premises. [Presidency Small Cause Courts Act (15 of 1882), S. 41, para 3].

One who occupies, or takes possession, one who has the actual use or is in the possession of a thing; one who takes possession or controls things actual; a person interested in the land which he possesses; a tenant in possession; a person holding a piece of property or office.

Occupant means a person holding the land in possession or actual enjoyment. *Amba Prasad* v. *Mahaboob Ali*, AIR 1965 SC 54, 58.

The term 'occupant' means a person in actual occupation. *Ramesh Kumar Satish Kumar and Sons* v. *Guru Singh Sabha,* (2001) 9 SCC 61, para 10 : AIR 2001 SC 1051.

A mortgagee in possession is not an occupant because he holds on behalf of the mortgagor. *Mustafa Khan* v. *Deputy Director of Consolidation,* AIR 1973 All 372, 373.

OCCUPANT AND OCCUPIER. A servant or employee claiming no title or interest in himself, or any right to the possession, is not occupant, within the meaning of the rules of law governing ejectments. He is acting under the control of another, and it is only in another's right that he occupies the premises.

A husband, though the head of the family, is not in any legal sense the possessor or occupant of the house or land owned by his wife, and in or upon which the family resides.

Occupantis fiunt derelicta. (*Maxim*) Things abandoned become the property of the (first) occupant.

Occupation. The principal business of one's life, vocation, calling, trade, the business which a man follows to procure a living or obtain wealth; that which occupies or engages one's time or attention, vocation, employment, calling, trade; the business in which a man is usually engaged, to the knowledge of his neighbour.

Occupation and profession. An occupation is a principal activity related to a job, work or calling that earns regular wages for a person and profession, on the other hand requires extensive training study and mastery of the subject, whether it is teaching students, providing legal advance or treating patients or diagnosing diseases. [*Employees' State Insurance Corporation's Medical Officer's Association* v. *Employees' State Insurance Corporation*, (2014) 16 SCC 182, para 11].

Actual holding or possession especially of a place or land. [IPC (45 of 1860), S. 157]; employment; business; a calling, trade [CrPC 1973 (2 of 1974), S. 133(1)(b) and Constitution of India, Art. 19(6)(i)]; temporary holding and control of a country or a part of a country by a foreign military force. [Air Force Act (45 of 1950), S. 4(1)(c)].

A territory is considered as occupied when it finds itself in fact placed under the authority of a hostile army. This means that occupation is by military authorities. *R. Monteivo* v. *State of Goa*, AIR 1970 SC 329 at 335. [Geneva Conventions Act (6 of 1960), Sch. IV, Art. 6]

The owner can occupy a place and make use of it in any manner. If the landlord on getting possession starts the work of demolition within the prescribed time, it would amount to occupation. Occupation in this sense would include occupation for demolition to make it fit for residence. *R.P. Mehta* v. *I.A. Sheth,* AIR 1964 SC 1676.

This word must be given its general meaning in which sense it would mean a person holding the land who is in actual enjoyment of the property. Between a landlord and a tenant and between a tenant and a sub tenant, the latter will be deemed to be the occupant. *Amba Parsad* v. *Mahaboob Ali,* AIR 1965 SC 54.

The word 'occupation' has a wide meaning such as any regular work, profession, job, principal activity, employment, business or a calling in which an individual is engaged. Sodan Singh v. N.D. Municipal Committee, (1989) 4 SCC 155, para 28, as cited in *T.M.A. Pai Foundation* v. *State of Karnataka,* (2002) 8 SCC 481, para 22.

Whatever else occupation may comprise, activity in a specific line of endeavor which engages or occupies time and attention of a person and which is carried on with a certain amount of continuity or regularity in the sense that it is not momentary, not 'an isolated or semi-occasional and temporary adventure' in that line of endeavour-would certainly constitute 'occupation'. *C.E.T.* v. *Ambalal Sarabai,* (1969) 73 ITR 78, 84, Guj. [Income-tax Act (43 of 1961), S. 28]

'Occupation' and 'possession'. There is a distinction between 'occupation' and 'possession, because there may be a legal or constructive possession where there is no actual occupation.

The word "occupy" is a word of uncertain meaning. Sometimes it indicates legal possession in the technical sense, as when occupation is made the test of rateability; and it is in this sense that it is said that the occupation of premises by a servant if such occupation is subservient and necessary to the service is the occupation of the master. At other times occupation denotes nothing more than physical presence in a place for a substantial period of time. 31 MLT 114 : 4 UPLR 97 (PC)

Occupation tax. It is not a tax upon property, but upon a pursuit which a man follows in order to acquire property and support his family.

Occupational disease. A disease that is contracted due to exposure to debilitating conditions or substances while in employment.

"Occupational disease" means a disease specified in the Third Schedule as a disease peculiar to the employment of the employee. [Code on Social Security, 2020 (36 of 2020), section 2(51)]

Occupational hazard. Danger or risk related to a particular occupation or calling.

Occupied. If the judgment-debtor himself chooses to let out a part of the house to tenants for occupation by them, that part cannot be treated as being occupied by the judgment-debtor. *Ude Bhan* v. *Kapoor Chand,* AIR 1967 Punj 53, (FB). [CPC (5 of 1908), S. 60(1)(ccc) (as added by S. 35), Punjab Relief and Indebtedness Act (7 of 1984)]

Occupier. "OCCUPIER" in relation to any institution generating bio-medical waste, which includes a hospital, nursing home, clinic dispensary, veterinary institution, animal house, pathological laboratory, blood bank by whatever name called, means a person who has control over that institution and/or its premises. [Bio-Medical Waste (Management and Handling) Rules, 1998, R. 3(8)]

"OCCUPIER" includes an owner in occupation of, or otherwise using his own land or building. [Cantonments Act (2 of 1924), S. 2(xxiii)]

"OCCUPIER", in relation to any factory or premises means a person who has control over the affairs of the factory or the premises and includes, in relation to any substance, the person in possession of the substance. [Environment (Protection) Act (29 of 1986), S. 2(f) and Air (Prevention and Control of Pollution) Act (14 of 1981), S. 2(m)]

"OCCUPIER", in relation to an establishment or a workshop, means the person who has the ultimate control over the affairs of the establishment or workshop. [Child Labour (Prohibition & Regulation) Act (61 of 1986), S. 2(vi)]

One who occupies. [Factories Act (63 of 1948), S. 2(n)].

"Occupier" in respect of a factory means the person who has ultimate control over the affairs of the factory. [Code on Social Security, 2020 (36 of 2020), section 2(52) and its proviso]

"Occupier" of a factory means the person who has ultimate control over the affairs of the factory. [Occupational Safety, Healthy & Working Conditions Code, 2020 (37 of 2020), section 2(1)(zs) and its proviso]

OCCUPIER is one who is in the use or enjoyment of a thing; person having the actual use or occupation.

"OCCUPIER" in relation to the premises where an insanitary latrine exists, or someone is employed as a manual scavenger, means the person who, for the time being, is in occupation of such premises. [S. 2(1)(j) of the Prohibition of Employment as Manual Scavengers & Their Rehabilitation Act, 2013 (25 of 2013)]

Occupier and **owner.** S. 4 of the Indian Easements Act (5 of 1882) shows that not merely the "owner" but even an "occupier", may acquire an easement and there is no *prima facie* reason why the enjoyment of a person as an "occupier" should not be tackled on under S. 15, to his enjoyment as "owner" if there is no interruption in his use.

The expression "occupier" is not to be equated with "owner". *John Donald Mackenzie* v. *Chief Inspector of Factories*, AIR 1962 SC 1351, 1352.

Occupier of factory. "OCCUPIER OF FACTORY" means the person who has ultimate control over the affairs of the factory,

Provided that—

(i) in the case of a firm or other association of individuals, any one of the individual partners or members thereof shall be deemed to be the occupier;

(ii) in the case of a company, any one of the directors shall be deemed to be the occupier;

(iii) in case of a factory owned or controlled by the Central Government or any State Government, or any local authority, the person or persons appointed to manage the affairs of the factory, as the case may be, shall be deemed to be the occupier;

Provided further that in the case of a ship which is being repaired, or on which maintenance work is being carried out, in a dry dock which is available for hire,—

(1) the owner of the dock shall be deemed to be the occupier for the purposes of any matter provided for by or under

(a) Section 6, Section 7, Section 7A, Section 7B, Section 11 or Section 12;

(b) Section 17, in so for as it relates to the providing and maintenance of sufficient and suitable lighting in or around the dock;

(c) Section 18, Section 19, Section 42, Section 46, Section 47 or Section 49, in relation to the workers employed on such repair or maintenance;

(2) the owner of the ship or his agent or master or other officer-in-charge of the ship or any person who contract with such owner, agent or master or other officer-in-charge to carry out the repair or maintenance work shall be deemed to be the occupier for the purposes of any matter provided for by or under Section 13, Section 14, Section 16 or Section 17 (save or otherwise as provided in this proviso) or Chapter IV (except Section 27) or Section 43, Section 44 or Section 45, Chapter VI, Chapter VII, Chapter VIII or Chapter IX or Section 108, Section 109 or Section 110, in relation to—

(a) the workers employed directly by him, or through any agency; and

(b) the machinery, plant or premises in use for the purpose of carrying out such repair or maintenance work by such owner, agent, master or other officer-in-charge or person. [Factories Act (63 of 1948), S. 2(n)]

"OCCUPIER OF A FACTORY" means the person who has ultimate control over the affairs of the factory, and where the said affairs are entrusted to a managing agent, such agent shall be deemed to be the occupier of the factory. [Employees Provident Funds and Miscellaneous Provisions Act (19 of 1952), S. 2(k)]

The word "occupier" in general means a person who occupies the factory either by himself or his agent. He may be an owner, he may be a lessee or even a mere licensee, but he must have the right to occupy the property and dictate how it is to be managed.

In case of a factory owned or controlled by the Central Government or any State Government, or any local authority, the person or persons appointed to manage the affairs of the factory, as the case may be, shall be deemed to be the occupier. *K.S.K. Union (Regd.)* v. *Union of India,* AIR 1988 SC 1965, 1969. [Factories Act (63 of 1948), S. 2(n) (iii)]

Occupier of land. An occupier is a person in use or enjoyment of the land, that is, a person having the actual use or occupation. *H.R. Rama Rao* v. *Collector,* AIR 1957 AP 1042, 1044.

Occupy. To take possession of, seize, employ, to take possession of and retain or keep. "To occupy" property denotes a physical possession; but "occupy" is a word which in one form and another is not infrequently used of an incorporeal hereditament.

To be in occupation of. [CPC (5 of 1908), O. XXI, R. 96]; [Army Act (46 of 1950), S. 3(1)(b)].

'Occupy' is to hold or keep for use, to possess, and to cover or fill. So to say that one occupies or has occupied land continuously is tantamount to saying that he has or had actual possession of the same.

Occur. To befall; to happen; to meet with; come to one's mind; to take place. As used in regard to losses insurance policies, the term has been held equivalent to arise, or accrue.

Occurrence. Happening; incident.

Occurrence rule. The rule which states that a limitation period begins to run when the alleged wrongful act or omission takes place, rather than when the plaintiff discovers the injury.

Octroi. Means a tax on the entry of goods into the limits of a municipal borough for consumption, use or sale therein. [Gujarat Municipalities Act, 1963 (34 of 1964), S. 2(16)]

A tax on commodities brought into a town or city; municipal customs. [Indian Carriage by Air Act (69 of 1972), Sch. I, Item 16(1)].

Oculist. Ontometrist. [Income-tax Act (43 of 1961), S. 80U, *Prov.* (a)].

Odiosa et inhonesta non sunt in lege praesumanda et in facto quod se habe ad bonum et malum, magis de bono quam de malo preasumendum est. (*Co. Lit. 78*). Odious and dishonest acts are not presumed in law; and in an act which partakes both of good and bad, the presumption is in favour of what is good.

ODR. (*abbr.*) Online Dispute Resolution. 1. The use of the internet to settle disputes through Alternative Dispute Resolution (ADR) processes. 2. resolution of dispute using information technology conducted at a distance usually *via* the Internet, independent from the physical location of the parties. (*Arbitration*)

Of. Owned by, as, property of another; belonging to, as clerk of the Court; from or proceeding from, as the cause, source, means, or agent, bestowing, belonging to; pertaining or relating to, as, in Court of the District; cause of accident; master of the house; concerning.

The word 'of' in the expression 'within six months of the seizure of the goods' should be read as 'from'. *Vasantilal* v. *Union of India,* AIR 1967 Bom 138, 142. [Customs Act (52 of 1962), Ss. 110(2) and 124]

The word 'of' is sometimes the equivalent of after. *In re* v. *S. Mehta* AIR 1970 AP 234 at 236. [Factories Act (63 of 1948), S. 106]

Of one opinion. Having the same view on any matter, issue or question.

Of the half blood. A phrase which necessarily signifies that the consanguinity is collateral rather than lineal.

Of the offence charged. It means offence complained of and not necessarily the first offence. *Ajit Singh* v. *Charan Singh Pardeshi,* AIR 1974 Punj 116, 118. [Trade & Mercandise Mark Act (43 of 1958), S. 92] [Now repealed & replaced by Act 47 of 1999]

Of their choice. These are key words in the Article and indicate that the extent of the right under the Article is to be determined not with reference to any concept of State necessity and general societal interest but with respect to the educational institutions themselves, *i.e.* with respect to the goal of making the institutions effective vehicles of education for the minority community or other persons who resort to them. Accordingly, the regulations imposed should be one designed to achieve such goal, without nullifying any part of the right of the management in substantial measure. *Frank Anthony P.S.E. Association* v. *Union of India,* AIR 1987 SC 311, 327. [Constitution of India, Art. 30(1)]

The expression 'of their choice' occurring in Article 30 includes not only the choice of the institution to be established and administered by the minorities, like institutions for elementary, primary, secondary, university, vocational and technical and medical education, but also the choice of the students who have to be imparted education in such institutions. *T.M.A. Pai Foundation* v. *State of Karnataka,* (2002) 8 SCC 481, para 253. [Constitution of India, Art. 30(1)]

"Off-Campus centre". Means centre of Institution Deemed to be University, approved by the Government and situated beyond its Campus within India. [UGC (Institutions Deemed to be Universities) Regulations, 2019, Regn. 2(2.14)].

OFF-CAMPUS CENTRE. Means a centre of the university located outside its main campus (within or outside the state where the deemed university is located) operated and maintained as its constituent unit by the resources of this university, having the centre's own compliment of facilities, faculty and staff. [Guidelines for Establishing New Departments within the Campus, Setting up of Off-Campus Centre(s)/Institution(s)/ Off-shore Campus and starting Distance Education Programmes by the Deemed to be Universities, 2004, Definitions (b) **as cited in** *Orissa Lift Irrigation Corporation Limited v. Rabi Shankar Patro,* (2018) 1 SCC 468, para 23.6].

Off-shore Campus. Means an institution, college, centre, school or campus of the University established outside the country. [S. 2(r) of the Rajiv Gandhi National Aviation University Act, 2013 (26 of 2013)]

Offence. "OFFENCE" means any act or omission made punishable by any law for the time being in force. [General Clauses Act (10 of 1897), S. 3(38)]

In this section, the word "offence" includes every act committed outside India which, if committed in India, would be punishable under this Sanhita. [(w. e. f. 1-7-2024) repealed & replaced by Bharatiya Nyaya Sanhita, 2023 (45 of 2023), section 1(5), Explanation]

"Offence", as used in this section, includes the abetment of, or attempt to commit, the offence. [(w. e. f. 1-7-2024) Bharatiya Sakshya Adhiniyam, 2023 (47 of 2023), section 24, Explanation I]

An offence means any act or omission made punishable by law. [*State of Rajasthan v. Bhagwan Das Agarwal,* (2013) 16 SCC 574, para 18].

"OFFENCE" means any act or omission made punishable by any law for the time being in force and includes any act in respect of which a complaint may be made under Section 20 of the Cattle Trespass Act (1 of 1871). [CrPC 1973 (2 of 1974), S. 2(n)]

A crime; an act or omission punishable by law.

The word 'offence' generally implies infringement of public duty as distinguished from mere private rights punishable under criminal law. *Depot Manager A.P.S.R.T.C.* v. *Mohd Yousuf Miya,* (1997) 2 SCC 699, para 8 : AIR 1997 SC 2232.

By the word 'offence' in Art. 20(1) Constitution of India is meant something which is a violation of a law in force and for the violation of which the law prescribes a penalty. *Raj Narain Singh* v. *Atmaram Govind,* AIR 1954 All 319, 339.

Even breaches of the customs laws entailing a monetary penalty or forfeitures of the goods concerned would be offences contemplated by Art. 20(3). *Collector of Customs* v. *Calcutta Motor and Cycle Co.,* AIR 1958 Cal 682, 685. [Constitution of India, Art. 20(3)].

Contempt of Court is not an offence within the meaning of S. 4 CrPC 1973 (2 of 1974). *State* v. *Padma Kant Malviya,* AIR 1954 All 523, 537 (FB).

Offence : Crime. The word "offence" is another name for crime. Crimes in the broad sense include not only the major crime (indictable offences) but also summary offences. The Latter regulate many trades and special activities (the so-called "regulatory offences"), as well as the conduct of ordinary people in their daily life. [GLANVILLE WILLIAMS : Criminal law, 2nd Edn. 1983, c. 1, S. 1.5, page 18]

Offence against the public peace. A crime which tends to disturb the peace. The common-law offences of this type were riot, unlawful assembly, dueling, rout, affray.

Offence of personation. The act of representing oneself to be someone else, with a criminal intention which is an offence under law.

Offences involving breach of peace. The words "offence involving a breach of the peace" in S. 106 of the CrPC (2 of 1974) refer not only to a necessary breach of the peace but also a probable breach of the peace.

Offend. To transgress the state laws or the moral or divine law.

Offender. A term constantly employed to indicate persons implicated in the commission of crime.

One who commits an offence. [IPC (45 of 1860), S. 21, Eighth].

The term 'offender' is confined to the offender who uses any deadly weapon. *Phoolkumar* v. *Delhi Administration*, AIR 1975 SC 905, 907. [IPC (45 of 1860), S. 397]

Offensive. Anything that causes displeasure, gives pain or unpleasant sensations. "The disturbing cause must however be real, not fanciful; something more than mere delicacy or fastidiousness."

(1) unpleasant or disgusting, as to the senses; (2) causing anger or annoyance; insulting; (3) for the purpose of attack rather than defence. [Collin's Dictionary as cited in *Shreya Singhal v. Union of India*, (2015) 5 SCC 1, para 51].

That which makes angry; to hurt the feelings of [Indian Evidence Act (1 of 1872), S. 152]; attacking, aggressive. [CrPC 1973 (2 of 1974), S. 52]; repugnant [Indian Railways Act (9 of 1890), S. 47(1)(c)]; harmful; causing injury or damage [Cantonments Act (2 of 1924), S. 116(d)].

Offensive matter. "OFFENSIVE MATTER" includes animal carcasses, kitchen or stable refuse, dung, dirt and putrid or putrefying substances other than sewage. [New Delhi Municipal Council Act (44 of 1994), S. 2(30); Delhi Municipal Corporation Act (66 of 1957), S. 2(35) and Maharashtra Municipalities Act, 1950 (11 of 1965), S. 2(29)]

Offensive weapon. An instrument of any kind used in warfare or combat or attack. [CrPC 1973 (2 of 1974), S. 52].

Offer. A proposal to give or to do something [Indian Evidence Act (1 of 1872), S. 155(2)]; to tender for acceptance or refusal; to hold out (a thing) to a person to take if he will [IPC (45 of 1860), S. 171B(2)]; to present.

An offer or, as it is sometimes called, a proposal means the signification by one person to another of his willingness to enter into a contract with him on certain terms. It may be express or may be implied from the conduct of the party. A mere statement of a person's intention or declaration of his willingness to enter into negotiation is not an offer, and cannot be accepted so as to form a binding contract. HALSBURY, 3rd Edn., Vol. 8, p. 69.

Offer document. "OFFER DOCUMENT" means any document by which a mutual fund invites public for subscription of units of a scheme. [SEBI (Mutual Funds) Regulations, 1996, Reg. 2(r)]

Offer for sale. "OFFER FOR SALE" includes a reference to an intimation by a person of the price proposed by him for the sale of any drug, made by the publication of a price list, by exposing the drug for sale in association with a mark indicating price, by the furnishing of a quotation or otherwise howsoever. [Drug (Control) Act (26 of 1950), S. 2(1)(c)]

Offer of bribery. It must be given a very wide meaning and not a narrow construction in order to ensure that elections are held in an atmosphere of absolute purity". *Ghasi Ram Majhi* v. *Omkar Singh,* AIR 1968 Ori 99 at 103. [Representation of the People Act (43 of 1951), S. 123(1)]

Offer period. "OFFER PERIOD" means the period between the date of public announcement of first offer and the date of closure of that offer. [SEBI (Sub. ACQ of shares and takeovers) Regulations, 1997, Reg. 2(f)]

Offer to the public. An offer to the public signifies an offer made by advertisement or circular to the general public or some section thereof, as distinguished from an offer made privately, that is, to a select and small circle of friends, customers or connections. Where a business is converted into a private company, shares offered by the vendors to their friends, relations or to selected customers, have not hitherto been regarded as having been offered to the public. *Palmer Company Precedents, 17th Edition, Part I, Page 58)* [Companies Act (1 of 1956), S. 69]

'Offered for sale' of properties means held for sale, though they had not been put on the market for sale. It does not require an actual proffer for sale to some particular person.

"It includes newspaper advertisements. The willingness to sell is to be inferred primarily from the fact of advertisement itself. Where the offer for sale in a newspaper advertisement was of a copyright infringing book then the offence of offering for sale is committed at all places where the newspaper circulates and the concerned Magistrates will have jurisdiction.

Offered in evidence. The words"*offered in evidence*" are synonymous with the word 'introduced' and mean that the evidence offered was introduced in evidence.

Offering. A presenting of something as an act of worship or donations. [Delhi Sikh Gurudwaras Act (82 of 1971), S. 2(g)(iii)].

Office. A position or place to which certain duties are attached more or less of a public character. A sort of permanent position held by successive incumbents. May be with or without remuneration. It is a right to exercise a public or private employment or to hold a position which has certain duties attached to it.

An office may be classed into *civil* and *military*. And civil may be classed into *political, judicial* and *ministerial*. *Political* are such as are not connected immediately with the administration of justice, or the execution of the mandates of a superior officer.

Judicial are those which relate to the administration of justice. *Ministerial* are those which give the officer no power to judge of the matter to be done, and require him to obey the mandates of a superior. (2 *Bouvier* 256; 4 *Jacob* 433; 2 *Tomlin* 665)

(1) A position of duty, trust, or authority, especially one conferred by a governmental authority for a public purpose (the office of attorney general). [Black's Law Dictionary as cited in *Urmila Devi v. Yudhvir Singh*, (2013) 15 SCC 624, para 53].

A position to which certain duties are attached, especially a place of trust, authority or service under constituted authority. [Oxford Shorter English Dictionary, 3rd Edn. As cited in *P.V. Narasimha Rao v. State*, (1998) 4 SCC 626 : 1998 SCC (Cri) 1108, para 60,152]. See also *Central Bureau of Investigation, Bank Securities and Fraud Cell v. Ramesh Gelli*, (2016) 6 SCC 788, para 34].

The word "office" does not necessarily imply that it must have an existence apart from the person, who may hold it. Cases are known, in which, in order to make use of the special knowledge, talent, skill or experience of certain persons, posts are created, which exist only for so long as they hold them. It will be difficult to hold that such persons are not holders of offices. *Deorao Laxman Anade* v. *Keshav Laxman Borkar,* AIR 1958 Bom 314, 316. [Constitution of India, Art. 191(1)(a)]

Appointment as a special government pleader to assist the Government Pleader is not appointment to an office. *Kanta Kathuria* v. *Manak Chand*, AIR 1970 SC 694 at 702. [Constitution of India, Art. 191 (1)(a)]

Office means a position which requires the person holding it to perform certain duties and discharge certain obligations. An office may not depend on any law, or any contract or any mandate from the State or any authority. [Income-tax Act (43 of 1961), S. 28]

A place for the transaction of business, often including the staff or denominating their department; the room, a department in which the business is done [Mines Act (35 of 1952), S. 64(a)]; official position to which duties and functions are attached; a position of authority. *Maharaj Shri Govindlalji Ranchhodlalji* v. *C.I.T.,* (1958) 34 ITR 92 (Bom). [CPC (5 of 1908), S. 123(4) and Constitution of India, Art. 18(4)].

Office bearer. "OFFICE BEARER" in relation to a trade union, includes any member of the executive thereof but does not include an auditor. [Industrial Disputes Act (14 of 1947), S. 2(iii)]

"Office-bearer", in relation to a Trade Union, includes any member of the executive thereof, but does not include an auditor. [Industrial Relations Code, 2020 (35 of 2020), section 2(zb)]

"OFFICE BEARER" means a *Panch, Sarpanch* or *Upsarpanch* of a *gram panchayat*, a member, a President or Vice President of a *Janpad Panchayat* or a member, or President or Vice President of *Zila Panchayat* as the case may be. [MP Panchayat Raj Adhiniyam, 1993 (1 of 1994), S. 2(xiii)]

"OFFICE BEARER" means an individual elected by the general body or the board of the Co-operative society to any office of such Co-operative society in accordance with its bye-laws. [Andhra Pradesh Mutually Aided Co-operative Societies Act (AP Act No. 30 of 1995), S. 2(q)]

Office copy. An authenticated or codified copy of an official or legal record; a copy made or kept to be used in office. [Mines Act (35 of 1952), S. 64(a)].

Office of Internet Enforcement. Division of the SEC that oversees securities offerings, trading, and fraudulent scams on the Internet. (*Cyber Law*)

Office of profit. The term 'office of profit' is frequently used to designate offices otherwise known as 'lucrative offices.' It describes an office to which salary, compensation, or fees are attached, and the amount of the salary or compensation is not material.

For the purposes of this article, a person shall not be deemed to hold any office of profit by reason only that he is the President or Vice-President of the Union or the Governor of any State or is a Minister either for the Union or for any State. [Constitution of India, Articles 58, *Explanation* and 66, *Explanation*]. *See also* Articles 102(1), *Explanation* and 191(1), *Explanation.*

An "office of profit" is an office which is capable of yielding a profit or pecuniary gain. The word "profit" has always been treated equivalent to or substitute to the term "pecuniary gain." The very context in which the word "profit" has been used after the words "office of" shows that not all the offices are disqualified but only those which yield pecuniary gains as profit other than mere compensatory allowances, to the holder of office. [U.C. Raman v. P.T.A. Rahim, (2014) 8 SCC 934, para 20].

'Office of profit' indicates an office which exists independently of the holder of the office. A contractor recognised under Govt. Department does not hold office of profit. *Tajneswar Bora* v. *Returning Officer, Panchayat, Raj Elections, Nowyong,* AIR 1975 Gauhati 61, 66, 68.

Merely because the committee of the Durgah Endowment or the members of the committee are removable by the Government of India or the committee can make bye-laws prescribing the duties and powers of its employees, it cannot convert the servants of the committee into holders of office of profit under the Government of India. The power of the Government to appoint a person to an office of profit or to continue him in that office or revoke his appointment at their direction and payment from out of Government revenue are important factors in determining whether that person is holding an office of profit under the Government though payment from a source other than Government revenue is not always a decisive factor. *Abdul Shakur* v. *Rikhab Chanel*, AIR 1958 SC 52, 55. [Constitution of India, Art. 58(1)]

A person who was a Pramukh at the time of filing of the nomination paper and who was drawing an honorarium of Rs. 300/- p.m. was not holding an office of profit. *Umrao Singh* v. *Yashwant Singh,* AIR 1970 Raj 134 at 141, 143. [Constitution of India, Art. 102(1)(a)]

The expression "office of profit" means an office capable of yielding a profit or from which a man might reasonably be expected to make a profit. The actual making of profit is not necessary. Profit means gain or any material benefit. *Deorao Laxman Anade* v. *Keshav Laxman Borkar,* AIR 1958 Bom 314, 318. [Constitution of India, Art. 191(1)(a)]

The post of the Principal of a Government aided educational institution is not an office of profit held under the State Government. *Rajender Kumar* v. *Vijay Singh,* AIR 1987 All 121, 124.

Provision made for daily allowance or travelling allowance cannot make an office of profit. Municipal membership is not an office of profit. *Pakanti Sudharishan Reddy* v. *District Collector, Warangal,* AIR 1964 AP 421, 424.

A medical practitioner working as a panel doctor appointed under the Employees' State Insurance Scheme does not hold 'office of profit' under the State Government. *Madhukar* v. *Jaswant,* AIR 1976 SC 2283.

A stamp vendor who does not get any fixed remuneration, but only gets a commission on the sales he conducts cannot be considered to be a person holding an office of profit. *Venkatappa* v. *S. Subba Rao,* AIR 1957 Mys 79, 80.

A person who is employed in an educational institution managed by a private society, and receiving a grant-in-aid from the Govt. is not a holder of an office of profit and therefore he is not disqualified to be chosen as Municipal Councilor. *Lalitha Bai* v. *Returning Officer, City Municipality Elections, Gulbargo,* AIR 1971 Mys 35, 36.

An office which is capable of yielding pecuniary gain. [Parliament (Prevention of Disqualification) Act (10 of 1959), Preamble and Constitution of India, Art. 58(2)].

Office of profit under the government. The Office of the Headmaster in a school receiving grant-in-aid from the State Government is not an office of profit under the Government.

Office of the mine. Means an office at the surface of the mine concerned. [Mines Act (35 of 1952), S. 2(1)(k)]

Office or place of profit. In section 188(1) of Act 18 of 2013, the expression 'office or place of profit' means any office or place—

(*i*) where such office or place is held by a director, if the director holding it receives from the company anything by way of remuneration over and above the remuneration to which he is entitled as director, by way of salary, fee, commission, perquisites, any rent-free accommodation, or otherwise;

(*ii*) where such office or place is held by an individual other than a director or by any firm, private company or other body corporate, if the individual, firm, private company or body corporate holding it receives from the company anything by way of remuneration, salary, fee, commission, perquisites, any rent-free accommodation, or otherwise. [*Explanation* (*a*) to section 188(1) of the Companies Act, 2013 (18 of 2013)]

Office : Post. The word 'post' and its previous counterpart the word 'office' mean position in service. Article 565(a) of the Civil Service Regulations spoke of 'office' and therefore F.R. 56(c)(i) and FR 56(f) spoke of 'post'. Post here means the place and position in service held by him. The words 'retains his post' mean first that he remains a member of the Indian Civil Service, and secondly, he is kept in that place or position and is allowed to remain there in service. (*P.R. Nayak* v. *Union of India,* AIR 1972 SC 554).

Office under Government. "OFFICE UNDER GOVERNMENT" includes any office or employment in or under any department of the Government or of the Government. [Official Secrets Act (19 of 1923), S. 2(6)]

Office under the State. To be an office a position or place has to satisfy three tests : (i) It must be a subsisting, permanent or substantive position; (ii) it must exist independently of the incumbent who occupies it, and (iii) it must be of a position of a more or less public character to which certain duties are attached. *State of U.P.* v. *Bhola Nath Srivastava,* AIR 1972 All 460, 464. [Constitution of India, Article 16(1)]

Office yearly premium. Means regular premium (excluding extra premiums which are required to be shown separately) payable by the policyholder to secure the basic benefits under the policy in a policy year. [Insurance Regulatory and Development Authority (Actuarial Report and Abstract) Regulations, 2000, Rgn. 2(j)]

Officer. "OFFICER" includes any director, managing agent, secretaries, and treasurers, manager or secretary, or any person in accordance with whose directions or instructions the Board of Directors or any one or more of the directors is or are accustomed to act, and also includes—

(a) where the managing agent or the secretaries and treasurers is or are a firm, any partner in them;

(b) where the managing agent or the secretaries and treasurers is or are a body corporate, any director or manager of the body corporate;

but save in Sections 477, 478, 539, 543, 545, 621, 625 and 633 does not include an auditor. [Companies Act (1 of 1956), S. 2(30)]

A person holding an office. [CPC (5 of 1908), S. 2(7)].

'OFFICER' means a person elected or appointed by a society to any office of such society according to its bye-laws : and includes a Chairman, Vice-Chairman, President, Vice-President, managing Director, manager, Secretary, Treasurer, Member of the Committee, and any other person elected or appointed under this Act, the rules or the byelaws, to give directions in regard to the business of such society. [Gujarat Cooperative Society Act, 1961 (10 of 1962), S. 2(14) as cited in *Vipulbhai M. Chaudhary v. Gujarat Cooperative Milk Marketing Federation Limited,* (2015) 8 SCC 1, para 36].

'OFFICER' means a person appointed to a public service or post in connection with the affairs of the State of Madhya Pradesh. [Madhya Pradesh Lokayukta Evam Uplokayukt Act (37 of 1981), S. 2(a) as cited in *Lokayukta, JusticeRipusudan Dayal v. State of Madhya Pradesh,* (2014) 4 SCC 473, para 9].The expression 'officer' in the dictionary sense means one who holds an office. In relation to companies or societies, it is a person who holds and takes part in the management or direction of a society or institution. *Sarbeswar Bardoloi* v. *V.K. Gohain,* AIR 1955 Ass 149. [Industrial Disputes Act (14 of 1947), S. 36(2)]

A person to be an officer must hold some office though it does not matter whether the office is humble or exalted and the remuneration must be paid by the Government. *Manshankar* v. *State,* AIR 1970 Guj 97 at 102. [IPC (45 of 1860), S. 161 (*omitted*)]

The liquidator of a company shall not be deemed to be an officer of the company within the meaning of sub-section (2). [Companies Act (18 of 2013), section 439, *Expln.*]

Under-Secretary to State Government is not an officer.

"OFFICER" for the purposes of section 336 of Act 18 of 2013, the term 'officer' includes any person in accordance with whose directions or instructions the directors of the company have been accustomed to act. [*Explanation* to Section 336 of the Companies Act, 2013 (18 of 2013); *Explanation* (*b*) to Section 339 of the Companies Act, 2013 (18 of 2013)]

"OFFICER" includes any director, manager or key managerial personnel or any person in accordance with whose directions or instructions the Board of Directors or any one or more of the directors is or are accustomed to act. [S. 2(59) of the Companies Act, 2013 (18 of 2013)]

Officer commanding the area. Means the Officer Commanding anyone of the areas into which India is for military purposes for the time being divided, or any sub-area which does not form part of any such area, or any area which the Central Government may, by notification in the Official Gazette, declare to be an area for all or any of the purposes of this Act. [Cantonments Act (2 of 1924), S. 2 (xxiv)]

Officer commanding the station. Means the military officer for the time being in command of the forces in a cantonment, or, if that officer is the Officer Commanding the Area or Officer Commanding-in-Chief, the Command, the military officer who would be in command of those forces in the absence of the Officer Commanding the Area and Officer Commanding-in-Chief, the Command. [Cantonments Act (2 of 1924), S. 2(xxiva)]

Officer, Commissioned. An officer of the armed forces holding a commission. [CrPC 1973 (2 of 1974), S. 131].

Officer conducting the prosecution. An officer, who handles the institution and carrying on of a legal proceeding against a person.

Officer de facto. One in actual possession of an office.

Officer de jure. One who has lawful right to the office, but who is not in present possession.

Officer-in-charge. Officer having the care, custody or superintendence.

Officer in charge of a police station. Includes, when the officer in charge of the police-station is absent from the station-house or unable from illness or other cause to perform his duties, the police officer present at the station-house who is next in rank to such officer and is above the rank of constable or when the State Government so directs, any other police officer so present. [CrPC 1973 (2 of 1974)), S. 2 (o)] [Now (w. e. f. 1-7-2024) repealed & replaced by Bharatiya Nagarik Suraksha Sanhita, 2023 (46 of 2023), S. 2(1)(r), same definition in new Sanhita].

An officer, who is incharge of or has immediate control over a police station. [CrPC 1973 (2 of 1974), S. 2(o) and 129(1)] [Now (w. e. f. 1-7-2024) repealed & replaced by Bharatiya Nagarik Suraksha Sanhita, 2023 (46 of 2023)].

An Assistant Sub-Inspector on duty in mofussil during investigation is not an officer-in-charge of the police station for purposes of S. 154, CrPC 1973 (2 of 1974) when the first information report is made, unless he comes within the strict terms of S. 3 (o) of that Code.

The expression 'officer in charge of a police station' occurring in Section 2(o) of the Code includes any other police officer, who is superior in rank to an officer in charge of a police station. *C.B.I.* v. *State of Rajasthan,* (2001) 3 SCC 333, para 11 : AIR 2001 SC 668. [CrPC, 1973 (2 of 1974), S. 2(o)]

When the Sub-Inspector and others senior officers were away on other duty, the clerk attached to the station may be said to be 'officer-in-charge' of the police station. *Pybi Yaccob* v. *State,* AIR 1953 TC 466, 469.

The fact that the police officer who is ordinarily in charge of a police station has left for attending to a raid would not lead to the inference that after his return from the raid he was not in charge of the police station. *The State* v. *Daulatrao,* MLJ : QD (1956-1960) Vol. II C1396 : AIR 1956 Bom 195 : 1956 CrLJ 481. [CrPC (5 of 1898), S. 173].

Officer-in-charge of jail. An officer, who is incharge of or has immediate control over a jail.

Officer-in-command. A person in an office by virtue of which he is commanding or exercising power of control or authority. [CrPC 1973 (2 of 1974), S. 130(2)].

Officer in default. For the purpose of any provision in this Act which enacts that an officer of the Company who is in default shall be liable to any punishment or penalty, whether by way of imprisonment, fine or otherwise, the expression "OFFICER WHO IS IN DEFAULT" means all the following officers of the company, namely—

(a) the managing director, or managing directors;

(b) the whole time director or whole time directors;

(c) the manager;

(d) the secretary;

(e) any person in accordance with whose directions or instructions the Board of directors of the company is accustomed to act;

(f) if any person charged by the Board with the responsibility of complying with that provision :

Provided that the person to charged has given his consent in this behalf to the Board;

(g) Where any company does not have any of the officers specified in clauses (a) to (c), any director or directors who may be specified by the Board in this behalf of where no director is so specified, all the directors :

Provided that where the Board excersis any power under clause (f) or clause (g), it shall, with in thirty days of the exercise of such powers, file with the Registrar a return in the prescribed form. [Companies Act (1 of 1956), S. 5, *substituted with new provisions specifying the officers by 1988 Amendment Act*]

"OFFICER IN DEFAULT" for the purpose of any provision in the Act, mean any officer who is knowingly guilty of any contravention, failure or refusal or who knowingly authorises or permits such contravention, failure or refusal. [West Bengal Societies Registration Act (26 of 1961), S. 2(f)]

Officer of Government. Means any Officer of the Central Government or of a State Government. [Influx from Pakistan (Control) Repealing Act (76 of 1952), S. 2(b)]

Officer of Parliament means any of the following officers, namely, the Chairman and Deputy Chairman of the Council of States and the Speaker and the Deputy Speaker of the House of the People. [Salaries and Allowances of Officers of Parliament (20 of 1953), S. 2]

Officer of police. "OFFICER OF POLICE" includes also village-watch-man. [Cattle Trespass Act (1 of 1871), S. 3]

Officer, Medical. A medical man, who holds any office by virtue of which he is incharge of health and treatment.

Officer of the Court. The person charged with upholding the law and the judicial system; the term includes a judge, clerk, bailiff, sheriff *etc.*; a lawyer has also been held to be an officer of the Court.

Officer of the Force. Means an officer of and above the rank of Assistant Sub-Inspector appointed to the Force and includes a superior officer. [Railway Property (Unlawful Possession) Act (29 of 1966), S. 2(c)]

Officer of the legislature. A person deployed by the Speaker for maintaining Law and Order in the Assembly is an 'officer' coming within the purview of Art. 212 (2). *Raghunatha Panicker* v. *Kunjala Thankappan*, AIR 1987 Ker 159, 163. [Constitution of India, Art. 212 (2)]

Officer of the mint. Any person holding an office in the place where money is coined under public authority.

Officer of the Post Office. The expression "*officer of the Post Office*" includes any person employed in any business of the Post Office or on behalf of the Post Office. (*Peloubet*)

Officer, Serving. The officer making the legal delivery of a process or writ.

Officer, Subordinate. Officer belonging to an inferior rank, grade, class or order.

Officer, Superior. An officer of higher rank or official station [position).

Officer who is in default. For the purpose of any provision in the Companies Act, 2013 (18 of 2013), which enacts that an officer of the company who is in default shall be liable to any penalty or punishment by way of imprisonment, fine or otherwise, means any of the following officers of a company, namely:—

(*i*) whole-time director;

(*ii*) key managerial personnel;

(*iii*) where there is no key managerial personnel, such director or directors as specified by the Board in this behalf and who has or have given his or their consent in writing to the Board to such specification, or all the directors, if no director is so specified;

(*iv*) any person who, under the immediate authority of the Board or any key managerial personnel, is charged with any responsibility including maintenance, filing or distribution of accounts or records, authorises, actively participates in, knowingly permits, or knowingly fails to take active steps to prevent, any default;

(*v*) any person in accordance with whose advice, directions or instructions the Board of Directors of the company is accustomed to act, other than a person who gives advice to the Board in a professional capacity;

(*vi*) every director, in respect of a contravention of any of the provisions of this Act, who is aware of such contravention by virtue of the receipt by him of any proceedings of the Board or participation in such proceedings without objecting to the same, or where such contravention had taken place with his consent or connivance;

(*vii*) in respect of the issue or transfer of any shares of a company, the share transfer agents, registrars and merchant bankers to the issue or transfer. [S. 2(60) of the Companies Act, 2013 (18 of 2013)]

Officers and employees of the Corporation. Includes,—

(i) the officers and employees who were in the service of the Burmah Shell Refineries and who continued to be in the service of the said company after it became a Government company; and

(ii) the officers and employees who were in the service of Burmah Shell and whose service were transferred to the corporation by Section 9 of the Burmah Shell (Acquisition of Undertaking in India) Act, 1976. [Bharat Petroleum Corporation Limited (Determination of Conditions of Service of Employees) Act (44 of 1988), S. 2(d)]

Official. The person who holds an office of or pertaining to the office held by one [IPC (45 of 1860) (*repealed*), S. 162]; employed in some public capacity [Indian Evidence Act (1 of 1872), S. 124]; prescribed or recognized as authorised (by government).

Of or relating to an office or position of trust or authority (official duties). [Black's Law Dictionary as cited in *Urmila Devi v. Yudhvir Singh*, (2013) 15 SCC 624, para 52].

Official act. Any act done by the officer in his official capacity, under colour and by virtue of his office.

Police officer failing to send for trial person arrested for offence under Excise Law would be forbearing to do an "official act".

Receiving illegal gratification cannot be an official act, that is an act done or purporting to be done in execution of duty.

The expression 'official act' means an act by a person while acting or purporting to act in the discharge of his official duty. *Chaman Lal* v. *Mulakh Raj,* AIR 1967 Punj 51, 52. [CrPC 1973 (2 of 1974), S. 197 (1)]

Official assignee. "OFFICIAL ASSIGNEE" includes an acting Official Assignee. [Presidency Towns Insolvency Act (3 of 1909), S. 2(*c*)] [Repealed by Act 31 of 2016]

A member appointed to wind up the estate of a defaulting debtor.

Official body. A government body. [Indian Evidence Act (1 of 1872), S. 74(1)(ii)].

Official capacity. The capacity in which a person acts, because he is an officer, lawfully appointed and qualified, or because he lawfully performs duties that are of an official character.

Position of enablement derived from or having the sanction of persons in office. [Registration Act (16 of 1908), S. 86].

Official character. Official position [Indian Evidence Act (1 of 1872), S. 79]; [Religious Endowments Act (20 of 1863), S. 22].

Official confidence. The words "communication in official confidence" in S. 124 of the Indian Evidence Act (1 of 1872) import no special degree of secrecy and no pledge or direction for its maintenance but include generally all matter communicated by one officer to another in the performance of his duties. Where a person seeks to put in evidence a report made by one officer to another and where its production is objected to on the ground of its being detrimental to public interest, it is a sufficient cause for a Court to refuse to compel its production. The public officer in charge of the record is the sole Judge of the detrimental character of the document and his assertion as to its character is final and binds the Court.

Documents produced or statements made under process of law cannot be said to be made in 'official confidence' under S. 123. [Indian Evidence Act (1 of 1872)]

Trust reposed on account of official position. [Indian Evidence Act (1 of 1872), S. 124].

Official duty. Official duties are the duties imposed on officers of the government.

The phrase 'faithful performance of official duty' as used in a bond requiring a faithful performance of official duty, should be construed as equivalent to a recital of all the statutory duties of the officer in the bond, and is a binding on the principal and sureties as if such duties were inserted in the bond.

The expression "official Duty" implies that the act or omission must have been done by the public servant in the course of his service and that it should have been done in discharge of his duty. [*General Officer Commanding, Rashtriya Rifles v. Central Bureau of Investigation*, (2012) 6 SCC 228, para 22].

"Official duty" denotes a duty that arises by reason of an office or position of trust or authority held by a person. [*Urmila Devi v. Yudhvir Singh*, (2013) 15 SCC 624, para 56].

The expression 'official duty' occurring in Section 197(1) of the Code implies that the act or omission must have been done by the public servant in the course of his service and that it should have been in discharge of his duty. *State of H.P.* v. *M.P. Gupta,* (2004) 2 SCC 349, 359, para 11. [CrPC 1973 (2 of 1974), S. 197(1)]

Official function. A function belonging to an office, whether exercised by the officer or by a subordinate acting for him.

A function belonging to an office. [IPC (45 of 1860) (*Repealed*), S. 163].

Official Gazette. "OFFICIAL GAZETTE" or "GAZETTE" shall mean the Gazette of India or the Official *Gazette* of a State. [General Clauses Act (10 of 1897), S. 3 (39)].

The words 'OFFICIAL GAZETTE' refer to the official Gazette of the State which enunciates the scheme and not to the Central Govt. Gazette. *Duley Singh* v. *State of U.P.*, AIR 1977 All 251, 155. [Motor Vehicles Act (4 of 1939), S. 68-D(1) and (3)] [Now Repealed & replaced by Act 59 of 1988]

Official house. "OFFICIAL HOUSE" in relation to a Marriage Officer, means—

(i) the official house of residence of the officer;

(ii) the office in which the business of the officer is transacted;

(iii) a prescribed place. [Foreign Marriage Act (33 of 1969), S. 2(e)]

Official liquidator. A liquidator appointed as such by the government.

"OFFICIAL LIQUIDATOR" means an Official Liquidator appointed under section 359(1) of the Companies Act, 2013 (18 of 2013). [S. 2(61) of the Companies Act, 2013 (18 of 2013)]

Official member. A member, who is also an officer of the government. [Food Corporations Act (37 of 1964), S. 19(5), Prov.].

Official misconduct. By 'Official misconduct' with reference to officers, is meant any un-lawful behaviour in relation to the duties of his office, wilful in its character, of the officer entrusted in any manner with the administration of justice or the execution of the laws; and under this head of official misconduct are included any wilful or corrupt failure, refusal, or neglect of an officer to perform any duty enjoined on him by law.

The phrase 'official misconduct' authorizing removal from office on account of official misconduct does not include drunkenness, inasmuch as drunkenness in itself does not indicate corruption or neglect of duty.

Official receiver. A Court officer entrusted with duties under the Insolvency Act, in connection with the winding up of an insolvent's estate.

Official record. A record prepared or maintained in official capacity. [Indian Evidence Act (1 of 1872), S. 123].

Official reserves. Gold and currency reserves kept by the government.

Official residence. "OFFICIAL RESIDENCES", in relation to a Governor, means such residences as may be specified by the President by notification in the official Gazette, as the official residence of the Governor and includes the staff quarters and other buildings appurtenant thereto and the gardens thereof. [Governors (Emoluments, Allowances & Privileges) Act (43 of 1982), S. 2(d)]

Official secret. The expression "OFFICIAL SECRET" in the Official Secrets Act, has reference to a secret of one or the other department of the Government or the state and not to any secret of a private office. The word official by itself has obtained the meaning attached to it in the Act and it cannot be held that the expression "official secret" is a wider term including secrets of a private institution.

Official signature. Signature made in official capacity. [CrPC 1973 (2 of 1974), S. 371].

Officially valid document. Means the passport, the driving licence, the permanent account number (PAN) Card, the Voter's Identity Card issued by the Election Commission of India, job card issued by NREGA duly signed by an officer of the State Government, the letter issued by the Unique Identification Authority of India or the National Population Register containing details of name, address and Aadhar number or any other document as notified by the Central Government in consultation with the Regulator. [Prevention of Money-Laundering (Maintenance of Record) Rules, 2005, R. 2(1)(d) **as cited in** *K. S. Puttaswamy* v. *Union of India,* (2019) 1 SCC 1, para 1445].

For the purpose of this clause, a document shall be deemed to an "officially valid document" even if there is a change in the name subsequent to its issuance provided it is supported by a marriage certificate issued by the State Government or Gazette notification, indicating such a change of name. [Prevention of Money Laundering (Maintenance of Records) Rules, 2005, R 2(1)(d), *Explanation*]

Official title. A name or designation given to one officially; the name of an office [Indian Evidence Act (1 of 1872), S. 76]; [CrPC 1973 (2 of 1974), S. 32(1)]; [General Clauses Act (10 of 1897), S. 17(1)].

Official trustee. The official Trustee mentioned in S. 6 of the Married Women's Property Act (3 of 1874) is not the legal person referred to in the Official Trustees Act (2 of 1913), S. 4 which is a corporation sole.

An official trustee appointed under Section 4 of the Official Trustees Act (2 of 1913)].

Official year. "OFFICIAL YEAR" shall mean the year commencing on the first day of April. [Bom Act III of 1901 (District Municipal), S. 3, cl. IV].

Officiate. To 'officiate' is 'to do the duty of an office,' and the extent of the duty will be exactly in proportion to the sphere of that duty.

Officiating. Acting in an official capacity, filling a position temporarily.

Officiating and **temporary.** The word 'officiating' is generally used when a servant having held one post permanently or substantively is appointed to a post in a higher rank, but not permanently or substantively. The word 'temporary' usually denotes a person appointed in the Civil service for the first time and the appointment is not permanent but temporary (*ie*) for the time being, with no right to the post. *Arun Kumar* v. *S. E. Railway*, AIR 1985 SC 482, 485. [Railway Establishment Manual, R. 312.]

Officiator. "OFFICIATOR" means the person actually performing the duties of an hereditary office for the time being, whether he be a representative watandar or a deputy or a substitute appointed under any of the provision of the Hereditary Offices Act. [Bom Act III of 1874 (Hereditary Offices), S. 4].

Officit conatus si effectus sequatur. (*Lat.*) (Jenk. Cent. 55) The attempt becomes of consequence, if the effect follows.

Offline verification. "offline verification" means the process of verifying the identity of the Aadhaar number holder without authentication, through such offline modes as may be specified by regulations. [Aadhaar (Targeted Delivery of Financial & Other Subsidies, Benefits & Services) Act (18 of 2016), section 2(pa)]

Offline verification-seeking entity. "Offline verification-seeking entity" means any entity desirous of undertaking offline verification of an Aadhaar number holder [Aadhaar (Targeted Delivery of Financial & Other Subsidies, Benefits & Services) Act (18 of 2016), section 2(pb)]

Offshore area. Means the territorial waters, continental shelf, exclusive economic zone and other maritime zones of India under the Territorial Waters, Continental Shelf, Exclusive Economic Zone and Other Maritime Zones Act, 1976. [Offshore Area Minerals (Development and Protection) Act, 2002 (17 of 2003), S. 4(n)]

Offshore installation. "OFF-SHORE INSTALLATION" means an installation, whether mobile or fixed, which is used or is intended to be used for underwater exploration or exploitation of crude oil, petroleum or other similar mineral oils, under lease, licence or any other form of contractual arrangement and includes—

(a) any installation which could be moved from place to place under its own motive power or otherwise; and

(b) a pipe-line. [Merchant Shipping Act (44 of 1958), S. 356B(i)]

Oil. Oil is a mineral, and being a mineral, is part of the realty. In this it is like coal or any other natural product which *in situ* forms part of the land. It may become, by severance, personality, or there may be a right to use or take it originating in custom or prescription. Nevertheless, whenever conveyance is made of it, whether that conveyance is called a lease or a deed, it is, in effect the grant of part of the corpus of the estate, and not of a mere incorporeal right.

"OIL" means any persistent hydro carbon mineral oil such as crude oil, fuel oil, heavy diesel oil, lubricating oil and whale oil, whether carried on board a tanker as cargo or fuel. [Merchant Shipping Act (44 of 1958), S. 352H(b) (*Substituted by Merchant Shipping (Amendment) Act, 2002*)]

"OIL" means petroleum in any form including crude oil, fuel oil, sludge, oil refuse and refined products. [Merchant Shipping Act (44 of 1958), S. 356B(j) (*Substituted by Merchant Shipping (Amendment) Act, 2003*)]

"Oil" means any edible oil carried on vessel as cargo or persistent oil such as crude oil, heavy diesel oil, lubricating oil and white oil, carried on board of a vessel as cargo or fuel. [Inland Vessels Act, 2021 (24 of 2021), section 3(ze)]

Oil does not include gas.

Vanaspathi is essentially an Oil although it is a different kind and which forms its basic ingredient. When it retains its essential properties in spite of certain processes which again do not convert it into a different substance even though it is being sold as un-hydrogenated form. *Champakital H. Thakkarr* v. *State of Gujarat*, AIR 1980 SC 1889, 1891. [Minimum Wages Act (11 of 1948), Sch., Part 1, Item 5]

Oil field. "OIL FIELD" any means area where any operation for the purpose of obtaining natural gas and petroleum, crude oil, refined oil, partially refined oil and any of the products of petroleum in a liquid or solid state, is to be or is being carried on. [Oil Fields (Regulation and Development Act (53 of 1948), S. 3(e)]

Oil industrial concern. Means any company, corporation or co-operative society, which is engaged or which is to engage in any activity referred to in clause (k). [Oil Industry (Development) Act (47 of 1974), S. 2(j)]

Oil industry. Includes all activities by way of prospecting or exploring for or production of mineral oil, refining, processing, transportation, storage, handling and marketing of mineral oil, production and marketing of all products, down-stream of an oil refinery and the production of fertilizers and petro-chemicals and all activities directly or indirectly connected therewith. [Oil Industry (Development) Act (47 of 1974), S. 2(k)]

Oil mixture. Means a mixture with any oil content. [Merchant Shipping Act (44 of 1958), S. 356B(k)]

Oil reception facilities. In relation to a port, means facilities for enabling vessels using the port to discharge or deposit oil residues. [Merchant Shipping Act (44 of 1958), S. 356B(m)]

Oil seed. An 'oil seed' botanically means a seed which is a flowering plants' unit of reproduction or germ capable of developing into another such plant. Seed which can yield oil is an 'oil seed'. If a seed by reason of application of a scientific method produces oil is not necessarily understood to be an 'oil seed' in a common parlance. If a commodity possesses all the qualities of an oil seed it cannot be excluded from the ambit of the expression 'oil seed'. *CST* v. *Popular Trading Co.*, AIR 2000 SC 1578 : 2000 AIR SCW 1297.

Oil seeds. The expression 'oil seeds' includes coconut and copra. *Kasturi Seshagiri Pai & Co.* v. *Deputy Commissioner of South Kanara,* AIR 1962 Mys 1, 3. [Central Sales Tax Act (74 of 1956), S. 14(vi)]

Groundnut is oil seed. *Anand Sugar Mills Ltd.* v. *Sales Tax Officer, Sitapur*, AIR 1973 SC 2440, 2441.

Oil tanker. Means a ship constructed or adapted primarily to carry oil in bulk in its cargo spaces and includes any combination carrier or any chemical tanker when it is carrying a cargo or part cargo of oil in bulk. [Merchant Shipping Act (44 of 1958), S. 356B(l) (*Substituted by Merchant Shipping (Amendment) Act, 2003*)]

Old chemical weapons. Means :

(a) Chemical weapons which were produced before 1925; or

(b) Chemical weapons produced in the period between 1925 and 1946 that have deteriorated to such extent that they can no longer be used as chemical weapons. [Chemical Weapons Convention Act (34 of 2000), Art. II 5]

Old machinery. In order to fall within the expression 'old machinery' in the entry, the machinery must be old machinery in the sense that it has become non-functional or non-usable. *Rainbow Steels Ltd.* v. *Sales Tax Commissioner, U. P.*, AIR 1981 SC 2101, 2104.

Oligarchy. A form of government in which supreme power is restricted to a few; a perverted form of aristocracy.

Oligopsony. A market where a few buyers have buying power.

OLR. (*abbr.*) Off-Line Reader. Enables information to be downloaded and read off-line without maintaining a connection to the Internet. Material may also be prepared for mailing and then sent in a Blink. (*Cyber Law*)

Ombudsman. A popular name (derived from Sweden) for an official appointed to receive and investigate the complaints of citizens about the government and its officials.

"OMBUDSMAN" means a person appointed as an Insurance Ombudsman under these rules. [Insurance Ombudsman Rules, 2017, R. 4(1)(g)].

Omina Praesumuntur rite et solemniter esse acta donec probetur in contrarium. All things are presumed to have been done regularly and with due formality until the contrary is proved.

Omissio eorum quae tacite insunt nihil operatur. (*Lat.*) The omission of those things which are tacitly implied is of no consequence.

Omission. "OMISSION" denotes as well a series of omissions as a single omission. [IPC (45 of 1860), S. 33] [Now (w. e. f. 1-7-2024) repealed & replaced by Bharatiya Nyaya Sanhita, 2023 (45 of 2023), section 2(25), same definition in new Sanhita]

"Omission" with reference to the performance of a duty involves the idea of conscious or wilful omission. "Act" includes omission.

"Omission" is nothing but a particular form of words evincing an intention to abrogate an enactment or portion thereof. [Halsbury's Laws of England as cited in *Shree Bhagwati Steel Rolling Mills v. Commissioners of Central Excise*, (2016) 3 SCC 643, para 13].

The expression 'omission' does not connote any obligation. 'Omission' is a colourless word which merely refers to the not doing of something and if the assessee in fact does not make a return, it is an omission on his part, whether the law casts any obligation upon him to make a return or not. *Pannalal Nandlal Bhandari* v. *CIT*, AIR 1956 Bom 557, 558.

A person cannot be said to have omitted or failed to disclose something when, of such thing, he had no knowledge. *P.R. Mukherjee* v. *CIT*, AIR 1956 Cal 197, 200.

Omit. Abstain from inserting, bypass, cast aside, count out, cut out, delete, discard, drop, exclude, fail to do, fail to include, fail to insert, fail to mention, leave out, leave undone, let go, let pass, let slip, miss neglect, omittere, pass over, praetermittere, skip, slight, transire. [Thesaurus as cited in *Shree Bhagwati Steel Rolling Mills v. Commissioners of Central Excise*, (2016) 3 SCC 643, para 13].

Omne accessorium sequitur suum principale. (*Maxim*) Every accessory thing follows its principal.

Omne actum ab intentione agentis est judicandum ; a voluntate procedit causa vitii atque virtutis. Every act is to be estimated by the intention of the doer : the cause of vice and virtue proceeds from the will.

Omne crimen ebrietas et incendit et detegit. (*Lat.*) Drunkenness kindles and exposes every crime.

Omne jus aut consensus fecit, aut necessitas constituit aut firmavit consuetudo. (*Lat.*) (D. I, 3, 40) Every right is either made by consent, or is constituted by necessity, or is established by custom.

Omne magnum exemplum habet aliquid ex iniquo, quod publica utilitate compensatur. Every great example has something of injustice, which is compensated by its public utility.

Omne majus continet in se minus. (*Maxim*) Every greater contains in itself the less. (*Black*)

Omne nimium vertitur in vitium. Every excess becomes a vice.

Omne principale trahit ad se accessorium. (*Maxim*) Every principal thing draws to itself the accessory. (*Bouvier*)

Omne quod solo inaedificatur solo cedit. (*Maxim*) Every thing which is built upon the soil passes with the soil. (*Latin for Lawyers*)

Omne sacramentum debet esse de certa scientia. (*Maxim*) Every oath ought to be founded on certain knowledge. (*Peloubet*)

Omne testamentum morte consummatum est. (*Maxim*) Every will is consummated by death. (*Latin for Lawyers*)

Omnes actiones in mundo infra certa tempora habent limitationem. All actions in the world are limited with certain periods.

Omnes licentiam habere his quae pro se indulta sunt renunciare. (*Lat.*) (C. I, 3, 51) It is a rule of the ancient law that all persons shall have liberty to renounce those privileges which have been conferred for their benefit.

Omnes prudentes illa admittere solent quae probantur iis qui in arte sua bene versati sunt. All prudent men are accustomed to admit those things which are approved by those who are well versed in the art.

Omnia deo grata, hominibus utilia, reipublicae honesta privatis justa et commoda probant leges, et pro viribus cuique imponunt. The laws approve all things agreeable to God, useful to men, honorable to the State, just and advantageous to private persons, and impose themselves upon every one according to his faculties.

Omnia honeste et ordine fiant. Let all things be done honestly and in order.

Omnia lascivia legibus vetita. (*Maxim*) All wantonness is contrary to law. (*Morgan*)

Omnia praesumuntur contra spoliatorem. (*Lat.*) (*Maxim*) All things are presumed against a "wrongdoer" or "despoiler". (*Bouvier*; *Wharton*)

Omnia praesumuntur Legitime facta donec probetur in contrarium. (*Lat.*) (*Maxim*) All things are presumed to be lawfully done, until proof be made to the contrary. (*Black*)

Omnia praesumuntur pro matrimonio. (*Maxim*) Where there is a ceremony followed by cohabitation as man and wife, a strong presumption arises that the parties are lawfully married.

Omnia praesumuntur rite esse acta. All things are presumed to have been done rightly.

Omnia praesumuntar rite it dowee probetur in contrarium solemniter esse acta. This Latin term means All the acts are presumed to have been done rightly and regularly. Applied in this case. [*Gian Chand v. State of Haryana*, (2013) 14 SCC 420, para 29].

Omnia praesumuntur rite et dowee probetur in contrarium solemiter esse acta. (*Maxim*) All acts are presumed to have been done rightly and regularly, applies.

Omnia prius verbis experiri quam armis sapientem decet. It is the part of wisdom to exhaust negotiation before resorting to arms.

Omnia quae jure contrahuntur contrario jure pereunt. (*Lat.*) (D. 50, 17, 100) All things which are contracted by law perish by a contrary law.

Omnia rite esse acta praesumuntur. All things are presumed to have been rightly done.

Omnibus. For all public vehicle "OMNIBUS" means any motor vehicle constructed or adopted to carry more than six persons excluding the driver. [Motor Vehicles Act (59 of 1988), S. 2(29)]

Omnibus claim. A specification claim claiming the invention as described with reference to the drawings or examples. (*Patents*)

Omnibus infra regnum orantibus legis remedium patet. The remedy of the law lies open to all within the kingdom who ask it.

Omnibus poenalibus judiciis et aetati est imprudentiae succurritur. (*Lat.*) In all criminal proceedings, age and ignorance are aided.

Omnis consensus tollit errorem. Every consent removes an error.

Omnis contractus turpitudinis legibus invisus. Every dishonorable contract is odious to the law.

Omnis indemnatus pro innoxio legibus habetur. Every uncondemned person is held by the law as innocent.

Omnis interpretatio si fieri potest ita fienda est in instrumentis ut omnes contrarietates amoveantur. (*Lat.*) (Jenk. Cent. 96) Every interpretation, if it can be done is to be so made in instruments as that all contradictions may be removed.

Omnis prohibitio mandato equipatatur. Every prohibition is equivalent to a command.

Omnis regula suas patitur exceptiones et omnis exceptio est regula. Every rule is subject to its own exceptions and every rule is subject to its own exceptions and every exception is a rule.

On a particular date. The legal connotation of the expression 'to quit on a particular day' is that the person required to quit can remain in occupation till the midnight of that day if he so desires. *Ananda Biah* v. *Hazi Orimuddier Sadagas,* AIR 1952 Ass 132. [T.P. ACT (4 of 1882), S. 106]

On a point of law. The term of point of law has been construed by High Courts in various decisions and includes an order of commitment rested upon on acceptable and valid evidence. *Marapureddigari* v. *State,* AIR 1952 Mad 821, 823.

On account of. Because of; by reason of; toward payment of.

Concerning. [T.P. Act (4 of 1882), S. 76(h)]; because of [Indian Contract Act (9 of 1872), S. 43, *Expln.*]; [CPC, O. XXI, R. 60].

On all fours. Squarely on point on both facts and law.

On any other ground. The expression "on any other ground" occurring in Section 19(3)(c), refer to and relates to all grounds that are available in proceedings under the Act other than grounds which relate to sanction granted by the authority. [*Asian Resurfacing of Road Agency Private Limited* v. *Central Bureau of Investigation,* (2018) 16 SCC 299, para 51.4] [Prevention of Corruption Act (49 of 1988), S. 19(3)(c)].

On bail. When a person is said to be 'on bail' or to have given bail, it is intended to apply as well to recognizances as to bail bonds.

On behalf of. The expression 'on behalf of' connotes some benefit to the person on whose behalf another person acts.

A contract by certain parties 'on behalf of' others *prima facie* imports that they made the contract only as agents.

The words 'on behalf of' connote an agency. A relative, authorised to file complaint by a wife, acts on behalf of the wife and after the death of the wife, the relative no longer acts on behalf of the wife. *State of Mysore* v. *Gangamma,* AIR 1965 Mys 235, 236. [CrPC 1973 (2 of 1974), S. 198]

The expression 'on behalf of' means that the holder of the property is only a representative of the real owner. *Kripashankar* v. *Commissioner of Wealth Tax,* AIR 1966 Pat 371, 372. [Wealth Tax Act (52 of 1957), S. 21]

On call. 'On call', as used in an instrument payable on call, is equivalent to the expression 'on demand' or 'when demanded'.

'ON CALL' as used in a bond which by its terms is payable call, signifies that it is payable immediately; money lent, either repayable on demand or at short notice.

On conviction. Upon or following the result of a criminal trial which ends in a judgment or sentence that the prisoner (accused) is guilty as charged. [CrPC 1973 (2 of 1974), S. 106].

On demand. When demanded. This phrase, when applied to payment, usually denotes a debt already due and actionable; but may be used to signify that demand is a condition precedent to the right to payment.

Except in case of negotiable instruments the words on demand require an actual demand before a right to the money arises.

In Promissory Note payable "*on demand*" the words "on demand" mean "at once" no demand is necessary prior to bringing an action. The reason of the above rule may be traced to the Law Merchant under which "the debtor is bound to have the money ready *on demand*".

A note which by its terms is payable on demand is payable immediately.

The words "*on demand*" do not necessarily mean that there must be an express demand. These words are merely equivalent to "forthwith" or "immediately".

Sometimes, the words 'on demand' indicate the cause of action to arise only after request.

In the case of an ordinary agreement providing for payment "demand," time runs from the date of the agreement and not from the date of demand.

The expression "on demand" in a promissory note has a technical meaning, viz., payable immediately or forthwith. In such cases, no actual demand is necessary to make the money due under the promissory note expiable. *Muthu Gounder* v. *Perumayyammal,* AIR 1961 Mad 347, 348. [Indian Stamp Act (2 of 1899), S. 2(22)]

When claimed (in the case of a negotiable instrument) immediately, forthwith. [CrPC 1973 (2 of 1974), S. 42(1)]; [Indian Evidence Act (1 of 1872), S. 76].

On duty. Officially engaged.

The officer taking the training and the officer giving the training are both regarded to be on duty.

On his behalf. From his side. [Indian Contract Act (9 of 1872), S. 199].

On its face. From its very appearance. [Indian Evidence Act (1 of 1872), S. 93].

On-line. Communications that provide a real-time connection. (*Information Technology*)

This term is actually used in association with using the Internet, referring to a service or information accessed through the telephone network via a modem. (*Cyber Law*)

The state of being in direct communication with a computer. It is usually used to describe (1) peripherals that are connected to a computer system and ready to operate, or (2) services, such as information services, that require direct communication between two computers connected by telephone. (*Computer*)

On-line information and database access or retrieval. Means providing data or information, retrievable or otherwise, to a customer, in electronic form through a computer network. [Finance Act (32 of 1994), S. 65(61) now repealed by Goods and Services Tax Act, 2017]

On merits. After the Court has heard and investigated the arguments and gone through the record and applied his mind.

An *ex-parte* decree passed by a foreign Court without examining points at controversy between the parties cannot be said a judgement 'on merits'. *International Woollen Mills* v. *Standard Wool,* (2001) 5 SCC 265, para 32 : AIR 2001 SC 2134. [CPC (5 of 1908), S. 13(b)]

On or about. Approximately.

On presentment. "In a promisory note or bill of exchange, the expressions "at sight" and "on presentment" mean on demand." [Negotiable Instruments Act (26 of 1881), S. 21]

On probation of good conduct. On a trial or test of good or proper personal behaviour, deportment or mode of action. [CrPC 1973 (2 of 1974), S. 360(1)].

On regular basis. The expression 'on a regular basis' means the appointment to the post on a regular basis in contradiction to appointment on *ad hoc* or stop-gap or purely temporary basis. *K. Madhavan* v. *Union of India*, AIR 1987 SC 2291, 2296. [Constitution of India, Art. 309]

On sale or return. With option to the the recipient that he may accept the goods as sold to him or return them to the supplier. [Sale of Goods Act (3 of 1930), S. 24].

On the date fixed for scrutiny. The expression "on the date fixed for scrutiny" means "on the whole of the day on which the scrutiny of nomination has to take place". *Pashupati Nath Singh* v. *Harihar Prasad Singh*, AIR 1968 SC 1064, 1067. [Representation of the People Act (43 of 1951), S. 36 (2)(a)]

On the door. The phrase 'on the door', in a statute requiring notice of a tax sale to be posted on the courthouse door, does not necessarily mean on the swinging panel which fills the opening or entrance to the building, but a conspicuous posting upon the building at the side of the opening, or upon a separate board or panel kept there for that purpose, is sufficient, to all reasonable intents and purposes.

On the face of it. Quite apparent. [Registration Act (16 of 1908), S. 33(4)].

On the face of the record. The expression "on the face of the record" means "what would appear on the face of the decree and the papers relevant for the purpose of understanding it". *Amabla* v. *Sarat*, 54 CLJ 593 [CPC (5 of 1908), S. 38]

On the first day of hearing of the suit. The words 'on the first day of hearing of the suit' do not mean the day fixed for return of the summons or the returnable day, but the day on which the Court applies its mind in the case, that is, when the issues are framed or evidence taken. *Ambalal* v. *Babldas,* AIR 1964 Guj 9, 2 0 .

On the occasion of charge. There can be no warrant forgiving the words 'on the occasion of charge' the same meaning as 'in consequence of' or 'to give effect to'. *J.K. Commercial Corporation Ltd.* v. *CIT, U.P. Lucknow,* AIR 1964 All 22, 24. [Excess Profits Tax Act (15 of 1940), S. 8 (3)]

On the pleadings. Rendering of a judgment without hearing or evaluating the full arguments of the parties.

On the spot. At the particular place itself [Indian Evidence Act (1 of 1872), S. 114, ill. (b) and Manoeuvres, Field Firing and Artillery Practices Act (5 of 1938), S. 6(2)].

On trial. Actually in progress before the Court (as) case on trial.

On whose behalf. The words "on whose behalf" mean in whose favour or for whose benefit. *Om Prabha Jain* v. *Gain Chand,* AIR 1959 SC 837, 841.

One man company. A company in which all the shares except those necessary for constituting a company, are held by one man, or in which one man is the moving spirit and has the control of the whole business.

One Person Company. Means a company which has only one person as a member. [S. 2(62) of the Companies Act, 2013 (18 of 2013)]

Onerous. Burdensome; oppressive.

Burdensome; having a legal obligation attached to it. [T.P. Act (4 of 1882), S. 127].

Onerous property. For the purposes of this section, the term "ONEROUS PROPERTY" means—

(*i*) any unprofitable contract; and

(*ii*) any other property comprised in the estate of the bankrupt which is unsaleable or not readily saleable, or is such that it may give rise to claim. [Insolvency and Bankruptcy Code (31 of 2016), S. 160, *Explanation*].

Ongoing project. "Ongoing project" means a multi-year project undertaken by a Company in fulfilment of its CSR obligation having timelines not exceeding three years excluding the financial year in which it was commenced, and shall include such project that was initially not approved as a multi-year project but whose duration has been extended beyond one year by the board based on reasonable justification. [Companies (Corporate Social Responsibility Policy) Rules, 2014, R. 2(1)(i)]

Online auctions. Buying and selling goods and services in an auction format using the Web. (*Cyber Law*)

Online Dispute Resolution. Means where conventional disputes or e-disputes are resolved using Alternative dispute resolution methods such as Mediation or conciliation or adjudication methods like arbitration through internet and computers. [Karnika Seth, *Computers Internet and New Technology Laws*, 2021, LexisNexis, Glossary of Legal Terms]

Online gaming. Means offering of a game on the internet or an electronic network and includes online money gaming. [Central Goods and Services Tax Act 2017 (12 of 2017), S. 2(80A)]

Online information and database access or retrieval services. "Online information and database access or retrieval services" means services whose delivery is mediated by information technology over the internet or an electronic network and the nature of which renders their supply involving minimal human intervention and impossible to ensure in the absence of information technology and includes electronic services such as,—

(i) advertising on the internet;

(ii) providing cloud services;

(iii) provision of e-books, movie, music, software and other intangibles through telecommunication networks or internet;

(iv) providing data or information, retrievable or otherwise, to any person in electronic form through a computer network;

(v) online supplies of digital content (movies, television shows, music and the like);

(vi) digital data storage; and

(vii) online gaming excluding the online money gaming as defined in clause (80B) of section 2 of the Central Goods & Services Tax Act, 2017 (12 of 2017; [The Integrated Goods and Services Tax Act, 2017 (13 of 2017), S. 2(17)]

Online mediation. Means online mediation referred to in section 30. [Mediation Act, 2023 (32 of 2023), S. 3(q)]

Online money gaming. Means online gaming in which players pay or deposit money or money's worth, including virtual digital assets, in the expectation of winning money or money's worth, including virtual digital assets, in any event including game, scheme, competition or any other activity or process, whether or not its outcome or performance is based on skill, chance or both and whether the same is permissible or otherwise under any other law for the time being in force. [Central Goods and Services Tax Act 2017 (12 of 2017), section 2(80B)]

Only. 'Liable *only* for the amount opposite his name', as used in a subscription contract providing that a subscriber shall be 'liable only for the amount opposite his name' is so construed as to make the contract a several obligation.

The significance of the word 'only' is that, other qualifications being equal, the race, religion or caste of a citizen should not be a ground of preference or disability. *Dorairajan* v. *State of Madras,* AIR 1951 Mad 120, 123 (FB). [Constitution of India, Art. 15(1) and 29(2)]

Onus. A burden; a load. Also, an encumbrance.

Onus probandi. The burden of proving; the burden of proof.

'Onus probandi' and 'animus attestandi'. The Latin expression '*onus probandi*' and '*animo attestandi'* are two basic features in the matter of the civil Court's exercise of testamentary jurisdiction. Whereas *onus probandi* lies in every case upon the party propounding a will, the expression *animo attestandi* means and implies *animus to attest* : in common parlance it means intent to attest. As regards the latter maxim, the attesting witness must subscribe with the intent that the subscription of the signature made stands by way of complete attestation of Will. *N. Kamalam* v. *Ayyasamy,* (2001) 7 SCC 503, 508, para 1. [Indian Succession Act (39 of 1925), S. 63(c)]

Oocyte means naturally ovulating oocyte in the female genetic tract. [Surrogacy (Regulation) Act, 2021 (47 of 2021), section 2(1)(v)]

Op. cit. (*abbr.*) Opera citato.

The book previously cited.

Open. Patent; visible; apparent. *As an adjective*, not closed; not concealed; not hidden; exposed to view; free from concealment, reserve, or disguise, not secret or secretive, plain and aboveboard; so public as to be practically avowed; *As a verb*, simply, to clear off obstructions.

The section covers only licences to open a market. The word 'open' in S. 203(1) of the Act applies only to the first or initial opening of the market. In cannot be said to be opened when the renewal of licence is granted after the expiry of a term mentioned in the earlier licence. *V. Ratna Mudaliar* v. *Contenment Board*, AIR 1958 Mad 513, 514. [Cantonments Act (2 of 1924), S. 203(1)]

Open access. Means the non-discriminatory provision for the use of transmission lines or distribution system or associated facilities with such lines or system by any licensee or consumer or a person engaged in generation in accordance with the regulations specified by the Appropriate Commission. [Indian Electricity Act (36 of 2003), S. 2(47)]

Open access in transmission. Open access in distribution. Implies freedom to the licensee to procure power from any source of his choice, open access in distribution means, freedom to the consumer to get supply from any source of his choice. The provision of open access to consumers ensure right of the consumer to get supply from a person other than the licensee of his area of supply using the distribution system of such distribution licensee. [*Brihanmumbai Electric Supply and Transport Undertaking v. Maharashtra Undertaking Regulatory Commission* (MERC), (2015) 2 SCC 438, para 22].

Open account. An open account is one in which some item of the contract is not settled by the parties, whether the account consists of one item or many, or where there have been running or current dealings between the parties, and the account is kept open with expectation of further dealings

An account which has not been settled or balanced. [Limitation Act (36 of 1963), Sch., Art. 1]

Open and notorious possession. The possession or control that is evident to others.

Open and Distance Learning. Mode means a mode of providing flexible learning opportunities by overcoming separation of teacher and learner using a variety of media, including print, electronic, online and occasional interactive face-to-face meeting with the presence of an High Educational Institution or Learner Support Services to deliver teaching-learning experiences, including practical or work experiences. [University Grants Commission (Open and Distance Learning) Regulations, 2017, Regn. 2(m)].

Open arrest. Means confinement within the precincts of any barracks, lines or camp for the time being occupied by any part of the force. [Central Reserve Police Force Act (66 of 1949), S. 2(e)]

Open bid. A bid which may be reduced by the bidder after submission in order to meet competing bids.

Open cast working. Means a quarry, that is to say, an excavation where any operation for the purpose of searching for or obtaining minerals has been or is being carried on, not being a shaft or an excavation which extends below superjacent ground. [Mines Act (35 of 1952), S. 2(1)(kk)] [Occupational Safety, Healthy & Working Conditions Code, 2020 (37 of 2020), section 2(1)(zu)]

Open Court. A sitting of Court at the transactions of which the public are free to be present. [Indian Evidence Act (1 of 1872), S. 119 and Constitution of India, Art. 145(4)].

Sessions Court holding trial within jail premises pursuant to order of High Court under S. 9(6), CrPC, 1973 (2 of 1974) having regard to the unprecedented violent situation then prevailing, held, deemed to be an open Court. (*Kehar Singh* v. *State (Delhi Admn.),* AIR 1988 SC 1883).

Open-credit. A credit given by a banker to his customer, because of his (customer's) high credit worthiness, without any security or guarantee.

Open end fund. A mutual fund which continually offers new shares and buys again the existing shares on demand.

Open-end mortgage. A mortgage allowing the mortgagor to borrow additional funds against the same property.

Open-ended equity oriented fund. Means—

(i) the Unit Scheme, 1964, made by the Unit Trust of India; and

(ii) such fund where the investible funds are invested by way of equity shares in domestic companies to the extent of more than fifty per cent of the total proceeds of such fund :

Provided that the percentage of equity share holding of the fund shall be computed with reference to the annual average of the monthly averages of the opening and closing figures; [Income-tax Act (43 of 1961), S. 115T *Expln.* (b)]

Open ended scheme. "OPEN ENDED SCHEME" means a scheme of mutual funds which offers units for sale without specifying any duration for redemption. [SEBI (Mutual Funds) Regulations, 1996, Reg. 2(s)]

Open market. If the transactions of sale and purchase are effected under conditions enabling every person desirous of purchasing the goods to place orders with such manufacturing unit and obtain supplies, they will constitute purchases form the open market. *Ahura Chemicals Products P. Ltd.* v. *Union of India*, AIR 1981 SC 1782, 1785.

Open market operation. A monetary policy instrument which is used by the reserve bank mainly with a view to affect the reserve base of the banks and thereby the extent of monetary expansion. Open market operations are by way of outright sale and purchase of securities through the securities department and repo and reverse repo transactions. [*M L Tannan Banking Law & Practice in India*, Vol. 2, 2021, LexisNexis, Dictionary of Banking Terminology]

Open minds. Readiness to weigh *pros* and *cons* of evidence.

Open or keep open. A private cart stand is "kept open" only if it is kept open to others in charge of vehicles besides the owner of the place, to keep their vehicles there to let their vehicles stand there. *A.B. Transport* v. *Dharampuram Municipality,* AIR 1957 Mad 781, 785.

Open shelter. "Open shelter" means a facility for children, established and maintained by the State Government, either by itself, or through a voluntary or non-governmental organization under sub-section (1) of Section 43, and registered as such, for the purposes specified in that section. [Juvenile Justice (Care and Protection of Children) Act, 2015 (2 of 2016), S. 2(41)].

Open space. "OPEN SPACE" means an area, forming an integral part of the site, at the ground level open to the sky. [W.B. Municipal (Building) Rules, 1996, R. 2(35)]

'OPEN SPACE' includes any public park, heath, common recreation ground, pleasure ground, garden, walk, ornamental enclosure or disused burial ground under the control and management of a local authority. [Ministry of Housing and Local Government Provisional Order Confirmation (Greater London Parks and Open Spaces) Act, 1967, S. 6]

Open University. Means a University which imparts education through distance education or Open and Distance Learning mode using variety of Information and Communication Technology educational aids i.e. online education in the form of Open Educational Resources (OERs) or Massive Open Online Courses (MOOCs) etc. [University Grants Commission (Open and Distance Learning) Regulations, 2017, Regn. 2(n)].

Opening statement. A party's overview of the case to be presented.

Openly enjoyed. Where the owner of a dominant tenement, with the intention of preventing the use of a way, creates an obstruction of a permanent nature rendering such use impossible, the way cannot be said, during the continuance of the obstruction to have been openly enjoyed. [Indian Easements Act (5 of 1882), S. 15].

Operand. Usually considered to be one of two major parts of an instruction, the operation code being the other. An operand is an item to be operated upon or is somehow involved in the operation specified by the operation code. An operand may be a memory address, a number to be added, a parameter of some type, *etc.* (*Computer*)

Operate. To put in action and supervise the working of; to perform a work of labour; to effect any result; to bring about a specified result; to produce the proper or intended effect.

The word 'operate' means to put into or to continue in operation or activity; to work as to operate a machine and is distinct from maintaining or keeping in repair.

To take effect; to be in activity; to work.

Operating agency. Means any group of experts consisting of persons having special knowledge of business or industry in which the sick industrial company is engaged and includes public financial institution, State level institution, scheduled bank or any other person as may be specified as the operating agency by the Tribunal. [Companies Act (1 of 1956), S. 2(31AA)]

"OPERATING AGENCY" means any public financial institution, State level institution, scheduled bank or any other person as may be specified by general or special order as its agency by the Board. [Sick Industrial Companies (Special Provisions) Act (1 of 1986), S. 3(1)(i)]

Operating cycle. An operating cycle is the time between the acquisition of assets for processing and their realisation in cash or cash equivalents. Where the normal operating cycle cannot be identified, it is assumed to have a duration of twelve months. [Companies Act (18 of 2013), Schedule III, Division I, Notes]

The operating cycle of an entity is the time between the acquisition of assets for processing and their realisation in cash or cash equivalents. When the entity's normal operating cycle is not clearly identifiable, it is assumed to be twelve months. [Companies Act (18 of 2013), Schedule III, Division II, Notes]

Operating expenses. Expenses incurred in running a business and producing output.

Operating right. Means the right of holder of a reconnaissance permit, or an exploration licence, or a production lease. [Offshore Areas Minerals (Development and Protection) Act, 2002 (17 of 2003), S. 4(o)]

Operating System. Software that controls the operation of a computer. An operating system whose functions include the control of the flow of data to or from a disk is commonly called a *Disk Operating System.* (DOS). (*Computer*)

Operation. The exertion of power, physical, mechanical or moral— action, as of an army or fleet— movement of machinery; exertion of power; method of working; process of operating.

The condition of being in force [Indian Evience Act (1 of 1872), S. 41 and Constitution of India, Art. 13(3)(b)]; the act or process of operating; action or movements [Army Act (46 of 1950), S. 3(1)(a)]; working [T.P. Act (4 of 1882), S. 2(d)]; [Damodar Valley Corporation Act (14 of 1948), S. 12(a)]; a surgical operation [IPC (45 of 1860), S. 88, ill.]; working to keep running [Motor Vehicles Act (59 of 1988), S. 63A(2)(a)].

It is not every business activity of a manufacturer that comes within the expression 'operation'. These provisions have no application unless according to the known and accepted business notions and usages the particular activity is regarded as a well defined business operation. Activities which are not well defined or are of a casual or isolated character would not ordinarily fall within the ambit of this rule. *Anglo French Textile Co. Ltd.* v. *Commissioner of Income Tax*, AIR 1953 SC 105, 108.

Operation code. A portion of an instruction or control word that specifies the function that the computer is to perform. Eventually translated into binary-form machine language, the operation code may be any one of several high-level forms, including a symbolic form, when entered by the programmer. (*Computer*)

Operation of law. A law is always in operation as long as it is the rule of conduct of the people upon which it is intended to operate, that is, as long as the people are bound to obey it, or conform their condition to its provisions. The operation of a law can be nothing more than the obligation of a law. The law ceases to operate when it is no longer obligatory, and as long as it is obligatory it is in full operation.

OPERATION OF LAW AND EXECUTION OF LAW. There is a great difference, between the operation of the laws, and the execution of the laws. A law may be in operation, and yet, from a defect of Courts or officers of justice, it may not be possible to carry it into execution. The operation of a law is a part of its very existence. It ceases to be a law when it is no longer operative.

Operation of law, By. By the action or working of law. [T.P. Act 4 of 1882), S. 2(d)].

Operation relating to prospecting. For the purposes of this section,—

"OPERATION RELATING TO PROSPECTING" means any operation undertaken for the purpose of exploring, locating or proving deposits of any mineral, and includes any such operation which proves to be infructuous or abortive. [Income-tax Act (43 of 1961), S. 35E(5)(a)]

Operational Certificate. A Digital Signature Certificate which is within its operational period at the present date and time or at a different specified date and time, depending on the context. (*Information Technology*)

Operational feasibility. The measure of how well the proposed e-commerce project will work in the organization and how internal and external customers will feel about the proposed e-commerce project. (*Cyber Law*)

Operational management. Refers to all business/ service unit management (*i.e.* the user management) as well as Information Technology management. (*Information Technology*)

Operational period. The period starting with the date and time a Digital Signature Certificate is issued (or on a later date time certain, if stated in the Digital Signature Certificate) and ending with the date and time on which the Digital Signature Certificate expires or is earlier suspended or revoked. (*Information Technology*)

Operational plan. "OPERATIONAL PLAN" means a schedule of irrigation deliveries with details of the mode and duration of supplies drawn up for regulation of irrigation in the command area of an irrigation system. [Andhra Pradesh Farmers Management of Irrigation Systems Act (AP Act No. 11 of 1997), S. 2(t)]

Operations security (OPSEC). A process of identifying critical information and subsequently analyzing friendly actions attendant to military operations and other activities.

Operations Zone. An area where access is limited to personnel who work there and to properly escorted visitors. Operations Zones should be monitored at least periodically, based on a threat risk assessment

(TRA), and should preferably be accessible from a Reception Zone. (*Information Technology*)

Operative. A workman; a labourer; one employed in a factory as workman : a skilled workman, an artisan, especially those who operate a machine in a mill or manufactory.

Operative part, of a document as distinguished from the introductory matter, recitals, *etc*., refers to that part of the document which is intended to create or transfer rights.

The operative part of a deed is that portion of it which expresses the effect.

Operator. "Every person generating, transmitting supplying or using energy referred to as the "OPERATOR"." [Indian Electricity Act (9 of 1910), S. 32(1)]

"OPERATOR" means a person employed directly or by or through any agency (including a contractor), whether as a regular worker or as a casual worker, with or without the knowledge of the principal employer, whether for remuneration or not, in the operation or cleaning of any dangerous machine or any part thereof or in any other kind of work incidental to, or connected with, the operation or cleaning of any dangerous machine or any part thereof. [Dangerous Machines (Regulation) Act (35 of 1983), S. 3(k)]

"OPERATOR" means the owner or bareboat charterer or any other natural or juridicial person to whom the responsibilities of the owner or bareboat charter have been formally assigned. [UN Convention on conditions for Registration of Ships, Geneva, Feb. 7, 1986, Art. 2]

"OPERATOR" in relation to an aircraft at any time, means the person who at the time has the management of the aircraft. [Tokyo Convention Act (20 of 1975), S. 2(g)]

Operator of a bio-medical waste facility. Means a person who owns, controls or operates a facility for the collection, reception, storage, transport, treatment, disposal or any other form of handling of bio-medical waste. [Bio-Medical Waste (Management and Handling) Rules, 1998, R. 3(9)]

Operator of a facility. "OPERATOR OF A FACILITY" means a person who owns or operates a facility for collection, segregation, storage, transportation, processing and disposal of municipal solid wastes and also includes any other agency appointed as such by the municipal authority for the management and handling of municipal solid wastes in the respective areas. [Municipal Solid Wastes (Management and Handling) Rules, 2000, R. 3(xvi)]

Opinio quae favet testamento est tenenda. That opinion is to be followed which favours the will.

Opinion. A view; estimation. [CrPC 1973 (2 of 1974), S. 95(1); Constitution of India, Art. 124(3)(c)].

The opinion which a witness is not allowed to give instead of a statement of fact is defined to be an inference of fact from observed facts.

"Opinion" means "the statement by a Judge or court of the decision reached in regard to a cause tried or argued before them, expounding the law as applied to the case, and detailing the reasons upon which the judgment is based." [Black's Law Dictionary as cited in *Natural Resources Allocation, In Re*, Special Reference No. 1 of 2012, (2012) 10 SCC 1, para 44].

Opinion means something more than mere retaining of gossip or of hearsay; it means judgment or belief, that is, a belief or a conviction resulting from what one thinks on a particular question. *Dolgorindu* v. *Nimai Charan*, AIR 1959 SC 914, 918.(*Of Court*). The 'opinion' of a Court is the reasons given for its judgment.

Opinion of Court and Decision of Court. There is a manifest difference between a mere opinion and a decision; the former is a statement given by the Court for its conclusions, while the latter is the judgment or conclusion of the Court.

Opinion of the majority. The view of the greater or larger number. [CrPC 1973 (2 of 1974), S. 96(5)]; [CPC (5 of 1908), O. XLVII, R. 6(2)].

Opinion poll. "OPINION POLL" means a poll taken to ascertain the wishes of the electors in pursuance of the provisions of this Act. [Goa, Daman and Diu (Opinion Poll) Act (38 of 1966), S. 2(g)]

"OPINION POLL" means any service designed to secure information on public opinion regarding social, economic, political or other issues. [Finance Act (32 of 1994), S. 65 (75a) (*Inserted by Finance (No.2) Act (23 of 2004), S. 90*) now repealed by Goods and Services Tax Act, 2017]

Opinion poll agency. Means any person engaged in providing any service in relation to opinion poll. [Finance Act (32 of 1994), S. 65 (75) (75b) (*Inserted by Finance (No.2) Act (23 of 2004), S. 90*) now repealed by Central Goods and Services Tax Act, 2017]

Opium. Includes also poppy-heads, preparations or admixtures of opium and intoxicating drugs prepared from the poppy.

'OPIUM' means—

(1) the capsules of the poppy (Papaver *somniferum* L), whether in their original form or cut, crushed or powdered and whether or not juice has been extracted therefrom;

(2) the spontaneously coagulated juice of such capsules which has not been submitted to any manipulations other than those necessary for packing and transport; and

(3) any mixture, with or without neutral materials, of any of the above forms of opium, and includes any derivative of opium. [Medicinal & Toilet Preparations (Excise Duties) Act (16 of 1955), S. 2(i)]

OPIUM means:—

(a) the coagulated juice of the opium poppy; and

(b) any mixture, with or without any neutral material, of the coagulated juice of the opium poppy,

but does not include any preparation containing not more than 0.2 per cent of morphine. [Narcotic Drugs and Psychotropic Substances Act (61 of 1985), S. 2(xv)]

Opium, as used in a life policy providing that the same should be void in case the insured should come to his 'death by opium,' means not the accidental or involuntary, but the rational and voluntary, use of opium.

Opium derivative. "OPIUM DERIVATIVE" means—

(a) medicinal opium, that is, opium which has undergone the processes necessary to adopt it for medicinal use in accordance with the requirements of the Indian Pharmacopoeia or any other pharmacopoeia notified in this behalf by the Central Government, whether in powder form or granulated or otherwise or mixed with neutral materials;

(b) prepared opium, that is, any product of opium obtained by any series of operations designed to transform opium into an extract suitable for smoking and the dross or other residue remaining after opium is smoked;

(c) phananthrene alkaloids, namely, morphine, codeine, thebaine and their salts;

(d) diacetylmorphine, that is, the alkaloid also known as dismorphine or heroin and its salts; and

(e) all preparations containing more than 0.2 per cent of morphine or containing any diacertylmorphine. [Narcotic Drugs and Psychotropic Substances Act (61 of 1985), S. 2(vi)]

Opium poppy. Means—

(a) the plant of the species *Papaver somniferum* L; and

(b) the plant of any other species of Papaver from which opium or any phenanthrene alkaloid can be extracted and which the Central Government may, by notification in the Official Gazette, declare to be opium poppy for the purpose of this Act. [Narcotic Drugs and Psychotropic Substances Act (61 of 1985), S. 2(xvii)]

Oportet legem brevem esse, quo facilius ab imperitis teneatur. Laws ought to be short, that they may be more readily comprehended by the unlearned.

Opportunity. Convenient time; suitable occasion; time or place favourable for executing the purpose of doing the thing in question; a fit or convenient time; a time favourable for the purpose; a convenience or fitness of time and place.

Chance; occasion. [Indian Evidence Act (1 of 1872), S. 7; Constitution of India, Art. 39(f)].

Opportunity cost. The cost in which the cost of acquired asset is measured by the value of an alternative investment that is foregone.

Opportunity of being heard. Proceeding further by the Income-tax Commissioner, without giving notice to the assessee of the serious allegations of fraud, collusion and conspiracy, interpolation of records *etc.* he found on inquiry, amounts to being heard without giving opportunity to the assessee. *Rampiyari* v. *I.T. Commissioner*, AIR 1964 Cal 367, 368. [Income-tax Act (11 of 1922), S. 33]

Opportunity of making representation. The right of being afforded the "earliest opportunity of making a representation against the order" is not confined to only a physical opportunity by supplying paper and pen only. In order that a representation can be made the person detained must first have knowledge of the grounds on which the authorities conveyed that they were satisfied about the necessity of making the detention order. It is, therefore, clear that if the representation has to be intelligible to meet the charges contained in the grounds, the information conveyed to the detained person must be sufficient to attain the object. (*State of Bombay* v. *Atma Ram Shridhar Vaidya,* AIR 1951 SC 157). [Constitution of India, Art. 22(5)]

Opportunity of showing cause. The expression "opportunity of showing cause', includes the principles of natural justice and also a right to be heard and make representations against the proposed action. *M.N. Bose* v. *District Magistrate, Alipore,* AIR 1978 Cal 197, 201. [Legal Practitioners Act (18 of 1879), S. 36(2)]

Opposed to. Set against. [T.P. Act (4 of 1882), S. 6(h)]; [T.P. Act (4 of 1882), S. 25].

Opposite party. 'OPPOSITE PARTY' means the person who answers complaint or claim. [Consumer Protection Rules, 1987, R. 2(f)]

The term "opposite party" in O. XXII, R. 10, CPC (5 of 1908) does not include an attaching creditor. The expression 'opposite party' means only a party who is interested in supporting the order which is sought to be received. [CPC (5 of 1908), O. XLVII, R. 4(2)(*a*)]

Opposition. A minority political party serving as a check on the party power, the party that opposes has a recognised position in the system of Parliamentary Government.

Oppression. An act of cruelty, severity, un-lawful exaction, domination, or excessive use of authority.

The word 'oppression' has not acquired a strictly technical meaning, and may be taken in its ordinary sense, which is an act of cruelty, or severity. When a revenue officer, under colour of law, wilfully and unlawfully takes the property of another, or subjects him to greater hardships than are necessary for the proper enforcement of the law, he is guilty of oppression. It is not essential that an unlawful act should be a serious injury to a person to make it oppressive. The exercise of unlawful power, or other means, in depriving an individual of his liberty or property against his will, is generally an act of oppression.

An act or omission may also amount to oppressive conduct if it is designed to achieve an unfair advantage. [Companies Act (1 of 1956), S. 397]

The person complaining of oppression must show that he had been constrained to submit to a conduct which is unfair to him and which causes prejudice to him in the exercise of his legal and proprietary rights as share-holder. *N.I.I. Ltd.* v. *N.I.N.I.H. Ltd.*, AIR 1981 SC 1298, 1321.

Oppression of minority. In company law, a Court will give relief if it finds that the acts of the management of a company are oppressive to the minority shareholders.

Oppressive. Unjustly severe, rigorous or harsh. [Companies Act (1 of 1956), S. 397]; [CPC (5 of 1908), O. XI, R. 7].

Opt for waiting. The phrase 'opt-for-waiting' means to forego a claim of his choice in first round of counselling by a higher meritted candidate and who had right to appear again in the second consulting. *Paramjeet Gambhir* v. *State of M.P.*, (2003) 4 SCC 276, para 5 : AIR 2003 SC 1338.

Optandum est ut li quo praesunt reipublicae legum similes sint, quae, ad puniendum, non iracundia sed acquitate ducuntur. It is desirable that those set in authority over the state shall be like the laws of the state, which, in inflicting punishment, are influenced not by anger, but by justice.

Opted. The word 'opt' means to make a choice, especially of nationality, when territory is transferred. *Abedakhatoon* v. *Ant. Custodian, E.P.*, AIR 1966 Pat 29, 32. [Administration of Evacuee Property Act (31 of 1950), S. 7(1)]

Optima est legis interpres consuetudo. (*Maxim*) Custom is the best interpreter of the law.

Optima est lex quae minimum relinquit arbitrio judicis, optimus judex qui minimum sibi. (*Maxim*) That system of law is best, which leaves least to the discretion of the Judge—that Judge states the best, who relies least on his own opinion. (*Broom*)

Optima evidentia rei praevalebit. The best evidence of the matter will prevail.

Optima legum interpres est consuetude. Custom is the best interpreter of the law.

Optima statuti interpretatrix est (omnibus particulis ejusdem inspectis) ipsum statutum. (*Lat.*) (8 Rep. 117) The best interpreter of a statute is (all the separate parts being considered) the statute itself.

Optimam esse legem quae minimum relinquit arbitrio judicis; id quod certitude ejus praestat. That law is the best which leaves the least discretion to the Judge; and this is an advantage which results from its certainty.

Optimus interpres rerum users. Usage is the best interpreter of things.

Optimus interpres rerum usus. (*Maxim*) Usage is the best interpreter of things. (*Broom*)

Optimus interpretandi modus est et sic interpretare et concordare leges legibus. (8 Rep 169) - The best mode of interpretation is so to interpret that laws may accord with laws. (*Latin for Lawyers*)

Optimus judex qui minimum sibi. He is the best Judge who relies least upon his own opinion.

Option. For the purposes of these guidelines—'OPTION' means a right but not an obligation granted to an employee to apply for shares at a pre-determined price. [Employees' Stock Option Plan or Schemes 2001, S. 7 *Expln* (iv)]

Power or liberty of choosing [Indian Contract Act (9 of 1872), S. 2(i)]; a right to buy or sell designated securities or commodities at a specified price during the period of the contract; a purchase of a put or call.

Option contract. A forward exchange contract in which the customer has the right to settle on any day within a specified period.

Option in goods. Means an agreement for the purchase or sale of a right to buy or sell, or a right to buy and sell, goods in future and includes a teji, a mandi, a teji-mandi, a galli, a put, a call or a put and call in goods. [Forward Contract (Regulation) Act (74 of 1952), S. 2(g)] [Now Repealed by s. 132 of Finance Act, 2015 (20 of 2015)]

Option in securities. Means a contract for the purchase or sale of a right to buy or sell, or a right to buy and sell, securities in future. The term includes a teji, a mandi, a teji-mandi, a galli, a put, a call, or a put and call in securities. [Securities Contracts (Regulation) Act (42 of 1956), S. 2(d)]

Option of, At the. According to the choice or liberty. [Indian Partnership Act (9 of 1932), S. 37].

Option premium. In this chapter, unless the context otherwise requires,—

"OPTION PREMIUM" means the premium payable by the purchaser of an "option in securities" at the time of such purchase. [Finance Act (23 of 2004), Chap. VII, S. 97(8)]

Optional. Not obligatory.

Not compulsory or obligatory; left to the discretion of one concerned. [Registration Act (16 of 1908), S. 32].

Optional trade. "Optional trade" means any trade or occupation or any subject field in engineering or non-engineering or technology or any vocational course as may be determined by the employer for the purposes of this Act. [Apprentices Act (52 of 1961), S. 2(1)(II) as inserted by Amending Act (29 of 2014)].

Options. Means the rights available to a policyholder under a policy. [Insurance Regulatory and Development Authority (Actuarial Report and Abstract) Regulations, Reg. 2(k)]

Or. The word "or" is a disjunctive particle that marks an alternative, generally corresponding to "either," as, "either this or that," a connective that marks an alternative, as "you may read or may write that is, you may do one of the things at your pleasure, but not both." A conjunction marking distribution or an alternative.

It is normally disjunctive, but sometimes it is read as conjunctive to give effect to the manifest intention of the legislature as disclosed from the context. *Municipal Council* v. *Bishandas Nathumal,* AIR 1969 MP 147 at 149.

The word "OR" occurring in Rule 18 cannot be given literal interpretation as that leads to various disastrous results and, therefore, this word has to be read as "and" as that is what was intended by the rule-maker in the scheme of things and to carry out the objectives of Rule 18 and also to bring it on a par with Rule 19. [*Spentex Industries Limited v. Commissioner of Central Excise*, (2016) 1 SCC 780, para 22] [Central Excise Rules, 2002, Rr. 18 and 19].

There may be circumstances where "or"/"and" are to be read as vice versa to give effect to manifest intention of the legislature as disclosed from the context. [*Spentex Industries Limited v. Commissioner of Central Excise*, (2016) 1 SCC 780, para 23].

These two words normally "or" and "and" are to be given their literal meaning unless some other part of the same statute or the clear intention of it requires that to be done otherwise. However, wherever use of such a word viz. "and"/"or" produces unintelligible or absurd results, the Court has the power to read the word "or" as "and" and vice versa to vie effect to the intention of the legislature which is otherwise quite clear. [*Spentex Industries Limited v. Commissioner of Central Excise*, (2016) 1 SCC 780, para 24].

The word 'or' has to be read to mean 'and'. *State of Bihar* v. *S.R. Roy*, AIR 1966 SC 1995, 1997. [Coal Mines Provident Fund and Bonus Schemes Act (46 of 1948), S. 2(*b*)]

The word 'or' must be read as 'and'. *State of Bihar* v. *S.R. Roy,* AIR 1966 SC 1995, 1997. [Industrial Disputes Act (14 of 1947), S. 16(2)]

The use of the expression 'or' is not disjunctive. Depending on the context, 'or' may be read as 'and' but the Court would not do it unless it is obliged because 'or' does not generally mean 'and' and 'and' does not generally mean 'or'. *R.S. Nayak* v. *A.R. Autulay*, AIR 1984 SC 684, 708. [IPC (45 of 1860), S. 21, Twelfth, (*a*)]

The word 'or' in cl. (*g*) must mean 'and', for the context regarding the qualification to be a member of the Board indicates that the members should be not only Hindus but also being to the denomination of Pushti-Margiya Vaishnavas. *Govindalalji Maharaj* v. *State of Rajasthan*, AIR 1963 SC 1638, 1652. [Rajasthan Nathdwara Temple Act (13 of 1959), S. 5(2)(*g*)]

The word 'or' in the proviso has the effect of 'and'. When there is a bar imposed in one circumstance or another, it means that the act barred cannot be done if either circumstance exists. *Raja Syed Mohammad Saadat Alikhan* v. *Wealth Tax Officer*, AIR 1963 All 488, 493. [Wealth Tax Act (27 of 1957), S. 25, proviso (a)]

Or at any time afterwards. The words 'or at any time afterwards' in S. 164 (1), CrPC 1973 (2 of 1974) obviously denote that if the confession was not made in the course of the investigation, then it must be made at any time afterwards but before the enquiry or trial commenced. If there has been no investigation at all, then the question 'or at any time afterwards' does not arise. *Rishi* v. *State of Bihar,* AIR 1955 Pat 425.

Or for any other purpose. Even where the duty has been fully paid and only the signature of Excise Inspector to the proforma and signature on gate passed to speed the movements of goods, bribes are paid not only to get unlawful things done but to get lawful things done promptly connotes 'for any other purpose'. *Som Prakash* v. *State of Delhi,* AIR 1974 SC 989. [Indian Evidence Act (1 of 1872), S. 161]

Or is otherwise invalid. The expression 'or is otherwise invalid' in S. 30(*c*), Arbitration Act (10 of 1940) (*repealed*) covers all objections to an award on the ground of invalidity from any cause whatsoever and does not refer to the invalidity of the kind referred to in the preceding clauses of the section. *Ismail* v. *Hansraj,* AIR 1955 Raj 153. [Now repealed & replaced by Act 26 of 1996]

Or : Nor. In a negative statement, "or" may be taken as equivalent to "nor" : following a negative, it has the same effect as "nor".

Or otherwise. The word "or" in "or otherwise" is a disjunctive that marks an alternative which generally corresponds to the word "either". An interpretation of the general words "or otherwise" limiting them to the matters and things of the same kind as the previous words would make the general words "or otherwise" following the preceding specific words, redundant. These words "or otherwise" are not words of limitation, but of extension so as to cover all possible ways in which title may vest in the land in the unauthorised occupation of the person concerned.

The Legislature, when it used the words 'or otherwise', apparently intended to cover other cases which may not come within the meaning of the preceding clauses. The rule of *ejusdem generis* is intended to be applied where general words have been used following particular and specific words of the same nature. *Lila Vati Bai* v. *State of Bombay*, AIR 1957 SC 521, 528, 529.

Expression covers all the other Directors who for one reason or the other cease to hold office and are immediately thereafter re-appointed as directors. *Laljibhata C. Kapadia* v. *Laliji B. Desai,* AIR 1972 Bom 276, 294. [Companies Act (1 of 1956), S. 264(1)]

"OR OTHERWISE" for the purposes of section 164(1)(d) and section 167(1)(f) of Act 18 of 2013, 'or otherwise' means any offence in respect of which he has been convicted by a Court under Act 18 of 2013 or the Companies Act, 1956 (1 of 1956). [R. 2(1)(s) of the Companies (Specification of Definitions Details) Rules, 2014]

Or such of those powers as the Court thinks fit. The words 'or such of those powers as the Court thinks fit' occurring in Order XV, Rule 1(d) would mean that the Courts have to exercise the discretion in the appointment of a receiver with care, caution and restraint so as to subserve the ends of justice but in the widest possible amplitude. *Industrial Credit & Investment Corpn. of India Ltd.* v. *Karnataka Ball Bearings Corpn. Ltd.*, (1999) 7 SCC 488, para 6. [CPC (5 of 1908), O. XV, R. 1(d)]

Or within the State. The words 'or within that State' in Art. 304 elucidate the words 'throughout the territory of India" in Art. 301 meaning that the freedom of trade, declared in Art. 301 is the freedom not only between one State and another, but also between different parts of the same state. *State* v. *Philipose Philip,* AIR 1954 TC 257. [Constitution of India, Arts. 301 and 304]

Oral. The word "oral" in S. 92, proviso 4 of the Indian Evidence Act (1 of 1872) is used in the sense of "not committed to writing", and includes all unwritten agreements whether come to by word of mouth or inferred from the acts and conduct of the parties.

Oral account. An oral report or description. [Indian Evidence Act (1 of 1872), S. 63(5)].

Oral admission. An admission made orally. [Indian Evidence Act (1 of 1872), S. 22].

Oral agreement includes all unwritten agreements whether they are oral or they are implied from the acts and conduct of parties.

An unwritten agreement. [Indian Evidence Act (1 of 1872), S. 92; T.P. Act (4 of 1882), S. 107].

Oral argument. Spoken presentation of a lawyer before a Court for or against the legal relief at issue.

Oral communication. Means any oral communication uttered by a person exhibiting an expectation that such communication is not subject to interception under circumstances justifying such expectation but such term does not include any electronic communication. [Prevention of Terrorism Act (15 of 2002), S. 36(c)]

Oral contract. An oral contract is a contract which is partly in writing and partly orally, or none of which is in writing.

Oral deposition. A deposition which is given in response to oral questioning by a lawyer.

Oral evidence. "A witness who is unable to speak may give his evidence in any other manner in which he can make it intelligible, as by writing or by signs, but such writing must be written and signs made in open Court. Evidence so given shall be deemed to be ORAL EVIDENCE." [Indian Evidence Act (1 of 1872), S. 119]

Evidence that is given orally. [Indian Evidence Act (1 of 1872), Ss. 3, 59 and 60].

Oral testimony. Oral testimony is that delivered from the lips of the witness.

Oral trust. Means a trust which is not declared by a duly executed instrument in writing including any wakf deed which is valid under the Mussalman Wakf Validating Act, 1913 (6 of 1913) and which is not deemed under Explanation 1 to be a trust declared by a duly executed instrument in writing. [Income-tax Act (43 of 1961), S. 160(1)(v) *Expln.* (2)]

Oral will. The making of a will by verbal declaration of the testator and which is usually dependent on oral testimony for proof.

Orally. Verbally. [CrPC 1973 (2 of 1974), S. 108(1)(i)].

Orchard. An enclosure or assemblage of fruit or nut-bearing trees.

The word 'orchard' under Section 2(5) of the Act means a compact area of land having fruit trees grown thereon or devoted to cultivation of fruit trees in such number that the main use to which the land is put is growing of fruits or fruit trees. *Manzoor Ahmad Magray* v. *Ghulam Hassan Aram*, (1999) 7 SCC 763, para 17 : AIR 2000 SC 191. [J&K Agrarian Reforms Act (26 of 1972), S. 2(5)]

Ordain. To appoint : to institute, to clothe with authority.

Ordeal (or Ordal). "An ancient manner of trial in criminal cases; for, when an offender being arragned pleaded "Not guilty", he might choose whether he would put himself for trial upon God and the country, by twelve men, as at this day, or upon God only; and then it was called "The Judgment of God", presuming that He would deliver the innocent. (*Termes de la Ley*, 9 Rep 32.)

Order. "ORDER" means the formal expression of any decision of a Civil Court which is not a decree. [CPC (5 of 1908), S. 2(14)]

'Order' means the formal expression of any decision of a civil court which is not a decree. [*Sinnamani v. G. Vettivel*, (2012) 5 SCC 759, para 9] [Civil Procedure Code (5 of 1908), S. 2(14)].

An authoritative direction, injunction, mandate; a decision of a Court or judge made or entered in writing [CPC (5 of 1908), S. 2(14) and Constitution of India, Art. 13(3)(a)]; sequence, succession of acts or events [Indian Evidence Act (1 of 1872), S. 3(2), ill. (a)]; public quiet; freedom from disturbance [IPC (45 of 1860), S. 21, fourth and Constitution of India, Art. 212(2)]; a religious society or fraternity living under a rule [Hindu Marriage Act (25 of 1955), S. 13(1)(vi)]; to give order [Indian Contract Act (9 of 1872), S. 50, ill. (a)].

The word 'order' in S. 26(2) Administration of Evacuee Property Act (31 of 1950) is used in its widest connotation and includes an act of confirmation of a sale. *Sun Dulari* v. *Addl. Custodian, Evacuee Property,* AIR 1953 All 718.

Order—*in commercial sense*, an order means a firm request for supply of definite goods emanating from a buyer, and indent placed by a purchaser. *M.S.P. Exports Pvt. Ltd.* v. *Coffee Board*, AIR 1980 SC 1468, 1482. [Central Sales Tax Act (74 of 1956), S. 5(3)]

An interlocutory finding is not an order and so is not appealable under Sec. 82 of the Act. *Jiwajirao Cotton Mills Ltd.* v. *Employees State Insurance Corporation Ltd.,* AIR 1960 MP 256, 257. [Employees' State Insurance Act (34 of 1948), S. 82(2)]

The words "notifications, orders, rules or bye-laws" have no reference to judicial orders the passing and cancellation whereof is subjected to and regulated by the procedural law of the land. Obviously, the words 'notifications, orders, rules and bye-laws" with which the expression 'orders' is associated must be deemed to limit the scope of the word 'orders' to non-judicial orders. *Bachchulal* v. *State,* AIR 1951 All 836. [General Clauses Act (10 of 1897), S. 21]

The term 'order' is general and is comprehensive enough to include all kinds of orders including a formal order'. *State of U.P.* v. *Mahendra Pratap Pitammah*, AIR 1956 All 585, 586. [Limitation Act (36 of 1963), S. 12(2)]

Formal Order drawn up as a result of Judgment of the Trial Court dismissing the application for condonation of delay was an order within the meaning of Sec. (2)(14) of CPC (5 of 1908) and Sec. 12(2) of Limitation Act (36 of 1963). *Shahjahan Begum* v. *Zahirul Hasan,* AIR 1972 All 511, 513.

Expression 'order' in Sec. 214(1)(*b*) means an 'order' already passed in favour of a deceased person which is sought to be executed. *Lakhan Mahto* v. *State of Bihar,* AIR 1972 Pat 37, 38. [Indian Succession Act (39 of 1925), S. 214(1)(*b*)]

Control Order is law within the meaning of Articles 302 and 304(*b*) of the Constitution of India. *Nani Gopal* v. *State of West Bengal,* AIR 1966 Cal 167, 176. [Constitution of India, Arts. 302, 304(*b*)]

"THE TERMS 'JUDGMENT,' 'DECREE,' 'DECISION,' AND 'ORDER' are more or less cognate as applied in legal proceedings, and closely allied in meaning. The term 'order' is not infrequently used in a more restricted sense than the word 'judgment'. It may be defined to be a command, direction, or decision of the Court or Judge on some intermediate point or issue in the case, but without finally disposing of the main issue or issues in the case. Then it is merely interlocutory. But the term is sometimes given a more extensive signification, even in legal controversies, and is occasionally used as a synonym of 'Judgment' or 'decree'.

ORDER (*in mercantile law*). An order is a brief note, resembling a bill of exchange, requesting the payment of money or the delivery of personalty to the bearer of the note.

The word 'order' *in a bill of exchange* has a positive fixed meaning and means an order endorsed on or accompanying the bill.

ORDER (*in parliamentary law*). A resolution or order is not a law, but merely the form in which the legislative body expresses an opinion. An ordinance cannot be replaced or sustained by an order or resolution.

Order affirming decision. An order dismissing an appeal as time-barred on the ground that it was not preferred within the period prescribed by the Limitation Act is an "*order affirming the decision*" of the lower Court.

Order has the force of a decree. The crucial test for determining the question whether an order has the force of a decree is not whether it is executable as a decree but whether it finally adjudicates on the rights that are in controversy in the proceedings before the Court concerned. An order granting letters of administration should be considered to be an order having the force of a decree. *Pancy Fernandas* v. *M.F. Deoros,* AIR 1963 All 153, 157, 158 (FB).

Order nisi. A provisional or conditional order, which allows a certain time within which to do some required act, on failure of which the order will be made absolute.

Order of commitment. The order by a magistrate sending up the accused to be tried by the Court of sessions.

Order of discharge. (*In Bankruptcy*) The discharge by order of Court of an insolvent from all debts and demands proveable in insolvency.

An order letting off the accused in a warrant case before the charge is framed. [CrPC 1973 (2 of 1974), S. 123(5)]

Order of dismissal. An order of rejection [CPC (5 of 1908), S. 2(2)(b)]; an order dismissing a person from his post.

Order of forfeiture. The order for deprivation of a person of his property as a penalty for some act or omission.

Order of government. The Governor is the head and symbol of the executive administration, and it is an order issued by or under his authority that constitutes an order of the Government. *Pioneer Motors* v. *O.M.A. Majeed,* AIR 1957 Mad 48, 57. [Constitution of India, Art. 166]

Order of performance. The sequence or succession of the accomplishment or carrying out or doing of any action or work. [Indian Contract Act (9 of 1872), S. 52]

Order of release. The order for setting free some person or property. [CrPC 1973 (2 of 1974), S. 442(1)]

Order of remand. An order sending back the accused to custody; and order passed by a superior Court of sending back the case to the lower Court with certain directions for re-trial.

Order of the State Government. Shall be construed as a reference to "order of the Central Government or the State Government, as the case may be." [Prevention of Terrorism Act (15 of 2002), S.49(3)(a)(ii)]

Order-on-default. An order granted on account of the default of the prosecution to complete the investigation and file the *challan* within the prescribed period is generally termed as an 'order-on-default'. (*Hitendra Vishnu Thakur* v. *State of Maharashtra,* AIR 1994 SC 2623.

Order, Original. The primary or initial or first order. [CrPC 1973 (2 of 1974), S. 123(7)].

Order passed on appeal. The phrase does not include an order refusing to admit an appeal after the period of limitation.

Order, Religious. A religious society or fraternity living under a rule. [Hindu Marriage Act (25 of 1955), S. 13(vi)].

Order sheet. The Order Sheet or *fard-akkahn* is no where noticed in the code. It is merely the creation of the General Rules (Criminal) framed by the Allahabad High Court for the guidance of subordinate Courts. Rule 3 of Chapter 4 of the General Rules requires an order-sheet to be maintained in the prescribed form, and further provides that upon it shall be recorded (1) every routine order passed by the Court in the case; (2) a notice of every other order regarding a document produced before the Court; and (3) a note of the date of such hearing and the proceedings on that date. *Shambu* v. *State,* AIR 1956 All 633, 634.

Order, standing. An instruction or prescribed procedure in force permanently or until specifically changed or cancelled.

Ordinance. A law, decree, or statute. (*Tomlin*)

Ordinance promulgated by the President of India under Art. 123, Const. or the Governor of any State under Art. 213, Const. when the legislature is not in session; a class of delegated legislation. [Constitution of India, Art. 13(3)(a)].

Ordinarily. The word "*ordinarily*" does not mean solely or in the main. It only means regularly and habitually, not casually, whether it be for a larger or a smaller portion of the day. (15 Bom LR 68.) See 30 Bom LR 387 : 109 IC 357 : 1928 Bom 140..

Ordinarily means non-exceptional or usual. It does not mean "primarily" nor does it mean 'universally'. It does not also mean "generally". *Municipal Board, Kanpur* v. *Janki Prasad,* AIR 1963 All 433, 435 (FB). [Prevention of Food Adulteration Act (37 of 1954), S. 2(*v*)(*a*)]

'Ordinarily' means normally and it is used where there can be an exception. It means in the large majority of cases but not invariably. 'Ordinarily' excludes 'extraordinary' or 'special circumstances'. [*Babubhai v. State of Gujarat,* (2010) 12 SCC 254, para 33 : (2011) 1 SCC (Cri) 336 as cited in *Mithilesh Kumar Singh v. State of Rajasthan,* (2015) 9 SCC 795, para 7].

Ordinarily employed. With reference to any establishment or part thereof, means the average number of persons employed per day in the establishment or part thereof during the preceding calendar year obtained by dividing the number of man days worked by the number of working days excluding rest days and other non-working days. [Occupational Safety, Healthy & Working Conditions Code, 2020 (37 of 2020), S. 2(1)(zv)]

Ordinarily lie. "Ordinarily lie" has reference to the Court to which appeals in the usual course lie as a matter of right. (*Anantram,* 11 Bom 438) [CrPC (5 of 1898), S. 195 (same Section in 1974 Code)].

Ordinarily prudent person. A hypothetical person who is used as a legal standard, specially to determine that someone acted negligently.

Ordinarily reside. The words 'ordinarily reside' for the purpose of Section 9 of the Act do not have same meaning as 'residents at the time of application'. [*Amrit Pal Singh* v. *Jasmit Kaur,* AIR 2006 Del 213, 215, para 8] [Guardians and Wards Act (8 of 1890), S. 9)].

Ordinarily resident in a constituency. The phrase 'ordinarily resident' in a constituency, as mentioned in Section 20 was held to mean a habitual resident of that place or a resident as a matter of fact in regular, normal or usual course permanently for a considerable length of time. *Election Commission of India* v. *Man Mohan Singh,* (2000) 1 SCC 591, para 9 : AIR 2000 SC 231. [Representation of People Act (43 of 1950), S. 20]

Ordinarily resides. The word 'ordinarily' has been intentionally used to bring in considerations other than that of mere factual residence. Mere factual residence at a place at the time of the proceeding is not sufficient to give jurisdiction to the place. *Jhala Harpalsinh* v. *Bal Arunkumar,* AIR 1954 San 13, 14. [Guardians and Wards Act (8 of 1890), S. 4(5)(*b*)(*ii*)]

Where a man has no permanent abode, he must be deemed to reside where he actually resides. It follows that his children must also be deemed to reside at the place where he happens to reside. *Sree Vimalabai* v. *Babu Rao Shamrao,* AIR 1951 Nag 179. [Guardians and Wards Act (8 of 1890), S. 9(1)]

Ordinarily residing. The expression 'ordinarily residing' at a particular place, means one must have an intention to stay at that place for a considerably long time. It would not include a flying visit or a short or casual presence at that place. *Union of India* v. *Dudhnath Prasad,* (2002) 2 SCC 20, para 16 : AIR 2000 SC 525. [Representation of People Act (43 of 1950), Ss. 20(1), 20(1-A), 20(7)]

A person who is residing in a particular district for a considerable long time, he will be treated to be 'ordinarily residing' in that district. The mere fact that he holds some property in another district will not affect his status as such. *Union of India* v. *Dudhnath Prasad,* AIR 2000 SC 525.

Ordinarily sold. "Ordinarily sold" would mean the normal practice or the practice followed by majority of persons in the wholesale trade in the goods concerned. [Elgi Equipment Ltd. v. CCE, (2007) 8

SCC 84, as cited in *Commissioner of Central Excise, Mumbai v. Fiat India Private Limited*, (2012) 9 SCC 332, para 44].

Ordinary. Regular, common, usual; methodical, according to established order; conforming to general order.

Of the usual kind; common. [T.P. Act (4 of 1882), S. 55(1)(a)].

The word 'ordinary' means 'normally', 'in the ordinary course'. *Y.K. Bammi* v. *Jawahar Lal Nehru University,* AIR 1993 Del 239, 245. [Jawaharlal Nehru University Act (53 of 1966), S. 13]

Ordinary capital. Means—in the case of a company, the amount of ordinary capital paid up and attributable to the undertaking of the licensee; in the other cases the net amount standing to the credit of the proprietor or proprietor's account or accounts whether in capital personal or any other account howsoever called and properly attributable to the business of electricity supply. [Electricity (Supply) Act (54 of 1948), Sch. 6 para (xvii)(5)]

Ordinary care. Ordinary care is the care usually bestowed on the matter in hand by persons accustomed to deal with such matters, and having the prudence of the general class of society to which the person, whose conduct is in question, belongs.

Ordinary caution. 'Ordinary caution,' means such caution as may naturally and reasonably be expected to exist under the circumstances of the particular case.

The expression 'ordinary prudence and caution' is but a synonym for 'ordinary care.'

Ordinary course. The usual or routine course. [Indian Partnership Act (9 of 1932), S. 26].

Ordinary course of business. "The ordinary course of business," as the term is used in the statement that an inability to pay debts in the ordinary course of business constitutes insolvency, does not mean an ability to turn out goods or other property to pay one's debts, without leaving in the debtor's hands assets to provide for other debts as they become due.

The usual course and routine of business.

Ordinary diligence. Ordinary diligence is that care which every prudent man exercises under the same or similar circumstances.

Ordinary election. Means an election held to fill a vacancy in the office of an elected member of a Board arising by efflux of time. [Cantonments Act (2 of 1924), S. 2(xxv)]

Ordinary jurisdiction. The expression "ordinary jurisdiction" is opposed to extraordinary jurisdiction which the Court may assume at its discretion upon special occasions and by special orders.

Ordinary law. The body of law which is derived from statute instead of constitutions or judicial decisions.

Ordinary or special resolution. Means an ordinary resolution, or as the case may be, special resolution referred to in section 114 of the Companies Act, 2013 (18 of 2013). [S. 2(63) of the Companies Act, 2013 (18 of 2013)]

Ordinary prudence. 'Ordinary prudence' means such care and prudence as the average prudent man would exercise under like surroundings and in the like situation.

Ordinary rate of wages. The expression 'ordinary rate of wages' means the ordinary, *i.e.* minimum rate for normal work (not over-time work) fixed under the Minimum Wages Act (11 of 1948), as contrasted with 'over-time rate'. *UOI* v. *B.D. Rathi,* AIR 1963 Bom 54, 57. [Minimum Wages (Central) Rules 1950, R. 25]

Ordinary repairs. All buildings are subject, more or less to natural and unavoidable decay : and 'ordinary repairs,' when used in reference to buildings, means expenses reasonably incurred in keeping the property in good condition and order.

Ordinary residence. The place of usual abode. [CPC (5 of 1908), O. III, R. 5].

Ordinary residence of the minor. Ordinary residence of the minor means not the permanent house of the minor but place where the minor ordinarily resides either in his family house or in a rented house and it need not be his own. *Lakshmi Devi* v. *Chandrakala Daroji,* AIR 1975 Pat 83, 88. [Guardians and Wards Act (8 of 1890), S. 10(1)(*a*)]

Ordinary resolution. A resolution which is passed by majority of shareholders in a company.

A resolution shall be an ordinary resolution if the notice required under this Act has been duly given and it is required to be passed by the votes cast, whether on a show of hands, or electronically or on a poll, as the case may be, in favour of the resolution, including the casting vote, if any, of the Chairman, by members who, being entitled so to do, vote in person, or where proxies are allowed, by proxy or by postal ballot, exceed the votes, if any, cast against the resolution by members, so entitled and voting. [Companies Act (18 of 2013), section 114(1)]

Ordinary share capital. In relation to a company, means all the issued share capital (by whatever name called) of the company, other than capital the holders whereof have a right to a dividend at a fixed rate but have no other right to share in the profits of the company. [Business Profits Tax Act (21 of 1947), S. 2(13)]

Ordinary shares. Equity shares with full voting rights and entitlement to dividends, rights and bonus issues.

Ordinary tenant. 'ORDINARY TENANT' means a tenant other than a *pakka* tenant and shall not include a sub-tenant [Madhya Bharat Land Revenue and Tenancy Act (Smvt 2007) (66 of 1950), S. 54(viii)]

Ordnance. Mounted guns; cannon; department for military stores.

Military supplies including weapons, ammunition, combat vehicles and the necessary maintenance tools and equipment.

Ore. Unwrought metal. [Indian Contract Act (9 of 1872), S. 19, ill. (d)].

Organ. "ORGAN" means

(a) any principal or subsidiary organ of an international organization, or

(b) any Commission, Committee or sub-group of any such organ, in which States are members. [Vienna Conventions on the Representation of States in their Relations with International Organizations of a Universal Character, 1975, Art. I(4)]

Organic food. Means food products that have been produced in accordance with specified organic production standards. [*Explanation* (3) to S. 22 of the Food Safety & Standards Act, 2006 (34 of 2006)]

Organic law. 'Organic law' is a term usually applied to the supreme law only, and it imports a high degree of authority.

Constitutional law.

Organisation. For the purposes of section 11 of Act 11 of 2011, 'organisation' means any Government industrial unit or public sector undertaking possessing melting facilities. [*Explanation* to section 11 of the Coinage Act, 2011 (11 of 2011)]

Organization. Formation; arrangement of parties; act of organizing; orderly connection of parts in and for a whole; organized body or system or society.

Organizational (intrabusiness) e-commerce. Using e-commerce functions and technologies for improving productivity within an organization. (*Cyber Law*)

Organize. To form with suitable organs to incorporate; establish; create; form. Give orderly structure; systematize; bring into working order.

Organized crime. Wide spread criminal activities co-ordinated and controlled by a syndicate of criminals.

'Organised crime' means any continuing unlawful activity by an individual, singly or jointly, either as a member of an organised crime syndicate or on behalf of such syndicate, by use of violence or threat of violence or intimidation or coercion, or other unlawful means, with the objective of gaining pecuniary benefits, or gaining undue economic or other advantage for himself or any other person or promoting insurgency. [Maharashtra Control of Organised Crime Act (30 of 1999), S. 2(l), as cited in *State of Maharashtra v. Vishwanath Maranna Shetty*, (2012) 10 SCC 561, para 8.] See also *Mahipal Singh v. CBI*, (2014) 11 SCC 282, para 7. Organised crime syndicate

Organised crime. Any continuing unlawful activity including kidnapping, robbery, vehicle theft, extortion, land grabbing, contract killing, economic offence, cyber-crimes, trafficking of persons, drugs, weapons or illicit goods or services, human trafficking for prostitution or ransom, by any person or a group of persons acting in concert, singly or jointly, either as a member of an organised crime syndicate or on behalf of such syndicate, by use of violence, threat of violence, intimidation, coercion, or by any other unlawful means to obtain direct or indirect material benefit including a financial benefit, shall constitute "ORGANISED CRIME". [(w. e. f. 1-7-2024) Bharatiya Nyaya Sanhita, 2023 (45 of 2023), S. 111(1)]

Organised crime syndicate. Means a group of two or more persons who, acting either singly or jointly, as a syndicate or gang indulge in any continuing unlawful activity. [(w. e. f. 1-7-2024) Bharatiya Nayaya Sanhita, 2023 (45 of 2023), S. 111(1), *Explanation* (i)]

'Organised crime syndicate' means a group of two or more persons who, acting either singly or collectively, as a syndicate or gang indulge in activities of organized crime. [Maharashtra Control of Organised Crime Act (30 of 1999), S. 2(f) as cited in *State of Maharashtra v. Vishwanath Maranna Shetty*, (2012) 10 SCC 561, para 8].

Origin. Beginning; source [Indian Evidence Act (1 of 1872), S. 90, *Expln.*]; constituting the product or model from which copies are made that which existed at first or has existed from the first; constituting a source, beginning or first reliance.

Origin, legitimate. An origin which is in accordance with law. [Indian Evidence Act (1 of 1872), S. 90, *Expln.*].

Original. "ORIGINAL", in relation to a design means originating from the author of such design and includes the cases which though old in themselves yet are new in their application. [Design Act (16 of 2000), S. 2(g)]

That which has served as a pattern of which a copy or translation is made; first hand; not imitative; novel in style, character or inventive.

Initial [CPC (5 of 1908), S. 105(1) and Constitution of India, Art. 131]; constituting the source [CPC (5 of 1908), S. 108].

Original assignor. A person who originally makes an assignment. [CPC (5 of 1908), O. XXI, R. 18(2)].

Original cost. "ORIGINAL COST" of an asset means the amount of expenses certified or determined under paragraph II to have been properly incurred on and incidental to the provision of the asset for the purposes of the undertaking, generating station or main transmission line, as the case may be. [Electricity (Supply) Act (54 of 1948), Sch. 4(1)(b)]

"ORIGINAL COST" means in respect of any asset the sum of—

(a) the cost of the asset to the licencee, including the cost of delivery and all charges properly incurred in erecting and bringing the asset into beneficial use;

(b) interest charge on capital expenditure incurred during the period between the date of grant of the licence and the date when the undertaking commences supply, from borrowed money and properly attributable to the assets as actually accrued up to the date of such supply, as well as incurred on outlays for subsequent expansions;

(c) a proper addition on account of supervision not exceeding fifteen per centum of the cost referred to in sub-paragraph (a),

so, however, that the original cost of any asset shall not in any case exceed the original cost attributed thereto in the book of the undertaking. [Electricity (Supply) Act (54 of 1948), Sch. 6th Paragraph (XVII) (6)] [Now repealed & replaced by Act 36 of 2003]

Original cost to the assessee. The cost to be calculated for the purpose of depreciation allowance is the cost to the assessee and not to the person who makes the sale. *Jogta Coal Co. Ltd.* v. *Commissioner of Income Tax*, AIR 1959 SC 1232, 1235.

Original equipment manufacturer. Means manufacturer of equipment or product using lead acid batteries as a component. [Batteries (Management and Handling) Rules, 2001, R. 3(m)]

Original jurisdiction. The phrase 'original jurisdiction' means jurisdiction to entertain cases in the first instance, as distinguished from appellate jurisdiction.

The jurisdiction of first instance; the authority of a Court to take cognizance of a controversy at the inception of legal proceedings thereon. [CrPC 1973 (2 of 1974), S. 193 and Constitution of India, Art. 131].

Original land owner. For the pupose Section 46 of Act 30 of 2013 'Original land owner' refers to the owner of the land as on 5-9-2011. [*Explanation* (a) to S. 46 of the Right to Fair Compensation & Transparency in Land Acquisition, Rehabilitation & Resettlement Act, 2013 (30 of 2013)]

Original literary work. "Original literary work" means that the work must be the expression of original or inventive thought. Copyright Act is not concerned with the originality of ideas, but with the expression of thought; and, in the case of 'literary work,' with the expression of thought in print or writing. The originality which is required relates to the expression of thought; but the Act does not require that the expression must be in an original or novel form, but that the work must not be copied from another work—that it should originate from the author.

The word 'original' in S. 13(a) does not imply any originality of ideas, but merely means that the work in question should not be copied from some other work but originate in the author, being the product of his labour and skill. [Copyright Act (14 of 1957), S. 13(a)]

Original petition. 'Original petition' means a petition whereby any proceeding other than a suit or appeal or a proceedings in execution of a decree or order, is instituted in a court. [Sinnamani v. G. Vettivel, (2012) 5 SCC 759, para 8] [Madras High Court Civil Rules of Practice and Circular Orders, R. 3(9)].

Original suit. Suit commenced in the first Court. The substitution of a plaintiff is not an original suit, but an incident of an existing one,—a step in it, and nothing more.

The suit at the first instance. [CPC (5 of 1908), O. XLI, R. 10(1)]

Original summons. A summons issued in the first place. [CPC (5 of 1908), O. V, R. 16 and App. B, Form No. 11(3)].

Original votes. 'ORIGINAL VOTES' in regard to any candidate means the votes derived from the ballot papers on which a first preference is recorded for such candidate. [Kerala Wakf Rules, 1996, R. 2(m)]

Originally. In the original time or in an original manner; primarily; from the beginning.

In the first place. [IPC (45 of 1860), S. 227].

Originating good. Means a good which qualifies as an originating good under provisions of the Customs Tariff (Determination of Origin of Goods under the Comprehensive Economic Partnership Agreement between the Republic of India and Japan) Rules, 2011 notified vide notification of the Government of India, Ministry of Finance, Department of Revenue, No. 55/2011—Customs (N.T.), dated the 1st August, 2011, published vide number G.S.R. 594(E), dated the 1st August, 2011. [India-Japan Comprehensive Economic Partnership Agreement (Bilateral Safeguard Measures) Rules, 2017, R. (1)(g)].

Originator. "ORIGINATOR" means a person who sends, generates, stores or transmits any electronic message or causes any electronic message to be sent, generated, stored or transmitted to any other person but does not include an intermediary. [Information Technology Act (21 of 2000), S. 2(1)(za)]

"ORIGINATOR" means the owner of a financial asset which is acquired by a securitisation company or reconstruction company for the purpose of securitisation or asset reconstruction. [Securitisation and Reconstruction of Financial Assets and Enforcement of Security Interest Act (54 of 2002), S. 2(1)(r)]

"ORIGINATOR" of a data message means a person by whom or on whose behalf, the data message purports to have been sent or generated prior to storage, if any but it does not include a person acting as an intermediary with respect to that data message. [United Nations : UNCITRAL Model Law on Electronic Commerce (Adopted Dec. 16, 1996), Art. 2(c)]

Orphan. "ORPHAN" means a person, none of whose parents is alive and is in receipt of monthly widow/widower pension. [Employee's Pension Scheme, 1995, S. 2(xi)]

"ORPHAN" means a Child—

(i) who is without biological or adoptive parents or legal guardian; or (ii) whose legal guardian is not willing to take, or capable of taking care if the child. [Juvenile Justice (Care and Protection of Children) Act, (2 of 2016) S. 2(42)].

Ossification test. An X-ray ossification test may provide a surer basis for determining the age of an individual than the opinion of a medical expert, but it can by no means be so infallible and accurate a test as to indicate the correct number of years and days he has lived. *Kishori Lal* v. *State,* AIR 1957 Punj 78, 79. [IPC (45 of 1860), Ss. 361, 363]

Ostensible. Ostensible means capable of being shown; proper or intended to be shown; exhibited; declared; avowed; professed.

Apparent; merely professed, pretended; often opposed to actual or real.

Ostensible owner. One, who holds himself out as an owner but is not really so. [T.P. Act (4 of 1882), S. 41].

Ostensible partner. A person holding himself out as partner in a firm or business but having no actual interest in the partnership.

Ostensibly. To all outward appearances. [T.P. Act (4 of 1882), S. 58(c)].

Ostracism, Social. Exclusion from society or common privileges. [Representation of the People Act (43 of 1951), S. 123(2)(a)(i)].

Ostrich instruction. In criminal case, it is an instruction which states that a defendant can be found to have acted knowingly if he or she deliberately avoided acquiring knowledge.

Other additional remuneration. The expression "other additional remuneration" refers to such remuneration which is payable at the will of the employer and it does not refer to any remuneration payable under the contract. *Willman (India) Pvt. Ltd.* v. *E.S.I.C.*, AIR 1994 SC 1037, 1044. [Employees' State Insurance Act (34 of 1948), S. 2(22)]

Other authorities. The words 'other authorities' mentioned in Art. 12, Constitution of India have reference to independent authorities having origin in a statute or other law. Thus, an institution, such as the Bank of Patiala, which is owned and controlled by the State Government comes within the meaning of 'State' as used in both the Articles 12 & 308 but not within the meaning of 'other authorities' used in Art. 12. *S. Mohan Singh* v. *Patiala and East Punjab States Union,* AIR 1954 Pepsu 136.

The expression 'other authorities' includes all public authorities, that is, authorities created by a statute endorsed with powers and functions in a given field of activity and for the control thereof, and having the power to make their own rules and regulations, having the force of law. *Mohanlal* v. *State of Rajasthan,* AIR 1966 Raj 1, 5.

Life Insurance Corporation does not fall within the expression "other authorities" in Art. 12 and is not State within the meaning of Art. 12. *Pramodrai Shamaldas Bhavsar* v. *LIC,* AIR 1969 Bom 337 at 340.

The expression 'other authorities' includes all constitutional or statutory authorities on whom powers are conferred by law. A company incorporated under the Companies Act and governed by the provisions of the Companies Act cannot be characterised as an authority. *Abdul Ahad* v. *Govt. Wollen Mill,* AIR 1979 J&K 57, 63, 66 (FB).

Other authority. Council of Scientific and Industrial Research is not an authority within the meaning of Art. 12 of the Constitution. *Subhajit Tewary* v. *Union of India*, AIR 1975 SC 1329, 1331. [Constitution of India, Art. 12]

The expression 'other authorities' occurring in Article 12, means that the entity should have been created by a statute or under a statute and functioning with liability and obligations to the public. *Pradeep Kumar Biswas* v. *Indian Institute of Chemical Biology*, (2002) 5 SCC 111.

"OTHER AUTHORITY" the expression 'other authority' appearing in rule 9(2) of the Railway Servants (Discipline and Appeal) Rules, 1968, is intended to cover a vast field and there is no indication of the mind of the framers that the expression must be given a restricted or a narrow meaning. It is possible that where the authority is vested in a person or a body as a result of delegation, then delegatee of such authority has to work strictly within the field delegated. *UOI* v. *Alok Kumar*, AIR 2010 SC 2735.

Other backward classes. Recruitment to judicial services in the State of Himachal Pradesh is governed by the HP Judicial Service Rules, 1973 framed by the Governor in consultation with the High Court and in exercise of the powers conferred by Article 234 read with Article 309 of the Constitution of India. These Rules do not make any provision for reservation in favour of Scheduled Castes, Scheduled Tribes and Other Backward Classes. These Rules also do not contemplate reservation in the category of ex-army personnel. Ex-army personnel is a category covered by "Other Backward Classes." (*A.C. Thalwal* v. *High Court of HP,* AIR 2000 SC 2732).

Other Backward Classes of Citizens. The expression 'other backward classes of citizens' under Section 2(b) means those backward classes of citizens specified in Schedule I to the Act. If any particular caste is added to the list by amendment after enactment of the Act as backward class, for all purposes, the Act commences in respect of the newly added caste from the date when the Amendment Act came into effect. [*U.P. Public Service Commission* v. *Satya Narayan Sheohare,* (2009) 5 SCC 473, 476, para 9] [U.P. Public Services (Reservation for Scheduled Castes, Scheduled Tribes and other Backward Classes) Act (4 of 1994), S. 2(b)]

Other categories of persons. Includes persons with disability as defined in the Persons with Disabilities (Equal Opportunities, Protection of Rights and Full Participation) Act, 1995 and who may not be gainfully employed; and also includes guardians who need insurance to protect spastic persons or persons, with disability. [Insurance Regulatory and Development Authority (Obligations of Insurers to Rural or Social Sectors) Regulations, 2000, Reg. 2(g)]

Other charges. The expression 'other charges' occurring in Section 13(2)(i) of the Act includes interest. *South Eastern Coalfields Ltd.* v. *State of M.P.*, (2003) 8 SCC 648, para : AIR 2003 SC 4482. [Mines and Minerals (Regulation and Development) Act (67 of 1957), S. 13(2)(i)]

Other dues. For the purposes of this section, the expression "OTHER DUES" means interest, penalty, fee or any other amount payable under this Act or the rules made thereunder. [Central Goods and Service Tax Act (12 of 2017), S. 49, *Explanation (b)(ii)*].

Other glass and glassware. Screens for fitting in motor vehicles, known as wind screens, rear screens and door screens, are only motor vehicle parts and they are not 'glass and glassware'. *Arul Glass Industries (P) Ltd.*, v. *Collector of Central Excise*, AIR 1986 SC 1730, 1736. [Central Excise and Salt Act (1 of 1944), Sch. 1, Tariff item Nos. 23-A(4) and 68]

Other goods. The expression "other goods" in Section 4(1)(b) evidently means those goods which are not governed by section 4(1)(a). [*State of Karnataka* v. *Durga Projects Inc.*, (2018) 4 SCC 633, para 17] [Karnataka Value Added Tax Act, 2003 (32 of 2004), Ss. 4(1)(a) & 4(1)(b)].

Other information. The words "other information" are wide enough to include an application by a private party. *R.H. Bhutani* v. *Mani J. Desai*, AIR 1968 SC 1444, 1449. [CrPC 1973 (2 of 1974), S. 145(1)]

Other injury of any kind. The expression 'injury' connotes an act or omission contrary to the law involving infringement of any right vested in some person. Instances of such cases are infringement of a copyright or of a trade mark or an obstruction to a right of easement or to the exercise of rights of property or of a right of public worship *etc.* All wrongs covered by the expression 'tort' would be within the scope of the expression but there has to be an injury and that injury would necessarily be a result of the wrong. *Kripa Nath Chakravarthy* v. *Roopchand Lunawat,* AIR 1955 Ass 156, 157. [CPC (5 of 1908), O. XXXIX, R. 2]

The expression 'other injury of any kind' comprehends any kind of legal injury, not necessarily an injury akin to a breach of contract. An obstruction to the exercise of rights of property is an injury. *Roshan Lal* v. *Rath,* AIR 1977 HP 10, 12.

Other intangible thing. The right of a simple mortgagee in the property mortgaged is only an intangible thing like a charge on immoveable property within the meaning of the S. 54, Transfer of Property Act (4 of 1882).

Other legal ground. The words "other legal ground" in S. 32, Parsi Marriage and Divorce Act (3 of 1936) construed on the principle of "*ejusdem generis*" mean any other legal ground which is of the same kind as those previously mentioned.

Other legal proceeding. This general expression coming after "suit" is of limited application, and must be construed on the principle of *ejusdem generis*, and does not include a criminal proceeding. [Presidency Towns Insolvency Act (3 of 1909), S. 17]

Other matters connected therewith. The words "other matters connected therewith" cover and include, although not very directly, the effectuation of separation of the evacuees' interest through the mode prescribed in Section 9(2). *Mahindra Engineering and Chemical Products Ltd.* v. *Union of India,* (1992) 1 SCC 727. [Evacuee Interest (Separation) Act (64 of 1951), S. 9]

Other modification. The words 'other modification' have to be read *ejusdem generic* with the words "distortion" and "mutiliation". Modification in the sense of permission of the original may amount to distortion or mutiliation. There can be modification simplicitor such as where "A" is changed to "B", both being quite distinct. *Mannu Bhandari* v. *Kata Vikas, Pictures (P.) Ltd.,* AIR 1987 Del 13, 16. [Copyright Act (14 of 1957), S. 57(1)(*b*)]

Other parties thereto. The other parties in the case of a promissory note will be parties other than the maker; in the case of a bill of exchange, it will be all parties other than the acceptor while in the case of a cheque other parties must be parties other than the drawee. *Manik Ratan Guru* v. *Prakash Chandra,* AIR 1955 Cal 338. [Negotiable Instruments Act (26 of 1881), S. 64]

Other person. These words will include persons who generate or supply electricity or who intend to establish or acquire a generating station or with whom the Electricity Board has entered into arrangements for the generation. *M.S.E. Board* v. *Telegaon Dabhade Municipality,* AIR 1967 Bom 75, 80. [Electricity (Supply) Act (54 of 1948), S. 76(1)] [Now repealed & replaced by Act 36 of 2003]

Other personal injuries not causing the death of the party. The expression includes the physical injuries also. *P.P. Kandaswamy* v. *Mariappa Stores,* AIR 1974 Mad 178, 179. [Indian Succession Act (39 of 1925), S. 306]

Other proceedings. The words 'other proceedings' in Art. 132. Constitution of India should not be construed '*ejusdem generis*' with what precedes. Those are words of wide amplitude and include all proceedings other than civil or criminal proceedings and thus include revenue proceedings. AIR 1950 SC 169 Ref. *Sriram Gulabdas* v. *Board of Revenue*, AIR 1954 Nag. 1, 5 (FB)

The words 'other proceeding' in S. 69(4)(b) relate to the proceedings of the nature of set-off and nothing else. These words do not apply to other judicial proceedings in contra-distinction to a suit and are limited to proceedings taken to claim a set-off and similar claim in a written statement. *Ram Lal Harnam Dass* v. *Bal Krishen,* AIR 1957 Punj 159, 160. [Indian Partnership Act (9 of 1932), S. 69(4)(b)]

The words "or other proceeding" immediately follow the words "a claim of set off". When words are used in such juxtaposition, the earlier words have a demonstrative or limiting effect. The earlier words are illustrative or demonstrative of the intention of the legislature. *Kajaria Traders (India) Ltd.* v. *Foreign Import and Export Trade Association,* AIR 1961 Bom 65, 68.

The expression 'other proceeding' is not un-restricted but is restricted to those proceedings which have been instituted for the purpose of enforcing a right arising from a contract. *Partabmull* v. *Phulchand K. & Co.,* AIR 1964 Cal 452, 457.

Other product raised on the land. Trees are not included with the meaning of 'other products raised on the land.' AIR 1973 SC 2498, 2503.

Other purposes. The words 'other purposes' have been extensively used in titles to statutes, reciting that they are for certain specified and *other purposes,* to cover any and every thing whether connected with the main questions indicated by the title or not.

Other reasonable cause. "Other reasonable cause", mentioned in cl. (*f*) of S. 13 of the Legal Practitioners Act (18 of 1879), is not restricted to matters *ejusdem generis* with the matters mentioned in cls. (*a*) to (*e*) of the section.

Other remedy. The term 'other remedy' means that the other remedy need not necessarily be one provided under any statute, ordinance, order, rule, regulation, bye-law *etc.* but it would be sufficient if the other remedy is provided for, by or under any other law for the time being in force which takes in common law as well. *Govt. of India* v. *National Tobacco Co.,* AIR 1977 AP 250, 263 (FB). [Constitution of India, Art. 226(3)]

Other services and posts. The expression 'other services and posts' cannot mean services and posts other than civil services. *A.D. Sundaram* v. *State,* AIR 1956 TC 158, 159. [Constitutions of India, Art. 320(3)(*e*), (Prov.)]

Other similar allowance. Any 'other similar allowance' must be of the same kind mentioned in the earlier part of the section *i.e.* dearness allowance, house-rent allowance, overtime allowance, bonus and commission and not the payment for the work done between the quota and the norm. *Jay Engineering Works Ltd.* v. *Union of India*, AIR 1963 SC 1480, 1483. [Employees' Provident Funds Act (19 of 1952), S. 2(*b*)(*ii*)]

Other similar forms of forced labour. The words "other similar forms of forced labour" should be construed *ejusdem generis*. The kind of forced labour that is contemplated in the constitutional prohibition has to be something in the nature of either traffic in human being or *begar*. *Dulal Samanta* v. *District Magistrate, Howrah,* AIR 1958 Cal 365, 372. [Constitution of India, Art. 23]

Other sufficient cause. The words "other sufficient cause' in O. XXIII, R. 1(3)(*b*), CPC (5 of 1908) do not include any cause whatever but only causes which are atleast analogous to a formal defect. AIR 1922 PC 112 **Rel. on** *Satyanarayan* v. *Chotelal,* AIR 1949 Nag 10.

It is well-settled that these words should be understood *ejusdem generis* with the two grounds immediately proceeding them. Being so it is enough to state that no other sufficient reason has been disclosed for review. *Board of Revenue* v. *P.K. Syed Akbar Sahib,* AIR 1973 Ker 285, 288. [CPC (5 of 1908), O. XLVII, R. 1]

Other sufficient ground. The words 'other sufficient grounds' in O. XXIII, R. 1 (3)(*b*), CPC (5 of 1908) has been interpreted to mean "grounds *ejusdem generis*" to those mentioned in cl. (*a*) or at least analogous to them. Insufficient evidence or a false geneological table or even the fraud of plaintiff's *vakil,* will not come under this clause. *Veeraswami* v. *Laxmidas,* AIR 1951 Mad 715.

Whether the grounds are to be of the same *genus* as a formal defect or whether the grounds are to be such as are at least analogous to a formal defect, there will be little difficulty in actual practice in distinguishing between cases to which the rule of *ejusdem generis* could be applied and those which are beyond its remedial operation. *Kancherla Sarveswara Rao* v. *Kancherla Veerraju,* AIR 1957 AP 303, 306. [CPC (5 of 1908), O. XXIII, R. 1 (2)(*a*)]

Other sufficient reason. The words "other sufficient reason" in O. XLVII, R. 1, CPC (5 of 1908) mean other sufficient reason of the kind mentioned in the earlier part of the section.

Other than medicines or medicine. The intention of the Legislature was to except from the definition of drug all medicines and substances which were either used exclusively or prepared for use exclusively in accordance with the Ayurvedic or Unani systems of medicine. *Ishwar Singh* v. *State of U.P.,* AIR 1966 All 168, 171. [Drugs and Cosmetics Act (23 of 1940), S. 3(1)]

Other welfare schemes. Means such Government schemes, in addition to the Targeted Public Distribution System, under which foodgrains or meals are supplied as part of the schemes. [S. 2(12) of the National Food Security Act, 2013 (20 of 2013)]

Otherwise. By other like means; contrarily; different from that to which it relates; in a different manner; in another way; in any other way; differently; in other respects; in different respects; in some other like capacity.

The word clearly indicates that it is open to the Court to base the judgment on statements made by a party not only in the pleadings but also *de hors* the pleadings. *Sikkarchand* v. *Bari Bai,* AIR 1974 MP 75, 77. [CPC (5 of 1908), O. XII, Rule 6]

The term 'otherwise' means in any manner whatsoever. *Murli Prasad* v. *Prasanth Prasad,* AIR 1967 Pat 191, 196. [Indian Electricity Act (9 of 1910), S. 9(2)]

The expression 'otherwise' means some kind of legal obligation or some transaction enforceable at law or in equity which, though not in the form of contract, may confer a benefit on the donor. *George* v. *Controller, Estate Duty, Mys.* AIR 1967 SC 849, 851.

The word 'otherwise' would cover a reference made by a rival claimants. *Anadi Charan Rout* v. *Collector of Cuttack,* AIR 1972 Ori 202, 203. [Rice Milling Industry (Regulation) Act (21 of 1958), S. 7]

The word 'otherwise' is not to be construed *ejusdem generis* with the preceding words 'circulars', 'advertisements'. *Siddharth Wheels (P.) Ltd.* v. *Berock Ltd.,* AIR 1988 Del 228, 236. [Trade and Merchandise Marks Act (43 of 1958), S. 120]

Otherwise adjusted. These words in O. XXI, R. 2(1), CPC (5 of 1908) are wide enough to include an oral adjustment of the decree.

Otherwise dealt with. From the words "otherwise dealt with" it does not necessarily mean something which is not included in the investigation, inquiry or trial and the word 'otherwise' points to the fact that the expression "dealt with" is all comprehensive and that investigation, inquiry and trial are some of the aspects dealing with the offence. *State of Punjab* v. *Babbir Singh*, AIR 1994 SC 1872, 1878. [CrPC 1973 (2 of 1974), S. 4]

Otherwise destroyed. For treating a will as having been "otherwise destroyed" under the latter part of Sec. 70, the act of destruction must be similar to "burning" or "tearing". *C.G. David Thakaran* v. *Lily Jacob,* AIR 1993 Ker 9, 15. [Indian Succession Act (39 of 1925), S. 70]

Ought to be admitted. The expression "ought to be admitted" means "should be admitted in the exercise of sound discretion". If the interest of justice requires the admission of additional evidence permission for its admission should be accorded. *Sumitra* v. *Mharaju,* AIR 1963 HP 21, 23. [CPC (5 of 1908), O. 41, R. 27(1)(*a*).]

Oust. Put out of possession; eject.

Ouster. An ouster is the wrongful dispossession or exclusion from real property of a party entitled to the possession thereof.

Ouster of jurisdiction. A condition which exists when a Court which once had jurisdiction over a matter ceases to retain its jurisdiction.

Ouster or dispossession. Is a wrong or injury that carries with it the notion of a change of possession, for, thereby, the wrong doer gets into the actual occupation of the land or hereditament, and obliges him that hath a right to seek his legal remedy in order to gain possession and damages for the injury sustained.

Out of and in the course of his employment. The expression 'in the course of employment' means not only the actual work which the man is employed to do but what is incident to it, in the course of his service. The expression applies to employment as such *i.e.* to its nature, its conditions, its obligations, and its incidents. It would include not only the period when he is doing the work actually allotted to him but also the time when he is at a place where he would not be but for his employment. *Works Manager C&W Shop* v. *Mahabir,* AIR 1954 All 132, 139. [Workmen's Compensation Act (8 of 1923), (S. 3(1))]

Out-of-Court settlement. The settlement and termination of pending suit arrived at without the participation of the Court.

Out of funds in his possession. The words 'out of funds in his possession' have reference only to the funds relatable to the particular evacuee against whom or against whose property, the claim for refund is made by a claimant. *Custodian, Evauee Property* v. *Rabia Bai*, AIR 1976 SC 2557, 2565. [Administration of Evacuee Property Act (31 of 1956), S. 10(2)(*n*)]

Out of pocket expense. An expense which is paid by a person from his own funds.

Out of employment. The expression "out of employment" conveys the idea that there must be a causal connection between the employment and the injury caused to the workman as a result of accident. [*Daya Kishan Joshi v. Dynemech Sysems Private Limited,* (2018) 11 SCC 642, para 8].

Outbreak. A sudden rise in the incidence of disease especially to epidemic or near epidemic proportions [Local Authorities Loans Act (9 of 1914), S. 3(1)(iii)]; a sudden or violent breaking out of activity; bursting forth.

Outdoor caterer. Means a caterer engaged in providing services in connection with catering at a place other than his own. [Finance Act (32 of 1994), S. 65 (76)(76a) (*Inserted by Finance Act (23 of 2004), S. 90*) now repealed by Central Goods and Services Tax Act, 2017]

Outgoing. Going outward; departing a person who is laying down an office.

Outgoings. Outlay; expense; charge [T.P. Act (4 of 1882), S. 69A(8)(i)].

Outhouse. A house or building belonging to and adjoining, and subsidiary to, a dwelling house. [IPC (45 of 1860), S. 445, *Expln.*].

Outlaw. One who is put out of the law, deprived of its benefits and protection. (*Burrill; Cowel.*)

By the unlearned the word 'outlawed' is often used as applying to notes, bills, and other evidences of debt invalid by lapse of time, or as tantamount to the legal language 'barred by the statute of limitations.' Thus, a barred note in popular phrase is said to be 'outlawed' and it will be given this sense in an agreement by one to pay a certain note in case the promissor therein did not pay it before it was 'outlawed.'

Outlawry. The being put out of the law. (*Cowell; Tomlin*)

OUTLAWRY is an old process of the common law for compelling a person to appear before a Court of justice and meet a charge or claim made against him, and for punishing him for his contempt in not appearing and for evading writs or warrants issued for his arrest. (*Tomlin*)

Outlawry, legally speaking, is a judicial proceeding, and no one can be outlawed but in such a proceeding, and by due process of law.

Outlay. Expenses.

Something that is laid out. [Land Acquisition Act (1 of 1894), S. 24, seventh].

Outlive. Live longer than or beyond another.

Outpost. The post or station of detachment. [Assam Rifles Act (5 of 1941), S. 2(1)].

Output. Amount of goods produced by manufacture.

Something that is put out or produced. [Mines Act (35 of 1952), S. 57(t)].

Output contract. A contract in which the buyer promises to buy all the goods which the seller can supply during a specific period and at a set price.

Output tax. Value added tax (VAT) charged (on taxable goods or services) by a trader registered for VAT.

"Output tax" in relation to a taxable person, means the tax chargeable under this Act on taxable supply of goods or services or both made by him or by his agent but excludes tax payable by him on reverse charge basis. [The Central Goods and Services Tax Act, 2017 (12 of 2017), S. 2(82)]

''Output tax'' in relation to a taxable person, means the Union territory tax chargeable under this Act on taxable supply of goods or services or both made by him or by his agent but excludes tax payable by him on reverse charge basis [The Union Territory Goods and Services Tax Act, 2017 (14 of 2017), S. 2(7)]

Outrage. A bold or wanton injury to person or property; wanton mischief; gross injury; aggravated wrong; forcible violation of other's rights, sentiments *etc.*; gross or wanton offence.

Outrage modesty. To flagrantly infringe modesty (of another). [IPC (45 of 1860), S. 354].

Outrage the modesty. The act of pulling a woman, removing her dress coupled with a request for sexual intercourse is such as would be an 'outrage to the modesty of a woman'. *Aman Kumar* v. *State of Haryana,* (2004) 4 SCC 379, 388, para 13.

Outrageous conduct. Conduct which exceeds all reasonable bounds of decency.

Outside sale—inside sale. Sales in which the goods delivered are for consumption in the State of first delivery or first destination are inside sales. Where goods are delivered for consumption in States other than the State of first delivery are outside sales. *Tobacco Manufacturers (India) Ltd.* v. *Sales Tax Commissioner*, AIR 1961 SC 402, 408. [Constitution of India, Art. 286]

Outstanding. Still unsettled prominent, conspicuous.

The expression 'outstanding' will have to be construed in the background of the phrase 'amount of tax—payable in consequence of an order' and in that context it must mean remaining unpaid after the obligation to pay is incurred. *Wealth Tax Commissioner* v. *Cotton Manufactures Ltd.*, AIR 1984 SC 946, 952. [Wealth Tax Act (27 of 1957), S. 2(*m*)]

Uncollected; unpaid; unsettled [CPC (5 of 1908), 1st Sch., App. D, form No. 17(9)]; standing out [Unit Trust of India Act (52 of 1963), S. 2(o)]; prominent.

Outstanding accounts. Such accounts as are due or unpaid.

Outstanding book debts. Unpaid debts recorded in a book of account. [CPC (5 of 1908), 1st Sch., App. D, form No. 21].

Outstanding claim. A claim that has not been settled or that remains unpaid.

Outstanding crop. Crop in the field, not gathered and stored.

Outstanding for the time being. Standing out at the time. [Unit Trust of India Act (52 of 1963), S. 2(o)].

Outstanding liabilities. Debts and liabilities due and unpaid.

Outward supply. "Outward supply" in relation to a taxable person, means supply of goods or services or both, whether by sale, transfer, barter, exchange, licence, rental, lease or disposal or any other mode, made or agreed to be made by such person in the course or furtherance of business [The Central Goods and Services Tax Act, 2017 (12 of 2017), S. 2(83)]

Outwork. Advanced or detached part of a fortress *etc.*

Outside work. [Minimum Wages Act (11 of 1948), S. 18(2)].

Outworker. A worker who works outside. [Minimum Wages Act (11 of 1948), S. 2(i)].

Overawe. The word 'overawe' in S. 121-A, IPC (45 of 1860) clearly imports more than the creation of apprehension or alarm or even perhaps fear. *Mir Hasan Khan* v. *State,* AIR 1951 Pat 60.

To keep in awe by supeior influence. [IPC (45 of 1860), S. 121-A].

Outward supply. In relation to a taxable person, means supply of goods or services or both, whether by sale, transfer, barter, exchange, licence, rental, lease or disposal or any other mode, made or agreed to be made by such person in the course or furtherance of business. [Central Goods and Service Tax Act (12 of 2017), S. 2(83)].

Outstanding debt. For the purposes of voting by persons who receive notice as shareholder or creditor under this rule, "OUTSTANDING DEBT" shall mean all debt owed by the company to the respective class or classes of creditors that remains outstanding as per the latest audited financial statement, or it such statement is more than six months old, as per provisional financial statement not preceding the date of application by more than six months. [Companies (Compromises, Arrangements and Amalgamations) Rules, 2016, R. 9, *Explanation (b)*].

Over Dimensional Cargo. For the purposes of this rule, the expression "Over Dimensional Cargo" shall mean a cargo carried as a single indivisible unit and which exceeds the dimensional limits prescribed in

Rule 93 of the Central Motor Vehicle Rulers, 1989, made under the Motor Vehicles Act, 1988 (59 of 1988). [Central Goods and Services Tax Rules, 2017, R. 138, *Explanation 2*].

Ovebreadth doctrine. The doctrine which states that if a statute is so broadly written that it deters free expression, then it can be struck down on its face because of its chilling effect, even if it also prohibits acts that may legitimately be forbidden. (*U.S.*)

Overdraft. A loan; the act of issuing cheques for more money than one has on deposit in a bank; an act by reason whereof the drawer obtains special credit from the bank upon his cheques; over-drawing of bank account; amount by which balance is overdrawn.

The action of overdrawing an account; the amount by which a draft exceeds the balance against which it is drawn. [Indian Contract Act (9 of 1872), S. 133, ill. (a)].

Overdraw. To draw upon a bank by bills or cheques to an amount in excess of the funds remaining to the drawer's credit.

To draw cheques upon (a Bank accout) in excess of the deposit balance of the drawer. [Indian Contract Act (9 of 1872), S. 133, ill. (a)].

Overdue. "OVERDUE" means an amount which remains unpaid beyond the due date [Securitisation Companies Reconstruction Companies Prudential Norms (Reserve Bank) Directions (54 of 2002), S. 3(iv)]

Past the time of payment.

Unpaid after the proper assigned time of payment [Negotiable Instruments Act (26 of 1881), S. 45-A].

Overhead expenses. Those general charges or expenses in a business which cannot be charged upon as belonging exclusively to any particular part of the work or product (*e.g.* rent, taxes, *etc.*) [Payment of Bonus Act (21 of 1965), 2nd Sch., Item 6(e)].

Overhead line. Means an electric line which is placed above the ground and in the open air but does not include live rails of a traction system. [Electricity Act (36 of 2003), S. 2(48)]

Overlapping. To lap over; to overlie partially; to cover and extend beyond.

Overleaf. On the other side of the leaf of a book.

Overpass. Over crossing. [Delhi Urban Art Commission Act (1 of 1974), S. 11(2)(f)].

Over migration limit. Means the maximum permitted amount of non-volatile substances released from a material or article into food simulants. [Food safety and Standards (Packaging) Regulations, 2018, Regn. 2(1)(d)].

Overpayment. Payment in excess of what is due. [Payment of Wages Act (4 of 1936), S. 7(2)(f)].

Override. Ride over enemy's country with armed force; trample under foot, claim superior authority.

To ride too much or too hard [Prevention of Cruelty to Animals Act (59 of 1960), S. 11(a)]; to dominate or prevail over [Companies Act (1 of 1956), S. 460(2)]; to pay a commission to (as a general agent or sales manager) on sales made by sub-ordinates.

Overriding. Sub-ordinating all others to itself. [Hindu Adoptions and Maintenance Act (78 of 1956), S. 4].

Overriding commission. Commission paid in addition to regular compensation. [Life Insurance Corporation Act (31 of 1956), Sch. III].

Overrule. Set aside decision or argument by superior authority or by a higher Court.

To set aside (a previous action or decision). [CrPC 1973 (2 of 1974), S. 404]; to decide or rule against.

Overruling. The word 'overruling' assumes to mean that a contrary decision is given on the same facts or law. *National Agricultural Coop. Marketing Federation of India Ltd.* v. *UOI,* (2003) 5 SCC 23, para 19 : AIR 2003 SC 1329.

Overrunning. To over run; to go or extend beyond limits; to be in excess [Factories Act (63 of 1948), S. 28(2)(c)].

Overseas corporate body (OCB). Means any institution, association or body, whether incorporated or not, established under the laws of a country outside India wherein any non-resident Indian has any interest. [Remittances of Foreign Exchange and Investment in Foreign Exchange Bonds (Immunities and Exemptions) Act (41 of 1991), S. 5(1)(c)]

OVERSEAS CORPORATE BODY (OCB) means a company, partnership firm, society and other corporate body owned directly or indirectly to the extent of at least sixty per cent by Non-resident Indians and includes overseas trust in which not less than sixty per cent beneficial interest is held by Non-resident Indians directly or indirectly but irrevocably. [Foreign Exchange Management (Deposit) Regulation, 2000, Reg. 2(xi), Foreign Exchange Management (Borrowing and Lending in Rupees) Regulations, 2000, Reg. 2(b) and Foreign Exchange Management (Transfer or Issue of Security by a Person Resident Outside India) Regulations, 2000, Reg. 2(viii)]

Overseas Custodian Bank. For the purposes of rule 13 of the Companies (Registration of Foreign Companies) Rules, 2014, 'Overseas Custodian Bank' means a banking company which is established in a country outside India and which acts as custodian for the equity shares of Issuing Company, against which IDRs are proposed to be issued by having a custodial arrangement or agreement with the Domestic Depository or by establishing a place of business in India. [*Explanation* (*iii*) to Rule 13(3) of the Companies (Registration of Foreign Companies) Rules, 2014]

Overseas Depositary Bank. Means a bank authorised by the issuing company to issue global depositary receipts against issue of Foreign Currency Convertible Bonds or ordinary shares of the issuing company. [Issue of Foreign Currency Convertible Bonds And Ordinary Shares (Through Depositary

Receipt Mechanism) Scheme, 1993, S. 2(e); Income-tax Act (43 of 1961), S. 115ACA (3), *Expln.* (d)]

Overseas financial organization. Means any fund, institution, association or body, whether incorporated or not, established under the laws of a country outside India, which has entered into an arrangement for investment in India with any public sector bank or public financial institution or a mutual fund specified under clause (23D) of Section 10 and such arrangement is approved by the Central Government for this purpose. [Income-tax Act (43 of 1961), S. 115 AB (2) *Expln.* (a)]

Overseas market. In relation to any goods, means the market in the country outside and in which such goods are intended to be sold. [FERA (46 of 1973), S. 2(n)]

Oversight. Inadvertent mistake; omission to notice; a casual overlooking of something that should have been seen.

Overt. Open; an opening. (*Tomlin*)

Overt act. An open act which by law must be manifestly proved. (*Tomlin*)

An overt act sufficient to justify the taking of human life must be some demonstration made by the deceased against the accused of such character as to impress upon him that he was in imminent danger of his life or some great bodily harm. In some instances the extent of the overt act which would induce the accused to act in self-defence is measured by the character of the deceased for a violent, quarrelsome, dangerous and turbulent disposition, notorious in the community or known to the accused.

Overtake. To pass another vehicle; to catch up with and pass.

Overtime. Beyond regular hours of work (as) overtime employment of workman in a factory.

Overtime work can only mean work in excess of the maximum hours of work permissible under the statute. *Philips India Ltd.* v. *Labour Court, Madras,* AIR 1985 SC 1034, 1040.

Overtime allowance. Allowance given for work done beyond normal working hours.

Overtime rate. Rate at which payment is made for the work in excess of a set time limit. [Minimum Wages Act (11 of 1948), S. 3(2)(d)].

Overwhelming. Irresistible by numbers of weight *etc.*

Overwhelming proof. Proof sufficient to remove every doubt from the mind.

Owelty. While effecting a partition it would not be possible to divide the properties by metes and bounds there being of necessity an allocation of properties of unequal values amongst the members of the joint family. In such cases there will have to be an adjustment of the values by providing for the payment by a person who gets properties of a larger value to properties of a smaller value. This provision for payment is called owelty. *T.S. Swaminatha Udayar* v. *Official Receiver*, AIR 1957 SC 577, 581.

Owing. Held under obligation of paying; due; absolutely and unconditionally bound to pay, (as) debt owing.

Own. To have a good legal title to; to hold as property; to possess; often used as synonymous with possess.

Own motion. Own instance. [CrPC 1973 (2 of 1974), S. 144(6)].

Owned capital. 'OWNED CAPITAL' means the paid up share capital, reserve fund, any other reserve which has been created out of profits and undistributed and unappropriated profits, if any. [Delhi Co-operative Society Rules, 1973, R. 2(xx)]

Owned fund. OWNED FUND means—

1. Paid-up equity capital
2. Preference shares which are compulsorily convertible into equity
3. Free reserves
4. Balance in share premium account
5. Capital reserves representing surplus arising out of sale proceeds of asset, excluding reserves created by revaluation of asset

Less Accumulated loss balance, book value of intangible assets and deferred revenue expenditure, if any. [Non-Banking Financial Companies Prudential Norms (Reserve Bank) Directions, 1998, Para 2(1)(xiii)]

"OWNED FUND" means aggregate of paid up equity capital, preference shares which are compulsorily convertible into equity and free reserves as reduced by accumulated balance of loss, deferred revenue expenditure, book value of intangible assets and under/short provision against NPA/ diminution in value of investments, and over-recognition of income, if any; and further reduced by book value of the company's investments in shares, bonds, debentures and outstanding loans and advances made to and deposits with related parties as defined in AS 18 of Institute of Chartered Accountants of India (ICAI), other than investments in joint ventures for asset reconstruction permitted by Reserve Bank of India. [Securitisation Companies /Reconstruction Companies Prudential Norms (Reserve Bank) Directions (54 of 2002), S. 2(v)].

Owner. "One who has dominion of a thing, real or personal, corporeal or incorporeal, which he has the right to enjoy and to do with it as he pleases—either to spoil or destroy it as far as the law permits—unless he be prevented by some law, agreement or covenant which restrains his right": one who owns; the rightful proprietor.

'OWNER' includes where the person in possession of the vehicle is minor, the guardian of such a minor, and in relation to a vehicle which is the subject of her-purchase agreement the person in possession of the vehicle under that agreement. [Assam Requisition and Control of Vehicle Act, 1968 (5 of 1969), S. 2(b) as cited in *Purnya Kala Devi* v. *State of Assam*, (2014) 14 SCC 142, para 7].

A registered owner and where the agreement on hire-purchase or an agreement of hypothecation has been entered into or lease agreement, the person in possession of the vehicle is treated as an owner. [Managing Director, Karnataka State Road Transport Corporation v. New India Assurance Company Limited, (2016) 2 SCC 382, para 10] [Motor Vehicles Act, (00 of 1988), S. 2(30)].

"OWNER" includes any person who is receiving or is entitled to receive the rent of any building or land whether on his own account or on behalf of himself and others or an agent or trustee, or who would so receive the rent or be entitled to receive it if the building or land were let to a tenant. [Cantonments Act (2 of 1924), S. 2(xxvi)]

"OWNER" in relation of any land planted with coffee plants, includes,—

(1) any agent of the owner, and

(2) a mortgagee, lessee or other person in actual possession of the land. [Coffee Act (7 of 1942), S. 3(i)]

"OWNER" when used in relation to a mine, means any person who is the immediate proprietor or lessee or occupier of the mine or of any part thereof and in the case of a mine the business whereof is being carried on by a liquidator or receiver such liquidator or receiver; but does not include a person who merely receives a royalty, rent or fine from the mine, or is merely by the proprietor of the mine, subject to any lease, grant or licence for the working thereof, or is merely the owner of the soil and not interested in the minerals of the mine but any contractor or sub-lessee for the working of a mine or any part thereof shall be subject to this Act in like manner as if he were an owner, but not as to exempt the owner from any liability. [Mines Act (35 of 1952), S. 2(1)(l)]

"Owner", in relation to a mine, means any person who is the immediate proprietor or lessee or occupier of the mine or of any part thereof and in case of a mine the business whereof is being carried on by a liquidator or receiver, such liquidator or receiver; but does not include a person who merely receives a royalty, rent or fine from the mine, or is merely the proprietor of the mine, subject to any lease grant or licence for the working thereof, or is merely the owner of the soil and not interested in the minerals of the mine; but any contractor or sub-lessee for the working of a mine or any part thereof shall be subject to this Code in like manner as if he were an owner but not so as to exempt the former from any liability. [Occupational Safety, Healthy & Working Conditions Code, 2020 (37 of 2020), section 2(1)(zw)]

"OWNER" in relation to commercial or an industrial concern means the person who, or the authority which, has the ultimate control over the affairs of the concern, and where the said affairs are entrusted to a manager, managing director or managing agent, such manager, managing director or managing agent shall be deemed to be the owner of the concern. [Collection of Statistics Act (32 of 1953), S. 2(e)]

"OWNER" includes any person who is receiving or is entitled to receive the rent of any building or land whether on his own account or on behalf of himself and others or as agent or trustee, or who would so receive the rent or be entitled to receive it if the building or land were let to a tenant. [Slum Areas (Improvement and Clearance) Act (96 of 1956), S. 2(g)]

"OWNER" includes—

(i) a joint owner invested with powers of management on behalf of himself and other joint owners and successor-in-title of any such owner; and

(ii) any manager or trustee exercising powers of management and the successor-in-office of any such manager or trustee. [Ancient Monuments And Archaeological Sites And Remains Act (24 of 1958), S. 2(g)]

"OWNER" —

(i) with reference to any factory the possession of which has been transferred by lease, mortgage or otherwise, means the transferee so long as his right to possession subsists;

(ii) with reference to any factory for which an agent, by whatever name called, is employed, means the agent if, and in so far as, he has been duly authorized by the owner in that behalf, and

(iii) with reference to any factory the management of which has been taken over by any person or body of persons under the Industries (Development and Regulation) Act, 1951, means that person or body of persons. [Sugar Export Promotion Act (30 of 1958), S. 2(e)]

"OWNER" means—

(i) the person registered as owner of the ship and includes the operator who for the time being is in charge of the ship and the master of the ship; or

(ii) in the absence of registration, the person owning the ship; or

(iii) in the case of a tanker owned by a foreign State, the person registered in that State as operator of the ship. [Merchant Shipping Act (44 of 1958), S. 352H(c) (*Substituted by Merchant Shipping Act, 2002*)]

"OWNER" used with reference to an animal, includes not only the owner but also any other person for the time being in possession or custody of the animal, whether with or without the consent of the owner. [Prevention of Cruelty to Animals Act (59 of 1960), S. 2(f)]

"OWNER", (i) in relation to goods, includes any consignor, consignee, shipper or agent for the sale, custody, loading or unloading of such goods (ii) in relation to any vessel or any aircraft making use of any port, includes any part-owner, character, consignee or mortgagee in possession thereof. [Major Port Trusts Act (38 of 1963), S. 2(o)]

"OWNER" in relation to an undertaking, means an individual Hindu undivided family, body corporate or other association of individuals, whether incorporated or not, trust (whether public or private or whether religious or charitable) who or which owns or controls, the whole or substantially the whole of such undertaking, and includes any association person who is a constituent of a group and who has the ultimate control over the affairs of such undertaking. [Monopolies and Restrictive Trade Practices Act (54 of 1969), S. 2(ja)] [Now repealed & replaced by Act 12 of 2003]

"OWNER" means the person who lets or has let, delivers or has delivered possession of goods, to a hirer under a hire-purchase agreement and includes a person to whom the owner's property in the goods or any of the owner's rights or liabilities under the agreement has passed by assignment or by operation of law. [Hire-Purchase Act (26 of 1972), S. 2(f)] [Now repealed by Act 31 of 2005]

"OWNER" in relation to any land planted with cardamom plants, includes—

(i) any agent of the owner,

(ii) or mortgagee, lessee or other person in actual possession the land. [Spices Board Act (10 of 1986), S. 2(j)]

"Owner" means any person in whose name a motor vehicle stands registered, and where such person is a minor, the guardian of such minor, and in relation to a motor vehicle which is the subject of a hire-purchase agreement or an agreement of lease or an agreement of hypothecation, the person in possession of the Vehicle under that agreement. [Motor Vehicles Act (59 of 1988), S. 2(30)]

"OWNER" means a person who owns, or has control over handling, any hazardous substance at the time of accident and includes,—

(i) in the case of a firm, any of its partners;

(ii) in the case of an association, any of its members;

(iii) in the case of a company, any of its directors, managers, secretaries or other officers who is directly in the charge of, and is responsible to, the company for the conduct of the business of the company. [Public Liability Insurance Act (6 of 1991), S. 2(g)]

"OWNER" means a person who owns, or has control over handling, any hazardous substance at the time of accident and includes,—

(i) in the case of a firm, any of its partners;

(ii) in the case of an association, any of its members; and

(iii) in the case of a company, any of its directors, managers, secretaries or other officers who is directly in charge of, and is responsible to, the company for the conduct of the business of the company. [National Environment Tribunal Act (27 of 1995), S. 2(q)]

The popular definition of the word 'owner' is one who has the right to own; exclusive right of possession; legal or just claim or title; proprietorship.

The word 'OWNER' includes any person using a boiler of which he is the agent of the owner. The definition cannot be pressed into service for the purpose of bringing within its mischief the directors of the company. [Indian Boilers Act (5 of 1923) S. 2(d)]

"OWNER" in relation to the premises where an insanitary latrine exists or someone is employed as a manual scavenger, means, the person who, for the time being has legal title to such premises. [S. 2(1)(k) of the Prohibition of Employment as Manual Scavengers & Their Rehabilitation Act, 2013 (25 of 2013)]

Owner, Absolute. A person capable of disposing the whole interest in immovable property although it is charged or encumbered. [CPC (5 of 1908), 1st Sch., App. A, form No. 13].

"Owner" and "Person interested." The expression "owner" which occurs in S. 49 of the Land Acquisition Act (1 of 1894) is no where defined in the Act, and though the expression "person interested" as explained in S. 3 must obviously include "owner," the connotation of the two terms are by no means coincident. A "person interested" who cannot be strictly considered an owner, cannot avail himself of the rights conferred by S. 49. *Province of Bengal* v. *Mahes Misser,* AIR 1941 Cal 625.

To claim to be a owner, besides producing the steamer receipt which can be treated as a document of title, one should prove that this receipt was handed over to him on payment of money. *Niranjan Lal* v. *R.S. Navigation Co.,* AIR 1967 A&N 74, 76. [Carriers Act (3 of 1865), S. 8]

A raising contractor of a mine under the terms of agreement who was in fact in actual physical possession and enjoyment of the colliery by virtue of being in possession in his own right and was not in possession on behalf of somebody, is an owner. *Industrial Supplies Pvt. Ltd.* v. *Union of India*, AIR 1980 SC 1858, 1862. [Coking Coal Mines (Nationalisation) Act (36 of 1972), S. 3(2), 4(1)]

Owner—mentioned Sec. 12(2) comprehends a person who has all right and incidences of ownership of the property. Such a person must have full control and dominion in any manner that suited him including the right to possess and the right to transfer the same. *Jamini Mohan Acharju* v. *Santosh Kumar Roy,* AIR 1983 Gau 88, 90. [Indian Electricity Act (9 of 1910), S. 12(2)]

For the purpose of Sec. 22, the owner must be that person who can exercise the rights of the owner, not on behalf of the owner but in his own right. *RR Jodha Mal Ruthiala* v. *C.I.T.*, (1971) 82 ITR 570, 575, 578 (SC). [Income Tax Act (43 of 1961), S. 22]

The words used by the lessee that he and his ancestors exercised permanent heritable and transferable rights to the land and they enjoyed the same with the consent of Govt. could not be deemed to be an assertion of absolute ownership sufficient to entail forfeiture of a permanent tenancy of the nature. *Mohd. Amir* v. *Municipal Board Sitapur,* AIR 1965 SC 1923, 1930.

A person who keeps in his possession or control a vehicle at a stage after the stage of manufacturing of the motor vehicle is the owner of the vehicle. *Hindustan Motors Ltd.* v. *State of Bengal,* AIR 1985 Cal 529, 532.

Owner of a lodging house. Means a person who receives or is entitled to receive whether on his own account or on behalf of himself and others or as an agent or a trustee for any other person, any monetary consideration from any person on account of board, lodging or other services provided in the lodging house. [Delhi Rent Act (33 of 1995), S. 2(i)]

Owner of a vehicle. 'OWNER OF A VEHICLE' includes where the person in possession of the vehicle is a minor, the guardian of such minor and in relation to a vehicle which is the subject of a hire purchase or a hypothecation agreement, the person in possession of the vehicle under that agreement. [Bihar Premises and Vehicles (Realisation) Act (X of 1978), S. 2(iv)]

Owner's risk rate. At owner's risk; on condition that the owner should bear the risk (as of loss, damage or delay). [Indian Railways Act (9 of 1890), S. 72(b)(i)].

Ownership. Ownership is the right by which a thing belongs to an individual, to the exclusion of all other persons.

Ownership denotes the relation between a person and an object forming the subject-matter of his ownership. It consists in a complex of rights, all of which are rights in rem, being good against all the world and not merely against specific persons. Thought in certain situations some of these rights may be absent, the normal case of ownership can be expected to exhibit the following incidents.

First, the owner will have a right to possess the thing which he owns….

Secondly, the owner normally has the right to use and enjoy the thing owned: the right to manage it i.e., the right to decide how it shall be used; and the right to the income from it. Whereas the right to possess is a right in the strict sense, these rights are in fact liberties: the owner has a liberty to use the thing i.e., he is under no duty not to use it, in contrast with others who are under a duty not to use or interfere with it." [Jurisprudence, by Salmond, p. 246, 12th End., para 44 as cited in *Monnet Ispat and Energy Limited v. Union of India,* (2012) 11 SCC 1, para 215].

Collection of rights to use and enjoy property, including right to transmit it to others. The right of one or more persons to possess and use a thing to the exclusion of others. The right by which a thing belongs to someone in particular, to the exclusion of all other persons. The exclusive right to possession, enjoyment, and disposal; involving an essential attribute the right to control, handle and dispose. [Black's Law Dictionary (6th Edn.) as cited in *Industrial Credit and Development Syndicate Limited v. Commissioner of Income Tax, Mysore,* (2013) 3 SCC 541, para 21].

The fact or state of being an owner; proprietorship. [T.P. Act (4 of 1882), S. 40].

Transfer of stolen property passes no ownership to buyer.

Owning. Who owns. [CrPC 1973 (2 of 1974), S. 133(1)].

Oyer and terminer. A Court or Commission of "Oyer and Terminer", is one to hears and determines. (*Termes de la Ley; Cowel; Jacob.*)

It was a commission directed to certain judges in England and other gentlemen of the county to which it was issued, by virtue whereof they had power to hear and determine reasons, and all manner of felonies and trespasses. (*Tomlin*)

Ozone depleting substance. Means the ozone depleting substances specified in column (2) of Schedule 1, whether existing by itself or in a mixture, excluding any such substance or mixture (blend) which is in a manufactured product other than a container used for the transportation or storage of such substance. [Ozone Depleting Substances (Regulation and Control) Rules, 2000, R. 2(i)].

Ozone layer. The 'OZONE LAYER' means the layer of atmospheric ozone above the planetary boundary layer. [Vienna Convention for the Protection of the Ozone Layer (1985), Art. 1]

P

Paci sunt maxime contraria, vis et injuria. Violence and injury are especially contrary to peace.

Package. "PACKAGE" means a box, bottle, casket, tin, barrel, case, receptacle, sack, bag, wrapper or other thing in which an article of food is placed or packed. [Prevention of Food Adulteration Act (37 of 1954), S. 2(x)]

'PACKAGE' means a box, bottle, casket, tin barrel, case receptacle, sack, bag, wrapper or other thing in which an insecticide is placed or packed. [Insecticides Act (46 of 1968), S. 3 (l)]

"PACKAGE" includes any case, box, container, covering, folder, receptacle, vessel, casket, bottle, wrapper, label, band, ticket, reel, frame, capsule, cap, lid, stopper and cork. [Trade Marks Act (47 of 1999), S. 2(1)(q) (Similar definition provided in Act 43 of 1958, now repealed by Act 47 of 1999) and Geographical Indications of goods (Registration and Protection) Act (48 of 1999), S. 2(1)(i)]

"PACKAGE" includes a wrapper, box, carton, tin or other container. [Cigarettes and other Tobacco Products (Prohibition of Advertisement and Regulation of Trade and Commerce, Production, Supply and Distribution Act (34 of 2003), S. 3(i)]

A number of things bound together convenient for handling and conveyance; a bundle; a quantity pressed or packed together; a bundle or bale made up for transportation; a bundle or parcel.

"PACKAGE" means a pre-packed box, bottle, casket, tin, barrel, case, pouch, receptacle, sack, bag, wrapper or such other things in which an article of food is packed. [S. 3(1)(zh) of the Food Safety & Standards Act, 2006 (34 of 2006)]

Package or container. Means a pre-packaged box, bottle, casket, tin, barrel, case, pouch, receptacle, sack, bag, wrapper or such other things in which an article of food is packed. [Food Safety and Standards (Packaging Regulations, 2018, Reng. 2(1)(e)].

Packaging activity. "PACKAGING ACTIVITY" means packaging of goods including pouch filling, bottling, labelling or imprinting of the package, but does not include any packaging activity that amounts to 'manufacture' within the meaning of clause (*f*) of Section 2 of the Central Excise Act, 1944. [Finance Act (32 of 1994), S. 65(76b) *as inserted by Finance Act (18 of 2005), S. 88(a)(xvii)* now repealed by Central Goods and Services Tax Act, 2017]

Packet. A bundle of data that travels over the network. A message may comprise many packages. It contains information about its source, destination and an identifier for the recipient to understand how it relates to other packets. (*Cyber Law*)

Packet filter firewall. A type of firewall that controls data traffic (the export and import of data) based on packets passing through the network. (*Cyber Law*)

Packet sniffer. A device or program that monitors the data travelling between computers on a network. (*Cyber Law*)

Packet sniffing. Packet sniffing is a technique in which attackers surreptitiously insert a software program at remote network switches or host computers. The program monitors information packets as they are sent through networks and sends a copy of the information retrieved to the hacker. By picking up the first 125 keystrokes of a connection, attackers can learn passwords and user identifications, which, in turn, they can use to break into systems. (*Cyber Law*)

Packet switching. Using packet switching, a message is transmitted by dividing it into fixed-length packets and then sending the individual packets to their destination. Connections don't need to be established before data transmission begins; in other words, no virtual circuit is needed. (*Cyber Law*)

The method used to move data around on the *Internet.* In packet switching, all the data coming out of a machine is broken up into chunks, each chunk has the address of where it came from and where it is going. This enables chunks of data from many different sources to co-mingle on the same lines and be sorted and directed along different routes by special machines along the way. This way many people can use the same lines at the same time. You might think of several caravans of trucks all using the same road system to carry materials. (*Matisse Enzer-Glossary of Internet Terms; Internet and E-commerce.*)

Packing. "Packing as in Section 2(k)(i) is the packing of the finished manufactured article which is done to facilitate or make possible its sale or transport for sale to customers". Where packing is of raw material as in this case bating of the grass it does not constitute packing as defined in Section 2(k)(i) of the act. *Sri Gopal Paper Mills Ltd.* v. *Inspector of Factories, U.P.*, AIR 1969 All 547 at 548. [Factories Act (63 of 1948), S. 2(k)(i) and (m)]

Pact. An agreement especially between nations.

Pacta conventa quae neque contra leges neque dolo malo inita sunt, omni modo observanda sunt. (*Lat.*) (C. 2, 3, 29) Contracts which are not illegal, and do not originate in fraud must in all respects be observed.

Pacta dant legem contractui. (*Maxim*) Agreements constitute the law of the contract. (*Latin for Lawyers*)

Pacta privata non derogant juri communi. Private agreements cannot derogate from common right (or law).

Pacta quae contra leges constitutionesque vel contra bonos mores fiunt nullam vim habere indubitati juris est. (*Lat.*) (C. 2, 3, 6) That contracts which are made against law or against good morals, have no force, is a principle of undoubted law.

Pacta quae turpem causam continent non sunt observanda. (*Maxim*) Agreements founded upon an immoral consideration are not to be observed. (*Black*)

Pacta reciproca vel utrosque ligant vel neutrum. Mutual bargains bind both parties or neither.

Pacta sunt servanda. Contracts must be kept.

Pacta traditione firmantur. Agreements are confirmed by delivery.

Pactum super hæreditate viventis. (*Lat.*) An agreement concerning the succession of a person still living.

Paediatrician. Means a person who possesses a post-graduate qualification in paediatrics. [Pre-Natal Diagnostic Techniques (Regulation and Prevention of Misuse) Act (57 of 1994), S. 2(h)]

Pageant. 1.It is an entertainment consisting of a procession of people in elaborate costumes, or an outdoor performance of a historical scene. 2 (also beauty pageant) a beauty contest. 3. historical a scene erected on a fixed stage or moving vehicle as a public show of unknown origin" [Oxford Concise English Dictionary as cited in *Dream Merchants* v. *State of Karnataka*, Writ Petition No. 48502/2017, decided on 30-1-2018, para 11]

Page view (PV). One surfer viewing one web site page. (*Cyber Law*)

Pager. Means an instrument, apparatus or appliance which is a non-speech, one-way personal calling system with alert and has the capability of receiving, storing and displaying numeric or alpha-numeric messages. [Finance Act (32 of 1994), S. 65(62) now repealed by Central Goods and Services Tax Act, 2017]

Paging system. A one-way mobile radio service where a user carries a small, lightweight miniature radio receiver capable of responding to coded signals. These devices, called "pagers," emit an audible signal, vibrate or do both when activated by recognising its own call sign. (*Telecommunication*)

Paid. Applied; settled; satisfied.

"It does not contemplate actual receipt of the dividend by the member of a company in general, when the company discharges its liability and makes the amount of dividend unconditionally available to the member entitled thereto, it is paid within the meaning of the term. *Benaras State Bank* v. *I.T. Commissioner*, AIR 1970 SC 281 at 282.

PAID means actual payment or offer to pay even if the employee spurns the offer of the management. *Presidency Talkies Private Ltd.* v. *Presiding Officer Labour Court,* AIR 1969 Mad 87 at 89. [Industrial Disputes Act (14 of 1947), S. 33(2)(*b*)]

The word 'paid' is not equivalent to 'offered' or 'tendered'.

Paid and allowed. The word 'paid' takes in every receipt by the employee from the employer, whether it is due to him or not. The term 'allowed' means fixed, taken into account, set apart, granted and it takes in perquisites given in cash or in kind or in money or money's worth and also amenities which are not convertible into money. *I.T. Commissioner* v. *LW Runnel*, AIR 1965 SC 49, 52.

Paid in full. The expression 'paid in full' means payment of the full amount as the creditor would be entitled to as if no order of adjudication has been passed against the debtor. *Jabrachand* v. *C. Oliver,* AIR 1965 Mys 117, 120.

Paid out of fund. Paid out of actual cash resources reserved or assigned to any particular or specified purpose. [T.P. Act (4 of 1882), S. 45].

Paid up capital. "PAID UP CAPITAL" includes capital credited as paid up. [Companies Act (1 of 1956), S. 2(32)]

For the purposes of this sub-section, "PAID-UP CAPITAL" means, in the case of an owner not being a company, the market value of all assets and stocks of the undertaking on the date of contract of insurance. [Public Liability Insurance Act (6 of 1991), S. 4(2A) *Expln.*]

That part of the subscribed capital of an undertaking which has been actually paid. [Industrial Development Bank of India Act (18 of 1964), S. 25(2)].

Paid-up share capital. Means such aggregate amount of money credited as paid-up as is equivalent to the amount received as paid-up in respect of shares issued and also includes any amount credited as paid-up in respect of shares of the company, but does not include any other amount received in respect of such shares, by whatever name called. [S. 2(64) of the Companies Act, 2013 (18 of 2013)]

"PAID UP SHARE CAPITAL" means such portion of the subscribed share capital as is actually paid-up in cash and/or credited as paid up. [Delhi Co-operative Society Rules, 1973, R. 2(xxi) Now repealed by the Delhi Co-operative Societies Rules, 2007].

Pain and suffering. Mean physical discomfort and distress and include mental and emotional trauma for which damages can be recovered in an accident claim.

Painful complaint. Any ailment which causes great agony or pain. [IPC (45 of 1860), S. 88, ill.].

Paint. Decoplast is a plastic emulsion paint. *Asian Paints Ltd.* v. *Collector of Central Excise*, AIR 1988 SC 1087, 1089. [Central Excises and Salt Act (1 of 1944), Sch. 1, Item 14(1)(3)(iv)]

Painter. One who represents the appearance of natural or other objects on a surface by the means of colours.

One who paints or does the work of painting pictures. [CPC (5 of 1908), 1st Sch., App. A, form No. 39].

Painting. A likeness, image, or scene depicted with paints. (*Cent. Dict.*)

A representation of an object or scene on a surface by means of colours. [CrPC 1973 (2 of 1974), S. 95(2)(b)].

Pairuvi. The word '*pairuvi*' denotes something more than giving mere information. It means taking active part in the prosecution by production of witnesses and doing all other things required for the success of the prosecution. *Amaldar Singh* v. *Sabhajit Singh,* AIR 1963 All 580, 581.

Pais. Assurance of land "by matter in pais, or deed; which is an assurance transacted between two or more private persons in pais in the country; that is upon the very spot to be transferred".

Palm jaggery. Palm jaggery is produced from the juice of palm tree. The tappers collect *neera* from palm and other trees and prepare jaggery by boiling neera without the aid of any machinery. (*Venkataraman* v. *State of Madras,* AIR 1970 SC 508).

Palm kernel. Palm kernel, cannot be included under the item 'palm seeds' as the two commodities are different as understood in commerce or trade. (*Priyanka Overseas (P.) Ltd.* v. *Union of India,* AIR 1991 SC 583)

Palm-sized computer. A computer small enough to be held comfortably in the hand, with either a miniature keyboard or a touch sensitive surface on which the user can input information. (*Computer*)

Palmyra Sugar. "PALMYRA SUGAR" that is to say, sugar manufactured from jaggery obtained by boiling the juice of the palmyra palm. [Sugar (Regulation of Production) Act (55 of 1961), S. 2(f)(ii)]

Pamphlet. A small treatise occupying fewer pages than would make a book composed and issued as a separate work. [IPC (45 of 1860), S. 292(a)].

Pan masala. In this Chapter, "Pan masala" means any preparation containing betel-nuts and any one or more of the following ingredients, namely:—

(i) lime; and
(ii) kattha (catechu),

but not tobacco, whether or not containing any other ingredients, such as cardamom, copra and menthol. [Central Excise Tariff Act (5 of 1986), I Sch., S. IV, Chap. 21, Note 3]

'Pan Masala' is a food within the meaning of S. 2(*v*). *K.G. Sharma* v. *Govt. of N.C.T. of Delhi,* (1996) 4 SCC 513. [Prevention of Food Adulteration Act (37 of 1954), S. 2(*v*)]

Panch. "PANCH" means a panch of a *gram panchayat.* [MP Panchayat Raj Adhiniyam, 1993 (1 of 1994), S. 2(xvi)]

Panchayat. "PANCHAYAT" means an institution (by whatever name called) of self-government constituted under Article 243B, for the rural areas. [Constitution of India, Art. 243(d)]

Panchayat is a body constituted for the local administration of a village under the Act.

Panchayat area. Means the territorial area of a Panchayat. [Constitution of India, Art. 243(e) and Manipur Panchayat Raj Act (26 of 1994), S. 2(l)]

Panchayat at intermediate level. "PANCHAYAT AT INTERMEDIATE LEVEL" means an institution (by whatever name called) of self-government constituted, at the intermediate level, under Article 243-B of the Constitution, for the rural areas in accordance with the provisions of Part IX of the Constitution. [Gram Nyayalayas Act, 2008 (4 of 2009), S. 2(f)]

Panchnama. So long as *panchnama* is a mere record of things heard and seen by *panchas* and does not constitute a statement communicated to a police officer in the course of investigation by him, it would not fall within the mischief of Section 162 of CrPC 1973 (2 of 1974). *Valibhai Omarji* v. *State,* AIR 1963 Guj 145, 147. [CrPC 1973 (2 of 1974), S. 162].

Panchnama is a document having legal bearings which records evidence and findings that an officer makes at the scene of offence/crime. However, it is not only the recordings of the crime but also of anywhere else which may be related to the crime/offence and from cohere incriminating evidence is likely to be collected. The document so prepared needs to be signed by investigating officer who prepares the same and at least by two independent and impartial witnesses called "panchas" as also by the party concerned. The witnesses are required to be not only impartial but also "respectable". "Respectable" here would mean a person who is not dis-reputed. One should also check if the witnesses are in their senses at the time of the panchnama proceedings. Only majors are to be taken as witnesses as minors' witnesses may not withstand the legal scrutiny. [*Yaqub Abdul Razak Memon* v. *State of Maharashtra,* (2013) 13 SCC 1, para 353].

Pandal or shamiana. Means a place specially prepared or arranged for organising an official, social or business function. [Finance Act (32 of 1994), S. 65(77a) (*Inserted by Finance (No.2) Act (23 of 2004), S. 90*) now repealed by Central Goods and Services Tax Act, 2017]

Pandal or shamiana contractor. Means a person engaged in providing any service, either directly or indirectly, in connection with the preparation, arrangement, erection or decoration of a pandal or shamiana and includes the supply of furniture, fixtures, lights and lighting fittings, floor coverings and other articles for use therein. [Finance Act (32 of 1994), S. 65(77b) (*Inserted by Finance (No.2) Act (23 of 2004), S. 90*) now repealed by the Central Goods and Services Tax Act, 2017]

Pandects. The books of the Civil Law, compiled by Justinian.

Panel. A group of persons selected for some job or duty.

Panic. Panic is a state of mind or reaction to fearsome or gruesome events or even creating unreasoning or hysterical fear, often spreading quickly. It is the effect, the cause being due to many situations. What creates panic can also create terror depending upon the acts with which a person is confronted. *Ramesh Roy* v. *State of West Bengal*, AIR 1972 SC 1678, 1679.

Panjis. (Pedigree tables) are maintained by *Panjikars* who are professional genealogists. They systematically maintain pedigree tables in the community of *Naithal Brahmins*. They go from place to place and periodically ascertain the genealogies of their clients and enter them in *Panjis* (Palm leaf manuscripts of genealogy) and add to them such fresh additions as occur in the family from time to time. They are considered important in this community because questions of marriage (who may marry whom) and relationship and caste turn on them. *Sitaji* v. *Bijendra Narain*, AIR 1954 SC 601, 603. [Indian Evidence Act (1 of 1872), Ss. 32, 33]

Paper. "PAPER" means any document, including a newspaper, other than a book. [Press and Registration of Books Act (25 of 1867), S. 1]

"PAPER" includes vellum, parchment or any other material on which an instrument may be written. [Indian Stamp Act (2 of 1899), S. 2(18)]

A written or printed document or instrument. [Indian Evidence Act (1 of 1872), S. 39]; [Constitution of India, Art. 105(2)].

Paper, whether lined or blank, means a material on which writing, printing, drawing *etc.* can be done. An exercise-book which is a collection of sheets or paper (blank of lined) stitched together by a piece of string or pinned together with pins of a stapler would fall within the item "paper". *Maharaja Book Department* v. *State of Gujarat* AIR 1979 SC 180, 183. [Essential Commodities Act (10 of 1955), S. 2(*a*)(*vii*)]

The word 'paper' is not synonymous with the word 'newspaper', because the Act has used the word 'newspaper' distinctly in several sections of the enactment and has even defined it. The word 'paper' was really intended to cover all those papers which could not be defined as 'books' or 'newspapers' but which had historical, cultural or literary value. *State* v. *Udit Narain,* AIR 1955 All 524, 525. [Press and Registration of Books Act (25 of 1867), S. 3]

The word 'paper' in the common parlance or in commercial sense means paper which is used for printing, writing, or packing purposes. *State of U.P.* v. *Kores (India) Ltd.*, AIR 1977 SC 132, 135.

'Paper' does not include ammonia paper or ferro paper being chemically coated paper used for obtaining prints and sketches of site plan. *Commissioner of Sales Tax* v. *Macheill & Barry Ltd.,* AIR 1986 SC 386.

Paper blockade. Blockade that lacks effectiveness and exists merely on paper.

Paper currency. 'Paper currency' designates notes or bills circulated by the authority of the government as money, and includes both treasury notes, and those issued for circulation by national banks.

Paper or papers. A manufactured substance composed of fibres adhering together, in form consisting of sheets of various sizes and different thicknesses, used for writing or printing; a substance used for writing and printing on; a written instrument, or document; any written paper or instrument; a writing; a printed sheet; a printed or written instrument; document, essay, or the like; a writing.

Papers laid on the table. Laying of Parliamentary papers or documents on the Table of both Houses of Parliament for bringing them on the record of the House. (*Constitutional and Parliamentary Term*)

Par, At. At exactly the nominal value.

Par in parem imperium non habet. (*Maxim*) An equal has no power over an equal. (*Bouvier*)

Paralegal. One who assists a lawyer in his practice of law but is not a trained or licensed attorney.

Parallel importation. Unauthorised importation of legally marketable patented goods from a country. (*Patents*)

Parallel imports. Imports taken into a country and sold at a lower price than the one that normally prevails there (because they are cheaper in the country of origin).

Paramedical. 'PARAMEDICAL' means any personnel qualified in paramedical subject and who helps in teaching or practice of medicine within the meaning of clause (i) of Section 2 of the Indian Council Act (1956). [M.P. Sah Chikiriy, Parishad Adhiniyam, 2000 (11 of 2001), S. 2(b)(i)]

Paramour. One with whom a person has illicit sexual relations; the illicit lover of a married woman.

Parapet. "PARAPET" means a low wall or railing built along the edge of a roof on a floor. [W.B. Municipal (Building) Rules, 1996, R. 2(36)]

Paraphernalia. Property which a wife was allowed to keep, in addition to her dowry, on the death of her husband.

Parcel. Means goods entrusted to a railway administration for carriage by a passenger or a parcel train. [Railways Act (24 of 1989), S. 2(27)]

Parcels train. Means a train intended solely or mainly for the carriage of coaching traffic other than passenger traffic. [Railways Red Tariff Rules, 1960, R. 2(m)]

Parcener : parcenary. Equivalents of co-parcener and co-parcency.

Pardanashin lady. A *pardanashin* lady, in the true sense of that term, is a lady living in seclusion, that is the *zenana*, and having no communication with any male strangers except from behind a screen. But a lady with a certain amount of education, who subscribes newspapers, manages her affairs and even appears in Courts is not a *pardanashin* lady.

A *Pardanashin lady* is one who does not expose her face to the public.

Parda-nishin. "PARDA-NISHIN" means a woman who, according to the custom of the country, might reasonably object to appear in a public office. [Ben. Act (1 of 1876) (Mohammedan Marriage and Divorce Registration), S. 2]

Pardon. A pardon is an act of grace proceeding from the power entrusted with the execution of the laws which exempts the individual on whom it is bestowed from the punishment the law inflicts for a crime he has committed. There are several kinds of pardons; thus, a pardon may be full and unconditional, partial or conditional.

A remission, either free or conditional of the legal consequences of a crime; the excusing of a fault. [CrPC 1973 (2 of 1974), S. 306(1) and Constitution of India, Art. 72(1)].

A 'pardon' is an act of grace, proceeding from the power entrusted with the execution of laws, which exempts the individual on whom it is bestowed from the punishment the law inflicts for a crime he has committed. A full pardon may blot out the guilt itself. It does not amount to acquittal. *State Govt. of NCT of Delhi* v. *Prem Raj,* (2003) 7 SCC 121, para 9.

Pardon and remission. The vital difference between a pardon and a mere remission of sentence lies in the fact that in the former case it affects both the punishment prescribed for the offence and the guilt of the offender: in other words, a full pardon may blot out the guilt itself; in the latter case the guilt of the offender is not affected nor is the sentence of the Court affected, except in the sense that the person concerned does not suffer incarceration for the entire period of the sentence, but is relieved from serving out a part of it. Pardon and remission, therefore stand on different footings and give rise to different conesquences. *Khagendranath* v. *Umesh Chandra Nath,* MLJ : QD (1956-1960) Vol. II C1765 : AIR 1958 Assam 183. [CrPC (5 of 1898), S. 401]

Pardon the error but not its repetition. Applying the maxim, the Apex Court observed that the strength of power of High Court over the district Courts and Courts subordinate thereto is not displayed solely in cracking a whip on errors, mistakes or failures; the power should be so wielded as to have propensity to prevent and to ensure exclusion of repetition if committed once innocently or unwittingly. *'K', A Judicial Officer, In re,* (2001) 3 SCC 54, para 15 : AIR 2001 SC 792.

Parens est nomen generale ad omne genus cognationis. (*Lat.*) (Co. Litt. 80b) Parent is a general name for every kind of relationship.

Parens patriae. Literally "Parent of the Country." (*Burill*)

In the case of Bhopal Gas tragedy, the victims were not in a position to look after their own interests effectively or purposefully and they needed State's protection and should come within the umbrella of State's sovereignty to assert, establish and maintain their rights against the wrong doers in this mass disaster. So, it is possible to apply the principle of *parens patrial* doctrine to the victims. *Charan Lal Sahu* v. *Union of India*, AIR 1990 SC 1480, 1535. [Bhopal Gas Disaster (Processing of Claims) Act (21 of 1985]

Parent. "PARENT" includes the father and mother of a legitimate child and the mother of an illegitimate child. [Vaccination Act (13 of 1880), S. 2]

"PARENT" shall include father and mother and grandfather and grandmother. [Indian Fatal Accidents Act (13 of 1955), S. 4]

"PARENT" in relation to any child, includes a guardian and every person who has the actual custody of the child. [Delhi Primary Education Act, 1960 (39 of 1960), S. 2(g)]

'PARENT' means the father or mother of a child and includes an adopted father or mother. [Tamil Nadu Compulsory Elementary Education (T.N. Act No. 33 of 1995), S. 2(7)]

A person, who has begotten or borne a child; father or mother [IPC (45 of 1860), S. 317]; one who, or that which produces; that from which anything springs or branches.

The word 'parent' or 'parents' may be held to mean one of both parents.

In the legal or ordinary acceptation of the term, 'parent' does not include a step-father or step-mother.

It may be reasonably contended that having regard to the context, the word 'parents' should necessarily mean 'male parent' and will not include the mother. *Wilson Reade* v. *C.S. Booth,* AIR 1958 Ass 128, 137. [Constitution of India, Art. 366(2); General Clauses Act (10 of 1897), S. 13]

Parentage. Parenthood; lineage; origin. [CrPC 1973 (2 of 1974), Ss. 263(e) and 355(d)].

Parent-alienation syndrome. A situation in which one parent has manipulated a child to fear or hate the other parent; a condition resulting from a parent's actions that are designed to poison a child's relationship with the other parent. Some mental health specialists deny that this phenomenon amounts to a "psychological syndrome".—Also termed *parental-alienation syndrome.* [Black's Law Dictionary, Deluxe Ninth Edition

Parent entity. For the purpose of this section, "parent entity" means a constituent entity, of an international group holding, directly or indirectly, an interest in one or more of the other constituent entities of the international group, such that—

(i) it is required to prepare a consolidated financial statement under any law for the time being in force or the accounting standards of the country or territory of which the entity is resident; or

(ii) it would have been required to prepare a consolidated financial statement had the equity shares of any of the enterprises were listed on a stock exchange,

and, there is no other constituent entity of such group which, due to ownership of any interest, directly or indirectly, in the first mentioned constituent entity, is required to prepare a consolidated financial statement, under the circumstances referred to in clause (i) or clause (ii), that includes the separate financial statement of the first mentioned constituent entity;

Parent University. Means the University to which the college concerned is affiliated, or of which the college concerned is a constituent. [University Grants Commission (Conferment of Autonomous Status upon Colleges and Measures for Maintenance of Standards in Autonomous Colleges) Regulations, 2018, Regn. 2 (2.9)].

Parental influence. 'Parental influence' is not terror and coercion, but kindness and affection, which may bias the child's mind and induce the child to do that which may be imprudent, and which, if the child were properly protected, it would never do.

Influence exercised (on the child) by a parent. [Indian Contract Act (9 of 1872), S. 16(3), ill. (a)].

Parental rights. A parent's rights which are concerned with one's child and includes the right to educate and discipline the child and also the right to control the child's earnings and property.

Parents. [Indian Succession Act (39 of 1925), S. 51(2)]; [Constitution of India, Art. 5(b)].

Parentum est liberos alere ctiam nothos. (*Maxim*) It is the duty of parents to support their children even when illegitimate. (*Bouvier*)

Pari causa. With equal right, upon equal footing.

Pari delicto. In a similar offence or crime; equal in guilt or in legal fault. (*Bouvier*)

Pari delicto potior est conditio defendentis. The principle that the Court will refuse to enforce an illegal agreement at the instance of a person who is himself a party to an illegality or fraud.

Pari materia. (*Lat.*) In the same matter.

Pari passu. (*Lat.*) With equal step; with simultaneous progress.

"Pari passu" means at an equal rate or pace, with simultaneous progress proportionately *etc.* This term is generally used in the context of creditors who, in marshalling assets, are entitled to receive out of the same fund without any precedence over each other. *N.D. Jayal* v. *Union of India,* (2004) 9 SCC 362, 389, para 39.

Parity. Being on a par with; analogy; close similarity (as) by party of reasoning.

Parity checking. The nontechnical meaning of "parity" has to do with maintaining equality. Applied to computer use, it means adding a bit to a unit of information so that the total number of 1s in the unit is either always odd or always even, depending upon which method is chosen. The bit added is called the parity bit, and it is a way of checking the accuracy of storage or transfer. (*Computer*)

Parking space. 'PARKING SPACE' means an area enclosed or unenclosed sufficient in size to park vehicles together with drive-way connecting parking spaces with a street or allow and permitting easy ingress and egress of the vehicles. [Delhi Cinematograph (Exhibition, of Film by VCR) Rules 1986, R. 2(xiv)]

Parlance. Way of speaking proper to a specified class or subject (as) in legal parlance; in common parlance; in medical parlance.

Parliament. The central legislature of India; the supreme legislature of United Kingdom.

Parliament may by law provide. The words "may by law provide" do not necessarily exclude delegation and it will have to be seen in each case how far the intention of the Constitution was that the entire provision should be made by law without recourse to any rules framed under the power of delegation. *D.S. Garewal* v. *State of Punjab*, AIR 1959 SC 512, 517. [Constitution of India, Art. 312]

Parliament : Prorogation of. Discontinue meetings (of Parliament *etc.*) without dissolving it.

Parlementaire. An agent employed by the commander of belligerent forces in the field to go in person within the enemy lines for the purpose of communicating or negotiating openly and directly with the enemy commander.

Parliamentarian. Skilled parliamentary debator.

Parliamentary Committee. Means a committee which is appointed or elected by the house or nominated by the speaker and works under the direction of the speaker and presents its report to the house or to the speaker and the Secretariat for which is provided by the Lok Sabha Secretariat. [Rules of Procedure and Conduct of Business in Lok Sabha (1952), (Ed. 7), R. 2(1)]

Parliamentary constituency. A constituency for the election of a member of Parliament.

Parliamentary Government. A system of Government having the real executive power vested in a cabinet composed of members of the Legislature who are individually and collectively responsible to the Legislature. (*Merriam Webster*)

Parliamentary law. 'Parliamentary law' as generally understood, means rules and usages of Parliament or of deliberative bodies. (*Webster*)

Parliamentary papers. The papers connected with the proceedings of the House as well as those presented to the House.

Parliamentary party. Parliamentary Wing of an organized political party; which consists exclusively of Members of Parliament.

Parliamentary privilege. The distinctive mark of a parliamentary privilege is its ancillary character. They are rights which a sovereign legislature must possess for the due execution of its powers. Some of them are enjoyed by the individual members of the House. *Raj Narain Singh* v. *Atma Ram Govind,* AIR 1954 All 319, 325. [Constitution of India, Art. 194(3)]

Parliamentary procedure. The procedure and rules adopted by the Parliament to regulate its conduct of business.

Parol. A word; speech; hence, oral or verbal; expressed or evidenced by speech only; not expressed by writing; not expressed by sealed instrument. Also used to distinguish contracts which are made verbally, or in writing not under seal, from those which are under seal. (*Bouvier*)

Parol evidence of a written document. Means extrinsic evidence, whether verbal or otherwise.

Parole. A parole is a form of conditional pardon, by which the convict is released before the expiration of his term, to remain subject, during the remainder thereof, to supervision by the public authority and to return to imprisonment on violation of the condition of the parole.

'Parole' means conditional enlargement of a prisoner from the jail under these rules. [Rajasthan Prisoners' Release on Parole Rules, 1958, R. 2(d) as cited in *Krishan Lal* v. *State of Rajasthan,* (2013) 11 SCC 395, para 11].

The promise of a prisoner upon his faith and honour to fulfil stated conditions (as to return to custody); the state or period of freedom resulting from a parole; a conditional and revocable release of a prisoner serving an unexpired sentence in a penal institution. [IPC (45 of 1860), S. 130, *Expln.*].

'Parole' is merely a conditional suspension of the sentence imposed and not its vacation. *Wooden* v. *Goheen, Ky,* 255 SW, 1000, 1002, as cited in *Sunil Fulchand Shah* v. *Union of India,* AIR 2000 SC 1023.

'Parole' and 'furlough'. Furlough is to be granted periodically for no particular reason, parole is to be granted only on a sufficient cause, such as cases of severe illness or death of any member of the prisoner's family. *Bhikhabai* v. *State of Gujarat,* AIR 1987 Guj 136, 146 (FB). [Prisons Act (9 of 1894), Rules 1959, Rr. 3, 4 (10) as (19)]

Parole or furlough. The expression 'parole or furlough' be stretched to the period during which the person was enlarged on bail, during pendency of trial or appeal or revision. *State of Haryana* v. *Sauratta Singh,* (2000) 3 SCC 514, para 11. [CrPC 1973, (2 of 1974), S. 428, 432]

Parsi. A "PARSI" means a Parsi Zoroastrain. [Parsi Marriage and Divorce Act (3 of 1936), S. 2(7)]

A worshipper of fire. (*Wil Gloss.*)

Part. "PART" shall means a part of the Act or Regulation in which the word occurs. [General Clauses Act (10 of 1897), S. 3(40)].

A fragment; a member; a piece; division; a section; a portion or moiety; a share; one of the portions, equal or unequal, into which anything is divided or regarded as divided.

In the context of an acquisition of land for running a factory on the private sector, the contribution by the Government was very little. In that context it was held that the word "part" does not necessarily mean a substantial part. *Somawanti* v. *State of Punjab,* AIR 1963 SC 151, 169. [Land Acquisition Act (1 of 1894), S. 6(1), *Proviso*]

Part-paid and part-promised, price. Only a certain portion of the price, debt, *etc.* actually paid. [T.P. Act (4 of 1882), S. 54].

Part performance. In order to justify a claim based on the doctrine of part performance of a verbal agreement for the sale of real estate, the acts of part performance relied on must be clearly, definitely, and satisfactorily shown, and it must appear that such facts were done with reference to and in pursuance of the contract.

The principle on which Courts enforce oral agreements on the ground of part performance is that, when one of the parties has been induced to alter his situation on the faith of the oral agreement to such an extent that a refusal to enforce it would result, not merely in the denial of the rights which the agreement was intended to confer, but in the infliction of an unjust and unconscientious injury and loss to him, the other party will be held estopped by force of his acts from setting up the statute; but the acts constituting such part performance must have been in reliance on and in pursuance of the oral agreement, and must be related to and connected with it, though such acts are not confined to doing what the contract stipulates.

To apply the doctrine of part performance to a particular case, it must be shown that the acts of part performance are unequivocally referable to the alleged agreement; in other words, part performance always supposes a completed agreement. There can be no part performance where there is no completed agreement in existence.

Part-time member. Means a Part-time Member of the Board appointed under Section 4, but does include an *ex officio* Member, the Nominated member or an elected Member. [Prasar Bharati (Broadcasting Corporation of India) Act (25 of 1990), S. 2(r)]

Partem aliquam recte intelligere nemo potest, antequam totum iterum atque iterum perlegerit. (*Lat.*) (3 Rep. 59) No one can rightly understand any part until he has read the whole over and over again.

Partes rei sunt favorabiliores. (*Lat.*) The condition of a defender is more favourable (than that of the pursuer).

Partial board. Partial provision of daily meals. [Indian Evidence Act (1 of 1872), S. 92, ill. (h)].

Partial disablement. Means, where the disablement is of a temporary nature, such disablement as reduces the earning capacity of a workman in any employment in which he was engaged at the time of the accident resulting in the disablement, and, where the disablement is of a permanent nature, such disablement as reduces the earning capacity in every employment which the workman was capable of undertaking at that time. [Workmen's Compensation Act (8 of 1923), S. 2(1)(g); War Injuries (Compensation Insurance) Act (23 of 1943), S. 2(e)]

Partiality. Inclination to favour a particular person or thing.

Partiality, Capricious. Capricious, not guided by steady judgment, intent or purpose. [Indian Succession Act (39 of 1925), S. 61, ill. (viii)].

Particeps criminis. (*Lat.*) One who assists another in any manner in carrying out a fraudulent purpose; an accomplice. One who has share in the crime.

Mere presence at the scene of the perpetration of a crime does not render a person a *particeps criminis.* To constitute him a party to the criminal act there must be not only presence upon the scene, but an actual *participation*—an aiding and abetting in the crime committed.

An unwilling or forced bribe-giver may not even be stigmatised as an accomplice in the strict sense of the term of '*particeps criminis*'. (*Maha Singh* v. *State (Delhi Administration),* AIR 1976 SC 449).

Participating Government. Means the Central Government, the State Government of Bihar and the State Government of West Bengal. [Damodar Valley Corporation Act (14 of 1948), S. 2(4)]

Participating financial institution. Means a financial institution empanelled with the Bureau, in accordance with the operations manual mentioned in clause (b) of sub-rule (3) of Rule 7, for participating in the Fund, such as scheduled commercial bank (other than regional rural bank) or public financial institutions [registered under Section 4-A of the Companies Act, 1956 (1 of 1956) or non-banking financial companies with the certificate of registration from Reserve Bank of India, registered under the category of non-deposit taking non-banking financial companies, Systemically Important Core Investment Company not raising public deposit or Infrastructure Finance Companies applying for guarantee facility under Partial Risk Guarantee Fund for Energy Efficiency. [Energy Conservation (Partial Risk Guarantee Fund for Energy Efficiency) Rules, 2016, R. 2(1)(s)].

Participating States. Means the States of Haryana, Rajasthan and Uttar Pradesh. [National Capital Region Planning Board Act (2 of 1985), S. 2(g)]

"PARTICIPATING STATES" means the parties participating in the Trade Expansion and Economic Co-operation Agreement concluded with India on the 23rd December, 1967. [Customs Tariff (Determination of Origin of the UAR and Yugoslavia) Rules, R. 1976, R. 3(a)]

Participation. Participation in a crime does not include mere consent, where no aid is given, and no encouragement rendered.

Participes plures sunt quasi unum corpus, in eo quod unum jus habent, et oportet quod corpus sit integrum et quod in nulla partesit defectus. (*Lat.*) (Co. Litt. 164a) Several partners are as one body, inasmuch as they have one right, and its necessary that the body be perfect, and that there be defect in no part.

Participient criminis. Sharer of crime.

Particular. *As an adjective*, sole, single, individual, specific; of or pertaining to a single person, class or thing, belonging to one only; not general, not common; hence personal, peculiar, singular. (*Webster*)

As a noun, a detail. *In the plural as a noun*, details; the details of a claim, or the separate items of an account; sometimes called a bill of particulars.

Distinctive among others of the same kind; specific; not general. [CrPC 1973 (2 of 1974), S. 407(1)(c)(ii)].

Particular instance. A special example cited to demonstrate the correctness or explain the significance of a proposition.

Particular knowledge. State or condition of understanding (something) which is special to a person. [Indian Evidence Act (1 of 1872), S. 15].

Particular lien. A lien upon specific property as security for the payment of a debt or the satisfaction of some other obligation arising out of a transaction or an agreement involving that property. [Indian Contract Act (9 of 1872), S. 170].

Particular temporary need. Particular and temporary needs may co-exist on a particular route. There may exist a temporary need for transport facilities on a particular route, even in case of permanent need for such facilities. *M.P.S. R.T. Corporation* v. *R.T. Authority*, AIR 1966 SC 156, 158.

Particulars. A statement that one has not heard the particulars of a transaction is contradicted by showing that he had heard the details. The words 'particulars' and 'details' are in fact synonymous, and in ordinary parlance convey the same meaning.

Actual details. [CrPC 1973 (2 of 1974), S. 407(1)(c)(ii)].

Parties. "PARTIES" means, unless the text otherwise indicates, parties to protocol. [Ozone Depleting Substances (Regulation and Control) Rules, 2000, R. 2(j)].

The words "parties" not confined to only plaintiffs and defendants in the suit but would include all those interested in the trust, the suit being representative in nature. R. *Venugopala Naidu* v. *Venkatarayulu Naidu Charities,* AIR 1990 SC 444. [CPC (5 of 1908), S. 92]

Parties concerned in such disputes. The words "the parties concerned in such dispute" in S. 145(1) CrPC 1973 (2 of 1974) must have been intended to extend to persons other than the actual disputants. *Ratan Singh* v. *Raghubir Singh,* AIR 1952 MB 165.

Parties interested. The expression 'parties interested' means those who are interested in the result of the suit and they need not be arraigned as defendants or plaintiffs. *Anadullah* v. *Lassa Beba,* AIR 1966 J&K 1, 7. [Arbitration Act (10 of 1940), S. 21]

Parties to the suit. 'Parties to the suit' in S. 47, CPC (5 of 1908), means 'parties who have been properly made parties in accordance with the provisions of the Code'.

The expression "parties to the suit" in S. 47, CPC (5 of 1908), clearly implies the parties opposed to each other.

Partisan. Strong adherent of a party, side or cause.

Partisan witness. A relative, though a partisan witness, may be a reliable witness. *Hari Ram* v. *State of U.P.,* (2004) 8 SCC 146, 153, para 22.

Even in the matter of the evidence of an accomplice corroboration is not required in every detail of the occurrence but corroboration in some of the material particulars alone might be sufficient to believe the evidence of the accomplice. In the case of a partisan witness it cannot be said that his evidence is tainted just as that of an accomplice. Some caution is of course required in the matter of the evidence of the partisan witness also, but the corroboration, may not be just of that type which is required in the case of an accomplice. Some corroboration in one or two material particulars inspire confidence in the evidence of a partisan witness. General observations made by the highest Courts are of course of great value, but it is the duty of the Court deciding a particular case to carefully examine the circumstances in the context of which those observations were laid down. In a bribery case it often becomes necessary to lay a trap and if simply on account of such a trap the evidence of the complainant and the police party is to be discarded, it would be very difficult to bring the offenders to book. Of course, as the complainant in a bribery case is interested like the complainants in other cases and the police officials are more or less anxious that the trap might succeed, it might be said that it is advisable that some corroboration from independent sources might be sought. But it cannot be said that in no case should the evidence of the complainant and the police officials of the raiding party be acted upon without corroboration. *Kishan Dayal* v. *State,* MLJ : QD (1956-1960) Vol. II C2852-2853 : 1958 Raj LW 596. [Evidence Act (1 of 1872), S. 133]

Simply because a witness is present when the amount to be offered as bribe is given to the complainant and is also present when the recovery is made, it cannot be held that he is to be taken as a partisan witness. It may happen by accident that both the events might take place in the presence of the same witness. It may also happen that some witnesses might be asked to witness the recovery of the amount of the bribery from the bribe-taker and thereafter the amount to be offered might be delivered by the officer in their presence to the complainant. *Kishan Dayal* v. *State,* MLJ : QD (1956-1960) Vol. II C2852 : 1958 Raj LW 596. [Evidence Act (1 of 1872), S. 133]

Partition. Act of dividing; state of being divided; division of an estate among the co-tenants in accordance with their shares in the estate. [Wealth-tax Act (27 of 1957), S. 20(1)].

The term "partition" in CPC (5 of 1908), S. 54 is not confined to the mere division of the lands into the requisite parts, but includes the delivery of the shares to their respective allottees.

Partition wall. "PARTITION WALL" means an interior non-load-bearing wall of storey or part storey weight. [W.B. Municipal (Building) Rules, 1996, R. 2(38)]

Partly. With respect to a part in some measure only and not wholly. [T.P. Act (4 of 1882), S. 58(d)].

Partner. Each of the persons who have entered into partnership with one another. [Indian Partnership Act (9 of 1932), S. 4].

Partner in a firm. [Indian Partnership Act (9 of 1932), S. 30(1); Collection of Statistics Act (32 of 1953), S. 9, ill. (b)].

Partners. Persons associated in the carrying on of a trade, industry or business jointly.

PARTNERS are where two or more persons agree to come into any trade or bargain in certain proportions agreed upon.

SLEEPING PARTNER. One who has money invested in a business, but takes no part in its management.

Partnership. "PARTNERSHIP" is the relation between persons who have agreed to share the profits of a business carried on by all or any of them acting for all. [Indian Partnership Act (9 of 1932), S. 4]

"PARTNERSHIP" is the relation which subsists between persons who have agreed to combine their property, labour or skill in some business, and to share the profits thereof between them. [Indian Contract Act (9 of 1872), S. 239 (*Repealed by Act 19 of 1932*) and VII Sch., list III, item 7, Constitution of India].

A partnership is a contract of two or more competent persons to place their money, effects, labour, and skill, or some or all of them, in lawful commerce or business and to divide the profit and bear the loss in certain proportions.

The members of a Hindu joint family carrying on a family business are not "partners" in view of the provisions of S. 5 of the Indian Partnership Act (9 of 1932).

Partnership and **co-ownership.** Co-ownership is not always the product of an agreement between the co-owners, whereas co-partnership can only come into existence by mutual agreement. *Hardayan Garodia* v. *Gangadhar Periwal,* AIR 1963 Cal 500, 503. [CPC (5 of 1908), O. XXI, R. 49]

Partnership at will. A partnership where no provision is made by contract between the partners for the duration or determination of their partnership. [Indian Partnership Act (9 of 1932), S. 7].

Partnership firm. 'Partnership firm' is an association of persons but every partner can have his own separate existence from the firm. *Shashi Kapila* v. *R.P. Ashwin,* (2002) 1 SCC 583, para 9.

Parts. Copies of an instrument which has been executed in as many identical copies as there are parties to it, each copy being treated as original and primary evidence of the transaction amongst the parties to it [Negotiable Instruments Act (26 of 1881),

S. 7]; the portions which along with other portion or portions make up a whole. [Indian Evidence Act (1 of 1872), S. 77].

Party. (*In practice*) A party to an action or suit is one who is directly interested in the subject matter in issue; who has set the Court in motion, or has a right to make a defence, control the proceedings, or appeal from the judgment.

"PARTY" means a party to an arbitration agreement. [Arbitration and Conciliation Act (26 of 1996), 2(1)(h)]

"PARTY" includes a consumer or an enterprise or a person or an information provider, or a consumer association or a trade association, or the Central Government or any State Government or any statutory authority, as the case may be, and shall include an enterprise or a person against whom any inquiry or proceeding is instituted; and any enterprise or person impleaded by the Commission to join the proceedings [Competition Act, 2002 (12 of 2003), section 2(ka)]

"PARTY" means a party to a works contract and includes its successors, executors, administrators or assignees. [Gujarat Public Works Contract Disputes Arbitration Tribunal Act (4 of 1992), S. 2(g)]

"PARTY" means a person who has signed an instrument as drawer, maker, acceptor, endorser or guarantor. [UN : Convention on International Bills of Exchange and International Promissory Notes, 1989 ILR 170, Art. 5(i)]

"PARTY" means a state which has consented to be bound by the treaty and for which the treaty is in force. [Vienna Convention on Succession of States in Respect of Treaties 1978, Art. 2(1)(g)]

'PARTY' means a state or any regional economic integration organization constituted by sovereign states which has competence in respect of the negotiation, conclusion and application of international agreements in matters covered by this convention for which this convention is in force. [Convention on the Conservation of Migratory Species of Wild Animals (1980), Art. I(k)]

A corporation may be a party as well as a natural person.

The word 'person' and 'party' and other word or words importing the singular number, shall be held to include firms, companies, associations and corporations.

A decree-holder by becoming a purchaser at a sale held in execution of his decree does not cease to be a party to the suit within the meaning of Section 47 of the CPC (5 of 1908).

The word 'party' in S. 9 of the Oaths Act (44 of 1969) includes a duly authourised agent, where a *vakalatnama* authorised a counsel to get statements recorded, to do *pairvi* in the case and to take such steps as he thought advisable and the client agrees to whatever he might do in the conduct of the case, the authority is sufficient to justify counsel, when no other step is open to him submitting the case to the test of oath of a man supposed to be honest.

Where in a suit the Court, instead of directing that a certain party should be struck out as having been improperly impleaded, erroneously makes an order dismissing suit as against him, such a person cannot properly be said to have been a party to that suit within the meaning of the Explanation to S. 47, CPC (5 of 1908).

The next friend of a minor plaintiff is not technically a party to the suit, but for the purpose of appointing a recognised agent to take some step in the suit the next friend is to be regarded as a party to the suit within the meaning of O. III, R. 1, CPC (5 of 1908).

Where a person is merely a *pro forma* party to the suit and has no dispute either with the plaintiff or defendant he is not a party interested in the suit.

The word 'party' is not confined to mean only a technical party in the suit or the appeal and in appropriate case, includes any beneficiary. *Jotindra Nath* v. *Jugal Chandra,* AIR 1966 Cal 637, 638. [CPC (5 of 1908), S. 144(1)]

When the word 'party' is used with reference to a proceeding in a Court, its primary meaning is a litigant. It means a person who has a part to play in the proceeding. *Sri Krishna* v. *Baijnath,* AIR 1953 All 698.

"PARTY" includes a person or a permanent establishment which participates or takes part in an arrangement. [(w.e.f. 1-4-2016) S. 102(6) of the Income-tax Act, 1961 (43 of 1961). Also see (still-born) Section 102(7) of the Income-tax Act, 1961 (43 of 1961) as inserted (w.e.f. 1-4-2014) by the Finance Act, 2012 (23 of 2012) and omitted (w.e.f. 1-4-2014) by the Finance Act, 2013 (17 of 2013)]

Party aggrieved. A party who has been injured or is having a grievance. [State Financial Corporations Act (63 of 1951), S. 32(9)].

Party, Appearance of. When the party is represented by a pleader, the test of the party's "appearance" whether he be present in person or not, is whether the pleader is in possession of full instructions to conduct the case, so far as it can be conducted at that hearing, and, if so whether he acts upon these instructions and does not either withdraw or demonstrate in some other manner his un-willingness to proceed further. If he does withdraw either expressly or constructively or reports no instructions, or otherwise ceases fully to represent his client, it makes no difference that the client may himself be present, unless it is clear that he assumes charge of his own case; because it may be assumed that a party who employs a pleader is not himself prepared, upon the pleader's withdrawal, to undertake his function.

Party in the case. If the State Government is impleaded to an appeal in the High Court as a contending party, it would be a party in the case and therefore if the decision is adverse to it, it would be entitled to appeal on the conditions mentioned in Art.

132. *State of U.P.* v. *Ram Swarup*, AIR 1974 SC 1570, 1578. [Constitution of India, Art. 132(3)]

Party interested. A person who makes a report or is injured on account of the commission of the crime or is related to the person injured or killed, does not thereby become a party interested. *N.C. Bose* v. *Probodh Dutta Gupta,* AIR 1955 Assam 116.

Party of the first part. A deed must be read according to the manifest intention of the parties, and if by mistake the words 'party of the first part' are written where 'party of the second part' should have been written, the mistake will not be permitted to defeat the intention of the parties, but the Court will give effect to the deed so as to carry out the intentions of the parties.

Party to an arrangement. For the purposes of Chapter X-A of Act 43 of 1961, a 'party to an arrangement' shall be an accommodating party, if the main purpose of the direct or indirect participation of that party in the arrangement, in whole or in part, is to obtain, directly or indirectly, a tax benefit (but for the provisions of Chapter X-A of Act 43 of 1961) for the assessee whether or not the party is a connected person in relation to any party to the arrangement. [(w.e.f. 1-4-2016) S. 97(3) of the Income-tax Act, 1961 (43 of 1961); (still-born) Section 97(3) of the Income-tax Act, 1961 (43 of 1961) as inserted (w.e.f. 1-4-2014) by the Finance Act, 2012 (23 of 2012) and omitted (w.e.f. 1-4-2014) by the Finance Act, 2013 (17 of 2013)]

Party to proceedings. It cannot be said that in a complaint proceeding the complainant and the accused are the only parties to the proceeding, a third party who intervenes and lays claim to the subject matter involved in those proceedings must also be regarded as a party to the proceeding for the Court has to adjudicate upon the title with regard to the subject matter. *Kachrulal* v. *P.H. Mawle,* AIR 1952 Hyd 7, 9.

Party to the proceeding. Any person whose involvement in the proceeding is such as to bind him by whatever may be the decision, determination or judgement in the case. [Indian Evidence Act (1 of 1872), S. 18].

Party wall. "PARTY WALL" means a wall forming part of a building and used or constructed to be used for the support or separation of adjoining buildings belonging to different owners, or constructed or adapted to be occupied by different persons. [Cantonments Act (2 of 1924), S. 2(xxvii)]

A party wall is a dividing wall between two houses to be used as an exterior wall for each.

A common or party wall is one which has been built at a common expense, or one which has been built by one party, but in which another has acquired an easement right. Every wall or separation between two buildings is presumed to be a common or party wall.

Pass. "PASS" means an authority given by a railway administration, or by an officer appointed by a railway administration in this behalf, and authorizing the person to whom it is given to travel as a passenger on a railway gratuitously. [Indian Railways Act (9 of 1890), S. 3(15)].

"PASS" means a duty, privilege or courtesy pass entitling the person to whom it is given to travel in a stage carrier gratuitously and includes a pass issued on payment for travel in a stage carrier for the period specified therein. [Motor Vehicles Act (59 of 1988), S. 124, *Expln.*(a)]

"PASS" means an authority given by the Central Government or a railway administration to a person allowing him to travel as a passenger, but does not include a ticket. [Railways Act (24 of 1989), S. 2(28)]

"PASS" means an authority given by the metro railway administration or by an officer appointed by that administration in this behalf, to a person allowing him to travel as a passenger on the metro railway, but does not include a ticket. [Delhi Metro Railway (Operation and Maintenance) Act (60 of 2002), S. 2(1)(n)]

To be allowed or approved by a Court or by a legislative or deliberative body; to be given or pronounced (in case of verdict, reference or judgement) [Companies (Profits) Surtax Act (7 of 1964), S. 11(4)]; to go by transfer or conveyance or to come by inheritance [Sale of Goods Act (3 of 1930), S. 26]; permit, ticket or order allowing one free transportation or free admission [Central Excises and Salt Act (1 of 1944), S. 25(b)] [Now repealed by Act 12 of 2017].

The word 'passing' used of notes, includes any delivery of a note to another, for value, with intent that it shall be put into circulation as money, and does not necessarily import that the notes are transferred as genuine.

'To pass counterfeit money' means delivery as money, or as known and conventional substitute for money, and does not necessarily mean to transfer for a valuable consideration received from the person to whom the bill is given.

The plain or ordinary and usual sense of the word 'pass,' as applied to coin or bank notes, is to deliver in exchange for something else, and is equally expressed by the words 'sell,' 'exchange', or 'deliver.'

In a written agreement for an exchange of real estate and other property, and providing that one of the parties should pay the taxes on his land up to passing of papers, the 'passing of papers' meant the execution and delivery of formal conveyances securing to each the title contracted for.

Pass book. "PASS BOOK" means a book issued by a bank reflecting the deposit of gold tendered under the Scheme and its withdrawal. [Gold Deposit Scheme, 1999, S. 2(v).]

A passbook used by a depositor in a savings bank is not negotiable paper, such as to justify the payment of the amount of the deposit to one having possession of the passbook.

A passbook is a book of the buyer or usually debtor party, in which he allows the other party to enter their mutual transactions, and thus these entries become in a great degree the written admissions of both parties. Whatever is entered there by one party is entered with the other's consent.

Pass judgment. Deliver judgment.

Pass sentence. Give decision and prescribe punishment in a criminal case.

Passage. A means or way of passing [Indian Railways Act (9 of 1890), S. 7(1)(a)]; [Delhi Municipal Corporation Act (66 of 1957), S. 2(57)]; a continuous but indefinite portion of a bank [Copyright Act (14 of 1957), S. 52(g)]; a portion of a writing [Indian Succession Act (39 of 1925), S. 102, ill. (ii)].

Passage benefit is not property. It is at best a right which the employee may be entitled to so long as he is in service and on terms as stated in the Statutory Rules. *N. Baksi* v. *Advocate General,* AIR 1957 Pat 515, 528.

Passage, Free. Unimpeded passage; to allow to pass without constraints. [Indian Easements Act (5 of 1882), S. 17(b)].

Passenger. "PASSENGER" includes any person carried in a mechanically propelled vessel other than the master and crew and the owner, his family and servant. [Inland Vessels Act (1 of 1917), S. 2(d)]

The word 'PASSENGER' occurring in Section 95(2) of the Motor Vehicles Act, cannot be held to be limited to the case of a person who travels in the vehicle either by remaining seated in the seating accommodation provided or by standing in vehicles where travel by standing is specially permitted. [Motor Vehicles Act (4 of 1939), S. 95(2)(b)(ii)]

"PASSENGER" means any person carried on board a ship except—

(a) a person employed or engaged in any capacity on board the ship on the business of the ship;

(b) a person on board the ship either in pursuance of the obligation laid upon the master to carry shipwrecked, distressed or other persons or by reason of any circumstances which neither the master nor the charterer, if any, could have prevented or forestalled;

(c) a child under one year of age. [Merchant Shipping Act (44 of 1958), S. 3(24)]

'PASSENGER' means any person travelling on a railway in any description or class of train or carriage on payment of his fare, whether at full rates or at concessional rates. [Railway Passengers Fares Act (46 of 1971), S. 2(b)]

"PASSENGER" mean any person boarding, at any aerodrome, an aircraft for performing an inland journey, but does not include,—

(i) a person who performs an iland journey on a through international ticket and which precedes, or forms part of a series of journeys preceding, or follows, or forms part of a series of journey following, a journey to or from a place outside India on the same ticket; or

(ii) a person employed or engaged in any capacity on board the aircraft on the business thereof. [Finance Act (13 of 1989), S. 41(f)]

For the purposes of this section "PASSENGER" includes a railway servant on duty. [Railways Act (24 of 1989), S. 124, *Expln.*]

"PASSENGER" includes—

(i) a railway servant on duty; and

(ii) a person who has purchased a valid ticket for travelling, by a train carrying passengers, on any date or a valid platform ticket and becomes a victim of an untoward incident. [Railways Act (24 of 1989), S. 124A *Expln.*]

One, who travels in some vessel or vehicle; a traveller by any public vehicles entered by fare.

One who enters upon depot grounds by the approaches furnished by the carrier is a passenger. The fare does not have to be paid, nor the train entered, but the person must merely enter within the control of the carrier at the depot through the usual channels of business, with intention of becoming a passenger by either paying fare before or after entering the train.

One who has railroad ticket and is present to take the train at the ordinary point of departure, is a passenger, though he has not entered the cars.

One in good faith coming to the depot to take passage on the cars is a passenger, though he has not bought a ticket.

Where one in good faith inquired of a railroad agent for a ticket for passage in a freight train, and was referred to the conductor, but was injured before getting upon the train, held, that the relation of passenger was established.

Where an employee of a railroad company, whose duties are not connected with the running of its trains, rides on one of its trains on a free pass, and is injured, the company is liable to him as to a passenger.

A bonafide passenger is one who travels on the basis of a pass or ticket or some other express or implied authority of Railway Administration. *Yashoda Devi* v. *UOI,* AIR 1979 All 287, 292. [Indian Railways Act (9 of 1890), S. 82-A]

A trespasser or a person travelling without ticket, pass or authority is not a passenger. *Sundri* v. *UOI,* AIR 1984 All 277, 278.

A Railway servant on duty is not a passenger. *Ram Ekbal Prasad* v. *UOI,* AIR 1988 Pat 130, 132.

PASSENGER, in the Indian Railways Act (9 of 1890), S. 118, is used in a restricted sense of denoting a person who, without the permission of a railway servant, enters any carriage of a railway for the purpose of travelling therein as a passenger.

The expression "passenger" in S. 109, Indian Railways Act (9 of 1890) includes a class of passengers.

Passenger ship. Means a ship carrying more than twelve passengers. [Merchant Shipping Act (44 of 1958), S. 3(25)]

Passenger train. "PASSENGER TRAIN" means a train intended solely or mainly for the carriage of passengers and other coaching traffic. [Railways Red Tariff Rules, 1960, S. 2(n)]

Passes. It means "changes hands". Where the *muafi* held by a person lapsed on his death it is not properly "passing" on his death. *Controller of Estate Duty* v. *Usha Devi Patankar,* AIR 1969 MP 229 at 232. [Estate Duty Act (34 of 1953), S. 5(1)]

Only when there is a change or shifting of beneficial possession or enjoyment of trust property from one person to another, the property settled 'passes on death'. *Mahendra* v. *Controller of Estate Duty,* AIR 1965 Guj 9, 17.

Passing of decree. The expression 'THE PASSING OF A DECREE' will mean 'the passing of a judgment'. *Balabhadra Pradhan* v. *Sundariwani Devi,* AIR 1995 Ori 180, 183. [Hindu Marriage Act (25 of 1955), S. 13(1-A)(ii)]

Passing off. The wrong committed by a person who sells goods or carries on business, *etc.* under such a name, mark, description or otherwise in such a manner as to mislead the public into believing that the goods or business *etc.* is that of another person. [Trade and Merchandise Marks Act (43 of 1958), S. 27(2)] [Now repealed & replaced by Act 47 of 1999].

The passing off doctrine operates on the general principle that no person is entitled to represent his or her business as business of other person. [*S. Syed Mohideen v. P. Sulochana Bai*, (2016) 2 SCC 683, para 32].

Passing to the buyer. Being actually transferred (from the seller) to the buyer [T.P. Act (4 of 1882), S. 55(4)(a)].

Passion. Any overpowering emotion. [Excep. 1, ill. (a), IPC (45 of 1860), S. 300].

Passive attack. A form of attack in which data is released (captured or obtained) from the target system. Attack that does not result in an unauthorized state change, such as an attack that only monitors and/or records data. (*Cyber Law*)

Passive personality principle of jurisdiction. Jurisdiction based on the nationality or national character of the person injured by the offense. (*Cyber Law*)

Passive threat. The threat of unauthorized disclosure of information without changing the state of the system. A type of threat that involves the interception, not the alteration, of information. (*Cyber Law*)

Passive trust. A trust in which the trustee has no active duty to perform.

Passive Website. A Website that transmits information only and doesn't solicit business. (*Cyber Law*)

Passport. "PASSPORT" includes a passport which having been issued by or under the authority of the government of a foreign country satisfies the conditions prescribed under the Passport (Entry into India) Act, 1920 (34 of 1920), in respect of the class of passports to which it belongs. [Passports Act (15 of 1967), S. 3, *Expln.* (a)]

Official document showing traveller's identity and commending him to protection in other countries.

A document issued by the Government to a citizen, certifying his status, to be used while travelling abroad.

A licence to go to a port or town or from one country to another. [Constitution of India, VII Sch., List I, item 19].

Passport is a document of identify, it is a *prima facie* evidence of nationality, controlling not only exit from the state to which one belongs but without it, with a few exceptions, it is not possible to enter another state. *Satwant Singh* v. *A.P.O. New Delhi*, AIR 1967 SC 1836, 1841.

Passport Authority. Means an officer or authority empowered under rules made under this Act to issue passports or travel documents and includes the Central Government. [Passports Act (15 of 1967), S. 2(c)]

Passport Seva Laghu Kendra. Means a small passport application processing centre under the Passport Seva Project. [Passports Application (Facilitation and Processing) Rules, 2010, R. 2(b)].

Password. (*Milit.*) Selected word or phrase distinguishing friends from enemies.

Watch word or countersign or secret word.

Confidential authentication information usually composed of a string of characters used to provide access to a computer resource. (*Information Technology*)

A code used to gain access (*login*) to a locked system. Good passwords contain letters and non-letters and are not simple combinations such as *virtue 7.* A good password might be : 5%df(29). But don't use that one! (*Matisse Enzer-Glossary of Internet Terms*)

A code used to gain access to a locked system. Good passwords contain letters and non-letters and are not simple combinations such as virtue 7. At good password might be: 27 rasgullas! [A 'Rasgulla' is a type of Indian sweet.] *See also*: Login. (*Internet and E-Commerce*)

"IMPOUNDING OF A PASSPORT". Can only be done by the passport authority under section 10(3) of the Passports Act, 1967. *Suresh Nanda* v. *CBI*, AIR 2008 SC 1414.

Password cracking/password theft. Password cracking is a technique used to surreptitiously gain system access by using another users account. Users often select weak password. The two major sources of weakness in passwords are easily guessed passwords based on knowledge of the user (wife's maiden name) and passwords that are susceptible to dictionary attacks (brute-force guessing of passwords using a dictionary as the source of guesses). Password cracking and theft is a technique in which attackers try to guess or steal passwords to obtain access to computer systems. Attackers have automated this technique; rather than attackers trying to guess legitimate users' passwords, computers can very efficiently and systematically do the guessing. For example, if the password is a dictionary word, a computer can quickly look up all possibilities to find a match. Complex passwords comprised of alphanumeric characters are more difficult to crack. However, even with complex passwords, powerful computers can use brute force to compare all possible combinations of characters until a match is found. (*Cyber Law*)

Password sniffing. A form of sniffing that entails sampling specific portions of the data stream during a session (collecting a certain number of initial bytes where the password can be intercepted in unencrypted form on common Internet services) so as to obtain password data that can then be exploited. (*Cyber Law*)

Pasteurised milk. Pasteurised is a process consisting in heating milk to temperature which destroys nearly all the microorganisms present without seriously affecting its composition or properties. *Narani Dass Daulaat Ram* v. *State of Haryana,* AIR 1978 P&H 310, 316. [Essential Commodities Act (10 of 1955), S. 3]

Pasture. To feed on growing grass or herbage. [Indian Forest Act (16 of 1927), S. 26(d)].

Patent. "PATENT" means a patent granted under the provisions of the Patents and Designs. [Patents and Designs Act (2 of 1911), S. 2(11)]

The word 'patent' means the exclusive privilege granted by the sovereign authority to an inventor with respect to his invention.

A grant from the government to a person or persons conferring for a certain definite time the exclusive privilege of making, using or selling some new invention. [CPC (5 of 1908), 1st Sch., App. F, Form No. 8].

Patent agent. "PATENT AGENT" means a person for the time being registered under this Act as a patent agent. [Patents Act (39 of 1970), S. 2(n)]

"An agent registered and authorised to conduct all proceedings in all matters relating to patents on behalf of the applicant. (*Patents*)

Patent ambiguity. A patent ambiguity is that which appears ambiguous on the face of the deed or instrument.

PATENT AMBIGUITY AND LATENT AMBIGUITY. A patent ambiguity is one which arises solely from the terms of the instrument, while a latent ambiguity is one not appearing on the face of the instrument, but which is developed by extrinsic evidence.

"Patent article" and "patented process". Mean respectively an article or process in respect of which a patent. [Patents Act (39 of 1970), S. 2(o)]

Patent Attorney. One specializing in the preparation of patent applications and in the search to determine that the invention is new and does not infringe on previous patents. (*Patents*)

Patent Cooperation Treaty. Means the Patent Cooperation Treaty done at Washington on the 19th day of June, 1970 as amended and modified from time to time. [Patents Act (39 of 1970), S. 2(oa)]

Patent defect. Plainly and obviously visible defect.

Patent error. Error open to view, readily visible or intelligible; evident error. [Ancient Monuments and Archaeological Sites and Remains Act (24 of 1958), S. 36].

A 'patent error' is an error which is self-evident which can be perceived or demonstrated without involving into any lengthy or complicated argument or a long-drawn process of reasoning where two inferences are reasonably possible, and the subordinate Court has chosen to take one view, the error cannot be called gross or patent. *Surya Dev Rai* v. *Ram Chander Rai*, (2003) 6 SCC 675, para 38(6) : AIR 2003 SC 675.

Patent of addition. 'PATENT OF ADDITION' means a patent granted in accordance with Section 54. [Patents Act (39 of 1970), S. 2(1)(q)]. *See also* Income-tax Act (43 of 1961), S. 80 RRB, Expln.(e).

Patent or proprietary medicine. Means,—

(i) in relation to Ayurvedic, Siddha or Unani Tibb systems of medicines all formulation, containing only such ingredients mentioned in the formulae described in the authoritative books of Ayurveda, Siddha or Unani Tibb systems of medicine specified in the first Schedule, but does not include a medicine which is administered by parenteral route and also a formulation included in the authoritative books as specified in Clause (a);

(ii) in relation to any other systems of medicine, a drug which is a remedy or prescription presented in a form ready for internal or external administration of human beings or animals and which is not included in the edition of the Indian Pharmacopœia authorised in this behalf by the Central Government after consultation with The Drugs Technical Advisory Board Constituted under S. 5. [Drugs and Cosmetics Act (23 of 1940), S. 3(h)]

Patent right. A patent right in its usual significance means a privilege granted by the government to the first inventor of a new and useful discovery or mode of manufacture that he shall be entitled during a limited period to the exclusive use and benefit thereof.

Patented article. Includes any article made by a patented process. [Patents Act (39 of 1970), S. 82(a)]

"Patented article" and "Patented process". Means respectively an article or process in respect of which a patent is in force. [Patents Act (39 of 1970), S. 2(o)]

Patentee. "PATENTEE" means the person, being the true and first inventor of the invention, whose name is entered on the patent register as the patentee, in accordance with the Patents Act, 1970, (39 of 1970) and includes every such person, being the true and first inventor of the invention, where more than one person is registered as patentee under that Act in respect of that patent. [Income-tax Act (43 of 1961), S. 80 RRB, *Expln* (d)].

"PATENTEE" means the person for the time being entered on the register as the grantee or proprietor of the patent. [Patents Act (39 of 1970), S. 2(p)]

"PATENTEE" includes an exclusive licensee. [Patents Act (39 of 1970), S. 82(b)]

Paternity. The state or condition of being father biologically.

Paternity proceeding. A Court proceeding to determine whether a particular person is the father of a child born out of wedlock.

Paternity test. The test to determine whether a particular person is a biological father of a particular child. The test involves DNA identification or tissue typing.

Patha-Samiti (Board of Studies). Means a Board constituted by the University for the regulation of studies. [Visva-Bharati Act (29 of 1951), S. 3(n)]

Patient. One who is under medical treatment. [Representation of the People Act (43 of 1950), S. 20(2)].

In the law relating to insane persons in lunatic asylums the word *Patient* means any person detained and taken care of as an insane person in the asylum.

Patriarch. Father or ruler of a family or tribe.

Patrimony. A hereditary estate or right descended from ancestors.

Patriotic purpose. The expression 'patriotic purpose' even if it be confined to purposes beneficial to the state, is not necessarily confined to charitable purposes and a gift for 'patriotic purposes' is so uncertain as to be void. *Laxman Balwant* v. *Charity Commissioner Bombay*, AIR 1962 SC 1589, 1599. [Bombay Public Trusts Act (19 of 1950), Sections. 2(13), 9(4), 11]

Patriotism. Love of one's country.

Patronage. "PATRONAGE" means the use of services offered by the Producer Company to its Members by participation in its business activities. [Companies Act (1 of 1956), S. 581A(h)); Companies Act (18 of 2013), section 378A(h)]

The action of a patron in supporting, encouraging or countenancing a person, institution *etc.*; the financial support given by customers in making use of a commercial concern.

Patronage bonus. Means payments made by a Producer Company out of its surplus income to the Members in proportion to their respective patronage. [Companies Act (1 of 1956), S. 581(A)(i)]

Patta. *(Tel.)* A measure of land in the northern *Sirkars*. [P. Ramanath Aiyar's, *The Law Lexicon*, 2017, LexisNexis]

"PATTA" shall have the same meaning as assigned to it in the relevant Central or State Acts or Rules or Regulations made thereunder. [S. 3(w) of the Right to Fair Compensation & Transparency in Land Acquisition, Rehabilitation & Resettlement Act, 2013 (30 of 2013)]

Pattern. Something designed or used as a model for making things; order.

Patti. Patti/pati has various contextual connotations including a strip of land detached from the original village though dependent on it; it is a sub-division of land. [*Sarjeet Singh* v. *Hari Singh*, (2015) 1 SCC 760, para 6].

Pauper. Defined, Act 5, 1908, Sch. I, O. XXXIII. R 1, *Expln*. I.

A person destitute of means except as are derived from charity; one allowed to sue in *forma pauperis*.

A pauper, is a poor person especially one so indigent as to depend on charity for maintenance or one supported by some public provision; one so poor that he must be supported at public expense. The words 'pauper' and 'poor' have nearly the same meaning and they both embrace several classes.

A very poor person.

Pauper leper. Means a leper—

(a) who publicity solicits alms or exposes or exhibits any sores, wounds, bodily ailment or deformity with the object of exciting charity or of obtaining alms, or

(b) who is at large without any ostensible means of subsistence. [Lepers Act (3 of 1898), S. 2(2)]

Pawn. A pledge or gage for payment of money lent. (*Tomlin*)

A thing given, deposited or left in another's keeping as a security for a debt or for the performance of some action. [IPC (45 of 1860), S. 378, ill. (k)].

The term 'pawn' is used in Art. 6(2) of the Indian Stamp Act (2 of 1899) in a much wider sense than it is used in S. 172 of the Indian Contract Act (9 of 1872). It covers contracts whereby all kinds of chattels and choses in action are made security for payment of a debt. No contract will however amount to a contract of pawn unless possession either actual or constructive is delivered to the pawnee.

Pawn and Lien. The contract of *pawn* is to be distinguished from a lien under which there is a mere right to retain possession by way of security and from a mortgage, in which (according to English law) the whole title in the property mortgaged is conveyed to the mortgagee (subject to the mortgagor's equity of redemption), and upon which possession may or may not be given to him.

Pawn-broker. One who lends money on goods which he receives on pledge.

PAWN BROKERS are persons who loan money in small sums on security of personal property.

A pawn-broker is one who pursues the business of lending money upon interest and receiving upon deposit as security for the payment of such loan and interest any personal property.

A pawnbroker has none of the characteristics of a broker and is not an agent at all. He contracts in his own name, has no employer, charges no brokerage, and always takes possession of the property. Neither does he deal in money, notes, and bills of exchange, like brokers, and his business is to lend money on the security of personal property pawned or left with him. The verbal coincidence of the last two syllables of the longer word being 'broker' is purely fortuitous, for a pawn-broker is not a broker at all. (*Ame. Words and Phrases*)

Pawn or pledge. A bailment of goods by a debtor to his creditor, to be kept till the debt is discharged.

A *pawn* or pledge is a bailment of personal property as a security for some debt or other engagement.

A pledge or pawn is property deposited with another as security for the payment of a debt.

Pawnee. The bailment of goods as security for payment of a debt or performance of a promise is called "pledge". The bailee is called the "pawnee". [Indian Contract Act (9 of 1872), S. 172]

"Pawnor" and "Pawnee". The bailment of goods as security for payment of a debt or performance of a promise is called "pledge". The bailor in this case is called the "pawnor". The bailee is called the "pawnee". [Indian Contract Act (9 of 1872), S. 172].

Pay. 'PAY' means basic pay plus special pay if any, sanctioned to a post but does not include various allowances. [Mulki Rules Act (79 of 1972), S. 2(h)]

PAY. The word "pay" in its ordinary significance in relation to service means "to give what is due for service done". Though in service jurisprudence, the term pay is assigned a definite connotation and is inclusive of various components and it includes pay, personal pay and special pay. [Oxford Dictionary as cited in *Association of Personal Assistants Private Secretaries and Senior Private Secretaries, High Court, Bombay . v The State of Maharashtra* Writ Petition 2134 of 2014, decided on 31-1-2018, para 14]

'PAY' means the amount drawn monthly by a government servant as—

(i) the pay, other than special pay or pay granted in view of his personal qualifications which has been sanctioned for a post held by him substantively or in an officiating capacity, or to which he is entitled by reason of his position in a cadre, and

(ii) overseas pay, special pay and personal pay, and

(iii) any other emoluments which may be specially classed as pay by the President. [Fundamental Rule, 9(21)]

'PAY' means basic wages, with dearness allowance, retaining allowance and cash value of food concessions admissible, if any. [Employer's Pension Scheme, 1995, S. 2(xiii)]

All sums payable to a man in respect of his services other than allowance; money paid for labour or service; to make payment.

The word 'pay' in its ordinary significance in relation to service means "to give what is due for services done". *SBI* v. *K.P. Subbaiah*, (2003) 11 SCC 646, 654, para 16.

"PAY" for the purpose of Pension, dearness allowance and special allowances do not form part of 'pay'. *N. D. P. Namboodripad* v. *UOI*, AIR 2007 SC 1782 : 2007 AIR SCW 2972.

Pay channel. "pay channel", in respect of a cable television network, means a channel for which subscription fees is to be paid to the broadcaster by the cable operator and due authorisation needs to be taken from the broadcaster for its re-transmission on cable [Cable Television Networks (Regulation) Act (7 of 1995), S. 4A Explanation (e)]

Pay load. 'PAY LOAD' in respect of a good vehicle means the registered laden weight less the unladen weight of the vehicle. [Gujarat Carriage of Goods Taxation Act (Guj Act No. 23 of 1962), S. 2(d)]

Payable. What is to be paid under any liability; liable to be paid. [T.P. Act (4 of 1882), S. 57(a)].

The word 'payable' is a descriptive word, meaning 'capable of being paid; suitable to be paid; admitting or demanding payment; justly due; legally enforceable.'

The term 'payable' means money payable in future on ascertainment under a decree passed by Court. *Selvambal Ammal* v. *Venkataram,* AIR 1966 Mad 460, 461. [CPC (5 of 1908), O. XXI, R. 1]

"PAYABLE" the term 'payable' in the context of the language of rule 4(1) of the Customs Valuation (Determination of Price of Imported Goods) Rules, 1988, must be read as referring to 'the particular transaction' and payability in respect of the transaction envisages a situation where payment of price may be deferred. *Commissioner of Customs* v. *Bureau Veritas*, AIR 2005 SC 1292.

Payable on demand. The words "payable on demand" occurring in a promissory note mean payable "at once".

Payable at once, forthwith or immediately. [CPC (5 of 1908), S. 20, ill. (b)].

Payable to bearer. A negotiable instrument is payable to bearer when it is drawn in favour of bearer or order of bearer or a specified person or bearer.

Payee. The person named in the instrument, to whom or to whose order the money is by the instrument directed to be paid, is called the "PAYEE." [Negotiable Instruments Act (26 of 1881), S. 7].

The person to whom a sum of money is to be paid; the person in whose favour a negotiable instrument has been drawn.

The term 'payee,' in a non-negotiable note providing that the failure to pay interest when due, at the election of the payee, should make the principal and interest at once due, would include an assignee of the instrument.

Paying capacity. The expression "PAYING CAPACITY" means the aggregate of the market value of all the attachable assets in India of the displaced debtor plus the income which is likely to accrue to him for the next three years succeeding, excluding from the computation of such income a sum calculated at the rate of two hundred and fifty rupees a month. [Displaced Persons (Debts Adjustment) Act (70 of 1951), S. 32(10) *Expln.*]

Paying debt, In. In satisfying the debt by payment. [Indian Partnership Act (9 of 1932), S. 48(b)(i)].

Paying guest. 'PAYING GUEST' means a person, not being a member of the family, who is given a part of the premises, in which the licensor resides on licence.

Paying-in slip. A printed form on which particulars and details of the amount are written when a customer pays a sum into a bank, indicating how it is made up.

Paying off. Paying any debt in full. [T.P. Act (4 of 1882), S. 93].

Payment. "PAYMENT" means payment in money's worth but does not include any payment for defraying or reimbursing—

(i) The cost of removing, transporting or preserving the human organ to be supplied; or

(ii) any expenses or loss of earnings incurred by a person so far as reasonably and directly attributable to his supplying any human organ from his body. [Transplantation of Human Organs Act (42 of 1994), S. 2(k)]

The act of paying. [IPC (45 of 1860), S. 64]; that which is paid [T.P. Act (4 of 1882), S. 36]; the action or an act of rendering to a person anything due or discharging an obligation.

(1) The act of paying. (2) Pay; requital; recompense. [Webster's Comprehensive Dictionary (International Edn.) Vol. 2 as cited in *Himachal Pradesh Housing and Urban Development Authority* v. *Ranjit Singh Rana*, (2012) 4 SCC 505, para 13].

The action of paying or the process of being paid (2) An amount paid or payable. [Concise Oxford English Dictionary (10th Edn., Revised) as cited in *Himachal Pradesh Housing and Urban Development Authority* v. *Ranjit Singh Rana*, (2012) 4 SCC 505, para 12].

Payment for honour. Payment of a protested bill or draft by someone other than the primary debtor made with the purpose of saving the credit of such debtor. [Negotiable instruments Act (26 of 1881), S. 101(f)].

Payment has actually been made. Means the actual payment of expenditure irrespective of the previous year in which the liability for the expenditure was incurred according to the method of accounting regularly employed by the assessee. [Income-tax Act (43 of 1961), S. 35ABB(1) *Expln. (i)*]

Payment in due course. "PAYMENT IN DUE COURSE" means payment in accordance with the apparent tenor of the instrument in good faith and without negligence to any person in possession thereof under circumstances which do not afford a reasonable ground for believing that he is not entitled to receive payment of the amount therein mentioned. [Negotiable Instruments Act (26 of 1881), S. 10].

Payment into Court. Means deposit into Court to the credit of the creditor party. A payment into Court is an admission of an indebtedness to the extent of the payment.

Payment by deposit with the Court. [CPC (5 of 1908), O. XXIV].

Payment out of. The words 'payment out of' when used in connection with the word 'fund' connote actual payment by taking the money out of the drawer or drawing a cheque on the bank. *R.K. Dalmia* v. *Delhi Administration*, AIR 1962 SC 1821, 1834.

Payment supra protest. A payment made after protest has been made denying all or part liability.

Payment towards principal and interest. Of a debt is to be treated as open payment.

Payout ratio. Ratio between the dividends per share and earning per share of a corporation.

Payroll. Paymaster's list of those entitled to wages or salary.

PC Card. A hardware token complaint with standards promulgated by the Personnel Computer Memory Card International Association (PCMCIA) providing expansion capabilities to computers, including the facilitation of information security. (*Information Technology*)

PCS. (*abbr.*) Pre-Carrier Selection. Registration of a subscriber with a TSP other than the one connecting him to the fixed telephone network. This registration allows the subscriber to telephone "by default" via the first TSP without resorting to his CSC. However, this option does not prevent the subscriber from using the CSCs of other competitors. (*Telecommunication*)

PDA. *Personal Digital Assistant*. Small, handheld devices which typically integrate with computers. The Psion and Palm product ranges include examples. A portable organiser, increasingly with Internet access and e-mail functions. (*Cyber Law*)

PDF. (*abbr.*) Portable Document Format. A file format designed to enable printing and viewing of documents with all their formatting (typefaces, images, layout, *etc.*) appearing the same regardless of what operating system is used, so a PDF document should look the same on Windows, Macintosh, Linux, OS/2, *etc.* The PDF format is based on the widely used postscript document-description language. Both PDF and Postscript were developed by the Adobe Corporation. (*Matisse Enzer-Glossary of Internet Terms*)

Peaceable possession. Peaceable possession is such as continues and is not interrupted by adverse suits to recover the estate.

Peaceably and openly enjoy. To enjoy in a peaceable and friendly manner, without strife or contention. [Limitation Act (36 of 1963), S. 25(1)].

Peat. A piece of turf cut for use as fuel. [Indian Forest Act (16 of 1927), S. 2(4)(b)(iv)].

Peccata contra naturam sunt gravissima. Crimes against nature are the most heinous. (*Latin for Lawyers*)

Whoever voluntarily has carnal intercourse against the order of nature with any man, woman, or animal, shall be punished under law.

Peccatum peccato addit qui culpae quam facit petrocinium defensionis adjungit. He adds fault to fault when he sets up his own wrongdoing as a defence. (*Latin for Lawyers*)

Pecuniary. Monetary; relating to money; consisting of money.

Of, belonging to, or having relation to money [IPC (45 of 1860), S. 161 (*Omitted*), *Expln.*]; in the form of money [Form No. 39(5), CPC (5 of 1908), 1st Sch., App. A].

Pecuniary ability. Where an Act provides that divorce may be decreed on petition of the wife when the husband, 'being of sufficient pecuniary ability to provide suitable maintenance for her, refuses or neglects to do so.' *Held*, that the words 'pecuniary ability,' as so used, mean the possession of property with which to furnish her maintenance, and do not include his capacity for acquiring property by means of labour.

Pecuniary bequest. A bequest of money.

Pecuniary compensation. A compensation in the form of money.

Pecuniary damage. 'Pecuniary' is a term of much narrower scope in the law of damages than the word 'necessary.' The latter embraces all those consequences of an injury usually denominated 'general damages' as distinguished from 'special damages,' whereas 'pecuniary' damages cover a smaller class of damages within the larger class of general damages.

Pecuniary demonstrative legacy. In order to constitute a pecuniary demonstrative legacy, two things are necessary: (1) There must be a gift of certain sum of money; (2) with reference to a particular fund as a primary, but not exclusive, source of payment.

Pecuniary jurisdiction. A jurisdiction as limited by the value of the subject-matter of the suit.

Pecuniary legacy. An annuity given by a will, whatever may be the direction as to the mode of its payment, is a 'pecuniary legacy.'

Pecuniary legatee. A receiver of money under a will. [CPC (5 of 1908), 1st Sch., App. A, Form No. 43].

Pecuniary liability. The words 'pecuniary liability' will cover any liability which is of a monetary nature. *Kaushalya Devi* v. *Pritam Sing*, AIR 1960 SC 1030, 1031. [Displaced persons (Debts Adjustment) Act (70 of 1951), S. 2(6)(c)]

Pecuniary limitation. Limits in terms of money. [CPC (5 of 1908), S. 16].

Pecuniary loss. A loss of money or of something having monetary value.

Pedigree. The term 'pedigree' means the 'lineage, descent, or succession of families.'

The term 'pedigree' embraces not only general questions of descent and relationship, but also the particular facts of birth, marriage, and death, and the times, when, either absolutely or relatively, these events happened, provided such facts are required to be proved for some genealogical purpose. (*Taylor on Evidence*)

Pedigree, Family. The origin and history of the family. A history of family succession.

Pelletisation. Means a process whereby pellets are prepared which are small cubes or cylindrical pieces made out of solid wastes and includes fuel pellets which are also referred as refuse derived fuel. [Municipal Solid Wastes (Management and Handling) Rules, 2000, R.3 (xvii).

Penal. Pertaining to punishment and penalty.

Penal action. A penal action is an action on a statute which gives a certain penalty to be recovered by any person who will sue for the same.

A penal action is one allowed in pursuance of public justice under particular laws.

An action for libel or slander is in the nature of a penal action.

Penal code. A systematic collection of legal provisions laying down penalties for various kinds of offences or transgressions.

Penal interest. The expression 'Penal interest' means an extraordinary liability incurred by a debtor on account of his being a wrongdoer of not making the payment in time and it may be charged only once for one period of default. *Central Bank of India* v. *Ravindra*, (2002) 1 SCC 367, para 38.

Penal law. A penal law is a statute which imposes a penalty.

A law providing for the punishment of offences.

Penal statute. A penal statute is one which imposes a pecuniary penalty or other punishment for an offence.

Penal sum. A penalty or penal sum is a sum of money payable as an equivalent for an injury.

Money payable as penalty. [CPC (5 of 1908), 1st Sch., App. A, Form No. 18(2)].

Penalty. (*In Contract*) Penalty is a liability composed as a punishment on the party committing the breach of contract. Agreement to pay at default interest at a higher rate does not amount to penalty.

(*In Criminal law*) A penalty is a punishment inflicted by a law for its violation.

'PENALTY' AND 'FINE' are not the same in law. A penalty is always recoverable in a civil action. A fine never is a penalty, when recovered, goes to the party suing; a fine, to the state. A fine is defined in law to be a pecuniary punishment imposed by a lawful tribunal upon a person convicted of a crime or misdemeanor. This definition is wholly inapplicable to a judgment in a civil suit.

The expression 'penalty' is a word of wide significance. Sometimes, it means recovery of an amount as a penal measure even in civil proceedings. An exaction which is not compensatory in character is also termed as a penalty. When penalty is imposed by an adjudicating officer, it is done so in 'adjudicatory proceedings' and not by way of fine as a result of prosecution of an accused for commission of an offence in a criminal Court. *Director of Enforcement* v. *MCTM Corpn. Pvt. Ltd.*, AIR 1996 SC 1100, 1104.

Penalty and forfeiture. The noun 'penalty' is defined 'forfeiture' or a sum to be forfeited for non-compliance with an agreement; a fine. (*Worcester*) These definitions show that in one sense, the words 'forfeit' and 'penalty' are substantially synonymous.

Penalty and punishment. 'Penalty' is synonymous with 'punishment,' in connection with crimes and is fixed by the law defining the criminal act.

Penalty of death. When the words 'penalty of death' are used, they are understood, in a somewhat figurative sense, to signify the forfeiture of life. It is less usual to say the penalty of imprisonment.

Pendency. State or condition of being pending or being undecided.

Pendente lite. A purchaser *pendente lite* is one who by purchase acquires an interest in the matter in litigation pending the suit.

Pending the law suit; during the actual progress of a suit; during litigation. (*Black*)

Matters "pendente lite" are contingent on outcome of litigation.

Pendente lite nihil innovetur. (*Lat.*) During a litigation nothing new should be introduced.

During a litigation no change in the position of things, or of parties, can be made.

Pending. The term 'pending' means nothing more than undecided.

'PENDING' is defined to mean depending; remaining undecided; not terminated.

An action is considered as pending from the time of its commencement of the proceeding.

A legal proceeding is "pending" as soon as commenced and until it is concluded, *i.e.* so long as the Court having original cognizance of it can make an order on the matters in issue, or to be dealt with, therein. *Asgarali Nazarali Singapore Walla* v. *State of Bombay*, AIR 1957 SC 503, 509.

A suit filed in a Court, on the averments in the suit giving jurisdiction to the Court to try the suit, but later on the averments giving jurisdiction having been found not correct, even then the suit was legally pending before the Court. [CPC (5 of 1908), S. 24]

A criminal case is pending against one as early as his arrest and commitment for a crime for which he is afterwards indicted.

Literally hanging in suspense; remaining undecided or awaiting settlement.

Pending judicial proceeding. A judicial proceeding is said to be pending—

(A) in the case of a civil proceeding, when it is instituted by the filing of a plaint or otherwise;

(B) in the case of a criminal proceeding under the Code of Criminal Procedure, 1898, or any other law—

  (i) Where it relates to the commission of an offence, when the charge-sheet or challan is filed, or when the Court issues summons or warrant, as the case may be against the accused, and

  (ii) in any other case, when the Court takes cognizance of the matter to which the proceeding relates, and in the case of a civil or criminal proceeding. [Contempt of Courts Act (70 of 1971), S. 3 *Expln.* (a)]

Pending proceeding. A legal proceeding is said to be pending as soon as it is commenced and until it is concluded.

"Penetrate" means 'find access into or through, pass through.' [Concise Oxford Dictionary as cited in *Suresh Kumar Koushal* v. *Naz Foundation*, (2014) 1 SCC 1, para 59.6].

Penetration. 'Penetration' as used in the rule that penetration only is necessary to be proved on a trial for rape, is a limitation upon and qualification of the meaning of the term 'carnal knowledge.' In limiting the 'carnal knowledge' mentioned in the definition of 'rape' to 'penetration' only, the Legislature intended to eliminate the question of 'emission' in such cases.

Insertion; the fact of passing, into or through. [IPC (45 of 1860), S. 375, fifthly, *Expln.*].

'Penetration' is the *sine qua non* for an offence of rape. In order to constitute 'Penetration', there must be evidence clear and cogent to prove that some part the virile member of the accused was within the labia of pudendum of the woman, no matter how little. *Aman Kumar* v. *State of Haryana*, (2004) 4 SCC 379, 386, para 7.

With regard to IW : A successful attack—the ability to obtain unauthorized (undetected) access to files and programs or the control state of a computer system. (*Cyber Law*)

Penetration signature. The description of a situation or set of conditions in which a penetration could occur or of system events which in conjunction can indicate the occurrence of a penetration in progress. (*Cyber Law*)

Penetrative sexual assault. A person is said to commit "Penetrative sexual assault" if—

(a) he penetrates his penis, to any extent into the vagina, mouth, urethra or anus of a child and makes the child to do so with him or any other person; or

(b) he inserts, to any extent any object or a part of the body, not being the penis, into the vagina, the urethra or anus of the child or makes the child to do so with him or any other person; or

(c) he manipulates any part of the body of the child so as to cause penetration into the vagina, urethra or anus or any part of the body of the child or makes the child to do so with him or any other person; or

(d) he applies his mouth to the penis, vagina or anus, urethra of the child or make the child to do so to such person or any other person. [Protection of Children from Sexual Offence Act (32 of 2012), S. 3].

Penitentiary. 'Penitentiary,' is a word in common use, denoting a prison or place of punishment, and means the place of punishment in which convicts sentenced to confinement and hard labour are confined by the authority of the law.

The word 'penitentiary' whenever the same is used in any of the laws of the state as a place of punishment for crime, shall be construed to mean and refer to the state prison.

Reformatory prison or house of correction [Geneva Conventions Act (6 of 1960), III Sch., Art. 22].

Penology. Study of punishment and prison discipline.

Pension. "PENSION" means a pension, whether contributory or not, of any kind whatsoever payable to or in respect of any person, and includes retired pay so payable, a gratuity so payable and any sum or sums so payable by way of the return, with or without interest thereon or any other addition thereto, of subscriptions to a provident fund. [Constitution of India, Art. 366(17)]

"PENSION" means a pension of any kind whatsoever payable to or in respect of a Judge, and includes any gratuity or other sum or sums so payable by way of death or retirement benefits. [High Court Judges (Conditions of Service) Act (28 of 1954), S. 2(gg)]

"PENSION" means and includes any amount of money to be paid periodically to an employee after retirement from and out of the Fund and includes gratuity, death-cum-retirement benefit and family pension *etc.* [Assam non-government (Deficit) College Control Pension and Provident Fund Act, 1997, S. 3(j)]

A periodical payment made by a government, company or an employer of labour in consideration of past services or the relinquishment of rights, claims or emoluments; regular payment to persons in order that they may maintain themselves. [Constitution of India, Art. 112(3)(d)(i)].

The word 'pension' implies periodical payments of money to a pensioner. Two essentials are necessary in order to constitute a pension: (1) it must be a periodical payment, and (2) it must be a grant not in respect of any right, privilege, perquisite or office but on political considerations or on account of past services or present infirmities or as a compassionate allowance. *Shaukat Hussain Beg Mirza* v. *State of Uttar Pradesh,* AIR 1959 All 769, 770. [Pensions Act (23 of 1871), S. 11]

The word 'pension' as used in S. 60(1)(*g*), CPC (5 of 1908) is wide enough to cover all sorts of periodical payments in whatever shape they are made by the Government. A *Jagir* that is realised in the shape of an assignment of land revenue is a pension within that clause, and is, therefore, exempt from attachment in execution of a decree.

The word 'pension' as used in the CPC (5 of 1908) "implies periodical payment of money by Government to the pensioner", and it does not apply to a person who draws rents not as a pensioner, but as a limited owner of the properties which yield them.

The term 'pension' includes gratuity except when the term 'pension' is used in contradistinction to gratuity, in consonance with the basic concept. *Jarnail Singh* v. *Secretary, Ministry of Home Affairs*, AIR 1994 SC 1484, 1487. [Central Civil Services (Pension) Rules, 1972, Rule 9]

Conceptually, pension is a reward for past service. It is determined on the basis of length of service and last pay drawn. Length of service is determinative of eligibility and quantum of pension. *State of Punjab* v. *Justice S.S. Dewan,* (1997) 4 SCC 569, 573.

Pension business. Includes business of effecting contracts to manage investments of pension funds or superannuation schemes or contracts to pay annuities that may be approved by the Authority in this behalf. [Insurance Regulatory and Development Authority (Registration of Indian Insurance Companies) Regulations, 2000, Rgn. 2(k)]

Pension fund. Means an intermediary which has been granted a certificate of registration under section 27(3) of Act 23 of 2013 by the Authority as a pension fund for receiving contributions, accumulating them and making payments to the subscriber in the manner as may be specified by regulations. [S. 2(1)(*l*) of the Pension Fund Regulatory & Development Authority Act, 2013 (23 of 2013)]

"Pension Fund" means the Pension Fund established under clause (*b*) of sub-section (*1*) of section 16. [Code on Social Security, 2020 (36 of 2020), section 2(57)]

'Pension fund' means the fund created for the purpose of transferring the total accumulated amount of University contribution in C.P.F (including the amount of loan taken out of it) and interest thereon as on date of commencement of these Regulations and monthly contribution made thereafter in respect of such employees who opted or are deemed to have opted the pension scheme under these Regulation. The pension paid to the retired employees shall be charged to this Fund. [Rajasthan University Pension Regulations, 1990, Regn. 3(5) as cited in *University of Rajasthan* v. *Prem Lata Agarwal*, (2013) 3 SCC 705, para 19].

Pension Schemes. For the purpose of these regulations shall include the pension schemes regulated by the Authority being the National Pension System (NPS), NPS-Lite-Swavalamban and Atal Pension Yojana (APY) regulated and administered by the Authority or any other pension scheme of the Government of India. [Pension Fund Regulatory and Development Authority (Point of Presence) Regulations, 2018, Regn. 2(1)(g)].

Pension Regulatory and Development Fund. Means the fund constituted under section 40(1) of Act 23 of 2013. [S. 2(1)(m) of the Pension Fund Regulatory & Development Authority Act, 2013 (23 of 2013)]

Pensionable office. "An office coming within the provisions of any Act authorizing the grant of a superannuation allowance.

Pensioner. Person who is receiving a pension. [T.P. Act (4 of 1882), S. 6(g)].

Penultimate. Last but one; as penultimate Saturday.

The last but one of any series.

People. The people, in a legal sense, must be understood to be those who are invested with political rights, and who will be the sole organs through which the will of the body politic will be expressed.

'PEOPLE,' when not used as the equivalent of 'state' or 'nation,' must apply to a body of persons less than a state or nation, and this meaning would be satisfied by considering it as applicable to any consolidated political body.

PEOPLE, NATION. People is the generic, and nation the specific. A nation is a people connected by birth; there cannot, therefore, strictly speaking, be a nation without a people.

PEOPLE, POPULACE, MOB. People is said of anybody supposed to be assembled, as well as really assembled : populace is said of a body only when actually assembled. The voice of the people cannot always be disregarded. Mob designate not only what is low, but tumultuous. A mob is at all times an object of terror.

People in general. The 'people in general' do not connote the inhabitants of any particular village but they signify all members of the public irrespective of any class, a community or any place of residence. *Ram Saran* v. *Narayan Chandra,* AIR 1954 Cal 125, 127.

Per. (*Lat.*) Through; by; for each; for every.

Per annum. Strictly speaking, the words 'per annum' mean by the year or through the year.

Per capita. Per head (counting) by heads. [Hindu Succession Act (30 of 1956), S. 7(2), *Expln.*].

Per capita : Per stirpes. Where distribution is to be *per capita*, the members of the class take the property to be distributed in equal shares, the individual alone being considered in the distribution. In distribution *per stirpes*, the stock or family is considered, and children do not take concurrently with their parents.

Per cent. Means the percentage of metals prescribed for any coin. [S. 2(i) of the Coinage Act, 2011 (11 of 2011)]

"PER CENT" is an abbreviation of the Latin term '*per centum.*' and means 'by the hundred.' It is so used and understood by mathematicians, accountants, and all persons having occasion to use it.

Per centum ad valorem. Percentage according to the value. [Mica Mines Labour Welfare Fund Act (22 of 1946), S. 2(1) omitted by the Finance Act , 2016 (28 of 2016)].

Per consequens. By consequence; consequently.

Per curiam. A 'per curiam' is the opinion of the count in a case in which the judges are all of one mind, and the question involved is so clear that it is not considered necessary to elaborate it by an extended discussion.

Per diem. By the day. Used chiefly relating to payments that are payable or paid or accrue by the day.

Per directum not permissible to be done per obliquum. Whatever is prohibited by law to be done directly cannot legally be effected by an indirect and circuitous contrivance.

Per incuriam. Through inadvertence or through want of care.

Through carelessness.

Through inadvertence. [*Hyder Consulting (U.K.) Limited* v. *Governor, State of Orissa*, (2015) 2 SCC 189, para 46].

A decision should be treated as given *per incuriam* when it is given in ignorance in terms of a statute, or of a rule having the force of a statute. *Municipal Corporation of Delhi* v. *Gurnam Kaur*, AIR 1989 SC 38.

'Per incuriam' means 'through want of care'. A decision of the Court which is mistaken. A decision of the Court is not a binding precedent if given *per incuriam, i.e.* without the Court's attention having been drawn to the relevant authorities, or statutes.

Per infortunium. (*Lat.*) By misadventure or mischance.

Per mensem. By the month.

Per rerum naturam factum negantis nulla probatio est. It is in the nature of things that he who denies a fact is not bound to give proof. (*Black*)

Per se. By himself or itself; inherently; in itself.

Per stirpes. A distribution of property "*per stirpes* and not *per capita*," means, that all the beneficiaries will not, necessarily or probably, take equal shares but, that the property is to be divided into as many parts as there are stocks and each stock will have one, and only one, of such parts though such stock may consist of many persons whilst another may consist of only one person. (*Stroud*)

By stocks in inheritance the children of each descendant divide only the share that would have been their parents.

According to the branch (of the family). [Hindu Succession Act (23 of 1956), S. 19(a)].

Perempt. To exercise a peremptory challenge.

Peremption. A nonsuit.

Peremptory. Imperative; absolute; not admitting of question; delay, or reconsideration; positive; final; decisive; not admitting of any alternative; self-determined; arbitrary.

Peremptory norm. In international law the principle or rule which is so fundamental that it binds all states and does not allow any exception.

Perfect trust. A trust which is complete and enforceable by the beneficiaries without further acts by the settlor.

Performance. "performance", in relation to performer's right, means any visual or acoustic presentation made live by one or more performers. [Copyright Act (14 of 1957), S. 2(q) as amended by 38 of 1994 (w.e.f 10-5-1995)]

"PERFORMANCE" in relation to performer's right, means any visual or acoustic presentation made live by one or more performers [Copyright Act (14 of 1957), S. 2(q)]

The action of performing [Indian Contract Act (9 of 1872), S. 8 and Constitution of India, Art. 71(2)]; doing [T.P. Act (4 of 1882), S. 33]; completion of contractual duty; to accomplish; to execute.

Performance evaluation. In relation to in vitro diagnostic medical device means any systematic investigation by which data is assessed and analysed to establish or verify performance of the in vitro diagnostic medical device for its intended use. [Medical Devices Rules, 2017, R. 3(zk)].

Performance bond. A type of guarantee which is an undertaking that should the seller fail to carry out the terms of the contract, then the buyer may claim a certain amount of money. [*M L Tannan Banking Law & Practice in India*, Vol. 2, 2021, LexisNexis, Dictionary of Banking Terminology].

Performer. Includes an actor, singer, musician, dancer, acrobat, juggler, conjurer, snake charmer, a person delivering a lecture or any other person who makes a performance. [Copyright Act (14 of 1957), S. 2(qq)]

"PERFORMERS" are actors, singers, musicians, dancers and other persons who act, sing, deliver, declaim, play in, interpret or otherwise perform literary or artistic works or expressions of folk-lore. [WIPO : Performances and Phonograms Treaty Adopted in Geneva Dec. 20, 1996, Art. 2(a)]

Performing animal. "PERFORMING ANIMAL" means any animal, which is used at, or for the purpose of any entertainment to which the public are admitted through sale of tickets. [Performing Animal Rules, 1973, R. 2(b)]

Performing purposes. 'PERFORMING PURPOSES' means any effort to force the animal to carry out-unnatural act including performance of circus tricks. [Central Zoo Authority and Recognition of Zoo Rules, 1992, R. 2(f)]

Performing rights society. Means a society, association or other body, whether incorporate or not, which carries on business in India of issuing or granting licence for the performance in India of works in which copyright subsists. [Copyright Act (14 of 1957), S. 2(r) Omitted by Act 38 of 1994 (w.e.f. 10-5-1995)]

Periculum rei venditae, nondum traditae, est emptoris. (*Lat.*) A thing sold and not yet delivered is the purchaser's.

Perils of the sea. Every kind of natural misfortune which may affect a maritime adventure, such as hurricane, shipwreck, stranding, and damage be heavy weather beyond the ordinary damage of wind and waves. The term extends also to acts attributable to the acts or fault of other parties such as loss or damage by collision, capture by pirates, or damage by rats. (*Walker*)

Perimeter. In case of challange inspection means the external boundary of the inspection site, defined by either geographic coordinates or description on a map. [Chemical Weapons Convention Act (34 of 2000), (verification Annex.), 21]

Period begins to run. [Limitation Act (36 of 1963), Sch., Column 3].

Period of Emergency. '*Period of Emergency*' means the period of operation of the proclamation under clause (1) of Art. 352 of the Constitution of India issued by the President on the 26th day of October 1962. [West Bengal Local Authorities (Postponement of Elections) Act (West Bengal Act No. 19 of 1963), S. 2(d)]

"PERIOD OF EMERGENCY" means, in relation to the Proclamation of Emergency issued under clause (1) of Article 352 of the Constitution,

(i) on the 26th day of October, 1962, the period beginning with the 26th day of October, 1962, and ending with the 10th day of January, 1968, that is to say, the date on which the said Emergency was declared, by notification of the Government of India in the Ministry of Home Affairs, No. G.S.R. 93, dated the 10th January 1968, to have come to an end;

(ii) on the third day of December, 1971, the period beginning with the 3rd day December, 1971, and ending with such date as the Central Government may, by notification in the Official Gazette, declare to be the date on which the said Emergency shall come to an end. [Personal Injuries (Compensation Insurance) Act (37 of 1963), S. 2(f); Personal Injuries (Emergency Provisions) Act (59 of 1962), S. 2(5)]

Period of inspection. For the purposes of Article IX, means the period of time from provision of access to the inspection team to the inspection site until its departure from the inspection site, exclusive of time spent on briefings before and after the verification activities. [Chemical Weapons Convention Act (34 of 2000), (Verification Annex.), 22]

"PERIOD OF INSPECTION", for the purposes of Articles IV, V and VI, means the period of time from arrival of the inspection team at the inspection site until its departure from the inspection site, exclusive of time spent on briefings before and after the verification activities. [Chemical Weapons Convention Act (34 of 2000), (Verification Annex.), 23]

Period of limitation. "PERIOD OF LIMITATION" means the period of limitation prescribed for any suit, appeal or application by the Schedule. [Limitation Act (36 of 1963), S. 2(j)].

For the purposes of this Chapter, unless the context otherwise requires, "period of limitation" means the period specified in section 514 for taking cognizance of an offence. [(w. e. f. 1-7-2024) Bharatiya Nagarik Suraksha Sanhita, 2023 (46 of 2023), section 513]

The time laid down by law within which an action can be brought, and after the expiry of which recourse to Courts cannot be had for any remedy. [Limitation Act (36 of 1963), S. 2(j)]; [Presidency-towns Insolvency Act (3 of 1909), S. 101-A].

Period of mere attendance. Means the period during which a person remains at his post solely in order to reply to possible calls or to resume action at the time fixed in the duty schedule. [Motor Transport Workers Act (27 of 1961), S. 2(f), *Expln.* (3)]

Period of residence on duty. Means the period during which a member resides at a place where a session of a House of Parliament or a sitting of a committee is held or where any other business connected with his duties as such member is transacted, for the purpose of attending such session or sitting or for the purpose of attending to such other business, and includes—

(i) in the case of session of a House of Parliament, a period of such residence, not exceeding three days, immediately preceding the commencement of the session and a period of such residence, not exceeding three days, immediately succeeding the [date on which the House of Parliament is adjourned sine die or for a period exceeding seven days], and

(ii) in the case of a sitting of a committee or any other business a period of such residence, not exceeding two days, immediately preceding the commencement of the business of the committee or other business and a period of such residence, not exceeding two days, immediately succeeding the conclusion of the business of the committee or other business;

Explanation.—A member who ordinarily resides at a place where a session of a House of Parliament or a sitting of a Committee is held or where any other business connected with his duties as such member is transacted shall, for the duration of the session or sitting or the time occupied for the transaction of other business (including the three or two days immediately preceding or succeeding), be deemed to reside at such place for the purpose of attending such session or, sitting or, as the case may be, for the purpose of attending to such other business. [Salary, Allowances & Pension of Members of Parliament Act (30 of 1954), S. 2(d)]

Period of life of the bond. "PERIOD OF LIFE OF THE BOND" means the period commencing from the date of issue of the bond and ending on the date of the maturity or redemption of such bond. [Income-tax Act (43 of 1961), S. 36(iiia) *Expln.* (*ii*) *as inserted by Finance Act (18 of 2005), S. 12(a)*]

Period of two years. S. 2(ii) of the Dissolution of Muslim Marriage Act (8 of 1939).

Period of the repayment plan. For the purposes of this section, "period of the repayment plan" means the period from the date of the order passed under Section 114 till the date on which the notice is given by the resolution professional under Section 117 or report submitted by the resolution professional under Section 118, as the case may be. Rights of secured creditors in relation to payment plan. [Insolvency and Bankruptcy Code (31 of 2016), S. 110, *Explanation*].

Periodical. Recurring at regular intervals; pertaining to period [CPC (5 of 1908), O. XXI, R. 33]; a serial publication usually produced at regular intervals of less than a year and containing at least some articles and/or news items, as distinct from legislation and case reports [Chartered Accountants Act (38 of 1948), S. 30(2)(m)].

Peripheral. Any part of a computer other than the CPU or working memory (RAM and ROM). For example, disks, keyboards, monitors, mice, printers, scanners, tape drives, microphones, speakers, and other such devices are peripherals. (*Cyber Law*)

An auxiliary device (such as a modem, monitor, or disk drive) that is connected to a computer. (*Computer*)

Perish. To come to an untimely end; to lose life; to suffer destruction. [T.P. Act (4 of 1882), S. 27, ill. (b)].

TO PERISH, DIE, DECAY. To perish expresses more than to die, and is applicable to many objects; for the latter is properly applied only to express the extinction of animal life, and figuratively to express the extinction of life or spirit in vegetables or other bodies. To perish expresses the end; to decay, the process by which this end is brought about.

Subject to quick deterioration; liable to perish. [CrPC 1973 (2 of 1974), S. 83(5)].

Perishable goods. Goods which decay or lose their value if not consumed soon : (as) fish, fruits, vegetables, confectionery, &c.

Perjury. Violation of a promise made on oath; the action of swearing to a statement known to be false. [IPC (45 of 1860), S. 165 (*omitted*), ill. (c)].

Perjury is an obstruction of justice. Deliberately making false statements which are material to the case, and that too under oath, amounts to crime of perjury. [*Kishorbhai Gandubhai Pethani* v. *State of Gujarat*, (2014) 13 SCC 539, para 9].

Permanent. 'PERMANENT' is defined to mean not temporary, or subject to change; abiding, remaining fixed, or enduring in character, state, or place.

Lasting or designed to last indefinitely without change. [T.P. Act (4 of 1882), S. 3(c)].

The appointment as a permanent servant does not mean that the tenure of office is guaranteed for any definite period. The word 'permanent' in the appointment order is descriptive of the nature of the appointment so as to distinguish it from a mere acting or temporary appointment. *Mookam Guseph Thomakutty* v. *Thomas,* AIR 1952 TC 104.

Permanent account number. Means a number which the Assessing Officer may allot to any person for the purpose of identification and includes a permanent account number allotted under the new series. [Income-tax Act (43 of 1961), S. 139A(8), *Expln.* (b)]

Permanent account number under the new series. Means a permanent account number having ten alphanumeric characters and issued in the form of a laminated card. [Income-tax Act (43 of 1961), S. 139(A)(8) *Expln.* (c)]

Permanent alimony. Permanent alimony is a provision for the support and maintenance of the wife out of her husband's estate during her life, according to her rank and condition in the community in which she resides.

Permanent appointment. 'Permanent appointment' does not mean that the tenure of office is guaranteed for any definite period. The word 'permanent' is used as a descriptive of the nature of the appointment so as to distinguish it from a mere acting or temporary appointment. Permanent appointment has a fixity of tenure though not for any fixed period. *Thomakutty* v. *Thomas,* AIR 1954 TC 104, 107.

Permanent disability. The 'Permanent disability' for which recovery may be had in an action for personal injuries is the permanent reduction of the injured person's power to earn money, resulting from the injury, caused by the negligent act of the other party.

Permanent employment. An agreement to give a person 'permanent employment' means nothing more than that the employment is to continue indefinitely, and until one or the other of the parties wishes for some good reason to sever the relation; it is opposed to temporary employment.

Permanent establishment. Referred to in clause (iii), includes a fixed place of business through which the business of the enterprise is wholly or partly carried on [Income-tax Act 1961, S. 92F(iiia). Also see S. 94A(6)(ii) of the Income-tax Act, 1961 (43 of 1961) as inserted (w.e.f. 1-6-2011) by the Finance Act, 2011 (8 of 2011)]

Permanent injunction. A permanent injunction means an injunction which shall remain in force until vacated by order of Court.

Permanent mission. "PERMANENT MISSION" means a mission of permanent character, representing the State, sent to an international organization by a State not a member of the organization. [Vienna Convention on the Representation of States in their Relations with International Organizations of a Universal Character, 1975, Art. 1(7)]

Permanent observer mission. "PERMANENT OBSERVER MISSION" means a mission of permanent character, representing the State, sent to an international organization by a State not a member of the organization. [Vienna Convention on Representation of States in their Relations with International Organizations of a Universal Character, 1975, Art. 1(8)]

Permanent partial disablement. Means such disablement of a permanent nature, as reduces the earning capacity of an employee in every employment which he was capable of undertaking at the time of the accident resulting in the disablement:

Provided that every injury specified in Part II of the Second Schedule shall be deemed to result in permanent partial disablement. [Employees' State Insurance Act (34 of 1948), S. 2(15-A)]

"Permanent partial disablement" means, where the disablement is of a permanent nature, such disablement as reduces the earning capacity of an employee in every employment which he was capable of undertaking at the time of the accident resulting in the disablement:

Provided that every injury specified in Part II of the Fourth Schedule shall be deemed to result in permanent partial disablement. [Code on Social Security, 2020 (36 of 2020), section 2(55)]

Permanent place of abode. The permanent place of abode is the one where a man has actually been living permanently and not merely as a temporary visitor or a temporary lodger. *Raj Rani* v. R. *Mool Raj,* AIR 1962 Punj 62, 63. [Indian Succession Act (39 of 1925), S. 276(2)]

Permanent representative. "PERMANENT REPRESENTATIVE" means the person charged by the sending state with the duty of acting as the head of the permanent mission. [Vienna Convention on the Representation of States in their Relations with International Organizations of a Universal Character, 1975, Art. 1(18)]

Permanent residence. The words 'permanent residence' would mean that the person has settled down at a particular place permanently and regularly for some purpose. [*Bhagwan Dass* v. *Kamal Abrol,* AIR 2005 SC 2583]

Permanent seasonal employee. A "PERMANENT SEASONAL EMPLOYEE" is one who has completed service for a period equal to ⅔rd of the duration or a season or three months whichever is less in a clear vacancy and shall be deemed to be permanent employee for the purpose of these orders. [M.P. Industrial Employment (Standing Orders) Act (26 of 1961), Standing order No. 2 (ii) **as cited in** *Ram Naresh Rawat* v. *Ashwini Ray,* (2017) 3 SCC 436, para 6].

Permanent structure. If a structure is such in quality that it is not easily removable, like a furnace or water tank then it is a permanent structure. *Duabhai Lalji Kalidas* v. *Ramnik Lal Somchand Mehta,* AIR 1975 Guj 213, 217.

Permanent character of structure has to be determined, having regard to the nature of the structure, materials used in the making of the structure and the manner in which the structure is erected, and in the light of the above considerations, structure made of bamboos and iron sheets is not permanent structure. *Ibrahim* v. *Khanmahamed,* AIR 1965 Guj 152, 154.

Permanent tenant. "PERMANENT TENANT" means a holder of *khoti* land who has a right of occupancy in such land. [Bom Act I of 1880 (Khoti Settlement), S. 3, cl. 8].

Permanent total disablement. Means such disablement of a permanent nature as incapacitates an employee for all work which he was capable of performing at the time of the accident resulting in such disablement.

Provided that permanent total disablement shall be deemed to result from every injury specified in Part I of the Second Schedule or from any combination of injuries specified in part II thereof where the aggregate percentage of the loss of earning capacity, as specified in the said Part II against those injuries, amounts to one hundred percent or more. [Employees' State Insurance Act (34 of 1948), S. 2(15-B)]

"Permanent total disablement" means such disablement of a permanent nature as incapacitates an employee for all work which he was capable of performing at the time of the accident resulting in such disablement:

Provided that permanent total disablement shall be deemed to result from every injury specified in Part I of the Fourth Schedule or from any combination of injuries specified in Part II thereof where the aggregate percentage of the loss of earning capacity, as specified in the said Part II against those injuries, amounts to one hundred per cent. [Code on Social Security, 2020 (36 of 2020), section 2(56)]

Permanent workman. To be a permanent workman, it is not necessary that the workman should be engaged throughout the year, but the work on which he is engaged should be of permanent nature and should last throughout the year. *Jaswant Sugar Mills Merut* v. *Badri Prasad,* AIR 1967 SC 513, 514.

Permanently. In a permanent manner; lastingly. [T.P. Act (4 of 1882), S. 33].

Permissible classification. It is now well established that while Art. 14 of the Constitution of India forbids class legislation, it does not forbid reasonable classification for the purposes of legislation. In order, however, to pass the test of permissible classification two conditions must be fulfilled, namely (i) that the classification must be founded on an intelligible differentia which distinguishes persons or things that are grouped together from others left out of the group; and (ii) that that differentia must have a rational relation to the object sought to be achieved by the statute in question. *Lachmandas* v. *State of Bombay,* AIR 1952 SC 235, 244.

Permission. The action of permitting or giving leave; liberty or licence granted to someone. [Indian Evidence Act (1 of 1872), S. 123].

The word 'permission' shows that he is granted leave to act in a particular way. The word 'permission' is a word of wide import, 'permission' means only leave to do some act which but for the leave would be illegal. Exemption is just one way of giving leave. *Dhanrajamal Gobindram* v. *Shamji Kalidas and Co.*, AIR 1961 SC 1285, 1290.

Permit. "PERMIT" means a permit granted under this Act or any rule made thereunder. [Wild Life (Protection) Act, 1972, S. 2(23)]

To grant permission; to give leave; to grant express licence or liberty to.

A written order giving permission [Emigration Act (31 of 1983), S. 24(1)(k)]; to allow the doing of something [Indian Evidence Act (1 of 1872), S. 154].

'Permit' conveys the idea of an allowance, a sufferance, a toleration, an authorization.

In deciding the true scope and effect of the relevant words in any statutory provision, the context in which the words occur, the object of the statute assumes relevance. Since the object of 71(4) is not to confer monopoly on the hand of one individual operator, temporary permits issued in favour of an applicant cannot be taken into consideration while computing the ceiling on permits. *Iarardan Pandan* v. *Regional Transport Authority,* AIR 1995 Ori 143, 145. [Motor Vehicles Act (59 of 1988), S. 71(4)]

Permit to be represented. To allow to be described as having a specified character or quality. [Indian Partnership Act (9 of 1932), S. 28(1)].

Permitted. Unless the Head of the Department has no objection and be so permitted, in question about permitting any evidence about the information relating to the affairs of the State, the Court would not order the production of those unpublished official records in the proceeding. *Raj Narain* v. *Indira Gandhi,* AIR 1974 All 324, 325. [Indian Evidence Act (1 of 1872), S. 123]

The word 'permitted' means accepted, allowed. *Nutan Kumar* v. *II Additional District Judge, Bander,* AIR

1994 All 298, 315. [Indian Contract Act (9 of 1872), S. 23]

Permitted currency. Means a foreign currency which is freely convertible. [Foreign Exchange Management (Manner of Receipt and Payments) Regulations, 2000, Reg. 2(v)]

Permitted use. In relation to a registered trade mark, means the use of trade mark—

(i) by a registered user of the trade mark in relation to goods or services—

(a) with which he is connected in the course of trade; and

(b) in respect of which the trade mark remains registered for the time being; and

(c) for which he is registered as registered user; and

(d) which complies with any conditions or limitations to which the registration of registered user is subject; or

(ii) by a person other than the registered proprietor and registered user in relation to goods or services—

(a) with which he is connected in the course of trade; and

(b) in respect of which the trade mark remains registered for the time being; and

(c) by consent of such registered proprietor in a written agreement; and

(d) which complies with any conditions or limitations to which such user is subject and to which the registration of the trade mark is subject. [Trade Marks Act (47 of 1999), S. 2(1)(r)]

"PERMITTED USE", in relation to a registered trade mark, means the use of the trade mark.—

(i) by a registered user of the trade mark in relation to goods—

(a) with which he is connected in the course of trade; and

(b) in respect of which the trade mark remains for the time being; and

(c) for which he is registered as registered user; and

(ii) which compiles with any conditions or restrictions to which the registration of the trade mark is subject. [Trade and Merchandise Marks Act (43 of 1958), S. 2(1)(m)]

Permittee. Means the person in whose name the reconnaissance permit is granted. [Offshore Areas Minerals (Development and Regulation) Act, 2002 (17 of 2003), S. 4(p)]

Perpetrate : Commit. One may commit offences of various degree and magnitude; but one perpetrates crimes only, and those of the more heinous kind. A lawless banditti, who spend their lives in the perpetration of the most horrid crimes, are not to be restrained by the ordinary course of justice; he who commits any offence against the good order of society exposes himself to the censure of others, who may be his inferiors in certain respects.

Perpetration. The act of one committing a crime either with his own hands, or by some means or instrument or through some innocent agent.

Perpetrator. The perpetrator (or, if you will, the "principal") means, and exclusively means the person who performs the offence. More precisely, the perpetrator is the person who, being directly struck at by the criminal prohibition, offends against it with the necessary *mens rea* or negligence (if either of these be required). He is normally indicated by the wording of the legal rule. In murder, he is the person who kills; in burglary the person who trespasses with the requisite intent; in forgery, the person who makes or uses the forged document. [GLANVILLE WILLIAMS : Criminal law, 2nd Edn., 1983, c. 15, S. 15-1, pp. 329, 330]

"(1) A principal in an offence is one who, with any necessary fault element, and possessing any qualification required for the offence, does the acts constituting the external elements of the offence. (2) A person does such an act not only when he does it himself but also when he—

(a) acts through an innocent agent; or

(b) is otherwise responsible for the act of another which constitutes an external element of an offence." [Law Commission Working Party on Codification, the words given in brackets are added by Glanville Williams : *See* GLANVILLE WILLIAMS : Criminal law, 2nd Edn., 1983, p. 330]

A perpetrator (or principal) is one who, being within the criminal prohibition, offends against it with any necessary fault element. He may act himself or through an innocent agent or instrumentality, and he is also a perpetrator whenever he is responsible for the act of another. [GLANVILLE WILLIAMS : Criminal law, 2nd Edn., 1983, c. 15, s. 15.1 (summary), p. 375]

Perpetua lex est, nullam legem humanam ac positivam perpetuam esse; et clausula quae abrogationem excludit, ab initio non valet. It is an everlasting law, that no human and positive law shall be perpetual; and a clause which excludes abrogation is invalid from its commencement. (*Latin for Lawyers*)

Perpetual. Lasting for ever; eternal. [Specific Relief Act (47 of 1963), S. 36].

Perpetual injunction. "An injunction granted upon the final trial is called a PERPETUAL INJUNCTION." [Specific Relief Act (47 of 1963), Ss. 36 and 37(2)].

Perpetual interest. A perpetual interest has a duration equal to that of the property.

Perpetual lease. The term "perpetual lease" can only mean one for years, wherein the lessee has the covenant of the lessor for perpetual renewals.

Perpetual management. The companies Act by enacting Section 255 shows that it does not disapprove of a person having power to appoint a succession of directors and in the case of a private company, a succession even of all the directors. Such a person would have what is described as 'perpetual management'. *Oriental Metal Pressing Works (P) Ltd.* v. *Bhaskar Kashnath Thakur*, AIR 1961 SC 573, 576. [Companies Act (1 of 1956), S. 255]

Perpetuities. A perpetuity as defined by Lewis in his well-known book on "Perpetuities" (p. 164) is 'a future limitation, whether executory, or by way of remainder, and of either real or personal property which is not to vest until after the expiration of, or will not necessarily vest within, the period fixed and prescribed by law for the creation of future estates and interests'. *Ram Baran* v. *Ram Mohit*, AIR 1967 SC 744, 747. [T.P. ACT (4 of 1882), S. 14].

Perpetuity. A perpetuity is a limitation of property which renders it inalienable beyond the period allowed by law.

The duration without limitation as to time [T.P. Act (4 of 1882), S. 105]; the condition of an estate limited so that it will not take effect or vest within the period fixed by law or so limited as to be or have a possibility of being inalienable either perpetually or beyond the bounds fixed by law. [T.P. Act (4 of 1882), S. 14].

Perquisite. A privilege, gain or profit incidental to an employment in addition to regular salary or wages. [Income-tax Act (43 of 1961), S. 17(1)(iv)].

Perquisites. 'Perquisites' means emolument, fee or profit attached to the office or position of an addition to salary or wages. The payment of compensatory city allowance is neither an emolument nor fee nor profit but it is a reimbursement of personal expenses required by a Government servant to be incurred on account of expenses of living at a particular place. *CIT* v. *D.R. Pathak,* (1975) 99 ITR 14 (Bom). [Income-tax Act (43 of 1961), S. 17(2)]

Persecution. Harassment. [Geneva Conventions Act (6 of 1960), IIIrd Sch., Art. 45].

Persistent default. One or two isolated cases of failure to act will not amount to persistent default. Even a single act of disobedience of the direction may, added to certain continuing circumstances, depending on the gravity of the matter, indicate persistence on the part of the defaulter. *Kerala Wakf Board* v. *State of Kerala,* AIR 1984 Ker 57, 62. [Wakf Act (29 of 1954) (*repealed by Act 43 of 1995*), S. 64(1)]

Persistent offender. A person who has repeatedly offended against the criminal law. Such an offender is normally punished more heavily than one who has not previously or has occasionally offended, and statutes sometimes expressly provide greater maximum penalties or special regimes, such as preventive detention, for persistent offenders. (*Walker*)

Persistently. Tenaciously. [Indian Partnership Act (9 of 1932), S. 44(d)].

'Persistently' connotes some degree of continuance or repetition.

Person. "The word "PERSON" shall include any Company or Association or body of persons, whether incorporated or not" [Indian Penal Code (45 of 1860), S. 11] and [General Clauses Act (10 of 1897), S. 3(42)].

The word "person" in Article 21 of Constitution of India is wide enough to cover not only citizens of this country but also foreigners who come to this country. [*Isaac Isanga Musumba* v. *State of Maharashtra*, (2014) 15 SCC 357, para 6].

"Person" includes—

(a) an individual;

(b) a Hindu Undivided Family;

(c) a company;

(d) a firm;

(e) a Limited Liability Partnership;

(f) an association of persons or a body of individuals, whether incorporated or not, in India or outside India;

(g) any corporation established by or under any Central Act, State Act or Provincial Act or a Government company as defined in clause (45) of S. 2 of the Companies Act, 2013;

(h) any body corporate incorporated by or under the laws of a country outside India;

(i) a co-operative society registered under any law relating to co-operative societies;

(j) a local authority;

(k) Central Government or a State Government;

(l) society as defined under the Societies Registration Act, 1860;

(m) trust; and

(n) every artificial juridical person, not falling within any of the above [The Central Goods and Services Tax Act, 2017 (12 of 2017), S. 2(84)]

"PERSON" does not include a body of persons. [Representation of the People Act (43 of 1950), S. 2(g)]

"PERSON" does not include any company or association or body of individuals, whether incorporated or not. (Citizenship Act (57 of 1955), S. 2(f)]

"PERSON" includes a Hindu undivided family or a company or an association or a body of individuals or persons, whether incorporated or not. [Gift-tax Act (18 of 1958), S. 2(xvii)]

"PERSON" includes—

(i) an individual,

(ii) a Hindu undivided family,

(iii) a company

(iv) a firm

(v) an association of persons or body of individuals, whether incorporated or not,

(vi) a local authority, and

(vii) every artificial juridical person, not falling within any of the preceding sub-clauses

Explanation.—For the purposes of this clause, an association of persons or a body of individuals or a local authority or an artificial juridical person shall be deemed to be a person, whether or not such person or body or authority or juridical person was formed or established or incorporated with the object of deriving income, profits or gains [Income-tax Act (43 of 1961), S. 2(31)]

"PERSON" includes the Government. [Patents Act (39 of 1970), S. 2(s)]

"PERSON" includes a foreigner. [National Security Act (65 of 1980), S. 2(1)(d)]

"PERSON" includes—

(i) every department of office.

(ii) every organisation established or constituted by Government.

(iii) every local authority within the territory of India.

(iv) every co-operative society.

(v) every other society registered under the societies Registration Act, 1860. [Standards of Weights and Measures Act (60 of 1976), S. 2(q)]

PERSON includes,—

(i) a firm whether registered or not;

(ii) a Hindu undivided family;

(iii) a cooperative society;

(iv) every other association of persons whether registered under the Societies Registration Act, 1860 (21 of 1860), or not. [Consumer Protection Act (68 of 1986),S. 2(m)] [Now repealed & replaced by s. 107(1) of Act 35 of 2019]

"PERSON" includes—

(i) an individual,

(ii) a Hindu undivided family,

(iii) a company,

(iv) a firm,

(v) an association; of person or a body of individuals, whether incorporated or not, and

(vi) every artificial juridical person, not falling within any of the preceding sub-clauses, but does not include a local authority. [Voluntary Deposits (Immunities and Exemptions) Act (47 of 1991), S. 2(d)]

"PERSON" means—

(i) an individual who is a citizen of India;

(ii) an association of individuals or body of individuals, whether incorporated or not, whose members are citizens of India;

(iii) a company as defined in section 3 of the Companies Act, 1956 (1 of 1956); [Cable Television Networks (Regulation), Act (7 of 1995), S. 2(e) as amended by Act 21 of 2011 (w.r.e.f. 25-10-2011)]

PERSON includes—

(i) an individual,

(ii) a Hindu undivided family,

(iii) a company,

(iv) a firm,

(v) an association of persons or a body of individuals, whether incorporated or not,

(vi) a local authority,

(vii) every artificial juridical person, nor falling within any of the preceding sub-clauses,

(viii) assessee, as defined in Rules 2 of Central Excise Rules, 1944,

(ix) exporter as defined in clause (20) of Section 2 of the Customs Act, 1962,

(x) importer as defined in clause (26) of Section 2 of the Customs Act, 1962,

(xi) any person against whom proceedings have been initiated and are pending under any direct tax enactment or indirect tax enactment, [Finance Act (No. 2) (21 of 1998), S. 87(k)]

"PERSON" includes—

(i) an individual,

(ii) a Hindu undivided family,

(iii) a company,

(iv) a firm,

(v) an association of persons or a body of individuals, whether incorporated or not,

(vi) every artificial juridical person, not falling within any of the preceding sub-clauses, and

(vii) any agency, office or branch owned or controlled by such person. [Foreign Exchange Management Act (42 of 1999), S. 2(u)]

"PERSON" includes.—

(i) an individual;

(ii) a Hindu undivided family;

(iii) a company;

(iv) a firm;

(v) an association of persons or a body of individuals, whether incorporated or not, in India or outside India;

(vi) any corporation established by or under any Central, State or Provincial Act or a Government company as defined in Section 2(45) of the Companies Act, 2013 (18 of 2013);

(vii) any body corporate incorporated by or under the laws of a country outside India;

(viii) a co-operative society registered under any law relating to co-operative societies;

(ix) a local authority;

(x) every artificial juridical person, not falling within any of the preceding sub-clauses. [Competition Act, 2002 (12 of 2003), S. 2(l)]

"PERSON" includes—

(i) an individual,

(ii) a Hindu undivided family,

(iii) a company,

(iv) a firm,

(v) an association of persons or a body of individuals, whether incorporated or not,

(vi) every artificial juridical person not falling within any of the preceding sub-clauses, and

(vii) any agency, office or branch owned or controlled by any of the above persons mentioned in the preceding sub-clauses; [Prevention of Money-Laundering Act (15 of 2003), S. 2 (1) (s)]

"PERSON" includes an individual, whether resident in India or outside India, a Hindu undivided family, co-operative society, a company, whether incorporated in India or outside India, a firm, proprietary concern, or an association of persons or body of individuals, whether incorporated or not, local authority and any agency, office or branch owned or controlled by such individual, Hindu undivided family, co-operative, association, body, authority or company. [Special Economic Zones Act (28 of 2005), S. 2(v)].

Legal entity that is recognised by law as the subject of rights and duties; an individual [IPC (45 of 1860), S. 11 and General Clauses Act (10 of 1897), S. 3(42) and Constitution of India, Art. 21]; the living body of an individual [Guardians and Wards Act (8 of 1890), S. 4(2)].

The natural and obvious meaning of the expression 'person' is a living human being, a man, woman or child, an individual of the human race. As used in law the word includes natural persons and artificial persons like corporations and joint stock companies, but it does not include a State or Government. *Shiv Prashad* v. *Punjab State,* AIR 1957 Punj 150, 151. [Constitution of India, Art. 14]

In the Excess Profits Tax Act, includes a Firm. *A.G. Pandu Rao* v. *Collector of Madras,* AIR 1954 Mad 1049. [Excess Profits Tax Act (15 of 1940), S. 2(17)]

A firm is a 'person'. A firm and an individual or group of individuals may form an association of persons within the meaning of S. 2(31) of the Income-tax Act. *M.M. Ipoh* v. *Commissioner of Income Tax*, AIR 1968 SC 317, 324. [Income-tax Act (43 of 1961), S. 2(31)]

The word 'person' is comprehensive enough to include a joint family. *Yeditha Satyanarayamurthy* v. *Tadi Subramanyam,* AIR 1959 AP 534, 535. [T.P. Act (4 of 1882), S. 53-A]

The word "person" in O. XXX refers, only to "individuals and not to corporations," because corporations are dealt with in O. XXIX of the Code and therefore only individual persons who are legal entities carrying on trade in a name are "person" under O. XXX. *Modi Vanaspati Manufacturing Company* v. *Kathiar Jute Mills (P.) Ltd.,* AIR 1969 Cal 496 at 511. [CPC (5 of 1908), O. XXXIII, R. 10]

"PERSON" in CPC (5 of 1908), O. XXXIII, R. 1 and 3 does not include a juridical person, such as a receiver.

A joint stock company which has gone into liquidation is a 'person' entitled to sue as a pauper. *Syed Ali* v. *Deccan Commercial Bank,* AIR 1951 Hyd 124.

The word 'person' in O. XXXIII, R. 1 includes juridical person like a public limited company. *Union Bank of India* v. *Khaders International Constructions Ltd.,* AIR 1993 Ker 31. [CPC (5 of 1908), O. XXXIII, R. 1]

The expression 'person' occurring in Rule 24 designates everyone in a group, defendant, his agent, servants and workmen and not for excluding any defendant against whom the order of injunction has primarily been passed. *Ram Prasad Singh* v. *Subodh Prasad Singh*, AIR 1983 Pat 278, 280. [CPC (5 of 1908), O. XXXIX, Rule 2-A]

The term "person" used in SS. 61 and 64 of the Indian Stamp Act (2 of 1899) includes the members of a trading partnership.

"The Municipal Corporation can be prosecuted for offences which are only punishable with fine for in the very nature of things imprisonment of a Municipal Council is out of question and hence for this limited purpose the Municipal Council is "person". *Girdharilal* v. *Lal Chand,* AIR 1970 Raj 145 at 149. [IPC (45 of 1860), S. 11]

The word 'person' in Art. 14, Constitution of India includes not only human beings but also juristic persons such as corporations. *R.M. Sheshadri* v. *Second Addl. Income-Tax Officer,* AIR 1954 Mad 806.

The word "person" cannot be so narrowly construed as to exclude the dead body of a human being who was killed in the course of the same transaction in which theft was committed. The matter would be different if a thing is stolen from dead body apart from the transaction in which death occurred. *Jamnadas Parashram* v. *State of M.P.,* AIR 1963 MP 106, 114. [IPC (45 of 1860), S. 392]

A corporate body cannot be treated as a person indictable for offences which can be committed only by individuals. *State of Maharashtra* v. *Syndicate Transport Co. (P.) Ltd.,* AIR 1964 Bom 195, 197. [IPC (45 of 1860), Ss. 2, 11]

"PERSON". Includes—

(i) an individual,

(ii) a company,

(iii) a firm,

(iv) an organization or an association of persons or a body of individuals, whether incorporated or not,

(v) every artificial juridical person, not following within any of the preceding sub-clauses, and

(vi) any agency, office or branch owned or controlled by any person falling within any of the preceding sub-clauses. [S. 2(ec) of the

Unlawful Activities (Prevention) Act, 1967 (37 of 1967) as inserted by the Unlawful Activities (Prevention) Amendment Act, 2012 (3 of 2013)]

"PERSON". Salmond defines the term 'person' as any being whom the law regards as capable of rights and duties or as a being, whether human or not, of which rights and duties are the attributes. Thus, the word 'person', in law, unless otherwise intended, refers not only to a natural person (male or female human being), but also any legal person (that is an entity that is recognized by law as having or capable of having rights and duties). *Ramanlal Bhailal Patel* v. *State of Gujarat*, AIR 2008 SC 1246.

"PERSON" the ordinary, popular and natural meaning of the word 'person' is a specific individual human being. But in law the word 'person' has a slightly different connotation, and refers to any entity that is recognized by law as having the rights and duties of a human being. *Ramanlal Bhailal Patel* v. *State of Gujarat*, AIR 2008 SC 1246.

"PERSON" the term 'person' for the purposes of Ceiling Act would include individuals as natural persons as well as group or body of individuals as artificial persons, as also a joint family and a family. *Ramanlal Bhailal Patel* v. *State of Gujarat*, AIR 2008 SC 1246.

"Person accountable" or "accountable person". Means the person accountable for estate duty within the meaning of this Act, and, includes every person in respect of whom any proceeding under this Act has been taken for the assessment of the principal value of the estate of the deceased. [Estate Duty Act (34 of 1953), S. 2(12-A)]

Person accused of an offence. A person against whom an FIR is lodged, is a person accused of an offence. *Ramanlal Bhogilal Shah* v. *D.K. Guha*, AIR 1973 SC 1196, 1200. [Constitution of India, Art. 20(3)]

Person accused of any offence. The expression, 'accused person' in Section 24 and the expression 'a person accused of any offence' in Section 25 have the same connotation and describe the person against whom evidence is sought to be led in a criminal proceeding. The expression 'accused of any offence' in Section 27, as in Section 25 is also descriptive of the person concerned against whom evidence relating to information alleged to be given by him is made provable by Section 27 of the Evidence Act. It does not predicate a formal accusation against him at the time of making the statement sought to be proved, as a condition of its applicability. *State of U.P.* v. *Deoman Upadhyaya,* MLJ : QD (1956-1960) Vol. II C2544 : 1960 All LJ 733 : (1960) 2 Ker LR 368 : 1960 CrLJ 1504 : AIR 1960 SC 1125 : 1960 All WR (HC) 568 : (1960) 2 SCA 371 : 1960 All CrR 361 : (1961) 1 SCR 14 : (1961) 2 SCJ 334 : (1961) 2 MLJ (SC) 90 : 1961 MLJ (Cri) 554 : (1961) 2 An WR (SC) 90. [Evidence Act 1 of 1872), Ss. 24, 25, 27]

The word information received from "a person accused of any offence" in Section 27 cannot be read to mean that he must be an accused when he gives the information but would include a person if he became subsequently an accused person, at the time when that statement is sought to be received in evidence against him. *State* v. *Memon Mohamad Hussain Ismail*, MLJ : QD (1956-1960) Vol. II C2564 : 61 Bom LR 715 : ILR (1959) Bom 1244 : 1959 CrLJ 1419 : AIR 1959 Bom 534. [Evidence Act (1 of 1872), S. 27]

Person acting in concert. Comprises,—(1) persons who, for a common objective or purpose of substantial acquisition of shares or voting rights or gaining control over the target company, pursuant to an agreement or understanding (formal or informal), directly or indirectly co-operate by acquiring or agreeing to acquire shares or voting rights in the target company or control over the target company. [Securities and Exchange Board of India (Substantial Acquisition of Shares and Takeovers) Regulations, 1997, regulation 2(1)(e). Also see *Explanation* to section 236(8) of the Companies Act, 2013 (18 of 2013)]

Person affected. The proximity of a cremation and burial ground to a site where houses would spring up is an injury to health and hygiene of the inmates of the houses and in that sense the owners of those adjacent sites are persons affected. *Valliammal* v. *State of Madras,* AIR 1967 Mad 332, 334.

Person aggrieved. The words "person aggrieved" unconditioned and unfettered as they are, mean that any person, whether he be the first informant, or the Department or the officer in charge of the Custodian Department, if he considers himself aggrieved, by an order passed under Secs. 7, 16 or 40, he has got a right of appeal under Section 24(1) of the Act. *Mohd. Shariffudin* v. *R.P. Singh,* AIR 1957 Pat 235, 239. [Administration of Evacuee Property Act (31 of 1950), S. 24(1)]

The State Bar Council is a person aggrieved for the purpose of filing appeal under S. 38, Advocates Act. *Bar Council of Maharashtra* v. *M.V. Dabhalkar*, AIR 1975 SC 2092, 2099. [Advocates Act (25 of 1961), Ss. 37, 28]

A person who feels disappointed with the result of a case is not a person aggrieved. The order must cause him a legal grievance by wrongfully depriving him of something. *Adi Pherozshah Gandhi* v. *H.M. Servai*, AIR 1971 SC 385. [Companies Act (1 of 1956), S. 10-F]

A person aggrieved must be a man who has suffered a legal grievance, a man against whom a decision has been pronounced which has wrongly deprived him of something or wrongfully refused him something or wrongfully affected his title to something. *Ex-parte Sidebotham, In re Sidebotham,* (1880) 14 Ch D 458 at 465 quoted, *V.D. Kumarappan* v. *Secretary Home Department,* AIR 1960 Ker 378, 380.

Wife, a person aggrieved on the date when the offence was committed, does not cease to be so, despite the fact that at a later date before the complaint is lodged in Court, there is a decree for divorce dissolving the marriage between her and her husband. *Balarani Kali*

v. *Jagannath,* AIR 1967 Cal 203, 204. [CrPC 1973 (2 of 1974), S. 198]

Prosecution made at the instance of a person empowered under the power of general attorney to act on behalf of Electricity Supply Company, is one made at the instance of the person aggrieved, within the meaning of S. 50, though actually the First Information Report was launched by another person at the instance of the above said person aggrieved. *Ramchandra* v. *State of Bihar*, AIR 1967 SC 349, 352. [Indian Electricity Act (9 of 1910), S. 50]

Insolvency Court declining to make complaint against debtor under S. 70. The Receiver cannot be considered to be an aggrieved person in respect of that order. *Official Receiver* v. *Chellappa Chettair,* AIR 1951 Mad 935 (FB). [Provincial Insolvency Act (5 of 1920), S. 75(1)]

A person who took no interest in the controversy in the election petition which was confined only to the election petitioner and another respondent, is not a person aggrieved by the order in the election petition. *Thamanna* v. *K. Veera Reddy*, AIR 1981 SC 116, 122. [Representative of the People Act (43 of 1951), S. 116-C]

A person against whom a suit for declaration of rights to the trade-mark in question has been filed and the proprietors of a trade mark applying for rectification of the register by cancelling the entry as to registered user will be 'persons aggrieved'. *B. Monappa* v. *R.S. Ramappa,* AIR 1956 Mad 184, 187.

Any trader or merchant who is in any way injured or restrained in his business or embarrassed by registration of a mark is a person aggrieved. *Chandra Bhan Agarwal* v. *Arjun Das Agarwal,* AIR 1974 Cal 183, 187. [Trade and Merchandise Marks Act (43 of 1958), S. 56]

Person and individual. Individual means a single man or woman, as contrasted from the species or body of which he or she is a member along with other individuals. An individual is different from a person. *Mathai Mathew* v. *C&B Syndicate,* AIR 1967 Ker 174.

Person associated with commercial organization. For the purposes of Section 8 and this section, 'A PERSON IS SAID TO BE ASSOCIATED WITH THE COMMERCIAL ORGANIZATION,' if such person performs services for or on behalf of the commercial organization irrespective of any promise to give or giving of any undue advantage which constitutes an offence under sub-section (1). [Prevention of Corruption Act (49 of 1988), S. 8 and 9 as substituted by Amending Act (16 of 2018)].

Person carrying on designated business or profession. Means,—

(i) a person carrying on activities for playing games of chance for case of kind, and includes such activities associated with casino;

(ii) a registrar or sub-registrar appointed under section 6 of the Registration Act, 1908 (16 of 1908), as may be notified by the Central Government;

(iii) real estate agent, as may be notified by the Central Government;

(iv) dealer in precious metals, precious stones and other high value goods, as may be notified by the Central Government;

(v) person engaged in safekeeping and administration of cash and liquid securities on behalf of other persons, as may be notified by the Central Government; or

(vi) person carrying on such other activities as the Central Government may, by notification, so designate, from time to time. [S. 2(1)(sa) of the Prevention of Money-Laundering Act, 2002 (15 of 2003) as inserted by the Prevention of Money-Laundering (Amendment) Act, 2012 (2 of 2013)]

Person claiming through a member. Before a person can be said to claim through a member, the claim should arise through a transaction or dealing which the member entered into with the society as a member. *L.R. Hingoriani* v. *Pravinchandra Kantilal Shah*, AIR 1972 SC 2161, 2162.

Person conducting a prosecution. One who conducts a prosecution.

Person dealing with the firm. The expression "persons dealing with a firm" equally applies to old and new customers of the firm but only to such of them as have dealt with the firm on the assumption that the person whom they wish to hold liable was a partner in that firm.

Person employed. If the employer in a tailoring establishment provides the sewing machines and has right to reject the end products if it does not conform to the instruction of the employer and has the right to control the manner of work, the persons employed under him would be considered as 'person employed' and there exists the relationship of master & servant. *Silver Jubilees Tailoring House* v. *Chief Inspector of Shops and Establishments*, AIR 1974 SC 37, 44, 45.

Person entitled to make an application. The words "person entitled to make an application," in S. 7 of the Limitation Act (36 of 1963), mean a person who is entitled to make an application on his own behalf.

Person familiar with the manner of communication of the child. Means a parent or family member of a child or a member of his shared household or any person in whom the child reposes trust and confidence, who is familiar with that child's unique manner of communication, and where presence may be required for or be conducive to more effective communication with the child. [Protection of Children from Sexual Offences Rules, 2012, R. 2(e)].

Person holding high political office. 'Person holding high political office' includes—

(i) member of the Council of Ministers and the Chief Minister;

(ii) any person falling under the definition of public servant under clause (c) of section 2 of the Prevention of Corruption Act, 1988 or under Section 21 of the Indian Penal Code, 1860 who has been appointed to discharge the executive functions of the State in any organization specified in the Explanation below clause (b) of Section 2 of the said Act and receiving pay or honorarium or allowances for the services so rendered. [Orrisa Special Courts Rules, 2007 (the 2007 Rules), R. 2(f) as cited in *Yogendra Kumar Jaiswal v. State of Bihar*, (2016) 3 SCC 183, para 10].

Person holding high public office. 'Person holding high public office'. Incudes a public servant falling within the meaning of clause (c) of Section 2 of the Prevention of Corruption Act, 1988 or under Section 21 of the Indian Penal Code, 1860 and belonging to Group A service of the Central or State Government or officers of equivalent rank in any organization specified in the Explanation below clause (b) of Section 2 of the said Act who was serving under or in connection with the affair of the State Government. [Orrisa Special Courts Rules, 2007 (the 2007 Rules), R. 2(e) as cited in *Yogendra Kumar Jaiswal v. State of Bihar*, (2016) 3 SCC 183, para 10]. Person having substantial interest in the business. A person shall be deemed to have a substantial interest in the business, if—

(a) in a case where the business is carried on by a company, such person is, at anytime during the financial year, the beneficial owner of equity shares carrying twenty per cent or more, of the voting power; or

(b) in any other case, such person is, at any time during the financial year, beneficially entitled to twenty per cent or more, of the profit of such business. [Income tax Act (43 of 1961), Chap. XA, S. 102(9)].

Person holding office under government. The Chairman of the Mines Board of Health is not a person holding an office under the Government. *Surya Kant* v. *I.H. Khan*, AIR 1975 SC 1053, 1055.

Person, In. Personally. [CrPC 1973 (2 of 1974), S. 287(2)].

Person in authority. A person holding an office by virtue of which he can wield power over others. [Indian Evidence Act (1 of 1872), S. 24]; [CrPC 1973 (2 of 1974), S. 163(1)].

A person in authority within the meaning of S. 24 should be one who by virtue of his position wields some kind of influence over the accused. *Nannhu Gobrya* v. *State of M.P.*, AIR 1960 MP 132, 134. [Indian Evidence Act (1 of 1872), S. 24]

Person-in-charge. Means,—

(a) in relation to a vessel, the master of the vessel;

(b) in relation to an aircraft, the commander or pilot-in-charge of the aircraft;

(c) in relation to a railway train, the conductor, guard or other person having the chief direction of the train;

(d) in relation to any other conveyance, the driver or other person-in-charge of the conveyance. [Customs Act (52 of 1962), S. 2(31)]

Person in charge of the property. Person having the charge or control of the property.

Person in loco parentis. A person acting in the place of a parent; a person who has assumed the obligations of a parent without formally adopting the child.

Person in occupation of property. The expression "person in occupation of property" includes every person including a contractual or a statutory tenant. *Rambai Manjanath Nayak* v. *Union of India*, AIR 1993 SC 342, 352, 350. [Income-tax Act (43 of 1961), S. 269-D(2)(a)]

Person in receipt of a pension. Means "a person who receives a pension."

Person interested. The expression "PERSON INTERESTED" includes all persons claiming an interest in compensation to be made on account of the acquisition of land under this Act; and a person shall be deemed to be interested in land if he is interested in an easement affecting the land. [Land Acquisition Act (1 of 1894), S. 3(b) repealed by Act 30 of 2013].

A "person interested" would be one who is… "engaged in, or in promoting research in the same field as that to which the invention relates". [*Aloys Wobben* v. *Yogesh Mehra*, (2014) 15 SCC 360, para 21] [Patents Act (39 of 1970) S. 2(1)(t)].

A "person interested" would include a person who has a direct, present and tangible interest with a patent, and the grant of the patent adversely affects his above rights. A "person interested" would include any individual who desires to make independent use of either the invention itself (which has been patented), or desires to exploit the process (which has been patented in his individual production activity). [*Aloys Wobben* v. *Yogesh Mehra*, (2014) 15 SCC 360, para 21].

The expression "PERSON INTERESTED" includes all persons claiming an in interest in compensation to be made on account of the imposition of restrictions upon the use and enjoyment of land under this Act; and a person shall be deemed to be interested in land if he is interested in an easement affecting the land. [Work of Defence Act (7 of 1903), S. 2(b)]

"PERSON INTERESTED" means the person who was in actual possession of the premises requisitioned under Section 7A immediately before the requisition, or where no person was in such actual possession, the owner of such premises. [Census Act (37 of 1948), S. 7(B) *Expln.*]

The expression "PERSON INTERESTED" in relation to any requisitioned land, includes all persons claiming an interest in the compensation to be paid on account of the requisitioning or acquisition of the requisitioned land under the provisions of Section 19 of the Defence of India Act, 1939, or Section 6 of the Requisitioned Land (Continuance of Power) Act, 1947. [Requisitioned Land (Apportionment of Compensation) Act (51 of 1949), S. 2(a)]

The expression "PERSON INTERESTED," in relation to any property, includes all persons claiming, or entitled to claim, an interest in the compensation payable on account of the requisitioning or acquisition of that property under this Act. [Requisitioning and Acquisition of Immovable Property Act (30 of 1952), S. 2(d)]

The expression "PERSON INTERESTED" includes all persons claiming an interested in compensation to be made on account of the acquisition of rights in or over land, under this Act. [Coal Bearing Areas (Acquisition and Development) Act (20 of 1957), S. 2(d)]

"PERSON INTERESTED", in relation to any immovable property, includes all person claiming or entitled to claim, an interest in the compensation payable on account of the acquisition of that property under this chapter. [Income-tax Act (43 of 1961), S. 269-A(g)]

"PERSON INTERESTED" includes a person engaged in, or in promoting, research in the same field as that to which the invention relates. [Patents Act (39 of 1970), S. 2(t)]

Beneficiary is a person interested to determine just and proper compensation and has a right to be heard by the collector or the Court. *Neyveli Lignite Corporation Ltd.* v. *Special Tehsildar (Land Acquisition) Neyveli,* AIR 1995 SC 1004. [Land Acquisition Act (1 of 1894), SS. 3(b) & 50(2)] [Now repealed & replaced by Act 30 of 2013]

Only the person who is entitled to compensation and can be bound by the award of compensation, is the person interested under the Act. (*Scindia Employees Union* v. *State of Maharashtra,* 1996 (10) SCC 150). [Land Acquisition Act (1 of 1894), S. 3(d) repealed by Act 30 of 2013] [Now repealed & replaced by Act 30 of 2013]

A 'person interested' who had not accepted the award has the right to insist on a reference to the District Court, if he had complied with the provisions of sub-sec. (2) of S. 18. A 'person interested' does not mean a person whose interest the collector is prepared to admit. *K.S. Govinda Pillai* v. *District Collector,* AIR 1952 Ker 152, 153. [Land Acquisition Act (1 of 1894), S. 3(*b*) repealed by Act 30 of 2013]

Where in pursuance to a notification issued under S. 12 of the Displaced Persons (Compensation and Rehabilitation) Act (44 of 1954), Central Government acquired the lessee rights and in a subsequent auction the land is sold, the purchaser will be a person interested. *Gen. Govt. Servants Co-operating Housing Society* v. *Wahab Uddin,* AIR 1981 SC 866, 867, 868.

A purchaser after notification under Section 4 or even declaration under Section 6 of the Act can be a 'person interested'. *Seethalakshmi Ammal* v. *State,* AIR 1993 1, 17 (FB). [Land Acquisition Act (1 of 1894), S. 3(*b*)] [Now repealed & replaced by Act 30 of 2013]

There are two types of persons interested, namely, a person interested in compensation in respect of his land acquired and a person interested in the land acquired. A person for whose benefit the land is acquired, is not one interested. *Neyveli Lignite Corporation Ltd.* v. *Rangaswamy,* AIR 1990 Mad 160, 170 (FB).

The expression 'person interested' within the meaning of S. 18 means person admittedly interested, or believed or found by the Collector to be interested in the land. *Gulap Singh* v. *Union of India,* AIR 1977 Gau 40, 41. [Land Acquisition Act (1 of 1894), S. 18]

Municipal Corporation of Bombay for whose benefit land was being acquired is not a person interested so as to give it a right to become a party to the acquisition proceedings. *Special L.A. Officer (1)* v. *Greater Bombay Municipal Corporation,* AIR 1988 Bom 9, 13. [Land Acquisition Act (1 of 1894), S. 18, 50(2)]

"PERSON INTERESTED" in S. 41 of the Transfer of Property Act (4 of 1882), means a person personally interested in the property. The guardian of a minor is not such a person.

Person interested must include his predecessorin-title or interest as long as there is organic continuity of title. *Karanpure Development Co.* v. *Union of India*, AIR 1988 SC 1478, 1484. [Coal Bearing Areas (Acquisition and Development Act (20 of 1957), S. 2(*d*)]

A secretary of a responsible social and cultural organisation who is running several homes to bring up deserted children or orphans and who *bona fidely* desires to oppose the application and others, himself to the appointed as guardian or *bona fidely* seeks the custody of the child for the purpose of bringing her up in Indian traditional manner, can be said to be a person interested. *Chaganlal Vijayyaawargiya* v. *Astor Quisth,* AIR 1972 AP 49, 52. [Guardians and Wards Act (8 of 1890), S. 10]

A tenant is not a 'person interested' as defined in Section 269-A(*g*). *Shantinory Ray* v. *Competent Authority,* (1984) 145 ITR 365, 371 (All). [Income-tax Act (43 of 1961), S. 269-A(g)]

"PERSON INTERESTED". Means—

(i) all persons claiming an interest in compensation to be made on account of the acquisition of land under Act 30 of 2013;

(ii) the Scheduled Tribes and other traditional forest dwellers, who have lost any forest rights recognized under the Scheduled Tribes and Other Traditional Forest Dwellers (Recognition of Forest Rights) Act, 2006 (2 of 2007);

(iii) a person interested in an easement affecting the land;

(iv) persons having tenancy rights under the relevant State laws including share-croppers by whatever name they may be called; and

(v) any person whose primary source of livelihood is likely to be adversely affected. [S. 3(x) of the Right to Fair Compensation & Transparency in Land Acquisition, Rehabilitation & Resettlement Act, 2013 (30 of 2013)]

"Person in default". Means the asset reconstruction company or any person which has committed any failure, contravention or default under this Act and any person in-charge of such company or such other person, as the case may be, shall be liable to be proceeded against and punished under Section 33 for such failure or contravention or default committed by such company or person. [Securitisation and Reconstruction of Financial Assets and Enforcement of Security Interest Act (54 of 2002), S. 30-A, *Explanation (ii)*].

"Person is deemed to be connected". If such person—

(i) is a company under the same management or group, or any subsidiary company thereof within the meaning of sub-section (1-B) of Section 370, or sub-section (11) of Section 372 of the Companies Act, 1956 (1 of 1956) or sub-clause (g) of Section 2 of the Monopolies and Restrictive Trade Practices Act, 1969 (54 of 1969) as the case may be; or

(ii) is an intermediary as specified in Section 12 of the Act, Investment Company, Trustee Company, Asset Management Company or an employee or Director thereof or an official of a stock exchange or of clearing house or corporation;

(iii) is a merchant banker, share transfer agent, registrar to an issue, debenture trustee, broker, portfolio manager, investment Adviser, sub-broker, Investment Company or an employee thereof, or a member of the Board of trustees of a mutual fund or a member of the Board of Directors of the Asset Management Company of a mutual fund or is an employee thereof who have a fiduciary relationship with the company;

(iv) is a Member of Board of Directors or an employee of a public financial institution as defined in Section 4-A of the Companies Act, 1956; or

(v) is an official or an employee of a Self-regulatory Organisation recognized or authorized by the Board of a regulatory body; or

(vi) is a relative of any of the aforementioned persons,

(vii) is a banker of the company;

(viii) relatives of the connected person; or

(ix) s a concern, firm, trust, Hindu undivided family, company or association of persons wherein any of the connected persons mentioned in sub-clause (i) of clause (c), of this regulation or any of the persons mentioned in sub-clause (vi), (vii) or (viii) of this clause have more than 10 percent of the holding or interest. [SEBI (Prohibition of Insider Trading) Regulations, 1992, Regn. 2(h), **as cited in** *Chintalapati Srinivasa Raju* v. *Securities and Exchange Board of India*, (2018) 7 SCC 443, paa 13.2].

Person interested in a wakf. Means any person who is entitled to receive any pecuniary or other benefit from the *wakf* and includes—

(i) any person who has a right to worship or to perform any religious rite in a mosque, *idgah*, *imambara*, *dargah*, *khanqah*, *maqbara*, graveyard or any other religious institution connected with the *wakf* or to participate in any religious or charitable institution under the *wakf*;

(ii) the *wakif* and any descendant of the *wakif* and the *mutawalli*. [Wakf Act (43 of 1995), S. 2(k)]

Person located in a notified jurisdictional area. In section 94A of Act 43 of 1961, 'person located in a notified jurisdictional area' shall include,—

(a) a person who is resident of the notified jurisdictional area;

(b) a person, not being an individual, which is established in the notified jurisdictional area; or

(c) a permanent establishment of a person not falling in sub-clause (a) or sub-clause (b), in the notified jurisdictional area. [S. 94A(6)(i) of the Income-tax Act, 1961 (43 of 1961) as inserted (w.e.f. 1-6-2011) by the Finance Act, 2011 (8 of 2011)]

Person of Indian Origin (PIO). Means a citizen of any country other than Bangladesh or Pakistan, if

(a) he at any time held Indian passport; or

(b) he or either of his parents or any of his grand-parents was a citizen of India by virtue of the Constitution of India or the Citizenship Act, 1955 (57 of 1955);

or

(c) the person is a spouse of an Indian citizen or a person referred to in sub-clause (a) or (b). [Foreign Exchange Management (Deposit) Regulations, 2004, Reg. 2(xii)]

PERSON OF INDIAN ORIGIN (PIO) means a citizen of any country other than Bangladesh or Pakistan or Sri Lanka, if

(a) he at any time held Indian passport; or

(b) he or either of his parents or any of his grandparents was a citizen of India by virtue of the Constitution of India or the Citizenship Act, 1955 (57 of 1955);

or

(c) the person is a spouse of an Indian citizen or a person referred to in sub-clause (a) or (b). [Foreign Exchange Management (Remittance of Assets) Regulations, 2000, Reg. 2(iii)]

PERSON OF INDIAN ORIGIN (PIO) means an individual (not being a citizen of Pakistan or Bangladesh or Sri

Lanka or Afghanistan or China or Iran or Nepal or Bhutan), who

(i) at any time, held Indian passport;

or

(ii) who or either of whose father or whose grandfather was a citizen of India by virtue of the [Constitution of India or the Citizenship Act, 1955 (57 of 1955)]. [Foreign Exchange Management (Investment in Firm or Proprietary Concern in India) Regulations, 2000, Reg. 2(vi)].

Person of ordinary prudence. A common discreet person; a person of ordinary forethought and deliberation. [Indian Partnership Act (9 of 1932), S. 21].

Person of unsound mind. "PERSON OF UNSOUND MIND" shall mean any person not a minor who, not having been found to be a lunatic, shall be incapable from infirmity of mind to manage his own affairs. [Trustees Act (27 of 1866), S. 2]

Person or authority. The words 'person or authority' are wide enough to include even Government. *Surajmal Arjundas Vaidya* v. *State of Madhya Pradesh,* AIR 1958 MP 103, 112 (FB). [Constitution of India, Art. 226]

Person resident in India. Means—

(i) a person residing in India for more than one hundred and eighty-two days during the course of the preceding financial year but does not include—

(A) a person who has gone out of India or who stays outside India, in either case—

(a) for or on taking up employment outside India, or

(b) for carrying on outside India a business or vocation outside India, or

(c) for any other purpose, in such circumstances as would indicate his intention to stay outside India for an uncertain period;

(B) a person who has come to or stays in India, in either case, otherwise than—

(a) for or on taking up employment in India, or

(b) for carrying on in India a business or vocation in India, or

(c) for any other purpose, in such circumstances as would indicate his intention to stay in India for an uncertain period;

(ii) any person or body corporate registered or incorporated in India,

(iii) an office, branch or agency in India owned or controlled by a person resident outside India.

(iv) an office, branch or agency outside India owned or controlled by a person resident in India. [Foreign Exchange Management Act (42 of 1999), S. 2(v)]

"PERSON RESIDENT IN INDIA" means—

(i) a citizen of India who has, at any time after the 25th day of March, 1947, been staying in India, but does not include a citizen of India who has gone out of, or stays outside, India, in either case—

(a) for or on taking up employment out India, or

(b) for carrying on outside India a business or vocation outside India, or

(c) for any other purpose, in such circumstances as would indicate his intention to stay outside India for an uncertain period;

(ii) a citizen of India, who having ceased by virtue of paragraph (a) or paragraph (b) or paragraph (c) of sub-clause (i) to be resident in India, returns to, or stays in India, in either case

(a) for or on taking up employment in India, or

(b) for carrying on in India a business or vocation in India, or

(c) for any other purpose, in such circumstances as would indicate his intention to stay in India for an uncertain period;

(iii) a person, not being a citizen of India, who has come to, or stays in, India in either case—

(a) for or on taking up employment in India; or

(b) for carrying on in India a business or vocation in India; or

(c) for staying with his or her spouse, such spouse being a person resident in India, or

(d) for any other purpose, in such circumstances as would indicate his intention to stay in India for an uncertain period;

(iv) a citizen of India, who not having stayed in India at any time after the 25th day of March, 1947, comes to India for any of the purposes referred to in paragraphs (a), (b), and (c) of sub-clause (iii) or for the purpose and in the circumstances referred to in paragraph (d) of that sub-clause or having come to India stays in India for any such purpose and in such circumstances.

Explanation—A person, who has, by reason only of paragraph (a) or paragraph (b) or paragraph (d) of sub-clause (iii) been resident in India, shall during any period in which he is outside India, be deemed to be not resident in India. [Foreign Exchange Regulation Act (46 of 1973), S. 2(p)] Now Repealed and replaced by the Foreign Exchange Management Act, 1999.

Person resident outside India. Means a person who is not resident in India. [Foreign Exchange Management Act (42 of 1999), S. 2(w)]

Person responsible for collecting. Means a person who is required to collect tax under this Act or is required to pay any other sum of money under this Act and includes—

(a) every person in respect of whom any proceeding under this Act have been taken, and

(b) every person who is deemed to be an assessee-in-default under any provision of this Act. [Expenditure-tax Act (35 of 1987), S. 2(8)]

Person shall be deemed to have a substantial interest in the business. A 'person shall be deemed to have a substantial interest in the business', if,—

(a) in a case where the business is carried on by a company, such person is, at any time during the financial year, the beneficial owner of equity shares carrying twenty per cent or more, of the voting power; or

(b) in any other case, such person is, at any time during the financial year, beneficially entitled to twenty per cent or more, of the profits of such business. [(w.e.f. 1-4-2016) S. 102(8) of the Income-tax Act, 1961 (43 of 1961). Also see (still-born) Section 102(9) of the Income-tax Act, 1961 (43 of 1961) as inserted (w.e.f. 1-4-2014) by the Finance Act, 2012 (23 of 2012) and omitted (w.e.f. 1-4-2014) by the Finance Act, 2013 (17 of 2013)]

Person suing. The expression 'person suing' means all the partners of the firm who are its partners at the time of the institution of the suit. *Shankar Housing Corporation* v. *Mohan Devi,* AIR 1978 Del 255, 262. [Indian Partnership Act (9 of 1932), S. 69(1 & 2)]

Person bringing an action.

Person under disability. Person under legal disqualification or incapacity. [CPC (5 of 1908), S. 147].

Person who has a substantial interest in the company. In relation to a company, means a person who is the beneficial owner of shares, not being shares entitled to a fixed rate of dividend whether with or without a right to participate in profits, carrying not less than twenty per cent of the voting power. [Income-tax Act (43 of 1961), S. 2(32)]

Persons with benchmark disability. Means a person with not less than forty per cent of a specified disability where specified disability has not been defined in measurable terms and includes a person with disability where specified disability has not been defined in measurable terms, as certified by the certifying authority]rights of Persons with Disabilities Act (49 of 2016), S. 2(r) **as cited in** *Justice Sunanda Bhandare Foundation* v. *Union of India,* (2017) 14 SCC 1, para 14].

Person with disability. For the purposes of this section, "PERSON WITH DISABILITY" means a person referred to in clause (t) of Section 2 of the Persons With Disabilities (Equal Opportunities, Protection of Rights and Full Participation) Act, 1995, or clause (j) of Section 2 of the National Trust for Welfare of Persons with Autism, Cerebral Palsy, Mental Retardation and Multiple Disabilities Act, 1999. [Income-tax Act (43 of 1961), S. 80U *Expln.* (c) (*Substituted by Finance Act (23 of 2004), S. 19 Expln. (c)*)]

"PERSON WITH DISABILITY" means a person suffering from any of the conditions relating to autism, cerebral palsy, mental retardation or a combination of any two or more of such conditions and includes a person suffering from severe multiple disability. [National Trust for Welfare of Persons with Autism, Cerebral palsy, Mental Retardation and Multiple Disabilities Act (44 of 1999), S. 2(j)]

"PERSON WITH DISABILITY" means a person suffering from not less than forty per cent of any disability as certified by a medical authority. [Persons with Disabilities (Equal Opportunities, Protection of Rights and Full Participation) Act 1995 (1 of 1996), S. 2(t). Also see S. 2(13) of the National Food Security Act, 2013 (20 of 2013)]

Person with intersex variations". Means a person who at birth shows variation in his or her primary sexual characteristics, external genitalia, chromosomes or hormones from normative standard of male or female body. [Transgender Persons (Protection of Rights) Act, 2019 (40 of 2019), section 2(i)]

Person with low vision. Means a person with impairment of visual functioning even after treatment or standard refractive correction but who uses or is potentially capable of using vision for the planning or execution of a task with appropriate assistive device. [Persons with Disabilities (Equal Opportunities, Protection of Rights and Full Participation) Act, 1995 (1 of 1996), S. 2(u)]

Person with severe disability. Means—

(i) a person with eighty per cent or more of one or more disabilities, as referred to in sub-section (*4*) of Section 56 of the Persons With Disabilities (Equal Opportunities, Protection of Rights and Full Participation) Act, 1995; or

(ii) a person with severe disability referred to in clause (*o*) of Section 2 of the National Trust for Welfare of Persons with Autism, Cerebral Palsy, Mental Retardation and Multiple Disabilities Act, 1999. [Income-tax Act (43 of 1961), S. 80DD, (*Substituted by Finance Act (23 of 2004), S. 16(d)*)]

Persona designata. A person pointed out or described as an individual, as opposed to a person ascertained as a member of a class, or as filling a particular character.

PERSONA DESIGNATA is a person selected to act in his private capacity and not in his capacity as a judge.

(The Chief Justice and the taxing judge while deciding a reference under S. 5 of the act are not *persona designata*). *Maharaja Dharmendra Prasad Singh* v. *State of U.P.*, AIR 1969 All 484 at 486. [Court Fees Act (7 of 1870), S. 5]

Persona grata. An acceptable person (in diplomatic parlance).

Persona non grata. Person not wanted; an undesirable person. In international law and diplomatic usage, a person not acceptable (for reasons peculiar to himself) to the Court or government to which it is proposed to accredit him in the character of an ambassador or minister. (*Black*)

An unacceptable person (in diplomatic parlance).

Personal. The word "personal", means pertaining to the person or bodily form.

Of or relating to a particular person [CPC (5 of 1908), S. 81]; exclusively for a given individual; relating to the person or body [Gold (Control) Act (45 of 1968) (*repealed*), S. 2(p)]; relating to an individual, his character, conduct, motives or private affairs. [CPC (5 of 1908), S. 60(1), prov. (a)].

Personal acknowledgement. An acknowledgement made by any one himself or personally. [T.P. Act (5 of 1882), S. 3].

Personal action. "Action personal" is such as one man brings against another on any contract for money or goods or on account of any offence or trespass; and it claims a debt, goods, chattels, &c, or damages."

The action of an individual. [CPC (5 of 1908), O. XXXIX, R. 5].

Personal appearance. Appearance of the person himself. [CPC (5 of 1908), S. 81].

Personal attendance. Attendance of the person himself. [CrPC 1973 (2 of 1974), Ss. 115 and 205(2)].

Personal attendance of the accused. For the purpose of this section, "personal attendance of the accused" includes attendance through audio-video electronic means. [(w. e. f. 1-7-2024) Bharatiya Nagarik Suraksha Sanhita, 2023 (46 of 2023), section 355, Explanation]

Personal character. The moral qualities and excellence of behaviour of any individual. [IPC (45 of 1860), S. 171G].

Personal claim. Means a claim resulting from loss of life or personal injury. [Merchant Shipping Act (44 of 1958), S. 352(f)]

Personal Communications Service (PCS). Any of several types of wireless, voice and/or data communications systems, typically incorporating digital technology. PCS licenses are most often used to provide services similar to advanced cellular mobile or paging services. However, PCS can also be used to provide other wireless communications services, including services that allow people to place and receive communications while away from their home or office, as well as wireless communications to homes, office buildings and other fixed locations. (*Telecommunication*)

Personal cultivation. "PERSONAL CULTIVATION" with its grammatical variations, means cultivation by a *raiyat* himself, or by members of his family or by servants or hired labourers on fixed wages payable in cash or kind but not in crop share under his personal cultivation or the supervision of any member of his family during a main agricultural operation. [Bihar Land Reforms (Fixation of Ceiling Area and Acquisition of Surplus Land) Act, 1961 (12 of 1962), S. 2(i)]

"Personal data" means any data about an individual who is identifiable by or in relation to such data. [Digital Personal Data Protection Act, 2023 (22 of 2023), section 2(t)]

Personal data breach. Means any unauthorised processing of personal data or accidental disclosure, acquisition, sharing, use, alteration, destruction or loss of access to personal data, that compromises the confidentiality, integrity or availability of personal data. [Digital Personal Data Protection Act, 2023 (22 of 2023), section 2(u)]

Personal decree. A decree is said to be personal only as distinguished from a decree which directs that the amount decreed is to be realized by the sale of specific property.

A decree by which relief has been granted against the person of the judgment debtor, without making any specific property liable for the same. [CPC (5 of 1908), 1st Sch., App. D, Form No. 5, Para 7].

Personal direction and superintendence of the judge. The instructions and supervision of the judge himself. [CPC (5 of 1908), O. XVIII, R. 4].

Personal effects. "Personal effects" are used to designate articles associated with person, as property having more or less intimate relation to person or possessor of such tangible opportunity as attends the person. Silver bars and bullion cannot be deemed to be "effects" meant for personal use. *Rana Hemant Singhji* v. *C.I.T. Rajasthan*, AIR 1976 SC 662, 664.

Personal estate. All of a person's property not coming under the denomination of real estate.

Personal expenses. "Personal expenses" of a candidate at an election includes "the reasonable travelling expenses of such candidate, and the reasonable expenses of his living at hotels or elsewhere, for the purposes of and in relation to such election."

Personal guarantor. Means an individual who is the surety in a contract of guarantee to a corporate debtor. [Insolvency and Bankruptcy Code (31 of 2016), S 5(22)].

Personal injuries. "PERSONAL INJURIES" includes any disease and any impairment of a person's physical or mental condition. [Interest Act (14 of 1978), S. 2(d)]

"Personal injuries", in a contract of insurance mean bodily injuries.

'Personal injuries' include not only bodily injuries but also defamation and the like tortious injuries. (*M.*

Veerappa v. *Evelyn Sequeira,* AIR 1988 SC 506). [Indian Succession Act (39 of 1925), S. 306]

Personal injury. "PERSONAL INJURY" means physical or mental injury or a disease, whether manifesting itself immediately or subsequently—

(a) caused by—

(i) the discharge of any missile (including liquid or gas or both), or

(ii) the use of any weapon, explosive or other noxious thing, or

(iii) the doing of any other injurious act, whether by the enemy or in combating the enemy or in repelling an imagined attack by the enemy; or

(b) caused by the impact, on any person or property, of any aircraft or any aircraft belonging to or held by any person on behalf of or for the benefit of the Government of India or any allied power, or any part of, or anything dropped from, any such aircraft; or

(c) caused by any explosion or fire which involves any explosives or munitions or other dangerous things, required for the purposes of defence against the enemy or which happens or is caused by, through, or in connection with, the manufacture, storage or transportation of any such explosives, munitions or other dangerous things. [Personal Injuries (Emergency Provisions) Act (59 of 1962), S. 2(6)]

The words 'personal injury' have a wider significance than the words 'physical injury' and they apply to all kinds of injury whether physical or otherwise. *Ratanlal Bhannalal Mahajan* v. *Baboolal Hajarailal Jain,* AIR 1960 MP 200, 202. [Indian Succession Act (39 of 1925), S. 306]

Personal interest. 'Personal interest' is not limited to private interest and it may well include official interest also. *Rameshwar Bhartia* v. *State of Assam*, AIR 1952 SC 405, 406.

Personal law. The law which governs certain aspects of a person's status or relationships or rights or privileges in regard to certain matters such as succession, marriage, etc, by virtue of his belonging to a particular community or group [IPC (45 of 1860), S. 732, *Expln.* II and General Clauses Act (10 of 1897), S. 3(20)].

Personal liberty. Personal liberty consists of the right of locomotion—to go where one pleases, and when—and to do that which may lead to one's business or pleasure, only so far restrained as the rights of others may make it necessary for the welfare of all other citizens.

It is a very wide term and includes the right of every person to move freely throughout the territory of India and to go abroad. Thus it covers the right guaranteed under Art. 19(1)(d). *Menaka Gandhi* v. *Union of India*, AIR 1978 SC 597, 622. [Constitution of India, Art. 19(1)(d)]

Personal liberty means liberty of every kind necessary to live as human being and to ensure all round development of one's personality and to live with dignity. The right to establish and administer educational institution of the choice of the citizen or groups of citizen is covered by 'personal liberty'. *Bapuji Educational Association* v. *State of Karnataka*, AIR 1986 Kant 119, 129. [Constitution of India, Arts. 21, 30]

Personal lines. Means an insurance policy taken or given in an individual capacity. [Insurance Ombudsman Rules, 2017, R.. 4(1)(h)].

Personal luggage. The expression 'personal luggage' means whatever a passenger takes with him for his personal use or convenience, either with reference to his immediate necessities or for his personal needs at the end of his journey. *State of Maharashtra* v. *M.H. George*, AIR 1965 SC 722, 744.

Personal notice. By "personal notice" is meant the delivery of a notice in writing to another in person.

Personal obedience. Obeying by the person himself. [CPC (5 of 1908), S. 16, *Prov.*].

Personal office. Personal office is a place where an outsider would not normally be admitted. *V.S. Talwar* v. *Prem Chandra Sharma*, AIR 1984 SC 664, 665, 666.

Personal property. "Personal property" as defined by Blackstone, is composed of property in possession and property in action.

In its general or ordinary signification the term "personal property" embraces all objects and rights which are capable of ownership, except estates in land and incorporeal hereditaments issuing thereout or exercisable within the same.

The words 'personal property' embrace not only goods, chattels, coin, bills and evidences of debt, but, in their strict and more appropriate legal definition signify the right and interest of the owner or owners in these articles.

Personal right. Means immunity from the jurisdiction of Courts except with the permission of government of India, exemption from custom duties, the privilege to carry fire-arms without licence, and various other rights and privileges which a ruler had prior to the inauguration of the Constitution of India." *Ahmadunnisa Begum* v. *UOI,* AIR 1969 AP 423 at 432. [Constitution of India, Art. 363]

Personal rights and privileges. The words 'personal rights and privileges' are sufficiently comprehensive to embrace an immunity from civil action. *Mohan Lal* v. *Samax Man Singhji*, AIR 1962 SC 73, 76. [Constitution of India, Art. 362 (*repealed*)]

Personal safety. The condition of being safe personally. [IPC (45 of 1860), S. 336].

Personal security. "PERSONAL SECURITY" means a security not on property.

Security given by a person. [Indian Trusts Act (2 of 1882), S. 54].

Personal service. The term "personal service" has a fixed and definite meaning in law. It is service by delivery of the process or notice to the defendant personally.

It seems that "personal service" ordinarily means service upon the defendant personally and does not include service by leaving a notice at his last and usual place of abode.

Personal service injury. In relation to a civil defence volunteer, means any physical or mental injury, or a disease, whether manifesting itself immediately or subsequently, shown to the satisfaction of the Central Government or other authority authorised to make payments under a scheme to have arises out of and in the course of the performance by the volunteer of his duties as a member of the Civil Defence Organisation to which he belonged at the time the injury was sustained or the disease was contacted, and (except in the case of personal injury) not to have arisen out of, and in the course of, his employment in any other capacity:

Provided that before being so satisfied, the Central Government or other authority authorised to make payments under a scheme shall have received from the civil defence organisation of which the volunteer concerned was a member at the time when the injury was sustained or the disease was contracted, a report, by an officer of the organisation authorised by the Central Government to make such reports, about the injury or the disease in question. [Personal Injuries (Emergency Provisions) Act (59 of 1962), S. 2(7)]

Personalised vehicle. "PERSONALISED VEHICLE" means a motor cycle (including moped, scooter and cycle with attachment for propelling the same by mechanical power) and a motor car with seating capacity of more than three but not exceeding five which are solely used for personal purpose. [Bihar Motor Vehicles Taxation Act, 1994 (8 of 1994), S. 2(h)]

Personally. As the rules require the application to be signed by the partner in person, the signature by an agent on his behalf is invalid. *Commissioner of Agricultural Income Tax* v. *Keshal Chandra*, AIR 1950 SC 265, **relied on** *Ravulu Subba Rao* v. *Commissioner of Income Tax*, AIR 1956 SC 604, 613.

Personally appeared. "Personally appeared" as used in an affidavit means that the signer appeared before the notary administering the oath.

Personally works for gain. The expression 'personally works for gain' refers to an individual person and not to a company or a corporation. *Standard Tubewell and Engineering Works Ltd.* v. *Jogendranath Sen,* AIR 1959 Cal 461.[CPC (5 of 1908), S. 20(*a*)]

Personam, In. In respect of a person; proceeding *in personam* is one directed against or with reference to a specific person.

Personate. To represent by fictitious or assumed character, so as to pass for the person represented. (*Tomlin*)

To create a wrongful appearance of being someone other than oneself, whether fictitious or real. [Registration Act (16 of 1908), S. 82(c)].

Personating a public servant. Pretending to hold any particular office as a public servant, knowing that one does not hold such office, or falsely personating any other person holding such office. [IPC (45 of 1860), S. 170]

Personation. The action of personating. [IPC (45 of 1860), S. 416].

Personation at election. Whoever at an election applies for a voting paper or votes in the name of any other person, whether living or dead, or in a fictitious name, or who having voted once at such election applies at the same election for a voting paper in his own name : and whoever abets, procures or attempts to procure the voting by any person in any such way, commits the offence of personation at an election. [IPC (45 of 1860), S. 171D] [(w. e. f. 1-7-2024) repealed and replaced by Bharatiya Nyaya Sanhita, 2023 (45 of 2023), section 172]

Personnel. Staff or hands of an institution or service or business as opposed to its equipment or plant.

Persons of a particular group; a body of persons employed in some service. [Army Act (46 of 1950), S. 32].

Persons claiming under them. The expression "persons claiming under them" in Section 35 widens the net of those whom arbitral award binds. It does so by reaching out not only to the parties but also to those who claim under them, as well. The expression "persons claiming under them" is a legislative recognition of the doctrine that besides the parties, an arbitral award binds every person whose capacity or position is derived from and is the same as a party to the proceedings. Having derived its capacity from a party and being in the same position as a party to the proceedings, binds a person who claims under it. [*Cheran Properties Limited* v. *Kasturi and Sons Limited,* (2018) 16 SCC 413, para 29] [Arbitration and Conciliation Act (26 of 1996), S. 35].

Persons employed for payment. S. 77 does not indicate by whom those persons must have been employed. But the gist of a corrupt practice as defined in Section 123(7) is that the employment of extra persons and the incurring or authorising of excess expenditure must be 'by' the candidate or his agent. *Rananja Singh* v. *Baijnath Singh*, AIR 1954 SC 749, 751. [Representation of the People Act (43 of 1951), S. 123(7)]

Persons entitled to practise. The words "persons entitled to practise'" would include determining or prescribing the qualifications and conditions that a person should possess and satisfy before becoming entitled to practise as an advocate before the Supreme Court or High Courts. *Bar Council U.P.* v. *State of*

U.P., AIR 1973 SC 231, 237. [Constitution of India, Art. 246, Sch. 7, List 1, Entries 77, 78]

Persons having a judicial background. For the purposes of this clause, the expression "persons having a judicial background" shall mean persons having knowledge and experience for at least a period of ten years as a presiding officer at the district level Court or any tribunal at equivalent level. [Consumer Protection Act (68 of 1986), S. 20 *Expln.*]

Persons in authority. Words have reference to a person who has authority to interfere in the matter under inquiry. Generally speaking 'person in authority' is one who is engaged in the apprehension, detention or prosecution of the accused or one who is empowered to examine him. AIR 1933 Pat 149 (DB). [Indian Evidence Act (1 of 1872), S. 24]

Person with benchmark disability. Means a person with not less than forty per cent of a specified disability where specified disability has not been defined in measurable terms and includes a person with disability where specified disability has been defined in measurable terms, as certified by the certifying authority. [Rights of Persons with Disabilities Act (49 of 2016), S. 2(r)].

Person with disability. Means a person with long term physical, mental, intellectual or sensory impairment which, in interaction with barriers, hinders his full and effective participation in society equally with others. [Rights of Persons with Disabilities Act (49 of 2016), S. 2(s)].

Person with disability having high support needs. Means a person with benchmark disability certified under clause (a) of sub-section (2) of Section 58 who needs high support. [Rights of Persons with Disabilities Act (49 of 2016), S. 2(t)].

Persons likely to be affected thereby. The expression 'persons likely to be affected thereby', means that they must be persons whom the bye-law when made is likely to affect by its own terms. *Bagalkot City Municipality* v. *Bagalkot Cement Co.*, AIR 1963 SC 771, 773.

Persuade. To induce a person to believe or do something. [Representation of the People Act (43 of 1951, S. 129(2)(a)]; [Indian Evidence Act (1 of 1872), S. 10, ill.].

Persuade, Entice, Prevail upon. *Persuade* is employed to express different means to the same end; namely, that of drawing any one to a thing: one persuades a person by means of words; one entices him either by words or actions; one may persuade either to a good or bad thing: but one *entices* commonly to that which is bad; one uses arguments to persuade, and arts to entice. Persuade and entice comprehend either the means or the end or both. *Prevail* upon comprehends no more than the end : we may persuade without prevailing upon, and we may prevail upon without persuading. Many will turn a deaf ear to all our persuasions, and will not be prevailed upon, although persuaded.

Persuasive authority. Authority that carries some weight but is not binding on a Court.

Pertaining to. The expression 'pertaining to' presupposes another subject-matter and it means to bring into association or connection with. *Doypack Systems (P) Ltd.* v. *Union of India*, AIR 1988 SC 782, 799. [Swadeshi Cotton Mills Co. Ltd. (Acquisition and Transfer of Undertakings) Act (30 of 1986), S. 3]

Perusal. The action of perusing. [CrPC 1973 (2 of 1974), S. 353(4)].

Peruse. The word 'peruse' in its ordinary dictionary meaning connotes "to examine in detail". The proper meaning would be "to go through critically", that is, to read attentively and examine critically in detail, one by one. *Sohan Mushar* v. *Kailash Singh,* AIR 1962 Pat 249, 251. [CrPC 1973 (2 of 1974), S. 145(4)]

To go through; to look at or look through fairly attentively. [CrPC 1973 (2 of 1974), S. 145(4)].

Pervasive. It means that which pervades/tends to pervade in such a way, so as to be, or become, prevalent or dominant." "Extensive or far reaching, spreading through every part of something". [*Balmer Lawrie & Company Limited* v. *Partha Sarathi Sen Roy*, (2013) 8 SCC 345, para 11].

Perverse. The expression 'perverse' occurring in Section 48 means that the findings of the subordinate authority are not supported by the evidence brought on record or they are against the law or suffer from the vice of procedural irregularity. *Gayadin* v. *Hanuman Prasad,* AIR 2001 SC 386. [U.P. Consolidation of Holdings Act, 1953 (5 of 1954), S. 48]

Perverse finding. "Perverse finding" means a finding which is not only against the weight of evidence but is altogether against the evidence itself. *Parrys (Cal) Employees' Union* v. *Parry and Co.,* AIR 1966 Cal 31, 42.

Perverse order. An order made in conscious violation of pleading and law is a perverse order. *Narayanagowde* v. *Girijamma,* AIR 1977 Kar 58, 60.

Pervert. To make use of, usually wilfully, in a wrong or improper way. [Limitation Act (36 of 1963), Sch., Art. 84].

Pest. 'PEST' means any insect or other invertebrate animal. [Gujarat Agricultural Pests and Diseases Act, 1980 (7 of 1980), S. 2(7)]

Pesticide residue. Means any specified substance in food resulting from the use of a pesticide and includes any derivatives of a pesticide, such as conversion products, metabolites, reaction products and impurities considered to be of toxicological significance and also includes such residues coming into food from environment. [*Explanation* (1) to S. 21 of the Food Safety & Standards Act, 2006 (34 of 2006)]

Petition. "PETITION" means a petition calling in question an election. [Disputed Elections (Prime Minister & Speaker) Act (16 of 1977), S. 2(g)]

A formal application in writing made to Court for judicial action for something that lies in its jurisdiction; a written application addressed to a superior, or to a person or body in authority, soliciting some favour, right or mercy or the redress of some wrong or grievance [CrPC 1973 (2 of 1974), S. 401(5)]; a document embodying formal written request [CPC (5 of 1908), O. XXXIII, R. 8].

The expression 'petition' means original petition filed for any of the substantive reliefs awardable under SS. 9 to 13-B. *Shyamali* v. *Ashin Kumar,* AIR 1988 Cal 124, 126. [Hindu Marriage Act (25 of 1955), S. 19]

Petition writer. A person who scribes petitions and other legal documents for others. [CrPC 1973 (2 of 1974), S. 477(1)(a)].

Petitioner. The word 'petitioner' refers to the applicant in the application and not in the original petition by which the proceedings under the Act were started. *Baburao* v. *Sushila Bai,* AIR 1964 MP 73, 75. [Hindu Marriage Act (25 of 1955), S. 24]

One who makes a petition. [Indian Lunacy Act (4 of 1912) (*repealed*), S. 6(4)].

Petitioner and **Respondent.** The words 'petitioner' and 'respondent' in S. 24 of the Act mean respectively the party who had made the application under this section and the party opposing the application or against whom a claim under this section is made. *Kamala* v. *Shama Rupchand,* AIR 1958 Bom 466, 467. [Hindu Marriage Act (25 of 1955), S. 24]

Petro-chemicals. Means chemicals whether organic or inorganic, derived from petroleum including crude oil, natural gas, condensates, refined petroleum fractions and refinery gases. [Oil Industry (Development) Act (47 of 1974), S. 2(l)]

'Petrochemicals' are derived from various chemical compounds, mainly hydrocarbons. These hydrocarbons are derived from crude oil and natural gas. Among the various factions produced by distillation of crude oil, petroleum gases, naphtha, kerosene and gas oil the main feedstock for the petrochemical industry. Ethane and natural gas liquids obtained from natural gas are the other important feedstocks used in the petrochemical industry. Olefins (ethylene, propylene and butadiene) and aromatics (benzene, toluene and xylenes) are the major building blocks from which most petrochemicals are produced. [Report of Working Group on Chemicals and Petrochemicals in the 11th Five Year Plan from 2007-2008 to 2011-2012 made by the Department of Chemicals and Petrochemicals as cited in *Pepsico India Holding Private Limited* v. *Grocery Market and Shops Board*, (2016) 4 SCC 493, para 12].

Petroleum. Means any liquid hydrocarbon of mixture of hydrocarbons, and any inflammable mixture (liquid, viscous or solid) containing any liquid hydrocarbon. [Petroleum Act (30 of 1934), S. 2(a); Indian Power Alcohol Act (22 of 1948), S. 3(b); Petroleum & Minerals Pipelines (Acquisition of Right of User in Land) Act (50 of 1962), S. 2(c) and Oil and Natural Gas Commission Act (43 of 1959), S. 2(f)]

Petroleum Class A. Means petroleum having a flash-point below twenty-three degrees centigrade. [Petroleum Act (30 of 1934), S. 2(b)]

Petroleum Class B. Means petroleum having a flash point of twenty-three degrees centigrade and above but below sixty-five degrees centigrade. [Petroleum Act (30 of 1934), S. 2(bb)]

Petroleum Class C. Means petroleum having a flash point of sixty-five degree centigrade and above but below ninety-three degree centigrade. [Petroleum Act (30 of 1934), S. 2(bbb)]

Petroleum product. Means any commodity made from petroleum or natural gas and includes refined crude oil, processed crude petroleum, residuum from crude petroleum, cracking stock, uncracked fuel oil, fuel oil, treated crude oil residuum, casing head gasoline, natural gas, gasoline, naphtha, distillate gasoline, kerosene, bitumen, asphalt and tar, waste oil, blended gasoline, lubricating oil, blends or mixture of oil with one or more liquid products or by-products derived from oil or gas and blends or mixtures of two or more liquid products or by-products derived from oil condensate and gas or petroleum hydrocarbon not specified herein-before. [Oil Industry (Development) Act (47 of 1974), S. 2(m)]

'PETROLEUM PRODUCT' means any commodity made from petroleum or natural gas and shall include refined crude oil, processed crude petroleum, residuum from crude petroleum, cracking stock, uncracked fuel oil, fuel oil, treated crude oil residuum, casing head gasoline, natural gas gasoline, naphtha, distillate gasoline, kerosene, waste oil, blended gasoline, lubricating oil, blends or mixture of oil with one or more liquid products or byproducts derived from oil condensate, gas or petroleum hydrocarbons, whether herein enumerated or not. [Petroleum and Natural Gas Rules, 1959, R. 3(n)]

Petty offence. A minor or insignificant crime.

"PETTY OFFENCES" includes the offences for which the maximum punishment under the Indian Penal Code (45 of 1860) or any other law for the time being in force is imprisonment up to three years. [Juvenile Justice (Care and Protection of Children) Act, 2015 (2 of 2016), section 2(45)]

For the purposes of this section, "petty offence" means any offence punishable only with fine not exceeding five thousand rupees, but does not include any offence so punishable under the Motor Vehicles Act, 1988 (59 of 1988), or under any other law which provides for convicting the accused person in his absence on a plea of guilty. [(w. e. f. 1-7-2024) Bharatiya Nagarik Suraksha Sanhita, 2023 (46 of 2023), section 229(2)]

Petty officer. "PETTY OFFICER" means a sailor rated as such and includes a chief petty officer and a master chief petty officer. [Navy Act (62 of 1957), S. 3(17)]

Petty organised crime. Whoever, being a member of a group or gang, either singly or jointly, commits any act of theft, snatching, cheating, unauthorised selling of tickets, unauthorised betting or gambling, selling of public examination question papers or any other similar criminal act, is said to commit petty organised crime. [(w. e. f. 1-7-2024) Bharatiya Nyaya Sanhita, 2023 (45 of 2023), section 112(1)]

An officer in the navy corresponding in rank to a non-commissioned officer in the Army [CrPC 1973 (2 of 1974), S. 132(3)(b) and Air force Act (45 of 1950), S. 4(xxiii)(b)].

Pharmaceutical products. For the purposes of this section, 'Pharmaceutical products' means any patented product, or product manufactured through a patented process, of the pharmaceuticals sector needed to address public health problems and shall be inclusive of ingredients necessary for their manufacture and diagnostic kits required for their use. [Patents Act (39 of 1970), S. 92A, *Expln.* As inserted by Patents (Amendment) Act (15 of 2005), S. 55]. [Patents (Amendment) Ordinance (7 of 2004), S. 54(3) *Expln.*]

Pharmaceutical substance. "PHARMACEUTICAL SUBSTANCE" means any new entity involving one or more inventive substance. [Patents Act (39 of 1970), S. 2(1)(ta) *as inserted by Patents Amendment Act (5 of 2005), S. 2(h)*]

Pharming. Pharming occurs where a cyber criminal redirects a user from a legitimate site to a fraudulent and malicious site where their machines are infected with malware. In order to engage in 'pharming,' a Personal Computer has to be contaminated with a Trojan horse program. The Trojan contains a keylogger which remains dormant until the user of the infected PC happens to visit one of the specified websites. At that time, the keylogger becomes activated and records the passwords/PINs typed in by the User in the legitimate website. Aparna Viswanathan, *Cyber Law: Indian & International Perspectives,* 2012, LexisNexis Butterworths at p. 21.

Pharsa. *Pharsa* is a sharp-edged weapon. Its blade resembles a *gandasa* blade or may even be curved like that of a battle-axe. *State of U.P.* v. *Shankar*, AIR 1981 SC 897, 903.

Phishing. Phishing is an attempt by a third party to solicit confidential information from an individual, group, or organization by mimicking (or spoofing) a specific brand, usually one that is well known, often for financial gain. Phishers attempt to trick users into disclosing personal data, such as credit card numbers, online banking credentials, and other sensitive information, which they may then use to commit fraudulent acts. ['Symantec Global Internet Security Threat Report: Trends in 2009' (Vol. XV), April 2010 at p. 65]

Phonogram. "PHONOGRAM" means the fixation of the sounds of a performance or of other sounds, or of a representation of sounds, other than in the form of a fixation incorporated in a cinemotographic or other audio visual work. [WIPO: Performances and Phonograms Treaty Adopted in Geneva Dec. 20, 1996, Art. 2(b)]

Phonograms convention country. "PHONO-GRAMS CONVENTION COUNTRY" means a country which has either ratified, or accepted, or acceded to the Convention for the Protection of Producers of Phonograms against Unauthorized Duplication of their Phonograms, done at Geneva on the twenty-ninth day of October, one thousand nine hundred and seventy-one, and includes a country mentioned in Part V of the Schedule of Order. [International Copyright Order, 1999, S. 2(c)]

"Phooka" or "doomdev". Includes any process of introducing air or any substance into the female organ of a milch animal with the object of drawing off from the animal any secretion of milk. [Prevention of Cruelty to Animals Act (59 of 1960), S. 2(g)]

Photograph. "PHOTOGRAPH" includes an undeveloped film or plate. [Official Secrets Act (19 of 1923), S. 2(7)]

"PHOTOGRAPH" includes photo-lithograph and any work produced by any process analogous to photography but does not include any part of the cinematography film. [Copyright Act (14 of 1957), S. 2(s)].

Photographs are the paper copies taken from the original plate called the "negative", made sensitively by chemicals, and printed by sunlight through the camera. It is the result of art guided by certain principles of science. Photographs are not the original likenesses. Their lines are not traced by the hand of the artist. A photograph like a portrait or miniature painted from life, and proved to resemble the person, is admissible in evidence to identify the person photographed.

"Photograph" includes an undeveloped film or plate.

A picture taken by the process of photography. [Indian Evidence Act (1 of 1872), S. 3, ill.].

"PHOTOGRAPHY" includes still photography, motion picture photography, laser photography, aerial photography or fluorescent photography. [Finance Act (32 of 1994), S. 65(78) now repealed by Central Goods and Services Tax Act, 2017]

The process or art of production of pictures by means of the chemical action of light on a sensitive film of paper, glass, metal, *etc.* [Indian Evidence Act (1 of 1872), S. 62, *Expln.* 2].

'Photography' is the science which relates to action of light on sensitive bodies in production of pictures, fixation of images and the like. [Words and Phrases as cited in *State of Karnataka* v. *Pro Lab*, (2015) 8 SCC 557, para 16].

Photography studio or agency. Means any professional photographer or a commercial concern engaged in the business of rendering service relating to photography. [Finance Act (32 of 1994), S. 65(79) now repealed by Central Goods and Services Tax Act, 2017]

Phracker. Individual who combines phone phreaking with computer hacking. Formed by a play on both phreaker and hacker. (*Cyber Law*)

Phreak/phone phreak. A term for hacking or cracking-type exploitation directed at the telephone system (as opposed to the data communications networks). When the intrusion or action involves both telephone and data communications networks, that portion of the intrusion activity directed toward manipulating the telephone system is typically called phreaking. (*Cyber Law*)

Phreaker. Individual fascinated by the telephone system. Commonly, an individual who uses his or her knowledge of the telephone system to make calls at the expense of another. (*Cyber Law*)

Phreaking. The word 'phreaking' is a combination of the two words 'phone' and 'freak.' Phreaking refers to people who tamper with systems of telecommunications such as the public telephone networks and various phone system audio frequencies. Aparna Viswanathan, *Cyber Law: Indian & International Perspectives,* 2012, LexisNexis Butterworths at p. 90

Physical. Of or relating to body [Minimum Wages Act (11 of 1948), S. 13(3)]; of or pertaining to material nature; material; corporeal. [Two-Member Constituencies (Abolition) Act (1 of 1961), S. 6].

Physical abuse. For the purposes of section 3 of Act 43 of 2005, 'PHYSICAL ABUSE' means any act or conduct which is of such a nature as to cause bodily pain, harm, or danger to life, limb, or health or impair the health or development of the aggrieved person and includes assault, criminal intimidation and criminal force. [*Explanation* I(i) to S. 3 of the Protection of Women from Domestic Violence Act, 2005 (43 of 2005)]

Physical harm. Any physical impairment of chattels, land, or the human body.

Physical impossibility. Impossibility which occurs due to the fact that the crime cannot be actually or physically accomplished, *e.g.*, trying to pick an empty pocket.

Physical incapacity. "Physical incapacity" as a ground for annulment of a marriage is such a physical defect or incurable disease existing at the time of marriage as will prevent sexual coition, and does not include pregnancy.

Physical infirmity. There is no reason to restrict the interpretation of the words "incapable of cultivation by reasons of physical infirmity" to mean that the tenant must be bed-ridden or paralysed or otherwise incapable of moving. The ordinary meaning is that physical infirmity has rendered the tenant incapable of performing all the necessary acts of cultivation.

Physical injury. The term "physical injury" is the synonym of "bodily harm" or "bodily hurt."

Physical obstruction. If the judgment-debtor and his men move in a defiant attitude against the process-server and show every intention of resisting by force the execution by him of the warrant of possession of immovable property that constitutes the physical obstruction required by S. 186. IPC (45 of 1860), even though no physical force is actually, brought into play at the time.

Physical or mental disability. Means physical or mental disability by reason of which the person subject to such disability is incapable of cultivating land by personal labour or supervision. [Gujarat Agricultural Lands Ceiling Act, 1960 (27 of 1961), S. 2(22)]

Physical possession. Personal and immediate possession. [Limitation Act (36 of 1963), Sch., Art. 97].

Physical safety. Physical safety would mean the likelihood of assault to physical existence of a person. [*Bihar Public Service Commission* v. *Saiyed Hussain Abbas Rizwi*, (2012) 13 SCC 61, para 27].

Picket. Small body of men on police duty where troops are quartered; man or party stationed by trade union to deter would be workers during strike.

Picketing. The meaning applied to the picketing of liquor shops is to intercept people going to the shop to buy liquor and prevail upon them to desist from doing so.

The word 'picketing' is not used in the sense of offerring resistance to the visitor—physical or otherwise—or even dissuading him, from entering the house of the suspect but merely of watching and keeping a record of the visitors. *Kharak Singh* v. *State of U.P.*, AIR 1963 SC 1295, 1300.

Pickpocket. A thief who steals money or property from another person.

Picture. An individual painting on a surface. [Indian Contract Act (9 of 1872), S. 37, ill. (b)].

PID Block. Means the Personal Identity Data element which includes necessary demographic and/or biometric and/or OTP collected from the Aadhaar number holder during authentication. [Aadhaar (Authentication) Regulations, 2016, Regn. 2(1)(n)].

Piece goods. Cloth fabrics that are sold from the bolt at retail in lengths specified by the customer. [Trade and Merchandise Marks Act (43 of 1958), Ss. 72 and 74(1)] [Now repealed & replaced by Act 47 of 1999].

Piece rate. The price per unit of production paid to a piece worker. [Minimum Wages Act (11 of 1948), S. 3(2)(d)].

Pieces of counterfeit coin. Counterfeit coins. [Indian Evidence Act (1 of 1872), S. 14, ill.(b)].

Pier. "PIER" shall include any stage, stairs, landing-place, jetty, floating-barge, transhipper or pontoon, and any bridges or other works connected therewith. [Ben. Act III of 1890 (Port, Calcutta), S. 6, cl. 7

A solid support of masonry or the like designed to sustain vertical pressure; a solid structure of stone or of earth faced with piles, extending into the sea or a tidal river, to protect or enclose a harbour and form a landing-stage [Aircraft Act (22 of 1931), S. 2(2) and Workmen's Compensation Act (8 of 1923), Sch. II, item (vii)(c)]; [Indian Electricity Act (9 of 1910), S. 31].

Pig iron. A product of iron ore made by the reduction of the ore in the large blast furnaces which are filled with layers of the charcoal or coke and flux [Employees' Provident Funds and Miscellaneous Provisions Act, Sch. 1, *Expln.* (b) and Central Sales Tax Act (74 of 1956), S. 14(iv)(a)].

Pigmentary colours. Colouring matter. [Motor Vehicles Act (59 of 1988), 1st. Sch., form III(d)].

Pilfer. Steal or thieve in a petty way.

Pilferage. A petty larceny. [Indian Railways Act (9 of 1890), S. 76F]. Now Repealed.

Pilgrim. "PILGRIM" means a person making a pilgrimage and, in the case of passenger on board a pilgrim ship, includes every person accompanying or travelling with the person making the pilgrimage. [Merchant Shipping Act (44 of 1958), S. 3(26)]

"PILGRIM" means a Muslim proceeding on or returning from pilgrimage to Saudi Arabia, Syria, Iraq Iran or Jordan. [Haj Committee Act (51 of 1959), S. 2(b)]

"PILGRIM" means a Muslim proceeding to, or returning from, Haj. [Haj Committee Act (35 of 2002), S. 2(f)]

Pilgrim ship. "PILGRIM SHIP" means a special trade passenger ship which makes a voyage to or from the Hedjaz, or, as the case may be, to or from any other place of pilgrimage declared as such by the Central Government in persuance of clause (27), during the season of the pilgrimage and which carries pilgrimage in the proportion of not less than one pilgrim for every one hundred tons of the gross tonnage of the ship. [Merchant Shipping Act (44 of 1958), S. 3(28)]

"PILGRIM SHIP" means a ship conveying or about to convey pilgrims from or to the port of Bombay to or from any port in the Red Sea other than Suez. [Haj Committee Act (51 of 1959), S. 2(c)]

Pilgrimage. "PILGRIMAGE" means pilgrimage to any holy place in the Hedjaz or to any other place declared by the Central Government to be a place of pilgrimage by notification in the Official Gazette. [Merchant Shipping Act (44 of 1958), S. 3(27)]

Pillage. Plunder [Navy Act (62 of 1957), S. 65]; [Geneva Conventions Act (6 of 1960), 1st Sch., Art. 12].

Pilot. "PILOT" means a person for the time being authorised by the Government to pilot vessels. [Indian Ports Act (15 of 1908), S. 3(3)]

"PILOT" means a person for the time being authorized by the Local Government to pilot vessels. [Bur Act IV of 1905 (Burma Port), S. 4, cl. 8].

One who flies or is qualified to fly an aeroplane [Foreigners Act (31 of 1956), S. 6(2)]; a person who is duly qualified and usually licensed to conduct a ship into and out of a port [Calcutta Port (Pilotage) Act (33 of 1948), S. 4]; a trial unit in experimenting or in testing apparatus or in checking technique or cost preparatory to full scale activity.

Pilot in command. In relation to an aircraft, means a person who for the time being is in charge of the piloting of the aircraft without being under the direction of any other pilot in the aircraft and responsible for the operation and safety of the aircraft during flight time. [Tokyo Convention Act (20 of 1975), S. 2(h)]

Pilotage. Fee of the pilot; function of the pilot.

Navigation of a ship or airplane by observation of land marks directly or by means of a radar.

Pilotage fees. Fees allowed as compensation for the services rendered by a pilot [Carriage by Air Act (69 of 1972), 1st Sch., item 20(2); Indian Ports Act (15 of 1908), Ss. 35(1) and 36].

Pimp. One who solicits customers for a prostitute.

PIN. A Personal Identification Number. Used similarly to a password to access and manipulate information electronically. (*Information Technology*)

PING. Package Internet Groper. A program used to test if Internet destinations exist and are operational. (*Cyber Law*)

Ping. To check if a server is running. From the sound that a sonar systems makes in movies, you know, when they are searching for a submarine. (*Matisse Enzer-Glossary of Internet Terms*)

Pin-money. Pin money was an allowance made by a husband to his wife for her separate personal expenses and was usually provided for in a settlement by a yearly rent charge on the husband's real estate. HALSBURY, 4th Edn., Vol. 22, para 1083, p. 672.

Personal allowance (usually from a parent or spouse) for buying small personal items. By extension it also refers to earned income (not needed for essential expenditure) that is spent merely on luxury or trivial items.

Pious purpose. (*Hindu Law*) A Hindu father or any other managing member has power to make a gift within reasonable limits of ancestral immovable property for pious puposes, but a gift by the father-in-law to the daughter-in-law at the time of marriage cannot by any stretch of reasoning be called a pious purpose. *Perumalakkal* v. *Kumaresan Balakrishnan*, AIR 1967 SC 569, 578.

Pipeline. Means a pipe (together with any apparatus and works associated therewith) or system of pipes (together with any apparatus and work associated therewith) for the conveyance of a hazardous chemical other than a flammable gas as set out in Column 2 of part II of Schedule 3 at a pressure of 1 less than 8 bars absolute; the pipeline also includes inter-state pipelines. [Hazardous Waste (Management and Handling) Rules, 1989, R 2(k); Manufacture, Storage and Import of Hazardous Chemicals Rules 1989, R. 2(k)]

"PIPELINE" means, a pipe (together with any apparatus and works associated therewith) or system of pipes (together with any apparatus and works associated therewith) for the conveyance of a hazardous chemical other than a flammable gas as set out in column 2 of Part II of Schedule I, at a pressure of less than 8 bars absolute. [Chemical Accidents (Emergency Planning, Preparedness, and Response) Rules, 1996, R. 2(j)]

Piracy. Piracy consists of those acts of robbery or depredation on the high seas which if committed on the land would have amounted to a felony, and is sometimes spoken of as a marine felony. It is therefore robbery on the high seas.

Depredation and robbery in the high seas. [Navy Act (62 of 1957), S. 67].

Pirates. A *pirate* is one who roves the sea in an armed vessel without any commission or passport from any government, solely on his own authority, and for the purpose of seizing by force, and appropriating to himself without discrimination every ship he may meet. For this reason pirates have always been compared to robbers. The only difference between them is that the sea is the theater of action for the one and the land for the other.

Pith and substance. (*Interpretation of Statutes*) The phrase raises in a convenient form an appropriate question in cases where the real issue is one of a subject-matter and it may also serve a useful purpose in the process of deciding whether a particular enactment is a law with respect to trade, commerce or intercourse as such or whether it is a law with respect to some other subject which incidentally trenches upon trade, commerce and intercourse. *State of Bombay* v. *R.M.D. Chamarbaugwala*, AIR 1957 SC 699, 721.

Its real nature, its pith and substance is that it imposes a tax on the sale of goods. No other succint description can be given of it except that it is a tax on the sale of goods. It is in fact a tax which according to ordinary canons of interpretation appears to fall precisely within Entry 48 of the Provincial Legislative List. [*Governor Generals-in-Council* v. *Province of Madras,* AIR 1945 PC 98 : 72 IA 91. See also *State of Karnataka* v. *Drive-in-Enterprises,* (2001) 4 SCC 60, 65, para 8]

PKI. A public key infrastructure comprising a set of technology components combined with practices, policies and a supporting legal framework which provide a highly trusted infrastructure. At its core is the application of asymmetric encryption techniques that ensure trust in the confidentiality and authentication of data and entities within electronic systems. (*Cyber Law*)

PKI (Public Key Infrastructure)/ PKI Server. A set of policies, processes, server platforms, software and workstations used for the purpose of administering Digital Signature Certificates and public-private key pairs, including the ability to generate, issue, maintain, and revoke public key certificates. (*Information Technology*)

PKI Hierarchy. A group of Certifying Authorities whose functions are organized according to the principle of delegation of authority and related to each other as subordinates and superior Certifying Authority. (*Information Technology*)

PKIX. (Public Key Infrastructure X. 509) : This is a working group of the Internet Engineering Task Force (IETF) concerned with defining standards for interoperatability of public key infrastructure components such as security administrators, certification authorities, users, and directories. (*Information Technology*)

Placard. A notice or other document, written or printed on one side of a single sheet, to be posted up, or otherwise publicly displayed. [Indian Evidence Act (1 of 1872), S. 62, *Expln.*, ill. 2].

Placate. Conciliate; propitiate.

Place. "PLACE" includes a house, building and other structure and premises, and also includes a tent, vehicle and a vessel. [Cinematograph Act (37 of 1952), S. 2(e) and Untouchability (Offences) Act (22 of 1955), S. 2(b)]

"PLACE" includes a house, building, tent, vehicle and vessel. [CrPC, 1973 (2 of 1974), S. 2(p)] [Now (w.e.f. 1-7-2024) repealed & replaced by Bharatiya Nagarik Suraksha Sanhita, 2023 (46 of 2023), S. 2(1)(s), same definition in new Sanhita]

"PLACE" means an open space without any building. [West Bengal Religious Building and Places Act (32 of 1985), S. 2(d)]

Locality; position. [Protection of Civil Rights Act (22 of 1955), S. 2(b)]; to put in any place.

The expression "place" will depend for its connotation on the context in which it is used. The word is generally found in conjunction with other words which give it a colour, and is usually controlled by its context. In clause of charter party requiring charterer to procure safe "place" for discharge of cargo, quoted word meant spot selected to drop anchor plus area over which tanker might swing on tide and charterer's duty was not fulfilled merely by selecting area containing both safe and unsafe berths. The words "place" as used in a statute relating to searching for stolen goods in any store, shop, warehouse, or other building or place in a town includes a steam boat or vessel moored at the wharf. (*Collector of Customs* v. *Sun Industries,* 1988 Supp SCC 342, 346).

Place of abode. Place of habitual residence.

Place of birth. The expression 'place of birth' occurring in Article 15(1) of the Constitution is not synonymous to the expression 'domicile' occurring in Article 16(2). *Saurabh Chaudri* v. *Union of India,* (2003) 11 SCC 146, 162, para 29. [Constitution of India, Arts. 15(1) & 16(2)]

Place of business. "PLACE OF BUSINESS" means any office, sub-office, , sub-pay office and any place of business at which deposits are received, cheques cashed or moneys lent. [Banking Regulation Act (10 of 1949),S. 11(5)(a)]

"Place of business" includes—

(a) a place from where the business is ordinarily carried on, and includes a warehouse, a godown or any other place where a taxable person stores his goods, supplies or receives goods or services or both; or

(b) a place where a taxable person maintains his books of account; or

(c) a place where a taxable person is engaged in business through an agent, by whatever name called [The Central Goods and Services Tax Act, 2017 (12 of 2017), S. 2(85)]

'PLACE OF BUSINESS' includes—

(i) in any case where a dealer carries on business through an agent (by whatever name called), the place of business of such agent;

(ii) a warehouse, godown or other place where a dealer stores his goods, and

(iii) a place where a dealer keeps his books of account. [Central Sales Tax Act (74 of 1956), S. 2(dd)]

'PLACE OF BUSINESS' includes an office or any other place which a hotelier uses for the purposes of his business or where he keeps his books of accounts. [Maharashtra Tax on Luxuries (in Hotels and Lodging Houses) Act (41 of 1987), S. 2(i)]

Place of effective management of the com pany. For the purposes of this section, "PLACE OF EFFECTIVE MANAGEMENT OF THE COMPANY" means—

(A) the place where the board of directors of the company or its executive directors, as the case may be, make their decisions; or

(B) in a case where the board of directors routinely approve the commercial and strategic decisions made by the executive directors or officers of the company, the place where such executive directors or officers of the company perform their functions. [Income-tax Act (43 of 1916), Chap. XII G, S. 115VC, *Expln.*

Place of heritage. "PLACE OF HERITAGE" means any such place of historical, archaelogical or artistic importance, which has been in existence for not less than one hundred years as may be prescribed. [Tamil Nadu Aquaculture (Regulation) Act (T.N. Act No. 60 of 1995), S. 2(j)]

Place of pilgrimage. Means a place where any temple, mosque, gurudwara, church or other place of public worship of renown throughout any State or States is situated. [Income Tax Act (43 of 1961), S. 80IA(12)(d), S. 80IB(14)(e)]

Place of public entertainment. "PLACE OF PUBLIC ENTERTAINMENT" includes any place to which the public are admitted and in which an entertainment is provided or held.

Explanation—"Entertainment" includes any exhibition, performance, game, sport and any other form of amusement. [Protection of Civil Rights Act (22 of 1955), S. 2(c)]

A place to which the public are admitted and where any kind of food and drinks are supplied for consumption in the premises, would undoubtedly come within the expression "place of public entertainment". [*Mohan H. Pai v. Commissioner of Police Bangalore*, (2013) 14 SCC 592, para 15].

Place of public worship. Means a place, by whatever name known, which is used as a place of public religious worship or which is dedicated generally to, or is used generally by, persons professing any religion or belonging to any religious denomination or any section thereof, for the performance of any religious service, or for offering prayers, therein, and includes—

(i) all lands and subsidiary shrines appurtenant or attached to any such place,

(ii) a privately owned place of worship which is, in fact, allowed by the owner thereof to be used as a place of public worship, and

(iii) such land or subsidiary shrine appurtenant to such privately owned place of worship as is allowed by the owner thereof to be used as a place of public religious worship. [Protection of Civil Rights (22 of 1955), S. 2(d)

Place of removal. Means—

(i) a factory or any other place or premises of production or manufacture of the excisable goods;

(ii) a warehouse or any other place or premises wherein the excisable goods have been permitted to be deposited without payment of duty,

from where such goods are removed. [Central Excise Act (1 of 1944), S. 4(3)(b)]

"PLACE OF REMOVAL" is the place or premises from where the excisable goods are to be sold after their clearance from the factory and from whose such goods are removed. [*Commissioner of Central Excise, Mumbai – III* v. *Emco Limited*, (2015) 10 SCC 321, para 12].

"Place of removal" has been defined to mean not only the premises of production or manufacture of excisable goods but also a warehouse or any other place or premises wherein such goods have been permitted to be deposited without payment of duty and from where such goods are ultimately removed. [*Commissioner of Customs and Central Excise, Nagpur* v. *Ispat Industries Limited*, (2016) 1 SCC 631, para 15] [Central Excise Act (1 of 1944) S. 4 (as amended in 1973)].

"Place of safety". Means any place or institution, not being a police lock-up or jail, established separately or attached to an observation home or a special home, as the case may be, to receive and take care of the children alleged or found to be in conflict with law, by an order of the Board or the Children's Court, both during inquiry and ongoing rehabilitation after having been found guilty for period and purpose as specified in the order. [Juvenile Justice (Care and Protection of Children) Act, 2015 (2 of 2016), S. 2(46)].

Place of residence. The expression 'place of residence' connotes a place where a person has his dwelling house, which need not necessarily be permanent or exclusive. *Sukh Lal* v. *State Bank of India, Calcutta,* AIR 1967 SC 543, 545. [Displaced Persons (Debts Adjustment) Act (70 of 1951), S. 2(6)]

Place of safety. "PLACE OF SAFETY" means any place or institution (not being a police station or jail), the person incharge of which is willing temporarily to receive or take care of a child and which in the opinion of the competent authority may be a place of safety for the child. [Children Act (60 of 1960), S. 2(nn)(*repealed)*]

"PLACE OF SAFETY" means any place or institution (not being a police station or Jail), the person in charge of which is willing temporarily to receive and take care of a Juvenile and which, in the opinion of the competent authority may be a place of safety for the Juvenile. [Juvenile Justice Act (53 of 1986), S. 2(o)]

"Place of safety" means any place or institution, not being a police lock-up or jail, established separately or attached to an observation home or a special home, as the case may be, the person in-charge of which is willing to receive and take care of the children alleged or found to be in conflict with law, by an order of the Board or the Children's Court, both during inquiry and ongoing rehabilitation after having been found guilty for period and purpose as specified in the order. [Juvenile Justice (Care and Protection of Children) Act, 2015 (2 of 2016), S. 2(46)].

"PLACE OF SAFETY" means any place or institution (not being a police lock-up or jail), the person incharge of which is willing temporarily to receive and take care of the juvenile and which, in the opinion of the competent authority, may be a place of safety for the juvenile. [Juvenile Justice (Care and Protection of Children) Act (56 of 2000), S. 2(q)]

Place of worship. "PLACE OF WORSHIP" means a temple mosque, *gurudwara,* Church, monastery or any other place of public religious worship of any religious denomination or any section thereof, by whatever name called. [Places of Worship (Special Provisions) Act (42 of 1991), S. 2(c)]

Place open to public view. "PLACE OPEN TO PUBLIC VIEW" includes any private place or building, monument, fence or balcony visible to a person being in, or passing along, any public place. [Himachal Pradesh Non-biodegradable Garbage (Control) Act (HP Act No. 15 of 1995), S. 2(i)]

Plagiarism. The act of publishing borrowed thoughts or literary work as originals.

Plagiarism. Means the practice of taking someone else's work or idea and passing them as one's own. [University Grants Commission (Promotion of Academic Integrity and Prevention Plagiarism in Higher Educational Institutions) Regulations 2018, Regn. 2(l)].

Plain-meaning rule. The principle that, in the interpretation of a constitutional or statutory provision, words should be given their ordinary and accepted meaning. (CRAIG R. DUCAT—*Constitutional Interpretation*)

Plaint. A "plaint" is the process by which proceedings in the Courts, are, generally commenced.

The statement in writing of a course of action in which the relief claimed is set out in detail. [CPC (5 of 1908), O. VI, R. 1 and Court-fees Act (7 of 1870), S. 7(iv)(f)].

A plaint in a Court is in the nature of an original writ. The first process in Court is a plaint.

Plaint means a statement in writing of the cause of action in a suit. *S.T. Corporation of India* v. *Ironside Ltd.,* AIR 1966 Bom 126, 131.

Plaint or memorandum of appeal. The words 'the plaint or memorandum of appeal', as used in Col. 3 of Art. 5 mean the plaint or memorandum of appeal which has given rise to the judgment under review and not any other plaint or morandum of appeal. *Narayan Tewari* v. *Vasudeo Narayan Missir,* AIR 1958 Pat 587, 589 (FB). [Court Fees Act (7 of 1870), Art. 5]

Plaintiff. "PLAINTIFF" includes—(i) any person from or through whom a plaintiff derives his right to sue; (ii) any person whose estate is represented by the plaintiff as executor, administrator or other representative. [Limitation Act (36 of 1963), S. 2(i)]

The party, who brings a suit to a Court of law. [CPC (5 of 1908), O. XXII, R. 2 and Companies Act (1 of 1956), S. 632].

By virtue of S. 146 it is open to a person deriving title through the plaintiff to apply under O. IX, R. 9 to set aside an order under R. 8. It therefore implies that the word 'plaintiff' in R. 9 should be construed as 'plaintiff and his representatives'. *Balaji Govinda Narain* v. *Hiralal,* AIR 1957 AP 364, 367. [CPC (5 of 1908), O. IX, Rr. 9 & 8 and S. 146]

The word 'plaintiff' includes the assignees and legal representatives of the plaintiff. *Suraj Rattan* v. *Azarabad Tea Co.*, AIR 1965 SC 295, 301.

'Plaintiff' and 'defendant'. The words 'plaintiff' and 'defendant' include persons from or through whom the plaintiff or defendant derives his right to sue or liability to be sued. The words "*plaintiff*" and "defendant" shall include, (*i*) a pleader duly appointed to act on behalf of such plaintiff or defendant, and (*ii*) the recognised agent of a plaintiff or defendant.

Plaintiff decree-holder. Plaintiff in whose favour the suit has been decreed. [CPC (5 of 1908), Sch. 1. App. G, form No. 2].

Plan. A plan is a design, a delineation, or projection on a plane surface of a structure, which is reduced in size, the relative position of which, and the proportions, being preserved.

A plan is a draft or form of representation of a horizental section of anything, as of a building or machinery. Its synonyms are "draft", "delineation", "sketch" and "design".

A drawing, sketch *etc.* of any object, made by projection upon a flat surface [Indian Evidence Act (1 of 1872), S. 83]; [Delivery of Books and Newspapers (Public Libraries) Act (27 of 1954), S. 2(a)]; a scheme for accomplishing a purpose, a proposed method [Unit Trust of India Act (52 of 1963), S. 19(cc)]; to design; to make a plan.

Planned economy. Economy in which some or all economic activity is planned and undertaken by the state, directly or indirectly, irrespective of the market forces of *supply and demand,* and without *private enterprise.*

Planning authority. Means an Urban Development Authority or any other authority in any city or town designated by the appropriate Government as responsible for regulating the land use by defining the precise extent of areas for any particular activity in the master plan or development plan or zonal plan or layout plan or any other spatial plan which is legally enforceable under the applicable Town and Country Planning Act or the Urban Development Act or the Municipal Act, as the case may be. [S. 2(1)(g) of the Street Vendors (Protection of Livelihood and Regulation of Street Vending) Act, 2014 (7 of 2014)]

Planning area. Means a planning area or a development area or a local planning area or a regional development plan area, by whatever name called, or any other area specified as such by the appropriate Government or any competent authority and includes any area designated by the appropriate Government or the competent authority to be a planning area for future planned development, under the law relating to Town and Country Planning for the time being in force and as revised from time to time. [Real Estate (Regulation and Development) Act (16 of 2016), S. 2(zh)]

Planning period. Means a period not exceeding 12 months from the date of acquisition of assets for reconstruction, allowed for formulating a plan for realisation of such assets. [Securitisation of Companies/ Reconstruction Companies Prudential Norms (Reserve Bank) Directions, 2002, S. 3(vi)]

Plant. "Plant" means the fixtures, machinery, tools, apparatus, appliances *etc.*, necessary to carry on any trade or mechanical business, or any mechanical operation or process.

"PLANT" includes ships, vehicles books, scientific apparatus and surgical equipment used for the purpose of the business or profession, but does not include tea bushes or livestock. [Income Tax Act (43 of 1961), S. 43(3)]

"PLANT" includes machinery, equipment or appliance, whether affixed to land or not. [Atomic Energy Act (33 of 1962), S. 2(c)]

"PLANT" (Production facility, Workshop) means a relatively self-contained area, structure or building containing one or more units with auxiliary and associated infrastructure, such as;

(i) Small administrative section;
(ii) Storage/handling areas for feedstock and products;
(iii) Effluent/waste handling/treatment area;
(iv) Control/analytical laboratory;
(v) First aid service/related medical section; and
(vi) Records associated with the movement into, around and from the site, of declared chemicals and their feedstock or product chemicals formed from them, as appropriate. [Chemical Weapons Convention Act (34 of 2000), (verification annex), 6(b)]

Fixtures, implements, machinery used in Industrial process [Coal Mines Provident Fund and Miscellaneous Provisions Act (46 of 1948), S. 2(b)(xii)]; a young tree, vine or shrub lately planted or suitable for planting [Central Sales Tax Act (74 of 1956), S. 14(v)].

The word 'plant' will not cover the container or the storage place of the stock-in-trade of the assessee. *Jayasing Rao Piraji Rao* v. *CIT,* AIR 1963 Bom 66, 68.

It includes sanitary fittings and pipelines installed in a hotel. *Commissioner of Income Tax, Andhra Pradesh* v. *Taj Mahal Hotel, Seemdrabad*, AIR 1972 SC 168, 171.

Plant will include any article or object fixed or movable, live or dead, used by a businessman for carrying on his business and it is not necessarily confined to an apparatus which is used for mechanical operations or processes or is employed in mechanical or industrial business. *Scientific Engineering House (P) Ltd.* v. *Commissioner of Income Tax*, (1986) 157 ITR 86, 96 (SC). [Income Tax Act (43 of 1961), S. 32]

Plant and machinery. An electric stove is both a plant and a machinery. Diesel engine fitted to a lorry is a machinery. *M. Ganesh Beedi Works* v. *CIT,* AIR 1964 Mys 235, 236, 237.

Plant installed. The term "plant installed" applies to motor vehicles, which are "inducted or introduced" into the business. [Income Tax Act (11 of 1922), S. 10(2)(vi-b)]

Plant material. "PLANT MATERIAL" means any propagation material used in raising the plant and includes Budwood, Scion, rootstack, seed and cutting. [Goa Fruit and Ornamental Plant-Nursuries (Regulation) Act, 1995 (13 of 1997), S. 2(j)]

Plant site (Works, Factory). Means the local integration of one or more plants, with any intermediate administrative levels, which are under one operational control, and includes common infrastructure, such as;

(i) Administration and other offices;
(ii) Repair and maintenance shops;
(iii) Medical centre;

(iv) Utilities;
(v) Central analytical laboratory;
(vi) Research and development laboratories;
(vii) Central effluent and waste treatment area; and
(viii) Warehouse storage. [Chemical Weapons Convention Act (34 of 2000), (Verification Annex), 6(a)]

Plantation. "PLANTATION" means any estate which is maintained for the purpose of growing cinchona, rubber, coffee or tea on which 25 or more persons are employed for that purpose. [Payment of Wages Act (4 of 1936), S. 2(iii)]

"PLANTATION" means any plantation to which this Act, whether wholly or in part, applies and includes offices, hospitals, dispensaries, schools, and any other premises used for any purpose connected with such plantation, but does not include any factory on the premises to which the provisions of the Factories Act, 1948, apply. [Plantations Labour Act (69 of 1951), S. 2(f)]

"PLANTATION" means—

(a) any land used or intended to be used for—
 (i) growing tea, coffee, rubber, cinchona or cardamom which admeasures five hectares or more
 (ii) growing any other plant, which admeasures five hectares or more and in which ten or more persons are employed or were employed on any day of the preceding twelve months, if, after obtaining the approval of the Central Government, the State Government, by notification, so directs. [Code on Social Security, 2020 (36 of 2020), section 2(59)] [Occupational Safety, Health & Working Conditions Code, 2020 (37 of 2020), section 2(1)(zx)]

'Plantation' means any land used by a person principally for the cultivation of tea, coffee, cocoa, rubber, cardamom or cinnamon (hereinafter in this referred to as 'plantation crops') and includes—

(a) land used by the said person for any purpose ancillary to the cultivation of plantation crops or for the preparation of the same for the market;
(b) land contiguous to, or in the vicinity of, or within the boundaries of, the area cultivated with plantation crops, not exceeding twenty per cent of the area so cultivated and reserved by the said person and fit for the expansion of such cultivation;
(c) agricultural land interspersed within the boundaries of the area cultivated by the said person with plantation crops, not exceeding such extend as may be determined by the Land Board or the Taluk Land Board, as the case may be as necessary for the protection and efficient management of such cultivation. [Kerala Land Reforms Act, 1963 (1 of 1964), S. 2(44) as cited in *N.K. Rajendra Mohan v. Thiruvambadi Rubber Company Limited*, (2015) 9 SCC 326, para 18].

The expression "PLANTATION" means any land not less than four hectares in extent which is being prepared for the production of, or actually produces, tea, coffee, pepper, rubber, cardamom, cinchona or such other products as the State Governments may, by notification in the Official Gazette specify and the expression "superintendent of the plantation" means the person having the charge or supervision of the labourers and work in the plantation, whether called a manager, superintendent or by any other name. [Registration of Birth and Death Act (18 of 1969), S. 9, *Expln.*]

The ordinary signification of the term "plantation" is a farm. These terms are nearly synonymous. A plantation is a place planted; land brought under cultivation; ground occupied by trees or vegetables, which have been planted.

Plate. "PLATE" includes any stereotype or other plate, stone, block, mould, matrix, transfer, negative duplicating equipment or other device used or intended to be used for printing or reproducing copies of any work, and any matrix or other appliance by which records for the acoustic presentation of the work are or are intended to be made. [Copyright Act (14 of 1957), S. 2(t)]

A prize as a cup or other piece of plate given to the winner in contest [Indian Contract Act (9 of 1872), S. 30]; a flat thin smooth piece on or from which something is or is to be embossed, moulded, engraved, gained, deposited or written. [IPC (45 of 1860), Ss. 473 and 485].

Platform work means a work arrangement outside of a traditional employer-employee relationship in which organizations or individuals use an online platform to access other organisations or individuals to solve specific problems or to provide specific services or any such other activities which may be notified by the Central Government, in exchange for payment. [Code on Social Security, 2020 (36 of 2020), section 2(60)]

Platform worker means a person engaged in or undertaking platform work. [Code on Social Security, 2020 (36 of 2020), section 2(61)]

Platinum. Means platinum, iridium, osmium, palladium, rhodium and ruthenium. [Customs Tariff Act (51 of 1975), I Sch., Import Tariff, S. XIV, Chap. 71, Note 4(b); Central Excise Tariff (5 of 1986), I Sch, S. XIV, Chap. 71, Note 3(b)]

Playing-off. Playing-off is a technical term in industry and means that due to the closure of certain departments some of the employees are asked to work for less hours than they were working before the closure and those employees are paid on the basis of the less work done by them. *Gambhirji* v. *Bind Basni Prasad,* AIR 1955 Bom 369.

PLC (also plc, Plc). (*abbr.*) Public limited company; Power Line Communication. Communication via domestic electrical power supply lines. (*Telecommunication*).

PLC connection. Connection allowing a subscriber to connect to public telecoms networks via domestic electricity power supply lines. (*Telecommunication*)

Plea. That which either party alleges for himself in Court, in a cause there depending to be tried. (*Tomlin*)

That which is pleaded in justification or excuse; that which is demanded by pleading [CrPC 1973 (2 of 1974), S. 246(3)]; [Reciprocity Act (9 of 1943), S. 4].

Plea bargaining. Plea bargaining in criminal cases is where the accused instead of defending his case in proper defence simply pleaded guilty under a promise or assurance that he would be let off lightly and then in appeal or revision to enhance the sentence. *Thippeswamy* v. *State of Karnataka*, AIR 1983 SC 747, 748. [CrPC 1973 (2 of 1974), Ss. 375, 229, 386, 401]

Plea of guilty. Is plea to the charge and does not necessarily amount to a confession of all the facts alleged.

A plea of guilty amounts to nothing more than an acknowledgment of the facts charged, and whether such facts constitute an offence is left open to be decided by the Court.

A plea of guilty, entered by one accused of crime, is a confession of the charge, and judgment is rendered thereon without a trial on any issue of law or of fact.

Plead. Address to the Court as an advocate or party; maintain a cause in Court; allege as a plea in proceedings in Court.

'Plead' means to address the Court as an advocate on behalf of either party. So a permanent Judge of the High Court can plead his own cause before the High Court and there is no bar. *J.P. Mitter* v. *H.K. Bose,* AIR 1963 Cal 178, 182. [Constitution of India, Art. 220]

Pleader. "PLEADER", when used with reference to any proceeding in any Court, means a person authorised by or under any law for the time being in force, to practice in such Court, and includes any other person appointed with the permission of the Court to act in such proceeding. [CrPC 1973 (2 of 1974), S. 2(q)].

"PLEADER" means any person entitled to appear and plead for another in Court, and includes an advocate, a *vakil* and an attorney of a High Court. [CPC (5 of 1908), S. 2(15)].

A category of legal practitioners authorised to plead in a law Court. [CPC (5 of 1908), S. 2(15)].

The 'pleader' appointed under Section 303 of CrPC is not necessarily to be a power-of-Attorney holder of the party in the case. What seems to be a condition precedent is that his appointment should have been preceded by grant of permission of the Court. *T.C. Mathai* v. *Distt. & Sessions Judge*, AIR 1999 SC 1385. [CrPC, 1973 (2 of 1974), Ss. 2(q) & 303]

Pleading. "PLEADING" shall include original applications, reply statements, rejoinders and additional statements supplementing the original applications and reply statements as may be permitted by the Tribunal. [Debts Recovery Tribunal Regulations of Practice, 1997, S. 3(vi)]

Plaint or written statement containing in a concise form, the material facts on which the party pleading relies for his claim or defence. [Indian Evidence Act (1 of 1872), S. 58].

"PLEADINGS" means and includes application including interlocutory application, petition, appeal, revision, reply, rejoinder, statement, counter claim, additional statement supplementing the original application and reply statement under these rules and as may be permitted by the Tribunal. [National Company Law Tribunal Rules, 2016, R. 2(19)].

Pleasure craft. In this chapter unless the context otherwise requires,—

"PLEASURE CRAFT" means a ship of a kind whose primary use is for the purposes of sport or recreation. [Income-tax Act (43 of 1961), Chap. XII G, S. 115V(f) (*Inserted by Finance Act (23 of 2004), S. 30*)]

Pleasure doctrine. In England, all public officers and servants of the Crown hold their appointments at the pleasure of Crown and their services can be terminated at will without assigning any cause. By the expression 'the pleasure' is conveyed this right of the Crown. [*Union of India* v. *Tulsiram Patel,* (1985) 3 SCC 398, 438, para 35]

Pleasure doctrine relates with the tenure of Government servant. *R.P. Raja* v. *State of Bihar,* AIR 1988 Pat 116, 121.

Pleasure of President. The tenure of office of a person serving under the Union is at the pleasure of the President. This pleasure should be exercised by the President or Governor, as the case may be, himself and cannot be delegated to any sub-ordinate authority. It would be open to the President to terminate his services according to his pleasure, with the one exception that this pleasure could not be exercised against or contrary to any express provision in the Constitution. *Shyam Behari* v. *UOI,* AIR 1963 Ass 94, 103 (FB). [Constitution of India, Arts. 310, 311]

Pleasure of the Governor. "We should not be taken to have accepted the submission of the learned Attorney-General who appeared for the respondent-State, that the provision in Art. 310(1) of the Constitution that "members of a Civil Service of a State hold office during the pleasure of the Governor", confer a power on the State Government to compel an officer to continue in service of the State against his will apart from service rules which might govern the matter even after the age of superannuation was reached, or where he was employed for a defined term, even after the term of his appointment was over. We consider that to construe the expression "the pleasure of the Governor" in that manner would be patently unwarranted besides being contrary to what this

Court said in *State of Bihar* v. *Abdul Majid,* AIR 1954 SC 245. (*S. Pratap Singh* v. *State of Punjab,* AIR 1964 SC 72 (81)). (*Service Laws*)

Plebiscite. Direct vote of all electors on a special issue.

Pledge. A pledge is defined to be a bailment of personal property as security for some debt or engagement.

The bailment of goods as a security for payment of a debt or performance of a promise is called "PLEDGE". [Indian Contract Act (9 of 1872), S. 172]

Pledged articles. Articles pledged with a bank cannot be held as securities and the question of obtaining succession certificate does not arise. *Branch Manager, State of Hyderabad* v. *G.R.B. Viswanadha Raju,* AIR 1993 AP 337, 338. [Indian Contract Act (9 of 1872), S. 174]

Pledgee. One who holds property as a pledge or with whom a pledge is deposited. [Indian Evidence Act (1 of 1872), S. 130].

Plenary. Not subject to limitation or exceptions; not incomplete (as) plenary powers.

Plenary cause. Green-leaf defines "plenary causes" as those in which the order and solemnity of the law are strictly observed in the regular contest of the suit, while summary proceedings are those in which its order and solemnity are, more or less, dispensed with.

Plenipotentiary. A person invested with full powers especially a special ambassador or envoy to some foreign country. [Geneva Conventions Act (6 of 1960), 1st Sch.].

Plinth. "PLINTH" means the part of a wall or structure between the ground level and the level of the lowest floor of a building above ground level. [WB Municipal (Building) Rules (1996), R. 2(40)]

Plot. 'PLOT' means a continuous portion of land held in one ownership. [Bombay Town Planning Act, 1954 (27 of 1955), S. 2(b)]

Plough. Is a tool which is pulled by bullock cart for furrowing the land and is considered as an agricultural implement. *U. P. State Agro Industrial Corporation Ltd.* v. *Kisan Upbhokta Parishad,* AIR 2008 SC 777.

Plug-and-play (PnP). A hardware and software specification developed by Intel that allows a PnP system and a PnP adapter to configure automatically. PnP cards generally have no switches or jumpers, but are configured via the PnP system's BIOS or with supplied software for non-PnP computers. (*Cyber Law*)

Plug-in. A (usually small) piece of software that adds features to a larger piece of software. Common examples are plug-ins for the Netscape® *browser* and web *server.* Adobe Photoshop® also uses plug-ins. (*Matisse Enzer-Glossary of Internet Terms*)

A (usually small) piece of software that adds features to a larger piece of software. Common examples are plug-ins for the Netscape browser and web server. Adobe Photoshop also uses plug-ins. The idea behind plug-in's is that a small piece of software is loaded into memory by the large program, adding a new feature, and that users need only install the few plug-ins that they need, out of a much larger pool of possibilities. Plug-ins are usually created by people other than the publishers of the software the plug-in works with. (*Internet and E-Commerce*)

Plunderage. Embezzling of goods on a ship.

Plus peccat auctor quam actor. The originator or instigator of a crime is a worse offender than the actual perpetrator of it.

Plus valet unus oculatus testis quam auriti decem. (4 *Inst.* 279) One eye witness is better than ten ear witnesses.

PNG. Portable Network Graphics. PNG is a graphics format specifically designed for use on the World Wide Web. PNG enable compression of images without any loss of quality, including high-resolution images. Another important feature of PNG is that anyone may create software that works with PNG images without paying any fees - the PNG standard is free of any licensing costs. (*Matisse Enzer-Glossary of Internet Terms*)

Poena. Punishment; a penalty.

Poena ad paucos, metus ad omnes perveniat. (22 *Vin. Abr.* 556) If penalty is imposed on some, a fear (of punishment) comes to all.

Poena ex delicto defuncti haeres teneri non debet. (2 *Inst.* 198) The heir is not to be bound by penal consequences arising out of the criminal acts of the deceased.

Poena non potest, culpa perennis erit. Punishment cannot be, crime will be, perpetual.

Point. The most important essential in some discussion. [CPC (5 of 1908), O. XLI, R. 29]; a step, a stage or degree in progress or development; something that is subject of discussion or attention; a matter in debate, under attention or to be taken into account [CPC (5 of 1908), O. VIII, R. 4]; a place or station.

Point for determination. The question to be decided upon. [CrPC 1973 (2 of 1974), S. 354(1)(b)]; [CPC (5 of 1908), O. XX, R. 4(1)].

Point of law. A distinct legal proposition at issue in a case.

Point of order. In parliamentary procedure, an objection to the proceedings raised while another member is speaking.

Point of presence. Means an intermediary registered with the Authority under section 27(3) of Act 23 of 2013 as a point of presence and capable of electronic connectivity with the central recordkeeping agency for the purposes of receiving and transmitting funds and instructions and pay out of funds. [S. 2(1)(n) of the Pension Fund Regulatory & Development Authority Act, 2013 (23 of 2013)]

Point of Presence sub-entity. Means an entity which has been assigned with any of the functions or obligations of a point of presence as specified under these regulations, by a registered point of presence and which has been approved by the Authority. [Person Fund Regulatory and Development Authority (Point of Presence) Regulations, 2018, Regn. 2(1)(h)].

Point of substance. Point of essence. [CPC (5 of 1908), O. VIII, R. 4].

Point of view, A confessional. [Geneva Conventions Act (6 of 1960), III Sch., Art. 37].

Point-to-point connection in an electronic data interchange environment. EDI partners establish a direct computer-to-computer link through a private network. (*Cyber Law*)

Point-to-point protocol (PPP). One of the TCP/IP services that performs error checking and recovery functions, it can handle synchronous as well as asynchronous communications. (*Cyber Law*)

Point-to-point tunneling protocol. One of the TCP/IP services creates secure connections between private networks over public networks. (*Cyber Law*)

Poles. Means 'a long slender piece of metal or wood commonly tapering and more or less rounded'. Electric poles being hollow ones, are not much different from pipes or tubes. [Central Excise and Salt Act (1 of 1944), item 26 AA and 68.]

Police. The word "POLICE" shall include all persons who shall be enrolled under the Police Act. [Police Act (5 of 1861), S. 1].

The civil force to which is entrusted the duty of maintaining public order *etc.* [CrPC 1973 (2 of 1974), S. 2(c), *Expln.* (b)].

Police custody. The expression '*police custody*' does not necessarily mean formal arrest. It also includes some form of police surveillance and restriction on the movements of the persons concerned by the police.

Police diary. A diary maintained by a police officer, particularly in respect of a crime under investigation. [CrPC 1973 (2 of 1974), S. 172(2)].

Police duties. The expression 'police duties' will include the detection, prevention and investigation of offence and other duties which have been specially imposed on them under the Act. *Delhi Administration* v. *Ram Singh*, AIR 1962 SC 63, 66. [Suppression of Immoral Traffic in Women and Girls Act (104 of 1956), S. 2(*i*)]

Police force. 'POLICE FORCE' includes any force charged with the maintenance of public order. [Police Force (Restriction of Rights) Act (33 of 1966), S. 2(b)]

POLICE FORCE is a term commonly understood to refer to the body of men appointed to preserve the peace and good order of a city or town.

Police officer. "POLICE OFFICER" means an officer in charge of a police station, a police officer making an investigation under Chapter XIV of the Code of Criminal Procedure, 1898, or any other police officer not below the rank of sub-inspector. [Identification of Prisoners Act (32 of 1920), S. 2(b)]

Any person holding an office usually above the rank of a constable in the police force of the country. [Indian Evidence Act (1 of 1872), S. 25; CrPC 1973 (2 of 1974), S. 2(c)].

"Police officer" shall have the same meaning as assigned to the expression "police" under the Police Act, 1861 (5 of 1861) [(w. e. f. 1-7-2024) Bharatiya Nayaya Sanhita, 2023 (45 of 2023), section 64(2), Explanation (c)]

One of the staff of men employed in cities and towns to enforce the laws and ordinances, for preserving the peace and good order of the community.

"Police officer" means the officer-in-charge of a police station or an officer not below the rank of Head Constable. [Criminal Procedure (Identification) Act, 2022 (11 of 2022), section 2(1)(c)]

The term "police officer" includes "*chowkidar*" and the confession made while the accused were in the custody of *chowkidar* becomes inadmissible by virtue of S. 26, Indian Evidence Act (1 of 1872).

Excise officer is also regarded as a police officer. *Raja Ram Jaiswal* v. *State of Bihar*, AIR 1964 SC 828, 837. [Indian Evidence Act (1 of 1872), S. 25]

"POLICE OFFICER" shall have the same meaning as assigned to the expression 'police' under the Police Act, 1861 (5 of 1861). [*Explanation* (c) to s. 376(2) of IPC, 1860 (45 of 1860), as substituted by the Criminal Laws (Amendment) Act, 2013 (13 of 2013)] Refer 'Police'.

Police power. The inherent power of Government to regulate its police affairs, to secure public peace, and enforce law and order.

"Police powers" and "eminent domain". The police and eminent domain powers are essentially distinct. Under the police power many restrictions may be imposed and the property may even be destroyed without compensation being given, whereas under the power of eminent domain, the property may be appropriated to public use on payment of compensation only. The distinction between the two powers is brought out clearly in the following passage in the *American Jurisprudence,* 2d Edn., Vol. 16, Art. 301, p. 592.

"The State, under the police power, cannot in any manner actually take and appropriate property for public use without compensation, for such action is repugnant to the constitutional guarantee that where private property is appropriated for public use, the owner shall receive reasonable compensation. Thus, there is a vital difference which is recognised by the authorities, between an Act passed with exclusive reference to the police power of the State, without any purpose to take and apply property to public uses, and an Act which not only declares the existence of a nuisance created by the condition of particular property, but in addition, and as the best means of accomplishing the end in view, authorizes the same property to be appropriated by the public." (*Deputy Commissioner & Collector* v. *Durganath Sarma,* AIR 1968 SC 394, 399).

Police report. The term '*Police report*' in S. 190, CrPC is not limited to the report mentioned in S. 170. A report made by the Police in a non-cognizable case under the order of a Magistrate is a Police report. 11 ALJ 331 : 19 IC 314 : 14 Cr LJ 218.

"Police report" means a report forwarded by a police officer to a Magistrate under sub-section (3) of section 193. [(w. e. f. 1-7-2024) Bharatiya Nagarik Suraksha Sanhita, 2023 (46 of 2023), S. 2(1)(t)]

Police report and report of Police officer. "Police report means a report forwarded by a police officer to a Magistrate under sub-section (2) of Section 173. [CrPC 1973 (2 of 1974), S. 3(r)]

A report to qualify itself to be a police report is required to contain only such facts as are mentioned in S. 173(2). *State of Haryana* v. *Mehal Singh,* AIR 1978 P&H 341, 344 (FB). [CrPC 1973 (2 of 1974), S. 173(2)]

The expression 'police report' as used in the code for reports of offence made by the Police carries a special meaning. The expression as used in S. 190(1)(*b*) means reports of cognizable offences or non-cognizable offences with regard to which there had been a direction by a Magistrate to investigate, made after an investigation under Chapter XIV. Other police reports were to be treated as complaints coming under S. 190(1)(*a*). *Premchand Khetry* v. *State,* AIR 1958 Cal 213, 216.

'Police report' means a formal charge-sheet or challan containing accusation of a cognizable offence, submitted by a police officer, after investigation. A challan, not making any accusation of a cognizable offence but mentioning that there is no case against the person, is not police report. *Shamlal* v. *State of Himachal Pradesh,* AIR 1965 HP 37, 39, 40.

Police station. "POLICE STATION" means any post or place declared, generally or specially, by the State Government to be a police station, and includes any local area specified by the State Government in this behalf. [CrPC 1973 (2 of 1974), S. 2(s)] [Now (w.e.f. 1-7-2024) repealed & replaced by Bharatiya Nagarik Suraksha Sanhita, 2023 (46 of 2023), S. 2(1)(u), same definition in new Sanhita].

Police witness. Where police officers while on patrol duty suddenly come across certain persons carrying prohibited liquor and arrest them on the spot, it would be open to the trial Court to accept the Police evidence and convict the accused if the Court is satisfied that the evidence is of a satisfactory character and the guilt of the accused is proved. *Koliganda Malu* v. *State,* MLJ : QD (1956-1960) Vol. II C1747 : 1956 CrLJ 775 : (S) AIR 1956 Sau 25. [CrPC (5 of 1898), S. 367]

Policeman : Police constable. The word "policemen" may be used as a generic term, and when so used may equally apply to any member of the police force whatever his rank or station; but this can only be true when the word is used alone as a generic term, and as descriptive of the whole police force—officers as well as men—and not when officers and men are carefully segregated from each other in meaning by apt terms of distinctive designation.

A person holding an office in the police force of the country; member of police force. [IPC (45 of 1860), S. 182, ill. (c)].

Policy. Where a Provident Insurance Society grants annuities upon human life, "POLICY" includes the instrument evidencing the contract to pay such an annuity, and "*policyholder*" includes annuitant. [Provident Insurance Societies Act (5 of 1912), S. 2(6)]

A course of action adopted as advantageous or expedient [Unit Trust of India Act (52 of 1963), S. 30]; a document containing an undertaking in consideration of a premium or premiums to pay a specified amount or part thereof in the event of a specified contingency [Indian Contract Act (9 of 1872), S. 212, ill. (c)].

Policy-holder. "POLICY-HOLDER." means the person who for the time being is the legal holder of the policy for securing the contract with the Provident Insurance Society. [Provident Insurance Societies Act (5 of 1912), S. 2(5)].

"POLICY-HOLDER" means the person who for the time being is the legal holder of the policy for securing the contract with the life assurance company. [Life Assurance Companies (6 of 1912), S. 2(7)]

POLICY-HOLDER includes a person to whom, the whole of the interest of the policy-holder in the policy is assigned once and for all, but does not include an assignee thereof whose interest in the policy is defeasible or is for the time being subject to any condition. [Insurance Act (4 of 1938), S. 2(2)]

Policy of assurance on human life. Means any instrument by which the payment of money is assured on death (except death by accident only) or the happening of any contingency dependent on human life or any instrument evidencing a contract which is subject to payment of premiums for a term dependent on human life. [Life Assurance Companies (6 of 1912), S. 2(b); Provident Insurance Societies (5 of 1912), S. 2(4)].

Policy of Assurance, or Insurance. An instrument entered into by insurers of lives, ships and merchandise, *etc.*, to the persons ensuring obligatory for the payment of the sum ensured, in case of death or loss. (*Tomlin*)

Policy of group insurance. Means any instrument covering not less than fifty or such smaller number as the Central Government may approve, either generally or with reference to any particular case, by which an insurer, in consideration of a premium paid by an employee or by an employer and his employees jointly, engages to cover, with or without medical examination and for the sole benefit of persons other than the employer, the lives of all the employees or of any class of them, determined by conditions pertaining to the employment, for amounts of insurance based upon a plan which precludes individual selection. [Indian Stamp Act (2 of 1899), S. 2(19-A)]

Policy of insurance. "POLICY OF INSURANCE" includes—(a) any instrument by which one person, in consideration of a premium, engages to indemnify another against loss, damage or liability arising from an unknown or contingent event; (b) a life-policy and any policy insuring any person against accident or sickness, and any other personal insurance. [Indian Stamp Act (2 of 1899), S. 2(19)]

Policy of sea insurance. "POLICY OF SEA-INSURANCE" or "SEA POLICY"—

(a) means any insurance made upon by any ship or vessel (whether for marine or inland navigation), or upon the machinery, tackle or furniture of any ship or vessel, or upon any goods, merchandise or property of any description whatever on board of any ship or vessel, or upon the freight of, or any other interest which may be lawfully insured in, or relating to, any ship or vessel, and

(b) it includes any insurance of goods, merchandise or property for any transit which includes, not a sea-risk within the meaning of clause (a), but also any other risk incidental to the transit insured from the commencement of the transit to the ultimate destination covered by the insurance.

Where any person, in consideration to any sum of money paid or to be paid for additional freight or otherwise, agrees to take upon himself any risk attending goods, merchandise or property of any description whatever while on board of any ship or vessel, or engages to indemnify the owner of any such goods, merchandise or property from any risk, loss or damage, such agreement or engagement shall be deemed to be a contract for sea-insurance. [Indian Stamp Act (2 of 1899), S. 2(20)]

Policy or Policy of Insurance. Means a contract of insurance issued under the Scheme and includes a policy of insurance and renewal endorsement. [Emergency Risks (Goods) Insurance Act (50 of 1971), S. 2(f)]

'POLICY' means a marine policy. [Marine Insurance Act (11 of 1963), S. 2(*g*)]

Political. Pertaining to the policy or the administration of a State or government. [CPC (5 of 1908), O. V, R. 26(a)]; [T.P. Act (4 of 1882), S. 6(g) and Constitution of India, preamble].

Political activity. Includes any activity promoting or propagating the aims or objects of a political party or any cause, issue or question of a political nature by organising meetings, demonstration, processions, collection or disbursement of funds, or by the issue of directions or decree, or by any other means, and includes also such activity or on behalf of a person seeking election as a candidate for any election of Parliament, any State Legislature or any local authority. [Religious Institutions (Prevention of Misuse Act (41 of 1988), S. 2(d)]

Political Agent. "POLITICAL AGENT" shall mean,—

(a) in relation to any territory outside India, the Principal Officer, by whatever name called, representing the Central Government in such territory; and

(b) in relation to any territory within India to which the act or regulation containing the expression does not extend, any officer appointed by the Central Government to exercise all or any of the powers of a Political Agent under that Act or Regulation. [General Clauses Act (10 of 1897), S. 3(43)]

The term "Political Agent" in S. 7 of the Extradition Act (34 of 1962) must be construed in the light of S. 3(43) of the General Clauses Act (10 of 1897), and so construed the term would include an "Assistant Political Agent."

Political and/or economic integration organization. "POLITICAL AND/OR ECONOMIC ORGANIZATION" means an organization constituted by sovereign state to which its member states have transferred competence in respect of matters governed by this convention and which has been duly authorised in accordance with its internal procedures to sign, ratify, accept, approve, formally confirm or accede to it. [Basic Convention on the Control of Transboundary Movements of Hazardous Wastes and their Disposal, 28 ILM 657 (1989), Art. 2(20)]

Political asylum. Refuge granted to a person on political grounds.

Political grounds. The expression 'political grounds' connotes vague and fanciful attitude. *Harbhajan Singh* v. *Union of India*, AIR 1987 SC 9, 15. [CPC (5 of 1908), Ss. 86, 87]

Political offence. Politics are about Government and therefore, a "political offence" is one committed with the object of changing the Government of a State or inducing it to change its policy. (*Rajender Kumar Jain* v. *State,* AIR 1980 SC 1510).

Political party. "POLITICAL PARTY" means an association or a body of individual citizens of India registered with the Election Commission as a political party under Section 29-A. [Representation of the People Act (43 of 1951), S. 2(f)]

"POLITICAL PARTY" means an association or body of persons—

(i) Which is, or is deemed to be, registered, with the Election Commission of India as a political party under the Election Symbols (Reservation and Allotment) Order, 1968, as in force for the time being; or

(ii) which has set up candidates for election to any legislature, but is not registered, or deemed to be registered, as a political party, under the Election Symbols (Reservation and Allotment) Order, 1968; or

(iii) organised to carry on any political activity or to acquire or exercise political power through election or otherwise. [Religious Institutions (Prevention of Misuse) Act (41 of 1988), S. 2(e)]

A political party is a voluntary association of voters who are desirous of promoting a common political end, or carrying out a certain line of public policy.

"POLITICAL PARTY" for the purposes of section 182 of Act 18 of 2013, 'political party' means a political party registered under section 29A of the Representation of the People Act, 1951 (43 of 1951). [*Explanation* to section 182 of the Companies Act, 2013 (18 of 2013)]

Political pension. Pension granted by the State to any one for some political reason; an allowance payable by the Government of India under an arrangement effected between the Government of India and another sovereign power. [CPC (5 of 1908), S. 60(1)(g)].

Political power. Political power embraces all governmental powers and functions, whether exercised by one department or another, or the officers of one or the other.

Political prisoner. A person in custody or imprisoned for a political offence.

Political rights. Are those which may be exercised in the formation or administration of the government; which consist in the power to participate, directly or indirectly, in the establishment or management of the government; those rights which belong to a nation, or to a citizen, or to an individual member of a nation, so distinguished from civil rights, namely, local rights of a citizen.

Political science. The science dealing with the organisation and government of states.

Politics. According to its true original meaning "politics" comprehends "everything that concerns the government of the country, of which the administration of justice makes a considerable part".

Poll. "Poll" means the number of aggregate of heads—a list or register of heads or individuals who may vote in an election—so that poll includes all who actually cast their votes at the election, those who stay away not being counted.

The entering of votes in order to their being counted. [Representation of the People Act (43 of 1951), S. 56]; [Companies Act (1 of 1956), S. 179(1)].

Polling agent. An agent appointed by a candidate to look after his interest and represent him at the poll. [Representation of the People Act (43 of 1951), S. 49(1)].

Polling station. "POLLING STATION" means any place appointed for holding election to a Municipality. [Kerala Municipality Act (20 of 1994), S. 2(28)]

Pollute. To make physically impure, foul or filthy [CPC (5 of 1908), 1st Sch., App. A, form No. 23(1)].

Polluter pays principle. The Polluter Pays Principle as interpreted by the Supreme Court of India means that the absolute liability for harm to the environment extends not only to compensate the victims of pollution but also the cost of restoring the environmental degradation. Remediation of the damaged environment is part of the process of "Sustainable Development" and as such the polluter is liable to pay the cost to the individual sufferers as well as the cost of reversing the damaged ecology.

Pollution. Means such contamination of water or such alteration of the physical, chemical or biological properties of water or such discharge of any sewage or trade effluent or of any other liquid, gaseous or solid substance, into water (whether directly or indirectly) as may, or is likely to create a nuisance, or render such water harmful or injurious to public health or safety, or to domestic, commercial, industrial, agricultural or other legitimate use, or to the life and health of animals or plants, or of aquatic organisms. [Water (Prevention and Control of Pollution) Act (6 of 1974), S. 2(e)]

Pollution damage. Means—

(i) loss or damage caused outside the ship by contamination resulting from escape or discharge of oil from the ship, wherever such escape or discharge occurs, provided that compensation for impairment of the environment other than losses or profit from such impairment shall be limited to costs of reasonable measures of reinstatement actually undertaken or to be undertaken;

(ii) the costs of preventive measures and further loss or damage caused by such measures. [Merchant Shipping Act (44 of 1958), S. 352H(f)]

Pollution of offshore environment. Means the introduction by any person, directly or indirectly, of substances or energy into the offshore environment which results, or is likely to result, in deleterious effect on living resources and marine life, hazards to human health, hindrance to marine activities, including fishing and other legitimate uses of the offshore areas and impairment of quality of sea water for use and reduction of amenities. [Offshore Area Minerals (Development and Regulation) Act, 2002 (17 of 2003), S. 4(q)]

Pollution of water. Means and implies, acts which make a thing physically impure and unclean, without leaving the water in its natural condition. Something is added or allowed to mix with water, which brings in change in its nature, resulting in its pollution. (*Halsbury's Laws of England* 1914 Edn Vol XVIIIP 432). (*Water Law*)

Polyarchy. Government by many persons.

Polygamia est plurium simul virorum uxorumve connubium. (*Lat.*) (3 Inst. 88.) Polygamy is the marriage of many husbands or wives at one time.

Polygamy. (*Polygamia*) The having a plurality of wives or husbands at once. (*Tomlin*)

The practice or custom according to which one man has or may have two or more wives. [Indian Contract Act (9 of 1872), S. 56, ill. (c)].

Polygarchy. Government by many persons.

Polytechnic. "POLYTECHNIC" means an institution in which instruction is provided for courses of study in technical education leading to a diploma of the Council. [W. Bengal State Council of Technical Education Act (21 of 1995), S. 2(g)]

Polygraph. A device or instrument used as a lie detector, which enables the investigator to test the truthfulness of a person.

Pondicherry. Means the union Territory comprising the territories of the former French Establishments. [Pondicherry (Administration) Act (49 of 1962), S. 2(f)]

Pontage. A payment made or toll levied for the repair of bridges.

Pool. "POOL" means any joint underwriting operation of insurance or reinsurance in which the participants assume a predetermined and fixed interest in all business written. [Insurance Regulatory and Development Authority (General Insurance—Reinsurance) Regulations, Rgn. 2(f)]

Combining of several persons of their separate resources in one large operation or to promote their joint business or undertaking.

Pooling arrangement. For the purposes of this sub-clause,—

"POOLING ARRANGEMENT" means an agreement between two or more persons for providing services through a pool or operating one or more ships and sharing earnings or operating profits on the basis of mutually agreed terms. [Income-tax Act (43 of 1961), Chap. XIIG, S. 115V-I 2(A) *Expln.* (*Inserted by Finance Act (23 of 2004), S. 30*)]

Poorer and working classes. The expression 'poorer and working classes' refers to such indigent and working people who need accommodation and cannot on their own make arrangements for reasonable accommodation. *Jabalpur Municipality* v. *Kishanlal*, AIR 1966 SC 207, 209.

Poorer sections. The expression 'poorer sections' denotes a division among socially and educationally backward classes on economic criterion. *Indira Sawhney* v. *Union of India*, AIR 1993 SC 477, 632. [Constitution of India, Art. 16(4)]

POP. Point of Presence—the point where a user can access the internet from a particular service provider. (*Penelope Lawrence*) (*Internet*)

Point of Presence, also Post Office Protocol. A Point of Presence usually means a city or location where a network can be connected to, often with dial up phone lines. So if an Internet company says they will soon have a POP in Belgrade, it means that they will soon have local phone number in Belgrade and/or a place where leased lines can connect to their network.

Poppy straw. Means all parts (except the seeds) of the opium poppy after harvesting whether in their original form or cut, crushed or powdered and whether or not juice has been extracted therefrom. [NDPS Act (61 of 1985), S. 2 (xviii)]

Popular Government. If the body of the nation keeps in its own hands through its representatives the Government of the country or the right of command, it is a popular Government.

Population. "POPULATION" means the population as ascertained at the last preceding census of which the relevant figures, have been published.

Provided that the reference in this *Explanation* to the last preceding census of which the relevant figures have been published shall, until the relevant figures for the first census taken after the year 2026 have been published, be construed as a reference to the 1971 census. [Constitution of India, Art. 55(3)]

"POPULATION" for the purposes of the proviso (*ii*) to section 2(1A)(c) of Act 43 of 1961, 'population' means the population according to the last preceding census of which the relevant figures have been published before the first day of the previous year. [(w.e.f. 1-4-2013) *Explanation* 4 to section 2(1A) of the Income-tax Act, 1961 (43 of 1961)]

Pornography. Material that depicts erotic behaviour and is intended to cause sexual excitement.

Port. "PORT" means any major port to which this Act applies within such limits as may, from time to time to be defined by the Central Government for the purposes of this Act by notification in the Official Gazette, and, until a notification is so issued, within such limits as may have been defined by the Central Government under the provisions of the Indian Ports Act. [Major Port Trusts Act (38 of 1963), S. 2(q)]

"Port" means generally a harbour or shelter to vessels from a storm.

A port is a place, for the lading and unlading of ships or vessels.

A harbour or place of shelter where ships arrive with their freight and customs for goods are taken; to carry or convey.

A term used for different points of entry into a single computer. For example, FTP, e-mail and WEB browsing may use different ports. However, the technicalities of ports are usually handled transparently as far as the user is concerned. (*Cyber Law*)

An external electrical connector used for attaching a peripheral to a computer. (*Computer*)

Port also refers to translating a piece of software to bring it from one type of computer system to another, *e.g.* to translate a Windows program so that is will run on a Macintosh. (*Matisse Enzer-Glossary of Internet Terms; Internet and E-commerce*)

Port approaches. In relation to a port, means those parts of the navigable rivers and channels leading to the port in which the Indian Ports Act is in force. [Major Port Trusts Act (38 of 1963), S. 2(r)]

Port authority. "PORT AUTHORITY" means—

(a) in relation to any major port, the Board of Trustees in respect of that port constituted under any law for the time being in force.

(b) in relation to any other port, the Conservator of the Port, within the meaning of Section 7 of the Indian Ports Act, 1908. [Merchant Shipping Act (44 of 1958), S. 356 I(4) *Expln.*]

"PORT AUTHORITY" means any authority administering a port. [Child Labour (Prohibition & Regulation) Act (61 of 1986), S. 2(vii)]

A local authority entrusted with the administration of a port. [CPC (5 of 1908), S. 60, *Expln.* III(i)].

Port of call. A port where vessels can call for stores or repairs. [Geneva Conventions Act (6 of 1960), Art. 37].

Port of registry. In relation to a ship or a sailing vessel, means the port at which she is registered or is to be registered. [Merchant Shipping Act (44 of 1958), S. 3(29)]

Port-officer. Is synonymous with master-attendant. [Indian Ports Act (15 of 1908), S. 3(5)]

Port services. Means any service rendered by a port or any person authorised by the port, in any manner, in relation to a vessel or goods. [Finance Act (32 of 1994), S. 65(1)(67) now repealed by Central Goods and Service Tax Act, 2017]

Port trust. A local authority entrusted with the administration of the affairs of a port. [Indian Trusts Act (2 of 1882), S. 20(d)].

Port trust security. Means debentures, bonds or stock certificates issued by a Board in respect of any loan contracted by it under the provisions of this Act or issued by any other authority for the payment of which the Board is liable under this Act. [Major Ports Trusts Act (38 of 1963), S. 2(s)]

Portal. A web site usually on a specific topic that acts as a gateway to linked topics. (*Penelope Lawrence*) (*Internet*)

Usually used as a marketing term to describe a Web site that is or is intended to be the first place people see when using the Web. Typically a "Portal site" has a catalogue of web sites, a search engine, or both. A portal site may also offer email and other service to entice people to use that site as their main "point of entry" (hence "portal") to the Web. (*Matisse Enzer-Glossary of Internet Terms; Internet and E-Commerce*)

Porterage. A fee charged by a dock company for using its porters' services.

Portfolio. "PORTFOLIO" means the total holdings of securities belonging to any person. [Securities and Exchange Board of India (Portfolio Managers) Rules, 1993, R. 2(d)]

Portfolio manager. "PORTFOLIO MANAGER" means any person who pursuant to a contract or arrangement with a client advises or directs or undertakes on behalf of the client (whether as a discretionary portfolio manager or otherwise) the management or administration of a portfolio of securities or the funds of the client, as the case may be. [SEBI (Portfolio Managers) Rules, 1993, R. 2(e)]

Portion of his claim. A right which a litigant does not know that he possesses or a right which is not in existence at the time of the first suit can hardly be regarded as a portion of his claim. *State of M.P.* v. *State of Maharashtra*, AIR 1977 SC 1466, 1472. [CPC (5 of 1908), O. II, R. 2]

Portrait. A figure drawn, painted or carved upon a surface to represent some object; especially a likeness of a person especially of the face made from life by drawing, painting, photograph, engraving, *etc.* [Indian Evidence Act (1 of 1872), S. 32(6)]; [CPC (5 of 1908), App. A Form 39].

Position-based bargaining. A sophisticated bargaining technique employed by an effective mediator in the mediation process to bring the parties in dispute to get a more realistic view of the settlement value of their claims and defences by narrowing their differences which ultimately result in mutually satisfactory agreement. This is done by the mediator by pointing out to them that they cannot both be completely correct in their insistence of a definite result in their favour because of (a) their weakness in their positions, (b) uncertainties of the legal process, (c) hidden costs of trial and (d) costs of protracted court proceedings and the disputants slowly acknowledging their weaknesses and yielding to the reality. (*Arbitration*)

Positive assertion. An assertion admitting of no doubt. [Indian Contract Act (9 of 1872), S. 18(1)].

Positive law. A system of law implemented and laid down by the political authority within a particular political community; it is an enacted law.

Positivism. The doctrine that all true knowledge is derived from observable phenomena, rather than speculation or reasoning.

Possible view. A possible view denotes a conclusion which can reasonably be arrived at regardless of the fact whether it is agreed upon or not by the higher court. [*Murugan* v. *State,* (2012) 10 SCC 383, para 34 **as cited in** *Hakeem Khan* v. *State of M.P.*, (2017) 5 SCC 719, para 12].

Possess. Is frequently used in the sense of "own" "entitled to."

Possess means. A person cannot be said to 'possess means' when he is merely entitled to claim a sum of money which may or may not be realised from the debtor. It cannot be assumed that a person so entitled to make a claim is necessarily possessed of means to the extent of the claim.

Possessed. The word 'possessed' is used in Section 14 in a broad sense and in the context 'possession' means 'the state of owning or having in one's hands or power'. It includes possession by receipt of rents and profits. Even if a trespasser is in possession of land belonging to a female owner on the date when the Act came into force, the female owner might conceivably be regarded as being in possession of the land, if the trespasser had not perfected his title by adverse possession before the Act came into force. *Gaddam Venkayamma* v. *Gaddam Veerayya,* AIR 1957 AP 280, 281. [Hindu Succession Act (30 of 1956), S. 14(1)]

If the Legislature has used the expression "any property possessed by a female Hindu" it is not to be confined only to present possession. *Ramsaroop Singh* v. *Hiralall Singh,* AIR 1958 319, 323. [Hindu Succession Act (30 of 1956), S. 14 (1)]

Possession referred to in S. 14 need not be actual physical possession or personal occupation of the property by the Hindu female but may be possession in law. The possession of a licensee, lessee or a mortgagee from the female owner or the possession of a guardian or a trustee or an agent of the female owner would be her possession for the purpose of S. 14. The word "possessed" is used in S. 14 in a broad sense and in the context, possession means the state of owning or having in one's hands or power. *Kotturuswami* v. *Setra Veeravva*, AIR 1959 SC 577, 581. [Hindu Succession Act (30 of 1956), S. 14]

The word "possessed" cannot be confined in its operation only to the possession of the Hindu female at the date of the enforcement of the Act either on a grammatical view or even in view of the texture of the section itself. *Ramsewak Ojha* v. *Sheopujan Pandey,* AIR 1959 Pat 75, 77. [Hindu Succession Act (30 of 1956), S. 14]

The term 'possessed' includes possession, either actual or constructive. *Anandi Bai* v. *Sundra Bai,* AIR 1965 MP 85, 92. [Hindu Succession Act (30 of 1956), S. 14]

'Possessed' and 'Held'. The words "possessed" and the word "held" used in S. 14(1) mean one and the same thing and the little controversy that has centred round the word "possessed" would have been availed if the parliamentary draftsman had used the same word "held" in both places. *Marudakkal* v. *Arumugha Gounder,* AIR 1958 Mad 255, 260. [Hindu Succession Act (30 of 1956), S. 14(1)]

Possessed by. The expression 'possessed by' connotes state of ownership. Section 14(1) will not apply at all to a case where a Hindu female has parted with her rights so as to place herself in a position where she could, in no manner, exercise her rights of ownership in the property any longer. *Mangal Singh* v. *Rattno*, AIR 1967 SC 1786, 1793. [Hindu Succession Act (39 of 1956), S. 14(1)]

Possessed by female Hindu. Where a female Hindu is in possession of joint family properties in lieu of maintenance, she is in possession of the property within the meaning of S. 14(1). *Limba* v. *Manikrao,* AIR 1978 Bom 83. [Hindu Succession Act (30 of 1956), S. 14(1)]

Possessed of. The word 'possession' should be given the widest possible interpretation. so as to cover not merely possession in fact, but possession in law as well. The words "possessed of" has been used implying title or ownership. The phrase 'possessed of' has been used in the sense of ownership. *Krishna Dassi Saha* v. *Akhil Ch. Saha,* AIR 1958 Cal 671, 674. [Hindu Succession Act (30 of 1956), S. 14(1)]

Possession. Physical control, whether actual or in the eyes of law, over property; the condition of holding at one's disposal [T.P. Act (4 of 1882), S. 66]; the area in one's possession.

There can be no possession without intention or consciousness or will.

Possession need not be physical possession but can be constructive, having power and control over the gun, while the person to whom physical possession is given holds it subject to that power or control. *Gunwantlal* v. *State of M.P.*, AIR 1972 SC 1756, 1759. [Arms Act (54 of 1959), Ss. 4 & 25(1)(a)]

The term "possession" consists of two elements. First, it refers to the corpus or the physical control and the second, it refers to the animus or intent which has reference to exercise of the said control. [*Mohan Lal* v. *State of Rajasthan*, (2015) 6 SCC 222, para 12].

Possession is an incidence of ownership and can be transferred by the owner of an immovable property to another such as in a mortgage or leave. A licensee holds possession on behalf of the owner. [*Maria Margarida Sequeira Fernandes* v. *Erasmo Jack De Sequeira*, (2012) 5 SCC 370, para 62].

Possession is a polymorphous term which may have different meanings in different contexts. The possession of a first arm must have the element of consciousness or knowledge of that possession and when there is no actual physical possession, a control or dominion over it, there is no possession. *Superintendent and Remembrancer of Legal Affairs, West Bengal* v. *Anil Kumar Bhunja*, AIR 1980 SC 52, 54. [Arms Act (54 of 1959), S. 29 (b)]

Obtaining a symbolic possession is in law equivalent to obtain actual physical possession and has the effect of terminating the legal possession of the person bound by the decree and order. *Umrao Singh* v. *UOI,* AIR 1975 Del 188, 191. [Land Acquisition Act (1 of 1894), S. 28] [Now repealed & replaced by Act 30 of 2013]

'Possession' and 'Acquired'. Possession need not be possession in the dictionary meaning of that expression, but in the legal sense of entitlement to secure such possession. Acquired is the right of entitlement to possess the property. R. *Narsimhachari* v. *Andalammal,* AIR 1979 Mad 31, 35. [Hindu Succession Act (30 of 1956), S. 14(1)]

Possession and control. "Possession" under the section means conscious possession but it need not always be manual possession, that is, possession by physically touching the incriminating object. "Control" is a somewhat wider concept than "possession" but there again the control must be actual control and not merely constructive or notional control. *State of Bihar* v. *Amir Hasan,* AIR 1951 Pat 638. [Explosive Substances Act (6 of 1908), S. 5]

Possession and occupation. Bare occupation and possession are two different things. The concept of possession, at any rate as it is understood in legal terminology, is a complex one which need not include actual occupation. It comprises rather the right to possess, and the right and ability to exclude others from possession and control coupled with a mental element, namely, the *animus possidendi*, that is to say, knowledge of these rights and the desire and intention of exercising them if need be. The adverse possession of which the law speaks does not necessarily denote actual physical ouster from occupation but an ouster from all those rights which constitute possession in law. It is true that physical occupation is ordinarily the best and the most conclusive proof of possession in this sense but the two are not the same. It is also true that there must always be physical ouster from these *rights* but that does not necessarily import physical ouster from *occupation* especially when this is of just a small room or two in a house and when this occupation is shared with others. The nature of the ouster and the *quantum* necessary naturally varies in each case.

The words 'possession' and 'occupy' are in common parlance used interchangeably. However, in law, 'possession' over a property may amount to holding it as an owner but to 'occupy' is to keep possession of being present in it. *Ramdass* v. *Davinder*, AIR 2004 SC 2162, 2164 para 7.

Possession and prescriptive title. The possession which is necessary as an element in the acquisition of title by prescription must have three qualities; it must be long (*i.e.*) for the period prescribed by law, continual and peaceable and as of right [Indian Easements Act (5 of 1882), S. 15].

KINDS OF POSSESSION, ACTUAL. That possession which exists where the thing is in the immediate occupancy of the party. Applied to land, the actual exercise by the owner of the present power to deal with the estate and exclude other persons from meddling with it.

CONSTRUCTIVE. That possession which exists in contemplation of law without actual personal occupation; that which the law annexes to the title, the possession of one claiming to hold by virtue of some title, without having the actual occupancy.

ADVERSE POSSESSION. Possession to be adverse, must be actual, visible, exclusive, hostile and continuous for the time necessary to create the bar.

POSSESSION IN FACT. Possession in fact is nothing more than a simple holding or detention of a thing which is under our power and control.

POSSESSION OF EXPLOSIVES. Possession must be conscious and intelligent possession and not merely the physical presence of the accused in proximity or even in close proximity of the offending object. These are the important elements which go to make up an offence under S. 4(*b*) of the Explosive Substances Act (4 of 1884).

POSSESSION OF LAND. Possession of land has been defined as the holding of it and exclusive dominion over it.

Possession and title. Possession is good evidence of title against all persons except the owner.

Possession of personal property is *prima facie* evidence of title, good against everybody but the rightful owner.

Possession, British. A territory subject to the British rule or government. [General Clauses Act (10 of 1897), S. 3(6)].

Possession, Immediate. Direct possession, as opposed to mediate possession [Specific Relief Act (47 of 1963), S. 8]; [R. 9, CPC (5 of 1908), O. XXXIX].

Possession : occupation (Distinction). Where title by adverse possession is set up, it is necessary to consider the distinction between possession and occupation. In some circumstances the defendant's occupation of a site would not necessarily be the denial of the plaintiff's possession. The concept of possession comprises the right to possess and the right and ability to exclude others from possession and could be coupled with a mental element, the *animus possidendi i.e.*, knowledge of these rights and the desire and intention of exercising them if need be. ILR 1942 Nag 564 **Rel.** *Nanhelal* v. *Singhai Nathuram*, MLJ : QD (1956-1960) Vol. III C2142 : 1958 MPLJ (Notes) 33. [Limitation Act (9 of 1908), Ss. 142-144]

Possession of unauthorised material. 'Possession of unauthorised material' by a candidate shall mean having any unauthorised material on his person or desk or chair or table or at any place within reach in the examination hall and its environs or having such material on him in urinal, toilet or passage thereto or therefrom at any time from the commencement of the examination till its end. [Allahabad University Ordinance, Chap. 28, Ordinance No. 1-2(B)]

Possessor. One who holds possession of property.

One who possesses. [Sale of Goods Act (3 of 1930), S. 2(4)]; [Companies Act (1 of 1956), S. 535(1)(c)].

POSSESSOR, PROPRIETOR, OWNER. The possessor has the full power, if not the right of the present disposal over the object of possession; the proprietor and owner have the unlimited right of transfer, but not always the power of immediate disposal. The proprietor and the owner are the same in signification, though not in application: the first term being used principally in regard to matters of importance; the latter on familiar occasions: the proprietor of an estate: the owner of a book is more becoming than the proprietor.

Possessory action. A real action to recover the possession of land.

Possessory title. A title gained by possession.

Possibility. A legal "possibility" as such term is used in connection with real estate, is an estate founded on a contingency which may or may not happen.

That which is possible. [T.P. Act (4 of 1882), S. 6(a)].

Possibility of reverter. The interest a transferor keeps when he transfers a fee simple determinable or a fee simple conditional.

Possible. Falling within the bounds of what may happen or may be done. [CPC (5 of 1908), S. 60(1), Prov. (m)].

'Possible' means (1) capable of existing, happening, or being achieved. (2) that may exist or happen, but that is not certain or probable. [Oxford English Dictionary as cited in *Murugesan* v. *State*, (2012) 10 SCC 383, para 33].

Possible right or interest. Right or interest that may possibly be acquired in future [CPC (5 of 1908), S. 60(1), prov. (m)]; possible to do so consistent with the nature and circumstances of the case, where it is [CPC (5 of 1908), O. XXXIIA, R. 3(1)].

Post. "POST" means a post, pole, standard, stray, strut or other above ground contrivance for carrying, suspending or supporting a telegraph line. [Indian Telegraph Act (13 of 1885), S. 3(5)]

"Post" means a post and includes a pole, tower, standard, stay, shut, cabined, pillar or any above ground contrivance for carrying, suspending or supporting any network infrastructure facility. [Cable Television Networks (Regulation) Act (7 of 1995), S. 2(e-i)].

"POST" means a post within or outside India. [Administrative Tribunal Act (13 of 1985), S. 3(k)]

A post is an employment, but every employment is not a post. A casual labourer is not the holder of a post. *State of Assam* v. *Kanak Choudra*, AIR 1967 SC 884, 886. [Constitution of India, Arts. 310, 311]

A place where armed men are permanently quartered for defensive or other purposes; a nation's organization or system for handling the transmission of letters and other matters; the matter so sent and received [Indian Contract Act (9 of 1872), S. 4, ill. (b)]; a position or appointment [Army Act (46 of 1950), S. 34(h)]; [Constitution of India, Art. 16(4)]; to put in post for onward transmission [Indian Evidence Act (1 of 1872), S. 114, ill. (f)].

Post date. To date after the real date of document. Assign or affix a latter date than the actual date (as) post dated cheque.

To date as of a time subsequent to that of execution; to assign a date subsequent to actual occurrence. [Indian Stamp Act (2 of 1899), S. 68(b)].

Post-dated cheque. A cheque which is dated subsequent to the actual date on which it is drawn, and which is issued before the date it bears, is called a 'post-dated cheque'. [*Thomson's Dictionary of Banking*, 12th Edn., at p. 463, **as cited in** *Ashok Yeshwant Badave* v. *Surendra Madhavrao Nighojakar*, (2001) 3 SCC 726, para 16 : AIR 2001 SC 1315.

When a 'post-dated cheque' is written or drawn, it is only a bill of exchange. It becomes a 'cheque' within the meaning of Section 138 of the Act on the date written thereon and the six months period has to be reckoned for the purposes of proviso (a) to Section 138 of the Act from the said date. *Ashok Yeshwant Badave* v. *Surendra Madhavrao Nighojakar,* AIR 2001 SC 1335 : (2001) 3 SCC 726, 734, para 20. [Negotiable Instruments Act (26 of 1881), S. 138]

Post-dating an instrument. The dating of an instrument as of a date after that on which it is executed.

Post-entry. Events or developments that occur after a company's entry into a stock market.

Post-epileptic mental ill-health. In this condition, stupor following the epileptic fits is replaced by automatic act of which the patient has no recollections. The patient is confused, fails to recognize his own relatives, and wanders aimlessly. He is terrified by visual and auditory hallucinations of a religious character and delusions of persecution, and consequently, may commit crimes of a horrible nature, such as thefts, incendiarism, sexual assaults and brutal murders. The patient never attempts to conceal them at the time of perpetration but on regaining consciousness may try to conceal them out of fear. [Medical Jurisprudence and Toxicology by Modi, 24th Edn., 2011 as cited in *State of Rajasthan v. Shera Ram*, (2012) 1 SCC 602, para 20].

Post free. Without fee for postage.

Post-graduate. Study carried on after getting the graduate degree. Belonging to study pursued after graduation. Holder of a Postgraduate degree.

Post-graduate Degree. "A Bachelor's Degree like B.T. or the LL.B. is not considered as Post-Graduate Degree eventhough these degrees can be taken only after graduation. It is the degrees like M. Ed. or LL.M. which are regarded as Post-Graduate Degrees. *Juthika* v. *State of Madhya Pradesh*, AIR 1976 SC 2534, 2536, 2537.

Post-graduate Training. The term "postgraduate training" used in the rule is in the sense of training received by a person holding a degree in medicine or science and not in the sense that such training must be imparted by a post-graduate institution. *M. Prasad* v. *Suresh Singh*, AIR 1976 SC 1404, 1407. [Drugs and Cosmetics Rules (1945), R. 49(c)]

Post-hearing briefs. Written documents requested by an arbitrator, or submitted to him by attorneys representing the parties in a dispute, as a supplement to the original presentation of the case, after hearings have already been held. Post-hearing briefs give the parties an opportunity to quote in full the relevant portions of Court decisions which pertain to the case as a means of reinforcing their oral evidence. (*Arbitration*)

Post letter. A letter with a fictitious address, dropped into the letter box of a post office receiving house, in order to test the honesty of an employee in the post office, is a "post letter."

Post litem motam. After the commencement of action. The phrase is used chiefly to denote statements made by the parties to the litigation or deceased persons after the commencement of the litigation.

Post mark. Official stamp on letters *etc.* with the name of the office, date and other details.

Any mark impressed by the post office on any article sent through the agency of the post office; a mark officially impressed upon letters or other postal packages; usually a mark giving the place, date and hour of dispatch or of the arrival of the mail. [Indian Evidence Act (1 of 1872), S. 21, ill. (c)].

The use of a post mark in evidence involves at least three distinct principles, In the first place, the question arises, if it may be inferred from the presence of what purports to be the official mark, that the mark was genuinely affixed by an officer of the Post Office concerned. This is a question of an authentication and may be answered in the affirmative. In the second place the question arises, whether, if the post mark be taken as genuine, it is evidence that the cover bearing it was stamped on the date the impression bears. The answer is in the affirmative. Thirdly the post mark, is evidence that the place or office mentioned therein was actually the place where it was affixed. The mere fact of a notice bearing a certain date is no proof that it was posted on that date.

Post-mortem. A post-mortem examination is an examination of a body after death, and does not necessarily imply an autopsy, which is an examination of a dead body, by dissection to ascertain the cause of death.

After death; an examination of a corpse made under the direction of the constituted authorities; an autopsy.

A "post mortem examination" as generally understood, means the dissection of the body, made within a few hours or at the furthest a few days after the death.

Post-natal. After birth.

Post-nuptial. After marriage.

Post-nuptial settlement. Such settlements are made by either party to the marriage in respect of their properties to determine the right in such properties in the event of death of either of them or divorce between them.

Post of Lok Ayukta. The 'post of Lok Ayukta' is an independent statutory post and it can not come under the purview of employment under the Government. It is a public authority which has public or statutory duties to perform and it is in no way under the control of the State Government. Once appointed, the Lok Ayukta, there is no relationship between the Government and the appointee. [*Sreenivasan Venugopalan* v. *M.M. Pareed Pillai*, AIR 2009 Ker 148, 150, paras 6, 7]

Post office. The expression "POST OFFICE" includes every house, building, room, carriage or place used for the purposes of the Post Office, and every letter-box provided by the Post Office for the reception of postal articles. [Indian Post Office Act (6 of 1898), S. 2(*h*)].

"The expression "the *Post Office"*, means the department established for the purpose of carrying the provisions of this Act into effect and presided over by the Director-General". [Indian Post Office Act (6 of 1898), S. 2(*k*)]

GENERAL POST OFFICE. The central office for transaction of postal business, of which there may be many branch offices.

Post-paid. Letter with postal stamp already affixed.

Post Office Protocol. Refers to a way that e-mail *client* software such as Eudora gets mail from a mail *server.* When you obtain an account from an Interest Service Provider (*ISP*) you almost always get a POP account with it, and it is this POP account that you tell your e-mail software to use to get your mail. Another protocol called IMAP is replacing POP for email. (*Matisse Enzer-Glossary of Internet Terms*)

(Point of Presence, also Post Office Protocol) - Two commonly used meanings: Point of Presence and Post Office Protocol. A Point of Presence usually means a city or location where a network can be connected to, often with dial up phone lines. So if an Internet company says they will soon have a POP in Mumbai, it means that they will soon have a local phone number in Mumbai and/or a place where leased lines can connect to their network. A second meaning, Post Office Protocol refers to the way email software such a Eudora gets mail from a mail server. When you obtain a SLIP, PPP, or shell account you almost always get a POP account with it, and it is this POP account that you tell your e-mail software to use to get your mail. (*Internet and E-Commerce*)

Postage. The expression "POSTAGE" means the duty chargeable for the transmission by post of postal articles [Indian Post Office Act (6 of 1898), S. 2(*f*)].

The fee charged by the post office for any article sent through its agency [CPC (5 of 1908), S. 143].

Postage-stamp. The expression "POSTAGE STAMP" means any stamp provided by the Central Government for denoting postage or other fees or sums payable in respect of postal articles under this Act and includes adhesive postage stamps and stamp printed, embossed, impressed or otherwise indicated on any envelope, wrapper, postcard or other article. [Indian Post Office Act (6 of 1898), S. 2(*g*)]

Adhesive stamp or label with which postage charges have to be paid.

Postal article. "The expression "POSTAL ARTICLE" includes a letter, postcard, newspaper, book, pattern or sample packet, parcel and every article or thing transmissible by post". [Indian Post Office Act (6 of 1898), S. 2(i)].

Postal ballot. "POSTAL BALLOT" includes voting by share holders by postal or electronic mode instead of voting personally by presenting for transacting businesses in a general meeting of the company. [Companies (Passing of the Resolutions by Postal Ballot) Rules, 2001, R. 2(b)]

"POSTAL BALLOT" means voting by post or through any electronic mode. [S. 2(65) of the Companies Act, 2013 (18 of 2013)]

Postal charges. Cost of postage; fee charged by the post office for any article sent through its agency. [CPC (5 of 1908), O. IX, R. 2].

Postal communication. Transmission by post. [CPC (5 of 1908), O. V, R. 25].

Postal employee. A person in the service of the postal department.

Posterior mortgagee. Subsequent mortgagee of any mortgaged property. [T.P. Act (4 of 1882), S. 94].

Posthumous child. A child born after his father's death. (*Tomlin*)

Posthumus pro nato habetur. A posthumous child is considered as though born (before the father's death).

Postmaster-General. "The expression "Postmaster-General" includes a Deputy Postmaster-General or other officer exercising the powers of a Postmaster-General". [Indian Post Office Act (6 of 1898), S. 2(j)]

Postpone. Defer; put off; keep for a later time; adjourn.

To put off to later time; to defer [CrPC 1973 (2 of 1974), S. 309(2)]; [Indian Trusts Act (2 of 1882), S. 38, ill(b)].

Postponement. The word "postponement" as used in speaking of the postponement of legal proceedings is synonymous with the word "continuance."

The word "postponement" is usually preferred to the word 'continuance' when the purpose is to obtain a continuance to another day during the term at which the case is fixed, rather than to a future term.

The action or fact of postponing or putting off to a later time [CrPC 1973 (2 of 1974), Ss. 202 and 309, *Expln.* 2]; the fact of being postponed [CPC (5 of 1908), O. IX, R. 6(2)].

Posts and vacancies. The expression "posts" and "vacancies" often used in the executive instructions are rather problematical. The word "post" means an appointment, job, office or employment. A position to which a person is appointed, 'Vacancy' means an unoccupied post of office. The plain meaning of the two expressions, make it clear that there must be a 'post' in existence to enable the 'vacancy' to occur. *R. K. Sabharwal* v. *State of Punjab*, AIR 1995 SC 1371, 1375. [Constitution of India, Art. 16(4)]

Post-trial access. Means making a new drug or investigational new drug available to a trial subject after completion of clinical trial through which the said drug has been found beneficial to a trial subject during clinical trial, for such period as considered necessary by the investigator and the Ethics Committee. [New Drugs and Clinical Trials Rules, 2019, R. 2(1)(cc)].

Potentia est duplex, remota et propinqua; et potentia remotissima et vana est quae nunquam venit in actum. Possibility is of two kinds, remote and near; that which never comes into action is a power the most remote and vain.

Potentia non est nisi ad bonum. Power is not conferred but for the (public) good.

Potentia propinqua. A common possibility which is likely to happen.

Potential. "Potential" means having latent power; endowed with energy adequate to a result; efficacious; existing in possibility, not in act.

The word "potential" means in possibility, not in act, not positively; in efficacy, not in actuality.

The word 'potential' means capable of coming into being, possibility. Naturally and probably expected to come into existence at some future time, though not now existing; for example the future product of grain or trees already planted, or the successive future instalments or payments on a contract or engagement. *Lucknow Development Authority* v. *M.K. Gupta*, AIR 1994 SC 787, 793. [Consumer Protection Act (68 of 1986), S. 2(o)]

'Potential' means 'existing in possibility but not in act. Naturally and probably expected to come into existence at some future time, though not now existing; for example, the future product of grain or trees already planted, or the successive future instalments or payments on a contract or engagement already made'. [Black's Law Dictionary as cited in *LDA* v. *M.K. Gupta*, (1994) 1 SCC 243, para 4]. See also *Narne Construction Private Limited* v. *Union of India*, (2012) 5 SCC 359, para 4.

'Potential' means 'capable of coming into being, possibility'. [Oxford Dictionary as cited in *LDA* v. *M.K. Gupta*, (1994) 1 SCC 243, para 4]. See also *Narne Construction Private Limited v. Union of India*, (2012) 5 SCC 359, para 4.

Potentially. "Potentially" means in possibility, and not in act, not positively; in efficiency, not in actuality; and hence mere ownership or possession of the soil does not carry with it the production of crops, potentially.

Potest quis renunciare pro se et suis jus quod pro se introductum est. One may relinquish for himself and his heirs a right which was introduced for his own benefit.

Potestas stricte interpretatur. A power is to be strictly construed.

Potior est conditio possedentis. The condition of the actual possessor is stronger.

Pottery. "Pottery" in a wide sense will take in all objects that are made from clay and hardened by fire, from crude earthen pots to delicate porcelain. (*South Gujarat Roofing Tiles Manufacturers Association* v. *State of Gujarat,* AIR 1977 SC 90).

Poultry. 'POULTRY' means domestic fowls, turkeys, geese, ducks, guinea-fowls, pigeons, pheasants and partridges. [Medicines Act, 1968, S. 132(1)]

Pour out. To fail to obtain damages or relief in law suit.

Power. "POWER" means electrical energy or any other form of energy which is mechanically transmitted and is not generated by human or animal agency. [Factories Act (63 of 1948), S. 2(g)]

"POWER" means any form of energy which is mechanically transmitted and is not generated by human or animal agency, and includes electrical energy. [Central Silk Board Act (61 of 1948), S. 3(d)]

"POWER" means electrical or mechanical energy, or any other form of energy which is mechanically transmitted into a dangerous machine. [Dangerous Machines (Regulation) Act, 1983 (35 of 1983), S. 2(l)]

Ability conferred upon a person by the law to alter, by his own will directed to that end, the rights, duties, liabilities or other legal relations either of himself or other persons [CrPC 1973 (2 of 1974), S. 91(1) and Constitution of India, Art. 161, margin]; electrical energy [Damodar Valley Corporation Act (14 of 1948), S. 22(2)(i)].

Basically power means authority, whether any discretion is left or not and whether any direction is imperative or directory relates to the manner and exercise of the power and not to the basic ingredient of the authority itself. Without authority, a valid act cannot be done irrespective of whether the act is discretionary on the part of the doer of the act, or he is bound to do it. In both situations, he must have authority. *Seth Lookasan Sethiya* v. *Ivan E. John,* AIR 1975 All 113, 121.

POWER AND AUTHORITY. Power is either physical or mental, public or private; in the former case it is synonymous with strength, in the latter with authority. Civil power includes in it all that which enables us to have any influence or control over the actions, persons, property, *etc.*, of others: authority is confined to that species of power which is derived from some legitimate source. Power exists independently of all right; authority is founded only on right. Power may be abused; authority may be exceeded. (*Crabb*)

Power alcohol. Means ethyl alcohol containing not less than 99.5 per cent by volume of ethanol measured at sixty degrees Fahrenheit corresponding to 77.4 over proof strength. [Indian Power Alcohol Act (22 of 1948), S. 3(c)]

"Power" and "Rights". Whether a case involves public law or private law rights depends upon the facts and circumstances of the case. The dichotomy between rights and remedies cannot be obliterated by any straitjacket formula. It would depend upon the factual matrix as to whether the case was one of arbitrary exercise of "power" or exercise of a "right" arising either under a contract or statute. However, such exercise of power cannot be dealt with by the State or the instrumentality of the State without informing and taking the affected into confidence. In such situations most often people feel aggrieved by exclusion of knowledge if not being taken into confidence. (*Mahabir Auto Stores* v. *Indian Oil Corporation,* AIR 1990 SC 1031.

Power density. Means the total energy output per unit bandwidth from a pulse or sequence of pules for which transmit power is at its maximum level, dividend by the total duration of the pulses. [Use of Low Power and Very Low Power Short Range Radio frequency Devices (Exemption from Licensing Requirement) Rules, 2018, R. 2(e); Use of Very Low Power Ultra-wideband Devices (Exemption from Licensing Requirements) Rules, 2018, R. 2(g)].

Power-of-attorney. "POWER OF ATTORNEY" includes any instrument (not chargeable with a fee under the law relating to court-fees for the time being in force) empowering a specified person to act for and in the name of the person executing it. [Indian Stamp Act (2 of 1899), S. 2 (21)].

A power of attorney is not an instrument of transfer in regard to any right, title or interest in an immovable property. The power of attorney is creation of an agency whereby the grantor authorises the grantee to do acts specified therein, on behalf of grantor, which when executed will be binding on the grantor as if done by him. It is revocable or terminable at any time unless it is made irrevocable in a manner known to law. Even an irrevocable attorney does not have the effect of transferring title to the grantee. [*Suraj Lamp and Industries Private Limited (2)* v. *State of Haryana*, (2012) 1 SCC, 656, para 20].

The term "power of attorney" indicates a power or authority under seal. A "power of attorney" is an instrument in writing by which one person, as principal, appoints another as his agent and confers upon him the authority to perform certain specified acts or kinds of acts on behalf of the principal. [*Shilpa Chaudhary* v. *Principal Judge*, AIR 2016 All 122, para 18].

A formal instrument by which one person empowers another to represent him or act in his stead for certain purposes [T.P. Act (4 of 1882) and S. 102, long title, Powers-of-Attorney Act (7 of 1882)].

A power-of-attorney is an authority given by a formal instrument whereby one person, who is called the donor or principal, authorises another person, who is called the donee, attorney, or agent, to act on his behalf.

A GENERAL POWER-OF-ATTORNEY is one by which authority is given to act for the principal in all matters, or in all matters of a particular nature, or concerning a particular business.

A general power-of-attorney must confer upon the donee of the power all necessary powers with regard to the business of the donor or at least with regard to a particular class of business of the donor, and even if one were prepared to take a liberal view of a general power-of-attorney, even so it must at least authorise the agent to act for the donor with regard to all his litigation in different Courts. What one has got to look at before one decides whether a power is general or special is what is the subject-matter in respect of which this power is conferred and if the Court comes to the conclusion that the subject matter is not general that it is restricted to something specific, something particular, then the power-of-attorney, would not be a general power-of-attorney. *Western India Theatres Ltd.* v. *Ishwarbhai Sonabhai Patel,* AIR 1959 Bom 386, 388, 390. [CPC (5 of 1908), O. III, R. 2]

A SPECIAL POWER-OF-ATTORNEY is one by which authority is given to do some particular specified act. The law relating to powers-of-attorney is a branch of the law of agency.

Power-of-attorney includes *vakalatnama*

Power of attorney holder. 'Power of attorney holder' is not a pleader to conduct the prosecution on behalf of legal heirs of complainant within the meaning of Section 2(q) of the Code. *Jimmy Jahangir Madan* v. *Bolly Cariyappa Hindley*, AIR 2005 SC 48, 52, para 10. [CrPC 1973 (2 of 1974), S. 2(q)]

Power of sale. A power of sale is not an ordinary accompaniment of a mortgage, but is a power coupled with an interest, in its nature irrevocable.

This word in the proviso to S. 17, Presidency Towns Insolvency Act (3 of 1909), refers to such powers as mortgagees and pledgees may have of selling the property mortgaged to or hypothecated with them without recourse to a suit, and the words "deal with his security" in same proviso refer to the rights they may have of transferring or assigning the debt due to, and the security in the possession or at the disposal of, the said creditors.

The words "power of sale" in S. 69(*c*) of the T.P. Act (4 of 1882), refer to a clause to be expressly included in the mortgage and must be understood to mean what is ordinarily known and understood in conveyancing by that expression. It is a well-known expression in conveyancing and is a technical one.

Power plant : Power project. The term 'power project' is not equated with the term power plant. The 'power plant' is set up to generate power for one's own requirement or captive consumption of the industrial unit, whereas as a 'power project' is set up by the Government to cater to the needs of the public by generating and distributing electricity generally. (*Union of India* v. *Indian Charge Chrome*, AIR 1999 SC 3504).

Power system. Means all aspects of generation, transmission, distribution and supply of electricity and includes one or more of the following, namely:—

(a) generating stations;

(b) transmission or main transmission lines;

(c) sub-stations;

(d) tie-lines;

(e) load despatch activities;

(f) mains or distribution mains;

(g) electric supply-lines;

(h) overhead lines;

(i) service lines;

(j) works. [Electricity Act (36 of 2003), S. 2(50)]

Power thresher. "POWER THRESHER" means a machine, operated with the aid of power for threshing one or more kinds of agricultural produce. [Dangerous Machines (Regulation) Act (35 of 1983), S. 2(m)]

Power to appoint property. Means power to determine the disposition of property of which the person invested with the power is not the owner. [Estate Duty Act (34 of 1953), S. 2(13)]

Power transmission system. In relation to each company specified in the First Schedule, means the main transmission lines (including extra high voltage alternative current (EHVAC) lines and high voltage direct current (HVDC) lines) and sub-stations owned by each such company. [National Thermal Power Corporation Limited, the National Hydroelectric Power Corporation Limited and the North Eastern Electric Power Corporation Limited (Acquisition and Transfer of Power Transmission System) Act (24 of 1993), S. 2(e)]

"POWER TRANSMISSION SYSTEM", in relation to the company, means the main transmission lines (including extra high voltage alternative current (EHVAC) lines and high voltage direct current (HVDC) lines) and sub-stations owned by the company. [Neyveli Lignite Corporation Limited (Acquisition and Transfer of Power Transmission System) Act (56 of 1994), S. 2(f)]

PPP. (*abbr.*) Point to Point Protocol. Allows, amongst other things, IP connections between a computer and access provider. Any dial-up service used with an access provider will use PPP, or SLIP, its predecessor. (*Cyber Law*)

Point to Point Protocol—is a way by which two computers communicate with each other. (*Internet*)

The most common protocol used to connect home computers to the Internet over regular phone lines.

Most well known as a protocol that allows a computer to use a regular telephone line and a *modem* to make *TCP/IP* connections and thus be really and truly on the *Internet*. (*Matisse Enzer-Glossary of Internet Terms*)

Practicable. The expression 'practicable' means possible or feasible with due diligence. *Karam Singh* v. *Transport Commissioner,* AIR 1965 J&K 53, 55.

Reasonably capable of being accomplished; feasible. [Black's Law Dictionary as cited in *C. N. Paramasivam* v. *Sunrise Plaza*, (2013) 9 SCC 460, para 25]. 'Capable of being put into practice, carried out in action, effected, accomplished, or done; feasible'. [Oxford English Dictionary as cited in *Union of India v. Tulsiram Patel*, (1985) 3 SCC 398 :

1985 SCC (L&S) 672, para 130]. See also *Reena Rani v. State of Haryana*, (2012) 10 SCC 215, para 9.

Practicable despatch. Feasible promptitude. [CPC (5 of 1908), O. XLI, R. 13(2)].

Practice. The word 'PRACTICE' means "exercise of any profession or occupation". [Chartered Accountants Act (38 of 1949), S. 22]

"PRACTICE" includes any practice relating to the carrying on of any trade by a person or an enterprise. [Competition Act, 2002 (12 of 2003), S. 2(m)]

The word 'Practice' means appear, act and plead, unless there is anything in the subject or context to limit its meaning. [*Re Powers-of-Advocates,* (1929) ILR 52 Mad 92 : 55 MLJ 551 : AIR 1928 Mad 1182 as cited in *Dasam Vijay Rana Rao* v. *M. Sai Sri*, AIR 2015 Hyd 191, para 10].

The word "practice" in Section 4 of the Legal Practitioners Act (18 of 1879) includes the right to appear, plead and act.

To "practice" is to exercise a calling or profession. It is the application of science or knowledge to the wants of man in the recording incidents of life, as the practice of law or medicine.

A member of the Institute under this provision shall be deemed to be in practice when he renders such other services as in the opinion of the council are or may be rendered by a chartered accountant. When a member agrees to work as a liquidator in pursuance to an order of the High Court, there can be no doubt that in working as such liquidator he was rendering services which in the opinion of the council may be rendered by a chartered accountant. *Council of The Institute of Chartered Accountants* v. *B. Mukherjea*, AIR 1958 SC 72, 75, 76. [Chartered Accountants Act (38 of 1949), S. 2(2)]

The usual mode or method of doing something [Gift-tax Act (18 of 1958), S. 5(xvi)(b), prov.]; usage [Inland Vessels Act (1 of 1917), S. 19Q and Central Sales Tax Act (74 of 1956), S. 2(h)]; performance or operation of something; conduct [Navy Act (62 of 1957), S. 41(b)]; be professionally engaged in.

Practice and **custom.** Both 'practice' and 'custom' are general or particular but the former is absolute, the latter relative; a practice may be adopted by a number of persons without reference to each other; but a custom is always followed by the imitation or prescription; the practice of gaming has always been followed by the vicious part of society, but it is to be hoped for the honour of man that it will never become a custom. [*Bhimashya* v. *Janabi,* (2006) 13 SCC 627, 636, para 29]

Practice and procedure. "Practice and procedure" are said to relate to the legal rules directing the manner of bringing parties into the Court, and the method of the Court after they are brought in, in hearing, dealing with, and disposing of, matters in dispute between them. [Words and Phrases, Vol. 33, published by West Publishing Company, page 188]

Practice directions. Statements by the judiciary which are usually noted in the law reports, with the intention of guiding the Courts and legal profession on matters of practice and procedure.

Practice of law. "Practice of law," as the term is generally understood, is the doing or performing services in a Court of justice, in any matter depending therein, throughout its various stages, and in conformity to the adopted rules of procedure. But in a larger sense it includes legal advice and counsel as the preparation of legal instruments and contracts by which legal rights are secured, although such matters may not be pending in a Court.

Practice of medicine. The practice of medicine may be said to consist in three things: First, in judging the nature, character and symptoms of the disease; second, in determining the proper remedy for the disease; and third, in giving or prescribing the application of the remedy to the disease.

The PRACTICE OF MEDICINE includes the application of knowledge of medicine, of disease, and of the loss of health. Thus the act entitled "To regulate the practice of medicine" is sufficiently broad and comprehensive to include within its scope the entire range of practice of the medical profession.

Practice of the Courts. Usual method of the working of the Courts. [CPC (5 of 1908), Sch. 1, App. D, form No. 17(13)].

Practice in its larger sense like procedure, denotes the mode of proceeding by which a legal right is enforced as distinguished from the law that gives and defines the right. 'Procedure' as defined in Wharton means the mode in which successive steps in litigation are taken. *State of Seraikella* v. *Union of India*, AIR 1951 SC 253, 266.

Practise in Court. To practise law in a Court. [CrPC 1973 (2 of 1974), S. 480].

Practising chartered accountant. Means a person who is a member of the Institute of Chartered Accountants of India and is holding a certificate of practice granted under the provisions of the Chartered Accountants Act, 1949 and includes any concern engaged in rendering services in the field of chartered accountancy. [Finance Act (32 of 1994), S. 65(68) now repealed by Central Goods and Services Tax Act, 2017]

Practising company secretary. Means a person who is a member of the Institute of Company Secretaries of India and is holding a certificate of practice granted under the provisions of the Company Secretaries Act, 1980 and includes any concern engaged in rendering services in the field of company secretary ship. [Finance Act (32 of 1994), S. 65(70) now repealed by Central Goods and Services Tax Act, 2017]

Practising cost accountant. Means a person who is a member of the Institute of Cost and Works Accountants of India and is holding a certificate of practice granted under the provisions of the Cost and Works Accountants Act, 1959 and includes any concern engaged in rendering services in the field of cost accountancy. [Finance Act (32 of 1994), S. 65(69) now repealed by Central Goods and Services Tax Act, 2017]

Pradhan. "PRADHAN" means the chairperson of a *Gram Nyayalaya.* [Madhya Pradesh Gram Nyayalaya Adhiniyam, 1996 (26 of 1997), S. 2(g)]

Praedium serviens. The words "praedium serviens" in the civil law, in reference to services which correspond to our easements, were used to designate what was known in our law as the servient estate.

Praescriptio est titulus ex usu et tempore substantiam capiens ab auctoritate legis. Prescription is a title derived from use and time, taking substance from the authority of the law. (*Latin for Lawyers*)

Praestat cautela quam medela. Prevention is better than cure.

Praesumitur pro legitimatione. The presumption is in favour of legitimacy.

Praesumptio, ex eo quod plerumque fit. Presumptions arise from what generally happens. (*Black*)

Praesumptio violenta valet in lege. Strong presumption avails in law.

Praesumptiones sunt conjecturae ex signo verisimili ad probandum assumptae. Presumptions are conjectures from probable proof, assumed for purposes of evidence.

Pramukh. "PRAMUKH" means *Sarpanch* of the *Gram Panchayat,* President of *Janpada Panchayat* or *Zila Pradhan* of the *Zilla Parishad* as the case may be. [Madhya Pradesh Panchayats (Procedure of Meeting and Conduct of Business) Rules, 1991, R. 2(d)]

Pratique. A health certificate issued to the master of a ship confirming that no infectious disease has been found on board.

Pray in aid. A phrase often used to signify "claiming the benefit of an argument."

Prayer for relief. A request which is addressed to the Court and appearing at the end of a pleading, specially a request for specific relief or damages.

Pre-contract. A contract made before another contract.

Pre-emption. A right to purchase property before or in preference to other person. [CPC (5 of 1908), O. XX, R. 14].

Pre-emption suit. A suit for the enforcement of a right of pre-emption. [CPC (5 of 1908), O. XX, R. 14(1)].

Pre-emptor. A pre-emptor is one who acquires a right to purchase land.

One who has exercised or exercises the right of pre-emption. [CPC (5 of 1908), O. XX, R. 14(2)(a)].

Pre-fill. Means the automated process of data input by the computer system from the database maintained in electronic registry of the Central Government. [R. 2(1)(n) of the Companies (Specification of Definitions Details) Rules, 2014]

Pre-adoption foster care. Means a stage when the temporary custody of a child is given to prospective adoptive parents, till the adoption order is granted by the competent court. [Adoption Regulations, 2017, Regn. 2(16)].

Pre-arrival document scrutiny. Refers to the scrutiny of documents submitted by the Food Importer to the Authorised Officer in advance, before the actual arrival of the articles of food to facilitate faster clearance of articles of food imported at the customs port. [Food Safety and Standards (Import) Regulations, 2017, Regn. 2(1)(q)].

Pre-incorporation/pre-operative expenses. Shall include amounts remitted to Investee Company's account, to the investor's account in India if it exists, to any consultant, attorney or to any other material/service provider for expenditure relating to incorporation or necessary for commencement of operations. [Foreign Exchange Management (Transfer of Issue of Security by a Person Resident Outside India) Regulations, 2000, Schedule 1, Para 2(5), *Explanation*].

Pre-natal diagnostic procedures. Means all gynaecological or obstetrical or medical procedures such as ultrasonography, foetoscopy, taking or removing samples of amniotic fluid, chorionic villi, embryo, blood or any other tissue or fluid of a man, or of a woman before or after conception, for being sent to a Genetic Laboratory or Genetic Clinic for conducting any type of analysis or pre-natal diagnostic tests for selection of sex before or after conception. [Pre-Natal Diagnostic Techniques (Regulation and Prevention of Misuse) Act (57 of 1994), S. 2(i)]

Pre-natal diagnostic techniques. Include all pre-natal diagnostic procedures and pre-natal diagnostic tests. [Pre-Natal Diagnostic Techniques (Regulation and Prevention of Misuse) Act (57 of 1994), S. 2(j)]

Pre-natal diagnostic test. Means ultrasonography or any test or analysis of amniotic fluid, chorionic villi, blood or any tissue of a pregnant woman conducted to detect genetic or metabolic disorders or chromosomal abnormalities or congenital anomalies or haemoglobinopathies or sex-linked diseases. [Pre-Natal Diagnostic Techniques (Regulation and Prevention of Misuse) Act (57 of 1994), S. 2(k)]

Pre-nuptial. Before marriage; pre-marital.

Pre-nuptial agreement. A before marriage agreement in respect to support and property in case of divorce or death of a spouse.

Pre-primary stage. "Pre-primary stage" means a stage of school education previous to the primary stage. [Delhi School Education Rules, 1973, R. 2(h)]

Pre-School Centre. PRE-SCHOOL CENTRE means an institution by whatever name called which provides education for children who have attained the age of three years but have not attained the age of six years. [Maharashtra Employees of Private Schools

(Conditions of Service) Regulation Act, 1977 (3 of 1978), S. 2(16)]

"PRE-SCHOOL CENTRE" means a private *Shishu Kendra-Balwary, Balwadi* or Kindergarten or any other private pre-school centre, by whatever name called, which is run for imparting pre-school informal education to the children. [Maharashtra Pre-School Centres (Regulation of Admission) Act, 1996 (29 of 1997), S. 2(g)]

Pre-shipment application. Are those treatments applied directly preceding and in relation to export, to meet the phytosanitary or sanitary requirements of the importing country or existing phytosanitary or sanitary requirements of the exporting country. [Hazardous Waste (Management and Handling) Rules, 1989, R. 2(k)]

Preamble. "PREAMBLE", in relation to any notification or order, means that part of the notification or order which refers to the powers in exercise or in pursuance of which such notification or order is issued or made. [Central Excise Laws (Amendment and Validation) Act (58 of 1982), S. 2(d)]

A recital at the beginning of some Acts to explain the mind of makers of the Acts, and the mischief they intend to remedy by the same; the introductory part of a statute, ordinance or regulation that states the reasons and intent of law or regulation or is used for explanatory purposes. [Indian Evidence Act (1 of 1872), Preamble].

Preamble has been defined in the Oxford English Dictionary to mean a preliminary statement in speech or writing; an introductory paragraph, section or clause; a preface, prologue, introduction. It has further been defined there as 'an introductory paragraph' or part in a statute, deed, or other document setting forth the ground and intention of it. The preamble thus betokens that which follows. *Dhananjoy Das* v. *District Magistrate*, AIR 1982 SC 1315, 1319.

Precatory. (Of words) requesting, recommending, or expressing a desire for action, but usually in a non-binding way.

Precaution. Care taken beforehand; a measure taken beforehand against possible danger, failure, *etc.*; caution exercised beforehand to provide against mischief or secure good results; prudent foresight. [IPC (45 of 1860), S. 443 and CrPC 1973 (2 of 1974), S. 109].

Precedence. Priority; higher or more honourable place.

Precedent. A decided case that forms the basis for determining subsequent cases involving similar facts and issues.

In law a precedent is an adjudged case or decision of a Court of justice, considered as furnishing a rule or authority for the determination of an identical or similar case afterwards arising, or of a similar question of law. The only theory on which it is possible for one decision to be an authority for another is that the facts are alike, or, if the facts are different, that the principle which governed the first case is applicable to the variant facts. WILLIAM M. LILE et al., *Brief Making and the Use of Law Books* 288 (3d ed. 1914).

Precedent, is an adjudged case or decision of a Court of justice, considered as furnishing an example or authority for an identical or similar case afterward arising or a similar question of law; also a draft or form of a conveyance, settlement, will, pleading, bill, or other legal instrument, which is considered worthy to serve as a pattern for future instruments of the same nature.

Precedent interest. As between two interests, the one which is earlier in time. [T.P. Act (4 of 1882), S. 23].

Precedent sub silentio. "It is not only from decided cases where the point has been raised upon argument, but also from the long-continued practice of the Courts, without objection made, that we collect rules of laws."

Though the practice of the Courts or forms of pleadings which pass *sub silentio*, doe not make a law, yet a constant practice of permitting certain acts to be done in Courts without opposition, is a great evidence of law."

Preceding. That precedes in order, time or movement. [CPC (5 of 1908), O. XXIII, R. 2].

Preceding calendar month. If the claim of the workmen is resisted on the ground specified in S. 25-A(1)(a), the period with reference to which that test has to be applied is the calendar month that preceded that point of time, the point of time when the statutory right conferred by S. 25-C arose. *Kohinoor Saw Mills Co. Ltd.* v. *State of Madras,* AIR 1957 Mad 410, 413. [Industrial Disputes Act (14 of 1947), S. 25-A (1)(a)]

Precept. Rule of conduct or action; maxims (as) precepts of law.

A written order or a mandate. [CPC (5 of 1908), S. 46].

Precinct. "PRECINCT" in relation to a temple includes any *mandap*, building and land appertaining to the temple and ordinarily used for any purpose connected with the worship in the temple or not, and the entire area of, land appertaining to the temple on which a *Jantra* or fair is held. [Gujarat Animals and Birds Sacrifices (Prevention) Act, 1972, S. 2(a)]

The term "precinct", in its general sense, indicates any district marked out and defined.

The space enclosed by the walls or other boundaries of a particular place or building [Employees' Provident Funds and Miscellaneous Provisions Act (19 of 1952), S. 2(g)].

The term 'precincts' is usually understood as a space enclosed by walls. *In Re K.V.V. Sharma,* AIR 1953 Mad 269. [Factories Act (63 of 1948), S. 2(m)]

Precinct. A 'precinct' cannot be a location since it is really an area. *Mass Holdings Pvt. Ltd.* v. *Municipal Corpn. of Greater Mumbai*, AIR 2006 SC 749 : 2006 AIR SCW 38.

Precincts of prison. The "precincts of the prison" within the meaning of a statutory provision that the warden and deputy warden of the state prison may serve legal processes within the precincts of the prison, embraces not only the prison building, but the grounds connected therewith.

Precints of the House. Means and includes the chamber the lobbies, the Galleries and such other places as the speaker may from time to time specify. [Rules of Procedure and Conduct of Business in Lok Sabha, R. 2(1)]

Precious metal. Means silver, gold and platinum. [Customs Tariff Act (51 of 1975), I Sch. Import Tariff, S. XIV, Chap. 71, Note 4(a); Central Excise Tariff Act (5 of 1986), I Sch. S. XIV, Chap. 71, Note 3(a)]

"PRECIOUS METAL" means gold, silver, platinum, palladium or rhodium or such other metal as may be notified by the Central Government. [S. 2(1)(sb) of the Prevention of Money-Laundering Act, 2002 (15 of 2003) as inserted by the Prevention of Money-Laundering (Amendment) Act, 2012 (2 of 2013)]

Precious stone. Includes pearl and semi-precious is stone and such other stone or gem as the Central Government may, for the purposes of this Act, notify in this behalf in the Official Gazette. [Foreign Exchange Regulation Act (46 of 1973), S. 2(r)]

PRECIOUS STONE OR STONE means ruby, spinel or sapphire, and includes any other stone which the local Government may, by notification in the official Gazette, declare to be a precious stone for the purpose of the Burma Ruby Regulation. [Bur. Regn. XII of 1887 (U.B. Rubies), S. 2, cl. 1].

"PRECIOUS STONE" means diamond, emerald, ruby, sapphire or any such other stone as may be notified by the Central Government. [S. 2(1)(sc) of the Prevention of Money-Laun-dering Act, 2002 (15 of 2003) as inserted by the Prevention of Money-Laundering (Amendment) Act, 2012 (2 of 2013)]

Precipice. A vertical, almost vertical or overhanging surface. [IPC (45 of 1860), S. 390, ill. (e)].

Precis. A concise summary of the essential points of the text.

Precise. Exact; to the point; without deviation. [Specific Relief Act (47 of 1963), S. 14(3)(c)(i)]; [CPC (5 of 1908), O. VI, R. 11].

Preclude. To close the door against; to shut out; to exclude; to render impracticable by anticipatory action [Indian Evidence Act (1 of 1872), S. 91, *Expln.* (3)]; to prevent [CrPC 1973 (2 of 1974), S. 145(5)]; [Oil Industry (Development) Act (47 of 1974), S. 6(2)(h)]; [Trade and Merchandise Marks Act (43 of 1958), S. 108(5)].

Precursor. Means any chemical reactant which takes part at any stage in the production by whatever method of a toxic chemical. This includes any key component of a binary or multi-component chemical system.

(For the purpose of implementing this Convention, precursors which have been identified for the application of verification measures are listed in Schedules contained in the Annex on Chemicals). [Chemical Weapons Convention Act (34 of 2000), Art. II 3]

Predatory pricing. Unlawful below cost pricing which is intended to eliminate specific competitors and reduce overall competition.

Predecessor. In the common acceptation "predecessor" means one who goes before or precedes another in a given state, position or office, and does not necessarily express any relation of legal privity.

One who has preceded another in any office or position [Specific Relief Act (47 of 1963), S. 15(e)]; one that precedes.

Predecessor State. "PREDECESSOR STATE" means the State which has been replaced by another State on the occurrence of a Succession of States. [Vienna Convention on Succession of States in Respect of Treaties, 1978, Art. 2(c)]

Predicate device. Means a device, first time and first of its kind, approved for manufacture for sale or for import by the Central Licensing Authority and has the similar intended use, material of construction, and design characteristics as the device which is proposed for licence in India. [Medical Devices Rules, 2017, R. 3(zm)].

Preference. "Preference" means the act of preferring one thing above another; estimation of one thing more than another; choice of one thing rather than another.

The expression 'preference' means an equitable apportionment of the vacancies reserved (for backward classes) among them. *Indra Sawhney* v. *Union of India*, AIR 1993 SC 477, 578. [Constitution of India, Art. 16(4)]

The word "preference" does not mean that the Railways trained apprentice (as held earlier) will have an exclusive right to the exclusion of all others to be considered for appointment. [*Abdul Hamid* v. *Union of India,* (2017) 16 SCC 346, para 11].

"Preference" means right or privilege to be conferred without any process of selection, and in the case of two or more applicants for grant of lease or licence, one who applied first in point of time is given preference. *Barium Chemical Ltd.* v. *Govt. of India,* AIR 1987 AP 267, 291 (FB). [Mines and Minerals (Regulation and Development Act) Act (67 of 1957), S. 11(2)]

Preference would mean that other things generally appearing to be qualitatively and quantitatively equal though not with mathematical accuracy, statutory provisions will tilt the balance in favour of the undertakings. *Sher Singh* v. *Union of India*, AIR 1984 SC 200, 204.

Preference Capital. Means the amount of paid up capital attributable to the undertaking of the licensee, issued on such preferred terms as are sufficient to qualify it for such description. [Electricity (Supply) Act (54 of 1998), Sixth Sch., Para XVII(7)]

Preference share. "PREFERENCE SHARE" means a share which carries, as respects dividends, a preferential right to be paid a fix amount or an amount calculated at a fixed rate. [Preference Shares (Regulation of Dividends) Act, 1960 (63 of 1969), S. 2(c)]

Guaranteed share and interest bearing share. [Companies Act (1 of 1956), S. 4(1)(b)(i)].

Preference share capital. For the purposes of section 43 of Act 18 of 2013, the expression 'preference share capital', with reference to any company limited by shares, means that part of the issued share capital of the company which carries or would carry a preferential right with respect to—

(*a*) payment of dividend, either as a fixed amount or an amount calculated at a fixed rate, which may either be free of or subject to income-tax; and

(*b*) repayment, in the case of a winding up or repayment of capital, of the amount of the share capital paid-up or deemed to have been paid-up, whether or not, there is a preferential right to the payment of any fixed premium or premium on any fixed scale, specified in the memorandum or articles of the company. [*Explanation (ii)* to section 43 of the Companies Act, 2013 (18 of 2013)]

''Preference share capital'', with reference to any company limited by shares, means that part of the issued share capital of the company which carries or would carry a preferential right with respect to—

(a) payment of dividend, either as a fixed amount or an amount calculated at a fixed rate, which may either be free of or subject to income-tax; and

(b) repayment, in the case of a winding up or repayment of capital, of the amount of the share capital paid-up or deemed to have been paid-up, whether or not, there is a preferential right to the payment of any fixed premium or premium on any fixed scale, specified in the memorandum or articles of the company; [Companies Act (18 of 2013), S. 43, Explanation (ii)].

"PREFERENCE SHARE CAPITAL" means with reference to any company limited by shares, whether formed before or after the commencement of the Companies Act, 1956, that part of the share capital of the company which fulfils both the following requirements, namely—

(a) that as respects dividends, it carries or will carry a preferential right to be paid a fixed amount or an amount calculated at a fixed rate, which may be either free of or subject to income-tax, and

(b) that as respects capital, it carries or will carry, on a winding up or repayment of capital, a preferential right to be repaid the amount of the capital paid up or deemed to have been paid up, whether or not there is a preferential right to the payment of either or both of the following amounts, namely—

(i) any money remaining unpaid, in respect of the amounts specified in clause (a) up to the date of the winding up or repayment of capital, and

(ii) any fixed premium or premium on any fixed scale, specified in the memorandum or articles of the company. [Companies Act (1 of 1956), S. 85(1) now replaced by Companies Act, 2013]

Preference share, Redeemable. Guaranteed redeemable share. [Companies Act (1 of 1956), S. 78(2)(d)].

Preferment. The act of bringing a bill of indictment before an appropriate Court.

Preferential Allotment. Includes issue of shares on preferential basis and/or through private placement made by a company in pursuance of a resolution passed under sub-section (1A) of Section 81 of the Companies Act, 1956 and issue of shares to the promoters and their relatives either in public issue or otherwise. [Unlisted Public Companies (Preferential Allotment) Rules, 2003, R. 3(1)]

Preferential offer. For the purposes of rule 13 of the Companies (Share Capital & Debentures) Rules, 2014, the expression 'preferential offer' means an issue of shares or other securities, by a company to any select person or group of persons on a preferential basis and does not include shares or other securities offered through a public issue, rights issue, employee stock option scheme, employee stock purchase scheme or an issue of sweat equity shares or bonus shares or depository receipts issued in a country outside India or foreign securities. [*Explanation* (*i*) to rule 13(1) of the Companies (Share Capital & Debentures) Rules, 2014]

Preferential qualification. 'Preferential qualification' in service law refers to numeric superiority. It is also essentially related to better mental capacity, ability and maturity to shoulder the responsibilities which are entrusted to the candidates after their selection to a particular post. [*Surinder Singh* v. *Union of India*, (2007) 11 SCC 599, 604, para 16]

Preferential treatment. For the purposes of this notification, "PREFERENTIAL TREATMENT" in relation to any product means the exemption granted under the notification of the Government of India in the Ministry of Finance (Department of Revenue), No. 26/2000 Customs, dated 1st March, 2000 and includes preferential concessions. [Customs Tariff Determination of origin of goods under the free trade agreement between the Democratic Socialistic Republic of Sri Lanka and the Republic of India, Rules 2000, R. 4 *Expln.*]

Preferential voting. The term is used to describe various systems under which the voter is permitted or required to express more than one choice for the same office. It differs from the proportional representation system in two leading respects: (1) A majority or plurality is required to elect, and (2) it is used more frequently in the election of individual officers than in the election of legislative or other governing boards or bodies. In some jurisdictions preferential voting is provided for by constitutional provision, and in others the validity of the statutes providing therefor has either been expressly upheld or impliedly recognized. But in still other jurisdictions such system has been held to be violative of constitutional guaranties. (18 Am Jur 317)

Preferred an appeal. If we read into the words "prefer an appeal" the sense of effectively prosecuting an appeal, then mere institution followed by withdrawal will cancel the effect, result in non-prosecution and obliteration of the appeal, which is the same as not preferring an appeal. Among available semantic options law prefers that which furthers the statutory objective. (*CIT (Central)* v. *B.N. Bhattacharjee,* 1979 (4) SCC 121). [Income-tax Act (43 of 1961), S. 245D(1), Proviso, *as it then stood*]

Pregnancy. The condition of being pregnant. [Maternity Benefit Act (53 of 1961), S. 3(j)]; the state of being with young [Maternity Benefit Act (53 of 1961), S. 4(3)]; gestation [Employees' State Insurance Act (34 of 1948), S. 2(3)].

Pregnant. Containing unborn young within the body [Maternity Benefit Act (53 of 1961), S. 6(2)]; [Employees' State Insurance Act (34 of 1948), S. 2(14B)]; [Maternity Benefit Act (53 of 1961), S. 3(j)]; full of meaning; fitting and to the purpose.

Pregnant with quick child. A woman is "pregnant with a quick child" when it has been "quickened" or in other words so moved in the mother's womb that she has felt the movement.

Prejudice. Injurious effect, injury to or impairment of a right, claim, statement *etc.* [Indian Contract Act (9 of 1872), S. 202]; to affect injuriously or unfavourably; [CrPC 1973 (2 of 1974), S. 216(3)]; favoured beforehand without due examination.

Prejudice. As per the Oxford English Dictionary, the word "prejudice" means a preconceived opinion or a harm or injury that results or may result from some action or judgment. Black's Law dictionary gives the meaning of the word "prejudice" to be a fore judgment, bias, partiality, preconceived opinion, and in respect of speedy trial, prejudice means actual prejudice to the defendant's ability to present effective defence. Prejudice, in the context of a delay in initiation of a disciplinary proceeding, has to be understood to mean that the delay in the initiation has resulted in a situation where, due to the change in the circumstance as because of the delay, the delinquent is in a less advantageous position to defend his case in the proceeding in comparison to what would have been, had the proceeding been initiated at an earlier point of time. [As cited in *Rabindra Nath Barman* v. *Gauhati High Court* 2017(2) GLT 773, para 43]

A preconceived judgment formed without being based on facts.

(i) a judgment or opinion, favourable or unfavourable, formed be forehand or without due examination... detriment arising from a hasty and unfair judgment; injury; harm. [Webster Comprehensive Dictionary (International Edn.) as cited in *Manharibahi Muljiibhai Kakadia* v. *Shaileshbhai Mohanbhai Patel*, (2012) 10 SCC 517, para 47.2].

Preconceived opinion that is not based on reason or actual experience. Unjust behaviour formed on such a basis. (2)harm or injury that results or may result from some action or judgment (v) (1) give rise to prejudice in (someone); make biased. (2) cause harm to (a state of affairs). [Concise Oxford English Dictionary (10th Edn., Revised) as cited in *Manharibhai Muljibhai Kakadia* v. *Shaileshbhai Mohanbhai Patel*, (2012) 10 SCC 517, para 47.1

Prejudice to accused. *Willie Slancy* v. *State of M.P*, AIR 1956 SC 116 quoted-in judging a question of prejudice, as of guilt, Courts must act with a broad vision and look to the substance and not to the technicalities, and their main concern should be to see whether the accused had a fair trial, whether he knew what he was being tried for, whether the main facts sought to be established against him were explained to him fairly and clearly and whether he was given a full and fair chance to defend himself. *Gurbachan Singh* v. *State of Punjab*, AIR 1957 SC 623, 626. [CrPC 1973 (2 of 1974), SS. 464, 465]

Prejudice, Without. When statements are made or letters written with the words "without prejudice" affixed, they cannot be afterwards used as evidence, should litigation follow.

Preliminary. Initiatory; temporary; provisional, as preliminary examination, injunction, articles of peace, *etc.*

Preparatory, introductory, preceding and leading up to the main subject. [CPC (5 of 1908), O. XX, R. 13(1)].

Preliminary decree. A preliminary decree is one which declares the rights and liabilities of the parties leaving the actual result to be worked and in further proceedings. *Shankar Balwant Lokhande* v. *Chandrakant Shanker Lokhande*, AIR 1995 SC 1211.

Preliminary examination. (*In criminal cases*) The object of a preliminary examination is two-fold: (1) to inquire touching the commission of crime and the accused's connection with it; (2) to perpetuate testimony. The state has an interest in both.

A preliminary hearing is in no sense a trial in which accused's rights in respect to his guilt or innocence are adjudged, determined, or prejudiced, whether the hearing results in a discharge of the accused person or in holding him for appearance at the proper Court to answer the accusations made against him. The examination is to ascertain *prima facie*, whether the crime charged has been committed, and, if such is found to be the case, to enforce his presence at the proper Court to answer the charge.

Preliminary : Final decrees. A "decree" is preliminary when further proceedings have to be taken before the suit can be completely disposed of. It is final where such adjudication completely disposes of the suit. It may be partly preliminary and partly final. [CPC (5 of 1908), S. 2(2), *Expln.*]

Preliminary hearing. A hearing in a criminal case to determine whether there is sufficient evidence to prosecute an accused.

Preliminary information memorandum. "Preliminary information memorandum" means a memorandum submitted by the corporate debtor under clause (*b*) of sub-section (1) of section 54G. [Insolvency and Bankruptcy Code (31 of 2016), section 5(23A)]

Preliminary injunction. A "preliminary injunction" or, as it is sometimes called "injunction *pendente lite*", is a provisional remedy, granted before the hearing on the merits for the purpose of preventing the perpetration of wrong or the doing of any act whereby the rights in controversy may be materially injured or endangered before the final adjudication; and its purpose is to preserve the subject of controversy until an opportunity is afforded for a full and deliberate investigation.

Preliminary inquiry. Means an inquiry conducted under Act 1 of 2014. [S. 2(1)(m) of the Lokpal & Lokayuktas Act, 2013 (1 of 2014)]

Preliminary meeting. A pre-hearing meeting called by the arbitrator, of all parties to an arbitration so as to formalise and finalise the procedures, arrangements and a time-table for the smooth progress of the arbitration reference. An Order for Directions is usually issued by the arbitrator to both parties after the preliminary meeting. Also termed as '*meeting for directions.*' (*Arbitration*)

Preliminary objection. A preliminary objection is one that challenges the competence of a Court to hear and decide a particular cause before it.

A preliminary objection is one that is raised to the sustainability of an application or action on the basis of the assumption of the truth of all the averments of fact made by the suitor in the application or plaint and is therefore one that can be taken into argument though not raised in the written defence. *Prabhakar Gerald Walter* v. *Chief Secretary,* AIR 1953 TC 286.

Preliminary point. The expression "preliminary point" in O. XLI, R. 23, CPC (5 of 1908) is not confined to such legal points only as may be pleaded in bar of suit, but comprehends all such points as may have prevented the Court from disposing of the case on the merits, whether such points are pure questions of law or pure questions of fact.

A point which, if determined in favour of the plaintiff, permits the progress of the suit, but when determined against him, brings the suit to an end leaving other issues undetermined. [CPC (5 of 1908), O. XLI, R. 23].

A 'preliminary point' means 'a point, the determination of which enables the trial Court to pass a decree and relieves it from the necessity of determining the other points, involved is the suits.' The expression 'preliminary point' does not mean the same thing as a 'preliminary issue'. *Bai* v. *Mahadu Marute,* AIR 1960 Bom 543, 547.

The words 'preliminary point' should not be narrowly construed so as to be confined to pleas like limitation and *res judicata* but should be given a liberal meaning so as to include any point connected or not connected with the merits of the case, a decision of which in some particular manner results in the disposal of the suit without the necessity of deciding other points actually arising in the case which or at any rate some of which must necessarily be decided for the disposal of the case in the event of a different decision on preliminary point not resulting in the disposal of the suit. *Abdul Ghanai* v. *Devi Lal,* AIR 1960 Raj 77, 79.

Pre-litigation mediation. Means a process of undertaking mediation, as provided under section 5, for settlement of disputes prior to the filing of a suit or proceeding of civil or commercial nature in respect thereof, before a court or notified tribunal under sub-section (2) of section 5. [Mediation Act, 2023 (32 of 2023), S. 3(u)]

Prematurity. The circumstance existing when the facts underlying a plaintiff's complaint do not yet create a live claim.

Premeditate. "Premeditated, wilful, malicious and deliberate" denote the intent with which killing must be done to make it murder in the first degree. Moreover they denote, not only the moral impulse, but peculiarly the mental process through which the crime is conceived and the act resolved upon.

Premeditated design. "A premeditated design to effect the death" of a person means that there was a design to kill the deceased fully formed in the mind of the slayer before the killing was done, and that such design had been thought over and meditated on, or before the fatal act was committed for any length of time, no matter how short.

"PREMEDITATED DESIGN" as used in a statutory definition of murder, means the same as "malice aforethought" in the common law definition.

"Premeditated design" as used in an Act defining murder as killing perpetrated on a person with a premeditated design to effect his death, is not an intention formed on the instant. The words "premeditated" and "design" both import forethought, careful reflection, and deliberately arranged purpose; ideas all involving in their structure essential elements of time—that is, a reasonable time, time for reflection, time to survey the contemplated deed in all its bearings and probable results, and to contrive and arrange, if so decided, the means and method and occasion of its deadly accomplishment.

An intention to kill, formed on the instant of striking the fatal blow, is not a "premeditated design" to commit murder.

"Premeditated design" as used in the statute defining murder in the first degree, means a previously formed intention to kill.

Premeditated killing. A premeditated killing is murder in the first degree, and can be nothing else because it implies the lying in wait and malice aforethought and settled design.

Premeditation. By the term "premeditation," or "premeditated" is meant thought of beforehand for any length of time, however short.

Previous deliberation as to action, planning and contriving; considering or planning an act beforehand. [IPC (45 of 1860), S. 300, *Excep*. 2].

Premier unit. A new industrial unit or industrial complex fulfilling the following criteria will be considered for granting status of a "Premier Unit"—

(a) The industrial unit shall have a project cost of Rs. 500 crores. Such units having project cost of Rs. 1000 crores and above shall be entitled for extended period to avail incentive as provided under para 6B.

(b) Only one unit per Taluka will be eligible for the premier unit status. In banned area no unit is permitted.

(c) The unit shall employ at least 100 workers on a regular basis and shall follow the employment policy of the State Government. [Capital Investment Incentive to Premier/Prestigious Unit Scheme, 1995-2000, Clause (v) as cited in *State of Gujrat v. Essar Oil Limited*, (2012) 3 SCC 522, para 5].

Premises. "PREMISES" means any land, shop, stall or place where any insecticide is sold or manufactured or stored or used, and includes any vehicle carrying insecticide. [Insecticide Act (46 of 1968), S. 3(m)]

'PREMISES' includes messuages, buildings and lands of any, tenure, whether open or enclosed, whether built on or not and whether public or private. [Bombay Municipal Corporation Act (3 of 1888), S. 3(gg) as cited in *Makarand Dattatreya Sugavkar* v. *Municipal Corporation of Greater Mumbai*, (2013) 9 SCC 136, para 17].

"PREMISES" means any land or any building or part of a building and includes—

(i) the garden, grounds and outhouses, if any, appertaining to such building or part of a building and

(ii) any fitting affixed to such building or part of a building for the more beneficial enjoyment thereof. [Public Premises (Eviction of Unauthorised Occupants) Act (40 of 1971), S. 2(c)]

"PREMISES" includes—

(i) a place where any business, industry, production or trade is carried on by a person, whether by himself or through an agent, by whatever name called,

(ii) a warehouse, godown or place where any weight, measure or other goods are stored or exhibited,

(iii) a place where any books of account or other document pertaining to any trade or transaction are kept,

(iv) a dwelling house, if any part therefore is used for the purpose of carrying on any business, industry, production or trade.

Explanation.—"Place" includes a vehicle or vessel or any other mobile device, with the help of which any trade or business is carried on, and also includes any measuring instrument mounted on a vehicle, vessel or other mobile device. [Standards of Weights and Measures Act (60 of 1976), S. 2(r)]

"PREMISES" means any land or building or part of a building and includes—

(a) the garden, ground and out-houses, if any, appertaining to a building or part of a building, and

(b) any fittings affixed to a building or part of a building for the more beneficial enjoyment thereof. [New Delhi Municipal Council Act (44 of 1994), S. 2(33) and Control of National Highways (Land and Traffic) Act, 2002 (13 of 2003), S. 2(j)]

PREMISES includes any land, building or structure. [Electricity Act (36 of 2003), S. 2(51)]

"PREMISES" means any land or building or part of a building, and includes—

(i) the garden, grounds and outhouses, if any, appertaining to such building or part of a building; and

(ii) any fittings affixed to such building or part of a building for more beneficial enjoyment thereof. [Airport Authority of India (Amendment) Act (43 of 2003), S. 8(c)]

"Premises" can refer to an entire area, which may have several separate buildings, within it, or which may correspond to an open yard. [as per Factories Act, 1948 and cited in *Mohan Singh* v. *Chairman, Railway Board*, (2015) 10 SCC 759, para 18].

"PREMISES" means any building or part of a building which is, or is intended to be, let separately for use as a residence or for non-residential use or for any other purpose, and includes—

(i) the garden, grounds and out-houses, if any, appertaining to such building or part of the building;

(ii) any fittings to such building or part of the building for the more beneficial enjoyment thereof;

but does not include a room in a hotel or a lodging house. [Delhi Rent Act (33 of 1995), S. 2(j)]

A house or building with adjoining grounds and other appurtenances [Requisitioning and Acquisition of

Immovable Property Act (30 of 1952), S. 2(e) and IPC (45 of 1860), S. 157].

Premises means any land not being used for agricultural purposes. The material date for ascertaining whether the plot is premises is the date of letting and not the date on which the application for fixation of the standard rent is made. *Subhadra* v. *Narsaji*, AIR 1966 SC 806, 808.

A stall like a cup-board hanging on outside wall of shop is not a premises. *A.K. Poraunderwala* v. *Gulam Husain Alibhai Nathani,* AIR 1974 Bom 288, 291.

Whatever is suitable or adaptable for residential uses, even by making some changes, can be designated 'residential premises'. *Busching Schnitz* v. *Menghani*, AIR 1977 SC 1569, 1576.

The word 'premises' in cl. (m) of S. 2, Factories Act (63 of 1948), means not only buildings but includes lands as well. *State* v. *Ardeshir Harmusji Bhimandiwala,* AIR 1956 Bom 219, 224.

The word "premises" refers to either land or buildings or to both depending on the context. Salt works would come within the meaning of the expression "premises" in the definition of the word "factory" and would be factory if the work carried on there comes within the definition of "manufacturing process". *Ardeshir H. Bhiwandiwala* v. *State of Bombay*, AIR 1962 SC 29, 30, 33.

The word 'premises' is defined to mean any land, any land would include agricultural land. *Hari Singh* v. *Military Estate Officer, Delhi Circle, Delhi Cantt. and Bharatia Hotel* v. *Union of India*, AIR 1972 SC 2205, 2212. [Public Premises (Eviction of Unauthorised Occupants Act (40 of 1971), S. 2(c)]

"PREMISES" include any shop, stall, hotel, restaurant, airline services and food canteens, place or vehicle or vessel where any article of food is sold or manufactured or stored for sale. [S. 3(1)(zi) of the Food Safety & Standards Act, 2006 (34 of 2006)]

"PREMISES" the word 'premises' as given in section 2(c) of the W.B. Government Premises (Tenancy Regulation) Act 19 of 1976 is a very comprehensive one and it not only means any building or hut or part of a building or hut and a seat in a room, let separately but also includes godowns, gardens and out-houses appurtenant thereto and also any furniture supplied or any fittings or fixtures affixed for the use of the tenant in such building, hut or seat in a room, as the case may be. *Associated Indem Mechanical (P.) Ltd.* v. *West Bengal S.S.I.D.C. Ltd.*, AIR 2007 SC 788 : 2007 AIR SCW 489.

Premises including precincts. The expression 'premises including precincts' merely shows that there may be some premises with precincts and some premises without precincts, where premises are buildings, they would include precincts. Where premises are lands they would have no precincts and there would be nothing to be included. The expression 'premises including precincts' would not exclude lands. *State* v. *Ardeshir Hormusji Bhiwandilala,* AIR 1956 Bom 219, 222. [Factories Act (63 of 1948), S. 2(m)]

Premium. "The price paid or promised in consideration of a lease of immoveable property is called the PREMIUM". [Transfer of Property Act (4 of 1882), S. 105]

A reward; the periodical payment for the insurance of life or property; a lump-sum or fine paid for the granting of a house; a sum paid in excess of the nominal value of shares of stock. [Deposit Insurance and Credit Guarantee Corporation Act (47 of 1961), S. 2(e)].

When shares are issued for consideration other than cash the value of the assets transferred in excess of the par value of shares issued would be regarded as premium. *I.T. Commissioner (Central) Calcutta* v. *Standard Vacuum Oil Co*., AIR 1966 SC 1393, 1397. [Business Profits Tax Act (21 of 1947), Sch. II, R.2(1)]

'Premium' means a sum of money paid as consideration for grant of lease. It represents capitalized rent which in fact is the difference between the actual rent and the rent which might otherwise be obtained by the lessor. *Govind Ram* v. *Rajphul Singh,* AIR 1973 P&H 94, 99. [Transfer of Property Act (4 of 1882), S. 60].

Premium term. Means the period during which premiums are payable. [Insurance Act (4 of 1938), Fourth Sch. Pt. 1(5) and Insurance Regulatory and Development Authority (Actuarial Report and Abstract) Regulations, 2000, Regn. 2(n)]

Prepaid expenses. Expenditure that results in a prepayment or deferred charge. For example, insurance premiums or rents already paid continue to provide benefit in the future (and as such are assets).

Prenuptial. Made or occurring before marriage.

Prenuptial gift. A gift from one spouse to another before marriage.

Prenuptial will. A will executed before marriage.

Preparation. "PREPARATION", in relation to a narcotic drug or psychotropic substance means any one or more such drugs or substances in dosage form or any solution or mixture, in whatever physical state, containing one or more such drugs or substances. [Narcotic Drugs and Psychotropic Substances Act (61 of 1985), S. 2(xx)]

The action of preparing or getting ready [Indian Evidence Act (1 of 1872), S. 8]; something that is prepared; something made for a specific purpose [IPC (45 of 1860), S. 276]; to make ready beforehand [Salt Cess Act (49 of 1953), S. 2(a)].

The word 'preparation' denotes not only the action or process of preparing the components to produce the compound but also that which is prepared. *Union of India* v. *Pesticides Mfg. & Fromulators Assn. of India*, (2002) 8 SCC 410, para 15.

Preponderance. The term "PREPONDERANCE OF EVIDENCE" generally signifies that which satisfies the conscience and carries conviction to an intelligent mind.

Superiority in importance, weight or influence.

PREPONDERANCE of evidence means to outweigh; to weigh more. A clear preponderance may mean that which may be seen, is discernible, and may be appreciated and understood; but it may also convey the idea of certainty beyond doubt.

By preponderance of evidence is not meant a preponderance in point of numbers of witnesses, but a preponderance of facts and circumstances that are convincing to the jury.

Preponderance of probability. Means an outweighing in the process of balancing however slight may be the tilt of the balance or the preponderance. *Rishi Kesh Singh* v. *State,* AIR 1970 All 51 at 90 (FB). [Indian Evidence Act (1 of 1872), S. 105]

Prerogative. The word "prerogative" properly implies sovereign right.

Prescribe. "To prescribe is to lay down authoritatively for direction; to give as a guide, direction, or rule of action; to impose as peremptory order; to direct."

'PRESCRIBE' means "to state authoritatively that something should be done in a particular way". [Oxford Dictionary as cited in *Accountant General, State of M.P.* v. *S.K. Dubey*, (2012) 4 SCC 578, para 67].

To appoint, ordain, direct, enjoin; to lay down by rules [Chartered Accountants Act (34 of 1949), S. 2(1)(f); CrPC 1973 (2 of 1974), S. 285(3) and Constitution of India, Art. 16(3)].

Prescribe to. To assert or claim anything by title or prescription.

Prescribed. Means prescribed by rules. [CPC (5 of 1908), S. 2(16)]

In this article, "PRESCRIBED" means,—

(i) until a Finance Commission has been constituted, prescribed by the President by order, and

(ii) after a Finance Commission has been constituted, prescribed by the President by order after considering the recommendation of the Finance Commission. [Constitution of India, Art. 270(3)]

"PRESCRIBED" means, in relation to proceedings before High Court, prescribed by rules made by the High Court, and in other cases, prescribed by the rules made under this Act. [Trade and Merchandise Marks Act (43 of 1958), S. 2(1)(n)]

"PRESCRIBED" means,—

(a) in relation to proceedings before a High Court, prescribed by rules made by the High Court;

(b) in relation to proceedings before the Appellate Board, prescribed by rules made by the Appellate Board; and

(c) in other cases, prescribed by rules made under this Act. [Patents Act (39 of 1970), S. 2(u)]

"PRESCRIBED", except in Chapter III, means prescribed by rules made by the State Government. [Wakf Act (43 of 1995), S. 3(l)]

"PRESCRIBED" means prescribed by rules made under this Act by the appropriate Government or the competent authority, as the case may be. [Freedom of Information Act (50 of 2003), S. 2(e)]

"PRESCRIBED" means prescribed from time to time by the Local Government by notification in the official Gazette. [Ben Act VIII of 1885 (Tenancy), S. 3(15)].

Prescribed authority. "Prescribed authority" means such authority or officer as the Administrator may, from time to time, by order to be published in the Official Gazette, prescribe:

Provided that the Administrator may prescribe different authorities or officers for different provisions of this Act. [Punjab Municipal Corporation Law (Extension to Chandigarh) Act (45 of 1994), S. 2(37A), Schedule-Part II]

The term 'prescribed authority' means the authority under S. 9(2) empowered to assess the tax. *K.M. Chopra & Co.* v. *Addl. Commissioner Sales Tax,* AIR 1967 MP 124, 125. [Central Sales Tax Act (74 of 1956), SS. 8 (1), (4) and 9 (2)]

Prescribed equipment. Means any property which the Central Government may, by notification, prescribe, being a property which in its opinion is specially designed or adapted or which is used or intended to be used for the production or utilisation of any prescribed substances, or for the production or utilisation of atomic energy, radioactive substance, or radiation, but does not include mining, milling, laboratory and other equipment not so specially designed or adapted and not incorporated in equipment used or intended to be used for any of the purposes aforesaid. [Atomic Energy Act (33 of 1962), S. 2(f)]

Prescribed manner. Includes the payment of the prescribed fee. [Patents Act (39 of 1970), S. 2(v)]

Prescribed period. "PRESCRIBED PERIOD" means the period of limitation computed in accordance with the provisions of this Act. [Limitation Act (36 of 1963), S. 2(j)].

Prescribed substance. Means any substance including any mineral which the Central Government may, by notification, prescribe, being a substance which in its opinion is or may be used for the production or use of atomic energy or research into matters connected therewith and includes uranium, plutonium, thorium, beryllium, deuterium or any of their respective derivatives or compounds or any other materials containing any of the aforesaid substances. [Atomic Energy Act (33 of 1962), S. 2(g)]

Prescribed therefor. The words 'prescribed therefor' mean prescribed for that particular suit, appeal or application. *Sehat Ali Khan* v. *Abdul Ravi Khan,* AIR 1956 273, 275 (FB).

Prescription. Rules established by long usage; extinction of a title or right by failure to claim or exercise it for a long (prescribed) period; so also acquisition by adverse possession.

A title acquired by use and time, and allowed by law; as when a man claims anything, because he, his ancestors, or they whose estate he hath, have had possession for the period prescribed by law. [Indian Easements Act (5 of 1882), S. 15; Limitation Act (36 of 1963), S. 25].

Prescription is a manner of acquiring the ownership of property, or discharging debts by the effect of time, and under the conditions regulated by law.

The definition of "prescription" is "a title acquired by use and time and allowed by law." Three things are necessary to establish a right by prescription: (1) use and occupation or enjoyment; (2) the identity of the thing enjoyed; and (3) that it should be adverse to the rights of some other person.

Acquisition of title by use and time as allowed by law. [Indian Easements Act (5 of 1882), S. 15 and CPC (5 of 1908), Sch., 1, App. A, form No. 49(10)].

Prescriptive right. A right acquired by prescription, *i.e.* uninterrupted use or possession from time immemorial, or for a period fixed by law. [CPC (5 of 1908), Sch. 1, App. A, form No. 49(10)].

Presence. The phrase "in his *presence*" in the statute providing that a police officer may make an arrest without a warrant when a public offence is committed in his presence, means in the sight of, or that the act is done in such a manner that the officer can detect it by sight or hearing, as the act of the accused. It does not apply to a case when he cannot detect the act, but has merely a suspicion.

The fact or condition of being present. [CrPC 1973 (2 of 1974), S. 109].

A statute requiring wills to be signed in the presence of the witnesses is satisfied if the subscribing witnesses were so situated that they could and would naturally see the signing.

One may be present in the eye of the law, though not actually present, as if several confederate to do a deed of death and one keeps guard at the door while the other inflicts the wound, the one on guard is present, in legal contemplation, participating in the act done, and is equally responsible with those actually present, doing the act. [IPC (45 of 1860), S. 114].

The term 'presence', as used in Section 273, does not mean actual physical presence but contemplates constructive presence. *State of Maharashtra* v. *Praful B. Desai (Dr.)*, AIR 2003 SC 2053. [CrPC, 1973 (2 of 1974), S. 273]

Present. Now existing; being at this time [Specific Relief Act (47 of 1963), S. 7, *Expln.* 2]; now in progress [Sale of Goods Act (3 of 1930), S. 6(3)]; in view; to appear; to bring one-self into the presence of; to deliver formally for acceptance [CrPC 1973 (2 of 1974), S. 378(1)]; the action of presenting [CPC (5 of 1908), O. XXXIII, R. 3]; to bring or place (a person *etc.*) before, into the presence of or under the notice of another [CPC (5 of 1908), O. VIII, R. 10]; to furnish or provide with something by way of present or gift; to make a present or donation [Indian Museum Act (10 of 1910), S. 7(c)]; to introduce formally in a Court [Income-tax Act (43 of 1961), S. 249(2)]; a gift [Constitution of India, Art. 18(4)].

The dictionary meaning of the word 'present' is to bring formally under notice, or submit or give thing to person as present *etc. Gopalkrishnan Iyer* v. *Padmanabhan,* AIR 1972 Ker 96, 97. [Provincial Insolvency Act (5 of 1920), S. 10(2)].

Present and Voting. "Present and voting" means persons who were physically present and voted and not those who withdrew from the House at the time of voting. *D. Jayaraman* v. *Govt. of Tamil Nadu,* AIR 1987 Mad 215, 220. [Constitution of India, Art. 169 (1)]

Present notice. A notice to take effect at once and not at a future time. [CPC (5 of 1908), Sch. 1, App. E, form No. 22].

Present value. A term used in discounting, and referring to a simple deduction of interest from the face value of a bill.

Presentation. The action of presenting [CPC (5 of 1908), S. 26]; being presented; the act of presenting usually in a formal manner for acceptance [Presidential and Vice-Presidential Elections Act (31 of 1952), S. 21(2)(d)]; the act of presenting to a sight or view [Copyright Act (14 of 1957), S. 2(q)].

"PRESENTATION" as used in a delivery order stating that certain goods were held, which would be delivered on the presentation of the order duly endorsed, meant delivering up the order, and not merely showing the same.

Presentence hearing. A proceeding at which a Judge receives and examines all relevant information regarding a convicted criminal and the offence related to him before passing the sentence.

Presentment. After sight; at sight; on presentment.

The act of presenting to an authority a formal statement of a matter to be dealt with [Negotiable Instruments Act (26 of 1881), S. 21]; [Provincial Insolvency Act (5 of 1920), S. 11, *Prov.*].

Presentment for payment. (*of bill of exchange*) to be sufficient, must be made (1) by the holder, or by some person authorised to receive payment on his behalf; (2) at a reasonable hour on a business day; (3) at a proper place; (4) to the person primarily liable on the instrument, or, if he is absent or inaccessible, to any person found at the place where the presentment is made.

Preservation. The act of keeping safe from injury, harm or destruction [Industrial Finance Corporation Act (15 of 1948) (*Repealed by Act 23 of 1993*), S. 2(c) and T.P. Act (4 of 1882), S. 17(2)(iii)]; [Salarjung Museum Act (26 of 1961), S. 16(2)(a)].

Preserve. The word "preserve" means to keep; to secure; to uphold; and when used in a statute intended to preserve the public peace it means to secure that quiet order and freedom from agitation or disturbance which is guaranteed by the laws.

To maintain (as state of things) [IPC (45 of 1860), S. 21, fourth]; to manage or retain for the rightful owner; to keep safe from harm or injury [Indian Contract Act (9 of 1872), S. 168; Companies Act (1 of 1956), S. 209(4A), Prov. and Constitution of India, Art. 60].

Preside. (*In Court*) When a judge "holds" Court he directs, controls, and governs it as the chief officer, and this is the extent of the meaning of the word "preside."

Presidency-town. "PRESIDENCY-TOWN" shall mean the local limits for the time being of the ordinary original civil jurisdiction of the High Court of Judicature at Calcutta, Madras or Bombay, as the case may be. [General Clauses Act (10 of 1897), S. 3(44)].

President. The constitutional head in a republican government; the President of India. [CPC (5 of 1908), S. 133(1)(i)]; the person selected to preside over the meetings of a body; the head of a body or institution [Cantonments Act (2 of 1924), S. 17(1)] [Now repealed & replaced by Act 41 of 2006].

"PRESIDENT" in Chapter XXVII of Act 18 of 2013, unless the context otherwise requires, 'President' means the President of the Tribunal. [S. 407(*d*) of the Companies Act, 2013 (18 of 2013)]

Presidential election. Means the election to fill the office of the President of India. [Presidential and Vice-Presidential Elections Act (31 of 1952), S. 2(f)]

Presiding. One who presides. [Industrial Finance Corporation Act (15 of 1948) (*Repealed by Act 23 of 1993*), S. 17(3)].

Presiding Judge. The term "presiding judge" is equivalent to that of "presiding Magistrate" or "judge" conducting proceedings in Court.

Presiding officer. The judicial officer, who presides over the Court; the officer who presides over a deliberative assembly, an officer appointed to superintend the polling at an election. [Representation of the People Act (43 of 1951), S. 26(1), Prov.]; [Industrial Disputes Act (14 of 1947), S. 7(C)].

Press. 'PRESS' means a printing press, and includes all plant, machinery, duplicators, types, implements and other materials used for the purpose of or in connection with printing or multiplying; documents. [Prevention of Publication of Objectionable Matter Act (27 of 1976), S. 2(g)]

Printing press; newspapers; the power exerted by newspapers on the public mind.

The machine for printing; printing house; printing establishment [CrPC 1973 (2 of 1974), S. 95(2)(a)]; to bring pushing or thrusting force to bear on by means of something in direct contact [Central Sales Tax Act (74 of 1956), S. 14(ii)]; an instrument by which garments are properly smoothed and creased; news reporters, publishers and broadcasters as group.

Press Registrar. Means the Registrar of newspapers for India appointed by the Central Government under Section 19-A and includes any other person appointed by the Central Government to perform all or any of the functions of the Press Registrar. [Press and Registration of Books Act (25 of 1867), S. 1]

Pressing social need. A concept, used by the European Court of Human Rights as the basis for assessing whether or not an interference with a qualified right is necessary in a democratic society.

Prestigious unit. 'Means a 'new industrial unit' first established in any Panchayat Samiti of the State during the period of this scheme in which investment in fixed capital exceeds Rs. 10 crores with a minimum permanent employment of 250 persons or a 'new industrial unit' having a fixed capital investment exceeding Rs. 25 crores and with a minimum permanent employment of 250 persons or a new electronic industrial unit having fixed capital investment exceeding Rs. 25 crores. [Rajasthan Sales Tax New Incentive Scheme for Industries, 1989, Clause 2(i) as cited in *Commercial Tax Officer, Rajasthan* v. *Binani Cements Limited*, (2014) 8 SCC 319, para 12].

Presume. To hold as proved until evidence to the contrary is forthcoming. [Indian Evidence Act (1 of 1872), S. 4].

PRESUME. The dictionary defines the word "presume" as: supposed to be true, take for granted; whereas "deem" as: regard, consider; and whereas "show" as: point out and prove. [Oxford Dictionary as cited in *Akhtar Rehman* v. *State of U.P.* Criminal Apppeal No. 5414 of 2004, decided on 19-4-2017, para 17]

"To believe or accept upon probable evidence"; "to take as proved until evidence to the contrary is forthcoming". [Black's Law Dictionary as cited in *Amit Kapoor* v. *Ramesh Chander*, (2012) 9 SCC 460, para 30].

Presumption (*Presumptio*). A legal or factual assumption drawn from the existence of certain facts.

A presumption is a conclusion drawn from the proof of facts or circumstances and stands as establishing facts until overcome by contrary proof.

'A presumption is a rule of law, statutory or judicial, by which finding of a basic fact gives rise to existence of presumed fact, until presumption is rebutted'. [Black's Law Dictionary, 5th Edn., 1979, p. 1067 as cited in *Heinz India Private Limited* v. *State of U.P.*, (2012) 5 SCC 443, para 40].

In law of evidence, a presumption is a conclusion or inference as to the truth of some fact in question, drawn from some other fact judicially noticed or proved or admitted to be true. [Indian Evidence Act (1 of 1872), S. 79].

'Presumption' in law of evidence is a rule indicating the stage of shifting of the burden of proof. From a certain fact or facts the Court can draw an inference and that would remain until such inference is either disproved or dispelled. *M. Narsinga Rao* v. *State of A.P.*, AIR 2001 SC 318.

Presumption of Constitutionality. An assumption made failing proof to the contrary that an enactment is in accordance with the Constitution. The presumption is always in favour of the constitutionality of an enactment and the burden is upon him who attacks it to show that there has been a clear transgression of the Constitutional principles. (*Constitutional and Parliamentary Term*)

Presumption of continuance. Presumption of fact suggesting that any proved state of affairs can be presumed to have continued for sometime.

Presumption of death. If one of the spouses remains continually absent and is not heard of being alive for a period of seven years, he or she may be presumed to be dead and the subsequent marriage will not amount to bigamy.

Presumption of fact. A presumption of fact is an inference of the existence of a certain fact arising from its necessary and usual connection with other facts which are known.

A presumption of fact is an inference which a reasonable man would draw from certain facts which have been proved. Its basis is in logic, and its source is probability.

"Presumption of facts" and "presumption of law". While "presumptions of fact" merely affect the 'burden of going forward with the evidence', 'presumptions of law', however go so far as to shift the legal burden of proof so that, in the absence of evidence sufficient to rebut in on a balance of probability a verdict must be directed. *Syad Akbar* v. *State of Karnataka,* AIR 1979 SC 1848.

Presumption of innocence. Every accused is to be presumed innocent until proved to be guilty.

The legal presumption of innocence arises in favour of the accused on the trial of every criminal case as a matter of evidence introduced by the law in his behalf.

Presumption of law. A presumption of law "is a presumption artificially made by annexing a rule at law or legal incident to a particular fact proved."

Presumption of legal knowledge. It is often said that the "presumption of legal knowledge" or knowledge of the laws of the state in every citizen is a positive rule of law. and applies to all cases where acts are knowingly done which are expressly forbidden by law, and gives rise to a conclusive presumption of criminal intent. If the word "conclusive", in this connection, means "irrebuttable" then such presumption is very unreasonable when applied to all criminal charges, and is not justified to that extent. "No man knows all the law. Judges differ in their legal decisions, and lawyers are continually discussing in the Courts doubtful and controverted questions of law. The presumption of legal knowledge is a general rule, and not accurately defined as to the extent of its application. It should be a very strong presumption, subject to some reasonable qualifications, in criminal trials where the life and liberty of the citizen are involved. In such cases the law should be literally construed, so as to give effect to all of its beneficent provisions, to avoid conflict of rules of law and secure the citizen against anything that would be unjust or oppressive.

Presumption of legitimacy. A child born during lawful wedlock is presumed to be legitimate.

Presumption of paternity. The presumption that a child born in wedlock is the child of the husband, except as it be proved that the husband did not have access to the wife. (*Ballentine's Law Dictionary, 3rd Edn.*)

Presumptive evidence. The term "presumptive evidence" consists in the proof of minor or other facts incidental to or usually connected with the fact sought to be proved, which, when taken together, inferentially establish or prove the fact in question to a reasonable degree of certainty.

Pretence. Professed rather than real intention or purpose [IPC (45 of 1860), S. 215]; [Pharmacy Act (8 of 1948), S. 41(2)(a)].

Pretend. The common and generally accepted meaning of the verb "pretend" is to hold out as true that which is false; to feign; to simulate.

To hold out, represent or assert falsely. [IPC (45 of 1860), S. 170].

Pretext. "Pretext" as is an ostensible reason or motive assigned as a colour or cover for the real reason or motive; false appearance; pretence.

Prevail. To be effectual as against another rule, direction *etc.* [T.P. Act (4 of 1882), S. 60A(2)].

Prevarication. The word originally signified the conduct of an advocate who betrayed the cause of his client, and by collusion assisted his opponent.

Prevent. "PREVENT" means to intercept; to hinder; to frustrate; to stop; to thwart; to hinder from happening by means of previous measures; ward off; to stop in advance from some act or operation; intercept or bar; check; restrain.

To hinder from doing something, to preclude, stop [Indian Evidence Act (1 of 1872), S. 8, ill. (e) and Constitution of India, Art. 15(3)]; [CrPC 1973 (2 of 1974), S. 149].

Refusal to give a sample even on payment is not the same thing as prevention which need not have an element of physical obstruction but it does involve some act which hinders an Inspector from taking a sample. *Bishan Dass Telu Ram* v. *State,* AIR 1957 Punj 99, 100. [Prevention of Food Adulteration Act (37 of 1954), S. 16(b)]

The word 'prevent' means to act before, in anticipation of or in preparation for (a future event, a point in time). *State of Maharashtra* v. *Umraniswaminathan Laxaman*, (1997) 11 SCC 426, para 3.

Prevention and deterrance. The term 'prevention' and 'deterrance' are not synonymous. In the first place, prevention does not mean only deterrance by physical force but by other means as well. Secondly, the distinction seems to be with reference to the stage of interference by the accused. *In re Ganapathia,* AIR 1953 Mad 936, 938. [IPC (45 of 1860), S. 353]

"It has to be given wide meaning where a person with the intent to prevent the Food Inspector to obtain sample from him by disappearing had made it impossible for the Food Inspector to obtain sample from him he has "prevented." An overt act in the form of physical obstruction, threat or assault is not necessary to constitute an offence under the section. *Teja Mohan* v. *Mangubhai,* AIR 1970 Guj 209 at 216.

Preventive. Devoted to or concerned with prevention. [heading, CrPC 1973 (2 of 1974), Ch. XI].

Preventive detention. Confinement or detention in a prison under the preventive law. [Prisoners (Attendance in Court) Act (32 of 1955), S. 2(a) and Constitution of India, Art. 22(3)(b)].

"Preventive detention" and "punitive detention". In case of 'punitive detention', the person concerned is detained by way of punishment after he is found guilty of wrongdoing as a result of a trial where he has the fullest opportunity to defend himself, while 'preventive detention' is not by way of punishment at all, but it is intended to preempt a person from indulging in any conduct injurious to the society. In case of preventive detention, he is detained merely on suspicion with a view to preventing him from doing harm in future and the opportunity that he has for contesting the action of the executive is very limited. *Francis Coralie Mullin* v. *Administrator, Union Territory of Delhi,* AIR 1981 SC 746.

Preventive justice. The portion of law which has reference to the direct prevention of offences.

Preventive measures. "PREVENTIVE MEASURES" means any reasonable measures taken by any person after the incident to prevent or minimise pollution damage. [Merchant Shipping Act (44 of 1958), S. 352H(g)]

Preventive relief. A relief intended to prevent an injury. [Specific Relief Act (47 of 1963), S. 36].

Previous. Going before in time.

Prior, antecedent; earlier [CPC (5 of 1908), S. 93]; [Sale of Goods Act (3 of 1930), S. 30(1)].

PREVIOUS, PRELIMINARY, PREPARATORY, INTRODUCTORY. Prudent people are careful to make every *previous* inquiry before they seriously enter into engagements with strangers: it is impolitic to enter into details until all *preliminary* matters are fully adjusted; one ought never to undertake any important matter without first adopting every *preparatory* measure that can facilitate its prosecution; in complicated matters it is necessary to have something *introductory* by way of explanation.

Previous approval. States Reorganisation Act (37 of 1956); S. 115 (7). AIR 1956 SC 138. (*N. Raghavendra Rao* v. *D.C. South Kauara*) quoted. The expression 'previous approval' would include a general approval to the variations in the conditions of service indicated by the Union Government. *Mohammad Shujat Ali* v. *UOI*, AIR 1974 SC 1631. 1630.

Previous company law. Means any of the laws specified below:—

(*i*) Acts relating to companies in force before the Indian Companies Act, 1866 (10 of 1866);

(*ii*) the Indian Companies Act, 1866 (10 of 1866);

(*iii*) the Indian Companies Act, 1882 (6 of 1882);

(*iv*) the Indian Companies Act, 1913 (7 of 1913);

(*v*) the Registration of Transferred Companies Ordinance, 1942 (Ordinance No. 54 of 1942);

(*vi*) the Companies Act, 1956 (1 of 1956); and

(*vii*) any law corresponding to any of the aforesaid Acts or the Ordinances and in force—

(*A*) in the merged territories or in a Part B State (other than the State of Jammu and Kashmir), or any part thereof, before the extension thereto of the Indian Companies Act, 1913 (7 of 1913); or

(*B*) in the State of Jammu and Kashmir, or any part thereof, before the commencement of the Jammu and Kashmir (Extension of Laws) Act, 1956 (62 of 1956), in so far as banking, insurance and financial corporations are concerned, and before the commencement of the Central Laws (Extension to Jammu and Kashmir) Act, 1968 (25 of 1968), in so far as other corporations are concerned;

(*viii*) the Portuguese Commercial Code, in so far as it relates to *sociedades anonimas*; and

(*ix*) the Registration of Companies (Sikkim) Act, 1961. [S. 2(67) of the Companies Act, 2013 (18 of 2013)]

Previous conviction. It has been the policy of the legislature since the mitigation of the severe punishments at one time imposed on criminals to provide for a gradual increase of severity of punishment in the case of habitual offenders.

A conviction (for any offence) to which a person has been subjected previously to his trial for the offence under examination. [CrPC 1973 (2 of 1974), S. 211(7)].

"PREVIOUS CONVICTION" S. 75 applies in cases of convictions prior to the conviction of the offence for the enhanced punishment of which S. 75 is to be invoked. But it does not provide for enhanced punishment in the case of convictions subsequent to the offence. The theft for which the accused was committed to the Court of Session was committed on 28th October, 1938. The accused had convictions subsequent to the commission of this offence the dates of these convictions being 26th June. 1939 and 20th July 1939. *Held,* that the previous convictions being subsequent to the commission of the offence for which the accused was committed could not be deemed "previous convictions" within the meaning of S. 75. [IPC (45 of 1860), S. 75].

Previous occasion. Earlier occasion. [Indian Evidence Act (1 of 1872), S. 155, ill (a)].

Previous or subsequent conduct. A conduct which precedes or follows the occurrence in question. [Indian Evidence Act (1 of 1872), S. 8].

Previous statement. A statement made at some time antecedent to the one at which any matter to which statement is relevant has come under consideration. [Indian Evidence Act (1 of 1872), S. 145].

Previous year. For the purposes of this Act, "previous year" means the financial year immediately preceding the assessment year:

Provided that, in the case of a business or profession newly set up, or a source of income newly coming into existence, in the said financial year, the previous year shall be the period beginning with the date of setting up of the business or profession or, as the case may be, the date on which the source of income newly comes into existence and ending with the said financial year. [Income-tax Act (43 of 1961), section 3]

"PREVIOUS YEAR" means twelve months expiring on 21st March immediately preceding the year in respect of which assessment is to be made. [MP Vritti Kar Adhiniyam (16 of 1995), S. 2(g)]

According to the definition in S. 2(11) "previous year" is the year which is previous to the year of assessment, and that means that there can be only one previous year to a given year of assessment. *Dhandhania Kedia & co.* v. *Commissioner of Income Tax*, AIR 1959 SC 219. 221.

The expression 'end of previous year' means the end of the accounting year expiring immediately preceding the date of discontinuance or succession. *Commissioner of Income Tax* v. *V.K. Srinivasan*, AIR 1953 SC 113, 118.

Previously. Antecedently. [T.P. Act (4 of 1882), S. 48]; [CPC (5 of 1908), S. 10]; [CrPC 1973 (2 of 1974), S. 211(7)].

Previously created right. A right which is antecedent to the one under creation or contemplation; any right that was created at a time earlier than the time when any matter to which that right is relevant comes up for consideration. [T.P. Act (4 of 1882), S. 48].

Price. "PRICE" means the money consideration for a sale of goods. [Sale of Goods Act (3 of 1930), S. 2(10)].

"PRICE", in relation to the sale of any goods or to the performance of any services, includes every valuable consideration, whether direct or indirect, or deferred, and includes any consideration which in effect relates to the sale of any goods or to the performance of any services although ostensibly relating to any other matter or thing. [Competition Act 2002 (12 of 2003), S. 2(q); M.R.T.P. Act (54 of 1969), S. 2(l)]

The price is the value which a seller places upon his goods for sale. It is not a fixed and unchangeable thing. It may be one thing today and another tomorrow and one valuation to one customer and a different one to another on the same day or hour. The price asked is the existing fact until it is changed. When the price asked is changed to another price, the former price is no longer an existing fact.

The price of an article which has its value in the market rises or falls accordingly as the relation between supply and demand changes.

The money (or other equivalent) for which anything is or is proposed to be bought or sold. [Sale of Goods Act (3 of 1930), S. 2(10)].

Sale as defined in S. 54 of the T.P. Act (4 of 1882), is a "transfer of ownership in exchange for a price paid or promised or part paid and part promised." The word "price" is used in the section in the sense of money. It does not include services present or future.

The word "price" is comprehensive enough to include not only cash consideration but also satisfaction of the outstanding debts includeing dower debts. But a consideration as not to contest a suit cannot be taken to be a price as contemplated by S. 54, Transfer of Property Act (4 of 1882). *Mahima Byasadeba Gadi* v. *Dinabandhu Mohanty,* AIR 1960 Ori 16, 18.

Price : Damages. 'Price' is a sum of money at which an article is sold. It is something which one ordinarily accepts voluntarily in exchange for something else.

The 'damages' are pecuniary consequence which the law imposes for the breach of some duty or the violation of some right. *Verendra Kumar* v. *State of U.P.,* AIR 1980 All 100, 103. [Indian Forest Act (16 of 1927), S. 82]

Price discrimination. The practice of charging different customers different prices for the same goods in order to exploit their different degrees of enthusiasm for it.

Price-sensitive information. For the purposes of section 195 of Act 18 of 2013, 'price-sensitive information" means any information which relates, directly or indirectly, to a company and which if published is likely to materially affect the price of securities of the company. [*Explanation (b)* to section 195(1) of the Companies Act, 2013 (18 of 2013) Repealed by Act 1 of 2018 (w.e.f. 9-2-2018]

Price sensitive information. Means any information which relates directly or indirectly to a company and which if published is likely to materially affect the price of securities of company.

Explanation.—The following shall be deemed to be price sensitive information—

(i) periodical financial results of the company;

(ii) intruded declaration of dividends (both interim and final);

(iii) issue of securities or buy-back of securities;

(iv) any major expansion plans or execution of new projects;

(v) amalgamation, mergers or takeovers;

(vi) disposal of the whole or substantial part of the undertaking; and

(vii) significant changes in policies, plans or operations of the company. [SEBI (Prohibition of Insider Trading) Regulations, 1992, Regn. 2(i) **as cited in** *Chintalapati Srinivasa Raju* v. *Securities and Exchange Board of India,* (2018) 7 SCC 443, para 13.2].

Prima facie. On the face of it; at first sight; arising at first sight; based on the first impression. [CPC (5 of 1908), O. XX, R. 17].

Prima facie case. A *prima facie* case is a case made out by proper and sufficient testimony.

Prima facie case is a case made out by sufficient testimony; one which is established by sufficient evidence. and can be overthrown only by rebutting evidence adduced on the other side.

Prima facie evidence. *Prima facie* evidence is that which suffices for the proof of a particular fact until contradicted and overcome by other evidence.

The term "*prima facie* evidence of title" means "evidence sufficient to establish title, unless some person shows a perfect title".

Evidence sufficient in law to raise a presumption of fact or establish the fact in question unless rebutted. [CPC (5 of 1908), O. XX, R. 17].

PRIMA FACIE EVIDENCE is generally synonymous with sufficient evidence.

Prima pars aequitatis aequalitas. The first ingredient of equity is equality.

Primage. Cost of loading or unloading a vessel, normally part of freight charges.

Primary. That which is first in order, rank or importance; anything from which something else arises or is derived. [Indian Evidence Act (1 of 1872), S. 62].

Primary adjustment. For the purposes of this section, *"primary adjustment"* to a transfer price, means the determination of transfer price in accordance with the arm's length principle resulting in an increase in the total income or reduction in the loss, as the case may be, of the assesse. [Income-tax Act (43 of 1961), S. 92-CE, *Explanation (iv)*].

Primary and secondary evidence. The terms 'primary and secondary evidence' apply to the kinds of proof that may be given to the contents of a document, irrespective of the purpose for which such contents, when proved, may be received. Primary evidence is an evidence which the law requires to be given first; secondary evidence is evidence which may be given in the absence of that better evidence subject to exceptions when a proper explanation of its absence has been given. *Cement Corpn. of India Ltd.* v. *Purya,* (2004) 8 SCC 270, 280, para 24. [Land Acquisition Act (1 of 1894), S. 51-A]

Primary conveyance. A conveyance which creates an estate, *e.g.,* feoffment, gift, grant, lease, exchange, and partition.

Primary education. "PRIMARY EDUCATION" means education up to such class or standard not beyond the eighth class or standard as may be prescribed. [Delhi Primary Education Act (30 of 1960), S. 2(i)]

'PRIMARY EDUCATION' means education imparted in such subjects and up to such standards as may be determined by the State Government, from time to time, located either in a primary or a secondary school. [Maharashtra Employees of Private School (Condition of Service) Regulation Act (3 of 1978), S. 2(18)]

Primary evidence. "PRIMARY EVIDENCE means the document itself produced for the inspection of the Court.

Explanation (1).—Where a document is executed in several parts each part is primary evidence of the document.

Where a document is executed in counterpart, each counterpart being executed by one or some of the parties only, each counterpart is primary evidence as against the parties executing it.

Explanation (2)—Where a number of documents are all made by one uniform process, as in the case of printing, lithography, or photography, each is primary evidence of the contents of the rest; but where they are all copies of a common original they are not primary evidence of the contents of the original." [Indian Evidence Act (1 of 1872), S. 62)

"Primary evidence" means the document itself produced for the inspection of the Court.

Explanation 1.—Where a document is executed in several parts, each part is primary evidence of the document.

Explanation 2.—Where a document is executed in counterpart, each counterpart being executed by one or some of the parties only, each counterpart is primary evidence as against the parties executing it.

Explanation 3.—Where a number of documents are all made by one uniform process, as in the case of printing, lithography or photography, each is primary evidence of the contents of the rest; but, where they are all copies of a common original, they are not primary evidence of the contents of the original.

Explanation 4.—Where an electronic or digital record is created or stored, and such storage occurs simultaneously or sequentially in multiple files, each such file is primary evidence.

Explanation 5.—Where an electronic or digital record is produced from proper custody, such electronic and digital record is primary evidence unless it is disputed.

Explanation 6.—Where a video recording is simultaneously stored in electronic form and transmitted or broadcast or transferred to another, each of the stored recordings is primary evidence.

Explanation 7.—Where an electronic or digital record is stored in multiple storage spaces in a computer resource, each such automated storage, including temporary files, is primary evidence. [(w. e. f. 1-7-2024) Bharatiya Sakshya Adhiniyam, 2023 (47 of 2023), section 57

Primary evidence is that kind of evidence which under every possible circumstance affords the greatest certainty of the fact in question. Thus a written instrument is itself the best possible evidence of its existence and contents.

Primary evidence is such as in itself does not indicate the existence of other and better proof.

Primary food. "PRIMARY FOOD" means any article of food, being a produce of agriculture or horticulture in its natural form. [Prevention of Food Adulteration (Amendment) Act (41 of 1971), S. 2(xii-a)]

"PRIMARY FOOD" means an article of food, being a produce of agriculture or horticulture or animal husbandry and dairying or aquaculture in its natural form, resulting from the growing, raising, cultivation, picking, harvesting, collection or catching in the hands of a person other than a farmer or fisherman. [S. 3(1)(zk) of the Food Safety & Standards Act, 2006 (34 of 2006)]

Primary gold. 'Primary gold' means gold in any unfinished or semi-finished form and includes ingots, bars, blocks, slabs, billets, shorts, pellets, rods, sheets, foils and wires. [Gold (Control) Act (45 of 1968) (*repealed*), S. 8(1)]

Primary produce. Means—

(i) produce of farmers, arising from agriculture (including animal husbandry, horticulture, floriculture, pisciculture, viticulture, forestry, forest products, re-vegetation, bee raising and farming plantation products), or from any other primary activity or service which promotes the interest of the farmers or consumers; or

(ii) produce of persons engaged in handloom, handicraft and other cottage industries;

(iii) any product resulting from any of the above activities, including by-products of such products;

(iv) any product resulting from an ancillary activity that would assist or promote any of the aforesaid activities or anything ancillary thereto;

(v) any activity which is intended to increase the production of anything referred to in sub-clauses (i) to (iv) or improve the quality thereof. [Companies Act (1 of 1956), S. 581A(j); Companies Act (18 of 2013), section 378A(j)]

Primary rural credit society. Means a cooperative society, by whatever name called,—

(i) which has as its object or business the provision of financial accommodation to its member for agriculture or agricultural operations or for the marketing of crops, or for rural development; and

(ii) the bye-laws of which do not permit admission of any other co-operative society as member;

Provided that this sub-clause shall not apply to the admission, as a member, of a co-operative society, which is a state co-operative bank or Central co-operative bank by reason of such bank subscribing to the share capital of the co-operative society out of funds provided by the State Government for the purpose. [National Bank for Agricultural and Rural Development Act (61 of 1981), S. 2(n)]

Primary stage. "PRIMARY STAGE" means a stage of education from classes I to V (both inclusive). [Delhi School Education Rules, 1973, R. 2(i)]

Prime mover. "PRIME-MOVER" includes any engine which derives its power from steam, a fly-wheel, first driving shaft or pulley attached to such engine, and every appurtenance necessary for the safe and efficient working thereof. [Bur. Act II of 1910 (Steam-boilers and Prime movers.), S. 3].

PRIME MOVER means any engine, motor or other appliance which generates or otherwise provides power. [Factories Act (63 of 1948), S. 2(h)]

"PRIME MOVER" means an engine, motor or other appliance which generates or otherwise provides power to a dangerous machine. [Dangerous Machine (Regulation) Act (35 of 1983), S. 3(o)]

Principal. An 'agent' is a person employed to do any act for another, or to represent another in dealing with third person. The person for whom such an act is done, or who is so represented, is called the 'PRINCIPAL'. [Indian Contract Act (9 of 1872), S. 182].

"Principal" means a person on whose behalf an agent carries on the business of supply or receipt of goods or services or both [The Central Goods and Services Tax Act, 2017 (12 of 2017), S. 2(88)]

One who employs another to act for him subject to his general control and instruction; the person from whom an agent's responsibility is derived [T.P. Act (4 of 1882), S. 3, *Expln.* 3, Prov.]; the original sum or capital sum invested or lent [Indian Contract Act (9 of 1872), S. 145, ill. (a)]; [Industrial Finance Corporation Act (15 of 1948), S. 5]; (*Repealed by Act 23 of 1993*) the first in rank or importance [CPC (5 of 1908), S. 92(1)]; the actual perpetrator (of a crime) [CrPC 1973 (2 of 1974), S. 306(1)]; the matter or thing of primary importance [Indian Partnership Act (9 of 1932), S. 58(1)(b)]; head of a college [Aligarh Muslim University Act (40 of 1920), S. 7(1)]; [University of Hyderabad Act (39 of 1974), S. 2(1)].

"Principal" means highest in rank, authority, character, importance, or degree; most considerable or important; chief; main (as) the principal officers of a government, the principal men of a state, the principal productions of a country; the principal arguments in a case.

(*In criminal law*) Those persons only are deemed principals who commit the overt act, while those who are present, aiding and abetting, are deemed accessories after the fact; and those who not being present had advised the felony are deemed accessories before the fact.

"PRINCIPAL" means the head of a college or an institution. [S. 2(s) of the Rajiv Gandhi National Aviation University Act, 2013 (26 of 2013)]

Principal agent. Means a person who, not being a salaried employee of an insurer, in consideration of any commission,—

(i) performs any administrative and organising functions for the insurer, and

(ii) procures general insurance business whether wholly or in part by employing or causing to be employed insurance agents on behalf of the insurer. [Insurance Act (4 of 1938), S. 2(15) now omitted by Act 5 of 2015 (w.r.e.f. 26-12-2014).]

Principal amount. The word 'principal sum' in S. 34 means the amount initially advanced including the interest added from the date of advance, on the date of the suit. *Indrajit Roy* v. *Bank of Baroda,* AIR 1991 Ori 44, 45. [CPC (5 of 1908), S. 34]

Principal debtor. In a 'contract of guarantee', the person in respect of whose default the guarantee is given is called the 'PRINCIPAL DEBTOR'. [Indian Contract Act (9 of 1872), S. 126].

The person who borrowed the original sum or money. [Indian Contract Act (9 of 1872), S. 145].

The principal debtor in respect of a guaranteed debt, is the person for whom a guarantee is given.

Principal employer. 'PRINCIPAL EMPLOYER' means a person for whom or on whose behalf any contract labour is engaged or employed in an establishment. [Beedi and Cigar Workers (Conditions of Employment) Act (32 of 1966), S. 2(m)]

"PRINCIPAL EMPLOYER" means—

(i) in relation to any office or department of the Government or a local authority, the head of that office or department or such other officer as the Government or the local authority, as the case may be, may specify in this behalf,

(ii) in a factory, the owner or occupier of factory and where a person has been named as the manager of the factory under the Factories Act, 1948, the person so named;

(iii) in a mine, the owner or agent of the mine and where a person has been named as the manager of the mine, the person so named;

(iv) in any other establishment, any person responsible for the supervision and control of the establishment.

Expln.—For the purpose of sub-clause (iii) of this clause the expressions "mine", "owner" and "agent" shall have the meanings respectively assigned to them in clause (j), clause (1) and clause (c) of sub-section (1) of Section 2 of Mines Act, 1952. [Contract Labour (Regulation and Abolition) Act (37 of 1970), S. 2(1)(g)]

"PRINCIPAL EMPLOYER", in relation to a dock worker employed or to be employed by or through any agency (including a contractor), means the person in connection with whose work he is employed or is to be employed by such agency. [Dock Workers (Safety Health and Welfare) Act (54 of 1986), S. 2(g)]

"PRINCIPAL EMPLOYER" means an employer who engages unprotected workers by or through a contractor in any scheduled employment. [Gujarat Unprotected Manual Workers (Regulation of Employment and Welfare) Act (25 of 1979), S. 2(8)]

'PRINCIPAL EMPLOYER ' means an employer who engages unprotected workers by or through a contractor in any scheduled employment. [Maharashtra Mathadi, Hamal and other Manual Workers (Regulation of Employment and Welfare) Act (30 of 1969), S. 2(7) as cited in *Pepsico India Holding Private Limited* v. *Grocery Market and Shops Board*, (2016) 4 SCC 493, para 8].

The definition of 'principal employer' in S. 2(17) includes an owner. *Inayat Husain* v. *Employees State Insurance Corporation,* AIR 1963 MP 130, 131. [Employees' State Insurance Act (34 of 1948), S. 2(17)]

Principal in first degree. (*In criminal law*) Whoever actually commits, or takes part in the actual commission of, a crime, is a principal in the first degree, whether he is on the spot when the crime is committed or not; and if a crime is committed partly in one place and partly in another, everyone who commits any part of it at any place is a principal in the first degree.

The general definition of a *Principal in the first degree* is, one who is the actor or actual perpetrator of the fact.

Principal in second degree. Whoever aids or abets the actual commission of a crime, either, at the place where it is committed or elsewhere, is a principal in the second degree in that crime.

Principal market yard. "PRINCIPAL MARKET YARD" means an enclosure, building or locality declared or deemed to be declared to be a principal market yard under this Act. [Gujarat Agricultural Produce Markets Act, 1963 (20 of 1964), S. 2(xvii)]

Principal money. "PRINCIPAL MONEY", in relation to a mortgage deed executed by an evacuee, means—

(i) in the case of a mortgage deed which has not been executed by way of renewal of a prior mortgage deed, the sum of money advanced by way of loan at the time of the execution of the mortgage deed;

(ii) in the case of a mortgage deed which has been executed at any time before the 1st day of January, 1940, by way of renewal of a prior mortgage deed, the consideration for which the renewed mortgage deed was executed;

(iii) in the case of a mortgage deed which has been executed at any time after 1st day of January, 1940, by way of renewal of a prior mortgage deed executed before that date, the sum of money which became due on the 1st day of January, 1940, on account of the money advanced on the prior mortgage deed and interest there-upon upto the said date;

(iv) in the case of a mortgage deed which was executed at any time after the Ist day of January, 1940, by way of renewal of a prior mortgage deed which was also executed after that date, the sum of money advanced by way of loan at the time of the execution of the prior mortgage deed;

Expln.—For the purpose of calculating the principal money in relation to any mortgage deed which has been executed by way of renewal of a prior mortgage deed, any sum of money advanced at the time of such renewal in addition to the sum of money which was due on the prior mortgage deed shall also be taken into account. [Evacuee Interest (Separation) Act (64 of 1951), S. 2(h)]

The original amount lent on interest [CPC (5 of 1908), S. 73(1), Prov. (c), (thirdly)].

Principal money expressed to be secured. The expression "principal money expressed to be secured" with reference to a suit for a partial redemption for the purposes of cl. ix of S. 7 of the Court Fees Act (7 of 1870), must be taken to be the proportionate amount of the debt for which portion of the property is liable.

Principal of original loan. "Means only the actual cash originally advanced as principal". *K. Manick Chand* v. *Elias Saleh Mohamed Sait*, AIR 1969 SC 671 at 673.

Principal of the loan. Principal of the loan means the money which the money-lender actually advanced to the borrower and not the amount for which the bond is executed.

Principal office. The "Principal Office" of a Co.—is the place at which the business of the Co. is managed and controlled as a whole.

Principal officer. "PRINCIPAL OFFICER", used with reference to a company, means the secretary, manager, managing agent or managing director of the company, and includes any person connected with the management of the affairs of the company upon whom the Assessing Officer has served a notice of his intention of treating him as the principal officer thereof. [Wealth Tax Act (27 of 1957), S. 2(o)]

"PRINCIPAL OFFICER", used with reference to a company or any association of persons means—

(a) the secretary and treasurer, manager, managing agent, managing director or agent of the company or association; or

(b) any person connected with the management of the affairs of the company or association upon whom the Assesssing Officer has served a notice of his intention of treating him as the principal officer thereof. [Gift-tax Act (18 of 1958), S. 2(xxi)]

"PRINCIPAL OFFICER", used with reference to a local authority or a company or any other public body or any association of persons or any body of individuals, means—

(a) the secretary, treasurer, manager or agent of the authority, company, association or body, or

(b) any person connected with the management or administration of the local authority, company, association or body upon whom the Assessing Officer has served a notice of his intention of treating him as the principal officer thereof. [Income-tax Act (43 of 1961), S. 2(35)]

"PRINCIPAL OFFICER" means—

(i) a secretary, manager or director of the body corporate, or

(ii) any person connected with the management or administration of the body corporate upon whom the Board has served notice of its intention of treating him as the principal officer thereof. [SEBI (Debenture Trustees) Regulations 1993, Reg. 2(f)]

"PRINCIPAL OFFICER" means any person connected with the management of the applicant or any other person upon whom the Authority has served notice of its intention of treating him as the principal officer thereof. [Insurance Regulatory and Development Authority (Registration of Insurance Companies) Regulations, 2000, Reg. 2(l)]

The chief officer. [Wealth-tax Act (27 of 1957), S. 2(o)].

A 'principal officer' of a corporation is one whose oversight or agency exists either over the whole or some particular department of the general business of the corporation; as a president, who has ordinarily a general oversight over its entire business, a secretary over its records or a treasurer over its moneys.

The agent of the local branch of a foreign company, is a "principal officer" of the Company, within the meaning of Order XXIX, R. 1 of the CPC (5 of 1908), and competent, as such to sign and verify the plaint.

Principal officer of the corporation. The words "principal officer of the corporation" in Order XXIX, Rule 1, CPC (5 of 1908) include an acting manager.

Principal place. Office at which the business of the company is managed [CPC (5 of 1908), O. XXX, R. 3(b)]; [Indian Partnership Act (9 of 1932), S. 58(1)(b)].

Principal place of business. Is where the governing power of the corporation is exercised, where those meet in council who have a right to control its affairs and prescribe what policy of the corporation shall be pursued, and not where the labour is performed in executing the requirements of the corporation in transacting its business.

"PRINCIPAL PLACE OF BUSINESS means the place of business specified as the principal place of business in the certificate of registration [The Central Goods and Services Tax Act, 2017 (12 of 2017), S. 2(89)]

"PRINCIPAL PLACE OF BUSINESS", means the place designated as the principal place of business of the corporation in its certificate of incorporation.

Principal successor State. Means—

(i) in relation to the existing State of Bombay, Madhya Pradesh, Madras or Rajasthan, the State with the same name; and

(ii) in relation to the existing states of Hyderabad, Madhya Pradesh, and Travancore-Cochin, the State of Andhra Pradesh, Madhya Pradesh and Kerala, respectively. [States Reorganisation Act (37 of 1956), S. 2(m)]

Principal sum. The sum that was originally lent or invested. [CPC (5 of 1908), S. 34(2)].

Principal sum adjudged. The expression "principal sum adjudged" would mean only the "principal sum". It will never include the interest whatever be the agreement between the parties. *Union Bank of India* v. *Dalpat Gaurishankar Upadhyay,* AIR 1992 Bom 482, 491 (FB). [CPC (5 of 1908), O. XXXIV, Rr. 2 and 11]

Principal Supply. means the supply of goods or services which constitutes the predominant element of a composite supply and to which any other supply forming part of that composite supply is ancillary [The Central Goods and Services Tax Act, 2017 (12 of 2017), S. 2(90)]

Principiorum non est ratio. (*Lat.*) *(2 Buls. 239)* There is no reasoning (required to prove) fundamental principles.

Principle. A general law or rule as a guidance to action. [Specific Relief Act (47 of 1963), S. 20(1)].

As opposed to any specific direction governing any particular or specific instance, transaction or situation a principle would be a guiding rule applicable generally to cases or class of cases. *Consolidated Coffee Ltd.* v. *Coffee Board*, AIR 1980 SC 1468, 1479. [Central Sales Tax Act (74 of 1956), S. 5(3)]

Principle of comity of courts. Means that courts of one State or jurisdiction will give effect to the laws and judicial decisions of another ,not as a matter of obligation but out of deference and mutual respect. [Black's Law Dictionary, 5th Edn. 1979 cited in *World Sport Group (Mauritius) Limited* v. *MSM Satellite (Singapore) PTE Ltd.*, (2014) 11 SCC 639, para 22].

The principle of the comity of courts is essentially a principle of self-restraint, applicable when a foreign court is seized of the issue of the custody of a child prior to the domestic court. There may be a situation where the foreign court though seized of the issue does not pass any effective or substantial order or direction. In that event, if the domestic court were to pass an effective or substantial order or direction prior in point of time then the foreign court ought to exercise self-restraint and respect the direction or order of the domestic court (or vice versa), unless there are very good reasons not to do so. [*Surya Vadanan v. State of T.N.*, (2015) 5 SCC 450, para 46].

Principle of ejusdem generis. The expression '*ejusdem generis*' means 'of the same kind' and the doctrine of *ejusdem generis* is of ancient vintage. According to it when general words follow particular and specific words in an enumeration describing the legal subject, the general words are intended to embrace only objects of the same species as are enumerated by the preceding specific words : the enumeration by specific words of course must not be exhaustive. The principle underlying this doctrine is designed to reconcile an incompatibility between specific and general words in view of other rules of construction, *e.g.,* all words in a statute have, if possible, to be given due effect, the legislature does not use superfluous words and all part of a statute are to be construed together. It is thus really a question of assumed intention of statute. The rule of *ejusdem generis* is accordingly not a rule of law, but merely a rule of construction often useful and convenient. Its application is thus presumptive and not pre-emptory. In order to attract this doctrine it may safely be said to be necessary that–(i) the Statute contains an enumeration of specific words which constitute a class (ii) the said class is not exhausted by the enumeration; (iii) the general words follow the specific words and (iv) the legislative intention is not clearly manifest in favour of according broader meaning to the general words. Since the class of enumeration may often be an artificial creation, the rule of *ejusdem generis* is at times described to be a dangerous yard-stick to measure the legislative intent with. It is, therefore, to be supplied with caution lest it is pushed too far. *Gurbachan Singh* v. *Ichhar Singh,* MLJ : QD (1961-1965) Vol III C3067 : 1965 Cur LJ 32 : (1965) ILR 1 Punj 532. [Interpretation of statutes]

Principle of equal pay for equal work. In granting relief while applying the principle of 'equal pay for equal work', the Court or Tribunal should be, very circumspect and until and unless it is established that the two posts are almost similar in all aspects, the Court or Tribunal should not venture to grant the relief sought for. [*Secretary to Government* v. *C. Muthu*, (2001) 10 SC 545 : (2000) 8 Supreme 551]

Principle of equity. 'Principle of equity' that a person cannot approbate and reprobate finds legislative recognition in Section 116 of Evidence Act (1 of 1872) and Section 111(g) of the Transfer of Property Act (4 of 1882). Court should construe the Section 10(2)(vii) of the Act in the light of this principle. [*C. Chandramohan* v. *Sengottaiyan,* AIR 2000 SC 568 : (2000) 1 SCC 451, para 17] [T.N. Buildings (Lease and Rent Control) Act, 1960, S. 10(2)(vii)]

Principle of escheat. Where on a determination of rights of the claimants before the Consolidation Authorities it was found that none of the claimants could be held to be the tenure holder of the property in question which belonged to a third person who was not heard of for more than seven years and was therefore treated as having died a civil death or who, in fact was dead without leaving any heir, the property would vest in the Gaon Sabha. This is the principle of escheat. [*Sheo Nand* v. *Dy. Director of Consolidation,* (2000) 3 SCC 103, 109, para 6 : AIR 2000 SC 1141]

Principle of estoppel. The principle of estoppel cannot be pressed into service to defeat the provision of Section 125 of the Code. [*Savitaben Somabhai Bhatiya* v. *State of Gujarat,* (2005) 3 SCC 636, 642, para 17] [CrPC (2 of 1974), S. 125]

Principle of fair trial. The 'principle of fair trial' now informs and energises many areas of the law. It is reflected in numerous rules and practices. It is constant, ongoing development process continually adopted to new changing circumstances, and exigencies of the situation—peculiar at times and related to the nature of crime, persons involved—directly or operating behind, social impact and social needs and even so many powerful balancing factors which may come in the way of administration of criminal justice system. [*Zahira Habibullah Sheikh (5)* v. *State of Gujarat,* (2006) 3 SCC 374, 394, para 33]

Principle of Law : Question of law. A principle of law means a rule or axiom of law, while a question of law is one which arises when a conclusion is reached on the application of the rules and principles of law to certain proved facts and circumstances. *Gulab Chand* v. *Kudi Lal (FB),* AIR 1959 MP 151.

Principle of legitimate expectation. The legitimacy of an expectation can be inferred only if it is founded on the sanction of law or custom or an established procedure followed in regular and natural sequence...... Such expectation should be justifiably legitimate and protectable. [*Union of India* v. *Hindustan Development Corporation,* (1993) 3 SCC 499, 540, para 28. See also *Chanchal Goyal (Dr.)* v. *State of Rajashtan,* (2003) 3 SCC 485, 499, para 19]

Principle of proportion. 'Principle of proportion' between crime and punishment is a principle of just desert that serves as the foundation of every criminal sentence that is justifiable. As a principle of criminal justice it is hardly less familiar or less important than the principle that only the guilty ought to be punished. Indeed, the requirement that punishment not be disproportionately great, which is a corollary of first desert, is dictated by the same principle that does not allow punishment of the innocent, for any punishment in excess of what is deserved for the criminal conduct is punishment without guilt. [*Lehna* v . *State of Haryana,* (2002) 3 SCC 76, 87, para 26. See also *Ruli Ram* v. *State of Haryana,* (2002) 7 SCC 691, 704, para 24-25]

Principle of proportionality. Proportion between crime and punishment is a goal respected in the 'principle of proportionality' and in spite of errant notions it remains a strong influence in the determination of sentences. The practice of punishing all serious crimes with equal severity is now unknown in civilized societies, but such a radical departure from the principle of proportionality has disappeared from the law only in recent times. Anything less than a penalty of greatest severity for any serious crime is thought to be a measure of tolerance that is unwarranted and unwise. [*Ruli Ram* v. *State of Haryana,* (2002) 7 SCC 691, 704, para 25. See also *Lehna* v . *State of Haryana,* (2002) 3 SCC 76, 87, para 26.

Under the 'principle of proportionality' the Court requires to see that the legislature and the administrative authority maintain a proper balance between the adverse effects which the legislation or administrative order may have on the rights, liberties or interests of persons keeping in mind the purpose which they were intended to serve. [*Om Kumar* v. *Union of India,* AIR 2000 SC 3689 : JT (2000) 53 SC 92 : (2000) 8 SLT 463]

Principle of res ipsa loquitor. The 'principle of *res ipsa loquitor'* is only a rule of evidence to determine the onus of proof in actions relating to negligence. The said principle has application only when the nature of the accident and the attending circumstances would reasonably lead to the belief that in the absence of negligence the accident would have not occurred. [*Mohammed Aynuddin* v. *State of A.P.,* (2000) 7 SCC 72, para 8 : AIR 2000 SC 2511]

Principle of res judicata. Stated in simple form, 'principle of *res judicata*' is that where once there has been a decision in a suit between the parties, the rule of *res judicata* will prevent a fresh suit between them for the same relief as was negativated by the previous decision. [AIR 1925 PC 34] It will include constructive *res judicata.* [(1973) 1 Andh WR 322 (324)] [CPC (5 of 1908), S. 11]

Principle of separation of powers. If under the guise of elimination of creamy layer, the legislature makes a law which is not indeed a true elimination but is seen by the Court to be mere cloak, then the Court will necessarily strike down such a law as violative of 'principle of separation of powers.' [*Indra Sawhney II* v. *Union of India,* AIR 2000 SC 498 : (2000) 1 SCC 168, 190-91, para 29]

Principle of severability. The principle was held to be not applicable in *A. Sowkath Ali* v. *Union of India,* AIR 2000 SC 2662 : (2000) 7 SCC 148, para 27.

Principle of social justice. The principle of social justice cannot be invoked contrary to the statute as the legislature would already have taken care of the same while fixing the compensation payable to the workmen on closing down the establishment. The High Court has no authority to grant *ex gratia* payment in addition to what is provided under the statute *i.e.* Industrial Disputes Act (14 of 1947) by invoking the 'principle of social justice'. [*Gordon Woodroffe Agencies (P) Ltd.* v. *Presiding Officer, Principal Labour Court,* (2004) 8 SCC 90, 94, para 13]

Principle of stare decisis. 'Apart from any question as to the Courts being of co-ordinate jurisdiction, a decision which has been followed for a long period of time, and has been acted upon by persons in the formation of contracts or in the disposition of their property, or in the general conduct of affairs, or in legal procedure or in other ways, will generally be followed by Courts of higher authority than the Court establishing the rule, even though the Court before whom the matter arises afterwards might not have given the same decision had the question come before it originally. But the Supreme Appellate Court will not shrink from overruling a decision, or series of decisions, which establish a doctrine plainly outside the statute and outside the common law, when no title and no contract will be shaken, no persons can complain, and no general course of dealing be altered by the remedy of a mistake. [**As referred in** *Saurashtra Cement & Chemical Industries Ltd.* v. *Union of India,* (2001) 1 SCC 91, 115, para 32. See also *Maktul* v. *Manbhari,* AIR 1958 SC 918.

Principle of sustainable development. The concept of 'SUSTAINABLE DEVELOPMENT' is to be treated as an integral part of life under Article 21 of the constitution. To ensure sustainable development is one of goals of Environment (Protection) Act (29 of 1986).

Principle of unjust enrichment. Where Section 11-B(2) of the Act which incorporates the principle of 'unjust enrichment' had come into force after deposit of excess duty, the provisions were held to be inapplicable in such a case. [*Hindustan Metal Pressing Works* v. *CCE,* (2003) 3 SCC 559, 561, para 6] [Central Excise Act (1 of 1944), S. 11-B(2)]

Principle of waiver. The principle of waiver is akin to the principle of estoppel. The difference between the two, is that whereas estoppel is not a cause of action but it is rule of evidence, on the other hand the waiver is contractual and may constitute a cause of action and it is an agreement between the parties and a party fully knowing of its right has agreed not to assert a right for consideration. [*Krishna Bahadur* v. *Purna Theatre,* (2004) 8 SCC 229, 233, para 9]

Principles and rules. The expression 'principles and rules' in S. 7 does not mean the grounds on which a suit or proceeding may be instituted. *Reynold Rajamani* v. *Union of India*, AIR 1982 SC 1261, 1263. [Indian Divorce Act (4 of 1869), SS. 7, 10]

Something impressed with a print or formed in a mould. [Wealth-tax Act (27 of 1957), S. 5(1)(xiii)].

Principles of constructive res judicata. The 'principles of constructive *res judicata*' were held to include the elements of the rule of *res judicata* referred to in the section, namely :

(i) that the previous decision must have been between the same parties; [1968 Pat LJR 554]

(ii) that the matter was directly and substantially in issue in the former proceeding either expressly or impliedly; [*Ashsaq Husain* v. *Gauri Sahai,* (1911) 33 All 264 (274) (PC)]

(iii) that the parties litigated under the same title in the previous proceeding; [(1906) 28 All 644]

(iv) that the Court in the previous proceeding was competent to decide the point; [AIR 1952 All 206]

(v) that the matter raised in the subsequent proceeding was heard and decided in the former proceeding, expressly or constructively; [*Rocky Tyres* v. *Ajit Jain,* AIR 1960 Ori 197 (FB)] [CPC (5 of 1908), S. 11]

Principles of natural justice. "Principles of natural justice" have an important place in modern Administrative Law. They have been defined to mean "fair play in action". While applying the principles of natural justice, it must be borne in mind that "they are not immutable but flexible" and they are not cast in a rigid mould and they cannot be put in a legal straitjacket. [*Ravi S. Naik* v. *Union of India,* 1994 Supp (2) SCC 641]

The rules of natural justice are not embodied rules. The question whether in given case the principles have been violated or not has to be found out on consideration as to whether the procedure adopted by appropriate authority is in accordance with law or not and further whether the delinquent knew what charges he is going to meet and whether the Tribunal has acted in good faith. If these requirements are satisfied then it cannot be said that the principles of natural justice has been violated. [*U.P. State Road Transport Corporation* v. *Ram Chandra Yadav,* (2000) 9 SCC 327 : JT (2000) 9 SC 198]

It is a fundamental requirement of law that the doctrine of natural justice be complied with and the same has, as a matter of fact, turned out to be an integral part of administrative jurisprudence of this country. As a matter of fact the doctrine is termed as a synonym of fairness in the concept of justice and stands as the most accepted methodology of a Government action. The judicial process itself embraces a fair and reasonable opportunity to defend but the same is dependent upon the facts and circumstances of each case. [*Kumaon Mandal Vikas Nigam Ltd.* v. *Girja Shankar Pant,* AIR 2001 SC 24 : (2001) 1 SCC 182]

The principles of natural justice, it is trite, cannot be put in a straitjacket formula. In a gives case the party should not only be required to show that he did not have a proper notice resulting in violation of principles of natural justice but also to show that he was seriously prejudiced thereby. [*Sohan Lal Gupta* v. *Asha Devi Gupta,* (2003) 7 SCC 492, 506, para 29]

Print : printing. Prints are impressions on paper or some substance or engravings on copper, steel, wood, or stone, *etc.*, representing some particular subject or composition. Prints, like paintings, embrace every variety of subjects, but differ very widely in the manner in which they are engraved.

Typewriting is given the same legal force, meaning, or effect as writing.

For some purposes, type-writing may be regarded as printing; but it is not the same as writing by hand.

Printed. Produced (a book, picture, *etc.*) by applying to paper, vellum, *etc.* in a press or machine, inked types, blocks, or plates bearing characters or designs. [CrPC 1973 (2 of 1974), S. 108(2)].

Printer (*of a paper*)**.** The term 'printer' means not one who merely performs the mechanical process of printing, but one having an interest as owner of the paper.

The word "printer," as used in a statute requiring proof of a publication in a newspaper to be made by the affidavit of the printer, *etc.*, does not mean the person who sets up the type. It is rather used as synonymous with "publisher," and such provision is satisfied when the affidavit is made by the editor of the paper.

One who prints or is engaged in the art or business of printing [CrPC 1973 (2 of 1974), S. 108(2)].

Printing. "PRINTING" includes cyclostyling and printing by lithography. [Press and Registration of Books Act (25 of 1867), S. 1]

The action of printing. [Indian Evidence Act (1 of 1872), S. 62, *Expln.* 2].

Prior. Preceding in time or order. [T.P. Act (4 of 1882), S. 27].

Prior art. Evidence that part or all of the invention was already in public circulation or use prior to filing for a patent. It renders the invention unpatentable. (*Patents*)

All usage or public knowledge relevant for deciding the novelty and clarity of an invention before the prior date. (*Patents*)

Prior disposition. A disposition earlier in time or higher in order of preference. [T.P. Act (4 of 1882), S. 27].

Prior interest. Any interest which had come into existence earlier. [T.P. Act (4 of 1882), S. 16].

Prior mortgagee. A mortgagee the mortgage in whose favour stands earlier in time. [T.P. Act (4 of 1882), S. 78].

Prior possessio cum titulo posteriore melior est priore titulo sine possessione. (*Lat.*) Prior possession with a subsequent title is better than a prior title without possession.

Prior restraint. A governmental restriction on speech or publication before its actual expression.

Prior use. Prior use is the use of an invention before the priority date of an application claiming the invention. (*Patents*)

Priority. A legal preference or precedence (as) priority of claims.

A precedence in claims; a preference in order of payment; the requirement that earlier attention is to be given to; an earlier action taken on any matter as against all other matters under consideration or needing action. [T.P. Act (4 of 1882), S. 69A(8)(ii); Companies Act (1 of 1956), S. 121(2)].

Priority households. Means households identified as such under section 10 of Act 20 of 2013. [S. 2(14) of the National Food Security Act, 2013 (20 of 2013)]

Priority of mortgages. The order in which two or more mortgages of the same property take effect.

Prison. "PRISON", means any jail or place used permanently or temporarily under the general or special orders of a State Government for the detention of prisoners, and includes all lands and buildings appurtenant thereto, but does not include (*a*) any place for the confinement of prisoners who are exclusively in the custody of the Police; (*b*) any place specially appointed by the State Government under S. 541 of the Code of Criminal Procedure, 1882; or (*c*) any place which has been declared by the State Government, by general or special order, to be a subsidiary jail. [Prisons Act (9 of 1894), S. 3(1)].

In this Chapter, "prison" includes,—

(i) any place which has been declared by the State Government, by general or special order, to be a subsidiary jail;

(ii) any reformatory, Borstal institution or other institution of a like nature. [(w. e. f. 1-7-2024) Bharatiya Nagarik Suraksha Sanhita, 2023 (46 of 2023), section 301(b)]

"PRISON" includes any place which has been declared by the State Government by general or special order, to be a subsidiary jail. [Prisoners Act (3 of 1900), S. 2(b)]

"PRISON" includes any subsidiary jail, judicial lock-up or police lock-up and any place used for the custody of persons who are ordered to be detained under any law for the time being in force. [Exchange of Prisoners Act (58 of 1948), S. 2(a)]

"PRISON" includes,—

(i) any place which has been declared by the State Government, by general or special order, to be a subsidiary jail;

(ii) any reformatory, Borstal institution or other institution of a like nature. [CrPC 1973 (2 of 1974), S. 266(b) and Prisoners (Attendance in Courts) Act (32 of 1955), S. 2(b)]

A place in which a person is kept in captivity or confinement as a result of a legal process. [CPC (5 of 1908), S. 135A(1)(d)].

Prisoner. "PRISONER" means any person committed to custody in a prison on or before the Ist day of August, 1948 under the writ, warrant or order of any Court or authority other than a civil Court or Court Martial. [Exchange of Prisoners Act (58 of 1948), S. 2(b)]

"PRISONER" means a person undergoing a sentence of imprisonment under an order passed by a criminal Court including the Courts established under the law for the time being in force in contracting States. [Repatriation of Prisoners Act (49 of 2003), S. 2(c)]

One who is confined or detained within a prison; one who is in custody as the result of a legal process [IPC (45 of 1860), S. 130].

Person kept in prison. A prisoner is a person deprived of his liberty by virtue of a judicial or other lawful process; a person committed to prison; a captive detained in some place of confinement.

Prisoner with mental illness. Means a person with mental illness who is an under-trial or convicted of an offence and detained in a jail or prison [The Mental Healthcare Act, 2017 (10 of 2017), S. 2(1) (w)]

Prisoner with mental illness. Means a person with mental illness who is an undertrial or convicted of an offence and detained in a jail or prison. [Mental Healthcare Act (10 of 2017), S. 2(1)(w)].

Prisoner under sentence of death. A prisoner can be said to be under sentence of death, only when the death sentence is beyond judicial scrutiny and would be operative without any interference from any other authority. *Sunil Batra* v. *Delhi Administration*, AIR 1978 SC 1675, 1730. [Prisons Act (9 of 1894), S. 30(2)]

Privacy. Freedom from unauthorised oversight or observation; seclusion. [IPC (45 of 1860), S. 509].

Private. Not public; not official; belonging or concerning to one or more individuals.

As opposed to public; apart from the State; not in public office; not open to public; [Indian Evidence Act (1 of 1872), S. 75]; own; peculiar to oneself; belonging to or concerning an individual person or company; relating to personal affairs. [Indian Contract Act (9 of 1872), S. 17, ill. (d)].

Private Act. For the purpose of section 354C of Act 45 of 1860, 'private act' includes an act of watching carried out in a place which, in the circumstances, would reasonably be expected to provide privacy and where the victim's genitals, posterior or breasts are exposed or covered only in underwear; or the victim is using a lavatory; or the victim is doing a sexual act that is not of a kind ordinarily done in public. [*Explanation* 1 to S. 354C of IPC, 1860 (45 of 1860), as inserted by the Criminal Laws (Amendment) Act, 2013 (13 of 2013)]

A private bill, Act, or law relates only to particular classes of men and their private concerns.

A British Parliamentary Act affecting the interest of a particular individual or corporation [Indian Evidence Act (1 of 1872), S. 81]; Act of Parliament not held to be of general application, it may be local or personal.

Private airport. Means an airport owned, developed or managed—

(i) any person or agency other than the Authority or any State Government, or

(ii) any person or agency jointly with the Authority or any State Government or both where the share of such person or agency, as the case may be, in the assets of the private airport is more than fifty per cent. [Airport Authority of India (Amendment) Act (43 of 2003), S. 4(nn)]

Private alienation. Alienation by oneself alone, not related to or dependent on official machinery. [CPC (5 of 1908), S. 64].

Private carrier. The motor service maintained by the Post and Telegraph Department is not maintained as a private carrier, as the work of the Central Govt. done under the Post Office Act is not for the purpose of making gains or profits and cannot be construed as carrying on business. *Mohd. Zafrul* v. *Birendra Lall*, AIR 1965 Bom 120, 122. [Motor Transport Workers Act (27 of 1961), S. 1(4)]

Private company. "PRIVATE COMPANY" means a company which, by its articles,—(a) restricts the right to transfer its shares, if any; (b) limits the number of its members to fifty, not including—(i) persons who are in the employment of the company; and (ii) persons who, having been formerly in the employment of the company, were members of the company while in that employment and have continued to be members after the employment ceased; and (c) prohibits any invitation to the public to subscribe for any shares in or debentures of, the company:

Provided that where two or more persons hold one or more shares in a company jointly they shall, for the purposes of this definition, be considered as a single member. [Companies Act (1 of 1956), S. 3(1)(iii)].

Company privately formed by members who subscribe the whole of the capital among themselves.

A company with restrictions on the number of shareholders, whose shares may not be offered to the general public. [Companies Act (1 of 1956), S. 2(35)].

"PRIVATE COMPANY" means a company having a minimum paid-up share capital as may be prescribed, and which by its articles,—

(*i*) restricts the right to transfer its shares;

(*ii*) except in case of One Person Company, limits the number of its members to two hundred:

Provided that where two or more persons hold one or more shares in a company jointly, they shall, for the purposes of this clause, be treated as a single member:

Provided further that—

(*A*) persons who are in the employment of the company; and

(*B*) persons who, having been formerly in the employment of the company, were members of the company while in that employment and have continued to be members after the employment ceased, shall not be included in the number of members; and

(*iii*) prohibits any invitation to the public to subscribe for any securities of the company. [S. 2(68) of the Companies Act, 2013 (18 of 2013) as amended by Act 21 of 2015]

Private debt. "PRIVATE DEBT" means any debt or liability other than a public debt. [U.P. Act I of 1903 (Encumbered Estates), S. 2, cl. (*a*)].

Private defence, Right of. A man's right to defend his or another's person or his or another's property as allowed by law. [IPC (45 of 1860), Ss. 96 and 106].

Private document. All documents which are not public documents are private documents. [Indian Evidence Act (1 of 1872), S. 75] [(w. e. f. 1-7-2024) repealed and replaced by Bharatiya Sakshya Adhiniyam, 2023 (47 of 2023), S. 74(2)]

Private dwelling house. "PRIVATE DWELLING HOUSE" means a house in which persons engaged in the manufacture of beedi or cigar or both reside. [Beedi and Cigar Workers (Conditions of Employment) Act (32 of 1966), S. 2(n)]

Private easement. A "private easement" is defined to be a privileged service or convenience which one neighbour has of another by prescription, grant, or necessary implication, without profit.

Private establishment. Means a company, firm, cooperative or other society, associations, trust, agency, institution, organization, union, factory or such other establishment as the appropriate Government may, by notification, specify. [Rights of Persons with Disabilities Act (49 of 2016), S. 2(v)]

Private forest. Lands on which firewood trees are grown for reasonable supply of fuel to factory employees, smoke houses and rubber or tea factories will not come under the definition of "private forests". *Pioneer Rubber Plantations* v. *State of Kerala*, AIR 1993 SC 192.

'PRIVATE FOREST' means the forest which is not owned by the Government, but does not include—

(i) areas which are waste and are not enclaves within wooded areas;

(ii) areas which are gardens or nilams;

(iii) areas which are planted with tea, coffee, cocoa, rubber, cardamom or cinnamon; and

(iv) other areas which are cultivated with proper areca nut, coconut, cashew or other fruit-bearing trees or are cultivated with any other agricultural crop. [Kerala Land Reforms Act, 1963 (1 of 1964), S. 2(47) as cited in *N.K. Rajindra Mohan v. Jhirvamadi Rubber Company Limited*, (2015) 9 SCC 326, para 18].

Private informer. "PRIVATE INFORMER" means any person including an officer of the Government Department other than an officer of the Forest Department who renders meritorious service to the Forest Department in the detention and prevention of forest offences. [Kerala Forest (Regulation of Rewards) Rules, 1995, R. 2(d)]

Private institution. Means an institution imparting education or training, established and administered or maintained by (any body of persons), and recognised as educational institution by the Government, and includes a college, a special institution and a minority educational institution, but does not include an educational institution—

(a) established and administered or maintained by the Central Government or the State Government or any local authority;

(b) established and administered by any University established by law; or

(c) giving, providing or imparting only religious instruction, but not any other instruction. [AP Education Act, 1982, S. 2(35)]

Private key. Means the key of a key pair used to create a digital signature. [Information Technology Act (21 of 2000), S. 2(1)(zc)]

A key for encryption and decryption that is paired with a Public Key and is kept secret by its owner. (*Information Technology*)

Private lane. A lane which is not open to the public for use. [CPC (5 of 1908), Sch. I, App. E, Form No. 6].

Private market. "PRIVATE MARKET" means a market which is not maintained by a Board and which is licensed by a Board under the provisions of this Act. [Cantonments Act (2 of 1924), S. 2 (xxviii)]

'PRIVATE MARKET' means a market which is not a municipal market, but does not include a market established for the purpose of any law for the time being in force regulating the marketing of agricultural and other produce in such markets. [Maharashtra Municipalities Act (40 of 1965), S. 2(37)(a)]

"PRIVATE MARKET" means a market which is not a municipal market. [New Delhi Municipal Council Act (44 of 1994), S. 2(35)]

Private member. "PRIVATE MEMBER" means a member other than a minister. [Rules of Procedure and Conduct of Business in Lok Sabha, 1952 (Ed. 7), R. 2(1)]

Member of the Legislature holding no Government office *i.e.* not being a Minister.

Private Member Bill. A bill proposed in the Parliament or State Legislature by a Private Member *i.e.* a member not being a Minister.

Private Members' Business. The business in a Legislature consisting of Bills and Resolutions initiated by Members other than Ministers; it is usually taken up on Fridays.

Private Member's Resolution. Resolutions moved by Private Members in the Parliament or State Legislature; they enable the Government to gauge the feelings of the House with regard to them. The last two-and-a-half hours of a sitting of the House on every alternate Friday are allotted for the discussion on such resolutions.

Private nuisance. A nuisance affecting some particular person or persons as distinguished from the public at large or any section thereof. [CPC (5 of 1908), Sch. 1, App. D, form No 14].

Private party. A party which does not hold a public capacity. [CPC (5 of 1908), O. XXVII, R. 8(2)].

Private person. A person who does not hold any public office. [CrPC 1973 (2 of 1974), S. 51].

Private property. Private property is that which is one's own; something that belongs or inheres exclusively in an individual person.

The property of a private charitable corporation, though charged with the maintenance of a college, hospital, or other public charity is "private property."

Private right. A right which vests in an individual or individuals as such and not as a member or members of the public. [*Expln.* (6), CPC (5 of 1908), S. 11].

Private right of way. A private right of way serves as a means of accommodation to a limited neighbourhood for local convenience. It has been defined to be that right which one man has of going over another's land, and is confined either to the inhabitants of a particular district, or to those occupying or owning certain estates, or it generally extends to one or more individuals.

Private road. "PRIVATE ROAD" means any street, road, square, Court alley or passage which is not a public road and includes a pathway made by the owner or premises on his own land to secure access to, or the convenient use of, such premises. [Manipur Municipalities Act (43 of 1994), S. 2(45); Sikkim Municipalities Act (Sikkim Act No. 6 of 1995), S. 2(xxix)]

Private school. "PRIVATE SCHOOL" means school which is not run by the Central Government, Administrator, a local authority or any other authority designated or sponsored by the Central Government, Administrator or a local authority. [Delhi School Education Act (18 of 1973), S. 2(r)]

'PRIVATE SCHOOL' means a recognised school established or administered by a management, other than the Government or a local authority. [Maharashtra Employees of Private School (Condition of Service) Regulation Act (3 of 1978), S. 2(20)]

Private sector. The sphere of private enterprise. [Payment of Bonus Act (21 of 1965), S. 2(15)].

Private security. "PRIVATE SECURITY" means security provided by person other than a public servant, to protect or guard any person or property or both and includes provision of armoured car service. [Private Security Agencies (Regulation) Act (29 of 2005), S. 2(f)].

Private security guard. "PRIVATE SECURITY GUARD" means a person providing private security with or without arms to another person or property or both an includes or supervisor. [Private Security Agencies (Regulation) Act (29 of 2005), S. 2(h)]

Private servant. A 'PRIVATE SERVANT' is a person who is in the domestic service of a member of the mission and who is not an employee of the sending state. [Diplomatic Relations (Vienna Convention) Act (43 of 1972), S. 2 & Sch., Art. (h)]

Private service vehicle. Means a motor vehicle constructed or adapted to carry more than six persons excluding the driver and ordinarily used by or on behalf of the owner of such vehicle for the purpose of carrying persons for, or in connection with, his trade or business otherwise than for hire or reward but does not include a motor vehicle used for public purposes. [Motor Vehicles Act (59 of 1988), S. 2(33)].

Private slaughter-house. "PRIVATE SLAUGHTER HOUSE" means a slaughter house which is not a municipal slaughter house. [Maharashtra Municipalities Act, 1965 (40 of 1985), S. 2(37)(b) and Manipur Municipalities Act (43 of 1994), S. 2(47)]

Private street. "PRIVATE STREET" means any street, which is not a public street and includes any passage securing access to two or more places belonging to the same or different owners. [New Delhi Municipal Council Act (44 of 1994), S. 2(36) and Delhi Municipal Corporation Act, 1957 (66 of 1957), S. 2(39)]

Private transfer. An act of parties by which the title to property is conveyed from one person to another. [CPC (5 of 1908), S. 64].

Private trust. A trust the beneficial interest in which is vested absolutely in one or more individuals who are, or within given time may be definitely ascertained. [Indian Trusts Act (2 of 1882), Preamble].

Private water. "PRIVATE WATERS" means waters-(*a*) which are the exclusive property of any person; or (*b*) in which any person has an exclusive right of fishery, and in which fish are not confined but have means of ingress or egress. [Ben. Act II of 1889 (Private Fisheries Protection), S. 2].

Private wrong : Public wrong. Private wrongs or civil injuries are an infringement or privation of the civil rights which belong to individuals, considered merely as individuals; public wrongs or crimes and misdemeanours are a breach and violation of the public rights and duties due to the whole community in its social aggregate capacity. [Blackstone, Commentaries on the Laws of England, edited by Wayne Morrison, Vol. 4, p. 5 as cited in *Subramanian Swamy* v. *Union of India*, (2016) 7 SCC 353, para 85].

Privatization. Act or process converting a government business or industry to the ownership and control of private hands.

Privatorum conventio juri publico non derogat. (*Lat.*) (9 Rep. 141) A private agreement does not derogate from the public right.

Privatum incommodum publico bono pensatur. (*Lat.*) (Jenk. Cent. 85) Private individuals should suffer public welfare.

Privies. Those who are partakers, or have an interest in any action or thing, or any relation to another. (*Tomlin*)

Privilege. A right or immunity granted as a peculiar benefit; advantage or favour; a peculiar or personal advantage or right, especially when enjoyed in derogation of a common right [CPC (5 of 1908), O. XI, R. 19(2) and Constitution of India, Art. 59(3)].

Privilege is a legal freedom on the part of one person as against another to do a given act or a legal freedom not to do a certain act. *Isha Valimohamed* v. *Haji Gulam Mohamad & Haji Data Trust*, AIR 1974 SC 2061, 2065.

Immunity from civil action may be described also as a privilege, because the word "privilege" is sufficiently wide to include an immunity. *Mohanlal* v. *Sawai Van Singhiji*, AIR 1962 SC 73, 75.

The word 'privilege' has been defined as a particular and peculiar benefit or advantage enjoyed by a person. *V. Pechimuthu* v. *Gowrammal*, AIR 2001 SC 2446.

Privilege of pre-emption. A right of pre-emption is only a prior right to purchase land pre-empted. It is not a claim of title, in any sense, but a naked right to effect a purchase and acquire a title.

Privileged communication. With reference to privileged communications being inadmissible in evidence, it is a settled rule of law that if the communication be to one who is at the time professionally employed, and occupies the attitude of a *legal adviser*, it is privileged, and the seal of silence is on it, subject to be broken by consent of the client only.

A communication cannot be considered as privileged because made in professional confidence, unless the person to whom it is made is acting for the time being in the character of a legal adviser of the person who makes it. The communication must also be made for the purpose of obtaining professional advice or aid in the matter to which the communication relates.

A *husband or wife* cannot be examined as to any communications made by one to the other during marriage, nor shall they be permitted, after the marriage relation ceases, to reveal any such communication. Such communications are also privileged.

Letters from a husband, found by the wife's administrator among her papers, which may be used against him in a suit in which he was then interested, would be privileged communications.

In order to make a *communication to a minister of the Gospel or priest* privileged it must be received in confidence. By this is not meant that it must be made under the express promise of secrecy, but, rather, that the communication was in confidence, and with the understanding, express or implied, that it should not be revealed to anyone. The mere fact that a communication is made to a person who is a priest does not of itself make such communication privileged. To have that effect, it must have been made in confidence of the relation, and under such circumstances as to imply that it should forever remain secret in the breast of the confidential adviser.

Privileged occupant. "PRIVILEGED OCCUPANT" means; (*a*) a *dharekari*, or (*b*) a quasi *dharekari*, or (*c*) a permanent tenant. [Bom Act I of 1880 (Khoti Settlement), S. 3, cl. 5)]

Privileged person. "PRIVILEGED PERSON" means a person—

(1) who is not a proprietor, tenure-holder, under-tenure-holder or a *Mahajan;* and

(2) who besides his homestead, holds no other land or holds any such land not exceeding one acre. [Bihar Privileged Persons Homestead Tenancy Act (4 of 1948), S. 2(i)]

Privilegium non valet contra rem publicam. A privilege avails not against the State.

Privity. A derivative kind of interest, founded upon or growing out of the contract of another, as that which subsists between an heir and his ancestor, between executor and testator, and between lessor and lessee and his assignee; a relation which creates an obligation.

The term "privity" denotes mutual or successive relationship to the same right of property.

A mutuality of interest.

Privity of contract. "To many students and practitioners of the common law *privity of contract* became a fetish. As such, it operated to deprive many a claimant of a remedy in cases where according to the *mores* of the time the claim was just. It has made many learned men believe that a *chose* in action *could not* be assigned. Even now, it is gravely asserted that a man cannot be made the debtor of another against his will. But the common law was gradually influenced by equity and by the law merchant, so that by assignment a debtor could become bound to pay a perfect stranger to himself, although until the legislature stepped in, the common law Courts characteristically made use of a fiction and pretended that they were not doing that which they really were doing." WILLIAM R. ANSON, *Principles of the Law of Contract* 335 (ARTHUR L. CORBIN ed., 3d Am. ed. 1919).

Privy. One who is a partner or has any part or interest in any action, matter or thing [CrPC 1973 (2 of 1974), S. 94(1)(e)]; toilet [Factories Act (63 of 1948), S. 11(1)]; [Beedi and Cigar Workers (Conditions of Employment) Act (32 of 1966), S. 8].

Privy Council. "PRIVY COUNCIL" shall mean the Lords and others for the time being of Her Majesty's Most Honourable Privy Council. [General Clauses Act (10 of 1897), S. 3(42) (*as it stood before amendment*)]

In Great Britain a body of advisers selected by the Sovereign, together with certain persons who are members by usage, as the princes of the blood, the archbishops and the chief officers of the present and past ministries of State. [Indian Evidence Act (1 of 1872), S. 78(3)].

Privy councillor. Member of the Privy Council.

Privy purse. Allowance from public revenue for the sovereign's private expenses.

Prize. "PRIZE" means anything which, subject to this Act and the rules made thereunder, may be subjected to adjudication and includes a ship or an aircraft and goods carried therein, irrespective of whether the ship is captured at sea or seized in port or whether the aircraft is on or over land or sea at the time of capture or seizure. [Naval and Aircraft Prize Act (59 of 1971), S. 2(h)]

The term 'prize' is used to designate the reward in a lottery, which the lucky person or persons will receive.

An honour or reward striven for in a competition or in contest of chance [Indian Contract Act (9 of 1872), S. 30]; property (as a ship) lawfully captured in times of war [Indian Trusts Act (2 of 1882), S. 1]; awarded or intended to be awarded as a prize. [Aligarh Muslim University Act (40 of 1920), S. 5(2)].

A vessel or cargo captured at sea or seized at the port by the forces of the nations which are at war (liable to be appropriated, it being an enemy property).

Prize amount. "PRIZE AMOUNT" means the difference between the chit amount and the discount, and in the case of a fraction of a ticket means the difference between the chit amount and the discount proportionate to the fraction of the ticket, and when the price amount is payable otherwise than in cash, the value of the price amount shall be the value at the time when it becomes payable. [Chit Funds Act (40 of 1982), S. 2(m)]

Prize chit. "PRIZE CHIT" includes any transaction or arrangement by whatever name called under which a person collects whether as a promoter, foreman, agent or in any other capacity, monies in one lumpsum or in instalments by way of contributions or subscriptions or by sale of units, certificates or other instruments or in any other manner or as membership fees or admission fees or service charges to or in respect of any savings, mutual benefit, thrift or any other scheme or arrangement by whatever name called, and utilises the monies so collected or any part thereof or the income accruing from investment or other use of such monies for all or any of the following purposes; namely:—

(i) giving or awarding periodically or otherwise to a specified number of subscribers as determined by lot, draw or in any other manner, prizes or gifts in cash or in kind, whether or not the recipient of the prize of gift is under a liability to make any further payment in respect of such scheme or arrangement,

(ii) refunding to the subscribers or such of them as have not won any prize or gift, the whole or part of the subscriptions, contributions or other monies collected, with or without any bonus, premium, interest or other advantage by whatever name called on the termination of the scheme or arrangement, or after the expiry of the period stipulated therein, but does not include a conventional chit. [Prize Chits and Money Circulation Schemes (Banning) Act (43 of 1978), S. 2(e)]

The giving away or awarding prizes or gifts to a specified number of subscribers is an essential element of a Prize Chit, as also refunding to the subscribers the whole or part of the amount of subscription and an Endowment Certificate Scheme is outside the Prize Chit. *Reserve Bank of India* v. *Peerless G. FR. I. Co. Ltd.*, AIR 1987 SC 1024, 1040. [Prize Chits and Money Circulation Schemes (Banning) Act (43 of 1978), S. 2(e)]

Prize Competition. Means any competition (whether called a crossword prize competition, a prize missing-word prize competition, a picture prize competition or by any other name) in which prizes are offered for the solution of any puzzle based upon the building up, arrangement, combination or permutation, of letters, words or figures. [Prize Competition Act (42 of 1955), S. 2(d)]

Prize Court. The Prize Court is the division of the Admiralty Court which has jurisdiction over prizes taken from a foreign power in time of war.

A Prize Court is in fact a Court of all the nations in the world, because all persons in every part of the world are concluded by its sentence in cases clearly coming within its jurisdiction.

A Prize Court is a Court having jurisdiction to adjudicate upon captures made at sea in time of war, and to condemn the property captured, if such a decree be proper. Prize Courts are not instituted to determine civil and private rights, but for the purpose of trying judicially the lawfulness of captures at sea according to the principles of public international law, with the double object of preventing and redressing wrongful captures, and of justifying the rightful acts of the captors in the eyes of other nations.

Prize goods. Prize goods are defined to be goods taken on the high seas, *jure belli*; taken out of the hands of the enemy.

Pro bono publico. For the public good, for the benefit of the community as a whole.

Pro forma. As a matter of form.

As per form; set up in advance to prescribe form or describe items.

Pro possessore habetur qui dolo injuriave desiit possidere. A person is considered a possessor who has ceased possession through fraud or injury.

Pro rata. According to a measure which fixes proportions; according to a certain part; in proportion; according to the rate; implying the disposition of a fund or sum indicated in proportion to same fixed rate or standard.

Pro re rata. To meet the emergency.

Pro tanto. For so much; to that extent; for as much as may be.

Pro tem. For the time being.

Pro tempore. For the time being; temporarily; provisionally.

Probability. A probability of the existence of a thing or condition is created when there is more evidence in favour of its existence than against it.

Probability means likelihood, appearance or resemblance of truth, and, in ordinary language, implies doubt, so that to instruct a jury that they may act on probabilities means that they may act on less than convincing evidence, or without the moral certainty required by law, and is erroneous.

The quality or fact of being probable; a probable event, circumstance, belief. [CPC (5 of 1908), O. XXV, R. 1(2)].

Probable. "Probable" means having more evidence for than against; supported by evidence which inclines the mind to believe, but leaves some room for doubt.

That may reasonably be expected to happen, or to prove true. [Indian Evidence Act (1 of 1872), S. 52].

Probandi necessitas incumbit illi qui agit. The necessity of proving lies upon him who brings the charge.

Probate. "PROBATE", means the copy of a will certified under the seal of a Court of competent jurisdiction with a grant of administration to the estate of the testator. [Indian Succession Act (39 of 1925), S. 2(*f*)]

The officially verified copy of a will together with the certificate of its having been proved, which is delivered to the executor. [Indian Evidence Act (1 of 1872), S. 41].

A judicial procedure to establish a testamentary document as a valid will.

Probate homestead. A homestead, exempt from creditors' claims, set apart for use by surviving spouse and minor children of a descendant.

Probate judge. A judge who has jurisdiction over probate, inheritance, guardianship and the like.

Probate jurisdiction. The jurisdiction exercised in probate matters *i.e.* probate and administration. [Indian Evidence Act (1 of 1872), S. 41].

Probation. Testing of a person's capacity, conduct or character, especially before he is admitted to regular employment or full membership of some society.

The action or process of testing or putting to proof; a system of releasing on suspended sentence, during good behaviour, young persons and especially first offenders, and placing them under the supervision of a probation officer who acts as a friend and adviser. [CrPC 1973 (2 of 1974), S. 360].

Probation, on. Mere use of the words 'on probation' is not conclusive to be a probationer. A person who is appointed against a post substantively vacant with definite conditions of probation, is a 'probationer'. [*High Court of Punjab and Haryana* v. *State of Haryana,* (1975) 1 SCC 843, 849-50 paras 20 and 23]

Probationer. A probationer holds only a temporary appointment till he has proved himself to be fit to fill the permanent appointment. A servant on probation is on trial during the period he is on probation and he passes into permanent service only after the lapse of the period during which he is on probation. *Harbilas* v. *I.T. Commissioner,* AIR 1963 Cal 359 (362). [Constitution of India, Art. 311(1)]

A person who continues in service after the expiry of the period of probation will not ordinarily get automatic confirmation in service. *Giovanola-Binny Limited* v. *Industrial Tribunal, Calicut,* AIR 1969 Ker 313 at 315. [Industrial Disputes Act (14 of 1947), S. 33]

A convict who is on probation.

A 'PROBATIONER' means an employee who is provisionally employed to fill a clear vacancy, and who has not completed six months' satisfactory service in the aggregate. [M.P. Industrial Employment (Standing Orders) Act (26 of 1961), Standing Order No. 2(iii) **as cited in** *Ram Naresh Rawat* v. *Ashwani Ray,* (2017) 3 SCC 436, para 6].

Probative. Tending or serving to prove or disprove.

Probative force. Probative force means a force serving for proof.

Probative value. The probative value of a piece of evidence means the weight to be given to it. This is something which has to be judged in accordance with the facts and circumstances of each case. *Ram Bihari Yadav* v. *State of Bihar,* AIR 1998 SC 1850.

Procedure. Mode of conducting business (as) Parliamentary procedure; legal procedure, *etc.*

The mode or form of conducting judicial (or other) proceedings. [CrPC 1973 (2 of 1974), S. 254].

"PROCEDURE" it is a hand-maiden to justice which should never be made a tool to deny justice or perpetuate injustice, by any oppressive or punitive use. The well recognized exceptions to this principle are : (*i*) where the statute prescribing the procedure, also prescribes specifically the consequence of non-compliance; (*ii*) where the procedural defect is not rectified, even after it is pointed out and due opportunity is given for rectifying it; (*iii*) where the non-compliance or violation is proved to be deliberate or mischievous; (*iv*) where the rectification of defect would affect the case on merits or will affect the jurisdiction of the court; (*v*) in case of Memorandum of Appeal, there is complete absence of authority and the appeal is presented without the knowledge, consent and authority of the appellant. *Uday Shankar Triyar* v. *Ram Kalewar Prasad Singh*, AIR 2006 SC 269 : 2006 AIR SCW 6044.

Procedure established by law. "Procedure established by law" is not synonymous with 'due process of law' which finds a place in the American Constitution nor is it synonymous with law in the sense '*Jus*' *i.e.* the principles of natural justice. The procedure therefore means procedure laid down by law or procedure prescribed by Art. 22. *Ajaile Singh Lehna Singh* v. *State of Punjab,* AIR 1962 Punj 309, 334 (FB). [Constitution of India, Art. 21]

Proceed. "Proceed" as used in a notice by a surety on a note after it became due, directing that the payee should at once proceed and collect the note, means to commence and carry on a legal process.

A stipulation not to proceed against a party is an agreement not to sue him.

To go on with an action or investigation. [CPC (5 of 1908), S. 22]; [CrPC 1973 (2 of 1974), S. 137(2)].

Proceeding. "PROCEEDING" includes any suit, appeal or application. [Soldiers Litigation Act (4 of 1925), S. 2(d)]

PROCEEDING. "Carrying on of an action at law, a legal action or process, any act done by authority of a court of law; any step taken in a cause by either party". The term "proceeding" is a very comprehensive term and generally speaking means a prescribed course of action for enforcing a legal right. It is not a technical expression with a definite meaning attached to it, but one the ambit of whose meaning will be governed by the statute. It indicates a prescribed mode in which judicial business is conducted. [Shorter Oxford Dictionary as cited in *Jagdish Narayan Tandon* v. *Onkar Nath Tandon,* 2017 (6) ADJ 707, para 10]

"PROCEEDING" means any proceeding under this Act in respect of any year which may be pending on the date on which the powers under this section are exercised or which may have been completed on or before such date and includes also all proceedings under this Act which may be commenced after such date in respect of any year. [Income-tax Act (43 of 1961), S. 133A (6) *Expln.* (b)]

The term 'proceeding' in Section 29 is a very wide term to mean a prescribed course of action to enforce the legal right. It indicates the prescribed mode in which the judicial business is conducted. The execution is a step in the judicial process. It seeks to enforce the final order to realise the result of the adjudication. *P. L. Kantha Rao* v. *State of A.P.*, AIR 1995 SC 807, 809 [Administrative Tribunals Act (13 of 1985), S. 29].

The word "proceedings" ordinarily relates to forms of law, to the modes in which judicial transactions are conducted.

A legal action or process; any act done by authority of a Court of law; any step taken by either party in a legal proceeding; a particular action or course of action [CrPC 1973 (2 of 1974), S. 263(j) and Constitution of India, Art. 88].

A "proceeding" is defined as the instrument whereby the party injured obtains redress for wrongs committed against him, either in respect to his personal contracts, his person, or his property.

A proceeding in a civil action is an act necessary to be done in order to attain a given end. It is a prescribed mode of action for carrying into effect a legal right.

In its general acceptation, "proceeding" means the form in which actions are to be brought and defended, the manner of intervening in suits, of conducting them, the mode of deciding them, of opposing judgments and of executing. Ordinary proceedings intend the regular and usual mode of carrying on a suit by due course of law.

Proceedings under Art. 226 of the Constitution also fall within the scope of the expression 'proceedings' in Art. 194 (2). *A.K. Subbiah* v. *Karnataka Legislative Council,* AIR 1979 Kant 24, 31. [Constitution of India, Art. 194(2)]

The expression 'proceedings' with reference to a case, would imply taking of steps in connection with the further progress of the case when a case is listed for hearing and the case is taken up by the Court and an order is made in the case, it would be proceedings in the case. It is not possible to confine the word 'proceedings' to the recording of evidence only. *Jai Ram* v. *State,* AIR 1937 All 137, 139. [CrPC 1973 (2 of 1974), S. 326]

A proceeding is a prescribed course of action for the enforcement of a legal right. The legal right of a person who has obtained preliminary decree is to apply for a final decree. *Reba Sircar* v. *Bisweswar Lal,* AIR 1980 Cal 328, 330. [CPC (5 of 1908), O. XXXIV, R. 5(3)]

The word 'proceeding' in S. 195(1)(b) is used in a wider sense than judicial proceeding and the section simply requires that there should be some relationship between the offence and the proceeding. *Hrishikesh Nag* v. *State,* AIR 1965 Tri 13, 14. [CrPC 1973 (2 of 1974), S. 195(1)(b)]

The word 'proceedings' must be interpreted, in its wider sense, as including, among other matters, appeals and revisions. *State of J&K* v. *Abdul Ghani Petwari,* AIR 1977 J&K 17, 19.

The word 'proceeding' in S. 69(3) Indian Partnership Act (9 of 1932) means something in the nature of a suit, that is, a proceeding which is instituted or initiated in a Court and does not cover a reference to arbitration aliunde the Court. *Babulal Dhandhania* v. *Gautham & Co.,* AIR 1950 Cal 391.

Proceedings closed. The order "proceedings closed" does not necessarily amount to dismissal.

Proceedings for the recovery. The 'proceedings for the recovery' start when the Income Tax Officer forwards the certificate to the collector. *Aruna Devi Jajodia* v. *Collector of Madras,* AIR 1952 Mad 794.

Proceedings in any Court of civil jurisdiction. It means proceedings covering original matters like probates, guardianships, divorce, insolvency. *Ratindra Nath Bose* v. *Jyoti Bikash Ghosh,* AIR 1975 Cal 377, 380. [CPC (5 of 1908), S. 141]

Proceeds. The word "proceeds" is one of equivocal import, and of great generality. It does not necessarily mean money, its meaning in each case depending very much upon the connection in which it is employed and the subject-matter to which it is applied.

That which proceeds from something; what is derived from something (as a sale, investment, levy, business) by way of total revenue; total amount brought in. [CrPC 1973 (2 of 1974), S. 83(5) and Constitution of India, Art. 27].

Strictly speaking it implies something that arises or leads out of or from another thing, and in its ordinary acceptation when applied to the income to be derived from real estate, it embraces the idea of issues, rents, profits, or produce. In a commercial sense it means the sum, amount or value of goods, or things sold and converted into money.

"PROCEEDS" mean produce, outcome, profit. An amount never received cannot be part of the proceeds. So where the commission of certain receivers was fixed at certain percentage of the "gross sale proceeds," the term does not include the trade discount which is invariably deducted before the sale price is arrived at.

Proceeds of crime. Means any property derived or obtained directly or indirectly, by any person as a result of criminal activity (including crime involving currency transfers) or the value of any such property. [CrPC, 1973 (2 of 1974), S. 105A(c)] [Now (w. e. f. 1-7-2024) repealed & replaced by Bharatiya Nagarik Suraksha Sanhita, 2023 (46 of 2023)]

In this Chapter, unless the context otherwise requires,--"proceeds of crime" means any property derived or obtained directly or indirectly, by any person as a result of criminal activity (including crime involving currency transfers) or the value of any such property. [(w. e. f. 1-7-2024) repealed & replaced by Bharatiya Nagarik Suraksha Sanhita, 2023 (46 of 2023)]

"PROCEEDS OF CRIME" means any property derived or obtained, directly or indirectly, by any person as a result of criminal activity relating to a scheduled offence or the value of any such property or where such property is taken or held outside the country, then the property equivalent in value held within the country. [Prevention of Money Laundering Act (15 of 2003), S. 2(1)(u)]

Proceeds of execution sale. The amounts collected by sale in execution of a decree. [CPC (5 of 1908), S. 73].

Proceeds of terrorism. Shall means all kinds of properties which have been derived or obtained from commission of any terrorist act or have been acquired through funds traceable to a terrorist act, and shall include cash irrespective of person in whose name such proceeds are standing or in whose possession they are found. [Prevention of Terrorism Act (15 of 2002), S. 2(1)(c)]

Proceeds of terrorism. Means,—

(i) all kinds of properties which have been derived or obtained from commission of any terrorist act or have been acquired through funds traceable to a terrorist act, irrespective of person in whose name such proceeds are standing or in whose possession they are found; or

(ii) any property which is being used, or is intended to be used, for a terrorist act or for the purpose of an individual terrorist or a terrorist gang or a terrorist organization.

Explanation.—For the purposes of Act 37 of 1967, it is hereby declared that the expression 'proceeds of terrorism' includes any property intended to be used for terrorism. [S. 2(g) of the Unlawful Activities (Prevention) Act, 1967 (37 of 1967) as substituted by the Unlawful Activities (Prevention) Amendment Act, 2012 (3 of 2013)]

Proces-verbal. (*Fr.*) Verbal trial.

Process. For the removal of doubts, it is hereby clarified that the expression "process" includes and shall be deemed to have always included transmission by satellite (including up-linking, amplification, conversion for down-linking of any signal), cable, optic fibre or by any other similar technology, whether or not such process is secret. [Income-tax Act (43 of 1961), section 9(1)(i), *Explanation 6*]

"PROCESS" includes any practice, treatment and mode of manufacture of any article. [Bureau of Indian Standard Act (63 of 1986), S. 2(o)]

A word which may be applied either to methods of action such as legal proceedings, or to the treatment of substance in transforming and reducing it to a different state and the means of such treatment.

"PROCESS" means "a continuous and regular action or succession of actions taking place or carried on in a definite manner and leading to the accomplishment of some result". [Oxford English Dictionary as cited in *Mamta Surgical Cotton Industries, Rajasthan* v. *Assistant Commissioner (Anti-Evasion), Bhilwara, Rajasthan*, (2014) 4 SCC 87, para 23].

(1) a series of operations performed during manufacture, etc. (2) a series of stages which a product, etc. passes through resulting in a development or transformation of it. [Chamber's 21st Century Dictionary as cited in *Mamta Surgical Cotton Industries, Rajasthan* v. *Assistant Commissioner (Anti-Evasion), Bhilwara, Rajasthan*, (2014) 4 SCC 87, para 23].

A summons, mandate or writ that serves as a means used to bring a person or thing into Court for litigation; a formal command or mandate [CPC (5 of 1908), S. 29]; the course of procedure in a judicial action or in a suit in litigation; a particular mode or system of doing something [IPC (45 of 1860), S. 68]; a particular method or system used in a manufacturing operation. [Indian Standards Institution (Certification Marks) Act (36 of 1952), S. 2(a)(i)].

A commission, issued to an *Ameen* to make a local investigation, is not a "process" within the meaning of S. 20 of the Court Fees Act (7 of 1870). Process has a well understood meaning within which such a commission cannot be included.

"PROCESS" for the removal of doubts, it is hereby clarified that the expression 'process' includes and shall be deemed to have always included transmission by satellite (including up-linking, amplification, conversion for down-linking of any signal), cable, optic fibre or by any other similar technology, whether or not such process is secret. [*Explanation 6* to section 9(1)(vi) of the Income-tax Act, 1961 (43 of 1961) as inserted (w.r.e.f. 1-6-1976) by the Finance Act, 2012]

Process of law. A particular mode of the operation or working of law. [IPC (45 of 1860), S. 68].

Process for bidding. The 'process for bidding' used in the Explanation to Section 3(3) would cover every stage from notice inviting tender till the award of contract and would also include all intermediate stages such as pre-bid clarification and bid notifications also. [*Excel Crop Care Limited* v. *Competition Commission of India,* 2013 CC Online Comp AT 149 **as cited in** *Excel Crop Care Limited* v. *Competition Commission of India,* (2017) 8 SCC 47, para 17] [Competition Act, 2002 (12 of 2003), S. 3(3), *Explanation*].

Process-server. One who serves in the manner prescribed by law a summons, mandate or writ issued by a Court of law [CPC (5 of 1908), Sch. I, App. B form No. 11]; [Employment Exchanges (Compulsory Notification of Vacancies) Act (31 of 1959), S. 2(i)(5)].

Processes. In this section the expression 'processes' includes summonses and commissions for the examination of witnesses and summonses to produce documents. [Arbitration and Conciliation Act (26 of 1996), S. 27(6)]

Processing. PROCESSING, in relation to marine products includes the preservation of such products such as canning, freezing, drying, salting, smoking, peeling or filleting and any other method of processing which the Authority may, by notification in the *Gazette of India,* specify in this behalf. [Marine Products Export Development Authority Act (13 of 1972), S. 3(l)].

'PROCESSING' in relation to fishing includes cleaning, beheading, filleting, shelling, peeling, icing, freezing, canning, setting, smoking, cooking, pickling, drying and otherwise preparing or preserving fish by any other method. [Maritime Zones of India (Regulation of Fishing by Foreign Vessels) Act (42 of 1981), S. 2(l)]

"PROCESSING" of a chemical means a physical process, such as formulation, extraction and purification, in which a chemical is not converted into another chemical. [Chemical Weapons Convention Act (34 of 2000), Art. II, 12(b)]

"PROCESSING" means the process by which solid wastes are transformed into a new or recycled products. [Municipal Solid Wastes (Management and Handling) Rules, 2000, R. 3(xviii)]

The blending of ore in the course of loading through the Mechanical Ore Handling Plant amounts to processing of ore within the meaning of S. 8(3) and R. 13. *Chowgule & Co. (P) Ltd.* v. *Union of India,* AIR 1981 SC 1014, 1029. [Central Sales Tax Rules (1957), R. 13; [Central Sales Tax Act (74 of 1956), S. 8(3)(a)].

Whenever a commodity undergoes a change as a result of some operation performed on it or in regard to it, such operation would amount to processing of the commodity. Whatever be the means employed for the purpose of carrying out the operation, it is the effect of the operation on the commodity that is material for the purpose of determining whether the operation constitutes 'processing'. *Chowgule & Co. Pvt. Ltd.* v. *Union of India,* (1981) 47 STC 124, 131, 132 (SC).

Preparing for market, manufacture or other commercial use by subjecting to some process. [Gold (Control) Act (45 of 1968) (*Repealed*), S. 2(c)].

"Processing" and "manufacturing". "Processing" means a sequence of operations or changes undergone. The term "Processing" merely has to be distinguished from "manufacturing" in the sense that a mere processing does not ordinarily make the original thing to undergo a change losing its original identity while under the process of 'manufacturing' the original article loses its identity and a thing or article differently known or recognized in common parlance comes into existence. (*Diamond Industries* v. *Comm. of Sales Tax,* 1994 MPLJ 257).

A very broad and a wide definition of the "processing" if applied, would include manufacture of a new or distinct product. In the present context (of a mineral), "processing" would mean activities in order to make the mineral mined marketable, saleable and transportable, without substantially changing the identity of the mineral, as mined. When there is substantial change at the mineral mined and the process results in a different commodity being produced or transforming and completely changing the mineral, it would fall outside the scope of the word "processing". [*Manganese Ore India Limited* v. *State of M.P.,* (2017) 1 SCC 8, paras 20 and 21].

Processing Fee. Means the charges that have to be paid by the applicant institution to the Commission along with the application for processing such application. [UGC (Institutions Deemed to be Universities) Regulations, 2019, Regn. 2(2.16)]

Processing for export. Means rendering a commodity suitable for export. In respect of 'fish', every process of freezing or applying chemical so long it is undertaken to make fish worthy for export, would be covered. *Regional Executive Kerala Fisherman's Welfare Fund Board* v. *Fancy Food,* AIR 1995 SC 1620.

Processing of goods. The expression 'PROCESSING OF GOODS' includes any art or process for producing, preparing or making an article by subjecting any material to a manual, mechanical, chemical, electrical or any other like operation. [State Financial Corporation Act (63 of 1951), S. 2(C) *Expln.*; Industrial Development Bank of India Act (18 of 1964), S. 2(c) *Expln.*; Bombay Stamp Act (60 of 1958), Sch. 1, Art. 36, *Expln.* III]

Procession. Procession is the action of a body of persons going or marching along in orderly succession in a formal or ceremonial way, especially as a religious ceremony or on a festive occasion.

Processor. "PROCESSOR" means a person who processes any agricultural produce on payment of charge. [Maharashtra Agricultural Produce Marketing (Regulation) Act, 1963 (20 of 1964), S. 2(n)]

'PROCESSOR' means a person engaged in any ancillary process subsequent to the production of cloth, such as dyeing, bleaching, mercerising, calendering, embroidering, printing, raising, cloth empossing or any other finishing process, but does not include a producer, and the expression 'process' shall be construed accordingly. [Handlooms (Reservation of Articles for Production) Act (22 of 1985), S. 2(e)]

Processor serial number. An authentification technology wherein a unique number is embedded in every central processing unit of computers. (*Cyber Law*)

Prochein Ami. Next friend, the latter term being defined as one who, without being appointed guardian, acts for the benefit of an infant, lunatic, married woman, or other person incapacitated person (*non sui juris*).

Proclaimed offender. "The expression "proclaimed offender" includes any person proclaimed as an offender by any Court or authority in any territory in India to which this Code does not extend, in respect of any act which, if committed in the territories to which this Code extends, would be an offence punishable under any of the following sections of the Indian Penal Code (45 of 1860), namely, 302, 304, 382, 392 to 399 (both inclusive), 402, 435, 436, 449, 450 and 457 to 460 (both inclusive). [CrPC 1973 (2 of 1974), S. 40(2)(ii)] [Now (w. e. f. 1-7-2024) repealed & replaced by Bharatiya Nagarik Suraksha Sanhita, 2023 (46 of 2023)]

The expression "proclaimed offender" includes any person proclaimed as an offender by any Court or authority in any territory in India to which this Sanhita does not extend, in respect of any act which if committed in the territories to which this Sanhita extends, would be an offence punishable under any of the offence punishable with imprisonment for ten years or more or with imprisonment for life or with death under the Bharatiya Nyaya Sanhita, 2023. [(w. e. f. 1-7-2024) Bharatiya Nagarik Suraksha Sanhita, 2023 (46 of 2023), S. 34(2)(ii)]

Proclamation. A formal public announcement made by the government.

Procreate. Produce offspring.

The word 'procreate' means capacity of a spouse to give birth as also rear up and bring up children. *Alka Sharma* v. *Abhinesh Chandra Sharma,* AIR 1991 MP 205, 212. [Hindu marriage Act (25 of 1955), S. 5(ii)(b)]

Procurator. An agent or attorney in fact.

Procure. The word "procure" means to acquire for one's self; to cause to come; to obtain by any means; to contrive; to bring about.

Procurement. The act of procuring; the purchasing, leasing, renting, or selling of materials, services, equipment, or construction.

Produce. 'PRODUCE' includes manufacture and all its grammatical variations and cognate expression shall be construed accordingly. [Monopolies and Restrictive Trade Practices Act (54 of 1969), S. 2(ll) repealed by Act 12 of 2003 (w.e.f. 1-9-2009]

To bring forward; to show or exhibit: to bring into view or notice; as, to produce books or writings at a trial in obedience to a subpoena; to bring forward; to offer to view or notice; to show; to manufacture; make.

The word "produce" is not necessarily confined to what is grown from the ground. It refers also to a finished article or a semi-finished article made from raw material. Thus mollases can fairly be called the produce of a sugar mill.

"TO PRODUCE" a thing or document to a person, means, to show it to him personally, and does not involve the idea that the possession of it is to be parted with (as) a railway passenger's duty to *produce* the ticket for inspection by the ticket examiner.

Produced. The word 'produced' appearing in entry No. 84 is used in juxtaposition with the word 'manufactured' and used in connection with a duty of excise and consequently it appears to contemplate some expenditure of human skill and labour in bringing the goods concerned into the condition which would attract the duty. They should be produced in the sense that some human activity should be spent on them and they should be subject to some processes in order that they may be brought to the state in which they may become fit for consumption. *Aluminium Corporation of India Ltd.* v. *Coal Board,* AIR 1959 Cal 222, 226. [Constitution of India, Sch. 7, List 1, Entry 84]

A document can be said to have been produced in a Court when it is not only produced for the purposes of being rendered in evidence but also for some other purpose. *Nirmaljit Singh Hoon* v. *State of W. B.*, AIR 1972 SC 2639, 2650. [CrPC 1973 (2 of 1974), S. 195(1)(b)(ii)]

Produced means to bring forth to bring into existence from elements for raw materials. *Deputy Commissioner of Agricultural Income Tax and Sales Tax, Central Zone, Ernakulam* v. *Palampadam Plantations Ltd, Kottayam,* AIR 1969 SC 930 at 931.

The word "produced" as used in S. 33 of the Indian Stamp Act (2 of 1899) means produced in the ordinary course of law and not produced under compulsion. Further a document is produced by a party only when it is sought to be proved and a witness is examined in respect thereof and not earlier. It is highly improper for a Court to compel a party to produce an original document with a view to impound the document, because the Court has been informed that it is not sufficiently stamped. The essentials required by the Indian Stamp Act which confers the authority to impound a document are either the document must be 'produced' or come before the judge 'in performance of his functions.' The word 'produce' has a technical meaning and means either produced in response to a summons or produced voluntarily for some judicial purpose, such, for instance as evidence. It cannot refer to a document which falls accidentally or incidentally into a judge's hands. It carries with it, when used in this connection, a mental element just as the word 'deliver.' There must be an intention to produce, just as there must be an intention to deliver. The mere physical act of production is not enough when there is no intention to produce. It is further necessary that the document should come before the judge, 'in the performance of his functions' *as a judge*. Hence where a witness summoned to produce a document produces it along with others not connected with the case before the Court, the latter cannot be impounded under the provisions of the Indian Stamp Act.

Produced or comes in the performance of his function. The phrase 'produced or comes in the performance of his functions' as used in S. 33, Indian Stamp Act (2 of 1899), could not have been intended by the Legislature to include the performance of functions by a Collector under S. 31. *Chunnilal Buruman* v. *Board of Revenue, U.P.*, AIR 1951 All 851, 852.

Producer. 'PRODUCER', includes a manufacturer. [Drugs (Control) Act (26 of 1950), S. 2(d)]

"Producer" means any person engaged in any activity connected with or relatable to any primary produce. [Companies Act (1 of 1956), S. 581A(k); Companies Act (18 of 2013), section 378A(k)]

"PRODUCER", in relation to a cinematograph film or sound recording, means a person who takes the initiative and responsibility for making the work. [Copyright Act (14 of 1957), S. 2(uu)]

'PRODUCER' in relation to a feature film, means,

(i) the producer of such film; or

(ii) where the application for a certificate in respect of such film under Section 4 of the Cinematograph Act, 1952 is made by any other person, such other person. [Cine-Workers Welfare Cess Act (30 of 1981), S. 2(d)]

'PRODUCER', in relation to a jute manufacture, means the producer of such jute manufacture. [Jute Manufacture Cess Act (28 of 1983), S. 2(c)]

"PRODUCER" in relation to a feature film, means the person by whom the arrangements necessary for making of such film (including the raising of finances and engaging cine workers for the making of such film) are undertaken. [Cine Workers and Cinema Theatre Workers (Regulation of Employment) Act (50 of 1981), S. 2(h); Cine-Workers Welfare Fund Act (33 of 1981), S. 2(f)]

'PRODUCER' means a person engaged in the production of cloth on any loom other than handloom, and shall include a person who owns, works or operates on, a loom for the production of cloth, and the expression 'produce' shall be construed accordingly. [Handlooms (Reservation of Articles for Production) Act (22 of 1985), S. 2(f)]

"PRODUCER", in relation to goods, means any person, who,—

(i) if such goods are agricultural goods, produces the goods and includes the person who processes or packages such goods;

(ii) if such goods are natural goods, exploits the goods;

(iii) if such goods are handicraft or Industrial goods, makes or manufactures the goods,

and includes any person who trades or deals in such production, exploitation, making or manufacturing, as the case may be, of the goods. [Geographical Indications (Registration and Protection) Act (48 of 1999), S. 2(1)(k)]

"PRODUCER" means a person carrying on the business of manufacturing sugar. [Essential Commodities (Amendment) Act (37 of 2003), S. 2, *Expln.* (a)]

One who manufactures or produces goods.

One who produces, grows, makes an article of consumption [Cotton Textiles Cess Act (7 of 1948), S. 2(b)].

Producer Company. Means a body corporate having objects or activities specified in Section 581B and registered as Producer Company under this Act. [Companies Act (1 of 1956), S. 581A(l)]

Producer institution. Means a Producer Company or any other institution having only producer or producers or Producer Company or Producer Companies as its member whether incorporated or not having any of the objects referred to in Section 581B and which agrees to make use of the services of the Producer Company or Producer Companies as provided in its articles. [Companies Act (1 of 1956), S. 581A(m)]

Producer of phonograms. 'PRODUCER OF PHONOGRAMS' means the person who, or the legal entity which, first fixes the sounds of a performance or other sounds. [International Convention for the Protection of Performers, Producers of Phonograms and Broadcasting Organisations (Rome, 26 Oct, 1961, Art. 3(c)]

Producible. That which can be brought forth, offered for inspection or consideration. [CPC (5 of 1908), O. XIII, R. 11].

Product. The word "product" imports an article which is made of something, and which, when made, has characteristics which are apparent to the senses. In judging as to the similarity of products (in Patent Law), the material of which a product is made and its appearance when made, may be taken into consideration.

"Product" means any article or goods or substance or raw material or any extended cycle of such product, which may be in gaseous, liquid, or solid state possessing intrinsic value which is capable of delivery either as wholly assembled or as a component part and is produced for introduction to trade or commerce, but does not include human tissues, blood, blood products and organs. [Consumer Protection Act, 2019 (35 of 2019), section 2(33)]

According to Webster's Comprehensive Dictionary, the word 'product' means "anything produced or obtained as a result" of some operation or work whether such derivation is by a simple physical process or by a chemical reaction would not make any difference to the end product. *Collector of C. E. Coimbatore* v. *Protein Products of India Ltd.*, AIR 1989 SC 627, 629. [Central Excises and Salt Act (1 of 1944), S. 37] [Now repealed by Act 12 of 2017]

A thing produced by nature or a natural process; something produced by physical labour or intellectual effort; the result of work or thought.

Product Liability. Liability of a manufacturer/wholesaler/dealer of a product for manufacturing/selling defective goods making them liable to pay monetary compensation to public for any injury caused to them due to the defects in goods. [Karnika Seth, *Computers Internet and New Technology Laws*, 2021, LexisNexis, Glossary of Legal Terms].

"Product liability" means the responsibility of a product manufacturer or product seller, of any product or service, to compensate for any harm caused to a consumer by such defective product manufactured or sold or by deficiency in services relating thereto. [Consumer Protection Act, 2019 (35 of 2019), section 2(34)]

Product manufacturer. Means a person who—

(i) makes any product or parts thereof; or

(ii) assembles parts thereof made by others; or

(iii) puts or causes to be put his own mark on any products made by any other person; or

(iv) makes a product and sells, distributes, leases, installs, prepares, packages, labels, markets, repairs, maintains such product or is otherwise involved in placing such product for commercial purpose; or

(v) designs, produces, fabricates, constructs or re-manufactures any product before its sale; or

(vi) being a product seller of a product, is also a manufacturer of such product. [Consumer Protection Act, 2019 (35 of 2019), section 2(36)]

Product under reference. Means the *product or activity* to which the Report relates. [Cost Audit Report Rules, 2001, R. 2(e)]

Production. 'PRODUCTION' with its grammatical variations and cognate expressions; includes—

(i) packing; labelling, re-labelling, of containers,

(ii) re-packing from bulk packages to retail packages, and

(iii) the adoption of any other method to render the product marketable. [Cigarettes (Regulation of Production, *etc.*) Act (49 of 1975), S. 2(k)]

'PRODUCTION' in relations to a feature film, includes any of the activities in respect of the making thereof. [Cine Workers and Cinema Theatre Workers (Regulations of Employment) Act (50 of 1981), S. 2(i)]

'PRODUCTION' means the separation of opium poppy straw, coca leaves or cannabis from the plants from which they are obtained. [N.D.P.S. Act (61 of 1985), S. 2(xxii)]

For the purpose of Article VI:

'PRODUCTION' of a chemical means its formation through chemical reaction. [Chemical Weapons Convention Act (34 of 2000), Art. II, 12(a)]

"PRODUCTION", with its grammatical variations and cognate expressions, includes the making of cigarettes, cigars, cheroots, *beedis,* cigarette tobacco, pipe tobacco, *hookah* tobacco, chewing tobacco, *pan masala* or any chewing material having tobacco as one of its ingredients (by whatever name called) or snuff and shall include—

(i) packing, labelling or re-labelling, of containers;

(ii) re-packing from bulk packages to retail packages; and

(iii) the adoption of any other method to render the tobacco product marketable. [Cigarettes and other Tobacco Products (Prohibition of Advertisement and Regulation of Trade and Commerce, Production, Supply and Distribution) Act (34 of 2003), S. 3(k)]

"PRODUCTION" in relation to any ozone depleting substance means the manufacture of an ozone depleting substance from any raw material or feedback chemicals, but does not include

(i) the manufacture of a substance that is used and entirely consumed (except for trace quantity) in the manufacture of other chemicals; or

(ii) quantities which are produced incidentally in the manufacture of other chemical substance; or

(iii) quantities which are recycled or reused; or

(iv) quantities which are destroyed by technologies to be specified by Central Government. [Ozone Depleting Substances (Regulation and Control) Rules, 2000, R. 2(l)]

"PRODUCTION" means the amount of controlled substances produced minus the amount destroyed by technologies to be approved by the parties. [Montreal Protocol on Substances that Deplete the Ozone Layer, 1987, Art I. 5]

The word "production" may designate as well a thing produced as the operation of producing; (as) production of commodities or the production of a witness.

The action of producing [Indian Evidence Act (1 of 1872), S. 131]; [Working Journalists and Other Newspaper Employees (Conditions of Service) and Miscellaneous Provisions Act (45 of 1955), S. 2(d)]; [Constitution of India, Art. 142(2)].

(*In Political Economy*) Creation of bringing into existence of objects which constitute wealth; thing produced. *In commerce* it means the bringing forward and offering of an article for sale.

(*In Copyright Law*) The term "production" has been used to describe the legal source of the proprietary rights of authorship, (as the literary production of an author). It is a species of occupancy, and is called "production" as distinguished from "invention."

The expression 'production' means a thing resulted from any action, process or effort. The action of a person purchasing an old car, removing parts therefrom and selling the same, without moulding, repairing or changing them does not amount to production.

PRODUCTION, PRODUCE, PRODUCT. Corn, hay, vegetables, and fruits in general are termed *products* of the earth; the naturalist examines all the *production* of nature; the husbandman looks to the *produce* of his land; the traveller inquires about the *products* of different countries.

Production capacity. Means: The annual quantitative potential for manufacturing a specific chemical based on the technological process actually used or, if the process is not yet operational, planned to be used at the relevant facility. It shall be deemed to be equal to the nameplate capacity or, if the nameplate capacity is not available, to the design capacity. The nameplate capacity is the product output under conditions optimized for maximum quantity for the production facility, as demonstrated by one or more test-runs. The design capacity is the corresponding theoretically calculated product output. [Chemical Weapons Convention Act (34 of 2000), Art. II, 10]

Production lease. Means a lease granted under Section 13 which confers an exclusive right for the purpose of undertaking production operation. [Offshore Areas Minerals (Development and Regulation) Act, 2002 (17 of 2003), S. 4(t)]

Production : manufacture. The word 'production' or 'produce' when used in juxtaposition with the word 'manufacture' takes in bringing into existence new goods by a process which may or may not amount to manufacture. The expressions 'manufacture' and 'produce' are normally associated with movable articles and goods, big and small but they are never employed to denote the construction activity regarding dam, bridge, road or building. *I.T. Commissioner, Orissa* v. *N. C. Budharaja & Co.*, AIR 1993 SC 2529, 2534. [Income-tax Act (43 of 1961), S. 80HH(2)(i)]

Production operation. Means any operation undertaken for the purpose of winning any mineral from the offshore area and includes any operation directly or indirectly necessary therefor or incidental thereto. [Offshore Areas Minerals (Development and Regulation) Act, 2002 (17 of 2003), S. 4(s)]

Production, Processing, Consumption of a Chemical. For the purposes of Article VI:

(a) "Production" of a chemical means its formation through chemical reaction;

(b) "Processing" of a chemical means a physical process, such as formulation, extraction and purification, in which a chemical is not converted into another chemical;

(c) "Consumption" of a chemical means its conversion into another chemical *via* a chemical reaction. [Chemical Weapons Convention Act (34 of 2000), Art. II 12]

Profess. To make open declaration of, as of one's knowledge or belief; to confess publicity.

To make an open declaration of; to avow; to make pretence of [T.P. Act (4 of 1882), S. 35]; to profess a religion.

The word 'profess' in the Presidential order appears to have been used in the sense of an open declaration or practice by a person of the Hindu (or the Sikh) religion. *Punjab Rao* v. *D. Meshram*, AIR 1965 SC 1179, 1184. [Constitution (Scheduled Castes) Order (1950), cl. 3]

TO PROFESS, DECLARE. A Christian *professes* to follow the doctrine and precepts of Christianity; a person *declares* that a thing is true or false, or he *declares* his firm belief in a thing.

Professes. The expression 'professes' in para 3 of Constitution (Scheduled Castes) Order, 1950 is intended to have the same meanings as the expression "belongs to". Mere sympathy with or admiration for particular tenets of any religion by a person who was not born in it and who has not been converted to it would not bring him within the meaning of the expression "professing a particular religion". *G. Michael* v. S. *Venkateswaran, Addl. Secretary to Govt. Madras,* AIR 1952 Mad 474, 478.

Professes a religion. Tomlin in his book "The Law Dictionary" says that the word "professions" was used particularly for entering into any religious order", The phrase "professes a religion" used in para 3 of the Order is used in this sense and in order to attract the provisions of this paragraph it has to be established that the person concerned has publicly entered a religion different from the Hindu or the Sikh religion. Mere declarations falling short of this would not be sufficient. *Narayan Waktu Karwadi* v. *Panjabsas Hakanu Shambarkar,* AIR 1958 Bom 296, 297. [Constitution (Scheduled Castes) Order, 1950, Para 3, Sch., Part IV, cl. (3), Item 13]

Profession. "PROFESSION" includes vocation. [Income Tax Act (43 of 1961), S. 2 (36)]

The term is applied to an occupation or calling which requires learned and special preparation in the acquirement of scientific knowledge and skill.

The occupation which one professes to be skilled in and to follow; any calling or occupation by which a person habitually earns his living [Income-tax Act (43 of 1961), S. 2(36) and Indian Evidence Act (1 of 1872), S. 150]; [North-Eastern Hill University Act (24 of 1973), S. 7].

A profession or occupation is carried on for the purpose of earning a livelihood and a profit motive does not underlie such carrying of profession or occupation. *L.M. Chitale* v. *Commissioner of Labour,* AIR 1964 Mad 131, 133. [Constitution of India, Art. 19(6)]

A 'profession' involves the idea of an occupation requiring either purely intellectual skill or if any manual skill, as in painting and sculpture or surgery, skill controlled by the intellectual skill of the operator, as distinguished from an occupation which is substantially the production or sale or arrangements for the production or sale of commodities. *C.I.T.* v. *Manmohan Das*, (1966) 59 ITR 699, 710 (SC) [Income Tax Act (43 of 1961), S. 28]

Profession and Trade or Business (distinction). There is a fundamental difference between 'profession' and 'trade or business'. The words 'trade' and 'business' do not mean the same thing. While all trades may be business, all business is not trade. The distinction between 'business' and 'profession' is emphasised in R. 40 of the Rules made by the Bar Council of India. The rule says that an advocate shall not personally engage in 'business' and he may be a sleeping partner in a firm, if in the opinion of the appropriate State Bar Council the nature of business is not inconsistent with the dignity of the profession. It is therefore clear that the two terms 'profession' and 'business' are not synonymous. An advocate is approached by his client in regard to his problems with reference to his property, his trade business or industry and sometimes with regard to problems relating to his freedom and it is expected that an advocate would be in a position to help him in his difficulties, to the best of his ability and not betray the confidence reposed in him. This is one of the elements which should be borne in mind in considering whether a particular person is practicing a 'profession' or is merely doing a 'business'. The profession of an advocate involves a high code of ethics and very considerable responsibility. The profession of an advocate constitutes a learned 'profession' which cannot be termed as 'business' within the definition of Section 10(3)(c)(iii) of the Tamil Nadu Buildings (Lease and Rent Control) Act. Therefore the landlord who is an advocate cannot apply under S. 10(3)(c)(iii) of the Act for eviction the tenant from the premises on the ground that the respondent requires the same for 'locating his office' (MAHESWARAN, J) *M/s Kolapur Traders* v. *Subramania Mudaliar,* MLJ: YD (1979) Suppl to Feb. p. 526 : (1979) ILR 2 Mad 440 : (1979) 2 Ren CR 129 : (1979) 11 Lawyer 94 : (1980) 1 Ren LJ 247: 92 Mad LW 290 : (1979) 2 Mad LJ 43.

'Profession', 'business' and 'occupation'. 'Profession' has be distinguished from 'business' or a mere 'occupation'. While in 'business' and to a certain extent in 'occupation', there is a profit motive, 'profession' is primarily a service to society wherein earning is secondary or incidental. [*P.A. Inamdar* v. *State of Maharashtra,* (2005) 6 SCC 537, 605, para 140]

Profession, business, vocation, occupation. The word "profession" is of still wider scope than 'business'. What may not amount to business may amount to 'profession' and what may not amount to 'profession' may amount to 'vocation' and what may not amount to 'vocation' may amount to 'occupation'. *Lala Indra Sen, In re*, (1940) 8 ITR 187, 204-5 (All). *Also see*, *B. Malick* v. *CIT*, (1968) 67 ITR 616 (All).

Profession : Commercial activity. Profession as distinguished with 'commercial' means a person who enters into a profession, it involves certain amount of skill as against commercial activity where it is more of a matter of things or business activity. In profession, it is purely use of skill activity. Therefore, two are distinct concepts in commercial activity—one works for gain or profit and as against this, in profession, one works for his livelihood. *Shiv Narayan* v. *M.P. Electricity Board*, AIR 1999 MP 246, 251-252.

Profession or occupation. Politics is a profession or occupation. *Commissioner of Expenditure Tax* v. *P. U. G. Raja*, AIR 1976 SC 140, 142. [Expenditure Tax Act (35 of 1987), S. 5(a)]

Profession or occupation or business. The words "profession or occupation or business" are of wide import and whether or not gain is made by an educational institution it cannot cease to be a business. *Sakharkherda Education Society* v. *State of Maharashtra,* AIR 1968 Bom 91, 95. [Constitution of India, Art. 19(2)(g)]

Profession or vocation. Teaching is a vocation if not a profession. Teaching of Vedanta is as much teaching and, therefore, a vocation as any other teaching. There is no reason why reading of Vedanta as a matter of religion is not carrying on of a vocation. In order to become a vocation, it is not essential that the activity must be organised. It is well-known that a single act may amount to the carrying on of a business of profession. It is not the motive of the person doing an act which decides whether the act done by him is the carrying on of a business, profession or vocation. If any business, profession or vocation in fact produces an income that is taxable income and nonetheless because it was carried on without the motive of producing any income. (1888) 3 Tax Cas 105, **Foll.** The question is, whether the activity has actually produced an income and it matters not whether that activity is called by the name of business, profession, vocation or by any other name or with what intention it was carried on. *P. Krishna Menon* v. *Commr. of Income-tax, Mysore, Travancore and Coorg, Bangalore,* MLJ : QD (1956-1960) Vol. III C909 : (1959) 35 ITR 48 : 1959 SCJ 96 : (1959) 1 MLJ (SC) 49 : (1959) 1 Andh WR (SC) 49 : 1959 Ker LT (SC) 4 : AIR 1959 SC 75 : 61 Bom LR 41 : 1959 Ker LJ 178 : ILR (1959) Ker 115 :

(1959) Supp (1) SCR 133. [Income-tax Act (11 of 1922), S. 10]

Profession tax. 'PROFESSION TAX' means the tax on professions, trades, callings and employments levied under this Act. [W.B. State Tax on Professions, Trades, Callings and employment Act (7 of 1979), S. 2(i)]

Profession, trade or calling. The expression 'profession, trade or calling' occurring in Section 21(1)(a) includes therein all activities wherein a person may usefully and/or gainfully engage himself. *Shanti Devi* v. *Swami Ashanand,* (2003) 2 SCC 26, para 5 : AIR 2003 SC 823. [U.P. Urban Buildings (Regulation of Letting, Rent and Eviction) Act (13 of 1972), S. 21(1)(a)]

Professional. "PROFESSIONAL" means a person who is having special expertise in a field which would promote the welfare of persons with disability. [National Trust for Welfare of Persons with Autism, Cerebral Palsy, Mental Retardation and Multiple Disabilities Act (44 of 1999), S. 2(l)]

"PROFESSIONAL" means a person who has at least ten years' experience in telecommunication or systems management. [Punjab Health Systems Corporation Act (Punj Act No. 6 of 1996), S. 2(h)]

Pertaining to, or connected with a profession. [Indian Evidence Act (1 of 1872), S. 32(2)].

Professional capacity. An application to an attorney to draw a deed is an application in a "professional capacity," making the same a privileged communication, which the attorney cannot divulge.

Professional College. "PROFESSIONAL COLLEGE" means a university, college or an affiliated college in which instruction is provided primarily for courses of study leading to any degree, diploma or certificate of the university in any professional subject and which is recognised under this Act as a professional college. [Burdwan University Act (28 of 1981), S. 2(16)]

Professional duty. A duty pertaining to or connected with one's profession [Indian Evidence Act (1 of 1872), S. 32(2)].

Professional employment. An occupation pertaining to or connected with one's profession [Indian Evidence Act (1 of 1872), S. 126].

Professional equipment. Means such portable equipments, instruments, apparatus and appliances as are required in his profession, by a carpenter, a plumber, a welder, a mason, and the like and shall not include items of common use such as cameras, cassette recorders, dictaphones, personal computers, typewriters, and other similar articles. [Customs Tariff, Baggage Rules, 1998, R. 2(V)]

Professional indemnity insurance. A type of insurance which is effected by various persons; *e.g.* solicitors, accountant, brokers, architects against their liability to pay damages to their clients by reason of their negligence in the performance of their professional duties.

Professional institution. Organisations which impart advanced learning in a particular field of profession such as law, medicine or engineering for attainment of special knowledge as distinguished from mere skill are professional institutions. *Kannamal Educational Trust* v. *University of Madras,* AIR 1966 Mad 303, 308.

Professional misconduct. The giving of improper legal advice may amount to professional misconduct. That however may not be so by the giving of wrong legal advice. *P. D. Khandekar* v. *Bar Council of Maharashtra,* AIR 1984 SC 110, 114. [Advocates Act (25 of 1961), S. 35(1)]

It suggests dishonesty or some conduct involving moral turpitude and not every irregularity or negligence on the part of the notary would amount to professional misconduct. *State Govt. of U.P.* v. *Kashi Prasad Saksena,* AIR 1969 All 363 at 364. [Notaries Act (53 of 1952), S. 10(d)]

Professional programs. Means a programme other than programmes in engineering, medicine, dental pharmacy, nursing, architecture, physiotherapy and programmes not permitted to be offered in distance mode by any Statutory Councils or Regultory Authorities to be conducted by the Higher Educational Institutions under Open and Distance Learning mode or Distance Education mode for the purposes of these regulations, if any, should be considered only if the same are approved by the respective Statutory Councils or Regulatory Authorities. [University Grants Commission (Open and Distance Learning) Regulations, 2017, Regn. 2(p)].

Professional or other misconduct. For the purposes of this Act, the expression "professional or other misconduct" shall be deemed to include any act or omission provided in any of the Schedules, but nothing in this section shall be construed to limit or abridge in any way the power conferred or duty cast on the Director (Discipline) under sub-section (1) of section 21 to inquire into the conduct of any member of the Institute under any other circumstances. [Chartered Accountants Act 1949 (38 of 1949), S. 22. Also see *Explanation* to section 132(4) of the Companies Act, 2013 (18 of 2013)]

Professional Standard. Means the standard of practice specified by the Institute of Actuaries of India by issue of guidance notes/Actuarial Practice Standard to its members. [Insurance Regulatory and Development Authority of India (Appointed Actuary) Regulations, 2017, Regn. 2(vi)].

Professional service. Service rendered by one who does a profession. [Chartered Accountants Act (38 of 1949), S. 2(2)(iii) and Indian Contract Act (9 of 1872), S. 16(3), ill. (b)].

Professional treatise. A book or other writing which treats a particular subject in a scientific manner, particularly, for the guidance of those in the profession. [Indian Evidence Act (1 of 1872), S. 159].

Professions : Trades : Callings and Employment. The expression 'persons practising any profession or art or carrying on any trade or calling, includes the persons in private employment of a bus syndicate.

Professor. A teacher at a university or college. [Aligarh Muslim University Act (40 of 1920), S. 2(k)].

Proficiency. Advancement toward the attainment of a high degree of knowledge or skill. [Apprentices Act (52 of 1961), S. 21(1) and Official Languages Act (19 of 1963), S. 3(4)].

Profiling. The use of various bits of information, possibly sourced separately, to build up a picture about a person, especially in relation to purchasing habits. (*Cyber Law*)

Profit. An advantage or benefit; the gain, the preliminary gain in any transaction [CrPC 1973 (2 of 1974), S. 145(2)].

'Profit' means accession of goods, valuable results, useful consequences, avail, gain, as an office of profit, excess of return over expenditures or excess of income over expenditure. [*U.S.* v. *Mintzes*, D.C. Md. 304 F Supp. 1305, 1312 **as cited in** *Karmchari Union, Agra* v. *Union of India*, AIR 2000 SC 1226]

Profit a prendre. A profit a prendre, is a right vested in one man of entering upon the land of another and taking therefrom a profit of the soil.

Right exercised by one man in the soil of another to participate in the profits of the soil thereof such as rights of pasture. Under the Act an easement includes but in England it excludes profits a prendre *e.g.* the right to graze cattle on another's land, to take leaves, quarry or soil from it. While natural rights are incident to the possession of every occupier of land, easements and profits a prendre have to be acquired by grant, prescription or custom.

"Profit a prendre" and "easement". "The chief distinction between 'an easement' and a profit a prendre is that whereas an easement only confers a right to utilise the servient tenement in a particular manner or to prevent the commission of some act on that tenement, '*a profit a prendre*' confers a right to take from the servient tenement some part of the soil of that tenement or minerals under it or some part of its natural produce or the animals *ferae noturae* existing upon it. What is taken must be capable of ownership, for otherwise the right amounts to a mere easement." (*Halsbury,* Fourth Edn., para 43 at pages 21 to 22).

A profit a prendre when granted in favour of the owner of a dominant heritage for the beneficial enjoyment of such heritage would, therefore, be an easement but it would not be so if the grant was not for the beneficial enjoyment of the grantee's heritage. *State of Orissa* v. *Titaghur Paper Mills Co. Ltd.,* 1985 Supp SCC 280, 283.

Profit bonus. A profit bonus is strictly not wages, at least not for the purpose of computing liability to income-tax. It is not an expense, in the ordinary sense of the term incurred for the purpose of earning profits. A *fortiori* profits have already been made. It is more like sharing of profits on the basis of a certain formula. (*C.I.T.* v. *Swadeshi Cotton and Flour Mills (Pvt.) Ltd.*, 1964, 53 ITR 134, 139 (SC). [Income Tax Act (43 of 1961), S. 36(1)(ii)]

Profit in lieu of salary. The phrase 'profit *in lieu* of salary' includes 'any payment' due to or received by an assessee from an employer, even though it has no connection with the profits of the employer. *Karmchari Union, Agra* v. *Union of India*, AIR 2000 SC 1226. [Income-tax Act (43 of 1961), S. 17]

Profit margin. The difference between the cost of something and the price for which it is sold.

Profit received in lieu of salary. If the object of a payment by the employer to the employee was unrelated to the relations between the employer and the employee, it would not fall within the expression "profit' received in lieu of salary". *I.T. Commissioner* v. *E.D. Sheppard,* AIR 1963 SC 1343, 1349.

Profit-sharing plan. A benefit plan of an employer which allows an employee to share in profits of the company.

Profitable contract. A Contract yielding profit. [Indian Contract Act (9 of 1872), S. 73, ill. (i)]

Profiteering. Making an exorbitant and unjustifiable profit, taking undue advantage of short supply of necessary commodities. [Representation of the People Act (43 of 1951), S. 8(3), *Expln.* (a)].

Profits. Profit is the gain made on any business or investment when both the receipts and payments are taken into consideration.

Profit is the acquisition beyond expenditure; excess of value received for producing, keeping or selling over cost; hence pecuniary gain in any transaction or occupation; emolument.

"PROFITS" imply a comparison of the value of an asset when the asset is acquired with the value of the asset when the asset is transferred and the difference between the two values is the amount of profit or gain made by a person. [*Topman Exports v. Commissioner of Income Tax, Mumbai*, (2012) 3 SCC 593, para 21].

The profits of a business mean the net proceeds of the concern after deducting the necessary outgoings without which those proceeds could not be earned. *Bharat Insurance Co. Ltd.* v. *CIT,* (1931) 1 Com Cases 192, 196 (Lah). [Companies Act (1 of 1956), S. 205]

Profits of the business. Means the profits of the business as computed under the head "Profits and gains of business or profession" as reduced by—

(1) ninety per cent of any sum referred to in clauses (*iiia*), (*iiib*) and (*iiic*) of Section 28 or of any receipts by way of brokerage, commission, interest, rent, charges or any other receipt of a similar nature included in such profits; and

(2) the profits of any branch, office, warehouse or any other establishment of the assessee situate outside India. [Income tax Act (43 of 1961), S. 80HHC (4C) *Expln.* (baa)]

Progeny. Children or descendants; offspring.

Program. A set of instructions written in a language understood by the computer, to perform a given task (*Information Technology*)

(1) A collection of computer instructions arranged so as to cause the computer to perform a specific task. (2) The act of selecting and placing in the proper order the instructions required for a given computer operation. (*Computer*)

Programme. "PROGRAMME" means any audio or visual matter, live or recorded, which is intended to be disseminated by transmission of electromagnetic waves through space or through cables intended to be received by the general public either directly or indirectly through the medium of relay stations. [Finance Act (32 of 1994), S. 65(86a) (*Inserted by Finance (No.2) Act (23 of 2004), S. 90*) now repealed by Central Goods and Service tax Act, 2017]

"PROGRAMME" means any television broadcast and includes—

(i) exhibition of films, features, dramas, advertisements and serials

(ii) any audio or visual or audio-visual live performance or presentation,

and the expression "programming service" shall be construed accordingly. [Cable Television Networks (Regulation) Act (7 of 1995), S. 2(g) as amended by Act 21 of 2011 (w.r.e.f. 25-10-2011)]

Programming language. A system of coding used for writing instructions for controlling the operation of a computer. *High-level languages* use recognizable words and commands with some similarity to a spoken language. (*Computer*)

Progress. An action of stepping or moving forward or onward; the going on; course or process (of action, events, *etc.*) [CPC (5 of 1908), O. XVII, R. 3].

Prohibit. The word "prohibit" when used in a grant of power to a city corporation, giving it a right to prohibit certain occupations, *etc.*, is not materially different from the word "prevent". In fact, "prevent" is the stronger word, conveying the idea of prohibition and use of means necessary to give it effect.

To forbid by authority or command. [Arms Act (54 of 1959), S. 14(1)(a)].

Prohibited ammunition. Means any ammunition containing or designed or adopted to contain any noxious liquid, gas or other such thing, and includes rockets, bombs, grenades, shells, missiles, articles designated for torpedo service and submarine mining and such other articles as the Central Government may, by notification in the Official Gazette, specify to be prohibited ammunition. [Arms Act (54 of 1959), S. 2(h)]

'Prohibited area' or 'regulated area' means an area near or adjoining a protected monument which the Central Government has, by notification in the Official Gazette, declared to be a prohibited area, from, as the case may be, a regulated area, for purposes of mining operation or construction or both. [Karnataka Ancient and Historical Monuments and Archaeological Sites and Remains Rules, 1966, R. 2(g) as cited in *K. Guruprasad Rao* v. *State of Karnataka*, (2013) 8 SCC 418, para 21].

Prohibited arms. 'PROHIBITED ARMS' means—

(i) firearms so designed or adopted that, if pressure is applied to trigger, missiles continue to be discharged until pressure is removed from the trigger or the magazine containing the missiles is empty, or

(ii) weapons of any description designed or adopted for the discharge of any noxious liquid, gas or other such thing,

and includes artillery, anti-aircraft and antitank firearms and such other arms as the Central Government may, by notification in the Official Gazette, specify to be prohibited arms. [Arms Act (54 of 1959), S. 2(i)]

Prohibited article. "PROHIBITED ARTICLE" means an article the introduction or removal of which into or out of prison is prohibited by any rule under that Act. [Prisons Act (9 of 1894), S. 3(9)]

Prohibited article of food. Means that articles of food which has been declared by the food authority from time to time as prohibited article of food and published on the website of the Food Authority. [Food Safety and Standards (Import) Regulations, 2017, Regn. 2(1)(r)].

Prohibited degrees of relationship or degrees of prohibited relationship. "Two persons are said to be within the "degrees of prohibited relationship."

(i) if one is a lineal ascendant of the other; or

(ii) if one was the wife or husband of a lineal ascendant or descendant of the other; or

(iii) if one was the wife of the brother or of the father's or mother's brother or of the grandfather's or grandmother's brother of the other; or

(iv) if the two are brother and sister, uncle and nice, aunt and nephew, or children of brother and sister, or of two brothers

or of two sisters." [Hindu Marriage Act (25 of 1955), S. 3 (g)]

Prohibited goods. Means any goods the import or export of which is subject to any prohibition under the Customs Act (52 of 1962), or any other law for the time being in force but does not include any such goods in respect of which the conditions subject to which the goods are permitted to be imported or exported have been complied with. [Customs Act (52 of 1962), S. 2(33)]

Prohibited place. "PROHIBITED PLACE" means—

(a) any work of defence, arsenal, naval, military or air-force establishment or station, mine, minefield, camp, ship or aircraft belonging to, or occupied by or on behalf of Government, any military telegraph or telephone so belonging or occupied, any wireless or signal station or office so belonging or occupied and any factory, dockyard or other place so belonging or occupied and used for the purpose of building, repairing, making or storing any munitions of war, or any sketches, plans, models or documents relating thereto, or for the purpose of getting any metals, oil or minerals of use in time of war;

(b) any place not belonging to Government where any munitions of war or any sketches, models, plans or documents relating thereto, are being made, repaired, gotten or stored under contract with, or with any person on behalf of. Government, or otherwise on behalf of Government;

(c) any place belonging to or used for the purpose of Government which is for the time being declared by the Central Government, by notification in the Official Gazetted to be a prohibited place for the purposes of this Act on the ground that information with respect thereto, or damage thereto, would be useful to an enemy, and to which a copy of the notification in respect thereof has been affixed in English and in the vernacular of the locality;

(d) any railway, road, way or channel, or other means of communication by land or water (including any works or structures being part thereof, or connected therewith) or any place used for gas, water or electricity works or other works for purposes of a public character, or any place where any munitions of war or any sketches, models, plans, or documents relating thereto, are being made, repaired, or stored otherwise than on behalf of Government, which is for the time being declared by the Central Government, by notification in the Official Gazette, to be a prohibited place for the purposes of this Act on the ground that information with respect thereto, or the destruction or obstruction thereof, or interference therewith, would be useful to an enemy, and to which a copy of the notification in respect thereof has been affixed in English and in the vernacular of the locality. [Official Secrets Act (19 of 1923), S. 2(8)]

Prohibited substance. Means the substance prohibited for handling. [Environment (Protection) Rules, 1986, R. 2(ee)]

Prohibition. The writ of prohibition is an extra-ordinary judicial writ issuing out of a Court of superior jurisdiction and directed to an inferior tribunal, or to an inferior ministerial tribunal possessing incidentally judicial powers and known as a *quasi*-judicial tribunal or even in extreme cases to a purely ministerial body, commanding it to cease abusing or usurping judicial functions.

The action of prohibiting by or as by authority [CPC (5 of 1908), O. XXXIII, R. 7(2) and Constitution of India, Art. 32(2)]; the forbidding by law of the transportation as well as the manufacture and sale of intoxicating liquors except for medicinal and sacramental purposes.

Prohibition order. Means an order issued under section 33 of Act of 34 of 2006. [S. 3(1)(zl) of the Food Safety & Standards Act, 2006 (34 of 2006)]

Section 33 (1) & (2) of Act 34 of 2006:

(1) If—

(a) any food business operator is convicted of an offence under this Act; and

(b) the court by or before which he is so convicted is satisfied that the health risk exists with respect to that food business,

the court, after giving the food business operator an opportunity of being heard, may by an order, impose the following prohibitions, namely:—

(i) a prohibition on the use of the process or treatment for the purposes of the food business;

(ii) a prohibition on the use of the premises or equipment for the purposes of the food business or any other food business of the same class or description;

(iii) a prohibition on the use of the premises or equipment for the purposes of any food business.

(2) The court may, on being satisfied that it is necessary so to do, by an order, impose a prohibition on the food business operator participating in the management of any food business, or any food business of a class or description specified in the order.

Prohibition State. Means any State which the Central Government may, by notification in the Official Gazette, specify as being a State in which or any part of which the consumption of alcoholic liquors is generally prohibited by law. [Spirituous Preparations (Inter-State Trade and Commerce) Control Act (39 of 1955), S. 2(c)]

Prohibitory order. A prohibitory order is one which operates in restraining a party from doing an act which if done will result in irreparable injury to the other side. In other words the gist of a prohibitory order lies in preventing a man from doing what he has already begun to do or intends to do. *N. Baksi* v. *O.K. Ghosh,* AIR 1957 Pat 528, 532. [Constitution of India, Arts. 215 and 226]

An order which operates in restraining a party from doing an act which if done will result in irreparable injury to the other side. [CPC (5 of 1908), Sch. I, App. E, form No. 21].

Project. "PROJECT" means a project for the construction of a building, road, dam, bridge or other structure or assembly or installation of any machinery or plant. [Finance Act (32 of 1985), S. 2(8), *Expln.* (ii)]

A planned undertaking. [Aligarh Muslim University Act (40 of 1920), S. 19(b)].

"PROJECT" means a project for which land is being acquired, irrespective of the number of persons affected. [S. 3(z) of the Right to Fair Compensation & Transparency in Land Acquisition, Rehabilitation & Resettlement Act, 2013 (30 of 2013)]

Project authority. 'PROJECT AUTHORITY' means an officer in whom the overall control and superintendence of the execution of the project vests and includes an officer whom the State Government may, by a general or special order, designate to be a project authority. [Maharashtra Project Affected Persons Rehabilitation Area Act (33 of 1989), S. 2(11)]

Project plan. "PROJECT PLAN" means a detailed plan prepared to implement one or more elements of the Regional plan, Sub-Regional plan or functional plan. [National Capital Regional Planning Board Act (2 of 1985), S. 2(i)]

Project report. A usually formal account of the results of an investigation given by a person or group authorised or delegated to make the investigation regarding a project. [Income-tax Act (43 of 1961), S. 35D(2)(a)(ii)].

Projectile. Capable of being hurled, thrown or projected with force similar to a missile. [Arms Act (54 of 1959), S. 2(1)(e)].

Projection. An extension beyond something else; a part that projects or juts out. [Cantonments Act (2 of 1924), S. 116(e)] [Now Repealed & replaced by Act 41 of 2006].

Projector. 'Projector' is a device for projecting a light beam, an apparatus for throwing illuminated images or motion pictures on the screen. *Collector of Central Excise* v. *Fusebase Eltoto Ltd.*, AIR 1994 SC 1289, 1291.

Proletariat. The lowest class of a community; the common people.

Prolix. Of long duration, lengthy wordy. [CPC (5 of 1908), O. XI, R. 7].

Prolixity. Excessive length or repetitiveness in statements of case, affidavits, or other documents.

Promiscuous. The word "promiscuous" implies "indiscriminate".

Promiscuous sexual intercourse. Sexual intercourse not restricted to one partner. [Immoral Traffic (Prevention) Act (104 of 1956), S. 2(e) omitted by Act 46 of 1978, sec. 2 (w.e.f. 2-10-1979)].

Promise. When the person to whom the proposal is made signifies his assent thereto, the proposal is said to be accepted. A proposal, when accepted, becomes a promise. [Indian Contract Act (9 of 1872), S. 2(b)]

A declaration made to another person with respect to the future, stating that one will do or refrain from some specified act or that one will give some specified thing [Indian Contract Act (9 of 1872), S. 2(b)]; to make a promise [Indian Contract Act (9 of 1872), S. 52, ill.].

To create a promise within the meaning of S. 25 of the Indian Contract Act (9 of 1872) it is not necessary that there should be an accepted proposal reduced to writing. It is enough that the writing expresses an intention to pay wholly or in part the debt referred to therein, and the document refers to the debt in such a way as to identify it.

Promise of secrecy. A promise to keep secrecy. [Indian Evidence Act (1 of 1872), S. 29].

Promise, Reciprocal. "Promises which form the consideration or part of the consideration for each other are called reciprocal promises." [Indian Contract Act (9 of 1872), S. 2(f)].

Promisee. The person accepting the proposal is called the 'promisee". [Indian Contract Act (9 of 1872), S. 2(c)]

Person to whom or in whose favour a promise is made.

The person to whom a promise is made [Indian Contract Act (9 of 1872), S. 2(c)].

Promisor. The person accepting the proposal is called the 'promisor'. [Indian Contract Act (9 of 1872), S.2(c)]

The person making the promise. [Indian Contract Act (9 of 1872), S. 2(c)].

One who makes a promise.

Promissory estoppel. It is quite fundamental that the doctrine of promissory estoppel cannot be used to compel the public bodies or the Government to carry out the representation or promise which is contrary to law or which is outside their authority or power. The doctrine cannot also be invoked if it is found to be inequitable or unjust in its enforcement. *Delhi Cloth and General Mills Ltd.* v. *Union of India*, AIR 1987 SC 2414, 2419, 2420. [Income Tax Act (43 of 1961), S. 143(3)]

Promissory estoppel, doctrine of. Where no representation had been made by the Union of India contrary to International Price Reimbursement Scheme, which could mislead the appellant into altering his position to his detriment, the doctrine of promissory estoppel would not apply. [*Larsen & Toubro Ltd.* v. *Union of India,* (2005) 3 SCC 654, 661, para 17]

Promissory estoppel, Principle of. To attract applicability of promissory estoppel' a contract in writing is not a necessary requirement. This principle is based on premise that no one can take advantage of its own omission or fault. [*State of Orissa* v. *Mangalam Timber Products Ltd.,* (2003) 9 SCALE 578 : (2003) 7 SLT 132]

Promissory note. A "PROMISSORY NOTE" is an instrument in writing (not being a bank-note or a currency-note) containing an unconditional undertaking signed by the maker, to pay a certain sum of money only to, or to the order of, a certain person or to the bearer of the instrument. [Negotiable Instruments Act (26 of 1881), S. 4].

"PROMISSORY NOTE" in the Stamp Act also includes a note promising the payment of any sum of money out of any particular fund which may or may not be available, or upon any condition or contingency which may or may not be performed or happen. [Indian Stamp Act (2 of 1899), S. 2(22)].

"PROMISSORY NOTE" includes a treasury bill. [Public Debt Act (18 of 1944), S. 2(4)]

"PROMISSORY NOTE" means any instrument whereby the maker engages absolutely to pay a specified sum of money to another at a time therein limited, or on demand, or at sight. [Limitation Act (36 of 1963), S. 2(k)]

A negotiable instrument promising to pay a specified sum on a specified date, to, or to the order of, a specified person.

A "promissory note" is defined to be a plain and direct acknowledgment, in writing, to pay a sum specified, at the time therein limited, to the person therein named or sufficiently indicated, or to his order or to bearer.

Promote. The use of the expression 'promote' suggests that power was conferred upon the University to encourage the study of Guajarati and Hindi and their use as media of instruction and examination. *Gujarat University* v. *Krishna*, AIR 1963 SC 703, 712. [Gujarat University Act, 1949, S. 4(27)]

The expression "promote" would not only connote publicity of the goods but also attempts and endeavours made in order to boost the sale of such goods. [*Videocon International Limited* v. *Nandakumar Naidu*, (2014) 14 SCC 337, para 19].

To contribute to the growth or enlargement [Industrial Disputes Act (14 of 1947), S. 3(2)]; [Representation of the People Act (43 of 1951), S. 125]; to advance in station, rank or honours [Cardamom Act (42 of 1965), S. 9(1)]; [Constitution of India, Art. 43]; to put forward [Indian Trusts Act (2 of 1882), S. 74].

Promoter. Means a person—

(*a*) who has been named as such in a prospectus or is identified by the company in the annual return referred to in section 92; or

(*b*) who has control over the affairs of the company, directly or indirectly whether as a shareholder, director or otherwise; or

(*c*) in accordance with whose advice, directions or instructions the Board of Directors of the company is accustomed to act:

Provided that nothing in sub-clause (*c*) shall apply to a person who is acting merely in a professional capacity. [S. 2(69) of the Companies Act, 2013 (18 of 2013)]

"PROMOTER" means a person and includes a partnership firm or a body or association of persons, whether registered or not who constructs or causes to be constructed a block or building of flats or apartments for the purpose of selling some or all of them to other persons, or to a company, cooperative society or other association of persons, and includes his assignees; and where the person who builds and the person who sells are different persons, the term includes both. [Maharashtra Ownership of Flats (Regulation of Construction, Sale Management and Transfer) Act, 1963, S. 2(c) as cited in *Esha Ekta Apartments Co-operative Housing Society Limited* v. *Municipal Corporation of Mumbai*, (2013) 5 SCC 357, para 49].

"PROMOTER" means a local authority or person in whose favour an order has been made and includes a local authority or person on whom the rights and liabilities conferred and imposed on the promoter by this Act and by the order and any rules made under this Act as to the construction, maintenance and use of the tramway, have devolved. [Indian Tramways Act (11 of 1886), S. 3(7)]

For the purpose of these guidelines—"PROMOTER" means:

(a) the person or persons who are in overall control of the company;

(b) the person or persons who are instrumental in the formation of the company or programme pursuant to which the shares were offered to the public;

(c) the person or persons named in the offer document as promoter(s);

Provided that a director or officer of the company, if he is acting as such only in his professional capacity will not be deemed to be a promoter.

Explanation.—Where a promoter of a company is a body corporate, the promoter of that body corporate shall also be deemed to be a promoter of the company. [Employees' Stock Option Scheme or Plan, 2001, S. 7, *Expln.* (v)]

"PROMOTER" means the authority, person or co-operative society, as the case may be, by which, or by whom, any multi-storeyed building has been constructed. [Delhi Apartment Ownership Act (58 of 1986), S. 2(w)]

"PROMOTER" means person or persons who take(s) part in the process of the organisation and promotion of a Co-operative Society and signs the application for registration. [Delhi Co-operative Societies Rules, 1973, R. 2(xxiv)]

"PROMOTERS" in relation to a lottery includes an organiser or any person having contract of a lottery. [M.P. Lottery Pratibandh Act, 1993 (8 of 1993), S. 2(c)]

(*of a company*) A person who employs himself in the preliminary work necessary to the flotation of a company.

In criminal law, the person who encourages or incites the commission of a crime.

Promoter group. For the purpose of these guidelines—

"PROMOTER GROUP" means:

(a) an immediate relative of the promoter (*i.e.*, spouse of that person, or any parent, brother, sister or child of the person or of the spouse);

(b) persons whose shareholding is aggregated for the purpose of disclosing in the offer document "shareholding of the promoter group". [Employees' Stock Option Plan or Scheme, 2001, S. 7, *Expln* (vi)]

Promotion. "PROMOTION" means to employ directly or indirectly any method of encouraging any person to purchase or use infant milk substitute, feeding bottle or infant food. [Infant Milk Substitutes, Feeding Bottles and Infant Food (Regulation of Production, Supply and Distribution) Act (38 of 2003), S. 2(j)]

"PROMOTION". A 'promotion' involves going to a higher grade. *State of Kerala* v. *P. V. Neelakandan Nair*, AIR 2005 SC 3066 : 2005 AIR SCW 3489.

Promotion money. Money paid to the promoters of a joint stock company, for their services in launching the concern.

Prompt. "Prompt", is convertible with "at once" and in its ordinary acceptation means at the same point of time; immediately; without delay; at one and the same time; simultaneously; directly.

Promulgate. The word 'promulgate' means to make known by public declaration; to publish; to disseminate or to proclaim. In essence the word connotes two ideas: (1) making known of an order, and (2) the means by which the order is made known must be by something done openly and in public. Private information will not be 'promulgation'. It may be by beat of drum; it may be by publication in Gazette; it may be by reading out an order openly in public. *State* v. *Tugla,* AIR 1955 All 423, 431. [CrPC 1973 (2 of 1974), S. 145]

(1) To declare or announce publicly; to proclaim. (2) To put (a law decree) into force or effect. (3) (Of an administrative agency) to carry out the formal process of rule making by publishing the proposed regulation, inviting public comments, and approving or rejecting the proposal. [Black's Law Dictionary (9th Edition 2009) as cited in *Presiding Officer, Court of Inquiry* v. *Sunil Issar*, (2013) 11 SCC 659, para 20].

When an order is notified, or is published by beat of drum or in a gazette or by reading it in open to public, the order can be said to be promulgated. *Nandlal Mitra* v. *State,* AIR 1968 Cal 523, 524. [IPC (45 of 1860), S. 188]

Promulgated. When a judgment or order is passed in open Court, it constitutes a formal declaration to the public of the decision of the Court in the case in which the order is given or the judgment is passed. *Ezaz Ahmad* v. *Kunwar Maheshwar Bakhsh Singh,* AIR 1953 All 257.

'PROMULGATED' means a public declaration by an authority that a certain order had been made with respect to certain property. *Ram Samugh* v. *State of U.P.,* AIR 1967 All 579, 580. [IPC (45 of 1860), SS. 188 and 474]

Promulgation. Promulgation is a word used to express the act of a state by which the existence of new laws is brought to the knowledge of a nation. In most countries laws are promulgated by publication in the official gazette of the State.

"Promulgation" means 'to make public or make widely known by act of final proclamation. [Oxford Advanced Dictionary as cited in *Presiding Officer, Court of Inquiry* v. *Sunil Issar* , (2013) 11 SCC 659, para 20].

In regard to the necessity of a railway company formulating and promulgating rules, "promulgate" means to make known; that the rules shall be brought to the attention of the service affected thereby, or that it be given such publicity as that the sevant, in the proper discharge of his duties, is bound to take notice of it.

The official publication of a new law, ordinance *etc.* [IPC (45 of 1860), S. 271].

Pronounce. "Pronounce" means to utter formally, officially or solemnly; to declare or affirm; as, pronounce a judgment or order.

To utter, declare or deliver (A sentence or statement) formally or solemnly. [CPC (5 of 1908), S. 33].

PRONOUNCING A JUDGMENT within the meaning of O. XX, CPC (5 of 1908) does not require a reading out of the whole judgment by the Court.

Pronounce judgement. The expression 'pronounce judgment' occurring in Section 17 of the Act would itself indicate judicial determination by reasoned order for arriving at the conclusion that the decree in terms of award be passed. *Union of India* v. *Manager, Jain and Associates*, AIR 2001 SC 809 : (2001) 3 SCC 277, 284, para 12. [Arbitration Act (10 of 1940), S. 17]

Pronouncement of talaq. A plea of previous divorce taken in the written statement by the husband cannot be treated as 'pronouncement of *talaq*' by him on the wife on the date of filing of written statement in the Court followed by delivery of copy thereof to the wife. *Shamim Ara* v. *State of U.P.,* (2002) 7 SCC 518, para 16.

Proof. "Proof" is merely that quantity of evidence which produces a reasonable assurance of the existence of the ultimate fact.

The word "proof" seems properly to mean anything which serves, either immediately or mediately, to convince the mind of the truth or falsehood of a fact or proposition; and as truths differ, the proofs adapted to them differ also. 'Proof' is also applied to the conviction generated in the mind by proof properly so called.

Anything which serves either immediately or mediately to convince the mind of the truth or falsehood of a fact or proposition [IPC (45 of 1860), S. 51]; an impression taken for correction (in printing).

PROOF AND EVIDENCE. Evidence is the medium of proof. Proof is the effect of evidence.

Proof beyond reasonable doubt. A reasonable doubt does not mean some light, airy, insubstantial doubt that may flit through the minds of any of us about almost anything at some time or other; it does not mean a doubt begotten by sympathy out of reluctance to convict; it means a real doubt, a doubt founded upon reasons. (*K. Gopal Reddy* v. *State of A.P.*, AIR 1979 SC 387)

The concepts of probability, and the degree of it, cannot obviously be expressed in terms of units to be mathematically enumerated as to how many of such units constitute proof beyond reasonable doubt. There is an unmistakable subjective element in the evaluation of the degrees of probability and the quantum of proof. Forensic probability must, in the last analysis, rest on a robust common sense and, intimately, on the trained intuitions of the Judge. *Krishnan* v. *State*, (2003) 7 SCC 56, *See also Ramakant Rai* v. *Madan Rai*, JT (2003) Supp 2 SCC 344 : AIR 2004 SC 77.

The concepts of probability, and the degrees of it, cannot obviously be expressed in terms of units to be mathematically enumerated as to how many of such units would constitute 'proof of beyond reasonable doubt'. There is an unmistakable subjective element in the evaluation of the degrees of probabilities and the quantum of proof. [*State of M.P.* v. *Dharkole,* (2004) 13 SCC 308, 313, para 12]

Proof of age. The age of a person may be proved by direct evidence, such as the testimony of someone present at the person's birth, and in some cases from his appearance. It is usually proved by producing a birth certificate, under the exception to the hearsay rule relating to statements in public documents, and evidence that the person in question is the one referred to in the birth certificate. (*Oxford Law Dictionary 5th Edn., 2003*)

Proof of handwriting. Handwriting may be proved by the testimony of the person whose handwriting it is or by that of someone who saw him execute the document in question. It may also be proved by the opinion of someone familiar with the handwriting of the alleged writer or by comparison with a proved example of the writer's handwriting. Expert testimony is also admissible. (*Oxford Law Dictionary 5th Edn., 2003*)

Propagate. The word 'propagate' means to transmit or spread one's religion by an exposition of its tenets. *Rev. Stainislans* v. *State of M.P.*, AIR 1977 SC 908, 911. [Constitution of India, Art. 25(1)]

Propeller. A mechanical device having one or more blades which when rotated about a central shaft produce a forward thrust due to the aerodynamic forces acting upon them. [Air Corporations Act (27 of 1953), Sch., para 11(f)].

Proper. Fit; apt; suitable [Indian Partnership Act (9 of 1932), S. 13(e)(i)]; appropriate.

Proper authority. "PROPER AUTHORITY" means the authority appointed by, or under the law of, a reciprocating territory to receive and transmit documents to which that Act applies. [Maintenance Orders Enforcement Act (18 of 1921), S. 2].

Proper channel. Proper course for anything to move outward. [CPC (5 of 1908), O. XXVII, R. 5].

Proper Court. The term "proper Court" means not merely a duly constituted tribunal, but one having authority over the subject-matter of the particular case in question.

Proper custody. Infants are said to be in the "proper custody" if they are in the place in which, and under the care of the person with whom, they should naturally be.

Proper form. The form in which anything can or ought to be done. [CPC (5 of 1908), O. XXXIII, R. 4(1)].

Proper indorsement. "Proper indorsement", as used with reference to an indorsement on a negotiable instrument, means such an indorsement as the law requires in order to authorise payment to the holder.

Proper instrument. 'Proper instrument' means an instrument which complies with all the formalities required by the Companies Act including the stamp duty required to be affixed. [Companies Act (1 of 1956), S. 108]

Proper law of contract. The expression 'proper law of a contract' refers to the legal system by which the parties to the contract intended their contract to be governed. If their intention is expressly stated or if it can be clearly inferred from the contract itself or its surrounding circumstances, such intention determines the proper law of the contract. *National Thermal Power Corpn.* v. *Singer Company,* (1992) 3 SCC 551, 560.

Proper notice. The expression 'proper notice' under Section 34(2) of the Act means 'sufficient notice'. [*SJP Motors* v. *TVS Motors Company Ltd.*, AIR 2009 (NOC) 311 (Ker.)]. [Arbitration and Conciliation Act (26 of 1996), S. 34(2)]

Proper officer. "Proper officer" in relation to any function to be performed under this Act, means the Commissioner or the officer of the central tax who is assigned that function by the Commissioner in the Board [The Central Goods and Services Tax Act, 2017 (12 of 2017), S. 2(91)]

Proper party. Proper parties are those without whom a substantial decree may be made, but not a decree which shall completely settle all the questions which may be involved in the controversy, and conclude the rights of all the persons who have any interest in the subject-matter of the litigation.

A proper party is a person whose presence would enable the court to completely, effectively and properly adjudicate upon all matters and issues, though he may not be a person in favour of or against whom a decree is to be made. [*Vidur Implex and Traders Private Limited* v. *Tosh Apartments Private Limited,* (2012) 8 SCC 384, para 41.3]

Proper return port. Means, in relation to a master, seaman or apprentice discharged or left behind, the port at which the master, seaman or apprentice was engaged, or the port agreed to as such by the master, seaman or apprentice, as the case may be. [Merchant Shipping Act (44 of 1958), S. 3(33)]

Proper time. S. 108 of the T.P. Act (4 of 1882) imposes an obligation on the tenant to pay and tender at the 'proper time and place' the rent to the landlord or to the landlord's agent. The expression 'proper time' appearing in this section means the time which has been fixed by the terms of the agreement or where there is no agreement or where the agreement is silent in regard to the time of payment, the time which has been orally agreed upon between the parties. When there is no written or oral agreement, the rent becomes payable at the end of the period for which it is reserved.

The time at which anything can and ought to be done. [T.P. Act (4 of 1882), S. 55(1)(d)].

Properly incurred. The words "*properly incurred*" in S. 90 of the Indian Trusts Act (2 of 1882) mean reasonably and suitably incurred.

Brought upon oneself in the due execution of the office or in the interest of the estate one holds. [T.P. Act (4 of 1882), S. 69(4)].

Property. "PROPERTY" shall include any moveable property, money or valuable security. [Police Act (5 of 1861), S. 1]

In this Chapter, unless the context otherwise requires,—"property" means property and assets of every description whether corporeal or incorporeal, movable or immovable, tangible or intangible and deeds and instruments evidencing title to, or interest in, such property or assets derived or used in the commission of an offence and includes property obtained through proceeds of crime. [(w. e. f. 1-7-2024) Bharatiya Nagarik Suraksha Sanhita, 2023 (46 of 2023)]

For the purposes of this section, "property" includes—

(a) property of any kind or document which is produced before the Court or which is in its custody;

(b) any property regarding which an offence appears to have been committed or which appears to have been used for the commission of any offence. [(w. e. f. 1-7-2024) Bharatiya Nagarik Suraksha Sanhita, 2023 (46 of 2023), section 497(1), Explanation]

"PROPERTY" includes, in the case of wife, any property to which she is entitled for an estate in remainder or reversion or as a trustee, executrix or administratrix; and the date of the death of the testator or intestate shall be deemed to be the time at which any such wife becomes entitled as executrix or administratrix. [Indian Divorce Act (4 of 1869), S. 3(10)]

"PROPERTY" includes any property over which or the profits of which any person has disposing power which he may exercise for his own benefit. [Provincial Towns Insolvency Act (5 of 1920), S. 2(*d*); Presidency Towns Insolvency Act (3 of 1909), S. 2(*e*)].

"PROPERTY" means the general property in goods, and not merely a special property. [Sale of Goods Act (3 of 1930), S. 2(11)]

"PROPERTY" means property of any kind, and includes any right or interest in such property. [Administration of Evacuee Property Act (31 of 1950), S. 2(i)]

"PROPERTY" means immovable property of any kind and includes any right in or over such property. [Requisitioning and Acquisitioning of Immovable Property (30 of 1952), S. 2(g)]

"PROPERTY" includes any interest in property, movable or immovable, the proceeds of sale thereof and any money or investment for the time being representing the proceeds of sale and also includes any property converted from species in another by any method.

Expln. 1. The creation by a person or with his consent of a debt or other right enforceable against him personally or against property which he was or might become competent to dispose of, or to charge or burden for his own benefit, shall be deemed to have been a disposition made by that person, and in relation to such a disposition the expression "property shall include the debt or right created."

Expln. 2. The extinguishment at the expense of the deceased of a debt or other right shall be deemed to have been a disposition made by the deceased in favour of the person for whose benefit the debt or right was extinguished, and in relation to such a disposition the expression "property" shall include the benefit conferred by the extinguishment of the debt or right. [Estate Duty Act (34 of 1953), S. 2(15)]

'PROPERTY' includes both movable and immovable property acquired by a female Hindu by inheritance or device, or at a partition or *in lieu* of maintenance or arrears of maintenance or by gift from any person, whether a relative or not, before, at or after her marriage or by her own skill or exertion, or by purchase or by prescription, or in any other manner whatsoever, and also any such property held by her as *stridhan* immediately before the commencement of this Act. [Hindu Succession Act (30 of 1956), S. 14(1) *Expln.*]

The expression "PROPERTY" includes any interest in property, movable or immovable, the proceeds of sale thereof and any money or investment for the time being representing the proceeds of sale thereof and where the property is converted into any other property by any method, such other property. [Wealth-tax Act (27 of 1957), S. 4, *Expln.* (c)]

"PROPERTY" includes any interest in property, movable or immovable. [Gift-tax Act (18 of 1958), S. 2(xxii)]

"PROPERTY" includes any interest in property, movable or immovable, the proceeds of sale thereof and any money or investment for the time being representing the proceeds of sale thereof and where the property is converted into any other property by any method, such other property. [Income-tax Act (43 of 1961), S. 64(2) *Expln.* 1]

"PROPERTY" means property and assets of every description, whether corporeal or incorporeal, movable or immovable, tangible or intangible and deeds and instruments evidencing title to, or interest in, such property or assets, derived from the illegal hunting and trade of wild life and its products. [Wild Life (Protection) Act (53 of 1972), S. 58B(h)]

"PROPERTY" means property and assets of every description whether corporeal or incorporeal, movable or immovable, tangible or intangible and deeds and instruments evidencing title to, or interest in, such property or assets derived or used in the commission of an offence and includes property obtained through proceeds of crime. [CrPC 1973 (2 of 1974), S. 105A(d)]

"PROPERTY" means property and assets of every description, whether corporeal or incorporeal, movable or immovable, tangible or intangible and deeds and instruments evidencing title to, or interest in, such property or assets, derived or obtained from the terrorist act and includes proceeds of terrorism. [Terrorist and Disruptive Activities (Prevention) Act (28 of 1987), S. 2(gg)]

"PROPERTY" means property of any kind, whether movable or immovable, tangible or intangible and includes any right or interest in such property. [Benami Transactions (Prohibition) Act (45 of 1988), S. 2(c)]

"PROPERTY" means property and assets of every description, whether corporeal or incorporeal, movable or immovable, tangible or intangible and deeds and instruments evidencing title to, or interest in, such property or assets and includes bank account. [Prevention of Terrorism Act (15 of 2002), S. 2(1)(d)]

"PROPERTY" means—

(i) immovable property;

(ii) movable property;

(iii) any debt or any right to receive payment of money, whether secured or unsecured;

(iv) receivables, whether existing or future;

(v) intangible assets, being know-how, patent, copyright, trade mark, licence, franchise or any other business or commercial right of similar nature. [Securitisation and Reconstruction of Financial Assets and Enforcement of Security Interest Act (54 of 2002), S. 2(1)(t)]

"PROPERTY" means any property or assets of every description, whether corporeal or incorporeal, movable or immovable, tangible or intangible and includes deeds and instruments evidencing title to, or interest in, such property or assets, wherever located. [Prevention of Money-Laundering Act (15 of 2003), S. 2(1)(v)]

"PROPERTY" means property and assets of every description, whether corporeal or incorporeal, movable or immovable, tangible or intangible and deeds and instruments evidencing title to, or interest in, such property or assets, and includes cash and bank account. [Unlawful Activities (Prevention) Act (37 of 1967), S. 2(1)(h) *as substituted by Unlawful Activities (Prevention) Amendment Act (29 of 2004), S. 4*]

'PROPERTY' includes goods, articles or things, and intangible property. [Income-Tax Rules, 1962, R. 10A(b)]

"PROPERTY" means the land, the multistoreyed building, all improvements and structures thereon, and all easements, rights and appurtenances belonging thereto, and all articles of personal property intended for use in connection therewith. [Delhi Apartments Ownership Act (58 of 1986), S. 2(x)]

Something that is or may be owned or possessed; an estate; intangible assets or intangible rights [T.P. Act (4 of 1882), S. 2(b) and Estate Duty Act (34 of 1963), S. 2(15)]; an exclusive right to possess, enjoy and dispose of; a quality or trait belonging to a person or thing.

Property has been defined as the right and interest which a man has in lands and chattels to the exclusion of others. The term "property" is a generic term of extensive application, and while strictly speaking it means only the right which a person has in relation to something, or that dominion or indefinite right of user and disposition which one may lawfully exercise over particular things or objects, it is frequently used to denote the subject of the property, or thing itself which is owned or in relation to which the right of property exists. In the former sense it extends to every species of valuable right or interest, in either real or personal property, or in easements, franchises, and incorporeal hereditaments, and in the latter to everything which is the subject of ownership, or to which the right of property may legally attach, or in other words every class of acquisitions which a man can own or have an interest in.

Property signifies every species of property. Comprehends all a man's worldly possessions.

MONEY is also property.

A *trade mark* is a species of property, which may be sold or transmitted by death, with the business in which it has been used.

Where a servant cannot sue his master for salary before it is earned, such *salary* is not "property" nor even a "debt" payable in future and as such is not liable to attachment under S. 60, CPC (5 of 1908).

The mere fact that the word 'property' is followed by words 'interest or dividend payable thereon cannot restrict its meaning only to movable property. *Kanhyalal Hanumantrao* v. *Reginald Mathaone,* AIR 1951 Nag 52. [CPC (5 of 1908), O. XXI, R. 52]

A claim for damages for breach of contract is 'property' and is capable of being vested in the transferee company. *New Central Jute Mills Co.* v. *Rivers Steam Navigation Co.,* AIR 1959 Cal 352.

The word 'property' is certainly large enough to include money. *Yusuf Maulvi* v. *Official Assignee,* AIR 1959 Mad 484, 487. [Presidency Towns Insolvency Act (3 of 1909), S. 33(4)]

The definition of the term 'property' contemplates that the power of disposition must be an unconditional power. Employees' Provident Fund is not property within this definition since the employees have no power of disposition over the same. *Trustees of the Provident Fund of the Tinplate Co. of India* v. *Muktilal Agarwal,* AIR 1951 Pat 488. [Provincial Towns Insolvency Act (5 of 1920), S. 2(d)] [Now Repealed by Act 31 of 2016]

The term 'property' is a generic term for all that a person has domain over. The word property cannot be held to be confined to the material object. The property may be owned by another but the lease-hold, mortgage or other rights over such property would also be regarded as 'property'. *In re Varikanti Aukanna,* AIR 1958 AP 120, 121, 122. [Provincial Towns Insolvency Act (5 of 1920), S. 2(d)]

The term 'property' envisaged under S. 28(5) refers to the tangible property and not to the extent the right of the insolvent therein. *Bati Mohan Lal* v. *Bakshi Ram,* AIR 1975 P&H 214, 217 (FB). [Provincial Towns Insolvency Act (5 of 1920), Ss. 28(2), 28(5) and 2(1)(d)]

PROPERTY, CORPOREAL AND INCORPOREAL. Property may be classified as being either corporeal or incorporeal, corporeal property being that which affects the senses and may be seen or handled, and incorporeal that which cannot be seen or handled, but which consists merely in legal right. The terms are used most frequently in connection with the term "hereditaments."

Property means the highest right a man can have to anything, being the right which one has to lands or tenaments, goods or chattels which does not depend on others' courtesy. It includes ownership, estates, and interests in corporeal things and also rights such as trade marks, copyrights, patents and rights in personam capable of transfer or transmission such as debts and signifies a beneficial right to or a thing considered as having money value with reference to transfer or succession and to their capacity of being injured. The expression "property" in Entry 42, List III of the Constitution includes assets, liabilities, organisations and obligations of a going concern as a unit. R. *C. Cooper* v. *Union of India*, AIR 1970 SC 564 at 591, 592. [Banking Companies (Acquisition and Transfer of Undertaking) Act (22 of 1969), S. 5]

The word 'property' should be given a liberal and a wide connotation and should be extended to those well recognised types of interest which have the insignia or characteristics of proprietory right. Both office and property and duties and personal interest of a Mahant are blended together. *Commissioner of H.R.E.* v. *Sri Lakshmindra Thirtha Swamiar of Sri Shirur Mutt*, AIR 1954 SC 282, 288.

The creditors have got the right to take the usufructs of trees till the debts are wiped out or to get back the amounts advanced by them. Such a right is property. *P.A. Syed Mohammad Koya* v. *UOI,* AIR 1972 Ker 85, 86.

The verified claim of a claimant under the Displaced Persons (claims) Act (44 of 1950), cannot possibly fall within any of the categories of "property"; it created no rights whatsoever. *Murat Singh* v. *Controller of Estate Duty,* AIR 1960 Punj 428, 430. [Estate Duty Act (34 of 1953), S. 2(15)]

The term 'property' in S. 7 of the Guardians and Wards Act (8 of 1890) is used in a generic sense. It has a wide connotation and is not restricted to the kind of property in which the minor has a beneficial enjoyment. The enjoyment is not an essential element to constitute 'property' within the purview of the Act. The word 'property' is a term of far-reaching conception. It is comprehensive enough to take in all types of proprietory rights. *Kanteti Sastrulu* v. *Madupalli Venkateswar Rao,* AIR 1959 AP 232, 233 (FB). [Guardians and Wards Act (8 of 1890), S. 7]

The term 'property' means the interest held by a Hindu widow. *Triloki Madar* v. *Dukhani Devi,* AIR 1966 Pat 259, 263. [Hindu Succession Act (30 of 1956), S. 14(1), *Expln.*]

Property acquired by a female Hindu in lieu of maintenance would be 'property acquired by her' within the meaning of Section 14. *Nanak Singh* v. *Chhindo,* AIR 1974 Punj 220. [Hindu Succession Act (30 of 1956), S.14]

Property includes realisation of the debt due to the partnership firm from a third party. *Baba Commercial Syndicate* v. *Channamasetti,* AIR 1988 AP 378 at 380. [Indian Partnership Act (9 of 1932), S. 69(3)(a)]

The word 'property' includes a chose in action. *Shivanarayan* v. *State of Maharashtra*, AIR 1980 SC 439, 441. [IPC (45 of 1860), S. 409]

A passport is property. *N. M. Chakraborty* v. *State of West Bengal*, AIR 1977 SC 1174, 1176. [Passport (Entry into India) Act (34 of 1920); S. 2, Passports Act (15 of 1967), S. 2(b)]

There is a juristic distinction between a right or legally protected interest and the '*res*' or object of that right. S. 2(11), Sale of Goods Act defines property in the sense of the right and not of the '*res*'. *State of Bihar* v. *Rameshwar Jute Mills Ltd.,* AIR 1953 Pat 236. [Sale of Goods Act (3 of 1930), S. 2(11)]

The word 'property' is used in S. 2(17) of the Indian Stamp Act (2 of 1899) in its widest and most generic legal sense, and embraces every kind of property whether movable or immovable. Actionable claim must be regarded as movable property.

When a Legislature with limited and restricted powers makes use of a word of such wide and general import as "property" the presumption must be that it is using it with reference to that kind of property with respect to which it is competent to legislate, and to no other.

"PROPERTY" for the removal of doubts, it is hereby clarified that 'property' includes and shall be deemed to have always included any rights in or in relation to an Indian company, including rights of management or control or any other rights whatsoever. [*Explanation* to section 2(14) of the Income-tax Act, 1961 (43 of 1961) as inserted (w.r.e.f. 1-4-1962) by the Finance Act, 2012 (23 of 2012)]

"PROPERTY" means,—

(*i*) the immovable property;

(*ii*) the movable property;

(*iii*) any debt or any right to receive payment of money, whether secured or unsecured;

(*iv*) the receivables;

(*v*) the intangible assets, being know-how, patent, copyright, design, trade mark, licence, franchise or any other business or commercial right of similar nature. [S. 2(o) of the Factoring Regulation Act, 2011 (12 of 2012)]

Property claim. Means any claim other than a personal claim arising from an occurrence. [Merchant Shipping Act (44 of 1958), S. 352(g)]

Property derived from the deceased. Means any property which was the subject-matter of a disposition made by the deceased, either by himself alone or in concert or by arrangement with other person, notwithstanding that the disposition was made for full consideration in money or money's worth paid to him for his own use or benefit, or which represented any of the subject-matter of such a disposition, whether directly or indirectly, and whether by virtue of one or more intermediate dispositions and whether any such intermediate disposition was or was not for full or partial consideration:

Provided that where the first mentioned disposition was for full consideration in money or money's worth paid to the deceased for his own use or benefit and is proved to the satisfaction of the Controller that the disposition was not part of associated operations which included—

(a) a disposition by the deceased, either by himself alone or in concert or by arrangement with any other person, otherwise than for full consideration in money or money's worth paid to the deceased for his own benefit, or

(b) a disposition by any other person operating to reduce the value of the property of the deceased; then, in considering whether estate duty should be charged the said first mentioned disposition shall be left out of account as if this provision did not apply in relation to it;

(c) "disposition" includes any trust, covenant, agreement or arrangement; and

(d) "subject matter" includes, in relation to any disposition, any annual or periodical payment made or payable under or by virtue of the disposition. [Estate Duty Act (34 of 1953), S. 16(2)]

Property in possession. When property is in the possession of a person's wife, clerk or servant, on account of that person, it is in that person's possession within the meaning of the IPC (45 of 1860), S. 27.

Property, Common. Property belonging to more than one person in common [T.P. Act (4 of 1882), S. 47].

Property mark. "A mark used for denoting that movable property belongs to a particular person is called a property mark." [IPC (45 of 1860), S. 479] (w. e. f. 1-7-2024) repealed and replaced by Bharatiya Nyaya Sanhita, 2023 (45 of 2023), S. 345(1)]

Property passing on death. "PROPERTY PASSING ON THE DEATH" includes property passing either immediately on the death or after any interval, either certainly or contingently, and either originally or by way of substitutive, limitation, and "on the death" includes "at a period ascertainable only by reference to the death. [Estate Duty Act (34 of 1953), S. 2(16)]

Share of a goodwill of a deceased partner in the assets of a firm passes on his death under the Estate Duty Act. *State* v. *Prem Nath,* AIR 1977 P&H 62, 75 (FB). [Estate Duty Act (34 of 1953), Ss. 2(16) and 5]

Property right. Any right to property real or personal, tangible or intangible.

Property specifically decreed. Property given under the decree and which has been exactly or precisely indicated. [CPC (5 of 1908), S. 51(a)].

Property Tax. "Property tax" means a tax simpliciter requiring no service at all and not in the nature of fee requiring service. [Karnataka Municipal Corporation Act (Karnataka Act 14 of 1976), S. 28B(2) Explanation as cited in *Bangalore Development Authority* v. *Aircraft Employees' Co-operative Society Limited*, (2012) 3 SCC 442, para 10].

Property which is not ordinary article of commerce. The expression does not contemplate an article manufactured or prepared at the instance or specification of a contracting party but means certain rare things which could not be produced or manufactured even at the specification or behest of the party. *Maheswari & Co. P. Ltd.* v. *The Corporation of Calcutta,* AIR 1975 Cal 165, 169. [Specific Relief Acts (47 of 1963), S. 10]

Prophylactic. (Medi.) Done or used as preventive against disease. Formulated to prevent something.

Guarding from or preventing the spread or occurrence of disease or infection". [Merriam-Webster's Medical Desk Dictionary, 579 (1993) as cited in *Commissioner of Central Excise* v. *Wockhardt Life Science Limited*, (2012) 5 SCC 585, para 19].

A biologic, chemical or mechanical agent that prevents the spread of disease. [Mosby's Dictionary, 1284 (4th Edn., 1994) as cited in *Commissioner of Central Excise* v. *Wockhardt Life Science Limited*, (2012) 5 SCC 585, para 19].

The word "prophylactic" derive from the Greek word "prophylactic" which means "to take precaution against" or "to keep guard before". [*Commissioner of Central Excise* v. *Wockhardt Life Sciences Limited*, (2012) 5 SCC 585, para 19].

Propinquity. Nearness of relationship. [Indian Succession Act (39 of 1925), S. 54(d)].

Proponent. The party who bears the evidential, and in some cases the persuasive, burden of proof in relation to an issue in litigation.

Proportion. The term "proportion" is synonymous with "*pro rata*".

The relation of one part to another or to the whole with respect to magnitude, quality or degree; ratio; a portion of share, of an actual or implied whole having a size or value relative to other portions or shares. [T.P. Act (4 of 1882), S. 45].

Proportional. Having or being in proportion. [IPC (45 of 1860), S. 69].

Proportional representation. Proportional representation system gives a choice to each elector of as many preferences as there are candidates in the field. *Surendra Pal* v. *Shamin Ahmad,* AIR 1985 Del 22, 28. [Representation of the People Act (43 of 1950), S. 27 H]

Proportionality. The principle that the use of force should be in proportion to the threat or grievance provoking the use of force and the punishment in proportion to the offence.

Jurisprudentially, "proportionality" can be defined as the set of rules determining the necessary and sufficient conditions for limitation of a constitutionally protected right by a law to be constitutionally permissible. [*Modern Dental College and Research Centre* v. *State of M.P.*, (2016) 7 SCC 353, para 60].

Proportionate. Being in proportion; proportionally adjusted. [T.P. Act (4 of 1882), S. 60].

Proportionately. In proportion. [Indian Contract Act (9 of 1872), S. 61]; [T.P. Act (4 of 1882), S. 47].

Proposal. "When one person signifies to another his willingness to do or to abstain from doing anything, with a view to obtaining the assent of that other to such act or abstinence, he is said to make a proposal." [Indian Contract Act (9 of 1872), S. 2(a)].

PROPOSAL. The expression "proposal" is defined as "an action of stating or propounding something"; "a course of action etc. proposed; a scheme, a plan, a motion; a suggestion, an idea". [Shorter Oxford English Dictionary as cited in *Suresh Sharma* v. *NTRO,* W.P.(C) 3937, 3948 and 3950/2017, decided on 18-8-2017, para 23]

Something put forward for consideration or acceptance.

"PROPOSAL" may mean an offer, as of marriage; an introduction; and it may also mean an expression of intention or design; and a statement in a letter that "I propose to settle" is the same as "I intend or mean to settle".

Proposal form. "PROPOSAL FORM" means a form to be filled in by the proposer for insurance, for furnishing all materials information required by the insurer in respect of a risk, in order to enable the insurer to decide whether to accept or decline, to undertake the risk, and in the event of acceptance of the risk, to determine the rates, terms and conditions of a cover to be granted.

Explanation.—"Material" for the purpose of these regulations shall mean and include all important, essential and relevant information in the context of underwriting the risk to be covered by the insurer. [IRDA (Protection of Policy Holders' Interest) Regulations, 2002, Regn. 2(1)(d)]

Propose. To "propose" is defined to be "to offer, as a plan or scheme; to put or hold before one's mind, as a design or determination; to form, as a purpose".

To lay before another or others as something which one offers to do or wishes to be done. [Indian Contract Act (9 of 1872), S. 4, ill. (a)]; [Indian Partnership Act (9 of 1932), S. 58(1)].

'Proposed to be listed' shall include securities of an unlisted company:

(i) if such unlisted company has filed offer documents or other documents, as the case may be, with the Board, stock exchange(s) or registrar of companies in connection with the listing; or

(ii) if such unlisted company is getting listed pursuant to any merger or amalgamation and has filed a copy of such scheme of merger or amalgamation under the Companies Act, 2013 [Securities and Exchange Board of India (Prohibition of Insider Trading) Regulation, 2015, Regn. 2(1)(ha)].

Proposition. A proposition does not become a contract until the maker or his agent is notified of its acceptance.

That which is propounded. [CPC (5 of 1908), O. XIV, R. 1(1)].

Propound. To offer for consideration, deliberation or debate. [CPC (5 of 1908), Sch. I, App. A, form No. 49(15)(6)].

Proprietary. 'Proprietary,' means belonging to; ownership; as proprietary rights; belonging or pertaining to a proprietor. 'Proprietor' is defined as one who has the legal right or exclusive title to anything, whether in possession or not; an owner.

Relating to property. [Indian Evidence Act (1 of 1872), S. 18(1)].

Proprietary company. Parent company holding lands or mining rights parts of which it sells or leases to others.

Proprietary estoppel. Where the requirements of proprietary estoppel are satisfied, the landowner is precluded from denying the existence of the rights in question, and may indeed be compelled to grant them. Because the estoppel precludes him from denying the existence of rights in property, it has come to be known as 'proprietary estoppel. (*Greasley* v. *Cooke*, (1980) 1 WLR 1306, 1311]

Proprietary interest. Any right, title *etc.* which one has by virtue of his being the holder of any kind of property or estate. [Indian Evidence Act (1 of 1872), S. 18(1)].

Proprietary right. (*In Hindu Law*) There are seven lawful modes of acquiring property, or proprietary rights, *viz.* inheritance, finding or friendly donation, purchase, conquest, lending at interest, the performance of work and the acceptance of gifts from virtuous men.

Proprietor. One who has exclusive right or title to the use or disposal of a thing; an owner. [CPC (5 of 1908), O. XXXIX, R. 9; Constitution of India, Art. 31A(2)(b)].

An owner is the person who has the legal right or exclusive title to anything, whether in possession or not.

The term 'proprietor' has a well-defined meaning, and, according to lexicographers, means 'one who has the legal right or exclusive title to anything, whether in possession or not; an owner; as the proprietor of a farm or mill'.

Proprietor, Landed. An owner of land. [Indian Contract Act (9 of 1872), S. 23, ill. (g)].

Proprietor of a new and original design. (*a*) where the author of the design, for good consideration, executes the work for some other person, means the person for whom the design is so executed; and (*b*) where any person acquires the design or the right to apply the design to any article, either exclusively of any other person or otherwise, means, in the respect and to the extent in and to which the design or right has been so acquired, the person by whom the design or right is so acquired; and (*c*) in any other case, means the author of the design; and where the property in, or the right to apply, the design has devolved from the original proprietor upon any other person, includes that other person. [Patents and Designs Act (2 of 1911), S. 2(14)]

Propriety. Fitness; suitability; conformity with requirement, rule or principle. [CPC (5 of 1908), O. XI, R. 3].

"Propriety" means "fitness; appropriateness; aptitude; suitability; appropriateness to the circumstances or conditions; conformity with requirement, rule or principle; rightness, correctness, justness, accuracy". [Oxford English Dictionary (Vol. III) as cited in *Hindustan Petroleum Corporation Limited* v. *Dilbahar Singh*, (2014) 9 SCC 78, para 16]

Proprietary and novel food. Means an article of food for which standards have not been specified but is not unsafe:

Provided that such food does not contain any of the foods and ingredients prohibited under this Act and regulations made thereunder. [*Explanation* (4) to S. 22 of the Food Safety & Standards Act, 2006 (34 of 2006)]

Proprio vigore. (*Lat.*) By its own force; by its intrinsic meaning.

Prorate. To divide or distribute proportionality.

Prorogation. The act of bringing a session of Parliament or other legislative assembly to an end.

'Prorogation' and 'Adjournment'. A 'prorogation' terminates a session; an 'adjournment' is an interruption in the course of one and the same session. [*May's Parliamentary Practice*, **as cited in** *Gujarat Assembly Election Matter, Election Commission,* (2002) 8 SCC 237, para 142]

Prorogue : Adjourn. Prorogue, from the Latin *prorogo*, signifies to put off, and is used in the general sense of deferring for an indefinite period.

Adjourn, signifies only to put off for a day, or some short period; the former is applied to national assemblies only; the latter is applicable to any meeting or sitting of Court.

Proscription. A prohibition or restriction.

Prosecute. To institute legal proceedings against (a person) for some offence [CPC (5 of 1908), S. 85(1)]; to follow onwards or pursue in order to reach or accomplish.

The expression "prosecuting" is generally applicable to proceedings by a person as a plaintiff or an applicant, and not to proceedings in which such person is merely resisting, as a defendant or respondent, the claim of another.

Prosecution. "PROSECUTION", in relation to a course of study, includes promotion from one part or stage of the course of study to another part or stage of the course of study. [University Grants Commission Act (3 of 1956), S. 12A(c)]

"Prosecution" means "a criminal action; a proceeding instituted and carried on by due course of law, before a competent tribunal, for the purpose of determining the guilt or innocence of a person charged with crime". [Black's Law Dictionary, 5th Edn as cited in *Dashrath Rupsingh Rathod* v. *State of Maharashtra*, (2014) 9 SCC 129, para 16.1].

"Prosecution" means a criminal action before a court of law for the purpose of determining "guilt" or "innocence" of a person charged with a crime. [*General Officer Commanding Rashtriya Rifles* v. *Central Bureau of Investigation*, (2012) 6 SCC 228, para 28].

Prosecution is the institution or commencement of a criminal proceeding the process of exhibiting formal charges against an offender before a legal tribunal, and pursuing them to final judgment on behalf of the state or government or by indictment or information. A prosecution exists until terminated in the final judgment of the Court, to write the sentence, discharge or acquittal.

The institution and carrying on of the legal proceedings against a person [CrPC 1973 (2 of 1974), S. 198]; the party by whom criminal proceedings are instituted or conducted; the act of prosecuting in any sense.

The word 'prosecution' in Art. 20(2), Constitution of India means judicial proceedings before a Court or a legal tribunal. It cannot have reference to departmental or disciplinary proceedings taken for inflicting departmental penalty or punishment on an officer belonging to the department for any misconduct. *Suresh Chandra* v. *Himangshu Kumar Roy,* AIR 1953 Cal 316, 319.

"PROSECUTION" AND "ACTION." The term "*prosecution*" is now used as signifying the procedure for obtaining the adjudication of a Court of Justice with respect to acts and omissions punishable by criminal or penal sanction; as "*action*" or suit describes the procedure for obtaining civil remedies for the alleged infraction of civil rights.

Prosecution and punishment. The words 'prosecution and punishment' in Art. 20(2) Constitution of India have reference to criminal offences and have the effect of limiting the scope of the article to criminal proceedings before a Court of law or judicial tribunal competent to deal with criminal cases. AIR 1953 Cal 316 **relied on.** *Raj Narain Singh* v. *Atmaram Govind,* AIR 1954 All 319, 334.

Prosecution of common object. Carrying out of common object. [IPC (45 of 1860), Ss. 146 and 149].

Prosecution witness. A witness appearing on behalf of the prosecution side. [CrPC 1973 (2 of 1974), S. 204(2)].

Prosecutor. One who institutes and carries on proceedings in a Court of law especially in a criminal Court. [CrPC 1973 (2 of 1974), S. 216(3) and IPC (45 of 1860), S. 486(b)].

To prosecute is to set the law in motion and the law is only set in motion by an appeal to some person clothed with judicial authority in regard to the matter in question. The gist of the action for malicious prosecution is that the defendant set the magistrate in motion. The answer to the question who is the "prosecutor" must depend upon the whole circumstances of the case. Where the defendant made a report to a Sub-Inspector of Police against the plaintiff and on his not taking any action moved the Superintendent of Police to direct the Sub-Inspector of Police to make an investigation and to prosecute the plaintiff, and eventually a *challan* was filed against the plaintiff under S. 454, IPC (45 of 1860), *held*, that the plaintiff was prosecuted by the defendant.

Prosecutrix. A woman who institutes and carries on proceedings in a Court of law especially in a criminal Court. [Indian Evidence Act (1 of 1872), S. 155(4)].

Prospect. "PROSPECT" means any party that enters or proposes to enter into an insurance contract directly, or through an insurance intermediary. [Insurance Regulatory and Development Authority (Insurance Advertisement and Disclosure) Regulations, Regn. 2(e)]

Prospecting. Searching for minerals with a view of further operations; making a search or investigation. [Oil Industry (Development) Act (47 of 1974), S. 2(k)].

Prospecting licence. Means licence granted for the purpose of undertaking prospecting operations. [Mines and Minerals (Regulation and Development) Act (67 of 1957), S. 3(g)]

"Prospecting licence-cum-mining lease" means a two stage concession granted for the purpose of undertaking prospecting operations followed by mining operations. [Mines and Minerals (Development and Regulation) Act (67 of 1957), S. 3(ga) as inserted by Amending Act (10 of 2015)].

Prospecting operations. Means any operations undertaken for the purpose of exploring, locating or proving mineral deposits. [Mines and Minerals (Development and Regulation) Act (67 of 1957), S. 3(h)]

Prospecting stage. The stage at which the actual operations have not started but exploratory investigation and tests are going on. [Payment of Bonus Act (21 of 1965), S. 16, *Expln.* III].

Prospective. Effective or operative in future.

Prospective overruling. The doctrine of "prospective overruling" has been borrowed from American Jurisprudence. The parameters of the power as far as this country is concerned were sought to be laid down in *Golak Nath* v. *State of Punjab*, AIR 1967 SC 1643: (1967) 2 SCR 762 itself when it was said, that as the Court for the first time was called upon to the apply the doctrine of prospective overruling evolved in a different country under different circumstances, the Court said laid down the following propositions:

(1) that doctrine of prospective overruling can be invoked only in matters arising under the Constitution of India.

(2) it can be applied only is the Supreme Court of India as it has the Constitutional jurisdiction to declare law binding on all the Courts of India.

(3) the scope of the retroactive operation of the law declared by the Supreme Court of India superseding its earlier decision is left to its discretion to be moulded in accordance with the justice of the cause or matter before it.

The expression 'prospective overruling' implies an earlier judicial decision on the same issue which was otherwise final. *Somaiya Organics (India) Ltd.* v. *State of U.P.,* (2001) 5 SCC 519, para 24 : AIR 2001 SC 1723.

'Prospective overruling' takes several different forms. In its simplest form 'prospective overruling' involves a Court giving a ruling of the character sought by the bank in the present case. Overruling of this simple or pure type has the effect that the Court ruling has an exclusively prospective effect. The ruling applies only to transactions or happenings occurring after the date of Court decision. [*National Westminster Bank Plc.* v. *Spectrum Plus Ltd.,* (2005) UKH2 41: (2005) 3 WLR 58, **relied on.** *P.V. George* v. *State of Kerala,* (2007) 3 SCC 557, 566-67, para 22]

Prospective purchaser. "Prospective purchaser" means a man who is ready to purchase, who is willing to purchase, subject to contract, and who has the necessary financial means to carry the purchase into effect.

Prospectively. Being operative with regard to the future. [T.P. Act (4 of 1882), S. 1].

Prospects. Expectation for something to come. [Representation of the People Act (43 of 1951), S. 123(3)].

Prospectus. Means any document described or issued as a prospectus and includes a red herring prospectus referred to in section 32 or shelf prospectus referred to in section 31 or any notice, circular, advertisement or other document inviting offers from the public for the subscription or purchase of any securities of a body corporate. [S. 2(70) of the Companies Act, 2013 (18 of 2013)]

"PROSPECTUS" means any prospectus, notice, circular, advertisement or other invitation, offering to the public for subscription or purchase of any shares or debentures of a company. [Companies Act (7 of 1911), S. 2(14)]

The outline of any plan submitted for public approval of a joint stock company [Industrial Finance Corporation Act (15 of 1948) *Repealed by Act 23 of 1993, S.* 41(2)]; [Companies Act (1 of 1956), S. 2(22)]; an account of the organisation of a school, college *etc.*

A document containing a statement of the property, business, undertaking, enterprise or project for the formation and development of a company for which an appeal is made to the public to subscribe for shares.

The school or college which issues a prospectus gives complete information about itself in it. The prospectus is the instrument through which the school or college 'holds out', its contents or 'represents' to the general public interested.

'PROSPECTUS' includes any publication, whether in print or otherwise, issued for providing fair and transparent information, relating to a higher educational institution and programmes, to the general public (including to those seeking admission in such Higher Educational Institutions) by the management of such Higher Educational Institutions or any authority or person authorized by such Higher Educational Institutions to do so. [University Grants Commission (Open and Distance Learning) Regulations, 2017, Reng. 2(q)].

Prosperous. Having continuous success or good fortune; flourishing. [T.P. Act (4 of 1882), S. 127, ill. (a)].

Prostitute. A female who offers her body for promiscuous sexual intercourse for hire, whether in money or in kind. [Immoral Traffic (Prevention) Act (104 of 1956), S. 2(e) omitted by Act 46 of 1978 (w.e.f. 2-10-1979)].

A woman is not a prostitute who indulges in illicit sexual intercourse with only one man; hence a man cannot be guilty of enticing a female away from her home for the purpose of prostitution, where the proof shows that he enticed her away for the purpose of having intercourse with her himself and not to induce her to have intercourse indiscriminately with other men. The most usual motive for indiscriminate sexual intercourse being the money paid therefor, prostitution is sometimes defined to be indiscriminate sexual commerce for gain. If, however, a woman submits to indiscriminate sexual intercourse, which she invites or solicits by word or act or any device, and without profit, she is as much a prostitute as one who does so solely for hire. Her vocation may be known from the manner in which she plies it, and not from the pecuniary charges and compensation gained.

PUBLIC PROSTITUTE. A *public prostitute* is a woman who is a prostitute by profession and whose trade is to let out her body on hire to all visitors or to all visitors of a specified class. When a woman rests content with one lover for years though she may have changed her lovers at intervals of some years, she is not a public prostitute.

Prostitution. "PROSTITUTION" means the sexual exploitation or abuse of persons for commercial purpose and the expression "prostitute" shall be constructed accordingly. [Immoral Traffic (Prevention) Act (104 of 1956), S. 2(f)]

The act of a female offering her body for promiscuous sexual intercourse for hire, whether in money or in kind. [Immoral Traffic (Prevention) Act (104 of 1956), S. 2(f) and IPC (45 of 1860), S. 372].

Protect. The word 'protect' means to cover, shield, or defend from injury, harm, or danger of any kind.

To defend or guard from injury or danger; to shield; to keep safe; take care of; to extend patronage to [Indian Evidence Act (1 of 1872), S. 126]; [Constitution of India, Art. 60]; [Indian Partnership Act (9 of 1932), S. 13(e)(ii) and Constitution of India, Art. 46].

Protected area. "PROTECTED AREA" means a geographically defined area which is designated or regulated and managed to achieve specific conservation objectives. [Convention on Biological Diversity, June 5, 1992, 31 ILM 818 (1992), Art. 2]

Protected activity. Includes reasonable opposition to a practice believed to violate sexual harassment laws on behalf of oneself or others such as participation in sexual harassment proceedings, cooperating with an internal investigation or alleged sexual harassment practices or acting as a witness in an investigation by an outside agency or in litigation. [All India Council for Technical Education (Gender Sensitization, Prevention and Prohibition of Sexual Harassment of Women Employees and Students and Redressal of Grievances in Technical Educational Institutions) Regulations, 2016, Regn. 2(j)].

Protected internee. Means a person protected by the Fourth Convention and interned in India. [Geneva Conventions Act (6 of 1960), S. 2(c)]

Protected monument. Means an ancient monument which is declared to be of national importance by or under this Act. [Ancient Monuments and Archaeological Sites and Remains Act (24 of 1958), S. 2(j)]

Protected prisoner of war. Means a person protected by the Third Convention. [Geneva Conventions Act (6 of 1960), S. 2(e)]

Protecting power. "PROTECTING POWER", in relation to a protected internee or a protected prisoner of war, means the power of organisation which is carrying out, in the interests of the power of which he is a national or of whose forces he is or was at any material time a member, the duties assigned to protecting power under the Third Convention or, as the case may be, the Fourth Convention. [Geneva Conventions Act (6 of 1960), S. 2(d)]

Protection. "PROTECTION" means the utilization of any weight or measure, or any reading obtained with the help of any weight or measure, for the purpose of determining whether or not any step is required to be taken to safeguard the well-being of any human being or animal, or to protect any commodity, vegetation or thing, whether individually or collectively. [Standards of Weight & Measures (Enforcement) Act (54 of 1985), S. 3(j)]

Immunity from prosecution granted to some class of persons such as public officers acting in discharge of their official duties [Industrial Finance Corporation Act (15 of 1948), S. 38A]; saving from danger of harm [Children Act (60 of 1960) (*repealed*), preamble and Constitution of India, Art. 20, margin]; [IPC (45 of 1860), S. 99].

Protection money. The expression 'protection money' relating to criminal world, means the money paid by businessman, land developers, persons carrying illegal activities in gambling dens, drug traffickers *etc.*, to the gangsters for resolving the disputes according to their will. *State of Maharashtra* v. *Bharat Ghaganlal Raghani,* (2001) 9 SCC 1, para 2.

Protection Officer. Means an officer appointed by the State Government under section 8(1) of Act 43 of 2005. [S. 2(n) of the Protection of Women from Domestic Violence Act, 2005 (43 of 2005)]

Protection order. Means an order made in terms of section 18 of Act 43 of 2005. [S. 2(o) of the Protection of Women from Domestic Violence Act, 2005 (43 of 2005)]

Section 18 of Act 43 of 2005:

The Magistrate may, after giving the aggrieved person and the respondent an opportunity of being heard and on being *prima facie* satisfied that domestic violence has taken place or is likely to take place, pass a protection order in favour of the aggrieved person and prohibit the respondent from—

(a) committing any act of domestic violence;

(b) aiding or abetting in the commission of acts of domestic violence;

(c) entering the place of employment of the aggrieved person or, if the person aggrieved is a child, its school or any other place frequented by the aggrieved person;

(d) attempting to communicate in any form, whatsoever, with the aggrieved person, including personal, oral or written or electronic or telephonic contact;

(e) alienating any assets, operating bank lockers or bank accounts used or held or enjoyed by both the parties, jointly by the aggrieved person and the respondent or singly by the respondent, including her stridhan or any other property held either jointly by the parties or separately by them without the leave of the Magistrate;

(f) causing violence to the dependants, other relatives or any person who give the aggrieved person assistance from domestic violence;

(g) committing any other act as specified in the protection order.

Protection under Art. 14. The word "protection" used in Art. 14 of the constitution cannot be invoked by a person whose claim is not that his rights or liberties be preserved from violation or abridgement, but that his obligations be curtailed by abridging another person's rights. *Hanuman Bank Ltd.* v. *P.T. Munia Servai,* AIR 1958 Mad 279, 280. [Constitution of India, Art. 14]

Protective headgear. "PROTECTIVE HEADGEAR" means a helmet which (a) by virtue of its shape, material and construction could reasonably be expected to afford to the person driving or riding on a motor cycle a degree of protection from injury in the event of an accident, and (b) is securely fastened to the head of the wearer by means of straps or other fastenings provided on the headgear. [Motor Vehicles Act (59 of 1988), S. 129, *Expln.*]

Protective home. "PROTECTIVE HOME" means an institution, by whatever name called (being an institution established or licensed as such under Section 21, in which persons who are in need of care and protection, may be kept under this Act, and where appropriate technically qualified persons, equipment and other facilities have been provided but does not include—

(i) a shelter where undertrials may be kept in pursuance of this Act, or

(ii) a corrective institution. [Immoral Traffic (Prevention) Act (104 of 1956), S. 2(g)]

Home for shelter. [Immoral Traffic (Prevention) Act (104 of 1956), S. 2(g)].

Protectorate. In international law, the relationship between a weaker nation and a stronger one when the weaker nation has transferred the management of its more important international affairs to the stronger nation.

Protest. When a promissory note or bill of exchange has been dishonoured by non-acceptance or non-payment, the holder may within reasonable time, cause such dishonour to be noted and certified by a notary public, such certificate is called a protest.

A written declaration made by the master of a ship attested by a Justice of the Peace or a Consul, stating the circumstances under which injury has happened to the ship or cargo, or under which officers or crew have incurred any liability [Indian Evidence Act (1 of 1872), S. 32, ill. (h)]; [Negotiable Instruments Act (26 of 1881), S. 100]; A complaint, objection or display of unwillingness usually to an idea or cause of action. [CPC (5 of 1908), O. XXX, R. 8].

Protest for better security. When the acceptor of a bill of exchange has become insolvent, or his credit has been publicly impeached, before the maturity of the bill, the holder may, within a reasonable time, cause a notary public to demand better security of the acceptor, and on its being refused may, within a reasonable time, cause such facts to be noted and certified as aforesaid. Such certificate is called a protest for better security. [Negotiable Instruments Act (26 of 1881), S. 100]

Protested. Bearing protest. [Negotiable Instruments Act (26 of 1881), S. 104].

Prothonotary. The title given to an officer who officiates as principal clerk of some Court. [CPC (5 of 1908), S. 128(2)(i)].

Protocol. "PROTOCOL" means the Protocol for the Suppression of Unlawful Acts Against the Safety of Fixed Platforms Located on the Continental Shelf adopted at Rome on the 10th day of March, 1988 as amended from time to time. [Suppression of Unlawful Acts against Safety of Maritime Navigation and Platform on Continental Shelf Act (69 of 2002), S. 2(f)]

"PROTOCOL" means the Montreal Protocol on Substances that deplete the Ozone Layer, adopted on 16th September 1987. [Ozone Depleting Substances (Regulation and Control) Rules, 2000, R. 2(m)]

The minutes of the proceedings of an international conference or drafts, signed by the delegates giving them finality.

It is also used for the rules of ceremonial followed in all writings which pass in the official relations.

A rough or preliminary draft of a contract or treaty. [Indian Carriage by Air Act (69 of 1972), S. 2(2)].

Originally, the word appears to have meant the original note or minute of a transaction, negotiation, agreement, or the like, drawn up by a recognised public official, notary *etc.*, and duly attested, which formed the legal authority for any subsequent deed, agreement, or the like based on it. The word 'protocol' also meant a formal or official statement of a transaction or proceeding.

Protocol State. Means a State Party to the Protocol. [Suppression of Unlawful Acts against Safety of Maritime Navigation and Platform on Continental Shelf Act (69 of 2002), S. 2(g)]

Provable debt. In bankruptcy proceedings any debt which a person can recover either in his own name or in the name of any other person, is a provable debt.

Prove. To establish (a thing) as true (as by argument or evidence) [IPC (45 of 1860), S. 482]; to subject to a testing process (any natural, prepared or manufactured substance or object) [Arms Act (54 of 1959), S. 5(a)].

Prove up. To present or show that one has fulfilled the legal requirements.

Proved. "A fact is said to be proved when, after considering the matters before it, the Court either believes it to exist, or considers its existence so probable that a prudent man ought, under the circumstances of the particular case, to act upon the supposition that it exists." [Indian Evidence Act (1 of 1872), S. 3] [Now (w. e. f. 1-7-2024) repealed & replaced by Bharatiya Sakshya Adhiniyam, 2023 (47 of 2023) & same definition in new Adhiniyam, section 2(1)(j)]

What is required even in criminal cases, is not absolute certainty. All that is required is material whereas the Court can reasonably act upon the supposition that a fact exists. *Anibharan Singh* v. *State,* AIR 1953 All 493.

"Proved", "disproved", "not proved". The definitions of the words "proved", "disproved" and "not proved" simply describe the degree of certainty to be arrived at before a fact can be said to be proved, disproved or not proved. The definitions are mere embodiment of a sound rule of common sense. Under the Evidence Act 'a fact is said to be proved when the Court considers its existence so probable on the available evidence that a prudent man ought to act upon the supposition that the fact exists. *Antoniswamy* v. *Anna Manickam,* AIR 1970 Mad 91]. [Indian Evidence Act (1 of 1872), S. 3]

Provide. To make a stipulation; to lay down a legal provision [Press Council Act (37 of 1978), S. 12(2)(h)]; to make provision [Children Act (60 of 1960) (*repealed*), S. 10(3) and Indian Evidence Act (1 of 1872), S. 8, *Expln.* 2, ill (e)].

Provided. A clause beginning with this word is usually termed a proviso. It may have various effects. Sometimes it is to be taken for a condition, sometimes for an explanation, sometimes for a covenant, sometimes for an exception, sometimes for a reservation. (*Ency. of the laws of England*)

Supplied with [Indian Evidence Act (1 of 1872), S. 8, *Expln.* 2, ill. (e)]; provision having been made; laid down by a legal provision [T.P. Act (4 of 1882), S. 6]; with the provision or condition [IPC (45 of 1860), S. 92].

Provided that. Denoting a condition on which any action, operation or transaction is to be taken; making an exception to the main legal provision by laying down a special provision for the case excepted from the operation of the main rule. [T.P. Act (4 of 1882), S. 10]; [Inland Vessels Act (1 of 1917), S. 19(2), prov.].

Provident fund. "PROVIDENT FUND" means a fund in which subscriptions or deposits of any class or classes of employees are received and held on their individual accounts, and includes any contributions credited in respect of subscriptions or deposits and any interest or increment accruing on such subscriptions, deposits or contributions under the rules of the Fund. [Provident Funds Act (29 of 1925), S. 2(*e*)].

Provident Fund means the Employees' Provident Fund established under clause (*a*) of sub-section (*1*) of section 16. [Code on Social Security, 2020 (36 of 2020), section 2(63)]

A fund in which the subscription or deposits of any class or classes of employees are received and held on their individual accounts, and includes contributions from the employer, if any, credited in respect of, and any interest accruing on, such subscriptions or deposits under the rules of the fund. [CPC (5 of 1908), S. 60(1), prov. (k)].

Provident Insurance Society. Means any person who, or body of persons whether corporate or unincorporate which, receives premiums or contributions for insuring money to be paid on the birth, marriage or death of any person or on the happening of such other contingency or class of contingency as may be prescribed. [Provident Insurance Societies Act (5 of 1912), S. 2(8)].

Provident society. "PROVIDENT SOCIETY" means, a person who or a body of persons (whether corporate or unincorporate) which, not being an insurer registered for the time being under Part II of this Act, carries on the business of insuring the payment, on the happening of any of the contingencies mentioned in sub-section (2) of—

(a) an annuity of or equivalent to one hundred rupees or less, payable for an uncertain period, or

(b) a gross sum of one thousand rupees or less, whether paid or payable in lump sum or in two or more installments over a certain period, exclusively in both cases (a) and (b) of any profits or bonus not being a guaranteed profits or bonus.

Explanation—For the purposes of this sub-section, a period is "certain" if its duration is ascertainable in advance and "uncertain" if its duration is not so ascertainable. [Insurance Act (4 of 1938), S. 65(1)]

A society making provision for the future. [Life Insurance Corporation Act (31 of 1956), S. 2(3)(ii), *Expln.*, III].

Providing credit facilities. The expression 'providing credit facilities' takes its colour from the activity of banking. A person who advances loans or supplies goods on credit in connection with and in the course of some other business of manufacture or purchase or sale of goods *etc.*, cannot be said to be carrying on the business of providing credit facilities. *Addl. CIT* v. *U.P. Cooperation Cane Union,* (1978) 114 ITR 70 (All). [Income Tax Act (43 of 1961), S. 80P(2)(a)(i)]

Provision. The expression 'PROVISION' shall, subject to sub-clause (2) shall mean any amount written off or retained by way of providing for depreciation, renewals or diminution in value of assets, or retained by way of providing for any known liability of which the amount cannot be determined with substantial accuracy. (*Sub. Cl (2))—Where—*

(a) any amount written off or retained by way of providing for depreciation, renewals or diminution in value of assets, not being an amount written off in relation to fixed assets before the commencement of this Act, or

(b) any amount retained by way of providing for any known liability;

is in excess of the amount which in the opinion of the Directors is reasonably necessary for the purpose, the excess shall be treated for the purpose of this Schedule as a reserve and not a provision. [Companies Act (1 of 1956), Pt. III, Schedule VI]

A provision is a distinct rule or principle of law in a statute which governs the situation covered by it. So an incomplete idea, even though stated in the form of a section of a statute, cannot be said to be a provision for, by its incompleteness, it cannot really be said to provide a whole rule or principle for observance by those concerned. *C. Vecttil Ammad* v. *Taluk Land Board*, AIR 1979 SC 1573, 1577.

Each of the clauses or divisions of a legal instrument laying down a rule for the regulation of some particular matter [IPC (45 of 1860), S. 2]; a stock of needed materials or supplies; a stock of food; victuals, eatables and drinkables [Navy Act (62 of 1957), S. 31(10)].

Provision and maintenance. The words 'provision' and 'maintenance' convey the same meaning and they cannot be read as meaning two different things. The liability of a former husband to his divorced wife to pay maintenance and make provision for her is confined to the *Iddat* period only. *Usmankhan Bashanani* v. *Fathirunnisa Begum,* AIR 1990 AP 225, 239 (FB). [Muslim Women (Protection of Rights on Divorce) Act (25 of 1986), S. 3(1)(a)]

Provision and reserve. A reserve is a stand-by erected out of profits of a business to meet contingencies which are unknown and which cannot be foretold on the basis of knowledge of current facts. A reserve is created by way of appropriation of profits. It is not a charge against profits. It does not go out of the business, but is retained as part of the capital. But a provision is a charge against profits. It is created to meet liabilities which are known and foreseeable, but whose exact timing, and hence whose quantification, alone are uncertain at the moment. *CIT* v. *Crompton Engineering Co. (Madras) Ltd.,* (1983) 140 ITR 320, 323 (Mad).

A reserve may be a general reserve or specific reserve and the amount should be kept apart for some purpose, either general or specific. The broad distinction between the words "reserve" and "provision" is that whereas a provision is a charge against the profits to be taken into account against gross receipts in the profit and loss account, a reserve is an appropriation of profits, the asset or assets by which it is represented being retained to form part of the capital employed in the business. *Vazir Sultan Tobacco Co. Ltd.* v. *CIT,* AIR 1981 SC 2105.

Provisional. Temporary, preliminary; tentative; taken or done by way of precaution or *ad interim*. (*Black*)

Not final; temporary in nature. [Companies (Profits) Surtax Act (7 of 1964), S. 7].

Provisional damages. Damages which are given in personal cases when the injuries sustained may cause in the future some serious disease or other serious deterioration in the physical or mental condition of the claimant.

Provisional Parliament. For the purposes of this section, 'Provisional Parliament' shall include the body which functioned as the Constituent Assembly of the Dominion of India immediately before the commencement of the Constitution. [Salary, Allowances and Pension of Members of Parliament Act (30 of 1954), S. 8AB, *Expln.* as inserted by Amending Act No. (40 of 2006), S. 9]

Provisions. 'Provisions' refer to the articles of food for human consumption, and does not embrace chop feed for animals.

Food, victuals eatables and drinkables. [Army Act (46 of 1950), S. 42(g)].

Proviso. A condition, exception, limitation or stipulation to a legal or formal document's validity or application.

The word "proviso" is used frequently to denote the clause the first words of which are "Provided that' inserted in deeds and instruments generally, and containing a condition or stipulation on the performance or non-performance of which, as the case may be, the effect of a proceeding clause or of the deed depends.

A clause inserted in a legal or formal document, making some condition, stipulation, exception or limitation or upon the observance of which the operation or validity of the instrument depends. [Indian Evidence Act (1 of 1872), S. 105].

A proviso is generally intended to restrain the enacting clause and to except something which would have otherwise been within it or in some measure to modify the enacting clause.

Proviso est providere praesentia et futura, non praeterita. (*Rep.* 72) A proviso is to provide for things present and future, not past.

Provocation. Provocation means, in law. that treatment by another which arouses anger or passion.

The action or an act of exciting anger, resentment or irritation. [IPC (45 of 1860), S. 153].

An action, insult etc. that a likely to provoke physical retaliation. [Oxford Dictionary as cited in *B.D. Khunte* v. *Union of India*, (2015) 1 SCC 286, para 15].

The provocation could be an act or series of acts done by the deceased to the accused resulting in inflicting of injury. [*Budhi Singh* v. *State of Himachal Pradesh*, (2012) 13 SCC 663, para 18] [Indian Penal Code (45 of 1860), S. 300, Exception I].

It is a defence to a charge of murder that the fatal act was committed in the heat of passion caused by sudden provocation, and before there was time for the passion to cool. But the defence does not amount to excuse or justification, and operates only to reduce the quantity of the offence and fails wholly if the accused acted after he had time to reflect and cool.

Provoke. 'To provoke is to excite, to arouse'. To incite or stimulate a person to action.

Provost. A governing officer of a university or college. [Aligarh Muslim University Act (40 of 1920), Sch., item (11)(1)].

Provost Marshal. Means a person appointed as such under S. 107 includes any of his deputies or assistants or any other person legally exercising authority under him or on his behalf. [Army Act (46 of 1950), S. 3(xx); Air Force Act (45 of 1950), S. 2(xxv); Navy Act (62 of 1957), S. 3(19)]

Proximate. Proximate means direct or immediate.

Proximate cause. An act which directly produced or concurred directly in producing an effect or injury; an immediate, or direct, or efficient cause of injury.

The loss which is produced by the direct efficient and predominating cause is the proximate cause of the loss in the Law of Marine insurance. *A. Akooji Jadwat P. Ltd.* v. *Oriental Fair and General Co. Ltd.*, AIR 1972 Cal 228, 237. [Marine Insurance Act (11 of 1963), S. 57]

That which, in a natural and continuous sequence, unbroken by any efficient intervening cause, produces injury and without which the result would not have occurred. *Wisniewski v. Great Atlantic & Pacific Tea Co.*, 226 Pa Super 574 : 323 A 2 d 744, p. 748 (1944). That which is nearest in the order of responsible causation. That which stands next in causation to the effect, not necessarily in time or space but in causal relation. The proximate cause of an injury is the primary or moving cause, or that which, in a natural and continuous sequence, unbroken by any efficient intervening cause, produces the injury and without which the accident could not have happened, if the injury be one which might be reasonably anticipated or foreseen as a natural consequence of the wrongful act. An injury or damage is proximately caused by an act, or failure to act, whenever it appears from the evidence in the case, that the act or omission played a substantial part in bringing about or actually causing the injury or damages; and that the injury or damage was either a direct result or a reasonably probable consequence of the act or omission." [Black's Law Dictionary (5th Edn.) as cited in *Sushil Ansal* v. *State*, (2014) 6 SCC 173, para 84].

Proximate security. Means protection provided from close quarters, during journey by road, rail, aircraft, water craft or on foot or any other means of transport and shall include the places of functions, engagements, residence or halt and shall comprise ring round teams, isolation cordons, the sterile zone around, and the rostrum and access control to the person or members of his immediate family. [Special Protection Group Act (34 of 1988), S. 2(g)]

Proximity. Closeness; nearness (as) proximity of blood; proximity of war.

Immediate nearness in time, place, relationship *etc.* [Destructive Insects and Pests Act (2 of 1914), S. 5(1) and Indian Electricity Act (9 of 1910), S. 32(2)].

Proximity-release door opener. A security device to control access to the computer room. Access to the computer area is gained through the use of a small audio transmitter located in the authorized employees' identification badges. When the authorized person comes to within a predetermined distance of the entry door, a radio signal sends a key number to the receiver, which unlocks the door for admittance. (*Cyber Law*)

Proxy. One acting for another; a writing authorizing a person to vote instead of another at a meeting *etc.*; a vote so given. [Representation of the People Act (43 of 1951), S. 59].

One who acts for another; written authorisation for such action.

A proxy is an authority or power to do a certain thing.

A proxy is a "lawfully constituted agent".

A proxy is a creature of law of agency, though with this difference that under the company law such an agent has to be appointed in a manner and provided thereunder. [Companies Act (1 of 1956), S. 391(2)]

Proxy bidding. Placing a maximum bid that is held in confidence by the online auction site. The system will use only as much of the maximum bid as is necessary to maintain the bidder's high-bid position. (*Cyber Law*)

Proxy contest. A struggle which occurs between two corporate factions so as to obtain the votes of uncommitted shareholders. A proxy contest usually occurs when a group of dissident shareholders mounts a battle against the corporation's managers.

Proxy server. A server that sits between a client application such as a web browser and a real server. It intercepts all requests to the real server to see if it can fulfill the request itself. It not, it forwards the request to the real server. (*Information Technology*)

A type of server used to store previously accessed web pages, making later retrieval much quicker. (*Cyber Law*)

A Proxy Server sits in between a *Client* and the "real" *Server* that a Client is trying to use. Client's are sometimes configured to use a Proxy Server, usually an *HTTP* server. The clients makes all of its requests from the Proxy Server, which then makes requests from the "real" server and passes the result back to the Client. Sometimes the Proxy server will store the results and give a stored result instead of making a new one (to reduce use of a *Network*). Proxy servers are commonly established on *Local Area Networks* (*Matisse Enzer-Glossary of Internet Terms*)

Proxy solicitation. A request that a corporate shareholder authorize another person to cast the vote of a shareholder at a corporate meeting.

Prudence. The degree of care required by the exigencies or circumstances under which it is to be exercised [Indian Contract Act (9 of 1872), S. 151]; wisdom applied to practice. [Life Insurance Corporation Act (31 of 1956), S. 15(1)].

Prudent. Having sound judgment in practical affairs, circumspect [Indian Contract Act (9 of 1872), S. 125(3)]; [Indian Evidence Act (1 of 1872), S. 3]; discreet, worldly wise [Companies Act (1 of 1956), Sch. 1, table A, Interpretation 87(2)].

Prudent man. A person having sound judgment in practical affairs. [Indian Evidence Act (1 of 1872), S. 3].

Prudentur agit qui praecepto legis obtemperat. (5 Rep. 49) He acts prudently, who obeys the command of the law.

Pseudonym. Fictitious name assumed, as by an author. [Copyright Act (14 of 1957), S. 23(3)(a)].

"Psychiatric hospital" or "psychiatric nursing home". Means a hospital or, as the case may be, a nursing home established or maintained by the Government or any other person for the treatment and care of mentally ill person and includes a convalescent home established or maintained by the Government or any other person for such mentally ill persons, but does not include any general hospital or general nursing home established or maintained by the Government and which provides also for psychiatric services. [Mental Health Act (14 of 1987), S. 2(q)]

Psychiatrist. Means a medical practitioner possessing a post-graduate degree or diploma in psychiatry awarded by an university recognised by the University Grants Commission established under the University Grants Commission Act, 1956, or awarded or recognised by the National Board of Examinations and included in the First Schedule to the Indian Medical Council Act, 1956, or recognised by the Medical Council of India, constituted under the Indian Medical Council Act, 1956, and includes, in relation to any State, any medical officer who having regard to his knowledge and experience in psychiatry, has been declared by the Government of that State to be a psychiatrist for the purposes of this Act [The Mental Healthcare Act, 2017 (10 of 2017), S. 2(1)(y)]

Means a medical practitioner possessing a post-graduate degree or diploma in psychiatry, recognized by the medical Council of India, constituted under the India Medical Council Act, 1956 and includes, in relation to any State, any medical officer who, having regard to his knowledge and experience in psychiatry, has been declared by the Government and which provides also for psychiatric services. [Mental Health Act (14 of 1987), S. 2(r)]

Psychopath. A person with a mental disorder characterized by an extremely antisocial personality which often leads to aggressive, perverted, or criminal behaviour.

Psychopathic disorder. "PSYCHOPATHIC DISORDER" means a persistent disorder or disability of mind (whether or not including subnormality of intelligence) which results in abnormally aggressive or seriously impossible conduct on the part of the defendant, and whether or not it requires or is susceptible to medical treatment. [Parsi Marriage and Divorce Act (3 of 1936), S. 32, *Expln.* (b)]

Psychotropic substance. Means coca leaf, cannabis (hemp), opium, poppy straw and includes all manufactured goods. [Narcotic Drugs and Psychotropic Substances Act 1985, 2 (xiv)]

Puberty : Sexual Maturity. The earliest age at which persons are capable of begetting or bearing children.

Public. The word "PUBLIC" includes any class of the public or any community. [IPC (45 of 1860), S. 12] [Now (w. e. f. 1-7-2024) repealed & replaced by Bharatiya Nyaya Sanhita, 2023 (45 of 2023), S. 2(27), same definition in new Sanhita]

The people; the general body of mankind [IPC (45 of 1860), S. 12]; [Indian Contract Act (9 of 1872), S. 74, *Expln.*]; of or belonging to the people; pertaining to a community or a nation; general [Representation of the People Act (43 of 1951), S. 126(1)]; unconcealed, not private [Indian Evidence Act (1 of 1872), S. 8, *Expln.* 2, ill. (a)].

The body of the people at large; the people of the neighbourhood; the community at large; the people; the whole body politic, or all the citizens of the state; the inhabitants of a particular place.

Pertaining to, or belonging to, the people; shares relating to a nation, state, or community; open to all the people; in or to be shared or participated in or enjoyed by people at large; not limited or restricted to any particular class of the community; of or pertaining to the people; belonging to the people.

Public account. The accounts of the expenditure of a nation.

Public accountant. The expression "PUBLIC ACCOUNTANT" means any person who as official Assignee or Trustee, or a sarbarahkar, is entrusted with receipt, custody or control of any moneys or securities for money, or the management of any lands belonging to any other person or persons, and for the purposes of Section 4 and 5 of this Act the expression shall also include any person, who, by reason of any office held by him in the service of the Central Government or the Government of a State, is entrusted with the receipt, custody or control of any moneys or securities for money, or the management of any lands belonging to such Government. [Public Accountant's Default Act (12 of 1850), S. 3]

Public accounts committee. A Parliamentary Committee for the examination of the accounts showing the appropriation of the sums granted by Parliament to meet the public expenditure and of such other accounts laid before parliament as the Committee may think fit.

Public and private nuisance (Distinction). A private nuisance is a civil wrong but a public nuisance is a criminal offence, an act not warranted by law or an omission to discharge a legal duty which act or omission, obstructs or causes inconvenience or damage to the public in the exercise of rights common to all the subject. Public and private nuisance are not in reality two species of the same genus at all. *Datta Mal Chiranji Lal* v. *L. Ladli Prasad,* MLJ : QD (1956-1960) Vol. IV C2489 : AIR 1960 All 632.

Public auction. A public sale of property conducted by bindings. [CPC (5 of 1908), Sch. 1, App. E, form No. 29].

Public authority. One of the distinguishing features of an authority not being a public authority, is profit-making. It is not incumbent that a body in order to be a public body must always be constituted by a statute. *Madan Mohan* v. *State of West, Bengal*, AIR 1966 Cal 23, 28, 29.

A public authority is a body which has public or statutory duties to perform, and which performs such duties and carries out its transactions for the benefit of the public, and not for private profit. [*Blamer Lawric & Company Limited* v. *ParthaSarathi Sen Roy*, (2013) 8 SCC 345, para 21].

"PUBLIC AUTHORITY" means the Central Government or State Government or a local authority; and, so far as regards tolls levied by a railway company under Section 4 of the Indian Guaranteed Railways Act, 1879 or Section 51 of the Indian Railways Act, 1890, includes such a railway company. [Indian Tolls (Army and Air Force) Act (2 of 1901), S. 2(i)]

"PUBLIC AUTHORITY" means any authority or body or institution of self-government established or constituted—

(a) by or under the Constitution;

(b) by any other law made by Parliament;

(c) by any other law made by State Legislature;

(d) by notification issued or order made by the appropriate Government,

and includes any—

(i) body owned, controlled or substantially financed;

(ii) non-Government organisation substantially financed,

directly or indirectly by funds provided by the appropriate Government. [Right to Information Act (22 of 2005), S. 2(h)] *See also* Companies (Corporate Social Responsibility Policy) Rules, 2014, rule 2(1)(j)

Having regard to the public purpose which the State Bank of India is meant to serve, extensive Govt. Control over the Bank, the statutory audit subject to Govt. Control and the Power of Central Government to wind up the Bank, State Bank of India is public authority. *V. Ramaih* v. *State Bank of India,* AIR 1964 Mad 335, 344. [Constitution of India, Art. 226]

Public carrier. An owner of a transport vehicle who transports or undertakes to transport goods, or any class of goods, for another person at any time and in any public place for hire or reward. [Motor Vehicles Act (59 of 1988), S. 2(23)].

Public charges. Any impost made by public authorities for any public purpose. [T.P. Act (4 of 1882), S. 55(1)(g)].

Public charitable purpose. Includes relief of the poor, education, medical relief and the advancement of any other object of general public utility within the territories of India. [Estate Duty Act (34 of 1953), S. 2(17)]

Public Cloud. A public cloud is one in which the infrastructure and other computational resources that it comprises are made available to the general public over the internet. [National Institute of Standards and Technology, *'Guidelines on Security and Privacy in Public Cloud Computing,' Draft Special Publication* 800-144., January 2011, p. 3]

Public company. "PUBLIC COMPANY" means a company which—

(a) is not a private company;

(b) has a minimum paid up capital of five lakh rupees or such higher paid-up capital, as may be prescribed;

(c) is a private company which is a subsidiary of a company which is not a private company. [Companies Act (1 of 1956), S. 3(iv)]

A company whose capital consists of shares publicly subscribed.

"PUBLIC COMPANY". Means a company which—

(*a*) is not a private company and;

(*b*) has a minimum paid-up share capital as may be prescribed:

Provided that a company which is a subsidiary of a company, not being a private company, shall be deemed to be public company for the purposes of this Act even where such subsidiary company continues to be a private company in its articles. [S. 2(71) of the Companies Act, 2013 (18 of 2013) as amended by Act 1 of 2018]

Public decency. Proper or becoming behaviour of a community or a general public. [Immoral Traffic (Prevention) Act (104 of 1956), S. 8(b)].

Public disclosure of private facts causing injury to reputation. One of four types of common law torts for the invasion of privacy; defined as revealing highly personal facts or information about another, leading to damage to their reputation. (*Cyber Law*)

Public document. The following documents are public documents— (1) documents forming the acts or records of the acts (*i*) of the sovereign authority; (*ii*) of official bodies and tribunals, and; (*iii*) of public officers, legislative, judicial and executive, of any part of India, or of The Commonwealth or of foreign country; (2) public records kept in any State of private documents. [Indian Evidence Act (1 of 1872), S. 74].

The following documents are public documents:—

(a) documents forming the acts, or records of the acts—

(i) of the sovereign authority;

(ii) of official bodies and tribunals; and

(iii) of public officers, legislative, judicial and executive of India or of a foreign country;

(b) public records kept in any State or Union territory of private documents. [(w. e. f. 1-7-2024) Bharatiya Sakshya Adhiniyam, 2023 (47 of 2023), section 74(1)]

A document which can be made use of by the general public by way of inspection or making copies *etc.* [Indian Evidence Act (1 of 1872), S. 74]

Public domain. "PUBLIC DOMAIN" means domain that has no restrictions upon dissemination of information within or from it; the existence of any legal rights to intellectual property in that information does not remove such information from being in public domain. [Weapon of Mass Destruction and Their Delivery Systems (Prohibition of Unlawful Activities) Act (21 of 2005), S. 4(i)]

Public drainage. The line of drains for the flow of rain water and dirty water which is maintained by public authorities. [IPC (45 of 1860), S. 432].

Public dues. In relation to a displaced person, includes—

(i) arrears of rent in respect of any property allotted or leased to the displaced person by the Central Government or a State Government or a Custodian;

(ii) any amount recoverable, whether in one lump sum or in instalments, from the displaced person on account of loans granted to him by the Central Government or a State Government or the Rehabilitation Finance Administration Act, 1948, and any interest on such loans;

(iii) the amount of purchase-money or any part thereof and any interest on such amount or part remaining unpaid and recoverable from the displaced person on account of transfer to him of any property of interest therein by—

(a) the Central Government; or

(b) any State Government; or

(c) any body corporate or other authority or person financed by the Central Government or a State Government for the purpose of the acquisition, development or construction of any immovable property for the rehabilitation of displaced person;

(iiia) any dues payable, whether in one lump sum or in instalments, to a co-operative society, registered as such under any law for the time being in force, by the displaced person on account of loans granted to him by the co-operative society, where such loans have been granted out of funds placed at the disposal of the co-operative society by the Central Government or a State Government and such dues have declared by the Central Government, by notification in the Official Gazette, to be public dues;

(iv) any other dues payable to the Central Government, a State Government or the Custodian which may be declared by the Central Government, by notification in the official Gazette, to be public dues recoverable from displaced person. [Displaced Persons (Compensation and Rehabilitation) Act (44 of 1954), S. 2(d)]

Public duty. "PUBLIC DUTY" means a duty in the discharge of which the State, the public or the community at large has an interest;

Explanation.—In this clause "State" includes a corporation established by or under a Central, Provincial or State Act, or an authority or a body owned or controlled or aided by the Government or a Government company as defined in Section 617 of the Companies Act, 1956 (1 of 1956). [Prevention of Corruption Act (49 of 1988), S. 2(b)]

Duty owed to the people in general; duty attaching to the office held under the State. [IPC (45 of 1860), S. 187].

Public embankment. "PUBLIC EMBANKMENT" means an embankment maintained by the officers of Government. [Ben. Act 2 of 1882, (Embankment), S. 3]

Public emergency. The expression 'public emergency' means one which raises problems concerning the interest of the public safety, the sovereignty and integrity of India, the security of the State, friendly relations with foreign states or public order or the prevention of incitement to the commission of an offence. *Hukum Chand* v. *Union of India*, AIR 1976 SC 789. [Indian Post Offices Act (6 of 1898), S. 26 and Indian Telegraph Act (13 of 1885), S. 5(1)]

"Public emergency" and **"Economic emergency".** 'Public emergency' within the contemplation of S. 5(1) is one which raises problems concerning the interest of the public safety, the sovereignty and integrity of India, the security of the State, friendly relations with foreign States or public order or the prevention of incitement to the commission of an offence. Economic emergency is not one of those matters expressly mentioned in the statute. Mere 'economic emergency' may not necessarily amount to a 'public emergency' and justify action under this section unless it raises problems relating to the matters indicated in the section. *Hukam Chand Shyam Lal* v. *Union of India,* AIR 1976 SC 789. [Indian Telegraph Act (13 of 1885), S. 5(1)]

Public facilities and services. Includes all forms of delivery of services to the public at large, including housing, educational and vocational trainings, employment and career advancement, shopping or marketing, religious, cultural, leisure or recreational, medical, health and rehabilitation, banking, finance and insurance, communication, postal and information, access to justice, public utilities, transportation. [Rights of Persons with Disabilities Act (49 of 2016), S. 2(x)].

Public finance. It is the study of the nature and effects of taxation, spending, and borrowing policies of a Government. It also includes the study of financial relations between different tiers of Government in a federal polity. (*Taxation*)

Public financial institution. Means

(a) the Industrial Credit and Investment Corporation of India Limited, a company formed and registered under Indian Companies Act, 1913;

(b) the Industrial Reconstruction Corporation of India Limited, a company formed and registered under the Companies Act, 1956, or;

(c) any other institution, being a company a defined in Section 617 of Companies Act, 1956 or a company

to which the provisions of Section 619 of that Act apply, which the Central Government may, having regard to the nature of the business carried on by such institution, by notification in the Official Gazette, specify to be a public financial institution for the purposes of this Act. [Public Financial Institutions (obligations as to Fidelity and Secrecy) Act (48 of 1983), S. 2(1)]

"PUBLIC FINANCIAL INSTITUTION". Means—

(*i*) the Life Insurance Corporation of India, established under section 3 of the Life Insurance Corporation Act, 1956 (31 of 1956);

(*ii*) the Infrastructure Development Finance Company Limited, referred to in section 4A(1)(vi) of the Companies Act, 1956 (1 of 1956), so repealed under section 465 of the Companies Act, 2013 (18 of 2013);

(*iii*) specified company referred to in the Unit Trust of India (Transfer of Undertaking and Repeal) Act, 2002 (58 of 2002);

(*iv*) institutions notified by the Central Government under section 4A(2) of the Companies Act, 1956 (1 of 1956), so repealed under section 465 of the Companies Act, 2013 (18 of 2013);

(*v*) such other institution as may be notified by the Central Government in consultation with the Reserve Bank of India:

Provided that no institution shall be so notified unless—

(*A*) it has been established or constituted by or under any Central or State Act other than this Act or the previous company law; or

(*B*) not less than fifty-one per cent. of the paid-up share capital is held or controlled by the Central

Government or by any State Government or Governments or partly by the Central Government and partly by one or more State Governments. [S. 2(72) of the Companies Act, 2013 (18 of 2013) as amended by Act 1 of 2018 (w.e.f. 9-2-2018).]

Public-forest land. "PUBLIC FOREST-LAND" means land at the disposal of the Government and not included in a reserved forest. [Bur Forest Act (4 of 1902), S. 3(10)]

Public-private partnership. "Public-private partnership" means such partnership under a scheme of the Central Government which provides for establishment of Institute involving collaboration between the Central Government, the State Government and industry partners [The Indian Institutes of Information Technology (Public Private Partnership) Act, 2017 (23 of 2017), S. 3(k)]

Public function. An act or duty of a public servant in his capacity as such. [CrPC 1973 (2 of 1974), S. 213, ill. (d)].

A body is performing a 'public function' when it seeks to achieve some collective benefit for the public or a section of the public and is accepted by the public or that section of the public as having authority to do so. Bodies therefore exercise public functions when they intervene or participate in social or economic affairs in the public interests. [Commentary on Judicial Review of Administrative Action (5th Edn.) by de Smith, Woolf and Jowell. In chapter 3, para 0.24 as cited in *Binny Limited v. V. Sadasivam*, (2005) 6 SCC 657, para 11 : 2005 SCC (L&S) 881]. See also *Jatya Pal Singh v. Union of India*, (2013) 6 SCC 452, para 51.

Public good. Anything conducive to the welfare of the community [IPC (45 of 1860), S. 499, Excep. 1].

Public highway. A way open to all the citizens as a matter of right. [CPC (5 of 1908), Sch. 1, App. A, form No. 25].

Public holiday. "The expression "PUBLIC HOLIDAY" includes Sunday; and any other day declared by the Central Government by notification in the Official Gazette, to be a public holiday." [Negotiable Instruments Act (26 of 1881), S. 25, *Expln.*]

"PUBLIC HOLIDAY" means a public holiday within the meaning of the Negotiable Instruments Act, 1881 (26 of 1881);

Provided that no day declared by the Central Government to be a public holiday shall be deemed to be such a holiday, in relation to any meeting, unless the declaration was notified before the issue of the notice convening such meeting. [Companies Act (1 of 1956), S. 2(38)]

Public interest. Means those interest which concern the public at large.

Matter of public interest "does not mean that which is interesting as gratifying curiosity or love of information or amusement; but that in which a class of the community have a pecuniary interest, or some interest by which their legal rights or liabilities are affected."

"Public interest" means the general welfare of the public that warrants recommendation and protection; something in which the public as a whole has a stake. [Black's Law Dictionary (8th Edn.) as cited in *Bihar Public Service Commission* v. *Saiyed Hussain Abbas Rizwi*, (2012) 13 SCC 61, para 22].

The expression "public interest" is not capable of precise definition and has not a rigid meaning and is elastic and takes its colours from the statute in which it occurs, the concept varying with the time and state for society and its needs. Thus what is 'public interest' today may not be so considered a decade later. *State of Bihar* v. *Kameshwar Singh*, AIR 1952 SC 252. [Companies Act (1 of 1956), S. 397]

The notion of public interest synonymises collective welfare of the people and public institution and is generally informed with the dictates of public trust doctrine—res communious, by everyone in common. [*Sayyed Ratanbhai Sayeed* v. *Shirdi Nagar Panchayat*, (2016) 4 SCC 631, para 58].

The expression 'public interest' occurring in Section 30, Prov. of the Act does not mean the interest of the persons, covered by illegal colonisation area alone but it may extend to the interest of the public of the entire town. *Administrator, Nagar Palika* v. *Bharat,* (2001) 9 SCC 232, para 5. [M.P. Vinirdishta Bhrastha Acharan Nivaran Adhiniyam (36 of 1982), S. 30, Proviso]

That which concerns welfare and rights of the community or a class thereof. [Indian Evidence Act (1 of 1872), S. 124 and Constitution of India, Art. 302].

A subject, in which the public or a section of the public is interested, becomes one of public interest. [IPC (45 of 1860), S. 499, Exception 1]

"PUBLIC INTEREST" the expression 'public interest' if it is employed in a given statute is to be understood and interpreted in the light of the entire scheme, purpose and object of the enactment but in the absence of the same it cannot be pressed into service to confer any right upon a person who otherwise does not possess any such right in law. *Meerut Development Authority* v. *Association of Management Studies*, AIR 2009 SC 2894.

Public interest litigation (PIL). The litigation at the instance of a public spirited citizen espousing the cause of others, as an exception to the traditional view that a petition could be maintained by the "aggrieved person".

Expression 'Public Interest Litigation' (PIL) means the legal action initiated in a Court of law for the enforcement of public interest or general interest in which the public or a class of the community have pecuniary interest or some interest by which their legal rights or liabilities are affected. *Janta Dal* v. *H.S. Chowdhary,* AIR 1993 SC 892; *Also see B. Singh* v. *Union of India,* AIR 2004 SC 1923, 1926, para 8.

Lexically the expression 'PIL' means a legal action initiated in a Court of law for the enforcement of public interest or general interest in which the public or a class of the community has pecuniary interest or some interest by which their legal rights or liabilities are affected. (*Janta Dal* v. *H.S. Chowdhary,* (1992) 4 SCC 305, 331). The principle of *res judicata,* is applicable to public interest litigation. (*Forward Construction Co.* v. *Prabhat Mandal etc.*, AIR 1986 SC 391).

'Public interest litigation' means the legal action initiated in a Court of law for the enforcement of public interest or general interest in which the public or a class of a community have a pecuniary interest or some interest by which their legal rights or liabilities are affected. There must be real and genuine public interest involved in litigation, and not merely an adventure of knight errant or poke one's nose into for a probe. *Ashok Kumar Pandey* v. *State of W.B.*, JT 2003 (9) SC 140 : 2003 (9) Scale 741.

The expression 'public interest litigation' means the legal action initiated in a Court of law for enforcement of public interest or general interest in which the public or a class of community have pecuniary interest or some interest by which their legal rights or liabilities are affected. [*Dattaraj Nathuji Thaware* v. *State of Maharashtra,* AIR 2005 SC 540]

'Public interest litigation' is a weapon which has to be used with great care and circumspection and the judiciary has to be extremely careful to see that behind the beautiful veil of public interest an ugly private malice, vested and/or publicity-seeking is not lurking. It is to be used as an effective weapon in the armoury of law for delivering social justice to the citizens. It should be aimed at redressal of genuine public wrong or public injury and not publicity oriented or founded on personal vendetta. It should not be used for suspicious products of mischief. [*Kushum Lata* v. *Union of India,* (2006) 6 SCC 180, 184-85, para 13]

Public key. Means the key part of a key pair used to identify a digital signature listed in the Digital Signature Certificate. [Information Technology Act (21 of 2000), S. 2(1)(zd)]

Public key infrastructure. The architecture, organization, techniques, practices, and procedures that collectively support the implementation and operation of a certificate based public key cryptographic system. It includes a set of policies, processes, server platforms, software and workstations, used for the purpose of administering Digital Signature Certificates and keys. (*Information Technology*)

Encryption and associated technologies in the issuance and management of digital credentials to provide multilayered security. (*Cyber Law*)

Public lamp. "An electric lamp used for the lighting of any street" [Indian Electricity Act (9 of 1910), S. 2(k)]. Now repealed by Act 36 of 2003, S. 2(53).

Public land mark. An object set up to mark a boundary line of public land or any other conspicuous object in the landscape, which serves as a guide [CrPC 1973 (2 of 1974), S. 152].

Public law. That body of laws which deals with the relations between private individuals and the Government; the laws affecting the general public.

Public library. "PUBLIC LIBRARY" means a library, which permits members of the public to use it for reference or borrowing without charging fee or subscriptions. [Goa Public Libraries Act, 1993 (Goa Act No. 4 of 1995), S. 2(h)]

Public lunatic asylum. A hospital for the reception and treatment of lunatics maintained out of the public funds [CrPC 1973 (2 of 1974), S. 338(1)].

Public matter. Something pertaining to the people of a country or locality.

Public mischief. A misdeameanour committed by a person wilfully interferring with the course of justice by an act or attempt which tends to the prejudice of the community.

Public morals. The basic moral structure of society.

Public nature. That which by its very nature affects the public in general or is rooted in their welfare. [Indian Evidence Act (1 of 1872), S. 37].

Public news. The expression "public news" means something such as "current happenings or alleged current happenings of interest or likely to be of interest to the public or to portion of the public". Anything new or unknown when communicated to another is news, and news which is intended for communicated to the general public, no matter what its nature, is public news. An item of news irrespective of its nature when reported in a paper published for the general public, would be a public news but if published only in a periodical intended for a small circle of readers interested in a particular subject would not be a public news. All news appearing in a periodical which is published for the general public is public news and the paper is a "newspaper."

The Law Reports publish recent judgments rendered by Supreme Court, High Court and the public are interested therein. As such, the reports are public news. *All India Reporter Karmachari Sangh* v. *AIR Ltd.*, AIR 1988 SC 1325, 1330. [Working Journalists & other Newspapers Employees (Conditions of Service) and Miscellaneous Provisions Act (45 of 1955), S.2 (b)]

Public notice. A notice given in such a manner as could bring it to the knowledge of all concerned and also the public in general. [Indian Evidence Act (1 of 1872), S. 14, ill. (h)]; [Carriers Act (3 of 1865), S. 6].

Public nuisance. "A person is guilty of a public nuisance who does any act or is guilty of an illegal omission which causes any common injury, danger or annoyance to the public or to the people in general who dwell or occupy property in the vicinity, or which must necessarily cause injury, obstruction, danger or annoyance to persons who may have occasion to use any public right." [IPC (45 of 1860), S. 268].

A nuisance (as obstructing a highway) that causes harm or annoyance to persons of particular locality in violation of their rights as members of the community. [IPC (45 of 1860), S. 268].

"The expression public nuisance" in S. 91(1). CPC (5 of 1908) does not include public nuisances in law or constructive public nuisances, *i.e.* acts which are nuisances merely because they contravene the provisions of an Act, and which but for the Act, would not be nuisances at all.

It includes an act which causes or which must necessarily cause injury, obstruction or annoyance to persons who may have occasion to use any public right. *Firm Pyarelal Satpal* v. *Sant Lal,* AIR 1972 Raj 103, 110. [CPC (5 of 1908), S. 91 (2)]

Public nuisance and Private nuisance (Distinction). All the persons of a particular locality should not be examined to prove public nuisance. But all the same if two neighbours have come and complained of any nuisance that by itself would not become a public nuisance but a private one for which a civil action is the proper remedy for which no criminal action can lie. (K.B. PANDA, J) *BerhampurMunicipality through the Executive Officer* v. *Oruganti Kondaya,* MLJ : YD (1977) Suppl to Oct C 2848 : (1977) 44 CLT 283 [W&P]

A person is guilty of a public nuisance who does any act or is guilty of an illegal omission which causes any common injury, danger or annoyance to the public or to the people in general who dwell or occupy property in the vicinity, or which must necessarily cause injury, obstruction, danger or annoyance to persons who may have occasion to use any public right but a common nuisance is not excused on the ground that it causes some convenience or advantage. [(w. e. f. 1-7-2024) Bharatiya Nyaya Sanhita, 2023 (45 of 2023), S. 270]

Public offer. For the purposes of Chapter III of Act 18 of 2013, 'public offer' includes initial public offer or further public offer of securities to the public by a company, or an offer for sale of securities to the public by an existing shareholder, through issue of a prospectus. [*Explanation* to section 23 of the Companies Act, 2013 (18 of 2013)]

Public office. Public office is one created by the Constitution of India or by any statute and invested with the power or charged with the duty of acting in execution or in enforcement of law. The office may be an elective office or one in respect of which a nomination or appointment is made. *P.S. Venkataswamy* v. *University of Mysore,* AIR 1964 Mys 159, 165.

Position involving exercise of governmental functions [T.P. Act (4 of 1882), S. 6(f)]; an office where public business is transacted. [CPC (5 of 1908), O. XIII, R. 5(2)].

Public officer. "PUBLIC OFFICER" means a person falling under any of the following descriptions, namely:—(a) every Judge; (b) every member of an All-India Service; (c) every commissioned or gazetted officer in the military or naval or air forces of the Union, while serving under the Government; (d) every officer of a Court of Justice whose duty it is, as such officer, to investigate or report on any matter of law or fact, or to make; authenticate or keep any document or to take charge or dispose of any property, or to execute any judicial process, or to administer any oath, or to interpret or to preserve order in the Court, and every person especially authorised by a Court of Justice to perform any of such duties; (e) every person who holds any office by virtue of which he is empowered to place or keep any person in confinement; (f) every officer of the Government whose duty it is, as such officer, to prevent offences, to give information of offences to bring offenders to justice, or to protect the public health, safety or convenience; (g) every officer whose duty it is, as such officer, to take, receive, keep or expend any property on behalf of the Government, or to make any survey, assessment or contract on behalf of the Government, or to execute any revenue-process, or to investigate, or to report on any matter affecting the pecuniary interests of the Government, or to make, authenticate or keep any document relating to the pecuniary interests of the Government, or to prevent the infraction of any law for the protection of the pecuniary interest of the Government; and (h) every officer in the service or pay of the Government, or remunerated by fees or commission for the performance of any public duty. [CPC (5 of 1908), S. 2(17)].

Where the officers of the Corporation are in service and pay of the Corporation and are paid out of the funds of Corporation they are not 'public officers' within the meaning of S. 80. *Kanta Prasad Singh* v. *Regional Manager, Road Corporation of India,* AIR 1974 Pat 376, 377. [CPC (5 of 1908), S. 2(17) (h) and 80]

The officers of Kerala Electricity Board, being in the service of the Board and paid by the Board and not performing any of the duties on behalf of Government, are not public officers. *V.P. Nair* v. *K.S.E. Board,* AIR 1989 Ker 86, 89.

The Provident Fund Commissioner holds the office of commissioner on appointment by Government and he is therefore, a public officer. *Coal Mines Provident Fund Commissioner*. v. *Ramesh Chander Jha*, AIR 1990 SC 648, 650. [Coal Mines Provident Fund and Miscellaneous Provisions Act (46 of 1948), Ss. 3, 3c(4) and 10-C]

A person holding an office in the pay of the public; a holder of a public office; everyone who is appointed to discharge a public duty and receives a compensation in whatever shape from the State or otherwise. [CPC (5 of 1908), S. 2(17)]; [Destruction of Records Act (5 of 1917), S. 3(2)(c)].

The members of a Court-Martial convened under the Army Act are public officers as defined by S. 2(17), CPC (5 of 1908).

Public or general interest. Interest of the public or of the people in general. [Indian Evidence Act (1 of 1872), S. 87].

Public or other official book. Any record or register maintained by a public authority or an officer. [Indian Evidence Act (1 of 1872), S. 35].

Public order. The word "public order' is virtually synonymous with public peace, safety and tranquility and the activities of a single individual in transport of grain cannot lead to disturbance of public peace, safety and tranquility. *Amar Singh* v. *State of Madhya Pradesh,* AIR 1965 MP 126, 128. [Defence of India Rules (1962), R. 30]

Public order means even tempo of the life of the community taking within its fold even a specified locality and a substantial section of the society. *Nagen Murmu* v. *State of W.B*, AIR 1973 SC 844, 845. [Maintenance of Internal Security Act (26 of 1971) (*repealed*), S. 3(1)(e)(iii)]

Forcing entry into school, setting fire to school building, attempting to throw a bomb at the police are all connected with public order. *Babul Mitra* v. *State of West Bengal*, AIR 1973 SC 197, 200.

Public order and law and order. A mere disturbance of law and order leading to disorder is not sufficient for action under the Defence of India Act but disturbances which subvert the public order are. One has to imagine three concentric circles. Law and order represents the largest circle within which is the next circle representing public order and the smallest circle represents security of State. *Ram Manohar* v. *State of Bihar*, AIR 1966 SC 740, 758. [Defence of India Rules (1962), R, 30(1)(b)]

'Public order' and 'public peace' and 'tranquility'. See also [*Baboolal Ramratan* v. *State of M.P.*, AIR 1955 NUC (Madh. B.) 3864]. [Preventive Detention Act (4 of 1950), S. 3]

Public order and **Public safety.** The expression 'public order' must be taken in a comprehensive sense so as to include 'public safety' in its relation to the maintenance of public order. The public safety mainly depends on public order. The maintenance of public order would result in public safety so that the two subjects are interdependent. *M.P. Menon* v. *State,* AIR 1953 TC 540.

The words "public safety" and "public order" are interchangeable terms. In this case these two words were considered in the context in which they were used under Section 6 of Ordinance No. IV of 1940 and Section 9 of Act No. III of 1950. "Public safety" ordinarily means security of the public or their freedom from danger. In that sense, anything which tends to prevent dangers to public health may also be regarded as securing public safety. The meaning of the expression must, however, vary according to the context. *Romesh Thapar* v. *The State,* AIR 1950 SC 124.

Public order and **Public tranquility.** Even if 'public order' and 'public tranquility' are not entirely co-extensive, there is no doubt that public tranquility is at least an essential constituent of 'public order'. *Ram Manohar Lohia* v. *State of U.P.,* AIR 1968 All 100, 109. [Constitution of India, Art. 19(2) & (3)]

'Public order' : 'Law and order' : 'Security of the State'. 'Public order', 'law and order' and the 'security of the State' fictionally draw three concentric circles, the largest representing law and order, the next representing public order and the smallest representing security of the State. Every infraction of law must necessarily affect order, but an act affecting law and order may not necessarily also affect the public order. Likewise an act may affect public order, but not necessarily the security of the state. The true test is not the kind, but the potentiality of the act in question. One act may affect only individuals while the other, though of a similar kind, may have such an impact that it would disturb even the tempo of the life of the community. This does not mean that there can be no overlapping, in the sense that an act cannot fall under two concepts at the same time. An act, for instance, affecting public order may have an impact that it would affect both 'public order' and the 'security of the State'. *Commer. of Police* v. *C. Anita,* (2004) 7 SCC 467, 472, para 10. See also *Kishori Mohan Bera* v. *State of W.B.,* (1972) 3 SCC 845.

Public peace. 'Public peace' as used in a statute pointing out the penalties to be imposed for breaches of the public peace, means 'that invisible sense of security which every man feels so necessary to his comfort, and for which all governments are instituted.'

The security and tranquility of the community in general. [CrPC 1973 (2 of 1974), S. 129(1)].

Public peace and public safety. The words 'public peace' and 'public safety' do not mean ordinary disturbance of law and order. Public safety means safety of the public at large and not safety of a few persons only. *Ganesh Chandra Bhatt* v. *District Magistrate Almora,* AIR 1993 All 291, 305. [Arms Act (54 of 1959), S. 14(1)(b)(ii)]

Public perception. There is no barometer to gauge the perception of the people. In a democracy there are many people who get elected by thumping majority to high legislative offices. Many a times 'public perception' of a class of society in regard to such people may be that they are not desirable to hold such post but can such a public opinion deprive such people from occupying constitutional or statutory offices without there being a law to the contrary. *People's Union for Civil Liberties* v. *UOI*, AIR 2005 SC 2419 : 2005 AIR SCW 2481.

Public performance. Performance of a copyrighted work in a place open to the public or where a substantial number of people outside a normal circle of family and social acquaintances are gathered. (*Cyber Law*)

Presenting a work in public places, where there are a substantial number of persons outside a normal circle of friends or family. (*Cyber Law*)

Public place. "PUBLIC PLACE" means any place intended for use by, or accessible to the public and includes any public conveyance. [Immoral Traffic (Prevention) Act (104 of 1956), S. 2(h)]

A 'PUBLIC PLACE' includes also property belonging to the State, camping grounds and ground left unoccupied for sanitary or recreative purposes. [CrPC, 1973 (2 of 1974), S. 133, *Expln.*] [Now (w. e. f. 1-7-2024) repealed & replaced by Bharatiya Nagarik Suraksha Sanhita, 2023 (46 of 2023), S. 152, Explanation, same definition in new Sanhita]

"PUBLIC PLACE" means a road, street, way or other place, whether a thoroughfare or not, to which the public have a right of access and includes any place or stand at which passengers are picked up or set down by a stage carriage. [Motor Vehicles Act (59 of 1988), S. 2(34)]

For the purposes of this sub-section, the expression "PUBLIC PLACE" includes any public conveyance, any hotel, any shop or any other place intended for use by, or accessible to the public. [Information Technology Act (21 of 2000), S. 80(1) *Expln.*]

"PUBLIC PLACE" means any place to which the public have access, whether as of right or not, and includes auditorium, hospital buildings, railway waiting room, amusement centres, restaurants, public offices, Court buildings, educational institutions, libraries, public conveyances and the like which are visited by general public but does not include any open space. [Cigarettes and other Tobacco Products (Prohibition of Advertisement and Regulation of Trade and Commerce, Production, Supply and Distribution) Act (34 of 2003), S. 3(l)]

"PUBLIC PLACE" means any place which is open to the use and enjoyment of the public, whether it is actually used or enjoyed by the public or not. [New Delhi Municipal Council Act (44 of 1994), S. 2(37)]

"PUBLIC PLACE" means a space, not being private property which is open to the use or enjoyment of the public whether such space is vested in a municipality or not. [Manipur Municipalities Act (43 of 1994), S. 2(48) and Sikkim Municipalities Act (Sikkim Act No. 6 of 1995), S. 2(xxvii)]

A place where the people in general have an access and wherein they congregate; a place owned by public authorities and open to the people in general. [CrPC 1973 (2 of 1974), S. 133(1)(a)]; [Immoral Traffic (Prevention) Act (104 of 1956), S. 2(h)].

PUBLIC PLACE means a road, street, way or other place whether a thoroughfare or not, to which the public are granted access or over which they have a right to pass.

A room of a hotel occupied by a customer, booked under his name remains a 'public place' like a hotel under Section 43 of the Act. *Ganga Bahadur Thapa* v. *State of Goa,* (2000) 10 SCC 312, para 3. [NDPS Act (61 of 1985), S. 43]

The link road or the parking area in the aerodrome premises are not public places. *Taxi Drivers' Union* v. *Kerala State Road Transport Corporation,* AIR 1983 Ker 69, 73 [Now Repealed & replaced by Act 59 of 1988].

A place belonging to a Public Works Department to which access had been granted to the workmen engaged in the construction of a bridge or a dam is a public place. *Lanka Sarmma* v. *Rajendra Singh,* AIR 1984 AP 32, 35.

The expression 'public place' means a place accessible to members of public whether permissive, limited, restricted or regulated by oral or written permission and available for their use, enjoyment, avocation or other purpose. *Pandurang* v. *New India LIC Ltd.,*1988 Bom 248, 252 (FB).

A public place is one which is in full view of the public and one to which the public have access.

Public policy. Principles in accordance with which actions of men and communities need to be regulated to achieve the good of the entire community or public. [prov., IPC (45 of 1860), S. 171B(1)].

Public policy is not a static concept. It varies with times and from generation is generation. But what is in public good and public interest cannot be opposed to public policy and vice versa. Fundamental Policy of Law would also constitute a facet of public policy. This would imply that all those principles of law that ensure justice, fair play and bring transparency and objectivity and promote probity in the discharge of public functions would also constitute public policy. Conversely, any deviation abrogation, frustration or negation of the salutary principles of justice, fairness, good conscience, equity and objectivity will be opposed to public policy. [*Board of Control for Cricket in India* v. *Cricket Association of Bihar*, (2015) 3 SCC 251, para 96].

The principles and matters which the legislature and the Courts broadly regard as being of fundamental concern to the state and the whole society; the principles violation of which is considered to be against the public good, interest of the State and community.

It is equivalent to the 'policy of the law'. It is applicable to the spirit as well as the letter. Whatever tends to injustice of operation, restraint of liberty, commerce and natural or legal right, obstruction of justice, violation of statute, against good morals is against Public Policy. *Kolaparti Venkatareddi* v. *Kolaparti Peda Venkatachalam,* AIR 1964 AP 465, 467. [Indian Contract Act (9 of 1872), S. 23]

Public policy is not the policy of a particular government. It connotes some matter which concerns the public good and the public interest. The principles governing public policy must be and are capable, on proper occasion, of expansion or modification. *General Inland Water Transport Corporation Ltd.* v. *Brojo Nath*, AIR 1986 SC 1571, 1612.

The concept of public policy is illusive, varying and uncertain. It is described as "untrustworthy guide", "unruly horse", *etc. P. Rathinam* v. *Union of India*, AIR 1994 SC 1844, 1864. [Indian Contract Act (9 of 1872), S. 23]

The words 'public policy' refer to the public policy of India and the recognition and enforcement of the award of the Arbitral Tribunal cannot be questioned on the ground that it is contrary to the public policy of the State of New York. *Renusagar Power Co. Ltd.* v. *General Electric Co.*, AIR 1994 SC 860, 885. [Foreign Award (Recognition and Enforcement) Act (45 of 1961), S. 7(1)(b)(i)]

Public policy of India. The phrase 'public policy of India' as used in Section 34(2)(b) of Arbitration and Conciliation Act (26 of 1996), in a wider sense means, 'some matter which concerns public good or public interest.' *ONGC Ltd.* v. *Saw Pipes Ltd.*, AIR 2003 SC 2629.

Public premises. Means—

(1) any premises belonging to, or taken on lease or requisitioned, or on behalf of, the Central Government, and includes any such premises which have been placed by that Government, whether before or after the commencement of the Public Premises (Eviction of Unauthorised Occupants) Amendment, 1980 under the control of the Secretariat of either Houses of Parliament for providing residential accommodation to any member of the staff of that Secretariat,

(2) any premises belonging to, or taken on lease by, or on behalf of,

(i) any company as defined in section 3 of [3][the Companies Act, 2013 (18 of 2013)], in which not less than fifty-one per cent. of the paid up share capital is held by the Central Government or any company which is a subsidiary (within the meaning of that Act) of the first-mentioned company;

(ii) any corporation (not being a company as defined in section 3 of the Companies Act, 2013 (18 of 2013), or a local authority) established by or under a Central Act and owned or controlled by the Central Government;

(iii) any company as defined in clause (20) of section 2 of the Companies Act , 2013 (18 of 2013) in which not less than fifty-one per cent. of the paid up capital is held partly by the Central Government and partly by one or more State Governments and includes a company which is a subsidiary (within the meaning of that Act) of the first-mentioned company and which carries on the business of public transport including metro railway.

Explanation. For the purposes of this item, metro railway shall have the same meaning as assigned to it in clause (i) of sub-section (1) of section 2 of the Metro Railway (Operation and Maintenance) Act, 2002 (60 of 2002);

(iiia) any University established or incorporated by any Central Act,]

(iv) any Institute incorporated by the Institutes of Technology Act , 1961 (59 of 1961);

[3][(v) any Board of Trustees or any successor company constituted under or referred to in the Major Port Trusts Act, 1963 (38 of 1963);]

(vi) the Bhakra Management Board constituted under section 79 of the Punjab Reorganisation Act, 1966 (31 of 1966), and that Board as and when re-named as the Bhakra-Beas Management Board under sub-section (6) of section 80 of that Act; [4][***]

[5][(vii) any State Government or the Government of any Union Territory situated in the National Capital Territory of Delhi or in any other Union Territory;

(viii) any Cantonment Board constituted under the Cantonments Act, 1924 (2 of 1924); and]

[6][(vii) any State Government or the Government of any Union Territory situated in the National Capital Territory of Delhi or in any other Union Territory;

(viii) any Cantonment Board constituted under the Cantonments Act, 1924 (2 of 1924); and]

(3) in relation to the [7][National Capital Territory of Delhi]

(i) any premises belonging to the [7][Council as defined in clause (9) of section 2 of the New Delhi Municipal Council Act , 1994 (44 of 1994) or Corporation or Corporations notified under sub-section (1) of section 3 of the Delhi Municipal Corporation Act , 1957 (66 of 1957)], of Delhi, or any Municipal Committee or notified area committee;

(ii) any premises belonging to the Delhi Development Authority, whether such premises are in the possession of, or leased out by, the said Authority;] [2][and]

(iii) any premises belonging to, or taken on lease or requisitioned by, or on behalf of any State Government or the Government of any Union Territory;]

[4][(iv) any premises belonging to, or taken on lease by, or on behalf of any Government company as defined in clause (45) of section 2 of the Companies Act, 2013 (18 of 2013).

Explanation. For the purposes of this clause, the expression, State Government occurring in clause (45) of the said section shall mean the Government of the National Capital Territory of Delhi.]

(4) any premises of the enemy property as defined in clause (c) of section 2 of the Enemy Property Act, 1968 (34 of 1968).]

[Public Premises (Eviction of Unauthorised Occupants) Act (40 of 1971), S. 2(e)*as substituted by act of 2015*]

Any premises which belong to or are taken on lease by a company in which not less than fifty one per cent of the paid up share capital is held by the General Government fall within the expression "public premises". *Bharat Petroleum Corporation Ltd.* v. *Union of India,* AIR 1992 P&H 248, 251. [Public Premises (Eviction of Unauthorised Occupants) Act (40 of 1971), S. 2(c)]

Public procession. Where a procession is taken out at a public place, it is going along a public thoroughfare to a meeting which is admittedly public *i.e.* a purpose of a party as opposed to a private purpose, and it is open to the public or a class of the public to join in the procession, the reasonable inference from the proved facts is that the procession is public. *Inderdeo Singh* v. *State,* AIR 1951 Pat 242.

Public procurement. Obtaining goods or services for the use of public sector.

Public property. 'PUBLIC PROPERTY' means any property belonging to Government or any local authority. [Assam Panchayat Act, 1994 (Assam Act No. 18 of 1994), S. 2(17)]

"PUBLIC PROPERTY" means any property, whether immovable or movable (including any machinery) which is owned by, or in the possession of, or under the control of—

(i) the Central Government; or

(ii) any State Government; or

(iii) any local authority; or

(iv) any corporation established by, or under, a Central, Provincial or State Act; or

(v) any company as defined in Section 617 of Companies Act, 1956, or;

(vi) any institution, concern or undertaking which the Central Government may, by notification in the official Gazette, specify in this behalf: Provided that the Central Government shall not specify any institution, concern or undertaking is financed wholly or substantially by funds provided directly or indirectly by the Central Government or by one or more State Governments, or partly by the Central Government and partly by one or more State Governments. [Prevention of Damage to Public Property Act (3 of 1984), S. 2(b)].

Property owned by the government or local bodies on behalf of the community in general [CrPC 1973 (2 of 1974), S. 37(c)]; [Constitution of India, Art. 51A(i)].

Public prosecutor. "PUBLIC PROSECUTOR" means any person appointed under S. 24, CrPC 1973 (2 of 1974), and includes any person acting under the directions of a public prosecutor. [CrPC 1973 (2 of 1974), S. 2(u)] [Now (w. e. f. 1-7-2024) repealed & replaced by Bharatiya Nagarik Suraksha Sanhita, 2023 (46 of 2023)]

A public official charged with the investigation and prosecution of punishable acts on behalf of a State or an international commission. [CrPC 1973 (2 of 1974), S. 2(u)].

"Public Prosecutor" means any person appointed under section 18, and includes any person acting under the directions of a Public Prosecutor. [(w. e. f. 1-7-2024) Bharatiya Nagarik Suraksha Sanhita, 2023 (46 of 2023), S. 2(1)(v)]

For the purposes of this Chapter, the expression "Public Prosecutor" has the meaning assigned to it under clause (*v*) of section 2 and includes an Assistant Public Prosecutor appointed under section 19. [(w. e. f. 1-7-2024) Bharatiya Nagarik Suraksha Sanhita, 2023 (46 of 2023), S. 298, *Explanation*]

"Public Prosecutor" is a holder of "public office" and he holds a "post" yet he is not in government service as the term is usually understood. [*Deepak Aggarwal* v. *Keshav Kaushik*, (2013) 5 SCC 277, para 85].

Public purpose. "The expression "PUBLIC PURPOSE" includes—(i) the provision of village-sites, or the extension, planned development or improvement of existing village sites; (ii) the provision of land for town or rural planning; (iii) the provision of land for planned development of land from public funds in persuance of any scheme or policy of Government and subsequent disposal thereof in whole or in part by lease, assignment or outright sale with the object of securing further development as planned; (iv) the provision of land for a corporation owned or controlled by the State; (v) the provision of land for residential purposes to the poor or landless or to persons residing in areas affected by natural calamities, or to persons displaced or affected by reason of the implementation of any scheme undertaken by Government, any local authority or corporation owned or controlled by the State; (vi) the provision of land for carrying out any educational, housing, health or slum clearance scheme sponsored by Government, or by any authority established by Government for carrying out any such scheme, or with the prior approval of the appropriate Government, by local authority, or a society registered under the Societies Registration Act, 1860 (21 of 1860), or under any corresponding law for the time being in force in a State, or a co-operative society within the meaning of any law relating to co-operative societies for the time being in force in any State; (vii) the provision of land for any other scheme of development sponsored by Government, or with the prior approval of the appropriate Government, by a local authority, (viii) the provision of any premises or building for locating a public office, but does not include acquisition of land for companies." [Land Acquisition Act (1 of 1894), S.3 (f)] [Now Repealed & replaced by Act 30 of 2013].

A purpose for the general good of the masses. [Land Acquisition Act (1 of 1894), S. 3(f)].

Even if only a section of the public is benefited by a land acquisition, the purpose would still be a public purpose and hence the acquisition of house sites for *Panchamas* is a public purpose.

The expression 'public purpose' would include a purpose in which the general interest of the community as opposed to the particular interest of individuals is directly and vitally concerned. *Somawanti* v. *State of Punjab*, AIR 1963 SC 151, 161. [Land Acquisition Act (1 of 1894), S. 2(f)] [Now Repealed & replaced by Act 30 of 2013]

The requisitioning of land for military purpose is a public purpose. *Dimboswar Dattu* v. *Deputy Commissioner Sibsagar,* AIR 1954 Ass 159. [Land Acquisition Act (1 of 1894), S. 3(f)] [Now Repealed & replaced by Act 30 of 2013]

The requirement of land for residential and commercial purposes and for development of the sector involves in it an element of general interest of the community and whatever furthers the general interest must be regarded as a "public purpose" as opposed to the particular interest of individuals. [*State of Haryana v. Vinod Oil and General Mills*, (2014) 15 SCC 410, para 13].

Where a Co-operative Society, in which the State has a major interest, wants to construct a factory for encouraging the local sugarcane growers and the industry and also for increasing the production of sugar to meet the acute shortage of sugar, 'public purpose' is involved in such a venture. *T. Subba Reddy* v. *State of A.P.,* AIR 1979 AP 127, 129.

If there is scheme for acquisition of land for cooperative societies and in implementation of the scheme, acquisition is made for a particular co-operative society, the acquisition would be for the public purpose. *Musamiyam Imam Haridarbux Razvi* v. *State of Gujarat,* AIR 1971 Guj 158, 164. [Land Acquisition Act (1 of 1894), S. 3(f), 4 and 6]

Use as a residential house for the Chief Minister is a public purpose. *Francisco Feweira Martins* v. *Union of India,* AIR 1985 Bom 312, 316.

Whenever a factory for manufacturing purposes is to be set up, dwelling houses will have to be constructed for others. Acquisition for building such dwelling houses though it would benefit only a fraction of the public will be a public purpose. *Barkya Thakurb* Case, AIR 1960 SC 1203 Relied on. [Land Acquisition Act (1 of 1894), Ss. 4 and 6]

The definition of "public purpose" in S. 6 of the Land Acquisition Act (1 of 1894), is a partially inclusive, no exhaustive definition.

The acquisition for the purpose of construction of the temples must be held to be a public purpose. *State of Bihar* v. *Kameshwar Singh* AIR 1952 SC 252.

The plan to provide healthy and properly planned development of the city is called 'public purpose'. *Matri Devi* v. *Chief Commissioner Delhi*, AIR 1975 SC 1699, 1702. [Land Acquisition Act (1 of 1894), S. 16]

General interest of the public requires industrial development to be made, so that not only some of the people living in the place are given employment and also their living standard may be upgraded and therefore, planned industrial development is for "public purpose". *Brij Bhushan Goswami* v. *State of U.P.,* AIR 1990 All 15, 16. [Land Acquisition Act (1 of 1894), S. 17(4)] [Now Repealed & replaced by Act 30 of 2013]

The mere fact that the Government will charge a moderate rent such rent as the letting value of the property cannot alter the essential character of a building as one used for a public purpose.

The general interest of the community was directly and vitally concerned with the efficiency of the Government servants because it would be to its benefit to have such servants and therefore providing living accommodation for them was a public purpose. *State of Bombay* v. *R.S. Nanji*, AIR 1956 SC 294, 297.

Acquisition for the purpose of enabling the teaching staff to live in close proximity to the university campus and afford to them the necessary convenience is a public purpose. *Al. C.T. Alagappa Chettiar* v. *Revenue Divisional Officer,* AIR 1969 Mad 183 at 186.

Whatever furthers the general interests of the community, as opposed to the particular interest of the individual must be regarded as a public purpose. The phrase has to be construed according to the spirits of the time in which the particular legislation is enacted. *State of Bihar* v. *Kameshwar Singh*, AIR 1952 SC 252. [Constitution of India, Sch. 7, Entry 36, List III, Entry 42]

To bring Govt. waste land under cultivation and also to allot the land to a landless member of the backward class for the purpose of his personal cultivation is a public purpose. *Sanadhiyala Gram Panchayat Bhavnagar* v. *State of Gujarat,* AIR 1985 Guj 105, 106.

To carry passengers along certain routes can hardly be described as a 'public purpose'. It may be conceded that such activity is in public interest. *Chandra Kishore* v. *State of Uttar Pradesh,* AIR 1963 All 301, 305.

The requisitioning of the property in question for the purpose of placing it at the disposal of the Lady Irwin

College was a public purpose. *Vinod Sagar* v. *Union of India,* AIR 1976 Del 76, 80. [Requisitioning and Acquisition of Immovable Property Act (30 of 1952), S. 3(1)]

Land, though acquired for resettlement of immigrants but used for the establishment of a hospital for crippled children is for 'public purpose'. *Collector 24 Parganas* v. *Lalit Mohan Mullick*, AIR 1986 SC 622, 626.

The conservation and the prudent and discriminating exploitation of minerals with a view to secure maximum benefit to the community is a public purpose. *State of Tamilnadu* v. *Hond Stone Etc.*, AIR 1981 SC 711, 716.

'Public purpose' and 'public necessity'. 'Public purpose' is wider than a 'public necessity'. Purpose is more pervasive than urgency. That which one sets before him to accomplish, an end, intention, aim, object, plan or project, is purpose. A need or necessity, on the other hand, is urgent, unavoidable, compulsive. 'Public purpose' should be liberally construed, not whittled down by logomachy. [*Sooraram Pratap Reddy* v. *District Collector*, (2008) 9 SCC 552, 586, para 79]

Public record. "PUBLIC RECORDS" includes—

(i) any document, manuscript and file;

(ii) any microfilm, microfiche and facsimile copy of a document;

(iii) any reproduction of image or images embodied in such microfilm (whether enlarged or not); and

(iv) any other material produced by a computer or by any other device. [Public Records Act (69 of 1993), S. 2(e)]

Record of transactions *etc.* maintained by public authorities. [Indian Evidence Act (1 of 1872), S. 35].

Public resort. A private house and garden where a sale by public auction takes place is for the time a 'place of public resort'. The place need not be a place of resort all the year round.

Frequent, habitual or general going or retiring to or visiting of general public. [Emigration Act (7 of 1922), S. 2(f)(iv)].

Public resort, Place of. A place at which the public assembles or to which they retire. [CPC (5 of 1908), O. XXI, R. 74, prov.].

Public revenue. The income of an organized public authority from each and every source whatever and from which expenses of that public body on all heads are met. [Indian Evidence Act (1 of 1872), S. 125, *Expln.*].

Public right. A right enjoyed by the public, as distinguished from a private or personal right attached to the personality of an individual. [Indian Evidence Act (1 of 1872), S. 32(4)].

Public right of way. Right to pass along a way enjoyed by the public. [Indian Evidence Act (1 of 1872), S. 42, ill.].

Public road. "PUBLIC ROAD" means any street, road, square, Court alley, passage or pathway over which the public have a right of way whether a thoroughfare or not, and includes—

(a) the roadway over any public bridge or causeway;

(b) the footway attached to any such road, public bridge or causeway; and

(c) the drains attached to any such road, public bridge or causeway, and the land, whether covered or not by any pavement, verandah or other structure, which lies on either side of the roadway up to the boundaries of the adjacent property whether that property is private property or Government property. [Manipur Municipalities Act (43 of 1994), S. 2(49)]

A road which is open to the public as a matter of right. [CPC (5 of 1908), Sch. I, App. A, form No. 37]; [Indian Railways Act (9 of 1890), S. 125(4)].

Public safety. 'Public safety' ordinarily means security of the public or their freedom from danger. In that sense anything which tends to prevent dangers to public health may also be regarded as securing public safety. *Romesh Thappar* v. *State of Madras*, AIR 1950 SC 124, 127.

The security of the public or their freedom from danger. [CrPC 1973 (2 of 1974), S. 116(3)]; [Arms Act (54 of 1959), S. 1(3)(b)].

Public sector. That part of the industry which is controlled fully or partly by a public undertaking. [Employment Exchanges (Compulsory Notification of Vacancies) Act (31 of 1959), S. 4(1)].

Public sector bank. The expression "PUBLIC SECTOR BANK" means the State Bank of India constituted under the State Bank of India Act, 1955, a subsidiary bank as defined in the State Bank of India (Subsidiary Banks) Act, 1959, a corresponding new bank constituted under Section 3 of the Banking Companies (Acquisition and Transfer of Undertakings) Act, 1970 or under Section 3 of the Banking Companies (Acquisition and Transfer of Undertakings) Act, 1980. [State Financial Corporation Act (63 of 1951), S. 2(da); Small Industries Development Act (39 of 1989), S. 2(la)]

"PUBLIC SECTOR BANK" means—

(i) a corresponding new bank specified in the First Schedule to the Banking Companies (Acquisition and Transfer of Undertaking) Act, 1970;

(ii) a corresponding new bank specified in the First Schedule to the Banking Companies (Acquisition and Transfer of Undertakings) Act, 198;

(iii) the State Bank of India constituted under the State Bank of India Act, 1955;

(iv) a subsidiary bank as defined in the State Bank of India (Subsidiary Banks) Act, 1959; [Banking Service Commission Act (44 of 1984), S. 2(j)]

Public securities. "PUBLIC SECURITIES" means—

(i) promissory notes, debentures, stock or other securities of the Central Government or of any State Government:

Provided that securities both the principal whereof and the interest whereon have been fully and unconditionally guaranteed by any such Government, shall be deemed, for the purposes of this clause, to be securities of such Government;

(ii) debentures or other securities of money issued by or on behalf of any municipal body, Improvement Trust or Port Trust under the authority of any law for the time being in force in India (including the Port Trust securities). [Major Port Trusts Act (38 of 1963), S. 2(u)] [Now Repealed by s. 75(1) of Act 1 of 2021].

"PUBLIC SECURITIES" means, any securities of the Central Government or a State Government or any securities guaranteed by the Central Government or a State Government or any securities issued under this Act or any debentures issued by the Bombay, Calcutta, Delhi or Madras Municipal Corporation. [New Delhi Municipal Council Act (44 of 1994), S. 2(38)]

Public security. Safety of the members of the community. [CrPC 1973 (2 of 1974), S. 130(1)].

Public servant. The words "public servant" denote a person falling under any of the descriptions hereinafter following, namely:—

* * *

Second.—Every Commissioned Officer in the Military, Naval or Air Forces * * * of India.

Third.—Every Judge including any person empowered by law to discharge, whether by himself or as a member of any body of persons, any adjudicatory functions;

Fourth.—Every officer of a Court of Justice (including a liquidator, receiver or commissioner) whose duty it is, as such officer, to investigate or report on any matter of law or fact, or to make, authenticate, or keep any document, or to take charge or dispose of any property, or to execute any judicial process, or to administer any oath, or to interpret, or to preserve order in the Court, and every person specially authorised by a Court of Justice to perform any of such duties;

Fifth.—Every juryman, assessor, or member of a panchayat assisting a Court of Justice or public servant;

Sixth.—Every arbitrator or other person to whom any cause or matter has been referred for decision or report by any Court of Justice, or by any other competent public authority;

Seventh.—Every person who holds any office by virtue of which he is empowered to place or keep any person in confinement;

Eighth.—Every officer of the Government whose duty it is, as such officer, to prevent offences, to give information of offences, to bring offenders to justice, or to protect the public health, safety or convenience;

Ninth.—Every officer whose duty it is, as such officer, to take, receive, keep or expend any property on behalf of the Government, or to make any survey, assessment or contract on behalf of the Government, or to execute any revenue process, or to investigate, or to report, on any matter affecting the pecuniary interests of the Government or to make, authenticate or keep any document relating to the pecuniary interests of the Government or to prevent the infraction of any law for the protection of the pecuniary interests of the Government

* * *

Tenth.—Every officer whose duty it is, as such officer, to take, receive, keep or expend any property, to make any survey or assessment or to levy any rate or tax for any secular common purpose of any village, town or district, or to make, authenticate or keep any document for the ascertaining of the rights of the people of any village, town or district;

Eleventh.—Every person who holds any office in virtue of which he is empowered to prepare, publish, maintain or revise an electoral roll or to conduct an election or part of an election;

Twelfth.—Every person—

(a) in the service or pay of the Government or remunerated by fees or commission for the performance of any public duty by the Government;

(b) in the service or pay of a local authority, a corporation established by or under a Central, Provincial or State Act or a Government company as defined in Section 617 of the Companies Act, 1956 (1 of 1956).

Explanation 1.—Persons falling under any of the above descriptions are public servants, whether appointed by the Government or not.

Explanation 2.—Wherever the words "public servant" occur, they shall be understood of every person who is in actual possession of the situation of a public servant, whatever legal defect there may be in his right to hold that situation.

Explanation 3.—The word "election" denotes an election for the purpose of selecting members of any legislative, municipal or other public authority, of whatever character, the method of selection to which is by, or under, any law prescribed as by election.

* * *

State Amendment.—[Rajasthan]. In its application to the State of Rajasthan, after clause *Twelfth,* add the following new clause, namely:—

Thirteenth—Every person employed or engaged by any public body in the conduct and supervision of any examination recognised or approved under any law".

Explanation.—The expression "public body" includes—

(a) a University, Board of Education or other body, either established by or under a Central or State Act or under the provisions of the Constitution of India or constituted by the Government; and

(b) a local authority.—Rajasthan Act 4 of 1993, Section 2 (*w.e.f.* 11-2-1993). [IPC (45 of 1860), S. 21] [Now (w. e. f. 1-7-2024) repealed & replaced by Bharatiya Nyaya Sanhita, 2023 (45 of 2023)].

"PUBLIC SERVANT" means—

(i) any person in the service or pay of the Government or remunerated by the Government by fees or commission for the performance of any public duty;

(ii) any person in the service or pay of a local authority;

(iii) any person in the service or pay of a corporation established by or under a Central, Provincial or State Act, or an authority or a body owned or controlled or aided by the Government or a Government company as defined in Section 617 of the Companies Act, 1956;

(iv) any Judge, including any person empowered by law to discharge, whether by himself or as a member of any body of persons, any adjudicatory functions;

(v) any person authorised by a Court of justice to perform any duty, in connection with the administration of justice, including a liquidator, receiver or commissioner appointed by such Court;

(vi) any arbitrator or other person to whom any cause or matter has been referred for decision or report by a Court of justice or by a competent public authority;

(vii) any person who holds an office by virtue of which he is empowered to prepare, publish, maintain or revise an electoral roll or to conduct an election or part of an election;

(viii) any person who holds an office by virtue of which he is authorised or required to perform any public duty;

(ix) any person who is the president, secretary or other office-bearer of a registered co-operative society engaged in agriculture, industry, trade or banking, receiving or having received any financial aid from the Central Government or a State Government or from any corporation established by or under a Central, Provincial or State Act, or any authority or body owned or controlled or aided by the Government or a Government company as defined in Section 617 of the Companies Act, 1956;

(x) any person who is a chairman, member or employee of any Service Commission or Board, by whatever name called, or a member of any selection committee appointed by such Commission or Board for the conduct of any examination or making any selection on behalf of such Commission or Board;

(xi) any person who is a Vice-Chancellor or member of any governing body, professor, reader, lecturer or any other teacher or employee, by whatever designation called, of any University or any person whose services have been availed of by a University or any other public authority in connection with holding or conducting examinations;

(xii) any person who is an office-bearer or an employee of an educational, scientific, social, cultural or other institution, in whatever manner established, receiving or having received any financial assistance from the Central Government or any State Government or local or other public authority.

Explanation 1.—Persons falling under any of the above sub-clauses are public servants, whether appointed by the Government or not.

Explanation 2.—Wherever the words "public servant" occur, they shall be understood of every person who is in actual possession of the situation of a public servant, whatever legal defect there may be in his right to hold that situation. [Prevention of Corruption Act (49 of 1988), S. 2(c)]

A holder of public office. [IPC (45 of 1860), S. 21].

A member of the Indian Administrative Service and Civil Servant working on deputation on a Co-operative Society is not a Public Servant. *S. S. Dhanoh* v. *Municipal Corporation Delhi*, AIR 1981 SC 1385, 1399.

An M.L.A. is not a public servant. *R.S. Nayak* v. *A.R. Antulay*, AIR 1984 SC 684, 717.

A 'public servant' is an authority who must be appointed by Government or a semi Governmental body and should be in the pay or salary of the same. Secondly, a 'public servant' is to discharge his duties in accordance with the rules and regulations made by the Government. *Ramesh* v. *State of Maharashtra*, AIR 1985 SC 1655, 1656.

An inspector in the Finger Print Bureau being in the service and pay of Government is a public servant, even if he is not performing the ordinary duties of a police officer.

To attract the protection conferred by S. 197, CrPC 1973 (2 of 1974) the public servant concerned must be, laid down by cl. (b) of sub-sec. (1) of S. 197, CrPC 1973 (2 of 1974), a person employed in connection with the affairs of a state. A *serpanch* or a *upasarpanch* is not a public servant since they hold office by election and not by employment. *Konkati Narayani* v. *Balakanti Veerayya,* AIR 1959 AP 27, 28. [CrPC 1973 (2 of 1974), S. 197]

"PUBLIC SERVANT". A person who is engaged by a competent authority to work on a fee or a fixed remuneration can be a 'public servant'. *UOI* v. *Alok Kumar*, AIR 2010 SC 2735.

"PUBLIC SERVANT" means a person referred to in clauses (a) to (h) of sub-section (1) of section 14 but does not include a public servant in respect of whom the jurisdiction is exercisable by any court or other authority under the Army Act, 1950 (45 of 1950), the Air Force Act, 1950 (46 of 1950), the Navy Act, 1957 (62 of 1957) and the Coast Guard Act, 1978 (30 of 1978) or the procedure is applicable to such public servant under those Acts. [S. 2(1)(o) of the Lokpal & Lokayuktas Act, 2013 (1 of 2014)]

"PUBLIC SERVANT". Section 21(12)(b) of the Indian Penal Code, 1860 and section 2(c)(iii) of the Prevention of Corruption Act, 1988, provide that a person in the service of a Corporation established by or under a Central, Provincial or State Act is a 'public servant'. *Dalco Engineering Private Ltd.* v. *Shree Satish Prabhakar Padhye*, AIR 2010 SC 1576.

Public servant concerned. "Whoever happened to occupy that post at the time of filing the complaint is the Public servant concerned". *Public Prosecutor* v. *Mohammed Ali,* AIR 1969 AP 41 at 43. [CrPC 1973 (2 of 1974), S. 195(1)(a)]

Public service commission. An independent body under the State entrusted with the task of recruitment of civil servants. (See Part XIV, Chapter II of Const. from Arts. 315-323)

Public service vehicle. "PUBLIC SERVICE VEHICLE" means any motor vehicle used or adopted to be used for the carriage of passengers for hire or reward, and includes a maxicab, a motorcar, contract carriage, and stage carriage. [Motor Vehicles Act (59 of 1988), S. 2(35)] [Now Repealed & replaced by Act 59 of 1988]

"PUBLIC SERVICE VEHICLE" means a vehicle which is used to carry passengers from one place to another. [Delhi Cinematograph (Exhibition of Film by VCR) Rules 1986, R. 2(xv)]

The term has not been defined anywhere. The word 'public' has got a well-known connotation and means a carriage to which any member of the public can have free access on payment of the usual charges. *Tata Engineering and Locomotions Co. Ltd.* v. *Sales Tax Officer*, AIR 1979 SC 343, 345.

Public share holding. "PUBLIC SHAREHOLDING" means shareholding in the Land of person(s) other than the acquirer and persons acting in concert with him. [SEBI (Sub. Acq. of Shares and Takeovers Regulations, 1997, Reg. 2(j)]

Public street. 'PUBLIC STREET" means any street heretofore levelled paved metalled, channelled, sewered or repaired by the corporation, and any street which becomes a public street under any of the provisions of the Municipal Act. [City Bombay Municipal Act (3 of 1988), S. 3(ix)]

"PUBLIC STREET" shall mean any street — (i) Over which the public have a right of way, or; (ii) heretofore levelled, paved, metalled, channelled, sewered or repaired out of municipal or other public funds; or (iii) which, is declared by the municipality to be, or under any other provisions of the Municipal Act becomes a public street. [Punjab Municipal Act (3 of 1911), S. 3(b)]

"PUBLIC STREET" means any street which vests in the Council as a public street or the soil below the surface of which vests in the Council or which under the provisions of this Act becomes, or is declared to be, a public street. [New Delhi Municipal Council Act (44 of 1994), S. 2(39)]

"PUBLIC STREET" means any street or the soil below the surface thereof which is specifically vested in the Corporation by an order of the Administrator issued in this behalf. [Punjab Municipal Corporation law (Extension to Chandigarh) (45 of 1994), S. 2(43), Schedule-Part II]

Street by which the public may pass as a matter of right. [CrPC 1973 (2 of 1974), Sch. II, form No. 24].

Even the private property which forms part of public street, is public street and stands vested in the Municipal Committee. *Municipal Committee Karnal* v. *Nirmal Devi*, AIR 1996 SC 892, 893.

Not only pavements but *varandahs* in front of the shops are part of the streets and public streets. *Banarsidas* v. *Ramkrishna,* AIR 1995 MP 147, 152.

Public tranquility, Disturb the. Disturbing the calmness or serenity concerning the people as a whole. [CrPC 1973 (2 of 1974), S. 107(1)]; [IPC (45 of 1860), S. 153A(1)(b)].

Public trust. 'PUBLIC TRUST' means an express or constructive trust for either a public religious or charitable purpose or both and includes a temple, a *math,* a *wakf,* church, synagogue, *agiary* or other place of public religious worship, a *dharmada* or any other religious or charitable endowment and a society formed either for charitable purpose, or for both and registered under the Societies Registration Act, 1860. [Bombay Public Trust Act (29 of 1950), S. 2(13)]

Public trust, doctrine. The 'public trust doctrine' primarily rests on the principle that certain resources like air, sea, waters and the forests have such great importance to the people as a whole that it would be wholly unjustified to make them a subject of private ownership. The said resources being a gift of nature, they should be made freely available to everyone irrespective of the status in life. The doctrine enjoins upon the Government to protect the resources for the enjoyment of the general public rather than to permit their use for private ownership or commercial purposes. [*Karnataka Industrial Areas Development Board* v. *C. Kenchappa,* (2006) 6 SCC 371, 389, para 87 : AIR 2006 SC 2038]

Our legal system includes the public trust doctrine as part of its jurisprudence. The state is the trustee of all natural resources which are by nature meant for public use and enjoyment. The State as a trustee is under a legal duty to protect the natural resources. [*Intellectuals Forum* v. *State of A.P.,* (2006) 3 SCC 549, 574, para 75, **relying on** *M.C. Mehta* v. *Kamal Nath,* (1997) 1 SCC 388, 413, para 34; *M.I. Builders (P) Ltd.* v. *Radhey Shyam Sahu,* (1999) 6 SCC 464]

The 'public trust' is more than an affirmation of State power to use public property for public purposes. It is an affirmation of the duty of the State to protect the people's common heritage of streams, lakes, marshlands and tidelands, surrendering the right only in those rare cases when the abandonment of the right is consistent with the purposes of the trust. [*National Audubon Society* v. *Superior Court of Alpine Country,* 33 Call 419 (S.C. of California)-**As referred in** *Intellectuals Forum* v. *State of A.P.*, (2006) 3 SCC 549, 575, para 76]

Public trustee. A trustee appointed by the Government. [Companies Act (1 of 1956), S. 153A].

Public use. A 'public use' must be for the general public, or some portion of it, and not a use by or for particular individuals or for the benefit of certain estates.

Public utility. Public utility means any work, project which is going to be useful to members of the public at large. The public benefit aimed at or intended to be secured need not be to whole community but to a considerable number of people. *B.B. Nirman Sahkari Samiti* v. *State of Rajasthan,* AIR 1979 Raj 209, 213.

Public utility service. Means any—

(i) transport service for the carriage of passengers or goods by air, road or water; or

(ii) postal, telegraph or telephone service; or

(iii) supply of power, light or water to the public by any establishment; or

(iv) system of public conservancy or sanitation; or

(v) service in hospital or dispensary; or

(vi) insurance service. [Legal Services Authorities Act (39 of 1987), S. 22A(b)]

"PUBLIC UTILITY SERVICE" means—

(i) any railway service or any transport service for the carriage of passengers or goods by air;

(ia) any service in, or in connection with the working of any major port or dock.

(ii) any section of an industrial establishment, on the working of which the safety of the establishment or the workmen employed therein depends;

(iii) any postal, telegraph or telephone service;

(iv) any industry which supplies power, light or water to the public;

(v) any system of public conservancy or sanitation;

(vi) any industry specified in the First Schedule which the appropriate Government may, if satisfied that public emergency or public interest so requires, by notification in the Official Gazette, declare to be a public utility service for the purposes of this Act, for such period as may be specified in the notification.

Provided that the period so specified shall not, in the first instance, exceed six months but may, by a like notification, be extended from time to time by any period not exceeding six months, at any one time if in the opinion of the appropriate Government public emergency or public interest requires such extension. [Industrial Disputes Act (14 of 1947), S. 2(m)]

"PUBLIC UTILITY SERVICE" means any undertaking which supplies power, light, gas or water to the public, or carries on a public transport, or maintains any system of public conservancy or sanitation and which is declared by notification in the Official Gazette, by the Central Government to be a public utility service to which this Act applies:

Provided that no such notification shall be issued unless the Central Government is satisfied that, having regard to the need of the Territorial Army, the persons employed in any such public utility service should, in the public interest, be made compulsorily liable for service in that Army under this Act. [Territorial Army Act (56 of 1948), S. 2(dd)]

Public view. 'PUBLIC VIEW' means anything which is visible to public view while they are in or passing along any public place. [Goa Prevention of Defacement of Property Act, 1988 (Goa Act No. 5 of 1990), S. 2(g)]

Public waqf. Means the permanent dedication by a person professing Islam of any immovable property for any purpose recognised by Muslim Law as a public purpose of a pious, religious or charitable nature. [Public Wakf (Extension of Limitation) Act (29 of 1959), S. 2]

Public water-course. "PUBLIC WATER-COURSE" means a water-course under the charge of the officers of Government. Ben. Act II of 1882 (Embankment), S. 3.

Public way. Way by which public have a right to pass. [Indian Evidence Act (1 of 1872), S. 32, ill. (i)]; [IPC (45 of 1860), S. 283].

Publication. The action of making publicly known; the issuing or offering to the public of a book, map, engraving, *etc.* [IPC (45 of 1860), S. 173].

Publication of defamatory matter involves the communication of it to some person other than the person to whom it is addressed. Normally there is no publication when a letter containing defamatory imputations is sent direct to the person defamed but when it is proved that the writer knew that the person defamed could not read when he sent the letter and the person defamed gets it read by a third person, it must be held that there is evidence of a publication to a third person, for in such a case the writer must have known that the letter would be read to the person defamed by some third person.

'Publication is the act of publishing anything; offering it to the public notice or rendering it accessible to public scrutiny; a making known of something to them for a purpose. *State of M.P.* v. *Ram Ragubir Prasad*, AIR 1979 SC 888, 895.

'Publication' means making a work available to the public by issue of copies or by communicating the work to the public. [The Copyright Act, 1957, S. 3].

Publication of order. Where an order is published in the Gazette, it may be presumed that the publication of the order by the Government is sufficient publication and it may be further presumed that publication was made in the Gazette in compliance with all the provisions including the provision as to the determination of the most suitable form of publication. *State Govt. Madhya Pradesh* v. *Seth Parasmal,* AIR 1952 Nag 10, 11. [Indian Evidence Act (1 of 1872), S. 114]

Publicly impeached. Called in question publicly [Negotiable Instruments Act (26 of 1881), S. 100].

Publicly placing another in a false light. One of four types of common law torts for the invasion of privacy; defined as falsely connecting a person to an immoral, illegal, or embarrassing situation resulting in damage to their reputation. (*Cyber Law*)

Publicum bonum privato est praeferendum. The public good is to be preferred to private advantage.

Publish. To make generally accessible or available; to place before or offer to public; to bring before the public for sale or distribution [Indian Contract Act (9 of 1872), S. 224, ill. (b)].

The literal meaning of the word 'publish' used in Section 499 means 'making known to others'. The use of the word 'publish' in S. 499 IPC does not contemplate those communications which one is bound to make to others in the normal course of his legal duties. *Brij Ballabh Goyal* v. *Shri Sata Dev,* AIR 1960 Raj 213, 214. [IPC (45 of 1860), S. 499]

Publisher. "Publisher" is one who, by himself or his agent, makes a thing publicly known; one engaged in the circulation of books, pamphlets, news or other papers.

The word "publisher" has been used in the Act in a restricted sense and does not include the vendor of the newspaper or book. But a man who causes a book to be printed and offers it to the public for sale is a publisher. *In re G. Alavandar,* AIR 1957 Mad 427, 429. [Press and Registration of Books Act (25 of 1867), S. 3]

Publishes. The word 'publishes' will not include the mere sending of anonymous letter to the Deputy Commissioner who is a person other than the person of whom it is written. *Kali Ram* v. *State,* AIR 1961 Punj 381.

Pucca structure. Means a structure with

(i) cemented, or wooden floor,

(ii) iron, brick or concrete posts, and

(iii) roof of reinforced concrete, or of galvanised iron, aluminium or asbestos sheets. [Assam Urban Areas Rent Control Act, 1961 (Assam Act No. 2 of 1962), S. 2(h)]

"Pucca structure" means any structure constructed mainly of brick, stone or concrete or any combination of the materials. [The Calcutta Thika Tenancy Act, 1949 (2 of 1949) (West Bengal Act, (29 of 1969)), S. 2(4-a) as cited in *Nemai Chandra Kumar* v. *Mani Square Limited,* (2015) 14 SCC 203, para 17].

Puisne. Junior or inferior in rank.

Puisne judge. A puisne judge is one of the Justices of the High Court other than the Chief Justice.

Puisne mortgagee. A person who holds a mortgage which is subsequent in date to another mortgage. [CPC (5 of 1908), O. XXXIV, R. 1, *Expln.*].

Pulley. A wheel turning about an axis, and receiving a rope chain, or band on its rim, used for raising weights, changing direction or pull transmission of power *etc.* [Factories Act (63 of 1948), S. 2(i)].

Pullican. A pullican is an instrument formerly used for extracting teeth by man force.

Pulp. The soft mass, obtained from the breaking and grinding of rags, wood *etc.* [Employees' Provident Funds and Miscellaneous Provisions Act (19 of 1952), Sch. I, item. 13]; [Income-tax Act (43 of 1961), Sch. V, item 16].

Punctuation. The division of words in a document by stops, commas *etc.*

Punishable. Liable to punishment. [CrPC 1973 (2 of 1974), S. 2(x)].

The word 'punishable' is ordinarily defined as deserving of or capable or liable to punishment; capable of being punished by law or fight, may be punished, or liable to be punished, and not must be punished. *Sube Singh* v. *State of Haryana*, AIR 1988 SC 2235.

Punishment. Punishment is the penalty for the transgression of the law.

Any damage or pain inflicted on an offender through judicial procedure. [IPC (45 of 1860), S. 53 and Constitution of India, Art. 34].

The punishments to which offenders are liable under the provisions of the Indian Penal Code are,—

First.—Death; *Secondly,*—Imprisonment for life; *Thirdly,*—(*Deleted*); *Fourthly,*—Imprison-ment, which is of two descriptions, namely:—(1) Rigorous, that is, with hard labour. (2) Simple; *Fifthly,*—Forfeiture of property; *Sixthly,*—Fine. [IPC (45 of 1860), S. 53].

Suspension would not be a punishment by itself. *Lakshmi Devi Sugar Mills Ltd.* v. *Pt. Ram Sarup*, AIR 1957 SC 82, 93. [Industrial Disputes (Appellate Tribunal) Act, 1950, S. 22(1)]

The word 'punishment' is wide enough to comprehend both the punishment of imprisonment and the punishment of fine. *Rajeshwari Prasad* v. *Ram Babu Gupta,* AIR 1961 Pat 19, 21. [Probation of Offenders Act (20 of 1958), S. 4]

Punishment, Cumulative. Punishment increased by succeeding additions.

Punitive action. Means action taken by a local authority under the relevant law against unauthorised development and shall include demolition, sealing of premises and displacement of persons or their business establishment from their existing location, whether in pursuance of court orders or otherwise. [S.

2(1)(g) of the National Capital Territory of Delhi Laws (Special Provisions) Act, 2011 (5 of 2011)]

"Punitive detention" and "preventive detention". There is a vital distinction between these two kinds of detention. In case of 'punitive detention' the person concerned is detained by way of punishment after he is found guilty of wrongdoing as a result of a trial where he has the fullest opportunity to defend himself, while 'preventive detention' is not by way of punishment at all, but it is intended to pre-empt a person from indulging in any conduct injurious to the society. In case of preventive detention, he is detained merely on suspicion with a view to preventing him from doing harm in future and the opportunity that he has for contesting the action of the executive is very limited. *Francis Coralie Mullin* v. *Administrator, Union Territory of Delhi,* AIR 1981 SC 746.

Purchase. Means any transfer of the possession of goods by one person to another in the ordinary course of trade or business for cash or deferred payment or other valuable consideration. [Central Excise and Salt Act (1 of 1944), S. 2(h)] Now Central Excise Act.

"Purchase" means the acquisition of property by a party's own act, as distinguished from acquisition by act of law.

To acquire property whether movable or immovable by paying money or its equivalent. [T.P. Act (4 of 1882), S. 101].

Purchase money. The money paid or stipulated to be paid as price for the purchase of any property movable or immovable. [T.P. Act (4 of 1882), S. 46, ill. (b)].

Purchaser. "PURCHASERS" include persons purchasing, consuming or using for the purpose or in course of trade or business or for public purposes; and references in this section to any one person include references to any two or more persons being inter-connected undertakings or individuals carrying on business in partnership with each other. [M.R.T.P. Act (54 of 1969), S. 38(2)]

One who purchases. [Indian Contract Act (9 of 1872), S. 23, ill. (i)].

As the term is used in the law of sales "purchaser" means the person buying the goods sold.

Purchaser, Innocent. One who by honest agreement purchases property or acquires an interest therein without knowledge or means of knowledge sufficient to charge him in law with knowledge of any infirmity in law in the title of the seller. [CrPC 1973 (2 of 1974), S. 453].

Purchasing Centre. "Purchasing Centre" means any place at which cane is purchased, delivered, weighed or paid for and includes such portion of the premises of the factory as is used for any of these purposes. [M.P. Sugarcane (Regulation of Supply and Purchase) Rules,1959, R. 2(f) as cited in *Krishi Upaj Mandi Samiti, Narsinghpur* v. *Shiv Shakti Khansari Udyog*, (2012) 9 SCC 368, para 17].

Purdanashin lady. It only means a woman who by habit or family usage does not come out in the open to conduct her affairs. *Shyam Lal* v. *Ranbir Singh,* AIR 1951 All 386, 390.

Purdanashin or Pardanashin. A lady who had no objection to communicate, when necessary, in matters of business, with men other than members of her own family, who was able to go to Court to give evidence and to attend at the Registrar's Office in person to acknowledge her deeds for the purpose of Registration is not a *purdanashin* lady.

Purge. To clear of moral defilement; to clear of accusation or the charge of a crime.

Purity. The quality or condition of being pure. [Gold (Control) Act (45 of 1968)(*repealed*), S. 2(k)].

Purport. The word "purport," as used in speaking of the purport of an instrument, means the substance thereof as it appears on the face thereof to every eye that reads it.

To mean; to have as its purport; to profess or claim by its tenor [T.P. Act (4 of 1882), S. 48]; substance; tenor.

"Purport" means to present, especially deliberately, the appearance of being; profess or claim, often falsely. It means to convey, Imply, Signify or Profess outwardly, often falsely. In other words, it means to claim (to be certain thing, etc.) by manner or appearance; intent to show; to mean; to intend. Purport also means "alleged". [Armed Forces (Jammu and Kashmir) Special Powers Act (21 of 1990), S. 7(ii) as cited in *General Officer Commanding, Rashtriya Rifles* v. *CBI*, (2012) 6 SCC 228, para 67].

Purporting. When power is given to do something "purporting" to have a certain effect, it will seem to prevent objections being urged against the validity of the act which might otherwise be raised. Thus when validity is given to anything "purporting" to be done in pursuance of a power, a thing done under it may have validity though done at a time when the power would not be really exercisable. [Armed Forces (Jammu and Kashmir) Special Powers Act, 1990 (21 of 1990), S. 2(ii) as cited in *Dicker* v. *Angerstein*, (1876) 3 Ch D 600]. See also *General Officer Commanding, Rashtriya Rifles* v. *CBI*, (2012) 6 SCC 228, para 67.

Purporting to authorise. Professing to endow with authority. [T.P. Act (4 of 1882), S. 137, *Expln.*].

Purporting to be done. Professing to be performed. [CrPC 1973 (2 of 1974), S. 132(1)].

The act must bear such relation of the duty that the person acting could by a reasonable but not a fanciful or propounded claim, say that he did it in the course of his performance of his duty. *Shyam Manohar Lal* v. *4th Additional District Judge,* AIR 1978 All 238, 240. [Constitution of India, Art. 226; Provincial Small Cause Courts Act (9 of 1887), Schedule II, Art. 1]

There must be something in the nature of the act that attaches it to his official character. Even if the act is not justified or authorised by law, he will still be purporting to act in the execution of his duty if he acts on a mistaken view of it. So it means that something is deficient or a miss : everything is not as it is intended to be. [Armed Forces (Jammu and Kashmir) Special Powers Act, 1990 (21 of 1990), S. 7(ii) as cited in *General Officer Commanding, Rashtriya Rifles* v. *CBI*, (2012) 6 SCC 228, para 67].

Purporting to be done by a public officer in his official capacity. An act 'purporting to be done by a public officer in his official capacity" means an act of a public officer which is intended by him to carry forth or convey to the minds of all persons who become aware of that act the impression that he did the act in his official capacity and not as an ordinary private individual and which has the effect of conveying such an impression by its seeming or appearance.

Purporting to be done under the Act. The expression 'purporting to be done under the Act' will not include an act which is wholly outside the provisions of the Act. *Balghat Municipality* v. *Meghraj,* AIR 1966 MP 104, 109.

Purports to effect sale. Professes to transact a sale. [T.P. Act (4 of 1882), S. 58(c)].

Purpose. The object which one has in view. [Indian Partnership Act (9 of 1932), S. 13(d)].

The word 'purpose' means "that which a person sets before himself as an object to be reached or accomplished; the end or aim to which the view is directed in any plan, manner, or execution; end, or the view itself; design; intention."

The expression 'purpose' implies 'the thing intended or the object' and not the motive behind the action. *Keralchand Nemchand Mehta* v. *CIT,* (1968) 67 ITR 804, 815. [Income-tax Act (43 of 1961), S. 57]

Purpose means the fundamental principles upon which the association was formed and the trust created. *Ram Charan Agarwal* v. *Sridhar Misra,* AIR 1962 All 610, 615. [Societies Registration Act (21 of 1860), SS. 1, 2, 12, 20]

Purpose and **object.** The word 'purpose' has been used in a wide or comprehensive sense, that is, in the sense of the main object or the central aim of the society as distinguished from its detailed activities which will naturally be directed towards the statement of that object. Purpose means the fundamental principles upon which the association is formed. *Ram Charan* v. *Shridhar,* AIR 1962 All 610, 614. [Societies Registration Act (21 of 1860), S. 20]

The words 'purpose' and 'objects' have been treated in the Act as synonymous words. *Shridhar Misra* v. *Jaichandra Vidyalankar,* AIR 1959 All 598, 601. [Societies Registration Act (21 of 1860), S. 12]

Purpose of business. The expression 'purpose of business' means that the expenditure incurred shall be for carrying on of the business and the assessee shall incur the expenditure in his capacity as a person carrying on the business. *CIT* v. *Standard Vacuum Oil Company,* AIR 1967 Cal 68, 73.

Purpose of sale. Object or aim of sale. [IPC (45 of 1860), S. 292(a)].

Purposes not prohibited under the Convention. Means—

(i) industrial, agricultural, research, medical, pharmaceutical or other peaceful purposes;

(ii) protective purposes namely those purposes directly related to protection against Toxic Chemicals and to protection against Chemical Weapons;

(iii) military purposes not connected with the use of Chemical Weapons and not dependant on the use of the Toxic Properties of Chemicals as a method of warfare; and

(iv) law enforcement including domestic riot control purposes. [Chemical Weapons Convention Act (34 of 2000), S. 2(k)]

Purposive interpretation. A purposive construction of an enactment in one which gives effect to the legislative purpose by—(a) following the literal meaning of the enactment where that meaning is in accordance with the legislative purpose, or

(b) applying a strained meaning where the literal meaning is not in accordance with the legislative purpose. [*Statutory Interpretation*, a book by FRANCIS BENNION, **as referred in** *National Insurance Co. Ltd.* v. *Laxmi Narain Dhut,* (2007) 3 SCC 700, 718, para 34]A purposive construction of an enactment in one which gives effect to the legislative purpose by—

(a) following the literal meaning of the enactment where that meaning is in accordance with the legislative purpose, or

(b) applying a strained meaning where the literal meaning is not in accordance with the legislative purpose. [Statutory Interpretation by Francis Bennion, **as referred in** *National Insurance Co. Ltd.* v. *Laxmi Narain Dhut,* (2007) 3 SCC 700, 718-19, para 34 (37); *Oriental Insurance Co. Ltd.* v. *Brij Mohan,* (2007) 7 SCC 56, 63, para 12]

Purser. A purser of a ship is the fiscal agent of the owners; a paymaster or cashier.

An officer charged with managing money matters and keeping accounts. [Seamen's Provident Fund Act (4 of 1966), S. 2(1)].

Pursuant to. In accordance with [Concise Oxford English Dictionary as cited in *Bharat Aluminium Company* v. *Kaiser Aluminium Technical Services Inc.*, (2016) 4 SCC 126, para 8].

The expression 'pursuant to or in pursuance of' have a restrictive interpretation and have been regarded as equivalent to 'in conformity with', and imply that what is done is in accordance with an instruction or direction. [Words and Phrases, Permanent Edn., Vol. 35-A as cited in *Bharat Aluminium Company* v.

Kaiser Aluminium Technical Services Ins., (2016) 4 SCC 126, para 8].

Pursuit. An activity that one engages in seriously and continually or frequently as a vocation or profession; the action of pursuing. [CrPC, 1973 (2 of 1974), S. 48].

Purveyor. "Purveyor" means a person who sells or deals in particular goods or he who spreads or promotes idea, views etc. or he who deals in traditional Christian values. [Oxford Dictionary (online) as cited in *Pepsico India Holding Pvt. Ltd.* v. *State of Punjab*, AIR 2012 P&H 163, para 14].

A person (purveyor) should be supplier or dealer of perched, fried or cooked food. [*Pepsico India Holding Pvt. Ltd.* v. *State of Punjab*, AIR 2012 P&H 163, para 15] [Punjab Agricultural Produce Markets (General) Rules, 1962, R. 18(1)(a)].

Purview. The meaning usually attached to the term "purview" by writers on law seems to be "the enacting part of a statute, in contradistinction to the preamble."

Scope; range [Delhi Administration Act (19 of 1966), S. 23]; field of activity or view. [Aligarh Muslim University Act (40 of 1920), Sch., item 21(a)].

Where a statute repeals a prior statute so far as the prior statute comes within the purview of the later one, the word "purview" applies to the enacting part, the body or subject of the act, in contradistinction from the other parts thereof, such as the preamble, the saving; and the proviso, and hence the repeal is not confined merely to such parts of the former act as are inconsistent with the provisions of the repealing act.

The word "purview" as used in the repealing clause of an act stating that all laws within the purview of this act are repealed, *etc.* means within the limit or scope of the act.

Push technology. The internet can be quite a passive experience, needing the user to log onto a site to determine if changes have occurred, or to download information. With push technology, the browser can be set to automatically download data from a set site. (*Cyber Law*)

Put up. To offer for some purpose. [CPC (5 of 1908), O. XXI, R. 74(2)].

Putative. Reputed; supposed; commonly esteemed.

Putative father. Commonly supposed to be father. [Children Act (60 of 1960) (repealed), S. 50(3)].

Putative marriage. A putative marriage is "a marriage which is in reality null, but which has been contracted in good faith by the two parties, or by one of them." Such marriages are so far valid as to impose a civil liability upon either party to the other party, if innocent.

Putative spouse. A spouse who believes in good faith that his or her invalid marriage is legally valid.

Putrefaction. Rotting.

Q

Q.B. Queen's Bench.

Q.B.D. Queen's Bench Division.

Qua. Considered as; in so far as; in the character or capacity of, for example "the trustee *qua* trustee (that is, in his character as trustee) is not liable", *etc.*

Quack. A "quack" is one who pretends to a skill or knowledge which he does not possess; an imposter; a boastful pretender to medical skill; and ignorant medical practitioner.

Quae ab initio non valent ex post facto convalescere non possunt. Things that are invalid from the beginning are not made valid by a subsequent act.

Quae accessionum locum obtinent, extinguuntur cum principales res peremptae fuerint. (*Lat.*) (2 Pothierob. 202) Things which are incidents are extinguished when the principals are extinguished.

Quae communi legi derogant stricte interpretantur. (*Lat.*) (*Jenk. Cent.* 221) Statutes that derogate from the common law are to be strictly construed.

Quae in testamento ita sunt scripta ut intelligi non possint, perinde sunt ac si scripta non essent. (*Lat.*) (D. 50, 17, 73). Words in a will so written that they are ambiguous (cannot be understood) have the same effect as if they had not been written at all.

Quae inter alios acta sunt nemini nocere debent, sed prodesse possunt. (6 *Rep.* 1). Transactions among strangers may benefit, but cannot injure, persons not parties thereto.

Quae legi communi derogant non sunt trahenda in exemplum. Things that derogate (or detract) from the common law are not to be drawn into precedent.

Quae mala sunt inchoata in principio vix bono peraguntur exitu. (*Lat.*) (4 Coke. 2) Things bad in principle at the commencement seldom achieve a good end.

Quae praeter consuetudinem et morem majorum fiunt, neque placent neque recta videntur. Things which are done contrary to the custom and usage of our ancestors neither please nor appear right.

Quae rerum natura prohibentur nulla lege confirmata sunt. What is prohibited by the nature of things can be confirmed by no law.

Quae sunt minoris culpae sunt majoris infamiae. Offenses which are of a lower grade of guilt are of a higher degree of infamy.

Quae sunt temporalia ad agendum, sunt per-petua ad excipiendum. (*Lat.*) Those things which afford a ground of action if raised within a certain time, may be pleaded at any time by way of exception.

Quaelibet concessio fortissime contra donatorem interpretanda est. Every grant is to be construed most strongly against the grantor. (*Latin for Lawyers*)

Quaelibet poena corporalis, quamvis minima, major est qualibet poena pecuniaria. (3 *Inst.* 220). Every corporal punishment, although the very least, is greater than any pecuniary punishment.

Quaeras de dubiis, legem bene discere si vis. Inquire into doubtful points, if you wish to understand the law well.

Quaerere dat sapere quae sunt legitima vere. To inquire into is the way to know what is really true.

Qualification. QUALIFICATION means a degree or any other qualification awarded by a University. [National Commission for Minority Educational Institution Act, 2004 (2 of 2005), S. 2(i)].

That which makes a man fit to hold an office; that which makes any person fit to do a certain act; also abatement, diminution. The circumstance or group of circumstances whereby an individual is rendered eligible for a post is called his qualification. Any incident annexed to a right, *e.g.*, an inherent reciprocal obligation is also called a qualification of the right.

Quality, accomplishment, *etc.* which qualifies or fits a person for some office or function; something that qualifies or restricts. [Representation of the People Act (43 of 1950), S. 20(3)]; [CPC (5 of 1908), 1st Sch., App. C, form No. 11].

Qualification shares. The number of shares or amount of stock which under a company's articles must be held by a person acting as Director.

Qualified. "Qualified" has a double sense, and means a condition or status of an officer, and is also often used to describe his act of taking an oath.

The word "qualified." when applied to any person elected or appointed to office, shall be construed to mean the performance by such person of those things which are required by law to be performed by him previous to his entering upon the duties of his office.

Endowed with qualities or possessed of accomplishments, which fit one for certain end, office or function. [CrPC 1973 (2 of 1974), S. 174(3)].

Qualified acceptance. "An acceptance is qualified— (a) where it is conditional, declaring the payment to be dependent or the happening of an event therein stated; (b) where it undertakes the payment of part only of the sum ordered to be paid; (c) where, no place of payment being specified on the order, it undertakes the payment at some other place and not otherwise or elsewhere; (d) where it undertakes the payment at a time other than that at which under the order or would be legally due." [Negotiable Instruments Act (26 of 1881), S. 86, *Expln.*]

An acceptance is general when it imports an absolute acceptance precisely in conformity to the tenure of the bill itself. It is unqualified when it contains no qualification, limitation, or condition different from what is expressed on the face of the bill or from what the law implies upon a general acceptance. It is qualified when the drawee absolutely accepts the bill, but makes it payable at a different time or place, or to a different firm, or in a different mode from that which is the tenure of the bill.

Qualified elector. As used in election law means, a person who is legally qualified to vote.

"Qualified financial market participant". Includes,—

(i) a banking institution, or a non-banking financial company, or such other financial institution which is subject to regulation or prudential supervision by the Reserve Bank of India;

(ii) an individual, partnership firm, company, or any other person or body corporate whether incorporated under any law for the time being in force in India or under the laws of any other country and includes any international or regional development bank or other international or regional organisation;

(iii) an insurance or reinsurance company which is subject to regulation or prudential supervision by the Insurance Regulatory and Development Authority of India established under the Insurance Regulatory and Development Authority Act, 1999 (41 of 1999);

(iv) a pension fund regulated by the Pension Fund Regulatory and Development Authority established under the Pension Fund Regulatory and Development Authority Act, 2013 (23 of 2013);

(v) a financial institution regulated by the International Financial Services Centres Authority established under the International Financial Services Centres Authority Act, 2019 (50 of 2019); and

(vi) any other entity notified by the relevant authority under clause (*b*) of section 4. [Bilateral Netting of Qualified Financial Contracts Act, 2020 (30 of 2020), section 2(1)(o)]

Qualified Foreign Investor. For the purpose of section 194LD of Act 43 of 1961, 'Qualified Foreign Investor' shall have the meaning assigned to it in the Circular No. Cir/IMD/DF/ 14/2011, dated 9-8-2011, as amended from time to time, issued by the Securities and Exchange Board of India, under section 11 of the Securities and Exchange Board of India Act, 1992 (15 of 1992). [(w.e.f. 1-6-2013) *Explanation* (*c*) to section 194LD of the Income-tax Act, 1961 (43 of 1961)]

Qualified institutional buyer. Means:

(i) a mutual fund, venture capital fund, Alternative Investment Fund and foreign venture capital investor registered with the Board;

(ii) a foreign institutional investor and sub-account (other than a sub-account which is a foreign corporate or foreign individual), registered with the Board;

(iii) a public financial institution as defined in section 4A of the Companies Act, 1956; (10 of 1956)

(iv) a scheduled commercial bank;

(v) a multilateral and bilateral development financial institution;

(vi) a state industrial development corporation;

(vii) an insurance company registered with the Insurance Regulatory and Development Authority;

(viii) a provident fund with minimum corpus of twenty five crore rupees;

(ix) a pension fund with minimum corpus of twenty five crore rupees;

(x) National Investment Fund set up by resolution no. F. No. 2/3/2005-DDII, dated November 23, 2005 of the Government of India published in the Gazette of India;

(xi) insurance funds set up and managed by army, navy or air force of the Union of India;

(xii) insurance funds set up and managed by the Department of Posts, India.

(xiii) systemically important non-banking financial companies. [Securities and Exchange Board of India (Issue of Capital and Disclosure Requirements) Regulations 2009, regulation 2(1)(zd) as amended by Notification dated dated 31-05-2017. Also see *Explanation II(i)* to section 42 of the Companies Act, 2013 (18 of 2013)]

QULAIFIED BUYER means a financial institution, insurance company, bank, state financial corporation, state industrial development corporation, trustee of asset reconstruction company which has been granted a certificate of registration under sub-section (4) of section 3 or any asset management company making investment on behalf of mutual fund] or a foreign institutional investor registered under the Securities and Exchange Board of India Act, 1992 (15 of 1992) or regulations made thereunder any category of non-institutional investors as may be specified by the Reserve Bank under sub-section (1) of section 7, or any other body corporate as may be specified by the Board; [Securitisation and Reconstruction of Financial Assets and Enforcement of Security Interest Act (54 of 2002), S. 2(1)(u) as amended Act No. 44 of 2016 (w.e.f. 1-9-2016)]

Qualified medical practitioner. Means any person registered under any Central Act, Provincial Act or an Act of the Legislature of a State, providing for the maintenance of a register of medical practitioners, or in any area where no such last-mentioned Act is in force, any person declared by the State Government, by notification in the Official Gazette, to be a qualified medical practitioner for the purposes of this Act. [Employee's Compensation Act (8 of 1923), S. 2(i)]

Qualified midwife. Means a midwife registered in any state in India under a law for the registration of midwives. [Orissa Clinical Establishments (Control and Regulation) Act (8 of 1990), S. 2(j)]

Qualified nurse. "QUALIFIED NURSE" means a person who holds a certificate/diploma of a recognised hospital/institution and who is employed on recommendations of the attending Medical Practitioner. [Scheme of Hospitalization and Domiciliary Hospitalization Benefit Policy, Specified for the purpose 80D of the Income-tax Act (43 of 1961).

Qualified ownership. The ownership of property is qualified : (1) When it is shared with one or more persons; (2) when the time of enjoyment is deferred or limited; (3) when the use is restricted.

Qualified person. Means a citizen of India who is ordinarily resident in India and who,—

(i) has obtained a recognised medical qualification within the meaning of Indian Medical Council Act, 1956, or

(ii) has obtained, or has passed an examination which entitles him to obtain, a degree of a University or its equivalent qualification in any branch of engineering or technology or both.

Expln. For the purpose of this Act, a qualified person who is resident in India shall be deemed to be ordinarily resident there unless—

(a) he is residing there only for the purposes of attending a course of education; or

(b) the circumstances of his residence there are otherwise such as to show that he is residing there for a temporary purpose only; or

(c) he, being a person who was born or domiciled in any country outside India, has been resident in India for less than two years. [National Service Act (28 of 1972), S. 2(f)]

Qualify. As the word "qualify" is used in an Act requiring state officers to "qualify," *etc*., it means the taking of the oath or affirmation constitutionally provided for.

To give the required qualities to; to fit especially for an office or privilege [Inland Vessels Act (1 of 1917), S. 28(i)]; to become legally capable; to limit or modify the meaning of [Capital Issues (Control) Act (29 of 1947), S. 3(4)]; to modify by attachment of condition.

An expert witness "qualifies" when he has read up, or otherwise masters, the details of the particular case on which he is to give evidence.

Qualifying date. In relation to the preparation or revision of every electoral roll means the 1st day of January of the year in which it is so prepared or revised. [Kerala Panchayat Act (Ker Act No. 13 of 1994), S. 2(xxxvi)]

Qualifying debt. Means amount due, which includes interest or any other sum due in respect of the amounts owed under any contract, by the debtor for a liquidated sum either immediately or at certain future time and does not include—

(*a*) an excluded debt;

(*b*) a debt to the extent it is secured; and

(*c*) any debt which has been incurred three months prior to the date of the application for fresh start process. [Insolvency and Bankruptcy Code (31 of 2016), S. 79(19)].

Qualifying examination. 'Qualifying examination' in the context of promotion refers to an examination which when passed, qualifies or makes the candidate eligible for promotion. An interview cannot generally be considered to be a qualifying examination. 'Qualifying examination' would necessarily refer to a written examination in absence of any specific provision prescribing interview as the means of ascertainment of fitness for promotion. [*Diploma Engineers Sangh* v. *State of U.P.,* (2007) 13 SCC 300, 310, para 10] [U.P. Service of Engineers (Building and Road Branch) Class II Rules 1936, R. 9(ii)]

Qualifying service. An earlier service less than five years, prior to the break, is not qualifying service, even if the interruption or break in service in condoned unconditionally. *Hans Raj* v. *State of Punjab*, AIR 1985 SC 69, 74. [Punjab Civil Services (Premature Retirement) Rules (1975), R. 2(3)]

Quality. "QUALITY", in relation to any article includes the state and condition of the article. [Agricultural Produce (Grading and Marking) Act (1 of 1937), S. 2(f)]

The degree of excellence [Indian Contract Act (9 of 1872), S. 38, ill. and Trade and Merchandise Marks Act (43 of 1958), S. 2(1)(c)]; the social status; rank; a mental or moral attribute; trait or characteristic. [Specific Relief Act (47 of 1963), S. 15(b), *Prov.*].

Quality assurance. Means the systematic measures applied and steps taken by manufacturers and packets of fortified food throughout the manufacturing or packing process to ensure that the finished food complies with the provisions of the act and regulations and standards specified there under. [Food Safety and Standards (Fortification of Foods) Regulations, 2018, Regn. 2(1)(g)].

Quality control. Means any activity having for its object the determination of the quality of a commodity (whether during the process of manufacture or production or subsequently) in order to ascertain whether it satisfies the standard specifications applicable to it or any other specification stipulated in the export contract and whether it may be accepted for the purposes of export. [Export (Quality Control and Inspection) Act (22 of 1963), S. 2(f)]

Quality Management System. Means requirements for manufacturing of medical devices as specified in the Fifth Schedule. [Medical Devices Rules, 2017, R. 3(zn)].

Quam rationabilis debet esse finis, non definitur sed omnibus circumstantiis inspectis pendet ex justiciariorum discretione. (11 Rep. 44). What a reasonable fine ought to be is not defined, but is left at the discretion to the judges all the circumstances being considered.

Quando aliquid conceditur, conceditur id sine quo illud fieri non possit. When anything is granted, that also is granted without which it cannot take effect.

Quando aliquid mandatur, mandatur et omne per quod pervenitur ad illud. (*Maxim*) When anything is commanded, everything by which it can be accomplished is also commanded.

Quando aliquid per se non sit malum, tamen si sit mali exempli, non est faciendum. When anything by itself is not evil, and yet if it is an example for evil, it is not to be done.

Quando aliquid prohibetur ex directo, prohibitur et per obliquum. When anything is prohibited directly, it is prohibited also indirectly.

Quando aliquid prohibetur, prohibetur et omne per quod devenitur ad illud. (*Maxim*) When anything is prohibited, everything by which it is reached is prohibited also.

To carry out effectually the object of a statute, it must be so construed as to defeat all attempts to do, or avoid doing, in an indirect or circuitous manner that which it has prohibited or enjoined:. [*Ankush Shivaji Gaikwad* v. *State of Maharashtra*, (2013) 6 SCC 770, para 57].

Quando aliquis aliquid concedit concedere videtur et sine quod res uti non potest. When a person grants anything, he is supposed to grant that also without which the thing cannot be used.

Quando charta continet generalem clausulam posteaque descendit ad verba specialia quae clausulae generali sunt consentanea, interpretanda est charta secundum verba specialia. When a deed contains a general clause and afterwards descends to special words which are agreeable to the general clause, the deed is to be interpreted according to the special words. (8 Coke, 154-b)

Quando de una et eadem re duo onerabiles existunt unus, pro insufficientia alterius, de integro onerabitur. When there are two persons liable for one and the same thing, one of them, in case of default of the other, shall be charged with the whole.

Quando dispositio referri potest ad duas res ita quod secundum relationem unam vitiatur et secundum alteram utilis sit, tum facienda est relatio ad illam ut valeat dispositio. (Coke 76). When a disposition may refer to two things so that by the latter it would be preserved, then the relation is to be made to the latter, so that the disposition may be valid.

Quando duo jura in una persona concurrunt aequum est ac si essent in deversis. (*Maxim*) When two rights concur in one and the same person, it is the same as if they were in separate persons.

Quando jus domini regis et subditi concurrunt jus regis praeferri debet. (9 Rep. 129) When the rights of the king and of the subject concur, those of the king are to be preferred.

Where the title of the king and the title of a subject concur, the king' title must be preferred. [Legal Maxims, 10th Edn., pp. 35-36 as cited in *Rana Girdars Limited* v. *Union of India*, (2013) 10 SCC 746, para 19].

Quando lex aliquid alicui, concedit, concedere videtur id sine quo res ipsa esse non potest. (*Lat.*) (5 Rep. 47) When the law gives a man anything, it gives him that also without which the thing itself cannot exist.

When the law gives anything to anyone, it also gives all those things without which the thing itself would be unavoidable. [*Amit Kapoor* v. *Ramesh Chander*, (2012) 9 SCC 460, para 20].

The principle embodied in the Section 482 of CrPC 1973 (2 of 1974) regarding inherent powers to make such orders as may be necessary to give effect to any order under the code, or to prevent abuse of the process of any Court or otherwise to secure the ends of justice, is based on this maxim. *Dinesh Dutt Joshi* v. *State of Rajasthan,* (2001) 8 SCC 570, para 6.

Quando lex est specialis, ratio autem generalis, generaliter lex est intelligenda. (*Lat.*) (2 Inst. 83) When a law is special but its reason (or object) is general, the law is to be understood generally. (*Latin for Lawyers*)

Quando plus fit quam fieri debet videtur etiam illud fieri quid faciendum est. (*Maxim*) When more is done than ought to be done that at least shall be considered as performed which should have been performed. (*Broom*)

Quantification. To carry out effectually the object of a statute, it must be so construed as to defeat all attempts to do, or avoid doing, in an indirect or circuitous manner that which it has prohibited or enjoined:. [*Ankush Shivaji Gaikwad v. State of Maharashtra,* (2013) 6 SCC 770, para 57].

Quantity. Applied to an estate, denotes the duration and extent of the holder's interest,—as for years, or for life or in fee.

Total amount, size or magnitude. [Sale of Goods Act (3 of 1930), S. 37].

Quantum. The sum total 8 of two or more particular sums or quantities; the aggregate; the whole quantity; a totality (as) *quantum* of damages.

Quantity; a certain amount. [Seamen's Provident Fund Act (4 of 1966), S. 14].

Quarantine. Is a period of (time theoretically forty days) during which a vessel, coming from a place where a contagious or infectious disease is prevalent, is detained by authority in the harbour of her port of destination, or at a station near it without being permitted to land or discharge her crew or passengers. Quarantine is said to have been first established at Venice in 1484. It is an isolation imposed on ship or person to prevent infection.

The fact or practice of isolating or being isolated as a precaution against the spread of any infectious disease; the period of such isolation, also the place where such isolated persons are detained. [IPC (45 of 1860), S. 271].

Quarantine application. With respect to Group VIII of Schedule I ozone depleting substance, are treatments to prevent the introduction, establishment and or spread of quarantine pests (including diseases), or to ensure their control as specified by the Central Government. [Ozone Depleting Substance (Regulation) Rules, 2000, R. 2(n)]

Quarry. "QUARRY" means to take from the surface as well as to extract from a quarry. [U. P. Act 5 of 1886, S. 3 cl. 5].

(*In mining law*) An open excavation where the works are visible at the surface; a place where stone, slate, marble, *etc.*, is dug out or separated from a mass of rock.

An excavation or system of excavations for the purpose of, or in connection with getting of minerals (whether in their natural stage or in solution of suspension) or products of minerals being neither mine nor merely a well or borehole or a well and borehole combined. [Coal Mines Provident Fund and Miscellaneous Provisions Act (46 of 1948), S. 2(b)(iv); Indian Forest Act (16 of 1927), S. 26(g)].

Quarter. "QUARTER" means the period of three months ending on the last day of March, June, September or December. [Banking Regulation Act (10 of 1949), S. 25(3)(c)]

"Quarter" shall mean a period comprising three consecutive calendar months, ending on the last day of March, June, September and December of a calendar year [The Central Goods and Services Tax Act, 2017 (12 of 2017), S. 2(92)]

"QUARTER" means a quarter of the English Calendar year. [West Bengal Motor Vehicles (Taxation of Goods and Passengers) Act (4 of 1985), S. 2(8)]

A fourth part; one of four equal or corresponding parts.

Fourth part of the year [Factories Act (63 of 1948), S. 64(4), *Expln.*]; S. 2(m), Emergency Risks (Undertakings) Act (51 of 1971)]; fourth part; a living accommodation.

Quash. To overthrow or annul, to make void; to abate. (*Tomlin*) (as) quashing a conviction.

To throw out as invalid; to put an end to a legal proceeding.

Quasi. As if; as it were analogous to; seemingly not really. This term is used in legal phraseology to indicate that one subject resembles another, with which it is compared, in certain characteristics, but that there are also intrinsic differences between them.

The word "*quasi*" marks the resemblance, and supposes a little difference, between two objects.

Quasi delict. *(Lat.)* Refers to an unlawful act, done through negligence, without malice.

Quasi easements. The term applies to those easements which not being easements of absolute necessity come into existence for the first time by presumed grant or operation of law on a severance of two or more tenements formerly united in the sole or joint possession or ownership of one or more persons.

Quasi-Governmental agency. The expression '*quasi* Governmental agency' means 'a Government sponsored enterprise or corporation'. *Pradeep Kumar Biswas* v. *Indian Institute of Chemical Biology,* (2002) 5 SCC 111, para 74.

Quasi-judicial. Of or relating to the adjudicative acts of an executive or administrative official.

When the law commits to an officer the duty of looking into certain facts not in a way which it specially directs, but after a discretion in its nature judicial, the function is *quasi*-judicial.

Sharing the qualities of and approximating to what is judicial; essentially judicial in character but not within the judicial power or function nor belonging to the judiciary as constitutionally defined. [CPC (5 of 1908), S. 128(2)(i)].

"Quasi-judicial" is a term which may not always be used with utmost clarity and precision. An authority which exercises judicial functions or functions analogous to the judicial authorities would normally be termed as "quasi-judicial" [Black's 7th Edn., 1999 as cited in *Namit Sharma* v. *Union of India*, (2013) 1 SCC 745, para 25].

Describing a function that resembles the judicial function in that it involves deciding a dispute and ascertaining the facts and any relevant law, but differs in that it depends ultimately on the exercise of an executive discretion rather than the application of law. [Oxford Law Dictionary, 5th Edn., 2003 as cited in *Namit Sharma* v. *Union of India*, (2013) 1 SCC 745, para 75].

The expression '*quasi* judicial' has been termed to be one which stands midway between a judicial and administrative function. If the authority has any express statutory duty to act judicially in arriving at the decision in question, it would be deemed to be *quasi*-judicial. *State of H.P.* v. *Raja Mahendra Pal,* AIR 1999 SC 1786.

Quasi-judicial act. A *quasi*-judicial act requires that a decision is to be given not arbitrarily or in the mere discretion of the authority, but according to the facts and circumstances of the case, as determined upon an enquiry held by the authority after giving an opportunity to the party to be affected of being heard and whenever necessary leading evidence in support of his contentions. *Avadhesh Pratap Singh* v. *U.P. State,* AIR 1952 All 63, 69. [Constitution of India, Art. 226]

Quasi-judicial authority. The primary test is as to whether a particular authority alleged to be a *quasi-judicial* one, has any express statutory duty to act judicially in arriving at the decision in question. If the reply is in the affirmative, the authority would be deemed to be a '*quasi* judicial authority' and if the reply is in the negative, it would not be so. [*State of H.P.* v. *Raja Mahendra Pal,* AIR 1999 SC 1786 : (1999) 4 SCC 43, 56, para 8]

Where there is a *lis* or two contesting parties making rival claims and the statutory authority under the statutory provision is required to decide such a dispute, in the absence of any other attributes of a *quasi*-judicial authority, such a statutory authority is *quasi* judicial authority. *Indian National Congress (India)* v. *Institute of Social Welfare,* (2002) 5 SCC 685.

Quasi-judicial decision and administrative act (distinction). The essential test of a *quasi*-judicial decision which distinguishes it from an administrative act is that the law empowering the *quasi*-judicial authority to make a decision requires a judicial approach, either expressly or by necessary implication. *Haji Abdual Shakoor* v. *Rent Control and Eviction Officer,* MLJ : QD (1956-1960) Vol. II C 338-339 : AIR 1959 All 440.

Quasi-judicial function. Where function to determine a dispute is exercised by virtue of an executive discretion rather than the application of law.

A '*quasi*-judicial function' has be termed to be one which stands midway between a judicial and an administrative function. [*State of H.P.* v. *Raja Mahendra Pal.* AIR 1999 SC 1786 : (1999) 4 SCC 43, 56, para 8]

Quasi-judicial order. The order lying in the file and styled as an order is not valid without signatures of the Officer concerned. *Kilasho Devi Burman* v. *Commissioner of Income Tax,* 1996 (7) SCC 613.

The Election Commission while exercising its power to register a political party under Section 29-A of the Act, acts '*quasi*-judicially' and decision rendered by it is a '*quasi*-judicial order'. *Indian National Congress* v. *Institute of Social Welfare,* (2002) 5 SCC 685, para 41(2) : AIR 2002 SC 2158. [Representation of The People Act (43 of 1951), S. 29-A]

Direction of Chief Justice of High Court for transferring of a writ petition from Lucknow Bench to Allahabad Bench by detailed and reasoned order after hearing the parties is at least a *quasi*-judicial order, if not judicial order and not an executive order. *Manju Verma* v. *State of U.P.,* (2004) 9 Scale 663. [CPC (5 of 1908), S. 24]

Quasi-judicial power. An administrative agency's power to adjudicate the rights of those who appear before it.

Quasi-judicial proceeding. A departmental proceeding is a *quasi*-judicial proceeding. The enquiry officer performs a *quasi*-judicial function. [*Roop Singh Negi* v. *Punjab National Bank,* (2009) 2 SCC 570, 577, para 14]

The matter of enquiry under Section 5(1)(b) is not a *quasi*-judicial proceeding hence reasons need not be stated in the notification fixing minimum wage. *U.P. Cinema Exhibitors Federation* v. *State of U.P.,* MLJ : YD (1977) Suppl to Oct 2147 : 1977 Lab IC. 993 (All).

Quasi-legislative power. An administrative agency's power to engage in rulemaking.

Quasi-marital. Partaking of the nature of marital in some respects but not amounting to marital itself. [IPC (45 of 1860)].

Quasi permanent. A certain class of temporary Government servants have been given some security of tenure by virtue of Rule 3 of Central Civil Service (Temporary Service) Rules 1949 by creating a separate class known as "*Quasi* Permanent". Rule 3 of these rules governing a servant says that (1) if he has been in continuous Government Service for more than three years and (2) if the appointing authority being satisfied as to his suitability in respect of age, qualification, work and character for employment in *quasi* permanent capacity has issued a declaration to that effect" he will acquire the status of a *quasi* permanent Government servant. Thus three years continuous service and a declaration under the rules confer a *quasi* permanent statutes on the civil servant concerned. *Champak Lal* v. *Union of India,* AIR 1964 SC 1854; *Prafulla Chander* v. *Union Territory,* AIR 1953 Tri 38.

Quay. Landing place. "A convenient place fitted on the shore for the loading and unloading of vessels; commonly called a wharf". (*Stroud*)

An artificial bank or landing place built; stone or other solid material, lying along or projecting into navigable water for convenience of loading and unloading vessels. [S. 5(1)(a), Indian Dock Labourers Act (19 of 1934), S. 372, *Expln.* II].

Queen. Female monarch of England when used in law. [Indian Partnership Act (9 of 1932), S. 58(3)].

The Queen is a woman who possesses the sovereignty and royal power in a country under a monarchical form of government; the wife of a king.

Question. (*In evidence*) An interrogation put to a witness, for the purpose of having him declare the truth of certain facts as far as he knows them. (*In practice*) A point on which the parties are not agreed and which is submitted to the decision of a judge and jury.

The interrogative statement on some point to be investigated or discussed [Indian Evidence Act (1 of 1872), S. 150]; [Unlawful Activities (Prevention) Act (37 of 1967), S. 2(f)].

"Question" means "a doubt' the raising of a doubt or objection; a problem requiring solution." [Concise Oxford Dictionary (10th Edn.) as cited in *Natural Resources Allocation, In Re,* Special Reference No. 1 of 2012, (2012) 10 SCC 1, para 28].

Question means anything inquired. [*Union of India* v. *Ibrahim Uddin,* (2012) 8 SCC 148, para 63].

Question hour. Parliamentary question serves as a technique of parliamentary surveillance over the administration practiced in representative parliamentary democracies. The first hour of every sitting in both the Houses of the Parliament and State Legislatures is devoted to asking and answering questions which is known as question hour.

The time fixed for asking and answering of oral questions in a sitting in a Legislature; it is fixed under the Rules of the House or Standing Orders. (*Constitutional and Parliamentary Term*)

Question, In. In dispute; at issue [Press Council Act (37 of 1978), S. 13(3)].

Question in dispute. A point on which the parties are at issue. [Indian Evidence Act (1 of 1872), S. 32(6)].

Question in issue. Question in dispute.

Question of fact. "The question "what is a reasonable time" is, in each particular case, a question of fact." [Indian Contract Act (9 of 1872), S. 46, *Expln.*]

"The question "what is a proper time and place" is, in each particular case, a question of fact." [Indian Contract Act (9 of 1872), S. 48, *Expln.*]

"Question of fact" is whether a particular factual situation exists or not. [*Union of India* v. *Ibrahim Uddin*, (2012) 8 SCC 148, para 63].

A question of fact is one capable of being answered by way of demonstration. A question of opinion is one that cannot be so answered. An answer to it is a matter of speculation which cannot be proved by any available evidence to be right or wrong. [*Union of India* v. *Ibrahim Uddin*, (2012) 8 SCC 148, para 63].

Question of fact and law. The question of the validity of execution/attestation of/in gift is a mixed question of fact and law, hence it cannot be raised at appellate stage for the first time. [*Brij Raj Singh* v. *Sewak Ram*, AIR 1999 SC 2203 : (1999) 4 SCC 331]

Question of jurisdiction. The 'question of jurisdiction' is a question of procedure and not of substantive law. [*Burhan Mirdha* v. *Khodeja Bibi*, AIR 1937 Cal 189 (SB)] [CPC (5 of 1908), S. 16]

Question of law. The proper effect of a proved fact is a question of law.

Question of private importance. By a question of being private importance is meant private importance to both parties to the litigation and not only to one of them. *Indian Trade and General Insurance Co. Ltd.* v. *Rajmal Pahar Chand,* AIR 1956 Punj 228, 230.

Question relating to evacuee property. The words 'question relating to evacuee property' are wide enough to bring questions arising in a suit for the enforcement of an agreement relating to evacuee property. *Sohan Singh* v. *Ram Nath,* AIR 1952 Punj 372. [Administration of Evacuee Property Act (31 of 1950), S. 50(1)]

Question relating to execution or discharge of satisfaction of the decree. A question between the auction-purchaser or his representative and the judgment-debtor or his representative, relating to the delivery of possession, is not a question relating to the execution or discharge of satisfaction of the decree.

Question, Starred. A question seeking oral answer in the House; distinguished by an asterisk. The order in which the Ministers and Private Members answer oral questions is decided by the Government. (*Constitutional and Parliamentary Term*)

Question, Supplementary. Questions asked by Members in the Legislature arising out of the answer to the main oral questions; these are asked to seek further elucidation of the answer given by the Minister. (*Constitutional and Parliamentary Term*)

Question, Unstarred. A question which seeks a written answer; it is not distinguished by an 'asterisk'; it is not asked orally. (*Constitutional and Parliamentary Term*)

Question, Withdrawal of. Withdrawal of a question by a member before it is due to be asked.

In the Lok Sabha a member can withdraw the question before the sitting for which his question has been placed on the list; he can also withdraw it by making a statement to that effect when his question is called by the Speaker. (*Constitutional and Parliamentary Term*)

Qui accusat integrae famae sit et non criminosus. Let him who accuses be of clear fame, and not criminal. (*Latin for Lawyers*)

Qui acquirit sibi acquirit haeredibus. He who acquires for himself acquires for his heirs. (*Trayner*)

Qui adimit medium, dirimit finem. He who takes away the means destroys the end.

Qui alienum fundum ingreditur, potest a domino, si is praeviderit, prohiberi ne ingrediatur. He who enters on another's land may be resisted by the owner if he shall have previously forbidden it.

Qui aliquid statuerit, parte inaudita altera, aequum licet dexerit, haud aequum facerit. He who determines any matter without hearing both sides, though he may have decided right, has not done justice.

Qui approbat non reprobat. He who approbates does not reprobate, (*i.e.* he cannot both accept and reject the same thing). (*Black*)

Interestingly the Apex Court also applied the maxim in Indian conditions as a basic inhibitory principle of law. *Velamuri Venkata Sivaprasad* v. *Kothuri Venkateswarlu,* AIR 2000 SC 434; *See also New Bihar Biri Leaves Co.* v. *State of Bihar,* AIR 1981 SC 679, paras 50 and 51.

Qui bene distinguit bene docet. (2 Inst. 470) He who distinguishes well teaches (learns) well

Qui contemnit praeceptum, contemnit praecipientem. He who contemns (contemptuously treats) a command contemns the party who gives it. (12 *Coke,* 97)

Qui destruit medium destruti finem. He who destroys the mans destroys the end.

Qui facit per alium facit per se. He who acts through another acts himself. (*i.e.*) the acts of an agent are the acts of the principal).

Qui haeret in litera haeret in cortice. (*Lat.*) He who considers merely the letter of an instrument goes but skin deep into its meaning.

Qui in suo utitur, nemini facit injuriam. He who uses his legal rights harms no one. (*Broom*)

Qui in utero est, pro jam nato habetur, quoties de ejus commodo quaeritur. He who is in the womb is considered as born wherever his benefit is concerned. (*Latin for Lawyers*)

Qui jure suo utituer neminem ladit. He who exercises his right injures no one.

Qui jussu judicis aliquod fecerit non videtur dolo malo fecisse, quia parere necesse est. Where a person does an act by command of one exercising judicial authority, the law will not suppose that he acted from any wrongful or improper motive, because it was his bounden duty to obey. (*Broom*)

Qui non negat fatetur. He who does not deny, admits. (*Trayner*)

Qui non obstat quod abstare potest, facere videtur. He who does not prevent (a thing) which he can prevent is considered to do (as doing) it.

Qui non prohibet quod prohibere potest assentire videtur. (*Lat.*) He who does not prohibit what he can prohibit is regarded as consenting.

Qui parcit nocentibus innocentibus punit. He who spares the guilty punishes the innocent.

Qui peccat ebrius lua sobrius. He who sins when drunk shall be punished when sober. (*Broom*)

Qui per alium facit per seipsum facere videur. He who does a thing by an agent is considered as doing it himself.

Qui prior est tempore, potior est jure. He who is before in time is the better in right. Priority in time gives preference in law. (*Broom; Story Eq. Jur.*)

He who is first in time has the strongest claim in law.

Qui prius jus suum insinuaverit præferetur. (*Lat.*) He is preferred whose right has been first recorded.

Qui S'excuse S'accuse. Excuses are born of a guilty conscience.

Qui sentit commodum sentire debet et onus ; et e contra. He who receives the advantage ought also to suffer the burden. (*Broom; Black*)

Qui sentit onus sentire debet et commodum. He who bears the burden of a thing ought also to experience the advantage arising from it.

Qui tacet consentire videtur. He who is silent is supposed to consent. The silence of a party implies his consent. (*Broom*) (*Latin for Lawyers*)

Qui tacet non utique fatetur, sed tamen verum est eum non negare. He who is silent does not indeed confess, but yet it is true that he does not deny.

Quick Transit Service. Means the special scheme of transit of goods consignments over the Indian Railway System in which the delivery of goods at destination is guaranteed within the stipulated time. [Customs Tariff Baggage (Transit to Customs Stations) Regulation, 1967, Rgn. 3(b) *Expln.*]

Quick unborn child. Unborn but moving foetus. [IPC (45 of 1860), S. 316].

Quick with child. "Quick with child" means having conceived.

In the state of pregnancy at which the motion of the foetus is felt. [IPC (45 of 1860), S. 312].

The common understanding of the words is that a woman is not quick with child until she has felt the child alive and quick within her.

Quickening. (*In medical jurisprudence*) The first motion of the foetus in the womb felt by the mother, occurring usually about the middle of the term of pregnancy.

Quicquid est contra normam recti est injuria. (3 Bulst 313). Whatever is against the rule of right is a wrong.

Quicquid fixatur solo, solo cedit. The maxim which means "whatever is fixed to soil, goes with or belongs to the soil" is a rule of the common law of England. But this rule has not been accepted in India. *Patnaik and Co.* v. *State of Orissa*, AIR 1965 SC 1655, 1658.

Quicquid judicis auctoritati subjicitur, novitati non subjicitur. Whatever is subject to the authority of a judge is not subject to innovation. (4 Inst. 66)

Quicquid inaedificatur solo, solo cedit. The maxim which means— whatever is affixed to the soil, belongs to the soil—is a rule of considerable antiquity and has been held to be inapplicable in this country. *Venkatasubbiah* v. *Thirupurasundari,* AIR 1965 Mad 185, 186. [T.P. Act (4 of 1882), S. 63]

Quicquid plantatur (or fixatur) solo, solo cedit. Fixture to the soil, goes with or belongs to the soil; whatever is planted on the soil goes with the soil.

There is no custom of Hindu (or other) law by which the maxim *quicquid plantatur* (*or aedificatur*) *solo, solo cedit* does not apply in India. The English law would apply unless it is clear that by local, customary, or other law applicable in this country, it does not. The Courts of India have not excluded the application of the maxim altogether, though they have held and the legislature has said in effect that there are substantial exceptions to the application of the maxim.

Quicunque jussu judicis aliquid fecerit non vidtur dolo malo fecisse, quia parere necesse est. Whoever does anything by the command of a judge is not reckoned to have done it with an evil intent, because it is necessary to obey.

Quid pro quo. The giving of one thing of value for another thing of value.

The literal meaning of the phrase '*quid pro quo*' is 'one for the other' meaning thereby— "you charge the fee for the service". Service to the mining area, factory, market or marketing operations are services to the payer of the fee. *Kewal Krishan* v. *State of Punjab*, AIR 1980 SC 1008, 1034.

Quid turpi ex causa promissum est non valet. A promise arising out of immoral causes is invalid.

Quiet and peaceable possession. Possession that is free from external disturbance and free from strife

[CPC (5 of 1908), 1st Sch., App. D, form No. 3A(2)(ii)].

Quilibet juri pro se introducto renunciare potest. (*Lat.*) Any one may renounce a right which has been introduced for his own advantage.

Quilibet potest renunciare juri pro se introducto. Every one may renounce or relinquish a right introduced for his own benefit. (*Wing. Max.*)

Quit. To leave; remove from : surrender possession of.

To depart from or out of. [Beedi and Cigar Workers (conditions of Employment) Act (32 of 1966), S. 26(2)].

To quit, as used in an Act requiring a landlord to give a tenant notice to quit, is synonymous with the word "to leave".

NOTICE TO QUIT. A written notice given by a landlord to his tenant, stating that the former desires to repossess himself of the demised premises and asking the tenant to remove himself from the same at a time designated, either at the expiration of the term, if the tenant is in under a lease, or immediately, if the tenancy is at will or by sufferance. [T.P. Act (4 of 1882), S. 106].

Quo warranto. By what authority. The name of a species of prerogative writ. A writ of *quo warranto* is one of the prerogative writs issued by a superior Court against a person who claims or who usurps any office, franchise or liberty, to enquire by what authority he supports his claim.

An order by which any person, who occupies or usurps an independent substantive public office or franchise or liberty, is asked to show by what right he claims it. [Constitution of India, Art. 32(2)].

Quo warranto (Requisites). Per SHIV DAYAL, C.J.— The only requisites which must be satisfied before a writ of '*quo warranto*' can be issued are: (i) the office must be public; (ii) the office must be substantive in character and independent in title; (iii) the office must have been created by a statute or by Constitution; and (iv) the office is held by usurper without legal authority. An office is usurped if the respondent is not entitled to that office or if the appointment of the respondent has not been made in accordance with law. AIR 1965 SC 491, **Foll.** [SHIV DAYAL, C.J. and J.S. VERMA, J.] *Sudhir Kumar Mishra* v. *Municipal Corporation, Jabalpur*, MLJ : YD 1978 Suppl C 577 : (1978) MPLJ 14 : (1978) Lab IC 294 : (1978) SCJ 238 : (1978) SLJ 34 : (1978) 1 Serv LR 604 (MP). [Constitution of India, Art 226]

Quod a quoque paenae nomine exactum est id eidem restituere nemo cogitur. That which has been exacted as a penalty no one is obliged to restore.

Quod ab initio non valet in tractu temporis non convalescit. That which is bad in its commencement improves not by lapse of time. (*Broom*)

Quod aedificatur in area legata cedit legato. Whatever is built on ground given by will goes to the legatee. (*Broom*)

Quod alias bonum et justum est, si per vim, vel fraudum petatur, malum et injustum efficitur. What otherwise is good and just, if it be sought by force and fraud, becomes bad and unjust.

Quod alias non fuit licitum, necessita licitum facit. What otherwise was not lawful, necessity makes lawful.

Quod approbo non reprobo. I cannot approve and reject at the same time. (*Broom*)

Quod contra legem fit, pro infecto habetur. (*Lat.*) That which is done against law is regarded as not done at all. (4 Rep. 31).

Quod contra rationem juris receptum est, non est producendum ad consequentias. That which has been received against the reason of the law is not to be drawn into a precedent.

Quod cunque aliquis ob tutelam corporis sui facerit, jure id fecisse videtur. Whatever any one does in defence of his person, that he is considered to have done legally. (*Latin for Lawyers*)

Quod semel aut bis existit proetereunt legislatores. Legislators pass by that which happens but once or twice.

The maxim was considered and in the context of a 'casus omissus' as the rule that a case left unprovided for, must be disposed of according to the law as it existed before a statute. *Union of India* v. *Rajiv Kumar*, (2003) 6 SCC 516, para 24.

Quod est necessarium est licitum. What is necessary is lawful.

Quod fieri non debet factum valet. That which ought not to be done, when done, is valid. (*Broom*)

Quod initio non valet, tractu temporis non valet. That which is void in the beginning, does not become valid by lapse of time.

Quod ipsis qui contraxerunt obstat et successoribus corum obstabit. That which bars those who have made a contract will bar their successor also.

Quod meum est sine facto meo vel defectu meo amitti vel in alium transferri non potest. That which is mine cannot be lost or transferred to another without any alienation or forfeiture. (*Broom*)

Quod naturalis ratio inter omnes homines constituit, vocatur jus gentium. That which natural reason has established among all men is called the "law of nations."

Quod necessitas cogit defendit. That which necessity compels, is justified.

Quod non apparet non est et non apparet judicialiter ante judicium. (*Lat.*) (2 *Inst.* 479) That which appears not is not, and nothing appears judicially before judgment.

Quod non habet principium non habet finem. That which has not beginning has not end. (*Wing. Max.*)

Quod nullius est, est domini regis. That which is the property of nobody, belongs to our Lord the King.

Quod nullius est, id ratione naturali occupanti conceditur. That which is the property of no one is, by natural reason, given to the (first) occupant.

Quod nullum est nullum producit effectum. That which is null produces no effect.

Quod per alluvionem agro tuo flumen adjecit. jure gentium tibi adquiritur. That which a river adds on your land by process of alluvion becomes yours by the law of nations.

Quod per me non possum nec per alium. What I cannot do by myself, I cannot by another.

Quod pure debetur praesenti die debetur. That which is due unconditionally is due now. (*i.e.*) at once. (*Trayner*)

Quod semel aut bis existit praetereunt legislatores. (*Lat.*) (D. 1, 3, 6) The legislature takes no notice of that which is only of occasional occurrence.

Quod semel placuit in electionibus amplius displicere non potest. What a party has once determined, in a case where he has an election cannot afterwards be disavowed. (*Black*)

Quod turpi ex causa promissum est, non valet. A promise founded on an illegal consideration is not binding.

Quod vanum et inutile est, lex non requirit. (*Lat.*) (*Co. Litt.* 319) The law requires not what is vain and useless.

Quod vero contra rationem juris receptum est, non est producendum ad consequentias. But what has been admitted contrary to the reason of law ought not to be drawn into precedents.

Quorum. The number of the members of an organized body of persons (as a legislative body or board of directors) that when duly assembled is legally competent to transact business in the absence of other members. [Industrial Finance Corporation Act (15 of 1948) (*repealed by Act 23 of 1993*), S. 17(2) and Constitution of India, Art. 100(3)].

When the word, 'quorum' is used in the context of a meeting, it would mean the presence of such minimum number of members as necessitated by the regulations of the body concerned, in order to make a meeting valid. [*Md. Ali Reza* v. *State of W.B.*, AIR 2012 Cal 86, para 9].

"Quorum denotes the minimum number of members of any body of persons whose presence is necessary in order to enable that body to transact its business validly, so that its acts may be lawful." *Punjab University* v. *Vijay Singh*, AIR 1976 SC 1441, 1443.

Quot homines, tot sententiae. There are as many opinions as there are men.

Quota. A certain proportional part or share; the share or proportion assigned to each on division.

Quotation. (*In legal Practice*) The production to a Court or judge of the exact language of a statute precedent, or other authority, in support of an argument or proposition advanced; (*in literary usage*) the transcription of part of a literary composition into another book or writing; (*in commerce*) a statement of the market price of one or more commodities; or the price specified to a correspondent.

Quoted company. A company whose name appears on the official list of a stock exchange.

Quotiens dubia interpretatio libertatis erit, secundum libertatem respondendum est. (D. 50 17. 20) As often as the interpretation of liberty is doubtful the answer should be on the side of liberty.

Quotiens idem sermo duas sententias exprimit : ea potissimum accipiatur, quae rei generendae aptior est. Whenever the same language expresses two meanings, that should be adopted which is the better fitted for carrying out the subject matter.

Quoties in stipulationibus ambigua oratio est, commodissimum est id accipi quo res de qua agitur in tuto sit. Whenever the language of stipulations is ambiguous, it is most fitting that, that (sense) should be taken by which the subject matter may be protected.

Quoties in verbis nulla est ambiguitas, ibi nulla expositio contra verba fienda est. When in the words there is no ambiguity, then no exposition contrary to the words is to be made.

Quum de lucro duorum quaeratur, melior est causa possidentis. When the question is as to the gain of two persons, the title of the party in possession is the better one.

Quum in testamento ambigue aut etiam perperam scriptum est, benigne interpretari est secundum id quod credible et cogitatum, credendum est. When in a will an ambiguous or even an erroneous expression occurs, it should be construed liberally and in accordance with what is thought the probable meaning of the testator. (*Broom*)

R

R. An abbreviation of regina, rex.

Race. Tribe, nation or people regarded as common stock; one of the great divisions of mankind having certain physical peculiarities in common. [T.P. Act (4 of 1882), S. 69(1)(a) and Constitution of India, Art. 23(2)].

Race club. "RACE CLUB" includes a body of persons, Corporate or incorporate, Society, Club or other association—

(i) formed for the purpose of promoting horse racing or pony racing or for holding race meeting, or

(ii) conducting or controlling such meetings. [Delhi Entertainments and Betting Tax Act, 1996 (8 of 1997), S. 2(p)]

Racial discrimination. Discrimination on the grounds of colour, race, nationality, or ethnic origins. It is dealt with by the Race Relations Acts of 1965, 1968, and 1976. The 1965 Act created an offence of incitement to racial hatred and made racial discrimination illegal in public places. The 1968 Act prohibits discrimination in respect of goods, services, facilities, employment, accommodation, and advertisements. The 1976 Act prohibits indirect racial discrimination, as well as discrimination in clubs with more than 25 members. It also prohibits the types of discrimination dealt with by the 1975 Sex Discrimination Act. The Race Relations (Amendment) Act 2000 extends coverage of the 1976 Act by prohibiting racial discrimination in the functions of the police and other public authorities not previously covered by that Act. It also places a general duty on public authorities to eliminate discrimination and promote racial equality. The Commission for Racial Equality has the power to conduct formal investigations into complaints. Individual complaints in the field of employment are dealt with by employment tribunals; other complaints are dealt with in specified county Courts. (*England*) (*Oxford Law Dictionary, 5th Edn., 2003*)

Rack-rent. "Rack-rent," is only a rent of the full value of the tenement, or near it."

Rent raised to the utmost: the full annual benefit of the property. [Presidency Small Cause Courts Act (15 of 1882), S. 41, 1st para].

It can only mean gross rent and not net rent. *Laxshmshi Hiralal and Co.* v. *Dhamji Khimji and Co.,* AIR 1969 Bom 73 at 74. [Presidency Small Cause Courts Act (15 of 1882), S. 41].

Racketeering. A system of organised crime that is traditionally involved in extortion of money from businessmen by intimidation, violence, or other illegal methods.

Radiation. Means gamma rays, x-rays and rays consisting of alpha particles, beta particles, neutrons, protons and other nuclear and sub-atomic particles, but not sound or radio waves, or visible, infra-red or ultra-violet light. [Atomic Energy Act (33 of 1962), S. 2(1)(h)]

Radio-diffusion. 'RADIO-DIFFUSION' includes communication to the public by means of wireless diffusion whether in the form of sounds or visual images or both. [Copyright Act (14 of 1957), (S. 2(v) *omitted* by Act (23 of 1983)]

Radio-set telegraph. A radio set receiving communications is a telegraph. *State of Bihar* v. *Mangal Sao,* AIR 1963 SC 445, 446. [Indian Telegraph Act (13 of 1885), S. 3(1)]

"Radio waves" or "Hertzian waves". Means electro-magnetic waves of frequencies lower than 3000 gigacycles per second propagated in space without artificial guide. [Indian Telegraphs Act (13 of 1885), S. 3(1AA) *Expln.* & Wireless Telegraphy Act (17 of 1933), S. 2(1)]

"Radioactive substance" or "radioactive material". Any substance or material which spontaneously emits radiation in excess of the levels prescribed by the Central Government. [Atomic Energy Act (33 of 1962), S. 2(1)(i)]

Radius. The term "radius" means a "Right line drawn or extended from the centre of a circle to its periphery," so that an agreement not to practice dentistry within a radius of ten miles of the town means from the center of the town; the town as a whole not being suitable as the centre implied by the term "radius".

Rag or Rag Pulp. "Rag" or "rag pulp" which is made from cotton waste or cotton textile material. [*Coastal Paper Limited* v. *Commissioner Central Excise, Visakhapatnam,* (2015) 10 SCC 664, para 31].

"Rag pulps"."Papermaking fibers made from new or old cotton textile cuttings. The term may also apply to cotton linters i.e., the short fibers which adhere to the cotton seed after the ginning process. Rag pulps are used in paper where permanence and durability are needed e.g., ledger, blueprint, map, currency paper, etc." [Dictionary of paper by Tappi as cited in *Coastal Paper Limited* v. *Commissioner of Central Excise, Visakhapatnam,* (2015) 10 SCC 664, para 29].

Papermaking fibers of cotton made from material like new or old cotton textile cuttings or cotton linters, mill run, fly cotton, cotton waste, etc. Rag pulps are used in papers where permanence and durability are needed, for example, ledger, blueprint, map, currency papers, etc. [Indian Standard Glossary of Terms used in Paper Trade and Industry-IS 4661 : 1999 as cited in *Coastal Paper Limited* v. *Commissioner of Central Excise, Visakhapatnam,* (2015) 10 SCC 664, para 30].

Ragging. Means causing inducing, compelling or forcing a student, whether by way of a practical joke or otherwise, to do any act which detracts from human dignity or violates his person or exposes him to ridicule or to forbear from doing any lawful act by intimidating, wrongfully restraining, wrongfully confining or injuring him or by using criminal force to him or by holding out to him any threat of such intimidation, wrongful restraint, wrongful confinement, injury or the use of criminal force. [Karnataka Education Act 1983 (10 of 1995), S. 2(29)]

"RAGGING" means doing an act which causes or is likely to cause insult or annoyance or fear or apprehension of threat or intimidation or outrage of modesty or injury to a student. [Andhra Pradesh Prohibition of Ragging Act (26 of 1997), S. 2(e)]

Rail travel agent. Means any person engaged in providing any service connected with booking of passage for travel by rail. [Finance Act (32 of 1994), S. 65(1)(72) now repealed by Central Goods and Services Tax Act, 2017]

Railroad. A railroad has been defined as a road specially laid out and graded, having parallel rails of iron or steel for the wheels of carriages or cars, drawn by steam or other motive power, to run upon.

A road laid with rails on which wheels of the wagons containing goods or pasengers are made to run by locomotives or any other engine. [CPC (5 of 1908), 1st Sch., App. A, form No. 29].

Railway. "RAILWAY" means a railway or any portion of a railway for the public carriage of passengers, animals or goods and includes—

(a) all land within the fences or other boundary-marks indicating the limits of the land appurtenant to a railway; (*b*) all lines of rails, sidings or branches worked over for purposes of, or in connection with, a railway; (*c*) all stations, offices, warehouses, wharves, workshops, manufactories, fixed plant and machinery and other works constructed for the purposes of, or in connection with, a railway; and (*d*) all ferries, ships, boats and rafts which are used in inland waters for the purposes of the traffic of a railway and belong to or are hired or worked by the authority administering the railway. [Indian Railways Act (9 of 1890), S. 3(4) Now repealed by the Railways Act, 1989 (24 of 1989)].

"RAILWAY" does not include—

(a) a tramway wholly within a municipal area, or
(b) any other line of communication wholly situate in one State and declared by Parliament by law not to be a railway. [Constitution of India, Art. 366(20)]

"RAILWAY" means a railway, or any portion of a railway, for the public carriage of passengers or goods, and includes—

(a) all lands within the fences or other boundary marks indicating the limits of the land appurtenant to a railway;
(b) all lines of rails, sidings, or yards, or branches used for the purposes of, or in connection with a railway;
(c) all electric fraction equipments, power supply and distribution installations used for the purposes of, or in connection with, a railway;
(d) all rolling stock, stations, officers, warehouse wharves, workshops, manufactories, fixed plant and machinery, roads and streets, running rooms, rest houses, institutes, hospitals, water works and water supply installation, staff dwellings and any other works constructed for the purpose of, or in connection with, railway;
(e) all vehicles which are used on any road for the purposes of traffic of a railway and owned, hired or worked by a railway; and
(f) all ferries, ships, boats and rafts which are used on any canal, river, lake or other navigable inland waters for the purposes of the traffic of a railway and owned, hired and worked by a railway administration, but does not include—
    (i) a tramway wholly within a municipal area; and
    (ii) lines of rails built in any exhibition ground, fair, park, or any other place solely for the purpose of recreation. [Railways Act (24 of 1989), S. 2(31)]

The word 'railway' in the ordinary sense, would not have meant a 'steamer' but it has been defined arbitrarily and given to it an artificial meaning, which otherwise it would not have conveyed ordinarily. Under the definition in S. 3(4) 'railway' includes a 'steamer'. *Mohd. Khaliluddin* v. *Union of India*, AIR 1962 Pat 109. [Indian Railways Act (9 of 1890), S. 3(4)]

A line or track consisting of iron or steel rails on which carriages or wagons carrying passengers or goods are moved by an engine; the whole organisation necessary for managing it. [Indian Contract Act (9 of 1872), S. 72, ill. (b)].

Railway-administration. "RAILWAY-ADMINI-STRATION" or "ADMINISTRATION," in the case of a railway administered by the Government or a Native State, means the manager of the railway and includes the Government or the Native State, and, in the case of a railway administered by a railway company means the railway company. [Indian Railways Act (9 of 1890), S. 3(6) Now repealed by the Railways Act, 1989 (24 of 1989)].

"RAILWAY ADMINISTRATION" means—

(i) any company administering a railway or tramway in any part of India either under a Special Act of Parliament of the United Kingdom or an Indian law, or under contract with the Government, or
(ii) the manager of any railway or tramway administered by the Central Government or by a State Government, and includes in any case referred to in sub-clause (ii) the Central

Government or the State Government, as the case may be. [Provident Funds Act (19 of 1925), S. 2(f)].

"RAILWAY ADMINISTRATION", in relation to —

(a) a Government railway, means the General Manager of a Zonal Railway; and

(b) a non-Government railway, means the person who is the owner or lessee of the railway or the person working the railway under an agreement. [Railways Act (24 of 1989), S. 2(32)]

The administration of the railway. [Sale of Goods Act (3 of 1930), S. 25(3), *Expln.*].

Railway authority. Means an authority administering railway land, as may be notified by the Central Government in this behalf. [S. 2(1)(m) of the Prohibition of Employment as Manual Scavengers & Their Rehabilitation Act, 2013 (25 of 2013)]

Railway claims tribunal. The Railway Claims Tribunal is the creature of the statute. So it is not a civil Court. *Birla Cement Works* v. *General Manager Western Railways*, AIR 1995 SC 1111, 1112. [Indian Railways Act (9 of 1890), S. 34] [Now Repealed & replaced by Act 24 of 1989]

Railway company. "RAILWAY COMPANY" includes any persons, whether incorporated or not, who are owners or lessees of a railway or parties to an agreement for working a railway. [Indian Railways Act (9 of 1890), S. 3(5)]. [Now Repealed & replaced by Act 24 of 1989]

"RAILWAY COMPANY" means a Company registered under the Indian Companies Act, 1882, and formed for the purpose of making and working, or making or working, a railway in India, whether alone or in conjunction with other purposes. [Railway Companies Act (10 of 1895), S. 2(3)]

A company-owning and operating a railway system. [Indian Contract Act (9 of 1872), S. 72, ill. (b)].

"Railway company" includes any persons whether incorporated or not, who are owners or lessees of a railway or parties to an agreement for working a railway. [Code on Social Security, 2020 (36 of 2020), section 2(67)]

Railway land. Means any land in which a Government railway has any right, title or interest. [Railways Act, 1989 (24 of 1989), S. 2(32A). Also see S. 2(1)(n) of the Prohibition of Employment as Manual Scavengers & Their Rehabilitation Act, 2013 (25 of 2013)]

Railway property. 'RAILWAY PROPERTY' includes any goods, money or valuable security or animal, belonging to, or in charge or possession of, a railway administration. [Railway Property (Unlawful Possession) Act (29 of 1966), S. 2(d); Railway Protection Force Act (23 of 1957), S. 2(e)]

Railway provident fund. "RAILWAY PROVIDENT FUND" means a Provident Fund constituted by the authority of a railway administration for any class or classes of its employees. [Provident Funds Act (19 of 1925), S. 2(g)]

Railway receipt. A receipt issued by the railway administration for goods accepted by the railway for assignment from one station to another. [T.P. Act (4 of 1882), S. 137, *Expln.*].

Railway servant. "RAILWAY SERVANT" means any persons employed by a railway administration in connection with the service of a railway. [Indian Railways Act (9 of 1890), S. 3(7)] [Now Repealed & replaced by Act 24 of 1989]

"RAILWAY SERVANT" means any person employed by the Central Government or by a railway administration in connection with the service of a railway. [Railways Act (24 of 1989), S. 2(34)]

Railway stores. Means any article which is the property of any railway administration and which is used or is intended to be used for the construction, operation or maintenance of a railway. [Railway Stores (Unlawful Possession) Act (51 of 1955), S. 2 Now repealed by the Railway Property (Unlawful Possession) Act, 1966 (29 of 1966)].

Raiyat. "RAIYAT" means primarily a person who has acquired a right to hold land for the purpose of cultivating it by himself, or by members of his family, or by hired servants, or with the aid of partners. [Ben. Act VI of 1908 (Chota Nagpur Tenancy), S. 6.]

"RAIYAT" means a person or an institution holding land for any purpose including non-agricultural land. [West Bengal Land Holding Revenue Act (44 of 1979), S. 2(k)]

Ration card. Means a document issued under an order or authority of the State Government for the purchase of essential commodities from the fair price shops under the Targeted Public Distribution System. [S. 2(16) of the National Food Security Act, 2013 (20 of 2013)]

Rajya Sabha. Council of States (Upper House of Indian Parliament).

RAM. (*abbr*) Random Access Memory. A data-storage device for which the order of access to different locations does not affect the speed of access. This is in contrast to magnetic disk or magnetic tape where it is much quicker to access data sequentially because accessing a nonsequential location requires physical movement of the storage medium rather than just electronic switching. The most common form of RAM in use today is built from semiconductor integrated circuits, which can either be static (SRAM) or dynamic (DRAM). (*Cyber Law*)

A type of memory formed by one or more chips whose contents can, at any time, be quickly changed by the computer. This type of memory loses its data when electrical power is removed. (*Cyber Law*)

Random access. The ability to gain access to any one storage location among many in an equal amount of time and effort and not depending upon any previous action. (*Computer*)

Range. "RANGE" means all the areas of land or water that a migratory species inhabits, stays in temporarily, crosses or overflies at any time on its normal migration route. [Convention on the Conservation of Migratory Species of Wild Animals, 1979, Art. I. 1(f)].

A series or chain of mountain peaks considered as forming one connected system. [Scheduled Areas (Assimilation of Laws) Act (16 of 1953), Sch.].

Rank. Row or line—especially of soldiers standing side by side.

A grade or status or dignity; an order. [CrPC 1973 (2 of 1974), S. 2(o)]; [Army Act (46 of 1950), S. 20(4)].

The word 'rank' means grade or status. *N.C. Dalwad's* v. *State of Gujarat*, AIR 1987 SC 1933, 1937.

Rank—Precedence. The word 'rank' in common parlance, as also in English diction refers to a position, especially an official one within a social organisation, of high social order or other standing status. Likewise, the word 'precedence' denotes the ceremonial order or priority to be observed on formal occasions, or a right to preferential treatment. *S.C. Advocates on Record Association* v. *Union of India*, AIR 1994 SC 268, 445.

Ranks. Common soldiers. [Army Act (46 of 1950), S. 71(f)].

Ransom. Ransom is a sum of money paid for redeeming a captive or prisoner of war, or a prize. It is also used to signify a sum of money paid for the pardoning of some great offence, and or setting the offender who was imprisoned, free.

The money, price or consideration paid or demanded for the release of a person or restoration of a thing. [Army Act (46 of 1950), S. 66].

Rap de femme. Rape of a woman.

Carnal knowledge of a woman without her legal consent. [IPC (45 of 1860), S. 375].

Rape. A man is said to commit 'rape' if he—

(a) penetrates his penis, to any extent, into the vagina, mouth, urethra or anus of a woman or makes her to do so with him or any other person; or

(b) inserts, to any extent, any object or a part of the body, not being the penis, into the vagina, the urethra or anus of a woman or makes her to do so with him or any other person; or

(c) manipulates any part of the body of a woman so as to cause penetration into the vagina, urethra, anus or any part of body of such woman or makes her to do so with him or any other person; or

(d) applies his mouth to the vagina, anus, urethra of a woman or makes her to do so with him or any other person,

under the circumstances falling under any of the following seven descriptions:—

First.—Against her will.

Secondly.—Without her consent.

Thirdly.—With her consent, when her consent has been obtained by putting her or any person in whom she is interested, in fear of death or of hurt.

Fourthly.—With her consent, when the man knows that he is not her husband and that her consent is given because she believes that he is another man to whom she is or believes herself to be lawfully married.

Fifthly.—With her consent when, at the time of giving such consent, by reason of unsoundness of mind or intoxication or the administration by him personally or through another of any stupefying or unwholesome Substance, she is unable to understand the nature and consequences of that to which she gives consent.

Sixthly.—With or without her consent, when she is under eighteen years of age.

Seventhly.—When she is unable to communicate consent.

Explanation 1.—For the purposes of this section, "vagina" shall also include *labia majora.*

Explanation 2.—Consent means an unequivocal voluntary agreement when the woman by words, gestures or any form of verbal or non-verbal communication, communicates willingness to participate in the specific sexual act:

Provided that a woman who does not physically resist to the act of penetration shall not by the reason only of that fact, be regarded as consenting to the sexual activity.

Exception 1.—A medical procedure or intervention shall not constitute rape.

Exception 2.—Sexual intercourse or sexual acts by a man with his own wife, the wife not being under fifteen years of age, is not rape. [S. 375 of IPC, 1860 (45 of 1860), as substituted by the Criminal Law (Amendment) Act, 2013 (13 of 2013)]

"RAPE". "A man is said to commit "RAPE" who, except in the case hereinafter excepted, has sexual intercourse with a woman under circumstances falling under any of the five following descriptions :

First.—Against her will.

Secondly.—Without her consent.

Thirdly.—With her consent, when her consent has been obtained by putting her in fear of death, or of hurt.

Fourthly.—With her consent, when the man knows that he is not her husband, and that her consent is given because she believes that he is another man to whom she is or believes herself to be lawfully married.

Fifthly.—With her consent, when at the time of giving such consent, by reason of unsoundness of mind or intoxication or administration by him personally or through another of any stupefying or unwholesome substance, she is unable to understand the nature or consequences of that to which she gives consent.

Sixthly.—With or without her consent, when she is under sixteen years of age.

Explanation.—Penetration is sufficient to constitute the sexual intercourse necessary to the offence of rape.

Exception.—Sexual intercourse by a man with his own wife, the wife not being under fifteen years of age, is not rape." [Indian Penal Code (45 of 1860), S. 375 [Now (w. e. f. 1-7-2024) repealed & replaced by Bharatiya Nayaya Sanhita, 2023 (45 of 2023)]

A man is said commit "RAPE" if he—

(a) Penetrates his penis, to any extent, into the vagina, mouth, urethra or anus of a woman or makes her to do so with him or any other person; or

(b) insets, to any extent, any object or a part of the body, not being the penis, into the vagina, the urethra or anus of a woman or makes her to do so with him or any person; or

(c) manipulates any part of the body of a woman so as to cause penetration into the vagina, the urethra, anus or any part of body of such woman or makes her to do so with him or any other person; or

(d) applies his mouth to the vagina, anus, urethra of a woman or makes her to do so with him or any person, under the circumstances falling under any of the following seven descriptions—

First.—Against her will

Secondly.—Without her consent.

Thirdly.—With her consent, when her consent has been obtained by putting her or any person in whom she is interested, in fear of death or of hurt.

Fourthly.—With her consent, when the man knows that he is not her husband and that her consent is given because she believes that he is another man to whom she is or believes herself to be lawfully married.

Fifthly.—With her consent when, at the time of giving such consent by reason of unsoundness of mind or intoxication or the administration by him personally or through another of any stupefying or unwholesome substance, she is unable to understand the nature and consequences of that to which she gives consent.

Sixthly.—With or without her consent, when she is under eighteen years of age.

Seventhly.—When she is unable to communicate consent.

Explanation 1.—For the purposes of this section "vagina" shall also include labia majora.

Exception 2.—Sexual intercourse or sexual acts by a man with his own wife, the wife not being under fifteen years of age, is not rape. [Indian Penal Code (45 of 1860), S. 375 as substituted by Amending Act (13 of 2013)].

Rape is the carnal knowledge of woman without her consent. It must not only be obtained by force and threats, but without the consent and against her will. It must be forcible and against the will of the prosecutrix.

The 'rape' in its simplest term is 'the ravishment of a woman, without her consent, by force, fear or fraud', or 'the carnal knowledge of a woman by force against her will'. *Bhupinder Sharma* v. *State of H.P.,* (2003) 8 SCC 551, para 10.

Rarest of rare case. 'Rarest of rare' doctrine has not only a statistical dimension *i.e.* incidence of particular type of murder, but rarest of rare benchmark can also be used in the context of other parameters such a brutality, planning, society's reaction *et al.* It can not conclusively said that murder of the wife for usurping property is a 'rarest of rare case' though it can be a rare case. [*Swamy Shraddananda* v. *State of Karnataka*, AIR 2007 SC 2531, 2549, para 97]

Rarest of rare case doctrine. A survey of the application of 'rarest of rare doctrine' in various courts will reveal that various Courts have given their own meaning to the doctrine. This variation in the interpretation of rarest of rare analysis may amount to be constitutionally infirm because of apparent arbitrariness on the count of content of the doctrine. Today it could be safely said in the context of Indian experience on death penalty that no standards can be culled out from the judge-made law which governs the selection of penalty apart from the broad overall guideline of rarest of rare under *Bachan Singh* case. [*Santosh Kumar Satishbhushan Bariyar* v. *State of Maharashtra,* (2009) 6 SCC 498, 547-48, paras 125, 126; *Bachan Singh* v. *State of Punjab,* (1980) 2 SCC 684 : 1980 SCC (Cri 580)]

Rarest of rare cases. The expression 'rarest of rare cases' used after the words 'sparingly and with circumspection' in Section 482 of the Code and merely emphasises and reiterates what is intended to be conveyed by the words 'sparingly and with circumspection'. It means that the power under Section 482 to quash proceedings should not be used mechanically or routinely, but with care and caution, only when a clear case for quashing is made out and failure to interfere would lead to a miscarriage of justice. It is not used in the sense in which it is used with reference to punishment for offence under Section 302 of IPC (45 of 1860). [*Som Mittal* v. *Govt. of Karnataka,* (2008) 3 SCC 574, 580k-81, para 9] [CrPC, 1973 (2 of 1974), S. 482]

Where though a person was held to be a ringleader and planned murderer of triple murder but in the circumstances of the case, the case did not fall within the ambit of the expression 'rarest of the rare cases' to award death sentence to him. [*Prithvi* v. *Mam Raj,* (2004) 13 SCC 279, 289, para 25]. See also *Ram Singh* v. *Sonia,* (2007) 3 SCC 1, 30, para 60.

A case where deceased victim died due to excessive bleeding after rape committed by the accused and not due to any specific overt act of the accused, cannot, come within the 'rarest of rare cases' for imposing a death sentence. [*Amrit Singh* v. *State of Punjab*, (2006) 12 SCC 79, 86, paras 21 & 22]

In a case following a sudden quarrel the accused who was drunk fired and killed three persons and injured four other persons within few minutes would not come within the expression 'rarest of rare cases' for imposing death sentence. [*Desh Raj* v. *State of Punjab,* (2007) 12 SCC 494, 502, para 12] [IPC (45 of 1860), S. 302]

Rash. Hasty; impetuous; acting without due consideration or regard for consequences. [IPC (45 of 1860), S. 279]; [Presidency-towns Insolvency Act (3 of 1909), S. 39(2)(f)].

Rash or negligent act. There is a distinction between a rash act and a negligent act. In the case of a rash act the criminality lies in running the risk of doing such an act with recklessness or indifference as to the consequence. Criminal negligence is the gross and culpable neglect or failure to exercise that reasonable and proper care and precaution to guard against injury either to the public generally or to an individual in particular, which having regard to all the circumstances out of which the charge has arisen, it was the imperative duty of the accused person to have adopted. Negligence is an omission to do something which a reasonable man, guided upon those considerations which ordinarily regulate the conduct of human affairs would do, or doing something which a prudent and reasonable man would not do. A culpable rashness is acting with the consciousness that the mischievous and illegal consequences may follow, but with the hope that they will not, and often with the belief that the actor has taken sufficient precautions to prevent their happening. The imputability arises from acting despite the consciousness. Culpable negligence is acting without the consciousness that the illegal and mischievous effect will follow, but in circumstances which show that the actor has not exercised the caution incumbent upon him and if he had he would have had the consciousness. The imputability arises from the neglect of the civic duty of circumspection. (*Bhalachandra Waman Pathe* v. *State of Maharashtra,* 1968 ACJ 38 and *S.N. Hussain* v. *State of A.P.,* AIR 1972 SC 685). [IPC (45 of 1860), S. 364-A]

Rashness. The state or condition of being rash. [Indian Evidence Act (1 of 1872), S. 14].

Rasure. A scraping off; the removal of words from an instrument by scraping off.

Rate. Rate is the standard of measure. [*State of U.P. v. Systematic Consom Limited*, (2014) 13 SCC 627, para 20].

"RATE" includes any fare, charge or other payment for the carriage of any passenger, animal or goods; as railway rate. [Indian Railways Act (9 of 1890), S. 3(13)] [Now Repealed & replaced by Act 24 of 1989]

"RATE" includes any toll, rent, rate, fee or charge leviable under this Act. [Major Port Trusts Act (38 of 1963), S. 2(x)] [Now Repealed by s. 75(1) of Act 1 of 2021]

"RATE" includes any fare, freight or any other charge for the carriage of any passenger or goods. [Railways Act (24 of 1989), S. 2(35)]

"RATE" includes any fare, charge, or other payment for the carriage of passengers, animals or goods. [Rajasthan Ropeways Act, 1996 (Raj Act No. 18 of 1997), S. 2(l)]

Local tax [IPC (45 of 1860), S. 21, tenth]; a charge per unit of public service, commodity *etc.* [IPC (45 of 1860), S. 263A(4)].

By the use of the expression 'rate' a relation between the taxable income and the tax charged is intended, but the relation need not be of the nature of proportion or fraction. The expression 'rate' is often used in the sense of a standard or measure. *Sundaram & Co.* v. *Commissioner of Income Tax*, AIR 1968 SC 124, 128.

RATE means the scale or amount of any other charges. *Union of India* v. *Motilal Padampat Sugar Mills Co. (Private) Ltd., Kanpur*, AIR 1969 SC 630 at 633. [Indian Railways Act (9 of 1890), S. 41(1)(c)]

Rate of exchange. "RATE OF EXCHANGE" means the rate of exchange determined or recognised by the Central Government for the conversion of Indian currency into foreign currency or foreign currency into Indian currency. [Income-tax Act (43 of 1961), S. 43A, *Expln.* 1(a)]

The price at which a bill drawn in one country upon another may be sold in the former.

The amout of one currency that will buy a given amount of another. [Negotiable Instruments Act (26 of 1881), S. 5].

Rate of interest. In common acceptation, the expression "rate of interest" refers to the percentage or amount of interest, and not to the manner of computing; and the phrase "rate of interest," in a statute providing that parties might agree on any rate of interest, meant the amount of interest, and did not refer to means of computation.

Rate of return. Amount of money made on an investment (in the form of interest or dividend), normally expressed as a percentage of the amount invested.

"Rate or rates in force" or "rates in force". In relation to an assessment year or financial year, mean—

(i) for the purposes of calculating income-tax under the first proviso to sub-section (5) of Section 132, or computing the income-tax chargeable under sub-section (4) of Section 172 or sub-section (2) of Section 174 or Section 175 or sub-section (2) of Section 176 or deducting income-tax under Section 192 from income chargeable under the head "Salaries" or computation of the "advance tax" payable under Chapter XVII-C in case not falling under Section 115A or Section 115B or Section 115BB or Section 115BBB or Section 115E or Section 164 or Section 164A or Section 167B, the rate or rates of income-tax specified in this behalf in the Finance Act of the relevant year, and for the purposes of computation of the "advance tax" payable under Chapter XVII-C in a case falling under Section 115A or Section 115B or Section 115BB or Section 115BBB or Section 115E or Section 164 or Section 164A or Section 167B, as the case may be, or the rate or rate of income-tax specified in this behalf in the Finance Act of the relevant year, whichever is applicable;

(ii) for the purposes of deduction of tax under Sections 193, 194, 194A, 194B, 194BB and 194D, the rate or rate of income-tax specified in this behalf in the Finance Act of the relevant year;

(iii) for the purposes of deduction of tax under Section 195, the rate or rates of income-tax specified in this behalf in the Finance Act of the relevant year or the rate or rates of income-tax specified in an agreement entered into by the Central Government under Section 90, whichever is applicable by virtue of the provisions of Section 90. [Income-tax Act (43 of 1961), S. 2(37A)]

Rate of tax of the said country. The expression "RATE OF TAX OF THE SAID COUNTRY" means income-tax and super-tax actually paid in the said country in accordance with the corresponding laws in force in the said country after deduction of all relief due, but before deduction of any relief due in the said country in respect of double taxation, divided by the whole amount of the income as assessed in the said country. [Income-tax Act (43 of 1961), S. 91(3), *Expln.* (iii)]

Rate payer. Means a person liable to pay any rate, tax, cess or licence fee under this Act. [New Delhi Municipal Council Act (44 of 1994), S. 2(41)]

Rateable. Made or reckoned to a proportionate rate. [CPC (5 of 1908), O. XXI, R. 90]

Rateable distribution. Distribution of assets held by a Court in proportion to the amounts due to various persons who have applied for execution of decrees for payment of money against the same judgement-debtor. [CPC (5 of 1908), O. XXI, R. 90(1)].

Rateable value. "RATEABLE VALUE" means the value of any land or building fixed in accordance with the provisions of the Act and the bye-laws made thereunder for the purpose of assessment to property taxes. [N.D.M.C. Act (44 of 1994), S. 2(42)]

Rateably. In accordance with the proportion to one's share. [Indian Partnership Act (9 of 1932), S. 48(b)(ii)]; [T.P. Act (4 of 1882), S. 82]; [CPC (5 of 1908), S. 73(1) and (2)]

Rates. The word "RATES" includes any toll, due, rent, rate, or charge leviable under the Port Trust Act. [Bom. Act VI of 1879 (Port Trust Act (Bom), S. 3, cl. 1].

Ratification. Confirmation; ratification is the adoption of a contract made on behalf of some one whom he did not authorize, which relates back to the execution of the contract, and renders it obligatory from the outset.

Approval, by word or conduct, of that which was improperly or unauthorisedly performed in the first instance; confirmation; formal sanction. [Indian Contract Act (9 of 1872), S. 196].

"Ratification" means "the making valid of an act already done". This principle is derived from the Latin maxim "ratihabitio mandato aequiparatur" meaning thereby "a subsequent ratification of an act is equivalent to a prior authority to perform such act." It is for this reason, the ratification assumes an invalid act which is retrospectively validated. [*National Institute of Technology v. Pannalal Choudhary*, (2015) 11 SCC 669, para 29].

A ratification, when fairly made, will have the same effect as an original authority has, to bind the principal, not only in regard to the agent himself but in regard to third persons; and the ratification relates back to the inception of the transaction, and has a complete retroactive efficacy.

Ratify. To make valid; to confirm; to sanction an act already done; to give sanction and validity to something done without authority; to give validity to the act of another; usually to approve or confirm by a principal what has been done by an agent or one assuming to act for another.

To confirm or make valid (an act, promise *etc.*) by giving consent, approval or formal sanction, especially to what has been done or arranged by another on one's behalf. [Indian Contract Act (9 of 1872), S. 196 and Specific Relief Act (47 of 1963), S. 27(2)(a)].

Ratihabitio mandato aequiparatur. Ratification is equivalent to express command. (*Black*)

Rating. The expression "RATE" OR RATING, OF VESSELS, as used in policies of assurance, means relative state in regard to insurable qualities.

An assignment in an occupational group within which a petty officer holds a rate. [Navy Act (62 of 1957), S. 82(14)].

Ratio. "Ratio" is variously defined to be the relation between two magnitudes of the same kind; the relation between two similar magnitudes in respect to quantity; the relation between two similar quantities in respect to how many times one makes so many times the other; especially the relation expressed by the division of one quantity by the other, by the factor that, multiplied into one, will produce the other; relative amount; proportion.

The relation between two similar magnitudes in respect to quantity.

Where a payment is to be made according to a certain ratio, the word "ratio" imports a payment in certain proportions.

Ratio decidendi. Reasons for deciding; the grounds of decision.

"Ratio decidendi is the opinion given by the judge and such opinion is necessary for the decision of a particular case".

A decision is only an authority for what it actually decides and not for what may logically follow from it. Every judgment must be read as applicable to the particular facts proved, since the generality of expressions, which may be found there, are not intended to be expositions of the whole law but governed or qualified by particular facts of the case in which such expressions are to be found. *C.D. Kamdar* v. *State of Orissa,* (1985) Tax LR 2497, 2499 (Ori). [Income-Tax Act (43 of 1961), S. 260]

The enunciation of the reason or principle upon which a question before a Court has been decided is alone binding as a precedent. This underlying principle is called the '*ratio decidendi*', namely the general reasons given for the decision or the general grounds upon which it is based, detached or abstructed from the specific peculiarities of the particular case which give rise to the decision. [*Halsbury's Laws of England* (Fourth Edition), Vol 37, para 1237, Vol 37 **as referred in** *Amar Kumar Mahto* v. *State of Bihar*, AIR 2010 Pat 19, 22, para 10]

'Ratio decidendi' and 'obiter dicta' (distinction). A precedent is a judicial decision which contains in itself a principle. The underlying principle which thus forms its authoritative elements is often termed the *ratio decidendi*. The concrete decision is binding between the parties to it, but it is the abstract *ratio decidendi* which alone has the force of law as regards the world at large.

The only judicial principles which are authoritative are those which are thus relevant in their subject matter and limited in their scope. All others, at the best, are of merely persuasive efficacy. They are not true *ratio decidendi* and are distinguished from them under the name of *dicta* or *obiter dicta*, things said by the way. The prerogative of judges is not to make law by formulating and declaring it—this pertains to the legislature—but to make law by applying it. Judicial declaration, unaccompanied by judicial application, is not of binding authority. Passages from SALMOND on *Jurisprudence,* 11th Edn. Pp. 223 and 224 quoted. *Obiter dicta* though they may have great weight as such, are not conclusive authority. *Obiter dicta* in this context means that what the words literally signify—namely, statements by the way. If a judge thinks it desirable to give his opinion on some point which is not necessary for the decision of the case, that has not the binding weight of the decision of the case and the reasons for the decision (1934) 2 KBD 132 (154), **foll.** *M. Shaik Dawood* v. *Collector of Central Excise, Madras,* MLJ : QD (1956-1960) Vol. IV C1085 : 73 Mad LW 491 : 1960 Mad LJ (Cri) 626 : (1960) 2 Mad LJ 230 : ILR (1960) Mad 961: 1961 CrLJ 96 : AIR 1961 Mad 1 (FB).

Ratio decidendi of a case. It is the rule deducible from the application of law to the facts and circumstances of a case which constituents its *ratio decidendi* and not some conclusion based upon facts which may appear to be similar. One additional or different fact can make a world of difference between conclusions in two cases even when the same principles are applied in each case to similar facts. (*Regional Manager* v. *Pawan Kumar Dubey,* AIR 1976 SC 1766)

Ratio est formalis causa consuetudinis. Reason is the formal cause of custom.

Ratio est legis anima, mutata legis ratione, mutatur et lex. Reason is the soul of law; the reason of the law being changed, the law is also changed. (*Latin for Lawyers*)

Ratio in jure aequitas integra. Reason in law is total equity.

Ratio potest allegari deficiente lege, sed vera et legalis et non apparens. Reason can be adduced when law is defective; but it must be true and legal reason, and not merely apparent.

Ration. The food allowance of one person or one animal for one day. [Navy Act (62 of 1957), S. 31(10)].

Rational. Based on, derived from reason or reasoning; agreeable to reason; reasonable; [Indian Evidence Act (1 of 1872), S. 118]; judicious.

Ravine. A ravine is a long, deep, and narrow hollow worn by a stream or torrent of water; a long, deep, and narrow hollow or pass through mountains; hence the presence of water at least occasionally, is almost inseparable from the idea of a ravine.

A deep, narrow gorge. [Indian Forest Act (16 of 1927, S. 35(c)(ii)].

Ravish. "Ravish", from the Latin word "rapuit", imports the use of force and an indictment for rape, charging that the defendant ravished a certain female against her consent, sufficiently alleges the crime, without an express allegation of the use of force.

The term "ravish" imports both force and resistance and includes the meaning of the phrase "carnally know by force and against her will."

To rape. [Indian Evidence Act (1 of 1872), S. 155(4)].

Raw materials. The term 'RAW MATERIALS' would include materials which physically enter into the composition of the finished product; materials like stores and fuel which assist the manufacturing process but do not physically enter into the composition of the finished product would not be included in raw materials. [ICAI, Statement on the Amendments to Schedule VI to the Companies Act (1 of 1956), para 6.3]

'Raw material' means:

(i) basic material which are needed for the manufacture of goods, but which are still in a raw, natural, unrefined or unmanufactured state; and

(ii) for a manufacturer, any materials or goods which are required for the manufacturing process, whether they have actually been previously manufactured or are processed or are still in a raw or natural state. [The Export and Import Policy 1997-2002, 3.41 as cited in *Meridian Industries Limited* v. *Commissioner of Central Excise*, (2015) 15 SCC 469, para 15].

Products before they have come into the process of manufacture, such as cotton, hemp *etc.*

An input or ingredient, getting burnt up or consumed in the chemical process of manufacture is raw material for the end product. The ingredient should go into the making of the end product in the sense that without the ingredient, the presence of the end product is rendered impossible. Sodium sulphate used in the manufacture of paper is raw material. *Collector of Central Excise, New Delhi* v. *Ballarpur Industries Ltd.*, AIR 1990 SC 196. [Central Excise Rules (1944), R. 8(1)]

"Raw material is one which is used in the process of manufacture. A printing machinery is not a raw material in relation to Newspaper Industry". *In re, K.T. Kosalram,* AIR 1968 Mad 113 at 116. [Imports and Exports (Control) Act (18 of 1947) (as amended by Act 4 of 1960), S. 5]

Raw materials. "Raw material" means any material or commodity capable of being used for manufacture of any other product specified in any authorization certificate as intended by the holder for use by him as raw material in the manufacture of goods in the state for sale by him but shall not include the following commodities, namely—

(*a*) tea, (*b*) coal, (*c*) liquefied petroleum gas, (*d*) plywood, (*e*) petrol, diesel oil and lubricants. [Assam Industries (Sales Tax Concession) Rules, 1988, R. 2(f) **as cited in** *Dugar Tea Industries Private Limited* v. *State of Assam,* (2016) 9 SCC 519, para 17].

"RAW MATERIAL" means goods used as ingredient in the manufacture of other goods and includes processing materials, consumable stores and materials used in the packing of the goods so manufactured but does not include fuels for the purpose of generation of electricity. [Gujarat Value Added Tax, 2003 (1 of 2005), S. 2(19) **as cited in** *State of Gujarat* v. *Reliance Industries Limited,* (2017) 16 SCC 28, para 14].

Re. In the matter of.

Re-arrest. To apprehend by legal authority for the second or at subsequent time. [CrPC 1973 (2 of 1974), S. 43(2)].

Re-attachment. Attachment again of property released from attachment. [CPC (5 of 1908), O. XXXVIII, R. 11].

Re-conditioner. Means a person involved in repairing of lead acid batteries for selling in the market. [Batteries (Management and Handling) Rules, 2001, R. 2(n)]

Re-employment. Re-employment is different from retention in service. Retention in service means continued employment in the service in which the employee has been serving, is a quite different thing from re-employment of an employee after he has retired.

Re-enactment. (*Interpretation of statutes*) When a provision in a statute has received a particular interpretation and the Legislature re-enacts that very provision inspite of that interpretation, such re-enactment is legislative recognition of the construction placed upon it by Courts.

Re-entry. The act of re-entering particularly upon possession of lands, tenements, *etc.* previously granted or let to another. [T.P. Act (4 of 1882), S. 65A(e)].

Re-erect. The expression "RE-ERECT" when used with reference to building, includes—

(a) the reconstruction of a building after more than one-half of its cubical extent has been taken down or burnt down or has fallen down;

(b) the conversion of one or more huts or temporary structures into a masonry or framed building;

(c) the conversion into place for human habitation of any building not originally constructed for such habitation; and

(d) the extension of a building. [Manipur Municipalities Act (43 of 1994), S. 2(46)]

Re-examination. "The examination of a witness, subsequent to the cross-examination by the party who called him, shall be called his re-examination". [Indian Evidence Act (1 of 1872), S. 137].

The questioning of a witness by the party who first called him after he has been crossexamined; re-examination is limited to clarifying what the witness has stated.

Re-examine. To examine (a witness) again after cross-examination for the purpose of explaining matters referred to in crossexamination or of introducing new matters with Court's permission. [CrPC, 1973 (2 of 1974), S. 200, 2nd prov.].

Re-hear the appeal. Hear (the arguments in) the appeal again. [CPC (5 of 1908), O. XLI, R. 21].

Re-heard. Means that the witnesses are to be fully heard again from the beginning (*i.e.*) to be examined-in-chief before cross-examination and re-examination. Further cross-examination of a reading of or a summary of the previous evidence will not do.

The word "re-heard" means that the witnesses should be heard afresh from the start (*i.e.*) they should be examined afresh in chief and then cross-examined, if the accused so desire. It is not enough merely to allow them to be cross-examined.

The word 're-heard' means that the whole of the evidence of the witness is to be recorded again *i.e.* he should be examined-in-chief, cross-examined and re-examined. Merely exhibiting the previous deposition of a witness or reading it over to him and asking him some further questions does not amount to re-hearing a witness.

Re-hearing. A "re-hearing" strictly speaking is simply a new hearing and a new consideration of the case by the Court in which the suit was originally heard, and upon the pleadings and depositions already in the case.

Re-imburse. To re-imburse is to pay back, and this primary meaning to the word is to be imputed to it, where the meaning is not controlled by context or contract stipulations.

Re-instate. To re-install; to re-establish; to place again in a former state, condition or office; to restore to a state or position from which the object or person had been removed. [T.P. Act (4 of 1882), S. 49]; [Indian Reserve Forces Act (4 of 1888), S. 7(1)].

Re-instatement. Establishing in former condition, post or authority.

Re-instatement means that a man is put back in his job. Re-instatement can only arise if a man is dismissed or removed from service or if otherwise his service has terminated and he is brought back to service. [Constitution of India, Art. 311]

Re-instatement and **re-employment.** Re-instatement results in replacing a person in the position from which he resigns or was dismissed. It means restoration of the *status quo ante,* the resignation or dismissal. The word 're' when used as prefix normally means again or back. Re-employment means taken back to the service or taken again into service. Whether the person is re-employed or re-instated would depend upon the facts of each case. *R.S. Maniyar* v. *State,* 1967 SLR 823.

Re-instating. To replace in an original or equivalent state. [T.P. Act (4 of 1882), S. 49]; restoring. [T.P. Act (4 of 1882), S. 72(e)].

Re-sale. A second sale.

Resale, for the purpose of O. XXI, R. 71 CPC (5 of 1908) means a sale that has finalised and has resulted in passing the judgment debtor's property, to the purchaser. If a sale, on objections having been raised or because of the necessary deposits having been made by the judgment debtor, is set aside it should be regarded as having never taken place. [CPC (5 of 1908), O. XXI, R. 71, 92]

Re-transfer. "RE-TRANSFER" means transfer of any item notified under this Act from any country or entity to which it has been exported from India, to yet another country or entity. [Weapons of Mass Destruction and Their Delivery Systems (Prohibition of Unlawful Activities) Act (21 of 2005), S. 4(k)]

To transfer back (the property) [T.P. Act (4 of 1882), S. 58(e)].

Re-try. To try (a person or case) again [CPC (5 of 1908), S. 24(2)].

Resummon. To call for on second or subsequent occasion by issue of summons. [CrPC 1973 (2 of 1974), S. 326(1), *Prov.*].

A second summons; the summons of a person a second time to answer an action, where the first summons is defeated.

Reach of the process of the Court, out of. Beyond the extent to which the process of a Court can go or be of effect. [Indian Evidence Act (1 of 1872), S. 65(a)].

Read/write head. A small unit capable of both producing and sensing magnetic fields. Used to record and play back information on magnetic tapes, disks, drums, and any other magnetic recording device. (*Computer*)

Reader. One who performs the act of reading; lecturer, especially a higher grade of university lecturer [Aligarh Muslim University Act (40 of 1920), S. 2(k) and Jawaharlal Nehru University Act (53 of 1966), S. 5(7)]; in Courts.

Readiness and willingness. To come within the expression "readiness and willingness" in S. 51 of the Contract Act (9 of 1872), it is not necessary for a person to prove that on the due date he had the goods actually in his possession. It is quite sufficient if he is able to prove that he had control of the requisite goods or that he had the capacity to deliver them to the purchaser when called upon to do so, in other words, that he was in a position to fulfil his part of the contract on the due date on a demand being made by the purchaser.

The expression 'readiness and willingness' means continuous readiness and willingness to pay the balance price as and when the appropriate occasion for the same arises and the expression cannot be treated as a strait jacket formula. *Sant Lal* v. *Shyam Dhawan,* AIR 1986 Del 275, 281. [Specific Relief Act (47 of 1963), S. 16]

Readings of a Bill. Three presentations of Bill in Parliament—1st for leave to introduce, 2nd for approval of principle and 3rd for acceptance with details settled.

Readmission of the appeal. Taking on the file of the Court again the appeal which was previously rejected by it. [CPC (5 of 1908), O. XLI, R. 19].

Ready. The word 'ready' means willing. [Specific Relief Act (47 of 1963), S. 16(c)]

Ready delivery contract. means a contract which provides for the delivery of goods and the payment of a price therefore, either immediately, or with such period not exceeding eleven days after the date of contract and subject to such conditions as the Central Government may, by notification in the Official Gazette, specify in respect of any goods, the period under such contract not being capable of extension by the mutual consent of the parties thereto or otherwise:

Provided that where any such contract is performed either wholly or in part;

(I) by realization of any such of money being the difference between the contract rate and the settlement rate or clearing rate or the rate of any offsetting contract; or

(II) by any other means whatsoever, and as a result of which the actual tendering of the goods covered by the contract or payment of the full price therefore is dispensed with, then such contract shall not be deemed to be ready delivery contract. [Securities Contracts (Regulation) Act (42 of 1956), S. 2(ea) as inserted by Finance Act (20 of 2015), S. 133].

Means a contract which provides for the delivery of goods and the payment of a price therefor, either immediately or within such period not exceeding eleven days after the date of the Contract and subject to such conditions as the central Government may, by notification in the Official Gazette, specify in respect of any goods, the period under such contract not being capable of extension by the mutual consent of the parties thereto or otherwise;

Provided that where any such contract is performed either wholly, or in part,—

(1) by tendering of the documents of title to the goods covered by the contract by any party thereto (not being a commission agent or a bank) who has acquired ownership of the said documents by purchase, exchange or otherwise, to any other person (including a commission agent but not including a bank); or

(2) by the realisation of any sum of money, being the difference between the contract rate and settlement rate or clearing rate or the rate of any offsetting contract; or

(3) by any other means whatsoever, and as a result of which the actual tendering of the goods covered by the contract and as a result of which the actual tendering of the goods covered by the contract or the payment of the full price therefor is dispensed with, then, such contract shall not be deemed to be a ready delivery contract.

Explanation.—For the purpose of this clause,—

(i) "Bank" includes any banking company as defined in the Banking Regulation Act, 1949, a co-operative bank as defined in the Reserve Bank of India Act, 1934, the State Bank of India and any of its subsidiaries and any corresponding new bank constituted under Section 3 of the Banking Companies (Acquisition and Transfer of Undertakings) Act, 1970;

(ii) "Commission agent" means a person who, in the ordinary course of business, makes contract for the sale or purchase of goods for the other for a remuneration (whether known as commission or otherwise) which is determined in the contract itself or determinable from the term of the contract, in either case only with reference to the quantity of goods or to the price therefor as stipulated in the contract. [Forward Contracts (Regulation) Act (74 of 1952), S. 2(i)]

Ready for storing. Prepared for storing. [CPC (5 of 1908), O. XXI, R. 75(1)].

Ready money. A deed of assignment, directing that the assigned property be disposed of for ready money, means for cash.

Money on hand or quickly available, especially money held ready for payment or actually paid at the time of a transaction. [Indian Contract Act (9 of 1872), S. 133, ill. (d)].

A bequest of "ready money" includes cash at the bankers whether balance on current account or on a deposit.

Reaffirmation. Approval of something previously decided or agreed to.

Real. Related to things, as distinct from humans.

Real audio/video. A client-server based system where both the browser and server must have real audio/video components to provide streaming media to visitors at your website without waiting for the clip to download. *(Cyber Law)*

"Real Estate Activity". Means any activity involving own or leased property for buying, selling and renting of commercial and residential properties or land and also includes activities either on a fee or contract basis assigning real estate agents for intermediating in buying, selling, letting or managing real estate. However, this would not include development of integrated township, purchase/long term letting of industrial land as part of new project/ modernization or expansion of existing units or any activity under 'infrastructure sub-sectors' as given in the Harmonised Master List of Infrastructure sub-sectors approved by the Government of India vide Notification F. No. 13/06/2009-INF, as amended/updated from time to time. [Foreign Exchange Management (Borrowing and Lending) Regulations, 2018, Regn. 2 (xii)].

Real estate agent. Means a person who is engaged in rendering any service in relation to sale, purchase, leasing or renting, of real estate and includes a real estate consultant. [Finance Act (32 of 1994), S. 65(1)(73) now repealed by Central Goods and Services Tax Act, 2017] [Also see S. 2(1)(va) of the Prevention of Money-Laundering Act, 2002 (15 of 2003) as inserted by the Prevention of Money-Laundering (Amendment) Act, 2012 (2 of 2013)]

Real estate business. Means buying and selling of real estate or trading in transferable development rights (TDRs) but does not include development of townships, construction of residential/ commercial premises, roads or bridges. [Foreign Exchange Management (Transfer or issue of any Foreign Security) Regulations, 2000]

'REAL ESTATE BUSINESS' shall not include development of townships, construction of residential/ commercial premises, roads or bridges. [FEM (Permissible Capital Account Transactions)

Regulations, 2000/FEM (Borrowing & Lending in Rupees) Regulations, 2000, Reg. 4, R. 6]

Real estate consultant. Means a person who renders in any manner, either directly or indirectly, advice, consultancy or technical assistance, in relation to evaluation, conception, design, development, construction, implementation, supervision, maintenance, marketing, acquisition or management, of real estate. [Finance Act (32 of 1994), S. 65(1)(74) now repealed by Central Goods and Services Tax Act, 2017]

"Real gross domestic product". Means gross domestic product, reckoned at constant prices, as published by the Central Statistics Office from time to time. [Fiscal Responsibility and Budget Management Act (39 of 2003), S. 2(ca) as substituted by Finance Act (13 of 2018)].

"Real output growth". Means growth in real gross domestic product. [Fiscal Responsibility and Budget Management Act (39 of 2003), S. 2(cb) as substituted by Finance Act (13 of 2018)].

Real owner. A person who is in fact, the owner of the property, even if for the sake of appearance the property is shown to stand in the name of another.

Real party in interest. In statutes requiring suits to be brought in the name of such party, the person who is actually and substantially interested in the subject-matter, as distinguished from one who has only a formal or technical interest in it, or connection with it; the party who is to be benefited or injured by the judgment in the case.

Real person. An actual person or a person in existence. [Indian Evidence Act (1 of 1872), S. 14, ill. (d)].

Real property. The word "land" and the phrases "real estate' and "*real property"* include lands, tenements, hereditaments, and all rights thereto and interests therein, equitable, as well as legal.

Real question. The point actually to be investigated or discussed. [CPC (5 of 1908), O. VI, R. 17].

Real security. A mortgage of the legal and equitable estate and interest in real estate.

Real time operation. Means action to be taken at a given time at which information about the electricity system is made available to the concerned Load Despatch Centre. [Electricity Act (36 of 2003), S. 2(54)]

Realisation. Conversion into actual cash of what was previously contingent or doubtful.

The action of obtaining or acquiring. [CPC (5 of 1908), S. 73(1)].

Realize. To convert into cash or into any form whereby it becomes available for immediate distribution.

To recover, to obtain or to acquire possession.

When used in connection with the conversion of claims or demands into money, "realize" is a very broad term, and may reasonably be said to include a realization of money by "compromise".

The word 'realise' has been used to enable the Corporation to recover possession of any portion of its debtor's property which may be in the custody of a third person. The word 'realise' was used to confer this power on the corporation and was not intended to grant the right of making a lease. *Vikram Cotton Mills Ltd.* v. *Jwala Pd. Radhakrishna,* AIR 1956 All 14, 16. [Industrial Finance Corporation Act (15 of 1948) (*repealed by Act 23 of 1993*), S. 28]

"REALIZED" In Provincial Insolvency Act (3 of 1907), S. 34 does not apply to money which had been attached but had not reached the Court which laid the attachment.

Under the terms of the trust, created by the former Nizam of Hyderabad, the trustees were sending the amounts to the beneficiaries to London. It means that the assessees had realised those amounts in India itself. *Prince Muttakhan Jah Bahadur* v. *Commissioner of Expenditure Tax, Hyderabad,* AIR 1973 SC 2346, 2347. [Expenditure Tax Act (29 of 1957), S. 5(0) (ii)]

The mere order sending for the moneys of the judgment debtor will not be an order realising the assets within the meaning of S. 51(1). *Mepatti Sambayya* v. *Official Receiver,* AIR 1952 Mad 256. [Provincial Insolvency Act (5 of 1920), S. 51(1)]

Realty. A brief term for real property; also for anything which partakes of the nature of real property.

Reason. The very life of law, for when the reason of a law once ceases, the law itself generally ceases, because reason is the foundation of all our laws. (*Wharton*)

A statement of some fact (real or alleged) employed as an argument to justify or condemn some act, prove or disprove some assertion, idea or belief; a ground or cause of or for something. [Indian Contract Act (9 of 1872), Ss. 16(2)(b) and 231].

Reason to believe. A person is said to have "reason to believe" a thing if he has sufficient cause to believe that thing but not otherwise. [section 26, Indian Penal Code (45 of 1860)] [Now (w. e. f. 1-7-2024) repealed & replaced by Bharatiya Nyaya Sanhita, 2023 (45 of 2023), S. 2(29), same definition in new Sanhita]

The words 'reason to believe' contemplate an objective determination based on intelligent care and deliberation involving judicial review, as distinguished from purely subjective consideration. *Melicio Fernandes* v. *Mohan,* AIR 1966 Goa 23, 27 (SB). [CrPC 1973 (2 of 1974), S. 93(1)]

The words mean a belief which a reasonable person would entertain on facts before him. *Jai Shankar (Lunatic) through Vijay Shankar* v. *State of Himachal Pradesh,* AIR 1972 SC 2267, 2272. [CrPC, 1973 (2 of 1974), S. 328]

Though the words 'reason to believe', are not in terms embodied in the authorisation, the phraseology used, in effect and substance, meant the same thing. *Gopikisan* v. *Asst. Collector, Customs, Raipur,* AIR

1967 SC 1298, 1299. [Customs Act (52 of 1962), S. 105]

The expression "reason to believe" is not synonymous with subjective satisfaction of the officer. The belief must be held in good faith; it cannot be merely a pretence. *Partap Singh* v. *Director of Enforcement F.E.R. Act*, AIR 1985 SC 989, 992. [Foreign Exchange Regulation Act (46 of 1973), S. 37, 38]

REASON TO BELIEVE means facts which *prima facie* will convince the Court that a reasonable man could, under the circumstances form a belief which will impel him to take action under the law. *Mamchand and Co.* v. *CIT West Bengal II,* AIR 1969 Cal 431 at 441. [Income Tax Act (43 of 1961), S. 132(1)]

The expression 'reason to believe' means the existence of rational and intelligible nexus between the reasons and the belief, so that on such reasons no one properly instructed on facts and the law could reasonably entertain the belief. *Ganga Saran & Sons* v. *I.T. Officer*, AIR 1981 SC 1363, 1367. [Income Tax Act (43 of 1961), S. 147]

The word 'believe' is a very much stronger word than 'suspect', and it involves the necessity of showing that the circumstances were such that a reasonable man must have felt convinced in his mind that the note with which he was dealing was a forged one. *Hamid Ali* v. *State,* AIR 1961 Tri 46, 48. [IPC (45 of 1860), Ss. 489-B, 489-C]

Reason to doubt. "Reason to doubt" does not mean "reason to suspect." A mere suspicion upon the correctness of the invoice produced by an importer is not sufficient to reject it as evidence of the value of imported goods. The doubt held by the officer concerned has to be based on some material evidence and is not to be formed on a mere suspicion or speculation. [*Commissioner of Customs, Vishakhapatnam v. Aggarwal Industries Limited*, (2012) 1 SCC 186, para 16].

Reason to suspect. The words 'reasons to suspect' in the context of the expression "reason to suspect the commission of an offence" would mean the sagacity of rationally inferring the commission of a cognizable offence based on the specific articulate facts mentioned in the first information report as well in the annexures, if any, enclosed and any attending circumstances which may not amount to proof. (*State of Haryana* v. *Bhajan Lal,* AIR 1992 SC 604. [CrPC, 1973 (2 of 1974), S. 157(1)]

Reasonable. Fair; proper; moderate under a particular circumstance.

Being in agreement with right judgment; not conflicting with reasons [T.P. Act (4 of 1882), S. 38]; endowed with reason.

'Reasonable' means *prime facie* in law reasonable in regard to those circumstances of which the actor, called upon to act reasonably, knows or ought to know. *Gujarat W.S. & S.B.* v. *Unique Erectors (Gujarat) (P) Ltd.*, AIR 1989 SC 973, 977.

The expression 'reasonable' is so wide and elastic that a Court should not ordinarily strike down any restrictive provision as void as being not reasonable unless it appears to the Court that a different view could not be taken with any justification. *P. Arumugam* v. *State of Madras,* AIR 1953 Mad 664, 671. [Constitution of India, Art. 19(5)]

The expression 'reasonable' means 'rational according to the dictates of reason and not excessive or immoderate'. An act is reasonable when it is conformable or agreeable to reason, having regard to the facts of the particular controversy. S. *Raghbir Singh Sandhawalla* v. *CIT,* AIR 1958 Punj 250, 254.

The word 'reasonable' has in law the *prima facie* meaning of reasonable in regard to those circumstances of which the actor, called on to act reasonably, knows or ought to know. *Delhi Municipal Corporation* v. *Jagan Nath Ashok Kumar*, AIR 1987 SC 2316, 2320.

It would be hard to give an exact definition of the word reasonable. Reason varies in its conclusions according to the idiosyncrasy of the individual and the times and circumstances in which he thinks; but frequently reasonableness belongs to the knowledge of the law and therefore to be decided by the Courts. *Collector* v. *P. Mangamma*, (2003) 4 SCC 488, para 6.

Reasonable accurate description. Description which is accurate to a fairly sufficient extent.

Reasonable Accomodation. "Reasonable accomodation' means necessary and appropriate modification and adjustments not imposing a disproportionate or undue burden, where needed in a particulate case, to ensure to persons with disabilities the enjoyment or exercise on an equal basis with others of all human rights and fundamental freedoms. [U.N. Convention on Protection and Promotion of the Rights and Dignity of Persons with Disabilities, 2008, Article 2 as cited in *Deaf Employee Welfare Association v. Union of India*, (2014) 3 SCC 173, para 13].

Reasonable and ***bona fide*** **requirements.** Reasonable means which is rational, just not excessive. *Bona fide* means honesty and not actuated by bad faith or oblique motive. *Mangaram Chuhanmal* v. *B.C. Patel,* AIR 1972 Bom 46, 48, 62. [Bombay Rents, Hotel and Lodging house Rates Control Act (57 of 1947), S. 5(1)(c)]

Reasonable and probable cause. A phrase used in connection with the defence to an action for false imprisonment, that the defendant had reasonable and probable cause for arresting the plaintiff.

Reasonable apprehension. Though confidence in the administration of justice is an essential element of good Government and reasonable apprehensions of failure of justice in the mind of the accused should be taken into consideration in dealing with the applications for transfer of criminal cases, at the same time, it must be remembered that the apprehension entertained by an accused must be such as a reasonable person placed in that situation would entertain. Mere fanciful apprehension on the part of an accused cannot be a ground for transfer of a criminal case. *B. N. Kuttappa* v. *State of Coorg,* MLJ : QD (1956-1960) Vol. II C2022 : 1956 CrLJ 628 : ILR (1956) Mys 64 : AIR 1956 Mys 38. [CrPC (5 of 1898), S. 526(1)(a)]

Reasonable apprehension of bias. "The proper test to be applied in a matter of this type was correctly expressed by the Court of Appeal . . . the apprehension of bias must be a reasonable one, held by reasonable and right minded persons, applying themselves to the question and obtaining thereon the required information. In the words of the Court of Appeal, that test is 'what would an informed person, viewing the matter realistically and practically—and having thought the matter through—conclude' . . . I can see no real difference between the expressions found in the decided cases, be they 'reasonable apprehension of bias' 'reasonable suspicion of bias' or 'real likelihood of bias'. . ." *Committee for Justice & Liberty* v. *Canada (National Energy Board)*, [1978] 1 SCR 369 at 394-5, 9 NR 115, 68 DLR. (3d) 716, de GRANDPRE J. (dissenting). (*Dukelow's Dict. of Canadian Law, 2nd Edn., 1999*)

Reasonable belief. "Reasonable belief" of impending danger, sufficient to justify homicide in self-defence, must be a belief begotten by attendant circumstances fairly creating it, and must be honestly entertained.

The circumstances 'reasonable belief' is entertained, have to be viewed from the experienced eye of the officer well equipped to interpret the suspicious circumstances and to form a reasonable belief in the light of the circumstances. *State of Gujarat* v. *Mohanlal*, AIR 1987 SC 1321, 1323. [Customs Act (52 of 1962), S. 123]

Reasonable care. The expression "reasonable care" means such care as an ordinary man of business or a person of ordinary prudence would take.

REASONABLE CARE is that care and foresight which men of ordinary prudence are accustomed to employ and which they probably would have employed under the exact circumstances of the particular case.

What is to be deemed "reasonable care" within S. 41 of the Transfer of Property Act (4 of 1882) so as to entitle the transferee from an ostensible owner to the benefit of that section, depends on the circumstances of each case.

THE REASONABLE AND ORDINARY CARE, SKILL, AND DILIGENCE which the law requires of physicians and surgeons are such as those in the same general line of practice in the same general locality ordinarily have and exercise in like cases. Surgeons should, however, keep up with the latest advance in medical science and use the latest and most improved methods and appliances, having regard to the general practice of the profession in the locality where they practice.

The term *"reasonable care"* is synonymous with the term *"ordinary care"*. The terms may be used interchangeably.

REASONABLE AND PROBABLE CAUSE in a suit for malicious prosecution means "an honest belief, in the guilt of the accused, based upon a full conviction founded upon reasonable grounds of the existence of a state of circumstances which, assuming them to be true, would reasonably lead any ordinarily prudent and cautious man placed in the position of the accused to the conclusion that the person charged was probably guilty of the crime imputed". The term "malice" in an action for malicious prosecution is not to be considered in the sense of spite or hatred against an individual, but of *malus animus,* and as denoting that the party is actuated by improper and indirect motives."

Reasonable and probable cause means an honest belief founded upon reasonable grounds, of the existence of a state of circumstances, which, assuming them to be true, would reasonably lead any ordinarily prudent and cautious man to the conclusion arrived at.

'Reasonable and probable cause' means simply reasonable cause, the word probable being with its original meaning of 'probable' and hence 'reliable'. The conjunction of the adjectives 'reasonable' and 'probable' is a heritage from the redundancies in which the old pleaders delighted. Salmond observes that probable is synonymous with reasonable and means a good cause and that *probabilis* cause was not unknown to classical Latin.

Reasonable and probable cause means a genuine belief, based on reasonable grounds, that the proceedings are justified.

REASONABLE AND PROPER CARE AND CAUTION is that degree of care and caution that reasonably prudent persons exercise.

Reasonable cause. As applied to human action, that which would constrain a person of average intelligence and ordinary prudence; probable cause; legal cause.

Reasonable cause for remand. "If sufficient evidence has been obtained to raise a suspicion that the accused may have committed an offence and it appears likely that further evidence may be obtained by a remand this is a REASONABLE CAUSE FOR A REMAND." [CrPC, 1973 (2 of 1974), S. 309, *Expln.* 1]

Reasonable certainty. Reasonable certainty means that which on a fair and reasonable construction may be called certain, without resorting to possible facts which do not appear.

"REASONABLE CERTAINTY" is the being free from reasonable doubt".

The expression "reasonable certainty" presupposes that the Court should be in a position to judge the exact nature of the transaction that is the subject matter of the document. *Kamala Bai Laxman Pattak* v. *Onkar Parshram Patil,* AIR 1995 Bom 113, 116. [Transfer of Property Act (4 of 1882), S. 53-A]

Reasonable charges. Charges that are agreeable to reason. [CPC (5 of 1908), 1st Sch., App. A, form No. 39].

Reasonable classification. Art. 14 does not forbid reasonable classification for the purpose of legislation. To pass the test of reasonable classification must be founded on an intelligible differentia which distinguishes persons or things that are grouped together from others left out of the group and the differentia must have a rational relation to the object sought to be achieved by the statute in question. *Budhan Chowdhury* v. *State of Bihar*, AIR 1955 SC 191. [Constitution of India, Art. 14]

Reasonable compensation. What is a reasonable compensation for physical and mental suffering is a question of fact depending on circumstances. Such compensation cannot be measured by any unvarying mathematical rule or standard.

The compensation not exceeding the amount named in a contract to be paid in case of breach, by way of damage or loss or penalty. [Indian Contract Act (9 of 1872), S. 74]

Reasonable cost. Reasonable price paid or payable for a thing. [CPC (5 of 1908), 1st Sch., App. A, form No. 8]; reasonable expense.

Reasonable custom. The period for ascertaining whether a particular custom is reasonable or not is the time of its possible inception and consequently the reasonableness or otherwise must be determined with reference to the period of its commencement and not of its present working. A custom which may be prejudicial to a class but beneficial only to a particular individual, is, no doubt, repugnant to the law of reason. But it is not logical to say that what may now appear to be unreasonable must have been so from its inception. Every judicial case where a custom has been upheld is evidence of its reasonableness.

Reasonable danger. "Reasonable danger" is defined, as a danger to be judged of by an exercise of reason and judgment.

Reasonable diligence. This phrase has only a relative signification : "It means reasonable attention to business; such diligence as a prudent man would exercise or employ as to his own affairs; such diligence as an ordinarily prudent and diligent person would exercise under similar circumstances."

Reasonable deligence means not the doing of everything possible, not necessarily the using of any means at the plaintiff's disposal, not even necessarily the doing of anything at all, but it means the doing of that which an ordinarily prudent buyer and possessor of a valuable work of art would do having regard to all the circumstances, including the circumstances of the purchase.

Reasonable doubt. A reasonable doubt is an honest misgiving generated by the insufficiency of the proof, which reason sanctions as a substantial doubt.

REASONABLE DOUBT is such a doubt as honest, conscientious, painstaking men may entertain upon a state of facts presented to them.

Reasonable doubt is not a Mere Imaginary, Captious, or Possible doubt, but a fair doubt, based on reason and common sense, and growing out of the testimony in the case.

The reasonable doubt that will justify and require an acquittal must be as to the guilt of the accused when the whole of the evidence is considered, and not as to any particular fact in the case.

It is an essential principle of our criminal law that criminal charge has to be established by the prosecution beyond reasonable doubt. The philosophy underlying this rule is the *oft-quoted maxim* that it is better that ten guilty persons should escape than one innocent suffer. The time honoured expression that the Court must be satisfied "beyond reasonable doubt" has been accepted in the Anglo Saxon world as the standard of proof in criminal cases. Lord GODDAR suggested in England that this phrase should be abandoned. But his view has not been accepted. The fourth edition of HALSBURY'S *Laws of England* goes so far as to say that the phrase "reasonable doubt" should be avoided. (HALSBURY, 4th Edn., Vol. II, para 298, p. 173).

"It is the doubt of the prudent man who is possessed of the capacity to "separate the chaff from the grain". It is the doubt of a reasonable, astute, and alert mind arrived at after due application of mind to every relevant circumstances of the case appearing from the evidence." *Rishikesh Singh* v. *State,* AIR 1970 All 51 at 85. [Indian Evidence Act (1 of 1872), S. 105]

Reasonable excuse. If the 'person liable' did not receive the notice because he was ill or abroad, the fact that he was ill or abroad would constitute reasonable excuse.

A woman of modern times is entitled to insist that her husband should treat her with dignity and self respect befitting the status of a wife that her life with her husband will be peaceful and happy. Whether the misbehaviour or misconduct of the husband is such as will entitle and give reasonable excuse the wife to refuse to cohabit with him. *Kanna Alias Mahalaxmi* v. *Krishnaswamy Achari,* AIR 1972 Mad 247, 249, 250. [Hindu Marriage Act (25 of 1955), S. 9(1)]

Reasonable expenses. Reasonable expenses which are allowable to a wife for the purpose of prosecuting an action for divorce should be construed to include her attorney's fees.

Reasonable ground. Means substantially probable cause.

Reasonable ground for believing. The expression 'reasonable ground for believing' occurring in Section 437(1) of CrPC, 1973 (2 of 1974) would mean whether there is a genuine case against the accused and the prosecution will be able to produce *prima facie* evidence in support of the charge. It does not mean to have the evidence establishing the guilt of the accused beyond reasonable doubt, at the stage of granting bail. *Prahlad Singh Bhati* v. *NCT Delhi,* AIR 2001 SC 1444. [CrPC, 1973 (2 of 1974), S. 437(1)]

Reasonable ground of suspicion. The reasonable ground of suspicion which will justify an officer arresting a person without a warrant is a deceptive appearance of guilt, arising from facts and circumstances misapprehended or misunderstood so far as to produce belief.

Reasonable hours. A term often used in commercial documents in regard to applications, presentments, *etc.*, and mainly to be decided by commercial custom.

Reasonable men. Reasonable men are those who think and reason intelligently.

Reasonable notice. Such notice or information of a fact as may be expected or required in the particular circumstances.

Reasonable opportunity. Once the opportunity to show cause is given, the Government is exonerated of its duty of giving reasonable opportunity to officer concerned. [*P. Joseph John* v. *State of Travancore-Cochin.*, AIR 1955 SC 160]

The second stage of giving an opportunity to show cause comes after the enquiry is over *i.e.* when the punishment is to be imposed. The authority who is competent to take the action after applying his mind to the gravity of the charges should ask the servant to show cause against one of three punishments which are proposed to be inflicted. This should be communicated to him and reasonable time should be given to him to make representation against the proposed punishment. *Khem Chand* v. *Union of India,* AIR 1958 SC 300. The authority competent to take the action should communicate to the accused officer firstly the punishment which is going to be inflicted and secondly the reasons on which the punishment is sought to be based and it should include the findings of the enquiry officer.

Reasonable opportunity of being heard in appeal. A personal hearing is not an indispensable and inreparable part of the reasonable opportunity within the meaning of the constitutional provision at every stage of the proceeding, when such personal hearing has already been given at the stage of the departmental enquiry. *District Collector of Stores* v. *Ram Govinda,* AIR 1964 Cal 68, 71. [Constitution of India, Art. 311(2)]

Reasonable opportunity of showing cause. The expression 'showing cause' was held to connote 'an opportunity of leading evidence in support of one's allegation and in controverting such allegations as are made against one'. *Ram Shankar Srivastava* v. *Divisional Supdt. Northern Railway,* AIR 1956 All 393, 394. [Constitution of India, Art. 311(2)]

Reasonable period. For the purposes of clause (iv), "REASONABLE PERIOD" shall be construed as a period not ordinarily exceeding a period of six months. [Patents Act (39 of 1970), S. 84(6) *Expln., as inserted by Patents Amendment Act (15 of 2005), S. 52(b)*].

Reasonable person. A hypothetical person who is used as a legal standard, specially to determine whether someone acted with negligence.

Reasonable possibility is no more than a possibility.

Reasonable precautions. In an instruction requiring defendant in an action for negligence to have used all *reasonable precautions,* no higher degree of care is required than reasonable care and caution.

Reasonable provocation. Is synonymous with "legal, lawful, or adequate provocation," and to constitute such provocation there must be an assault, personal violence, or other good cause for provocation.

Reasonable requirement. The words 'reasonable requirement' postulate that there must be an element of need, as opposed to a mere desire or wish. If the premises is required by the person owning it for augmenting his income, as the income so far received by him is not sufficient to make two ends meet, it is a case of real requirement or genuine need. *Bega Begum* v. *Abdul Alad Khan*, AIR 1979 SC 272, 276. [Jammu and Kashmir Houses and Shops Rent Control Act (34 of 1966), S. 11(1)(L)]

The expression 'reasonable requirement' connotes something more than desire although much less than absolute necessity, and the landlord must have a genuine present need for the portion. *Petroleum Workers Union* v. *A. Mohammad & Co.,* AIR 1967 Mad 33, 35.

Reasonable restriction. The phrase 'reasonable restriction' connotes that the limitation imposed on a person in enjoyment of the right should not be arbitrary or of an excessive nature, beyond what is required in the interest of the public. The word 'reasonable' implies intelligent care and deliberation, that is the choice of a course which reason dictates. Legislation which arbitrarily or excessively invades the right cannot be said to contain the quality of reasonableness and unless it strikes a proper balance between the freedom guaranteed in Art. 19(1) (2) and the social control permitted by cl. (6) of Art. 19, it must be held to be wanting in that quality. *Chintaman Rao* v. *State of M.P.*, AIR 1951 SC 118; *Bishamber Dayal Chandra Mohan* v. *State of U.P.*, AIR 1982 SC 33, 35.

It is open to the State Government to place restrictions on the plying of public buses, to confine the use of public highways for running public buses to only such persons as have been granted permits under the Motor Vehicle Act and to cancel or refuse to renew permits held by an operator or a class of operators. *State Transport Co.* v. *State of Madhya Pradesh,* AIR 1952 Nag 353.

Reasonable return. Means—

In respect of any year of account, the sum of the following—

(a) the amount found by applying the standard rate to the capital base at the end of the year;

(b) the income derived from investment other than those included in the capital base under the provisions of clause (d) of sub-para (1);

(c) an amount equal to one-half of one percentum on any loans advanced by the Board;

(c-1) an amount equal to one-half of onepercentum on the amounts borrowed from organisations or institutions approved by the State Government;

(c-2) an amount equal to one-half of one percentum on the amounts realised by the issue of debentures;

(d) an amount equal to one-half of one per centum on the accumulations in the Development Reserve created under para VA of this Schedule;

(e) such other amount as may be allowed by the Central Government having regard to the prevailing tax structure on the country. [Electricity (Supply) Act (54 of 1948), Sixth Sch., Para XVII (9)]

Reasonable suspicion. Reasonable suspicion is the amount of knowledge about the suspected criminal sufficient to induce on ordinary prudent and cautious man to believe that a criminal act was going to be committed.

Reasonable time. "REASONABLE TIME" is defined to be so such time as is necessary, under the circumstances, to do conveniently what the contract or duty requires should be done in a particular case.

Reasonable use. Reasonable use is that which does not unreasonably prejudice the rights of others.

Reasonableness. Fairness in the circumstances. All executive action must be reasonable in the circumstances.

"Reasonableness" as a pervasive concept arising out of the totality of fundamental rights and expressed in the preamble and inspired by the directive principles can be used to adjudge constitutionality without relying on any particular fundamental right. [*Kasturilal Lakshmi Reddy* v. *State of Jammu and Kasmir,* MLJ : YD (1981) p. 505 : (1980) 4 SCC 1]. [Constitution of India, Arts. 13 and 32]. See also *R.K. Garg* v. *Union of India,* (1981) 4 SCC 675, 689, para 6.

Reasonably. In a reasonable manner; to a fairly sufficient extent. [IPC (45 of 1860), S. 99]; [CPC (5 of 1908), O. I, R. 8(2)].

Reasonably certain. As used with regard to degree of proof, is equivalent to "beyond reasonable doubt."

Reasonably due. Reasonably due is more akin to 'morally due' than the expression 'legally due'. Time barred rent is something which is due morally from the tenant to the landlord. *Children's Educational Uplift Society* v. *Kaushalaya Govind Singh Moral,* AIR 1981 Bom 364, 369.

Reasonably expected. The expression "reasonably expected" occurring in Regulation 2(e)(i) cannot be mere ipse dixit—there must be material show that such person can reasonably be so expected to have access to unpublished price sensitive information. [*Chintalapati Srinivasa Raju* v. *Securities and Exchange Board of India*, (2018) 7 SCC 443, para 18] [SEBI (Prohibition of Insider Trading) Regulations, 1992, Regn. 2(e)(i)].

Reasonably practicable. Which is "reasonably practicable" is no more nor less than what is capable of being done to make roofs and sides secure within the limits of what it is reasonable to do and it cannot be reasonable to do for this purpose anything more than that which appears necessary and sufficient to do according to the best assessment of what is necessary and sufficient that can be made at the relevant time. *Marshall* v. *Gotham Co. Ltd.*, (1952) 2 All ER 1044, 1051 (CA). [Metaliferous Mines General Regulations 1938, Reg. 7(3)]

Reasons. Reasons is a faculty of mind by which it distinguishes truth from falsehood, good from evil and which enables the possessor to deduce inferences from facts or from propositions. (*R.B. Jodhmal & Co. Pvt. Ltd.* v. *DDA,* 1995 (58) DLT 315)

"Reasons" are the links between the materials on which certain conclusions are based and the actual conclusions. They disclose how the mind is applied to subject matter for a decision whether it is purely administrative or *quasi*-judicial. They should reveal a rational nexus between the facts considered and the conclusions reached. Only in this way can opinion and decisions recorded be shown to be manifestly just and reasonable. *Union of India* v. *M.L. Capoor,* AIR 1974 SC 87 **as referred in** *Sharda Oil Industries Pvt. Ltd.* v. *Appellate Authority/Superintending Engineer, U.P. State Electricity Board,* AIR 1994 All 386, 389. See also *Gurdial Singh Fijji* v. *State of Punjab,* (1979) 2 SCC 368, 376-77, para 18.

Reasons of state. Political justification.

Reasons of State connected with defence. The expression "reasons of State connected with defence" and the expression 'reasons connected with the maintenance of public order' in Entry No. 1 of List I and entry No. I of List No. II of Sch. VII of the Constitution are wide enough to include "public safety or interest".

Reasons to believe. In the sphere of disciplinary action taken against the erring members of the legal profession, what factors would weigh with the Bar Council, which is constituted of professional men elected by the whole body of the Bar, cannot be conveniently categorised and anticipated. It would not be proper to lay down a law by interpreting or construing Section 35 of the Advocates Act (25 of 1961), which would be so narrow or rigid as to create such limitations on the powers of the Bar Council that the very purpose for which it has been constituted is frustrated. The use of the words 'reasons to believe' in Section 35 of that Act cannot be construed in a manner similar to Section 147 of the Income-tax Act (43 of 1961). It is obvious that the object to be achieved under Section 147 of the Income-tax Act and under other Acts are quite different from the one to be achieved by Section 35 of the Advocates' Act. [K.B. Asthana, C.J. and Gopinath, J.] *P.C. Chaturvedi* v. *Bar Council of U.P., Allahabad*, YD 1977 Suppl to Oct C 7 : (1977) CrLJ 897 : (1977) AWC 45.

Reasons which should be compelling. The meaning of the expression 'reasons which should be compelling' was explained in. [*Harbans Singh* v. *State of Punjab,* AIR 1962 SC 439]

Reasons, Necessity to give. Our Courts have laid down that all orders which are appealable or liable to be challenged either under Art. 226 of the Constitution, or Art. 136 of the Constitution, must contain reasons. In effect, this means that all orders must contain reasons.

Rebate. A reduction from a sum of money to be paid; a discount. [Payment of Bonus Act (21 of 1965), Sch. 1, item 2(c)].

"The etymological or dictionary meaning of the term includes any discount or deduction from a stipulated payment, charge, or rate not taken as in advance of payment, but handed back to the payer after he has paid the stipulated sum, even when such discount or deduction is equally applied to all from whom such payment is demandable." [Corpus Juris Secundum, Vol. 52 CJ, p. 1189 as cited in *State of U.P. v. Jaiprakash Associates Limited*, (2014) 4 SCC 720, para 40].

"Rebate" is "discount", to allow as a deduction from a gross amount. It is a discount repaid to the payer. [New International Webster's Pocket Dictionary and Bloomsbury Concise English Dictionary as cited in *State of U.P. v. Jaiprakash Associates Limited*, (2014) 4 SCC 720, para 40].

Rebel. One who opposed authority or restraint; one who breaks with established customs or traditions; one who participates in a rebellion. [Army Act (46 of 1950), S. 3(x)].

Rebellion. Taking up arms by the citizens or subjects of a state to resist or overthrow the existing Government.

Rebut. To repel by counter-proof; to refute (evidence or charge *etc.*). [Indian Evidence Act (1 of 1872), S. 9].

In pleadings and evidence, to defeat, refute, or take away the effect of something. When a plaintiff in an action produces evidence which raises a presumption of the defendant's liability, and the defendant adduces evidence which shows that the presumption is ill-founded, he is said to 'rebut it'." [Black's Law Dictionary, 5thEdn., 1979, p. 1139 as cited in *Heinz India Private Limited v. State of U.P.*, (2012) 5 SCC 443, para 41].

Rebuttable presumption. A presumption which may be rebutted by evidence.

Rebuttal. The introduction of rebutting evidence; the stage of the trial at which such evidence may be introduced; also the rebutting evidence itself.

Rebutting evidence. Is "a term particularly applied to that evidence given by plaintiff to explain or repel the evidence given by defendant; evidence adduced to rebut a presumption of fact or of law, that is, to avoid its effect; and evidence adduced to destroy the effect of prior evidence, whether by explanation or direct denial."

Rebuttal evidence. Rebuttal evidence is that which is given to explain, repel, counteract, or disprove facts given in evidence by the adverse party. Anything may be given as re-buttal evidence which is a direct reply to that produced by the other side.

Recall of witness. The further examination of a witness who has given his evidence. This practice is permitted by the Court to allow evidence in rebuttal.

Recapitalization. A process whereby stock, bonds or other securities of a corporation are adjusted or restructured as to type, amount, income or priority. Recasting of capital structure (e.g. exchange of bonus for stock) within frame work of existing corporation. (*Black*)

Recaption. The right which a person has to retake goods or chattels or which he has been wrongfully deprived of by another.

Recapture. The recovery by force of property captured by the enemy.

Receipt. "RECEIPT" includes any note, memorandum or writing—(*a*) whereby any money, or any bill of exchange cheque or promissory note is acknowledged to have been received, or (*b*) whereby any other moveable property is acknowledged to have been received in satisfaction of a debt, or (*c*) whereby any debt or demand or any part of a debt or demand, is acknowledged to have been satisfied or discharged, or (*d*) which signifies or imports any such acknowledgment, and whether the same is or is not signed with the name of any person. [Indian Stamp Act (2 of 1899), S. 2(23)]

Written acknowledgement of money or goods received [T.P. Act (4 of 1882), S. 137, *Expln.*]; the act of receiving [CPC (5 of 1908), 1st Sch., App. F, form No. 9].

RECEIPT is an acknowledgment of payment or delivery; an acknowledgment of the fact of payment or other settlement between debtor and creditor; a written acknowledgment of something received as of right by the party writing; a written admission made by the party signing it, of the fact which it recites.

The word 'receipts' does not connote *mesne profits*. *Narayan Prasad* v. *Radhakant Prasad*, AIR 1967 Pat 5, 6. [Transfer of Property Act (4 of 1882), S. 76(i)]

Receipt and disbursement. That which has been received and that which has been paid out. [CPC (5 of 1908), 1st Sch., App. F, form No. 9].

Receipt of amount and **receipt of payment.** The terms 'receipt of payment' and 'receipt of amount' is without difference. *Somasundaram* v. *District Collector,* AIR 1967 AP 126, 127. [Land Acquisition Act (1 of 1894), S. 31(2), Proviso]

Receipt of notice. Receipt of notice need not be a physical service. If communication cannot be had by a physical service of notice, notice can be served by affixture. *Narayanan Nair* v. *State of Kerala,* AIR 1980 Ker 153, 155.

Receivables. Mean all or part of or undivided interest in any right of any person under a contract including an international contract where either the assignor or the debtor or the assignee is situated or established in a State outside India; to payment of a monetary sum whether such right is existing, future, accuring, conditional or contingent arising from and includes, any arrangement requiring payment of toll or any other sum, by whatever name called, for the use of any infrastructure facility or services. [S. 2(p) of the Factoring Regulation Act, 2011 (12 of 2012)]

Receive. To receive means to get by a transfer, as, to receive a gift, to receive a letter, or to receive money and involves an actual receipt.

To accept. [IPC (45 of 1860), S. 207]; to take [CrPC 1973 (2 of 1974), S. 142(2)]; to get [Indian Partnership Act (9 of 1932), S. 13(a)]; to take delivery. [Indian Railways Act (9 of 1890), S. 27].

Received. An amount which has been deposited cannot be said to have been received within the meaning of O. XXI, R. 89(1), CPC (5 of 1908). Received means received free from qualifying adverbs and cannot mean "virtually or constructively received".

Received any advantage. After the contract terminated in a transfer of property the transaction went out of the dominion of contract and the tenant is not entitled to any refund for the amount which he obtained earlier for obtaining the tenancy. *Ram Anjore* v. *Sadanand,* AIR 1967 All 262, 263. [Indian Contract Act (9 of 1872), S. 65]

Receiver. A receiver is one who receives the money of another to render an account.

One who receives [Indian Partnership Act (9 of 1932), S. 6, *Expln.* 2(d)]; [CrPC 1973 (2 of 1974), S. 110(b)]; one who has been appointed by Court to receive and conserve property that is the subject of litigation, to administer it under the supervision of the Court as its agent and to apply, manage and dispose of it in accordance with the orders and decrees of the Court. [CPC (5 of 1908), O. XL, R. 1].

A receiver is an indifferent person, standing between the parties to a case, appointed by the Court to receive and preserve the property or funds in litigation *pendente lite,* when it does not seem reasonable to the Court that either party shall hold it. A receiver is not the agent of either party.

Receiver in the suit. Receiver appointed in that particular suit. [CPC (5 of 1908), 1st Sch., App. D, form No. 17(9)].

Receiver *pendente lite*. A receiver *pendente lite* is a person appointed to take charge of the fund or property to which the receivership extends while the case remains undecided.

Receives or retains any stolen property. Doubtless there is a real distinction between receipt and retention. In some instances receipt of property may be honest, but subsequently when the offender comes to know that the property is stolen property and yet continues in possession of the same he may be said to retain the same. But in Sections 411 and 412, the words "receives" and "retains" occur side by side and the collocation of receipt and retention of stolen property is obviously intended to do away with the necessity of proving the presence of dishonesty at the time of its possession. As both receiving and retaining constitute one offence, the accused is not entitled to claim the nature of his possession specified and it is sufficient if he is charged for receiving or retaining and evidence is adduced to prove guilty knowledge at some period antecedent to its recovery by the police. *Bama Jena* v. *State*, MLJ : QD (1956-1960) Vol. IV C977 : ILR (1958) Cut 131 : 1958 CrLJ 657 : AIR 1958 Orissa 106. [IPC (45 of 1860), Ss. 411, 412]

Receiving stolen goods. The crime of receiving stolen goods includes generally the receiving, buying, concealing or aiding in concealing goods stolen or embezzled, with knowledge that they were so stolen or embezzled, and with fraudulent intent to deprive the true owner thereof.

Receptacle. Any container or vessel [IPC 45 of 1860), S. 481; Produce Cess Act (15 of 1966), S. 16(2); Income-tax Act (43 of 1961), S. 132(1)(c)(ii) and Trade and Merchandise Marks Act (43 of 1958), S. 2(1)].

Reception. The act of receiving [long title and preamble, Exchange of Prisoners Act (58 of 1948)]; to receive as inmates [Children Act (60 of 1960) (*repealed*), S. 9(2)]; adoption in whole or in part of the law of one jurisdiction by another jurisdiction [Indian Carriage of Goods by Sea Act (26 of 1925), Sch. I, Art. III(c)]; taking in [Income-tax Act (43 of 1961), S. 10(22A)]; formal receiving of guests; a type of special defence. In this case the owner can use the necessary force for taking his goods.

Reception facilities. In relation to a port, means facilities for enabling tankers or ships using the port to discharge or deposit residue or mixture of any substance subject to control by the Convention. [Merchant Shipping Act (44 of 1958), S. 356 B(m) (*Substituted by Merchant Shipping (Amendment) Act, 2003*)]

Reception order. Means an order made under the provisions of the Lunacy Act for the reception into an asylum of a lunatic other than a lunatic so found by inquisition. [Lunacy Act (4 of 1912), S. 3 Lunacy Act, 1912 has been repealed by the Mental Health Act, 1987 (14 of 1987) and further Mental Health Act, 1987 has been repealed by the Mental Healthcare Act, 2017 (10 of 2017)].

"RECEPTION ORDER" means an order made under the provisions of this Act for the admission and detention of a mentally ill person in a psychiatric hospital or a psychiatric nursing home. [Mental Health Act (14 of 1987), S. 2(s)]

Recess. The word 'recess' when applied to a legislative body, means a temporary dismissal, and not an adjournment *sine die*, and means only the intermission between sittings of the same body at its regular or adjourned session, and not to the interval between the final adjournment of one body and the convening of another at the next regular session.

Recession. The period of a sharp slow-down in economic activity, declining employment, and decrease in investment and consumer spending.

Recidivism. Habitual relapse into crime.

Recidivist. A habitual offender; one convicted of numerous offences; a repeat offender.

Recipe. Directions for making something, especially a food or drink; a prescription. [Drugs and Cosmetics Act (23 of 1940), S. 18, *Expln*.].

Recipient.

"Recipient" of supply of goods or services or both, means—

(a) where a consideration is payable for the supply of goods or services or both, the person who is liable to pay that consideration;

(b) where no consideration is payable for the supply of goods, the person to whom the goods are delivered or made available, or to whom possession or use of the goods is given or made available; and

(c) where no consideration is payable for the supply of a service, the person to whom the service is rendered, and any reference to a person to whom a supply is made shall be construed as a reference to the recipient of the supply and shall include an agent acting as such on behalf of the recipient in relation to the goods or services or both supplied [The Central Goods and Services Tax Act, 2017 (12 of 2017), S. 2(93)]

"RECIPIENT" means a person into whom any human organ is, or is proposed to be, transplanted. [Transplantation of Human Organs Act (42 of 1994), S. 2(m)]

One who or that which receives. [Income-tax Act (43 of 1961), S. 197(1)]; [Estate Duty Act (34 of 1953), S. 7(4)].

Recipient (of a Digital Signature). A person who receives a digital signature and who is in a position to rely on it, whether or not such reliance takes place. [*Information Technology*]

Recipient credit. For the purposes of this section, the expression "RECIPIENT OF CREDIT" means the supplier of goods or services or both having the same Permanent Account Number as that of the Input Service Distributor. [Central Goods and Services Tax Act (12 of 2017), S. 20, *Explanation* (*b*)].

Recipient system. "RECIPIENT SYSTEM" means the part of the environment such as soil, water, air or other which receives the pollutants. [Environment Protection Rules, 1986, R. 2(f)]

Reciprocal contract. Bi-lateral contract; a contract consisting the consideration of mutual promises.

Reciprocal promise. "Promises which form the consideration or part of the consideration for each other, are called reciprocal promises". [Indian Contract Act (9 of 1872), S. 2(f)].

Reciprocal will. The term "reciprocal will" is used to designate wills made by two or more persons in which they make reciprocal testamentary provisions in favour of each other, whether they unite in one will or each executes a separate one.

Reciprocating. Giving and receiving in return or mutually. [CPC (5 of 1908), S. 44A(1)].

Reciprocity. The relation existing between two States when each of them gives the subjects of the other certain privileges.

Mutual or bilateral action; mutual concession of advantages and privileges in commercial or diplomatic relations; mutuality.

Recital. An account or description of something, fact or incident; the statement in a formal or legal document of some fact or facts closely connected with the matter or purpose of the document itself. [Indian Evidence Act (1 of 1872), S. 37]; [*Expln*., Registration Act (16 of 1908), S. 17(2)].

A specific statement recited in a document or statute.

A recital is the setting down or report of something done before.

RECITAL is the rehearsal or making mention in a deed or writing of something which has been done before.

Recitals in a document means statement in a deed, agreement or other formal instrument, introduced to explain or lead upto the operative part of the instrument. *Ram Charan* v. *Girija Nandini*, AIR 1966 SC 323, 327.

A recital in a deed is a notice to a purchaser of the fact recited.

The term "RECITAL", as used in the law of estoppel, applies to all material statements of fact contained in the instrument. A particular recital states some fact definitely. Particular and definite recitals are conclusive evidence of the material facts stated.

Recite. To give account or description of something [CrPC 1973 (2 of 1974), 2nd Sch., form No. 24]; to read aloud; to narrate.

To state specifically in a document or a statute, generally in the form of consecutive items, which forms part of the document or statute itself or constitute the reasons for issuing it.

Reckless. Characterized by the creation of a substantial and unjustifiable risk of harm to others and by a conscious (and sometimes deliberate) disregard for or indifference to that risk; heedless; rash. Reckless conduct is much more than mere negligence: it is a gross deviation from what a reasonable person would do. [Black's Law Dictionary, 7th Edn., 1999 as cited in *State v. Sanjeev Nanda*, (2012) 8 SCC 450, para 38].

Reckless disregard. 'A reckless disregard for safety' means doing or omitting to do something when one recognises that one's act or omission is likely to cause serious injury and one does not care whether it does or not.

Reckless driving. A criminal offense; a basis of liability for injury to the person or property of another. Driving under circumstances showing a reckless disregard of the consequences; driving carelessly and heedlessly in wilful or wanton disregard of the rights or safety of others, or without due caution and circumspection and at a speed or in a manner endangering person or property. (*Ballentine's Law Dictionary, 3rd Edn.*)

Driving a motor-vehicle in a manner showing conscious indifference to the safety of others.

Reckless manslaughter. This form of manslaughter requires the prosecution to prove that the defendant caused the death in question by an act or omission, amounting in either case to what is called recklessness (in a special sense) a breach of a duty of care. [GLANVILLE WILLIAMS : Criminal law, 2nd Edn., c. 12, S. 12.2, p. 259]

Recklessly. "Recklessly" (London Lighterage Clause), unlike "negligently", does not connote a legal duty but must be taken at its ordinary meaning, *i.e.* "with gross carelessness". (*Shawinigan* v. *Vokins & Co.*, [1961] 3 All ER 396 (QB).

Reckless, Recklessly, Recklessness. "Recklessness" is synonymous with "heedlessness" and "indifference".

"RECKLESSNESS", in a moral sense, means a certain state of consciousness with reference to the consequences of one's acts. No matter whether defined as indifference to what those consequences may be, or as a failure to consider their nature or probability as fully as the party might and ought to have done; it is understood to depend on the actual condition of the individual's mind with regard to consequences, as distinguished from mere knowledge of present or past facts or circumstances from which some one, or everybody else, might be led to anticipate or apprehend them if the supposed act were done.

'RECKLESS' means no more than 'very careless' and 'recklessly' mean 'in a reckless manner'. "Recklessness" is an indifference whether wrong done or not; an indifference to the rights of others. In popular use "recklessness' is a stronger term than mere or ordinary negligence.

Recklessness. Extreme negligence in as much as the person is wholly indifferent to the risk involved in his act. Such indifference is often equated with an intention to do the act.

Reckon. To arrive at or estimate by calculation; to compute. [Limitation Act (36 of 1963), S. 6(1) and Constitution of India, Art. 108(2)]; [General Clauses Act (10 of 1897), S. 3(35)].

Reclamation. "RECLAMATION" includes cultivation, afforestation or any other improvement of land. [Rajasthan Soil and Water Conservation Act, 1964 (1 of 1965), S. 2(l)]

"RECLAMATION" means reprocessing and upgrading of a recovered ozone depleting substance through such methods as filtering, drying, distillation and, or chemical treatment in order to restore the substance to a specified standard a performance. [Ozone Depleting Substances (Regulation and Control) Rules, 2000, R. 2(p)]

The word 'reclamation' means the bringing into cultivation of land not previously cultivated.

Reclusion. Reclusion means incarceration under a sentence to undergo an infamous punishment, including civil degradation.

A formal admission to show that a person, entity or thing has a particular status.

Recognised association. Means an association to which recognition for the time being has been granted by the Central Government, under Section 6 in respect of goods or classes of goods specified in such recognition. [Forward Contracts (Regulation) Act 1952, S. 2(j). Also see (w.e.f. 1-4-2014) *Explanation 2(iii)* to section 43(5) of the Income-tax Act, 1961 (43 of 1961)]

Recognised chamber of commerce. Means a Chamber of Commerce recognised by the Government of its country as being competent to issue certificates of origin, and includes other associations similarly recognised. [Commercial Documents Evidence Act (30 of 1939), S. 4]

Recognised dealer. Means a person carrying on the business of purchasing, selling or distributing sugar. [Essential Commodities (Amendment) Act (37 of 2003), S. 2, *Expln.* (b)]

Recognised examination. "RECOGNISED EXAMINATION" means an examination specified in the Schedule and includes evaluation, tabulation, publication of results and all other matters connected therewith. [Orissa Conduct of Examination Act (2 of 1988), S. 2(a-4)]

Recognised group. Means,—

(i) in relation to the Council of States, every party which has a strength of not less than fifteen members and not more than twenty-four members in the Council;

(ii) in relation to the House of the People, every party which has a strength of not less than thirty members and not more than fifty-four members in the House. [Leaders and Chief whips or Recognised Parties and Groups in Parliament (Facilities) Act, 1998 (5 of 1999), S. 2(a)]

Recognised home. Means a home in respect of which a certificate has been granted. [Orphanages & Other Charitable Homes (Supervision & Control) Act (10 of 1960), S. 2(g)]

Recognised Institution. "RECOGNISED INSTITUTION" means an institution of higher learning maintained or recognised by, or associated with, the University. [Jawaharlal Nehru University Act (53 of 1966), S. 2(c)]

'Recognised institution' means, an institution which imparts the course of instruction prescribed or recognized by the Department or the Intermediate Board or University, and satisfies one or more of these authorities, as the case may be, in the matter of efficiency. Such an institution is open to periodical inspections by an officer or officers of the Department and its students are eligible for admission to public examinations conducted by the Department, or the Intermediate Board, or a University. [Educational Code of Uttar Pradesh (Revised 1958 Edn.), Para 1(x)(a) as cited in *State of U.P. v. Pawan Kumar Divedi*, (2014) 9 SCC 692, para 22]

"RECOGNISED INSTITUTION" means an institution admitted to the privileges of the University for imparting education in aviation studies or its associated disciplines. [S. 2(t) of the Rajiv Gandhi National Aviation University Act, 2013 (26 of 2013)]

Recognised language. "RECOGNISED LANGUAGE" means—

(i) Hindi written in the Devnagri script, or

(ii) English, if the debtor so desires in writing, or

(iii) Where both the parties speak the same language, that language. [Rajasthan Money Lenders Act, 1963 (1 of 1964), S. 2(13)]

Recognised party. Means,—

(i) in relation to the Council of States, every party which has a strength of not less than twenty-five members in the Council;

(ii) in relation to the House of the People, every party which has a strength of not less than fifty-five members in the House. [Leaders and Chief Whips of Recognised Parties and Groups in Parliament (Facilities) Act, 1998 (5 of 1999), S. 2(b)]

Recognised political party. The expression 'recognised political party' as occurring in the first proviso to sub-section (1) Section 33 of the Act means a political party registered with the Election Commission under Section 29-A of the Act. *Krishna Mohini* v. *Mohinder Nath Sofat*, (2000) 1 SCC 145, para 28 : AIR 2000 SC 317 : [Representation of People Act (43 of 1951), Ss. 33, 29A and Election Symbols (Reservation & Allotment) Order, 1968, para 13]

Recognised provident fund. Means a provident fund which has been and continues to be recognised by the Chief Commissioner or Commissioner in accordance with the rules contained in Part A of the Fourth Schedule, and includes a Provident Fund established under a scheme framed under the Employees' Provident Fund Act (19 of 1952). [Income-tax Act (43 of 1961), S. 2(38)]

Recognised stock exchange. Means, in relation to any provision of this Act in which it occurs, a stock exchange, whether in or outside India, which is notified by the Central Government in the Official Gazette as a recognised stock exchange for the purposes of that provision. [Companies Act (1 of 1956), S. 2(39)]

"RECOGNISED STOCK EXCHANGE" means a stock exchange which is for the time being recognised by the Central Government. [Securities Contracts (Regulation) Act (42 of 1956), S. 2(f)] [Also see S. 2(73) of the Companies Act, 2013 (18 of 2013)]

Recognised teachers. Means such persons as are recognised by the University for the purpose of imparting instructions in a college or an institution admitted to the privileges of the University. [S. 2(u) of the Rajiv Gandhi National Aviation University Act, 2013 (26 of 2013)]

"RECOGNISED TEACHERS" means person working in any recognised institution or in any Institution associated with the University and recognised by the University for the purpose of imparting instruction or conducting research or both. [University of Hyderabad Act (39 of 1974), S. 2(n)]

Recognition. Formal acknowledgement as conveying approval or sanction. [Indian Evidence Act (1 of 1872), S. 78(4)].

'Recognition' and **'approval'.** The word 'recognition' as employed is NCTEA and 'approval' as mentioned in Section 10(k) of the AICTE Act and Section 10-A of I.M.C.

Act would give the same meaning in legal parlance having regard to the object of those provisions contained in the respective enactment. [*Bharathidasan University* v. *Dhanalakshmi Srinivasan E. & C. Trust*, AIR 2005 Mad 377, 390-91, para 24] [National Council for Teacher Education Act (73 of 1993), S. 14; All-India Council for Technical Education Act (52 of 1987), S. 10(1)(k) and Indian Medical Council Act (102 of 1956), S. 10-A]

Recognizance or **Recognisance.** An obligation of record, entered into before a Court or officer duly authorized for that purpose, with condition to do some act required by law, is a recognizance.

A bond or obligation entered into and recorded before a Court or magistrate by which a person engages himself to perform some act or observe some condition (as to appear when called upon); also a sum of money pledged as security for such performance. [CrPC 1973 (2 of 1974), S. 445].

Recognize. The word "recognize", according to the best lexicographers, signifies to admit; to acknowledge something existing before.

To acknowledge the status or legality of [Jawaharlal Nehru University Act (53 of 1966), S. 5(7)]; [General Clauses Act (10 of 1897), S. 3(30)]; [Indian Evidence Act (1 of 1872), S. 13(a)]; admit [Arbitration (Protocol and Convention) Act (6 of 1937), Sch. I, Art. I].

RECOGNIZE, ACKNOWLEDGE. To recognize is to take cognizance of that which comes again before our notice, to acknowledge is to admit to one's knowledge whatever comes fresh under our notice.

Recognized. That which has been accorded recognition. [Payment of Wages Act (4 of 1936), S. 5(2), *Prov.*].

Recognized by Government. Recognition is an acknowledgment by the Government of the title of a grantee expressly or by some unequivocal act on its part. Acquiescence in the context of certain surrounding circumstances may amount to a recognition, but it must be such as to lead to that inevitable conclusion. *T.V.V. Narasimhamam* v. *State of Orissa*, AIR 1963 SC 1227, 1232.

Recognized stock exchange. For the purpose of these guidelines—

"RECOGNISED STOCK EXCHANGE" means stock exchange in India recognised by the Securities and Exchange Board of India or stock exchange outside India recognised by similar regulatory authorities of countries outside India. [Employees' Stock Option Scheme or Plan, 2001, S. 7, Expln (viii)]

Recollection. The mental operation by which objects or ideas are revived in mind. [Indian Evidence Act (1 of 1872), S. 160].

Recommendation. A statement expressing commendation, or a message of this nature. [Constitution of India, Art. 109(2)].

"Recommendation" will mean a complete and valid recommendation after an application for grant of mining lease is made under Rule 22 with all full particulars in accordance with law. [*Monnet Ispat and Energy Limited v. Union of India*, (2012) 11 SCC 1, para 277] [Mineral Concession Rules, 1960, R. 22].

Recommended. Recommended means suggested as fit for employment. *A. Pandurangam Rao* v. *State of Andhra Pradesh*, AIR 1975 SC 1922, 1924. [Constitution of India, Art. 233(2)]

Recopense. Compensation; repayment, or retribution for some loss, injury or damage.

Reconciliation. The restoration to friendship or harmony. [Hindu Marriage Act (25 of 1955), S. 14(2)].

Renewal of amicable relations between two persons, having been in conflict.

Reconduction. The renewal of a lease.

Reconnaissance operations. Means any operations undertaken for preliminary prospecting of a mineral through regional, aerial, geophysical or geochemical surveys and geological mapping, but does not include pitting, trenching, drilling (except drilling of boreholes on a grid specified from time to time by the Central Government) or subsurface excavation. [Mines and Minerals (Regulation and Development) Act (67 of 1957), S. 3(ha)]

"RECONNAISSANCE OPERATION" means any preliminary geo-scientific survey undertaken for the purpose of searching or locating mineral deposits. [Offshore Areas Minerals (Development and Regulation] Act, 2002 (17 of 2003), S. 4(u)]

Reconnaissance permit. Means a permit granted for the purpose of undertaking reconnaissance operations. [Mines and Minerals (Regulation and Development) Act (67 of 1957), S. 3(bb) and Offshore Areas Minerals (Development and Regulation) Act, 2002 (17 of 2003), S. 4(v)]

Reconsideration. Reconsideration, in parliamentary law, is defined to be taking up for renewed consideration that which has been passed or acted on previously.

Reconstituted. Constituted afresh. [Indian Partnership Act (9 of 1932), S. 32(2)].

Reconstituted plot. 'RECONSTITUTED PLOT' means a plot which is in any way altered by the making of a town planning Scheme. [Bombay Town Planning Act, 1954 (27 of 1955), S. 2(9)]

"RECONSTITUTED PLOT" means a plot which is altered in ownership or in any other way by the framing of a town development scheme under this Act. [Punjab Regional and Town Planning and Development Act (11 of 1995), S. 2(zd)]

Reconstruction company. Means a company formed and registered under the Companies Act, 1956 for the purpose of asset reconstruction. [Securitisation and Reconstruction of Financial Assets and Enforcement of Security Interest Act (54 of 2002), S. 2(v)]

Reconvert. A person, converted again to a former religion. [Hindu Marriage Act (25 of 1955), S. 2, *Expln.* (c)].

Reconvey. To convey back. [CPC (5 of 1908), 1st Sch., App. D, form No. 3(4)(ii)].

Record. "RECORD" means any disc, tape, perforated roll or other device in which sounds are embodied so as to be capable of being reproduced therefrom, other than a sound track associated with a cinematograph film. [Copyright Act (14 of 1957), S. 2(w)]

"RECORD" includes the records maintained in the form of books or stored in a computer or in such other form as may be determined by regulations. [Depositories Act (22 of 1996), S. 2(1)(i)]

"RECORD" includes—

(i) any document, manuscript and file;

(ii) any microfilm, microfiche and facsimile copy of a document;

(iii) any reproduction of image or images embodied in such microfilm (whether enlarged or not); and

(iv) any other material produced by a computer or by any other device. [Right to Information Act (22 of 2005), S. 2(i)]

A memorial or remembrance; an authentic testimony in writing. A memorial of a thing done; a writing preserved as evidence; a transcription into something permanent for preservation as a memorial.

An authentic or official report of the proceedings in any cause coming before a Court; copy of the material points, pleadings and issues between plaintiff and defendant on a matter of law constituting the case to be decided by the Court; an account of some fact or event preserved in writing or other permanent form; any document that is specially created as being authentic evidence of a matter of legal importance [IPC (45 of 1860), S. 192]; to make a written note of [Indian Partnership Act (9 of 1932), S. 63(1)]; any disc, tape perforated roll or other device in which sounds are embodied so as to be capable of being reproduced therefrom; a performance or occurrence not recorded to have been surpassed.

A record is a memorial of what has been done; authentic written evidence, considered as either public or private but usually public.

"RECORDS" include the records maintained in the form of books or stored in a computer or apes or discs or in any other electronic form or transcribe information. [Fugitive Economic Offenders (Forms, Search and Seizure and the Manner of Forwarding the Reasons and Material to the Special Court) Rules, 2018, R. 2(1)(g)].

"RECORDS" include the records maintained in the form of books or stored in a computer or tapes or discs or in any other electronic or transcribed information. [Fugitive Economic Offenders (Forms, Search and Seizure and the Manner of Forwarding the Reasons and Material to the Special Court) Rules, 2018, R. 2(1)(d)].

Record date. Means such date as may be fixed by—

(i) a company for the purposes of entitlement of the holder of the securities to receive dividend; or

(ii) a Mutual Fund or the Administrator of the specified undertaking or the specified company as referred to in the *Explanation* to clause (35) of Section 10, for the purposes of entitlement of the holder of the units to receive income, or additional unit without any consideration, as the case may be. [Income-tax Act (43 of 1961), S. 94 *Expln* (aa) (*Substituted by Finance Act (23 of 2004), S. 25(c)(aa)*)]

"RECORD DATE" means the date agreed upon by the secured creditors representing not less than three-fourth in value of the amount outstanding on such date. [Securitisation and Reconstruction of Financial Assets and Enforcement of Security Interest Act (54 of 2002), S. 13 *Expln.* (a)]

Record of any proceeding. A record of any proceeding, that is not governed by or held under the provisions of the code, cannot be called for and examined under S. 435 even if it is held by an inferior Criminal Court. *Mathan* v. *Municipal Board of Orai*, AIR 1956 All 351, 354. [CrPC 1973 (2 of 1974), S. 397]

Record of rights. "RECORD OF RIGHTS" includes the supplementary administration paper prepared at or after the time of making a settlement. [C.P. Act XVIII of 1881. (Land Revenue), S. 4, Cl. 17].

Record of the case. The expression 'record of the case' occurring in Section 227 of the CrPC, 1973 (2 of 1974) does not indicate the right of accused to file any material at stage of framing of charge. It relates to the record of case and documents referred in Section 209 of the CrPC, 1973 (2 of 1974). *State of Orissa* v. *Debendra Nath Padhi*, JT 2004 (10) SC 303 : 2004 (7) SLT 339.

Recorda sunt vestigia vetustatis et veritatis. Records are the vestiges of antiquity and of truth.

Recordation. The act or process of recording an instrument in the public registration office.

Recording. "RECORDING" means the aggregate of the sounds embodied in and capable of being reproduced by means of record. [Copyrights Act (14 of 1957), S. 2(x) (*Substituted by the definition of "Reprography"*)]

A record of sound or images made for later reproduction on magnetic tape, film or gramophone disc. [Copyright Act (14 of 1957), S. 2(d)(v)].

Recording officer. Means any officer duly empowered to make or amend entries in the settlement-register or other settlement records. [Bom Act I of 1880 (Khoti Settlement), S. 3(11)].

Recording reasons in writing. The natural meaning of S. 87 of the CrPC 1973 (2 of 1974) is that the Court should record its reasons in writing. The adoption of a stereotyped printed form is not a sufficient compliance with the imperative language of the section.

Records. For the purpose of rule 27 of the Companies (Management & Administration) Rules, 2014, the term 'records' means any register, index, agreement, memorandum, minutes or any other document required by Act 18 of 2013 or the rules made there under to be kept by a company. [*Explanation* to rule 27(2) of the Companies (Management & Administration) Rules, 2014]

"RECORDS" include the records maintained in the form of books or stored in a computer or such other form as may be prescribed. [Prevention of Money-Laundering Act (15 of 2003), S. 2(1)(w)]

Records creating agency. "RECORDS CREATING AGENCY" includes,—

(i) in relation to the Central Government, any ministry, department or office of that Government;

(ii) in relation to any statutory body or corporation wholly or substantially controlled or financed by the Central Government or commission or any committee constituted by that Government, the offices of the said body, corporation, commission or committee;

(iii) in relation to a Union territory Administration, any department or office of that Administration;

(iv) in relation to any statutory body or corporation wholly or substantially controlled or financed by Union territory Administration or commission or any committee constituted by that Administration, the offices of the said body, corporation, commission or committee. [Public Records Act (69 of 1993), S. 2(f)]

Recount. Count again. [Representation of the People Act (43 of 1951), S. 169(2)(g)].

Recoup. To make good; to indemnify.

To compensate for something; to make good. [Indian Trusts Act (2 of 1882), S. 32].

Recourse. The act of seeking help or advice; enforcement or method of enforcing a right.

Recover. The word "recover" has a technical meaning in law whereby it signifies, to recover by action and by the judgment of the Court.

To get back again into one's possession or hand; [IPC (45 of 1860), S. 215]; to gain by legal process; to get or obtain (money) [CPC (5 of 1908), O. XXI, R. 19]; to recoup from illness *etc.*

Recoverable. The plain, ordinary and natural meaning of the word "recoverable" is that which is able to be, or is capable to be, or is capable of being recovered; obtainable from a debtor or possessor, as by legal process. It means that which can be recovered as a matter of legal right.

Capable of being recovered; which can be got into possession or hand. [Indian Partnership Act (9 of 1932), S. 44(e)]; [T.P. Act (4 of 1882), S. 95].

The action of recovering. [CPC (5 of 1908), O. II, R. 4]; [CPC (5 of 1908), S. 60(1)(p)].

Recovery. RECOVERY means collection and storage of ozone depleting substances from machinery, equipment, or containment vessel during servicing or prior to disposal. [Ozone Depleting Substance (Regulation) Rules, 2000, R. 2(o)]

A thing secured by the process of law.

Recovery Officer. Means any officer of the Central Government, State Government or the Corporation, who may be authorised by the Central Government, by notification in the Official Gazette, to exercise the power of a Recovery officer under this Act. [Employees' State Insurance Act (34 of 1948), S. 45-I(b)]

Recreative purpose. Purpose of recreation or enjoyment. [CrPC 1973 (2 of 1974), S. 133(2), *Expln.*].

Recrimination. A counter-accusation; an accusation made by an accused party against the accuser.

Countercharge. [Representation of the People Act (43 of 1951), S. 97].

Recruit. Recruit is a newly enlisted and not yet trained soldier; a person who newly joins a society or organization.

Recruit., "Recruit" means enlist; enroll; and recruitment has been defined to mean action of recruiting people. [Concise Oxford English Dictionary, Indian Edition as cited in *Mahendranath Mudoi and Ors.* v. *State of Assam and Ors.* decided on 31-7-2017, para 68]

A soldier or other newly recruited person. [Foreign Recruiting Act (4 of 1874), S. 3].

Recruiting agent. Means a person engaged in India in the business of recruitment for an employer and representing such employer with respect to any matter in relation to such recruitment including dealings with persons so recruited or desiring to be so recruited. [Emigration Act (31 of 1983), S. 2(1)(l)]

Recruitment. "RECRUITMENT" includes entering into any agreement or other arrangement for recruitment and all its grammatical variations and cognate expressions shall be construed accordingly. [Inter-State Migrant Workmen (Regulation of Employment and Conditions of Service) Act (30 of 1979), S. 2(h)]

"RECRUITMENT" includes the issuing of any advertisement for the purpose of recruitment, the offering by advertisement to secure or assist in securing any employment in any country or place outside India and the entering into any correspondence, negotiation agreement or arrangement with any individual in any country or place outside India. [Emigration Act (31 of 1983), S. 2(1)(m)]

"Recruitment" and "Appointment". The term "recruitment" connotes and clearly signifies enlistment, acceptance, selection or approval for appointment. Certainly, this is not actual appointment or posting in service. In contradistinction the word "appointment" means and actual act of posting a person to a particular office. Recruitment is just an initial process. That may lead to eventual appointment in the service. (*Prafulla Kumar Swain* v. *Prakash Chandra Misra,* 1993 (1) SLR 565 (SC)).

Recruitment and placement service. Means any person, company, institution, agency or other organisation, in the public or private sector which is engaged in recruiting seafarers on behalf of employers or placing seafarers with employers. [Merchant Shipping Act (44 of 1958), S. 95(3) *Expln.* (a) (*Inserted by Merchant Shipping (Amendment) Act, 2002*)]

Recruitment by transfer. Is a method of recruitment to a service, in the same service initially and thereafter to a different service altogether. Once an employee undergoes a transfer by way of a recruitment to a different cadre or to a different service, the employee loses his lien in the parent cadre/service. In that process, there is an induction of a new cadre and sometimes with a different type of duty. Such induction has distinct consequences on the career of the employee different from what would have been in the normal course, had he continued in the parent service. [*V. Jagannadha Rao* v. *State of A.P.,* (2001) 10 SCC 401 : 2002 SCC (L&S) 872 and *B. Thirumal* v. *Ananda Sivakumar,* (2014) 16 SCC 593 : (2015) 3 SCC (L&S) 379 **as cited in** *Palure Bhaskar Rao* v. *P. Ramaseshaiah,* (2017) 5 SCC 783, para 15].

Recruitment year. "RECRUITMENT YEAR" in relation to a vacancy means a period of twelve months commencing on the first of January of a year within which the process of direct recruitment against such vacancy is initiated. [MP Lok Seva (Anusuchit Jation Anusuchit Jan Jation aur Anya Pichhade Vargon ke liye Arakshan) Adhiniyam (MP Act No. 24 of 1994), S. 2(h)]

Rectification. 'Rectification' implies the correctness of an error or removal of defects or imperfections. It implies prior existence of error, mistake or defect, which after rectification is made right, and corrected by removal of the flaws.

The action or process of rectifying. [Specific Relief Act (47 of 1963), Ch. III]; [Estate Duty Act (34 of 1953), 61, *Prov.*].

Rectify. "Rectifying", means correcting; amending; refining by distillation; purifying; adjusting. Rectifying is not a process of manufacture. *Benarsi Das Saraf* v. *Dalmia Dadri Cement Ltd.,* AIR 1959 Punj 232, 235.

To make or set right. [Specific Relief Act (47 of 1963), S. 26(1)(a)].

Recurring. Means a happening again and again; not that which occurs only once.

Occurring or coming again specially, frequently or periodically. [Limitation Act (36 of 1963), Art. 136].

Recurring period. Period that is periodically occurring. [Limitation Act (36 of 1963), Art. 136].

Recusancy, In the case of. Persistent refusal to accept or obey a constituted authority. [Guardians and Wards Act (8 of 1890), S. 45(1)].

Recycler. Means an occupier who processes used lead acid batteries or components thereof for recovering lead. [Batteries (Management and Handling) Rules, 2001, R. 2(o)]

Recycling. "RECYCLING" means the process of transforming segregated solid wasted into raw materials for producing new products, which may or may not be similar to the original products. [Municipal Solid Wastes (Management and Handling) Rules, 2000, R. 2(xix)]

Red-handed. In the act of crime (as) a thief caught red-handed.

Red herring prospectus. For the purposes of S. 32 of Act 18 of 2013, the expression 'red herring prospectus' means a prospectus which does not include complete particulars of the quantum or price of the securities included therein. [*Explanation* to S. 32 of the Companies Act, 2013 (18 of 2013)]

Red list. The list of extinct species.

Red sandalwood. 'Red sandalwood' is a species of Petrocarpus native of India seen nowhere in the world which is also known as Lal Chandan/RaktaChandan in Hindi which is an endemic and endangered species. Red sandalwood passes medical properties viz. and anticoagulant, improves local circulation and used on traumatic wounds, aberration and bruises. [*T.N. Godvaraman Thirumulpad* v. *Union of India*, (2012) 4 SCC 362, para 43].

Red-tapism. The system of formal routine in Government and other public offices.

Redaction. A revised or edited document.

Reddendo singula singulis. (*Lat.*) A phrase which indicates that different words in one part of a deed or other instrument are to be applied respectively to their appropriate objects in another part.

Reddendum. In conveyancing, rendering; yielding. The technical name of that clause in a conveyance by which the grantor creates or reserves some new thing to himself, out of what he had before granted; that clause in a lease in which a rent is reserved to the lessor, and which generally commences with the word "yielding".

Reddere, nihil aliud est quam acceptum restituere : seu, reddere est quasi retre dare; et redditur dicitur a redeundo, quia retro it. (*Co. Lit. 142*). To restore is to make restitution, or to give back again; and it is called from returning because it goes back again.

Redeem. To free mortgaged property by payment of the amount due or by fulfilling some obligation. [T.P. Act (4 of 1882), Ss. 60, 67 and 91]; [CPC (5 of 1908), O. XXI, R. 49(3)].

Redeemable. Capable of being redeemed. [Indian Trusts Act (2 of 1882), S. 20A(1)].

Redeemable rights. Rights which return to the conveyor or disposer of land & c., upon payment of the sum for which such rights are granted.

Redemption. A repurchase; a buying or getting back. By a mortgagor, a buying back of the legal estate after it has passed to the mortgagee.

The action of redeeming; the action of clearing off a liability. [CPC (5 of 1908), S. 16(c)].

"Redemption" means cancellation of the units at the prevailing unit price of the segregated funds offered in the products, in case of partial withdrawals, switches, surrender, maturity etc. [Insurance Regulatory and Development Authority (Linked Insurance Products) Regulations, 2013, Regn. 1-A(t)].

Redemption of mortgage. Paying off the principal sum, and interest due on a mortgage, and thereby redeeming the charge.

Redemption value. The amount which has to be paid redeeming a security. [Indian Trusts Act (2 of 1882), S. 20A(1)].

Redlining. The process of creating a new draft of a document showing suggested revisions explicitly alongside the text of an earlier version.

Redress. To set right; to compensate; to make amend to; relief; reparation.

Reparation of, satisfaction of, compensation for a wrong sustained or the loss resulting from this. [CPC (5 of 1908), O. I, R. 7; Payment of Wages Act (4 of 1936), S. 15(4)(d)].

REDRESS, RELIEF. Redress is said only with regard to matters of right and justice; relief to those of kindness and humanity.

Reduce. The word 'reduce' includes punishment of stoppage of increments.

To lower, diminish, lessen; to deduct a smaller quantity from a bigger one; to bring into a lower state, rank, *etc.* [Army Act (46 of 1950), S. 20(2)].

Reduce to possession. To "reduce to possession" is to change a right existing as an actionable claim into actual custody and enjoyment.

Reduction. The word 'reduction' in the context of cl. (ii) is not necessarily confined to abolition, and keeping certain parts in abeyance comes within the expression. *K.S. Srinivasan* v. *Union of India*, AIR 1958 SC 419, 426. [Central Civil Services (Temporary Service) Rules, 1949, R. 6 (ii)]

The action of reducing [T.P. Act (4 of 1882), S. 76(f) and Constitution of India, Art. 117(1), prov.]; [Indian Contract Act (9 of 1872), S. 50, ill. (c)]; [Payment of Wages Act (4 of 1936), S. 7, *Expln.* 2(ii)].

The word 'reduction' can only be used when something is left after reduction. To speak of abolition as a reduction of the whole thing does not sound sensible or reasonable. *Motor Transport Controller* v. *Provincial Rashtriya Motor Karngar Union,* AIR 1964 SC 1690, 1692.

Reduction in rank. The words 'reduction in rank' under Art. 311, Constitution of India must be in the nature of a punishment or penalty. In the case of a person officiating in a higher post, if he is reverted to his original post in the normal course, (for example for inefficiency) there is no question of a punishment or penalty being imposed. *Jitindra Nath Biswas* v. R. *Gupta,* AIR 1954 Cal 383, 385.

Reduction in rank and Reversion. Reduction in rank and reversion are not synonymous. A reversion of a civil servant shall be to a post held by him earlier. But reduction in rank of a civil servant by way of penalty need not necessarily be a post held by him earlier. [*R. Gopal Rao* v. *The Commissioner of Incometax, Madras II,* MLJ : Digest (1984), p. 39 : (1983) 2 MLJ 478]. [Central Civil Services (Classification Control and Appeal), Rules 1957, Rule 13(iv)]

Redundancy. Dismissal from employment through no fault of the employee, which in the UK entitles a full-time ex-employee to compensation ranging from half a week's pay to one-and-a-half week's pay per year of employment, depending on the age of the exemployee (after two years service).

Refer. To allude or direct attention to something [Metal Corporation of India (Acquisition of Undertaking) Act (44 of 1965), S. 10(b) and Constitution of India, Art. 76(2)]; to send or direct for treatment, aid, information or decision. [Indian Contract Act (9 of 1872), S. 28, *Excep.* 1].

Referee. Arbitrator; umpire; person chosen to decide between opposing parties.

Reference. "REFERENCE" means a reference to arbitration. [Arbitration Act (10 of 1940), S. 2(e)]

Reference, Court of. A Court having jurisdiction to entertain and dipose of references from other Courts.

Reference standard. Means the set of standard weight or measure which is made or manufactured by or on behalf of the Central Government for the verification of any secondary standard. [Standards of Weights and Measures Act (60 of 1976), S. 2(t)]

References. Submission of a contractual dispute to arbitration; direction to where the information may be found.

The action of referring; the thing referred. [T.P. Act (4 of 1882), S. 59A].

KINDS OF REFERENCES. References are divisible into references by consent of the parties, and compulsory references. They are further divisible into : (1) references to hear and determine all the issues; (2) references to hear and determine part of the issues; (3) references merely to take and state an account; (4) references to report on a particular question of fact involved; and (5) references merely to take testimony.

No written reference need be made to an arbitrator who is appointed by naming him in the written agreement of arbitration itself or subsequently. *M.P. Tejari* v. *Kulsumbai,* AIR 1967 Bom 300, 307. [Arbitration Act (10 of 1940) (*repealed*), S. 2(e)]

Referendum. A method of submitting an important legislative measure to the direct vote of the whole people; system by which a question is submitted to the direct vote of the whole electorate; taking of plebiscite.

Refiner. One who refines a metal, *etc.* [Gold (Control) Act (45 of 1968)(*repealed*), S. 2(s)].

Refinery. A building and equipment for refining or purifying metals, *etc.* [Gold (Control) Act (45 of 1968)(*repealed*), S. 2(t)].

Reform. To create; to make anew; to rectify.

Reformation. The act of reforming what is defective or evil, or the state of being reformed; correction or amendment.

The action of reforming; improvement. [Children Act (60 of 1960) (*repealed*), S. 10(3)].

Reformatory. Any place in which persons voluntarily assemble or are forcibly detained for purpose of instruction and discipline.

An institution to which juvenile offenders are sent with a view to their reformation.

Refractory plant. Means the refractory manufacturing plant, owned by the company, situated near Ramgarh in the State of Bihar. [Assam Sillimanite Limited (Acquisition and Transfer of Refractory Plant) Act (22 of 1976), S. 2(d)]

Refrain. To hold back; to abstain; to keep oneself from one act or feeling. [Indian Contract Act (9 of 1872), S. 27, *Excep.*, (1)].

Refreshing memory. A witness, under examination, may refresh his memory by referring to a document or memorandum made by him or from a note written by some one else, as long as he adopts it as his own.

Refugee. One who flees for refuge to another country especially from religious prosecution or political commotion.

Refund. "REFUND" includes rebate of duty of excise on excisable goods exported out of India or on excisable material used in the manufacture of goods which are exported out of India. [Central Excise and Salt Act (1 of 1944), S. 11A(3)(i)]

To repay; to give back; to restore; reimburse. The amount refunded [Companies (Profits) Surtax Act (7 of 1964), S. 13(5)]; to make return or restitution of a sum received or taken; to hand back; repay; restore [Indian Contract Act (9 of 1872), S. 65, ill. (d)]; [Unit Trust of India Act (52 of 1963), S. 4(3)].

Refusal. The act of refusing; a denial. [CrPC 1973 (2 of 1974), S. 373].

Refusal to deal. Includes any agreement which restricts, or is likely to restrict, by any method the persons or classes of persons to whom goods are sold or from whom goods are bought. [Competition Act, 2002 (12 of 2003), S. 3(4) *Expln.* (d)]

Refuse. To decline positively; to express or show a determination not to do something [T.P. Act (4 of 1882), S. 127, ill. (a)]; to decline to take or accept; to reject [CPC (5 of 1908), O. XXI, R. 32(4)]; that which is rejected or left as worthless [Coal Mines (Taking Over of Management) Act (15 of 1973), S. 2(g)(v)].

Refuses to order the document to be registered. The words "refuses" to order the document to be registered" cover both cases, that is to say, where the Registrar refuses to order the registration of a document in his own office or where he refuses to direct that the Sub-Registrar should register it.

Regal function. The term 'sovereign functions' appeared to be derived from the term 'regal functions'.

Construction of a building and manufacture of arms and ammunition could not be said to be part of the tradition regal functions of the state. *Bakhtawar Singh* v. *UOI*, AIR 1983 Del 201, 210.

Regiment. A considerable body of troops, more or less permanently organised under the command of a superior officer, and foming a definite unit of an army or military force. [CrPC 1973 (2 of 1974), S. 475(1), *Expln.* (a)].

Regimental and other debts in camp or quarters. Includes—

(i) in relation to any person subject to the Army Act, 1950, moneys due as military debts, namely, sums due in respect of or of any advance in respect of—

(a) quarters;

(b) mess, band and other regiments, not exceeding a sum equal to three months' pay of the deceased and having become due within eighteen months before the date of his death; and

(ii) in relation to any person subject to the Air Force Act, 1950, moneys due as air force debts, namely, sums due in respect of or of any advance in respect of—

(a) quarters;

(b) mess, band and service accounts;

(c) air force clothing, appointments and equipments, not exceeding a sum equal to three months pay of the deceased and having become due within eighteen months before the date of his death. [Army and Air Force (Disposal of Private Property) Act (40 of 1950), S. 2(3)]

Region. A large tract of land; a country; a district; an administrative area.

A tract of country. [North-Eastern Hill University Act (24 of 1973), Preamble].

Regional centre. "REGIONAL CENTRE" means a centre established or maintained by the University for the purpose of co-ordinating and supervising the work of Study Centres in any region and for performing such other functions as may be conferred on such centre by the Board of Management. [Indira Gandhi National Open University Act (50 of 1985), S. 2(j)]

"REGIONAL CENTRE" means a centre established as such by the University for maintaining records regarding enrolment of students, despatching teaching materials, making arrangements for holding lectures in the classes in the study centres and dealing with other allied matters. [Netaji Subhash University Act (W.B. Act No. 19 of 1997), S. 2(14)]

Regional Director. For the purposes of section 441 of Act 18 of 2013, 'Regional Director' means a person appointed by the Central Government as a Regional Director for the purposes of the Companies Act, 2013 (18 of 2013). [*Explanation* (*b*) to section 441(2) of the Companies Act, 2013 (18 of 2013)]

"REGIONAL DIRECTOR" means the person appointed by the Central Government in the Ministry of Corporate Affairs as a Regional Director. [R. 2(1)(e) of the Companies (Authorised to Registered) Rules, 2014 & R. 2(1)(j) of the Companies (Registration Offices and Fees) Rules, 2014]

Regional economic integration organisation.

"REGIONAL ECONOMIC INTEGRATION ORGANISATION" means an organisation constituted by Sovereign States of a given region to which its member States have transferred competence in respect of matters governed by this convention and which has been duly authorised, in accordance with its internal proceedings, to sign, ratify, accept, approve or accede to it. [Convention on Biological Diversity, 1992, Art. 2]

Regional Electricity Board. Means any of the Boards as constituted immediately before the commencement of the [Electricity Laws (Amendment) Act, 1991] by resolution of the Central Government for ensuring integrated operation of constituent system in the region. [Electricity (Supply) Act (54 of 1948), S. 2(9A)] [Now repealed & replaced by Act 36 of 2003]

Regional Load Despatch Centre. Means the Centre so designated where the operation of each of the Regional Electricity Grids constituting the country's power system is coordinated. [Electricity (Supply) Act (54 of 1948), S. 2(9B)]

Regional plan. Means the plan prepared under this Act for the development of the National Capital Region and for the control of land-uses and the development of infrastructure in the National Capital Region. [National Capital Region Planning Board Act (2 of 1985), S. 2(j)]

Regional Power Committee. Means a committee established by resolution by the Central Government for a specified region for facilitating the integrated operation of the power systems in that region. [Electricity Act (36 of 2003), S. 2(55)]

Register. A book in which regular entry is made of details of any kind sufficiently important to be exactly recorded; a written record thus formed [Indian Evidence Act (1 of 1872), S. 35]; to make a formal entry (of a document, fact, name *etc.*) in a particular register; to enter in a register.

Register of companies. Means the register of companies maintained by the Registrar on paper or in any electronic mode under the Companies Act, 2013 (18 of 2013). [S. 2(74) of the Companies Act, 2013 (18 of 2013)]

Register of mutations (*Dakhil kharij*). This is the important register of changes, by aid of which the *jamabandi* is kept correct. There is an abstract statement made out from it, giving the year's total of transactions both as regards owners and hereditary (or occupancy) tenants. It will be observed that there are details in the Rules as to what transactions are entered, and no mutation is incorporated in the *jamabandi* till a revenue officer has passed orders on the register, allowing the fact. A copy of all entries attested in this way is attached to each yearly *jamabandi* as a voucher for the changes noted in it.

Registered. "REGISTERED" means registered in any part of the territories to which this Act extends under the law for the time being in force regulating the registration of documents. [Transfer of Property Act (4 of 1882), S. 3]

"Unless there be something repugnant in the subject or context "REGISTERED" means registered under the law for the registration of documents for the time being in force." [Indian Stamp Act (2 of 1899), S. 3].

"REGISTERED" used with references to a document, shall mean registered in India under the law for the time being in force for the registration of documents. [General Clauses Act (10 of 1897), S. 3(49)].

Entered in the register in accordance with the provisions of law relating to registration of documents, or associations or individuals, *etc.* [T.P. Act (4 of 1882), S. 3 and General Clauses Act (10 of 1897), S. 3(49)].

Registered axle weight. Means, in respect of the axle of any vehicle, the axle weight certified and registered by the registering authority as permissible for that axle. [Motor Vehicles Act (59 of 1988), S. 2(26)]

Registered consumers' association. "REGISTERED CONSUMERS' ASSOCIATION" means a voluntary association of persons registered under the Companies Act (1 of 1956) or any other law for the time being in force which is formed for the purpose of protecting the interests of consumers generally and is recognised by the Central Government as such association on an application made in this behalf in such form and such manner as may be prescribed. [Monopolies and Restrictive Trade Practices Act (54 of 1969), S. 2(n)]

"Registered dentist", "registered dental hygienist" and **"registered dental mechanic".** Shall mean, respectively, a person whose name is for the time being registered in a register of dentists, a register of dental hygienists and a register of dental mechanics. [Dentists Act (16 of 1948), S. 2(l)]

Registered document. The term "registered document" means document registered under the law prevailing in India. *Ramanathan* v. *Somasundaram,* AIR 1964 Mad 527, 530. "Registered entity" means any entity, including designated consumers, registered for carbon credit trading scheme specified under clause (w) of section 14. [Energy Conservation Act (52 of 2001), section 2(qa)]

Registered firm. "REGISTERED FIRM" means a firm constituted under an instrument of partnership specifying the individual shares of the partners of which the prescribed particulars have been registered with the Income tax officer in the prescribed manner. [Income-tax Act (11 of 1922), S. 2(14)]

A firm which has been registered under the law relating to registration of firms. [Indian Partnership Act (9 of 1932), S. 60(1)].

Registered Foreign Institutional Investor (RFII). Means a foreign institutional investor registered with SEBI. [Foreign Exchange Management (Transfer or Issue of Security by a Person Resident Outside India) Regulation, 2000, Reg. 2(iii) and Foreign Exchange Management (Foreign Exchange Derivative Contracts) Regulations, 2000, Reg. 2(vi)]

Registered instrument. Any formal legal document in writing which has been registered under the law for the time being in force regulating the registration of documents. [T.P. Act (4 of 1882), S. 3, *Expln.* 1].

Registered layout-design. Means a layout-design which is actually on the register. [Semi-conductor Integrated Circuit Layout Design Act (37 of 2000), S. 2(n)]

Registered medical practitioner. "REGISTERED MEDICAL PRACTITIONER" means any person,—

(i) who holds a qualification granted by an authority specified in, or notified under, Section 3 of the Indian Medical Council Act, 1956; or

(ii) who is entitled to be registered as a medical practitioner under any law for the time being in force in any State to which this Act extends relating to the registration of medical practitioners. [Drugs and Magic Remedies (Objectionable Advertisements) Act (21 of 1954), S. 2(cc)]

"REGISTERED MEDICAL PRACTITIONER" means a medical practitioner who possesses any recognised medical qualification as defined in clause (h) of Section 2 of the Indian Medical Council Act, 1956, whose name has been entered in a State Medical Register and who has such experience or training in gynaecology and obstetrics as may be prescribed by rule made under this Act. [Medical Termination of Pregnancy Act (34 of 1971), S. 2(d)]

Registered office. The office of a company which is registered according to law. [CPC (5 of 1908), O. XXIX, R. 2(b)].

Registered organization. Means an association of persons with disability or an association of parents of persons with disability or a voluntary organisation, as the case may be, registered under Section 12. [National Trust for Welfare of Persons with Autism, Cerebral Palsy, Mental Retardation and Multiple Disabilities Act (44 of 1999), S. 2(m)]

Registered owner. Means a depository whose name is entered as such in the register of the issuer. [Depositories Act (22 of 1996), S. 2(1)(f)]

Registered person. Means a person who is registered under Section 25 but does not include a person having a Unique Identity Number. [Central Goods and Services Tax Act (12 of 2017), 2(94)].

Registered pharmacist. Means a person whose name is for the time being entered on the register of the State in which he is for the time being residing or carrying on his profession or business of pharmacy. [Pharmacy Act (8 of 1948), S. 2(i)]

Registered practitioner. "REGISTERED PRACTITIONER" means a medical practitioner whose name is for the time being entered in the register, but does not include a person whose name is provisionally entered in the register. [Gujarat Medical Council Act, 1967 (10 of 1968), S. 2(i)]

Registered proprietor. A proprietor whose name has been entered in the register [CPC (5 of 1908), O. XXI, R. 14]; [Trade and Merchandise Marks Act (43 of 1958), S. 2(1)(q)].

Registered recycler. Means a recycler registered with the Ministry of Environment and Forests or an agency designated by it for reprocessing used lead acid batteries or components thereof. [Batteries (Management and Handling) Rules, 2001, R. 2(p)]

Registered society. In the Co-operative Societies Act means a society registered or deemed to be registered under that Act. [Co-operative Societies Act (2 of 1912), S. 2(e)].

Registered talukdar. "REGISTERED TALUQDAR" means a sole *taluqdar*, or the eldest or principal of several co-sharers of a *taluqdari* estate, whose name is authorizedly entered in the Government records as holding such estates, or as the representative of the several co-sharers holding the same. Bom Act VI of 1888 (Guzarat Taluqdars), S. 2, cl. (b).

Registered trade mark. Means a trade mark which is actually on the register and remaining in force. [Trade Marks Act (47 of 1999), S. 2(1)(w)]

"Registered Trade Union". Means a Trade Union registered under this Code. [Industrial Relations Code, 2020 (35 of 2020), section 2(zf)]

Registered trader. "REGISTERED TRADER" means a person whose name is, for the time being, registered in the register for the respective trade. [Bombay Metropolitan Region Specified Commodities Markets (Regulation of Location) Act (42 of 1983), S. 2(12)]

Registered user. Means a person who is for the time being registered as such under section 49. [Trade Marks Act, 1999 (47 of 1999), S. 2(x)]

Registering authority. "REGISTERING AUTHORITY" means any authority competent under any law for the time being in force to register any company, firm or other body of persons, or any trade mark or design, or to grant a patent. [Bureau of Indian Standards Act (63 of 1986), S. 2(p)]

Registering officer. The officer, who makes the registration. [Registration Act (16 of 1908), S. 88(3)]; [Income-tax Act (43 of 1961), S. 230A(1)].

Registering officer means an officer appointed as such under section 15. [Antiquities & Art Treasures Act (52 of 1972), section 2(1)(e)]

Registrable documents. Documents which are to be or may be registered. [long title, Registration Act (16 of 1908)].

Registrar. "REGISTRAR" means—

(i) a Registrar of Trade Union appointed by the appropriate Government under Section 3, and includes any Additional or Deputy Registrar of Trade Unions; and

(ii) in relation to any Trade Union the Registrar appointed for the State in which the or registered Office, as the case may be, of the Trade Union is situated. [Trade Unions Act (16 of 1926), S. 2(f)]

"REGISTRAR" means a Registrar, or an Additional, a Joint, a Deputy or an Assistant Registrar, having the duty of registering companies under this Act. [Companies Act (1 of 1956), S. 2(40)]

"REGISTRAR" means the Registrar of Chits appointed under Section 61, and includes an Additional, a Joint, Deputy or an Assistant Registrar appointed under this section. [Chit Funds Act (40 of 1982), S. 2(o)]

An official recorder or keeper of records; an officer whose duty is to make a registration; an officer in Courts entrusted with executive duties and some judicial functions; an official of an educational institution charged with registering students, keeping academic records and issuing official information *etc.* [University of Hyderabad Act (39 of 1974), S. 10(5)].

A registrar of deeds is a public officer authorised and required by law to keep records of instruments in writing, especially instruments affecting the title to real property. Notwithstanding the performance of his duties requires, to some extent, the exercise of judgment and discretion, the office of register of deeds is essentially a ministerial one.

"REGISTRAR" means a Registrar, an Additional Registrar, a Joint Registrar, a Deputy Registrar or an Assistant Registrar, having the duty of registering companies and discharging various functions under the Companies Act, 2013 (18 of 2013). [S. 2(75) of the Companies Act, 2013 (18 of 2013)]

Registrar (LLP). Means the Registrar dealing with the matters relations to Limited Liability Partnership. [R. 2(1)(f) of the Companies (Authorised to Registered) Rules, 2014]

Registrar's Facilitation Office. Means an office maintained by the Central Government or an agency authorised by it to facilitate e-filing of documents into the electronic registry and their inspection and viewing. [R. 2(1)(k) of the Companies (Registration Offices and Fees) Rules, 2014]

Registrar's Front Office. Means an office maintained by the Central Government or an agency authorised by it to facilitate e-filing of documents into the electronic registry and their inspection and viewing. [R. 2(1)(o) of the Companies (Specification of Definitions Details) Rules, 2014]

Registration. The act of entering in register maintained for the purpose of keeping an official record of any transaction of which a record is required to be kept by law or customary practice. [T.P. Act (4 of 1882), S. 3].

The term "registration" includes the getting made and the making of certain endorsements, making the certificate of registration and the copying of the documents in the register book and the filing of the map or plan, if any, in the Registrar's office books. The substantial portion is apparently complete with the making of the certificate of registration.

Registration amounts to notice.

Registration-cum-Membership, Certificate". Means the membership certificate issued by Export Promotion council for Expert Oriented Units and Special Economic Zones. [Special Economic Zones Rules, 2006, R. 2(zg)].

Registration office. The office where registration takes place. [Registration Act (16 of 1908), S. 8(1)].

Registry. REGISTRY means the registry of the Court [Supreme Court Rules, 1966, R. 2(1)(n)].

Act of registering; enrolment; registration; place where public registers are kept; an official record book or entry in the same.

Regress. The right or liberty of going back; reentry.

Regula est, juris quidem ignorantiam unique nocere, facti vero ignorantiam non nocere. (1) 22, 6, 9). (*Lat.*) The rule is that ignorance of the law is harmful (or prejudicial) to anyone, but ignorance of a fact is not. Ignorance of a fact may excuse a party from the legal consequences of his conduct, but not ignorance of law.

Regular. Conformable to rule; periodical; recurring or repeated at fixed times or uniform intervals; properly constituted; normal; marked by steadiness or uniformity of action, procedure or occurrence.

Regular army. The expression "REGULAR ARMY" means officers and other ranks who, by their commission, terms of enrolment or otherwise, are liable to render continuously for a term military service under the Army Act, 1950. [Territorial Army Act (56 of 1948), S. 2(e)]

"REGULAR ARMY" means Officers, Junior commissioned officers, Warrant officers, noncommissioned officers and other enrolled persons who, by their commission, warrant, terms of enrolment or otherwise, are liable to render continuously for a term military service to the Union in any part of the world, including persons belonging to the Reserve Forces and the Territorial Army when called out on permanent service. [Army Act (46 of 1950), S. 3(xxi)]

Regular employment. Shall not include employment provided by the industrial unit to daily wagers or casual employees. [Central Excise Tariff Act, 1985 (5 of 1986), Gen. Exemption No. 48, 3(2) *Expln.* (b)]

Regular forces. "REGULAR FORCES" means the Royal Navy, the Royal Marines, the regular army and the regular air force or any reserve or auxiliary force which has been called out on permanent service or which has been embodied. [Reserve Forces (Safeguard of Employment) Act, 1985, S. 20(1)]

Regular income-tax. In Chapter XII-BA of Act 43 of 1961, 'regular income-tax' means the income-tax payable for a previous year by a person on his total income in accordance with the provisions of Act 43 of 1961 other than the provisions of Chapter XII-BA of Act 43 of 1961. [S. 115JF(d) of the Income-tax Act, 1961 (43 of 1961) as inserted (w.e.f. 1-4-2012) by the Finance Act, 2011 (w.e.f. 1-4-2012) amended by the Finance Act, 2012 (23 of 2012) (w.e.f. 1-4-2013)]

Regular suit. Probate proceedings, both original and appellate, do not fall within the meaning of a "regular suit".

Regularisation. The words 'regular' or 'regularisation' do not connote permanence. They are terms calculated to condone any procedural irregularity and are meant to cure only such defects as are attributable to the methodology followed in making the appointments. They cannot be construed so as to convey an idea of the nature of tenure of the appointments. *B.N. Nagrajan* v. *State of Karnataka*, AIR 1979 SC 1676, 1681. [Constitution of India, Arts. 309, 162]

Regularisation and **permanence.** Regularisation of an appointment is not the same thing as permanent appointment. An appointment to be permanent requires confirmation. *State of Mysore* v. *S.V. Narayanappa*, 1967 SLR 117.

Regularity. The state or charcter of being regular. [Indian Evidence Act (1 of 1872), S. 114, ill. (e)].

"Regularity" means the procedure being followed in accordance with the principles of natural justice and fair play. [*Hindustan Petroleum Corporation Limited v. Dilbahar Singh*, (2014) 9 SCC 78, para 29.4].

Regularly. "Regularly" implies a uniform order, at certain intervals of periods, as by day and night.

In a regular manner. [Indian Evidence Act (1 of 1872), S. 160, ill.].

'REGULARLY' does not mean exact or mathematical punctuality in depositing rents, but means a reasonable punctuality. *M.L. Heder* v. *Noormohamad Adam Shaikh*, AIR 1988 SC 1111, 1115.

The word 'regularly' means payment of rent in a uniform and consistent manner without any breach or default. *Raj Kanta* v. *Financial Commissioner, Punjab*, AIR 1980 SC 1464, 1466.

Regularly kept. "Regularly kept" means— account kept in accordance with certain fixed methods or form referring to system. (*Pit Ram Singh* v. *Vimla Devi,* AIR 1992 Raj 149).

Test of regularity of keeping accounts by shopkeeper who has daily transactions cannot be same as that of broker in real estates. (*CBI* v. *V.C. Shukla,* 1998 (72) DLT 302 at 320). [Indian Evidence Act (1 of 1872), S. 34]

The expression 'regularly kept' occurring in S. 34 of the Act would mean that the book has been regularly and systematically maintained. *C.B.I.* v. *V.C. Shukla*, (1998) 3 SCC 410, para 31 : AIR 1998 SC 1406. [Indian Evidence Act (1 of 1872), S. 34]

'Regularly kept' books of account. It is not possible to accept the view that an entry must necessarily be made in the book of account at or about the time the related transaction took place so as to enable the book to pass the test of 'regularly kept'. The rule fixes no precise time and each case must depend upon its own circumstances. *CBI* v. *V.C. Shukla,* AIR 1998 SC 1406. (*Evidence*)

Regularly kept in the course of business. Books are regularly kept in the course of business within the meaning of the provisions of Section 34, Indian Evidence Act (1 of 1872) if they are kept in pursuance of some continuous and uniform practice in the current routine of the business of the particular person to whom they belong.

Maintained continuously and uninterruptedly to keep correct and proper record of the transactions taking place from day to day in the flow of business.

"Books of account regularly kept in the course of business" in S. 34 of the Indian Evidence Act (1 of 1872) are not confined to books entered up from day to day, or from hour to hour, as transactions take place. The time of making the entries may affect the value of them, but should not, if not made from day to day or from hour to hour, make them entirely irrelevant. If the view that the words in S. 34, "books of account regularly kept in the course of business" are confined to books entered up from day to day, or from hour to hour, as transactions take place, were correct merchants' and bankers' books regularly kept would in many cases be excluded from being used as corroborative evidence.

Regularly performed. The words 'regularly performed' mean done with due regard to form and procedure. *Nishan Singh* v. *State,* AIR 1955 Punj 65, 73.

Done with due observance of regularity. [Indian Evidence Act (1 of 1872), S. 114, ill. (e)].

Regularly stamped agreement. An agreement which bears the stamps necessary for the purpose according to the prevalent law. [Indian Evidence Act (1 of 1872), S. 92, ill. (h)].

Regulate. To regulate means to adjust by rule, method, of established mode; to direct by rule of restriction; to subject to governing principles or laws.

To correct by control; to control, govern or direct by rules or regulations; to adjust in respect of time, quantity, *etc.* with reference to standard or purpose.

"Regulate" is variously defined as meaning to adjust; to adjust, order, or govern by rule, method, or established mode; to adjust or control by rule, method, or established mode, or governing principles or laws; to govern; to govern by rule; to govern by, or subject to, certain rules or restrictions; to govern or direct according to rule; to control, govern, or direct by rule or regulations.

"Regulate" is also defined as meaning to direct; to direct by rule or restriction; to direct or manage according to certain standards, laws or rules; to rule; to conduct; to fix or establish; to restrain; to restrict. [Corpus Juris Secundum, Vol. 76, p. 611 as cited in *Bharat Sanchar Nigam Limited v. Telecom Regulatory Authority of India*, (2014) 3 SCC 222, para 83]. [*Omkar Agency v. Food Safety and Standards Authority of India*, AIR 2016 Pat 160, para 88]

'Regulate' means, 'to control, govern, or direct by rule or regulation; to subject to guidance or restrictions'. [Shorter Oxford Dictionary as cited in *Narinder S. Chandha v. Municipal Corporation of Greater Mumbai*, (2014) 15 SCC 689, para 24].

The meaning of the word "regulate" would also include controlling entry of undeserving or weak students into the profession who cannot be groomed in normal circumstances as good physicians or doctors or dentists. The term "regulate" would normally mean to control something by means of rules or by exercise of control over a system. It is an admitted fact that one of the functions of these apex bodies of the professionals is to regulate the system of education. [*Christian Medical College, Vellore v. Union of India*, (2014) 2 SCC 305, para 196].

"Regulate" and **"prohibit".** 'Regulation' promotes the freedom or the facility which is required to be regulated in the interest of all concerned, whereas 'prohibition' obstructs or shuts off, or denies it to those to whom it is applied. Word "regulate" does not include prohibition. *State of UP* v. *Hindustan Aluminium Corpn.*, AIR 1979 SC 1459.

Regulated assets. Means the assets and properties, both tangible and intangible, owned, leased or developed by and other rights belonging to, the central recordkeeping agency. [S. 2(1)(p) of the Pension Fund Regulatory & Development Authority Act, 2013 (23 of 2013)]

Regulating slaughter houses. The words 'regulating slaughter houses' mean laying down the term and conditions according to which the slaughter houses shall be worked but it does not mean that any particular kind of animal shall or shall not be slaughtered in the slaughter house. *Balla* v. *State of U.P.*, AIR 1956 All 335.

Regulation. "Regulation" means 'the act of regulating, or the state of being regulated.' [Shorter Oxford Dictionary, 3rd Edn., as cited in *D.K. Trivedi and Sons v. State of Gujrat*, 1986 Supp SCC 20, para 31]. See also *Monnet Ispat and Energy Limited v. Union of India*, (2012) 11 SCC 1, para 110].

"REGULATION" shall mean a Regulation made by the Presidence under Art. 240 of the Constitution and shall include a Regulation made by the President under Art. 243 thereof and a Regulation made by the Central Government under the Government of India Act, 1870, or the Government of India Act, 1915, or the Government of India Act, 1935. [General Clauses Act (10 of 1897), S. 3(50)].

The action of regulating [long title, Dock Workers (Regulation of Employment) Act (9 of 1948)]; rule prescribed for the management of some matter; rule or order having the force of law issued by an executive authority of a government usually under power granted by the Constitution. [General Clauses Act (10 of 1897), S. 3(50) and Constitution of India Art. 13(3)(a)].

The term "regulations" implies a rule for a general course of action, but does not apply to a case in which specific instructions are to be given applicable to that case alone.

"Regulation" promotes the freedom or the facility which is required to be regulated in the interest of all concerned whereas "prohibition" obstructs or shuts off, or denies it to those to whom it is applied. *State of U.P.* v. *Hindustan Aluminium Corporation*, AIR 1979 SC 1459, 1466.

The 'power to regulate' will not include the 'power to prohibit'. *Purxotoma* v. *UOI*, AIR 1970 Goa 35 at 44. [Essential Commodities Act (10 of 1955), S. 3]

The word "regulation" also means prohibition. *K. Ramanathan* v. *State of Tamil Nadu*, AIR 1985 SC 660, 669.

Regulation of trade and commerce. A regulation of trade and commerce may achieve some public purpose which affects trade and commerce incidentally but without impairing the freedom. If the regulation itself amounts to restriction, the restriction must be reasonably in the public interest. *Automobile Transport* v. *Rajasthan State*, AIR 1962 SC 1406, 1462. [Constitution of India, Art. 301, 304(b)]

Regulations of a fund. Means the special body of regulations governing the constitution and administration of a particular provident fund. [Income-tax Rules (1962), Sch IV, Part A, R. 2(g)]

Rehabilitation. "REHABILITATION" refers to a process aimed at enabling persons with disabilities to reach and maintain their optimal physical, sensory, intellectual, psychiatric or social functional levels. [Rehabilitation Council of India Act (34 of 1992), S. 2(1)(ma) and Persons with Disabilities (Equal Opportunities, Protection of Rights and Full Participation) Act 1995 (1 of 1996), S. 2(w)]

A restoring to former ability. (*Tomlin*)

Improving a criminal's character so that he can live in the society without committing further crime.

Rehabilitation professionals. "REHABILITATION PROFESSIONALS" means—

(i) audiologists and speech therapists;
(ii) clinical psychologists;
(iii) hearing aid and ear mould technicians;
(iv) rehabilitation engineers and technicians;
(v) special teachers for educating and training the handicapped;
(vi) vocational counsellors, employment officers and placement officers dealing with handicapped;
(vii) multi-purpose rehabilitation therapists, technicians; or
(viii) such other category of professionals as the Central Government may, in consultation with the Council, notify from time to time. [Rehabilitation Council of India Act (34 of 1992), S. 2(1)(n)]

Rei depositæ proprietas apud deponentem manet; sed et possessio. (*Lat.*) The right of property in a thing deposited remains with the depositor, and also the possession.

Rei turpis nullum mandatum est. There is no mandate for a thing immoral (or illegal). Hence, there is no action for failing to act upon such a mandate.

Reinstate. "Reinstate" means to place again (as in possession or in a former position, to restore to a previous effective state. [Merriam-Webster

Dictionary as cited in *Deepali Gundu Surwase v. Kranti Junior Adhyapak Mahavidyalaya*, (2013) 10 SCC 324, para 21].

"Reinstate" means to reinstall or re-establish (a person or thing in a place, station, condition, etc.); to restore to its proper or original state. [Shorter Oxford English Dictionary, Vol. 2, 3rd Edn., as cited in *Deepali Gundu Surwase v. Kranti Junior Adhyapak Mahavidyalaya*, (2013) 10 SCC 324, para 21].

To reinstall; to re-establish; to place again in a former state, condition or office; to restore to a state or position from which the object or person had been removed. [T.P. Act (4 of 1882), S. 49; Indian Reserve Forces Act (4 of 1888), S. 7(1)]

Reinstate a case. To reinstate a case means simply to place again in the position enjoyed prior to dismissal. An order of Court granting a motion to reinstate the case does not say that the plaintiff shall be permitted to file a new complaint, or that he shall be entitled to a new trial. (*United States* v. *Green (CCA Mont)*, 107 Fed (2d) 19).

"Reinstatement" means:

"To reinstall, to re-establish, to place again in a former state, condition, or office; to restore to a state or position from which the object or person had been removed." [Black's Law Dictionary, 6th Edn. as cited in *Deepali Gundu Surwase v. Kranti Junior Adhyapak Mahavidyalaya*, (2013) 10 SCC 324, para 21].

"Reinstatement" means the action of the reinstating; re-establishment. [Shorter Oxford English Dictionary, Vol. 2, 3rd Edn., as cited in *Deepali Gundu Surwase v. Kranti Junior Adhyapak Mahavidyalaya*, (2013) 10 SCC 324, para 21].

Reject. To refuse to hear, receive or admit; to refuse to grant or accede to; to throw or cast away [CPC (5 of 1908), O. XLI, R. 10(2)]; [CrPC 1973 (2 of 1974), S. 340(2)]; to refuse to accept [CrPC, 1973 (2 of 1974), S. 121 and Constitution of India, Art. 108(1)(a)].

Reject the appeal. To refuse to entertain an appeal. [CPC (5 of 1908), O. XLI, R. 10(2)].

Rejected evidence. Evidence *i.e.* testimony of witness or a document which the Court has refused to admit. [Indian Evidence Act (1 of 1872), S. 167].

Rejection. Referred to in the definition of a decree in S. 2(2), CPC (5 of 1908), is such rejection as is permissible under the Code. Before an order can amount to a "rejection" it must be a rejection authorised by some provision of the Code. If a plaint of a memorandum of appeal is rejected for a cause for which the code does not empower the Court to do so, it will not be a decree as defined by the Code, though the Court may use the word "reject" in disposing of the suit or appeal.

The action of rejecting. [Beedi and Cigar Workers (Conditions of Employment) Act (32 of 1966), S. 4(4)(b)]; [Indian Evidence Act (1 of 1872), S. 167].

Rejoinder. In the law of pleadings, rejoinder is a reply to the plaintiff's replication.

Related. Persons shall be deemed to be "RELATED" if—

(i) they are inter-connected undertakings;

(ii) they are relatives;

(iii) amongst them the buyer is a relative and a distributor of the assessee, or a sub-distributor of such distributor; or

(iv) they are so associated that they have interest, directly or indirectly, in the business of each other. [Central Excise Act (1 of 1944), S. 4(3(b)]

"RELATED" means related by legitimate kinship :

Provided that illegitimate children shall be deemed to be related to their mother and to one another, and their legitimate descendants shall be deemed to be related to them and to one another; and any word expressing relationship or denoting a relative shall be construed accordingly. [Hindu Succession Act (30 of 1956), S. 2(j)]

Related party. For the purposes of Section 2(76)(ix) of Act 18 of 2013, a director or key managerial personnel of the holding company or his relative with reference to a company, shall be deemed to be a 'related party'. [R. 3 of the Companies (Specification of Definitions Details) Rules, 2014]

"RELATED PARTY". With reference to a company, means—

(*i*) a director or his relative;

(*ii*) a key managerial personnel or his relative;

(*iii*) a firm, in which a director, manager or his relative is a partner;

(*iv*) a private company in which a director or manager is a member or director;

(*v*) a public company in which a director or manager is a director or holds along with his relatives, more than two per cent of its paid-up share capital;

(*vi*) any body corporate whose Board of Directors, managing director or manager is accustomed to act in accordance with the advice, directions or instructions of a director or manager;

(*vii*) any person on whose advice, directions or instructions a director or manager is accustomed to act:

Provided that nothing in sub-clauses (*vi*) and (*vii*) shall apply to the advice, directions or instructions given in a professional capacity;

(*viii*) any company which is—

(*A*) a holding, subsidiary or an associate company of such company; or

(*B*) a subsidiary of a holding company to which it is also a subsidiary;

(*ix*) such other person as may be prescribed. [S. 2(76) of the Companies Act, 2013 (18 of 2013)]

Related person. "RELATED PERSON" means a person who is so associated with the assessee that they have interest directly or indirectly, in the business of each other and includes a holding company, a subsidiary company, a relative and a distributor of the assessee, and any sub-distributor of such distributor.

Expln. In this clause "holding company", "subsidiary company" and "relative" have the same meaning as the Companies Act, 1956 (1 of 1956). [Central Excise and Salt Act (1 of 1944), S. 4(4)(c)] [Now repealed by Act 12 of 2017]

The criteria for establishing the related person concept are that the buyer should hold company or subsidiary company or relative of the manufacturer. *Collector, Central Excise, Madras* v. *T.I. Millers Ltd.*, AIR 1988 SC 1154, 1157. [Central Excise and Salt Act (1 of 1944), S. 4(4)(c)]

Relates to the existence of any relationship. The wording of S. 32(5) of the Indian Evidence Act (1 of 1872), "relates to the existence of any relationship", is wide enough to include statements about the birth and death of relatives which events either commence or terminate the relationship.

Relates to the suit. Merely because what is agreed to be done is consideration for a compromise, it cannot be said that what is to be done is a matter that "relates to the suit" within the meaning of O. XXIII, R. 3, CPC (5 of 1908). The expression "so far as it relates to the suit" is somewhat wider than the words "so far as it relates to so much of the subject matter of the suit as is dealt with by the compromise". There are matters which may not, strictly speaking, be the subject matter of the suit itself as brought, and yet they may relate to the suit.

Relating to. The phrase "relating to" as it occurs in an enactment restrictive of the right to sue, must be construed strictly, *i.e.*, in favour of the right to proceed.

Relating to any matter in question. It is sufficient if the documents would be relevant for the purpose of throwing light on the matter in controversy. Every document which will throw any light on the case is a document relating to a matter in dispute in the proceedings, though it might not be admissible in evidence. *Shri M.L. Sethu* v. *R.P. Kapur*, AIR 1972 SC 2379, 2383. [CPC (5 of 1908), O. XI, R. 12]

Relating to execution. The words "relating to execution" in S. 47, CPC (5 of 1908), are doubtless very general, but they must be restricted to "the contents of the order made or to how far it has been carried out" and do not therefore include an agreement not to execute the decree.

The words *"relating to execution"* are wide enough to include an order relating to stay of execution.

Relatio semper fiat ut valeat dispositio, et quando ad duas res referri potest dispositio, ita quod secundum unam vitiatur et secundum alterm utilis est, tunc facienda est relatio ut valeat dispositio. (*6 Rep. 76*) Let reference be made always in such a manner, that the disposition may avail; and when the disposition may be referred to two things, so that by one it may be vitiated, and by the other it may stand, then let the reference be made to that by which the disposition may avail.

Relation. "Relation" is a very indefinite word, which has often perplexed Courts. In a broad sense there are relations by affinity as well as by consanguinity, though as used in statutes "a relative" has been held to be one related by blood. The word "family" as used in a statute of descents has been construed to mean those who have the blood relationship, such as "kindred", "children" and parent and may also include relations growing out of the adoption of a child.

A person connected by consanguinity or affinity [T.P. Act (4 of 1882), S. 6(a)]; relationship; the mode in which one entity stands to another. [Indian Partnership Act (9 of 1932), S. 4].

Relation of things. The feature or attribute of things which is involved in considering them in comparison or contrast with each other; the particular way in which one thing is thought of in connection with another; any condition, correspondence or association which can be conceived as naturally existing between things. [Indian Evidence Act (1 of 1872), S. 3].

Relationship. RELATIONSHIP includes,—

(a) relationship by half or uterine blood as well as by full blood;

(b) illegitimate blood relationship as well as legitimate;

(c) relationship by adoption as well as by blood; and all terms of relationship in this Act shall be construed accordingly. [Special Marriage Act (43 of 1954), S. 2, *Expln. I*]

The state of being related; a condition or character based upon this [Indian Evidence Act (1 of 1872), S. 109]; being related by blood or affinity. [Indian Evidence Act (1 of 1872), S. 32(5)].

"RELATIONSHIP" is described by lexicographers as kindred, affinity, or other allegiance. "RELATIONSHIP", as used in the bye-laws of a beneficial association, providing that the applicant for membership shall enter upon his application the relationship or dependence of the members of his family or those depending upon him to whom he desires the benefit to be paid, refers to the connection between him and the member or members of his family upon whom the benefit is to be conferred.

All words expressive of RELATIONSHIP apply to a child in the womb who is afterwards born alive. [Indian Succession Act (39 of 1925), S. 99(i)]

Relative. Having relation; conditional; opposed to absolute.

'Relative' includes any person related by blood, marriage or adoption and living with the respondent. [Domestic Violence Bill 2002, S. 2(i) as cited in *Deoki Panjhiyara* v. *Shashi Bhushan Narayan Azad*, (2013) 2 SCC 137, para 7].

A person related to another by blood or affinity [Estate Duty Act (34 of 1953), S. 17(4)(iii), *Expln.* and Companies Act (1 of 1956), S. 2(41)]; in relation to.

"RELATIVE" includes any person related by blood, marriage or adoption. [Lunacy Act (4 of 1912) (*repealed*), S. 3]

The expression "RELATIVE" means a husband, wife, ancestor, lineal descendant, brother or sister. [Estate Duty Act (34 of 1953), S. 17(4)(iii), *Expln. (a)*]

"RELATIVE" means in relation to the deceased,

(a) the wife or husband of the deceased,

(b) the father, mother, children, uncles and aunts of the deceased, and

(c) any issue of any person falling within either of the preceding sub-clauses and the other party to a marriage with any such person or issue. [Estate Duty Act (34 of 1953), S. 27(7)(i)]

A person shall be deemed to be a RELATIVE of another if, and only if,—

(a) they are members of a Hindu undivided family; or

(b) they are husband and wife; or

(c) the one is related to the other in the manner indicated in Schedule I-A. [Companies Act (1 of 1956), S. 6]

"RELATIVE" in relation to an individual, means the husband, wife, brother or sister or any lineal ascendant or descendant of that individual. [Income-tax Act (43 of 1961), S. 2(41) and FEM (Acquisition & Transfer of Immovable Property Outside India) Regulations, 2000, R. 5, *Expln.*]

"RELATIVE" in relation to an individual means—

(a) the mother, father, husband or wife of the individual, or

(b) a son, daughter, brother, sister, nephew or niece of the individual, or

(c) a grandson or grand-daughter of the individual, or

(d) the spouse of any person referred to in sub-clause (*b*). [Income-tax Act (43 of 1961), S. 80 B(8), omitted by Act 4 of 1988 w.e.f. 1.4.1989]

"RELATIVE" means —

(1) spouse of the person;

(2) brother or sister of the person;

(3) brother or sister of the spouse of the person;

(4) any lineal ascendant or descendant of the person;

(5) any lineal ascendant or descendant of the spouse of the person;

(6) spouse of a person referred to in sub-clause (2), sub-clause (3), sub-clause (4) or sub-clause (5);

(7) any lineal descendant of a person referred to in sub-clause (2) or sub-clause (3). [Narcotic Drugs and Psychotropic Substances Act (61 of 1985), S. 68B(i)]

"RELATIVE" includes any person related to the mentally ill person by blood, marriage or adoption. [Mental Health Act (14 of 1987), S. 2(t)]

For the purpose of these guidelines—"RELATIVE" means immediate relative namely spouse, parent, brother, sister or child of the person or the spouse. [Employees' Stock Option Scheme or Plan, 2001, S. 7, *Expln* (vii)]

An illegitimate son of the father of a lunatic is not a relative of the lunatic and so he cannot file an application under S. 63 of the Lunacy Act. *Laxmikutty* v. *Mohandas,* AIR 1990 Ker 78, 84. [Lunacy Act (4 of 1912) (*repealed*), S. 3(11)]

"RELATIVE". In the absence of any statutory definition, the term 'relative' must be assigned a meaning as is commonly understood. Ordinarily, it would include father, mother, husband or wife, son, daughter, brother, sister, nephew or niece, grandson or granddaughter of an individual or the spouse of any person. The meaning of the word 'relative' would depend upon the nature of the statute. It principally includes a person related by blood, marriage or adoption. *U. Suvetha* v. *State*, AIR 2009 SC (Supp) 1451.

"RELATIVE" means,—

(i) in case of an individual—

(A) spouse of the individual;

(B) brother or sister of the individual;

(C) brother or sister of the spouse of the individual;

(D) brother or sister of either of the parents of the individual;

(E) any lineal ascendant or descendant of the individual;

(F) any lineal ascendant or descendant of the spouse of the individual;

(G) spouse of the person referred to in items (B) to (F); and

(ii) in case of a Hindu undivided family, any member thereof. [*Explanation* (*e*) to section 56(2)(vii) of the Income-tax Act, 1961 (43 of 1961) as substituted (w.r.e.f. 1-10-2009) by the Finance Act, 2012 (23 of 2012). Also see (w.e.f. 1-4-2016) S. 102(7) of the Income-tax Act, 1961 (43 of 1961); (still-born) Section 102(8) of the Income-tax Act, 1961 (43 of 1961) as inserted (w.e.f. 1-4-2014) by the Finance Act, 2012 (23 of 2012) and omitted (w.e.f. 1-4-2014) by the Finance Act, 2013 (17 of 2013)]

"RELATIVE" with reference to any person, means anyone who is related to another, if—

(*i*) they are members of a Hindu Undivided Family;

(*ii*) they are husband and wife; or

(*iii*) one person is related to the other in such manner as may be prescribed. [S. 2(77) of the Companies Act, 2013 (18 of 2013)]

"RELATIVES IN TERMS OF SECTION 2(77) OF ACT 18 OF 2013". A person shall be deemed to be the relative of another, if he or she is related to another in the following manner, namely:—(1) Father: *Provided* that the term 'Father' includes step-father; (2) Mother: *Provided* that the term 'Mother' includes the step-mother; (3) Son: *Provided* that the term 'Son' includes the step-son; (4) Son's wife; (5) Daughter; (6) Daughter's husband; (7) Brother: *Provided* that the term 'Brother' includes the step-brother; (8) Sister: *Provided* that the term 'Sister' includes the step-sister. [R. 4 of the Companies (Specification of Definitions Details) Rules, 2014]

Relax. To make less severe or strict. [Cardamom Act (42 of 1965)(*repealed*), S. 32(2)].

Relay. A set of persons [Mines Act (35 of 1952), S. 2(1)(p) and Factories Act (63 of 1948), S. 2(r)]. "Relay" means a set of two or more persons carrying out the same kind of work during different periods of the day and each such period is called a "shift". [Occupational Safety, Health & Working Conditions Code, 2020 (37 of 2020), section 2(1)(zzd)]

Release. The action of releasing or the state of being released [Indian Contract Act (9 of 1872), S. 44]; to set free from restraint, confinement or servitude; to set at liberty; to give up (a claim, right, title) in favour of another [CrPC 1973 (2 of 1974), S. 118]; to free a thing from attachment. [Army Act (46 of 1950), S. 179(d)].

A release is a discharge of an existing obligation or right of action by the person in whom the obligation or right is vested to the person against whom it exists.

Released on bail. "Released on bail", as used in criminal practice relating to the accused who had been "released on bail", implies that the person so released is not in prison after such release.

Relevancy. "Relevancy", as that term is used by writers on the law of evidence, omitting metaphysical distinctions, is that which "conduces to prove a pertinent theory in a case", or one which influences or controls the case.

The quality or fact of being relevant *i.e.* bearing upon, connected with, pertinent to the matter in hand. [Indian Evidence Act (1 of 1872), S. 3].

Relevancy : Admissibility. Facts though not in issue, are so connected with a fact in issue as to form part of the same transaction, are relevant, whether they occurred at the same time and place or different times and places.

Admissibility of evidence has to be decided by the Court; should be decided as it arises, should not be reserved until judgment in the case is given. [Indian Evidence Act 1872 (Act 1 of 1872), Ss. 5 & 6]

More often the expressions 'relevancy' and 'admissibility' are used as synonyms but their legal implications are distinct, and different for more often than not facts which are relevant may not be admissible. For *eg.* communication made by spouses during marriage or between an advocate and his client, though relevant, are not admissible. (*Ram Bihari Yadav* v. *State of Bihar,* AIR 1998 SC 1850 at 520). [Indian Evidence Act (1 of 1872), Ss. 3 and 5]

Relevant. "One fact is said to be relevant to another when the one is connected with the other in any of the ways referred to in the provisions of this Act relating to the relevancy of facts." [Indian Evidence Act (1 of 1872), S. 3]. [Now (w. e. f. 1-7-2024) repealed & replaced by Bharatiya Sakshya Adhiniyam, 2023 (47 of 2023)]

A fact is said to be relevant to another when it is connected with the other in any of the ways referred to in the provisions of this Adhiniyam relating to the relevancy of facts. [(w. e. f. 1-7-2024) Bharatiya Sakshya Adhiniyam, 2023 (47 of 2023), section 2(1)(k)]

Pertinent [Indian Evidence Act (1 of 1872), Ss. 3, 6 and 7 and Indian Partnership Act (9 of 1932), S. 6].

Logically connected and having a tendency to prove or disprove a matter in issue.

The meaning of the word "relevant", as applied to testimony, is that it directly touches upon the issue which the parties have made by their pleadings, so as to assist in getting at the truth of it.

Relevant activity. "RELEVANT ACTIVITY" means,—

(i) the development, production, handling, operation, maintenance, storage or dissemination of a nuclear, chemical or biological weapon; or

(ii) the development, production, maintenance, storage or dissemination of missiles specially designed for delivering any such weapon. [Weapons of Mass Destruction and Their Delivery Systems (Prohibition of Unlawful Activities) Act (21 of 2005), S. 4(j)]

Relevant assessment year. "RELEVANT ASSESSMENT YEARS" means any assessment year falling within a period of ten consecutive assessment years referred to in this section. [Income Tax Act (43 of 1961), S. 10A *Expln.*2(vi)]

"RELEVANT ASSESSMENT YEARS" means the ten consecutive years beginning with the year in which the industrial undertaking begins to manufacture or produce articles or things. [Income Tax Act (43 of 1961), S. 10 (*Expln.*) (iv)]

"RELEVANT ASSESSMENT YEARS" means any assessment year falling within a period of fifteen consecutive assessment years referred to in this section. [Income-tax Act (43 of 1961), S. 10AA *Expln.* (iv) *as inserted by Special Economic Zones Act (28 of 2005), Second Schedule (c)*]

Relevant date. Means,—

(a) in the case of excisable goods on which duty of excise has not been levied or paid or has been short-levied or short-paid—

(i) where under the rules made under this Act a monthly return, showing particulars of the duty paid on the excisable goods removed during the month to which the said return relates, is to be filed by a manufacturer or producer or a licensee of a warehouse as the case may be, the date on which such return is so filed;

(ii) where no monthly return as aforesaid is filed, the last date on which such return is to be filed under the said rules;

(iii) in any other case, the date on which the duty is to be paid under this Act or the rules made thereunder;

(b) in a case where duty of excise is provisionally assessed under this Act or the rules made thereunder, the date of adjustment of duty after the final assessment thereof;

(c) in the case of excisable goods on which duty of excise has been erroneously refunded, the date of such refund. [Central Excise and Salt Act (1 of 1944), S. 11A(3)(ii)]

For the purposes of this section "RELEVANT DATE" means,—

(i) in the case of taxable service in respect of which service tax has not been levied or paid or has been short-levied or short-paid—

(a) where under the rules made under this Chapter, a periodical return, showing particulars of service tax paid during the period to which the said return relates, is to be filed by an assessee, the date on which such return is so filed;

(b) where no periodical return as aforesaid is filed, the last date on which such return is to be filed under the said rules;

(c) in any other case, the date on which the service tax is to be paid under this Chapter or the rules made thereunder;

(ii) in a case where the service tax is provisionally assessed under this chapter or the rules made thereunder, the date of adjustment of the service tax after the final assessment thereof;

(iii) in a case where any sum, relating to service tax, has erroneously been refunded, the date of such refund. [Finance Act (32 of 1994), S. 73(6) (*Substituted by Finance (No.2) Act (23 of 2004), S. 90*) now repealed by Central Goods and Services Tax Act, 2017]

"RELEVANT DATE". For the purposes of section 327 of Act 18 of 2013, the expression 'relevant date' means—

(*i*) in the case of a company being wound up by the Tribunal, the date of appointment or first appointment of a provisional liquidator, or if no such appointment was made, the date of the winding up order, unless, in either case, the company had commenced to be wound up voluntarily before that date; and

(*ii*) in any other case, the date of the passing of the resolution for the voluntary winding up of the company. [*Explanation* (*c*) to section 327 of the Companies Act, 2013 (18 of 2013)]

Relevant debentures. For the purposes of section 194 of Act 18 of 2013, 'relevant debentures' mean shares and debentures of the company in which the concerned person is a whole-time director or other key managerial personnel or shares and debentures of its holding and subsidiary companies. [*Explanation* to section 194 of the Companies Act, 2013 (18 of 2013)]

Relevant evidence. Evidence tending to prove or disprove a matter in prove.

Relevant financial year. "RELEVANT FINANCIAL YEAR" means the financial year of the company in respect of which exemption from branch audit is to be determined. [Companies (Branch Audit Exemption) Rules, 1961, R. 2(b)]

Relevant geographic market. "RELEVANT GEOGRAPHIC MARKET" means a market comprising the area in which the conditions of competition for supply of goods or provision of services or demand of goods or services are distinctly homogenous and can be distinguished from the conditions prevailing in the neighbouring areas. [Competition Act 2002 (12 of 2003), S. 2(s)]

Relevant information. For the purposes of this section, "RELEVANT INFORMATION" means the information required by the resolution applicant to make the resolution plan for the corporate debtor, which shall include the financial position of the corporate debtor, all information related to disputes by or against the corporate debtor and any other matter pertaining to the corporate debtor as may be specified. [Insolvency and Bankruptcy Code (31 of 2016), S. 29, *Explanation*].

Relevant law. Means in case of—

(*i*) the Delhi Development Authority, the Delhi Development Act, 1957 (61 of 1957);

(*ii*) the Municipal Corporation of Delhi, the Delhi Municipal Corporation Act, 1957 (66 of 1957); and

(*iii*) the New Delhi Municipal Council, the New Delhi Municipal Council Act, 1994 (44 of 1994). [S. 2(1)(h) of the National Capital Territory of Delhi Laws (Special Provisions) Act, 2011 (5 of 2011)]

Relevant market. "RELEVANT MARKET" means the market which may be determined by the Commission with reference to the relevant product market or the relevant geographic market or with reference to both the markets. [Competition Act 2002 (12 of 2003), S. 2(r)]

Relevant period. For the purposes of this section, the "RELEVANT PERIOD" shall be—

(*i*) if the recipients of credit have turnover in their States or Union Territories in the financial year preceding the year during which credit is to be distributed, the said financial year; or

(*ii*) if some or all recipients of the credit do not have any turnover in their States or Union Territories in the financial year preceding the year during which the credit is to be distributed, the last quarter for which details of such turnover of all the recipients are available, previous to the month during which credit is to be distributed. [Central Goods and Services Tax Act (12 of 2017), S. 20, *Explanation (a)*].

Relevant port. In relation to any claim, means a port where the event giving rise to the claim occurred, or if that event did not occur in that port, the first port of call after the event occurred and includes in relation to a claim for loss of life or personal injury or for damage to cargo, the port of disembarkation or discharge. [Merchant Shipping Act (44 of 1958), S. 352D(5)(b)]

Relevant previous years. Means the fourteen previous years beginning with the previous year in which such expenditure is incurred or, where such expenditure is incurred before the commencement of the business, the fourteen previous years beginning with the previous year in which the business commenced :

Provided that where the rights commenced, that is to say, became effective, in any year prior to the previous year in which expenditure on the acquisition thereof was incurred by the assessee, this clause shall have effect with the substitution for the reference to fourteen years of a reference to fourteen years less the number of complete years which, when the rights are acquired by the assessee, have elapsed since the commencement thereof, and if fourteen years have elapsed as aforesaid, of a reference to one year. [Income-tax Act (43 of 1961), S. 35A(1) *Expln.* (1)]

"RELEVANT PREVIOUS YEARS" means—

(A) in a case where the licence fee is actually paid before the commencement of the business to operate telecommunication services, the previous years beginning with the previous year in which such business commenced;

(B) in any other case, the previous years beginning with the previous year in which the licence fee is actually paid, and the subsequent previous year or year during which the licence, for which the fee is paid, shall be in force. [Income-tax Act (43 of 1961), S. 35 ABB(1) *Expln* (i)]

Relevant product market. "RELEVANT PRODUCT MARKET" means a market comprising all those products or services which are regarded as interchangeable or substitutable by the consumer, by reason of characteristics of the products or services, their prices and intended use. [Competition Act, 2002 (12 of 2003), S. 2(t)]

Relevant question. Any question which relates to matters which are pertinent to a proper decision being reached in the case. [T.P. Act (4 of 1882), S. 55(1)(c)].

Relevant shares. For the purposes of section 194 of Act 18 of 2013, 'relevant shares' mean shares of the company in which the concerned person is a whole-time director or other key managerial personnel or shares and debentures of its holding and subsidiary companies. [*Explanation* to section 194 of the Companies Act, 2013 (18 of 2013)]

Reliable evidence. S. 173(2) CrPC 1973 (2 of 1974), lays down that a Magistrate in an enquiry under S. 133 has to find if there is any reliable evidence in support of the denial of the party alleged to cause the obstruction. Reliable evidence is evidence of reliable persons. What is really meant is that the Magistrate should weigh the evidence produced by both sides and then come to the conclusion which he believes or which he prefers, but the Magistrate should take the evidence as it stands and see whether on the face of it if there was no evidence to the contrary, he could come to the conclusion that the evidence was false and therefore unreliable.

The expression 'reliable evidence' in S. 137(2), CrPC 1973 (2 of 1974) means evidence on which a competent Court places reliance. *Atul Krishna* v. *State of Bengal,* AIR 1966 Cal 215, 216.

Relief. Deliverance from some hardship, burden or grievance. [T.P. Act (4 of 1882, S. 114]; [Courts-fees Act (7 of 1870), S. 19B]; legal redress or remedy [Presidential and Vice-Presidential Elections Act (31 of 1952), S. 16]; the lightening or removal of any burden [Income-tax Act (43 of 1961), Ch. 18].

Relief agency. An agent appointed by a candidate for the purpose of relieving his other agents at the election. [Representation of the People Act (43 of 1951), S. 46].

Relief sought. The words 'relief sought' in S. 7(iv)(f), Court Fees Act (7 of 1870) do not refer to the consequential relief merely, but they mean the relief sought as a whole, that is, the declaratory decree or order with the consequential relief. *Madan Mohan* v. *T.G.C.H.S. Assn.,* AIR 1949 All 207.

Relief works. Public buildings or other works started to give work to the unemployed in period of agricultural famine or trade depression.

Relieve. To free or clear (a person) from an obligation. [CPC (5 of 1908), O. XXI, R. 89(3)]; [Indian Railways Act (9 of 1890), S. 71F].

Religion. A system of faith and worship. [IPC (45 of 1860), S. 295 and Constitution of India, Art. 15(1)].

Religion incorporates the particular belief(s) that a group of people subscribe to. [*Adi Saiva Sivachariyargal NalaSangam* v. *Government of Tamil Nadu*, (2016) 2 SCC 725, para 1].

"Before dilating further on the issue, it is also necessary to discuss about the meaning of religious rights, spiritual rights, temporal and secular rights.

The belief in and worship of a superhuman controlling power, especially a personal God or gods: ideas about the relationship between science and religion. • details of belief as taught or discussed: children should be taught religion in schools. • a particular system of faith and worship: the world's great religions. • a pursuit or interest to which someone ascribes supreme importance: consumerism is the new religion. [Oxford Dictionary as cited in *K.S. Varghese and Ors.* v. *ST. Peter's and Paul's Syrian Orth. and Ors.* 2017 (7) SCALE 450, para 98]

A system of faith and worship usu. involving belief in a supreme being and usu. containing a moral or ethical code; esp. such a system recognised and practiced by a particular church, sect, or denomination. In construing the protections under the Establishment Clause and the Free Exercise Clause, courts have interpreted the term religion quite broadly to include a wide variety of theistic and nontheistic beliefs. [Black's Law Dictionary as cited in *K.S. Varghese and Ors.* v. *ST. Peter's and Paul's Syrian Orth.,* 2017 (7) SCALE 450, para 98]

Religion is certainly a matter of faith with individuals or communities and it is not necessarily theistic. There are well known religions in India like Buddhism and Jainism which do not believe in God or in any Intelligent First Cause. A religion undoubtedly has its basis in a system of beliefs or doctrines which are regarded by those who propose that religion as conducive to their spiritual well-being, but it would not be correct to say that religion is nothing else but a doctrine of belief. *Commissioner H.R.E.* v. *Lakshmindra Thirtha Swamiar, Sri Shrirur Mutt.*, AIR 1954 SC 282, 290.

The teachings of Sri Arubindo is only philosophy and not religion. *S.P. Mittal* v. *Union of India*, AIR 1983 SC 1, 4, 33. [Constitution of India, Art. 25, 26].

The expression "religion" mentioned in cl. (b) of Art. 26, includes not only the philosophical side of religion, but also religious practices as laid down in the tenets of any religious sect. *Ram Chandra Deb* v. *State of Orissa,* AIR 1959 Ori 5, 10. [Constitution of India, Art. 26 (b)]

The word 'religion' means the distinct religion and all recognised practices thereof. [Constitution of India, Art. 30 (1)]

Religion, freedom of. The Constitution guarantees to all persons freedom of conscience and the right to profess, practice and propagate religion; this right is subject to the requirements of public order. The secular and other activities associated with religion can, however, be regulated, and the State can enact measures of social welfare and reform and throw open Hindu temples to all classes and sections of Hindus.

The Fundamental Right extends to the right to establish and maintain religious and charitable institutions, to manage its own affairs in matters of religion and buy and administer property; this right can, however, be regulated in the interests of public order, morality and health.

No tax can be levied for the purpose of any particular religion and religous instruction cannot be provided in an institution wholly maintained out if State funds.

Religious. Of or relating to religion; concerned with religion. [IPC (45 of 1860), S. 295-A].

"Devoted to religion; exhibiting the spritual or practical effects of religion following the requirements of religion; pious, godly, devout." [Shorter Oxford English Dictionary as cited in *Commissioner of Income Tax, Ujjain* v. *Dawoodi Bohara Jamat*, (2015 16 SCC 222, para 33].

Religious community. 'Religious community' means a community which denotes abiding by a particular faith. [*Shantagauri Ramniklal Trust* v. *CIT*, (1999) 239 ITR 528 (Guj)]

Religious denomination. A religious sect or body having a common faith and organisation and designated by a distinctive name, which enjoys certain rights pertaining to the establishment, management *etc.* of its own religious and charitable institutions.

Neither Aurobindo Society nor Auroville Township constitutes a religious denomination. *S.P. Mittal* v. *Union of India*, AIR 1983 SC 1, 30. [Constitution of India, Articles 25, 26]

Religious endowments. 'Religious endowments' are of two kinds, public and private. In a public endowment, the dedication is for the use or benefit of the public at large or a specified class. But when property is set apart for the worship of a family god, in which the public is not interested, the endowment is a private one. [*State of W.B.* v. *Sri Sri Lakshmi Janardan Thakur*, (2006) 7 SCC 490, 494, para 14]

Religious faith and religious belief. Essentially religion is a matter of personal faith and belief, of personal relation of an individual with what he regards as his Maker or his Creator or the higher agency which he believes regulates the existence of sentient beings and the forces of the Universe. *Ratilal* v. *State of Bombay,* AIR 1953 Bom 242, 252. [Constitution of India, Arts. 25 and 26]

Religious feeling. Religious feeling means nothing more or less than feeling associated with a person's religious creeds. Feeling of Hindus against cow-slaughter is religious feeling. *Kitab Ali* v. *Santi Ranjan,* AIR 1965 Tri 23, 24. [IPC (45 of 1860), S. 298]

Religious institution. "RELIGIOUS INSTITUTION" means any place, by whatever name known, which is used as a place of religious worship or which is dedicated to or used as of right by the public generally or any community or section thereof, for religious purposes. [Madhya Pradesh Anugrahik Tatha Sevarth Nagad Anudan Sampati Adhiniyam 1982 (11 of 1983), S. 2(b)]

"RELIGIOUS INSTITUTION" means an institution for the promotion of any religion or persuation and includes any place or premises used as a place of public religious worship by whatever name or designation known. [Religious Institution (Prevention of Misuse) Act (41 of 1988), S. 2(f)]

Religious instruction. The expression 'religious instruction' used in Art. 28(1) has a restricted meaning. It conveys that teaching of customs, ways of worship, practices or rituals cannot be allowed in educational institutions wholly maintained out of State funds. *Aruna Roy* v. *Union of India*, (2002) 7 SCC 368, 404, para 81 [Constitution of India, Art. 28(1)].

Religious liberty. Religious liberty does not include the right to introduce and carry out every scheme or purpose which persons see fit to claim as part of their religious system. No one can stretch his own liberty so as to interfere with that of his neighbours and violate the peace.

Religious minority. Religious minority is to be determined only in relation to the particular legislation which is sought to be impugned, namely that if it is the state legislature these minorities have to be determined in relation to the population of the state. *D.A.V. College, Jullunder* v. *State of Punjab*, AIR 1971 SC 1737, 1742. [Constitution of India, Art. 30]

Religious or charitable foundation. An endowment for development, maintenance, propagation, *etc.*, of religion or for charity. [Indian Evidence Act (1 of 1872), S. 49].

Religious or charitable purposes. A private gift to one's own self or kith and kin may be meritorious and pious but is not a charity in the legal sense. *Fazlul Rabbi* v. *State of W.B.*, AIR 1965, SC 1722, 1728.

Religious order. A religious society or fraternity living under a rule. [Hindu Marriage Act (25 of 1955), S. 13(vi)].

Religious place. For the purpose of this notification, "RELIGIOUS PLACE" means a place which is meant for conduct of prayers or worship pertaining to a religion. [Central Excise Tariff Act, 1985 (5 of 1986), Appendix IX, Service Tax (c)(iv), *Expln.*]

Religious rites or ceremonies. Rites or ceremonies of the nature of, pertaining or appropriate to, concerned or connected with religion. [CPC (5 of 1908), S. 9, *Expln.*I].

Religious sect. "People believing in the same religious doctrines, who are more or less closely associated or organized to advance such doctrines and increase in the number of believers therein," constitute a religious sect.

Religious service. A performance of religious worship. [Geneva Conventions Act (6 of 1960), III Sch., Art. 34].

Religious symbol. The calf and cow symbol is not a religious symbol. *Bhartendra Singhi* v. *Ramasahai Pandey,* AIR 1972 MP 167, 179. [Representation of the People Act (43 of 1951), S. 123 (3)]

Relinquish. To give over possession or control of; to leave off [T.P. Act (4 of 1882), S. 35]; [Indian Partnership Act (9 of 1932), S. 19(2)(c)]; [Presidency-towns Insolvency Act (3 of 1909), S. 12(2)].

Relinquishment. A forsaking, abandoning, or giving over. (*Tomlin*)

A release of a claim or portion of it; the act of relinquishing [CPC (5 of 1908), O. XX, R. 12(1)(c)(ii)]; [Registration Act (16 of 1908), S. 90(1)(e)].

Relinquishment of tenancy. The relinquishment of a tenancy is equivalent to surrender by the lessee or tenant of his rights as such. *W.H. King* v. *Republic of India*, AIR 1952 SC 156.

Rely. To depend upon a person or thing with full trust or confidence; to rest upon assurance. [CPC(5 of 1908, O. VI, R. 12].

Rely/Reliance (On a Certificate and Digital Signature). To accept a digital signature and act in a manner that could be detrimental to oneself were the digital signature to be ineffective (See also relying party : recipient). [*Information Technology*]

Relying Party. A recipient who acts in reliance on a certificate and digital signature (See also recipient : rely or reliance on a certificate and digital signature). [*Information Technology*]

Remain. "Remain" means to continue; to stay; to be left; to be left after another or others have gone.

To be left upon the removal or appropriation of some part, number or quantity. [CPC (5 of 1908), S. 52(2)].

Remain due. Remain owing or payable [CPC (5 of 1908), 1st Sch., App. A, form No. 18(3)].

Remain in force. Remain operative. [CPC (5 of 1908), O. XXI, R. 53(6)].

Remainder. An expectant portion, remnant, or residue of interest, which on the creation of a particular estate, is at the same time limited over to another, who is to enjoy it after the determination of such particular estate [CPC (5 of 1908), 1st Sch., App. A form No. 15]; that which is left when part has been taken away, used or dealt with [CPC (5 of 1908), S. 60(1)(i)]; [Constitution of India, Art. 55(2)(b)].

(*estate in*). Residual interest in estate; right of succession to an estate or title on holder's decease.

A future interest arising in a estate in a third person *i.e.* other than the creator or creator's heirs on natural termination of the preceding estate.

Remainder-man. The owner of an estate in remainder; person entitled to an expectant estate.

A person who holds or is entitled to a legal remainder. [Specific Relief Act (47 of 1963), S. 15(d)].

Remaining. Left after the removal or appropriation of some part, number or quantity [T.P. Act (4 of 1882), S. 84 and Industrial Finance Corporation Act (15 of 1948) (*Repealed by Act 23 of 1993*), S. 4A(2)].

Remaining interest. An interest which is left after the prior estate or interest has come to an end in one way or another. [T.P. Act (4 of 1882), S. 13].

Remaining witnesses. The words 'any remaining witnesses' for the prosecution in S. 246(6) CrPC

1973 (2 of 1974) are wide enough to include any witness, who according to the prosecution, is able to support its case, though he has not been summoned, provided that he is not sprung upon the defence all of a sudden and sufficient opportunity is given to the latter to prepare for the cross-examination of the witness. *Rewa Chand* v. *State,* AIR 1955 Raj 113.

The words do not refer only to those witnesses who were in the first list. They refer to witnesses who had not been examined or those whose names have not been disclosed in the list before the charge was framed. *V.R. Shenoy* v. *S.A. Prabhu,* AIR 1967 Ker 233, 234.

Remand. After a preliminary or partial hearing before a Court or Magistrate, to send a prisoner back to the custody, to be kept until the hearing is resumed or the trial comes on; to remit or send back a cause to the Court from which it was removed, appealed, or transferred into another Court, in order that some further action may be taken upon it in the original Court.

The act of sending back (a prisoner) into custody, specially in order that further evidence on the charge may be obtained; the act of sending back a case or suit or an appeal to the lower Court or authority for rehearing [CPC (5 of 1908), S. 105(2) and CrPC 1973 (2 of 1974), S. 309(2), *Expln.*]; to send back.

Remanent. The name given to a cause, the trial of which has been postponed from one sitting to another.

Remargining. In *Securities law*, the act or process of depositing additional cash or collateral with a broker when the equity in a margin account falls to an insufficient level.

Remarks. Comments. [Contempt of Courts Act (70 of 1971), S. 16(2)].

Remedial Act. A remedial Act is one made from time to time to supply defects in the existing law, arising from the inevitable imperfection of legislation, mistake or other cause, and the words of a remedial statute are to be construed largely and beneficially, so as to suppress the mischief sought to be remedied.

Remedial law. A law passed to correct or modify an existing law.

Remedial statute. A statute providing a remedy for an injury.

A remedial statute has for its object either to redress some existing grievance or to introduce some new regulation or proceeding conducive to the public good.

Remedy. "REMEDY" means variation from the standard weight and fineness. [Coinage Act (11 of 2011), S. 2(k)].

Something that corrects or counter-acts an evil, disease, *etc.*; the legal means to recover a right or to prevent or obtain redress for a wrong; legal redress. [Indian Contract Act (9 of 1872), S. 139].

As a legal term means to recover a debt or enforce a right; a mode prescribed by law to enforce a duty or redress a wrong; that which gives relief to the party aggrieved; the means by which the obligation is effectuated; the means employed to enforce a right or redress an injury; the mode or procedure by which the liability of property to the satisfaction of a debt is enforced; the particular result to obtain which an action is brought; the action or means given by law for the recovery of a right.

"REMEDY" means variation from the standard weight and fineness. [S. 2(k) of the Coinage Act, 2011 (11 of 2011)]

Remise. To release a claim; to surrender.

Remission. 'Remission' is reduction of the amount of a sentence without changing its character. *State (Govt. of NCT of Delhi)* v. *Prem Raj,* (2003) 7 SCC 121, para 10.

The action of remitting or giving up partially or wholly a tax, debt, penalty, *etc.*, [IPC (45 of 1860), S. 227 and Constitution of India, Art. 110(1)(a)]; remission of land revenue, *etc.*

In India this power is exercised by the President of India under Art. 72 of Const., in respect of Central laws and by the Governor under Art. 161 of Const., in respect of State laws.

A remission is an act of justice, and cannot be obtained until the entire innocence of the petitioner be established, not by his testimony taken *ex parte*, but after full notice to the proper officer of government. A pardon, on the other hand, imports an act of mercy and favour, and generally supposes its object guilty.

Remission and **remit.** The expression "remission" with regard to punishment and "remit" in relation to sentence. *Ashok Kumar* v. *Union of India*, AIR 1991 SC 1792, 1804.

Remission of sentence. An act of executive clemency by which the sentence of a person convicted of a crime is reduced. In India, the power can be exercised by the President or the Governor of a State.

Remission system. "REMISSION SYSTEM" means the rules for the time being in force regulating the award of marks to, and the consequent shortening of sentences of, prisoners in jail. [Prisons Act (9 of 1894), S. 3(5)]

Remit. To "remit" money means, to send the money in the ordinary manner.

To give up partially or wholly a tax, debt, penalty, *etc.* [Registration Act (16 of 1908), S. 70; IPC (45 of 1860), S. 405, ill. (c) and Constitution of India, Art. 72(1)]; to send (money) to a person or place [Indian Trusts Act (2 of 1882), S. 15, ill. (a)]; [Indian Contract Act (9 of 1872), S. 212, ill. (a)].

The word 'remit' is not a term of art. Some of the meanings of the word 'remit' are to pardon; to refrain from inflicting; to give up. *Deputy Inspector General of Police* v. *D. Rajaram,* AIR 1960 AP 259, 262. [CrPC 1973 (2 of 1974), S. 432]

Remittance. "REMITTANCE" means remittance made in foreign exchange by any person resident outside India to a person resident in India on or after the date of commencement of this Act but before the specified date, in the form of drafts, traveller's cheques, cheques drawn on banks situated outside India, telegraphic transfers, mail transfers, money orders or by way of transfer from Non-resident (External) Account, Foreign Currency Non-resident Account or Foreign Currency Non-resident Special Deposit Account maintained in India under the rules made under the Foreign Exchange Regulation Act, 1973. [Remittances of Foreign Exchange and Investment in Foreign Exchange Bonds (Immunities and Exemptions) Act (41 of 1991), S. 2(b)]

Remittance of assets. Means remittance outside India of funds representing a deposit with a bank or a firm or a company, provident fund balance or superannuation benefits, amount of claim or maturity proceeds of Insurance policy, sale proceeds of shares, securities, immovable property or any other asset held in India in accordance with the provisions of the Act or rules or regulations made thereunder. [Foreign Exchange Management (Remittance of Assets) Regulations, 2000, Reg. 2(iv)]

Remote. Opposite or proximate. A remote cause is the antithesis of proximate cause. Remote damages are those "remotely resulting from the act complained of".

Far removal in place, time, chain of causation or relation. [Indian Contract Act (9 of 1872), S. 73].

Remote cause. A remote cause is one which is inconclusive in reasoning, because from it no certain conclusion can be legitimately drawn. In other words, a remote cause is a cause the connection between which and the effect is uncertain, vague, or indeterminate. Although the existence of the remote cause is necessary for the effect (for, unless there be a remote cause there may be no effect), still the existence of the remote cause does not necessarily imply the existence of the effect. The remote cause being given, the effect may or may not follow. It differs from a proximate cause, which is one in which is involved the idea of necessity. It is one the connection between which and the effect is plain and intelligible. It is one that can be used as a term by which a proposition can be demonstrated; that is, one that can be reasoned from conclusively. A proximate cause being given, the effect must follow.

Remote damages. Alike in actions on contract and tort the damages, which the plaintiff is entitled to, must result directly from the wrongful act of the defendant and not to be remote. That is the basis of the principle of the rule that plaintiff should avoid or diminish the damages as far as he can.

Remoteness. Want of close connection between a wrong and the injury, as cause and effect, whereby the party injured cannot claim compensation from the wrong doer. (*Wharton*)

Remoteness of damage. The extent of which a defendant is liable for the consequences of his wrongful act or omission.

Removable from appointment. The words "removable from appointment" in the Public Servants (Inquiries) Act, 1850 merely indicates removal from the appointment in the sense of office or post held by the officer and not removal from service. (*R.P. Kapur* v. S. *Pratap Singh Kairon,* AIR 1964 SC 295).

Removal. The act of taking away entirely [Taxation Laws (Continuation and Validation of Recovery Proceedings) Act (11 of 1964), S. 3(2)]; the act of conveying or shifting from one place to another; the fact of being so transferred [Representation of the People (Miscellaneous Provisions) Act (88 of 1956), S. 2 and Constitution of India, Art. 92(1)]; [IPC (45 of 1860), S. 421 and Constitution of India, Art. 49].

"Removal" in relation to goods, means—(a) dispatch of the goods for delivery by the supplier thereof or by any other person acting on behalf of such supplier; or

(b) collection of the goods by the recipient thereof or by any other person acting on behalf of such recipient [The Central Goods and Services Tax Act, 2017 (12 of 2017), S. 2(96)]

The term "removal" means a discharge, the act of removing from office, or putting an end to an employment.

The term "removal" means the act of removing from office or putting an end to an employment. [*State of Uttrakhand* v. *Yogendra Nath Arora*, (2013) 14 SCC 299, para 11].

The punishment of 'removal' is not something as 'condoning misconduct and merely discharging from service' as provided in para 22(v)(e) of the rules. *State Bank of India* v. *T.J. Paul,* AIR 1999 SC 1994. [Bank of Cochin Service Code, Ch. VII, para 22(v)(e)]

The word 'removal' is not used in its widest connotation in Art. 311 of Constitution of India. It refers only to a removal which is for some fault or misconduct of the employee himself which he may try to explain. *Shyam Lal* v. *State of U.P.,* AIR 1954 All 235.

The word 'removal' is not used in its wider sense of termination of service but is used in its restricted sense of removal by way of punishment. The compulsory retirement of a government servant is not a 'removal'. *Raj Kishore* v. *State of U.P.,* AIR 1954 All 343.

A termination of service has not been held to be a removal. *Anant Ram Misra* v. *A.N. Dixit,* AIR 1956 All 527, 528.

Removal is defined as take off or away from place occupied, convey to another, place, change, situation of get rid of, dismiss. *Ramkrishna Gangaram Nathi* v. *Kishan Zingaraj Madke*, AIR 1971 Bom 305, 310.

Removal and dismissal. 'Removal' and 'dismissal' in the context of Section 240(3) of the Act are synonymous terms. [*U.P. Government* v. *Sabir Hussain,* (1975) 4 SCC 703, 706, para 7] [Govt. of India Act, 1935, S. 240(3)]

Under S. 39 of the Municipal Act as well as the Punjab Civil Services Rules, a clear distinction is made between renewal and dismissal, and it is not possible to say that 'dismissals' and 'removal' are synonymous terms. 'Dismissal' also includes 'removal', but the converse cannot be said to be true because the dismissal is a much more serious and drastic punishment than removal because dismissal involves disqualification from future service. *Municipal Committee, Ambala* v. *Mangal Sain,* MLJ : QD (1961-1965) Vol IV C1433 : 63 Pun LR 870 [Punjab Municipal Act (3 of 1911), S. 39]

Removal or dismissal. The order of retirement in the case is not an order of dismissal or removal. The authority lower in rank is competent to pass the order of retirement in public interest. [J.S. VERMA and G.P. SINGH, JJ.] *Ghanshyam Das Srivastava* v. *Chief Conservator of Forests (General), Madhya Pradesh,* MLJ : YD 1978 Suppl C 634 : (1978) SLJ 109 : (1978) MPLJ 59. [Constitution of India, Art 311].

Removal, dismissal and reduction in rank. The terms 'removal', 'dismissal' and 'reduction in rank' as used in Art. 311 have a technical meaning and must be understood in the same sense in which they have been used in the relevant rules of the appropriate civil services rules setting out the various penalties to which a civil servant can be subjected for indiscipline or misconduct and must be based on misconduct or indiscipline. *Prem Biharilal* v. *State of Madhya Bharat,* AIR 1954 MB 49. [Constitution of India, Art. 311]

Removal from custody. The words 'removal from custody' would cover refusal by person to deliver child to its natural guardian when asked to do so. *Lachmi Ram* v. *Prabhoo,* AIR 1964 HP 12. [Guardians and Wards Act (8 of 1890), S. 25]

Removal from service. The only distinction between dismissal proper and dismissal in the shape of removal from service was that the former ordinarily disqualified from future employment but the latter did not do so. The word 'dismissal' is comprehensive enough to include removal from service. *CAD Souza* v. *State of Madhya Pradesh,* AIR 1961 MP 261, 266. [Constitution of India, Arts. 226, 311]

Remove. The word 'remove' means to take off or away from the place occupied. *State of Mysore* v. *Chikkavenkatappa,* AIR 1965 Mys 253, 255. [CrPC 1973 (2 of 1974), S. 197]

To move from or out of the place occupied [IPC (45 of 1860), S. 421]; to take away entirely; to dismiss from office or post. [Army Act (46 of 1950), S. 20(1)].

Removed from custody. Custody includes legal or formal custody. Refusal by a person who has the actual custody to hand over minor to a person appointed as guardian under S. 7 would be removal from custody. Application under S. 25 lies. *Chandrapal* v. *Mungia,* MLJ : QD (1961-1965) Vol III C918 : AIR 1961 All 549 [Guardians and Wards Act (8 of 1890), S. 7, 25]

Removed from service. The term in its ordinary meaning means nothing more or less than the termination of a person's office. *Prasadi* v. *Works Manager*, AIR 1957 Cal 4; *Moti Ram* v. *N.E. Frontier Rly*, AIR 1964 SC 600.

The term is synonymous with termination of service. *R.P. Kapur* v. *Pratap Singh,* AIR 1964 SC 295.

Remuneration. Means the basic wage or salary, and any additional emoluments whatsoever payable, either in cash or in kind to a person employed in respect of employment or work done in such employment. If the terms of the contract of employment, express or implied, were fulfilled. [Equal Remuneration Act (25 of 1976), S. 2(g)]

Payment for services rendered or work done. [Constitution of India, Art. 76(4)].

In the Banking Act the word 'remuneration' has been used in the widest sense. In that sense, it undoubtedly includes bonus. *Central Bank of India* v. *Their Workmen*, AIR 1960 SC 12, 24.

The expression 'remuneration' in its ordinary connotation means "reward, recompense, pay, wages or salary" for service rendered. *Accountant General Bihar* v. *N. Bakshi*, AIR 1962 SC 505, 509. [Constitution of India, Art. 314]

The word 'remuneration' though it includes 'wages' may mean payment, which srictly speaking may not be called 'wages'. It is a term of much wider import including 'recompense', 'reward', 'payment' *etc. I.T. Commissioner* v. *Calcutta A.S.E. Assa.*, AIR 1959 SC 763, 768.

"REMUNERATION". For the purposes of Schedule V of Act 18 of 2013, 'remuneration' means remuneration as defined in section 2(78) of Act 18 of 2013 and includes reimbursement of any direct taxes to the managerial person. [*Explanation VI(B)* to section IV of Part II of Schedule V of the Companies Act, 2013 (18 of 2013)]

"REMUNERATION" means any money or its equivalent given or passed to any person for services rendered by him and includes perquisites as defined under the Income-tax Act, 1961 (43 of 1961). [S. 2(78) of the Companies Act, 2013 (18 of 2013)]

Render. To yield, or return; to give up; to surrender; to make up and exhibit, as an account; to determine upon and announce, as a verdict or judgment.

The word 'render' sometimes means "bestow or provide; furnish; give in answer to requirement of duty or demand".

Render due accounts. To submit or lay before another (for consideration or approval) true accounts. [Indian Partnership Act (9 of 1932), S. 9].

Rendered illegal. The words "rendered illegal" do not mean 'held illegal'. *Labour Commissioner* v. *Burhanpur Tapti Mills Ltd.*, AIR 1964 SC 1687, 1689.

Rendition. Surrender of a suspected or convicted person under *inter se* arrangements.

Renege. To fail to keep a promise or commitment; to back out of a deal.

Renewable. What is capable of being renewed in terms of the grant or under the provisions of law. [T.P. Act (4 of 1882), S. 72(e)].

"Renewable Energy Implementing Agency". Means a company or entity designated by the Central Government or the State Government to act as Intermediary Procurer to select and buy power from Renewable Energy Generating Station(s) and sell the same to one or more distribution licensees or any other person in accordance with the Guidelines issued from time to time by the Ministry of Power, Government of India or the Ministry of New and Renewable Energy. Government of India or the State Government. [Central Electricity Regulatory Commission (Grant of Connectivity, Long-term Access and Medium-term Open Access in inter-State Transmission and Related Matters) Regulations, 2009, Regn. 2(1)(b) (ka)].

"Renewable Energy Generating Station". Shall mean a generating station based on any renewable source of energy, and shall include Renewable Hybrid Generating Station. [Central Electricity Regulatory Commission (Grant of Connectivity, Long-term Access and Medium-term Open Access in inter-State Transmission and Related Matters) Regulations, 2009, Regn. 2(1)(ra)].

"Renewable Power Park Developers". Shall mean a Solar Power Park developer or Wind Power Park Developer or Renewable Hybrid Power Park Developer. [Central Electricity Regulatory Commission (Grant of Connectivity, Long-term Access and Medium-term Open Access in inter-State Transmission and Related Matters) Regulations, 2009, Regn. 2(1)(r-d)].

Renewal. A change of something old for something new.

An act of renewing any permission, grant, *etc.* [T.P. Act (4 of 1882), S. 71].

Renewal of permit. The word 'renewal' is not a term of art. The word 'renewal' is merely used to enable the Government to give preference to the previous permit holders who are quite properly, to be treated on a different footing from the new applicants. *Ch. Anjaiyah* v. *Regional Transport Officer,* AIR 1957 AP 470, 471.

Renoncant. A native resident of former French possessions in India who has renounced his personal law and adopted the French civil law. [Child Marriage Restraint Act (19 of 1929), S. 1(2)].

Renounce. To give up a right; surrender; abandon; refuse to recognise any longer (as) to renounce treaty principles, authority, heirship, *etc.*

To give up. [T.P. Act (4 of 1882), S. 111(g)(2) and Constitution of India, Art. 51A(e)].

Renounce the world. To withdraw from worldly interests in order to lead a spiritual life. [Hindu Marriage Act (25 of 1955), S. 13(vi)].

Renouncing. Making formal resignation of some right or trust especially of one's position as heir or executor. [Indian Contract Act (9 of 1872), S. 201].

Rent. For the purposes of this section,— "RENT" means any payment, by whatever name called, under any lease, sub-lease, tenancy or any other agreement or arrangement for the use of any land or any building (including factory building), together with furniture, fittings and the land appurtenant thereto, whether or not such building is owned by the payee. [Income-tax Act (43 of 1961), S. 1994, *Expln* (i)]

In the first instance, it means any payment which is made under any lease, sub-lease, tenancy. Once the payment is made under lease, sub-lease or tenancy, the nomenclature which is given is inconsequential. Such payment under lease, sub-lease and/or tenancy would be treated as "rent". In the second place, such a payment made even under any other "agreement or arrangement for the use of any land or any building" would also be treated as "rent". Whether or not such building is owned by the payee is not relevant. [*Japan Airlines Company Limited* v. *Commissioner of Income Tax, New Delhi*, (2015) 10 SCC 591, para 14].

"RENT" in relation to any public premises means the consideration payable periodically for the authorised occupation of the premises and includes—

(i) any charge for electricity, water or any other services in connection with the occupation of the premises,

(ii) any tax (by whatever name called) payable in respect of the premises, where such charge or tax is payable by the Central Government or the corporate authority. [Public Premises (Eviction of Unauthorised Occupants) Act (40 of 1971), S. 2(f)]

"RENT", in relation to any airport premises, means the consideration payable periodically for the authorised occupation of the premises, and includes—

(i) any charge for electricity, water or any other service in connection with the occupation of the premises; and

(ii) any tax, by whatever name called, payable in respect of the premises. [Airports Authority of India Act (55 of 1994), S. 28A(d)].

A return made by a tenant or occupant of land or corporeal hereditaments to the owner for the possession and use thereof; a pecuniary sum agreed upon between a tenant and his landlord and paid at fixed intervals by the tenant to the landlord for the use of land or its appendages; a fixed periodical profit in money, provisions, chattels or services arising out of lands and tenements in payment for use. [T.P. Act (4 of 1882), S. 105 and Indian Succession Act (39 of 1925), S. 167, *Expln.*].

The word 'rent' as used in Art. 8 of the Schedule, properly speaking, relates to rent for immovable property only, and has not been used to cover suits relating to hire for movables. *Pukhraj* v. *Mohammad*

Ali, AIR 1957 Raj 279, 281. [Provincial Small Causes Courts Act (9 of 1887), Sch. II, Art. 8]

The word 'rent' means payment to a landlord by a tenant for the demised property and does not include payments made by licensees. *State of Punjab* v. *British India Corporation Ltd.*, AIR 1963 SC 1459, 1464.

In its wider sense rent means any payment made for the use of land or buildings and thus includes the payment by a licensee in respect of the use, and occupation of any land or building. *Ramamurthy Subudhi* v. *Gopinath Naik*, AIR 1968 SC 919, 922. [T.P. Act (4 of 1882), S. 105].

Rental value. The term "rental value" as applied to realty is but another form of saying the value of the use, and means simply the value of the use of the land for any purpose for which it is adapted in the hands of a prudent and discreet occupant upon a judicious system of husbandry.

"Renting" means allowing, permitting or granting access, entry, occupation, use or any such facility, wholly or partly, in an immovable property, with or without the transfer of possession or control of the said immovable property and includes letting, leasing, licensing or other similar arrangements in respect of immovable property. [Finance Act (32 of 1994), S. 65B(41) now repealed by Central Goods and Services Tax Act, 2017].

Renunciation. The action of renouncing, giving up or surrendering (a possession, right, title, *etc.*) [Indian Contract Act (9 of 1872), S. 207]; [long title, Dissolution of Muslim Marriage Act (8 of 1939)].

Repair. Restoration of some material thing or structure by the renewal of decayed or worn out parts, by refixing what has become loose or detached [T.P. Act (4 of 1882), S. 108(f)]; to restore by replacing a part or putting together what is torn or broken.

A workman who is whitewashing a building is doing something which would fall within the meaning of the term 'repair' as used in heading VIII of Sch. II to the Workman's Compensation Act (8 of 1923).

All replacements or renewals need not necessarily be repairs. Restoration of stability or safety of subordinate or subsidiary part or a portion of a building is repair but not the reconstruction of the entirety of the building. *Shadi Lal & Sons, Shamli* v. *I.T. Commissioner, Kanpur*, AIR 1988 SC 424, 427. [Income Tax Act (43 of 1961), S. 24(1)(i)]

In case of a thatched old shed made of very flimsy materials like bamboo and arecanut stem repair implies renewal and replacement of parts that have decayed. *Augustin* v. *Chandy,* AIR 1953 TC 462.

Repairer. Includes a person who adjusts, cleans, lubricates or paints any weight or measure or renders any other service to such weight or measure to ensure that such weight or measure conforms to the standards established by or under this Act. [Standards of Weights and Measures Act (60 of 1976), S. 2(u)]

Repairs and renovation. Renovation means demolition of old structure and building a new one on the same site. Repair, whenever a thing or a part of a thing is worn out and a new thing is replaced in its place, such replacement of new thing amounts to repair. *Khimchand Parshottam* v. *Shah Bhupatray Nathalal*, AIR 1971 Guj 81, 83. [Saurashtra Rent Control Act (22 of 1951), S. 13(1) and 16]

Repatriate. Restore or return to one's country of origin, allegance or citizenship. [Passports Act (15 of 1967), S. 6(2)(h)].

Repatriate to India. Means bringing into India the realised foreign exchange and—

(i) the selling of such foreign exchange to an authorised person in India in exchange for rupees, or

(ii) the holding of realised amount in an account with an authorised person in India to the extent notified by the Reserve Bank,

and includes use of the realised amount for discharge of a debt or liability denominated in foreign exchange and the expression "repatriation" shall be construed accordingly. [Foreign Exchange Management Act (42 of 1999), S. 2(y)]

Repatriation. Return or restoration of some person by a foreign country to his native country, particularly a refugee or a criminal.

Repatriation expenses. Means expenses incurred in returning a distressed seaman to a proper return port and in providing him with necessary clothing and maintenance until his arrival at such port, and includes in the case of a shipwrecked seaman the repayment of expenses incurred in conveying him to port after shipwreck and maintaining him while being so conveyed. [Merchant Shipping Act (44 of 1958), S. 3(36)(a)]

Repay. To pay back; to refund (a sum of money *etc.*) [T.P. Act (4 of 1882), S. 58(e)]; [Indian Contract Act (9 of 1872), S. 45, ill.].

Repayment. The act of repaying; payment back of (money, debt *etc.*) [Indian Contract Act (9 of 1872), S. 133, ill. (e)].

"Repayment account". Means the bank account to which a debtor is obliged to repay its debt, as recorded in an information utility. [Insolvency and Bankruptcy Board of India (Information Utilities) Regulations, 2017, Regn. 2(1)(m)].

"Repayment plan". Means a plan prepared by the debtor in consultation with the resolution professional under Section 105 containing a proposal to the committee of creditors for restructuring of his debts or affairs. [Insolvency and Bankruptcy Code (31 of 2016), S. 79(20)].

Repeal. A revocation; as the repealing of a statute is the revoking or disannulling it. (*Tomlin*)

Abrogation of any law. [Indian Partnership Act (9 of 1932), S. 74 and Constitution of India, Art. 395, margin].

"Repeal" means to abolish, abrogare, abrogate, annual, avoid, cancel, countermand, declare null and void, delete, formally withdraw, invalidate, make void, negate, nullify, obliterate, officially withdraw, override, overrule, quash, recall, render invalid, rescind, rescindere, retract, reverse, revoke, set aside, vacate, void, withdraw. [Thesaurus as cited in *Shree Bhagwati Steel Rolling Mills* v. *Commissioner of Central Excise*, (2016) 3 SCC 643, para 12].

A repeal signifies the abrogation of one statute by another.

The primary meaning of the word "repealed", as used in speaking of the repeal of a statute, is, as its etymology imports, that the statute has been recalled or revoked.

Repeal and Amendment. Amendment includes abrogation or a deletion of a provision in an existing statute. If the amendment of an existing law is small, the Act professes to amend; if it is extensive, it repeals and reenacts it. *Bhagat Ram* v. *Union of India*, AIR 1988 SC 740, 746. [General Clauses Act (10 of 1987), Ss. 6, 21 and 24]

Repel. Repulse; ward off; refuse acceptance. To drive, to resist or oppose effectively; to drive off or back.

Repentance. State of being penitent; sorrow for what one has done or omitted to do.

Repetition. The fact of occurring, appearing or being repeated again. [CPC (5 of 1908), O. XXXIX, R. 2].

Replace. To put back [Industrial Finance Corporation Act (15 of 1948). (*Repealed by Act 23 of 1993*), S. 29(e)].

Replacement. A person or thing taking the place of another. [Factories Act (63 of 1948), S. 6(3), *Expln.*]; [Income-tax Act (43 of 1961), S. 10(30)].

Replanting. To plant at another place. [Cardamom Act (42 of 1965) (*repealed*), S. 9(2)(c)].

Replegiare est, rem apud allum detentam cautione legitima interposita, redimere. (*3 Bl. Comm. 146*): Replevin is to redeem, with lawful security, any thing detained by another.

Replevin. Replevin is a form of action which lies to regain possession of personal chattels which have been unlawfully taken or detained, and also for damages for taking and detention.

Repelvin is an action to recover the possession of personal property. The right to recover possession in an action of repelvin depends upon the question who has the right of possession.

Replication. (*In pleadings*) A replication which corresponds to the modern reply was the plaintiffs answer to the defendants' original plea; the plaintiff's answer or reply to the defendant's plea or answer.

Report. The 'report' mentioned in cl. (2) of S. 14, Act (8 of 1890), Guardians and Wards Act does not mean a judicial reference; it indicates a purely ministerial act.

Something which gives information; an account or statement of a legal case heard and of the decision and opinion of the Court or *quasi*-judicial administrative agency determining the case; a record of the speeches delivered and actions taken during a session of any deliberative body as formally published; a formal and official statement giving the conclusion and recommendations of a person or group authorised to consider a proposal; formal account of the results of an investigation given by a person authorised to make the investigation. [Indian Evidence Act (1 of 1872), S. 84; IPC (45 of 1860), S. 219 and Constitution of India, Art. 105(2)].

Reports (*in law*) are collections of the authoritative expositions of the law by the regularly constituted judicial tribunals supplemented and arranged by an officer called the Court reporter.

Each volume of reports usually consists of a title page, of a statement of the entry of copy right; of a list of the Judges composing the Court, of a table of cases reported in the volume arranged in alphabetical order, of an index to all subjects judicially considered, arranged alphabetically, often consisting substantially of a production of the headnotes of the cases reported, and principally of the reported cases themselves. In addition it may and frequently does contain appropriate cross reference and footnotes.

Report of decisions. A published account of a legal proceedings giving a statement of the facts, the arguments on both sides, and the reasons the Court gave for its judgment. [Indian Evidence Act (1 of 1872), S. 84].

Reportable injury. Means any injury other than a serious bodily injury which involves, or in all probability will involve, the enforced absence of the injured person from work for a period of seventy-two hours or more. [Mines Act (35 of 1952), S. 2(pp)]

Reporter. A reporter of a newspaper is a person employed "in reporting proceedings of Courts, public meetings, legislative assemblies, and other services of a kindred character for the newspaper".

LAW REPORTERS AND OFFICIAL REPORTERS A reporter is a person who reports the decisions upon the questions of law in the case adjudged in the Courts of law; and an official reporter has been defined to be an official who edits and publishes decisions of the highest Courts of the state.

An official reporter is a public officer, and presumption of faithfulness and honesty must be indulged in his favour as in the case of other public officers.

Reporting authority. "REPORTING AUTHORITY" means such authority or authorities supervising the performance of member of the service reported upon as may be specifically empowered in this behalf by the Government. [All India Services (Confidential Rolls) Rules, 1970, R. 2(e)]

Reporting entity. Means a banking company, financial institution, intermediary or a person carrying on a designated business or profession. [S. 2(1)(wa) of the Prevention of Money-Laundering Act, 2002 (15 of 2003) as inserted by the Prevention of Money-Laundering (Amendment) Act, 2012 (2 of 2013)]

Repose. To give rest to. [Indian Trusts Act (2 of 1882), S. 3].

Repository. A repository is a place where things are or may be deposited for safety or preservation; a depository; a store-house; a magazine; a "place where things are kept for sale; a shop, as a carriage repository".

Represent. To represent a person is to stand in his place, to act his part, to exercise his right, or to take his share.

To act the part of, in place of or for (another) [Indian Contract Act (9 of 1872), S. 182]; to be accredited deputy or substitute for (a number of persons) in a legislative or deliberative assembly; to place a fact clearly before another with a view to influencing action or conduct [Indian Partnership (9 of 1932), S. 28(1)]; to make a formal statement of facts, reasons or arguments with a view to affecting some action *etc.*

To represent means to stand in the place of; and so insurance money represents the property insured, so that, where the property is exempt from execution, the insurance money is also.

Representation. "REPRESENTATION" includes probate, letters of administration, with or without the will annexed and succession certificate, constituting a person executor or administrator of the estate of a deceased person or authorising him to receive or realise the assets of a deceased person. [Army & Air Force (Disposal of Private Property) Act (40 of 1950), S. 2(4)]

"REPRESENTATION" means probate of a will or letters of administration. [Estate Duty Act (34 of 1953), S. 2(18)]

Likeness; picture; model [IPC (45 of 1860), S. 499]; a statement or account especially made to convey a particular view or impression of something with the intention of influencing action [IPC (45 of 1860), S. 118]; the action of representing (another) [Industrial Development Bank of India Act (18 of 1964), S. 25(3)]; a formal and serious statement of facts, reasons or arguments made with a view to effecting some change, preventing some change, preventing some action *etc.* [Minimum Wages Act (11 of 1948), S. 5(2)].

A fiction of the law, the effect of which is to put the representative in the place, degree, or right of the person represented. In the law of contracts in general, a statement, incidental to a contract, relative to some fact having reference thereto, and upon the faith of which the contract is entered into.

Representation need not be in any particular form. Sometimes silence in answer to a question or a nod or a smile is held to be sufficient. A representation could be by word of mouth or by a document. *Ganeshdas* v. *Kamalabai,* AIR 1952 Nag 29. [T.P. Act (4 of 1882), S. 43]

Representation suit. The suit by any two or more representing numerous persons interested in prosecuting or defending a civil proceeding.

Representative. "REPRESENTATIVE" includes the guardian of a minor and the committee or other legal curator of a lunatic or idiot. [Registration Act (16 of 1908), S. 2(10)].

"REPRESENTATIVE" means any person who has taken out representation, but does not include an Administrator-General. [Army and Air Force (Disposal of Private Property) Act (40 of 1950), S. 2(5)]

One who represents another as agent, delegate, substitute, successor or heir; a person appointed to represent his sovereign or government in a foreign Court or country; one that represents a constituency as a member of a legislative or other governing body. [Indian Evidence Act (1 of 1872), Ss. 86 and 115 and Constitution of India, Art. 80(1)(b)].

The word 'representative' in S. 2(10) of the Registration Act (16 of 1908) includes the *de facto* guardian of a minor. AIR 1930 Mad 425.

The term "representative" in S. 115 of the Indian Evidence Act (1 of 1872) is not limited to a gratuitous transferee or to a subsequent transferee for value with notice. It includes a *bona fide* assignee for value without notice of the circumstances creating an estoppel.

The word "representative" in S. 47, CPC (5 of 1908) does not include a person who had purchased from the judgment-debtor property against which the decree was sought to be executed, but which was not affected until an order for sale in execution of the decree was made.

The word 'representative' in S. 47. CPC (5 of 1908), has a much wider meaning than the words 'legal representative' used in S. 50 of the Code in as much as it includes not only a legal representative but any representative in interest (*i.e.*) any transferee of the interest of a party.

Besides wife, husband, parent and child, the expression 'representative' includes also a person who is entitled to succeed to the estate of the deceased. *Anita Rani* v. *State of Punjab,* AIR 1988 P&H 141, 143. [Fatal Accidents Act (13 of 1855), S. 1 A]

Persons who are properly constituted to be the agents and capable of acting in the transactions possessing primordial authority from his principal not only to act for him but also to give good discharge by accepting consideration of it was a case of a sale *inter vivos*. *Gram Seva Mandal Wardha* v. *Collector of Wardha,* AIR 1975 Bom 73, 76. [Land Acquisition Act (1 of 1894), S. 12 (2)]

The term "representative" means persons who are entitled to represent the person executing of claiming. *Sakinabai* v. *Sakinabai,* AIR 1963 MP 286, 289. [Registration Act (16 of 1908), Ss. 2 (10), 32]

Representative assessee. Assessee as in the capacity of a representative. [Income-tax Act (43 of 1961), S. 139(4A)].

Representative capacity. The term "representative capacity" is a well-understood term, and only applies to a party acting for and on behalf of some other party or estate, and not for himself personally.

Representative in interest. The purchaser at a sale in execution of decree is a "representative in interest" of a judgment-debtor within the meaning of S. 21 of the Indian Evidence Act (1 of 1872).

The expression "representatives in interest" includes privies in estate.

One who represents the interest of another by virtue of inheritance, transfer, *etc*.. [Indian Evidence Act (1 of 1872), S. 21].

Representative in parliament. "Representative in parliament is a phrase synonymous with member of parliament".

Representative of a party. The expression "representative of a party" in the last paragraph of S. 47, CPC (5 of 1908), does not mean the representative of a party to the execution proceedings but it means the representative of a party to the suit.

Representative of the Government of India. "An officer who with respect to any territory or place not forming part of India or Her majesty's Dominions, is a Political Agent therefor, as defined in S. 3, clause 43, of the General Clauses Act, 1897, shall for the purposes of this section, be deemed to be representative of the Central Government in and for the country comprising that territory or place." [Indian Evidence Act (1 of 1872), S. 86]

Represented. Exhibited by artificial resemblance or delineation. [Indian Evidence Act (1 of 1872), S. 36].

Represented by him. (The person or estate) for whom he is acting. [CPC (5 of 1908), O. XXXIII, R. 3].

Reprieve. Temporary postponement of the execution of a criminal sentence especially a death sentence; respite.

Reprimand. To reprove severely, especially, publicy or officially. [Army Act (46 of 1950), S. 71(i)].

A form of punishment awarded by Legislature to those who commit a breach of its privilege.

Reprisal. The taking one thing in satisfaction for another.

Seizures in retaliation. [Naval and Aircraft Prize Act (59 of 1971), S. 4(3)].

Reproach. The word "reproach" is synoymous with the words "censure" and "obloquy". Reproof.

Reproachful. Deserving censure. [Navy Act (62 of 1957), S. 48(b)].

Reprobate. Reject; to disapprove of; condemn. To REPROBATE, CONDEMN. To reprobate is much stronger than to condemn; we always condemn when we reprobate, but not *vice versa*; to reprobate is to condemn in strong and reproachful language. We reprobate all measures which tend to sow discard in society and to loosen the ties by which men are bound to each other; we condemn all disrespectful language towards superiors.

Reproducing. Producing again. [General Clauses Act (10 of 1897), S. 3(65)].

Reproduction. The action or process of bringing again before the mind in the same form. The Action or process of repeating in a copy. A copy or counterpart. A copy of a picture or other work of art by means of engraving or some other process and finally a representation in some form or by some means of the essential features of a thing. *B.C.S. Bureau* v. *United Concern,* AIR 1967 Mad 381, 387. [Copyright Act (14 of 1957), S. 2(m) (iv)]

Reprography. Reprography means the making of copies of a work, by photocopying or similar means. [Copyright Act (14 of 1957), S. 2(x)]

Reprography consists of the process of photocopying of graphic material; Reproduction in the form of a copy on paper or an assimilated medium by means of a photographic process or one having equivalent effect permitting direct reading. [French Code, Article L. 122-10] (*Copyright*)

Republic. A republic is a government for the protection of the citizens against the exercise of all unjust power. It is a government administered by a few, as the representatives of the people and for their benefit.

Republican government. A government in the republican form; a government of the people; a government by representatives chosen by the people. *In re Duncan*, 139 US 449 : 11 S Ct 573 : 35 L Ed 219.

Repudiate. To reject (a charge *etc.*) with denial, as being quite unfounded or inapplicable; to disown or disavow. [Indian Contract Act (9 of 1872), S. 215 and S. 215, ill. (b)].

Repudiate the suit. To disown or disavow the suit. [CPC (5 of 1908), O. XXXII, R. 13(1)].

Repudiation. The renunciation of a right, contract or obligation.

Repugnance. One meaning given of "repugnance" is "inconsistency." These words, though not exactly synonymous, may be and often are used interchangeably.

Repugnancy. Repugnancy between two statutes may be ascertained on the basis of the following three principles; (1) whether there is direct conflict between the two provisions; (2) whether the parliament intended to lay down an exhaustive code in respect of the subject matter replacing the Act of the State Legislature; and (3) whether the law made by parliament and the law made by the state legislature occupy the same field. *Deb Chand* v. *State of U.P.*, AIR 1959 SC 648, 665. [Constitution of India, Art. 254]

To the extent of contradiction.

Repugnant. Contrary or contradictory (to); inconsistent or incompatible (with) [T.P. Act (4 of 1882), S. 3; Companies Act (1 of 1956), S. 9(b) and Indian Railways Act (9 of 1890), S. 3].

The concurrent list is not a forbidden field to the State Legislature and the mere fact that the State Legislature has legislated on a matter in the Concurrent List is not enough to attract the mischief of Art. 254. There must be actual repugnancy between such legislation and existing law as required by Art. 254 (1). *Mangtulal* v. *Radha Shyam,* AIR 1953 Pat 14, 20. [Constitution of India, Art. 254]

'Repugnant to' really means 'inconsistent with'. One law is inconsistent with another law when the command or power or provision in the one law conflicts directly with the command or power or provision in the other. *Vishnu Vishnu Bhattathiripad* v. *Poulopoulo,* AIR 1953 TC 327, 335.

Repugnant in the subject or context. Contrary or contradictory to the subject or context. [CPC (5 of 1908), S. 2 and General Clauses Act (10 of 1897), S. 4(1)].

Reputatio est vulgaris opinio ubi non est veritas. Reputation is a common opinion where there is no certain knowledge.

Reputation. Credit, honour, character, good name.

The common or general estimate of a person with respect to character or other qualities. [Indian Evidence Act (1 of 1872), S. 55, *Expln.* and IPC (45 of 1860), S. 44].

"To have a good name; the credit, honour, or character which is derived from a favourable public opinion or esteem and character by report." Personal rights of a human being include the right of reputation. [*Umesh Kumar v. State of A.P.*, (2013) 10 SCC 591, para 18].

Reputation is a sort of right to enjoy the opinion of others and it is a personal right and an enquiry to reputation is a personal injury. Thus, scandal and defamation are injurious to reputation. [*Umesh Kumar v. State of Andhra Pradesh*, (2013) 10 SCC 591, para 18].

Reputation is fundamentally a glorious amalgam and unification of virtues which makes a man feel proud of his ancestry and satisfies him to bequeath it as a part of inheritance on posterity. It is a nobility in itself for which a conscientious man would never barter it with all the tea of China or for that matter all the pearls of the sea. The said virtue has both horizontal and vertical qualities. When reputation is hurt, a man is half-dead. It is an honour which deserves to be equally preserved by the downtrodden and the privileged. The aroma of reputation is an excellence which cannot be allowed to be sullied with the passage of time. The memory of nobility no one would like to lose; none would conceive of it being atrophied. It is dear to life and on some occasions it is dearer than life. [*Om Prakash Chautala v. Kanwar Bhan*, (2014) 5 SCC 417, para 1].

Repute. Reputation; distinction; honour; credit [University Grants Commission Act (3 of 1956), S. 5(3)(c)(iii)].

Reputed owner. One who has, to all appearances, the right of ownership or actual possession of property.

An insolvent not stopping business long prior to filing of insolvency petition but was active till the filing the petition, is not a reputed owner. *In the Matter of P.K. Pattbiraman,* AIR 1989 Mad 271, 274. [Presidency Towns Insolvency Act (3 of 1909), S. 52(2)(c)]

Request. A demand or requirement.

The act on the part of a specified person of asking for some service *etc.*; the expression of one's desire directly addressed to the person or persons able to gratify it to ask or ask for (something). [Indian Contract Act (9 of 1872), S. 145, ill. (b)].

Require. "Require" means "to make necessary; to demand; to ask as of right."

To demand as neccessary or essential on general principles or in order to comply with some regulation. [T.P. Act (4 of 1882), S. 37, ill. (b)].

Required. Called for or demanded as appropriate or suitable in the particular case. [CrPC 1973 (2 of 1974), S. 52].

Required to give evidence. The words 'required to give evidence' denote not voluntary act of giving evidence by a party in his favour, but required to do so by the other side or the Court. *Syed Yasin* v. *Syed Mohd. Hussain,* AIR 1967 Mys 37, 39. [CPC (5 of 1908), O. XVI, R. 21]

Requirement. That which is required; a need; a want; the act of requiring; a request.

Requiring body. Means a company, a body corporate, an institution, or any other organization or person for whom land is to be acquired by the appropriate Government, and includes the appropriate Government, if the acquisition of land is for such Government either for its own use or for subsequent transfer of such land is for public purpose to a company, body corporate, an institution, or any other organization, as the case may be, under lease, licence or through any other mode of transfer of land. [S. 3(zb) of the Right to Fair Compensation & Transparency in Land Acquisition, Rehabilitation & Resettlement Act, 2013 (30 of 2013)]

Requisite. The word 'requisite" is a strong word; it may be regarded as meaning something more than the word required. It means "*properly required.*" *Santimoney Dey* v. *Suriya Properties Pvt. Ltd.,* AIR 1976 Cal 81, 82, 83.

Required by the circumstances or the nature of things [T.P. Act (4 of 1882), Ss. 34 and 103]; [CPC (5 of 1908), O. XXVI, R. 9].

Requisite majority. With regard to Special Resolution means votes cast in favour of the business is three times more than the votes cast against, with regard to ordinary resolution, votes cast in favour is more than the votes cast against. [Companies (Passing of the Resolutions by Postal Ballot) Rules, 2001, R. 2(c)]

Requisition. The formal demand by one government upon another of the surrender of a fugitive criminal.

A requirement; the act of formally requiring one to perform some action, discharge some duty *etc.* [CrPC 1973 (2 of 1974), S. 41(i)]; [T.P. Act (4 of 1882), S. 60A(2)]; the taking of possession of property for a limited period for the purpose of the State or for such purposes as may be specified in the statute [Defence and Internal Security of India Act (42 of 1971), S. 3(2)(31)].

"Requisition" and "Acquisition". Requisition is not included in acquisition but it is separate and distinct from acquisition. 'Acquisition' is used only in the sense of compulsory acquisition of land which is enacted in the Land Acquisition Act (I of 1894) or the compulsory purchase of land which is known to English Law. 'Requisition' is always understood to mean a dominion or control of the property and not the acquisition of the rights of ownership.

The word 'requisition' in S. 41(1)(i) of the CrPC 1973 (2 of 1974) is quite general and clearly covers a message communicated by telephone or wireless. *Roshan Lal* v. *Supt. Central Jail,* AIR 1950 MB 83.

The word 'requisition' in S. 41(1)(i) CrPC 1973 (2 of 1974) is of wide import. The words 'it appears therefrom' in the clause indicate that the requisition must be in writing; the words do not go well with a verbal requisition. *State* v. *Ram Chandra,* AIR 1955 All 438, 442.

"Requisition" is the term used where the title in the property remains unaffected, but the titleholder is deprived of its use for a time. In such a case, the compensation being for loss of profits, becomes a revenue receipt. *Commissioner of Income-tax* v. *Sudhanshu Mazumdar,* AIR 1971 SC 1594. [Land Acquisition Act (1 of 1894), Ss. 3 & 4]

Requisition order. An order passed by the State taking possession of a property passed for a temporary period; such orders are generally passed during an emergency.

Requisition to supply. The words 'requisition to supply' is not confined to requisitions made after the commencement of Section 47-A, but would also include requisitions made prior to it. *Mirzapur Electric Supply Co. Ltd.* v. *State of U.P.,* AIR 1975 All 29, 33. [Electricity (Supply) Act (54 of 1948), S. 47-A]

Requisitioned land. The expression "REQUISITIONED LAND" means any immovable property which is, or was, subject to any requisition effected under the rules made under the Defence of India Act, 1939, or continued under the Requisition Land (Continuance of Powers) Act, 1947. [Requisitioned Land (Apportionment of Compensation) Act (51 of 1949), S. 2(b)]

Requisitioning. In relation to any property means "take possession of the property or require the property to be placed at the disposal of the requisitioning authority" [Naval and Aircraft Prize Act (59 of 1971), S. 7(d)]; to require some one to perform some action.

Requisitioning and acquisition. Requisitioning and acquisition are two different concepts in law, requisitioning implying only a temporary deprivation of the owner, of the use and possession of a property, acquisition implying a transference of the property, or all rights thereto. In requisitioning, the title remains with the owner, but he is excluded by the State from the right to the possession or enjoyment of the property, but acquisition is the acquiring of the entire title of the expropriated owner whatever the nature or extent of that title may be. *Ouseph Martha* v. *State of Kerela,* MLJ : QD (1961-1965) Vol I C1940 : (1960) 1 Ker LR 364 : ILR (1960) Ker 464 [Travancore-Cochin Requisitioning and Acquisition of Property Act (1 of 1956), S. 1]

Res. In the civil law, a term said to signify a thing an object.

"Res" means "everything that may form an object of rights and includes an object, subject-matter or status." [*Dr. Subramanian Swami v. State of T.N.*, (2014) 5 SCC 75, para 39].

Res accessoria cedit rei principalii. An accessory thing belongs to the principal thing.

Res accessoria sequitur rem principalem. (*Lat.*) The accessory follows the principal. (*Latin for Lawyers*)

Res adjudicata. "*Res adjudicata*" means that if an action be brought, and the merits of the question be discussed between the parties, and a final judgment be obtained by either party, the parties are concluded, and cannot agitate the same question in another action. It is founded upon two maxims of the law, one of which is that a man should not be twice vexed for the same cause, and the other that it is for the public good that there be an end of litigation.

RES ADJUDICATA is a matter adjudged; a thing judicially acted on or decided. The principle is that the decision of a Court of competent jurisdiction upon a point which is or should have been construed as necessarily involved is final and conclusive. [CPC (5 of 1908), S. 11]

Matters once determined by a Court of competent jurisdiction can never be questioned. It matters not under what form the question be presented. Whenever the same question recurs between the same parties, the plea of *res adjudicata* estops.

Res communes. Common things; things common to all by the law of nature

Things common to all.

Res derelicta. Property that has been abandoned by its owner.

Res est misera ubi jus est vagum et incertum. *(2 Salk. 512).* It is a miserable state of things where the law is vague and uncertain.

Res gestae. Things done, or liberally speaking, the facts of the transaction; the facts of a transaction, explanatory of an act or showing a motive for acting; matters incidental to a main fact and explanatory of it, including acts and words which are so closely connected with a main fact as will constitute a part of it, and without a knowledge of which the main fact might not be properly understood; events speaking for themselves through the instinctive words and acts of participants, not the words and acts of participants when narrating the events; the circumstances, facts and declarations which grow out of the main fact, or are contemporaneous with it and serve to illustrate its character; those circumstances which are the automic and undersigned incidents of a particular litigated act, and are admissible when illustrative of such act.

Acts; declarations and incidents accompanying or explaining the fact in issue or which are deemed to constitute the fact in issue; facts so connected with a fact in issue as to form part of the same transaction.

The test of whether or not declaration are *res gestae* is, were the the facts talking through the party or the party's talk about the facts? Instinctiveness is the requisite, and when this exists the declarations are admissible.

Res immobiles. Immovable things.

Res incorporales. Incorporeal things.

Res integra. Matter not yet decided.

Res inter alios acta alteri nocere non debet. A thing done between others ought not to injure another.

Res inter alios judicatae nullum aliis praejudicium faciunt. Things adjudged in a cause do not prejudice those who were not parties to it.

Res ipsa loquitur. A phrase meaning "The thing speaks for itself"; "the affair speaks for itself;" a general way of saying that the circumstances attendant upon an accident are of themselves of such a character as to justify in inferring negligence as the cause of that accident.

The principle of '*res ipsa loquitur*' may be applied to infer negligence but it cannot be applied to infer misconduct. [Indian Railways Act (9 of 1890), Ss. 74-C, 72].

This rule generally applies only to those cases where the exact cause of the accident is unknown. The maxim is merely a rule of evidence, affecting onus.

This maxim suggests that on the circumstances of a given case the *Res* speaks and is elequent because the facts stand unexplained, with the result that the natural and reasonable inference from the facts—not a conjectural inference—shows that the act is attributable to some person's negligent conduct. The effect of this maxim, however depends on the cogency of the inferences to be drawn and must therefore vary in each case.

The maxim '*res ipsa loquitur*' means that an accident by its nature be more consistent with its being caused by negligence. In such a case, the mere fact of the accident is *prima facie* evidence of the negligence.

The maxim *res ipsa loquitur* (the thing speak for itself) applies to a motor accident caused by the breaking down of the spindle of front wheel of a bus.

This maxim is applicable in actions for injury by negligence where no proof of negligence is required beyond the accident itself, which is such as necessarily involves negligence.

"RES IPSA LOQUITUR" imports that the plaintiff has made out a *prima facie* case without any direct proof of actionable negligence.

The thing speaks for itself; this maxim means that in certain cases one fact raises *prima facie* presumption of another fact unless and until the contrary is proved. This phrase is used in actions for injury occasioned by negligence where no proof is required of negligence beyond the accident itself.

Res judicata. A matter adjudged; the legal principle that prevents interminable relitigation of the merits of a case by foreclosing other than the pertinent appellate tribunals from deciding the merits of a case once a Court of competent jurisdiction has rendered judgment. (CRAIG R. DUCAT—*Constitutional Interpretation*)

"*Res Judicata*" means "a matter adjudged; a thing judicially acted upon or decided; a thing or matter settled by judgments". [*Dr. Subramanian Swami v. State of T.N.*, (2014) 5 SCC 75, para 39].

Corpus Juris explains that res judicata is a rule of universal law pervading every well-regulated system of jurisprudence, and is put upon two grounds, embodies in various maxims of the common law; the one, public policy and necessity, which makes it to the interest of the State that there should be an end to litigation; and other, the hardship on the individual that he should be vexed twice for the same cause. [*State of T.N. v. State of Kerala*, (2014) 12 SCC 696, para 163] [Corpus Juris].

A case or suit already decided. [CPC (5 of 1908), S. 11].

Res judicata ; Res adjudicata. A matter adjudged; a thing judically acted upon or decided; a thing or matter settled by judgment; a thing definitely settled by judicial decision, the thing adjudged.

Res judicata" literally means a "thing adjudicated" or "an issue that has been definitely settled by judicial decision". The principle operates as a bar to try the same issue once over. It aims to prevent multiplicity of proceedings and accords finality to an issue, which directly or substantially had arisen in the former suit between the same parties or their privies and was decided and has become final, so that the parties are not vexed twice over; vexatious litigation is put to an end to and valuable time of the court is saved. [*Nagabhushammal* v. *C. Chandikeshwaralingam,* (2016) 4 SCC 434, para 15].

'*Res judicata*' and 'estoppel' (distinction). Sometimes the doctrine of *res judicata* is considered as branch of law of estoppel. There is distinction between doctrine of *res judicata*, principle of 'issue estoppel' and 'rule estoppel' under S. 115 of the Act. Doctrine of *res judicata* creates legal embargo on the hands of the Court to a judicial determination of deciding the same question over again even though earlier determination may be demonstrably erroneous. When the proceedings between the same parties have attained finality, they are bound by the judgment and cannot be permitted to reagitate the same *lis*. The determination of the issue in the same set of the facts in the previous *lis* between the parties would give rise to an issue estoppel. It operates in any subsequent proceedings between the same parties.

The doctrine of *res judicata* is based on rule of procedure. However doctrine of mere estoppel is based on rule of evidence. In case of estoppel under S. 115 of the Act, there is embargo on the party to plead or prove a particular fact whereas in case of *res judicata*, the prohibition is operative against the Court to deal with the same kind of issue again and again. [*Yamunabai Purushottam Deogirikar* v. *Mathurabai Nilkanth Choudhari*, AIR 2010 (NOC) 109 (Bom) : 2009 (5) AIR Bom R 742] [CPC (5 of 1908), S. 11 and Evidence Act (1 of 1872), S. 115]

Res judicata pro veritate accipitur. A matter adjudged is taken for truth.

The full maxim which has, over the years, shrunk to mere 'res judicata', which means that res judicata is accepted for truth. [*Dr. Subramanian Swami v. State of T.N.*, (2014) 5 SCC 75, para 39].

Res judicata pro veritate habetur. An adjudicated matter shall be deemed correct.

Res loquitur. The phrase "*res loquitur*," which literally translated, means that "the thing speaks for itself," is merely a short way of saying that the circumstances attendant upon an accident are, of themselves, of such a character as to justify a jury in inferring negligence as the cause of that accident.

Res nullius. Things belonging to no one; the property of nobody. A thing which has no owner.

Res sua nemini servit. (*Lat.*) No one can have a servitude over his own property.

Res sub judice. Matters pending judicial inquiry.

Resale price maintenance. Includes any agreement to sell goods on condition that the prices to be charged on the resale by the purchaser shall be the prices stipulated by the seller unless it is clearly stated this prices lower than those prices may be charged. [Competition Act, 2002 (12 of 2003), S. 3(4) *Expln.*(e)]

Rescind. To rescind is to abrogate, annul, avoid, or cancel a contract.

To do away with; to annul; to cancel [Institutes of Technology Act (59 of 1961), S. 6(1)(i)]; [Indian Evidence Act (1 of 1872), S. 92, *Prov*., (4)].

Rescission. The undoing of a thing.

The action of rescinding or the fact of being rescinded. [CPC (5 of 1908), 1st Sch., App. A, form No. 34].

Rescue. A rescue is defined to be "when a man lawfully arrested and taken is set at large wrongfully."

"RESCUE, is the act of forcibly freeing a person from custody against the will of those who have him in custody. If the person rescued is in the custody of a private person, the offender must have notice of the fact that the person rescued is in such custody." (*Steph. Cr. Law* 99, 100.)

RESCUE OF PERSONS. Rescue at law is forcibly and knowingly freeing another from arrest or imprisonment. Rescue consists in a high contempt of the law in preventing the operation of its process. The rescuers are, in any event, whether the party rescued be convicted or not, guilty of obstructing public justice. The essential element of the offence, at law, are (1) valid arrest; (2) actual custody; (3) the forcibly and knowingly freeing a person from arrest or custody; and (4) escape of the prisoner.

RESCUE OF PROPERTY. Rescue of property is the taking away and setting at liberty of a distrained animal against law, or the recaption of goods distrained.

RESCUE AND AIDING ESCAPE BY PRISONER. A rescue takes place where there is no effort on the part of the prisoner to escape, but his delivery is effected by the interference of others without his co-operation, whereas the offence of aiding a prisoner to escape consists inciting, supporting, and re-enforcing his exertions in his own behalf tending to the accomplishment of the object.

Research. "RESEARCH" means study or systematic investigation of any biological resource or technological application, that uses biological systems, living organisms or derivatives thereof to make or modify products of processes for any use. [Biological Diversity Act 2002 (18 of 2003), S. 2(m)]

An investigation directed to the discovery of some fact; careful study of a subject. [Payment of Bonus Act (21 of 1965), Sch. II, item 3(d)].

Research Advisory Committee. Means the Research Advisory Committee of the University. [S. 3(o) of the Rani Lakshmi Bai Central Agricultural University Act, 2014 (10 of 2014)]

Resemble. Being similar or like. [CPC (5 of 1908), App. F, form No. 8]; [Drugs and Consmetics Act (23 of 1940), S. 9(2)].

Reservation. "RESERVATION" means reservation of posts in the services for the members of schedules castes, the scheduled tribes and other backward classes. [Madhya Pradesh Lok Seva (Anusuchit Jatiyon, Anusuchit Jan Jation Aur Anya Pichhade Vargon ke liye Arakshan) Adhiniyam (M.P. Act No. 21 of 1994), S. 2(c)]

"RESERVATION" means a unilateral statement, however phrased or named, made by a state, when signing, ratifying, accepting, approving or acceding to a treaty, whereby it purports to exclude or to modify the legal effect of certain provisions of the treaty in their application to that state. [Vienna Convention on Succession of States in Respect of Treaties, 1978; Vienna Convention on the Law of Treaties (1969), Art. 2(d)]

A keeping aside, or providing as when a man lets or parts with his land, but reserves or provides for himself a rent out of it for his own livelihood; sometimes it has the force of a saving or exception. (*Co. Litt.* 143; *Tomlin*)

The action of reserving or the fact of being reserved. [T.P. Act (4 of 1882), S. 48 and Constitution of India, Art. 16(4)].

Reservation : Selection. 'Reservation' was something different from the 'selection' of permissible area. The two terms were not only not synonymous but were mutually exclusive. 'Selection' of permissible area was allowed only to a landlord who had not exercised his right of 'reservation'. *Lajpat Rai* v. *State of Punjab,* AIR 1981 SC 1401.

Reserve. Money or its equivalent kept in hand or set apart usually to meet a specified liability or anticipated liabilities [Companies (Profits) Surtax Act (7 of 1964), Sch. II, R. 1(v), *Expln.*]; to retain or secure some right or profit for oneself or another by formal stipulation; to set apart a thing for some purpose or with some end in view; to keep for some use [Sale of Goods Act (3 of 1930), S. 23(2)]; something specially kept apart for future use or for a specific occasion [Motor Vehicles Act (59 of 1988), S. 48(3)(xvi)].

One ordinary natural meaning of the word 'reserve' is "to set apart for some purpose or with some end in view, to keep for some use". *Commissioner of Income Tax Business Profits Tax* v. *Vasantha Mills Ltd.,* AIR 1958 Mad 326, 330. [Business Profits Tax Act (21 of 1947), Sch. 2, R. 2 (1) *Expln.*]

A reserve can only mean profit earned by a company and not distributed as dividend to the shareholders but kept back by the directors for any purpose to which it may be put in future. *First National City Bank* v. *I.T. Commissioner*, AIR 1961 SC 812, 816.

In its ordinary meaning the expression 'reserve' means something specially kept apart for future use or for a specific occasion. Earned surplus, an account in which the net profits less the appropriations are added year after year, represents reserve. *I.T. Commissioner (Central) Calcutta* v. *Standard Vacuum Oil Co.*, AIR 1966 SC 1393, 1401, 1402.

The Institute of Chartered Accountants, England has defined, 'reserve' as 'amount set aside out of profits and other surpluses, which is not designed to meet any liability, contingency, commitment or diminution in value of assets known to exist as at the date of the balance sheet. *Recommendations on Accounting Principles*, No. VI, Para 43. [Companies Act (1 of 1956), S. 217]

Reserve Bank. Means the Reserve Bank of India constituted under S. 3 of the Reserve Bank of India Act, 1934 (2 of 1934). [S. 2(q) of the Factoring Regulation Act, 2011 (12 of 2012)]

Reserve forces. Reserve force is a force which is not intended to become operative ordinarily, but would become operative whenever the situation demands. *State of Bengal* v. *Tarun Kumar Sen Gupta,* AIR 1974 Cal 39, 43. [Central Reserve Police Force Act (66 of 1949), S. 3]

Reserve forest. "RESERVED FOREST" means and includes a forest and every part of a forest—(*a*) declared to be a reserved forest under the provisions of this Act or the corresponding S. of any enactment previously in force; or (*b*) declared to be a reserved forest under the provisions of any rules in force, [Bur. Act IV of 1902 (Forests), S. 3, cl. 11]

Reserve fund. A fund set apart by a company, firm or institution, over and above its capital, to provide for contingencies. [Companies (Profits) Surtax Act (7 of 1964), Sch. I, R. 1(xi)(a)]; [Income-tax Act (43 of 1961), S. 236(2), *Expln.*].

Reserve Price. It is the price with which the public auction starts and the auction bidders are not permitted to give bids below the said price i.e., the minimum bid at auction. [*State of U.P.* v. *Shiv Charan Sharma*, 1981, Supp SCC 85 : AIR 1981 SC 1722 as cited in *Ram Kishun* v. *State of U.P.*, (2012) 11 SCC 511, para 19].

Reserve; reserved. The expression 'RESERVE' shall not, subject to aforesaid, include any amount written off or retained by way of providing for depreciation, renewals or diminution in value of assets or retained by way of providing for any known liability. [Companies Act (1 of 1956), Part III, Sch. VI]

Reserved bidding. An amount below which a property put up for auction is not to be sold. [CPC (5 of 1908), 1st Sch., App. D, form No. 21].

Reserved price. A price announced at an auction as the least that will be entertained. [Indian Contract Act (9 of 1872)), S. 237, ill. (a)].

Reserves. The expression reserves cannot be given any technical meaning but must be construed in its 'plain natural meaning,—A reserve can only mean profit earned by a company and not distributed as dividend to the share-holders but kept back by the directors for any purpose to which it may be put in future. *Commissioner of Income Tax* v. *Century Spinning and Manufacturing Co.*, AIR 1951 Bom 420.

Reservoir. In common speech, a "reservoir" often signifies the water kept, not the structure in which it is kept.Place where something is kept in store; a tank. [Cantonments Act (2 of 1924), S. 134(1)].

"A pond, lake or basin, either natural or artificial, for the storage, regulation and control of water." [Glossary of Irrigation and Hydro-Electric Terms and Standard Notations used in India, 3rd Edn., published by the Central Board of Irrigation and Power as cited in *State of Andhra Pradesh* v. *State of Maharashtra*, (2013) 5 SCC 68, para 56.5].

Resettlement. The act of settling again. [Damodar Valley Corporation Act (14 of 1948), S. 22(3)]; [Constitution of India, Art. 7, prov.].

Resettlement area. Means an area where the affected families who have been displaced as a result of land acquisition are resettled by the appropriate Government. [S. 3(zc) of the Right to Fair Compensation & Transparency in Land Acquisition, Rehabilitation & Resettlement Act, 2013 (30 of 2013)]

Reside. "RESIDE",—

(a) a person shall be deemed to "RESIDE" in any dwelling-house which or some portion of which he sometimes, although not uninterruptedly, uses as a sleeping apartment, and

(b) a person shall not be deemed to cease to 'RESIDE' in any such dwelling house merely because he is absent from it or has elsewhere another dwelling-house in which he resides, if there is the liberty of returning to it at any time and no abandonment of the intention of returning to it. [New Delhi Municipal Council Act (44 of 1994), S. 2(44)]

Reside and residing together. The word 'reside' connotes some degree of continuity of stay in a place and the words 'residing together' consequently mean that the persons residing together have continuously stayed together in the same dwelling for some time. *Clearance* v. *Raicheel,* AIR 1964 Mys 67, 69. [Indian Divorce Act (4 of 1869), S. 3(3)]

The word 'resided' does not refer to permanent residence. It implies something more than a brief visit but not such a continuity as to amount to domicile. *Sampoornam* v. *N. Sundaresan,* AIR 1953 Mad 78. [CrPC, 1973 (2 of 1974), S. 126(1)]

Reside : Residence. The word "reside" is used in two senses—the one, constructive, technical, legal; the other, denoting the personal, actual habitation of individuals. When a person has a fixed abode, where he dwells with his family, there can be no doubt as to the place where he resides. The place of his personal and legal residence is the same, so that when a person has no permanent habitation or family, but dwells in different places, as he happens to find employment, there can be no doubt as to the place where he resides. He must be considered as residing where he actually or personally resides. But some individuals have permanent habitations where their families constantly dwell, yet pass a great portion of their time in other places. Such persons have a legal residence with their families, and a personal residence in other places; and the word "reside" may, with respect to them, be used to denote either their personal or their legal residence.

A person who has an abode elsewhere, but who comes to a place for a short period and with a fixed purpose for being within the jurisdiction of a Court cannot be said to "reside" there.

The word "reside", as used in S. 2 of the Indian Divorce Act (4 of 1869) implies a dwelling either of a permanent nature or for some considerable time. It cannot therefore apply to the stay of a person who has a permanent abode elsewhere and who merely comes to India for the purpose of filing a suit under the Act with the intention of returning to his permanent abode on the conclusion of the litigation.

Intention of the spouses to live together in a place is not necessary. If the purpose of the spouse is to have company each other and to eat, drink and sleep together, it will constitute residence of the spouse, the visit of the spouse, the visit of the spouses to each other even for short duration being immaterial. S. *Saroja* v. *P.G. Emmanuel,* AIR 1965 Mys 12, 15. [Indian Divorce Act (4 of 1869), S. 3(3)]

The word "resided" is not defined by the Act. In its dictionary sense of the word, 'to reside', means, to dwell permanently or for a long period, temporary place of residence or a casual place of stay is thus excluded from being called a residence. *T. Sareetha* v. *T. Venkata Subbaiah,* AIR 1983 AP 356, 361. [Hindu Marriage Act (25 of 1955), S. 19(iii)].

Where both the parties are working at two different places having their separate residential houses, both places would be fit for the residence of the spouses. if they visit each other, such visits cannot be termed as casual or flying, and they would come under the terms 'resides' and 'resided'. *Pritma Sharma* v. *Mohinder S. Bharadwaj,* AIR 1984 P&H 305, 307.

Residence. "RESIDENCE" includes the staff quarters and other buildings appurtenant thereto, and the garden thereof, and "maintenance" in relation to a residence includes the payment of local rates and taxes and the provision of electricity and water. [Salaries and Allowances of Ministers Act (58 of 1952), S. 4(2) *Expln.*; Salaries and Allowances of Officers of Parliament Act (20 of 1953), S. 4(b), *Expln.*]

"RESIDENCE" means the use for human habitation of any land or building or part thereof including gardens, grounds, garages, stables and out-houses, if any, appertaining to such building, and the expression 'residential' shall be construed accordingly. [W.B. Town and Country (Planning and Development) Act (13 of 1979), S. 2(24)]

The fact or act of dwelling in a place for sometime [T.P. Act (4 of 1882), S. 106 and Constitution of India, Art. 16(2)]; a temporary or permanent dwelling place.

Every person has in law a residence or domicile. In determining the place of residence the following rules should be observed; (1) It is the place where one remains when not called elsewhere for labour or other special or temporary purpose, and to which he returns in seasons of repose. (2) There can only be one residence. (3) A residence cannot be lost until another is gained. (4) The residence of the father during his life and after his death and the residence of the mother while she remains unmarried, is the residence of an unmarried minor child. (5) The residence of the husband is the residence of the wife. (6) The residence can be changed only by the union of act and intent.

A person is to be deemed to reside at the place where he actually and voluntarily resides and carries on business; and he cannot be said to reside at a place where he has the family home and which he only occasionally visit.

The word 'residence' may receive a larger or more restricted meaning according to what the Court believes the intention of the legislature to have been in framing the particular provision in which the word is used. The word in O. XXV, R. 1, CPC (5 of 1908) was intended by the legislature to mean a residence under such circumstances as would afford reasonable probability that the plaintiff would be forthcoming when the suit was decided.

"Residence" connotes something more than stay; it implies some intention to remain at a place and not merely to pay it a casual visit. By staying in a particular place, the intention must be to make it his or their abode or residence either permanent or temporary. *Ponnen* v. *Rathi Varghese,* AIR 1967 Ker 1, 12 (FB). [Indian Divorce Act (4 of 1869), S. 3(3)]

Where by choice a particular place is made an abode permanently or even temporarily it is a residence. It excludes the place where his family eat, drink and sleep. *Paster J.S. Singh* v. *Jyotsama Singh,* AIR 1982 MP 123, 124.

Resides must mean the actual place of residence and not a legal or constructive residence. It certainly does not connote the place of origin. The word 'resides' is a flexible one and has many shades of meaning, but it must take its colour and content from the context in which it appears and cannot be read in isolation. *Jeewanti Pandey* v. *Krishan Chandra Pandey*, AIR 1982 SC 3, 5. [Hindu Marriage Act (25 of 1955), S. 19, Cl. (ii)]

An established home where a person's wife and children live is undoubtedly his residence for the purposes of S. 106. T.P. Act even though he may be employed elsewhere. A place is a person's residence if he has lived there and has freely exercised his intention of remaining there permanently or for a length of time. *Manoharlal Naneemal* v. *Mohanlal Krishunlal,* AIR 1960 MP 167, 168. [Transfer of Property Act (4 of 1882), S. 106]

"RESIDENCE". A 'residence' ordinarily means a place where one resides; the act or fact of abiding or dwelling in a place for some time; an act of making one's home in a place. *Associated Indem Mechanical (P.) Ltd.* v. *West Bengal S.S.I.D.C. Ltd.*, AIR 2007 SC 788 : 2007 AIR SCW 489.

'Residence' and 'domicile'. Etymologically, 'residence' and 'domicile' carry the same meaning, in as much as both refer to the permanent home but under private international law, 'domicile' carries a little different sense and exhibits many facets. In spite of having a permanent home, a person may have a commercial, a political or forensic domicile. 'Domicile' and 'residence' are relative concepts and have to be understood in the context in which these words are used. [*Union of India* v. *Dudh Nath Prasad,* (2000) 2 SCC 20, 30, 31]

Residence order. Means an order granted in terms of S. 19(1) of Act 43 of 2005. [S. 2(p) of the Protection of Women from Domestic Violence Act, 2005 (43 of 2005)]

Section 19(1) of Act 43 of 2005 : (1) While disposing of an application under sub-section (1) of section 12, the Magistrate may, on being satisfied that domestic violence has taken place, pass a residence order—

(a) restraining the respondent from dispossessing or in any other manner disturbing the possession of the aggrieved person from the shared household, whether or not the respondent has a legal or equitable interest in the shared household;

(b) directing the respondent to remove himself from the shared household;

(c) restraining the respondent or any of his relatives from entering any portion of the shared household in which the aggrieved person resides;

(d) restraining the respondent from alienating or disposing off the shared household or encumbering the same;

(e) restraining the respondent from renouncing his rights in the shared household except with the leave of the Magistrate; or

(f) directing the respondent to secure same level of alternate accommodation for the aggrieved person as enjoyed by her in the shared household or to pay rent for the same, if the circumstances so require:

Provided that no order under clause (b) shall be passed against any person who is a Woman.

Resident. The word "RESIDENT" denotes the chief civil officer at Aden appointed by the Government, by whatever designation such officer may be called, and includes any Acting Resident or officer acting temporarily as such chief civil officer. [Bom. Act II of 1864 (Aden Civil & Cri. Justice), S. 1].

"RESIDENT" means a person holding a valid passport issued under the Passports Act, 1967 (15 of 1967) and normally residing in India. [Baggage Rules, 2016, R. 2(1)(iv)]

The word "resident" has the same meaning as "inhabitant," and means one who dwells or resides permanently in a place.

The words "RESIDENT" AND 'INHABITANT' are not synonymous; the latter implying a more fixed and permanent abode than the former.

Resident abroad. One who resides permanently abroad. [Indian Contract Act (9 of 1872), S. 230(1)].

Resident in India. A person who is residing in India. [Income-tax Act (43 of 1961), S. 2(42)].

"RESIDENT IN INDIA". For the purpose of Schedule V of Act 18 of 2013, 'resident in India' includes a person who has been staying in India for a continuous period of not less than twelve months immediately preceding the date of his appointment as a managerial person and who has come to stay in India,—

(*i*) for taking up employment in India; or

(*ii*) for carrying on a business or vacation in India. [*Explanation I* to Part I of Schedule V of the Companies Act, 2013 (18 of 2013)]

For the purposes of this rule, the term "resident in India" means a person who has stayed in India for a period of not less than one hundred and twenty days during the immediately preceding financial year. [Companies (Incorporation) Rules, 2014, rule 3(1), *Explanation I*]

"RESIDENT IN INDIA". For the purposes of rule 3 of the Companies (Incorporation) Rules, 2014, the term 'resident in India' means a person who has stayed in India for a period of not less than one hundred and eighty two days during the immediately preceding one calendar year. [*Explanation* to Rule 3(1) of the Companies (Incorporation) Rules, 2014]

Resident of India. An Indian employed abroad comes back to his country and lives in his home for a certain period. During that period, he is 'residing in India' within the meaning of the term. *Mary Kurian* v. *T.T. Joseph,* AIR 1980 Ker 131, 134. [Indian Divorce Act (4 of 1869), S. 2]

A person who is a resident of India. [Cost and Works Accountants Act (23 of 1959), S. 4(1)(i)].

Resident within Jurisdiction. The expression "any person within the local limits" in S. 110 of the CrPC 1973 (2 of 1974), means any person who is within the local limits at the time the Magistrate takes action under the section. The object of the section is to prevent crime and that object would be defeated if its scope were restricted to persons *residing* within the jurisdiction of the Magistrate. Consequently, a Magistrate has jurisdiction to take security from a person who resides outside the jurisdiction of the Magistrate but is found within the local limits of his jurisdiction.

A person residing with his wife, within the jurisdiction of a Magistrate can be tried by him under section 110, CrPC 1973 (2 of 1974), though he happens to be outside the jurisdiction when arrested under section 41(2), CrPC 1973 (2 of 1974).

Residential. The word 'residential' and other cogerate expressions such as, 'reside', 'residing', 'resident', 'residence', 'residences' and 'occupy' occurring in several statutes have variously shaded but elastic meaning. A person is ordinarily said to 'reside' where he lives with his family. The word 'residence' connotes two elements, (1) actual or physical habitation and (2) the intention to remain there permanently that is, for an unlimited time. In its ordinary sense, the word 'reside' carries with it the idea of permanence, that is for any length of time, as well as, continuity. The word 'residence' denotes a dwelling house where a person lives in a settled abode. *Firm Gangaram Kishore Chand* v. *Firm Jai Ram Bhagat Ram,* AIR 1957 Punj 293, 296. [CPC (5 of 1908), S. 60(1), proviso (c)]

"RESIDENTIAL". Ordinarily means used, serving or designed as a residence or for occupation by residents; relating to or connected with residence. *Associated Indem Mechanical (P.) Ltd.* v. *West Bengal S.S.I.D.C. Ltd.*, AIR 2007 SC 788 : 2007 AIR SCW 489.

Residential building. A seat in a room or gardens or godowns by themselves do not qualify to be called a 'residential building'. *Associated Indem Mechanical (P.) Ltd.* v. *West Bengal S.S.I.D.C. Ltd.*, AIR 2007 SC 788 : 2007 AIR SCW 489.

'Residential building' refers to any building in which sleeping accommodation is provided for normal residential purpose with or without cooking or dining or both facilities and includes one or two or multi-family dwelling, lodging or rooming houses, dormitories, apartment houses, flats and hostels. [Noida Building Regulations and Directions, 2006 Regn. 3.12(h) as cited in *R.K. Mittal* v. *State of Uttar Pradesh*, (2012) 2 SCC 232, para 22].

Residential complex. "RESIDENTIAL COMPLEX" means any complex comprising of—

(i) a building or buildings, having more than twelve residential units;

(ii) a common area; and

(iii) any one or more of facilities or services such as park, lift, parking space, community hall, common water supply or effluent treatment system, located within a premises and the layout of such premises is approved by an authority under any law for the time being in force, but does not include a complex which is constructed by a person directly engaging any other person for designing or planning of the layout, and the construction of such complex intended for personal use as residence by such person.

Explanation.—For the removal of doubts, it is hereby declared that for the purposes of this clause,—

(a) "personal use" includes permitting the complex for use as residence by another person on rent or without consideration;

(b) "residential unit" means a single house or a single apartment intended for use as a place of residence. [Finance Act (32 of 1994), S. 65(91a) *as inserted by Finance Act (18 of 2005), S. 88(a)(xviii)* now repealed by Central Goods and Services Tax Act, 2017]

Residential purposes. *Held* that the purchasing of a plot of ground for the purpose of having a house built upon it in which the purchaser intended to reside would undoubtedly be a purchase for "residential purposes", but the purchases of plots of ground as a speculation for having dwelling houses for tenants upon them may not be treated as "purchases" of that kind.

Residential use. 'Residential use' means the use of any land or building or part thereof for human habitation and such other uses incidental to residential uses. [Noida (Preparation and Finalisation of Plan) Regulations, 1991, Regn. 2(1)(k) as cited in *R.K. Mittal* v. *State of Uttar Pradesh*, (2012) 2 SCC 232, para 19.1].

Residential unit. For the purposes of this section, "RESIDENTIAL UNIT" means an independent housing unit with separate facilities for living, cooking and sanitary requirements, distinctly separated from other residential units within the building, which is directly accessible from an outer door or through an interior door in a shared hallway and not by walking through the living space of another household. [Income-tax Act (43 of 1961), S. 80-IBA (6), *Explanation (c)*].

Resides. The word resides must be taken to refer to natural persons and not to legal entities such as limited companies or governments. *Azizuddin & Co.* v. *UOI,* AIR 1955 Mad 345. [CPC (5 of 1908), S. 20]

"The terms "RESIDES" AND "LAST RESIDED" in S. 126(1), CrPC 1973 (2 of 1974), mean both permanent as well as a temporary residence.

A person resides in a place if he through choice makes it his abode permanently or even temporarily. If the word 'resides' includes temporary residence, the expression 'last resided' means the place where the person had his last temporary residence. The verb 'is' in between the above two expressions connotes the presence or the existence of the person in the district when the proceedings are taken. *Jagir Kaur* v. *Jaswant Singh*, AIR 1963 SC 1521, 1524, 1525.

Residing. Dwelling permanently or for a consierable period. [CrPC 1973 (2 of 1974), S. 100(1)].

Residing in compensability. A person is said to be "residing in compensability" with the tenant if he is living jointly with him, having a common mess, without paying for his food, and without paying any rent to him. *Ram Chander* v. *Chanderwati Ram Mohan,* AIR 1962 Punj 474, 475.

Residual doubt. "Residual doubt" is a mitigating circumstance, sometimes used and urged before the jury in the United States and, generally, not found favour by the various courts in the United States. [*Ashok Debbarma* v. *State of Tripura*, (2014) 4 SCC 747, para 32].

Residual value. The net amount which an enterprise expects to obtain for an asset at the end of its useful life after deducting the expected costs of disposal.

Residuary bequest. A residuary bequest is one which, if valid, carries all the personal property not otherwise disposed of.

Residuary clause. A clause in a will by which the testator disposes of such part of his estate as remains undisposed of by previous devises or bequests.

Residuary devisee. The person named in a will, who is to take all the real property remaining over and above the other devisees.

Residuary estate. The part of a testator's estate which remains after payment of debts and legacies.

Residuary legacy. A residuary legacy embraces only that which remains after all the bequests of the will are discharged.

Residuary legatee. The person to whom the residue of the estate of a testator is given after distributing legacies *etc.* or charges against the estate. [CPC (5 of 1908), 1st Sch., App. D, form No. 18(3)]; [Indian Succession Act (39 of 1925), S. 232].

Residuary powers. The powers conferred on the Speaker to regulate matter not specifically provided for in the rules as well as questions relating to the detailed working of the rules also powers of the Parliament not enumerated in the lists of Seventh Schedule. [Constitution of India, Art. 246.]

Residue. Something that remains after a part is taken, separated, removed or designated. [Indian Stamp Act (2 of 1899), S. 28(4)]; the part of a testator's estate or of any part thereof, remaining after the satisfaction of all debts, charges of administration, statutory allowances for support of a widow and children and previous devises and bequests. [CPC (5 of 1908), App. D, form No. 18(3)].

Residues of veterinary drugs. Include the parent compounds or their metabolites or both in any edible portion of any animal product and include residues of associated impurities of the veterinary drugs concerned. [*Explanation* (2) to S. 21 of the Food Safety & Standards Act, 2006 (34 of 2006)]

Residuum. A residuum is what is left after a process of separation.

Resign. With regard to an office "resign" "implies that the party resigning has been elected into the office which he resigns; a man cannot '*resign*' that which he is not entitled to."

To give up an office. [CPC (5 of 1908), S. 123(4) and Working Journalists and Other Newspaper Employees (Conditions of Service) and Miscellaneous Provisions Act (45 of 1955), S. 5(1)(b)].

Resignatio est juris propril spontanea refu-tatio. Resignation is a spontaneous relinquishment of one's own right.

Resignation. A resignation of an office to be complete, implies the consent of the incumbent.

"RESIGNATION" implies that the person resigning has been elected into the office he resigns. One cannot resign that which he is not entitled to, and which he has no right to occupy.

Only the acceptance of a resignation makes an office vacant and not the resignation. This applies to the case of an Honorary Magistrate also. [AIR 1924 Mad 395].

'Resignation' and **'retirement'.** In the case of 'resignation', the relationship of employer and employee terminates on acceptance of 'resignation' and in the case of 'retirement', voluntary or superannuation, the relationship continues for the purposes of payment of retiral benefits. *Jaipal Singh* v. *Sumitra Mahajan*, AIR 2004 SC 2066, 2069, para 10. *See also UCO Bank* v. *Sanwar Mal,* AIR 2004 SC 2135, 2140, para 9.

Resignation in writing. The phrase "by writing" cannot by any stretch of imagination, be considered as requiring the person resigning to write, the resignation in his own hand. The phrase "by writing under his hand" is used to indicate that the resignation cannot be oral and it must be in writing and must be by hand *i.e.* it must bear his signature. When the letter is typed or typewritten, there is no infirmity. *Vikram Singh* v. *Ram Ballabhji Kasat,* AIR 1995 MP 140, 145. [Constitution of India, Art. 190(3)(b)]

Resile. To withdraw from.

Resist. To oppose; to oppose with force; to prevent; to hinder.

To exert oneself to counteract or defeat; to oppose. [IPC (45 of 1860), S. 141, Second].

Resist an officer. Personally to resist; to resist directly and actively and by force not merely to hinder or interrupt an officer.

Resist arrest. To refuse to go with the officer who assumes to make an arrest.

Resistance. A mere objection to Police Officer taking away property does not amount to offering resistance within the meaning of S. 188. IPC (45 of 1860). *Ragi* in the possession of the accused was, during their absence, seized by the Police and kept loaded in a cart for being taken away. The three accused and others, hearing about it, came from the opposite direction and stood before the cart, and raising their hands said that the cart should not be driven and that they objected to the property being taken. No force was used and nothing was done by the accused. *Held,* that no offence was committed. [*In Re : Rangaswami Goundan*, AIR 1944 Mad 45].

Resistance is a much wider word than obstruction and objection taken in any tangible and identifiable form will constitute resistance. *Bharat Plywood and Timber Products (P.) Ltd.* v. *Kerala State Electricity Board, Trivendrum,* AIR 1972 Ker 47, 55. [Indian Telegraph Act (13 of 1885), S. 16]

Passive and active opposition. [Ss. 224 and 225, IPC (45 of 1860)].

Resolution. Something that is resolved; something that is determined upon. [Companies Act (1 of 1956), S. 9].

Any proposal made at a meeting and put to the vote; the judgment of a Court; the form in which the legislative body expresses an opinion; only a less solemn or less usual form of an ordinance; according to ordinary parliamentary practice, merely a suggestion or direction in writing, concurred in by the two houses of the legislature if there be two houses, or passed by one house if there be but one, and not submitted to the executive for approval, ordinarily passed without the forms and delays which are generally required as prerequisites of the enactment of valid laws or ordinances.

A resolution is a procedural means available to the members of the Parliament or State Legislatures and the Ministers to raise a discussion in a House on a matter of public interest. It is a substantive motion. It is in the form of a declaration of opinion or a recommendation or in the form so as to record either approval or disapproval by the House of an act or Government Policy or convey a message; or commend, urge or request an action or call attention to a matter or situation for consideration by the Government, or in such other forms as the Speaker or Chairman may consider appropriate.

"Resolution applicant". Means any person who submits a resolution plan to the resolution professional. [Insolvency and Bankruptcy Code (31 of 2016), S. 5(25)].

"RESOLUTION APPLICANT" means a person, who individually or jointly with any other person, submits a resolution plan to the resolutions professional pursuant to the invitation made under clause (*h*) of sub-section (2) of section 25. [Insolvency and Bankruptcy Code (31 of 2016), S. 5(25) as substituted by Amending Ordinance (7 of 2017)].

"RESOLUTION APPLICANT" means a person, who individually or jointly with any other person, submits a resolution plan to the resolution professional pursuant to the invitation made under clause (*h*) of sub-section (2) of Section 25. [Insolvency and Bankruptcy Code (31 of 2016), S. 5(25) as substituted by Amending Act (8 of 2018)].

"Resolution professional". For the purposes of this part, means an insolvency professional appointed to conduct the corporate insolvency resolution process and includes an interim resolution professional. [Insolvency and Bankruptcy Code, 2016, S. 5(27) **as cited in** *Innoventive Industries Limited* v. *ICICI Bank,* (2018) 1 SCC 407, para 19].

"Resolution professional". For the purposes of this Part, means an insolvency professional appointed to conduct the corporate insolvency resolution process and includes an interim resolution professional. [Insolvency and Bankruptcy Code (31 of 2016), S. 5(27)].

Resoluto jure concendentis, resolvitur jus concessum. Where the right of the grantor is extinguished, the right granted is extinguished.

Resolve. To express an opinion or determination by resolution or vote.

Resort. "Resort" is the "act of visiting; assembly; meeting concourse; frequent assembly".

To make one come or go up especially habitually or frequently to a person or place. [CrPC 1973 (2 of 1974), S. 40(1)(b)]; concourse.

Respectable inhabitants. The word 'respectable' in 'respectable inhabitants' is to be emphasised and not respectable inhabitants of the locality and in that view, the *serpanch* of *Ganbhari Panchayat* and a ward member of the village are respectable. *State of Orissa* v. *Satyanarayan,* AIR 1965 Ori 136, 138. [CrPC 1973 (2 of 1974), S.100 (4)]

Respectable inhabitants of the locality. The persons selected should be absolutely unprejudiced and uninterested in the result of what they have to take part in. *In Re, Rajabather,* AIR 1959 Mad 450, 452. [CrPC 1973 (2 of 1974), S. 100(4)]

Respective. Proper or relating to particular persons or things each to each. [CPC (2 of 1974), O. XX, R. 13(2)]; [CrPC 1973 (2 of 1974), S. 145(1)].

Respective terms. Respective periods or determined or prescribed times. [CPC (5 of 1908), 1st Sch., App. F, form No. 8].

Respectively. Relatively to each of several things in the order in which they are specified.

Respondeat superior. Literally "Let the principal answer". A general rule which charges the master with liability for the servant's negligence in the master's business causing injury to third persons; founded on this principle, that he who expects to derive advantage from an act which is done by another for him must answer for any injury which a third person may sustain from it.

Respondent. 'RESPONDENT' includes an intervener. [Supreme Court Rules, 1966, R. 2(1)(o)]

A party called upon to respond or answer a petition, a claim or an appeal. [CPC (5 of 1908), O. XXII, R. 11].

The expression 'respondent' appearing in S. 24, refers to the respondent in the application under S. 24 and not the original proceedings taken under the Act. *Babu Rao* v. *Sushila Bai,* AIR 1964 MP 73, 74. [Hindu Marriage Act (25 of 1955), S. 24]

The word 'respondent' is used not in the orthodox sense in which the word is generally used in matrimonial cases, but in the sense of an opposite party to a petition. *Sachindra Nath Biswas* v. *Banamala Biswas,* AIR 1960 Cal 575, 576. [Hindu Marriage Act (25 of 1955), S. 25(1)]

"RESPONDENT" means any adult male person who is, or has been, in a domestic relationship with the aggrieved person and against whom the aggrieved person has sought any relief under this Act:

Provided that an aggrieved wife or female living in a relationship in the nature of a marriage may also file a complaint against a relative of the husband or the male partner. [S. 2(q) of the Protection of Women from Domestic Violence Act, 2005 (43 of 2005)]

Respondentia bond. A bond executed in a foreign port, by the master of a vessel, for the repayment of advance to supply the necessaries of the ship together with such interest as may be agreed upon. [Indian Stamp Act (2 of 1899), S. 29(a), No. 56].

Responsibility. The state or fact of being responsible; something for which anyone is responsible or accountable. [Indian Contract Act (9 of 1872), Ss. 44, and 164].

Responsible. Able to respond; able to pay a sum for which a person may become liable. Liable to answer for; accountable. [Indian Contract Act (9 of 1872), S. 129, ill. (a)].

Responsible litigant. 'Responsible litigant' means—

(i) That litigation will not be resorted to for the sake of litigating.

(ii) That false pleas and technical points will not be take and shall be discouraged.

(iii) Ensuring that the correct facts and all relevant documents will be placed before the court.

(iv) That nothing will be suppressed from the court and there will be no attempt to mislead any court or tribunal. [National Litigation Policy, 2010 as cited in *Punjab State Power Corporation Limited, Patiyala* v. *Atma Singh Grewal*, (2014) 13 SCC 666, para 10].

Responsible situation. A position of responsibility. [CPC (5 of 1908), 1st Sch., App. A, form No. 22].

Restaurant. Means premises in which is carried on principally or wholly the business of supplying meals or refreshments to the public or a class of the public for consumption on the premises but does not include a restaurant attached to a theatre. [Weekly Holidays Act (18 of 1942), S. 2(c)]

"RESTAURANT" means any premises, not being a restaurant situated in a hotel referred to in clause (1) of Section 3, in which the business of sale of food or drink to the public is carried on and such premises, at the beginning of any month, are equipped with, or have access to, facilities for air conditioning. [Expenditure-tax Act (35 of 1987), S. 2(9A)].

Restitutio in integrum : To restore parties to their original position. Restitution to the original condition; applied to parties on the rescinding of a contract, and to a cause in which a second hearing is granted.

Restitution. The act of restoring or a condition of being restored; restoration of a person to a former position or status; restoration of a thing or institution to its original state or form. [CPC (5 of 1908), S. 144(1)]; [CrPC 1973 (2 of 1974), S. 453].

It is open to the Court in the exercise of its inherent power to make an order for restitution for the purpose of doing justice between the parties concerned even in a case which may not come under S. 144, CPC (5 of 1908).

The concept of restitution is virtually a common law principle and it is a remedy against unjust enrichment or unjust benefit. The core of the concept lies in the conscience of the court which prevents a party from retaining money or some benefit derived from another which it has received by way of an erroneous decree of court. [*State of Gujarat* v. *Essar Oil Limited*, (2012) 3 SCC 522, para 61].

The word 'restitution' in its etymological sense means restoring to a party on the modification, variation or reversal of a decree what has been lost to him in execution of the decree or in direct consequence of the decree. *Zafarkhan* v. *Board of Revenue, U.P.*, AIR 1985 SC 39, 46.

Restitution of conjugal rights. The compelling of a husband or wife, who has withdrawn and lives separate without cause, to live with the other.

Restoration. The act of being restored or reinstated. [Specific Relief Act (47 of 1963), S. 28(2)(b)].

Restoration of child. For the purposes of this section "RESTORATION OF CHILD" means restoration to—

(a) parents;

(b) adopted parents;

(c) foster parents. [Juvenile Justice (Case and Protection of Children) Act (56 of 2000), S. 39(*Expln.*)]

Restoration and protection of a child. For the purposes of this section, "Restoration and Protection of a Child"

means restoration to—

(a) parents;

(b) adoptive parents;

(c) foster parents;

(d) guardian; or

(e) fit person. [Juvenile Justice (Care and Protection of Children) Act, 2015 (2 of 2016), S. 40, Explanation].

Restore : Restoration. To give back; to make return or restitution of (anything previously taken away or lost); to put back into a former or original state. [T.P. Act (4 of 1882), S. 108(m)]; [Indian Contract Act (9 of 1872), S. 64].

The term 'restoration' does not mean that a person should restore the goods to another person by delivering the same to him. As long as there is intimation by the person restoring the goods to the other person that he can take back the goods, the person restoring evinces intention of restoration. *Union of India* v. *Sita Ram*, AIR 1977 SC 329, 331. [Indian Contract Act (9 of 1872), S. 70]

Restrain. To hold back a person from action, procedure or course. [T.P. Act (4 of 1882), S. 40]; [CPC (5 of 1908), O. XXXIX, R. 2(1)].

Restrain : Restrict. To restrain is an act of power; but to restrict is an act of authority or law; the will or the actions of a child are restrained by the parent; but a patient is restricted in his diet by a physician, or any body of people may be restricted by laws.

Restraining order. An order in the nature of an injunction.

Restraint. Whosoever voluntarily obstructs any person so as to prevent that person from proceeding in any direction in which that person has a right to proceed, is said wrongfully to restrain that person.

Exception—The obstruction of a private way over land or water which a person in good faith believes himself to have a lawful right to obstruct, is not an offence within the meaning of this section. [IPC (45 of 1860), S. 339]

The action of restraining. [IPC (45 of 1860), S. 105].

Any limitation imposed on the exercise of fundamental right given to a citizen is restraint. [Court Fees Act (7 of 1870), S. 19(xvii)]

Restraint of trade. S. 27 of the Indian Contract Act (9 of 1872) has abolished the distinction between partial and total restraints of trade. Whether the restraint is general or partial, unqualified, or qualified, if it is in the nature of a restraint of trade, it is void.

Restrict. To restrain by prohibition. [CrPC 1973 (2 of 1974), S. 432 (6)].

Restrict and modify. The power of introducing necessary restrictions and modifications is incidental to the power to apply or adapt the law. The modifications are to be made within the framework of the Act and they cannot be such as to affect its identity or structure or the essential purpose to be served by it. *Rajnarain Singh* v. *Chairman Committee*, AIR 1954 SC 569, 573. [Constitution of India, Art. 245] AIR 1951 SC 332 quoted.

Restricted estate. If along with the creation of a life estate certain valid, restrictions are put, then what is created is a 'restricted estate'. *Veerabhadra Rad* v. *Lakshmi Devi,* AIR 1965 AP 367, 370. [Hindu Succession Act (30 of 1956), S. 14(2)]

Restricted End Uses. Shall mean end uses where borrowed funds cannot be deployed and shall include the following:

(*a*) In the business of chit fund or Nidhi Company;

(*b*) Investment in capital market including margin trading and derivatives;

(*c*) Agricultural or plantation activities;

(*d*) Real estate activity or construction of farm houses; and

(*e*) Trading in Transferable Development Rights (TDR), where TDR shall have the meaning as assigned to it in the Foreign Exchange Management (Permissible Capital Account Transactions) Regulations, 2015. [Foreign Exchange Management (Borrowing and Lending) Regulations, 2018, Regn. 2(xiv)].

Restricted substance. Means the substance restricted for handling. [Environment (Protection) Rules, 1986, R. 2(ff)]

Restriction. Restriction includes and covers total prohibition. *Gotiram* v. *Sonabai,* AIR 1970 Bom 73, 77. [Indian Succession Act (39 of 1925), S. 307(2)]

A limitation placed on the use or enjoyment of real or other property; confinement within bounds [IPC (45 of 1860), S. 100 and Constitution of India, Art. 15(2)].

Restriction and **regulation.** The distinction between the power to regulate and the power to restrict will be apparent from a scrutiny of Art. 25(2)(a) where the words 'regulating' and 'restricting' occur in juxtaposition thereby indicating unmistakably that the framers of the constitution intended to convey two different meanings by the two words. The expression 'restriction' in Art. 19(6) cannot be held to be synonymous with 'regulation'. *Lokanath Mishra* v. *State of Orissa,* AIR 1952 Ori 42, 45. [Constitution of India, Arts. 19 & 2(2)(a)]

Restrictive endorsement. Is one which destroys the negotiability of a bill of exchange.

Restrictive trade practice. "RESTRICTIVE TRADE PRACTICE" means a trade practice which tends to bring about manipulation of price or its conditions of delivery or to affect flow of supplies in the market relating to goods or services in such a manner as to impose on the consumers unjustified costs or restrictions and shall include—

(a) delay beyond the period agreed to by a trader in supply of such goods or in providing the services which has led or is likely to lead to rise in the price;

(b) any trade practice which requires a consumer to buy, hire or avail of any goods or, as the case may be, services as condition precedent to buying, hiring or availing of other goods or services. [Consumer Protection Act (68 of 1986), S. 2(1)(nnn)]

"RESTRICTIVE TRADE PRACTICE" means a trade practice which has or may have the effect of preventing, distorting or restricting competition in any manner and in particular:

(i) which tends to obstruct the flow of capital or resources into the stream of production, or

(ii) which tends to bring about manipulation of prices or conditions of delivery or to affect the flow of supplies in the market relating to goods or services in such a manner as to impose on the consumers unjustified costs or restrictions. [Monopolies and Restrictive Trade Practices Act (46 of 1969), S. 2(o)]

Restructuring and streamlining. In relation to the organisational and functional set-up of the National Dairy Development Board includes—

(i) opening or closing of units or offices;

(ii) revision of the organisational and functional set-up;

(iii) declaration of staff required;

(iv) integration of posts, fixation of seniority and pay scales;

(v) integration of required personnel in the revised set-up and issuance of appointment orders in that behalf;

(vi) declaration or demarcation of duties and responsibilities attendant to posts;

(vii) declaration of posts equivalent to one another; and

(viii) any other matter that may be necessary or incidental to meet the organisational or functional needs of the National Dairy Development Board. [National Dairy Development Board Act (37 of 1987), S. 3(k)]

Resulting company. "RESULTING COMPANY" means one or more companies (including a wholly owned subsidiary thereof) to which the undertaking of the demerged company is transferred in a demerger and, the resulting company in consideration of such transfer of undertaking, issues shares to the shareholders of the demerged company and includes any authority or boy or local authority or public sector company or a company established, constituted or formed as a result of demerger. [Income-tax Act (43 of 1961), S. 2(41A)]

Resumption. The action of beginning again [CrPC, 1973 (2 of 1974), S. 331]; [Hindu Marriage Act (25 of 1955), S. 13(1A)(i)].

'Resumption' connotes the idea that the land resumed is not the property of the persons from whom it is taken back by the rightful owner. *Raj Rajendra Malojirao Shitole* v. *State of Madhya Bharat,* AIR 1953 MB 97, 121 (FB).

Retail. The sale of goods in small quantities to unltimate consumers [Cardamom Act (42 of 1965) (*repealed*), S. 20(1)(a)]; [Poisons Act (12 of 1919), S. 2(1)].

Retail dealer. "RETAIL DEALER" in relation to any commodity in packaged form means a dealer who directly sells such packages to the consumer and includes, in relation to packages as are sold directly to the consumer, a wholesale dealer who makes such direct sale to the consumer. [Legal Metrology (Packaged Commodities) Rules, 2011, R. 2(j)]

Retail package. "RETAIL PACKAGE" means the packages which are intended for retail sale to the ultimate consumer for the purpose of consumption of the commodity contained therein and includes the imported packages:

Provided that for the purposes of "retail food package", the definition of the same contained in the rules or regulations made under the Food Safety and Standards Act, 2006 (34 of 2006) shall apply. [Legal Metrology (Packaged Commodities) Rules, 2011, R. 2(k)]

Retail sale. "RETAIL SALE", in relation to a commodity, means the sale, distribution or delivery of such commodity through retail sales shops, agencies or other instrumentalities for consumption by an individual or a group of individuals or any other consumer. [Legal Metrology (Packaged Commodities) Rules, 2011, R. 2(l)]

RETAIL SALE is to sell goods in small parcels and not in gross.

Retail sale price. 'RETAIL SALE PRICE' means the maximum price at which the commodity in packaged form may be sold to the ultimate consumer and the price shall be printed on the package in the manner given below;

'Maximum or Max. retail price Rs. ..../ Rs............ inclusive of all taxes or in the form MRP Rs. ..../Rs............ incl., of all taxes after taking into account the fraction of less than fifty paise to be rounded off to the preceding rupee and fraction of above 50 paise and up to 95 paise to the rounded off to fifty paise. [Legal Metrology (Packaged Commodities) Rules, 2011, R. 2(m).]

Retain an attorney. Engaging an attorney for attending to any single case or to all cases which may arise and need to be attended to in a Court of law [Indian Evidence Act (1 of 1872), S. 126, ill. (c)].

Retain possession. To continue to hold possession even though the term may have expired. [Indian Evidence Act (1 of 1872), S. 102, ill. (a)].

Retained. The word 'retain' in the *Vakalatnama* had a legal significance. The English concept of retainer for lawyers is thus not without purpose, introduced in the Indian *Vakalatnama*. A retainer is the engagement of a pleader or an advocate to give his service to a client, and involves the payment of a fee—the acceptance of a retainer binds pleader or advocate to accept a brief on behalf of the client who retains him and not to accept a brief from his opponent. *State* v. *Jaganand Panigrahi,* AIR 1962 Ori 67, 68 (FB). [Legal Practitioners Act (18 of 1879), S. 13(a)]

Retainer. "Retainer" may be defined as 'the act of a client by which he engages an attorney to manage his cause", and also as "the retaining fee".

Retaining fee. A preliminary fee given to a counsel, along with the retainer, in order to ensure his advocacy.

Retention. "RETENTION" means the portion of the risk which an insurer/reinsurer assumes for his own account. [Insurance Regulatory and Development Authority (General Insurance Reinsurance) Regulations, 2016, Reg. 2(o)]

The right of retaining property until a debt due from the owner is paid.

Keeping in one's own possession or control. [T.P. Act (4 of 1882), S. 57(b)]; [Indian Easements Act (5 of 1882), S. 2(a)].

The expression 'to retain' is 'to hold or keep in possession', 'to keep from departure or escape', to detain and 'not to lose or part with'. The word 'retention' contemplates as continuity of the right in the outgoing proprietor, or in other words, the right of possession over the lands which were in the proprietor from before are allowed to continue as such even after the vesting of the estate. *Brijnandan Singh* v. *Jamuna Prasad,* AIR 1958 Pat 589, 594.

Retention and re-employment. Retention in service, which means continued employment in the service in which an employee has been serving is quite a different thing from reemployment of an employee after he has retired. *Basanta Kumar Pal* v. *Chief Electrical Engineer,* AIR 1958 Cal 657, 658.

Retinue. A number or company of persons retained in the service or attached to or following someone, especially a sovereign noble or person in authority. [CPC (5 of 1908), S. 86(4)(c)].

Retire. To withdraw from office, generally on superannuation; to withdraw from business [Indian Partnership Act (9 of 1932), S. 32(1)]; to withdraw to or into a place for seclusion; retire from service.

Retired partner. Partner who has withdrawn from the partnership. [Indian Partnership Act (9 of 1932), S. 33(2)].

Retirement. "RETIREMENT" means termination of the service of an employee otherwise than on superannuation. [Payment of Gratuity Act (39 of 1972), S. 2(q)]

"RETIREMENT" means giving up of practice as an advocate which is communicated to and recorded by the Bar Council. [Gujarat Advocates Welfare Fund Act (14 of 1991), S. 2(m) and Goa Advocates Welfare Fund Act, 1995 (Goa Act No. 2 of 1997), S. 2(n)]

The act of retiring; the state or condition of being retired [Indian Partnership Act (9 of 1932), S. 32(2)]; [Air Force Act (45 of 1950), S. 189(2)(a)]; [CPC (5 of 1908), O. XXXII, R. 8(1)]; retirement from service.

"Retirement Benefits". Means any payment due to the depositor on account of his retirement whether on superannuation or otherwise and includes following payments:—

(i) Balance at the credit of employee in any of the contributory provident funds, including employer's share.

(ii) Retirement/superannuation gratuity.

(iii) Cash equivalent of leave.

(iv) Savings element of Group Savings Linked Insurance Scheme payable by employer to the employee on retirement.

(v) Retirement-cum-withdrawal benefit under the Employees' Family Pension Scheme, 1971.

(vi) Commuted value of pension, if any, payable by the public sector company. [Deposit Scheme for Retiring Employees of Public Sector Companies, 1991, S. 3(e). Discontinued with effect from 9-7-2004 vide Notification F. No. 15-01/2004-NS. II (i), dated 9-7-2004.]

Retiring director. For the purposes of sections 152 and 160 of Act 18 of 2013, the expression 'retiring director' means a director retiring by rotation. [*Explanation* to section 152 of the Companies Act, 2013 (18 of 2013)]

Retiring partner. A partner who leaves a partnership.

Retract bid. To withdraw, recall, revoke or rescind an offer to purchase. [Sale of Goods Act (3 of 1930), S. 64(2)].

Retraction. The act of taking or withdrawing back.

Retraction right. The author's right to withdraw from circulation a published work so that he can revise it to reflect his changed opinions or views. (*Copyright*)

Retrenchment. "RETRENCHMENT" means the termination by the employer of the service of a workman for any reason whatsoever, otherwise than as a punishment inflicted by way of disciplinary action, but does not include—

(a) voluntary retirement of the workman; or

(b) retirement of the workman on reaching the age of superannuation if the contract of employment between the employer and the workman concerned contains a stipulation in that behalf; or

(bb) termination of service of the workman as a result of non-renewal of the contract of employment between the employer and the workman concerned on its expiry or of such contract being terminated under a stipulation in that behalf contained therein; or

(c) termination of the service of a workman on the ground of continued illhealth. [Industrial Disputes Act (14 of 1947), S. 2(oo)]

If retrenchment means in ordinary parlance, discharge of the surplus, it cannot include discharge on closure of business. *Pipraich Sugar Mills Ltd.* v. *Paraich Sugar Mills Mazdoor Union*, AIR 1957 SC 95, 104. [Industrial Dispute Act (14 of 1947), S. 2(oo) and S. 25-F]

The definition makes 'retrenchment' a termination of service. A service cannot be said to be terminated unless it was capable of being continued. If it is not capable of being continued in the same manner in which it had been going on before, and it is, therefore, brought to an end, that is not a termination of the service. *Workmen of the Bangalore Woollen Cotton and Silk Mills Co. Ltd.* v. *Management of the Bangalore Woollen Cotton and Silk Mills Co. Ltd.*, AIR 1962 SC 1363, 1366.

The discharge of a workman on the ground that the workman did not pass the test which would have entitled the workman to be confirmed is 'retrenchment'. *Santosh Gupta* v. *State Bank of Patiala*, AIR 1980 SC 1217, 1223.

The word 'retrenchment' means the discharge of surplus labour or staff by the employer for any reason whatsoever, otherwise than as a punishment inflicted by way of disciplinary action, and it has no application where the services of all workmen have been terminated by the employer on a real and *bona fide* closure of business or where the services of all workmen have been terminated by the employer on the business or undertaking being taken over by another employer. *Hariprasad Shivshankar Shukla* v. *A.D. Divelkar*, AIR 1957 SC 121, 132. [Industrial Disputes Act (14 of 1947), S. 25-FF]

Discharge from service of an employee, consequent upon the transfer of an undertaking in which he was employed, is not retrenchment.

The term 'retrenchment' does not apply to a case of *bona fide* closure of business.

Retrenchment compensation. The compensation payable to an employee on account of his retrenchment [Payment of Bonus Act (21 of 1965), S. 2(21)(vi)].

Retribution. In criminal law, the theory that a criminal should be punished in proportion to his offence.

Retroactive. Acting backward; affecting what is past.

"Retroactive" Acting backward; affecting what is past. (of a statute, ruling, etc.) extending in scope or effect to matters that have occurred in the past. [Black's Law Dictionary, 7th Edn., 1999 as cited in *State Bank's Staff Union (Madras Circle)* v. *Union of India*, (2005) 7 SCC 584 : (2005) SCC (L&S) 994, para 21] See also *Swami Vivekanand College of Education* v. *Union of India*, (2012) 1 SCC 642, para 35.

Retrocession. "RETROCESSION" means the transaction whereby a reinsurer cedes to another insurer or reinsurer all or part of the reinsurance it has previously assumed. [Insurance Regulatory and Development Authority (General Insurance-Reinsurance) Regulations, Reg. 2(g)]

Retrospective. Having operation from a past time.

Looking back; contemplating what is past. 'Retrospective' means 'looking backwards' having reference to a state of things existing before the act in question. A retrospective statute contemplates the past and gives to a previous transaction some different legal effect from that which it had under the law when it occurred or transpired. *Ram Parkash* v. *Savitri Devi,* AIR 1958 Punj 87, 90 (FB).

"Retrospective", when used with reference to an enactment may mean (i) affecting an existing contract; or (ii) reopening up of past, closed and completed transaction; or (iii) affecting accrued rights and remedies; or (iv) affecting procedure. [Judicial Dictionary (13th Edn.) by K.J. Aiyar, Butterworth, p. 857, as cited in *State Bank's Staff Union (Madras Circle)* v. *Union of India*, (2005) 7 SCC 584 : 2005 SCC (L&S) 994, para 20]. See also *Swami Vivekanand College of Education* v. *Union of India*, (2012) 1 SCC 642, para 35.

'Retrospective or retroactive law' is one which takes away or impairs vested or accrued rights acquired under existing laws. A retroactive law takes away or impairs vested rights acquired under existing laws, or creates a new obligation, imposes a new duty, or attaches a new disability, in respect to transactions or considerations already past. [Words and Phrases, permanent Edn., Vol. 37-A, pp. 224-25 as cited in *State Bank's Staff Union (Madras Circle)* v. *Union of India*, (2005) 7 SCC 584 : 2005 SCC (L&S) 994, para 20]. See also *Swami Vivekanand College of Education* v. *Union of India*, (2012) 1 SCC 642, para 35.

'Retrospective' is somewhat ambiguous and that good deal of confusion has been caused by the fact that it is used in more senses than one. In general, however, the courts regard as retrospective any statute which operates on cases or facts coming into existence before its commencement in the sense that it affects, even if for the future only, the character or consequences of transactions previously entered into or of other past conduct. Thus a statute is not retrospective merely because it affects existing rights; nor is it retrospective merely because a part of the requisite for its action is drawn from a time antecedent to it passing. [Halsbury's Law of England, 4th Edn., Vol. 44, p. 570, para 921 as cited in *State Bank's Staff Union (Madras Circle)* v. *Union of India*, (2005) 7 SCC 584 : 2005 SCC (L&S) 994, para 21]. See also *Swami Vivekanand College of Education* v. *Union of India*, (2012) 1 SCC 642, para 35.

Retrospective law. One which is made to affect acts or facts transpiring, or rights accruing before it came into force.

Retrospective law is a law which looks back; a law which contemplates or affects an act done, or a right accrued before its passage.

Retrospective legislation. Legislation which operates on matters taking place before its enactment.

Retrospective operation. The use of the expression "retrospective operation" is at times vague and misleading. In a broad general sense it may be right to say that a statute has retrospective operation when it purports to touch facts or events which took place before the enactment came into force. It is sometimes used in a different sense when vested rights are sought to be affected. It is sometimes loosely used in the context of certain fictions of law which the law maker deems it necessary to introduce in existing laws for the purpose of setting certain matters right or avoiding certain mischief which might be possible but for the change in the law; and this is done by laying down that certain facts or things which did not in fact exist shall be deemed to have existed. This last need not necessarily be called retrospective legislation. *New Shorrock Spinning and Manufacturing Co. Ltd.* v. *N.V. Raval Income-tax Officer,* AIR 1959 Bom 477, 480.

Retrospective statutes. 'A statute which is to be deemed to be retrospective, which takes away or impairs any vested right acquired under existing laws, or creates a new obligation, or imposes a new duty, or attaches a new disability in respect to transactions or considerations already past'. [CRAIES *on Statute Law,* 7th Edn. p. 387 **as referred in** *State Bank's Staff Union (Madras Circle)* v. *Union of India,* 2005 SCC 3446, 3451, para 21]

Retrospectively. With retrospective effect. [T.P. Act (4 of 1882), S. 1].

Retrospectivity and **Declaratory laws.** An assessment under a fiscal statute creates vested rights. A retrospective law has the effect of reopening a liability which has become barred by limitation. Unless an amending Act is retrospective in effect, the assessee cannot be subjected to reassessment. A declaratory Act can be construed as retrospective. But, such laws usually seek to set right that which is construed by the Parliament as a judicial error. Such laws also contain the word "declared" to remove any ambiguity. *National Steel Industries Ltd.* v. *CCE,* 2000 (126) ELT 709(T).

Return. A report of a formal or official character giving information as to the number, amounts *etc.* of the subjects of inquiry [CPC (5 of 1908), O. V, R. 18]; the action of returning [Sale of Goods Act (3 of 1930), S. 25(3)]; [Indian Contract Act (9 of 1872), S. 168]; to give or render back (to a person); to elect.

Signing a prescribed form without date and without filling up the columns and writing the word "blank" against the item of "total", accompanied by a letter stating that the assessee did not carry on any business would not constitute a 'return' for the purpose of assessment under the Income Tax Act.

Return a verdict. The expression of opinion finally and authoritatively.

Return day. The day on which a writ is appointed or required to be returned.

Returned as juryman. Entered in an official report or return as having been selected as a juror. [IPC (45 of 1860), S. 229].

Returned candidate. "RETURNED CANDIDATE" means a candidate whose name has been published under Section 67 of the Representation of the People Act, 1951, as duly elected at an election in the case of Prime Minister or as the case may be, an election in the case of Speaker. [Disputed Elections (Prime Minister & Speaker) Act (16 of 1977), S. 2(i)]

A returned candidate is one who has been elected. *Harswarup* v. *Brij Bhushan*, AIR 1976 SC 836, 838. [Representation of the People Act (43 of 1951), S. 82(a)]

Returning officer. One who conducts and announces result of an election.

Returns. Proceeds; income in relation to the means by which it is produced.

Revaccination. "REVACCINATION" means vaccination of a person who has been successfully vaccinated previously. [Maharashtra Vaccination Act (35 of 1984), S. 2(m)]

Revalidation. The expression 'revalidation' does not mean 'extension of the period'. *Rajeshwar Parshad* v. *Municipal Corporation of Delhi,* AIR 1991 Del 71, 79.

Reveal. To disclose; to divulge. [Drugs and Cosmetics Act (23 of 1940), S. 17(a)].

Revenge. Vindictive retaliation.

Revenue. The word "REVENUE" includes every sum annually payable to Government by the proprietor of any estate or tenure in respect thereof, and every sum payable to Government in respect of *takkavi*, or of any money advanced by Government to proprietors of land for making or repairing embankments, reservoirs or water-courses, or other improvements on the land held by them. [Ben. Act VII of 1868 (Land-Revenue Sales), S. 1]

"REVENUE" means whatever is lawfully payable by *raiyat* under the provisions of this Act in respect of his land holdings. [West Bengal Land Holding Revenue Act, 1979 (44 of 1979), S. 2(o)]

The annual or periodical yield of taxes, excises, customs, duties and other sources of income that a nation, state or municipality collects and receives into the treasury for public use [CPC (5 of 1908), S. 135(2)]; income from any source [Income-tax Act (43 of 1961), S. 2(1-A)(a)].

Income, annual profits received from land or other funds.

Revenue comprehends only assessments, quit rents, ground rents or any other charge upon the land payable to Government. Property Tax collectable by a Municipality is not 'revenue'. *Ramdarjee Varu* v.

Tripathi Devasthanam, AIR 1965 AP 334, 336. [CPC (5 of 1908), O. XXI, R. 66(2)(b)]

The expression 'revenues' means "the income of the nation derived from its taxes, duties or other sources, for the payment of the nation's expenses". It is a term generally "used in referring to income of a government or governmental sub-division and as so used means all the public moneys which the state collects and receives from whatever source and in whatever manner. [Constitution of India, Art. 266]

Revenue agent. A person admitted under the Legal Practitioners Act (18 of 1879), as a revenue agent. [CPC (5 of 1908), S. 135(2)].

Revenue assessed. The amount determined as revenue. [CPC (5 of 1908), 1st Sch., App. E, form No. 29].

Revenue deficit. Means the difference between revenue expenditure and revenue receipts which indicates increase in liabilities of the Central Government without corresponding increase in assets of that Government. [Fiscal Responsibility and Budget Management Act (39 of 2003), S. 2(e)]

Revenue expenditure. If the expenditure is made not for the purpose of bringing into existence any asset or advantage but for running the business or working it with a view to produce profits it is a revenue expenditure. *Assam Bengal Cement Co.* v. *I.T. Commissioner, West Bengal*, AIR 1955 SC 89, 96.

Revenue-free property. "REVENUE-FREE PROPERTY" means any land not subject to the payment of land revenue which is included under one entry in any part of the general register of revenue-free lands. [Ben. Act III of 1876 (Land Registration). S. 3, Cl. (10)]

Revenue office. "REVENUE OFFICE", includes all Courts (other than Civil Courts) trying suits under any Act for the time being in force relating to landholders and their tenants or agents. [Legal Practitioners Act (18 of 1879), S. 3]

Revenue officer. An officer employed in or about the business of any branch of the public revenue. [Indian Evidence Act (1 of 1872), S. 125, *Expln.*].

Revenue process. A process issued in connection with the collection of revenue. [CPC (5 of 1908), S. 2(17)(g)].

Revenue sale. Sale of the property of one who has defaulted in the payment of revenue or against whom any revenue arrears are outstanding. [T.P. Act (4 of 1882), S. 73].

Revenues of the Government. Means, in respect of any part of India, in which the powers and duties of government under this Act are exercised and discharged by a Local Government, the revenues allocated to that Government under the Government of India Act. [Act III of 1913 (Administrator-Generals), S. 4, cl. (1); Act II of 1913 (Official Trustees), S. 2, cl. (7)]

Reversal. The action of reversing. [CPC (5 of 1908), S. 144(1)]; [Indian Evidence Act (1 of 1872), S. 167].

Reversal of onus. When a patent claims a process for making the compound, the compound is presumed to be made by the patented process unless it is proved otherwise. (*Patents*)

Reverse Charge. Means the liability to pay tax by the recipient of supply of goods or services or both instead of the supplier of such goods or services or both under sub-section (3) or sub-section (4) of Section 9, or under sub-section (3) or sub-section (4) of Section 5 of the Integrated Goods and Services Tax Act. [Central Goods and Services Tax Act (12 of 2017), S. 2(98)].

Reversal : alteration. Reversal of the order implies its obliteration, whereas alteration would imply no more than modification and not its obliteration. [*State of U.P.* v. *Thadi Narayana,* AIR 1962 SC 240, para 12 : (1962) 1 Cri LJ 207 **as cited in** *State of H.P.* v. *Nirmala Devi,* (2017) 7 SCC 262, para 62].

Reverse. To turn back; to act in an opposite direction; to undo, annul (as) to reverse the judgment of the lower Court.

To undo; to annul. [CPC (5 of 1908), S. 144(1)]; [Constitution of India, Art. 134(1)(a)].

The word 'reverse' means setting aside of the order of the decree by the Court which passed it and also by the Court of higher forum, either in appeal or revision. *Jagat Bandhu* v. *Ram Nagina,* AIR 1977 Cal 281, 283. [CPC (5 of 1908), S. 144 (1) and O. IX, R. 13]

Reversible. Fit to be reversed or annulled. [CrPC, 1973 (2 of 1974), S. 465].

Reversion. Right to property or benefit, the enjoyment of which does not come into operation until the happening of a certain event or the expiration of a certain period.

The returning of an estate upon its termination to its former owner or his successor in interest; the action of reverting; the right of succeeding to the possession of something after another has done with it or simply obtaining it at some future time. [T.P. Act (4 of 1882), S. 54 and S. 46, ill. (b)].

Reversionary interest. A term generally applied to a deferred interest in land, money or personal property.

Interest of a reversioner. [Indian Trusts Act (2 of 1882), S. 16].

Reversionary lease. A lease to take effect in future. A second lease to commence after the expiration of the former lease.

Reversioner. One that has or is entitled to reversion; one entitled to succeed on the termination of an exising interest on the basis of his being an heir to the previous owner. [Specific Relief Act (47 of 1963), S. 15(e)].

Revert. To return to the former possesser or proprietor or his heirs. [T.P. Act (4 of 1882), S. 35].

Review. The power of a Court or a superior Government officer or agency to examine and either to confirm, modify or annul, a regulation or determination of an inferior Court or official, or of an administrative agency; Court's power to examine a proposed act of an administrative agency.

A review is a proceeding which exists by virtue of statute. It is in its nature a new trial of the issue previously tried between the parties, the cause of action being brought into Court again for trial by a new petition.

The process under which a Court in certain circumstances can reconsider its own judgment; a general survey or re-examination; a retrospective survey of past actions *etc*. [CPC (5 of 1908), O. XLVII, R. 1(2)].

The term 'review' means a judicial re-examination of the case in certain specified and prescribed circumstances. *Parduman Singh* v. *State of Punjab,* AIR 1958 Punj 63, 68.

Review application fee. Means the fee levied by the food authority towards disposal of review application submitted by the Food Importer against the order of Authorised Officer pertaining to clearance of import of articles of food. [Food Safety and Standards (Import) Regulations, 2017, Regn. 2(1)(t)].

Review his own order. Does not mean particular person passing the order. [Administration of Evacuee Property Act (31 of 1950), S. 26(2)]

Reviewing authority. "REVIEWING AUTHORITY" means such authority or authorities supervising the performance of the reporting authority as may be specifically empowered in this behalf by the Government. [All India Services (Confidential Rolls) Rules, 1970, R. 2(f)]

'REVIEW AUTHORITY' is the Deputy Governor in charge of Rural Planning and Credit Department of the Reserve Bank, who shall review the award of a Banking Ombudsman subject to satisfaction of the issues raised before him and shall also be responsible for implementing such Award as per the Scheme. [Banking Ombudsman Scheme, 2002, S. 3(7)]

Revised emoluments. "REVISED EMOLUMENTS" means the basic pay of a Government servant in the revised scale and includes the revised non-practicising allowance if any admissible to him, in addition to the pay in the revised scale. [CCS (Revised Pay) Rules, 1986, R. 3(4)]

Revision. The act of examining again in order to remove any defect or grant relief against the irregular or improper exercise or non-exercise of jurisdiction by a lower Court. [CPC (5 of 1908), S. 115].

Revisional Court. A Court exercising revisional jurisdiction. [CPC (5 of 1908), S. 18(2)].

Revisional and **appellate jurisdiction—Distinction.** An appeal is only the continuation of the original proceeding and the powers of the appellate Tribunal are co-extensive with those of original Tribunal. The revisional jurisdiction is circumscribed by the statute conferring such jurisdiction and extent of such power is regulated by the statute. *Rohtas Industries* v. *State of A.P.,* MLJ : QD (1961-1965) Vol V C16 : (1961) 1 An WR 28 : (1961) 12 STC 693 [A.P General Sales Tax Act (6 of 1957) S. 20]

Revival. The revival of a suit, which is either abated or made defective by the death of a party interested, is not a new suit, but is still the same suit, in which both parties are entitled to the benefit of all former proceedings.

An application for transmission of a decree from the High Court to the District Court is not by itself a revival of the decree within the meaning of the Act inasmuch as it is a mere ministerial act of an officer of the Court and not the judicial act of a Judge.

Revive. The primary meaning of the word "revive" is to give life again.

The return to consciousness or life [Hindu Minority and Guardianship Act (32 of 1956), S. 9(2)]; to become operative again; to restore to consciousness or life; to make operative again. [CPC (5 of 1908), O. XXI, R. 33(3)].

Revivor. In order to constitute a revivor of a decree there must be expressly or by implication a determination that the decree is still capable of execution and the decree-holder is entitled to enforce it. An order of attachment of the properties of the judgment-debtor after notice to them under O. XXI, R. 22, CPC (5 of 1908), amounts to a revivor of the decree although the notice to one of the judgment-debtors who is a minor is not served on the proper guardian of the minor, but on a wrong guardian.

Revocable. Capable of being revoked. [T.P. Act (4 of 1882), S. 126].

Revocation. The act of revoking [Indian Contract Act (9 of 1872), S. 3 and Indian Easements Act (5 of 1882), S. 61].

The undoing of a thing granted; or a destroying or making void of some deed that had existence until the act of revocation made it void.

Revocation only means revocation of an order which is otherwise valid and operative. "Revocation includes cancellation of all orders invalid as well as valid". *Hadibandhu Das* v. *District Magistrate, Cuttack*, AIR 1969 SC 43 at 48. [Preventive Detention Act (4 of 1950), S. 13(2)]

The word, 'revocation' means annulling rescinding, withdrawing. *Pradip Kumar Das* v. *State of West Bengal*, AIR 1974 SC 2151, 2153. [Maintenance of Internal Security Act (27 of 1978) (*Repealed*), S. 14]

POWER OF REVOCATION. A power granted or reserved to revoke an appointment is called a power of revocation.

Revocation of will. The cancellation of a will.

By "REVOCATION OF A WILL" is generally understood an act by which the will ceases to have any effect or efficacy.

Revoke. Means to re-call, to take back, or to repeal.

To call back; to rescind; to cancel; to annul by recalling or taking back [T.P. Act (4 of 1882, S. 42]; [Indian Contract Act (9 of 1872), S. 5, ill.].

"To revoke" sometimes denotes the right to annul, rescind, or abolish.

The word 'revoke' means 'to call back; to withdraw.' *R.P. Kapur* v. *UOI,* AIR 1967 Punj 417, 419.

The true meaning of the verb 'revoke' and its noun signify that revocation is a process of recall of what had been done. *Ibrahim Bachu Bafan* v. *State of Gujarat*, AIR 1985 SC 697, 700. [Conservation of Foreign Exchange and Prevention of Smuggling Activities Act (52 of 1974), S. 11(1) and (2) and (3)]

Revoked licence. "A licence is deemed to be revoked—(a) when, from a cause preceding the grant of it, the grantor ceases to have any interest in the property affected by the licence; (b) when the licensee releases it, expressly or impliedly, to the grantor or his representative; (c) where it has been granted for a limited period, or acquired on condition that it shall become void on the performance or non-performance of a specified act, and the period expires, or the condition is fulfilled; (d) where the property affected by the licence is destroyed or by superior force so permanently altered that the licensee can no longer exercise his right; (e) where the licensee becomes entitled to the absolute ownership of the property affected by the licence; (f) where the licence is granted for a specified purpose and the purpose is attained or abandoned, or becomes impracticable; (g) where the licence is granted to the licensee in holding a particular office, employment or character, and such office, employment or character ceases to exist; (h) where the licence totally ceases to be used as such for an unbroken period of twenty years and such cessation is not in pursuance of a contract between the grantor and the licensee; (i) in the case of an accessory licence, when the interest or right to which it is accessory, ceases to exist." [Indian Easements Act (5 of 1882), S. 62]

Revolt. A rebellion, insurrection. [Extradition Act (34 of 1962), 2nd Sch., item 15].

Reward. The term "reward" is usually applied to a sum paid for the performance of some specific act to some person or persons.

A recompense or grant tor service rendered or merit displayed [IPC (45 of 1860), S. 116, ill. (a)]; [IPC (45 of 1860), S. 378, ill. (1)]; [Contract Labour (Regulation and Abolition) Act (37 of 1970), S. 2(i)].

A "reward" is a recompense or a premium offered by a government or an individual in return for special or extraordinary services to be performed.

Rex. In old English law, King; a king.

Rex debet esse sub lege, quia lex facit regem. The king ought to be under the law, because the law makes the king.

Rex est major singulls, minor universis. The king is greater than any single person; less than all. (*Latin for Lawyers*)

Rex non potest peccare. The king cannot do wrong; the king can do no wrong.

Rex nunquam moritur. The king never dies.

RFC. (*abbr.*) Request For Comments. The name of the result and the process for creating a standard on the *Internet.* New standards are proposed and published on the Internet, as a Request For Comments. The proposal is reviewed by the Internet Engineering Task Force, a consensus-building body that facilitates discussion, and eventually a new standard is established, but the reference number/ name for the standard retains the acronym RFC, *e.g.* the official standard for *e-mail* message formats is RFC 822. (*Matisse Enzer-Glossary of Internet Terms*)

Rice mill. Means the plant and machinery with which, and the premises including the precincts thereof, in which, or in any part of which, rice milling operation is carried on. [Rice Milling Industry (Regulation) Act (21 of 1958), S. 2(i), The Act repealed by Act (28 of 1997)]

Rider. Any separate addition to a document, or addition to a resolution attached to the original, a piece of parchment containing an added clause tacked to a bill in parliament after the bill has been read a third time.

Any separate addition to a document. [Registration Act (16 of 1908), S. 2(5)].

"Riders" or "Rider Benefits". Means add-on benefits, which are in addition to basic benefits under a policy. [Insurance Regulatory and Development Authority (Actuarial Report and Abstract) Regulations, 2000, Reg. 2(o)]

Right. A claim or title to any subject matter whatsoever; legal title. [T.P. Act (4 of 1882), S. 2(c)]; proper; fit; suitable; correct [CPC (5 of 1908), O. XIV, R. 1(5)].

The term "right", in civil society, is defined to mean that which a man is entitled to have or to do, or to receive from others, within the limits prescribed by law.

A right is an interest which is recognised and protected by law. As it is recognised by law a man is entitled to have it. As it can be protected by law the possessor can enforce it by an appropriate action in a Court. Immunity is one aspect of right and entitles the possessor to see that no one interferes with it. It also furnishes him with a complete answer to any action intended to interfere with that right. *Raj Rajendra Sardar Maloji Narsing Rao* v. *Shankar Saran,* AIR 1958 All 775, 787.

'Right' in S. 74 of the Indian Partnership Act (9 of 1932) means 'substantive rights' and not merely 'right to sue'. *Nand Kishore* v. *Firm Mahswari Mills,* AIR 1953 MB 42, 43.

Right in rem. A right in a thing, whether by ownership of the whole or of an interest. (*Ballentine's Law Dictionary, 3rd Edn.*)

"A right *in rem* need not relate to a tangible *res.* Thus a right that one's reputation should not be unjustifiably attacked is today described as a right *in rem,* since it is a right that avails against persons generally. This shows how far the conception has developed from the

Roman notion of *actio in rem,* for one who sues to protect his reputation is not asking for judgment for a specific *res.* It should also be noticed that on breach of a right *in rem,* a right *in personam* arises against the aggressor." GEORGE WHITECROSS PATON, *A Textbook of Jurisprudence* 300 (G.W. PATON & DAVID P. DERHAM eds. 4th ed. 1972).

Right in rem and **Right in personam.** The security as to life and limb, and indemnity against personal injuries occasioned by the negligence, fraud, or violence of others, is a right in *rem,* as distinguished from a right which avails against a particular individual or a determinate class of persons, which is a right *in personam;* for example, the indemnity which the law affords against assaults by other is a right *in rem,* while the right which one may obtain by contract to secure an indemnity from another for assault by a stranger is a right *in personam.*

Right, liability or relief. The procedure, by which a right or liability may be determined or enforced, or a relief may be obtained is not a *right, liability or relief* within the meaning of S. 2*(c)* of the Transfer of Property Act (4 of 1882).

Right of action. Right of claiming or suing for a debt or obligation due to another.

Right of assembly. A fundamental right of the people to assemble peacefully and without arms for public expression of political ideas and grievaness. [Constitution of India, Art. 19(1)(b)].

Right of audience. A right to appear and be heard in a given Court.

Right of pre-emption. A contractual right of a potential buyer to have the first opportunity to buy at a specified price, if the seller chooses to sell.

Right of privacy. The so-called "right of privacy" is, as the phrase suggests founded upon the claim that a man has the right to pass through this world, if he wills, without having his picture published, his business enterprises discussed, his successful experiments written up for the benefit of others, or his eccentricities commented upon, either in hand bills, circulars, catalogues, periodicals, or newspapers; and necessarily the things which may not be written and published of him must not be spoken of him by his neighbours, whether the comment be favourable or otherwise. Such right does not exist in law, and is not enforceable in equity.

Right of property. Consists in the free use, enjoyment, and disposition of a person's acquisitions without any control or diminution, save only by the law of the land; the right to acquire power and enjoy it in any way consistent with the equal rights of others and the just exactions and demands of the state.

The right to distribute the offerings is a right to property, though the trustees may not have any personal interest in the offerings. [CPC (5 of 1908), S. 9, *Expln.* I]

Right of publicity. The right to the commercial value of identity of a person, including the name of a person, likeness, voice or other indicators of identity.

Right of redemption. Is an agreement by which the mortgagor or vendor reserves to himself the power of taking back the thing sold by returning the loan or price paid.

Right of retainer. Rights of a personal representative to retain debts due to him in preference to paying other creditors of the same degree.

Right of search. The right of a belligerent to examine and inspect the papers of a neutral vessel on the high seas, and the goods contained in her, to see whether she is neutral or an enemy, and to ascertain whether she has contraband of war or enemies property on board.

Right of self defence. The right of self-defence is a high-prized gift granted to the citizens to protect themselves by effective selfresistance against unlawful aggression. No man is expected to fly away when he is attacked. He can fight back and when he apprehends death or grievous hurt he can see that his adversary is vanquished without modulating his defence step by step. Faced with dangerous adversary, no man can possibly act with a detached reflection and under such circumstances if he travels a little beyond the limit, the law protects him and hence Courts should not place more restrictions on him than the law demands. *Chacko Mathai* v. *State of Kerala,* MLJ : QD (1961-1965) Vol IV C1968 : 1964 (2) CrLJ 297 : ILR (1963) 1 Ker 458 : 1963 Ker LT 450 : (1963) 1 Ker LR 468 : AIR 1964 Ker 222.

Right of trade competition. It is the right of every person to engage in a trade or occupation available to him under the law. It may happen that his doing so and competing with another causes loss to the latter but he is not liable for such damage.

Right of way. This phrase has (1) a legal, and (2) a popular, meaning. In its legal sense, it connotes the right of easement which one man has over the land of another, and, in that sense a man cannot have a right of way over his own land; but in its popular sense, "right of way" means, the right of passing over a particular road or place which, of course, is inherent in the ownership of such road or place. The public have a general right of way over all streets and highways.

Right or power to realise property of a dissolved firm. The expression any "right or power to realise the property of a dissolved firm" in S. 69(3), Indian Partnership Act (9 of 1932), would include a suit to recover the outstandings of the dissolved firm. The outstandings are property and a suit to recover the same would be a suit to realise the property. Such right or power is not limited to turning the property into money by sale.

Right to begin. The right to open a case, or the evidence in a case, at the trial.

Right to counsel. The right under which by the constitutions of many of the States, everyone accused of crime is entitled to have the assistance of counsel for his defence; in some jurisdictions the right is confined to capital cases.

Right to die. The right of a terminally ill person to refuse life-sustaining treatment.

Right to education. The State shall provide free and compulsory education to all children of the age of six to fourteen years in such manner as the State may, by law, determine. [Constitution of India, Art. 21-A]

Right to information. "RIGHT TO INFORMATION" means the right to information accessible under this Act which is held by or under the control of any public authority and includes the right to—

(i) inspection of work, documents, records;

(ii) taking notes, extracts or certified copies of documents or records;

(iii) taking certified samples of material;

(iv) obtaining information in the form of diskettes, floppies, tapes, video cassettes or in any other electronic mode or through printouts where such information is stored in a computer or in any other device. [Right to Information Act (22 of 2005), S. 2(j)]

Right to know. Of, relating to, or being a law requiring businesses (as chemical manufacturers) producing or importing hazardous substances to provide information about the substances to the community and inform and train employees who handle it. (*Merriam Webster Dictionary*)

Right to life. The 'right to life' enshrined in Article 21 is not mere survival or existence but it guarantees a right of persons to life with human dignity. All the aspects of life which go to make a person's life meaningful, complete and worth living are included therein. Anyone who wishes to live in peace, comfort and quiet within his house has a right to prevent noise as pollutant reaching him. [*Noise Pollution (V), In Re,* (2005) 5 SCC 733, 745, para 10] [Constitution of India, Art. 21]

'Right to life' for the purpose of Article 21 will not include right to employment. [*Secretary, State of Karnataka* v. *Umadevi*, AIR 2006 SC 1806, 1826, para 42] [Constitution of India, Art. 21]

The 'right to life' under Article 21 of the Constitution embraces within its sweep not only physical existence but the quality of life. [*Confederation of Ex-serviceman Assn.* v. *Union of India*, (2006) 8 SCC 399, 429, para 61] [Constitution of India, Art. 21]

The expression 'right to life' occurring in Article 21 includes 'opportunity'. [*Reliance Energy Ltd.* v. *Maharashtra State Road Development Corpn. Ltd.*, (2007) 8 SCC 1, 21, para 36] [Constitution of India, Art. 21]

Right to light. Every owner of land or building has a natural right to the light vertically coming to his property. But he has no natural right to the light coming laterally to him as it would involve a serious restriction of the natural right of the owner of adjacent land to build it as he pleases.

Right to marry. A right set out in Article 12 of the European Convention on Human Rights and now part of UK law as a consequence of the Human Rights Act. The right is not a particularly strong one; it only exists subject to the national laws governing the exercise of this right. (*Oxford Law Dictionary, 5th Edn., 2003*)

Right to privacy. The right to be let alone; the right of a person to be free from unwarrantd publicity. Term 'right of privacy' is generic term encompassing various rights recognised to be inherent in concept of ordered liberty.

The expression 'right to privacy' would certainly include telephone conversation in the privacy of one's home or office. It is a part of the right to 'life' and personal liberty under Article 21 of the Constitution. *People's Union for Civil Liberties* v. *Union of India,* AIR 1997 SC 568. [Constitution of India, Art. 21]

Right to profess, practise and propagate religion. The fundamental 'right to profess, practise and propagate religion' under Article 25 is subject to public order, morality and health. No person has right to make a claim of curing the ailments and to improve health on the basis of his right to freedom of religion. [*Rajesh Kumar* v. *A.P. Verma,* AIR 2005 All 175, 180, para 19] [Constitution of India, Art. 25]

Right to property. It has been observed in Section 9 that a 'right to property' is a civil right, and where a plaintiff claims a right to property the civil Courts will have jurisdiction to decide the claim though a caste question is incidentally raised in the suit. (1902) 26 Bom 174 (DB) [CPC (5 of 1908), S. 9]

The right of trustees of a Dargah to distribute the offerings made to the Dargah amongst persons entitled thereto is a right to property though the trustees may not have any personal interest in the offerings. The words "right to property" cannot be narrowly construed to mean only "right of ownership of property". *Saruddin Allisahed Mutaval* v. *Hajarat Peer Shamma Meer Saheb Dargar*, MLJ : YD 1977 Suppl to Oct C 131 : AIR 1977 Bom 38. [CPC (5 of 1908), S. 9]

Right to shelter. Right to shelter therefore, was supposed to include adequate living space, safe and decent structure, clean and decent surroundings, sufficient light, pure air and water, electricity, sanitation and other civic amenities like roads so as to have easy access for attending daily avocation. It was concluded that the right to shelter does not mean a right to a mere roof over one's head but right to all the infrastructure to enable human beings to live and develop as human beings. this was found to be an essential requisite to right to live and should be deemed to have been guaranteed as a fundamental right. Reference was also made to the Directive Principles of State Policy and it was ultimately concluded that the State should be deemed to be under an obligation to secure for its citizens, subject to economic budgeting, a decent shelter. *Chameli Singh* v. *State of U.P.*, AIR 1996 SC 105.

Right to sue. The expression "the right to sue" means the right to bring a suit asserting a right.

The words "right to sue" when applied to appeals mean "right to obtain relief".

A claim for unliquidated damages for breach of a contract, after the breach, is not an actionable claim but is a mere right to sue.

The words 'right to sue' are equivalent to right to seek relief when applied to appeals. *Ratanlal Bhannalal Mahajan* v. *Baboolal Hajarilal Jain,* AIR 1960 MP 200, 202. [CPC (5 of 1908), O. XXII, R. 1]

The words "right to sue" mean a right to seek relief, that is a right to prosecute by law, to obtain relief by means of legal procedure; in other words a 'right to sue' accrues when a cause of action arises. *Maheshwar Mahto* v. *Bati Mahatain,* 1994 (1) BLJR 630 at 633.

Right to vote. 'Right to vote' means right to exercise the right in favour of or against the motion or resolution. Such a right implies right to remain neutral as well. [*Mohinder Singh Gill* v. *Chief Election Commr.,* (1993) 4 SCC 234, 236-37, para 2. See also *People's Union for Civil Liberties* v. *Union of India,* (2009) 3 SCC 200, 203, para 4]

Right to worship. 'Right to worship', is a civil right, interference with which raises a dispute of civil nature, but not disputes which are in respect of rituals or ceremonies alone if they are not essentially connected with civil rights of an individual or a sect. *Ugam* v. *Kesrimal,* AIR 1971 SC 2540. [CPC (5 of 1908), S. 9, *Expln.* I]

Rightfully. In conformity with right; in a rightful manner. [Indian Contract Act (9 of 1872), S. 145].

Rights arising from a contract. Basically the rights arising out of a contract must be the rights specifically laid down by it. The correct test is to consider as to whether the right arises either directly or indirectly from the contract itself or it is a right *de hors*. *Partabmull Rameshwar* v. *Fulchand Kanahayilal and Co.,* AIR 1964 Cal 452, 458. [Indian Partnership Act (9 of 1932), S. 69(3)].

Rights in personam. Easement rights created by the decree are contractual obligations which are rights *in personam* enforceable only against the individual owner who expressly or impliedly enters into a contract to respect them. Against the person who thus covenants, an equitable right is created which binds the covenantor, his heirs, assigns or successors. *Lachhaman Ram* v. *Jagbandho Sahu,* MLJ : QD (1961-1965) Vol III C11 : (1962) 4 Orissa JD 349 [Easements Act (1882)]

Rights Management Information. Means,

(a) the title or other information identifying the work or performance;

(b) the name of the author or performer;

(c) the name and address of the owner of rights;

(d) terms and conditions regarding the use of the rights; and

(e) any number or code that represents the information referred to in sub-clauses (a) to (d),

but does not include any device or procedure intended to identify the user. [S. 2(xa) of the Copyright Act, 1957 (14 of 1957) as inserted (w.e.f. 21-6-2012) by the Copyright (Amendment) Act, 20l2 (27 of 2012)]

Rigor juris. Strictness of law. Rigor of the law.

Rigor mortis. Temporary stiffening of a body's joints and muscles after death whose onset may vary from 15 minutes to several hours after death depending on the condition of the dead body and the atmosphere.

Rigorous. Characterised by rigour; rigidly severe or unbending. [CrPC, 1973 (2 of 1974), S. 122(8)].

Rigorous imprisonment. Is defined to mean, imprisonment "with hard labour".

Imprisonment under which the convict has to do hard labour [Fourthly, IPC 1973 (45 of 1860), S. 53]; [CrPC, 1973 (2 of 1974), S. 426(3)].

Riot. A riot is a tumultuous disturbance of the peace by five or more persons, assembled and acting with a common intent; either in executing a lawful private enterprise in a violent and turbulent manner, to the terror of the people, or in executing an unlawful enterprise in a violent and turbulent manner.

A violent disturbance of peace by an assembly or body of persons; an outbreak of active lawlessness. [IPC (45 of 1860), S. 146 and CrPC 1973 (2 of 1974), S. 144(1)].

Riot Control Agent. Means : Any chemical not listed in a Schedule, which can produce rapidly in humans sensory irritation or disabling physical effects which disappear within a short time following termination of exposure. [Chemical Weapons Convention Act (34 of 2000), Art. 2(7)]

Rioting. Whenever force or violence is used by an unlawful assembly, or by any member thereof, in prosecution of the common object of such assembly, every member of such assembly is guilty of the offence of rioting. [IPC (45 of 1860), S. 146]

Riparian. A term used to describe the rights of owners of uplands along running streams or rivers; relating to the bank of a stream or other water river, lake, or sea; pertaining to or situated on the bank of a river; or pertaining to the bank of a river.

Riparian states. States whose jurisdictions are bounded by the banks of a river.

Rising of Court. Final adjournment of a term of a Court; temporary break or recess in Court's business such as the end of the day.

Risk. (*In Insurance Law*) Peril, hazard, or danger; chance of loss.

With specific regard to data or information systems—accidental or unpredictable exposure of information, or violation of operations integrity due to the malfunction of hardware or incomplete or incorrect software design. (*Cyber Law*)

The danger of damage to a system or peripherals attached with the system, due to both security threat and vulnerability. (*Information Technology*)

The chance or hazard of commercial loss; hazard. [IPC (45 of 1860), S. 81, *Expln.* and S. 87].

"RISK" in relation to any article of food, means the probability of an adverse effect on the health of consumers of such food and the severity of that effect, consequential to a food hazard. [S. 3(1)(zm) of the Food Safety & Standards Act, 2006 (34 of 2006)]

Risk analysis. The operation of verifying the security risks, their level and locating the areas for which the safeguards are needed. (*Information Technology*)

"RISK ANALYSIS" in relation to any article of food, means a process consisting of three components, *i.e.*, risk assessment, risk management and risk communication. [S. 3(1)(zn) of the Food Safety & Standards Act, 2006 (34 of 2006)]

Risk assessment. An analysis of system assets and vulnerabilities to establish an expected loss from certain events based on estimated probabilities of the occurrence of those events. (*Information Technology*)

"RISK ASSESSMENT" means a scientifically based process consisting of the following steps : (i) hazard identification,(ii) hazard characterisation; (iii) exposure assessment, and (iv) risk characterization. [S. 3(1)(zo) of the Food Safety & Standards Act, 2006 (34 of 2006)]

Risk-based random sampling. Means the activity of drawing samples randomly based on the risk criteria identified and the compliance history of the importer. [Food Safety and Standards (Import) Regulations, 2017, Regn. 2(1)(v)].

Risk communication. Means the interactive exchange of information and opinions throughout the risk analysis process concerning risks, risk-related factors and risk perceptions, among risk assessors, risk managers, consumers, industry, the academic community and other interested parties, including the explanation of risk assessment findings and the basis of risk management decisions. [S. 3(1)(zp) of the Food Safety & Standards Act, 2006 (34 of 2006)]

Risk management. The total process of identifying, controlling, and eliminating or minimizing uncertain events that may affect Information Technology System resources. (*Information Technology*)

"RISK MANAGEMENT" means the process, distinct from risk assessment, of evaluating policy alternatives, in consultation with all interested parties considering risk assessment and other factors relevant for the protection of health of consumers and for the promotion of fair trade practices, and, if needed, selecting appropriate prevention and control options. [S. 3(1)(zq) of the Food Safety & Standards Act, 2006 (34 of 2006)]

Ritual. Means pertaining or relating to, connected with rites. Rite is a formal procedure or act in a religious or other solemn observance. [*Muniandi Kone* v. *Ramanatha Setupathi Hereditary Trustee of Arulmighu Mangalanathaswami Temple,* AIR 1982 Mad 170, 172, 174. [CPC (5 of 1908), S. 9, *Expln. I*].

River. The word "river" is defined to be a large stream of water flowing in a channel on land toward the ocean, lake, or other river.

"RIVER" includes any stream, canal, creek or other channels, natural or artificial. [Indian Forest Act (16 of 1927), S. 2(5)].

"RIVER" includes its tributaries. [Rajasthan Flood Plain Zoning Act, 1990 (Raj Act No. 15 of 1997), S. 2(i)]

RLAN. (*abbr.*) Radio Local Area Network. Also called RLAN which is the abbreviation of radio local area network. This system allows an extension of the local area computer network without the need of cable (*e.g.* wireless internet access in airports with laptops). (*Telecommunication*)

Road. "ROAD" means the way of a road, street, thoroughfare, passage or place along or across which a tramway authorized under this Act is, or is intended to be, laid, and includes the surface-soil and sub-soil of a road, and the footway, berms, drains and ditches of a road, and any bridge, culvert or causeway forming part of a road. [Indian Tramways Act (11 of 1886), S. 3(2)]

An ordinary line of communication between different places used by horses, travellers on foot or vehicles [Indian Evidence Act (1 of 1872), S. 32, ill. (i); Delhi Muncipal Corporation Act (66 of 1957), S. 57 and Constitution of India, Art. 15(2)(b)].

"A foot path, a foot track, bridge path, tramway track, speedway, autobahn and railway track or railroad will all be roads", notwithstanding their use or exclusive use by a pedestrian, rider, tramway, fast moving vehicles or a railway engine, wagon or compartment. *UOI* v. *Authority Under the Minimum Wages Act, 1948, for Neval Area*, AIR 1969 Bom 310, 314. [Minimum Wages Act (11 of 1948), Sch. I, Part I, Entry 7]

Road Ambulance. Means a specially equipped and ergonomically designed vehicle for transportation and/or emergent treatment of sick or injured people and capable of providing out of hospital medical care during transit or when stationary, commensurate with its designated level of care when appropriately staffed. [Central Motor Vehicles Rules, 1989, R. 2(zb)].

Road safety works. Means the works on State roads (other than Rural Roads) for rectification of identified road accident black spots based on road accident or fatality data or the works based on the recommendations of specialized bodies or expert committees set up for this purpose. [Central Road Fund (State Roads) Rules, 2014, R. 2(1)(gb)].

Road marking. Means the lines, patterns, words except road signs which are applied or attached to the carriageway or kerbs or to objects within or adjacent to the carriageway for controlling, warning, guiding and informing the road users. [Motor Vehicles (Driving) Regulations, 2017, Regn. 2(1)(n)].

Road-authority. "ROAD-AUTHORITY", in relation to a road, means—

(a) if a local authority maintains and repairs the road, then that authority;

(b) if a local authority does not maintain and repair the road, and the road is neither vested in Government nor maintained and repaired by Government, then the person in whom the road is vested; and

(c) if an authority does not maintain and repair the road, and the road is vested in Government or maintained and repaired by Government, then the Government for whose purposes a road is so vested or by which the road is maintained and repaired, as the case may be. [Indian Tramways Act (11 of 1886), S. 3(3)]

Road transport service. Means a service carrying passengers or goods or both by road in vehicles for hire or reward. [Road Transport Corporations Act (64 of 1950), S. 2 (e)]

Roaming. Contracts between operators enabling customers to use other mobile telephony networks. (*Telecommunication*)

The use of a wireless phone outside of the "home" service area defined by a service provider. Higher per-minute rates are usually charged for calls made or received while roaming. Long distance rates and a daily access fee may also apply. (*Telecommunication*)

Robbed. One against whom robbery has been committed [Indian Evidence Act (1 of 1872), S. 8, ill. (f)]; deprived of something by unlawful force or the exercise of superior power [Indian Evidence Act (1 of 1872), S. 8, ill. (k)].

Robber. One who indulges in robbery as defined in the Indian Penal Code.

Robbery. Extortion is robbery if the offender, at the time of committing the extortion, is in the presence of the person put in fear, and commits the extortion by putting that person in fear of instant death, or instant hurt, or of instant wrongful restraint to that person, or to some other person, and, by so putting in fear, induces the person so put in fear then and there to deliver up the thing extorted." [IPC (45 of 1860), S. 390].

In all robbery there is either theft or extortion. Theft is "robbery" if, in order to the committing of the theft, or in committing the theft, or in carrying away or attempting to carry away property obtained by the theft, the offender, for that end, voluntarily causes or attempts to cause to any person death or hurt or wrongful restraint, or fear of instant death or of instant hurt, or of instant wrongful restraint.

The word "robbery" when used in the expression "robbery from a running train" need not be interpreted with reference to the definition of "robbery" contained in the Indian Penal Code (45 of 1860).

"Robbery" means what "robbery" is defined to mean in the Indian Penal Code; even if this is not correct it must mean something more than mere theft by stealth from a train, running or otherwise.

Rod. A bar. [Gold (Control) Act (45 of 1968) (*repealed*), S. 2(r)].

Roll. "ROLL" means the electoral roll for a ward. [Kerala Municipalities (Registration of Electors) Rules, 1994, R. 2(f)]

Rolling-stock. "ROLLING-STOCK" includes locomotive engines, tenders, carriage, wagons, trucks and trollies of all kinds. [Indian Railways Act (9 of 1890), S. 3(10)]

"ROLLING STOCK" includes locomotives, tenders, carriages, wagons, rail-cars, containers, trucks, trolleys and vehicles of all kinds moving on rails. [Indian Railways Act (24 of 1989), S. 2(37)]

"ROLLING STOCK" includes locomotives, engines carriages (whether powered or not), wagons, trollies and vehicles of all kind moving or intended to move on rails. [Metro Railways (Construction of Works) Act (33 of 1978), S. 2(q)]

ROM. (*abbr.*) Read-only memory. A type of data-storage device that is manufactured with fixed contents. The term is most often applied to semiconductor-integrated circuit memories. ROM is inherently nonvolatile storage—it retains its contents even when the power is switched off, in contrast to RAM. It is used in part for storage of the lowest level bootstrap software (firmware) in a computer.

The word 'ROM' is an acronym for 'Read Only Memory', a type of unchangeable memory residing in chips or the ICs on the motherboard. ROM contains bare minimum of instructions needed to start computer. ROMs are generally called firmware. [*Aanjaleem Enterprises (P) Ltd.* v. *CCE,* (2006) 2 SCC 336, 347, para 19]

Roman catholic. "ROMAN CATHOLIC" means and applies to the Church which regards the Pope of Rome as its spiritual head. [(Indian) Christian Marriage Act (15 of 1872), S. 3]

Room. "ROOM" includes a suite of rooms which is ordinarily hired out as one unit. [Bihar Taxation on Luxuries in Hotels Act (5 of 1988), S. 2(n)]

Room charges. Means the charges for a unit of residential accommodation in a hotel and includes the charges for—

(a) furniture, air conditioner, refrigerator, radio, music, telephone, television and

(b) such other services as are normally included by a hotel in room rent, but does not include charges, for food, drinks, any services other than those referred to in sub-clauses (a) and (b). [Expenditure-tax Act (35 of 1987)], S. 2(10)]

Room in a hotel. A room in a hotel must fulfil two conditions (1) it must be part of a hotel in the physical sense and (2) its user must be connected with general purpose of the hotel of which it is a part. The space let out to an hairdresser is an amenity for the residents of the hotel. So it will be a room in a hotel. *Associated Hotels of India Ltd.* v. *R.N. Kapoor*, AIR

1959 SC 1262, 1264. [Delhi Ajmer Merwara Rent Control Act (19 of 1947), S. 2(b)]

Rootkits. Rootkits are programmes designed to capture the 'root access' or take control of the system while avoiding detection from anti-virus scans. In other words, a rootkit is a virus which seeks to hide the fact that the computer is compromised from the operating system and therefore from the user. ['Symantec Internet Security Threat Report Trends for 2010', April 2011]

Root stock. "ROOT STOCK" means a fruit and ornamental plant or part thereof on which any portion of fruit and ornamental plant has been grafted or budded. [Goa Fruit and Ornamental Plant Nurseries (Regulation) Act, 1995 (Goa Act No. 13 of 1997), S. 2(n)]

Rope. "ROPE" includes any cable, wire, rail or way, whether flexible or rigid, used for suspending, carrying or hauling a carrier. [Rajasthan Ropeways Act, 1996 (Raj. Act No. 18 of 1997), S. 2(m)]

Rosewood tree. "ROSEWOOD TREE" includes blackwood, rose wood, Indian rosewood and includes Malabar blackwood, their stumps and brush woods and also includes rose wood trees when they have fallen or have been felled and all rose wood whether cut up or fashioned or hollowed out for any purpose or not. [T.N. Rosewood Trees Conservation Act, 1994 (1 of 1995), S. 2(4)]

Rotational transfer. It means transfer from one post to another and after the member has spent some time in the post to which he has been transferred he should be brought back to the original post. *P.C. Joshi* v. *The Director General, Posts & Telegraphs, New Delhi*, AIR 1975 SC 1, 5.

Round trip financing. For the purposes of section 97(1) of Act 43 of 1961, 'round trip financing' includes any arrangement in which, through a series of transactions—

(a) funds are transferred among the parties to the arrangement; and

(b) such transactions do not have any substantial commercial purpose other than obtaining the tax benefit (but for the provisions of this Chapter),

without having any regard to—

(A) whether or not the funds involved in the round trip financing can be traced to any funds transferred to, or received by, any party in connection with the arrangement;

(B) the time, or sequence, in which the funds involved in the round trip financing are transferred or received; or

(C) the means by, or manner in, or mode through, which funds involved in the round trip financing are transferred or received. [(w.e.f. 1-4-2016) S. 97(2) of the Income-tax Act, 1961 (43 of 1961); [(still-born) Section 97(2) of the Income-tax Act, 1961 (43 of 1961) as inserted (w.e.f. 1-4-2014) by the Finance Act, 2012 (23 of 2012) and omitted (w.e.f. 1-4-2014) by the Finance Act, 2013 (17 of 2013)]

Route. "ROUTE" means a line of travel which specifies the highway which may be traversed by a motor vehicle between one terminus and another. [Motor Vehicles Act (59 of 1988), S. 2(38)]

"Route" and "Highway". A route is a line of travel between one terminus and another but it is not distinct from the highway traversed. *Adarsh Travels Bus Service* v. *State of U.P.*, AIR 1986 SC 319, 322.

Route or area. The word 'route' means the national line and also the actual road on which the omnibuses run. The words 'route' and 'area' mean the same thing. *CPC Motor Services* v. *State of Mysore*, AIR 1966 SC 1661, 1665.

Route, road, course. Route is to road as the species to the genus; a route is a circular kind of road; it is chosen as the circuitous direction towards a certain point; the road may be either in a direct or indirect line; the route is always indirect; the route is chosen only by horsemen, or those who go to a considerable distance; the road may be chosen for the shortest distance; the route and road are pursued in their beaten track; the course is often chosen in the unbeaten track; an army or a company go by a certain route; foot passengers are seen to take a certain course over fields.

Royalty. "ROYALTY", in respect of a patent, means consideration (including any lump sum, consideration but excluding any consideration which would be the income of the recipient chargeable under the head "Capital gains" or consideration for sale of product manufactured with the use of patented process or of the patented article for commercial use) for—

(i) the transfer of all or any rights (including the granting of a licence) in respect of a patent; or

(ii) the imparting of any information, concerning the working of, or the use of, a patent; or

(iii) the use of any patent; or

(iv) the rendering of any services in connection with the activities referred to in sub-clauses (*i*) to (*iii*). [Income tax Act (43 of 1961), S. 80 RRB *Expln.* (g)]

Dues payable to a land for mining rights; sums paid for the use of a patent; percentage paid to an author by a publisher on the sale of his book. [Coal Mines (Nationalisation) Act (26 of 1973), S. 22(2)(a) and Indian Stamp Act (2 of 1890), S. 26].

ROYALTY has several meanings : (1) percentages or dues payable to land owners for mining rights; (2) sums paid for the use of a patent; (3) percentages paid to an author by a publisher on the sales of a book.

Royalty, a payment reserved by the grantor of a patent, lease of a mine or similar right, and payable proportionately to the use made of the right by the grantee. It is usually a payment of money, but may be a payment in kind, that is, of part of the produce of the exercise of the right. *State of Orissa* v. *Titaghur Paper Mills Co. Ltd.*, AIR 1985 SC 1293, 1336.

Royalty means a share of the product or profit reserved by the owner for permitting another to use the property.

Royalty is a tax on forest produce grown on private lands. *District Council of Jowei Autonomous District* v. *D Wet Singh*, AIR 1986 SC 1930, 1938.

"ROYALTY". For the removal of doubts, it is hereby clarified that the 'royalty' includes and has always included consideration in respect of any right, property or information, whether or not—

(a) the possession or control of such right, property or information is with the payer;

(b) such right, property or information is used directly by the payer;

(c) the location of such right, property or information is in India. [*Explanation 5* to section 9(1)(vi) of the Income-tax Act, 1961 (43 of 1961) as inserted (w.r.e.f. 1-6-1976) by the Finance Act, 2012 (23 of 2012)]

'Royalty' and 'dead rent'. Royalty is a kind of rent which the lessor of a mine charges from the lessee, varying with the quantity of the minerals produced.

Dead rent is the minimum guaranteed amount of royalty per year payable as per rules or agreements under a mining lease. *Atma Ram Bilochi* v. *State of Rajasthan,* AIR 1981 Raj 197, 200. [Mines and Minerals (Regulation and Development) Act (67 of 1957), S. 15]

RSA. A cryptographic system of public key invented by Rivest, Shamir and Adelman. (*Information Technology*)

RSS. Rich Site Summary or RDF Site Summary or Real Simple Syndication. A commonly used protocol for syndication and sharing of content, originally developed to facilitate the syndication of news articles, now widely used to share the contents of *blogs*.

RSS is an *XML*-based summary of a web site, usually used for syndication and other kinds of content-sharing.

There are RSS "feeds" which are sources of RSS information about web sites, and RSS "readers" which read RSS feeds and display their content to users.

RSS is being overtaken by a newer, more complex protocol called *Atom.* (*Matisse Enzer-Glossary of Internet Terms*)

Rubber. "RUBBER", means—

(i) crude rubber, that is to say, rubber prepared from the leaves, bark or latex of any rubber plant;

(ii) the latex of any rubber plant whether fluid or coagulated, in any stage of the treatment to which it is subjected during the process of conversion into rubber;

(iii) latex (dry rubber content) in any state of concentration, and includes scrap rubber, sheet rubber, rubber in powder and all forms and varieties of crepe rubber, but does not include contained in any manufactured article. [Rubber Act (24 of 1947), S. 3(h)]

Rubber means crude rubber, the latex of any rubber plant, latex (dry rubber content) and includes scrap rubber, sheet rubber, rubber in powder and all forms and varieties of crepe rubber. *Madras Rubber Factory Ltd.* v. *Rubber Board, Kottayam,* AIR 1982 Ker 257. [Rubber Act (24 of 1947), S. 3(h)]

Rubber plant. Includes plants, trees, shrubs or vines of any of the following: —

(i) Hevea Braziliensis (Para Rubber),

(ii) Maniaot Glaziovii (Ceara Rubber),

(iii) Castillio elastica,

(iv) Ficus elastica (Rambong), and

(v) Any other plant which the Board may, by notification in the Gazette of India, declare to be a rubber plant for the purpose of this Act. [Rubber Act (24 of 1947), S. 3(i)]

Rubbish. "RUBBISH" means broken brick, mortar, broken glass, kitchen or stable refuse, or refuse of any kind whatsoever not included in the term "offensive matter". [Bengal Municipal Act (3 of 1884), S. 6(14)]

Rubrics. "Rubrics" was a name given in England to the titles of Acts of Parliament, and were so called because written in red ink.

Rule making. The process which is used by an administrative agency to formulate, amend, or repeal a rule or regulation.

Rule nisi. A rule which will become imperative and final unless cause be shown against it.

Rule nisi and rule absolute. An order made by the Court on motion requiring a person to show cause why he should not do some particular act, or commanding the performance of the particular act forthwith. When the rule is to show cause, it is called a *rule nisi*, which is served on the opposite party and when it comes on for hearing the Court, having heard counsel, discharges the rule or makes it absolute. When it directs the performance of the act forthwith, it is called a *rule absolute*.

Rule of course. A rule granted as matter of routine without application to the judge, or with only a formal application; otherwise called *office rule.* (*Kinney*)

Rule of exclusion. (*Interpretation of Statutes*) The rule of exclusion is merely an anxiliary rule of construction adopted for the purpose of ascertaining the intention of the law giver. It is neither conclusive nor of universal application and is to be applied with great caution. It may be applied only when in the natural association of ideas the contract between what is provided and what is left out leads to an inference that the latter was intended to be excluded; it may accordingly be held inapplicable if there exists a plausible reason for not including what is left out. *C.W. Co-operative Transport Society* v. *Punjab State*, AIR 1962 Punj 94, 98.

Rule of law. The rule of law permeates the entire fabric of the constitution and indeed forms one of its basic features. The rule of law excludes arbitrariness; its postulate is 'intelligence without passion' and 'reason freed from desire'. *Bachan Singh* v. *State of Punjab*, AIR 1982 SC 1325, 1336. [Constitution of India, Article 14, 21].

The term rule of law in brief connotes the undisputed supremacy of law and envisages a state of things in which everyone respects the law and where law is to be followed by everyone collectively and individually by the citizens as well as the State. [Sale of Goods Act (3 of 1930), S. 66(e)]

The rule of law means that decisions should be made by the application of known principles and rules and, in general, such decisions should be predictable and the citizen should know where he is. *Jaisinghani* v. *Union of India*, AIR 1967 SC 1427, 1434.

Rule of procedure. Rules made by any judicial or legislative body, as to the mode and manner of conducting the business of the body.

Rule of strict construction. The rule that a fiscal statute must be construed strictly means only this much that if the words construed reasonably create a liability it is not for the Court to determine the wisdom of enactment; but if the words do not indicate the liability of the subject, the tax must be disallowed. *Shriram Gulabdar* v. *Board of Revenue*, AIR 1952 Nag 378.

Rule or rules. "RULE" shall mean a rule made in exercise of a power covered by an enactment, and shall include a regulation made as a rule under any enactment. [General Clauses Act (10 of 1897), S. 3(51)].

"RULES" include prescribed forms. [Extradition Act (15 of 1903), S. 2]

"RULES" and "RULE" mean, respectively the rules made or to be made and notified by the Local Government under the authority of any Act, and any one of such rules. [Pun. Act III of 1911 (Municipal), S. 3 cl. 12.]

"RULES" with reference to the rules relating in general to the constitution and management of an association, includes in the case of an incorporated association its memorandum and article of association. [Forward Contracts (Regulation) Act (74 of 1952), S. 2(k)]

That which is prescribed or laid down as a guide to conduct; that which is settled by authority or custom; a regulation; a prescription; a minor law; a uniform course of things; the regulation adopted by a deliberative body for the conduct of its proceedings.

A prescribed, suggested or self-imposed guide for conduct or action; a principle; a kind of regulation or bye-law; a principle regulating some action. [General Clauses Act (10 of 1897), S. 3(51) and Constitution of India, Art. 13(3)(a)].

A "rule" is a definite regulation prescribed as a law of conduct.

A rule is one which prescribes or lays down a general standard or guide to conduct. Such a general standard or guide to conduct having behind it the sanction of a statutory provision is a statutory rule having the force of law. *Saksena* v. *State of M.P.*, AIR 1964 MP 248, 252. [Constitution of India, Art. 309, *Prov.*].

Ruler. "RULER" means the Prince, Chief or other person who, at any time before the commencement of the Constitution (Twenty-sixth Amendment) Act, 1971, was recognised by the President as the Ruler of an Indian State or any person who, at any time before such commencement, was recognised by the President as the successor of such Ruler. [Constitution of India, Art. 366(22)]

"RULER" includes the Prince, Chief or other person recognised before such commencement by His Majesty or the Government of the Dominion of India as the Ruler of any Indian State. [Constitution of India, Art. 363(2)(b)]

"RULER", in relation to a foreign state, means the person who is for the time being recognised by the Central Government to be the head of that State. [CPC (5 of 1908), S. 87A(1)(b)]

One who rules over a nation or people. [Indian Evidence Act (1 of 1872), S. 113].

Rules. "RULES", in a legal sense, mean "laws".

"Rules" include prescribed forms.

Statutory rules, when validly made within the powers conferred by the Act, must be regarded as part of the Act itself and made with the full authority of the Legislature. The rules must be held to be a part of the Parent Act, and can do anything it can do if within its scope.

Rules and Regulations. Includes any rule or regulation (by whatever name called) which the Institute is competent to make in the exercise of the powers conferred on it under the Societies Registration Act, 1860, but shall not include any bye-laws or standing orders made under the rules and regulations for the conduct of its day-to-day administration. [Indian Statistical Institute Act (57 of 1959), S. 2 (c)]

"RULES AND REGULATIONS" includes any rule or regulation by whatever name called which the sabha is competent to make in the exercise of the powers conferred on it under the Societies Registration Act 1860 but shall not include any bye-laws or standing orders made under the rules and regulations for the conduct of its work. [Dakshina Bharat Hindi Prachar Sabha Act (14 of 1964), S. 2(b)]

Rules committee. A Parliamentary Committee appointed to consider matters of procedure and conduct of business in the House; recommends amendments or additions to the Rules.

Rules made. Under the Code there are two classes of rules, *i.e.* Rules contained in the First Schedule which may be annulled, altered or added to by the High Court and other rules which do not form part of the

First Schedule but will have the same force and effect as if they had been contained in the First Schedule. *Pappathi Ammal* v. *Sivagnanam Pillai,* AIR 1954 TC 526, 531 (FB). [Code of Civil Procedure (Amendment) Act, 1951, S. 20(2)]

Rules of Court. The rules of practice and rules to regulate procedure and facilitate the administration of justice which Courts have the inherent power to prescribe as they may deem necessary, independently of statute giving them authority to do so. [Constitution of India, Art. 145].

Rules of natural justice. The expression 'rules of natural justice' has not been completely or absolutely defined although some principles have been laid down, which are widely accepted. Two of those principles are generally applicable to all departmental enquiries and they are (1) a person must be told clearly and specifically of the offences with which it is intended to charge him, and (2) he must not be condemned unheard. 1911 AC 179 : 1915 AC 120 : (1946) 1 KB 621 : AIR 1952 Cal 594 : AIR 1951 Mad 1003 : (1951) 2 MLJ 96 : AIR 1955 Cal 166 and 59 CalWN 794, **relied on**. *Ramesh Chandra Verma* v. R. *D. Verma,* MLJ : QD (1956-1960) Vol. II C692 : AIR 1958 All 532 : ILR (1958) 1 All 577. [Constitution of India, Art. 311]

Rules of procedure. The expression 'rules of procedure' means rules regulating the procedure and conduct of business of the legislature. *Godavaris Misra* v. *Nand Kishore Das,* AIR 1953 Ori 111, 115. [Constitution of India, Art. 208 (2)]

Rules of the organization. "RULES OF THE ORGANIZATION" means, in particular the constituent instruments relevant decisions and resolutions and established practice of the organization. [Vienna Convention on the Presentation of State in their Relation with International Organizations of a Universal Character, 1975, Art. I (34)]

Ruling. A judicial decision; an authoritative pronouncement.

Ruling chief. The chief who is ruling. [CPC (5 of 1908), O. XXXII, R. 16].

Rummage. A thorough search, especially among a variety or confusion of objects or into every section of an area [Gold (Control) Act (45 of 1968) (*repealed*), S. 61(a)].

Rumour. A statement or report circulating in a community of the truth of which there is not clear evidence. [IPC (45 of 1860), S. 505].

Runner. A law office employee who delivers papers between offices and files papers in Court.

Running account. Current account; *i.e.* an account between two parties having a series of transactions not covered by evidence of indebtedness (as notes or certificates) and usually subject to settlement at stated intervals (as monthly or quarterly). [T.P. Act (4 of 1882), S. 79].

Running days. Consecutive days, including Sundays and holidays.

Running down case. An action for damages against the driver or owner of a vehicle for colliding with another vehicle or person.

Running time. In relation to a working day means the time from the moment a transport vehicle starts functioning at the beginning of the working day until the moment when the transport vehicle ceases to function at the end of the working day, excluding any time during which the running of the transport vehicle is interrupted for a period exceeding such duration as may be prescribed during which period the persons who drive, or perform any other work in connection with the transport vehicle are free to dispose of their time as they please or are engaged in subsidiary work. [Motor Transport Workers Act (27 of 1961), S. 2(f) *Expln.* (1)]

Running trains. A "running train" means a train in motion between stations.

The expression "running train" includes a train temporarily stopped at a signal between stations.

Runway. A path for aircraft to land on or to take off from. [Factories Act (63 of 1948), S. 29(3), *Expln.* (a)].

Rural area. Means any area other than—

(i) an area which is comprised within the jurisdiction of a municipality (whether known as a municipality, municipal corporation, notified area committee, town area committee or by any other name) or a cantonment board and which has a population of not less than ten thousand according to the preceeding census of which relevant figures have been published before the first day of the previous year; or

(ii) an area within such distance not being more than fifteen kilometers from the local limits of any municipality or cantonment board referred to in sub-clause (i), as the Central Government may, having regard to the stage of development of such area (including the extent of, and scope for, urbanisation of such area) and other relevant considerations specify in this behalf by notification in the Official Gazette. [Income-tax Act (43 of 1961), S. 80 IA (12)(e)] and [Income-tax Act (43 of 1961), S. 80B (14)(f)]

"RURAL AREA" means the area comprised in any village and includes the area comprised in any town the population of which does not exceed ten thousand or such other figure as the Reserve Bank may specify from time to time. [National Bank for Agriculture and Rural Development Act (61 of 1981), S. 2(q)(b)]

"RURAL AREA" means any area in a State except those areas covered by any urban local body or a cantonment board established or constituted under any law for the time being in force. [S. 2(17) of the National Food Security Act, 2013 (20 of 2013)]

Rural artisan. "RURAL ARTISAN" means a person who being resident in a rural area, earns his livelihood in such area by practising any craft by his own labour or by the labour of the members of his family and whose annual income during the year immediately preceeding the appointed day does not exceed two thousand and four hundred & four rupees. [Gujarat Rural Debtors (Temporary Relief) Act (15 of 1976), S. 2(i)]

Rural development. Means development of rural areas through many activities conducive to such development;

(a) activities conducive to development of rural areas include activities relating to production of goods or provision of services in rural areas and activities for the promotion of cottage and village industries, industry in the tiny and decentralised sector and small-scale industry and handicrafts and other rural crafts;

(b) "rural area" means the area comprised in any village and includes the area comprised in any town the population of which does not exceed ten thousand or such other figure as the Reserve Bank may specify from time to time. [National Bank for Agriculture and Rural Development Act (61 of 1981), S. 2(q)]

Rural sector. Shall mean any place as per the latest census which has—

(i) a population of not more than five thousand;

(ii) a density of population of not more than four hundred per square kilometre; and

(iii) at least seventy-five per cent of the male working population is engaged in agriculture. [Insurance Regulatory and Development Authority (Obligations of Insurers to Rural or Social Sectors) Regulations, 2000, *Regn.* 2(c)]

Ryot. Peasant, subject, tenant of land.

The tenant of an old waste which is not *ryoti* land does not come under the definition of *ryot*. 21 IC 532 (533).

The word '*ryot* has the same meaning as under the Madras Estates Land Act, 1908 and the question as to who is a *ryot* can arise only in respect of *ryoti* land. [*Bobbili Sriramamurthy* v. *Batchu Dhanraju*, AIR 1957 AP 495, 497]. [Madras Estates (Abolition and Conversion into Ryotwari) Act (26 of 1948), S 56]

Ryotwari. Arrangement about rent made annually in India, directly between the Government and the ryots.

S

SAARC. "SAARC" means an organisation known as the South Asian Association for Regional Co-operation established by the Charter of the South Asiȧn Association for Regional Co-operation signed on eighth day of December, 985. [South Asian University Act, 2008 (8 of 2009), S. 2(t)]

"SACFA". Means Standing Advisory Committee for Frequency Allocation. [Flight and Maritime Connectivity Rules, 2018, R. 2(1)(m)].

Sabotage. Malicious destruction or damage to property with the intention of injuring a business or impairing the economic system or weakening a government or nation especially at war or national emergency. [Payment of Bonus Act (21 of 1965), S. 9(c)].

Sacita quaedam habentur pro expressis. Certain things though unexpressed are considered as expressed.

Sacramentum habet in se tres comites, veritatem, justitiam et judicum : veritas habenda est in jurato; justitia et judicium in judice. (*Lat.*) (3 Inst. 160) An oath implies or requires three attendant circumstances truth, justice and judgment; truth is to be observed in the partly sworn, justice and judgment in the judge (before whom the oath is taken).

Sadar. Principal, chief; eminence; superiority; supreme; the chief seat of Government; the presidency as opposed to the provinces or mofussil.

Sadr adalat. The Supreme Court, the name of the highest Court established under the East India Company in each Presidency.

Sadr diwani adalat. The chief Civil Court under the East India Company.

Sadr nizamat and diwani adalat. The Supreme Criminal and Civil Court; the title of a Supreme Court and Court of final appeal established under the East India Company.

Saepe constitutum est. res inter alios judicatas aliis non praejudicare. It has often been determined that matters adjudged between other parties do not prejudice.

"Safai karamchari" means a person engaged in, or employed for, manually carrying human excreta or any sanitation work. [National Commission for Safai Karamcharis Act (64 of 1993), S. 2(e)] and [Maharashtra State Commission for Safai Karamcharis Act (44 of 1997), S. 2(e)]

Safe. Free from danger or hurt [IPC (45 of 1860), S. 431]; affording protection from danger; securing from harm; secure or affording security [CPC (2 of 1974), 1st Sch. App. F, form No. 7]; a chest or closet. [Income-tax Act (43 of 1961), S. 132(c)(ii)].

"SAFE", as used in the statement that employers are bound to furnish safe machinery, safe appliances, safe places to work, etc. does not have an absolute or unqualified meaning, since they would operate to make an employer an absolute insurer of the safety of his employees. The word "safe", as so used, means merely to require the exercise of care with regard to safety.

Safe and secure custody. A custody in which there is safety and protection from danger. [CPC (5 of 1908), 1st Sch., App. F, form No. 7].

Safe harbour. An area or means of protection. A provision (as in a statute or regulation) that affords protection from liability or penalty.

Guidelines for conduct which, if followed, mean that one will not be prosecuted.

Safety. The quality or condition of being safe; exemption from danger or hurt. [IPC (45 of 1860), S. 21, *Eighth*].

Safety Convention. Means the Convention for the Safety of Life at Sea signed in London on the [1st day of November, 1974] as amended from time to time. [Merchant Shipping Act (44 of 1958), S. 3(37)]

Safety convention certificate. Means,—

(i) a passenger ship safety certificate,

(ia) a special trade passenger ship safety certificate,

(ib) a special trade passenger ship space certificate,

(ii) a qualified passenger ship safety certificate,

(iii) a cargo ship safety construction certificate,

(iv) a qualified cargo ship safety construction certificate,

(v) a cargo ship safety equipment certificate,

(vi) a qualified cargo ship safety equipment certificate,

(vii) a cargo ship safety radio telegraphy certificate,

(viii) a cargo ship safety radio telephony certificate,

(ix) an exemption certificate,

(x) a nuclear passenger ship safety certificate,

(xi) a nuclear cargo ship safety certificate, issued under Part IX or, as the case may be, Part IXA. [Merchant Shipping Act (44 of 1958), S. 3(38)]

Safety glass. 'SAFETY GLASS' means glass conforming to the specifications of the Bureau of Indian Standards or any International Standards [***]] and so manufactured or treated that if fractured, it does not fly or break into fragments capable of causing severe cuts;

(ii) any windscreen or window at the front of the vehicle, the inner surface of which is at an angle [more than thirty degrees] to the longitudinal axis of the vehicle shall be deemed to face to the front.

[Central Motor Vehicle Rules, 1989, R. 100(1) *Expln.* (i)]

Safety in coal mines. Includes the safety of any railway situated on the surface above a coal mine. [Coal Mines (Conservation & Development) Act (28 of 1974), S. 3(i)]

Sagol. Means cement obtained by heating limestone and burnt coal in a kiln. [Customs Tariff Act (51 of

1975), I Sch., Import Tariff, S. V, Chap. 25, Note 4, Supplementary note, heading No. 2523; Central Excise Tariff Act, 1985 (5 of 1986), Sch. I, S. V, Chap. 25, Note 3, heading No. 25.02]

Sagotra. A kinsman; one allied by community of name and descent; a gentile relation. (*Wil. Gloss.*)

Sailing vessel. Means any description of vessel provided with sufficient sail area for navigation under sails alone, whether or not fitted with mechanical means of propulsion and includes a rowing boat or canoe but does not include a pleasure craft. [Merchant Shipping Act (44 of 1958), S. 3(39)]

Sailor. "SAILOR" means a member of the Coast Guard other than an officer, a subordinate officer or other enrolled person. [Coast Guard Act (30 of 1978), S. 2(t)]

One who is professionally occupied with navigation; a member of a ship's company below the rank of officer; member of the naval force. [CrPC, 1973 (2 of 1974), S. 475(2)].

Salaried servant of Government. 'SALARIED SERVANT OF THE GOVERNMENT' does not include a retired servant of the Government in receipt of a pension or a person in receipt of a salary from the Government who is not a full time servant of the Government. [Gujarat Municipalities Act, 1963 (34 of 1964), S. 2(24)]

Salaries. The 'salaries' received by Judges of Supreme Court and High Courts under Arts. 125 and 225 respectively comes within the expression 'salaries' under Section 15 of the Act. *Justice Deoki Nandan Agarwala* v. *Union of India*, AIR 1999 SC 1951. [Income-tax Act (43 of 1961), S. 15]

Salaries and wages. Means the sums expended for salaries and wages and any contributions made by the owner of the station for pensions, provident fund, superannuation and insurance of officer and servants less the proportion of such sums properly attributable to the cost of fuel under cl. (d) and to the cost of repairs, maintenance and renewals under clause (f). [Electricity (Supply) Act (54 of 1948), Ninth Sch. I (g)] [Now repealed & replaced by Act 36 of 2003]

Salary. "SALARY" means the total monthly emoluments, excluding any allowance declared exempt from attachment under the provisions of cl. (l), derived by a person from his employment whether on duty or on leave. [CPC (5 of 1908), S. 60, *Expl.* II]

"SALARY" includes—

(i) wages;

(ii) any annuity or pension;

(iii) any gratuity;

(iv) any fees, commission, perquisites or profits *in lieu* of or in addition to any salary or wages;

(v) any advance of salary;

(va) any payment received by an employee in respect of any period of leave not availed of by him;

(vi) the annual accretion to the balance at the credit of an employee participating in a recognised provident fund, to the extent to which it is chargeable to tax under Rule 6 of Part A of the Fourth Schedule; and

(vii) the aggregate of all sums that are comprised in the transferred balance as referred to in sub-rule (2) of Rule 11 of Part A of the Fourth Schedule of an employee participating in a recognised provident fund, to the extent to which it is chargeable to tax under sub-rule (4) thereof.

(viii) the contribution made by the Central Government or any other employer in the previous year, to the account of an employee under a pension scheme referred to in section 80CCD; [Income-tax Act (43 of 1961), S. 17(1)]

For the purposes of this section, "SALARY" includes dearness allowance, if the terms of employment so provide, but excludes all other allowances and perquisites'. [Income-tax Act (43 of 1961), S. 80 CCD *Expln.* (Inserted by Finance Act (23 of 2004), S. 15].

'Salary' of a teacher or employee means the aggregate of the emoluments, including dearness or any other allowance, for the time being payable to him at the rate approved for the purpose of payment of maintenance grant. [Uttar Pradesh Junior High Schools (Payment of Salaries of Teachers and Other Employees) Act, 1978, S. 2(i) as cited in *State of U.P. v. Pawan Kumar Divedi*, (2014) 9 SCC 692, para 28].

"SALARY" includes dearness allowance, if the terms of employment so provide, but excludes all other allowances and perquisites. [Income Tax Rules (1962), Sch IV, Part A, R. 2(h)]

Fixed payment made periodically to a person as compensation for regular work (now usually for non-manual work). [T.P. Act (4 of 1882), S. 6(f)].

The word 'salary' as used in proviso (i) to S. 60(1), CPC (5 of 1908), must be construed as meaning the total monthly emoluments to which a public servant is entitled, including any sum which may be required for the payment of taxes or payments or repayments to a Provident Fund, even though these may be recovered by deduction from his salary. AIR 1943 Lah 60.

The term 'salary' takes in all emoluments excluding any allowance declared exempt from attachment. *Kausalya Devi* v. *Praveen Bankers,* AIR 1980 Ker 148, 149. [CPC (5 of 1908), S. 60(1), *Expln.* II]

SALARY AND HONORARIUM. Salary is a reward or recompense for service performed. It is usually applied to the reward paid to a public officer for the performance of his official duties. Salary is also applied to the reward paid for the performance of other services; but if it be not fixed for each month or year it is called *honorarium*.

SALARY AND PRICE. There is difference between salary and price; the former is the reward paid for services or for the hire of things; the latter is the consideration paid for a thing sold.

SALARY AND WAGES. Salary seems to denote a higher degree of employment and is suggestive of a large compensation for more important services than wages.

Salary is generally regarded as a per month or per annum compensation, while wages are defined as compensation paid or to be paid by the day, week *etc.*

Both salary and wages are emoluments paid to an employee by way of recompense for his labour. Salary is remuneration paid to an employee whose period of engagement is more or less permanent in character. Both may be paid weekly, fortnightly or monthly, though remuneration for the day's work is not ordinarily termed 'salary'. *Mohmaedalli* v. *Union of India*, AIR 1964 SC 980, 985. [Employees' Provident Funds Act (19 of 1952), S. 2(b)]

Conceptually 'salary' and 'wages' connote one and the same thing, namely, remuneration or payment for work done or services rendered but the former expression is generally used in connection with services of a higher or non-manual type while the latter is used in connection with manual services. *Gestetner Duplicators (P) Ltd.* v. *Commissioner of Income Tax*, AIR 1979 SC 607, 613.

"SALARY". For the purposes of section 36(1)(iva) of Act 43 of 1961, 'salary' includes dearness allowance, if the terms of employment so provide, but excludes all other allowances and perquisites. [*Explanation* to section 36(1)(iva) of the Income-tax Act, 1961 (43 of 1961) as inserted (w.e.f. 1-4-2012) by the Finance Act, 2011 (8 of 2011)]

Salary or wage. Means all remuneration (other than remuneration in respect of overtime work) capable of being expressed in terms of money, which would, if the terms of employment, express or implied, were fulfilled, be payable to an employee in respect of his employment or of work done in such employment and includes dearness allowance (that is to say all cash payments, by whatever name called, paid to an employee on account of a rise in cost of living), but, does not include—

(i) any other allowance which the employee is, for the time being, entitled to;

(ii) the value of any house accommodation or of supply of light, water, medical attendance or other amenity or of any service or of any concessional supply of food grains or other articles;

(iii) any travelling concession;

(iv) any bonus (including incentive, production and attendance bonus);

(v) any contribution paid or payable by the employer to any pension fund or provident fund or for the benefit of the employee under any law for the time in force;

(vi) any retrenchment compensation or any gratuity or other retirement benefit payable to the employee or any *ex gratia* payment made to him;

(vii) any commission payable to the employee,

Expln.—Where an employee is given *in lieu* of the whole or part of the salary or wage payable to him, free food allowance or free food by his employer, such food allowance or the value of such food shall, for the purpose of this clause, be deemed to form part of the salary or wage of such employee. [Payment of Bonus Act (21 of 1965). S. 2(21)]

Sale. "SALE is a transfer of ownership in exchange for a price paid or promised or part-paid and part-promised". [T.P. Act (4 of 1882), S. 54].

"A contract of sale of goods is a contract whereby the seller transfer or agrees to transfer the property in goods to the buyer for a price. There may be contract of sale between one part-owner and another." [Sale of Goods Act (3 of 1930), S. 4]

'SALE' with its grammatical variations and cognate expressions, means any transfer of property in goods (otherwise than by way of a mortgage, hypothecation, charge or pledge) for cash or deferred payment or other valuable consideration, and includes—

(i) a transfer, otherwise than in pursuance of a contract, of property in any goods for cash, deferred payment or other valuable consideration;

(ii) a transfer of property in goods (whether as goods or in some other form) involved in the execution of a works contract; (iii) the delivery of goods on hire purchase or any system of payment by instalments;

(iv) a transfer of the right to use any goods for any purpose (whether or not for a specified period) for cash, deferred payment or other valuable consideration;

(v) the supply of goods by any unincorporated association or body of persons to a member thereof for cash, deferred payment or other valuable consideration; and

(vi) the supply, by way of or as port of any service or in any other manner whatsoever, of goods, being food or any other article for human consumption or any drink (whether or not intoxicating) where such supply or service is for cash or deferred payment or other valuable consideration. [U.P. Trade Tax Act, 1948, S. 2(h) as cited in *State of U.P. v. Jaiprakash Associates Limited*, (2014) 4 SCC 720, para 22].

"SALE" with its grammatical variations and cognate expressions, means the sale of any article of food, whether for cash or on credit or by way of exchange and whether by wholesale or retail, for human consumption or use, or for analysis and includes an agreement for sale, an offer for sale, the exposing for sale, or having in possession for sale of any such article and includes also an attempt to sell any such article. [Prevention of Food Adulteration Act (37 of 1954), S. 2(xiii)]

A sale of goods made within the State for cash or deferred payment or other valuable consideration, does not include a mortgage, hypothecation, charge of pledge. [*Larsen and Taurbo Limited v. State of Karnataka*, (2014) 1 SCC 708, para 115] [Maharashtra Value Added Tax Act, (9 of 2005), S. 2(24)].

"SALE", with its grammatical variations and cognate expressions, means any transfer of property in goods by one person to another for cash or deferred payment or for any other valuable consideration, and includes,—

(i) a transfer, otherwise than in pursuance of a contract, of property in any goods for cash, deferred payment or other valuable consideration;

(ii) a transfer of property in goods (whether as goods or in some other form) involved in the execution of a works contract;

(iii) a delivery of goods on hire-purchase or any system of payment by instalments;

(iv) a transfer of the right to use any goods for any purpose (whether or not for a specified period) for cash, deferred payment or other valuable consideration;

(v) a supply of goods by any unincorporated association or body of persons to a member thereof for cash, deferred payment or other valuable consideration;

(vi) a supply, by way of or as part of any service or in any other manner whatsoever, of goods, being food or any other article for human consumption or any drink (whether or not intoxicating), where such supply or service, is for cash, deferred payment or other valuable consideration. [Central Sales Tax Act (74 of 1956), S. 2(g)]

"SALE", with its grammatical variations and cognate expressions, means the sale of any insecticide, whether for cash or on credit and whether by wholesale or retail, and includes an agreement for sale, an offer for sale, the exposing for sale or having in possession for sale of any insecticide and includes also an attempt to sell any such insecticide. [Insecticides Act (46 of 1968), S. 3(p)]

"SALE" with its grammatical variations and cognate expressions, means transfer of property in any weight, measure or other goods by one person to another for cash or for deferred payment or for any other valuable consideration, and includes a transfer of any weight, measure or other goods on the hire purchase system or any other system of payment by instalment, but does not include a mortgage or hypothecation of, or a charge or pledge on, such weight, measure or other goods. [Standards of Weights and Measures Act (60 of 1976), S. 2(v)]

"SALE," with its grammatical variations and cognate expressions, means any transfer of property in goods by one person to another, whether for cash or on credit, or by way of exchange, and whether wholesale or retail, and includes an agreement for sale, and offer for sale and exposure for sale. [Cigarettes and Other Tobacco Products (Prohibition of Advertisement and Regulation of Trade and Commerce, Production, Supply and Distribution Act (34 of 2003), S. 3(m)]

A transfer of property whether movable or immovable, made by one person to another for a price paid or promised or other monetary consideration. [T.P. Act (4 of 1882), S. 54].

If all the members of a society jointly authorise the society to pool their goods and sell them and pay the sale price to them in the manner prescribed by them, the society does not cease to be an agent and the transaction is not a sale by the members to the society. *Khedut Sahakeri Ginning and Pressing Society Ltd.* v. *State of Gujarat*, AIR 1972 SC 1786, 1789.

The phrase 'compulsory sale' is a contradiction in terms. The word 'sale' in its ordinary meaning means a voluntary transaction and therefore a compulsory sale is really a contradiction and is no sale at all. *Calcutta Backtime Supply Corporation Ltd.* v. *CIT,* AIR 1951 Cal 151, 153.

Hire purchase agreements are not conditional sales. When all the terms of the agreement are satisfied and the option to purchase is exercised, a sale takes place of the goods which till then had been hired. *K. L. Johar And Co.* v. *Deputy Commercial Tax Officer*, AIR 1965 SC 1082, 1089, 1090. [Entry 54, of List II, Schedule 7, Constitution]

If an incorporated club supplies its property to its members at a fixed tariff, the transaction would be deemed to be one for sale, even if the transaction is on a non-profit basis; where the club is merely acting on behalf of the members to make available to them refreshments, beverages and other articles, the transaction will not be regarded as sale. *J. Officer Madras* v. *Y. M. A. Madras*, AIR 1970 SC 1212, 1216.

The term 'sale' also includes a sale to Food Inspector. *Usman Ali* v. *State of U.P.,* AIR 1965 All 39, 40. [Prevention of Food Adulteration Act (37 of 1954), S. 2(13)]

In a case where sale is effected, as per the conditions in a written order of Statutory Authority, no element of mutual consent or agreement between the assessee and allottee is necessary and the transaction effected is 'a sale'. *Union Territory of Chandigarh* v. *Amrit Roller Flour Mills*, AIR 1985 SC 1199, 1201. [Punjab General Sales Tax Act (46 of 1948), S. 3]

Acquisition of land is not a sale. *Awami Kumar v. of Rajasthan,* AIR 1977 Raj All 63, 66.

The term 'Sale' in S. 69 does not take within its embrace a statutory sale held under the Land Revenue Act. *NID Contract* v. *State of U.P.,* AIR 1977 All 63, 66. [T.P. Act (4 of 1882), S. 69]

SALE AND BARTER. A sale is an exchange of goods or property for money paid or to be paid, as distinguished from barter, which is an exchange of one commodity or article of property for another; an exchange of goods; a commutation; transmutation or transfer of goods for other good.

"SALE". With its grammatical variations and cognate expressions, means the sale of any article of food, whether for cash or on credit or by way of exchange and whether by wholesale or retail, for human consumption or use, or for analysis, and includes an agreement for sale, an offer for sale, the exposing for sale or having in possession for sale of any such article, and includes also an attempt to sell any such article. [S. 3(1)(zr) of the Food Safety & Standards Act, 2006 (34 of 2006)]

"SALE" means any transfer of property in goods for cash, deferred payment or other valuable consideration, and includes—

(*a*) any transfer, otherwise than in pursuance of a contract, of property in any goods for cash, deferred payment or other valuable consideration;

(*b*) any delivery of goods on hire-purchase or any system of payment by instalments;

(*c*) any transfer of right to use any goods for any purpose (whether or not for a specified period) for cash, deferred payment or other valuable consideration;

(*d*) any supply, by way of, or as a part of, any service or in any other manner whatsoever, of goods, being food or any other article for human consumption or any drink (whether or not intoxicating), where such supply or service in for cash, deferred payment or other valuable consideration;

(*e*) any supply of goods by any unincorporated association or body of persons to a member thereof for cash, deferred payment or other valuable consideration, and such transfer, delivery or supply of any goods shall be deemed to be a sale of those goods by the person or unincorporated association or body of persons making the transfer, delivery or supply and a purchase of those goods by the person to whom such transfer, delivery, or supply is made, but does not include a mortgage, hypothecation, charge or pledge.

Explanation.—A sale shall be deemed to take place in West Bengal if the goods are within West Bengal—

(*a*) In the case of specific or as curtained goods, at the time of the contract of sale is made; and

(*b*) In the case of unascertained or future goods, at the time of their appropriation to the contract of sale by the seller, whether the assent of the buyer to such appropriation is prior or subsequent to the appropriation:

Provided that where there is a single contract of sale in respect of goods situated in West Bengal as well as in places outside West Bengal, provisions of this Explanation shall apply as if there were a separate contract of sale in respect of the goods situated in West Bengal. [West Bengal Sales Tax Act, 1994, S. 2(30) **as cited in** *State of W.B. v. Calcutta Club Limited,* (2017) 5 SCC 356, para 10].

Sale and mortgage. When a bill of sale is executed as security, it is generally held to be a mere mortgage. Thus, in cases where there has been no change of possession, or the sale is accompanied by a defeasance, or provides for redemption, or a re-conveyance, the transaction is ordinarily held to be merely a mortgage.

SALE AND OFFER TO SELL. An offer to sell imposes no obligations until accepted according to its terms; and an offer rejected cannot be afterwards accepted.

'Sale' and "purchase". With their grammatical variations and cognate expressions, mean any transfer of the possession of goods by one person to another in the ordinary course of trade or business for cash or deferred payment or other valuable consideration. [Central Excise Act (1 of 1944), S. 2(h)]

Sale and sold. Sale is a transfer of property for a price, and adjustment of the rights of the partners in a dissolved firm is not a transfer nor it is for a price. *Commissioner of Income Tax* v. *Dewar Cine Corporation*, AIR 1968 SC 676, 678.

Sale by description. Sale of goods by the description thereof under contract for sale of the goods implying that the goods shall correspond with description. [Sale of Goods Act (3 of 1930), S. 15].

Sale by sample. A sale by sample is where a small quality of any commodity is exhibited by the vendor as a fair specimen of a larger quantity called the 'bulk', which is not present, and there is no opportunity for a personal examination. To constitute such sale, it must appear that the parties contracted solely with reference to the sample, and mutually understood that they were so dealing in regard to the quality of the bulk.

A sale of goods with reference to a sample implying that the goods supplied will be in accordance with the sample. [Sale of Goods Act (3 of 1930), S. 17].

Sale in enforcement of mortgage. Sale to enforce the charge under a mortgage. [CPC (5 of 1908), O. XXI, R. 83(3)].

Sale-note. A memorandum given by a broker to a seller or buyer of goods, stating the fact that certain goods have been sold by him on account of a person called the seller to another person called the buyer.

Sale-notes are also called bought and sold notes.

Sale of goods and purchase of goods. *Gannon Dunkerley's case* AIR 1958 SC 560 Quoted-"In order to constitute a sale, it is necessary that there should be an agreement between the parties for the purpose of transferring title to goods and it must be supported by money consideration and as a result of the transaction, property must actually pass in the goods". On a parity of reasoning, to constitute a purchase of goods, there must be an agreement for purchase of goods and the passing of property pursuant to such an agreement. *Andhra Sujarb Ltd.* v. *State of A.P.*, AIR 1968 SC 599, 602. [Constitution of India, Sch. 7, List 2, Entry 54]

Sale on credit. A sale is not one on credit, where no time was given for payment of the price, or leave given to take the property away without payment.

Sale on trial. If it is sale on trial, it is said to be a sale on condition precedent to buy if satisfied; the title does not pass until the condition prescribed is fully performed, although the possession is delivered, being rather a bailment with the option to buy than a sale.

Sale or purchase in the course of export. A purchase for the purpose of export even though such purchase is effected to implement orders for the export of these goods is not "a sale or purchase in the course of export". *State of Madras* v. *K.H. Chambers Ltd.,* AIR 1955 Mad 314, 324. [Constitution of India, Art. 286]

Sale or selling. 'SALE OR SELLING' includes any transfer including gift. [Andhra Pradesh Prohibition Act (A.P. Act No. 17 of 1995), S. 2(15)]Omitted by A.P. Act No. 35 of 1995.

Sale or transfer. A sale or transfer presupposes the existence of the property which is sold or transferred. It presupposes the transfer from one person to another of the right in property. *Provident Investment Co. Ltd.* v. *CIT,* AIR 1954 Bom 95.

Sale price. "SALE PRICE" means the amount payable to a dealer as consideration for the sale of any goods, less any sum allowed as cash discount according to the practice normally prevailing in the trade, but inclusive of any sum charged for anything done by the dealer in respect of the goods at the time of or delivery thereof other than the cost of freight or delivery or the cost of installation in cases where such cost is separately charged. [Central Sales Tax Act (74 of 1956), S. 2(h)]

The amount recovered by a dealer from the purchasers in respect of sales tax must under the definition of 'sale price' be regarded as part thereof and that it has to be taken into account while arriving at a dealer's taxable turnover. *Jethalal Virajlal* v. *State of M.P.,* AIR 1953 Nag 194.

Sale proceeds. The total amount brought in by a sale (of goods or property). [T.P.Act (4 of 1882), S. 73(1)]; [CrPC, 1973 (2 of 1974), S. 145(8)].

Sale promotion employee. Means any person by whatever name called (including an apprentice) employed or engaged in any establishment for hire or reward to do any work relating to promotion of sale or business, or both, but does not include any such person—

(i) who, being employed or engaged in a supervisory capacity, draws wages exceeding sixteen hundred rupees per month; or

(ii) who is employed or engaged mainly in a managerial or administrative capacity.

Explanation—For the purposes of this clause, the wages per mensem of a person shall be deemed to be the amount equal to thirty times his total wages (whether or not including, or comprising only of, commission) in respect of the continuous period of his service falling within the period of twelve months immediately preceding the date with reference to which the calculation is to be made, divided by the number of days comprising that period of service. [Sales Promotion Employees (Conditions of Service) Act (11 of 1976), S. 2(d)]

Saleable. Capable of being sold. [CPC (5 of 1908), S. 60(1)].

Sales guaranteed. The term "sales guaranteed", is used in a contract for the sale of goods, means that if the goods were not sold, or if they proved to be not sellers, the purchaser might return them and have credit for their value.

Sales tax law. Means any law for the time being in force in State or part thereof which provides for the levy of taxes on the sale or purchase of goods generally or on any specified goods expressly mentioned in that behalf. [Central Sales Tax (74 of 1956), S. 2(i)]

Sales within shape. 'Sales within shape' includes 'sales determined to be inside the state'. *Instalment Supply Co.* v. *S. T. O. Ahmedabad*, AIR 1974 SC 1105, 1109.

Salt. "SALT" includes swamp salt, spontaneous salt and salt or saline solutions made or produced from any saline substances or from salt earth. [Central Excises and Salt Act (1 of 1944), S. 2(i) and Salt Cess Act (49 of 1953), S. 2(b)].

Salt-factory. 'SALT FACTORY' includes—

(i) a place used or intended to be used in the manufacture of salt and all embankments, reservoirs, condensing and evaporating pans, buildings and waster places situated within the limits of such place, as defined from time to time by the Collector of Central Excise;

(ii) all drying grounds and storage platforms and store-houses appertaining to any such place; and

(iii) land on which salt is spontaneously produced. [Central Excises and Salt Act (1 of 1944), S. 2(j)]

"SALT FACTORY" includes—

(i) a place used or intended to be used for the manufacture of salt and all embankments, reservoirs, condensing and evaporating pans, buildings & waste places situated within the limits of such place,

(ii) all drying grounds and storage platforms and store-houses appertaining to any such place;

(iii) land on which salt is spontaneously produced. [Salt Cess Act (49 of 1953), S. 2(c)]

Salt-revenue officer. "SALT-REVENUE-OFFICER" means any officer of the Northern India Salt

Department and also includes any person invested by the Local Government with any of the powers of a Salt-revenue officer under this Act. [Salt Act (12 of 1882), S. 3]

Saltpetre. "SALTPETRE" includes *rasi*, *sajji* and all other substances manufactured from saline earth, and *kharinun* and every form of sulphate or carbonate of soda. [Salt Act (12 of 1884), S. 3; Salt Cess Act (49 of 1953), S. 2(a), *Expln.* and Central Excise and Salt Act (1 of 1944), S. 2(i)]

Salus populi est suprema lex. The welfare of the people is the supreme law.

Safety of the people is the supreme law. [*Prithipal Singh v. State of Punjab*, (2012) 1 SCC 10, para 25].

This phrase is based on the implied agreement of every member of the society that his own individual welfare shall, in cases of necessity, yield to that of the community; and that his property, liberty and life shall, under certain circumstances, be played in jeopardy or even sacrificed for the public good." [A Selection of Legal Maxims by Herbert Broom as cited in *Sayyed Ratanbhai Sayeed v. Shirdi Nagar Panchayat*, (2016) 4 SCC 631, para 56].

The welfare of the people is the supreme law. [*Lala Ram v. Union of India*, (2015) 5 SCC 813, para 8].

It connotes that health, safety and welfare of the public is the supreme in law. [*Sayyed Ratanbhai Sayeed v. Shirdi Nagar Panchayat*, (2016) 4 SCC 631, para 56].

Salus reipublicae suprema lex. (Lat.) The welfare of the public is the supreme law. The safety of the State is the supreme law, coexist. [*Prithipal Singh v. State of Punjab*, (2012) 1 SCC 10, para 7].

Salvage. "SALVAGE" includes all expenses properly incurred by the salvor in the performance of salvage services. [Merchant Shipping Act (44 of 1958), S. 3(40)]

The action of saving a ship or its cargo from wreck, capture, *etc.* [CPC (5 of 1908), S. 140(1)].

Salvage charges. 'SALVAGE CHARGES' means 'charges recoverable under maritime law by a salvor independently of contract. They do not include the expenses of services in the nature of salvage rendered by the assured or his agents or any person employed for hire by them, for the purpose of averting a peril insured against'. ....[Marine Insurance Act (11 of 1963), S. 65(2)]

Salvage operations. For the purpose of this clause, "SALVAGE OPERATIONS" includes—

(i) the raising, removal, destruction or the rendering a ship harmless which is sunk, wrecked, stranded or abandoned including anything that is or has been on board such ship;

(ii) the removal, destruction or rendering the cargo of a ship harmless; and

(iii) the measures taken to avert or minimise loss to a ship or its cargo or both. [Merchant Shipping Act (44 of 1958), S. 352(h) *Expln.*]

Salvage or salvage money. A reward which is payable by owners of ships and good saved at sea from pirates, enemies or the perils of the sea, to those who have saved them.

Salved vessel. A vessel to which salvage services are rendered.

Salvo. (*Lat.*) Saving; excepting; without prejudice to.

Salvor. "SALVOR" means any person rendering services in direct connection with salvage operations. [Merchant Shipping Act (44 of 1958), S. 352(h), *inserted by Amending Act (63 of 2002), S. 16*]

Samadhi. Means the structure built in token of reverence for Mahatama Gandhi at Rajghat on the western bank of the Jamuna in Delhi, and includes the premises described in the Schedule with all buildings contained therein, together with all additions thereto or alterations thereof which may be made after the commencement of this Act. [Rajghat Samadhi Act (41 of 1951), S. 2(b)]

Same. Identical with what has been indicated [CPC (5 of 1908), O. VIII, R. 6(1)]; [CPC (5 of 1908), S. 88]; [CrPC, 1973 (2 of 1974), S. 300(1)]; one and the same [CrPC, 1973 (2 of 1974), S. 223(a)].

Same and **similar.** Although the word 'same' is frequently loosely used in the sense of 'similar', the word 'similar' never means 'same'. *Deva Sharma* v. *Laxmi Narain Gaddodia,* AIR 1956 Punj 49, 55. [Indian Partnership Act (9 of 1932), S. 54]

Same business. A common control, that is, the unity of control, and common management by the same Board of Directors in respect of business of import and the business of export carried on by the asessee constitute the same business. *B. R. Ltd.* v. *I. T. Commissioner, Bombay*, AIR 1977 SC 1320. 1326.

Same cause of action. A suit based on a defective title deed and another suit based on a rectified deed cannot be considered to be based on the same cause of action. *Sudarsan Swami* v. *Jagannatha Routh,* AIR 1972 Ori 112, 114. [CPC (5 of 1908), O. IX, R. 9]

Same interest. The expression 'same interest' implies a joint and inseparable interest. It is not a distinct individual interest even though arising out of or taken away by the same act or transaction. S. *Avtar Singh* v. *State of J&K,* AIR 1980 J&K 50, 52. [CPC (5 of 1908), O. I, R. 8]

'The same interest' means that the interest of the husband shall devolve on his widow to the same extent, *i.e.* subject to the rights and obligations which that interest has at the time of her husband's death. *Kunja Sahu* v. *Bhaglan Mohantry,* AIR 1951 Ori 35.

Same judgment-debtor. Where a decree is obtained against a person, and another decree is obtained against the legal representative of the judgment-debtor, although the estate of the deceased judgment-debtor may be liable in the case of both the decrees, it cannot be said that the two decrees are against the same judgment-debtor within the meaning of S. 73. CPC (5 of 1908).

Same manner. The phrase "in the same manner" has a well-understood meaning in legislation, and that meaning is not one of restriction or limitation, but of procedure. It means by similar proceedings, so far as such proceedings are applicable to the subject matter.

Same network. For the purposes of the Companies (Audit and Auditors) Rules, 2014, the expression 'same network' includes the firms operating or functioning, hitherto or in future, under the same brand name, trade name or common control. [*Explanation I* to rule 6 of the Companies (Audit and Auditors) Rules, 2014]

Same offence. In CrPC, 1973 (2 of 1974), S. 223 (a), the words imply that both the accused should have acted in concert or association. They do not apply to a case in which the allegations against the two accused are mutually exclusive.

Same transaction. What amounts to "same transaction" is a question of fact to be decided in the circumstances of each case.

Separate offences by individual conspirators which are not committed in pursuance of the conspiracy, but which are isolated acts committed individually during the continuance of the conspiracy are not part of the same transaction with the conspiracy itself and with those acts which are alleged to have been the subject of the conspiracy.

Where the accusation against all the accused persons is that they carried out a single scheme by successive acts done at intervals but there was complete unity of project, and the whole series were all linked together by one motive and design, it constitutes "one and the same transaction" within the meaning of S. 223(a) of the CrPC, 1973 (2 of 1974).

It is a question of fact in each case whether the acts are so connected together as to form part of the same transaction. The word transaction must be read as meaning a completed act. Mere interval of days will not disturb the oneness of the transaction, nor necessarily the fact that different sets of persons were engaged on different occasions. But if the aim of the accused on the different occasions is directed towards effecting different purposes, the transactions are different.

In order to determine whether the various acts alleged from the same transaction, the proximity of time between different acts is not an essential factor; but it is necessary to see how one act is related to the other. If they are related in point of purpose, as cause and effect or as principal and subsidiary acts so as to constitute one continuous act, they will be deemed to form the same transaction. *Raj Kishore Tervari* v. *Rex,* AIR 1949 All 139. *In re Saroje Narayana Bhatta*, AIR 1949 Mad 9 (*FB*)

The expression 'same transaction' implies a community of purpose and continuity of action. *Umar Bin* v. *State,* AIR 1954 San 15. [CrPC, 1973 (2 of 1974), S. 223(a)]

In order that a series of acts may constitute the "same transaction", the essential condition is the continuity of action which involves essentially, continuity or proximity of time; in other words the series of acts must be so connected together as to form a single and entire transaction, clearly, therefore, continuity of action or proximity of time is a very essential element in connecting a series of acts so as to form part of the same transaction. Where the accused visited a brothel for the purpose of committing theft and in the course of committing theft from the prostitute also committed rape upon her, both the acts must be held to form part of the same transaction. ILR 1945 Kar. 100. In Ss. 235 and 239, CrPC (5 of 1898). (Now Ss. 220 and 223 of 1974 Code.) 25 Pat 503 : 1946 PWN 179 : 27 Pat LT 173.

Same work or work of similar nature. "SAME WORK OR WORK OF A SIMILAR NATURE" means work in respect of which the skill, effort and responsibility required are the same, when performed under similar working conditions, by a man or a woman and the differences, if any, between the skill, effort and responsibility required of a man and those required of a woman are not of practical importance in relation to the terms and conditions of employment. [Equal Remuneration Act (25 of 1976), S. 2(h)]

The expression "same work or work of similar nature" contemplates similarity of skill, effort and responsibility when performed under similar conditions. *State of Madhya Pradesh* v. *Pramod Bhartiya*, AIR 1993 SC 286, 292. [Equal Remuneration Act (25 of 1976), S. 2(h)]

Sample. A small quantity of commodity exhibited.

A relatively small quantity of material or an individual object from which the quality of the mass or group or species *etc.* which it represents may be inferred [IPC (45 of 1860), S. 415, ill. (c); Sale of Goods Act (3 of 1930), S. 17].

The word "sample", both in its legal and popular acceptation, means that which is taken out of a large quantity is a fair representation of the whole; a part shown as a specimen.

"SAMPLE" means a sample of any article of food taken under the provisions of Act 34 of 2006 or any Rules and Regulations made thereunder. [S. 3(1)(zs) of the Food Safety & Standards Act, 2006 (34 of 2006)]

Sanction. That part of a law which inflicts a penalty for its violation or bestows a reward for its observance. Sanctions are of two kinds,—those which redress civil injuries, called civil sanctions, and those which punish crimes, called penal sanctions.

An express authorisation, permission or recognition (*e.g.* of an action, custom, institution, *etc.*) [CrPC, 1973 (2 of 1974), S. 132(1)(a)].

Sanction of the Governor. The expression 'sanction of the Governor' under Rule 9(2)(b)(i) of the Rules would not mean the personal sanction of the Governor. It includes a decision to sanction prosecution taken by the Council of Ministers. [*State* *of M.P.* v. *Yashwant Trimbak (Dr.),* (1996) 2 SCC 305, 312-13, para 19] [M.P. Civil Services Pension Rules, 1976, R. 9(2)(b)(i)]

Sanction to prosecute. A sanction to prosecute is quite distinct from a direction to prosecute. A sanction leaves the private prosecutor to exercise his unfettered discretion as to whether he will proceed or not. An order expressly ordering a prosecution is, therefore, not a sanction to prosecute.

The order of a Magistrate ordering a prosecution *suo motu* is not a sanction.

A Collector ordering the prosecution of a person for an offence under S. 182, IPC (45 of 1860), for making false allegations against one of his subordinates in a written petition puts himself in the position of a prosecutor and is disqualified from performing the judicial function of deciding whether to grant a sanction or not. His order is a mere executive order.

Sanctioned. The word 'sanctioned' in S. 2(b) cannot be construed to mean sanctioned by the award and not by settlement. *Union of India* v. *Majur Mahajan Mandal*, AIR 1977 SC 714, 719. [Additional Emoluments (Compulsory Deposit) Act (37 of 1974), S. 2(b)]

Sandalwood. "SANDALWOOD" means the food derived out of any part of chandan tree and includes chips, dust or powder of such wood. [Orissa Forest Act (14 of 1972), S. 2(m)]

Sandpapering. A lawyer's general preparation of a witness before a deposition or trial.

Sandwich course student. "SANDWICH COURSE STUDENT" means a student undergoing a sandwich course of studies at any of the technical institutions recognised for the purpose and leading to the award of degree or diploma in engineering or technology. [Apprenticeship Rules, 1991, R. 2(7)]

Sandwich lease. A lease in which the lessee subleases the property to a third party, especially for more rent than under the original lease.

Sane. Whole; sound; in healthful state. It is applicable equally to the mind and to the body. (*Den* v. *Vancieve*, 5 NJL 661).

Sanitary board. "SANITARY BOARD" means the persons for the time being appointed, either by name or by official designation, by the Local Government by notification in the Gazette to constitute a Sanitary Board for any local area. [Ben. Act III of 1884 (Municipal), S. 6, cl. (14-a)]

Sanitary fittings. Sanitary fittings means such pipes and materials as are used in lavatories, urinals, or bathrooms of private houses or public buildings and they do not include heavy pipes which are laid underground as mains for carrying water supply from one area to another. *Deputy Commissioner of Sales Tax (Law) Board of Revenue (Taxes) Ernakulam* v. *G. S. Pai & Co.*, AIR 1980 SC 611, 613.

"Sanitary fittings" means such pipes or materials as are used in lavatories, urinals or bathrooms of private houses or public buildings. Even where a huge pipe is used for carrying the excreted material from the commode to the septic tank that may be treated as sanitary fittings. *State of U.P.* v. *Indian Hume Pipe Co. Ltd.*, AIR 1977 SC 1132, 1134.

Sanitary latrine. Means a latrine which is not an 'insanitary latrine'. [S. 2(1)(o) of the Prohibition of Employment as Manual Scavengers & Their Rehabilitation Act, 2013 (25 of 2013)]

Sanitary purposes. Free from, or effective in preventing or checking an agent (as filth or infection) injurious to health. [CrPC, 1973 (2 of 1974), S. 133(2), *Expln.*].

Sanitation worker. "SANITATION WORKER" means a person employed in collecting or removing filth or in cleaning drains, latrines or slaughter houses. [Kerala Municipality Act (20 of 1994), S. 2(41), *as amended by Kerala Act (8 of 1995)*]

Sanity. The state of a person who has a sound understanding; the reverse of insanity.

"SANITY" is the presence of reason, thought, and comprehension.

"Sanity, when used as a test of criminal responsibility, is the ability of a person to distinguish between right and wrong in reference to the act which he is about to commit. The true test is not, as is some times laid down, the capacity merely to distinguish between the rightfulness and wrongfulness of the act committed, but there must also be sufficient will power to choose whether he shall do or refrain from doing it.

Sanity being the normal and usual condition of the mind, the law presumes that every individual is in that state.

Sapinda. A kinsman connected by offerings of balls of rice or of meat to common ancestors; the affinity extends to three individuals only in descent from the common ancestor; some authorities extend it to seven persons in both the ascending and the descending line. (*Wil. Gloss.*)

The expression '*sapinda*' is peculiar to traditional Hindu law and it would be altogether in opposite in the context of citizens of Muslim or Christian faith. *Jagat Singh* v. *Karan Singh*, AIR 1987 SC 1279, 1280.

Sapinda relationship. With reference to any person extends as far as the third generation (inclusive) in the line of ascent through the mother, and the fifth (inclusive) in the line of ascent through the father, the line being traced upwards in each case from the person concerned, who is to be counted as the first generation. [Hindu Marriage Act (25 of 1955), S. 3(f)(i)]

Sapindas. Are of two classes; (*a*) *Gotraj* and (*b*) *Bhandhus*. *Gotraj* comprise *Gotraja Sapinda* and *Samanodakas* who are the preferential heirs, failing whom the succession devolves on the *Bhandhus* or *Bhinna gotra Sapindas*.

SAPTA. Means the Agreement on SAARC Preferential Trading Arrangement, signed at Dhaka, Bangladesh on the 11th day of April, 1993. [Customs

Tariff (Determination of origin of goods under the agreement on SAARC Preferential Trading Arrangement) Rules, 1995, R. 3(a)]

Saptapadi. The seven steps. Part of the Brahmanical marriage, ceremony on completion of which the marriage is irrevocable. (*Moore's Malabar Law*)

Sarai/Serai. (*Persian*). "SARAI" means any building used for the shelter and accommodation of travellers, and includes, in any case in which only part of a building is used as a sarai, the part so used of such building. It also includes a purao so far as the provisions of this Act are applicable thereto. [Sarais Act (22 of 1867), S. 2]

Satellite. Any device in extra terrestrial space capable of transmitting signals. [Article 1(iii), Satellite Convention]; Any satellite operating on frequency bands which, under telecommunications law, are reserved for the broadcast of the signals for reception by the public, or which are reserved for closed point-to-point communication. [Article 1(1), Satellite Broadcasting and Cable Retransmission Directive] (*Copyright*)

A radio relay station that orbits the earth. A complete satellite communications system also includes earth stations that communicate with each other *via* the satellite. The satellite receives a signal transmitted by an originating earth station and retransmits that signal to the destination earth station(s). Satellites are used to transmit telephone, television and data signals originated by common carriers, broadcasters and distributors of cable TV program material. (*Telecommunication*)

Satellite earth station (Hub/Gateway). Earth station for making transmissions to satellites or receiving transmissions from satellites. Allows access to terrestrial networks. (*Telecommunication*)

Satellite GSO. (*abbr.*) Geostationary Orbit Satellite. Satellite placed in geostationary orbit at an altitude of 36,000 km. (*Telecommunication*)

Satellite Home Viewer Improvement Act of 1999 (SHVIA). An Act modifying the Satellite Home Viewer Act of 1988, SHVIA permits satellite companies to provide local broadcast TV signals to all subscribers who reside in the local TV station's market. SHVIA also permits satellite companies to provide "distant" network broadcast stations to eligible satellite subscribers. (*Telecommunication*)

Satellite LEO. (*abbr.*) Low Earth Orbit satellite. Satellite placed in low orbit at an altitude of approx. 1,000 km. (*Telecommunication*)

Satellite Master Antenna Television (SMATV). A satellite dish system used to deliver signals to multiple dwelling units (*e.g.*, apartment buildings and trailer parks). (*Telecommunication*)

Satellite MEO. (*abbr.*) Medium Earth Orbit satellite. Satellite placed in medium orbit at an altitude of approx. 10,000 km. (*Telecommunication*)

Sati. (*Sanskrit*) "SATI" means the burning or burying alive of—

(i) any widow along with the body of her deceased husband or any other relative or with any article, object or thing associated with the husband or such relative; or

(ii) any woman along with the body of any of her relatives, irrespective of whether such burning or burying is claimed to be voluntary on the port of the widow or the woman or otherwise. [Commission of Sati (Prevention) Act, 1987 (3 of 1988), S. 2(c)]

Satisfaction. The payment of a debt or discharge of an obligation in full; the state of being satisfied; contented [T.P. Act (4 of 1882), S. 69A(6)]; dissipation of doubt; removal of doubt [CrPC, 1973 (2 of 1974), S. 81(1), prov.]; carrying out the terms of.

Acceptance by the creditor of the consideration of an accord extinguishes the obligation, and is called "satisfaction."

Equivalent or compensation; that which satisfies; indemnification; reward; remuneration; requital; amends; atonement; recompense. In law, release and discharge of the obligation in reference to which it is given; payment of a legal debt or demand; the discharging or cancelling or a judgment or a mortgage, by paying the amount of it.

The satisfaction contemplated by S. 47, CPC (5 of 1908), must have arisen out of some transaction between the parties subsequent to the decree.

Satisfaction of claim. The fulfilment of a claim. [CPC (5 of 1908), O. XXIV, R. 1].

Satisfaction of Governor or President. 'The satisfaction of the Governor or President" referred under Art. 311(2) proviso (c) is not with respect to the allegations leveled against the public servant that those allegations merit his dismissal or removal from service. Whatever may be the nature of charges against the Government servant, the satisfaction of the Governor should be with regard to the holding of enquiry contemplated in clause (2) of Art. 311 being not expedient: and that too for the reason that it is not in the interest of the security of State. [*B. Bhaskar Reddy* v. *The Govt. of Andhra Pradesh, Hyderabad,* MLJ : YD (1982), p. 178 : 1981 Lab IC 18] [Constitution of India, Art. 311(2), prov. (c)]

Satisfactorily account. The Legislature has advisedly used the expression "satisfactorily account". The emphasis must be on the word "satisfactorily", and the Legislature has, thus, deliberately cast a burden on the accused not only to offer a plausible explanation as to how he came by his large wealth, but also to satisfy the Court that his explanation was worthy of experience. *C.S.D. Swami* v. *State*. AIR 1960 SC 7, 10. [Prevention of Corruption Act (2 of 1947), S. 5(3)]

Satisfactory. A contract for the sale of machinery "warranted to perform in a satisfactory manner" means satisfactory to the defendant. Capable of dispelling doubt; that which is adequate for the needs of a case.

Satisfied. The word 'satisfied' is a term of considerable expensiveness. The term 'satisfied' has been understood to mean, free from anxiety, doubt, perplexity, suspense or uncertainty. In this context, it is synonymous with "convince the understanding; or, convince beyond a reasonable doubt." *Faquir Chand Sultani Ram* v. *Bhana Ram Mausa Ram,* AIR 1957 Punj 303, 304. [CrPC, 1973 (2 of 1974), S. 145(1)]

The word 'satisfied' means satisfied on preponderance of probabilities and not satisfied beyond a reasonable doubt. *Gauri Dey* v. *Bidhu Bhushan Dey,* AIR 1986 Gau 22, 23.

Satisfy. To meet a financial obligation in full; to put an end to doubt or to set free from doubt or uncertainty; to carry out the terms of. [CrPC, 1973 (2 of 1974), S. 288(2)].

Satius est petere fontes quam sectari rivulos. (*Maxim*) It is better to seek the fountains than to follow out the streams.

Satyameva Jayate. "Satyameva Jayate" (literally "truth stands invincible") is a mantra from the ancient scripture Mundaka Upnished. Upon Independence of India, it was adopted as the national motto of India. It is inscribed in Devanagari script at the base of the national emblem. The meaning of the full mantra is as follows:

"Truth alone triumphs; not falsehood. Through truth the divine path is spread out by which the sages whose desires have been completely fulfilled, reach where that supreme treasure of truth resides." [*Maria Margaride Sequeira Fernandes v. Erasmo Jack De Sequeira*, (2012) 5 SCC 370, para 43].

Save as otherwise expressly provided. Except when otherwise expressly provided. [Contempt of Courts Act (70 of 1971), S. 12(1)].

Save as otherwise prescribed. Except when otherwise prescribed. [CPC (5 of 1908), O. XXI, R. 65].

Save as otherwise provided by or under this act. The expression means save as otherwise expressly barred by or under the Act. *State of Rajasthan* v. *Shri Noor Mohammad*, AIR 1973 SC 2729, 2732.

Saving. That which is saved; something laid up or kept from being expended; preservation from loss; exception; reservation (as a saving clause in a section of an enactment).

A reservation; saving clause. [T.P. Act (4 of 1882), S. 137].

Saving clause. A saving clause is an exception of a special thing out of general things mentioned in a statute.

A "saving clause" is ordinarily a restriction in a repealing Act and saves rights, pending proceedings, penalties, *etc.*, from the annihilation which would result from unrestricted repeal.

In a legal instrument, a saving clause is a clause exempting something which might otherwise be subjected to the operation of the instrument. In an act of parliament, a saving clause which is repugnant to the body of such act is void.

Savings bank book. A savings bank book has a peculiar character. It is not a mere pass book or the statement of an account. It is issued to the person in whose name the deposit is made, and with whom the bank has made its contract. It is his voucher, and the only security he has as evidence of his debt. The book is the instrument by which alone the money can be obtained, and its possession is thus some evidence of title in the person presenting it at the bank.

Savings banks. Institutions for the safe custody and increase of the small savings of the people designed for the encouragement of industry and thrift.

A banking institution organised to receive savings accounts only on which accrued interest is periodically paid to the depositors. [Payment of Wages Act (4 of 1936), S. 7(2)(k)].

Saw mill. "SAW MILL" means the plant and machinery with which and the premises including the precincts thereof in which or in any part of which sawing is carried on with the aid of electrical or mechanical power. [Orissa Saw Mills and Saw Pits (Control) Act, 1991 (11 of 1992), S. 2(h)]

Saw pit. "SAW PIT" means a place where wood is sawn by manually operated saws. [Orissa Saw Mills and Saw Pits (Control) Act, 1991 (11 of 1991), S. 2(i); Bihar Saw Mill (Regulation) Act (19 of 1990), S. 2(h).]

Sawing. With its grammatical variations and cognate expressions means operations of sawing, cutting, converting, fashioning or seasoning wood and includes preservation and treatment thereof either by mechanical process with the aid of electrical or mechanical power or manually operated saws. [Bihar Saw Mill (Regulation) Act (19 of 1990), S. 2(i)]

Sayer/Sayer. "Sayer/Sayer" literally refers to movables' it also concerns miscellaneous levies apart from the land revenue. [*Sarjeet Singh v. Hari Singh*, (2015) 1 SCC 760, para 6].

Sayar or Sayer are variable imposts on movable property and thus, are distinct from land revenue. [*Sarjeet Singh v. Hari Singh*, (2015) 1 SCC 760, para 6].

Scaffolding. Temporary framework of platforms and poles constructed to accommodate workmen and their materials during the erection, repairing *etc.* of building. [Indian Contract Act (9 of 1872), S. 54, ill. (b)].

Scale. A standard of measurement, calculation or estimation. [Mines Act (35 of 1952), S. 58(f)].

Scale of expenses. Degree or proportion of expenses. [CPC (5 of 1908), O. XVI, R. 2(3)].

Scam. A trick; a ruse; a swindle; a fraud; a racket; a story; a rumour; information; perpetrate a fraud; cheat; trick or swindle (a person, firm, *etc.*)

SCAM means to get money or property from, another, under false pretences, by gaining the confidence of the victim, also includes; swindle; defraud.

Scandal. A report on rumour, whereby one is affronted in public. (*Tomlin*)

Scandalising the Court. The 'scandalising' might manifest itself in various ways but in substance it is an attack on individual Judges or the Court as a whole with or without reference to particular cases casting unwarranted and defamatory aspersions upon the character and ability of the Judges. (*State of M.P.* v. *Revashankar,* AIR 1959 SC 102, 105, 107; *Brahma Prakash Sharma* v. *State of U.P.*, AIR 1954 SC 10).

The expression 'scandalising the Court' would mean hostile criticism of judges as judges or judiciary. Any personal attack upon a judge in connection with the office he holds is dealt with under law of libel or slander. [*D.C. Saxena (Dr.)* v. *Chief Justice of India,* (1996) 5 SCC 216, 247, para 40 : AIR 1996 SC 2481]

The scandalisation within the meaning of Section 2(c)(i) of the Act must be in respect of the Court or the Judge with reference to administration of justice. It was held to be a species of contempt which may take several forms. The dilemma of the law of contempt arises because of the constitutional need to balance two great but occasionally conflicting principles—Freedom of expression, and fair and fearless justice. [*Arundhati Roy, in Re*, (2002) 3 SCC 343, 360, para 16, Contempt of Courts Act (70 of 1971), S. 2(c)(i)]

Attributing improper motive to a Judge or scurrilous abuse of a Judge would amount to 'scandalising the Court'. [*Rajesh Kumar Singh* v. *High Court of Judicature of M.P.*, AIR 2007 SC 2725, 2729, para 13] [Contempt Courts Act (7 of 1971), S. 2(c)]

Scandalous. A pleading is said to be 'scandalous', if it alleges anything unbecoming the dignity of the Court to hear, or is contrary to good manners, or which charges a crime immaterial to the issue. But the statement of a scandalous fact that is material to the issue is not a scandalous pleading.

Of the nature of a scandal, containing defamatory information. [Indian Evidence Act (1 of 1872), S. 151].

Facts not material to the decision are impertinent, and, if reproachful, are scandalous.

The term "scandalous", as applied to the pleading of scandalous matter, cannot be applied to any matter which is not also impertinent and unnecessary.

Scandalous matter. (*In pleading*) The matter that is not only grossly disgraceful or defamatory but also irrelevant to the cause or defence.

Scandalous statement. A statement which is irrelevant and abuse.

Scanner. A computer input device that converts images into computer data. Some scanners, for example, are used to convert photographs into digital information that can be placed in a computer document. Other scanners are used to input bar codes or other codes designed for identifying products. Yet other scanners are used to scan printed material that is then converted into computer text with technology called optical character recognition. (*Computer*)

An optical character recognition machine which consists of a scan head, a computer processor, and an output device. Used for interpreting documents, invoices, bar-codes, and photos for use in Color separations. (*Advertising law*)

A radio receiver that moves across a wide range of radio frequencies and allows audiences to listen to any of the frequencies. (*Telecommunication*)

Scavenge/scavenging. Searching through object residue (discarded disks, tapes, or paper) to acquire sensitive data without authorisation. (*Cyber Law*)

Schedule. "SCHEDULE" means a schedule to the Act or Regulation in which the word occurs. [General Clauses Act (10 of 1897), S. 3(52)].

A small scroll; list summary, index, or inventory; a writing, additional or appendant.

An appendix to an Act of legislature or to legal instrument containing a statement of details or taking the form of a detailed list or relevant matter. [General Clauses Act (10 of 1897), S. 3(52)].

Schedule feasibility. Determining whether the e-commerce project will be ready within the time frame needed by an organization. (*Cyber Law*)

Scheduled Act. Means an Act specified in the First Schedule and is in force on the commencement of this Act in the territories to which such Act extends generally, and includes the rules made thereunder. [Labour Laws (Exemption from Furnishing Returns and Maintaining Registers by Certain Establishments) Act (51 of 1988), S. 2(d)]

Scheduled air transport service. Means an air transport service undertaken between the same two or more places and opened according to a published time table or with flights so regular or frequent that they constitute a recognisably systematic series, each flight being open to use by members of the public. [Air Corporations Act (27 of 1953), S. 2(viii)]

Scheduled and tribal areas. Areas in any State other than Assam, Meghalaya, Tripura and Mizoram declared by the President in an order are scheduled areas.

Scheduled animal article. Means an article made from any scheduled animal and includes an article or object in which the whole or any part of such animal has been used but does not include tail feather of peacock, an article or trophy made therefrom and snake venom or its derivative. [Wild Life (Protection) Act (53 of 1972), S. 49A(b)]

Scheduled area. Means the scheduled areas as defined in section 2 of the Provisions of the Panchayats (Extension to the Scheduled Areas) Act, 1996 (40 of 1996). [S. 3(zd) of the Right to Fair Compensation & Transparency in Land Acquisition, Rehabilitation & Resettlement Act, 2013 (30 of 2013)]

Scheduled Areas. Means the Scheduled Areas as referred to in Article 244(1) of the Constitution. [S. 2 of the Provisions of the Panchayats (Extension to the Scheduled Areas) Act, 1996 (40 of 1996)]

Scheduled Bank. In this Scheme, unless the context otherwise requires,—

"SCHEDULED BANK" means the State Bank of India constituted under the State Bank of India Act, 1955 (23 of 1955), a subsidiary bank as defined in the State Bank of India (Subsidiary Banks) Act, 1959 (38 of 1959), a corresponding new bank constituted under Section 3 of the Banking Companies (Acquisition and Transfer of Undertakings) Act, 1970 (5 of 1970), or under Section 3 of the Banking Companies (Acquisition and Transfer of Undertakings) Act, 1980 (40 of 1980), or any other bank being a bank included in the Second Schedule to the Reserve Bank of India Act, 1934 (2 of 1934). [Investment Deposit Account Scheme, 1986, S. 2(g); Finance Act (18 of 2005), Ch. VII, S. 94(7)]

"SCHEDULED BANK" means a bank included in the Second Schedule. [Reserve Bank of India Act 1934, S. 2(*e*). Also see S. 2(80) of the Companies Act, 2013 (18 of 2013)]

Scheduled Caste/Tribe. A 'Scheduled Caste/ Tribe' person who migrates from the State of his origin to another State in search of employment or for educational purposes or the like, cannot be treated as a person belonging to the 'Scheduled Caste/ Tribe' of the State to which he migrates and hence, he cannot claim benefit as such in the latter state. *U.P. Public Service Commission, Allahabad* v. *Sanjay Kumar Singh*, (2003) 7 SCC 657, 662 para 13.

Scheduled castes. "SCHEDULED CASTES" in relation to the union territory means such castres, races or tribes or parts of or groups within such castes, race or tribes as are deemed under Article 341 to be scheduled castes in relation to that Union Territory. [Government of Union Territories Act (20 of 1963), S. 2(f)]

Such castes, races or tribes as are deemed under Article 341 of the Constitution of India to be scheduled castes for the purposes of the Constitution.

Scheduled district. "SCHEDULED DISTRICT" shall mean a "Scheduled District" as defined in the Scheduled Districts Act, 1874. [General Clauses Act (10 of 1897), S. 3(53)].

Scheduled employment. "SCHEDULED EMPLOYMENT" means an employment specified in the Schedule, or any process or branch of work forming part of such employment. [Minimum Wages Act (11 of 1948), S. 2(g)]

'Scheduled employment' means any employment specified in the Schedule hereto or any process or branch of work forming part of such employment. [Maharashtra Mathadi, Hamal and Other Manual Workers (Regulation of Employment and Welfare) Act (30 of 1969), S. 2(9) as cited in *Pepsico India Holding Private Limited v. Grocery Market and Shops Board*, (2016) 4 SCC 493, para 8].

Scheduled offence. "SCHEDULED OFFENCE" means an offence specified in the schedule being an offence forming part or arising out of, or connected with, any such disturbance as is referred to in Section 3. [Disturbed Areas (Special Courts) Act (77 of 1976), S. 2(d)]

"SCHEDULED OFFENCE" means an offence specified in the Schedule being an offence committed in a terrorist affected area. [Terrorist Affected Areas (Special Courts) Act (61 of 1984), S. 2(f)]

"SCHEDULED OFFENCE" means,—

(i) the offences specified under Part A of the Schedule; or

(ii) [the offences specified under Part B of the Schedule if the total value involved in such offences is Footnote 4[one crore rupees or more; or

(iii) the offences specified under Part C of the Schedule. Inserted by Act 20 of 2005]. [Prevention of Money Laundering Act (15 of 2003), S. 2(1)(y)]

Scheduled product. Means any of the agricultural or processed food products included in the Schedule. [Agricultural & Processed Food Products Export Development Authority Act. (2 of 1986), S. 2(i)]

Scheduled tribes. Such castes, races or tribes as are deemed under Article 342 of the Constitution of India to be scheduled tribes for the purposes of the Constitution. [Hindu Minority and Guardianship Act (32 of 1956), S. 3(2)].

"SCHEDULED TRIBES" in relation to the Union Territory mean such tribes or tribal communities or parts of or groups within such tribes or tribal communities as are deemed under Article 342 to be scheduled tribes in relation to that Union Territory. [Government of Union Territories Act (20 of 1963) S. 2(g)]

Scheme. "SCHEME" means a scheme formulated by the National Housing Bank under National Housing Bank Act, 1987 for the purpose of enabling—

(i) any person to make deposit with that Bank;

(ii) such Bank to credit forty per cent of the amount of such deposit to a special fund created for financing slum clearance and low cost housing for the poor; and

(iii) the depositor to utilise the net deposit for any purpose specified by him. [Voluntary Deposits (Immunities and Exemptions) Act (47 of 1991), S. 2(e)]

"SCHEME" means a scheme inviting subscription to security receipts proposed to be issued by a asset reconstruction company under that scheme. [Securitisation and Reconstruction of Financial Assets and Enforcement of Security Interest Act (54 of 2002), S. 2(1)(y)]

In this scheme, unless the context otherwise requires,—

"SCHEME" means the Securities Lending Scheme, 1997, for lending of securities through an approved intermediary to a borrower under an agreement for a specified period with the condition that the borrower will return equivalent securities of the same type or class at the end of the specified period along with the corporate benefits accruing on the securities borrowed. [Securities Lending Scheme, 1997, S. 3(g)]

"SCHEME" means a scheme for corporatisation or demutualisation of a recognised stock exchange which may provide for—

(i) the issue of shares for a lawful consideration and provision of trading rights *in lieu* of membership cards of members of a recognised stock exchange;

(ii) the restrictions on voting rights;

(iii) the transfer of property, business, assets, rights, liabilities, recognitions, contracts of the recognised stock exchange, legal proceedings by, or against, the recognised stock exchange, whether in the name of the recognised stock exchange or any trustee or otherwise and any permission given to, or by, the recognised stock exchange;

(iv) the transfer of employees of a recognised stock exchange to another recognised stock exchange;

(v) any other matter required for the purpose of, or in connection with, the corporatisation or demutualisation, as the case may be, of the recognised stock exchange. [Securities Contracts (Regulation) Act (42 of 1956) S. 2(ga) *as inserted by Securities Contracts (Regulation) Act (42 of 1956), S. 2*]

A plan; a purpose; a specific organization for some end; a combination of things by design.

A system of correlated things, institution, arrangement, *etc.*; the manner in which such a system is organised. [CPC (5 of 1908), S. 92(1)(g) and Constitution of India, Art. 39A].

A 'scheme' under the Act means a proposal prepared and published by a State Transport Undertaking indicating the nature of the services proposed to be run and operated by the undertaking in relation to any area or route whether to the exclusion, complete or partial of other persons or otherwise. *M.P. State Road Transport Corporation* v. *State Transport Authority, M.P. Gwalior,* AIR 1975 MP 181, 183.

"SCHEME" means a scheme of pension fund approved by the Authority under Act 23 of 2013. [S. 2(1)(o) of the Pension Fund Regulatory & Development Authority Act, 2013 (23 of 2013)]

Scholarship. An aid granted to a scholar. [University of Hyderabad Act (39 of 1974), S. 5(13)].

School. "SCHOOL" includes a pre-primary, primary, middle and higher secondary school, and also includes any other institution which imparts education or training below the degree level, but does not include an institution which imparts technical education. [Delhi School Education Act (18 of 1973), S. 2(u)]

"SCHOOL" means a primary school, secondary school, higher secondary school, junior college of education or any other institution by whatever name called including technical, vocational or art institution or part of any such school, college or institution, which imparts general, technical, vocational, art or, as the case may be, special education or training in any faculty or discipline or subject below the degree level.. [Substituted by Mah. 32 of 1990 Maharashtra Employees of Private Schools (Conditions of Service) Regulation Act, 1977 (3 of 1978), S. 2(24)]

"SCHOOL" means any recognised school imparting elementary education and includes—

(i) a school established, owned or controlled by the appropriate Government or a local authority;

(ii) an aided school receiving aid or grants to meet whole or part of its expenses from the appropriate Government or the local authority;

(iii) a school belonging to specified category; and

(iv) an unaided school not receiving any kind of aid or grants to meet its expenses from the appropriate Government or the local authority. [Right of Children to Free and Compulsory Education Act 2009 (35 of 2009), S. 2(n)].

"SCHOOL" means a School of Studies of the University. [S. 2(v) of the Rajiv Gandhi National Aviation University Act, 2013 (26 of 2013)]

School leaving certificate. As the very expression indicates, is issued by the school since the pupil leaves the school. [Hina v. Union of India, (2016) 6 SCC 293, para 6].

School education. "SCHOOL EDUCATION" means primary, upper primary, non-formal, adult and secondary education. [A.P. School Education (Community Participation) Act (13 of 1998), S. 2(11)]

School property. "SCHOOL PROPERTY" means all movable and immovable property belonging to, or in possession of, the school and all other rights and interests in, or arising out of such property, and includes land, building and its appurtenances, play grounds, hostels, furniture, books, apparatus, maps, equipment, utensils, cash, reserve fund, investments and bank balances. [Delhi School Education Act (18 of 1973), S. 2(v)]

Science. A branch of study that is concerned with observation and classification of facts and specially with the establishment or strictly with the quantitative formulation of verifiable general laws chiefly by induction and hypothesis. [Indian Evidence Act (1 of 1872), Ss. 45 and 57(13) and Constitution of India, Art. 80(3)].

The word 'science' is wide enough to meet the requirement of treating the opinion of a typewriter expert as an opinion evidence under section 45 of the Indian Evidence Act. *State* v. *S.J. Choudhary*, AIR 1996 SC 1491, 1496. [Indian Evidence Act (1 of 1872), S. 45]

Scientific or technical consultancy. Means any advice, consultancy, or scientific or technical assistance, rendered in any manner, either directly or indirectly, by a scientist or a technocrat, or any science or technology institution or organisation, to any person, in one or more disciplines of science or technology. [Finance Act (32 of 1994), S. 65(1)(92) now repealed by Central Goods and Services Tax Act, 2017].

Scientific research. "SCIENTIFIC RESEARCH" means any activities for the extension of knowledge in the fields of natural or applied science including agriculture, animal husbandry or fisheries. [Income-tax Act (43 of 1961), S. 43(4)]

Scientific Opinion. Means a scientific output given by the Scientific Committee or Scientific Panel. [Food safety and Standards Authority of India (Transaction of Business and Procedures for the Scientific Committee and Scientific Panels) Regulations, 2016, Regn. 2(1)(h)].

Scion. "SCION" means a portion of a fruit plant which is grafted or budded on to a root stock. [U.P. Fruit Nurseries (Regulation) Act (21 of 1976), S. 2(i)]

Scope. Design, aim, or purpose, extent, limits, *etc.*

Ambit; general extent [Indian Contract Act (9 of 1872), S. 228]; [Industrial Finance Corporation Act (15 of 1948), S. 34(4)]; the range of operation; subject under consideration [Arbitration (Protocol and Convention) Act (6 of 1936), S. 7(2)(c)]; room for action.

Scrap. "SCRAP" means waste and scrap from the manufacture or mechanical working of materials which is definitely not usable as such because of breakage, cutting up, wear and other reasons. [Income-tax Act (43 of 1961), S. 206C, *Expln.* (b)]

Screening. Sheltering or shielding (an offender) with the object of saving him from punishment. [IPC (45 of 1860), S. 213].

Scrip. A certificate or schedule; also evidence of the right to obtain shares in a public company, sometimes called "scrip-certificate", to distinguish it from the real title to shares.

Script. The original or principal instrument, where there are part and counterpart; a writing.

Scripts. Scripts are programs written to run with your Web pages and perform a specific task in response to visitor actions such as clicking a button. For example, a Perl script counts the visits to this page, and a Javascript makes the buttons change colours when you put your mouse pointer over them. Scripts can be written in Perl, Java, JavaScript, VBScript, and a dozen other programming languages. (*Cyber Law*)

Scroll. A mark which supplies the place of a seal.

To move an image on the display screen vertically or sideways. Scrolling brings unseen areas of the image into view on the screen. (*Computer*)

Scrutiny. (*Of Voting Papers*) An examination of voting papers.

Examination of anything; an official examination of the votes cast at an election in order to eliminate any votes that are invalid and to rectify or confirm the numbers stated in the return. [Representation of the People Act (43 of 1951), S. 30(c)].

Sculptor. An artist who produces works of sculpture. [Indian Evidence Act (1 of 1872), S. 98, ill.].

SDRAM. Stands for synchronous dynamic random access memory. SDRAM incorporates new features that make it faster than standard DRAM and EDO memory. (*Cyber Law*)

SDSL. (*abbr.*) Symmetric Digital Subscriber Line. A version of *DSL* where the upload speeds and download speeds are the same. (*Matisse Enzer-Glossary of Internet Terms*)

Sea. "SEA" includes bay, inlet, creek or an arm of the sea. [Gujarat Khar Lands Act, 1963 (17 of 1964), S. 2(g)]

Seafarer. "Seafarer" means any person who is employed or engaged or works in any capacity on board a sea going ship, but does not include—

(i) the employment or engagement or work on board in any capacity of any person in a ship of war; or

(ii) any Government ship used for military or non-commercial purposes. [Merchant Shipping Act (44 of 1958), S. 88A(d) as inserted by Amending Act (32 of 2014)].

Sea-going. In relation to a vessel, means a vessel proceeding to sea beyond inland waters or beyond waters declared to be smooth or partially smooth waters by the Central Government by notification in the Official Gazette. [Merchant Shipping Act (44 of 1958), S. 3(41)]

Sea going ship. In this chapter unless the context otherwise requires,—"SEAGOING SHIP" means a ship if it is certified as such by the competent authority of any country. [Income-tax Act (43 of 1961), Chapter XII, G, S. 115V(i), *Inserted by Finance Act (23 of 2004), S. 30*].

Sea mark. A conspicuous object distinguishable at sea which serves to guide or warn sailors in navigation. [IPC (45 of 1860), S. 433].

"Sea policy" or "policy of sea insurance".—

(a) means any insurance made upon any ship or vessel (whether for marine or inland navigation), or upon the machinery, tackle or furniture of any ship or vessel, or upon any goods, merchandise or property of any description whatever on board of any ship or vessel or upon the freight of, or of any other interest which may be lawfully insured in, or relating to any ship or vessel; and

(b) includes any insurance of goods, merchandise or property for any transit which includes, not only a sick risk within the meaning of clause (a), but also any other risk incidental to the transit insured from the commencement of the transit to the ultimate destination covered by the insurance;

Where any person, in consideration of any sum of money paid or to be paid for additional freight or otherwise, agrees to take upon himself any risk attending goods, merchandise or property of any description whatever while on board of any ship or vessel, or engages to indemnify the owner of any such goods, merchandise or property from any risk, loss or damage, such agreement or engagement shall be deemed to be contract for sea insurance. [Indian Stamp Act (2 of 1899), S. 2(20)]

Sea wall. A wall or embankment to prevent the encroachment of sea *etc.* [Indian Evidence Act (1 of 1872), S. 46, ill. (b)].

Seafarer Means any person who fulfills the conditions to be employed or engaged in any capacity on board a sea-going ship other than a government ship used for military or non-commercial purposes. [Merchant Shipping (Amendment) Act (63 of 2002), S. 4(iv) *Expln.* (b)]

Seafaring profession. The profession of a sailor. [Seamen's Provident Fund Act (4 of 1966), S. 19].

Seal. Means a device or process by which a stamp is made, and includes any wire or other accessory which is used for ensuring the integrity of any stamp. [Standards of Weights and Measures Act (60 of 1976), S. 2(w)]

Seal is taken either for wax impressed with a device and attached to deeds, & c., or for the instrument with which the wax is impressed. In law, the former is the most usual sense. (*Tomlin*)

An indication or mark of office; an engraved stamp of metal or other hard material to make an impression [Indian Evidence Act (1 of 1872), S. 57(6) and IPC (45 of 1860), S. 472]; to set a seal to; to stamp; to set one's seal to; to fasten with a seal.

SEAL is an impression upon wax, wafer, or some other tenacious substance capable of being impressed.

GREAT SEAL. The state seal of the United Kingdom.

PRIVY SEAL. Official seal appended to royal grants.

SET ONE'S SEAL. To give one's authority or assent to.

UNDER SEAL. Authenticated in a formal manner.

Sealed. The word 'sealed' has acquired an enlarged meaning, even when applied in the law. In the earlier times wax, upon which some impression was made, was understood by the act of sealing. Gradually, however some symbol adopted by the maker in lieu of the actual seal was allowed in law, and this, ought to be the crucial test in such matters, namely, the adoption by the party who is required to seal of something in its stead."

Bearing the mark of a seal [First, IPC (45 of 1860), S. 464]; [Indian Evidence Act (1 of 1872), S. 76]; confirmed or made secure by or as if by a seal. [Registration Act (16 of 1908), S. 42].

Sealed container. Sealed container means a container which is so closed that access 'to the contents' is impossible without breaking the fastening. *Marland Diary and Farm* v. *Union of India*, AIR 1975 SC 1492, 1493. [Central Sales Tax Act (74 of 1956), S. 6]

Seaman. "SEAMAN" means any person forming part of the crew of any ship, but does include the master of the ship. [Employee's Compensation Act (8 of 1923), S. 2(k)]

"SEAMAN" means every person (except a master, pilot or apprentice) employed or engaged as a member of the crew of a ship under this Act, but in relation to Section 178 to 183 (inclusive) includes a master. [Merchant Shipping Act (44 of 1958), S. 3(42)]

"SEAMAN" means a person employed or engaged as a member of the crew of a ship under the Merchant Shipping Act, but does not include a master navigating or engineering officer, radio officer, medical officer, welfare officer, pursuer, electrician, nurse, musician, pilot, apprentice or dock barber. [Seamen's Provident Fund Act (4 of 1966), S. 2(e)]

Search. An examination of a man's house, premises, or person for the purpose of discovering proof of his guilt in relation to some crime or misdemeanour of which he is accused.

Examination or scrutiny for the purpose of finding a person or thing; to look into or over carefully or thoroughly in an effort to find or discover. [CrPC, 1973 (2 of 1974), S. 51; T.P. Act (4 of 1882), S. 3(c)].

Proceedings for the search and seizure of property stolen or illegally withheld are in most instances of a criminal nature and are usually ancillary to the prosecution of some particular offence, but may or may not be accompanied by a criminal prosecution depending upon the nature of the facts disclosed, if any.

In the registration law, an examination made in the proper office for mortgages, liens, judgments, or other incumbrances against real estate. The certificate given by the officer as to the result of such examination is also called a *search certificate*.

Search and seizure. The executive power of 'search and seizure' is a necessary concomitant of a welfare State. It tends to promote the well-being of the nation. *Bishamber Dayal Chandra Mohan Etc.* v. *State of U.P.*, AIR 1982 SC 33, 34.

Search engine. A computer program that utilises key word identification to find websites and establish hypertext links to them. (*Information Technology*)

A (usually web-based) system for searching the information available on the *Web.* Some search engines work by automatically searching the contents of other systems and creating a database of the results. Other search engines contain only material manually approved for inclusion in a database, and some combine the two approaches. (*Matisse Enzer-Glossary of Internet Terms*)

Search, Right of. (*In International Law*) *In times of peace,* the right of a public vessel to visit and search private vessels for the purpose of investigating their character. Within the territorial waters of a State, it may be exercised by the public vessels of said State for the enforcement of revenue and other domestic laws. As it is a police measure it cannot, apart from treaty stipulations, be exercised upon the high seas, except after pursuit of an offending vessel which has escaped from the territorial waters of the state, and by public vessels generally where there is a well-grounded suspicion of piracy.

In times of War, the right of a belligerent to visit and search neutral merchant vessels. It is exercised, first, as an incident to the belligerent right to capture, upon the high seas, private property of enemy subjects. Secondly, it is exercised as an incident to the recognized belligerent right to prevent the carriage of contraband by neutral vessels to the enemy and to punish breaches of blockade.

Search warrant. A search warrant is generally defined to be an order in writing signed by a Magistrate and directed to an officer, commanding him to search for personal property and bring it before the Magistrate.

An order by a magistrate directing any person, generally a police officer above the rank of a constable to search any place mentioned in it in order to seize a document or a thing. [Heading, CrPC, 1973 (2 of 1974), S. 93].

SEARCH WARRANT is granted by a justice of the peace for the searching of a house, shop or other premises, for stolen or unlawful goods.

Search warrant is a warrant requiring the officer to whom it is addressed to search a house or other place, therein specified for property therein alleged to have been stolen, and, if the same shall be found upon such search, to bring the goods so found, together with the body of the person occupying the same, who is named, before the justice or other officer granting the warrant or some other justice of the peace, or other lawfully authorized officer.

Seasonal and intermittent. A seasonal industrial establishment, that is, an industrial establishment, which normally works only during defined periods or seasons of the year, will obviously be an industrial establishment which works intermittently, the expression 'intermittent' being used here in relation to a given period, annual or otherwise. In the context of Section 25-A(2), the expressions 'seasonal' and intermittent would appear to indicate that it should be seasonal or intermittent under normal conditions. *Kohinoor Saw Mills Co. Ltd.* v. *State of Madras,* AIR 1957 Mad 410, 415. [Industrial Disputes Act (14 of 1947), S. 25-A(2)]

Seasonal factory. Means a factory which is exclusively engaged in one or more of the following manufacturing processes, namely, cotton ginning, cotton or jute pressing, decortication of groundnuts, the manufacture of coffee, indigo, lac, rubber, sugar (including gur) or tea or any manufacturing process which is incidental to or connected with any of the aforesaid processes and includes a factory which is engaged for a period not exceeding seven months in a year—

(a) in any process of blending, packing or repacking of tea or coffee; or

(b) in such other manufacturing process as the Central Government may, by notification in the official Gazette, specify. [Employees' State Insurance Act (34 of 1948), S. 2(19A)]

Seaward artillery practice. Means artillery practice or coastal firing towards the sea, whether within or beyond the territorial waters and includes air armament practice. [Seaward Artillery Practice Act (8 of 1949), S. 2(1)(c)]

Seaworthiness. 'A ship is deemed to be seaworthy when she is reasonably fit in all respects to encounter the ordinary perils of the sea of the adventure insured.' [Marine Insurance Act (11 of 1963), S. 41(4)]

Seaworthy. A term applied to a ship, indicating that she is, in every respect fit for undertaking a voyage.

Secession of a part of the territory of India from the Union. Includes the assertion of any claim to determine whether such part will remain a part of the territory of India. [Unlawful Activities (Prevention) Act (37 of 1967), S. 2(1)(i) *as substituted by Unlawful Activities (Prevention) Amendment Act (29 of 2004), S. 4*]

'Second assured career progression scale' with reference to—

(i) Government servant means the revised scale as mentioned in Column 4 of Part I of Schedule I against the name of post(s) in column 2 of Part I of Schedule I, on which the government servant was recruited as a direct recruited fresh entrant in the Government service.

(ii) all other Government servants not covered in sub-clause (i) above but on whom these Rules apply, the pay scale as mentioned in Column 4 of Part II of Schedule I against the pay scale mentioned in Column 2 of Part II of Schedule I, as the corresponding existing pay scale prescribed for the post against which such government servant was recruited as a direct recruited fresh entrant in the Government service:

Provided that the Second Assured Career Progression scale may also be referred to as second ACP scale or ACP-II scale. [Haryana Civil Service (Assured Career Progression) Rules, 1998, R. 3(q) as cited in *State of Haryana v. Sita Ram,* (2013) 16 SCC 677, para 4].

Second offence. Second offence means an offence which the offender has committed after he has been convicted for the first offence. The terms 'third offence' and 'subsequent offence' convey the similar meanings. *State of Rajasthan* v. *Badri,* AIR 1965 Raj 152, 155. [Prevention of Food Adulteration Act (37 of 1954), S. 16(1)(ii)]

The words 'second offence' mean any act which is an offence under any of the clauses in the sub-section which has been done later in point of time after a conviction for the offence under the Act no matter whether the acts or omissions constituting the two offences are of the same type or not. *Jagdish Prasad* v. *State of U.P.*, AIR 1966 SC 290, 292.

Second stage dealer. Means a dealer who purchases the goods from a first stage dealer. [CENVAT Credit Rules, 2002, R. 2(k)]

Secondary adjustment. For the purposes of this section, "SECONDARY ADJUSTMENT" means an adjustment in the books of accounts of the assessee and its associated enterprise to reflect that the actual allocation of profit between the assessee and its associated enterprise are consistent with the transfer price determined as a result of primary adjustment, thereby removing the imbalance between cash account and actual profit as assessee. [Income-tax Act (43 of 1961), S. 92-CE, *Explanation (v)*].

Secondary food packaging. Means packaging material which encloses the primary food packaging and does not come in direct contact with food products. [Food Safety and Standards (Packaging) Regulations, 2018, Regn. 2(1)(h)].

Secondary evidence. "SECONDARY EVIDENCE means and includes—(1) certified copies given under the provisions hereinafter contained; (2) copies made from the original by mechanical processes which in themselves insure the accuracy of the copy, and copies compared with such copies; (3) copies made from or compared with the original; (4) counterparts of documents as against the parties who did not execute them; (5) oral accounts of the contents of a document given by some person who has himself seen it." [Indian Evidence Act (1 of 1872), S. 63]

SECONDARY EVIDENCE is such as from necessity in some cases is substituted for stronger and better proof.

"SECONDARY EVIDENCE" is that which is inferior to primary. Thus, a copy of an instrument or oral evidence of its contents is secondary evidence of the instrument and its contents.

Secondary standard. Means the set of standard weight or measure which is made or manufactured by or on behalf of the Central or State Government for the verification of any working standard. [Standards of Weights and Measures Act (60 of 1976), S. 2(x)]

Secrecy. The quality of being secret. [Deposit Insurance and Credit Guarantee Corporation Act (47 of 1961), S. 39].

Secret. The word a "secret," in a statute making it a ground for attachment that the debtor has secreted his property with intent to defraud creditors, means to hide it or to put it where the officer of the law will probably not be liable to find it.

Confidential, concealed.

Secretarial standards. For the purpose of section 205 of Act 18 of 2013, the expression 'secretarial standards' means secretarial standards issued by the Institute of Company Secretaries of India constituted under section 3 of the Company Secretaries Act, 1980 (56 of 1980), and approved by the Central Government. [*Explanation* to section 205(1) of the Companies Act, 2013 (18 of 2013)]

Secretary. "SECRETARY" means,—

(i) in the case of a Post Office Savings Bank, the Postmaster-General appointed for the area in which the Post Office Savings Bank is situated, or any officer of the Government as the Central Government may, by general or special order, specify in this behalf; and

(ii) in the case of a banking company or other company or institution, an officer of that banking company or other company or institution, as the case may be, or any officer of the Government or any other person as the Central Government may, by general or special order, specify in this behalf. [Government Savings Bank (5 of 1873), S. 3(bb) (*substituted by Finance Act (23 of 2004), S. 116*)].

"SECRETARY" means a Company Secretary within the meaning of clause (c) of sub-section (1) of Section 2 of the Company Secretaries Act, 1980 (56 of 1980), and includes any other individual possessing the prescribed qualifications and appointed to perform the duties which may be performed by a secretary under this Act and any other ministerial or administrative duties. [Companies Act (1 of 1956), S. 2(45)]

One who is employed to conduct correspondence, to keep records and (usually) to transact other business for another person, or for a society, corporation or public body. [Khadi and Village Industries Commission Act (61 of 1956), S. 2(g) and Constitution of India, Art. 31 A(1)(d)].

One entrusted with the management of business.

The "secretary" of a corporation is one of the general managing agents of the company, and when in the discharge of the duties of his office, he represents the corporation itself. Therefore, the representations by him in the course of the business of the corporation are binding on it.

"SECRETARY" means a company secretary as defined in section 2(1)(*c*) of the Company Secretaries Act, 1980 (56 of 1980), who is appointed by a company to perform the functions of a company secretary under the Companies Act, 2013 (18 of 2013). [S. 2(24) of the Companies Act, 2013 (18 of 2013)]

Secretary-General. Means the Secretary General to the Council and includes any person for the time being performing the duties of the Secretary-General. [Rules of Procedure and Conduct of Business in the Council of States (Rajya Sabha), R. 2(1)]

Secreted. The word 'secreted' means documents which are kept not in the normal or usual places with a view to conceal them. In other words documents or things which a person is likely to keep out of the way or to put it in a place where the officer of law cannot find it. *Durgaprasad* v. *Superintendent (Prev.) Central Excise, Nagpur*, AIR 1966 SC 1209, 1216. [Customs Act (52 of 1962), S. 105(1)]

Secretes. To secrete means to hide. In connection with a postal article addressed to some person the fact that it is retained in his possession by an officer of the post office in an almirah and that too for an inordinately long period would be tantamount to hiding that article. *Radha Kishan* v. *State of Uttar*

Pradesh, AIR 1963 SC 822, 825. [Indian Post Office Act (6 of 1898), S. 52]

Sect. A "sect" is a body of persons distinguished by peculiarities of faith and practice from other bodies adhering to the same general system.

A separately organised religious body having its distinctive name and its own place of worship. [T.P. Act (4 of 1882), S. 69(1)(a)].

A sect is a class of people holding in effect the same religious faith and associating together in the same form of religious discipline, and worship. Mere difference in faith with regard to doctrinal points seemingly does not constitute a sectarian difference, but the test lies in the similarity of discipline and worship, though there be diversity of opinion in regard to doctrine.

It represents a religious denomination and also represents a sub-division of that religious community or section of the electorate. *Hari Ram Sri Harkesh* v. *Election Tribunal,* AIR 1970 All 146 at 150.

Section. "SECTION" shall mean a section of the Act or Regulation in which the word occurs. [General Clauses Act (10 of 1897), S. 3(54)]

The word "SECTION" denotes one of those portions of a Chapter of this Code which are distinguished by prefixed numeral figures. [IPC (45 of 1860), S. 50]

A part separated from the rest; a division; a portion as, specifically, a distinct part of a book or writing; the sub-division of a chapter; the division of a law or other writing; a paragraph.

A sub-division of a statute [IPC (45 of 1860), S. 50 and General Clauses Act (10 of 1897), S. 3(54)]; one of the parts into which anything may be considered as divided or of the parts into which anything may be considered as divided or of which it may be built up [Industrial Disputes Act (14 of 1947), S. 2(n)(ii)]; [Indian Iron and Steel Company (Taking Over of Management) Act (50 of 1972), S. 3(2)].

Sector. The tracks on a disk are divided into sectors. Clusters contain from 1 to 64 sectors. (*Cyber Law*)

Sectoral cap. Means the maximum investment including both foreign investment on a repatriation basis by persons resident outside India in capital instruments of a company or the capital of an LLP, as the case may be, and indirect foreign investment, unless provided otherwise. This shall be the composite limit for the Indian investee entity;

Explanation.—

(*a*) FCCBs and DRs having underlying of instruments being in the nature of debt shall not be included in the sectroal cap.

(*b*) Any equity holding by a person resident outside India resulting from conversion of any debt instrument under any arrangement shall be reckoned under the sectoral cap. [Foreign Exchange Management (Transfer or Issue of Security by a Person Resident outside India) Regulations, 2017, Regn. 2(xxxix)].

Secular. The word "secular" means temporal or worldly; also, opposed to spiritual or holy; temporal things; things of the world.

Secular state. 'Secular state' means non-religious and not irreligious State. *Perunchithiranar* v. *State of Tamil Nadu,* AIR 1986 Mad 83, 86. [Constitution of India, Art. 15]

Secularism. Secularism is a system of utilitarian ethics, seeking to maximise human happiness or welfare quite independently of what may be either religious or the occult. (*Ziyauddin Burhanuddin Bukhari* v. *Brijmohan Ramdass Mehra,* AIR 1975 SC 1788)

'Secularism' means religious tolerance and equal treatment to all religions. (*S.R. Bommai* v. *Union of India,* AIR 1994 SC 1918). See also *T.M.A Pai Foundation* v. *State of Karnataka,* (2002) 8 SCC 481; *R.C. Poduyal* v. *Union of India*, (1994) Supp. 1 SCC 324.

Secundum allegata et probata. (*Maxim*) According to what is alleged and proved.

According to the pleadings and the proofs.

Secure. Safe; free from apprehension of distress; to give security for (any debt) [T.P. Act (4 of 1882), S. 58(a)]; to make sure [long title, Jayanti Shipping Company (Taking Over of Management) Act (63 of 1971)]; to get hold of [Navy Act (62 of 1957), S. 17(a)].

"To secure" is to make safe; to protect from danger; to ensure; to enclose effectually.

Secure Channel. An encoded communications way that saves messages against anticipated security threats. (*Information Technology*)

Secure Electronic Transactions (SETs). Industry standards of cryptography governing commercial transactions. (*Cyber Law*)

Secure server (SSL). One method of ensuring that information entered through your Web site is protected. Information submitted via a secure form is sent to the server in encrypted mode. This is most commonly used for credit card transactions. (*Cyber Law*)

Secure sockets layer (SSL). Introduced by Netscape Corporation, a relatively secure method to encrypt data transmitted over a public network such as the Internet. (*Cyber Law*)

Secure system. Means computer hardware, software, and procedure that—

(a) are reasonably secure from unauthorised access and misuse;

(b) provide a reasonable level of reliability and correct operation;

(c) are reasonably suited to performing the intended functions; and

(d) adhere to generally accepted security procedures. [Information Technology Act (21 of 2000), S. 2(1)(*ze*)] [Also see *Explanation* (ii) to rule 20(2) of the Companies (Management & Administration) Rules, 2014]

'Secure system means' computer hardware, software, and procedure that—(*a*) are reasonably secure from unauthorized access and misuse; (*b*) provide a reasonable level of reliability and correct operation; (*c*) are reasonably suited to performing the intended functions; and (*d*) adhere to generally accepted security procedures. [Information Technology Act (21 of 2000), S. 2(1)(*ze*)]

Secured advance. Means a loan or advance made on the security of assets the market value of which is not at any time less than the amount of such loan or advance; and unsecured loan or advance means a loan or advance not so secured . [Banking Regulation Act (10 of 1949), S. 5(n)]

Secured asset. Means the property on which security interest is created. [Securitisation and Reconstruction of Financial Assets and Enforcement of Security Interest Act (54 of 2002), S. 2(1)(*zc*)]

Secured creditor. "SECURED CREDITOR" includes a landlord who under any enactment for the time being in force has a charge on land for the rent of that land. [Presidency Towns Insolvency Act (3 of 1909), S. 2(*g*)]

"SECURED CREDITOR, means a person holding a mortgage, charge or lien on the property of the debtor or any part thereof as a security for a debt due to him from the debtor. [Provincial Towns Insolvency Act (5 of 1920), S. 2(*e*)].

Secured creditor is one, who has some mortgage, charge or lien on the company's property... A solicitor who holds a lien on documents of a liquidating company for his costs against the company is a secured creditor, and must mention his lien in his proof. [Palmer's Company Law, 21st Edn. at p. 765 as cited in *Bombay Stock Exchange* v. *V.S. Kandalgaonkar*, (2015) 2 SCC 1, para 31].

"SECURED CREDITOR" means—

(i) any bank or financial institution or any consortium or group of banks or financial institutions holding any right, title or interest upon any tangible asset or intangible asset as specified in clause (1);

(ii) debenture trustee appointed by any bank or financial institution; or

(iii) an asset reconstruction company whether acting as such or managing a trust set up by such asset reconstruction company for the securitisation or reconstruction, as the case may be; or

(iv) debenture trustee registered with the Board appointed by any company for secured debt securities; or

(v) any other trustee holding securities on behalf of a bank or financial institution, in whose favour security interest is created by any borrower for due repayment of any financial assistance. [Securitisation and Reconstruction of Financial Assets and Enforcement of Security Interest Act (54 of 2002), S. 2(1)(zd) as substituted by Amending Act (44 of 2016)].

"SECURED CREDITOR" means any bank or financial institution or any consortium or group of banks or financial institutions and includes—

(i) debenture trustee appointed by any bank or financial institution; or

(ii) securitisation company or reconstruction company; or

(iii) any other trustee holding securities on behalf of a bank or financial institution, in whose favour security interest is created for due repayment by any borrower of any financial assistance. [Securitisation and Reconstruction of Financial Assets and Enforcement of Security Interest Act (54 of 2002), S. 2(1)(zd)]

A creditor holding security the realisation of which would satisfy his claim.

A "secured creditor" is one who has security for his debt.

The definition of the term 'secured creditor' is to be understood as confined to his capacity '*qua*' the secured debt and not comprehending his capacity as regards debts for which there is no security. *G. Guruswami Pillai* v. *Shri Chitra Cardamons Co-op. Society, Bank Ltd.*, AIR 1954 TC 419.

Secured debt. Means a debt which is secured by any security interest. [Securitisation and Reconstruction of Financial Assets and Enforcement of Security Interest Act (54 of 2002) S. 2(1)(*ze*)]

"Security interest" means right, title or interest of any kind, other than those specified in Section 31, upon property created in favour of any secured creditor and includes—

(i) any mortgage, charge, hypothecation, assignment or any right, title or interest any kind, on tangible asset, retained by the secured creditor as an owner of the property, given on hire or financial lease or conditional sale or under any other contract which secures the obligation to pay any unpaid portion of the purchase price of the asset or an obligation incurred or credit provided to enable the borrower to acquire the tangible asset; or

(ii) such right, title or interest in any intangible asset or assignment or licence of such intangible asset which secures the obligation to pay any unpaid portion of the purchase price of the intangible asset or the obligation incurred or any credit provided to enable the borrower to acquire the intangible asset or licence of intangible asset. [Securitisation and Reconstruction of Financial Assets and Enforcement of Security Interest Act (54 of 2002), S. 2(1)(zf) as substituted by Amending Act (44 of 2016)].

Secured loan. Means a loan made on the security of assets the market value of which is not at any time less than the amount of such loan. [Banking Regulation Act (10 of 1949), S. 5(n)]

Secured loan or advance. Means a loan or advance made on the security of assets the market value of which is not at any time less than the amount of such loan or advance. [Banking Regulation Act (10 of 1949), S. 5(n)]

Securing property. Where the instrument makes a property secure or safe, as far as the beneficiary is concerned, it is an instrument securing property. *Chief Inspector of Stamps* v. *U.P. Sugar Works,* AIR 1967 All 242, 244. [Court Fees Act (7 of 1870), S. 7 (iv-4) (U.P.)]

Securities. "SECURITIES" means any of the following instruments issued or to be issued, or created or to be created, by or for the benefit of a company, namely—

- (i) shares, stocks and bonds;
- (ii) debentures;
- (iii) mortgage deeds, instruments of pawn, pledge or hypothecation and other instrument, creating or evidencing a charge or lien on the assets of the company; and
- (iv) instruments acknowledging loan to or indebtedness of the company and guaranteed by a third party or entered into jointly with third party. [Capital Issues (Control) Act (29 of 1947), S. 2(l)].

"SECURITIES" includes stock. [Constitution of India, Art. 366(26)]

"SECURITIES" means any of the following instruments issued or to be issued, or created or to be created, by or for the benefit of a company, namely,—

"SECURITIES" includes shares, scrips, stocks, bonds, debentures, debenture stocks or other marketable securities of a like nature in or of any incorporated company or other body corporate and also Government securities. [Forward Contract (Regulations) Act (74 of 1952), S. 2(l)]

"SECURITIES" include, (i) shares, scrips, stocks, bonds, debentures, debenture stock or other marketable securities of a like nature in or of any incorporated company or other body corporate; (ia) derivatives; (ib) units or any other instrument issued by any collective investment scheme to the investors in such schemes; (ii) Government securities; (iii) such other instruments as may be declared by the Central Government to be securities; and (iv) rights or interest in securities. [Securities Contracts (Regulation) Act (42 of 1956), S. 2(h)] [Also see *Explanation* (a) to section 112(1) of the Income-tax Act, 1961 (43 of 1961) as substituted (w.e.f. 1-4-2013) by the Finance Act, 2012 and [S. 2(81) of the Companies Act, 2013 (18 of 2013)]

"SECURITIES" includes,—

- (i) shares, scrips, stocks, bonds, debentures, debenture stock, units of the Unit Trust of India or any other mutual fund or other marketable securities of a like nature in or of any incorporated company or other body corporate:
- (ii) Government securities; and
- (iii) rights or interests in securities. [Special Court (Trial of Offences Relating to Transactions in Securities) Act (27 of 1992), S. 2(c)]

Documents entitling the holder to specified realisable rights in land, money, stocks, shares, bonds, mortgages, *etc.*

"SECURITIES". For the purposes of Chapter XII-EA of Act 43 of 1961, 'securities' means debt securities issued by a Special Purpose Vehicle as referred to in the guidelines on securitisation of standard assets issued by the Reserve Bank of India. [(w.e.f. 1-6-2013) *Explanation* (*b*) to section 115TCA of the Income-tax Act, 1961 (43 of 1961)]

Securities and Exchange Board. Means the Securities and Exchange Board of India established under section 3 of the Securities and Exchange Board of India Act, 1992 (15 of 1992). [S. 2(82) of the Companies Act, 2013 (18 of 2013)]

Securities Appellate Tribunal. Means a Securities Appellate Tribunal established under section 15K(1) of the Securities and Exchange Board of India Act, 1992 (15 of 1992). [S. 2(1)(p) of the Pension Fund Regulatory & Development Authority Act, 2013 (23 of 2013)]

Securities transaction tax. In this chapter, unless the context otherwise requires, "SECURITIES TRANSACTION TAX" means tax leviable on the taxable securities transactions under the provisions of this Chapter. [Finance (No.2) Act (23 of 2004), Chapter VII, S. 97(11)]

Securitisation. Means acquisition of financial assets by any asset reconstruction company from any originator, whether by raising of funds by such asset reconstruction company from qualified buyers by issue of security receipts representing undivided interest in such financial assets or otherwise. [Securitisation and Reconstruction of Financial Assets and Enforcement of Security Interest Act (54 of 2002), S. 2(1)(*z*)]

"SECURITISATION" means acquisition of debt or receivables by any special purpose distinct entity from any originator or originators for the purpose of issuance of securitised debt instruments to investors based on such debt or receivables and such issuance. [Securities and Exchange Board of India (*Public Offer and Listing of Securitised Debt Instruments*) *Regulations 2008, regulation 2(1)(r)*].

"SECURITISATION". For the purposes of section 10(23DA) of Act 43 of 1961, 'securitisation' shall have the same meaning as assigned to it,—

- (i) in clause (r) of sub-regulation (1) of Regulation 2 of the Securities and Exchange Board of India (Public offer and Listing of Securitised Debt Instruments) Regulations, 2008, made under the Securities and Exchange Board of India Act, 1992 (15 of 1992) and the Securities Contracts (Regulation) Act, 1956 (42 of 1956) ; or
- (ia) in clause (z) of sub-section (1) of section 2 of the Securitisation and Reconstruction of

Financial Assets and Enforcement of Security Interest Act, 2002 (54 of 2002); or [Inserted by the Act No. 28 of 2016]

(*ii*) under the guidelines on securitisation of standard assets issued by the Reserve Bank of India. [(w.e.f. 1-4-2014) *Explanation* (*a*) to section 10(23DA) of the Income-tax Act, 1961 (43 of 1961)]

Securitisation trust. For the purposes of Chapter XII-EA of Act 43 of 1961, 'securitisation trust' means a trust, being a—

(*i*) 'special purpose distinct entity' as defined in regulation 2(1)(u) of the Securities and Exchange Board of India (Public Offer and Listing of Securitised Debt Instruments) Regulations, 2008, made under the Securities and Exchange Board of India Act, 1992 (15 of 1992), and the Securities Contracts (Regulation) Act, 1956 (42 of 1956), and regulated under the said regulations; or

(*ii*) 'special purpose vehicle' as defined in, and regulated by, the guidelines on securitisation of standard assets issued by the Reserve Bank of India, which fulfils such conditions, as may be prescribed. [(w.e.f. 1-6-2013) *Explanation* (*d*) to section 115TC of the Income-tax Act, 1961 (43 of 1961). Also see (w.e.f. 1-4-2014) *Explanation* (*b*) to section 10(23DA) of the Income-tax Act, 1961 (43 of 1961) and (w.e.f. 1-4-2014) *Explanation* to section 10(35A) of the Income-tax Act, 1961 (43 of 1961)]

Securitised debt instrument. Means any certificate or instrument, by whatever name called, of the nature referred to in sub-clause (ie) of clause (h) of section 2 of the Act issued by a special purpose distinct entity. [Securities and Exchange Board of India (Public Offer and Listing of Securitised Debt Instruments) Regulations 2008, regulation 2(1)(s)]

"SECURITISED DEBT INSTRUMENT". For the purposes of Chapter XII-EA of Act 43 of 1961, 'securitised debt instrument' shall have the same meaning as assigned to it in regulation 2(1)(s) of the Securities and Exchange Board of India (Public Offer and Listing of Securitised Debt Instruments) Regulations, 2008, made under the Securities and Exchange Board of India Act, 1992 (15 of 1992), and the Securities Contracts (Regulation) Act, 1956 (42 of 1956). [(w.e.f. 1-6-2013) *Explanation* (*c*) to section 115TCA of the Income-tax Act, 1961 (43 of 1961)]

Security. The state of being protected from unauthorized access or uncontrolled losses or effects. Absolute security is impossible to achieve in practice and the quality of a given security system is relative. Within a state-model security system, security is a specific "State" to be preserved under various operations. (*Information Technology*)

Security is defined as : 1. Collateral given or pledged to guarantee the fulfillment of an obligation, esp. the assurance that a creditor will be repaid (usually with interest) any money or credit extended to a debtor 2. A person who is bound by some type of guaranty; surety. 3. The state of being secure, esp. from danger or attack. 4. An instrument that evidences the holder's ownership rights in a firm (e.g. a stock), the holder's creditor relationship with a firm or government (e.g., a bond) or the holder's other rights (e.g. an option)" [Black's Law Dictionary as cited in *Nutan Thakur v. State of U.P.*, 2017(11)ADJ471, para 62]

"SECURITY" means the shares, stocks, bonds, debentures, debentures stock, Government securities as defined in Public Debt Act (18 of 1944) Savings Certificates to which the Government Savings Certificates Act (46 of 1959) applies, deposits receipts in respect of deposit of securities, and units or sub-units of Unit Trust and includes certificates of title to securities, but does not include bills of exchange or promissory notes other than Government promissory notes. [FERA (46 of 1973), S. 2(u)]

"SECURITY" means shares, stocks, bonds and debentures, Government securities as defined in the Public Debt Act, 1944, savings certificates to which the Government Savings Certificates Act, 1959 applies, deposit receipts in respect of deposits of securities and units of the Unit Trust of India established under sub-section (1) of Section 3 of the Unit Trust of India Act, 1963 or of any mutual fund and includes certificates of title to securities, but does not include bills of exchange or promissory notes other than Government promissory notes or any other instruments which may be notified by the Reserve Bank as security for the purposes of this Act. [Foreign Exchange Management Act (42 of 1999), S. 2(za)]

Property deposited or made over, or bonds, recognizances, or the like entered into, by or on behalf of a person in order to secure his fulfilment of an obligation and forfeitable in the event of non-fulfilment; a document held by a creditor as guarantee or his right to payment; hence, any form of investment guaranteed by such documents. [CrPC, 1973 (2 of 1974), S. 110]; the condition of being protected from or not exposed to danger, safety.

That which renders a matter sure; an instrument which renders certain the performance of a contract. A person who becomes the surety for another, or who engages himself for the performance of another's contract.

The word 'security' is a word of general import meaning nothing more than an assurance. Anything that makes the money more assured in its payment or more readily recoverable and may range from a mere personal bond or promissory note or guarantee, or even a mere pledge of something of no intrinsic value, to a mortgage of property from out of which the money can be realised. *Palai Central Bank* v. *Jacob P. Cherian,* AIR 1963 Ker 128, 134. [Transfer of Property Act (4 of 1882), S. 134]

COLLATERAL SECURITY is security given for the payment of a debt or the performance of some other act.

Security agency. Means any person engaged in the business of rendering services relating to the security of any property, whether movable or immovable, or of any person, in any manner and includes the services of investigation, detection or verification, of any fact or activity, whether of a personal nature or otherwise, including the services of providing security personnel. [Finance Act (32 of 1994), S. 65(1)(94) now repealed by Central Goods and Services Tax Act, 2017].

Security agreement. Means an agreement, instrument or any other document or arrangement under which security interest is created in favour of the secured creditor including the creation of mortgage by deposit of title deeds with the secured creditor. [Securitisation and Reconstruction of Financial Assets and Enforcement of Security Interest Act (54 of 2002), S. 2(1)(*zb*)]

Security audit. A search through a computer system for security problems and vulnerabilities. (*Cyber Law*)

Security bond. 'SECURITY BOND' in the sense it is used in Art. 57, is an instrument executed by way of security for the due execution of an office, or to account for money or other property received by virtue thereof, or executed by a surety to secure the due performance of a contract. [Indian Stamp Act (2 of 1899), Art. 57]

A bond executed to secure the performance of a personal obligation. [CPC (5 of 1908), 1st. Sch., App. G, form No. 2].

Security breach. A violation of controls of a particular information system such that information assets or system components are unduly exposed. (*Cyber Law*)

Security Certificate. A chunk of information (often stored as a text file) that is used by the *SSL* protocol to establish a secure connection. (*Matisse Enzer-Glossary of Internet Terms*)

A chunk of information (often stored as a text file) that is used by the SSL protocol to establish a secure connection.

Security Certificates contain information about who it belongs to, who it was issued by, a unique serial number of other unique identification, valid dates, and an encrypted ''fingerprint'' that can be used to verify the contents of the certificate. In order for an SSL connection to be created both sides must have a valid Security Certificate. (*Internet and E-Commerce*)

Security for costs. In certain cases, a Court may order the plaintiff to furnish security for the costs of the defendant; this is done, *eg*, if the plaintiff is resident outside the jurisdiction of the Court.

Security interest. Means right, title or interest of any kind, other than those specified in section 31, upon property created in favour of any secured creditor and includes—

(i) any mortgage, charge, hypothecation, assignment or any right, title or interest of any kind, on tangible asset, retained by the secured creditor as an owner of the property, given on hire or financial lease or conditional sale or under any other contract which secures the obligation to pay any unpaid portion of the purchase price of the asset or an obligation incurred or credit provided to enable the borrower to acquire the tangible asset; or

(ii) such right, title or interest in any intangible asset or assignment or licence of such intangible asset which secures the obligation to pay any unpaid portion of the purchase price of the intangible asset or the obligation incurred or any credit provided to enable the borrower to acquire the intangible asset or licence of intangible asset;

[Substituted by Act 44 of 2016 Securitisation and Reconstruction of Financial Assets and Enforcement of Security Interest Act (54 of 2002), S. 2(1)(*zf*)]

"SECURITY INTEREST" means mortgage, charge, hypothecation, assignment or any other right, title or interest of any kind whatsoever upon property, created in favour of any bank or financial institution and includes—

(*a*) such right, title or interest upon tangible asset, retained by the bank or financial institution as owner of the property, given on hire or financial lease or conditional sale which secures the obligation to pay any unpaid portion of the purchase price of the asset or an obligation incurred or any credit provided to enable the borrower to acquire the tangible asset; or

(*b*) such right, title or interest in any intangible asset or licence of any intangible asset, which secures the obligation to pay any unpaid portion of the purchase price of the intangible asset or the obligation incurred or any credit extended to enable the borrower to acquire the intangible asset or licence of intangible asset. [Recovery of Debts Due to Banks and Financial Institutions Act (51 of 1993), S. 2(lb)].

"SECURITY INTEREST" means right, title or interest of any kind, other than those specified in section 31, upon property created in favour of any secured creditor and includes—

(*i*) any mortgage, charge, hypothecation, assignment or any right, title or interest of any kind, on tangible asset, retained by the secured creditor as an owner of the property, given on hire or financial lease or conditional sale or under any other contract which secures the obligation to pay any unpaid portion of the purchase price of the asset or an obligation incurred or credit provided to enable the borrower to acquire the tangible asset; or

(*ii*) such right, title or interest in any intangible asset or assignment or licence of such intangible asset which secures the obligation to pay any unpaid portion of the purchase price of the intangible asset or the obligation incurred or any credit provided to enable the borrower to acquire the intangible asset or licence of intangible asset; [Securitisation and Reconstruction of Financial Assets and Enforcement of Security Interest Act (54 of 2002), S. 2(1)(zf)].

"SECURITY INTEREST" means right, title or interest or a claim to property, crated in favour of, or provided for a secured creditor by a transaction which secures payment of performance of an obligation and includes mortgage, charge, hypothecation, assignment and encumbrance or any other agreement or arrangement securing payment or performance of any person:

Provided that security interest shall not include a performance guarantee. [Insolvency and Bankruptcy Code (31 of 2016), S. 3(31)].

"SECURITY INTEREST" means right, title or interest or a claim to property, created in favour of, or provided for a secured creditor by a transaction which secures payment or performance of an obligation and includes mortgage, charge, hypothecation, assignment and encumbrance or any other person:

Provided that security interest shall not include a performance guarantee. [National Company Law Tribunal Rules, 2016, R. 2(27)].

Security of India. For the purpose of this section, the expression "SECURITY OF INDIA" includes any action necessary for the security of India which—

(i) relates to fissionable materials or the materials from which they are derived; or

(ii) relates to the traffic in arms, ammunition and implements of war and to such traffic in other goods and materials as is carried on directly or indirectly for the purpose of supplying a military establishment; or

(iii) is taken in time of war or other emergency in international relations. [Patents Act (39 of 1970), S. 157A, *Expln.*]

Security of the state. The words 'security of the state' do not and cannot mean merely danger to the security of the entire country, nor can it be restricted to an upheaval or a rebellion endangering the security of the entire country. *Indulal K. Yagrik* v. *State,* AIR 1960, Bom 399, 402. [Constitution of India, Art. 19(2)]

Security policy. A document which articulates requirements and good practices regarding the protections maintained by a trustworthy system. (*Information Technology*)

'Security policy' means documented business rules and processes for protecting information and the computer resource. [Information Technology (Procedure and Safeguard for Monitoring and Collecting Traffic Data or Information Rules, 2009, R. 2(o)]

Security procedure. This means the security procedure prescribed under Section 16 of the Information Technology Act, 2000.

Security receipt. Means a receipt or other security, issued by an asset reconstruction company to any qualified buyer pursuant to a scheme, evidencing the purchase or acquisition by the holder thereof, of an undivided right, title or interest in the financial asset involved in securitisation. [Securitisation and Reconstruction of Financial Assets and Enforcement of Security Interest Act (54 of 2002), S. 2(1)(*zg*)]

Security Services. Services provided by a set of security frameworks and performed by means of certain security mechanisms. Such services include, but are not limited to, access control, data confidentiality and data integrity. (*Information Technology*)

Security tokens. Also called digipasses; another means to authenticate users. (*Cyber Law*)

Security Zone. An area to which access is limited to authorised personnel and to authorised and properly escorted visitors. Security Zones should preferably be accessible from an Operations Zone, and through a specific entry point. A Security Zone need not be separated from an Operations Zone by a secure parameter. A Security Zone should be monitored 24 hours a day and 7 week by security staff, other personnel or electronic means. (*Information Technology*)

Sedition. An offence, tending towards treason, but wanting the overt act. The raising commotions or disturbances in the State; it is a revolt against legitimate authority.

An insurrectionary movement tending towards treason but wanting an overt act; attempts made by meetings or speeches or by publications to disturb the tranquility of the State. [IPC (45 of 1860), S. 124 A].

The word 'sedition' occurring in Section 124-A of the Code means a crime against society nearly allied to that of treason. It embraces all those practices, whether by word, deed or writing, which are calculated to disturb the tranquillity of the State, and lead ignorant persons to endeavour to subvert the Government and laws of the country. *Nazir Khan* v. *State of Delhi*, (2003) 8 SCC 461, para 37. [IPC (45 of 1860), S. 124-A]

Seditious. Pertaining to or exciting sedition.

Seditious libel. Libel which is made with the intent of inciting sedition.

Seduce, seduction. To "seduce" is to draw aside from the path of rectitude and duty in any manner; to entice to evil; to lead astray; to tempt and lead to iniquity; to corrupt; to deprave.

To induce to surrender chastity; act of a man enticing of woman to have unlawful intercourse with him by means of persuasion, solicitation, promises, bribes, or other means without employment of force [IPC (45 of 1860), S. 366]; to persuade (a vessel, servant, soldier *etc.*) to desert his allegiance or service; to lead (a person) astray in conduct or belief; to tempt, entice or beguile to do something wrong, foolish [IPC (45 of 1860), S. 131 and Army Act (46 of 1950), S. 37(e)].

On each occasion when a woman is persuaded to indulge in illicit intercourse, she is being tempted into sin and so "seduced" consequently, though a woman has lost her chastity and become a prostitute, she can be "seduced" again for the purpose of S. 366-A of the IPC (45 of 1860).

The action of seducing. [Limitation Act (36 of 1963), Sch., Art. 77].

There are three principal ingredients of the offence.

(a) that a minor girl below the age of 18 years is induced by the accused.

(b) that she is induced to go from any place or do any act, and.

(c) that she is so induced with intent that she may be or knowing that it is likely that she will be forced or seduced to illicit intercourse with another person. [IPC (45 of 1860), S. 366]

Seduction is the act of a man in enticing a woman to have unlawful intercourse with him by means of persuasion, promises, bribes, or other means without the employment of force.

Seed. "SEED" means any of the following classes of seeds used for sowing or planting—

(i) seeds of food crops including edible oil-seeds and seeds of fruits and vegetables;

(ii) cotton seeds;

(iii) seeds of cattle fodder;

(iv) jute seeds

and includes seedings, and tubers and bulbs, rhizomes, roots, cuttings, all types of grafts and other vegetatively propagated material, of food crops or cattle fodder. [Seeds Act (54 of 1966), S. 2(11)]

"SEED" means a type of living embryo or propagule capable of regeneration and giving rise to a plant which is true to such type. [Protection of Plant Varieties and Farmers' Rights Act (53 of 2001), S. 2(x)]

"To kill *seeds,*" means, to destroy, by artificial means, the vitality or germinating power of such seeds.

Seed money. Start-up money for a business venture.

Seen. The word "seen" in Indian Evidence Act (1 of 1872), S. 63(5), means something more than the mere sight of the document. The clause clearly contemplates the evidence of a person who, having seen and examined the document, is in a position to give direct evidence of the contents thereof.

An oral account of the contents of a document given by an illiterate person who has merely seen it with his eyes is not secondary evidence within the meaning of S. 63(5) of Indian Evidence Act (1 of 1872). The word 'seen' means something more than the mere sight of the document.

Segregate. To separate from others.

Segregation. "SEGREGATION" means to separate the municipal solid wastes into the groups of organic, inorganic, recyclables and hazardous wastes. [Municipal Solid Wastes (Management and Handling) Rules, 2000, R. 3(xxi).

"SEGREGATION" means sorting and separate storage of various components of solid waste namely biodegradable wastes including agriculture and dairy waste, non biodegradable wastes including recyclable waste, non-recyclable combustible waste, sanitary waste and non recyclable inert waste, domestic hazardous wastes, and construction and demolition wastes;

The separation or isolation of individuals or groups from a large group of society. [Lepers Act (3 of 1898), Preamble]; [Epidemic Diseases Act (3 of 1897), S. 2(2)(b)].

Seisin. Actual possession. Formal legal ownership as opposed to mere possession or beneficial interest.

'Seize' and 'impound'. The words 'seize' and 'impound' convey different meaning 'seizure' is done at a particular moment of time and after seizing of a property or document is retained for some period of time, then such retention amounts to impounding of the property or document. [*Suresh Nanda* v. *C.B.I.*, AIR 2008 SC 1414, 1417, para 12]

Seize : seized. To take possession forcibly or in pursuance of a warrant, order of Court or other legal process. [Indian Contract Act (9 of 1872), S. 223, ill. (a)].

The word 'seize' was used in S. 102 in consonance with the dictionary meaning of the word, *i.e.* taking in actual physical custody. *Textiles Traders Syndicate Ltd.* v. *State of U.P.*, AIR 1960 All 405, 407. [CrPC, 1973 (2 of 1974), S. 102]

In the context in which it is used in the Act in S. 178-A, the word 'seized' means 'take possession of contrary to the wishes of the owner of the property.' *Gian Chand* v. *State of Punjab*, AIR 1962 SC 496, 499. [Sea Customs Act, 1878, S. 178-A]

Seizure. The legal definition of the word "seizure" is the taking possession of property by an officer under legal process.

The action of seizing. [CrPC, 1973 (2 of 1974), S. 83(3)(a)].

Seizure notes. Notes made out by a customs officer on discovering and taking possession of goods fraudulently obtained or bearing fraudulent trade marks.

Select. Chosen for excellence; picked out as best and most suitable.

To choose or pick out in preference to another or others. [Indian Trusts Act (2 of 1882), S. 74].

To select an item is to identify to the computer one or more files or folders that you wish to do something with. This is usually done by pointing to an item with the screen pointer, and then quickly pressing and releasing the left mouse button once. (*Cyber Law*)

Select committee. A parliamentary committee, composed of certain members appointed by the House to consider or inquire into any matters, and to report their opinion for the information of the House.

Select Committee on Bill(s). [A Parliamentary Committee composed of member specially named and appointed from time to time to consider, inquire into or deal with Bills.] (*Constitutional and Parliamentary Term*)

Select list. In relation to the grades of Principal Director, Director, Joint Director, Deputy Director, Section Officer or Assistant Section Officer means the Select List prepared every year for promotion to the respective grades to fill the existing and anticipated vacancies likely to occur during the year and are decided to be filled by promotion. [Armed Forces Headquarters Civil Service Rules, 2018, R. 2(o)].

Selection and Reservation. The expressions 'reservation' and 'selection' involve the same process and to some extent they are convertible for one can reserve land by selection and another can select land by reservation. *Gurbax Singh* v. *State of Punjab*, AIR 1967 SC 502, 506.

Self-control. Control of one's self, one's desires *etc.* [Indian Evidence Act (1 of 1872), S. 105, ill. (b)]; [IPC (45 of 1860), S. 300, *Excep*. 1].

Self-defence. The protection of one's person or property against some injury attempted by another; the right of such protection. [IPC (45 of 1860), S. 79, ill.].

Right to defend, even to the extent of homicide, one's person, the members of one's family and property against attacks.

Self-governing dominion. Means the Dominion of Canada, the Commonwealth of Australia, the Dominion of New Zealand, the Union of South Africa, and Newfoundland. [Copyright Act (14 of 1957), S. 35]

Self-incrimination. Acts or declarations by which a person explicitly or implicitly admits his connection with a crime.

Self-Signed Public Key. A data structure that is constructed the same as a Digital Signature Certificate but that is signed by its subject. Unlike a Digital Signature Certificate, a self-signed public key cannot be used in a trustworthy manner to authenticate a public key to other parties. (*Information Technology*)

Sell. To dispose of by sale. [T.P. Act (4 of 1882), S. 37, ill. (a); Sale of Goods Act (3 of 1930), S. 47(1)(b)].

When more than one person is involved in the sale, only a person possessing the animus to sell is liable for the sale and as such an employee is not seller. R. *Venkatakrishnan* v. *Food Inspector (HQS) F&D Administrary, Pondicherry,* AIR 1989 Mad 35. [Prevention of Food Adulteration Act (37 of 1954), Ss. 7, 17]

Seller. "SELLER" means a person who sells or agrees to sell goods. [Sale of Goods Act (3 of 1930), S. 2(13)]

"SELLER" means the Central Government, a State Government or any local authority or corporation or authority established by or under a Central, State or Provincial Act, or any company or firm or cooperative society and also includes an individual or a Hindu undivided family whose total sales, gross receipts or turnover from the business or profession carried on by him exceed the monetary limits specified under clause (*a*) or clause (*b*) of Section 44AB during the financial year immediately preceding the financial year in which the goods of the nature specified in the Table in sub-section (*1*) are sold. [Income tax Act (43 of 1961), S. 206C, *Expln.* (*c*)]

One who disposes of a thing in consideration of money; a vendor. This term is more usually applied in the sale of chattels and the term *vendor* in the sale of lands and estates.

One who sells. [Sale of Goods Act (3 of 1930), S. 31].

"SELLER" is the term used in the law of sales to designate the person selling goods which are the subject of the sale.

Manufacturer, manufacturing not for his consumption but for sale, is seller. *Tillo Ram* v. *State of Delhi,* AIR 1967 Del 71, 72. [Prevention of Food Adulteration Act (37 of 1954), S. 7]

Seller of goods. 'SELLER OF GOODS' includes a seller of goods acting as an agent. [Emergency Risks (Goods) Insurance Act (62 of 1962), S. 2(d)]

Seller's lien. Charge in favour of the seller upon the property sold for the amount of the purchase money or any part thereof remaining unpaid and for interest thereon from the date of delivery of possession, where the ownership of the property has passed to the buyer before payment of the whole of the purchase money. [Heading, Sale of Goods Act (3 of 1930), S. 47].

Seller's option. "Seller's option" means that the seller should first intimate to the buyer of the availability of goods and the readiness to deliver, and until the seller exercises that option the buyer cannot do anything and therefore, the important factor is the communication of the date of the seller when the goods will be delivered, in which case alone the buyer can apply for delivery. *Sundaram Iyer & Co.* v. *M. Mudaliar,* AIR 1957 Mad 228, 231.

Seller's risk. Chances of hazards of commercial loss which a seller has to ordinarily undertake. [Sale of Goods Act (3 of 1930), S. 26].

Semen. "SEMEN" wherever it occurs in this Act, means the semen or ovum of male and female human being, as the case may be. [Delhi Artificial Insemination (Human) Act, 1995 (12 of 1996), S. 2(h)]

Semen Bank. "SEMEN BANK" means any premises used or intended to be used for storage, sale, donation or supply of semen. [Delhi Artificial Insemination (Human) Act, 1995 (12 of 1996), S. 2(i)]

Semi-skilled. The word 'semi-skilled' seems to describe a person who falls between the two categories, *i.e.*, (*i*) skilled and (*ii*) unskilled as he is not fully skilled and also is not completely unskilled but has some amount of skill for the work for which he is employed. The word 'unskilled' cannot, therefore, be understood dissociated from the words 'skilled' and 'semi-skilled' to read and construe it to include in it all categories of employees irrespective of the nature of employment. *Ahmedabad Pvt. Primary Teachers' Association* v. *Administrative Officer*, AIR 2004 SC 1426 : 2004 AIR SCW 356.

Semi-trailer. Means a vehicle not mechanically propelled (other than a trailer), which is intended to be connected to a motor vehicle and which is so constructed that a portion of it is super-imposed on, and a part of whose weight is borne by, that motor vehicle. [Motor Vehicles Act (59 of 1988), S. 2(39)]

Semiconductor integrated circuit. Means a product having transistors and other circuitry elements which are inseparably formed on a semiconductor material or an insulating material or inside the semiconductor material and designed to perform an electronic circuitry function. [Semiconductor Integrated Circuit Layout-Design Act (37 of 2000), S. 2(r)]

Semiconductor topography. Etching on a computer chip otherwise known as a mask work or right.

Semper in dubiis benigniora praeferenda sunt. In doubtful cases, the more favourable constructions are always to be preferred.

Semper in dubiis id agendum est, ut quam tutissimo loco res sit bona fide contracta, nisi quum aperte contra leges scriptum est. In doubtful cases, such a course should be taken that a contract made *bona fide* should be in the safest condition (most carefully upheld), unless when it has been openly made against law.

Semper in obscuris quod minimum est sequimur. In things obscure we always follow the least obscure.

Semper necessitas probandi incumbit ei qui agit. The suitor is always bound to prove. The burden of proof is on the claimant.

Semper praesumitur pro legitimatione puerorum. The presumption always is in favour of the legitimacy of children.

Semper praesumitur pro matrimonio. The presumption is always in favour of the validity of a marriage.

Semper praesumitur pro-negante. The pre-sumption is always in favour of the one denying.

Semper praesumitur pro sententia. The presumption always is in favour of a sentence.

Semper sexus masculinus etiam faemininum continet. The male sex always includes the female.

Semper specialia generalibus insunt. Species are always included in generals.

Send. The expression "send", used in the O. V, R. 25, CPC (5 of 1908), means that the service shall be deemed to be effected by properly addressing, pre-paying and posting by registered post, a letter containing the document, and, unless the contrary is proved, to have been effected at the time at which the letter would be delivered.

Sending state. "SENDING STATE" means the state which sends:

(a) a mission to the organization at its seat or to an office of the organization, or

(b) a delegation to an organ or delegation to a conference, or

(c) an observer delegation to an organ or an observer delegation to a conference. [Vienna Convention on the Representation of States in their Relations with International Organisations of a Universal Character, 1975, (14 May, 1975), Art. I. 1(16)]

Senior advocate. Means any advocate so designated under sub-section (2) of Section 16 of the Advocates Act, 1961 (25 of 1961), and all such advocates whose names were borne on the roll of the senior advocates of the Court immediately before the commencement of Chapter III of the Advocates Act, 1961. [Supreme Court Rules, 1966, R. 2(1)(q)]

Senior Basic School. 'Senior Basic School' or 'Junior High School' means either a school preparing students for the Junior High School Examination of the Department or a school teaching Classes I to VIII or VI to VIII (middle section). [Educational Code of Uttar Pradesh (Revised 1958 Edn.) Para 1(xxvi)(c) as cited in *State of U.P. v. Pawan Kumar Divedi*, (2014) 9 SCC 692, para 22].

Senior citizen. For the purposes of section, "Senior Citizen" means an individual resident in India who is of the age of sixty years or more at any time during the relevant previous year. [Income-tax Act (43 of 1961), S. 80D (5), Explanation (i) as inserted by Finance Act (20 of 2015), S. 19]

Senior citizen. Means an individual resident in India who is of the age of sixty years or more at any time during the relevant previous year. [Income-tax Act (43 of 1961), S. 80 DDB *Expln.* (iv)]

"SENIOR CITIZEN" means any person being a citizen of India, who has attained the age of sixty years or above. [Maintenance and Welfare of Parents and Senior Citizens Act 2007, S. 2(h). Also see S. 2(19) of the National Food Security Act, 2013 (20 of 2013)]

Senior management. The expression 'senior management' means personnel of the company who are members of its core management team excluding Board of Directors comprising all members of management one level below the executive directors, including the functional heads. [*Explanation* to section 178 of the Companies Act, 2013 (18 of 2013)]

Seniority. One of the attributes of regular service is what is called the seniority. Seniority means a longer life than of another thing or person taken for comparison. In the case of Government service, it means the length of service. *N. Chandramauli* v. *State of Mysore,* AIR 1971 Mys 53, 54, 57. [State Reorganisation Act (37 of 1956), S. 115]

Sensation. An operation of any of the senses; a physical feeling. [Indian Evidence Act (1 of 1872), S. 3, ill. (d)].

Sense of feeling. Faculty of perception or sensation [IPC (45 of 1860), S. 350, ill. (g)].

Sensitive personal data or information. "Sensitive personal data or information" means such personal information as may be prescribed by the Central Government in consultation with such professional bodies or associations as it may deem fit. [Information Technology Act (21 of 2000), S. 43A, *Expln.* (iii) as inserted by amending Act (10 of 2009), S. 22]

Sensor-to-shooter. A descriptive phrase employed to connote the cumulative feedforward of data and information through an operational military system, from initial acquisition of novel data elements (via the sensors) through to the element(s) effecting instrumental response as needed (the shooter). A loose descriptor for the scope of processing for intrasystemic functions to obtain advantage in a theater of operations. (*Cyber Law*)

Sensus ex causa dicendi accipiendus est ; et sermones semper accipiendi sunt secundum subjectam materiam. The sense of words is to be taken from the occasion of speaking them, and discourses are always to be interpreted according to the subject-matter.

Sensus verborum est anima legis. The true meaning of the words is the soul of the law.

Sentence. This term is now applied to the judgment of a Court of criminal jurisdiction imposing on a person convicted a punishment, such as fine or imprisonment.

The judicial determination of the punishment to be inflicted on a convicted criminal. [IPC (45 of 1860), Ss. 55 and 60 and Constitution of India, Art. 136(1)].

A sentence is the judgment of a Court. It is the final determination of a criminal Court; the pronouncement by the judge of the penalty or punishment as the consequence to the defendant of the fact of his guilt.

"SENTENCE", as the term is used in criminal law, is the appropriate word to denote the action of the Court before which the trial is had, declaring the consequences to the convict of the fact thus ascertained.

SENTENCE; JUDGMENT. A judgment, or judicial declaration made by a judge in a cause.

The term *judgment* is more usually applied to civil, and *sentence* to criminal, proceedings.

A sentence is a judgment on conviction for crime; and any proceeding that may end in a sentence is substantially criminal in its nature.

Sententia facit jus, et res judicata pro veritate accipitur. The judgment creates the right, and what is adjudicated is taken for truth.

SEO. (*abbr.*) Search Engine Optimization. The practice of designing web pages so that they rank as high as possible in search results from *search engines.*

There is "good" SEO and "bad" SEO. Good SEO involves making the web page clearly describing its subject, making sure it contains truly useful information, including accurate information in *Meta tags*, and arranging for other web sites to make links to the page. Bad SEO involves attempting to deceive people into believing the page is more relevant than it truly is by doing things like adding inaccurate Meta tags to the page. (*Matisse Enzer-Glossary of Internet Terms*)

Separate. Distinct; divided; separate from another (as) separate estate.

Parted, divided or withdrawn from others; considered or reckoned by itself, single; individual. [T.P. Act (4 of 1882), S. 45].

Separate and independent proceeding. An application for injunction pending a suit or an application for stay of the order of the trial Court pending an appeal would certainly be a separate and independent proceeding in the sense that it is not a part of the proceeding leading to the termination of the suit or the appeal. *Ajaibul Hasan* v. *Chiranji Lal,* AIR 1951 All 564, 565. [CPC (5 of 1908), S. 115]

Separation. A cessation of cohabitation of husband and wife by mutual agreement.

The action of separating. [O. XXVI, R. 13, CPC (5 of 1908)].

A "separation" between husband and wife implies the consent of both parties to be affected thereby, and is not synonymous with "desertion", the very idea of which is to leave without consent of the other and in violation of duty. The word "separate" means "to part from each other".

Separation deed. A separation deed is one by which, either directly or through the medium of some third person, acting as a trustee, provision is made by a husband for the support of his separated wife.

Separation of powers. A theory that the three organs of a Government—legislature, executive and judiciary—should function without encroaching upon one another's field.

Septic tank. Means a water-tight settling tank or chamber, normally located underground, which is used to receive and hold human excreta, allowing it to decompose through bacterial activity. [S. 2(1)(p) of the Prohibition of Employment as Manual Scavengers & Their Rehabilitation Act, 2013 (25 of 2013)]

Sepulture. A burial place. S. 297, IPC (45 of 1860)].

Serial. The organization of a unit so that only one part of an element is available at a time. Used to describe the way in which data are transferred or processed, such as only one bit of a byte being available at a time. To handle or process in sequence rather than simultaneously. (*Computer*)

Serial access. The ability to reach information in storage only sequentially. Tape units are serial-access storage units in that the tape must be moved past the read/write head until the desired location is reached. (*Computer*)

Serial line Internet protocol (SLIP). One of the TCP/IP services that provides a reasonably fast, low overhead service that is typically used to connect to UNIX hosts and Internet service providers. (*Cyber Law*)

Series. A succession, sequence, or continued course. [Indian Evidence Act (1 of 1872), S. 39]; [CrPC, 1973 (2 of 1974), S. 220(1)]; [Companies Act (1 of 1956), S. 128].

Series of letters. A set of letters, having certain features in common. [Indian Evidence Act (1 of 1872), S. 39].

Serious adverse event. Means an untoward medical occurrence that leads to,—

(*i*) a death; or

(*ii*) a serious deterioration in the health of the subject that either—

(a) resulted in a life-threatening illness or injury; or

(b) resulted in a permanent impairment of a body structure or a body function; or

(c) required in-patient hospitalisation or prolongation of existing hospitalization; or

(d) resulted in medical or surgical intervention to prevent life threatening illness or injury or permanent impairment to a body structure or a body function; or

(*iii*) foetal distress, foetal death or a congenital abnormality or birth defect. [Medical Devices Rules, 2017, R. 3(zq)].

"SERIOUS ADVERSE EVENT" means an untoward medical occurrence during clinical trial resulting in death or permanent disability, or hospitalization of the trial subject where the trial subject is an outdoor patient or healthy person, prolongation of hospitalization where the trial subject is an indoor-patient, persistent or significant disability or incapacity, congenital anomaly, birth defect or life threatening event. [New Drugs and Clinical Trials Rules, 2019, R. 2(1)(ff)].

Serious bodily injury. Means any injury which involves, or in all probability will involve, the permanent loss of any part or section of a body or the use of any part or section of a body, or the permanent loss of or injury to the sight or hearing or any permanent physical incapacity or the fracture of any bone or one or more joints or bones of any phalanges of hand or foot [Mines Act (35 of 1952), S. 2(1)(q)]

Serious Fraud Investigation Office. Means the office referred to in section 211 of the Companies Act, 2013 (18 of 2013). [S. 2(83) of the Companies Act, 2013 (18 of 2013)]

Serious injury. "SERIOUS INJURY" means an injury causing significant overall impairment in the position of a domestic industry. [Customs Tariff Act (51 of 1975), S. 8B]

Servant. A personal or domestic attendant [CPC (5 of 1908), 1st Sch., App. A, form No. 25]; one who is under the obligation to render certain services to, and to obey the orders of a person or a body of persons especially in return for wages or salary. [IPC (45 of 1860), S. 14].

Serve. To perform service. As applied to a summons of Court to deliver it with judicial effect; in such manner as to charge the person with the receipt of it.

To attend upon (as a servant does); to wait upon, minister to the comport of; to make legal delivery of a process. [Plantations Labour Act (69 of 1951), S. 11(2)(c)]; to suffice for; to satisfy; to undergo (a sentence).

Serve and service. To serve means "to perform function, do what is required for". An officer in the service of the Government, by virtue of his service, is appointed by the Government as Commissioner and he performs public duties. He is in the service of the Government. *Coal Mines Provident Fund Commissioner* v. *Ramesh Chander Jha*, AIR 1990 SC 648, 649.

Server. A computer system on a network which provides services to Client applications. For example : a Gopher application requires both Client and Server applications which communicate with each other. (*Cyber Law*)

A computer that provides shared resources to network users. (*Information Technology*)

A computer, or a software package, that provides a specific kind of service to *client* software running on other computers. The term can refer to a particular piece of software, such as a *WWW* server, or to the machine on which the software is running, *e.g.* "Our mail server is down today, that's why e-mail isn't getting out". A single server machine can (and often does) have several different server software packages running on it, thus providing many different servers to *clients* on the *network.* Sometimes server software is designed so that additional capabilities can be added to the main program by adding small programs known as *servlets.* (*Matisse Enzer-Glossary of Internet Terms*)

Server-based LAN. A LAN with a central computer that provides application, file, security and communications services. (*Cyber Law*)

Server side includes (SSI). Allows the server to understand and respond to special page commands. As an example, if you had a footer you wanted on all your pages that may change from time to time, you can create a text file with the desired footer and place it in your document. On each page you put a simple include to read the file and place it at the bottom of the desired pages. Then changing the footer on all your pages would be just as simple as changing the one text file. (*Cyber Law*)

Service. "SERVICE" means service of any description which is made available to potential users and includes, but not limited to, the provision of facilities in connection with banking, financing, insurance, transport, processing, supply of electrical or other energy, board or lodging or both, housing construction, entertainment, amusement or the purveying of news or other information, but does not include rendering of any service free of charge or under a contract of personal service. [Consumer Protection Act (68 of 1986), S.2(1)(o)]

"Services" means anything other than goods, money and securities but includes activities relating to the use of money or its conversion by cash or by any other mode, from one form, currency or denomination, to another form, currency or denomination for which a separate consideration is charged [The Central Goods and Services Tax Act, 2017 (12 of 2017), S. 2(102)]

"SERVICE" means service which is made available to potential users and includes the provision of facilities in connection with banking, financing, insurance, chit fund, real estate, transport, processing, supply of electrical or other energy, board or lodging, or both, entertainment, amusement or the purveying of news or other information, but does not include the rendering of any service free of charge or under a contract of personal service;

Explanation.—For the removal of doubts, it is hereby declared that any dealings in real estate shall be included and shall be deemed always to have been included within the meaning of "service". [Monopolies and Restrictive Trade Practices Act (54 of 1969), S. 2(r)]

For the purposes of this clause—"SERVICE" means service of any description which is made available to potential users and includes the provision of services in connection with business of any industrial or commercial nature such as accounting, banking, communication, conveying of news or information, advertising, entertainment, amusement, education, financing, insurance, chit funds, real estate, construction, transport, storage, processing, supply of electrical or other energy, boarding and lodging. [Income-tax Act (43 of 1961), S. 28(va), *Expln.* (*ii*)]

"Service" means any activity carried out by a person for another for consideration, and includes a declared service, but shall not include—

(a) an activity which constitutes merely—

(i) a transfer of title in goods or immovable property, by way of sale, gift or in any other manner; or

(ia) such transfer, delivery or supply of any goods which is deemed to be sale within the meaning of clause (29A) of Article 366 of the Constitution; or

(ii) a transaction in money or actionable claim;

(b) a provision of service by an employee to the employer in the course of or in relation to his employment;

(c) fees taken in any Court or tribunal established under any law for the time being in force.

Explanation 1.—For the removal of doubts, it is hereby declared that nothing contained in this clause shall apply to,—

(A) the functions performed by the Members of Parliament, Members of State Legislature, Members of Panchayats, Members of Municipalities and Members of other local authorities who receive any consideration in performing the functions of that office as such member; or

(B) the duties performed by any person who holds any post in pursuance of the provisions of the Constitution in that capacity; or

(C) the duties performed any person as a Chairperson or a Member or a Director in a body established by the Central Government or State Governments or local authority and who is not deemed as an employee before the commencement of this section.

Explanation IA:—For the purposes of this clause, transaction in money shall not include any activity relating to the use of money or its conversion by cash or by any other mode, from one form, currency or denomination to another form, currency or denomination for which a separate consideration is charged.

Explanation 2.—For the purposes of this clause, the expression "transaction in money or actionable claim" shall not include

(i) Any activity relating to the use of money or its conversion by cash or by any other mode, from one form, currency or denomination to another form, currency or denomination for which a separate consideration is charged;

(ii) Any activity carried out, for a consideration, in relation to, or for facilitation of, a transaction in money or actionable claim, including the activity carried out—

(a) By a lottery distributor or selling agent on behalf of the State Government, about promotion, marketing, organizing, selling of lottery or facilitating in the organizing lottery of any kind, in any other manner, by the provisions of the Lotteries (Regulation) Act, 1998 (17 of 1998);

(b) By a foreman of chit fund for conducting or organizing a chit in any manner.].

Explanation 3.—For the purposes of this chapter—

(a) an unincorporated association or a body of persons, as the case may be, and a member thereof shall be treated as distinct persons;

(b) an establishment of a person in the taxable territory and any of his other establishment in a non-taxable territory shall be treated as establishment of distinct persons.

Explanation 4.—A person carrying on business through a branch or agency or representational office in any territory shall be treated as having an establishment in that territory. [Finance Act (32 of 1994), S. 65B(44) now repealed by Central Goods and Services Tax Act, 2017].

"SERVICE" means period of employment of a seaman under the agreement with the crew and includes any period in respect of which wages are paid or are payable to him. [Seamen's Provident Act (4 of 1966), S. 2(m)]

"SERVICE" means service within or outside India. [Administrative Tribunals Act (13 of 1985), S. 3(p)]

"SERVICE" means any service connected with recording of allotment of securities or transfer of ownership of securities in the record of a depository. [Depositories Act (22 of 1996), S. 2(1)(m)]

"SERVICE" means service of any description which is made available to potential users and includes the provision of facilities in connection with banking, financing, insurance, medical assistance, legal assistance, chit fund, real estate, transport, processing, supply of electrical or other energy, boarding or lodging or both, entertainment, amusement or the purveying of news or other information, but does not include the rendering of any service free of charge or under a contract of personal service. [Foreign Exchange Management Act (42 of 1999), S. 2(zb)]

"SERVICE" means service of any description which is made available to potential users and includes the provision of services in connection with business of any industrial or commercial matters such as banking, communication, education, financing, insurance, chit funds, real estate, transport, storage, material treatment, processing, supply of electrical or other energy, boarding, lodging, entertainment, amusement, construction, repair, conveying of news or information and advertising. [Trademarks Act (47 of 1999), S. 2(1)(z) and Competition Act, 2002 (12 of 2003), S. 2(u)]

The action of serving, helping or benefiting; conduct tending to the welfare or advantage of another; a branch of public employment [IPC 1973 (45 of 1860), S. 21, twelfth and Constitution of India, Art. 19(6)(ii)]; the action or an act of serving (a writ, notice *etc.*) upon a person [CrPC, 1973 (2 of 1974), S. 63]; a regularly scheduled transport trip over a public transportation route [Motor Vehicles Act (59 of 1988), S. 48(3)(iii)]; a good turn, benefit to another.

Applied to the commencement of a suit, that notice given to the defendant, which makes him a party to the proceeding, and makes it incumbent upon him to appear and answer to the cause, or run the risk of having a valid judgment rendered against him in consequence of his default; serving the defendant with a copy of the process, the particular act of the officer by which the copy of the citation was communicated; the judicial delivery or communication of papers; execution of process; the delivery or communication of a pleading, notice, or other paper in a suit, to the opposite party, so as to charge him with the receipt of it, and subject him to its legal effect.

Repair charges during warranty period do not come within the meaning of 'service' during warranty period. *C.C.E.* v. *Eicher Tractors Ltd.*, (2004) 9 SCC 22. [Central Excise and Salt Act (1 of 1944), S. 4]

Service only means "judicial service" as defined by Art. 236 (b). *Behariji Dass* v. *Chandra Mohan,* AIR 1969 All 594 at 597. [Constitution of India, Art. 233 (2)]

The word "service" implies formal communication of the order after it has been passed on termination of the proceedings, so that the party to whom it is communicated, may, if aggrieved, seek redress in a higher forum in the manner prescribed by law. *Commissioner of Sales Tax, U.P.* v. *Mangal Sen Sharam Lal, Bhagwan Lebsing*, AIR 1975 SC 1106, 1110.

"SERVICE". The provision of facilities in connection with supply of electrical energy is a 'service'. *Karnataka Power Transmission Corpn. Ltd.* v. *Ashok Iron Works Pvt. Ltd.*, AIR 2009 SC 1905.

Service an office. To discharge the duties of an office.

Service by post. A document is served "by post", "by properly addressing, prepaying and posting, a letter containing the document, and (unless the contrary is proved) to have been effected at the time at which the letter would be delivered in the ordinary course of post."

Service centre. In these regulations, unless the context otherwise requires—

"SERVICE CENTRE" means the place specified by the Commissioner of Customs where data entry, for the purpose of lodgement of declaration or submission of any information, is carried out. [Bill of Entry (Electronic Declaration) Regulation 1995, Regn. 2(f)]

Service family pension fund. A pension fund created for the benefit of the families of persons who are in service. [CPC (5 of 1908), S. 60(1), *Prov.* (g)].

Service for pension. Includes—

(i) actual service;

(ii) time spent by a Judge of a High Court in attending the sittings of the Supreme Court as an *ad hoc* Judge under Art. 127 of the Constitution, if he is subsequently appointed as a Judge;

(iii) the amount, actually taken, of each period of leave on full allowances at a rate equal to the monthly rate of the salary .[Supreme Court Judges (Salaries and Conditions of Service) Act (41 of 1958), S. 2(h)]

"SERVICE FOR PENSION" includes—

(i) actual service;

(ii) the amount actually taken of each period of a leave on full allowances at a rate equal to the monthly rate of salary;

(iii) joining time on return from leave out of India. [High Court Judges (Conditions of Service) Act (28 of 1954), S. 2(1)(h)]

Service line. "SERVICE LINE" means any electric supply-line through which electricity is, or is intended to be, supplied—

(a) to a single consumer either from a distributing main or immediately from the Distribution Licensee's premises; or

(b) from a distributing main to a group of consumers on the same premises or on contiguous premises supplied from the same point of the distributing main. [Electricity Act (36 of 2003), S. 2(61)]

The transformer is not a part and parcel of the 'service line'. *U.P.S.E. Board* v. *Lakshmi Devi,* AIR 1977 All 499, 502. [Indian Electricity Act (9 of 1910), S. 2(l)] Now repealed by Act 36 of 2003.

Service matters. "SERVICE MATTERS" in relation to a person, means all matters relating to the conditions of his service in connection with the affairs of the Union or of any State or of any local or other authority within the territory of India or under the control of the Government of India, or, as the case may be, of any corporation owned or controlled by the Government, as respects—

(i) remuneration (including allowances), pension and other retirement benefits;

(ii) tenure including confirmation, seniority, promotion, reversion, premature retirement and superannuation;

(iii) leave of any kind;

(iv) disciplinary matters; or

(v) any other matter whatsoever. [Administrative Tribunals Act (13 of 1985), S. 3(q)]

Service of legal process. Under the law of Parliament, service of legal process on its Members within the precincts of the House when it sits constitutes a breach of privilege of the House.

Service of notice. When the Legislature used the word 'notice', it must be presumed to have borne in mind that it means not only a formal intimation but also an informal one. Similarly, it must be deemed to have in mind the fact that service of a notice would include constructive or informal notice. *Nilkantha Sidramappa Ningashetti* v. *Kashinath Somanna Ningashetty*, AIR 1962 SC 666, 669.

Service of process. The delivery of notice of any cause or suit being instituted or of any steps being taken therein to the party affected thereby or having an interest in the subject matter of the suit.

Service of summons. A letter containing the summons sent by registered post and returned with the endorsement "refused" is *prima facie* good evidence that the defendant had an opportunity of accepting it and amounts to due and proper service.

"Service passage" or "lane" or "bye-lane". Means a passage or strip of land constructed, set apart or utilised for the purpose of serving as or carrying a drain or electricity cable (undergrond or overhead) and any electrical and other allied installations or any other civil services by municipal employees or other person employed in the service thereof. [New Delhi Municipal Council Act (44 of 1994), S. 2(48)]

Service Plan. The rate plan you select when choosing a wireless phone service. A service plan typically consists of a monthly base rate for access to the system and a fixed amount of minutes per month. (*Telecommunication*)

Service provider. Means the Government as a service provider and includes a licensee. [Telecom Regulatory Authority of India Act (24 of 1997), S. 2(j)]

"SERVICE PROVIDER" means an entity registered under section 10(1) of Act 43 of 2005. [S. 2(r) of the Protection of Women from Domestic Violence Act, 2005 (43 of 2005)]

Services. 'SERVICES' includes—

(i) providing personnel (including skilled or unskilled workmen and persons for rendering technical or other services) for the purpose of any work or project (by whatever name called) or any activity;

(ii) transferring of technology, including transferring, or securing the transfer of rights, knowhow, expertises or other skill with respect to any patent, invention, model, design, secret formula or process or similar property;

(iii) furnishing any information, blueprints, plans or advice with respect to any matter, and

(iv) making available any other resources. [Export-Import Bank of India Act (28 of 1981), S. 2(j)]

"SERVICES" means such tradable services which,—

(i) are covered under the General Agreement on Trade in Services annexed as IB to the Agreement establishing the World Trade Organisation concluded at Marrakesh on the 15th day of April, 1994;

(ii) may be prescribed by the Central Government for the purposes of this Act; and

(iii) earn foreign exchange. [Special Economic Zones Act (28 of 2005), S. 2(z)]

Servient estate or tenement. The term "servient estate", in the law of easements, is used to designate the estate in which another owns an easement.

Servient heritage. "The land on which the liability is imposed is called the servient heritage." [Indian Easements Act (5 of 1882), S. 4]

Servient owner. "The land on which the liability is imposed is called the servient heritage, and the owner or occupier thereof the servient owner." [Indian Easements Act (5 of 1882), S.4].

Servient tenant. One who holds a servient estate and is therefore, burdened by an easement.

Serving. Serving means holding employment as distinguished from actually performing the duties of service. A member of Air Force on leave is "serving" within the meaning of the section. *Ajit Singh* v. *State,* AIR 1970 P&H 351 at 357 (FB). [Air Force Act (45 of 1950), S. 9]

Serving officer. An officer of the Court whose duty is to make legal delivery of writ or summons, notice or any other process of the Court. [CrPC, 1973 (2 of 1974), S. 62(3)].

Servitude. A servitude or easement is a right which the owner of one estate, the dominant, has over another estate, the servient, which does not belong to him. They are charges of one estate for the benefit of another, and are rights in *alieno solo* as distinguished from rights of ownership proper.

Session. A periodical sitting of Justices of the Peace or Sessions or Assistant or Additional Sessions Judges. [CrPC, 1973 (2 of 1974), S. 7(1)].

Sitting of Court, Parliament or other deliberative body to carry on its business.

Session hijacking. Taking over an authorized user's terminal session, either physically when the user leaves his or her terminal unattended, or electronically when the intruder carefully connects to a just-disconnected communications line. (*Cyber Law*)

Sessions division. "Every State shall be a sessions divisions or shall consist of sessions divisions; and every sessions division shall, for the purposes of this Code, be a district or consist of districts:

Provided that every metropolitan area shall, for the said purposes, be a separate sessions division and district." [CrPC, 1973 (2 of 1974), S.7(1)].

One of the divisions into which a state has been divided under the Code of Criminal Procedure, 1974 for the purpose of trial of sessions cases. [CrPC, 1973 (2 of 1974), Ss. 7(1) and 9(1)].

Sessions Judge. "SESSIONS JUDGE" means the Judge appointed to the Court of Session for a sessions division within which a Gram Nyalaya is situate and shall include an Additional Sessions Judge appointed to the Court of Session. [Madhya Pradesh Gram Nyayalaya Act, 1996 (26 of 1997), S. 2(h)]

Set. A collection or number of things; a number of things grouped together according to a system of classification or conceived as a whole. [Indian Contract Act (9 of 1872), S. 57, ill.]; studded [Gold (Control) Act (45 of 1868) (*repealed*), S. 2(p)].

Set aside. When it is said that a voluntary deed is void as against the creditors of a grantor, or will be set aside, the terms "void" and "set aside' are to be understood as meaning only that the conveyance, while good as against all others, shall not operate to defeat the equality of the creditors of the grantor.

To annul, quash, render void or negatory [CrPC, 1973 (2 of 1974), S. 96]; [Income-tax Act (43 of 1961), S. 178(3)(b)].

Set forth. To express in words; to give an account or statement of; to present fully and clearly. [Army Act (46 of 1950), S. 44].

Set-off. An item or amount which is or should be set off against another in the settlement of accounts; a counter claim or a counter balancing debt pleaded by the defendant in an action to recover the money due. [heading, CPC (5 of 1908), O. VIII]; to make a set-off.

Set-off signifies the subtraction or taking away of one demand from another opposite or cross-demand, so as to distinguish the smaller demand and reduce the greater by the amount of the less; or, if the opposite demands are equal, to extinguish both. It was also, formerly, sometimes called stoppage, because the amount to be set-off was stopped or deducted from the cross-demand. [A Treatise on the Law of Set-off, Recoupment, and Counterclaim by Thomas W. Waterman as cited in *Jitendra Kumar Khan v. Peerless General Finance and Investment Company Limited,* (2013) 8 SCC 769, para 14].

'Set-off' means a debtor's right to reduce the amount of a debt by any sum the creditor owes the debtor; the counterbalancing sum owed by the creditor. [Black's Law Dictionary (7th Edn., 1999) as cited in *Jitendra Kumar Khan v. Peerless General Finance and Investment Company Limited,* (2013) 8 SCC 769, para 14].

The right of set-off is the right of a defendant in an action for a fixed and ascertained sum of money, where he has himself a liquidated demand against the plaintiff; to set one demand against the other.

Where there are mutual debts between the plaintiff and defendant, or if either party sues or be sued by the other one debt may be set against the other.

SET-OFF is a claim for debt or damages set up by the defendant against the plaintiff in reduction of his claims.

A set-off is a cross-action by the defendant against the plaintiff, which is allowed by statute to avoid a multiplicity of suits when the debts are mutual that is, when the parties are the same, and the debts are due in the same right.

The essence of a set-off is that the defendant should have a cause of action against the plaintiff apart from the suit and not merely as a defence to the plaintiff's claim. The set-off is in the nature of a cross-action which could be seperately entertained. *Pramada Prasad* v. *Sagarmal,* AIR 1954 Pat 439, 441. [CPC (5 of 1908), O. VIII, R. 6]

Set-off against his income, profits or gains. These words can only apply to income which has not already suffered tax but income in respect of which tax could be levied and collected. The word used is 'income' and not 'total income'. The loss sustained by the assessee in a speculation business cannot be set-off against the taxed share income received by the assessee as a partner of an unregistered firm. *CIT* v. *Ratanshi Bhavanji,* AIR 1953 Mad 358.

Set out. The use of the words "set out" in reference to the facts necessary to be set out in an indictment, means no more than the word 'aver" or "allege."

Laid down. [Industrial Employment (Standing Orders) Act (20 of 1946), S. 15(2)(b)].

Set up. Unless a factory is erected and the plants and machinery installed therein, it cannot be said to have been set up. [Wealth Tax Act (27 of 1957), S. 5(1)(xxi) and 2nd proviso]

The meaning of the words "set up" is "ready to commence business." *V.K. Namboodiri* v. *UOI,* AIR 1965 Ker 183, 184.

The word "set up" is equivalent to the word established but operations for establishment cannot be equated with the establishment of the unit itself of its setting up. *Commissioner of Wealth Tax* v. R. S. *Cottom Mills*, AIR 1967 SC 509, 511.

Set up an alibi. Where a defendant in a criminal prosecution sought to break the prosecution case by testimony tending to show that he was elsewhere at the time of the commission of the offence charged in the indictment, in common expression he is said to "set up an *alibi*."

Setting of business. Only when a business is established and is ready to commence business, it can be said of that business that it is set up. *Western India Vegetable Products Ltd.* v. *CIT,* (1954) 26 ITR 151, 158 (Bom).

Setting up a title. Putting forward a title. [T.P. Act (4 of 1882), S. 111(g)].

Settle. To adjust or ascertain; to pay.

To decide upon; to decide by arrangement between the contesting parties; [T.P. Act (4 of 1882), S. 54]; to settle accounts [Indian Trusts Act (2 of 1882), S. 35]; to settle assessment of land; settle property; to dispose of; to make final payment; to establish residence [Indian Succession Act (39 of 1925), S. 10, ill. (i)].

IN CONTRACTS. An agreement by which two or more persons who have dealings together so far arrange their accounts as to ascertain the balance due from one to the other; payment in full.

Settled. "SETTLED" when used with reference to a village or any other area, means the village or other area in respect of which settlement or resettlement of rent or revenue or both has been made. [Rajasthan Land Reforms and Acquisition of Land Owners, Estates Act, 1963 (11 of 1964), S. 2(h)]

Settled accounts. A statement of money received and paid with calculation of balance which has been finally decided between the parties. [CPC (5 of 1908), 1st Sch., App. D, form No. 21].

Settled property. Means property which stands limited to, or in trust for, any persons, natural or juridical, by way of succession, whether the settlement took effect before or after the commencement of this Act. [Estate Duty Act (34 of 1953), S. 2(19)]

Settlement. "SETTLEMENT" means any non-testamentary disposition, in writing, of moveable or immovable property made—(a) in consideration of marriage, (b) for the purpose of distributing property of the settlor among his family or those for whom he desires to provide, or for the purpose of providing for some person dependent on him, or (c) for any religious or charitable purpose; and includes an agreement in writing to make such a disposition and, where any such disposition has not been made in writing, any instrument recording, whether by way of declaration of trust or otherwise, the terms of any such disposition. [Indian Stamp Act (2 of 1899), S. 2(24)]

"SETTLEMENT" means the settlement referred to in section 48A [Competition Act 2002 (12 of 2003), section 2(ua)]

"SETTLEMENT" means a settlement arrived at in the course of conciliation proceeding and includes a written agreement between the employer and worker arrived at otherwise than in the course of conciliation proceeding where such agreement has been signed by the parties thereto in such manner as may be prescribed and a copy thereof has been sent to an officer authorised in this behalf by the appropriate Government and to the conciliation officer. [Industrial Relations Code, 2020 (35 of 2020), section 2(zi)]

"SETTLEMENT" means any instrument (other than a will or codicil as defined by the Indian Succession Act (39 of 1925), whereby the distination or devolution of successive interests in moveable or immovable property is disposed of or is agreed to be disposed of. [Specific Relief Act (1 of 1877), (Section 2(b) of Specific Relief Act (47 of 1963)]

'SETTLEMENT' means a settlement arrived at in the course of conciliation proceeding and includes a written agreement between the employer and workmen arrived at otherwise than in the course of conciliation proceeding where such agreement has been signed by the parties thereto in such manner as may be prescribed and a copy thereof has been sent to an officer authorised in this behalf by the appropriate Government and the Conciliation Officer. [Industrial Disputes Act (14 of 1947), S. 2(p)]

A decision of a question, dispute, *etc*., the settling (of accounts) [Indian Contract Act (9 of 1872), S. 50, ill. (b)]; to fix definitely; to ascertain [CPC (5 of 1908), O. V, R. 5]; the process of assessing the government land-tax over a specific area; the act of settling property upon a person or persons, in particular the terms of such an arrangement; the deed or instrument by which it is effected [Specific Relief Act (47 of 1963), S. 2(b)]; disposition [Apprentices Act (52 of 1961), S. 20]; the act of deciding disputes between parties. [Industrial Disputes Act (14 of 1947), S. 18].

Settlement by conciliation. *'Settlement by 'conciliation'* means the process by which a conciliator who is appointed by parties or by the Court, as the case may be, conciliates the disputes between the parties to the suit by the application of the provisions of the Arbitration and Conciliation Act, 1996 (26 of 1996) insofar as they relate to conciliation, and in particular, in exercise of his powers under Sections 67 and 73 of that Act, by making proposals for a settlement of the dispute and by formulating or reformulating the terms of a possible settlement; and has a greater role than a mediater. [Civil Procedure Alternative Dispute Resolution and Mediation Rules, 2003, R. 4 as **referred in** *Salem Advocate Bar Assn.* v. *Union of India,* (2005) 6 SCC 344, 381, para 65]

Settlement of accounts. A "settlement of accounts" is a contract between two parties by means of which they ascertain the state of the accounts between them and strike a balance.

The word "settlement" of accounts does not necessarily mean payment or satisfaction, though it may mean that. It means liquidation of amount, arrangement of difficulties, adjustment, *etc.*

Settlement of issues. Ascertainment by the Court of points of dispute in regard to proposition of law or fact between the parties in a civil case. [CPC (5 of 1908), O. V, R. 5].

Settlement-officer. "SETTLEMENT-OFFICER" means the Collector or any officer in charge of the revenue jurisdiction of a district, and includes any Assistant Commissioner, Deputy Collector or Sub-Deputy Collector whom the Collector or other officer as aforesaid may authorize to conduct the inquiries and proceedings connected with any settlement of land-revenue, and any officer who may be appointed by the State Government to make any such settlement. [Bengal Rent Settlement Act (8 of 1879), S. 3]

Settlements. Settled colonies. [Tea Act (29 of 1953), S. 17(3)].

Settling a scheme. The action of establishing or arranging permanently a plan for accomplishing an object. [CPC (5 of 1908), S. 92(1)(g)].

Sever. To separate; to disjoin.

Severable. Capable to being separated [Sale of Goods Act (3 of 1930), S. 38(2)]; capable of being divided [Sale of Goods Act (3 of 1930), S. 13(2)].

Several. More than one [CPC (5 of 1908), O. VIII, R. 7]; existing apart; separate [Indian Trusts Act (2 of 1882), S. 27]; distinct. [CPC (5 of 1908), O. XX, R. 18(1)].

Severally. Separately; individually. [T.P. Act (4 of 1882), S. 37, ill. (b)]; [CPC (5 of 1908), O. I, R. 1]; [Indian Partnership Act (9 of 1932), S. 25].

Severance. The division of a joint estate into different parts. [T.P. Act (4 of 1882), S. 37]; putting apart.

In pleading, the adoption by several defendants of separate pleas instead of joining in the same plea. In estates, the destruction of any one of the joint unities of a joint tenancy. The term is also used to signify the cutting of crops or the separating of anything from the realty.

Severe. Rigorous; strict or stern in dealings. [IPC (45 of 1860), S. 320, *Eighthly*].

Severe disability. Means disability with eighty per cent, or more of one or more of multiple disabilities. [National Trust for Welfare of Persons with Autism, Cerebral Palsy, Mental Retardation and Multiple Disabilities Act (44 of 1999), S. 2(o)]

Severing. The action of separating one from the other or connected parts. [Indian Partnership Act (9 of 1932), S. 30(4)].

Sewage. "SEWAGE" means night-soil and other contents of privies, latrines, urinals, cesspools and drains, and includes polluted water from sink, bathrooms, stables, cattle-sheds and other like places and also discharges from manufactories of all kinds. [Manipur Municipalities Act (43 of 1994). S. 2(55)]

"SEWAGE" means night-soil and other contents of latrines, urinals, cesspools or drains, and polluted water from sinks, bath-rooms, stables, cattle sheds and other like places and includes trade effluents and discharges from factories of all kinds. [New Delhi Municipalities Council Act (44 of 1994), S. 2(49)]

Sewage effluent. Means effluent from any sewerage system or sewage disposal works and includes sullage from open drains. [Water (Prevention and Control of Pollution) Act (6 of 1974), S. 2(g)]

Sewer. "SEWER" means any conduit pipe or channel, open or closed, carrying sewage or trade effluent. [Water (Prevention and Control of Pollution) Act (6 of 1974), S. 2(gg)]

"SEWER" means an underground conduit or pipe for carrying off human excreta, besides other waste matter and drainage wastes. [S. 2(1)(q) of the Prohibition of Employment as Manual Scavengers & Their Rehabilitation Act, 2013 (25 of 2013)]

Sewerage-connection. Includes—(a) any sewer between any water-closet, latrine, urinal, privy, bathroom cook-room, sink, sulliage-tray, manhole or trap on the one hand, and any sewer set apart by a committee for sewage and other offensive matter on the other hand; and (b) any cistern, flush-tank, land, building, machinery, work or thing constructed or used for collecting and passing any sewage into any sewer vested in a committee. [Bur. Act III of 1898 (Municipalities), S. 2, cl. (11)]

Sex. One of the two divisions of organic beings, especially human beings, respectively designated male and female. [Guardians and Wards Act (8 of 1890), S. 10(1)(a) and Constitution of India, Art. 15(1)].

Sex non-cogit and impossibilia and innutilia. The maxim '*sex non-cogit and impossibilitia and innutilia* (the law does not compel the impossible) applies to persons from whom exact cause of accident could be obtained having been injured and having been incapable of making a statement for a number of days after the accident. *Pooma Electric Supply Co.* v. *State of Maharashtra,* AIR 1967 Bom 23, 33. [Indian

Electricity Act (9 of 1910), S. 33(1)] Now repealed by Act 36 of 2003.

Sex selection. Includes any procedure, technique, test or administration or prescription or provision of anything for the purpose of ensuring or increasing the probability that an embryo will be of a particular sex. [Pre-Natal Diagnostics Techniques (Regulation and Prevention of Misuse) Act (57 of 1994), S. 2(o)]

Sexual abuse. For the purposes of section 3 of Act 43 of 2005, 'sexual abuse' includes any conduct of a sexual nature that abuses, humiliates, degrades or otherwise violates the dignity of woman. [*Explanation I(ii)* to S. 3 of the Protection of Women from Domestic Violence Act, 2005 (43 of 2005)] For the purposes of this section, "sexual abuse" includes any conduct of a sexual nature that abuses, humiliates, degrades or otherwise violates the dignity of a woman. [Protection of Women from Domestic Violence Act (43 of 2005), S. 3, *Explanation I(ii)* **as cited in** *Hiralal P. Harsora v. Kusum Narottamdas Harsora,* (2016) 10 SCC 165, para 19].

Sexual harassment. A type of discrimination in employment consisting of verbal or physical abuse of sexual nature.

Sexual harassment is not a fiction and the gender-based violation is discrimination and it violates a woman's basic human rights. Sexual integrity of a woman is her basic and fundamental right, says Supreme Court of India. *Vishaka* v. *State of Rajasthan,* (1997) 2 SCC 241.

"SEXUAL HARASSMENT" includes any one or more of the following unwelcome acts or behaviour (whether directly or by implication) namely—(i) physical contact and advances; or (ii) a demand or request for sexual favours; or (iii) making sexually coloured remarks; or (iv) showing pornography; or (v) any other unwelcome physical, verbal or non-verbal conduct of sexual nature. [S. 2(n) of the Sexual Harassment of Women at Workplace (Prevention, Prohibition & Redressal) Act, 2013 (14 of 2013)]

(1) A man committing any of the following acts—

(i) physical contact and advances involving unwelcome and explicit overtures; or

(ii) a demand or request for sexual favours, or

(iii) showing pornography against the will of a woman; or

(iv) making sexually coloured remarks, shall be guilty of the offence of 'SEXUAL HARASSMENT'.

(2) Any man who commits the offence specified in clause (i) or clause (ii) or clause (iii) of sub-section (1) shall be punished with rigorous imprisonment for a term which may extend to three years, or with fine, or with both.

(3) Any man who commits the offence specified in clause (iv) of sub-section (1) shall be punished with imprisonment of either description for a term which may extend to one year, or with fine, or with both.] [Indian Penal Code (45 of 1860), S. 354A as inserted by Amending Act, (13 of 2013)].

A person is said to commit 'SEXUAL HARASSMENT' upon a child when such person with sexual intent,—

(i) utters any word or makes any sound, or makes any gesture or exhibits any object or part of body with the intention that such word or sound shall be heard, or such gesture or object or part of body shall be seen by the child; or

(ii) makes a child exhibit his body or any part of his body so as it is seen by such person or any other person; or

(iii) shows any object to a child in any form or media for pornographic purposes; or

(iv) repeatedly or constantly follows or watches or contacts a child either directly or through electronic, digital or any other means; or

(v) threatens to use, in any form of media, a real or fabricated depiction through electronic, film or digital or any other mode, of any part of the body of the child or the involvement of the child in a sexual act; or

(vi) entices a child for pornographic purposes or gives gratification therefore.

Explanation.—Any question which involves "sexual intent" shall be a question of fact. [Protection of Children from Sexual Offences Act (32 of 2012), S. 11].

"SEXUAL HARASSMENT" includes any one or more of the following unwelcome acts or behaviour (whether directly or by implication) namely.—

(i) physical contact and advances; or

(ii) demand or request for sexual favours; or

(iii) making sexually coloured remarks; or

(iv) showing pornography; or

(v) any other unwelcome physical, verbal or non-verbal conduct of sexual nature. [Sexual Harassment of Women at Workplace (Prevention, Prohibition and Redressal) Act (14 of 2013), S. 2(n)].

"SEXUAL HARASSMENT" includes any one or more of the following acts or behaviour (whether directly or by implication), namely—

(i) physical contract and advances; or

(ii) a demand or request for sexual favours; or

(iii) making sexually coloured remarks; or

(iv) showing pornography; or

(v) any other unwelcome physical, verbal, non-verbal conduct of a sexual nature. [Central Civil Services (Conduct) Rules, 1964, R. 3-C, Explanation 1(a) as substituted by Second Amending Rules, 2014].

"SEXUAL HARASSMENT" includes any one or more of the following unwelcome acts or behaviour (whether directly or by implication) namely—

(i) physical contact and advances;

(ii) a demand or request for sexual favours;
(iii) making sexually coloured remarks;
(iv) showing or exhibiting pornography and/or sexually explicit material by any means;
(v) sending undesirable sexually coloured oral or written massages, text messages, e-mail messages, or any such messages by electronic, manual or other means;
(vi) stalking or consistently following aggrieved woman in the Supreme Court precincts and outside;
(vii) voyeurism including overt or tacit observation by the Respondent by any means of the aggrieved woman in her private moments;
(viii) any conduct whereby the Respondent takes advantage of his position and subjects the aggrieved woman to any form of sexual harassment and seeks sexual favours specially while holding out career advancements whether explicitly or implicitly, as an incentive or a natural result of submitting to the insinuations/demands of the Respondent;
(ix) any other unwelcome physical, verbal or non-verbal conduct of sexual nature;
(x) implied or explicit promise of preferential Treatment in her legal career;
(xi) implied or explicit threat of detrimental treatment in her legal career;
(xii) implied or explicit threat about her present or future legal career;
(xiii) interferes with her work or creating an intimidating or offensive or hostile work environment for her; or
(xiv) any treatment having a sexual colour or content likely to affect her emotional and/or physical health or safety. [Gender Sensitisation and Sexual Harassment of Women at the Supreme Court of India (Prevention, Prohibition and Redressal) Regulations, 2013, Regn. 2(k)].

"SEXUAL HARASSMENT". (1) A man committing any of the following acts – (i) Physical contact and advances involving unwelcome and explicit sexual overtures; or (ii) a demand or request for sexual favours; or (iii) showing pornography against the will of a woman; or (iv) Making sexually coloured remarks, shall be guilty of the offence of sexual harassment. [Indian Penal Code 1860, S. 354A (1), as inserted by the Criminal Law (Amendment) Act 2013 (13 of 2013)]

Sexual intercourse. Means actual contact of the sexual organs of a man and a woman and an actual penetration into the body of the latter.

Carnal copulation of male and female, implying actual penetration. [IPC (45 of 1860), S. 372, *Expln.* II and CrPC, 1973 (2 of 1974), S. 198(6)].

In this section, "SEXUAL INTERCOURSE" shall mean any of the act mentioned in clauses (a) to (d) of section 375. [Indian Penal Code (45 of 1860), S. 376B, Explanation as substituted by Amending Act (13 of 2013)]. [Now (w. e. f. 1-7-2024) repealed & replaced by Bharatiya Nayaya Sanhita, 2023 (45 of 2023)]

In this section, "sexual harassment" shall mean any of the acts mentioned in clauses (a) to (d) of section 63. [(w. e. f. 1-7-2024) Bharatiya Nayaya Sanhita, 2023 (45 of 2023), section 67, *Explanation*, section 68, *Explanation 1*, and section 120, *Explanation*]

"SEXUAL INTERCOURSE". In section 376B of Act 45 of 1860, 'sexual intercourse' shall mean any of the acts mentioned in clauses (a) to (d) of section 375 of Act 45 of 1860. [*Explanation* to S. 376B of IPC, 1860 (45 of 1860), as substituted by the Criminal Law (Amendment) Act, 2013 (13 of 2013)]. Refer 'Rape'.

Sexual orientation. "SEXUAL ORIENTATION" is understood to refer to each-person's capacity for profound emotional, affectional and sexual attraction to and intimate and sexual relations with individuals of a different gender or the same gender or more than one gender. [Yogyakarta Principles **as cited in** *Navtej Singh Johar v. Union of India,* (2018) 10 SCC 1, para 153].

Sexual orientation refers to an enduring pattern of emotional, romantic and/or sexual attraction to men, women or both sexes. Sexual orientation also refers to a person's sense of identity based on those attractions, related behavior, and membership in a community of others who share those attractions. Research over several decades has demonstrated that sexual orientation ranges along a continuum, from exclusive attraction to the other sex to exclusive attraction to the same sex. [American Psychological Association **as cited in** *Navjej Singh Johar* v. *Union of India,* (2018) 10 SCC 1, para 154].

Sexual penetration. Includes sexual intercourse, cunnilingus, fellatio, anal intercourse or any other intrusion, no matter how slight, into the victim's genital, oral or anal openings by the suspect's body or by an object. An emission of semen is not required. (*Criminal*)

Sexually transmitted disease. A disease which is transmitted only or chiefly by engaging in sexual acts with an infected person. Gonorrhea and Syphilis are the common examples of sexually transmitted disease.

Shake the credit. To bring about impairment of the credibility. [Indian Evidence Act (1 of 1872), S. 153].

Shall. In common parlance, a term which, it is said, has always a compulsory meaning, and in its common and ordinary usage, unless accompanied by qualifying words which show a contrary intent, always refers to the future; but it may be used in the sense of "must" of which it is a synonym. As used in statutes, the word is generally mandatory; although it is not always imperative but may be consistent with an exercise of discretion. Thus, it may be construed to mean "may" when no right or benefit to any one depends on its imperative use; when no advantage is lost, when no right is destroyed, when no benefit is sacrificed, either to the public or to any individual by giving it that construction; or when it is absolutely necessary to prevent irreparable mischief, or to construe a direction so that it shall not interfere with mental branches of government; and it also means 'may' when used by a legislature in a grant of authority to a Court. (*Ame. Cyc.*)

The word "shall" in its ordinary signification is mandatory though there may be considerations which would influence the Court in holding that the intention of the legislature was to give a discretion.

The use of the word "shall" would not by itself make a provision of the Act mandatory. It is to be construed with reference to the context in which it issued.

The word 'shall' in context similar to the provisions of clause 2 in the First Schedule has often been interpreted as merely being directory. *Union of India* v. *Allied Trading Co.,* AIR 1956 Punj 7, 9. [Arbitration Act (10 of 1940) (*repealed*), Sch. I, R. 2]

The employment of the auxiliary verb "shall" is inconclusive and similarly the mere absence of the imperative is not conclusive either. *Collector Monghyr* v. *Keshav Prasad Goenka*, AIR 1962 SC 1694, 1701.

The word "shall" in S. 12, CPC (5 of 1908) is imperative on the suitor and not upon the Court for whose benefit it is intended.

The word "shall" in O. XLVI, R. 7, CPC (5 of 1908), has only a directory sense, and is not mandatory.

Where the word 'shall' is used in a statute, the presumption is that its use is imperative and not merely directory, particularly when it is addressed to a Court or a public servant and when a right or benefit depends on its imperative use. *Pratap Singh Kaison* v. *Gurmej Singh,* AIR 1958 Punj 409, 411. [CPC (5 of 1908), O. XIV, R. 2]

The word shall in R. 27(2) of O. XIV is not mandatory and the omission to record reasons for allowing additional evidence does not vitiate such admission. *Ramgauda* v. *Form by Name "Gonhal Basangauda Basavarajappa Rajendra Gunj Raichur",* AIR 1969 Mys 111, 112 at 113. [CPC (5 of 1908), O. XLI, R. 27]

The word "shall" is in the context only directory and not mandatory and the non-compliance with the direction would not render a promotion or a transfer otherwise regularly and validly made any way ineffective or inoperative. *C.P. Mary* v. *State of Travancore Cochin,* AIR 1958 Ker 85, 87. [Constitution of India, Art. 320].

The word "shall" in S. 82, Representation of the People Act (43 of 1951) casts on the petitioner a duty to implead all the duly nominated candidates as respondents. *Collector of Customs* v. *Calcutta Cycle Syndicate,* AIR 1964 Cal 225, 230.

The use of word 'shall' in a statute though generally taken in a mandatory sense, does not necessarily mean that in every case it shall have that effect, that is to say, that unless the words of the statute are punctually followed, the proceeding or the outcome of the proceeding, would be invalid. It is not always correct to say that where the word 'may' has been used, the statute is only permissive or directory in the sense that non-compliance with those provisions will not render the proceeding invalid. *State of U.P.* v. *Manbodhan Lal Srivastava*, AIR 1957 SC 912, 917.

The use of the expression "shall" *prima facia* makes the inquiry or the investigation, as the case may be, by the Magistrate mandatory. The word "shall" is ordinarily mandatory but sometimes, taking into account the context or the intention, it can be held to be directory. The use of "shall" in all circumstances in not decisive. Bearing in mind the aforesaid principle, when looked upon the intention of the legislature, it is found that it is aimed to save innocent persons from harassment by unscrupulous persons from false complaints. Hence, the use of the expression "shall" and the background and the purpose for which the amendment has been brought, there is no doubt that inquiry <u>or</u> the investigation, as the case may be, is mandatory before summons are issued against the accused living beyond the territorial jurisdiction of the Magistrate. [*Vijay Dhanuka v. Najima Mumtaj,* (2014) 14 SCC 638, para 12 **as cited in** *Abhijit Pawar v. Hemant Madhukar Nimbalkar,* (2017) 3 SCC 528, para 24] [Criminal Procedure Code, 1973 (2 of 1974), S. 202, 2005 Amendment].

Shall also be liable to fine. The legislature has given the discretion to Court to impose imprisonment and the discretion to impose fine also. It is not necessary that fine must be imposed in every case of conviction under the section. *Tetar* v. *Gananuri,* AIR 1968 Pat 287 at 288. [IPC (45 of 1860), S. 325]

Shall and Must. It is well settled law that every use of the word 'shall' or 'must' does not render the provision mandatory. It should be found out from the rules under consideration as to what are the consequences and non-consequences with that particular provision. If non-compliance is not visited with any adverse consequences it shall not be mandatory, but only directory. *P.M. Doraiswamy Reddy* v. *Election Authority and Director of Marketing Andhra Pradesh,* AIR 1977 AP 286, 288.

Shall be allowed. The expression "shall be allowed" cannot be construed to mean "shall be admitted' or "shall be entertained". To admit the application is not the same thing as to allow it.

Shall be annulled. Construed as discretionary and not mandatory.

Shall be compelled to be a witness. The term "to be a witness" means even in all cases where the accused is compelled to furnish any material which may be used against him for the purpose of convicting him. If the accused is forced to give his thumb impression, he can take protection under the guarantee bestowed upon him in the provisions of Art. 20(3). *Bhalik Behera* v. *State,* AIR 1957 Ori 172, 176. [Constitution of India, Art. 20(3)]

Shall be compelled to give. The words "SHALL BE COMPELLED TO GIVE" in S. 132 of the Indian Evidence Act (1 of 1872) apply to pressure put upon a witness after he is in the box, and when he asks to be excused from answering a question.

Shall be deemed. The word "deemed" means "supposed", "considered", "construed", "thought", "taken to be", or "presumed". The word "deemed" refers to "what is supposed to be", not to "what actually is". It rather suggests that something is being assumed as true for certain purposes though really it is not. *A.G. Goel* v. *First National Bank Ltd.,* AIR 1960 Punj 476, 477. [Companies Act (1 of 1956), S. 441]

Shall be deemed to contract. The use of the expression "shall be deemed to contract" in S. 55 (2) of the T.P. Act (4 of 1882) makes it clear that the contract so deemed to have been entered into should be taken as part and parcel of the transaction of sale, and where the circumstances require a writing registered, as embodied in such writing.

Shall be deemed to have been done. When a statute enacts that something shall be deemed to have been done which in fact and truth was not done, the Court is entitled and bound to ascertain for what purposes and between what persons the statutory fiction is to be resorted to and full effect must be given to the statutory fiction and it should be carried to its logical conclusion. *Federal Bank of India Ltd.* v. *Durga Das Kapur,* AIR 1954 Punj 21.

Shall be final. Where in the same Act the decisions under two sections are final with respect to the matters mentioned therein and in one of the sections, it is specifically stated that decision cannot be questioned in a Court of law and in the other section there is no such prohibition, the ordinary and legitimate inference is that where there is no such prohibition in a section, the Court of law can question the legality, although the decision may be final as between the parties. S. *Ananda Rao* v. *Labour Officer,* AIR 1957 Ker 55, 56.

Shall be held. Just because the words used in this section are "shall be held", it does not necessarily follow that merely on that account these words have no reference back to the past and that, therefore, the section applies only to properties which are possessed by a Hindu female at the commencement of the Act or which may be acquired and possessed by her subsequent to the enforcement of the Act. *Ramsewak Ojha* v. *Sheopujan Pandey,* AIR 1959 Pat 75, 78. [Hindu Succession Act (30 of 1956), S. 14(1)]

Shall be laid before the Parliament. Where the statute makes the laying of the rules before Parliament a condition precedent or the resolution of the Parliament a condition subsequent, there is no difficulty as, in the former case, the rule has no legal force at all till the condition precedent is complied with and in the latter case, it ceased to have force from the date of non-compliance with the condition subsequent. *D.K. Krishnan* v. *Secretary, Regional Transport Authority,* AIR 1956 AP 129, 137.

Shall be presumed. The term "shall be presumed" means that the Court is bound to take the fact as proved until evidence is adduced to disprove it and the party interested in disproving it must produce such evidence if he can. *Public Prosecutor* v. *A. Thomas,* AIR 1959 Mad 166, 171. [Prevention of Corruption Act (2 of 1947), S. 4]

Shall be punishable. The expression "punishable" does not confer a discretion on the Court whether to award a punishment or not. *State of Maharashtra* v. *J. Lal,* AIR 1966 SC 940, 942. [Suppression of Immoral Traffic in Women and Girls Act (104 of 1956), S. 3(1)]

Shall be rejected. The phrase "his plaint shall be rejected" read with the provision as to an extension of time means that the plaint shall be rejected if the Court should not deem it proper to allow further time.

Shall be stamped at the time of execution. The expression "shall be stamped at the time of execution" means that the signing and affixing of the stamp are practically simultaneous. *K. Markose* v. *Varkey,* AIR 1966 Ker 315.

Shall be void. The words "shall be void" are to be interpreted to mean that such laws which are inconsistent with the provisions of Part III, Fundamental Rights, will "become void" from the date of the commencement of the Constitution and not from the very inception. Article 13(1) of the Constitution is not retrospective but prospective. *Abdul Khader* v. *State of Mysore,* AIR 1951 Mys 72, 86 (FB). [Constitution of India, Art. 13(1)]

Shall presume. "Whenever it is directed by this Act that the Court shall presume a fact, it shall regard such fact as proved, unless and until it is disproved." [Indian Evidence Act (1 of 1872), S. 4]

The legislature has chosen to use the words "shall presume" and not "may presume", the former a presumption of law and latter of fact. It is a presumption of law and therefore, it is obligatory on the Court to raise this presumption in every case brought under S. 4 of the Prevention of Corruption Act, because unlike the case of presumption of fact, presumptions of law constitute a branch of jurisprudence. *State of Madras* v. *A. Vaidyanatha Iyer*, AIR 1958 SC 61, 65. [Prevention of Corruption Act (2 of 1947), S. 4]

Shall presume : May presume. The expression "may presume" is compendiously known as "factual presumption" or "discretionary presumption", and "shall presume" as "legal presumption" or compulsory presumption. "The expression" shall be presumed used in Section 4 of Prevention of Corruption Act, 1947, is to be understood as in terrorem, *i.e.* having some import of compulsion that the accused accepted gratification as a motive or reward or for bearing to do any official act. *State of A.P.* v. *V. Vasudeva Rao*, 2004 CrLJ 620, pp. 623,

624 (SC). [Prevention of Corruption Act (2 of 1947), S. 4)]

Sham. Good in appearance but false in fact, as a sham plea or answer.

The word "sham" is defined by lexicographers as false, counterfeit, or pretended, and it has received the same interpretation when applied to pleadings.

Sham marriage. A marriage which is entered into for some ulterior motive, without the intention of cohabiting with the other party.

Sham transaction. A sham transaction is one which was always intended and devised to be a fraud of a provision of the statute concerned in relation to which it is alleged to be a fraud. [*Mettur Beardsell Ltd.* v. *Workmen*, (2006) 9 SCC 488, 499, p. 19]

Shamilat. "Shamilat" connotes commonality or possession, in contradistinction to ownership individually or severally. [*Sarjeet Singh v. Hari Singh*, (2015) 1 SCC 760, para 6]. Shamilat-banjar

Shamilat-banjar. Portions of common land—Kanara. 'Shamilat banjar' means common uncultivable lands. [*Sarjeed Singh v. Hari Singh*, (2015) 1 SCC 760, para 6].

'Shamilat deh' are common or village lands. [*Sarjeet Singh v. Hari Singh*, (2015) 1 SCC 760, para 6].

Share. "SHARE" means share in the share capital of a company, and includes stock except where a distinction between stock and shares is expressed or implied. [Companies Act (1 of 1956), S. 2(46)]

Share is a right to a specified amount of the share capital of a company carrying out certain rights and liabilities. In other words, shares are bundles of intangible rights against the company. Shares are to be regarded as situate in the country in which it is incorporated and a register is kept. Shares are transferable like any other movable property under the Companies Act and the Transfer of Property Act. [*Vodafone International Holdings BV v. Union of India*, (2012) 6 SCC 613, para 270].

The part or portion (of something) which is allotted or belongs to an individual, when distribution is made among a number; also, the portion or quota which is contributed by an individual; a definite portion of the capital of a company; to get a share. [Indian Partnership Act (9 of 1932), S. 48(iv)].

A portion of anything. Sometimes shares are equal, at other times they are unequal.

The word "share" ordinarily means a part or definite portion of a thing owned by a number of persons in common. It contemplates something owned in common by two or more persons, and has reference to that part of the undivided interest which belongs to some one of them.

A share is not a sum of money, but represents an interest measured by a sum of money and made up of diverse rights contained in the contract evidenced by the articles of association of company. *I.T. Commissioner (Central) Calcutta* v. *Standard Vacuum Oil Co. Ltd.*, AIR 1966 SC 1393, 1397. [Business Profits Act (21 of 1947), Sch. II, R. 2(1)]

A share is undoubtedly moveable property. It is incorporeal in its nature, and it consists merely of a bundle of rights and obligations. Everyone of these rights and obligations is created by a statute or under statutory instruments or powers which also define their extent, scope, boundaries and incidents. S. *Vishwanathan* v. *East India Distillaries and Sugar Factories Ltd.,* AIR 1957 Mad 341, 342.

"SHARE" means a share in the share capital of a company and includes stock. [S. 2(84) of the Companies Act, 2013 (18 of 2013)]

Share Capital. "SHARE CAPITAL" means the subscribed share capital including Government Share Capital. [H.P. Co-op Societies Rules, 1971, R. 2(ix)]

Share in a corporation. "SHARE IN A CORPORATION" shall be deemed to include stock, debenture stock, debentures or bonds. [CPC (5 of 1908), S. 2(19)]

Share warrant. A document certifying that the bearer owns the shares specified and that they are fully paid up.

A warrant certificate issued by a corporation evidencing the right of its holder to receive a specified number of paid up shares of the stock of the corporation. [Companies Act (1 of 1956), S. 2(27)]; [Indian Stamp Act (2 of 1899), S. 62(2)].

Shared household. Means a household where the person aggrieved lives or at any stage has lived in a domestic relationship either singly or along with the respondent and includes such a household whether owned or tenanted either jointly by the aggrieved person and the respondent, or owned or tenanted by either of them in respect of which either the aggrieved person or the respondent or both jointly or singly have any right, title, interest or equity and includes such a household which may belong to the joint family of which the respondent is a member, irrespective of whether the respondent or the aggrieved person has any right, title or interest in the shared household. [S. 2(s) of the Protection of Women from Domestic Violence Act, 2005 (43 of 2005)]

"SHARED HOUSEHOLD" means a household where the person charged with the offence lives or has lived at any time in a domestic relationship with the child. [(w.e.f. 14-11-2012) S. 2(1)(k) of the Protection of Children from Sexual Offences Act, 2012 (32 of 2012)].

Shareholder. In this Schedule, "SHAREHOLDER" means any person who immediately before the appointed day is registered as the holder of a share in the Imperial Bank. [State Bank of India Act (23 of 1955), Sch. I, Para 1]

Shareholder means only a registered shareholder. Only the person whose name is entered in the register of shareholders of the company as the holder of the shares who can be said to be a shareholder.

Rameshwar Lal Sanwarmal v. *Commissioner of Income Tax, Assam*, AIR 1980 SC 372, 376.

Shareholders' agreement. Shareholders Agreement ("SHA") is essentially a contract between some or all other shareholders in a company, the purpose of which is to confer rights and impose obligations over and above those provided by the company law. SHA is a private contract between the shareholders compared to the articles of association of the company, which is a public document. Being a private document, it binds parties thereof and not the other remaining shareholders in the company. [*Vodafone International Holdings BV v. Union of India*, (2012) 6 SCC 613, para 261].

The expression "shareholder" means a shareholder registered in the books of the company. A Hindu undivided family can be a registered shareholder of the company. *Commissioner of I.T.* v. *Shakuntala*, AIR 1966 SC 719, 722.

Shareholding. For the purposes of voting by persons who receive the notice as shareholder or creditor under this rule, "shareholding" shall mean the shareholding of the members of the class who are entitled to vote on the proposal. [Companies Compromises, Arrangement and Amalgamations) Rules, 2016, R. 9, *Explantion (a)*].

Shareholder director. "Shareholder director" means a director who represents the interest of shareholders, and elected or nominated by such shareholders. [Securities and Exchange Board of India (Depositories and Participants) Regulations, 2012, Regn. 2(1)(fa) as inserted by 2012 Amendment].

Shares. Means shares in the share capital of a company carrying voting rights and includes—

(i) any security which entitles the holder to receive shares with voting rights;

(ii) stock except where a distinction between stock and share is expressed or implied. [Competition Act, 2002 (12 of 2003), S. 2(v)]

"Shares" means the equity shares of the company carrying voting rights, and includes any securities, such as depository receipts, which entitles the holder thereof to exercise voting rights. [Companies (Compromises, Arrangements and Amalgamations) Rules, 2016, rule 3(5), *Explanation I*]

Shares of any member in a company is a movable property and can be transferred in the manner provided by the articles of association of the company. [*Vodafone International Holdings BV v. Union of India*, (2012) 6 SCC 613, para 269].

"SHARES" means shares in the share capital of a company carrying voting rights and includes any security which would entitle the holder to receive shares with voting rights. [SEBI (Substantial Acquisition of Shares and Takeovers) Regulation, 1997, Reg. 2(k)]

Shares and **Share scrips.** Shares are not the same thing as share scrips. Share scrips are documents of title and they are of no value to a third party. Only in the shareholder himself transferring the shares to a third party, the third party becomes owner of the shares. Share scrips are moveable property. *Rajbans* v. *Janki Devi,* AIR 1965 Punj 314, 315. [Court Fees Act (7 of 1870), S. 7(iv)(a)]

Shares in a corporation. A definite portion of the capital in a corporation. [CPC (5 of 1908), Ss. 2(19) and 60(1)]; [Income Tax Act (43 of 1961), Sch. II, item 1(g)].

Shares or other securities. For the purposes of rule 13 of the Companies (Share Capital & Debentures) Rules, 2014, the expression, 'shares or other securities' means equity shares, fully convertible debentures, partly convertible debentures or any other securities, which would be convertible into or exchanged with equity shares at a later date. [*Explanation* (*ii*) to rule 13(1) of the Companies (Share Capital & Debentures) Rules, 2014]

Shareware. Software that is distributed free of charge or for a small fee to encourage its use on a trial basis. A person who likes the program and continues to use it is expected to pay a nominal fee to the program's owner. (*Computer*)

Sharing. Dividing into shares and taking of each a portion. [Indian Contract Act (9 of 1932), S. 43].

Shed. Means a slight or temporary structure for shade or shelter. [New Delhi Municipal Council Act (44 of 1994), S. 2(50) and Cantonments Act (2 of 1924), S. 2(xxxiii)]

Sheering. Sheering involves assortment and variety of processes, representing a number of sub-species of operations which may or may not alter the nature of the 'grey' fabric. *Maftlal Firm Spinning of Manufacturing Co. Ltd.* v. *Collector, C.E. Bombay*, AIR 1989 SC 784, 787. [Central Excise Rules (1944), R. 49-A (1)(b) and (2)]

Shelf prospectus. For the purposes of section 31 of Act 18 of 2013, the expression 'shelf prospectus' means a prospectus in respect of which the securities or class of securities included therein are issued for subscription in one or more issues over a certain period without the issue of a further prospectus. [*Explanation* to section 31 of the Companies Act, 2013 (18 of 2013)]

Shelf-life. Means the period between the date of manufacture and the "Best Before" or "Date of expiry" whichever is earlier as printed on the label. [Food Safety and Standards (Import) Regulation, 2017, Regn. 2(1)(w)].

Sheltered accommodation. Means a safe and secure accommodation option for persons with mental illness, who want to live and manage their affairs independently, but need occasional help and support. [Mental Healthcare (Right of Persons with Mental Illness) Rules, 2018, R. 2(1)(h)].

Shelter home. Means any shelter home as may be notified by the State Government to be a shelter home for the purposes of Act 43 of 2005. [S. 2(t) of the

Protection of Women from Domestic Violence Act, 2005 (43 of 2005)]

Shell companies. A company which exists only on paper, but in reality, they are investments companies. [*Vodafone International Holdings BV v. Union of India*, (2012) 6 SCC 613, para 318].

Shia wakf. Means a *wakf* governed by Shia law. [Wakf Act (43 of 1995), S. 3(n)]

Shift. Where work of the same kind is carried out by two or more sets of workers working during different periods of the day, each of such sets is called a "group" or "relay" and each of such periods is called a "SHIFT." [Factories Act (63 of 1948), S. 2(r)]

Change (as) working by shifts in a factory.

A group of people who work or occupy themselves in turn with other groups; the time of working of such group. [Mines Act (35 of 1952), S. 2(1)(p)].

Shifting burden of proof. Changing the burden of proof from one party to another.

Ship. "SHIP" shall include every description of vessel used in navigation not exclusively propelled by oars. [General Clauses Act (10 of 1897), S. 3(55)].

"SHIP" means any vessel used for the carriage of goods by sea, [Indian Carriage of Goods by Sea (26 of 1925), Sch, Art 1(*d*)].

"SHIP" means any sea-going vessel and sea borne craft of any type whatsoever constructed or adapted for the carriage of oil in bulk as cargo, provided that a ship capable of carrying oil and other cargoes shall be regarded as a ship only when it is actually carrying oil in bulk as cargo and during any voyage following such carriage unless it is proved that it has no residues of such carriage of oil in bulk aboard. [Merchant Shipping Act (44 of 1958), S. 352H(h) *as substituted by Amending Act (63 of 2002), S. 23*]

Large vessel [General Clauses Act (10 of 1897), S. 3(55)]; to put, receive or take on board [Tea Act (29 of 1953), S. 18(1)].

"Ship" and **"vessel".** Under the (U.K.) Merchant Shipping Acts a distinction has been drawn between "VESSEL" and "SHIP". A vessel includes any ship or boat or other description of vessel used in navigation. Ship includes every description of vessel used in navigation not propelled by oars. The statutory definitions are intended to enlarge the meaning of ship. To be a ship a vessel must be used in navigable waters, either inland or at sea and although she must be constructed for navigation, it is not necessary to the definition that she should be able to navigate and under her own power. HALSBURY, 4th Edn., Vol. 43, para 91.

Ship of war. "SHIP OF WAR" means any ship belonging to the Armed Forces and includes any armed ship in the service of the Armed Forces and any other ship used as transport or auxiliary or in any other way for the purpose of prosecuting or aiding hostilities. [Naval and Aircraft Prize (59 of 1971), S. 2(j)]

Ship papers. Includes all books, passes, sea briefs, charterparties, bills of lading, customs receipts, manifests, certificates, licences, lists, tickets, notes, letters and other documents and writings delivered up or found on board a ship captured at sea or seized in port. [Naval and Aircraft Prize Act (59 of 1971), S. 2(k)]

Ship-owner. Means owner, charterer, manager and operator of a sea-going ship. [Merchant Shipping Act (44 of 1958), S. 352(i) *as inserted by* Amending Act (63 of 2002), S. 16]

"SHIPOWNER" means a person of the description mentioned in Section 21 of the Act or who had obtained loans or financial assistance in any other form from the Committee. [Shipping Development Fund Committee (Abolition) Act (66 of 1986), S. 2(g)]

Shipper. "SHIPPER" means any person by whom or in whose name or on whose behalf a contract of carriage of goods by sea has been concluded with a carrier, or any person by whom or in whose name or on whose behalf the goods are actually delivered to the carrier in relation to the contract of carriage by sea. [Hamburg Rules, Part 1, Art. 1, R. (3)]

Shipping concern. "SHIPPING CONCERN" means any concern engaged in the business of shipping, owned, controlled or managed by a ship owner. [Shipping Development Fund Committee (Abolition) Act (66 of 1986), S. 2(h)]

Shipping Corporation of India. Means the Shipping Corporation of India Limited, being a Government company as defined in the Companies Act, 1956, having its registered office at Bombay. [Jayanti Shipping Company (Acquisition of Shares) Act (63 of 1971), S. 2(d)]

Shipping line. Means any person who owns or charters a ship and includes an enterprise which operates or manages the business of shipping. [Finance Act (32 of 1994), S. 65(1)(97) now repealed by Central Goods and Services Tax Act, 2017]

Shipping master. Means the shipping master referred to in Section 11; but in relation to any seaman for the purposes of Sections 178 to 183 (inclusive) means a shipping master appointed—

(i) for the port at which the seaman entered into, or is believed to have entered into, an agreement, or

(ii) where the seaman did not enter into his agreement in India, for the port to which the seaman has returned, or is expected to return, on the completion of his latest voyage. [Merchant Shipping Act (44 of 1958), S. 3(46)]

Shock. A sudden agitation of body or mind; a sudden and violent blow, impact or collision, tending to overthrow or to produce internal oscillation in a body subject to it; also the disturbance of equilibrium or the internal oscillation resulting from this. [IPC (45 of 1860), S. 93 ill.].

Shooting. Letting fly or causing to be driven forward with force from a weapon. [Indian Evidence Act (1 of 1872), S. 14, ills. (i) and (o)].

Shoots. The word "shoots" means discharges a fire arm or other weapon." It does not mean going for shooting.

The word "shoot" is frequently— perhaps usually— employed in the sense of "skill".

Shop. "SHOP" includes any premises where any retail trade or business is carried on, including the business of a barber or hair dresser, and retail sales by auction, but excluding the sale of programmes, catalogues and other similar sales at theatre. [Weekly Holidays Act (1842), S. 2(d)]

"SHOP" means any premises where goods are solid either wholesale or by retail or both wholesale and by retail and includes—

(i) any place from where goods are sold by a hawker or vendor or from a mobile van or cart,

(ii) a laundry and a hair cutting saloon,

(iii) any other place where services are rendered to customers. [Protection of Civil Right Act (22 of 1955), S. 2(e)]

The word shop appears to be derived from the old high German 'schopf' or 'scopf' which meant a building without a front wall. It is a term of various significance, and has many definitions, and it may have different meanings when used with different texts. In its popular sense, as well as its legal meaning, the term shop is not confined to a store, and it may include both a store and a workshop. The word shop may denote a place where goods are sold, a place, building or room in which things are sold; and expressing this concept, the term is defined as meaning a place kept and used for the sale of goods; a place where goods are sold for retail;..." [Corpus Juris Secundum, Vol. LXXX as cited in *Bangalore Turf Club Limited v. Regional Director, Employees' State Insurance Corporation*, (2014) 9 SCC 657, para 38.5].

The word shop means a room or building in which the making, preparing, or repairing of any article is carried on, or in which any industry is pursued; the place where anything is made; the producing place or source. [Words and Phrases, Permanent Edn., Vol. 39 as cited in *State v. Sabo*, 140 NE 499, p. 500 : 108 Ohio St 200 (1923)]. See also *Bangalore Turf Club Limited v. Regional Director, Employees' State Insurance Corporation*, (2014) 9 SCC 657, para 38.4

SHOP is a place kept and used for the sale of goods. A building as distinguished from a place of sale which is open like a stall. In order to constitute a shop, there must be some structure of a more or less permanent character.

Employing only three persons for manufacturing spare parts to be delivered to the customer at his place. No selling takes place in the place where the spare parts are manufactured. Such a place is not a 'shop'. *Kalidas Dhanjibhai* v. *State of Bombay,* AIR 1955 SC 62.

'Shop' means a place where the trading activities connected with the buying and selling of goods are carried on, negotiations of the terms of sale, carrying on of the survey of the goods imported, arranging for the delivery of the goods sold, collection of the price of the goods sold *etc.* being trading activities. It is not necessary that the delivery of the goods should take place at the premises of the business to constitute the premises as 'shop'. *International Ore and Fertilisers (India (P) Ltd.* v. *E.S. I. Corporation*, AIR 1988 SC 79, 81. [Employees' State Insurance Act (34 of 1948), S. 1(5), A.P. Govt. Notification in G.O. Ms. No. 297, dt. 25-3-75]

The place where a person carries on stevedoring, clearing and forwarding operations is a shop. *Cochin Shipping Co.* v. *E.S.I. Corporation*, AIR 1993 SC 252, 258. [Employees' State Insurance Corporation Act (34 of 1948), S. 1(5), Notification dt. 18-9-74, Entry (v)]

Shop-keeper. "SHOP-KEEPER" means a person owning or having charge of the business of a shop, and includes an agent or manager of, and any other person acting on behalf of such person in the general management or control of a shop. [West Bengal Shops and Establishments Act (13 of 1963), S. 2(14)]

One who keeps shop for the sale of goods. [Indian Evidence Act (1 of 1872), S. 114, as to ill. (a)].

Shoplifting. Stealing goods from a shop.

Short duration question. A device available to private members of the Parliament to bring to the notice of the Houses matters of urgent public importance for a discussion for short duration. For raising such a discussion, a member has to give notice to the Secretary General specifying the matter precisely and explaining clearly the reasons thereof. Such notice should also be signed by at least two other members of the Parliament.

Short international voyage. Means an international voyage in the course of which a ship is not more than 200 miles from a port or place in which the passengers and crew could be placed in safety, and which does not exceed 600 miles in length between the last port of call in the country in which the voyage begins and the final port of destination. [International Conference on Safety of Life at Sea, 1974, Art. VI, Part A, Reg. 2(a)]

Short notice questions. A short notice question is that Parliamentary question which relates to the matter of urgent public importance and can be asked with a shorter notice than the ten days prescribed for an ordinary question.\

Short period."Short period" means duration of few days or few months. It cannot be few years. [*Shreenidhi Kumar v. Union of India*, (2012) 1 SCC 669, para 14].

Short title. The abbreviated title by which an Act is officially designated. [Indian Evidence Act (1 of 1872), S. 1 and Constitution of India, Art. 393, margin].

Short-term use. Means intended continuous use of a medical device for not less than sixty minutes but not more than thirty days. [Medical Devices Rules, 2017, R. 3(zr)].

Show. "Show" means to make clear or apparent, as by evidence, testimony, or reasoning; to prove.

To expose or exhibit to view, to make clear or evident as by evidence or reasoning [CrPC, 1973 (2 of 1974), S. 144(7)]; an act of showing; an exhibition; an entertainment.

"Showing" a case to be within the purview of a statute consists of a disclosure of the facts which prove it within such statute.

Show cause. Article 311 of the Constitution requires the showing of a cause before person is punished. This expression implies that adequate opportunity to the person concerned to establish his innocence and to controvert the contentions raised against him, is afforded. Not only this, where necessary opportunity to cross examine the witnesses of the opposite party should also be given. (*Shyam Lal* v. *State*, AIR 1954 All 235)

The opportunity given to the Government servant should be a reasonable one. He should have an opportunity to say what his case is and that he has not been guilty of any misconduct to merit any punishment at all and also that the particular punishment proposed is much more drastic and severe than what he deserves. (*Sarangthem* v. *State*, AIR 1956 Mani 34)

Show-trial. A trial usually in a non-democratic country, that is staged primarily for propagandistic purposes, with the outcome predetermined.

Showing cause. The expression does not imply that a mere opportunity of submitting an explanation is enough. It implies that adequate opportunity of leading evidence in support of the contentions raised against him must be given and where necessary, opportunity of cross-examining witnesses of the other side and of addressing arguments should also be afforded. *Shyamlal* v. *State of U.P.*, AIR 1954 All 235, 243. [Constitution of India, Art. 311].

Shrinkwrap agreement. An agreement formed with a customer wherein some terms of agreement are packed inside the package of a product such as a software. Generally in case of Shrinkwrap agreements, if the product's sale and purchase terms are not acceptable to a user after he opens the package, the product can be returned within a specified time window. [Karnika Seth, *Computers Internet and New Technology Laws*, 2021, LexisNexis, Glossary of Legal Terms]

Shrink-wrap licence. Terms of a contractual licence that are not available for review until after the product is opened and the shrinkwrap packaging is removed. (*Cyber Law*)

Si duo in testamento pugnantia reperientur, ultimum est ratum. (*Lat.*) If two provisions in a will are found to be repugnant (to each other) the last one is to be observed (given effect to).

Si quidem in nomine, cognomine, praenomine legatarii testator erraverit, cum de persona constat, nihilominus valet legatum. (*Lat.*) Though a testator may have made a mistake in the proper name or in the surname of the legatee, when it is certain who is the person meant, the legacy is nevertheless valid.

Si quis cum totum petiisset partem petat, exceptio rei judicatae vocet. If a party, when he could have sued for the entirety, sues only for a part, the judgment is *res judicata* against another suit. No one is allowed to split his cause of action.

Si quis praegnantem uxorem reliquit, non videtur sine liberis decessisse. If a man dies, leaving his wife pregnant, he shall not be considered as having died childless. (*Principia legis*)

Sic. In brackets after a word expression in a quoted passage, it indicates the quotation being exact.

Thus; in such manner; so. The word is used in the sense that the apparent error in a quotation is to be found in the original text and that the quotation itself correctly reproduced.

Sic interpretandum est ut verba accipiantur cum effectu. (A statute) is to be so interpreted that the words may be taken with effect.

Sick bays. Compartments for sick and wounded on a ship. [Geneva Conventions Act (6 of 1960), Second Sch., Art. 28].

Sick industrial company. Means an industrial company which has—

(i) the accumulated losses in any financial year equal to fifty per cent, or more of its average net worth during four years immediately preceding such financial year; or

(ii) failed to repay its debts within any three consecutive quarters on demand made in writing for its repayment by a creditor or creditors of such company. [Companies Act (1 of 1956), S. 2(46AA)]

Sick textile undertaking. Defines a 'sick textile undertaking' to mean "a textile undertaking taken over by the Central Govt. under the Industries (Development and Regulation) Act, 1951 or vested in the Central Govt. under the Sick Textile Undertakings (Taking over of Management) Act, 1972". *Kothandram Spinning Mills (P) Ltd.* v. *Union of India*, AIR 1989 SC 1331, 1332. [Sick Textile Undertakings (Nationalised) Act (57 of 1974), Ss. 2(j) and 2(f)]

A mill not resuming work by the appointed day, it having been closed for more than three months before the appointed day, and suffering continuous losses is a 'sick textile undertaking'. *Govt. of Tamil Nadu* v. *Ahobila Matam*, AIR 1987 SC 244, 245.

Sickness. "SICKNESS" means a condition which requires medical treatment and attendance and necessitates abstention from work on medical grounds. [Employees' State Insurance Act (34 of 1948), S. 2(20)]

Sickness, ailment. Insurance Contracts — Whatever the terms 'ailment' or 'sickness' may mean in the medical sense, or in accordance with their dictionary meaning, they cannot embrace merely transitory and temporary illness in its accepted sense, as they are not material to the risk insured. These terms refer to disorders of substantially serious nature affecting general health and do not include passing indisposition which do not affect the applicant's general health. *Laxmi Insurance Co. Ltd.* v. *Bibi Padmawati,* AIR 1961 Punj 253, 263.

Sight. A drawee's acceptance of a draft (payable after sight).

Sign. "SIGN" with its grammatical variations and cognate expressions shall, with reference to a person who is unable to write his name, include "mark" with its grammatical variations and cognate expressions. [General Clauses Act (10 of 1897), S. 3(56)]

"SIGN" in relation to a person who is unable to write his name means authenticate in such manner as may be prescribed. [Representation of the People Act (43 of 1951), S. 2 (1)(i)]

The definition of the word 'sign' in S. 2(1)(i) clearly envisages that an illiterate person can be a proposer and a candidate for the purpose of signing the form. [Representation of the People Act (43 of 1951), S. 2(1)(i)]

To affix a signature to; to ratify by hand or seal, to subscribe in one's own handwriting.

A signal [CrPC, 1973 (2 of 1974), S. 96(3)]; a gesture expressing a meaning [Representation of the People Act (43 of 1951, S. 130(1)(e)]; a signature (to) [CrPC, 1973 (2 of 1974), S. 64].

Where a person is unable to write his name, he may place his mark on the instrument or other paper and the requirements of law are complied with, provided he puts the mark in the presence of the Returning Officer or the presiding officer or such other officer as may be specified in this regard by the Election Commission and such officer on being satisfied as to the identity attests the mark as being the mark of that person. *Ram Dayal* v. *Brijraj Singh*, AIR 1970 SC 110 at 112. [Representation of the People Act (43 of 1951), S. 2(1)(i)]

If a testator is capable of writing but on account of weakness is unable to put his signature, he can execute the will by affixing a mark. *Sushilal Bala Saha* v. *Sarathwathi Mundal,* AIR 1991 Cal 166, 172. [Indian Succession Act (39 of 1925), S. 63(a)]

The actual signing of a written instrument in a legal sense may imply more than the clerical act of writing the name. The element of intent may enter into the act, not the intent merely to place the name on the paper, but to affix it to the instrument in token of an intention to be bound by its conditions; for a signing consists of both the act of writing a person's name and the intention in doing this to execute, authenticate, or to sign as a witness.

Significant beneficial owner. Means an individual referred to in sub-section (1) of section 90 (holding ultimate beneficial interest of not less than ten per cent.) read with sub-section (10) of section 89, but whose name is not entered in the register of members of a company as the holder of such shares, and the term 'significant beneficial ownership' shall be construed accordingly;

Explanation I.—For the purpose of this clause, the significant beneficial ownership, in case of persons other than individuals or natural persons, shall be determined as under—

(*i*) where the member is a company, the significant beneficial owner is the natural person, who, whether acting alone or together with other natural persons, or through one or more other persons or trusts, holds not less than ten per cent. share capital of the company or who exercises significant influence or control in the company through other means;

(*ii*) where the member is a partnership firm, the significant beneficial owner is the natural person, who, whether acting alone or together with other natural persons, or through one or more other persons or trusts, holds not less than ten per cent. of capital or has entitlement of not less than ten per cent. of profits of the partnership;

(*iii*) where no natural person is identified under (i) or (ii), the significant beneficial owner is the relevant natural person who holds the position of senior managing official;

(*iv*) where the member is a trust (through trustee), the identification of beneficial owner(s) shall include identification of the author of the trust, the trustee, the beneficiaries with not less than ten per cent. interest in the trust and any other natural person exercising ultimate effective control over the trust through a chain of control or ownership;

Explanation II.—It is hereby clarified that instruments in the form of global depository receipts, compulsorily convertible preference shares or compulsorily convertible debentures shall be treated as 'shares' for the purpose of this clause. [Companies (Significant Beneficial Owners) Rules, 2018, R. 2(1)(e)].

"SIGNIFICANT BENEFICIAL OWNER" in relation to a reporting company means an individual referred to in sub-section (1) of section 90, who acting alone or together, or through one or more persons or trust, possesses one or more of the following rights or entitlements in such reporting company, namely:—

(*i*) holds indirectly, or together with any direct holdings, not less than ten per cent. of the shares;

(*ii*) holds indirectly, or together with any direct holdings, not less than ten per cent. of the voting rights in the shares;

(*iii*) has right to receive or participate in not less than ten per cent. of the total distributable dividend, or any other distribution, in a financial year through indirect holdings alone, or together with any direct holdings;

(*iv*) has right to exercise, or actually exercises, significant influence or control, in any manner other than through direct holdings alone:

Explanation I.—For the purpose of this clause, if an individual does not hold any right or entitlement indirectly under sub-clauses (i), (ii) or (iii), he shall not be considered to be a significant beneficial owner.

Explanation II.—For the purpose of this clause, an individual shall be considered to hold a right or entitlement directly in the reporting company, if he satisfies any of the following criteria, namely.—

(*i*) the shares in the reporting company representing such right or entitlement are held in the name of the individual;

(*ii*) the individual holds or acquires a beneficial interest in the share of the reporting company under sub-section (2) of section 89, and has made a declaration in this regard to the reporting company.

Explanation III.—For the purpose of this clause, an individual shall be considered to hold a right or entitlement indirectly in the reporting company, if he satisfies any of the following criteria, in respect of a member of the reporting company, namely:—

(*i*) where the member of the reporting company is a body corporate (whether incorporated or registered in India or abroad), other than a limited liability partnership, and the individual,—

(*a*) holds majority stake in that member; or

(*b*) holds majority stake in the ultimate holding company (whether incorporated or registered in India or abroad) of that member;

(*ii*) where the member of the reporting company is a Hindu Undivided Family (HUF) (through karta), and the individual is the karta of the HUF;

(*iii*) where the member of the reporting company is a partnership entity (through itself or a partner), and the individual,—

(*a*) is a partner; or

(*b*) holds majority stake in the body corporate which is a partner of the partnership entity; or

(*c*) holds majority stake in the ultimate holding company of the body corporate which is a partner of the partnership entity.

(*iv*) where the member of the reporting company is a trust (through trustee), and the individual,—

(*a*) is a trustee in case of a discretionary trust or a charitable trust;

(*b*) is a beneficiary in case of a specific trust;

(*c*) is the author or settlor in case of a revocable trust.

(*v*) where the member of the reporting company is,—

(*a*) a pooled investment vehicle; or

(*b*) an entity controlled by the pooled investment vehicle, based in member State of the Financial Action Task Force on Money Laundering and the regulator of the securities market in such member State is a member of the International Organization of Securities Commissions, and the individual in relation to the pooled investment vehicle,—

(a) is a general partner; or

(b) is an investment manager; or

(c) is a Chief Executive Officer where the investment manager of such pooled vehicle is a body corporate or a partnership entity.

Explanation IV.—Where the member of a reporting company is,

(*i*) a pooled investment vehicle; or

(*ii*) an entity controlled by the pooled investment vehicle,

based in a jurisdiction which does not fulfil the requirements referred to in clause (v) of Explanation III, the provisions of clause (i) or clause (ii) or clause (iii) or clause (iv) of Explanation III, as the case may be, shall apply.

Explanation V.—For the purpose of this clause, if any individual, or individuals acting through any person or trust, act with a common intent or purpose of exercising any rights or entitlements, or exercising control or significant influence, over a reporting company, pursuant to an agreement or understanding, formal or informal, such individual, or individuals, acting through any person or trust, as the case may be, shall be deemed to be 'acting together'

Explanation VI.—For the purposes of this clause, the instruments in the form of global depository receipts, compulsorily convertible preference shares or compulsorily convertible debentures shall be treated as 'shares'.

(i) "significant influence" means the power to participate, directly or indirectly, in the financial and operating policy decisions of the reporting company but is not control or joint control of those policies'. [Companies Significant Beneficial Owners) Rules, 2018, R. 2(1)(h)].

Significant economic presence. For the removal of doubts, it is hereby clarified that the significant economic presence of a non-resident in India shall constitute "business connection" in India and "significant economic presence" for this purpose, shall mean—

(*a*) transaction in respect of any goods, services or property carried out by a non-resident in India including provision of download of data or software in India, if the aggregate of payments arising from such transaction or transactions during the previous year exceeds such amount as may be prescribed; or

(*b*) systematic and continuous soliciting of business activities or engaging in interaction with such number of users as may be prescribed, in India through digital means:

Provided that the transactions or activities shall constitute significant economic presence in India, whether or not,—

(*i*) the agreement for such transactions or activities is entered in India; or

(*ii*) the non-resident has a residence or place of business in India; or

(*iii*) the non-resident renders services in India:

Provided further that only so much of income as is attributable to the transactions or activities referred to in clause (a) or clause (b) shall be deemed to accrue or arise in India. [Income-tax Act (43 of 1961), S. 9(1)(i), *Explanation 2-A* inserted by Finance Act (13 of 2018)].

Significant-risk. Means—

(*a*) the presence of significant-risk body substances;

(*b*) a circumstance which constitutes significant-risk for transmitting or contracting HIV infection; or

(*c*) the presence of an infectious source and an uninfected person.

Explanation.—For the purpose of this clause,—

(*i*) "significant-risk body substances" are blood, blood products, semen, vaginal secretions, breast milk, tissue and the body fluids, namely, cerebrospinal, amniotic, peritoneal, synovial, pericardial and pleural;

(*ii*) "circumstances which constitute significant-risk for transmitting or contracting HIV infection" are—

(a) sexual intercourse including vaginal, anal or oral sexual intercourse which exposes an uninfected person to blood, blood products, semen or vaginal secretions of an HIV-positive person;(B) sharing of needles and other paraphernalia used for preparing and injecting drugs between HIV-positive persons and uninfected persons;

(b) the gestation, giving birth or breast feeding of an infant when the mother is an HIV-positive person;

(c) transfusion of blood, blood products, and transplantation of organs or other tissues from an HIV-positive person to an uninfected person, provided such blood, blood products, organs or other tissues have not been tested conclusively for the antibody or antigen of HIV and have not been rendered non-infective by heat or chemical treatment; and

(d) other circumstances during which a significant-risk body substance, other than breast milk, of an HIV-positive person contacts or may contact mucous membranes including eyes, nose or mouth, non-intact skin including open wounds, skin with a dermatitis condition or abraded areas or the vascular system of an uninfected person, and including such circumstances not limited to needle-stick or puncture wound injuries and direct saturation or permeation of these body surfaces by the significant-risk body substances:

Provided that "significant-risk" shall not include—

(*i*) exposure to urine, faeces, sputum, nasal secretions, saliva, sweat, tears or vomit that does not contain blood that is visible to the naked eye;

(*ii*) human bites where there is no direct blood to blood, or no blood to mucous membrane contact;

(*iii*) exposure of intact skin to blood or any other blood substance; and

(*iv*) occupational centres where individuals use scientifically accepted Universal Precautions, prohibitive techniques and preventive practices in circumstances which would otherwise pose a significant-risk and such techniques are not breached and remaining act. [Human Immunodeficiency Virus and Acquired Immune Deficiency Syndrome (Prevention and Control) Act (16 of 2017), s. 2(v)].

"Sign" and "Subscribe". Although of a different derivation than "subscribe", and although its literal meaning may have a shade or two of difference, the two words are substantially the same, except where, in a statute, or connection with a context some peculiar or additional meaning to the words is indicated. (*Ame Words and Phrases*))

Sign manual. The signature or 'Royalhard' of the sovereign, as distinguished from the signing of documents by the signet. [Indian Evidence Act (1 of 1872), S. 57(5)].

Signal intelligence (SIGINT). A category of intelligence comprising—either individually or in combination—all communications intelligence, electronics intelligence, and foreign instrumentation signals intelligence, however transmitted. (*Cyber Law*)

Signal security (SIGSEC). A generic term that includes both communications security and electronic security. (*Cyber Law*)

Signatory. Signing party of document or a treaty, personally or through an agent.

Signature. A sign or mark impressed upon anything; a stamp; a mark; the name of a person written and subscribed by himself.

Signature analysis. A biometric security measure of the user's pattern, pressure deviation, acceleration, and the length of the time needed to sign his or her name. (*Cyber Law*)

Signature, Authenticating. A signature that authenticates. [Indian Evidence Act (1 of 1872), S. 82].

Signature or sig. The personal tag used at the end of an e-mail message or posting. May include name, tel, fax, e-mail, business, *etc.* Anything from one to seven lines. Users with excessively large signatures, especially in relation to the text of their message, are often accused of having a low signal to noise ratio. In other words, the useful content is small, the noise, their sig, is large. (*Cyber Law*)

Signed. "SIGNED", save in the case of a judgment or decree includes stamped. [CPC (5 of 1908), S. 2(20)]

For the purposes of this section, "SIGNED", with its grammatical variations and cognate expressions, shall, with reference to a person, mean affixing of his hand written signature or any mark on any document and the expression "signature" shall be construed accordingly. [Information Technology Act (21 of 2000), S. 5, *Expl.*]

Signed copy. So long as there is the signature of the arbitrator or umpire on the copy of the award filed in Court and it shows that the person signing authenticated the accuracy or correctness of the copy, the document would be a signed copy of the award. *Hindustan Construction* v. *Union of India*, AIR 1967 SC 526, 527. [Arbitration Act (10 of 1940) (*repealed*), S. 14(2)]

Significant accounting transaction. For the purposes of section 455 of Act 18 of 2013, 'significant accounting transaction' means any transaction other than—

(*a*) payment of fees by a company to the Registrar;

(*b*) payments made by it to fulfil the requirements of this Act or any other law;

(*c*) allotment of shares to fulfil the requirements of this Act; and

(*d*) payments for maintenance of its office and records. [*Explanation* (*ii*) to section 455(1) of the Companies Act, 2013 (18 of 2013)]

Significant influence. For the purposes of section 2(6), the expression 'significant influence' means control of at least twenty per cent of total voting power, or control of or participation in business decisions under an agreement.. [*Explanation* to S. 2(6) of the Companies Act, 2013 (18 of 2013)]

Signify. To make known; intimate.

Signing. 'Signing' a judgement does not mean initialling but means the writing of the full name of the Magistrate or the judge.

Signing means writing one's name on some document or paper. [General Clauses Act (10 of 1897), S. 3(56)] has extended its meaning with reference to a person who is unable to write his name to include 'mark' with its grammatical variations and cognate expressions. *Hindustan Construction Co.* v. *Union of India*, AIR 1967 SC 526, 527. [Arbitration Act (10 of 1940) (*repealed*), S. 14(2).

Silence. The state of a person who does not speak, or one who refrains from speaking.

The act of abstaining or forbearing from speech or utterance, the state or condition resulting from this. [Indian Contract Act (9 of 1872), S. 17, *Expln.*].

Silence estoppel. Mere silence cannot amount to any assent. It does not even amount to any representation on which any plea of estoppel may be founded. *Bank of India* v. *R.F. Cowarjee,* AIR 1955 Bom 419, 430. [Indian Contract Act (9 of 1872), S. 3]

Silver. 'SILVER' includes silver bullion or ingot, silver sheets and plates which have undergone no process of manufacture subsequent to rolling and uncurrent silver coin which is not legal tender in India or elsewhere and jewellery or articles made wholly or mainly of silver. [Foreign Exchange Regulation Act, 1947, S. 2(l)]

SIM. (*abbr.*) Subscriber Identification Module. Plastic card which is placed in the back of a mobile phone and allows you to store information on your phone. (*Cyber Law*)

Similar. Sameness in essential particulars. Similar denotes partial resemblance, and may also denote sameness in all essential particulars. Similar offence may mean an offence identical in kind.

Similitudo legalis est casuum diversorum inter se collatorum similis ratio ; quod in uno similium valet, valebit in altero. Legal similarity is (consists in) the like reason of different cases when compared together, that which has force in one of the like cases shall have force in the other.

Simple. With nothing added as distinguished from rigorous [CrPC, 1973 (2 of 1974), S. 426(3)]; as distinguished from compound. [Indian Trusts Act (2 of 1882), S. 23].

Simple counter. Graphical count of visitors to your Web site, which appears on your Web page. (*Cyber Law*)

Simple imprisonment. That variety of imprisonment in which the convict is not required to work or labour. [CrPC, 1973 (2 of 1974), S. 426(3)].

Simple interest. That interest on the amount of which no interest is added. [Indian Trusts Act (2 of 1882), S. 23].

Simple mortgagee. "Where, without delivering possession of the mortgaged property, the mortgagor binds himself personally to pay the mortgage money, and agrees expressly or impliedly, that in the event of his failing to pay according to his contract, the mortgagee shall have a right to cause the mortgaged property to be sold and the proceeds of sale be applied, so far as may be necessary, in payment of the mortgage-money, the transaction is called a simple mortgage and the mortgagee is a SIMPLE MORTGAGEE." [T.P. Act (4 of 1882), S.58(b)]

A person in whose favour a simple mortgage is made. [T.P. Act (4 of 1882), S. 58(b)].

Simple obligation. An obligation which does not depend for its execution on any event provided for by the parties; one not based on a contingency.

Simple trust. The simple trust is where property is vested in one person upon trust for another; and the nature of the trust, not being prescribed by the settlor, is left to the "construction of law". (*Lewin*)

Simulation prototyping. Allows e-commerce specialists to quickly analyze and predict the performance of the e-commerce site before its final implementation. (*Cyber Law*)

Simultaneous execution. Execution of two or more things at the same time. [CPC (5 of 1908), O. XXI, R. 21].

Simultaneously. At the same time; in a simultaneous manner. [Hindu Succession Act (30 of 1956), S. 16, R. 1 and S. 21].

Sine die. Without appointment of a day to appear again.

Without day; without assigning a day for a further meeting or hearing. Hence, a legislative body adjourns *sine die*, when it adjourns without appointing a day on which to appear or assemble again.

Sine qua non. An indispensable condition. An indispensable requisite.

Sine scripto jus venit, quod usus approbavit, nam diuturni mores consensu utentium comprobati legem imitantur. (1 Bl. Comm. 74). Writing is not necessary to make that law which custom has rendered binding; for customs of long duration, sanctioned by common consent, resemble or stand in the place of law.

Single judge. One judge when acting judicially or when presiding over a Court of justice. [Constitution of India, Art. 145(2)].

Single member constituency. A constituency from which one member is to be elected. [Two Member Constituencies (Abolition Act (1 of 1961), S. 6].

Singular. "Unless contrary appears from the context, the words importing singular number include the plural number, and the words importing the plural number include the singular number." [IPC (45 of 1860), S. 9]

Sink. "SINK" with all its grammatical variations and cognate expressions in relation to a well includes any drilling, boring, or digging of a new well or deepening carried out to an existing well. [A.P. Ground Water (Regulation for Drinking Water Purposes Act (7 of 1996), S. 2(10)]

"SINK" means any process, activity or mechanism which removes a green house gas, an aerosol or a precursor of a green-house from the atmosphere. [U.N. Framework Convention on Climate Change, 1992, Art. 1(8)]

Sinking fund. A fund set up and accumulated by usually regular payments or interest earning deposits for paying off the principal of a debt when it falls due; a fund formed by periodically setting aside revenue to accumulate at interest usually for the purpose of reducing the principal of a national, municipal or company's debt. [Indian Trusts Act (2 of 1882), S. 20(b)].

A fund arising from particular taxes, imposts or duties which is appropriated towards the payment of the interest due on a public loan and for the gradual payment of the principal.

Site. Means, any location where hazardous chemicals are manufactured or processed, stored, handled, used, disposed of and includes the whole of an area under the control of an occupier and includes pier, jetty or similar structure whether floating or not. [Chemical Accidents (Emergency Planning, Preparedness, and Response) Rules, 1996, R. 2(k) and Rule 2(k) of the Manufacture, Storage and Import of Hazardous Chemicals Rules, 1989, R. 2(m)]

'SITE' means the ground or the land on which the house stands and would not include a terrace or other open portion of the building on which an additional construction is made. *Dattatraya son of B. Bhalerao* v. *State of Maharashtra*, AIR 1986 Bom 295, 298. [C.P. and Berar Letting of Houses and Rent Control Order (1949), Clauses 2(3) and 30]

The word 'site' connotes a place habitually devoted to some purpose. *Biss* v. *Smallburgh Rural District Council*, (1964) 2 All ER 543, 554 (CA). [Caravan Sites and Control of Development Act, 1960, S. 1(4), S. 13(a)]

Site marketing. A combination of traditional and Web marketing tools used to promote the e-commerce site. (*Cyber Law*)

Site office. Means a sub-office of the Project office established at the site of a project but does not include a Liaison office. [Foreign Exchange Management (Establishment in India of Branch or Office or Other Place of Business) Regulations, 2000, Reg. 2(g)]

Site formation and clearance, excavation, and earthmoving and demolition. "SITE FORMATION AND CLEARANCE, EXCAVATION AND EARTHMOVING AND DEMOLITION" includes,—

(i) drilling, boring and core extraction services for construction, geophysical, geological or similar purposes; or

(ii) soil stabilization; or

(iii) horizontal drilling for the passage of cables or drain pipes; or

(iv) land reclamation work; or

(v) contaminated top soil stripping work; or

(vi) demolition and wrecking of building, structure or road,

but does not include such services provided in relation to agriculture, irrigation, watershed development and drilling, digging, repairing, renovating or restoring of water sources or water bodies. [Finance Act (32 of 1994), S. 65 (97a) *as inserted by Finance Act (18 of 2005), S. 88(a)(xix)* now repealed by Central Goods and Services Tax Act, 2017]

Site submission. Submits your site information to a database of over 1600 search engines, link engines, and directories. (*Cyber Law*)

Sitting. The active presence or meeting of a body of persons in their seats with authority to transact business. [Constitution of India, Art. 91(2)].

Sitting in a suit. When two or more Judges of the Small Cause Court are sitting together for the purpose of exercising the jurisdiction conferred by S. 38 of the Presidency Small Cause Courts Act (15 of 1882) they are sitting in a suit within the meaning of those words in S. 61.

Sitting member. In relation to either House of Parliament or of the Legislature of the existing State of Madhya Pradesh means a person who immediately before the appointed day, is a member of that House. [Madhya Pradesh Reorganisation Act (28 of 2000), S. 2(i)]

Sittings in camera. Sittings other than sittings in open Court. This course is often adopted for the hearing of cases where a public hearing would defeat the ends of justice, or on the ground of public decency.

Situate. The word, "situate", means to set, place, locate. [*Vodafone International Holding BV v. Union of India*, (2012) 6 SCC 613, para 397].

Situated. Located. [T.P. Act (4 of 1882), S. 3, *Expln.* 1].

Situation awareness (SA). Sometimes termed "situational awareness." The perception of the elements in the environment within a volume of time and space, the comprehension of their meaning, and the projection of their status in the near future. This term is broadly used to denote the state of awareness that a subject (operator; pilot) has in the course of a task at a given point in time. (*Cyber Law*)

Situation, responsible. A position of responsibility [CPC (5 of 1908), 1st Sch., App. A, form No. 22].

Skelp and strips. Skelp—a plate of wrought iron or steel used for making pipe or tubing by rolling the skelp into shape and lap welding or rivetting edges together. Strip—a flat, rolled product of smaller cross-section than sheet or bar. *Union of India* v. *Tata Iron and Steel Co. Ltd.*, AIR 1975 SC 769, 771. [Central Excises and Salt Act (1 of 1944), Schedule 1, item 26-AA (iii)]

Sketch. "SKETCH" includes any photograph or other mode of representing any place or thing. [Official Secrets Act (19 of 1923), S. 2(9)]

Skilful person. A person having skill. [Indian Evidence Act (1 of 1872), S. 21, ill. (e)].

Skill. The art of doing a thing as it ought to be done.

Practical knowledge in combination with ability. [Indian Contract Act (9 of 1872), S. 212].

Skilled employee. A trained teacher is not described in industrial field or service jurisprudence as a 'skilled employee'. Such adjective generally is used for employee doing manual or technical work. *Ahmedabad Pvt. Primary Teachers' Association* v. *Administrative Officer*, AIR 2004 SC 1426 : 2004 AIR SCW 356.

Skilled witness. A person called to give evidence in a matter relating to his own trade or profession.

Skipper "SKIPPER" means a subordinate officer in command of a ship. [Coast Guard Act (30 of 1978), S. 2(v)]

Slander. Defamatory words spoken of another. [Limitation Act (36 of 1963), Sch., Art. 76].

The maliciously defaming of a man in his reputation, profession or livelihood, by words. (*Tomlin*)

Oral defamation. (*Cyber Law*)

Slander per se. Categories of oral defamation in which damages to reputation are presumed to exist. (*Cyber Law*)

Slaughter. "SLAUGHTER" means killing by any method whatsoever and includes maiming and inflicting of personal injury which in the ordinary course will cause death. [Orissa Prevention of Cow Slaughter Act, 1960 (Orissa Act No. 5 of 1961), S. 2(e) and Goa, Daman & Diu Prevention of Cow Slaughter Act (13 of 1978), S. 2(d)]

Slaughter-house. "SLAUGHTER HOUSE" means any place ordinarily used for the slaughter of animals for the purpose of selling the flesh thereof for human consumption. [Cantonments Act (2 of 1924), S. 2(xxxiv) and Manipur Municipalities Act (43 of 1994), S. 2(56)]

A house or place where the animals are killed for food. [CPC (5 of 1908), 1st Sch., App. A, form No.. 36].

"SLAUGHTER-HOUSE" means any place used for the slaughter of cattle, sheep, goats, kids or pigs for the purpose of selling the flesh thereof as meat.

SLIP. (*abbr.*) *Serial Lin, Internet Protocol.* Allows devices to use IP over communications links-being superseded by PPP. (*Cyber Law*)

Slowdown. An organized effort by the workers to decrease production with a view to pressurise the employer to fulfil their demand.

Slum areas. Highly congested urban residential areas characterised by deteriorated unsanitary buildings, poverty and social disorganisation. [Delhi (Delegation of Powers) Act (23 of 1964), Sch., item 5].

Slum clearance. Means the clearance of any slum area by the demolition or removal of buildings therefrom. [Slum Areas (Improvement and Clearance) Act (96 of 1956), S. 2(i) and Gujarat Slum Areas (Improvement Clearance and Redevelopment) Act (11 of 1973), S. 2(m)]

Slum dwellers. The term 'slum dwellers' includes poor inhabiting a crowded place in a city. Persons belonging to the low and middle income groups and living in abodes in crowded places in a city, no better than slums, are slum dwellers in a sense. *Sivaprakasa* v. *State of Madras,* AIR 1964 Mad 115, 117.

Slump. A sudden serious fall of prices, business, *etc.*

Slump sale. Means the transfer of one or more undertakings as a result of the sale for a lump sum consideration without values being assigned to the individual assets and liabilities in such sales. [Income-tax Act (43 of 1961), S. 2(42C)]

Slurry. 'Slurry' is a residue, rejector waste of an industrial process consisting of mud, ash, oily substances, water and carbonaceous ingredients. *Kundori Labour Co-operative Society Ltd.* v. *State of Bihar*, AIR 1986 Pat 242, 246. [Mines and Minerals (Regulation and Development) Act (67 of 1957), S. 3(a)]

Slush fund. Money set aside for some unspecified purpose.

Small cause. Means a suit of the nature cognizable by a Court of Small Causes.

Small Cause Court. A category of Court having jurisdiction to try civil cases summarily. [CPC (5 of 1908), O. L, R. 1(a)(i)].

Small Cause Court judgment. A Court of Small Causes need not give reasons for its decision and need not give even a concise statement of the case.

Small coin. Means any coin of the value of less than one rupee, which is legal tender under the Indian Coinage Act, 1906. [Small Coins (Offences) Act (52 of 1971), S. 2(b)]

Small company. Means a company, other than a public company,—

(*i*) paid-up share capital of which does not exceed fifty lakh rupees or such higher amount as may be prescribed which shall not be more than ten crore rupees; or

(*ii*) turnover of which as per profit and loss account for the immediately preceding financial year does not exceed two crore rupees or such higher amount as may be prescribed which shall not be more than one hundred crore rupees:

Provided that nothing in this clause shall apply to—

(*A*) a holding company or a subsidiary company;

(*B*) a company registered under section 8; or

(*C*) a company or body corporate governed by any special Act. [S. 2(85) of the Companies Act, 2013 (18 of 2013)]

"Small company" means a company, other than a public company,—

(i) paid-up share capital of which does not exceed fifty lakh rupees or such higher amount as may be prescribed which shall not be more than five crore rupees; or

(ii) turnover of which as per its last profit and loss account does not exceed two crore rupees or such higher amount as may be prescribed which shall not be more than twenty crore rupees:

Provided that nothing in this clause shall apply to—

(A) a holding company or a subsidiary company;

(B) a company registered under section 8; or

(C) a company or body corporate governed by any special Act. [Companies Act (18 of 2013), S. 2(85)].

Small farmer. "SMALL FARMER" means a farmer who possesses more than two hectares but less than four hectares if he is a member of any of the Scheduled Tribes, and more than one hectare but less than two hectares in other cases of land, either as an owner or as a *raiyat* or as a share cripper. [West Bengal Relief of Rural Indebtedness Act (41 of 1975), S. 2(m)]

"SMALL FARMER" means a cultivator with an unirrigated land holding up to two hectares or with an irrigated land holding up to one hectare, but more than the holding of a marginal farmer. [S. 3(ze) of the Right to Fair Compensation & Transparency in Land Acquisition, Rehabilitation & Resettlement Act, 2013 (30 of 2013)]

Small holder. "SMALL HOLDER" means an agriculturist cultivating less than one-ninth of the ceiling area and who earns his livelihood principally by agriculture, or by agricultural labour. [Maharashtra Agricultural Lands (Ceiling on Holdings) Act (27 of 1961), S. 2(29) deleted by Mah. 21 of 1975].

Small quantity. In relation to narcotic drugs and psychotropic substances, means any quantity lesser than the quantity specified by the Central Government by notification in the Official Gazette. [Narcotic Drugs and Psychotropic Substance Act (61 of 1985), S. 2(xxiiia).

Small scale industrial concern. Means an industrial concern in which the investment in plant and machinery is not in excess of seven and a half lakhs of rupees or such higher amount not exceeding twenty lakhs of rupees, as the Central Government may, by notification in the Official Gazette, specify in this behalf having regard to the trends in industrial development and other relevant factors. [Banking Regulation Act (10 of 1949), S. 5(na)]

Small scale industrial undertaking. Means means an industrial undertaking which is, as on the last day of the previous year, regarded as a small-scale industrial undertaking under section 11B of the Industries

(Development and Regulation) Act, 1951 (65 of 1951). [Income-tax Act (43 of 1961), S. 80IB (14)(g)]

Small scale industry. "SMALL SCALE INDUSTRY" means industrial concerns in the small scale sector and "industrial concern in the small scale sector" means an industrial concern—

(i) in which the investment in machinery and plant is not in excess of rupees twenty lakhs or such higher amounts as the Central Government may specify by notification in this behalf having regard to trend in industrial development and other relevant factors and

(ii) which is not an industrial concern in the tiny and decentralised sector. [National Bank for Agriculture and Rural Development Act (61 of 1981), S. 2(t) omitted by Act 7 of 2018].

Small shareholders. For the purposes of section 151 of Act 18 of 2013, 'small shareholders' means a shareholder holding shares of nominal value of not more than twenty thousand rupees or such other sum as may be prescribed. [*Explanation* to section 151 of the Companies Act, 2013 (18 of 2013)]

Smaller grower. Means an owner whose estate does not exceed fifty acres in area. [Rubber Act (24 of 1947), S. 2(k)]

Smart card. A hardware token that incorporates one or more Integrated Circuit (IC) Chips to implement cryptographic functions and that possesses some inherent resistance to tampering. (*Information Technology*)

Stored financial value and other important personal and financial information used for online payments. (*Cyber Law*)

Similar to tokens, they have the added feature of portability; users may access data even at offsite computers. (*Cyber Law*)

S/MIME. A specification for E-Mail security exploiting a cryptographic message syntax in an Internet MIME environment. (*Information Technology*)

Smilies or Emoticons. Punctuation used to impart emotions within e-mail messages. Particularly in Newsgroups. When viewed at ninety degrees, they represent the human face. For example:-) = happy,:—(= sad, :-o = amazement. (*Cyber Law*)

Smoking. Means smoking of tobacco in any form whether in the form of cigarette, cigar, *beedis* or otherwise with the aid of a pipe, wrapper or any other instruments. [Cigarettes and other Tobacco Products (Prohibition of Advertisement and Regulation of Trade, Commerce, Production, Supply and Distribution Act (34 of 2003), S. 3(n); Himachal Pradesh Prohibition of Smoking and Non-smoking Health Protection Act (H.P. Act No. 17 of 1997), S. 2(g)]

SMTP. (*abbr.*) Simple Mail Transfer Protocol. The Internet protocol for transporting mail. (*Information Technology*)

The standard set of rules for transferring e-mail messages from one computer to another. (*Cyber Law*)

The main protocol used to send electronic mail from to *server* on the Internet. SMTP is defined in *RFC* 821 and modified by many later RFC's. (*Matisse Enzer-Glossary of Internet Terms*)

The main protocol used to send electronic mail on the Internet.

SMTP consists of a set of rules for how a program sending mail and a program receiving mail should interact.

Almost all Internet email is sent and received by clients and servers using SMTP, thus if one wanted to set up an email server on the Internet, one would look for email server software that supports SMTP. (*Internet and E-commerce*)

Smuggle. Convey clandestinely into (or out of) a country or district in order to avoid payment of duties imposed by law or in contravention of some enactment. [Indian Contract Act (9 of 1972), S. 58, ill.].

Smuggled goods. Smuggled goods mean goods which have been imported by avoiding the payment of the customs duty leviable thereon, or by evading the legal order of prohibition or restriction on the import of such goods. *Sitaram Agarwalla* v. *State,* AIR 1962 Cal 370, 373.

Smuggling. "SMUGGLING", in relation to goods, means any act or omission which will render such goods liable to confiscation under S. 111 or S. 113 of the Customs Act. [Customs Act (52 of 1962), S. 2(39)]

The word 'smuggling' means not only going out of the country and coming back with goods which are contraband or to evade duty but also to encourage such activities as well by dealing in such goods. *Sitthi Zuraina Begum* v. *Union of India,* (2002) 10 SCC 448, para 9. [COFEPOSA Act (52 of 1974), S. 3(1)(i)]

Snatching. Theft is snatching if, in order to commit theft, the offender suddenly or quickly or forcibly seizes or secures or grabs or takes away from any person or from his possession any movable property. [(w. e. f. 1-7-2024) Bharatiya Nyaya Sanhita, 2023 (45 of 2023), section 304(1)]

Sniff/Sniffing. The act of surreptitiously monitoring data streams so as to intercept and capture exploitable information. (*Cyber Law*)

Sniffer. A tool used to intercept potentially exploitable data from the traffic on a network. A program to capture data across a computer network. Used by hackers to capture user-ID names and passwords. Software tool that audits and identifies network traffic packets. (*Cyber Law*)

SNMP. (*abbr.*) Simple Network Management Protocol. A set of standards for communication with devices connected to a TCP/IP *network.* Examples of these devices include *routers,* hubs, and switches.

SNMP is defined in *RFC* 1089 (*Matisse Enzer Glossary of Internet Terms*)

A set of standards for communication with devices connected to a TCP/IP network. Examples of these devices include routers, hubs, and switches.

A device is said to be "SNMP compatible" if it can be monitored and/or controlled using SNMP messages, SNMP messages are known as "PDU's"-Protocol Data Units.

Devices that are SNMP compatible contain SNMP "agent" software to receive, send, and act upon SNMP messages.

Some SNMP software is designed to handle a wide variety of devices. (*Internet and E-commerce*)

So. In this manner or degree; thus; on this account; in a high degree. "So COMPLETED", or "so ALTERED" — imports the doing of the thing in the manner and so as to satisfy the requirements previously prescribed.

So far as may be. To the extent possible. [CrPC, 1973 (2 of 1974), S. 250(4)].

So far as may be practicable. To the extent a thing is capable of being carried out in action or feasible. [CPC (5 of 1908), S. 158].

So help me God. The formula with which an oath concludes when the words of it are repeated by the person swearing.

So help you God. The formula with which the administration of an oath always concludes.

So long as. During and up to the end of the time that; as long as [CrPC, 1973 (2 of 1974), S. 389(3)]; [Industrial Finance Corporation Act (15 of 1948) (*Repealed by Act 23 of 1993*), S. 32(2), *Prov*.].

Social audit. Means the process in which people collectively monitor and evaluate the planning and implementation of a programme or scheme. [S. 2(20) of the National Food Security Act, 2013 (20 of 2013)]

Social boycott. "Social boycott" means a refusal to permit a person to render to other person or receive from him any customary service or to abstain from social relations that one would maintain with other person or it isolate him from other. [Schedule Castes and the Scheduled Tribes (Prevention from Atrocities) Act (33 of 1989), S. 2(1)(eb) as inserted by Amending Act (1 of 2016)].

Social engineering. A term that denotes criminal intent of stealing information from vulnerable people on the internet who reveal passwords or other information on social networking sites or otherwise. The technique is rampantly used on the internet by cybercriminals to commit net banking and credit card thefts through phishing or baiting unsuspecting internet users or in other words, netizens. [Karnika Seth, *Computers Internet and New Technology Laws*, 2021, LexisNexis, Glossary of Legal Terms].

Social justice. Social justice has been attained in the Indian Constitution by abolition of all sorts of discrimination which originates from wealth, race, caste, religion or title. It is these factors which tend to increase exploitation of one class by another. By giving social justice in the shape of various Articles, this has been avoided. Social justice tends to harmonise the rival claim and interests of different classes in society. It is only by giving social justice to masses that we can really fulfil the dream of welfare State. *Crown Aluminium Work* v. *Workmen,* AIR 1958 SC 30; *Muir Mills* v. *Suti Mills Union,* (1955) 1 SCR 991; *Express Newspaper* v. *Union of India,* AIR 1958 SC 578; *R.S. Swamiji* v. *State of Mysore,* AIR 1966 SC 1172 at 1175.

Social justice adjudication. Prof. (Dr.) N.R. Adhava Menon has explained the meaning and contour of social justice adjudication as the application of equality jurisprudence evolved by Parliament and the Supreme Court in myriad situations presented before courts where unequal parties are pitted in adversarial proceedings and where courts are called upon to dispense equal justice. Apart from the socio-economic inequalities accentuating the disabilities of the poor in an unequal fight, the adversarial process itself operates to the disadvantage of the weaker party. In such a situation the court has to be not only sensitive to the inequalities of the parties involved but also positively undivided to the weaker party, if the imbalance were not to result in miscarriage of justice. The courts, in such situations, generally invoke the principle of fairness and equality which are essential for dispensing justice. Purposive interpretation is given to subserve the ends of justice particularly when the cases of vulnerable groups are decided. The court has to keep in mind the "problem solving approach" by adopting therapeutic approaches to the maximum extent the law permits rather than "just deciding" cases, thereby bridging the gap between law and life, between law and justice. The notion of access to justice is to be taken in a broader sense. The objective is to render justice to the needy and that means fair solutions to the conflict thereby providing real access to "justice". [*Narendera* v. *State of U.P.*, (2017) 9 SCC 426, para 11].

Social network. Is a group of individuals connected socially over a network due to common interests, friendship, dislike or views on a subject. Individual participants in a network are sometimes referred to as 'Nodes'. Facebook and Twitter form two of the most popular social networks in the cyberspace that allows one to invite and add new contacts in the network to share views and ideas about any topic of one's interest. [Karnika Seth, *Computers Internet and New Technology Laws*, 2021, LexisNexis, Glossary of Legal Terms].

Social sector. Includes unorganised sector, informal sector, economically vulnerable or backward classes and other categories of persons, both in rural and urban areas. [Insurance Regulatory and Development Authority (Obligations of Insurers to Rural or Social Sectors) Regulations, 2000, Rgn. 2(d)]

"Social security". Means the measures of protection afforded to employees, unorganised workers, gig workers and platform workers to ensure access to health care and to provide income security, particularly in cases of old age, unemployment, sickness, invalidity, work injury, maternity or loss of a breadwinner by means of rights conferred on them and schemes framed, under this Code. [Code on Social Security, 2020 (36 of 2020), section 2(78)]

Socialist. The term 'socialist' occurring in Preamble of the Constitution has both an economic as well as a political content. It is incorporated in the Preamble not for mere ornamentation but it is put with a definite object. The basic needs of a citizen in a civilized country with any form of government are food, clothing, education and health services. [*Lakshmi Charan Sen* v. *A.K.M. Hassan*, (1985) 4 SCC 689, 711, p. 32]

Socially and economically backward. If the cast is to be taken into consideration then for finding out socially and economically backward class, creamy layer of the caste is to be eliminated for granting benefit of reservation because that creamy layer cannot be termed as 'socially and economically backward'. [*Indra Sawhney* v. *Union of India,* (2000) 1 SCC 168, 200]

Socially and economically backward classes. The backward classes mentioned in Article 16(4) refers to weaker sections of the citizens as contemplated by Articles 16(4), Article 46 and Article 340 of the Constitution of India. (*V.H. Pillai* v. *State,* 1967 SLR 553)

Socially and educationally backward. In considering the scope and extent of the expression "backward classes" under Article 15(4) of Constitution of India, it is necessary to remember that the concept of backwardness is not intended to be relative in the sense that any classes who are backward in relation to the most advanced classes of the society should be included in it. If such relative tests were to be applied by reason of the most advanced classes, there would be several layers or strata of backward classes and each one of them may claim to be included under Article 15(4). [*M.R. Balaji and others* v. *State of Mysore*, (1963) Supp 1 SCR 439]

Socially and educationally backward classes. The expression 'socially and educationally backward classes' occurring in Article 15(4) of the Constitution is comparable to Scheduled Castes and Scheduled Tribes. The homogeneity of the class of citizens is social and educational backwardness. These are groups other than groups based on caste. [*State of U.P.* v. *Pradip Tandon*, (1975) 1 SCC 267, 274, p. 16 *See also M.R. Balaji* v. *State of Mysore*, AIR 1963 SC 649 : (1963) Supp 1 SCR 439. [Constitution of India, Art. 15(4)]

Society. 'SOCIETY' includes a company, institution, club or other association of persons by whatever name called. [Delhi Entertainments and Betting Tax Act, 1996 (8 of 1997), S. 2(q)]

An association organised under law for some recognised civil or business purpose [Land Acquisition Act (1 of 1894), S. 3(cc)]; the aggregate of persons living together in a more or less ordered community.

Socket. A receptacle, usually on a motherboard, that processors or chips can be inserted into. (*Cyber Law*)

Sodomite. One who has been guilty of sodomy.

Sodomy. Sodomy, in its broadest meaning, is the carnal copulation by human beings with each other against nature or with a beast, in which sense it includes the crime against nature, bestiality, and buggery. In its narrower sense, sodomy is the carnal copulation between two male human beings, *per* anus.

Carnal copulation committed by a human being with another human being *per* anus. [Hindu Marriage Act (25 of 1955), S. 13(2)(ii)].

"Sodomy" means "carnal intercourse against the order of nature". [*Suresh Kumar Koushal* v. *Naz Foundation*, (2014) 1 SCC 1, para 60].

Sodomy is non-coital, carnal copulation with a member of the same or opposite sex *e.g. per* anus or *per os*. A man may indulge in sodomy even with his own wife. *Grace Jayamani* v. *E.P. Peter,* AIR 1962 Kant 46, 48, 49. [Indian Divorce Act (4 of 1869), S. 10]

Soft coke. Means all coke which is unsuitable for being used in metallurgical industriest. [Coal Mines (Conservation and Safety) Act (12 of 1952), S. 3(i)]

Software. Means any computer programme, database, drawing, design, audio/video signals, any information by whatever name called in or on any medium other than in or on any physical medium. [Foreign Exchange Management (Export of Goods and Services) Regulations, 2000, Reg. 2(*viii*)]

A 'software' is a computer programme. It consists of instructions that make hardware work. There are two type of softwares, namely, system software which controls the working of the computer and application software such as word processing programme, databases, etc., which perform the tasks for which we use computers. [*Commr. of Custom* v. *Hewlett Packard India Sales (P) Ltd.*, (2007) 8 SCC 404, 410, para 17]

If software is required to load a program on the computer, then the program which has to be loaded on the computer continues to be 'software'. Simply because the 'motion capture animation files' requires another software known as 'soft image' to get the final result does not detract the goods from being 'software'. [*Commr. of Customs* v. *Pentamedia Graphics Ltd.* (2006) 9 SCC 502, 506, p. 12] [Customs Tariff Act (51 of 1975), Exemption Notification No. 20/99 Cus. Dated 28.2.1999]

Software piracy. This is the act of duplicating and distributing copyright-protected materials without authorization from or payment to the copyright owner. (*Cyber Law*)

Software technology park. Means any park set up in accordance with the Software Technology Park Scheme notified by the Government of India in the Ministry of Commerce and Industry. [Income Tax Act (43 of 1961), S. 10A(vii)]

Solatium. Consolation; compensation; sentimental damages.

Sold. Includes a transfer by way of exchange or a compulsory acquisition under any law for the time being in force but does not include a transfer, in a scheme of amalgamation, of any asset by the amalgamating company to the amalgamated company where the amalgamated company is an Indian Company. [Income-tax Act (43 of 1961), S. 42(2)]

Soldier. "SOLDIER" means any person who is a soldier or a sailor or an airman subject to the Army Act, 1950, the Navy Act, 1957 or the Air Force Act, 1950 as the case may be, and who is not a military officer. [Cantonments Act (2 of 1924), S. 2(xxxv)]

Sole. Alone, single, used in contradistinction to joint or married (as) *feme sole* or corporation sole.

Sole or principal office. The only or main office. [CPC (5 of 1908), S. 20].

Solely responsible. Exclusively responsible. [T.P. Act (4 of 1882), S. 69A(3)].

Sole proprietorship. Means a business that legally has no separate existence from its owner and the income and losses are taxed on the individual's personal income tax return. [Insurance Ombudsman Rules, 2017, R. 4(1)(j)].

Solemn. Formal; in regular form.

Solemn affirmation. Statements made upon solemn affirmation must be taken to be statements upon solemn declaration.

An affirmation made with due formality or ceremony. [IPC (45 of 1860), S. 51].

Solemnisation. A ceremony before some authorised person. [Child Marriage Restraint Act (19 of 1929), preamble]; [Special Marriage Act (43 of 1954), S. 4].

Solemnised. Performed with the ceremony or according to legal forms. [Hindu Marriage Act (25 of 1955), S. 5].

Solemnize. The word 'solemnize' means, in connection with a marriage, 'to celebrate the marriage, with proper ceremonies and in due form', according to the shorter Oxford Dictionary. *Bhaurao Shankar Lokhande* v. *State of Maharashtra*, AIR 1965 SC 1564, 1565. [Hindu Marriage Act (25 of 1955), S. 17]

Solicit. To entreat (a person) for or to do something; to importune. [IPC (45 of 1860), S. 363A(4)(a)(ii)].

Solicitation. Asking repeatedly; request.

Solicitor. One properly qualified and formally admitted to practise as a law-agent in any Court. [Indian Evidence Act (1 of 1872), S. 32, ill. (c)].

Solicitor-General. The Solicitor-General in England is one of the law officers of the Crown. He is not a member of the Cabinet; but is a Minister of the Crown, and a member of the House of Commons, and the duration of his office depends upon the continuance in power of the party to which he belongs. He is an *ex officio* member of the General Council of the Bar. His duties are substantially the same as those of the Attorney-General to whom he is subordinate. He has full power to represent the Crown in the absence of the Attorney-General; and the whole business and authority of the A.G. during a vacancy in his office devolve upon the Solicitor General. (*R* v. *Wilkes*, (1770) 4 Burr. 2554)

Solitary confinement. That variety of imprisonment during which a convict is segregated from other convicts and kept alone. [IPC (45 of 1860), Ss. 73 and 74].

In a general sense, the separate confinement of a prisoner, with only occasional access to any other person, and that only at the discretion of the jailor; in a stricter sense, the complete isolation of prisoner from all human society, and his confinement in a cell so arranged that he has no direct intercourse with or sight of any human being, and no employment or instruction.

Solo cedit, quicuid solo plantatur. What is affixed to the soil belongs to the soil. (*Latin for Lawyers*)

Solo cedit quod solo implantatur. (*In the civil Law*) That which is planted in the soil belongs to the soil.

Solo cedit quod solo inaedificatur. That which is built upon the soil belongs to the soil.

Solvency. Ability to discharge debts and obligations in full; the state of a person who is able to pay all his debts; as also such state of his property as may be reached and subjected by process of law, without his consent, to the payment of such debts.

Ability to discharge all debts and obligations in full. [T.P. Act (4 of 1882), S. 133].

Solvent. One who has sufficient means to pay his debts and all obligations.

Able to discharge one's debts and obligations in full [Indian Evidence Act (1 of 1872), S. 14, ill. (f)]; anything that dissolves another. [Income-tax Act (43 of 1961), 5th Sch. item 31].

Some person executing. The expression 'some person executing' means the person actually and in fact executing the document and it does not refer to the principal who may be considered to be executing the document by means of an agent. *Ram Gopal* v. *L. Mohan Lal,* AIR 1960 Punj 226, 229. [Registration Act (16 of 1908), S. 32(a)]

Some portion of the property. The expression "some portion of the property" in S. 28 of the Registration Act (16 of 1908) means not a substantial portion, but any portion of the property.

Somnambulism. Sleep-walking. The mental condition in this affection is not very unlike that of dreaming. Many of their phenomena are the same; and the former differs from the latter chiefly in the larger number of the functions involved in the abnormal process. In addition to the mental activity common to both, the somnambulist enjoys the use of his senses in some degree, and the power of locomotion. He is thereby enabled to perform manual operations as well, frequently as in his waking state.

Usually, however the action of the senses is more or less imperfect, many of the impressions being incorrectly or not at all perceived. The person walks against a wall, or stumbles over an object in his path;

he mistakes some projections for a horse, strides across it, and imagines himself to be riding; he hears the faintest sound connected with what he is doing, while the voices of persons near him, and even the blast of a trumpet are entirely unnoticed. For the most part, he operates asleep, groping about in the dark, endeavouring to make his way out of the house through doors or windows, making some inarticulate sounds, perhaps, and all the while unconscious of persons or things around. The power of the perceptive faculties, as well as that of the senses, is sometimes increased in a wonderful degree.

The somnambulist always, awakes suddenly, and has but a faint conception, if any, of what he has been thinking and doing. If conscious of anything, it is of an unpleasant dream imperfectly remembered. This fact, not being generally known will often enable us to detect simulated somnambulism. If the person on waking continues the same train of thought and pursues the same plans and purposes which he did while asleep, there can be no doubt that he is feigning the affection. When a real somnambulist for some criminal purpose undertakes to simulate a paroxysm, he is not at all likely to imitate one of his own previous paroxysms, for the simple reason that he knows less than others how he appeared while in them. If, therefore, somnambulism is alleged in any given case, with no other proof than the occurrence of former paroxysms unquestionably genuine, it must be viewed with suspicion if the character of the alleged paroxysm differs materially from that of the genuine ones. In one way or other, a case of simulation would generally be detected by means of a close and intelligent scrutiny, so difficult is it to imitate the mixture of consciousness and unconsciousness, of dull and sharp perceptions, which somnambulism presents. The history of the individual may throw some light on the matter.

The legal consequences of somnambulism should be precisely those of insanity, which it so nearly resembles. The party should be exempt from punishment for his criminal acts. (Tayl. Med. Jur. 744. See Grey Med. Jur. 265; Whart & S. Med. Jur, 492; *Rush on the Mind 302, 18 Am Journ. of Ins 236; Ency of the Laws of England; Ame Cyc.*)

Son. "SON", in the case of any one whose personal law permits adoption, shall include an adopted son. [General Clauses Act (10 of 1897), S. 3(57)].

In the absence of any definition or explanation to the effect that the word 'son' would also include a step-son, that word should be given its natural meaning, if so, a son of a deceased female would mean a male issue of the body of that deceased female. *Mallappa Fakirappa Sauna Nagashetti* v. *Shivappa,* AIR 1962 Mys 140, 146. [Hindu Succession Act (30 of 1956), S. 15(1)(a)]

The term 'son' should be the son of the female Hindu, even though she might have been married once or more than once and might have given birth to children from these marriages. *Gurnam Singh* v. *Kaur,* AIR 1977 P&H 103, 108.

'Sons in Mitakshara Chapter II, 6 (1) includes grandson'.

"Sons" in Cl. (a) of S. 15(1) do not include steps sons and step sons fall in the category of heirs of the husband referred to in Cl. (b) thereof. *Lachman Singh* v. *Kripasingh*, AIR 1987 SC 1616, 1619. [Hindu Succession Act (30 of 1956), S. 15(1)(a)]

Sonologist or imaging specialist. Means a person who possesses any one of the medical qualifications recognised under the Indian Medical Council Act, 1956 or who possesses a post-graduate qualification in ultrasonography or imaging techniques or radiology. [Pre-Natal Diagnostic Techniques (Regulation and Prevention of Misuse) Act (5 of 1994), S. 2(p)]

Sons and daughters. Illegitimate Children cannot be included within the meaning of the words 'son' and 'daughter' in Class I of Schedule to the Act. *Dadoo* v. *Raghunath,* AIR 1979 Bom 176, 181. [Hindu Succession Act (30 of 1956), S. 8(1) read with Ss. 3(i) and 4, Sch. Class I]

The expression 'sons and daughters' in S. 15(1)(a) can only mean sons and daughters of the female Hindu dying intestate and it cannot by any stretch of imagination include sons and daughters of the husband of that female Hindu. *Kishori Bala* v. *Tribhanga,* AIR 1980 Cal 334, 337. [Hindu Succession Act (30 of 1956), S. 15 (1)(a)]

Soon. Within a reasonable time.

Soon after. The words 'soon after' imply that the interval should not be much between the time of death and that of the recovery. *Kishan Sama* v. *State of Assam,* AIR 1968 A&N 13, 14. [Indian Evidence Act (1 of 1872), S. 114, as to ill (a)]

Soon before. Where the death of a woman is caused by any burns or bodily injury or occurs otherwise than under normal circumstances within 7 years of her marriage and it is shown that soon before her death she was subjected to cruelty or harassment by her husband or his relatives in connection with demand of dowry, such death will be considered as 'DOWRY DEATH'. [IPC, (45 of 1860) S. 304-B(1)]

'Soon before' as used in Section 32(1) of the Act is a relative term which is required to be considered under specific circumstances of each case and no straitjacket formula can be laid down by fixing any time limit. This term is pregnant with the idea of proximity test. It is not synonymous with the term, immediately before and is opposite of the expression 'soon after' as used and understood in Section 114, illustration (a) of the Act. It would imply that the interval should not be too long between the time of making the statement and death. [*Kans Raj* v. *State of Punjab,* (2000) 5 SCC 207, 222, para 15] [Evidence Act (1 of 1872), Ss. 32, 114]

The expression 'soon before' occurring in Section 113-B of Evidence Act and in Section 304-B of IPC would normally imply that the interval should not be much between the cruelty or harassment concerned and the death in question. *Hiralal* v. *State (Govt. of*

NCT.), Delhi, (2003) 8 SCC 80, para 9 : AIR 2003 SC 2865. [Indian Evidence Act (1 of 1872), S. 113-B and IPC (45 of 1860), S. 304-B]

The expression 'soon before' occurring in Section 113-B of the Act does not mean 'immediately before'. The expression is pregnant with the idea of proximity test. It would normally imply where the interval between the cruelty or harassment concerned and the death in question should not be much. [*Kailash* v. *State of M.P.*, AIR 2007 SC 107, 109, para 11] [Indian Evidence Act (1 of 1872), S. 113-B]

The expression 'soon before' would normally imply that interval should not be much between the concerned cruelty and death in question. The period which can come within the term 'soon before' is left to be determined by the Courts on the facts of each case. [*Prem Kanwar* v. *State of Rajasthan,* AIR 2009 SC 1242, 1246, para 12] [IPC (45 of 1860), S. 304-B; Evidence Act (1 of 1872), S. 113-B]

The expression 'soon before' appearing in Section 304-B of the Code and Section 113B of the Act would normally imply that the interval should not be much between the concerned cruelty or harassment and death in question. There must be existence of a proximate and line link between the effect of cruelty based on dowry demand and the concerned death. [*Baldev Singh* v. *State of Punjab,* AIR 2009 SC 913, 918, para 13] [IPC (45 of 1860), S. 304-B; Evidence Act (1 of 1872), S. 113-B]

Soon before her death. The expression 'soon before her death' occurring in Section 113-B of the Act and Section 304-B of the Code is a relative term and it would depend upon facts and circumstances of each case what would constitute a period of soon before the occurence. It would normally imply that the interval should not be much between the concerned cruelty or harassment and the death in question. *Kaliyaperumal v. State of T.N.,* JT (2003) 7 SC 392 : 2003 (5) SLT 1 : 2003 (3) Crimes 374 (SC). [Indian Evidence Act (1 of 1872), S. 113-B and IPC (45 of 1860), S. 304-B]

The expression 'soon before her death' occurring in Section 304-B of the Code does not necessarily mean immediately before her death. It is an elastic expression and it can refer to a period either immediately before death or within few days or few weeks before death of the deceased. But there should be perceptible nexus between the death of the deceased and the dowry related harassment or cruelty inflicted on her. [*Raja Lal Singh* v. *State of Jharkhand,* AIR 2007 SC 2154, 2156, para 18] [IPC (45 of 1860), S. 304-B]

"SOON BEFORE HER DEATH". The expression 'soon before her death' used in section 304B of Indian Penal Code, 1860, cannot be given a restricted or a narrower meaning. It must be understood in its plain language and with reference to its meaning in common parlance. *Ashok Kumar* v. *State of Haryana,* AIR 2010 SC 2839.

Sought. That is or has been searched for, desired *etc.* [Limitation Act (36 of 1963), Sch., Art. 131].

Sound. Free from defect; in good condition or repair [Indian Evidence Act (1 of 1872), S. 20, ill.]; free from disease, abnormality or defect founded in law; solidly or securely based [Specific Relief Act (47 of 1963), S. 20(1)]; noise without meaning; to give an impression on hearing; to mean.

Sound mind. That state of mind which can understand the nature of the (man's) action from a judgment of his own. [Indian Contract Act (9 of 1972), S. 11 and CPC (5 of 1908), O. XXXII, R. 4(1)].

The word 'sound mind' does not mean that the testator should have his mental faculties in their fullest vigour, but he should have the capacity to understand the nature of his property, the memory to remember the relations and persons normally having claims on his bounty and also a judgment of his own in making the dispositions. R. *Kamleswara Rao* v. *B. Surya Prakasa Rao,* AIR 1962 AP 178, 184. [Indian Succession Act (39 of 1925), S. 59]

Sound recording. Means recording of sound on any media or device including magnetic storage device, and includes services relating to recording of sound in any manner such as sound cataloguing, storing of sound and sound mixing or re-mixing or any audio post-production activity. [Finance Act (32 of 1994), S. 65(98) *as substituted by Finance Act 2005,* now repealed by Central Goods and Services Tax Act, 2017].

"SOUND RECORDING" means a recording of sounds from which such sounds may be produced regardless of the medium on which such recording is made or the method by which the sounds are produced. [Copyright (Amendment) Act (38 of 1994), S. 2(xx)]

'Sound recording' means recording of sound on any media or device including magnetic storage device, and includes services relating to recording of sound in any manner such as sound cataloguing, storing of sound and sound mixing or re-mixing or any audio post production activity. [Finance Act (32 of 1994), S. 65(98) as substituted by Finance Act (18 of 2005), S. 88(a)(xx) now repealed by Central Goods and Services Tax Act, 2017]

Sound Recording Studio or **Agency.** Means any person engaged in the business of rendering any service relating to sound recording. [Finance Act (32 of 1994), S. 65(99) now repealed by Central Goods and Services Tax Act, 2017]

Sound spectrograph. 'Sound spectrograph' is an electromagnetic instrument which produces a graphic display of speech in the parameters of time, frequency and intensity. The display is called a sound spectrogram. [Scientific Evidence in Criminal Cases by Andre A. Moenssens, Ray Edward Moses and Fred E. Inbau as cited in *Ritesh Sinha v. State of U.P.*, (2013) 2 SCC 357, para 38].

Soundtrack. Signals which are recorded in electronic form in videotape or in the lateral portions of filmstrip recordings which permit sounds to be heard along with the moving picture patterns when converted and displayed as images. (*Copyright*)

Source. "SOURCE" means any process or activity which releases a green house gas, an aerosol or a precursor of a green house gas into the atmosphere. [U.N. Framework on Climate Change, Art. 1(9)]

"SOURCE" means the published primary and secondary material from any source whatsoever and includes written information and opinions gained directly from other people, including eminent scholars, public figures and practitioners in any form whatsoever as also data and information in the electronic form be it audio, video, image or text; Information being given the same meaning as defined under Section 2(1)(v) of the Information Technology Act, 2000 and reproduced here in Regulation 2(1). [University Grants Commission (Promotion of Academic Integrity and Prevention of Plagiarism in Higher Educational Institutions) Regulations, 2018, Regn. 2(p)].

Source of income. 'Source' means not a legal concept but which a practical man would regard as a real source of income. *Commission of Income Tax* v. *Kandhanbax*, AIR 1970 SC 691, 693.

Sources of the law. The authority from which the laws derive their force. A term used to include all the reliable testimonials of what constitutes the law.

Those repositories of legal rules to which lawyers especially judges turn in order to discover what the law is.

Sovereign. One who has supremacy or rank above or authority over others, a superior; a ruler; governor; lord or master (of persons *etc.*) the recognised supreme rule of a people or country under monarchical government, monarch, a king or queen. [Indian Evidence Act (1 of 1872), S. 57(5)]; possessed of controlling power [Indian Evidence Act (1 of 1872), S. 74(1)(i)]; [IPC (45 of 1860), S. 230 and Constitution of India, preamble].

Sovereign authority. The power in a State to which none other is supeior or equal and which includes all the specific powers necessary to accomplish legitimate ends and purpose of government. [Indian Evidence Act (1 of 1872), S. 74(1)(i)].

Sovereign Democratic Republic. By the Constitution of India, 1950, India has been constituted a Sovereign Democratic Republic. The expression means that the absolute power vested in the people of India under the Constitution is to be exercised by them through their duly elected representatives. (*Ram Nandan* v. *State,* AIR 1959 All 101)

Sovereign functions. One of the tests to determine whether the executive function is sovereign in nature is to find out whether the State is answerable for such action in Courts of law. Acts like defence of the country, raising armed forces and maintaining it, making peace or war, foreign affairs, power to acquire and retain territory, are functions, which are indicative of external sovereignty and are political in nature. They are, therefore, not amenable to the jurisdiction of ordinary civil Court inasmuch as the State is immune in such matters. [*Chief Conservatior of Forests* v. *Jagannath Maruti Kondhare,* (1996) 2 SCC 293]

Sovereign immunity. A historical doctrine of law in certain jurisdictions under which sovereign Governments may not be sued or their assets seized.

The doctrine that Government cannot be sued without its consent. (CRAIG R. DUCAT— *Constitutional Interpretation*)

Sovereign power, or sovereignty. Sovereign power gives the States sufficient authority to enact law, subject to the limitations of the Constitution, to discharge its functions. The sovereign power is plenary and inherent in every State to do all things which may promote the health, peace, morals, education and good order of people. [Constitution of India, Preamble]

Police power is not independent power, but part of the power of the State to legislate with respect to the matters enumerated in the State and Concurrent Lists subject to constitutional limitations. *Synthetics & Chemicals Ltd.* v. *State of U.P.*, AIR 1990 SC 1927, 1946, 1949.

Sovereign State. 1. A people permanently occupying a fixed territory, bound together by common laws, habits, and customs into one body politic, exercising through the medium of an organized government, independent sovereignty and control over all persons and things within its boundaries, capable of making war and peace, and of entering into international relations with other communities. 2. In the United States, each State constitutes a distinct and independent sovereignty, and consequently the laws of one State do not operate of their own force in any other State. (*Ballentine's Law Dictionary*)

Sovereignty. The supreme power which governs the body politic that constitutes the State; a term used to express the supreme political authority of an independent State or nation; power by which any state is governed.

Sovereignty means supremacy in respect of power, dominion or rank; supreme dominion authority or rule. It implies supreme, absolute, uncontrollable power by which any State is governed. *Govindrao and* v. *State of M.P.*, AIR 1982 SC 1201, 1204.

Sovereignty of Parliament. The constitutional principle that the legislative competence of Parliament is unlimited. No Court in the UK can question its power to enact any law that it pleases. In practice, however, Parliament does not assume unlimited authority; it can legislate only for territories that are recognized by international law to be within its competence, *i.e.* the UK, the Channel Islands and the Isle of Man, and UK dependencies. The Welsh Assembly, Scottish Parliament, and Northern Ireland Assembly have devolved power in certain areas. (*Oxford Law Dictionary, 5th Edn., 2003*)

Sovereignty of the people. 'Sovereignty of the people' can only be related to the political sovereignty of the people recognised by the preamble to our Constitution where the people are described as the Constitution makers who gave the Constitution unto themselves. This does not mean that the people retained unto themselves any residue of legal sovereignty. [*Indira Nehru Gandhi* v. *Raj Narain,* (1975) Supp SCC 1, 219, para 578] [Constitution of India, Preamble]

Space service. A radio communication service between earth stations are space stations or between space stations, or between earth stations when the signals are re-transmitted by space stations, or transmitted by reflection from objects in space, excluding reflection or scattering by the ionosphere or within the earth's atmosphere. (*Telecommunication*)

Space station. A station in the space service located on an object which is beyond, is intended to go beyond, or has been beyond, the major portion of the earth's atmosphere. (*Telecommunication*)

Spam. An inappropriate attempt to use a mailing list, or USENET or other networked communications facility as if it was a broadcast medium (which it is not) by sending the same message to a large number of people who did not ask for it. The term comes from a Monty Python sketch which featured the word "spam" repeated over and over. (*Information Technology*)

Spamming. Sending unsolicited bulk e-mail advertisements. (*Cyber Law*)

The way of sending unwanted information to a number of computers at the same time. (*Internet*)

An inappropriate attempt to use a *mailing list,* or *USENET* or other networked communications facility as if it was a broadcast medium (which it is not) by sending the same message to a large number of people who didn't ask for it. The term probably comes from a famous Monty Python skit which featured the word spam repeated over and over. The term may also have come from someone's low opinion of the food product with the same name, which is generally perceived as a generic content-free waste of resources. (Spam® is a registered trademark of Hormel Corporation, for its processed meat product.) (*Matisse Enzer-Glossary of Internet Terms*)

Speaker. "SPEAKER" means the speaker of the House of the people. [Judges (Inquiry) Act (51 of 1968), S. 2(e)]

The official designation of the person presiding over certain legislative bodies, especially, the House of People (Lok Sabha) in the Centre and the Legislative Assemblies in the States in India [CPC (5 of 1908), S. 133(1)(vii)]; one who speaks.

Speaker Pro Tem. A member of a Legislative House appointed to perform the duties of the office of the Speaker when the offices of both the Speaker and the Deputy Speaker are vacant, the Speaker *pro tem* continues in office till the Speaker is elected.

Speaker's Eye, Catching The. A well-established Parliamentary practice to attract the attention of the Speaker in order to be called to speak. When several members of the House rise, hoping to catch the Speaker's eye, it is the Speaker who decides and whom his eyes see first is given precedence. (*Constitutional and Parliamentary Term*)

Speaking award. An award with reasons. Also termed as a *motivated* or *reasoned award.* (*Arbitration*)

Speaking order. An order which contains matter which is explanatory or illustrative of the direction which is given by it is sometimes thus called.

An intelligible order; an order that tells its own story and is clear-cut.

Special. The term "special" includes species and sub-species of fish, wildlife and plants as well as geographically distinct populations of vertebrate wildlife even though the species as a whole may not be endangered. [*T.N. Godavarman Thirumulpad v. Union of India*, (2012) 4 SCC 362, para 48].

Special agent. "SPECIAL AGENT" means a person who, not being a salaried employee of an insurer, in consideration of any commission, procures life insurance business for the insurer whether wholly or in part by employing or causing to be employed insurance agents on behalf of the insurer, but does not include a chief agent. [Insurance Act (4 of 1938), S. 2(17) omitted by Act 5 of 2015].

Special audit. "SPECIAL AUDIT" means an audit of accounts pertaining to a specified item or series of items requiring thorough examination. [Gujarat Local Fund Act (49 of 1963), S. 2(h)]

"SPECIAL AUDIT" means an audit of accounts pertaining to a specified item or series of items requiring thorough examination, and includes re-audit of the accounts for a period already covered by audit as specified by the Director. [Kerala Local Fund Audit Act (14 of 1994), S. 2(j)]

Special agreement. For the purposes of this sub-section, the expression "SPECIFIED AGREEMENT" means a registered agreement in which a person owning land or building or both, agrees to allow another person to develop a real estate project on such land or building or both, in consideration of a share, being land or building or both in such project, whether with or without payment of part of the consideration in cash. [Income-tax Act (43 of 1961), S. 45(5-A), *Explanation (ii)*].

Special category States. For the purposes of the section, the expression "special category States" shall mean the States as specified in sub-clause (g) of clause (4) of Article 279-A of the Constitution. [Central Goods and Services Tax Act (12 of 2017), S. 22, *Explanation (iii)*].

Special Certificate of Airworthiness. Means a document issued by the Director-General to an aircraft which has a restricted type certificate or complies with airworthiness specifications as specified by the Director-General for ensuring adequate safety. [Aircraft Rules, 1937, R. 3(51-B)].

Special category explosive substance. The expression "SPECIAL CATEGORY EXPLOSIVE SUBSTANCE" shall be deemed to include research development explosive (RDX), penta erythritol tetra nitrate (PETN), high melting explosive (HMX), trinitro toluene, (TNT), low temperature plastic explosive (LTPE), composition exploding (CE) (2, 4, 6 phenyl methyl nitramine or tetryl), OCTOL (mixture of high melting explosive and tri nitro toluene), plastic explosive kirkee-1 (PEK-1) and RDX/TNT compounds and other similar type of explosives and a combination thereof and remote control devices causing explosion and any other substance and a combination thereof which the Central Government may, by notification in the Official Gazette, specify for the purposes of this Act. [Explosive Substance Act (6 of 1908), S. 2(b)]

Special bench. A bench consisting of three or more judges of the Court convened under some rule or enactment to hear or decide some intricate point of law or fact. [CrPC, 1973 (2 of 1974), S. 96(2)].

Special case. Case reserved; statement in writing of facts proved or settled between the parties to obtain the opinion of the Court in. [Heading, CPC (5 of 1908), S. 90].

Special circumstances. "Special circumstances" connotes something exceptional in character, extraordinary, significant, uncommon. It is an antonym of common, ordinary and general, it is neither practicable nor advisable to enumerate such circumstances. Non-service of summons will undoubtedly be a special circumstances. [*Rajni Kumar v. Suresh Kumar Malhotra*, (2003) 5 SCC 315, para 9 as cited in *TVC Skyshop Limited v. Reliance Communication and Infrastructure Limited*, (2013) 11 SCC 754, para 10].

Special conditions. Special terms [Indian Trusts Act (2 of 1882), S. 38]; special circumstances.

Special Court. Means the court of a Special Judge appointed under section 3(1) of the Prevention of Corruption Act, 1988 (49 of 1988). [S. 2(1)(s) of the Lokpal & Lokayuktas Act, 2013 (1 of 2014)]

Special damage. Special damage does not mean serious damage in the sense of irreparable loss but damage affecting the plaintiff individually or peculiar to the plaintiff or damage beyond what is suffered by him in common with the owners of other houses opening into the lane. *Ramabrahma Sastri* v. *Laxminarasimham,* AIR 1957 AP 44, 47. [CPC (5 of 1908), S. 91(1)(b)]

The damage sustained by wrongful act, for which damages beyond general damages may be claimed; the damage which must be pleaded and proved by a party in order to be entitled to be compensated therefor; the damage peculiar to the plaintiff because of his particular condition, or the particular circumstances in which he finds himself. [CPC (5 of 1908), S. 91(1)].

Special employment exchange. Means any office or place established and maintained by the Government for the collection and furnishing of information, either by keeping of registers or otherwise, respecting—

(i) persons who seek to engage employees from amongst the persons suffering from disabilities;

(ii) persons with disability who seek employment;

(iii) vacancies to which person with disability seeking employment may be appointed. [Persons with Disabilities (Equal Opportunities, Protection of Rights, Full Participation) Act, 1995 (1 of 1996), S. 2(x)].

Special exception. An exception to a particular provision as distinguished from a general exception which applies to the provisions in general. [Indian Evidence Act (1 of 1872), S. 105].

Special hardship. Unusual or extraordinary difficulty. [CPC (5 of 1908), O. XLV, R. 7(1)(b), *Prov.*].

Special home. "Special home" means an institution established by a State Government or by a voluntary or non-governmental organization, registered under section 48, for housing and providing rehabilitative services to children in conflict with law, who are found, through inquiry, to have committed an offence and are sent to such institution by an order of the Board. [Juvenile Justice (Care and Protection of Children) Act, 2015 (2 of 2016), S. 2(56)].

Special Indian Law. The expression 'Special Indian Law' means a special Indian Law enacted by the Indian Legislature and Banking Companies Act is a special Indian Law. *Bank of India* v. *Vijay Transport*, AIR 1988 SC 151, 154, 155. [Banking Companies (Acquisition and Transfer of Undertakings) Act (5 of 1970), S. 3]

Special juvenile police unit. "Special juvenile police unit" means a unit of the police force of a district or city or, as the case may, any other police unit like railway police, dealing with children and designated as such for handling children under section 107. [Juvenile Justice (Care and Protection of Children) Act, 2015 (2 of 2016), S. 2(55)].

Special law. Is a law applicable to a particular subject. [IPC (45 of 1860), S. 41]

[Now (w. e. f. 1-7-2024) repealed & replaced by Bharatiya Nyaya Sanhita, 2023 (45 of 2023), section 2(30), same definition in new Sanhita]

Special leave to appeal. A discretionary power of the highest Court to grant appeal from any decision on any matter by any Court or tribunal.

Special local meeting. Means a meeting of the shareholders whose names are registered in a branch register, convened for the transaction of some particular business specified in the notice convening the meeting. [Imperial Bank of India (47 of 1920), S. 2(j)]

Special local resolution. Means a resolution passed at a special local meeting. [Imperial Bank of India (47 of 1920), S. 2(k)]

Special means of knowledge. "Special means of knowledge" does not necessarily mean that the person should be himself engaged in a particular business or be a member of an establishment or that the means of his knowledge should be confined to his own experience. All that is required is that he had opportunities for acquiring knowledge of a usage or custom and that he acquired the necessary knowledge.

The expression "special means of knowledge" does not necessarily mean that the person giving evidence should himself engage in a particular business or that he himself should be a member of a particular class of people. It is sufficient that he has special means of knowledge regarding the meaning of words or terms used in a particular district or by a particular class of people. *Kanubhai Prabhudas* v. *State of Gujarat*, MLJ : QD (1961-1965) Vol III C408 : 1963(2) CrLJ 87 : (1963) 4 Guj LR 733 [Evidence Act (1 of 1872), S. 49]

Special messenger. A person particularly engaged to carry a particular message or messages. [CPC (5 of 1908), O. V, R. 30(3)].

Special Notice. A 'special notice' required to be given to the company shall be signed, either individually or collectively by such number of members holding not less than one percent of total voting power or holding shares on which an aggregate sum of not less than five lakh rupees has been paid up on the date of the notice. [R. 23(1) of the Companies (Management & Administration) Rules, 2014]

Special or adequate reasons. The grounds for reduction of sentence, that 'accused was an unsophisticated and illiterate citizen belonging to a weaker section of the society', and that he was chronic addict to drinking and he committed rape in the state of 'intoxication' and that his family comprising of 'an old mother, a wife and children were dependant upon him, were held neither special nor adequate. *State of Karnataka* v. *Krishnappa,* (2000) 4 SCC 75 para 18 : AIR 2000 SC 1470. [IPC (45 of 1860), S. 376, Proviso]

Special or local law. The types of law covered by the above phrase are such as the Opium Act or the Gambling Act and not a vast system like the English common law.

Special order. An order having a limited application, object or intention or devoted to distinct cases. [CrPC, 1973 (2 of 1974), S. 57].

Special police officer. Means a police officer appointed by or on behalf of the State Government to be in charge of police duties within a specified area for the purpose of the Suppression of Immoral Traffic in Women and Girls Act (104 of 1956). [Suppression of Immoral Traffic in Women and Girls Act (104 of 1956), S. 2(i)]

Special purpose vehicle. For the purposes of this clause, "SPECIAL PURPOSE VEHICLE" means an Indian company in which the business trust holds controlling interest and any specific percentage of shareholding or interest, as may be required by the regulations under which such trust is granted registration. [Income-tax Act (43 of 1961), S. 10 (23-FC), Explanation as inserted by Finance Act, (No. 2) (25 of 2014), S. 5].

Special property. That of a bailee, or officer in possession of the goods. That property in a thing which gives a qualified or limited right.

A property, right or qualified interest in property subordinate to the general or absolute interest or ownership. [Sale of Goods Act (3 of 1930), S. 2(11)].

Special purpose distinct entity. Means a trust which acquires debt or receivables out of funds mobilized by it by issuance of securitised debt instruments through one or more schemes, and includes any trust set up by the National Housing Bank under the National Housing Bank Act, 1987 (53 of 1987) or by the National Bank for Agriculture and Rural Development under the National Bank for Agriculture and Rural Development Act, 1981 (61 of 1981). [Securities and Exchange Board of India (Public Offer and Listing of Securitised Debt Instruments) Regulations 2008, regulation 2(1)(u). Also see (w.e.f. 1-6-2013) *Explanation* (*d*)(*i*) to section 115TC of the Income-tax Act, 1961 (43 of 1961)]

Special purpose vehicle. Means as defined in, and regulated by, the guidelines on securitisation of standard assets issued by the Reserve Bank of India. [(w.e.f. 1-6-2013) *Explanation* (*d*)(*ii*) to section 115TC of the Income-tax Act, 1961 (43 of 1961)]

Special reasons. The expression 'special reasons' means special to the accused in the case or special to the facts and the circumstances of the case in which the sentence is being awarded. *Meet Singh* v. *State of Punjab*, AIR 1980 SC 1141, 1143. [Prevention of Corruption Act (2 of 1947), S. 5(2), Proviso]

An amalgamation of the circumstances connected with both, the crime in question as also the criminal. [Bachan Singh v. State of Punjab, (1980) 2 SCC 684 : 1980 SCC (Cri) 580 as cited in *B. Kumar v. Inspector of Police*, (2015) 2 SCC 346, para 21].

"Special reasons" means exceptional; particular; peculiar; different from others; designed for a particular purpose, occasion, or person; limited in range; confined to a definite field by action. [*State of Rajasthan v. Vinod Kumar*, (2012) 6 SCC 770, para 9].

"Special reasons" obviously means "exceptional reasons" founded on the exceptionally grave circumstances of the particular case relating to the crime as well as the criminal. [*Mohinder Singh v. State of Punjab*, (2013) 3 SCC 294, para 37.2].
Special resolution

Special school. "SPECIAL SCHOOL" means any institution which imparts such primary education as in the opinion of the State Government or the local authority is suitable for children suffering from any physical or mental defect. [Gujarat Compulsory

Primary Education Act (Guj. Act No. 41 of 1961), S. 2(l)]

Special tax. "Special tax" is sometimes held to mean an additional tax; and above the general tax. [*State of U.P. v. Systemetic Consom Limited*, (2014) 13 SCC 627, para 20].

Special trade. Means the conveyance of large number of passengers by sea within prescribed sea areas. [Merchant Shipping Act (44 of 1958), S. 3(47A)]

Special trade passenger. Means a passenger carried in special trade passenger ship in spaces on the weather deck or upper deck or between decks which accommodate more than eight passengers and includes a pilgrim or a person accompanying a pilgrim. [Merchant Shipping Act (44 of 1958), S. 3(47B]

Special trade passenger ship. Means a mechanically propelled ship carrying more than thirty special trade passengers. [Merchant Shipping Act (44 of 1958), S. 3(47C)]

Specialia generalibus derogant. (*Lat.*) Special provisions derogate from general.

Specialised arbitration. An arbitration touching on specialised matters or subjects which requires persons with specialised knowledge to be appointed as arbitrators, e.g., commodity or maritime arbitrations. (*Arbitration*)

Specialised equipment. Means :

(i) The main production train, including any reactor or equipment for product synthesis, separation or purification, any equipment used directly for heat transfer in the final technological stage, such as in reactors or in product separation, as well as any other equipment which has been in contact with any chemical specified in Article II, paragraph 8(a)(i), or would be in contact with such a chemical if the facility were operated;

(ii) Any chemical weapon filling machines;

(iii) Any other equipment specially designed, built or installed for the operation of the facility as a chemical weapons production facility, as distinct from a facility constructed according to prevailing commercial industry standards for facilities not producing any chemical specified in Article II, paragraph 8(a)(i), or corrosive chemicals, such as : equipment made of highnickel alloys or other special corrosion resistant material; special equipment for waste control, waste treatment, air filtering, or solvent recovery; special containment enclosures and safety shields; non-standard laboratory equipment used to analyse toxic chemicals for chemical weapons purposes; custom-designed process control panels; or dedicated spares for specialized equipment. [Chemical Weapons Convention Act (34 of 2000), (Verification Annex), 5(a)]

Specialist. "SPECIALIST" means a medical practitioner with post-graduate qualification in any of the disciplines relating to medical sciences. [Punjab Health Systems Corporation Act (Punj Act No. 6 of 1996), S. 2(i)]

One who devotes himself to the particular study or practice of a special subject.

Specially appointed. The word 'specially' has reference to the special purpose of appointment and is not used to convey the sense of a special as against a general appointment. The word 'specially' connotes the appointment of an officer or officers to perform functions which ordinarily a collector would perform under the Act. *Abdul Hussain Tayabali* v. *State of Gujarat*, AIR 1968 SC 432, 436. [Land Acquisition Act (1 of 1894), S. 3(c)]

Specially denatured spirit. The specially denatured spirit is different from denatured spirit only because of the difference in the quantity and quality of the denaturants. *State of U.P.* v. *V. Synthetics & Chemicals Ltd.*, AIR 1980 SC 614, 626.

Specially empowered. The words 'specially empowered' mean specially empowered with reference to the power conferred. *C.V.M. Mannadiar* v. *District Collector,* AIR 1970 Ker 50 at p. 52. [Preventive Detention Act (4 of 1950), S. 3(2)(b)]

Specie. Metallic money issued by public authority. This term is used in contradistinction to paper money, which in some countries is issued by the government, and is a mere engagement which represents specie (as) specie payments; remitted in specie.

Gold or silver coins. [Banking Regulation Act (10 of 1949), S. 8, *Expln*.].

Species. Visible image [Estate Duty Act (34 of 1953), S. 2(15)]; kind, sort.

Specific Anti Avoidance Rules (SAAR). Are used by tax administrations to prevent particular tax avoidance behavior that is abusive. The Indian tax law has several SAAR provisions, introduced over the years comprising rules to address specific classes of structures or transactions. For instance, there are rules to prevent unaccounted money being received as share capital, loans, interest, or dividend, understatement of consideration for transfer of immovable property, excessive payments to related parties, expenditure in cash, and transfer pricing for international transactions. [Parthasarthi Shome, *Taxation Principles and Applications A compendium*, 2014, LexisNexis, at p. 540].

Specific bequest. A bequest of specific item or cash amount.

'Specific date' means the date of the coming into force of the amending Act of 1972. [Gujarat Agricultural Lands Ceiling Act, 1960 (after the amendment), S. 2(27A) as cited in *State of Gujarat v. Manoharsinhji Pradyumansinhji Jadeja*, (2013) 2 SCC 300, para 34].

Specific delivery contract. Means a forward contract which provides for the actual delivery of specific qualities or types of goods during a specified future period at a price fixed thereby or to be fixed in the manner thereby agreed and in which the names of both the buyer and the seller are mentioned. [Forward Contracts (Regulation) Act (74 of 1952), S. 2(m)]

"Specific delivery contract" means a commodity derivative which provides for the actual delivery of specific qualities or types of goods during a specified future period at a price fixed thereby or to be fixed in the manner thereby agreed and in which the names of both the buyer and the seller are mentioned. [Securities Contracts (Regulations) Act (42 of 1956), S. 2(ha) as inserted by Finance Act, (20 of 2015), S. 133].

Specific goods. The goods identified and agreed upon at the time a contract of sale is made. [Sale of Goods Act (3 of 1930), S. 20].

Specific injury. The expression 'specific injury' has been used with a view to distinguish a case where death has been caused in the natural course of disease. The disease must be attributable to the work that the workman was doing in the course of his employment. *M. Mackenzia & Co.* v. *Habiba,* AIR 1967 Bom 404, 407. [Workman Compensation Act (8 of 1923), S. 3(4)]

Specific legacy. A bequest of a particular identifiable and existing thing or part of a testator's estate. [CPC (5 of 1908), 1st Sch., A, form No. 42].

Specific legatee. A person to whom a thing of particular nature or class is given under legacy or in a will. [CPC (5 of 1908), 1st Sch., App. A, form No. 42].

Specific performance. The performance of a contract exactly or substantially according to its terms.

SPECIFIC PERFORMANCE of contracts is a remedy by which a party to a contract is compelled to do or omit the very acts which he has undertaken to do or omit. In general, the contract must have the essentials of a contract valid and binding at law in order to be enforceable. It must be a concluded contract; there must have been a clear mutual understanding and a positive assent on both sides as to the terms of the contract; it must be sufficiently definite and certain; the parties must have the capacity to contract; it must be upon a valuable consideration; and it must not be illegal.

Specific relief. A particular relief to which a person is entitled in the first instance as distinguished from compensatory relief.

Specifically. Specifically is used in contradistinction to the word generally. [Indian Evidence Act (1 of 1872), S. 68]

Specifically denied. Explicitly or particularly denied. [CPC (5 of 1908), O. VIII, R. 5].

The words "specifically denied" in S. 68, Indian Evidence Act (1 of 1872) evidently mean specifically denied by the party against whom the document is sought to be used and not only by the executant. *Zaharul Hussain* v. *Mahadeo Ramji,* AIR 1949 Nag 149.

Specification. "SPECIFICATION" means a description of an article or process as far as practicable by reference to its nature, quality, strength, purity, composition, quantity, dimensions, weight, grade, durability, origin, age, material, mode of manufacture or other characteristics to distinguish it from any other article or process. [Bureau of Indian Standards Act, 1986, (63 of 1987), S. 2(s)]

A particular and detailed list or account of a thing; of work to be done or of goods to be supplied in the carrying out of order or contract.

Explicit or detailed enumeration, mention or statement of something. [CPC (5 of 1908), O. XXI, R. 13(a)].

Detailed statement or making a detailed statement.

Specified agency. Means—

(i) the Reserve Bank of India constituted under the Reserve Bank of India Act, 1934; or

(ii) the State Bank of India constituted under the State Bank of India Act, 1955; or

(iii) such other Bank or institution as may be specified in this behalf by the Central Government. [Research & Development Cess Act (32 of 1986), S. 2(g)]

Specified amount. Means one thousand and five hundred rupees, or, as the case may be, the fixed amount by the Corporation under the third Proviso to sub-sec (1). [Deposit Insurance and Credit Guarantee Corporation (47 of 1961), S.16(4)(b)]

Specified area. Includes the Indian customs water, and such inland area not exceeding one hundred kilometres in width from any coast or other border of India, as the Central Government may, having regard to the vulnerability of that area to smuggling, by notification in the Official Gazette, specify in this behalf :

Provided that where a part of any village, town or city falls within a specified area, the whole of such village, town or city shall, notwithstanding that the whole of it is not within one hundred kilometres from any coast or other border of India, be deemed to be included in such specified area. [Customs Act (52 of 1962), S. 11H(c)]

Specified asset. Means any of the following assets, namely—

(i) shares in an Indian company;

(ii) debentures issued by an Indian company which is not a private company as defined in the Companies Act, 1956 (1 of 1956);

(iii) deposits with an Indian Company which is not a private company as defined in the Companies Act, 1956 (1 of 1956);

(iv) any security of the Central Government as defined in clause (2) of Section 2 of the Public Debt Act, 1944 (18 of 1944);

(v) such other assets as the Central Government may specify in this behalf by notification in the

Official Gazette. [Income-tax Act (43 of 1961), S. 115C(f)]

Specified assesse. For the purposes of this section, "SPECIFIED ASSESSE" means a person other than,—

(i) a domestic company; or

(ii) a fund or institution or trust or any university or other educational institution or any hospital or other medical institution referred to in sub-clause (iv) or sub-clause (v) or sub-clause (vi) or sub-clause (vi-a) of clause (23-C) of Section 10; or

(iii) a trust or institution registered under Section 12-A or Section 12-AA. [Income-tax Act (43 of 1961), S. 115-BBDA, *Explanation (b)*].

Specified bank note. Means a bank note of the denominational value of five hundred rupees or one thousand rupees of the series existing on or before the 8th day of November, 2016. [Specified Bank Notes (Cessation of Liabilities) Ordinance (10 of 2016), S. 2(1)(e)].

Specified company. Means a company to be formed and registered under the Companies Act, 1956 and whose entire capital is subscribed by such financial institutions or banks as may be specified by the Central Government, by notification in the Official Gazette, for the purpose of transfer and vesting of the undertaking. [Unit Trust of India (Transfer of Undertaking and Repeal) Act (58 of 2002), S. 2(h)]

"SPECIFIED COMPANY". For the purpose of section 194LC of Act 43 of 1961, 'specified company' means an Indian company. [*Explanation* (b) to section 194LC of the Income-tax Act, 1961 (43 of 1961) as inserted (w.e.f. 1-7-2012) by the Finance Act, 2012 (23 of 2012)]

"SPECIFIED COMPANY". [Also see (w.e.f. 1-6-2013) *Explanation* (*i*) to section 115R(2) of the Income-tax Act, 1961 (43 of 1961)]

Specified date. "SPECIFIED DATE" means—

(a) in respect of income chargeable under the head "Salaries", the last day of the month immediately preceding the month in which the salary is due, or is paid in advance or in arrears;

(b) in respect of income [by way of "interest on securities"], the last day of the month immediately preceding the month in which the income is due;

(c) in respect of income chargeable under the heads "Income from house property", "Profits and gains of business or profession" [not being income referred to in clause (*d*)] and "Income from other sources" (not being income by way of dividends and "interest on securities"), the last day of the previous year of the assessee.

(d) in respect of income chargeable under the head "Profits and gains of business or profession" in the case of a non-resident engaged in the business of operation of ships, the last day of the month immediately preceding the month in which such income is deemed to accrue or arise in India;

(e) in respect of income by way of dividends, the last day of the month immediately preceding the month in which the dividend is declared, distributed or paid by the company;

(f) in respect of income chargeable under the head "Capital gains", the last day of the month immediately preceding the month in which the capital asset is transferred.

Provided that the specified date, in respect of income referred to in sub-clauses (*a*) to (*f*) payable in foreign currency and from which tax has been deducted at source under Rule 26, shall be [the date on which the tax was required to be deducted under the provisions of Chapter XVII-B. [Income-Tax Rules, 1962, R. 115(1) *Expln.* (2)]

Specified date. For the purposes of section 271AAB of Act 43 of 1961, 'specified date' means the due date of furnishing of return of income under section 139(1) or the date on which the period specified in the notice issued under section 153A for furnishing of return of income expires, as the case may be. [*Explanation* (a) to section 271AAB of the Income-tax Act, 1961 (43 of 1961) as inserted (w.e.f. 1-7-2012) by the Finance Act, 2012 (23 of 2012)]

Specified distance. "SPECIFIED DISTANCE" means the distance specified in any licence or where no such distance is specified, a distance of twenty kilometers measured in either case by the shortest surface route from any place. [West Bengal Government Premises (Regulation of Occupancy) Act, (21 of 1984), S. 2(l)]

Specified domestic transaction. For the purposes of section 92BA and sections 92, 92C, 92D and 92E of Act 43 of 1961, 'specified domestic transaction' in case of an assessee means any of the following transactions, not being an international transaction, namely:—

(ii) any transaction referred to in section 80A;

(iii) any transfer of goods or services referred to in section 80-IA(8);

(iv) any business transacted between the assessee and other person as referred to in section 80-IA(10);

(v) any transaction, referred to in any other section under Chapter VI-A or section 10AA, to which provisions of section 80-IA(8) or section 80-IA(10) are applicable; or

(vi) any other transaction as may be prescribed, and where the aggregate of such transactions entered into by the assessee in the previous year exceeds a sum of twenty crore rupees. [Section 92BA of the Income-tax Act, 1961 (43 of 1961) as inserted (w.e.f. 1-4-2013) by the Finance Act, 2012 (23 of 2012]

Specified end-use. "Specified end-use" means any of the following end-uses and the expression "SPECIFIED END-USER" shall with its grammatical variations be construed accordingly,—

(i) production of iron and steel;

(ii) generation of power including the generation of power for captive use;

(iii) washing of coal obtained from a mine;

(iv) cement;

(v) such other end-use as the Central Government may, by notification, specify. [Coal Mines (Special Provisions) Act (11 of 2015), S. 3(1)(v)].

Specified finance transaction. For the purposes of sub-section (1), "SPECIFIED FINANCIAL TRANSACTION" means any—

(a) transaction of purchase, sale or exchange of goods or property or right or interest in a property; or

(b) transaction for rendering any service; or

(c) transaction under a works contract; or

(d) transaction by way of an investment made or an expenditure incurred; or

(e) transaction for taking or accepting any loan or deposit; which may be prescribed:

Provided that the Board may prescribe different values for different transactions in respect of different persons having regard to the nature of such transaction:

Provided further that the value or, as the case may be, the aggregate value of such transactions during a financial year so prescribed shall not be less than fifty thousand rupees. [Income-tax Act (43 of 1961), S. 285BA (3) (*Inserted by Finance Act (23 of 2004), S. 63*].

Specified foreign company. In section 115BBD of Act 43 of 1961, 'specified foreign company' means a foreign company in which the Indian company holds twenty-six per cent or more in nominal value of the equity share capital of the company. [S. 115BBD(3)(ii) of the Income-tax Act, 1961 (43 of 1961) as inserted (w.e.f. 1-4-2012) by the Finance Act, 2011 (8 of 2011)]

Specified income. For the purposes of section 10(46) of Act 43 of 1961, 'specified income' means the income, of the nature and to the extent arising to a body or authority or Board or Trust or Commission (by whatever name called) referred to in this clause, which the Central Government may, by notification in the Official Gazette, specify in this behalf. [*Explanation* to section 10(46) of the Income-tax Act, 1961 (43 of 1961) as inserted (w.e.f. 1-6-2011) by the Finance Act, 2011 (8 of 2011)]

Specified knowledge based industry or service. Means—

(i) information technology software;

(ii) information technology service;

(iii) entertainment service;

(iv) pharmaceutical industry;

(v) bio-technology industry;

(vi) any other industry or service, as may be specified by the Central Government, by notification in the Official Gazette. [Income-tax Act (43 of 1961), S. 115 ACA(1), *Expln.* (a)]

Specified land. "SPECIFIED LAND" means the land held for carrying out excavation for the purpose of obtaining mineral oils or for extraction of mineral oils. [Gujarat Rural Development Cess Act (4 of 1984), S. 2(f)]

Specified IFSC Public Company. For the purpose of this rule, a 'SPECIFIED IFSC PUBLIC COMPANY' means an unlisted public company which is licensed to operate by the Reserve Bank of India or the Securities and Exchange Board of India or the Insurance Regulatory and Development Authority of India from the International Financial Services Centre located in an approved multi services Special Economic Zone set-up under the Special Economic Zones Act, 2005 (28 of 2005) read with the Special Economic Zones Rules, 2006:

Provided further that the maximum limit in respect of deposits to be accepted from members shall not apply to following classes of private companies, namely—

(i) a private company which is a start-up, for five years from the date of its incorporation;

(ii) a private company which fulfills all of the following conditions, namely—

(a) which is not an associate or a subsidiary company of any other company;

(b) the borrowings of such a company from banks or financial institutions or any body corporate is less than twice of its paid up share capital or fifty crore rupees, whichever is less; and

(c) such a company has not defaulted in the repayment of such borrowings subsisting at the time of accepting deposits under Section 73:

Provided also that all the companies accepting deposits shall file the details of monies so accepted to the Registrar in Form DPT-3. [Companies (Acceptance of Deposits) Rules, 2014, R. 3(3), *Explanation*].

Specified manner. For the purposes of this rule, the term "specified manner" shall mean service of documents as specified under Section 20 of the Act and rules made thereunder and details in respect of address (including electronic mail ID) provided in the KYC documents filed in the registry shall be used for communication under this rule. [Companies (Adjudication of Penalties) Rules, 2014, R. 3(15), *Explanation 1*].

Specified persons. Includes any person other than—(i) appropriate Government; (ii) Government company; (iii) association of persons or trust or society as registered under the Societies Registration Act, 1860 (21 of 1860), wholly or partially aided by the appropriate Government or controlled by the appropriate Government. [*Explanation* (b) to S. 46 of the Right to Fair Compensation & Transparency in Land Acquisition, Rehabilitation & Resettlement Act, 2013 (30 of 2013)]

Specified place. It is a phrase intended to mean a place so described as would enable the holder of a note to go to it with a reasonable certainty of being able to find the drawer of the note to present the note to him. *Dungramull Missenlal* v. *Sambhu Charan Pandey,* AIR 1951 Cal 55, 61. [Negotiable Instruments Act (26 of 1881), S. 69]

When a specified place is referred to in Section 69, Negotiable Instruments Act (26 of 1881), it must have been intended to refer not to a vast area in general terms like a big city, but a place indicated with sufficient precision to enable the person, who wants to charge the maker with liability, to resort to him readily. *V.C. Jayaram Mudaliar* v. *C.M. Sivaram,* AIR 1963 Mad 294, 296.

Specified previous year. For the purposes of section 271AAB of Act 43 of 1961, 'specified previous year' means the previous year—

(i) which has ended before the date of search, but the date of furnishing the return of income under Section 139(1) for such year has not expired before the date of search and the assessee has not furnished the return of income for the previous year before the date of search; or

(ii) in which search was conducted. [*Explanation* (b) to Section 271AAB of the Income-tax Act, 1961 (43 of 1961) as inserted (w.e.f. 1-7-2012) by the Finance Act, 2012]

Specified securities. For the purposes of sections 68 and 70 of Act 18 of 2013, 'specified securities' includes employees' stock option or other securities as may be notified by the Central Government from time to time. [*Explanation I* to Section 68 of the Companies Act, 2013 (18 of 2013)]

Specified security. For the purposes of this section "SPECIFIED SECURITIES" includes employees' stock option or other securities as may be notified by the Central Government from time to time. [Companies Act (1 of 1956), S. 77A *Expln. (b)*]

Specified undertaking. Includes all business, assets, liabilities and properties of the Trust representing and relatable to the schemes and Development Reserve Fund specified in the Schedule I. [Unit Trust of India (Transfer of Undertaking and Repeal) Act (58 of 2002), S. 2(i)]

Specified warning. "SPECIFIED WARNING" means the following warning, namely "cigarette smoking is injurious to health." [Cigarettes (Regulation of Production-Supply and Distribution) Act (48 of 1975), S. 2(m)]

"SPECIFIED WARNING" means such warnings against the use of cigarettes or other tobacco products to be printed, painted or inscribed on packages of cigarettes or other tobacco products in such form and manner as may be prescribed by rules made under this Act. [Cigarettes and Other Tobacco Products (Prohibition of Advertisement and Regulation of Trade, Commerce, Production, Supply and Distribution Act (34 of 2003), S. 3(q)]

Specify. "SPECIFY" means to specify by regulations made under this Act and the expression "specified" shall be construed accordingly. [Foreign Exchange Management Act (42 of 1999), S. 2(zd)]

To mention definitely or explicitly; to make specific.

Specimen. "SPECIMEN" means an individual example of a species of wild animal or wild plant or part of a wild plant. [African Convention on the Conservation of Nature and Natural Resources, 1968, Art. III(2)]

The object or portion serving as a sample especially for purposes of study or collection. [Oilfields (Regulation and Development) Act (53 of 1948), S. 6(2)(f)].

Spectator. One who looks on. [Dramatic Performances Act (19 of 1876), S. 6(c)].

Spectrum management. Planning, coordinating, and managing joint use of the electro-magnetic spectrum through operational, engineering, and administrative procedures, with the objective of enabling electronic systems to perform their functions in the intended environment without causing or suffering unacceptable interference.

Speculation. More or less risky investment of money for the sake of, and in expectation of unusually large profits.

Act of speculating or its result. [Presidency Towns Insolvency Act (3 of 1903), S. 39(2)(f)]; [Urban Land (Ceiling and Regulation Act (33 of 1976), preamble].

Speculative transactions. "SPECULATIVE TRANSACTION" means a transaction in which a contract for purchase or sale of any commodity, including stocks and shares, is periodically or ultimately settled otherwise than by the actual delivery or transfer of the commodity or scrips.

Provided that for the purposes of this clause—

(a) a contract in respect of raw materials or merchandise entered into by a person in the course of his manufacturing or merchanting business to guard against loss through future price fluctuations in respect of his contracts for actual delivery of goods manufactured by him or merchandise sold by him; or

(b) a contract in respect of stocks and shares entered into by a dealer or investor therein to guard against loss in his holdings of stocks and shares through price fluctuations; or

(c) a contract entered into by a member of a forward market or a stock exchange in the course of any transaction in the nature of jobbing or arbitrage to guard against loss which may arise in the ordinary course of his business as such member;

(d) an eligible transaction in respect of trading in derivatives referred to in clause (ac) of section

2 of the Securities Contracts (Regulation) Act, 1956 (42 of 1956) carried out in a recognised stock exchange; or

(e) an eligible transaction in respect of trading in commodity derivatives carried out in a recognised association, which is chargeable to commodities transaction tax under Chapter VII of the Finance Act, 2013 (17 of 2013), hall not be deemed to be a speculative transaction. [Income-tax Act (43 of 1961), S. 43(5)]

Unless the transaction was settled by actual delivery or transfer of the commodity, it would be a speculative transaction. *Jute Investment Co.* v. *I.T. Commissioner W.B.*, AIR 1980 SC 483, 485.

A transaction cannot be described as a "speculative transaction" where there is a breach of the contract and on a dispute between the parties, damages are awarded as compensation by an arbitration award. *I.T. Commissioner Bombay* v. *Shantilal Pvt. Ltd.*, AIR 1983 SC 952, 954.

Speculator. One who practises speculation in trade or business of any kind.

Speech. A discourse; oration; talk [Copyright Act (14 of 1957), S. 2(n)]; the power of speaking. A formal discourse in public.

Speed. The rate at which the distance is covered; quickness.

Speed boat. Means a motor boat driven by a high speed internal combustion engine capable of propelling the boat at a speed exceeding 24 kilometres per hour in still water and so designed that when running at a speed it will plane, *i.e.,* its bow will rise from the water. [Income-tax Rules, 1962, App. I, Note (4)]

Speedy trial. 1. A right of an accused. [21 Am J2d Crim L § 241] A trial conducted according to fixed rules, regulations, and proceedings of law, free from vexatious, capricious, and oppressive delays. 2. The constitutional and statutory right of one accused of a criminal offence to a speedy trial is a right which is personal to the accused alone and one in which the State has no special interest, and it has been held without question that he may waive his right in that respect. (*Ballentine's Law Dictionary*)

Spes Successionis. *(Lat.)* 'Hope of succession'. The chance of an heir apparent succeeding to an estate.

Spices. "SPICES" means the spices specified in the Schedule:

Provided that the Central Government may, if satisfied that it is necessary or expedient in the public interest so to do, by notification in the official Gazette, add any other spice to the Schedule or omit any spice therefrom. [Spices Board Act (10 of 1986), S. 2(n)]

Spirit. "SPIRIT" means any liquor, containing alcohol obtained by distillation. [Excise Act (12 of 1896), S. 3]

"SPIRIT" means any liquor containing alcohol and obtained by distillation whether it is denatured or not. [Andhra Pradesh Prohibition Act (AP Act No. 17 of 1995), S. 2(15) omitted by A.P. Act No. 35 of 1995].

The soul; essence; real meaning; a distilled liquid; an aequeous solution of ethyl alcohol.

Spiritual.

"1. of, relating to, or affecting the human spirit or soul as opposed to material or physical things: I'm responsible for his spiritual welfare | the spiritual values of life. • (of a person) not concerned with material values or pursuits. 2. of or relating to religion or religious belief; Iran's spiritual leaders.

(also negro spiritual) A religious song of a kind associated with black Christians of the southern US, and thought to derive from the combination of European hymns and African musical elements by black slaves." [Oxford Dictionary as cited in *K.S. Varghese v. ST. Peter's and Paul's Syrian Orth,*. 2017 (7) SCALE 450, para 100]

A spiritual person is one who seeks to value and connect himself to higher power or simply his higher self.

"The word 'spiritual' has been defined to mean as of or relating to ecclesiastical rather than secular matters." [Black's Law Dictionary as cited in *K.S. Varghese.* v. *ST. Peter's and Paul's Syrian Orth,*. 2017 (7) SCALE 450, para 100]

Spirituous liquor. "SPIRITUOUS LIQUOR" means any fermented liquor, any wine or any alcoholic liquid obtained by distillation of the sap of any kind of palm tree, and includes any other liquid containing alcohol which the Central Government, may, by notification in official Gazette, declare to be a spirituous liquor for the purpose of this Act. [Cantonments Act (2 of 1924), S. 2(xxxvi)]

Spirituous preparation. Means—

(i) any medicinal preparation containing alcohol, whether self-generated or otherwise; or

(ii) any mixture or compound of wine with medicinal substances, whether the wine is fortified with spirit or not; or

(iii) any other substance notified to be spirituous preparation. [Spirituous Preparations (Inter-State Trade and Commerce) Control Act (39 of 1955), S. 2(d)]

Splash screen. An initial web site page used to capture the surfer's attention for a short period, and which usually directs the surfer to the web site. (*Cyber Law*)

Spoliatus debet ante omnia restitui. The party dispossessed ought first of all to be restored.

Spondeat superior. (*Lat.*) Let the master answer or be responsible.

Sponsor. "SPONSOR" means any person holding not less than ten per cent of the paid up equity capital of a asset reconstruction company. [Securitisation and Reconstruction of Financial Assets and Enforcement of Security Interest Act (54 of 2002), S. 2(zh)]

"SPONSOR" means a person who, acting alone or in combination with another body corporate, establishes a mutual funds. [SEBI (Mutual Funds) Regulations, 1996, R. 2(x)]

Sponsor group. Includes:

(i) the sponsor(s);

(ii) in case the sponsor is a body corporate;

(a) entities or person(s) which are controlled by such body corporate;

(b) entities or person(s) who control such body corporate;

(c) entities or person(s) which are controlled by person(s) as referred at clause (b).

(iii) in case sponsor is an individual:

(a) an immediate relative of such individual (i.e., any spouse of that person, or any parent, brother, sister or child of the person or of the spouse); and

(b) entities or person(s) which are controlled by such individual. [Securities and Exchange Board of India (Real Estate Investment Trusts) Regulations, 2014, Regn. 2(1)(zta)].

Sponsoring body. Means a body being a charitable or a not-for-profit Society or Trust or Company under Section 8 of Companies Act, 2013 making an application for declaring an institution under its administrative, academic and financial control as a Deemed to be University. [UGC (Institutions Deemed to be Universities) Regulations, 2019, Regn. 2(2.18)].

Spontaneous. Produced of itself; of one's free will. [Mines Act (35 of 1952), S. 23(1)(b)].

Spoofing. Spoofing occurs where one computer on a network pretends to have the identity of another computer on the network. [*Symantec Global Internet Security Threat Report: Trends for 2009,* (Vol. XV) April 2010]

Sport. Hunting or shooting for sport or amusement [Arms Act (54 of 1959), S. 13(3)(a)(i)]; some game or play 10(23), Income-tax Act (43 of 1961)].

Spot. A particular small area, part or definite point in any surface or body. [CrPC, 1973 (2 of 1974), S. 157(1)] [Plantations Labour Act (69 of 1951), S. 5(c)].

Spot delivery contract. Means a contract which provides for—

(a) actual delivery of securities and the payment of a price therefor either on the same day as the date of the contract or on the next day, the actual periods taken for the dispatch of the securities or the remittance of money therefor through the post being excluded from the computation of the period aforesaid if the parties to the contract do not reside in the same town or locality;

(b) transfer of the securities by the depository from the account of a beneficial owner to the account of another beneficial owner when such securities are dealt with by a depository. [Securities Contract (Regulation) Act (42 of 1956), S. 2(i)]

Spouse. Bride; wife; husband or wife as the case may be; married pair.

Spouse means a wife or a husband and the use of the term cannot be limited to a spouse married under Special Marriage Act. *Uma Charan Roy* v. *Kajal Coy,* AIR 1971 Cal 307, 309. [Special Marriage Act (43 of 1954), S. 4]

Spread-over. "SPREAD OVER" means the period between the commencement of duty on any day and the termination of duty on that day. [Motor Transport Workers Act (27 of 1961), S. 2(k)]

Spring. An outflow of water from the earth; an elastic contrivance usually for setting in motion or for reducing shocks.

Sprinkle. To scatter in small drops or particles. [Drugs and Cosmetics Act (23 of 1964), S. 3].

Spun silk. Means silk yarn spun from pierced or spoilt cocoons, fluff from cocoons, pieces of silk, coils, or other silk waste. [Central Silk Board Act (61 of 1958), S. 3(f)]

Spurious. The word "spurious" means (1) not genuine, not proceeding from true source, (2) not legitimate. *Chaitanya Kumar* v. *Sushila*, AIR 1975 SC 1718, 1721.

Spurious goods and services. Mean such goods and services which are claimed to be genuine but they are actually not so. [Consumer Protection Act (68 of 1986), S. 2(1)(oo)]

Spyware. A somewhat vague term generally referring to software that is secretly installed on a users computer and that monitors use of the computer in some way without the users' knowledge or consent.

Most spyware tries to get the user to view advertising and/or particular *web pages.* Some spyware also sends information about the user to another machine over the Internet.

Spyware is usually installed without a users' knowledge as part of the installation of other software, especially software such as music sharing software obtained *via download.* (*Matisse Enzer-Glossary of Internet Terms*)

Spying. Watching; secretly listening and gathering information about the activities and movements of the enemy and transmitting the same to one's own government or group.

The act of secret agent employed to watch others or to collect information especially of a military nature. [Navy Act (62 of 1957), S. 38].

SQL. (*abbr.*) Structured Query Language. A specialized language for sending queries to databases. Most industrial-strength and many smaller database applications can be addressed using SQL. Each specific application will have its own slightly different version of SQL implementing features unique to that application, but all SQL-capable databases support a common subset of SQL. (*Internet and E-commerce*)

SELECT name, email FROM people-table WHERE contry='uk' (*Matisse Enzer Glossary of Internet Terms*)

Square. An open space, commonly but not necessarily of that shape. [Indian Electricity Act (9 of 1910), S. 2(m); Delhi Municipal Corporation Act (66 of 1957), S. 2(57)].

Squatter. One who settles on the lands of others without any legal authority; this term is applied particularly to persons who settle on the public land.

SSL. (*abbr.*) Secure Sockets Layer : a protocol designed by Netscape Communications to enable encrypted, authenticated communications across the Internet. SSL is used mostly (but not exclusively) in communications between web browsers and web servers. URLs that begin with "https" (rather than "http") indicate that an SSL connection will be used.

SSL, provides 3 important things: Privacy, Authentication, and Message Integrity.

In an SSL, connection each side of the connection must have a Security Certificate, which each side's software sends to the other. Each side then encrypts what it sends using information from both its own and the other side's Certificate, ensuring that only the intended recipient can de-crypt it, and that the other side can be sure the data came from the place it claims to have come from, and that the message has not been tampered with. (*Internet and E-commerce; Information Technology*)

Stab. To make a wound with a pointed instrument. A stab differs from a cut or a wound.

To wound (often to kill) with a thrust of pointed weapon. [IPC (45 of 1860), S. 108, *Expln.* 2, ill. (b)].

Stabit praesumptio donec probetur in contrarium. The presumption shall stand until it be proved to the contrary.

Staff. Body of officers attached to a commander for the purpose of keeping the parts of an army, *etc.*, in relation; body of assistants by whom an institution or business is carried on (as) the regimental staff; staff officers.

A person who is a pharmacist and designated as dresser will not come under the definition of 'artisan'. If he is engaged on a monthly salary basis discharging the duties of a dresser, he has to be considered as one of the members of the staff of the Tea Garden. *Cabhar Cha Sramik Union* v. *Manager, Manjhegram Tea Estate,* AIR 1960 Ass 123, 125.

The personnel responsible for the functioning of an institution or the establishment or the carrying out of an assigned task under an overall discretion of a head. [CPC (5 of 1908), S. 86(4)(c)]; [CPC (5 of 1908), O. XXVIII, R. 1(2)].

Staff employment. Employing a body of persons in different parts in any establishment. [CPC (5 of 1908), O. XXVIII, R. 1(2)].

Stage carriage. "STAGE CARRIAGE" means a motor-vehicle constructed or adapted to carry more than six passengers excluding the driver for hire or reward at separate fares paid by or for individual passengers, either for the whole journey or for stages of journey. [Motor Vehicles Act (59 of 1988), S. 2(40)]

"STAGE CARRIAGE *VIS-À-VIS* CONTRACT CARRIAGE". 'Stage carriage' is intended to meet the requirements of the general public travelling from one destination to another having different purposes whereas a 'contract carriage' is meant for those who want to hire a public service vehicle as a whole collectively for their transport from one destination to another having the same purpose. *Hardeo Motor Transport* v. *State of M.P.*, AIR 2007 SC 839 : 2007 AIR SCW 556.

Stakeholder. A person with whom money or other property is deposited by the parties to a bet or wager pending the decision of the event on which the bet has been made.

Stalking. (1) Any man who—

(i) follows a woman and contacts, or attempts to contact such woman to foster personal interaction repeatedly despite a clear indication of disinterest by such woman; or

(ii) monitors the use by a woman of the internet, email or any other form of electronic communication,

commits the offence of stalking:

Provided that such conduct shall not amount to stalking if the man who pursued it proves that—

(i) it was pursued for the purpose of preventing or detecting crime and the man accused of stalking had been entrusted with the responsibility of prevention and detection of crime by the State; or

(ii) it was pursued under any law or to comply with any condition or requirement imposed by any person under any law; or

(iii) in the particular circumstances such conduct was reasonable and justified. [Indian Penal Code 1860, S. 354D(1), as inserted by Criminal Law (Amendment) Act, 2013 (13 of 2013)].

Stamp. "STAMP" means any mark, seal or endorsement by any agency or person duly authorised by the State Government, and includes an adhesive or impressed stamp, for the purposes of duty chargeable under this Act. [Indian Stamp Act (2 of 1899), S. 2(26) (*Substituted by Finance Act (23 of 2004), S. 117*) now repealed by Goods and Service Tax Act, 2017]

"STAMP" means a mark, which is made on, or in relation to, any weight or measure with a view to—

(1) Certifying that such weight or measure conforms to the standard specified by or under this Act, or,

(2) Indicating that any mark which was previously made thereon certifying that such weight or

measure conforms to the standards specified by or under this Act, has been obliterated.

Explanation.—A stamp may be made by impressing, casting, engraving, etching, branding or any other process. [Standard of Weights and Measures Act (60 of 1976), S. 2(y)]

An impression; an official mark or seal set on something (as a warrant or deed) or on papers legally requiring execution to signify that the duty or tax has been paid [Indian Evidence Act (1 of 1872), S. 82 and Indian Stamp Act (2 of 1899), S. 10]; to impress with a stamp; imprint [Indian Stamp Act (2 of 1899), S. 18(2)].

"STAMP" means a mark, made by impressing, casting, engraving, etching, branding, affixing pre-stressed paper seal or any other process in relation to, any weight or measure with a view to—

(i) certifying that such weight or measure conforms to the standard specified by or under this Act, or

(ii) indicating that any mark which was previously made thereon certifying that such weight or measure conforms to the standards specified by or under this Act, has been obliterated. [Legal Metrology Act, 2009 (1 of 2010), S. 2(t)]

Stamp duty. A tax on documents dealing with such matters as transfer of property, shares, debentures, and insurance policies. If unstamped, these documents become invalid. (*Taxation*)

Stamp paper. A paper containing an embossed or impressed mark to certify that the amount stated in it has been paid to government. [CPC (5 of 1908), O. VII, R. 11(c)].

Stand mute. Defendant's refusal to enter a plea in criminal trial.

Stand alone system. Means the electricity system set-up to generate power and distribute electricity in a specified area without connection to the grid. [Indian Electricity Act (36 of 2003), S. 2(63)]

Stand-of-barrier. "STAND OF BARRIER" means a physical barrier set back from the outer edge of an enclosure barrier. [Recognition of Zoo Rules, 1992, R. 2(g)]

Standard. Something that is established by authority, custom or general consent as a model or example to be followed. [Beedi and Cigar Workers (Conditions of Employment) Act (32 of 1966), S. 18(4), *Expln.*]; a criterion [Mines Act (35 of 1952), S. 58(d)]; [Press Council Act (37 of 1978), S. 12(1)]; an upright post/pillar; stick [Workmen's Compensation Act (8 of 1923), Sch. II, item (ix)].

"STANDARD". In relation to any article of food, means the standards notified by the Food Authority. [S. 3(1)(zu) of the Food Safety & Standards Act, 2006 (34 of 2006)]

"Standard" means "a model accepted as correct by custom, consent, or authority; a criterion for measuring acceptability, quality or accuracy." [Black's Law Dictionary (10th Edn.) as cited in *Modern Dental College & Research Centre v. State of M.P.*, (2016) 7 SCC 353, para 127.]

"Standard" means " A level of quality or attainment, a required or agreed level of quality or attainment (in elementary schools) a grade of proficiency tested by examination, something used as a measure, norm or model in comparative evaluation." [Concise Oxford English Dictionary (10th Edn., Revised) as cited in *Modern Dental College and Research Centre v. State of M.P.*, (2016) 7 SCC 353, para 127].

Standard Asset. Means the asset in respect of which no default in repayment of principal or payment of interest has occurred or is perceived and which has neither shown signs of any problem relating to repayment of principal sum or interest nor does it carry more than normal risk attached to the business. [R. 3(1)(f) of the Nidhi Rules, 2014]

Standard equipment. "STANDARD EQUIPMENT" means :

(i) Production equipment which is generally used in the chemical industry and is not included in the types of specialized equipment;

(ii) Other equipment commonly used in the chemical industry, such as : fire-fighting equipment; guard and security/ safety surveillance equipment; medical facilities, laboratory facilities; or communications equipment. [Chemical Weapons Convention Act (34 of 2000), (Verification Annex), 5(b)]

Standard export figure. Means such quantity as the Central Government may, by notification in the Official Gazette, specify pursuant to any international agreement in this behalf. [Tea Act (29 of 1953), S. 3(m)]

Standard family. Means a family consisting of the employee, his or her spouse, and two children requiring in all three adult consumption units. [Beedi and Cigar Workers (Condition of Employment) Act (32 of 1966), S. 18(4), *Expln.* I]

Standard foot or **inch.** One-third part of the standard yard shall be called a STANDARD FOOT, and one-thirty-sixth part of such a yard shall be called a STANDARD INCH. [Measures of Length Act (11 of 1889), S. 4]

Standard mark. "STANDARD MARK" means the Bureau of Indian Standards Certification Mark specified by the Bureau to represent a particular Indian Standard and also includes any Indian Standards Institutions Certification Mark specified by the Indian Standards Institution. [Bureau of Indian Standards Act (63 of 1987), S. 2(t)]

"Standard Mark" means the mark specified by the Bureau, and includes Hallmark, to represent conformity of goods, article, process, system or service to a particular Indian Standard or conformity to a standard, the mark of which has been established, adopted or recognized by the Bureau and is marked on the article or goods as a Standard Mark or on its covering or label attached to such goods or article so marked. [Bureau of Indian Standards Act (11 of 2016), S. 2(40)].

Standard Milk. Means cow milk, buffalo milk or sheep milk or goat milk or a combination of any of these milk has been standardized to fact and solid-not-fat percentage given in the Table below in 2.1.1:1 by the adjustment of milk solids. Standardised milk shall be pasteurized and shall show a negative phosphatase test. [Food Safety and Standards (Food, Products and Food Additives) Regulations, 2011, Regn. 1.2.21 **as cited in** *Swami Achutanand Tirtha* v. *Union of India,* (2016) 9 SCC 699, para 43].

Standard pay scale .'Standard pay scale' (as it is or with the prefix 'First" or 'Second', as the case may be) with respect to any government servant means the scale of pay, other than the existing pay scale prescribed for the post on which such government servant is working, in which the government servant was drawing his pay prior to 31-12-1995 and also and pay scale granted to him for the purposes of drawing his pay as 'pay scale as a personal measure to him' as defined under these Rules through any other order/notification of the Government or with any other reason. [Haryana Civil Services (Assured Career Progression) Rules, 1990, R. 3(r) as cited in *State of Haryana v. Sita Ram*, (2013) 16 SCC 677, para 4].

Standard of proof. Indicates the extent or benchmark to which a particular fact is required to be proved. [Karnika Seth, *Computers Internet and New Technology Laws*, 2021, LexisNexis, Glossary of Legal Terms].

Standard quality. The expression "STANDARD QUALITY" means—

(a) in relation to a drug, that the drug complies with the standard set out in the Second Schedule;

(b) in relation to a cosmetic, that the cosmetic complies with such standard as may be prescribed. [Drugs And Cosmetics Act (23 of 1940), S. 8(1)]

Standard rate. In respect of any year of account means—

(a) in relation to that part of the capital base for that year of account which is equivalent to the capital base as on the 31st day of March 1955, seven per centum per annum;

(b) in relation to the remaining capital base for that year, the Reserve Bank ruling at the beginning of that year plus—

(i) two per centum for investments made up to the date of the commencement of the Electricity Laws (Amendment) Act, 1991; and

(ii) five per centum for investments made thereafter;

Provided that the Central Government may, by notification in the Official Gazette, and with effect from such date as may be specified therein, increase or decrease the standard rate specified in clause (b), if after consultation with the Authority, that Government considers it necessary so to do to ensure that any rise or fall in the Reserve Bank rate does not affect the reasonable return in any subsequent year of account in relation to that part of the capital base which is equivalent to the capital base as computed on the last date of the previous year of account. [Electricity (Supply) Act (54 of 1948), Sch. Sixth, Para XVII (10)]

Standard weight. Means the weight prescribed for any coin. [Coinage Act (3 of 1906), S. 2(e)] [Also see S. 2(l) of the Coinage Act, 2011 (11 of 2011)]

Standard weight or measure. 'STANDARD WEIGHT OR MEASURE' means a weight, measure or number which confirms to the standards established in relation thereto by or under the standards act. [Standards of Weights & Measure Act (Enforcement) Act (54 of 1985), S. 2(l)]

Standardisation. The act of standardising; making uniform. [Industrial Disputes Act (14 of 1947), Sch. IV, item 10].

Standing. "STANDING" means the period of actual practice after the commencement of this Act. [Gujarat Advocate Welfare Fund Act (14 of 1991), S. 2(o)]

"STANDING" means the period of actual practice from the date of enrollment as advocate and sanad obtained from the Bar Council or appropriate authority. [Goa Advocates Welfare Fund Act, 1995, (Goa Act No. 2 of 1997), S. 2(p)]

Position or grade General Clauses Act in profession, university or society [Employees' State Insurance Act (34 of 1948), S. 74(3)]; erect; permanent].

Standing committee. A standing committee is a sub-unit of a political or deliberative body established in a permanent fashion to aid the parent assembly in accomplishing its duties, usually by providing focused attention on one particular subject matter.

Standing orders. Procedure Rules for Parliament or other Legislative bodies.

Standing timber. Trees, the wood of which can be used for building or repairing houses or for other industrial purposes and implies an intention, sooner or later; to sever the trees from the soil. [T.P. Act (4 of 1882), S. 3].

Staple foods. Means articles of food intended for mass consumption on a daily basis and include rice, wheat, wheat flour, atta, maida, oil, salt, milk, and such other articles of food as may be designated staple foods under these regulations. [Food Safety and Standards (Fortification of Foods) Regulations, 2018, Regn. 2(1)(h)].

Star chamber. A chamber at Westminster so called, because at first the ceiling thereof was adorned with images of gilded stars. (*Tomlin*)

A civil and Criminal Court noted for arbitrary procedure.

Star-shaped structure. An organizational structure consisting of only decision makers and unskilled labor. It eliminates middle-management personnel.

Stare decisis. Abide by the decisions; a Latin phrase meaning "to stand by decided cases; to uphold precedents; to maintain former adjudications."

To stand by things decided; to abide by precedents where the same points come again in litigation.

'To stand by decision and not to disturb what is settled'. [*Shakher Raju v. Union of India*, (2011) 2 SCC 132 : (2011) 1 SCC (L&S) 161, para 10 as cited in *Purbanchal Cables and Conductors Private Limited v. Assam State Electricity Board*, (2012) 7 SCC 462, para 72].

To adhere to precedent and not to unsettle things which are settled.[*Purbanchal Cables and Conductors Private Limited v. Assam State Electricity Board*, (2012) 7 SCC 462, para 69].

Stare decisis, et non quieta movere. It is best to adhere to decisions and not to disturb questions put at rest.

Starred questions. The Parliamentary questions that are to be answered on the floor of the Parliament or the State Legislature which may be followed by supplementary questions by members. They are known by the name because of being always distinguished by an asterisk.

Start-up. Normally used to describe a company that is beginning from scratch. A start-up often needs *venture capital* financing to help it on its way.

"Start-up" means an entity, where—

(i) more than five years have not lapsed from the date of its incorporation of registration;

(ii) the turnover for any of the financial years, out of the aforementioned five years, did not exceed Rupees Twenty-five crores; and

(iii) it is working towards innovation, development, deployment or commercialization of new products, processes or services driven by technology or intellectual property:

Provided that any such entity formed by splitting up or reconstruction of a business already in existence shall not be considered as a start-up:

Provided further that the mere act of developing—

(a) products or services or processes which do not have potential for commercialization, or

(b) undifferentiated products or services or processes, or

(c) products or services or processes with no or limited incremental value for customers or workflow,

would not be covered under this definition.

Explanation 1.—An entity shall cease to be a start-up on completion of five years from the date of its incorporation/or registration or if its turnover for any previous year exceeds Rupees Twenty-five crores.

Explanation 2.—Entity means a private limited company (as defined in the Companies Act, 2013), or a registered partnership firm registered under Section 59 of the Partnership Act, 1932 or a limited liability partnership under the Limited Liability Partnership Act, 2002.

Explanation 3.—The term "Turnover" shall have the same meaning as defined in the Companies Act, 2013 (18 of 2013).

Explanation 4.—An entity is considered to be working towards innovation, development, deployment or commercialization of new products, processes or services driven by technology or intellectual property if it aims to develop and commercialise a new product or service or process, or a significantly improved existing product o service or process that will create or add value for customers or workflow.

Explanation 5.—The reference rates of foreign currency of the Reserve Bank of India shall prevail. [Patent Rules, 2003, R. 2(fb)].

For the purpose of this sub-regulation a 'START-UP' means an entity which complies with the conditions laid down in Notification No. G.S.R. 180(E), dated February 17, 2016 issued by Department of Industrial Policy and Promotion, Ministry of Commerce and Industry, Government of India. [Foreign Exchange Management (Foreign Currency Accounts by a Person Resident in India) Regulations, 2015, Regn 5(E), *Explanation*].

"STARTUP" means:

(i) an entity in India recognized as a startup by the competent authority under Startup India initiative,

(ii) In case of a foreign entity, an entity fulfilling the criteria for turnover and period of incorporation/registration as per Startup India initiative and submitting declaration to that effect.

Explanation.—In calculating the turnover reference rates of foreign currency of Reserve Bank of India shall prevail. [Trade Marks Ruls, 2017, R. 2(1)(x)].

"STARTUP" means an entity which complies with the conditions laid down in Notification No. G.S.R. 180(e) dated February 17, 2016 issued by Department of Industrial Policy and Promotion, Ministry of Commerce and Industry, Government of India. [Foreign Exchange Management (Transfer or Issue of Security by a Person Resident Outside India) Regulations, 2017, Regn. 2(xli)].

"START-UP" means an entity which complies with the conditions laid down in Notification No. G.S.R. 180(E), dated February 17, 2016, as amended/updated from time to time, issued by Department of Industrial Policy and Promotion. Ministry of Commerce and Industry, Government of

India. [Foreign Exchange Management (Borrowing and Lending) Regulations, 2018, Regn. 2(xvi)].

Start-up company. Usually a new company that is beginning from scratch. It may need *venture capital* to help it on its way.

For the purpose of this Regulation, a 'STARTUP COMPANY' means a private company incorporated under the Companies Act, 2013 or Companies Act, 1956 and recognized as such in accordance with notification number G.S.R. 180(E), dated February 17, 2016 issued by the Department of Industrial Policy and Promotion, Ministry of Commerce and Industry. [Foreign Exchange Management (Transfer or Issue of Security by a Person Resident Outside India) Regulations, 2000, Regn. 6-D, *Explanation*; Companies (Acceptance of Deposits) Rules, 2014, R. 2(1)(c)(xvii), *Explanation I*].

"STARTUP COMPANY" means a private company incorporated under the Companies Act, 2013 and recognized as such in accordance with notification number G.S.R. 180(E) dated February 17, 2016 issued by the Department of Industrial Policy and Promotion, Ministry of Commerce and Industry, Government of India and complies with the conditions laid down by it. [Foreign Exchange Management (Transfer or Issue of Security by a Person Resident Outside India) Regulations 2017, Regn. 2(xlii)]

Stat pro rationed voluntas reasons. 'Stat pro rationed voluntas reasons'. A claim devoid of reasons.[*Ravi YashwantBhoir v. District Collector, Raigad*, (2012) 4 SCC 407, para 59].

State. "STATE" includes a Union Territory having a Legislative Assembly but does not include the State of Jammu and Kashmir. [Delimitation Act (13 of 2002), S. 2(f)]

A body politic, or society of men, united together for the purpose of promoting their mutual safety and advantage, by the joint efforts of their combined strength. (*Cooley, Const. Lim. 1*)

State" includes the Government and Parliament of India and the Government and Legislature of each State as well as "all local or other authorities within the territory of India or under the control of the Government of India". [*K.K. Saksena v. International Commission on Irrigation and Drainage*, (2015) 4 SCC 670, para 33].

The body politic as organised for supreme civil rule and government [General Clauses Act (10 of 1897), S. 3(58) and Constitution of India, Art. 3, *Expln.* I]; the condition; manner of existence; mode of existence; status; stationing in life [Mines Act (35 of 1952), S. 7(c)]; [Sale of Goods Act (3 of 1930), S. 2(12)]; [Air Force Act (45 of 1950), S. 48(1)]; to put into words; to set forth; to express the details.

The word 'State' include a Union Territory. *Ramkishore* v. *Union of India*, AIR 1966 SC 644, 648. [Constitution of India, Art. 3]

'The State' includes its Income Tax Department. *Bidi Supply Co.* v. *Union of India*, AIR 1956 SC 479, 484. [Constitution of India, Art. 12]

The Port Trust would fall within the extended definition of the State under Art. 12, Constitution of India because it would be a local authority. R. *Sarangapani* v. *Madras Port Trust,* AIR 1961 Mad 234, 239.

The expression "the State" used in Art. 50 has to be construed in the distributive sense as including the Government and Parliament of India and the Government and the Legislature of each State and all local or other authorities within the territory of India or under the control of the Government of India. *S.C. Advocates on Record Association* v. *Union of India*, AIR 1994 SC 268, 318. [Constitution of India, Arts. 50, 12]

Merely because the Government is giving 25% subsidy to a private company for setting up a plant does not mean that the company is a 'State'. *Jothi & Co.* v. *Tamilnadu Pollution Control Board,* AIR 1994 Mad 50, 53. [Constitution of India, Arts. 12]

Electricity Board is 'STATE'. *Electricity Board, Rajasthan* v. *Mohan Lal*, AIR 1967 SC 1837, 1863; *Surya Narain Yadav* v. *B.S.E. Board*, AIR 1985 SC 941, 944.

Life Insurance Corporation of India is purely autonomous business body. It employs servants as any private house does and enforces discipline amongst its servants as that house. Life Insurance Corporation does not fall within the ambit of "State" as contemplated by Article 12 of the Constitution. Having regard to the Constitution and nature of its legal entity and the measure of State Control, Gusgaeon Gramin Bank is an instrumentality of the State and is made of the State's Own flesh and bones and the Bank is 'State' within the meaning of Art. 12 of the Constitution. *M.K. Agarwal* v. *Gargeon Gramin Bank*, AIR 1988 SC 286, 288.

A Society to be "State", should undertake Government business or perform public obligation of the State and Institute of Constitutional and Parliamentary Studies, not being an agency or instrumentality of the State, is not 'State'. *Tekraj* v. *Union of India*, AIR 1988 SC 469, 481.

An authority forming an instrumentality or agency of the Government, is State. Regional Rural Banks, being under deep and persuasive control of the Central Govt. and having been established as the instrumentality of the Govt. are 'State'. *Chairman, Prathama Bank, Moradabad* v. *Vijay Kumar*, AIR 1989 SC 1977, 1982.

The National Council of Educational Research and Training is not 'State' within the meaning of Art. 12. *Chandra Mohan Khanna* v. *NCERT*, AIR 1992 SC 76, 80.

The word 'State' in Art. 131 contemplates a State as a constituent unit of the Union along with its territory and permanent institutions. *State of Rajasthan* v. *Union of India*, AIR 1977 SC 1361, 1431. [Constitution of India, Art. 131]

State Act. Shall mean an Act passed by the Legislature of a State established or continued by the Constitution. [General Clauses Act (10 of 1897), S. 3(59)]

State aided society. "STATE AIDED SOCIETY" means a society which receives or has received aid or grant or loan from Central Government or State Government or any other statutory body. [Madhya Pradesh Society Registrikaran Adhiniyam (44 of 1973), S. 3(f)]

State Bank of India. Means the State Bank of India constituted under section 3 of the State Bank of India Act, 1955 (23 of 1955). [S. 2(r) of the Factoring Regulation Act, 2011 (12 of 2012)]

State Blood Transfusion Council. "STATE BLOOD TRANSFUSION COUNCIL" means a society registered, in consultation with the National Blood Transfusion Council, under the Societies Registration Act, 1860 or under any law corresponding to that Act in force in any part of the India and has Secretary to the Government of that State dealing with the Department of Health, as its Chairman, by whatever name called. [Income-tax Act (43 of 1961), S. 80G(2)(a)(iiih) *Expln.*(b)]

State Board. Means, —

(i) in relation to a State in which the Water (Prevention and Control of Pollution) Act, 1974, is in force and the State Government has constituted for that State a State Pollution Control Board under Section 4 of that Act, the said State Board; and

(ii) in relation to any other State, the State Board for Prevention and Control of Air Pollution constituted by the State Government under Section 5 of this Act. [Air (Prevention and Control of Pollution) Act (14 of 1981), S. 2(o)]

'State cadre' means the sanctioned strength of the nongazetted posts borne on the establishment of the headquartered offices of the departments having jurisdiction over the whole State but does not include the posts borne on the divisional and district cadres. [Jammu and Kashmir Subordinate Services Recruitment Rules, 1992, R. 3(vi) as cited in *Vinod Kumar Koul v. State of J&K*, (2012) 11 SCC 247, para 4].

State Commission. Means a Consumer Disputes Redressal Commission established in a State under clause (b) of Section 9. [Consumer Protection Act, 1986 (68 of 1986), S. 2(1)(p)]

"STATE COMMISSION" means the State Food Commission constituted under section 16. [S. 2(21) of the National Food Security Act, 2013 (20 of 2013)]

State co-operative bank. Means the principal co-operative society in a State, the primary object of which is the financing of other co-operative societies in the State. [Industrial Reconstruction Bank of India Act, 1984 (62 of 1985), S. 2(t)]

"STATE CO-OPERATIVE BANK" means the principal co-operative society in a State, the primary object of which is the financing of other co-operative societies in the State :

Provided that in addition to such principal society in a State, or where there is no such principal society in a State, the State Government may declare any one or more co-operative societies carrying on business in that State to be also or to be a State co-operative bank or State co-operative banks within the meaning of this definition. [National Bank for Agriculture and Rural Development Act (61 of 1981), S. 2(u)]

State concerned. In relation to the acquired territories referred in Part I, Part II and Part III of the First Schedule, means respectively, the State of Assam, the State of Punjab and State of West Bengal; and "State Government concerned" shall be construed accordingly. [Acquired Territories (Merger) Act (64 of 1960), S. 2(g)]

State Goods and Services Tax Act. Means the law to be made by the State Legislature for levy and collection of tax by the concerned State on supply of goods and services or both. [Goods and Services Tax (Compensation to States) Act (15 of 2017), S. 2(1)(o)].

State Government. In relation to a Union territory, means the Administrator thereof appointed under article 239 of the Constitution. [S. 2(22) of the National Food Security Act, 2013 (20 of 2013)]

"STATE GOVERNMENT". In relation to a Union territory, means the Administrator thereof appointed under article 239 of the Constitution. [S. 2(1)(r) of the Prohibition of Employment as Manual Scavengers & Their Rehabilitation Act, 2013 (25 of 2013)]

State Government undertaking. For the purposes of section 40(*a*)(*iib*) of Act 43 of 1961, a 'State Government undertaking' includes—

(i) a corporation established by or under any Act of the State Government;

(ii) a company in which more than fifty per cent of the paid-up equity share capital is held by the State Government;

(iii) a company in which more than fifty per cent of the paid-up equity share capital is held by the entity referred to in clause (i) or clause (ii) (whether singly or taken together);

(iv) a company or corporation in which the State Government has the right to appoint the majority of the directors or to control the management or policy decisions, directly or indirectly, including by virtue of its shareholding or management rights or shareholders agreements or voting agreements or in any other manner;

(v) an authority, a board or an institution or a body established or constituted by or under any Act of the State Government or owned or controlled by the State Government. [(w.e.f. 1-4-2014) *Explanation* to section 40(*a*)(*iib*) of the Income-tax Act, 1961 (43 of 1961)]

"State Government" includes—

(a) in relation to a Union territory with legislature, the Government of the Union territory; and

(b) in relation to a Union territory without legislature, the administrator appointed under article 239 of the Constitution as an administrator thereof. [Code on Social Security, 2020 (36 of 2020), section 2(80)]

State land development bank. Means the co-operative society which is the principal land development bank (by whatever name called) in a State and which has as its primary object the providing of long-term finance for agricultural development:

Provided that, in addition to such principal land development bank in a State, or where there is no such bank in a State, the State Government may declare any co-operative society carrying on business in that State and authorized by the bye-laws of such co-operative society to provide long-term finance for agricultural development to be also or to be a State land development bank within the meaning of this definition. [National Bank for Agriculture and Rural Development (61 of 1981), S. 2(v)]

State level co-operative society. In this Part, unless the context otherwise requires, "STATE LEVEL CO-OPERATIVE SOCIETY" means a co-operative society having its area of operation extending to the whole of a State and defined as such in any law made by the Legislature of a State. [Constitution of India, Part IXB, Article 243ZH(h)].

State Medical Council. Means a medical council constituted under any law for the time being in force in any State regulating the registration of practitioners of medicine. [Indian Medical Council Act (102 of 1956), S. 2(j)]

State of export. "STATE OF EXPORT" means a party from which a transboundary movement of hazardous wastes or other wastes is planned to be initiated or is initiated. [Basel Convention on the Control of Transboundary Movements of Hazardous Wastes and Their Disposal, (1989), Art. 2.10]

State of import. "STATE OF IMPORT" means a party to which a transboundary movement of hazardous wastes or other wastes is planned or takes place for the purpose of disposal therein or for the purpose of loading prior to disposal in an area not under the national jurisdiction of any State. [Basel Convention on the Control of Transboundary Movements of Hazardous Wastes and Their Disposal, (1989), Art. 2.11]

State of intoxication. "A person as a result of his consumption of intoxicating liquor whereby his physical and mental faculties were appreciably and materially impaired in the conduct of ordinary affairs or acts of daily life is said to be in a state of intoxication. *Hari Charan* v. *State,* AIR 1968 Ori 31 at 32. [Indian Railways Act (9 of 1890), S. 120]

State of mind. The condition or capacity of a mind of a person.

State of quarantine. The condition of being in compulsory isolation or detention to prevent spread of contagion or infection. [IPC (45 of 1860), S. 271].

State of the ship's registry. "STATE OF THE SHIP'S REGISTRY', in relation to registered or unregistered ships, means the State of registration of the ship, or as the case may be, the State whose flag the ship is flying'. [Merchant Shipping Act (44 of 1958), S. 352H(i)]

State of transit. "STATE OF TRANSIT" means any State, other than State of export or import through which a movement of hazardous wastes or other wastes is planned or takes place. [Basel Convention on the Control of Transboundary Movements of Hazardous Wastes and Their Disposal, (1989), Art. 2.12]

State party. "STATE PARTY" means a signatory or acceding State to the Convention whose instrument of ratification or accession has been deposited with the Depository of the Convention. [Chemical Weapons Convention Act (34 of 2000), S. 2(l)]

State premises. "STATE PREMISES" means any premises belonging to or taken on lease or licence or requisitioned by, or on behalf of the State Government. [West Bengal Premises (Regulation of Occupancy) Act (21 of 1984), S. 2(n)]

State sponsored scheme. 'STATE SPONSORED SCHEME' means a scheme sponsored by way of financial assistance by the State Government under which the State Government either—

(i) advances money to a banking company or Government company for the purposes of disbursing loans, advances or grants or for the purposes of sale of goods on credit or hire purchase; or

(ii) guarantees or agrees to guarantee the repayment of a loan, advance or grant or the payment of the price of goods sold on credit or hire purchase. [M.P. Public Moneys Recovery of Dues Act (1 of 1988), S. 2(h)]

State transport undertaking. Means any undertaking providing road transport service, where such undertaking is carried on by—

(i) the Central Government or a State Government;

(ii) any Road Transport Corporation established under Section 3 of the Road Transport Corporation Act, 1950;

(iii) any municipality or any corporation or company owned or controlled by the Central Government or one or more State Governments, or by the Central Government and one or more State Government;

(iv) Zilla Parishad or any other similar local authority.

Explanation—For the purposes of this clause, "road transport service" means a service of motor vehicles carrying passengers or goods or both by road for hire or reward. [Motor Vehicles Act (59 of 1988), S. 2(42)]

Stated. Put into words [Sale of Goods Act (3 of 1930), S. 38(2)]; (of account) which have been stated with the consensus of all the parties that they are correct. [Limitation Act (36 of 1963), Sch., Art. 26].

Statement. The act of stating, reciting, or presenting verbally or on paper.

Something that is stated; an allegation; declaration [IPC (45 of 1860), S. 199]; a document setting forth information on any point; usually submitted periodically.

The term '*statement*' is of more general import than the term 'writing'. The former in the absence of anything to the contrary may include both oral and written statements but the latter can by no possible stretch of its meaning include an oral statement.

Statement means the formal statement to be made under the provisions of the Act and cannot be constructed so as to include all enquiries and all kinds of information. *State of Gujarat* v. *Acharya Shri Devendra prasadji Pande*, AIR 1969 SC 373 at 377.

"Statement" in Section 162, CrPC, 1973 (2 of 1974) is the entirety of the facts stated by the witness to a police officer during the investigation. All these facts whenever and wherever stated go to constitute his "statement". *Maninajappa* v. *State of Mysore,* AIR 1958 Mys 138, 140. [CrPC, 1973 (2 of 1974), S. 162]

The expression "statement made in the ordinary course of business" in S. 32(2) of the Indian Evidence Act (1 of 1872) means a statement made during the course not of any particular transaction of an exceptional kind, but of business or professional employment in which the deceased was ordinarily or habitually engaged.

A 'statement' under Section 157 means only "something that is stated" and the element of communication to another person is not necessary before "something that is stated" becomes a statement under that section. *Bhogilal Chunilal Pandya* v. *State of Bombay*, AIR 1959 SC 356, 359. [Indian Evidence Act (1 of 1872), S. 157]

Statement made to police officer. The words 'statement made to police officer' mean that there must be communication of the statement to the police officer and in the light of the above consideration, a letter recovered from the pocket of an accused person when he was unconscious due to pellet injuries does not amount to a statement made to police officer. *Himatsingh* v. *State of Gujarat,* AIR 1965 Guj 302, 306. [CrPC, 1973 (2 of 1974), S. 162]

A *batta* which was addressed by the constable to Station House Officer was in the nature of narration of what he has been told by the accused. It will amount to a statement made to a police officer. *Kali Ram* v. *State of Himachal Pradesh*, AIR 1973 SC 2773, 2780.

Statement of accounts. In this Scheme unless the context otherwise requires,—

"STATEMENT OF ACCOUNTS" means a statement reflecting the credit of gold tendered by the depositor and its debit, where such account is being maintained in a dematerialized form. [Gold Deposit Scheme, 1999, S. 2(iii)]

Statement of fact. A 'statement of fact' for the purpose of S. 123(4) can be one which is capable of proof as 'false' and which the maker either 'believed to be false' or did not believe to be true' at the time of making it. *Y.K. Gadakh* v. *Balasaheb Vikhe Patil*, AIR 1994 SC 678, 694. [Representation of the People Act (43 of 1951), S. 123(4)]

Statement of objects and reasons. A statement explaining the contents and objects of a Bill in non-technical language.

Statement of Truth. (In civil proceedings) A statement made by a party (or his authorized agent, *e.g.* lawyer) that he believes the content of the document in which the Statement of Truth appears is true.

Statement or confession. The use of the expression 'statement' or 'confession' in S. 80 in juxtaposition to a prisoner or an accused person, and the context in which those words occur, point to the conclusion that it was intended that a statement as well as a confession of a prisoner or an accused person duly taken by a Magistrate was to be presumed to be genuine. It is not correct to say that the word 'statement' occurring in S. 80 has reference to a statement made by a witness as distinguished from a 'confession' made by a prisoner or an accused person. *Ram Sanehi* v. *State,* MLJ : QD (1961-1965) Vol III C439 : AIR 1963 All 308 : 1963 (2) CrLJ 1 [Evidence Act (1 of 1872), S. 80]

Station. "STATION" means any broadcasting station with studios or transmitters or both and includes a relay station. [Prasar Bharti (Broadcasting Corporation of India) Act (25 of 1990), S. 2(v) and Prasar Bharti (Broadcasting Corporation of India) Amendment Second Ordinance, 1977 (29 of 1997), S. 2(s)]

"STATION" means a railway station and includes any reservation office or booking office. [Railway Passengers (Cancellation of Tickets and Refund of Fares) Rules, 1990, R. 2(7)]

When used with reference to railways or military. [Navy Act (62 of 1957), S. 97(3) and Inland Vessels Act (1 of 1917), S. 54A(2)]; when used with reference to the police force; when used with reference to the radio, television *etc.*; a habitat; a place.

Station house. Police station.

Station master. "STATION MASTER" means a railway employee by whatever name called, in overall charge of a railway station and includes any other railway employee authorised to grant refund of fare at a station. [Railway Passengers (Cancellation of Tickets and Refund of Fares) Rules, 1990, R. 2(8)]

Station to station road. Means a special reduced rate applicable to a specific commodity booked between specified stations. [Indian Railways Act (24 of 1989), S. 2(38)]

Stationary. Still; unmoving; fixed. [Factories Act (63 of 1948), S. 14(2)].

Stationary vendors. Means street vendors who carry out vending activities on regular basis at a specific location. [S. 2(1)(k) of the Street Vendors (Protection of Livelihood and Regulation of Street Vending) Act, 2014 (7 of 2014)]

Statistics. A collection of facts and figures regarding the condition of a people, class *etc.*; the science which treats of the collection and arrangement of facts bearing on the social, moral and material condition of the people.

The science of statistics [Collection of Statistics Act (32 of 1953), S. 4]; numerical facts or data collected and classified [Cardamom Act (42 of 1965) (*repealed*), S. 9(2)(i)].

Status. "STATUS" means the category under which the assessee is assessed as "individual", "Hindu undivided family" and so on. [Income-tax Act (43 of 1961), S. 293A, *Expln.* (*b*)]

The status of an individual means the legal position of the individual in or with regard to the rest of the community. The rights, duties capacities and incapacities which determine a person to a given class, constitute his status. (*Campb. Austtin 137.*)

Legal standing or position of a person; position or standing in society; profession or the like. [Indian Partnership Act (9 of 1932), S. 5]; [Constitution of India, Art. 38(2)].

The status of a person means his personal legal condition only so far as his personal rights and burdens are concerned. *Duganna* v. *Ganeshayya,* AIR 1965 Mys 97, 101. [Indian Evidence Act (1 of 1872), S. 41]

The fact of a person being legally nominated as junior, having a peculiar relationship with the senior is status, and the capacity to succeed to the head is the incident of that status. The status, when created by a nomination, cannot be withdrawn or cancelled at the mere will of the parties. *Mahalinga Thambiran* v. *Arulnandi Thambiran*, AIR 1974 SC 199, 206.

Status quo. The existing state of things at any given date.

Existing condition.

"*Status quo*" or more fully "*Status quo* ante" means simply the existing state of things" existing before a particular point of time. For that to be of any help, it is necessary to answer the question : Existing when? Before what point of time? For the answer may be different, according as you look at the existing state of things at the date when the defendant did the act, or the first act, which is alleged to have been wrongful, or the date when the plaintiff ought first to have been aware of that act; or the date when the plaintiff complained to the defendant; or the date when he issued his writ. I think the relevant point of time for purposes of the '*status quo*' may well vary in different cases." *Alfred Dunhill* v. *Sunoptic,* (1979) FSR 337, p. 376.

Statuta pro publico commodo late interpretantur. (Jenk. Cent. 21). Statutes made for the public good ought to be liberally construed. (*Principia legis*)

Statuta suo claudunter territorio, nec ultra territorium disponunt. Statutes are limited (in their operation) to their own territory and have no extra-territorial effect.

Statute. Signifies an Act of the legislature. (*Tomlin*)

A written law as distinguished from a customary law or law of use and want; a type of subordinate legislation applied generally to be framed by university. [Indian Contract Act (9 of 1972), S. 1]; [Aligarh Muslim University Act (40 of 1920), S. 28(1)].

Statute law. "Statute law" is frequently used interchangeably with statute; but the term is broader in its meaning, and includes not only statutes as already defined, but also the judicial interpretation and application of such statutes.

Statutory arbitration. When arbitration is conducted in accordance with the provisions of a certain special Statute/ Act which provides for arbitration in respect of disputes arising on matters covered by that Statute/Act, it is called statutory arbitration. (*Arbitration*)

Statutory authority. "STATUTORY AUTHORITY" means any authority, board, corporation, council, institute, university or any other body corporate, established by or under any Central, State or Provincial Act for the purposes of regulating production or supply of goods or provision of any services or markets therefor or any matter connected therewith or incidental thereto. [Competition Act, 2002 (12 of 2003), S. 2(w)]

A 'STATUTORY AUTHORITY' cannot, in absence of the provisions of a statute, be treated to be an agency of the State. It is one thing to say that the State exercises statutory control over the functions of a statute but it is another thing to say that thereby an agency is created which would be separate in entity over which the State exercises control. *Deewan Singh* v. *Rajendra Pd. Ardevi*, AIR 2007 SC 767 : 2007 AIR SCW 461.

Statutory body. "STATUTORY BODY" means corporation, committee, commission, council, board or other body of persons, whether incorporated or not, established by or under any law for the time being in force. [Parliament (Prevention of Disqualification) Act (10 of 1959), S. 2(b)]

A statutory body is an institution owing its very existence to a statute which would be the fountain head of its powers. *Vaish Degree College* v. *Lakshmi Narain*, AIR 1976 SC 888, 893.

Statutory damages. Payment entitled by plaintiff *in lieu* of actual damages. (*Cyber Law*)

Statutory deduction. "STATUTORY DEDUCTION" means an amount equal to fifteen percent of the capital of the company as computed in accordance with the provisions of the second schedule, or an amount of two hundred thousand rupees, whichever is greater. Provided that where the previous year is longer or shorter than a period of twelve months, the aforesaid amount of fifteen percent or, as the case may be, of two hundred thousand rupees shall be increased or decreased proportionately.

Provided further that where a company has different previous years in respect of its income, profits and gains, the aforesaid increase or decrease, as the case may be, shall be calculated with reference to the length of the previous year of the longest duration. [Companies (Profits) Surtax Act (7 of 1964), S. 2(8)]

A deduction according to a statute. [Companies (Profits), Surtax Act (7 of 1964), S. 2(8)].

Statutory definition. Generally, ordinary meaning is to be assigned to any word or phrase used or defined in a statute. Therefore, unless there is any vagueness or ambiguity, no occasion will arise to interpret the term in a manner which may add something to the meaning of the word which ordinarily does not so mean by the definition itself, more particularly, where it is restrictive definition. *Feroze N. Dotivala* v. *P.M. Wadhwani*, (2003) 1 SCC 433 443, para 14.

Statutory interpretation. The act or process of interpreting a statute.

Statutory liabilities. Excise dues are not the statutory liabilities which arise out of the land and or the plant and machinery. Statutory liabilities arising out of the land and building could be in the form of the property tax or other types of cess relating to property, etc and those arising out of the plant and machinery could be the sales tax, etc. payable on the said machinery. [*Rana Girders Limited v. Union of India*, (2013) 10 SCC 746, para 23].

Statutory liabilities. Excise dues are not the statutory liabilities which arise out of the land and or the plant and machinery. Statutory liabilities arising out of the land and building could be in the form of the property tax or other types of cess relating to property, etc and those arising out of the plant and machinery could be the sales tax, etc. payable on the said machinery. [*Rana Girders Limited v. Union of India*, (2013) 10 SCC 746, para 23].

A lien arising solely by force of statute upon specified circumstances or conditions, but does not include any lien provided by or dependent upon an agreement to give security, whether or not such lien is also provided by or is also dependent upon statute and whether or not the agreement or lien is made fully effective by statute." [Black's Law Dictionary, 5th Edn. as cited in *Bombay Stock Exchange* v. *V.S. Kandalgaonkar*, (2015) 2 SCC 1, para 38].

A lien arising solely by force of statute upon specified circumstances or conditions, but does not include any lien provided by or dependent upon an agreement to give security, whether or not such lien is also provided by or is also dependent upon statute and whether or not the agreement or lien is made fully effective by statute." [Black's Law Dictionary, 5th Edn. as cited in *Bombay Stock Exchange v. V.S. Kandalgaonkar*, (2015) 2 SCC 1, para 38].

Statutory Liquidity Ratio. The amount of liquid assets, for example cash, that a financial institution must maintain in its reserves. [S S Tarapore, *S S Tarapore's Interpreting Financial Policies for the Common Person*, 2013, LexisNexis, Glossary at p. 185].

Statutory meeting. Every company limited by shares, and every company limited by guarantee and having share capital, shall, within a period of not less than one month nor more than six months from the date at which the company is entitled to commence business, hold a general meeting of the members of the company, which shall be called "the STATUTORY MEETING". [Companies Act (1 of 1956), S. 165(1)]

Statutory reserve. Reserve required by law.

Statutory Rules are to be considered as part of the Act under which they are made.

Statutory Rules and Bye-laws. Rules framed under an Act are parts of the Act and when they are made and published, they have effect as if enacted in the Act. A statutory rule cannot be challenged on the ground that it is unreasonable, whereas a bye-law is open to challenge on the ground that it is unreasonable. Several statutes give to the local authorities the power to enact bye-laws for good rule, administration and government. *Dukhram Gupta* v. *Co-operative Agricultural Association Ltd.,* AIR 1960 MP 272, 276. [Co-operative Societies Act (2 of 1912), S. 43(2)(*c*)]

Statutory tenancy. If a contractual tenancy determines for any cause, and the tenant or the previous tenant under the contractual tenancy remains in possession of the property not under the terms of the contract but pursuant to the provisions of statute like the Rent Act, his possession from the date of the determination of the contractual tenancy, when he starts maintaining the same under the provisions of a statute, is termed a statutory tenancy. This term is not used in the statute itself. *Nihal Chand* v. *Shiv Narain,* AIR 1958 Punj 263, 265.

Stay. Overstaying is a continuous idea, because stay itself is a continuous idea. In the context, 'stay' means 'dwell' which again is a continuous act and not a repetition of several acts.

To stop; arrest; delay; prevent.

'Stay' and 'Injunction'. 'Stay' means suspension of enforcement of Judgment or order until something else happens 'Injunction' is a Judicial order restraining person from commencing or continuing action. Order of 'stay' is in nature of prohibitory order and is addressed to Court carrying out execution. Order of 'injunction' is issued to party forbidding the party from doing certain acts. (*N. Bhat* v. *Mahajasawamy Varaho Devarau,* 1998 (4) Kant LJ 186 at). [Madras Hindu Religious and Charitable Endowments Act, 1951, S. 62]

Stay order. Stay of operation of an order only means that the order which has been stayed would not be operative from the date of the passing of the stay order and it does not mean that the said order has been wiped out from existence. *Shree Chamundi Mopeds Ltd.* v. *Church of South India Trust Association, Madras*, AIR 1992 SC 1439, 1444.

Stay of the action or proceeding. The words "stay of the action or proceeding" have been widely interpreted by the Supreme Court and mean that any type of the orders passed by the Supreme Court would be an inhibitive action on the part of the authorities to proceed further. [*Abhey Ram* v. *Union of India,* (1997) 5 SCC 421, para 9]. See also *Raj Kumar Gandhi v. Gandhigiri Administration*, (2018) 7 SCC 763, para 11.

Staying proceedings. The suspension of an action. Proceedings are stayed absolutely or conditionally.

Every Court has inherent power to temporarily suspend the proceedings in any action where the plaintiff is in default or has disobeyed any lawful order of the Court. In addition, large powers of staying proceedings are given to the Court by various statutes rules, and orders.

Steam-pipe. Means any pipe through which steam passes from a boiler to a prime mover or other user or both, if—

(i) the pressure at which the steam passes through such pipe exceeds 3.5 kilograms per square centimeter above atmospheric pressure; or

(ii) such pipe exceeds 254 millimeters in internal diameter;

and includes in either case any connected fitting of steam pipe. [Indian Boilers Act (5 of 1923), S. 2(f)]

Steamer agent. "STEAMER AGENT" means any person who undertakes, either directly or indirectly,—

(a) to perform any service in connection with the ship's husbandry or dispatch including the rendering of administrative work related thereto; or

(b) to book, advertise or canvass for cargo for or on behalf of a shipping line; or

(c) to provide container feeder services for or on behalf of a shipping line. [Finance Act (32 of 1994), S. 65(1)(100) now repealed by Central Goods and Services Tax Act, 2017]

Steel encasement. A heavy-gauge, welded steel security device designed to fit over the entire computer. Only the security administrator or another designated person has access to the key.

Steel furniture. Operation tables are not furniture and therefore, they cannot be considered to be steel furniture. *Elpro International Ltd.* v. *Jt. Secretary, Govt. of India*, AIR 1985 SC 380, 381. [Central Excises and Salt Act (1 of 1944), Sch. I, item 40]

Steeping. To wet thoroughly; a soaking process. [Salt Cess Act (49 of 1953), S. 2(a)].

Stenography. The art of writing in cipher or secret characters.

Process of hiding messages *within* text or graphics.

Step. Includes a measure or an action, particularly one of a series taken in order to deal with or achieve a particular thing or object in the arrangement. [(w.e.f. 1-4-2016) S. 102(9) of the Income-tax Act, 1961 (43 of 1961); (still-born) Section 102(10) of the Income-tax Act, 1961 (43 of 1961) as inserted (w.e.f. 1-4-2014) by the Finance Act, 2012 and omitted (w.e.f. 1-4-2014) by the Finance Act, 2013]

Step-father. The husband of one's mother by virtue of a marriage subsequent to that of which the person spoken of is the offspring.

The husband of one's mother but not being one's natural father. [Hindu Minority and Guardianship Act (32 of 1956), S. 6, *Expln.*].

Step-in-aid of execution. The words "take some step-in-aid of the execution of a decree," mean to obtain some order of the Court in furtherance of the execution of the decree.

Step-mother. The wife of one's father by virtue of a marriage subsequent to that of which the person spoken of is the offspring.

The wife of one's father, but not being one's mother. [Hindu Minority and Guardianship Act (32 of 1956), S. 6, *Expln.*].

Step-son. The son of one's wife by a former husband or of one's husband by a former wife.

According to Collins English Dictionary, a 'son' means a male off-spring and 'step-son' means a son of one's husband or wife by a former union. *Lachman Singh* v. *Kirpa Singh*, AIR 1987 SC 1616, 1619.

Steps in the proceedings. "Taking any step in the proceedings" means some step which indicates an intention on the part of a party to the proceedings that he desires that the action should proceed and has no desire that the matter should be referred to arbitration. *Bansidhar Narayanji* v. *E.B. Sikhia,* AIR 1957 MP 24, 25. [Arbitration Act (10 of 1940) (*repealed*), S. 34]

Taking other steps in the suit proceedings connotes the idea of doing something in aid of the progress of the suit or submitting to the jurisdiction of the Court for the purpose of adjudication on the merits of the controversy in the suit. *The State of U.P.* v. *Janki Sasan Kailash Chandra and Another*, AIR 1973 SC 2071, 2075, 2076.

Service of copy of plaint without being asked for does not mean that the defendant has taken a step in the proceeding. *Satpal Anand* v. *R.K. Ahuja,* AIR 1973 P&H 197, 199.

Stereotype. A solid metallic plate for printing, cast, a plastic mould of movable types. [Copyright Act (14 of 1957), S. 2(t)].

Sterilisation. The process by which all types of microorganism (including spores) are destroyed. This is achieved by the use of heat, radiation, chemicals, or filtration. [Oxford Dictionary of Nursing as cited in *Servo-Med Industries Private Limited v. Commissioner of Central Excise, Mumbai*, (2015) 14 SCC 47, para 29].

Sterling Worth. "Sterling worth" would mean a witness worthy of credence, one who is reliable and truthful. This has to be gathered from the entire statement of the witnesses and the demeanour of the witness, if any, noticed by the court. Linguistically, "sterling worth" means "thoroughly excellent" or "of great value". This term, in the context of criminal jurisprudence cannot be of any rigid meaning. It must be understood as a generic term. It is only an expression that is used for judging the worth of the statement of a witness. [*Kureija v.State of Rajasthan*, (2012) 10 SCC 433, para 24].

Stevedore. A stevedore is a mere handler of goods in the maritime movement of commodities. *Provident Fund Commissioners* v. *B. Paul Abrao,* AIR 1965 Ker 239, 240.

The person who carry on the business of supplying tally clerks cannot be called stevedors. The words 'employer' and stevedors' are not synonymous. Roughly speaking, the work of stevedoring is mainly concerned with the stowing and discharge of cargo. *Kesab Lal Banerjee* v. *Calcutta Dock Labour Board,* AIR 1960 Cal 166, 169, 170.

Stevedors employers. Employers, who employ persons to load or unload a ship.

Steward. 'STEWARD' in relation to a race club includes any person—

(i) connected with the organisation of the race club; or

(ii) responsible for, or for the time being in charge of the management thereof. [Delhi Entertainments and Betting Tax Act, 1996 (8 of 1997), S. 2(r)]

Sthanam. A station, rank or dignity. (*Moore's Malabar Law*)

A position of dignity, generally in the property attached to the position for the maintenance of the dignity and for the fulfilment of the duties attached to that position, the holder is called *sthanee*, prevalent in Kerala. [Estate Duty Act (34 of 1953), S. 7(4), *Expln.*].

Stigma. Loss of confidence by the employer in the employee is a feat which certainly affects the character or reputation of the employee and so the allegation of loss of confidence amounted to stigma. *Kamal Kishore* v. *Management P.A.W. Airways*, AIR 1987 SC 229, 231.

A mark of infamy, a disgrace or reproach attached to anyone.

Stile. An upright member in framing or panelling. [Indian Railways Act (9 of 1890), S. 13(c)].

Still birth. Means foetal death where a product of conception has attained at least the prescribed period of gestation. [Registration of Births and Deaths Act (18 of 1869), S. 2(g)]

Stipend. A provision made for the support of the clergy; salary; settled pay.

A fixed periodical payment of any kind, *e.g.* pay, pension or allowance. [T.P. Act (4 of 1882), S. 6(g)].

Stipendiary judges. Judges who are paid for their work as such. [Representation of the People Act (43 of 1951), S. 123(7)(b)].

Stipulate. To arrange or settle definitely, as agreement or covenant; to contract; make a bargain. [Indian Contract Act (9 of 1972), S. 74, ill. (e)].

Stipulated dividend. Means in relation to a preference share, means the fixed amount or the amount calculated at a fixed rate which the holder of such share has a preferential right to be paid as dividend. [Preference Shares (Regulation of Dividends) Act (63 of 1960), S. 2(e)]

Stipulation. A material term or article in an agreement.

The action or an act of stipulating; an agreement; the term of an agreement.

Stock. "STOCK" means any fund, annuity or security transferable in books kept by any company or society established or to be established, or transferable by deed alone, or by deed accompanied by other formalities, and any share or interest therein. It shall also include shares in ships registered under the Merchant Shipping Act, 1854, or at any port in British India. [Trustees Act (27 of 1866), S. 2]

The progenitor of a family and his descendants; the whole of descendants of one individual; the source of a line of descent; the original progenitor [Indian Succession Act (39 of 1925), S. 26(d)].

STOCK includes the national debt of a country, and fully paid up shares in a company.

In Mercantile Law, stock is the capital of a merchant, tradesman, or other person, including his merchandise money, and credits. The goods and wares he has for sale and traffic.

'Stock' means 'to keep'. *S.K. Amir* v. *State of Maharashtra*, AIR 1974 SC 469, 470. [Drugs and Cosmetics Act (23 of 1940), S. 18(*a*) and (*c*), 27(*a*)]

Stock-broker. "STOCK-BROKER" means a stock-broker who has either made an application for registration or is registered as a stock-broker in accordance with the rules and regulations made under the Securities and Exchange Board of India Act, 1992. [Finance Act (32 of 1994), S. 65(1)(101) now repealed by Central Goods and Services Tax Act, 2017]

"STOCK-BROKER" means a person, who has either made an application for registration or is registered as a stock-broker or sub-broker, as the case may be, in accordance with the rules and regulations made under the Securities and Exchange Board of India Act, 1992. [Finance Act (32 of 1994), S. 65(101) (Substituted by Finance Act (23 of 2004), S. 90) now repealed by Central Goods and Services Tax Act, 2017]

"STOCK BROKER" means a member of a stock exchange. [SEBI (Stock brokers and Sub brokers) Rules 1992, R. 2(e)]

Stock exchange. "STOCK EXCHANGE" means—

(a) anybody of individuals, whether incorporated or not, constituted before corporatisation and demutualisation under Sections 4A and 4B, or

(b) a body corporate incorporated under the Companies Act, 1956 whether under a scheme of corporatisation and demutualisation or otherwise. [Securities Contracts (Regulation) Act (42 of 1956), S. 2(j) as Substituted Securities Contracts (Regulation) Act (42 of 1956), S. 2]

A society of stock-brokers and stock-jobbers. In the transaction of business, they are governed by certain usages and by rules framed by the committee of the stock exchange. Also, the place where they meet to transact business.

"STOCK EXCHANGE" means any body of individuals, whether incorporated or not, constituted for the purpose of assisting, regulating, or controlling the business of buying, selling or dealing in securities. [Securities Contracts (Regulation) Act (42 of 1956), S. 2(j)]

'*Stock Exchange*' means any body of individuals whether incorporated or not, constituted for the purpose of assisting or controlling the business of buying, selling or dealing in securities. *Madhubhai* v. *Union of India*, AIR 1961 SC 21, 22.

Stock in trade. All such chattels as are acquired for the purpose of being sold, or let to hire in a person's trade. [Indian Contract Act (9 of 1972), S. 52, ill. (b)].

Stock-jobber. A dealer in stock; one who buys and sells stock on his own account on speculation.

Stockist. "STOCKIST" means a person who has, in customary course of business, in his possession of, or control over, a stock of luxuries whether manufactured, made or processed by him in West Bengal, or brought by him into West Bengal, either on his own account or on account of others from any place outside West Bengal, for stocking, vending, supplying or distributing such luxuries in West Bengal"; [W.B. Luxury Tax Act, 1994, S. 2(i)]

Stolen property. "Property, the possession whereof has been transferred by theft, or by extortion, or by robbery, and property which has been criminally misappropriated or in respect of which criminal breach of trust has been committed, is designated as "stolen property," whether the transfer has been made, or the misappropriation or breach of trust has been committed, within or without India. But, if such property subsequently comes into the possession of a person legally entitled to the possession thereof, it then ceases to be stolen property." [IPC (45 of 1860), S. 410].

The expression 'stolen property or property fraudulently obtained' denotes three ingredients (1) possession of the property or conveyance or offering of the property by the accused for sale or pawn (2) reason of Court to believe that the property is stolen or fraudulently obtained and (3) the accused unable to account for his possession. *Champaklal* v. *State of Maharashtra*, AIR 1975 SC 160, 162.

Stone. The word 'stone' has been defined in the Shorter Oxford Dictionary as a 'piece of rock or hard mineral substance (other than metal) of a small and moderate size'. Therefore, a piece of pure metal would not partake of the nature of a stone, nor, would a small piece of stone containing some quantity of metal or mineral, for that reason, cease to be a stone. *Madhya Pradesh Mineral Industry Association* v. *Regional Labour Commissioner (Central) Civil Lines,* AIR 1958 Bom 332, 334.

Stop-gap. If an appointment is made to meet the contingency on account of delay in completing the process for regular recruitment to the post due to any reason and it is not possible to leave the post vacant till then, such an appointment can appropriately be called as a 'stopgap' arrangement. *Rudra Kumar Sain* v. *Union of India*, (2000) 8 SCC 25, para 19 : AIR 2000 SC 2808.

Stop-gap arrangement. A stop-gap arrangement cannot last for eight years. (*D.R. Nim* v. *Union,* 1967 SLR 221)

Stoppage in transit. Intercepting and detaining (the goods) while they are in transit. [Sale of Goods Act (3 of 1930), S. 50].

Storage. "STORAGE" means keeping hazardous wastes for a temporary period, at the end of which the hazardous waste is treated and disposed off. [Hazardous Waste (Management and Handling) Rules, 1989, R. 2(t)]

The word 'storage' covers all kinds of storages maintained under different conditions for different purposes. The ordinary meaning of the word is a place for storing. *C.H.O. & C. Storage Co. Ltd.* v. *Prafullachandra,* AIR 1967 Bom 126, 135.

The action of storing; the condition or fact of being stored [Food Corporations Act (37 of 1964), S. 13(1)]; [CPC (5 of 1908), 1st Sch., App. A, form No. 39].

The term 'storage' means storage of the article for sale and not for any other purpose. *Rameshwar Das* v. *State of Punjab*, AIR 1967 Pun 132, 136. [Prevention of Food Adulteration Act (37 of 1954), S. 16].

Storage and warehousing. "STORAGE AND WAREHOUSING" includes storage and warehousing services for goods including liquids and gases but does not include any service provided for storage of agricultural produce or any service provided by a cold storage. [Finance Act (32 of 1994), S. 65(1)(87) now repealed by Central Goods and Services Tax Act, 2017]

Store. The expression 'store' means storing for the sale. *Girdhari* v. *Calcutta Corporation*, AIR 1966 Cal 634, 636. [Prevention of Food Adulteration Act (37 of 1954), Ss. 7 and 16(1)(*a*)].

Stores. "STORES" means goods for use in a vessel or aircraft and includes fuel and spare parts and other articles of equipment, whether or not for immediate fitting. [Customs Act (52 of 1962), S. 2(38)]

Stowage. Money paid for a room where goods are laid.

Stowing. Means the operation of filling with sand or any other material, or with both, spaces left underground in a coal mine by the extraction of coal. [Coal Mines (Conservation and Development) Act (28 of 1974), S. 3(j)]

Stowing expenses. Stowing is an operation carried out in the process of extraction of coal and unless it is carried out, extraction of coal is not possible irrespective of the fact whether depillaring has been done or not. The stowing expenditure is a revenue expenditure. *Commissioner of Income Tax Bihar & Orissa* v. *Kirkand Coal Co.*, AIR 1970 SC 1586, 1587.

Straight Through Process. Means the process in which an e-from is approved through system without manual interruption. [R. 2(1)(*l*) of the Companies (Registration Offices and Fees) Rules, 2014]

Straight voting. A system of voting for corporate directors in which each shareholder may cast one vote for each share of stock owned for each seat in contention.

Stranded. Driven on shore; left helpless without further recourse [Navy Act (62 of 1957), S. 55(1) and Marine Insurance Act (11 of 1963), Sch., para 5].

Stranger. One not privy or party to an act; one not standing towards another in some relation implied in the context [CPC (5 of 1908), O. XVI, R. 14]; a person with whom one is not acquainted [Indian Evidence Act (1 of 1872), S. 10. ill.].

Straw man. An intermediary for a transaction.

Stream. "STREAM" includes—

(i) river;

(ii) water course (whether flowing or for the time being dry;

(iii) inland water (whether natural or artificial);

(iv) sub-terranean waters;

(v) sea or tidal waters to such extent or, as the case may be, to such point as the State Government may, by notification in the Official Gazette, specify in this behalf. [Water (Prevention and Control of Pollution) Act (6 of 1974), S. 2(j)]

The idea conveyed is that the body of water flows through a defined channel having a bed and banks on both the sides. [Indian Easements Act (5 of 1882), S. 17(c)]

Streedhanam. *Streedhanam* given on the occasion of marriage being taken as a gift to a female. *Vedamen Patarra* v. *Ummini Nadar Kochukrishnan,* AIR 1974 Ker 11.

Street. Includes any way, road, lane, square, Court, alley, or passage in a cantonment, whether a thoroughfare or not and whether built upon or not, over which the public have a right of way and also the road way or foot way over any bridge or cause way. [Cantonments Act (2 of 1924), S. 2(xxxvii)]

Street is a general term, including all urban ways which can be, and are generally, used for the ordinary purposes of travel. A "street" is a way upon land, more properly a paved way, lined, or proposed to be lined, by houses on each side.

The word "street", as it is generally used, includes the roadway, the gutters, and the sidewalks, though it is no doubt often used in a more restricted sense, so as to include only the roadway.

The parking place attached to the road would be part of the road and cannot be treated something separate therefrom. *Harpal Singh* v. *State of Punjab,* AIR 1992 P&H 314, 317.

When a varenda in front of a shop is being used for passing and repassing by the public at large, it is a "street". *Gobind Pershad Jagdish Pershad* v. *New Delhi Municipal Committee*, AIR 1993 SC 2313, 2316.

Street alignment. 'STREET ALIGNMENT' means a line dividing the lands comprised in forming part of a street from the adjoining land. [Kerala Municipality Act (20 of 1994), S. 2(46), As amended by Kerala Act (8 of 1995)]

Street vendor. Means a person engaged in vending of articles, goods, wares, food items or merchandise of everyday use or offering services to the general public, in a street, lane, side walk, footpath, pavement, public park or any other public place or private area, from a temporary built up structure or by moving from place to place and includes hawker, peddler, squatter and all other synonymous terms which may be local or region specific; and the words "street vending" with their grammatical variations and cognate expressions, shall be construed accordingly. [S. 2(1)(*l*) of the Street Vendors (Protection of Livelihood and Regulation of Street Vending) Act, 2014 (7 of 2014)]

'Street vendor/hawker' is a person who offers goods for sale to the public at large without having a permanent structure/place for his activities. Some street vendors/hawkers are stationary in the sense that they occupy space on the pavements or other public/provide places while others are mobile in the sense that they move from place to place carrying their wares on pushcarts or in baskets on their heads. [*Maharashtra Ekta Hawkers Union v. Municipal Corporation, Greater Mumbai*, (2014) 1 SCC 490, para 1].

Strength (of board). The number of members of a body. [Seamen's Provident Fund Act (4 of 1966), S. 6(2)].

Strict construction. "STRICT CONSTRUCTION" is that which refuses to expand the law by implications or equitable considerations, and confines its operation to cases which are clearly within the letter of the statute, as well as within its spirit or reason. When the sense of the law is manifest, and leads to nothing absurd, there can be no reason not to adopt it. Statutes exercising the power of taxation in any of its forms, or delegating the power to political sub-divisions, are to be strictly construed.

Strict constructionism. An interpretation which considers only the literal words of a writing.

Strict interpretation. "Strict interpretation" of statutes relating to crime means this : "Such statutes are to reach no further in meaning than their words. No person is to be made subject to them by implication, and all doubts concerning their interpretation are to preponderate in favour of the accused. Only those transactions are covered by them which are within both their spirit and their letter."

Strict liability. Liability without fault; where a man acts at his peril, he is responsible for accidental harm, without taking into consideration his wrongful intent or negligence.

Stridhan. (*In Hindu Law*) The property held by a Hindu woman unconditionally, and subject to no restrictions is *stridhan* property devolving upon her own heirs. "That alone is her peculiar or *stridhan* property, which she has power to give, sell, or use—independently of her husband's control" (*Dayabhaga*).

STRIDHANA means "what was given to a woman by the father, mother, husband or brother or received by her at the nuptial fire or presented to her on her husband's marriage to another wife and the like is denominated woman's property.

When a Hindu woman dies possessed of *stridhan* property called *anavadhaya* (a gift subsequent to marriage), and the claimants to that property are her sons and daughters, these all become entitled to share the property equally as heirs; with this difference however, as to daughters, that the unmarried have preference over the married.

Strike. "STRIKE" means a cessation of work by a body of persons employed in any industry acting in combination, or a concersted refusal, or a refusal under a common understanding, of any number of persons who are or have been so employed to continue to work or to accept employment. [Industrial Disputes Act (14 of 1947), S.2(q)]

"Strike" means a cessation of work by a body of persons employed in any industry acting in combination, or a concerted refusal, or a refusal, under a common understanding, of any number of persons who are or have been so employed to continue to work or to accept employment and includes the concerted casual leave on a given day by fifty per cent. or more workers employed in an industry. [Industrial Relations Code, 2020 (35 of 2020), section 2(zk)]

A combined withdrawal from work of a body of workers, for the purpose of obtaining better terms or higher wages from their employers.

To deal (a person, an animal) a blow; to hit with some force either with the hand or with a weapon [IPC (45 of 1860), S. 300, ill. (f)]; to engage in a temporary stoppage of work by a body of workers designed to enforce compliance with demands on employer; to annul; to remove; a temporary stoppage of work by a body of workers designed to enforce compliance with demands. [Industrial Disputes Act (14 of 1947), S. 2(q)].

Strike down. To annul.

Strike price. In this chapter, unless the context otherwise requires,—"STRIKE PRICE" means the price at which the "option in securities" may be exercised on the expiry date of such option. [Finance (No. 2) Act (23 of 2004), Chap. VII, S. 97(12)]

Stringency. Strictness. [Indian Contract Act (9 of 1972), S. 16(3), ill. (d)].

Structural alteration, addition or renewal. Shall not be deemed to include any renewal or replacement of a petty nature when the part or fitting used for replacement is not inferior in strength, efficiency or otherwise to the replaced part or fitting. [Indian Boilers Act (5 of 1923), S. 2(g)]

Structure. "Structure" is defined to be that which is built or constructed; an edifice or a building of any kind; in the widest sense, any production or piece of work artificially built up or composed of parts and joined together in some definite manner; any construction.

The process of building or construction; a fabric or framework of material parts put together. [T.P. Act (4 of 1882), S. 108(p) and Constitution of India, Art. 31A, prov.]; a thing constructed.

Student. "STUDENT" means a person enrolled in the University for undergoing a course of studies for obtaining a degree, diploma or other academic distinction duly instituted. [Central Agricultural University Act (40 of 1992), S. 2(q)] [S. 3(q) of the Rani Lakshmi Bai Central Agricultural University Act, 2014 (10 of 2014)]

"STUDENT" means a student of the University and includes any person who has enrolled himself for pursuing any course of study of the university. [Netaji Subhash Open University Act (W.B. Act No. 19 of 1997), S. 2(19); Indira Gandhi National Open University (50 of 1985), S. 2(n)]

"STUDENT" means a person who is admitted to an educational institution and whose name is lawfully borne on the attendance register thereof. [Andhra Pradesh Prohibition of Ragging Act (Act No. 26 of 1997), S. 2(f)]

Student of the University. "STUDENT OF THE UNIVERSITY" means a person enrolled in the University for taking a course of study for degree, diploma or other academic distinction duly instituted. [Rajasthan Agriculture University Act (18 of 1962), S. 2(i)]

Study. The application of mind to the acquisition of learning. [Industrial Development Bank of India Act (18 of 1964), S. 9(1)(h)].

Study centre. "STUDY CENTRE" means a centre established, maintained or recognised by the university for the purpose of advising or counselling or for rendering such other assistance in the activities of the University as may be required by the students. [Netaji Subhash Open University Act (19 of 1997), S. 2(20)]

Stupefying. That which deprives of apprehension, feeling or sensibility. [IPC (45 of 1860), S. 328].

Style. A legal, official or honorific title; the proper name or recognized application of a person, family or trading firm; ceremonial classification. [CPC (5 of 1908), O. XXX, R. 10].

Sub-account. "SUB ACCOUNT" includes those institutions, established or incorporated outside India and those funds or portfolios, established outside India whether incorporated or not, on whose behalf investments are proposed to be made in India by a Foreign Institutional Investor. [SEBI (Foreign Institutional Investors) Regulations 1995, Regn. 2(k)]

Sub-agent. "A 'SUB-AGENT' is a person employed by, and acting under the control of the original agent in the business of the agency." [Indian Contract Act (9 of 1872), S. 191]

An agent appointed by one who is himself an agent. [Indian Contract Act (9 of 1972), S. 190].

Sub-broker. "SUB BROKER" means any person not being a member of a stock exchange who acts on behalf of a stock broker as an agent or otherwise for assisting the investors in buying, selling or dealing in securities through such stock brokers. [SEBI (Stock Brokers and Sub-brokers) Rules, 1992, R. 2(f)]

"SUB-BROKER" means a sub-broker who has either made an application for registration or is registered as a sub-broker in accordance with the rules and regulations made under the Securities and Exchange Board of India Act, 1992. [Finance Act (32 of 1994), S. 65(1)(103) omitted by Finance (No. 2) Act, 2004 now repealed by Central Goods and Services Tax Act, 2017]

Sub-district. A division or sub-division of a district. [T.P. Act (4 of 1882), S. 3(c), *Expln.* 1].

Sub-division of a survey number. "SUB DIVISION OF A SURVEY NUMBER" means a portion of a survey number of which the area and assessment are separately entered in the land records under an indicative number subordinate to that of the survey number of which it is a portion. [Maharashtra Land Revenue Code (41 of 1966), S. 2(35)]

Sub-divisional Magistrate. A magistrate incharge of a sub-division. [CrPC, 1973 (2 of 1974), S. 23(1)].

Sub-divisional Officer. "SUB-DIVISIONAL OFFICER" means the officer in charge of a sub-division of a district as constituted for revenue and general purposes.

The expression "Sub-divisional Officer" is an expression commonly in use to describe an Assistant Collector of the first class incharge of sub-division. *Kedar Nath* v. *S.N. Misra (FB),* AIR 1957 All 484, 486.

Sub-judice. Before a judge or Court; pending decision of a competent Court. In course of trial.

Sub-lease. A lease by a tenant to another person of a part of the premises held by him.

A lease granted by one who is a lessee or tenant; an underlease. [T.P. Act (4 of 1882), S. 108(j)].

Sub-let. The word, sub-let takes in the letting even to licensees or their occupation at the instance of the tenant either for some consideration like rent or premium. *Dattatraya Kaluram Jadhar* v. *Narayandas Badridas Rathi,* AIR 1974 Bom 189, 191.

Sub-market yard. "SUB-MARKET YARD" means an enclosure, building or locality declared or deemed to be declared to be a sub-market yard under this Act. [Gujarat Agricultural Produce Markets Act, 1963 (20 of 1964), S. 2(xxi)]

Sub-mortgage. The mortgagee himself mortgaging the mortgaged property to another person. [CPC (5 of 1908), 1st Sch., App. D, form No. 11(2)(ii)].

Sub-ordinate. Belonging to an inferior rank, grade, class or order; dependent upon the authority or power of another. [Indian Evidence Act (1 of 1872), S. 121]; a person or thing that is ranked lower.

The word 'sub-ordinate' in Art. 311(1), Constitution of India means subordination in rank and not subordination of function. *Mahadev Prasad Roy* v. *S.N. Chaterjee,* AIR 1954 Pat 285.

By the use of the word 'sub-ordinate' without any qualifying words, the legislature has expressed its legislative intention of making punishable such sub-ordinates also who have no connection with the functions with which the business or transaction is concerned. An Assistant Controller of Imports in the office of the Joint Chief Controller of Imports and Exports is a sub-ordinate of the Joint Chief Controller though the acceptance of the bribe has nothing to do with the appeal pending before the Joint Chief Controller. *R.G. Jacob* v. *Republic of India*, AIR 1963 SC 550, 553.

Sub-ordinate Court. "SUB-ORDINATE COURT" means all Courts sub-ordinate to the High Court, including Courts of Small Causes. [Legal Practitioners Act (18 of 1879), S. 3]

Sub-ordinate officer. The test whether officers are "sub-ordinate" or not is not whether a review of such of their determinations as are *quasi*-judicial may be had, but whether in the performance of their various duties, they are subject to the direction and control of a superior officer, or are independent officers, subject only to such discretions as the statutes give.

Sub-ordination. Submission and obedience to authority; the condition of being subordinate. [CrPC, 1973 (2 of 1974), S. 19].

Sub-ordination of Courts. Court of Additional District Magistrate would not seem to be sub-ordinate to High Court within Section 195 (3). *Santokh Singh* v. *Izhar Hussain*, AIR 1973 SC 2190, 2191. [CrPC, 1973 (2 of 1974), S. 195(4)]

Sub-region. "SUB-REGION" means such part of the National Capital Region as falls entirely within the limits of a participating State or the Union territory. [National Capital Region Planning Board Act (2 of 1985), S. 2(l)]

Sub-rule. A sub-division of a rule. [CPC (5 of 1908), O. XIII, R. 4(1)].

Sub-sale. A sale by buyer. [Sale of Goods Act (3 of 1930), S. 53(1)].

Sub-section. "SUB-SECTION", shall mean a sub-section of the section in which the word occurs. [General Clauses Act (10 of 1897), S. 3(61).

A sub-division of a section (of a law). [General Clauses Act (10 of 1897), S. 3(61)]

Sub-silentio. Under silence.

Sub-soil. The stratum of weathered material that underlies the surface soil [Northern India Canal and Drainage Act (8 of 1873), S. 14].

Sub-standard. An article of food shall be deemed to be 'sub-standard' if it does not meet the specified standards but not so as to render the article of food unsafe. [S. 3(1)(zx) of the Food Safety & Standards Act, 2006 (34 of 2006)]

Sub-standard asset. "SUB-STANDARD ASSET" means—

(a) an asset, which has been classified as non-performing asset for a period of not exceeding two years;

(b) an asset where the terms of the agreement regarding interest and/or principal have been renegotiated or rescheduled after commencement of operations, until the expiry of one year of satisfactory performance under the renegotiated or rescheduled terms. [Non-Banking Financial Companies Prudential Norms (Reserve Bank) Directions, 1998, Para 2(1)(xvi)]

Sub-station. "SUB-STATION" means a station for transforming or converting electricity for the transmission or distribution thereof and includes transformers, converters, switchgears, capacitors, synchronous condensers, structures, cable and other appurtenant equipment and any buildings used for that purpose and the site thereof. [Electricity Act (36 of 2003), S. 2(69)]

Sub-tenant. One who leases all or a part of rented premises from the original lessee for a term less than that held by the latter.

Sub-wholesaler. 'SUB-WHOLESALER' means an appointed dealer who purchases any one or more of the notified articles from the wholesaler and sells to such retailers at such prices, in such quantities and at such intervals of time as may be directed by the licensing Authority. [Assam Public Distribution of Articles Order, 1982, cl. 2(m)]

Sub-delegated legislation. Legislation made under powers conferred by delegated legislation or by subdelegated legislation itself (in which case it is technically sub-subdelegated legislation).

Subjacent. Located underneath or below (the land's subjacent support).

Subjacent and adjacent soil. "Land is in its natural condition when it is not excavated and not subjected to artificial pressure; and the "subjacent and adjacent soil" mentioned in this illustration means such soil only as in its natural condition would support the dominant heritage in its natural condition." [Indian Easements Act (5 of 1882)], S.7, ill. (e), *Explanation*].

Subject. Topic; matter of discourse [Indian Partnership Act (9 of 1932), S. 2]; matter for any action or operation [CrPC, 1973 (2 of 1974), S. 145(1)]; one who is subject. [CrPC, 1973 (2 of 1974), S. 22].

Subject-matter. The matter in a dispute; matter presented for consideration. *Kaloot Sao* v. *Munni Sao,* AIR 1977 Pat 90, 92. [Indian Evidence Act (1 of 1872), S. 18(1)].

The subject-matter of a suit cannot be equated with the property in respect of which the parties quarrel. The term 'subject-matter' includes the cause of action also.

Subject matter jurisdiction. Means power of the court to hear and decide specific cases that can be categorized in a subject matter domain. [Karnika Seth, *Computers Internet and New Technology Laws*, 2021, LexisNexis, Glossary of Legal Terms].

Subject-matter of the suit. Whether a particular matter is the subject-matter of or relates to a suit is primarily a question of fact depending upon the circumstances of each case. Although a matter is not strictly the subject matter of a suit, it may relate to or have reference to the suit if it forms part of the consideration.

The equity of redemption by the mortgage property in a suit for recovery of money on the basis of the mortgage is exempt from the subject-matter of the suit, as contemplated under *Expln.* 1(*a*) of R. 1 of O. XXXIII, CPC. [CPC (5 of 1908), O. XXXIII, R. 1, *Expln.* 1(*a*)] *G. Sreeramulu* v. *M. Adinarayana Rao,* AIR 1985 AP 62, 64.

As the subject-matter in the suit cannot be construed as comprehending the entire property but only the right of tenancy, the suit premises cannot be taken as 'subject-matter of the suit.' *S.Z. Zare* v. *P.V. Muralidhar,* AIR 1979 AP 107, 110. [CPC (5 of 1908), O. XXXIII, R. 1]

'Subject-matter of the suit' cannot be read as subject-matter of the plaint nor even as a subject-matter in dispute in the suit or proceeding. *C. Muthuvel Pillai* v. *Hazrath Syed Shahmiam Shakkala Sahib Kadhiri Thaikal,* AIR 1974 Mad 199, 203.

Subject of the sale. The phrase "the subject of the sale" does not admit of physical possession, does not refer to anything other than the nature of the property conveyed by the sale and has no reference to the ability or inability of the vendor to place the vendee in actual physical possession of the property sold, from whatever cause that inability may arise.

Subject thereto. The use of the expression 'subject thereto' cannot attribute to the previous operation of the repealed statute an overriding effect, so as to deprive the authorities constituted under the repealing Act of their power to entertain appeals or revision applications. *Bishanbar Nath* v. *State of U.P.*, AIR 1966 SC 573, 579. [Administration of Evacuee Property Act (31 of 1950), S. 58(3)]

Subject to. The effect of the words "subject to" in a deed is to introduce condition or proviso. Under the control or influence of some one or something, subordinate to. [Sale of Goods Act (3 of 1930), S. 16]; [Motor Transport Workers Act (27 of 1961), S. 40(1)].

The use of the word "subject to" in a transfer of property subject to an existing agreement, was construed to mean subject, not only to the disadvantages imposed by such agreement, but also to the advantages given thereby.

The meaning of the expression "subject to" is not to make the transfer conditional. It simply means that the sale is in consideration of payment of money. *Dayal Singh* v. *Collector of Stamps,* AIR 1972 Del 131, 133. [Indian Stamp Act (2 of 1899), S. 24]

Subject to Jurisdiction. Only those who are subject by their birth, naturalization or residence are within the terms of this phrase.

Subject to the Jurisdiction Thereof. The phrase "*subject to the jurisdiction thereof*" means those who are within the dominion of the State and under the protection of its laws, with the consequent obligation to obey them when obedience can be rendered. (*Ame. Words and Phrases*)

Subject to the approval. 'Subject to the approval' means that the appointment is valid, and effective until disapproved by the District Council. It does not mean the same thing as subject to the permission or with the approval. *U.G. Koring Singh Lyngdoh* v. *Executive Committee, District Council U.K. Hills District, Shillong,* AIR 1971 Ass 129, 136.

Subject to the duty of excise. The words 'subject to the duty of excise' indicate present liability in duty and not liability to duty in future. *Madho Charan* v. *State,* AIR 1963 Pat 211, 213. [Medicinal and Toilet Preparation (excise duties) Act (16 of 1955), S. 2(*c*)]

Subject to the other provisions of this constitution. The words 'subject to the other provisions of this Constitution' in Art. 372 do not mean that law which had been passed by the Central Legislature before 26-1-50, automatically ceases to have effect because the subject was now being made a State subject. *Dulal Samanta* v. *District Magistrate, Howrah,* AIR 1958 Cal 365, 373. [Constitution of India, Art. 372]

Subject to the process of the Court. Against which or whom a process of the Court can be enforced. [Indian Evidence Act (1 of 1872), S. 65(a)].

Subject to the provisions of this Act. The words 'subject to the provisions of this Act' mean that the Code of Civil Procedure is applicable only subject to the provisions of S. 23(2) and S. 32. *Indian Minerals Co.* v. *Northern India Lime Marketing Association,* AIR 1958 All 692, 695. [Arbitration Act (10 of 1940) (*repealed*), S. 41] [Now repealed & replaced by Act 26 of 1996]

Subjective. Pertaining or peculiar to an individual subject or his mental operations; personal; individual; pertaining or relating to one who is subject.

Subjective. The word "subjective" is defined to mean dependent on the mind or on an individual's perception for its existence. The subjective satisfaction is the satisfaction of a reasonable man which can be arrived at on the basis of some material, influenced by or based on personal beliefs or feelings rather than on objective facts. [Oxford Dictionary as cited in *Hanuman Rajaram Mhatre v. The Commissioner of Police, Thane,* LNIND 2018 BOM 125, para 8]

Subjoin. To add afterwards.

Subjugate. To bring under one's power or dominion; to conquer.

Subjugation. "Subjugation puts an end to the state of war and destroys the source of authority of the existing government. It is one of the modes of acquiring title and in it not only the *de facto* but also the *de jure* rights passes to the conqueror. R. *Monteiro* v. *State of Goa*, AIR 1970 SC 329 at 336. [Geneva Conventions Act (6 of 1960), Sch. IV, Art. 6]

Sublata causa tollitur effectus. The cause being removed, the effect comes to an end. (*Latin for Lawyers*)

Subletting. The granting of a sublease.

Submersion. The act of putting under the surface of liquid. [Damodar Valley Corporation Act (14 of 1948), S. 25].

Submission. "SUBMISSION" means a written agreement to submit present or future differences to arbitration, whether an arbitrator is named therein or not. [Indian Arbitration Act (9 of 1899), S. 4(b)]

That act is called a "submission" by which parties refer any matter in dispute between them to the decision of a third person, the person to whom the reference is made is an "arbitrator," and the judgment pronounced by the arbitrator is an "award."

The act of submitting; the act of yielding or surrendering [CrPC, 1973 (2 of 1974), S. 46(1)]; the act of sending or committing for consideration, study or decision [Oilfields (Regulation and Development) Act (53 of 1948), S. 6(2)(j)]; [Drugs and Cosmetics Act (23 of 1940), S. 6(2)(d)]; the act of agreeing.

The term 'submission' connotes an actual submission of the dispute to arbitration or a completed reference to arbitration, prior to the date of the institution of the suit. *Food Corporation, India* v. *Mardestine Compania Naviera,* AIR 1977 Ker 108, 109. [Foreign

Awards (Recognition and Enforcement) Act (45 of 1961), S. 3]

Submission agreement. An agreement to arbitrate existing disputes. (*Arbitration*)

Submission to requisition. Complying with the requisition. [CrPC, 1973 (2 of 1974), S. 348].

Submission of information. Includes updating of information, as the context may require. [Insolvency and Bankruptcy Board of India (Information Utility) Regulations, 2017, Regn. 2(1)(q)].

Submit. To refer to the judgment of another. To put forward as a contention or proposition; to urge or represent with deference [Indian Partnership Act (9 of 1932), S. 19(2)(a)]; to send or commit for consideration, study or decision [Dock Workers (Regulation of Employment) Act (9 of 1948), S. 6A(1)]; to surrender (oneself to); to agree [CrPC, 1973 (2 of 1974), S. 348].

The word 'submit' in S. 19(2) also includes 'agreement to refer'. *National S.I. Corporation* v. *Punjab T.P. & Industries,* AIR 1979 Del 58, 60. [Partnership Act (9 of 1932), S. 19(2)]

Subordinate Court. "SUBORDINATE COURT" means all Courts subordinate to the High Court, including Courts of Small Causes. [Legal Practitioners Act (18 of 1879), S. 3.]

Subordinate legislation. The compendious term "subordinate legislation" refers to notifications, orders, schemes, rules and bye-laws referred to in Ss. 20 and 21 of the General Clauses Act (10 of 1897). (*Sukhdev Singh* v. *Bhagat Ram,* AIR 1975 SC 1331)

A delegate of the legislature is conferred with the power to make rules and regulations to carry out the purposes of the legislation and such rules and regulations are called delegated legislation or subordinate legislation. [*Swami Vivekanand College of Education v. Union of India*, (2012) 1 SCC 642, para 26].

Subordinate officer. "SUBORDINATE OFFICER" means a person appointed as an acting sub-lieutenant, a midshipman or a cadet in any branch of the Indian Navy or the Indian Naval Reserve Forces but does not include a cadet whilst under training in a joint service institution. [Navy Act (62 of 1957), S. 3(23)]

Subordinate service or post. Means any service or post, appointments to which are not notified in the Official Gazette but includes any service of *tehsildars*. [Public Employment (Requirement as to Residence) Act (44 of 1957), S. 3(2)(aa)]

'Subordinate service' means and includes all non-gazetted ports under the Government whether grouped into organized service or not. [Jammu and Kashmir Subordinate Services Recruitment Rules, 1992, R. 3(v) as cited in *Vinod Kumar Koul v. State of Jammu and Kashmir*, (2012) 11 SCC 247, para 4].

Subornation. Submission and obedience to authority; the condition of being subordinate. [CrPC 1973 (2 of 1974), S. 19].

Subornation of perjury. Where the crime of perjury is committed at the instigation or procurement of another, it is termed "subornation of perjury."

Subpoena. Under a penalty; a judicial writ commanding appearance of a person under a penalty.

A judicial writ commanding appearance of a person (generally a witness) under a penalty. [IPC (45 of 1860), S. 174, ill. (a)].

Affirmative order by a Court to produce specific records or to appear as a witness in Court.

Subreption. Obtaining property through misrepresentation or the concealing of facts.

Subrogated. Substituted to a right or claim. [CPC (5 of 1908), O. XXXIV, R. 4(4)]

Subrogated to the rights. Substituted to the rights. [CPC (5 of 1908), O. XXXIV, R. 4(4)].

Subrogation. "Subrogation" is a substitution of one person or thing for another.

The substitution of one person in place of another with reference to a lawful claim, demand or right. [T.P. Act (4 of 1882), S. 92].

Subscribe. To contribute to a fund or society [Indian Contract Act (9 of 1872), S. 30]; to contribute money for shares *etc.* [Industrial Finance Corporation Act (15 of 1948) (*repealed by Act 23 of 1993*), S. 4(2)]; to sign [Indian Evidence Act (1 of 1872), S. 76]; to make a signed promise of payment for [Companies Act (1 of 1956), S. 3(iii)(c)]; to put one's name down as a purchaser.

The use of the word 'subscribe' would show that the oath repeated orally should be reduced to writing and be signed by the person taking it, in token of his acceptance. *G. Vasantha Pai* v. *C.K. Ramaswamy,* AIR 1978 Mad 342, 357. [Constitution of India, Art. 188]

Subscribe and deliver. The distinction between the two words 'subscribe' and 'deliver' is clearly indicated. If any elector subscribes more than one nomination paper at the same election, whether as a proposer or seconder, then his signature shall be inoperative on any nomination paper other than the one which has been first delivered to the Returning Officer. *Mithilesh Kumar Sinha* v. *Returning Officer*, AIR 1993 SC 20, 34. [Presidential and Vice-Presidential Elections Act (31 of 1952), S. 5-B(1)(*a*)(5)]

Subscribed. The word 'subscribed' means an oath repeated orally, reduced the same to writing and signed by the person taking the oath in token of his adhesion to what is written. *Shabbir* v. *State of U.P.*, AIR 1965 All 97, 105. [Constitution of India, Art. 219]

Subscribed capital. Means such part of the capital which is for the time being subscribed by the members of a company. [S. 2(86) of the Companies Act, 2013 (18 of 2013)]

Subscriber. "SUBSCRIBER" includes a person who holds a fraction of a ticket and also a transferee of a ticket or fraction thereof by assignment in writing or by operation of law. [Chit Funds Act (40 of 1982), S. 2(r)]

"SUBSCRIBER" means a person to whom any service of a telephone connection or a facsimile or a leased circuit or a pager or a telegraph or a telex has been provided by the telegraph authority. [Finance Act (32 of 1994), S. 65(89) now repealed by Central Goods and Services Tax Act, 2017]

"SUBSCRIBER" means any individual, or association of individuals, or a company, or any other organisation or body who receives the signals of cable television network at a place indicated by him or it to the cable operator, without further transmitting it to any other person. . [Cable Television Networks (Regulation) Act (7 of 1995), S. 2(i) substituted by Act 21 of 2011].

"SUBSCRIBER" means a person in whose name the Electronic Signature Certificate is issued. [Information Technology Act (21 of 2000), S. 2(1)(zg)]

One who put his signature to a document either as an executant or as an attesting witness.

One that subscribes. [Tax on Postal Articles Act, 1971 S. 2(b)].

An individual who is the holder of the Digital Signature Certificate. (*Information Technology*)

Any customer who has concluded a contract with a telecommunications service provider, relating to the use of these service. (*Telecommunication*)

"SUBSCRIBER" includes a person who subscribes to a scheme of a pension fund. [S. 2(1)(q) of the Pension Fund Regulatory & Development Authority Act, 2013 (23 of 2013)]

Subscriber agreement. The agreement executed between a subscriber and a Certifying Authority for the provision of designated public certification services in accordance with this Certification Practice Statement. (*Information Technology*)

Subscriber information. Information relating to the applicant given in the application, to a Certifying Authority for the issuance of a Digital Signature Certificate. (*Information Technology*)

Subscriber information means any information held by a service provider relating to subscribers of its services, other than traffic or content data, by which it can be established: (1) the type of communication service used, the technical provisions and the period of service, (2) the subscriber's identity, postal or geographic address, telephone and other access number, billing and payment information and (3) any other information on the site of the installation of communication equipment. [The European Convention on Cyber Crime, Art. 15]

Subscriber Line Charge (SLC). A monthly fee paid by telephone subscribers that is used to compensate the local telephone company for part of the cost of installation and maintenance of the telephone wire, poles and other facilities that link your home to the telephone network. These wires, poles and other facilities are referred to as the "local loop". The SLC is one component of access charges. (*Telecommunication*)

Subscribing witness. One who writes his name under an attesting clause; one who sees a writing executed or hears it acknowledged and at the request of the party thereupon signs his name as a witness; one who was present when the instrument was executed, and who at that time, at the request or with the assent of the party, subscribed his name to it, as a witness of the execution.

Subscription. The word "subscription" includes a mark, the name being written near the mark and witnessed.

Something that is subscribed; a sum subscribed [Provident Funds Act (19 of 1925), S. 2(a)]; [Salarjung Museum Act (26 of 1961), S. 19(1)(c)]; sign specially as a witness, a subscribing witness is the same thing as an attesting witness.

SUBSCRIPTION, (*to a deed*) indicates consent by signature.

A subscription of a will, within the meaning of the statutes in reference to subscribing witnesses, is satisfied by the act of the witness in affixing his mark to his name.

A SUBSCRIPTION FOR SHARES in a corporation is an agreement to take them upon the conditions prescribed for the same and subjects the subscriber to those liabilities only which are imposed by the law or rules under which the corporation is organized.

A subscription for shares is defined as implying a promise to pay for them.

A "subscription" to the stock of a corporation implies an agreement to pay for the shares.

Subsequent. A thing which occurs next to another thing or follows another thing in point of time.

Subsequent suit. A suit filed after a previous one; later suit. [CPC (5 of 1908), S. 35A(4)].

Subsequently. Later on. [T.P. Act (4 of 1882), S. 42].

Subsidiary. A subordinate; one who or that which aids or supplies.

"SUBSIDIARY". For the purposes of section 129(3) of Act 18 of 2013, the word 'subsidiary' shall include associate company and joint venture. [*Explanation* to section 129(3) of the Companies Act, 2013 (18 of 2013)]

Subsidiary Bank. Means any new bank and includes the Hyderabad Bank and the Saurashtra Bank. [State Bank of India (Subsidiary Banks) Act, 1959 (38 of 1959), S. 2(k). Also see Factoring Regulation Act, 2011(12 of 2012), S. 2(s)]

Subsidiary company. "For the purposes of this act, a company shall, subject to the provisions of sub-section (3), be deemed to be a subsidiary of another if, but only if,—(a) that other controls the composition of its Boards of Directors; or (b) that other—(i) where the first mentioned company is an existing company in respect of which the holders of preference shares issued before the commencement of this Act have the same voting rights in all respects as the holders of equity shares, exercises or controls more than half of the total voting power of such company; (ii) where the first mentioned company, holds more than a half in nominal value of its equity share capital; or (c) the first mentioned company is a subsidiary of any company which is that other's subsidiary." [Companies Act (1 of 1956), S.2(47)] and S. 4]

A company which is controlled by a parent company which owns majority of the shares in the company which is controlled.

One of which another company holds most of the shares. [Companies Act (1 of 1956), S. 2(47)].

Merely because there are common directors for two companies, does not mean that one company is the subsidiary company of the other. *Shree Cement Ltd.* v. *Official Liquidator,* AIR 1994 Cal 90, 95. [Companies Act (1 of 1956), S. 4]

"SUBSIDIARY COMPANY". In relation to any other company (that is to say the holding company), means a company in which the holding company—

(*i*) controls the composition of the Board of Directors; or

(*ii*) exercises or controls more than one-half of the total voting power either at its own or together with one or more of its subsidiary companies:

Provided that such class or classes of holding companies as may be prescribed shall not have layers of subsidiaries beyond such numbers as may be prescribed.

Explanation.—For the purposes of this clause,—

(*a*) a company shall be deemed to be a subsidiary company of the holding company even if the control referred to in sub-clause (*i*) or sub-clause (*ii*) is of another subsidiary company of the holding company;

(*b*) the composition of a company's Board of Directors shall be deemed to be controlled by another company if that other company by exercise of some power exercisable by it at its discretion can appoint or remove all or a majority of the directors;

(*c*) the expression "company" includes any body corporate;

(*d*) "layer" in relation to a holding company means its subsidiary or subsidiaries. [S. 2(87) of the Companies Act, 2013 (18 of 2013)]

Subsidiary motion. The motions of the Parliament that depend upon or relate to other motions or follow up on some proceedings in a House. They, by themselves, have no meaning and are not capable of stating the decision of the House without reference to the original motion or proceeding of the House.

Subsidiary works. "SUBSIDIARY WORK" means work in connection with a transport vehicle, its passenger or its load which is done outside the running time of the transport vehicle, including in particular;

(i) work in connection with accounts, the paying in of cash, the signing of register, the handing in of service sheets, the checking of tickets and other similar work;

(ii) the taking over and garaging of the transport vehicle;

(iii) travelling from the place where a person sign on to the place where he takes over the transport vehicle and from the place where he leaves the transports vehicle to the place where he signs off;

(iv) work in connection with the upkeep and repair of the transport vehicle; and

(v) the loading and unloading of the transport vehicle. [Motor Transport Workers Act (27 of 1961), S. 2(f) *Expln.* (2)]

Subsidiary works in the Minor Canals Act. Mean all works required for the control or maintenance of the supply to a canal or for the maintenance of a canal in proper condition or for the regulation of the irrigation therefrom or for the prevention of floods or for the provision of proper drainage, in connection with such irrigation, and include also the land required for such work. [Pun. Act III of 1905 (Minor Canals), S. 3, cl. (11).]

Subsidy. A government grant to any enterprise whose promotion is considered to be in public interest.

Subsist. To have an existence as a reality. [T.P. Act (4 of 1882), S. 43 and S. 55(2)].

Subsistence allowance. An allowance for maintenance granted under special circumstances. [CPC (5 of 1908), S. 57]; [CPC (5 of 1908), O. XXI, R. 39].

Subsistence grant. An authoritative bestowal of such sum to meet the minimum requirements of life; a grant given in advance (as to a solider or workman) to meet the basic needs of life while awaiting a pay day.

Subsisting. Existing as a reality; remaining in existence [Sale of Goods Act (3 of 1930), S. 60]; [Metal Corporation of India (Acquisition of Undertaking) Act (36 of 1966), S. 8]; [Indian Easements Act (5 of 1882), S. 4, *Expln.*].

Substance. Essence [Cattle-trespass Act (1 of 1871), S. 21]; that of which a physical thing consists; the material of which a body is formed [IPC (45 of 1860), S. 476]; a particular kind of corporeal matter [CrPC, 1973 (2 of 1974), S. 133(1)(c)].

The expression 'substances' means things. Absorbent cotton wool, roller bandages and gauze are substances intended to be used for or in the treatment of diseases of human beings or animals. *Chimanlal Jagjivandas Sheth* v. *State of Maharashtra*, AIR 1963 SC 665, 666. [Drugs Cosmetics Act (23 of 1940), S. 3(*b*)]

"SUBSTANCE" includes any natural or artificial substance or other matter, whether it is in a solid state or in liquid form or in the form of gas or vapour.

[S. 3(1)(zw) of the Food Safety & Standards Act, 2006 (34 of 2006)]

Substance of the information. The words 'substance of the information' means such or so much of the information as would enable the party to know under what clause of section 110 he is charged or to what particular class of offenders he is said to belong. *Raghunath Singh* v. *State,* AIR 1953 Pat 1. [CrPC, 1973 (2 of 1974), S. 112]

Sub-Standard Asset. Means a borrowal account which is a non-performing asset:

Provided that reschedulement or renegotiation or rephasement of the loan instalment or interest payment shall not change the classification of an asset unless the borrowal account has satisfactorily performed for at least twelve months after such reschedulement or renegotiation or rephasement. [R. 3(1)(g) of the Nidhi Rules, 2014]

Substantial. 'Substantial' is not the same as "not unsubstantial" *i.e.* just enough to avoid the *de minimis principle*. One of the primary meanings of the word is equivalent to considerable, solid, or big.

The word 'substantial' when used with reference to an injury caused or likely to be caused by a nuisance only means 'actual' or 'real' as opposed to 'trivial', not serious, temporary, occasional, unimportant, imaginary or seeming.

Of importance and value [CPC (5 of 1908), O. XXI, R. 90, *Prov.*]; relating to or proceeding from the essence of a thing [CPC (5 of 1908), O. VI, R. 13]; of ample or considerable amount or quantity.

'Substantial' means of real worth and importance; of considerable value; valuable. Belonging to substance; actually existing; real; not seeming or imaginary; not illusive; solid; true; veritable. ... Something worthwhile as distinguished from something without value or merely nominal. ... Synonymous with material. [Black's Law Dictionary (6th Edn.) as cited in *Thalappalam Service Cooperative Bank Limited v. State of Kerala*, (2013) 16 SCC 82, para 47].

"Substantial" means 'of ample or considerable amount or size; sizable, fairly large; having solid worth or value, of real significance; solid; weighty; important, worthwhile; of an act, measure, etc. having force or effect, effective, thorough." [Shorter Oxford English Dictionary (5th Edn.) as cited in *Thalappalam Service Cooperative Bank Limited v. State of Kerala*, (2013) 16 SCC 82, para 47].

The word "substantial" is not synonymous with "dominant" or "majority". It is closer to "material" or "important" or "of considerable value". "Substantially" is closer to "essentially" both words can signify varying degrees depending on the context. [*Thalappalam Service Cooperative Bank Limited v. State of Kerala*, (2013) 16 SCC 82, para 47].

Substantial and compelling reasons. The term 'substantial and compelling reasons' in the context of appeal against acquittal is not intended to restrict the power of the Appellate Court to appreciate the evidence on which acquittal order is based. In case the order of acquittal is to be set-aside, there should be express reasons for doing so. [*Sonwant Singh* v. *State of Rajasthan,* AIR 1962 SC 715]

Substantial cause. The discovery after filing of an appeal, of fresh evidence not known to and not available to the appellant after due diligence in the first Court is a substantial cause within the meaning of O. XLI, R. 27, CPC (5 of 1908) and such evidence can be admitted at the hearing of the appeal.

The words 'substantial cause' can be construed to mean that the power to allow additional evidence is exercised when any point is required to be cleared up in the interests of justice. *Wasawa Singh* v. *Jagir Singh,* AIR 1965 Punj 494, 496. [CPC (5 of 1908), O. XLI, R. 27(*b*)]

Substantial damage. "The doing of any act likely to injure the plaintiff by affecting the evidence of the easement, or by materially diminishing the value of the dormant heritage, is substantial damage within the meaning of this section and Section 34." [Indian Easements Act (5 of 1882), S. 33, *Expln.*1]

"SUBSTANTIAL DAMAGE" shall mean such damage as shall involve an expenditure equivalent to six months' rent or more of the premises or such less expenditure as the Rent Authority is satisfied, keeping in view, the special nature of damage, justifies the same to be treated as substantial damage for carrying out the repairs for such damage. [Delhi Rent Act (33 of 1995), S. 22(2)(l), *Expln.*]

Substantial error. Any mistake having important and material bearing on the subject.

Substantial evidence. Evidence which a reasonable man will accept as adequate for coming at the decision in a case.

Substantial expansion. Means the expansion of an existing industrial undertaking which substantially increases the productive capacity of the undertaking, or which is of such a nature as to amount virtually to a new industrial undertaking, but does not include any such expansion as is normal to the undertaking having regard to its nature and the circumstances relating to such expansion. [Industries (Development and Regulation) Act (65 of 1951), S. 13(2) *Expln*]

"SUBSTANTIAL EXPANSION" means increase in the investment in the plant and machinery by at least fifty per cent of the book value of plant and machinery (before taking depreciation in any year), as on the first day of the previous year in which the substantial expansion is undertaken. [Income-tax Act (43 of 1961), S. 80 IC (8)(ix)]

Substantial failure of justice. The word 'substantial failure of justice' used in Cl. (c) of Art. 226(1) of the Constitution of India is a relative term. Any order which is not in conformity with the principles of natural justice or is not in consonance with the statute under which it is passed may amount to a substantial failure of justice to a person in given circumstances. [D.S. TEWATIA and TIWANA, JJ.] *Suresh Chand* v.

Ved Parkash, MLJ : YD 1979 Suppl to Feb p. 889 : (1979) 81 Punj LR 96.

Substantial interest. "SUBSTANTIAL INTEREST",—

(i) in relation to a company means the holding of a beneficial interest by an individual or his spouse or minor child, whether singly or taken together, in the shares thereof, the amount paid upon which exceeds five lakhs of rupees or ten per cent of the paid-up capital of the company, whichever is less;

(ii) in relation to a firm, means the beneficial interest held therein by an individual or his spouse or minor child whether singly or taken together, which represents more than ten per cent of the total capital subscribed by all the partners of the said firm. [Banking Regulation Act (10 of 1949), S. 5(ne)]

Holding of a beneficial interest by individual or his spouse or minor child, whether singly or taken together in the shares of a company, the amount paid up on which exceeds 10% of the paid up capital of the company; or the capital subscribed by all the partners of a partnership firm. [Non-Banking Financial Companies Prudential Norms (Reserve Bank) Directions, 1998, para 2(1) (xviii)]

Actual and valuable right to have the advantage accruing from anything material or legal concern in anything. [CPC (5 of 1908), O. XIV, R. 7(b)]; [Specific Relief Act (47 of 1963), S. 14(3)(c), *Prov.* (ii)].

Substantial loss. The loss which is material and appreciable either in quantity or quality.

Substantial part. Material and appreciable portion of a thing. [CPC (5 of 1908), S. 51, *Prov.* (b)].

Substantial question of law. Any question of law affecting the rights of parties would not by itself be a substantial question of law. The important or difficult question would of course be a substantial question; but even if a question is not important or difficult, if there is room for reasonable doubt or difference of opinion on the question, then it would be a substantial question of law within the meaning of Art. 133, Constitution of India. *Subba Rao* v. *Veeraja,* AIR 1951 Mad 969, 978 (FB).

Substantial renovation and modernisation. For the purposes of this sub-clause, "SUBSTANTIAL RENOVATION AND MODERNISATION" means an increase in the plant and machinery in the network of transmission or distribution lines by at least fifty per cent of the book value of such plant and machinery as on the 1st day of April, 2004. [Income-tax Act (43 of 1961), S. 80-IA(4) (*Substituted by Finance Act (23 of 2004), S. 17(c) Expln.*)].

Substantial similarity. A strong resemblance occurring between a copy righted work and alleged infringement, thereby creating an inference of unauthorized copying.

Substantially. In a substantial manner; so as to be substantial; essentially. [T.P. Act (4 of 1882), S. 26].

"Substantially" means "essentially; without material qualification; in the main; in substance; materially." [Black's Law Dictionary (6th Edn.) as cited in *Thalappalam Service Cooperative Bank Limited v. State of Kerala*, (2013) 16 SCC 82, para 47].

Substantially the whole of the undertaking. For the purposes of section 180(1)(a) of Act 18 of 2013, the expression 'substantially the whole of the undertaking' in any financial year shall mean twenty per cent or more of the value of the undertaking as per the audited balance sheet of the preceding financial year. [*Explanation (ii)* to section 180(1)(a) of the Companies Act, 2013 (18 of 2013)]

Substantiate. To prove or confirm. [Provincial Insolvency Act (5 of 1920), S. 49(2)].

Substantive. Of or relating to a matter of substance as opposed to form or procedure; affecting rights, duties, or causes of actions, existing in its own right; specifically of or relating to a substantive crime.

Substantive and permanent. The phrase "substantive and permanent" as applied to an appointment is more descriptive of the nature and character of the appointment than indicative of the duration of that appointment. *Bimalacharan* v. *Trustees Museium,* AIR 1930 Cal 404.

Substantive basis. The expression 'substantive basis' is used in the service jurisprudence in contradistinction with *ad hoc* or purely stopgap or fortuitous. There is difference between substantive post as *contra* distinguished from temporary post and appointment of an incumbent to these posts could be made either on substantive basis or on *ad hoc* or stopgap basis. *Ramesh K. Sharma* v. *Rajasthan Civil Services,* AIR 2001 SC 362 : (2001) 1 SCC 637, para 4.

Substantive evidence. Evidence which is offered to support a fact in issue, as opposed to impeachment or corroborating evidence.

A confession of an accused under Section 15(1) of the Act is substantive evidence against the co-accused, abettor or conspirator jointly tried with the accused. *State* v. *Nalini*, AIR 1999 SC 2640. [TADA Act (28 of 1987), S. 15(1)]

Substantive law. That part of law which creates and defines rights; not adjective law, which defines methods of enforcing rights.

Substantive motions. A motion of the Parliament which is self-contained independent proposal submitted for approval of the House and is drafted in such a way as to be capable of expressing a decision of the House. It neither depends nor arises out of another motion. The Motion of thanks on the President's address, motions for election or removal of the Speaker or Deputy Speaker of the Lok Sabha or the Vice Chairman of the Rajya Sabha *etc.* are substantive motions.

Substantive sentence. A sentence awarding punishment principally or in the first instance as distinguished from that awarded in case of default (of payment of fine). [CrPC, 1973 (2 of 1974), S. 30(1)(b)].

Substantive vacancies. Substantive vacancies are to be regarded as synopsis with permanent posts under the A.P. State and Subordinate Service Rules. (*A.K. Nazeer Saheb* v. *A.P. Public Service Commission,* (1998) 9 SCC 453).

Substitute. To put (one) in place of another; to replace [Indian Contract Act (9 of 1972), S. 62]; one, who acts in the place of another; [Customs Tariff Act (51 of 1975), Sch. 1, Ch. 3, note (c)].

In some cases, the word 'substitute' may be employed to mean replacement by cancellation of the previous one. It might also mean the replacement of one by another, which might be equal to it, but differently expressed. *N.N. Chakravarty* v. *State of Assam,* AIR 1960 Ass 11, 15.

Substitute motions. The motions of the Parliament moved in substitution of the original motion and proposing an alternative are called substitute motions.

Substituted Agent. "Where an agent, holding an express or implied authority to name another person to act for the principal in the business of the agency, has named another person accordingly, such person is not a sub-agent, but an agent of the principal for such part of the business of the agency as is entrusted to him." [Indian Contract Act (9 of 1872)], S. 194]

Substituted service. Service of process authorised by the Court to be made on some other person, or in some other manner than direct personal service when the party cannot be found or evades service.

The service of process (on a defendant) otherwise than in the ordinary way of personal service, by publication and/or by affixing a copy thereof in some conspicuous part of the house where he is known to have last resided or carried on business or personally worked for gain. [CPC (5 of 1908), O. V, R. 20].

SUBSTITUTED SERVICE is the machinery by which where prompt personal service cannot be effected, leave may be obtained for service by post; or upon some person known to be in communication with the party to be served; or by advertisement, or affixing to the outer door of the last known residence or otherwise.

Substitution. The word 'substitution' does not connote two severable steps, one of repeal and another of a fresh enactment, but it means adding by way of amendment to remove an existing anomaly. *Bhagat Ram* v. *Union of India*, AIR 1988 SC 740, 747.

Substitution of parties. The provisions of CPC (5 of 1908), O. I, R. 10, which enables the substitution of right persons as plaintiffs, can be applied to a case in which the original plaintiff has no right to sue, provided the suit has been commenced through a *bona fide* mistake. The words "if the suit is brought in the name of the wrong person as plaintiff" cannot be construed as excluding altogether persons who may institute the suit without any right to do so.

Subsurface right. A landowner's right to the minerals and water below the property.

Subversive activities. Subversive activity must amount to actively pursuing such activities as are calculated to subvert the Government established by law. *V.S. Menon* v. *Union of India*, AIR 1963 SC 1160, 1164.

Succeed. To come after in time or sequence [IPC (45 of 1860), S. 37, ill. (c)]; to come next after and take the place of another either by descent, election or appointment in a position of rule or ownership. [T.P. Act (4 of 1882), S. 6(a)].

Successful. Resulting in success; having the desired effect or termination.

Succession. "SUCCESSION" includes both intestate and testamentary succession. [Ben. Act VIII of 1885 (Tenancy), S. 3]

The process by which one person succeeds another in the occupation or possession of any estate or the like [Hindu Succession Act (30 of 1956), Ss. 25 and 26]; the act or process of following in order of time or place.

The act or right of legal or official investment with a predecessor's officer, dignity, possessions, or functions; a series of persons following one another; a lineage; an order of descendants. In the law of descent, the coming in of another to take the property of one who dies without disposing of it by will.

Succession certificate. A certificate entitling the holder to collect the debts of the deceased or obtain rights to his shares and securities.

Succession of States. "SUCCESSION OF STATES" means the replacement of one State by another in the responsibility for the international relations of territory. [Vienna Convention on Succession of States in Prospect of Treaties, 1978, Art. 2(1)(b)]

Successive. Coming one after another in an uninterrupted sequence; following one another in order [CPC (5 of 1908), O. II, R. 2(3), *Expln.*]; [T.P. Act (4 of 1882), S. 94].

Successive claims. Claims following one after another in a line or series. [CPC (5 of 1908), O. II, R. 2(3), *Expln.*].

Successively. In a successive manner, in a series, following in order or uninterrupted course [T.P. Act (4 of 1882), S. 13, ill.]; [Indian Evidence Act (1 of 1872), S. 15, ill. (a)].

In a successive manner; in a series; in an order; following in order or uninterrupted course.

Successor. One, who takes the place which another has left; one who succeeds another in office, function, position, or estate [Ancient Monuments and Archaeological Sites and Remains Act (24 of 1958), S. 2(g)]; [Industrial Finance Corporation Act (15 of 1948)(*Repealed by Act 23 of 1993*), S. 11(2)].

The word "successor" is an apt and appropriate term to designate one to whom property descends, and in association with the words "heirs, administrators, and assignees" plainly imports a devolution or charge upon the obligator's estate.

The word "successor" includes a heir as well as a transferee.

Successor in business. Means,—

(i) where there has been an amalgamation of a company with another company, the amalgamated company;

(ii) where the first-mentioned person is succeeded by any other person in that business or profession, the other person;

(iii) where a firm carrying on a business or profession is succeeded by another firm, the other firm.

(iv) where there has been a demerger, the resulting company. [Income-tax Act (43 of 1961), S. 41(1), *Expln.* 2]

Successor state. "SUCCESSOR STATE", in relation to an existing State, means any State to which the whole or any part of the territories of that existing State is transferred by the provisions of Part II, and includes in relation to the existing State of Madras, also that State as territorially altered by the said provisions and the Union. [State Reorganisation Act (37 of 1956), S. 2(o)]

"SUCCESSOR STATE" means the State which has replaced another State on the occurrence of a succession of States. [Vienna Convention an Succession of States in Respect of Treaties, 1978, Art. 2. 1(d)]

Succour. To aid in distress; to relieve. [Employees' State Insurance Act (34 of 1948), S. 51D].

Such. The word "such" indicates something just before specified or spoken of, proximately and not merely previously. The word "such" occurring in the expression "such revocation or renunciation" in S. 206 will refer only to the revocation and renunciation dealt with in S. 205. *Bright Bros. (P.) Ltd.* v. *J.K. Sayani,* AIR 1976 Mad 55, 59. [Indian Contract Act (9 of 1872), S. 206]

'Such' means 'having the particular quality or character specified; certain; representing the object as already particularised in terms which are not mentioned'. [Webster as cited in *Dr. Subramanian Swamy v. State of T.N.*, (2014) 5 SCC 75, para 22].

'Such' means 'of a kind previously or about to be mentioned or implied; of the same quality as something just mentioned (used to avoid the repetition of one word twice in a sentence); of a degree or quantity stated or implicit; the same as something just mentioned (used to avoid repetition of one word twice in a sentence); that part of something just stated or about to be stated'. [New Webster's Dictionary and Thesaurus as cited in *Dr. Subramanian Swamy v. State of T.N.*, (2014) 5 SCC 75, para 22].

Such condition. When the Standing Committee of a Municipal Corporation is given powers to accord sanction for a layout plan on such conditions as it may think fit, the expression 'such conditions' has to be understood so as to advance the objective of the provision and the purpose for which it has been enacted and such a condition cannot mean asking the owner to surrender a portion of the land and transfer it to the Corporation. *Chet Ram Vashist* v. *Municipal Corporation of Delhi*, AIR 1995 SC 431, 434. [Delhi Municipal Corporation Act (16 of 1957), S. 313]

Such Court. Such Court means Court in which suit is pending. *Shaukat Hussain Ali Akram* v. *Bhuvaneshwari Devi*, AIR 1973 SC 528, 532. [CPC (5 of 1908), Or. XXI, R. 29]

Such Court means the very Court before which a party to a proceeding in that Court has produced or tendered in evidence a document in respect of which the offence is alleged to have been committed. *Nirmaljit Singh Hoon* v. *State of W.B.*, AIR 1972 SC 2639, 2651. [CrPC, 1973 (2 of 1974), S. 195(4), *Prov.*]

Such further evidence as may appear necessary. In CrPC 1973 (2 of 1974), S. 116 (1), is evidence *ejusdem generis* with the evidence described in the words which immediately precede it, *i.e.*, evidence as to the truth of the information on which action was taken.

Sudden. Happening or coming without warning or premonition; taking place or appearing all at once; abrupt; sharp. [IPC (45 of 1860), S. 358]; [Land Acquisition Act (1 of 1894), S. 17(3)].

'Sudden' means an action which must be quick and unexpected so far as to provoke the appellant. [*Sukhlal Sarkar v. Union of India*, (2012) 5 SCC 703, para 9] [Indian Penal Code (45 of 1860), S. 300, Exception I]

Sudden fight. A 'sudden fight' implies mutual provocation and blows on each side. *Ghappoo Yadav* v. *State of M.P.*, (2003) 3 SCC 528, para 10 : AIR 2003 SC 1620; *Dhirajbhai Gorakhbhai Nayak* v. *State of Gujarat,* (2003) 9 SCC 322, para 11. [IPC (45 of 1860), S. 300 *Excep. 4*]

Sudden quarrel. It is not possible to enunciate any general rule as to what shall be deemed to be a sudden quarrel. It is a question of fact and whether quarrel is sudden or not must necessarily depend upon the proved facts of each case. [*Prakash Chand* v. *State of H.P.*, (2004) 11 SCC 381, 384, para 7. See also *Sridhar Bhuyam* v. *State of U.P.*, (2004) 11 SCC 395, 397, para 8] [IPC (45 of 1860), S. 300 Exception-4]

Sudder. The chief seat of Government, contradistinguished from mofussil or interior of the country. The Presidency. (*Fifth Report*)

Sudder Dewanny Adawlut. The chief Civil Court of Justice under the East India Company's Government, held at the Presidency. (*Fifth Report*)

Sudder Nizamut Adawlut. The chief Criminal Court of Justice under the East India Company's Government. (*Fifth Report*)

Sue. To institute a suit. [T.P. Act (4 of 1882), S. 6(e)].

In the context in which the word 'sues' is used in S. 4(1), we do not think that the legislature intended this word to mean also 'or is a defendant in a suit'. The right conferred by Section 4 should accrue to the member of the undivided family only in the event of the transferee seeking to obtain partition of his share in the dwelling house. *Sakhawat Ali* v. *Ali Hussain,* AIR 1957 All 356, 358 (FB). [Partition Act (4 of 1893), S. 4]

The word 'sue' means taking any legal proceeding in accordance with the provisions of the Code of Civil Procedure. *Maharama Bhagwat Singh* v. *State of Rajasthan,* AIR 1963 Raj 22, 23. [CPC (5 of 1908), S. 86]

Sues for partition. Section 4 refers to a suit of partition and it is well-known that a party in a particular suit, whether a plaintiff or a defendant, is at the same time a plaintiff as well as a defendant. This dual capacity arises from the very nature of a partition proceeding where each party is entitled to ask for partition of his share and separate allotment. It will not be very inappropriate to speak of a defendant in a partition suit as 'suing for partition' and thus, the transferee-defendant may well come within the phrase 'and such transferee sues for partition'. *Haradhone Haldar* v. *Ushacharan Karunakar,* AIR 1955 Cal 292. [Partition Act (4 of 1893), S. 4]

Suffer further damage. To sustain further damage. [Sale of Goods Act (3 of 1930), S. 59(2)].

Sufferance. Passive consent; the state of one holding land without owner's consent; toleration.

Sufficiency. The quality or condition of being sufficient for its purpose or for the end in view. [CPC (5 of 1908), O. VI, R. 9].

Sufficient. "Sufficient", means adequate to suffice.

Competent; equal to the end proposed; adequate to a certain purpose or object. [Indian Evidence Act (1 of 1872), S. 24].

Sufficient cause. Perusal of different remedy like filing application under Art. 227, than appeal on wrong advice by counsel constitutes sufficient cause. *State of West Bengal* v. *Administrator Howrah Municipality*, AIR 1972 SC 749, 757.

Sufficient cause. "Sufficient cause" is the cause for which the defendant cannot be blamed for his absence. The meaning of the word "sufficient" is "adequate" or "enough", inasmuch as maybe necessary to answer the purpose intended. Therefore, the word "sufficient" embraces no more than that which provides a platitude, which when the act done suffices to accomplish the purpose intended in the facts and circumstances existing in a case, duly examined from the view point of a seasonal standard of a cautions man. In this context, "sufficient cause" means that the party should not have acted in a negligent manner or there was a want of *bona fide* on its part in view of the facts and circumstances of a case or it cannot be alleged that the party has 'not acted diligently' or "remained inactive". [*Basawaraj v. Special Land Acquisition Officer*, (2013) 14 SCC 81, para 9].

Perusal of a different remedy like filing application under Art. 227, than appeal on wrong advice by counsel constitutes sufficient cause. *State of West Bengal v. The Administrator Howrah Municipality*, AIR 1972 SC 749, 757.

An appeal against the award of enhanced compensation for land acquisition was filed beyond the limitation due to bona fide miscalculation of the period of limitation. This wrong calculation is sufficient cause to condone the delay. *Punjab University etc. v. Acharya Swami Ganesh*, AIR 1972 SC 1973, 1975.

Where the plaintiff who was throughout appearing in the suit through his pleader could not be informed of the date of hearing owing to the sudden illness of his pleader, there was sufficient cause for his non-appearance. *Motichand* v. *Ant Ram,* AIR 1952 Bho 33. [CPC (5 of 1908), O. IX, R. 9]

With reference to the question as to what is "sufficient cause" within the meaning of CPC (5 of 1908), O. XXII, R. 9 and other similar provisions, it cannot be laid down as a general proposition that ignorance of law can never be considered, but it should be allowed as such only in very special cases. *Hardial Singh* v. *Bagga Singh,* AIR 1972 Punj 343, 345.

A person who had no knowledge of the pending suit, and files a petition to implead himself, there is no question of any negligence on his part and so absence of knowledge is sufficient cause. *Nripti Nath* v. *Rajalakshmi,* AIR 1978 Cal 394, 396.

The expression 'sufficient cause' implies the presence of legal and adequate reason. The word 'sufficient' means 'adequate', 'en-ough', 'as much as may be necessary to answer the purpose intended.' It embraces no more than that which provides a plentitude which, when done, suffices to accomplish the purpose intended in the light of existing circumstances and when viewed from reasonable standard of practical and cautious men. *Benarsi Das Saraf* v. *Dalwier Dadri Cement Ltd.,* AIR 1959 Punj 232, 235.

An appeal against the award of enhanced compensation for land acquisition was filed beyond the limitation due to *bona fide* miscalculation of the period of limitation. This wrong calculation is sufficient cause to condone the delay. *Punjab University etc.* v. *Acharya Swami Ganesh*, AIR 1972 SC 1973, 1975.

Sufficient cause, means some cause beyond the control of the party and for successfully invoking the aid of the Court, the claimant must have acted with due care and attention. *Hemlata Devi* v. *S.K. Loman,* AIR 1974 Ori 24, 26.

SUFFICIENT CAUSE FOR NON-APPEARANCE. If a person has no knowledge of the suit or the final decree proceedings on the date of the hearing, he can be taken to have shown sufficient cause for non-appearance. *R.M.T.S.S. Dhanasekaran* v. *State Bank of India,* AIR 1977 Mad 252, 254. [CPC (5 of 1908), O. IX, R. 13]

Sufficient evidence. By "sufficient evidence" is meant that amount of proof which ordinarily satisfies an unprejudiced mind beyond reasonable doubt.

Sufficient ground. Sufficient basis or foundation. [CrPC, 1973 (2 of 1974), S. 204(1)].

Sufficient means. While determining whether the applicant is possessed of "sufficient means" within the meaning of the *Explanation 1* of O. XXXIII, R. 1, CPC (5 of 1908), the correct mode of approach is to determine whether the applicant is possessed of realizable assets. This is a question of fact and must be determined in each case according to the facts and circumstances.

The test to find out whether a person possessed sufficient means is not his power to raise money but whether he can succeed in raising anything substantial by exercising it. *Rani Ammal* v. *Rathnasabapathi,* AIR 1967 Mad 424, 426. [CPC (5 of 1908), O. XXXIII, R. 1]

If a person who can enable himself to pay the prescribed fee and if he can raise the requisite amount on some property, he will be considered, as having 'sufficient means' to pay the Court fee and he would not be allowed to sue as a pauper. *Sanyukta* v. *Prem Kumar Madan,* AIR 1974 Punj 203, 204.

Sufficient reason. Though it is difficult and perhaps undesirable to attempt to define precisely the meaning of the words "any other sufficient reason" in O. XLVII, R. 1, CPC (5 of 1908), yet, from the earlier part of the clause it is clear that a point which might have been, but which was not, discovered at the trial by the exercise of due diligence, was not intended by the section to afford any sufficient reason for review.

Sufficient security. Sufficient security, means adequate security, and it makes no difference whether it is personal or real security. The fact that the real estate offered as security had a previous mortgage upon, is no legal objection to its sufficiency. It might notwithstanding be abundantly adequate.

Sufficient time. A guaranty of a machine, stating that if, on starting the machine, it should in any way prove defective or fail to work, the purchaser should give prompt written notice to the agent from whom he purchased and allow "sufficient time" for a person to be sent to put it in order, and the defective part, if any, replaced, means a reasonable time under the circumstances.

Suffrage. A vote; the act of voting; the right or privilege of casting a vote at public elections; a vote in approbation or assent.

Sugar. "SUGAR" means—

(i) any form of sugar containing more than ninety percent of sucrose, including sugar candy;

(ii) Khandsari sugar or bura sugar or crushed sugar or any sugar in crystalline or powdered form. [Essential Commodities Act (10 of 1955), S. 2(e)]

(iii) sugar in process in vacuum pan sugar factory or raw sugar produced therein.

"SUGAR" means any form of sugar containing more than ninety per cent, of sucrose. [Sugar Export Promotion Act (30 of 1958), S. 2(f); Sugarcane Act (15 of 1934), S. 2(3)]

"SUGAR" means any form of sugar, whether wholly or partially manufactured, but does not include—

(i) "Khandsari sugar", that is to say, sugar in the manufacture of which neither a vacuum pan nor a vaccuum evaporator is employed; or.

(ii) "palmyra sugar", that is to say, sugar manufactured from jaggery obtained by boiling the juice of the palmyra palm. [Sugar (Regulation of Production) Act (55 of 1961), S. 2(f) and Sugar (Special Excise Duty) Act (58 of 1959), S. (c)]

"SUGAR" means any form of sugar including crushed sugar or sugar in crystallised or powder form, containing ninety percent or more of sucrose and produced by the vacuum pan process and includes raw sugar produced by the said process. [Sugar Cess Act (3 of 1982), S. 2(d)]

"SUGAR" includes plantation white sugar, raw sugar and refined sugar, whether indigenously produced or imported. [Essential Commodities (Amendment) Act (37 of 2003), S. 2, *Expln.* (a)]

Sugar factory. Means any premises (including the precincts thereof) in any part of which sugar is manufactured by vacuum pan process. [Sugar Cess Act (3 of 1982), S. 2(c)]

Sugar undertaking. Means an undertaking engaged in the manufacture or production of sugar by means of vacuum pans and with the aid of mechanical power. [Sugar Undertaking (Taking Over of Management) Act (49 of 1978), S. 2(f)]

Sugar year. "SUGAR YEAR" means the period of twelve months commencing on the 1st day of October and ending with the 30th day of September next following. [Sugar Undertakings (Taking over of Management) Act (47 of 1978), S. 2(g)]

Suggest. To put forward in a suggestion [Indian Contract Act (9 of 1972), S. 17(1)]; [Indian Evidence Act (1 of 1872), S. 17].

Sui juris (*Of his own right*) A person who can validly contract and bind himself by legal obligation, uncontrolled by any other person, is said to be *sui juris*; in other words, a person not subject to any incapacity, such as non-age, or insanity; possessing full social and civil rights; not under any legal disability, or the power of another or guardianship.

A phrase used to denote a person who is under no disability affecting his legal power to make conveyances of his property, to bind himself by contracts and to sue and be sued as opposed to persons wholly or partially under disability, as minors, mentally disordered persons, *etc.* [Estate Duty Act (34 of 1953), S. 3(1)(a)].

Suicide. "Suicide" means self-killing. It is not restricted to mean a wrongful act of self-murder. It means self-killing to the same extent as homicide means killing any one else.

The word "*suicide*" and the words "TO DIE BY HIS OWN HAND", Or "BY HIS OWN ACT", Or "TO TAKE HIS OWN LIFE", mean the same thing, and each conveys the idea of voluntary, intentional self-destruction.

A suicide "is one who deliberately puts an end to his own existence, or commits any unlawful malicious act, the consequence of which is his own death, as if, attempting to kill another, he runs upon his antagonist's sword, or, shooting at another, the gun bursts and kills himself.

A death by accident even though it be the result of one's own act is not suicide, and upon this principle self-destruction by an insane man or a lunatic is not an act of suicide within the meaning of the law.

ATTEMPT TO COMMIT SUICIDE. If the act of suicide fails to accomplish its purpose, it constitutes an attempt to commit suicide, which is an offence.

'Suicide' and 'euthanasia'. The view that distinction between 'suicide' and 'euthanasia' is logically inconsistent may not be quite incorrect, because in passive euthanasia, wherever it has been accepted as legally permissible, consent of the patient, if he be in a sound mental condition, has been regarded as one of the prerequisites. So, if one could legally commit suicide, he could also give consent for his being allowed to die. But then, the legal and other questions relatable to euthanasia are in many ways different from those raised by suicide. One would, therefore, be right in making a distinction logically and in principle between suicide and euthanasia, though it may be that if suicide is held to be legal, the persons pleading for legal acceptance of passive euthanasia would have a winning point. *P. Rathinam* v. *Union of India,* AIR 1994 SC 1844.

Suit. "SUIT" includes counter-claim and set off. [Marine Insurance Act (11 of 1963), S. 2(i)] "SUIT" does not include an appeal or an application. [Limitation Act (36 of 1963), S. 2(l)]

"SUIT" means a civil suit triable by a *Nyaya Panchayat.* [West Bengal Panchayat Act (41 of 1973), S. 2(q)]

A process instituted in a Court of justice for recovery or protection of a right, the enforcement of a claim, or the redress of a wrong. [CPC (5 of 1908), S. 85].

Prosecution or pursuit of some claim, demand or request; attempt to attain a certain result; the act of suing; the process by which one gains an end or object; an action or process for the recovery of a right or claim; the prosecution of some demand in a Court of Justice; any proceeding in a Court of Justice in which plaintiff pursues his remedy to recover a right or claim; the mode and manner adopted by law to redress civil injuries; a proceeding in a Court of Justice for the enforcement of a right.

The expression "suits" used in Cl. (*ix*) of S. 7, Court Fees Act (7 of 1870) means "appeal" as well, as the expression has been used to cover the entire litigation from its beginning to the end.

The word "suit" in the last clause of para 2, S. 11, Court Fees Act (7 of 1870), does not mean the entire suit. It can fairly be construed as the suit or claim in respect of the mesne profits.

A suit and all appeals made therein are to be regarded as one legal proceeding.

The plain and grammatical meaning of the word would include the whole of the suit and not a part of the suit or an issue in a suit. *Gulab Bai* v. *Manphool Bai*, AIR 1962 SC 214, 217. [CPC (5 of 1908), S. 11]

The word "suit" will include execution proceedings.

The word 'suit' in S. 4 of the Pensions Act (23 of 1871), could not be deemed to include execution proceedings.

A land acquisition proceeding is not a "suit" within the meaning of S. 11, CPC (5 of 1908), so as to render a decision come to therein binding when the same question arises in what is strictly a suit.

The term 'suit' as used in S. 21 of the Act has to be construed in its wider sense as including an appeal. *Bundi Municipal Board* v. *Bundi Electric Supply Co. Ltd.,* AIR 1957 Raj 278, 279. [Arbitration Act (10 of 1940) (*repealed*), S. 21]

The word 'suit' means a proceeding instituted in a civil Court by the presentation of a plaint.

A proceeding under Section 54 of the Co-operative Societies Act is not a suit and consequently Section 22 of the Payment of Wages Act cannot operate as a bar to such a proceeding being taken. *Farkhundah Namuhay* v. *V.B. Potdar*, AIR 1962 Bom 162, 164 (FB) [Payment of Wages Act (4 of 1936), S. 22].

Suit and appeal. The only difference between a suit and an appeal is that an appeal "only reviews and corrects the proceedings in a cause already constituted but does not create the cause." *Daywati* v. *Inderjit*, AIR 1966 SC 1423, 1427.

SUIT : CASE. The use of the word "cases" instead of "suits" in S. 115, CPC (5 of 1908) shows that the section contemplates legal proceedings which are not suits in the strict sense but which are governed by the provisions of the CPC.

Suit dismissed "for default". Dismissed "for want of prosecution."

Suit for an account in Provincial Small Cause Courts Act (9 of 1887), Art. 31, is a special form of suit. It does not mean every case in which accounts have to be looked into in order to ascertain the correctness or otherwise of the amount claimed by the plaintiff.

The words "suit for account" occurring in the first para of S. 11 of the Court Fees Act (7 of 1870), would be applicable to such portion of any suit as claims that relief, viz., relief by way of account.

A suit for an account is that suit where the defendant is under an obligation to render accounts to the plaintiff, the relationship between them being more than a debtor and creditor such as agent or bailee or receiver or trustee or partner or mortgagee. *Girija Prasad* v. *Sardribh Singh,* AIR 1977 Pat 241, 242. [Provincial Small Cause Courts Act (9 of 1887), Sch. II, Art. 31]

Suit for determination of any right to or interest in, immovable property. A suit of recovery of unpaid purchase-money under a contract for the sale of land is a suit "for the determination of any other right to or interest in immovable property."

The expression "suit for determination of any right to or interest in immovable property" in S. 19, Cl. (*g*) of the Presidency Small Cause Courts Act (15 of 1882), refers only to suits expressly brought for the purpose of obtaining a decree determining a right or interest in immovable property, and not suits for money or moveable property in which a question of title to immovable property may be raised by the defendant.

Suit for foreclosure. "A suit to obtain a decree that a mortgagor shall be absolutely debarred of his right to redeem the mortgaged property is called a suit for disclosure." [Transfer of Property Act (4 of 1882), S. 67]

Suit for recovery of money. Where in a suit by the landlord for eviction on the ground of non-payment of rent, the tenant deposited the rent and then made a claim for a set-off, it was held that a set-off can only be claimed in a suit for recovery of money and not in a suit for ejectment. *L. Manoharlal Nathanmal* v. *Madan Lal Murari Lal,* AIR 1956 Punj 190, 192. [CPC (5 of 1908), O. 8, R. 6]

Suit for redemption. "The right conferred by this section is called a right to redeem and a suit to enforce it is called a suit for redemption." [Transfer of Property Act (4 of 1882), S. 60]

Suit of a civil nature. "A suit in which the right to property or to an office is contested is a suit of a civil nature, notwithstanding that such right may depend entirely on the decision of questions as to religious rites or ceremonies." [CPC (5 of 1908), S. 9, *Expln.* II]

Suit of the nature cognisable in Courts of Small Causes. The construction of the words a "suit of the nature cognisable in Courts of Small Causes" in S. 102, CPC (5 of 1908) does not depend upon the tribunal in which the suit is brought and is equally applicable whether the suit be brought in a Court of Small Causes or in any other Court.

Suit or proceeding. The words "suit," "proceeding," and words of similar connotation have different meanings in different statutes and it is not possible to lay down a general rule of interpretation which would be applicable to all cases. In each particular case, the question has to be examined in reference to the context and that meaning is to be preferred which will best fit in with it.

Suit relating to recovery of possession. The expression would include a suit for an injunction, which may be necessitated because of the act of the landlord in trying to recover possession of the premises from the tenant by force. *A.K. Poraunderwal & Sons* v. *Ghulam Hussain Alibhai Nathani,* AIR 1974 Bom 288, 293.

Suit to which this Act applies" means any suit,—

(a) for the recovery of a loan made after the commencement of this Act; or

(b) for the enforcement of any security taken or any agreement, whether by way of settlement of account or otherwise, made, after the commencement of this Act in respect of any loan made either before or after the commencement of this Act; or

(c) for the redemption of any security given after the commencement of this Act in respect of any loan made either before or after the commencement of this Act. [Usurious Loans Act (10 of 1918), S. 2(3)]

Suitable employment. In relation to the holder of any certificate, means employment in a capacity for which the holding of such certificate is an essential qualification. [Merchant Shipping Act (44 of 1958), S. 87A(d)]

Suitor. A plaintiff in a suit. [Indian Evidence Act (1 of 1872), S. 18].

"Suits" and **"legal proceeding".** The word "suit" in S. 171 of the Companies Act means a proceeding which is instituted with the presentation of a plaint in a Court of original jurisdiction. The expression "legal proceeding" in this section is coupled with "suit" and obviously means proceedings *ejusdem generis*, that is to say, original proceedings in a Court of first instance, analogous to a suit initiated by means of a petition similar to a plaint. It does not include proceedings taken in the course of the suit, nor proceedings arising from the suit and continued in a higher Court, like an appeal from an interlocutory order or final order passed in the suit.

Suits pending. The expression 'suits pending' means a live suit, whether in the Court of first instance or in an appeal where the judgment of the Court of first instance is being considered. *Daywati* v. *Inderjit*, AIR 1966 SC 1423, 1427. [Usurious Loans Act (10 of 1918), S. 3 *as amended by S. 5, Punjab Relief of Indebtedness Act (7 of 1934)*]

Sum. A quantity or amount of money [T.P. Act (4 of 1882), S. 57(a)(1)]; [Indian Partnership Act (9 of 1932), S. 48(b)].

In a suit on the note, the "SUM DEMANDED" is not only the principal of the note, but also the interest on the same.

In acts relating to jurisdiction, "SUM IN CONTROVERSY" has precisely the same meaning as "sum demanded". The demand of a sum is the sum in controversy.

In English Law—A summary or abstract; a compendium; a collection. Several of the old law treatises are called 'sum'. Lord Hale applies the term to summaries the statute law. Burrill. The sense in which the term is most commonly used in 'money'; a quantity of money or currency; any amount indefinitely, a sum of money, a small sum, or a large sum. [Black's Law Dictionary as cited in *Hyder Consulting (UK) Limited v. State of Orissa*, (2015) 2 SCC 189, para 6].

While the word 'sum' must be construed in connection with the context, it has a definite meaning appropriate to use with reference to dollars and cents, and, except where a different meaning plainly appears, it is restricted in its application to money, and in sense it is lexically defined as meaning money, and this is said to be the sense in which the word is most commonly used. [Corpus Juris Secumdum, Vol. 83 as cited in *Hyder Consulting (UK) Limited v. Governor, State of Orissa*, (2015) 2 SCC 189, para 72.4]

Sum certain. An amount that can be determined with certainty from the information presented without resort to outside sources.

Sum up his case. To give a summary of relevant facts, evidence and law at the close of the case. [Navy Act (62 of 1957), S. 111(8)].

Summarily. In a summary manner. [T.P. Act (4 of 1882), S. 76(c)].

Summarily sold. The expression 'summarily sold' implies that the proceeding for realisation of rent by sale of the mortgaged property is of a summary nature such as a certificate proceeding under the Public Demands Recovery Act. *Jay Prasad Choubey* v. *Jasoda,* AIR 1958 Pat 649, 651. [Transfer of Property Act (4 of 1882), S. 76(c)]

Summary. Hasty; provisional. Performed or effected by a short method; done without delay; carried out rapidly by the omission of certain formalities [CrPC, 1973 (2 of 1974), S. 421(2)]; containing or comprising the chief points or the sum and substance of a matter.

Summary procedure. Short and concise procedure followed in suits of particular class. [CPC (5 of 1908), S. 128(2)(f)].

Summary proceedings. A proceeding without following the strict rules of procedure for trials.

Summary process. "Summary", as applied to process, means immediate, instantaneous, in contradistinction from the ordinary course, by emanating and taking effect without intermediate applications or delays.

Summary suits. The suits or class of suits in which summary procedure is followed. [CPC (5 of 1908), 1st Sch., App. B, form No. 4].

Summary trial. A trial of offences not raising complicated issues which can be tried by adopting a simplified procedure so that a speedy result is obtained.

'Summary trial' is a speedy trial by dispensing with unnecessary formalities or delay. (*Bindeshwari,* AIR 1959 Pat 46) [CrPC (5 of 1898), S. 260 (same Section in 1974 Code)]

Summon. To call upon. [CrPC, 1973 (2 of 1974), S. 62(2)]; [Constitution of India, Art. 85(1)].

Summon or prorogue. To call upon or to adjourn.

Summoning. To call (by a summons). [Army Act (46 of 1950), S. 135].

Summons. A "summons" is a process issued from the office of a Court of Justice requiring the persons to whom it is addressed to attend the Court for the purpose therein stated.

An authoritative call to attend a specified place for a specified purpose; an order by which a person is called to appear before a Court, judicial officer *etc.* [IPC (45 of 1860), Ss. 172, 173 and 174].

A "summons" is a process issued by a court calling upon a person to appear before a Magistrate. It is used for the purpose of notifying an individual of his legal obligation to appear before the Magistrate as a response to violation of law. In other words, the summons will announce to the person to whom it is directed that a legal proceeding has been started against that person and the date and time on which the person must appear in court. A person who is summoned is legally bound to appear before the court on the given date and time. [*Bhushan Kumar v. State (NCT of Delhi)*, (2012) 5 SCC 424, para 12].

The order fixing the date for filing written statement and for final hearing should be treated as summons. *Srinath Agarwal* v. *Santosh Kumar,* AIR 1981 All 400, 404.

Summons-case. "SUMMONS-CASE" means a case relating to an offence, and not being a warrant-case. [CrPC, 1973 (2 of 1974), S. 2(w)] [Now (w. e. f. 1-7-2024) repealed & replaced by Bharatiya Nagarik Suraksha Sanhita, 2023 (46 of 2023), section 2(1)(x), same definition in new Sanhita]

Summons and **warrant case (Difference).** The criterion in determining whether a case is summons case or a warrant case is the punishment provided for an offence. *Public Prosecutor* v. *Shaik Dawood,* MLJ : QD (1956-1960) Vol. II C1594 : 1956 Andhra LT 392 : AIR 1957 AP 977. [CrPC (5 of 1898), S. 247]

Summum jus, summa injuria. (*Lat.*) (Hob. 125) Extreme law is extreme injury.

Sunnah. (*A.*) Traditional law, the name of a compilation of the sayings and practices of Muhammad, made about a hundred years after his death, to supplement the Koran when that was found insufficient to regulate the affairs of the then greatly extended empire. The *sunnah* is invested with the force of law and some of the authority of inspiration.

Sunnat. (*H.*) The traditional law of mohammadans based upon the sayings and doings of Mohammad, and of scarcely inferior authority to the text of the Koran in the estimation of the Sunnis, although not recognised by the Shias : also any obligatory religious ceremony, a circumcision. (*Wilson's Gloss.*)

Sunni. (*A.*) A follower of the *sunnah*; the name of the first great division of the Muhammadans.

A follower of the traditions; the designation of one of the two great divisions of the Mohammadans, characterized not only by the difference which the members pay to tradition, but by their affirmation of the lawful succession of the first four khalifs, Abubakr, Omar Othman, and Ali, in opposition to the Shias, who denounce the three first as usurpers. (*Wilson's Gloss,* 494)

Sunni waqf. "SUNNI WAKF" means a *wakf* governed by Sunni law. [Wakf Act (43 of 1995), S. 3(q)]

Suo motu. Of one's own motion. The expression implies a considerable discretion and option. The Court initiates proceedings *suo motu i.e.* on its own without any party approaching for it. Mostly the Court intervenes so as to check the abuse of power by the executive often in cases of violation of human rights and in cases of public interest. Use of their powers *suo motu* by higher Courts, seems to be inherent in them.

Taking *suo motu* cognizance of the illegal felling of forest trees which are of immense importance to the existence of mankind, the Rajasthan High Court sent notice to the responsible officials of the forest department to appear and explain the situation. Being not satisfied with their explanation, the Court directed them to file detailed reply to the queries of the Court and in the meantime directed them to prevent felling of trees in the forest areas and trees which are not exempt under the Rajasthan Forest (Produce Transit) Rules, 1957. *Suo Motu* v. *Principal, Chief Conservator, Forest, Jaipur,* AIR 2005 Raj 30. [Rajasthan Forest (Produce Transit) Rules (1954), R. 2]

Super specialist. 'SUPER SPECIALIST' means a medical practitioner with any higher qualification than a post-graduate qualification in any one of the disciplines relating to medical sciences eg. specialisation in heart surgery, neuro-surgeon and cancer cure it. [Punjab Health System Corporation Act (6 of 1996), S. 2(j)]

Superannuation. "SUPERANNUATION", in relation to an employee who is a member of the Pension Scheme, means the attainment, by the said employee, of such age as is fixed in the contract or conditions of service as the age on the attainment of which such employee shall vacate the employment. [Coal Mines Provident Fund and Miscellaneous Provisions Act (46 of 1948), S. 2(j)]

"SUPERANNUATION", in relation to an employee, who is the member of the Pension Scheme means the attainment, by the said employee, of the age of fifty-eight years. [Employees' Provident Fund and Miscellaneous Provisions Act (19 of 1952), S. 2(ll)]

"SUPERANNUATION", in relation to an employee means the attainment by the employee of such age as is fixed in the contract or conditions of service as the age on the attainment of which the employee shall vacate the employment. [Payment of Gratuity Act (39 of 1972), S. 2(r)]

"Superannuation", in relation to an employee, means the attainment by the employee of such age as is fixed in the contract or conditions of service, as the age on the attainment of which the employee shall vacate the employment:

Provided that for the purposes of Chapter III, the age of superannuation shall be fifty-eight years. [Code on Social Security, 2020 (36 of 2020), section 2(82)]

Superannuation allowance. 'SUPERANNUATION ALLOWANCE' includes, any pension on superannuation, or other retiring allowance".

Allowance for expenses on clothes and food. [Companies Act (1 of 1956), S. 321(3)].

"Superannuation" and **"Termination".** *Superannuation* and *termination* are two entirely different matters. *Superannuation* takes place automatically on an employee reaching a particular age for which no notice is required, hence *termination* cannot include *superannuation.* The import of two expressions is entirely different. [1975 Lab IC 1484 (1486, 1487) (Punj)]

Superficial contents. Contents appearing on the surface. [Registration Act (16 of 1908), S. 21(3)].

Superficies solo cedit. Whatever is attached to the land forms part of it. The surface goes with the land.

Superintendence. "Superintendence" means the act of superintending, care, and oversight, for the purpose of direction, and with authority to direct.

The exercise of supervision over; the act of superintending. [CrPC, 1973 (2 of 1974), S. 275(1)].

The word "superintendence" seems properly to imply the exercise of some authority or control over the person or thing subjected to oversight.

Superintendence of the High Court is not confined to administrative superintendence, it also includes judicial superintendence and the High Court has power to correct any decision of a tribunal within its jurisdiction through its power of superintendence. *A.R. Sarin* v. *B.C. Pabil,* AIR 1951 Bom 423. [Constitution of India, Art. 227]

The word includes administrative as well as judicial superintendence. *Jagannath* v. *Puniya,* AIR 1952 MB 51.

Superintendence connotes supervision which implies a hierarchy, viz., supervisor and the one supervised. It would mean keeping a check, watch over the work of another who may be a subordinate in a hierarchy of authority. It would also imply giving of direction, guidance, even instructions, and in a given case and in a given situation asking one who is being supervised to forbear from doing a thing and directing someone else to do that thing. *State of Bihar* v. *J.A.C. Saldame* , AIR 1980 SC 326, 333.

Superintendent. One who superintends.

A "superintendent" is one who has the oversight and charge of something, with the power of direction.

"SUPERINTENDENT". In relation to a jail, remand home or other place of custody or a women's or children's institution, includes a person holding any other office in such jail, remand home, place or institution by virtue of which such person can exercise any authority or control over its inmates. [*Explanation 3* to S. 376C of IPC, 1860 (45 of 1860), as substituted by the Criminal Law (Amendment) Act, 2013 (13 of 2013)] [Now (w. e. f. 1-7-2024) repealed & replaced by Bharatiya Nayaya Sanhita, 2023 (45 of 2023), section 68, Explanation 3, same as defined in new Sanhita]

Superintendent of Police. "SUPERINTENDENT OF POLICE" includes any police-officer of a like or superior rank, and any person upon whom the powers of a Superintendent of police are for the purposes of this Act conferred by the Central Government. [Official Secrets Act (19 of 1923), S. 2(10).]

Superintendent of the plantation. The expression "SUPERINTENDENT OF THE PLANTATION" means the person having the charge or supervision of the labourers and work in the plantation, whether called a manager, superintendent or by any other name. [Registration of Birth and Deaths Act (18 of 1969), S. 9 *Expln.*]

Superior. Higher in degree, quality, importance or other respect; higher in rank or dignity. [IPC (45 of 1860), S. 76, ill. (a)].

Superior authority. The power of the head of the State to dismiss or remove is not affected by Art. 311 of the Constitution. (*N.W.F. Provinces* v. *Suraj Narain,* AIR 1949 PC 112)

An authority superior to the appointing authority can dismiss or remove from service the servant concerned. (*Parshotam Lal Dhingra* v. *Union of India,* AIR 1958 SC 36)

Superior officer. "SUPERIOR OFFICER," when used in relation to or person subject to this Act, includes a warrant officer and a non-commissioned officer and as regards person serving under such conditions as may be prescribed, an officer, junior commissioned officer, warrant officer, petty officer and non-commissioned officer of the regular Army or the Navy. [Air Force Act (45 of 1950), S. 4(xxvii)] and Army Act (46 of 1950), S. 3(xxxiii)]

"SUPERIOR OFFICER" means any officer, junior commissioned officer, warrant officer or non-commissioned officer of the regular Army or of the Territorial Army. [Lok Sahayak Sena Act (53 of 1956), S. 2(d)]

"SUPERIOR OFFICER" means any of the officers appointed under Section 4 and includes any other officer appointed by the Central Government as a superior officer of the Force. [Railway Protection Force Act (23 of 1957), S. 2(1)(f)]

Higher in rank, status, *etc.* [IPC (45 of 1860), S. 76, ill. (a)].

When used in relation to a person subject to naval law, this term means any officer or petty officer who is senior to that person under regulations made under the Navy Act, 1957, any officer or petty officer who, though not so senior to that person, is entitled under the Navy Act or regulations made thereunder to give a command to that person. [Navy Act (62 of 1957), S. 2(24)]

Superior soldier. When used in relation to a person subject to this Act, includes a warrant officer and a non-commissioned officer, and as regards persons serving under such conditions as may be prescribed, an officer, junior commissioned officer, warrant officer, petty officer and non-commissioned officer of the Regular Army or the Navy. [Air Force Act (45 of 1950), S. 4(xxvii)]

Superscription. The action of superscribing. [Registration Act (16 of 1908), S. 43(1)].

Supersede. To make void; annual; repeal by replacing.

Superseded. Set aside; replaced by [Industrial Finance Corporation Act (15 of 1948) (*Repealed by Act 23 of 1993*), S. 6(5)].

Superseding motions. Those subsidiary motions are moved in the course of debate on another question and seek to supersede that question even though they are independent in form *e.g.* a motion seeking recommittal of a Bill to a Committee or recirculation to elicit further opinion or adjournment of the debate on the Bill. Most of them are dilatory in nature.

Supersession. The word 'supersession' has been used in the sense of removal and replacement, and the notification does not have effect of wiping out tax liability under the previous notifications. *State of Orissa* v. *Titaghur Paper Mills Co. Ltd.*, AIR 1985 SC 1293, 1316.

Supervise. The word 'supervise' covers manual work coupled with a power of inspection and superintendence of the manual work of others. *R.B. Employees' Association* v. *Reserve Bank*, AIR 1966 SC 305, 314. [Industrial Disputes Act (14 of 1947), S. 2(s)]

Supervise: Monitor. To supervise would mean to observe and direct the execution of a task whereas to monitor would only mean to maintain surveillance. [*Manohar Lal Verma v. Principal Secretary*, (2014) 2 SCC 532, para 39].

To oversee with the powers of direction and decision; to superintend. [Specific Relief Act (47 of 1963), S. 14(1)(d)].

Supervisor. A surveyor or overseer. (*Tomlin*) Clerks in the audit department doing the work of checking up books of accounts and entries made therein are not supervisors. *Lloyds Bank, New Delhi* v. *Panna Lal Gupta*, AIR 1967 SC 428, 432.

Supervisory officer. Means any of the officers appointed under Section 4 and includes any other officer appointed by the Central Government as a supervisory officer of the Force. [Central Industrial Security Force Act (50 of 1968), S. 2(1)(i)]

Supplement. A "supplement" is that which supplies a deficiency; that which fills up, completes, or makes an addition to something already organised, arranged or set apart; a part added to or a continuation of something. It is used sometimes as a synonym of "appendix".

"SUPPLEMENT" is a supplying by addition of what is wanting.

Supplemental. Furnishing a supplement to the deficiency in; supplying (a deficiency); of the nature of forming or serving as a supplement. [T.P. Act (4 of 1882), S. 4 and Constitution of India, Art. 4(1)].

Supplemental Register. Publication of the PTO that provides constructive notice of ownership to companies in all fifty States that you are using a trademark not yet registrable. (*Cyber Law*)

Supplementary grants. Grants sought in the event of authorised amount for a service being found to be insufficient for the current financial year or when need has arisen during the current financial year for supplementary or additional expenditure upon some 'new service' not contemplated in the annual financial statement for that year.

Suppliant. The party preferring a petition of right.

Supplied on credit. Given on the condition of the price being paid later.

Supplier. The term SUPPLIER in relation to supply of any goods, means a person who supplies goods to any person for the ultimate purpose of re-sale and include a wholesaler. [Monopolies and Restrictive Trade Practices Act (54 of 1969), S. 39(3) *Expln.*]

"Supplier" in relation to any goods or services or both, shall mean the person supplying the said goods or services or both and shall include an agent acting as such on behalf of such supplier in relation to the goods or services or both supplied [The Central Goods and Services Tax Act, 2017 (12 of 2017), S. 2(105)]

"SUPPLIER" means an ancillary industrial undertaking or a small scale industrial undertaking holding a permanent registration certificate issued by the Directorate of Industries of a State or Union territory. [Interest on Delayed Payments to Small Scale and Ancillary Industrial Undertakings Act (32 of 1993), S. 2(f)]

Supplier of goods. 'SUPPLIER OF GOODS' means a person carrying on a business in the course of which he supplies goods for the purpose of, or in pursuance of contracts made by him for work, labour and materials. [Emergency Risks (Goods) Insurance Act (62 of 1962), S. 2(e); Emergency Risks (Goods) Insurance Act, (50 of 1971), S. 2(j)]

Supply. "Supply" in relation to electricity, means the sale of electricity to a licensee or consumer. [Electricity Act (36 of 2003), S. 2(70)]

Supply chain. The integrated network of suppliers, transportation companies, and brokers that provide materials and services to the customers (businesses and consumers). (*Cyber Law*)

Supply-chain management. The active participation and cooperation of supply-chain suppliers and other companies to improve products, services, procedures, and processes using information systems and e-commerce technologies. (*Cyber Law*)

Supply curve. A line on a price-output graph showing the relationship between a good's price and the quantity supplied at a given time.

Supply of water for domestic purposes. A "*supply of water for domestic purposes*" does not include a supply of water for cattle, or for horses, or for washing carriages, where the cattle, horses or carriages are kept for sale or hire or by a common carrier, or a supply for any trade, manufacture or business, or for watering gardens, or for fountains or for any ornamental purpose. [Bur. Act XIX of 1884 (Rangoon Water works), S. 2, cl. (8).]

Supply of rail coaches to railways if sale. The mere manufacture and supply of railway coaches to Railway Board by assessee Hindustan Aeronautic Ltd cannot be a sale, since the difference between the price of a coach and the cost of material can only be the cost of services rendered by the assessee. *Commissioner of Commercial Taxes Mysore Bangalore* v. *Hindustan Aeronautics Ltd.*, AIR 1972 SC 744, 749.

Support. Not only does the word "support" include "bearing weight" but it is also used by the student and understood in common phraseology as covering "to keep from falling" and other kindred expressions.

The action of supplying of a living thing with what is necessary for subsistence [Guardians and Wards Act (8 of 1890), S. 24]; to strengthen the position of one by assistance; to stand by; to back up [Indian Evidence Act (1 of 1872), S. 46]; to prop up [CrPC, 1973 (2 of 1974), S. 133(1)(d)].

"Support services" means infrastructural, operational, administrative, logistic, marketing or any other support of any kind comprising functions that entities carryout in ordinary course of operations themselves but may obtain as services by outsourcing from others for any reason whatsoever and shall include advertisement and promotion, construction or works contract, renting of immovable property, security, testing and analysis. [Finance Act (32 of 1994), S. 65-B(49)] Omitted by the Finance Act, 2015 and now repealed by Central Goods and Services Tax Act, 2017]

Supported accommodation. Means a living arrangement whereby a person, in need of support, who has a rented or ownership accommodation, but has no live-in caregiver, gets domiciliary care and a range of support services from a caregiver of an agency to help him live independently and safely in the privacy of his home. [Mental Healthcare (Rights of Persons with Mental Illness) Rules, 2018, R. 2(1)(i)].

Supporting manufacturer. Means a person being an Indian company or a person (other than a company) resident in India, manufacturing (including processing) goods or merchandise and selling such goods or merchandise to an Export House or a Trading House for the purposes of export. [Income-tax Act (43 of 1961), S. 80HHC (4C) *Expln.* (d)]

Suppose. To presume.

Supposed. Presumed. [IPC (45 of 1860), S. 141, *Fourth*].

Supposition. An assumption of something being true without proof of its veracity.

In an instruction that "if the evidence, though in part circumstantial, is to your mind consistent with the supposition that defendant is guilty of this charge and inconsistent with the supposition that he is innocent of it", *etc.*, "it is your duty to find him guilty," the word "supposition" is used in the sense of hypothesis and as meaning primarily what is not known to be true and not proved and hence, the instruction is not erroneous.

Hypothesis. [Indian Evidence Act (1 of 1872), S. 3].

Suppress. To put down by force or authority; to quell [IPC (45 of 1860), S. 154]; to hold back, especially from publication, divulgation *etc.*

Suppressio veri. *Supressio veri* implies previous knowledge and there can be no *suppressio veri* in vacuum. *Suppressio veri* means withholding of information. *J.J.S. Rodrignes* v. *UOI,* AIR 1967 Goa 169, 172.

Suppressio veri, expressio falsi. Suppression of the truth is equivalent to the expression of falsehood.

Suppressio veri, suggestio falsi. Suppressing the truth; suggesting the false.

Suppression. Where there is an obligation to speak a failure to speak, will constitute the "suppression of a fact" but where there is no obligation to speak silence cannot be termed "suppression".

Suppression of documents. The dishonest destruction, hiding, or defacing of any valuable security (*i.e.* almost any document creating, extinguishing, or transferring a right in money or property), will or similar document, or any original document (but not a copy) belonging to or filed in any Court or governmental department.

Suppression of evidence. Destruction of evidence; refusal to give evidence or to testify; ruling of the trial judge that the evidence sought to the admitted be excluded because of having been illegally acquired.

Suppression of fact. The expression 'suppression of facts,' would mean a deliberate or conscious omission to state a fact with the intention of deriving wrongful gain. *Collector of Customs* v. *Tin Plate Co. of India Ltd.,* (1997) 10 SCC 538, para 5. [Customs Act (52 of 1962), S. 28(1), *Proviso*]

Supra protest. After protest. [Negotiable Instruments Act (26 of 1881), S. 7].

Supreme Court. The Supreme Court of the United Kingdom is the High Court of Parliament, consisting of King, Lords, and Commons, who are invested with a kind of omnipotency in making new laws, repealing and reviving old ones; and it is on the right balance of these three depends the well-being, and indeed the very being, of the constitution.

The highest Court of justice in India. [CrPC, 1973 (2 of 1974), S. 2(e)(iii)]; [Constitution of India, Part V, Chap. IV].

"Supreme Court of India precincts" means the whole premises of the Supreme Court including the Court Block, open grounds, parking, old and new Chamber Blocks, libraries, canteens, bar-rooms, health centres and/or any other part of the premises under the control of the Hon'ble Chief Justice of India. [Gender Sensitisation and Sexual Harassment of Women at the Supreme Court of India (Prevention, Prohibition and Redressal) Regulations, 2013, Regn. 2(l)].

Surcharge. 'SURCHARGE' means an additional charge for payment. [Assam Panchayat Act (18 of 1994), S. 2(31)]

'SURCHARGE' means an amount for which the auditor, in exercise of the powers vested in him under this Act makes, a person liable for loss, waste, misapplication or misappropriation of any money or other property belonging to any local authority. [Kerala Local Fund Audit Act (14 of 1994), S. 2(l)]

An overcharge of what is just and right; to overburden; in equity practice, to add an item to an account; an overcharge, beyond what is just and right. (*Merch. Dict.*; *Tomlin*)

The expression "surcharge" in the context of taxation means an additional imposition which results in enhancement of the tax and the nature of the additional imposition is the same as the tax on which it is imposed as surcharge. *Sarojini Tea Co. (P) Ltd.* v. *Collector of Dibrugarh*, AIR 1992 SC 1264, 1269.

Surcharge stands for an additional or extra charge or payment. It is a super added charge, a charge over and above the usual or current dues. *Bisra Stone lime Co.* v. *O. S.E. Board*, AIR 1976 SC 127, 130. [Electricity (Supply) Act (54 of 1948), S. 49]

Surety. "The person who gives the guarantee is called the SURETY." [Indian Contract Act (9 of 1872), S. 126]

A person who binds himself for the payment of a sum of money or for the performance of something else for another who is already bound for the same. [Indian Contract Act (9 of 1872), S. 126].

Suretyship. A primary undertaking to answer for the debt, default, or miscarriage of another.

The position or function of a surety. [Indian Contract Act (9 of 1872), S. 133, ill. (a)].

Surf. To browse the Internet without any particular destination in mind. (*Cyber Law*)

Surgeon. One who practises the art of healing by manual operation. [IPC (45 of 1860), S. 88, ill.]; [Mines Act (35 of 1952), S. 11(1)].

Surgical Operation means :

(i) cutting operation (not including any lancing operations or injections)

(ii) any operation involving the reducing of fractures

(iii) any treatment or adjustment in respect of or any dislocation or joints or bones, orthopaedic or neuro-surgery or plastic surgery by qualified surgeon

(iv) stitching of wounds. [Scheme of Hospitalisation and Domiciliary Hospitalisation Benefit Policy, Specified for the purpose of S. 80D of the Income-tax Act (43 of 1961)]

Surname. A family or additional name. [Trade and Merchandise Marks Act (43 of 1958), S. 9(1)(d)].

Surplus. "SURPLUS" means the net excess of income over the expenditure. [Andhra Pradesh Mutually Aided Co-operative Societies Act (A.P Act No. 30 of 1995), S. 2(s)]

"SURPLUS" means the number by which the value of the votes original and transferred, of any candidate exceeds the quota. [Bar Council of West Bengal Election Rules, 1986, R. 2(u)]

"Surplus" is defined as "over plus"; that which remains when use is satisfied; excess beyond what is prescribed or wanted in law; the residue of an estate after the debts and legacies are paid.

That which remains when use or need is satisfied. [CPC (5 of 1908), S. 73, *Prov.* (a)].

Surplus assets. What is left of a company's property after payment of debts and repayment of the whole of the preference and ordinary capital.

Surrender. 'SURRENDER' means the selling of foreign exchange to an authorised person in India in exchange of rupees. [Foreign Exchange Management (Realisation, Repatriation And Surrender of Foreign Exchange) Regulations, 2000, Reg. 2(iv)]

To give up in favour of or for the sake of another; to give up (something) out of one's own possession or power into that of another who has or asserts a claim to it. [ill., T.P. Act (4 of 1882), S. 111(f)].

Surrender : transfer. In general the words "surrender of the demised estate" mean yielding up of the estate to the landlord, so that the leasehold interest becomes indistinct by mutual agreement between the parties or by operation of law. It does not involve alienation of an estate. Under a surrender the landlord resumes possession of the property without opposition from the tenant. This term is well known to law and is generally distinguished from abandonment which is another term that does not involve transfer. *Mubarak Hussain* v. *Custodian General of Evacuee Property,* AIR 1957 Punj 197, 200. [Administration of Evacuee Property Act (31 of 1950), S. 40]

Surrender value. (*In Insurance Law*) The value of a life insurance policy at any given time when the person insured, because of inability to continue paying premiums desires a lump sum to be paid to him in consideration of what he has already paid. The cash value of an insurance policy.

Surrendered child. "Surrendered child" means a child, who is relinquished by the parent or guardian to the Committee, on account of physical, emotional and social factors beyond their control, and declared as such by the Committee. [Juvenile Justice (Care and Protection of Children) Act, 2015 (2 of 2016), S. 2(60)].

Surrogacy. The role of a woman (a surrogate mother) who is commissioned to bear a child by a married couple unable to have children themselves.

Surrogate. A substitute; a person appointed to act for another.

A deputy of an ecclessiastical judge. [Indian Christian Marriage Act (15 of 1872), S. 73].

Surveiliance. Police investigative technique involving visual or electronic observation or listening directed at a person or place.

Close watch kept over one or more persons. [Punjab Laws Act (4 of 1872), S. 46].

Survey. A general appraisal of something; a general view; a close examination or inspection to ascertain condition, quantity or quality.

"SURVEY" means a survey of manual scavengers undertaken in pursuance of section 11 or section 14 of Act 25 of 2013. [S. 2(1)(s) of the Prohibition of Employment as Manual Scavengers & their Rehabilitation Act, 2013 (25 of 2013)]

Survey and exploration of mineral. Means geological, geophysical or other prospecting, surface or sub-surface surveying or map making service, in relation to location or exploration of deposits of mineral, oil or gas. [Finance Act (32 of 1994), S. 65(104a) (Inserted by Finance (No.2) Act (23 of 2004), S. 90) now repealed by Central Goods and Services Tax Act, 2017]

Survey and map-making. "SURVEY AND MAPMAKING" means geological, geophysical or any other prospecting, surface, sub-surface or aerial surveying or map-making of any kind, but does not include survey and exploration of mineral. [Finance Act (32 of 1994), S. 65(104b) *as inserted by Finance Act (18 of 2005), S. 88(a)(xxi)* now repealed by Central Goods and Services Tax Act, 2017]

Survey-mark. "SURVEY-MARK" means any pillar, pipe, post or other mark erected or placed above or below the surface by or by order of any officer appointed by the Local Government to make a survey of any land on or within the boundaries such land for the purpose of indicating survey points or lines. [Bur. Act V of 1880 (Burma Boundaries), S. 1-A.]

Surveyor. 'SURVEYOR' means a person whose business is to survey a consignment of agricultural produce for sale in regard to quality, refraction, adulteration and such other purposes. [Bihar Agricultural Produce Markets Act (16 of 1960), S. 2(u)]

One that makes a survey. [Indian Contract Act (9 of 1872), S. 195, ill. (a)].

Survive. The word "survive" in its popular signification may mean "over living a specified individual," or "living beyond a specified event," or it may mean "still living" or "living at some designated period of time."

To continue to live after the death of another, or after the end or cessation of something or condition or the occurrence of some event (expressed or implied)

[T.P. Act (4 of 1882), S. 24, ill.]; [CPC (5 of 1908), O. XXII, R. 3(1)]; [Income-tax Act (43 of 1961), S. 159(2)(b)].

Surviving defendant. When there are more than one defendant in a suit and some of them have died, the remaining defendant. [CPC (5 of 1908), O. XXII, R. 2].

Survivor. One who survies. [T.P. Act (4 of 1882), S. 24, ill.].

Survivorship. The right of a person to property by reason of his having survived another person who had an interest in it; the state or condition of being a survivor. [CPC (5 of 1908), S. 60(1)(m)].

Suspect. Someone believed to have committed or having been connected with the commission of a wrong.

Suspend. To dely; to debar from any privilege, office or emolument, for some time.

To put a stop for the time being; to debar or cause to withdraw temporarily from any privilege, office or function or subject to suspension [CPC (5 of 1908), O. XXI, R. 33(3)]; [Constitution of India, Art. 72(1)].

"Suspend" is defined to mean to interrupt; to cause to cease for a time; to stay and delay; to hinder the proceeding for a time.

Suspend—it refers to or comprehends both types of suspension, viz : suspension by way of punishment and suspension pending a disciplinary enquiry.

The term "suspend" would mean to debar usually, for a time, from any privilege, the execution of an office or from the enjoyment of an income." It is temporary deprivation of office or privilege. By reason of suspension, the powers, functions and privileges remain in abeyance but one continues to be subjected to the same discipline and penalties and to the same authorities. [*State of Punjab v. Jaswant Singh Kanwar*, (2014) 13 SCC 622, para 11].

Suspending payment. The expression 'suspending payment' is a well-known commercial expression; and a merchant suspends payment when he ceases to discharge his mercantile obligations in due course. In ordinary parlance, the terms 'insolent' and 'suspending payment' have practically the same meaning.

Suspense account. An account of transactions which it is impossible to enter in the books in the regular way, and they have to be held in suspense.

It is an expression in banking business where a person whose money is held in suspense is entitled to withdraw it any moment he likes, though he neither gets a pass book nor is entitled to draw any cheques or to be paid interest in respect of the amount. *CIT* v. *K.R.M.T.T. Thiagaraja Chetty & Co.,* AIR 1952 Mad 305, 322.

Suspension. Suspension literally means 'the act of debarring for a time from a function or a privilege'. It means a temporary deprivation of one's office or position. *Dandapani Gouda* v. *State of Orissa,* AIR 1953 Ori 329. [Constitution of India, Art. 311(2)]

Suspension of payment. When traders, firms or companies, unable to cope with their liabilities, decide to cease paying further debts, and announce the fact to their creditors, it is called a "suspension of payment."

Suspension of practice. "SUSPENSION OF PRACTICE" means voluntary suspension of practice as an advocate or suspension of an advocate by a State Bar Council for misconduct. [Advocates' Welfare Fund Act (45 of 2001), S. 2(s)]

Suspensory award. When an accident had caused an injury to a workman and the injury, although it did not affect the present earning capacity, was likely to affect the capacity in future, it is essential to make a declaration of the employer's liability when the evidence was fresh and then adjourn the matter reserving to each of the parties thereto liberty to make such further application as they might be advised to make in future. Such an order is called suspensory award. *Sukhai* v. *Hukum Chand Jute Mills,* AIR 1957 Cal 601, 604.

Suspicious circumstance. A circumstance would be suspicious when it is not normal or is not normally expected in a normal situation or is not expected of a normal person. The suspicious circumstances may be as to the genuineness of the signatures of the testator, the condition of the testator's mind, the dispositions made in the will being unnatural. *Indu Bala* v. *Manindra Chandra*, AIR 1982 SC 133, 134.

Suspicious circumstances. Circumstances open to deserving of or exciting suspicion. [CrPC, 1973 (2 of 1974), S. 40(1)(d)].

Sustain. To hold of; maintain; prove; sanction.

Sustainable development. Development that meets the needs and aspirations of the current generation without compromising the ability to meet those of future generations. (*Biodiversity*)

'Sustainable development' means the type or extent of development that can take place and which can be sustained by nature/ecology with or without mitigation. [*Narmada Bachao Andolan* v. *Union of India,* (2000) 10 SCC 664]

"Sustainable development is the development that meets the needs of the present without compromising the ability of future generations to meet their own needs." [The United Nations Commission on Environment and Development as cited in *Centre for Environmental Law, World Wide Fund-India* v. *Union of India*, (2013) 8 SCC 234, para 45].

"Sustainable development" covers the development that meets the needs of the person without compromising with the ability of the future generation to meet their own needs. It means the development, that can take place and which can be sustained by nature/ecology with or without mitigation. [*Tirupur Dyeing Factory Owners Assn.* v. *Noyyal River Ayacutdars Protection Assn.*, (2009) 9 SCC 737, 747, para 26]

Sustainable use. "SUSTAINABLE USE" means the use of components of biological diversity in such manner and at such rate that does not lead to the long-term decline of the biological diversity thereby maintaining its potential to meet the needs and aspirations of present and future generations. [Biological Diversity Act, 2002 (18 of 2003), S. 2(o); Convention on Biological Diversity, June 5, 1992, Art. 2]

Sustenance. "Sustenance" is that which supports life; food; victuals; provisions.

Suzerainty. The dominion, authority or relationship of suzerain with regard to a subject, person or State especially in the matter of control over the foreign affairs of such State. [General Clauses Act (10 of 1897), S. 3(28)(a)].

Swathanthryam. "Swathanthryam" means liberty, freedom, independence, etc. [*Mathai Samual* v. *Eapen Eapen*, (2012) 13 SCC 80, para 26].

Swear. "SWEAR", with its grammatical variations and cognate expressions, shall include affirming and declaring in the case of persons by law allowed to affirm or declare instead of swearing. [General Clauses Act (10 of 1897), S. 3(62)].

To take an oath; to make a solemn declaration [General Clauses Act (10 of 1897), S. 3(62)]. The term "swear" includes every mode authorised by law for administering an oath.

By statute is generally provided that the words "swear" or "sworn" shall include the words "affirm" or "affirmed".

Sweat equity share. "SWEAT EQUITY SHARES" means equity shares issued by a company to its employees or directors at a discount or for consideration other than cash for providing know-how or making available rights in the nature of intellectual property rights or value additions, by whatever name called. [Companies Act (1 of 1956), S. 79A *Expln.* 2]

"Sweat equity shares" means such equity shares as are issued by a company to its directors or employees at a discount or for consideration, other than cash, for providing their knowhow or making available rights in the nature of intellectual property rights or value additions, by whatever name called. [Companies Act (18 of 2013), S. 2(88)].

Sweat equity shares. Means such equity shares as are issued by a company to its directors or employees at a discount or for consideration, other than cash, for providing their know-how or making available rights in the nature of intellectual property rights or value additions, by whatever name called. [S. 2(88) of the Companies Act, 2013 (18 of 2013)]

Swift. Society for worldwide interbank financial telecommunication is a co-operative organization by more than 70 banks to provide a communications network for the speedy transmission of international payment by messages. It enables members to transmit between themselves international payment statements, and outer messages connected with international banking. It enables a bank to send money by mail, cable, or telex faster more efficiently and safely. [*M L Tan Banking Law & Practice in India*, Vol. 2, 2021, LexisNexis, Dictionary of Banking Terminology].

Swindle. To cheat under the pretence of fair dealing.

Syllabus. A head note to a decision; a note prefixed to the report of an adjudged case, containing an epitome or brief statement of the rulings of the Court upon the point or points decided in the case.

An abstract or outline of a course of study.

M.P. Prathmik, Middle School Tatha Madhyamik Shiksha (Pattiya Pustakon Sambandhi Uyavastha) Adhiniyam (13 of 1973), S. 2(d). 'Sylliabi' means—there must be sufficient information for those concerned to know generally what courses of instruction are broadly covered under the heading mentioned, so that they may offer text-books for such courses. *State of Madhya Pradesh* v. *Ram Ragubir Prasad*, AIR 1979 SC 888, 894.

Symbol. Outward emblem or sign of a person, cause, quality *etc.* [Representation of the People Act (43 of 1951), S. 123(3)].

Symbolic delivery. The constructive delivery of the subject matter of a sale by actual delivery of an article which represents the item, that renders access to it possible, or which is the evidence of the purchaser's title to it, such as the key to the warehouse or a bill of lading for good on ship-board.

Symmetric cryptography. An encryption/decryption system in which knowledge of the encryption key is equivalent to knowledge of the decryption key. (*Information Technology*)

Symptom. A (bodily or mental) phenomenon, circumstance or change of condition from and accompanying a disease or affliction and constituting an indication or evidence of it; sign of something. [Indian Evidence Act (1 of 1872), S. 7, ill. (c)].

Synallagmatic contract. A reciprocal contract *i.e.* characterised by mutual rights and duties.

Syndicate. A group organized to carry out a particular transaction or enterprise; an association of organized criminals.

Synonymous. The word "synonymous" means conveying the same or approximately the same meaning.

Synopsis. A view of the whole together; a general view of a single subject.

"Synopsis" means to cut short, diminish, reduce; a brief or partial statement, less than the whole; an epitome.

Sysop (*abbr.*) System Operator. Anyone responsible for the physical operations of a computer system or network resource. For example, a System Administrator decides how often backups and maintenance should be performed and the System Operator performs those tasks. (*Matisse Enzer Glossary of Internet Terms*)

System administrator. An individual who gives the rights to the users for the use of the computer system as well as controls designs and manages the system. (*Information Technology*)

System disk. A floppy disk that contains all the essential files needed to run DOS. If anything happens to your hard disk, you can start your PC using a system disk, helping you to fix the problem without losing any data. (*Cyber Law*)

System files. Special description files, which control how your PC starts up. (*Cyber Law*)

System : method. System expresses more than method, which is but a part of system : system is an arrangement of many single or individual objects according to some given rule, so as to make them coalesce. Method is the manner of this arrangement or the principle upon which this arrangement takes place. All sciences must be reduced to system; and without system there is no science; all business requires method; and without method little can be done to any good purpose.

System of work. The term 'system of work' is a comprehensive term including not merely hours of work but other conditions of work and the entire system of work under which an adult worker works in any particular factory. *State* v. *Manilal Bhikalal,* AIR 1963 Guj 105, 106. [Factories Act (63 of 1948), S. 61(10)]

System registry. The system configuration files used by Windows 95, 98 and NT to store settings about user preferences, installed soft-ware, hardware and drivers, and other settings required for Windows to run correctly. The system updates the registry every time you add new hardware or a new program to your system. When the registry becomes "broken," it can cause serious system problems. (*Cyber Law*)

System security. Where the use of the computer network, computer system or objects is restricted to certain users, by a system function. (*Information Technology*)

System software. Application—independent software that supports the running of application software. It is a software that is part of or made available with a computer system and that determines how application program are run; *e.g.* an operating system. (*Information Technology*)

Systematic. Arranged or conducted according to plan or organised method; [Income-tax Act (43 of 1961), S. 94(3)(b)].

The expression 'systematic' would involve an element of planning, of method, of some continuity or persistence. *Sudhir Laxman Hendre* v. *Shripat Amrit Dange,* AIR 1960 Bom 249, 261.

Systemic failure. For the purposes of this section, "SYSTEMIC FAILURE" with respect to a country or territory means that the country or territory has an agreement with India providing for exchange of report of the nature referred to in sub-section (2), but—

(i) in violation of the said agreement, it has suspended automatic exchange; or

(ii) has persistently failed to automatically provide to India the report in its possession in respect of any international group having a consistent entity resident in India. [Income-tax Act (43 of 1961), S. 286, *Explanation (l)*].

Systems interference. Systems interference is defined as the serious hindering, without right, of the functioning of a computer system by inputting, transmitting, damaging, deleting, deteriorating, altering or suppressing computer data. [The European Convention on Cyber Crime, Art. 5]

T

Table. "TABLE" means the Table of the Council of States (Rajya Sabha). [Rules of Procedure and Conduct of Business in the Council of States (Rajya Sabha), R. 2(1)]

A systematic list of facts, figures, *etc.* arranged according to a definite file. [Representation of the People Act (43 of 1950), S. 2(ff) omitted by the North-Eastern Areas (Reorganisation) (Adaptation of Laws on Union Subjects) Order, 1974].

Table of cases. An alphabetical list of cases cited, referred to, or digested in a legal textbook, volume of reports, or digest, with references to the section, page, or paragraph where each case appears.

Tacit. Unspoken; implied; not expressed (as) tacit consent.

"TACIT" is said of that which, although not expressed, is understood from the nature of the thing, or from the provision of the law.

Tacit acceptance. Acceptance is tacit, when some act is done by a person which necessarily supposes his intention to accept, and which he would have no right to do but in his acceptance.

Tacita quaedam habentur pro expressis. (8 *Rep*. 40). Things silent are sometimes considered as expressed.

Tack. Duty, rent reserved upon a lease; a lease or contract of location; also an addition, supplement.

Tacking. The doctrine known by the name of tacking (*i.e.*) consolidating and priorizing two or more claims.

Uniting a third or subsequent encumbrance to the first whereby it acquires priority over an intermediate mortgage. [T.P. Act (4 of 1882), S. 93].

The uniting securities given at different times, so as to prevent any intermediate purchaser from claiming a title to redeem or otherwise discharge on lien, which is prior, without redeeming or discharging the other liens also, which are subsequent to his own title.

Tacking a mortgage. Is the doctrine that enables a mortgagee who is secured by the legal estate, to tack on to that security, another security which he holds on the same property and so give the latter security priority over a mesne incumbrance prior in date thereto, if he took his other security without notice of the mesne incumbrance to be so displaced.

Tactical internet. A battlefield communication system networked together using commercially based internet protocols. (*Cyber Law*)

Tahsil. Collection especially of the public revenue derived from the land; the revenue collected. The office of the Tahsildar. (*Wil. Gloss.*)

Tahsildar. Officer in chief executive charge of a tahsil.

Taint. To contaminate; to corrupt; to tinge or affect slightly for the worse.

"The word 'taint' can be expressed to mean a 'trace', 'stain' or a 'blemish'. It denotes some evil quality, a contaminating or corrupting influence. It can lead to mean an imbue with any thing objectionable or to contaminate or infect. The word 'taint' when used as a verb means dishonest, destroy integrity, vitiate, tarnish and degenerate morally." [New Shorter Oxford English Dictionary (Vol. II) as cited in *Joginder Pal v. State of Punjab*, (2014) 6 SCC 644, para 23].

Tainted evidence. Evidence which is inadmissible as it was directly or indirectly obtained by illegal means.

Take care of. As used in an undertaking whereby one agrees to support and take care of another, is to be construed according to the various circumstance of the party, and does not necessarily imply that the person to be supported is not to use any exertions to support himself.

Take evidence. The phrase 'take evidence' denotes a capacity to call for evidence and not merely to record what is adduced by the parties. *Zonal Manager L.I.C.* v. *City Munsif,* AIR 1968 All 270, 271.

Take in adoption. To take a child as one's adopted son or daughter. [Hindu Adoptions and Maintenance Act (78 of 1956), S. 7].

Take into consideration. The words "take into consideration" mean "take into consideration for the purpose of arriving at a conclusion of fact." R. v. *Bayaji*, Bom HC Cr Ruling, 18th November 1886 : 14 Ind NS 384.

Take it or leave it contract. A standard form contract which is prepared by one party, to be signed by the party in a weaker position, usually a consumer, who has little choice about the terms.

Take-or-pay contract. A contract which requires the buyer to either purchase and receive a minimum amount of product at a set price ("take") or pay for this minimum without taking immediate delivery ("pay").

Take out of the keeping. The use of the word 'keeping' connotes the idea of charge, protection, maintenance and control of the guardian. *State of Haryana* v. *Raja Ram*, AIR 1973 SC 819, 822. [IPC (45 of 1860), S. 361]

Take-off. A phase of flight from the application of takeoff power to an altitude of final take-off segment. [Environment (Protection) Rules, 1986, Schedule I, Sl. No. 111, Definitions (f)].

Take possession. Enter into possession; take delivery of.

Take proceedings. The words 'take proceedings' cannot be interpreted to mean "order proceedings to be taken". *Mangalal Chemical* v. *Manilal Majaulal*, AIR 1968 SC 822, 824.

Taken cognizance of the offence. Once the Court on perusal of the complaint is satisfied that the complaint discloses the commission of offence and there is no reason to reject the complaint at that stage, and proceeds further in the matter, it must be held to have 'taken cognizance of the offence'. One should not confuse taking of cognizance with issuance of process. [*Cref Finance Ltd.* v. *Shree Shanthi Homes (P.) Ltd.*, (2005) 7 SCC 467, 471, para 10]

Takeover. Succeed to the charge of.

Takeover offer for a company. The acquisition of a business by another through purchase, exchange of capital stock, or any other device.

Takes or entices. The word "takes" means to cause to go, to escort or to get into possession, when the accused takes the minor with him, whether she was willing or not, the act of taking is complete. The word "entice" involves an idea of inducement by exciting hope or desire in the other. *In re Khalandar Saheb,* AIR 1955 Andhra 59, 61. [IPC (45 of 1860), S. 361]

Taking. "TAKING" means taking, hunting, fishing, capturing, harassing, deliberate billing or attempting to engage in any such conduct. [Convention on the Conservation of Migratory Species of Wild Animals, 1979, Art. I(*i*)]

The taking need not be by force, actual or constructive and it is immaterial whether the girl consents or not. The word "take" means to cause to go, to escort or to get into possession. *Chajju Ram* v. *State,* AIR 1968 Punj 439 at 440. [IPC (45 of 1860), S. 361]

Taking and retaining possession. The dichotomy between taking and retaining indicates that they are mutually exclusive and apply to two different situations. The word "taking" applies to a person taking possession of a land otherwise than in accordance with the provisions of the law, while the word "retaining" to a person taking possession in accordance with the provisions of the law but subsequently retaining the same illegally. *Bhinka* v. *Charan Singh*, AIR 1959 SC 960, 965.

Taking any part in the publication of any advertisement. Includes (i) the printing of the advertisement, (ii) the publication of any advertisement outside the territories to which this Act extends by or at the instance of a person residing within the said territories. [Drugs and Magic Remedies (Objectionable Advertisements) Act (21 of 1954), S. 2(d)]

Taking away. To constitute "taking away" within the meaning of S. 498, IPC (45 of 1860) there must be some influence, physical or moral, brought to bear by the accused to induce the wife to leave her husband in order that her leaving may amount to taking away by the accused. To bring the section into operation, there must be some influence operating on the woman, or co-operating with her inclination at the time the final step is taken which causes a severance of the woman from her husband, for the purpose of causing such step to be taken.

In order that a person should be made liable for an offence under S. 498, it is not necessary that there should be any enticement. All that is required is that if any person 'takes away' another man's wife with the intent that she may have illicit intercourse with him, then the offence is completed. *In Re Akkiravu Sanvasi,* AIR 1950 Mad 13, 14. [IPC (45 of 1860), S. 498]

Taking by force. "Taking by force" as applied to the action of trespass, is taking without right or permission, in violation of the lawful possession of another.

Taking charge. "TAKING CHARGE" means that the goods have been handed over to and accepted for carriage by the multimodal transport operator. [Multimodal Transportation of Goods Act (28 of 2000), S. 2(s)]

Taking cognizance. Taking cognizance does not involve any formal action, or indeed action of any kind, but occurs as soon as a Magistrate, as such, applied his mind to the suspected commission of an offence. The word "cognizance" is used in the Code to indicate the point when a Magistrate or a Judge first takes judicial notice of an offence. It is a different thing from the initiation of proceedings rather it is the condition precedent to the initiation of proceedings by the Magistrate. Cognizance is taken of case, not of persons, and there seems to be nothing in theory to prevent a Magistrate from taking cognizance of a case even where the offenders are unknown. The fact that a Magistrate has taken cognizance does not necessarily mean that there will be judicial proceedings against any one. Therefore cognizance is something prior to and does not necessarily mean the commencement of judicial proceedings against any one.

'Taking of cognizance' means the point in time when a Court or a Magistrate takes judicial notice of an offence with a view of initiating proceedings in respect of such offence which appears to have been committed. At the stage of taking of cognizance of offence, the court has only to see whether *prima facie* there are reasons for issuing the process and whether the ingredients of the offence are there on record. [*Nupur Talwar v. Central Bureau of Investigation, Delhi*, (2012) 2 SCC 188, para 20 and 21].

The expression 'Taking cognizance' means that the Magistrate takes cognizance of an offence and not the offenders. *Raghubans Dubey* v. *State of Bihar*, AIR 1967 SC 1167, 1169. [CrPC 1973 (2 of 1974), S. 190]

Taking cognisance/cognizance of offence. When on receiving a complaint, the Magistrate applies his mind for the purposes of proceeding under S. 200 and the succeeding sections in Chapter XV of the Code of 1973, he is said to have taken cognizance of the offence within the meaning of S. 190(1)(a). *Devarapally Lakshminarayana Reddy* v. *V. Narayan Reddy*, AIR 1976 SC 1672. [CrPC, 1973 (2 of 1974), S. 190] See also *Tula Ram* v. *Kishore Singh*, AIR 1977 SC 2401.

'Taking cognizance' does not involve any formal action of any kind. It occurs as soon as a Magistrate applies his mind to the suspected commission of an offence. Cognizance is taken prior to commencement of criminal proceedings. Taking the cognizance is thus a sina qua non or condition precedent for holding a valid trial. Cognizance is taken of an offence and not of an offender. Whether or not a Magistrate has taken cognizance of an offence depends on the facts and circumstances of each case and no rule of universal application can be laid down as to when a Magistrate can be said to have taken cognizance. [*Chief Enforcement Officer v. Videocon International Limited,* (2008) 2 SCC 492, para 11 as cited in *Sarah Mathew v. Institute of Cardio Vascular Diseases,* (2014) 2 SCC 62, para 24].

The expression 'taking cognizance of an offence' under Section 190 of the Code would mean the action taken by the Court for initiating judicial proceedings against the offender in respect of the offence regarding which the complaint is filed. Before it can be said that any Magistrate or Court has taken cognizance of an offence, it must be shown that he has applied his mind to the facts for the purpose of proceeding further in the matter at the instance of the complainant. [*Narsingh Das Tapadia* v. *Govardhan Das Partani,* (2000) 7 SCC 183, 186, para 8. *See also Narayandas Bhagwandas Madhavdas* v. *State of W.B.,* AIR 1959 SC 1118] [CrPC, 1973 (2 of 1974), S. 190]

Taking for public use. The phrase "TAKING FOR PUBLIC USE" is defined to be the actual seizing or direct taking of specific property for public use.

A taking of property for a public use "means a taking altogether; an entire change of ownership."

Private property is "taken for public use" when it is appropriated to the common use of the public at large.

Taking out. 'Taking out' does not mean 'in the process of taking out'. *Mohd. Akram* v. *State,* AIR 1951 Ass 17. [Imports and Exports (Control) Act, (18 of 1947), S. 2(b)].

Taking out of India. The expression "taking out... to a place outside India" in R. 2(c) of the Rules would include taking out to the high seas as high seas would also mean a place outside India if it is beyond the territorial waters of India. In international trade the ship beyond the territorial waters of a country would be a place outside the country, if the goods are taken to that place, that is, a situation outside the territorial waters of a country and the title to the goods passes to the purchasers. *Collector of Customs* v. *Sun Industries,* 1988 Supp SCC 342. [Customs and Central Excise Duties Drawback Rules, 1971, R. 2(c)]

Taking over management of an institution. "TAKING OVER MANAGEMENT OF AN INSTITUTION" with its grammatical variations and cognate expression means the taking over of the management of the institution and the property of the institution used in relation to such management. [Maharashtra Educational Institutions (Management) Act (13 of 1976), S. 2(vii)]

Taking over the management or control. A mortgagee taking possession of the mortgaged properties, on the basis of covenants in the mortgage deed between the parties, does not mean taking over the management or control. *National Sugar Mills* v. *State of West Bengal,* AIR 1967 Cal 609, 611. [Industries (Development and Regulation) Act (65 of 1951), S. 20]

Talaq. Divorce, unilateral repudiation of his wife by a husband.

"*Talaq* is the power given by Islam to the husband. The wife is not vested with such a power except in the case of *Tafweez i.e.,* the delegation by the husband. *Khula* divorce can be effected like other cases of *Talaq* when so pronounced by the husband". PLD 1967 AJ&K 32 (*Pak*) (*Legal Terms & Phrases*—ILYAS KHAN)

Talaq-e-tafwiz. A Muslim wife is entitled, at the time of marriage or subsequently, to make a contract with her husband. Such a contract may lay down the terms upon which marital life is to be regulated. It may also provide for dissolution of marriage by wife. If the husband violates the agreement, the wife is entitled to divorce herself without the intervention of the court. [Dr Kauser Edappagath, *Divorce and Gender Equity in Muslim Personal Law of India,* 2014, LexisNexis.]

Talaqnama. A written proforma of Talaq.

Talbana. It means "process fee" only and it does not include "subsistence-allowance". *Kodu* v. *Banmali,* AIR 1969 MP 20 at 21. [CrPC 1973 (2 of 1974), S. 204(4)]

Talis interpretatio semper fienda est, ut evitetur absurdem, et inconveniens, et ne judicium sit illusorium. (*Lat.*) (1 Rep. 52) Interpretation is always to be made in such a manner that what is absurd and inconvenient is to be avoided, and so that the judgment be not illusory.

Tally. To tally is to see that two things agree or correspond and if it is checking, it must be presumed to be correct.

Taluk. "TALUK" means a revenue *taluk* but excluding there from the limits of a larger urban area, smaller urban area, transitional area or an industrial township specified] under any law for the time being force. e. [Karnataka Panchayat Raj Act, 1993, S. 2(38) substituted by Act 29 of 1997.

"TALUK" means a revenue taluk. [Kerala Panchayat Raj Act, (*Ker Act No.* 13 of 1994), S. 2(xliii)]

Taluka or **Taluqa.** The word *"taluqa"* means any local area for which a *taluqa* local board is established, inclusive of the portion of such area, if any, for the time being within a municipal district or a military cantonment. [Bom Act I of 1884 (Local Boards), S. 3, cl. (4)]

Talukdar. "TALUQDAR" includes a *thakur, mehwassi, kasbati* and *naik* and a *mulgameti* who holds land directly from Government. [Bom Act VI of 1888 (Guzrat Taluqdars), S. 2, cl. (*a*)]

Taluqa. Means an estate in Oudh to which the permissions of the Oudh Estates Act, 1869, apply. [U.P. Act III of 1899 (Court of Wards), S. 3, cl. (3)]

Tamper with. To meddle [Defence and Internal Security of India Act (42 of 1971), S. 3(2)(3)]; to interfere so as to misuse, alter or corrupt [Trade and Merchandise Marks Act (43 of 1958), S. 78(f)]; to alter for an improper purpose or in an improper way. [Representation of the People Act (43 of 1951), S. 58(a)].

Tampering. Meddling or interfering with (a thing) so as to misuse, alter, corrupt or pervert it [IPC (45 of 1860), S. 489]; bringing improper influence to bear upon a witness as by bribery or intimidation; altering for a improper purpose or in an improper way [Indian Railways Act (9 of 1890), S. 100B].

Tan. To convert into leather by steeping in vegetable solutions containing mineral salts or synthesised chemicals for tanning. [Khadi and Village Industries Commission Act (61 of 1956), Sch., item (5)].

Tangible. That which can be touched; material; objective. [T.P. Act (4 of 1882), S. 54].

Tangible assets. Appreciable assets like immovable property, valuable machinery and cash.

Tangible form. The expression 'tangible form' refers to a specific physical form or shape as applied to an article and not the mere ability to replicate, convert and give a physical shape to the design, though of course to fall under the expression 'tangible form', it is not necessary that the article should have been used. [*Reckitt Benkiser India Ltd. v. Wyeth Ltd.*, AIR 2013 Del 101, para 18(i)(FB)].

Tangible immovable property. The words "tangible immovable property" in S. 54 of the Transfer of Property Act (4 of 1882) includes an undivided share in a house or shop.

It is quite easy to give possession of an undivided share in immovable property either directly or by handing over to the purchaser a proportionate share in the rent and for that reason such share is tangible immovable property within the meaning of S. 54 of the T. P. Act (4 of 1882).

By 'tangible property' is meant lands, buildings, etc. which immediately or through the medium of tenants may be the subject of possession deliverable by the seller to the buyer. By the phrase 'reversion or other intangible thing' it is apparently intended to denote all the various interests which are included under the general title immovable property, but do not any more than choses in action involve possession.

Tangible securities. Corporeal securities.

Tank. A large basin or cistern; a reservoir of water [Factories Act (63 of 1948), S. 36(1)]; a pool; a pond; [Constitution of India, Art. 15(2)(b)].

All the following three together, namely (1) the underground or the land underneath, on which water is stored (ii) the embankment or the *bandh* which serves the purpose of keeping the water confined within its boundary and (iii) the bed or pit of the tank, is known as tank. *Sobharam Mahato* v. *Raja Mahton,* AIR 1957 Pat 278, 283.

Tank includes a well.

(*Milit.*) Steel box travelling by motor power containing crew and guns and serving as peripatetic fort in battle.

"TANK". A pond or pool, or lake; a tank is often of many acres in extent; an irrigation reservoir, a dammed up ravine or other suitable place for collecting the water. All the following three together, namely (*i*) the underground or the land underneath, on which water is stored; (*ii*) the embankment or the bandh which serves the purpose of keeping the water confined within its boundary and (*iii*) the bed or pet of the tank, is known as 'tank'. *K. N. Farms Industries (Pvt.) Ltd.* v. *State of Bihar*, AIR 2009 SC 3031.

Tanker. Means a cargo ship constructed or adapted for the carriage in bulk of liquid cargoes of an inflammable nature. [Merchant Shipping Act (44 of 1958), S. 3 (48A)]

"TANKER" means a ship in which greater part of the cargo space is constructed or adopted for the carriage of liquid cargoes in bulk and which is not, for the time being carrying a cargo other than oil in that part of its cargo space. [Merchant Shipping Act (44 of 1958), S. 356 B(l)]

Tantum habent de lege, quantum habent de justitia. Precedents have value in the law to the extent that they represent justice.

Tantum operatur fictio in casu ficto quantum veritas in casu vero. (*Lat.*) A legal fiction operates to the same extent and effect in the supposed case as the truth does in a real case.

Tantum prescriptum quantum possessum. The doctrine of '*tantum prescriptum quantum possessum*' (the title acquired by adverse possession is limited to the area actually possessed) is confined to a mere trespasser who claims title only by possession without any claim or colour of title. *Onkarmal Agarwalla* v. *Bireswar Hazra*, AIR 1959 Cal 195, 200. [Limitation Act (9 of 1908), Arts. 142 and 144]

Tap. To pierce so as to let out fluid [Indian Forest Act (16 of 1927), S. 26(f)]; secretly to attach a receiver to a telephone wire in order to overhear a conversation; a hole or short pipe with a value for running off a fluid.

Tape. A ribbon of paper printed by a recording instrument, as in telegraphy.

Tape-recording. Record of sound imprinted on magnetic tape.

Target company. "TARGET COMPANY" means a listed company whose shares or voting rights or control is directly or indirectly acquired or is being acquired. [SEBI (Sub. Area of Shares and Takeovers) Regulations, 1997, Reg. 2(q)]

Targeted Public Distribution System. Means the system for distribution of essential commodities to the ration card holders through fair price shops. [S. 2(23) of the National Food Security Act, 2013 (20 of 2013)]

Tari. "TARI" means the sap of any kind of palm-tree. [Excise Act (12 of 1896), S. 3]

Tariff. Duties or customs to be paid on imports or exports, such duties collectively; law imposing these duties.

'Tariff' includes within its ambit not only the fixation of rates but also the rules and regulations relating to it. [*PTC India Ltd. v. Central Electricity Regulatory Commission*, (2010) 4 SCC 603, para 17 as cited in *Jharkhand State Electricity Board v. Laxmi Business and Cement Company Private Limited*, (2014) 5 SCC 236, para 9].

Tarwad. (*Mal.*) A group of persons forming a joint family with community of property governed by *Marumakkattayam* law of inheritance. [Estate Duty Act (34 of 1953), S. 7(3)]

Tax. "TAX" in relation to the assessment year commencing on the 1st day of April, 1965, and any subsequent assessment year means income-tax chargeable under the provisions of this Act, and in relation to any other assessment year income-tax and super-tax chargeable under the provisions of this Act prior to the aforesaid date and in relation to the assessment year commencing on the 1st day of April, 2006, and any subsequent assessment year includes the fringe benefit tax payable under section 115 WA. [Income-tax Act (43 of 1961), S. 2(43)]

'TAX' means entertainment tax, betting tax or the totalizator tax, as the case may be, and includes surcharge, penalty or any other charge levied under this Act. [Delhi Entertainments and Betting Tax Act, 1996, Delhi Act No. (8 of 1997), S. 2(t).]

'TAX' means a tax, cess, rate or other import leviable under this Act but does not include a fee. [Bombay Village Panchayat Act, 1958, S. 3(23)]

A compulsory contribution to the support of the government levied on persons, income, commodities, transaction, etc. [IPC (45 of 1860), S. 21, *Tenth*]; to fix the amount of (costs to be fixed in the decree).

Tax admitted. Admission to be considered is the one made before assessing authority and not which is made before appellate authority. *Kanpur Vanaspati Stores, Kanpur* v. *The Commissioner of Sales Tax, U.P. Lucknow*, AIR 1973 SC 2373, 2376.

Tax admittedly payable. The expression "tax admittedly payable" means the tax which is payable, *inter alia*, according to the return filed by the dealer. *Commissioner of Sales Tax* v. *Qureshi Cruchible Centre*, AIR 1994 SC 25.

Tax advantage. For the purposes of this section, "TAX ADVANTAGE" includes,—

(i) the determination of the allowance for any expense or interest, or the determination of any cost or expense allocated or apportioned, or, as the case may be, which has the effect of reducing the income or increasing the loss, as the case may be, from activities other than tonnage tax activities chargeable to tax, computed on the basis of entries made in the books of account in respect of the previous year in which the transaction was entered into; or

(ii) a transaction or arrangement which produces to the tonnage tax company more than ordinary profits which might be expected to arise from tonnage tax activities. [Income-tax Act (43 of 1961), Chap. XII G 115 VZB(2) *Expln.* (*Inserted by Finance Act (23 of 2004), S. 30*)]

Tax and fee. In the case of fee there is correlation between it and the services rendered. [*Hingir Rampur Coal Co. Ltd.* v. *State of Orissa*, AIR 1961 SC 459]

It is true that between a tax and a fee there is no generic difference. Both are compulsory exactions of money by public authorities; but whereas a tax is imposed for public purposes, a fee is levied essentially for services rendered and as such there is an element of *quid pro quo* between the person who pays the fee and the public authority which imposes it. If specific services are rendered to a specific area or to a specific class of persons or trade or business in any local area, and as a condition precedent for the said services or in return for them, cess is levied against the said area or the said class of persons or trade or business, the cess is distinguishable from a tax and is described as a fee. There is, however, an element of compulsion in the imposition of both tax and fee. Whether or not a particular cess levied by a statute amounts to a fee or tax would always be a question of fact to be determined in the circumstances of each case. *Hingir Rampur Coal Co. Ltd.* v. *State of Orissa,* MLJ : QD (1961-1965) Vol. II C833 : AIR 1961 SC 459 : (1961) 1 SCA 210.

Commissioner H.R. E. v. *Lakashmindra Tirtha Swamiar*, AIR 1954, SC 282, 295 quoted. The distinction between a tax and a fee lies primarily in the fact that tax is levied as a part of a common burden while a fee is payment for special benefit or privilege. *Anem Pedda* v. *Executive Officer, Berhampur Municipality,* AIR 1957 Ori 285, 286.

Tax and licence fee (Distinction). A licence fee is an imposition or exaction on the right to use or dispose of property, to pursue a business, occupation or calling or to exercise a privilege. A licence fee is imposed primarily with the object of reimbursing the State for the services rendered by it, while a tax is exacted with the object of providing revenue for the State and enabling it to carry on the duties of Government. It is necessary also to ascertain the power, whether regulatory or taxing, under which the amount is demanded and the purpose for which the demand is made. The amount of the imposition or exaction must be also taken into consideration. The amount of licence fee need not be confined to the mere expenses of issuing the licence but may include any reasonably proper cost of supervision, inspection, examination and regulation of the business, in respect of which the licence is issued. It is not possible to lay down any hard and fast rules for the purpose of determining whether a particular fee is reasonable or otherwise. *Gopi Parshad* v. *State of Punjab,* MLJ : QD (1956-1960) Vol. I C2395 : 58 Punj LR 480 : ILR (1957) Punj 184 : (S) AIR 1957 P&H 45. [Constitution of India, Art. 19(6) and 265]

Tax arrear. "Tax arrears" would mean the determined amount of duties as due or payable which would include drawback of duty, credit of duty or any amount representing duty, cesses, interest, fine or penalty determined. [*Union of India v. Nitdip Textile Processors Private Limited*, (2012) 1 SCC 226, para 28].

Tax arrear means,—

(i) in relation to direct tax enactment, the amount of tax, penalty or interest determined on or before the 31st day of March, 1998 under that enactment in respect of an assessment year as modified in consequence of giving effect to an appellate order but remaining unpaid on the date of declaration;

(ii) in relation to indirect tax enactment,—

(a) the amount of duties (including drawback of duty, credit of duty or any amount representing duty), cesses, interest, fine or penalty determined as due or payable under that enactment as on the 31st day of March, 1998 but remaining unpaid as on the date of making a declaration under Section 88; or

(b) the amount of duties (including drawback of duty, credit of duty or any amount representing duty) cesses, interest, fine or penalty which constitutes the subject matter of a demand notice or a show-cause notice issued on or before the 31st day of March, 1998 under the enactment but remaining unpaid on the date of making a declaration under Section 88, but does not include any demand relating to erroneous refund and where a show-cause notice is issued to the declarant in respect of seizure of goods and demand of duties, the tax arrear shall not include the duties on such seized goods where such duties on the seized goods have not been quantified.

Explanation—Where a declarant has already paid either voluntarily or under protest, any amount of duties, cesses, interest, fine or penalty specified in this sub-clause, on or before the date making a declaration by him under Section 88 which includes any deposit made by him pending any appeal or in pursuance of a Court order in relation to such duties, cesses, interest, fine or penalty, such payment shall not be deemed to be the amount unpaid for the purposes of determining tax arrear under this sub-clause. [Finance Act (21 of 1998), S. 87(m) now repealed by Goods and Services Tax Act, 2017].

Tax base. Form of income upon which tax is calculated. For example, the tax base for income tax is a person's taxable income, for corporation tax a company's profits.

Tax benefit. Includes,—

(a) a reduction or avoidance or deferral of tax or other amount payable under this Act; or

(b) an increase in a refund of tax or other amount under this Act; or

(c) a reduction or avoidance or deferral of tax or other amount that would be payable under this Act, as a result of a tax treaty; or

(d) an increase in a refund of tax or other amount under this Act as a result of a tax treaty; or

(e) a reduction in total income; or

(f) an increase in loss,

in the relevant previous year or any other previous year. [(w.e.f. 1-4-2016) S. 102(10) of the Income-tax Act, 1961 (43 of 1961); (still-born) Section 102(11) of the Income-tax Act, 1961 (43 of 1961) as inserted (w.e.f. 1-4-2014) by the Finance Act, 2012 (23 of 2012) and omitted (w.e.f. 1-4-2014) by the Finance Act, 2013 (17 of 2013)]

"Tax benefit" means—

(a) a reduction or avoidance or deferral of tax or other amount payable under this Act; or

(b) an increase in the refund of tax or other amount under this Act; or

(c) a reduction or avoidance or deferral tax or other amount that would be payable under this Act, as a result of a tax treaty; or

(d) an increase in a refund of tax or other amount under this Act as a result of a tax treaty; or

(e) a reduction in total income including increase in loss, in relevant previous year or any other previous year. [Income-tax Act (43 of 1961), Chap. X-A, S. 102(11)].

Tax bracket. The percentage of a person's income that he or she pays in tax depends on the level of income. Incomes are divided into brackets (ranges) for the purpose of calculating tax.

Tax credit. Tax credit (or tax rebate) is a legal provision permitting taxpayers to deduct specified sums from their tax liability.

Tax credit certificate. Means a tax credit certificate granted to any person in accordance with the provisions of Chapter XXII-B and any scheme made thereunder. [Income-tax Act (43 of 1961), S. 2(43A)]

Tax due. the expression 'tax due' includes penalty, interest or any other sum payable under the 1961 Act. [(w.e.f. 1-6-2013) *Explanation* to section 167C of the Income-tax Act, 1961 (43 of 1961); (w.e.f. 1-6-2013) *Explanation* to section 179 of the Income-tax Act, 1961 (43 of 1961)]

Tax evasion. Action by a person to avoid, in whole or in part, a tax lawfully exigible from him, as by not declaring or under-declaring income or taxable transactions. Such conduct is criminal and subject to heavy penalties. (*Walker*)

Tax-free security. Means any security of the Central Government issued or declared to be income-tax free, or any security of a State Government issued income-tax free, the income-tax whereon is payable by the State Government. [Finance Act (38 of 1993), S. 2(e) now repealed by Goods and Services Tax Act, 2017]

Tax fraction. Means the fraction calculated in accordance with formula, r / (r + 100) where 'r' is the percentage rate of tax applicable to the sale under this Regulation. [Andaman and Nicobar Islands Value Added Tax Regulation (6 of 2017), S. 2(1)(zh)].

Tax haven. An offshore financial centre having legal mechanisms to reduce or eliminate taxes on income, wealth, profits and inheritance or to accumulate tax free income offshore pending repatriation to a taxable jurisdiction. [*M L Tannan Banking Law & Practice in India*, Vol. 2, 2021, LexisNexis, Dictionary of Banking Terminology].

The term "tax haven" is sometimes described as a state with nil or moderate level of taxation and/or liberal tax incentives for undertaking specific activities such as exporting. The expression "tax haven" is also sometimes used as a "secrecy jurisdiction". [*Vodafone International Holdings BV v. Union of India*, (2012) 6 SCC 613, para 318]. Tax legislation

Tax on luxuries. "The concept of a tax on 'luxuries' in Entry 62, List II cannot be limited merely to tax things tangible and corporeal in their aspect as 'luxuries'. It is true that while frugal or simple food and medicine may be classified as necessities; articles such as jewellery, perfume, intoxicating liquor, tobacco, *etc.*, could be called articles of luxury. But the legislative entry cannot be exhausted by these cases, illustrative of the concept. The entry encompasses all the manifestations or emanations, the notion of 'luxuries' can fairly and reasonably (sic) can be said to comprehend the element of extravagance of indulgence that differentiates 'luxury' from 'necessity' cannot be confined to goods and articles. There can be elements of extravagance or indulgence in the quality of services and activities." *Express Hotel* v. *State of Gujarat*, (1989) 3 SCC 677, 690.

Tax period. "Tax period" means the period for which the return is required to be furnished [The Central Goods and Services Tax Act, 2017 (12 of 2017), S. 2(106)]

Tax Recovery Officer. Means any Income-tax Officer who may be authorised by the Principal Chief Commissioner or Chief Commissioner or Principal Commissioner or Commissioner by general or special order in writing, to exercise the powers of a Tax Recovery Officer and also to exercise or perform such powers and functions which are conferred on, or assigned to, an Assessing Officer under this Act and which may be prescribed. [Income-tax Act (43 of 1961), S. 2(44)]

"TAX RECOVERY OFFICER", in relation to any scheduled Act, means a Tax Recovery Officer and where there is no such definition, means an officer (by whatever name called) to whom a certificate for the recovery of arrears of Government dues may be issued under that Act. [Taxation Laws (Continuation and Validation of Recovery Proceedings) Act (11 of 1964), S. 2(e)]

Tax return. An income tax form to report or submit income, deductions, exemptions and tax, liability; also known as 'return or income tax return'.

Tax; taxation. A 'tax' is a compulsory exaction of money by public authority for public purposes enforceable by law and is not payment for services rendered. *Commissioner H.R. E.* v. *Lakshmindra Thirtha Swamiar of Sri Shirur Mutt*, AIR 1954 SC 282, 295. [*Mathews v. Chicory Mktg. Board (Vic)*, (1938) 60 CLR 263, 276 (Aus), para 9 by C.J., Latham as cited in *Delhi Race Club Limited v. Union of India*, (2012) 8 SCC 680, para 32].

Tax includes any levy. *Shyam Sunder* v. *Gift Tax Officer*, AIR 1967 All 19, 23.

TAXATION is the act of laying a tax, or imposing these burdens or charges upon persons or property, or in other words, the process or means by which the taxing power is exercised.

Fixing the amount of (costs to be fixed in the decree) [CPC (5 of 1908), S. 118]; to lay a tax on [Companies (Profits) Surtax Act (7 of 1964), S. 24A(b)].

Tax treaty. Means an agreement referred to in section 90(1) or section 90A(1) of Act 43 of 1961. [(w.e.f. 1-4-2016) S. 102(11) of the Income-tax Act, 1961 (43 of 1961); (still-born) Section 102(12) of the Income-tax Act, 1961 (43 of 1961) as inserted (w.e.f. 1-4-2014) by the Finance Act, 2012 (23 of 2012) and omitted (w.e.f. 1-4-2014) by the Finance Act, 2013 (17 of 2013)]

Taxable banking transaction. "TAXABLE BANKING TRANSACTION" means—

(a) a transaction, being withdrawal of cash (by whatever mode) on any single day from an account (other than a savings bank account) maintained with any scheduled bank, exceeding,—

(i) twenty-five thousand rupees, in case such withdrawal is from the account maintained by any individual or Hindu undivided family;

(ii) one lakh rupees, in case such withdrawal is from the account maintained by a person other than any individual or Hindu undivided family; or

(b) a transaction, being receipt of cash from any scheduled bank on any single day on encashment of one or more term deposits, whether on maturity or otherwise, from that bank, exceeding,—

(i) twenty-five thousand rupees, in case such term deposit or deposits are in the name of any individual or Hindu undivided family;

(ii) one lakh rupees, in case such term deposit or deposits are by any person other than any individual or Hindu undivided family. [Finance Act (18 of 2005), Ch. VII, S. 94(8)

Taxable commodities transaction. Means a transaction of sale of commodity derivatives in respect of commodities, other than agricultural commodities, traded in recognised associations. [Finance Act 2013, S. 116(7). Also see (w.e.f. 1-4-2014) *Explanation* to section 36(1)(xvi) of the Income-tax Act, 1961 (43 of 1961)]

Taxable expenditure. Means the total expenditure of an assessee liable to tax under this Act. [Expenditure-tax Act (29 of 1957), S. 2(o)]

Taxable income. That portion of income against which tax rates are applied to compute tax to be paid by an individual or entity. This amount comprises of gross income of business or individuals after deducting expenses and exemptions available under law. [Karnika Seth, *Computers Internet and New Technology Laws*, 2021, LexisNexis, Glossary of Legal Terms]

Taxable profit (tax loss). "TAXABLE PROFITS" means the amount by which the profits during a chargeable accounting period exceed the abatement in respect of that period. [Business Profits Tax Act (21 of 1947), S. 2(17)]

Taxable securities transaction. In this chapter "TAXABLE SECURITIES TRANSACTION" means a transaction of—

(a) purchase or sale of an equity share in a company or a derivative or a unit of an equity oriented fund, entered into a recognised stock exchange; or

(b) sale of a unit of an equity oriented fund to the Mutual fund. [Finance Act (23 of 2004), Chapter VII, S. 97(13)].

Taxable service. Means any [service provided or to be provided]—

(a) [to any person], by a stock-broker in connection with the sale or purchase of securities listed on a recognised stock exchange;

(d) to a [policy holder or any person], by an [insurer, including re-insurer] carrying on general insurance business in relation to general insurance business;

(e) [to any person], by an advertising agency in relation to advertisement, in any manner;

(f) 80[to any person], by a courier agency in relation to door-to-door transportation of time sensitive documents, goods or articles;

[(g) to any person, by a consulting engineer in relation to advice, consultancy or technical assistance in any manner in one or more disciplines of engineering including the discipline of computer hardware engineering.

Explanation:—For the purposes of this sub-clause, it is hereby declared that services provided by a consulting engineer in relation to advice, consultancy or technical assistance in the disciplines of both computer hardware engineering and computer software engineering shall also be classifiable under this sub-clause;] engineering but excluding the discipline of computer software engineering]; [Finance Act (32 of 1994), S. 65(105) now repealed by Central Goods and Services Tax Act, 2017].

'Taxable turnover'. Means that part of turnover which remains after deducting therefrom the aggregate amount of the proceeds of sale of goods—

(i) on which no tax is leviable under this Act,

(ii) which take already been subjected to tax under this Act,

(iii) which have been sold to persons outside the State for consumption outside the State, and

(iv) which are taxable at a point of sale within the State subsequent to the sale by the dealer and such sale is covered by a declaration as may be required under any provision of this Act or the rules made thereunder:

Provided that where a dealer in goods which are exempted from tax unconditionally, sells any bardana, container or any other packing material received along with such goods at the time of purchase thereof by him, the taxable turnover in respect of such sales shall, at the option of such dealer to be exercised in the prescribed manner, be one percent of the aggregate amount of the sale prices received or receivable by him in respect of the sale or supply of such goods and of such bardona, container or material. [Rajasthan Sales Tax Act (29 of 1954), S. 2(s) as cited in *Assistant Commissioner, Commercial Taxes, Rajasthan v. M.B. and Company*, (2012) 13 SCC 401, para 10].

Taxable territory. Means the territory to which the provisions of this Act apply. [Central Goods and Services Tax Act (12 of 2017), S. 2(109)].

Taxable vehicle. "TAXABLE VEHICLE" means a motor vehicle carrying or adapted to carry goods for hire or reward or a public service vehicle. [Madhya Pradesh Motor Vehicles (Taxation of Goods) Act, 1962, S. 2(8)]

Taxation. Includes the imposition of any tax or impost, whether general or local or special. [Constitution of India, Art. 366(28)]

'Taxation' is a mode of raising revenue for public purposes. In exercise of the power to tax, the purpose always is that a common burden shall be sustained by common contributions, regulated by some fixed general rules, and apportioned by the law according to some uniform ratio of equality. [*Union of India v. Nitdip Textile Processors Private Limited*, (2012) 1 SCC 226, para 25].

'Taxation' is a mode of raising revenue for public purposes. The term is ordinarily used to express the exercise of the sovereign power to raise revenue for the expenses of the Government. [*State of U.P. v. Systematic Consom Limited*, (2014) 13 SCC 627, para 20].

Taxation, Direct And Indirect. A direct tax is one which is demanded from the very person who it is intended or desired should pay it. Indirect taxes are those which are demanded from one person in the expectation and the intention is that he shall indemnify himself at the expense of another.

Taxes on income. "TAX ON INCOME" includes a tax in the nature of an excess profits tax. [Constitution of India, Art. 366(29)]

Taxes and Tolls. Tolls for the actual use of passage over land or water highways cannot be treated as taxes. They are not levied on the property or on persons as their share of any public burden laid on the people, but they are a fixed compensation for the use of that which has value and which is actually used to advantage. Thus, taxes levied on those who used a stream, which had been improved for logging purposes by the state, is not a tax.

Taxidermy. "TAXIDERMY", with its grammatical variations and cognate expressions, means the curing, preparation or preservation or mounting of trophies. [Wildlife (Protection) Act (53 of 1972), S. 2(30)]

Taxing Authority. In relation to any scheduled Act, means an officer (by whatever name called) empowered to serve upon an assessee a notice of demand in respect of any Government dues under that Act. [Taxation Laws (Continuation and Validation of Recovery Proceedings) Act (11 of 1964), S. 2(d)]

Taxing officer. The officer who determines the amount of costs to be taxed in the decree. [CPC (5 of 1908), O. XI, R. 3].

Taxing power. The "taxing power" is one of the attributes or incidents of sovereignty. It is and must be inherent in every form of Government. The necessity for the exercise of the power rests wholly in the discretion of the Legislature, and that discretion extends to the selection of the subjects of taxation or the things to be taxed, whether it be persons or property, business or vocation.

TCP. (*abbr.*) Transmission Control Protocol. A higher level of protocol than IP. IP is concerned with packets of data. TCP is concerned with messages which may comprise numerous packets. Almost universally used together and referred to as TCP/IP. (*Cyber Law*)

TCP/IP (Transmission Control Protocol/ Internet Protocol). A set of rules used to connect to other computers. (*Cyber Law*)

This is the suite of protocols that defines the *Internet.* Originally designed for the *UNIX* operating system, TCP/IP software is now included with every major kind of computer operating system. To be truly on the *Internet*, your computer must have TCP/IP software. (*Matisse Enzer-Glossary of Internet Terms*)

Tea. Means the plant Camellia Sinensis (L) O. Kuntze as well as all varieties of the product known commercially as tea made form the leaves of the plant Camelia Sinensis (L) O. Kuntze including green tea. [Tea Act (29 of 1953], S. 3(n)].

Tea estate. Means an estate, situated in the tea districts, any part of which is used or is intended to be used for the cultivation or manufacture of tea or for any purpose connected therewith. [Tea Districts Emigrant Labour Act, 1932 (Repealed by Act 50 of 1972), S. 2(b)]

Tea grown. The words 'tea grown' has the same meaning as grown by the process of agriculture. *Maharaj Prashad Jain* v. *I.T.C., Lucknow,* AIR 1967 All 12, 14.

Tea seed. Includes seeds, roots, stumps, cuttings, buds and any living portion of the plant *Camellia sinensis (L) O. kuntze,* which may be used to propagate that plant [Tea Act (29 of 1953), S. 3(o)]

Teacher. "TEACHERS" means a salaried professor, reader, lecturer or tutor who imparts instruction in a Faculty of, or in a college maintained by, the University and includes any other person who is declared to be a teacher by the Academic Council. [Banaras Hindu University Act (16 of 1915), S. 2(i)]

"TRAINED TEACHERS". Are not skilled, semi-skilled, unskilled, manual, supervisory, technical or clerical employees. They are also not employed in managerial or administrative capacity. Occasionally, even if they do some administrative work as part of their duty with teaching, since their main job is imparting education, they cannot be held employed in managerial or administrative capacity. *Ahme-dabad Pvt. Primary Teachers' Association* v. *Administrative Officer*, AIR 2004 SC 1426 : 2004 AIR SCW 356.

'Teacher' of an institution means a Headmaster or other teacher in respect of whose employment maintenance grant is paid by the State Government to the institution. [Uttar Pradesh Junior High Schools (Payment of Salaries of Teachers and Other Employees) Act, 1978, S. 2(h) as cited in *State of U.P. v. Pawan Kumar Divedi*, (2014) 9 SCC 692, para 28].

"TEACHER" means a member of the regular faculty at the levels of Professor, or Associate Professor or Assistant professor, and includes adjunct faculty and faculty on a long-term contract of not less than three years. [UGC (Institutions Deemed to be Universities) Regulations, 2019, Regn. 2(2-20)].

Teacher education. "TEACHER EDUCATION" means programmes of education, research or training of persons for quipping them to teach at pre-primary, primary, secondary and senior secondary stages in schools, and includes non-formal education, part-time education, adult education and correspondence education. [National Council for Teachers Education Act (73 of 1993), S. 2(l)]

Teacher education qualification. "TEACHER EDUCATION QUALIFICATION" means a degree, diploma or certificate in teacher education awarded by a University or examining body in accordance with the provisions of this Act. [National Council for Teachers Education Act (73 of 1993), S. 2(m)]

Teachers. Means Professors, Associate Professors, Assistant Professors, Teaching Faculty Members and their equivalent appointed for imparting instruction or conducting research or extension education programmes or combination of these in the University, college or any institute maintained by the

University and designated as teachers by the Ordinances. [S. 3(r) of the Rani Lakshmi Bai Central Agricultural University Act, 2014 (10 of 2014)]

"TEACHERS". The definition of the term 'teachers' under section 2(35) of the Maharashtra University of Health Sciences Act, 1999 (10 of 1999), is wide enough to include even unapproved teacher. In fact, the said definition has two parts, the *first part* deals with full time approved Demonstrators, Tutors, Assistant Lecturers, Lecturers, etc., and the *second part* deals with other persons teaching or giving instructions on full time basis in affiliated colleges or approved institutions in the University. *Maharashtra University of Health Sciences* v. *Satchikitsa Prasarak Mandal*, AIR 2010 SC 1325.

Teachers of the University. "TEACHERS OF THE UNIVERSITY" means Professors, Readers, Lecturer and such other persons as may be appointed for imparting instruction or conducting research in the University and are designated as teachers by the Ordinances. [Jamia Milla Islamia Act (58 of 1988), S. 2(n); Tezpur University Act (45 of 1993), S. 2(u); Babasaheb Bhimrao Ambedkar University Act (58 of 1994), S. 2(t); Maulana Azad National Urdu University Act, 1996 (2 of 1997), S. 2(q); Mahatma Gandhi Antarrashtriya Hindi Vishwavidyalaya Act, 1996 (3 of 1997), S. 2(q) and Mizoram University Act (8 of 2000), S. 2(t)]

"TEACHERS OF THE UNIVERSITY" means Professors, Associate Professors, Assistant Professors, Readers, Senior Lecturers, Lecturers and such other persons as may be appointed or recognised for imparting instruction or conducting research in the University or in any college or institution maintained by the University or for giving guidance to students for any course of study of the University are designated as teachers by the Statutes. [S. 2(x) of the Rajiv Gandhi National Aviation University Act, 2013 (26 of 2013)]

Technical. Peculiar to a particular art, science or craft (as) technical skill; technical school or education.

Appropriate or peculiar to or characteristic of; a particular art, science, profession, or occupation [Indian Evidence Act (1 of 1872), S. 98]; [Industrial Finance Corporation Act (15 of 1948) (*repealed by Act 23 of 1993*), S. 43(2)(n)].

Technical attack. An attack that can be perpetrated by circumventing or nullifying hardware and software protection mechanisms, rather than by subverting system personnel or other users. (*Cyber Law*)

Technical defect. A 'technical defect' in law is one which may come within the four corners of it, but in fact it does not affect the merits of the case. It is a mistake which does not go to the core of the matter. *Gangadhar Bandwate* v. *Premchand Kashyap,* AIR 1958 MP 182, 184.

Technical education. Means programmes of education, research and training in engineering, technology, architecture, town planning, management, pharmacy and applied arts and crafts and such other programme or areas as the Central Government may, in consultation with the Council, by notification in the Official Gazette, declare. [All India Council for Technical Education Act (52 of 1987), S. 2(g)]

Technical fraud. Fraud committed by means of technological systems. (*Cyber Law*)

Technical institution. Means an institution, not being a University, which offers courses or programmes of technical education, and shall include such other institutions as the Central Government may, in consultation with the Council, by notification in the Official Gazette, declare as technical institutions. [All India Council for Technical Education Act (52 of 1987), S. 2(h)]

Technical intelligence (TECHINT). Intelligence derived from exploitation of foreign material, produced for strategic, operational, and tactical level commanders. Technical intelligence begins when an individual service member finds something new on the battlefield and takes the proper steps to report it. The item is then exploited at succeedingly higher levels until a countermeasure is produced to neutralize the adversary's technological advantage. (*Cyber Law*)

Technical know-how. The very meaning of "technical know-how" is the knowledge which would enable a company receiving such know-how to do the project. A techno-economic feasibility study relating to a project for setting up a sponge iron plant with electric steel-making and continuous billet casting plant amounts to "technical know-how". *Lurgi India Co. P. Ltd.* v. *C.B.D.T.,* (1980) 121 ITR 287 (Del). [Income Tax Act (43 of 1961), S. 80 MM (*omitted by Finance Act, 1983*)]

Technical Member. In Chapter XXVII of Act 18 of 2013, unless the context otherwise requires, 'Technical Member' means a member of the Tribunal or the Appellate Tribunal appointed as such. [S. 407(*e*) of the Companies Act, 2013 (18 of 2013)]

Technical service. The expression "technical services" has a very broad connotation and it has been used elsewhere in the statute also so widely as to comprehend professional services: vide S. 9(1)(vii). Whatever may be the position regarding other 'professional services', services involving specialised knowledge, experience and skill in the field of constructional operations are "technical services". The question whether "professional services" would be "technical services" or not has no impact on the point viz that in order to say that a person is rendering such services to another, it is not necessary that the services should be rendered by the former personally and not through the medium of others. *Continental Construction Ltd.* v. *C.I.T.*, AIR 1992 SC 803. [Income Tax Act, 1961, Ss. 80-O & 9(1)(vii), *Expln.* 2]

The expression 'technical services' always includes 'professional services' *Central Board of Direct Taxes* v. *Oberoi Hotels (India) Pvt. Ltd.*, AIR 1998 SC 1666. [Income-tax Act (43 of 1961), S. 80(o)]

Technician. For the purposes of this clause, "TECHNICIAN", means a person having specialised knowledge and experience in—

(i) constructional or manufacturing operations, or in mining or in the generation of electricity or any other form of power, or

(ii) agriculture, animal husbandry, dairy farming, deep sea fishing or ship building, or

(iii) such other field as the Central Government may, having regard to availability of Indians having specialised knowledge and experience therein, the needs of the country and other relevant circumstances, by notification in the Official Gazette, specify,

who is employed in India in a capacity in which such specialised knowledge and experience are actually utilised. [Income-tax Act (43 of 1961), S. 10(5B), *Expln.*]

Technical committee. Means a committee constituted by the Bureau under sub-section (3) of Section 10 of the Act and includes a Division Council, sectional committee, sub-committee, panel, working group or any other committee. [Bureau of Indian Standards Rules, 2017, R. 2(10(i)].

Technician (vocational) apprentice. Means an apprentice who holds or is undergoing training in order that he may hold a certificate in vocational course involving two years of study after the completion of the secondary stage of school education recognised by the All-India Council and undergoes apprenticeship training in any designated trade.. [Apprentices Act (52 of 1961), S. 2(pp)]

Technology. "TECHNOLOGY" means any special or technical knowledge or any special service required for any purpose whatsoever by an industrial concern under any foreign collaboration, and includes designs, drawings, publications and technical personnel. [Research and Development Cess Act (32 of 1986), S. 2 (h)]

"TECHNOLOGY" means any information (including information embodied in software) other than information in the public domain, that is capable of being used in—

(i) the development, production or use of any goods or software;

(ii) the development of, or the carrying out of, an industrial or commercial activity or the provision of a service of any kind.

Explanation.—When technology is described wholly or partly by reference to the uses to which it (or the goods to which it relates) may be put, it shall include services which are provided or used, or which are capable of being used, in the development, production or use of such technology or goods. [Weapons of Mass Destruction and Their Delivery Systems (Prohibition of Unlawful Activities) Act (21 of 2005), S. 4(l)]

"Technology" means:

"(1) Theoretical knowledge of industry and the industrial arts.

(2) The application of science to the arts.

(3) That branch of ethnology which treats of the development of the arts." [Webster's Comprehensive Dictionary as cited in *Association of Management of Private Colleges v. All India Council for Technical Education*, (2013) 8 SCC 271, para 62.1].

"Technology" means:

"any information (including information embodied in software) other than information in the public domain, that is capable of being used in—

(i) the development, production or use of any goods or software;

(ii) the development of, or the carrying out of, an industrial or commercial activity or the provision of a service of any kind." [Encyclopedic Law Lexicon as cited in *Association of Management of Private Colleges v. All India Council for Technical Education*, (2013) 8 SCC 271, para 62.3].

"Technology" means:

"1. (a) The branch of knowledge that deals with the mechanical arts of applied sciences; a discourse or treaties on (one of) these subjects. Orig. on an art or arts.

(b) The terminology of a particular subject; technical nomenclature.

2. (a) The mechanical arts or applied sciences collectively; the application of (any of) these.

(b) A particular mechanical art or applied science." [New Shorter Oxford English Dictionary as cited in *Association of Management of Private Colleges v. All India Council for Technical Education*, (2013) 8 SCC 271, para 62.4].

Technology transfer. The sale or licensing of intellectual property.

Telecast rights. Means a licence or contract to exhibit motion pictures or television programmes over a television network either through terrestrial transmission or through a satellite broadcast in a specified territory. [Income-Tax Act (43 of 1961), S. 80HHF, *Expln.* (g)]

Telecommunication service. "TELECOMMUNICATION SERVICE" means service of any description (including electronic mail, voice mail, data services, audio tax services, video tax services, radio paging and cellular mobile telephone services) which is made available to users by means of any transmission or reception of signs, signals, writing, images and sounds or intelligence of any nature, by wire, radio, visual or other electromagnetic means but shall not include broadcasting services. [Telecom Regulatory Authority of India Act (24 of 1997), S. 2(1)(k)]

"Telecommunication service" means service of any description (including electronic mail, voice mail, data services, audio text services, video text services, radio paging and cellular mobile telephone services) which is made available to users by means of any transmission or reception of signs, signals, writing, images and sounds or intelligence of any nature, by wire, radio, visual or other electromagnetic means [The Central Goods and Services Tax Act, 2017 (12 of 2017), S. 2(110)]

Telecommunications Relay Service (TRS). A free service that enables persons with TTYs, individuals who use sign language and people who have speech disabilities to use telephone services by having a third party transmit and translate the call. (*Telecommunication*)

Telecopier. A machine used for transmitting over telephone lines an exact copy of a printing or handwriting.

Telegram. "TELEGRAM" means written matter intended to be transmitted by telegraph. [Tax on Postal Articles Act, (47 of 1971), S. 2(f)]

A telegram is any message or other communication transmitted or intended for transmission by telegraph. (*Ame. Cyc.*)

A telegram by itself is not an authentic document. It is like an unsigned anonymous communication. Unless a telegram is confirmed by a subsequent signed application, representation or an affidavit, the contents of the telegrams have no authenticity at all and the same cannot be taken into consideration for assessing the value of the other authentic documents on the record. *District Magistrate* v. *G. Jothisankar*, AIR 1993 SC 2633, 2635.

Telegraph. "TELEGRAPH" means any appliances, instrument, material, or apparatus used or capable of use for transmission or reception of signs, signals, writing, images and sounds or intelligence of any nature by wire, visual or other electro-magnetic emissions, Radio waves or Hertzian waves, galvanic, electric or magnetic waves. [Indian Telegraph Act (13 of 1885), S. 3 (1AA)]

An apparatus for transmitting communication by means of electric signal. [CrPC 1973 (2 of 1974), S. 37(c)]; [Indian Electricity Act (9 of 1910), S. 2(a)].

In its general legal significance, the term "*telegraph*" is used to designate any apparatus for transmitting communications by means of electric signals. Such apparatus generally consists of an extended wire, to the ends of which are attached certain instruments, respectively used for sending and receiving signals transmitted through the wire, and which instruments are connected with batteries producing electric currents.

Telegraph authority. Means the Director General of Posts and Telegraphs, and includes any officer empowered by him to perform all or any of the functions of the telegraph authority under this Act. [Indian Telegraph Act (13 of 1885), S. 3(6)]

Telegraph line. Means a wire or wires used for the purpose of a telegraph, with any casing, coating, tube or pipe enclosing the same and any appliances and apparatus connected therewith for the purpose of fixing or insulating the same. [Indian Telegraph Act (13 of 1885), S. 3(4)]

"Telegraph lines" means a wire or wires used for the purpose of an appliance or apparatus for using telegraphic or other communications by means of electricity. *Senior Electric Inspector* v. *Lakminarayan Chopra*, AIR 1962 SC 159, 161. [Indian Telegraph Act (13 of 1885), S. 3(1) & (4)]

Telegraph office. "TELEGRAPH OFFICE" includes a Government telegraph office and a licenced telegraph office, but does not include a military field telegraph office. [Tax on Postal Articles Act (47 of 1971), S. 2(g)]

Telegraph officer. Means any person employed either permanently or temporarily in connection with a telegraph established, maintained or worked by the Central Government or by a person licenced under this Act. [Indian Telegraph Act (13 of 1885), S. 3(2)]

Telegraph wire. Means any copper wire the diameter of which in millimeters, is—

(i) not less than 2.43 and not more than 2.53; or

(ii) not less than 2.77 and not more than 2.87; or

(iii) not less than 3.42 and not more than 3.52 [Telegraph Wires (Unlawful Possession) Act (74 of 1950), S. 2(b)].

Telegraphic message. A message by telegraph. [Indian Evidence Act (1 of 1872), S. 88].

Telegraphic transfer selling rate. In relation to a foreign currency means the rate of exchange adopted by the State Bank of India constituted under the State Bank of India Act, 1955 (23 of 1955), for selling such currency where such currency is made available by that bank through telegraphic transfer. [Income-Tax Rule, 1962, R. 115 A *Expln.*]

Telegraphy. Telegraphy has been defined as the transaction of business over or through wires.

A system of telecommunications which is concerned in any process providing transmission and reproduction at a distance of documentary matter, such as written or printed matter or fixed images, or the reproduction at a distance of any kind of information in such a form. For the purposes of the Radio Regulations, however, unless otherwise specified therein, telegraphy shall mean "a system of telecommunications for the transmission of written matter by the use of a signal code". (*Telecommunication*)

Telemarketing. Marketing technique that uses telephone contact with prospective customers. (*Cyber Law*)

Telemarketer. For the purpose of these Regulations, is an entity registered with Telecom Regulatory Authority of India under chapter III of The Telecom Commercial Communications Customer Preference Regulations, 2010 (as amended from time to time). [Insurance Regulatory and Development Authority of

India (Insurer Web Aggregators) Regulations, 2017, Regn. 2(n)].

Telemarketing and Consumer Fraud and Abuse Act of 1994. Federal law that allows the FTC to regulate the content of telemarketing calls. (*U.S.*) (*Cyber Law*)

Telemedicine. Means use of internet and computers to diagnose, advise and / or offer treatment to a patient about a medical condition by a doctor who is virtually present but may be physically based in a far away geo location. [Karnika Seth, *Computers Internet and New Technology Laws*, 2021, LexisNexis, Glossary of Legal Terms].

Telephone connection. The expression 'telephone connection' would mean in common parlance 'connecting two telephone apparatus so as to enable the caller to avail the speech transmission facility with a desired person'. *N. Krishna Devaraya* v. *UOI*, AIR 1996 Kant 189, 192.

Telephone Consumer Protection Act (TCPA) of 1991. Extends privacy rights to several aspects of telephone marketing activities. (*Cyber Law*)

Federal law that regulates telemarketing activities including automatic dialing, unsolicited faxes, and telemarketing lists. (*U.S.*) (*Cyber Law*)

Telephone tapping. The practice of listening to, and frequently also of recording, telephone conversations.

Telephony. The word used to describe the science of transmitting voice over a telecommunications network. (*Telecommunication*)

Television news software. Means a collection of sounds and images, reportage, data and voice of actualities broadcast either through terrestrial transmission, wire or satellite, live or pre-recorded on video cassettes or digital media. [Income-Tax Act (43 of 1961), S. 80HHF, *Expln.* (h)]

Television set. The word 'television' would include a device having a screen operating on television technology and it is not necessary the screen must be built in the device and that it cannot be separated from the apparatus. *Shankar Video* v. *State of Maharashtra*, AIR 1993 SC 2111, 2115.

Teleworking. Working at home but linked to one's employer through fax, telephone or computer modem.

Telex. "TELEX" means a typed communication by using teleprinters through telex exchanges. [Finance Act (32 of 1994), S. 65(1)(112) now repealed by Central Goods and Services Tax Act, 2017].]

Telnet. A protocol which allows you to connect over the Internet to another computer in such a way as to appear as a local user of that computer. Requires the use of a terminal emulator simulating your view of the remote computer. This is steadily being superseded by the WWW. (*Cyber Law*)

The command and program used to *login* from one *Internet* site to another. The telnet command/program gets you to the login : prompt of another host. (*Matisse Enzer Glossary of Internet Terms*)

Telnet account. Telnet allows real-time access to the command line of your server (similar to the C:\ prompt in DOS) to run programs and install and configure scripts. Most cgi scripts can be installed without Telnet unless you need it for debugging purposes. (*Cyber Law*)

Temple. "TEMPLE" includes any building or other structure whether roofed or not, constructed or made to preserve the memory of a person in respect of whom *sati* has been committed or used or intended to be used for the carrying on of any form of worship or for the observance of any ceremony in connection with such commission. [Commission of Sati (Prevention) Act, 1987 (3 of 1988), S. 2(e)]

Building treated as the dwelling place or devoted to the worship of God.

The exclusion of others or outsiders from interference with the management of the institution by the founders will not take away the institution from the definition of a "temple". So long as there was no intention on the part of the founders to exclude the right of worship, the restriction of the right of outsiders to interfere in the management of the temple is not a determining factor in considering whether the temple is a public or private temple.

An institution will be a temple if it is a place of public religious worship and it is dedicated to, or is for the benefit of, or is used as of right by, the Hindu Community, or any section thereof, as a place of religious worship. *P.F. Sadavarthy* v. *Commissioner, H.R. & C.E.*, AIR 1963 SC 510, 512.

A place would be temple if it be used as a place of public religious worship. *Nivas Das* v. *Surjanaryan*, AIR 1967 SC 256, 260.

A place creating reverence that God resides there or an edifice dedicated to service of God is a temple. *T.V.D. Naidu* v. *Commissioner H.R. & C.E. (Admn.) Department*, AIR 1989 Mad 60, 66.

Temporal. Wordly; earthly. [Indian Evidence Act (1 of 1872), S. 24].

The word temporal' has been defined as :

1. Relating to worldly as opposed to spiritual affairs; secular. 2. of or relating to time. • relating to or denoting time or tense. [Oxford Dictionary as cited in *K.S. Varghese v. ST. Peter's and Paul's Syrian Orth*, 2017 (7) SCALE 450, para 105]

Temporal means worldly, earthly.

The word 'temporal" is defined to mean civil or political power as distinguished from ecclesiastical power. [Black Law Dictionary as cited in *K.S. Varghese, v. ST. Peter's and Paul's Syrian Orth*, 2017 (7) SCALE 450, para 105]

Temporary officer. In relation to any grade means a person holding a temporary or officiating appointment in that grade on the basis of his being regularly approved for such appointment or an officer appointed to agrade who is yet to be removed from probation. [Armed Forces Headquarters Civil Service Rules, 2018, R. 2(q)].

Temporarily. The expression "for the time" and "for the time being" are equivalent to the word "temporarily", and each constitutes a good definition of that word.

For the time or for the time being. [Indian Contract Act (9 of 1872), S. 16(2)(b)].

Temporary disablement. Means a condition resulting from an employment injury which requires medial treatment and renders an employee, as a result of such injury, temporarily incapable of doing the work which he was doing prior to or at the time of the injury. [Employees' State Insurance Act (34 of 1948), S. 2(21)]

"Temporary disablement" means a condition resulting from an employment injury which requires medical treatment and renders an employee, as a result of such injury, temporarily incapable of doing the work which he was doing prior to or at the time of the injury. [Code on Social Security, 2020 (36 of 2020), section 2(83)]

Temporary lecturer. 'TEMPORARY LECTURER' means a lecturer appointed in the pay scale prescribed by the university concerned for lecturers and on temporary basis as stopgap arrangement but shall not include lecturers appointed on contract basis or those in foreign service and serving the university concerned on deputation. [Rajasthan University Teachers (Absorption of Temporary Lecturers) Act (7 of 1979), S. 2(iv)]

Temporary loans. For the purposes of section 180(1)(c) of Act 18 of 2013, the expression 'temporary loans' means loans repayable on demand or within six months from the date of the loan such as short-term, cash credit arrangements, the discounting of bills and the issue of other short-term loans of a seasonal character, but does not include loans raised for the purpose of financial expenditure of a capital nature. [*Explanation* to section 180(1)(c) of the Companies Act, 2013 (18 of 2013)]

Temporary occupation. In relation to any public premises, means occupation by any person on the basis of an order of allotment made under the authority of the Central Government, a State Government, the Government of a Union Territory or a statutory authority for a total period (including the extended period, if any) which is less than thirty days. [Public Premises (Eviction of Unauthorised Occupants) Act (40 of 1971), S. 2(fb)]

Temporary restraining order. A Court order which preserves the *status quo* until the application of a plaintiff for a preliminary or permanent injunction can be heard.

Temporary workman. "TEMPORARY WORKMAN" means a workman who has been appointed in a factory for a limited period for work which is of an essentially temporary nature or who is employed temporarily as an additional workman in connection with temporary increase in work of a permanent nature. [Maharashtra Unemployment Allowance Payment to Workmen in Factories (For Temporary Period) Act (16 of 1976), S. 2(f) and Gujarat Payment of Unemployment Allowance to Workmen in Factories Act (Guj Act No. 20 of 1981), S. 2(g)]

Ten clear days. Notice of ten clear days means ten days exclusive of date on which notice is given and date of on which meeting is held. *Harish Chandra Singh* v. *State of Bihar,* AIR 1971 Pat 406, 407.

Tenable. Capable of being retained, kept or defended. [Trade and Merchandise Marks Act (43 of 1958), S. 87(1)(a)].

Tenancy. 'TENANCY' means the relationship of landlord and tenant. [Goa, Daman and Diu Agricultural Tenancy Act (7 of 1964), S. 2(22).

The condition of a tenant; the temporary possession of land or house belonging to another.

A holding of a tenant; occupancy of lands or tenements under a lease. [T.P. Act (4 of 1882), S. 106].

A tenancy exists where one has let real estate to another to hold of him as landlord. When duly created and the tenant put in possession, he is the owner of an estate for the time being, and has all the usual rights and remedies of an owner to defend his possession. But a tenancy does not necessarily imply a right to complete and exclusive possession. It might, on the other hand, be created with implied or express reservation of a right to possession on the part of the landlord, for all purposes not inconsistent with the privileges granted to the tenant.

No particular form of words is necessary to create a tenancy. Any words that show an indication of the lessor to divest himself of the possession and confer it on another, subject to his own title, is sufficient.

A tenancy-in-common, there is unity of possession but no unity of title i.e. the interests are differently held and each co-tenant has different shares over the estate. Thus tenancy rights, being the proprietary rights, by applying the principle of inheritance, the shares of heirs are different and ownership leasehold rights would be confined to the respective shares of each heir and none will have title to the entire lease property. Therefore, the estate shall be divided among the co-tenants and each tenant in common has an estate in the whole of the single tenancy. Consequently, the privity exists between the landlord exists between the landlord and the tenant in common in respect of such estate. [*Suresh Kumar Kohli* v. *Rakesh Jain,* (2018) 6 SCC 708, para 15].

In 'tenancy-in-common' there may be unity of possession and commencement of title but the other two features as to unity of title and interest are missing. [*Ram Awalamb* v. *Jata Shankar,* 1968 SCC On Line All 178 : AIR 1969 All 702 **as cited in** *T. Ravi* v. *B. Chinna Narasimha,* (2017) 7 SCC 342, para 64].

Tenancy at will. A tenancy that can be terminated at any time by either the landlord or the tenant.

Tenancy by estoppel. A tenancy which exists despite the fact that the person who granted it had no legal right to do so.

Tenancy for a term. A tenancy whose duration is known in years, weeks, or days from the moment of its creation.

Tenancy from year to year. A tenancy from year to year arises by express agreement or operation of law (*e.g. S.* 106 of the TP Act (4 of 1882) and continues for successive period of one year each, until determined at the end of a year of tenancy by a proper notice.

Tenancy in common. A tenancy by two or more persons, in equal or unequal undivided shares, each person having an equal right to possess the whole property but no right of survivorship.

Tenancy in perpetuity. A tenancy in perpetuity is created by express grant or by a presumed grant and continues until determined by forfeiture.

Tenancy rights. The tenancy rights in a flat which a company had, may not be an asset for the purpose of liquidation proceedings. *Nirmala R. Bafna* v. *Khandesh Spinning & Weaving Mills Co. Ltd.*, AIR 1993 SC 1380, 1384.

Tenant. "TENANT" means any person by whom or on whose account rent is payable for any premises and includes such sub-tenants and other person as have derived title under the tenant under any law for the time being in force. [Requisitioning and Acquisition of Immovable Property Act (30 of 1952), S. 2(h).]

"Tenant" means an agriculturist who cultivates personally the land he holds on lease from a landlord and includes—

(i) a person who is deemed to be a tenant under section 4;

(ii) a person who was protected from eviction from any land by the Karnataka Tenants (Temporary Protection from Eviction) Act, 1961;

(ii-a) a person who cultivates personally any land on lease under a lease created contrary to the provisions of section 5 and before the date of commencement of the amendment Act;

(iii) a person who is a permanent tenant; and

(iv) a person who is a protected tenant. [Karnataka Land Reforms Act, 1961 (10 of 1962), S. 2(A)(34) as cited in *Harsha V. Rai v. State of Karnataka*, (2013) 10 SCC 484, para 10].

"Tenant" means a person who holds land under another person, and is, or but for a special contract would be, liable to pay rent for that land to that other person; but it does not include—

(a) an inferior landowner; or

(b) a mortgagee of the rights of a landowner; or

(c) a person to whom a holding has been transferred, or an estate or holding has been let in farm under the Punjab Land Revenue Act, 1887 (17 of 1887), for the recovery of an arrear of land revenue or of a sum recoverable as such an arrear; or

(d) a person who takes from the Government a lease of unoccupied land for the purpose of subletting it. [Punjab Tenancy Act, 1887, S. 4(5) as cited in *Shyam Lal v. Deepa Dass Chela Ram Chela Garib Dass*, (2016) 7 SCC 572, para 3].

'TENANT' means a person who holds land under another person and is, or but for a special contract would be, liable to pay rent for that land to that person. [Orissa Tenancy Act, 1913, S. 3(23)]

'TENANT' means the person by whom rent is or but for a contract express or implied, would be payable and except when the contrary intention appears includes a sub tenant but does not include a mortgagee of proprietary or under proprietary rights a grove holder, a rent free grantee, a grantee at a favourable rate of rent or except as otherwise expressly provides by this Act, as under proprietor, a permanent lessee or a Kadar. [United Provinces Tenancy Act (17 of 1939), S. 3(23)].

A person lawfully cultivating any land belonging to another person shall be deemed to be a TENANT if such land is not cultivated personally by the owner and if such person is not:—

(a) a member of the owner's family, or

(b) a servant on wages payable in cash or kind but not in crop share or a hired labourer cultivating the land under the personal supervision of the owner or any member of the owner's family, or

(c) a mortgagee-in-person. [Bombay Tenancy and Agricultural Land Act, 1948, S. 4].

The term 'TENANT' includes any person deriving title to the land or the building erected upon such land from the tenant whether by operation of law or by transfer *inter-vivos*. [Delhi Municipal Corporation Act (66 of 1957), S. 120(2) *Expln.*]

"Tenant" has the meaning assigned to it in the Punjab Tenancy Act, 1887 (16 of 1887), and includes a sub-tenant, and self-cultivating lessee, but shall not include a present holder, as defined in section 2 of the Resettlement Act. [Punjab Security of Land Tenures Act, 1953 (10 of 1953), S. 2(6) as cited in *Shyam Lal v. Deepa Dass Chela Ram Chela Garib Dass*, (2016) 7 SCC 572, para 2].

'TENANT' with its grammatical variations and cognate expressions includes—

(i) a person who, as lessee, sub-lessee, mortgagee or sub-mortgagee or in good faith believing himself to be lessee, sub-lessee, mortgagee of land, is in possession thereof,

(ii) a person who with the *bona fide* intention of attorning and paying a reasonable rent to the person entitled to cultivate or let waste-land, but without permission of such person, brings such land, under cultivation and is in occupation thereof as cultivator, and

(iii) a person who comes into possession of land belonging to another person and makes improvements thereon in the *bona fide* belief that he is entitled to make such improvements. [Kerala Compensation for Tenants Improvements Act (29 of 1958), S. 2(d)]

'TENANT' means any person by whom or on whose account or behalf the rent of any premises is, or, but for a special contract, would be, payable. [Delhi Rent Control Act (59 of 1958), S. 2(l)]

'TENANT' means a person who on or after the date of commencement of this Act holds land on lease and cultivates it personally and includes a person who is deemed to be a tenant under this Act. [Goa, Daman and Diu Agricultural Tenancy Act (7 of 1964), S. 2(23)]

'TENANT' means any person by whom or on whose account rent is payable for a building and includes the surviving spouse, or any son, or daughter, or the legal representative of a deceased tenant who had been living with the tenant in the building as a member of the tenant's family up to the death of the tenant and a person continuing in possession after the termination of the tenancy in his favour, but does not include a person placed in occupation of a building by its tenant or a person to whom the collection of rents or fees in a public market, cart-stand or slaughterhouse or of rents for shops has been framed out or leased by a municipal council. [Pondicherry Buildings (Lease and Rent Control) Act (5 of 1969), S. 2(10)]

"TENANT" means any person by whom or on whose account or behalf the rent of any premises is or, but for a special contract, would be payable, and includes—(i) a sub-tenant; (ii) any person continuing in possession after the termination of his tenancy, but does not include—(i) any person against whom an order or decree for eviction has been made, except where such decree or order for eviction is liable to be re-opened under the proviso to Section 3 of the Delhi Rent Control (Amendment) Act, 1976; (ii) any person to whom a licence as defined in Section 52 of the Indian Easements Act, 1882 has been granted. [Delhi Rent Act (33 of 1995), S. 2(n)]

One who holds land, a house, etc., by lease [T.P. Act (4 of 1882), S. 6(i)]; in the case of house, open land, etc., on rent.

The party to whom a lease is made is called the "tenant".

One who holds land by any kind of title, whether for years, for life, or in fee, is a tenant.

The word 'tenant' could not include 'subtenant'.

The expression 'tenant' includes a tenant continuing in possession after the termination of the tenancy in his favour. *Manisubrat Jain* v. *Raja Ram Vohra*, AIR 1980 SC 299, 300.

The expression 'tenant' also includes members of the family of a deceased tenant living with the deceased at the time of his death. *Purificaco* v. *Hango Vicent De Ferpetuo,* AIR 1985 Bom 202, 207.

Son of an original tenant, the tenancy being heritable, is a tenant liable to pay rent. *K.S. R. Setty* v. *L.S. Vasudevamurthy,* AIR 1977 Kant 50, 52.

'TENANT' means any person by whom or on whose account rent is payable for a building and includes the surviving spouse, or any son or daughter, of a deceased tenant who had been living with the tenant in the building as a member of the tenant's family up to the death of the tenant and person continuing in possession after the termination of the tenancy in his favour, but does not include a person placed in occupation of a building, by its tenant or a person to whom the collection of rents or fees in a public market, cart-stand or slaughter house or of rents for shops has been framed out or leased by a local authority. [A.P. Buildings (lease, Rent and Eviction) Control Act (15 of 1960), S. 2(ix) **as cited in** *Noorunnissa Begum* v. *Brij Kishore Sanghi,* (2015) 17 SCC 128, para 13].

Tenant and Licensee distinction. The fundamental difference between a tenant and a licensee is that a tenant, who has exclusive possession, has an estate in land, as opposed to a personal permission to occupy. If, however, the owner of the land proves that he never intended to accept the occupier as tenant, then the fact that the occupier pays regular seems for his occupation does not make the occupier a tenant. [*The Law of Landlord and Tenant*, 4th Edn., page 33, by EVANS & SMITH, **as cited in** *C.M. Beena* v. *P.N. Ramchandra Rao*, (2004) 3 SCC 595, 600, para 10]

Tenant at a fixed rate. The expression "*tenant at fixed rates*" means a tenant holding land the rent of which under the laws in force or the customs prevailing in the family domains is not liable to enhancement, but does not include a tenant paying rent in kind. [U.P. Act III of 1904 (Benares Family Domains), S. 2, cl. (6).]

Tenant by courtesy. The holder of an estate by courtesy.

Tenant by sufferance. After a lease is terminated if the tenant continues in possession without the consent or acquiescence of the lessor, such a tenant is a 'tenant by sufferance'. *Mogilopuvu Annapurnaiah* v. *Malampati Narsimhan Rao,* AIR 1982 AP 253, 254.

Tenant for life. A "tenant for life" of estates is one to whom lands or tenements are granted or devised, or to which he derives title by operation of law, for the term of his own life or the life of another.

Tenant for years. One who holds lands or tenements under a demise for a term of certain number of years agreed on.

Tenant from year to year. One who holds lands or tenements under a demise where no certain term has been fixed, but an annual rent has been reserved.

Tenant holding over. 'Tenant holding over' has been used in wider sense so as to include a tenant-at-sufferance. It means a tenant who holds over or continues to remain in possession of the premises after the termination of the tenancy. *Harish Chandra Golcha* v. *Jiwaji Rao Cotton Mills Ltd.,* AIR 1972

MP 150, 151. [Court fees Act (7 of 1870), S. 7(xi) (cc)]

Tenant in fee simple. One who has lands and tenements to hold to him and his heirs for ever generally absolutely.

Tenant inferior to the tenant of the first degree. 'A TENANT INFERIOR TO THE TENANT OF THE FIRST DEGREE' means a tenant holding immediately or mediately under a tenant of the first degree. [West Bengal Premises Rent Control (Temporary Provisions) Act (17 of 1950), S. 13 *Expln.* (b)]

Tenants-in-common. Have several interests, where joint tenants, whether a law or in equity, have one interest. The tenants-in-common may be entitled to equitable shares in the land in unequal shares and for interests which may be unequal in duration; different shares would be subject to different limitations and the limitation may entailed interests. [Halsbury's Laws of England, 5th Edn,, Vol. 87, para 221 **as cited in** *T. Ravi* v. *B. Chinna Narasimha,* (2017) 7 SCC 342, para 56].

Tenant of building. Where the landlord lets the residential building together with its appurtenant land, the tenant is a tenant of building. *V. Sanjeevaraya Mudaliar* v. *N. A. Ragavachari*, AIR 1969 SC 435 at 438.

Tenant of land. Where the landlord let the appurtenant land separately and retained the building, the letting is of land only and the tenant is a tenant of land. *V Sanjeevaraya Mudaliar* v. *N.A. Ragavachari*, AIR 1969 SC 435 at 438.

Tenant of the first degree. 'A TENANT OF THE FIRST DEGREE' means a tenant who does not hold under any other tenant. [West Bengal Premises Rent Control (Temporary Provisions) Act (17 of 1950), S. 13, *Expln.* (a)]

Tenant on sufferance. A tenant on sufferance is one who wrongly continues in possession after the extinction of a lawful title. There is very little difference between him and a trespasser.

Tenants-in-common. Are such as hold by several and distinct titles, but by unity of possession; because none knoweth his own severality, and therefore they all occupy promiscuously. (*Tomlin*)

Persons who hold property in common [Hindu Succession Act (30 of 1956), S. 19(b)].

Tendency. The fact or quality of tending to something. [CrPC 1973 (2 of 1974), S. 161(2)].

Tender. Offer; proposal for acceptance; offer to pay a specified sum or do certain acts; the offering of money or any other thing in satisfaction. (*Termes de la ley*; *Tomlin*)

A formal offer duly made by one party to another, especially an offer of money, or, the like, in discharge of a debt or liability especially an offer which thus fulfils the terms of the law and of the liability; an offer of a bid for contract [T.P. Act (4 of 1882), S. 55(1)(d)]; the action of tendering [C.PC (5 of 1908), O. V, R. 18]; to make a formal offer to another [Sale of Goods Act (3 of 1930), S. 50]; soft, delicate, sensitive [Indian Evidence Act (1 of 1872), S. 118]; give, present [Indian Railways Act (9 of 1890), S. 74(1)]; a vehicle attached to the rear of a locomotive for carrying a supply of fuel or water [Indian Railways Act (9 of 1890), S. 3(10)].

Tender years. The phrase "minor of tender years", used in various connections in pleadings may embrace as well minors of 20 years as of 20 months. It cannot be said absolutely what is or is not a tender age, and applying to the rule that a pleading is to be taken most strongly against the pleader, little more effect can apparently be given to the phrase "minor of tender years" than that it indicates a minor not endowed with the discretion of maturity. (*Ame. Words and Phrases*) Immature age. [Indian Evidence Act (1 of 1872), S. 118].

Tender-years doctrine. In family law, the doctrine which holds that the custody of very young children should generally be awarded to the mother in a divorce unless she is found to be unfit.

Tending. Watching over and waiting upon (the sick of helpless. [Indian Railways Act (9 of 1890), S. 55(2)].

Tenement. "TENEMENT" means a building or part of a building let or intended to be let or occupied separately. [Gujarat Education Cess Act (15 of 1962), S. 2(xiii)]

House occupied or capable of being occupied by a tenant.

The word "tenement" in legal acceptation means property held by a tenant.

Tenets. A doctrine, dogma, principle or opinion in religion, philosophy, politics or the like held by a school, sect., party or person. [Indian Evidence Act (1 of 1872), S. 49].

Tenor. The exact words of the document; the actual wording of a legal document, what appears on the face of the instrument to be the intention of the parties [Negotiable Instruments Act (26 of 1881), S. 10]; the time between the date of issue or acceptance of a note or draft and the maturity date; in ordinary parlance, it means 'purport'.

Although in ordinary language in speaking of the tenor of a document only its general purport or substance may be meant, in law the word has a strict, technical meaning. Technically it signifies an exact copy of the particular document.

"Tenor" of an instrument imports identity.

Tentative trust. A revocable trust which is created by one's deposit of money in one's own name as a trustee for another.

Tenure. The mode or system or the action or fact of holding land or tenement [CPC (5 of 1908), O. XXI, R. 3]; time of holding; [Cardamom Act (42 of 1965), S. 7(4), *Prov.*]; [Salarjung Museum Act (26 of 1961), S. 13].

Tenure-holder. "Tenure-holder" means all or any of the holders of a tenure.

TENURE-HOLDER is an individual or a person who is the "holder of the holding" and the fact that the land is not recorded in the name of that person is of no consequence. *Upper Ganges Sugar Mills Ltd.* v. *Civil Judge Bijner,* AIR 1970 All 130, at 134, 135 (FB).

Tenure of office. Period fixed for the holding of the office.

Terabyte. 1000 gigabytes. (*Matisse Enzer Glossary of Internet Terms*)

Term. Appointed limit; limited period; period during which university, school, or judicature is at work.

A fixed period; a determined or prescribed time [IPC (45 of 1860), Ss. 40 and 53A(2)]; limiting condition, condition or stipulation, as to what is proposed to be granted or done [IPC (45 of 1860), S. 29, *Expln.* (1), ill.]; an expression [Negotiable Instruments Act (26 of 1881), S. 4, ill.].

Term loan. "TERM LOAN" means a loan advanced to an agriculturist for meeting outlay relating to the replacement or maintenance of wasting assets including machineries or for capital investment designed to increase the crop output and is repayable within any period exceeding fifteen months but not exceeding twenty years. [West Bengal Agricultural Credit Operations Act (34 of 1973), S. 2(i)]

Term loans. A loan may be made for a specified period (a term loan). In such a case, repayment is due at the end of the specified period and, in the absence of any express provision or implication to the contrary, no further demand for repayment is necessary. [Chitty on Contracts, Vol. II, 30th Edn., p. 913 as cited in *Keshavlal Khemchand and Sons Private Limited* v. *Union of India*, (2015) 4 SCC 770, para 31].

Advances/Loans made by creditors to businessmen and industrialists are generally not repayable on demand but repayable in accordance with a fixed time schedule agreed upon by the parties known as "term loans" [*Keshavlal Khemchand and Sons Private Limited v. Union of India*, (2015) 4 SCC 770, para 31].

The expression 'term loan' in context of banking parlance implies the grant of loan for a fixed term. [*Canara Bank* v. *P.R. N. Upadhyaya*, AIR 1998 SC 3000).

Term of art. Word or phrase having specific significance in a particular art, craft or department of knowledge i.e. technical term. [Indian Succession Act (39 of 1925), S. 74].

Term of office. "TERM OF OFFICE" means,— (a) in relation to a person who is a member at the commencement of this Act, the period beginning with such commencement and ending with the date on which his seat becomes vacant; (b) in relation to a new member,—(i) where such new member is the member of the Council of States elected in the biennial election, or nominated to that House, the period beginning with the date of publication of the notification in the Official Gazette notifying his name under S. 71 of the Representation of People Act (43 of 1951), or (ii) where such new member is a member of the House of the People elected in a general election held for the purpose of constituting a new House of the People, the period beginning with the date of publication of the notification of the Election Commission under S. 73 of the said Act; or (iii) where such new member is a member of either House of Parliament elected in bye-election to that House or a member nominated to the House of the People the period beginning with the date of his election referred to in S. 67-A of the said Act or, as the case may be, the date of his nomination. [Salary, Allowances and Pension of Members of Parliament Act (30 of 1954), S. 2(e)]

"Term of office" means the period or limit of time during which the incumbent is permitted to hold.

Term of years. An estate for years is an interest in lands or tenements for some determinate and fixed period, the right to the possession of the lands being acquired by contract.

Terminable. Liable to terminate or be terminated. [T.P. Act (4 of 1882), S. 106].

Terminable interest. An interest that may be terminated upon the lapse of time or upon the occurrence of some condition.

Terminal. A device that allows you to send commands to a computer somewhere else. At a minimum, this usually means a keyboard and a display screen and some simple circuitry. Usually you will use terminal software in a personal computer—The software pretends to be (emulates) a physical terminal and allows you to type commands to a computer somewhere else. (*Matisse Enzer Glossary of Internet Terms*)

The word "terminal" refers not to the destination or origin of the goods but to the *termini* of the Municipal limits. 'Terminus' means the point to which motion or action tends; goal; end finishing point; sometimes that from which it starts; starting point. An end; extremity; the point at which something comes to an end. *Central India Spinning and Weaving and Manufacturing Co. Ltd. The Express Mills* v. *Municipal Committee Wardha*, AIR 1958 SC 341, 347.

Terminal charges. Railway charges for loading, unloading, and otherwise handling goods entrusted to them for transportation.

Terminal tax. Taxes leviable on goods 'imported or exported' from municipal limits denoting thereby that they are connected with the traffic of goods.

Terminals. "TERMINALS" includes charges in respect of stations, sidings, wharves, depots, warehouses, cranes and other similar matters, and of any services rendered thereat. [Indian Railways Act (9 of 1890), S. 3(14)]

As the wharfage and demurrage are charges in respect of goods unloaded from wagons and kept at the station, and also in respect of goods kept on platforms of the station, the said charges are charges in respect of the station and they are "terminals" within the meaning of the definition. *Raichand Amulakh Shah* v. *Union of India*, AIR 1964 SC 1268, 1271. [Indian Railways Act (9 of 1890), S. 3(14) and 46C (d) and (h)]

Terminated. Brought or come to a close. [Indian Contract Act (9 of 1872), S. 162].

Termination. The expression 'termination' contained in the order of delegation is used in the limited sense of simple contractual termination and not termination by way of removal or dismissal as penalty or punishment for misconduct. *Devraj Urs* v. *General Manager, Mysore State Road Transport Corporation, Bangalore,* AIR 1971 Mys 99, 106. [Road Transport Corporation Act (64 of 1950), Ss. 14, 34, and 45]

Termination installation. Means any site for the storage of oil in bulk which is capable of receiving oil from waterborne transportation, including any facility situated off-shore and linked to such site. [Merchant Shipping Act (44 of 1958), S. 352S(g) (*Inserted by Merchant Shipping (Amendment) Act, 2002*)]

Termination of a suit. A suit can ordinarily be said to terminate when there is nothing more to be done in it except execution.

Termination of services. There is clear distinction between the 'termination of services' of person under the terms of a contract governing him and the termination of his services in accordance with the terms of his conditions of service. *Hartwell Prescott Singh* v. *State of Uttar Pradesh,* AIR 1957 SC 886.

Where the appointment of a teacher and extension granted to him provides that the appointment would terminate on a specified date, and appointee has been permitted to continue upto the specified date, the services come to an end automatically. When he is informed that his services are no longer required, the same does not amount to 'termination' of his services, which would give him a right of action. [R. N. MISRA and B.K. RAY, JJ.] *The Managing Committee Mahavir Ucha Vidyapiths* v. *Baishnab Charan Nayak*, MLJ : YD 1978 Suppl C 987 : (1978) 46 CLT 436. [Orissa Education Act (15 of 1969), S. 10]

Termination of the present hostilities. Means such date as the Central Government may, by notification in the Official Gazette, declare to be the date on which the said hostilities terminated. [War Injuries (Compensation Insurance) Act (23 of 1943), S. 2(ff)]

Termination—removal. 'Termination' is interchangeable with the word 'removal'. *Managing Committee of the Digambar College, Dibai* v. *Vice Chancellor, Meerut University,* AIR 1975 All 445, 448.

Terminus. "Terminus" means the point to which motion or action tends, goal, end, finishing, point; sometimes that from which it starts; starting point. An end; extremity; the point at which something comes to an end. *Empress Mills* v. *Municipal Committee Wardha*, AIR 1958 SC 341, 347.

Terminus a quo. "*Terminus a quo*" is the point or place from which the grantee of a private right of way is to set out any order to use the way.

Place of beginning; point of beginning.

Terminus ad quem. "*Terminus ad quem*" is the place where a private right of way ends.

"Terminus", "terminal" and "terminal tax". "Terminus" means the point to which main action tends, goal, end, finishing point, the point at which something comes to an end. The word "terminal" in connection with transportation means the fixed beginning or ending point of a given run. Thus, a terminal tax could be levied only by the Corporation or the State which is the final destination of the goods sent from any other area. *Man Mohan Tuli* v. *Municipal Corporation of Delhi*, AIR 1981 SC 991.

Terms and conditions of service. The words 'terms and conditions of service' in Art. 309, Constitution of India may not include conditions regulating recruitment or initial appointment. But once recruitment or appointment has taken place, all disciplinary matters, including terms relating to removal from service and dismissal, would be governed by the conditions of service applicable to that person subject to special provisions in the constitution. *Laxmi Devi Sugar Mills Ltd.* v. *U.P. Government,* AIR 1954 All 705, 714.

The expression 'terms and conditions of service' means tenure of service. *D. C. Saxena* v. *State of Haryana*, AIR 1987 SC 1463, 1466.

Terms cash. "Terms cash" as used in a bill of goods purchased, in which the words stand by themselves, mean *prima facie* that the sale is for cash, but may be shown to have been used in a different meaning by the parties, in accordance with a usage by which the word had a different meaning, as only requiring a cash payment after the expiration of a given time.

Terms of contract. The expression 'terms" must relate to statements, assertions, or representations contained in a written contract which relate to the subject matter of the contract and to something to be done or not to be done under the contract and has no application to a provision in the nature of a condition precedent to the very existence or formation of a contract. *P.S. Bhatt* v. *V.R. Thakkar,* AIR 1972 Bom 365, 367. [Indian Evidence Act (1 of 1872), Ss. 91 and 92]

Territorial. Relating to or in connection with a part of a country or territory. [CrPC 1973 (2 of 1974), S. 7].

Territorial nexus. The standing invitations in respect of the prize competition, the filling up of the forms and the payment of money take place within the State of Bombay. The tax is on gambling although collected from the promoters. All these constitute sufficient territorial nexus which entitles the State of Bombay to impose a tax on the gambling that takes place within its boundaries and the law cannot be struck down on the ground of extra territorialitiy. *State of Bombay* v. *R.M.D. Chamarbangwala*, AIR 1957 SC 699, 711. [Constitution of India, Art. 245]

Territorialism. The traditional approach to choice of law, whereby the place of injury or of contract formation determines which State's law will be applied in a case. (*Black*)

Territory. The land or country belonging to or under the dominion of a ruler or State. [IPC (45 of 1860) and Art. 1(2), Constitution of India, S. 18].

Territory of a state. Comprises its ports and harbours, the mouths of its rivers, and its landlocked bays. By the usage of nations, the territorial jurisdictions extend also to a marine league seawards. This belt of sea is known as territorial waters. (*Ency. of the Laws of England.*)

Territory of India. The phrase 'territory of India', wherever employed, in every Article means the territory of India for the time being as falls within Art. 1(3). *N. Masthan Sahib* v. *Chief Commissioner of Pondicherry*, AIR 1962 SC 797, 803. [Constitution of India, Art. 142]

Terror. "Terror" signifies more than "alarm" or "force". It is agitating of excessive fear, which usually benumbs the faculties. It is one of the passions the existence of which will sometimes reduce a homicide from murder to manslaughter, but it is never necessarily an element of self-defence.

Terrorism. The term "terrorism" is a concept that is commonly and widely used in everyday parlance and is derived from the Latin word "terror" which means the state of intense fear and submission to it. There is no particular form of the terror, hence, anything intended to create terror in the minds of general public in order to endanger the lives of the members and damage to public property may be termed as a terrorist act and a manifestation of terrorism. [*Yakub Abdul Razak Memon v. State of Maharashtra*, (2013) 13 SCC 1, para 809].

Use of violence for political ends. 'Terrorism' may be described as use of violence when its most important result is not merely the physical and mental damage of the victim but the prolonged psychological effect, it produces or has the potential of producing on the society as a whole. There may be death, injury, or destruction of property or even deprivation of individual liberty in the process but the extent and reach of the intended terrorist activity travels beyond the effect of an ordinary crime capable of being punished under the ordinary penal law of the land and its main objective is to overawe the Government or disturb the harmony of the society or 'terrorise' people and the society and not only those directly assaulted, with a view to disturb the even tempo, peace and tranquillity of the society and create a sense of fear and insecurity. *Madan Singh* v. *State of Bihar*, AIR 2004 SC 3317, 3324, para 16.

"Terrorism" means "the use or threat of violence to intimidate or cause panic, especially as a means of affecting political conduct."]Black's Law Dictionary (8th Edn., p. 1512) as cited in *Yakub Abdul Razak Memon v. State of Maharashtra*, (2013) 13 SCC 1, para 809].

Terrorism is the use or threatened use of force designed to bring about political change. [Brain Jenkins as cited in *Nazir Khan v. State of Delhi*, (2003) 8 SCC 461, para 15 : 2003 SCC (Cri) 2033]. See also *Yakub Abdul Razak Memon v. State of Maharashtra*, (2013) 13 SCC 1, para 826. Terrorism is the unlawful use of force or violence against persons or property to intimidate or coerce a government, the civilian population, or any segment thereof, in furtherance of political or social objectives. [FBI definition as cited in *Nazir Khan v. State of Delhi*, (2003) 8 SCC 461, para 15 : 2003 SCC (Cri) 2033]. See also *Yakub Abdul Razak Memon v. State of Maharashtra*, (2013) 13 SCC 1, para 826.

Terrorism is the premediated, deliberate, systematic murder, mayhem, and threatening of the innocent to create fear and intimidation in order to gain a political or tactical advantage, usually to influence an audience. [James M. Poland as cited in *Nazir Khan v. State of Delhi*, (2003) 8 SCC 461, para 15 : (2003) SCC (Cri) 2033]. See also *Yakub Abdul Razak Memon v. State of Maharashtra*, (2013) 13 SCC 1, para 826.

Terrorism constitutes the illegitimate use of force to achieve a political objective when innocent people are targeted. [Walter Laqueur as cited in *Nazir Khan v. State of Delhi*, (2003) 8 SCC 461, para 15 : 2003 SCC (Cri) 2033]. See also *Yakub Abdul Razak Memon v. State of Maharashtra*, (2013) 13 SCC 1, para 826.

Terrorist. "TERRORIST" means a person who indulges in wanton killing of persons or in violence or in disruption of services or means of communications essential to the community or in damaging property with a view to—

(i) putting the public or any section of the public in fear; or

(ii) affecting adversely the harmony between different religious, racial, language or regional groups or castes or communities; or

(iii) coercing or overawing the Government established by law; or

(iv) endangering the sovereignty and integrity of India. [Terrorist Affected Areas (Special Courts) Act (61 of 1984), S. 2(h)]

"TERRORIST" means any person who, with intent to over-awe the Government as by law established or to strike terror in the people or any section of the people or to alienate any section of the people or to adversely affect the harmony amongst different sections of the people, does any act or thing by using bombs, dynamite or other explosive substances or inflammable substances or firearms or other lethal weapons or poisons or noxious gases or other chemicals or any other substances (whether biological or otherwise) of a hazardous nature, in such a manner as to cause, or as is likely to cause, death of, or injuries to, any person or persons or damage to, or destruction of, property or disruption of any supplies or services essential to the life of the community.

[National Security Guard Act, 1986 (47 of 1986), S. 2(y)]

An advocate or practitioner of terror as a means of coercion. [Bengal Suppression of Terrorist Outrages (Supplementary) Act (24 of 1932), S. 1].

Terrorist act. 'Terrorist acts' are meant to destabilize the nation by challenging its sovereignty and integrity to raze the constitutional principles, to create a psyche of fear and anarchism among common people, to tear apart the secular fabric, to overthrow democratically elected government, to promote prejudice and bigotry, to demoralize the security forces, to thwart the economic progress and development and so on. Terrorism cannot be equated with a usual law and order problem within a State. [*People's Union for Civil Liberties* v. *Union of India*, AIR 2004 SC 456, 465, para 9]

"Criminal acts, including against civilians, committed with the intent to cause death or serious bodily injury, or taking of hostages, with the purpose to provoke a state of terror in the general public or in a group of persons or particular persons, intimidate a population or compel a Government or an international organization to do or to abstain from doing any act, which constitute offences within the scope of and as defined in the international conventions and protocols relating to terrorism, are under no circumstances justifiable by considerations of a political, philosophical, ideological, racial, ethic, religious or other similar nature, ..." [The United Nations Security Council in its 2004 Resolution as cited in *Yakub Abdul Razak Memon v. State of Maharashtra*, (2013) 13 SCC 1, para 816].

Whoever does any act with the intent to threaten or likely to threaten the unity, integrity, sovereignty, security, or economic security of India or with the intent to strike terror or likely to strike terror in the people or any section of the people in India or in any foreign country,—

(a) by using bombs, dynamite or other explosive substance or inflammable substance or firearms or other lethal weapons or poisonous or noxious gases or other chemicals or by any other substance (whether biological, radioactive, nuclear or otherwise) of a hazardous nature or by any other means of whatever nature to cause or likely to cause,—

(i) death of, or injury to, any person or persons; or

(ii) loss of, or damage to, or destruction of, property; or

(iii) disruption of any supplies or services essential to the life of the community in India or in any foreign country; or

(iv) damage to, the monetary stability of India by way of production or smuggling or circulation of counterfeit Indian paper currency, coin or of any other material; or

(v) damage or destruction of any property in India or in a foreign country used or intended to be used for the defence of India or in connection with any other purposes of the Government of India, any State Government or any of their agencies; or

(b) overawes by means of criminal force or the show of criminal force or attempts to do so or causes death of any public functionary or attempts to cause death of any public functionary; or

(c) detains, kidnaps or abducts any person and threatening to kill or injure such person or does any other act in order to compel the Government of India, any State Government or the Government of a foreign country or an international or inter-governmental organisation or any other person to do or abstain from doing any act,

Commit a TERRORIST ACT. [(w. e. f. 1-7-2024) Bharatiya Nyaya Sanhita, 2023 (45 of 2023), section 113(1)]

Terrorist gang. "TERRORIST GANG" means any association, other than terrorist organisation, whether systematic or otherwise which is concerned with, or involved in terrorist act. [Unlawful Activities (Prevention) Act (37 of 1967), S. 2(1)(l) *as substituted by Unlawful Activities (Prevention) Amendment Act (29 of 2004), S. 4*]

Terrorist organizations. 'TERRORIST ORGANISATION' means an organisation listed in the Schedule or an organisation operating under the same name as an organisation so listed. [Unlawful Activities (Prevention) Act (7 of 1967), S. 2(1)(m) as substituted by Unlawful Activities (Prevention) Amendment Act (29 of 2004), S. 4]

"Terrorist"; "terrorism"; "disruption" and "disruptive". *Disruption* means the act of bursting and tearing asunder. *Disruptive* means producing or resulting from or attending disruption. *Terrorism* means the act of terrorising; unlawful acts of violence committed in an organized attempt to overthrow a Government or like purposes. *Terrorist* means one who adopts or supports the policy of terrorism. The *terrorist and disruptive activities* are naturally disruptive of public place, tranquillity and development. *State of Punjab* v. *Sukhpal Singh,* AIR 1990 SC 231. [Terrorist and Disruptive Activities (Prevention) Act, 1985, S. 2(1)(c) and (f)]

Terry stop. The act of a police officer's stopping a person whose behaviour is reasonably considered suspicious and frisking that person for weapons.

Test. A critical trial; a trial of fitness or an examintion. [Sale of Goods Act (3 of 1930), S. 22]; [Arms Act (54 of 1959), S. 5(a)].

Test certificate. A Digital Signature Certificate issued by a Certifying Authority for the limited purpose of internal technical testing. Test certificates may be used by authorized persons only. (*Information Technology*)

Testament. A "testament" is a testimonial in which is contained and set forth the will of him who makes it, establishing or appointing his heirs, and disposing as he thinks fit of his property after death.

Testamenta cum duo inter se pugnantia reperiuntur, ultimum ratum est; sic est, cum duo inter se pugnantia reperiuntur in eodem testamento. When two conflicting wills are found, the last one prevails; the same principle applies when two clauses in a will are found to conflict. (*Principia legis*)

Testamenta latissimam interpretationem habere debent. Wills ought to have the broadest interpretation.

Testamentary. Relating to testament or will; of the nature of a testament. [IPC (45 of 1860), S. 31].

Testamentary capacity. Mental condition such as to admit of the making of a valid will.

Testamentary causes. Causes or matters relating to the probate of wills.

Testamentary gift. A gift which is made by will.

Testamentary guardian. A guardian appointed by the last will of the father.

A guardian appointed by a will. [Guardians and Wards Act (8 of 1890), S. 28].

Testamentary instrument. A "testamentary instrument" is one which declares the present will of the maker as to disposal of his property after death, without attempting to declare or create any rights therein prior to such event.

Testamentary intention. The principle that a person's will must reflect his true wishes.

Testamentary trust. A trust which is created by a will and takes effect when the testator dies.

Testamentum est voluntatis nostrae justa sententia, de eo quod quis post mortem suam fieri velit. A testament is the just expression of our will concerning that which any one wishes done after his death.

Testamentum omne morte consummatum. Every will is completed by death.

Testate. Having left a will.

Testator. He who makes a will or testament. One who makes a will. [CPC (5 of 1908), O. XXXI, R. 2].

Testatrix. A woman who has left a will.

Testibus deponentibus in pari numero dignioribus est credendum. When the number of witnesses is equal on both sides, the more worthy are to be believed. (*Latin for Lawyers*)

Testify. "Testifying" is making a solemn declaration on oath or affirmation for the purpose of establishing or making proof of some fact. To affirm or declare solemnly or on oath; to bear witness. [Indian Evidence Act (1 of 1872), S 118]; [Aligarh Muslim University Act (40 of 1920), Sch., item 29(4)].

The word "testify" has three definitions: (1) To make a statement or declaration in confirmation of some fact; to bear witness. (2) To give evidence or testimony in regard to a case pending in a Court or tribunal. (3) In law, to make a solemn declaration under oath or affirmation, before a tribunal, Court, Judge, or Magistrate, for the purpose of proving some fact.

Every mode of oral statement under oath or affirmation is embraced by the term "testify."

Testifying expert. An expert who is identified by a party as a potential witness at trial.

Testimoignes ne poent testifie le negative, mes l'affirmative. Witnesses cannot testify to a negative; they must testify to an affirmative.

Testimonia ponderanda sunt, non enumeranda. Proofs are to be weighed, not numbered.

Testimonial evidence. Evidence which is elicited from a witness.

Testimony. The word "testimony" in its ordinary meaning, means the statement made by a witness under oath.

Personal or documentary evidence or attestation in support of a fact or statement; hence, any form of evidence or proof. [Indian Evidence Act (1 of 1872), S. 157].

The words "EVIDENCE" AND "TESTIMONY" are synonymous in meaning, though evidence includes testimony as well as all other kinds of proof.

Testis de visu praeponderat aliis. An eye-witness is of more weight than others.

Testis incertus. A doubtful witness; a witness who testifies from hearsay.

Testis lupanaris sufficit ad factum in lupanari. (*Moor. 817*) A strumpet is a sufficient witness to a fact committed in a brothel. (*Principia legis; Latin for Lawyers*)

Testis nemo in sua causa esse potest. (*Maxim*) No one can be a witness in his own cause.

Testis occulatus unus plus valet quam auriti decem. One eye-witness is worth more than ten ear-witnesses.

TETRA. (*abbr.*) 'Terrestrial Trunked Radio. Professional radio-communication standard approved by ETSI. These types of network are generally used for business communications and communications between security forces. (*Telecommunication*)

TETRAPOL. (*abbr.*) Terrestrial Trunked Radio for security services. Professional radio-communication standard developed specially to meet the requirements of security services. (*Telecommunication*)

Text. A short passage from the Holy Books, when used with reference to Hindu Law [Hindu Minority and Guardianship Act (32 of 1956), S. 5(a)]; the actual words of a book, poem etc. in their original form or any form they have been transmitted in or transmitted into.

The word "text", in its dictionary meaning, means, "subject or theme", when an enactment amends the text of another, it amends the subject or theme of it, though sometimes it may expunge unnecessary words without altering the subject. The word 'text' is comprehensive enough to take in the subject as well as the terminology used in a statute. *Jethamanad Betab* v. *State of Delhi*, AIR 1960 SC 89, 92. [General Clauses Act (10 of 1897), S. 6-A]

Textbook. "TEXTBOOK" means any book or other printed material prescribed, recommended or otherwise approved by the Board for study in any affiliated institution. [H.P. Board of School Education Act (14 of 1968), S. 2(u)]

Textile machinery. Means the equipment employed directly or indirectly for the processing of textile fibre into yarn and for the manufacture of fabric therefrom by weaving or knitting and includes equipment used either wholly or partly for the finishing, folding or packing of textiles. [Textiles Committee Act (11 of 1963), S. 2(f)]

Textile process. The entire process from the receipt of the cotton or yarn to the final stage when it is ready to go on to the market should be included in what we call the textile process. *Workers in United Bleachers (P.) Ltd.* v. *Management of United Bleachers (P.) Ltd.,* AIR 1960 Mad 131, 132. [Industrial Disputes Act (14 of 1947), Sch. I, Item 5]

Textiles. "TEXTILES" means any fabric or cloth or yarn or garment or any other any article under wholly or in part of—(i) cotton; or (ii) wool; or (iii) silk; or (iv) artificial silk or other fibre; and includes fibre. [Textiles Committee Act (41 of 1963), S. 2(g)]

"TEXTILES" includes yarn or fabrics made either wholly, or partly of cotton, wool, jute, synthetic and artificial (man-made) fibres. [Textiles Undertakings (Nationalisation) Act (39 of 1995), S. 2(1)(k)]

The meaning of 'textile' as a noun is a fabric which is or may be woven, a fabric made by weaving, a woven fabric, or a material suitable for weaving; textile material. *Shree Meenakshi Mills* v. *Union of India*, AIR 1974 SC 366, 371.

Rayan yarn and nylon yarn are made of fibres and they come within the purview of the term "textiles". *Sirsilk Ltd.* v. *Textiles Committee*, AIR 1989 SC 317, 331. [Textiles Committee Act (41 of 1963). sec. 2(g)]

The word 'textiles' is derived from the Latin '*texere*' which means to weave and it means any woven fabric. When yarn whether cotton, silk, woolen, rayon, nylon or of any other description or made out of any other material is woven into a fabric, what comes into being is a 'textile'. *Porrits & Spencer (Asia) Ltd.* v. *State of Haryana*, AIR 1979 SC 300, 302.

Thag or Thug. A cheat; a knave; an impostor : latterly applied to a robber and assassin of a peculiar class, who rallying forth in a gang and in the characters of wayfarers either on business or pilgrimage fall in with other travellers on the road, and having gained their confidence, take a favourable opportunity of strangling them by throwing their turbans or handkerchiefs round their necks, and then plundering them and burying their bodies : it has also been applied to child stealing and robbery. (*Wil. Gloss.*)

Thakur. "THAKUR" means also *taluqdar*, *jagirdar* and *kasbati*, and such other classes of holders of estates as the Local Government may, with the previous sanction of the Governor-General in Council, declare to be thakurs for the purposes of this Act. [Bom. Act (21 of 1881), S. 3]

The. "The" is the word used before nouns, with a specifying or particularizing effect opposed to the indefinite or generalising force of "a" or "an."

The article "THE" directs what particular thing or things we are to take or assume as spoken of. It determines what particular thing is meant; that is, what particular thing we are to assume to be meant.

Article 'THE' before word 'agreement' would refer to that agreement which is implicit in the sale occasioning the export. And the agreement spoken of must be the agreement with foreign buyer. *Consolidated Coffee Ltd.* v. *Coffee Board Bangalore*, AIR 1980 SC 1468, 1482. [Central Sales Tax Act (74 of 1956), S. 5 (3)]

"THE" is the word used before nouns, with a specifying of particularising effect opposed to the indefinite or generalising force of 'a' or 'an'. It determines what particular thing is meant; that is, what particular thing one has to assume to be meant. 'The' is always mentioned to denote particular thing or a person. 'The' would, therefore, refer implicitly to a specified bank and not any bank. 'The bank' referred to in clause (*a*) to the proviso to section 138 of the Negotiable Instruments Act, 1881 (26 of 1881), would mean the drawee-bank on which the cheque is drawn and not all banks where the cheque is presented for collection including the bank of the payee, in whose favour the cheque is issued. *Shri Ishar Alloys Steels Ltd.* v. *Jayaswals NECO Ltd.*, AIR 2001 SC 1161 : 2001 AIR SCW 837.

The Company. Means the Orissa Mineral Development Company Limited, a Company formed and registered under the Companies Act and having its registered office at Chartered Bank Buildings, Calcutta in the State of West Bengal. [Bolani Ores Limited (Acquisition of Shares) and Miscellaneous Provision Act (42 of 1978), S. 2(e)]

The cost of such staff. The expression, 'the cost of such staff' occurring in Section 58-A of Bombay Prohibition Act (25 of 1949), includes all the costs incurred by State Government for the purpose of disbursing pay and other allowances to the Government employees posted for supervision, whether recovered in advance or in due course the additional amounts which become recoverable on account of upward revision of pay scales with retrospective effect. [*Govt. of Maharashtra* v. *Deokar's Distillery*, AIR 2003 SC 1216]

The date of the said order. 'The date of the said order' within the meaning of Rule 8 of the Payment of Wages (Procedure) Rules, is the date on which the order is actually made, if it is made in the presence of the parties or after previous notice to them of the date on which the order will be made, or it is made in the absence of parties and without previous intimation to them, the date on which it is communicated to them or on which they acquire actual or constructive knowledge of the order. *Sitaram Mulchand Transport Co.* v. *Bashir Ahmad Stattoo,* AIR 1961 Bom 73, 74. [Payment of Wages (Procedure) Rules 1957, R. 8(3), Prov.]

The day of acceptance. Means,—

(a) the day of the actual delivery of goods or the rendering of services; or

(b) where any objection is made in writing by the buyer regarding acceptance of goods of services within thirty days from the day of the delivery of goods or the rendering of services, the day on which such objection is removed by the supplier. [Interest on Delayed Payments to Small Scale and Ancillary Industrial Undertakings Act (32 of 1993), S. 2(b) *Expln.* (i)]

The day of deemed acceptance. Means, where no objection is made in writing by the buyer regarding acceptance of goods or services within thirty days from the day of the delivery of goods or the rendering of services, the day of the actual delivery of goods or the rendering of services. [Interest on Delayed Payments to Small Scale and Ancillary Industrial Undertakings Act (32 of 1993), S. 2(b) *Expln.* (ii)]

The expected revenue from charges. In this section, "the expected revenue from charges" means the total revenue which a licensee is expected to recover from charges for the level of forecast supply used in the determination under sub-section (5) above in any financial year in respect of goods or services supplied to customers pursuant to a licensed activity. [A.P. Electricity Reforms Act (30 of 1998), S. 26, *Explanation* (a) **as cited in** *Sai Bhaskar Iron Limited* v. *A.P. Electricity Regulatory Common,* (2016) 9 SCC 134, para 8].

The owner or the person in possession of the property. The phrase "the owner or the person in possession of the property" ought to be construed as indicating the person who is in actual occupation of the premises to be requisitioned. *Jhansi Electric Supply Co. Ltd.* v. *District Magistrate,* AIR 1968 All 135, 138.

The ozone layer. "THE OZONE LAYER" means the layer of atmospheric ozone above the planetary boundary layer. [Vienna Convention for the Protection of the Ozone Layer, (1985), Art. 1.1]

The premises. Premises means any land not being used for agricultural purposes and any building or a part of a building let separately. *Raja Bahadur Motilal Bombay Mills Ltd.* v. *Govind Ram Brothers (P) Ltd.*, AIR 1974 SC 1708, 1712.

The relevant date. Under sub-section (8) of Section 530, for the purposes of Section 530: the expression 'THE RELEVANT DATE' means—

(i) in the case of a company ordered to be wound up compulsorily, the date of the appointment (or first appointment) of a provisional liquidator, or if no such appointment was made, the date of the winding up order, unless in either case the company had commenced to be wound up voluntarily before that date; and

(ii) in any case where sub-clause (*i*) does not apply, the date of the passing of the resolution for the voluntary winding up of the company. [Companies Act (1 of 1956), S. 530(8)]

The result of the election has been materially affected. The words 'the result of the election has been materially affected' indicate that the result should not be judged by the mere increase or decrease in the total number of votes secured by the returned candidate but by proof of the fact that the wasted votes would have been distributed in such a manner between contesting candidates as would have brought about the defeat of the returned candidate. *Vashist Narain Sharma* v. *Dev Chandra*, AIR 1954 SC 513, 515. [Representation of the People Act (43 of 1951), S. 100(1)(d)]

The service. The term 'the service' means judicial service. *Chandramohan* v. *State of U.P.*, AIR 1966 SC 1987, 1994. [Constitution of India, Arts. 233(2), 234, 236]

The State. In this part, unless the context otherwise requires, "THE STATE" includes the Government and Parliament of India and the Government and the Legislature of each of the States and all local or other authorities within the territory of India or under the control of the Government of India. [Constitution of India, Art. 12]

The Territory of India. THE TERRITORY OF INDIA shall comprise—

(a) The territories of the States;

(b) The Union territories specified in the First Schedule; and

(c) Such other territories as may be acquired. [Constitution of India, Art. 1(3)]

The two companies. Means—

(i) Parel Investment and Trading Private Limited, a company within the meaning of the Companies Act, 1956, having its registered office at 53/57, Lakshmi Insurance Buildings, Sir Phirozshah Mehta Road, Bombay-1;

(ii) Domestic Gas Private Limited, a company within the meaning of the Companies Act 1956, having its registered office at 3464, Rashtrapti Road, Secunderabad. [Parel Investments and Trading Private Limited and Domestic Gas Private Limited (Taking over of Management) Act (29 of 1979), S. 2(f)]

The undertaking. Means the undertaking in India of the Kosangas company the right, title and interest to which have, on the dissolution of that firm, vested in Gocul Gas Private Limited as sole proprietor thereof. [Kosangas Company (Acquisition of Undertaking) Act (28 of 1979), S. 2(e)]

Theatre. "THEATRE" includes any premises intended principally or wholly for the presentation of moving pictures, dramatic performances or stage entertainments. [Weekly Holidays Act (18 of 1942), S. 2(e)]

A building for dramatical performance usually with stage at one end [Indian Contract Act (9 of 1872), S. 56, ill. (e)]; [Weekly Holidays Act (18 of 1942), Preamble].

Theft. "Whoever, intending to take dishonestly any moveable property out of the possession of any person without that person's consent, moves that property in order to such taking, is said to commit THEFT". [IPC (45 of 1860), S. 378] [(w. e. f. 1-7-2024) repealed & replaced by Bharatiya Nyaya Sanhita, 2023 (45 of 2023), section 303(1)]

For the purposes of this sub-section "theft" includes trick theft, theft from vehicle, dwelling house or business premises, cargo theft, pick pocketing, theft through card skimming, shoplifting and theft of Automated Teller Machine. [(w. e. f. 1-7-2024) Bharatiya Nyaya Sanhita, 2023 (45 of 2023), section 112(1), Explanation]

Theft (ingredients). Before the offence of theft is made out, it has to be established that (1) the accused was not legally entitled to the property alleged to be stolen and that the complainant was wrongfully deprived of the property, (2) the means employed to take possession were unlawful and (3) the taking was without consent. *Pooran Mal* v. *Sadho Ram,* MLJ : QD (1961-1965) Vol IV C2188 : 1965 All LJ 214 : 1964 All CrR 483 [IPC (45 of 1860), S. 378]

Theft and Robbery. Theft is robbery if, in order to the committing of the theft, or in committing the theft, or in carrying away or attempting to carry away property obtained by the theft, the offender, for that end voluntarily causes or attempts to cause to any person death or hurt or wrongful restraint, or fear of instant death or of instant hurt, or of instant wrongful restraint. [(w. e. f. 1-7-2024) Bharatiya Nyaya Sanhita, 2023 (45 of 2023), section 309(2)]

Dispossessing one of the movables without his consent and with a dishonest intention is "theft". If in the act of dispossession, the person in possession of the movable resists and the offender causes or attempt to cause death, hurt or wrongful resistance or fear of instant death or instant hurt or of instant wrongful restraint to any person, then the offence will be "robbery". [*Devassia Joseph* v. *State of Kerala,* MLJ : YD (1982), p.1295 : (1982) KLT 20] [IPC (XLV of 1860), Ss. 394 and 379]

Then. The word "then" means, when used as a word of reasoning, "in that event", or "in that case", or "therefore". It also means "at that time" or "immediately afterwards".

The word "then" as an adverb means at that time, referring to a time specified, either past or future. It has no power in itself to fix a time.

The word 'then' in S. 235(2) stands for what is subsequently to follow in point of sequence. *Jangir Singh* v. *State,* AIR 1952 Pepsu 161. [CrPC 1973 (2 of 1974), S. 235(2)]

Then and there. "Then and there" as used in indictments specifying the time and place of the commission of the crime, is sufficient as the allegation that all the acts alleged in the indictment occurred at such time. "It is undoubtedly a rule in criminal pleadings that every material fact must be alleged with the venue and be charged as done at some time and place. This is usually done after the time and place have been definitely stated, by the words 'then and there'.

Then in force. "Then in force" as used in an Act providing that the provisions of the Act should not apply to any actions commenced nor to any cases where the rights of action should have accrued before the time when the Act took effect, but that the same should remain subject to the "laws then in force" means the laws in force when the statute was passed and has no reference to the laws in force at the time of the accrual of a cause of action.

Therapeutic. "To prevent, to guard against it, before, in medicine, preventive protecting against disease."; guarding against disease, a preventive of disease; a condom; preventive treatment against diseases." [Webster's New 20th Century Dictionary as cited in Commissioner of *Central Excise v. Wockhardt Life Sciences Limited*, (2012) 5 SCC 585, para 30].

"Therapeutic" and "prophylactic"."To prevent, the guard against it, before, in medicine, preventive protecting against disease."; "Guarding against disease, a prevention of disease; a condom; preventive treatment against diseases." And; "Serving to cure or heal, curative concerned in discovering and applying remedies for diseases." [Webster's New 20th Century Dictionary and Chambers English Dictionary as cited in *Commissioner of Central Excise v. Wockhardt Life Science Limited*, (2012) 5 SCC 585, para 30].

Therapeutic practice. 'Therapeutic practice' means "contributing to use of disease". [*Mohd.Sahabuddin v. State of Assam*, (2012) 13 SCC 491, para 11].

Therapeutic purposes. "THERAPEUTIC PURPOSES" means systematic treatment of any disease or the measures to improve health according to any particular method or modality. [Transplantation of Human Organs Act (42 of 1994), S. 2(p)]

There be, and hereby is granted. "There be, and hereby is granted" as used in an Act which declares that there be, and hereby is, granted certain lands, etc., should be construed as words which import a grant *in praesenti*, and not in future, or the promise of a grant.

There is hereby appropriated. The phrase "there is hereby appropriated the sum" etc., is customarily used in bills appropriating money for the payment of salary and other expenses of government.

Thereafter. "Thereafter' as used in a note promising to pay on demand and after a certain date, and interest at a certain rate thereafter, limits the interest period; for, without it, interest would have run from the date of the note.

Subsequently; after that in time, order or sequence. [CPC (5 of 1908), S. 35(1)].

Thereby. By that means; in consequence of that, or because of that; through that. [IPC (45 of 1860), S. 28, *Expln.* II].

Thereby causes loss or injury to the consumer. The expression occurring in S. 36-A MRTP Act (54 of 1969) means 'actual loss and injury to the consumers must be caused thereby'. *Hindustan Ciba Giegy* v. *Union of India*, (2003) 1 SCC 134, para 10.

Therefor. For it or for them; for that thing or action; for those things or actions.

Therein. In that thing or circumstance.

Thereon. On that.

Theretofore. The word "theretofore" as used in an indictment alleging that defendant on a certain date, having theretofore fraudulently devised a scheme to defraud, etc., means "before then."

Thereunder. Under that or it.

Thereunto. To that or them.

Thereupon. Upon that; in consequence of that. [CPC (5 of 1908), O. XIV, R. 1(5)]; [Employment of Children Act (26 of 1938), S. 3A]; [National Bank for Agriculture and Rural Development Act (16 of 1981), S. 10].

"Thereupon" is defined as meaning (1) upon that; (2) in consequence of that; (3) immediately after that and without delay.

Thief. "Thieves" in law, as in common parlance, means those who have committed larceny.

One who commits theft. [Indian Evidence Act (1 of 1872), S. 114(a), ill.].

Thika Tenant. "Thika Tenant" means any person who occupies, whether under a written lease or otherwise, land under another person, and is or but for a special contract would be liable to pay rent, at a monthly or at any other periodical rate, for that land to that another person and has created or acquired by purchase or gift any structure on such land for residential, manufacturing or business purpose and includes the successors-in-interest of such person. [Calcutta Thika and Other Tenancies and Lands (Acquisition and Regulation) Act, 1981 [West Bengal Act (37 of 1981)] S. 3(8) as cited in *Nemai Chandra Kumar v. Mani Square Limited*, (2015) 14 SCC 203, para 21].

Thin. "Thin" is defined as slender, slight or flimsy.

Thing. The word "thing" is of extensive signification, and in common parlance may intend all matters of substance, in contradistinction to person.

An admission on a point of law is not an admission of a "thing" so as to make the admission matter of estoppel within the meaning of S. 115 of the Indian Evidence Act (1 of 1872).

Thing adjudged. "Thing adjudged" is said of that which has been decided by a final judgment, from which there can be no appeal, either because the appeal did not lie, or because the time fixed by law for appealing has elapsed, or because it has been confirmed on the appeal.

Things in Indian Evidence Act (1 of 1872), S. 115] cover estoppel in connection with representation only of "things." That is, facts, and not also representations in law.

Things done and omitted to be done. The words 'things done and omitted to be done' in S. 1(3) mean acts or omissions and all that the expression saves is the liability or the immunity, as the case may be, in respect of such acts or omission. *Ram Prasad Shaw* v. *Govt. of West Bengal,* AIR 1955 Cal 374. [Preventive Detention Act (4 of 1950), S. 1(3)]

Think. To hold or form an opinion; to judge; to consider; to believe.

Third degree. Term used to describe the process of securing a confession or information from a suspect or prisoner by prolonged questioning, the use of threats, or actual violence. (*Black*)

Third party. "THIRD PARTY" used in relation to a firm or to a partner therein means any person who is not a partner in the firm. [Indian Partnership Act (9 of 1932), S. 2(d)]

"THIRD PARTY" means a person other than the person making a request for information and includes a public authority. [Right to Information Act (22 of 2005), S. 2(n)]

The person, who is not a party to a contract of agreement or any matter in which the actual parties are concerned [Indian Partnership Act (9 of 1932), Ss. 2(d) and 27]; a party numbered as third [T.P. Act (4 of 1882), S. 60A].

The expression "third party" does not take within its sweep anybody and everybody involved in an accident wherein a vehicle insured is involved. The insurer has no liability in respect of a gratuitous passenger in a goods vehicle. *Jitanandana Mohanty* v. *Artabrana Misra,* AIR 1992 Ori 110, 115.

Third Party Harassment. Refers to a situation where sexual harassment occurs as a result of an act or omission by any third party or outsider, who is not an employee or a student of the TI, but a visitor to the TI in some other capacity or for some other purpose or for some other purpose or reason. [All India Council for Technical Education (Gender Sensitization, Prevention and Prohibition of Sexual Harassment of Women Employees and Students and Redressal of Grievances in Technical Educational Institutions) Regulations, 2016, Regn. 2(m)].

Third party information. "THIRD PARTY INFORMATION" means any information dealt with by an intermediary in his capacity as an intermediary. [Information Technology Act (21 of 2000), S. 79(3)

Expln. as Substituted by amending Act (10 of 2009), S. 40]

Third party risks. A form of insurance to cover the death or injury to other parties. In motor insurance, it is compulsory for cover to be obtained for the death or injury of other persons.

Third person. The words "third person" include all who are not parties to the obligation or transaction concerning which the phrase is used.

One who is a stranger to transaction, instrument or proceeding [T.P. Act (4 of 1882), S. 60]; [Indian Contract Act (9 of 1872), S. 182]; one who is numbered as third [Indian Contract Act (9 of 1872), S. 132].

Third reading. The final reading of a Bill in Parliament or The State Legislature before it is passed into law.

Thought disorders. 'Thought disorders' are unusual or dysfunctional ways of thinking. One form of thought disorder is called "disorganized thinking". This is when a person has trouble organizing his or her thoughts or connecting them logically, a person with a thought disorder might make up meaningless words, or "neologisms". [*Veer Pal Singh v. Secretary, Ministry of Defence*, (2013) 8 SCC 83, para 14.1].

Thoroughfare. A public way or street.

The term "thoroughfare", in its ordinary sense, cannot be applied to road that has no outlet at one end thereof.

For a place to be thoroughfare, there must be unobstructed transit. That is to say, the place must be used as a passage for the people to pass through. *Antarjami Mohanty* v. *State of Orissa,* AIR 1951 Ori 51.

The essential idea of a thoroughfare is the right of the public to pass and repass over it. It is not essential that the public should have a right to ride or drive over it, it is enough if they have a right to walk across but the right to pass and repass is essential. *Public Prosecutor* v. *K.G. Sivaswamy,* AIR 1954 Mad 249.

Thread of a stream. The thread of a stream is the middle line of a channel; that is, of the hollow bed of running water, when the water is at its ordinary stages.

Threat. A threat in criminal law is a menace or declaration of one's purpose or intention to work injury to the person, property or rights of another.

Declaration of one's purpose or intention to work injury to the person, property or right of another with a view to restraining such person's freedom of action [Indian Evidence Act (1 of 1872), S. 24]; a source of danger.

Where striking employees had been enjoined from interfering with other employees by the use of threats or intimidation, a simple request to do or not to do a thing made by one or more of a body of strikers under circumstances calculated to convey a threatening intimidation with a design to hinder or obstruct employees in the performance of their duties, is a direct threat and intimidation, and will be punished as such.

Mere vulgar and abusive epithets do not constitute "threats".

The language, in order to amount to a threat, need not necessarily be aimed at causing bodily injury or hurt. It is enough if the language is calculated to cause injury to the reputation so as to restrain the freedom of action of that person. *Damayanti* v. S. *Vaney,* AIR 1966 Bom 19, 27.

Threat : Menace. We may be threatened with either small or great evils; but we are menaced only with great evils. One individual threatens to strike another; a general menaces the enemy with an attack. We are menaced by persons only : a person is threatened with a look; he is menaced with a prosecution by his adversary.

A threat "is any menace of such a nature and extent as to unsettle the mind of the person on whom it operates and to take away from his acts that free, voluntary action which alone constitutes consent."

Threat of serious injury. "THREAT OF SERIOUS INJURY" means a clear and imminent danger of serious injury. [Custom Tariff Act (51 of 1975), S. 8B(6)(d)]

Threaten. Seem to impend evil (as) threaten person with penalty or prosecution or punishment.

To intimidate by threats. [Indian Contract Act (9 of 1872), S. 15].

Threatened species. "Threatened species" are those likely to become endangered "within a foreseeable time." [*T.N. Godavarma Thirumulpad v. Union of India*, (2012) 4 SCC 362, para 48].

Threatening behaviour. An offence committed towards other person by threatening, abusing or using insulting words.

Through. Between distant or important points, without regard to intervening spaces (as) through journey; through passenger; through traffic; through train, etc.

By the instrumentality of. [CPC (5 of 1908), O. XVI, R. 16(2)].

"Through" does always mean from end to end or from side to side, but frequently means simply within.

In common parlance, the word 'through' connotes 'medium', agency', or 'instrument'. The word is also used to express 'direction' or to indicate and emphasise intervening or intermediate state. *Rajnath Bajaj* v. *Public Commission,* AIR 1955 MB 56.

"THROUGH". For the removal of doubts, it is hereby clarified that the expression 'through' shall mean and include and shall be deemed to have always meant and included "by means of", "in consequence of" or "by reason of". [*Explanation 4* to section 9(1)(i) of the Income-tax Act, 1961 (43 of 1961) as inserted (w.r.e.f. 1-4-1962) by the Finance Act, 2012]

Through traffic. "THROUGH TRAFFIC", means traffic which is carried over the railways of two or more railway administrations [Indian Railways Act (9 of 1890), S. 3(12)].

Throughout the territory of India. The words 'throughout the territory of India' in Art. 19(1)(d), Constitution of India indicate that free movement from one state to another within the Union is protected. *A. K. Gopalan* v. *State of Madras*, AIR 1950 SC 27.

Thrown away votes. Votes polled by a person can be regarded as 'thrown away votes', only where the electors concerned have knowledge or notice that the person is ineligible for filling the seat. *Chandappa* v. *Laxman Naik,* AIR 1967 Mys 182 190.

Thug. "Whoever, at any time after the passing of this Act, shall have been habitually associated with any other or others for the purpose of committing robbery or child-stealing by means of or accompanied with murder, is a THUG". [IPC (45 of 1860), S. 310]

Thuggery. Practices of the Thugs.

Thus enforce his rights. These words in Indian Contract Act (9 of 1872), S. 28, mean the enforcement "by the usual legal proceedings in the ordinary tribunals."

Ticket. "TICKET" (in the Railways Act) includes a single ticket, a return ticket and a season ticket. [Indian Railways Act (9 of 1890), S. 3(16)]

"TICKET" means the share of a subscriber in a chit. [Chit Fund Act (40 of 1982), S. 2(s)]

"TICKET" means person desirous of travelling on a railway shall upon payment of the fare, be supplied with a ticket by a railway servant or an agent authorised in this behalf and such ticket shall contain the following particulars, namely (i) the date of issue; (ii) the class of carriage, (iii) the place from and the place to which it is issued and (iv) the amount of the fare. [Indian Railways Act (24 of 1989), S. 50, cl. (1)]

"TICKET" means a single journey ticket or any half of a return ticket and excludes season ticket. Indrail pass ticket and special ticket for a reserved carriage or a tourist car/saloon or a special train. [Railway Passengers (Cancellation of Tickets and Refund of Fares) Rules, 1990, R. 2(9)]

A slip usually of paper or cardboard, bearing the evidence of the holder's title to some service or privilege, to which it admits him. [Indian Evidence Act (1 of 1872), S. 106, ill. (b)].

Card or paper securing admission to its holder (as) in a theatre, or railway or for a lottery, etc.

Document giving particulars of shares sold and given to a purchaser by his broker.

The word "ticket" has no legal or other fixed and determinate meaning. There are tickets of various description and for various purposes, such as lottery tickets, playhouse tickets, or admission tickets at public exhibitions or private parties, or to a seat in a stage, or for a passage in a steam-boat, etc.

Tidal land. 'TIDAL LAND' means such parts of the bed or shore of the tidal water as are covered and uncovered by the flow and ebb of the tide at ordinary spring tides together with the adjoining bed or shore not exceeding two furlongs in distance from the spring tide mark. [Gujarat Khar Lands Act, 1963 (17 of 1964), S. 2(h)]

Tidal water. "TIDAL WATER" means any part of the sea and any part of a river within the ebb and flow of the tide at ordinary spring tides and not being a harbour. [Merchant Shipping Act (44 of 1958), S. 3(49)]

"TIDAL WATER" means any part of the sea or river within the flow and ebb of the tide at ordinary spring tides. [Gujarat Khar Lands Act, 1963, (17 of 1964), S. 2(i)]

Tie-in arrangement. Includes any agreement requiring a purchaser of goods, as a condition of such purchase, to purchase some other goods. [Competition Act, 2002 (12 of 2003), S. 3(4), *Expln.*(a)]

Tie-in-clause. Tie-in-clause requires the licensee to buy even unpatented materials from the licensor in licensing agreements of patent. (*Patents*)

Tie line. Means a line for the transfer of electricity between two power systems together with switchgear and other works necessary to, and used for, the control of such line. [Electricity (Supply) Act (54 of 1948), S. 2(11B)]

Tie-out-clause. Tie-out-clause requires the licensee not to buy material from competitors in licencing agreements of patents. (*Patents*)

Tied product. A less desirable product that must be purchased in order to be able to purchase a more desirable tying product.

Tier-II capital. Includes the following —

(a) preference shares other than those which are compulsorily convertible into equity;

(b) revaluation reserves at discounted rate of fifty five per cent;

(c) general provisions and loss reserves to the extent these are not attributable to actual diminution in value or identifiable potential loss in any specific asset and are available to meet unexpected losses, to the extent of one-and-one-fourth per cent of risk weighted assets;

(d) hybrid debt capital instruments; and

(e) subordinated debt,

to the extent the aggregate does not to exceed Tier-I capital. [Non-Banking Financial Companies Prudential Norms (Reserve Bank) Directions, 1998. Para 2 (1) (xx)].

Ties. A bond that constrains or restrains; connecting link. [Hindu Adoptions and Maintenance Act (78 of 1956), S. 12].

Till. A money box etc. in a shop or bank in which cash for daily transaction is temporarily kept; to the time of; to.

Tillage. "Tillage" means husbandry; the cultivation of the land, particularly by the plough.

Timber. "Timber" includes trees when they have fallen or have been felled, and all wood whether cut up or fashioned or hollowed out for any purpose or not. [Indian Forest Act (16 of 1927), S. 2(6)].

Wood meant for building or such like use. [T.P. Act (4 of 1882), S. 3].

The word "timber" of commerce is squared sticks of wood used in building. The trees from which they were cut became known as "timber tress". The word "timber" may mean wood suitable for building houses or ships or for use in carpentry, etc,; trees cut and squared, or capable of being squared and cut into beams, rafters, planks, boards, etc.; growing trees, yielding wood suitable for constructive uses; trees generally; woods.

Having regard to the use to which *Babul* tree is put in India, it would come within the scope of the expression "timber" and its cutting down by a lessee or mortgagee would amount to an act of waste.

The subsidiary of Eucalyptus Tree sold in heaps after the '*Ballies* and Poles' are separated cannot be called timber. *Mukesh Kumar Aggravel & Co.* v. *State of M.P.*, AIR 1988 SC 563, 566.

Time-barred. Right barred on account of non-action for the period prescribed under the law of limitation.

Time being. The phrase "for the time being" may, according to its context mean the time present, or denote a single period of time; but its general sense is that of time indefinite, and refers to an indefinite state of facts which will arise in the future, and which may (and probably will) vary from time to time.

Time bomb. A logic bomb that is specifically triggered by a temporal even (a predetermined date/time). A logic bomb that is triggered by reaching some preset time, either once or periodically. A variant of the Trojan horse in which malicious code is inserted to be triggered later. (*Cyber Law*)

Time deposits. For the purposes of section 80TTA of Act 43 of 1961, 'time deposits' means the deposits repayable on expiry of fixed periods. [*Explanation* to section 80TTA of the Income-tax Act, 1961 (43 of 1961) as inserted (w.e.f. 1-4-2013) by the Finance Act, 2012(23 of 2012)]

For the purposes of this section, "Time Deposits" means the deposits repayable at the expiry of the fixed periods. [Income-tax Act (43 of 1961), S. 80-TTA(2), Explanation].

Time draft. A *draft* that is payable on a specified date in the future.

Time immemorial. From time whereof the memory of man runneth not to the contrary.

Time liabilities. Means liabilities which are not demand liabilities. [Banking Regulation Act (10 of 1949), S. 5(f)]

Time limited by law. The period fixed by law after which an action will not lie in any Court or before any authority. [CPC (5 of 1908), O. XXII, R. 3(2)].

Time loan. A loan with a specified due date, and such a loan typically cannot be repaid before maturity without incurring a penalty.

Time note. A note which is payable only at a specified time and not on demand.

Time out. A security feature that logs off a user if any entry is not made at the terminal within a specified period of time. (*Information Technology*)

(1) A specific interval in which an event must occur or the operation is considered in error or ended is called a 'time-out.' (2) The act of allowing this interval to elapse is called a 'time-out.' (*Computer*)

Time out of mind. Time beyond legal memory.

Time policy. (*In Marine Insurance*) Policy in respect of goods in transit, and limited to a specified period.

A time policy as the term is used in the law of marine insurance is a policy on a vessel for any prescribed time which covers the vessel during such time on any voyage she may undertake.

A "policy on time" as the term is used in mar- ine insurance insures on specific voyage but covers any voyage within the prescribed time."

Time requisite. The expression "time requisite" in S. 12(2) of the Limitation Act (36 of 1963) does not mean the time actually taken in obtaining a copy of the decree but means the time properly required for such purpose and does not include time taken unnecessarily by the appellant. In applying this rule, the Court has to consider whether the appellant has exercised reasonable and proper diligence in obtaining a copy of the order appealed against.

Any failure in reasonable diligence which produces unnecessary delay at one or more of the several stages in obtaining copy of the order will disentitle an appellant to claim the whole of the time actually occupied in obtaining the copy. The time unnecessarily occupied is not time "requisite" within the meaning of S. 12 of the Limitation Act (36 of 1963). *Kanji Devji* v. *Velji Haridas,* AIR 1950 Bom 350.

Time necessarily spent in the preparation of the decree and time necessarily spent in the preparation of the copy. *Kerhar Sugar Works* v. *R.C. Sharma,* AIR 1951 All 122, 135 (FB).

The expression 'time requisite' must be understood to mean time properly and reasonably required. The 'time requisite' is not always the time actually spent in securing the copies. *Lala Bal Mukand* v. *Lajwanti,* AIR 1975 SC 1089, 1092.

In the case of more than one application made for obtaining copy of the order, judgment or decree within the period of limitation, the period between the date of the first application and the date on which the first copy of the order, judgment or decree was obtained is the 'time requisite'. *State of U.P.* v. *Maharaj Narain,* AIR 1965 All 443, 445.

The expression 'time requisite' means the time properly required for getting a copy of the decree, in the facts and circumstances of each particular case, and in respect whereof there would be no default or negligence on the part of the person applying for a copy of the decree. *Annada Sundari* v. *Manoharan,* AIR 1981 Cal 365, 378.

Time requisite for obtaining copy of decree. The expression 'time requisite for obtaining copy of decree' includes the time taken by the Court to prepare the decree before an application for the copy of the decree is made. *Thirumala* v. *Anavoma Reddi,* AIR 1934 Mad 307. [Limitation Act (36 of 1963), S. 12]

Time-sharing. An arrangement whereby people buy time during which they are entitled to use a property (such as a two-week time share in a holiday villa abroad).

Time sheet. Document that records the time a worker or machine spends on each activity in a particular period, used mainly for costing purposes.

Timely. Occurring or appearing in good time. [T.P. Act (4 of 1882), S. 72(e), prov.].

Timing. "Timing" means the way anything is timed. Timing involves choice of the moment for doing a particular act. "Timing" conveys the idea of one vehicle preceding or succeedding the other, thereby making a planned programme of arrivals and departure of stage carriages. *K. Mohammed Sadique* v. *Secretary, R.T.A. Kozhikode,* AIR 1994 Ker 1, 5.

Tindal. "TINDAL" means the person in command or charge of a sailing vessel. [Merchant Shipping Act (44 of 1958), S. 3(50)]

Tinted. The word "tinted" means shade or hue as per the dictionary. The rear and front and side glasses of vehicles are provided with such shade or tint, and therefore, they are widely referred to as "tinted glasses", which is different from "black films". The glasses of the vehicles having a coating of black films cannot be termed as "tinted glasses" because they are not manufactured as such. [*Avishek Goenka v. Union of India*, (2012) 5 SCC 321, para 4].

Tipper. In securities law, one who possesses material inside information and who selectively discloses that information for trading or other personal purposes.

Tirni. "TIRNI" means the dues payable to the Khan of *Teri* for the time being for the grazing of sheep, goats and camels by the owners of the same in the estates held by the said Khan on *istamrari* tenure. [Pun. Regn, IV of 1902 (Teri), S. 2. cl. (*b*)]

Tissue. Means a group of cells, except blood, performing a particular function in the human body. [Transplantation of Human Organs and Tissues Act 1994, S. 2(oa) as inserted by Act 16 of 2011, S. 5]

Title. A general head, comprising particulars, as in a claim of right. It is the means whereby an owner possesses his property justly; evidence of ownership.

A legal right (particularly to the possession of property) [Indian Evidence Act (1 of 1872), S. 41]; a description, name; a distinctive appellation [Trade Unions Act (16 of 1926), S. 5(1)(c)]; an appellation of dignity, honour, distinction or pre-eminence attached on a hereditary or acquired basis [Registration Act (16 of 1908), S. 2(1) and Constitution of India, Art. 18(1)] [Companies Act (1 of 1956), S. 303, *Expln.* (2)]; the name of a book, poem, table picture or a section in a law book [Indian Standards Institution (Certification Marks) Act (36 of 1952), S. 7(c)].

"TITLE" is the means whereby a person's right to property is established.

The term "title" in S. 11, CPC (5 of 1908), refers to the capacity or interest of a party that is to say, whether he sues or is sued for himself, in his own interest or for himself as representing the interest of another or as representing the interest of others along with himself. It has nothing to do with the particular cause of action on which he sues or is sued.

Title by adverse possession. "Title by adverse possession" is not merely an equitable but a complete legal title. The law creates and confers the title arising from adverse possession. It does not flow from a contract between the parties which could be reduced to writing and put on record. There is no privity between the possessor and him who is dispossessed, and the right of the former does not result from any act of the latter, but is the effect given by the law to his possession.

Title by descent. "Title by descent" is a title by which one person upon the death of another acquires real estate of the latter as his heir at law. Property acquired by descent is property which the law, upon the death of the ancestor, casts on the heir.

Title-deed. A deed or document containing or constituting evidence of title. [Indian Evidence Act (1 of 1872), S. 130].

Title member. A partner whose name appears in the name of partnership.

Title search. A search of public records to determine the condition of title to real property usually that is the subject of a transaction.

Titular. Such in name with the reality (as) titular Sovereignty.

Titulus est justa causa possidendi id quod nostrum est. Title is the just cause of possessing that which is ours.

To. In designating boundaries, the word "to" without the word "inclusive" excludes the object to which the line runs. [General Clauses Act (10 of 1897), S. 9(1)]

The words "FROM", "TO" AND "AT" may be taken inclusively, according to the subject-matter.

The word 'to' would include any action towards the final goal of the action. *Hindustan Lever Ltd.* v. *Ashok V. Kate*, AIR 1996 SC 285, 299.

To any other person in whom director is interested. For the purposes of section 185 of Act 18 of 2013, the expression 'to any other person in whom director is interested' means—

(*a*) any director of the lending company, or of a company which is its holding company or any partner or relative of any such director;

(*b*) any firm in which any such director or relative is a partner;

(*c*) any private company of which any such director is a director or member;

(*d*) any body corporate at a general meeting of which not less than twenty-five per cent of the total voting power may be exercised or controlled by any such director, or by two or more such directors, together; or

(*e*) any body corporate, the Board of directors, managing director or manager, whereof is accustomed to act in accordance with the directions or instructions of the Board, or of any director or directors, of the lending company. [*Explanation* to section 185(1) of the Companies Act, 2013 (18 of 2013)]

To attend a recognized primary school. "TO ATTEND A RECOGNIZED PRIMARY SCHOOL" means to be present for instruction at such school on such days in the year at such time or times, and for so many hours on each day of attendance as may be fixed by the prescribed authority. [HP Compulsory Primary Education Act (7 of 1954), S. 2(11)]

To be a witness. The protection afforded to an accused in so far as it is related to the phrase 'to be a witness" is not merely in respect of testimonial compulsion in the Court room but may well extend to compelled testimony previously obtained from him. *Admin* v. *State,* AIR 1958 All 293, 302. [Constitution of India, Art. 20(3)]

To be a witness against himself. "To be a witness against himself" would mean "to furnish evidence against himself". Such evidence can be furnished as much by word of mouth as by hand. *M. P. Sharma* v. *Satish Chandra*, AIR 1956 SC 300. [Constitution of India, Art. 20(3)]

To cultivate. "TO CULTIVATE" with its grammatical variations and cognate expressions, means to till or husband land for the purpose of raising or improving agricultural produce, whether by manual labour or with the use of cattle or by machinery, or to carry on any agricultural operation thereon.

Explanation.—A person who enters into a contract to cut grass on any land, shall not on that account only be taken to cultivate such land. [Maharashtra Agricultural Lands (Ceiling on Holdings) Act (27 of 1961), S. 2(8)]

'To cultivate' with its grammatical variations and cognate expressions means to till or husband the land for the purpose of raising or improving agricultural produce, whether by manual labour or by means of cattle or machinery or to carry on any agricultural operation thereon;

Explanation.—A person who enters into a contract only to cut grass or to gather the fruits or other produce of trees, on any land, shall not on that account only, be deemed to cultivate such land. [Gujarat Agricultural Lands Ceiling Act, 1960 (27 of 1961), S. 2(11) as cited in *State of Gujarat v. Manoharsinghji Pradyumansingji Jadeja*, (2013) 2 SCC 300, para 33].

To cultivate personally. 'To cultivate personally' means to cultivate land on one's own account—

(i) by one's own labour, or

(ii) by the labour of any member of one's family, or

(iii) under the personal supervision of oneself or any member of one's family. by hired labour or by servants on wages payable in cash or kind but not in crop share;

Explanation I.—A widow or a minor or a person who is subject to any physical or mental disability, or a serving member of the armed forces shall be deemed to cultivate land personally, if such land is cultivated by her or his servants or hired labour;

Explanation II.—In the case of a joint family, land shall be deemed to be cultivated personally, if it is so cultivated by any member of such family. [Gujrat Agricultural Lands Ceiling Act, 1960 (27 of 1961), S. 2(12) as cited in *State of Gujarat v. Manoharsinhji Pradyumansinhji Jadeja*, (2013) 2 SCC 300, para 33].

To decide. To decide means settle (question, issue, dispute) by giving victory to one side; give judgment (between, for in favour of, against); bring, come, to a 'resolution' and 'decision' means settlement, (of question etc); conclusion; formal judgment; making up, one's mind; resolve; resolveness; decided character. *Nirmala Beru Tatel* v. *Indersingh Bagi,* AIR 1977 Ori 211, 213.

To enforce the right to share in the property. The words 'to enforce the right to share in the property' imply that the plaintiff has been excluded from the enjoyment of such property and are inapplicable to a case in which he has not been so excluded. *Mahadeo Ganesh* v. *Sadashiv Khanderao,* AIR 1953 MB 151, 182. [Court Fees Act (7 of 1870), S. 7(iv)(b)]

To enquire. To enquire means to make investigation. That is, to examine systematically in detail and it can never mean that conclusions of the investigation would have any binding force or be conclusive. *Hirendra Nath* v. *of India,* AIR 1976 Cal 88, 96.

To erect. "TO ERECT", in relation to any building, includes—

(i) any material alteration or enlargement of such building,

(ii) conversion, by structural alteration, into a place for human habitation of such building not originally constructed for human habitation.

(iii) conversion into more than one place for human habitation of such building originally constructed as one such place,

(iv) conversion of two or more places of human habitation in such building into a greater number of such places,

(v) such alteration of such building as would alter the drainage or sanitary arrangements therein or would materially affect its security, and

(vi) the addition of any rooms in such building. [Metro Railways (Construction of Works) Act (33 of 1978), S. 2(1)(r)]

"TO ERECT" with its grammatical variations means to construct, reconstruct, re-erect extend, or alter any building. [Poona Mutna River Flood Limits (Prohibition of Building) and Provision for Alternative Building Sites Act (Mah Act 37 of 1961), S. 2(g)]

To establish. The expression 'to establish' occurring in Art. 30 means to set up on permanent basis. *T.M.A. Pai Foundation* v. *State of Karnataka*, (2002) 8 SCC 481, para 254. [Constitution of India, Art. 30]

To export from India. With its grammatical variations and cognate expressions means to take out of India to a place outside India. [Narcotic Drugs and Psychotropic Substances Act (61 of 1985), S. 2(xxvi)]

To export inter-state. "TO EXPORT INTER STATE" means to take out of a State or Union Territory in India to another State or Union Territory in India. [Narcotic Drugs and Psychotropic Substances Act (61 of 1985), S. 2(xxvii)]

To extend and to enlarge. To extend a certain period is the same thing as to enlarge that period. The words 'to extend' and 'to enlarge' are synonymous, whenever any period fixed for doing a certain thing is extended, the extension would commence from the point of time when the earlier period ends. *J.K. Iron & Steel Co. Ltd.* v. *Labour Appellate Tribunal,* AIR 1953 All 624, 626.

To fell a tree. "TO FELL A TREE" includes burning or cutting or lopping a tree to cause substantial damage or destruction thereto. [Maharashtra Felling of Trees (Regulation) Act (36 of 1984), S. 2(e)]

To give evidence. The expression 'to give evidence' includes the act of furnishing the statements or information. *Ambalal* v. *State of Maharashtra,* AIR 1966 Bom 243, 252. [Defence of India (Amendment) Rules (163), R. 126 L]

To hold. With its grammatical variations, in relation to any vacant land, means—

(i) to own such land; or

(ii) to possess such land as owner or as tenant or as mortgagee or under an irrevocable power of attorney or under a hire-purchase agreement or partly in one of the said capacities and partly in any other of the said capacity or capacities. [Urban Land (Ceiling and Regulation) Act (33 of 1976), S. 2(l)]

To hold elections. In its wide connotation, the phrase 'to hold elections' will include all steps such as the delimitation of constituencies, the compilation of electoral rolls etc., which are a necessary preliminary to the actual conduct of elections. *State of Gujarat* v. *Jamnadas G. Pabin*, AIR 1974 SC 2233, 2237.

To hold land. In every case in which the landlord or the owner continues in actual possession of the land, he must be held to hold the land. *Godavari Sugar Mills Ltd. Bombay* v. S. *Ramamurthy,* AIR 1979 Bom 225, 228.

To import. Petroleum means to bring it into India by land, sea or air, otherwise than during the course of transport. [Petroleum Act (30 of 1934), S. 2(e)]

To import inter-state. "TO IMPORT INTERSTATE" means to bring into a State or Union Territory in India from another State or Union territory in India. [Narcotic Drugs and Psychotropic Substances Act, (61 of 1985), S. 2(xxiv)]

To import into India. With its grammatical variations and cognate expressions, means to bring in to India from a place outside India and includes the bringing into any port or airport or place in India of a narcotic drug or a psychotropic substance intended to be taken out of India without being removed from the vessel, aircraft, vehicle or any other conveyance in which it is being carried.

Explanation.—For the purposes of this clause and clause (xxvi), "India includes the territorial waters of India." [Narcotic Drugs and Psychotropic Substance Act (61 of 1985), S. 2(xxv)]

To let. A distinction must be drawn between the expression 'TO LET' and the expression "TO PLY FOR HIRE" though the two expressions are often used together to denote one and the same thing. The implications are different in the two expressions; there can be cases where there may be a letting of a motor vehicle without plying for hire and *vice versa*.

To manage its own affair in matters of religion. To manage its own affairs in matters of a religion can only mean that in domestic matters of a religious denomination, where those matters are concerned with questions of religion, the Legislature cannot interfere unless the denomination is managing its affairs in such a way as to interfere with public order, morality and health. *Svyedna Taher Saifuddin* v. *Tyebhai Moosaji Koicha,* AIR 1953 Bom 183, 188. [Constitution of India, Art. 26]

To pay ransom. To pay a ransom, in ordinary sense means to pay the price or demand for ransom. This would show that the demand has to be communicated. [*Akram Khan v. State of W.B.*, (2012) 1 SCC, para 28].

To permit. The ordinary meaning of 'to permit' is to give leave for an act to be done which the person permitting has power to prevent.

'To possess' or **'To retain'.** Means to possess or to retain in physical form and the words 'possession' or 'retention' shall be construed accordingly. [Foreign Exchange Management (Possession and Retention of Foreign Currency) Regulations, 2000, Reg. 2(ii)]

To recur. "To recur" simply means "to occur again" or to repeat, the word connotes distinct and different repetitions of the same act. *Rasool* v. *State of Mysore,* AIR 1959 Mys 136, 138.

To set aside. "To set aside" means no more than "to designate" and means "to separate to a particular use". *Imporial Chit Funds* v. *I.T. Department,* AIR 1979 Ker 23, 30 (FB). [Income-Tax Act (43 of 1961), S. 178(3)(b)]

To show cause. The term "to show cause" does not merely mean to allege cause, nor even to make out that there is room for argument, but to allege cause and to prove it to the satisfaction of the authority issuing the showcause notice. *Baruagar Electric Supply and Industries Co. Ltd.* v. *State of M.P.,* AIR 1963 MP 41, 46. [Indian Electricity Act (9 of 1910), S. 4(3)]

The expression "to show cause" in S. 3(1)(a), of Requisitioning and Acquisition of Immovable Property Act (30 of 1952), means the right to be heard in person or by counsel. *Pannalal* v. *State of Delhi,* AIR 1954 Punj 251.

To state reasons. 'To state reasons' must necessarily mean that there should be an indication that evidence has been considered. (*Shamlal,* 33 CrLJ 729) [CrPC (5 of 1898), S. 370 (S. 355 in 1974 Code)]

To store. Petroleum means to keep it in any one place, but does not include any detention happening during the ordinary course of transport. [Petroleum Act (30 of 1934), S. 2(f)]

To sue. The words 'to sue' signify not only 'to prosecute' but also 'to defend' or "to do something which the law requires for the better prosecution or defence of the cause". *Haradhone Haldar* v. *Usha Charan Karanakar,* AIR 1955 Cal 292.

The expression 'to sue' includes proceedings other than suits, if the proceedings are for dissolution of a firm or for the accounts of a dissolved firm. *Iqbal Singh* v. *Ram Narain,* AIR 1977 All 352, 354. [Indian Partnership Act (9 of 1932), S. 69(3)(a)]

To the best of judgment. The clause 'to the best of his judgment' implies a consideration of something that is before the assessing officer. He should exercise his judgment. It should not be the result of pure guess work.

To transport. "TO TRANSPORT" means to take from one place to another within the same State or Union territory. [Narcotic Drugs and Psychotropic Substances Act (61 of 1985), S. 2(xxviii)]

To transport petroleum. Means to move petroleum from one place to another in India and includes moving from one place to another in India across a territory which is not part of India. [Petroleum Act (30 of 1934), S. 2(d)]

To withdraw or not to withdraw from being a candidate at an election. The expression means whether there can be withdrawal after the time for withdrawal has expired. *Mohd. Yunus Saleem* v. *Shivakumar Shastri,* AIR 1974 SC 1278, 1223. [Representation of the People Act (43 of 1951), S. 123(1(A)(a)]

To withhold services. 'To withhold services' would mean not merely to resign from the force but deliberately refuse, to forbear or to refrain from performing tasks and duties enjoined upon the members of the force by the rules governing them. 'To withhold services', means something more aggravated than even committing breach of a disciplinary rule. *Indulal K. Yagnik* v. *State,* AIR 1960 Bom 399, 403. [Police (Incitement to Disaffection) Act (22 of 1922), S. 3]

Tobacconist. "TOBACCONIST" means a person who supplies whether by way of sale or otherwise luxuries, like, tobacco products manufactured by him or purchased from other States or from other persons in this State and includes any person who for the purpose of Business gets the manufacturing done from any person whether or not on job work basis". [A.P. Tax on Luxuries Act, 1987, S. 2(kkk) (*as amended by A.P. Act No. 28 of 1996*)]

"TOBACCONIST" means :—

(i) a manufacturer whose turnover of receipts in a year exceeds one lakh rupees who supplies tobacco by way of sale or otherwise and includes any person who for the purpose of business gets the manufacturing done from any other person, whether or not on job work basis, but does not include any person who manufactures tobacco only on job work basis without obtaining any proprietary right over it at any stage;

(ii) any person who for the purpose of business brings or causes to be brought tobacco in the State or to whom any tobacco is dispatched from any place outside the State and who supplies such tobacco by way of sale or otherwise;

(iii) any person who supplies tobacco from a place within the State to any place outside the State by way of sale or otherwise;

(iv) any person who does not buy or otherwise obtain unmanufactured tobacco under a brand name but supplies by way of sale or otherwise such unmanufactured tobacco in a sealed container under a brand name;

Explanation.—For the removal of doubts, it is clarified that a person—

(1) who exclusively supplies unmanufactured tobacco whether or not in a sealed container but not under a brand name; or

(2) not being a person referred to in sub-clause (iii) who exclusively obtains tobacco by way of purchase or otherwise from a registered tobacconist;

shall not be deemed to be a tobacconist for the purposes of this clause. [U.P. Tax on Luxuries Act 1995 (U.P. Ordinance No. 8 of 94), S. 2(h)]

Together. "Together" means in "company"; "into or in union with each other as wholes or parts, so as to be combined or joined with each other; conjointly; in the same place or at the same spot with each other locally, as in company; at the same moment of time;

simultaneously; contemporaneously; mutually; reciprocally."

"Together" means "as well as" or "along with" [*Assam SEB v. Shanti Conductors (P) Ltd.*, (2002) 2 Gau LR 550, para 12 as cited in *Modern Industries v. SAIL*, (2010) 5 SCC 44 : (2010) 2 SCC (Civ) 280, para 41]. See also *Purbanchal Cables and Conductors Private Limited v. Assam State Electricity Board*, (2012) 7 SCC 462, para 16.

The words "the husband and wife reside or last resided together" in S. 3, Indian Divorce Act (4 of 1869) indicate clearly that "together" must be read with "last resided" only.

"TOGETHER", The word 'together' ordinarily means conjointly or simultaneously. *Modern Industries* v. *Steel Authority of India Ltd.*, AIR 2010 SC 1625.

Toilet preparation. Means any preparation which is intended for use in the toilet of the human body or in the perfuming apparel of any description, or any substance intended to cleanse, improve or alter the complexion, skin, hair or teeth, and includes deodorants and perfumes. [Medicinal and Toilet Preparations (Excise Duties) Act (16 of 1955), S. 2(k)]

Toilet soap. "Toilet soap" as used in Tariff Act will not include a medical soap containing 20 per cent of carbolic acid, and used for curative purposes.

Toilet soap which is being used for everyday household use for the purpose of the bath would fall within the meaning of 'household soap'. *Oswal Agro Mills Ltd.* v. *Collector of Central Excise*, AIR 1993 SC 2288, 2295. [Central Excises and Salt Act (1 of 1944), Sch. I, Item 15]

Token. "TOKEN" means a ticket to be displayed on a motor vehicle as an indication that the tax has been duly paid or that no tax is payable. [Delhi Motor Vehicles Taxation Act (57 of 1962), S. 2(h)]

A "token" is defined to be a sign or mark. Something that serves to indicate a fact, event, object, feeling etc., a symbol. [IPC (45 of 1860) and S. 42, Mines Act (35 of 1952), S. 171].

Token grant. A grant of a token sum made by Parliament to meet the proposed expenditure on a new service.

Tokyo convention. "TOKYO CONVENTION" means the convention on offences and certain other acts committed on board aircraft signed at Tokyo on the fourteenth day of September, 1963. [Tokyo Convention Act (20 of 1975), S. 2(1)(i)]

Tola. "TOLA" means a weight of one hundred and eighty Troy Grains. [Excise Act (12 of 1896), S. 3]

Tolerate. Allow the existence or occurrence of anything; leave unmolested; put up with (as) to tolerate poligamy; to tolerate infringement of copyright.

The word "tolerate" is defined thus; "To allow, so as not to hinder; to hinder; to permit, as something not wholly approved; to suffer; to endure; to admit." It implies knowledge of the thing tolerated.

Toll. "TOLL" includes any charge leviable in respect of the use of a tramway. [Indian Tramways (11 of 1886), S. 3(10)]

"TOLLS" includes duties, dues, rates, fees and charges, but does not include customs duties levied under the Indian Tariff Act, 1934, octroi duties or town duties on the import of goods, or fares paid for the conveyance of passengers on a tramway. [Indian Tolls (Army and Air Force) Act (2 of 1901) S. 2(j)]

'Toll' is a tax levied for the use of the public roads and it cannot be imposed on the vehicles going out of the limits of the Municipal Board.

'Toll' means a definite payment exacted by the state or the local authority; by virtue of sovereignty or lordship, or in return of protection; more especially for permission to pass somewhere, do some act, or perform some function. *Hansraj & Sons* v. *State of J&K.*, AIR 2002 SC 2692.

Toll-Collector. "TOLL-COLLECTOR" means a person appointed by the superintendent to levy tolls at a public ferry the right to levy the tolls of which has not been let. [Bur. Act II of 1898 (Ferries), S. 3, cl. (7).]

Toll-through. The expression 'toll-through' means the toll prescribed by a town for every beast that goes through their town. *Hansraj & Sons* v. *State of J&K*, AIR 2002 SC 2692.

Tollitur omnis obligatio solutione ejus quod debitur. Every obligation is dissolved by the payment of what is due.

Tom delivery. Means delivery of foreign exchange on a working day next to the day of transaction. [Foreign Exchange Management (Foreign Exchange Derivative Contracts) Regulations, 2000, Reg. 2(ix)]

Tomb-stone. A stone or slab standing or laid over grave usually with epitaph. [Indian Evidence Act (1 of 1872), S. 32(6)].

Ton. "TON" means a ton as determined or determinable by the rules made under S. 74 of the Merchant Shipping Act, 1958, for regulating the measurement of the gross tonnage of ships. [Indian Ports Act (15 of 1908), S. 3(6)]

"TON", in relation to oil, means a metric ton. [Merchant Shipping Act (44 of 1958), S. 352 S(h)]

Tonnage. "TONNAGE" means the tonnage of a ship determined in accordance with the provisions of Section 352B and where it is not so determinable, it means forty percent of the weight in tons of oil cargo the ship is capable of carrying. [Merchant Shipping Act (44 of 1958), S. 352H(f). Also see S. 356Q(e)]

Tonnage tax company. In this chapter unless the context otherwise requires, —"TONNAGE TAX COMPANY" means a qualifying company in relation to which tonnage tax option is in force. [Income-tax Act (43 of 1961), Chapter XII G, S. 115V(l) (*Inserted by Finance (No. 2) Act (23 of 2004), S. 30*)]

Tonnage tax scheme. In this chapter unless the context otherwise requires, —"TONNAGE TAX SCHEME" means a scheme for computation of profits and gains of business of operating qualifying ships under the provisions of this Chapter. [Income-tax Act (43 of 1961), Chapter XII, G S. 115V(m) (*Inserted by Finance (No. 2)Act (23 of 2004), S. 30*)]

Tonne. Means metric ton, *i.e.,* 1,000 kg. [Chemical Weapons Convention Act (34 of 2000), (Verification Annex), 26]

Tontine. 'Tontine' means an annuity with benefit of survivorship among several persons. (19 *Halsbury's Laws* (4th edn.,) para 104 n).

Tools. Things designed to help the hand in work, especially in industrial operations.

A sewing machine owned by a tailor is a tool of an artisan and therefore, exempt from attachment. [CPC (5 of 1908), S. 60 (1), Prov. (b)]

The term 'tools' cannot be restricted to simple implements used by artisans for purpose of their trade. *T.R. Punuavanam* v. *U. Muthuswami,* AIR 1962 Mad 444, 446. [CPC (5 of 1908). 60(1), Prov. (b)]

A barber's chair and mirror, when used by him in his business, are exempt as being tools of a mechanic used in his occupation.

Law books are also common tools of trade of a lawyer.

Tools and instruments, within the meaning of a Code exempting the tools and instruments necessary for the exercise of the trade or profession of the debtor from seizure, being intended to encourage such trade or profession by enabling the debtor to sustain himself and family by his own men; the law books of a lawyer are perhaps not any less necessary to the proper exercise of his profession than the tools of a mechanic are to the latter, and enable him to carry on his trade.

Tools of artisan. A musician is not an artisan and his musical instruments are not "the tools of an artisan" exempt from attachment under S. 60(1), *Prov.*, CPC (5 of 1908).

"Tools or implements", within the meaning of the statute exempting from execution the tools and implements of a debtor, include various machines for making boots, owned by the debtor and used in his shop, although he employs four or five men to help him.

"Tools", as used in a statute exempting tools from execution includes the surgical instruments of a physician.

A typewriter is not exempt from execution as a tool or apparatus belonging to the profession of a physician, though he uses it in correspondence and advertising his business.

Tools of trade. A workman's tools, which he is entitled to keep if he is made bankrupt.

Topography. A detailed study, description or features of a limited area. [Income-tax Act (43 of 1961), S. 33A(8)].

Torment. In laws relating to cruelty to animals, the word "torment" includes every act, omission, or neglect whereby unjustifiable physical pain, suffering or death is caused or permitted.

Torpedo. A bomb, cartridge, case of explosives or detonator of various kinds used in warfare etc. [Official Secrets Act (19 of 1923), S. 2(5)].

Torrent. Rushing stream—especially one that dries up in summer.

Tort. "TORT" means a civil wrong which is not exclusively the breach of a contract or the breach of a trust. [Limitation Act (36 of 1963), S. 2(m)].

An injury or a wrong committed with or without force to the person or property of another, and such injury may arise by either the non-feasance, malfeasance, or misfeasance of the wrongdoer.

Tort action : Criminal prosecution. A 'tort action' is instituted by an individual seeking redress for the wrong done to him. A 'criminal prosecution' is normally instituted by the Crown or some other body expressly authorised by statute to bring criminal prosecution for specific offences. [Clerk & Lindsell on Torts, 17th Edn., 1995, c. 1, para 1-14, p.13]

Tort and **Contract.** 'Contract' is concerned with voluntary obligations and 'tort' with involuntary obligations. (*Atiyah*, The Rise and Fall of Freedom of Contract, (1979), p. 408).

Tort : Crime. An act is a 'tort or other civil wrong' means that it can be followed by a civil action for damages, or other civil redress. To say that it is a crime means that it can be followed by a criminal prosecution. [GLANVILLE WILLIAMS : Criminal law, 2nd Edn., 1983, c. 1, S. 1.6, page 27]

The 'crime' inheres in the agreement to act unlawfully (*Mulcahy* v. *R.,* (1868) L.R. 3 H.L. 306 at 317]; but the 'tort' arises when damage is caused or threatened by the combination. [*Midland Bank Trust Co. Ltd.* v. *Green,* (No. 3), (1979) Ch. 496, per OLIVER J.]

'Tort' and 'crime' both serve to impose obligations of universal application designed to protect the good order of the society. Tort may primarily be concerned with the loss to specific victims of past wrongdoing, but also plays an important role in preventing future wrongdoing. [Law Commission Consultation Paper No. 132, Aggravated, Exemplary and Restitutionary Damages, (1993)]

Tort-feasor. Wrongdoer; a trespasser. One who commits or is guilty of a tort.

Tortious. The word "tortious" is a synonym of the word 'unlawful'. Constituting a tort : recognized as a tort.

Tortuous liability. Tortious liability arises from the breach of a duty primarily fixed by the law; such duty is towards persons generally and its breach is redressible by an action for unliquidated damages. [Winfield, Province of the Law of Tort, (1931), p. 32]

Torture is, where inflicted at all, inflicted for one of two purposes; (1) as a means of eliciting evidence from a witness or from an accused person, (2) as a part of the punishment.

The infliction of excruciating pain. [IPC (45 of 1860), S. 330, ill. (a)]; [Stage Carriage Act (16 of 1861), S. 9].

Torture is a wound in the soul so painful that sometimes you can almost touch it, but it is also so intangible that there is no way to heal it. Torture is anguish squeezing in your chest, cold as ice and heavy as a stone, paralysing as sleep and dark as the abyss. Torture is despair and fear and rage and hate. It is a desire to kill and destroy including yourself. [Adriana P. Bartow as cited in *D.K. Basu v. State of W.B.*, (1997) 1 SCC 416 : 1997 SCC Cri 92 : AIR 1997 SC 610]. See also *Mehmood Nayyar Azam v. State of Chhatisgarh*, (2012) 8 SCC 1, para 18].

The term "torture" also engulfs the concept of torment. The word "torture" in its denotative concept includes mental and psychological harassment. The accused in custody can be put under tremendous psychological pressure by cruel, inhuman and degrading treatment. [*Mahmood NayyarAzam v. State of Chhattisgarh*, (2012) 8 SCC 1, para 22].

Total and whole. 'Total' and 'whole' are synonymous. Whole is total and *vice versa*. *Mangala Prasad Jaiswal* v. *District Magistrate,* AIR 1971 All 77, 81.

Total disablement. Means such disablement, whether of a temporary nature, as incapacitates an employee for all work which he was capable of performing at the time of the accident resulting in such disablement. [Employee's Compensation Act (8 of 1923), S. 2(l); Employee's State Insurance Act (34 of 1948), S. 2 (24)]

"TOTAL DISABLEMENT" means such disablement whether of a temporary or permanent nature, as incapacitates a workman for all work which he was capable of performing at the time the injury was sustained:

Provided that permanent total disablement shall be deemed to result from every injury, or from any combination of injuries, specified in the Schedule, where the percentage, or the aggregate percentage, of disability as specified in the Schedule against such injury, or combination of injuries, amounts to one hundred per cent or more. [Personal Injuries (Compensation Insurance) Act (37 of 1963), S. 2(h)]

A carpenter fell down during the course of employment and suffered injuries resulting in the amputation of his left arm. *Held :* The injury was of such a nature as to cause permanent disablement and it incapacitated him from performing all work which he was capable of performing, *viz.* that of a carpenter. *Pratap Narain Singh Deo* v. *Srinivas Sabata,* AIR 1976 SC 222. [Workmen's Compensation Act (8 of 1923), S. 2(l)(l)]

Total debt. For the purposes of this sub-regulation, 'TOTAL DEBT' is the sum of—

(*a*) the amount of debt due to the creditors listed in sub-regulation 2(*a*);

(*b*) the amount of the aggregate debt due to workmen under sub-regulation 2(*b*); and

(*c*) the amount of the aggregate debt due to employees under sub-regulation 2(*c*). [Insolvency and Bankruptcy Board of India (Insolvency Resolution Process for Corporate Persons) Regulations, 2016, Regn. 16(3), *Explanation*].

Total full time earnings. "In this sub-section, the expression "TOTAL FULL TIME EARNINGS" includes the cash equivalent of the advantage accruing through the concessional sale to the employees of foodgrains and other articles, as the employee is for the time-being entitled to, but does not include bonus." [Beedi and Cigar Workers (Conditions of Employment) Act (32 of 1966), S. 27 (1), *Expln. I*]

Total full time earnings, in the case of house-workers will be daily average hours of work done by home worker during the last month before leave provided such average does not exceed the daily period of work as prescribed in a notice under Section 32. *Mangalore Ganesh Beedi Works* v. *Union of India*, AIR 1974 SC 1832, 1833. [Beedi and Cigar workers (Conditions of Employment) Act (32 of 1966), S. 27, *Explanation I*]

Total inability to labour. "Total inability to labour" does not confine the capability of the member's earning capacity to the same employment as that in which he was engaged at the time of becoming incapacitated, but requires such member to engage in any work or employment for which he is fitted, or which he is capable of performing.

Total income. "TOTAL INCOME" means total amount of income, profits and gains from all sources to which this (Income) Act applies computed in the manner laid down in that Act. [Income Tax Act (11 of 1922), S. 2(15)]

Total income of any previous year. "The total income of any previous year of a person who is a resident includes all income from whatever source derived which—(a) is received or is deemed to be received in India in such year by or on behalf of such person; or (b) accrues or arises or is deemed to accrue or arise to him in India during such year; or (c) accrues or arises to him outside India during such year.

Provided that in the case of a person not ordinarily resident in India within the meaning of sub-section (6) of section 6, the income which accrues or arises to him outside India shall not be so included unless it is derived from a business controlled in or a profession set up in India.

The total income of any previous year of a person who is a non-resident includes all income from whatever source derived which—(a) is received or is deemed to be received in India in such year by or on behalf of such person; or (b) accrues or arises or is deemed to accrue or arise to him in India during such year.

Explanation 1.—Income accruing or arising outside India shall not be deemed to be received in India within the meaning of this section by reason only of the fact that it is taken into account in a balance-sheet prepared in India.

Explanation 2.—For the removal of doubts, it is hereby declared that income which has been included in the total income of a person on the basis that it has accrued or arisen to him shall not again be so included on the basis that it is received or deemed to be received by him in India." [Income Tax Act (43 of 1961), S. 5]

Total loss. Total loss does not exclude loss of the entire cargo on account of jettisoning. *General Insurance Society Ltd., Calcutta* v. *M.S. Sivasami,* AIR 1974 Mad 257, 259. [Marine Insurance Act (11 of 1963), S. 7]

Total number of directors. For the purposes of section 152(6) of Act 18 of 2013, 'total number of directors' shall not include independent directors, whether appointed under the Companies Act, 2013 (18 of 2013), or any other law for the time being in force, on the Board of a company. [*Explanation* to section 152(6) of the Companies Act, 2013 (18 of 2013)]

Total Share Capital. For the purposes of section 2(6) and section 2(87) of Act 18 of 2013, means the aggregate of the—(a) paid-up equity share capital; and (b) convertible preference share capital. [R. 2(1)(r) of the Companies (Specification of Definitions Details) Rules, 2014]

Total strength. For the purposes of section 174 of Act 18 of 2013, 'total strength' shall not include directors whose places are vacant. [*Explanation (ii)* to section 174(4) of the Companies Act, 2013 (18 of 2013)]

Total turnover. "TOTAL TURNOVER" shall not include freight or insurance attributable to the transport of the goods or merchandise beyond the customs station as defined in the Customs Act, 1962. [Income-tax Act (43 of 1961), S. 80 HHC (4), *Expln.*(ba)]

"TOTAL TURNOVER" shall not include—

(A) any sum referred to in clauses (*iiia*), (*iiib*) and (*iiic*) of Section 28;

(B) any freight, telecommunication charges or insurance attributable to the delivery of the film software, music software, telecast rights, television news software, or television software as defined in clauses (*d*), (*e*), (*g*), (*h*) or (*i*), as the case may be, outside India;

(C) expenses, if any, incurred in foreign exchange in providing the technical services outside India. [Income-tax Act (43 of 1961), S. 80 HHF (6) *Expln* (j)]

Total sales. Means total turnover less—

(*i*) the amount specified in clause (*a*) of sub-rule (1) of Rule 3, and

(*ii*) the deductions specified in clause (*e*) of sub-rule (2) of Rule 3,

(*iii*) the aggregate of sale prices received or receivable in respect of subsequent sale in the course of inter-state trade or commerce of any goods, purchased in the course of inter-state trade or commerce during their inter-state movement,

(*iv*) the aggregate of sale prices received or receivable in respect of sale in the course of export out of territory of India of any goods purchased in the course of export; and

(*v*) the aggregate of sale prices received or receivable in respect of sale in the course of import into the territory of India of any goods purchased in the course of import. [Karnataka Value Added Tax Rules, 2005, R. 131(4)(b) **as cited in** *State of Karnataka* v. *M.K. Agro Tech. Private Limited,* (2017) 16 SCC 210, para 14].

Total power control. Means a mechanism to reduce the amount of power to that necessary for successful communication. [Use of Very Low Power Ultra-wideband Devices (Exemption from Licensing Requirements) Rules, 2018, R. 2(u)].

Total voting power. In regard to any matter relating to a body corporate, means the total number of votes which may be cast in regard to that matter on a poll at a meeting of such body, if all the members thereof and all other persons, if any, having a right to vote on that matter are present at the meeting, and cast their votes. [Companies Act (1 of 1956), S. 2(48)]

"TOTAL VOTING POWER". In relation to any matter, means the total number of votes which may be cast in regard to that matter on a poll at a meeting of a company if all the members thereof or their proxies having a right to vote on that matter are present at the meeting and cast their votes. [S. 2(89) of the Companies Act, 2013 (18 of 2013)]

Total world income. 'TOTAL WORLD INCOME' includes all incomes wherever accruing or arising, except incomes which are not included in the total income under any of the provisions of Chapter III and except any capital gains which are not includable in the total income of an assessee. [Income-tax Act (43 of 1961), S. 2(46)]. (*Omitted by* Act 10 of 1965, S. 4.)]

Totalizator. 'TOTALIZATOR' means a totalizator in an enclosure which the stewards controlling a race meeting have set apart for the purpose, and includes any instrument, machine or contrivance known as the totalizator or any other instrument; machine or contrivance of a like nature, or any scheme for enabling any number of persons to make belts with one another on like principles but does not include a book maker. [Delhi Entertainments and Betting Tax Act, 1996 (Delhi Act No.8 of 1997), S. 2(v)]

Totting up. Term applied to the procedure for disqualification from driving for repeated driving offences whereby each offence carries certain penalty points and disqualification must normally follow the achieving of a certain number of points. (*England*).

Totum praefertur unicuique parti. The whole is preferable to any single part.

Touch. (*In Maritime law*) The word "touch" and its derivatives is in a sense a nautical phrase. It is defined thus : "To come or to attain to; to arrive at; to reach, as, to touch their naval shore". And its use is illustrated as follows: "To touch at; arrive at; or come to this state".

Where a vessel makes irregular and transient visitation to a port in course of her voyage to various ports, she is said to touch at each of the ports which she visits. A vessel plies between two places; she may touch at many.

Touching. It is one thing to state that 'touching' may be synonymous with 'concerning' and another thing to contend that 'touching' would be equivalent to 'affecting' howsoever remote it might be. *Himangsha Bhusun Chakrabarthi* v. *Nirmal Kumar Das,* AIR 1962 Cal 488, 490.

The dictionary meaning of the word 'touching' is 'in reference or relation to, respecting, regarding, or concerning'.

Touching the business of the society. The word "touching" would include any matter which relates to, concerns or affects the business of the society. *Farkhundhali Namhay* v. *V.B. Potdar,* AIR 1962 Bom 162, 163 (FB).

Tour. Means a journey from one place to another irrespective of the distance between such places. [Finance Act (32 of 1994), S. 65(1)(113) now repealed by Central Goods and Services Tax Act, 2017].]

Tour operator. "TOUR OPERATOR" means any person engaged in the business of planning, scheduling, organising or arranging tours (which may include arrangements for accommodation, sightseeing or other similar services) by any mode of transport, and includes any person engaged in the business of operating tours in a tourist vehicle or a contract carriage by whatever name called, covered by a permit, other than a stage carriage permit, granted under the Motor Vehicles Act, 1988(59 of 1988) or the rules made there under.. [Finance Act (32 of 1994), S. 65(115) (*Substituted by Finance Act 2008]* now repealed by Central Goods and Service Tax Act, 2017].

Touring cinematograph. "TOURING CINEMATOGRAPH" means a cinematograph apparatus which is constructed so that it can be taken from place to place for the purpose of giving cinematograph exhibitions. [Delhi Cinematograph Rules 1981, R. 2(xvii) and HP Cinemas (Regulation) Rules, 1979, R. 2(x)]

Tourism industry. Means, hotels, travel agents, tour operators or tourist transport operators, who are certified as Export House or Trading House or Star Trading House or Super Star Trading House in terms of notification of the Government of India in the Ministry of Commerce, No. 33 (RE-98) 1997-2002, dated the 26th November, 1998. [Customs Tariff Act (51 of 1975), Gen. Exemption No. 63(3), *Expln.* (7)]

Tourist. "TOURIST" means a person not normally resident in India, who enters India for a stay of not more than six months in the course of any twelve months period for legitimate non-immigrant purposes, such as touring, recreation, sports, health, family reasons, study, religious pilgrimage or business. [Customs Tariff, Baggage Rules, 1998, R. 2(iii)]

For purpose of clause (b) of this proviso, the word "TOURIST" means a person who not being a citizen of India visits India for a period not exceeding six months with no other object than recreation, sightseeing, or participation in a representative capacity in meetings convened by the Central Government or in international conferences, associations or other bodies. [Arms Act (54 of 1959), S. 10(b), *Expln.*]

Tourist transport operator. 'TOURIST TRANSPORT OPERATOR' means a company or an individual engaged in the business of promotion of tourist circuits, recognised by the Department of Tourism of the Government of India. [Motor Vehicles (All India Permit of Tourist Transport Operators) Rules, 1993, R. 2(g)]

Tournament. Medieval tilting match between two sides; contest in any game of skill or exercise with selective competitors.

Tout. "TOUT" means a person—(a) who procures, in consideration of any remuneration moving from any legal practitioner, the employment of the legal practitioner in any legal business; or who proposes to any legal practitioner or to any person interested in any legal business any business to procure, in consideration of any remuneration moving from either of them, the employment of the legal practitioner in such business; or (*b*) who for the purposes of such procurement frequents the precincts of Civil or Criminal Courts or of revenue-offices, or railway stations, landing stages lodging places or other places of public resort. [Legal Practitioners Act (18 of 1879), S. 3]

'TOUT" means a person who procures, in consideration of any remuneration moving from an advocate or from any person acting on his behalf, the employment of such advocate in any legal business, or who proposes to or procures any advocate, in consideration of any remuneration moving from such advocate or from any person on his behalf, the employment of the advocate in such business, or who, for purposes of such procurement, frequents the precincts of the Court. [Supreme Court Rules, 2013, Order IV, R. 14(1), Explanation].

One who looks out for custom in an obstructive way; one who solicits clients for an advocate.

Tout ce que la loi ne defend pas est permis. Everything is permitted which is not forbidden by law.

Toute exception non surveillee tend a prendre la place du principle. Every exception not watched tends to assume the place of the principle.

Towage. The towing or drawing a ship or barge along the water by another ship or boat fastened to her; or by men or horses, etc., on land : it is also money which is given by bargemen to the owner of the ground next to a river where they tow a barge or other vessel. (*Tomlin*)

The action of pulling or dragging (such as a boat on water). [CPC (5 of 1908), S. 140(1)].

Town. "TOWN" means a town which has a population not exceeding one lakh according to the last preceding census of which the relevant figures have been published before the first day of the previous year. [Income-tax Act (43 of 1961), S. 80 G(2)(a)(iiih) *Expln.*]

An assemblage of buildings, public or private, larger than a village, and having more complete and independent local government. [CPC (5 of 1908), S. 8].

Township-officer. "TOWNSHIP OFFICER", means the officer in charge of a township as constituted for revenue and general purposes. [Bur. Act (6 of 1907), (Villages), S. 4, cl. (5)]

Toxic chemical. "TOXIC CHEMICAL" means : Any chemical which through its chemical action on life processes can cause death, temporary incapacitation or permanent harm to humans or animals. This includes all such chemicals, regardless of their origin or of their method of production, and regardless of whether they are produced in facilities, in munitions or elsewhere.

[(For the purpose of implementing this Convention, toxic chemicals which have been identified for the application of verification measures are listed in Schedules contained in the Annex on Chemicals]. [Chemical Weapons Convention Act (34 of 2000), Art. II (2)]

Toxic tort. A tort in which there is personal injury or property damage due to exposure to toxic substances.

Toxicologist. A person, who deals with the science that treats the origin, nature, properties etc. of poisons. [Insecticides Act (46 of 1968), S. 4(3)(xvi)].

Toxicology. The science which treats of poisons, their effects, antidotes and recognition of poisons.

Trace routine. A program intended to assist programmers in locating flaws during the program-testing process. A trace routine allows the programmer to execute one instruction at a time in order to examine the results of that instruction, the inputs provided, and the contents of the most significant registers involved. (*Computer*)

Tracing. "TRACING" means determining the nature, source, disposition, movement, title or ownership of property. [CrPC, 1973 (2 of 1974), S. 105-A(e))] [Now (w. e. f. 1-7-2024) repealed & replaced by Bharatiya Nagarik Suraksha Sanhita, 2023 (46 of 2023)] and Wild Life (Protection) Act (53 of 1972), S. 2(j); Narcotic Drugs and Psychotropic Substances (61 of 1985), S. 68B(j)]

In this Chapter, unless the context otherwise requires,—"tracing" means determining the nature, source, disposition, movement, title or ownership of property. [(w. e. f. 1-7-2024) Bharatiya Nagarik Suraksha Sanhita, 2023 (46 of 2023), section 111(e)]

Trackball. A computer input device that has a ball that the user rolls with the fingers or the palm of the hand to position a cursor on the display of a computer. (*Computer*)

Tract. A precise, defined or definable area. [Registration Act (16 of 1908), S. 1(2)].

Tractor. "TRACTOR" means a motor vehicle which is not itself constructed to carry any load (other than equipment used for the purpose of propulsion); but exludes a road roller. [Motor Vehicles Act (59 of 1988), S. 2(44)]

Trade. "TRADE" means any trade, business, industry, profession or occupation relating to production, supply, distribution, storage or control of goods and includes the provision of any services. [M.R.T.P. Act (54 of 1969), S. 2(s); Competitions Act, 2002 (12 of 2003), S. 2(x)]

The business of buying and selling or bartering commodities. [Indian Contract Act (9 of 1872), S. 27]; [Trade Unions Act (16 of 1926), S. 2(g)].

The connotation of "trade" is not limited to an occupation which primarily concerns itself with sale and purchase of goods. Pursuit of a skilled employment with a view to earn profit, such employment not being in the nature of a learned profession or agriculture must be regarded as engaging, in "trade" within the meaning of Art. 276 of the Constitution. A skilled occupation which involves the application of manufacturing processes to a commodity submitted to the person carrying on the occupation must be regarded as trade. *Municipality of Chopala* v. *Motilal Manakchand,* AIR 1958 Bom 487, 489. [Constitution of India, Art. 276]

'Trade' means 'leading, movements of goods, transactions linked with merchandise or flow of goods, the promotion of buying and selling advance, borrowings, discounting bills and mercantile documents, banking and other forms of supply of funds'. *Fatechand Himmatlal* v. *State of Maharashtra*, AIR 1977 SC 1825. 1834. [Constitution of India, Arts. 392, 301]

The word 'business' is a wider term than 'trade' and it includes any occupation. The two words are not necessarily used in an analogous sense. *National Union of Commercial, Employees* v. *M.R. Meher,* AIR 1960 Bom 22, 24. [Industrial Disputes Act (14 of 1947), S. 2(j)]

The word 'trade' bears the meaning which may be taken from Halsbury's Laws of England, Third Edition Vol. 38, p. 8 (a) exchange of goods for goods or goods for money, (b) any business carried on with a view to profit, whether manual or mercantile, as distinguished from the liberal arts or learned professions and from agriculture. *Secretary, Madras*

Gymkhana Club Employees' Union v. *Management of The Gymkhana Club*, AIR 1968 SC 554, 562.

The expression trade should not be construed in its technical sense. The business of making plans and estimates for profits as consulting sanitary engineers and contractors would be included within the expression 'trade'. *Mulshanker* v. *Govt. of Bombay,* AIR 1951 Bom 233. [IPC (45 of 1860), S. 168]

Trade in its primary meaning is the exchanging of goods for goods or goods for money; in its secondary meaning it is repeated activity in the nature of business carried on with a profit motive, the activity being manual or mercantile, as distinguished from the liberal arts or learned professions or agriculture. *State of Punjab* v. *Bajaj Electricals Ltd.*, AIR 1968 SC 739, 741.

Trade allowance. "TRADE ALLOWANCE" includes an allowance having the sanction of custom in the notified market area concerned and market charges payable to various functionaries. [H.P. Agricultural Produce Markets Act 1969 (9 of 1970), S. 2(q)]

"TRADE ALLOWANCE" means anything realised in cash or kind, by the purchaser from the seller in any transaction relating to agricultural produce either by deduction from the price agreed upon or otherwise; *Explanation*—In is clause 'purchaser' includes a commission agent. [W.B. Agricultural Produce Marketing (Regulation) Act (35 of 1972), S. 2(u)]

The question whether a particular payment is a trade allowance or not, depends on the facts of each case. Firstly, it must be a deduction in any transaction in respect of commercial crops. If it is a deduction out of the price or commodity agreed to be paid or transferred., it would be a trade allowance. On the other hand, if the payment is '*de hors*' the terms of the transaction but made towards consideration for the use of the premises or services rendered, it would not be a deduction from the price or in any transaction. *Arunachala Nadar* v. *State of Madras,* AIR 1959 SC 300. 308.

Trade association. "TRADE ASSOCIATION" means a body of persons (whether incorporated or not) which is formed for the purpose of furthering the trade interests of its members or of persons represented by its members. [M.R.T.P. Act (54 of 1969), S. 2(t)]

An association of business organizations having similar problems and engaged in similar fields formed for mutual protection, interchange of ideas and statistics and for maintenance of standards within their industry.

Trade : Business. Business is a much wider term than trade. Business covers a continuous occupation involving liabilities to others, and involving dealings carried on frequently and systematically and over a considerable period and should be deemed to exist from the time of the commencement and till all the assets are realised and liabilities are discharged or otherwise settled. It includes any trader, commerce, a manufacture, or any adventure or concern in the nature of trade, commerce or manufacture. *B. C. Munirathinam Naidu* v. *Meena Financiers, Madras*, AIR 1978 Mad 46, 48. [Presidency Towns Insolvency Act (3 of 1909), S. 9]

Trade card. A card containing a short description as to the composition, date of manufacturer, manufacture's name or any information, instruction or notice regarding any commodity which is affixed or attached or given with the things sold by the manufacturer or dealer. [CPC (5 of 1908), 1 Sch., App. F, form No. 8].

Trade, commerce and intercourse. There is apparently an element of gambling or chance which is the outstanding feature of a Chit Fund Scheme where, on payment of every installment by all the subscribers of a particular Chit, there is an auction and the prize goes to the lowest bidder *i.e.*, one who offers highest sacrifice or the largest discount not exceeding 25 percent. of the Chit value. The limit having been fixed, if more than one subscriber offers to take the Chit at the maximum discount allowed, the offer is decided by casting lots. Essentially, therefore, such a scheme is one of a prize competition which does not involve skill in any substantial degree and cannot, therefore, constitute 'trade, commerce or intercourse' within the meaning of Art. 301, Constitution of India. AIR 1957 SC 699, **relied on.** [SHIV DAYAL, C.J. and S. S. SHARMA, J.] *Sudarshan Finance Corporation, Madras* v. *State of Madhya Pradesh,* MLJ : YD (1977) Suppl. to Oct. C. 2089 : 1977 MPLJ 74 : 1977 Jab LJ 554 : AIR 1977 MP 74. [MP Dhan Parichalan Skeem (Pratishedh) Adhiniyam (1975), S. 1]

Trade : Commerce : Business. "Trade" in its primary meaning is the exchanging of goods for goods or goods for money; in its secondary meaning, it is repeated activity in the nature of business carried on with a profit motive, the activity being manual or mercantile as distinguished from the liberal arts or learned professions or agriculture [*State of Punjab* v. *Bajaj Electricals Ltd.*, (1968) 70 ITR 730, 732 (SC)]. If a person buys goods with a view to selling them at profit, it is an ordinary case of 'trade'. If the transactions are on a large scale, it is called 'commerce' [*Gannon Dunkerley & Co.* v. *State of Madras*, (1954) 5 STC 216, 244 (Mad)], and it is the continuous repetition of such transactions which will constitute a 'business'.

Trade Credit. Refer to the credits extended by the overseas supplier, bank/financial institution for imports into India in accordance with the Trade Credit framework decided by the Reserve Bank in consultation with the Government of India;

Explanation.—Depending on the source of finance, such trade credits include both suppliers' credit relates to the credit for imports into India extended by the overseas supplier, while buyers' credit refers to loans for payment of imports into India arranged by the importer from overseas bank or financial institution. Imports should be as permissible under the extant Foreign Trade Policy of the Director-

General of Foreign Trade (DGFT). [Foreign Exchange Management (Borrowing and Lending) Regulations, 2018, Regn. 2(xvii)].

Trade description. "TRADE DESCRIPTION" means any description, statement or other indication, direct or indirect,—(i) as to the number, quantity, measure, gauge or weight of any goods; or (ii) as to the standard of quality of any goods or services according to a classification commonly used or recognised in the trade; or (iii) as to fitness for the purpose, strength, performance or behaviour of any goods, being "drug" as defined in the Drugs and Cosmetics Act, 1940, or "food" as defined in the Prevention of Food Adulteration Act, 1954; or (iv) as to the place or country in which or the time at which any goods or services were made, produced or provided, as the case may be; or (v) as to the name and address or other indication of the identity of the manufacturer or of the person providing the services or of the person for whom the goods are manufactured or services are provided; or (vi) as to the mode of manufacture or producing any goods or providing services; or (vii) as to the material of which any goods are composed; or (viii) as to any goods being the subject of an existing patent, privilege or copyright, and includes—(a) any description as to the use of any mark which according to the custom of the trade is commonly taken to be an indication of any of the above matters; (b) the description as to any imported goods contained in any bill of entry or shipping bill; (c) any other description which is likely to be misunderstood or mistaken for all or any of the said matters. [Trade Marks Act (47 of 1999), S. 2(1)(za) and Trade and Merchandise Marks Act (43 of 1958), S. 2(1)(u)]

The phrase "all rights reserved" in the outer cover of the spurious edition was held to be a trade description under S. 2 of Trade and Merchandise Marks Act (4 of 1889).

Where a motor car is offered for sale when the mileage recorded on the millimeter is 23000 odd miles, that recorded mileage is capable of amounting to a trade description applied by the seller at the time of the offer for sale.

Trade discounts. Discount allowed in the trade (by whatever name such discount is described) should be allowed to be deducted from the sale price having regard to the nature of the goods, if established under agreements or under terms of sale or by established practice, the allowance and the nature of the discount being known at or prior to the removal of the goods. Such trade discounts shall not be disallowed only because they are not payable at the time of each invoice or deducted from the invoice price. [*Union of India v. Bombay Tyres International (P) Limited*, (2005) 3 SCC 787, para 3 as cited in *IFB Industries Limited v. State of Kerala*, (2012) 4 SCC 618, para 25].

Trade dispute. "TRADE DISPUTE" means any dispute between employers and workmen or between workmen and workmen, or between employers and employers which is connected with the employment or non-employment, or the terms of employment or the conditions of labour, of any person, and "workmen" means all persons employed in trade or industry whether or not in the employment of the employer with whom the trade dispute arises. [Trade Unions Act (16 of 1926), S. 2(g)].

Trade dress. The overall appearance and image in the marketplace of a product or a commercial enterprise.

Trade effluent. Includes any liquid, gaseous or solid substances which is discharged from any premises used for carrying on any industry, operation or process or treatment and disposal system, other than domestic sewage. [Water (Prevention and Control and Pollution) Act (6 of 1974), S. 2(k)]

"TRADE EFFLUENT" means any liquid either with or without particles of matter in suspension therein, which is wholly or in part produced in the course of any trade or industry carried on at trade premises, and in relation to any trade premises means any such liquid as aforesaid which is so produced in the course of any trade or industry carried on at those premises, but does not include domestic sewage. [New Delhi Municipal Council Act (44 of 1994), S. 2(52)]

Trade libel. A false statement that disparages the quality or reputation of another's product or business.

Trade mark. "TRADE MARK" means—(i) in relation to Chapter X (other than S. 81), a registered trade mark or a mark used in relation to goods for the purpose of indicating or so as to indicate a connection in the course of trade between the goods and some person having the right as proprietor to use the mark; and (ii) in relation to other provisions of this Act, a mark used or proposed of indicating or as to indicate a connection in the course of trade between the goods and some person having the right, either as proprietor or as registered user, to use the mark whether with or without any indication of the identity of that person, and includes a certification trade mark registered as such under the provisions of Chapter VIII. [Trade and Merchandise Marks Act (43 of 1958), S. 2(i)(v)]

"TRADE MARK" means a mark capable of being represented graphically and which is capable of distinguishing the goods or services of one person from those of others and may include shape of goods, their packaging and combination of colours; and—(i) in relation to Chapter XII (other than S. 107), a registered trade mark or a mark used in relation to goods or services for the purpose of indicating or so as to indicate a connection in the course of trade between the goods or services, as the case may be, and some person having the right as proprietor to use the mark (ii) in relation to other provisions of this Act, a mark used or proposed to be used in relation to goods or services for the purpose of indicating or so to indicate a connection in the course of trade between the goods or services, as the case may be, and some person having the right, either as proprietor or by way of permitted user, to use the mark whether with or without any indication of the identity of that person, and includes a certification trade mark or collective mark. [Trade Marks Act (47 of 1999), S. 2(1)(zb)]

"TRADE MARK" means a mark used or proposed to be used in relation to goods for the purpose of indicating, or so as to indicate a connection in course of trade between the goods and some person having the right, either as proprietor or as registered user to use the mark, whether with or without any indication of the identity of that person. [Bureau of Indian Standards Act (63 of 1986), S. 2(u)]

A trade-mark is the name, symbol, figure, letter, form or device adopted and used by the manufacturer or merchant in order to designate the goods that he manufactures or sells, and to distinguish them from those manufactured or sold by another, to the end that they may be known in the market as his, and thus enable him to secure such profits as result from a reputation for superior skill, industry, or enterprise.

A mark (now one secured by legal registration) used by a manufacturer or trader to distinguish his goods from the goods of other concerns.

'Trade mark' and 'Domain name'. There is distinction between 'trade mark' and a 'domain name'. A 'trade mark' is protected by the laws of a country where such trade mark may be registered. Consequently, a 'trade mark' may have multiple registration in many countries throughout the world. On the other hand, since the internet allows for access without any geographical limitation, a 'domain name' is potentially accessible irrespective of the geographical location of the consumers for which the national laws might be inadequate to effectively protect a domain name. This lacuna necessitated international regulation of the domain name system. *Satyam Infoway Ltd.* v. *Sifynet Solutions (P) Ltd.*, AIR 2004 SC 3540 : (2004) 6 SCC 145, 152, para 18.

Trade-mark medicine. "Trade-mark medicine" must be held to be medicine as to which a similar monopoly to that of patent and proprietary medicines has been secured, by the use of a trade-mark or trade name under which it is prepared and sold.

Trade name. That name which is used by manufacturers, industrialists and merchants to identify their businesses, which actually symbolizes reputation of business. (*Black*)

A name or style by which the trade is carried on. [Sale of Goods Act (3 of 1930), S. 16(1), *Prov.*].

Trade or business. The word 'business' which is used as synonymous with 'trade' connotes some real, substantial and systematic or organised course of activity with a set purpose and dealing in liquor is business. AIR 1955 SC 176 quoted. *Krishnan Kumar* v. *J & K. State*, AIR SC 1368, 1371. [Constitution of India, Art. 19(1)(g)]

The word 'business' should be seen in a wider context than the word 'trade'. Business always involves continuous exercise of activity and so long as the liabilities incurred in the course of business remain undischarged, the business activity should be deemed to be continued. *In the Matter of P.K. Pattabiraman*, AIR 1989 Mad 271, 274. [Presidency Town Insolvency Act (3 of 1909), S. 52(2)(c)]

Business is a much wider term than trade. Business covers a continuous occupation involving liabilities to others, and involving dealings carried on frequently and systematically and over a considerable period and should be deemed to exist from the time of the commencement and till all the assets are realised and liabilities are discharged or otherwise settled. It includes any trade, commerce, a manufacture, or any adventure or concern in the nature of trade, commerce or manufacture. [Presidency Towns Insolvency Act (3 of 1909), S. 9]

Trade or calling. 'Trade' has a wider meaning of engaging into any kind of activity which may result in profit. As to the following of the calling by a workman, he is only an employee of the company. There may be cases where some special skill may be required in doing a particular job and in that case the particular workman may be said to follow a particular calling. But if the workman is employed by a company, the company will also be carrying on the calling. The pressing of bales was trade or calling. The petitioner on his own showing did not do any trade in wool and therefore, this part of his business of pressing wool into bales on certain charges could rightly be said to be a trade or calling. A company could not be said to be carrying on that trade or calling when it pressed its own goods in order to make them marketable. *Mahalaxmi Mills Co., Ltd.* v. *Chief Commr., State of Ajmer*, MLJ : QD (1956-1960) Vol. IV C160 : 1958 Raj LW 304 : ILR (1958) 8 Raj 195. [Ajmer-Marwara Municipalities Regulation (1925), S. 76(b)]

Trade practice. "TRADE PRACTICE" means any practice relating to the carrying on of any trade, and includes—(*i*) anything done by any person which controls or affects the price charged by, or the method of trading of, any trader or any class of traders, (ii) a single or isolated action of any person in relation to any trade. [M.R.T.P. Act (54 of 1969), S. 2(u)]

Trade premises. "TRADE PREMISES" means any premises used or intended to be used for carrying on any trade or industry. [New Delhi Municipal Council Act (44 of 1994), S. 2(53)]

Trade refuse. "TRADE REFUSE" means the refuse of any trade or industry. [New Delhi Municipal Council Act (44 of 1994), S. 2(54)]

Trade repository. "Trade repository" means a person who is engaged in the business of collecting, collating, storing, maintaining, processing or disseminating electronic records or data relating to such derivatives or financial transactions, as may be specified by the Reserve Bank from time to time. [Payment and Settlement Systems Act (51 of 2007), S. 2(r) as inserted by Amending Act (18 of 2015).

Trade secret. A "trade secret" as protected from misappropriation, may consist of any formula, pattern, device of compilation of information which is used in one's business, and which gives a person an opportunity to obtain an advantage over competitors who do not know or use it; or it may be a formula or a chemical compound, a process of manufacturing, treating or preserving materials, a pattern for a machine or other device, or a list of customers. (*Black*)

Trade Tax. 'Trade tax' means a tax payable under this Act on sales or purchases of goods, as the case may be. [Uttar Pradesh Trade Tax Act, 1948, S. 2(bb) as cited in *State of U.P. v. Jaiprakash Associates Limited*, (2014) 4 SCC 720, para 22].

Trade unions. "TRADE UNION" means any combination, whether temporary or permanent, formed primarily for the purpose of regulating the relations between workmen and employers, or between workmen and workmen, or between employers and employers, or for imposing restrictive conditions on the conduct of any trade or business, and includes any federation of two or more trade Unions. [Trade Unions Act (16 of 1926), S. 2(h)].

Organisation of workmen formed for mutual protection and assistance and for the purpose of improving their condition in employment.

Trade unions upto a certain point have been recognised now as organs for good. They are the only means by which workmen can protect themselves from the tyranny of those who employ them. But the moment that trade unions become tyrants in their turn, they are engines for evil; they have no right to prevent people from working on any terms that they choose.

Trader. "TRADER" in relation to any goods means a person who sells or distributes any goods for sale and includes the manufacturer thereof, and where such goods are sold or distributed in package form, includes the packer thereof. [Consumer Protection Act (68 of 1986), S. 2 (q)]

The mere description as trader does not prevent a person from showing that he is an agriculturist.

One whose business is to trade or commerce or who is engaged in trading. [Indian Contract Act (9 of 1872), S. 17, ill. (d)].

One engaged, in merchandise or commerce.

A trader is a person who buys agricultural produce from the agriculturist and sells the same, either in the same form or after processing the same, to a customer or another dealer. The Steel Authority of India Ltd., incidentally purchasing wood, an agricultural product, for manufacture of steel and iron and not for the propose of selling it in the same form or in the transformed form is only a consumer and not a 'trader'. *Steel Authority of India Ltd.* v. *Bihar Agriculture Produce Market Board,* AIR 1990 Pat 146, 154 (FB).

The expression 'trader' means a person who 'in his normal course of business' 'buys or sells' any notified agricultural produce.

Tradesman. Shopkeeper.

One whose business is trade. [Indian Contract Act (9 of 1872), S. 70, ill. (a)].

Trading. "TRADING" means purchase of electricity for resale thereof and the expression "TRADE" shall be construed accordingly. [Indian Electricity Act (36 of 2003), S. 2(71)]

Traffic. "TRAFFIC" includes rolling stock of every description, as well as passengers, animals and goods. [Indian Railways Act (9 of 1890), S. 3(11)]

Illegal or disreputable business or activity [IPC (45 of 1860), S. 371]; the passing to and fro of persons or of vehicles etc. along routes of transport.

Trade; coming and going of persons, goods etc. by road, railroad or water (as) railroad traffic; motor traffic, etc.

Traffic includes goods as well as passenger traffic. [Indian Railways Act (9 of 1890), S. 42]

"TRAFFIC" includes vehicles of every description and other carriages and conveyances, pedestrians, processions, ridden or herded animals, and all other forms of road traffic using any road or highway for the purpose of travel. [Motor Vehicles (Driving Regulations, 2017, Regn. 2(1)(s)].

Traffic data. 'Traffic data' means any data identifying or purporting to identify any person, computer system or computer network or location to or from which the communication is or may be transmitted and includes communications origins, destination, route, time, date, size, duration or type of underlying service or any other information. [Information Technology Act (21 of 2000), S. 69B, *Expln.* (ii) as inserted by Amending Act (10 of 2009), S. 34]

Traffic sign. "TRAFFIC SIGNS" includes all signals, warning sign posts, direction posts, markings on the road or other devices for the information, guidance or direction of drivers of motor vehicles. [Motor Vehicles Act (59 of 1988), S. 2(45)]

Trafficking. Trafficking means carrying on a trade, buying or selling, often with a sinister implication, and is used in a disparaging sense or in a sense of dealing considered improper.

Trafficking in trade marks. It is guard against unauthorised, spurious, and miscellaneous use of a trade mark by a person or authority or institution other than the registered proprietor thereof. [Trade and Merchandise Marks Act (43 of 1958), S. 48]

Trafficking of person. (1) Whoever, for the purpose of exploitation, (a) recruits, (b) transports, (c) harbours, (d) transfers, or (e) receives, a person or persons, by—

First.— using threats, or

Secondly.— using force, or any other form of coercion, or

Thirdly.-by abduction, or

Fourthly.— by practising fraud, or deception, or

Fifthly.— by abuse of power, or

Sixthly.— by inducement, including the giving or receiving of payments or benefits, in order to achieve the consent of any person having control over the person recruited, transported, harboured, transferred or received, commits the offence of trafficking.

Explanation 1.—The expression "exploitation" shall include any act of physical exploitation or any form of sexual exploitation, slavery or practices similar to slavery, servitude, or the forced removal of organs.

Explanation 2.—The consent of the victim is immaterial in determination of the offence of trafficking. [Indian Penal Code (45 of 1860), S. 370, as substituted by the Criminal Law (Amendment) Act, 2013 (13 of 2013)]. [(w. e. f. 1-7-2024) repealed and replaced by Bharatiya Nyaya Sanhita, 2023 (45 of 2023), section 143(1)]

Trailer. "TRAILER" means any vehicle, other than a semi-trailer and a side-car, drawn or intended to be drawn by a motor vehicle. [Motor Vehicles Act (59 of 1988), S. 2(46)]

Tramway. "TRAMWAY" means a tramway constructed under the Indian Tramways Act, or any special Act relating to tramways. [Indian Railways Act (9 of 1890), S. 3(1)]

Tranquility. The quality or state of being free from agitation or disturbance; being calm, placid, quiet, peaceful (of things or actions). [IPC (45 of 1860), S. 505(b)].

Transaction. "TRANSACTION" includes an arrangement, understanding or action in concert,—

(A) whether or not such arrangement, understanding or action is formal or in writing; or

(B) whether or not such arrangement, understanding or action is intended to be enforceable by legal proceeding.' [Income-tax Act (43 of 1961), S. 92F(v)]. [Also see S. 94A(6)(iii) of the Income-tax Act, 1961 (43 of 1961) as inserted (w.e.f. 1-6-2011) by the Finance Act, 2011]

'TRANSACTION' includes a number of closely linked transactions. [Income-tax Rules, 1962, R. 10A(d)]

"Transaction" in the Usurious Loans Act (10 of 1918) is wide enough to include a course of dealings by way of advances and repayments. The word cannot be restricted to the transaction on which the suit is based ignoring the earlier dealings or settlements of accounts which have led up to such transaction.

TRANSACTION has a very wide meaning and can be applied to any particular act done in the carrying on of a business. It includes the carrying on or completion of an action or a course of action.

'Transaction' is the doing or performing of any business; management of any affair; performance; that which is done; an affair. A 'transaction' is something already done and completed. A 'transaction', in the ordinary sense of the word, is some business or dealing which is carried on, or transacted between two or more persons. A 'transaction' as the derivation denotes something which has been concluded between persons by a cross or reciprocal action as it were. *Chamnoo Mahto* v. *Jang Bahadur Singh,* AIR 1957 Pat 293, 297. [Indian Evidence Act (1 of 1972), S. 13. (a)]

The word 'transaction' is derived from the word 'transact' which means to do something. Partial partitioning of joint family is certainly an act and so is the starting of the partnership business. *Sohan Pathak & Sons* v. *ITC,* AIR 1950 All 643. [Excess Profits Tax Act (15 of 1940), S. 10A(1)]

The formation of a new firm and the division of the gold sovereign assets of the *sarrafa shop* were transactions within the meaning of S. 10-A of Excess Profits Tax Act (15 of 1940). *Kunjilal Nawal Bihari* v. *CIT,* AIR 1955 All 333, 337.

Transaction includes matters relating to affairs of partnership. It does not merely refer to commercial transaction of purchase and sale. *Saligram Ruplal Khanna* v. *Kanwar Rajnath*, AIR 1974 SC 1094, 1105. [Indian Partnership Act (9 of 1932), S. 47]

Transaction value. Means the price actually paid or payable for the goods, when sold, and includes in addition to the amount charged as price, any amount that the buyer is liable to pay to, or on behalf of, the assessee, by reason of, or in connection with the sale, whether payable at the time of the sale or at any other time, including, but not limited to, any amount charged for, or to make provision for, advertising or publicity, marketing and selling organization expenses, storage, outward handling, servicing, warranty, commission or any other matter; but does not include the amount of duty of excise, sales tax and other taxes, if any, actually paid or actually payable on such goods. [Central Excise Act (1 of 1944), S. 4(3)(d)]

"Transaction value" means the price actually paid or payable for the goods, when sold, and includes any amount that the buyer is liable to pay to the assesse in connection with the sale, whether payable at the time of sale or at any other time, including any amount charged for, or to make provisions for advertising or publicity, marketing and selling, and storage, etc., but does not include duty of excise, sales-tax, or any other taxes, if any, actually paid or payable on such goods. Therefore, each removal is a different transaction and duty is charged on the value of each transaction. [*Commissioner of Central Excise, Mumbai v. Fiat India Private Limited*, (2012) 9 SCC 332, para 76].

Transactions in Securities. The issue of debentures and also the redemption of debentures are transactions in securities.

Transboundary movement. "TRANSBOUNDARY MOVEMENT" means any movement of hazardous wastes or other wastes from are area under the national jurisdiction of one State to or through an area under the national jurisdiction of another State or to or through an area not under the national jurisdiction of any State, provided at least two States are involved in the movement. [Basel Convention on the Control of Transboundary Movements of Hazardous wastes and Their Disposal (1989), Art. 2.3]

Transcribe. To make a copy of something in writing [Indian Evidence Act (1 of 1872), S. 63, ill. (c)]; [CPC (5 of 1908), O. XLV, R. 7(1)(b)]; [Registration Act (16 of 1908), S. 43(1)].

Transcript is the copy of any original writing, or deed, etc, where it is written over again, or exemplified, (*Tomlin*); anything written from an original.

A copy of any original writing or deed etc.; anything written from an original. [Navy Act (62 of 1957), S. 108].

Transec. Acronym for transmission security (communications security). (*Cyber Law*)

Transfer. "TRANSFER" shall mean the execution and performance of every deed and act by which a person entitled to stock or Government securities can transfer such stock or Government securities from himself to another. [Trustees Act (27 of 1866), S. 2]

'Transfer' means every mode, direct or indirect, absolute or conditional, voluntary or involuntary, of disposing of or parting with property or with an interest in property, including retention of title as a security interest and foreclosure of the debtor's equity of redemption. [Black's Law Dictionary as cited in *Bombay Stock Exchange v. V.S. Kandalgaonkar*, (2015) 2 SCC 1, para 22].

"TRANSFER" with its grammatical variations and cognate expressions, includes letting on hire, lending, giving and parting with possession. [Arms Act (45 of 1959), S. 2(1)(k)]

"TRANSFER" means a transfer intervivos, and does not include a transfer by operation of law. [Government Savings Certificates Act (46 of 1959), S. 2(d)]

"TRANSFER", in relation to a capital asset, includes.—

(i) the sale, exchange or relinquishment of the asset; or

(ii) the extinguishment of any rights therein; or

(iii) the compulsory acquisition thereof under any law; or

(iv) in a case where the asset is converted by the owner thereof into, or is treated by him as, stock-in-trade of a business carried on by him, such conversion or treatment; or

(v) any transaction involving the allowing of the possession of any immovable property to be taken or retained in part performance of a contract of the nature referred to in Section 53A of the Transfer of Property Act, 1882 (4 of 1882); or

(vi) any transaction (whether by way of becoming a member of, or acquiring shares in, a co-operative society, company or other association of person or by way of any agreement or any arrangement or in any other manner whatsoever) which has the effect of transferring or enabling the enjoyment of, any immovable property.

Explanation.—For the purpose of sub-clauses (v) and (vi) "immovable property" shall have the same meaning as in clause (d) of Section 269UA. [Income-tax Act (43 of 1961), S. 2(47)].

"TRANSFER",—

(*i*) in relation to any immovable property referred to in sub-clause (*i*) of clause (*e*), means transfer of such property by way of sale or exchange or lease for a term of not less than twelve years, and includes allowing the possession of such property to be taken or retained in part performance of a contract of the nature referred to in Section 53A of the Transfer of Property Act, 1882 (4 of 1882).

Explanation.—For the purposes of this sub-clause, a lease which provides for the extension of the term thereof by a further term or terms shall be deemed to be a lease for a term of not less than twelve years if the aggregate of the term for which such lease has been granted and the further term or terms for which it can be so extended is not less than twelve years;

in relation to any immovable property of the nature referred to in sub-clause (*ii*) of clause (*e*), means the doing of anything (whether by way of transfer of shares in a co-operative society or company or by way of any agreement or arrangement or in any other manner whatsoever) which has the effect of transferring, or enabling the enjoyment of, such property. [Income-tax Act (43 of 1961), S. 269A(h)]

"TRANSFER" includes sale, purchase, exchange, mortgage, pledge, gift, loan or any other form of transfer of right, title, possession or lien. [Foreign Exchange Management Act (42 of 1999), S. 2(ze)]

"TRANSFER" includes sale, purchase, mortgage, pledge, gift, loan or any other form of transfer of right, title, possession or lien. [Prevention of Money Laundering Act (15 of 2003), S. 2(1)(za)]

An act of the parties, or of the law, by which the title to property is conveyed from one person to another [T.P. Act (4 of 1882), S. 44]; to convey title or interest in property to another [Indian Partnership Act (9 of 1932), S. 19(2)(g)]; to transfer from one place to another.

To convey; to make over from one to another; to remove. Document whereby one person transfers property, securities, or rights to another.

A transfer is an act or transaction by which property of one person is by him vested in another.

The relinquishment of his rights by a coparcener in favour of another coparcener cannot be strictly said to be a transfer within the meaning of S. 53 of the Transfer of Property Act (4 of 1882).

It is true that a partition is not a transfer, but since in AIR 1978 All 173 it was held that S. 109, T. P. Act is attracted to the case of partition also which the lower appellate Court should have followed in the absence of a centre decision of larger bench, partition is a transfer. *Mohar Singh* v. *Devi Charan*, AIR 1988 SC 1365, 1368. [T.P. Act (4 of 1882), S. 109]

Order allotting a Judge from a High Court to another High Court does not amount to transfer under Art. 222(1). *U. B. Raju* v. *State of Gujarat*, AIR 1980 SC 2075, 2077. [Constitution of India, Art. 222 (1)]

The word 'transfer' includes within its scope transfers both of the voluntary and involuntary. *Mangolore Electric Supply Co.* v. *C.I.T. W.B.*, AIR 1978 SC 1272, 1274.

"TRANSFER" for the removal of doubts, it is hereby clarified that 'transfer' includes and shall be deemed to have always included disposing of or, parting with an asset or any interest therein, or creating any interest in any asset in any manner whatsoever, directly or indirectly, absolutely or conditionally, voluntarily or involuntarily, by way of an agreement (whether entered into in India or outside India) or otherwise, notwithstanding that such transfer of rights has been characterised as being effected or dependent upon or flowing from the transfer of a share or shares of a company registered or incorporated outside India. [*Explanation 2* to section 2(47) of the Income-tax Act, 1961 (43 of 1961) as inserted (w.r.e.f. 1-4-1962) by the Finance Act, 2012 (23 of 2312)]

Transfer and Sale. The word 'transfer' is a larger word and the word 'sale' is a specific word. A transfer may be by means of lease, mortgage or sale or in any other mode. *Union of India* v. *Maqsood Ahmed,* AIR 1963 Bom 110, 114. [Administration of Evacuee Property Act (31 of 1950), S. 10(2), C1. (o)]

Transfer by indorsement. The term, "transfer by indorsement", when used in reference to bills of exchange or promissory notes, means not only the making of the written indorsement on the instrument, but also includes the delivery of the instrument.

Transfer charges. Means the amount to be paid from time to time by the transferee to the State Government as notified in accordance with the provisions of sub-rule (1) of Rule 6. [Minerals (Transfer of Mining Lease Granted otherwise than through Auction for Captive Purpose) Rules, 2016, R. 2(1)(b)].

Transfer from and to. 'Transfer' must necessarily be accompanied by the hand from which and the hand to which something is to be transferred, that is to say, "Transfer must carry with it 'from and to'. If either of them is wanting there can be no transfer". *Deepchand Nayak* v. *M.P. State Road Transport Corporation, Baisagarh, Bhopal,* AIR 1977 MP 42, 46. [Motor Vehicles Act (59 of 1988), S. 110, (1)(2)]

Transfer inter vivos. Transfer between living persons. [Government Savings Certificates Act (46 of 1959), S. 2(d)].

Transfer of business. These words in CPC (5 of 1908), S. 150, cover not only transfers made under special provisions of the Civil Procedure Code but also cases where the whole business of a Court might be transferred to another Court without any order of transfer being passed by a superior Court under S. 24 or any other section of the Code either as regards a particular case or as regards all the cases pending in a particular Court.

Transfer of commodity. To effect a valid transfer of commodity, it is not necessary that the transfer in question should be followed up by actual delivery of the goods to the transferee. Even if the goods are delivered to transferees, the first transfer also will be a valid transfer of commodity. *Raghunath Prasad Paddar* v. *Commission of Income Tax, Calcutta*, AIR 1973, SC 2061, 2062.

Transfer of property. "TRANSFER OF PROPERTY" means an act by which a living person conveys property, in present or in future, to one or more other living persons, or to himself and one or more other living persons; and "to transfer property" is to perform such act.

In this section "LIVING PERSON" includes a company or association or body of individuals, whether incorporated or not, but nothing herein contained shall affect any law for the time being in force relating to transfer of property to or by companies, associations or bodies of individuals. [T.P. Act (4 of 1882), S. 5]

"TRANSFER OF PROPERTY" includes a transfer of any interest in property and the creation of any charge upon property. [Provincial Insolvency Act (5 of 1920), S. 2(f); Presidency Towns Insolvency Act (3 of 1909), S. 2(i)]

The term "Transfer of Property Act" in S. 5 of the Transfer of Property Act is a general one and is not confined to transfers of a contractual and literal character. Besides including a conveyance or assignment of a contractual character, it appears, from the definition of "Transfer of Property" given in S. 5 to include the exercise of a power of appointment under a settlement.

Transfer of risk. The passing from the seller of property to the buyer of the incidence of the loss if the property is damaged or destroyed.

Transfer of venue. The transfer of a lawsuit from one Court to another, usually on the questions of fairness. Also called *change of venue.*

Transfer payments. Within a national economy, payments made by the Government or the wealthier sectors of a population to the poorer people in the country, as through social security payments, unemployment benefits and widows' pensions.

Transfer price. Within a group of companies, the price at which goods or services are sold by one subsidiary to another.

Transferable deposit. Means a deposit in which an evacuee has any right or interest, to the extent of that right or interest. [Transfer of Evacuee Property Act (15 of 1954), S. 2(f)]

Transferable development rights. Means certificates issued in respect of category of land acquired for public purpose either by Central or State Government in consideration of surrender of land by the owner without monetary compensation, which are transferable in part or whole. [Foreign Exchange Management (Borrowing and Lending in Rupees) Regulation, 2000, Reg. 2(d) and Foreign Exchange Management (Transfer or Issue of Security by a Person Resident Outside India) Regulations, 2000, Reg. 2(xi)]

Transferable interest. Any interest which is assignable or negotiable. [CPC (5 of 1908), O. XXI, R. 14].

Transferable securities. Means those classes of securities which are negotiable on the capital market, with the exception of instruments of payment, such as:

(*i*) shares in companies and other securities equivalent to shares in companies, partnerships or other entities, and depository receipts in respect of shares,

(*ii*) bonds or other forms of securitized debt, including depository receipts in respect of such securities;

(*iii*) any other securities giving the right to acquire or sell any such transferable securities or giving rise to a cash settlement. [EU council Regulation 833 of 2014 dated 31-7-2014, Article I, Regn. (f) **as cited in** *Arcelormittal India Private Limited* v. *Satish Kumar Gupta,* (2019) 2 SCC 1, para 103].

Transferable prisoner. Means—

(i) in the State of Punjab as it existed before Ist November, 1956, any prisoner who being a Muslim, is willing to be transferred to Pakistan under the Provision of this Act, and

(ii) in any other part in India, any prisoner of such category as the Central Government may specify by notification in the Official Gazette who, being a Muslim, is willing to be transferred to Pakistan under the provisions of this Act. [Exchange of Prisoner's Act (58 of 1948), S. 2(d)]

Transferable property. Property which is capable of being transferred. [T.P. Act (4 of 1882), S. 7].

Transferable specific delivery contract. Means a specific delivery contract which is not a non-transferable delivery contract. [Forward Contracts (Regulation) Act (74 of 1952), S. 2(n)]

"Transferable specific delivery contract" means a specific delivery contract which is a non-transferable specific delivery contract and which is subject to such conditions relating to its transferability as the Central Government may by notification in the Official Gazette, specify in this behalf. [Securities Contracts (Regulation) Act (42 of 1956), S. 2(k) as inserted by Finance Act (20 of 2015), S. 133].

"Transferred application" or "transferred petition". Means any proceeding which has been transferred to the Tribunal from the Company Law Board, the High Court, District Court, Board for Industrial and Financial Reconstruction as provided in clauses (*a*), (*c*) and (*d*) of sub-section (1) of Section 434 of the Act. [National Company Law Tribunal Rules, 2016, R. 2(29)].

Transferred territory. "Transferred territory", means so much of the territories comprised in the India-Bangladesh agreement and its protocol and referred to in the Second Schedule as are demarcated for the purpose of being transferred by India to Bangladesh in pursuance of the agreement and its protocol referred to in clause (c). [Constitution (One Hundredth Amendment) Act, 2015, S. 2(d)].

Transferee. "Where immovable property passed by operation of law, the persons from and to whom it so passes are, for the purpose of this section, to be deemed respectively, the transferor and transferee." [Indian Easements Act (5 of 1882), S. 13]

One to whom a transfer is made. [T.P. act (4 of 1882), S. 48].

Person to whom a transfer is made. A person by being a decree-holder of the decree-holder does not become a "transferee" of the decreeholder 'by operation of law.'

Transferee company. "TRANSFEREE COMPANY" means the company to which the undertakings of a dissolved company or of a transferred unit, as the case may be, stand transferred by virtue of the provisions of this Act. [Public Sector Iron and Steel Companies (Restructuring) and Miscellaneous Provisions Act (16 of 1978), S. 2(f)]

Transferee for consideration and without notice. A person the transfer in whose favour is for consideration and who, at the time of the transfer, has no knowledge of any defect in the title of the transferor, such as any encumbrance or lien etc. [T.P. Act (4 of 1882), S. 39].

Transferee for value. One to whom a transfer is made for a valuable consideration [Specific Relief Act (47 of 1963), S. 19(b)].

Transferee with notice. The person to whom a transfer is made where he has the knowledge or information of any previous charge, lien or encumbrance attached to the thing, transferred to him [Heading, CPC (5 of 1908), 1st Sch., App. A, form No. 33].

Transferor. "Where immovable property passed by operation of law, the persons from and to whom it so passes are, for the purpose of this section, to be deemed respectively, the transferor and transferee." [Indian Easements Act (5 of 1882), S. 13]

Person who makes a transfer.

Transferring partner. One member of a partnership firm who is making over his share in the partnership to anybody [Indian Partnership Act (9 of 1932), S. 29(1)].

Transhipment. "TRANSSHIPMENT" means to remove goods from the conveyance on which they were brought into India and to place the goods on the same or another conveyance for the purpose of taking them out of India, where these acts are carried out on a "through bill of lading", "through airway bill" or "through manifest".

Explanation.—"Through bill of lading", "through airway bill" and "through manifest" means respectively a bill of lading, airway bill and manifest, for the consignment of goods from a place outside India to a destination which is also outside India without a consignee in India. [Weapons of Mass Destruction and Their Delivery Systems (Prohibition of Unlawful Activities) Act (21 of 2005), S. 4(n)].

To transfer from one conveyance or line to another [Trade and Merchandise Marks Act (43 of 1958), S. 117(5)].

Transit. The passage or carriage of persons or goods from one place to another. [Sale of Goods Act (3 of 1930), S. 52].

Goods on lorries which arrived at the consignee's depot after working hours, and were taken into the depot but not unloaded, were still "in transit" within the terms of the carriage agreement.

Transient use. Means a device intended for continuous use for less than sixty minutes. [Medical Devices Rules, 2017, R. 3(zv)].

Transition date. Shall mean in respect of any state, the date on which the state Goods and Services Tax Act of the concerned state comes into force. [Goods and Services Tax (Compensation to States) Act (15 of 2017), S. 2(1)(q)].

Transition period. Means a period of five years from the transition date. [Goods and Service Tax (Compensation to States) Act (15 of 2017), S. 2(1)(r)].

Translate—Translation. To translate is to give the sense or equivalent of, as a word, expression or an entire work, in another language or dialect, (*Stand. Dict.*); hence to explain by clearer terms, or to express in a different form or style of language. Generally speaking, a translation need not consist of transferring from one language into another. It may apply to the expression of the same thoughts in other words of the same language.

To turn into another language. [CPC (5 of 1908), O. XLV, R. 7(1)(b)].

In the common sense of the word, signifies a version out of one language into another. (*Tomlin*)

The conversion of one form of code to another. For example, source statements are "translated" to machine language by assemblers and compilers; operation codes are translated into commands by decoders in the control units; and a code such as EBCDIC held in storage is translated to ASCII for transmission to another system. (*Computer*)

Translator. One who translates. [Indian Evidence Act (1 of 1872), S. 162].

"Transmissible agent". For the purpose of classification of in vitro diagnostic medical device, means an agent capable of being transmitted to a person, which causes communicable, infectious or contagious disease. [Medical Devices Rules, 2017, R. 3(zw)].

Transmission. "TRANSMISSION" means transmission by operation of law, devolution on the personal representation of a deceased person or any other mode transfer not being assignment. [Semiconductor Integrated Circuit Layout Design Act (37 of 2000), S. 2(t)]

The action of transmitting or the fact of being transmitted; conveyance from one person or place to another [Indian Contract Act (9 of 1872), S. 4]; [Indian Evidence Act (1 of 1872), S. 88]; [Employees' Provident Funds and Miscellaneous Provisions Act (19 of 1952), 1st Sch., item 5].

Transmission by operation of law. The expression "transmission by operation of law" covers a case where a person or authority acquires an interest in the property by operation of law, without any voluntary act on his part. *M. K. Sugar Mills* v. *I. K. Sugar Mills*, AIR 1965 All 135, 140. [Companies Act (1 of 1956), S. 108(1), Proviso 2]

Transmission capacity. Data transfer rate (64 kbit/s, 2 Mbit/s, *etc.*) on a certain bandwidth. (*Telecommunication*)

Transmission lines. Means all high pressure cables and overhead lines (not being an essential part of the distribution system of a licensee) transmitting electricity from a generating station to another generating station or a sub-station, together with any step-up and step-down transformers, switch-gear and other works necessary to and used for the control of such cables or overhead lines, and such buildings or part thereof as may be required to accommodate such transformers, switch-gear and other works. [Electricity Act (36 of 2003), S. 2(72)]

Transmission machinery. Means any shaft, wheel, drum, pulley, system of pulleys, coupling, clutch, driving belt or other appliance or device by which the motion of the prime mover is transmitted to or received by any machinery or appliance. [Factories Act (63 of 1948), S. 2(i)]

Transmission of shares. A transfer of shares that occurs automatically, by operation of law, upon bankruptcy (from the bankrupt to his trustee in bankruptcy) or upon death (to the personal representatives of the deceased).

Transmission utility. "TRANSMISSION UTILITY" means any generating company, board, licensee or other person engaged in the transmission of energy. [Electricity Regulatory Commission Act (14 of 1998), S. 2(k)]

Transmit. "TRANSMIT" means conveyance of electricity by means of transmission lines and the expression "transmission" shall be construed accordingly. [Electricity Act (36 of 2003), S. 2(74)]

To cause to be conveyed to another person or place. [CPC (5 of 1908), O. XXVI, R. 12(1) and Constitution of India, Art. 108(1)].

Transplantation. "TRANSPLANTATION" means the grafting of any human organ from any living person or deceased person to some other living person for therapeutic purposes. [Transplantation of Human Organs Act (42 of 1994), S. 2(q)]

Transport. "TRANSPORT" means to remove from one place to another within the territories administered by the same Government. [Opium Act (1 of 1878), S. 3]

"TRANSPORT" means movement of hazardous wastes by air, rail, road or water [Hazardous Waste (Management and Handling) Rules, 1989, R. 3(u)]

"TRANSPORT" means, movement of hazardous chemicals by any means over land, water or air. [Chemical Accidents (Emergency Planning, Preparedness and Response) Rules, 1996, R. 2(i)].

Transport vehicle. Means a public service vehicle, a goods carriage, an educational institution bus or a private service vehicle. [Motor Vehicles Act (59 of 1988), S. 2 (47)].

Transportation. "TRANSPORTATION" means conveyance of municipal solid wastes from place to place hygienically through specially designed transport system so as to prevent foul odour, littering, unsightly conditions and accessibility to vectors. [Municipal Solid Wastes (Management and Handling) Rules, 2000, R. 3(xxiv)].

Transporter. "TRANSPORTER" means a person engaged in the off-site transportation of hazardous waste by air, rail, road, or water. [Hazardous Waste (Management and Handling) Rules, 1989, R. 2(v)]

"TRANSPORTER" means a conveyance of municipal solid wastes from place to place hygienically through specially designed transport system so as to prevent foul odour, littering, unsightly conditions and accessibility to vectors. [Municipal Solid Wastes (Management and Handling) Rules, 2000, R. 2(xxiv)]

In these regulations, unless the context otherwise requires;—"TRANSPORTER" means the Railways, the owner of the vessel, the owner of the aircraft or, as the case may be, the owner of the motor vehicle, in which the goods imported are transported for the purposes of transhipment. [Goods Imported (Conditions of Transhipment) Regulations, 1995, Rgn. 2(c)]

Trap door. A hidden software or hardware mechanism used to circumvent security control. (*Cyber Law*)

Traveller's cheque. A draft issued by a bank, express company etc. having the bearer's signature and payable when the bearer signs it again in order to cash it. [Banking Regulation Act (10 of 1949), S. 6(1)(a)].

Travelling. The action of travel; making a journey.

Travelling and other expenses. The expenses required for travelling and other purposes connected with it. [CPC (5 of 1908), 1st Sch., App. B, form No. 13].

Traverse. To pass through, across or over [Indian Railways Act (9 of 1890), S. 11(2)]; a crossing or passage across. [Factories Act (63 of 1948), S. 25].

Treachery. Conduct that assists an enemy.

Treason. Attempt to overthrow the government of the State of which one owes allegiance by resorting to war against it or by helping the enemies.

Treasure. "TREASURE" means anything of any value hidden in the soil, or in anything affixed thereto. [Treasure Trove Act (6 of 1878), S. 3]

Money, bullion or other valuables found hidden in the earth or elsewhere; accumulated wealth (which is hidden) [Indian Contract Act (9 of 1872), S. 56, ill. (a)]; wealth stored up; anything much valued.

Treasurer. An officer to whom the treasure of another is committed to be kept, and truly disposed of. One who is responsible for the funds of any public body, or corporation or association. [Registration Act (16 of 1908), S. 17(2)(xa)]; [Constitution of India, Art. 31A(1)(d)].

Treasury. 'TREASURY' includes a sub treasury. [Punjab Reorganisation Act (37 of 1966), S. 2(o); Madhya Pradesh Re-organisation Act (28 of 2000), S. 2(l); Uttar Pradesh Reorganisation Act (29 of 2000), S. 2(l) and Bihar Reorganisation Act (30 of 2000), S. 2(l)]

Place where public monies are kept; the office of treasurer. (*Tomlin*)

A repository of treasures; place where public monies are kept. [IPC (45 of 1860), S. 405, ill. (e)].

Treasury bench. A name given to the bench occupied by the Ministers that is, the front bench extending up to the gangway on the right of the Speaker; also called government bench.

Treasury bills. Negotiable Government acknowledgments of loans made payable after a fixed period.

Treasury warrant. An order made in the form of a cheque on which government disbursements are made.

Treating. (*in Election Law*) Means that form of bribery where the gratification consists in food, drink, entertainment, or provision. [IPC (45 of 1860), S. 171-E]

Subjecting to a process [Factories Act (63 of 1948), S. 2(k)(i)]; to provide hospitality; to stand a drink or other gratification to [IPC (45 of 1860), S. 171-E, prov.]; or regard (as something or in a particular way) and act toward or deal with accordingly.

Treatise. A book or writing which treats of some particular subject [Indian Evidence Act (1 of 1872), S. 60, prov.]; [Drugs and Magic Remedies (Objectionable Advertisements) Act (21 of 1954), S. 14(b)]

Treatment. "TREATMENT" means a method, technique or process, designed to change the physical, chemical or biological characteristics or composition of any hazardous waste so as to render wastes harmless. [Environment (Protection) Act, 1986, R. 2(d)].

The action or manner of dealing with something often in a specialised way [Emigration Act (31 of 1983), S. 4(d)]; the action or manner of treating a patient medically or surgically [Employees' State Insurance Act (34 of 1948), S. 22(b)]; behaviour towards anyone [Industrial Employment (Standing Orders) Act (20 of 1946), Sch., item 10]; something used in treatment [Drugs and Magic Remedies (Objectionable Advertisements) Act (21 of 1954), S. 3(d), prov. (i)].

Treaty. 'TREATY' means an international agreement concluded between states in written form and governed by international law whether embodied in a single instrument or in two or more related instruments and whatever its particular designation. [Vienna Convention on the Law of Treaties, 1969, Art. 2.1(a)]

The TREATY means the Treaty for the Limitation of Naval Armament and for the Exchange of Information concerning Naval Construction signed in London on behalf of His Majesty on the twenty-fifth day of March, 1936. [Indian Naval Armament (7 of 1923), S. 2(c)]

"TREATY" means a reinsurance arrangement between the insurer and the reinsurer, usually for one year or longer, which stipulates the technical particulars and financial terms applicable to the reinsurance of some class or classes of business. [Insurance Regulatory and Development Authority (General Insurance-Reinsurance) Regulations, Regn. 2(i)]

A formal agreement especially between States [Customs Act (52 of 1962), S. 11(2)(q) and Constitution of India, Art. 73(1)(b)].

A treaty is a contract between two or more independent States, signed by or on behalf of their sovereign authorities. When relating to rights and duties of subjects or citizens of the respective States in one another's possessions, treaties are generally called conventions.

"Treaty" in the law of nations, "is an agreement or contract between two or more nations or sovereigns, entered into by agents appointed for that purpose, and duly sanctioned by the supreme powers of the respective parties".

A "treaty" is a contract between independent nations, or communities having the right of self-government. The only requisite is that each of the contracting parties shall possess the right of self-government and the power to perform the stipulations of the treaty.

'TREATY' means a reinsurance arrangements between the cedant and the reinsurer, usually for one year or longer, which stipulates the technical particulars and financial terms applicable to the reinsurance of defined class or classes of business. [Insurance Regulatory and Development Authority of India (General Insurance-Reinsurance) Regulations, 2016, Regn. 2(q)].

Treaty for the sale. Discussion of terms or negotiations for the sale. [Indian Contract Act (9 of 1872), S. 229, ill. (a)].

Treaty of cession. "TREATY OF CESSION" means the treaty concluded between France and India on the 28th day of May, 1956 establishing the cession of the French Establishments by France to India in full sovereignty. [Pondicherry (Administration) Act (49 of 1962), S. 2(g)]

A transfer usually evidenced by a treaty of Sovereignty over territory by one Sovereign State to another Sovereign apparently willing to accept it.

Treaty State. Means a foreign State with which an extradition treaty is in operation. [Extradition Act (34 of 1962), S. 2(j)]

Tree. "TREE" includes palms, skumps, brushwood and canes. [Indian Forest Act (16 of 1927), S. 2(7)]

A tree, strictly speaking, is that which is growing or standing in the ground, whether dead or alive. There are dead and alive trees, both standing; but, when the trunk is severed from the root and felled to the earth, it is no longer, properly speaking, a tree. It becomes timber or lumber, according to the use to which it can be applied.

A tree is a woody plant, whose branches spring from and are supported upon a trunk or body and the tree may be young or old, small or great and cannot be denominated as a "shrub" or undergrowth; for a shrub is a low, small plant, whose branches grow directly from the earth, without any supporting trunk or stem, while "undergrowth" is a term applicable to plants growing under or below other greater plants.

'TREE' means any of the following species of trees, namely—

Sandalwood (Santalum album), Teak (Tectonagrandis), Rosewood (Dalbergialatifolia), Irul (XyliaXylocarpa), Thempavu (Terminalia tomantosa), Kampakam (Hopeaparviflora), Chempakam (Micheliachempa), Chadachi (Grewiatiliaefolia), Chandanavempu (Cedrelatoona), Cheeni (Tetramelesnudiflora). [Kerala Preservation of Trees Act (35 of 1986), S. 2(e) as cited in *State of Kerala v. Abdul Ali*, (2013) 15 SCC 274, para 6].

Trespass. Doing of unlawful act or of lawful act in unlawful manner to the injury of another's person or property or any violation or transgression of the law; passing beyond some limit; an encroachment, intrusion on or upon. [IPC (45 of 1860), S. 297].

The word trespass in common English acceptation means and implies unlawful or unwarrantable intrusion upon land. In other words, it is a transgression of law or right. [*Bibek Motors v. Pyarimohan & Pramila Trust*, AIR 2012 Ori 87, para 11].

A forcible entry on the land of another with strong hand and against the will of the owner constitutes a trespass.

The term "trespass" in S. 297, IPC (45 of 1860), appears to mean any violence or injurious act committed in such place and with such knowledge or intention as is defined in that section.

Trespass and Nuisance. Trespass differs from 'nuisance' in that it is direct as opposed to a consequential injury, and is actionable without proof of damage, whereas damage must be proved in nuisance. [CLERK & LINDSELL *on Torts,* 17th Edn., 1995, c. 17, para 17-07, p. 840]

Trespasser. One who commits trespass; especially one who trespasses the lands of another. [IPC (45 of 1860), S. 443].

Trespasser is a person, who enters the premises of another with knowledge that his entrance is in excess of the permission that has been given to him. [*Bibek Motors v. Pyarimohan & Pramila Trust*, AIR 2012 Ori 87, para 11].

Trial. "TRIAL" means any hearing before the Court at which evidence is taken. [Banker's Books Evidence Act (18 of 1891), S. 2(7)]

A judicial examination, in accordance with law, of a cause either civil or criminal, of the issues between the parties, whether of law or fact, before a Court that has jurisdiction over it [CrPC, 1973 (2 of 1974), S. 407(1)(c)(iii)]; the subjugation of a person or thing to test or examination.

The examination by court of issues of fact and law in a case for the purpose of rendering the judgment relating to some offences committed. [*Ashwani Kumar Saxena v. State of M.P.*, (2012) 9 SCC 750, para 30].

TRIAL is the examination before a competent Court according to law of the facts or law put in issue in a cause.

It is a judicial examination of issues between the parties, whether they be of law or fact.

When charge has been read and explained to the accused and he pleads to it, the inquiry becomes a trial.

The trial in a warrant case commences when the Magistrate takes his seat in Court with the accused in the dock in front of him and not when the Magistrate frames a charge and the accused claims to be tried. *Emperor* v. *Ramchandra Narhar,* AIR 1944 Bom 14.

In quite a number of sections in the CrPC (5 of 1898), S. 494 (now S. 40 (1) of 1974 Code) the words 'trial' or 'tried' have been used in the sense of reference to a stage after the inquiry. That meaning attaches to the words in those sections having regard to the context in which they are used. There is no reason why where these words are used in another context in the Code, they should necessarily be limited in their connotation and significance. *State of Bihar* v. *Ram Naresh Pandey*, AIR 1957 SC 389, 394.

The word 'trial' occurring in Section 40(1) includes period from filing of first information report till the end of the trial. *Bipinchandra Parshottamdas Patel (Vakil)* v. *State of Gujarat,* AIR 2003 SC 2256. [CrPC 1973 (2 of 1974), S. 40(1)]

The trial mentioned in S. 98 is not the only stage in the proceedings in which evidence is taken and arguments are heard. The word clearly means the entire proceeding before a Tribunal from the reference to it by the Election Commission to the conclusion. *Om Prabha Jain* v. *Gian Chand*, AIR 1959 SC 837, 839. [Representation of the People Act (43 of 1951), S. 98]

Trial at the bar. A trial before all the judges at the bar of the Court.

Trial by battle. A method of trying the guilt of an accused or any dispute to tittle or a debt by making the opposite parties to fight each other, the loser was punished or he lost the claim.

Trial by jury is a trial presided over by a judge aided by a jury chosen according to law.

Trial by ordeal. A formerly used criminal trial in which the guilt or innocence of the accused was determined by subjection to dangerous or painful tests believed to be under divine control. (*Merriam Webster*)

Trial commenced. The trial before the General Court Martial commences the moment the General Court Martial (GCM) assembles to consider the charge and examines whether they would proceed with the trial. *Union of India* v. *Madan Lal Yadav*, AIR 1996 SC 1340, 1348. [Army Act (46 of 1950), Section 123]

Trial de novo. Means trial of the entire case anew.

Trial on merits. Trial on the substantive issues of a case.

Trial subject. Means a person who is either a patient or a healthy person to whom investigational product is a administered for the purposes of a clinical trial. [New Drugs and Clinical Trials Rules, 2019, R. 2(10(jj)].

Triangular merger. A merger in which the target corporation is absorbed into the acquiring corporation's subsidiary, with the target's shareholders receiving stock in the parent corporation.

Tribal areas. Means the tribal areas of Tochi and Kurram and includes such other Tribal areas adjoining the North West Frontier Province as may be specified in this behalf by an order of the Central Government. [Displaced Persons (Claims) Supplementary Act (12 of 1954), S. 2(e)]

Tribe. A race of people. [T.P. Act (4 of 1882), S. 69(1)(a)].

Tribunal. "TRIBUNAL" means the Registrar or, as the case may be, the High Court before which the proceeding concerned is pending. [Trade and Merchandise Marks Act (43 of 1958), S. 2(1)(x)]

The expression 'tribunal' as used in Art. 136., Constitution of India does not mean the same thing as 'Court' but includes, within its ambit all adjudicating bodies, provided they are constituted by the State and are invested with judicial as distinguished from purely administrative or executive functions. The Courts or tribunals established by or under any law relating to the Armed Forces are exempted. AIR 1950 SC 188 Rel. on. *Durga Shankar Mehta* v. *Raghuraj Singh*, AIR 1954 SC 520.

A judicial assembly; a judicial authority. [Indian Evidence Act (1 of 1872), S. 74(1)(ii)].

The tribunal as distinguished from the Court, exercises judicial power and decides matters brought before it judicially or *quasi* judicially, but it does not constitute a Court in the technical sense. *Engineering Mazdoor Sabha* v. *Hind Cycles Ltd.*, AIR 1963 SC 874, 878. [Constitution of India, Art. 136(1)]

The word 'tribunal' means the High Court or the Registrar before whom proceedings are pending. *Registrar, Trade Marks Kumar Ranjan,* AIR 1966 Cal 311, 314. [Trade and Merchandise Marks Act (43 of 1958), S. 56(4)]

"TRIBUNAL". Means the National Company Law Tribunal constituted under section 408 of the Companies Act, 2013 (18 of 2013). [S. 2(90) of the Companies Act, 2013 (18 of 2013)]

Tried jointly. The words "tried jointly" mean legally tried jointly, and not simply tried jointly as a matter of fact. R. v. *Jagat*, 22 Cal 50.

Trivial. Trifling; unimportant [CrPC 1973 (2 of 1974), S. 360(3)].

Trojan horse. A Trojan horse is an independent program that, when called by an authorized user, performs a useful function, but also performs unauthorized functions, often usurping the privileges of the user. (*Cyber Law*)

Programs that have the ability to hide and replicate themselves. (*Cyber Law*)

A computer program is either hidden inside another program or that masquerades as something it is not in order to trick potential users into running it. For example, a program that appears to be a game or image file but in reality performs some other function. The term "Trojan Horse" comes from a possibly mythical ruse of war used by the Greeks sometime between 1500 and 1200 B.C.

A Trojan Horse computer program may spread itself by sending copies of itself from the host computer to other computers, but unlike a *virus* it will (usually) not infect other programs. (*Matisse Enzer-Glossary of Internet Terms*)

Troll. The act of subverting a forum by deliberately posting provocative (especially provocatively stupid) messages with the intention of distracting others into response. (*Cyber Law*)

Troops. A body of soldiers. [Indian Evidence Act (1 of 1872), S. 6, ill.(b)].

Trophy. "TROPHY" means the whole or any part of any captive animal or wild animal, other than vermin, which has been kept or preserved by any means, whether artificial or natural, and includes—

(a) rugs, skins and specimens of such animal mounted in whole or in part through a process of taxidermy; and

(b) antler, bone, carapace, shell, horn, rhinoceros horn, hair, feather, nail, tooth, tusk, musk, eggs, nests and honeycomb [Wild Life (Protection) Act (53 of 1972), S. 2(31) substituted by Act 16 of 2003].

"TROPHY" means any dead animal specimen or part thereof whether included in a manufactured or processed object or otherwise dealt with, unless it has lost its original identity— also nests, eggs and egg shells. [African Convention on the Conservation of Nature and Natural Resources, 1968, Art. III(3)]

Trouble. Disturbance of mind or feelings; worry; vexation; affliction [Indian Contract Act (9 of 1872), S. 73, ill. (b)].

Trover. An action which lies where one man gets possession of the goods of another by delivery, finding or otherwise, and refuses to deliver them to the owner, or sells or converts them to his own use, without the consent of the owner, for which the owner, by this action, recovers the value of his goods. (*Tomlin*)

Truancy. The act or state of shirking responsibility.

Truce. A league or cessation of arms. (*Tomlin*)

True account. Correct account [Indian Partnership Act (9 of 1932), S. 9]; correct narration of facts [CrPC 1973 (2 of 1974), S. 164(4)].

True and correct. Authentic; accurate; unaltered.

True and first inventor. Does not include either the first importer of an invention into India, or a person to whom an invention is first communicated from outside India. [Patents Act, 1970, S. 2(y)]

Truncated cheque. "A TRUNCATED CHEQUE" means a cheque which is truncated during the course of a clearing cycle, either by the clearing house or by the bank whether paying or receiving payment, immediately a generation of an electronic image for transmission, substituting the further physical movement of the cheque in writing. [Negotiable Instruments Act (26 of 1881), S. 6 *Expln.*(1)(b)]

Trust. A "TRUST" is an obligation annexed to the ownership of property, and arising out of a confidence reposed in and accepted by the owner, or declared and accepted by him, for the benefit of another, or of another and the owner. [Indian Trusts Act (2 of 1882), S. 3]

"TRUST" includes every species of express, implied or constructive fiduciary ownership. [Specific Relief Act (1 of 1877), S. 3]

"TRUST" includes any other legal obligation. [Wild Life Protection Act (53 of 1972), S. 58B(k); Wealth-tax Act (52 of 1963), S. 21A(b)]

"TRUST" means an irrevocable public charitable or religious trust registered under any law for the time being in force and represented by its trustees, in whom the trust property is vested, as members. [Companies (Authorised to Register) Rules, 2014, rule 2(1)(i)]

To repose confidence in [Indian Evidence Act (1 of 1872), S. 14, ill. (f)]; responsibility.

A confidence which one man reposes in another. (*Tomlin*)

TRUST means only the "trust" created by an employer for the purpose of transferring the provident fund for the benefit of employees and it does not include a "trust" created by a Statute. *United Merchantile Co. Ltd. (P.) Ltd.* v. *C.I.T. Kerala,* AIR 1969 Ker 227 at

232. [Income Tax Act (43 of 1961), Sch. 4, Part A, R. 14 (1)]

"Trust" includes endowments for religious and charitable purposes.

The person who reposes or declares the confidence of trust is called the "AUTHOR OF THE TRUST" : the person who accepts the confidence is called the "TRUSTEE" : the person for whose benefit the confidence is accepted is called the "BENEFICIARY" : the subject matter of the trust is called "TRUST PROPERTY" or "TRUST MONEY" : the "BENEFICIAL INTEREST" OR "INTEREST" of the beneficiary is his right against the trustee as owner of the trust-property : and the instrument, if any, by which the trust is declared is called the "INSTRUMENT OF TRUST" : a breach of any duty imposed on a trustee, as such, by any law for the time being in force, is called a "BREACH OF TRUST". [Indian Trusts Act (2 of 1882), S. 3]

Trust company. A company which acts as a trustee for individuals and entities and which sometimes also operates as a commercial bank.

Trust documents. Documents in the possession of trustees *qua* trustees, containing trust information which beneficiaries are entitled to know and in which they have a proprietary interest.

Trust fund. A fund held by one person, the trustee, for the benefit of another, the affairs of the trust being conducted in accordance with the provisions of a formal trust agreement.

Trust, In. By way of trust [Indian Trusts Act (2 of 1882), S. 16, ill. (b)].

Trust instrument. The instrument by which a trust is declared is called the instrument of trust or trust instrument. [Indian Trust Act (2 of 1882), S. 3]

"Trust-money" or "Trust-property". "The subject-matter of the trust is called "trust property" or "trust money". [Indian Trust Act (2 of 1882), S. 3]

Trusted Third Party. In general, an independent, unbiased third party that contributes to the ultimate security and trustworthiness of computer based information transfers. A trusted third party does not connote the existence of a trustor-trustee or other fiduciary relationship. (*Information Technology*)

Trustee. The person who accepts the confidence (reposed or declared by the author of the trust) is called the TRUSTEE." [Indian Trust Act (2 of 1882), S. 3] [Also see R. 2(1)(i) of the Companies (Acceptance of Deposits) Rules, 2014]

"TRUSTEE", in relation to a part, means a member of the Board constituted for the port. [Major Port Trusts Act (38 of 1963), S. 2(y)]

"TRUSTEE" includes every person holding property in trust [Specific Relief Act (47 of 1963), S. 2(c)]

"TRUSTEE" does not include a *benamider,* a mortgagee remaining in possession after the mortgage has been satisfied, or a person in wrongful possession without title. [Limitation Act (36 of 1963), S. 2(n)]

"TRUSTEE" means a person who holds the property of the mutual fund in trust for the benefit of the unit-holders and includes a trustee company and the directors of the trustee company. [SEBI (Mutual Funds) Regulations 1996, R. 2(y)]

One to whom property is entrusted to be administered for the benefit of another. [Indian Trusts Act (2 of 1882), S. 3].

BOARD OF TRUSTEES. A constituted body of persons to whom the administration of a trust is entrusted.

Trustee Bank. Means a banking company as defined in the Banking Regulation Act, 1949 (10 of 1949). [S. 2(1)(v) of the Pension Fund Regulatory & Development Authority Act, 2013 (23 of 2013)]

Trustee de son tort is one who, of his own authority, enters into the possession or assumes the management of property which belongs beneficially to another.

Trusteeship. The office, status or function of a trustee; in international law, administration or supervision of a territory by one or more countries.

Trusts. An arrangement whereby several companies are placed under one control, mainly with a view to regulate the production and to beat down competition.

TRANSGRESSIVE TRUSTS. Trusts which transgress the rule against perpetuities are called "transgressive trusts".

Trusty. A convict or prisoner who is considered trustworthy by prison authorities and therefore given special privileges.

Truth : Veracity. Truth belongs to the thing; veracity to the person; the truth of the story is admitted upon the veracity of the narrator.

Try. To examine or determine (a cause or question) judicially; to determine the guilt or otherwise (of an accused person) by consideration of the evidence. [CrPC 1973 (2 of 1974), S. 260(1)].

Try and trial. The words 'try' and 'trial' have no fixed or universal meaning but they are words which must be construed with regard to the particular context in which they are used and with regard to the scheme and purpose of the measure concerned.

TTP. The abbreviation for a Trusted Third Party; an independent individual, firm or company set up or licensed by the State to provide, amongst other things, escrow services and certification or verification services for public and private key algorithms or codes used in cryptographic software, and providing authentication services in respect of digital signatures used in e-commerce. (*Cyber Law*)

TTY. A type of machine that allows people with hearing or speech disabilities to communicate over the phone using a keyboard and a viewing screen. It is sometimes called a TDD. (*Telecommunication*)

'TUFS' means Technology Upgradation Fund Scheme announced by the Government of India in the form of a resolution of the Ministry of Textiles, *vide* No.

28/1/99-CTI of 31st March, 1999. [Income-Tax Rules, 1962, App. I, Note (3B)]

Turnkey. Situation, especially in the computer and construction industries, in which a supplier provides a complete customized package to a customer.

Turnover. "TURNOVER" used in relation to any dealer liable to tax under this Act means the aggregate of the sale prices received and receivable by him in respect of sales of any goods in the course of inter-State trade or commerce made during any prescribed period and determined in accordance with the provisions of this Act and the rules made thereunder. [Central Sales Tax (74 of 1956), S. 2(j)]

"TURNOVER" includes value of sale of goods or services. [Competition Act, 2002 (12 of 2003), S. 2(y)]

Turnover is the amount of money turned over or drawn in a business, as in a retail shop, in a given time.

Excise duty though paid by the purchaser to meet the liability of the appellant, is a part of the consideration for the sale and is includible in the turnover. *Mc. Dowell & Co. Ltd.* v. *Commercial Tax Officer*, AIR 1986 SC 649, 659.

If any discount is given by a trader by way of trade discount, that could be excluded from the turnover. *Tungabhadra Industries Ltd.* v. *Commercial-tax Officer,* AIR 1986 SC 649, 659.

In calculating the total turnover, there is nothing wrong in treating the tax as part of the turnover, because "turnover" means the amount of money which is turned over in the business. *George Oakes (P) Ltd.* v. *State of Madras*, AIR 1962 SC 1352, 1355.

"TURNOVER" means the aggregate value of the realisation of amount made from the sale, supply or distribution of goods or on account of services rendered, or both, by the company during a financial year. [S. 2(91) of the Companies Act, 2013 (18 of 2013)]

'Turnover' means the aggregate amount for which goods are either bought or sold, supplied or distributed by a dealer, either directly or through another, on his own account or on account of others, whether for cash or for deferred payment or other valuable consideration. [Kerala General Sales Tax Act 15 of 1963, S. 2(xxvii) as cited in *IFB Industries Limited v. State of Kerala*, (2012) 4 SCC 618, para 18].

"Any cash or other discount on the price allowed in respect of any sale and any amount refunded in respect of articles returned by customers shall not be included in the turnover. [*IFB Industries Limited v. State of Kerala*, (2012) 4 SCC 618, para 18] [Kerala General Sales Tax Act (15 of 1963), S. 2(xxvii), Explanation 2(ii)].

'TURNOVER' means, the aggregate amount for which goods are supplied or distributed by way of sale or are sold, by a dealer, either directly or through another, on his account or on account of others, whether for cash or deferred payment or other valuable consideration. [Uttar Pradesh Trade Tax Act 15 of 1948, S. 2(i) as cited in *State of U.P. v. Systematic Conscom Limited*, (2014) 13 SCC 627, para 12].

"Turnover" means the aggregate amount for which the goods are bought or sold or distributed or delivered or otherwise disposed of in any of the ways referred to in clause (t) by a dealer, either directly or through another, on his own account or on account of others, whether for cash or for deferred payment or other valuable consideration. [Karnataka Sales Tax Act (25 of 1957), S. 2(v) **as cited in** *Larsen and Toubro Limited* v. *Additional Deputy Commissioner of Commercial Taxes,* (2016) 9 SCC 780, para 9].

"TURNOVER" means the aggregate amount for which goods are sold or distributed or otherwise disposed of in any of the ways referred to in clause (29) by a dealer, either directly or through another, on his own account or on account of others, whether for cash or for deferred payment or other valuable consideration, and includes the aggregate amount for which goods are purchased from a person not registered under the Act and the value of goods transferred or despatched outside the state otherwise than by way of sale, and subject to such conditions and restrictions as may be prescribed the amount for which goods are sold shall include any sums charged for anything done by the dealer in respect of the goods sold at the time of or before the delivery thereof.

Explanation.—For value of the goods transferred or despatched outside the State otherwise than by way of sale, shall be the amount for which the goods are ordinarily sold by the dealer or the prevailing market price of such goods where the dealer does not ordinarily sell the goods. [Karnataka Value Added Tax Act, 2003 (32 of 2004), S. 2(36) **as cited in** *Southern Motors* v. *State of Karnataka,* (2017) 3 SCC 467, para 11].

Turnover in State. "Turnover in State" or "turnover in Union territory" means the aggregate value of all taxable supplies (excluding the value of inward supplies on which tax is payable by a person on reverse charge basis) and exempt supplies made within a State or Union territory by a taxable person, exports of goods or services or both and inter-State supplies of goods or services or both made from the State or Union territory by the said taxable person but excludes central tax, State tax, Union territory tax, integrated tax and cess [The Central Goods and Services Tax Act, 2017 (12 of 2017), S. 2(112)]

Turnover of receipts. "TURNOVER OF RECEIPTS" (i) in the case of a hotelier means the aggregate of the amounts of valuable consideration received or receivable by a hotelier or by his agent in respect of the luxuries provided in a hotel during a given period; and. [Maharashtra Tax on Luxuries (In Hotels and Lodging Houses) Act (41 of 1987), S. 2(p) substituted by Mah. 16 of 1995]

"Turnover in State" or **"turnover in Union Territory".** Means the aggregate value of all taxable supplies (excluding the value of inward supplies on which tax is payable by a person on reverse charge basis) and exempt supplies made within a State or Union Territory by a taxable person, exports of goods or services or both and inter-State supplies of goods or services or both made from the State or Union Territory by the said taxable person but excludes Central Tax, State Tax, Union Territory tax, integrated tax and cess. [Central Goods and Services Ta Act (12 of 2017), S. 2(112)].

Turnover in Union Territory. §§ See under "TURNOVER IN STATE".

Turnover of zero-rated supply of goods. Means the value of zero-rated supply of goods made during the relevant period without payment of tax under bond or letter of undertaking. [Central Goods and Services Tax Rules, 2017, R. 89(4)(c)].

Turnover of zero-rated supply of services. Means the value of zero-rated supply of services made without payment of tax under bond or letter of undertaking, calculated in the following manner, namely—

Zero-rated supply of services is the aggregate of the payments received during the relevant period for zero-rated supply of services and zero-rated supply of services where supply has been completed for which payment had been received in advance in any period prior to the relevant period reduce by advances received for zero-rated supply of services for which the supply of services has not been completed during the relevant period. [Central Goods and Services Tax Rules, 2017, R. 89(4)(d)].

Turnover of stock of luxuries. "TURNOVER OF STOCK OF LUXURIES" in relation to a stockist in respect of any prescribed period or part thereof means the aggregate of the values of stock luxuries. [Orissa Luxury Act (11 of 1995), S. 2(i)]

Tutoring a man to give false evidence. To tutor a man to give false evidence would amount to what S. 192, IPC (45 of 1860), describes as the "causing of circumstance to exist" and such a person can be convicted under S. 194, IPC (45 of 1860).

(Two) 2G mobile systems. (*abbr.*) Second generation mobile systems. Mobile systems based on GSM (see GSM). (*Telecommunication*)

Two companies. Means—

(i) the Assam Oil Company Limited a company incorporated in the United Kingdom and having its registered office at Burmah House, Pipers, Way; Swindon, England; and

(ii) "the Burmah Oil Company (India Trading) Limited" a company incorporated in Scotland and having its registered office at 48, St. Vincent Street, Glasgow, Scotland, being foreign companies within the meaning of Section 591 of the Companies Act, 1956. [Burmah Oil Company (Acquisition of Shares of Oil India Ltd. and of the Undertaking in India or Assam Oil Company Ltd. and the Burmah Oil Company (India Trading) Ltd. Act (41 of 1981), S. 2(h)]

Two-member constituency. "TWO-MEMBER CONSTITUENCY" means a two member parliamentary constituency specified in the First Schedule, or a two member assembly constituency specified in the Second Schedule, to the Delimitation order. [Two Member Constituencies (Abolition) Act (1 of 1961), S. 2(e)]

A constituency from which two members are to be elected.

Two months. Does not mean 60 days. The calculation of the period must be made month-wise. *Laxmi Narain Ram Narain* v. *State of Bihar,* AIR 1977 Pat 73, 77. [CPC (5 of 1908), S. 80]

Two months next before the date of order. The expression 'two months next before the date of order' can be invoked only, if the party has been forcibly and wrongfully dispossessed within two months prior to the date of the preliminary order. *Athiappa Gounder* v. S. *A. Athiappa,* AIR 1967 Mad 445, 449 (FB). [CrPC, 1973 (2 of 1974), S. 145(4), *proviso*]

Two persons. The two persons referred to in S. 92, CP Code (5 of 1908), are two individuals and the fact that the two persons are father and son and members of a joint Hindu family will not convert them into one person for the purpose of that section.

(Two point five) 2.5G mobile systems. (*abbr.*) 2.5 generation mobile systems. Mobile systems based on GPRS (see GPRS) and HSCSD (see HSCSD). (*Telecommunication*)

Two witness rule. A rule requiring the testimony of at least two witnesses in order to convict for perjury.

Tying product. A desirable product that buyers can purchase only if they also purchase a tied product.

Type. "Type" means "a group of people or things with similar qualities or features that make them different from other groups". [Macmillan Dictionary as cited in *State of Jharkhand v. La Opala R.G. Limited*, (2014) 15 SCC 136, para 26].

"Types" means "kind, class, breed, group, family, genus". [Oxford Dictionary as cited in *State of Jharkhand v. La Opala R.G. Limited*, (2014) 15 SCC 136, para 26].

Type (Of Certificate). The defining properties of a Digital Signature Certificate, which limit its intended purpose to a class of applications uniquely, associated with that type. (*Information Technology*)

Typewriter ribbon. Typewriter ribbon is an accessory and not part of the typewriter, though it may not be possible to use the machine without the ribbon, just as aviation petrol is not a part of the aeroplane nor diesel is a part of bus. *State of U.P. and another* v. *Kores (India) Ltd.*, AIR 1977 SC 132, 135. [U.P. Sales Tax Act (15 of 1948), S. 3A]

Typographical error. 'Typographical error' is defined as a mistake made in the printed/typed material during a printing/typing process. The term includes errors due to the mechanical failure or slips of the hand or finger, but usually excludes errors of ignorance. Therefore, the act of neglecting to perform an action which one has an obligation to do cannot be called as a typographical error. [*J. Samuel v. Gattu Mahesh*, (2012) 2 SCC 300, para 21].

U

"UA marker". Means an age-based indicator for a film which has received or is intended to receive a "UA" certificate under section 4 and such indicator may be "UA 7+" or "UA 13+" or "UA 16+"

Provided that where the Central Government is satisfied that it is necessary or expedient so to do in public interest, it may, by an order published in the Official Gazette and for the reasons to be recorded in writing, declare such other indicators. [Cinematograph Act, 1952 (37 of 1952), S. 2(i)]

Uberrima fides. Most abundant faith; mutual good faith between persons in a particularrelationship, as guardian and ward, attorney and client, parent and child, physician and patient, confessor and penitent.

In certain contracts (contracts of marine, fire, and life insurance, contracts for the sale of land, for family settlements, and for the allotment of shares in companies) in which one of the parties is presumed to have means of knowledge not accessible to the other, that party is bound to treat the other with *uberrima fides,* and tell him everything which may be supposed to affect his judgment. In these cases non-disclosure of a material fact, even in the absence of misrepresentation or fraud, may make the contract voidable at the instance of the party to whom the *uberrima fides* is due.

Ubi aliquid conceditur, conceditur et id sine quo res ipsa esse non potest. When anything is granted, that also is granted without which the thing granted cannot exist.

Ubi aliquid impeditur propter unum, eo remoto, tollitur impedimentum. When anything is impeded by one single cause, if that be removed, the impediment is removed.

Ubi cessat remedium ordinarium ibi deccuritur ad extraordinarium. When a common remedy ceases to be of service, recourse must be had to an extraordinary one.

Ubi damna dantur victus victori in expensis condemnari debet. (*Lat.*) (2 Inst. 289) Where damages are given, the losing party should be adjudged to pay the costs of the victor.

Ubi eadem ratio ibi idem jus. Where the reason is the same, there the law will be the same.

Ubi eadem ratio ibi idem jus; de similibus idem est judicium. Where there is the same reason, there is the same right; and of things similar, the judgment is similar.

Ubi factum nullum, ibi fortia nulla. Where there is no act, there are no strong points.

Ubi jus ibi idem remedium (Ubi jus ibi remedium. (Lat.). Where there is a right there is a remedy.

Applying the maxim as a basic principle of jurisprudence the Apex Court held that Courts must always aim to preserve and protect the rights of the parties and extend help to enforce them rather than deny relief and thereby render the rights themselves otiose. Sardar Amarjit Singh Kalra v. Pramod Gupta, (2003) 3 SCC 272, para 33.

Every grievance has a remedy in law. [*Laxmi Devi v. State of Bihar*, (2015) 10 SCC 241, para 20].

Ubi jus incertum, ibi jus nullum. Where the law is uncertain, there is no law.

Ubi lex aliquem cogit ostendere, causam, necesse est quod causa sit justa et legitima. Where the law compels a man to show cause, it is necessary that the cause be just and legal. (*Latin for Lawyers*)

Ubi lex est specialis, et ratio eius generalis generaliter accipiendi est. Where the law is special and the reason of it is general, it ought to be taken as being general.

Ubi non est directa lex, standum est arbitrio judicis, vel procedandum ad similia. Where there is no direct law, the judgment of the judge must be depended upon, or reference made to similar cases.

Ubi non est manifesta injustitia judices habentur pro bonisviris, et judictum pro veritate. Where there is non manifest injustice the judges are to be regarded as honest men, and their judgment as truth.

Ubi non est principalis, non potest esse accessorius. Where there is no principal, there can be no accessory. (*Latin for Lawyers*)

Ubi nulla subest causa propter conventionem. Where there is no consideration for the promise or undertaking by one of the contracting parties, there is no obligation incurred. (*Broom,* 716)

Ubi periculum, ibi et lucrum collocatur. He at whose risk a thing is, should receive the profits arising from it.

Ubi pugnantia inter se in testamento juberentur, neutrum ratum est. Where two directions conflicting with each other are given in a will, neither is held valid.

Ubi quis delinquit ibi punietur. Let a man be punished where he commits the offence.

Ubi remeduim ibi jus. Whenever there is a right there should also be an action. A right pertains to substantive law and the remedy to procedural law which means that where a right is provided by a statute, a remedy, though not expressly provided for may necessarily be implied. The converse that suspension of the remedy cannot abrogate the right is however not true and cannot be invoked in modern times. *Makhan Singh* v. *State of Punjab,* AIR 1964 SC 38.

UCITA. (*abbr.*) Set of commercial rules designed to regulate transactions of computer information and licensing of software. (*Cyber Law*)

UDP. (*abbr.*) User Datagram Protocol. One of the protocols for data transfer that is part of the *TCP/IP* suite of protocols. UDP is a "stateless" protocol in that UDP makes no provision for acknowledgement of packets received. (*Matisse Enzer-Glossary of Internet Terms*)

Ulterior. Subsequent in time. [T.P. Act (4 of 1882), S. 27]; beyond what is seen or avowed.

Ulterior disposition. A transfer of property which is subsequent in time or which is to take effect subsequently. [T.P. Act (4 of 1882), S. 27].

Ultima voluntas testatoris est perimplenda secundum veram intentionem suam. The last will of a testator is to be fulfilled according to its true intention. (*Latin for Lawyers*)

Ultimate. Final, beyond which nothing is contemplatted or intended, that concludes a process or course of action or series; no longer alterable; definitive. [Collection of Statistics Act (32 of 1953), S. 2(e)].

'Ultimate' means 'beyond which no other exists or is possible; last or final; from which everything is derived; basic or fundamental; that cannot be surpassed or improved upon; greatest *etc.*' [*Oxford Advanced Learner's Dictionary of Current English,* Encyclopedic Edn. (1992) **as cited in** *J.K. Industries Ltd.* v. *Chief Inspector of Factories & Boilers*, (1996) 6 SCC 665, 683, p. 20]

'Ultimate': 'last; final; elemental; fundamental; basic or essential; highest; furthest or greatest thing.' [COLLINS *Dictionary of English Language*, **as referred in** *J.K. Industries Ltd.* v. *Chief Inspector of Factories & Boilers*, (1996) 6 SCC 665, 683, p. 20]

The word 'ultimate' means last or final beyond which no other exists or is possible. [*J.K. Industries Ltd.* v. *Chief Inspector of Factories & Boilers*, (1996) 6 SCC 665, 683, p. 20]

"Ultimate" and "final" are synonymous (*Re Wales* (1934) VLR 297).

Ultimate consumer. The DOT, MTNL and BSNL who have purchased the telephone instruments for supply to their customers on rental basis or on some other basis would come within the meaning of the expression 'ultimate consumers' under Rule 2(r) of the Rules. [*Jayanti Food Processing (P.) Ltd.* v. *CCE,* (2007) 8 SCC 34, 62, para 65] [Standard Weight and Measures (Packaged Commodities) Rules, 1977, R. 2(r)]

Ultimate facts. Facts which are absolutely necessary to decide any dispute in a court of law.

Ultimately. In the end. [CrPC, 1973 (2 of 1974), S. 389(4)].

Ultra posse non potest esse et vice versa. What is beyond possibility cannot exist, and the reverse (what cannot exist is not possible).

Ultra vires. Beyond one's powers.

Ultra vires only means that something has been done by a person or body of persons which was beyond his or their power.

The term '*ultra vires*' simply means 'beyond powers' or 'lack of power'. The term '*ultra vires*' signifies a concept distinct from illegality.

"Ultra-wideband device or equipment". Means a short-range device having a bandwidth of at least 50 MHz. [Use of Very Low Power Ultra-wideband Devices (Exemption from Licensing Requirements) Rules, 2018, R. 2(c)].

Ultrahazardous activity. Certain inherently dangerous forms of activity, such as using explosives and keeping wild animals.

Umpire. A submission to arbitration usually provides that in case of arbitrators not agreeing in an award, the matters should be decided by a third person, who is called an umpire.

The term 'umpire' truly means a third person who is to decide a controversy or question submitted to arbitrators in case of their disagreement. *Maganlal* v. *Ramji Bondarji*, AIR 1966 MP 177, 182. [Arbitration Act (10 of 1940) (*repealed*), S. 9]

Where an arbitration agreement contemplates the appointment of three "arbitrators" one by each party to the dispute and the third by the two arbitrators so appointed, that third appointee is obliged to function as an umpire. *D.R. Bharaduraj* v. *Nathibai Thackersay Women's University*, AIR 1992 Bom 253, 256.

Unable. Not able; not having sufficient strength, power or skill. [CPC (5 of 1908), O. X, R. 4(1)].

Unable to maintain itself. A Mohammedan girl who is of an age between 15 and 16 is not a child able to maintain herself and therefore is entitled to maintenance under S. 125(1), CrPC, 1973 (2 of 1974).

The words "UNABLE TO MAINTAIN ITSELF", in S. 125(1), CrPC, 1973 (2 of 1974) relate to the absence of sufficient maturity in physical and mental development in the child rendering it in consequence unable to earn its livelihood by its own exertions and do not refer to inability through poverty or absence of means. (25 MLJ 355 : 14 MLT 223 : 1913 MWN 997 : 21 IC 469).

Unabsorbed depreciation. Means so much of the allowance for depreciation of the predecessor firm or the proprietary concern or the amalgamating company or the demerged company, as the case may be, which remains to be allowed and which would have been allowed to the predecessor firm or the proprietary concern or amalgamating company or demerged company, as the case may be, under the provisions of this Act, if the reorganization of business or amalgamation or demerger had not taken place. [Income-tax Act (43 of 1961), S. 72A(7)(b)]

For the purposes of this section,—"UNABSORBED DEPRECIATION" means so much of the allowance for depreciation of the amalgamating banking company which remains to be allowed and which would have been allowed to such banking company if amalgamation had not taken place. [Income-tax Act

(43 of 1961), S. 72AA, Explanation (iv) *as inserted by Finance Act (18 of 2005), S. 19*]

Unacceptable tax avoidance. Unacceptable tax avoidance typically involves the creation of complex artificial structures by which, as though by the wave of a magic wand, the taxpayer conjures out of the air a loss, or a gain, or expenditure, or whatever it may be, which otherwise would never have existed. [Lord Goff in Ensign Tankers, (1992) 1 AC 655 : (1992) 2 WLR 469 : (1992) 2 All ER 275 (HL) as cited in *Vodafone International Holdings BV v. Union of India*, (2012) 6 SCC 613, para 175].

Unanimity. State of being of one mind; agreeing in opinion.

Unanimous. In taking a decision by a body of persons, 'unanimous' means that almost all of them voted in favour of an issue and none voting against it.

Unapplied. Which has not been applied or used. [Indian Trusts Act (2 of 1882), S. 83, ill. (c)].

Unascertained goods. Goods which have not been ascertained. [Sale of Goods Act (3 of 1930), S. 18].

Unattested. Not bearing attestation (as) unattested deed.

Unauthorised. "Done without the authority made without actual, implied or apparent authority". [Black's Law Dictionary as cited in *Executive Engineer, Southern Electricity Supply Company of Orissa Limited (SOUTHCO) v. Sri Seetaram Rice Mill*, (2012) 2 SCC 108, para 29].

Unauthorised act. An act for which there is no authority. [Indian Contract Act (9 of 1872), S. 199].

Unauthorised development. Means use of land or use of building or construction of building or development of colonies carried out in contravention of the sanctioned plans or without obtaining the sanction of plans, or in contravention of the land use as permitted under the Master Plan or Zonal Plan or layout plan, as the case may be, and includes any encroachment. [S. 2(1)(j) of the National Capital Territory of Delhi Laws (Special Provisions) second Act, 2011 (20 of 2011)]

Simpliciter misuse may not fall within the ambit of unauthorized development under the provisions of the Delhi Development Act, 1957. *Executive Engineer, Southern Electricity Supply Company of Orissa Limited (SOUTHCO) v. Sri Seetaram Rice Mill*, (2012) 2 SCC 108, para 29. [Delhi Development Act, 1957, S. 31-A].

Unauthorised material. 'UNAUTHORISED MATERIAL' shall mean any material whatsoever related to the subject of the examination printed-typewritten or otherwise, on paper, cloth, wood, or other material, in any language or in the form of a chart diagram, map or drawing. [Allahabad University Ordinance, Chap. 28, Ordinance No. 1.2(c)]

Unauthorised occupant. Where a landlord or tenant ceases to occupy a building or part thereof, no person shall occupy it in any capacity on his behalf, or otherwise than under an order of allotment or release u/s. 16, and if a person so purports to occupy it, he shall, without prejudice to the provisions of S. 31, be deemed to be an UNAUTHORISED OCCUPANT of such building or part. [U.P. Urban Buildings (Regulation of Letting, Rent and Eviction Act (13 of 1972), S. 13]

Unauthorised occupation. In relation to any public premises, means the occupation by any person of the public premises without authority for such occupation, and includes the continuance in occupation by any person of the public premises after the authority (whether by way of grant or any other mode of transfer) under which he was allowed to occupy the premises has expired or has been determined for any reason whatsoever. [Public Premises (Eviction of Unauthorised Occupants) Act (40 of 1971), S. 2(g) and Airport Authority of India (Amendment) Act (43 of 2003), S. 8(f) (*in relation to any airport premises*)]

"UNAUTHORISED OCCUPATION" means any occupation of the highway land, without permission under this Act for such purpose, by a person who—

(i) is trespasser on the Highway; or

(ii) for the time being is paying or is liable to pay to other person rent or any portion of the rent of the premises on a Highway; or

(iii) lives in or otherwise uses any premises on a Highway; or

(iv) is a rent-free tenant of any premises on a Highway; or

(v) is a licensee of any premises on a Highway for its possession; or

(vi) is liable to pay damages to the owner of any premises on a Highway for the use or possession of such premises. [Control of National Highways Act, 2002 (13 of 2003), S. 2(m)]

Unauthorised occupation 'is' obviously is used in the present perfect tense rather than in the present tense and 'is in unauthorised occupation' means that the occupation was unauthorised to start with and continued to be unauthorised throughout the time that the person was in possession.

The term 'unauthorised occupation' means the occupation by a person of the public premises without authority for such occupation and also includes the continuation by any person in occupation after the lease is determined. *Jain Ink Manufacturing Co. Ltd.* v. *L.I.C of India*, AIR 1981 SC 670, 672. [Public Premises (Eviction of Unauthorised Occupants) Act (40 of 1971), S. 2(2)(g)]

Unauthorised person. "UNAUTHORISED PERSON" means any person (whether duly empowered in this behalf by the evacuee or otherwise) who, after the 14th day of August, 1947, has been occupying, supervising or managing the property of an evacuee without the approval of the custodian. [Administration of Evacuee Property Act (31 of 1950), S. 2(j)]

A person who does not have authority (to do a particular thing). [Indian Contract Act (9 of 1872), S. 200, ill. (b)].

Unauthorised use of electricity. 'Unauthorised use of electricity' means use of electricity in a manner not authorised by the licensee of the Board. [*Executive Engineer, Southern Electricity Supply Company of Orissa Limited (SOUTHCO) v. Sri Seetaram Rice Mill*, (2012) 2 SCC 108, para 27].

Where there is no theft of electricity but the electricity is being consumed in violation of the terms and conditions of supply leading to malpractices, it may squarely fall within the expression "unauthorised use of electricity. [*Executive Engineer, Southern Electricity Supply Company of Orissa Limited (SOUTHCO) v. Sri Seetaram Rice Mill*, (2012) 2 SCC 108, para 15] [Electricity Act, (36 of 2003) S. 126].

Unavoidable. Inevitable; (as) unavoidable accident is an act of God; that may not be rendered null and void.

Incapable of being avoided. [*Prov.*, Registration Act (16 of 1908), Ss. 25(1) and 34].

Unbiased. Free from bias or prejudice; impartial.

Unbuilt area. In relation to the aggregate area of the plot of land on which the property is constructed, means that part of such aggregate area on which no building has been erected. [Wealth-tax Act (27 of 1957), III Sch, Part B, 6(c) *Expln.* (c)]

Uncalled capital. Money owing to a company on *partly-paid shares.* Uncalled capital exists as a reserve to be called upon at any time by the directors of a company.

Uncancelled. Which has not been cancelled. [T.P. Act (4 of 1882), S. 55(3), *Prov.*].

Uncertain. For the purposes of this sub-section, a period is "UNCERTAIN" if its duration is not so ascertainable. [Insurance Act (4 of 1938), S. 65(1)(b) *Expln.*]

Not fixed in point of time or occurrence; not sure to happen; of doubtful issue or tendency. [T.P. Act (4 of 1882), S. 21].

Uncertain but non negligible risk. If the environmental risks being run by regulatory inaction are in some way "uncertain but non negligible", then regulatory action is justified. This will lead to the question as to what is the "non negligible risk". In such a situation, the burden of proof is to be placed on those attempting to alter the *status quo.* If insufficient evidence is presented by them to alleviate concern about the level of uncertainty, then the presumption should operate in favour of environmental protection. *A.P. Pollution Control Board* v. *Prof. M.V. Nayudu,* AIR 1999 SC 812.

Uncertainty. Where the words of a deed or will are so vague that no definite meaning can be assigned to them, the grant or gift is void for uncertainty.

UNCITRAL. Internationally agreed on model standard for developing a coherent global regulatory system in electronic commerce. (*Cyber Law*)

Unclaimed article of food. Means an imported articles of food consignment not having a claimant or bill of entry or both up to thirty days after unloading. [Food Safety and Standards (Import) Regulations, 2017, Regn. 2(1)(z)].

Unclassed suit. "UNCLASSED SUIT" means a suit which is neither a land suit nor a small cause. [Pun. Reg. VII of 1901 (NWFP Law & Justice), S. 2(1) cl. (f).]

Unconditional. Not limited by or subject to conditions or stipulations. [Indian Contract Act (9 of 1872), S. 38(1) and Negotiable Instruments Act (26 of 1881), S. 5].

Unconditionally. In an unconditional manner. [Income-tax Act (43 of 1961), S. 2(18)(b) and Sale of Goods Act (3 of 1930), S. 23(1)].

Unconclusive (*proof*). Not conclusive.

Unconscionable. Irreconcilable with what is right or reasonable. [Indian Contract Act (9 of 1872), S. 16(3), ill. (c)]

Unconscionable bargain. Is one which no man in his senses, not under a delusion, would make on the one hand, and which no fair and honest man would accept on the other.

Irreconcilable with what is right or reasonable.
[Indian Contract Act (9 of 1872), S. 16(3), ill. (c)].

Unconscionable contract. Agreement that is so outrageously unfair to one party that a Court refuses to enforce it in a Court of law.

Unconscionable transaction. The circumstance that a grand-father made a gift of a portion of his properties to his only grandson a few years before his death is not on the face of it an unconscionable transaction. *Subhas Chandra* v. *Ganga Prasad*, AIR 1967 SC 878, 884. [Indian Contract Act (9 of 1872), S. 16(3)]

Unconstitutional. Contrary to, in conflict with or violative of the provisions of the constitution.

Uncontrolled transaction. Means a transaction between enterprises other than associated enterprises, whether resident or non-resident. [Income-tax Rules, 1962, R. 10A(ab)]

Uncorroborated. That which is not corroborated. [Indian Evidence Act (1 of 1872), S. 133].

Uncorroborated testimony. Testimony which is not corroborated; evidence standing alone.

Uncured trophy. Means the whole or any part of any captive animal or wild animal, other than vermin, which has not undergone a process of taxidermy and includes freshly killed wild animal, omleergris, musk and other animal products. [Wild Life (Protection) Act (53 of 1972), S. 2(32)]

Undefaced. Not disfigured. [T.P. Act (4 of 1882), S. 55(3), Prov.].

Undefended. When a person sued in a civil cause or accused of a crime has no counsel to speak for him on his trial, and has to make his defence himself, he is sometimes said to be undefended.

Under. In a position lower than, below; at a less cost than (as) "under five rupees".

The mere use of the word 'under' preceding the words "law in force in India" would not necessarily mean that you have to find a statutory provision or a provision of law which specifically deals with the subject of particular legal relationship being commercial in nature. *European Grain & Shipping Ltd.* v. *Bombay Extractions (P) Ltd.*, AIR 1983 Bom 36, 44. [Foreign Awards (Recognition and Enforcement) Act (45 of 1961)]

The concept of "under" can be relevant only when there are two entities one of which may be under the other. The mere fact that the State Bank of India and the Nationalised Banks are different entities cannot be a circumstance to show that they cannot be establishments under the Central Government. *C.V. Raman* v. *Management of Bank of India*, AIR 1988 SC 1369, 1377.

UNDER, BELOW, BENEATH. We live under the protection of Government; the sun disappears when it is below the horizon; we are apt to tread upon that which is altogether beneath us.

The word "under" used in the expression "under the management or control of such person" in Section 29-A(c) would seem to suggest positive or proactive control, as opposed to mere negative or reactive control. [*Arcelormuttal India Private Limited* v. *Satish Kumar Gupta,* (2019) 2 SCC 1, para 53].

Under a law. The words "under a law" signify those cases where the disqualification to stand for election is not to be found in the parliamentary statute itself but is imposed by virtue of powers enabling this to be done; in other words, where it is imposed by a law made by a subordinate law-making authority. *'Anjar' Municipality* v. *J.M. Vyas*, AIR 1999 Guj 298, 306. [Constitution of India, Art. 191 (1) (e)]

Under any law for the time being in force. The intention of the legislature was that all decrees and orders made by the Court in a proceeding under the Act shall be appealable and the words "under any law for the time being in force" were added to indicate that the forum where the appeal would lie *viz.* to the District Judge or the High Court, and such other matters as regards procedure for the hearing of the appeals would be decided by the law on the subject for the time being in force. *Sobhana Sen* v. *Amar Kanta Sen*, AIR 1959 Cal 455, 457. [Hindu Marriage Act (25 of 1955), S. 28]

The words 'Under any law for the time being in force' refer to the appealability of decrees and orders should be determined by the provisions of the code of civil procedure. *Prithviraj Singhji* v. *Bai Shinprabhakumari*, AIR 1960 Bom 315, 317.

The right of appeal against the decrees under the Act cannot be subject to the limitation that such right of appeal should exist under any other law for the time being in force. Most of the remedies provided for under the Act were unknown before. The words "under any law for the time being in force" contained in that section only regulated the forum as to where the appeal had to be filled. (*Sobhana* v. *Amar Kanta*, AIR 1959 Cal 455; *D. S. Seshadri* v. *Jayalakshmi*, AIR 1963 Mad 283, 285.

Under colour. The act done "under colour" of an office is an act having some relation to the office which the accused pretends to hold. A mere promise to appoint some person to an office or a writing on paper which is unintelligible and non-sense cannot be regarded as an act done "under colour" of an office.

Under colour of duty. The words "under colour of duty" include acts done under the cloak of duty, even though not by virtue of duty. When a police officer prepares a false *panchanama* or report he is clearly using the existence of his legal duty as a veil to his falsehood and he must be held to have done it "under colour of duty". *Virupaxappa Veerappa* v. *State of Mysore*, AIR 1963 SC 849, 852.

Under colour of the office. The words "under colour of the office" do not mean the something "by virtue of". Any rightful act in office is "by virtue of office" and any wrongful act in office may be "under colour of office". Any act may none the less be under colour of the office however unreasonable it might be and although it might be done in mistaken exercise of duty or authority. [MLJ : FYD (01-50), V. 2, p. 156 : AIR 1948 Bom 197]. [Bombay District Police Act (1890), S. 80].

"Under-Graduate and Post-Graduate Dental Education Board". Means the Board constituted under section 16. [National Dental Commission Act, 2023 (21 of 2023), section 2(zb)]

Under his hand. The phrase 'under his hand' ordinarily means that it is a writing signed by the person concerned. (*Words and Phrases,* permanent edition, Vol. 43 **as cited in** *Vice Chairman Maranbeed Village Panchayat* v. *Channabassappa B. Gaddi*, AIR 1985 Kant 252; *Vikram Singh* v. *Shri Ram, Ballabhji Kasat,* AIR 1995 MP 140, 144.)

Under lease or sub-lease. A transaction whereby a tenant grants an interest in the demised premises less than his own retaining to himself a reversion. [Indian Stamp Act (2 of 1899), Sch. I, item 35].

Under lessee. A sub-lessee, one to whom an under lease has been granted. [T.P. Act (4 of 1882), S. 115].

Under letting. Letting to a sub-tenant. [T.P. Act (4 of 1882), S. 114A(b)].

Under-officer. "UNDER OFFICER" means a person appointed to the Force as a Head Constable, Naik or Lance Naik. [Central Industrial Security Force (50 of 1968), S. 2(j); Railway Protection Force Act (23 of 1957), S. 2(1)(fa)]

Under proprietor. means in Oudh a person possessing a heritable and transferable right in land who is, or but for a judicial decision or contract would be, liable to pay rent therefor. [U.P. Act III of 1901 (Land Revenue), S. 4 cl. (15)]

Under protest. Payment under protest. The phrase signifies a payment of money accompanied by a declaration that the demand is illegal or in excess of what is justly due, and implying the need of a future rectification.

The value of the phrase "under protest" is to safeguard the position of the person who makes the payment and to ensure that it may not be said that the payment he made was a voluntary one. (AIR 1935 Mad 625)

If upon the offer being made tendering payment, the person concerned states in an application that he is prepared to receive it but only under protest, it is sufficient and the protest need not be recorded upon the receipt. *Union of India, Delhi* v. *Sajwa*, AIR 1973 Del 278, 279. [Land Acquisition Act (1 of 1894), S. 31(2), *Proviso* 1] [Now repealed & replaced by Act 30 of 2013]

Under-tenant. "UNDER-TENANT" means any holder of a heritable and transferable intermediate tenure between the Government and the *raiyat* other than a *zamindar*. [Ben. Act VIII of 1879 (Rent Settlement), S. 3]

Under the authority of. The words "under the authority of" mean pursuant to the authority, such as where an agent or a servant acts under or pursuant to the authority of his principal or master. *H. E. M. Union* v. *State of Bihar*, AIR 1970 SC 82 at 85, 86. [Industrial Disputes Act (14 of 1947), S. 2(a)]

Under the authority of Central Government. The phrase 'under the authority of the Central Government' must mean and is intended to apply to industries carried on directly under the authority of the Central Government. Industries which are carried on for their own purposes by incorporated commercial corporations which are governed by their own constitutions, as authorised by the Indian Companies Act cannot be described as carried on under the authority of the Central Government. *Abdul Rehman* v. *E. Paul*, AIR 1963 Bom 267, 268. [Industrial Disputes Act (14 of 1947), S. 2 (a) (i)]

Under the Act. The words "under the Act" would signify what is not directly to be found in the statute itself but is conferred or imposed by virtue of powers enabling this to be done. [*Indramani Pyarelal Gupta* v. *V.R. Natu,* AIR 1963 SC 274, para 15]. See also *BSNL* v. *TRAI,* (2014) 3 SCC 222, para 90; *Lok Prahari* v. *Union of India,* (2018) 4 SCC 699, para 47.

Under the colour of office. Unless there is a reasonable connection between the act complained of and the powers and duties of the office, it cannot be said that the accused officer, under the colour of his office, did the act. [*State of Maharashtra* v. *Narharrao,* (1966) 3 SCR 880].

Under-trial prisoner. When an under-trial prisoner complains to a court that he is not treated in accordance with the provisions of the Prisons Act and the rules thereunder, the Court has jurisdiction to enquire into such a complaint and pass necessary orders. The position of a subordinate Court is not different in this respect from that of the High Court. In such cases however the Court will not insist on a public inquiry if public interests are likely to suffer thereby.

Under value. The value below the real worth. [Indian Contract Act (9 of 1872), S. 19, ill. (d)].

Undergo. To be subjected to; to endure; suffer (as to undergo imprisonment).

Undergoing punishment. To suffer punishment. [Indian Succession Act (39 of 1925), S. 16, *Excep*.].

Underground. A secret place, movement or a body of people.

Understanding. An agreement or stipulation.

Undertake. To give a formal promise or pledge. [Indian Contract Act (9 of 1872), S. 74, ill. (e)]; [CPC (5 of 1908), O. XIII, R. 9(1)(b)]; to take upon oneself [Beedi and Cigar Workers (Conditions of Employment) Act (32 of 1966), S. 2(d)]; [Indian Contract Act (9 of 1872), S. 48].

Undertaking. "UNDERTAKING" means an enterprise which is, or has been, or is proposed to be, engaged in the production, storage, supply, distribution, acquisition or control of articles or goods, or the provision of services, of any kind, either directly or through one or more of its units or divisions, whether such unit or division is located at the same place where the undertaking is localised or at a different place or at different places.

Explanation I.—In this clause,—

(a) "article" includes a new article and "service" includes a new service; (b) "unit" or "division" in relation to an undertaking includes,—(i) a plant or factory established for the production, storage, supply, distribution, acquisition or control of any article or goods; (ii) any branch or office established for the provision of any service.

Explanation II.—For the purpose of this clause, a body corporate, which is , or has been, engaged only in the business of acquiring, holding, under-writing or dealing with shares, debentures, or other securities of any other body corporate shall be deemed to be an undertaking.

Explanation III.—For the removal of doubts, it is hereby declared that an investment company shall be deemed, for the purposes of this Act, to be an undertaking. [M.R.T.P. Act (54 of 1969), S. 2(v)] [Now repealed & replaced by Act 12 of 2003]

"UNDERTAKING" includes all moveable and immoveable property of the promoter suitable to and used by him for the purposes of the tramway. [Tramway Act (11 of 1986), S. 3(8)]

In this Scheme, unless the context otherwise requires,—

"UNDERTAKING" means any undertaking which is engaged in the business of developing, developing and operating or maintaining and operating an industrial park notified by the Central Government in accordance with this Scheme. [Industrial Park Scheme, 1999, S. 2(h)]

A promise, engagement or stipulation. [Sale of Goods Act (3 of 1930), S. 14]; [Registration Act (16 of

1908), S. 2(7)]; [CPC (5 of 1908), 1st Sch., App. F, form No. 8]; an enterprise. [Indian Partnership Act (9 of 1932), S. 8]; any business or project engaged in. [Electricity (Supply) Act (54 of 1948), S. 20(1)] [Now repealed & replaced by Act 36 of 2003]

UNDERTAKING is a promise, engagement or stipulation. The term is frequently used in the special sense of a promise given in the court of legal proceedings, by a party or his counsel, generally as a condition of obtaining some concession from the court on opposite party.

"It means the entire organisation. A company whether it has got a plant or an organisation is considered as one whole unit and the entire business of the going concern is embraced within the term and it includes all debts due by and performance of outstanding contracts." *R.C. Cooper* v. *Union of India*, AIR 1970 SC 564 at 630. [Banking Companies (Acquisition and Transfer of Undertaking) Act (22 of 1969), S. 5]

"It is an activity of a man engaged in, with a view to earn profit. *Bank of Maharashtra Ltd.* v. *Official Liquidator*, AIR 1969 Mys 280 at 291. [Companies Act (1 of 1956), S. 293(1)(a)]

The word 'undertaking' is used in the sense of an enterprise which can be owned and transferred. A solicitor's work which depends entirely on his own personal intellectual ability, is not capable of being transferred. Consequently it would not be an 'undertaking' within the meaning of the Act. *National Union of Commercial Employees* v. *M.R. Meher*, AIR 1960 Bom 22, 24. [Industrial Disputes Act (14 of 1947), S. 2(j)]

The word 'undertaking' must be defined as 'any business or any work or project which one engages in or attempts as an enterprise analogous to business or trade. *Secretary, Madras Gymkhana Club Employees Union* v. *Management of the Gymkhana Club*, AIR 1968 SC 54, 563.

The expression 'undertaking' means a separate and distinct business or industrial activity and does not comprehend an infinitesimally small part of manufacturing process. Painting section of a factory is not "undertaking". *A. S. Production Agencies* v. *Ind. Tribunal, Haryana*, AIR 1979 SC 170, 179, 180.

Undertaking means an enterprise engaged in production, sale or control of goods etc. *Carew & Co.* v. *Union of India*, AIR 1975 SC 2260, 2263. [Monopolies and Restrictive Trade Practices Act (54 of 1969), S. 2(v)] [Now repealed & replaced by Act 12 of 2003]

Even if it is solitary transaction, the act of storage would come within the meaning of an undertaking. *Balabhadra Rajguru Mohapatra* v. *State*, AIR 1954 Ori 25.

The expression 'undertake' has come to acquire through long practice, a technical meaning.

In all orders and decrees of the Court, whenever the expression 'a party undertakes' has been used, it has always borne the meaning that the undertaking has been to the Court. *Bairanglal Khemku* v. *Kapurchand Ltd.*, AIR 1950 Bom 363, 338.

"UNDERTAKING". For the purposes of section 180(1)(a) of Act 18 of 2013, 'undertaking' shall mean an undertaking in which the investment of the company exceeds twenty per cent of its net worth as per the audited balance sheet of the preceding financial year or an undertaking which generates twenty per cent of the total income of the company during the previous financial year. [*Explanation (i)* to section 180(1)(a) of the Companies Act, 2013 (18 of 2013)]

Undertakings of the company. Means—

(i) the industrial unit owned by the company and located at Bhavnagar in the State of Gujarat (hereinafter referred to as the Bhavnagar); and

(ii) the industrial unit owned by the company and located in Bombay in the State of Maharashtra (hereinafter referred to as the Bombay unit). [Alcock Ashdown Company Limited (Acquisition of Undertakings) Act (56 of 1973), S. 2(b)]

Underwater battery. Means a lead acid battery consisting of cells connected in series or parallel combination to produce power to submarine vessels including Torpedo and Chariot. [Central Excise Tariff Act (5 of 1986), Gen Exemption No. 24, 1(11) *Expln. (i)*]

Underworld. The lower or inferior world.

The world of gangsters is popularly known as the 'underworld' which comprises of various gangs headed by notorious dons. Deaths are sold by these dons at their asking price and purchased by those who resort to have immediate results for their enrichment with the deflation of their otherwise inflated money bags. *State of Maharashtra* v. *Bharat Chaganlal Raghani,* (2001) 9 SCC 1, para 1.

Underwrite. Deliver policy of insurance; practice marine insurance.

The expression 'underwrite' signifies "accept liability under". Acceptance must be signified by some act or acts agreed on by the parties or from which the law raises a presumption of acceptance. *LIC of India* v. R. *Vasireddy*, AIR 1984 SC 1014, 1018. [Indian Contract Act (9 of 1872), Ss. 7 & 8]

Underwriter. One who insures ships against loss; marine insurer.

One who underwrites an insurance policy, one who carries on an insurance business, especially of shipping.

An investment banker, giving guarantee of the sale of the newly issued securities by purchasing all or part of the shares for re-sale to the public.

A person joining with others in entering into a policy of insurance as an insurer.

Underwriting. "UNDERWRITING" means contract, with or without conditions, to subscribe for stocks, shares, bonds or debentures of an industrial concern with a view to the resale of the whole or any part thereof.

[State Financial Corporations Act (63 of 1951), S. 2(g)]

Agreeing to buy all or part of the new securities to be offered for re-sale to public.

Underwriting agreement. An underwriting agreement is a contract that the underwriter will either himself purchase or procure purchasers for the shares underwritten by him. *Nain Gopal Lahiri* v. *State of Uttar Pradesh*, (1965) 35 Com. Cases 30 (SC).

Underwriting commission. The expression 'underwriting commission' in context of Section 76 of the Act means the consideration for the contract of underwriting for taking the risk in the placing of shares before the public. *CIT* v. *U.P. State Industrial Development Corpn.*, AIR 1997 SC 2214. [Companies Act (1 of 1956), S. 76]

Undisclosed income. "UNDISCLOSED INCOME" includes any money, bullion, jewellery or other valuable article or thing or any income based on any entry in the books of account or other documents or transactions, where such money, bullion, jewellery, valuable article, thing, entry in the books of account or other document or transaction represents wholly or partly income or proerty which has not been or would not have been disclosed for the purposes of this Act. [Income-tax Act (43 of 1961), S. 158B(b)]

"UNDISCLOSED INCOME". For the purposes of section 271AAB of Act 43 of 1961, 'undisclosed income' means—

(i) any income of the specified previous year represented, either wholly or partly, by any money, bullion, jewellery or other valuable article or thing or any entry in the books of account or other documents or transactions found in the course of a search under section 132, which has—

(A) not been recorded on or before the date of search in the books of account or other documents maintained in the normal course relating to such previous year; or

(B) otherwise not been disclosed to the Chief Commissioner or Commissioner before the date of search; or

(ii) any income of the specified previous year represented, either wholly or partly, by any entry in respect of an expense recorded in the books of account or other documents maintained in the normal course relating to the specified previous year which is found to be false and would not have been found to be so had the search not been conducted. [*Explanation* (c) to section 271AAB of the Income-tax Act, 1961 (43 of 1961) as inserted (w.e.f. 1-7-2012) by the Finance Act, 2012 (23 of 2012)]

Undisposed of. Which has not been disposed of or settled or finally dealt with. [CPC (5 of 1908), 1st Sch., D, form No. 17(6)].

Undisputed. Not disputed; uncontested. [Indian Evidence Act (1 of 1872), S. 142].

Undivided estate. A joint estate; the interest of two or more persons in land, tenement or other effects which has not been partitioned or divided. [CPC (5 of 1908), S. 54].

Undivided family. A family in which separation or partition has not taken place. [T.P. Act (4 of 1882), S. 44].

Undivided family includes a group of persons who live in one house under one head. There must be only one house undivided amongst its members. Even if undivided members raised independent structure on undivided homestead, it constitutes dwelling house of undivided family. *Bhim Singh* v. *Ratnakar Singh*, AIR 1971 Ori 198, 201. [T.P. Act (4 of 1882), S. 44]

Collective body of persons living together within the same cartilege, subsisting in common, and directing their attention to a common object and to the promotion of their mutual interests and social happiness. *Satyendu Kurdu* v. *Amarnath Ghosh*, AIR 1964 Cal 52, 55.

UNDIVIDED FAMILY in Partition Act (4 of 1893, S. 4) is not equivalent to 'a joint Hindu family' but merely means 'a family which owns the property but has not divided it.'

It cannot be held as a matter of law that two Mohammedan sisters married or unmarried cannot form an undivided family within the meaning of S. 4 of the Partition Act. The phrase "undivided family" in the section is used in a very wide and general sense and two Mohammedan married daughters too may be regarded members of an undivided family within the meaning of the Act if the house is undivided and if one of them permanently occupies the house and the other though she lives mostly with her husband, has not permanently abandoned all intention of occupying the house should it become necessary to do so.

The expression 'undivided family' means a family not divided *qua* the dwelling house. Where the members of a family are in joint occupation of a dwelling house, the house not having been partitioned by metes and bounds, the family would be undivided family with respect to the house. *Santosh Kr. Mitra* v. *Kalipada Das*, AIR 1981 Cal 278, 282. [Partition Act (4 of 1893), S. 4]

Undivided share. If any meaning is to be given to the word "undivided", it must be "not divided and indivisible." *Azizum Nisa* v. *Asst. Custodian*, AIR 1957 All 561, 573. [Evacuee Interest (Separation) Act (64 of 1951), S. 2(d) (i)]

Undo. Annul.

Undue. The word means something which is not merited by the conduct of the claimant or is very much disproportionate to it. *Sterling General Insurance Co. Ltd.* v. *Planters Airways P. Ltd.*, AIR 1975 SC 415, 419. [Arbitration Act (10 of 1940) (*repealed*), S. 37 (4)]

Improper; unsuited to time, place or occasion. [CrPC, 1973 (2 of 1974), S. 165(1)].

Undue advantage. The expression 'undue advantage' as used in Section 300, *Exception* 4 of IPC (45 of 1860) means unfair advantage. *Sachehey Lal Tiwari* v. *State of U.P.*, AIR 2004 SC 5039, 5042, para 9.

"UNDUE ADVANTAGE" means any gratification whatever, other than legal remuneration.

Explanation.—For the purposes of this clause,—

(*a*) the word "gratification" is not limited to pecuniary gratifications or to gratifications estimable in money;

(*b*) the expression "legal remuneration" is not restricted to remuneration paid to a public servant, but includes all remuneration which he is permitted by the Government or the organisation, which he serves, to receive. [Prevention of Corruption Act (49 of 1988), S. 2(d)].

Undue influence. "A contract is said to be induced by 'UNDUE INFLUENCE' where the relations subsisting between the parties are such that one of the parties is in a position to dominate the will of the other and uses that position to obtain an unfair advantage over the other." [Indian Contract Act (9 of 1872), S. 16(1)]

"UNDUE INFLUENCE is unfair persuasion of a party who is under the domination of the person exercising the persuasion or who by virtue of the relation between them is justified in assuming that the person will not act in a manner inconsistent with his welfare." [Restatement (Second) of Contracts, S. 177(1)(1981)].

An improper or wrongful constraint, machination, or urgency or persuasion whereby the will of a person is overpowered and he is induced to do or forbear an act which he would not do or forbear if left to act freely; coercion produced by importunity or by silent resistless power, which a strong will often exercises over the weak and infirm. [Indian Contract Act (9 of 1872), S. 16(1)].

The word "undue" when qualifying 'influence' has a legal meaning of 'wrongful' as opposed to, 'excessive, inordinate or disproportionate'. Undue influence is understood to be held, when it overpowers the will without convincing the judgment. It is a grip on another's mind subjugating his will to that of the other. It is an influence which acts to the injury of a person, who is swayed by it, and is exerted by exercising an ascendency or power, which results in a person being impelled or compelled to do what he would not have done, if he had been a free agent. *Karnal Distillery Co. Ltd.* v. *Ladli Prasad Jaiswal*, AIR 1958 Punj 190, 203. [Indian Contract Act (9 of 1872), S. 16]

Undue influence at elections. (1) Whoever voluntarily interferes or attempts to interfere with the free exercise of any electoral right commits the offence of undue influence at an election.

(2) Without prejudice to the generality of the provisions of sub-section (1) whoever—

(*a*) threatens any candidate or voter, or any person in whom a candidate or voter is interested, with injury of any kind, or

(*b*) induces or attempts to induce a candidate or voter to believe that he or any person in whom he is interested will become or will be rendered an object of Divine displeasure or of spiritual censure,

shall be deemed to interfere with the free exercise of the electoral right of such candidate or voter, within the meaning of sub-section (1).

(3) A declaration of public policy or a promise of public action, or the mere exercise of a legal right without intent to interfere with an electoral right, shall not be deemed to be interference within the meaning of this section. [Section 171C, Indian Penal Code (45 of 1860)] [(w. e. f. 1-7-2024) repealed and replaced by Bharatiya Nyaya Sanhita, 2023 (45 of 2023), section 171]

(4) Whoever voluntarily interferes or attempts to interfere with the free exercise of any electoral right commits the offence of undue influence at an election. (2) Without prejudice to the generality of the provisions of sub-section (1), whoever—(a) Threatens any candidate or voter, or any person in whom a candidate or voter is interested, with injury of any kind, or (b) Induces or attempts to induce a candidate or voter to believe that he or any person in whom he is interested will become or will be rendered an object of divine displeasure or of spiritual censure, shall be deemed to interfere with the free exercise of the electoral right of such candidate or voter, within the meaning of sub-section (1). (3) A declaration of public policy or promise of public action, or the mere exercise of a legal right without intent to interfere with an electoral right, shall not be deemed to be interference within the meaning of this section. (Election Offences and Enquiries Act, section 2).

Unearned income. Income received from investments (and not from the provision of goods or services), including *dividends* and *interest* payments.

Unencumbered. Free from encumbrance (as) lien, charge, mortgage, etc.

Without encumbrance. [Specific Relief Act (47 of 1963), S. 13(1)(c)].

Unencumbered approved securities. Includes the approved securities lodged by the housing finance institution with another institution for an advance or any other arrangement to the extent to which such securities have not been drawn against or availed of or encumbered in any manner. [National Housing Bank (53 of 1987), S. 29B *Expln.*(ii); RBI Act (2 of 1934), S. 45-IB, *Expln.* (ii)]

Unenforceable. (Of a contract) valid but incapable of being enforced.

Unenforceable contract. A contract having some legal consequences, but that may not be enforced in an action for damages or specific performance in the face of certain defenses, such as the statute of frauds.

Unequitable. Not equitable; inequitable.

Unexhausted. Not exhausted or finished up. [Indian Trusts Act (2 of 1882), S. 83].

Unexhausted paper. The expression 'UNEXHAUSTED PAPER' means a ballot paper on which a further preference is recorded for a continuing candidate. [U.P. Zila Panchayats (Election of Adhyaksha and Upadhyaksha and settlement of Election Disputes) Rules 1994, Sch. II, cl. (4)]

Unexpired. Not expired; not come to end. [Indian Evidence Act (1 of 1872), S. 92, ill. (f)]; [CrPC, 1973 (2 of 1974), S. 123(7)]; [Income-tax Act (43 of 1961), 1st Sch., 5(c)].

Unfair. Not fair; marked by injustice, partiality or deception; not equitable in business dealings. [Indian Contract Act (9 of 1872), S. 16(1)].

Unfair advantage or hardship. Mere inadequacy of consideration or the mere fact that the contract is onerous to the defendant or improvident in its nature will not constitute 'unfair advantage or hardship'. *Surjeet Singh* v. *Kartar Singh*, AIR 1988 P&H 53, 60. [Specific Relief Act (47 of 1963), S. 20(2), Cl. (a), (b), *Expln. 1*]

Unfair competition. The stimulation by one person of the name, materials, colour, scheme, symbols, patterns, or devices employed by another for purpose of deceiving the public, or substitution of goods, or wares of one person for those of another, thus falsely inducing purchase of goods and obtaining benefits belonging to competitor. (*Black*)

Unfair contract. Means a contract between a manufacturer or trader or service provider on one hand, and a consumer on the other, having such terms which cause significant change in the rights of such consumer, including the following, namely:—

(i) requiring manifestly excessive security deposits to be given by a consumer for the performance of contractual obligations; or

(ii) imposing any penalty on the consumer, for the breach of contract thereof which is wholly disproportionate to the loss occurred due to such breach to the other party to the contract; or

(iii) refusing to accept early repayment of debts on payment of applicable penalty; or

(iv) entitling a party to the contract to terminate such contract unilaterally, without reasonable cause; or

(v) permitting or has the effect of permitting one party to assign the contract to the detriment of the other party who is a consumer, without his consent; or

(vi) imposing on the consumer any unreasonable charge, obligation or condition which puts such consumer to disadvantage. [Consumer Protection Act, 2019 (35 of 2019), S. 2(46)]

Unfair means. A candidate shall be deemed to have used 'UNFAIR MEANS' if the candidate is in possession of unauthorised material or if he has transcribed any part or whole of the unauthorised material or if he intimidates or threatens or manhandles or uses violence against any invigilator or person on duty in the examination or if the leaves the examination hall without surrendering his examination scrip to an invigilator or if he is found communicating with other examinees or anyone else inside or outside the examination hall. [Allahabad University Ordinance, Chap. 28, Ordinance No. 1.2(A)]

Unfair or misleading advertisement. Will mean and include any advertisement:

(i) that fails to clearly identify the product as insurance;

(ii) makes claims beyond the ability of the policy to deliver or beyond the reasonable expectation of performance;

(iii) describes benefits that do not match the policy provisions;

uses words or phrases in a way which hides or minimizes the costs of the hazard insured against or the risks inherent in the policy;

omits to disclose or discloses insufficiently, important exclusions, limitations and conditions of the contract;

gives information in a misleading way; illustrates future benefits or assumptions which are not realistic nor realisable in the light of the insurer's current performance;

where the benefits are not guaranteed, does not explicitly say so as prominently as the benefits are stated or says so in a manner or form that it could remain unnoticed;

implies a group or other relationship like sponsorship, affiliation or approval, that does not exist;

makes unfair or incomplete comparisons with products which are not comparable or disparages competitors. [Insurance Regulatory and Development Authority (Insurance Advertisements and Disclosure) Regulations, 2000, Rgn. 2(d)]

Unfair practice. The expression 'unfair practice' also means enjoyment or exercise by women of fundamental constitutional rights, or of human rights. [*Joseph* v. *State of Kerala,* AIR 2006 Ker 191, 192, para 7]. [Kerala Women's Commission Act, 1990, S. 2(i)]

Unfair prejudice. Unfair conduct on the part of those entrusted to run and control a company in respect of company members.

Unfair trade practice. "UNFAIR TRADE PRACTICE" means a trade practice which, for the purpose of promoting the sale, use or supply of any goods or for the provision of any service, adopts any unfair method or unfair or deceptive practice including any of the following practices, namely :—

(1) the practice of making any statement, whether orally or in writing or by visible representation which,—

(i) falsely represents that the goods are of a particular standard, quality, quantity, grade, composition, style or model;

(ii) falsely represents that the services are of a particular standard, quality or grade;

(iii) falsely represents any re-built, second-hand, renovated, reconditioned or old goods as new goods;

(iv) represents that the goods or services have sponsorship, approval, performance, characteristics, accessories, uses or benefits which such goods or services do not have;

(v) represents that the seller or the supplier has a sponsorship or approval or affiliation which such seller or supplier does not have;

(vi) makes a false or misleading representation concerning the need for, or the usefulness of, any goods or services;

(vii) gives to the public any warranty or guarantee of the performance, efficacy or length of life of a product or of any goods that is not based on an adequate or proper test thereof:

Provided that where a defence is raised to the effect that such warranty or guarantee is based on adequate or proper test, the burden of proof of such defence shall lie on the person raising such defence;

(viii) makes to the public a representation in a form that purports to be—

(i) a warranty or guarantee of a product or of any goods or services; or

(ii) a promise to replace, maintain or repair an article or any part thereof or to repeat or continue a service until it has achieved a specified result, if such purported warranty or guarantee or promise is materially misleading or if there is no reasonable prospect that such warranty, guarantee or promise will be carried out;

(ix) materially misleads the public concerning the price at which a product or like products or goods or services, have been or are, ordinarily sold or provided, and, for this purpose, a representation as to price shall be deemed to refer to the price at which the product or goods or services has or have been sold by sellers or provided by suppliers generally in the relevant market unless it is clearly specified to be the price at which the product has been sold or services have been provided by the person by whom or on whose behalf the representation is made;

(x) gives false or misleading facts disparaging the goods, services or trade of another person. [Consumer Protection Act (68 of 1986), S. 2(1)(r)]

Unfasten. To make loose; to detach [IPC (45 of 1860), S. 462]; to open. [IPC (45 of 1860), S. 445, *Sixthly*].

Unfavourable. Not favourable. [Indian Evidence Act (1 of 1872), S. 114, ill. (g)].

Unfetter. To set at liberty; to take the fetters from.

Unfinished. Which has not been completed. [Indian Partnership Act (9 of 1932), S. 47].

Unfit. The word "unfit" may be interpreted not merely as physically incapable, for instance partially blind or partially paralysed, but also as covering a case wherein the applicant contends that there has been a breach of trust on the part of the trustee.

Unsuitable; not fitted (for some purpose, action or end, to do something or to be done something to); not qualified. [T.P. Act (4 of 1882), S. 108(e)]; to make unfit.

Unfit person. A person not fit for some purpose or something; an unsuitable person. [CrPC, 1973 (2 of 1974), S. 121(1)].

Unforeseen. Not seen before hand; not expected. [IPC (45 of 1860), S. 464, ill. (j)]; [Land Acquisition Act (1 of 1894), S. 17(2)].

Unfriendly suitor. A person or business that attempts to take control of a corporation, against its wishes, by buying its stock and replacing its management.

Unguided power. A power granted without laying down the guidelines for the exercise of it; power not defined under a law.

Uni-cameral legislature. A legislature consisting of only one house.

Uniform Unvariable; conforming to one rule or mode.

Uniform process. A process showing a single form, degree or character in all occurrences or manifestations. [Indian Evidence Act (1 of 1872), S. 62, *Expln. 2*].

Uniform Resource Locator (URL). A standardized device for identifying and locating certain records and other resources located on the world wide web. (*Information Technology*)

Uniformly. In a uniform manner. [Hindu Succession Act (30 of 1956), S. 3(1)(d)].

Unilateral. One-sided.

Unilateral contract. When the party to whom an engagement is made makes no express agreement on his part, the contract is called unilateral contract, binding only one party.

Unilateral discharge. In a contract, the terms of which are carried out by first party but not by the other party, hence the other party is released from his obligations by the first party.

Unimpaired. Not impaired; not damaged or made less. [Land Acquisition Act (1 of 1894), S. 49(1)].

Unimpeachable. Free from fault; blameless; not capable of being impeached.

Uninhabitable. Unfit for habitation or residing. [CPC (5 of 1908), O. XXI, R. 32(5), ill.].

Union. "UNION" includes a Union Territory, whether having a Legislative Assembly or not. [Comptroller and Auditor-General's (Duties Powers and Conditions of Service) Act (56 of 1971), S. 2(e)]

An association or league of persons or states formed for some purpose or action. [Preamble, Representation of the People Act (43 of 1950)].

Union purposes. Means the purposes of Government relatable to any of the matters mentioned in the Union List in the Seventh Schedule to the Constitution. [Chandernnagore (Merger) Act (36 of 1954), S. 2(g)]

Union territories. UNION TERRITORY shall mean any "Union Territory specified in the First Schedule to the Constitution and shall include any other territory comprised within the territory of India but not specified in that Schedule." [General Clauses Act (10 of 1897), S. 3(62A)]

"UNION TERRITORY"

(i) the Andaman and Nicobar Islands;

(ii) Lakshadweep;

(iii) Dadra and Nagar Haveli and Daman and Diu;

(iv) Ladakh;

(v) Chandigarh; or

(vi) other territory.

Explanation.—For the purposes of this Act, each of the territories specified in sub-clauses (i) to (vi) shall be considered to be a separate Union territory. [Union Territory Goods and Services Tax Act (14 of 2017), S. 2(8)]

"UNION TERRITORY", in relation to the existing State of Jammu and Kashmir, means the Union territory of Jammu and Kashmir or Union territory of Ladakh, as the case may be. [Jammu & Kashmir Reorganisation Act, 2019 (34 of 2019), S. 2(n)]

Unique Identification Number (Aadhaar). "Unique Identification Number (Aadhaar)" means a unique identification number issued by the Unique Identification Authority of India. [Liquefied Petroleum Gas (Regulation of Supply and Distribution) Order, 2000, Clause 2(r)].

Unit. "UNIT" includes—

(a) any body of officers and airmen for which a separate authorised establishment exists;

(b) any separate body of persons subject to this Act employed on any service and not attached to a unit as aforesaid;

(c) any other separate body of persons composed wholly or partly of persons subject to this Act, and specified as a unit by the Central Government. [Air Force Act (45 of 1950), S. 4(xxviii); Indo-Tibetan Border Police Force Act (35 of 1992), S. 2(1)(y)]

Cambridge Advanced Learner's Dictionary (3rd Ed.) defines it as a single thing or a separate part of something larger. Webster's New Explorer College Dictionary (2003) defines "unit" as a single thing, person, or group that is a constituent of a whole. [*The Professional Couriers, Administrative Office vs. Employees Provident Fund Appellate Tribunal and Ors.*, 2017 (4) KLT 870, para 38.]

"UNIT" (Production unit, Process unit) means the combination of those items of equipment, including vessels and vessel set up, necessary for the production, processing or consumption of a chemical. [Chemical Weapon Convention Act (34 of 2000), (Verification Annex), b(c)]

"UNIT" means any self-contained portion of an industrial plant or any self-contained portion of a project specified under the said Heading No. 98.01 and having an independent function in the execution of the said project. [Customs Tariff, Project Import Regulations, Regn. 3(d)]

"UNIT" means a Unit set up by an entrepreneur in a Special Economic Zone and includes an existing Unit, an Offshore Banking Unit and a Unit in an International Financial Services Centre, whether established before or established after the commencement of this Act. [Special Economic Zones Act (28 of 2005), S. 2(zc)]

In this section—"unit" includes a regiment, corps, ship, detachment, group, battalion or company. [(w. e. f. 1-7-2024) Bharatiya Nagarik Suraksha Sanhita, 2023 (46 of 2023), section 521, Explanation (a)]

A single thing or person. [Cardamom Act (42 of 1965), S. 5(g)]; [Air Force Act (45 of 1950), S. 106(1)]; [Constitution of India, Art. 40]

Unit capital. Means the aggregate of the face value of the units sold under a unit scheme and outstanding for the time being. [Unit Trust of India Act (52 of 1963), S. 2(o)]

Unit certificate. "UNIT CERTIFICATE" means a certificate issued to the purchaser of a unit under a unit scheme. [Unit Trust of India Act (52 of 1963), S. 2(p)]

A certificate of holding a unit of the Unit Trust of India. [Unit Trust of India Act (52 of 1963), S. 2(g)].

Unit holder. Means a person for the time being recognised by the Trust as the holder of a unit certificate under a unit scheme. [Unit Trust of India (52 of 1963), S. 2(q)]

Unit sale price. 'UNIT SALE PRICE' means the retail sale price per specified unit of weight, measure or number. [Standard of Weight and Measures (Packaged Commodities) Rules, 1977, R. 2(u)]

Unit trust. Fund where money subscribed by many people are pooled and then used to purchase a variety of investments.

United Nations. An international organization formed on June 26, 1945 at San Fransisco after the Second World War to establish world community and peace, for preventing war, providing justice to nations and promoting human rights and welfare.

United States of America. The contiguous states bounded on the north by Canada and the Great Lakes, and on the south by Mexico and the Gulf of Mexico, and extending from the Atlantic to the Pacific Ocean, and the states of Alaska and Hawaii, united under one national government, having a national constitution adopted in 1787, and amended from time to time since. At present there are 50 states. (*The Law Dictionary*)

Unity. Making unto one. [Registration of Births and Deaths Act (18 of 1969), S. 3(3)].

Unity of time. Where an estate comes into the ownership of two or persons at the same moment.

Unity of title. Where an estate comes into the ownership of two or more persons by the same title.

Universal copyright convention country. "UNIVERSAL COPYRIGHT CONVENTION COUNTRY" means a country which has either ratified, or accepted, or acceded to the Universal Copyright Convention, and includes a country mentioned either in Part III or in Part IV of the Schedule of the order. [International Copyright Order, 1999, S. 2(e)]

Universal design. Means the design of products, environments, programmes and services to be usable by all people to the greatest extent possible, without the need for adaptation or specialized design and shall apply to assistive devices including advanced technologies for particular group of persons with disabilities. [Rights of Persons with Disabilities Act (49 of 2016), S. 2(ze)].

Universal Precautions. Means control measures that prevent exposure to or reduce, the risk of transmission of pathogenic agent (including HIV) and includes education, training, personal protective equipment such as gloves, gowns and masks, hand washing, and employing safe work practices. [Human Immunodeficiency Virus and Acquired Immune Deficiency Syndrome (Prevention and Central) Act (16 of 2017), S. 2(j)].

Universal defence. A defence which is good against every possible claimant, including a holder in due course.

Universal donee. A donee of the donor's whole property. [T.P. Act (4 of 1882), S. 128].

Universal malice. The state of mind of a person who determines to take a life on slight provocation, without knowing or caring who may be the victim.

Universal Service Obligation. Means the obligation to provide access to basic telegraph services to people in the rural and remote areas at affordable and reasonable prices. [Indian Telegraph (Amendment) Act (8 of 2004), S. 2(1A)]

University. For the purposes of this clause, "UNIVERSITY" means a University established or incorporated by or under a Central, State or Provincial Act and includes an institution declared under Section 3 of the University Grants Commission Act, 1956 (3 of 1956), to be a University for the purposes of that Act. [Income-tax Act (43 of 1961), S. 47(ix) *Expln*]

"UNIVERSITY" shall have the same meaning as assigned to it in clause (*f*) of section 2 of the University Grants Commission Act, 1956 (3 of 1956) and includes a health University. [National Dental Commission Act, 2023 (21 of 2023), S. 2(zc)]

"UNIVERSITY" shall have the same meaning as assigned to it in clause (*f*) of section 2 of the University Grants Commission Act, 1956 (3 of 1956) and includes a health University. [National Medical Commission Act, 2019 (30 of 2019), S. 2(x)]

University appointed teacher. "UNIVERSITY APPOINTED TEACHER" means a teacher appointed by the University for imparting instruction and conducting research in the University or any other College or institution maintained by the University. [University of Allahabad Act (26 of 2005), S. 3(w)]

University corps. Means any corps of the Indian Territorial Force constituted for the appointment thereto of students of, and other persons connected with, a University established by law in British Indian or colleges affiliated to such a University. [Territorial Force Act (48 of 1920), S. 2]

University Grants Commission. Means the Commission established under section 4 of the University Grants Commission Act, 1956 (3 of 1956). [S. 2(z) of the Rajiv Gandhi National Aviation University Act, 2013 (26 of 2013)]

University recognized teacher. "UNIVERSITY RECOGNIZED TEACHER" means a teacher recognized by the University for imparting instruction and conducting research in a college or institution admitted to the privileges of the University. [University of Allahabad Act (26 of 2005), S. 3(z)]

UNIX. A host operating system which supports multiple users sharing resources. Many host computers use UNIX Servers to provide their e-mail, FTP and Web services. (*Cyber Law*)

An operating system that is especially suited for use by a computer network with multiple users. (*Computer*)

A computer operating system (the basic software running on a computer, underneath things like word processors and spreadsheets). Unix is designed to be used by many people at the same time (it is multi-user) and has *TCP/IP* built-in. It is the most common operating system for *servers* on the *Internet.*

Apple computers' Macintosh operating system, as of version 10 ("Mac OS X"), is based on Unix. (*Matisse Enzer-Glossary of Internet Terms*)

Unjust. Contrary to justice or one's right; enjoyment of rights contrary to the code of conduct prescribed by statutes.

Not just; characterised by injustice; deficient in justice and fairness.

Unjust enrichment. The retention of a benefit conferred by another, without offering compensation, in circumstances where compensation is reasonably expected.

Unladen weight. "UNLADEN WEIGHT" means the weight of a vehicle or trailer including all equipments ordinarily used with the vehicle or trailer when working, but excluding the weight of a driver or attendant. [Motor Vehicle Act (59 of 1988), S. 2(48)]

Unlawful. "UNLAWFUL" means without the authority of the Central Government and the expression "unlawfully" shall be construed accordingly. [Weapons of Mass Destruction and Their Delivery Systems (Prohibition of Unlawful Activities) Act (21 of 2005), S. 4(o)]

That which is contrary to law or unauthorised by law; prohibited by law; irregular; against rule. [IPC (45 of 1860), S. 141].

The word "*unlawful*" means "contrary to the law laid down in the statute."

Unlawful access to stored communications. Access to data stored in computers on RAM or disk drives, prohibited by the *Electronic Communications Privacy Act.* (*Cyber Law*)

Unlawful activity. In relation to an individual or association, means any action taken by such individual or association (whether by committing an act or by words, either spoken or written, or by signs or by visible representation or otherwise),—

(i) which is intended, or supports any claim to bring about, on any ground, whatsoever, the cession of a part of the territory of India or the secession of a part of the territory of India from the Union, or which incites any individual or group of individuals to bring about such cession or secession.

(ii) which disclaims, questions, disrupts or is intended to disrupt the sovereignty and territorial integrity of India. [Unlawful Activities (Prevention) Act (37 of 1967), S. 2(f)]

"UNLAWFUL ACTIVITY", in relation to an individual or association, means any action taken by such individual or association (whether by committing an act or by words, either spoken or written or by signs or by visible representation or otherwise);

(i) which is intended, or supports any claim, to bring about, on any ground whatsoever, the cession of a part of the territory of India or the secession of a part of the territory of India from the Union, or which incites any individual or group of individuals to bring about such cession or secession; or

(ii) which disclaims, questions, disrupts or is intended to disrupt the sovereignty and territorial integrity of India; or

(iii) which causes or is intended to cause disaffection against India. [Unlawful Activities (Prevention) Act (37 of 1967), S. 2(1)(o) *as substituted by Unlawful Activities (Prevention) Amendment Act (29 of 2004), S. 4*]

Unlawful assembly. "An assembly of five or more persons is designated an 'UNLAWFUL ASSEMBLY' if the common object of the persons composing that assembly is :—

First.—To overawe by criminal force, or show of criminal force the Central Government or any State Government or Parliament or the Legislature of any State, or any public servant in the exercise of the lawful power of such public servant; or

Second.—To resist the execution of any law, or of any legal process; or

Third.—To commit any mischief or criminal trespass, or other offence; or

Fourth.—By means of criminal force, or show of criminal force to any person, to take or obtain possession of any property, or to deprive any person of the enjoyment of a right of way, or of the use of water or other incorporeal right of which he is in possession or enjoyment, or to enforce any right or supposed right; or

Fifth.—By means of criminal force, or show of criminal force, to compel any person to do what he is not legally bound to do, or to omit to do what he is legally entitled to do.

Explanation.—An assembly which was not unlawful when it assembled, may subsequently become an unlawful assembly." [IPC (45 of 1860), S. 141] [(w. e. f. 1-7-2024) repealed and replaced by Bharatiya Nyaya Sanhita, 2023 (45 of 2023), S. 189(1)]

An assembly does not become unlawful by reason of its lawful acts exciting others to do unlawful acts. But an assembly lawful in its inception may become unlawful by its acts. When a body of men are determined to vindicate their rights or supposed rights, by unlawful force and when they engage in a fight with men who, on the other hand, are equally determined to vindicate by unlawful force their rights or supposed rights, no question of self-defence arises, for neither side is trying to get the better of the other, and in such a case the assembly is unlawful.

Unlawful association. "UNLAWFUL ASSOCIATION" means any association—

(i) which has for its object any unlawful activity, or which encourages or aids persons to undertake any unlawful activity, or of which the members undertake such activity; or

(ii) which has for its object any activity which is punishable under Section 153A or Section 153-B of the India Penal Code, or which encourages or aids persons to undertake any such activity, or of which the members undertake any such activity.

Provided that nothing contained in sub-clause (ii) shall apply to the State of Jammu and Kashmir. [Unlawful Activities (Prevention) Act (37 of 1967), S. 2(p), *as substituted by the Unlawful Activities (Prevention) Amendment Act (29 of 2004), S. 4*]

Unlawful detaining. Detaining contrary to law. [Indian Contract Act (9 of 1872), S. 15].

Unlawful entry. The crime of entering another's property, by fraud or illegal means without the consent of the owner; Crossing of border of a country by an alien without proper documents.

Unlawful force. Action which constitutes an offence or actionable tort directed against a person without the consent of that person.

Unlawful possession of drugs. Possession of dangerous drugs which are subject to criminal regulation.

Unlawful trusts. Trusts which are liable to be declared void.

Unlawfully at large. Term applied to one who has escaped from lawful arrest, prison, detention centre, *etc.*

Unless. Promising to do or not to do a thing with a reservation or option about the happening of an event for doing or not doing the thing.

Unless and until. *Unless* means—if it be not that; if it be not the case that; if not, supposing not; if it be not; except. *Until* means up to the time of. A word of limitation used ordinarily to restrict that which precedes to what immediately follows, and its office is to fix some point of time or some event upon the arrival or occurrence of which what precedes will cease to exist. *Peirce, Leslie & Co. Ltd.* v. *Industrial Tribunal*, AIR 1962 Ker 220, 227.

Unlimited Company. Company that consists of members who are all liable for the total of the company's debts.

"UNLIMITED COMPANY" means a company not having any limit on the liability of its members. [S. 2(92) of the Companies Act, 2013 (18 of 2013)]

Unlisted company. Also called an unquoted company, a company whose shares are not traded on a major stock exchange.

For the purposes of the proviso to clause (52) of section 2 of the Act, the following classes of companies shall not be considered as listed companies, namely:—

(a) Public companies which have not listed their equity shares on a recognized stock exchange but have listed their—

(i) non-convertible debt securities issued on private placement basis in terms of SEBI (Issue and Listing of Debt Securities) Regulations, 2008; or

(ii) non-convertible redeemable preference shares issued on private placement basis in terms of SEBI (Issue and Listing of Non-Convertible Redeemable Preference Shares) Regulations, 2013; or

(iii) both categories of (i) and (ii) above.

(b) Private companies which have listed their non-convertible debt securities on private placement basis on a recognized stock exchange in terms of SEBI (Issue and Listing of Debt Securities) Regulations, 2008;

(c) Public companies which have not listed their equity shares on a recognized stock exchange but whose equity shares are listed on a stock exchange in a jurisdiction as specified in sub-section (3) of section 23 of the Act. [Companies (Specification of Definitions Details) Rules, 2014, rule 2A]

Unlisted securities. For the purposes of section 112(1) of Act 43 of 1961, 'unlisted securities' means securities other than listed securities. [*Explanation* (*ab*) to section 112(1) of the Income-tax Act, 1961 (43 of 1961) as introduced (w.e.f. 1-4-2013) by the Finance Act, 2012 (23 of 2012)]

Unliquidated. Not specified or determined or ascertained.

Unliquidated damages. Amount of damages determined by a Court, rather than specified by a contract.

Unliquidated debt. An obligation, the money

Unmarketable. Not salable; not suitable for the market.

Unmarketable title. Title which a reasonable buyer would refuse to accept because of possible conflicting interests in or litigation over the property.

Unmarried. The dictionary meaning of the word "unmarried" is "not married"; the popular and more usual sense is "never having been married". The word is commonly used in either sense and is therefore a flexible or equivocal term so that the meaning must in all cases be discovered from the context. In the case of deeds and wills where there is no context, where the document is completely colourless, the popular sense will usually be adopted.

Unmerchantable. Not fit for market; not saleable; not pertaining to trade. [Sale of Goods Act (3 of 1930), S. 17(2)(c)].

Unnatural death. Death under circumstances not natural. [CrPC, 1973 (2 of 1974), S. 40(1)(d)].

Unnatural offences. Voluntarily having carnal intercourse against the order of nature with any man, woman, or animal. [IPC (45 of 1860), S. 377]

Unnatural will. A will which distributes the estate of a testator to strangers instead of testator's relatives, without apparent reason.

Unnecessary. Not required under certain circumstances.

Not necessary. [CrPC, 1973 (2 of 1974), S. 56].

Unnecessary hardship. A deprivation of an owner's right to the beneficial use of property that is caused when a zoning ordinance makes it impossible to receive a reasonable return from the property.

Unobtainable. Not obtainable. [T.P. Act (4 of 1882), S. 52, *Expln.*].

Unopposed. Not opposed; not contested (as) a suit or application unopposed by the opposite party.

Unorganised sector. Includes self-employed workers such as agricultural labourers, bidi workers, brick kiln workers, carpenters, cobblers, construction workers, fishermen, hamals, handicraft artisans, handloom and khadi workers, lady tailors, leather and tannery workers, papad makers, powerloom workers, physically handicapped self-employed persons, primary milk producers, rickshaw pullers, safai karmacharis, salt growers, sericulture workers, sugarcane cutters, tendu leaf collectors, toddy tappers, vegetable vendors, washerwomen, working women in hills, or such other categories of persons. [Insurance Regulatory and Development Authority (Obligations of Insurers to Rural or Social Sectors) Regulations, 2000, Rgn. 2(e)]

"UNORGANISED SECTOR". In relation to a workplace means an enterprise owned by individuals or self-employed workers and engaged in the production or sale of goods or providing service of any kind whatsoever, and where the enterprise employs workers, the number of such workers is less than ten. [S. 2(p) of the Sexual Harassment of Women at Workplace (Prevention, Prohibition & Redressal) Act, 2013 (14 of 2013)]

"UNORGANISED SECTOR" Means an enterprise owned by individuals or self-employed workers and engaged in the production or sale of goods or providing service of any kind whatsoever, and where the enterprise employs workers, the number of such workers is less than ten. [Unorganised Workers Social Security Act 2008 (33 of 2008), S. 2(l)]

"UNORGANISED SECTOR" means an enterprise owned by individuals or self-employed workers and engaged in the production or sale of goods or providing service of any kind whatsoever, and where the enterprise employs workers, the number of such workers is less than ten. [Code on Social Security, 2020 (36 of 2020), section 2(85)]

Unorganised worker. Means a home-based worker, self-employed worker or a wage worker in the unorganised sector and includes a worker in the organised sector who is not covered by any of the Acts mentioned in Schedule II to this Act. [Unorganised Workers Social Security Act 2008 (33 of 2008), S. 2(m)]

"Unorganised worker" means a home-based worker, self-employed worker or a wage worker in the unorganised sector and includes a worker in the organised sector who is not covered by the Industrial Disputes Act, 1947 (14 of 1947), or Chapters III to VII of this Code. [Code on Social Security, 2020 (36 of 2020), section 2(86)]

Unpaid. Not paid. [Sale of Goods Act (3 of 1930), S. 45].

Unpaid seller. "The seller of goods is deemed to be an "unpaid seller" within the meaning of this Act—

(a) when the whole of the price has not been paid or tendered;

(b) when a bill of exchange or other negotiable instrument has been received as conditional payment and the condition on which it was received has not been fulfilled by reason of the dishonour of the instrument or otherwise." [Sale of Goods Act (3 of 1930), S. 45(1)]

A seller, who has not been paid the price of the thing sold by him. [Sale of Goods Act (3 of 1930), S. 45].

Unparliamentary. Contrary to the usages of proceedings in Parliament; not such as can be spoken in Parliament or Legislative Assemblies.

Unparliamentary expressions. Expressions contrary to the usages of Parliament containing accusations or imputations against a Member of either House which are abusive in nature and are not to be used in Parliamentary debate. The use of such language is a breach of order and, if the member using it does not immediately withdraw the offensive words at the request of the Speaker, he may be called upon to withdraw from the House or 'named'. (*Constitutional and Parliamentary Term*)

Unperformed. Not performed. [Specific Relief Act (47 of 1963), S. 12(2)(b)(i)].

Unprocessed. The expression "any other process" is used in the context of what constitutes manufacture and the expression "unprocessed" in the exempting notification draws its meaning from that context. *Siddeshwari Cotton Mills (P) Ltd.* v. *Union of India*, AIR 1989 SC 1019, 1023. [Central Excise and Salt Act (1 of 1944), S. 2(f)(v)]

Unproductive. Not productive; unprofitable.

Unprofessional conduct. Behaviour which is immoral, unethical, or dishonourable, either generally or when judged by the standards of specific profession.

Unprotected child. "UNPROTECTED CHILD" means a child who has not been protected from small-pox by having had that disease either naturally or by inoculation, or by having been successfully vaccinated, and who has not been certified under the Vaccination Act to be insusceptible to vaccination. [Vaccination Act (13 of 1880), S. 2]

Unprotected worker. 'Unprotected worker' means a manual worker who is engaged or to be engaged in any scheduled employment. [Maharashtra Mathadi, Hamal and Other Manual Workers [Regulation of Employment and Welfare) Act, (30 of 1969), 2(11) as cited in *Pepsico India Holding Private Limited v. Grocery Market and Shops Board*, (2016) 4 SCC 493, para 5].

Unpublished. Not published. [Indian Evidence Act (1 of 1872), S. 123].

Unpublished record. It does not mean only those documents or papers which are printed for general circulation. Even if a secret document or a part of it is revealed, the document will lose the sanctity as an unpublished record, because there cannot be any guarantee as to when and in what contingency the other parts may also be made known. *Raj Narain* v. *Indira Nehru Gandhi*, AIR 1974 All 324, 334. [Indian Evidence Act (1 of 1872), S. 123]

Unqualified. Not modified, limited or restricted. [Indian Contract Act (9 of 1872), S. 7(1)]; not having the qualification.

Unquoted share or security. For the purposes of this rule, "unquoted share or security" in relation to share or security means share or security which is not a quoted share or security. [Black Money (Undisclosed Foreign Income and Assets) and Imposition of Tax Rules, rule 3, *Expln. 1(e)*]

Unreasonable. Opposite of reasonable; not agreeable to reason.

Not reasonable; irrational. [Indian Evidence Act (1 of 1872), S. 32].

Unreasonable search. A search made without legal authority.

Unreasonableness. The quality of being unreasonable. [CPC (5 of 1908), O. XXXII, R. 14(2)].

Unreasonably. In an unreasonable manner. [CPC (5 of 1908), O. XI, R. 3]; [Damodar Valley Corporation Act (14 of 1943), S. 13].

Unregistered company. For the purposes of Part II of Chapter XXI of Act 18 of 2013, the expression 'unregistered company'—

(*a*) shall not include—

(*i*) a railway company incorporated under any Act of Parliament or other Indian law or any Act of Parliament of the United Kingdom;

(*ii*) a company registered under this Act; or

(*iii*) a company registered under any previous companies law and not being a company the registered office whereof was in Burma, Aden, Pakistan immediately before the separation of that country from India; and

(*b*) save as aforesaid, shall include any partnership firm, limited liability partnership or society or co-operative society, association or company consisting of more than seven members at the time when the petition for winding up the partnership firm, limited liability partnership or society or co-operative society, association or company, as the case may be, is presented before the Tribunal. [*Explanation* to section 375 of the Companies Act, 2013 (18 of 2013)]

"Unregulated Deposit Scheme". Means a Scheme or an arrangement under which deposits are accepted or solicited by any deposit taker by way of business and which is not a Regulated Deposit Scheme, as specified under column (3) of the First Schedule. [Banning of Unregulated Deposit Schemes Act, 2019 (21 of 2019), S. 2(17)]

Unrelated offence. A crime which is independent from the charged offence.

Unrepealed. Not repealed. [Indian Partnership Act (9 of 1932), S. 3].

Unreported cases. Transcripts of cases which do not appear in the published law reports.

Unsafe. Not safe; exposed to danger or risk. [Indian Contract Act (9 of 1872), S. 150, ill. (b)].

Unsafe food. Means an article of food whose nature, substance or quality is so affected as to render it injurious to health:—

(i) by the article itself, or its package thereof, which is composed, whether wholly or in part, of poisonous or deleterious substance; or

(ii) by the article consisting, wholly or in part, of any filthy, putrid, rotten, decomposed or diseased animal substance or vegetable substance; or

(iii) by virtue of its unhygienic processing or the presence in that article of any harmful substance; or (iv) by the substitution of any inferior or cheaper substance whether wholly or in part; or

(v) by addition of a substance directly or as an ingredient which is not permitted; or

(vi) by the abstraction, wholly or in part, of any of its constituents; or

(vii) by the article being so coloured, flavoured or coated, powdered or polished, as to damage or conceal the article or to make it appear better or of greater value than it really is; or

(viii) by the presence of any colouring matter or preservatives other than that specified in respect thereof; or

(ix) by the article having been infected or infested with worms, weevils, or insects; or

(x) by virtue of its being prepared, packed or kept under insanitary conditions; or

(xi) by virtue of its being mis-branded or substandard or food containing extraneous matter; or

(xii) by virtue of containing pesticides and other contaminants in excess of quantities specified by regulations. [S. 3(1)(zz) of the Food Safety & Standards Act, 2006 (34 of 2006)]

Unsatisfactory. That does not satisfy. [Indian Evidence Act (1 of 1872), S. 149, ill. (d)].

Unsatisfied. Undischarged or unfulfilled obligation; not satisfied of something desired. [CPC (5 of 1908), O. XXI, R. 48(2)].

Unseaworthy. Unfit for voyage. [Indian Contract Act (9 of 1872), S. 195, ill. (a)].

Condition of a ship when it is unsafe to load it or send it on a voyage.

Unsecured. Having no security or assurance or indemnification behind it.

Unsecured advance. Means an advance not made on the security of assets the market value of which is not at any time less than the amount of advance. [Banking Regulation Act (10 of 1949), S. 5(n)]

Unsecured bond. A bond which is backed only by the general credit and financial reputation of the corporate issuer, not by the lien on the assets of the corporation.

Unsecured claim. A claim which is held by a creditor who does not have the lien or a right of set off against the property of a debtor.

Unsecured creditor. Person who has made a loan but received no security (and therefore has no protection against non-payment).

Unsecured deposits. Where a company does not secure the deposits or secures such deposits partially, then, the deposits shall be termed as "unsecured deposits" and shall be so quoted in every circular, form, advertisement or in any document related to invitation or acceptance of deposits. [Companies Act (18 of 2013), S. 73(2), *proviso*]

Unsecured loan. "UNSECURED LOAN" means a loan not made on the security of assets the market value of which is not at any time less than the amount of such loans. [Banking Regulation Act (10 of 1949), S. 5(n)]

Unsecured note. A note which is not backed by a collateral.

Unsettled. Undecided; undetermined. [CPC (5 of 1908), O. VII, R. 2.].

Unsettled account. The account which has not been determined or decided. [CPC (5 of 1908), O. VII, R. 2].

Unskilful. Not skilful.

Unskilfulness. The quality or condition of being unskilful. [CPC (5 of 1908), App. A, plaint No. 29, para. 3].

Unskilled. The word 'unskilled' is opposite of the word 'skilled' and the word 'semi-skilled' seems to describe a person who falls between the two categories, i.e., he is not fully skilled and also is not completely unskilled but has some amount of skill for the work for which he is employed. The word 'unskilled' cannot, therefore, be understood dissociated from the words 'skilled' and 'semi-skilled' to read and construe it to include in it all categories of employees irrespective of the nature of employment. *Ahmedabad Pvt. Primary Teachers' Association* v. *Administrative Officer*, AIR 2004 SC 1426 : 2004 AIR SCW 356.

Unskilled office work. Means work done in an establishment by any of the following categories of employees, namely :—

1. daftari;
2. jamadar, orderly and peon;
3. dusting man or farash;
4. bundle or record lifter;
5. process server;
6. watchman;
7. sweeper;
8. any other employee doing any routine or unskilled work which the Central Government may, by notification in the Official Gazette, declare to be unskilled office work. [Employment Exchanges (Compulsory Notification of Vacancies) Act (31 of 1959) S. 2(i)]

Unskilled work. Includes engaging in agriculture.

Unsolicited Commercial Communications. 'Unsolicited Commercial Communication' means a communication in any form with commercial content that is sent to a recipient who has not requested it. [Telecom Unsolicited Commercial Communication Regulations, 2007, Reg. 2(q), Chapter 1]

Unsound mind. "A person is said to be of UNSOUND MIND for the purpose of making a contract; if, at the time when he makes it, he is incapable of understanding it and of forming a rational judgment as to its effect upon his interest." [Indian Contract Act (9 of 1872), S. 12]

Not mentally sound or moral; not sane. [IPC (45 of 1860), S. 84 and Constitution of India, Art. 102(i)(b)].

Unsoundness of mind. For the purposes of S. 12 of the Indian Contract Act (9 of 1872), the test of unsoundness of mind is whether the person is incapable of understanding the business concerned and its implications and mere weakness of mind is not sufficient.

State of not being mentally sound or normal. [Indian Evidence Act (1 of 1872), Ss. 3, ill. and 105, ill. (a)].

Unspecified. Not specified. [Indian Contract Act (9 of 1872), S. 34].

Unsponsored depository receipts. "Unsponsored depository receipts" mean depository receipts issued without specific approval of the issuer of the underlying permissible securities. [Depository Receipts Scheme, 2014, R. 2(1)(k)]

Unstamped. Not stamped. [IPC (45 of 1860), S. 230, ill. (b)].

Unstarred question. A parliamentary question whose answer, unlike a starred question, is not given orally but in a written form. So no supplementary questions can be asked thereon. It is so named as it is not marked with an asterisk.

Unsustainable. Not supporatable; that which is not maintainable.

Unsworn evidence. Evidence which is not given on oath or by affirmation.

Unsworn statement. Statement which is made by accused without being sworn.

Until evicted therefrom in due course of law. The expression 'until evicted therefrom in due course of law' occurring in Section 145(6) of CrPC 1973 (2 of 1974) means the eviction of the party successful before the Magistrate, consequent upon the adjudication of title or right to possession by a competent Court; that does not necessarily mean a decree of eviction. *Shanti Kumar Panda* v. *Shakuntala Devi,* AIR 2004 SC 115, 121, para 17.

Until further order. Upto the time of any other order; till another order in passed. [CPC (5 of 1908), 1st. Sch., App. F, form No. 5].

Untouchability. Article 17 places the word 'untouchability' in inverted commas; accordingly, the subject-matter of the article is not untouchability in its literal or grammatical sense but the practices as it has developed historically in India. *Jai Singh* v. *UOI*, AIR 1993 Raj 177, 181 (FB). [Constitution of India, Art. 17]

A literal construction of the term would include persons who are treated as untouchable either temporarily or otherwise for various reasons, such as their suffering from an epidemic or contagious disease or on account of social observances such as are associated with birth or death or on account of social boycott resulting from caste or other disputes. The imposition of untouchability in such circumstances has no relation to the causes which relegated certain classes of people beyond the pale of the caste system. Such relegation has always been based on the ground of birth in certain classes. *Devarajiah* v. *B. Padmanna*, AIR 1958 Mys 84, 85. [Untouchability Offences Act, 1955, Ss. 3, 4]

Untoward incident. "UNTOWARD INCIDENT" means—

(1) (i) the commission of a terrorist act within the meaning of sub-section (1) of Section 3 of the Terrorist and Disruptive Activities (Prevention) Act, 1987; or

(ii) the making of a violent attack or the commission of robbery or dacoity; or

(iii) the indulging in rioting, shootout or arson, by any person in or on any train carrying passengers, or in a waiting hall, cloak room or reservation or booking office or on any platform or in any other place within the precincts of a railway station; or

(2) the accidental falling of any passenger from a train carrying passengers. [Railways Act (24 of 1989), S. 123(c)]

Untransferable. Not transferable. [T.P. Act (4 of 1882), S. 6(i)].

Untruth, Falsehood, Fasity, Lie. Children are apt to speak *untruths* for want of understanding the value of words; travellers from a love at exaggeration are apt to introduce *falsehoods* into their narrations; it is the nature of a *lie* to increase itself to a tenfold degree; one *lie* must be backed by many more. *Falsehood* is also used in the abstract sense for what is false. *Falsity* is never used but in the abstract sense.

Unumquodque est id quod est principalius in ipso. That which is the principal part of a thing is the thing itself.

Unumquodque principiorum est sibimet ipsi fides; et perspicua vera non sunt probanda. Every principle is its own evidence and plain truths are not to be proved.

Unusual. Not usual; abnormal.

Unusual danger. A danger which is not usually found in carrying out the task in hand. The danger should be such that it is unreasonable conduct on the part of the occupier to expose the particular visitor to it.

Unwholesome. The words "UNWHOLESOME" and "noxious" when used in relation to an article of food mean respectively that the article is harmful to health or repugnant to human use. [Prevention of Food Adulteration Act (37 of 1954), S. 2(xv)]

Unwilling. Not willing. [T.P. Act (4 of 1882), S. 69A(2)].

Unworkmanlike manner, In. Manner not suited to or charcteristic of a good workman; incompetent manner. [CPC (5 of 1908), 1st Sch. App. A, form No. 17(3)].

Unworthy. Undeserving; not worthy. [Indian Evidence Act (1 of 1872), S. 155(1)]; [Indian Evidence Act (1 of 1872), S. 114, ill. (b)].

Unworthy of credit. One not deserving to be believed. [Indian Evidence Act (1 of 1872), S. 114, ill. (b); Indian Evidence Act (1 of 1872), S. 155(1)].

Unwritten law. Law, which, although never enacted in the form of a statute or ordinance, has the sanction of custom.

Unwrought. Not shaped into finished form; not processed for use. [Gold (Control) Act (45 of 1968) (*repealed*), S. 2(j)].

Up-to-date. In order that the employment register can properly be said to be *up-to-date*, it is necessary that it should contain, day by day, the names of the persons employed in the factory, their hours of work and the nature of their employment.

Upload. Making available of data from a computer to another on the Internet. (*Internet*)

To send a file from a small computer to a large computer or from a nearby computer to a distant computer. If is the opposite of *download.* (*Computer*)

Upon supposition. Upon a conjecture based upon possibility or, probability that a thing could or may have occurred, without proof that it did occur. [Indian Evidence Act (1 of 1872), S. 3].

Upset price. 'UPSET PRICE' means the price below which a privilege shall not be granted. [T.N. Liquor (Retail Vending) Rules, 1989, R. 2(z)

Price that must be reached at auction to effect sale. [Sale of Goods Act (3 of 1930), S. 64(5)].

Upset/reserve price. The term 'upset/ reserve price', in a sale by auction of a property is not synonymous with valuation of the property. It means lowest selling price. *Anil Kumar Srivastava* v. *State of U.P.*, AIR 2004 SC 4299, 4304, paras 11, 12 & 13]

Upstream merger. A merger of a subsidiary corporation into its parent.

Upstreaming. A parent corporation's use of a subsidiary's cash flow or assets for purposes unrelated to the subsidiary.

Upto. The word "upto" may include the last day or may not, and if it is in consonance with justice to interpret it in one of the ways permissible, there can be no complaint on the other side.

Upto not more than. The words "upto not more than" merely fix the maximum percentage of rank promotees in the category, leaving it to the appointing authorities to adopt any percentage below this figure. *State of Andhra* v. *Venkatappaya*, AIR 1961 SC 779, 782.

Urban agglomeration:

(A) in relation to any State or Union Territory specified in column (1) of Schedule I means,—

(i) the urban agglomeration specified in the corresponding entry in column (2) thereof and includes the peripheral area specified in the corresponding entry in column (3) thereof; and

(ii) any other area which the State Government may, with the previous approval of the Central Government, having regard to its location, population (population being more than one lakh) and such other relevant factors as the circumstances of the case may require, by notification in the Official Gazette, declare to be an urban agglomeration and any agglomeration so declared shall be deemed to belong to category D in that Schedule and the peripheral area therefor shall be one kilometre;

(B) in relation to any other State or Union Territory, means any area which the State Government may, with the previous approval of the Central Government having regard to its location, population (population being more than one lakh) and such other relevant factors as the circumstances of the case may require, by notification in the Official Gazette, declare to be an urban agglomeration and any agglomeration so declared shall be deemed to belong to category D in Schedule I and the peripheral area therefor shall be one kilometre. [Urban Land (Ceiling and Regulation) Act (33 of 1976), S. 2(n)]

Urban areas. "URBAN AREA" means any such area within the limits of a municipal corporation or municipality as the Central Government may, having regard to the population, concentration of industries, need for proper planning of the area and other relevant factors, by general or special order, declare to be an urban area for the purposes of this sub-section. [Income-tax Act (43 of 1961), S. 54G(1) *Expln.*]

Urban consumers co-operative society. For the purposes of this section, an "URBAN CONSUMERS CO-OPERATIVE SOCIETY" means a society for the benefit of the consumers within the limits of a municipal corporation, municipality, municipal committee, notified area committee, town area or cantonment. [Income-tax Act (43 of 1961), S. 80P(2)(f) *Expln.*]

Urban immovable property. 'URBAN IMMOVABLE PROPERTY' shall mean immovable property within the limits of a town, other than agriculture land. For the purpose of this Act a specified place shall be deemed to be a town (a) if so declared by the Local Government by notification in the official Gazette, or (b) if so found by the Courts. [Pun. Act II of 1905 (Pre-emption) S. 3, cl. (3).]

Urban infrastructure. Means a project for providing potable water supply, sanitation and sewerage, drainage, solid waste management, roads, bridges and flyovers or urban transport. [Income-tax Act (43 of 1961), S. 11(5)(ix a) *Expln.*(c)]

Urban land. "URBAN LAND" means land situate—

(i) in any area which is comprised within the jurisdiction of a municipality (whether known as a municipality, municipal corporation, notified area committee, town area committee, town committee or by any other name) or a cantonment board and which has a population of not less than ten thousand according to the last preceding census of which the relevant figures have been published before the valuation date; or

(ii) in any area within such distance, not being more than eight kilometres from the local limits of any municipality or cantonment board referred to in sub-clause (i), as the Central Government may, having regard to the extent of, and scope for, urbanisation of that area and other relevant considerations, specify in this behalf by notification in the Official Gazette,

but does not include land on which construction of a building is not permissible under any law for the time being in force in the area in which such land is situated or the land occupied by any building which has been constructed with the approval of the appropriate authority or any unused land held by the assessee for industrial purposes for a period of two years from the date of its acquisition by him or any land held by the assessee as stock-in-trade for a period of ten years from the date of its acquisition by him. [Wealth-tax Act (27 of 1957), S. 2(ea)(vi) *Expln.* (b)]

"URBAN LAND" means,—

(i) any land situated within the limits of an urban agglomeration and referred to as such in the master plan; or

(ii) in a case where there is no master plan, or where the master plan does not refer to any land as urban land, any land within the limits of an urban agglomeration and situated in any area included within the local limits of a municipality (by whatever name called), a notified area committee, a town area committee, a city and town committee, a small town committee, a cantonment board or a panchayat, but does not include any such land which is mainly used for the purpose of agriculture. [Urban Land (Ceiling and Regulation) Act (33 of 1976), S. 2(o)]

"URBAN LAND". Means land situate—

(*i*) in any area which is comprised within the jurisdiction of a municipality (whether known as a municipality, municipal corporation, notified area committee, town area committee, town committee, or by any other name) or a cantonment board and which has a population of not less than ten thousand; or

(*ii*) in any area within the distance, measured aerially,—

(I) not being more than two kilometres, from the local limits of any municipality or cantonment board referred to in sub-clause (i) and which has a population of more than ten thousand but not exceeding one lakh; or

(II) not being more than six kilometres, from the local limits of any municipality or cantonment board referred to in sub-clause (i) and which has a population of more than one lakh but not exceeding ten lakh ; or

(III) not being more than eight kilometres, from the local limits of any municipality or cantonment board referred to in sub-clause (i) and which has a population of more than ten lakh,

but does not include land classified as agricultural land in the records of the Government and used for agricultural purposes or land on which construction of a building is not permissible under any law for the time being in force in the area in which such land is situated or the land occupied by any building which has been constructed with the approval of the appropriate authority or any unused land held by the assessee for industrial purposes for a period of two years from the date of its acquisition by him or any land held by the assessee as stock-in-trade for a period of ten years from the date of its acquisition by him.

Explanation.—For the purposes of clause (*b*) of *Explanation 1*, 'population' means the population according to the last preceding census of which the relevant figures have been published before the date of valuation. [(w.e.f. 1-4-2014) *Explanation 1*(*b*) to section 2(ea) of the Wealth-tax Act, 1957 (27 of 1957)]

Urbanisable land. Means land situated within an urban agglomeration, but not being urban land. [Urban Land (Ceiling and Regulation) Act (33 of 1976), S. 2(p)]

Urge forward. The word "urge forward" means to advise or try hard to persuade somebody to do something, to make a person to move quickly in the particular direction, especially by pushing or forcing such person. [*Pawan Kumar* v. *State of H.P.,* (2017) 7 SCC 780, para 37].

Urgency. Providing sites to siteless people, ordinarily no urgent purpose. [Land Acquisition Act (1 of 1894), S. 17(1)]

Urgency and emergency. 'Urgency' relates to a situation demanding prompt action while 'emergency' indicates a situation suddenly arising and demanding prompt action. 'Emergency' is a stronger word than 'urgency'. *Major S. Arjun Singh* v. *State of Punjab*, AIR 1959 Punj 530, 543. [Land Acquisition Act (1 of 1894), S. 17]

Urgent. Demanding prompt action. [Indian Evidence Act (1 of 1872), S. 9, ill. (c)].

URI. (*abbr.*) Uniform Resource Identifier. An address for a resource available on the Internet. The first part of a URI is called the "scheme". The most well known scheme is *http*, but there are many others. Each URI scheme has its own format for how a URI should appear.

Here are examples of URIs using the *http, telnet*, and *news* schemes: http://www.economictimes.net/files/glossary. htm.l telnet://eco.sf.ca.us. news:new.newusers.questions (*Matisse Enzer-Glossary of Internet Terms*)

Urine specimen. A specimen of urine used for analysis in cases involving drunken driving.

URL. (Universal resource locator). A naming convention that identifies an e-commerce site or a web site. For example, the URL of Amazon.com is : <http./www.amazon. com>. (*Cyber Law*)

An attempt to standardise address details of Internet resources. Most commonly used with www pages. For example, the home page for the Natural History Museum is: http://www.nhm.ac .uk/. (*Cyber Law*)

The term URL is basically synonymous with *URI.* URI has replaced URL in technical specifications. (*Matisse Enzer-Glossary of Internet Terms*)

URL. (Uniform Resource Locator)—The standard way to give the address of any resource on the Internet that is part of the World Wide Web (WWW). A URL looks like this. The most common way to use a URL is to enter into a WWW browser program, such as Netscape, or Lynx. (*Internet and E-commerce*)

URN. (*abbr.*) Uniform Resource Name. A *URI* that is supposed to be available for a long time. For an address to be a URN some institution is supposed to make a commitment to keep the resource available at that address. (*Matisse Enzer-Glossary of Internet Terms*)

Usage. The expressions "custom" and "USAGE" signify any rule which, having been continuously and uniformly observed for a long time, has obtained the force of law among Hindus in any local area, tribe, community, group or family :

Provided that the rule is certain and not unreasonable or opposed to public policy; and

Provided further that, in the case of a rule applicable only to a family, it has not been discontinued by the family. [Hindu Adoptions and Maintenance Act (78 of 1956), S. 3(a)]

The law by which the signification or import of words is fixed and settled, and the shades of difference in their meaning is marked and defined.

Habitual use; established practice; customary mode of action on the part of a number of persons; an established or recognised mode or procedure, action or conduct. [Indian Evidence Act (1 of 1872), S. 49 and Constitution of India, Art. 13(3)(a)].

Use. "USE" in relation to narcotic drugs and psychotropic substances, means any kind of use except personal consumption. [Narcotic Drugs and Psychotropic Substances Act (61 of 1985), S. 2(xxviiia)]

Utilization. [C.PC (5 of 1908), 1st. Sch., App. A, form No. 23].

'Use' of the mark does not postulate actual sale of the goods bearing such a mark. 'Use' can be in any form or way and does not necessarily mean and imply actual physical sale and even mere advertisement without having even the existence of the goods can be said to be an use of the mark. *J.N. Nicholas (Vcints) Ltd.* v. *Rose and Thistle*, AIR 1994 Cal 43, 50. [Trade and Merchandise Marks Act (43 of 1958), Sections 26(1), 46(1)(b)]

Use a child. For the purposes of section 13 of Act 32 of 2012, the expression 'use a child' shall include involving a child through any medium like print, electronic, computer or any other technology for preparation, production, offering, transmitting, publishing, facilitation and distribution of the pornographic material. [(w.e.f. 14-11-2012) Explanation to S. 13 of the Protection of Children from Sexual Offences Act, 2012 (32 of 2012)]

Use of child for pornographic purposes. Whoever uses a child in any form of media (including programme or advertisement telecast by television channels or internet or any other electronic form or printed form, whether or not such programme or advertisement is intended for personal use or for distribution), for the purposes of sexual gratification, which includes—

(a) representation of the sexual organs of a child;

(b) usage of a child engaged in real or simulated sexual acts (with or without penetration);

(c) the indecent or obscene representation of a child, shall be guilty of the offence of using a child for pornographic purposes.

Explanation.—For the purposes of this section, the expression "use of a child" shall include involving a child through any medium like print, electronic, computer or any other technology for preparation, production, offering, transmitting, publishing facilitation and distribution of the pornographic material. [Protection of Children from Sexual Offence Act (32 of 2012), S. 13].

Use by date. "Use by date" or "recommended last consumption date" or "expiry date" means the dates which signifies the end of the estimated period under any stated storage conditions, after which product probably will not have the quality attributes normally expected by the consumers and the food shall not be marketable. [Prevention of Food Adulteration Rules, 1955, R 32, *Expln* VIII-C as inserted by 5th Amendment of Rules, 2008, R. 3(viii)]

For the purposes of this sub-rules, the expression "USE BY DATE" means the date which signifies the end of the estimated period under any stated storage conditions after which the product shall not have the quality attributes normally expected by the consumers and after this date, the commodity should not be regarded as marketable. [Legal Metrology (Packaged Commodities) Rules, 2011, R. 6(da), *Explanation (b)*].

Use of motor vehicles. The expression "use" of motor vehicle covers a very wide field, a field more extensive than which might be called traffic use of the motor vehicle and that the use of a vehicle is not confined to the periods when it was in motion or was moving and a vehicle would still be in use even when it was stationary. [*Shivaji Dayanu Patil* v. *Vatschala Uttam More,* (1991) 3 SCC 530]. See also *Kalim Khan* v. *Fimidabee,* (2018) 7 SCC 687, para 11

Used batteries. Means used, damaged and old lead acid batteries or components thereof. [Batteries (Management and Handling) Rules, 2001, R. 3(r)].

Useful to the public. A hospital, a public reading room or a library or an educational institution open to the public or such other work, as the public may directly use, are works which are useful to the public. *R.L. Arora* v. *State of Uttar Pradesh*, AIR 1962 SC 764, 774. [Land Acquisition Act (1 of 1894), Ss. 40, 41]

USENET. A world-wide system of discussion groups, with comments passed among hundreds of thousands of machines. Not all USENET machines are on the *Internet*. USENET is completely decentralized, with over 10,000 discussion areas, called *newsgroups*. (*Matisse Enzer-Glossary of Internet Terms*)

User. An authorized entity that uses a certificate as applicant, subscriber, recipient or relying party, but not including the Certifying Authority issuing the Digital Signature Certificate. (*Information Technology*)

Continued use or enjoyment of a right.

A user of a telecommunication service provided by a telecommunication services provider, who is not necessarily a subscriber (example : user of a GSM network through national or international roaming). (*Telecommunication*)

"USER" means a subscriber, issuer or requester of the Digital Locker system. [Information Technology (Preservation and Retention of Information by Intermediaries Providing Digital Locker Facilities) Rules, 2016, R. 2(1)(v)].

"USER" means a person who avails of the services of an information utility. [Insolvency and Bankruptcy Board of India (Information Utilities) Regulations, 2017, Regn. 2(1)(s)].

User and usage. The term 'user' means to act of using. The word 'usage' means uniform practice. A usage must be established, that is it must be known, certain, uniform, reasonable and not contrary to law; but it may be of very recent origin.

User agency. Means any person, organisation or company or department of the Central Government or State Government making a request for diversion or de-notification of forest land for non-forest purpose or using forest land for non-forest purpose in accordance with the provisions contained in the Forest (Conservation) Act, 1980 (69 of 1980) and the rules made and guidelines issued, thereunder. [Compensatory Afforestation Fund Act (38 of 2016), S. 2(p)].

User 'as of right'. In deciding whether the user of a certain way is of right or not, the Court should consider the character of the ground, the space for which the right is claimed, the relations between the parties, and the circumstances under which the user took place. The mere fact of a frequent or even constant user of the defendants *than* by plaintiffs, who were relatives and neighbours is not proof of user as of right.

User friendly. A term used to describe a computer system that is relatively easy to use. (*Computer*)

Uses. The word "*uses*" in S. 397 of the IPC (45 of 1860) should be construed in a wide sense so as to include not merely cutting, stabbing, shooting (as the case may be) but also carrying the weapon for the purpose of overawing the person robbed.

When the Legislature used the word 'uses' in the section they did not intend that the knife must be actually used for stabbing any person. If it was used for the purpose of producing such an impression upon the mind of a person that he would be compelled to part with his property, that would amount to 'using' the weapon within the meaning of Section 397. *Govind Dipaji More* v. *State*, AIR 1956 Bom 353. [IPC (45 of 1860), S. 397]

Using a false property mark. "Whoever marks any movable property or goods or any case, package or other receptacle containing movable property or goods, or uses any case, package or other receptacle having any mark thereon, in a manner reasonably calculated to cause it to be believed that the property or goods so marked, or any property or goods contained in any such receptacle so marked, belong to a person to whom they do not belong, is said to use a false property mark.". [IPC (45 of 1860), S. 481] [(w. e. f. 1-7-2024) repealed and replaced by Bharatiya Nyaya Sanhita, 2023 (45 of 2023), S. 345(2)]

Using a false trade mark. "Whoever marks any goods or any case, package or other receptacle containing goods, or uses any case, package or other receptacle with any mark thereon, in a manner reasonably calculated to cause it to be believed, that the goods so marked, or any goods contained in any such receptacle so marked, are the manufacture or merchandise of a person whose manufacture or merchandise they are not, *is said to use a false trade mark.*" [IPC (45 of 1860), S. 480]

Persons who stock goods wrapped in wrappers bearing marks which can be said to be a colourable imitation of genuine marks could not be held to have used any false trade mark. *Kundan Lal Agarwal* v. *State*, AIR 1958 All 643, 644. [IPC (45 of 1860), S. 482]

Using of unfair means. 'Using of unfair means' has a nexus with the employment of prohibited material and taking help of an outside agency. Using of a palm of the hand or the desk for rough work is not using of unfair means. *Sunil Kumar Jain* v. *Board of High School and Intermediate Education, U.P., Allahabad*, AIR 1973 All 27.

Usque ad filum aquae. Upto the middle thread of the water.

Usque ad medium filum aquae (viae). As far as the middle of the stream (or road).

Usual. Means according to usage; ordinary; customary; general; regular.

Usual place of abode. The place where a person is normally known to be living.

Usual place of custody. The place where ordinarily or generally people are kept in detention or charge or things are kept in charge or control or care and keeping. [CPC (5 of 1908), O. XI, R. 17].

Usual place of residence. "usual place of residence" means—

(a) in case of an individual, the place where he ordinarily resides;

(b) in other cases, the place where the person is incorporated or otherwise legally constituted [The Central Goods and Services Tax Act, 2017 (12 of 2017), S. 2(113)]

Usual way. Habitual or ordinary or customary mode or method. [Indian Partnership Act (9 of 1932), S. 19(1)].

Usually. In an usual manner, according to customary, established or frequent usage; as rule. [Indian Contract Act (9 of 1872), S. 12].

Usucaption. The acquisition of ownership by prescription.

Usufruct. Right of enjoying the use or advantages, of another's property, short of destroying or wasting its substance.

Usufructuary. One that hath the use, and reaps the profit of a thing.

Usufructuary mortgage. "Where the mortgagor delivers possession or expressly or by implication binds himself to deliver possession of the mortgaged property to the mortgagee, and authorises him to retain such possession until payment of the mortgagemoney, and to receive the rents and profits accruing from the property or any part of any such rents and profits and to appropriate the same in lieu of interest or in payment of the mortgage-money, the transaction is called an usufructuary mortgage and the mortgagee an usufructuary mortgagee." [T.P. Act (4 of 1882), S. 58(d)]

Usufructuary mortgagee. A person in whose favour there is a usufructuary mortgage.

Usura est commodum certum quod propter usum rei mutuatae recipitur. **(5 Rep.** 70) Usury is a certain benefit which is received for the use of a thing lent.

Usurer. One who lends money at a rate of interest greater than what the law allows.

Usurious. Pertaining to usury; partaking of the nature of usury.

Usurious contract. USURIOUS CONTRACT is one which stipulates for the payment of more than lawful interest, for the use of money or forbearance of a debt.

Usury. Reward taken for use of money; excessive interest.

Ut poena ad paucos, metus ad omnes perveniat. That punishment may happen to a few, the fear of it affects all.

Ut res magis valeat quam pereat. That the thing may rather have effect than be destroyed.

The provision of a statute must be so construed as to make it effective and operative on the principle of '*ut res magis valeat quam pereat*'. *Tinsukia Electric Supply Co. Ltd.* v. *State of Assam*, AIR 1990 SC 123, 152.

The maxim means that it is better to validate a thing than to invalidate it. There is a presumption that the legislature does not exceed its jurisdiction. Applying the maxim it was held that the Courts shall act to make a legislation effective and operative. *Welfare Assn.* v. *Ranjit P. Gohil,* AIR 2003 SC 1266. [Applied in *Executive Engineer, Southern Electricity Supply Company of Orissa Limited (SOUTHCO)* v. *Sri Seetaram Rice Mill*, (2012) 2 SCC 108, para 10].

It is better for a thing to have effect than for it to be made void i.e., a statute must be construed in such a manner so as to make it workable. [*State of Gujarat v. Justice R.A. Mehta*, (2013) 3 SCC 1, para 96].

Ut res valeat potius quam pereat. That construction should be preferred which makes the machinery workable. It is better for a statute to have effect, than to be made void. *Commissioner of Income-tax* v. *Shree Jagan Nath Maheshwary*, AIR 1957 P&H 226, 233.

Uterine. Pertaining to the womb; born of the same mother (as) uterine brother, or uterine sister.

Uterine blood. Being descended from a common female. Two persons are said to be related to each other by uterine blood when they are descended from a common ancestress but by different husbands. [Special Marriage Act (43 of 1954), S. 2(a), *Expln.* I and Hindu Succession Act (30 of 1956), S. 3(1)(e)].

Uterine brother. A brother born of the same mother.

Utilitarian theory. An ethical theory that examines the consequences of a given action and defines an action as morally right and ethical if it produces greatest amount of good for the greatest number of people.

Utilitarianism. A philosophy that the goal of public action should be the greatest happiness to the greatest number of people.

Assesses the applicability of policies and legislation to promote the 'happiness' of those citizens affected by them.

Utility. "UTILITY" means any person or entity engaged in the generation, transmission, sale, distribution or supply, as the case may be, of energy. [Electricity Regulatory Commission Act (14 of 1998), S. 2(l)]

"UTILITY" means the electric lines or electrical plant, and includes all lands, buildings, works and materials attached thereto belonging to any person acting as a generating company or licensee under the provisions of this Act. [Electricity Act (36 of 2003), S. 2(75)]

Utility statement. Part of a patent specification listing out its specific uses. (*Patents*)

Utmost care. Conveys a stronger and more significant meaning than the word "extreme care". It means all the care and diligence possible in the nature of the case.

Utopian. Imaginary; visionary; one who advocates impracticable reform, or who expects an impossible state of perfection in society.

Utter. Put (notes, base coin) in circulation.

Utterer of coin. One who utters (counterfeits) coins. [IPC (45 of 1860), S. 241, ill.].

Uuencode. Many file formats are 8-bit (also called binary), which means that the basic unit of information—a byte—comprises 8 on/off signals. E-mail, however, is a 7-bit (or text) medium, preventing the transfer of 8-bit data. Uuencoding compensates for this restriction by converting 8-bit data to 7-bit data. Uuencode accomplishes this by joining all of the file's bits together into a single stream, and then dividing the stream into 7-bit chunks. The data are then e-mailed and received by someone who must UUdecode it. (*Cyber Law*)

(Unix to Unix Encoding)—A method for converting files from Binary to ASCII (text) so that they can be sent across the Internet via e-mail. (*Internet and E-commerce*)

Uxor. Wife.

Uxoricide. One who kills his wife.

Uxorious. Excessively fond of one's wife.

V

Vacancies likely to occur. The expression 'vacancies likely to occur' occurring in 8(1) of the Rules would mean the vacancies which in all probability, would occur due to superannuation but it does not include the vacancies on account of death, compulsory retirement, voluntary retirement, removal, dismissal and appointment of officers as Judge of High Court. *Srikant Tripathi* v. *State of U.P.*, (2001) 10 SCC 237, para 34. [U.P. Higher Judicial Services Rules, 1975, R. 8(1)]

Vacancy. "VACANCY" includes a newly created post which has not been filled in. [Banking Service Commission Act (44 of 1984), S. 2(n)]

'Vacancy' cannot mean or include occupation. Consequently where an impecunious tenant fails to pay the rent, the house cannot be treated as not having been let at all. Nor can unrealised or unrealisable rent be treated as rent which did not accrue.

The state or condition of being unoccupied; the fact or condition of an office being vacant. [Industrial Disputes Act (14 of 1947), S. 5(4)]; [T.P. Act (4 of 1882), S. 69A(2)].

"VACANCY", for the purposes of Chapter XIII, means an unoccupied post (including newly created post, post of trainee, post to be filled through apprentice or any unoccupied post created in an establishment by any other means) in a cadre or occupation for the purpose of employing a person and carrying remuneration. [Code on Social Security, 2020 (36 of 2020), S. 2(87)]

Vacancy year. Shall be as per the instructions issued by the Government from time to time. [Armed Forces Headquarters Civil ServiceRule, 2018, R. 2(r)].

Vacancy and abeyance. There is certainly a difference between vacancy simpliciter and the post being kept in abeyance. In the case of vacancy it is available to be filled up at any time; in the case of a post kept in abeyance the post has to be brought into life from the stage of dormancy and then a vacancy created to be filled up. Otherwise put, when the post is kept in abeyance, there is no vacancy because there is no post to be filled up. (1960) 2 MLJ 75. **Rel. on.** [R.N. MISRA and P.K. MOHANTI, JJ.]. *Ramachandra Misra* v. *Additional Director of Public Instruction (Schools),* MLJ : YD (1979) Suppl. to Feb. p. 843 : (1979) 47 CLT 306 : AIR 1979 Ori 141 (DB).

'Vacancy' and **'Post'.** In service law the words 'vacancy' and 'post' are usually used interchangeably. Every direct recruitment and promotion, appointment is made only against a vacant post. *P.G.I. of Medical Education & Research* v. *K.L. Narasimhan,* (1997) 1 SCC 283, para 18.

Vacant. Unfilled; empty; unclaimed.

Unoccupied. [CPC (5 of 1908), O. XX, R. 8 and Constitution of India, Art. 89(2)]; empty.

The word 'vacant' used in this Act means that the tenant should have ceased to occupy the accommodation with the intention of not coming back to it again. *Mahabir Prasad* v. *Kawal Krishna,* AIR 1953 All 441.

Vacant land. "VACANT LAND" means land, not being land mainly used for the purpose of agriculture, in an urban agglomeration, but does not include.—(i) land on which construction of a building is not permissible under the building regulations in force in the area in which such land is situated; (ii) in an area where there are building regulations, the land occupied by any building which has been constructed before, or is being constructed on, the appointed day with the approval of the appropriate authority and the land appurtenant to such building; and (iii) in an area where there are no building regulations, the land occupied by any building which has been constructed before, or is being constructed on, the appointed day and the land appurtenant to such building:

Provided that where any person ordinarily keeps his cattle, other than for the purpose of dairy farming or for the purpose of breeding of live-stock, on any land situated in a village within an urban agglomeration (described as a village in the revenue records) then so much extent of the land as has been ordinarily used for the keeping of such cattle immediately before the appointed day shall not be deemed to be vacant land for the purposes of this clause [Urban land (Ceiling and Regulation) Act (33 of 1976), S. 2(q) (Repealed by Act 15 of 1999, sec. 2 (w.e.f. 18-3-1999)].

The cemented platform which is used for drying pulses and which has been constructed with the approval of the authority is not a vacant land. *Nanhumal Srilal* v. *District Judge, Aligarh,* AIR 1992 All 219, 220 [Urban Land (Ceiling and Regulation) Act (33 of 1976), S. 2(q)(ii) (Repealed by Act 15 of 1999, sec. 2 (w.e.f. 18-3-1999)].

The extent of land which is grove having fruit bearing trees will be treated as agricultural land and not as a vacant land. *Chand Jain* v. *Competent Authority, Urban Ceiling,* AIR 1993 All 19, 22 [Urban Land (Ceiling and Regulation) Act (33 of 1976), S. 2(q) (Repealed by Act 15 of 1999, sec. 2 (w.e.f. 18-3-1999)].

Mere non-cultivation cannot make agricultural land a vacant one. It should be shown that the owner could cultivate the land but did not cultivate the same. *Pratima Paul* v. *Competent Authority,* AIR 1990 Cal 185, 189 [Urban Land (Ceiling and Regulation) Act (33 of 1976), S. 6, *Expln.* (ii) (Repealed by Act 15 of 1999, sec. 2 (w.e.f. 18-3-1999)].

The expression 'vacant land' will not mean land mainly used for the purpose of agriculture, which includes horticulture and the land on which no construction can be made under the Building Regulations of the Calcutta Corporation. *Gautam Roy* v. *State,* AIR

1993 Cal 266, 270. [Urban Land (Ceiling and Regulation) Act (33 of 1976), S. 2(q)(Repealed by Act 15 of 1999, sec. 2 (w.e.f. 18-3-1999)]

Vacant possession. Property which has been abandoned, vacated and forsaken by any tenant or third party.

Vacantia bona. (*Lat.*) Goods unclaimed, or without an owner; goods escheated.

Vacate. It implies a unilateral act, and for that purpose all that is necessary is that the person in possession should give up possession.

To make or leave empty [Cardamom Act (42 of 1965) (*repealed by Act 10 of 1986*), R. 10(2)(a)]; to quit; to annul; to make void; to make of no authority or validity.

Vacates his office. The words 'remove' and 'vacate his office' convey the same meaning, *viz.*, to take off or away from the place occupied. Taking away from the office of President or Vice President will happen by the act of removal by the Govt. or by the act of the President or the Vice President vacating his office on an appropriate resolution being passed by the Municipal Council. *The State of Mysore* v. *Chikkavenkatappa*, AIR 1965 Mys 253, 255. [Criminal Procedure Code (5 of 1898), S. 197]

Vacation. "VACATION" means such period or period during a year as may be fixed as vacation by or under the rules of Supreme Court made with the prior approval of the President. [Supreme Court Judges (Salaries and Conditions of Services) Act (41 of 1958), S. 2(b)(i)]

Vacation Bench. Means a Bench duly constituted in discharging the functions of the Tribunal during the vacation. [Debts Recovery Tribunal Regulations of Practice, 1997, S. 3(vii)]

Vacation of seats. [Delhi Administration Act (19 of 1966), S. 18(b)(i) and Constitution of India, Art. 101, margin]; [Representation of the People Act (43 of 1951), S. 69].

Vaccination area. "VACCINATION AREA" means man or domestic animal of microorganisms that have previously been treated to make them harmless for the purpose of inducing the development of immunity.

Vaccination-circle. "VACCINATION-CIRCLE" means one of parts into which a municipality or cantonment has been divided under the Vaccination Act for the performance of vaccination. [Vaccination Act (13 of 1880), S. 2(6)]

Vaccination season. Means the period from time to time fixed by the State Government for any local area under its administration by notification in the Official Gazette, during which alone vaccination may be performed under this Act. [Vaccination Act (13 of 1880), S. 2(8)]

Vaccinator. "VACCINATOR" means any vaccinator appointed under this Act to perform the operation of vaccination, or any private person authorised in any manner hereinafter provided to perform the same operation, and includes a "SUPERINTENDENT OF VACCINATION". [Vaccination Act (13 of 1880), S. 2(7)]

Vadose water. Water which occurs between the ground, surface and the water table that is the unsaturated zone. [Municipal Solid Wastes (Management and Handling) Rules, 2000, R. 2(xxv)]

Vagina. For the purposes of section 375 of Act 45 of 1860, 'vagina' shall also include labia majora. [*Explanation 1* to S. 375 of IPC, 1860 (45 of 1860), as substituted by the Criminal Laws (Amendment) Act, 2013 (13 of 2013)]

Vagrancy. Vagrancy at common law was defined as the wandering or going about from place to place by an idle person who has no lawful, visible means of support, and who subsists on charity and does not work for a living though able so to do.

Vagrant. "VAGRANT" means a person of European extraction found asking for alms or wandering about without any employment or visible means of subsistence. [European Vagrancy Act (9 of 1874), S. 3]

Vague. Vague is the antonym of definite. If the ground which is supplied is incapable of being understood or defined with sufficient certainty it is vague. If on reading the grounds furnished it is capable of being intelligently understood and sufficiently definite to furnish materials to enable detained person to make any representation against the order of detention it is not vague. *Haribandhu Das* v. *District Magistrate*, AIR 1968 Ori 148 at 154.

Vakalatnama. Includes memorandum of appearance or any other document by which an advocate is empowered to appear or plead before any Court, tribunal or other authority. [Advocates' Welfare Fund Act (45 of 2001), S. 2(u)]

Valid. Good or adequate in law; legally binding or efficacious. [T.P. Act (4 of 1882), S. 30]; [CPC (5 of 1908), O. XXI, R. 80(3)].

Valid certificate. For the purposes of this chapter,— "VALID CERTIFICATE" means,—

(i) in case of ships registered in India—

  (a) having a length of less than twenty-four meters, a certificate issued under the Merchant Shipping (Tonnage Measurement of Ship) Rules, 1987 made under the Merchant Shipping Act, 1958;

  (b) having a length of twenty-four meters or more, an international tonnage certificate issued under the provisions of the Convention on Tonnage Measurement of Ships, 1969 as specified in the Merchant Shipping (Tonnage Measurement of Ship) Rules, 1987 made under the Merchant Shipping Act, 1958;

(ii) in case of ships registered outside India, a licence issued by the Director General of Shipping under Section 406 or Section 407 of the Merchant Shipping Act, 1958 specifying the net tonnage on the basis of Tonnage Certificate issued by the Flag State Administration where the ship is registered or any other evidence acceptable to the Director-General of Shipping produced by the ship owner while seeking permission for chartering in the ship. [Income-tax Act (43 of 1961), Chapter XII G, S. 115VX(b), (*Inserted by Finance Act (23 of 2004), S. 30*)]

Valid cession. A surrender or assignment (of territory) which is binding in law. [Indian Evidence Act (1 of 1872), S. 113].

Valid international load line certificate. Means a certificate purporting to have been issued in accordance with the Load Line Convention in respect of a ship, other than an Indian ship, by the Government of the country in which the ship is registered. [Merchant Shipping Act (44 of 1958), S. 3(53)]

Valid marriage. When the fact of celebration of marriage is established it will be presumed in the absence of evidence to the contrary that all the rites and ceremonies to constitute a 'valid marriage' have been gone through. *Koppisetti Subbharao alias Subramaniam* v. State of A. P., AIR 2009 SC 2684.

Valid safety convention certificate. Means a certificate purporting to have been issued in accordance with the Safety Convention in respect of a ship, other than an Indian ship, by the Government of the country in which the ship is registered. [Merchant Shipping Act (44 of 1958), S. 3(54)]

Valid sanction. A valid sanction means sanction given after a consideration of all relevant facts. *Indu Bhusan Chatterjee* v. *State*, AIR 1955 Cal 430. [Prevention of Corruption Act (2 of 1947), S. 6]

Valid return. Means a return furnished under sub-section (1) of Section 39 on which self-assessed tax has been paid in full. [Central Goods and Services Tax Act (12 of 2017), S. 2(117)].

Validate. To make valid. [Specific Relief Act (47 of 1963), S. 13(1)(b)].

Validate a certificate. The process performed by a recipient or relying party to conform that an end user subscriber Digital Signature Certificate is valid and was operational at the date and time a pertinent Digital Signature was created. (*Information Technology*)

Validating act. An act or statute enacted to cure or make valid transactions of the past.

Validation Act. "Validation Act" means "a law that is amended either to remove errors or to add provisions to conform to constitutional requirements". [Black's Law Dictionary (9th Edn., p. 1545) as cited in *Amarendra Kumar Mohapatra* v. *State of Orissa*, (2014) 4 SCC 583, para 22].

"Validation Act" removes actual or possible voidness, disability or other defect by confirming the validity of anything which is or may be invalid. [ITW Signode India Limited v. CCE, (2004) 3 SCC 48, para 44 as cited in *Amarendra Kumar Mohapatra* v. *State of Orissa*, (2014) 4 SCC 583, para 22].

Validation (Of Certificate Application). The process performed by the Certifying Authority or its agent following submission of a Digital Signature Certificate application as a prerequisite to approval of the application and the issuance of a Digital Signature Certificate. (*Information Technology*)

Validity. The word "validity" in S. 28, Court Fees Act (7 of 1870) is confined to the purposes of the Act in which it is found.

The word 'validity' would also include the question of limitation because a claim barred by limitation, is no longer valid. *Mury Exportation* v. *D. Khaitain & Sons Ltd.*, AIR 1956 Cal 644, 648.

Valuable. Of worth or value. [IPC (45 of 1860), S. 30].

Valuable consideration. A consideration which the law regards as an equivalent, as money, goods, lands, services on marriage.

A 'valuable consideration' in the sense of law, may consist either in some right interest, profit or benefit accruing to the one party, or some forbearance, detriment, loss or responsibility, given. suffered or undertaken by the other. *Kanak Sunder Bibi* v. *Ram Lakhan Pandey*, AIR 1955 Pat 458, 462.

Valuable security. "The words "VALUABLE SECURITY" denote a document, which is, or purports to be, a document whereby any legal right is created, extended, transferred, restricted, extinguished or released or whereby any person acknowledges that he lies under legal liability, or has not a certain legal right". [IPC (45 of 1860), S. 30] [Now (w. e. f. 1-7-2024) repealed & replaced by Bharatiya Nyaya Sanhita, 2023 (45 of 2023)]

"Valuable security" means a document which is, or purports to be, a document whereby any legal right is created, extended, transferred, restricted, extinguished or released, or whereby any person acknowledges that he lies under legal liability, or has not a certain legal right.

Illustration

A writes his name on the back of a bill of exchange. As the effect of this endorsement is to transfer the right to the bill to any person who may become the lawful holder of it, the endorsement is a "valuable security". [(w. e. f. 1-7-2024) Bharatiya Nyaya Sanhita, 2023 (45 of 2023), S. 2(31)]

A receipt for an insured parcel dispatched by post does not come with the definition of valuable security contained in S. 30. [IPC (45 of 1860), S. 30].

A certificate forged to get admission in college is not valuable security. *Shaikh Noor Mohammad* v. *State of Maharashtra,* AIR 1981 SC 297, 298.

Valuation. The action of valuing, value or worth. [CPC (5 of 1908), S. 128(2)(c)].

Valuation date. In relation to any year for which an assessment is to be made under this Act, means the last day of the previous year as defined in Section 3 of the Income-tax Act, if an assessment were to be made under that Act for that year.

Provided that—

(ii) in the case of a person who is not an assessee within the meaning of the Income-tax Act, the valuation date for the purposes of this Act shall be the 31st day of March immediately preceding the assessment year;

(iii) where an assessment is made in pursuance of Section 19A, the valuation date shall be the same valuation date as would have been adopted in respect of the net wealth of the deceased if he were alive. [Wealth-tax Act (27 of 1957), S. 2(q)]

"VALUATION DATE" means as respects any valuation the date as at which the valuation is made. [Insurance Regulatory and Development Authority (Actuarial Report and Abstract) Regulations, 2000, Regn. 2(p)]

Valuation Officer. Means a person appointed as a valuation Officer under Section 12A, and includes a Regional Valuation Officer, a District Valuation Officer and Assistant Valuation Officer. [Wealth-tax Act (27 of 1957), S. 2(r)]

Value. The expression "VALUE" in relation to any goods shall be deemed to be the wholesale cash price for which such goods of the like kind and quality are sold or are capable of being sold for delivery at the place of manufacture and at the time of their removal therefrom, without any abatement or deduction whatever except trade discount and the amount of duty then payable. [Industries (Development and Regulation) Act (60 of 1951), S. 9(1) *Expln*]

"Value" means intrinsic worth or cost or price for sale of a thing/property. [*Union of India* v. *Bombay Tyre International Ltd.,* (1984) 1 SCC 467 : 1984 SCC (Tax) 17 and *Gurbachan Singh* v. *Shivalak Rubber Industries,* (1996) 2 SCC 626 : AIR 1996 SC 3057 as cited in *Ram Kishu* v. *State of U.P.*, (2012) 11 SCC 511, para 18].

"VALUE" means the difference between the fair market value and the cost for acquiring specified securities. [Income Tax Act (43 of 1961), S. 17. *Expln.*(d)]

"VALUE" means the fair market value of any property on the date of its acquisition by any person, or if such date cannot be determined, the date on which such property is possessed by such person. [Prevention of Money Laundering Act (15 of 2003), S. 2(1)(zb)]

"VALUE", used with reference to a suit, means the amount or value of the subject-matter of the suit. [Punj. Act (18 of 1884), (Punjab Courts), S. 3(4)]

The material or monetary worth of a thing. [Customs Act (52 of 1962), S. 2(41) and T.P. Act (4 of 1882), S. 42, ill.].

The value of a thing means the quantity of some other thing, or of things in general, which it can exchange for.

The value of the property partitioned must be computed, for the purpose of the Stamp Act, with reference to its market value, and not according to the rules laid down in the Court-Fee Act for determining the fee payable on plaints and appeals. *Board of Revenue* v. *K.R. Venkatarama Iyer*, AIR 1950 Mad 738 (FB).

The value of an annuity for determining the amount of probate-fee payable thereon under the Court-Fee Act (7 of 1870), is the market value, and not ten times the annual payment.

Value added products. "VALUE ADDED PRODUCTS" means products which may contain portions or extracts of plants and animals in unrecognizable and physically inseparable form. [Biological Diversity Act, 2002 (18 of 2003), S. 2(p)]

Value added tax (VAT). A tax which is assessed at each stage of production and distribution on the amount of value contributed at each stage to the final product.

Value addition. Means anticipated economic benefits derived by the enterprise from expert and/or professional for providing know-how or making available rights in the nature of intellectual property rights, by such person to whom sweat equity is issued for which the consideration is not paid or included in—

(a) the normal remuneration payable under the contract of employment, in the case of an employee and/or

(b) monetary consideration payable under any other contract, in the case of non-employee. [Unlisted Companies (Issue of Sweat Equity Shares) Rules, 2003, R. 2(v)]

Value additions. For the purposes of rule 8 of the Companies (Share Capital & Debentures) Rules, 2014, the expression 'value additions' means actual or anticipated economic benefits derived or to be derived by the company from an expert or a professional for providing know-how or making available rights in the nature of intellectual property rights, by such person to whom sweat equity is being issued for which the consideration is not paid or included in the normal remuneration payable under the contract of employment, in the case of an employee. [*Explanation* (*ii*) to rule 8(1) of the Companies (Share Capital & Debentures) Rules, 2014]

Value additions. The expression 'VALUE ADDITIONS' means actual and anticipated economic benefits derived or to be derived by the company from an expert or a professional for providing know-how or making available rights in the nature of intellectual property rights, by such person to whom sweat equity is being issued for which the consideration is not paid or included in the normal remuneration payable under the contract of employment, in the case of an employee. [Companies (Share Capital and Debentures) Rules, 2014, R. 8(1), Explanation (ii)].

Value of exempt supply. For the purposes of this sub-section, the expression "VALUE OF EXEMPT SUPPLY" shall not include the value of activities or transactions specified in Schedule III, except those specified in

Paragraph 5 of the said Schedule. [Central Goods and Services Tax Act (12 of 2017), S. 17(3), *Explanation*].

"Value of goods". Means the fair market value of the goods at the time including insurance charges, excise duties, countervailing duties, tax paid or payable under the Central Sales Tax Act, 1956 (74 of 1956) in respect of the sale, transport charges, freight charges and all other charges incidental to the transaction of the goods. [Andaman and Nicobar Islands Value Added Tax Regulation (6 of 2017), S. 2(1)(zm)].

"Value of the goods" shall mean the purchase value of such goods that is to say, the purchase price at which a dealer has purchased the goods inclusive of charges bone by him as cost of transportation, packing, forwarding and handling charges, commission, insurance, taxes, duties and the like, or if such goods have not be purchased by him, the prevailing market price of such goods in the local area. [Karnataka Tax on Entry o Goods At (27 of 1979), S. 2(A)(8-a) **as cited in** *Hindustan Lever Limited* v. *State of Karnataka,* (2016) 16 SCC 177, para 2].

Value of stock of luxuries. "VALUE OF STOCK OF LUXURIES" means—

(i) in respect of any stockist, being a manufacturer of any of the luxuries, the value of such luxuries calculated at the ex-factory price at the time of receipt or entry thereof in his stock, and:

(ii) in respect of any stockist, being an importer of any of the luxuries, the value of such luxuries, calculated at the price thereof as per consignor's bill, invoice or consignment note or other document of like nature.

And shall include—

(A) excise duty and central sales tax, if any, paid or payable on such luxuries by the manufacturer or importer thereof, as the case may be, and

(B) transport charges and insurance charges, if any, for carrying such luxuries to any premises, godown, warehouse or any other place for delivery to a wholesaler, dealer, retailer, distributor or any other person. [W.B. Luxury Tax Act, 1994, S. 2(m)]

Value of the subject-matter of the suit. For the purpose of valuation the value of the subject matter in a suit for partition, is the value of the whole of the estate which it is sought to partition, and not merely of the particular share which one of the parties may claim.

Value received. A phrase used in bills or notes to show that there is valuable consideration and that the paper is not mere accommodation paper.

Valuer. A person whose business is to appraise or set a value upon property.

One that values. [Employees' State Insurance Act (34 of 1948), S. 37].

Vanaspathi. *Vanaspati* is essentially an oil although it is a different kind of oil than rapeseed oil, cotton seed oil, ground-nut oil, soybean oil or any other oil which forms its basic ingredient. *Champaklal* v. *State of Gujarat*, AIR 1980 SC 1889, 1891. [Minimum Wages Act (11 of 1948), Sch. II, Item 5]

Vandalism. Defacing or damaging property.

Vani timoris justa excusatio non est. A frivolous fear is not a legal excuse.

Vanishing company. For the purposes of clause (iii), the expression "VANISHING COMPANY" means a company, registered under the At or previous company law or any other law for the time being in force and listed with Stock Exchange which has failed to file its returns with the Registrar of Companies and Stock Exchange for a consecutive period of two years, and is not maintaining its registered office at the address notified with the Registrar of Companies or Stock Exchange and none of its directors are traceable. [Companies (Removal of Names of Companies from the Register of Companies) Rules, 2016, R. 3(iii), *Explanation*].

Variable annuity. An annuity which makes payments in varying amounts depending on the success of investment strategy.

Variable cost. The cost which varies in the short run in close relationship with changes in output.

Variable rate. An interest rate which fluctuates according to the correct market rate.

Variance. Variation; difference; divergence. [Indian Contract Act (9 of 1872), S. 133].

Variation. "VARIATION" shall include abrogation. [Companies Act (1 of 1956), S. 2(50)] The act of varying. [T.P. Act (4 of 1882), S. 65A(3)]; change in the form. [General Clauses Act (10 of 1897), S. 3(1)].

Variety. Means a sub-division of a kind identifiable by growth, yield, plant, fruit, seed or other characteristic. [Seeds Act (54 of 1966), S. 2(16)]

Various. Of different kinds; diverse; several.

Varishta Panchayat. Means the Varishta Panchayat as in existence immediately before the appointed day, and as reconstituted from time to time in accordance with law. [Dadra & Nagar Haveli Act (35 of 1961), S. 2(d)]

Varnish. Varnish is a generic name given to a homogeneous solution of gums or resins in alcohol, linseed oil or the like which is coated on various articles for protective or decorative purposes. *Akhtar Abbas* v. *Asst. Collector*, *Central Excise*, AIR 1961 MP 353, 356. [Central Excises and Salt Act (1 of 1944), Sch. I, item 22]

Vary. "VARY" shall include abrogate. [Companies Act (1 of 1956), S. 2(50)]

To change, alter or modify. [State Financial Corporation Act (63 of 1951), S. 37(7)(b)]; [Indian Trusts Act (2 of 1882), S. 40]; [Constitution of India, Art. 114(2)].

Vegetable. Sugar-cane is not a vegetable though it may be an agricultural product. *Saraswati Sugar Mills* v. *Haryana State Board*, AIR 1992 SC 224, 230.

Green ginger is a vegetable which is grown in the kitchen garden or in a farm or is used for the table, even though not as a principal item but as part of the meal as a subsidiary item. *State of West Bengal and others* v. *Washi Ahmed Etc.*, AIR 1977 SC 1638, 1639.

The word 'vegetables' in taxing statutes is to be understood as in common parlance i.e. denoting class of vegetables which are grown in a kitchen garden or in a farm and are used for the table. *Ramavatar* v. *Asst. Sales Tax Officer*, AIR 1961 SC 1325, 1327.

Chillies and lemons are vegetables. *Mangulu Sathu Ramachari Sahu* v. *Sales Tax Officer Ganjam*, AIR 1974, SC 390, 391.

The word 'vegetable' does not include *Pan* (betel leaves). *Ram Bux Chaturbhuj* v. *State of Rajasthan*, AIR 1963 SC 351, 352.

Vegetable oil. Means any oil produced from oilseeds, or any other oil bearing material of plant origin, and containing glycerides but does not include any such vegetable oil which has been subjected to any processing subsequent to the recovery of oil. [National Oilseeds and Vegetable Oils Development Board Act (29 of 1983), S. 3(h)]

Vegetable products. Latex is not a vegetable product. *Harisons Malayalam Ltd.* v. *Kerala State, Pollution Control Board*, AIR 1992 Ker. 168, 174. Water (Prevention and Control of Pollution) Cess Act (36 of 1977), Sch. I, Item 15]

Vegetarian food. 'VEGETARIAN FOOD' means any article of food other than Non-Vegetarian Food as defined in Explanation IX of this Rule. [Prevention of Food Adulteration Rules, 1955, R. 32, *Expln.* X]

Vehicle. A carriage; conveyance. [Road Transport Corporations Act (64 of 1950), S. 2(f)].

"VEHICLE" shall include bi-cycles, tri-cycles, and auto-motor cars, and every wheeled conveyance which is used or is capable of being used on a public street. [Bom. Act III of 1901 (Dist. Mun.), S. 3, cl. 17.]

"VEHICLE" includes every description of wheeled conveyance except perambulators and other conveyances designed for the carriage of children. [Bur. Act IV of 1899 (Rangoon Police), S. 5, cl. 4.]

"VEHICLE" means motor vehicle, for the carriage of Liquefied Petroleum Gas (LPG) between Bangladesh and India. [Central Motor Vehicles (Regulation of Petroleum Products Supply to Bottling Plant in Tripura from Bangladesh) Rules, 2018, R. 2(f)].

"VEHICLE" means a wheeled conveyance of any description which is capable of being used on a street, and includes a motor car, motor lorry, motor omnibus, cart, locomotive, tram car, hand cart, truck, motorcycle, bicycle, tricycle and rickshaw. [Cantonments Act (2 of 1924), S. 2(xxxviii)]

"VEHICLE" means any mechanically propelled vehicle, used or capable of being used for the purpose of road transport, and includes a tram-car, a trolley vehicle and a trailer. [Road Transport Corporations Act (64 of 1950), S. 2(f)]

"VEHICLE" means conveyance of any kind used on land and includes a vehicle. [Customs Act (52 of 1962), S. 2(42)]

"VEHICLE" means any conveyance used for movement on land, water or air and includes buffalo, bull, bullock, camel, donkey, elephant, horse and mule. [Wild Life (Protection) Act (53 of 1972), S. 2(33)]

"VEHICLE" means any mode of surface transport other than railways. [Public Liability Insurance Act (6 of 1991), S. 2(j)]

Hand-trollies running on rails laid on a public street and used by contractors for the purpose of carrying materials to fill up a tank, are vehicles.

An agricultural tractor is not used to convey anything and it is employed for agricultural operations. So it is not a vehicle. *State of Madras* v. *Messon Marshall Sons & Co.*, AIR 1954 Mad 884.

Vehicle could be read to include boat. *Mohan Lal Ganguly* v. *State of Bengal*, AIR 1978 Cal 12, 15.

Vehicular homicide. The act of killing another person by one's unlawful or negligent operation of a motor vehicle.

Vein. A zone or belt of mineral or mineral bearing rock with defined boundaries.

Vend. To sell.

Vendee. One to whom anything is sold.

One who purchases anything. [Cattle-trespass Act (1 of 1871), S. 10].

Vendens eandem rem duobus falsarius est. He is fraudulent who sells the same thing to two separate buyers.

"Vending zone" means an area or place or a location designated as such by the local authority, on the recommendation of the Town Vending Committee, for the specific use by street vendors for street vending and includes footpath, side walk, pavement, embankment, portions of a street, waiting are for public or any such place considered suitable for vending activities and providing services to the general public. [Street Vendors (Protection of Livelihood and Regulations of Street Vending) Act (7 of 2014), S. 2(1)(n)].

Vendor. "VENDOR" means person who sells foodstuffs as defined above packaged and stored in plastic carry bags and containers. [Recycled Plastic Manufacture and Usage Rules, 1999, R. 2(c)]

A settler; one who sells.

One who sells anything. [Specific Relief Act (47 of 1963), S. 28(2)(a)].

Vendor and **Vendee.** Vendor is the person who sells anything and vendee the person to whom it is sold. (*Tomlin*)

Vendor's lien. The lien of an unpaid vendor of personal property, unless it has been surrendered or passed into the hands of the *bona fide* purchaser. In application of this lien the vendor can stop the property in transit.

Venereal disease. A contagious disease that is typically acquired in sexual intercourse. [Hindu Marriage Act (25 of 1955), S. 13(1)(v)].

Veniae facilitas incentivum est delinquendi. Facility of pardon is an incentive to crime.

Vent. Outlet. [Factories Act (63 of 1948), S. 37(2)].

Ventilated. Exposed to air and especially to a current of fresh air. [Mines Act (35 of 1952), S. 20(2)].

Ventilation. [Beedi and Cigar Workers (Conditions of Employment) Act (32 of 1966), S. 9].

Venture capital company. Means such company as has made investments by way of acquiring equity shares of venture capital undertakings in accordance with the prescribed guidelines. [Income Tax Act (43 of 1961), S. 10 (23F) *Expln.*(b)]

"VENTURE CAPITAL COMPANY" means such company—

(i) which has been granted a certificate of registration under the Securities and Exchange Board of India Act, 1992, and regulations made thereunder;

(ii) which fulfils the conditions as may be specified, with the approval of the Central Government, by the Securities and Exchange Board of India, by notification in the Official Gazette, in this behalf. [Income Tax Act (43 of 1961), S. 10(23 FB) *Expln.*(a)]

"VENTURE CAPITAL COMPANY". For the purposes of section 10(23FB) of Act 43 of 1961, 'venture capital company' means a company which—

(A) has been granted a certificate of registration, before the 21st day of May, 2012, as a Venture Capital Fund and is regulated under the Securities and Exchange Board of India (Venture Capital Funds) Regulations, 1996 (hereinafter referred to as the Venture Capital Funds Regulations) made under the Securities and Exchange Board of India Act, 1992 (15 of 1992) ; or

(B) has been granted a certificate of registration as Venture Capital Fund as a sub-category of Category I Alternative Investment Fund and is regulated under the Securities and Exchange Board of India (Alternative Investment Funds) Regulations, 2012 (hereinafter referred to as the Alternative Investment Funds Regulations) made under the Securities and Exchange Board of India Act, 1992 (15 of 1992), and which fulfils the following conditions, namely:—

(i) it is not listed on a recognised stock exchange ;

(ii) it has invested not less than two-thirds of its investible funds in unlisted equity shares or equity linked instruments of venture capital undertaking ; and

(iii) it has not invested in any venture capital undertaking in which its director or a substantial shareholder (being a beneficial owner of equity shares exceeding ten per cent of its equity share capital) holds, either individually or collectively, equity shares in excess of fifteen per cent of the paid-up equity share capital of such venture capital undertaking. [(w.e.f. 1-4-2013) *Explanation* (*a*) to section 10(23FB) of the Income-tax Act, 1961 (43 of 1961). Also see *Explanation* (*b*) to section 56(2)(viib) of the Income-tax Act, 1961 (43 of 1961) as inserted (w.e.f. 1-4-2013) by the Finance Act, 2012 (23 of 2012)]

Venture capital fund. Means such fund, operating under a trust deed registered under the provisions of the Registration Act, 1908, established to raise monies by the trustees for investments mainly by way of acquiring equity shares of a venture capital undertaking in accordance with the prescribed guidelines. [Income Tax Act (43 of 1961) S. 10(23F) *Expln.* (a)]

"VENTURE CAPITAL FUND" means such fund—

(i) operating under a trust deed registered under the provisions of the Registration Act, 1908;

(ii) which has been granted a certificate of registration under the Securities and Exchange Board of India Act, 1992, and regulations made thereunder;

(iii) which fulfils the conditions as may be specified, with the approval of the Central Government, by the Securities and Exchange Board of India, by notification in the Official Gazette, in this behalf. [Income Tax Act (43 of 1961), S. 10(23 FB) *Expln.*(b)]

VENTURE CAPITAL FUND means a fund established in the form of a trust, a company including a body corporate and registered under the Securities and Exchange Board of India (Venture Capital Fund) Regulations, 1996, which has a dedicated pool of capital raised in a manner specified under the said Regulations and which invests in Venture Capital Undertakings in accordance with the said Regulations. [Foreign Exchange Management (Transfer or Issue of Security by a Person Resident Outside India) Regulations, 2000, Reg. 2(xia)]

"VENTURE CAPITAL FUND" for the purposes of section 10(23FB) of Act 43 of 1961, 'venture capital fund' means a fund—

(A) operating under a trust deed registered under the provisions of the Registration Act, 1908 (16 of 1908), which—

(I) has been granted a certificate of registration, before the 21st day of May, 2012, as a Venture Capital Fund and is regulated under the Venture Capital Funds Regulations ; or

(II) has been granted a certificate of registration as Venture Capital Fund as a sub-category of Category I Alternative

Investment Fund under the Alternative Investment Funds Regulations and which fulfils the following conditions, namely:—

(i) it has invested not less than two-thirds of its investible funds in unlisted equity shares or equity linked instruments of venture capital undertaking;

(ii) it has not invested in any venture capital undertaking in which its trustee or the settler holds, either individually or collectively, equity shares in excess of fifteen per cent of the paid-up equity share capital of such venture capital undertaking; and

(iii) the units, if any, issued by it are not listed in any recognised stock exchange; or

(B) operating as a venture capital scheme made by the Unit Trust of India established under the Unit Trust of India Act, 1963 (52 of 1963). [(w.e.f. 1-4-2013) *Explanation* (*b*) to section 10(23FB) of the Income-tax Act, 1961 (43 of 1961). Also see *Explanation* (*b*) to section 56(2)(viib) of the Income-tax Act, 1961 (43 of 1961) as inserted (w.e.f. 1-4-2013) by the Finance Act, 2012 (23 of 2012)]

Venture capital undertaking. "VENTURE CAPITAL UNDERTAKING" means such domestic company whose shares are not listed in a recognised stock exchange in India and which is engaged in the manufacture or production of such articles or things (including computer software) as may be notified by the Central Government in this behalf. [Income-tax Act (43 of 1961), S. 10(23F), *Expln.*(c)]

"VENTURE CAPITAL UNDERTAKING" means a domestic company—

(i) whose shares are not listed in a recognised stock exchange in India;

(ii) which is engaged in the business for providing services, production or manufacture of an article or thing but does not include such activities or sectors which are specified, with the approval of the Central Government, by the Securities and Exchange Board of India, by notification in the Official Gazette, in this behalf. [Income Tax Act (43 of 1961), S. 10(23 FB) *Expln.*(c)] [Also see *Explanation* (*b*) to section 56(2)(viib) of the Income-tax Act, 1961 (43 of 1961) as inserted (w.e.f. 1-4-2013) by the Finance Act, 2012]

VENTURE CAPITAL UNDERTAKING". For the purposes of section 10(23FB) of Act 43 of 1961, 'venture capital undertaking' means—

(i) a venture capital undertaking as defined in regulation 2(n) of the Venture Capital Funds Regulations; or

(ii) a venture capital undertaking as defined in regulation 2(1)(aa) of the Alternative Investment Funds Regulations. [(w.e.f. 1-4-2013) *Explanation* (*c*) to section 10(23FB) of the Income-tax Act, 1961 (43 of 1961)]

Venue. Place of trial of a law-suit.

Veracity. The quality or character in persons of speaking or stating the truth; habitual observance of the truth. [IPC (45 of 1860), S. 499, *Fifth* excep., ill. (b)].

Verba accipienda sunt secundum subjectam materiam. (*Lat.*) (6 Rep. 62) Words are to be interpreted according to the subject-matter.

Verba ambigua fortius accipiuntur contra profer entem. Ambiguous words are to be taken most strongly against the person making use of them.

Verba attendenda, non os loquitur. (TAYLER, 566)–Words should be regarded, not the speaker.

Verba chartarum fortius accipiuntur contra proferentem. (*Lat.*) (Co. Litt. 36b) The words of deeds are to be taken most strongly against the person offering it.

If the term applied by one party are an under, an interpretation against the party is preferred. [*RashtriyaIspat Nigam Limited* v. *Dewan Chand Ram Saran*, (2012) 5 SCC 306, para 28].

Verba cum effectu accipienda sunt. Words are to be interpreted so as to give them effect.

Verba generalia generaliter sunt intelligenda. General Words are to be generally understood. (*Latin for Lawyers*)

Verba in differenti materia per prius, non per posterius, intelligenda sunt. Words referring to different subjects are to be interpreted by what goes before, not by what follows.

Verba intentioni non e contra. (*Maxim*) The words should be made subservient and not contrary, to the intention of the Legislature. *CIT* v. *Jagannath Maheshwary*, AIR 1957 Punj 226, 233.

Verba ita sunt intelligenda ut res magis valeat quam pereat. (*Lat.*) Words are to be so understood that the subject-matter may have effect rather than fail.

Verba posteriora propter certitudinem addita ad priora quae certitudine indigent sunt referenda. (*Lat.*) (Wing) Subsequent words added for the purpose of certainty are to be referred to preceding words in which certainty is wanting. (*Latin for Lawyers*)

Verba relata hoc maxime operantur per referentiam ut in eis inesse videntur. (*Lat.*) (Co. Litt. 359a) Words to which reference is made in an instrument have the same effect and operation as if they were inserted in the clause referring to them.

Verba sunt indices animi. Words are indications of the intention.

Verbal. Oral. [Indian Evidence Act (1 of 1872), S. 92, ill. (g)].

Verbal and emotional abuse. For the purposes of section 3 of Act 43 of 2005, 'verbal and emotional abuse' includes—

(a) insults, ridicule, humiliation, name calling and insults or ridicule specially with regard to not having a child or a male child; and

(b) repeated threats to cause physical pain to any person in whom the aggrieved person is interested. [*Explanation 1* (iii) to S. 3 of the Protection of Women from Domestic Violence Act, 2005 (43 of 2005)]

Verbal statements. A person was convicted of murder. The victim whose throat was cut by the accused was alive for some time and being questioned regarding the offence and the person who committed it, she answered the questions by signs, being unable to speak. She described the accused by signs and when she was asked whether that person was the accused she showed assent by a nod. The question arose whether her statement was relevant and admissible against the accused. *Held,* that the statement made by the deceased constituted a verbal statement resembling the case of a dumb person and was relevant and admissible in evidence. *Sudhama* v. *King Emperor*, AIR 1949 Nag 405, 406.

Verbals. Any remarks that an accused person has made in the presence of the police.

Verbatim. Word for word.

Verbatim et literatim. Word for word, and letter for letter.

Verbia legis non recedendum est. From the words of law there should be no departure.

'Verbis Legis non est Recedendum' means, "from the words of law, there must be no departure" [*Hardeep Singh* v. *State of Punjab*, (2014) 1 SCC 92, para 42].

Verbis standum ubi nulla ambiguitas. (*Lat.*) One must abide by the words where there is no ambiguity.

Verdict. A decision of a jury in a civil or criminal cause upon an issue which has been submitted to their judgment; a finding, conclusion or judgment upon some matter or subject. [IPC (45 of 1860), S. 219].

Verification. "VERIFICATION", with its grammatical variations and cognate expressions includes, in relation to any weight or measure, the process of comparing, checking, testing or adjusting such weight or measure with a view to ensuring that such weight or measure conforms to the standards established by or under this Act, and also includes re-verification and calibration. [Standards of Weights and Measures Act (60 of 1976), S. 2(zb) repealed by the Legal Metrology Act, 2009 (1 of 2010), sec. 57 (w.e.f. 1-4-2011)]

Making out to be true; a formula with which all affirmative pleadings are required to conclude.

Formal assertion of truth; the action of establishing or testing the truth. [T.P. Act (4 of 1882), S. 83].

Verified. Proved by good evidence or valid testimony; testified or affirmed formally or upon oath. [T.P. Act (4 of 1882), S. 83].

Verified claim. "VERIFIED CLAIM" means any claim registered under the Displaced Persons (Claims) Act, 1950 in respect of which a final order has been passed under that Act or under the Displaced Persons (Claims) Supplementary Act, 1954 and includes any claim registered on or before the 31st day of May, 1953 under the East Punjab Refugees (Registration of Land Claims) Act, 1948 or under the Patiala Refugees (Registration of Land Claims) Ordinance, 2004 and verified by any authority appointed for the purpose by the Government of Punjab, the Government of Patiala or the Government of Patiala and East Punjab State Union, as the case may be, which has not been satisfied wholly or partially by the allotment of any evacuee land under the relevant notification specified in S. 10 of this Act, but does not include—

(i) any such claim registered in respect of property held in trust for a public purpose of a religious or charitable nature;

(ii) Except in the case of Banking company for the purpose of sub-clause (b) of sub-sec. (3) of S. 6 only—

(a) any such claim made by or on behalf of any company or association, whether incorporated or not;

(b) any such claim made by a mortgagee or other person holding a charge or lien on immovable property belonging to a displaced person in West Pakistan. [Displaced Persons (Compensation and Rehabilitation) Act (44 of 1954), S. 2(e)]

A person would be holding a verified claim or would hold such a claim when he has a title to that claim and as entitled to the rights and benefits which may accrue under it. *Gurbachan Singh* v. *UOI*, AIR 1968 Punj 242 at 249. [Compensation and Rehabilitation Act (44 of 1954), S. 2(e)]

Verified copy. A duplicate of an original, usually official, document, certified as an exact reproduction by the officer responsible for issuing or keeping the original.

Verify. "VERIFY" in relation to a digital signature, electronic record or public key, with its grammatical variations and cognate expressions means to determine whether—

(a) the initial electronic record was affixed with the digital signature by the use of private key corresponding to the public key of the subscriber;

(b) the initial electronic record is retained intact or has been altered since such electronic record was so affixed with the digital signature. [Information Technology Act (21 of 2000), S. 2(1)(zh(b))]

To assent or approve to be true; to ascertain, confirm or test the truth or accuracy of.

Veritas est justitiae mater. Trust is the mother of justice.

Veritas habenda est in juratore; justitia et judicium in judice. Truth is the desideratum in a juror; justice and judgment in a judge.

Veritas nihil veretur nisi abscondi. (*Lat.*) (9 Rep. 20) Truth fears nothing but concealment.

Veritas nimium altercando amittitur. (*Lat.*) (Hob. 334) By too much altercation truth is lost.

Veritas nominis tollit errorem demonstrationis. (*Lat.*) (Bac. Max. Reg. 24) The truth of the name takes away the error of description.

Veritas, quae minime defensatur opprimitur; et qui non improbat, approbat. Truth which is not sufficiently defended is overpowered; and he who does not disapprove, approves.

Vermi composting. Is a process of using earthworms for conversion of bio-degradable water into compost. [Municipal Solid Wastes (Management and Handling) Rules, 2000, R. 2(xxvi)]

Vermin. Noxious, mischievous or disgusting animals of small size, of common occurrence and difficult to control. [Drugs and Cosmetics Act (23 of 1940), S. 3(b)(ii)].

"VERMIN" means any wild animal notified under section 62. [Wild Life (Protection) Act (53 of 1972), S. 2(34)]

Vernacular. The language spoken by the people of a country or any part thereof. [Indian Partnership Act (9 of 1932), S. 72(a)]; [Registration Act (16 of 1908), S. 79].

Versus. Against.

Vertical agreements. Agreements between businesses at different levels of trade; for example, agreements between suppliers and distributors or between wholesalers and retailers.

Vertical integration. Amalgamation of companies involved in different stages of production in the same industry, *e.g.*, to produce one company capable of extracting raw materials, using them to produce goods and then distributing and selling the manufactured product.

Very senior citizen. For the purposes of this section, "VERY SENIOR CITIZEN" means an individual resident in India who is of the age of eighty years or more at any time during the relevant previous year. [Income-tax Act (43 of 1961), S. 80D(5), Explanation (ii) as inserted by Finance Act (20 of 2015), S. 19].

Very small establishment. Means establishment in which not more than nine persons are employed or were employed on any day of the preceding twelve months. [Labour Laws (Exemption from Furnishing Returns and Maintaining Registers by Certain Establishments) Act (51 of 1988), S. 2(f)]

Vessel. "The word "VESSEL" denotes anything made for the conveyance by water of human being or of property. [IPC (45 of 1860), S. 48] [Now (w. e. f. 1-7-2024) repealed & replaced by Bharatiya Nayaya Sanhita, 2023 (45 of 2023), S. 2(32), same definition in new Sanhita]

For the purpose of this Act, the term "VESSEL" shall be deemed to include also every article or thing or collection of things being or forming part of the tackle, equipment, cargo, stores or ballast of a vessel; and any proceeds arising from the sale of a vessel, and of the cargo thereof, or of any other property recovered therefrom, shall be regarded as common fund. [Obstructions in Fairways Act (16 of 1881), S. 7]

"Vessel" includes any ship, boat, sailing vessel or other description of vessel used or constructed for use in navigation by water, whether it is propelled or not, and includes a barge, lighter or other floating vessel, a hovercraft, an off-shore industry mobile unit, a vessel that has sunk or is stranded or abandoned and the remains of such a vessel. Explanation.—A vessel shall not be deemed to be a vessel for the purposes of this clause, when it is broken up to such an extent that it cannot be put into use for navigation, as certified by a surveyor. [The Admiralty (Jurisdiction and Settlement of Maritime Claims) Act, 2017 (22 of 2017), S. 2(1)(l)]

"VESSEL" includes any ship, boat, sailing vessel, or other description of vessel used in navigation, whether propelled by oars or otherwise and anything made for the conveyance, mainly by water, of human beings or of goods and a caisson. [Explosives Act (4 of 1884), S. 4(j)]

"VESSEL" shall include any ship or boat or any other description of vessel used in navigation. [General Clauses Act (10 of 1897), S. 3(63)]

"Vessel" includes every description of water craft used or capable of being used in inland waters or in coastal waters, including any ship, boat, sailing vessel, tug, barge or other description of vessel including non-displacement craft, amphibious craft, wing-in-ground craft, ferry, roll-on-roll-off vessel, container vessel, tanker vessel, gas carrier or floating unit or dumb vessel used for transportation, storage or accommodation within or through inland waters and coastal waters. [Energy Conservation Act (52 of 2001), S. 2(tb)]

"Vessel" includes every description of water craft used or capable of being used in inland waters, including any ship, boat, sailing vessel, tug, barge or other description of vessel including non-displacement craft, amphibious craft, wing-in-ground craft, ferry, roll on-roll-off vessel, container vessel, tanker vessel, gas carrier or floating unit or dumb vessel used for transportation, storage or accommodation within or through inland waters. [Inland Vessels Act, 2021 (24 of 2021), S. 3(zu)]

"VESSELS" shall refer to the fishing vessels engaged in commercial fishing, registered in the country of the Contracting Party and operated by a citizen or citizens of the Contracting Party or partnership, corporation or association, duly registered in such country, at least sixty per cent of equity of which is owned by a citizen or citizens and/or Government of such Contracting Party or seventy-five per cent by citizens and/or Government of the Contracting Parties. However, the goods taken from vessels engaged in commercial fishing under Bilateral

Agreements which provide for chartering/leasing of such vessels and/or sharing of catch between Contracting Party will also be eligible for Preferential treatment. In respect of vessels or factory ships operated by Government agencies, the requirements of flying the flag of the Contracting Party does not apply. [Customs Tariff (Determination of Origin of Goods under the free trade agreement between the Democratic Socialistic

Republic of Sri Lanka and the Republic of India) Rules, 2000, R. 4 *Expln.*]

A usually hollow structure used on or in water for the purpose of navigation [IPC (45 of 1860), S. 48 and General Clauses Act (10 of 1897)], S. 3(63); utensil [Trade and Merchandise Marks Act (43 of 1958), Ss. 2(1)(1) and 11 Repealed by the Trade Marks Act, 1999 (47 of 1999)]; receptacle; container.

Vest. To place in possession; to take possession of; to take an interest in property when a named period or event occurs.

(1) To give a person a legally fixed, immediate right or personal or future enjoyment of (an estate), to grant, endow, clothe with a particular authority, right of property, (2) To become legally vested; (TP Act) [Legal Glossary, published by the Official Language (Legislative) Commission, 1970 Edn., p. 302 as cited in *State of U.P.* v. *Hari Ram*, (2013) 4 SCC 280, para 25].

To place or give into the possession or discretion of some person or authority [the regulation of the waterways… to give to a person a legally fixed immediate right of present or future enjoyment of (as an estate) (a deed that vests a title estate in the grantee and a remainder in his children)

The word "vest has two connotations-the first and primary one relates to possession of land; and the second, an adjunctory one, pertains additionally to the title of that land. [*Laxmi Devi* v. *State of Bihar*, (2015) 10 SCC 241, para 12].

The word 'vest' is a word of variable import. The word 'vest' has not got a fixed connotation, meaning in all cases that the property is owned by the person or the authority in whom it vests. It may vest in title, or it may vest in possession, or it may vest in a limited sense, as indicated in the context in which it may have been used in a particular piece of legislation. *Fruit & Vegetable Merchants Union* v. *Delhi Improvement Trust*, AIR 1957 SC 344, 353.

The word 'vest' has to be understood in the different contexts. The vesting of the disputed area in the Central Government is limited, as a statutory receiver, with the duty of its management and administration according to Section 7 till it is handed over in terms of the adjudication made in the suits. *M. Ismail Faruqui* v. *Union of India*, AIR 1995 SC 605, 645. [Acquisition of Certain Area at Ayodhya Act (33 of 1993), Ss. 3 & 6]

Fixed; accrued; settled; absolute; complete. Having the character or given the rights of absolute ownership; not contingent; not subject to be defeated by a condition precedent. Rights are 'vested' when rights to enjoyment present or prospective, has become property of some particular person or persons as present interest; mere expectancy of future benefits, or contingent interest in property founded on anticipated continuance of existing laws, does not continue 'vested right'. *Vaughn* v. *Nade,* 228 Kan469 : 618 P 2d 778 (1980).

See also accrue; Vest, and specific types of vested interests, infra." [Black's Law Dictionary (6th Edn.), 1990, p. 1563 as cited in *State of U.P.* v. *Hari Ram*, (2013) 4 SCC 280, para 26].

Vested estate. An estate with a present right of enjoyment or a present fixed right of future enjoyment.

Vested interest. An interest is said to be a 'vested interest' when there is immediate right of present enjoyment or a present right for future enjoyment. [*Usha Subbarao* v. *B.E. Vishveswaraiah*, (1996) 5 SCC 201, 208, para 8]

[Where, on a transfer of property, an interest therein created in favour of a person without specifying the time when it is to take effect, or in terms specifying that it is to take effect, forthwith or on the happening of an event which must happen, such INTEREST IS VESTED, unless a contrary intention appears from the terms of transfer.

[A vested interest is not defeated by the death of the death of the transferee before he obtains possession.

Explanation—An intention that an interest shall not be vested is not to be inferred merely from a provision whereby the enjoyment thereof is postponed, or whereby a prior interest in the same property is given or reserved to some other person, or whereby income arising from the property is directed to be accumulated until the time of enjoyment arrives, or from a provision that if a particular event shall happen the interest shall pass to another person.] [T.P. Act (4 of 1882), S. 19]

[Where, on a transfer of property, an interest therein is created in favour of a person to take effect only on the happening of a specified uncertain event, or if a specified uncertain event shall not happen, such person thereby acquires a contingent interest in the property. Such interest becomes a vested interest in the former case, on the happening of the event, in the latter, when the happening of the event becomes impossible.

[*Exception*—Where, under a transfer of property, a person becomes entitled to an interest therein upon attaining a particular age, and the transferor also gives to him absolutely the income to arise from such interest before he reaches that age, or directs the income or so much thereof as may be necessary to be applied for his benefit, such interest is not contingent.] [T.P. Act (4 of 1882), S. 21]

Vested interest and contingent interest. Interest is vested when it is to take effect on the happening of an event which is certain. Interest is contingent when the right depends on the happening of an uncertain event which may or may not happen. Kapuri Kuer v. Sham Narain Prasad, MLJ : QD (1961-1965) Vol V C619 : AIR 1962 Pat 149 [Succession Act (39 of 1925), Ss. 119, 120]

Vested rights. The expression 'vested right' means an absolute or indefeasible right. It is an immediate fixed right in present or future enjoyment in respect of property. The claim based on the vested right or settled expectation to obtain sanction cannot be set up against statutory provisions. It cannot be countenanced against public interest and conveniences which are sought to be served. *Howrah Municipal Corpn.* v. *Ganges Rope Co. Ltd.*, (2004) 1 SCC 663, 680, para 37. [Howrah Municipal Corporation Act (58 of 1980), S. 175]

Rights are 'vested' when right to enjoyment, present or prospective, has become property of some particular person or persons as present interest; mere expectancy of future benefits, or contingent interest in property founded on anticipated continuance of existing laws, does not constitute vested rights. [Bibi Sayeeda v. State of Bihar, (1996) 9 SCC 516, para 17 as cited in *Purbanchal Cables and Conductors Private Limited* v. *Assam State Electricity Board*, (2012) 7 SCC 462, para 40].

Vested right is a right independent of any contingency. Such a right can arise from a contract, statute or by operation of law. A vested right can be taken away only if the law specifically or by necessary implication provide for such a course. *[J.S. Yadav v. State of U.P.*, (2011) 6 SCC 570, para 22 : AIR 2011 SC (Supp) 659 as cited in *Anand Kumar Sharma* v. *State of U.P.*, AIR 2014 All 106, para 26 (FB)].

"Vested rights", or "Accrued rights". The expressions "vested rights" or "accrued rights" have been used in the context of a right flowing under the relevant rule which was sought to be altered with effect from an anterior date and thereby taking away the benefits available under the rule in force at that time. Such an amendment having retrospective operation which has the effect of taking away a benefit already available to the employee under the existing rule is arbitrary, discriminatory and violative of the rights guaranteed under Articles 14 and 16 of the Constitution. *Chairman, Railway Board* v. *C.R. Rangadhamaiah,* AIR 1997 SC 3828, 3837.

Vesting. Mere transference of management or control is not enough to constitute vesting.

The word 'vest' not only includes vesting of possession but vesting of other rights too, that is intangible or abstract rights. *Unnee Shankar* v. *Saliq Ram*, AIR 1975 All 36, 47.

Vesting of a property in the Court or the receiver not only gives the Court or the receiver the right to take possession of the property and deal with it in a certain manner but amounts to legal transfer of the right, title and interest of the insolvent in the Court or the receiver as the case may be. *Kripa Nath* v. *Ganga Prasad,* AIR 1962 All 256, 260. [Provincial Insolvency Act (5 of 1920), S. 28(2))]

Vesting orders. A vesting order is an order of a Court under statutory authority, whereby property is transferred to and vested, without conveyance, in some person or persons, either solely or jointly with the original holder or holders, or some of them.

An order under statutory authority whereby property is transferred to and vested, without conveyance in some person or persons. [T.P. Act (4 of 1882), S. 57(b)]; [CPC (5 of 1908), O. XXI, R. 81].

Veterinary institution. Means any University or other institution within or without India which grants degree, diplomas or licences in veterinary science and animal husbandry. [Indian Veterinary Council Act (52 of 1984), S. 2(j)]

Veterinary medicine. Means scientific veterinary medicine in all its branches and includes veterinary surgery and obstetrics. [Indian Veterinary Council Act (52 of 1984), S. 2(k)]

Veterinary practitioner. The expression "INSPECTOR" and "VETERINARY PRACTITIONER", means, respectively the officers appointed as such under this Act, acting within the local limits for which they are so appointed. [Dourine Act (5 of 1910), S. 2(1)]

Veto. I forbid; the power of the head of the executive of negating bills which have been passed by the legislature.

Any authoritative prohibition; the power of rejecting or forbidding; the right of any one of the five permanent members of the Security Council of the United Nations to prevent the Council taking action on any matter other than purely procedural.

Vexation. The action of troubling or harassing by aggression or interference; the action of troubling or irritating by physical means. [CrPC, 1973 (2 of 1974), S. 217(a)].

Vexatious. An accusation cannot be said to be vexatious unless the main intention of the complainant was to cause annoyance to the person accused, and not merely to further the ends of justice.

Causing or likely to cause vexation. [CPC (5 of 1908), S. 35A].

The word "vexatious" means "harassment by the process of law", "lacking justification" or which "intention the harass". It signifies an action not having sufficient grounds, and which therefore, only seeks to annoy the adversary. The hallmark of a vexatious proceeding is that it has no basis in law (or at least no discernible basis): and that whatever the intention of the proceeding may be, its only effect is to subject the other party to inconvenience, harassment and expense, which is so great, that it is disproportionate to any gain likely to accrue to the claimant; and that it involves an abuse of process of the court. [*Ravinder Singh* v. *Sukhbir Singh*, (2013) 9 SCC 245, para 24].

Vexatious litigation or **suit.** The litigation initiated deliberately for the purpose of annoying someone.

Viability. Ability of a person, a company or even a country to support itself, or of a product to survive in a market and generate a profit.

Viable. Capable of independent existence or standing.

Vicarious. Done or suffered by one person on behalf of another.

Vicarious immunity. Principle that an agent performing a contract is entitled to any immunity conferred on his principal.

Vicarious infringement. Form of infringement liability for a third party not actually involved in infringement due to close relationship or responsibility for actions of the infringer.

Vicarious liability. Liability which falls on some person as a result of action of some other person e.g. that of the master for the actions of his servant.

Where the driver of a motor omnibus employed by the owner thereof to ply the same for hire by carrying passengers, allows an unlicensed and unskillful person to drive it, when there are passengers in it, the driver, *i.e.*, the servant carries out the duty for which he is employed negligently; and if such negligence results in an accident causing injury to a passenger, the owner, *i.e.* the master is liable in damages to the injured passenger. It is no valid defence to a suit for damages for the owner to say that the servant (driver) acted against the master's (owner's) express directions.

Vicarious performance of contract. Performance of a contract which is based on the delegation of work to a third person.

Vice. Fault; defect; also, in one's place or steed; used also to denote delegated or deputed authority (as) vice-principal or vice-chancellor.

Vice-admiralty. The maritime branch of the administration of justice for the British possessions overseas. [CPC (5 of 1908), S. 140(1)].

Vice-admiralty jurisdiction. The area or sphere of legal authority or power of the administration of justice relating to maritime branch for the British possessions overseas. [CPC (5 of 1908), S. 112(2)].

Vice-Chairman. "VICE-CHAIRMAN" means the Vice-Chairman of a Tribunal.

Explanation—In the case of a Tribunal having two or more Vice-Chairmen, references to the Vice-Chairman in this Act shall be construed as a reference to each of those Vice-Chairmen. [Administrative Tribunals Act (13 of 1985), S. 3(u)]

Vice-Consul. The deputy of consul. [General Clauses Act (10 of 1897), S. 3(16)].

Vice crime. A crime of immoral conduct, such as prostitution, gambling, or child pornography.

Vice versa. The other way round.

The word 'vice versa' means the order of relation being inverted, the other way round. *L.J. Razdam* v. *State of Jammu and Kashmir*, AIR 1966 J&K 9, 11. [Jammu and Kashmir Town Area Act (17 of 2011) as amended by Act (10 of 1965), S. 14-A]

Victim. "VICTIM" means a person who has suffered any loss or injury caused by reason of the act or omission for which the accused person has been charged and the expression "victim" includes his or her guardian or legal heir. [Cr PC, 1973 (2 of 1974), Section 2 (wa) as inserted by Amending Act No. (5 of 2009), Section 2] [Now (w. e. f. 1-7-2024) repealed & replaced by Bharatiya Nagarik Suraksha Sanhita, 2023 (46 of 2023)]

"VICTIM" means a person who has suffered any loss or injury caused by reason of the act or omission of the accused person and includes the guardian or legal heir of such victim. [(w. e. f. 1-7-2024) Bharatiya Nagarik Suraksha Sanhita, 2023 (46 of 2023), S. 2(1)(y)]

Victim-impact statement. A statement which is read into the record during sentencing to inform the Judge about the financial, physical, and psychological impact of the crime on the victim and the family of the victim.

Victimisation. Means one of two things. The first is where the workman concerned is innocent and yet he is being punished because he has in some way displeased the employer, for example, by being an active member of an union of workmen who were acting prejudicially in the employer's interest. The second case is where an employee has committed an offence but he is given a punishment quite out of proportion to the gravity of the offence simply because he has incurred the displeasure of the employer in a similar manner as mentioned above. *National Tobacco Co. of India Ltd.* v. *Fourth Industrial Tribunal*, AIR 1960 Cal 249, 257.

The word 'victimisation' in its normal meaning means being the victim of unfair and arbitrary action. *Workmen of Williamson Magor and & Co. Ltd.* v. *Williamson Magor & Co. Ltd.*, AIR 1982 SC 78, 81.

"VICTIMISATION" means any unfavourable treatment meted out to person with an implicit or explicit intention to obtain sexual favour. [All India Council of Technical Education (Gender Sensitization, Prevention and Prohibition of Sexual Harassment of Women Employees and Students and Redressal of Grievances in Technical Educational Institutions) Regulations, 2016, Regn. 2(n)].

Victimless crime. A crime which is considered to have no direct victim, usually because only consenting adults are involved, like possession of drugs and deviant sexual intercourse between consenting adults.

Vide. See.

Video. "Video" is the transmission and reception of a televised image. It is television image or the electric signals corresponding to it. It pertains to the picture portion of the televised programme. *Collector of Central Excise* v. *Fusebase Eltoto Ltd.*, AIR 1994 SC 1289, 1291.

Video-cinema. Exhibition of moving pictures given by means of VCR/VCP and a video projector fall within the ambit of the definition of a 'video cinema'. *Shankar Video* v. *State of Maharashtra*, AIR 1993 SC 2111, 2118.

Video-conferencing. 'Video-conferencing' is an advancement in science and technology which permits one to see, hear and talk with someone far away, with the same facility and ease. *State of Maharashtra* v. *Praful B. Desai,* AIR 2003 SC 2053.

Video conferencing or other audio visual means. For the purposes of rule 3 of the Companies (Meetings of Board and its Powers) Rules, 2014, 'video conferencing or other audio visual means' means audio visual electronic communication facility employed which enables all the persons participating in a meeting to communicate concurrently with each other without an intermediary and to participate effectively in the meeting. [*Explanation* to rule 3 of the Companies (Meetings of Board and its Powers) Rules, 2014]

Video Description. An audio narration for television viewers who are blind or visually disabled, which consists of verbal descriptions of key visual elements in a television program, such as settings and actions not reflected in dialog. Narrations are inserted into the program's natural pauses, and are typically provided through the Secondary Audio Programming channel. (*Telecommunication*)

Video evidence. Evidence from witnesses provided on video, either through live video link or prerecorded.

Video Privacy Protection Act of 1988 (VPPA). Federal law that protects information about rental and purchase of videos. (*U.S.*) (*Cyber Law*)

Expands the CCPA to prohibit the use and disclosure of personal information about the video-cassettes and related products an individual rents or buys. (*Cyber Law*)

Video production agency. "VIDEO PRODUCTION AGENCY" means any professional videographer or any commercial concern engaged in the business of rendering services relating to video-tape production. [Finance Act (32 of 1994), S. 65(119) Repealed by Central Goods and Services Tax Act, 2017]

Video recording. Any disc or magnetic tape containing information by the use of which the whole or part of a video work may be produced.

Video-tape production. "VIDEO-TAPE PRODUCTION" means the process of any recording of any programme, event or function on a magnetic tape and includes editing thereof, in any manner. [Finance Act (32 of 1994), S. 65(120)Repealed by Central Goods and Services Tax Act, 2017]

"VIDEO-TAPE PRODUCTION" means the process of any recording of any programme, event or function on a magnetic tape or on any other media or device and includes services relating thereto such as editing, cutting, colouring, dubbing, title printing, imparting special effects, processing, adding, modifying or deleting sound, transferring from one media or device to another, or undertaking any video post-production activity, in any manner. [Finance Act (32 of 1994) Repealed by Central Goods and Services Tax Act, 2017, S. 65(120) *as substituted by Finance Act (18 of 2005), S. 88(9)(xxiii)*]

View. An examination; inspection; survey; an act of looking or beholding; mode or manner of looking at or regarding something; a scene.

Vigilance Committee. Means a committee constituted under section 29 of Act 20 of 2013 to supervise the implementation of all schemes under Act 20 of 2013. [S. 2(24) of the National Food Security Act, 2013 (20 of 2013)]

Vigilantibus, et non dormientibus jura subveniunt. Equity comes to the aid of the vigilant and not the slumbering.

Equity aids only the vigilant and not the ones who sleep over their rights, will be highly appropriate. [*Chandigarh Administration* v. *Jasmine Kaur*, (2014) 10 SCC 521, para 33.6].

Law assists those who are vigilant and not those who sleep over their rights). [*H.Dohil Constructions Company Limited* v. *Nahar Exports Limited*, (2015) 1 SCC 680, para 20].

Village. Art. 243(g) defines 'village' to mean a village specified by the Governor by Public Notification to be a village for the purposes of Part IX and includes a group of villages so specified. The village so specified is a village for the purposes of carrying out the provisions of Part IX of the Constitution and not for any other purpose. *State of U.P.* v *Pradhan Singh Kshetra Samiti*, AIR 1995 SC 1512, 1516. [Constitution of India, Art. 243(g)]

"Village" includes—(a) a village-community; (b) village-lands; (c) rivers passing through or by village-lands; and (d) a group of villages.

Village. Includes village lands. [(w. e. f. 1-7-2024) Bharatiya Nagarik Suraksha Sanhita, 2023 (46 of 2023), S. 34(2)(i)]

The expression "village' connotes ordinarily an area occupied by a body of men mainly dependent upon agriculture or occupations subservient thereto. When the area is occupied by persons who are engaged mainly in commercial pursuits, rural areas in the vicinity of a town grow into a suburb of the town.

Village artisan. The expression 'VILLAGE ARTISAN' means who does not hold any agricultural land and whose main source of livelihood is manufacture or repair of traditional tools, implements and other articles or things used for agriculture or purposes ancillary thereto and includes a carpenter, weaver, potter, blacksmith, silversmith, goldsmith, barber, washerman, cobbler, or any other person who normally earns his livelihood by practising a craft either by his own labour or by the labour of any member of his family in any rural area.

Provided that no person shall be deemed to be a village artisan whose total income (including income of his or her spouse and minor children) exceeds two thousand four hundred rupees in a year. [U.P.Z.A. & Act (1 of 1951), S. 122-C, *Expln.* II]

Village-cess. "VILLAGE-CESS" includes any cess, contribution or due which is customarily leviable within an estate and is neither a payment for the use of private property or for personal service nor imposed by or under any enactment for the time being in force. [Punj. Act XVII of 1887 (Land-Revenue), S. 3, cl. (10)]

Village channel. "VILLAGE CHANNEL" means any channel by which water is led from a canal directly into the fields to be irrigated, and includes all subsidiary works connected with any such channel, except the sluice or outlet through which water is supplied from a canal to such channel. [Ben. Act III of 1876 (Irrigation), S. 3, cl. (2)]

Village immovable property. "VILLAGE IMMOVABLE PROPERTY" shall mean immovable property within the limits of village sites other than agricultural land. [Punj. Act II of 1905 (Pre-emption), S. 3 cl. (2)]

Village industry. Means,—

(i) any industry located in a rural area which produces any goods or renders any service with or without the use of power and in which the fixed capital investment per head of an artisan or a worker does not exceed fifteen thousand rupees or such other sum as may, by notification in the Official Gazette, be specified from time to time by the Central Government; Provided that any industry specified in the schedule and located in an area other than a rural area and recognised as a village industry at any time before the commencement of the Khadi and Village Industries Commission (Amendment) Act, 1987 shall, notwithstanding any, thing contained in the sub-clause, continue to be a village industry under this Act;

(ii) any other non-manufacturing unit established for the sole purpose of promoting, maintaining, assisting, servicing (including mother units) or managing any village industry. [Khadi & Village Industries Commission Act (61 of 1956), S. 2(h)]

Village officer. "VILLAGE-OFFICER" means a chief headman, headman or *patwari* of a village. [Punj. Act XVII of 1887 (Land Revenue), S. 3, cl. (11)]

Village tract. "VILLAGE-TRACT" means the local area under the jurisdiction of a headman, including a village or group of villages and adjacent lands. [Bur. Act VI of 1907 (Villages), S. 4, cl. (8)]

Vindicate. To clear a person or thing from suspicion, criticism, blame or doubt.

Violate. To break; disregard; infringe. [Specific Relief Act (47 of 1963), S. 16(b)].

Violation. The action of violating; the state of being violated. [IPC (45 of 1860), S. 405].

Violence. The exercise of physical force so as to inflict injury on, or damage to, persons or property; action or conduct characterised by this. [T.P. Act (4 of 1882), S. 108(e)].

Unwarranted use of force. Use of force against public liberty to cause injury, loss or damage.

Violent. Characterised by violence. [Payment of Bonus Act (21 of 1965), S. 9(b)].

Violent disorder. An offence committed when three or more persons, present together, use or threaten unlawful violence.

Vires. Powers; forces; capabilities; natural powers; powers granted or limited. Authority; power. (*Black*)

Virgin. (*Of metals*) produced directly from one or by primary smelting. [Gold (Control) Act (45 of 1968) (*repealed*), S. 2(j)].

Virtual battlespace. The ether occupied by communications impulses, databases, and computer codes. In this usage, the term is synonymous with cyber medium, cyberspace, and infosphere. (*Cyber Law*)

"Virtual digital asset". Means—

(a) any information or code or number or token (not being Indian currency or foreign currency), generated through cryptographic means or otherwise, by whatever name called, providing a digital representation of value exchanged with or without consideration, with the promise or representation of having inherent value, or functions as a store of value or a unit of account including its use in any financial transaction or investment, but not limited to investment scheme; and can be transferred, stored or traded electronically;

(b) a non-fungible token or any other token of similar nature, by whatever name called;

(c) any other digital asset, as the Central Government may, by notification in the Official Gazette specify:

Provided that the Central Government may, by notification in the Official Gazette, exclude any digital asset from the definition of virtual digital asset subject to such conditions as may be specified therein.

Explanation.—For the purposes of this clause,—

(a) "non-fungible token" means such digital asset as the Central Government may, by notification in the Official Gazette, specify;

(b) the expressions "currency", "foreign currency" and "Indian currency" shall have the same meanings as respectively assigned to them in clauses (h), (m) and (q) of section 2 of the Foreign Exchange Management Act, 1999 (42 of 1999). [Income-tax Act, 1961 (43 of 1961), section 2(47A)]

"VIRTUAL DIGITAL ASSET" Shall have the same meaning as assigned to it in clause (47A) of section 2 of the Income-tax Act, 1961 (43 of 1961). [Central Goods and Services Tax Act (12 of 2017), section 2(117A)]

Virtual private network (VPN). A new value added network that runs on the Internet and appears to the user as a private network. (*Cyber Law*)

Virtual reality. A computer-generated illusion in which a person has the experience of existing in a realistic, but artificial, environment. The illusion is accomplished by creating three-dimensional images that a person views through a dedicated viewing device, such as a helmet connected by wire to the computer. In most virtual reality systems, the image displayed changes with movements that the user makes, so that the user has the illusion of interacting with the computer-generated environment. (*Computer*)

Virtual realm. A synonym for information realm or cyberspace. (*Cyber Law*)

Virtual representation doctrine. The principle which states that a judgment may bind a person who is not a party to the litigation if one of the parties is so closely aligned with the nonparty's interests that the non-party has been adequately and effectively represented by the party in Court.

Virtual wallet. Stores the money in the software and not on the smart card. Once the account is opened, the customer enters their identification code and password whenever he intends to make a purchase.. [Karnika Seth, *Computers Internet and New Technology Laws*, 2021, LexisNexis, Glossary of Legal Terms].

Virulent. Any leprosy that led to deformity and unfitness for social intercourse could be considered virulent. *Swarajja Lakshmi* v. *Padma Rao*, AIR 1974 SC 165, 167. [Hindu Marriage Act (25 of 1955), S. 13(1)(iv)]

Virulent form. A form characterized by severity. [Hindu Marriage Act (25 of 1955), S. 13(1)(iv)].

Virus. The generic label for a unary set of code that is designed to operate so as to cause mischief or other subversive effect in a target computer system.

VIRUS means any computer instruction, information, data or programme that destroys, damages, degrades or adversely affects the performance of a computer resource or attaches itself to another computer resource and operates when a programme, data or instruction is executed or some other event takes place in that computer resource. (*Information Technology*)

A short program that copies itself and secretly "infects" (joins itself to) useful programs, usually for some malicious purpose. For example, a virus can be designed to alter data or destroy files in a computer after an infected program is run. A virus spreads from computer to computer by means of computer networks or through the use of diskettes containing programs that have been infected. (*Computer*)

A chunk of computer programming Code that makes copies of itself without any conscious human intervention. Some viruses do more than simply replicate themselves, they might display messages, install other software or files, delete software of files, *etc.*

A virus requires the presence of some other program to replicate itself. Typically viruses spread by attaching themselves to programs and in some cases files, for example the file formats for Microsoft word processor and spreadsheet programs allow the inclusion of programs called "macros" which can in some cases be a breeding ground for viruses. (*Matisse Enzer-Glossary of Internet Terms*)

Virus writing. The act of writing programs that have the ability to attach themselves to other programs in other computers and thereby replicate themselves.

Vis-a-vis. Opposite to; in relation to; facing each other.

Vis major. Irresistible force; Act of God.

VIS MAJOR to be regarded in law, as *vis major* or the act of God, an occurrence must be overwhelming and not only unforeseen but incapable of being foreseen, and absolutely incapable of being prevented or guarded against.

Visa. A notation or indorsement on a passport by an official who grants entry into a country.

Visible means of support. Without any ostensible ability to support himself though he is able bodied to take to any avocation.

Visible representation. A representation (i.e. image, portrait etc.) which is perceptible by the sense of sight. [IPC (45 of 1860), S. 124A].

Vision. [Personal Injuries (Compensation Insurance) Act (37 of 1963), Sch.].

Visit. To go and see [Reformatory Schools Act (8 of 1897), Ss. 7(2) and 26(1)(ii)]; to make social call upon; to go and see and care for as a charitable work.

Visitation. "Visitation" means that a non-custodial parents period of access to a child. [Black's Law Dictionary, 10th Edn. As cited in *Roxann Sharma* v. *Arun Sharma*, (2015) 8 SCC 318, para 6].

Visitation order. A visitation order means on order establishing the visitation times for a non-custodial parent with his or her children. [Black's Law Dictionary, 10th Edn. as cited in *Roxann Sharma* v. *Arun Sharma*, (2015) 8 SCC 318, para 6].

Visitor. One who visits officially for the purpose of inspection or supervision, in order to prevent or remove abuses or irregularities [CrPC, 1973 (2 of 1974), S. 337]; a person of eminence serving as the highest authority of a university [Aligarh Muslim University Act (40 of 1920), S. 13]; one who visits.

Visual inspection. Means the process of inspection by the Authorised Officer or an officer deputed by him for the purpose by which the physical condition of the food consignment, scrutiny of documents and compliance of packaging and labeling regulations are ascertained for the food safety compliance prior to drawing of samples. [Food Safety and Standards (Import) Regulations, 2017, Regn. 2(1)(ab)].

Visual recording. Means the recording in any medium, by any method including the storing of it by any electronic means, of moving images or of the representations thereof, from which they can be perceived, reproduced or communicated by any method. [S. 2(xxa) of the Copyright Act, 1957 (14 of

1957) as inserted (w.e.f. 21-6-2012) by the Copyright (Amendment) Act, 2012 (27 of 2012)]

Visually handicapped. "VISUALLY HANDICAPPED" means a person who suffers from any of the following conditions, namely:—

(i) total absence of sight;

(ii) visual acuity not exceeding 6/60 or 20/200 (snellen) in the better eye with the correcting lenses; or

(iii) limitation of the field of vision subtending and angle of degree or worse. [Rehabilitation Council of India Act (34 of 1992), S. 2(1)(o)]

Vitiate. Deprive of efficacy; be a fatal flaw.

To make bad, impure or defective. [CrPC, 1973 (2 of 1974), S. 460]; [Presidency-Towns Insolvency Act (3 of 1909), S. 118(2)].

Viva voce. With living voice or word of mouth.

Viva voce and **interview.** An interview is a meeting of the interviewer and the interviewed face to face, especially for the purpose of formal conference on some point, whereas a viva voce examination is something very different. It is an oral examination in a specified subject. *K.N. Chandrasekhara* v. *State of Mysore*, AIR 1963 Mys 292, 302.

Viva-voce examination. Oral examination or testing by verbal questions and answers instead of in writing. [CPC (5 of 1908), O. XI, R. 11].

Voice print. A voice print is a visual recording of voice. [*Ritesh Sinha* v. *State of U.P.*, (2013) 2 SCC 357, para 38].

'Voiceprint identification of voice' involves measurement of frequency and intensity of sound waves. [*Ritesh Sinha* v. *State of U.P.*, (2013) 2 SCC 357, para 39].

Expressed on conducted by word of mouth; oral.

Void. Not valid; of no effect; invalid.

Null; ineffectual; having no legal force or binding effect; incapable of being enforced by law. [T.P. Act (4 of 1882), S. 10 and Constitution of India, Art. 13(1)].

A thing which is void is "non-est" and it is not necessary that it be set aside though it may be sometimes convenient to do so. *Suresh Chandra* v. *State of W.B.*, AIR 1976 Cal 110, 113.

'Void' means ineffectual; nugatory, having no legal force or legal effect; unable in law to support the purpose for which it was intended. [Black's Law Dictionary as cited in *Rajasthan State Industrial Development and Investment Corporation* v. *Subhash Sindhi Cooperative Housing Society, Jaipur*, (2013) 5 SCC 427, para 17].

Void and not being valid. There is no real difference between transfer being void or not being valid. Sanction obtained from the charity commission subsequent to the sale transaction is not valid. *Chandra Bhan* v. *Shrawan Kumar*, AIR 1980 Bom 48, 53.

The word 'void' in Art. 13 (1) can't be read in the sense of 'repealed.' *Edward Ezra* v. *State*, AIR 1953 Cal 263, 275. [Constitution of India, Art. 13(1)]

The word 'void' in Art. 13(1), Constitution of India, so far as existing laws are concerned cannot be held to obliterate them from the statute book, and could not make such laws void altogether, because Art. 13, has not been given any retrospective effect. After the coming into force of the Constitution however the effect of Art. 13 (1) on such repugnant laws is that it nullifies them and makes them ineffectual and nugatory and devoid of any legal force or binding effect. *Behram Khurshid Pesikaka* v. *State of Bombay*, AIR 1955 SC 123, 145.

The expression 'void' in relation to a juristic act means without legal force, effect or consequence; not binding; invalid; null; worthless; cipher; useless; and ineffectual etc. *Nutan Kumar* v. *II Addl. District Judge Band*, AIR 1994 All 298, 303 (FB). [Indian Contract Act (9 of 1872), S. 23]

Mere use of word 'void' is not determinative of its legal impact. The word 'void' has a relative rather than an absolute meaning. It only conveys the idea that the order is invalid or illegal. It cannot be avoided. *State of Kerala* v. *M.K. Kunhikannan Nambiar*, AIR 1996 SC 906, 908.

Void agreement. "An agreement not enforceable by law is said to be void." [Indian Contract Act (9 of 1872), S. 2(g)]

Void and voidable. Void means that an instrument or transaction is so nugatory and ineffectual that nothing can cure it; voidable when an imperfection or defect can be cured by the act or confirmation of him who could take advantage of it.

A contract is void which is destitute of all legal effect, while a voidable contract is one which may be affirmed or rejected at the will of one of the parties.

Void contract. "A contract which ceases to be enforceable by law becomes void when it ceases to be enforceable." [Indian Contract Act (9 of 1872), S. 2(j)]

Void decree or order. Where a Court lacks inherent jurisdiction in passing a decree or making an order, a decree or order passed by such Court would be without jurisdiction, *non-est* and void *ab initio.* Validity of such decree or order can be challenged at any stage, even in execution or collateral proceedings. *Balwant N. Viswamitra* v. *Yadav Sadashiv Mule,* AIR 2004 SC 4377. [CPC (5 of 1908), Ss. 2(2), 33, 47.

Void judgment. One which has no legal force or effects, invalidity of which may be asserted by any person whose rights are affected, at any time and at any place, directly or collaterally. *Tranglobi Pisciculture Co-operative Stores Ltd.* v. *Chief Commissioner*, AIR 1969 Manipur 84 at 89.

Void jurisdiction and Ultra vires. The word 'void' means a mere nullity and may be ignored even in collateral proceedings. The expression 'jurisdiction' means inherent jurisdiction, competency and quasi-jurisdictional facts, without allegations of which the Court cannot be set in motion and without proof of which a decree should not be pronounced. The word '*ultra vires*' implies absence of jurisdiction or absence of competency. *Madhavan* v. *State of Kerala*, AIR 1966 Ker 212, 214 (FB).

Voidability. The quality or state of being voidable. [Indian Contract Act (9 of 1872), S. 19].

Voidable. Does not always mean voidable in entirety.

That may be avoided, or declared void, though not *ab initio* void. [Indian Contract Act (9 of 1872), S. 2(i) and T.P. Act (4 of 1882), S. 41].

Voidable contract. "An agreement which is enforceable by law at the option of one or more of the parties thereto, but not at the option of the other or others, is a VOIDABLE CONTRACT.". [Indian Contract Act (9 of 1872), S. 2(i)]

Voidable marriage. A marriage which is initially invalid but which remains in effect unless terminated by the order of the Court.

Voidable preference. A prebankruptcy transfer made by an insolvent debtor to or for the benefit of a creditor, thereby allowing the creditor to receive more than its proportionate share of the debtor's assets.

Volenti non fit injuria. He who consents cannot receive an injury.

That to which a man consents cannot be considered an injury.

To succeed under the maxim it is necessary for the defendant to prove that the person injured knew of the danger, appreciated it and voluntarily took the risk. That he had some knowledge of the danger is not sufficient. A man cannot voluntarily undertake a risk, the extent of which he does not appreciate.

In actions founded on tort the leave and licence of the plaintiff to do the act complained of usually constitutes a good defence; and as a rule a man must bear loss arising from acts to which he assented. On this principle, when a man connives at or condones the adultery of his wife, he cannot in such a case obtain damages from the seducer, nor sustain a petition for divorce. A railway company usually owes a duty to a passenger to take reasonable care of him, but he cannot demand such care if he expressly agrees, in consideration of free pass, to travel at his own risk. (*Latin for Lawyers*)

Volition. One's decision or choice made after due consideration or deliberation. [Specific Act (47 of 1963), S. 14(1)(b)].

Volitional test. In criminal law, a test for the insanity defence, which holds that a person is not criminally responsible for an act when mental disease prevented the person from controlling his or her conduct.

Volume. One of a number of books (of register) forming a related set or series. [Delivery of Books and Newspapers (Public Libraries) Act (27 of 1954), S. 2(A) and Indian Partnership Act (9 of 1932), 1st Sch.]; bulk; size or dimensions of a thing; a quantity; bulk. [Sick Textile Undertakings (Taking Over of Management) Act (72 of 1972), S. 7(1)].

Voluntarily. "A person is said to cause an effect "VOLUNTARILY" when he causes it by means whereby he intended to cause it, or by means which, at the time of employing those means, he knew or had reason to believe to be likely to cause it." [IPC (45 of 1860), S. 39] [Now (w. e. f. 1-7-2024) repealed & replaced by Bharatiya Nayaya Sanhita, 2023 (45 of 2023)]

"VOLUNTARILY" a person is said to cause an effect "voluntarily" when he causes it by means whereby he intended to cause it, or by means which, at the time of employing those means, he knew or had reason to believe to be likely to cause it.

Illustration

A sets fire, by night, to an inhabited house in a large town, for the purpose of facilitating a robbery and thus causes the death of a person. Here, A may not have intended to cause death; and may even be sorry that death has been caused by his act; yet, if he knew that he was likely to cause death, he has caused death voluntarily. [(w. e. f. 1-7-2024) Bharatiya Nayaya Sanhita, 2023 (45 of 2023), section 2(33)]

The expression 'VOLUNTARILY' is used in this section to mean 'naturalisation' in the narrow sense of that term and excluding compulsory, involuntary or collective naturalisation which some states have adopted at different times. [Citizenship Act (57 of 1955), S. 9(1)]

VOLUNTARILY means doing of something as the result of the free exercise of the will but not something done under a legal duty." "Where a person obtained a passport acted on his own volition and knew the nature of his act and did not act in performance of a legal duty, nor due to coercion or fraud or misrepresentation or mistake he has acted voluntarily. [Citizenship Rules (1956), R. 30]

Voluntarily causing grievous hurt. Whoever voluntarily causes hurt, if the hurt which he intends to cause or knows himself to be likely to cause is grievous, hurt and if the hurt which he causes is grievous hurt, is said "voluntarily to cause grievous hurt."

Explanation.—A person is not said voluntarily to cause grievous hurt except when he both causes grievous hurt and intends or knows himself to be likely to cause grievous hurt. But he is said voluntarily to cause grievous hurt, if intending or knowing him to be likely to cause grievous hurt of one kind, he actually causes grievous hurt of an other kind. [IPC (45 of 1860), S. 322]

Voluntarily causing hurt. "Whoever does any act with the intention of thereby causing hurt to any person, or with the knowledge that he is likely thereby to cause hurt to any person, does thereby cause hurt to any person, is said "voluntarily to cause hurt." [IPC (45 of 1860), S.321]

Voluntarily retired. Unless the termination of the service is the result of a voluntary move on the part of the employee, he cannot be said to have 'voluntarily retired'. A mere submission of the employees to the termination of service by the employer cannot be said to be a voluntary act of the former. *Desikachari* v. *Associated Publishers*, AIR 1962 Mad 327, 331. [Industrial Disputes Act (14 of 1947), S. 2 (oo) (a)].

Voluntary. Of one's free will, impulse or choice; not constrained by another; acting voluntarily or willingly. [Sale of Goods Act (3 of 1930), S. 2(2)]; [Constitution of India, Art. 101(3), *Prov.*].

Voluntary appearance. An appearance which is entered by a party's own will, without the service of process.

Voluntary assignment. Assignment of a debtor's property for the benefit of all the assignor's creditors, instead of only a few.

"Voluntarily causing hurt", defined. Act 45, 1860, Section 321. Act 15, 1887, Section 3(6); Act 5, 1892, Section 2(6); Reg. 2, 1888, Section 2(4); Reg. 4, 1890, S. 3(5).

"Whoever does any act with the intention of thereby causing hurt to any person, or with the knowledge that he is likely thereby to cause hurt to any person, does thereby cause hurt to any person, is said 'VOLUNTARILY TO CAUSE HURT." [Indian Penal Code (45 of 1860), S. 321] [(w. e. f. 1-7-2024) repealed and replaced by Bharatiya Nyaya Sanhita, 2023 (45 of 2023), S. 115(1)]

Voluntarily causing hurt and grievous hurt. The requirement of Explanation to Section 325 will be satisfied if the offender had the knowledge that by his act he was likely to "cause grievous hurt" . Explanation to Section 325 makes it clear that either the ingredient of intention or of knowledge must be essentially present in order to constitute the offence of hurt. [*Dhalapati Majhi v State,* Mad LJ : YD (1983), p. 181 : (1982) 53 Cut LJ 856 (Bom)]. [IPC (45 of 1860), S. 325]

Voluntarily causing grievous hurt. Whoever voluntarily causes hurt, if the hurt which he intends to cause or knows himself to be likely to cause is grievous hurt, and if the hurt which he causes is grievous hurt, is said "voluntarily to cause grievous hurt".

Explanation.—A person is not said voluntarily to cause grievous hurt except when he both causes grievous hurt and intends or knows himself to be likely to cause grievous hurt. But he is said voluntarily to cause grievous hurt, if intending or knowing himself to be likely to cause grievous hurt of one kind, he actually causes grievous hurt of another kind. [(w. e. f. 1-7-2024) Bharatiya Nyaya Sanhita, 2023 (45 of 2023), S. 117(1)]

Voluntary conduct. Conduct which results from the exercise of one's will.

Voluntary euthanasia. Euthanasia which is performed with the consent of terminally ill person.

Voluntary intoxication. A willing ingestion of alcohol or drugs to the point of impairment done with the knowledge that one's physical and mental capabilities would be impaired.

Voluntary manslaughter. An act of murder which is reduced to manslaughter because of extenuating circumstances, *eg.,* adequate provocation.

Voluntary retirement. Where conditional request for retirement was made and it was found that the charge was handed over under protest, it was held that an Industrial dispute arose and voluntary nature of retirement could be determined. (*B.N. Cotton Mills* v. *J. Bastian,* AIR 1960 SC 1110)

Article 465 of the Civil Service Regulations in its application to Government servants in the service of the Uttar Pradesh Government does not give any absolute right to a Government servant to retire on merely indicating his option to do so. (*Suraj Pal Singh* v. *State of U.P.,* 1967 SLR 49)

'Voluntary retirement' and **'resignation'.** The 'voluntary retirement' and 'resignation' involve voluntary acts on the part of employee to leave service. One of the basic distinctions between the two is that in case of resignation, it can be tendered at any time but in the case of voluntary retirement , it can only be sought for after rendering prescribed period of qualifying service. Further, in the case of resignation a prior permission is not mandatory while in the case of voluntary retirement, permission of the employer concerned is a requisite condition. Under R. 16, an employee who seeks voluntary retirement has to give three months notice to enable the employer to complete the designated mode of acceptance. Resignation may be unilateral whereas voluntary retirement is bilateral. In the case of resignation the relationship of employer and employee terminates on acceptance of resignation. Whereas in the case of retirement, voluntary or superannuation, the relationship continues for the purposes of payment of retrial benefits. *Jaipal Singh* v. *Sumitra Mahajan*, (2004) 4 SCC 522, 528, para 18. See also *UCO Bank* v. *Sanwar Mal*, (2004) 4 SCC 412 and *Reserve Bank of India* v. *Cecil Dennis Solomon* (2004) 9 SCC 461. [All India Services (Death-cum-Retirement Benefits) Rules, 1958, p. 16]

Voluntary sale or transfer. In 'voluntary sale or transfer' of the land, the owner is free to settle terms of transfer and choose the buyer as also to appoint the point of time when he would be receiving consideration and parting with his title and possession over the land. *Sunder* v. *Union of India,* (2001) SCC 211, para 22.

Voluntary waste. Waste which results from some positive act of destruction.

Voluntas in delictis non exitus spectatur. In offences, the will and not the consequences are to be looked to. (*Latin for Lawyers*)

Voluntas testatoris ambulatoria est usque ad mortem. The will of a testator is ambulatory until his death (that is he may change it at any time).

Voluntas testatoris habet interpretationem latam et benignam. The will of the testator should receive a broad and liberal interpretation.

Voluntas ultima testatoris est perimplenda secundum veram intentionem suam. The last will of a testator is to be fulfilled according to his true intention.

Volunteer. A person who receives a voluntary conveyance, (*i.e.*) a conveyance without consideration.

Vote. Wish, choice or opinion of a person expressed in some authorized way, (as) by ballot or *viva voce*.

VOTE, SUFFRAGE, VOICE. The vote is the wish itself, whether expressed or not; a person has a vote, that is, the power of wishing; but the suffrage and the voice are the wish that is expressed; a person gives his suffrage or his voice. The voice is the settled and fixed wish, it is that by which the most important concerns in life are determined; the suffrage is a vote given only in particular cases; the voice is a partial or occasional wish, expressed only in matters of minor importance. The vote and voice are given either for or against a person or thing; the suffrage is commonly given in favour of a person; in all public assemblies the majority of votes decide the question; members of Parliament are chosen by the suffrage of the people; in the execution of a will every executor has a voice in all that is transacted.

Vote by secret ballot. A vote by ballots cast in such a manner that a person expressing a choice cannot be identified with the choice expressed.

Vote casting. Vote that decides between the two equal parties. Deciding vote in a deliberative or parliamentary assembly cast by the Presiding Officer in the event of a tie. (*Constitutional and Parliamentary Term*)

Voters list. 'Voters list' is a public document and it can be used as a substantive piece of evidence. [*Gopi Kishan* v. *Shankerlal Dakot,* AIR 2005 Raj. 114, 118, para 15]

Voting of demands for grants. Putting to the vote of the House demands for grants for approval.

Vote of no confidence. A constitutional method by which a legislature by a majority of vote forces the cabinet or ministry to resign.

Voter. One who has a right to voice or vote; an elector. [IPC (45 of 1860), S. 171-C(2)(b)].

Voting by electronic means. For the purposes of rule 20 of the Companies (Management & Administration) Rules, 2014, the expression 'voting by electronic means' means a 'secured system' based process of display of electronic ballots, recording of votes of the members and the number of votes polled in favour or against, such that the entire voting exercised by way of electronic means gets registered and counted in an electronic registry in a centralized server with adequate 'cyber security'. [*Explanation* (*i*) to rule 20(2) of the Companies (Management & Administration) Rules, 2014]

Voting paper. A ballot paper. [IPC (45 of 1860), S. 171-D].

Voting right. Means the right of a member of a company to vote in any meeting of the company or by means of postal ballot. [S. 2(92) of the Companies Act, 2013 (18 of 2013)]

Vouch. Guarantee or make oneself responsible for a thing represented as true or reliable or existent.

Declared to be true. [CPC (5 of 1908), O. XX, R. 17].

Voucher. Document establishing payment of money or truth of accounts.

"Voucher" means an instrument where there is an obligation to accept it as consideration or part consideration for a supply of goods or services or both and where the goods or services or both to be supplied or the identities of their potential suppliers are either indicated on the instrument itself or in related documentation, including the terms and conditions of use of such instrument [The Central Goods and Services Tax Act, 2017 (12 of 2017), S. 2(118)]

A receipt, acquaintance or release, which may serve as evidence of payment or discharge of debt. [T.P. Act (4 of 1882), S. 76(g)].

Vouching of accounts. The production of proper vouchers for the various items in an account.

Vox populi vox Dei. The voice of the people is the voice of God.

Voyage. "VOYAGE" means the whole distance between a vessel's place of departure and her final place of arrival; but the return of a vessel from any place shall, notwithstanding the terms of any charter party, be deemed a distinct voyage, [Bur. Act IX of 1879 (Coast lights), S. 3].

"VOYAGE" includes the plying of a mechanically propelled vessel at or about any place. [Inland Vessels Act(1 of 1917), S. 2(1)(h)]

"VOYAGE" for the purposes of Part VIII, means the whole distance between the ship's port or place of departure and her final port or place of arrival. [Merchant Shipping Act (44 of 1958), S. 3(56)]

The passage of a vessel from one port to another or others.

Voyage charter. Charter agreement (relating to a ship or its cargo space) for a particular voyage.

Voyeurism. Any man who watches, or captures the image of a woman engaging in a private act in circumstances where she would usually have the expectation of not being observed either by the perpetrator or by any other person at the behest of the perpetrator or disseminates such image shall be punished on first conviction with imprisonment of either description for a term which shall not be less than one year, but which may extend to three years, and shall also be liable to fine, and be punished on a second or subsequent conviction, with imprisonment of either description for a term which shall not be less than three years, but which may extend to seven years, and shall also be liable to fine. [Indian Penal Code 1860, S. 354C, as inserted by Criminal Law (Amendment) Act 2013].

A man who watches, or captures the image of a woman engaging in a private act in circumstances where she would usually have the expectation of not being observed either by the perpetrator or by any other person at the behest of the perpetrator or disseminates such image (commits the offence of VOYEURISM).

Explanation 1.—For the purposes of this section "private act" includes an act of watching carried out in a place which, in the circumstances, would reasonably be expected to provide privacy and where the victim's genitals, posterior or breasts exposed or covered only in underwear; or the victim is using a lavatory; or the victim is doing a sexual act that is not of a kind ordinarily done in public.

Explanation 2.—Where the victim consents to capture of images or any acts but not to their dissemination to third persons and where such image or act is disseminated, such dissemination shall be considered an offence under this section. [Indian Penal Code (45 of 1860), S. 354C as inserted by Amending Act (13 of 2013)].

Whoever watches, or captures the image of a woman engaging in a private act in circumstances where she would usually have the expectation of not being observed either by the perpetrator or by any other person at the behest of the perpetrator or disseminates such image (commits the offence of VOYERISM).

Explanation 1.—For the purposes of this section, "private act" includes an act of watching carried out in a place which, in the circumstances, would reasonably be expected to provide privacy and where the victim's genitals, posterior or breasts are exposed or covered only in underwear; or the victim is using a lavatory; or the victim is doing a sexual act that is not of a kind ordinarily done in public.

Explanation 2.—Where the victim consents to the capture of the images or any act, but not to their dissemination to third persons and where such image or act is disseminated, such dissemination shall be considered an offence under this section. [(w. e. f. 1-7-2024) Bharatiya Nyaya Sanhita, 2023 (45 of 2023), section 77]

Vulnerability. A weakness that could be exploited to cause damage to the system or the assets it contains. (*Information Technology*)

With specific regard to IW—a known or suspected flaw in the hardware or software or operation of a system that exposes the system to penetration or its information to accidental disclosure.

Vulnerable. Capable of being wounded; liable to injury or criticism.

W

Wage. The giving of a security for the performance of anything.

Money paid for labour or services usually according to specified interval of work.

"Wage ceiling". Means such amount of wages as may be notified by the Central Government, for the purposes of becoming a member under Chapter III and Chapter IV. [Code on Social Security, 2020 (36 of 2020), S. 2(89)]

Wage period. In relation to the employee means the period in respect of which wages are ordinarily payable to him whether in terms of the contract of employment, express or implied otherwise. [Employee's State Insurance Act (34 of 1948), S. 2(23)]

Wage war. Carry on actions that constitute or promote war. [IPC (45 of 1860), S. 121].

Wage worker. Means a person employed for remuneration in the unorganised sector, directly by an employer or through any contractor, irrespective of place of work, whether exclusively for one employer or for one or more employers, whether in cash or in kind, whether as a home-based worker, or as a temporary or casual worker, or as a migrant worker, or workers employed by households including domestic workers, with a monthly wage of an amount as may be notified by the Central Government and State Government, as the case may be. [Unorganised Workers Social Security Act, 2008 (33 of 2008), S. 2(n)].

"WAGE WORKER" means a person employed for remuneration in the unorganised sector, directly by an employer or through any contractor, irrespective of place of work, whether exclusively for one employer or for one or more employers, whether in cash or in kind, whether as a home-based worker, or as a temporary or casual worker, or as a migrant worker, or workers employed by households including domestic workers, with a monthly wage of an amount as may be notified by the Central Government and the State Government, as the case may be. [Code on Social Security, 2020 (36 of 2020), S. 2(90)]

Wager. Something (especially a sum of money) laid down and hazarded on the issue of an uncertain event; a stake. [Indian Contract Act (9 of 1872), S. 30].

Wager of law. A number of oaths in support of one's innocence. A defendant discharging himself from the claim on his own oath, bringing with him at the same time into Court elevent of his neighbours to swear that they believe his denial to be true.

Wager policy. An insurance policy which is issued to a person who has no insurable interest in the person or property covered by the policy.

Wagering contract. To constitute a wagering contract, it is necessary to establish that it was not the intention of either of the parties, to deliver or to take delivery of the commodity. In other words, if it is proved to the satisfaction of the Court, that the parties were merely contemplating a nominal contract, dealing only in differences, and agreeing either of receiving or pay differences according to the rise and fall in the market, and if, as a matter of fact, neither of the parties intended to deliver or receive the commodity, the contract is null and void.

To constitute a wagering contract there must be proof that contract was entered into upon terms that the performance of the contract should not be demanded, but only the difference in prices should be paid. *Gherulal Parakh* v. *Mahdeodas,* AIR 1959 SC 781, 784.

Though in form an agreement for sale purports to contemplate delivery of the goods and the payment of the price, if there is no delivery of the goods and what is received is only the difference between the contract prices and the prices on a later day, it makes the contract a wagering contract. *B & C Exchange Ltd.* v. *State of Punjab,* AIR 1961 SC 268, 270.

Wages. "WAGES" includes any privilege or benefit which is capable of being estimated in money, other than a travelling allowance or the value of any travelling concession or a contribution paid by the employer of a workman towards any pension or provident fund or a sum paid to a workman to cover any special expenses entailed on him by the nature of his employment. [Workmen's Compensation Act (8 of 1923), S. 2(m)]

"WAGES" means all remuneration capable of being expressed in terms of money, which would, if the terms of employment, express or implied, were fulfilled, be payable to a workman in respect of his employment, or of work done in such employment, and includes—(i) such allowances (including dearness allowance) as the workman is for the time being entitled to; (ii) the value of any house accommodation, or supply of light, water, medical attendance or other amenity or of any service or of any concessional supply of foodgrains or other articles; (iii) any travelling concessions; (iv) any commission payable on the promotion of sales or business or both;

but does not include—(a) any bonus; (b) any contribution paid or payable by the employer to any pension fund or provident fund or for the benefit of the workman under any law for the time being in force; (c) any gratuity payable on the termination of his service. [Industrial Disputes Act (14 of 1947), S. 2(rr)]

"WAGES" means all remuneration (whether by way of salary, allowances or otherwise) expressed in terms of money or capable of being so expressed which would, if the terms of employment, express or implied, were fulfilled, be payable to person employed in respect of his employment or of work done in such employment and includes—(a) any remuneration payable under any award or settlement between the parties or order of a Court; (b) any remuneration to which the person employed is entitled in respect of overtime work or holidays or any leave period; (c) any additional remuneration payable under the terms of employment (whether called a bonus or by any other name); (d) any sum which by reason of termination of employment of the person employed is payable under any law, contract or instrument which provides for the payment of such sum, whether with or without deductions, but does not provide for the time within which the payment is to be made; (e) any sum to which the person employed is entitled under any scheme framed under any law for the time being in force;

but does not include—(1) any bonus (whether under a scheme of profit-sharing or otherwise) which does not form part of remuneration payable under the terms of employment or which is not payable under any award or settlement between the parties or order of a Court; (2) the value of any house-accommodation, or of the supply of light, water, medical attendance or other amenity or of any service excluded from the computation of wages by a general or special order of the State Government; (3) any contribution paid by the employer to any pension or provident fund, and the interest which may have accrued thereon; (4) any travelling allowance or the value of any travelling concession; (5) any sum paid to the employed person to defray special expenses entailed on him by the nature of his employment, or (6) any gratuity payable on the termination of employment in cases other than those specified in sub-clause (d). [Payment of Wages Act (4 of 1936), S. 2(vi)]

"WAGES" means all remuneration, capable of being expressed in terms of money, which would, if the terms of the contract of employment, expressed or implied, were fulfilled, be payable to a person employed in respect of his employment or of work done in such employment and includes house rent allowance but does not include—

(i) the value of

(a) any house-accommodation, supply of light, water, medical attendance, or

(b) any other amenity or any service excluded by general or special order of appropriate Government;

(ii) any contribution paid by the employer to any Pension Funds or Provident Fund or under any scheme of social insurance;

(iii) any travelling allowance or the value of any travelling concession;

(iv) any sum paid to the person employed to defray special expenses entailed on him by the nature of his employment; or

(v) any gratuity payable on discharge. [Minimum Wages Act (11 of 1948), S. 2(h)]

"WAGES" means all remuneration paid or payable, in cash to an employee, if the terms of the contract of employment, express or implied, were fulfilled and includes any payment to an employee in respect of any period of authorised leave, lock-out, strike which is not illegal or lay-off and other additional remuneration, if any, paid at intervals not exceeding two months, but does not include—

(a) any contribution paid by the employer to any pension fund or provident fund, or under this Act;

(b) any travelling allowance or the value of any travelling concession;

(c) any sum paid to the person employed to defray special expenses entailed on him by the nature of his employment; or

(d) any gratuity payable on discharge. [Employees State Insurance Act (34 of 1948), S. 2(22)]

"WAGES" includes emoluments. [Merchant Shipping Act (44 of 1958), S. 3(57)]

"WAGES" means all remuneration paid or payable cash to a woman, if the terms of the contract of employment, express or implied, were fulfilled and includes—

(1) such cash allowances (including dearness allowance and house rent allowance) as a woman is for the time being entitled to;

(2) incentive bonus; and

(3) the money value of the concessional supply of food grains and other articles, but does not include—

(i) any bonus other than incentive bonus;

(ii) over-time earnings and any deduction or payment made on account of fines;

(iii) any contribution paid or payable by the employer to any pension fund or provident fund or for the benefit of the woman under any law for the time being in force; and

(iv) any gratuity payable on the termination of service. [Maternity Benefit Act (53 of 1961), S. 3(n)]

"WAGES" means the basic wages for the time being payable to a seaman under the agreement with the crew and includes—

(i) any remuneration to which he is entitled in respect of holidays or any leave period;

(ii) any increase of such wages in accordance with such agreement or any other agreement between the parties : but does not include the overtime allowance. [Seamen's Provident Fund Act (4 of 1966), S. 2(n)]

"WAGES" means all emoluments which are earned by an employee while on duty or on leave in accordance with the terms and conditions of his employment and which are paid or are payable to him in cash and includes dearness allowance but does not include any bonus commission, house rent allowance, overtime wages and any other allowance. [Payment of Gratuity (39 of 1972), S. 2(s)]

"WAGES" means all emoluments which are payable to a worker in accordance with the terms of the contract of employment in cash, but does not include—

(i) the cash value of any food concession;

(ii) any dearness allowance (that is to say, all cash payments whatever name called, paid to a worker on account of a rise in the cost of living or on account of his being required to work in a place other than the place where he is normally residing), house rent allowance, overtime allowance, bonus commission or any other similar allowance payable to the worker in respect of his employment or of work done in such employment;

(iii) any contribution paid or payable by the employer to any pension fund or provident fund or for the benefit of the worker under any law for the time being in force;

(iv) any gratuity payable on the termination of his contract. [Cine-Workers & Cinema Theatre Workers (Regulation of Employment) Act (50 of 1981), S. 2(k)]

Bonus does not come under the definition of 'wages' as the bonus is not remuneration paid or payable in cash to an employee in terms of the contract of employment, expressed or implied and also additional remuneration paid at intervals not exceeding two months. *Regional Director, E.S.I. Corporation* v. *Bata Shoe Co. (P) Ltd.,* AIR 1986 SC 237, 240. [Employees' State Insurance Act (34 of 1948), S. 2(22)]

Broadly speaking wages have been classified into three categories viz., (1) the living wage, (2) the fair wage and (3) the minimum wage. The concept of all the three items are discussed in detail. *Express Newspaper Ltd.* v. *Union of India,* AIR 1958 SC 578, 600. [Industrial Disputes Act, (14 of 1947), S. 2(rr)]

The night shift allowance does not automatically form part of the wages of a workman. It is not such an allowance which flows to him as his entitlement, not restricted to his service. *Bharat Electronics Ltd, Bangalore* v. *Industrial Tribunal, Karnataka,* AIR 1990 SC 1080, 1086.

The lay-off compensation paid to an employee under S. 25-C(1). Industrial Disputes Act is not wages as defined in the Employees' State Insurance Act (34 of 1948). *Nutan Mills* v. *Employees State Insurance Corporation*, AIR 1956 Bom 336, 340. [Industrial Disputes Act (14 of 1947), S. 25-C(1)] Payment for unavailed portion of privilege and casual leave will be wages. When the management improperly stopped working and during this period, the workmen were prepared to work, the payment for this period would also be wages. *Lakshmi Devi Sugar Mills Ltd.* v. *Labour Appellate Tribunal,* AIR 1956 All. 401, 402. [Industrial Disputes (Appellate Tribunal) Act, 1950, Ss. 2(f) and 7(1)(b)(1)]

The word 'wages' does not include house rent allowance or the value of any house accommodation supplied by the employer to the employee. *Divisional Engineer G.I.P. Railway* v. *Mahadeo Raghoo,* AIR 1955 SC 295. [Payment of Wages Act (4 of 1936), S. 2(vi)]

Wages means remuneration, which an employer is liable to pay, if the terms of the contract of employment are fulfilled. As the amount of maternity benefit is payable even if the terms of employment are not fulfilled, it cannot be said to be wages within the meaning of this term given in the Payment of Wages Act. *Ganpatlal Mulchandji Joshi* v. *First Civil Judge, Class I*, AIR 1958 Bom 262, 264.

The definition of "wages" does not confine that expression to contractual wages. 'Minimum wages' are also wages under the Payment of Wages Act. *Balram Abaji Patil* v. *M.C. Rajojiwalia*, AIR 1961 Bom 59, 60, 61.

The expression 'wages' includes remuneration and loans payable under the awards and also some categories of gratuity. *Purshotham* v. *V.B. Potdar,* AIR 1966 SC 856, 859. [Payment of Wages Act (4 of 1936), S. 2(vi)(d) (Maharashtra Amendment)]

The attendance bonus payable to the employees under the terms of the settlement which has become a part of the contract of employment will fall within the first part of the definition of 'wages' under Section 2(22). *Wellman (India) Pvt. Ltd.* v. *E.S.I.C.*, AIR 1994 SC 1037, 1041. [Employees' State Insurance Act (34 of 1948), S. 2(22)]

Waging war. The expression 'waging war' can only mean waging war in the manner usual in war. *Nazirkhan* v. *State of Delhi*, (2003) 8 SCC 461, para 34.

Wagon. An open railway truck or closed railway van. [Explosives Act (4 of 1884) Substituted by Act 32 of 1978, S. 4(4)].

Wagon and other undertaking. Means the undertaking which is engaged in the manufacture of railway wagons and other goods. [Britannia Engineering Company Limited (Mokameh Unit) and The Arthur Butler and Company Muzaffarpore) Limited (Acquisition and Transfer of Undertaking) Act (41 of 1978), S. 2(j)]

WAIS. (*abbr.*) Wide Area Information Servers. Developed in the early 1990s WAIS was the first truly large scale system to allow the indexing of huge quantities of information on the *Web*, and to make those indices searchable across *networks* such as the *Internet.* WAIS was also pioneering in its use of ranked (scored) results where the software tries to determine how relevant each result it. (*Matisse Enzer Glossary of Internet Terms*)

A commercial software package that allows the indexing of huge quantities of information, and then making those indices searchable across networks such as the Internet. A prominent feature of WAIS is that the search results are ranked (scored) according to how relevant the hits are, and that subsequent searches can find more stuff like that last batch and thus refine the search process. (*Internet and E-Commerce*)

Wait. To defer action until some event has taken place; to continue in expectation of; to continue stationary or quiescent in expectation of. [Sale of Goods Act (3 of 1930), S. 60].

Waiting list. A 'waiting list' prepared in service matters by the competent authority is a list of eligible and qualified candidates who in order of merit are placed below the last selected candidate. A waiting list prepared in an examination conducted by the Gujarat Public Service Commission does not furnish a source of recruitment. It is operative only for the contingency that, if any of the selected candidate does not join, then the person from the waiting list may be pushed up and appointed in the vacancy so caused or if there is some extreme exigency the Government may as a matter of policy decision pick up persons in order of merit from the waiting list. *Gujarat State Deputy Executive Engineers Association* v. *State of Gujarat* (1994) Supp 2 SCC 591. *See also Shankarsan Dash* v. *Union of India,* (1991) 3 SCC 47 : (2003) 6 Supreme 196 : AIR 1994 SC 1804.

Waiting period. A time period which must expire before some legal right or remedy can be enjoyed or enforced.

Waive. To relinquish either by express declaration or by some intentional act which by law is equivalent to this. [CPC (5 of 1908), S. 86(2)(d)].

Waiver. Declining to take advantage of irregularities in proceedings.

The intentional or voluntary relinquishment of a known right; the act or an action of waiving. [T.P. Act (4 of 1882), S. 35].

A waiver is the renunciation or abandonment of a right, whereby right is lost or extinguished and may be either express or implied.

A waiver is an intentional relinquishment of a known right, or such conduct as warrants an inference of the relinquishment of such right. No one can acquiesce in a wrong, while ignorant that it has been committed and that the effect of his action will be to confirm it.

To constitute 'waiver' there must be an intentional relinquishment of a known right or the voluntary relinquishment or abandonment of a known existing legal right, or conduct such as warrants an inference of the relinquishment of a known right or privilege. Waiver differs from estoppel in the sense that it is contractual and is an agreement to release or not to assert a right. *Basheshar Nath* v. *C.I.T.,* (1959) 35 ITR 190, 234 (SC).

A waiver is an intentional relinquishment of a known right. There can be no waiver unless the person against whom the waiver is claimed had full knowledge of his rights and of facts enabling him to take effectual action for the enforcement of such rights. *Associated Hotels of India Ltd.* v. *S.B. Sardar Ranjit Singh,* AIR 1968 SC 933, 937. [T.P. Act (4 of 1882), S. 113]

Waiver is an intentional relinquishment of a know right, and that therefore, unless there is clear intention to relinquish a right that is fully known to a party, a party cannot be said to waive it. [*All India Power Engineer Federation* v. *Sasan Power Limited,* (2012) 1 SCC 487, para 21].

Waiver is an agreement to release or not to assert a right. *Satyanarayana* v. *Yelloji Rao,* AIR 1965 SC 1405, 1410.

"Waiver" and **"public interest".** Waiver will not be given effect to if it is contrary to public interest. [*All India Power Engineer Federation* v. *Sasan Power Limited,* (2012) 1 SCC 487, para 21].

Waiver of immunity. The act of giving up the right against self-incrimination and proceeding to testify.

Waiver of privilege. The absolute privilege accorded to statements or proceedings which may be waived to permit evidence to be adduced in an action for defamation.

Waiver of tort. "A person upon whom a tort has been committed and who brings an action for the benefits received by the tortfeasor is sometimes said to 'WAIVE THE TORT'." [Restatement of Restitution, S. 525 (1937)].

Wakalat-nama. Credentials; letter of authority; power of attorney. A letter appointing a *vakil* or representative; a power of attorney. (*Will. Gloss.*)

Wakf. "Trusts. There is a vast difference between Muslim wakfs and trusts created by Muslims. The basic difference is that wakf properties are dedicated to God and the "wakif" or dedicator does not retain any title over the wakf properties. As far as trusts are concerned, the properties are not vested in God. Some of the objects of such trusts are for running charitable organisations such as hospitals, shelter homes, orphanages and charitable dispensaries, which acts, though recognized as pious, do not divest the author of the trust from the title of the properties in the trust, unless he relinquishes such title in favour of the trust or the trustees, at times, the dividing line between public trusts and wakf may be thin, but the main factor always is that while wakf properties vest in God Almighty, the trust properties do not vest in God and the trustees in terms of deed of trust are entitled to deal with the same for the benefit of the trust and its beneficiaries. [*Maharashtra State Board of Wakfs v. Yusuf Bhai Chawla*, (2012) 6 SCC 328, para 28].

WAKF" means the permanent dedication by a person professing Islam, of any movable or immovable property for any purpose recognised by the Muslim law as pious, religious or charitable and includes—

(i) "a *Wakf* by user but such *wakf* shall not cease to be a *wakf* by reason only of the user having ceased irrespective of the period of such cesser;

(ii) "grants" including *mashart-ul-khidmat* for any purpose recognised by the Muslim law as pious, religious or charitable; and

(iii) a *wakf-alal-aulad* to the extent to which the property is dedicated for any purpose recognised by Muslim law as pious, religious or charitable, and "*waki*" means any person making such dedication. [Wakf Act (43 of 1995), S. 3(r)]

The word '*wakf*' is borrowed from Mahomedan Law and implies permanent dedication of property for religious or charitable purposes. When property is declared wakf, the original owner is divested of it and it vests in Almighty God.

It is not necessary for the creation of a valid *wakf* that the word *wakf* should be used in the document.

"WAQF" means the permanent dedication by any person, of any movable or immovable property for any purpose recognised by the Muslim law as pious, religious or charitable and includes—

(i) a waqf by user but such waqf shall not cease to be a waqf by reason only of the user having ceased irrespective of the period of such cesser;

(ii) a Shamlat Patti, ShamlatDeh, JumlaMalkkan or by any other name entered in a revenue record;

(iii) "grants", including mashrat-ul-khidmat for any purpose recognised by the Muslim law as pious, religious or charitable; and

(iv) a waqf-alal-aulad to the extent to which the property is dedicated for any purpose recognised by Muslim law as pious, religious or charitable, provided when the line of succession fails, the income of the waqf shall be spent for education, development, welfare and such other purposes as recognised by Muslim law,

and "waqif" means any person making such dedication. [S. 3(r) of the Wakf Act, 1995 (43 of 1995) as substituted by the Wakf (Amendment) Act, 2013 (27 of 2013)]

Wakf-alal-aulad. A wakf-alal-aulad is a gift of property to God, almighty for certain purposes. *Mohd. Ismail* v. *Sabir Ali,* AIR 1962 SC 1722, 1727.

Wakf deed. "WAKF DEED" means any deed or instrument by which a *wakf* has been created and includes any valid subsequent deed or instrument by which any of the terms of the original dedication have been varied. [Wakf Act (43 of 1995), S. 3(s)]

Wakf Nama. A written deed of endowment. *Wakf* deed.

Wakif. "WAKIF" means any person making such dedication (wakf). [Wakf Act (43 of 1995), S. 3(r)]

Walkout. Strike; the action of leaving a meeting or organization as an expression of disapproval.

WAN. (*abbr.*) Wide Area Network. Any *internet* or *network* that covers an area larger than a single building or campus. (*Matisse Enzer Glossary of Internet Terms*)

Want. Poverty; penury; destitution.

Deficiency, shortage or lack (of something desirable or necessary); absence [Indian Evidence Act (1 of 1872), S. 92, prov. (1)]; to desire [CrPC, 1973 (2 of 1974), S. 92(1)]; need or requirement.

WANT, NEED, LACK. He who wants nothing is a happy man; he who needs nothing may be happy if he wants no more than he has, for then he lacks that which alone can make him happy, which is contentment.

Want of due execution. Deficiency in the due performance of all formalities, as signing, sealing etc. necessary to give validity to a legal instrument. [Indian Evidence Act (1 of 1872), S. 92, *Prov.* (1)].

Want of jurisdiction and **excess of jurisdiction.** There is a distinction between "want of jurisdiction" and "excess of jurisdiction" where the officer has no jurisdiction at all his act would be *ultra vires* but where, on an investigation of the circumstances which would give him jurisdiction, an officer decides or acts in a particular manner, any mistake as to the facts of the deciding factor would not oust his jurisdiction. *Chintamani* v. *Paika Samal*, AIR 1958 Ori 136, 138.

Wanton. Uncalled for or reckless conduct in utter disregard of the rights of other persons.

Wanton misconduct. An act, or a failure to act when there is a duty to do so, in reckless disregard of the rights of another, coupled with the knowledge that injury will probable result.

Wanton negligence. A conscious voluntary act or omission in reckless disregard of a legal duty and of the consequences to another party, who may typically recover exemplary damages.

Wantonly. The expression "wantonly" means recklessness with regard to the consequences of a particular act done. *State of Orissa* v. *R.C. Chowla*, AIR 1966 Ori 192, 194. [IPC (45 of 1860), S. 153] Light heartedly; recklessly; lewdly. [IPC (45 of 1860), S. 153].

Wantonness. Conduct which indicates that the actor is aware of the risks but indifferent to the results.

WAP. "WAP" or "Wireless Application Protocol" means an open protocol for wireless multimedia messaging. [Mobile Banking (Quality of Service) Regulations, 2012, Regn. 2(r)].

Waqf. "Waqf" means the permanent dedication by any person, of any movable or immovable property for any purpose recognized by the Muslim law as pious, religious or charitable and includes—

(i) a waqf by user but such waqf shall not cease to be a waqf by reason only of the user having ceased irrespective of the period of such cesser;

(ii) a Shamlat Patti, Shamlat Deh, Jumla Malkkan or by any other name entered in a revenue record;

(iii) "grants", including mashrat-ul-khidmat for any purpose recognized by the Muslim Law as pious, religious or charitable; and

(iv) a waqf-alal-aulad to the extent to which the property is dedicated for any purpose recognised by Muslim law as pious, religious or charitable, provided when the line of succession fails, the income of the waqf shall be spent for education, development, welfare and such other purposes as recognised by Muslim law. [Waqf Act (43 of 1995), S. 3(r) as substituted by Amending Act (27 of 2013)].

War crime. Conduct which violates international laws governing war, *eg;* killing of hostages, abuse of civilians in occupied territories, abuse of prisoners of war, and devastation not justified by military necessity.

War dialer. A cracking tool, a program that calls a given list or range of numbers and records those that answer with handshake tones (and so might be entry points to computer or telecommunications systems). (*Cyber Law*)

War period. Means the period commencing on the 3rd day of September, 1939, and ending on the 31st day of March 1946. [Indian Matrimonial Causes (War Marriages) Act (40 of 1948), S. 2(c)]

Ward. "WARD" means a minor for whose person or property, or both, there is a guardian. [Guardians and Wards Act (8 of 1890), S. 4(3)]

A person, who by reason of minority; lunacy or other incapacity is under the protection or control of a guardian [Guardians and Wards Act (8 of 1890), S. 4(3)]; a room with several beds in a hospital etc.; a body of guards.

A person under the care of a guardian; a division of a city—so called because under the care of an alderman.

"WARD" is wide enough to include every minor who has a guardian.

Ward of Court. A minor under the care of a guardian, appointed by the parents or the Court, who exercises rights and duties over the child subject to the general control and discretion of the Court.

Warehouse. Means a public warehouse licensed under section 57 or a private warehouse licensed under section 58 or a special warehouse licensed under section 58A. [Customs Act (52 of 1962), S. 2(43)].

A warehouse is, properly speaking, a building used for the purpose of storing goods.

Warehouse keeper. Warehouse man; a man employed in or having the charge of a warehouse. [IPC (45 of 1860), S. 407].

Warehouse-keeper's certificate. Warehouse receipt; a document of title to goods lying in a warehouse signed or certified on behalf of the warehouse-keeper. [Sale of Goods Act (3 of 1930), S. 2(4)].

Warehouse to warehouse. The expression "warehouse to warehouse" in a policy indicates the period during which the policy would remain in force and has nothing to do about the type of the risk policy covered. *Bihar Supply Syndicate* v. *Asiatic Navigation,* AIR 1993 SC 2054, 2060. [Marine Insurance Act (11 of 1963), S. 3]

Warehoused goods. Means goods deposited in a warehouse. [Customs Act (52 of 1962), S. 2(44)]

Warn. To give cautionary notice or advice with regard to action or conduct.

Warning. A previous intimation or threat of impending evil or danger; an advice to beware of a person or thing. [Indian Evidence Act (1 of 1872), S. 8, ill. (h)].

Warning of caveat. A notice given to a person who has entered a caveat warning him to appear and state what his interest is.

Warrant. An order issued by some authority, empowering an officer to make an arrest, seizure or search or to execute a judicial sentence [IPC (45 of 1860), S. 6, ill. (b)]; to furnish good and sufficient ground for [CrPC, 1973 (2 of 1974), S. 245(1)]; authorised or attested [Indian Contract Act (9 of 1872), S. 18(1)]; to give a warranty [T.P. Act (4 of 1882), S. 133]; an official certificate inferior to a commission. [Army Act (46 of 1950), S. 109 and Constitution of India, Art. 124(2)].

A precept under hand and seal to some officer, to take up any offender or seize property to be dealt with according to due course of law.

A warrant is a written authority for doing an act.

In matters of trade or business such documents as dock warrants or dividend warrants are authorities or vouchers for delivery of the goods or for payment of the money named therein; and Treasury Warrants are used as the equivalent of cheques drawn on behalf of the National Government.

In law the term "warrant" is most frequently used to express the written authority of a judicial functionary directing or empowering the person named in it to do an act which without such authority would be an actionable wrong, *e.g.*, to make an arrest, or enter on the land of another or take possession of his goods.

Warrant case. "WARRANT CASE" means a case relating to an offence punishable with death, imprisonment for life or imprisonment for a term exceeding two years. [CrPC, 1973 (2 of 1974), S. 2(x)] [Now (w. e. f. 1-7-2024) repealed & replaced by Bharatiya Nagarik Suraksha Sanhita, 2023 (46 of 2023), S. 2(1)(z), same definition in new Sanhita]

Warrant of arrest. An order issued by some authority empowering an officer, ordinarily a police officer, for restraining the liberty of a man's person that is to take a man into custody. [CrPC, 1973 (2 of 1974), S. 70(1)].

Warrant of committal. A written order by a magistrate or Court sending a person for his trial by a competent Court. [CrPC, 1973 (2 of 1974), S. 298(b)].

Warrant-officer. "WARRANT OFFICER" means a person appointed, gazetted or in pay as a warrant officer of the Air Force and includes an acting warrant officer, a master warrant officer, and a warrant officer of any Air Force, Reserve or the Auxiliary Air Force who is for the first time being subject to this Act. [Air Force Act (45 of 1950), S. 4(xxix)]

Warrant the genuineness. To give a warranty regarding genuineness. [T.P. Act (4 of 1882), S. 121].

Warrantless arrest. An arrest, without a warrant, which is based on probable cause of a felony, or for a misdemeanor committed in the presence of a police officer.

Warranty. A promise that a proposition of fact is true; a covenant annexed to a conveyance of real estate, by which the vendor warrants the security of the title conveyed. [T.P. Act (4 of 1882), S. 133].

WARRANTY—EXPRESS AND IMPLIED. A warranty is a statement or representation made by the seller of goods, contemporaneously with and as a part of the contract of sale, although collateral to the express object of it, having reference to the character, quality, or title of the goods, and by which he promises or undertakes to insure that certain facts are or shall be as he then represents them. A warranty is express when the seller makes an affirmation with respect to the article to be sold pending the treaty of sale, upon which it is intended that the buyer shall rely in making the purchase. A warranty is implied when the law derives it by implication or inference from the nature of the transaction, or the relative situation or circumstances of the parties. A warranty is not one of the essential elements of a sale, but is a collateral undertaking.

Warranty deed. A deed which expressly guarantees the grantor's good, clear title and which contains covenants concerning the quality of title, including warranties of seisin, quiet enjoyment, right to convey, freedom from encumbrances, and defence of title against all claims.

Wash sale. The simultaneous selling and buying of the same asset, specially stock, by the same person so as to create the impression of market activity.

Washing. Means such process or combination of processes as may be approved in this behalf by the Central Government by which the whole or any part of the shaley and mineral matter found in the coal is removed therefrom. [Coal Mines (Conservation & Development) Act (28 of 1974), S. 3(k)]

Waste. Useless expenditure or consumption; squandering (of money, time etc.) [T.P. Act (4 of 1882), S. 66]; to expend uselessly [CPC (5 of 1908), O. XXXIX, R. 1(a)]; devastation; superfluous; left over.

Waste and arable lands. Waste land does not mean barren land. Arable land means cultivated or capable of being cultivated. *Baldeo Singh* v. *State of U.P.*, MLJ : QD (1961-1965) Vol IV C90 : AIR 1965 All 433 [Land Acquisition Act (1 of 1894), S. 17]

Waste land. Waste land means lands which are desolate, abandoned, and not fit ordinarily for use for building purposes. Waste land means barren or desolate lands which are unfit for any use or which are worthless. *State of Gujarat* v. *Gujarat Revenue Tribunal*, AIR 1980 SC 91.

The expression "waste land" means land which was neither developed, nor used as arable land, but land which was undeveloped and unproductive and which in any event could not be made productive unless it was developed. *Bejay Laxmi Cotton Mills Ltd.* v. *State of West Bengal*, AIR 1960 Cal 113, 118.

Waste land and Arable land. Arable land means land mainly used for ploughing and for raising crops. Waste land means land which is unfit for cultivation or habitation, desolate and barren land with little or no vegetation thereon. *Raja Anand* v. *State of U.P.*, AIR 1967 SC 1081, 1085.

Wasting. Undergoing gradual loss, diminution or decay. [Indian Trusts Act (2 of 1882), S. 16].

Wasting asset. Natural resource which is subject to *depletion* through the process of extraction or use *e.g.* mines, quarries.

Wasting property. A right to or an interest in something which is consumed in its normal use, like wasting asset, a leasehold interest, or a patent right.

Wasting trust. A trust in which the corpus is gradually depleted by periodic payment to the beneficiary.

Watan property. Unless there be something repugnant in the subject or context,— "WATAN PROPERTY" means the moveable or immoveable property held, acquired or assigned for providing remuneration for the performance of the duty appertaining to an hereditary office; it includes a right to levy customary fees or perquisites, in money or in kind, whether at fixed times or otherwise; it includes cash payments in addition to the original watan property made voluntarily by Government and subject periodically to modification or withdrawal. [Bom Act III of 1874 (Hereditary Offices), S. 4]

Watch. To stand sentry, or attend as a guard, etc. (*Tomlin*)

To be on the alert or guard against [Aligarh Muslim University Act (40 of 1920), Sch., item 6(5)(e)]; act or state of remaining on the alert or of observing vigilantly; surveillance.

Water dispute. Means any dispute or difference between two or more State Governments with respect to—

(i) the use, distribution or control of the water of, or in, any inter-State river or river valley; or

(ii) the interpretation of the terms of any agreement relating to the use, distribution or control of such waters or the implementation of such agreement; or

(iii) the levy of any water rate in contravention of the prohibition contained in Section 7. [Inter-State River Water Disputes Act (33 of 1956), S. 2(c)]

Water-mark. Faint translucent design in paper serving as trade mark, etc.

WATER-MARK means when referred to as a boundary, the mark to which water ordinarily ascends or descends (as) high water-mark; low water-mark.

Water-ordeal. (*In Old English Law*) The ordeal or trial by water, which was plunging the bare arm up to the elbow in boiling water, or by casting the person suspected into a river or pond of cold water.

Water pollution. Industrial and institutional waste, and other harmful or objectionable material in sufficient quantities to result in a measurable degradation of the water quality.

Water right. The right to use water from a natural stream or from an artificial canal for irrigation, power, domestic use and the like.

Water-seal latrine. "WATER-SEAL LATRINE" means a pour-flush latrine, water flush latrine or a sanitary latrine with a minimum water seal of 20 millimeters diameter in which human excereta is pushed in or flushed by water. [Employment of Manual Scavengers and Construction of Dry Latrines (Prohibition) Act (46 of 1993), S. 2(n)]

Water supply and sanitary fittings. The expression "water supply and sanitary fittings" means such pipes or materials as are meant for use for supply of water to or in lavatories, urinals or bathrooms of private houses or public buildings and they do not include heavy pipes which are laid underground as mains for carrying water supply from one area or place to another. *Deputy Commissioner of Sales Tax* v. *G.S. Pai & Co.,* AIR 1980 SC 611, 613.

Water-tank. Tank is not a vacant land within the meaning of S. 2(q) of the Act. *Srila Moitra* v. *State of West Bengal*, AIR 1981 Cal 126, 129. [Urban Land (Ceiling and Regulation Act (33 of 1976), S. 2(q) and Cl. (1)]

Water-trough. A vessel for watering or feeding animals. [Prevention of Cruelty to Animals Act (59 of 1960), S. 9(d)].

Water-works. "WATER WORKS" includes all lakes, tanks, streams, cisterns, springs, pumps, wells, reservoirs, aqueducts, water trucks, sluices, main pipes, culverts hydrants, stand pipes, and conduits and all machinery, lands, buildings, bridges and things, used for, or intended for the purpose of, supplying water to a cantonment. [Cantonments Act (2 of 1924), S. 2(xxxix)]

Water year. Unless the context otherwise requires, "WATER YEAR" means the year commencing with the first of June of a calendar year and ending with the thirty-first of May of the next calendar year. [Karnataka Cauvery Basin Irrigation Protection Ordinance, 1991, S. 2(d) **as cited in** *State of Karnataka* v. *State of T.N.,* (2018) 4 SCC 1 para 37

Watercourse. "WATERCOURSE" means any channel which is supplied with water from a canal, but which is not maintained at the cost of Government, and all subsidiary works belonging to any such channel. [CP Act VIII of 1873 (Northern India Canal and Drain), S. 3(2)]

"WATERCOURSE" includes any river, stream or channel whether natural or artificial. [New Delhi Municipal Council Act (44 of 1994), S. 2(56)]

A stream of water usually flowing in a defined channel, and discharging itself into some other stream or other body of water.

Way. Passage, street or road [Indian Electricity Act (9 of 1910), S. 2(m)]; manner or method. [Indian Partnership Act (9 of 1932), S. 19(1)].

Waybill. Document, normally drawn up by the carrier of goods, describing the goods, naming the sender and addressee, and the conditions of carriage.

Ways and means. Parliamentary expression relating to the provision of revenue to meet national expenditure.

Weaker sections of society. The expression "weaker section of society" includes also citizens of 'backward classes' who are covered by notification issued in pursuance to Arts. 15 (4) and 16 (4) of the Constitution. *Laxmi Narayan* v. *Madan Mohan*, AIR 1988 MP 142, 144. [Constitution of India, Arts. 15(4) & 16(4), Govt. notification No. F. 8-5-25-4-84, dt. 26-12-84]

A 'means test' that is, income of the family of a person, can be adopted for identifying the person as belonging to the weaker sections of the society and the income of a such person can be varied by State Government, taking into consideration the fall of the value of the rupee, general improvement in the income of people and other relevant factors. *Shantistar Builders* v. *Narayan Khinalal Totame,* AIR 1990 SC 630, 635. [Constitution of India, Arts. 46, 136]

Weaker sections of the people. The expression "weaker sections of the people" used in Article 46, however, is not confined to the "backward class" in Article 16(4) but also includes other backward classes as well, whether they are socially and educationally backward or not and whether they are adequately represented in the services or not. The expression "weaker sections" can also take within its compass, individuals who constitute weaker sections or weaker parts of the society. *Indra Sawhney* v. *Union of India,* AIR 1993 SC 477 [Constitution of India, Arts. 46 and 16(4)]

Wealth maximization. An economic situation in which a change in the allocation of resources benefits the winner.

Wealth-tax. For the purposes of this sub-clause, "WEALTH-TAX" means wealth-tax chargeable under the Wealth-tax Act, 1957 (27 of 1957), or any tax of a similar character chargeable under any law in force in any country outside India or any tax chargeable under such law with reference to the value of the assets of, or the capital employed in, a business or profession carried on by the assessee, whether or not the debts of the business or profession are allowed as a deduction in computing the amount with reference to which such tax is charged, but does not include any tax chargeable with reference to the value of any particular asset of the business or profession. [Income-tax Act (43 of 1961), S. 40(a)(iia) (*Expln*)]

Weapon. "WEAPON" includes ammunition, bows and arrows, explosives, firearms, hooks, knives, nets, poison, snares and traps and any instrument or apparatus capable of anaesthetizing, decoying, destroying, injuring or killing an animal. [Wild Life (Protection) Act (53 of 1972), S. 2(35)]

Weapon is an instrument of offensive or defensive combat.

An instrument of any kind used in warfare or combat to attack or defend. [CrPC, 1973 (2 of 1974), S. 174(1)]; [Arms Act (54 of 1959), S. 2(1)(c)].

Weapon of offence. Any offensive weapon or any article which is made, adapted, or intended for incapacitating someone, *e.g.* a rope to tie someone with or pepper to make him sneeze.

Weapons of mass destruction. "WEAPONS OF MASS DESTRUCTION" means any biological, chemical or nuclear weapons. [Weapons of mass Destruction and Their Delivery Systems (Prohibition of Unlawful Activities Act (21 of 2005), S. 4(p)]

Wear and Tear. Means deterioration or loss in value occasioned by usual use of the machinery.

Wearing or damaging due to ordinary usage; deterioration in the condition of a thing through constant use or service [T.P. Act (4 of 1882), S. 108(m)]; [Requisitioning and Acquisition of Immovable Property Act (30 of 1952), S. 6(1)].

Wearing apparel. Dress or personal clothing intended for wearing must be deemed to be wearing apparel. *Hiralal Choudhary* v. *Hariram Khetan*, AIR 1974 Pat 39. [CPC (5 of 1908), Sec. 60]

Articles of clothing collectively. [CrPC, 1973 (2 of 1974), S. 51(1)]; [Income-tax Act (43 of 1961), S. 2(14)(ii)].

Weather. The condition of the atmosphere (at a given place and time) with respect to heat or cold; presence or absence of rain, etc. [CrPC, 1973 (2 of 1974), S. 174(3)].

Web-based Telnet. Invoke a telnet session directly from your web browser. There's no need for any other applications or software. (*Cyber Law*)

Web browser. A software used to locate and display web pages from the internet. (*Information Technology*)

Web bugs. Technology designed to track Web users' browsing habits and product interests. (*Cyber Law*)

Web hosting. Administration of a client's website. (*Cyber Law*)

Web-hosting services. Third-party companies who offer complete e-commerce services including design and implementation of an e-commerce site. (*Cyber Law*)

Web page. A document designed for viewing in a *web browser*. Typically written in *HTML*. A *web site* is made of one or more web pages. (*Matisse Enzer Glossary of Internet Terms*)

Web portal. A portal or gateway for the World Wide Web that serves as an information search organizer. Portals provide single point integration and navigation through the Web. Portals creating an information community that can be customized for an individual or a corporation. (*Cyber Law*)

Web server. A type of server configured to store HTML, pages for access over the Internet. (*Cyber Law*)

Webcast. The making available, to one or more persons simultaneously, of information such as moving pictures and sound transmitted via the Internet. (*Cyber Law*)

Broadcasting from a website by means of streaming audio or video. (*Cyber Law*)

Webcasting. This is the internet trying to be older like TV or radio. Instead of viewing pages, you view a stream of data in the form of radio or video. Unfortunately, the infrastructure is lacking to make this a popular alternative to TV and radio. (*Cyber Law*)

Website. The individual electronic location making the material available to accessors through the World Wide Web. (*Copyright*)

"WEBSITE" means a location connected to the internet that maintains one or more web pages. [Limited Liability Partnership Rules, 2009, R. 2(xvi)]

The entire collection of *web pages* and other information (such as images, sound, and video files, *etc.*) that are made available through what appears to users as a single web server. Typically all the pages in a web site share the same basic *URL*, for example the following URLs are all for pages within the same web site:

http://www.baytherapy.com/

http://www.baytherapy.com/whatis/

http://www.baytherapy.com/teenagers/

The term has a somewhat informal nature since a large organization might have separate "web sites" for each division, but someone might talk informally about the organizations' "web site" when speaking of all of them. (*Matisse Enzer Glossary of Internet Terms*)

"WEBSITE" is a set of related web pages served from a single web domain. A website is hosted on a least one web server, accessible via a network such as the Internet or a private local area network through an Internet address known as a uniform resource locator. The word "website" includes a web portal and/or a mobile site for the purpose of these regulation. [Insurance Regulatory and Development Authority of India (Insurance Web Aggregators) Regulations, 2017, Regn. 2(p)].

Website Defacement. Website defacement is usually carried out by the substitution of the home page of a site by a system cracker that breaks into a web server and alters the hosted website creating one of its own. The hacker usually replaces the site matter with his own message or completely destroys the site's content. Aparna Viswanathan, *Cyber Law: Indian &*

International Perspectives, 2012, LexisNexis Butterworths at p. 16.

Wednesbury Principle. The principle that statutory discretion can not be exercised in a manner which can be held to be unlawful. The Principle is attracted where it is shown that an authority exercising the discretion has taken a decision which is devoid of plausible justification and any authority having reasonable persons could not have taken the said decision. (*Administrative law*) *Delhi Science Forum* v. *UOI*, (1996) 2 SCC 405, paras 10 & 11.

Wednesbury principles. To judge the validity of any administrative order or statutory discretion, normally the Wendnesbury test is to be applied to find out if the decision was illegal or suffered from procedural improprieties or was one which no sensible decision maker could, on the material before him and within the framework of the law, have arrived at. The Court would consider:

1. whether relevant matters had not been taken into account; or
2. whether irrelevant matters had been taken into account or whether the action was not *bona fide*;
3. whether the decision was absurd or perverse.
4. court would not however go into the correctness of the choice made by the administrator amongst the various alternatives open him.
5. the Court would not substitute its decision to that of the administrator. This is the 'Wednesbury test'. *Union of India* v. *G. Ganayutham (dead) by LRs.* AIR (1977) SC 3387.

Wednesbury unreasonableness. From the doctrine of wednesbury unreasonableness, the Court is leaning towards the doctrine of proportionality. The constitutional requirement for judging the question of reasonableness and fairness on the part of the statutory authority must be considered having regard to the factual matrix obtaining in each case. [*M.P. Gangadharam* v. *State of Kerala,* (2006) 6 SCC 162, 174, para 34]

Wednesbury unreasonableness (*Doctrine*). The action of state in not renewing the tenure of the Public Prosecutor or the District Counsel, can be subjected to judicial scrutiny *inter alia* on the ground that the same is arbitrary. The jurisdiction of the Court in a case of this nature would be to invoke the doctrine of 'Wednesbury unreasonableness as developed in *Associated Provincial Picture Houses Ltd.* v. *Wednesbury Corpn.,* (1947) 2 All ER 680. [*State of U.P.* v. *Johri Mal,* (2004) 4 SCC 714, 735, para 40]

Week. "WEEK" means a period of seven days beginning at midnight on Saturday night or such other night as may be approved in writing for a particular area by the Chief Inspector of Factories. [Factories Act (63 of 1948), S. 2(f)]

"WEEK" means a period of seven days beginning at midnight on Saturday. [Weekly Holidays Act (18 of 1942), S. 2(f); Beedi & Cigar Workers (Conditions of Employment) Act (32 of 1966), S. 2(p)]

Seven day period reckoned generally from Saturday midnight to next Saturday midnight.

The term "week" has to be taken to signify a cycle of seven days including Sundays. *B. Shah* v. *Presiding Officer, Labour Court Coimbatore and Others*, AIR 1978 SC 12, 16. [Maternity Benefit Act (53 of 1961), Sec. 5]

Weigh. To ascertain the weight of. [IPC (45 of 1860), S. 264].

Weighing or measuring instrument. Means any object, instrument, apparatus or device, or any combination thereof, which is, or is intended to be, used, exclusively or additionally, for the purpose of making any weighment or measurement and includes any appliance, accessory or part associated with any such object, instrument, apparatus or device. [Standards of Weights and Measures Act (60 of 1976), S. 2(zc)]

Weight. "WEIGHT" means the total weight transmitted from the time being by the wheels of a vehicle to the surface on which the vehicle rests or moves. [Motor Vehicles Act (59 of 1988), S. 2(49)]

A standard of quantity determined by or employed in weighing; a standard of weight [CrPC, 1973 (2 of 1974), S. 153(1)]; the heaviness of a thing especially as determined by weighing.

Weight of the evidence. The persuasiveness of some evidence relative to other evidence.

Weir. A contrivance placed in a flume for the purpose of regulating the amount of water passing from the feeder through the flume and something used to prevent a consumer from receiving more water than the amount to which he is entitled. [Northern India Canal; Drainage Act (8 of 1873), S. 3(3)].

Welfare. Keeping good health and enjoying all good things in life.

The state or condition of doing or being well. [Children Act (60 of 1960) (*repealed*), Preamble].

Welfare state. The state in which Government undertakes various welfare programmes for its people such as insurance, old age pension, provident fund scheme, exgratia payment in calamities etc.

A welfare state denotes a concept of Government, in which the State plays a key role in the protection and promotion of the economic and social well-being of all of its citizens, which may include equitable distribution of wealth and equal opportunities and public responsibilities for all those, who are unable to avail for themselves, minimal provisions for a decent life. It refers to "greatest good of greatest number and the benefit of all and the happiness of all." [*Lala Ram v. Union of India*, (2015) 5 SCC 813, para 9].

Well-founded. Based on good or sure grounds or reasons. [Indian Evidence Act (1 of 1872), S. 149].

Well-known trade mark. "WELL-KNOWN TRADE MARK", in relation to any goods or services, means a mark which has become so to the substantial segment of the public which uses such goods or receives such services that the use of such mark in relation to other goods or services would be likely to be taken as indicating a connection in the course of trade or rendering of services between those goods or services and a person using the mark in relation to the first-mentioned goods or services. [Trade Marks Act (47 of 1999), S. 2(1)(zg)]

Welsh mortgage. A mortgage in which there is no condition or proviso for repayment at any specified time.

West Pakistan. Means the territories of Pakistan excluding the Province of East Bengal and includes the tribal areas of Tochi and Kurram and such other tribal areas adjoining the North-West Frontier Province as may be specified in this behalf by order of the Central Government. [Displaced Persons (Compensation and Rehabilitation) Act (44 of 1954), S. 2(g)]

Western Medical Science. In this Act "WESTERN MEDICAL SCIENCE" means the western methods of Allopathic medicine, Obstetrics and Surgery, but does not include the Homeopathic or Ayurvedic or Unani system of medicine. [Medical Degrees Act (7 of 1916), S. 2]

Wharf. "WHARF" includes any wall or stage and part of the land or foreshore that may be used for loading or unloading goods, or for the embarkation or disembarkation of passengers and any wall enclosing or adjoining the same. [Major Port Trust Act (38 of 1963), S. 2(za)]

Wharfage. "WHARFAGE" means the charge levied on goods for not removing them from the railway after the expiry of the free time for such removal. [Railways Act (24 of 1989), S. 2 (41)]

Money paid for landing goods; duty paid for the privilege of using a wharf.

The charge for the use of wharf. [Indian Railways Act (9 of 1890), S. 45(1)(b)]; [Payment of Wages Act (4 of 1936), S. 7(2)(n)].

Wharfage is a charge in respect of goods unloaded from wagons and kept at the station and also in respect of goods kept on platforms of the station. *Raichand* v. *Union of India,* AIR 1964 SC 1268, 1271. [Indian Railways Act (9 of 1890), S. 3(14)]

Wharfinger. An owner or manager of a wharf. [IPC (45 of 1860), S. 407].

Whatever sum he has rightfully paid. The expression "whatever sum he has rightfully paid" occurring in S. 145 of the Indian Contract Act (9 of 1872), includes not only coin, but also property of whatever kind which is parted with in lieu of money, but not the mere incurring of a pecuniary obligation to the creditor in lieu or discharge of the debt owing him.

Wheel conspiracy. A conspiracy in which several independent conspiracies are linked by a common member, who is the only party liable for all of the conspiracies.

Wheeling. Means the operation whereby the distribution system and associated facilities of a transmission licensee or distribution licensee, as the case may be, are used by another person for the conveyance of electricity on payment of charges to be determined under Section 62. [Electricity Act (36 of 2003), S. 2(76)]

When the goods should have been delivered. The date 'when the goods should have been delivered' is the date when the ship by which the goods were contracted to be carried has left the port at which delivery was to be made. *East & West Steamship Co* v. *S.K. Ramalingam*, AIR 1960 SC 1058, 1067.

When the proper officer has reasons to belief. These words suggest that the belief must be that of an honest and reasonable person based upon relevant materials and circumstances. *Asst. Collector of Customs for Prevention* v. *New Control Mills. Co. Ltd.*, AIR 1973 Cal 91, 94. [Customs Act (52 of 1962), Sec. 105]

When the right to sue accrues. The words "when the right to sue accrues" may be taken to mean when the cause of action arises.

When the suit is called for hearing. The expression "when the suit is called for hearing" refers to the date which is stated in the summons issued to the defendant for appearing in Court. *Japal Singh* v. *Municipal Corporation of Delhi*, AIR 1972 Del 230, 232. [CPC (5 of 1908), O. IX, R. 8]

Whenever it thinks fit. The word 'whenever' means at whatever time or at what time so ever. *Haridoss* v. *Provincial Govt. C.P. and Berar*, AIR 1949 Nag 201. [CPC (5 of 1908), O. XXII, R. 4 (4)]

Whenever the Appropriate Govt. so directs. It refers to the taking of possession and not to the declaration of urgency. *Jetmull Bhogaraj* v. *State of Bihar and others,* AIR 1972 SC 1363, 1366. [Land Acquisition Act (1 of 1894), Sec. 17(1)]

Where an instrument has been admitted in evidence. If a document is provisionally admitted subject to final orders that may be passed in a revision case or subject to objections that may be raised under any other enactment like the Registration Act there is no actual admission of the document. *K. Manavala Naicker* v. *K.R. Gopala Krishnaiah Chetty*, AIR 1969 AP 417 at 419. [Indian Stamp Act (2 of 1899), S. 36]

Where and in so far as a decree is varied or. In S. 144, CPC (5 of 1908), must be construed as meaning where the decree is reversed either temporarily or finally.

Where no express provision has been made in this code for the punishment of such a conspiracy. These words in S. 120-B, IPC (45 of 1860) do not mean that when there is proof of an abetment of an offence, the charge should be for such an abetment.

Whereas. A word which implies a recital of a past fact or facts.

In view of consideration of the fact that; for as much as; in as much as; introducing a statement of fact in contrast or opposition to that expressed by the principal clause. [T.P. Act (4 of 1882), Preamble].

Whereby. By which; through which; in accordance with which.

Whether defended or not. The use of words "whether defended or not" does not mean that Court can pass decree in matrimonial matters, in the absence of the defendant, and a decree passed in the absence of the defendant is still an *ex parte* decree. *Jang Bahadur* v. *Mukta,* AIR 1986 Del 422, 427. [Hindu Marriage Act (25 of 1955), S. 23]

Whether it amounts to a confession or not. The expression "*whether it amounts to a confession or not*" appears to mean no more than this that if in the course of a confession to the police acknowledging guilt for the crime, any information is given which *distinctly* relates to the discovery of a fact and that fact is actually discovered by search made in consequence of the information, that portion only of the information which resulted in such discovery may be deposed to even though the sum total of the statement made amounts to a confession which is wholly excluded by one or other of the preceding sections. (See the observations of BHAGWATI, J, since made in *Ram Kishan Mithanlal* v. *State of Bombay,* AIR 1955 SC 104, 116 : (1955) 1 SCR 903, which are to the same effect.

Which is entered into. The expression "is entered into" is at the worst ambiguous and is capable of meaning either only those entered into after the date of the notification or as meaning "is or has been entered into" i.e. including a contract which having been entered into before is subsisting on that date. *Raghubar Dayal Jai Prakash* v. *Union of India,* AIR 1962 SC 263, 273. [Forward Contracts (Regulation) Act (74 of 1952), S. 15(1)] [Now repealed by s. 132 of the Finance Act, 2015 (20 of 2015]

Which is liable to be contradicted. The words "which is liable to be contradicted" in S. 155(3), Indian Evidence Act (1 of 1872) mean "which is relevant to the issue".

Which ought to have been passed. Means "which ought in law to have been passed." *Giani Ram* v. *Ramji Lal,* AIR 1969 SC 1144 at 1147. [CPC (5 of 1908), O. XLI, R. 33]

Whip. An official of a political party whose duty is to see that the party is as fully represented as possible at parliamentary divisions; directive to this effect issued by the whip.

To strike with a lash.

Whipping. To punish with lashes. [Air Force Act (45 of 1950), S. 71(a)].

White collar crime. A crime involving no violence such as cheating, fraud, bribery, dishonesty in commercial matters.

The crime committed by a person of high socio-economic status and respectability in the course of his occupation or profession. The criminal behaviour must be directly related to the occupational activities of the person.

White flag. Flag hoisted as a sign of surrender or a flag of truce.

White paper. Command papers published by the Government for the consideration of Parliament; it contains statements of policy or explanations of proposed legislation.

White phosphorus. Means the substance commonly known as white or yellow phosphorus. [White Phosphorus Matches Prohibition Act (5 of 1913), S. 2]

Whitehorse case. A reported case with facts which is virtually identical to those of the instant case, so that the reported case should determine the outcome of the instant case.

Who cannot be found. A person may be said to have been not found when it is known who he was and, in spite of search, was not found or was found to have been dead. But he may equally be said not to have been found if his identity cannot be traced or found and who therefore on account of the absence of his identity cannot be found. *Dogar Mal* v. *Sunam Ram,* AIR (31) 1944 Lah 58, para 62 f, g, h and 63a.

Whoever. The word "Whoever" in IPC (45 of 1860), Ss. 482 and 486, does not refer only to a definite individual or definite individuals and can apply to a corporate body.

The word 'whoever' means any person who commits a contravention of S. 12 without exception and it includes any association of persons such as a partnership firm. *Rai Bahadur Seth Shreeram Durgaprasad* v. *Director of Enforcement,* AIR 1987 SC 1364, 1367. [Foreign Exchange Regulation Act (7 of 1947), Ss. 23 (1), 23(c), 12(c) (*as stood prior to Amendment Act (39 of 1957)*)]

The word "whoever" in S. 202 refers to a person other than the offender and has no application to the person who is alleged to have committed the principal offence. *W.S. Thaod* v. *State of Gujarat,* AIR 1979 SC 1232, 1233. [IPC (45 of 1860), S. 202]

Whole blood. Kinship by descent from the same pair of ancestors.

Whole number or total number. 'WHOLE NUMBER' or 'TOTAL NUMBER' when used with reference to the members of a Board, means the total number of members holding office at the time. [Rajasthan Municipalities Act, 1959 (38 of 1959), S. 3(36)]

Whole of India. To the entire extent of India. [IPC (45 of 1860), S. 1].

Whole subject matter of the reference. The expression 'whole subject matter of the reference' means that the decision in the suit or legal proceeding one way or the other will decide the whole matter referred to the arbitrators. *Banwarilal Garodia* v.

Joylal Hargulal, AIR 1956 Cal 467, 470. [Arbitration Act (10 of 1940) (*repealed*), S. 35]

Wholesale. Of, relating to, or engaged in the sale of goods in quantity for resale. [Poisons Act (12 of 1919), S. 2(1)].

WHOLESALE is sale in a whole or unbroken quantity; opposed to retail sale.

The word 'wholesale' means primarily a sale in large quantities; where a trader sells the whole or a large part of his produce direct at fixed price to customers, that price also can be described as the 'wholesale price'.

Wholesale cash price. These words mean the potentiality of the articles being sold on a wholesale basis. *A.K. Roy* v. *Voltas Ltd.*, AIR 1973 SC 225, 228. [Central Excise and Salt Act (1 of 1944), Sec. 4(a)] [Now repealed by Act 12 of 2017]

The wholesale price of the goods manufactured by the seller is the wholesale price at which the seller sells those goods to the buyer, and it is not the wholesale price at which the buyer sells those goods to others. *Union of India* v. *Cibatal Ltd.,* AIR 1986 SC 281, 283.

Wholesale dealer. "WHOLESALE DEALER" means a person who buys or sells excisable goods wholesale for the purpose of trade or manufacture, and includes a broker or commission agent who, in addition to making contracts for the sale or purchase of excisable goods for others, stocks such goods belonging to others as an agent for the purpose of sale. [Central Excise Act (1 of 1944), S. 2(k) repealed]

A trader who stores bags and sells grain by the bulk without breaking the bags is a wholesale dealer.

"WHOLESALE DEALER" is a person who keeps for wholesale to traders a commodity for the purposes of trade.

Wholesale price. 'Wholesale price' means, the price which a wholesale dealer charges for his goods when he sells them in wholesale units, either in the wholesale market or if there is no whole sale market at the site of the factory. *Amco Batteries (P) Ltd.* v. *Asst. Collector, Central Excise*, AIR 1963 Mys 216, 218. [Central Excises and Salt Act (1 of 1944), S. 4(a)] [Now repealed by Act 12 of 2017]

Wholesaler. In relation to the sale of any goods, means a person who sells the goods, either in bulk or in large quantities, to any person for the purposes of re-sale. [Monopolies and Restrictive Trade Practices Act (54 of 1969), S. 2(x)] [Now repealed & replaced by Act 12 of 2003]

Wholesome. Conducive to bodily or spiritual health. [Mines Act (35 of 1952), S. 19(1)].

Wholetime. Full time. [Unit Trust of India Act (52 of 1963), S. 10(f), *Prov.*].

"Whole-time director" includes a director in the whole-time employment of the company. [Companies Act (18 of 2013), S. 2(94)].

Whole-time key managerial personnel. The following are the whole-time key managerial personnel:—

(i) managing director, or Chief Executive Officer or manager and in their absence, a whole-time director;

(ii) company secretary; and

(iii) Chief Financial Officer. [Companies Act (18 of 2013), S. 203(1)]

Wholly. The word 'wholly' means entirely, completely, fully, totally and in every respect and, to put a fetter to the right of female heir to claim partition of the dwelling house must be entirely, completely, totally and fully occupied by the members of the family. *Usha* v. *Sumriti*, AIR 1988 Cal 115, 117. [Hindu Succession Act (30 of 1956), S. 23]

As a whole; in its entirety; in full; completely. [Plantations Labour Act (69 of 1951) Substituted by The Plantations Labour (Amendment) Act, 1960, S. 2(f); T.P. Act (4 of 1882), S. 17].

Wholly and exclusively for purposes of such business. The expenditure of a capital nature is certainly not an expenditure which is deductible for compulsory profits though it may be an expenditure wholly and exclusively laid out for the purpose of the business. *Commissioner of Income Tax, Kerala* v. *Travancore Sugar & Chemicals Ltd.*, AIR 1973 SC 982, 986.

Wholly disabled. Does not mean complete physical incapacity. It only means inability to do substantial or material acts necessary to pursue an occupation.

Wholly for religious or charitable purpose. The expression 'wholly for religious and charitable purpose' means that the property under trust is held wholly for religious or charitable purposes. *Sadayapillai Trust* v. *Agricultural I.T. Officer*, AIR 1967 Mad 396, 397.

Wholly or in part dependent. In cases of poor working families particularly those living jointly, the earnings of all of them may be quite insufficient, in which case the parent can be said to be a dependent on the son. *Ponnuswami Gounder* v. *Rengaswamy*, AIR 1953 Mad 766. [Workmen's Compensation Act (8 of 1923), S. 2(1)(d)(iii)]

Where the earnings of the deceased workman far from being an asset to the family were not sufficient to maintain him and the father had to spend considerable portion of his earnings on the maintenance of his deceased son, the father was not wholly or in part dependent on the son. *St. Joseph's Automobile and Mechanical Works* v. *Maria Soosai Pillai*, AIR 1953 Mad 206. [Workmen's Compensation Act (8 of 1923), S. 2(1)(d) (iii)]

Wholly-owned subsidiary. "WHOLLY OWNED SUBSIDIARY (WOS)" means a foreign entity formed, registered or incorporated in accordance with the laws and regulations of the host country, whose entire capital is held by the Indian party. [Foreign Exchange Management (Transfer or Issue of any Foreign

Security) Regulations, 2000, Reg. 2(q) and Foreign Exchange Management (Transfer or Issue of Security by a Person Resident Outside India) Regulations, 2000, Reg. 2(vii)]

Wholly owned subsidiary abroad. Means a foreign concern formed, registered or incorporated in a foreign country in accordance with the laws and regulations of that country and whose entire capital is owned by an Indian entity. [Foreign Exchange Management (Borrowing or Lending in Foreign Exchange) Regulations, 2000, Reg. 2(h)]

Widow. A woman whose husband is dead and who has not married again. [T.P. Act (4 of 1882), S. 38, ill.].

Widowed mother. The expression "widowed mother" in S. 2 of Workmen's Compensation Act (8 of 1923) does not include a "widowed step-mother".

A widowed mother includes an adoptive widowed mother for the purposes of the Workmen's Compensation Act (8 of 1923), S. 2 where there has been a valid adoption of a son in accordance with the personal law of the parties.

A mother whose husband is dead and who has not married again. [Workmen's Compensation Act (8 of 1923) as amended by Act 8 of 1959, S. 2(1)(d)(iii)(b)].

Widower. A man whose wife is dead and who has not married again. [Hindu Adoptions and Maintenance Act (78 of 1872), S. 14(3)].

Wife. "WIFE" shall mean a married woman domiciled in India, who shall have completed the age of sixteen years; and shall not be a Christian, a Muhammadan nor a Jew. [Converts' Marriage Dissolution Act (21 of 1866), S. 3]

"WIFE" mean a Parsi wife. [Parsi Marriage and Divorce Act (3 of 1936), S. 2(9)]

For the purposes of this Chapter, "wife" includes a woman who has been divorced by, or has obtained a divorce from, her husband and has not remarried. [(w. e. f. 1-7-2024) Bharatiya Nagarik Suraksha Sanhita, 2023 (46 of 2023), S. 144(1), *Explanation*]

A woman joined to a man by marriage; a woman who has a husband living and undivorced. [Indian Evidence Act (1 of 1872), S. 120].

Wife and husband. The expression 'wife and husband' means a person claiming to be a wife or husband. The expression cannot be given a strict meaning as to convey only legally married wife and husband. *Laxmibai* v. *Ayodhya Prasad*, AIR 1991 MP 47, 51. [Hindu Marriage Act (25 of 1955), S. 24]

The terms 'wife' and 'husband' in S. 25(1) merely refer to parties who have gone through a ceremony of marriage and they do not signify an existing relationship as spouses. *Ratnaprabha* v. *Shadokharaiah*, AIR 1982 Kant 170, 172. [Hindu Marriage Act (25 of 1955), S. 25(1)]

Wife if includes widow. Under S. 125(1) Cl (b), CrPC, 1973 (2 of 1974), the wife continues to be a wife within the meaning of the provisions of the code, even though she has been divorced by her husband or has otherwise obtained a divorce and has not remarried. *Zohara Khatoon* v. *Mohd Ibrahim,* AIR 1981 SC 1243, 1248. [CrPC, 1973 (2 of 1974), S. 125(1), Cl (b) and S. 127(3)]

'Wife' includes a woman who has been divorced by, or has obtained a divorce from her usband and has not re-married. 'Wife' means a wife as defined, irrespective of the religion professed by her or by her husband. *Mohd. Ahmed Khan* v. *Shah Banu Begum,* AIR 1985 SC 945, 949.

The marriage of a woman according to Hindu rites to a man having a living spouse is a nullity and so she will not be entitled to the status of a wife. *Yamuna Bai* v. *Anantrao,* AIR 1988 (SC) 644, 648.

"Wi-Fi". Means a facility that allows computers, smartphones, or other devices to connect to the Internet or communicate with one another wirelessly within a particular area. [Flight and Maritime Connectivity Rules, 2018, R. 2(1)(u)].

Wild animal. Means any animal found wild in nature and includes any animal specified in Schedule I or Schedule II and found wild in nature [Wild Life (Protection) Act (53 of 1972) as amended by Act 16 of 2003, S. 2(36)]

Wild life. "WILD LIFE" includes any animal, Bees, butterflies, crustacea, fish and moths, aquatic or land vegetation which forms part of any habitat. [Wildlife (Protection) Act (53 of 1972) as amended by Act 16 of 2003,S. 2(37)]

Wildcat strike. Sudden unofficial strike action by workers.

Wilful. If the result in the result of compelling circumstances under which it was not possible to report or perform duty, such absence cannot be held to be willful. Absence from duty without any application or prior permission may amount to unauthorized absence, but it does not always mean wilful. [*Krushnakant B. Parmar v. Union of India*, (2012) 3 SCC 178, para 17].

"Wilful" means knowingly intentional, conscious, calculated and deliberate with full knowledge of consequences flowing therefrom. It excludes usual, accidental, bona fide or unintentional acts or genuine inability. [*Ram Kishan v. Tarun Bajaj*, (2014) 16 SCC 204, para 10].

Wilful abstention from inquiry and search. The words 'wilful abstention from enquiry and search' must be taken to mean, such abstention from enquiry or search as would show want of *bona fides*.

Wilful act. An act done intentionally, knowingly and purposely with supine indifference or without justifiable excuse so distinguish from an act done carelessly, thoughtlessly, needlessly, or inadvertently would come within the expression 'wilful act'. A 'wilful act' is different from negligent act and is a positive act unlike the latter which is negative. [*Krushnalal Buxi* v. *Sudarshan Pani* (1995) Supp(4) SCC 238]

'Wilful act' does not encompass involuntarily or negligent actions. The act has to be done with a "bad purpose or without justifiable excuse or stubbornly, obstinately or perversely". Wilful act is to be distinguished from an act done carelessly, thoughtlessly, heedlessly or inadvertently. It does not include any act done negligently or involuntarily. [*Ram Kishan v. Tarun Bajaj*, (2014) 16 SCC 204, para 10].

Wilful defaulter. Means an issuer who is categorized as a willful defaulter by any bank or financial institution or consortium thereof, in accordance with the guidelines on willful defaulters issued by the Reserve Bank of India and includes as issuer whose director or promoter is categorized as such. [Securities and Exchange Board of India (Issue and Listing of Debt Securities) Regulations, 2008, Regn. 2(1)(n); Securities and Exchange Board of India (Issue of capital and Disclosure Requirements) Regulations, 2009, Regn. 2(1)(zn)].

"WILFUL DEFAULTER" means any person who is categorized as a willful defaulter by any bank or financial institution or consortium thereof, in accordance with the guidelines on willful defaulters issued by the Reserve Bank of India and includes any person whose director, promoter or partner is categorized as such. [Securities and Exchange Board of India (Substantial Acquisition of Shares and Takeovers) Regulations, 2011, Regn. 2(1)(ze); Securities and Exchange Board of India (Intermediaries) Regulations, 2008, Regn. 2(1)(n)].

Wilful disobedience. If the disobedience is the result of some compelling circumstances under which it was not possible to comply with the order, it is not 'wilful disobedience'. *Niaz Mohammed* v. *State of Haryana*, AIR 1995 SC 308, 311. [Contempt of Courts Act (70 of 1971), S. 2(b)]

Wilful default. Wilful default in the payment of rent means that the default was intentional, deliberate, calculated and conscious with full knowledge of its consequences. *R.R.R. Gopala Rao* v. *N.G. Seharарao*, AIR 1989 SC 2185, 2187.

Wilful neglect. The expression "wilful neglect" means that the act is done deliberately and intentionally and not by accident or inadvertence, but so that the mind of the person who does the act goes with it.

The term "wilful neglect" in the section covers constructive desertion and means that the guilty spouse has been acting knowingly or has been consciously failing in a reprehensible manner in the discharge of his or her marital obligations.

Wilful neglect to maintain. Deliberate withholding of maintenance.

Wilful negligence. The phrase "wilful negligence" means that the officer in question is consciously acting or failing to act in a reprehensible manner. He would not be protected if he simply failed to give any consideration at all to the question of his duties if he acted recklessly and without caring whether he was fulfilling them or not. But such an officer will be excused if through mere inadvertence or error of judgment and while endeavouring honestly to carry out his duty he does or omits to do something which apart from these words might have rendered him liable. Thus the director of a company may be ignorant but if his ignorance arises from his wilfully shutting his eyes to the fact, which are before him, he is equally guilty. (*Govind* v. *Rangnath,* AIR 1930 Bom 572-74. 226)

Wilful refusal to consummate. The unjustified decision not to consummate a marriage, which may be grounds for annulment of the marriage.

Wilful, wilfully. The question whether an act or omission is wilful arises oftener in criminal than in civil causes; since in the former the general principle requiring the presence of *mens rea* excludes from criminality acts done accidentally and unintentionally and even acts done intentionally under honest but mistaken belief in the existence of facts which, if true, would have made the acts lawful or excusable.

An intending result which actually comes to pass; designed; not accidental or involuntary; intentional. [T.P. Act (4 of 1882), S. 3].

"Wilful" means deliberate or intentional and not accidental or by inadvertance. *Kedarnath* v. *State of U.P.*, AIR 1965 All 233, 236. [IPC (45 of 1860), S. 405]

Wilfully. The expression "wilfully" in O. XXI, R. 32, CPC (5 of 1908) cannot be construed as unreasonably. The refusal of the judgment debtor to live with her husband, expressed in unequivocal terms, is wilful. *Novkaratinam* v. *Suryanarayanan*, AIR 1949 Mad 374.

In a wilful manner; purposely; intentionally; deliberately. [Army Act (46 of 1950), S. 35(b)].

Wilfully presupposes a conscious action, while even by negligence one can allow another to do a thing. *Om Prakash Gupta* v. *State of U.P.,* AIR 1957 SC 458, 464. [IPC (45 of 1860), S. 405]

Wilfully means "intentionally"or "deliberately". S. *Harnam Singh* v. *State,* AIR 1976 SC 2140, 2145. [IPC (45 of 1860), S. 477-A]

Wilfully detains or delays. The word 'wilful' was used in S. 53 to mean only such detention which was deliberate and for some purpose. *Ramchandra* v. *State of Mysore,* AIR 1964 SC 1701, 1703. [Post Office Act (6 of 1898), S. 53]

Wilfully fails. Wilful failure means not an unintentional failure; not a failure by inadvertance, but a deliberate failure where the mind has been brought into play and the person has, after taking the facts into consideration, abstained. *State* v. *Awtarkrishna*, (1957) 8 STC 244. [Income Tax Act (43 of 1961), Sec. 276-D]

Will. "The words "A WILL" denote any testamentary document." [IPC (45 of 1860), S. 31] [Now (w. e. f. 1-7-2024) repealed & replaced by Bharatiya Nayaya Sanhita, 2023 (45 of 2023), S. 2(34), same definition in new Sanhita]

"WILL" means the legal declaration of the intention of the testator with respect to his property which he desires to be carried into effect after his death. [Indian Succession Act (39 of 1925), S. 2(h)]

"WILL" shall include a codicil and every writing making a voluntary posthumous disposition of property. [General Clauses Act (10 of 1897), S. 3(64)]

A will is the testament of the testator. It is a posthumous disposition of the estate of the testator directing distribution of his estate upon his death. It is not a transfer inter vivos. The two essential characteristics of a will are that it is intended to come into effect only after the death of the testator and is revocable at any time during the lifetime of the testator. It is said that so long as the testator is alive a will is not worth the paper on which it is written, as the testator can at any time revoke it. If the testator, who is not married, marries after making the will, by operation of law, the will stands revoked. Registration of a will does not make it any more effective. [*Suraj Lamp and Industries Private Limited* (2) v. *State of Haryana*, (2012) 1 SCC 656, para 14].

A person's formaldeclaration (in writing) of his intention as to the disposal of his property or other matters to be performed after his death [General Clauses Act (10 of 1897), S. 3(64)]; desire; wish; longing; inclination; disposition (to do anything). [IPC (45 of 1860), S. 86].

A will or testament is, "the legal declaration of a man's intentions of what he wills to be performed after his death", a will or testament being of no force till after the death of the testator, or person making it.

DOUBLE WILLS. The term "double will" has been applied to a testamentary instrument executed by two persons and giving the property of one dying first to the survivor, or giving their separate property to survivor for life and then to third persons.

HOLOGRAPH WILL is a will written entirely by the testator.

INOFFICIOUS WILL, is one disposing of property away from the natural heirs.

JOINT WILL is a testamentary instrument executed by two or more persons, in pursuance of a common intention, for the purpose of disposing their several interests in property owned by them in common, or of their separate property treated as a common fund, to a third person or persons.

MUTUAL OR RECIPROCAL WILLS are those in which two or more persons make mutual or reciprocal provisions in favour of each other, as by providing that the property of one dying first shall go to the survivor or survivors.

Will and **gift (Distinction).** The essential characteristic of a will is that it is a mere declaration of an intention so long as the testator is alive, a declaration that may be revoked or varied according to the variations in his intention; a disposition that require the testator's death for its consummation and is but ambulatory or without fixed effect until the happening of that event. A gift on the other hand is a transfer of property that is voluntary, gratuitous and absolute conferring immediate rights. *Parvathy Nadachy Umayaparvathy Nadachy* v. *Ramalakshmy Seethalakshmy,* MLJ : QD (1956-1960) Vol. IV C2000 : 1955 Ker LT 891 : AIR 1956 Trav.-Co. 127. See also *Mandakini Naik* v. *G.K. Naik*, AIR 2004 AP 525, 527, para 23. [Succession Act (39 of 1925), S. 2(h).]

Willful blindness. Deliberate failure to make a reasonable inquiry of wrongdoing despite suspicion or an awareness of the high probability of its existence.

Willful misconduct. Misconduct committed voluntarily and intentionally.

Willing. Having a ready will; disposed to consent or comply. [T.P. Act (4 of 1882), S. 69A(2)].

Willingly. Of one's own accord or free will; without reluctance.

Willingness. The state or condition of having a ready will or disposed to consent or to comply. [Indian Contract Act (9 of 1872), S. 2(a) and T.P. Act (4 of 1882), S. 83].

Winding up. Closing up a company's concerns, which may be by reason of insolvency or otherwise.

"Winding up" means winding up under this Act or liquidation under the Insolvency and Bankruptcy Code, 2016, as applicable. [Insolvency and Bankruptcy Code, 2016, S. 2(94A)]

To settle the accounts and liquidate the assets of partnership or corporation for the purpose of making distribution and dissolving the corporation.

The words 'winding up' must be given the widest possible amplitude, viz., to control the proceedings of a textile company which is in liquidation by the Central Government. *M.S.T. Corporation* v. *Official Liquidator,* AIR 1978 SC 476, 479. [Sick Textile Undertakings (Taking over of Management) Act (72 of 1972), S. 8]

Winding up an estate. Putting the estate in liquidation for the purpose of distributing the assets among the creditors and others who may be found entitled.

Winding-up order. A order of a Court which brings end to the activities of the company.

Wind-down plan. For the purpose of this regulation 'WIND-DOWN PLAN' means a process or plan of action employed, for transfer of the beneficial owner accounts and other operational powers of the depository to an alternative institution that would take over the operations of the depository in scenarios such as erosion of net-worth of the depository or its insolvency or its inability to provide critical depository operations or services. [Securities and Exchange Board of India (Depositories and Participants) Regulation, 1996, Regn. 35-B, *Explanation*].

Winner. One, who or that which wins. [Indian Contract Act (9 of 1872), S. 30].

Winning. The expression "winning" in a constitutional provision should be given a wider meaning as the Constitution makers would be using it to cover cases which deal with the obtaining of minerals and in that case that wider meaning would be to get or extract the mineral from the mine. *Gujarat Pottery Works* v. *B.P. Sood,* AIR 1967 SC 964, 967. [Constitution of India, Art. 31A(1) (e)]

Winning a mineral means getting or extracting it from the mine. *Bihar Mines Ltd* v. *Union of India,* AIR 1967 SC 887, 892. [Mines and Minerals (Regulation and Development) Act (67 of 1957), S. 3(d)]

Wireless communication. Means any transmissions emission or reception of sign, signals, writing, images and sounds, or intelligence of any nature by means of electricity, magnetism, or Radio waves of Hertzian waves, without the use of wires or other continuous electrical conductors between the transmitting and the receiving apparatus:

Explanation—"Radio waves" or "Hertzian waves" means electromagnetic waves of frequencies lower than 3,000 gigacycles per second propagated in space without artificial guide. [Indian Wireless Telegraphy Act (17 of 1933) Subs. by Act 15 of 1961, S. 2(1)]

Wireless e-commerce. Conducting e-commerce activities using mobile and wireless networks. (*Cyber Law*)

Wireless local loop (WLL). Today, technologies provide WLL services *i.e.* wireless access for home and business users to carriers and service provider network.

According to *Encyclopedia of Networking and Telecommunications* by Tom Sheldon, wireless local loop (WLL) refers to a variety of technologies for connecting subscribers to the public-switched telephone network (PSTN) using wireless links, rather than copper wire. WLL is a practical solution for connecting subscribers in countries/areas that do not have the wired infrastructure. It is also practical in rural areas as an alternative to laying cable. WLL is primarily a fixed wireless service (the subscriber generally stays in one place), while cellular systems offer mobile communication and roaming among different systems. [*Tata Teleservices Ltd.* v. *Bharat Sanchar Nigam Ltd.*, (2008) 10 SCC 556, 567 para 9 (ix)]

Wireless telegraphy apparatus. Appliance, instrument or material used or capable of use in wireless communication and includes any articles determined by rule made under Section 10 to be wireless telegraphy apparatus, but does not include any such apparatus, appliance, instrument or material commonly used for other electrical purposes, unless it has been specially designed or adapted for wireless communication or forms part of some apparatus, appliance, instrument or material specially so designed or adopted, not any article determined by rule made under Section 10 not to be wireless telegraphy apparatus. [Indian Wireless Telegraphy Act (17 of 1933), S. 2(2) **as cited in** *Star India Private Limited* v. *Department of Industrial Policy and Promotion,* (2019) 2 SCC 104, para 32].

Wireless transmitter. Means any apparatus, appliance, instrument or material used or capable of use for transmission or emission of wireless communication. [Indian Wireless Telegraphy Act (17 of 1933) Subs. by Act 15 of 1961, S. 2(2A)]

Wiretap orders. An order that is granted by a court allowing Police and other law enforcement agency to listen and record telephonic conversations. [Karnika Seth, *Computers Internet and New Technology Laws*, 2021, LexisNexis, Glossary of Legal Terms].

Wiretapping. A form of electronic or mechanical weaves dropping where upon Court order, law enforcement officials surreptitiously listen to phone calls or other conversations or communications of persons.

With a view of. With the object or design of. [Registration Act (16 of 1908), S. 2(2)].

With costs. Where the order of the Court was that the appeal be allowed 'with costs' that clearly means the costs of that Court.

With hard labour. Accompanied by hard labour. [, IPC (45 of 1860), S. 53(1), *Fourthly*].

With reasonable diligence. *Prima facie* with reasonable diligence means reasonable in regard to those circumstances of which the actor called on to act reasonably, knows or ought to know. [Limitation Act (36 of 1963), S. 17(1)]

With reference to. With regard to. [General Clauses Act (10 of 1897), S. 3(56)]; [Navy Act (62 of 1957), S. 3(1)(b)].

With respect to. The words 'with respect to the legislature' and 'in relation to the legislature' have wider significance than the words 'in the legislature'. The former words which are found in Cl. 2 of Art. 208 would include within their scope not only the rule dealing with procedure and conduct of business during the actual session of the legislature but all other incidental or ancillary matter. *Godavarts Misra* v. *Nand Kishore Das*, AIR 1953 Ori 111, 114.

Withdraw. To take back or a way something that has been given, allowed, possessed, experienced or enjoyed; to draw away [CPC (5 of 1908), O. XXIII, R. 1(3)]; [CrPC, 1973 (2 of 1974), S. 257]; to retire; to go away [Children Act (60 of 1960) (*repealed*), S. 28(2)].

Withdrawal. The act of withdrawing [T.P. Act (4 of 1882), S. 84, prov.]; (as in the case of candidature) [Representation of the People Act (43 of 1951), S. 37]; (as in the case of amount out of a fund or deposit) [Employees' Provident Funds and Miscellaneous Provisions Act (19 of 1952), Sch. II, item 7]; [Constitution of India, Art. 110(1)(c)].

Withdrawal of question. In the Lok Sabha a member can withdraw the question before the sitting for which his question has been placed on the list; he can also withdraw it by making a statement to that effect when his question is called by the Speaker.

Withheld price. "WITHHELD PRICE" means part of the price due and payable for goods supplied by any Member to the Producer Company; and as withheld by the Producer Company for payment on a subsequent date. [Companies Act (1 of 1956), S. 581A(n)]

Withhold. Withhold connotes withdrawal or deprivation of essential supply or services of some indirect or negative act on part of the landlord, i.e., by his failing to do what he was bound to do and what was within his power and control to do. *J. Satyavarte* v. *Mohamed Bhai Abdul Hussain Sadiq Buherinwalla*, AIR 1982 Bom 50, 60.

To keep back, refrain from granting or giving [Indian Evidence Act (1 of 1872), S. 123 and CPC (5 of 1908), O. XXI, R. 48(1)(a)]; [Employees' State Insurance Act (34 of 1948), S. 83].

Within. The word 'within' in relation to a period of time does not usually mean 'during' or throughout the whole of; it is more frequently used to delimit a period 'inside which' certain events may happen. *D.M. Thippaswamy* v. *Mysore Revenue Appellate Tribunal Bangalore*, AIR 1972 Mys 50, 53.

Within one month. The words "within one month" in O. XLI, R. 22, of the CPC (5 of 1908) mean "not beyond one month." The respondent has a right to file cross objections at any time up to one month after the date of service of the notice of the appeal.

Within precincts of. The phrase 'within the precincts' does not restrict the area of operation by the workman to the area contained within the four walls of the warehouse. It includes the space that may be required for the loading and unloading of goods within the warehouse or without warehouse. *K. Ramaswami Mudalir* v. *Poongavanam*, AIR 1954 Mad 218, 220. [Workmen's Compensation Act (8 of 1923), Sch II., Item 26]

Within so many days after an Act. Means so many clear days after it.

Within that state. The expression "within that state" includes freedom of trade within the state. It refers to trade, commerce or intercourse between other States or the citizens living under those States, and the State or the citizens of the State which under Article 305, has the authority to impose restrictions as the freedom of trade, commerce and intercourse. *Atma Ram Budhia* v. *State of Bihar*, AIR 1952 Pat 359, 373. [Constitution of India, Art. 304 (a)]

Within the jurisdiction. The words "within the jurisdiction" in S. 151, Cl (1) of the Army Act (46 of 1950) refers to "actions" and not to "persons".

Within the local limits. The words "within the local limits of his jurisdiction" are not equivalent to "residing within the local limits". It is sufficient to give the Magistrate jurisdiction, if the evil habits of the accused were practised and evil reputation acquired within the local limits of his jurisdiction.

Within the local limits of whose jurisdiction any substantial part of the subject matter of the trust estate to situate. 'It does not mean major parts and the word 'substantial' cannot be equated with the word 'major'. *Sukhlal Chandakmull Karnania Trust* v. *Shew Kunwar Karnami*, AIR 1973 Cal 444, 447. [Charitable and Religious Trust Act (14 of 1920), Sec. 7]

Without breaking bulk. Transferring the product from the drums by breaking seal of the drums to bottles is not without breaking bulk. *H.M.M. Ltd.* v. *Administrator, Bangalore City Corporation,* AIR 1990 SC 47, 51.

Without interruption. The words 'without interruption' mean a covenant for quiet enjoyment in an unqualified form. *Jabbar Sahib* v. *V.R. Ramu*, AIR 1964 Mad 514, 515. [T.P. Act (4 of 1882), S. 108(c)]

Without notice application. A procedure in civil litigation by which one party may apply for an order of Court to be made without the other party being aware of it.

Without prejudice. Without adversely affecting. [CPC (5 of 1908), O. XXXIII, R. 14].

An action taken without prejudice to one's right cannot necessarily mean that the entire action can be ignored by the party taking the same. In the context it only means that the party reserved to itself the right to contend before the arbitrator that a dispute raised on the claim made by the contractor was not covered by the arbitration clause. *Tarapore & Co.* v. *Cochin Shipyard Ltd., Cochin,* AIR 1984 SC 1072, 1086.

Without prejudice means (1) that the cause or the matter has been decided on merits (2) that fresh proceedings according to law were not barred. *Superintendent (Tech.) Central Excise, I.D.D. Jabalpur and Others* v. *Pratap Raj,* AIR 1978 SC 1244, 1246. [Customs Act (52 of 1962), Ss. 122, 128]

Without reasonable excuse. In a proceedings of the restitution of conjugal rights, the residence of the aged parents of the husband under the same roof with him is not provocative of creating circumstances grave enough to leave the matrimonial house and is without reasonable excuse of refusal to live with the husband. *K. Kantimathi* v. S. *Parameshwara Iyer*, AIR 1974 Ker 124, 127. [Hindu Marriages Act (25 of 1955), S. 9]

Without recourse. Words used in an indorsement of a negotiable instrument, meaning that the indorser assumes no liability or responsibility in case the negotiable instrument is dishonoured.

Witness. One who gives evidence in a cause; an indifferent person to each party, sworn to speak the truth, the whole truth, and nothing but the truth.

One who gives or is to give evidence in a cause; a person sworn to speak the truth in a trial; one who attests a document; one that is cognizant of something by direct experience. [Indian Evidence Act (1 of 1872), S. 137]; [Immoral Traffic (Prevention) Act (104 of 1956), S. 15(2), *Prov.*].

'Witness' means a person who is capable of providing information by way of deposing as regards relevant facts, via an oral statement, or a statement in writing, made or given in the court, or otherwise. [*Rohtash Kumar v. State of Haryana*, (2013) 14 SCC 434, para 26].

Witness cannot be found. A heavy responsibility is cast upon the Courts of law to satisfy themselves that there exist circumstances which make the previous deposition admissible under the section. The satisfaction of the Court is to be in the form of a proof. In other words, therefore, before a deposition can be admitted under S. 33, all the reasonable steps should be taken to secure the attendance of the witness. If the Court is informed by the police or through any other agency that a witness has shifted to a particular station, an attempt should be made to serve that witness at that station. The whereabouts of a person can be said to be unknown when he cannot be found at all the places which he had, or was informed to have, visited either permanently or for a temporary stay. *Tulsi Ram* v. *State,* MLJ : QD (1956-1960) Vol. II C2591 : 1956 CrLJ 1290 : AIR 1956 Bhopal 52. [Evidence Act (1 of 1872), S. 33]

Witness in attendance. A witness who is present and waiting in the Court.

Witness stand. The space in a Courtroom, usually a boxed area, occupied by a witness while testifying.

Witness, Tamper with. To endeavour to induce to give false evidence or to suppress the truth or to endeavour directly or indirectly to deter or hinder any person from appearing or giving evidence. (*Constitutional and Parliamentary Term*)

Witnesses for defence. The words "witnesses for defence" are wide enough to cover evidence extracted by cross-examination from witnesses for the prosecution.

WLAN. (*abbr.*) Wireless Local Area Network. Also called RLAN which is the abbreviation of radio local area network. This system allows an extension of the local area computer network without the need of cable (*e.g.* wireless internet access in airports with laptops). (*Telecommunication*)

WLL. (*abbr.*) Wireless local loop.

'WLL' is a generic term for radio based telecommunication technologies and the respective devices which can be implemented using a different wireless and to radio technologies. 'WLL' is a technology and it cannot be equated to WLL (M) which is a service. World over WLL is used to provide fixed wireless access for speedy roll out of fixed services. [*Tata Telesrevices Ltd.* v. *BSNL,* (2008) 10 SCC 556, 584, para 35]

WLL Connection. WLL connection allowing a subscriber to connect to public telecoms networks *via* a wireless link. (*Telecommunication*)

Woman. "The word "WOMAN" denotes a female human being of any age." [IPC (45 of 1860), S. 10] [Now (w. e. f. 1-7-2024) repealed & replaced by Bharatiya Nayaya Sanhita, 2023 (45 of 2023), S. 2(35), same definition in new Sanhita]

"WOMAN" means a female who has completed the age of eighteen years. [Women's and Children's Institutions (Licensing) Act (105 of 1956), S. 2(e); Orphanages and Other Charitable Homes (Supervision and Control), Act (10 of 1960), S. 2(i)]

"WOMAN" means a woman employed, whether directly or through any agency, for wages in any establishment. [Maternity Benefit Act (53 of 1961), S. 3(o)]

An adult female human being. [Immoral Traffic (Prevention) Act (104 of 1956) Subs. by Act 44 of 1986, S. 2(f) and IPC (45 of 1860), S. 10].

"WOMAN" means a woman employed, whether directly or through any contractor, for wages in any establishment:

Provided that for the purposes of Chapter IV, a woman who is or was an employee in respect of whom contribution is or were payable under the said Chapter and who is by reason thereof, entitled to any of the benefits provided under the said Chapter shall be called "insured woman" and shall include—

(i) a commissioning mother who as biological mother wishes to have a child and prefers to get embryo implanted in any other woman;

(ii) a woman who legally adopts a child of up to three months of age. [Code on Social Security, 2020 (36 of 2020), S. 2(91)]

The word 'woman' under S. 10 of the IPC (45 of 1860), denotes a female human being of any age, so that for the purpose of S. 354, a girl of 6 years is a woman within that section.

Woman with child. Pregnant woman. [S. 312, IPC (45 of 1860)].

Women's or children's institution. Means an institution, whether called an orphanage or a home for neglected women or children or a widow's home or an institution called by any other name, which is established and maintained for the reception and care of women or children. [*Explanation (d)* to S. 376(2) of IPC, 1860 (45 of 1860), as substituted by the Criminal Law (Amendment) Act, 2013 (13 of 2013). Also see *Explanation 4* to S. 376C of IPC, 1860 (45 of 1860), as substituted by the Criminal Law (Amendment) Act, 2013 (13 of 2013)]] [Now (w. e. f. 1-7-2024) repealed & replaced by Bharatiya Nayaya Sanhita, 2023 (45 of 2023), S. 64(2), *Explanation (d)*, same definition in new Sanhita]

Wood. 'WOOD' means and includes trees when they have fallen or have been felled, and all wood of any species whether cut, converted, fashioned, sawn or hollowed out for any purpose or not. [Bihar Saw Mill (Regulation) Act (19 of 1990), S. 2(k)

Trees cut down or felled, not growing.

A forest [S. 31, ill. (a), T.P. Act (4 of 1882)]; trees cut or sawed; timber.

Woollen fabrics. The term means not only woollen garments, but also woollen material used as covering or for similar purposes. *Union of India* v. *Gujarat*

Woollen Fert. Mills, AIR 1977 SC 1548, 1550. [Central Excises and Salt Act (1 of 1944), Sch. 1, Entry 21]

Word. One of the basic units of information processed by the computer. Most often, a word is considerably larger than a byte. A computer may use a sixteen-bit, thirty-two-bit, or forty-eight-bit word as its basic unit of information. (*Computer*)

Word of art. A word or phrase which has a specific, precise meaning in a given specialty, apart from its general meaning in ordinary contexts.

Word processing program. A computer program designed primarily for working with text, allowing the user to readily enter, format, edit, and print out text to create many different kinds of documents. (*Computer*)

Words and phrases. Are symbols that stimulate mental references to referents. *UOI* v. *Braj Nandan Singh*, AIR 2005 SC 4403 : 2005 AIR SCW 5383.

Words spoken. Words uttered. [S. 28(1), Indian Partnership Act (9 of 1932)].

Work. "WORK" means any of the following works, namely :—

(i) a literary, dramatic, musical or artistic work;

(ii) a cinematograph film;

(iii) a (sound recording. [Copyright Act (14 of 1957) as amended by Act 38 of 1994, S. 2(y)]

For the purposes of this section, the expression "WORK" shall also include—

(a) advertising;

(b) broadcasting and telecasting including production of programmes for such broadcasting or telecasting;

(c) carriage of goods and passengers by any mode of transport other than by railways;

(d) catering. [Income-tax Act (43 of 1961), S. 194C, *Expln.* (iv)]

"WORK" means—

(i) any unskilled work, including any form of industrial or agricultural labour;

(ii) any domestic service;

(iii) any service not being a service in a managerial capacity in any hotel, restaurant, tea-house or other place of public resort;

(iv) work as a driver of truck or other vehicle, mechanic, technician or skilled labourer or artisan;

(v) work as an office assistant or accountant or typist or stenographer or sales man, or nurse or operator of any machine;

(vi) work in connection with, or for the purposes of, any cinema, exhibition or entertainment;

(vii) any such work of professional or of any other nature as the Central Government may, having regard to the need for the protection of citizens of India and other relevant circumstances, specify by notification.

Provided that the Central Government may, if satisfied that it is necessary so to do having regard to the conditions of service applicable with respect to employment in any of the aforementioned categories of work or any sub-category thereof, whether generally or in relation to any particular country or place and other relevant circumstances, declare by notification that such category of work or sub-category of work shall not be deemed to be work within the meaning of this definition. [Emigration Act (31 of 1983), S. 2(1)(o)]

'Work' means a structure or apparatus of some kind; architecture or engineering structure, a building edifice. [*Larsen and Toubro Limited v. State of Karnataka*, (2014) 1 SCC 708, para 73].

Something that is done; task [S. 2(ii)(g), Payment of Wages Act (4 of 1936) and S. 14, ill. (g), Indian Evidence Act (1 of 1872)]; [S. 54, ill. (b), Indian Contract Act (9 of 1872)]; any production of art as a literary composition.

The word 'work' has a very wide meaning. It is really used in two senses of bestowing labour and that upon which labour has been bestowed. When used in plural the word certainly means some outstanding or important result of the labour that has been bestowed and large industrial and scientific establishment are called works. *Radha Raman* v. *State of Uttar Pradesh*, AIR 1954 All 700, 702. [Land Acquisition Act (1 of 1894), S. 40(1)(aa)]

Work-charged employees. The expression 'work-charged employees' means employees engaged on a temporary basis for the execution of a specified work. *State of Rajasthan* v. *Kunji Raman,* AIR 1997 SC 693.

Work-charged establishment. A work charged establishment means an establishment of which the expenses including the wages and allowances of the staff, are chargeable to "works." (*State of Maharashtra* v. *Pursottam,* AIR 1996 SC 2225).

Work for hire. A copyrightable work which is produced either by an employee within the scope of employment or by an independent contractor under a written agreement.

Work mine. To make an excavation in the earth, for the purpose of obtaining metals or minerals. [S. 108(o), T.P. Act (4 of 1882)].

Work of architecture. Means any building or structure having an artistic character or design, or any model for such building or structure. [Copyright Act (14 of 1957) Subs. by Act 38 of 1994, S. 2(b)]

Work of artistic craftsmanship. A certain work is a work of artistic craftsmanship if it has, whether one admires it or not, distinctive characteristics of shape, form and finish.

Work of improvement. Includes, in relation to any building in a slum area, the execution of any one or more of the following works, namely:—

(i) necessary repairs;

(ii) structural alterations;

(iii) provision of light points, water taps and bathing places;
(iv) construction of drains, open or covered.
(v) provision of latrines, including conversion of dry latrines into water-borne latrines;
(vi) provision of additional or improved fixtures or fittings;
(vii) opening up or paving of Courtyards;
(viii) removal of rubbish; and
(ix) any other work including the demolition of any building or any part thereof which in the opinion of the competent authority is necessary for executing any of the works specified above. [Slum Areas (Improvement and Clearance) Act (96 of 1956), S. 2(j)]

Work of joint authorship. Means a work produced by the collaboration of two or more authors in which the contribution of one author is not distinct from the contribution of the other author or authors. [Copyright Act (14 of 1957), S. 2(z)]

Work of permanent character. A *Kachcha* thatched house may be "a work of permanent character" within the meaning of S. 60(b) of the Indian Easements Act (5 of 1882), although the thatch of the house is renewed from time to time.

Work of sculpture. "WORK OF SCULPTURE." includes casts and models. [Copyright Act (14 of 1957), S. 2(za)]

Work product. Tangible material or its intangible equivalent, in unwritten or oral form, which was either prepared by or for a lawyer or prepared for litigation, either planned or in progress.

Work-release programme. A correctional programme which allows prison inmates, primarily those who are being readied for discharge, to hold job outside.

Worker. "WORKER" means a person employed, directly or by or through any agency (including a contractor) with or without the knowledge of the principal employer, whether for remuneration or not in any manufacturing process or in cleaning any part of the machinery or premises used for a manufacturing process, or in any other kind of work incidental to, or connected with, the manufacturing process, or the subject of the manufacturing process but does not include any member of the armed forces of Union. [Factories Act (63 of 1948), S. 2(l)]

"WORKER" means a person employed in plantation for hire or reward, whether directly or through any agency, to do any work, skilled, unskilled, manual or clerical, but does not include—

(i) a medical officer employed in the plantation;
(ii) any person employed in the plantation (including any member of the medical staff) whose monthly wages exceed rupees seven hundred and fifty;
(iii) any person employed in the plantation primarily in a managerial capacity, notwithstanding that his monthly wages do not exceed rupees three hundred; or
(iv) any person temporarily employed in the plantation in any work relating to the construction, development or maintenance of buildings, roads, bridges, drains or canals. [Plantation Labour Act (69 of 1951) Subs. by Act 34 of 1960, S. 2(k)]

"WORKER" means any person who is employed for wages in any kind of work and who gets his wages directly from the employer but shall not include an apprentice referred to in clause (aa). [Apprentices Act (52 of 1961) Subs. by Act 29 of 2014, S. 2(r)]

'Worker' means a person who is engaged or to be engaged directly or through any agency, whether for wages or not, to do manual work in any scheduled employment and, includes any person not employed by any employer or a contractor, but working with the permission of, or under agreement with the employer or contractor; but does not include the members of an employer's family. [Maharashtra Mathadi, Hamal and Other Manual Workers (Regulation of Employment and Welfare) Act (30 of 1969), S. 2(12) as cited in *Pepsico India Holding Private Limited v. Grocery Market and Shops Board*, (2016) 4 SCC 493, para 5].

"WORKER" means a person employed under a contract of service or apprenticeship. [Insecticides Act (46 of 1968), S. 3(r)]

According to the definition it must be shown that there were persons employed directly or through any agency, whether for wages or not. 'Employed' has been interpreted to mean that there must be a contract between the management and the person employed so as to bring them within the definition of 'worker'. *J. Manicka Gounder* v. *Inspector of Factories*, AIR 1959 Mad 430, 431. [Factories Act (63 of 1948), S.2 (l)]

Partners of a concern cannot be considered as workers even though the partners also may be doing some work in the factory. *State* v. *S.S. Pinto*, AIR 1960 Bom 236, 237.

Workers' compensation. Payments to workers who are injured at work or contract a work related illness.

Working capital. The money in circulation, acquired through cash balances, daily cash sales or short term borrowings and used to run day-to-day affairs of a business organisation.

Working class. Those persons within a community who exchange their labour power for a wage.

Working day. A day when work is normally done as distinguished from Sundays and legal holidays. [Mines Act (35 of 1952) Subs. by Act 62 of 1959, S. 52(8)]; [Payment of Wages Act (4 of 1936), S. 5(2)].

WORKING DAYS exclude Sundays and holidays, but not rainy or stormy day.

Working group. Means the Group constituted by the Reserve Bank for the purpose of considering proposals of export of goods and services on deferred payment terms or in execution of a turnkey project or a civil construction contract. [Foreign Exchange Management (Export of Goods and Services), Regulations, 2000, Reg. 2(x) now omitted by G.S.R. 434(E), dated 12-6-2014 (w.e.f. 8-7-2014)]

Working journalist. "WORKING JOURNALIST" means a person whose principal avocation is that of a journalist and who is employed as such in, or in relation to, any newspaper establishment, and includes an editor, a leader, writer, news-editor, sub-editor, feature-writer, copy-tester, reporter, correspondent, cartoonist, news-photographer and proof-reader, but does not include any such person who—

(i) is employed mainly in a managerial or administrative capacity; or

(ii) being employed in a supervisory capacity, performs, either by the nature of the duties attached to his office or by reason of the power vested in him, functions mainly of a managerial nature. [Working Journalists and Other Newspaper Employees (Conditions of Service) and Miscellaneous Provisions Act (45 of 1955), S. 2(f)]

"WORKING JOURNALIST" means a person whose principal avocation is that of a journalist and who is employed as such, either whole-time or part-time, in, or in relation to, one or more newspaper establishment, or other establishment relating to any electronic media or digital media such as newspaper or radio or other likemedia and includes an editor, a leader-writer, news editor, sub-editor, feature-writer, copy-tester, reporter, correspondent, cartoonist, news-photographer and proof-reader, but does not include any such person who is employed mainly in a managerial, supervisory or administrative capacity. [Occupational Safety, Health & Working Conditions Code, 2020 (37 of 2020), S. 2(1)(zzm)]

Working on the post. "Working on the post" means performing the duties and discharging the functions assigned to the post and not the capacity in which the post is held. *State of Madhya Pradesh* v. *Lakshmishankar Mishra,* AIR 1979 SC 979.

Working order. A condition of a machine in which it functions according to its nature and purpose. [Motor Vehicles Act (59 of 1988), S. 30].

Working partner. "WORKING PARTNER" shall a firm means a partner thereof who is required by the terms of the contract of partnership to devote substantially the whole of his time to the business of the firm. [Business Profits Tax Act (21 of 1947), S. 2(18)]

"WORKING PARTNER" means an individual who is actively engaged in conducting the affairs of the business or profession of the firm of which he is a partner. [Income-tax Act (43 of 1961), S. 40(b) *Expln.* 4]

Working standard. Means the set of standard weight or measure which is made or manufactured by or on behalf of Government for the verification of any standard weight or measure, other than a national prototype or national reference or secondary standard. [Standard of Weights and Measures Act (60 of 1976), S. 2(ze)]

Workman. "WORKMAN" means any person (other than a person whose employment is of casual nature and who is employed otherwise than for the purposes of the employer's trade or business who is—(i) a railway servant as defined in clause 34 of Section 2 of the Railways Act, 1989 (24 of 1989), not permanently employed in any administrative, district or sub-divisional office of a railway and not employed in such capacity as is specified in Schedule II, or (i-a) (a) a master, seaman or other member of a ship, (b) a captain or other member of the crew of an aircraft, (c) a person recruited as driver, helper, mechanic, cleaner or in any other capacity in connection with motor-vehicle, (d) a person recruited for work abroad by a company,

and who as employed outside India in any such capacity as is specified in Schedule II and the ship, aircraft or motor vehicle, or company, as the case may be, is registered in India, or (ii) employed in any such capacity as is specified in Schedule II,

Whether the contract of employment was made before or after the passing of this Act and whether such contract is express or implied, oral or in writing; but does not include any person working in the capacity of a member of the Armed Forces of the Union and any reference to a workman who has been injured shall, where the workman is dead, include a reference to his dependants or any of them. [Workmen's Compensation Act (8 of 1923), S.2 (1)(n) now omitted by Act 45 of 2009]

"WORKMAN" means any person who has entered into, or works under a contract of, service or apprenticeship with an employer whether by way of manual labour, clerical work or otherwise, and whether the contract is expressed or implied, oral or in writing. [Employee's Liability Act (24 of 1938), S. 2(a)]

"WORKMAN" means any person (other than whose employment if of a casual nature and who is employed otherwise than for the purposes of the employer's trade or business) who is employed in any of the employments specified in Section 6. [War injuries (Compensation Insurance) Act (23 of 1943), S. 2(j)]

"WORKMAN" means any person (including an apprentice) employed in any industry to do any manual, unskilled, skilled, technical, operational, clerical or supervisory work for hire or reward, whether the terms of employment be express or implied, and for the purpose of any proceedings under this Act in relation to an industrial dispute, includes any such person who has been dismissed, discharged or retrenched in connection with or as a consequence of, that dispute, or whose dismissal, discharge or retrenchment has led to that dispute, but does not include any such person—

(i) who is subject to the Air-Force Act, 1950, or the Army Act, 1950, or the Navy Act, 1957; or

(ii) who is employed in the police service or as an officer or other employee or other employee of a prison, or

(iii) who is employed mainly in a managerial or administrative capacity, or

(iv) who, being employed in a supervisory capacity draws wages exceeding one thousand six hundred rupees *per mensem* or exercise, either by the nature of the duties attached to the office or by reason of the powers vested in him, functions mainly of a managerial nature. [Industrial Disputes Act (14 of 1947), S. 2(s) substituted by Act 46 of 1982]

"WORKMAN" means any person employed in or in connection with the work of any establishment to do any skilled, semi-skilled or un-skilled manual, supervisory, technical or clerical work for hire or reward, whether the terms of employment be express or implied, but does not include any such person—

(a) who is employed mainly in a managerial or administrative capacity; or

(b) who, being employed in a supervisory capacity draws wages exceeding five hundred rupees *per mensem* or exercises, either by the nature of the duties attached to the office or by reason of the powers vested in him, functions mainly of a managerial nature; or

(c) who is an out-worker, that is to say, a person to whom any articles or materials are given out by or on behalf of the principal employer to be made up, cleaned, washed, altered, ornamented, finished, repaired, adopted or otherwise processed for sale for the purposes of trade or business of the principal employer and the process is to be carried out either in the home of the outworker or in some other premises under the control and management of the principal employer. [Contract Labour (Regulation and Abolition) Act (37 of 1970), S. 2(1)(i)]

"WORKMAN" means any person employed in or in connection with the work of any establishment to do any skilled, semi-skilled or unskilled, manual, supervisory, technical or clerical work for hire or reward whether the terms of employment be express or implied, but does not include any such person—

(i) who is employed mainly in a managerial or administrative capacity; or

(ii) who, being employed in a supervisory capacity, draws wages exceeding five hundred rupees *per mensem,* or exercises, either by nature of the duties attached to the office or by reason of the powers vested in him, functions mainly of managerial nature. [InterState Migrant Workmen (Regulation of Employment and Condition of Service) Act (30 of 1979), S. 2(1)(j)]

A senior assistant editor of a newspaper who has to display qualities of initiative and independence, is not a workman u/s. 2(s), Industrial Disputes Act (14 of 1947). *Sri Vinaya Nath Narayan Sinha* v. *Bihar Journals Ltd.,* AIR 1954 Pat 1.

One who labours; a man engaged to do a work or manual labour. [Workmen's Compensation Act (8 of 1923), S. 2 (1)(n) now omitted by Act 45 of 2009].

The doctor and the compounder are not workmen. *Lakshimi Devi Sugar Mills* v. *State of Uttar Pradesh,* AIR 1955 All 578, 579.

A person employed to collect octroi duty in octroi department of a municipality is a workman. *Municipal Committee* v. *Ram Lal,* AIR 1965 Punj 15, 17.

A workman performing supervisory duties, will not cease to be a workman, but he must be engaged in a supervisory capacity. *Arkal Govind Raj Rao* v. *Ciba Geigy of India Ltd., Bombay,* AIR 1985 SC 985, 987.

An employee doing the supervisory wok is not 'workman' and an internal auditor doing the duty of reporting and checking up on behalf of the management and having no independent right or authority to take decision is not, a supervisor and therefore is 'workman'. *National Engineering Industries Ltd.* v. *Shrikishan,* AIR 1983 SC 329, 332.

Maintenance Engineer supervising the work of Maintenance Department is, therefore, not a 'workman'. *Vimal Kumar* v. *Labour Court, Kanpur,* AIR 1988 SC 384.

Teachers employed by educational institutions, whether the institutions are imparting primary, secondary, graduate or post-graduate education, are not workmen. *A. Sundarambal* v. *Govt. of Goa, Daman & Diu,* AIR 1988, SC 1700, 1704.

The construction of a godown for the purposes of storing grain is so vitally connected with the business of dealing in grain, there can be not doubt that a mason constructing it was employed for the purposes of the employer's trade or business. *Hirjibhai Lakshmsibhai* v. *Damodar,* AIR 1957 MP 49, 50. [Workmen's Compensation Act (8 of 1923), S. 2(1)(n)]

Lorry Drivers, cleaners and *harmlis* are workmen within the meaning of Workmen's Compensation Act (8 of 1923), Sec. 2(1)(n). *Oriental Fire & General Insurance Co. Ltd.* v. *UOI,* AIR 1975 AP 222, 224.

Workman and tributor. There is a distinction between a workman under the Workmen's Compensation Act and a tributor. A tributor is a person who is engaged upon his own business and not upon the business of his master. A workman is a person who is engaged on the business of his master and not on his own business. If persons are allowed to do work of their own in their own time and are not subject to the orders of any master as to the way in which, or the time at which, they shall do it, they do not fall within the scope of the Workmen's Compensation Act. The fact that a person is not paid daily wages but according to the amount of work done is not a circumstance which is to be taken into account at all to decide whether a man is tributor or a workman, because it is quite possible for a workman to be paid by piece work and still remain under the orders of his employer.

Tributors who work at dump picking, or searching for overlooked or, and receive payment therefor either at the Mine Office or at the hands of the contractor, are licensees merely and their written permit to enter the mine premises is a document which shows that they are removed from the category of trespassers. They are not workmen within the meaning of the Act.

A daily labourer travelling in her employer's motor lorry for loading and unloading the lorry with bricks was the victim of an accident while riding in the lorry as a result of which she died. *Held* (1) that the labourer was a "workman" within the meaning of the term as defined in of the Workmen's Compensation Act; (2) that the labourer was killed in the course of her employment.

In order to take a person out of the definition of a workman as defined in the Workmen's Compensation Act, what is required is that his employment should be both of a casual nature and that it should be otherwise than for the purpose of the employer's trade or business.

Workmen's dues. In relation to a company, means the aggregate of the following sums due from the company to its workmen, namely:—

(i) all wages or salary including wages payable for time or piece work and salary earned wholly or in part by way of commission of any workman, in respect of services rendered to the company and any of the provisions of the Industrial Disputes Act, 1947 (14 of 1947);

(ii) all accrued holiday remuneration becoming payable to any workman, or in the case of his death to any other person in his right, on the termination of his employment before, or by the effect of, the winding up order or resolution;

(iii) the company is being wound-up voluntarily merely for the purposes of reconstruction or of amalgamation with another company, or unless the company has, at the commencement of the winding up, under such a contract with insurers as is mentioned in Section 14 of the Workmen's Compensation Act, 1923 (8 of 1923), rights capable of being transferred to and vested in the workman, all amount due in respect of any compensation or liability for compensation under the said Act in respect of the death or disablement of any workman of the company;

(iv) all sums due to any workman from a provident fund, a pension fund, a gratuity fund or any other fund for the welfare of the workmen, maintained by the company. [Companies Act (1 of 1956), S. 529(3)(b)]

Workmen's dues. For the purposes of sections 325, 326 and 327 of Act 18 of 2013, 'workmen's dues', in relation to a company, means the aggregate of the following sums due from the company to its workmen, namely:—

(*i*) all wages or salary including wages payable for time or piece work and salary earned wholly or in part by way of commission of any workman in respect of services rendered to the company and any compensation payable to any workman under any of the provisions of the Industrial Disputes Act, 1947 (14 of 1947);

(*ii*) all accrued holiday remuneration becoming payable to any workman or, in the case of his death, to any other person in his right on the termination of his employment before or by the effect of the winding up order or resolution;

(*iii*) unless the company is being wound up voluntarily merely for the purposes of reconstruction or amalgamation with another company or unless the company has, at the commencement of the winding up, under such a contract with insurers as is mentioned in section 14 of the Workmen's Compensation Act, 1923 (8 of 1923), rights capable of being transferred to and vested in the workmen, all amount due in respect of any compensation or liability for compensation under the said Act in respect of the death or disablement of any workman of the company;

(*iv*) all sums due to any workman from the provident fund, the pension fund, the gratuity fund or any other fund for the welfare of the workmen, maintained by the company. [S. 325(3)(*b*) of the Companies Act, 2013 (18 of 2013)] See also Black Money (Undisclosed Foreign Income and Assets) and Imposition of Tax Act (22 of 2015), S. 34(8)(b); Insolvency and Bankruptcy Code (31 of 2016), S. 53, *Explanation (ii)*.

Workmen's portion. In relation to the security of any secured creditor of a company, means the amount which bears to the value of the security the same proportion as the amount of the workmen's dues bears to the aggregate of—

(i) the amount of workmen's dues; and

(ii) the amounts of the debts due to the secured creditors. [Companies Act (1 of 1956), S. 529(3)(c)]

"WORKMEN'S PORTION". For the purposes of sections 325, 326 and 327 of Act 18 of 2013, 'workmen's portion', in relation to the security of any secured creditor of a company, means the amount which bears to the value of the security the same proportion as the amount of the workmen's dues bears to the aggregate of the amount of workmen's dues and the amount of the debts due to the secured creditors.

Illustration.—The value of the security of a secured creditor of a company is Rs. 1,00,000. The total amount of the workmen's dues is Rs. 1,00,000. The amount of the debts due from the company to its secured creditors is Rs. 3,00,000. The aggregate of the amount of workmen's dues and the amount of debts due to secured creditors is Rs. 4,00,000. The workmen's portion of the security is, therefore, one-fourth of the value of the security, that is Rs. 25,000. [S. 325(3)(*c*) of the Companies Act, 2013 (18 of 2013); Section 325 now repealed by Insolvency and Bankruptcy Code, 2016]

Workout loan. Loan that is not being repaid according to the terms of its contract (*e.g.* payments may be overdue).

Workplace. Includes—

(i) any department, organization, undertaking, establishment, enterprise, institution, office, branch or unit which is established, owned, controlled or wholly or substantially financed by funds provided directly or indirectly by the appropriate Government or the local authority or a Government company or a corporation or a co-operative society;

(ii) any private sector organization or a private venture, undertaking, enterprise, institution, establishment, society, trust, non-governmental organization, unit or service provider carrying on commercial, professional, vocational, educational, entertainmental, industrial, health services or financial activities including production, supply, sale, distribution or service;

(iii) hospitals or nursing homes;

(iv) any sports institute, stadium, sports complex or competition or games venue, whether residential or not used for training, sports or other activities relating thereto;

(v) any place visited by the employee arising out of or during the course of employment including transportation provided by the employer for undertaking such journey;

(vi) a dwelling place or a house. [S. 2(o) of the Sexual Harassment of Women at Workplace (Prevention, Prohibition & Redressal) Act, 2013 (14 of 2013)]

"WORKPLACE" means the campus of a TI, includes—

(*a*) any department, organisation, undertaking, establishment, enterprise, institution, office, branch or unit which is established, owned, controlled or wholly or substantially financed by funds provided directly or indirectly by the appropriate Tis;

(*iii*) any sports institute, stadium, sports complex or competition or games venue, whether residential or not used for training, sports or other activities relating thereof in TIs;

(*iv*) any place visited by the employee arising out of or during the course of employment including transportation provided by the employer for undertaking such journey for study in TIs. [All India council for Technical Education (Gender Sensitization, Prevention and Prohibition of Sexual Harassment of Women Employees and Students and Redressal of Grievances to Technical Educational Institutions) Regulations, 2016, Regn. 2(o)].

Works. "WORKS" includes electric line, and any building, plant, machinery, apparatus and any other thing of whatever description required to transmit, distribute or supply electricity to the public and to carry into effect the objects of a licence or sanction granted under this Act or any other law for the time being in force. [Indian Electricity Act (36 of 2003), S. 2(77)]

Structure or apparatus of some kind; engineering or architectural structures of building. [Indian Electricity Act (9 of 1910), S. 2(n) and IPC (45 of 1860), S. 430].

Works means some sort of construction of a permanent nature and it must be in existence on the date on which the ceiling is going to be fixed. *Mohd. Fakruddin* v. *State of Bihar*, AIR 1976 Pat 382, 384.

'Works' means a manufacturing establishment including buildings and equipment. [Webster's Comprehensive Dictionary, International Edition as cited in *Larsen and Toubro Limited* v. *State of Karnataka*, (2014) 1 SCC 708, para 73].

'Works' means architectural or engineering operations, a fortified building, a defensive structure, fortification or any of the several parts of such structures. [*Larsen and Toubro Limited* v. *State of Karnataka*, (2014) 1 SCC 708, para 73].

The general word 'works' in S. 35(5) is limited to something material in the sense of buildings, structures and such like improvements. Merely fencing a vacant plot of land does not come with the expression 'works'. *Indira B. Gokhale* v. *UOI*, AIR 1990 Bom 98, 103. [Defence of India Act (51 of 1962), S. 36(5)]

The plural 'works' is used in the sense of operations, projects, scheme, plan such as building works, irrigation works etc. and the licence to vend liquor in retail is not a contract for execution of works undertaken by Government. *Ram Raj Tewari* v. *Vijaiya Laxmi*, AIR 1986 All 325, 328. [Representation of the People Act (43 of 1951), S. 9A]

Works contract. "Works contract" means a contract for building, construction, fabrication, completion, erection, installation, fitting out, improvement, modification, repair, maintenance, renovation, alteration or commissioning of any immovable property wherein transfer of property in goods (whether as goods or in some other form) is involved in the execution of such contract [The Central Goods and Services Tax Act, 2017 (12 of 2017), S. 2(119)]

'WORKS CONTRACT' means an agreement in writing for the execution of any work relating to construction, repair, or maintenance of any building or superstructure, dam, weir, canal, reservoir, tank, lake, road, well, bridge, culvert, factory, workshop, powerhouse, transformers or such other works of the State Government or public undertakings as the State

Government may be notification, specify in this behalf at any of its stages, entered into by the State Government or by an official of the State Government or public undertaking or its official for and on behalf of such public undertaking and includes an agreement for the supply of goods or material and all other matters relating to execution of any of the said works. [M.P. Madhyasthan Adhikaran Adhiniyam (29 of 1983), S. 2(i)]

"Works Contract" means a contract wherein transfer of property in goods involved in the execution of such contract is leviable to tax as sale of goods and such contract is for the purpose of carrying out construction, erection, commissioning installation, completion, fitting out, repair, maintenance, renovation, alteration of any movable or immovable property or for carrying out any other similar activity or a part thereof in relation to such property. [Finance Act (32 of 1994), S. 65B(54) now repealed by Central Goods and Services Tax Act, 2017].

'Works Contract' means "any agreement for carrying out for cash or for deferred payment or other valuable consideration, the construction, fitting out, improvement or repair of any building, road, bridge or other immovable property or the fitting out, improvement or repair of any movable property." [Madras General Sales Tax, 1939 as amended by Madras General Sales Tax (Amendment) Act 25 of 1947, S. 2(i) as cited in State of Madras v. Gannon Dunkerly & Co. (Madras) Ltd. (1), AIR 1958 SC 560]. See also *Kone Elevator India Pvt. Ltd. v. State of T.N.*, (2014) 7 SCC 1, para 16.

"WORKS CONTRACT" is nothing but a contract in which one of the parties is obliged to undertake or to execute works. Such activity of construction has all the characteristics or elements of works contract [*Larson and Toubro Limited v. State of Karnataka*, (2014) 1 SCC 708, para 93].

'Works Contract' is an agreement for carrying out for cash, deferred payment or other valuable consideration, the building construction, manufacture, processing, fabrication, erection, installation, fitting out, improvement, modification, repair or commissioning of any movable or immovable property. [*Larsen and Tourbo Limited v. State of Karnataka*, (2014) 1 SCC 708, para 102, 120] [Maharashtra Value Added Tax (9 of 2005), S. 2(24), Explanation (b)(ii)].

"WORKS CONTRACT" means a contract for building, construction, fabrication, completion, erection, installation, fitting out, improvement, modification, repair, maintenance, renovation, alteration or commissioning of any immovable property wherein transfer of property in goods (whether as goods or in some other form) is involved in the execution of such contract. [Central Goods and Services Tax Act (12 of 2017), S. 2(119)].

"WORKS CONTRACT" includes any agreement for carrying out for cash or for deferred payment or for valuable consideration, the building construction, manufacture, processing, fabrication, erection, installation, fitting out, improvement, repair or commissioning of any movable or immovable property. [Andaman and Nicobar Islands Value Added Tax Regulation (6 of 2017), S. 2(1)(zn)].

Workshop. "WORKSHOP" means any premises (including the precincts thereof) wherein any industrial process is carried on, but does not includes any premises to which the provisions of Section 67 of the Factories Act, 1948, for the time being, apply. [Child Labour (Prohibition & Regulation) Act (61 of 1986), S. 2(x)]

Room or building in which manufacture is carried on.

World Anti-Doping Agency. Means an international agency established on 10th November, 1999 in Switzerland which adopts and amends the Code for giving effect to anti-doping policies and international standards. [National Anti-Doping Act, 2022 (15 of 2022), S. 2(zi)]

World Bank or **IBRD.** "WORLD BANK" means the International Bank for Reconstruction and Development Bank referred to in the International Monetary Fund and Bank Act, 1945. [Income-tax Act (43 of 1961), S. 80 HHBA(2) *Expln.* (b)]

World Trade Organization Country. "WORLD TRADE ORGANISATION COUNTRY" means a country which is a member of the World Trade Organisation and which has either ratified, or accepted, or acceded to the Agreement on Trade Related Aspects of Intellectual Property Right, 1994, and includes a country mentioned in Part VI of the Schedule of International Copyright Order 1999. [International Copyright Order, 1999, S. 2(f)]

World Wide Web (www). A hypertext-based, distributed information system in which users may create, edit or browse hypertext documents. A graphical document publishing and retrieval medium; a collection of linked documents that reside on the Internet. (*Information Technology*)

A feature of the Internet that provides access to interlinked documents. Documents on the Web use Hypertext Markup Language (HTML) to include pictures and other graphical elements as well as a means of identifying terms that provide the links to other Web documents. (*Computer*)

The World-Wide Web, or WWW, is the part of the Internet that you're using to view a particular Web page. The Web is just a set of protocols, or standards, for transferring data from one computer to another; just one aspect of the Internet, but by far the most popular. Telnet, FTP, Veronica, and Archie are some other Internet data-transfer protocols. Without protocols, computers wouldn't be able to communicate with or understand each other. (*Cyber Law*)

World Wide Web navigational agents. These agents allow the user to navigate the vast resources available on the Web, providing better results in finding information. (*Cyber Law*)

Worship. The reverence or veneration tendered to a divine being or supernatural power. [Constitution of India of India, Preamble].

Worth. The quality of a thing which gives it value. [T.P. Act (4 of 1882), S. 35, ill.]; [Obstruction in Fairways Act (16 of 1881), S. 2(b)].

Wound. Injury done to living tissue by cut or stab or blow or tear; injury to reputation; pain inflicted on feelings.

Injury done to living tissue by cut, stab, blow or tear; an injury in which the skin or other tissue is broken, cut, torn etc. [Indian Evidence Act (1 of 1872), S. 155, ill. (b)]; injury done to the feelings etc.

Wounding and maiming. Aggravated forms of battery.

Wreck. "WRECK" includes the following when found in the sea or in tidal water or on the shores thereof—

(a) goods which have been cast into the sea and then sink and remain under water;

(b) goods which have been cast or fall into the sea and remain floating on the surface;

(c) goods which are sunk in the sea, but are attached to a floating object in order that they may be found again;

(d) goods which are thrown away or abandoned, and

(e) a vessel abandoned without hope or intention of recovery. [Merchant Shipping Act (44 of 1958), S. 3(58)]

The destruction or injury to a vessel by being cast on shore or on rocks or by being disabled or sunk by the force of winds or waves or by other accident [Indian Evidence Act (1 of 1872), S. 32, ill. (h)]; to break up completely [Indian Contract Act (9 of 1872), S. 23, ill. (c)]; shipwrecked property [Customs Act (52 of 1962), S. 21]; remains of anything ruined.

"WRECK" means a state of any vessel, or goods or a part or property of such vessel or carried on the vessel,—

(i) which have been cast into or have fallen into the inland waters and then sunk and remain under water or remains floating on the surface; or

(ii) which have sunk in the inland waters, but are attached to a floating object in order that they may be found again; or

(iii) which are intentionally thrown away or abandoned without hope or intention of recovery; or

(iv) which by its presence in inland waters, is a hazard or causes impediment to navigation, or adversely affects safety of life or causes pollution. [Inland Vessels Act, 2021 (24 of 2021), S. 3(zv)]

Writ. A written command, precept, or formal order issued by a Court, directing or enjoining the person or persons to whom it is addressed to do or refrain from doing some act specified therein. [IPC (45 of 1860), S. 345].

Writ of certiorari. A judicial order operating in personam and made in original legal proceedings, directed by the Supreme Court or the High Court to any constitutional, statutory or non-statutory body or person, requiring the records of any action to be certified by the Court or dealt with according to law.

Writ of execution. A mandatory precept issued from a Court of justice to put in force its judgment, decree or order [CPC (5 of 1908), O. XLIX, R. 1]; [Presidency Small Cause Courts Act (15 of 1882), S. 89].

Writ of habeas corpus. A judicial order issued by the Supreme Court or a High Court by which a person who is confined by public or private agency may secure his release. It is in the form of an order calling upon the person confining him to let the Court know the legal justication for his detention or to release him.

Writ of mandamus. A judicial order issued by the Supreme Court or a High Court to any constitutional, statutory or a non-statutory agency to do or to forbear from doing some specific act which that agency is obliged to do or refrain from doing under the law and which is in the nature of a public or a statutory duty.

Writ of mandamus (Executive and ministerial act) distinction. If a statute directs a public officer to perform an act in regard to which no discretion is committed to him then that act would be ministerial although depending upon a statute which requires in some degree a construction of its language by the officer concerned. If, however, the duty is not plainly prescribed or if the law confers discretion on the respondent to do or not to do a certain act he may choose, the duty must be regarded involving the exercise of judgment or discretion which cannot be controlled by *mandamus* even though the construction of the officer may be erroneous. This is particularly so when the statute by which the duty is imposed is couched in permissive terms. In such a case discretion can obviously not be controlled by *mandamus* unless the decision is so manifestly arbitrary and capricious. *Karnal Kaithal Co-Operative Transport Society, Ltd.* v. *State of Punjab,* MLJ : QD (1956-1960) Vol. II C132 : 60 Punj LR 425 : (1958-1959) 15 FJR 49 : AIR 1959 Punj 75 : (1959) 1 Lab LJ 274 : ILR (1958) Punj 2061. [Constitution of India, Art. 226]

Writ of mandamus and certiorari (Distinction). There is an essential distinction between a writ of certiorari and writ of mandamus. A writ of certiorari is available for the removal of any judicial act or *quasi* judicial act of an inferior. Tribunal whereas a writ of mandamus is issued to compel the performance of duties of a public nature. The condition that the act complained of should be a judicial act applies to the former relief and not to the latter. *T. Venkateswara Rao* v. *State of Andhra Pradesh,* MLJ : QD (1956-1960) Vol. II C41 : (1958)

1 Andh WR 480 : AIR 1958 AP 458 : ILR (1958) AP 466. [Constitution of India, Art. 226]

Writ of prohibition. A judicial order issued by the Supreme Court or a High Court to any constitutional, statutory or non-statutory agency to prevent these agencies from continuing their proceeding in excess or abuse of their jurisdiction or in violation of the principles of natural justice or in contravention of the law of the land.

Writ of quo warranto. A judicial order issued by the Supreme Court or a High Court by which any person who occupies or usurps an independent public office or franchise or liberty is asked to show by what right he claims it, so that the title to the office, franchise or liberty may be settled and any unauthorised person ousted.

Write protected. (of a computer disk) having been protected from accidental writing or erasure. [*Collins Dictionary* **as cited in** *Tarun Tyagi* v. *Central Bureau of Investigation,* (2017) 4 SCC 490, para 12].

To protect the data on a computer disk so that it cannot be changed or removed by a user. [Cambridge Dictionary **as cited in** *Tarun Tyagi* v. *Central Bureau of Investigation,* (2017) 4 SCC 490, para 11].

Write off. To carry or remove.

Writing. Expressions referring to "WRITING" shall be construed as including references to printing, lithography photography and other mode of representing or reproducing words in a visible form. [General Clauses Act (10 of 1897), S. 3(65)]

"WRITING" includes, *inter alia,* telegram and telex. [Hamburg Rules, Art. 1, R. (8)]

The expression 'writing' appearing in Sec. 145 refers to the tangible object that appeals to the sense of right and that which is susceptible of being reproduced by printing, lithography, photography etc. It is not wide enough to include a statement appearing on a tape which can be reproduced through the mechanism of a tape recorder. *Rup Chand* v. *Mahabir Prasad*, AIR 1956 Punj 173. [Indian Evidence Act (1 of 1872), S. 145; General Clauses Act (10 of 1897), S. 3(65)] Written form. [Indian Evidence Act (1 of 1872), S. 73]; [General Clauses Act (10 of 1897), S. 3(65)].

Writing, In. In a written form. [CrPC, 1973 (2 of 1974), S. 108(1)(i)].

Writing under his hand. A type written letter of resignation duly signed by the person tendering the resignation also means 'writing under his hand'. *Vice Chairman, Village Panchayat* v. *Channabashappa Bgeddi*, AIR 1985 Kant 252, 256.

Writing under their hands. A writing bearing their signature. [Indian Evidence Act (1 of 1872), S. 58].

"WRITTEN AGREEMENT" means a mutual understanding or an arrangement about relative rights and duties by the parties. [*General Manager, Sri Siddheshwara Cooperative Bank Limited v. Ikbal,* (2013) 10 SCC 83, para 18].

Written down cost. Means—

Original cost less the amounts set aside or written off on account of depreciation in the books of the undertaking. [Electricity (Supply) Act (54 of 1948), Sixth Sch., Para XVII point 11]

Written law. Statute law.

Written statement. The pleading filed by the defendant in a suit stating his grounds of defence. [CrPC, 1973 (2 of 1974), S. 145(1)].

Wrong. Any damage or injury, contrary to right. (*Tomlin*)

Violation of a right or of law.

A violation; transgression or infringement of law; invasion of right to the damage or prejudice of another or others [Indian Evidence Act (1 of 1872), S. 10]; deviating from justice, equity and goodness; not morally right or equitable [IPC (45 of 1860), S. 84]; incorrect; mistaken [Companies (Profits) Surtax Act (7 of 1964), S. 5(3)]; whatever is not right or just. [Army Act (46 of 1950), S. 26].

The term 'wrong' in S. 23(a) means an act causing injury to the other side. A wife living separately from her husband cannot be considered to cause, thereby an injury to her husband. [Hindu Marriage Act (25 of 1955), S. 23(a)]

Wrong doer. One who commits wrongful,unjust or blameworthy acts; one who is guilty of a wrong, tort or trespass; a law breaker. [IPC (45 of 1860), S. 103].

Wrongful. Injurious; unjust. [IPC (45 of 1860), S. 418].

Wrongful act. Any act which unlawfully infringes upon the rights of another [CrPC, 1973 (2 of 1974), S. 107(2)]; [Requisitioning and Acquisition of Immovable Property Act (30 of 1952), S. 6(6), *Prov.*].

Wrongful confinement. "WHOEVER WRONGFULLY restrains any person in such a manner as to prevent that person from proceeding beyond certain circumscribing limits is said "wrongfully to confine" that person." [IPC (45 of 1860), S. 340] [(w. e. f. 1-7-2024) repealed and replaced by Bharatiya Nyaya Sanhita, 2023 (45 of 2023), S. 127(1)]

Wrongful gain. "WRONGFUL GAIN" is gain by unlawful means of property to which the person gaining is not legally entitled. [IPC (45 of 1860), S. 23]] [Now (w. e. f. 1-7-2024) repealed & replaced by Bharatiya Nayaya Sanhita, 2023 (45 of 2023), S. 2(36), same definition in new Sanhita]

Wrongful gain covers temporary wrongful gain.

"WRONGFUL GAIN". For the purposes of section 447 of Act 18 of 2013, 'wrongful gain' means the gain by unlawful means of property to which the person gaining is not legally entitled. [*Explanation* (*ii*) to section 447 of the Companies Act, 2013 (18 of 2013)]

Wrongful loss. "WRONGFUL LOSS", is the loss by unlawful means of property to which the person losing it is legally entitled. [IPC (45 of 1860), S. 23] Now (w. e. f. 1-7-2024) repealed & replaced by

Bharatiya Nayaya Sanhita, 2023 (45 of 2023), S. 2(37), same definition in new Sanhita

Wrongful loss covers temporary wrongful loss.

"WRONGFUL LOSS". For the purposes of section 447 of Act 18 of 2013, 'wrongful loss' means the loss by unlawful means of property to which the person losing is legally entitled. [*Explanation* (*iii*) to section 447 of the Companies Act, 2013 (18 of 2013)]

Wrongful manner. For the purposes of rule 11(b) of the Companies (Appointment and Qualification of Directors) Rules, 2014, the expression 'wrongful manner' means if the DIN is obtained on the strength of documents which are not legally valid or incomplete documents are furnished or on suppression of material information or on the basis of wrong certification or by making misleading or false information or by misrepresentation. [*Explanation* (*i*) to rule 11 of the Companies (Appointment & Qualification of Directors) Rules, 2014]

Wrongful restraint. "Whoever voluntarily obstructs any person so as to prevent that person from proceeding in any direction in which that person has a right to proceed, is said wrongfully to restrain that person." [IPC (45 of 1860), S. 339] [(w. e. f. 1-7-2024) repealed and replaced by Bharatiya Nyaya Sanhita, 2023 (45 of 2023), S. 126(1)]

Wrongfully. In a wrongful manner. [CPC (5 of 1908), Sch. I, App. A, form No. 15(3)]; [Indian Contract Act (9 of 1872), S. 180]; [Industrial Disputes Act (14 of 1947), Sch. II, item 3].

Wrongfully sold in the execution of decree. The words "wrongfully sold in execution of decree" in O. XXXIX, R. 1 of the CPC (5 of 1908), include a case where the property of the applicant is in danger of being sold in execution of a decree against another person.

Wrongly taking. The expression 'wrongly taking' is a wide one and it comprises not only of an act which would amount to conversion but also an act which would amount to trespass to goods. It thus includes wrongful impounding of cattle. *All Malna Kurmi* v. *Civil Judge Class I*, AIR 1953 Nag 213.

WWW. (*abbr.*) World Wide Web. World Wide Web (or simply Web for short) is a term frequently used (incorrectly) when referring to "The Internet", WWW has two major meanings:

First, loosely used : the whole constellation of resources that can be accessed using *Gopher, FTP, HTTP, Telnet, USENET, WAIS* and some other tools.

Second, the universe of hypertext *servers (HTTP Servers)*, more commonly called "web servers", which are the servers that serve *web pages* to web *browsers.* ((*Matisse Enzer Glossary of Internet Terms*)

X

X-509. A standard which specifies the format of Digital certificates, to provide a way to securely tie a name to a Public Key. (*Information Technology*)

The ITU-T (International Telecommunications Union-T) standard for Digital Signature Certificates. X. 509 V3 refers to certificates containing or capable of containing extensions. (*Information Technology*)

The ITU-T (International Telecommunications Union-T) standard for Digital Signature Certificates. X. 509 V3 refers to certificates containing or capable of containing extensions. (*Information Technology*)

xDSL. (*abbr.*) x Digital Subscriber Line— HDSL, ADSL & VDSL. Set of Techniques and equipment used on a subscriber line enabling the subscriber to set up links with high data rates. (*Telecommunication*)

XML (extensible markup language). A subset of the standard generalized markup language (SGML), XML is a recent and flexible technology for creating common information formats and shares both the format and the information on the e-commerce infrastructure. (*Cyber Law*)

Similar to HTML in that it describes the contents of a web page. XML also enables the interpretation of the value or nature of the data being described. (*Cyber Law*)

Extensible mark-up language—a coded language used to create more interactive and adaptable web pages. (*Penelope Lawrence*) (*Internet*)

A widely used system for defining data formats. XML provides a very rich system to define complex documents and data structures such as invoices, molecular data, news feeds, glossaries, inventory descriptions, real estate properties, *etc.* As long as a programmer has the XML definition for a collection of data (often called a "schema") then they can create a program to reliably process any data formatted according to those rules. (*Matisse Enzer-Glossary of Internet Terms*)

XMLRPC. XML Remote Procedure Call). A *protocol* for *client-server* communication that sends and receives information "on top of" *HTTP*. The data sent and received is in a particular *XML* format specifically designed for use with XMLRPC. (*Matisse Enzer Glossary of Internet Terms*)

XPFE. (*abbr.*) Cross Platform Front End. A suite of technologies used to create applications that will work and look the same on different computer operating systems. A widely used XPFE application is the Mozilla web browser and its derivities, such as the Netscape web browser in version 7 and later. The primary technologies used in creating XPFE applications are *Javascript, Cascading Style Sheets*, and *XUL*. (*Matisse Enzer Glossary of Internet Terms*)

XUL. XUL used to define what the user interface will look like for a particular piece of software. XUL is used to define what buttons, scrollbars, text boxes, and other user-interface items will appear, but it is not used to define how those items will look (*e.g.* what color they are). The most widely used example of XUL use is probably in the Mozilla web browser, where the entire user interface is defined using the XUL language (*Matisse Enzer-Glossary of Internet Terms*)

XYY-chromosome defence. In criminal law whereby the male defendant defends his criminal behaviour as it being due to his genetic abnormality of having an extra Y chromosome which causes him to have uncontrollable aggressive impulses.

Y

Yarn. Means any fibre, or wool, silk, flax, cotton, nylon etc. spun into strands for weaving, knitting or making thread. *Gwalior R.S. Manufacturing (Wvg.) Co.* v. *Textile Committee, Bombay,* AIR 1980 MP 69, 71. [Textiles Committee Act (41 of 1963), S. 2(g)(f)]

The yarn produced 'from 100% waste cotton' is still yarn produced from cotton. *State* v. *Dhanraj Mills Ltd.*, AIR 1960 Bom 453, 456. [Cotton Textiles (Control) Order, 1948, Cla. 21(3)(c)]

Year. "YEAR" shall mean a year reckoned according to the British calendar. [General Clauses Act (10 of 1897), S. 3(66)]

"YEAR" mean the year commencing on the first day of April. [Cantonment Act (2 of 1924), S. 2(xl)]

"YEAR" means the period of twelve months beginning with the first day of July and ending with thirtieth day of June next following. [Coffee Act (7 of 1942), S. 3(n)]

"YEAR" means, in relation to the Board or a Generating Company, the year commencing on the 1st day of April. [Electricity (Supply) Act (54 of 1948), S. 2(13)]

"YEAR" means the period commencing on the 1st day of April of any year and ending on the 31st day of March of the succeeding year. [Chartered Accountants Act (38 of 1949), S. 2(i)]

YEAR, in relation to a dealer, means the year applicable in relation to him under the general sales tax law of the appropriate State, and where there is no such year applicable the financial year. [Central Sales Tax Act (74 of 1956), S. 2(k)]

"YEAR" means the year beginning on the first day of May. [Sugar Export Promotion Act (30 of 1958), S. 2(g)]

"YEAR" means the year beginning on the first day of November and ending on the thirty- first day of October in the following year. [Sugar (Regulation of Production) Act (55 of 1961), S. 2(g)]

"YEAR" mean the financial year. [Food Corporations Act (37 of 1964), S. 2(f)]

A cycle in the Gregorian Calendar having 365 or 366 days divided into 12 months beginning with January and ending with December; a period of twelve months. [IPC (45 of 1860), S. 49 and General Clauses Act (10 of 1897), S. 3(66)].

Wherever the word "year" or the word "month" is used, it is to be understood that the year of the month is to be reckoned according to the British calendar. [IPC (45 of 1860), S. 49] [Now (w. e. f. 1-7-2024) repealed & replaced by Bharatiya Nyaya Sanhita, 2023 (45 of 2023)]

Wherever the word "year" is used, it is to be understood that the year is to be reckoned according to the British calendar. [(w. e. f. 1-7-2024) Bharatiya Nyaya Sanhita, 2023 (45 of 2023), S. 2(20)]

Year of account. Means, in relation to a licensee his financial year. [Electricity (Supply) Act (54 of 1948), S. 2(14)]

Year of commercial production. For the purposes of this section—

"YEAR OF COMMERCIAL PRODUCTION" means the previous year in which as a result of any operation relating to prospecting, commercial production of any mineral or any one or more of the minerals in a group of associated minerals specified in Part A or Part B, respectively, of the Seventh Schedule, commences. [Income-tax Act (43 of 1961), S. 35 E(5)(b)]

Year to year. From year to year (as in the case of tenancy). [T.P. Act (4 of 1882), S. 107].

Yeas and nays. The affirmative and negative votes on a bill or resolution before a legislature.

Yellow book. Popular term for a publication entitled *Admission and Securities Listing,* issued by the London Stock Exchange Council, setting out regulations of admission to the Official list and the obligations of securities admitted.

Yellow flag. Flag of ship with infectious disease; hospital ship; ship in quarantine.

Yes/No authentication facility. Means a type of authentication facility in which the identity information and Aadhaar number securely submitted with the consent of the Aadhaar number holder through a requesting entity, is then matched against the data available in the CIDR, and the Authority responds with a digitally signed response containing "Yes" or "No", along with other technical details related to the authentication transaction, but no identity information. [Aadhaar (Authentication) Regulations, 2016, Regn. 2(1)(p)].

Yield. The dividend expressed as a percentage of current prices.

Young Person. "YOUNG PERSON" means a person who is either a child or an adolescent. [Factories Act (63 of 1948), S. 2(d); Plantation Labour Act (69 of 1951), S. 2(l)]

"YOUNG PERSON" means a person under the age of twenty years. [Young Persons (Harmful Publications) Act (93 of 1956), S. 2(c)]

"YOUNG PERSON" means a person under eighteen years of age. [Merchant Shipping Act (44 of 1958), S. 3(59)]

"YOUNG PERSON" means a person who has completed fourteen years of age but has not completed eighteen years of age. [Beedi and Cigar Workers (Condition of Employment), Act (32 of 1966), S. 2(q)]

Youth. Being young; the period between childhood and adult age.

The fact or state of being young especially the early part of life; the period between childhood and the adult age. [IPC (45 of 1860), S. 491].

Youthful offender. "Youthful offender" means any boy who has been convicted of any offence punishable with imprisonment and who, at the time of such conviction, was under the age of fifteen years. [Reformatory Schools Act (8 of 1897), S. 4(a) and 31(2)]

Z

Zamindar. "ZAMINDAR" means all or any of the holders of any estate. [Ben Act (5 of 1875), (Survey), S. 2].

The word "ZAMINDAR" shall mean the person whose name is registered in the general register of estates paying revenue directly to Government as the proprietor of an estate so paying revenue, or the person whose name is registered in the general register of rent-free tenures as proprietor of a rent-free tenure. [Ben. Act (6 of 1870), (Village Chaukidari), S. 1]

The holder of large estate or *jagir;* landed proprietor; shareholder in estate.

Zamindari. The estate of a *zamindar* or pertaining to a *zamindar*.

Zap. In critical legal studies, a so called spontaneous moment of shared intuition.

Zealous witness. A witness who displays undue favouritism towards one party in the case.

Zero coupon bond. 'ZERO COUPON BOND' means a bond—

(*a*) issued by any infrastructure capital company or infrastructure capital fund or infrastructure debt fund or public sector company or scheduled bank on or after the 1st day of June, 2005;

(*b*) in respect of which no payment and benefit is received or receivable before maturity or redemption from infrastructure capital company or infrastructure capital fund or infrastructure debt fund or public sector company or scheduled bank; and

(*c*) which the Central Government may, by notification in the Official Gazette, specify in this behalf.

Explanation 1.—For the purposes of this clause, the expression "scheduled bank" shall have the meaning assigned to it in clause (*ii*) of the *Explanation* to sub-clause (*c*) of clause (*viia*) of sub-section (1) of section 36.

Explanation 2.—For the purposes of this clause, the expression "infrastructure debt fund" shall mean the infrastructure debt fund notified by the Central Government in the Official Gazette under clause (*47*) of section 10. [Income-tax Act (43 of 1961), S. 2(48)]

Zero Hour. The time immediately following the Question Hour in the Houses of the Parliament or the State Legislature is popularly known as Zero Hour, in one sense because it is a non-existent hour as it starts at twelve noon which is a Zero Hour of the day and the other because of its duration generally being of an hour. Any member may rise and ask questions on public matters to the Government and raise issues of national importance.

Zero-rated supply. A supply which is within the scope of value-added tax but is charged at a nil rate, *e.g.* are food (excluding restaurant and take-away meals), books and journals, and children's clothes; all exports are also zero-rated.

Zero-rating. Relief from payment of value added tax on the supply of certain goods and services.

Zihar. *(Arabic)* Divorce consequent upon a man's comparing his wife to some female relative with whom marriage is prohibited; under Mahommedan Law a separation must take place until proper explanation has been made. [*Wilson's Gloss* **quoted in** *P. Ramanath Aiyar's, The Major Law Lexicon*, 2010, LexisNexis].

Zila. (*H.*) Side, part, a division, a district under the British administration a province, a tract of country constituting the jurisdiction of a collector and the extent of a chief collectorate.

Ziladar. (*H.*) The officer in charge of a *Zila*, a provincial governor sometimes applied to the European collector or judge, whose authority extends over the *Zila* : in the Delhi territory the title was also given to the head of a village, who was chosen to superintend the revenue affairs of several adjacent villages, united under him for the convenience of revenue arrangement; in the *Maratha* country, a petty revenue officer, having jurisdiction over several villages, comprising a *taraf*, or other small division of country subordinate to the officer in charge of a *Pargana*. (*Wilson's Gloss. 567*)

ZIP. A way of compressing files to minimise transmission times over the Internet. Programs are available to ZIP files up (compress them) and UNZIP them (restore them to their original form) after transmission across the Internet. (*Cyber Law*)

The most popular method of compressing files so they can be sent over the internet. The only problem being when they arrive in the user's mailbox, they need unzipping. A special software is needed to do this operation of zipping and unzipping. (*Penelope Lawrence*) (*Internet*)

Zip archive. An archive of one or more Zip-compressed files. When used as a noun, Zip is typically capitalized. Compressed files can come in many formats besides Zip. (*Cyber Law*)

Zip file. A Zip archive that Windows presents as a single file. In general, the contents cannot be accessed unless the archive is decompressed, except when you are running Zip-Magic 2000. (*Cyber Law*)

Zone of influence. Means that part of the catchment area of the wetland or wetland complex, developmental activities in which induce adverse changes in ecosystem structure, and ecosystem services. [Wetlands (Conservation and Management) Rules, 2017, R. 2(1)(j)].

Zoning variance. A licence or official authorization to depart from a zoning law.

Zoo. Means an establishment, whether stationary or mobile, where captive animals are kept for exhibiting to the public or ex-situ conservation and includes a circus and off-exhibit facilities such as rescue centres and conservation breeding centres, but does not include an establishment of a licensed dealer in captive animals. [Wild Life (Protection) Act (53 of 1972), S. 2(39)]

I SAY NO TO PIRACY
Genuine Knowledge relies on Genuine Content
Scan and know Why it is necessary to buy ORIGINAL
Watch out for more signs of piracy
• Inferior print and paper quality
• Missing scratch label/access code for ebooks
• Outdated content
• Missing hologram sticker of LexisNexis logo/ wordmark on the cover (In local titles)